# CONGRESSIONAL QUARTERLY

## Almanac

## 102nd CONGRESS
## 2nd SESSION . . . 1992

## VOLUME XLVIII

**Congressional Quarterly Inc.**

1414 22nd Street N.W.
Washington, D.C. 20037

# Congressional Quarterly Inc.

Congressional Quarterly Inc. is a publishing and information services company and a recognized leader in political journalism. For almost half a century, CQ has served clients in the fields of news, education, business and government with timely, complete, unbiased and accurate information on Congress, politics and national issues.

At the heart of CQ is its acclaimed publication, the Weekly Report, a weekly magazine offering news and analyses on Congress and legislation. The CQ Researcher (formerly Editorial Research Reports), with its focus on current issues, provides weekly balanced summaries on topics of widespread interest.

Congressional Quarterly Inc. publishes the Congressional Monitor, a daily report on Congress and current and future activities of congressional committees, and several newsletters, including Congressional Insight, a weekly analysis of congressional action.

Congressional Quarterly Inc. also publishes a variety of books including political science textbooks under the CQ Press imprint and public affairs paperbacks to keep journalists, scholars and the public abreast of developing issues and events. CQ Books publishes highly regarded information directories and reference books on the federal government, national elections and politics, including the Guide to the Presidency, the Guide to Congress, the Guide to the U.S. Supreme Court, the Guide to U.S. Elections, Politics in America, the Federal Regulatory Directory and Washington Information Directory. The CQ Almanac, a compendium of legislation for one session of Congress, is published each year. Congress and the Nation, a record of government for a presidential term, is published every four years.

Washington Alert, Congressional Quarterly's online congressional and regulatory tracking service, provides immediate access to both proprietary and public databases of legislative action, votes, schedules, profiles and analyses.

Library of Congress Catalog Number 47-41081
ISBN: 0-87187-931-X ISSN: 0095-6007

*"By providing a link between the local newspaper and Capitol Hill we hope Congressional Quarterly can help to make public opinion the only effective pressure group in the country. Since many citizens other than editors are also interested in Congress, we hope that they too will find Congressional Quarterly an aid to a better understanding of their government.*

*"Congressional Quarterly presents the facts in as complete, concise and unbiased form as we know how. The editorial comment on the acts and votes of Congress, we leave to our subscribers."*

Foreword, Congressional Quarterly, Vol. I, 1945
Henrietta Poynter, 1901-1968
Nelson Poynter, 1903-1978

# SUMMARY TABLE OF CONTENTS

## APPENDIXES

## INDEXES

# TABLE OF CONTENTS

# Chapter 1 — 102nd Congress

# Chapter 2 — Economics & Finance

# Chapter 3 — Government/Commerce

# Chapter 4 — Energy/Environment/Science

# Chapter 5 — Law & Judiciary

# Chapter 6 — Labor/Housing/Veterans

# Chapter 7 — Health/Education/Human Services

# Chapter 8 — Defense

# Chapter 9 — Foreign Policy

# Chapter 10 — Appropriations

# Appendixes

# Indexes

# 102nd CONGRESS

# House Scandals Grab Hill's Attention

## *Much legislation is thwarted by internal problems, partisan inflexibility and charges of 'gridlock'*

The 102nd Congress, sharply partisan to the end of the second session, lurched to a close Oct. 9.

Lawmakers sent the White House a flurry of major last-minute bills and overrode a veto by President Bush for the first time. But the session was marked most clearly by scandals in the House and denunciations of congressional "gridlock" by presidential candidates — Democrats, Republicans and independents alike. Members called it quits earlier in the year than usual so that they could go home and fight for re-election in the most anti-incumbent year in decades.

"I think many people will be happy to see us go," House Speaker Thomas S. Foley, D-Wash., said Oct. 5.

The Senate worked through the Yom Kippur holiday until 9:46 p.m. Oct. 8 to quash filibustering obstructionists. The House convened for four minutes on Oct. 9 to officially end the second session of the 102nd Congress at 10:04 a.m., three days after it finished its legislative work.

In its final days, Congress cleared measures to provide billions in new aid to the former Soviet republics and Israel, cut defense spending and recast U.S. energy policy with an eye toward curbing oil imports.

Members also overrode Bush's veto of a bill to reregulate the cable television industry, breaking his flawless veto record. Congress had not overturned a veto since March 22, 1988, when it enacted a civil rights bill over President Ronald Reagan's objections. *(Vetoes, p. 6)*

But activist legislators in both parties were disappointed by legislative stalemate on topics such as taxes, health care, education, campaign finance and crime.

Among the bills atop the Democratic agenda that died by veto were a family leave bill to let workers take unpaid leave to care for a new child or ill relative, a "motor voter" bill to allow people to register to vote when they renewed their driver's licenses, a tax bill that included urban aid, and campaign-finance legislation to cap spending on congressional elections.

The House was preoccupied for the first part of the year by investigations into members' practice of writing overdraft checks at the House's internal bank. There was also a criminal investigation into possible wrongdoing by members at the House Post Office. The scandal-charged atmosphere led the House to hire a professional administrator to run many of its operations. *(House bank, p. 23; post office, p. 47; administrator, p. 55)*

Also inhibiting action was a shortage of money. The federal deficit climbed to $290.2 billion in 1992. A 1990 agreement left Congress with little flexibility to rearrange spending priorities and little incentive to cut deeper. "The 1990 budget deal created a zero-sum game — revenue neutrality — that in itself creates deadlock," said James A. Thurber, a congressional scholar at American University.

Democratic leaders had promised at the end of 1991 that the second session would be more productive than the first, but in retrospect, many observers said the high point of the Congress was its opening debate on the Persian Gulf War in January 1991.

One way the 102nd Congress did make history was in setting a record for retirements and primary defeats among its members. Congressional approval ratings hit record low levels in public opinion polls, and 53 House members and eight senators quit. Voters rejected 19 representatives and one senator in the primaries. *(Political report, p. 1-A)*

When general elections came Nov. 3, however, the voters did not deliver the blanket of pink slips that incumbents had feared. Four of the 26 Senate incumbents on the ballot lost; 24 House members were defeated in a year in which many representatives had to run in new and unfamiliar districts.

"Congress had a crisis of confidence in itself," said former Republican Bill Frenzel of Minnesota, who retired at the end of the 101st Congress. "The result was as poor a legislative session as I can remember, and it was painful and unpleasant for members."

In hopes of finding improvements, Congress set up an internal commission to propose institutional reforms by the end of 1993. *(Reform, p. 56)*

### RELATIONS WITH BUSH

Looming over the year was the prospect of the presidential election. Bush looked like a lock for re-election in March 1991 after the end of the Persian Gulf War, but a weakening economy gave Democrats hope as 1992 began.

Bush faced his Jan. 28 State of the Union address with the New Hampshire primary three weeks later looking unusually competitive. He had the lowest approval ratings of his presidency, and political commentator Patrick J. Buchanan was mounting a primary challenge from the right.

In the speech, touted in a Bush-Quayle campaign memo beforehand as the "defining event" of his presidency, Bush set the stage for confrontation with Congress. He equated reviving the economy to driving Saddam Hussein from Kuwait. "This will not stand," Bush vowed, echoing his language of a year before. "We can bring the same courage and sense of common purpose to the economy that we brought to Desert Storm." *(Text, p. 7-E)*

Much as he did then, Bush set a goal and a deadline. He asked Congress to pass measures he said would revive the economy, including a substantial cut in the capital gains tax, and he demanded action by March 20. "From the day after that, if it must be, the battle is joined," Bush said.

Before surveying the state of the union, Bush surveyed a world wrought by "changes of almost biblical proportion." It is a safer place to live, he said, where strategic bombers no longer stand on constant alert. "Communism died this year," Bush said, and he didn't hesitate to claim credit for its demise in the name of the nation. "By the grace of God, America won the Cold War."

Bush said the military budget could be pruned, but only so far, and he laid down markers for spending the peace dividend peripherally in his speech and more fully the next day when he proposed a fiscal 1993 budget. He ruled out transferring the money into domestic discretionary spending, per the rules established by the 1990 budget deal. *(Bush budget, p. 85)*

The centerpiece of Bush's speech was a three-tiered plan for the economy: initiatives he would take on his own; short-term items Congress should pass by March 20; and long-term initiatives.

● Bush ordered a 90-day moratorium on new regulations that could retard economic growth; a halt to "regulatory overkill" by banking regulators that he said was contributing to a "credit crunch"; and an adjustment to tax withholding tables to give workers a slight increase in take-home pay.

● To boost the economy in the short term, Bush proposed letting business depreciate certain plant and equipment purchases faster; giving first-time home buyers a tax credit of up to $5,000; allowing withdrawals from Individual Retirement Accounts for a first-time home purchase; permitting commercial real estate developers to use losses from rental properties to offset non-rental income, the so-called passive loss provision; and, finally, cutting the tax rate on capital gains to 15.4 percent.

Bush had sought to lower the capital gains tax rate for three previous years. "This time, at this hour, I cannot take no for an answer; you must cut the capital gains tax for the

## Membership Changes
### 102nd Congress, 2nd Session

#### SENATE

| Member | Party | Died |
|--------|-------|------|
| Quentin N. Burdick, N.D. | D | 9/8/92 |
| (Jocelyn Birch Burdick, D, was sworn in on 9/16/92.) | | |

#### HOUSE

| Member | Party | Died |
|--------|-------|------|
| Ted Weiss, N.Y. | D | 9/14/92 |
| Walter B. Jones, N.C. | D | 9/15/92 |

## 102nd Congress Leaders

### SENATE

President Pro Tempore — Robert C. Byrd, D-W.Va.
Majority Leader — George J. Mitchell, D-Maine
Majority Whip — Wendell H. Ford, D-Ky.
Secretary of the Democratic Conference — David Pryor, D-Ark.

Minority Leader — Bob Dole, R-Kan.
Assistant Minority Leader — Alan K. Simpson, R-Wyo.
Chairman of the Republican Conference — Thad Cochran, R-Miss.
Secretary of the Republican Conference — Bob Kasten, R-Wis.

### HOUSE

Speaker — Thomas S. Foley, D-Wash.
Majority Leader — Richard A. Gephardt, D-Mo.
Majority Whip — David E. Bonior, D-Mich..
Chairman of the Democratic Caucus — Steny H. Hoyer, D-Md.

Minority Leader — Robert H. Michel, R-Ill.
Minority Whip — Newt Gingrich, R-Ga.
Chairman of the Republican Conference — Jerry Lewis, R-Calif.
Chairman of the Republican Policy Committee — Mickey Edwards, R-Okla.

people of our country," he said.

● For the longer term, Bush urged Congress to hew to free trade. He called for passage of his New American Schools program; for a permanent research and development tax credit (it had to be extended each year); for more money to enroll preschoolers in Head Start; and for regulatory and tax relief to businesses that invested in poor neighborhoods.

Not all of the political maneuvering in Bush's speech was directed at Democrats. He also sought to keep peace with Republicans in Congress and to stare down Buchanan.

Buchanan had molded his campaign around the theme "America First," saying the country should curtail sharply its obligations abroad in the post-Cold War era. Bush argued that America had to continue its world leadership role "not out of arrogance, not out of altruism, but for the safety and security of our children." With a nod to phrasing once used by Barry Goldwater, he added, "This is a fact: Strength in the pursuit of peace is no vice; isolationism in the pursuit of security is no virtue."

Bush's capital gains proposal was partially directed at House Republicans, who had been complaining that Bush was not asking for generous enough capital gains relief. Bush then asked for his lowest rate ever and followed up with a visit to Republicans on Capitol Hill on Jan. 29.

Democrats demurred on Bush's deadline as well as his substance. "There is certainly no need to hurry and pass this plan," said Sen. Robert C. Byrd, D-W.Va., chairman of the Appropriations Committee. "It is the wrong course for America."

In the Democratic response, Speaker Thomas S. Foley, D-Wash., promised that Democrats would work with the president — but only to a point. "We will also stand our ground when basic principles are at stake," Foley said. "We will not

agree to do the wrong thing simply for the sake of doing something. In short, we seek a fundamental change from the unsuccessful economic policies of the past 12 years."

Even though they had once derided Bush's deadline, Democratic leaders in the end raced to beat it, ramming a final version of a $77.5 billion tax bill through Congress on March 20. Bush announced that he had signed his veto message even before receiving the bill, saying Democrats "could not resist their natural impulse to raise taxes." *(First tax bill, p. 133)*

Bush ran his re-election campaign as much against Congress as against Clinton. In his acceptance speech Aug. 20 in Houston, for instance, he chided "the gridlock Democrat Congress." Recalling his inaugural speech in 1989, he said, "I extended my hand to the congressional leaders, the Democratic leaders, and they bit it. . . . Every day, Congress puts politics ahead of principle and above progress."

The anti-Congress theme was also used by independent candidate Ross Perot, who kept both parties on their toes even after suspending his active campaigning July 16.

At the end of the session, leaders of both parties blamed their rivals for congressional inaction. "The president's repeated, gratuitous use of the veto and meaningless deadlines were major sources of gridlock," House Majority Leader Richard A. Gephardt, D-Mo., said.

Senate Republican leader Bob Dole of Kansas offered a different retrospective: "The congressional Democrat majority achieved its primary objective: Bash Bush every day. That didn't help make much legislation, but it did help make a lot of headlines, and it also provided a convenient smoke screen for House Democrats to obscure their hot checks," he said, referring to the House bank scandal.

Bush's relations with Congress were mirrored in members' votes. He ended up winning a dismal 43 percent of the roll call votes on which he took a stand in 1992 in Congressional Quarterly's annual vote study. It was the worst score recorded in the survey's 39 years. *(Vote studies, p. 3-B)*

"What's coming home to roost for Bush is his failure to enunciate a clear legislative agenda," said Cary Covington, a political scientist at the University of Iowa. "When presidents propose an agenda and get it to the floor, they win 90 percent of the time. . . . Where they lose is when they try to block someone else's initiative."

## INTERNAL RELATIONS

The lack of an affirmative legislative agenda intensified the spotlight on the powerful negative images of the 102nd Congress — the House bank and Post Office scandals in 1992, and Clarence Thomas' Supreme Court nomination hearings and the Keating Five investigation in 1991.

More than 60 percent of House members were found to have overdrafts at the bank, and members were hounded all spring by questions about their accounts. The affair was kept hot by a criminal investigation by a special Justice Department counsel. Also in the spring, leaders confronted a scandal at the House Post Office involving allegations that members had converted public funds into cash.

The scandals put Foley on the defensive and led to speculation about whether he could hang on to his job.

Democratic critics were especially furious about Foley's handling of the bank affair, arguing that he should have moved more decisively after learning of the problem back in 1989. That complaint dovetailed with a broader critique of Foley — that he was not aggressive enough in advancing Democrats' legislative interests.

---

## Second Session at a Glance

If the second session of the 102nd Congress was not marked by legislative achievement, it was notable for its brevity. The earliest in 16 years, the 102nd Congress officially ended at 10:04 a.m. on Oct. 9 when the House adjourned sine die. The Senate had adjourned sine die the night before at 9:46 p.m.

Convened on Jan. 3, 1992, the second session lasted 281 days — two days more than the second session of the 101st Congress but 84 days less than the 365 days of the first session of the 102nd. The Senate was in session for only 129 days, the lowest total since 1956, when senators were in session for 119 days. The House was in session for 126 days, the lowest since 1984. In 1991 the Senate met for 158 days, and the House for 154. The relatively early adjournment gave members nearly four full weeks to campaign for re-election compared with nine days that separated adjournment and the election in 1990.

There were 4,258 bills and resolutions introduced during the session, compared with 7,758 in 1991, 6,963 in 1990 and 7,390 in 1989. A total of 347 bills cleared by Congress in 1992 became public law.

President Bush vetoed 21 bills for a total of 46 during his four years in office; only one veto was overridden, the cable TV re-regulation bill (S 12). *(Vetoes, p. 6)*

During 1992, the House took 488 roll call votes and quorum calls, 44 more than the previous year. The Senate took 270 roll call votes, 10 less than in 1991 and the least since 1969.*

| Year | House | Senate | Total |
|------|-------|--------|-------|
| 1992 | 488 | 270 | 758 |
| 1991 | 444 | 280 | 724 |
| 1990 | 536 | 326 | 862 |
| 1989 | 379 | 312 | 691 |
| 1988 | 465 | 379 | 844 |
| 1987 | 511 | 420 | 931 |
| 1986 | 488 | 359 | 847 |
| 1985 | 482 | 381 | 863 |
| 1984 | 463 | 292 | 755 |
| 1983 | 533 | 381 | 914 |
| 1982 | 488 | 469 | 957 |
| 1981 | 371 | 497 | 868 |
| 1980 | 681 | 546 | 1,227 |
| 1979 | 758 | 509 | 1,267 |
| 1978 | 942 | 520 | 1,462 |

*\* Figures are for roll call votes and quorum calls in each chamber. In previous Almanacs (through 1987), tabulations in the House were for roll call votes only, and, in the Senate, en bloc treaty votes were counted just once.*

---

In the heat of the checking scandal, backbencher John Bryant of Texas took to the House floor to call on Foley to step down. Two moderate Democrats, Charles W. Stenholm of Texas and Dave McCurdy of Oklahoma, openly talked to colleagues about whether to challenge Foley.

Foley struggled to quell the institutional crisis first by pushing in-house reforms: curbing perquisites, overhauling the way the House was administered, and endorsing a panel to propose reforms in legislative procedures. He leaned on committee chairmen to get major legislation

*Continued on p. 8*

# President Bush's Vetoes . . .

President Bush vetoed 21 bills in 1992 — 11 direct vetoes and 10 pocket vetoes. The 21 vetoes in 1992 brought Bush's total for his four-year presidency to 46, but that included several pocket vetoes that were not recognized by Congress. *(1991 Almanac, p. 10; 1990 Almanac, p. 17; 1989 Almanac, p. 6)*

Under Article I, Section 7, of the U.S. Constitution, the president had 10 days (Sundays excepted) after receiving a bill passed by Congress to sign the measure into law or veto it, returning it to Congress with his objections. Any bill neither signed nor vetoed within those 10 days "shall be a law ... unless the Congress by their adjournment prevent its return, in which case it shall not be a law." The latter case constituted a pocket veto. *(Glossary, p. 6-D)*

Congress could override a veto by a two-thirds vote of each chamber.

It took nearly four years, but Congress finally did override a Bush veto, on a cable television reregulation bill (S 12). The override came on one of the last days of the 102nd Congress — on Bush's 11th veto of the year and on lawmakers' last override attempt in 1992.

Bush's final record of 45-1 on vetoes throughout his presidency, or a 97.8 percent success rate, was not much different from the historic average. From 1789 to 1992, presidents had vetoed 2,515 bills, and Congress had overridden just 104, or 4.1 percent, of them.

The override of the cable bill deprived Bush of being one of just a handful of presidents who never had a veto overridden. Only four presidents who had vetoed more than 10 bills had perfect records. William McKinley Jr. (in office from 1897-1901) had the most vetoes without an override, 42. He was followed by Lyndon B. Johnson (1963-69), with 30; John F. Kennedy (1961-63), 21; and Andrew Jackson (1829-37), 12.

Grover Cleveland had issued the most vetoes in one term — 414, while Franklin D. Roosevelt, who served as president for three terms, had vetoed the most measures — 635. Seven presidents had issued no vetoes during their tenures.

## 1989

| Bill | Description | Vetoed | Outcome |
|------|-------------|--------|---------|
| HR 2 | Minimum wage increase | June 13 | House sustained, 247-178 |
| S J Res 113 | FS-X plane co-development | July 31 | Senate sustained, 66-34 |
| H J Res 390 [1] | Thrift-bailout bill enrollment rules | Aug. 16 | No override attempt |
| HR 2990 | Labor, HHS, Education fiscal 1990 appropriations | Oct. 21 | House sustained, 231-191 |
| HR 3026 | District of Columbia fiscal 1990 appropriations | Oct. 27 | No override attempt |
| HR 2939 | Foreign aid fiscal 1990 appropriations | Nov. 19 | No override attempt |
| HR 3610 | District of Columbia fiscal 1990 appropriations | Nov. 20 | No override attempt |
| HR 1231 | Eastern Airlines strike resolution | Nov. 21 | House sustained, 261-160 |
| HR 1487 | State Department authorization | Nov. 21 | No override attempt |
| HR 2712 [2] | Chinese immigrant status | Nov. 30 | House overrode, 390-25 Senate sustained, 62-37 |

## 1990

| Bill | Description | Vetoed | Outcome |
|------|-------------|--------|---------|
| HR 2364 | Amtrak authorization | May 24 | House overrode, 294-123 Senate sustained, 64-36 |
| HR 20 | Hatch Act amendments | June 15 | House overrode, 327-93 Senate sustained, 65-35 |
| HR 770 | Parental/medical leave | June 29 | House sustained, 232-195 |
| HR 4328 | Textile import quotas | Oct. 5 | House sustained, 275-152 |
| H J Res 660 | Continuing appropriations | Oct. 6 | House sustained, 260-138 |
| S 2104 | Civil rights | Oct. 22 | Senate sustained, 66-34 |
| HR 4638 [3] | Orphan drug amendments | Nov. 8 | No override attempt |

# ...A Near-Perfect Record

## 1990 (cont'd)

| Bill | Description | Vetoed | Outcome |
|------|-------------|--------|---------|
| S 321 [3] | Indian Preference Act | Nov. 16 | No override attempt |
| HR 4653 [3] | Export controls authorization | Nov. 16 | No override attempt |
| HR 3134 [4] | Relief of Joan R. Daronco | Nov. 16 | No override attempt |
| S 2834 [3] | Intelligence authorization | Nov. 30 | No override attempt |

## 1991

| Bill | Description | Vetoed | Outcome |
|------|-------------|--------|---------|
| HR 2699 [2] | District of Columbia fiscal 1992 appropriations | Aug. 17 | No override attempt |
| S 1722 | Unemployment benefits | Oct. 11 | Senate sustained, 65-35 |
| HR 2707 | Labor, HHS, Education fiscal 1992 appropriations | Nov. 19 | House sustained, 276-156 |
| S 1176 [1] | Morris K. Udall Foundation | Dec. 20 | No override attempt |

## 1992

| Bill | Description | Vetoed | Outcome |
|------|-------------|--------|---------|
| HR 2212 | Conditional MFN status for China | March 2 | House overrode, 357-61 / Senate sustained, 60-38 |
| HR 4210 | Tax bill | March 20 | House sustained, 211-215 |
| S 3 | Campaign finance | May 9 | Senate sustained, 57-42 |
| S 2342 | Sioux Indian claims | June 16 | No override attempt |
| HR 2507 | Fetal tissue research/NIH | June 23 | House sustained, 271-156 |
| S 250 | Motor voter | July 2 | Senate sustained, 62-38 |
| S 5 | Family leave | Sept. 22 | Senate overrode, 68-31 / House sustained, 258-169 |
| S 323 | Family planning | Sept. 25, 1992 | Senate overrode, 73-26 / House sustained, 266-148 |
| HR 5318 | Conditional MFN status for China | Sept. 28, 1992 | House overrode, 345-72 / Senate sustained, 59-40 |
| HR 5517 | District of Columbia FY 1993 appropriations | Sept. 30, 1992 | No override attempt |
| S 12 | Cable TV reregulation | Oct. 3, 1992 | House overrode, 308-114 / Senate overrode, 74-25 |
| S 3095 [3] | Jena Band of Choctaws status | Oct. 21, 1992 | No override attempt |
| HR 5452 [5] | Delaware River Port Authority development | Oct. 27, 1992 | No override attempt |
| HR 2859 [3] | Lynn, Mass., study authorization | Oct. 27, 1992 | No override attempt |
| HR 5021 [3] | Wild and Scenic Rivers amendments | Oct. 27, 1992 | No override attempt |
| HR 5061 [3] | Dry Tortugas National Park | Oct. 27, 1992 | No override attempt |
| HR 2109 [3] | Revere Beach study authorization | Oct. 28, 1992 | No override attempt |
| HR 6185 [6] | Federal courts | Oct. 30, 1992 | No override attempt |
| HR 6138 [3] | Farm loan and grant eligibility rules amendments | Oct. 31, 1992 | No override attempt |
| S 3144 [3] | Abortion at military hospitals | Oct. 31, 1992 | No override attempt |
| HR 11 [7] | Tax bill | Nov. 5, 1992 | No override attempt |

[1] Bush asserted that he had pocket-vetoed these bills, although some members in Congress dispute that on the grounds that bills can be pocket-vetoed only after Congress has adjourned, not during a recess. H J Res 390 was moot, and Congress sent a new version of S 1176, which Bush signed.

[2] Bush said these were pocket vetoes but sent the bills back to Congress, where they were treated as regular vetoes.

[3] Pocket veto after final adjournment.

[4] Pocket veto. Similar provisions were put in HR 5316, signed Dec. 1 (PL 101-650).

[5] Pocket veto. Bush signed companion Senate bill (S 2964-PL 102-544) the same day.

[6] Pocket veto. Bush signed into law a similar bill (S 1569 - PL 102-572) on Oct. 29, 1992.

[7] Pocket veto. Bush on Nov. 4 sent a "memorandum of disapproval" to Congress.

*Continued from p. 5*
to the floor, arguing that the best way for the House to put the scandals behind it was to do its legislative business.

And Foley began trying to reinforce his personal bond with fellow Democrats by inviting small groups of members to private dinners to discuss the House and its leadership. Foley also talked to almost every Democratic nominee for the House and contributed money to many.

By the end of the session, with Bill Clinton riding high in the polls and Democrats eager for unity, all talk of a challenge to Foley had vanished. No one ran against him when Democrats met to organize for the next Congress. *(Organization, p. 12)*

The scandal-charged atmosphere brought down two of the House's top officers. Sergeant at Arms Jack Russ, whose office ran the House bank, resigned March 12, just as debate was beginning over whether to release the names of all members who had overdrawn their accounts. House Postmaster Robert V. Rota resigned March 19, in the midst of a Justice Department investigation into wrongdoing at the Post Office. Many of their functions were turned over to the new office of the House administrator.

The Senate was not immune from scandal. Brock Adams, D-Wash., abruptly gave up his bid for re-election March 1, the day The Seattle Times detailed the stories of eight unidentified women who accused him of serious sexual misbehavior. The Senate Ethics Committee on Aug. 12 formally rebuked Mark O. Hatfield, R-Ore., for misreporting gifts. After the session ended, The Washington Post published a long article detailing allegations by 10 women that Bob Packwood, R-Ore., made unwanted sexual advances toward them. *(Ethics cases, p. 51)*

The Senate tied up a loose end from the Keating Five investigation July 2 when it adopted by voice vote a resolution (S Res 273) to spell out when a senator could properly intervene with federal agencies in behalf of constituents.

Senate Majority Leader George J. Mitchell, D-Maine, had appointed a task force in April 1991 to review Senate rules governing "constituent service" in the wake of the Keating affair, in which five senators were accused of intervening improperly with federal regulators to help former savings and loan operator Charles H. Keating. *(1991 Almanac, p. 26)*

The measure was criticized by the government watchdog group Common Cause as flawed, partly because it did not attempt to spell out what was improper use of influence. The resolution said only that "the decision to provide assistance to petitioners may not be made on the basis of contributions or services, or promises of contributions or services, to the member's political campaigns or to other organizations in which the member has a political, personal or financial interest."

### Whitten Forced To Step Aside

The leadership structure remained stable in both cham-

---

## Public Laws

A total of 347 bills cleared Congress in 1992 and became public laws. Following is a list of the number of public laws enacted since 1972:

| Year | Public Laws |
|------|-------------|
| 1992 | 347 |
| 1991 | 243 |
| 1990 | 410 |
| 1989 | 240 |
| 1988 | 471 |
| 1987 | 242 |
| 1986 | 424 |
| 1985 | 240 |
| 1984 | 408 |
| 1983 | 215 |
| 1982 | 328 |
| 1981 | 145 |
| 1980 | 426 |
| 1979 | 187 |
| 1978 | 410 |
| 1977 | 223 |
| 1976 | 383 |
| 1975 | 205 |
| 1974 | 402 |
| 1973 | 247 |
| 1972 | 383 |

---

bers. The only significant change came in the House, where Appropriations Chairman Jamie L. Whitten, D-Miss. — who early in the year set a record for longest service in the House — was forced by illness to give up most of his duties. *(Whitten record, 1991 Almanac, p. 12)*

Whitten was hospitalized early in the year and returned in March, but he was visibly weakened. By June, he came under heavy pressure to resign. He attempted to chair a House-Senate conference committee session June 4, but his voice was so faint that many in the room could not hear him. Facing a humiliating vote by the House Democratic Caucus to force him out, he gave William H. Natcher, D-Ky., a letter June 9 asking him to step in.

Whitten, 82, kept the Appropriations title he had held since 1979 but let Natcher (seven months older than Whitten) take over day-to-day leadership.

Whitten tried to reclaim his power for the 103rd Congress, but he was stripped both of his full committee gavel and the chairmanship of the Agriculture Subcommittee, which he had headed since 1949. *(Whitten, p. 22)*

In the Senate, the death of Quentin N. Burdick, D-N.D., on Sept. 8 opened up the chairmanship of the Environment and Public Works Committee. But Burdick, who was 84, had been ailing for some time, and the committee was used to running without a strong chairman's hand. *(Burdick, p. 73)*

## END OF THE SESSION

As the session's finale approached, the air was thick with election-year politicking. House Republicans made floor speeches painting Democratic presidential candidate Bill Clinton as an unpatriotic draft-dodger, and Senate Democrats slammed Bush's prewar policy toward Iraq.

Lawmakers had worked through the night of Oct. 5-6, approving most bills by voice vote. But as noon approached Oct. 6, House Republicans grew restless, complaining that they knew little about what was in the bills they were letting pass. They vented their anger by trying to block a minor bill by Peter H. Kostmayer, D-Pa., ordering a Delaware River study. Just as Kostmayer was ready to bring up his bill, Jon Kyl, R-Ariz., proposed adjourning for the day. But Democrats voted down the proposal, 97-250, and Kostmayer's bill passed 256-84.

Foley then asked the House to allow Jack Brooks, D-Texas, to offer one last measure to be approved by unanimous consent — a small, uncontroversial chunk of the doomed anti-crime package. Hoping to halt procedural delays, the Speaker announced that he would not oppose another adjournment resolution — and reminded members that any such step would prevent them from delivering the speeches of tribute to retiring members that many had planned to give after the end of regular business.

Rep. William E. Dannemeyer, R-Calif., called Foley's

# Senate Cloture Votes in 1992

The Senate invoked cloture 14 times in 1992 of the 28 times it voted on such debate-limiting motions. Cloture motions require a three-fifths majority of the Senate, or 60 yea votes for all such motions in 1992.

The 28 cloture votes taken in 1992 brought to 345 the number taken since 1917, when the Senate's filibuster rule was adopted; the 14 successful votes in 1992 brought to 126 the number of successful votes.

Following is a list of all 1992 votes. Successful votes are indicated in **boldface** type. Some of the cloture votes were on the bill, some were on amendments to the bill, and some were on motions to proceed to the bill.

| Bill | Date | Vote | Story |
|------|------|------|-------|
| **School Improvement Bill (S 2)** | **Jan. 21** | **93-0** | **p. 455** |
| **National Energy Strategy (S 2166)** | **Feb. 4** | **90-5** | **p. 231** |
| **Joint Ventures Antitrust (S 479)** | **Feb. 25** | **98-0** | **p. 306** |
| Lumbee Tribe Recognition (HR 1426) | Feb. 27 | 58-39 | —— |
| **Corp. for Public Broadcasting (S 1504)** | **March 3** | **87-7** | **p. 187** |
| Crime Bill (HR 3371) | March 19 | 54-43 | p. 311 |
| Defense/Domestic Spending Walls (S 2399) | March 26 | 50-48 | p. 104 |
| **NIH Reauthorization/ Fetal Tissue Research (HR 2507)** | **March 31** | **98-2** | **p. 413** |
| **Motor-Voter Bill (S 250)** | **May 7** | **61-38** [1] | **p. 75** |
| Motor-Voter Bill (S 250) | May 12 | 58-40 | p. 75 |
| **Drug Abuse Mental Health (S 1306)** | **June 9** | **84-9** | **p. 422** |
| Striker Replacement (S 55) | June 11 | 55-41 | p. 361 |
| Striker Replacement (S 55) | June 16 | 57-42 | p. 361 |
| Gov't Sponsored Enterprises/ Balanced Budget Amendment (S 2733) | June 30 | 56-39 | p. 123 |
| Gov't Sponsored Enterprises/ Balanced Budget Amendment (S 2733) | July 1 | 56-39 | p. 123 |
| National Energy Strategy (HR 776) | July 23 | 58-33 | p. 231 |
| **National Energy Strategy (HR 776)** | **July 28** | **93-3** | **p. 231** |
| **Edward Carnes Nomination** | **Sept. 9** | **66-30** | **p. 319** |
| Product Liability (S 640) | Sept. 10 | 57-39 | p. 210 |
| Product Liability (S 640) | Sept. 10 | 58-38 | p. 210 |
| **School Improvement Bill (S 2)** | **Sept. 15** | **85-6** | **p. 455** |
| Labor/HHS/ Education Appropriations (HR 5677) | Sept. 16 | 56-38 | p. 651 |
| **START Treaty (Treaty Doc. 102-20, 102-32)** | **Sept. 29** | **87-6** | **p. 513** |
| School Improvement Bill (S 2) | Oct. 2 | 59-40 | p. 455 |
| Crime Bill (HR 3371) | Oct. 2 | 55-43 | p. 311 |
| **NIH Reauthorization/ Fetal Tissue Research (S 2899)** | **Oct. 2** | **85-12** | **p. 413** |
| **National Energy Strategy (HR 776)** | **Oct. 8** | **84-8** | **p. 231** |
| **Tax Bill (HR 11)** | **Oct. 8** | **80-10** | **p. 140** |

[1] *First successful vote occurred on the motion to proceed to the bill.*

bluff, and his adjournment motion passed, 268-38, shortly after 12:30 p.m. That left Brooks standing at the podium.

Although most House members headed home, the chamber remained officially open for business — but only by unanimous consent in the House. It soon became clear that this would not be forthcoming.

The Senate bogged down over several bills:
● Alfonse M. D'Amato, R-N.Y., on Oct. 5-6 staged a one-man 15-hour-and-15-minute filibuster — the sixth longest in Senate history — to protest the removal of a provision from an urban aid tax bill that he said could have restored jobs at a New York typewriter plant.
● Nevada Democratic Sens. Richard H. Bryan and Harry

Reid threatened to do the same to the energy bill because it contained a provision that would have made it easier to put a nuclear waste dump in their state.
● To delay action on a water projects bill opposed by farmers in his state, John Seymour, R-Calif., on Oct. 6 forced a Senate clerk to read the bill aloud for hours.

Senate leaders eventually whipped the members back into line. D'Amato and Seymour, both in tough races, each agreed to deals in which they introduced free-standing bills addressing their concerns, which the Senate passed knowing that they would die in the House. Bryan and Reid conceded defeat for the year after being soundly defeated on a cloture vote Oct. 8.

■

# Members of the 102nd Congress, Second Session...

*(As of Oct. 31, 1992)*

## Representatives
## D 266; R 166; I 1; 2 Vacancies

### A

Abercrombie, Neil, D-Hawaii (1)
Ackerman, Gary L., D-N.Y. (7)
Alexander, Bill, D-Ark. (1)
Allard, Wayne, R-Colo. (4)
Allen, George F., R-Va. (7)
Anderson, Glenn M., D-Calif. (32)
Andrews, Michael A., D-Texas (25)
Andrews, Robert E., D-N.J. (1)
Andrews, Thomas H., D-Maine (1)
Annunzio, Frank, D-Ill. (11)
Anthony, Beryl Jr., D-Ark. (4)
Applegate, Douglas, D-Ohio (18)
Archer, Bill, R-Texas (7)
Armey, Dick, R-Texas (26)
Aspin, Les, D-Wis. (1)
Atkins, Chester G., D-Mass. (5)
AuCoin, Les, D-Ore. (1)

### B

Bacchus, Jim, D-Fla. (11)
Baker, Richard H., R-La. (6)
Ballenger, Cass, R-N.C. (10)
Barnard, Doug Jr., D-Ga. (10)
Barrett, Bill, R-Neb. (3)
Barton, Joe L., R-Texas (6)
Bateman, Herbert H., R-Va. (1)
Bellenson, Anthony C., D-Calif. (23)
Bennett, Charles E., D-Fla. (3)
Bentley, Helen Delich, R-Md. (2)
Bereuter, Doug, R-Neb. (1)
Berman, Howard L., D-Calif. (26)
Bevill, Tom, D-Ala. (4)
Bilbray, James, D-Nev. (1)
Bilirakis, Michael, R-Fla. (9)
Blackwell, Lucien E., D-Pa. (2)
Bliley, Thomas J. Jr., R-Va. (3)
Boehlert, Sherwood, R-N.Y. (25)
Boehner, John A., R-Ohio (8)
Bonior, David E., D-Mich. (12)
Borski, Robert A., D-Pa. (3)
Boucher, Rick, D-Va. (9)
Boxer, Barbara, D-Calif. (6)
Brewster, Bill, D-Okla. (3)
Brooks, Jack, D-Texas (9)
Broomfield, William S., R-Mich. (18)
Browder, Glen, D-Ala. (3)
Brown, George E. Jr., D-Calif. (36)
Bruce, Terry L., D-Ill. (19)
Bryant, John, D-Texas (5)
Bunning, Jim, R-Ky. (4)
Burton, Dan, R-Ind. (6)
Bustamante, Albert G., D-Texas (23)
Byron, Beverly B., D-Md. (6)

### C

Callahan, Sonny, R-Ala. (1)
Camp, Dave, R-Mich. (10)
Campbell, Ben Nighthorse, D-Colo. (3)
Campbell, Tom, R-Calif. (12)
Cardin, Benjamin L., D-Md. (3)
Carper, Thomas R., D-Del. (AL)
Carr, Bob, D-Mich. (6)
Chandler, Rod, R-Wash. (8)
Chapman, Jim, D-Texas (1)
Clay, William L., D-Mo. (1)
Clement, Bob, D-Tenn (5)
Clinger, William F., R-Pa. (23)
Coble, Howard, R-N.C. (6)
Coleman, Ronald D., D-Texas (16)
Coleman, Tom, R-Mo. (6)
Collins, Barbara-Rose, D-Mich. (13)
Collins, Cardiss, D-Ill. (7)
Combest, Larry, R-Texas (19)
Condit, Gary, D-Calif (15)
Conyers, John Jr., D-Mich. (1)
Cooper, Jim, D-Tenn. (4)
Costello, Jerry F. D-Ill. (21)
Coughlin, Lawrence, R-Pa. (13)

Cox, C. Christopher, R-Calif. (40)
Cox, John W. Jr., D-Ill. (16)
Coyne, William J., D-Pa. (14)
Cramer, Bud, D-Ala. (5)
Crane, Philip M., R-Ill. (12)
Cunningham, Randy "Duke," R-Calif. (44)

### D

Dannemeyer, William E., R-Calif. (39)
Darden, George "Buddy," D-Ga. (7)
Davis, Robert W., R-Mich. (11)
DeFazio, Peter A., D-Ore. (4)
de la Garza, E. "Kika," D-Texas (15)
DeLauro, Rosa, D-Conn. (3)
DeLay, Tom, R-Texas (22)
Dellums, Ronald V., D-Calif. (8)
Derrick, Butler, D-S.C. (3)
Dickinson, Bill, R-Ala. (2)
Dicks, Norm, D-Wash. (6)
Dingell, John D., D-Mich. (16)
Dixon, Julian C., D-Calif. (28)
Donnelly, Brian, D-Mass. (11)
Dooley, Calvin, D-Calif. (17)
Doolittle, John T., R-Calif. (14)
Dorgan, Byron L., D-N.D. (AL)
Dornan, Robert K., R-Calif. (38)
Downey, Thomas J., D-N.Y. (2)
Dreier, David, R-Calif. (33)
Duncan, John J. "Jimmy" Jr., R-Tenn. (2)
Durbin, Richard J., D-Ill. (20)
Dwyer, Bernard J., D-N.J. (6)
Dymally, Mervyn M., D-Calif. (31)

### E

Early, Joseph D., D-Mass. (3)
Eckart, Dennis E., D-Ohio (11)
Edwards, Chet, D-Texas (11)
Edwards, Don, D-Calif. (10)
Edwards, Mickey, R-Okla. (5)
Emerson, Bill, R-Mo. (8)
Engel, Eliot L., D-N.Y. (19)
English, Glenn, D-Okla. (6)
Erdreich, Ben, D-Ala. (6)
Espy, Mike, D-Miss. (2)
Evans, Lane, D-Ill. (17)
Ewing, Thomas W. R-Ill. (15)

### F

Fascell, Dante B., D-Fla. (19)
Fawell, Harris W., R-Ill. (13)
Fazio, Vic, D-Calif. (4)
Feighan, Edward F., D-Ohio (19)
Fields, Jack, R-Texas (8)
Fish, Hamilton Jr., R-N.Y. (21)
Flake, Floyd H., D-N.Y. (6)
Foglietta, Thomas M., D-Pa. (1)
Foley, Thomas S., D-Wash. (5)
Ford, Harold E., D-Tenn. (9)
Ford, William D., D-Mich. (15)
Frank, Barney, D-Mass. (4)
Franks, Gary, R-Conn. (5)
Frost, Martin, D-Texas (24)

### G

Gallegly, Elton, R-Calif. (21)
Gallo, Dean A., R-N.J. (11)
Gaydos, Joseph M., D-Pa. (20)
Gejdenson, Sam, D-Conn. (2)
Gekas, George W., R-Pa. (17)
Gephardt, Richard A., D-Mo. (3)
Geren, Pete, D-Texas (12)
Gibbons, Sam M., D-Fla. (7)
Gilchrest, Wayne T., R-Md. (1)
Gillmor, Paul E., R-Ohio (5)
Gilman, Benjamin A., R-N.Y. (22)
Gingrich, Newt, R-Ga. (6)
Glickman, Dan, D-Kan. (4)
Gonzalez, Henry B., D-Texas (20)
Goodling, Bill, R-Pa. (19)
Gordon, Bart, D-Tenn. (6)
Goss, Porter J. R-Fla. (13)
Gradison, Bill, R-Ohio (2)
Grandy, Fred, R-Iowa (6)
Green, Bill, R-N.Y. (15)
Guarini, Frank J., D-N.J. (14)
Gunderson, Steve, R-Wis. (3)

### H

Hall, Ralph M., D-Texas (4)
Hall, Tony P., D-Ohio (3)
Hamilton, Lee H., D-Ind. (9)
Hammerschmidt, John Paul, R-Ark. (3)
Hancock, Mel, R-Mo. (7)
Hansen, James V., R-Utah (1)
Harris, Claude, D-Ala. (7)
Hastert, Dennis, R-Ill. (14)
Hatcher, Charles, D-Ga. (2)
Hayes, Charles A., D-Ill. (1)
Hayes, Jimmy, D-La. (7)
Hefley, Joel, R-Colo. (5)
Hefner, W. G. "Bill," D-N.C. (8)
Henry, Paul B., R-Mich. (5)
Herger, Wally, R-Calif. (2)
Hertel, Dennis M., D-Mich. (14)
Hoagland, Peter, D-Neb. (2)
Hobson, David L., R-Ohio (7)
Hochbrueckner, George J., D-N.Y. (1)
Holloway, Clyde C., R-La. (8)
Hopkins, Larry J., R-Ky. (6)
Horn, Joan Kelly, D-Mo. (2)
Horton, Frank, R-N.Y. (29)
Houghton, Amo, R-N.Y. (34)
Hoyer, Steny H., D-Md. (5)
Hubbard, Carroll Jr., D-Ky. (1)
Huckaby, Jerry, D-La. (5)
Hughes, William J., D-N.J. (2)
Hunter, Duncan, R-Calif. (45)
Hutto, Earl, D-Fla. (1)
Hyde, Henry J., R-Ill. (6)

### I

Inhofe, James M., R-Okla. (1)
Ireland, Andy, R-Fla. (10)

### J

Jacobs, Andrew Jr., D-Ind. (10)
James, Craig T., R-Fla. (4)
Jefferson, William J., D-La. (2)
Jenkins, Ed, D-Ga. (9)
Johnson, Nancy L., R-Conn. (6)
Johnson, Sam, R-Texas (3)
Johnson, Tim, D-S.D. (AL)
Johnston, Harry A., D-Fla. (14)
Jones, Ben, D-Ga. (4)
Jontz, Jim, D-Ind. (5)

### K

Kanjorski, Paul E., D-Pa. (11)
Kaptur, Marcy, D-Ohio (9)
Kasich, John R., R-Ohio (12)
Kennedy, Joseph P. II, D-Mass. (8)
Kennelly, Barbara B., D-Conn. (1)
Kildee, Dale E., D-Mich. (7)
Kleczka, Gerald D., D-Wis. (4)
Klug, Scott L. R-Wis. (2)
Kolbe, Jim, R-Ariz. (5)
Kolter, Joe, D-Pa. (4)
Kopetski, Mike, D-Ore. (5)
Kostmayer, Peter H., D-Pa. (8)
Kyl, Jon, R-Ariz. (4)

### L

LaFalce, John J., D-N.Y. (32)
Lagomarsino, Robert J., R-Calif. (19)
Lancaster, H. Martin, D-N.C. (3)
Lantos, Tom, D-Calif. (11)
LaRocco, Larry, D-Idaho (1)
Laughlin, Greg, D-Texas (14)
Leach, Jim, R-Iowa (1)
Lehman, Richard H., D-Calif. (18)
Lehman, William, D-Fla. (17)
Lent, Norman F., R-N.Y. (4)
Levin, Sander M., D-Mich. (17)
Levine, Mel, D-Calif. (27)
Lewis, Jerry, R-Calif. (35)
Lewis, John, D-Ga. (5)
Lewis, Tom, R-Fla. (12)
Lightfoot, Jim Ross, R-Iowa (5)
Lipinski, William O., D-Ill. (5)
Livingston, Robert L., R-La. (1)
Lloyd, Marilyn, D-Tenn. (3)
Long, Jill L., D-Ind. (4)
Lowery, Bill, R-Calif. (41)
Lowey, Nita M., D-N.Y. (20)
Luken, Charles, D-Ohio (1)

### M

Machtley, Ronald K., R-R.I. (1)
Manton, Thomas J., D-N.Y. (9)
Markey, Edward J., D-Mass. (7)
Marlenee, Ron, R-Mont. (2)
Martin, David O'B., R-N.Y. (26)
Martinez, Matthew G., D-Calif. (30)
Matsui, Robert T., D-Calif. (3)
Mavroules, Nicholas, D-Mass. (6)
Mazzoli, Romano L., D-Ky. (3)
McCandless, Al, R-Calif. (37)
McCloskey, Frank, D-Ind. (8)
McCollum, Bill, R-Fla. (5)
McCrery, Jim, R-La. (4)
McCurdy, Dave, D-Okla. (4)
McDade, Joseph M., R-Pa. (10)
McDermott, Jim, D-Wash. (7)
McEwen, Bob, R-Ohio (6)
McGrath, Raymond J., R-N.Y. (5)
McHugh, Matthew F., D-N.Y. (28)
McMillan, Alex, R-N.C. (9)
McMillen, Tom, D-Md. (4)
McNulty, Michael R., D-N.Y. (23)
Meyers, Jan, R-Kan. (3)
Mfume, Kweisi, D-Md. (7)
Michel, Robert H., R-Ill. (18)
Miller, Clarence E., R-Ohio (10)
Miller, George, D-Calif. (7)
Miller, John, R-Wash. (1)
Mineta, Norman Y., D-Calif. (13)
Mink, Patsy T., D-Hawaii (2)
Moakley, Joe, D-Mass. (9)
Molinari, Susan, R-N.Y. (14)
Mollohan, Alan B., D-W.Va. (1)
Montgomery, G. V. "Sonny," D-Miss. (3)
Moody, Jim, D-Wis. (5)
Moorhead, Carlos J., R-Calif. (22)
Moran, James P. Jr., D-Va. (8)
Morella, Constance A., R-Md. (8)
Morrison, Sid, R-Wash. (4)
Mrazek, Robert J., D-N.Y. (3)
Murphy, Austin J., D-Pa. (22)
Murtha, John P., D-Pa. (12)
Myers, John T., R-Ind. (7)

### N

Nagle, Dave, D-Iowa (3)
Natcher, William H., D-Ky. (2)
Neal, Richard E., D-Mass. (2)
Neal, Stephen L., D-N.C. (5)
Nichols, Dick, R-Kan. (5)
Nowak, Henry J., D-N.Y. (33)
Nussle, Jim, R-Iowa (2)

### O

Oakar, Mary Rose, D-Ohio (20)
Oberstar, James L., D-Minn. (8)
Obey, David R., D-Wis. (7)
Olin, Jim, D-Va. (6)
Olver, John, D-Mass. (1)
Ortiz, Solomon P., D-Texas (27)
Orton, Bill, D-Utah (3)
Owens, Major R., D-N.Y. (12)
Owens, Wayne, D-Utah (2)
Oxley, Michael G., R-Ohio (4)

### P

Packard, Ron, R-Calif. (43)
Pallone, Frank Jr., D-N.J. (3)
Panetta, Leon E., D-Calif. (16)
Parker, Mike, D-Miss. (4)
Pastor, Ed, D-Ariz. (2)
Patterson, Liz J., D-S.C. (4)
Paxon, Bill, R-N.Y. (31)
Payne, Donald M., D-N.J. (10)
Payne, Lewis F. Jr., D-Va. (5)
Pease, Don J., D-Ohio (13)
Pelosi, Nancy, D-Calif. (5)
Penny, Timothy J., D-Minn. (1)
Perkins, Carl C., D-Ky. (7)
Peterson, Collin C., D-Minn. (7)
Peterson, Pete, D-Fla. (2)
Petri, Tom, R-Wis. (6)
Pickett, Owen B., D-Va. (2)
Pickle, J. J., D-Texas (10)
Porter, John, R-Ill. (10)
Poshard, Glenn, D-Ill. (22)

# ...Governors, Supreme Court, Cabinet-Rank Officers

Price, David, D-N.C. (4)
Pursell, Carl D., R-Mich. (2)

## Q, R

Quillen, James H., R-Tenn. (1)
Rahall, Nick J. II, D-W.Va. (4)
Ramstad, Jim, R-Minn. (3)
Rangel, Charles B., D-N.Y. (16)
Ravenel, Arthur Jr., R-S.C. (1)
Ray, Richard, D-Ga. (3)
Reed, John F., D-R.I. (2)
Regula, Ralph, R-Ohio (16)
Rhodes, John J. III, R-Ariz. (1)
Richardson, Bill, D-N.M. (3)
Ridge, Tom, R-Pa. (21)
Riggs, Frank, R-Calif. (1)
Rinaldo, Matthew J., R-N.J. (7)
Ritter, Don, R-Pa. (15)
Roberts, Pat, R-Kan. (1)
Roe, Robert A., D-N.J. (8)
Roemer, Tim, D-Ind. (3)
Rogers, Harold, R-Ky. (5)
Rohrabacher, Dana, R-Calif. (42)
Ros-Lehtinen, Ileana, R-Fla. (18)
Rose, Charlie, D-N.C. (7)
Rostenkowski, Dan, D-Ill. (8)
Roth, Toby, R-Wis. (8)
Roukema, Marge, R-N.J. (5)
Rowland, J. Roy, D-Ga. (8)
Roybal, Edward R., D-Calif. (25)
Russo, Marty, D-Ill. (3)

## S

Sabo, Martin Olav, D-Minn. (5)
Sanders, Bernard, I-Vt. (AL)
Sangmeister, George E., D-Ill. (4)
Santorum, Rick, R-Pa. (18)
Sarpalius, Bill, D-Texas (13)
Savage, Gus, D-Ill. (2)
Sawyer, Tom, D-Ohio (14)
Saxton, H. James, R-N.J. (13)
Schaefer, Dan, R-Colo. (6)
Scheuer, James H., D-N.Y. (8)
Schiff, Steven H., R-N.M. (1)
Schroeder, Patricia, D-Colo. (1)
Schulze, Dick, R-Pa. (5)
Schumer, Charles E., D-N.Y. (10)
Sensenbrenner, F. James Jr., R-Wis. (9)
Serrano, Jose E., D-N.Y. (18)
Sharp, Philip R., D-Ind. (2)
Shaw, E. Clay Jr., R-Fla. (15)
Shays, Christopher, R-Conn. (4)
Shuster, Bud, R-Pa. (9)
Sikorski, Gerry, D-Minn. (6)
Sisisky, Norman, D-Va. (4)
Skaggs, David E., D-Colo. (2)
Skeen, Joe, R-N.M. (2)
Skelton, Ike, D-Mo. (4)
Slattery, Jim, D-Kan. (2)
Slaughter, Louise M., D-N.Y. (30)
Smith, Bob, R-Ore. (2)
Smith, Christopher H., R-N.J. (4)
Smith, Lamar, R-Texas (21)
Smith, Lawrence J., D-Fla. (16)
Smith, Neal, D-Iowa (4)
Snowe, Olympia J., R-Maine (2)
Solarz, Stephen J., D-N.Y. (13)
Solomon, Gerald B. H., R-N.Y. (24)
Spence, Floyd D., R-S.C. (2)
Spratt, John M. Jr., D-S.C. (5)
Staggers, Harley O. Jr., D-W.Va. (2)
Stallings, Richard, D-Idaho (2)
Stark, Pete, D-Calif. (9)
Stearns, Cliff, R-Fla. (6)
Stenholm, Charles W., D-Texas (17)
Stokes, Louis, D-Ohio (21)
Studds, Gerry E., D-Mass. (10)
Stump, Bob, R-Ariz. (3)
Sundquist, Don, R-Tenn. (7)
Swett, Dick, D-N.H. (2)
Swift, Al, D-Wash. (2)
Synar, Mike, D-Okla. (2)

## T

Tallon, Robin, D-S.C. (6)
Tanner, John, D-Tenn. (8)
Tauzin, W. J. "Billy," D-La. (3)
Taylor, Charles H., R-N.C. (11)

Taylor, Gene, D-Miss. (5)
Thomas, Bill, R-Calif. (20)
Thomas, Craig, R-Wyo. (AL)
Thomas, Lindsay, D-Ga. (1)
Thornton, Ray, D-Ark. (2)
Torres, Esteban E., D-Calif. (34)
Torricelli, Robert G., D-N.J. (9)
Towns, Edolphus, D-N.Y. (11)
Traficant, James A. Jr., D-Ohio (17)
Traxler, Bob, D-Mich. (8)

## U, V, W

Unsoeld, Jolene, D-Wash. (3)
Upton, Fred, R-Mich. (4)
Valentine, Tim, D-N.C. (2)
Vander Jagt, Guy, R-Mich. (9)
Vento, Bruce F., D-Minn. (4)
Visclosky, Peter J., D-Ind. (1)
Volkmer, Harold L., D-Mo. (9)
Vucanovich, Barbara F., R-Nev. (2)
Walker, Robert S., R-Pa. (16)
Walsh, James T., R-N.Y. (27)
Washington, Craig, D-Texas (18)
Waters, Maxine, D-Calif. (29)
Waxman, Henry A., D-Calif. (24)
Weber, Vin, R-Minn. (2)
Weldon, Curt, R-Pa. (7)
Wheat, Alan, D-Mo. (5)
Whitten, Jamie L., D-Miss. (1)
Williams, Pat, D-Mont. (1)
Wilson, Charles, D-Texas (2)
Wise, Bob, D-W.Va. (3)
Wolf, Frank R., R-Va. (10)
Wolpe, Howard, D-Mich. (3)
Wyden, Ron, D-Ore. (3)
Wylie, Chalmers P., R-Ohio (15)

## X, Y, Z

Yates, Sidney R., D-Ill. (9)
Yatron, Gus, D-Pa. (6)
Young, C. W. Bill, R-Fla. (8)
Young, Don, R-Alaska (AL)
Zeliff, Bill, R-N.H. (1)
Zimmer, Dick, R-N.J. (12)

## Delegates

Blaz, Ben, R-Guam
de Lugo, Ron, D-Virgin Islands
Faleomavaega, Eni F.H., D-Am. Samoa
Norton, Eleanor Holmes, D-D.C.

## Resident Commissioner

Colorado, Antonio J., Pop. Dem.-
Puerto Rico

## Senators

### D 57; R 43

Adams, Brock, D-Wash.
Akaka, Daniel K., D-Hawaii
Baucus, Max, D-Mont.
Bentsen, Lloyd, D-Texas
Biden, Joseph R. Jr., D-Del.
Bingaman, Jeff, D-N.M.
Bond, Christopher S., R-Mo.
Boren, David L., D-Okla.
Bradley, Bill, D-N.J.
Breaux, John B., D-La.
Brown, Hank, R-Colo.
Bryan, Richard H., D-Nev.
Bumpers, Dale, D-Ark.
Burdick, Jocelyn Birch, D-N.D.
Burns, Conrad, R-Mont.
Byrd, Robert C., D-W.Va.
Chafee, John H., R-R.I.
Coats, Daniel R., R-Ind.
Cochran, Thad, R-Miss.
Cohen, William S., R-Maine
Conrad, Kent, D-N.D.
Craig, Larry E., R-Idaho
Cranston, Alan, D-Calif.
D'Amato, Alfonse M., R-N.Y.
Danforth, John C., R-Mo.
Daschle, Tom, D-S.D.

DeConcini, Dennis, D-Ariz.
Dixon, Alan J., D-Ill.
Dodd, Christopher J., D-Conn.
Dole, Bob, R-Kan.
Domenici, Pete V., R-N.M.
Durenberger, Dave, R-Minn.
Exon, Jim, D-Neb.
Ford, Wendell H., D-Ky.
Fowler, Wyche Jr., D-Ga.
Garn, Jake, R-Utah
Glenn, John, D-Ohio
Gore, Al, D-Tenn.
Gorton, Slade, R-Wash.
Graham, Bob, D-Fla.
Gramm, Phil, R-Texas
Grassley, Charles E., R-Iowa
Harkin, Tom, D-Iowa
Hatch, Orrin G., R-Utah
Hatfield, Mark O., R-Ore.
Heflin, Howell, D-Ala.
Helms, Jesse, R-N.C.
Hollings, Ernest F., D-S.C.
Inouye, Daniel K., D-Hawaii
Jeffords, James M., R-Vt.
Johnston, J. Bennett, D-La.
Kassebaum, Nancy Landon, R-Kan.
Kasten, Bob, R-Wis.
Kennedy, Edward M., D-Mass.
Kerrey, Bob, D-Neb.
Kerry, John, D-Mass.
Kohl, Herb, D-Wis.
Lautenberg, Frank R., D-N.J.
Leahy, Patrick J., D-Vt.
Levin, Carl, D-Mich.
Lieberman, Joseph I., D-Conn.
Lott, Trent, R-Miss.
Lugar, Richard G., R-Ind.
Mack, Connie, R-Fla.
McCain, John, R-Ariz.
McConnell, Mitch, R-Ky.
Metzenbaum, Howard M., D-Ohio
Mikulski, Barbara A., D-Md.
Mitchell, George J., D-Maine
Moynihan, Daniel Patrick, D-N.Y.
Murkowski, Frank H., R-Alaska
Nickles, Don, R-Okla.
Nunn, Sam, D-Ga.
Packwood, Bob, R-Ore.
Pell, Claiborne, D-R.I.
Pressler, Larry, R-S.D.
Pryor, David, D-Ark.
Reid, Harry, D-Nev.
Riegle, Donald W. Jr., D-Mich.
Robb, Charles S., D-Va.
Rockefeller, John D. IV, D-W.Va.
Roth, William V. Jr., R-Del.
Rudman, Warren B., R-N.H.
Sanford, Terry, D-N.C.
Sarbanes, Paul S., D-Md.
Sasser, Jim, D-Tenn.
Seymour, John, R-Calif.
Shelby, Richard C., D-Ala.
Simon, Paul, D-Ill.
Simpson, Alan K., R-Wyo.
Smith, Robert C., R-N.H.
Specter, Arlen, R-Pa.
Stevens, Ted, R-Alaska
Symms, Steve, R-Idaho
Thurmond, Strom, R-S.C.
Wallop, Malcolm, R-Wyo.
Warner, John W., R-Va.
Wellstone, Paul, D-Minn.
Wirth, Tim, D-Colo.
Wofford, Harris L. Jr., D-Pa.

## Governors

### D 28; R 20; I 2

Ala.—Guy Hunt, R
Alaska—Walter J. Hickel, I
Ariz.—Fife Symington, R
Ark.—Bill Clinton, D
Calif.—Pete Wilson, R
Colo.—Roy Romer, D
Conn.—Lowell P. Weicker Jr., I
Del.—Michael N. Castle, R

Fla.—Lawton Chiles, D
Ga.—Zell Miller, D
Hawaii—John Waihee III, D
Idaho—Cecil D. Andrus, D
Ill.—Jim Edgar, R
Ind.—Evan Bayh, D
Iowa—Terry E. Branstad, R
Kan.—Joan Finney, D
Ky.—Brereton Jones, D
La.—Edwin W. Edwards, D
Maine—John R. McKernan Jr., R
Md.—William Donald Schaefer, D
Mass.—William F. Weld, R
Mich.—John Engler, R
Minn.—Arne Carlson, R
Miss.—Kirk Fordice, R
Mo.—John Ashcroft, R
Mont.—Stan Stephens, R
Neb.—Ben Nelson, D
Nev.—Bob Miller, D
N.H.—Judd Gregg, R
N.J.—James J. Florio, D
N.M.—Bruce King, D
N.Y.—Mario M. Cuomo, D
N.C.—James G. Martin, R
N.D.—George Sinner, D
Ohio—George V. Voinovich, R
Okla.—David Walters, D
Ore.—Barbara Roberts, D
Pa.—Robert P. Casey, D
R.I.—Bruce Sundlun, D
S.C.—Carroll A. Campbell Jr., R
S.D.—George S. Mickelson, R
Tenn.—Ned McWherter, D
Texas—Ann W. Richards, D
Utah—Norman H. Bangerter, R
Vt.—Howard Dean, D
Va.—L. Douglas Wilder, D
Wash.—Booth Gardner, D
W.Va.—Gaston Caperton, D
Wis.—Tommy G. Thompson, R
Wyo.—Mike Sullivan, D

## Supreme Court

Rehnquist, William H.—Va., Chief Justice
Blackmun, Harry A.—Minn.
Kennedy, Anthony M.—Calif.
O'Connor, Sandra Day—Ariz.
Scalia, Antonin—Va.
Souter, David H.—N.H.
Stevens, John Paul—Ill.
Thomas, Clarence—Ga.
White, Byron R.—Colo.

## Cabinet

Alexander, Lamar—Education
Barr, William P.—Attorney General
Brady, Nicholas F.—Treasury
Card, Andrew H.—Transportation
Cheney, Dick—Defense
Derwinski, Edward J.—Veterans Affairs [1]
Eagleburger, Lawrence S.—State (Acting) [2]
Franklin, Barbara H.—Commerce
Kemp, Jack F.—HUD
Lujan, Manuel Jr.—Interior
Madigan, Edward—Agriculture
Martin, Lynn—Labor
Sullivan, Louis W.—HHS
Watkins, James D.—Energy

## Other Executive Branch Officers

Darman, Richard G.—OMB Director
Hills, Carla A.—U.S. Trade Representative
Martinez, Bob—Director, Drug Policy
Quayle, Dan—Vice President
Baker, James A. III—Chief of Staff [2]

---

[1] Derwinski resigned his post Sept. 26, 1992.
No replacement was named.
[2] Eagleburger was appointed Acting Secretary of State on Aug. 13, 1992, when Baker was moved to the White House as Chief of Staff to replace Samuel K. Skinner, who had held that post since Dec. 5, 1991.

# Clinton's Win Spurs Rapid Organization

Party caucuses moved quickly to organize for the 103rd Congress, electing leaders, taking steps toward updating congressional procedures and beginning the task of absorbing the large group of freshmen elected in 1992.

At their organizing caucus Dec. 7-10, House Democrats accomplished in days what typically took weeks or months. With the aim of having the House humming before Bill Clinton was sworn in, Democrats unanimously re-elected their entire leadership, approved every anointed committee chairman, doled out scores of new panel assignments and adopted a controversial series of rule changes.

Activist conservatives tightened their grip on the House Republican Conference during their organizational meetings Dec. 7-9.

Few changes were made on the Senate side during meetings Nov. 10. Both parties kept their Senate leadership teams virtually intact. Senate committees did not fill their seats before the 103rd Congress began.

## HOUSE DEMOCRATS' ORGANIZATION

The House Democrats' meetings Dec. 7-10 focused on proposals to change House rules. To Democrats, the rules changes were designed to streamline the legislative process and enhance leadership power to direct it. Louise M. Slaughter, D-N.Y., who chaired the leadership subcommittee of the caucus that drafted the proposals, saw the changes as the key to fulfilling Clinton's pledge to make the next Congress "one of the most productive in history."

But Republicans depicted several rules changes as a transparent effort to bind and gag them. They focused on one proposal to limit the time available for "special orders," which members used to address the House after the conclusion of regular business, and on another to give the five delegates from the U.S. territories and the District of Columbia — all Democrats — power to vote on key questions on the floor. *(Delegates' votes, p. 14)*

Democrats approved these changes, but late in the week their leaders began softening their positions. They set up a task force to rethink the delegate voting rules, and House Speaker Thomas S. Foley directed the caucus to reverse its position on the special orders limits.

The new rules — minus the special orders and with a compromise on delegate voting to keep their votes from being decisive — were approved by the House on Jan. 5, 1993, on a largely party-line vote of 221-199.

As approved by the House, the rules package made these changes in the way the House went about its business:

● **Subcommittees.** The eight major committees and the Government Operations and House Administration panels were limited to six subcommittees, rather than eight; the remaining committees could have five. The exclusive committees, Appropriations and Ways and Means, were exempt from the limits. The Foreign Affairs Committee sought a waiver to have seven subcommittees to ensure a panel devoted to Africa, which was demanded by the Congressional Black Caucus.

Members were limited to no more than five subcommittee assignments — including select committees and task forces, except for the Select Intelligence Committee.

● **Committee meetings.** Panels would henceforth be allowed to meet while the House or the Committee of the Whole was in session. Previously, the "five-minute rule" had prevented committees from meeting without permission of the House while the House was debating amendments. Democrats said that rule made it difficult to schedule committee meetings and routine floor action. Republicans argued that the new rule would discourage floor participation and permit chairmen to abuse the system.

● **Rolling quorums.** Committee chairmen were allowed to declare the quorum needed to draft legislation once a majority of members has been in attendance for some part of the session. Previously, a bill could be ruled out of order on the House floor if the quorum had not been present at the same time.

● **Conferees.** The Speaker was given power to remove any House conferee from a House-Senate conference or to add additional members. Democrats said the power would prevent deadlock. Republicans said it would give the Speaker too much power.

● **Privileged motions.** The Speaker was given power to delay for two legislative days debate on privileged motions dealing with the rights of the House collectively and the integrity of its proceedings. Previously, these motions took precedence over other floor action. An exception was provided for the majority and minority leaders, whose motions would receive immediate attention. Privileged motions regarding an individual member's rights were not affected.

Republicans argued that by threatening to bring up privileged motions on the House bank, they persuaded the Democrats to release key information. *(House bank scandal, p. 23)*

● **Teller votes.** Once a principal method of voting, "teller votes" — in which members filed past stations where the number for and against a question was counted — were abolished on the grounds that they wasted time.

● **Authorizing language on appropriations bills.** The chairmen of the authorizing committees, who frequently complained about the Senate's adding legislation to appropriations bills that the House could not, were given an opportunity to offer a preferential motion to insist on disagreement with the Senate in consideration of a conference report.

### Caucus Debates Committees

In terms of changing the way the House wrote legislation, the most significant change was probably the decision to eliminate 16 subcommittees. The cuts were approved by the Democratic Caucus on a division vote of 87-35. An effort by Benjamin L. Cardin, Md., to eliminate seven more subcommittees was defeated by voice vote.

The House's select committees temporarily survived a push by Cardin and several other members to do away with them. At a last-minute meeting of the leadership rules panel Dec. 7, Cardin won approval of a plan to phase out the five select committees, which were not authorized to write legislation. Charles B. Rangel, D-N.Y., who chaired the Select Narcotics Abuse and Control Committee, strenuously opposed the plan. After a heated debate, the caucus agreed to strike Cardin's proposal to limit the committees' reauthorization to one year. At the beginning of the new Congress, however, the committee's future was again uncertain.

The caucus adopted rules for its own proceedings af-

fecting the way chairmen were chosen and retained. Under the new rules, if 14 of the 35 members of the Steering and Policy Committee voted against a chairman, an open vote would be held with nominations open to the floor. Steering and Policy also was given the power to declare the chairmanship of a committee or a subcommittee vacant, and the matter would go to the full caucus for a vote. Any committee member could be removed by the same process.

The caucus voted to establish a party policy council to set an agenda. The 20-member panel, officially called the Speaker's Working Group on Policy Development, would be handpicked by the Speaker, with half of its members coming from the Steering and Policy Committee.

That was a compromise, reached Dec. 3, between different factions within the party that had been jockeying throughout the fall for a strong role in setting an agenda for the House.

The Democratic Study Group (DSG), a liberal organization, proposed changes the week of Sept. 28 that infuriated many sitting committee chairmen. Some activist Democrats wanted to wrest control of the agenda from the committee chairmen who, they complained, ran separate fiefdoms. The DSG called for priorities to be set by a working group on policy made up primarily of leaders and rank-and-file Democrats. The chairmen asked that all 21 of them be included in any policy group.

The compromise gave power to the Speaker and dropped a proposal by Slaughter's panel to call the group the Democratic Policy Council, which some members felt implied that it would have power to set an agenda for which committee chairmen would be held accountable.

The caucus added a fourth chief deputy whip: Bill Richardson, D-N.M.

Democrats did an about-face on speaking privileges during the week. On the morning of Dec. 9, the caucus voted 174-35 to set strict limits on special orders. Under the rules change, the speeches could not have gone on for more than three hours or after 9 p.m., whichever came first.

Republicans objected strongly. They viewed the speeches, which were broadcast nationwide on C-SPAN, as a rare and essential chance for the minority to be heard.

Republican whip Newt Gingrich of Georgia said limits would "poison the well" for all future interparty dealing.

Democrats cited a Congressional Research Service report saying that it cost $800,000 to print the special orders in 1991 and a House clerk's memo saying utilities, videotape and printing amounted to $3,700 an hour to keep the House open late at night.

But the Democratic leadership was unwilling to risk Republican guerrilla warfare over it. Within an hour of the caucus vote to limit special orders, Foley sat down with Minority Leader Robert H. Michel, R-Ill., to discuss it. The next morning, at Foley's behest, the caucus reversed its position. It also retreated from a rules change that would have limited each party to 10 one-minute speeches at the beginning of the day.

## HOUSE REPUBLICAN ORGANIZATION

During GOP organizational meetings Dec. 7-9 in the Cannon Caucus Room, activist conservatives aided by a freshman class bent on change dethroned the incumbent House Republican Conference chairman, retained control over every other top post below Michel, imposed term limits and other restrictions on GOP committee leaders to check the moderate tendencies of some, and curbed the

---

## Leaders for 103rd Congress

### SENATE

President Pro Tempore — Robert C. Byrd, D-W.Va.
Majority Leader — George J. Mitchell, D-Maine
Majority Whip — Wendell H. Ford, D-Ky.
Secretary of the Democratic Conference — David Pryor, D-Ark.

Minority Leader — Bob Dole, R-Kan.
Assistant Minority Leader — Alan K. Simpson, R-Wyo.
Chairman of the Republican Conference — Thad Cochran, R-Miss.
Secretary of the Republican Conference — Trent Lott, R-Miss.

### HOUSE

Speaker — Thomas S. Foley, D-Wash.
Majority Leader — Richard A. Gephardt, D-Mo.
Majority Whip — David E. Bonior, D-Mich.
Chairman of the Democratic Caucus — Steny H. Hoyer, D-Md.

Minority Leader — Robert H. Michel, R-Ill.
Minority Whip — Newt Gingrich, R-Ga.
Chairman of the Republican Conference — Dick Armey, R-Texas
Chairman of the Republican Policy Committee — Henry J. Hyde, R-Ill.

---

power of members to free-lance with the Democratic majority.

A rump movement to oust numerous committees' ranking minority members failed, but House Administration's Bill Thomas of California barely survived.

"The loyal opposition just strengthened itself," said Robert S. Walker, Pa., one of the House's most confrontational conservatives.

From the opposite side, Marge Roukema, N.J., was forlorn: "The leadership is now unduly weighted toward the ideological right wing of the party."

In each of three contested leadership elections for the 103rd Congress, the more conservative candidate prevailed on secret ballots during the closed-door proceedings.

Dick Armey of Texas unseated Republican Conference Chairman Jerry Lewis, Calif., 88-84 on Dec. 7. The next day, Conference Vice Chairman Bill McCollum, Fla., beat Nancy L. Johnson, Conn., 93-70, and Tom DeLay, Texas, beat Bill Gradison, Ohio, 95-71, for the vacant conference secretary post. Gradison did not campaign actively, and early in the 103rd Congress he resigned his seat to work for a health insurance organization.

Michel of Illinois was re-elected by acclamation, but it was clear that he was the lone moderate in an influential position. Michel's designee on the Budget Committee, Alex McMillan, N.C., was beaten by the more activist John R. Kasich, Ohio, for the panel's ranking Republican post.

Also re-elected without challenge were Gingrich, the activists' point man, and Research Committee Chairman Duncan Hunter, Calif. Promoted to the leadership unopposed were Henry J. Hyde, Ill., the new Policy Committee chairman, and Bill Paxon, N.Y., the new chairman of the

*Continued on p. 16*

# House Grants Voting Privileges...

Democrats decided in 1993 that beginning the next year, they would give key floor-voting privileges to the delegates sent by the U.S. territories and the District of Columbia. The action outraged Republicans, who said it would effectively cut in half the gains they had made in 1992 elections, and set the stage for floor confrontations and court tests of the constitutionality of the move.

Under the new rule, the delegates were given the right to vote whenever the House was considering legislation in the Committee of the Whole — a parliamentary framework under which the entire House met to debate and amend important legislation; the procedure allowed for faster action. The delegates already had the right to vote in the House's regular committees.

Democrats approved the proposal, an amendment to the rules of the House, on Dec. 9 as they organized for the 103rd Congress. It was approved Jan. 5, 1993, by the full House as part of a package of rules changes. Leaders made a key modification shortly before the rule was formally adopted in January, allowing the House to revote on any issue decided by the delegates' votes. *(Organization, p. 12)*

The architect of the proposal was Del. Eleanor Holmes Norton of the District of Columbia. She convinced her fellow Democrats that there was no legal distinction between voting in committees and voting on the floor in the Committee of the Whole.

Other beneficiaries were Ron de Lugo of the Virgin Islands, Robert J. Underwood of Guam, Eni F. H. Faleomavaega of American Samoa and Carlos Romero-Barcelo, the resident commissioner of Puerto Rico. All five were Democrats.

Republicans objected strenuously Feb. 3, 1993, when the House held its first roll call votes on which the previously non-voting delegates were allowed to participate. They demanded two re-votes on amendments to a family-leave bill, votes they were entitled to because House rules allowed members to demand a new vote on any amendment adopted in the Committee of the Whole. Republicans also challenged the constitutionality of the rules in a suit in federal court. *(Family leave, p. 353)*

"It's a joke. It's an abuse of power," said Minority Whip Newt Gingrich, R-Ga. "They know they're wrong."

## BACKGROUND

The origin of the office of the territorial delegate could be traced to 1789, when the First Congress ratified the Northwest Ordinance. That act provided that the government of the"[t]erritory of the United States north-west of the river Ohio [could] elect a delegate to Congress, who shall have a seat in Congress, with a right of debating, but not voting during this temporary government."

Historians trace the origin of committee participation, and thus voting, to the first delegate from the Northwest Territories, James White. William Henry Harrison, who was elected as the nation's second delegate in 1799 and later became president, chaired several committees and steered passage of the Land Act of 1800.

Records from a House committee in 1841 state: "With the single exception of voting, the delegate enjoys every other privilege and exercises every other right of a representative. He can act as a member of a standing or select committee and vote on the business before said committees, and he may thus exercise an important influence on those initiatory proceedings by which business is prepared for the action of the House."

In an 1871 change in House rules, delegates traded their right to vote in committee for assurance that they would serve on the committees most important to them: the Committee on the District of Columbia and the Committee on the Territories.

The House restored one delegate's power to participate in committee votes in an amendment to the 1970 Legislative Reorganization Act. The amended House Rule XII stated, "The Resident Commissioner [of Puerto Rico] ... shall possess in such committees the same powers and privileges as the other members." In 1971, H Res 5 extended the privileges to the delegate from the District of Columbia. In 1973, the language was generalized to apply to "each delegate to the House." Delegates had been commonly referred to as "non-voting delegates" since the Northwest Ordinance.

## NORTON TAKES THE LEAD

Norton, a former law professor at Georgetown University, came to Congress in 1991 as the chief proponent of statehood — and full voting rights in both the House and Senate — for the District of Columbia. She said the idea to ask for a vote in the Committee of the Whole as an interim step occurred to her during her first campaign. She began by getting a Congressional Research Service legal opinion on the constitutional or statutory problems that could result from the rule change. In its Nov. 16 opinion, the research service's American Law Division concluded: "Since Congress has arguably treated the Committee of the Whole as if it were not the full House for purposes of a quorum, and since Congress has previously allowed delegates to vote in committees, allowing a delegate to vote in the Committee of the Whole is apparently consistent with present congressional interpretation of its constitutional authority."

Most Democrats first got wind of the proposal in December, when it was presented to the Democratic Caucus for approval. But few seriously thought through the implications, politically or legally.

Several members said later that in private discussions there was considerable skittishness over the idea. "Many members of the caucus have constitutional and political difficulties with this," said David E. Skaggs, D-Colo.

The skittishness came principally from allowing delegates who represented thinly populated territories such as American Samoa (population 47,000) to have virtually the same power on many House votes as the single at-large representative of Montana (population 799,000).

To the public, there was little visible distinction between the full House and the Committee of the Whole. The latter procedure was used chiefly for considering amendments to legislation. It allowed actions to proceed with a smaller quorum (100 members instead of 218) and had an

# . . .To Delegates From D.C., Territories

automatic 5-minute limit on debate on amendments.

Some Democrats wanted to draw a distinction that would allow voting privileges for the District's 607,000 residents, who, unlike residents of the territories, paid federal income taxes, or Puerto Rico's 3.6 million.

But few Democrats wanted to go on record against the idea of voting privileges, partly because they liked Norton and her legislative activism, a contrast to the last years of her predecessor, Walter E. Fauntroy.

Skaggs offered an amendment to require the House to revisit any issue decided by delegate votes in the Committee of the Whole. He withdrew it after pleas from party leaders, who said they were not sure how a vote would go.

The Democratic Caucus approved Norton's proposal by voice vote Dec. 9, but misgivings continued to grow. Later that week, Democratic leaders announced that they had set up a task force to re-examine the issue before the full House considered it in January.

Republicans greeted news of the Democrats' decision with outrage. "The votes of our constituents are being significantly diluted," said House Minority Leader Robert H. Michel, R-Ill. "The 10-vote increase that we got [in the November election] is already cut in half."

"It's just a terrible way to start a Congress where Clinton needs bipartisan support and the American people want bipartisan cooperation," said Steve Gunderson, R-Wis.

## CONGRESS' OPENING FIGHT

By January, it was evident that a majority of Democrats had serious reservations about Norton's proposal. Some members feared that it might be unconstitutional, while others expressed concern about fairness. Between the caucus meeting and the convening of the full House, Democratic leaders sent staff members into the chamber to remove a newly installed panel that would have listed delegate names on the vote tally scoreboard above the House floor. More important, they put out word that they were open to a compromise.

Skaggs revived his amendment, which provided that whenever a question was decided on the strength of delegate votes, regardless of whether it was approved or rejected, the committee would dissolve and the House would immediately vote on the issue without the delegates. The House would then turn itself back into the Committee of the Whole.

Four questions were decided by five or fewer votes in 1992.

The Democratic Caucus held a series of votes on the issue Jan. 5 before the House convened. It first voted 186-16 for the Skaggs amendment and then voted 170-45 for the amended proposal to allow the delegate votes. In addition to the 45 votes against the leadership compromise, 43 Democrats did not vote. The caucus then voted 173-28 to pass the entire package.

### Bitter Floor Action

When the swearing-in ceremonies ended and the floor fight over the rules proposals began, Republicans spared no fire. The maiden speeches of many Republican freshmen set a sharply partisan tone.

"Many a wayward politician embarked on the wrong path when he started to stuff the ballot box," said Rep. Ernest Jim Istook, R-Okla.

Roscoe G. Bartlett, R-Md., called the rule "wrongheaded and manifestly unfair." Steve Horn, R-Calif., said the leadership was "poisoning the waters."

Republicans dusted off a 1970 quote by Speaker Thomas S. Foley, D-Wash., opposing such delegate votes. They declared that it took legislation rather than a rule change to give the delegates votes on committees. And they ridiculed the Skaggs amendment.

"When they vote when it counts, it does not count," Rep. Robert S. Walker, R-Pa., said of the delegates, "and when it does not count, it counts."

Democrats joined the war of words, but the defense fell primarily to Norton, the other delegates and a handful of key leadership loyalists. The freshmen were notably silent.

Del. Faleomavaega noted that he was a Vietnam veteran, and Del. de Lugo reminded colleagues that three of his constituents were among the first to die in the Persian Gulf War.

The debate was harsher than most opening-day proceedings, but in the end the votes were neither close nor surprising. The House voted 224-176, with 10 Democrats and no Republicans defecting, to kill a GOP amendment to set up a task force to study the delegate question.

After a subsequent vote, in which all but three Democrats and no Republicans voted to cut off debate and amendments, the House voted 187-238 against a Republican motion to strike the delegate language from the rules package and impose term limits on committee chairmen and ranking members.

The House then approved the rules package including the delegate proposal on a largely party-line vote of 221-199.

On Jan. 7, House Minority Leader Michel and a group of fellow Republicans filed suit in U.S. District Court in Washington challenging the new rule.

U.S. District Judge Harold H. Greene held a hearing on the suit Feb. 9. Republicans offered three main arguments on why they felt the delegate voting procedure was unconstitutional:

● The Committee of the Whole was not a committee, as the majority claimed. It was, they said, tantamount to the full House and should be governed by the Constitution's provisions detailing House powers.

● A vote in the Committee of the Whole effectively franchised citizens of the territories and the District of Columbia at the expense of state citizens and their representatives, whose voting power was diminished by the greater vote totals.

● Delegates were granted committee voting privileges by law, not House rule, and the House could not expand those powers without statutory authority granted by the full Congress and the president.

On March 8, 1993, Judge Greene ruled that the delegate voting procedure was constitutional because "the votes . . . are meaningless." Without the second vote in close calls, the rule would have plainly been unconstitiutional," he wrote.

*Continued from p. 13*
Republican Congressional Campaign Committee.

The Lewis-Armey race for the No. 3 spot in the leadership was the week's key fight. Both had been campaigning for months. Armey's challenge was based mainly on his charge that Lewis was too cozy with the Democrats. Though Armey said he did not focus on ideology, Lewis was considered more moderate.

The conference voted to limit the terms of ranking minority members to three two-year terms, not counting service prior to the 103rd Congress. Proposed by Rep.-elect John Linder, Ga., it was approved 82-44 on Dec. 8 after a motion to study the issue failed 65-76. Opposing it were mostly senior members, including Bud Shuster, Pa., who was due to take over the top GOP spot on the Public Works Committee in 1993, and Don Young, Alaska, the top Republican on the Interior Committee since 1985.

The new rule required a complete turnover of every full committee's ranking Republican position in 1999, at the start of the 106th Congress. (Subcommittees would not be affected.)

That would represent a fundamental shift for Republicans, who even more than Democrats usually gave their top committee posts to each panel's most senior member.

"Now the ball's in the Democrats' court," said Rep.-elect Robert W. Goodlatte, Va.

The Democrats' chief proponent of term limits for committee chairmen, Dave McCurdy, Okla., considered offering a proposal during his party's caucus the week of Dec. 7 to limit the terms of chairmen and ranking Republicans and give the Speaker and minority leader more power in naming them. But he dropped the idea, saying he did not have the votes.

Young predicted that his colleagues would reverse course within the next six years, once it became clear that the Democrats would not budge. "If it were both sides, it would work," said Young. "If they don't do it, we're silly to do it."

In other action, the conference:

● Prohibited most committees' ranking Republicans from serving as the top GOP member of any subcommittee starting in 1995 with the 104th Congress. Proposed by Rep. John A. Boehner of Ohio, it passed 63-56.

The move was designed to empower junior members at the expense of senior members, including some moderates, such as Bill Goodling, Pa., the top Republican on the Education and Labor Committee and its grade-school subcommittee. Goodling said he would fight to repeal the rule.

● Declined to force indicted ranking minority committee members to step aside, as the Democrats required of indicted chairmen. The caucus instead, by voice vote, set up a task force to study the issue.

The proposal would have forced Joseph M. McDade, Pa., to give up his job as top Republican on the Appropriations Committee while fighting a corruption indictment. The change was proposed by Rep.-elect Peter G. Torkildsen, Mass., who had promised to push for it in his campaign to unseat indicted Rep. Nicholas Mavroules, D-Mass.

● Gave freshman classes a spot in the leadership, which previously included just the eight elected leaders plus the top Republicans on the Rules, Ways and Means, Appropriations and Budget committees. The proposal, approved by voice vote, evidenced the strength of the 47-member freshman GOP class, which elected as its leader Michael D. Crapo of Idaho.

● Passed a rule, by voice vote, aimed at preventing moderate Republicans from conspiring with Democrats to offer what sponsor Dana Rohrabacher, Calif., called "sweetheart motions" on the floor that blocked conservative Republicans from offering their own proposals.

The rule required that whenever the Republicans were granted a preferential motion — to instruct conferees to adopt a certain position in negotiation with the Senate, for example — the leadership would have to pick the proposal that best reflected the views of the GOP caucus and leaders.

## HOUSE COMMITTEE ORGANIZATION

Congress' seniority system emerged almost unscathed during a week of House politicking Dec. 7-11 over committee chairmen, ranking Republicans and new committee assignments.

With one exception, every committee chairman who won re-election retained his presiding seat. In the Republican Conference, all former ranking members held on to their posts, and 12 new ranking members moved up to fill vacancies.

The Democrats' Steering and Policy Committee the week of Dec. 7 made its recommendations for who should sit on the major committees, with the freshman class, women and minorities making inroads into the three most popular — Appropriations, Ways and Means, and Energy and Commerce. The Republicans' Committee on Committees finished making its committee assignments by the end of the week.

Playing out a drama that began when Jamie L. Whitten, D-Miss., suffered a stroke early in 1992, Steering and Policy on Dec. 8 stripped the ailing 82-year-old of his chairmanship of the Appropriations Committee, and the committee took away his post heading its Agriculture Subcommittee by a vote of 7-29 the next day after he refused to step aside voluntarily. *(Whitten retirement, p. 22)*

Steering and Policy gave the chairmanship to William H. Natcher, D-Ky., who had been running the committee on an acting basis since the spring.

There had been rumors among appropriators of a younger member, David R. Obey, D-Wis., challenging Natcher. But no one ran against Natcher, who got credit for delivering every fiscal 1993 appropriations bill on time and under President Bush's budget request.

Richard J. Durbin, D-Ill., won the Agriculture Subcommittee chairmanship on the next ballot, with 35 votes for him and one abstention.

Altogether, the Democrats got three new committee chairmen. Besides Natcher, Lee H. Hamilton, D-Ind., stepped up from the second slot on Foreign Affairs to succeed retiring Dante B. Fascell, D-Fla., and Norman Y. Mineta, D-Calif., became chairman of Public Works and Transportation due to the retirements of two more senior members.

There was almost a fourth new chairman, but Veterans' Affairs chief G. V. "Sonny" Montgomery, D-Miss., eked out a victory over Lane Evans, D-Ill., by 127-123.

Montgomery almost lost his colleagues' support because of his conservative votes and thin support for the Democratic leadership. He had ruled the Veterans' Affairs Committee with an iron hand, making more liberal Democrats such as Evans feel left out.

The Democratic Caucus re-elected Leon E. Panetta, D-Calif., chairman of the Budget Committee on Dec. 8. Two days later, as expected, President-elect Clinton nominated him for director of the Office of Management and Budget.

The Budget chairmanship was filled Jan. 6, 1993, when Democrats chose Martin Olav Sabo, D-Minn, over the more conservative John M. Spratt Jr., D-S.C., by 149-112 in a closed-door vote.

### Republican Challenge

On the GOP side of the aisle, one member came perilously close to losing his ranking position.

In an attack led by Minority Whip Gingrich, the Committee on Committees dropped Bill Thomas as the ranking member of House Administration and recommended Paul E. Gillmor, Ohio, instead.

"There was a perception that Bill may have been too willing to compromise, make deals with the Democrats," said one GOP member of the House Administration panel, who said he did not agree with that analysis.

The ouster of Thomas was short-lived because Gillmor did not want the job, although he did not withdraw his name from a vote.

"It's not a plum, it's something you do for the good of the institution and the caucus," Gillmor said.

After the Republican Conference rejected Gillmor by a 12-vote margin, the Committee on Committees recommended Thomas for the job.

In addition to the returning members, 12 others moved up the ladder to become ranking Republicans.

In the biggest change, John R. Kasich of Ohio was picked for the ranking spot on the House Budget Committee, taking over from Gradison, who stepped down after two years. Kasich won the top spot by dispatching Alex McMillan, N.C., to the Committee on Committees.

The other new ranking members were: Pat Roberts, Kan., on Agriculture; Floyd Spence, S.C., on Armed Services; Jim Leach, Iowa, on Banking; Carlos J. Moorhead, Calif., on Energy and Commerce; Benjamin A. Gilman, N.Y., on Foreign Affairs; William F. Clinger Jr., Pa., on Government Operations; Jack Fields, Texas, on Merchant Marine and Fisheries; John T. Myers, Ind., on Post Office; Bud Shuster, Pa., on Public Works; Jan Meyers, Kan., on Small Business; and Fred Grandy, Iowa, on Ethics.

### Committee Assignments

Altogether, nine freshman Democrats received appointments to the three most sought-after committees — Appropriations, Ways and Means, and Energy and Commerce. Republicans appointed two to Appropriations and two to Energy and Commerce and none to Ways and Means.

The Democratic leadership also made a concerted effort to increase the number of women and minorities on the major committees. Of the 12 Democrats joining the Appropriations Committee, three were Hispanic and three were women, one of whom, Carrie Meek of Florida, was black. Of the eight new Republicans, one was Hispanic and one was a woman.

Of the 10 new Democrats on Ways and Means, three were black, including lone freshman Mel Reynolds, Ill. Of the five new Republicans, all were white men.

On Energy and Commerce, five of the seven new Democrats were freshmen. One new member was black, and three were women. Previously, there were only one woman on that committee, Cardiss Collins, D-Ill. Of the seven new Republicans, two were freshmen, and one was black.

As far as policy went, the changes indicated that Energy and Commerce would have an easier time reporting out abortion rights legislation in the 103rd Congress compared with past years. All of the new Democratic members

supported abortion rights. Previously, the committee had had only a hairsbreadth majority in favor of abortion rights. On the Republican side, an anti-abortion activist — Crapo of Idaho — joined the committee.

### Black Caucus Chairman

The Congressional Black Caucus, dramatically enlarged by the 1992 elections, chose Democratic Rep. Kweisi Mfume of Maryland as its chairman over Rep. Craig Washington, D-Texas, in a closed-door caucus meeting Dec. 9. The vote was reportedly 27-9 before Mfume was chosen by acclamation. (Black caucus, p. 18)

Aside from non-voting delegates, the caucus membership expanded to include 38 representatives and one senator in the 103rd Congress. That was an increase from the 25 black representatives who served in 1992.

Mfume, re-elected to represent Baltimore for a fourth term, had been the caucus vice chairman. That position traditionally was a steppingstone to the chairmanship.

## SENATE PARTIES' ORGANIZATION

Senate party organizations changed almost nothing when they organized for the 103rd Congress on Nov. 10. All leaders who ran for another term either went unchallenged or beat their opponents. In the only close race during the closed-door sessions, Texas Sen. Phil Gramm won his bid to continue leading the National Republican Senatorial Committee by one vote — despite some members' concern that his presidential ambitions could pose a conflict.

Each party gave an open low-level leadership post to a conservative Southerner, broadening the ideological mix in the upper echelons of both parties.

There were no contested races on the Democratic side. Majority Leader George J. Mitchell of Maine, Majority Whip Wendell H. Ford of Kentucky and Conference Secretary David Pryor of Arkansas all were re-elected.

John B. Breaux of Louisiana, one of the Senate's more conservative Democrats, was uncontested for the chief deputy whip's position held by Alan J. Dixon, who was defeated in the Illinois Democratic primary.

Mitchell left two positions unfilled until the beginning of the 103rd Congress. Barbara A. Mikulski, Md., was named assistant floor leader, a post left vacant by the defeat of Georgia Democrat Wyche Fowler Jr. Mitchell named Bob Graham, Fla., as chairman of the Democratic Senatorial Campaign Committee.

On the Republican side, Minority Leader Bob Dole of Kansas was re-elected by acclamation. Alan K. Simpson of Wyoming, the assistant Republican leader, or whip, beat a long-shot challenge by Slade Gorton of Washington on a 25-14 vote.

Republican Conference Chairman Thad Cochran, Miss., was re-elected without opposition, as was Policy Committee Chairman Don Nickles, Okla.

Trent Lott of Mississippi won the single open race, replacing the defeated Bob Kasten, Wis., as conference secretary. Lott's main opponent, Christopher S. Bond, Mo., got 14 votes, while five voted for Frank H. Murkowski of Alaska.

Discussion of Gramm's bid to retain control of the GOP's campaign committee for an unprecedented second two-year term focused on his well-known interest in running for president in 1996. Mitch McConnell of Kentucky had been vying for the spot since Gramm beat him in 1990 by 26-17. This time he was edged out on a 20-19 vote. ∎

# Black Caucus Grows, Moves Toward Center

It was apparent before the start of the 103rd Congress that new African-American members would swell the ranks of the Congressional Black Caucus by half, heighten diversity within the caucus and hasten its move toward the political middle.

The caucus' 16 new House members elected in 1992 ensured that it could no longer be described as a small cadre of liberal activists, identified with big cities and an urban perspective. But the newcomers' moderate ideology represented not so much a sharp break for the caucus as a maturing of a trend.

Most of the freshmen came from sprawling, predominantly rural districts in the South, where five states sent blacks to Congress for the first time since Reconstruction.

This growth and the potential for power also led to a rare contest for chairmanship of the caucus. Rep. Kweisi Mfume, D-Md., elected chairman Dec. 9, acknowledged the difficulty of keeping the group focused as it became more diversified.

"I realize this is a challenge," Mfume said. "[But] I honestly believe that the task is manageable. We can grow and diversify and evolve while at the same time increasing our effectiveness."

Mfume oversaw the largest Congressional Black Caucus in history. Aside from non-voting delegates, membership increased from 25 representatives in the 102nd Congress to 38 House members and one senator in the 103rd Congress.

But the heightened presence was only the most obvious change:

● Most of the districts represented by the freshmen were as new as their representatives. Of the 16 new black members, 13 were from predominantly black districts created in 1992 from reapportionment. (The other three were replacing retiring or defeated black incumbents from urban districts).

● The newly created seats gave the caucus more of a Southern flavor. All of the 13 seats created in reapportionment were in a triangle stretching from the Washington suburbs to Miami to Dallas. This was the first time since the Reconstruction era that a black was among House delegations from Alabama, Florida, North Carolina, South Carolina and Virginia.

● The term freshman belied the political experience of the newcomers. All but one of the 16 new caucus members had previously held public office. About two-thirds of the 25 black members already serving had entered Congress with comparable experience.

● Women were gaining seats in minority districts much as elsewhere. Three years earlier, there was only one black woman in Congress; by January there were 10.

## New Southern Districts

The drawing of Southern districts to achieve black voting majorities resulted from judicial interpretations of the Voting Rights Act (as amended in 1982). These rulings mandated gerrymandering to maximize black voting strength — creating historic opportunities for African-Americans to elect fellow blacks as their representatives.

Naturally, the Congressional Black Caucus appreciated the outcome. Rep. Julian C. Dixon, D-Calif., called the influx of black members "a fine tribute to the Voting Rights Act."

The freshmen expressed similar feelings. "All of us are children of the Voting Rights Act," said Rep. Cynthia McKinney, D-Ga. "This is a testimony to the correctness of that legislation and the need for continued diversity."

The new Southern districts typically combined predominantly black neighborhoods of several cities with large swatches of rural communities.

This mix of urban, suburban and even rural territory had not been the predominant pattern for black districts in the 20th century. African-Americans elected during Reconstruction came from the South, where the great majority of blacks lived. But the last of this group left Congress in 1901. (Black caucus history, p. 20)

As recently as the late 1980s, nearly all of the House's "black districts" were in big-city ghettos.

The differences between the new and old districts held by blacks could lead to differences within the caucus.

Even the new members with city districts brought a different set of local concerns. Rep.-elect Carrie Meek, D-Fla., whose district included the impoverished Miami communities of Overtown and Liberty City, wanted more federal aid to ensure that an influx of Haitian refugees would not overburden local schools in the way that the mass migration of Cubans did.

## Signs of Change

One sign of change in the Congressional Black Caucus was the rising number of women members. The newcomers included Democrat Carol Moseley-Braun of Illinois, the first black in the Senate since the 1970s and the first black woman in Senate history.

"The diversity that women bring to the caucus will add to its clout," said McKinney, who welcomed "an opportunity for women to be seated at the table when policy-making is being conducted."

Another striking aspect of the black freshmen was their allegiance to President Clinton. Each of eight freshmen interviewed said he wanted to help the president keep his campaign promises.

Latching on to Clinton's agenda was one easy way for a freshman to have a program and a set of priorities for a first term.

At the same time, Mfume, not an early Clinton supporter, seemed to be cautioning caucus members not to become too closely allied with the new president.

A caucus member's role, he said, was "to be vigilant, to maintain oversight, to be supportive and to maintain independence [from] this or any other administration."

With all the emphasis on team play, some of the black freshmen predicted a new spirit of activism within their ranks. Rep. Bobby L. Rush, D-Ill., said that "the CBC has not done all it could do in promoting the interests of African-American constituents."

Several of the freshmen spoke of forming coalitions with women, Hispanics and liberals within the House.

New and veteran black lawmakers alike seemed to have more flexibility early in 1993 than when they were seen first and foremost as black leaders. Ron Walters of Howard University said that with such Democratic veterans as John Conyers Jr. of Michigan, Louis Stokes of Ohio and William L. Clay of Missouri gaining seniority, caucus members were acquiring "institutional responsibility that takes them

# African-Americans Who Served in Congress

As of the end of the 102nd Congress, 69 black Americans had served in Congress, three in the Senate and 66 in the House.

Following is a list of the black members, their parties and states, and the years in which they served. In addition, John W. Menard, R-La., won a disputed election in 1868 but was not permitted to take his seat in Congress. Walter E. Fauntroy, D (1971-91), and Eleanor Holmes Norton, D (1991- ), served as non-voting delegates from the District of Columbia.

## Senate

| | |
|---|---|
| Hiram R. Revels (R-Miss.) | 1870-71 |
| Blanche K. Bruce (R-Miss.) | 1875-81 |
| Edward W. Brooke (R-Mass.) | 1967-79 |

## House

| | |
|---|---|
| Joseph H. Rainey (R-S.C.) | 1870-79 |
| Jefferson F. Long (R-Ga.) | 1870-71 |
| Robert B. Elliott (R-S.C.) | 1871-74 |
| Robert C. De Large (R-S.C.) | 1871-73 |
| Benjamin S. Turner (R-Ala.) | 1871-73 |
| Josiah T. Walls (R-Fla.) | 1871-76 |
| Richard H. Cain (R-S.C.) | 1873-75; 1877-79 |
| John R. Lynch (R-Miss.) | 1873-77; 1882-83 |
| James T. Rapier (R-Ala.) | 1873-75 |
| Alonzo J. Ransier (R-S.C.) | 1873-75 |
| Jeremiah Haralson (R-Ala.) | 1875-77 |
| John A. Hyman (R-N.C.) | 1875-77 |
| Charles E. Nash (R-La.) | 1875-77 |
| Robert Smalls (R-S.C.) | 1875-79; 1882-83; 1884-87 |
| James E. O'Hara (R-N.C.) | 1883-87 |
| Henry P. Cheatham (R-N.C.) | 1889-93 |
| John M. Langston (R-Va.) | 1890-91 |
| Thomas E. Miller (R-S.C.) | 1890-91 |
| George W. Murray (R-S.C.) | 1893-95; 1896-97 |
| George H. White (R-N.C.) | 1897-1901 |
| Oscar De Priest (R-Ill.) | 1929-35 |
| Arthur W. Mitchell (D-Ill.) | 1935-43 |
| William L. Dawson (D-Ill.) | 1943-70 |
| Adam C. Powell Jr. (D-N.Y.) | 1945-67; 1969-71 |
| Charles C. Diggs Jr. (D-Mich.) | 1955-80 |
| Robert N. C. Nix (D-Pa.) | 1958-79 |
| Augustus F. Hawkins (D-Calif.) | 1963-91 |
| John Conyers Jr. (D-Mich.) | 1965- |
| Louis Stokes (D-Ohio) | 1969- |
| William L. Clay (D-Mo.) | 1969- |
| Shirley Chisholm (D-N.Y.) | 1969-83 |
| George W. Collins (D-Ill.) | 1970-72 |
| Ronald V. Dellums (D-Calif.) | 1971- |
| Ralph H. Metcalfe (D-Ill.) | 1971-78 |
| Parren J. Mitchell (D-Md.) | 1971-87 |
| Charles B. Rangel (D-N.Y.) | 1979- |
| Yvonne Brathwaite Burke (D-Calif.) | 1973-79 |
| Cardiss Collins (D-Ill.) | 1973- |
| Barbara C. Jordan (D-Texas) | 1973-79 |
| Andrew Young (D-Ga.) | 1973-77 |
| Harold E. Ford (D-Tenn.) | 1975- |
| Julian C. Dixon (D-Calif.) | 1979- |
| William H. Gray III (D-Pa.) | 1979-91 |
| Mickey Leland (D-Texas) | 1979-89 |
| Bennett McVey Stewart (D-Ill.) | 1979-81 |
| George W. Crockett Jr. (D-Mich.) | 1981-91 |
| Mervyn M. Dymally (D-Calif.) | 1981-93 |
| Gus Savage (D-Ill.) | 1981-93 |
| Harold Washington (D-Ill.) | 1981-83 |
| Katie Hall (D-Ind.) | 1983-85 |
| Charles A. Hayes (D-Ill.) | 1983-93 |
| Major R. Owens (D-N.Y.) | 1983- |
| Edolphus Towns (D-N.Y.) | 1983- |
| Alan Wheat (D-Mo.) | 1983- |
| Alton R. Waldon Jr. (D-N.Y.) | 1986-87 |
| Mike Espy (D-Miss.) | 1987-93 [1] |
| Floyd H. Flake (D-N.Y.) | 1987- |
| John Lewis (D-Ga.) | 1987- |
| Kweisi Mfume (D-Md.) | 1987- |
| Donald M. Payne (D-N.J.) | 1989- |
| Craig Washington (D-Texas) | 1990- |
| Maxine Waters (D-Calif.) | 1991- |
| Gary Franks (R-Conn.) | 1991- |
| William Jefferson (D-La.) | 1991- |
| Barbara-Rose Collins (D-Mich.) | 1991- |
| Lucien E. Blackwell (D-Pa.) | 1991- |

[1] *Confirmed as Agriculture secretary January 1993*

SOURCES: Maurice Christopher, *America's Black Congressmen* (Thomas Y. Crowell Co., 1971), 267-269; U.S. Congress, Joint Committee on Printing, *Biographical Directory of the American Congress, 1774-1989* (Washington, D.C.: U.S. Government Printing Office, 1989); and Congressional Quarterly Weekly Report.

away from their previous role of being another civil rights organization."

Even junior members had more flexibility to pursue their own agenda because there were more black officials in state and local office. Members of Congress no longer bore the responsibility of being the only black elected official their constituents could look to.

Given all these changes, it was uncertain whether these black freshmen could establish as strong a political hold on their districts as black members traditionally had.

The political strength of veteran black members was evident when examining the record of the 25 incumbents with the most overdrafts at the former House bank. Of the 18 incumbents who were white, only five were re-elected; eight other retired, and five were defeated. The seven black members with a large number of problem checks fared much better: Six were re-elected, and only one was defeated.

Most of the veteran black caucus members had relatively compact districts with a high percentage of black residents in a one-media market.

But the unusual contours of the new black-majority districts made their political outcomes less certain. Most of the black Southern freshmen represented a far-flung collection of communities in different media markets, and those freshmen generally had a lower proportion of black voters than their city-based colleagues. ∎

# The Spoils of the Civil War

In any discussion of African-Americans in Congress, the phrase "since Reconstruction" inevitably recurs — recalling a traumatic and ultimately tragic passage in American history.

Black participation in federal lawmaking began in the aftermath of the Civil War. After the 13th Amendment had abolished slavery in 1865, the 14th Amendment conferred citizenship regardless of race in 1868.

And the 15th Amendment, ratified in 1870, guaranteed the vote regardless of race (overturning restrictions in effect in many Northern states as well as Southern).

Thus enfranchised, African-Americans entered the process on a mass scale and profoundly altered the political order.

### Gaining Political Offices

The more than 4 million blacks (in a population of less than 40 million) were heavily concentrated in the states of the defeated Confederacy.

In five states — Alabama, Mississippi, South Carolina, Louisiana and Florida — blacks outnumbered whites. In some localities, they outnumbered whites by as much as 10-to-1.

Although these numbers were not often translated into a proportionate share of political offices, they did earn African-Americans a substantial share — at least for a time.

In the 1870s, the 14th and 15th amendments were generally enforced throughout the South, where state and local governments had been reconstituted under the Military Reconstruction Act of 1867.

In Mississippi, for example, the Reconstruction legislature of 1870 was only about one-third black. But this group worked successfully with white Republican members (elected in the era when former Confederate soldiers or officials could not vote).

The Mississippi legislature of 1870 elected Hiram Rhoades Revels as the first black member of the U.S. Senate.

Although born in North Carolina in 1827, Revels had never been a slave. He had been an itinerant preacher in several states, serving churches from Baltimore to St. Louis before settling in Vicksburg.

Revels was seated despite the livid protests of several senators who questioned his citizenship and the legitimacy of his election.

He served just 13 months, filling out the unexpired term that Jefferson Davis had suspended a decade earlier when he left to become president of the Confederacy.

THE FIRST COLORED SENATOR AND REPRESENTATIVES
In the 41st. and 42nd. Congress of the United States

**An 1872 Currier & Ives print depicted the first African-Americans to serve in Congress. The first black senator, Hiram R. Revels of Mississippi, is seated at left.**

Mississippi's Reconstruction legislature also elected the first full-term African-American senator, Blanche Kelso Bruce, who came to the Senate in 1875. Bruce, who was born in slavery, had escaped to the North and attended Oberlin College in Ohio.

Driven out of office when white Democrats took control of the post-Reconstruction legislature, Bruce served in the federal government and became the District of Columbia register of deeds.

### Changes in the House

On the House side, Joseph H. Rainey of South Carolina broke the color bar in 1870 by winning a special election.

Rainey was re-elected without opposition in 1872, but the results of his re-election victories in 1874 and 1876 were subjected to protracted challenge in the House.

Other lawmakers elected in the 1870s, including several from South Carolina alone, experienced similar struggles to be seated. Josiah Walls of Florida was seated in 1871 but unseated before he could finish his term.

Elected in 1872, Walls was denied his seat by a committee dominated by Democrats. (All 22 of the black members who served during the Reconstruction period were Republicans.)

John Mercer Langston, until 1992 the only black elected from Virginia, was denied his seat for nearly two years. A distinguished lawyer and educator, he was elected in 1888 but not seated until shortly before the next election.

But by the 1880s, the prospect of political office was becoming more remote, not less, for African-Americans. Military reconstruction ended in 1877, and reinstated ex-Confederates moved swiftly to reclaim the state legislatures.

Restrictions on voting, designed to bar black participation, cropped up across the region (persisting until the federal government moved to enforce the 15th Amendment in the 1960s).

Candidates were discouraged by various means, often including violence.

The campaign intensified in the 1890s. By the time George Henry White, a lawyer and state legislator, was elected from North Carolina in 1896, he was the only black member in Congress.

White left office in 1901. It would be 28 years before another African-American took the oath on Capitol Hill, and it would be 72 years before another black from the South did so.

# 103rd's Hispanic Contingent Largest Ever

More than 170 years after Rep. Joseph Hernandez came to Congress as the territorial representative for Florida, the 103rd Congress welcomed the largest class of Latino freshmen ever.

Nine new faces boosted Hispanic representation to 19 (including delegates from the U.S. Virgin Islands and Puerto Rico whose voting privileges are limited), the largest Hispanic delegation ever. *(See list, below)*

But Rita Elizondo, executive director for the Congressional Hispanic Caucus Institute, noted that while Hispanics were proliferating, they remained underrepresented.

Hispanics constituted about 9 percent of the U.S. population, but only 4.4 percent of Congress. And the Senate had not had a Hispanic member since Joseph M. Montoya, a Democrat who represented New Mexico from 1964 to 1977.

"We have a long way to go, but it's a start," said Elizondo.

"The Hispanic caucus will become more visible and will have a louder voice because of the increased numbers," said Frank Tejeda, a Democrat elected in November in Texas' 28th District (San Antonio).

Members also gained greater authority.

For the first time, three Hispanics were to serve on the House Appropriations Committee: Democrats Esteban E. Torres of California, Ed Pastor of Arizona and José E. Serrano of New York.

Another caucus member, Rep. Bill Richardson, D-N.M., was elected one of the Democratic Caucus' four chief deputy whips.

And the caucus' two non-voting members, Resident Commissioner Carlos Romero-Barceló of Puerto Rico and Delegate Ron de Lugo of the U.S. Virgin Islands, became eligible to participate in floor votes in 1993 when the House met as a Committee of the Whole. *(D.C. delegates, p. 14)*

Serrano was elected unanimously Dec. 8 to chair the Congressional Hispanic Caucus despite some members' concern that the liberal congressman from the Bronx would give the group too much of a liberal bent. Serrano had worked closely with the more liberal black caucus to boost his own group's leverage in Congress.

"I am personally liberal, but I will lead the caucus by consensus," Serrano said. "On very emotional issues that we disagree on, we just won't go into them in the caucus."

Two such issues had been Cuba and abortion rights.

Most of the new Hispanic members came from districts designed under the Voting Rights Act to elect a Hispanic representative. But the new arrivals also credited their elections to their tenacity and years of involvement in local and state politics.

Most of the Hispanic freshmen came with strong credentials. Democrat Robert Menendez was a former mayor of Union City, N.J., and a former state senator. Two Los Angeles-area Democrats, Xavier Becerra and Lucille Roybal-Allard, served in the California State Assembly. GOP freshman Lincoln Diaz-Balart was a Florida state senator from Miami.

Previously, most of the Hispanics in Congress were Mexican-American Democrats from the urban areas of the Southwest and Southern California. While the urban emphasis remained, the Class of 1992 included Cubans, Puerto Ricans and Hispanic Republicans. Several, including Democrats Menendez and Luis V. Gutierrez of Illinois, were the first Hispanics to represent their state.

The new members were wary of calling themselves a new breed, stressing their appreciation for those who preceded them. Yet many said they were elected in a different atmosphere.

"We've got a mandate from the public to reform government," said Becerra, a newly elected Democrat from California's 30th District. "A little more is expected immediately from us." ∎

# Hispanic Members of Congress

As of the end of 1992, 23 Hispanics had served in Congress; two in the Senate and 21 in the House. Following is a list of the Hispanic members, their parties and states, and the years in which they served.

Not included are Hispanics who served as territorial delegates (10), resident commissioners of Puerto Rico (13), or non-voting delegates of Guam (one) or the Virgin Islands (one).

### Senate

| | |
|---|---|
| Dennis Chaves (D-N.M.) | 1935-62 |
| Joseph M. Montoya (D-N.M.) | 1964-77 |

### House

| | |
|---|---|
| Romualdo Pacheco (R-Calif.) | 1877-78 |
| | 1879-83 |
| Ladislas Lazaro (D-La) | 1913-27 |
| Benigno Cardenas Hernandez (R-N.M.) | 1915-17 |
| | 1919-21 |
| Nestor Montoya (R-N.M.) | 1921-23 |
| Joachim Octave Fernandez (D-La.) | 1931-41 |
| Antonio Manuel Fernandez (D-N.M.) | 1943-56 |
| Henry B. Gonzalez (D-Texas) | 1961- |
| Edward R. Roybal (D-Calif.) | 1963- |
| E. "Kika" de la Garza (D-Texas) | 1965- |
| Manuel Lujan Jr. (R-N.M.) | 1969-89 |
| Herman Badillo (D-N.Y.) | 1971-77 |
| Robert Garcia (D-N.Y.) | 1978-90 |
| Tony Coelho (D-Calif.) | 1979-89 |
| Matthew G. Martinez (D-Calif.) | 1982- |
| Solomon P. Ortiz (D-Texas) | 1983- |
| Bill Richardson (D-N.M.) | 1983- |
| Esteban E. Torres (D-Calif.) | 1983- |
| Albert G. Bustamante (D-Texas) | 1985- |
| Ileana Ros-Lehtinen (R-Fla.) | 1989- |
| José E. Serrano (D-N.Y.) | 1990- |
| Ed Pastor (D-Ariz.) | 1991- |

SOURCES: Congressional Quarterly Weekly Report and Congressional Hispanic Caucus.

# The Source of Whitten's Power

When House Democrats deposed Jamie L. Whitten as chairman of the Appropriations Committee on Dec. 8, they dethroned one of the oldest and most powerful members of Congress. The very next day, Whitten's colleagues on the spending panel wrote his political obituary.

On a 7-29 vote Dec. 9, the 82-year-old Mississippi Democrat was unceremoniously dumped as chairman of the Appropriations Subcommittee on Agriculture — the post he held since 1949 and the source

R. MICHAEL JENKINS

**Since 1949, Jamie L. Whitten had been the man to come to on agriculture.**

of his power. Whitten ran the subcommittee single-handedly and single-mindedly, and for the past four decades, used it to become a pre-eminent power broker in all manner of congressional spending issues.

From deciding where to build roads, dams and inland waterways to telling the White House how to run its internal affairs, Whitten called the shots from his seemingly invisible perch on the Agriculture Subcommittee. He understood arcane and labyrinthine farm programs, some of which he helped to create, better than anyone else.

He also understood — and practiced — a key tenet of politics better than anyone. "All anybody wants is a fair advantage," Whitten liked to say. And as he uncharacteristically confessed a few years ago, "The way to get a fair advantage is to pass a law declaring it fair. . . . That's the contest that goes on around here all the time."

It was Whitten who defied Ronald Reagan's era of cost-cutting in the mid-1980s to give Democrats their most potent legislative tool to maintain their spending preferences. He controlled something called the Commodity Credit Corporation (CCC), a paper entity the Agriculture Department used to funnel all price- and income-support payments to farmers.

The explosive cost of farm subsidies in the early 1980s meant the CCC was in constant danger of running out of funds. No one in Washington wanted the blame for that, especially Republicans, who counted on the Farm Belt for much of their electoral support as well as their six-year control of the Senate.

So when the CCC ran out of money in the middle of the fiscal year, which happened routinely, it was Whitten's job to prepare an "emergency supplemental" appropriations bill. Congress turned these must-pass events into an annual excuse for piling on not-so-urgent riders. The man who brokered and shepherded these riders was, of course, Whitten.

Bob Traxler, D-Mich., once recalled going to Whitten with a special plea for drought-stricken farmers in his district. This was the era of Gramm-Rudman, when any new spending requests made all other spending programs subject to stiff penalties. Yet Whitten was sanguine:

"I've been here a long time," he told Traxler. "And I've never seen a disaster that wasn't an opportunity."

A few months later, the House approved $135 million in drought-relief funds, which, as a rider to Whitten's $6.7 billion supplemental for the CCC, was all but hidden from view. President Reagan signed it with fanfare.

The CCC was a product of the New Deal, as was the Soil Conservation Service, the Rural Electrification Administration and the Farmers Home Administration. All survived intact despite repeated assaults by the Reagan and Bush administrations and by other members of Congress — especially urban Democrats — who objected to expensive giveaways to rural America.

But to Whitten, these classic, pump-priming programs provided the fuel for the U.S. economy's revival from the Depression. "When we put the federal government in, is when our rural areas became wealthy," he said.

Whitten truly believed the corn fields of Iowa, the cotton rows of Mississippi and the fruit orchards of California — and their neighboring rural communities — merited spending priority. "Agriculture affects 84 percent of the geography of this country," he would say repeatedly. "I'm proud to have my name on rural electricity, water systems, telephones and high service roads in 84 percent of this country."

That view defined his role in Congress and made him more than open to suggestions and requests from other members. Though never a back slapper or, as modern politicians call it, a "coalition builder," Whitten nevertheless reveled in retail legislative politics. He dealt with members one on one, in private, but with an abiding sense of where each one came from.

"We have tried to deal fairly with members and their problems," he said in 1991 when unveiling the last spending bill that he personally oversaw. "And when I say members I mean sections of the United States."

But even as Whitten's ability to get pet projects into the enacted bill made him invaluable to members, it also may have contributed to his demise.

After his stroke early in 1992, shortly after he set a record for longest House service, Whitten became severely weakened. For the first time in 40 years, someone else wrote the agriculture appropriations bill. Though Whitten's health improved, members apparently wanted assurance that their needs, which Whitten had cultivated for so long, were taken care of. *(1991 Almanac, p. 12)*

"The majority didn't think he was strong enough to do it," said Neal Smith, D-Iowa, a longtime Appropriations colleague. That was the only reason, Smith said, that Whitten lost the position that really mattered to him.

# Voters Enraged Over House Bank Abuses

Revelations that hundreds of sitting and former House members for years had routinely overdrawn their House bank accounts without penalty shook the House throughout 1992. The scandal, which touched more members than any ethics controversy in congressional history, drove some members to retire and helped defeat others in primary or general elections.

The House ethics committee in April published the overdraft totals of 325 sitting and former House members. The disclosures had a devastating political impact.

Of the 269 sitting members with overdrafts, 77 — more than one in four — retired or were defeated in primary or general election bids for the House or other offices. That was a far higher casualty rate than other members suffered. Only 28 of 166 members (about one in six) with clean bank records had their political careers cut short.

The more overdrafts members had, the more likely they were to be defeated or to retire.

Only six of the 17 sitting members accused by the ethics committee of having "abused their banking privileges" were re-elected.

At year's end, a handful of lawmakers remained on edge as a criminal investigation into the entire mess continued. But most of those involved had received letters from the special counsel appointed to investigate the case exonerating them of any criminal wrongdoing.

### The Story in Brief

The scandal erupted swiftly after the General Accounting Office (GAO) disclosed Sept. 18, 1991, that 8,331 bad checks had been written against members' accounts at the House bank during a 12-month period ending June 30, 1990. The House voted Oct. 3, 1991, to close the bank and order the Committee on Standards of Official Conduct, the chamber's ethics panel, to look into its operations. *(1991 Almanac, p. 39)*

Democrats originally lined up behind a plan by the ethics committee, announced March 5, 1992, to identify only the two dozen worst overdrafters and to declare that they had "abused their banking privileges." But Republicans rebelled, calling for full disclosure, and the Democrats folded after much public hand-wringing. Under heavy pressure, the House on March 13 approved by 426-0 a resolution (H Res 396) ordering the release of the names of all members who overdrew their checking accounts at the House bank.

The ethics committee's plan (H Res 393) also was approved. Under that resolution, the panel on April 1 released the names of 17 sitting and five former members it

---

**THE UNFOLDING SCANDAL**

*See also the following stories:*

➡ **Abusers List.** The House Committee on Standards of Official Conduct on April 1 released a list of the 22 sitting and former members who had abused their privileges at the House bank............. p. 29.

➡ **The Complete List.** The panel then released a list April 16 that also included the other 303 overdrafters. ............ p. 32.

➡ **McHugh Quits.** Rep. Matthew F. McHugh, D-N.Y., who steered the House ethics committee through the investigation, announced May 4 that he would retire from the House at year's end. ..... p. 37.

➡ **Ackerman Flap.** Rep. Gary L. Ackerman, D-N.Y., who was accused by other members of leaking the list of top abusers, resigned July 28 from the ethics committee............... p. 40.

➡ **Bank History.** The House bank operated for more than 150 years outside the system of checks and balances. Its history reveals an institution plagued by scandal from just after its inception until its unhappy end. ......... p. 43.

---

said had abused their banking privileges. On April 16, the committee released the names of everyone else with overdrafts during the 39 months under review — 252 sitting and 51 former members. Both lists, which included check totals, contained powerful members of both parties, though the majority were Democrats. In all, 325 sitting and former members were named.

The check-kiting scandal infuriated voters, who saw it as further proof that members of Congress refused to play by the rules that governed everyone else.

Many members tried to blame the bank's managers for their problems. Sergeant at Arms Jack Russ, whose office ran the bank, resigned March 12 as the House began debating the issue.

Just as the House was trying to end the affair by naming names, Attorney General William P. Barr on March 20 appointed a special counsel to investigate whether crimes had been committed. Malcolm R. Wilkey, a retired federal appeals judge, wasted no time. On April 21, he subpoenaed the House bank's records — prompting another debate over whether the House should disclose its internal records. The Republicans again won, over the objections of Democratic leaders, with the House on April 29 voting 347-64 to comply.

On Sept. 9, Wilkey began sending letters to individual members clearing them of criminal wrongdoing. All but about two dozen sitting members had received such letters before the Nov. 3 general election.

## THE ETHICS COMMITTEE INVESTIGATION

The Committee on Standards of Official Conduct decided to turn over responsibility for investigating the bank mess to a six-member subcommittee headed by Matthew F. McHugh, D-N.Y., who also served as acting chairman of the full committee during the probe because the permanent chairman, Louis Stokes, D-Ohio, acknowledged having overdrawn his own account at the bank.

The committee was under orders from the House to determine whether anyone had abused the bank by "routinely and repeatedly" writing checks that were bad by "significant" amounts.

The six-member subcommittee interviewed GAO officials, outside banking experts and all House bank principals, including Sergeant at Arms Russ. It met twice a week for months.

The subcommittee first had the GAO compile a list of accounts that had had any bad checks since July 1988 — the period covered by the House's Oct. 3, 1991, charge to

the committee. Officials said the list showed how many bad checks each account had and the total face value of those checks (though not by how much they were short). From that list, the panel requested details on accounts with the most checks and the biggest total face values. That data included every bad check's face value; how much the account was short; and how long it took the member to make the check good.

Subcommittee members said they had no idea whose accounts they were studying. "We are dealing solely with coded numbers," said McHugh. "All the judgments . . . will be made without reference to names."

## Russ Blamed by Some

While the investigation was under way, many edgy House members tried to blame any overdrafts on sloppy management of the bank. They pointed to Russ, the sergeant at arms, who declined to serve as the fall guy.

"If I had created this system, if it had been my system, fine," he said of the bank's policy of routinely honoring members' bad checks. "The perception is that I changed all this to accommodate members, and I really wanted to clarify that I inherited this."

Russ insisted that he had little to do with the day-to-day operations of the House bank. In a mid-February interview, he explained that he placed virtually total control of the operation in the hands of Charles A. Mallon, the bank's longtime director.

"It was a gentleman's agreement that he would run the bank and I would handle all other duties of this office," said Russ, whose job also involved helping run the Capitol Police force, maintaining order in the chamber and escorting dignitaries. "The bank was something I supervised with very few meetings."

Russ, 46, had worked for the House nearly 25 years, starting out on the payroll of his congressman and family friend, William M. Colmer, D-Miss. (1933-73), who offered him a low-level staff job. He soon was made a House doorman, and five years later, in 1972, was appointed chief page. In 1976 he became deputy doorkeeper.

When the sergeant at arms job opened up in the early 1980s, Russ put together a coalition of influential members that included Parren J. Mitchell, D-Md. (1971-87), Dan Rostenkowski, D-Ill., and John P. Murtha, D-Pa. Russ won approval from the full House on Jan. 3, 1983.

Russ said that before the scandal blew up in 1991 he had attempted to make some changes in the House bank's long-established procedures.

"We were told flatly: 'It ain't broke; don't fix it,' " he said.

Although the sergeant at arms maintained to the end that the bank mess was not his fault, he ultimately bowed to the political exigencies of the situation and resigned his post March 12.

Members on both sides were preparing moves to force a vote to fire Russ when he took the matter into his own hands.

Russ' situation was clouded by the fact that he had suffered a bullet wound to the cheek during what he told police was a mugging in a Capitol Hill park March 1. Some news accounts said police suspected that Russ might have staged the robbery. Russ called such talk "ludicrous."

Russ said in a statement: "It is my sincere hope that my resignation will help put this matter to rest and allow the House of Representatives to move forward and address the important issues of the day without further distraction."

## An Attempt at Damage Control

On March 5, the ethics committee voted 10-4 to recommend that just 24 people — 19 sitting House members and 5 former members — be exposed for abusing their banking privileges. The panel said it would ask the House to approve a resolution authorizing disclosure of the offenders' names and records of their banking transgressions.

"This has been a thorough investigation designed to both ensure the integrity of the House and be fair to individual members," said McHugh.

But critics branded the committee's recommendation a whitewash. The panel's four dissenting members — Republicans Jim Bunning of Kentucky, David L. Hobson of Ohio, Nancy L. Johnson of Connecticut and Jon Kyl of Arizona — and other critics said they would offer for floor consideration at least one alternative recommendation that would disclose more members' bank records.

"This thing isn't going to end with 19," said W. G. "Bill" Hefner, D-N.C. "We're all going to have to 'fess up."

The ethics subcommittee's investigation covered a 39-month period from July 1, 1988, to Oct. 3, 1991. The subcommittee — which like the full committee was evenly divided between Democrats and Republicans — reached unanimous agreement on its recommendations, which were approved without change by the divided full committee.

The investigation uncovered practices that left many slack-jawed with astonishment. The panel said that nearly 20,000 bad checks were written during the period in question, some of them in the six-figure range. One of the worst offenders overdrew his checking account by thousands of dollars in 35 out of the 39 months analyzed.

"I was rather shocked," McHugh said. "I don't know how some of these folks slept at night given the kind of books that they kept."

## Too Lax a Test

The committee's job was complicated by the fact that there were no clear House rules against overdrafts at the bank. The key decision made by the committee was the standard it set to draw a line between abuses that were "routine, repeated and significant" — the standard set by the 1991 resolution that began the inquiry — and lesser offenses that would not be disclosed.

Under its complex standard, the panel singled out members who had been substantially overdrawn in at least 20 percent of the months in which they had an account (eight months for those with an account throughout the 39-month period studied). For each month, the shortfall had to exceed the member's net monthly salary — which McHugh said ranged between about $2,300 and $6,000, depending on deductions.

McHugh acknowledged that no commercial bank would tolerate deficiencies near that magnitude. But he said the committee took account of the fact that the House bank had a longstanding practice of not notifying members of a deficiency unless an overdraft exceeded the amount of their next paycheck.

Dissenting members of the committee said the standard was too lenient because it overlooked some egregious abuses. For example, some people wrote 800 bad checks but would not be named because the overdrafts did not exceed their monthly salary. And some members overdrew their accounts by far more than their next month's salary but would escape scrutiny because they did so fewer than eight times.

McHugh acknowledged that the standard was arbitrary. "Reasonable people can differ," he said, "and we cannot

say that they're wrong and we're right."

House Speaker Thomas S. Foley, D-Wash., in a private meeting of Democratic colleagues, urged support for the panel's expected recommendation. Many members said they planned to take refuge behind the authority of the ethics committee in opposing broader disclosure.

But the committee's authority was undermined by the fact that its judgment was not unanimous and by McHugh's acknowledgement that the line drawn was arbitrary.

"I think if you are going to disclose some names, you should disclose all the names," said Stephen J. Solarz, D-N.Y. "On what basis do you distinguish?"

Opposition was mounting from dissenting Republican members of the ethics committee, from a band of freshman Republicans known as the "Gang of Seven," who had been calling for full disclosure, and from some members of the Republican leadership, including House GOP Whip Newt Gingrich of Georgia.

## REVOLT IN THE HOUSE

With the drumbeat of GOP criticism mounting, House Democrats abandoned efforts to limit the disclosures to a small list of abusers. In the early morning hours of March 13, the full House voted unanimously to disclose the identity and records of all those who wrote bad checks during the preceding three years.

"I hope it will be clear to the country that we are not hiding any information, embarrassing as it may be, misleading as it may be, in many cases unjust to members as it may be," said House Speaker Foley.

Others saw it differently — and relished the consequences. "There will be many, many members who will be taken out, lose their re-election because of their record of bounced checks," said Michigan Rep. Guy Vander Jagt, chairman of the House Republicans' campaign committee. "I am absolutely overjoyed." (In the end, Vander Jagt himself lost his bid for re-election.) *(Political report, p. 15-A)*

Since the GAO first revealed abuses at the House bank, about 90 members had admitted writing bad checks and offered excuses. More than a dozen of those came forth shortly before and after the House voted for full disclosure.

"I called in the posse and gave myself up," Rep. Charles Wilson, D-Texas, told reporters March 12, acknowledging 75 or more overdrafts. (Wilson eventually was listed with 81.)

Some members who previously had denied floating checks or refused to say began confessing. "I was an industrial strength overdraft protection user," said Duncan Hunter, R-Calif. (Hunter was listed with 399.)

### The Votes for Disclosure

The vote to name all check-floaters came after midnight and followed a frantic day of negotiation, recrimination and consternation March 12.

Until that day, top Democrats pushed hard for the ethics committee's more limited disclosure plan. But the leaders reversed themselves after numerous party members jumped ship. Rank-and-file Democrats openly questioned Foley's handling of the scandal.

The House passed two resolutions. The first (H Res 393), approved 391-36 about 11 p.m. on March 12, required the naming of 19 current and five former members deemed by the ethics committee to have "abused their banking privileges." Detailed data was also to be released. *(Vote 44, p. 12-H)*

The second resolution (H Res 396), approved 426-0 at about 1:15 a.m. on March 13, called for exposure of the other sitting and former members who floated checks during the 39-month period. Each member's total number of bad checks was also to be disclosed. *(Vote 45, p. 12-H)*

Republicans drove the process with a vengeance. Most lambasted the ethics committee's limited disclosure plan as a cover-up, saying members who floated many hundreds of checks would escape. The Republicans denied purely political motives, but Democrats had more to lose from full disclosure because they held a 268-166 edge in the House.

Editorial writers and talk show hosts also called for a fuller accounting, whipping up voter outrage. "The public is just demanding it — calls are just pouring in," said Sherwood Boehlert, R-N.Y.

### Leadership Miscalculation

Foley predicted confidently on Monday, March 9, that the committee's limited-disclosure plan would be approved. His two top deputies, Majority Leader Richard A. Gephardt, Mo., and Whip David E. Bonior, Mich., also announced support. Democrats reported intense lobbying by the leadership in favor of the committee plan.

Key Republicans, however, were drumming up support for fuller disclosure, and GOP leader Robert H. Michel of Illinois remained notably mum.

Republican leaders met March 10. Conference Chairman Jerry Lewis, Calif., vowed to offer a full disclosure proposal if no one else did. Said Michel with a shrug: "The names are going to come out anyway, we might as well do it now."

Pressuring the leaders were the "Gang of Seven," the freshman Republicans who had been clamoring for the names since the scandal broke.

Said Jim Nussle of Iowa: "If constituents across the country are as angry as mine, then a little bit of tar is being boiled and feathers are being readied."

Vice President Dan Quayle lent a hand that night, calling the scandal a "national disgrace" on network television while commenting on primary election results. President Bush called for full disclosure the next morning.

The ethics committee report on its inquiry was officially released March 11. The report included mitigating circumstances — that some members apparently believed that they were allowed to overdraw their accounts; that no money was lost by recent overdrafts because members eventually covered the checks; that, in the committee's view, other members' money, not public funds, was used to cover overdrafts.

But the report also provided ammunition for those trying to force greater disclosure. "No doubt," it said of one of the panel's abuse standards, "many who are unfamiliar with how the House bank operated for many years will find this definition of 'significant amount' generous. It is."

Shortly after the report's release, many Democrats started publicly saying they leaned toward full disclosure.

Romano L. Mazzoli, D-Ky., took to the floor first: "I desperately wish I could support the committee's recommendation, but I cannot." A cross-section of Democrats agreed.

At a Democratic whip organization meeting March 12, Foley was verbally pummeled by members who favored full disclosure or saw the fight as a sure loser. The leadership caved.

Talks between leaders of both parties resulted in agreement on what was eventually approved. The full member-

ship of both parties met in the late afternoon. That was when many members realized that there was a good chance they would be named — months after many of them had either refused to comment or denied floating checks.

"Both Republicans and Democrats had caucuses that more closely resembled brawls," said Fred Grandy, R-Iowa. "Once they found out what full disclosure meant, there was open trembling."

Final details were worked out after the House recessed at 4:05 p.m.

While the House was out, the Senate, in rare comment on the affairs of the other chamber, approved on a 95-2 vote a measure sponsored by Jesse Helms, R-N.C., and Minority Leader Bob Dole, R-Kan., declaring that the Senate had nothing to do with the House bank scandal and had no such bank in its chamber. It also implicitly endorsed full disclosure. *(Vote 41, p. 7-S)*

### A Grim Recognition

The House reconvened at 8:25 p.m. for the final debate.

The first order of business was the reading of Russ' surprise resignation letter after nine years as sergeant at arms. Foley appointed longtime aide Werner W. Brandt acting sergeant and swore him in amid funeral-like silence.

Well-liked by members, Russ could not withstand the criticism the ethics committee had leveled at him. The panel blamed him for the bank's management, which it called unprofessional, haphazard and lax. Russ pursued reforms "in a halfhearted and untimely fashion." Worse, he "clearly misused" his position by cashing bad checks for himself totaling $56,300.

The mood on the floor was somber. Few voiced opposition to what was being done.

Even members who planned to vote against full disclosure fell in line. Hunter said his father called to persuade him to change his mind. "He said, 'The issue now is public trust: You must vote yes,'" Hunter recalled. "I'm going to vote yes."

The night was punctuated with occasional hisses from both sides, but the things really got heated when Gingrich took the floor and decried the "chutzpah, the hubris, the gall" of the Democrats for claiming bipartisanship on the final resolution, when in fact they had been forced to surrender. He laid the blame for the scandal at the Democrats' feet and called it a symptom of the corruption endemic to longtime one-party rule: "If we go down the same road, with the same one-sided appointments ... the same secrecy, the same arbitrariness, we'll be back at the same stand with another scandal and another scandal."

After the second resolution passed, Mickey Edwards, R-Okla., offered a resolution (H Res 397) calling for reconstructing all bank account histories and releasing that information within 20 days, even though ethics leaders insisted that it would take months.

An effort to sidetrack the resolution failed, 150-275. Leaders were forced to calm their troops, and they later rallied to bury the measure in committee by 244-133. *(Votes 46, 47, p. 12-H)*

## THE WAIT FOR THE WORST

The fog of the bank scandal spread throughout the Capitol the week of March 16, up the street to Pennsylvania Avenue and beyond the Beltway.

House members, humiliated by revelations of mismanagement of their personal finances, headed home to confess and contain the political damage.

The confessions ranged from California Democrat Barbara Boxer's "I feel like a fool" to Minnesota Republican Vin Weber's "I operated within the rules of the bank."

The scandal claimed its first electoral victim. In Illinois' March 17 primary, Democrat Charles A. Hayes, who was on the unofficial but widely publicized list of the 24 most serious abusers, lost his bid for renomination. Another member on the list, Democrat Robert L. Mrazek of New York, decided March 20 to end his campaign for U.S. Senate.

Attorney General William P. Barr on March 20 appointed a retired federal appeals judge, Malcolm R. Wilkey, to conduct a preliminary inquiry into whether the House bank affair involved any federal crimes. Barr acted four days after the local U.S. Attorney, Jay B. Stephens, announced that his office had been studying the question for five months.

Meanwhile, new allegations emerged of possible criminal activity at the House Post Office, and the House postmaster resigned. Federal prosecutors had been investigating that office since the summer of 1991. *(Post office investigation, p. 47)*

Foley, insisting "there is no spreading scandal," said March 20 that he would seek to end or alter time-honored member perquisites. Foley said he would close the House pharmacy and recommend quadrupling fees for the House gym. Foley also said he would push for a House administrator to oversee management. *(House administrator, p. 55)*

### Cabinet Officers Confess

On March 17, three Cabinet officers revealed that they would be on the list of House overdrafters. Two Republican senators also owned up to floating checks when they were in the House.

Defense Secretary Dick Cheney (R-Wyo., 1979-89), Agriculture Secretary Edward Madigan (R-Ill., 1973-91) and Labor Secretary Lynn Martin (R-Ill., 1981-91) each acknowledged overdrafts.

"As recently as last Thursday night, I was still telling jokes about the House bank," Cheney told reporters. "It doesn't seem quite as funny today."

Cheney said the House ethics committee told him that he had 25 "problem checks," but he said he was missing a bank statement and could verify only 21 of them.

Madigan reported having written 49 bad checks, totaling around $30,000. Martin issued a written statement acknowledging that she wrote 16 bad checks totaling $5,125.20.

Echoing now-familiar themes, all three Bush Cabinet members said they were never notified of overdrafts.

Bush directed his counsel to retrieve records from his own service in the House (1967-71) to see whether he had bounced any checks.

Vice President Dan Quayle said his bank statements during his House service (1977-81) indicated that his account was in balance; but as many members discovered, that was not necessarily accurate.

Bush invoked Congress' scandal-scarred image March 20 as he announced his veto of a tax bill just passed by Congress. Taunting that Democratic lawmakers "cannot manage a tiny bank or a tiny post office," Bush launched a broadside against Capitol Hill reminiscent of Harry S Truman's 1948 campaign against the "do-nothing Congress." "It is time for a new Congress," Bush said. "You give me the right lawmakers, and I'll give you the right laws."

## Campaign Loans, Personal Investments

Some members accused of exploiting the House bank lent thousands of dollars to their re-election campaigns or profited from personal investments while leaving their accounts in the red for hundreds of days over a three-year period, records showed.

Three on the ethics committee's list of the two-dozen top offenders admitted using overdraft checks to help finance their money-strapped re-election efforts.

They were Charles Wilson, D-Texas, former Rep. Doug Walgren, D-Pa. (1977-91), and former Rep. Jim Bates, D-Calif., who was in a nasty comeback fight for an open seat. All denied doing anything wrong.

Campaign records showed that four others who allegedly abused their banking privileges lent personal funds to their election efforts during the 39 months reviewed by the House Committee on Standards of Official Conduct. They were Harold E. Ford, D-Tenn.; James H. Scheuer, D-N.Y.; Edolphus Towns, D-N.Y.; and former Rep. Douglas Bosco, D-Calif.

All but a few on the ethics panel's abuser list profited from some type of investments or attempted to do so while they were, in effect, getting interest-free loans from the House bank by writing overdraft checks, according to a review of their annual financial disclosure statements. At least two bought and sold investments heavily.

Only one of the 24, Mrazek, appeared to have used House bank checks in business deals. An aide said Mrazek had used House bank checks in connection with his management of a partnership that had purchased an island in the Bahamas. He did not know if the checks were overdrafts.

Wilson, the only sitting member who admitted using his House bank account to finance his campaign, lent his campaigns a total of $40,000 between Oct. 18, 1990, and Jan. 4, 1991.

An aide to the Texas Democrat said all $40,000 came from House bank checks. Only one, for $10,000, led directly to an overdraft, said spokeswoman Elaine Lang. Wilson had a negative balance one of every five days, ethics committee records show.

Of the two dozen worst offenders, 21 reported unearned income — money made on investments, including interest, stock dividends and other profits — on their financial disclosure statements for 1988, 1989 and 1990. The three who did not were Robert W. Davis, R-Mich.; Edwards, R-Okla.; and Hayes, D-Ill.

Seven of the 21 acquired potentially profitable assets during the three years reviewed by the ethics committee. In addition to Mrazek, they were:

● Bill Alexander, D-Ark., who in 1989 acquired an interest in a Florida business venture for less than $5,000. The transaction was related to several dealings Alexander had over the years that sparked controversy in 1991 when it was reported that he had helped funnel federal appropriations to a nonprofit foundation run by his partners.

● Bosco, who bought a piece of property in late 1988 for more than $250,000.

● William L. Clay, D-Mo., who bought stocks, bonds or both in all three years. Clay declined to comment.

● Edward F. Feighan, D-Ohio, who was involved in the 1989 island deal with Mrazek. During the three years, Feighan also bought and sold numerous stocks and properties. The congressman did not return phone calls.

● Former Rep. Tommy Robinson, R-Ark., bought a significant amount of farmland in 1988. He could not be

reached for comment.

● Scheuer, whose financial disclosure statements included numerous pages of financial transactions involving income-producing assets.

## Deposit Delay Claimed

Members trying to persuade the ethics committee to absolve them of some or all of their overdrafts at the House bank claimed that deposits were not credited to their accounts fast enough. But committee members said that excuse was generally not valid.

"It's a problem, but it's getting overplayed," said James V. Hansen of Utah, the top Republican on the ethics panel.

Members were trying hard to convince the committee that their bad-check counts should be reduced before it released their names and overdraft totals. The panel had a big stack of appeal letters when the deadline for filing them came March 27.

The most frequent complaint was that commercial bank checks deposited into the House bank were held for days before being posted to members' accounts.

But bank officials insisted that all deposits were posted the same day or the next business day, depending on how late in the day the deposit was made.

Some members also complained that their monthly pay was not always deposited on the first of each month, but it was the bank's longstanding policy to credit accounts the first business day of each month.

Any delays beyond that, in either salary or other deposits, were explained by the fact that the bank sometimes closed when business was slow before or after holidays or when the computers were down, bank officials said. On such days, they added, neither credits nor debits were posted to members' accounts, so no overdrafts would have occurred.

## GOP Members Stung Too

Although the ethics committee planned to brand only four Republicans as abusers of the House bank, the GOP's successful push for full disclosure in the affair drew several other top Republicans into a wider net of big-time over-drafters.

Edwards of Oklahoma, chairman of the Republican Policy Committee, was the only leadership member of either party on the list of top abusers. But the ethics committee found that five other top Republicans — two leadership members, two committee leaders and an influential appropriator — had numerous overdrafts at the bank, each writing between 119 and 575 such checks during the 39 months.

Democrats still bore the brunt of the scandal. Twenty of 24 on the initial committee list of top offenders were Democrats, and many others, including some in leadership positions, admitted numerous overdrafts.

Both parties tried to score points with the scandal. Republicans released a biting television ad blaming the whole mess on the Democrats, and Democrats responded with a newspaper ad lambasting "hypocrites" attempting to capitalize on a scandal that brushed them.

The second tier of offenders — those who just missed making the first list or those with more than 100 overdrafts — included:.

● **Republicans**: Two junior members of the GOP leadership, Conference Secretary Weber of Minnesota and Research Committee Chairman Hunter of California; Chalmers P. Wylie of Ohio, ranking member on the Banking Committee; Bill Thomas of California, ranking member on

the House Administration Committee, which had jurisdiction over the bank; and Bill Lowery of California, an Appropriations Committee member.

● **Democrats**: Two Senate candidates, Wayne Owens of Utah and Boxer of California; Charles W. Stenholm of Texas, a leading conservative; Gary L. Ackerman, N.Y., an ethics committee member; and Gerry Sikorski, Minn., a member of the powerful Energy and Commerce Committee.

## OFFICIAL LIST OF ABUSERS

On April 1, the ethics committee completed the dirty job that the House handed it the previous October: deciding who abused the now-closed bank by "routinely and repeatedly" overdrawing their accounts by a "significant amount."

The subcommittee granted reprieves to two members — Democrats Charles Wilson of Texas and Scheuer of New York — who were on an initial list of 24 alleged abusers, but it tarred a broad swath of top Democrats and several important Republicans in naming the 22 others.

The panel tried to soften the blow, saying in a statement that it was "by no means clear" that "the people on this list intended to abuse banking privileges," given the bank's longstanding practice of covering almost all overdraft checks until members made them good.

Those on the list, however, insisted they had been unfairly burned in a political rush to judgment by a subcommittee so fearful of being accused of a cover-up that it created retroactive rules and then refused to listen to reason. *(Abuser list, p. 29)*

Particularly outraged were two members, Joseph D. Early, D-Mass., and Edwards, R-Okla., who were kept on the list by virtue of a 3-3 tie vote in the subcommittee.

It was clear that many members who escaped the abuser list still faced serious political difficulties. By the committee's initial count, an additional 279 current members and 54 former members had from one to 851 overdrafts. More than 200 had already confessed in public, although many refused to offer specifics.

Members got a taste of the recriminations to come after the committee released its list.

Shortly after acting ethics Chairman McHugh filed the list with the House clerk, five of the members on it launched blistering personal attacks on panel members.

"They ran like rats!" snarled Early, furious at being denied the chance to confront the subcommittee's leaders in public.

Clay used each of following words to describe the panel or its decision: disgraceful, callous, cavalier, unconscionable, libelous, arbitrary, pious, pompous, hypocritical, audacity, charade, shameful, malign, flimsy, unethical, unfair and erroneous. On top of that, some of the six subcommittee members lied to him, he charged, claiming that four had told him privately that they voted to take him off the list.

Perhaps the most aggrieved was Hayes, whose presence on the list had been leaked a few days before the March 17 Illinois primary, which he lost. "Even before I could adequately respond, I was tried and convicted in the press," he said. "I was the first official victim of this so-called check-kiting scandal."

At the weekly meeting of the Democrats' whip organization April 2, members complained bitterly to leaders that the subcommittee was uncompromising.

"The whip meeting was very rough," said Eckart. One member, Marty Russo, Ill., stormed out, and another, John Bryant of Texas, afterward called for Speaker Foley to step down at the end of the year.

McHugh and others vigorously defended the subcommittee's work, but declined to give much of a public reply to the attacks. "I felt some of the comments were unduly personal and wrong, but it doesn't do the institution any good to engage in a tit-for-tat debate on these other things," McHugh said.

### Edwards, Early Lose Appeals

The subcommittee had close votes on three members' cases — those of Early, Edwards and Bill Goodling, R-Pa.

Edwards' and Early's cases involved the same basic issue. The panel's overdraft abuse standard was based on the amount of each member's monthly net salary deposit. Early and Edwards had the bank automatically take money from their pay every month to pay bills — a mortgage for Edwards and children's tuition for Early. The money was deducted before their pay was credited. Edwards said that left him with a monthly net deposit as small as $1,600 instead of up to $6,000.

The subcommittee conceded this put them "at some disadvantage for purposes of this inquiry" because it meant that Edwards, for instance, could only get away with writing overdrafts up to $1,600 a month, while members without such automatic deductions could write up to $6,000 or so without breaking the threshold. But the panel, on 3-3 votes, declined to remove Edwards and Early from the list, deciding that the two should have known from their pay stubs and monthly bank statements how much was being put into their account.

Early and Edwards tried to appeal to the full committee but were turned down shortly before the list was released. "The full committee discussed the particulars of Joe's case and others; I'm fairly confident that those cases would not have been reversed by the full committee," said Grandy.

Edwards protested: "Nobody has ever questioned my integrity — ever — and I stand here today humiliated like this because the committee was not willing to reconsider the definition of a net deposit."

Goodling's case involved close calls on when deposits were posted. Though he managed to get nine of 439 overdraft checks and two of 11 months removed from the GAO tallies, he did not persuade the panel to remove the two additional months it would have taken to get off the list.

"Petty timing differences would seem to be an anomaly to the term 'flagrant abuser,'" Goodling said. "I do not consider myself a 'flagrant abuser.'"

### A Sour Spring Break

House members escaped Washington in early April for spring recess, but they could not escape the smoke of scandal spiraling from four inquiries into the House's post office and bank.

Weber declared his retirement in a surprise announcement April 9; he had acknowledged 125 overdrafts. Mrazek, who was on the list of 22 abusers, gave up his foundering campaign for the Senate the same day. Sen. Tim Wirth, D-Colo., said on April 8 that the prospect of an ugly campaign helped him decide not to run; he had been hammered for proposing a similar bank in the Senate.

Leaders of the subcommittee that handled the House bank inquiry announced April 10 that they had finished considering appeals of 150 members who contested the

# 22 Cited for Abuse of Bank

The House Committee on Standards of Official Conduct on April 1 listed 22 current and former members who, it concluded, had abused their privileges at the House bank.

The committee released official data in accordance with a resolution passed by the House on March 12. Additional information about these accounts was gleaned from a preliminary report on 66 accounts reviewed by the General Accounting Office (GAO).

The unofficial data was taken from the earlier GAO document by matching numbers where they were identical. In the five cases where the committee's final figures were different, footnotes indicate the changes.

All data was based on the 39-month period from July 1, 1988, to Oct. 3, 1991, that was reviewed by the GAO and the House committee.

## Official Data

The following information was released by the ethics committee on April 1:

● **Months overdrawn:** The number of separate months (of the 39) in which the member's account was overdrawn at any time by more than the member's next monthly net salary deposit.

● **Overdraft checks:** The number of checks for which the member's account did not have sufficient funds.

● **Bounced checks:** The number of overdraft checks that the House bank refused to cover and bounced.

● **Outside overdrafts:** The number of checks from outside financial institutions that were given to the bank for cashing or deposit and were bounced back to the House bank for lack of funds in the other institution.

## Unofficial Data

This information was taken from the earlier GAO chart. Footnotes denote the cases in which the committee's totals differed from the earlier data.

● **Face value:** The aggregate face value of the overdraft checks. This figure does not reflect the size of the overdrafts — only the size of the checks.

● **Biggest overdraft:** The highest negative balance — the largest amount the account was overdrawn at a single point in time.

● **Days in red:** The number of days (not necessarily continuous) during the study period (1,187 days for the 39 months) that the member's account was overdrawn.

● **Days over $1,000:** The number of days that the member's account was overdrawn by more than $1,000.

| | Official Data | | | | Unofficial Data | | | |
|---|---|---|---|---|---|---|---|---|
| | Months Overdrawn | Overdraft Checks | Bounced Checks | Outside Overdrafts | Face Value | Biggest Overdraft | Days in Red | Days Over $1,000 |
| **Sitting Members** | | | | | | | | |
| Charles Hatcher, D-Ga. | 35 | 819 | 2 | 0 | $273,361 | $10,746 | 1,052 | 963 |
| Harold E. Ford, D-Tenn. | 31 | 388 | 11 | 4 | 552,447 | 20,743 | 1,003 | 583 |
| Stephen J. Solarz, D-N.Y. | 30 | 743 | 53 | 11 | 594,646 | 23,019 | 917 | 855 |
| Robert J. Mrazek, D-N.Y. | 23 | 920 | 0 | 1 | 351,609 [1] | 27,398 [1] | 642 [1] | 531 [1] |
| Ronald D. Coleman, D-Texas | 23 | 673 | 6 | 1 | 275,849 | 9,409 | 927 | 825 |
| Bill Alexander, D-Ark. | 19 | 487 | 0 | 2 | 208,546 [2] | 10,957 [2] | 804 [2] | 322 [2] |
| Edolphus Towns, D-N.Y. | 18 | 408 | 0 | 0 | 176,503 | 12,964 | 560 | 424 |
| Mary Rose Oakar, D-Ohio | 18 | 213 | 0 | 1 | 227,598 [3] | 18,515 [3] | 667 [3] | 547 [3] |
| Charles A. Hayes, D-Ill. | 15 | 716 | 0 | 9 | 296,681 | 9,474 | 1,005 | 915 |
| Joseph D. Early, D-Mass. | 15 | 140 | 0 | 0 | 182,119 | 5,449 | 318 | 200 |
| Carl C. Perkins, D-Ky. | 14 | 514 | 25 | 28 | 565,651 | 41,200 | 506 | 436 |
| Robert W. Davis, R-Mich. | 13 | 878 | 0 | 0 | 344,450 | 13,416 | 756 | 372 |
| Mickey Edwards, R-Okla. | 13 | 386 | 0 | 1 | 54,299 | 5,385 | 409 | 195 |
| Bill Goodling, R-Pa. | 9 | 430 | 0 | 0 | 188,016 [4] | 25,078 [4] | 379 [4] | 242 [4] |
| William L. Clay, D-Mo. | 9 | 328 | 0 | 0 | 188,136 [5] | 33,766 [5] | 519 [5] | 219 [5] |
| John Conyers Jr., D-Mich. | 9 | 273 | 0 | 0 | 108,386 | 7,319 | 489 | 330 |
| Edward F. Feighan, D-Ohio | 8 | 397 | 0 | 0 | 218,994 | 13,978 | 711 | 533 |
| **Former Members** | | | | | | | | |
| Tommy F. Robinson, R-Ark. | 16 of 33 | 996 | 0 | 0 | 251,609 | 28,036 | 544 | 499 |
| Doug Walgren, D-Pa. | 16 of 31 | 858 | 0 | 0 | 226,161 | 14,478 | 633 | 560 |
| Douglas H. Bosco, D-Calif. | 13 of 32 | 124 | 0 | 4 | 537,985 | 75,723 | 215 | 126 |
| Tony Coelho, D-Calif. | 12 of 18 | 316 | 0 | 0 | 292,603 | 60,625 | 295 | 226 |
| Jim Bates, D-Calif. | 9 of 31 | 89 | 0 | 1 | 170,686 | 3,436 | 492 | 33 |

[1] *Based on 972 overdraft checks and 23 months in preliminary data*
[2] *Based on 499 overdraft checks and 20 months in preliminary data*
[3] *Based on 217 overdraft checks and 21 months in preliminary data*
[4] *Based on 439 overdraft checks and 11 months in preliminary data*
[5] *Based on 329 overdraft checks and 10 months in preliminary data*

panel's count of their overdrafts.

Preliminary data had indicated that the bigger list would include 333 names of current and former members with anywhere from one to 851 overdrafts. Officials estimated that the subcommittee removed no more than 20 or so from the list, rejecting members' defenses in most cases.

At an April 10 news conference, McHugh offered the soon-to-be-exposed overdrafters political cover by saying, "The people on this list did nothing wrong. They did not abuse their banking privileges." Top committee Republican Hansen observed, " 'Nothing wrong' is like beauty is to the eye of the beholder."

Public opinion polls indicated that, in the eyes of many voters, there was little difference between those with many overdraft checks and those who made the abuser list.

Wilkey, the Justice Department's special counsel investigating the House bank affair, hinted at an aggressive inquiry in interviews April 6-7. He told The New York Times that some members "may very well be prosecuted." He also said that he might investigate what members bought with overdrafts — something that the ethics committee refused to do. That raised the prospect of further embarrassing details about financial transactions members thought were private.

McHugh said that Wilkey had requested all of the committee's records on the matter. Congressional officials predicted that the House would resist such a broad request on separation-of-powers grounds. "My hope is that there will be an accommodation reached," McHugh said.

## OVERDRAFTERS ARE NAMED

On April 16, the House ethics committee finally released the names of 252 sitting and 51 former lawmakers who overdrew their checking accounts.

The list included 188 Democrats, 114 Republicans and one independent — a partisan breakdown that was close to the parties' representation in the House as a whole.

Even before the committee's announcement, more than 200 members had acknowledged writing overdrafts. But release of the complete list laid bare the magnitude of the problem that had been seized upon by many voters as an emblem of what was wrong with Congress.

The list included more than half the Democratic and GOP leadership and 15 out of 22 standing committee chairmen. Also hit were nine former members — all Republicans — who were in President Bush's Cabinet or in the Senate.

The committee made its disclosure in Washington in the middle of a two-week congressional recess, when many members were at home in their districts. That put them in a good position to assess hometown repercussions and respond to voters.

In the Capitol, dozens of reporters descended on the press gallery to snap up the long-awaited list. House Speaker Foley, one of the few members remaining in Washington to respond to reporters, moved with uncharacteristic aggressiveness to control the damage by portraying members as victims of sloppy bank practices and misleading news accounts.

In an April 17 column he wrote for The New York Times, Foley said: "The members named yesterday did not abuse their banking privileges. It would be more accurate to say that most members were abused by the bank."

And McHugh, the ethics chairman, said many members had never realized they were overdrawn at the bank.

"Written notice of an overdraft was not provided, and oral notice was haphazard," he said in releasing the list April 16. "Many members were never notified that their checks had been held," he added, and because the bank did not post negative balances on members' monthly statements, "some members were genuinely surprised to find that the bank had attributed overdrafts to their accounts."

### The Surprises

The list of 303 represented a broad cross section of the House: committee chairmen and freshmen, anonymous time-servers and rising stars.

The banking habits it adumbrated varied widely. Thirty-six of those listed floated 100 or more checks; 40 members wrote only one overdraft. Because the list gave only the number of checks each member wrote on insufficient funds, it was impossible to distinguish between members who overdrew by large and small amounts.

Some members on the full list wrote more bad checks than the 22 identified by the ethics committee as abusers of the bank, but they escaped the short list because their overdrafts did not exceed their paycheck often enough to meet the committee's standard of "abuse."

Many, if not most, members on the list said they had no idea they had ever overdrawn their accounts, because the bank often held checks until a deposit was made without telling account holders, and monthly statements did not show a negative balance for held checks.

Topping the new list with 851 checks was Ronald V. Dellums, D-Calif., chairman of an important Armed Services subcommittee and a leading member of the Congressional Black Caucus. Dellums responded angrily to the committee report, saying its finding was "beyond comprehension."

Although Dellums voted for the resolution calling for disclosure of all overdrafters' names, he called the report "an unwarranted intrusion into our private family life, an intrusion that any private citizen would not tolerate."

Among the surprises was the news that the ethics committee's chairman — Louis Stokes, D-Ohio — overdrew his account 551 times. Stokes, who became chairman of the ethics committee for the second time in 1991, had recused himself from the bank investigation after acknowledging that he had overdrawn his account "on occasions." But he had given no hint of the magnitude of the problem.

Another surprise was Henry A. Waxman, D-Calif., chairman of a powerful Energy and Commerce subcommittee, who overdrew his account 434 times. Waxman said his overdrafts violated no rules or laws but said, "I deeply regret the damage this controversy has caused to the House. Public confidence is eroded and legislation is at a standstill."

A leaked committee document showing details of 66 accounts but no names allowed reporters and opponents to match members with check numbers to cull additional information about the top overdrafters' banking habits.

For example, the document showed that Dellums just missed being named an abuser because he overdrew his account by more than his monthly net salary deposit seven times — one shy of the number used to identify abusers. Stokes' account, the document indicated, was in the red for more than 40 percent of the 39 months studied — sometimes by more than $1,000 and once by more than $8,000.

### Leaders of Both Parties Involved

Leaders of both parties had been slinging mud at each other for the House bank scandal, but the final list of

overdrafters made plain that neither side was untainted. Eight leaders — evenly divided between Democrats and Republicans — were among the current and former lawmakers who overdrew their House bank accounts.

Republicans had been trying to blame the whole imbroglio on the Democratic leadership, saying it was responsible for the lax bank practices that allowed members to overdraw their accounts with impunity.

But some GOP leaders were throwing stones from glass houses. Three of them overdrew their accounts more than 100 times: Research Chairman Duncan Hunter, R-Calif. (399); Policy Chairman Mickey Edwards, R-Okla. (386); and Conference Secretary Vin Weber, R-Minn. (125).

Among the leaders on the list was Minority Whip Gingrich, who had 22 overdrafts with a face value totaling $26,891. Gingrich retained an accountant to certify that none of the checks was used for personal investment or political purposes.

Gingrich was the only elected leader of either party who did not disclose his overdraft record until the day the ethics committee released its list. Tony Blankley, Gingrich's spokesman, said there was some uncertainty about the check total until the week of April 6 because Gingrich was appealing the ethics committee's original count. Blankley said Gingrich succeeded in reducing his check total by two or three.

The Democratic Congressional Campaign Committee (DCCC) had taken aim at Gingrich, who was a leading proponent of using the bank scandal as a political issue against Democrats and who was a key figure in driving former Speaker Jim Wright of Texas out of office under an ethics cloud. The DCCC on April 15 began airing a radio advertisement in Georgia that made much of the fact that Gingrich initially had said he had written only three bad checks and later said the total would be between 20 and 30. "Come on Newt, count the totals, tell the truth. And take your medicine like a man," the ad said.

But the Democratic majority leader, Richard A. Gephardt of Missouri, found himself in the similar position of having to change earlier statements about his bank account. Gephardt announced in 1991 that he had only three overdrafts, but that was based on a one-year period. On April 14, Gephardt acknowledged that the ethics committee's review of three years found 28 overdrafts.

In a lengthy statement, Gephardt blamed many of his overdrafts on the bank's "mismanagement." To bolster his contention that he did not abuse his bank privileges, Gephardt issued statements from an accountant he hired to look at his bank records and from a banking lobbyist.

Among the leaders who never overdrew their accounts were two of the parties' most partisan figures: campaign committee chairmen Guy Vander Jagt, R-Mich., and Vic Fazio, D-Calif.

The other leaders who had no overdrafts were Minority Leader Robert H. Michel of Illinois, GOP Conference Chairman Jerry Lewis of California and Bill McCollum of Florida, vice chairman of the Republican Conference.

Speaker Foley had two overdraft checks — one for $540 in 1990, another for $477 in 1989.

Republicans began rallying around the GOP leader hardest hit by the scandal — Edwards of Oklahoma, who was cited April 1 by the ethics committee as one of the 22 abusers of the bank. A letter signed by Michel, Gingrich and Lewis urged fellow Republicans to contribute to Edwards' re-election campaign fund, saying he is facing "a race for his survival" with little campaign cash.

## Chairmen Hit Hard

The House's committee chairmen proved more likely than not to have overdrawn their accounts. Fifteen of 22 committee chairmen had overdrafts — as did 11 ranking Republicans.

Near the top of the list were Agriculture Chairman E. "Kika" de la Garza, D-Texas, with 284 overdrafts, and John Paul Hammerschmidt of Arkansas, ranking Republican on Public Works, who had 224 overdrafts. Others on the list were Interior Chairman George Miller of California (99 checks) and Rules Chairman Joe Moakley of Massachusetts (90 checks), both Democrats.

But among those who had no overdrafts were two of the House's most powerful chairmen: Ways and Means Chairman Dan Rostenkowski, D-Ill., and Appropriations Chairman Jamie L. Whitten, D-Miss.

Also absent from the list of overdrafters was Charlie Rose, D-N.C., chairman of the House Administration Committee that oversaw the House bank. But the panel's ranking Republican, Bill Thomas of California, had 119 overdrafts.

Several influential subcommittee chairmen floated more than 100 checks: Waxman; Bob Traxler, Mich., an Appropriations subcommittee chairman (201); and Philip R. Sharp of Indiana, an Energy and Commerce subcommittee chairman (120).

## Freshmen, Blacks, Former Members

Twenty-six members on the list already had announced their retirement from politics, including three of the most frequent overdrafters: Hammerschmidt, Lowery and Dennis M. Hertel, a Michigan Democrat who wrote 547 overdrafts.

Sixteen freshmen managed to incur some overdrafts even though they were in Congress for only nine of the 39 months investigated by the ethics committee.

Among them were two members of the "Gang of Seven" — the band of freshman Republicans who were in the forefront of demands that the ethics committee disclose the names of all members who overdrew their accounts. Scott L. Klug of Wisconsin wrote three bad checks, as did Frank Riggs, Calif.

The investigation hit the black caucus hard. Twenty-two of the 26 blacks in Congress were found to have overdrawn their accounts, including five who were among the 22 abusers. The only blacks found not to have written overdrafts were Lucien E. Blackwell, D-Pa., Barbara-Rose Collins, D-Mich., Julian C. Dixon, D-Calif., and Delegate Eleanor Holmes Norton, D-D.C.

Of the 29 women in Congress, 19 were identified as overdrafters. Mary Rose Oakar, D-Ohio, wrote the most; with 213 checks, she was identified as one of the 22 abusers.

The 52 former members on the list included three Cabinet members who had acknowledged problems — Defense Secretary Dick Cheney, Labor Secretary Lynn Martin and Agriculture Secretary Edward Madigan. Also included was Housing and Urban Development Secretary Jack F. Kemp, with one overdraft.

The panel cited five senators, all Republicans, who had previously been House members: Hank Brown of Colorado, Larry E. Craig of Idaho, Daniel R. Coats of Indiana, James M. Jeffords of Vermont and Robert C. Smith of New Hampshire.

## Seeking Cover From Lobbyists

Even before the final list of overdrafters was released, House leaders had turned for succor to banking industry

# Overdrafts Listed From Most to Least . . .

Following is a list of 325 sitting and former House members (including non-voting delegates) who were found by the House Committee on Standards of Official Conduct to have had overdrafts at the House bank between July 1, 1988, and Oct. 3, 1991. It includes the committee's April 1 list of 22 members found to have abused banking privileges and the April 16 list of 303 other overdrafters. Former members are in *italics*. (* On April 1 list of abusers.)

| Name | Count |
|---|---|
| *Tommy F. Robinson, R-Ark.* * | 996 |
| Robert J. Mrazek, D-N.Y. * | 920 |
| Robert W. Davis, R-Mich. * | 878 |
| *Doug Walgren, D-Pa.* * | 858 |
| Ronald V. Dellums, D-Calif. | 851 |
| Charles Hatcher, D-Ga. * | 819 |
| Stephen J. Solarz, D-N.Y. * | 743 |
| Charles A. Hayes, D-Ill. * | 716 |
| Gerry Sikorski, D-Minn. | 697 |
| Ronald D. Coleman, D-Texas * | 673 |
| Louis Stokes, D-Ohio | 551 |
| Dennis M. Hertel, D-Mich. | 547 |
| Chalmers P. Wylie, R-Ohio | 515 |
| Carl C. Perkins, D-Ky. * | 514 |
| Bill Alexander, D-Ark. * | 487 |
| Henry A. Waxman, D-Calif. | 434 |
| Bill Goodling, R-Pa. * | 430 |
| Edolphus Towns, D-N.Y. * | 408 |
| Duncan Hunter, R-Calif. | 399 |
| Edward F. Feighan, D-Ohio * | 397 |
| Harold E. Ford, D-Tenn. * | 388 |
| Mickey Edwards, R-Okla. * | 386 |
| William L. Clay, D-Mo. * | 328 |
| *Tony Coelho, D-Calif.* * | 316 |
| Bill Lowery, R-Calif. | 300 |
| E. "Kika" de la Garza, D-Texas | 284 |
| John Conyers Jr., D-Mich. * | 273 |
| John Paul Hammerschmidt, R-Ark. | 224 |
| Mary Rose Oakar, D-Ohio * | 213 |
| Bob Traxler, D-Mich. | 201 |
| Mike Espy, D-Miss. | 191 |
| Bob McEwen, R-Ohio | 166 |
| Lawrence J. Smith, D-Fla. | 161 |
| Carroll Hubbard Jr., D-Ky. | 152 |
| Thomas J. Downey, D-N.Y. | 151 |
| *Walter E. Fauntroy, D-D.C.* | 145 |
| Barbara Boxer, D-Calif. | 143 |
| *Donald E. "Buz" Lukens, R-Ohio* | 142 |
| Joseph D. Early, D-Mass. * | 140 |
| *Jim Wright, D-Texas* | 138 |
| James H. Scheuer, D-N.Y. | 133 |
| *Morris K. Udall, D-Ariz.* | 128 |
| Chester G. Atkins, D-Mass. | 127 |
| John Lewis, D-Ga. | 125 |
| Vin Weber, R-Minn. | 125 |
| *Douglas H. Bosco, D-Calif.* * | 124 |
| Michael A. Andrews, D-Texas | 121 |
| Philip R. Sharp, D-Ind. | 120 |
| Bill Thomas, R-Calif. | 119 |
| Gary L. Ackerman, D-N.Y. | 111 |
| Beryl Anthony Jr., D-Ark. | 109 |
| *John G. Rowland, R-Conn.* | 108 |
| Ron de Lugo, D-Virgin Islands | 106 |
| *Bill Grant, R-Fla.* | 106 |
| Dan Glickman, D-Kan. | 105 |

| Name | Count |
|---|---|
| Jim Ross Lightfoot, R-Iowa | 105 |
| Dale E. Kildee, D-Mich. | 100 |
| George Miller, D-Calif. | 99 |
| Byron L. Dorgan, D-N.D. | 98 |
| Bill Paxon, R-N.Y. | 96 |
| Edward J. Markey, D-Mass. | 92 |
| Joe Moakley, D-Mass. | 90 |
| *Jim Bates, D-Calif.* * | 89 |
| Jerry Huckaby, D-La. | 88 |
| Richard E. Neal, D-Mass. | 87 |
| Wayne Owens, D-Utah | 87 |
| Charles W. Stenholm, D-Texas | 86 |
| Alan Wheat, D-Mo. | 86 |
| Les AuCoin, D-Ore. | 83 |
| Larry J. Hopkins, R-Ky. | 83 |
| Charles Wilson, D-Texas | 81 |
| Tom Petri, R-Wis. | 77 |
| David E. Bonior, D-Mich. | 76 |
| *Steve Bartlett, R-Texas* | 73 |
| Brian Donnelly, D-Mass. | 70 |
| Howard L. Berman, D-Calif. | 67 |
| Frank McCloskey, D-Ind. | 65 |
| Pat Williams, D-Mont. | 66 |
| David R. Obey, D-Wis. | 64 |
| Charles B. Rangel, D-N.Y. | 64 |
| Pete Stark, D-Calif. | 64 |
| Walter B. Jones, D-N.C. | 63 |
| Eni F. H. Faleomavaega, D-American Samoa | 63 |
| John T. Myers, R-Ind. | 61 |
| *William H. Gray III, D-Pa.* | 60 |
| Barbara B. Kennelly, D-Conn. | 60 |
| John Miller, R-Wash. | 58 |
| David E. Skaggs, D-Colo. | 57 |
| Don Young, R-Alaska | 57 |
| John Bryant, D-Texas | 55 |
| Sam Gejdenson, D-Conn. | 51 |
| Peter H. Kostmayer, D-Pa. | 50 |
| Jim Slattery, D-Kan. | 50 |
| George J. Hochbrueckner, D-N.Y. | 49 |
| *Edward Madigan, R-Ill.* | 49 |
| John D. Dingell, D-Mich. | 48 |
| Major R. Owens, D-N.Y. | 48 |
| John M. Spratt Jr., D-S.C. | 46 |
| *Robert E. Badham, R-Calif.* | 45 |
| Dennis Hastert, R-Ill. | 44 |
| Doug Bereuter, R-Neb. | 39 |
| Andy Ireland, R-Fla. | 38 |
| Ben Blaz, R-Guam | 36 |
| George "Buddy" Darden, D-Ga. | 35 |
| James T. Walsh, R-N.Y. | 34 |
| Robert A. Borski, D-Pa. | 33 |
| Bud Shuster, R-Pa. | 32 |
| John J. Rhodes III, R-Ariz. | 32 |
| Doug Barnard Jr., D-Ga. | 30 |
| Albert G. Bustamante, D-Texas | 30 |

| Name | Count |
|---|---|
| Richard A. Gephardt, D-Mo. | 28 |
| Nancy Pelosi, D-Calif. | 28 |
| Robert G. Torricelli, D-N.J. | 27 |
| George E. Brown Jr., D-Calif. | 26 |
| William E. Dannemeyer, R-Calif. | 26 |
| *Dick Cheney, R-Wyo.* | 25 |
| Robert T. Matsui, D-Calif. | 25 |
| *Arlan Stangeland, R-Minn.* | 25 |
| Jack Fields, R-Texas | 22 |
| Newt Gingrich, R-Ga. | 22 |
| Steve Gunderson, R-Wis. | 22 |
| Eliot L. Engel, D-N.Y. | 21 |
| Jill L. Long, D-Ind. | 21 |
| Ronald K. Machtley, R-R.I. | 21 |
| *Peter Smith, R-Vt.* | 21 |
| Paul B. Henry, R-Mich. | 20 |
| Ron Marlenee, R-Mont. | 20 |
| Gerald B. H. Solomon, R-N.Y. | 20 |
| Dick Armey, R-Texas | 19 |
| *Robert Garcia, D-N.Y.* | 19 |
| *Kenneth J. Gray, D-Ill.* | 19 |
| Matthew G. Martinez, D-Calif. | 19 |
| *Hank Brown, D-Colo.* | 18 |
| Cardiss Collins, D-Ill. | 18 |
| Ralph M. Hall, D-Texas | 18 |
| Solomon P. Ortiz, D-Texas | 18 |
| Christopher Shays, R-Conn. | 18 |
| *Denny Smith, R-Ore.* | 18 |
| *Ronnie G. Flippo, D-Ala.* | 17 |
| Thomas J. Manton, D-N.Y. | 17 |
| Carl D. Pursell, R-Mich. | 17 |
| *Tom Tauke, R-Iowa* | 17 |
| *Lynn Martin, R-Ill.* | 16 |
| Michael R. McNulty, D-N.Y. | 15 |
| Ralph Regula, R-Ohio | 14 |
| F. James Sensenbrenner Jr., R-Wis. | 14 |
| Gene Taylor, D-Miss. | 14 |
| Don Edwards, D-Calif. | 13 |
| Mike Parker, D-Miss. | 13 |
| Richard J. Durbin, D-Ill. | 12 |
| Kweisi Mfume, D-Md. | 12 |
| Alan B. Mollohan, D-W.Va. | 12 |
| Leon E. Panetta, D-Calif. | 12 |
| Floyd D. Spence, R-S.C. | 12 |
| *Wes Watkins, D-Okla.* | 12 |
| Bud Cramer, D-Ala. | 11 |
| Tom DeLay, R-Texas | 11 |
| Edward R. Roybal, D-Calif. | 11 |
| Mike Synar, D-Okla. | 11 |
| Bernard J. Dwyer, D-N.J. | 10 |
| Bill Green, R-N.Y. | 10 |
| Clyde C. Holloway, R-La. | 10 |
| Richard H. Lehman, D-Calif. | 10 |
| John P. Murtha, D-Pa. | 10 |
| Gerry E. Studds, D-Mass. | 10 |

# ...According to House Ethics Committee

| | |
|---|---|
| Sonny Callahan, R-Ala. | 9 |
| *Larry E. Craig, R-Idaho* | 9 |
| *Mike DeWine, R-Ohio* | 9 |
| Lane Evans, D-Ill. | 9 |
| *Robert W. Kastenmeier, D-Wis.* | 9 |
| Greg Laughlin, D-Texas | 9 |
| *Claudine Schneider, R-R.I.* | 9 |
| Ike Skelton, D-Mo. | 9 |
| Cliff Stearns, R-Fla. | 9 |
| Curt Weldon, R-Pa. | 9 |
| William J. Jefferson, D-La. | 8 |
| Tom Lewis, R-Fla. | 8 |
| Marilyn Lloyd, D-Tenn. | 8 |
| David O'B. Martin, R-N.Y. | 8 |
| Dave McCurdy, D-Okla. | 8 |
| David Price, D-N.C. | 8 |
| Matthew J. Rinaldo, R-N.J. | 8 |
| Dana Rohrabacher, R-Calif. | 8 |
| Richard Stallings, D-Idaho | 8 |
| Howard Wolpe, D-Mich. | 8 |
| *Jack Buechner, R-Mo.* | 7 |
| Jim Cooper, D-Tenn. | 7 |
| Gary Franks, R-Conn. | 7 |
| Ben Jones, D-Ga. | 7 |
| Paul E. Kanjorski, D-Pa. | 7 |
| Stephen L. Neal, D-N.C. | 7 |
| Timothy J. Penny, D-Minn. | 7 |
| Jose E. Serrano, D-N.Y. | 7 |
| *D. French Slaughter Jr., R-Va.* | 7 |
| Les Aspin, D-Wis. | 6 |
| Richard H. Baker, R-La. | 6 |
| Beverly B. Byron, D-Md. | 6 |
| Dave Camp, R-Mich. | 6 |
| Bill Emerson, R-Mo. | 6 |
| William D. Ford, D-Mich. | 6 |
| Bart Gordon, D-Tenn. | 6 |
| *John Hiler, R-Ind.* | 6 |
| Austin J. Murphy, D-Pa. | 6 |
| Michael G. Oxley, R-Ohio | 6 |
| Donald M. Payne, D-N.J. | 6 |
| Bill Richardson, D-N.M. | 6 |
| Robert A. Roe, D-N.J. | 6 |
| Bill Sarpalius, D-Texas | 6 |
| Dan Schaefer, R-Colo. | 6 |
| Lindsay Thomas, D-Ga. | 6 |
| Anthony C. Beilenson, D-Calif. | 5 |
| Elton Gallegly, R-Calif. | 5 |
| H. Martin Lancaster, D-N.C. | 5 |
| *Thomas A. Luken, D-Ohio* | 5 |
| Susan Molinari, R-N.Y. | 5 |
| Jim Ramstad, R-Minn. | 5 |
| Marge Roukema, R-N.J. | 5 |
| Bernard Sanders, I-Vt. | 5 |
| Patricia Schroeder, D-Colo. | 5 |
| *Robert C. Smith, R-N.H.* | 5 |
| *Virginia Smith, R-Neb.* | 5 |
| W. J. "Billy" Tauzin, D-La. | 5 |
| Tim Valentine, D-N.C. | 5 |

R. MICHAEL JENKINS
**License on car parked near Capitol**

| | |
|---|---|
| Maxine Waters, D-Calif. | 5 |
| Charles E. Bennett, D-Fla. | 4 |
| Tom Bevill, D-Ala. | 4 |
| Tom Campbell, R-Calif. | 4 |
| Gary Condit, D-Calif. | 4 |
| Jim Jontz, D-Ind. | 4 |
| *Mike Lowry, D-Wash.* | 4 |
| Raymond J. McGrath, R-N.Y. | 4 |
| Alex McMillan, R-N.C. | 4 |
| Dave Nagle, D-Iowa | 4 |
| *Bill Nichols, D-Fla.* | 4 |
| *Howard C. Nielson, R-Utah* | 4 |
| Ron Packard, R-Calif. | 4 |
| Pat Roberts, R-Kan. | 4 |
| Marty Russo, D-Ill. | 4 |
| Gus Savage, D-Ill. | 4 |
| Dick Schulze, R-Pa. | 4 |
| Sidney R. Yates, D-Ill. | 4 |
| Glenn M. Anderson, D-Calif. | 3 |
| Jim Bacchus, D-Fla. | 3 |
| *Lindy (Mrs. Hale) Boggs, D-La.* | 3 |
| *Joseph E. Brennan, D-Maine* | 3 |
| Thomas R. Carper, D-Del. | 3 |
| *Daniel R. Coats, R-Ind.* | 3 |
| *George W. Crockett Jr., D-Mich.* | 3 |
| Norm Dicks, D-Wash. | 3 |
| Floyd H. Flake, D-N.Y. | 3 |
| *Jaime B. Fuster,* | |
| *  Pop. Dem.-Puerto Rico* | 3 |
| Joseph M. Gaydos, D-Pa. | 3 |
| Pete Geren, D-Texas | 3 |
| Joel Hefley, R-Colo. | 3 |
| Frank Horton, R-N.Y. | 3 |
| Steny H. Hoyer, D-Md. | 3 |
| Scott L. Klug, R-Wis. | 3 |
| Robert J. Lagomarsino, R-Calif. | 3 |
| Norman Y. Mineta, D-Calif. | 3 |
| James P. Moran Jr., D-Va. | 3 |
| Frank Riggs, R-Calif. | 3 |
| John Tanner, D-Tenn. | 3 |
| Bruce F. Vento, D-Minn. | 3 |
| Craig Washington, D-Texas | 3 |
| Ted Weiss, D-N.Y. | 3 |
| *Edward P. Boland, D-Mass.* | 2 |
| Bill Brewster, D-Okla. | 2 |
| Terry L. Bruce, D-Ill. | 2 |

| | |
|---|---|
| Thomas S. Foley, D-Wash. | 2 |
| *Bill Frenzel, R-Minn.* | 2 |
| Dean A. Gallo, R-N.J. | 2 |
| Henry J. Hyde, R-Ill. | 2 |
| Nancy L. Johnson, R-Conn. | 2 |
| *Delbert L. Latta, R-Ohio* | 2 |
| William O. Lipinski, D-Ill. | 2 |
| James L. Oberstar, D-Minn. | 2 |
| *Charles "Chip" Pashayan Jr., R-Calif.* | 2 |
| Liz J. Patterson, D-S.C. | 2 |
| Tom Ridge, R-Pa. | 2 |
| H. James Saxton, R-N.J. | 2 |
| *Norman D. Shumway, R-Calif.* | 2 |
| Neal Smith, D-Iowa | 2 |
| Don Sundquist, R-Tenn. | 2 |
| Robin Tallon, D-S.C. | 2 |
| Barbara F. Vucanovich, R-Nev. | 2 |
| Bill Archer, R-Texas | 1 |
| Sherwood Boehlert, R-N.Y. | 1 |
| Rick Boucher, D-Va. | 1 |
| Bob Carr, D-Mich. | 1 |
| Rod Chandler, R-Wash. | 1 |
| Bob Clement, D-Tenn. | 1 |
| Jerry F. Costello, D-Ill. | 1 |
| Lawrence Coughlin, R-Pa. | 1 |
| Randy "Duke" Cunningham, R-Calif. | 1 |
| *Chuck Douglas, R-N.H.* | 1 |
| *Wayne Dowdy, D-Miss.* | 1 |
| Mervyn M. Dymally, D-Calif. | 1 |
| Glenn English, D-Okla. | 1 |
| Dante B. Fascell, D-Fla. | 1 |
| Bill Gradison, R-Ohio | 1 |
| Joan Kelly Horn, D-Mo. | 1 |
| Earl Hutto, D-Fla. | 1 |
| Andrew Jacobs Jr., D-Ind. | 1 |
| *James M. Jeffords, R-Vt.* | 1 |
| Harry A. Johnston, D-Fla. | 1 |
| *Jack F. Kemp, R-N.Y.* | 1 |
| Gerald D. Kleczka, D-Wis. | 1 |
| *Marvin Leath, D-Texas* | 1 |
| Nita M. Lowey, D-N.Y. | 1 |
| Nicholas Mavroules, D-Mass. | 1 |
| Matthew F. McHugh, D-N.Y. | 1 |
| *Bruce A. Morrison, D-Conn.* | 1 |
| Jim Olin, D-Va. | 1 |
| Owen B. Pickett, D-Va. | 1 |
| John Porter, R-Ill. | 1 |
| Richard Ray, D-Ga. | 1 |
| Steven H. Schiff, R-N.M. | 1 |
| Lamar Smith, R-Texas | 1 |
| Olympia J. Snowe, R-Maine | 1 |
| *Fofō I. F. Sunia, D-Am. Samoa* | 1 |
| Dick Swett, D-N.H. | 1 |
| Ray Thornton, D-Ark. | 1 |
| Jolene Unsoeld, D-Wash. | 1 |
| Fred Upton, R-Mich. | 1 |
| Harold L. Volkmer, D-Mo. | 1 |

lobbyists who often needed their help on legislation. The American Bankers Association and the Independent Bankers Association of America both issued statements in behalf of members seeking to downplay the scandal.

"There were abusers but the issue is badly overblown and should be put in a better perspective," the Independent Bankers Association of America (IBAA) said in its weekly newsletter March 20. "It is very common for good bank customers to have overdraft privileges. What's the big deal?"

Left unsaid was the fact that members' overdrafts were covered interest- and penalty-free until members made them good.

The article, written after inquiries to the IBAA from House members' offices, was quoted by members in statements on the scandal, including de la Garza's explanation for his 284 overdrafts.

Kenneth A. Guenther, the IBAA's top lobbyist, said the article came from the IBAA's heart: "If my guys didn't believe it, they wouldn't have done it."

The American Bankers Association weighed in with letters to members and fact sheets distributed to reporters through the Democratic Congressional Campaign Committee. The ABA's conclusion — that many checks were improperly considered overdrafts — repeatedly had been cited by Speaker Foley in defending his colleagues.

A top ABA lobbyist said in one letter that if the House bank had followed industry laws and standards, "a significant number of the checks alleged to have been written with insufficient funds would have been, in fact, fully covered because deposits would have been previously credited to the relevant accounts."

The letter was written by Floyd E. Stoner, a top ABA lobbyist and former aide to two Democratic congressmen. He said he based his conclusion on members' assertions that the bank frequently improperly delayed posting deposits to their accounts — a claim that bank officials denied and House ethics members disputed or discounted.

"I talked to members and drew conclusions," Stoner said. He denied any conflict in providing political cover to members whose influence he frequently courted. "I was responding to requests for information. I responded based on what I knew."

The letter was originally meant for Larry LaRocco, D-Idaho, but was later re-addressed at the request of Majority Leader Gephardt and sent to his office. Gephardt included it with his explanation for 28 overdrafts to bolster his case that many of the overdrafts were the bank's fault.

The Independent Bankers Association, chafing under what it considered Congress' penchant for overregulation in the aftermath of the savings and loan scandal, hoped the episode helped its case in Congress. "We hope Congress would take this and see that whole institutions — and whole industries — should not be ruined by the sins of a few." (Resolution Trust Corporation, p. 115)

## HOUSE ACTION

With the list of overdrafters in the public domain, attention shifted once again to the special counsel's investigation.

Armed with a sweeping subpoena, the Justice Department demanded all the bank's microfilm records, putting House leaders into a political box.

Foley alerted members in a letter April 24 and indicated that he considered the demand too broad.

"The records," Foley wrote, "include all banking transactions over a 39-month period — every single check (whether it caused an overdraft or not), deposit slips and monthly statements — of each member or former member of the House, whether he or she had overdrafts or not. The subpoenas also seek every check of every person who used the former bank during that period: employees, members of the press, members' spouses and even some members of the public."

"It is unprecedented in its sweep and scope," said House Counsel Steven R. Ross, who was in charge of defending the chamber's institutional prerogatives.

But Wilkey said in a letter to Foley: "When reviewing the operations of a bank which is conceded to have been abused, no request or subpoena for such basic records as checks and bank statements can be dismissed as overbroad."

Wilkey, a former federal judge, said he wanted even more: records from the ethics committee's deliberations in the matter and from the General Accounting Office, an investigative arm of Congress. If enforced with another, future subpoena, that would raise the stakes even higher.

Minority Leader Robert H. Michel, R-Ill., agreed that the subpoena was overly broad, aides said. In a letter to GOP colleagues, he suggested giving Wilkey copies of only those checks that resulted in overdrafts.

### Foley Spars With Wilkey

Foley took umbrage at the wide scope of Wilkey's requests for evidence. At a meeting April 13, the Speaker told Wilkey and Attorney General William P. Barr that House leaders from both parties would cooperate with the inquiry only if Wilkey agreed to respect the rights of individual members and the House.

"This meant, specifically, that the investigation could not proceed on the terms Judge Wilkey had proposed . . . as an open-ended and undefined inquiry into the general financial activities of all members," the Speaker said.

In his April 21 letter to Foley, Wilkey said he believed "that the vast majority of House members, if not all, will be found to have committed no crime, but I can only make such a determination by reviewing the bank's records."

Wilkey offered to limit the initial scope of his inquiry to those who had overdrafts and to exclude other members' checks in his review. But Foley said that "the plain language of the subpoenas requests all bank records contained on the microfilm rolls."

How the House would respond was unclear at first. "The consensus is that it's an outrage, but the question is how much you fight it because of the political considerations," said one Democratic aide.

Said a GOP aide: "Politically it would be difficult not to agree to turn everything over to them."

### 'A Classic Check-Kiting Scheme'

Wilkey pressured House members to comply in a combative public letter to lawmakers on April 27.

His letter compared the defunct House bank to "a failed S&L or a fraudulently operated BCCI" — referring to the troubled Bank of Credit and Commerce International. Rejecting Foley's protest that his request was too broad, he said investigators decide what is relevant, "not the objects of the inquiry."

One by one, Wilkey cast doubt on each claim used by members to minimize the scandal — that no public funds were involved, that no money was lost and, most signifi-

cantly, that no laws were broken. "How can anyone possibly make such a claim?" he asked. "As a matter of fact, our preliminary inquiry has already unearthed evidence that a classic check-kiting scheme may have occurred."

Democrats blanched at the suggestion. "How he reaches that conclusion is unexplained," said McHugh. "Based on everything I know, there was no evidence of such a thing," he added, conceding that his panel did not look for criminal activity.

"The Dictionary of Finance and Investment Terms" defined kiting as "depositing and drawing checks between accounts at two or more banks and thereby taking advantage of the float — that is, the time it takes the bank of deposit to collect from the paying bank."

In an interim report to the House in 1991, McHugh said that in some "very limited cases" bad checks on commercial banks were deposited at the House bank "to cover overdrafts the bank was already holding." The ethics panel's final report on the scandal said 60 members cashed or deposited 134 commercial bank checks at the House bank that ultimately bounced.

## Privacy Concerns

For the Republican-controlled Justice Department, the bank records represented the political equivalent of captured enemy documents. They included more than three years' of personal banking records for about 500 current and former members — checks, deposit slips, balance statements and, most important, records showing the overdrafts at the heart of the scandal.

"With that kind of ammunition in their hands, they would be able to bludgeon members," said Dave Nagle, D-Iowa, a leader of the anti-compliance Democrats.

Of paramount concern to Democrats was the danger of leaks, even though Wilkey promised to "meticulously guard" the information.

"I don't believe this, 'Trust me. I won't tell anybody,' " Nagle said. "We've got people who've got marital difficulties — all this is now open," he added. "Did you write a check for a marriage counselor? Did you write a check for a psychiatrist? Did you write a check for alcoholism? Did you write a check for a pharmacist for tranquilizers? Nobody should believe there's going to be any — quote — 'secrecy.' "

Wilkey insisted that he planned to use the information only to determine who, if anyone, committed crimes in using or running the House bank.

Some Republicans also seemed uneasy about Wilkey's tack. Weber, R-Minn., who retired in part because of his 125 overdrafts, said Wilkey was "on a fishing expedition . . . rigged and geared and ready to go after people."

Sounding most uneasy was Michel. In an impromptu talk with reporters on April 27, he agreed with the Democrats' main concerns, suggesting that Wilkey was on "a broad fishing expedition."

Of lawmakers' individual rights, he said, "What right does he have to invade members' privacy?" Of leaks, he said, "Once it's in the Department of Justice, you never know what can happen." Of constitutional considerations, he said he would tell his party's more combative members: "Before you get all carried away here, there are certain institutional prerogatives that we have as a co-equal branch of government."

The bottom line: Michel said he wanted to take the subpoena to court. "I'd want to test that baby," he said. "That's just too broad-sweeping."

## The House Gives In

But Michel and Foley looked increasingly isolated.

The Democrats' hope of standing up to Wilkey evaporated April 28, when Michel, facing a revolt in his own ranks, reversed himself and announced support for full compliance. He had been pummeled by members of his own party, who demanded that he back their call for compliance.

"I think he made a big misstep," said Shays. "He has taken the correct position now, and I wish he had taken that position initially."

A last-minute effort to rally Democrats failed as scores of members bolted in fear. "We simply do not need to appear to be stonewalling," said Timothy J. Penny, D-Minn.

Not helping was the party's leading presidential candidate, Arkansas Gov. Bill Clinton. "My advice would be to comply," he said, flanked by congressional leaders at a news conference April 29. The day before, President Bush had called for "full cooperation."

Despite members' concerns over institutional power and individual rights, the House on April 29 capitulated and voted to give the bank records to Wilkey.

First the House defeated, 131-284, a Democratic proposal (H Res 440) to ask the courts to rule on the matter. Republicans voted as a bloc; Democrats split. (Vote 91, p. 22-H)

Members then voted 347-64 to approve a Republican-sponsored resolution (H Res 441) to turn over the information. (Vote 92, p. 22-H)

Foley and other Democrats tried to argue that their proposal was for "full compliance" — but subject to a court's order. Left unclear was exactly what the House's lawyers would ask the court to do to the subpoena — quash it? Narrow it?

Republicans denounced the plan.

"This resolution is not neutral; it is in opposition to the subpoena," said Jon Kyl, R-Ariz. "We should, therefore, preserve the House's power by making that decision ourselves rather than deferring to another branch of government to make that decision for us."

On the floor, most GOP members, even the combative whip, Gingrich of Georgia, muted their rhetoric.

Hansen conceded that the Democratic proposal "may be the right thing to do." But he said it would take too long to implement. "And every time it comes up, people are going to talk about it," he said. "We are going to rip that scab off every time it happens and we are going to bleed, bleed, bleed, all the way until the first Tuesday in November."

By 11:30 p.m., the Democrats' proposal had been trounced, the Republicans' overwhelmingly approved. And House Republicans had again gained the upper hand by asserting that anything less than full capitulation would be a cover-up of Watergate proportions.

"The bottom line is, Congress isn't any more above the law than Nixon was," said Shays.

In defeat, Democrats said they feared that Wilkey's appetite for internal House documents would prove insatiable, prompting battles with even higher stakes. As for the long haul, Democratic institutionalists called the measure giving up the records a dangerous precedent that could severely weaken Congress at a crucial moment in its 203-year-old power struggle with the executive branch.

"It is a dismal document that we are going to be ashamed of for a long time," said Don Edwards, D-Calif.

The iconoclastic James A. Traficant Jr., D-Ohio, was blunter: "Under stress, Congress has turned into a bunch of constitutional wimps."

As an institution, however, the House decided the public's interest in a scandal-free Congress outweighed concerns over the balance of power and individual rights. "We simply cannot perfectly reconcile those conflicting principles," Michel said in a floor speech. "Complying with the special counsel's request is the surest way to both protect the reputation of the House and ensure that justice is done."

Included in the records subpoenaed were those of 170 members with no overdrafts — the fact that most troubled members from both parties.

To appease those with no overdrafts, Wilkey promised to produce a paper copy of the microfilm, segregate the records for the 170 accounts and return them "unreviewed by us."

### Court Challenge Filed

That was not enough for five Democrats who decided to ask a federal court to quash the subpoena. Moving first, on April 29, were Henry B. Gonzalez, Texas, chairman of the Banking Committee, who had no overdrafts, and Sidney R. Yates, Ill., who had four.

"You cannot waive my rights ... no matter what the collective vote of the House may be," Gonzalez wrote Foley and Michel. He called Wilkey "an unscrupulous opportunist" bent on "trying to bring down the House [and] destroy the fragile co-equality of the federal balance of powers."

Joining the action were Jolene Unsoeld, D-Wash., who overdrew her account once for 38 cents; Ted Weiss, D-N.Y., who had three overdrafts; and Craig Washington, D-Texas, a junior member with three. Their lawyer was Alan B. Morrison, director of the Public Citizen Litigation Group. Morrison was a leading constitutionalist who had won several major separation-of-powers cases, sometimes fighting for Congress, sometimes for the executive branch.

House officials prepared to deliver the records (41 microfilm rolls) to Wilkey on May 4 but hoped that it wouldn't be necessary. U.S. Judge John Garrett Penn said he would rule May 4 on the challenge to the subpoena.

A second struggle with Wilkey seemed possible. The special counsel had requested just about every document gathered or produced by the ethics committee during its seven-month inquiry.

Included in his request were the General Accounting Office's reconstructions of members' accounts and transcripts of all the panel's closed hearings — including those at which some of the most frequent overdrafters appealed the committee's decision to brand them abusers.

Some members said a subpoena of those records could violate the Constitution's ban on members being "questioned" for "any speech or debate."

Republican ethics members seemed willing to give Wilkey just about anything he wanted. "I don't see how we can withhold it," said Fred Grandy, R-Iowa. "How can we go back and negotiate when we've already unconditionally surrendered?"

### Wilkey's Watergate Past

Wilkey was no stranger to high-profile cases involving special prosecutors seeking sensitive documents, or to constitutional confrontations between the branches of government over separation of powers. He was a significant player in the granddaddy of them all: the Watergate tapes case.

In 1973, as a judge on the U.S. Court of Appeals for the District of Columbia, Wilkey was on the losing side in a 5-2 ruling that forced Richard M. Nixon to comply with Special Prosecutor Archibald M. Cox's subpoena and turn over to a judge the tapes that eventually forced Nixon to resign.

Some Democrats attacked Wilkey for trying to force a Democratic Congress to do what he tried to protect a Republican president from having to do.

"The one judge who thought that Richard Nixon should keep the tapes is not the one person who should be running this investigation," said Rep. Sam Gejdenson, D-Conn.

"I only wish Judge Wilkey remembered his own words from 1973," said Gonzalez, one of the plaintiffs in the suit to quash Wilkey's subpoena. "This independence cannot be a one-way street."

A close reading of Wilkey's 1973 dissent revealed no inconsistency. It turned on one basic position: that each branch of government should be the sole judge of whether to give its own material to another branch — which is what the House did in its April 29 vote.

"It was and is the president's right to make that decision [regarding the tapes] initially, and it is the American people who will be the judge as to whether the president has made the right decision," Wilkey wrote.

Nonetheless, at a May 1 hearing on the Gonzalez suit, Wilkey stepped back from his dissent. In light of subsequent facts, many learned only after the forced release of the Watergate tapes, he said, "I do not believe that I could have in July of '74 written the opinion on the Nixon case that I wrote in October of '73."

Wilkey's dissent in the Watergate case included language relevant to the House bank flap:

● **Forcing disclosure.** "I know of no case where the court has ever made the Senate or the House surrender records from its files, or where the executive has made the legislative branch surrender records from its files — and I do not think either one of them could."

● **Public interest.** "Of course one can imagine innumerable instances in which a court, Congress, or the executive ought to disclose the documents in the public interest, and probably would. . . . But the more certain it is that the holder of the documents — the holder of the privilege — will decide to disclose does not alter the fact that it is the holder of the constitutional privilege who decides."

● **Possibility of leaks.** "As the circle of 'secrecy' widens, it will dissolve and vanish. All human experience teaches this — particularly in Washington, D.C."

● **Compromise.** "Congressional demands for executive papers are as numerous as autumn leaves, and frequently fall due to a frost between the two ends of Pennsylvania Avenue. . . . But our history is full of examples of situations in which direct confrontations between two or more of the co-equal branches were avoided by one of the branches deciding not to push its position to the limit."

### Court Sides With Wilkey

Rejecting applications for a stay, jurists in three courts decided that Gonzalez and the other House members fighting to quash the Wilkey subpoena had little chance of success. "Movants cannot demonstrate that they are likely to prevail on the merits," wrote Judge Penn.

The members had argued that the subpoena was too broad, invaded their privacy and violated the separation-of-powers doctrine.

Penn turned them down at noon on May 4 — just as the House-approved deadline for turning over the records

# Acting Ethics Chairman Calls It Quits

Rep. Matthew F. McHugh, D-N.Y., who steered the House ethics committee through the most difficult and sweeping investigation in its history, stunned his colleagues May 4 by announcing he would retire from the House at the end of the year.

Elected in 1974, McHugh, 53, came to Congress with 74 other Democrats with a mandate for reform in the aftermath of Watergate. Nearly two decades later, he oversaw an ethics inquiry that plunged the House into turmoil, contributing to an exodus that dwarfed 1974's turnover. He was tapped to serve as acting chairman of the Committee on Standards of Official Conduct when the panel's regular chairman, Louis Stokes, D-Ohio, acknowledged having overdrafts at the House bank.

Although McHugh's announcement came the day the House turned over its bank records to a special counsel investigating possible criminal conduct in the scandal, McHugh insisted his decision to retire was not connected to the House bank affair.

"I know it's hard to believe," McHugh said. "Coming on the wake of the House bank, it's understandable that it looks that way. But it isn't."

Colleagues from both parties were shocked by McHugh's decision. "The banshees and monkeys are staying, and the sequoias are falling," said David R. Obey, D-Wis.

In an interview, McHugh explained his conflicted decision to leave the House at the end of the 1990-1992 term.

He noted that he had "very compelling political reasons to stay." His Republican-leaning district seemed amazingly comfortable with a liberal congressman. In the House, McHugh was likely soon to assume a powerful Appropriations subcommittee chairmanship. Though the House bank affair probably made him some enemies, he remained widely liked and respected, and a leadership bid was in the realm of possibility. "It's not a time when one traditionally leaves the Congress," he conceded.

But McHugh surveyed the political landscape and saw an America paralyzed by parochial interests. Looking at things from a partisan perspective, he called the 1980s a decade of "fundamental mistakes" — tax cuts for the rich, unchecked entitlement spending and a huge defense buildup. The country was paying the price: towering debt and recession.

"People are upset and angry," he said. "But there are a lot of people who, while they want change, are not prepared to compromise their own interests." He said President Bush was unwilling to confront them and Congress was unwilling to risk displeasing them.

The problem was worse than ever, he said, because the interest groups — the lobbyists in Washington and their grass-roots networks outside the Beltway — were stronger. "You have many members of Congress who are unwilling to take the risk. Why? It's going to hurt back home more than it used [to], and we're not going to win anyway."

"In a sense," he added, "all of us are to blame — the people and the leaders."

## Looking Homeward

McHugh weighed his view of the political reality against his desire for a more normal life with his wife, Alanna, and their three grown daughters and granddaughter. "It's a close call — you know, 52-48," he said, as if it were an election. "Literally every hour I'm kind of confronted with the emotion of it — is this the right thing to do?"

He didn't want anyone to think he was leaving in utter frustration, "wringing my hands" in anguish. He felt he had accomplished a fair amount as a pragmatic liberal, fighting for humanitarian foreign aid and domestic nutrition assistance programs. He pointed optimistically to what he saw as a general feeling in the nation "that something is wrong . . . that we have to do something."

"I'm not saying there's no hope, and I'm not saying I can't accomplish anything," he said. "I'm saying I may not be able to accomplish enough to justify, after 18 years, continuing to put my family through this. Not just my family — me."

McHugh had all but made his decision a week before he announced it. "Until I actually sat down with my staff, there was still a chance that I would go forward," he recalled. He told his staff April 30.

That was the day after the House voted to comply with a Justice Department subpoena for its bank records, a decision McHugh opposed.

"But it's not the reason I announced my decision to retire," he said. "It was coincidental."

passed. The judge said he was unwilling to interfere with the House's decision.

"The movants do not have a legitimate expectation of privacy in the records," Penn wrote. "The members took the same risk as ordinary depositors in a standard bank when they transacted business" at the House bank. The subpoena was not too broad, Penn ruled, because "the underlying facts certainly establish a basis for the materials subpoenaed."

Shortly after Penn ruled, four House officials — Sergeant at Arms Werner W. Brandt, two lawyers representing both parties' leaders and a Capitol Police officer — set out for an FBI office in Northern Virginia with 41 rolls of House bank microfilm in three boxes.

As the House officials watched, FBI agents unsealed the boxes and checked the contents. The boxes were then resealed, and House and FBI officials initialed the tape. "It was all very cordial," said Brandt.

The boxes were resealed because Wilkey had agreed to allow House employees to watch over the handling of the microfilm as it was copied into paper form and collated. The agreement was meant to assure members that federal agents would not review information from 170 accounts that had no overdrafts.

About 3 p.m., Penn denied Gonzalez's and Yates' request for a stay, saying delivery of the microfilm made the matter moot. Lawyers for Gonzalez and Yates appealed to the Court of Appeals and again asked for a stay, but the

request was turned down by 5 p.m.

On May 6, Gonzalez's lawyers asked U.S. Chief Justice William H. Rehnquist to order the records returned or sealed pending appeal; the chief justice turned him down within hours.

### Financial Disclosure Reports

The May 15 deadline for filing financial disclosure forms for 1991 posed a sensitive quandary for the Committee on Standards of Official Conduct. Members wanted to know whether overdrafts at the House bank for more than $10,000 met the threshold for reporting loans set in the Ethics in Government Act.

The law required lawmakers to disclose the approximate value of liabilities that totaled more than $10,000 at any time in the year.

Generally, the only exceptions were mortgages on residences, loans from certain relatives and loans secured by a car, furniture or appliances.

The House in 1992 twice voted for resolutions calling for what sponsors said was "full disclosure" in the bank mess.

In March, members voted to reveal all who had overdrafts in a 39-month period. In April, they voted to turn over bank records to the Justice Department so it could continue a criminal inquiry.

Nevertheless, the actual dollar amount of members' overdrafts had never been officially disclosed. The public would get a clearer picture if members had to report big overdrafts on their disclosure forms.

A leaked document showed that as many as 28 current members had $10,000-plus overdrafts at some point. The document summarized the results of an ethics committee reconstruction of 66 current and former members' accounts (out of a total of 325 who had overdrafts). Most, if not all, members with overdrafts of $10,000 or more were among the 66.

The committee on May 7 voted 12-1 not to require members to disclose overdrafts as loans — or as gifts or income. Its rationale was twofold: Complying would be too difficult, and it would not serve the purpose financial disclosure was meant to address — revealing potential conflicts of interest.

"It would be very difficult for members to comply," said McHugh, because many members did not know exactly how much they were overdrawn.

Said top ethics Republican James V. Hansen, Utah: "The 66 could do it; for the rest of these poor guys, it's just totally impossible to do.... The practical argument overwhelms the legal argument by far."

Besides, added McHugh, "While an overdraft is technically a loan, it is not the kind of transaction financial disclosure is designed to reach — who's the lender?"

The sole dissenter was Jim Bunning, R-Ky., an ardent advocate of openness during past bank fights. He favored following the financial disclosure law literally.

The decision was significant because the ethics law barred the Justice Department from seeking civil fines against members who filed false financial disclosures if they followed committee advice.

"This may give a little cover to members, but it wasn't meant to," said Hansen.

Panel leaders May 8 issued a long letter on the decision. "Further reporting of overdraft information would add little of substance to what is already publicly available," they wrote.

### More Bank Files Released

The House on May 28 voted 396-5 to turn over to the Justice Department additional documents related to the House bank. Wilkey requested the documents as part of his investigation of whether members violated criminal laws by overdrawing their accounts. *(Vote 145, p. 36-H)*

The documents included some records already provided to Wilkey on microfilm by a vote of the House on April 29 in response to a controversial subpoena. Members of the House ethics committee said they had reviewed most of the newly requested material in their investigation of members' overdrafts.

The information included the bank's balance ledgers; its daily settlement sheets, which listed overdrafts; any lists of members or others whose check privileges had been suspended or restricted; lists of individuals who were allowed to write checks against accounts of members who had overdrafts; and computer files showing overdrafts.

Also included were records about short-term loans made to members by the National Bank of Washington through the early 1980s. The House bank acted as an intermediary in setting up the loans.

The resolution (H Res 471) also authorized the bipartisan leadership of the House to respond to Wilkey's future requests without having to put the matter to a House vote — unless the leaders could not agree among themselves.

## WILKEY'S CLEARANCE LETTERS

By mid-October all but about two dozen of the 325 current and former lawmakers who overdrew their House bank accounts had received letters from the Justice Department clearing them of criminal wrongdoing.

Those left empty-handed had to sweat as Election Day approached and opponents continued to harp on their overdrafts.

The first letters were hand-delivered to members' offices by FBI agents who fanned out across Capitol Hill early Sept. 9. By the end of that week, The Associated Press reported that at least 137 of the 269 current members who overdrew their accounts said they had received what the Justice Department called "clearance letters."

Members still waiting put on a brave face.

"The letter doesn't mean anything — most of America hasn't received a letter from the Justice Department that says they haven't committed a crime," said Gary L. Ackerman, D-N.Y., who overdrew his account 111 times during the 39 months under review and faced a tough primary on Sept. 15.

Those who got a letter reported mixed feelings. "I'm glad I got this, obviously," said Peter H. Kostmayer, D-Pa., but "I don't think it helps. It just brings the issue up again."

The front-page headline in one of his home-state newspapers proclaimed: "Kanjorski, Kostmayer Cleared." Kostmayer replied: "As if I had been accused of something." Kostmayer had 50 overdrafts; fellow Pennsylvania Democrat Paul E. Kanjorski had seven.

Wilkey, the special counsel investigating the bank scandal, said in a statement that the "vast majority" of overdrafters eventually would be absolved of criminal wrongdoing.

A source familiar with Wilkey's plans said all but about three dozen would get letters in the initial batch. Additional letters would follow as work on the more complex accounts continued, officials said.

In a statement, the Justice Department stressed that the lack of a clearance letter to a member "is not necessarily indicative of him or her being under criminal investigation."

But the statement also stressed that Wilkey's letter only dealt with criminal culpability — while "not otherwise addressing the propriety of a member's actions."

Wilkey did not say what crimes he thought might have been committed, although he had said earlier that he had found evidence that "a classic check-kiting scheme may have occurred."

The Justice Department said that Wilkey had delivered an interim report to Attorney General Barr "discussing specific criminal statutes with their application to evidence gathered to date."

## Resentment Lingers

Reaction in Congress to Wilkey's initial round of letters was mostly negative, though generally muted, possibly because many members were still waiting to see if they would get one.

Speaker Foley, who got a letter, said in a statement: "We believe that Judge Wilkey's stated purpose of eliminating public speculation concerning members who used the former House Bank is laudable, but we have never seen the need to buttress what has always been evident to us — that no member has violated any law in this matter."

Even some Republicans who received letters were critical of Wilkey's tack. GOP Whip Gingrich, who had 22 overdrafts and got one, called Wilkey's approach "unfortunate" and "exactly backward to the American tradition. The American tradition is you're innocent until proven guilty."

Henry J. Hyde, R-Ill., who had two overdrafts and got a letter, added: "Not getting a letter amounts to a quasi-conviction without due process of law."

Others had harsher words.

Ben Jones, D-Ga., whose seven overdrafts contributed to his July 21 primary defeat, said of his letter in a floor speech: "I appreciate it, but it's a little late, since this whole matter didn't help me in my re-election bid. Now, with all due respect, the good judge can take this letter, fold it four ways, tie a ribbon around it and put it [pause] wherever he wants to."

Like many others, Scheuer, who had 133 overdrafts and had not yet received a letter, accused the administration of using the probe to defeat Democrats.

"It's the cheapest kind of politicization of the Justice Department that I've seen in my lifetime," he said.

The Justice Department denied having political motives.

"What the Justice Department is doing is attempting to be as fair as possible with individuals who have been unfairly tainted," said spokesman Paul McNulty.

One congressman who was especially grateful was Chalmers P. Wylie, R-Ohio, who had 515 overdrafts. He and Duncan Hunter, R-Calif., who had 399, were the only members with more than 200 overdrafts who reported receiving letters.

"I called Judge Wilkey to thank him for it," Wylie said. "He said, 'I don't think thanks are in order.'"

Wylie said Wilkey told him his account was one of the easiest to evaluate because most of his checks appeared to be for everyday household expenses — an indication that Wilkey was at least partly focusing on how members used overdraft checks.

## Gambling Allegation

As the 102nd Congress neared its close, the House bank story took one odd twist. Robert S. Walker, R-Pa., alleged in a floor speech Sept. 30 that some of the bad checks cashed at the House bank by former Sergeant at Arms Russ were used to pay members' gambling debts.

Walker, an outspoken critic of House Democratic leaders' handling of the bank scandal, did not name the members, explaining in an interview that he was not sure who they were.

"A number of those very, very substantial checks were written to pay gambling debts of members of the House," Walker said. He mentioned four checks worth a total of $35,000 that were short of funds in the summer of 1989.

Several Democrats challenged Walker to reveal the source of his information. Walker said his allegation was based on testimony given to the House ethics committee.

Russ could not be reached for comment, and ethics committee officials declined to comment.

Russ, who supervised the bank until he resigned March 12, cashed 20 bad checks (written on commercial bank accounts) worth more than $50,000. Asked about the checks in February, Russ said: "It's a personal matter between myself and a member who is no longer here. . . . I assumed money would be placed in my account that afternoon, and to make a long story short, it wasn't."

# ELECTION RESULTS

In the end, the House bank proved an effective though by no means perfect weapon for challengers across the country.

Along the Rio Grande, Texas Democratic Rep. Albert G. Bustamante's 30 *cheques calientes* (hot checks) helped doom his re-election bid. On Long Island, Thomas J. Downey, D-N.Y., fell in an upset Nov. 3 while trying to convince voters that his 151 overdrafts had nothing to do with his wife's job title (misleading, he said) — House bank auditor. Ohio Democrat Mary Rose Oakar's claim that she really had only 19 overdrafts — not 213 — did little but give her GOP opponent an easy opening.

"Ms. Oakar," Martin R. Hoke told her during a nationally televised encounter, "you are still in denial."

Overall, overdrafts were a significant factor in 1992 — especially when primary defeats and retirements were taken into account.

Only six of 17 current members accused of having "abused their banking privileges" by the House ethics committee were re-elected. Of the 46 members with 100 or more overdrafts, 25 (54 percent) retired or were defeated. Of the 389 with fewer than 100 overdrafts or none at all, 80 (21 percent) retired or were defeated.

## Some Weather the Storm

Most of the damage came in the primary season.

On Nov. 3, challengers beat 24 incumbents, far fewer than predicted by many political observers. All but five of the defeated had overdrawn their House bank accounts at least once during the 3¼ years studied by the ethics committee. Five had at least 140 overdrafts.

Some won despite many overdrafts — Jim Ross Lightfoot, R-Iowa (105 overdrafts); Bill Goodling, R-Pa. (430); Ronald D. Coleman, D-Texas (673); Dan Glickman, R-Kan. (105); and Charles Wilson, D-Texas (81).

Still, the House bank affair was a key, and perhaps decisive, issue in many of the incumbent losses.

# Ackerman Resigns House Ethics Panel

Rep. Gary L. Ackerman, D-N.Y., accused by other members of leaking a list of the top abusers of the House bank, resigned July 28 from the ethics committee.

His resignation came just days before the panel, officially called the Committee on Standards of Official Conduct, met to discuss whether to begin a full-scale investigation of the leak in March of the 24-member list of those who had most "abused" their banking privileges.

Ackerman said he decided to resign because the panel was too politicized and he was concerned that any future leaks would be blamed on him. Ackerman called the panel's work a "thankless task" and said, "It was more political than I'd like, so I got off."

Other members, who asked not to be identified, said that the resignation was part of a deal with Chairman Louis Stokes, D-Ohio, to avoid an ethics inquiry into whether he leaked the list. Ackerman, who denied the charge, said no deal had been made with Stokes. Stokes refused comment.

"I think he certainly should have resigned," said Charles Wilson, D-Texas, who was cited on the leaked list but not in the official report. "The circumstantial evidence that he did the leaking is overwhelming."

### Panel Divided Over Leak Probe

The ethics panel met for six hours on July 30 but put off a decision on whether to pursue a full-scale probe.

Most members wanted to put the bank scandal behind them. But the investigation was requested and was being pushed by several members cited as abusers, and Democrats were wary of looking as though they were engaged in a whitewash.

At the completion of the House bank investigation in March, the ethics committee compiled a preliminary list of the 24 worst abusers.

The list was supposed to remain secret for at least 10 days so members could be notified and given a chance to appeal. But the list was leaked to several media organizations before the appeals process could begin.

One member on the list, Democrat Charles A. Hayes, lost a primary just days after the names were revealed. Two other members, Wilson and James H. Scheuer, D-N.Y., successfully appealed and were not on the official 22-member list released by the ethics panel April 1.

Early on, Ackerman was suspected of being the source of the leak by Scheuer and Robert J. Mrazek, Democratic rivals of Ackerman in the New York House delegation.

A complaint against Ackerman was filed on July 8, demanding to know why he received a copy of the list from a staff member and requested an investigation of whether he leaked it. Although the complaint was filed by Hayes and Edward F. Feighan, D-Ohio, members said it was engineered by Scheuer and Mrazek.

Ackerman contended that the complaint was a political move by Scheuer because the two were slated to face each other in a 5th District primary. Scheuer later decided not to seek re-election.

### Matter Dropped

Ethics panel members were tight-lipped about the debate over a full-scale probe, but others monitoring the deliberations said the committee was divided on whether to close the case or open a full-scale inquiry.

James V. Hansen, Utah, the ranking Republican on the panel, was giving a lot of latitude to Stokes and other Democrats. "We kind of left that up to the Democrats," he said.

While Stokes was pushing to avoid a formal investigation, one source said that at least two Democrats on the panel — Jim McDermott, Wash., and Benjamin L. Cardin, Md. — wanted a probe.

In the end, the committee decided to drop the matter. On Sept. 17, the panel announced it would take no action against Ackerman.

One of the complainants, Hayes, said he was disappointed by the decision. "The leak raises serious questions about the integrity of the body," Hayes said. "That's been my concern all along."

---

Bustamante had been re-elected several times with more than 60 percent before Republican challenger Henry Bonilla depicted the overdrafts en español. Gerry Sikorski, D-Minn., had seemed secure before his 697 overdrafts helped Republican Rod Grams win by a wide margin. Though he had long represented a GOP-majority district, Downey had consistently won with 55 percent or more until Rick A. Lazio seized on his bank troubles. Despite previous ethics scrapes, Oakar had not polled under 70 percent since coming to Congress in 1976.

Bob McEwen, R-Ohio, had polled 70 percent or better for three elections in a row until his 166 overdrafts handed Democrat Ted Strickland an easy issue. Joseph D. Early, D-Mass., had run unopposed three times before Republican state Rep. Peter I. Blute struck a chord highlighting his 140 overdrafts.

Some had additional baggage weighing them down.

Former abortion opponent Sikorski's conversion to an abortion rights stance hurt him. Oakar also was tainted by the House Post Office scandal. Bustamante had been under investigation by a federal grand jury on other matters for three years and galled low-income constituents by purchasing a $500,000 home. Pennsylvania Democrat Peter H. Kostmayer had long been considered vulnerable in his solidly Republican district. His 50 overdrafts may have been just enough to put GOP state Sen. James C. Greenwood over the top.

A handful of overdrafters also were hurt by redistricting, most notably Jerry Huckaby, D-La., who had 88 overdrafts and lost to a fellow incumbent, the GOP's Jim McCrery, in a conservative district.

Even members with few or no checks were hurt by the scandal. Defeated GOP Reps. Don Ritter, Pa., and Tom Coleman, Mo., were nailed for using perks — especially after they showered their district with franked mail to announce that they had no overdrafts.

Dave Nagle, D-Iowa, who had four overdrafts, was criticized for trying to persuade House colleagues to resist a

federal subpoena of House bank records. Iowa Republican Jim Nussle, one of the so-called Gang of Seven GOP freshmen who clamored to close the bank, used the episode to paint Nagle as a leadership toady — and beat him. (Another of the Gang of Seven, Frank Riggs, R-Calif., who had three overdrafts, was defeated.)

In other races pitting incumbents against each other, the House bank played little or no role because both candidates had overdrafts. In Louisiana, Republican Richard H. Baker (six overdrafts) beat fellow Republican Clyde C. Holloway (10). In Montana, the man with more overdrafts, Democrat Pat Williams (66), beat Republican Ron Marlenee, who had 20.

The House bank was a factor in several Senate races. Democratic Reps. Barbara Boxer of California and Byron L. Dorgan of North Dakota were both able to win despite their overdrafts, 143 and 98, respectively. The check scandal helped incumbent GOP Sen. Bob Packwood of Oregon beat back a challenge by Democratic Rep. Les AuCoin, who had 83 overdrafts. Likewise, Democratic Sen. John Glenn of Ohio was able to deflect criticism of his role in the Keating Five affair by pointing to former Rep. Mike DeWine's nine overdrafts.

## THE FINAL STAGE

As 1992 drew to a close, a few current and former members faced full-blown criminal investigations, and a source involved in the probe said some probably would be indicted. No names were disclosed.

On Dec. 16 special counsel Wilkey concluded his 8½-month preliminary inquiry of the bank scandal and resigned his post.

"Actual criminal conduct by some members appears to have taken place, but it is quite limited," Wilkey said in a report to Attorney General Barr. "Where criminal violations were indicated, a full-scale investigation will be undertaken."

Wilkey ended his investigation without pursuing his initial request for transcripts of the House ethics committee's meetings or for General Accounting Office records prepared for the committee's internal use.

Barr immediately set up a special unit of five prosecutors and seven FBI agents in the Criminal Division's Public Integrity Section to conduct the investigation. Wilkey's chief of staff, Thomas J. Eicher, an assistant U.S. attorney from Philadelphia, was put in charge.

### About 20 Lack Letters

The department declined to name the roughly 20 former and current members Wilkey believed might have committed crimes or to give a precise count, saying only that "a very few individuals" were under suspicion, including some former House employees.

"The process of the investigation goes on, and some of these people will be cleared," Wilkey said in an interview. "It just takes time."

Only three members re-elected on Nov. 3 had not announced receiving letters: Harold E. Ford, D-Tenn., who had been under indictment since 1987 on unrelated federal corruption charges; Charles Wilson, D-Texas, who said in March that one of his overdrafts was used to loan $10,000 to his re-election campaign; and Charles B. Rangel, D-N.Y., who told The Associated Press that investigators were looking at whether there was a connection between his 64 overdrafts and his campaign treasury.

Thirteen defeated or retiring members also had not yet reported receiving exoneration letters, not counting Walter B. Jones, D-N.C., who died Sept. 15. (*Obituaries, p. 73*)

It was unclear how many former members remained without letters, but two of five former members identified as bank abusers by the ethics committee said they had not received letters, while two others — including former Democratic Whip Tony Coelho, Calif. — said they had.

### Possible Crimes

The Justice Department's criminal investigation was expected to focus on four types of violations:

● Check-kiting, in which bad checks at one bank were covered with bad checks from another bank. This could apply to any member who tried to cover overdrafts at the House bank with bad checks from another bank.

"This did occur in a number of members' accounts," Wilkey's report said. "Whether it occurred with the intent necessary to constitute a provable criminal offense can only be determined by a close examination of an individual member's account." The House bank's lax policies offered members "a golden opportunity" for a check-kiting scheme, Wilkey said.

The ethics committee said in March that 60 members had bounced a total of 134 commercial bank checks at the House bank. Among them were several of those still under scrutiny by the Justice Department, according to the ethics committee's list of so-called abusers.

Ford bounced four; Solarz, 11; retiring Rep. Carl C. Perkins, D-Ky., 28; defeated Rep. Charles A. Hayes, D-Ill., nine; former Rep. Douglas H. Bosco, D-Calif., four; defeated Rep. Bill Alexander, D-Ark., two; and defeated Rep. Mary Rose Oakar, D-Ohio, and former Rep. Jim Bates, D-Calif., one each.

● Conversion of public funds to personal use. Any such charge would be based on Wilkey's theory that the House bank's money was government property — a contention House leaders flatly rejected. Prosecutors likely would pursue such a charge against a member only if large sums were involved and if they could prove criminal intent.

Foley said in a statement that Wilkey told him Dec. 16 that "overdrafts at the former bank, in and of themselves, would not be sufficient" grounds for prosecution. "That has always been my view," Foley added.

But Wilkey said in an interview that Foley overstated his position slightly. "That is basically correct, unless the overdrafts were for huge amounts and there were several of them where you had obvious intent," Wilkey said.

Each of the 11 abusers still under scrutiny at least once had a negative balance in the thousands of dollars. Those with the highest negative balances were: Bosco, $75,723; Perkins, $41,200; Stephen J. Solarz, D-N.Y., $23,019; and Ford, $20,743.

One possible target of a conversion charge could be former Sergeant at Arms Russ, whose office ran the House bank. The ethics committee concluded that Russ and a former bank teller "misused their positions ... by cashing a number of bad checks" drawn on commercial banks at the House bank. Russ cashed 19 bad checks with a total value of $56,100, the ethics panel said. All eventually were made good. Russ was contacted but declined to comment.

Without addressing any particular circumstance, Wilkey in his report took pains to note that "simply because embezzled money has been replaced does not mean that an embezzlement has not taken place at a given point in time."

• Misuse of campaign money. Prosecutors probably planned to see whether any members converted campaign funds to personal use by depositing them into their House bank account.

• False campaign reports and financial disclosures.

Wilkey's report said investigators checked Federal Election Commission (FEC) reports and financial disclosure statements filed under ethics laws "to determine whether transactions were being concealed."

The report disclosed that in April when Wilkey was trying to persuade the House to turn over its bank records, Rep. Hansen of Utah, the top Republican on the ethics committee, told him "that a number of members were quite concerned that disclosure of their account records would reveal possible violations" of campaign and financial disclosure laws.

Even those who received clearance letters from Wilkey might still have worries in this regard: The report said that evidence of civil violations of such laws had been referred "to the appropriate agency" — presumably the FEC or the Justice Department's civil division.

## The Wilkey Report

At times testy and defensive, Wilkey's 49-page report offers a scathing critique of the House bank scandal and members' attempts to explain it away as much ado about nothing.

Wilkey defended his decision to clear individual members, which many criticized as a backward approach to prosecution implying that all were guilty until proved innocent.

"I believed that the unique clientele of this bank ... called for a reversal of the usual priorities," Wilkey said. Going after the most obvious criminal cases while doing nothing to exonerate the "clearly innocent," he said, "would have been grossly unfair to the vast majority of the members of the House, particularly those seeking re-election."

By Election Day, Wilkey said, all but nine members seeking re-election had exoneration letters. Three lost: Bustamante, Oakar and Nicholas Mavroules, D-Mass., who had just one overdraft but was also under indictment on unrelated federal corruption charges.

The inquiry, Wilkey said, involved examining 611,516 documents from the House bank and entering those dealing with overdrafters into a data base. Each overdrafter's account was reviewed by FBI agents and prosecutors. Some members submitted to interviews or provided prosecutors supplemental information.

"To date, there has been no hint of any leak," Wilkey said, referring to a major concern of members when he subpoenaed the records.

Several pages were dedicated to defending Wilkey's conclusion that the bank "dealt exclusively with public funds." Wilkey argued that the bank's assets, though made up of members' salary and other deposits held at the U.S. Treasury, "belonged to the United States until the Sergeant at Arms actually disbursed it." He buttressed his case with numerous court decisions and GAO opinions that reached the same conclusion and the fact that the House three times appropriated public funds to replenish money stolen from its bank.

House leaders had long insisted that the bank's money — which was kept in a Treasury account called "Members Balances With/At the Sergeant at Arms, House of Representatives" — was the sole property of the members. The leaders argued that members' salary and other deposits covered all the overdrafts, which in recent years were all eventually made good, and the Treasury account never had a negative balance overall.

In his Dec. 16 statement, Foley said, "I do not agree with Judge Wilkey's legal conclusion that public funds were involved in the operation of the former bank, and I remain firmly convinced that no losses resulted to the public because of its operation or closure."

Wilkey belittled other assertions that members offered to minimize the scandal. Of those members who said they were not notified of overdrafts, he said that "this could be true for a limited number of members" with a few small overdrafts, but that "habitual overdrafters were habitually notified."

Wilkey also did not agree with those who said there were no House checks that bounced. "There certainly were," the report said. "The abuse of the facility by some members grew so bad that they were advised that their checks would not be honored" unless they had sufficient funds on account, and the bank bounced at least five members' checks. Four of them still had not been cleared by Wilkey: The House bank bounced 53 of Solarz's House bank checks, 11 of Ford's, 25 of Perkins' and two of Hatcher's, the ethics committee said.

On the other hand, Wilkey defended members against arguments that all overdrafters should be prosecuted. Most members, Wilkey said, "fall into the categories of either innocent of any intentional wrongdoing or responsible for only ethical violations." He explicitly noted that few if any violated the District of Columbia's bad-check statute because the bank routinely honored overdrafts, shielding members from a law that required knowledge that the check in question would not be honored.

"The House bank permitted members to engage in conduct that would have been impossible (and, in some circumstances, even criminal) for the general public," Wilkey said.

Wilkey sharply criticized the management and oversight of the bank. The bank's vault, usually containing $200,000, was left open during bank hours, and tellers were allowed to replenish their cash drawers on an honor system. Bad checks were carried on the books "as mutilated money or cash," he said.

Check-cashing rules, Wilkey said, were rarely put to paper, and when they were, they were "abandoned or forgotten," apparently never circulated to bank employees or members. "The House bank particularly avoided creating written records concerning members' overdrafts," Wilkey said.

House bank employees knew in advance when the GAO would come for audits and "surprise" cash counts, Wilkey said. Even after auditors discovered Russ and a teller had cashed bad checks for themselves, a 1988 GAO audit reported finding no "material weakness" at the bank.

Members' overdrafts were criticized in secret GAO reports from 1949 to 1977, Wilkey said, but once the GAO started releasing the reports publicly, references to them became cryptic. It was not until the GAO decided to make an issue of the overdraft problem in public reports issued in 1990 and 1991 that a huge outcry prompted the House to close the bank.

"The credo of the House bank was to serve the House of Representatives and never embarrass a member," Wilkey wrote. "This credo, which underlay the bank's policies, indeed its very existence, ultimately led to its downfall." ∎

# History of the House Bank

Until its demise in 1991, the House bank operated for more than 150 years outside the system of checks and balances. Too often, there were plenty of checks but not enough balances. Its history reveals an institution that was plagued by scandal from just after its inception until its unhappy end.

Rapscallions of the past repeatedly made off with large sums from the members-only bank, which was run by the Office of the Sergeant at Arms. One cashier bolted with his mistress to Canada after cramming 20 times his annual salary into a valise, never to be heard from again. A former Florida congressman floated bad checks at the bank for years to speculate in real estate and to finance his comeback campaign. One sergeant at arms, Kenneth Romney, ripped off the bank repeatedly for two decades until he was caught and thrown behind bars.

Three times the bank was caught short by thousands of dollars — sums that in the 1990s would have been worth at least $2 million. Each time, the House enacted minimal reforms. But institutional memory always proved too short, and scandal again erupted in the face of startled leaders.

Records show that as far back as 1831, members were overdrawing their accounts — the focus of the 1991-92 inquiry by the House ethics panel. Decades before Sergeant at Arms Jack Russ reportedly floated a $10,000-plus check at the bank, two previous sergeants cashed bad checks for themselves.

The bank's history raised questions relevant to contemporary circumstances:
• Were taxpayer funds at risk? No, said sitting House leaders. "If the members' money was embezzled by an employee, the members were at risk of total loss," said a House Administration Committee task force in its 1991 report on the bank and its history.

But each of the three times the bank came up short, the House appropriated public funds to make up the loss — a fact not noted by the House Administration panel's report.
• Who owned the House bank's money? Majority Leader Richard A. Gephardt, D-Mo., gave his answer Oct. 3, 1991: "No taxpayer funds were used to cover insufficiencies; the funds of other members were employed."

Though the intricacies of the members' payroll system had changed, courts twice ruled in past decades that money in the hands of the House sergeant at arms was public money until given to the members who earned it. Indeed, past members used those rulings to justify covering losses with public funds, and, until the bank closed in 1991, the Treasury used members' deposits as if they were the government's money.

## Arrangements of Convenience

The House bank's roots stretched back almost to the First Congress and early attempts to set up a payroll system for members. Starting in 1789, the first congressional pay acts required members to go to the Treasury for their salary. But the law proved inconvenient for members and the Treasury.

So starting in the early 1790s, one of the first Speakers made an unofficial agreement with the Treasury that the money would be advanced to him so he could pay the members himself. This proved cumbersome for the Speaker, so he eventually turned to his underlings for help. For much of the early 1800s, the sergeant at arms did the paperwork, while the assistant doorkeeper fetched the money and paid the members.

About 1830, Speaker Andrew Stevenson of Virginia consolidated the system under the Office of the Sergeant at Arms. At first merely a disbursing office, it quickly turned into a place members could keep money on deposit, cash checks and, at times, arrange for loans. It had been known as the House bank since at least the 1930s and referred to as such in the official Congressional Directory since 1965.

It was always a scandal waiting to happen.

## 1832: 'THE UNFORTUNATE DEFALCATION'

John Oswald Dunn was the first sergeant at arms whose job it was to collect members' salaries and travel allowances from the Treasury and pay them their due. He was also the first to help himself to some of the cash.

Dunn was the House's third sergeant at arms, having succeeded his father when Thomas Dunn died in 1824. John Dunn was a former assistant doorkeeper, so he was familiar with the members' payroll system. It was he whom Speaker Stevenson turned to in about 1830 when he decided to consolidate the system.

By the time John Dunn took over, it already was becoming clear that the system had serious flaws.

There were long debates in 1829-30 over how to stop members from cheating on travel allowances. One member said his colleagues overcharged the government for $28,000 a year.

There was also a minor dust-up at about that time over revelations that the Bank of the United States — through a deal with the Treasury initiated by the Speaker — was advancing pay interest-free to members before the funds were appropriated. During debate on the issue in 1832, Stevenson disclosed that some members also "had unintentionally overdrawn their accounts" the previous year. He reminded members that "they cannot draw in advance."

Little on record explains exactly what Dunn was up to. This much is known: As in modern times, members let their salaries accumulate. Dunn kept track of how much money each had. When asked for cash, he wrote a check and had the member endorse it and the Speaker certify it. Dunn then cashed it and gave the members their money.

In the summer of 1832, however, Dunn stopped returning with the money. Or returned with only some. Or hiked the request and kept the change. Confronted, Dunn resigned June 25, 1832. He offered the House a humble letter of confession: "I have fallen into unexpected misfortunes, which I am but too sensible have led me into error."

## Making Good the Losses

There appears to have been sharp disagreement over whether the members should recoup the loss from taxpayer funds, but only scant details were noted in the House Journal and newspapers.

The House initially voted June 26 to reimburse members from House funds. But opposition to that idea grew later in the day. The opponents apparently argued that Dunn was the members' private agent; if he ran off with their money, tough luck.

Those out money insisted otherwise. "I fully believed

... the sergeant at arms was the agent of the House or the government," said Rep. John Dickson of New York, whom Dunn had taken for $1,504.

Opponents killed the reimbursement plan on a 71-97 vote, and the Committee on Accounts (now House Administration) was ordered to study the matter. But two days later, the House reversed itself on a 104-49 vote. The victims collected $8,668 — which would be equivalent today to $125,000.

It took several more years — and another scare — for the House to pass reforms. In January 1838, members were told that the office of Sergeant at Arms Roderick Dorsey was short by $3,887. But an inquiry cleared Dorsey, finding that the Bank of the Metropolis had made "an unintentional error" in furnishing his office with money. The bank repaid the money.

That episode, coupled with the "unfortunate defalcation of a former sergeant in 1832," the Accounts Committee said in a report, proved to all that the system was "dangerous to the public."

But the reforms, approved by the House later in 1838, were limited: The committee proposed sanctioning the system in House rules. To protect the taxpayers, the House required the sergeant at arms to post a bond of $5,000 to $10,000; that was later increased to $50,000.

## 1889: 'A RIFLED SAFE'

At about 4:20 p.m. on Wednesday, Dec. 4, 1889, a very worried John P. Leedom decided that it was time to open his Capitol office's huge two-vault safe and count the money.

Leedom, the House sergeant at arms, had feared the worst about the fate of his missing cashier, Craven E. Silcott. "He was afraid Mr. Silcott had been sandbagged," a fellow employee testified.

Leedom had good reason to suspect that Silcott had been robbed and killed: Silcott had told him the previous Saturday that he was going to New York City to collect a large debt. Silcott had told his wife that he would take the 11:40 p.m. train and return on Monday. He left home with only a nightshirt stuck in his overcoat pocket.

He was last seen carrying a new brown valise.

It was not just Leedom's long friendship with Silcott that made him dread that he had been mugged. Silcott was in charge of tens of thousands of dollars of members' money. The Republicans had just taken control of the House, which meant Democrats Silcott and Leedom (a defeated House member from Ohio) would soon have to account for the money and turn over the office to their GOP successors.

Silcott had assured Leedom the previous Saturday morning that nothing was amiss: "You will find the cash all right in the drawer." Leedom had not bothered to count the cash in his employees' hands in years.

But a few hours later, Silcott told Leedom of his trip to New York. He said he needed to fetch $12,000 owed him by another former Ohio member, David R. Paige, before settling the House bank's accounts.

The reason: Members regularly got advances on their $416-a-month salaries in a scheme that allowed Leedom to profit from interest he charged for borrowing his office's funds. "Some members are overdrawn," Silcott said. "We may not have enough there to make it up."

Silcott's friends and co-workers later testified that they considered him to be an honest family man (father of three) whose only vices were moderate betting at the horse races and temperate drinking.

A few knew, however, that he kept company with a local prostitute of French-Canadian descent, Herminie Thiebault, alias Louise "Lulu" Barrett. And one friend's description of moderate betting involved wagers of up to $50 — just short of a full week's salary for Silcott, who made $3,000 a year.

Monday came and went with no sign of Silcott. On Tuesday, the first day of the 51st Congress, Leedom sent two urgent telegrams to former Rep. Paige. No answer. Leedom sent two more Wednesday. Again, no reply.

That morning, everybody was jittery. Bookkeeper J. D. Selzer told teller Henry L. Ballentine that he suspected Silcott. Ballentine broached the matter with Leedom: "I feel distressed." Leedom replied: "You do not feel any more distressed than I do."

### The Jig Is Up

It was several hours later that Leedom decided to check the money in the safe. "If it is here," he told Ballentine, "Silcott is killed. If it is not here, then he has taken the money and gone."

Ballentine first opened the safe's outer door, then the outer vault, and finally, reading the combination off a slip of paper Silcott had given him four years earlier, the inner vault.

Inside were two bundles of money. They looked like two $10,000 packages of $100 bills, but they were actually stacks of $1 bills topped with a single $100 bill.

Said Leedom: "Ballentine, the jig is up."

They counted the rest. Silcott's vault was short by well over $50,000. There was panic in the office. Selzer heard the news when he returned from dinner. "If a clap of thunder had struck in the room, then I could not have been more surprised; it struck me dumb and speechless," Selzer said later.

Leedom sent for Isaac R. Hill, the deputy sergeant at arms and one of Silcott's best friends. "The first thing Mr. Leedom said was, 'This office is $50,000 short. Mr. Silcott has run away with a whore with the money,'" Hill recalled.

Later testimony confirmed that. Silcott had left his wife with some spending money, ostensibly to tide her over for a day or so; she counted it days later — $1,200. The bit about collecting from a former member turned out to be a ruse. Hill urged Leedom to keep the matter secret and to try to cover the shortage with his own funds, his $50,000 bond and, if necessary, private contributions. Hill said he had been told by a Democratic friend that the money "could be raised in town on a few hours' notice."

"You must adopt that course to save yourself and the Democratic Party from scandal," Hill told Leedom.

Leedom went sleepless that night. He woke up a top Democratic congressman at about 5:30 a.m. to ask advice. He woke up the cashier of the National Metropolitan Bank, where his office kept some money, and made him count those deposits. He concluded that the House bank was about $71,000 short (today's equivalent of $1.2 million).

Finally, at about 8 a.m. on Thursday, he went to the home of Rep. John G. Carlisle, D-Ky., the Speaker during the previous three Congresses, and told him the bad news. Carlisle told him to come clean.

At noon, a letter from Leedom to the new Speaker, Thomas B. Reed, R-Maine, was read on the floor, officially informing members of the matter. Most already knew: The Washington Post had published an extra edition on the

embezzlement a half-hour earlier. The House by voice vote created a special inquiry committee.

The scandal was front-page news the next day. "A Rifled Safe," blared The Washington Post. The New York Times' headline: "Congressmen Are Robbed, Their Salaries Gone with Cashier Silcott."

The press focused on Silcott's affair with Thiebault. She had been in town three years and worked out of "a house of ill-fame of the better sort," the Post said, until Silcott took her as his mistress in November 1888 and put her up in a two-room flat. Some of Thiebault's neighbors thought Silcott was married to her, while his close friends and co-workers knew little or nothing of her.

The House approved a $5,000 reward for Silcott's arrest, but to no avail. Newspapers soon placed the couple in Montreal, where they were seen at the home of Thiebault's sister. But by the time a local detective traced them there, "the birds had flown," the Post reported.

### Who Pays the Loss?

The inquiry panel began its investigation Dec. 6. Its sessions were closed to the public. "Many members of Congress have received advances," the Post explained, "and it would be embarrassing to those who have been thus accommodated to have these transactions publicly portrayed."

The inquiry panel's chairman, George E. Adams, R-Ill., admitted to taking a $200 advance. The hearing records, with detailed accounts of members' personal finances, eventually were made public. They showed overdrafts totaling more than $4,000.

But that was the least of the committee's discoveries. Between Silcott's malfeasance and Leedom's non-feasance, the House bank was nothing less than a fiscal cesspool.

Leedom's own money was mingled with members' deposits. Checks, some by Leedom, were left unredeemed for long periods. Office books showed that House bank officials thought they had more deposited at National Metropolitan Bank than they did.

And finally, Leedom's bond insuring the House bank's money was deemed invalid; contrary to House rules, it had expired in March 1889, at the end of the 50th Congress. Silcott's bond was further out of date.

The committee quickly pieced together Silcott's crime: On three separate days in late November, he withdrew a total of $133,442 from the Treasury. The money was supposed to be for members' monthly pay, due Dec. 4.

He used $14,560 to repay the National Metropolitan Bank for 35 salary-advance loans taken out in members' names. Silcott had forged most of the notes and taken the money months earlier. (For this he was indicted on 112 criminal charges in mid-December.) Silcott turned another $58,067 over to the House bank and made off with $60,815, for a total embezzlement of $75,375.

The bottom line was this: Most members stood to lose money — up to several thousand dollars for some.

The inquiry hearings ended Dec. 18. The panel voted 5-2 for a bill to appropriate up to $75,000 to make up the shortage. Raucous debate on Jan. 14-15 divided members into three camps:

● Some agreed with the committee, which argued that even though the sergeant at arms (unlike the secretary of the Senate) was nowhere recognized in statute as a government disbursing officer, he was one de facto. Therefore, the loss should fall to the taxpayers, just as it had in 1832.

● Others argued that Leedom was the private agent of members who, through his employees, collected their salaries as a favor. That meant the loss should fall to them, not the taxpayers. This side pointed out that none other than former President James A. Garfield, R-Ohio, as minority leader years earlier, had urged Congress to make the sergeant at arms a disbursing officer so the Treasury would reimburse members in case of loss.

The House in 1882 passed just such a bill, but it died in the Senate, prompting one member to shout during the 1890 debate, "Then the senators ought to pay the loss."

● The third camp wanted to turn the whole mess over to the U.S. Court of Claims to decide.

The outcome was summed up in a Jan. 16, 1890, headline in The New York Times: "Silcott's Victims Are Sad — No Money And No Reference to the Courts." The proposal to send the matter to the courts was rejected on a tie vote, 136-136. The spending bill fell 127-141.

As the outcome became clear, the Post reported, "there was a rush down the main aisle, and several members who had voted 'aye' changed to 'no.' They felt, as the bill had been defeated, they could afford to join the virtuous opposition."

### The Court Decides

Rep. William H. Crain, D-Texas, refused to take no for an answer. He sued the government in the Court of Claims — and won. "The sergeant at arms acted as a public officer," the court ruled in March 1890. "We all agree that judgment shall be entered in the plaintiff's favor."

Armed with the decision a week later, Rep. Adams brought his committee's spending bill back to the floor. It was approved by a stand-up vote of 160-15. The opponents tried forcing a recorded vote but failed. The Senate concurred without debate, and President Benjamin Harrison signed it.

Silcott was apparently never heard from again. As for Leedom, the inquiry panel severely condemned him for neglect, and he returned to Ohio. He died a few years later at age 47.

The panel's last act was to propose reforms. It brought a bill to the floor Sept. 25, 1890, that was quickly enacted.

Again, the changes were minimal: The bill explicitly stated that the sergeant at arms "shall be a disbursing officer" to make clear that the money in his hands was public. It enshrined his duties in law (as opposed to House rule) and required a $50,000 bond that could not lapse. He would also have to submit regular balance statements to the House and the Treasury. The General Accounting Office (GAO) was later added to the list.

The balance statements were accepted without question for almost 57 years, when the Republicans again took over the House and decided it was time for an audit.

## 1947: 'RUBBER CHECKS REPORTED'

Long before he was found out, Kenneth Romney knew that former Rep. John H. Smithwick, D-Fla., was leading him to ruin. "If you had never come to Congress," Romney wrote Smithwick, "I would not be in trouble today."

The letter was dated Dec. 3, 1931 — four days before Romney, then the House bank's cashier, was promoted to sergeant at arms by the Democrats, who had just taken control of the House. Romney's troubles had just begun. He would be thrown in prison before it was over.

Romney moved to Washington from Montana in 1914 as a newspaper reporter. He was hired by the House sergeant at arms office a year later. He was promoted to cashier in 1917, when he was about 30 years old.

By then, the House bank was operating much as it did in 1991. Members could have their paychecks delivered to them or to the private bank of their choice, but most kept their salaries on deposit with the sergeant at arms, who issued them checks and kept money from the Treasury on hand to cash those and other checks for members.

In Romney's tenure, members who needed money could get short-term 6 percent loans from the National Bank of Washington, according to a 1947 newspaper account. The sergeant at arms acted as middleman.

This practice was discontinued after Romney got in trouble but was later resumed. The 1991 House Administration Committee report said the House bank in the 1960s and '70s arranged short-term loans with the National Bank of Washington any time members wrote bad checks for more than $50. The National Bank of Washington stopped offering such loans in 1983.

But even as far back as the early 1950s, hundreds of members were getting interest-free loans simply by overdrawing their accounts, according to GAO reports of the time.

Decades earlier, Smithwick pioneered this practice with a vengeance. A Georgia lawyer, he moved to the Florida Panhandle in 1906 and was elected to Congress in 1918, serving from 1919 to 1927.

In 1925, Smithwick and Romney began speculating in Florida real estate together. They found an easy way to finance the deals: They wrote tens of thousands of dollars' worth of bad checks, which cashier Romney cashed. They made money on their first two deals. When Florida's land boom went bust, however, they took a bath. Smithwick was not doing well politically, either. He had been beaten in the 1926 primary and tried unsuccessfully to make a comeback in 1928 — a campaign financed with $25,000 in bad checks.

By late 1931, the House bank was holding $60,000 worth of Smithwick's bad checks, and Romney started to panic. He wrote to his partner "to call you back to bitter realities."

"The checks held and 'kited' through this office would easily approximate a million dollars and made possible all your operations," Romney wrote. "We have been jointly guilty of fraud. You know that as well as I do."

From there, things snowballed. Smithwick attempted to make up his losses in Florida with land speculation in Maryland — also financed with bad checks at the House bank. Two other bank employees, apparently taking advantage of Romney's predicament, joined the embezzling game. One made off with $8,000.

The other was Frank J. Mahoney, who made off with $25,000. After Mahoney was caught in 1938, Romney fired him, made him sign a confession and asked the House Speaker, William B. Bankhead, D-Ala., what to do. Instead of demanding that Mahoney be prosecuted and his bond seized, Bankhead told Romney to try to raise the money from his sponsors in the New York congressional delegation, Romney said later. The money was never raised. Mahoney moved to Honolulu.

In the meantime, Romney came up with a scheme to pay off the bank's other shortages. He started collecting paycheck kickbacks from his employees, including his daughter-in-law and niece. He stuffed this money, more than $20,000, into an envelope.

## The Truth Comes Out

The Democrats lost control of the House in the Nov. 5, 1946, election. His tenure about to expire, Romney two days later put the kickback money into the House bank's cash drawer to reduce shortages that by then totaled more than $140,000 — equivalent today to more than $800,000.

All this was uncovered when Romney's Republican successor, William F. Russell, demanded a General Accounting Office audit before taking over the House bank. The Washington Post broke the story Jan. 5, 1947: "Rubber Checks Reported," said a headline.

The GAO found the bank $125,563 short: three Romney checks totaling $22,965; 20 Smithwick checks totaling $64,573; Mahoney's embezzlement of $25,066; the other bank employee's $8,000; $1,376 in bad notes from a man described only as a "promoter"; and member overdrafts totaling $3,583, which were eventually made good. (Testimony at Romney's trial indicated that members' monthly overdrafts often totaled $20,000 or more.)

Everybody but Romney got off because of the statute of limitations. (Smithwick maintained his innocence until he died in December 1948.) Romney was convicted in May 1947 of three criminal counts for making false statements about the House bank's accounts to the GAO in 1946. He was sentenced to one to three years.

Romney appealed using an old argument — that the money was not the government's funds. It belonged to the members, his lawyer argued; therefore, he could not be convicted under laws that require officials to account truthfully for public money.

Romney lost. "Cash in the hands of such an official manifestly continues to be the property of the government until it has actually been disbursed by him to persons lawfully entitled to receive it," said the U.S. Court of Appeals for the District of Columbia Circuit in 1948. "It was public money which was embezzled."

The Supreme Court refused to review the case. Romney served a year in prison. He died in 1952 at age 66.

As for the missing money, some was collected on Romney's bond. The rest was made up in the summer of 1947 when Congress quietly included $83,879 for money "due and unpaid to members of the House" in a big supplemental spending bill.

## GAO Audits Begin

The GAO started doing twice-yearly audits of the House bank. Congress in 1949 made them mandatory.

Reports on these audits were secret until 1978, according to the House Administration Committee, and nobody paid much mind to members' bad-check habits — 5,660 overdrafts in fiscal 1963, 10,369 in 1969 and 12,309 in 1972.

"The reports for these years note, rather matter-of-factly, that the sergeant at arms considered the overdrafts to be an advance on salary," said the House ethics committee in a 1991 report.

A GAO report caused a minor stir in 1990, when it was disclosed that Sergeant at Arms Jack Russ had himself floated checks. Speaker Thomas S. Foley ordered reforms. But the GAO released a report Sept. 18, 1991, that for the first time in years included the number of members' bad checks (8,331 in a year). A blizzard of negative press followed, and two weeks later, the House voted to close the bank for good.  ■

# Post Office Probe Hints at Larger Scandal

The House Post Office matter began as an investigation of embezzlement and drug dealing among postal clerks, but it soon mushroomed into a full-scale scandal that included allegations that members used the facility to convert campaign checks or House expense vouchers to cash through sham transactions made to look like stamp purchases.

Postmaster Robert V. Rota resigned in March as federal and congressional investigators broadened their probe into corruption at the post office. Several postal workers admitted embezzling money and dealing drugs.

A federal grand jury subpoenaed voluminous expense account records of three House Democrats, including Dan Rostenkowski of Chicago, the chairman of the tax-writing Ways and Means Committee. News reports questioned why Rostenkowski had purchased $55,000 in stamps at the post office from 1986 to 1992.

A post office supervisor told federal investigators that he helped members of Congress get thousands of dollars in cash through phony transactions disguised as stamp purchases.

Democrats and Republicans on a special House Administration Committee task force that conducted its own investigation came up with some different conclusions, but both sides agreed that the post office was run in a slipshod manner.

The scandal prompted the House to do away with the postmaster's position and shift the postal operations to the U.S. Postal Service.

## BACKGROUND

The post office had previously been the subject of controversy in the House. In 1976, scandals involving members' abuse of House administrative services led Democratic leaders to curtail the $1,140 allowance for stamps that members had received.

The stamps were deemed unnecessary in view of the frank. Members were using stamps for mail, such as Christmas cards, that was not allowed to be franked, and there was evidence that some members were trading in stamps for cash.

The change in policy came about after leaders, fearful that negative publicity was taking the sting out of their Watergate-inspired attacks on Republicans, appointed a task force to improve the "propriety and appearance of propriety" of the members' official expense account system.

The task force focused on the lucrative — and controversial — practice by members of converting funds from the three annual allowances (stationery, travel and official expenses outside Washington) to cash for personal use. House members had the legal authority to simply pocket the money, called cash-outs, regardless of whether the corresponding expense actually was incurred.

The stamp allowance had a purpose stated in law: Stamps were to be used for airmail and special delivery, which provided faster service than franked mail, which traveled overland like other first-class shipments. But many members were trading in their airmail and special delivery stamps for first-class stamps.

Some members apparently were trading their stamps for cash at the House Post Office. Rules in effect at the time did not say whether this was permissible.

The task force fashioned sweeping changes in the allowance system. It proposed stripping House Administration of most its power to increase allowances, eliminating cash-outs and consolidating the allowances into a general office budget for each member and requiring the disclosure of members' expenditures in quarterly reports.

The task force also recommended that the postage allowance be abolished. Because the franking privilege covered all official domestic first-class mail, overseas, insured, certified and other special postal services could be paid for with the new consolidated office budget. A later report explained that "only a minimal allowance" for such services was required because airmail was discontinued as a separate class in 1977.

In implementing the reforms, little attention was paid to stamps. The House Administration Committee issued orders ending cash-outs for the three allowances where they had been specifically permitted — but remained silent on cashing out stamps. When the system of consolidated budgets took full effect in 1978, there was no limit on using official funds to buy stamps.

Moreover, at least initially, there was no regulation limiting what members could do with stamps, though the new voucher system required that members certify by signature that they would be used only "by my office in the discharge of my duties."

Stamp purchases grew after the reforms were enacted. Members explained that they were using them, in the words of one aide, for "anything that's not frankable."

After 15 retiring members in 1980 had procured stacks of stamps just before departing, the House Administration Committee passed a regulation that said that "unused postage stamps shall be forwarded to the clerk of the House prior to the end of a member's service."

By 1985, the committee's regulations prohibited using stamps purchased with official funds "in lieu of the frank." Personal or campaign funds could be used for mail that was ineligible for franking. The only permissible uses for official stamps explicitly allowed by the regulation were foreign, express, certified, registered and insured mail, and self-addressed stamped envelopes.

Prosecutors at one point in the late 1970s tried to determine whether members engaged in stamps-for-cash chicanery. A secretary to Postmaster Rota was fired after getting into a fist fight in the office. Apparently angry at being let go, the woman wrote a letter making allegations about the House Post Office.

The letter prompted federal investigators to question at least one former clerk about post office matters — including whether members used their stamp vouchers to get cash. Nothing ever came of that earlier probe.

## FEDERAL PROBE

The federal investigation began in mid-1991 as a little-noticed inquiry by Jay B. Stephens, U.S. attorney for the District of Columbia, of stamp clerks suspected of embezzlement and drug dealing.

Postal clerks told auditors in 1991 that employees regularly used postal money to pay personal bills or make loans to House employees. One former clerk under indictment

# Post Office Inquiry Leads to Scrutiny

Members of the House could mail almost anything official by using their signature on the envelope — the so-called franking privilege. But when it came to spending their office money on stamps purchased from the House Post Office, their approaches were vastly different.

Some members bought several thousand stamps a year, while many got by with far fewer or none.

"I can't really understand why anyone here needs a lot of stamps because we have the frank," said James V. Hansen, R-Utah, whose office had spent less than $20 a year on stamps.

Congressional Quarterly reviewed records of members' stamp purchases listed in House spending reports from 1986 through March 1992, the same period prosecutors were examining. (CQ's review did not include stamp purchases by members' campaign committees, which were also under scrutiny.)

The review showed the following:

● Members varied widely in the amount they spent on postage. Of 296 members in office for the previous six years, a handful reported spending nothing on stamps since 1986 and half spent less than $350 a year. Others purchased thousands of dollars worth a year, some buying as many as 10,000 stamps at a time. The disparities did not correlate with seniority, positions of power or other factors.

The average expenditure of the 296 members was about $550 a year, or $3,436 over 6¼ years. That meant the House's 435 members likely had been spending more than $200,000 a year on stamps in addition to the tens of millions of dollars that franked mail cost each year.

● The three members under scrutiny were among the House's top stamp-buyers. Illinois Democratic Rep. Dan Rostenkowski reported buying far more than anyone else had, purchasing $29,672 worth of stamps during the period reviewed. That averaged $4,748 a year — more than enough to mail 50 first-class letters every day for more than six years. Pennsylvania Rep. Joe Kolter, D, also under investigation, was fourth with $17,374. The other member under scrutiny, Austin J. Murphy, D-Pa., ranked 25th, with $9,244.

● When asked why they needed lots of stamps, many members described uses that seemed to violate House regulations that prohibited using stamps in lieu of the frank. Some members explained that their constituents objected to the frank as an unnecessary perk, so they put stamps on much of their mail. Not lost on some members was marketing research that showed a stamped letter was more likely to be opened than one with any other kind of postage.

Such practices had mattered little before because it cost taxpayers just as much to mail a stamped parcel as

a franked one. But if the practice continued, it would allow members to skirt recently enacted laws that limited each member's use of the frank.

Some members said they misunderstood the rules; others seemed to have disregarded them.

● Some members used taxpayer-funded stamps on mail — sympathy notes, anniversary and birthday greetings — that was not considered official business and so was barred under franking law. Others, however, were so careful about franking rules that they bought all stamps out of their own pockets. "We always pay for those out of my own personal budget, not out of my office budget," said Timothy J. Penny, D-Minn., who said he had not bought a stamp with taxpayer funds in years.

● Senators did not spend nearly as much on stamps as House members. CQ did not review Senate postage expenditures in detail, but several officials reported no large expenditures such as those found in the House.

"No member to my knowledge has ever bought more than a roll or two rolls at a time," said Senate Postmaster Gayle Cory. An aide with the Senate Rules Committee, which audited senators' expenditures, confirmed this: "We see stamps purchased, but not in any great amount," he said. "It's infrequent and in small amounts" of $30 or so at a time.

## Rules of the Road

Until 1985, regulations issued by the House Administration Committee were vague on how stamps procured with official funds from the House Post Office could be used. But the regulations were gradually clarified.

The regulations said: "Such postage or postage stamps are not to be used in lieu of the frank, but rather when the frank was insufficient, i.e., to pay the cost of certified, registered, insured, or Express Mail; to mail an item to a foreign country; or when the member provided a stamped self-addressed envelope to recover documents or materials related to the conduct of official business."

The New Member Orientation Handbook issued in December 1990 worded the regulation slightly differently: "Postage stamps are to be used only when the frank is insufficient. . . ."

Several House officials familiar with the regulation said it left little room for interpretation: Members were not supposed to put stamps on mail that was frankable unless they wanted to use some special service for which the U.S. Postal Service did not honor the frank. And since the frank was supposed to cover almost anything having to do with official business, members were not supposed to use taxpayer-financed stamps to send mail not considered official business under franking laws.

told investigators that he supplied drugs to one of his superiors. More than $33,000 in shortages were found.

Eventually, four clerks, a supervisor and the post office's chief of staff pleaded guilty to various charges.

The matter came into public view in 1992 when on May 14 the House learned that a federal grand jury looking into the matter had subpoenaed voluminous expense accounts of three Democrats: Ways and Means Committee Chair-

man Rostenkowski and Pennsylvanians Joe Kolter and Austin J. Murphy.

Each of the members denied wrongdoing and pledged cooperation. "Like many people, I am interested in learning what this is all about," Rostenkowski said.

"Based upon the type of information requested . . . I do not believe that my office is the subject or target of any inquiry," Murphy said.

# Of Franking Privileges, Stamp Purchases

"That to me, on the face of it, seems obvious," said Hansen, the top Republican on the House Committee on Standards of Official Conduct.

An aide to the ethics panel, who was allowed to speak to reporters only if he was not identified, summed up the regulation this way: "If it's frankable, don't use your stamps for it.... It's a fairly straightforward prohibition." Conversely, the aide adds, "You can't circumvent franking prohibitions by using stamps."

The House Commission on Congressional Mailing Standards, a bipartisan panel of six members, oversaw franking matters, but its aides said the panel had no jurisdiction over how members used stamps.

When asked to interpret the stamp regulation, however, two aides agreed with ethics committee officials' assessment: Official stamps should not be used for items that could be franked unless special postal services were required, and stamps could not be used for items banned under franking law. Said one aide: "That's pretty black-and-white."

To some, it's not.

"You could interpret it that way, but I would say in practice we have a broader interpretation," said Charlie Rose, D-N.C., who since 1991 had been chairman of the House Administration Committee, which oversaw members' expense allowances. As Rose saw it: "It's OK to use your stamps, just as you use your frank, for any official business.... I don't think it's illegal or improper or in violation of any of the rules to use a stamp."

House Administration Committee aides explained Rose's interpretation by saying that the regulations did not define when the frank was "insufficient."

"Insufficient is a judgment term," said Heidi M. Pender, special counsel to the chairman. "In the chairman's view, if someone made a decision that the frank was insufficient, he doesn't have a problem with that."

## 'My People Don't Like Franked Mail'

Rose reported spending $14,139 on stamps since 1986 — more than all but six members. He said his aides regularly put stamps on letters that were clearly frankable — almost everything but mass mailings. (No member reports using stamps for mass mailings.) On envelopes with a pre-printed signature, Rose said, aides stuck the stamp right over the frank.

He gave two reasons:

First, his aides believed the U.S. Postal Service sometimes gave franked mail inferior service. The Postal Service responded that there was no difference in the way franked and stamped mail was processed.

Second, Rose said his constituents did not like the frank; they saw it as a wasteful perk designed to give incumbents free political advertising. "That's the impression that many have given my staff, and that's the reason they have given me for that practice," Rose said.

William H. Natcher, D-Ky., who had a reputation as being frugal with office expenses, cited the same reason in explaining why he spent $20,431 on stamps.

"My people don't like franked mail," Natcher said. "I have people in my district who think all mail should have stamps on it." Natcher would not detail what types of letters his office puts stamps on, saying only, "When it's permissible to use stamps, I use stamps." Informed of regulations limiting the use of stamps, he insisted, "We don't violate any regulations in this office."

The only member to spend more than Natcher and less than Rostenkowski was Gus Yatron, D-Pa., who reported spending $23,450 on stamps since 1986. "We use them on everything congratulatory," said Yatron's administrative assistant, Joseph P. Gemmell. He said his boss was one of many members who regularly sent notes to high school and college graduates.

"Somewhere along the line, I read a ruling that for that kind of mailing, you use stamps and not the frank," Gemmell said. He could not remember where he read that. Officials with the House Administration Committee and the House franking commission said they knew of no such ruling. Since the 1970s, franking law had explicitly allowed members to frank mail expressing congratulations to a person for a "public distinction." Franking commission guidelines for years had cited graduation as allowable.

Other big postage buyers ($10,000 or more over 6¼ years) whose offices said they used some of their stamps for mail that should be franked included Don Sundquist, R-Tenn.; Floyd D. Spence, R-S.C.; Carlos J. Moorhead, R-Calif.; Patricia Schroeder, D-Colo.; E. "Kika" de la Garza, D-Texas; Joseph D. Early, D-Mass.; and Republican leader Robert H. Michel, Ill.

"We use stamps on our congratulatory letters," said Michel spokeswoman Michelle C. Tessier. "We know that it's frankable, but he has always used a stamp." She said the office was once told that "if something is frankable, you can also use official stamps.... We were obviously misinformed."

Several offices said they used stamps for things that were not, under franking law, considered official business and were therefore not frankable.

Gemmell said Yatron's office put stamps on sympathy letters, as did de la Garza's, according to aide Bernice McGuire. Moorhead said he also used stamps for sympathy letters. C. W. Bill Young, R-Fla., said he sent birthday and anniversary greetings with officially purchased stamps.

---

Kolter: "I welcome this investigation because I have done nothing wrong. I view this as an opportunity to exonerate myself."

The subpoenas were issued May 6. But they remained a tightly held secret among top Democratic officials and did not become public until May 14, when Republicans demanded that the House be notified. In an embarrassing rebuke to Speaker Thomas S. Foley, D-Wash., the House voted 324-3 for a GOP-sponsored resolution ordering him to produce the subpoenas and explain the delay. Foley apologized for not informing Republicans earlier and said the House would comply with the subpoenas. *(Vote 126, p. 32-H)*

In addition to the members' records, the grand jury demanded records from Werner W. Brandt, Jack Russ' successor as sergeant at arms, and House Clerk Donnald

K. Anderson, who kept most House records and was the chamber's main disbursing officer. Russ resigned March 12 in the midst of a separate scandal, one that involved the writing of bad checks by more than 300 House members. *(House bank scandal, p. 23)*

The subpoenas demanded the following records from House officers and the three members from Jan. 1, 1986, through April 15, 1992:

● All vouchers showing expenses charged to the officials' office accounts or signed by them, "including but not limited to vouchers for postal stamps."

● All records "regarding the status of" or "relating to overdrafts on" the officials' office accounts.

● Documents "regarding the proper use of stamp allotments" for lawmakers' and the sergeant at arms' offices.

### Stamp Scam Surfaces

A key witness in the investigation was a post office supervisor, James C. Smith, who reportedly told federal investigators that he helped members of Congress get thousands of dollars in cash through phony transactions disguised as stamp purchases. His allegations were reported to have led to the subpoenas of the three members' records.

Public records showed that, during the period under scrutiny, Rostenkowski, Kolter and Murphy made relatively large purchases of stamps from the post office with office funds.

House Administration Committee Chairman Charlie Rose, D-N.C., was skeptical that Rostenkowski could be involved in a stamp scam. "The notion that the chairman of the tax-writing committee in the most powerful nation on Earth, who at the time had some $2 million in his campaign funds, would ask a House employee to improperly give him cash ... just strains credibility to the breaking point," he said.

"That's ridiculous," Rostenkowski said May 21, when asked if he ever got cash from the post office. A spokesman for Kolter responded, "He certainly doesn't know if staff did, but he said he did not do that."

In December, the Chicago Sun-Times reported that Rostenkowski's campaign and a political action committee (PAC) he controlled had reported buying $26,000 worth of stamps from the House Post Office. Those purchases were in addition to the previously disclosed $29,672 in taxpayer funds Rostenkowski's congressional office reported spending for stamps from the House Post Office from 1986 through the first quarter of 1992.

The Sun-Times said that 27 of Rostenkowski's $55,000-plus in campaign and congressional stamp transactions involved purchases of $1,000 or more.

The federal investigation also looked into the unlawful use of postal workers. Griff Williams, the son of Rep. Pat Williams, D-Mont., told the grand jury that his bosses ordered him to fetch five lawmakers' campaign-related mail from postal boxes that were rented off Capitol Hill to avoid laws restricting the receipt of political donations in federal office buildings.

Federal law prohibited members from asking donors to send campaign contributions to their congressional offices, which was why some members rented postal boxes off Capitol Hill for collecting money. Federal law also prohibited paying an employee from public funds to do something unrelated to official duties.

Williams said he complained about the pickups because he thought the practice might be improper and eventually refused to continue making them.

### Subpoenas Issued

Rostenkowski, Kolter and Murphy were subpoenaed in person July 22, but they invoked the Fifth Amendment to avoid testifying and called the probe politically motivated. In a statement, the three members called the criminal probe a "fishing expedition and political witch hunt."

Federal prosecutors sidestepped a public confrontation by agreeing to excuse the three congressmen from appearing before a grand jury. But they did subpoena eight aides to the three Democrats.

The investigation intensified in September, when post office Chief of Staff Joanna G. O'Rourke agreed to cooperate with authorities. She agreed to plead guilty to two misdemeanors of embezzlement and misusing public funds on Sept. 17 as part of a deal with federal investigators to unravel what prosecutors said was a criminal conspiracy to provide unofficial favors to members.

Prosecutors said, and O'Rourke concurred, that the alleged conspiracy's goal was to give members and others "personal and campaign services," including pickup of political donations, Express Mail for personal property, falsified postmarks, the cashing of "large campaign and personal checks" and unspecified "other monetary services."

In a statement, her lawyer said, "Ms. O'Rourke has accepted responsibility for undertaking certain actions which were inappropriate for a federal manager."

## HOUSE INQUIRY

The House initiated its own inquiry into alleged wrongdoing at the post office. Despite initial pledges for bipartisanship, Democrats and Republicans on a special House Administration task force were unable to agree on key matters and released separate reports on July 22.

The investigation was set in motion Feb. 5, when on a 254-160 party-line vote the House approved a resolution (H Res 340) giving the House Administration panel the authority to continue an investigation begun in the spring of 1991. *(Vote 6, p. 2-H)*

Democrats, with only one defection, voted to reject a GOP alternative (H Res 341) by 250-161 that would have created a new committee made up of five members from each party to investigate the allegations and whether the Democratic leadership sought to cover up the scandal. *(Vote 7, p. 2-H)*

During the five-month probe, Democratic and Republican investigators rarely acted in concert, and witnesses were questioned behind closed doors.

The separate paths the two sides took was apparent when they met on July 7 to exchange draft reports. The two versions were vastly different in scope and tone, with each side citing members of the other party for possible wrongdoing.

On July 22, the task force returned a split verdict — a more detailed, harsher tome by its three Republicans placing much of the blame on Democrats and a shorter, more forgiving missive by its three Democrats blaming post office managers.

While the Republicans' task force report pointedly left unresolved the stamp-scam allegations, the Democrats' version dismissed them as "unfounded."

The three subpoenaed members said in a letter to Speaker Foley that the report negated the need for a criminal probe because it found "no merit whatsoever to any allegations that we or anyone else abused the stamp procurement process."

The two sides agreed that the office was badly mismanaged under Postmaster Rota. The two reports blamed the patronage system for producing a bloated, low-quality work force of employees more beholden to their political sponsors than their supervisors and a management team more capable of doling out favors to members and select lobbyists than running an efficient mail room.

"The task force heard consistent and abundant testimony that the patronage system caused a substantial portion of the dysfunction . . . in the House Post Office," said the Democrats' 64-page report. The Republicans' 93-page version said the office "was more akin to a feudal system than a modern business."

Both parties said their reports were incomplete because three top officials — Rota, Chief of Staff O'Rourke and stamp clerk supervisor Smith — invoked the Fifth Amendment to avoid testifying.

The following were some of the key conclusions made by the two reports:

**Cash for Stamps.** The allegation that members got cash from the post office received relatively scant mention in the two reports.

Both of the task force reports said the post office cashed checks for members and others in violation of U.S. Postal Service rules. As for Smith's reported allegations, Democrats said that when the task force interviewed him he "offered no indication that this occurred." Rostenkowski issued a statement July 22 proclaiming "total exoneration. . . . I thank the task force for removing this cloud and restoring my reputation."

Republicans said they found evidence that campaign checks may have been cashed. Their report said a review of 10 months' worth of checks submitted to the office, including some campaign checks, showed several "denominated in even dollar amounts of $50 or $100 or more" that were not "divisible by postage stamp denominations."

The Republicans concluded that lax procedures "may have permitted some members' personal and campaign offices to convert official funds to personal use by exchanging stamps for cash."

**Mail Boxes.** Republicans focused most of their efforts on exposing special favors provided by the Post Office to members and others. Their most significant find was a service set up in the mid-1970s to help members avoid breaking election laws that prohibit them from soliciting political contributions to be sent to congressional offices. Members' campaigns would rent postal boxes off Capitol Hill; House Post Office couriers would pick up the mail, including donations, and deliver them to the members' offices.

The Democrats said scores of members had boxes and violated no law or rule in doing so. But task force members recommended that the service be halted "for appearance purposes."

Republicans took a different view: "The post office boxes may become a concern when House employees are utilized" to service them.

The GOP report named five Democrats who had boxes in 1992 when the practice was first publicly disclosed — Mary Rose Oakar and Edward F. Feighan of Ohio; Nicholas Mavroules, Mass.; Jim Moody, Wis.; and Dennis M. Hertel, Mich. Also named were several members who previously maintained boxes: Republican Jan Meyers of Kansas and Democrat Rostenkowski, and former Democratic Reps. Mario Biaggi and Samuel S. Stratton of New York and Fernand J. St Germain of Rhode Island.

All who responded to the report denied wrongdoing. Most said they knew nothing about House couriers picking up their mail.

Both reports also said that post office employees were ordered to answer phones in members' offices during parties and to give members rides. The GOP report said postal employees also gave rides to lobbyists and Rota and ran personal errands for Rota and other House officials.

**Ghost Employees.** Democrats reported finding "no conclusive evidence" of "ghost employees" — paid workers who never showed up. Republicans, however, said two workers fell into the "no-show category." The Democrats conceded that many witnesses said the two were frequently absent. The Democrats referred the matter to the ethics committee.

The issue loomed large after the Cleveland Plain Dealer published stories in April reporting that Oakar quit her post on the task force after allegations arose that she had ghost employees on the payroll. Oakar sued the paper for libel. The Democrats' report specifically exonerated her of being connected to ghost employees.

The GOP report did not accuse her of having ghost employees. It did suggest that her House Administration Subcommittee on Personnel and Police helped engineer a reorganization of the post office that resulted in three Oakar-connected individuals getting jobs paying $51,000 a year or more.

Oakar denied ill motives and insisted that Pat Roberts, R-Kan., head of the GOP task force, had fully participated in the reorganization. Democrats pointedly noted in public statements — but not in their report — that Roberts, who was in charge of his party's patronage committee, and Bill Thomas of California, ranking Republican on the House administration Committee, had both had relatives on the House payroll.

The House voted 414-0 on July 22 to refer the matter to the Committee on Standards of Official Conduct and to make the secret files from the House Administration's task force available to the Justice Department. The ethics committee established a special task force in August that began to investigate whether any there were any violations of House rules. It did not report by the end of the year. (Vote 292, p. 72-H) ∎

# Cloud of Scandal Hovers Over Capitol Hill

The House bank and Post Office scandals topped the news, but individual lawmakers had their share of ethics problems in 1992:

## HATFIELD REBUKED

The Senate Ethics Committee rebuked Mark O. Hatfield, R-Ore., on Aug. 12 for accepting and failing to report gifts worth nearly $43,000 between 1983 and 1988 as well as three unspecified travel reimbursements.

The committee found that Hatfield had violated the 1978 Ethics in Government Act and Senate rules, and deemed his actions "improper conduct reflecting upon the Senate." It did not recommend discipline by the full Senate, closing the case on Hatfield.

Most of the gifts cited by the committee were from Dr.

James B. Holderman, former president of the University of South Carolina. While Hatfield chaired the Appropriations Committee in 1986, Congress approved a $16.3 million grant to the school.

In the course of its 15-month investigation, the ethics panel did not find evidence of criminal violations or willful wrongdoing by Hatfield, and it found no connection between Hatfield's official actions and acceptance of the gifts. His shortcomings were instead attributed to "negligence" and "inattention."

Seemingly as a warning to others, the committee pointedly noted that even if the gifts were not linked to Hatfield's official actions, they were "inappropriate and cannot be condoned."

Chairman Terry Sanford, D-N.C., and Vice Chairman Warren B. Rudman, R-N.H., said that the transgressions were serious and that the committee's action was a significant discipline. "I think particularly with a person with a long public service record, that he would find this very serious," said Sanford. "It is a serious rebuke," added Rudman.

After the panel's decision, Hatfield said, "I accept and agree with the committee's judgment.... My mistakes were many and my omissions serious."

The Justice Department began an inquiry into criminal and civil charges against Hatfield. Asked about the inquiry, Rudman said, "My sense is that their conclusion evidently must be such as ours, or else I think we would have heard otherwise."

By accepting the Ethics Committee's decision, Hatfield forestalled any further hearings or action against him by the Senate in the case.

For Hatfield, the decision brought to an end an unpleasant chapter in a career that began in the Oregon House in 1951 and included two terms as governor. He was re-elected to a fifth Senate term in 1990, several months before newspapers in South Carolina and Oregon began reporting on the free-spending ways Holderman used to promote his school. *(1991 Almanac, p. 43)*

After the allegations were made, Hatfield filed amended financial disclosure reports, changed his office's procedures for filling out financial disclosure forms and said he would no longer accept gifts from anyone except family members and close friends who had no stake in his official duties.

In addition to the gifts enumerated in the resolution, the committee reviewed the propriety of Hatfield's acceptance of low- and no-interest loans and his son's acceptance of a scholarship to the University of South Carolina estimated to be worth at least $15,000.

The committee did not officially mention — and thus did not object to — the loans themselves or reports that John Dellenbeck, a former House member who forgave more than $75,000 of his loans to Hatfield, had at one point discussed federal grants for a coalition of Christian colleges with Hatfield. It only objected to Hatfield's failure to disclose interest forgiveness.

Asked whether Dellenbeck lobbied Hatfield, Sanford said, "I think that depends on your definition of lobbying."

Similarly, the panel did not object to forgiveness of a $58,000 loan from banker Charles E. Cook, or a $50,000 loan from L. David and James E. Carley, developers who relied heavily on a Housing and Urban Development program Hatfield supported. Both had more than a passing interest in matters before Congress but apparently did not directly lobby Hatfield.

Moreover, the panel found no impropriety in the schol-

arship for Hatfield's son. Rudman and Sanford noted that Hatfield was informed of the scholarship after it was awarded. Rudman also said that Hatfield's son was an "emancipated person" — over 18 and financially independent — at the time he received the funds.

The committee, divided equally between Democrats and Republicans, voted 5-1 for the resolution to rebuke Hatfield. Democratic Sen. Richard H. Bryan of Nevada said that while he agreed with the outcome, he wanted stronger language in the resolution.

While Bryan refused to elaborate on his objections, his dissenting vote was highly unusual, a first according to Bryan. Typically the panel did not go public until its findings were unanimous.

The committee rebuke of Hatfield was a stronger action than that taken against four of the five senators involved with savings and loan magnate Charles H. Keating Jr. The committee found them guilty of poor judgment and issued letters to that effect.

The rebuke was not as strong as the action taken against the fifth senator, Alan Cranston, D-Calif., who was "reprimanded" before the Senate in Nov. 20, 1991, in an unusual action that did not require a vote. *(1991 Almanac, p. 26)*

## PACKWOOD ACCUSED OF HARASSMENT

Oregon Republican Sen. Bob Packwood came under pressure to resign after a number of women accused him of sexual harassment. The Washington Post on Nov. 22 published a long article detailing allegations by 10 women that Packwood made unwanted sexual advances toward them while most were working for the senator. Without admitting to any specific misbehavior, Packwood issued an apology. Several Oregon women's groups called for an investigation and demanded that he resign.

When confronted by Post reporters just before the election against Rep. Les AuCoin, D-Ore., Packwood denied the women's allegations and attempted to discredit his accusers, the paper said. After Packwood beat AuCoin 52 percent to 48 percent, he issued an apologetic statement:

"I will not make an issue of any specific allegation. If any of my comments or actions have indeed been unwelcome or if I have conducted myself in any way that has caused any individual discomfort or embarrassment, for that I am sincerely sorry. My intentions were never to pressure, to offend, nor to make anyone feel uncomfortable, and I truly regret if that has occurred with anyone either on or off my staff," he said.

Packwood then entered an alcohol treatment facility on Nov. 30 for an evaluation. "I hope my past conduct is not unforgivable," his statement said. "Upon reflection, I realize I have problems and will seek professional advice in connection with my use of alcohol."

In an unprecedented move, the Senate Ethics Committee on Dec. 1 began a "preliminary inquiry" into the allegations. It was the first time the panel was publicly known to have undertaken a sexual harassment investigation.

The irony of the charges against Packwood was that he had long been considered a champion of women's issues, leading the fight for abortion rights before many Democrats, much less a pro-choice Republican, ever took a public position. He also won praise from women's groups for hiring and promoting women in his office.

According to the Post article, the 10 women said Packwood "was abrupt, grabbing them without warning, kissing them forcefully and persisting until they made clear that

they were not interested or had pushed him away."

Most of the incidents dated to the late 1970s and early 1980s; frequently, the article said, they occurred when Packwood seemed to have been drinking. Some female aides told the Post that senior women on Packwood's staff warned them against working alone with the senator.

Packwood's former wife, Georgie Packwood, told the Post: "I have been aware of these allegations for many years. It does not come as any surprise to me."

More allegations quickly surfaced. Holly Pruett, executive director of the Oregon Coalition Against Domestic and Sexual Violence, said that her group had recently received calls from five women "with direct, personal experiences of Sen. Packwood's sexually inappropriate behavior."

Packwood came under intense pressure to resign. "For the sake of the country as a whole as well as for the institution, I call on his colleagues not to tolerate this," said Mary Nolan, a Democrat who was past president of the Oregon chapter of the National Abortion Rights Action League. The state Democratic Party called for Packwood to step down.

"I am not going to resign under any circumstances," Packwood told a crowded Capitol Hill news conference Dec. 10. "What I did was not just stupid or boorish," he said. "My actions were just plain wrong, and there is no other better word for it."

He urged Oregon voters to allow him to repair "the bond of trust between us," which he acknowledged "is stretched thin right now."

The quick decision to investigate the matter by the usually slow Ethics Committee followed pressure by Senate leaders for fast action, reflecting their sensitivity after the 1991 firestorm over the chamber's handling of harassment allegations against Clarence Thomas during hearings on his Supreme Court nomination.

Gloria Allred, a Los Angeles sexual harassment lawyer who heads a group called the Women's Equal Rights Legal Defense and Education Fund, filed a formal complaint with the Ethics Committee in a letter dated Nov. 25 and received Nov. 30.

"The American people have a right to know whether the allegations are true or false," her complaint said.

Senate Majority Leader George J. Mitchell, D-Maine, and Minority Leader Bob Dole, R-Kan., called for quick action on Packwood. "The allegations are serious and should be taken seriously," Mitchell said. "I expect there will be a prompt and thorough investigation."

The Ethics Committee responded to Allred's complaint the day after it was received, saying it had begun a preliminary inquiry. Under the panel's rules, a "preliminary inquiry" was the first phase of its process for handling unsworn complaints, followed by an "initial review" and finally a formal "investigation."

Sexual discrimination activists greeted the announcement with wary praise. "It's the first time in history that the Ethics Committee is dealing with sexual harassment, so we're glad that they're treating it seriously," said Jean Dugan, a member of the Capitol Hill Women's Political Caucus' Sexual Harassment Task Force.

## ADAMS DROPS RE-ELECTION BID

Following a Seattle Times account that portrayed him as habitually prone to sexual misconduct, Democratic Sen. Brock Adams of Washington ended his bid for a second term March 1.

"This is the saddest day of my life," said Adams at an emotional news conference in Seattle. "I have ... never harmed anyone."

The Senate Ethics Committee on May 22 dismissed an ethics complaint against Adams because the allegations were based on anonymous sources and because the alleged incidents occurred before he was a senator.

It was not the first time Adams, a former House member and Transportation secretary, had been accused of sexual misconduct. Allegations surfaced in 1988 that he had drugged and molested Kari Tupper, a 26-year-old family friend, at his Washington, D.C., home. Adams denied those charges.

While Adams weathered Tupper's allegations, the Seattle Times story was insurmountable. It presented detailed and similar accounts by eight women who said Adams had made unwanted and inappropriate sexual advances toward them. Some women accused him of drugging them. One woman, described as a Democratic activist, said that in the early 1970s Adams drugged and raped her, leaving $200 as he departed.

In not pursuing the complaint, the Ethics Committee said that Tupper never gave "any indication of a desire to initiate proceedings" in the five years since the incident. But Tupper's lawyer said that she was willing to cooperate, but had not been contacted by the committee.

Norleen Koponen, president of the Washington state chapter of the Nation Organization for Women, which filed the complaint, criticized the panel's decision. "This tells us again that these men just don't get it. They don't understand how devastating assault, harassment and rape can be."

## McDADE INDICTED

Rep. Joseph M. McDade, R-Pa., was charged on May 5 with running his office as a criminal enterprise by enriching himself over five years with more than $100,000 worth of extorted favors, bribes and illegal gratuities.

The five-count indictment by a federal grand jury in Philadelphia focused on his work in behalf of defense firms seeking government contracts, some for work in his unemployment-plagued district.

McDade, a lawyer, denied wrongdoing and vowed "to stay and fight" the charges. "I am innocent of these charges, and I look forward to taking the oath of office with you next January," McDade said in a May 4 letter telling colleagues of the pending indictment.

McDade faced 34 years in prison and $1.25 million in fines if convicted of all counts.

Despite the indictment, McDade breezed through the election, winning 91 percent of the vote with no major-party opposition.

After he was charged, some House Republicans pressed McDade to relinquish his post as ranking Republican on the Appropriations Committee. McDade left it up to Minority Leader Robert H. Michel, R-Ill., who decided against forcing him to give up the post. When House GOP members organized in December for the 103rd Congress, the Republican Conference rejected a proposed rule that would have forced any GOP committee leader to give up his post while under indictment.

McDade's troubles were first detailed in a front-page story in The Wall Street Journal on Dec. 1, 1988, three months after the Justice Department began its probe.

The newspaper reported that the FBI was investigating

the lawmaker's ties to United ChemCon Corp. (UCC), a company with headquarters in the southern Pennsylvania city of Lancaster and a factory in McDade's district. Prosecutors had said that officials and associates of the bankrupt and then-defunct firm defrauded the government of $12 million.

Much of the McDade indictment stemmed from that investigation, which had produced guilty pleas from a dozen UCC associates who were cooperating with prosecutors. Among them: Raymond S. Wittig, a one-time aide to McDade (when he was ranking Republican on the Small Business Committee) who later became a UCC lobbyist.

McDade helped the once-tiny company get its first big government contracts in the mid-1980s to bring jobs to the recession-wracked Allegheny Mountain town of Renovo. "I did nothing other than help a town in my district that was faced with 85 percent unemployment," McDade said.

The indictment also included allegations related to five other contractors, two of which were involved in earlier defense procurement scandals.

In addition to the conspiracy and illegal gratuity charges, the indictment accused McDade of violating the Racketeer Influenced and Corrupt Organizations (RICO) act, a law originally meant to make it easier to convict mobsters.

McDade said U.S. Attorney Michael M. Baylson, who headed the Philadelphia office, "intends to stretch and misuse the RICO statute to cover up his evidentiary deficiencies. This is perhaps the greatest outrage of this case."

Implying that the case was built on legal technicalities, McDade accused prosecutors of harassing him to enhance their careers. He also charged Baylson with an "obvious conflict of interest." As the 1986 campaign treasurer for Sen. Arlen Specter, R-Pa., Baylson accepted campaign contributions from some of the same UCC-connected individuals as McDade.

"I know some will question whether a political motive truly exists in this case," McDade said. "After all, (Baylson) and I belong to the same political party. Perhaps it is pure ambition; the scalp of a sitting member of Congress would certainly not hurt one's political career at the Department of Justice."

Baylson said he would respond if and when McDade "makes these allegations in motions filed with the court."

## MAVROULES INDICTED

Rep. Nicholas Mavroules, D-Mass., was indicted on Aug. 27 on 17 counts of extortion, racketeering, tax evasion and abuse of office.

The indictment, returned by a federal grand jury, accused Mavroules of soliciting and accepting free cars and cash for a variety of favors during 20 years in public office. "Congressman Mavroules used the power of his office to enrich himself," said U.S. Attorney A. John Pappalardo.

Mavroules denied the charges, calling them politically motivated and designed to hurt him just three weeks before the Democratic primary.

Mavroules won the primary but lost in the general election to Republican Peter G. Torkildsen.

"I simply and firmly declare my innocence and say I am confident that in the end I will be vindicated," Mavroules said in a news conference shortly before the indictment was announced.

Mavroules had acknowledged accepting the free use of cars from a local dealership during his years in Congress.

He had said his failure to report the cars on House financial disclosure forms or annual tax forms was an oversight.

But the 25-page indictment stated that Mavroules solicited the use of the cars — valued at $75,000 — and for four years asked that they be put under a false name.

Federal prosecutors also alleged that as mayor of Peabody, Mavroules extorted $25,000 from the owners of a liquor store for his assistance in securing a license. The indictment also said Mavroules arranged for a job in the store for his brother.

He was also charged with extorting $12,000 in 1985 in return for arranging a prison transfer for a convicted drug trafficker and soliciting and receiving a discount for the use of a beach house. Mavroules faced penalties in the millions of dollars and 20 years or more in jail if convicted on all counts.

## LEGAL CLOUD LIFTED FROM ROBB

After a 19-month investigation that damaged Sen. Charles S. Robb's straight-arrow image, a federal grand jury on Jan. 12, 1993, voted not to indict the Virginia Democrat on conspiracy and obstruction of justice charges.

Robb maintained his innocence throughout the investigation, even after after three aides implicated him in plea agreements they made to criminal charges. The case centered on the release of an illegally recorded cellular phone call involving Gov. L. Douglas Wilder, D-Va.

Robb himself had predicted that he would be indicted after a repeat appearance before the grand jury Dec. 17, 1992.

Robb's testimony might have helped convince the grand jurors that he was innocent, but it did not stop them from indicting an associate of his, Virginia Beach businessman Bruce Thompson, on three felony charges, including witness tampering, related to the case.

Also issued Jan. 12, 1993, the Thompson indictment included allegations that Robb declined to listen to the tapes, although he knew their contents, in order to maintain "plausible deniability." Similar allegations were contained in the earlier plea agreements.

The case involved an alleged scheme to disclose a taped phone conversation that Robb aides perceived as damaging to Wilder, a longtime rival. In the tape, recorded in October 1988, Wilder speculated that rumors about Robb's attendance at Virginia Beach parties where cocaine was used would ruin his career.

The tape was leaked to the media more than two years later, when rumors about Robb's private life were refueled by a beauty queen's claim that she had had an affair with Robb.

Robb's aides apparently believed that the rumors would be discounted if they could be traced to a rival, particularly when they seemed so inconsistent with the image of Robb, a square-jawed former Marine.

## DIXON NOT TIED TO KEATING AFFAIR

The Senate Ethics Committee on Feb. 26 announced that it had considered and rejected suggestions that Sen. Alan J. Dixon, D-Ill., might have taken steps to help thrift operator Charles H. Keating Jr. The panel looked at a memo to Keating saying that someone named "Dickson" had talked with other senators involved in the Keating Five affair about helping Keating. Dixon said he never had any involvement with Keating, and the committee concluded that the memo was "incorrect and inaccurate." *(1991 Almanac, pp. 26, 38)*

## INOUYE FACES ALLEGATIONS

On Dec. 1, the Senate Ethics Committee announced that it had considered opening an investigation into Sen. Daniel K. Inouye's conduct with women, but that it had "not yet determined that there is adequate evidence to warrant an inquiry" of the Hawaii Democrat.

In the fall campaign, Inouye's opponent, Republican state Sen. Rick Reed, raised questions about Inouye's behavior toward women in campaign advertisements. He taped Inouye's hairdresser saying the senator had sexually harassed her 17 years before. After Inouye denied the charges and the woman said she did not realize she was being tape-recorded, Reed removed the ads.

Afterwards, Hawaii state Rep. Annelle Amaral, a Democrat, said she had been contacted by nine women with complaints about Inouye, but none were willing to be named. Inouye publicly denied any wrongdoing. ∎

# House Approves Hiring of Professional Administrator

Following a rash of scandals involving the management of the House, lawmakers approved a resolution (H Res 423) to overhaul the House's internal operations and hire a professional administrator.

After a six-month search, House leaders on Oct. 23 named Leonard P. Wishart III, a retired Army lieutenant general, to be the director of non-legislative and financial services.

The establishment of a professional administrator position to run the House's day-to-day operations was hailed by Democratic proponents as an important step toward solving problems exposed by scandals at the House bank and Post Office. But Republicans portrayed it as cosmetic reform and called, unsuccessfully, for far-reaching changes in the legislative balance of power.

Leaders said one of the measure's main goals was to end the traditional system of patronage used to fill hundreds of House jobs, which they said was at the root of the problems in House operations. But the resolution did not explicitly affect about two-thirds of the House's positions.

The House also agreed to create the post of inspector general, who was responsible for auditing the House's administrative functions. The resolution eliminated the position of postmaster and abolished the House Post Office.

## BACKGROUND

The idea for a House administrator had been around since 1977, when it was part of a reform package that Speaker Thomas S. Foley, D-Wash., supported. A united House Republican Conference opposed it at that time. *(1977 Almanac, p. 792)*

Although the idea had circulated for years, it was not until a series of scandals surrounding House operations surfaced that it was approved. First came embarrassing revelations in October 1991 that House members had not paid a quarter of a million dollars in overdue bills at House restaurants. Then came the House bank and Post Office scandals, which exposed that two of the basic services of the House were run in a slipshod fashion. *(House bank*

*scandal, p. 23; post office investigation, p. 47)*

To bring professionalism to House operations, members turned to the idea of an administrator. Much like a county executive or town manager, the administrator was to oversee the House buildings, police force and subway system, as well as such services as the House hair salons, car washes and restaurants. The administrator would also supervise the financial and management operations of House officers: the clerk, doorkeeper and sergeant at arms.

David R. Obey, D-Wis., one of the architects of the proposal, said, "The plan assumes the existing office structure won't stand. We expect the functions and offices to be consolidated."

## PARTISAN FIGHT MARKS DEBATE

The House approved H Res 423 on April 9 on a 269-81 vote, after a bitter partisan fight. *(Vote 84, p. 20-H)*

It was the same day the House approved the final version of a campaign finance bill (S 3), which Democrats also promoted as a significant reform in the political system, and engaged in several skirmishes over the post office investigation. *(Campaign finance bill, p. 63)*

The debate over the administrator bill frequently deteriorated into shouting matches. Republicans loudly proclaimed the changes to be cosmetic reform and called for far-reaching changes in the legislative balance of power — including banning proxy voting and putting more Republicans on the Rules Committee.

GOP members contended that the measure did not go far enough toward bipartisanship in administrative matters. They said the director would still be accountable to Democrats because deadlocks in the bipartisan subcommittee the administrator reported to were referred to the full House Administration Committee, where Democrats dominated. (This program was changed at the start of the 103rd Congress.)

"It is a sham and a charade," said Republican leader Robert H. Michel of Illinois. "The real scandal is the way Congress does its legislative business."

Democrats countered that the measure represented a major reform that would bring House management into the modern era and allow members to get back to legislative business. "We were not sent here as members of the House to count the silverware in the House dining room," said Richard J. Durbin, D-Ill. "This is the most far-reaching reorganization of the non-legislative activities of the House of Representatives in the history of the country," said Foley.

Obey, who headed the commission that recommended the 1977 administrator bill, said House management was riddled with anomalies. One office was responsible for installing curtains in congressional offices, while another handled venetian blinds. One office serviced outside locks while another took care of inside locks. One office handled fluorescent lamps, another handled incandescent bulbs.

Some members said internal changes — even the more drastic ones that Republicans sought — would not raise the public's low esteem of Congress. "Rearranging things inside this building is not what voters' frustration is all about," said Rod Chandler, R-Wash. "How many people you have on the Rules Committee? People at home could care less."

Republicans offered a substitute bill that was a sweeping agenda of long-sought changes to overhaul committee and floor procedures that Republicans believe put the minority at an unfair disadvantage.

Democrats argued that issues of legislative power did

not belong in a bill about administrative matters. The substitute was rejected on a 159-254 party-line vote. *(Vote 83, p. 20-H)*

The bill gave the Republicans some voice: It allowed the minority leader to have a say in appointing the administrator, along with the Speaker and the majority leader.

## DEADLOCK DELAYS APPOINTMENT

Although leaders said an administrator would be named quickly, the position remained unfilled for six months because Foley, Majority Leader Richard A. Gephardt, D-Mo., and Michel were unable to agree on a candidate.

The three were finally able to agree on Wishart, a retired Army lieutenant general, and his appointment was announced Oct. 23. Wishart came into the job with a reputation as a nonpartisan straight-talker, which his supporters said would help make him immune to political pressures. "He'll tell them what they need to hear, not what they want to hear," said retired Gen. John W. Foss, who was Wishart's supervising officer from 1989 to 1991. "He's very direct."

The job required Wishart to oversee the offices of 440 House members, 1,100 congressional district offices and 11,000 employees.

Wishart acknowledged that at first outsiders may wonder how a man accustomed to giving orders to subordinates was going to run the House, a base designed to support 435 very important people.

"I think some people automatically assume that if you're military, you would run things like a battalion or a ship. You can't," said Wishart. "On the pure military side, you issue an order and you expect it to be carried out. But as a senior military officer, you deal more and more with people and institutions that are civilian."

Wishart's term was for two years. Under the resolution, he could be fired by the Speaker or through a vote of the full House.

## PATRONAGE STILL AN ISSUE

Speaker Foley declared in March that the "days of patronage are over." But the resolution establishing Wishart's position prohibited patronage only for jobs controlled by the new administrator. The bill listed a variety of functions big and small that would fall under Wishart's purview — the child-care center, the computer system, members' payroll, the finance office, the barbershop and beauty salon, the restaurants, the mailroom and the typewriter repair shop, among others.

Before the resolution passed, the House was home to more than 600 patronage jobs. While a handful were filled by the Republicans, the Democratic Personnel Committee (known as the patronage committee) controlled the rest. Only about 200 of them were expressly turned over to the House administrator — roughly 160 in the House Post Office and 35 in the clerk's office, according to a patronage committee tally.

The resolution did not mention several entities that employed the majority of patronage workers, including much of the House's biggest single patronage shop, the House Doorkeeper's Office. Doorkeeper James T. Molloy's operation employed about 160 workers in the the Publications Distributions Service (the so-called folding room), 40 doormen and 25 document room workers — all patronage jobs, according to a Democratic Personnel Committee aide.

Republican chief deputy whip Robert S. Walker of Pennsylvania said Republicans had tried to get the doorkeeper jobs transferred to the new House administrator. "That was not something that was overlooked — it was specifically rejected" by the Democrats when the reform resolution was being drafted, Walker said. "All this talk about eliminating patronage has not produced real results, at least not yet," Walker said.

Likewise unaffected were more than 20 House elevator operators under the Architect of the Capitol, about 65 pages and about 100 Capitol Police jobs — all of which were officially designated patronage jobs. (House officials said that the police jobs were patronage slots in name only and that the personnel panel had had no role in filling them in years.)

Democratic leadership aides predicted that most of the remaining patronage positions eventually would be put under Wishart's control. According to the reform resolution, the administrator must fill all his jobs "without regard to political affiliation and solely on the basis of fitness to perform the duties involved."

Democratic leadership aides said they did not know why the doorkeeper jobs were left out of the resolution.

The panel to which Wishart would answer, the House Administration Committee, had the authority to give Wishart additional tasks beyond those assigned to him by the resolution. The committee was directed to establish in the 103rd Congress a new Subcommittee of Administrative Oversight, with equal numbers of Republican and Democratic members, to oversee the administrator's performance.

The law at first required tie votes to be automatically referred to the full committee, where Democrats held a 15-9 edge in the 102nd Congress. But after Republicans objected, the procedure was changed on the first day of the 103rd Congress so that a proposal would die on a tie vote. ∎

# Lawmakers Look for Ways To Improve Operations

Battered by scandal, scorned by an unforgiving public, abandoned by some of its most talented members, Congress in 1992 plunged into a period of introspection.

Some of the most respected members in the House and Senate called for major changes in the way Congress did legislative business. Frustrated members put forth proposals that would streamline committees, give more power to party leaders and simplify the budget process.

"We could do a lot better," said Rep. Lee H. Hamilton, D-Ind. "We must prepare for the challenges and opportunities of the coming decade."

Hamilton helped shepherd through both chambers a bill to create a special House-Senate committee to study Congress. The Joint Committee on the Organization of Congress was authorized to review Congress and make recommendations by the end of 1993 on how to improve its operations.

## CONGRESS LOOKS INWARD

The House bank and Post Office scandals that erupted in 1992 were just the latest in a long line of ethics problems for members of Congress. *(House bank scandal, p. 23; post office investigation, 47)*

In 1989, House Speaker Jim Wright, D-Texas, resigned under an ethics cloud. In 1990 and 1991, the Senate investigated five of its members — the so-called Keating Five — for their intercession with federal regulators in behalf of thrift operator Charles H. Keating Jr., a campaign donor. With scandal seemingly dominating the news from Capitol Hill, it was no surprise that public opinion of Congress was at an all-time low. *(1989 Almanac, p. 36; 1990 Almanac, p. 78; 1991 Almanac, p. 26)*

Hamilton joined up with Republican Rep. Bill Gradison, Ohio, and Sens. David L. Boren, D-Okla., and Pete V. Domenici, R-N.M., to propose the special committee to look into reform proposals. That was the same approach that produced significant changes in 1946 and 1970.

The bill received a lukewarm response when Hamilton introduced the bill (H Con Res 192) in July 1991. Powerful committee chairmen were suspicious that changes would decrease their clout. Speaker Foley said he feared that it would distract energy from substantive legislative business.

But the idea picked up steam after the House was beset by scandals, and members looked for ways to show the public that they were cleaning up the institution. Foley endorsed the bill in March 1992.

The House voted 412-4 on June 18 to approve the measure to create the Joint Committee on the Organization of Congress. *(Vote 205, p. 50-H)*

The Senate followed suit shortly after, approving the measure by voice vote on July 30 after removing a provision that would have allowed House members serving on the panel to make interim recommendations before the two parties' caucuses met in December 1992 to organize for the 103rd Congress.

Warning that early reporting requirements could enmesh the panel in election-year politics, Senate sponsors inserted a provision specifying that no official work be conducted before Nov. 15, 1992.

The measure then went back to the House for final voice-vote approval on Aug. 6.

The resolution specified that the panel include 28 members of the House and Senate, equally divided among Democrats and Republicans. The House and Senate majority and minority leaders were the only members of the panel specified. The rest were chosen by the party leaders.

Boren and Domenici were selected as the respective chairman and vice chairman for the Senate members. Hamilton and Gradison were chosen to serve those respective roles on the House side.

Under the resolution, the panel was specified to study: the committee system; the relationship between the House and Senate; the relationship between Congress and the executive branch; and the responsibilities and powers of the congressional leadership.

Gradison acknowledged that institutional change was no panacea, but they said that Congress' structural infirmities clearly exacerbated its political problems. "If we don't find an effective way to channel these energies toward strengthening the institution, the exact opposite will happen," said Gradison. "We have a system that minimizes the opportunity to be courageous and wilts the willpower to address tough issues," said Domenici.

The whole concept of changing Congress as an institution was met with skepticism in many quarters. Sen. Robert C. Byrd, D-W.Va., who first joined Congress in 1953, said, "There is a basic change we have seen here taking place, and institutional so-called reforms will not deal with them. They are miniature reforms."

Party leaders filled out the membership on the committee in October. Senate Majority Leader George J. Mitchell, D-Maine, named the following Democrats: Jim Sasser, Tenn.; Wendell H. Ford, Ky.; Harry Reid, Nev.; Paul S. Sarbanes, Md.; and David Pryor, Ark. Senate Minority Leader Bob Dole, R-Kan., appointed the following GOP members: Nancy Landon Kassebaum, Kan.; Trent Lott, Miss.; Ted Stevens, Alaska; William S. Cohen, Maine; and Richard G. Lugar, Ind.

On the House side, Speaker Foley named five Democrats: David R. Obey, Wis.; Al Swift, Wash.; John M. Spratt Jr., S.C.; Sam Gejdenson, Conn.; and Eleanor Holmes Norton, D.C. Minority Leader Robert H. Michel, R-Ill., named these Republicans: Robert S. Walker, Pa.; Gerald B. H. Solomon, N.Y.; David Dreier, Calif.; Bill Emerson, Mo.; and Wayne Allard, Colo.

In December, G. Kim Wincup, a longtime Hill aide who also served as assistant secretary of the Air Force, was named staff director. From 1974 to 1989, Wincup had served as counsel and staff director of the House Armed Services Committee. Walter J. Oleszek of the Congressional Research Service was named policy director.

Gradison resigned from the House on Jan. 31, 1993, to head a health insurance association. Dreier took over as leader of House Republicans; the vacancy was filled by Jennifer Dunn, R-Wash. ∎

# Nuclear Bunker Draws Flak

Among the congressional perks to come under scrutiny in 1992 was the Greenbrier bunker. Built at the height of the Cold War to allow the nation's legislature to continue operating in the event of nuclear attack, it was located beneath a West Virginia resort famous for its luxurious golf courses and fancy eating spots. By the end of the year, Congress had cut its ties to the outdated facility.

First reports of the bunker appeared in the May 29 edition of *The Washington Times*, apparently spurred by the scheduled publication May 31 of a feature article on it in *The Washington Post Magazine*. The stories publicized the facility and detailed efforts by House Speaker Thomas S. Foley, D-Wash., and others to keep the bunker's existence secret.

In a joint statement, the bipartisan congressional leadership said that the usefulness of the facility, constructed beneath a wing of the Greenbrier Hotel in the late 1950s, had been jeopardized by the publicity. However, in a separate statement, House Majority Leader Richard A. Gephardt, D-Mo., acknowledged the seeming inappropriateness of the underground complex and called it "a relic of the Cold War which probably ought to be mothballed."

Only a few top lawmakers and government officials knew about the Greenbrier bunker, built for $14 million, leaders said. It was part of a plan to relocate and keep the federal government operating during a nuclear war.

The Greenbrier Hotel's owner, the CSX Corp., was paid about $50,000 to $60,000 a year in rent from the government for maintaining the exclusive space as a potential retreat in the case of war. The facility reportedly had its own power plant and was equipped with food, medical supplies, computers and communications equipment. It was not designed to sustain a direct nuclear hit. ∎

# Madison Amendment Surprises Lawmakers

It may have been the first time in history that a constitutional amendment crept up on Congress by surprise. But the May 7, 1992, ratification of a 203-year-old amendment prohibiting midterm pay raises did just that.

The Madison Amendment had just 24 words: "No law varying the compensation for the services of the Senators and Representatives shall take effect, until an election of Representatives shall have intervened."

Named for James Madison, who proposed and wrote the amendment in 1789, the amendment was first sent to the states in September 1789 as part of a package of 12 proposed amendments. Ten became the Bill of Rights, but the pay raise amendment was ratified by only six states between 1789 and 1792, and then languished until 1873, when Ohio affirmed it. (The other amendment in the package, dealing with apportionment of the House, was never ratified.)

The amendment was revived in the late 1970s, and 33 states approved it between 1978 and 1992, as congressional pay raises became the target of vocal public hostility.

Michigan pushed it over the required three-quarters threshold May 7. The final ratification was controversial, with lawmakers at first hesitant to accept the drawn-out process as legal. But, unwilling to oppose such a popular measure during an election year, both chambers on May 20 passed resolutions embracing the new amendment.

## BACKGROUND

Ironically, the arrival of the pay-raise amendment was not immediately precipitated by a salary boost by members.

On the House side, lawmakers stressed that the Madison procedure was followed for their latest raise. When they voted themselves a pay raise in 1989 (part of the larger Ethics Reform Act limiting honoraria and outside compensation) it did not take effect until 1991, after an election. In 1991, the Senate voted to raise its own pay during a late-night session. It went into effect the same year, bumping lawmakers in both chambers to annual salaries of $129,500. But by May, the hubbub surrounding the Senate raise had died down. *(1989 Almanac, p. 51; 1991 Almanac, p. 22)*

But voting among the state legislators remained active. The latest push for the Madison Amendment began in August 1991 when 35 House members introduced a resolution calling on state legislatures to re-examine the amendment. Freshman members dubbed it their "class project."

The results began rolling in May 5, when Missouri and Alabama ratified the amendment. On May 7, Michigan cast the decisive 38th vote, with New Jersey becoming the 39th state to ratify just a few hours later. Illinois made it 40 during the week of May 11.

Statutes require that once the state legislatures approve a new amendment it be taken to the archivist of the United States. Don W. Wilson, the archivist, could have: declared the amendment constitutional; delayed issuing a certification pending guidance from Congress; or issued a conditional certification of ratification pending congressional action. At first it appeared that Congress would at least exercise its power to review the timeliness question, but after Wilson announced May 13 that he found it constitu-

tional, opposition melted.

Most amendments proposed in modern times had been sent to the states with a deadline for ratification, usually seven years. But the Madison amendment and the 11 others sent to the states in 1789 had no deadline. Therefore, supporters argued, the extensive gaps between state ratifications did not invalidate the proposal.

The Supreme Court ruled in earlier cases that the decision on whether the time span between introduction and ratification was too long was up to Congress.

In the 1939 decision in *Coleman v. Miller*, the majority concluded that questions of timeliness on this issue were political in nature and not within the jurisdiction of the courts.

Earlier, in a 1921 decision, *Dillon v. Gloss*, the court had suggested that a long delay made ratification untenable.

## LEGISLATIVE ACTION

The new amendment snuck up on the Hill with little fanfare or warning, throwing legislators into a legal thicket from which the only politically possible escape was to accept the new proposal, hoping that the precedent was not damaging.

Word came on May 7 that the 38th state had ratified the amendment. In the following days, House Speaker Thomas S. Foley, D-Wash., and Sen. Robert C. Byrd, D-W.Va., a former majority leader and Senate institutionalist, suggested hearings in the Judiciary committees to explore whether too much time had lapsed for the amendment to be valid.

In the House, Don Edwards, D-Calif., chairman of the Judiciary Subcommittee on Civil and Constitutional Rights, suggested having Congress urge the seven states that acted before 1978 to vote again, removing any doubt of their support.

But by May 14, the day after the archivist's decision, Foley said that he expected the House to accept the amendment outright.

"I now recognize it as an amendment," Foley said, backing away from earlier skepticism about its validity. "I think as a practical matter, it will be considered a part of the Constitution."

Foley's comments made it clear that Congress was reluctant to challenge the amendment's validity, even though legal scholars had for decades considered it dead because it had been around too long.

After Foley's acceptance of the amendment, the Judiciary Committee canceled plans for hearings.

### 27th Amendment Certified

The 27th Amendment was officially certified by the United States Archivist on May 18, printed in the Federal Register on May 19 and became, for all relevant purposes, part of the Constitution.

On the Senate side, the move to accept the ratification of 40 states came from Byrd. Following Archivist Wilson's decision to certify ratification, the Senate leader acknowledged that the time had come for Congress to accept the amendment as well.

"In most circumstances, I believe that a lapse of this length would be too great to sustain ratification of an

amendment," Byrd said. "The congressional pay amendment deserves a different fate."

Byrd, considered a stickler for institutional rectitude, scolded Wilson for not following "historic tradition." When questions arose in the past about the validity of ratification, he said, certification by the archivist or secretary of State was postponed pending congressional discussion and resolution.

In addition to a resolution accepting the language as the 27th Amendment, Byrd also asked colleagues to declare four long-outstanding amendments to be invalid. Such language, he maintained, would prevent centuries of delay from becoming precedent.

The four amendments were sent to the states without a deadline and remain unratified. They include a proposal to change the apportionment of the House of Representatives (sent to the states in 1789), a stricture forbidding American officials from accepting titles of nobility (1810), language prohibiting federal laws against slavery (1861) and a proposal allowing Congress to regulate child labor (1924).

Two proposals to recognize the 27th Amendment (S Con Res 120, S Res 298) were approved 99-0 on May 20. The resolution to invalidate the lingering amendments was referred to the Judiciary Committee. *(Votes 99, 100, p. 14-S)*

On the House side, a somewhat ceremonial debate was held May 19, a day before a resolution (H Con Res 320) similar to Byrd's passed, 414-3. *(Vote 131, p. 32-H)*

House passage was accompanied by vocal support from members, many of whom argued that the passage of time had not robbed the amendment of its relevance.

"Our predecessors in 1789 offered wisdom by which this body can live in 1992 and beyond," said Jack Brooks, D-Texas, chairman of the Judiciary Committee. Brooks was joined by ranking committee Republican Hamilton Fish Jr., N.Y., who said that the "rash of recent ratifications" is enough to validate the timeliness of the proposal.

Don Edwards, D-Calif., said the long delay should be considered "an exception, not a precedent."

Only one member spoke against the amendment. Neal Smith, D-Iowa, argued that Congress was accepting the new amendment without questioning the long lapses between ratifications, risking damage to the integrity of the Constitution.

"The principle of contemporary consensus . . . is just too important to ever waive just because it appears popular at the moment," Smith told his colleagues.

Some outside scholars agreed with Smith, arguing that the amendment's political attractiveness overshadowed more substantive issues.

"I think there is reason to be concerned about what appears to be a very casual amendment," said Walter E. Dellinger, a professor of constitutional law at Duke University.

Dellinger said the process followed in this case might "lower the resistance to amending the Constitution."

Dellinger said that Madison, ironically, was not enthusiastic about the proposal that now bears his name. When the pay raise language was being debated in the 1st Congress, concern was expressed that the political popularity of low salaries could preclude good men from entering politics.

" 'Much inconvenience and very little good would result from this amendment,' " Dellinger read, quoting a participant in the early debates. " 'It might serve as a tool for designing men, they might reduce the wages very low, much lower than it was possible for any gentleman to serve

without injury to his private affairs, in order to procure popularity at home.' "

## COURT ACTION

Although the year ended without a challenge to the constitutionality of the ratification process, a federal judge in Washington on Dec. 16 ruled on whether or not previously approved cost of living adjustments (COLAs) were valid under the new amendment.

The challenge, filed by a group of plaintiffs including some legislators, called the congressional pay increases that went into effect Jan. 1, 1993, unconstitutional.

However, U.S. District Judge Stanley Sporkin rejected claims that the 3.2 percent COLA violated the 27th Amendment.

More than two dozen members of the 102nd and 103rd Congresses and assorted citizens' groups had urged Sporkin to block the COLA, which raised basic congressional salaries from $129,500 to $133,600 per year.

They based their challenge on the effective date of the COLA and of a slightly smaller increase (3 percent) in congressional pension benefits.

Both took effect Jan. 1 — four days before members of the 103rd Congress, elected Nov. 3, were scheduled to be sworn in. So even though "an election of Representatives" had intervened, defeated or retiring members of the outgoing 102nd Congress would also benefit from the increases. The effect would be felt primarily in lifetime pension benefits, which were based on the highest three years of pay.

Sporkin, however, said that nothing in the constitutional amendment implied that only a new Congress could take advantage of a change in pay. The sole requirement, he said, was for an intervening election between the time Congress approved the raise and the time the increase took effect.

"Automatic annual adjustments to congressional salaries meet both the language and the spirit of the 27th Amendment," Sporkin said.

Sporkin said the law as a whole was "as salutary a piece of government legislation as any enacted in modern times."

"The increase in question — 3.2 percent, or roughly $4,100 annually — is a small price to pay for good, honest government and for preventing reversion to a system of special interest payoffs," he declared in a 15-page opinion issued an hour after the conclusion of oral arguments in the case.

The plaintiffs had argued that the 1989 pay act did not adequately fulfill terms of the 27th Amendment. Lawmakers should have to vote publicly on every pay raise, including cost of living increases, counsel John C. Armor contended.

But in his decision, Sporkin maintained that voters had an opportunity to accept or reject members who supported the 1989 law during the 1990 and 1992 elections.

"One way to maintain high-quality government is to provide our elected officials with a living wage that automatically changes to reflect changed economic conditions," Sporkin said.

Armor also challenged part of the 1989 law calling for a citizens' commission, with presidential approval, to review and recommend changes to members' base salaries every four years. If the Madison Amendment is to mean anything, Armor said, it must require a new law and vote each time.

But Sporkin ruled that because the commission's recommendations must be voted on by Congress and go into effect only after the next election, the quadrennial review process also complied with the 27th Amendment. ∎

# Senators Benefit From Honoraria Loophole

A legal loophole permitted a cash windfall of nearly $9,000 for senators in 1991 — and nearly half of them took advantage of it, according to financial disclosure reports filed in 1992.

When the Senate voted itself a $23,200 pay hike in 1991, the increase was explained to voters as the price of a prohibition on honoraria — money paid directly to senators by special interests for speeches and appearances. *(1991 Almanac, p. 22)*

But while the salary increase took effect immediately — Aug. 14, 1991 — senators were allowed to keep honoraria they had already earned. That created the potential for a one-time windfall for senators who kept a full year's honoraria limit while accepting the part-year pay raise.

Thirteen senators collected the full year's honoraria limit, $23,068; 32 managed to make over $1,000 more than what they would have in 1991 had the Senate not acted on the honoraria-pay raise proposal. *(Chart, this page)*

Passage of the prohibition apparently did inspire six senators who accepted honoraria in 1990 to reject them the following year, including Hank Brown, R-Colo., and Patrick J. Leahy, D-Vt., both of whom collected more than

$20,000 in 1990. A total of 40 senators refused speaking fees in 1991.

The total honoraria collected by senators declined by a third in 1991, falling from $1.5 million in 1990 to approximately $1 million.

But three senators reversed course, accepting honoraria in 1991 after taking none the previous year. They were John Kerry, D-Mass., who kept $3,500; Strom Thurmond, R-S.C, who kept $8,500; and Lloyd Bentsen, D-Texas, who reported a Steuben glass sculpture valued at $604.

A House ban on honoraria took effect at the start of 1991, along with a pay raise. That seemed to have led to a substantial decline in fees for speeches — and, consequently, in charitable contributions of those fees made by House members.

In 1990, the top 10 recipients of honoraria in the House gave more than $730,000 to charity from fees they collected in excess of the limit they were permitted to keep. With no personal honoraria permitted last year, their money donated to charity dropped by more than half.

The top recipient in 1991, as in 1990, was Dan Rostenkowski, D-Ill., chairman of the powerful Ways and Means Committee. But the total of his speech fees fell by $200,000 to $110,000.

Colorado Democrat Patricia Schroeder was the No. 2 honoraria recipient in 1990, and she continued near the top in 1991. In 1990, she collected nearly $158,000 — $131,000 going to charity. In 1991, Schroeder's charitable contributions fell to $60,450.

These and other details emerged from the annual financial disclosure reports members submitted. They were released to the public June 11 and 12.

**New Loan**

The reports provided vast detail on members' assets, liabilities and gifts. Many members were quizzed by voters and reporters about golf trips and jaunts to faraway places; those with past financial problems were most carefully scrutinized.

The 1991 reports showed a new loan to Republican Sen. Mark O. Hatfield of Oregon from a friend who once lobbied the senator. The Justice Department and the Senate Ethics Committee began probing Hatfield's personal finances in 1991 after it was disclosed that he had accepted valuable gifts and favorable loans from friends who had more than a passing interest in the work of the Senate. *(1991 Almanac, p. 43)*

The new loan of between $15,001 and $50,000 came from former Rep. John R. Dellenback, R-Ore., raising Hatfield's debt to Dellenback to between $45,003 and $150,000, according to broad ranges listed on Hatfield's report.

Over the years, Dellenback lent Hatfield more than $250,000, forgave $83,059 of the senator's debts and provided him with gifts including a Hawaiian vacation and below-market rent on a farm.

Dellenback was once president of the Christian College Coalition and, in that capacity, persuaded Hatfield to sponsor a floor amendment for the schools.

Hatfield also reported owing between $50,001 and $100,000 in legal fees to the law firm of his attorney, John W. Nields Jr., and accepting $30,020 for a legal defense fund he set up the previous July.　　　　　　　■

## Senators' Honoraria

| Senator | Kept 1990 | Kept 1991 | Senator | Kept 1990 | Kept 1991 |
|---------|------|------|---------|------|------|
| Baucus | $27,000 | 14,500 | Inouye | 13,000 | 11,000 |
| Bentsen | 0 | 604 | Jeffords | 16,900 | 19,500 |
| Biden | 25,850 | 17,850 | Johnston | 27,000 | 22,000 |
| Bond | 23,598 | 15,400 | Kasten | 27,075 | 21,315 |
| Boren | 27,337 | 23,068 | Kerry (Mass.) | 0 | 3,500 |
| Breaux | 27,222 | 18,960 | Leahy | 27,305 | 0 |
| Brown | 27,000 | 0 | Lott | 27,337 | 23,068 |
| Bryan | 15,000 | 0 | Lugar | 24,713 | 21,592 |
| Bumpers | 25,800 | 10,900 | Mack | 24,500 | 23,000 |
| Burns | 27,303 | 22,900 | McConnell | 27,250 | 22,700 |
| Byrd | 9,000 | 0 | Mikulski | 6,700 | 8,750 |
| Coats | 18,380 | 23,000 | Mitchell | 30,000 | 18,850 |
| Chafee | 27,028 | 23,140 | Moynihan | 26,900 | 14,650 |
| Cohen | 11,950 | 21,300 | Murkowski | 24,800 | 15,275 |
| Conrad | 26,940 | 15,000 | Nickles | 27,300 | 22,200 |
| Craig | 26,750 | 23,000 | Nunn | 27,337 | 23,068 |
| D'Amato | 27,325 | 11,000 | Packwood | 27,215 | 23,000 |
| Danforth | 200 | 350 | Pressler | 27,300 | 23,068 |
| Daschle | 27,125 | 22,980 | Pryor | 27,337 | 15,500 |
| Dixon | 27,300 | 23,068 | Riegle | 16,500 | 16,000 |
| Dole | 30,400 | 24,508 | Roth | 27,337 | 23,068 |
| Domenici | 25,050 | 17,050 | Rudman | 27,300 | 20,000 |
| Durenberger | 24,159 | 23,000 | Sarbanes | 20,965 | 8,700 |
| Ford | 25,000 | 22,000 | Sasser | 27,337 | 23,068 |
| Fowler | 26,036 | 22,786 | Shelby | 27,000 | $21,500 |
| Garn | 27,300 | 23,000 | Simon | 12,000 | 19,750 |
| Gore | 27,337 | 10,750 | Simpson | 26,932 | 23,068 |
| Gorton | 23,300 | 6,900 | Specter | 3,000 | 0 |
| Gramm | 27,325 | 23,050 | Stevens | 20,000 | 17,000 |
| Hatch | 23,135 | 23,068 | Symms | 27,337 | 23,068 |
| Hatfield | 22,600 | 18,000 | Thurmond | 0 | 8,500 |
| Heflin | 26,150 | 17,000 | Wallop | 25,200 | 23,068 |
| Helms | 14,000 | 10,000 | Wellstone | 200 | 0 |
| Hollings | 26,988 | 22,900 | | | |

*NOTE: Does not include senators who kept no honoraria in either year.*

SOURCE: Senate Financial Disclosure Forms

# House Tightens Limits on Franked Mail

Under heavy pressure from challengers and faced with an embarrassing decision by a federal appeals court, House leaders curtailed one of the most potent advantages of incumbency in a redistricting year when members needed it most — free mail to new constituents.

Democratic leaders on July 30 announced that the House would no longer allow the franking privilege to be used for mass mail to constituents outside their current districts in order to head off a rebuff on the floor. The new rule ended the tradition of House members targeting "franked" mass mail at voters in the newly drawn districts they expected to represent after the election.

The House had twice voted to ban the practice. But on a practical level, many members of both parties were reluctant to give up the perk. Neither vote for a ban occurred on a bill likely to become law in time to affect the 1992 elections.

House challengers had agitated for a rule change throughout this redistricting year, arguing that out-of-district mailings amounted to nothing more than taxpayer-financed electioneering. Republicans, who stood to gain House seats if the grip of incumbency could be weakened, took up the cause. But until a federal appeals court ruled that most out-of-district mass mail was unconstitutional, it appeared that Democrats would delay action until too late for 1992.

"It took two House votes and a court ruling to get this change made administratively," said Bill Thomas of California, ranking Republican on the House Administration Committee, who had argued for the ban since January. "It's a major victory. The only sad part is that we lost seven months."

## APPEALS COURT ACTION

Just hours before the rule change was announced in the House, the U.S. Appeals Court for the District of Columbia issued a 2-1 decision finding it unconstitutional for members to send "postal patron" mailings — unaddressed mail to every household in a postal zone — to voters outside the existing borders of their districts. That ruling overturned a June 26 lower court decision upholding the practice.

"Any such statute which provides financial support to an incumbent against a major party challenger must receive heightened scrutiny," wrote Circuit Court Judge Laurence H. Silberman. "Whatever Congress' motive in passing the disputed provision, there is no showing of a substantial government interest in financing this sort of communication with voters."

"It is no different from a provision giving every incumbent $100,000 to hold campaign rallies in the new area," wrote Judge A. Raymond Randolph, adding that it "promotes the incumbent's re-election, without enhancing his capacity to serve his constituents."

Lawyers for the House had defended the constitutionality of non-district mail, arguing that voters shifted to a new district might otherwise not get legislative mail.

Ironically, the House votes to repeal language permitting out-of-district mail were influential in the court's reasoning. "It is worth noting that the *only* explanation advanced by the House for that repeal was that [out-of-district mail] is a 'taxpayer financed, indirect way to campaign at taxpayer expense,' " wrote Silberman.

The House first voted 408-8 to ban non-district mail April 8 as part of the campaign finance bill, which faced a certain veto. The second vote was equally lopsided, this time 417-2, and equally meaningless. On June 24, the House added similar repeal language to the legislative appropriations bill, but it was not expected to be enacted in time to have any effect. House rules had long prohibited all mass mail within 60 days of an election. *(Campaign finance, p. 63; appropriations, p. 633)*

A spokesman for Speaker Thomas S. Foley, D-Wash., said the court decision would not be appealed.

The suit was filed by the Coalition to End the Permanent Congress, the National Taxpayers Union and Public Citizen, and was joined by five House challengers — three Democrats and two Republicans.

## PRACTICAL IMPACT

With the legal victory in hand, Republicans pushed the House beyond the parameters of the court decision. Technically, the federal panel prohibited only out-of-district postal patron mailings, mailings that were sent without an individual name and address. Thomas wanted a ban on all out-of-district mass mail — which was defined as unsolicited, nearly identical letters of 500 or more, regardless of whether they were individually addressed.

When Thomas first offered a motion on July 30, shortly after word of the court decision, to ban all such mail, he was ruled out of order. That touched off a backroom skirmish in which Republicans threatened to offer an embarrassing motion complaining that the House counsel had misused taxpayer dollars by defending a rule that the House had voted twice to abolish.

Democratic leaders relented. In a colloquy between House Administration Committee Chairman Charlie Rose, D-N.C., and Thomas, the panel's ranking Republican, Rose made clear that no funds would be spent on any mass mailing, postal patron or otherwise, sent outside the district a member was elected to serve.

August was typically a heavy mail month, and advocates said stopping out-of-district mail immediately was meaningful. "The pattern is for those letters to stack up in the weeks before the election cutoff," said Cliff Arnebeck, president of the the Coalition to End the Permanent Congress. "This shows that Congress can't just do whatever it wants."

The National Taxpayers Union cited figures showing that House use of the franking privilege was 83 percent higher in the first quarter of 1992 than it had been in the first quarter of the previous year. "As the new congressional district lines became law around the country, House members have dumped millions of pieces of mail aimed at raising their name identification in the new districts," said David Keating, executive vice president of the National Taxpayers Union.

Congress had put other curbs on franking in 1990. *(1990 Almanac, p. 75)*   ∎

# Clinton Announces New Ethics Standards

Soon after he was elected president, Bill Clinton issued new ethics guidelines designed to curb influence peddling by former top government officials, a Washington practice he strongly attacked during the campaign.

The new standards, which would apply to 1,100 of the president-elect's 3,500 appointees, prohibited officials from lobbying their former agencies for five years and from ever representing foreign governments or foreign political parties before the U.S. government.

Clinton's transition director, Warren M. Christopher (later picked as secretary of State), announced the new guidelines Dec. 9, one day before Clinton made his first Cabinet nominations. New appointees were asked to sign a pledge agreeing to the ethics standards, making them contractually binding. The standards were made official in the first executive order issued by President Clinton, on Jan. 20, 1993.

Christopher on Nov. 13, 1992, had issued a set of rules for those working on the Clinton transition team designed to forestall conflicts of interest. Transition staff were required to sign a pledge that they would not lobby any agency for six months for which they had responsibility in the transition. They also were required to fill out financial disclosure forms and to recuse themselves from decisions that could conflict with their financial interest or those of their families or business interests.

## Slowing the Revolving Door

Administration officials acknowledged that the rules would not totally eliminate the "revolving door" through which many top officials went to earn large amounts of money using their former government contacts. But Christopher said the rules were designed to make such activities more difficult for top officials without discouraging too many qualified applicants from seeking administration jobs. "It's a matter of balance, of wanting to be able to attract the most outstanding people in government and yet preventing any possible vice that's inherent in the system as it now exists," Christopher said at a Little Rock, Ark., news conference Dec. 9.

Christopher noted that the restrictions went much further than existing law, which prohibited former officials from lobbying their agencies for one year after leaving the government. "Taxpayers need to know that public servants whose salaries they pay are working for them and not for special interests," Christopher said.

The 1978 Ethics in Government Act prohibited certain executive branch officials from lobbying their agencies for a year after leaving government. *(1978 Almanac, p. 835)*

Christopher called the new guidelines "just the beginning of Gov. Clinton's efforts to give the government back to the people." Clinton had also pledged to seek new legislation toughening campaign finance and lobbying laws.

However, Christopher hedged when asked if the president-elect would, as he promised in the campaign, push Congress to extend the new post-employment lobbying restrictions to former lawmakers. In 1989, Congress for the first time applied the one-year lobbying limit to its own members and staff. *(1989 Almanac, p. 53)*

"Gov. Clinton has got a very heavy agenda of legislative activities ahead. . . . I think we'll have to arrange the priorities," he said.

Critics of lobbying practices applauded the new guidelines, although some said they needed to be toughened. "They're a good start, but they don't go far enough," said Pat Choate, author of "Agents of Influence," a book that chronicled widespread lobbying for foreign interests by former U.S. government employees.

Choate said that without legislation to back up the executive order, the guidelines would be hard to enforce and could easily be rescinded by subsequent administrations. He also noted that the lifetime ban on foreign lobbying would not prohibit former U.S. officials from representing foreign corporations, foundations or other organizations.

"What we require is a loophole-free set of ethics," said Choate.

## Key Provisions

The new guidelines included three main provisions:

● Top officials were required to sign a pledge stating that they would not lobby their former agencies for five years after they left government. White House officials would be banned from lobbying both the Executive Office of the President and any department over which they had "substantial personal responsibility."

The five-year prohibition, which applied generally to those with salaries of $104,800 and higher, would not cover lobbying before Congress or agencies over which the official had no responsibility.

Exempted from the restrictions were career civil servants, former officials who went to work for the federal, state or local governments, and scientists or others who worked for nonprofit organizations and relied on federal grants for their work. In addition, legal representation in criminal or civil suits would not be restricted.

● The 1,100 officials were required to pledge that they would never lobby for any foreign government or foreign political party before the federal government.

● Trade negotiators were required to pledge not to "represent, aid or advise" foreign governments or foreign business entities in matters before the federal government for five years after they participated in a negotiation.

To enforce the rules in the event of a violation, Clinton aides said the new administration would seek a court injunction against the lobbying activities and would sue to recoup the former official's lobbying income. In addition, violators would be prohibited from lobbying their former agency for another five years.

Sen. Carl Levin, D-Mich., sponsor of legislation (S 2766) to toughen lobby registration and disclosure laws, praised the new rules. "No one has a God-given right to 'cash in' on his or her public service," Levin said in a statement.

The senator reintroduced his bill as S 349 in 1993. It had been approved in 1992 by the Governmental Affairs Committee and was endorsed by Clinton and Vice President Al Gore as a likely vehicle for the Clinton administration's lobbying reforms. ■

# Bush Rejects Campaign Finance Legislation

Buffeted by scandal, congressional Democrats moved quickly in 1992 to push through both chambers and send to the White House the most far-reaching attempt to reform federal election law in two decades. But — lacking bipartisan backing — it all came to naught by mid-May when President Bush vetoed the measure and the Senate fell nine votes short of overriding the veto.

The legislation sought to provide public funding and other incentives to congressional candidates who agreed to limit their campaign spending. The last time such a sweeping campaign finance bill had cleared was 1974, when Congress limited spending on presidential campaigns and imposed limits on contributions for all federal elections.

The bill, various forms of which had been kicking around for more than a decade, got new legs in the House in 1992 as that chamber was rocked by scandal over perks and privileges.

Until then, Bush's long-standing threat to veto any bill that included public funding of campaigns and the vast differences between the bills each chamber passed in 1991 seemed to reduce the likelihood of serious consideration.

Then scandals at the House bank and Post Office sent Democratic leaders on a reform mission and reignited the campaign finance bill. Conferees reconciled differences between the chambers' bills April 2 by letting each live by its own rules. The House also went along with the Senate's more restrictive language on "soft money," money raised under state law and then used to influence federal campaigns.

Under the bill, House candidates' spending would have been capped at $600,000 per election cycle; the ceiling for Senate candidates would have varied between $1.6 million and $8.9 million, depending on state population.

House candidates who complied with the spending limits and other restrictions would have gotten up to $200,000 in federal matching funds; Senate candidates would have received taxpayer-financed vouchers to buy discounted TV advertising time worth up to 20 percent of the state spending limit.

Bush and many Republicans objected to nearly every facet of the bill. They argued that spending limits skewed the system against challengers, that federal financing was too expensive and that the political action committee (PAC) restrictions did not go far enough.

The conference report passed the House April 9 by a 259-165 vote; the Senate cleared it April 30, 56-42. But on Saturday afternoon, May 9, Bush quietly vetoed the bill. Four days later, when the Senate tried but failed to override the veto, the measure was dead for the year.

Democrats contended that Bush killed the most sweeping overhaul of the campaign finance system in nearly two

---

## BOXSCORE

➡ **Campaign Finance (S 3, HR 3750).** Legislation to provide public funding and other incentives to congressional candidates who agreed to limit their campaign spending.

**Reports:** S Rept 102-37; H Rept 102-340; conference report H Rept 102-487.

### KEY ACTION

April 2 — **House-Senate** conference completed.

April 9 — The **House** adopted conference report on S 3, 259-165.

April 30 — The **Senate** cleared conference report, 56-42.

May 9 — President Bush vetoed S 3.

May 13 — The **Senate** failed to override veto by nine votes.

---

decades — one that would have restricted political action committees and curtailed the money marathon congressional candidates were running.

Republicans countered that the Democratic proposal was little more than an incumbent-protection plan that would have cost taxpayers millions and denied challengers the ability to compete.

## BACKGROUND

Major new laws to overhaul the campaign finance system to limit the influence of money in politics came only after scandals: Teapot Dome in the 1920s, Watergate in the 1970s. In the early 1990s, much of the impetus came from the well-publicized abuse of congressional perks following on the heels of the Keating Five. *(1991 Almanac, p. 26)*

Congress had been examining how to curb the ability of interest groups to dominate the flow of campaign money and attempting to establish a level playing field for all candidates since the first law regulating campaigns was enacted during the administration of Theodore Roosevelt.

In 1925, the Teapot Dome scandal yielded the Federal Corrupt Practices Act, an extensive statute governing the conduct of federal campaigns. But that law was so riddled with loopholes that it was ineffectual. It took Congress another four decades to adopt two pieces of legislation containing some of the ground rules under which elections were conducted into the 1990s.

President Richard M. Nixon reluctantly signed the Revenue Act of 1971 (PL 92-178), allowing the $1 tax checkoff for presidential campaign financing to take effect after almost five years of debate.

As a condition for his signature, however, Nixon insisted on postponing the measure until after the 1972 election. *(1971 Almanac, p. 430)*

During his re-election campaign, Nixon signed the Federal Election Campaign Act (FECA) on Feb. 7, 1972 (PL 92-225). The law required comprehensive disclosure for contributions and expenditures by candidates for federal office. *(1972 Almanac, p. 161)*

But FECA ultimately had a limited impact on controlling campaign spending. And in the wake of the Watergate scandal, Congress passed the FECA Amendments of 1974 (PL 93-443). The law set limits on contributions and expenditures for congressional and presidential elections, established an independent Federal Election Commission to oversee federal election laws and created a specific framework for providing presidential candidates with public financing. *(1974 Almanac, p. 611)*

### Buckley v. Valeo

The Supreme Court ruled in 1976 on a constitutional challenge to FECA in the case of *Buckley v. Valeo*. The

court upheld FECA's disclosure requirements, contribution limitations and public financing of presidential elections. But it struck down spending limits for congressional and presidential races, including restraints on using a candidate's personal assets, except for presidential candidates who accepted public financing, as unconstitutional limits on free speech. It also struck down limits on independent expenditures.

Subsequent congressional efforts to change the campaign finance system were driven largely by the desire to find a way to limit congressional campaign spending without violating the mandates of the *Buckley* decision.

What emerged was a move to offer public financing to candidates who adhered to optional limits on campaign spending, despite a large degree of skittishness about the issue. House members rejected public financing in 1974, and the subject did not return to the floor for 16 years.

House and Senate proposals (HR 5400, S 137) to reduce campaign spending and limit the influence of PACs died at the end of the 101st Congress, victims of sharp differences between the two parties over the best approach to take. paign system flaws that year because of the ongoing investigation into the so-called Keating Five — five senators suspected of doing favors for a wealthy campaign contributor, Charles H. Keating Jr. *(1990 Almanac, p. 59)*

House and Senate proposals (HR 5400, S 137) to reduce campaign spending and limit the influence of PACs died at the end of the 101st Congress, victims of sharp differences between the two parties over the best approach to take.

### 1991 Action

Congress successfully set the stage early in the 102nd Congress for sending President Bush the first overhaul of campaign finance legislation since the 1974 post-Watergate reforms. Outside groups cited congressional ethics problems and low ratings for Congress in public opinion polls to galvanize movement on Capitol Hill.

The Senate moved first, passing S 3 by a 56-42 vote on May 23. The House passed its version, HR 3750, 273-156, on Nov. 25. Bush held the trump card because it was apparent that neither chamber could muster the votes to overturn a presidential veto. And Bush made it clear that he would veto any bill that he felt favored Democrats over Republicans. *(1991 Almanac, p. 13)*

Both bills threatened the GOP: They imposed an artificial ceiling on spending and gave public funds to candidates. They also created separate systems for House and Senate candidates, which Bush said he would not accept.

Republicans and Democrats not only disagreed on how to fix the system, they also could not agree on what was wrong.

Democrats insisted that any new law had to limit campaign spending. Money they would take away from candidates, by limiting or banning PACs, they would replace with public subsidies.

Republicans, rather than capping spending, proposed curbing specific sources, such as PACs and large out-of-state contributions. They wanted to encourage political parties to spend even more in behalf of their candidates. What Republicans feared most was that locking in spending levels would lock in a Democratic majority.

Yet, there were plenty of reasons to keep fueling the momentum for campaign finance proposals. Common Cause, the public interest lobbying group, made the issue a centerpiece of its appeals to members. The Ralph Nadar-affiliated group, Public Citizen, and the labor-affiliated group, Citizen Action, also pushed for an overhaul of the law so that tax dollars would replace PAC dollars. The 33

million-member American Association of Retired Persons joined the coalition in favor of the legislation.

The Keating Five savings and loan investigation of 1990-91 provided another impetus, as it became referred to as the "smoking gun" that proved the corruption of the election finance system.

The House bank and Post Office scandals consumed Congress early in 1992, contributing to a wave of retirements, a fear of defeat and even a threat to the speakership of Thomas S. Foley, D-Wash. In this environment, House Democratic leaders began grasping for reform measures large and small, and campaign finance again was an obvious target. *(House bank, p. 23; post office, p. 47)*

But while the rush to move the two campaign finance bills through conference at the start of the second session of the 102nd Congress created a whirlwind of activity, it was in the vacuum of a continuing stalemate between the two parties.

## CONFERENCE ACTION

Democrats proudly claimed paternity for the campaign finance overhaul approved by a House-Senate conference late the night of April 2, but the measure was a child of scandal and it was apparent early on that the measure was unlikely to survive an expected veto.

Although Bush had vowed repeatedly to veto legislation resembling either of the bills (S 3, HR 3750) passed by the House and Senate in 1991, House leaders worked relentlessly the week of March 30 to ready a proposal for rapid floor action.

The drive to get a conference agreement was partisan from the outset. The conference met in a pro forma session March 31, when Democratic and Republican members gave opening statements reiterating old rhetoric. But it was evident that intense behind-the-scenes negotiating already had taken place. The majority staff distributed recommendations to Democratic members that day. With a few modifications, those recommendations were adopted.

The push for the bill so clearly came from the House that when the meeting was finally rescheduled, senators, including conference Chairman Wendell H. Ford, D-Ky., were not immediately informed. No senators ultimately attended the second meeting. Nor did many House members.

Nonetheless, by agreeing to the Senate's restrictive language on so-called soft money spent by state parties, House Democrats met their goal. Foley called the bill "the most fundamental reform of a generation" and predicted passage.

"This is a bill that pushes reform to the limit of where we had votes," said Sam Gejdenson, D-Conn., who headed a House task force on campaign finance.

The bill was never a good bet to become law because of Bush's objections to its spending limits, public funding for congressional candidates and creation of separate systems for House and Senate campaigns. The measure contained all three.

The final measure stripped a ban on political action committees previously adopted by the Senate. It also did not include a mechanism to pay for public financing, which was derided by Sen. Mitch McConnell, Ky., and other Republicans.

"While the public is screaming about mismanagement and overdrafts at the House bank, this bill writes the biggest rubber check in history to finance our campaigns for re-election," said McConnell.

### Spending Limits Proposed

Spending limits were at the heart of Democratic proposals for campaign finance reform. The Democrats main

# President Bush's Veto Message

*On May 9, President Bush vetoed legislation to overhaul campaign finance laws. Following is the text of the veto message he sent to the Senate.*

I am returning herewith without my approval S 3, the Congressional Campaign Spending Limit and Election Reform Act of 1992. The current campaign finance system is seriously flawed. For three years, I have called on the Congress to overhaul our campaign finance system in order to reduce the influence of special interests, to restore the influence of individuals and political parties, and to reduce the unfair advantages of incumbency. S 3 would not accomplish any of these objectives. In addition to perpetuating the corrupting influence of special interests and the imbalance between challengers and incumbents, S 3 would limit political speech protected by the First Amendment and inevitably lead to a raid on the Treasury to pay for the act's elaborate scheme of public subsidies.

In 1989, I proposed comprehensive campaign finance reform legislation to reduce the influence of special interests and the powers of incumbency. My proposal would abolish political action committees (PACs) subsidized by corporations, unions and trade associations. It would protect statutorily the political rights of American workers, implementing the Supreme Court's decision in *Communications Workers v. Beck*. It would curtail leadership PACs. It would virtually prohibit the practice of bundling. It would require the full disclosure of all soft money expenditures by political parties and by corporations and unions. It would restrict the taxpayer-financed franking privileges enjoyed by incumbents. It would prevent incumbents from amassing campaign war chests from excess campaign funds from previous elections.

These are all significant reforms, and I am encouraged that S 3 includes a few of them, albeit with some differences. If the Congress is serious about enacting campaign finance reform, it should pass legislation along the lines I proposed in 1989, and I will sign it immediately. However, I cannot accept legislation, like S 3, that contains spending limits or public subsidies, or fails to eliminate special interest PACs.

Further, as I have previously stated, I am opposed to different rules for the House and the Senate on matters of ethics and election reform. In several key respects, S 3 contains separate rules for House and Senate candidates, with no apparent justification other than political expediency.

S 3 no longer contains the provision that the Senate passed last year abolishing all PACs. Although that provision was overbroad in banning issue-oriented PACs unconnected to special interests, S 3 would not eliminate any PACs. Instead, the act provides only a reduced limit on individual PAC contributions to Senate candidates and no change in the status quo in the House. Moreover, the limit on aggregate PAC contributions to House candidates to one-third of the spending limit, $200,000, is not likely to diminish the heavy reliance of members on PAC contributions. The average amount a member of Congress raised from PACs in the last election cycle was $209,000.

The spending limits for both House and Senate candidates will most likely hurt challengers more than incumbents, especially because S 3 does little to reduce the advantages of incumbency. Inexplicably, there is no parallel House provision to the sensible Senate provision restricting the use of the frank in an election year. In the last election cycle, the amount incumbent House members spent on franked mail was three times the total amount spent by all House challengers. The system of public benefits, designed to induce candidates to agree to abide by the spending limits, is unlikely in many cases to overcome the inherent favors of incumbency.

S 3 contains several unconstitutional provisions, although none more serious than the aggregate spending limits. In *Buckley v. Valeo*, the Supreme Court ruled [that] to be constitutional, spending limits must be voluntary. There is nothing "voluntary" about the spending limits in this act. The penalties in S 3 for candidates who choose not to abide by the spending limits or to accept Treasury funds are punitive — unlike the presidential campaign system — as well as costly to the taxpayer. For example, if a nonparticipating House candidate spends just $1 over 80 percent of the spending limit, the participating candidate may spend without limit and receive unlimited federal matching funds. The subsidies provided for in S 3 could amount to well over $100 million every election cycle, yet the act is silent on how these generous government subsidies would be financed. It seems inevitable that they would be paid for by the American taxpayer. I understand why members of Congress would be reluctant to ask taxpayers directly to subsidize their re-election campaigns, but given the significant costs of S 3, its failure to address the funding question is irresponsible.

Our nation needs campaign finance laws that place the interests of individual citizens and political parties above special interests and that provide a level playing field between challengers and incumbents. What we do not need is a taxpayer-financed incumbent protection plan. For these reasons, I am vetoing S 3.

tained that the ever-increasing cost of campaigns was the most significant problem with the system. They pointed to polls that showed Americans disapproved of the vast sums of money spent on elections.

The bill sought to cap spending in House campaigns at $600,000 per election cycle. The limit for Senate campaigns was to vary according to a state's population.

Campaign reform without spending limits, said David L. Boren, D-Okla., the bill's chief Senate sponsor, "is like telling the doctor you can examine the patient, but you can't cure the patient."

But Republicans objected on two counts. They maintained that spending limits unfairly disadvantaged challengers who lacked the benefits of incumbency, such as high name recognition. The GOP also disapproved of the cost of spending limits: public financing.

The 1976 Supreme Court ruling against mandatory spending limits made it impossible to construct a bill that limited spending without luring candidates into compliance. Public financing was the lure.

The House bill included a matching fund system similar to that used in presidential campaigns. The Senate version offered candidates federally funded vouchers to purchase television advertising. House-Senate negotiators agreed early on to let each chamber design its own rules and left these provisions essentially intact.

But some Democrats were skittish about sending taxpayers the tab for even part of their campaigns, particularly when Congress was under fire for a series of disclosures about corrupt financial practices at the House bank.

Party leaders held Democratic votes by stripping the conference report of directives on how to pay for the bill. Neither the House nor the Senate bill said explicitly how to pay for public financing. The conference agreement was even less precise. Virtually all directions on how tax writers should fund the public financing provisions were stripped by conferees.

The conference report even suggested how not to pay for it. The measure included a sense of the Congress resolution that funding should not: come from general revenues, increase the federal budget deficit or decrease spending on other programs.

While this made it easier for Democrats to round up floor votes, particularly from Southerners, it fed Republican outrage. "You have to fund your public financing scheme," said Rep. James T. Walsh, R-N.Y.

### PAC Money

Republicans, led by Bush, argued that the major problem with the existing campaign finance system was special interest money funneled through political action committees. Republicans had long sought to ban PAC money, a step aimed at diminishing the role of unions that heavily favored Democrats.

Under existing rules, PACs could give a candidate $5,000 per election. Senate Democrats, who were less dependent on PAC contributions than were their House counterparts, supported an outright PAC ban in their 1991 bill. The House measure, by contrast, capped a candidate's PAC contributions at an aggregate of $200,000, an amount equal to one-third of the spending limit.

Conferees made no effort to reconcile differences between the House and Senate systems. The $200,000 aggregate House limit was to remain, and PACs could continue to make $5,000 contributions.

But Senate Democrats in 1992 backed away from the ban they had bravely supported in 1991. "A lot of questions were raised about the constitutionality of total abolition [of PACs]," Boren said.

The final measure proposed to limit PAC contributions to Senate candidates to an amount equal to 20 percent of the spending limit. This language originally was part of a backup provision that Senate Democrats included in the event a PAC ban was found unconstitutional. The backup proposal also called for limiting a PAC's contribution to an individual campaign to $1,000, the same limit that applied to contributions from individuals. But senators pressed for a higher limit, and the conference upped it to $2,500.

### Soft Money

To get Senate Democrats to accelerate consideration of campaign finance legislation, House leaders agreed to language that would sharply restrict the way state parties raised and spent money. Called soft money, these funds were used to influence federal elections but were raised under state law, which traditionally was more lenient than federal law.

While the original House bill essentially codified existing law, the Senate proposal that was included in the final measure placed restrictions on federal candidates in raising soft money — something both Bush and Democratic presidential nominee Michael S. Dukakis accomplished proficiently in the 1988 election. The Senate proposal also restricted state party electioneering and required state parties basically to comply with federal contribution limits.

Democratic state party chairmen strongly opposed the Senate language, and they pointed to the 1990 election of Texas Democratic Gov. Ann W. Richards as an example of why the existing system was essential to their work. Richards faced an opponent who raised much more money than she did, in part because of large personal contributions to his campaign. According to Texas Democrats, the funds the party raised to run a campaign that was coordinated with congressional candidates' efforts enabled Richards to win.

Rep. Martin Frost, D-Texas, helped whip Democratic votes for the original House bill. But he said he was inclined to oppose the conference agreement. "I can't support a bill that's going to destroy my party," Frost said. (He ultimately voted against the conference report.)

Democratic state party chairmen were not the only ones upset about the soft money provisions; Bush shared their concern. According to a statement issued by the White House on April 3: "Increasing the amounts political parties can spend on behalf of congressional candidates would permit candidates to spend less time fund-raising."

## HOUSE ACTION

Approved on a largely party-line vote on the eve of a two-week congressional recess, the bill to overhaul campaign finances became fodder for both parties. Democrats said it showed voters that they were reforming the way they did business; Republicans said it was a ruse.

Both parties agreed, however, that the measure was headed for a veto. The conference report was approved April 9 on a vote of 259-165. *(Vote 79, p. 20-H)*

The House vote was 24 short of the two-thirds majority that it would take to override a veto. Democrats defended the bill's spending caps as the best means to clean up the existing system. Such limits, said House Majority Leader Richard A. Gephardt, D-Mo., would replace "the foot race for financing with a competition for ideas."

Republicans contended that limits put challengers who needed more money to become known at a disadvantage with incumbents. Republicans also opposed the public funding it took to legally compel compliance with spending caps.

On the floor, House Minority Whip Newt Gingrich, R-Ga., said the public funding provisions amounted to "a new House bank with a new line of credit."

The bill's cost had been debated frequently, in part because it depended on so many variables, including how many candidates participated in the system. The Congressional Budget Office put a biennial price tag of $100 million to $150 million on the measure. Republicans put the figure slightly higher, at $200 million per election cycle.

Republicans attempted to send the bill back to conference with instructions to strip out all public subsidies, but the procedural motion was rejected on a largely party-line vote of 179-243. *(Vote 78, p. 20-H)*

Despite the veto threat, backers of overhauling the campaign finance system said that the vote was a benchmark.

"It is a mistake to think this is just an exercise," said Fred Wertheimer, president of Common Cause. "It took 17 years to get a vote in the House [on campaign finance legislation]. It took 16 years in the Senate. The last stage is the president."

Democratic leaders lost just 20 votes, and several of them were over the new language governing state parties. Only 19 Republicans strayed from the fold on final passage.

### Franking Privileges

House Republicans seized the opportunity to air their objections to the use of the congressional frank for mass mailings. Repeatedly during the debate, Republicans said that the $130 million House members spent on franking in 1991 was more than double what all House challengers spent for all campaign expenses in the 1990 elections.

Complaints about congressional use of franking were emphasized because of a drafting mistake in the initial

*Continued on p. 69*

# Campaign Finance Bill Provisions

*The 1992 campaign finance bill (S 3) represented the most far-reaching attempt to reform campaign law in nearly two decades. Though it was vetoed by the president May 9, the measure's Democratic supporters maintained that its provisions would be the point of departure for future legislation. The Senate and House negotiated the following regulations:*

## HOUSE CAMPAIGNS

### Compliance Requirements

● **Eligibility.** To qualify for federal aid in running for a House seat, candidates would have to win their primary and face a general-election opponent. Candidates also would have to agree to the spending limit and other restrictions. To receive benefits, a candidate would first have to raise $60,000 in contributions of $250 or less. The first $250 of any larger contribution also would count.

Those who complied would become "eligible" candidates and would be entitled to benefits including public funds. Eligible candidates could exceed the spending limit and still get these benefits under certain circumstances designed to punish opposing candidates who did not agree to the limit.

### Spending Limits

● **Limit.** The optional spending limit would be $600,000 for House candidates in each two-year election cycle.

● **Primary election.** There would be no separate spending limit for the primary. The spending limit would increase by $100,000 in case of a runoff primary.

● **General election.** No more than $500,000 could be spent during the general-election period, which would begin immediately after the primary.

● **Special election.** No more than $500,000 could be spent on a special election.

● **Personal funds limited.** Eligible candidates could spend no more than $50,000 of their own money. Any personal funds a candidate contributed to the campaign would count against the $200,000 limit placed on donations of more than $200.

The $50,000 limit on personal funds would not apply if: 1) an eligible candidate had an opponent who did not agree to the spending limit; and 2) this opponent raised or spent $250,000.

● **Exceptions.** The limit would increase in these cases:

**Free-spending opponent.** If an eligible candidate had an opponent who did not agree to the spending limit, the limit could increase and additional public funds become available.

**Independent expenditures.** The spending limit would rise, dollar for dollar, after an independent campaign spent $10,000 against an eligible candidate or for his opponent in the general election.

**Compliance fund.** Contributions to and expenditures from a separate fund to pay for a campaign's legal and accounting costs would be exempt from the limits but could not exceed $200,000. State and local taxes also could be paid out of this fund.

**Fundraising/overhead.** A campaign committee's spending for fundraising or overhead would be exempt from the limit, up to an amount equal to 5 percent of the limit.

**Close primaries.** Candidates who won their primaries by a margin of 10 percent or less could spend an additional $150,000 for the general election. This allowance was added to assuage fears that a costly primary fight could leave a candidate vulnerable in the general election.

### Benefits

● **Public matching funds.** A candidate would receive matching public funds for the first $200 of any contribution, with an aggre-

gate cap of $200,000 on the match.

● **Postage.** Participating candidates could mail up to one piece of mail per eligible voter at the lowest third-class nonprofit rate. (Identical provision for House and Senate candidates.)

● **Contingency money.** An eligible candidate with a non-complying opponent could begin to raise money in excess of spending limits and collect matching funds without regard to the $200,000 cap once the opponent raised more than $250,000 (50 percent of the general-election limit). If the non-complying opponent spent more than $400,000 (80 percent of the limit), the eligible candidate could begin to spend above the limit.

Eligible candidates would qualify for triple matching funds if their opponents personally contributed an amount of money equal to 50 percent of the spending limit to their campaigns. Eligible candidates would receive public money to match any independent expenditure made against them or for their opponent that exceeded $10,000 in the general election.

### Contribution Limits

● **PAC contributions to candidates.** House candidates could accept no more than $5,000 from any one PAC and no more than $200,000 in aggregate from PACs. The aggregate limit would rise by $50,000 in the event of a close primary (when the margin of victory was 10 percent or less) and $50,000 in case of a primary runoff.

● **Large individual contributions.** Candidates could accept no more than $200,000, in aggregate, in contributions of more than $250 from individuals. This limit would rise by $50,000 in the event of a close primary and $50,000 in the event of a primary runoff.

● **Party Contributions.** Candidates could not accept more than a total of $5,000 from national, state and local parties. This measure was aimed at stopping state party committees from all over the country from pouring money into a tight contest, a practice that had become more frequent. (Identical provision for Senate.)

## SENATE CAMPAIGNS

### Compliance Requirements

● **Eligibility.** To qualify for federal aid in running for a Senate seat, a candidate would have to win his or her primary and face a general-election opponent. The candidate also would have to agree to the spending limit and certain other restrictions. To receive benefits, a candidate would have to raise $250,000 or 10 percent of the general election spending limit, whichever was less, in contributions of $250 or less, and raise at least half of this sum from in-state donors.

Those who complied would become "eligible" candidates and would get certain benefits, including government vouchers, to purchase television advertising. Eligible candidates could exceed the spending limit and still get these benefits under certain circumstances designed to punish opposing candidates who did not agree to the limit.

### Spending Limits

● **Limit.** Optional spending limits for Senate candidates would vary by state. The high would be an $8.9 million limit for candidates in California who face opponents in both the primary and general elections. The low would be $636,500 for a small-state candidate facing a primary challenge but no general-election contest.

● **Primary election.** The spending limit for primaries would be 67 percent of the general-election limit or $2.75 million, whichever was less. The primary limit would not fall below $636,500. The limit for a runoff election would be 20 percent of the general-election limit.

● **General election.** The general-election limit would be set by the following formula: $400,000 plus 30 cents multiplied by the state's voting-age population up to 4 million, plus 25 cents multiplied by the voting-age population above 4 million. The general-

election limit would not fall below $950,000 or exceed $5.5 million.

● **Personal funds limited.** Eligible candidates could contribute or lend up to 10 percent of the general-election limit, but no more than $250,000, of their own or their family's money.

● **Exceptions.** The limit would rise in these cases:

**Free-spending opponent.** If an eligible candidate had an opponent who did not agree to the spending limit, the limit could increase. Additional public funds could then become available.

**Independent expenditures.** The limit would rise, dollar for dollar, after an independent campaign spent $10,000 against an eligible candidate or for his general election opponent.

**Compliance/incidental fund.** Candidates could exceed their state spending limit by the lesser of 15 percent of the limit or $300,000 to pay for legal and accounting expenses necessary to comply with this law.

**Television.** In states with no more than one VHF television station, such as New Jersey, the spending limit would be set by the following formula: $400,000, plus 80 cents multiplied by the voting-age population up to 4 million, plus 70 cents multiplied by the voting-age population beyond 4 million.

### Benefits

● **Public funds/vouchers.** Eligible candidates would receive a government voucher equal to 20 percent of the spending limit to be used to purchase television time.

● **Postage.** Participating candidates could mail up to one piece of mail per eligible voter at the lowest third-class nonprofit rate. (Identical provision for House and Senate.)

● **Discount broadcasting rates.** Television and radio broadcasters would be required to sell advertising time to candidates at a 50 percent discount from the most favorable terms offered any other advertiser for a comparable ad. The rates would apply throughout the general-election campaign and for the last 45 days of a primary.

● **Disclaimer.** A non-participating Senate candidate would be required to have a disclaimer on all advertising stating that he or she did not abide by spending limits.

● **Contingency money.** Eligible candidates would receive public funds to match spending above the limit by a non-complying opponent. Once a non-complying opponent exceeded the limit — either in funds raised or spent — the eligible candidate would get an additional federal subsidy of one-third of the general election limit. If the opponent exceeded the limit by more than one-third but less than two-thirds, the eligible candidate would get an additional subsidy of one-third of the limit. And if the opponent topped the spending limit by two-thirds or more, the eligible candidate would get an additional subsidy equal to another third. An eligible candidate facing a non-complying opponent could raise additional funds equal to the spending limit and begin to spend that money when the opponent had spent double the limit. Combined with the contingent federal subsidy, this could have effectively tripled the total spending limit for that candidate. Eligible candidates would receive public money to match any independent expenditure made against them or for their opponent that exceeded $10,000 in the general election.

### Contributions/PACs

● **PAC contributions to Senate candidates.** Senate candidates could accept no more than an aggregate of 20 percent of the general-election spending limit from PACs and not more than $2,500 from any one PAC. Limits would be raised for inflation and by 20 percent in the event of a runoff.

● **Party contributions.** Candidates could not accept more than a total of $5,000 from national, state and local parties. This measure was aimed at stopping state party committees from all over the country from pouring money into a tight contest, a practice that had become more frequent. (Identical provision for House.)

## INDEPENDENT EXPENDITURES

The bill would define independent expenditures as spending for an ad or communication that, as a whole, expressed support for or opposition to an eligible candidate and was made without the participation or cooperation of that candidate or campaign.

The measure specifically would prohibit independent expenditure campaigns by party committees and any political committee affiliated with an organization or person registered as a lobbyist, such as the American Medical Association or the National Rifle Association.

The bill would preclude virtually all contact between a candidate and an organization or individuals running an independent expenditure campaign for or against the candidate's campaign. The independent campaigner could not maintain a relationship with any political consultant who had a relationship with any of the candidates the independent campaigner supported or opposed.

An independent campaigner would have to inform a broadcaster of an intent to purchase broadcast time. The station in turn would have to inform the other candidates, who would be sold time to respond immediately afterward.

A television ad run in an independent campaign would have to carry notification of the sponsor of the ad in clear and readable type. Similar notices would have to be aired on radio or printed in newspaper ads.

The bill would require the reporting of independent expenditures of $10,000 or more within 48 hours to the Federal Election Commission (FEC) and the secretary of state of the state involved. The intent to spend more than $5,000 on an independent expenditure in the last 20 days of an election would have to be reported before that time, and the FEC would have to notify candidates of it within 24 hours.

## 'BUNDLING'

The bill would prohibit the following from serving as conduits or intermediaries: all political committees connected to organizations, such as those associated with unions, corporations and trade associations; party committees; all businesses, unions, trade associations and national banks; and all employees, officers or agents thereof. Registered lobbyists would be prohibited as intermediaries. This was designed to prevent the bundling of contributions to a candidate by interests that could benefit from legislation or other favors.

A candidate's representative, a fundraiser working under contract or a volunteer hosting a house party would not be considered an intermediary. The law would expressly permit joint fundraisers by two or more federal candidates.

## PARTY SOFT MONEY

In general, the bill would have limited spending by local, state and federal party committees for electioneering during federal election periods, which the bill defined as beginning April 1 in presidential election years and June 1 in other years when federal candidates are on the ballot. Further, all of this money would be subject to federal law for spending, contributions and disclosure requirements.

● **Limits.** A state party's spending to elect the presidential ticket, including get-out-the-vote and voter registration activities, would be limited to approximately 10 cents multiplied by the voting-age population of the state. The amount would be indexed for inflation.

Any money raised or spent for get-out-the-vote, voter registration or other specified activities that would influence a federal election during the election period would be brought under federal spending and contribution restrictions as well as federal reporting rules.

State-level campaign activities conducted by federal, state or local party committees — even those that did not mention federal candidates specifically — would be subject to a maximum spending limit of 30 cents multiplied by the voting-age population of the state.

National party committees, federal officeholders and all federal candidates would be prohibited from soliciting contributions in behalf of state parties not subject to the limits and reporting requirements of federal law.

● **Disclosure.** Political parties — federal, state and local —

would be required to itemize and disclose to the FEC all receipts and disbursements in excess of $200.

Money contributed for a party's building fund — i.e., for mortgage, equipment and other capital expenses — would not be subject to limits, only to disclosure.

## MISCELLANEOUS

● **Franking.** Senators would be prohibited from sending franked mail in election years. House members would be prohibited from sending franked mail outside their districts.

● **Broadcast rates.** Broadcasters would have to sell advertising to participating and non-participating candidates based on the lowest charge of the station for the same amount of time on the same date for any other advertiser. These lowest-unit rates would apply 45 days before the general election and 30 days before the primary. (Those rates would be cut in half for eligible Senate candidates.)

● **Advertising disclosure.** Candidates would have to state clearly their responsibility for their campaign ads. The bill would set minimum standards for doing so in print ads, on radio and on television. For example, the candidate's image would have to appear on the television screen for four seconds.

● **Closed-caption advertising.** Participating candidates would be required to provide closed-captioned television advertising for the hearing impaired.

● **Candidate fundraising.** A federal candidate would be prohibited from raising money for a tax-exempt organization if a significant portion of its mission was voter registration or get-out-the-vote campaigns. A federal candidate or officeholder also would be prohibited from raising funds for other candidates or party committees, state or federal, unless the money was in amounts and from sources permitted by federal law. This was designed to prevent candidates from helping themselves by raising money for another committee that could in turn spend it in a fashion beneficial to the candidate.

● **Candidate names.** Candidates would have to include their name in their campaign committee. Only authorized committees could use a candidate's name. Unauthorized committees would be barred from using a candidate's name in any fundraising context that would suggest that the committee was authorized.

● **Penalties.** Eligible candidates who broke the spending limit by less than 2.5 percent would pay an equal amount in civil penalties. If the overspending was between 2.5 percent and 5 percent, the payment would be triple the overspending. If the overspending exceeded 5 percent, the payment would equal triple the overspending plus an additional civil penalty assessed by the FEC.

● **Expedited review.** An appeal of any court ruling addressing the constitutionality of the act could be taken directly to the Supreme Court, which was directed to expedite its review.

● **Reporting requirements.** Individuals making contributions in excess of $10,000 would have to report that they had reached that figure and thereafter report every additional $5,000 increment.

Expenditures reported by candidates to political consultants would have to include the names and amounts paid to subcontractors.

● **Constitutional amendment.** The provision said it is the sense of Congress that an amendment to allow mandatory campaign spending limits be considered.

● **Ballot initiatives.** Committees that spend more than $1,000 for state initiatives that affect interstate commerce, federal elections, federal taxation or constitutional rights would have to register and report to the FEC all contributions over $50. The bill also would limit individual contributions to ballot initiative committees to $100 or less. (This was primarily a response to term-limit ballot initiatives being funded by out-of-state interests.)

● **Excess campaign funds.** At the end of an election cycle, candidates would be able to put remaining contributions up to the spending limit into an account for a future election. Federal matching funds not spent within 120 days of an election would have to be returned to the Treasury. When the bill was first implemented, incumbents would be able to put funds above the spending limit in an escrow account to be used for political purposes other than the incumbent's own election activities.

● **Post-election fundraising.** Candidates would be prohibited from paying off personal loans or loans from family members with contributions collected after a campaign ended.

● **Leadership PACs.** Federal candidates and officeholders would be barred from controlling any political committee other than their campaign committee, party committee or a joint fundraising committee.

● **Foreign nationals.** Foreign nationals would be prohibited from directly or indirectly influencing federal, state or local elections. PACs and party committees would be required to include a statement on all solicitation material stating that it is unlawful for foreign nationals to contribute. This was aimed in part at preventing foreign nationals from participating in U.S. elections through PACs affiliated with foreign-owned companies.

● **Telephone voting for disabled.** The FEC would be directed to conduct a feasibility study on telephone voting options for the disabled.

● **Government aircraft.** Candidates could not fly on government aircraft in connection with a federal election. The president and vice president would be permitted to use Air Force One and Two on campaign trips but would be required to reimburse the federal Treasury for the actual cost of all political travel.

● **Debates.** Candidates for president whose campaigns took federal funds would have to agree to four debates before the general election. Vice presidential candidates would have to agree to one debate.

● **Individual contributions to party committees.** Individuals would be permitted to contribute up to $20,000 to national party committees and up to $10,000 to the federal account of state party committees, but the aggregate could not exceed $30,000.

● **PAC contributions to party committees.** PACs could contribute up to $15,000 to national party committees and up to $10,000 to a state party committee's federal account.

● **Polling data.** A contribution of polling data would be valued at a fair market rate — with no more than 1 percent depreciation per day from the day the poll was completed.

● **Inflation.** Spending limits would be indexed annually for inflation.

● **Funding.** The bill authorized no funds to pay for the benefits. It would become effective only after separate legislation to fund the bill was enacted. ■

---

*Continued from p. 66*
conference report. As Democrats were preparing to bring it to the floor, they discovered that a provision barring senators from using the frank for mass mailings in the calendar year of a re-election campaign inadvertently had been applied to all members of Congress.

This compelled House Democrats to send the bill back to conference to exclude the House from the provision.

On a 7-3, party-line vote in the Rules Committee on April 7, Democrats denied a Republican request to offer instructions to conferees to ban members from franking outside their districts — a widely used privilege in redistricting years.

Republican members characterized the practice as helping Democrats hold onto their majority by introducing themselves to new voters in their districts.

When the matter came to the floor the following day, Republicans threatened an embarrassing showdown on franked mail. Democrats relented.

Bill Thomas, R-Calif., offered a motion to instruct conferees to include the provisions of HR 4104, a bill he had introduced in January to prohibit congressional funding of franked mail sent outside a member's current district.

No Democrat spoke against the Thomas amendment, and it was approved 408-8 on April 8. *(Vote 75, p. 18-H)*

## Bush Dinner Feeds Coffers, Fuels Political Debate

On April 28, George Bush raised nearly $11 million for his presidential campaign and other Republican interests. As a one-day record, this was good news for the GOP, but it also gave the Democrats ammunition to use against Bush in the debate over a campaign finance bill he threatened to veto.

An estimated $9 million was collected at an annual gala dubbed the "President's Dinner" at which individual guests contributed as much as $400,000 and corporations delivered bundles of $1,500 contributions from employees. That same day, the Senate was debating a Democratic campaign finance bill (S 3) that would crack down on such big-ticket contributions. (Campaign finance, p. 63)

Hours before the dinner, Bush also collected nearly $1.9 million in public funds for presidential campaigns — a system Bush said was anathema for congressional campaigns.

Altogether it was an embarrassing juxtaposition for a president who had tried to make the campaign finance system a staple of his recent attacks on Congress.

Under existing law, individuals could give up to $25,000 in limited amounts to federal candidates and campaign committees. But there were no federal limits on gifts to state parties for voter contact that indirectly influenced House, Senate and presidential elections. Fundraisers working on the President's Dinner encouraged donors to direct a minimum of $92,000 to various GOP causes.

---

The measure approved by the House included both the technical correction to the conference report and the Thomas language. (Franking ban, p. 61)

### SENATE ACTION

Both political parties agreed that the bill that the Senate cleared for Bush on April 30, after three days of partisan but desultory debate, was unlikely to become law. Bush had repeatedly vowed to veto S 3, saying it favored Democrats, disadvantaged challengers and gouged taxpayers.

The Senate approved the conference report by a party-line vote of 58-42, well short of the two-thirds majority needed to override a veto. The vote reflected only a few switched positions from the 56-42 tally on the Senate bill passed May 23, 1991. (Vote 82, p. 12-S)

Senate Minority Leader Bob Dole, R-Kan., said, "We're ready to adopt real campaign reform . . . and there is still time in 1992." But he emphasized that "bipartisan reform" would not include public financing of congressional campaigns.

Among the senators who changed their positions from 1991 were Quentin N. Burdick, D-N.D., and the two Democrats from Louisiana, J. Bennett Johnston and John B. Breaux, all of whom voted for the conference report. Two Republicans, William S. Cohen of Maine and Larry Pressler of South Dakota, voted against the conference report

after having initially supported S 3.

"The bill the Senate passed last May eliminated PACs [political action committees] entirely. The conference report does not," said Pressler. He also criticized the conference committee for having "cut and pasted together two separate sets of campaign rules, one for the Senate and one for the House."

Those absent from the 1991 vote, David Pryor, D-Ark., and Jesse Helms, R-N.C., each voted with their parties in 1992.

Only three Republicans voted for the bill; two Democrats voted against it.

Though no filibuster was threatened and amendments were not permitted to be added to a conference report, the debate continued from April 28 through the afternoon of the 30th in part because both parties saw partisan advantage in talking about the measure.

Republicans used the debate as a forum to lambaste Democrats for proposing taxpayer financing of congressional campaigns — Mitch McConnell, R-Ky., called it "food stamps for politicians" — while Democrats sought to tar Bush for "Watergate style" campaign contributions. (Bush fundraiser, this page)

"The low esteem in which Congress is now held is in part traced back to a feeling that this institution no longer belongs to the people," said Boren, a chief Senate architect of the bill. "It is too much serving the interests of those narrow special interest groups that are providing more and more of the money necessary to run political campaigns."

### FINAL ACTION

The coup de grâce for the campaign finance bill (S 3) came quietly May 13 as the Senate failed to override President Bush's May 9 veto of the Democratic plan to restrict spending and provide public funding for congressional campaigns.

The 57-42 vote, nine short of the two-thirds majority needed to overturn a veto, returned the issue to the political realm, where both Democrats and Republicans aggressively argued that the other side stymied their efforts at reform. (Vote 88, p. 12-S)

Alan K. Simpson, R-Wyo., called the bill a "turkey," and Bush said in his veto message that it would "inevitably lead to a raid on the Treasury to pay for the Democrats' elaborate scheme of public subsidies." (Text, p. 65)

In passing the bill, neither House nor Senate Democrats ever had the votes to override, and the override attempt was scheduled primarily to draw attention to what they called Bush's stealth veto. His Saturday afternoon veto message came without fanfare and was scarcely noted in the major media.

The vote to sustain the president remained largely along party lines. The only senator to switch his vote since the vote to clear the bill was John McCain, R-Ariz. He voted for the bill on April 30 but supported the veto.

Democrats Ernest F. Hollings, S.C., and Richard C. Shelby, Ala., broke party ranks on both votes to oppose the bill. Republicans Dave Durenberger, Minn., and James M. Jeffords, Vt., supported the bill and voted to override the veto.

The vote left intact Bush's unbroken string of 28 successful vetoes. (Vetoes, p. 6)

Despite the veto, bill sponsors said congressional passage of the legislation set an important benchmark, and Boren, who has championed the issue for years, said, "We'll be back again and again until we get it passed into law." ■

# Voters Embrace Congressional Term Limits

In a backlash against career politicians, voters in 14 states on Nov. 3 approved initiatives to limit the length of service of their House members and senators.

In most cases, the support was overwhelming. Nearly 21 million Americans supported term limits, a 200-year-old concept energized in recent years by congressional scandal and public discontent with career politicians.

"There is at least one clear and unequivocal mandate from the voters this election," said Cleta Mitchell, director of the Term Limits Legal Institute. "This mandate is that we limit terms."

The 14 states joined Colorado, which already had approved a term-limit initiative. In some of the states, House members were required to step aside in as little as six years, while all the states limited senators to 12 years. (See box, below)

Legal obstacles remained. Only hours after Florida approved a term-limit initiative, a suit was filed in a U.S. District Court challenging its constitutionality. Term-limit supporters planned to press Congress to approve a constitutional amendment to impose term limits on lawmakers from all 50 states.

## BACKGROUND

Colorado in 1990 became the first state to limit members' terms, voting for 12-year caps on House and Senate tenures. Numerous other states put similar limits on state officeholders. (1990 Almanac, p. 13)

Political experts said that the term-limit movement was driven by the public's low opinion of government. Thomas E. Mann of the Brookings Institution called it "a visceral crying out against the system." Not until federal and state governments regained the confidence of the electorate would support for term limits begin to ebb, he said.

Paul Jacob, from U.S. Term Limits, said that limits were needed to stop the permanent incumbency that House and Senate members enjoyed. "The only way an incumbent gets in trouble these days is if he gets his hand caught in the till."

Term-limit opponents argued that the initiatives would sharply decrease a state's clout. For example, members might think twice about electing a leader whose length of service was shortened by a term limit, said Norman Y. Mineta, D-Calif. "Why put them in the leadership track if they are going to be out in six years?" he asked.

Before 1992, public support for term limits and passage by a state of an initiative imposing them on their lawmakers were two different matters, as Washington state found out in 1991. An initiative in Washington was ridding high in the polls until Speaker Thomas S. Foley, D-Wash., and other lawmakers barnstormed across the state to defeat it. (1991 Almanac, p. 12-A)

Foley warned voters that term limits would deprive Washington state of power and allow California to grab the state's water resources. After being up by as many as 40 points in the polls, the initiative lost, 55 percent to 45 percent.

National term-limit supporters blamed the language in the initiative for its defeat. It counted previous service, meaning that Foley and all other House members would have had to retire in 1995.

At the heart of the debate was whether state-imposed term limits were constitutional. Many legal experts said they were not. "It's hard for me to see the Supreme Court upholding it," said Georgetown University law Professor Mark Tushnet.

Walter E. Dellinger, a law professor at Duke University, said it was clear that states could not add to the three basic qualifications for federal office set forth in the U.S. Constitution — age, residency and citizenship.

In 1969, the Supreme Court ruled in *Powell v. McCormack* that the House could not refuse to seat Rep. Adam Clayton Powell, D-N.Y., accused of abusing his office, because he met the basic qualifications set out in the Constitution. (1991 Almanac, p. 13-A)

But others argued that the case was not applicable because term limits were being imposed by voters in the state, not by Congress. Term-limit proponent Cleta Mitchell said the courts might not be willing to consider the issue because it was more political than legal. Even if they did, she contended, history suggested that the Supreme Court would uphold state-mandated limits on congressional service.

"The U.S. Supreme Court has, through the years and through many decisions, upheld the right of the states to regulate elections, including the electoral procedures related to the candidacies of persons seeking federal office," she wrote in a brief filed in December 1991 when opponents in Florida tried to keep the initiative off the ballot.

## TERM LIMITS WIN

The term-limit movement scored a perfect 14-for-14, winning in every state in which an initiative was on the ballot. Counting Colorado, 181 House and Senate members entered the 103rd Congress with term limits.

The anti-incumbent mood, driven by congressional scandals and frustration over the inability of Congress and President Bush to agree on legislation, proved the perfect setting for term-limit supporters to press their case.

## Term Limits on Nov. 3 Ballot

| State | Senate | House | Percentages: For/Against |
|---|---|---|---|
| Arizona | 12 years | 6 years | 74-26 |
| Arkansas | 12 years | 6 years | 60-40 |
| California | 12 years | 6 years | 63-37 |
| Florida | 12 years | 8 years | 77-23 |
| Michigan | 12 years | 6 years | 59-41 |
| Missouri | 12 years | 8 years | 74-26 |
| Montana | 12 years | 6 years | 67-33 |
| Nebraska | 12 years | 8 years | 68-32 |
| North Dakota | 12 years | 12 years | 55-45 |
| Ohio | 12 years | 8 years | 66-34 |
| Oregon | 12 years | 6 years | 69-31 |
| South Dakota | 12 years | 12 years | 63-37 |
| Washington | 12 years | 6 years | 52-48 |
| Wyoming | 12 years | 6 years | 77-23 |

SOURCE: Associated Press

House and Senate challengers made term-limit pledges a key plank in their race. Bush endorsed a constitutional amendment to limit lawmakers' terms.

Democratic consultant Vic Kamber, who worked to defeat term-limit initiatives in several states, laid the blame for his side's poor showing at the feet of Democratic congressional leaders. Foley and other members did not do enough to repair Congress' image, Kamber said, and were more interested in saving their political hides than taking on term limits.

"If the leadership is not willing to defend Congress, then maybe these bozos deserve it," he said.

Few incumbents, many facing tough races for the first time in years, chose to risk the political backlash and campaign against the initiatives. Foley, who was held to 58 percent of the vote, did not tour the state campaigning against term limits, as he did in 1991. Instead, he focused on overturning any initiative in court on the grounds that it was unconstitutional. "Surviving a constitutional test, which I think is a clear and absolute barrier to any state imposing term limits on members of Congress, is the final answer," he said.

There were competitive races in only a few states.

Washington, which recrafted its initiative to disregard previous service, approved the new version, 52 percent to 48 percent. Sherry Bockwinkel, campaign manager of the term-limit group LIMIT, said she learned from the mistakes of 1991, when the campaign ran out of money in the final week.

In 1992, Bockwinkel said the group spent most of the $190,000 it had allocated for media in the last 10 days, when most voters make up their minds.

Money was often the key to success. The national group, U.S. Term Limits, was able to parcel out more than $1.1 million to state campaigns, including $364,000 in Michigan and about $600,000 in California.

U.S. Term Limits contributed money in 11 of the 14 states, including $135,000 in Arkansas. Term-limit opponent Barbara Pardue, campaign director of Arkansans for Representative Democracy, said the contributions should have raised eyebrows. "The money coming out of Washington raises questions about whether it truly is a legitimate grass-roots effort," she said. Other term-limit opponents charged that U.S. Term Limits was being secretly financed by conservative and Libertarian groups, including billionaire brothers Charles and David Koch. ∎

# Anita Hill Leak Inquiry Unsuccessful

A special counsel hired by the Senate to investigate leaks of information to the media said that he was unable to identify the sources of leaks that ignited a public furor over Anita F. Hill's 1991 allegation that Supreme Court nominee Clarence Thomas had sexually harassed her.

After a four-month investigation that included interviews with more than 200 witnesses — but stopped short of a collision with the media over First Amendment rights — New York lawyer Peter J. Fleming Jr. in May said that it was a mystery to him who disclosed Hill's sworn personal statement to the Judiciary Committee to two media organizations.

Fleming also reported that he was unable to identify the source of numerous leaks involving the Senate Ethics Committee's 1990-91 inquiry into five senators' relationships with thrift executive Charles H. Keating Jr.

Though exhaustive, the 171-page report added little new substantive information to either case, and it did not fault Senate handling of confidential information involved in the leaks.

## BACKGROUND

Although the Judiciary Committee was deadlocked 7-7 on whether to endorse Thomas for the job, he was on his way to a relatively easy confirmation by the full Senate when National Public Radio (NPR) and New York Newsday made Hill's allegations public on Oct. 6, 1991. *(1991 Almanac, p. 274)*

The charges brought a storm of criticism of the Senate for its handling of sexual harassment accusations. The Senate postponed its scheduled Oct. 8 vote on Thomas and the Judiciary Committee reopened the hearings.

After a second round of hearings, in which Hill and Thomas delivered some of the most extraordinary testimony ever heard by a congressional committee, the full

Senate voted 52-48 to confirm Thomas. It was the closest vote on a Supreme Court nominee in more than a century.

Republicans were furious over the leak of Hill's statement. Saying that lawmakers could not be trusted, President Bush announced on Oct. 24 that FBI reports would no longer remain on Capitol Hill and that staff would not be permitted to read them. He rescinded that order five months later.

Sen. John C. Danforth, R-Mo., and others focused suspicions on Sen. Howard M. Metzenbaum, D-Ohio, a leading Thomas opponent, and his staff. Metzenbaum's aides initiated the talks with Hill that eventually led to an FBI inquiry and subsequent leaks to reporters. Metzenbaum denied guilt: "That is wrong. That is untrue. Let me say emphatically again, nothing could be further from the truth."

GOP members demanded that a special counsel be hired to investigate the leaks. On Oct. 24, 1991, the Senate voted 86-12 to investigate them. Democrats broadened the probe to include leaks of confidential information concerning the so-called Keating Five case, in which four Democratic and one Republican senator were accused of inappropriately interceding with federal thrift regulators in behalf of Keating, a campaign donor.

## LEAK SOURCES NOT FOUND

Fleming's report shed little light into who leaked Hill's statement to NPR reporter Nina Totenberg or who tipped off Newsday reporter Timothy Phelps about its contents. During the course of the investigation, Fleming subpoenaed Totenberg, Phelps and Bill Buzenberg, vice president for news and information at NPR, with regard to their stories about Hill's allegations. He also subpoenaed Paul M. Rodriguez of The Washington Times for stories he had written about the Keating Five investigation.

All four maintained that they would not reveal their sources on First Amendment grounds. Fleming also sought the telephone records of Totenberg and Phelps, saying that the records could point to the person responsible for leaking information.

But after lawyers for the two reporters protested, and some senators appeared startled by the maneuver, Fleming backed off, saying he would wait until the Senate Rules Committee ruled on the matter.

Rules Committee Chairman Wendell H. Ford, D-Ky., and Ted Stevens, Alaska, the panel's ranking Republican, decided March 25 in favor of the reporters. They blocked enforcement of the subpoenas that sought to compel reporters to reveal their sources and the telephone company to turn over the journalists' phone records.

"The traditions of the Senate regarding the press and the First Amendment require us to carefully balance the competing demands presented by this case," said Ford in a written statement. He added that the requests "could have a chilling effect on the media and could close a door where more doors need opening."

Ford encouraged the special counsel to "vigorously pursue" his investigation and said he would be inclined to uphold subpoenas issued to congressional employees who may have willfully disclosed secret information to the news media in violation of Senate rules.

The decision ended any possibility that Fleming would learn the source of the leaks. The final report, released May 4, did clear up one point: whether the FBI report on Hill's allegations was leaked to the media. According to Fleming, it was not. Only Hill's statement to the Judiciary Committee was leaked.

The report speculated that Totenberg's source was someone in the Senate, exonerating Hill and various activists who opposed the Thomas nomination. All the report could say about Phelps' source was that it probably was "not a Republican."

The report confirmed Hill's reluctance to go public with her allegations. The Judiciary Committee repeatedly said that it did not initially press the investigation because Hill did not want her name made public, but the Fleming report suggested that staff members were aware that there may have been some "misunderstanding" about Hill's request for confidentiality.

According to the report, Hill told at least two Senate staff members that she was reluctant to go public with her concerns because "a single complainant would not be believed, and that it would be important to have others corroborate her charges."

The report also revealed much about individual senators and the mores of the institution. The report notes that Strom Thurmond of South Carolina, the ranking Republican on the Judiciary Committee, never read Hill's statement and did not provide copies of it to fellow GOP committee members.

The Fleming report also noted that Hill's statement made it into Washington's social scene before it made the news columns: "The allegations were mentioned during at least two dinner parties on Saturday evening (Sept. 28) and made their way back to the Judiciary Committee."

In the Keating Five case, Fleming speculated that there were likely several sources of what he dubbed "a sea of leaks." While Fleming went out of his way to mention the "good reputations" of Sen. John McCain, R-Ariz., and his counsel, the report repeatedly noted that McCain was the beneficiary of many favorable news accounts based on leaked information. McCain and his staff denied being the source of leaks. ∎

# Three Die in September: Burdick, Jones, Weiss

Democratic Sen. Quentin N. Burdick, who died Sept. 8 at age 84, was a North Dakota institution during 32 years in the Senate, renowned for his ability to garner federal funds for his state.

Questions about Burdick's health and advancing age, which dogged him during his 1988 re-election campaign, resurfaced after Burdick entered a hospital in July complaining of fatigue and chest pains. A poll indicated that 76 percent of state residents thought he should resign. But to the end, he held on to his seat and to his chairmanship of the Environment and Public Works Committee.

Jocelyn Birch Burdick on Sept. 16 became North Dakota's first woman senator when she was sworn in as an interim successor to her husband. Her appointment put the number of women in the Senate at three, the most who had ever served at one time. Seven women had succeeded their husbands, the first in 1931.

Mrs. Burdick, 70, filled the seat until a special election was held Dec. 4.

Democratic Sen. Kent Conrad cruised to victory in the year's final Senate race, wrapping up an unlikely comeback in a year in which he had previously announced his retirement. He defeated Jack Dalrymple in the special election. Conrad had announced in April that he was retiring. He said he would follow through on a 1986 campaign pledge not to seek re-election unless the federal deficit was dramatically reduced. But he changed his mind after Burdick's death and decided to run for the open seat. The term was to expire in 1994.

At his death, Burdick ranked third in Senate seniority. His early political career was marked by a series of losses until he finally won a House seat in 1958, succeeding his father, Usher Burdick, a 20-year House veteran. Like his father, the younger Burdick started out as a Republican, and he also ran under the old populist Non-Partisan League banner. He became a Democrat in 1946.

His House tenure was brief; he won a special election for the Senate in 1960 after Republican William Langer died.

Burdick concentrated on constituent service and protecting state interests. When he gained the chairmanship of an Appropriations subcommittee, he said, "I will get everything North Dakota is entitled to now."

He viewed as his major accomplishment in Congress the 1965 authorization of the Garrison Diversion project in North Dakota, a large public works project that came under fire for being unaffordable. He stirred up criticism in 1990 by obtaining a $500,000 grant to help build a German-Russian museum in Strasburg, N.D., the birthplace of band leader Lawrence Welk. The project was derided as an example of pork barrel politics and eventually was withdrawn.

Burdick generally ducked the heavy responsibility of

committee chairmanship, and when he took over the Environment panel in 1987 he usually let his subcommittee chairmen run things. His voting record was fairly consistently liberal; he was an early critic of the Vietnam War and a strong backer of major civil rights legislation.

### Committee Changes

Burdick's death triggered a series of changes in the agenda of the Environment and Public Works Committee, starting with the elevation of Daniel Patrick Moynihan, D-N.Y., known as an energetic intellectual, to the chair.

Environmentalists and business representatives alike mourned the loss of the senior senator from North Dakota, with whom they had had an amicable and productive relationship. But they were also pleased at the prospect of a committee led by Moynihan.

The leadership of the committee changed again early in 1993 after President Clinton picked Sen. Lloyd Bentsen, D-Texas, as his Treasury secretary, opening up the chairmanship of the more powerful Finance Committee. Moynihan moved to that position, and Montana Democrat Max Baucus took the helm at Environment and Public Works.

Since the panel's creation from the old Public Works Committee in 1977, the unusually wide sweep of the panel's jurisdiction had prompted previous chairmen to give its subcommittee chairmen wide latitude. The self-effacing North Dakotan was happy to continue the tradition.

So although Burdick's committee presided over two significant pieces of legislation — the 1990 amendments to the Clean Air Act and the 1991 highway and transit reauthorization — subcommittee chairmen crafted those measures and built the coalitions that allowed them to become law: Environmental Protection Subcommittee Chairman Baucus handled the clean air legislation; Water Resources, Transportation and Infrastructure Subcommittee Chairman Moynihan shepherded the $151 billion surface transportation bill.

Burdick's death reverberated in another committee as well. As chairman of the Senate Appropriations Subcommittee on Agriculture, Rural Development and Related Agencies, he had given wide latitude to Mississippi Republican Thad Cochran, who had chaired the committee when the Republicans had control of the Senate during the Reagan administration.

In 1992, Arkansas Democrat Dale Bumpers guided the fiscal 1993 agriculture spending bill through committee as acting chairman after Burdick suffered a heart attack. Bumpers, the senior Democrat on the panel, was elevated to chairman.

## WALTER B. JONES

Nearly a year after Walter B. Jones decided to retire at the end of the 102nd Congress, the longtime North Carolina Democrat — chairman of the House Merchant Marine and Fisheries Committee — died on Sept. 15 at the age of 79.

His son, State Rep. Walter B. Jones Jr., sought the Democratic nomination but lost to a black county commissioner, Eva Clayton.

In his Oct. 4, 1991, announcement, Jones blamed the configuration of his congressional district under North Carolina's proposed redistricting plan for forcing his retirement. Legislators redrew his northeastern 1st District to create a majority-black district.

First elected in 1966, Jones had been ill for several years. He suffered from gout and diabetes, and often appeared in a wheelchair because of a circulatory problem. In recent years, he had been blamed for the committee's diminished standing in House politics. "He retired years ago and didn't tell anyone about it," complained one Democrat in 1988.

Jones had been chairman of the Merchant Marine and Fisheries Committee — the only committee assigned to monitor a single industry — since 1981. The panel, established in 1887, had no full committee counterpart in the Senate, only the Merchant Marine Subcommittee of the Commerce Committee.

The House Merchant Marine Subcommittee had long been known for its close ties to the maritime industry, including shipbuilders, seafarers' unions and shippers. Four of the previous six chairmen had been investigated for criminal links to the industry, the most recent being Mario Biaggi, a New York Democrat, who was convicted on racketeering charges in 1988 and resigned from Congress. *(1988 Almanac, p. 34)*

During his tenure, Jones, who replaced Biaggi as subcommittee chairman in 1987, had cleaned up the panel ethically, though the full committee still retained its sympathy for the industry.

Jones' retirement opened the way for second-ranking Democrat Gerry E. Studds of Massachusetts to take the committee's chairmanship. After winning a close re-election in the Nov. 3 election, Studds got the chairmanship position for the 103rd Congress.

Studds was expected by many Democrats to reinvigorate the panel with his aggressive advocacy of environmental issues. Studds had led the Fisheries and Wildlife Conservation and the Environment Subcommittee. In recent years, he had been active in passing legislation restricting drift net fishing and coastal water pollution and in protecting biological diversity.

An argumentative, articulate liberal with a piercing wit, Studds complemented the Interior Committee's new, assertive environmentalist chairman, George Miller, D-Calif. During consideration of legislation in the 101st Congress to increase federal liability limits of oil spillers, Miller joined Studds to push for tougher environmental amendments.

## TED WEISS

Rep. Ted Weiss, a liberal New York Democrat, died on Sept. 14 of heart failure.

State Rep. Jerrold Nadler was chosen by Manhattan Democratic officials Sept. 23 as their nominee in New York's 8th District, which assured him of election to succeed Weiss in a district that included Manhattan's liberal West Side.

Weiss, 64, had become a fixture in the Manhattan-based seat and appeared on his way to an easy re-election when he died on the eve of the September Democratic Primary.

Primary voters endorsed him nonetheless, giving party officials the right to pick a successor.

Nadler began serving the remainder of Weiss' term immediately after the November election, and in January 1993 began a full two-year term in his own right.

Weiss had advocated liberal interests, using his chairmanship of the Government Operations Subcommittee on Human Resources and Intergovernmental Relations as his personal soapbox. It had wide berth to oversee several federal departments and gave Weiss an outlet for crusading on health-care issues. ■

# Bush Rejects 'Motor Voter' Legislation

Legislation aimed at boosting the ranks of eligible voters across the nation encountered strong Republican opposition and a presidential veto as it moved through the 102nd Congress to its defeat.

The national voter registration bill (S 250) was popularly known as the "motor voter" bill because it sought to link voter registration to applying for a driver's license and other public certificates. The measure enjoyed broad support from voter-recruiting groups such as the League of Women Voters.

The Democratic leadership in the 103rd Congress made a nearly identical bill (HR 2) a top priority. Placed on a fast track, HR 2 sped through the House Feb. 4, 1993, on a 259-160 vote. Senate leaders planned similarly swift action and President Clinton said he would sign the measure.

But President Bush had maintained that while the intent of S 250 was commendable, it would have opened the door to election fraud and dumped heavy administrative costs on states.

Bush found strong allies in the Senate, where opponents used a number of delaying tactics to slow the bill's journey through Congress.

In addition to their concerns about costs and fraud, critics of the bill argued that the existing registration process was not complicated and that making it too easy to register might dilute the quality of the national electorate by including more people who knew little about the issues or the candidates.

## BACKGROUND

Efforts to increase voter registration and turnout had met with varying degrees of success in different states. But overall, civic leaders were less than inspired by the turnout on Election Day.

Federal Election Commission data indicated that even as the voting age population had increased by millions since the early part of the century, the actual percentage of those who turned out at the polls remained largely the same, roughly about 50 percent.

The situation led voter registration groups and lawmakers to suggest ways to make the registration process easier. One proposal that gained ground and had been implemented in a handful of states by the mid-1980s was to couple the registration process with other normal civic duties, such as getting a driver's license.

By May of 1992, 27 states had some type of motor-voter system in place.

Motor-voter legislation started its journey through Congress in 1989. But the path was not without detours and obstacles.

The House easily passed similar legislation in the 101st Congress only to see it languish and die on the Senate calendar. *(1990 Almanac, p. 71)*

---

### BOXSCORE

➡ **National voter registration (S 250).** The legislation would allow citizens to register to vote while applying for a driver's license or other public certificates.

**Report:** S Rept 102-60

#### KEY ACTION

May 7 — The **Senate** voted to limit debate on S 250, 61-38.

May 20 — The **Senate** passed S 250, 61-38.

June 16 — The **House** passed S 250, 268-153.

July 2 — President Bush vetoed S 250.

Sept. 22 — The **Senate** sustained the president's veto, 62-38.

---

important victories.

### Ford Scores Success

Stymied by the inability to cut off debate in previous years, Ford scored his first success on the voter registration bill on May 7 when he rounded up enough support to limit initial debate on the bill. The 61-38 vote allowed the Senate to proceed to the bill, although Republicans still could offer debilitating amendments. *(Vote 86, p. 12-S)*

Four Republicans voted to limit debate along with all 57 Democrats. A key GOP switcher was Bob Packwood, R-Ore.

But Bob Kasten, R-Wis., put the brakes on the bill immediately after the cloture vote by offering, in the form of an amendment, GOP-backed legislation (S 640) that sought to impose uniform federal standards on state product liability laws. *(Product liability, p. 210)*

Sponsors then pulled the legislation from consideration, waiting to return to it later with enough votes to kill the Kasten amendment.

A May 12 cloture vote to limit amendments failed, 58-40, two votes short of the 60 needed, forcing Majority Leader George J. Mitchell, D-Maine, to pull the bill from floor consideration for a second time. *(Vote 87, p. 12-S)*

Then two days later, on May 14, Mitchell returned to the motor-voter bill with enough votes to kill the Kasten amendment. The Senate voted, 53-45, on a motion by John D. Rockefeller IV, D-W.Va, to table the Kasten amendment. *(Vote 89, p. 13-S)*

Also on May 14, members rejected, 37-57, a GOP substitute amendment offered by Ted Stevens, R-Alaska, that would have made the bill's provisions voluntary and authorized $25 million for fiscal 1992-94 to assist states that wanted to implement motor-voter systems. *(Vote 90, p. 13-S)*

The next obstacle in the bill's path was put forward by Phil Gramm, R-Texas, who offered the GOP anti-crime package as an amendment. This forced Mitchell to again shelve the

House sponsors of the bill said they would wait on Senate action in the 102nd Congress before taking up the issue again. The Senate Rules Committee approved the bill on April 24, 1991, by a 7-4 vote. Two attempts on July 18, 1991, to break off Senate debate failed. *(1991 Almanac, p. 48)*

## SENATE FLOOR ACTION

Majority Whip Wendell H. Ford, D-Ky., chairman of the Rules Committee and the main sponsor of S 250, faced a strong current of GOP opposition all the way. His principal opponent was his own Kentucky colleague, Mitch McConnell, R, who fought the bill tirelessly in committee and on the floor.

At one point in Senate debate, McConnell jokingly retagged the bill as "auto-fraudo" legislation, because of what he said would be an increase in fraudulent voting if the bill became law.

But despite the stream of opposition from the GOP, Ford scored some

# President Bush's Veto Message

*On July 2, President Bush vetoed legislation that would allow citizens to register to vote while applying for a driver's license or other public certificates. Following is the text of his veto message.*

I am returning herewith without my approval S 250, the National Voter Registration Act of 1992.

This administration strongly supports the goal of increasing participation in the electoral process. We have worked with leaders of both parties in an attempt to produce legislation that would accomplish that purpose. S 250, however, would impose unnecessary, burdensome, expensive and constitutionally questionable federal regulation on the states in an area of traditional state authority. It would also expose the election process to an unacceptable risk of fraud and corruption without any reason to believe that it would increase electoral participation to any significant degree.

No justification has been demonstrated for the extensive procedural requirements — and significant related costs — imposed on the states by this bill. The proponents of S 250 simply have not made the case that requiring the states to make voter registration easier will translate into increased voter participation at the polls. Indeed, a recent study by the Federal Election Commission suggests that registration requirements have no significant effect on participation rates. In addition, to the extent that state registration requirements discriminate against minority groups, the Voting Rights Act already provides an adequate remedy.

S 250 would exempt from compliance with its requirements any state adopting an Election Day registration system. This exemption could create a compelling incentive for a state to adopt such a system, under which verification of voter eligibility is difficult. Thus, the bill would increase substantially the risk of voting fraud. It would not, however, provide sufficient authority for federal law enforcement officials to respond to any resulting increases in election crime and public corruption.

It is critical that the states retain the authority to tailor voter registration procedures to unique local circumstances. S 250 would prevent the states from doing this by forcing them to implement federally mandated and nationally standardized voter registration procedures. It would also restrict severely their ability to remove from the voter rolls the names of persons who have not voted in several years and who thus can be presumed fairly to have died or moved out of the jurisdiction. Enactment of S 250 would deny the states their historic freedom to govern their own electoral processes and would contravene the important principles of federalism on which our country was founded.

S 250 is constitutionally suspect. Although the Supreme Court has recognized that the Congress has general power to regulate federal elections to the extent necessary to prevent fraud and preserve the integrity of the electoral process, there has been no suggestion that S 250 would serve that goal. Nor has there been any showing that the bill is necessary to eliminate discriminatory practices. Accordingly, there is a serious constitutional question whether the Congress has the power to enact this legislation.

I support legislation that would assist the states in implementing appropriate reforms in order to make voter registration easier for the American public. I cannot, however, accept legislation that imposes an unnecessary and costly federal regime on the states and that is, in addition, an open invitation to fraud and corruption.

For the reasons discussed above, I am returning S 250 without my approval.

---

motor-voter bill and retreat for further negotiations.

Republicans later agreed to bring the standoff to an end, banking on the veto strategy to thwart the bill.

On May 19 the Senate returned to the bill and rejected a series of Republican amendments, most of which Ford said would have killed his bill.

● Members voted, 55-40, to table an amendment by John McCain, R-Ariz., that would have banned registration at agencies that provided public benefits to the needy, such as welfare and unemployment offices. McCain argued that the civil rights of the nation's poor might be harmed if they felt pressured into registering to vote before picking up a benefits check. *(Vote 91, p. 13-S)*

● Members tabled, 57-39, an amendment by McConnell that would have made voting fraud a federal crime punishable by a maximum prison sentence of 10 years and a $10,000 fine. (The bill as passed would make vote fraud a federal offense with a maximum penalty of five years in prison.)

Opponents argued that the amendment would have given federal election officials too much power over states in prosecuting voting fraud cases. *(Vote 92, p. 13-S)*

● The Senate also tabled, 61-36, another McConnell amendment that would have automatically discontinued the bill's requirements in states in which voter turnout in the 1996 election rose less than 2 percent from the 1992 election. *(Vote 93, p. 13-S)*

● Senators tabled, 55-41, an amendment by Don Nickles, R-Okla., that would have suspended implementation of the bill until Congress provided money to states to pay for it. *(Vote 94, p. 13-S)*

On May 20, the Senate passed the bill, 61-38, sending the measure to the House. *(Vote 98, p. 14-S)*

## HOUSE FLOOR ACTION

Al Swift, D-Wash., chairman of the House Administration Subcommittee on Elections, vowed to move quickly on a companion House bill (HR 4366) once the Senate hurdle had been cleared.

But as the session began drawing to a close, Swift encouraged House leaders to take up the Senate bill, noting that S 250 was not substantially different than the House companion and that the House had already held its own hearings on the matter in the 101st Congress.

Despite an almost certain presidential veto, the House cleared the bill on June 16. The vote was a 268-153, which was 13 votes shy of the two-thirds that would have been needed to override a veto. *(Vote 194, p. 48-H)*

Bill Thomas, R-Calif., offered an unsuccessful substitute bill on behalf of Minority Leader Robert H. Michel of Illinois that would have created a $25 million block grant program to help states increase voter registration. The proposal was defeated, 133-290. *(Vote 193, p. 48-H)*

After passing the motor-voter bill, Democrats stepped up pressure on Bush to sign the measure into law.

But a June 16 letter from the Office of Management and Budget said the bill was flawed and that White House advisers would recommend a veto.

"It's going to be vetoed, and the veto will be sustained," said bill foe Thomas.

## BUSH VETO

In a move that did not surprise either supporters or opponents of S 250, President Bush vetoed the bill on July 2. It was his 31st veto.

"I cannot . . . accept legislation that imposes an unnecessary and costly Federal regime on the states and that is, in addition, an open invitation to fraud and corruption," he said. He added that despite his veto, he did want to support "legislation that would assist the states in implementing appropriate reforms in order to make voter registration easier for the American public."

Arkansas Gov. Bill Clinton, then well on his way to winning the Democratic nomination for president, quickly issued a statement July 2. "Today's veto is nothing less than a slap in the face to American democracy," Clinton said. "The bill would have made it easier for millions of Americans, particularly young Americans, to participate in this election. But President Bush is clearly more interested in his own re-election than in making democracy work."

And undeclared independent candidate Ross Perot also criticized Bush. "The only reason to veto this bill is to try to keep people away from the polls this fall," Perot said.

### Veto Sustained

The Senate on Sept. 22 sustained the veto. The vote was 62-38, well short of the two-thirds needed. Bill backers gained the vote of Lloyd Bentsen, D-Texas, who had not voted on the final passage. Otherwise, the votes remained the same. *(Vote 226, p. 30-S)*

Sponsors of the bill planned to introduce similar legislation in the 103rd Congress. And the election of Clinton as president clearly lifted the spirits of bill backers. Clinton was strongly supportive of the measure and indicated that he would sign a similar bill as president. ∎

# Hit Film Prompts Release Of Kennedy Documents

Stirred to action by the publicity surrounding a 1991 movie about the 1963 assassination of President John F. Kennedy, Congress passed legislation late in the second session creating a special new commission with the authority to make public hundreds of thousands of pages of secret government documents, testimony and evidence surrounding the shooting and follow-up investigations into the president's death.

The measure (S 3006) established an independent commission to review government records and release all except those that would still violate privacy or national security concerns. The bill's aim was to deflate the many conspiracy theories that surrounded the shooting of the president, which were rekindled by the film "JFK," produced by Oliver Stone.

Since the assassination, much of the work of congressional and executive agencies had been kept secret. The administration objected to the initial legislation, which would have set up a board appointed by the judicial branch, on grounds that the disclosure requirements would unconstitutionally undercut the president's right to protect confidential information and intelligence sources and would violate the executive branch's appointment powers.

However, in the end President Bush signed the bill, which had been amended to let the White House appoint the five-member commission, subject to Senate confirmation.

## BACKGROUND

The movie "JFK" opened on Dec. 20, 1991, creating a stir with its premise that Lee Harvey Oswald was a bit player in a far-reaching government plot to kill the president. The movie sparked renewed debate over the Kennedy assassination and served as the major impetus for the legislation to make the files public.

Measures to release the thousands of pages of documents and records on the assassination were introduced by Sen. David L. Boren, D-Okla., and Rep. Louis Stokes, D-Ohio. The latter had served as chairman of a special House committee that investigated the assassination in 1976-79. At that time, a majority of panel members concluded that the president "was probably assassinated as a result of a conspiracy" but declared themselves unable to identify who besides Oswald was involved. *(Congress and the Nation, Vol. V, p. 734)*

That controversial conclusion disputed the Warren Commission's finding that "Oswald acted alone." The Warren Commission had been appointed on Nov. 29, 1963.

Headed by then-Chief Justice Earl Warren, the commission was directed by President Lyndon B. Johnson to investigate all circumstances relating to the Kennedy assassination. It issued its report on Sept. 27, 1964.

In introducing H J Res 454, Stokes called the movie "fiction and fantasy," and said that disclosure of an array of sealed files that had been compiled since the shooting in Dallas would dispel the air of conspiracy that had surrounded the tragedy. Among the files covered by the bill were documents maintained or gathered by the CIA, the FBI, the Secret Service, the Warren Commission and the so-called Church Committee, a Senate panel headed by the late Frank Church, D-Idaho, that investigated U.S. intelligence work in the mid-1970s.

While many historians disputed the movie's findings, Stone's film popularized the theory that more than one gunman took shots at the president and that Oswald had

---

### BOXSCORE

▸ **JFK Assassination Documents (S 3006, H J Res 454).** The bill created an independent commission to review and release to the public most government records collected during various investigations into the assassination of John F. Kennedy. The executive branch was given authority to choose commission members, and a strict timetable was set up to ensure final release of all documentation relevant to the shooting death of the president, except for material that greatly compromised national security or an individual's privacy.

**Reports:** H Rept 102-625 Parts 1, 2; S Rept 102-328

### KEY ACTION

**July 27** — The **Senate** passed S 3006 by voice vote.

**Aug. 12** — The **House** passed H J Res 454 by voice vote.

**Sept. 30** — The **House** passed S 3006 by voice vote.

**Oct. 26** — President Bush signed S 3006 — PL 102-526.

been recruited by U.S. military leaders as a scapegoat for the shooting. The Warren Commission concluded that there were only three shots, all fired from the sixth floor of the Texas School Book Depository. In declaring the probability of a conspiracy, the House committee chaired by Stokes cleared the U.S. government and the Soviet Union and Cuba but said "individual members" either of groups opposing Cuban leader Fidel Castro or of organized crime "may have been involved."

## HOUSE ACTION

Two House committees worked simultaneously on legislation to reopen the files related to the Kennedy assassination, producing versions with a few significantly different provisions.

The Government Operations Committee approved a measure (H J Res 454) on June 3 that gave the executive branch significant control over the records' release. After receiving a letter April 28 in which the Justice Department stressed that the executive branch should choose the panel members and have final say over which documents would be released, the Government Operations panel passed legislation to allow the executive branch to choose the review commission members.

The House Judiciary Committee approved a different version of the bill July 1 that called for representatives of the U.S. Court of Appeals to name and appoint a document review board. The Judiciary bill also contained provisions, added at the request of the national archivist, to allow the National Archives to exempt certain files and materials from review and permit the agency to charge standard reproduction fees for copies, even those obtained under the Freedom of Information Act.

After moving through both committees, the versions remained unreconciled. Rep. Jack Brooks, D-Texas, chairman of the Judiciary Committee, resisted the Government Operations proposal to allow the executive branch to choose commission members. He believed compromising on the JFK bill would set a bad precedent for a different legislative effort that he hoped to launch later in the year to reauthorize the law that permitted judicial panels to appoint special counsels to investigate wrongdoing in the executive branch. The Justice Department had opposed such appointments on the same grounds that applied to the JFK commission. *(Independent counsel, p. 315)*

Brooks also said that a court-appointed panel would allow its members to avoid "any appearance of conflict of interest."

### Floor Action

On Aug. 12, the House passed H J Res 454 by voice vote, preserving the language of Brooks' committee on having the courts, not the executive branch, appoint the members of the review board.

The House deleted provisions that had been added at the request of the Archivist of the United States, Don W. Wilson. The deleted language would have kept the seal on many of the records held in presidential libraries by excluding materials given to the government under a deed of gift, and could have increased the costs of accessing the files by exempting the National Archives from fee limits set by the Freedom of Information Act.

## SENATE ACTION

On the Senate side, the bill's first incarnation, as S J Res 282, included a provision calling for judicial branch appointment of the commission members. At hearing of the Governmental Affairs Committee on May 12, the heads of the CIA and FBI offered their support for releasing most documents. They maintained, however, that their agencies should control the flow.

FBI Director William S. Sessions said his agency wanted to keep the seal on about half the FBI's 499,000 files that he said concerned unrelated organized crime and criminal investigations, and to hold back information that would reveal law enforcement techniques and sources.

A Justice Department official indicated that his department was open to a compromise over control of the board.

The Governmental Affairs Committee on June 25 approved by voice vote draft legislation based on the resolution.

The measure, which was later reported out as an original bill and numbered S 3006, required that relevant government offices gather, review and make public documents related to the assassination. All released material was to be transferred to the National Archives. The bill agreed to let the five-member review board be appointed by the president, with the Senate's consent.

The committee also approved, by voice vote, language proposed by Chairman John Glenn, D-Ohio, to set strict timetables for reviewing documents. The amendment required a periodic review for all materials deemed unreleasable, and all withheld documents were to be released 25 years after enactment.

### Floor Action

With little debate, the bill (S 3006) passed the full Senate by voice vote on July 27.

The Senate bill set up a procedural maze for preparing the materials for the National Archives, where the public would have access. The process included the following steps:

● Government offices would organize and review their records within 10 months of the law's enactment, recommending what should be withheld.

The rest would be released immediately through the Archives.

● A five-member independent board would be created to review the records that had been recommended for continued protection.

The board would have up to three years to go through all the materials. The president would appoint the members, subject to Senate confirmation.

● The president could override the board's decision on executive branch files. Congress would have to adopt rules determining eventual release if it wanted records withheld.

● Material withheld would be reviewed periodically for disclosure. All material would be released within 25 years of enactment.

## FINAL ACTION

With time running short in the session, Judiciary Chairman Brooks set aside his doubts about executive branch control over the review board, paving the way for the House to pass the Senate version by voice vote on Sept. 30, thus avoiding a House-Senate conference and clearing the bill.

Although the administration had initially expressed reluctance to support the bill, the Senate version satisfied the administration's concerns, and the president signed the bill (PL 102-526) into law on Oct. 26. ∎

# Senate Suspends Action on Lobbying Rules

Legislation (S 2766) designed to force lobbyists to comply with stricter reporting and disclosure standards failed to make it to the Senate floor during the 102nd Congress, although supporters said they were laying the groundwork for action in the 103rd Congress.

The prospects for action were improved Nov. 3 when Bill Clinton was elected president. Clinton pledged during the campaign to seek new legislation toughening lobbying laws, and he imposed new ethics guidelines on his own appointees. (*Ethics guidelines, p. 62*)

S 2766, sponsored by Sen. Carl Levin, D-Mich., sought to establish more rigorous financial disclosure requirements for lobbyists and to require them to file a semiannual report revealing the income received for lobbying on behalf of a client. Although the legislation had bipartisan support among members of the Senate Governmental Affairs Committee, backers ran out of time in the last few months of the 102nd Congress to get the bill to the Senate floor. No companion measure moved in the House.

## BACKGROUND

The role of lobbyists in Congress became a crucial talking point during the presidential election of 1992, when independent candidate Ross Perot chided Congress and the Bush administration for being overly influenced by lobbyists who wore "alligator shoes" and spoke on behalf of foreign governments.

But even before the presidential debates, there was some movement in Congress for reform of the regulations governing the practice of lobbying. In May, Levin, chairman of the Senate Governmental Affairs Subcommittee on Oversight of Government Management, called for regulation of lobbyists in an effort to restore faith in Congress.

The Federal Regulation of Lobbying Act of 1946 — which required all people hired for the principal purpose of lobbying Congress to register with the House and Senate — had long been considered ineffective. This became especially true after the Supreme Court, in its 1954 ruling in *U.S. v. Harris*, narrowly interpreted its key provisions, ensuring that almost anyone could minimize reporting or avoid it altogether.

Equally loose, according to backers of S 2766, was the Foreign Agents Registration Act of 1938, which required anyone representing a foreign government or principal to register with the Department of Justice.

Supporters of S 2766 contended that these laws were vague and riddled with loopholes, making enforcement impossible.

## LEGISLATIVE ACTION

The first version of a disclosure reform bill (S 2279) was introduced in February, and there was a hearing on the measure in March. During that hearing before Levin's sub-

---

## BOXSCORE

➡ **Lobbying Disclosure Rules (S 2766, formerly S 2279).** The legislation sought to establish more rigorous financial disclosure requirements for lobbyists.

**Report:** S Rept 102-354.

### KEY ACTION

June 25 — The **Senate** Governmental Affairs Committee approved S 2766.

---

committee, the Bush administration registered its support.

The deputy director of the Office of Management and Budget, Frank Hodsoll, said lobby reporting laws were "so complicated and riddled with loopholes as to be neither enforced or enforceable."

The bill provisions subsequently were altered, and Levin, along with Sens. Herb Kohl, D-Wis., and William S. Cohen, R-Maine, introduced a new version, S 2766.

### Committee Action

S 2766 was approved by voice vote by the Senate Governmental Affairs Committee on June 25.

"These loopholes are breeding a disrespect for the law," Levin said. "About 70 percent of the people listed in 'Washington Representatives' [a guide to Washington lobbyists] are not listed as lobbyists under our laws."

The committee also approved by voice vote an amendment offered by Chairman John Glenn, D-Ohio. The amendment would have required those who worked in the executive or legislative branch in the two years before registering as lobbyists to disclose the details of their government service.

While the measure enjoyed the full support of committee members in attendance, Ted Stevens, R-Alaska, warned his colleagues that the Department of Justice had some concerns about the bill that had not been addressed by the committee. He said the department considered the definition of lobbying in the measure to be vague and confusing.

After the bill was reported out of committee, no further action was taken to bring it to the floor before the end of the session.

This did not come as a surprise to bill backers, who had said after the markup that there were not enough legislative days remaining to finish work on the bill.

### Provisions

As passed by committee, S 2766 substituted for the existing statutes a single, uniform rule, requiring anyone engaged in lobbying the executive or legislative branch to register with an Office of Lobbying Registration and Public Disclosure, unless these activities were incidental to the job.

Registered lobbyists were to issue a semiannual report revealing the income received for lobbying on behalf of a client or, if representing themselves, provide a good-faith estimate of the amount spent on lobbying activities.

Each report also was required to contain a list of issues the lobbyist worked on and the federal agencies and congressional committees contacted.

The bill created an Office of Lobbying Registration and Public Disclosure in the Justice Department to administer the statute. Its duties included providing interested parties with registration and reporting information as well as investigating and determining non-compliance. The bill established civil penalties for lobbying violations as high as $10,000. ∎

# House Considers Possible Presidential Vote

If public opinion polls had proved an accurate indicator, millions of Americans would have cast their votes for Ross Perot as the 42nd president. If they had, the election might have wound up in the House of Representatives at a time when Congress was riding particularly low in the public's esteem.

Faced with the possibility, House leaders dusted off studies of how the chamber should proceed if no candidate won a majority of the electoral votes in the Nov. 3 election. But after Perot suspended his campaign in mid-summer, interest in revisiting the rules waned. Perot ended up with 19 percent of the popular vote and no electoral votes.

In a close election, a Perot victory in one large state such as Texas — his home — could have kept either President Bush or Arkansas Gov. Bill Clinton from winning a majority of the 538 Electoral College votes.

Each state's Electoral College votes equaled its number of House districts plus its two senators. In 1992, the District of Columbia had three votes. If there was no Electoral College majority, the Constitution decreed that the president be chosen by the House and the vice president by the Senate. But the process was fraught with ambiguities — technical and political.

The House had been forced to elect a president only twice — in 1801 and 1825, when it chose Thomas Jefferson and John Quincy Adams, respectively. The country had changed enormously since then, yet the constitutional framework remained the same:

Each state got one vote, making a small state such as Rhode Island as important as California. House members from each state were polled, and the candidate who got the most support got the vote of that state. If the state's delegation was tied, it did not vote. The candidate who won the vote of 26 states was elected president.

No one truly believed the election would be thrown into the House, but Rep. Dan Glickman, D-Kan., said Congress should be prepared.

Glickman on May 13 wrote the Speaker and House Judiciary Committee Chairman Jack Brooks, D-Texas, urging them to hold hearings on the issue.

"We have an obligation to the American people to provide a smooth transition from one president to the next," Glickman said.

Speaker Thomas S. Foley, D-Wash., said he had brushed up on the two occasions that the presidential decision was thrown into the House. And he noted that Martin Frost, D-Texas, a House Rules Committee member, in 1980 already had explored many of the issues. Frost looked into the matter when former GOP Rep. John B. Anderson of Illinois was running as an independent against President Jimmy Carter and Republican Ronald Reagan. His research was never needed. Reagan won in a landslide; Anderson drew 6.6 percent and did not carry a single state.

## Questions Abound

If the 1992 election had wound up in the House, Clinton appeared to have the advantage. Democrats in 1992 controlled the House delegations of 32 states. Republicans had a majority in 10 states, seven states were evenly divided and one, Vermont, was represented by an independent.

However, the presumption was that the 103rd Congress would elect the president, with realigned party delegations if the election had gone to the House.

Regardless of a delegation's partisan makeup, Glickman said members were under enormous pressure to vote for the candidate who won in their district or state. But what would a member do if one candidate won the district but another won the state?

That was just one of the uncertainties. Following are some of the questions explored by Frost in his study of 1980:

**Who decides?** Under the Constitution, the members of Congress elected Nov. 3 were to be sworn into office Jan. 3, 1993 (although that was a Sunday, and the ceremony did not occur until Jan. 5). A federal statute required that the Senate and House count the Electoral College votes Jan. 6. Although the outcome was apparent long before then, the election was not official until that point.

Frost said the counting of Electoral College votes could theoretically be moved up, giving the outgoing Congress the right to choose the next president if no candidate had a majority. But such a move would require enactment of a new law and would undoubtedly precipitate an enormous public outcry.

**Would the House vote in public?** In the only presidential elections decided by the House, the balloting was secret, and the voting took place behind closed doors. But in an era when all House floor proceedings were televised, a secret proceeding seemed inconceivable.

"It would be dangerous for the House as an institution to attempt to impose a high degree of secrecy given the current mood of the public regarding distrust of government," Frost had written 12 years earlier. Presumably, delegations would be under tremendous pressure to reveal how each member voted.

**Who would write the rules for the House election?** After the elections of 1800 and 1824, a special committee was established to write them, but that was before the creation of a House Rules Committee. Frost said the panel was the logical one for the task. But because the majority Democrats dominated the Rules Committee, Republicans would have objected. Democrats held a 9-4 edge on the panel, significantly greater than their margin of control in the House at large.

**Would a candidate need a majority of a delegation's votes to win its support or only a plurality?** The rules used in the 19th century required a candidate to capture a majority of each delegation. Frost proposed rules in 1980 to let a state be awarded to the candidate with a plurality.

**What if the House deadlocked?**

If a decision was not made by Inauguration Day on Jan. 20, the incoming vice president would become acting president. But that assumed that the Senate was able to choose a vice president.

The Senate was to choose between the top two candidates for vice president. Each senator got a vote, and a majority of the whole Senate was needed to win. But lawmakers said the Senate would be reluctant to elect a vice president until the House had elected a president.

If the Senate was unable to decide on a vice president, the Constitution left it to Congress to decide who should serve as acting president until the House picked a president. ∎

# House Calls and Close Calls

The choice of a new president had fallen to the House of Representatives only twice in American history. Both times, it was a messy business indeed.

The Constitution originally stipulated that the person receiving the most votes in the Electoral College would become president, and the runner-up would be vice president. Electors had two votes — one each for their choice for president and vice president — but there was no distinction between the ballots.

Early on, the development of political parties and nominating tickets for president and vice president led to confusion.

In 1800, in the country's fourth presidential election, a caucus of the Democratic-Republican Party nominated Thomas Jefferson for president and Aaron Burr for vice president. The Federalists renominated President John Adams, with Charles Cotesworth Pinckney as his running mate.

The Democratic-Republicans won but failed to withhold one electoral vote for Burr. That meant Jefferson and Burr, who were running mates, finished in a tie for the presidency with 73 electoral votes each — an outcome that automatically sent the election to the House.

On Feb. 11, the House, which was dominated by the Federalists, appeared ready to elect Burr, but he would not give assurances that he would run the country as a Federalist.

After six days and 36 ballots, the House elected Jefferson president. Burr was automatically elected vice president.

## 12th Amendment Added, Tested

After that close call, the 12th Amendment, which changed the system, was added to the Constitution. It forced electors to specify their presidential and vice presidential choices. It also mandated that candidates receive the majority of electoral votes to win the presidency and vice presidency.

In 1824, the presidential election was decided by the House after a four-way contest ended with Andrew Jackson winning the most electoral votes, 99, but falling 32 short of the majority needed.

John Quincy Adams finished second with 84 votes, William H. Crawford won 41 votes and Henry Clay trailed with 37 electors. Because the 12th Amendment says the top three candidates are to be considered by the House, Clay was out of the race. Too bad for Clay; he was Speaker of the House.

A scandal ensued when a Philadelphia newspaper published an anonymous letter alleging that Clay had promised to give his votes to Adams in return for being appointed secretary of State.

Clay denied the charge, but he did support Adams, who won the support of 13 states, the minimum needed to be elected. Adams later appointed Clay as secretary of State, prompting Jackson to write, "Was there ever witnessed such a bare-faced corruption in any country before?"

## More Snafus

Those two elections were not the only ones Congress had to take an active role in deciding.

In 1837, the Senate was forced to choose a vice president. Democrat Martin Van Buren won 170 electoral votes, enough to be elected president, but his running mate, Richard M. Johnson, received only 147 because of a boycott by Virginia electors, who objected to Johnson's open relationship with a slave, with whom he had two daughters.

The Senate voted 33-16 to elect Johnson over Whig Francis Granger, who was the runner-up in the Electoral College vote.

The 1876 presidential election was a squeaker, with Republican Rutherford B. Hayes appearing to garner 185 electoral votes to Democrat Samuel J. Tilden's 184 votes on Election Day.

In several states, there were numerous allegations of popular-vote fraud by both parties. That led to uncertainty over which candidate was entitled to the electoral votes of those states. Four states submitted two separate sets of electoral votes to Congress — one from each party.

Unable to simply tally the Electoral College votes and declare a winner, the House and Senate jointly created a 15-member commission to decide how to count the disputed electoral votes.

Republicans had a one-vote advantage on the commission, which they used to uphold Hayes' electoral votes. The Democratic-controlled House voted to overturn the commission's findings, but the Republican Senate did not.

With time running out, Hayes made a deal with Democrats, agreeing that as president he would withdraw all federal troops from the South and end Reconstruction. On March 4, two days after the deadlock was resolved, Hayes was sworn in as president.

Although the House has not had to choose a president since 1824, there have been several close calls. For instance, if Richard M. Nixon had lost California in 1968, he would have fallen nine electoral votes short of a majority. Likewise, the 1960 election would have been undecided if John F. Kennedy had not won New York.

# Chapter 2

# ECONOMICS & FINANCE

# Hill Wrangles Over '93 Budget

## Democrats eager to spend defense savings fought an uphill battle for domestic programs

As Congress moved into the third year of the five-year budget deal struck in 1990, the budget peace that had prevailed in 1991 seemed a distant memory. Democratic leaders were eager to get access to defense savings for use in funding popular domestic programs. But that meant changing the 1990 budget rules, which erected "walls" between defense, domestic and international programs and barred Congress from taking discretionary money from one to aid another.

The scramble for money was expected to be particularly intense because the discretionary spending caps enacted as part of the 1990 budget deal were set to become much tighter in fiscal 1993. Moreover, appropriators had set themselves up for a tough year when they decided in 1991 to delay the obligation of more than $4 billion in fiscal 1992 spending authority into fiscal 1993.

In the end, however, the walls remained in place. Democratic leaders had not reckoned on strong opposition from defense-minded Democrats — who stood to lose hometown jobs if defense spending was significantly cut — or from conservative, Democratic "deficit hawks," who argued that any savings from defense cuts should go to deficit reduction.

Despite the tight caps, all 13 spending bills were fin-

ished on time. Democrats even agreed to cut several of them to meet President Bush's demand late in the year that the measures not exceed a freeze on discretionary spending that he had proposed as part of his January budget.

Efforts to enforce future budget discipline by amending the Constitution to require a balanced federal budget collapsed.

The balanced-budget fight was the only comprehensive attempt Congress made in 1992 to attack the deficit. House Budget Committee Chairman Leon E. Panetta, D-Calif., tried to work out a bipartisan deficit reduction plan, but negotiations with House Republicans collapsed.

While the 1990 budget deal had put strict limits on appropriated spending and required a pay-as-you-go offset for any tax cuts or new or expanded entitlement programs, it had grandfathered existing entitlements. The rapid growth in those programs — particularly Medicaid and Medicare and anti-recession aid such as unemployment benefits and food stamps — contributed to the prodigious growth in the deficit. As a result, fiscal 1992 ended with a deficit of $290.2 billion — far below the $403.8 billion predicted by the Office of Management and Budget in January but still more than the previous record of $268.7 billion chalked up in fiscal 1991.

# Bush Proposes $1.5 Trillion Budget

With his popularity badly eroded and the economy in what he described as a free fall, President Bush combined his annual State of the Union address and the fiscal 1993 budget in a rare one-two punch Jan. 28-29.

Declaring war on the recession and on any Democrat who dared oppose his recovery plan, Bush gave Congress a 52-day deadline to pass the core of his proposals. The budget, issued the morning after the speech, provided details of the package and much more. The $1.5 trillion fiscal 1993 budget proposed a lengthy list of tax cuts, defense cuts and spending shifts that included much to infuriate Democrats and draw a bright line between the parties nine months before the election.

It also virtually guaranteed prolonged warfare on a variety of fronts throughout the year.

Flashpoints included:

● **Taxes.** A steep reduction in the top capital gains tax rate from 28 percent to 15.4 percent for assets held three years or longer was the flagship of Bush's fleet of tax proposals. Other less controversial proposals included a

$500-per-child increase in the personal tax exemption, a new $5,000 tax credit and penalty-free withdrawals from individual retirement accounts (IRAs) for first-time home buyers, penalty-free IRA withdrawals for medical and educational expenses, and "passive loss" rules for active real estate investors. *(Box, p. 87)*

● **Defense cuts.** Bush bowed to political pressure and the new, post-Soviet military reality by proposing a $50.4 billion cut in defense spending authority by 1997. Bush threw his congressional opponents a curve by insisting that the savings — about $27.4 billion in outlays over 1992-97 — be used for deficit reduction or a tax cut, not for the increased domestic spending many Democrats wanted.

Specifically, White House budget director Richard G. Darman said that Bush would consider using the defense cuts to balance the cost of his proposed $500-per-child increase in the personal tax exemption if Congress were unwilling to accept a plan to offset the revenue loss with a series of controversial accounting changes and reductions in mandatory spending programs. He added, however, that

Bush would accept such a trade-off only if the five-year defense cuts went no deeper than $50.4 billion, the overall caps on discretionary spending (PL 101-508) were adjusted downward to reflect the shift, and individual caps on defense, domestic and international spending were extended through 1997. (*1990 Almanac, p. 129*)

Those caps, enacted as part of the 1990 budget agreement, were anathema to Democrats because they prevented them from shifting defense funds to other uses. The individual caps were slated to expire in fiscal 1994, to be replaced by a single, overall limit on discretionary spending. Democratic leaders in both chambers wanted to drop the caps a year early, and certainly not extend them.

Meanwhile, Democrats on the Appropriations committees wanted to use any savings from defense to boost domestic programs, not fund tax cuts.

● **Spending freeze.** Bush wanted to take back some of the substantial new spending authority he agreed to give appropriators in the 1990 budget-summit agreement.

He proposed a freeze in budget authority for discretionary domestic programs and a cutback in overall discretion

ary spending authority. Although he did not emphasize the proposal at the time, he resurrected it during the Republican National Convention in August. He threatened to veto appropriations bills that did not conform, and Democrats, eager to get out of town to campaign, caved in and trimmed spending bills to meet his criterion.

● **Spending shifts.** Within the $202.9 billion in spending authority that Bush proposed to allocate to domestic discretionary programs under his freeze plan, the budget offered hundreds of shifts to reflect White House priorities. These included increases for children's health and education programs, research and development, highway construction, federal prisons and prosecutors, and aid to the former Soviet republics.

Bush wanted to offset the increases by terminating or reducing 330 programs and killing more than 4,100 projects. Among targets familiar from past budgets were Amtrak, the Low-Income Home Energy Assistance Program and mass transit spending, all slated for cutbacks, and the Economic Development Administration, which was once again proposed for extinction.

● **Health-care revision.** Proposals to overhaul the nation's health-care system were to be a featured part of the budget proposal, but a rebellion by House Republicans touched off last-minute revisions, temporarily halting the printing of the budget and delaying the release of Bush's revamped health proposals until Feb. 6.

● **Mandatory spending.** Bush and congressional Democrats agreed that runaway mandatory spending programs — chiefly entitlement benefits such as Medicare, Medicaid, food stamps and farm subsidies — were the primary reason a balanced budget was unlikely in the remainder of the 20th Century. But there the agreement ended.

Both sides had fought bitterly over how and whether to cut politically sensitive programs such as Medicare during the 1990 budget summit. Democrats had hoped for a respite, but Darman doggedly pushed new mandatory spending cuts in the fiscal 1992 budget. Although those proposals went nowhere, Darman recycled many of them in the fiscal 1993 budget, including cuts in Medicare and agriculture subsidies for high-income beneficiaries that Democrats ignored in 1991.

If mandatory spending programs grew at a rate equal to the expansion of the eligible population plus inflation, the budget said, five-year savings would amount to $390 billion and the deficit could turn into a surplus. Darman did not propose going that far, but he did suggest imposing a cap on the growth rate of mandatory programs, particularly Medicare and Medicaid. Under this plan, the excess would trigger a reconciliation process to offset the overspending, and, if that failed, there would be an automatic spending cut in entitlement programs.

● **Accrual accounting.** In a new and even more controversial wrinkle, the budget proposed shifting deposit insurance and the Pension Benefit Guaranty Corporation from a cash-based system to accrual accounting. Accrual accounting, in effect, would have eliminated the need to show on budget the entire process involved when the government acquired and later sold the assets of a failed thrift or bank, a procedure that could take years. Instead of recording first an expense and later a gain, both on budget, accrual accounting would have moved the process off budget, recording only the net cost, upfront.

Bush projected that his proposed reforms, coupled with the change to accrual accounting, would have saved $13.7 billion in fiscal 1992-93 and $38 billion by 1997, enough to

# Revenue Changes Proposed by Bush

*(In billions of dollars, by fiscal year; totals may not add due to rounding)*

| | 1993 | 1993-97 | | 1993 | 1993-97 |
|---|---|---|---|---|---|
| **RECEIPTS** | | | Penalty-free IRA withdrawals | | |
| **First-year revenue gainers** | | | for first-time home buyers | −0.1 | −0.5 |
| Capital gains rate cut | 3.8 | 6.3 | Health insurance deduction for self-employed | −0.2 | −0.5 |
| Flexible IRAs | 0.5 | −2.9 | Tax credit to first-time home buyers | −2.1 | −4.9 |
| Extension of hospital insurance | | | Deductible loss on sale of principal residence | −0.4 | −1.9 |
| coverage to state, local employees | 1.6 | 7.6 | Other | 0.2 | — |
| Charitable contributions, revised rules | 0.1 | 0.6 | **TOTAL** | **−3.7** | **−19.4** |
| Securities inventories, accounting changes | 0.6 | 3.8 | **USER FEES/OTHER OFFSETTING COLLECTIONS** | | |
| Bar interest deductions for loans secured | | | **Discretionary** | | |
| by corporate life insurance policies | 0.3 | 2.4 | Food Safety Inspection Service | 0.1 | 0.3 |
| Bar certain deductions by thrifts | | | Elk Hills Naval Petroleum Reserve | 1.2 | −0.1 |
| getting federal aid | 0.4 | 0.6 | Energy enrichment plants | 0.2 | 0.9 |
| Equalize tax treatment | | | Medicare, Medicaid survey and certification | 0.3 | 1.2 |
| of large credit unions, thrifts | 0.2 | 1.0 | FDA product review, seafood inspection | 0.2 | 1.1 |
| Interest on certain annuities | 0.2 | 1.6 | Social Security processing of state payments | 0.1 | 0.9 |
| Communications excise tax | 0.1 | 0.5 | Hardrock mining claim holding | 0.1 | 0.4 |
| FCC processing fees | 0.1 | 0.5 | Interior receipt sharing | 0.1 | 0.3 |
| Abandoned mine reclamation fees | — | 0.5 | America the Beautiful passports | * | 0.2 |
| Increased employee contribution | | | Park Service entrance fees | * | 0.1 |
| to civil service retirement | 0.4 | 5.1 | Justice Department prisoner fee | * | 0.2 |
| Pension distribution changes | * | 1.1 | Veterans medical copayments | 0.1 | 0.7 |
| | | | Veterans home loan guarantee fees | 0.2 | 0.8 |
| **First-year revenue losers** | | | Commodity Futures Trading Commission | 0.1 | 0.3 |
| Increase personal exemption | −4.4 | −23.9 | Pesticide registration fees | * | 0.1 |
| Passive loss for real estate | −0.4 | −2.3 | SEC registration fee | 0.1 | 0.6 |
| Investment tax allowance | −1.6 | 4.2 | Small Business Administration loan guarantee | * | 0.3 |
| Alternative minimum tax depreciation | −0.4 | −1.4 | **Mandatory** | | |
| R&E credit | −0.8 | −7.7 | Arctic National Wildlife Refuge leasing | * | 2.1 |
| R&E allocation rules | −0.5 | −0.8 | Veterans home loan guarantee fees | * | 0.2 |
| Low-income housing credit | −0.2 | −1.7 | Corps of Engineers recreation site fee | * | 0.1 |
| Targeted jobs credit | −0.2 | −0.5 | FCC spectrum auction | — | 3.8 |
| Mortgage revenue bonds | −* | −0.4 | Other | — | 0.1 |
| Enterprise zones | −* | −1.8 | | | |
| Student loan interest deduction | −0.4 | −3.5 | **TOTAL FEES** | **2.8** | **14.6** |
| Penalty-free IRA withdrawals | | | | | |
| for medical, education expenses | −0.1 | −0.5 | | | |

*Amounts less than $50 million.*

SOURCE: Fiscal 1993 Budget

offset the revenue loss from many of the administration's tax-cut proposals.

## Projections for the Economy

The economic forecasts contained in the budget presented a stark contrast between what the White House said the economy would look like under "business as usual," meaning without Bush's proposals, and the economy it said would result under the president's program.

The administration forecast that real gross domestic product (GDP) would grow by 2.2 percent in 1992 and 3 percent in 1993 if Bush's budget were enacted — compared with an anemic 1.6 percent and 2.4 percent, respectively, if it were not. (GDP is an inflation-adjusted measure of the total output of goods and services within the borders of the United States.)

The administration's assumptions about life without the Bush budget tended to be far grimmer than key outside forecasts indicated, and its projections assuming enactment of Bush's plans did little more than match what others said the economy would be like anyway.

Both the Congressional Budget Office (CBO) and a

consensus of about 50 business, professional and academic economists that made up the Blue Chip Economic Indicators assumed stronger growth in 1992, and CBO saw a more robust recovery in 1993 as well. Consistent with its somewhat lower growth forecast, the administration also anticipated somewhat lower inflation and interest rates, but about the same level of unemployment as CBO and the Blue Chip.

This was not the first time in recent years that the administration put forth a more pessimistic outlook than other forecasters. But the size of the disparity was unusual, as was the attention that the administration gave to portraying its budget as a tool for stimulating the economy.

## Boos and Rave Reviews

Though expected, the notices from Democrats were still tough, and they gave no indication that the White House and Democrats could find much common ground anytime soon.

House Budget Committee Chairman Leon E. Panetta, D-Calif., called the budget "a dismal failure when it comes
*Continued on p. 98*

# Fiscal 1993 Budget by Function

*(Figures for 1992 and 1993 are estimates; in millions of dollars †)*

| | BUDGET AUTHORITY | | | OUTLAYS | | |
|---|---|---|---|---|---|---|
| | 1991 | 1992 | 1993 | 1991 | 1992 | 1993 |
| **NATIONAL DEFENSE** | | | | | | |
| Military defense | $ 290,904 | $ 276,223 | $ 267,156 | $ 262,389 | $ 294,640 | $ 277,933 |
| Atomic energy defense activities | 11,578 | 11,980 | 12,132 | 10,004 | 11,685 | 11,901 |
| Defense-related activities | 1,092 | 968 | 1,212 | 899 | 980 | 1,180 |
| TOTAL | 303,574 | 289,170 | 280,499 | 273,292 | 307,306 | 291,014 |
| **INTERNATIONAL AFFAIRS** | | | | | | |
| International security assistance | 9,061 | 7,651 | 6,642 | 9,823 | 7,783 | 7,007 |
| International development/humanitarian assistance | 6,778 | 7,443 | 7,847 | 5,141 | 6,154 | 6,385 |
| Conduct of foreign affairs | 3,238 | 3,686 | 4,292 | 3,282 | 3,560 | 4,108 |
| Foreign information and exchange activities | 1,243 | 1,308 | 1,384 | 1,253 | 1,343 | 1,384 |
| International financial programs | 2,369 | 13,208 | 404 | −3,648 | −1,029 | −904 |
| TOTAL | 22,689 | 33,297 | 20,569 | 15,851 | 17,811 | 17,981 |
| **GENERAL SCIENCE, SPACE AND TECHNOLOGY** | | | | | | |
| General science and basic research | 3,472 | 4,142 | 4,705 | 3,154 | 3,612 | 4,069 |
| Space flight, research and supporting activities | 13,046 | 13,213 | 13,714 | 12,957 | 12,761 | 12,964 |
| TOTAL | 16,519 | 17,356 | 18,418 | 16,111 | 16,373 | 17,033 |
| **ENERGY** | | | | | | |
| Energy supply | 4,220 | 3,631 | 4,203 | 1,170 | 3,000 | 3,442 |
| Energy conservation | 461 | 506 | 491 | 386 | 463 | 495 |
| Emergency energy preparedness | 336 | 282 | 60 | −235 | 336 | 381 |
| Energy information, policy and regulation | 369 | 264 | 278 | 340 | 226 | 241 |
| TOTAL | 5,386 | 4,683 | 5,032 | 1,662 | 4,026 | 4,560 |
| **NATURAL RESOURCES AND ENVIRONMENT** | | | | | | |
| Pollution control and abatement | 6,150 | 6,685 | 7,013 | 5,853 | 6,131 | 6,383 |
| Water resources | 4,370 | 4,675 | 4,432 | 4,366 | 4,729 | 4,425 |
| Conservation and land management | 3,912 | 4,433 | 4,483 | 4,047 | 4,374 | 4,602 |
| Recreational resources | 2,482 | 2,617 | 2,516 | 2,137 | 2,474 | 2,599 |
| Other natural resources | 2,309 | 2,566 | 2,531 | 2,148 | 2,522 | 2,456 |
| TOTAL | 19,224 | 20,976 | 20,976 | 18,552 | 20,231 | 20,464 |
| **AGRICULTURE** | | | | | | |
| Farm income stabilization | 14,734 | 14,958 | 12,836 | 12,924 | 14,670 | 13,113 |
| Agricultural research and services | 2,497 | 2,716 | 2,601 | 2,259 | 2,550 | 2,621 |
| TOTAL | 17,232 | 17,675 | 15,437 | 15,183 | 17,219 | 15,735 |
| **COMMERCE AND HOUSING CREDIT** | | | | | | |
| Mortgage credit | 7,816 | 2,834 | 2,131 | 5,362 | 3,201 | 3,950 |
| Postal Service subsidy (on budget) | 511 | 511 | 161 | 511 | 511 | 161 |
| Postal Service (off budget) | 3,301 | 2,226 | 4,509 | 1,317 | 825 | 1,647 |
| Deposit insurance | 72,789 | 50,680 | 51,371 | 66,394 | 47,825 | 55,704 |
| Other advancement of commerce | 2,132 | 2,546 | 2,322 | 2,054 | 2,380 | 2,160 |
| TOTAL | 86,548 | 58,797 | 60,494 | 75,639 | 54,741 | 63,623 |
| (On budget) | (83,247) | (56,571) | (55,985) | (74,321) | (53,917) | (61,975) |
| (Off budget) | (3,301) | (2,226) | (4,509) | (1,317) | (825) | (1,647) |
| **TRANSPORTATION** | | | | | | |
| Ground transportation | 19,096 | 23,247 | 25,249 | 19,545 | 21,090 | 21,663 |
| Air transportation | 8,932 | 10,018 | 10,754 | 8,184 | 9,042 | 9,762 |
| Water transportation | 3,122 | 3,242 | 3,389 | 3,148 | 3,633 | 3,396 |
| Other transportation | 251 | 270 | 332 | 223 | 270 | 317 |
| TOTAL | 31,401 | 36,776 | 39,723 | 31,099 | 34,035 | 35,138 |
| **COMMUNITY AND REGIONAL DEVELOPMENT** | | | | | | |
| Community development | 3,694 | 3,786 | 3,318 | 3,543 | 3,911 | 4,047 |
| Area and regional development | 4,061 | 3,749 | 2,781 | 2,743 | 3,148 | 3,012 |
| Disaster relief and insurance | 1 | 1,337 | 527 | 525 | 478 | 556 |
| TOTAL | 7,757 | 8,872 | 6,626 | 6,811 | 7,537 | 7,615 |
| **EDUCATION, TRAINING, EMPLOYMENT, SOCIAL SERVICES** | | | | | | |
| Elementary, secondary and vocational education | 13,130 | 14,173 | 14,904 | 11,372 | 13,052 | 13,841 |
| Higher education | 12,374 | 12,841 | 14,882 | 11,961 | 11,140 | 14,102 |
| Research and general education aids | 1,914 | 2,078 | 2,184 | 1,773 | 1,969 | 2,141 |
| Training and employment | 5,771 | 5,771 | 5,730 | 5,388 | 5,792 | 5,870 |
| Other labor services | 808 | 894 | 966 | 788 | 871 | 942 |
| Social services | 11,735 | 12,043 | 12,950 | 11,526 | 12,204 | 12,667 |
| TOTAL | 45,732 | 47,800 | 51,617 | 42,809 | 45,028 | 49,563 |

# Fiscal 1993 Budget by Function

*(Figures for 1992 and 1993 are estimates; in millions of dollars †)*

| | BUDGET AUTHORITY | | | OUTLAYS | | |
|---|---|---|---|---|---|---|
| | 1991 | 1992 | 1993 | 1991 | 1992 | 1993 |
| **HEALTH** | | | | | | |
| Health-care services | $ 63,880 | $ 83,039 | $ 96,962 | $ 60,723 | $ 82,810 | $ 95,973 |
| Health research and training | 9,877 | 10,724 | 10,939 | 8,899 | 10,070 | 10,643 |
| Consumer and occupational health and safety | 1,646 | 1,764 | 1,582 | 1,560 | 1,724 | 1,563 |
| TOTAL | 75,402 | 95,527 | 109,483 | 71,183 | 94,605 | 108,179 |
| **MEDICARE** | 103,208 | 118,515 | 128,834 | 104,489 | 118,638 | 129,342 |
| **INCOME SECURITY** | | | | | | |
| General retirement and disability insurance | 5,911 | 6,537 | 6,154 | 4,945 | 3,737 | 6,503 |
| Federal employee retirement and disability | 56,954 | 59,110 | 61,572 | 56,106 | 57,718 | 60,193 |
| Unemployment compensation | 24,258 | 29,249 | 27,422 | 27,084 | 36,396 | 29,727 |
| Housing assistance | 19,746 | 21,158 | 20,365 | 17,200 | 19,463 | 21,815 |
| Food and nutrition assistance | 29,435 | 33,058 | 39,531 | 28,481 | 33,561 | 34,064 |
| Other income security | 39,963 | 45,137 | 47,680 | 37,030 | 45,145 | 47,230 |
| TOTAL | 176,266 | 194,249 | 202,723 | 170,846 | 196,020 | 199,532 |
| **SOCIAL SECURITY** | 272,490 | 290,518 | 305,028 | 269,015 | 286,732 | 302,251 |
| (On budget) | (2,722) | (6,078) | (6,434) | (2,619) | (6,078) | (6,434) |
| (Off budget) | (269,768) | (284,440) | (298,593) | (266,395) | (280,654) | (295,817) |
| **VETERANS' BENEFITS AND SERVICES** | | | | | | |
| Income security | 17,490 | 17,231 | 17,744 | 16,961 | 17,193 | 17,381 |
| Education, training and rehabilitation | 830 | 409 | 463 | 427 | 696 | 840 |
| Housing | 730 | 866 | 175 | 85 | 1,153 | 365 |
| Hospital and medical care | 13,194 | 14,189 | 14,884 | 12,889 | 13,727 | 14,653 |
| Other benefits and services | 1,060 | 1,015 | 1,054 | 987 | 1,050 | 1,059 |
| TOTAL | 33,303 | 33,709 | 34,321 | 31,349 | 33,819 | 34,297 |
| **ADMINISTRATION OF JUSTICE** | | | | | | |
| Federal law enforcement activities | 5,952 | 6,629 | 7,074 | 5,661 | 6,422 | 6,668 |
| Federal litigative and judicial activities | 4,614 | 5,051 | 5,723 | 4,352 | 5,029 | 5,648 |
| Federal correctional activities | 1,728 | 2,051 | 2,187 | 1,600 | 1,901 | 2,202 |
| Criminal justice assistance | 853 | 870 | 774 | 663 | 709 | 876 |
| TOTAL | 13,147 | 14,601 | 15,758 | 12,276 | 14,061 | 15,394 |
| **GENERAL GOVERNMENT** | | | | | | |
| Legislative functions | 2,021 | 2,181 | 2,311 | 1,916 | 2,230 | 2,237 |
| Executive direction and management | 188 | 224 | 262 | 190 | 197 | 254 |
| Central fiscal operations | 6,257 | 6,951 | 7,503 | 6,097 | 6,790 | 7,293 |
| General property and records management | 2,095 | 748 | 505 | 657 | 704 | 1,474 |
| Central personnel management | 164 | 171 | 660 | 138 | 167 | 178 |
| General-purpose fiscal assistance | 2,138 | 2,133 | 2,120 | 2,100 | 2,158 | 2,130 |
| Other general government | 1,469 | 1,418 | 1,433 | 1,280 | 1,505 | 1,382 |
| Deductions for offsetting receipts | −718 | −914 | −925 | −718 | −914 | −925 |
| TOTAL | 13,613 | 12,912 | 13,869 | 11,661 | 12,838 | 14,022 |
| **NET INTEREST** | | | | | | |
| Interest on the public debt | 286,004 | 294,485 | 315,848 | 286,004 | 294,485 | 315,848 |
| Interest received by on-budget trust funds | −50,976 | −53,371 | −55,380 | −50,976 | −53,371 | −55,380 |
| Interest received by off-budget trust funds | −20,222 | −23,853 | −26,998 | −20,222 | −23,853 | −26,998 |
| Other interest | −20,698 | −16,913 | −18,786 | −20,266 | −16,948 | −18,848 |
| TOTAL | 194,109 | 200,348 | 214,684 | 194,541 | 200,313 | 214,621 |
| (On budget) | (214,331) | (224,201) | (241,682) | (214,763) | (224,166) | (241,619) |
| (Off budget) | (−20,222) | (−23,853) | (−26,998) | (−20,222) | (−23,853) | (−26,998) |
| **ALLOWANCES** | — | −96 | −464 | — | −96 | −426 |
| **UNDISTRIBUTED OFFSETTING RECEIPTS** | −39,356 | −38,761 | −41,628 | −39,356 | −38,761 | −41,628 |
| (On budget) | (−33,553) | (−32,665) | (−35,144) | (−33,553) | (−32,665) | (−35,144) |
| (Off budget) | (−5,804) | (−6,095) | (−6,484) | (−5,804) | (−6,095) | (−6,484) |
| **TOTAL** | $ 1,398,243 | $ 1,456,925 | $ 1,501,999 | $ 1,323,011 | $ 1,442,477 | $ 1,498,311 |
| (On budget) | (1,151,199) | (1,200,207) | (1,232,378) | (1,081,324) | (1,190,947) | (1,234,328) |
| (Off budget) | (247,043) | (256,718) | (269,621) | (241,687) | (251,530) | (263,983) |

† *Figures may not add due to rounding.*

SOURCE: Fiscal 1993 Budget

# Administration Economic Assumptions

*(Calendar years; dollar amounts in billions)* [1]

| | Actual 1990 | Projections | | | | | | |
|---|---|---|---|---|---|---|---|---|
| | | 1991 | 1992 | 1993 | 1994 | 1995 | 1996 | 1997 |
| **Gross domestic product** | | | | | | | | |
| Dollar levels: | | | | | | | | |
| Current dollars | 5,514 | 5,675 | 5,926 | 6,307 | 6,712 | 7,141 | 7,589 | 8,054 |
| Constant (1987) dollars | 4,885 | 4,848 | 4,919 | 5,066 | 5,218 | 5,374 | 5,532 | 5,689 |
| Implicit price deflator (1987 = 100), annual average | 112.9 | 117.1 | 120.5 | 124.5 | 128.6 | 132.9 | 137.2 | 141.6 |
| Percent change, fourth quarter over fourth quarter: | | | | | | | | |
| Current dollars | 4.1 | 3.5 | 5.4 | 6.5 | 6.4 | 6.4 | 6.2 | 6.1 |
| Constant (1987) dollars | -0.1 | 0.2 | 2.2 | 3.0 | 3.0 | 3.0 | 2.9 | 2.8 |
| Implicit price deflator (1987 = 100) | 4.2 | 3.3 | 3.2 | 3.4 | 3.3 | 3.3 | 3.2 | 3.2 |
| Percent change, year over year: | | | | | | | | |
| Current dollars | 5.1 | 2.9 | 4.4 | 6.4 | 6.4 | 6.4 | 6.3 | 6.1 |
| Constant (1987) dollars | 1.0 | -0.8 | 1.5 | 3.0 | 3.0 | 3.0 | 2.9 | 2.8 |
| Implicit price deflator (1987 = 100) | 4.1 | 3.7 | 2.9 | 3.3 | 3.3 | 3.3 | 3.2 | 3.2 |
| **Gross national product** | | | | | | | | |
| Dollar levels: | | | | | | | | |
| Current dollars | 5,524 | 5,689 | 5,938 | 6,319 | 6,726 | 7,156 | 7,604 | 8,070 |
| Constant (1987) dollars | 4,895 | 4,860 | 4,929 | 5,076 | 5,228 | 5,385 | 5,544 | 5,701 |
| Implicit price deflator (1987 = 100), annual average | 112.9 | 117.1 | 120.5 | 124.5 | 128.6 | 132.9 | 137.2 | 141.6 |
| **Incomes** | | | | | | | | |
| Personal income | 4,680 | 4,832 | 5,037 | 5,378 | 5,712 | 6,084 | 6,458 | 6,854 |
| Wages and salaries | 2,739 | 2,810 | 2,943 | 3,134 | 3,335 | 3,548 | 3,771 | 4,002 |
| Corporate profits before tax | 332 | 313 | 341 | 423 | 456 | 493 | 524 | 556 |
| **Consumer Price Index (all urban)** [2] | | | | | | | | |
| Level (1982-84 = 100), annual average | 130.7 | 136.2 | 140.2 | 144.8 | 149.4 | 154.2 | 159.2 | 164.1 |
| Percent change, fourth quarter over fourth quarter: | 6.2 | 2.9 | 3.1 | 3.3 | 3.2 | 3.2 | 3.2 | 3.1 |
| Percent change, year over year | 5.4 | 4.2 | 3.0 | 3.3 | 3.2 | 3.2 | 3.2 | 3.1 |
| **Unemployment rate, civilian** [3] | | | | | | | | |
| Fourth-quarter level | 5.9 | 6.9 | 6.8 | 6.4 | 6.0 | 5.7 | 5.3 | 5.3 |
| Annual average | 5.5 | 6.7 | 6.9 | 6.5 | 6.1 | 5.8 | 5.4 | 5.3 |
| **Federal pay raise, January (percent)** | 3.6 | 4.1 | 4.2 | 3.7 | 4.7 | 4.7 | 4.5 | 3.5 |
| **Interest rate (percent)** [4] | | | | | | | | |
| 90-day Treasury bills | 7.5 | 5.4 | 4.1 | 4.9 | 5.3 | 5.3 | 5.2 | 5.1 |
| 10-year Treasury notes | 8.6 | 7.9 | 7.0 | 6.9 | 6.7 | 6.6 | 6.6 | 6.6 |

[1] *Based on data available as of Jan. 10, 1992.*
[2] *CPI for urban consumers. Two versions of the CPI were published. The index shown here was that used, as required by law, in calculating automatic adjustments to individual income tax brackets.*
[3] *Percent of civilian labor force, excluding armed forces residing in the United States.*
[4] *Average rate on new issues within period*

SOURCE: Fiscal 1993 Budget

# Budget Authority, Outlays by Agency

*(Fiscal years; in millions of dollars †)*

| AGENCY | BUDGET AUTHORITY | | | OUTLAYS | | |
|---|---|---|---|---|---|---|
| | 1991 actual | 1992 estimate | 1993 proposed | 1991 actual | 1992 estimate | 1993 proposed |
| Legislative Branch | $2,498 | $2,684 | $2,855 | $2,296 | $2,760 | $2,788 |
| The Judiciary | 2,110 | 2,389 | 2,833 | 1,989 | 2,371 | 2,763 |
| Executive Office of the President | 190 | 226 | 264 | 193 | 199 | 255 |
| Funds Appropriated to the President | 15,729 | 25,135 | 11,691 | 11,724 | 11,482 | 11,316 |
| Agriculture | 60,075 | 62,163 | 64,840 | 54,119 | 61,794 | 59,373 |
| Commerce | 2,649 | 2,938 | 2,829 | 2,585 | 2,869 | 2,883 |
| Defense — Military | 290,440 | 276,020 | 266,996 | 261,925 | 294,422 | 277,786 |
| Defense — Civil | 26,492 | 28,015 | 29,221 | 26,543 | 27,890 | 29,250 |
| Education | 27,503 | 29,441 | 32,339 | 25,339 | 26,528 | 30,410 |
| Energy | 16,110 | 16,868 | 17,070 | 12,479 | 15,719 | 16,292 |
| Health and Human Services, except Social Security | 222,913 | 264,623 | 290,418 | 217,969 | 263,409 | 289,342 |
| Health and Human Services, Social Security | 269,768 | 284,440 | 298,593 | 266,395 | 280,654 | 295,817 |
| Housing and Urban Development | 27,634 | 25,165 | 24,323 | 22,751 | 24,184 | 28,141 |
| Interior | 6,884 | 7,007 | 6,333 | 6,097 | 7,098 | 6,542 |
| Justice | 8,966 | 9,873 | 10,745 | 8,244 | 9,367 | 10,354 |
| Labor | 32,565 | 37,855 | 35,601 | 34,040 | 42,286 | 38,443 |
| State | 4,354 | 4,683 | 5,381 | 4,252 | 4,539 | 5,175 |
| Transportation | 30,964 | 36,103 | 38,963 | 30,503 | 33,371 | 34,495 |
| Treasury | 276,222 | 292,239 | 313,734 | 274,295 | 290,613 | 312,114 |
| Veterans Affairs | 33,152 | 33,578 | 34,192 | 31,214 | 33,603 | 34,109 |
| Environmental Protection Agency | 6,004 | 6,504 | 6,785 | 5,769 | 5,948 | 6,164 |
| General Services Administration | 1,959 | 598 | 347 | 487 | 444 | 1,183 |
| National Aeronautics and Space Administration | 14,016 | 14,321 | 14,994 | 13,878 | 13,819 | 14,088 |
| Office of Personnel Management | 36,782 | 36,830 | 39,786 | 34,808 | 36,141 | 37,593 |
| Small Business Administration | 464 | 1,173 | 738 | 613 | 455 | 297 |
| Other independent agencies | 92,354 | 72,132 | 75,372 | 83,060 | 66,593 | 76,547 |
| Allowances | | −96 | −464 | | −96 | −426 |
| Undistributed offsetting receipts | −110,555 | −115,986 | −124,808 | −110,555 | −115,986 | −124,808 |
| (On budget) | (−84,529) | (−88,036) | (−91,326) | (−84,529) | (−88,036) | (−91,326) |
| (Off budget) | (−26,026) | (−29,948) | (−33,482) | (−26,026) | (−29,948) | (−33,482) |
| **TOTAL** | **$1,398,243** | **$1,455,425** | **$1,501,160** | **$1,323,011** | **$1,440,977** | **$1,497,472** |

*† Excludes comprehensive health reform; figures may not add to totals due to rounding; undistributed offsetting receipts not included above.*

SOURCE: Fiscal 1993 Budget

# Function-by-Function Highlights

*President Bush submitted his fiscal 1993 budget according to broad functional categories. Some of the $1.5 trillion in budget authority requested was to be spent in future fiscal years, and some of the $1.5 trillion in outlays came from money appropriated in previous fiscal years. The following summaries refer to outlays unless otherwise designated.*

## DEFENSE

Bush proposed $291 billion in defense-related outlays for the Pentagon and other agencies in fiscal 1993, a $16.3 billion reduction from estimated spending for fiscal 1992.

Excluding the budgetary aftereffects of the Persian Gulf War, he requested $281 billion in budget authority for the Defense Department itself — $10 billion less than the level he had projected a year before. The Pentagon calculated that this would lead to actual outlays of $286 billion in fiscal 1993 — a reduction of $6 billion.

Bush's approach to defense budget-cutting produced a gap between long-range reductions and immediate savings. The president offered no significant cuts in the budget for the military payroll — beyond the five-year, 25 percent reduction already under way — or for operations and maintenance.

Cutting uniformed manpower more rapidly would have required involuntary discharges on a large scale, which Pentagon officials said would shatter the morale of personnel. And they argued that the projected budget for operations and maintenance was essential so that the smaller force that was in the offing could retain its fighting edge.

Instead, Bush accelerated his previously planned cutbacks by cutting more deeply into weapons procurement and development. But because money for such military hardware was doled out to contractors in installments over several years, cuts in budget authority for procurement and research yielded much smaller cuts in immediate outlays.

Of the $281 billion in requested budget authority, $268 billion was earmarked for military programs of the Defense Department (excluding the public works budget of the Army Corps of Engineers).

Defense-related programs conducted by the Energy Department accounted for $12.1 billion. They included $4.8 billion to develop and manufacture nuclear warheads and $4.6 billion to clean up radioactive and other hazardous waste at defense-related Energy Department installations.

The remaining $1.2 billion was for miscellaneous defense-related programs of other agencies.

### Procurement Shift

Bush linked his hardware-heavy defense cuts to the demise of the Soviet Union in two ways:
- Because Russian President Boris N. Yeltsin and leaders of the other former Soviet republics had agreed to radical reductions in nuclear weaponry, Bush proposed a sharp cutback in the production of strategic arms, including: ending production of the B-2 stealth bomber after 20 planes and canceling outright production of long-range, bomber-launched cruise missiles and of powerful nuclear warheads for Trident II submarine-launched missiles.
- On the assumption that Pentagon planners no longer needed to anticipate a massive Soviet weapons program aimed at nullifying the technical superiority of U.S. conventional arms, the budget request assumed a fundamental shift in the Pentagon's weapons procurement strategy.

Under the new approach, Defense Secretary Dick Cheney announced, the Pentagon would continue to fund the development of new prototypes intended to push back the frontiers of weapons technology. But not all of those new weapons would be rushed to the assembly line. Some of the prototypes' novel features would be incorporated into existing designs. Other designs would go into production only after a painstaking development-and-testing pro-

gram had ensured their technical maturity.

Bush sought to cancel production plans for the *Seawolf*-class nuclear submarine and for the Army's Comanche helicopter. On the other hand, he wanted to continue planned production of other high-tech weapons, including Aegis destroyers for the Navy and the Air Force's C-17 cargo plane, as well as to continue development of the Air Force's new F-22 fighter, with the expectation of full-scale production beginning in 1996.

Allowing for changes due to declining inflation, the budget sought to trim $50 billion in budget authority from the $1.7 trillion six-year defense plan Bush unveiled the previous year for fiscal 1992-97. For the same period, the inflation-adjusted reduction in defense outlays was expected to total $27 billion.

### Personnel and Operations

Bush's request for $77.1 billion in budget authority for military personnel costs in fiscal 1993 assumed that the number of active-duty service members would decline from 2 million at the end of fiscal 1991 to 1.86 million at the end of fiscal 1992 and 1.77 million by the end of 1993.

Similarly, Bush proposed slicing the number of National Guard and reserve personnel to slightly more than 1 million, a reduction of 131,000 from the number on the rolls at the end of fiscal 1991. He proposed to fund a 3.3 percent pay raise for both uniformed personnel and civilian employees.

For operations and maintenance (O&M), Bush requested $86.5 billion in budget authority. This would allow combat units to continue training at their existing "operating tempo."

The O&M request also earmarked:
- $9.5 billion for the Pentagon's far-flung health-care program for military personnel and retirees and their dependents;
- $1.5 billion for environmental cleanup;
- $1.3 billion for drug interdiction efforts by the armed services.

### Weapons

For the array of anti-missile defense research programs that made up the Strategic Defense Initiative (SDI), Bush requested a total of $5.3 billion in budget authority, including $1 billion earmarked for defenses against short-range (or "tactical") missiles.

To bring the total fleet of operational B-2 bombers to 20, he sought $2.6 billion in budget authority for four more planes in fiscal 1993 and congressional approval to spend $1 billion that was appropriated for an additional plane in fiscal 1992 but which could not be spent without express congressional approval.

The Navy's procurement request included $3.4 billion in budget authority for four additional destroyers equipped with the Aegis anti-aircraft system. And it included $832 million for a nuclear power plant and other components to be used in an aircraft carrier slated for inclusion in the fiscal 1995 budget.

Major budget requests for aircraft programs included:
- $2.7 billion for eight additional C-17 cargo planes;
- $1.8 billion for 48 F/A-18 fighters plus $1.1 billion to develop a larger version of that plane;
- $2.2 billion to continue development of the F-22 fighter; and
- $443 million to continue development of the Comanche "scout" helicopter.

## AGRICULTURE

Bush requested slightly less in farm subsidies and other agriculture programs — $15.7 billion, or about $1.5 billion less than the estimated cost of the programs in fiscal 1992.

Much of the reduction resulted from a change in the way both Congress and the Bush administration accounted for federal loan guarantees. For example, although the Farmers Home Administration (FmHA) was slated to spend nearly $1.6 billion less in fiscal 1993, most of that could be attributed to the new loan accounting

practices as set out in the 1991 Credit Reform Act (PL 101-508). Under the new law, the budget had to reflect the expected loss to the government from loans in the year they were issued.

The largest portion of the agriculture budget was for the Commodity Credit Corporation, the agency that funneled price- and income-support payments to farmers. The budget assumed about $11.7 billion in outlays in fiscal 1993, compared with nearly $12 billion in fiscal 1992.

However, spending for farm subsidies actually was slated to increase $1 billion in fiscal 1993, mainly because more than $1 billion spent on disaster assistance to farmers in fiscal 1992 was not expected to be needed again and could be shifted to the subsidies.

In contrast to previous years, Bush did not propose any major changes to existing farm law. His budget did include a proposal to stop any federal payments to farmers with non-farm income that exceeded $100,000 a year. Bush estimated that this would save $65 million in fiscal 1993.

Bush left two major export programs unchanged from fiscal 1992. He proposed to allow $5.7 billion in new loan commitments under the Export Credit program, which provided loan guarantees for commodity sales abroad. And he recommended that the Export Enhancement Program use $1.2 billion in government-owned commodities to encourage exporters to lower their prices — the same amount as in fiscal 1992.

Some farm-state lawmakers had hoped the president would include more funds for export programs in his budget to send a signal to other foreign exporters, mainly the European Community, where governments heavily subsidized their farmers. If negotiations under the General Agreement on Tariffs and Trade (GATT) to reduce farm subsidies worldwide did not succeed by June 30, 1992, the secretary of Agriculture was required to increase export spending by $1 billion beginning in fiscal 1994.

Some members of Congress — most notably Rep. Pat Roberts, R-Kan. — had hoped that the president would include that $1 billion in the fiscal 1993 budget to spur negotiations and reassure American farmers.

Bush did include an extra $80 million in loan guarantee money that Agriculture Department officials called a "GATT adjustment." Should the negotiations fail, the administration could use the $80 million to fund up to $2.6 billion in export credit loans, officials said. *(1990 Almanac, p. 344)*

Domestically, the budget included $136 million in fiscal 1993 outlays — the estimated cost associated with FmHA programs to extend up to $2.7 billion in farm operating and land loans. The administration wanted to continue its shift toward providing fewer direct government loans and instead offering to guarantee more private loans.

## COMMERCE/COMMUNITY DEVELOPMENT

On the surface, the $71.2 billion that Bush requested for these two budget functions looked like a major reduction from the $99.2 billion he sought the year before. But the lower figures were based on credit reforms enacted in 1990 and on proposed changes in the way the government kept track of deposit insurance funds. Those funds constituted the bulk of the money sought for commerce, housing credit, and community and regional development.

● **Deposit Insurance.** Net outlays by the Federal Deposit Insurance Corporation (FDIC) to cover the cost of closing failed banks were projected to increase to $22.5 billion in fiscal 1993 from $12.5 billion in 1992.

The administration warned that unless the banking overhaul proposal that Congress rejected in 1991 was enacted, the costs of bank failures over the next five years could outstrip available resources, in turn requiring a taxpayer bailout for the FDIC similar to the one under way for failed savings and loans associations.

For the Resolution Trust Corporation (RTC), the agency created in 1989 to close failed thrifts, net outlays were projected to fall from $25 billion in 1992 to $19 billion in 1993. The administration renewed its call for Congress to give the RTC another $55 billion.

In the case of both the FDIC and the RTC, net outlays repre-sented losses incurred covering deposits in failed banks and thrifts, as well as costs and income associated with the purchase and eventual sale of assets in those institutions.

The outlay estimates reflected the administration's proposal to move the treatment of deposit insurance costs to so-called accrual accounting and away from the budget's traditional cash accounting method, which recorded income and receipts in the year they actually occurred. Instead, costs would have "accrued" before they were actually paid. The result was that some future costs would be swept into earlier years, and some costs (which would be offset by future collections) would not show on the government's books.

Bush warned that if Congress did not overhaul banking laws to allow banks to become more profitable, the $30 billion Congress allowed the industry to borrow in 1991 would not be enough to cover bank failures through 1997, as originally estimated. Without changes in federal law — for example, to allow banks to open branch offices across state lines — losses could be as much as $11 billion higher, the administration said.

● **Housing credit.** The president's budget allowed a slight increase — from $74.8 billion to $77.7 billion — in the amount of securities guaranteed by the Government National Mortgage Association (Ginnie Mae), the federal secondary market for home loans pooled by the Federal Housing Administration and the Department of Veterans Affairs. Under new accounting rules for loan guarantees, the White House estimated that Ginnie Mae guarantees would result in $6.9 million in fiscal 1993 outlays, up from $6.6 million in outlays in fiscal 1992.

● **Community development.** The budget assumed $3.3 billion in outlays for fiscal 1993 for the Community Development Block Grant program, administered by the Department of Housing and Urban Development. That was a $200 million increase over fiscal 1992 outlays. However, the outlay estimates did not reflect Bush's proposal to cut back the program, which was very popular among state and local governments. For fiscal 1993, Bush proposed $2.9 billion in new budget authority, down from $3.4 billion in budget authority in fiscal 1992.

● **Small Business Administration.** Bush sought to trim the Small Business Administration budget to $297 million in fiscal 1993 from $455 million in outlays in fiscal 1992. Much of the cuts were to be absorbed by the business loan program. The proposal attempted to lower the 19 percent default rate on guaranteed loans by increasing the share of default risk borne by private lenders.

● **Postal Service.** The budget assumed $122 million in outlays to reimburse the Postal Service for revenue lost through a subsidized mail program, a $348 million reduction from the fiscal 1992 level. Savings were to be achieved by tightening eligibility rules for recipients of postage rate subsidies. Nonprofit groups that received postage subsidies also would have been required to pay about 68 percent of overhead costs, at an estimated savings of $265 million.

● **Federal Communications Commission.** Bush proposed to expedite the transfer of 45 megahertz of government-held radio spectrum to the private sector. The frequencies were to be allocated by auction, rather than the existing method of lottery. Receipts from the auction would not have showed up until fiscal 1995.

## EDUCATION/TRAINING

Bush's budget assumed $49.6 billion in fiscal 1993 spending for education and training programs covered by the Departments of Education and Labor, up from $45 billion in estimated outlays for fiscal 1992. Spending for all of the Education Department's elementary, secondary, vocational and higher education programs was expected to reach $30.4 billion in outlays in fiscal 1993, up from $26.5 billion in outlays in fiscal 1992.

Nearly $8 billion of the fiscal 1993 Education budget was to cover the costs of mandatory programs such as the guaranteed student loan program, for which the government's obligations were set by law.

For most existing elementary and secondary education programs, Bush targeted moderate increases. Spending for the Chapter 1 compensatory education program, for example, rose to $6.6 billion in outlays in fiscal 1993, up from $6.2 billion.

Bush continued to hammer away at the theme of school "choice," offering proposals to send money to both public and private schools. Some of the largest increases in the Education budget were to fund his so-called America 2000 programs. Education Secretary Lamar Alexander said he would resubmit legislation to Congress to create and fund Bush's America 2000 initiatives with $767.5 million in new budget authority in fiscal 1993.

Of that, $500 million was to go for matching choice grants of $500 per child for families earning under approximately $40,000 a year, with states expected to provide another $500 per child. Families could use the $1,000 to send their child either to a public or private school.

Spending for higher education programs was also expected to rise under the Bush budget, from $11.1 billion in fiscal 1992 outlays to $14.1 billion in fiscal 1993 outlays.

Much of that increase was the result of previous appropriations. But Bush also sought increases for the future. In his requests for guaranteed student loans, Pell grants and other higher education aid programs, he asked for $13.7 billion in new budget authority in fiscal 1993, a 17 percent increase over the $11.7 billion enacted in fiscal 1992.

The largest increase was for Pell grants, named for Sen. Claiborne Pell, D-R.I. Bush asked for $6.6 billion in new budget authority, up from $5.5 billion in fiscal 1992. He wanted to raise the maximum Pell grant from $2,400 to $3,700 per student. And in a major switch from the 1992 budget, in which Bush proposed to limit grants only to families earning less than $10,000 a year, he also wanted to provide Pell grants to students from families earning up to $50,000 a year (for a family of four). At the time, eligibility was limited to families earning $30,000 or less.

For training and employment programs administered by the Labor Department, the budget showed virtually no increase in spending, allocating $5.9 billion in outlays for fiscal 1993 compared with $5.8 billion in fiscal 1992.

Bush proposed killing the $72 million Trade Adjustment Assistance program, created in 1988 to train workers who lost their jobs due to foreign competition.

## ENERGY

Although Congress had not endorsed the administration's national energy strategy, it was assumed in the energy portions of Bush's budget.

The budget called for boosting some energy research programs, as directed by the strategy. And it assumed that the administration would soon draw revenue from oil and gas leases in the Arctic National Wildlife Refuge, although the refuge was still legally off-limits.

Bush assumed $4.6 billion in energy related outlays for fiscal 1993, a 13.3 percent increase over the administration's projected fiscal 1992 spending. But some of that boost was related to expenses at the Tennessee Valley Authority, which was self-financing.

The budget recommended $4 billion in new budget authority, a 4.7 percent increase, for energy supply research and development. But the administration wanted to terminate 10 science-related university building projects with a combined $85 million price tag that congressional appropriators inserted in the Energy Department's fiscal 1992 spending bill.

Within that overall research funding, proposed spending on solar and renewable energy research would have roughly kept pace with inflation. Conservation research and development was to rise to $366 million in spending authority, but the administration also wanted to cut some conservation assistance grants.

Coal-related research and development was to be cut almost in half, to $154 million in budget authority for fiscal 1993. But full funding, $500 million in budget authority, was requested for an ongoing series of public-private demonstration programs to promote cleaner ways to burn coal.

Bush requested $360 million, close to a 7 percent increase in budget authority, for fusion energy. However, the administration abandoned plans to build its own fusion reactor, called the Burn-

ing Plasma Experiment, and was focusing on participation in an international fusion energy project.

● **Power marketing authorities.** Bush revived controversial plans to raise the interest rates the five power marketing companies paid the Treasury on past federal hydropower loans. That would have boosted electric rates for customers of the five agencies, which sold power from those hydropower projects and brought in an estimated $399 million in fiscal 1993.

● **Uranium enrichment.** The Energy Department produced enriched uranium and sold it as fuel for nuclear power plants. The budget would have slowed spending on a promising new enrichment technology while Congress debated whether to turn the enterprise into a private corporation. It also proposed assessing a cleanup fee on nuclear power producers to help cover cleanup costs at enrichment facilities.

● **Strategic Petroleum Reserve.** The budget anticipated buying 9.1 million additional barrels for the oil stockpile in fiscal 1993, a fill rate that would have left the reserve far short of Congress' 1 billion-barrel goal. However, the administration also planned to explore alternative financing arrangements to fill the reserve.

## ENVIRONMENT

Environmental and natural resource programs, which received no mention in Bush's State of the Union address, were slated to grow a modest 1.2 percent to $20.5 billion in fiscal 1993 outlays.

Bush assumed a fair amount of dollar shuffling, enabling outlays to be boosted to $2.6 billion for recreation programs governmentwide and to $6.4 billion for anti-pollution programs.

Despite administration calls for relaxing wetlands protections, Bush proposed $812 million, a 35 percent increase, in budget authority for wetlands programs.

The bulk of the proposed new spending was for a key wetlands conservation program at the Agriculture Department aimed at encouraging farmers to remove wetlands from farm production and an Interior Department program that sought to restore coastal wetlands.

Bush proposed $229 million in budget authority for the Environmental Protection Agency (EPA) to implement and enforce the requirements of the 1990 Clean Air Act amendments. That was a $42 million increase in budget authority over fiscal 1992. Bush proposed $539.4 million in total budget authority to implement and enforce the original Clean Air Act.

Bush's proposed increases for anti-pollution programs covering sewage, oil spills and hazardous wastes at federal facilities and elsewhere. That included $340 million approved by Congress in fiscal 1992 for direct grants to six large cities — Boston, New York, Los Angeles, San Diego, Seattle and Baltimore — to construct secondary wastewater-treatment plants.

The budget proposed $1.8 billion in budget authority for the hazardous-waste cleanup program known as "superfund" — 8 percent more than Congress approved in fiscal 1992.

Bush recommended $1.9 billion in budget authority to continue the "America the Beautiful" program, which provided money to plant trees and buy land in national parks and recreation areas. This represented a 17 percent increase over funding levels approved by Congress in fiscal 1992. It included 1,000 more seasonal park rangers and $139 million to meet Bush's 1988 campaign goal of planting a billion trees a year.

Bush recommended $1.4 billion in budget authority for the Interior Department's National Park Service, $10 million less than the fiscal 1992 level. The agency planned to ask Congress to increase entrance fees at 10 major national parks to $10 in an effort to raise $13 million in fiscal 1993. Bush assumed $2.6 billion in total outlays for recreational resources, a 5 percent increase.

A program to repair federal parks, called Legacy 99, was to get $800 million in spending authority.

## FOREIGN AFFAIRS

After reaffirming the U.S. victory in the Cold War during his State of the Union address, Bush sent a budget to Congress that contained a substantial increase in aid for adversaries from that

conflict, the former republics of the Soviet Union.

That aid initiative and increased contributions for United Nations peacekeeping forces were the most significant signs of change in Bush's request for international affairs. He sought $18 billion in outlays in fiscal 1993.

The budget function covered the State Department's operations and U.S. participation in a host of international organizations, in addition to economic and military assistance programs.

In its initiative for the post-Soviet era, the administration sought $620 million in new budget authority for technical and humanitarian aid over two years to help the newly independent republics ease their transition to democracy. Most of the assistance, $470 million, was included in the fiscal 1993 budget request.

The administration sought $700 million in new budget authority over two years for U.N. operations to support peace agreements in El Salvador, Cambodia and elsewhere. The first half of the money was sought as an amendment to the still-pending foreign aid request for fiscal 1992.

But Bush also asked to continue high levels of military and economic aid for longtime allies in the struggle against global communism, particularly the handful of countries that hosted NATO military bases.

He requested loans and grants totaling more than $1 billion in assistance for Turkey, Greece and Portugal, about the level provided in fiscal 1991, the most reliable basis for comparisons since a foreign aid appropriations bill had not yet been enacted for fiscal 1992.

Longstanding technical differences between procedures used by the State Department and OMB in calculating the international affairs budget also complicated comparisons. According to the State Department, outlays in the fiscal 1993 request amounted to $20.6 billion, with new budget authority of $22.1 billion.

The administration had requested a $12.2 billion increase in the U.S. contribution to the International Monetary Fund (IMF) in fiscal 1992, pushing the overall international affairs budget for that year to $34.5 billion, according to the State Department. Excluding IMF funding, the request for budget authority in fiscal 1993 was virtually unchanged from the 1992 request, according to department officials.

State Department officials said that budget authority for military aid had been reduced by 11 percent from the administration's fiscal 1992 budget request to help fund new initiatives. But the $4.5 billion request in budget authority for all forms of military assistance in fiscal 1993, including loans, represented a slight increase over the amount provided in the fiscal 1992 foreign operations bill approved by the House in 1991 (HR 2621).

The administration sharply reduced its military aid request for three countries: Pakistan, the Philippines and El Salvador. Most aid for Pakistan had been cut off since 1990, when Bush failed to certify that Islamabad did not possess a nuclear device. Under law, that certification was required for aid to be provided.

The administration, which had sought $100 million in military aid for Pakistan in fiscal 1992, requested no such assistance in fiscal 1993. Because of budget constraints, military aid for Pakistan "really just couldn't make the cut," said Robert Bauerlein, an aide to Deputy Secretary of State Lawrence S. Eagleburger.

Aid for the Philippines had declined in importance because of the ongoing closure of U.S. bases in that country. The State Department reduced its request for military aid to the Philippines from $200 million in fiscal 1992 to $47.5 million. The military aid request for El Salvador was more than halved, from $85 million to $41.4 million, after a peace agreement was concluded ending the country's long-running civil war.

But the administration reduced military aid only slightly for three of the remaining "base rights" countries — Greece, Turkey and Portugal. In addition, Bush requested $27 million in military assistance for Jordan, which was roundly condemned on Capitol Hill for siding with Iraq during the Persian Gulf War.

As in past years, Israel and Egypt dominated the aid budget, receiving a combined $5.3 billion in military and economic assistance under the administration's request — about one-third of the total funding for foreign aid.

Bush's budget did not mention Israel's controversial request for $10 billion in U.S. loan guarantees.

## HEALTH/MEDICARE

Bush's health budget was most notable for what was left behind on the cutting room floor — a long-awaited plan to overhaul the nation's health-care system was eliminated at the last minute after complaints, both substantive and political, from congressional Republicans.

What remained, however, was one of the largest functions in the budget — a total of $237.5 billion in outlays for fiscal 1993, an increase of more than 11 percent from the estimated $213 billion in fiscal 1992 outlays.

By far the most far-reaching health proposal in the budget was a cap on the growth of most mandatory federal programs, including the huge and fast-growing Medicare and Medicaid. Medicare, projected to cost $129.3 billion in outlays in fiscal 1993, provided health coverage to 34 million elderly and disabled recipients. Medicaid, a joint federal-state program providing health services for an estimated 31 million poor people, was expected to cost of $84.5 billion in fiscal 1993 outlays, more than twice the $34.6 billion the program cost as recently as fiscal 1989.

A White House fact sheet suggested that a new entitlement cap would work by combining all such programs (except Social Security), adjusting the total each year for increases in eligible participants and general inflation, then allowing a specific growth rate above that. The growth rate would be higher (an average of 2.5 percent) before enactment of "comprehensive health reform" than after, when it would drop to an average of 1.6 percent annually.

Under the plan, projected increases above the cap required Congress to go back and trim the programs to bring them into compliance, and failure to make those cuts triggered automatic cuts.

While both Republicans and Democrats agreed that the spiraling costs of Medicare and Medicaid needed to be brought under control, few suggested that such a politically perilous remedy as capping total costs was likely to be approved in an election year.

Another Bush proposal, first put forward in 1991, was to triple the premium paid by higher-income beneficiaries for the optional portion of Medicare. Under existing law, beneficiaries in the so-called Part B program, which underwrote physician and outpatient services, paid a monthly premium equal to 25 percent of the program's costs. In fiscal 1992 the amount was $31.80 a month. The remaining 75 percent of the program was covered by general revenues.

Bush proposed to turn that around by requiring individuals with annual incomes higher than $100,000 and couples with earnings over $125,000 to pay a monthly premium equal to 75 percent of the cost of the program ($95.40 in 1992), thus reducing the government's subsidy to 25 percent. The proposal was expected to raise an estimated $313 million in fiscal 1992 outlays and a total of $3.1 million over six years.

Another oft-proposed and oft-rejected change was to require all state and local government workers and their employers to pay for the hospital insurance portion of Medicare. Under existing law, only those hired after March 31, 1986, were required to pay the 1.45 percent payroll tax. The proposal was expected to generate an estimated $1.25 billion in fiscal 1993 outlays.

Bush also renewed proposals for two user-fees. One was to require nursing homes and other health facilities to pay for government inspections required for participation in Medicare and Medicaid; the other was to underwrite the costs to the Food and Drug Administration for processing new drug applications.

As was often the case in election years, the budget included increases of varying sizes for popular programs.

The National Institutes of Health, for example, were to get a nearly 5 percent boost to $9.4 billion in new budget authority, up from $8.9 billion in new budget authority in fiscal 1992.

Also pegged for increases were programs aimed at preventing disease — including ones to screen low-income women for breast and cervical cancer ($70 million in new budget authority, up from

$50 million in fiscal 1992) and to provide childhood immunizations ($349 million in new budget authority, up from $297 million in fiscal 1992).

Finally, the plan included increases of $155 million in new budget authority to expand the availability of health care through such programs as community health centers (up $90 million to $684 million), and the National Health Service Corps, which placed doctors in rural, inner-city and other underserved areas ($120 million, up from $100 million in fiscal 1992).

Bush also sought to more than double the "Healthy Start" program, a pilot project to decrease infant mortality in 15 selected areas around the country. Bush asked for $143 million in new budget authority, up from $64 million in fiscal 1992. He asked for $139 million the previous year, but Congress was reluctant to fund the initiative because the administration proposed taking some of the money out of other infant-mortality programs.

## INCOME/SOCIAL SECURITY

Income security programs, including food, nutrition, housing and unemployment compensation, were slated to receive a small increase, resulting in outlays of $501.8 billion in fiscal 1993 compared with $482.8 billion in 1992. However, Bush wanted to cut a number of individual programs, such as low-income energy assistance and some housing initiatives for the poor.

He called for a slight increase for Social Security from an administration estimate of $286.7 billion in outlays in fiscal 1992 to $302.3 billion in fiscal 1993. The increase included a projected 3 percent cost of living adjustment.

Other spending categories included:

● **Unemployment.** Bush budgeted $29.7 billion in outlays in fiscal 1993 to cover the cost of federal and state unemployment benefits, compared with estimated spending of $36.4 billion in outlays in fiscal 1992. These figures represented not only the federal extended benefits program and pending legislation to boost those benefits, but also the states' unemployment benefits program and federal and state administrative costs.

● **Housing.** Bush continued to stress economic empowerment of the poor while killing some existing programs and cutting the overall housing budget.

The housing assistance fund, which covered subsidized housing, public housing operating subsidies, emergency shelter for the homeless and new initiatives, was budgeted for $21.8 billion in outlays in fiscal 1993, a slight increase from $19.5 billion in fiscal 1992. However, outlays in housing mainly reflected previous funding requests. Bush requested $20.4 billion in new budget authority, a decrease from the $21.2 billion in new budget authority in fiscal 1992.

The president's budget eliminated new construction of public and American Indian housing, housing for people with AIDS and subsidized rental certificates.

He asked for a big boost for his new HOPE program — Homeownership and Opportunity for People Everywhere — which helped low-income and public housing tenants buy apartments and houses. Bush asked for $1 billion in new budget authority for HOPE, with fiscal 1993 outlays estimated at $118 million. In fiscal 1992, Congress appropriated $361 million in budget authority for HOPE, although only $7 million of that was expected to result in fiscal 1992 outlays.

By contrast, Congress appropriated $1.5 billion in new budget authority for fiscal 1992 for the HOME Investment Partnerships program, a Democratic initiative providing matching block grants to states and local governments to build or renovate affordable housing. Never a fan of the HOME program, Bush asked for only $700 million in new budget authority.

Bush also proposed to cut several other housing programs, including subsidized housing for low-income families, public housing operating subsidies, low-rent public housing loans and transitional housing and emergency shelters for the homeless. He requested $8.1 billion in budget authority for subsidized housing programs, such as Section 8 vouchers, down from $8.3 billion in fiscal 1992.

Construction grants to build Section 202 housing for the elderly and disabled decreased dramatically under Bush's plan. He proposed spending $54.4 million to build 822 units in fiscal 1993. But in fiscal 1992, budget authority of $430.5 million was allocated to build 6,727 units.

● **LIHEAP.** As in previous years, Bush requested controversial cuts in the popular Low Income Home Energy Assistance Program, which provided grants to states, Indian tribes and U.S. territories to help low-income families pay heating, cooling and weatherization costs. He assumed $1.07 billion in budget authority for the program, down from $1.5 billion in fiscal 1992.

Although Congress had regularly provided more for LIHEAP than Bush requested, funding had decreased since fiscal 1991, when spending totaled $1.6 billion in budget authority.

● **Nutrition.** Bush expected spending for the food stamp program to hover at $22.7 billion in fiscal 1993 outlays, the same as the 1992 spending level. But that figure did not reflect an additional $5.3 billion in new budget authority that he requested to hold "in reserve" for the program in case economic tough times pushed more people onto the food stamp rolls.

Bush included some boosts in nutrition programs as part of his theme of increasing funding to assist poor children. Spending for the Women, Infants and Children program was slated to increase to $2.8 billion in outlays for 1993, a slight increase over the 1992 figure of $2.6 billion.

Bush included $6.9 billion in outlays for subsidies for other child nutrition programs, such as the school lunch and breakfast programs and day-care homes for poor children, an increase of $340 million, or 5 percent, over fiscal 1992.

● **Pensions.** The administration proposed a change in the accounting procedure for the Pension Benefit Guaranty Corporation, the federal agency that safeguarded employee pension plans, reducing outlays by $2.5 billion in fiscal 1993 and a total of $15.6 billion over five years, including 1992.

● **Federal employees.** Federal employees were to receive a small increase in benefits under civilian retirement and disability programs, raising outlays from $34.4 billion in fiscal 1992 to $35.4 billion in 1993. Military retirement benefits were to increase from $24.3 billion in outlays in 1992 to $25.6 billion in 1993.

## LAW

Once again stressing America's siege of drugs and crime, Bush requested $15.4 billion in outlays for federal law enforcement and other justice programs, up from $14.1 billion in fiscal 1992.

The budget included $1.9 billion in net outlays for the FBI, $1.8 billion for prisons and $801 million for U.S. attorneys. Spending for prisons and U.S. attorneys was slated to go up 10 percent and 11 percent, respectively. The FBI, which had grown significantly in recent years, was to receive only 2 percent more.

Overall, Bush did not seek as high a percentage increase for agencies engaged in the administration of justice as he had in the past. The 9.5 percent increase in fiscal 1993 outlays contrasted with a 15 percent increase in Bush's 1992 budget and a 20 percent increase in his 1991 request. The smaller increase was in part an acknowledgment of the growing sentiment on Capitol Hill that law enforcement agencies could only absorb money so fast. Since Bush took office in 1989, the Justice Department's budget had risen nearly 70 percent, according to department officials.

In a policy change that required congressional approval, Bush wanted convicts to pay for their first year in prison. The administration estimated that it cost the Treasury $18,000 a year per inmate (excluding construction costs) and that about one-fifth of all the newly sentenced inmates could afford to pay the cost. The first-year "user fee" could raise $48 million a year, the White House said.

## SCIENCE/TECHNOLOGY

Bush again proposed boosting spending on science and technology programs, although the requested increases were less dramatic than they were the year before.

His request for outlays in the science and technology portion of

the budget rose about 4 percent, to $17 billion for fiscal 1993.

About three-fourths of that, or $13 billion, was for space flight and related programs. The remainder was for science programs run by the National Science Foundation, the Energy Department and, to a much lesser extent, the Defense Department.

Overall federal research and development, which cut across several departments and budget categories, was slated to rise enough to keep pace with inflation. Bush requested $76.6 billion in new budget authority for research and development, a 3 percent increase. Civilian research would continue to grow as a percentage of that spending, although defense-related research continued to represent more than half the total.

Research spending on advanced materials rose about 10 percent to $1.8 billion, reflecting a proposed new interagency-initiative.

● **NASA.** Bush requested just under $15 billion in new budget authority for the National Aeronautics and Space Administration, a 5 percent increase over fiscal 1992.

Much of that boost was in an 11 percent increase in budget authority, to $2.25 billion, for the space station *Freedom.* To accommodate that increase, NASA officials cut an advanced solid rocket motor program favored by Congress and a comet and asteroid exploration mission. The rocket motor program was to have speeded construction of the space station by lifting larger loads of equipment into space.

NASA also sought funding for preparations for two new robotic missions to the moon to provide mapping information in advance of Bush's stated goal of a manned mission.

The budget included $250 million in spending authority for developing a new launch system, with the money split evenly between NASA and the Defense Department. NASA's budget also included $80 million for its share of a national aerospace plane, another joint project with the Pentagon. The project aimed to design a plane capable of taking off from a conventional airport and going straight into low Earth orbit, similar to the space shuttle. Congress nearly eliminated proposed spending for this project in 1991.

Space shuttle operations were to receive $3.1 billion in spending authority, for a planned eight missions during fiscal 1993.

● **Superconducting super collider.** Bush wanted funding for the giant atom smasher to shoot up 34 percent to $650 million in fiscal 1993 budget authority.

● **Human genome.** Bush recommended $175 million in new spending authority for the government's intricate gene-mapping project, a 7 percent increase — $110 million for the National Institutes of Health and $65 million for the Energy Department.

● **Global change.** The budget included $1.4 billion in spending authority for an interagency program to study the Earth's climate, a 24 percent increase. NASA was to supply $891 million of that funding. NASA's Mission to Planet Earth program, including its Earth Observing System, was a key participant in the project.

● **National Science Foundation.** Bush once again slated the foundation for a large increase, up 17.6 percent to more than $3 billion in spending authority. However, some of the increase resulted from shifting a program out of Defense.

● **Supercomputers.** Bush allotted $803 million in budget authority for an interagency high-performance computing project, a 23 percent increase. Nine agencies worked on the project, which sought to advance supercomputer systems.

## TRANSPORTATION

Bush's request included $35.1 billion in fiscal 1993 outlays for transportation programs, 3.2 percent more than the $34 billion administration estimate of fiscal 1992 spending. Most of this proposed spending fell within the Transportation Department, which proposed outlays of $34.5 billion.

Bush recommended just $3 billion in budget authority for mass transit, compared with the $3.8 billion Congress appropriated in fiscal 1992. The proposed level was far below the $5.2 billion authorized in the landmark 1991 surface transportation reauthorization (PL 102-240) signed into law in December 1991. *(1991 Almanac, p. 137)*

Most of the cut was due to a longstanding request to eliminate operating assistance to urban areas with 500,000 or more people. Acting Transportation Secretary James B. Busey said local mass transit systems could still receive an additional $10 billion because the 1991 law provided new flexibility that allowed states to shift funds from roads to mass transit.

A pleasant surprise to a largely displeased transit industry was an administration proposal to encourage commuting on mass transit by raising the cap on tax-free transit fares offered as an employment benefit from $21 a month to $60 a month, bringing it on equal footing with similar parking benefits.

Bush proposed $17.6 billion in outlays for highway construction, safety and maintenance and called on Congress to raise to $18.9 billion the spending limit on the Highway Trust Fund. That represented a 13 percent increase over the $16.8 billion spending limit set in fiscal 1992.

The administration estimated that the highway funds would create 1 million jobs in fiscal 1993.

For the second year, the administration requested operating and capital subsidies for the passenger rail system Amtrak, but at levels below what Amtrak estimated was needed. Bush wanted $343 million in budget authority for Amtrak in fiscal 1993, $163 million less than it got in 1992. He requested no funds to improve the rail line in the Northeast corridor, a favorite project among East Coast lawmakers on the Appropriations committees.

Bush also ignored a provision in the surface transportation law that authorized a new program to develop a prototype magnetic levitation train system. Although Congress authorized $45 million for the program, Bush requested no funding for it. Instead, he recommended $28 million in budget authority for the Federal Railroad Administration and the Army Corps of Engineers to complete safety studies on high-speed rail options.

Bush wanted to boost budget authority for aviation programs to $9.4 billion, up from $8.9 billion in fiscal 1992, and increase outlays for the Federal Aviation Administration (FAA) trust fund to $7.3 billion, up from $5.7 billion in fiscal 1992. FAA operations got $4.6 billion in outlays, up from $4.4 billion in fiscal 1992, in part to provide for 150 more air traffic controllers.

Bush proposed a $1.9 billion cap on the Airport and Airways Trust Fund obligations for airport grants, the same level as in fiscal 1992, and assumed that airports would raise an additional $1 billion through new passenger facility charges levied on airline passengers.

## VETERANS

Bush budgeted $34.3 billion in outlays for veterans programs in fiscal 1993, a slight increase over the $33.8 billion spent in fiscal 1992.

For the third year in a row, he assumed an increase of nearly $1 billion to beef up medical care for veterans, bringing outlays for hospital and medical care to $14.7 billion.

The Department of Veterans Affairs (VA) had been plagued by charges that the quality of health care at some of its hospitals was substandard. About $58.6 million of the money was to go for hiring more health-care workers to help limit the work hours of VA physicians.

The proposal also sought to convert 787 hospital beds to nursing home care to accommodate the rising number of veterans who required long-term medical care.

Bush included $840 million in proposed outlays for fiscal 1993 for veterans' education, training and rehabilitation, up from $696 million in outlays in fiscal 1992.

The total VA budget included a 3 percent cost of living adjustment for disabled veterans and for spouses and children of veterans who died of service-related injuries. That figure, based on the Consumer Price Index, was the same as the annual increase for Social Security beneficiaries.

The budget included $365 million in outlays in fiscal 1993 for housing programs for veterans, a drop from $1.2 billion in fiscal 1992. The administration wanted to achieve the savings through proposed legislation it said would make VA housing programs more cost-efficient. ∎

## Deficit Projections

*(Fiscal years; dollar amounts in billions †)*

The following shows the final deficits for 1991-92 and the Office of Management and Budget projections for 1992-97 assuming enactment of President Bush's budget. The revised deficit reflects the actual 1992 number and OMB midsession estimates for later years; changes are due primarily to reduction in anticipated costs for the savings and loan bailout.

|  | 1991 | 1992 | 1993 | 1994 | 1995 | 1996 | 1997 |
|---|---|---|---|---|---|---|---|
| Outlays | 1,323.0 * | 1,475.6 | 1,515.0 | 1,474.0 | 1,536.0 | 1,608.6 | 1,685.2 |
| Revenues | 1,054.3 * | 1,071.8 | 1,159.1 | 1,257.6 | 1,337.5 | 1,421.9 | 1,496.8 |
| Deficit | 268.7 * | 403.8 | 356.0 | 216.4 | 198.6 | 186.7 | 188.4 |
| Deficit (Revised) |  | 290.2 * | 341.0 | 274.2 | 218.4 | 217.7 | 236.7 |

† Totals include Social Security, which was off budget; totals may not add due to rounding.
* Actual

SOURCE: 1992 Budget

*Continued from p. 87*

to meeting the fundamental, long-term needs of the nation's economy and society" and derided the proposal for providing "a little something for everyone in the short run, to be paid for by our children in the long-run."

Senate Budget Chairman Jim Sasser, D-Tenn., called the Bush proposals "the ultimate trickle-down package" that "will produce, I think, virtually no immediate economic stimulus." He criticized Bush's attempts to offset his recovery package with "unrealistic entitlement cuts and user fees ... [that] have been rejected by the Congress time after time after time, some starting back as far ago as 1981."

Republicans sprang to Bush's defense. Pete V. Domenici of New Mexico, a key Senate pragmatist and ranking Republican on the Budget Committee, praised Bush for coming up with a "budget-neutral approach" that has "some very significant incentives.... When you add all of these up together, we have a very positive budget approach."

### Deficit Ignored

While both parties were policing each other for strict adherence to the budget rules, neither had to pay much attention to the overall size of the deficit. The rules penalized willful overspending, but they were indifferent to the year-to-year growth of the deficit.

Nothing drove that point home more starkly than Bush's announcement in his State of the Union address that he was immediately reducing the amount withheld from employee paychecks in an attempt to give consumers more spending money. Darman said the change, which did not require congressional approval, would lower tax receipts substantially enough to raise the fiscal 1992 deficit by as much as $15 billion.

A voluntary $15 billion boost to the deficit would have been unthinkable under the old Gramm-Rudman antideficit rules, but the new rules imposed no penalty on a deficit increase that did not result from legislation. The idea was to avoid holding Congress responsible for deficit-boosting forces beyond its control, such as recessions. But the byproduct was to make the deficit a political non-issue.

After incorporating the effect of the withholding change, the Office of Management and Budget (OMB) raised its estimate of the fiscal 1992 deficit to an unprecedented $403.8 billion, more than $130 billion higher than the record $268.7 billion deficit recorded in 1991. OMB projected that the deficit would drop to $356.0 billion in fiscal 1993, making it the second-largest deficit in history.

While Congress chafed at the limits imposed by the budget rules, junking them would have removed the insulation that protected members from charges that they were not trying to cut the deficit. The alternative would have been to make another real stab at deficit reduction, something congressional and White House negotiators had done only with enormous difficulty and political anguish in 1990, and which few wanted to try again in a presidential election year. ■

# Budget Passed After Near-Defeat in House

Tight limits set under the 1990 budget rules were supposed to make the work of putting together a fiscal 1993 budget resolution — Congress' blueprint for the year's tax and spending decisions — relatively easy. But the task was complicated early in the year by disputes over how much to cut from defense, and how to use the savings — the so-called peace dividend.

Much of the Democratic leadership yearned to celebrate the collapse of the Soviet military threat by shifting billions of dollars from the defense budget to domestic spending projects such as roads, schools, child nutrition and job training.

The White House sharply disagreed, insisting that the savings go to deficit-reduction; top Senate Democrats were deeply split on the issue.

Moreover, under the budget rules Democrats could not get their hands on defense savings for anything other than reducing the deficit unless they could clear, and get President Bush's signature on, a bill explicitly allowing such a shift.

As a result, the budget resolution became intertwined with efforts to pass a bill tearing down the so-called walls between domestic, defense and international spending that had been erected as part of the 1990 budget deal. It turned out, however, that Democratic leaders had overestimated rank-and-file enthusiasm for their approach. Efforts to pass a bill removing the walls failed. *(Budget walls, p. 104)*

Congress' final $1.5 trillion budget resolution (H Con Res 287 — H Rept 102-529) cut defense $11 billion below the spending caps set in the 1990 budget deal — more than Bush wanted, but less than Democratic leaders originally had proposed.

And all the savings were to be devoted to deficit-reduction.

## HOUSE BUDGET COMMITTEE

The House Budget Committee approved a peace-dividend budget Feb. 27 that would have used defense savings to pay for a wide variety of domestic spending programs.

But in a concession to conservative Democrats — and to reality — the committee also approved an alternative fiscal 1993 budget that abandoned use of the peace dividend for anything but deficit reduction and stayed within the restrictive spending caps set in the 1990 budget summit agreement.

In an unusual move, the Budget Committee approved both budget blueprints — Plan A with peace dividend-spending and Plan B without — in a single budget resolution. Approval came by voice vote after a series of largely party-line votes in which the panel's Democratic majority defeated Republican attempts to rewrite the resolution.

If Congress failed to pass a bill tearing down the budget walls — or if Bush carried through on his threat to veto the bill — the House was to automatically switch to the fallback plan in time for a conference with Senate budget drafters.

Both budget options provided $274.4 billion in budget authority and $287.2 billion in outlays for defense. That meant defense cuts of $14 billion in spending authority and $9 billion in actual spending for fiscal 1993. Those numbers, recommended by House Armed Services Committee Chairman Les Aspin, D-Wis., were roughly double Bush's proposed cuts of $8 billion in budget authority and $5.3 billion in outlays.

House Democratic leaders sought to use the deeper defense cuts to draw a distinction between their party and the GOP, but they immediately ran into problems with their own rank and file. Some Democrats complained that the cuts were too small, while others, particularly those whose districts would have lost defense-related jobs, said they were too big.

But the most serious difficulty was a move by conservative Democrats to devote any defense cuts made solely to deficit reduction, rather than using the money for domestic programs.

### Two Possible Paths

The lack of unanimity among House Budget Committee Democrats clearly played a part in the decision by Chairman Leon E. Panetta, D-Calif., to produce two budget plans. Charles W. Stenholm, D-Texas, and fellow committee member Jerry Huckaby, D-La., said during the markup session Feb. 27 that they and other committee conservatives favored the plan that devoted the entire peace dividend to deficit reduction.

Facing pressure like that, Panetta adjusted even the peace-dividend budget plan to provide some deficit reduc-

---

## BOXSCORE

➤ **Fiscal 1993 Budget Resolution (H Con Res 287).** The $1.5 trillion budget resolution, Congress' blueprint for spending and tax bills, cut defense $11 billion below spending caps set in the 1990 budget deal — more than Bush wanted, but less than Democratic leaders originally had proposed — with all the savings devoted to deficit-reduction.

**Reports:** H Rept 102-450; conference report H Rept 102-529.

### KEY ACTION

**March 5** — The **House** passed H Con Res 287, Plan A, by a vote of 215-201 and H Con Res 287, Plan B, 224-191.

**April 10** — The **Senate** amended and approved H Con Res 287, 54-35.

**May 21** — The **House** approved conference report, H Rept 102-529, 209-207; the **Senate** approved it, 52-41.

---

tion, splitting defense savings about 75-25 between domestic spending and deficit cutting.

On the spending side, the peace-dividend budget would have increased spending for education, health, mass transit, highways, job training, housing and other programs by $12.5 billion more than Bush's budget. At the same time, it would have cut below fiscal 1991 levels in non-priority domestic spending, including a 5 percent cut for the legislative branch, the White House, and Cabinet and sub-Cabinet offices.

The fallback budget was much less generous, but still sought to stake out some differences from Bush. For instance, while the peace-dividend budget boosted spending for the Women, Infants and Children nutrition program by $160 million more than the Bush budget, the fallback plan provided a $60 million increase.

On the other hand, the fallback budget tracked Bush spending levels in many areas. It abandoned the peace-dividend budget's $200 million increase in Head Start, for instance, opting to stay at the Bush level.

Overall, both plans were confined to discretionary spending, which amounted to only a little more than a third of the $1.52 trillion fiscal 1993 budget. Left untouched was the half of the budget going to mandatory spending for entitlement programs such as Medicare, Medicaid, farm subsidies and the like. The other 14 percent of the budget went to interest on the national debt.

Democratic budget drafters rejected Bush's proposals to trim entitlements, either piecemeal or with an overall cap. Instead, the committee approved bipartisan language that expressed concern about out-of-control entitlement spending.

## HOUSE FLOOR ACTION

The House approved the two separate 1993 budgets March 5. However, party leaders were barely able to contain a rebellion by conservative Democrats who wanted any peace dividend to go to deficit reduction and by moderates and liberals who worried that deep defense cuts would cost jobs in their districts.

The leadership had planned to offer the two budgets as a single, budget resolution (H Con Res 287), but in a surprise move, Budget Committee ranking Republican Bill Gradison of Ohio invoked an obscure House rule that forced separate votes on each package. Gradison's plan was to showcase the rifts between Democrats; it worked.

The House first voted 215-201 to approve the Democrats' Plan A budget that split the peace dividend about 25-75 between deficit reduction and domestic spending. A total of 44 Democrats voted no. *(Vote 41, p. 10-H)*

The House then voted 224-191 for the Democrats' Plan B, the fallback budget that devoted all of the peace dividend to deficit reduction. The 39 Democrats voting no included a handful of liberals who wanted increased spending for domestic programs. After the votes, the two plans

# Budget Rules

*The following budget rules were enacted as part of the 1990 budget-reconciliation bill (PL 101-508) governed budget, tax and spending decisions for fiscal 1993.*

**Discretionary spending caps.** The budget rules set individual caps for three categories of discretionary spending — defense, domestic and international — and barred shifting money across categories. Thus defense savings could not be used for domestic programs; any savings in defense would simply reduce the deficit. The caps were set to last throughout fiscal 1993 before collapsing into a single cap on all discretionary spending for fiscal 1994-95.

**Pay-as-you-go restrictions.** So-called PAYGO rules covered tax cuts and mandatory spending (chiefly for entitlement programs such as Medicare, Medicaid and food stamps). Any changes had to be deficit neutral: A tax cut, a new entitlement program or a change that increased spending in an existing entitlement program had to be offset in the same year by a tax increase or a cutback in entitlement spending.

PAYGO rules also barred Congress from using savings made in discretionary accounts, such as defense, to pay for a tax cut.

**Maximum deficit targets.** The 1990 budget deal included maximum deficit targets, but the limits were toothless at least through fiscal 1993. Lawmakers were not held responsible for deficit increases that resulted from forces beyond their control — the recession or the savings and loan bailout, for example.

The only way Congress could trigger the penalty of across-the-board cuts (known as a sequester) for fiscal 1993 was by exceeding the discretionary spending caps or violating the PAYGO rules.

**Suspending the budget rules.** A vote on suspending the budget rules was mandatory after two back-to-back quarters of low or negative economic growth. The Senate had overwhelmingly rejected three such motions to shelve the budget rules in 1991.

were automatically rejoined in the single budget resolution originally brought to the floor by the House Budget Committee. *(Vote 42, p. 10-H)*

The decision on which plan would prevail came later in the month, when the House decisively defeated the separate bill to allow a defense-to-domestic shift, leaving Plan B as the House budget resolution.

### Democratic Rift

During debate on the twin budget resolutions, senior Democrats divided sharply over the defense cuts, which had drawn criticism earlier in the week from Defense Secretary Dick Cheney. Cheney charged that they would force him to cut an additional 300,000 men and women from the armed forces.

Armed Services Committee Chairman Aspin defended the Budget Committee's proposal, saying his panel "can and will make responsible defense cuts" that would not reduce personnel below the levels assumed in Bush's budget. But Defense Appropriations Subcommittee Chairman John P. Murtha, D-Pa., called the reductions "too much," saying he would vote for the plans only because he expected the cuts to be moderated when the Senate drew up its budget resolution. "There's no way we can accept the type of cuts we have here," he said.

The Congressional Black Caucus and the House Progressive Caucus joined to offer a budget that would have cut defense by $49.6 billion in spending authority and $20.7 billion in actual spending in 1993. The proposal was rejected, 77-342. *(Vote 40, p. 10-H)*

A majority of House Republicans appeared to opt for no budget resolution at all, rejecting the two Budget Committee plans, the Black Caucus budget, the president's budget and a substitute sponsored by arch-conservative Budget Committee member William E. Dannemeyer, R-Calif.

Dannemeyer offered the lowest spending levels of any of the five budgets considered during the debate March 4-5. His amendment would have frozen all domestic discretionary spending at fiscal 1992 levels, reduced foreign aid by 25 percent and put a strict cap on Medicare and Medicaid. It also assumed savings of $24 billion in 1993 by requiring the Treasury Department to begin refinancing the public debt with low-interest instruments such as gold-backed bonds. The measure was rejected 60-344. *(Vote 38, p. 10-H)*

Bush's budget garnered even fewer votes, failing 42-370, with 119 Republicans voting no. Republicans said they were put off by many of the specifics in the plan, including higher taxes on credit unions and annuities and controversial cuts in Medicare. "The president's budget is a real budget . . . it is detailed, it is specific," said Minority Leader Robert H. Michel, R-Ill., in a futile attempt to win GOP backing. "Of course, the detailed budget opens up the president to criticism. The Democrats, of course, are not required to offer all that many details." *(Vote 39, p. 10-H)*

## SENATE BUDGET COMMITTEE

The Senate Budget Committee waited until after the fate of the budget-walls bill had been determined before taking up the budget resolution. The committee approved its budget blueprint (H Con Res 287) by a vote of 11-10 on April 2, after the Senate had failed to cut off a filibuster on the walls bill and the House had rejected the measure.

The size of the cuts in defense was virtually the only substantive item on the committee's agenda.

Bowing to what Chairman Jim Sasser, D-Tenn., said was heavy White House pressure, including phone calls to wavering senators from Defense Secretary Cheney, the Budget panel upheld the Bush defense budget by a vote of 11-10, providing $280.4 billion in spending authority and $290.9 billion in outlays. The committee rejected, 9-12, a plan by Sasser to more than double the size of the defense cuts.

Sasser's proposal was scuttled by solid GOP opposition and the same coalition of Democratic deficit and defense hawks and moderate-to-liberal Democrats worried about jobs that helped kill the walls bill.

Conservative Democrats Jim Exon of Nebraska and Ernest F. Hollings of South Carolina opposed Sasser's cuts on the grounds that they were too deep or hit the wrong items. Liberal Christopher J. Dodd, D-Conn., said he

voted against the Sasser plan for fear that it cut too deeply, too quickly, and might jeopardize Connecticut's defense jobs, including construction of the *Seawolf* submarine in Groton.

Jobs were also a focus of Republican opponents. Ranking member Pete V. Domenici of New Mexico said Sasser's cuts could worsen already painful job losses and weaken U.S. defenses before it was certain that the military threat of the former Soviet Union had disappeared."What's so bad about waiting three or four years before we dramatically reduce defense?" he asked.

Sasser's draft resolution would have reduced the 1993 defense budget to $273 billion in spending authority — well below the $289 billion ceiling set in the budget rules and $2 billion lower than House budget resolution's $275 billion.

An Exon amendment to set the level at $273.4 billion by leaving big-ticket items such as the B-2 bomber alone and instead cutting back on scores of smaller weapons failed on a 10-11 vote.

The committee finally adopted an amendment by Hollings and Domenici to set the level at $281 billion, which they said was identical — except for estimating differences — to Bush's budget request.

The committee discussed setting a cap on mandatory spending programs such as Medicare, Medicaid and agriculture subsidies but took no action. Domenici said it was impossible to place broad controls on entitlements through the budget resolution.

Other items approved as part of Sasser's budget proposal included:

● A freeze in new spending authority for domestic appropriations at the 1992 enacted level, minus $2.1 billion in cuts that would come from reducing the size of government and attacking waste, fraud and abuse;

● A reduction in international appropriations by $1.3 billion in spending authority and $800 million in actual spending below the 1993 cap level;

● About $2 billion in mandatory spending savings, including increased user fees and plans to cut Medicare waste, fraud and abuse.

### Action on Amendments

The committee also:

● Approved, 14-7, an amendment by Phil Gramm, R-Texas, to restore a 60-vote point of order on the Senate floor against any legislation that exceeded the maximum deficit amount set by the budget resolution (Gramm insisted this was a technical matter.);

● Approved, 11-9, an amendment by Hank Brown, R-Colo., to state the sense of Congress that the Budget Committee be required to use the more conservative of the economic forecasts provided by the Congressional Budget Office and OMB;

● Approved, 21-0, an amendment by Trent Lott, R-Miss., to phase out the Coast Guard user fee enacted as part of the 1990 budget summit agreement;

● Rejected, 4-17, an amendment by Gramm that would have restored a 60-vote point of order against any budget resolution floor amendment that reduced the Social Security surplus;

● Rejected, 6-15, an amendment by Brown that would have barred agriculture subsidies to producers with incomes of more than $120,000 a year;

● Rejected, 3-18, a substitute budget resolution offered by Kent Conrad, D-N.D., that would have cut the 1993 deficit by $51.1 billion through a combination of discretionary spending cuts, restraints on entitlement programs and increases in taxes.

## SENATE FLOOR ACTION

Unable to use defense savings for anything other than deficit reduction, the Senate yielded to worries about job loss and a rapid defense reduction and decided April 10 to stick with Bush's moderate defense cuts for fiscal 1993. By a vote of 54-35, senators approved a budget resolution that included $280.4 billion in spending authority for defense — a cut of about $8 billion in spending authority and $5.3 billion in outlays below caps set in the 1990 budget summit. *(Vote 80, p. 11-S)*

The decisive vote on defense came April 9; the Senate rejected, 45-50, an amendment by Exon to roughly double Bush's defense cuts. A nearly solid bloc of Republicans joined with 13 Democrats to hold the line, warning that deeper cuts would threaten both hometown defense jobs and national security. *(Vote 69, p. 10-S)*

Exon characterized his rider as a modest and reasonable attempt to save a small amount of additional defense money by leaving big-ticket weapons systems such as the B-2 bomber and a proposed aircraft carrier alone, instead cutting increases in procurement and research and development costs for scores of smaller projects.

Arguing that the defense budget could be cut "without pink-slipping troops by the tens of thousands," Exon charged that arguments about job loss were an "artful, emotionally charged, yet inherently dishonest snow job."

But Ted Stevens, R-Alaska, among others, argued that Exon's cuts "would seriously harm our present defense posture" by disrupting an orderly transition to a peacetime military.

### Debate Over Entitlements

Despite a lengthy debate, the Senate sidestepped efforts to change politically sensitive mandatory spending programs, which made up more than half of federal spending.

And save for the defense debate and a largely symbolic move to cut legislative and executive branch spending by 25 percent over the next two years, the Senate resolution sought only minor modifications to the one-third of the budget devoted to discretionary spending.

Debate on the final day centered on a bitterly controversial amendment by Budget Committee ranking Republican Domenici to cap spending for entitlement programs such as Medicare, Medicaid, farm subsidies and food stamps. While virtually all sides agreed that limiting entitlement spending was critical to getting control of the deficit, there was no consensus on how to do it. The plan, sponsored by Domenici, Armed Services Chairman Sam Nunn, D-Ga., Warren B. Rudman, R-N.H., and Charles S. Robb, D-Va., tracked a proposal first aired in Bush's 1993 budget and pushed by White House budget director Richard G. Darman.

The amendment would have imposed a cap on all mandatory spending, except for Social Security and interest on the debt, beginning in 1994. It would have allowed increases to accommodate population growth, inflation and an additional factor starting at 2 percent in 1994 and falling to zero by 1997. Any violation would have presumably triggered unspecified, across-the-board cuts in all nonexempted entitlements, although that process would have to be determined by subsequent legislation.

# Fiscal 1993 Budget Resolution

*(In billions of dollars; totals may not add due to rounding)*

| | Bush's Budget [1] | House Passed | Senate Passed | Final |
|---|---|---|---|---|
| **National Defense** | | | | |
| Budget Authority | $ 281.0 | $ 274.4 | $ 280.4 | $ 277.4 |
| Outlays | 292.2 | 287.2 | 290.9 | 289.1 |
| **International Affairs** | | | | |
| Budget Authority | 19.4 | 19.7 | 19.0 | 19.6 |
| Outlays | 17.5 | 17.4 | 16.6 | 17.2 |
| **Science and Space** | | | | |
| Budget Authority | 18.4 | 17.1 | 17.1 | 17.1 |
| Outlays | 17.0 | 16.2 | 16.3 | 16.2 |
| **Energy** | | | | |
| Budget Authority | 5.6 | 5.9 | 6.0 | 5.9 |
| Outlays | 5.0 | 5.4 | 5.4 | 5.4 |
| **Natural Resources** | | | | |
| Budget Authority | 21.3 | 20.9 | 21.3 | 21.1 |
| Outlays | 21.0 | 20.6 | 20.9 | 20.8 |
| **Agriculture** | | | | |
| Budget Authority | 16.2 | 16.2 | 16.5 | 16.3 |
| Outlays | 15.8 | 16.0 | 16.1 | 16.1 |
| **Commerce and Housing** | | | | |
| Budget Authority | 83.0 | 82.4 | 82.4 | 82.4 |
| Outlays | 75.4 | 75.4 | 75.4 | 75.4 |
| **Transportation** | | | | |
| Budget Authority | 39.7 | 41.0 | 40.9 | 41.0 |
| Outlays | 35.2 | 35.4 | 35.2 | 35.5 |
| **Community Development** | | | | |
| Budget Authority | 6.2 | 6.9 | 7.4 | 7.2 |
| Outlays | 7.0 | 7.1 | 7.2 | 7.2 |
| **Education and Social Services** | | | | |
| Budget Authority | 51.8 | 51.7 | 50.7 | 51.9 |
| Outlays | 49.4 | 49.6 | 49.8 | 49.8 |
| **Health** | | | | |
| Budget Authority | 104.5 | 105.2 | 104.3 | 105.2 |
| Outlays | 103.7 | 104.5 | 104.0 | 104.5 |
| **Medicare** | | | | |
| Budget Authority | 130.9 | 132.2 | 132.2 | 132.2 |
| Outlays | 129.2 | 130.4 | 130.4 | 130.4 |
| **Income Security** | | | | |
| Budget Authority | 196.8 | 199.5 | 198.6 | 199.4 |
| Outlays | 195.0 | 196.7 | 196.8 | 196.7 |
| **Social Security** | | | | |
| Budget Authority | 306.2 | 306.2 | 306.2 | 306.2 |
| Outlays | 303.2 | 303.2 | 303.1 | 303.3 |
| **Veterans Benefits** | | | | |
| Budget Authority | 34.8 | 35.3 | 36.5 | 35.7 |
| Outlays | 34.4 | 35.0 | 35.8 | 35.2 |
| **Justice** | | | | |
| Budget Authority | 15.8 | 15.2 | 14.6 | 15.2 |
| Outlays | 15.9 | 15.3 | 14.8 | 15.3 |
| **General Government** | | | | |
| Budget Authority | 13.5 | 12.3 | 12.2 | 12.3 |
| Outlays | 14.1 | 12.9 | 12.8 | 12.9 |
| **Net Interest** | | | | |
| Budget Authority | 213.8 | 213.8 | 213.8 | 213.8 |
| Outlays | 213.8 | 213.7 | 213.8 | 213.7 |
| **Allowances** | | | | |
| Budget Authority | −0.5 | −2.3 | −5.9 | −4.1 |
| Outlays | −0.4 | −3.5 | −4.9 | −4.8 |
| **Offsetting Receipts** | | | | |
| Budget Authority | −41.5 | −40.6 | −39.9 | −39.9 |
| Outlays | −41.5 | −40.6 | −39.9 | −39.9 |
| **TOTALS** | | | | |
| Budget Authority | $ 1,516.8 | $ 1,513.0 | $ 1,514.3 | $ 1,515.9 |
| Outlays | 1,503.0 | 1,497.9 | 1,500.5 | 1,500.0 |
| Revenues | 1,171.2 | 1,173.4 | 1,173.4 | 1,173.4 |
| Deficit | 331.8 | 324.5 | 327.1 | 326.6 |

[1] *Congressional Budget Office re-estimate*

SOURCES: Congressional Budget Office, House and Senate Budget committees

---

Domenici said the plan was the only way to constrain out-of-control entitlement spending that threatened the nation with bankruptcy. But critics warned that capping entitlements would harm elderly and needy Americans who depended on such programs for survival. They argued that the real problem was rapid growth in Medicare and Medicaid, and the real solution was comprehensive health-care reform that constrained costs. Countered Domenici: "You will never get cost containment until you set a target for the money that is available for health-care expenditures by the federal government."

Domenici withdrew the amendment after the Senate approved, 66-28, what promised to be the first of a series of amendments exempting veterans and other groups from the cap. "The handwriting was on the wall," said Rudman. *(Vote 75, p. 11-S)*

**Amendments Considered**

During floor debate the Senate also:

● Approved, 94-3, an amendment by Lloyd Bentsen, D-Texas, to impose a 60-vote point of order against any budget-resolution floor amendment that raised Social Security benefits without increasing the payroll tax or cut the tax without cutting benefits. There was a 60-vote point of order against any budget resolution that came to the floor containing such a provision, but a floor amendment with the same language could be approved by a simple majority vote. *(Vote 68, p. 10-S)*

● Approved, by voice vote, an amendment by John C. Danforth, R-Mo., expressing the sense of the Senate that the U.S. government should not condone foreign trade subsidies that harmed U.S. industries. Danforth said the amendment was intended to repudiate a tentative agreement by the U.S trade representative to abandon further action on subsidies by European governments to their commercial aircraft consortium, Airbus Industrie — subsidies that Danforth said hurt Missouri-based aircraft manufacturer McDonnell Douglas.

● Approved, by voice vote, an amendment by Don Nickles, R-Okla., to express the sense of the Senate that senators should approve by June 5 a constitutional amendment requiring a balanced budget.

The Senate first voted 84-11 to approve an amendment by Robert C. Byrd, D-W.Va., adding a requirement

that the president submit a balanced budget every year. Then the Senate voted 63-32 to waive a budget act point of order that would have declared the Nickles amendment out of order. *(Votes 71, 72, p. 10-S)*

● Agreed, by a vote of 36-62, not to waive the Budget Act to allow an amendment by Bill Bradley, D-N.J., that would have cut defense spending authority $7 billion below Bush's request for fiscal 1993 and split the proceeds equally between high-priority domestic spending programs and deficit reduction. Bradley's amendment was then ruled out of order. *(Vote 70, p. 10-S)*

● Approved, by voice vote, an amendment by Brown of Colorado to require a study of all mandatory spending programs, except for Social Security and interest on the debt, to determine who received the benefits of those programs.

● Tabled (killed), by a vote of 53 to 40, an amendment by Tom Harkin, D-Iowa, that would have cut defense spending authority $6 billion below the president's request. *(Vote 73, p. 11-S)*

● Approved, 52-42, an amendment by John Seymour, R-Calif., as further amended by Sasser, to reduce the congressional and executive branch budgets 25 percent below the 1992 level over the following two years. Seymour proposed the reduction in Congress' budget, while Sasser added the identical executive-branch cut on a voice vote. *(Vote 74, p. 11-S)*

## FINAL ACTION

Congress adopted a final 1993 budget May 21, but not before the unpopular measure was nearly defeated on a chaotic House vote that some saw as a harbinger of the difficult votes to come on a constitutional amendment requiring a balanced federal budget.

As time on the House vote expired, the measure was losing by at least two votes and Democratic leaders had to twist arms to get two members to switch their votes to "yea." With the House floor in an uproar, one more member rushed into the chamber to vote against the budget, and Speaker Thomas S. Foley, D-Wash., cast one of his extremely rare floor votes to ensure a 209-207 victory. *(Vote 139, p. 34-H)*

Rep. Richard J. Durbin, D-Ill., blamed the close House vote on the fact that the budget seemed to have something for everyone to dislike. It spent too much on defense for some and too little for others, for instance, and it contained a deficit well in excess of $300 billion.

"The easiest vote was no," said House Budget Chairman Panetta. "As always with a budget resolution, there are members who can find any number of reasons not to vote for [it]."

A senior aide said Republicans, who voted without exception against the budget, were concerned about voting for a budget that did little or nothing to eliminate the deficit when they would be voting for a balanced budget amendment in a few weeks.

But Democrats scoffed, predicting that when it came to making the actual cuts to begin balancing the budget, Republicans would shy away.

"If the resolution had failed, it would just feed into the public perception of this place that we can't get our act together to get anything done," Panetta said.

The Senate later approved the resolution on a much less dramatic 52-41 vote. That completed action; budget resolutions did not go to the president for signature. *(Vote 110, p. 15-S)*

Passage cleared the way for the House and Senate Appropriations committees to make 1993 spending allocations to their 13 subcommittees and begin moving spending bills to the floor.

### Conference Decisions

The budget resolution came up for floor votes after conferees meeting in private agreed to split the difference between the House and Senate on defense spending, drop a Senate plan to trim domestic appropriations spending authority, and go most of the way toward restoring a Senate cut in foreign aid. The trade-offs made the budget — unpopular in the best of times — even less attractive for many members.

Though the changes at issue were comparatively minor, they touched off disputes among the conferees:

● **Defense spending.** It was a foregone conclusion that there would be cuts below the defense spending caps set in the 1990 budget agreement; the question was how much. In the end, conferees split the difference, providing $277.4 billion in budget authority and $289.1 billion in outlays for fiscal 1993. That represented cuts of roughly $11 billion in budget authority and $7.1 billion in outlays below the caps. (The Senate had approved cuts of roughly $8 billion and $5.3 billion respectively; the House had gone deeper, cutting $14 billion and $9 billion below the caps.

● **Domestic discretionary spending.** During the conference, Senate negotiators sought a $1 billion cut below the caps in spending authority for domestic appropriations. They argued that the 1990 spending caps created more spending authority than appropriators could use in outlays unless they resorted to gimmicks such as pushing 1993 outlays into 1994. But House appropriators in particular balked at ceding what they saw as their right to make such decisions, and the conferees finally agreed to stick to the domestic caps.

● **International discretionary spending.** The House budget duplicated Bush's request for foreign aid, which was $597 million below the cap in spending authority but equal to the outlay cap. The Senate would have cut both numbers by roughly another three-quarters of a billion dollars, but the two sides compromised, moving back closer to the House version. The final numbers represented a cut of $180 million in spending authority and $189 million in outlays below the House-Bush numbers.

In another key area, the compromise budget resolution assumed $2 billion a year in cuts from entitlements — which included such politically sensitive programs as Medicare, Social Security and farm subsidies — but made no specific recommendations for achieving those savings. The budget rejected all Bush's proposed entitlement cuts, however, and the cuts assumed in the resolution were not mandatory. ■

# Budget Walls Survive Battering

After President Bush challenged Congress to pass his economic agenda in a combative State of the Union address Jan. 28, congressional Democratic leaders decided to try to retake the political momentum by confronting Bush over a series of economic issues.

In addition to a tax bill and a budget resolution that would spell out their, not his, priorities, leaders planned to move quickly to knock down the budget "walls" that prohibited shifting defense money to domestic spending programs.

By changing the terms of the 1990 budget agreement, Democratic leaders hoped to allow a shift of defense savings into cash-short domestic programs. A Bush veto of such a bill, while virtually certain, would just sharpen the differences between what Democrats saw as their own invest-in-America policy and what they criticized as Bush's outmoded Cold War priorities.

But leaders failed to reckon on dissension in their own ranks. Trouble surfaced early when conservative Democrats on the House Budget Committee forced the panel to produce two budget proposals: a walls-down, leadership budget resolution that devoted most defense savings to domestic programs; and a walls-up, conservative budget resolution that would use any defense cuts for deficit reduction.

Senate Democrats ran into similar resistance from conservatives on their side. Senate Budget Committee Chairman Jim Sasser, D-Tenn., found support so shaky that he decided not even to move his measure (S 2399) through his own committee, opting instead to bring it straight to the Senate floor, where it encountered trouble that would prove fatal.

Sasser and other proponents of the measure argued that with the collapse of the Soviet military threat, it was time to invest a bigger-than-anticipated peace dividend in domestic programs.

But critics wondered how Sasser could talk about a peace dividend at a time when the nation was running enormous budget deficits.

Sasser responded that the bill would simply authorize a shift of money that would have been spent anyway from the defense account to the domestic account, with no net impact on the anticipated deficit. But critics insisted Congress should seize any chance to save money.

In the end, Senate Majority Leader George J. Mitchell, D-Maine, was unable to shut down a filibuster against the measure. On March 26, eight Democrats joined 40 Republicans to hold Mitchell and Sasser a critical 10 votes below the 60 they needed to stop the talkathon. The motion to invoke cloture (and thereby end the filibuster) was rejected, 50-48.

House leaders had no better luck. Worried about support among their rank and file, Democratic leaders repeatedly postponed a scheduled vote on the walls bill (HR

---

## BOXSCORE

➡ **Remove budget walls (HR 3732, S 2399).** The bills would have removed the "walls" erected by the 1990 budget agreement between defense and domestic appropriations, permitting appropriators to apply defense savings to increased domestic spending.

**Reports:** H Rept 102-446, Parts I and II.

### KEY ACTION

March 26 — The **Senate** rejected motion to cut off debate on S 2399, 50-48.

March 31 — The **House** rejected HR 3732, 187-238.

---

3732) that had been drawn up by House Government Operations Committee Chairman John Conyers Jr., D-Mich. When they finally brought the bill to a vote, they were beaten overwhelmingly. Republicans voted unanimously against the measure, and 76 Democrats crossed the line to join them in a 187-238 rout.

The anatomy of the Democratic coalition against the walls bill was a study in strange bedfellows. On one side were mostly conservative deficit hawks worried about budget discipline and defense hawks concerned about opening the floodgates between defense and domestic spending categories. On the other side were Democrats, including moderates and liberals, who worried about the loss of hometown defense jobs that might result if defense funds were heavily cut.

## BACKGROUND

The 1990 budget summit agreement walled off defense, domestic and international appropriations into separate, inviolable categories for the first three years of the deal (fiscal 1991-93), essentially to put a floor under defense spending. *(1990 Almanac, p. 129)*

While nothing barred Congress from cutting defense, any savings could only be used for deficit reduction, a psychological barrier that White House negotiators figured would safeguard defense funds from a Congress that might want to raid defense if it could spend the money on domestic projects.

The disintegration of the former Soviet Union and the collapse of the once-potent Soviet military fueled a conviction among Democratic leaders that the priorities set by the 1990 summit were obsolete.

Democratic strategists felt that a move to shift defense funds to cash-short domestic programs would draw a clear distinction between Democrats and Republicans during the presidential election year — demonstrating, they hoped, that Democrats were committed to investing in critical homefront programs, while the Bush White House and the congressional GOP were still locked into outmoded Cold War thinking. Bush had threatened to veto any bill to knock down the walls, but Democratic leaders figured a veto would simply draw the political distinctions that much more sharply.

Democratic leaders in both the House and the Senate had strong support for the walls bills from appropriators, who found that the discretionary spending caps set by the 1990 budget deal were beginning to pinch extremely tight. Appropriators who were beginning to put together the fiscal 1993 domestic spending bills realized they would have to cut spending in some instances below prior-year levels. Although the walls would come down the following year for fiscal 1994, that was no help for the appropriators' immediate problem, and they supported the move for a defense-to-domestic spending transfer now.

The failure of the walls bill, particularly in the House, was one of several times during the year when Democratic leaders appeared to miscalculate the strength of the conservatives in their party ranks.

In the House, "Boll Weevil" Democrats led by Rep. Charles W. Stenholm, D-Texas, turned out to be a potent force on fiscal issues on several occasions. On this and other key issues, conservative Democrats were able to briefly form a working majority with unified House Republicans to push the House in a more fiscally conservative direction than Democratic leaders wanted it to go. Although the conservatives were joined in this instance by moderates and liberals worried about hometown defense jobs, the vote margins showed they probably could have prevailed without them.

## HOUSE COMMITTEE ACTION

The House Government Operations Subcommittee on Legislation and National Security met Feb. 18 to approve a measure (HR 3732) drafted by committee Chairman Conyers to knock down the walls between defense, domestic and international spending in time for fiscal 1993 appropriations.

Committee ranking Republican Frank Horton of New York read a letter from White House budget director Richard G. Darman that warned the bill would draw a presidential veto, but subcommittee Democrats were unfazed.

The subcommittee approved the measure on a 7-4 vote, and the full Government Operations Committee followed suit the next day, Feb. 20, rejecting a Horton substitute 13-25 and approving the Conyers bill on a voice vote.

Horton's amendment embodied Bush's proposal to use the peace dividend to pay for deficit reduction and a tax cut.

A week later, the House Budget Committee approved a peace dividend budget Feb. 27 that would take advantage of the Conyers bill — should it pass — to use defense savings to pay for a wide variety of domestic spending programs.

But in a concession to reality — and to conservative Democrats — the committee also approved an alternative fiscal 1993 budget that abandoned use of the peace dividend for anything but deficit reduction and stayed within the restrictive spending caps set in the 1990 budget summit agreement.

Key Democrats conceded that Congress would almost certainly be forced to fall back on the alternative budget unless they could overcome a veto threat and change budget law in an election year — a task even optimists said seemed impossible now.

"Ultimately, we'll be squeezed into the caps," said House Budget Chairman Leon E. Panetta, D-Calif.

## SENATE COMMITTEE ACTION

Although Budget Committee Chairman Sasser ended up bypassing his own committee to bring his budget walls bill (S 2399) to the Senate floor, much of the skirmishing over the issue took place before the matter came before the full Senate.

Before Senate Democrats could agree to back a bill to knock down the budget walls, they had to resolve an internal dispute over how to spend the peace dividend.

While House Democrats seemed to agree early on to devote the peace dividend to domestic spending, top Senate Democrats were deeply split: Finance Committee Chairman Lloyd Bentsen, D-Texas, favored spending at least part of any new cuts in defense appropriations on a tax cut. Appropriations Chairman Robert C. Byrd, D-W.Va., flatly opposed using the money for anything but increased domestic discretionary spending.

Byrd disagreed so strongly with Bentsen that he refused to join a high-level task force convened by Majority Leader Mitchell to thrash out the issue.

The 11-senator group was chaired by Bentsen, which would have given him leverage in forcing Byrd to deal on any ultimate agreement. "The task force might come up with a package that I might not be able to fully support," said the Appropriations chairman, explaining why he turned down Mitchell's invitation to join.

Lest there be any doubt as to how he felt about turning over defense appropriations savings to the Senate Finance Committee to bankroll a tax cut, Byrd spelled out his sentiments before the Senate Budget Committee in testimony Feb. 5.

"I'm against that, not 99 percent but 100 percent," he said. "I shall oppose any attempt — and I will oppose it to the utmost of my ability . . . to use defense savings for tax cuts.

"Now, the wagon may run over me, but I ain't gettin' on that wagon," he said.

Instead, Byrd proposed an immediate lowering of the wall between defense and domestic spending to allow appropriators to shift defense money into domestic infrastructure projects that would boost economic growth and productivity.

Sasser indicated that he planned to grant at least part of Byrd's wish by quickly introducing a bill to knock down the walls between defense and domestic appropriations in time for Byrd to use defense money to beef up domestic appropriations in fiscal 1993 spending bills.

But Pete V. Domenici of New Mexico, ranking Republican on the Budget Committee, signaled GOP opposition to such a move, insisting that any agreement to shift money out of defense ought to come at the price of extending the three individual appropriations caps for at least two or three more years. Domenici said he told Bush the same thing, and he warned Democrats that if they wanted to fiddle with the wall between defense and domestic spending, "you've got to have the president on board."

The split over the peace dividend among top Democrats disappeared Feb. 20 when Bentsen said he no longer intended to try to capture some of the money for tax cuts, ending his feud with Byrd. Bentsen and House counterpart Dan Rostenkowski, D-Ill., chairman of the Ways and Means Committee, both indicated they intended to offset any tax cuts with revenue increases.

Meanwhile, the White House was offering to deal on the peace dividend, but on terms so odious to Democrats that it appeared there was no prospect of compromise. White House budget director Darman put two proposals on the table.

The first, outlined in the president's budget, would allow any defense savings to be split equally between deficit reduction and a tax cut — specifically, to offset the cost of Bush's proposed $500-per-child increase in the personal tax exemption.

But Democrats who wanted defense savings for domestic spending — chiefly Byrd — rejected that proposal, especially because Bush also conditioned it on an agreement by Congress to extend the life of the walls that separated defense, domestic and international appropria-

tions. Since the walls were set to come down the following year anyway, Democrats said they'd be fools to fall for any peace dividend offer if the price were more years of walls.

Darman insisted that the walls be extended through fiscal 1997. Democrats wanted the walls down a year early — in time for the fiscal 1993 appropriations bills they were writing in 1992 — and they wanted them down for good.

Darman put the second of Bush's proposals on the table Feb. 18 at a hearing of the Senate Appropriations Committee. He signaled that the administration would consider a defense-to-domestic shift if Congress were willing to put an enforceable cap on mandatory spending, which went primarily for entitlement programs such as Medicare, Medicaid, food stamps, farm subsidies and the like.

The idea of controlling mandatory spending was catnip to appropriators, whose share of the budget was being relentlessly squeezed by the skyrocketing growth of entitlement programs.

There was broad agreement that mandatory spending was out of control but little consensus on how to rein it in. Democrats and Republicans alike winced at the pain involved in cutting back on politically sensitive programs such as Medicare.

Critics said a cap would penalize low-growth entitlement programs for the explosive growth of Medicare and Medicaid, which many felt could not be controlled without a major plan for medical-cost containment, likely to come only as part of comprehensive health-care reform.

Some viewed Darman's proposal as a cynical ploy. Budget Committee Chairman Sasser, who also sat on Appropriations, said he thought Darman was out to drive a wedge between Democrats, specifically between Byrd's appropriators and Finance Committee Chairman Bentsen's tax writers, who controlled entitlement spending.

It eventually became apparent to Sasser that he would have grave difficulty moving his walls bills through the Budget Committee.

Sasser calculated that he could lose no more than one Democratic vote on the committee without losing his majority. He faced problems from Budget conservatives and from Christopher J. Dodd, D-Conn., who was battling Bush administration proposals to cut *Seawolf* submarine construction — and thousands of jobs — in Groton, Conn.

Besides Dodd, two other committee Democrats had refused to co-sponsor Sasser's bill: Ernest F. Hollings of South Carolina and Jim Exon of Nebraska. If all committee Republicans voted against the bill, as expected, Sasser would have to hold at least two of those Democrats to pass his bill.

In the end, he elected not to try to move the bill through the committee. He said later he could have secured the votes he needed but wanted to avoid a time-consuming joint referral to the Senate Governmental Affairs Committee.

## SENATE FLOOR ACTION

Sasser moved the bill directly to the full Senate, but he was ultimately unable to overcome a filibuster against the motion to take it up. After weeks of delay and uncertainty over the issue, Senate Democrats on March 26 fell a decisive 10 votes short of the 60 they needed to shut down a GOP-led filibuster against Sasser's bill to tear down the budget walls. The vote was 50-48. *(Vote 56, p. 8-S)*

Sasser had argued that the bill would only open the way for a transfer of money from one spending category to another, doing nothing to increase the deficit. "Are we going to move decisively to invest a portion of our peace dividend?" Sasser asked. "Or are we going to maintain Cold War policy and Cold War sacrifices after the Cold War is over?"

But Sasser's opponents ridiculed the notion that the government ought to spend the peace dividend on anything other than deficit reduction at a time when it was borrowing more than $300 billion to pay its bills. "What peace dividend?" asked John C. Danforth, R-Mo., during the Senate floor debate. "How can we talk about an election-year gift to the American people when we're broke?"

Republicans and Democrats alike criticized the measure for ignoring the deficit and jeopardizing defense spending.

"There's only one guaranteed result to a change in the budget deal, and that's to increase the deficit," said Armed Services Committee Chairman Sam Nunn, D-Ga. "If we pass this amendment . . . the defense budget will become the equivalent of the House bank." Nunn's pointed barb alluded to the ongoing check-kiting scandal at the by-then-closed House bank.

Budget Committee ranking Republican Domenici insisted that the Senate stick to the budget rules. "A deal is a deal," he said.

But Sasser said it was high time to change the 1990 deal, which he argued was completed before anyone realized the extent of the changes taking place in the former Soviet Union.

"The unreconstructed old Cold Warriors strap on their rusty armor and come over here on the floor and tell us, 'Oh, no, you can't reduce this military spending.' "

Although the bill by itself would not reduce defense spending, Sasser insisted, it was critical to knock down the wall to allow excess spending to go where it would do far more good. "It would be foolish not to seize this opportunity," he said. "It is time to go back to a policy of investing in America."

Sasser said that holding 1993 spending bills to the budget agreement's limits would keep domestic spending $6.7 billion below the level needed to keep pace with inflation, and he orchestrated warnings from appropriators that major projects would be in danger as a result.

"If the fire walls do not come down, we might have to shrink or even cancel the space station," said VA-HUD Subcommittee Chairman Barbara A. Mikulski, D-Md.

J. Bennett Johnston, D-La., chairman of the Energy, Water Subcommittee, said the money shortage would threaten Bush's planned increase for the superconducting super collider. "I am frank to say right now I don't know where the money's coming from," he said.

The Senate defeat, engineered in part by eight Democrats who voted to keep the filibuster going, underscored critical divisions among Democrats on this and other high-profile economic issues. It came only a day after House leaders were unable to muster even a majority in their attempt to override Bush's veto of the Democratic tax-cut bill. *(First tax bill, p. 133)*

It was one more lost skirmish in the surprising unraveling of Democratic plans to confront Bush on economic issues and seize back the momentum he gained in his combative State of the Union speech.

The Senate's failure to shut down the filibuster on the walls bill effectively killed the measure there. Proponents said it might be revived in some form if House Democrats managed to pass their own walls bill, but that never happened.

## HOUSE FLOOR ACTION

Democratic leaders had originally scheduled a vote on the House budget walls bill the week of March 2, but they ran into a storm of opposition from three groups of rank-and-file Democrats: conservatives who wanted all of the peace dividend to go to deficit reduction, conservatives who feared that the defense cuts would be too deep and a group that included moderates and liberals worried about the loss of defense-related jobs in their districts.

House Democratic leaders struggled to play catch-up in the face of a well-organized effort from those allies to defeat the bill.

In an indication of just how seriously they regarded the threat, backers of the Conyers bill wheeled out most of the House Democrats' big guns in a March 5 letter signed by 15 committee chairmen and 12 of the 13 Appropriations subcommittee chairmen. Included were Appropriations Chairman Jamie L. Whitten, Miss., Ways and Means Chairman Rostenkowski and Energy and Commerce Chairman John D. Dingell, Mich.

The letter urged members to vote for the Conyers bill to permit "critical domestic investments," warning that leaving the walls in place "will hurt economic growth." Of the Appropriations "cardinals," only Defense Subcommittee Chairman John P. Murtha, D-Pa., declined to sign. Worried that defense cuts would deepen, he opposed taking down the walls.

The House debated the walls bill March 12 but postponed a final vote. Backers released no vote counts, but they conceded they were behind. "There's some work to be done," said House Budget Committee Chairman Panetta.

Opponents took the delay as clear proof the leadership was playing a losing hand. "They have been beaten and they know it," said Gerald B. H. Solomon of New York, ranking Republican on the Rules Committee.

Panetta said the bill could be rewritten before the final vote in an attempt to peel off wavering Democrats, possibly by leaving the walls intact and instead lowering the defense cap while raising the domestic cap. Backers of the bill calculated that that might reassure conservatives that defense cuts would go no deeper.

Others said the bill might be recast to increase the amount of any peace dividend that would go to deficit reduction. Under one of the two budget resolutions the House approved March 5, any cut in 1993 defense spending was to be split roughly 75-25 between domestic spending and deficit reduction. Some suggested that a rewritten walls bill would alter that split to 50-50 to placate deficit hawks. *(Budget resolution, p. 98)*

As March progressed with no vote on the bill, Democratic leaders found their vote counts showing them behind and their rank and file badly distracted by the check-kiting scandal.

Stenholm, coordinator of the House's Conservative Democratic Forum and a leader of the effort to block the bill, said his vote count showed 50 "solid" Democratic votes against the measure, plus another 20 to 30 leaning his way. "The 20 or 30 leaning are more than just leaning," he said. "We would prevail by 20 votes today," he said on March 18. If all Republicans voted against the bill, opponents would need 52 Democratic "nay" votes to beat the measure.

House Speaker Thomas S. Foley, D-Wash., predicted that the bill would survive. "I think there are still the votes to take those walls down," he said. "We are gaining votes all the time."

Leadership efforts to win passage were complicated by the politically disastrous check-kiting scandal.

"It was a tough enough vote when you weren't dealing with the atmosphere created by the bank situation," said Budget Committee Chairman Panetta. "It becomes a near-impossible vote in the atmosphere that now pervades this institution. . . . Members don't want to be put in a position of changing the terms of the budget agreement when they're basically fighting for their own survival."

Panetta said Democratic leaders might have to abandon their defiant, veto-based strategy for confronting Bush and explore a compromise with Republicans if they wanted any new money for domestic appropriations in fiscal 1993. While emphasizing that he did not endorse the idea, he suggested Democrats think about a GOP proposal to trade some extra 1993 money for domestic programs for an extension of the budget walls into 1994-95, when they were set to expire. "I'm not so sure that isn't something worth exploring," he said. "Other than that, I don't see how there is going to be any opportunity . . . [to] make transfers from defense to domestic" spending.

House appropriators immediately rejected the idea, saying it would be foolish to trade a one-year spending increase for two more years of walls. "I do not support that concept," said House VA-HUD Appropriations Subcommittee Chairman Bob Traxler, D-Mich. "We'd pay far too high a price."

Traxler said he would prefer to cope with the below-inflation funding available for his subcommittee for fiscal 1993 in exchange for defense-to-domestic transfers when the walls came down in fiscal 1994-95.

After postponing a vote for four weeks in a row, leaders finally scheduled a March 31 showdown.

Leadership aides said they planned to pull out the stops to turn wayward Democrats around. Leaders warned the rank and file that big-ticket projects such as NASA's hyperexpensive space station and the multibillion-dollar superconducting super collider would be in dire straits if no way were found to increase domestic appropriations.

Transportation Appropriations Subcommittee Chairman William Lehman, D-Fla., sent a letter to his colleagues March 23 warning that the highway and mass transit funding they authorized in the 1991 surface transportation bill (HR 2950 — H Rept 102-404) would be slashed unless the House opened the way for more domestic spending. *(1991 Almanac, p. 137)*

A House aide familiar with the whip count said March 26 that bill proponents had only about 200 of the 218 votes they needed and would try over the intervening weekend before the vote to shift about a dozen Democrats.

But an angry Stenholm, who led opposition to the bill, insisted that the postponements had not helped the leadership gain ground. "Every day we're gaining," he said of his amorphous coalition of deficit hawks, defense hawks and moderates and liberals worried about the loss of hometown defense jobs. Stenholm blasted the House leadership for having "reneged" on commitments to hold a vote on the measure earlier in March. "When agreements don't stick, that's bad business," he said.

Finally, in a long-expected but nonetheless embarrassing defeat for top House Democrats, Republicans joined conservative Democratic deficit hawks March 31 to reject the bill.

The defeat came on a decisive 187-238 vote that marked the second time in two weeks that Democratic leaders had been unable to muster a majority in the overwhelmingly Democratic House to support a key component of their election-year program. *(Vote 66, p. 16-H)*

A week earlier, an attempt to marshal a two-thirds vote to override Bush's veto of the Democrats' tax-cut bill failed on a 211-215 vote.

In the end, 76 of 268 House Democrats voted against the measure, joining 162 Republicans.

Despite the setback, however, top House Democrats predicted that opponents in Congress and at the White House, which had threatened to veto the bill, would change their minds when they saw how tight spending would be for domestic projects. "This could ultimately force a negotiation with the White House, because their priorities are just as likely to get cut," said Budget Committee Chairman Panetta.

Failure to lower the walls left appropriators no choice but to work within the defense, domestic and international spending limits dictated by the 1990 budget deal.

Democrats could still argue that a majority of their members favored investing the peace dividend in domestic programs. But the defection of many Democrats weakened their case. "They control this place by over 100 votes," said Budget Committee ranking Republican Bill Gradison of Ohio. "Frankly, I don't understand why they bring this bill out. . . . All they're doing is exposing their own differences."

Democratic leaders said they had no choice but to bring the bill up for a sure defeat because they had promised conservative party members a vote on the matter in exchange for sticking with leaders on two controversial budget resolutions early in March.

Passage of the walls bill would have activated the budget resolution that directed most defense savings to domestic spending, but the bill's defeat meant the House would automatically stick with the fallback budget resolution that stayed within the 1990 spending caps.

Stenholm argued during floor debate that spending the peace dividend made no sense at a time when the nation was running a deficit projected as high as $400 billion. "There is no peace dividend, because we have borrowed 100 percent of the money that we have been spending on defense," he said. "A company $400 billion in debt cannot pay a dividend."

But bill author and Government Operations Chairman Conyers argued that Congress must devote some of the cutbacks in defense spending to domestic initiatives. "Our economic competitors are clobbering our brains out in manufacturing and trade, and we're debating whether it makes sense to spend a little more money educating the next generation, ensuring a healthy work force, rebuilding our infrastructure and discovering new technologies," he said.

Proponents of deficit reduction saw the failure of the walls bill as a sign that a Congress was increasingly concerned about the size of the deficit. Deficit hawks like Pete Geren, D-Texas, thought that would help them with the balanced-budget amendment they planned to bring to a House vote later in the year. "The [walls] bill is an indication of the strength of the deficit as an issue now," Geren said.

But others saw defeat of the bill as the natural reaction of members trying to strike a fiscally conservative pose to deflect voter ire in the highly charged atmosphere caused by scandals over the House bank and the House Post Office.

"Unfortunately, it all comes at a time when the House is under siege and members are running for cover from every tough decision that has to be made," Panetta said. "It would have been a much closer vote on this issue if it were not balled up in the guilt of this institution." ∎

# Balanced-Budget Amendment Defeated

The year's most dramatic clash over the budget came when a coalition of Republicans and mostly conservative Democrats sought to pass an amendment to the Constitution (HJ Res 290, SJ Res 18) requiring a balanced federal budget. Although the momentum at first seemed unstoppable, Democratic leaders in the House managed to erode enough support for the measure to defeat it. A last-ditch attempt to revive it in the Senate also failed.

The balanced-budget fight was the only comprehensive attempt Congress made in 1992 to attack the deficit, which had grown prodigiously despite the spending limits imposed by the 1990 budget deal.

The amendment itself would have done nothing to actually cut the deficit; that would have required separate implementing legislation. House Budget Committee Chairman Leon E. Panetta, D-Calif., tried to work out a bipartisan plan for reducing the deficit, with or without a constitutional amendment, but he was unsuccessful.

## BACKGROUND

To become part of the Constitution, an amendment must be approved by a two-thirds vote in each chamber of Congress and then win approval of three-fourths, or 38, of the state legislatures. (Amendments could also be drafted by a constitutional convention petitioned by two-thirds of the states, but that process had never been used.)

Proposals for a balanced-budget amendment had been kicked around for years in conservative circles. Presidents Ronald Reagan and George Bush had each called for such a change to the Constitution. But the issue had come to the floor of either chamber only four times in the previous two decades. In 1982, the Senate passed an amendment on a 69-31 vote, two more than the necessary two-thirds majority. The same year, the House fell 46 votes short, rejecting an amendment 236-187. In 1986, the Senate fell one vote short of the two-thirds needed, defeating an amendment 66-34. And in 1990, the House fell seven short with a vote of 279-150. *(1990 Almanac, p. 174)*

### New Debate

In May of 1992, the idea of amending the Constitution suddenly began gaining converts. Despite the budget agreement hammered out in 1990, deficits had continued to go up; the January estimate from the White House budget office for the fiscal 1992 deficit was roughly $400 billion. Meanwhile, public regard for Congress and its ability to handle the nation's finances was sinking in a critical election year. Democrats who had long opposed the idea were changing their minds out of sheer desperation.

One of the first signs that support was bubbling up from the rank and file came in April, when Speaker Thomas S. Foley, D-Wash., was quoted in the national press as telling home-state constituents that the House might pass a balanced-budget amendment in 1992.

On May 6, in a test of sorts, the House voted 322-66 in

favor of language in the Senate version of the fiscal 1993 budget resolution (H Con Res 287) that exhorted the Senate to adopted a balanced-budget amendment by June 5. *(Vote 107, p. 26-H)*

"In principle, I'm against it," said Sen. Warren B. Rudman, R-N.H., whose frustration over the deficit had already prompted him to announce that he would not seek re-election. "But this situation has me petrified.... A lot of very reasonable people have come to this conclusion."

The growing support was all the more surprising because there had been little in recent years of the grassroots clamor for a balanced budget that had been a hallmark of the late 1970s. The last time a state legislature had passed a resolution calling for a constitutional convention to write a balanced-budget amendment was in 1983. Congressional committees had paid only a smattering of attention to the issue, and there was little up-to-date analysis of how an amendment would work — if it would work at all.

### Stenholm, Simon Proposals

The two proposals getting the most attention in Congress were put forward by Rep. Charles W. Stenholm, D-Texas, and Sen. Paul Simon, D-Ill. Both closely tracked amendments that had been defeated in prior Congresses. Both seemed to enjoy broad support. And both were criticized by some Republicans as not going far enough.

Stenholm's amendment (H J Res 290) would have required Congress and the president to agree on an estimate of total receipts for a given year, enacting a law devoted solely to that subject. Government outlays (actual spending) could not exceed that revenue estimate. It would have taken three-fifths of the total membership (not just those present and voting) of each chamber to override this requirement. Even then, the deficit could not rise freely: Congress would have to approve a specific amount by which outlays could exceed receipts.

No bill to increase revenue could have been enacted unless it were approved by a majority of the total membership of each chamber.

The president would have been required to submit a balanced budget to Congress for each fiscal year.

Stenholm also would have required a three-fifths majority in both chambers to pass a bill to increase the limit on the federal debt. The debt limit — a statutory ceiling on the government's total accumulated deficits — had to be increased periodically to accommodate additional borrowing. Under existing law, raising the debt limit required only a simple majority. Those requirements could have been waived if a declaration of war was in effect.

Simon's proposal (S J Res 18) was the simpler of the two. It would have required that total outlays not exceed the government's total receipts for a given year. A three-fifths majority of the total membership (not just those present and voting) of each chamber would have been required to override this requirement. Congress would have had to specify the amount of the new deficit.

Simon's amendment would have required the president

---

### BOXSCORE

➡ **Balanced-Budget Amendment (H J Res 290, S J Res 18).** The measures would have approved a constitutional amendment requiring the president to submit and Congress to approve a balanced federal budget each fiscal year.

**Report:** S Rept 102-103.

#### KEY ACTION

June 11 — The **House** defeated H J Res 290, 280-153; a two-thirds majority was required for passage.

June 30 — The **Senate** voted 56-39, four votes shy of the 60 needed to stop a filibuster and allow a vote on the amendment.

July 1 — The **Senate** again failed, 56-39, to invoke cloture.

---

to submit a balanced budget for each fiscal year. A bill to increase revenue could be enacted only if it were approved by a majority of the entire membership of the House and Senate. Congress could waive the requirements in the event of a declared war or when an enacted law declared that an ongoing military conflict threatened national security.

### EARLY HOUSE ACTION

With interest in an amendment growing, longtime deficit hawk Stenholm had no trouble collecting the 218 signatures he needed on a "discharge petititon" that allowed the amendment to bypass the Judiciary Committee, which had failed to report the bill.

A furious few weeks of maneuvering and debate on the measure took place in May, before the amendment reached the House floor.

Budget Chairman Panetta, who opposed the amendment, launched a series of hearings, promising to air thoroughly all questions about the need for and efficacy of amending the Constitution. "This is a serious step, and we need to evaluate its implications for the Constitution, as well as for this body," he told the House on May 6.

Although a balanced-budget amendment had largely been a Republican cause in the past, many Republicans worried that the Democratic-sponsored version would erect only the smallest of barriers to using tax increases to offset the deficit. Bush insisted that an amendment include "safeguards against a resort to higher taxes as the means of complying with the constitutional mandate."

But the most intense debate was over whether a balanced-budget amendment should be linked to a companion deficit-reduction bill that set deficit targets leading to a balanced budget no later than the end of the decade, mandating spending cuts and tax increases to ensure that the targets were met.

### Panetta's Ploy

Panetta wanted to force House members to immediately confront the hard choices that would be necessary to bring the budget into balance. He thought that allowing a vote solely on a constitutional amendment, without going public with a specific plan to balance the budget, would give members a free vote. "I can't stop hypocrisy. But I hope at least I can expose it," Panetta said May 14, sounding increasingly exasperated at the force behind the amendment juggernaut. *(Deficit-reduction plan, p. 112)*

"That's a strategy devised purely to defeat the balanced-budget amendment," Stenholm said May 14.

Not everyone in Stenholm's camp agreed. "There's a group on both sides of the balanced-budget debate that wants to focus on a plan to get us there, and it will be a tough plan," said amendment supporter Timothy J. Penny, D-Minn. "We ought to be forced to take tough votes," he said.

But intensive efforts by Majority Leader Richard A Gephardt, D-Mo., to find a compromise ended in a standoff.

Panetta pressed his views further May 26, unveiling three scenarios designed to show just how painful it would be to implement a balanced-budget amendment. He warned it would take a staggering $560 billion in spending cuts, tax increases or both over five years, starting in fiscal 1993, to balance the budget by 1997, when an amendment approved by Congress in 1992 would likely have taken effect.

Panetta's scenarios described deep cuts in such politically hypersensitive areas as Medicare, Social Security and veterans' health care. Without tax increases, the cuts would have been enormous; if revenues were part of the mix, it would have taken substantial increases in corporate and individual income taxes or the creation of a national sales tax to bring a $350 billion deficit to zero by 1997.

"I'm not trying to scare anybody, but I'm also not trying to kid anybody," Panetta said. "If you're serious about doing a constitutional amendment, then you have to be serious about making these kinds of choices."

The White House immediately shot back that Panetta was "crying wolf." Spokesman Marlin Fitzwater said "wise" spending cuts coupled with economic growth would balance the budget with no tax increases and without endangering essential programs. But even some Republicans privately dismissed that as a naive view, warning that any attempt to balance the budget by 1997 would require painful measures.

Panetta also unveiled his version of the enforcement statute (HR 5272) that would be required to implement any balanced-budget amendment. In a variation on the Gramm-Rudman anti-deficit law first passed in 1985, Panetta's bill would have laid out yearly deficit-reduction targets and punished any failure to meet them by imposing harsh, across-the-board spending cuts or automatic surcharges on corporate and individual income taxes.

### House Leaders, Others Weigh In

In an effort to draw votes away from Stenholm, House Democratic leaders proposed their own amendment, requiring a balanced budget but exempting Social Security from spending cuts and revenue estimates. Gephardt insisted that his plan, cosponsored by Majority Whip David E. Bonior, D-Mich., David R. Obey, D-Wis., and others, was "a far better, more thoughtful and effective approach" than Stenholm's.

Stenholm immediately assailed the Gephardt measure as an attempt to provide members cover by immunizing them against attack if they voted against his amendment. "Most members will see through it, that it is not a sincere effort," he charged. "This definitely is a much weaker amendment than ours. We make it much more difficult to deficit spend; they make it easier."

Gephardt also outlined an enforcement plan, which would have set fixed deficit targets between 1992 and 1997 and punished overspending with a 60-40 mix of across-the-board spending cuts and surcharges on individual and corporate income taxes.

Organized labor weighed in, launching a national lobbying campaign to head off the amendment. The AFL-CIO began running radio commercials warning that the "balanced-budget hoax would hurt all of us" by raising taxes and cutting government benefits, including Social Security and veterans benefits. The spots also charged that the amendment would "destroy" 3 million jobs a year and push up state and local taxes. AFL-CIO spokesman David Saltz said the campaign would soon spread to an additional seven states.

The Children's Defense Fund, Common Cause, the League of Women Voters, Public Citizen and the Religious Action Center of Reform Judaism sent a joint letter to members of Congress warning that the amendment would involve the courts in economic policy and undermine majority rule in Congress by requiring a three-fifths vote for deficit spending.

Finally, there was the Byrd factor. Senate Appropriations Chairman Byrd gave amendment opponents a crucial lift in late May when he made it clear that he vehemently opposed the amendment and planned to devote a great deal of energy to trying to stop it. In a May 20 floor speech, Byrd warned that the amendment would shift fiscal power from Congress to the White House and the courts, and he virtually promised a filibuster. "Unlimited debate is one of the cornerstones [of] this institution," he said. "There are some of us who intend to have our say before the die is cast."

## HOUSE FLOOR ACTION

Still, barely a week before the vote, House passage seemed certain. But a combination of hard lobbying by the Democratic leadership and outside interest groups and a creeping uneasiness about tinkering with the Constitution left backers of the amendment nine votes short of the two-thirds majority they needed.

The House began the debate June 9, taking up a proposed balanced-budget law that was similar to a bill that had passed the House in 1990 as an alternative to a constitutional amendment. The measure (HR 5333) would have required the president to submit a balanced budget, and the House and Senate Budget committees to send balanced budgets to the floor of both chambers, beginning in fiscal 1998. The House Democratic caucus supported the measure in a closed meeting on June 4, but the bill died on a 199-220 vote, not winning even a simple majority, much less the two-thirds needed because it was brought up under a special procedure that prevented amendments. (Vote 174, p. 42-H)

Stenholm cheered the defeat as proof that "there were no cheap votes." Sponsor Barbara B. Kennelly, D-Conn., rejected assertions that the bill was introduced to provide political cover for those opposing the constitutional amendment. Of the 189 Democrats who voted for the bill, however, 121 later voted against the amendment.

The next day, the House engaged in general debate on the merits of a balanced-budget amendment, with both supporters and opponents saying the anticipated vote was too close to call.

Then on June 11, in a king-of-the-hill process, the House voted on a series of four balanced-budget amendment proposals, with the last one adopted by a majority vote submitted to the House for a final vote, requiring a two-thirds majority. The four alternatives were:

● By Jon Kyl, R-Ariz. His amendment, like the others, would have required that all government outlays not exceed total receipts. But it had two other significant provisions: It would have restricted total outlays to 19 percent of the country's total output of goods and services for the year, measured by the gross national product (GNP), and it would have given the president authority to veto all or part of individual provisions of bills that appropriated money or otherwise obligated the Treasury.

Bills resulting in deficits or in outlays in excess of the GNP ceiling would have required support of three-fifths of

the total membership of the House and Senate.

The amendment was rejected 170-258, on a nearly party-line vote. *(Vote 183, p. 46-H)*

• By Joe L. Barton, R-Texas. This amendment largely tracked Stenholm's, with one significant wrinkle. It would not have allowed government revenues to increase at a rate greater than that of total growth in national income, unless a bill to that effect supported by three-fifths of both chambers was enacted into law.

Barton's amendment won strong Republican support and drew more Democrats than Kyl's, but it was rejected 200-227. *(Vote 184, p. 46-H)*

• By Gephardt. It would have required the president to submit a balanced budget and Congress to produce one unless the president issued a "declaration of national urgency" and a majority of Congress voted to approve it. It would have required only a majority of both the House and Senate to permit a deficit. But it would have capped outlays at the level proposed by the president, and it would have excluded Social Security from deficit calculations, which Gephardt contended would have protected that program from cuts.

Some Democratic opponents of Stenholm were clearly enamored of this version, if only to show their support either for a balanced budget or for Social Security.

But some raised serious questions about ceding power to the president by letting him set a ceiling on outlays. "Not even two-thirds of the House and two-thirds of the Senate are empowered to [spend more than the president proposes]," said Tom Campbell, R-Calif. "For the first time, this would be an absolute veto.... This is very, very dangerous."

The amendment appeared to have the desired effect of muting Democratic support for Stenholm. "The decision to put Gephardt in brought about 35 votes," Nagle said. In all, 47 Democrats voted for Gephardt and against Stenholm; six of them had been Stenholm cosponsors.

The amendment was rejected 103-327, with a significant majority of Democrats and virtually all Republicans opposed. *(Vote 185, p. 46-H)*

• By Stenholm. His alternative preserved the basic terms of H J Res 290 as originally introduced — including three-fifths majorities to permit deficit spending or an increase in the federal debt. But it incorporated the military emergency waiver, a requirement that Congress enforce the amendment by statute and a later effective date of fiscal 1988. The substitute was first adopted by a vote of 279-153. *(Vote 186, p. 46-H)*

It then failed on final passage — when a two-thirds majority was required — by 280-153. The difference was that Walter B. Jones, D-N.C., voted no on the substitute and yes on passage, and Foley, who has voted only 14 times in 1992, voted no on passage. In a bitter twist for Stenholm, 12 cosponsors of his original amendment were persuaded to vote against the final version, three more than his losing margin. *(Vote 187, p. 46-H)*

Lobbyists from labor unions, advocacy groups representing senior citizens and low-income people, religious organizations and the citizens lobby Common Cause crowded the hallway outside the chamber. As the amendment was defeated, a cheer arose first in the chamber and then among the lobbyists. But it seemed clear that the efforts of Foley, Panetta and most of the rest of the Democratic leadership were more important to the outcome than those of outside lobbyists.

It might have helped, however, that traditional anti-deficit lobbyists such as the Chamber of Commerce of the United States opposed the amendment, chiefly because they feared it would be used to justify a tax increase. And several members mentioned the opposition of presumed presidential candidate Ross Perot as a factor. Perot announced his opposition on the NBC "Today" show the morning of the vote.

## SENATE ACTION

A longtime enthusiast of writing a balanced-budget requirement into the Constitution, Simon had secured Judiciary Committee approval for his amendment the previous year. The panel had approved the measure in a little-noticed vote of 11-3 on May 23, 1991. *(1991 Almanac, p. 56)*

As chances for passage in the House suddenly improved in the spring of 1992, a core of Senate backers — mostly Democrats who previously were governors — appeared before television cameras May 14 to call attention to the growing support in their chamber for a constitutional amendment.

It appeared that the biggest fight in the Senate would be over an administration-backed Republican effort to require more than a simple majority to approve future tax increases. Simon's plan would have required a simple majority of the total membership of the House and Senate. But Bob Kasten, R-Wis., and others preferred that three-fifths of the total membership of each chamber be required. Simon and other Democratic supporters of the amendment opposed Kasten, however, and it appeared unlikely that the GOP effort would prevail.

But thanks to the one-man wrecking crew of Appropriations Chairman Bryd, the Senate drive behind the amendment fell apart a week before the House was scheduled to vote on the matter.

"In the final analysis, Congress will not propose this amendment," Byrd predicted June 2, and many of his colleagues concurred. "Once members are really informed on the mischief this amendment could do, the damage it could do ... I have a feeling that there's enough character to this Senate" to defeat it.

While Majority Leader Mitchell and others in the Senate worked to reverse the amendment juggernaut, it seemed to be chiefly Byrd's efforts that turned the tide. "The chairman of the Appropriations Committee is working my colleagues very, very hard," Simon said. "All of us have things in the Appropriations Committee we'd like to get through."

Byrd flatly denied using his position as chairman to bludgeon amendment supporters, though he admitted to having called in many of his fellow Democrats for chats. He merely argued the merits, he said. But others noted that Byrd obviously did not have to remind his colleagues of his position of power.

Byrd made it clear he intended to filibuster the measure for as long as he could, offering a series of amendments in hope of ladening it with unacceptable baggage. "It's going to require some talk to inform the country that this is just an effort to seek an easy way out," he said. "There will be amendments offered, no doubt."

Concerned that the amendment's backers might defeat amendments and get the 60 votes they needed to cut off debate, Mitchell put off floor action to allow opposition to solidify.

He never had to schedule a vote. Immediately after the

House defeated Stenholm's amendment, Mitchell said that he would not call Simon's measure up, apparently killing any chance for the amendment in 1992. Before the House vote, Simon later said, his vote count had shown 63 senators for the amendment, four shy of the 67 needed to garner the necessary two-thirds.

### Last Gasp

Two weeks later, Phil Gramm, D-Texas, and other die-hard supporters tried to bring the amendment back to life by attaching it to an unrelated bill regulating government-sponsored enterprises (S 2733). The partisan tone of the debate splintered what had been a strong, bipartisan coalition in favor of the amendment. Simon said the attempt to bring it up after the House had effectively killed it had "something of a partisan twist" to it, adding that he had told his Democratic allies that he would release them from their pledges to support the measure.

Byrd vowed to talk the measure to death if necessary, and on June 25 began speaking at length. During three hours of criticism, Byrd called the amendment "a dagger at the throat of the people's branch. The grand strategy of some is to erode the people's power and put it in the hands of the executive branch and the judiciary."

In identical 56-39 votes June 30 and July 1, the Senate fell four votes shy of the 60 it would have taken to choke off the Democratic filibuster. Byrd called the cloture vote whose failure finally killed the measure the most important such vote he had cast in his 34-year Senate career. *(Votes 135, 136, p. 34-H)*

"This is the end of the debate for the year," said Minority Leader Bob Dole, R-Kan. "I'm not totally happy with the result, but the Senate has spoken." Dole said a clear majority wanted a vote on the amendment, however, and he said he hoped the measure would fare better the following year.

### EPILOGUE

The defeat of the balanced-budget amendment looked briefly as if it would set Congress up for a summerlong series of tests of fiscal self-discipline. Budget-cutters in both parties hoped they could turn their defeat into an opportunity for a new assault on the deficit, backed by members eager to demonstrate that, despite their vote against the amendment, they were committed to deficit-reduction. "There will be a groundswell, and I think it will accomplish what many of us wanted," said Rep. David Dreier, R-Calif., an amendment supporter.

"This has been a wake-up call," said Jim Slattery, D-Kan., a strong advocate for spending restraint who opposed the amendment. "There will be a lot of key votes in the next 10 days" as appropriations bills begin to come to the floor.

And, in a rare floor speech June 11, House Speaker Thomas S. Foley, D-Wash., urged support for Panetta's deficit-cutting bill. "If half of the courage expressed in the rhetoric presented here today in support of this amendment will stand behind a proposal, which the Committee on the Budget will shortly produce on the floor, we can establish the process to reduce the deficit," he said.

But the budget-cutting fever quickly waned. After an unexpected House vote to end funding for the hyperexpensive superconducting super collider, the two chambers contented themselves primarily with a series of amendments that trimmed overhead and administrative

spending. Most of the money for the supercollider was eventually restored.

Panetta tried to work out a bipartisan deficit-reduction plan, but negotiations with House Republicans collapsed, and his bill died without being reported by any of the three committees (Rules, Government Operations, Ways and Means) to which it was referred. ∎

# Deficit-Reduction Plan: Panetta's Holy Grail

House Budget Committee Chairman Leon E. Panetta, D-Calif., had long made congressional adoption of a serious deficit-reduction plan the Holy Grail of his congressional career, but in 1992 he had added motivation. Panetta was worried that Congress would adopt a balanced-budget amendment to the Constitution and think that that alone would somehow balance the budget.

In May, just as balanced-budget fever was beginning to sweep Congress, Panetta unveiled a plan designed to implement a balanced budget — and, not coincidentally, to show his colleagues just how tough that would be.

Both the House and the Senate shortly thereafter failed to adopt the balanced-budget amendment, but Panetta kept on trying to assemble a major deficit-reduction plan. *(Balanced-budget amendment, p. 108)*

Such a plan would have offered cover to Democrats who opposed the balanced-budget amendment. And because a truly tough plan was widely assumed to be going nowhere in Congress in 1992, it also was an exercise to help lay the groundwork for the serious attempt at deficit reduction that many assumed would be coming in 1993, after the presidential elections.

When negotiations with House Republicans broke down, Panetta introduced his own plan (HR 5676), which was designed to balance the budget by 1998. Essentially a procedural bill, it provided a mechanism for Congress and the president to meet deficit-reduction targets each year through a combination of spending cuts and revenue increases. Its tough enforcement process included the potential for automatic tax increases and cutbacks in Social Security.

In the end, the medicine was too tough and the political need to cut the deficit not acute enough to force action. Although subcommittees of the Rules Committee and the Government Operations Committee held hearings on the measure late in the session, the measure died without coming to a vote in either panel.

### LEGISLATIVE ACTION

Panetta's action on the bill began as part of a coordinated effort by House Democrats and others to head off the balanced-budget amendment.

On May 26, Panetta unveiled three scenarios designed to show just how painful it would be to implement such an amendment. Panetta warned that it would take a staggering $560 billion in spending cuts, tax increases or both over five years, starting in fiscal 1993, to balance the budget by 1997, which is when most thought any amendment approved by Congress in 1992 would take effect.

Panetta's scenarios described deep cuts in such politi-

cally hypersensitive areas as Medicare, Social Security and veterans health care. Without tax increases, the cuts would be enormous; if revenues were part of the mix, it would take substantial increases in corporate and individual income taxes or the creation of a national sales tax to bring a $350 billion deficit to zero by 1997.

"I'm not trying to scare anybody, but I'm also not trying to kid anybody," Panetta said. "If you're serious about doing a constitutional amendment, then you have to be serious about making these kinds of choices."

The White House immediately shot back that Panetta was "crying wolf." Spokesman Marlin Fitzwater said "wise" spending cuts coupled with economic growth would balance the budget with no tax increases and without endangering essential programs. But even some Republicans privately dismissed that as a naive view, warning that any attempt to balance the budget by 1997 would require painful measures.

### Balanced-Budget Enforcement Statute

Panetta also unveiled his version of the enforcement statute (HR 5272) that would be required to implement any balanced-budget amendment. The Constitutional amendment itself could not force the detailed congressional action necessary to match spending to revenues. In a variation on the Gramm-Rudman anti-deficit law first passed in 1985, Panetta's bill laid out yearly deficit-reduction targets and proposed to punish any failure to meet them by imposing harsh, across-the-board spending cuts or automatic surcharges on corporate and individual income taxes.

With the failure of House efforts to pass the balanced-budget amendment in June, Panetta switched gears. In an effort some outsiders viewed as noble but quixotic, he held closed-door meetings of the Budget Committee in late June to try to put together a broad deficit-reduction package that could come to the House floor with bipartisan support.

The mere fact that Republicans and Democrats were bargaining at all was counted as at least a partial victory, given the poisonous partisan atmosphere that prevailed as the presidential campaign began to tighten.

Panetta, who was widely regarded as holding the process together almost by sheer force of will, declared the job "three-quarters done" and said the talks had moved far enough to make it worthwhile to brief top leaders from both parties to get their input for the final push.

But while committee members had outlined a tentative procedural plan to balance the budget by 1998, they had done little more than talk about core issues such as whether to raise taxes and how to cut entitlement spending for programs such as Medicare.

"It's an interesting discussion, but it's not clear that it's going to be very productive," said White House budget director Richard G. Darman, who, like many outside the talks, saw more problems than opportunities for serious deficit reduction. "We're in the midst of a partisan political period, and it's not going to get done right now."

The last serious budget negotiations, in 1990, required an all-out commitment from the White House and leaders from both parties in the House and Senate. Panetta hoped he could build enough momentum to force the White House and the Senate to join in this time, but both were keeping their distance. Senate Budget Committee Chairman Jim Sasser, D-Tenn., said that the Senate would only be "spinning its wheels" if it tried to undertake a serious deficit-reduction effort in 1992.

A hardheaded view of the remaining congressional schedule in this election-shortened year revealed little of the political or temporal space necessary for the lengthy process of shaping a deficit-reduction package, however. "Time is not on our side," said Rep. John Lewis, D-Ga., a chief deputy majority whip. "Members want to sort of play it safe."

But Panetta remained optimistic. "My experience is that if you don't push on these things," he said, "you never get anything." Democratic leaders were sending encouraging signals. House Speaker Thomas S. Foley, D-Wash., said he thought a deficit-reduction bill could get to the House floor in July.

Panetta planned to try to find consensus for a bill in the Budget Committee, but the panel had no legislative jurisdiction. Instead, the bill would be referred to the Government Operations, Rules, and Ways and Means committees, where its prospects were murky.

Government Operations Committee Chairman John Conyers Jr., D-Mich., for example, was not enthusiastic. While saying he did not want to prejudge Panetta's effort, Conyers said he had "never been enamored of budget-enforcement measures in the Congress."

### Bipartisan Bill Effort Collapses

Panetta's efforts to forge a bipartisan bill collapsed July 9, when House Republicans pulled out of formal negotiations.

The withdrawal came in a letter from House Minority Leader Robert H. Michel, R-Ill., who criticized Democrats for failing to live up to the existing budget agreement and said there was no point to continued formal talks.

Democrats had expected the GOP withdrawal and said beforehand that they planned to bring a package to the House floor nonetheless.

Budget Committee Republicans had been negotiating with committee Democrats for weeks, but GOP leaders, including Michel and Ohio's Bill Gradison, ranking member on Budget, concluded that their differences with Democrats over taxes and other budget items were too great to warrant continued talks.

Republicans also said they did not want to be part of an effort by Democrats to provide cover for members who voted against the balanced-budget amendment.

In his sharply worded July 9 letter that essentially said Democrats were not to be trusted when they made budget deals, Michel told Foley that Republicans saw "little benefit in pursuing *formal* negotiations with little prospect of producing any meaningful legislative enactment at this time."

Michel noted that the Senate had no intention of considering a deficit-reduction plan in 1992 and that in any event, there was little time left in the session. But he suggested that Republicans might be willing to continue "informal discussions" to see if they could work out differences.

He accused the Democrats of consistently violating the terms of the 1990 budget agreement and said that dismal history had convinced him that "any bipartisan effort in this Congress to address budget enforcement will be met with widespread skepticism and derision."

Michel cited the House Democrats' move early in 1991 to shift scorekeeping authority over certain spending programs from the White House's Office of Management and Budget to the Congressional Budget Office. He also charged Democrats with having repeatedly used emergency spending exemptions or Rules Committee waivers to get around budget enforcement rules.

Given that record, Michel said, "you can surely understand our skepticism about the sincerity of the majority to live up to any budget enforcement agreement."

Gephardt said he found it "strange" that Republicans were not interested in pursuing talks. "It looks to me like they're after a press release and not any concrete action that would achieve anything," he said.

### Panetta Unveils Democrats-Only Plan

On July 23, Panetta unveiled a tough, Democrats-only plan to balance the budget by 1998 and said he hoped to see the House vote on it in the next few months.

Panetta had an uphill fight from the start. In addition to opposition from the White House and indifference from Senate Democrats, it was far from clear that House Democrats would want to vote in an election year for a plan that contained potential tax increases and cutbacks in Social Security. Budget Committee ranking Republican Gradison said he looked forward to hammering Democrats on those and other features of the plan if it came to the floor.

"If you just want to talk about reducing the deficit and not do it, then obviously you're not going to support an approach like this," Panetta said.

Panetta's proposal was essentially an update of the pre-1990 Gramm-Rudman deficit-reduction law, which set annual deficit targets and imposed across-the-board spending cuts if Congress exceeded the targets. The 1990 budget deal temporarily removed the targets and year-end spending cuts in favor of tight restraints on spending.

Instead of deficit limits, Panetta's new package set annual deficit-reduction goals, to be met through a combination of cuts in appropriations and entitlements, possibly coupled with tax increases. The specifics of how to reach each year's deficit targets would be worked out by Congress and the president.

Appropriations would be limited by a single overall cap.

Proposed reductions in entitlements and increases in taxes would be set by the congressional budget resolution, and a "spinoff bill" assigning those targets to specific committees would go to the president for his signature.

If the president signed the bill, the panels that failed to meet their deficit-reduction goals would face cuts in their entitlement programs or imposition of a personal and corporate surtax.

If no spinoff bill were enacted, enforcement would occur through an across-the-board freeze on all spending and tax indexing, coupled with a temporary tax increase on those with incomes of more than $250,000. Unlike the Gramm-Rudman enforcement mechanism, which provided for numerous exemptions, this plan would hit all spending, including heretofore sacred programs such as Social Security.

Panetta's plan had the support of Budget Committee Democrats, including key conservative Charles W. Stenholm of Texas.

Gradison and fellow Budget Committee Republican Alex McMillan of North Carolina said they would develop a GOP alternative that could be considered if Panetta's plan made it to the floor. Gradison said his chief objections were Panetta's inclusion of possible tax increases, his failure to protect Social Security, and his abandonment of separate caps for defense, domestic and international spending.

Although House Speaker Foley continued to send encouraging signals about the prospects for the measure, it quickly became clear that there was far too little enthusiasm for the politically and fiscally tough bill among Democrats to get it to the floor. ∎

# Small Step Toward Line-Item Veto

Fiscal conservatives who had tried in vain for years to give the president increased authority to cut individual items out of large appropriations bills celebrated a partial victory in 1992 with House passage of a bill that would have given the president the equivalent of a weak line-item veto.

Although the measure died without Senate action when Congress adjourned, the House vote signaled increasing momentum for the concept, which later won qualified support from President-elect Bill Clinton.

The measure fell far short of the full line-item veto some conservatives wanted. Instead, it built on authority the president already had to propose that Congress rescind previously appropriated spending. Under law, Congress could ignore such presidential "rescission" proposals; if it did, the proposals expired after 45 days.

The bill (HR 2164) would have forced Congress to vote on the president's rescission proposals. If both the House and Senate approved them by majority votes, the spending would be cut.

The "expedited rescission" measure was introduced in May 1991 by Rep. Thomas R. Carper, D-Del. Congressional appropriators bitterly opposed virtually any proposal to increase the president's power to tamper with appropriations bills, and Democratic leaders had generally bowed to the appropriators' wishes to keep such proposals from the floor.

In this instance, however, Carper and other backers managed to force the House leadership to schedule a vote by holding hostage a short-term continuing resolution (CR) that Congress had to pass to keep the government going while the House and Senate finished the final fiscal 1993 appropriations bills.

The House later voted under suspension of the rules on Oct. 3 to pass the expedited rescissions bill. But House backers knew they were sending the bill to its death in the Senate, where Appropriations Committee Chairman Robert C. Byrd, D-W.Va., opposed it strongly enough to keep it from ever reaching the floor. When Congress adjourned on Oct. 9, the Carper measure died with other unfinished business.

But the measure picked up momentum and important backing that promised to make it an issue later on. House Speaker Thomas S. Foley, D-Wash., despite what conservative Democrats said were his initial efforts to keep the measure off the floor, endorsed and voted for the measure. And shortly after Clinton was elected president, he told reporters that he and Foley had discussed the possibility of compromising over Clinton's desire for a line-item veto — possibly through some form of expedited rescissions measure.

## BACKGROUND

Backers argued that giving the president some form of line-item veto or beefed-up rescission authority over appropriations bills would help control the deficit by giving the chief executive the power to weed out pork-barrel spending and other questionable items buried in big spending bills.

But critics argued that the line-item veto simply shifted too much power over spending from Congress to the president. They further contended that even an aggressively wielded line-item veto would likely save little real money in a time of $300 billion deficits, since Congress and the

administration usually agreed on the vast bulk of appropriations and fought their battles only at the margins.

Without a line-item veto, presidents who wanted to root out specific spending items had to veto entire appropriations bills or use their authority to propose that Congress rescind specific items in bills that had already been passed.

These so-called rescission proposals did not give the president much clout; Congress was free to ignore them, and if it did, the proposals expired after 45 days.

Backers of increased presidential clout over spending bills had proposed three different forms of legislation:

● **Line-item veto.** This would enable the president to veto individual line items in appropriations bills, instead of having to veto entire bills. Congress could override a line-item veto only with a two-thirds vote of both the House and the Senate.

● **Enhanced rescission authority.** This would strengthen the president's existing rescission authority by shifting the burden to Congress to disapprove rescission proposals, which would go into effect unless both the House and the Senate voted by majority to reject them. The president could veto a congressional disapproval resolution, again setting up a situation in which Congress would have to muster a two-thirds vote of both the House and the Senate to override the president.

● **Expedited rescission authority.** This compromise leaves the burden on the president to get Congress to approve his rescission proposals, and it satisfied some critics who contended that Congress should never put itself in a situation where the president could dictate spending policy with only a one-third-plus-one minority of Congress to back him up. Expedited rescission authority would maintain majority rule by requiring that any rescission proposal be approved by majority votes of both the House and the Senate. The one major change it would make would be to force Congress to vote on proposals it could ignore. If the House passed a rescission proposal by a majority vote, the Senate would have to vote on it. If the Senate approved, also by a majority, the rescission would go into effect.

## LEGISLATIVE ACTION

With the deficit increasingly an issue in the presidential campaign, fiscal conservatives in Congress had tried throughout the year to pass bills giving the president new authority to strip items out of appropriations bills. None succeeded until a bipartisan group of House members forced the House leadership to schedule HR 2164 for a vote at the very end of the session.

The House leadership had sought to avoid bringing the matter to the floor at all but faced a rebellion by conservative Democrats on Sept. 30 during a chaotic vote on the rule governing floor consideration of a short-term continuing resolution, a must-pass bill to fund the government while Congress finished the 1993 appropriations bills.

Angry that House leaders would not agree to give them a floor vote on the expedited rescission bill, conservative Democrats teamed with Republicans to oppose the rule. House leaders thought they could tough out the vote, but with all time expired, the rule was losing by six votes or more.

At that point, Majority Leader Richard A. Gephardt, D-Mo., sued for peace, promising bill sponsor Carper and key ally Charles W. Stenholm, D-Texas, that they would have their floor vote. Carper, Stenholm and some of their allies then switched their votes to aye, and the rule passed, 213-204. *(Vote 439, p. 108-H)*

Carper's measure would have allowed the president to veto all funding for any unauthorized project but only 25 percent of the money for an authorized project.

The House would have been required to vote on the proposal within 10 days, but it could also vote on an alternative rescission proposal from the Appropriations Committee. A mandatory Senate vote would follow if the House passed the rescission measure.

Carper and Stenholm's power play recalled Stenholm's similar success in rallying conservative Democrats to oppose a House leadership plan earlier in the year to break down the budget "walls" between defense and domestic spending. Then, as this time, Democratic leaders miscalculated their support on an issue of particular appeal to fiscal conservatives in their own party. *(Budget walls, p. 104)*

The House voted 312-97 on Oct. 3 to pass the Carper measure under suspension of the rules. Having done that, however, the House sent the bill to its death in the Senate, where it was opposed by Byrd. The measure died when Congress adjourned on Oct. 9. *(Vote 459, p. 112-H)*

During House debate, proponents said the measure would be a small but important step toward deficit reduction. Opponents argued that it was unnecessary, since Congress had approved more rescissions than the White House had requested since the process was codified in the 1974 Budget Act — although lawmakers had often substituted their own cuts for those proposed by the president. Some critics further argued that giving the president the power to threaten to cut individual projects would give him enormous new leverage to force individual members of Congress to vote with him on unrelated issues. ■

# S&L Bailout Funding Dries Up

The 102nd Congress adjourned for the year without replenishing the savings and loan bailout; the effort died after political gamesmanship in the House and a lack of firm White House prodding by the Bush administration led to an impasse. As a result, the Resolution Trust Corporation (RTC), the thrift salvage agency, was forced to virtually shut down. The agency said the delay was costing taxpayers $6 million a day.

The Senate was able to muster a bare majority for a bill (S 2482) that would have appropriated $43 billion more for the bailout — $25 billion plus $18 billion that had been appropriated in 1991 but had since reverted to the Treasury. But on April 1, the House overwhelmingly rejected a bill (HR 4704) that would have provided just the unspent $18 billion.

A separate House bill providing $43 billion (HR 4241) was approved by the House Banking Committee but went no further, after it was apparent it could not pass.

After HR 4704 went down to defeat, President Bush weighed in again with a July 29 letter to House Democratic

and Republican leaders that urged prompt action on the bill. The impasse, however, was not broken.

## BACKGROUND

The main thrift cleanup law, the Financial Institutions Reform, Recovery and Enforcement Act of 1989, gave the taxpayer-financed RTC the task of cleaning up the thrift debacle of the 1980s. *(1989 Almanac, p. 117)*

In 1989, lawmakers gave the RTC an initial grant of $50 billion ($18.8 billion of it from taxpayers). Congress voted twice in 1991 to replenish the agency's coffers with taxpayer money: $30 billion in the spring and up to $25 billion in November. But the November grant had a catch: The RTC could spend as much of the $25 billion as it needed through April 1, 1992. On that date, $18 billion of the money remained unspent; it reverted to the Treasury, and the RTC became virtually moribund. *(1991 Almanac, p. 98)*

It was widely acknowledged that, one way or another, the bailout eventually had to be funded — otherwise the government would renege on its 59-year-old promise to guarantee deposits. And there was near-universal agreement that Congress was negligent in allowing the funding to lapse.

"I cannot believe the political cowardice of these folks," said Herbert Sandler of World Savings and Loan in California, one of the nation's largest thrifts. "You don't have to be a rocket scientist to figure out that this is the right thing to do."

But there were plenty of reasons for individual members to vote no.

Those from districts whose local thrifts had remained generally healthy found it galling to vote to bail out thrifts that were concentrated in pockets elsewhere in the country, including Florida and the Southwest. In addition, the thrift agency had few fans in Congress and was under attack for the way it had been running the bailout. Critics said the RTC was cutting fire-sale deals as it disposed of the assets of failed thrifts, that it offered generous guarantees on mortgage-backed securities sold by the agency that exposed the taxpayers to huge risk if the underlying loans went bad, and that it wasted millions in payments to outside lawyers and accountants.

"On the whole, members are very unhappy with the RTC," said Rep. Bill McCollum, R-Fla.

So, apparently, was Democratic presidential candidate Bill Clinton.

In his campaign manifesto, "Putting People First," he said he could save $17 billion in 1993-96 through "RTC management reform."

The debate over RTC funding came as those responsible for the cleanup said it was almost complete and that the industry has regained its footing. "The challenge I accepted — to help clean up the thrift industry and restore it to profitability and stability — is virtually complete," said Office of Thrift Supervision (OTS) Director Timothy Ryan, who stepped down in December.

Near year's end, the RTC had dispatched 653 institutions; 74 more were under agency control and were awaiting

---

### BOXSCORE

➡ **RTC Financing (HR 4704, S 2482).** The House bill would have allowed the Resolution Trust Corporation (RTC), the agency responsible for the savings and loan salvage operation, to spend $18 billion in already appropriated funds that had reverted to the Treasury. The Senate version would have provided $43 billion.

#### KEY ACTION

**April 1** — The **House** rejected HR 4704 by a vote of 125-298.

**March 26** — The **Senate** passed S 2482, 52-42.

---

resolution. As the thrift cleanup neared completion, the RTC was slated to go out of business. Under existing law, the agency could no longer take control of failing thrifts after Sept. 30, 1993, but it had until the end of 1996 to resolve such thrifts' losses and sell off assets.

## HOUSE COMMITTEE ACTION

The Banking Subcommittee on Financial Institutions Subcommittee voted 25-11 on Feb. 27 in favor of a bill (HR 4241) to pump another $43 billion into the savings and loan salvage operation. It would have freed up the unused $18 billion and provided an additional $25 billion through April 1, 1993.

The $25 billion in new money was well shy of what the Treasury Department said was needed to finish the job.

Treasury Secretary Nicholas F. Brady had asked Congress to provide a $55 billion cash infusion to the RTC, but a Republican-led effort to reduce that amount to $25 billion prevailed.

RTC chief executive Albert V. Casey wrote the subcommittee on Feb. 26 to say that an additional $25 billion would be sufficient to carry the agency through April 1, 1993. His letter came after testimony given to the subcommittee the same day by the General Accounting Office (GAO). GAO officials urged Congress to keep the RTC on a short financial leash, providing it with enough money to last until the spring of 1993. The GAO, which had been sharply critical of RTC management, said it was impossible to know how much the agency would need to complete its task.

Some administration officials were plainly unhappy with the subcommittee's decision. "This [letter] has undercut everybody; we were about to get the money," fumed one.

But Deputy Treasury Secretary John E. Robson said he was pleased with the outcome. "Everybody would prefer the full amount necessary to finish the job. But you take what you get in this world," Robson said.

Several subcommittee Democrats, including Gerald D. Kleczka of Wisconsin and Peter Hoagland of Nebraska, said they believed the subcommittee had been willing to vote for at least $55 billion.

Hoagland and Doug Barnard Jr., D-Ga., offered an amendment to give the RTC as much as it needed through April 1, 1994, with no dollar cap. They argued that repeated trips to the congressional well merely caused delay and uncertainty and drove up the cost of the bailout.

House Speaker Thomas S. Foley, D-Wash., shared their view. But critics argued that an unlimited appropriation would amount to a blank check and would restrict congressional oversight. The amendment was defeated on a voice vote.

The vote came after one of the tamer markup sessions on the thrift bailout. Subcommittee Chairman Frank Annunzio, D-Ill., refused to allow consideration of 18 amendments, many of them controversial, sparing the panel most of the partisan rancor that had caused several prior bailout

bills to implode in committee or on the floor.

### Full Committee Approval

The full House Banking Committee approved HR 4241 by a 30-17 vote on March 12, after a debate that was notable for its brevity and lack of divisiveness.

That was because Chairman Henry B. Gonzalez, D-Texas, and ranking minority member Chalmers P. Wylie, R-Ohio, stood together to oppose all amendments. Members had drafted at least nine, many of which would have been controversial. But the committee voted 34-11 to shut off debate before any were considered.

In the past, RTC financing bills had attracted dozens of amendments that would have altered the agency's asset-disposition policies (often in contradictory fashion), imposed race and gender requirements on its contracting practices, or required it to take special actions to protect environmentally or historically sensitive property.

## FULL HOUSE ACTION

Although the bill had made it out of committee, floor action was stalled by opposition from a majority of Republicans. GOP Whip Newt Gingrich of Georgia was promoting a plan to strip most of the money if the bill came to the floor.

When it became clear that the measure would not pass the House, Gonzalez and Wylie introduced a new, radically trimmed-down bill (HR 4707) that would have merely lifted the April 1 deadline by which the RTC had to spend the rest of the $25 billion appropriated in 1991. The bill was introduced March 31 and went to the House floor the next day, where it was resoundingly defeated by a vote of 125-298. *(Vote 69, p. 18-H)*

The bill failed after Republicans began to abandon it. They did so after the Rules Committee sent the bill to the floor under a closed rule that allowed no amendments, including one by Bill McCollum, R-Fla., to aid scores of thrifts whose cushion of capital reserves was impaired by an accounting change enacted in the 1989 law inaugurating the bailout.

Republican Whip Gingrich cited McCollum's amendment and the closed rule and led a revolt against the bill, giving an out to members who knew that a vote to spend money on the bailout was politically risky. Without Republican support, Democrats were unwilling to walk the plank alone and a majority also jumped ship, leaving the RTC without money to finance the closing of failed thrifts and to cover depositor losses in those institutions. RTC officials were forced to suspend their thrift closing operations with about 50 thrifts awaiting shutdown.

McCollum's amendment would have earmarked $2.5 billion to buy back so-called supervisory good will from about 53 weak thrifts. Good will was an intangible asset that was acquired by these institutions in the mid-1980s when they bought failing thrifts from the government. They originally were entitled to count it toward a minimum capital requirements, but the 1989 thrift bailout law revoked that privilege.

McCollum argued that if the government had replaced the good will with cash, these thrifts would have been profitable and met minimum capital requirements. Without that action, he said, the thrifts would fail at a much higher cost to taxpayers. The administration argued strenuously against McCollum's proposal as a giveaway, and members of both parties opposed it.

Barney Frank, D-Mass., summed up the feelings of many Democrats: "What we have here are a lot of people on the other side who hope they can vote no so the rest of us will vote yes, and they can have their cake and eat it, too. That is not going to happen today."

## SENATE ACTION

The Senate worked late into the night March 26 before a bare majority of the membership voted to give the RTC another $43 billion. By a 52-42 vote, the Senate passed a bill (S 2482) to provide the extra money and make some significant changes in the bailout. Some of the non-financing provisions of the Senate bill — which were added almost entirely at the insistence of Democrats on the Senate Banking Committee — drew fire from Republicans and consumer groups. *(Vote 59, p. 9-S)*

"None of us want to spend this money; it's an enormous waste of money," said Tim Wirth, D-Colo., during floor debate. Republicans Phil Gramm, Texas, and Jake Garn, Utah, argued strenuously in favor of stripping out all language beyond the financing provisions. Gramm's amendment to do so was killed on a tabling motion that passed 58-36. A similar amendment failed in committee on a 10-11 vote. *(Vote 58, p. 9-S)*

The Senate also refused to go along with a proposal by John Kerry, D-Mass., that the balance of the bailout be financed with either tax increases or spending cuts — instead of through additional borrowing. Kerry's pay-as-you-go amendment was rejected when the Senate voted 45-48 not to waive a parliamentary point of order that the provision had not been considered and reported by the Senate Budget Committee. The waiver motion required a 60-vote majority. *(Vote 57, p. 9-S)*

Perhaps the most controversial provision in the Senate bill would have earmarked $1.85 billion for a program to put taxpayer money into weakened institutions to finance mergers with healthier thrifts. Shareholders of the weak thrifts would not lose their investments, as they did when an institution failed. Terry Sanford, D-N.C., was the author of the provision, which was added during committee markup.

The money — taken from what was provided to the RTC — would be handed over to the Office of Thrift Supervision (OTS), a separate agency that regulated all functioning thrifts. The OTS decided when to close an institution that was failing, and under the program it could decide to shore up one up instead of closing it. OTS Director Ryan had been pushing the idea.

Sanford's proposal was similar to the House proposal put forth by McCollum. He defended it by noting that a large number of weak thrifts were profitable but technically undercapitalized because of accounting changes in the 1989 thrift bailout law. Those thrifts were candidates for closure because of their low capital. If the government infused them with capital, Sanford argued, many would survive and eventually return a profit to the government.

But Treasury officials doubted that the plan would save money. And they said it could wrongly benefit shareholders of badly run institutions. Consumer groups shared Treasury's concern that similar policies in the past had merely delayed the inevitable closure of failing institutions.

Although the Senate stood reluctant but ready to provide the RTC money, the defeat of the much slimmer bill in the House spelled the end for efforts to replenish the agency in 1992. ∎

# Credit Reform Dies in House

A bill to significantly beef up federal regulation of the nation's credit-reporting industry made it as far as the House floor, but sponsors killed the measure (HR 3596) after suffering a white-knuckle defeat on a key amendment. The Senate Banking Committee did not act on a similar bill (S 2776).

The House bill contained several provisions designed to make it easier for consumers to obtain their own credit reports and correct inaccurate information. Most importantly, if a customer disputed information in his credit report, the credit bureau would have had to reinvestigate within 30 days and delete all information that could not be verified within that time.

But at no stage in the legislative process were the bill's sponsors, Banking Committee Chairman Henry B. Gonzalez, D-Texas, and Esteban E. Torres, D-Calif., able to win language that would have allowed states to preserve credit-reporting laws that were more stringent than the federal rules proposed in the bill. Supporters of the credit reporting and banking industries prevailed, and the bill retained language that would have made the federal statute pre-empt state laws. Bill supporters said that the provision would have gutted the bill because it would have rolled back about 20 more stringent state laws.

After losing a seesaw 203-207 vote during floor consideration Sept. 24, Torres and Gonzalez pulled the bill. *(Vote 426, p. 104-H)*

But even had the bill passed the House without the pre-emption language, its prospects were decidedly mixed in the Senate. The Senate bill included the language, and any attempt to pass a House-passed bill without it would have drawn opposition, which in all probability would have been fatal given the lateness of the session.

## BACKGROUND

Except for the pre-emption provision, there was wide support for the bill and a sense among members that something needed to be done to rein in the nation's credit bureaus.

Since the Fair Credit Reporting Act became law in 1970, the credit-reporting industry had grown enormously. But with that growth and the greater automation of the industry came horror stories about consumers who had errors in their reports and great difficulties in getting them corrected. Bill sponsors said that up to 50 percent of credit reports contained errors, and the Federal Trade Commission fielded about 10,000 complaints about the industry the previous year.

Critics of the industry said that it ran roughshod over consumers and made it next to impossible to fix incorrect information.

"Credit bureaus and their customers have inflicted pain and suffering on people of virtually all walks of life," Torres said. "Whether you apply for credit, try to rent an apartment, buy a house, or apply for a job — a mistake in your credit report can ruin your life."

Consumer groups had made the bill a priority in 1992, saying that inaccurate information in credit reports had led millions of consumers to be turned down for loans, credit cards or jobs. In one high-profile mistake, 1,500 residents of Norwich, Vt., were mistakenly labeled as tax deadbeats.

That error led Vermont to enact one of the toughest laws in the nation.

## HOUSE ACTION

The credit-reporting industry had blocked attempts in previous years to pass legislation. But tough state laws and a spate of lawsuits led them to seek relief through the pre-emption provision, said Charles E. Schumer, D-N.Y.

Action on the bill kicked off in the Banking Committee's Consumer Affairs Subcommittee, which approved the bill by voice vote March 5, and credit bureaus, department stores and banks seemed content with it. But Consumers Union and other groups complained that it had been "eviscerated" in subcommittee.

Torres, who chaired the subcommittee, lost several votes during subcommittee markup.

By a 9-7 tally, Doug Barnard Jr., D-Ga., and full committee Ranking Republican Chalmers P. Wylie of Ohio prevailed on an amendment to insert the language to pre-empt state credit-reporting laws. And on another 9-7 vote, the subcommittee deleted a section of the bill requiring credit-reporting agencies to provide a free copy of their credit reports to consumers each year.

Under the bill, if a customer disputed information in his credit report, the credit bureau would have had to reinvestigate within 30 days and delete all information that could not be verified within that time.

For the first time, banks and retailers would have been required to follow procedures aimed at ensuring the accuracy of the information they provided to credit agencies.

The bill also would have barred businesses from negligently providing false information to a credit-reporting agency. And it would have required reporting agencies to set up toll-free telephone lines for consumers who wanted to attempt to correct their reports.

### Full Committee

The Banking Committee approved the bill by voice vote June 18, almost three months after a five-hour markup on March 25 that adjourned after Gonzalez and Torres lost again on the pre-emption language.

In response to an objection that not enough members were present to form a voting quorum, Gonzalez quickly gaveled the meeting to a close, saying that work on the bill would resume later.

Bernard Sanders, I-Vt., registered the parliamentary point of order. He and Gonzalez had been on the losing side of a 24-27 vote on the pre-emption provision.

The action angered some members, who believed Gonzalez had gone beyond his prerogatives as chairman; several said they could not remember the last time a nearly completed markup was aborted due to lack of a quorum. And in the three-month interregnum, bill sponsors were unable to turn around enough votes to change the outcome.

At the March 25 session, several amendments were made to the subcommittee bill, including one that would have given states the authority to enforce the law.

As amended by the committee, it would have given consumers the right to review their credit history files for a fee of no more than $8. Consumers could also have obtained free of charge any credit report that was the basis

for an adverse ruling on a credit application. The bill would have established procedures and a 30-day deadline for investigating and, if necessary, correcting items in a credit report that a consumer contended were incorrect. It would have barred prospective employers from using credit reports without a job applicant's express authorization. And it would have permitted consumers to file civil damage lawsuits against banks and other institutions that negligently and willfully provided false information to credit-reporting agencies.

Backed by Gonzalez and others, consumer groups pressed the full committee to adopt several amendments, including the language barring federal pre-emption. But credit-reporting companies and lenders were vigorous in their opposition, and the consumer advocates lost nearly every major vote.

Credit bureaus argued that they were being asked unfairly to absorb costs and other liabilities. Al McCandless, R-Calif., who along with Barnard led the fight against the consumer amendments, repeatedly said he was sympathetic to the consumer groups' concerns but argued that their requests would raise costs or be cumbersome or impossible to implement.

On a series of votes, the committee refused to require credit bureaus to give consumers annual copies of their credit histories free or for less than $8.

The committee refused to require lenders to establish procedures that would ensure the transfer of accurate information to credit bureaus and to reduce the burden of proof required to hold lenders liable for errors. It also declined to set new privacy standards for the use of information about consumers by lenders; the committee did agree to stiffen the privacy standards that applied to credit bureaus.

### House Floor

The bill came to the floor Oct. 24, but Torres said before floor consideration that unless he was successful in stripping out the pre-emption language, he would kill the bill. For several moments it looked as though he and Gonzalez would prevail as the vote stood at 204-202, with Democratic Whip David E. Bonior of Michigan gesturing for the gavel to come down.

But sitting in the chair was amendment opponent Edward F. Feighan, D-Ohio, — whom Torres had counted in his corner — and Feighan held the vote open long enough for the tide to turn.

The credit-reporting industry, banks, credit card companies and retailers had lobbied hard to keep the pre-emption language in the bill. On the floor, Banking Committee Republicans argued that a patchwork of different state laws would be too burdensome on the credit reporting industry and on lenders, and ultimately would worsen the credit crunch. They also argued that killing the bill over the pre-emption issue would deprive consumers in states without credit reporting laws of the relief provided in the bill.

Gonzalez and Torres then pulled the bill from the floor, and it saw no further action. ∎

# Commemoratives OK'd But Redesign Rejected

During his final months in Congress, Sen. Alan Cranston, D-Calif., did his best to pass a pet project: the redesign of U.S. coins. Despite Cranston's vociferous lobbying, however, the House refused to approve several new commemorative coins until his redesign provisions were dropped. Once they were stripped out, Congress cleared the coin bill (HR 3337), and Bush signed the measure May 13 (PL 102-281).

The law authorized the minting of coins marking the 200th anniversary of the White House, James Madison, the 500th anniversary of the voyage of Christopher Columbus, the 1994 World Cup soccer games and the American soldiers who served in the Persian Gulf War.

In the end, it was Cranston's personal commitment to the issue — he had shepherded the bill through the Senate 13 times since 1987 — that alienated some lawmakers. Several House members expressed annoyance at Cranston's persistence and at the seeming frivolity of spending so much time on this issue. Others said the lobbying had paid off. "I think I'll vote for it just so Alan Cranston doesn't call me anymore," said Thomas J. Downey, D-N.Y.

### BACKGROUND

Cranston had been trying since 1987 to require the U.S. Mint to redesign the tail sides of the half-dollar, quarter, dime, nickel and penny. Behind the redesign movement was Diane Wolf, a former member of the U.S. Commission of Fine Arts. She called the old designs "ordinary and boring" and said the public would be happy to see them replaced. She took up the issue as a personal cause in 1987, and while serving on the Arts Commission recruited Cranston and Rep. Henry B. Gonzalez, D-Texas, to her redesign mission.

Wolf, Cranston and coin collectors — who favored a change — stressed that the mint was authorized to change the back sides of all coins after they had been in circulation 25 years. All five major coins were well past their 25th anniversaries in 1992; the oldest extant design, on the quarter, dated to 1932.

Except for 1976-77, when the backs of the quarter and half dollar were temporarily changed to commemorate the bicentennial of the Declaration of Independence, there had been no major coin redesign since 1964, when the John F. Kennedy half-dollar was first minted.

The House passed HR 3337 in 1991; in the Senate, Cranston attached his proposal to the measure on the last day of the session. There was no time to send the amended bill to conference before the first session ended. *(1991 Almanac, p. 106)*

### HOUSE ACTION

In the first vote of 1992 on the coin bill, a testy House of Representatives on Feb. 19 rejected the Senate proposal to require redesign of the back sides of all circulating coins. The vote was 172-241. *(Vote 16, p. 4-H )*

When the bill went to conference, Cranston was more successful. On March 12, House and Senate conferees agreed — after three hours of trading offers and counteroffers — to require that the back sides of two coins, the quarter and half-dollar, be changed within the next two years to commemorate the bicentennials of the Constitution and the Bill of Rights.

The next move came when the conference report (H Rept 102-485) went to the House floor April 1. Al McCandless, R-Calif., moved to send the measure back to the conference committee with instructions to House conferees to insist that the redesign provision be dropped. The motion carried 206-199. *(Vote 70, p. 18-H)*

On April 2, the conference reconvened and dropped the redesign, though Cranston tried to persuade House members to accept a scaled-back version. House conferees argued that the four commemoratives, which would raise money for the White House, the Olympics and the World Cup soccer tournament, were too important to jeopardize with further design fights.

On April 8, the House adopted the new conference report by a vote of 414-0. *(Vote 74, p. 18-H)*

### SENATE ACTION

Cranston had refused to sign the second conference report, but in preparation for a filibuster attempt, Bob Graham, D-Fla., collected signatures from 65 of his colleagues to signal that he had the necessary 60 votes to break any filibuster effort.

On April 8, Cranston blocked the Senate Banking Committee's plans to recommend confirmation of David J. Ryder as director of the U.S. Mint. The job had been vacant since July 1991. At the time, Jake Garn of Utah, the committee's ranking Republican, lamented Cranston's tying coin redesign to Ryder's confirmation. "I wish it were possible to break that legislation loose," he said. A Treasury spokesman called Cranston's action "absolutely outrageous."

Despite Cranston's efforts, the Senate on April 28 cleared the commemorative coin bill, minus the redesign language, by a vote of 75-22. *(Vote 81, p. 12-S)* ■

# Greenspan Confirmed

As expected, the Senate on Feb. 27 confirmed Alan Greenspan for a second four-year term as chairman of the Federal Reserve Board of Governors. Senators gave their approval — by voice vote and without debate — despite the unhappiness that many had expressed over high unemployment, higher-than-desired long-term interest rates and the general course of the Fed's monetary policy.

The Senate Banking Committee had recommended Greenspan's reconfirmation Feb. 26 by a 20-1 vote. Alfonse M. D'Amato, R-N.Y., was the lone dissenter.

Banking Committee members pressed Greenspan hard during a hearing Feb. 25, when the Fed chairman presented his semi-annual monetary policy report. He made a similar appearance before the House Banking Committee on Feb. 19.

At the time, Greenspan told the Senate committee that he remained optimistic that the economy would begin a modest recovery during the spring months of 1992.

Many senators lectured Greenspan that monetary policy should be used aggressively to boost the economy, particularly since Greenspan had been counseling Congress not to enact tax cuts or spending increases to do so.

Greenspan continued to draw criticism throughout the spring and summer from legislators concerned about the nation's high unemployment rate and the tepid effect that lower long-term interest rates had had on the country's continuing recession. ■

# Red Tape Cut for Banks

A set of mostly non-controversial "regulatory relief" initiatives aimed at cutting red tape on the nation's banks and thrifts became law in 1992.

Hoping to ease what they saw as a regulatory burden on financial institutions, members of the House and Senate Banking committees added several low-profile regulatory relief provisions to a bill (HR 5334 — H Rept 102-1017) to reauthorize federal housing programs. The action occurred Oct. 2 during the housing bill conference. President Bush signed the measure into law Oct. 28 (PL 102-550).

Action on the regulatory relief issues presaged a more ambitious effort in 1993. Supporters said that various regulatory requirements enacted in previous years had swamped banks and that many of the rules could have been changed without affecting the ability of regulators to ensure safe banking operations. The banking industry said that the new regulations were forcing banks to curb lending.

The provisions were "a minipackage of some things that could be done this year," said Edward L. Yingling, chief lobbyist for the American Bankers Association. "We have a broader relief agenda next year."

The red-tape package, said proponents, represented some of the clearest and least controversial examples of regulatory overkill. One of the provisions eased a requirement that certified appraisers examine property before banks could make loans. The provision clarified that bank regulators had the authority to allow banks to make real estate loans of up to $100,000 without obtaining a certified appraisal. The banking industry argued that the requirement for such appraisals for smaller loans was too burdensome on small and rural banks and that it was mainly large loans for commercial developments, not individual mortgages, that posed risks to the safety of a bank.

Another provision allowed regulators, on a case-by-case basis, to give savings and loan institutions more time to either sell or fully capitalize their real estate subsidiaries. Under the existing regulations, most thrifts chose to sell their real estate operations, but thrifts argued that the deadlines had hurt them because of a slump in the real estate market. Under the provision, regulators first had to determine that the additional flexibility did not pose a risk to the thrift's financial soundness. The provision was to expire in 1996.

Other parts of the package included:
● Scaling back a provision of the 1991 deposit-insurance overhaul law (PL 102-242) that let regulators limit executives' pay at weak institutions. The language clarified that pay could be limited only if a clear safety and soundness issue was involved or if an enforcement action was under way.
● Easing existing restrictions on loans to bank officers and other insiders. The restrictions would be lifted if the loans were fully secured.
● Delaying for three months, from March to June 1993, the implementation of the truth-in-savings provisions of the 1991 bank bill. The law was aimed at making it easier for consumers to understand and shop for interest rates, but banks said that the regulations had only recently been issued and that they needed extra time to comply.

The language made it onto the housing bill after some senators threatened to block the bill unless the regulatory relief provisions were added. During floor consideration of the housing bill, Senate Banking Committee Chairman Donald W. Riegle Jr., D-Mich., promised to tack the provisions onto the bill in conference. *(Housing bill, p. 367)* ■

# Money-Laundering Bill Finally Gets Through

A money-laundering bill (HR 6018) that had been approved in different forms by both chambers in 1991 languished through much of the 1992 session but got a jump start in October and rode to enactment after being attached to an unrelated housing bill (HR 5334 — PL 102-550).

The legislation, which set stiff penalties on banks and bank officers found guilty of money laundering, was a swan song for its principal sponsor, retiring Rep. Frank Annunzio, D-Ill., second-ranking Democrat on the Banking Committee. "Money laundering is a crime which makes the illegal drug business profitable," said Annunzio. "Without a place to launder cash, drug dealers would be left with a vast pile of worthless paper."

The bill had gotten its start in the wake of the Bank of Credit and Commerce International (BCCI) scandal, in which the Luxembourg-based BCCI had been convicted of laundering millions of dollars in Florida for Colombian drug cartels but had been allowed to remain open. The House voted overwhelmingly for nearly identical money-laundering bills in 1990 and 1991. The non-controversial measure had passed the Senate in various forms as well. However, the bill had been snake-bit by Senate politics and, for the third year in a row, was subject to last-minute maneuvering.

In 1990, both chambers passed money-laundering bills, but the Senate version also included a variety of unrelated banking provisions. An end-of-the-session attempt by the House to move a clean bill failed after Senate Republicans blocked consideration. *(1990 Almanac, p. 187)*

In 1991, the House voted 406-0 in favor of a money-laundering bill (HR 26). In the Senate, a conflict over unrelated issues led Banking Chairman Donald W. Riegle Jr., D-Mich., to avoid considering a separate money-laundering bill, instead attaching the provisions to the Senate's version of a broad overhaul of banking law (S 543). But the provisions were dropped in conference in an effort to slim down the bill. *(1991 Almanac, p. 105)*

In 1992, the Senate added the laundering language to a bill (S 2733) to tighten federal regulation of two government-sponsored enterprises that helped finance the mortgage market. But supporters of that bill wanted to remove unrelated provisions to ensure passage. *(GSEs, p. 123)*

In a late-session effort to enact the money-laundering legislation, negotiators ironed out minor differences between House and Senate versions, and the agreed upon language was introduced as a new bill (HR 6048). The House passed the new bill by voice vote on Sept. 29; the Senate did not act on it before adjournment.

To be safe, the money-laundering provisions were also incorporated into the conference report on the housing bill, and it was in that form that it became law. *(Housing bill, p. 367)*  ∎

# Banking Rules Eased In Disaster Areas

In an effort to speed redevelopment in areas devestated by Hurricanes Andrew and Iniki and the Los Angeles riots, Congress cleared legislation (HR 6050) on Oct. 8 to ease certain banking regulations in those locales. President Bush signed the measure into law on Oct. 23 (PL 102-485).

The bill eased credit requirements for lenders aiding disaster victims. Supporters said that regulations written for normal times impeded banks from making loans in devastated communities. For example, rules that required banks to make appraisals before issuing real estate loans were difficult to comply with in devastated areas.

The bill gave regulators the authority to lift such appraisal requirements in disaster areas. Such authority would last for up to three years after the disaster.

In addition, the new law allowed banks to exclude big infusions of deposits attributable to insurance payments when calculating their capital requirements. Large and quick accumulations of deposits from such sources could have lowered capital ratios.

The bill was a scaled-back version of a proposal sent to the Hill by the Treasury Department. The administration's original request was far too sweeping for Senate Banking Committee Chairman Donald W. Riegle Jr., D-Mich. He said the original bills (HR 5999, S 3242) would have allowed regulators far too much authority to lift regulations, even in areas unaffected by disasters.

"I had hoped the administration would not use these national tragedies as vehicles to advance its broad deregulatory agenda for America's financial institutions," Riegle said.

The bills were not marked up by the Banking committees and came directly to the House floor on Oct. 3 and passed by voice vote. The Senate cleared the measure on Oct. 8. Bank regulators issued rules to implement the legislation before the end of the year.  ∎

# Government Securities Bill Is Quashed

A jurisdictional and procedural fight between the House Energy and Commerce and Banking committees scuttled a bill (S 1699) to rein in the largely unregulated $2.6 trillion market in government securities.

The fight spilled onto the House floor Sept. 16, with Energy Committee Chairman John D. Dingell, D-Mich., on the losing end of the vote.

The bill grew out of a 1991 bid-rigging scandal in which Salomon Brothers Inc. bought larger-than-permitted stakes of government debt. Energy and Commerce Committee members blamed the scandal on lax oversight by Treasury and the Federal Reserve.

The bill contained a variety of provisions aimed at preventing fraud in the trading of government securities and would have made it easier for the Securities and Exchange Commission (SEC) and other regulators to discover and prosecute such violations.

Over vehement protests from House Banking Committee Chairman Henry B. Gonzalez, D-Texas, the leadership of the Energy and Commerce and Ways and Means committees brought the bill to the floor under suspension of the rules — a process that barred amendments and cut the Banking Committee's contribution from the bill.

With members of the Banking Committee protesting what they called a turf grab and amid a growing sense that the bill did not belong on the so-called suspension calendar, the measure went down to a big defeat.

In 1991, the Senate had passed a much narrower, administration-backed version of the bill that would have clarified that violations of Treasury Department bidding rules on bond sales were illegal under federal securities laws.

## BACKGROUND

The legislative effort came in the wake of a bid-rigging scandal that rocked the federal government bond market in mid-1991. The Wall Street firm of Salomon Brothers Inc. had admitted repeatedly submitting false bids in order to acquire larger portions of certain bond offerings. By increasing its share of a particular issue, Salomon might have been able to control the resale of those bonds in the secondary market.

Even before the scandal broke, Congress was moving to reauthorize the Government Securities Act of 1986, which gave the Treasury Department limited authority to regulate the financial capacity and related activities of firms that traded in government bonds.

### 1991 Action

The Senate passed a bill (S 1247) in July 1991 that would have extended the Government Securities Act and

---

## BOXSCORE

➡ **Government Securities Act Reauthorization. (S 1247, HR 3927).** The House bill would have significantly stiffened federal oversight of the largely unregulated market in government bonds; the Senate passed a much narrower measure in 1991. Action came in the wake of a 1991 bid-rigging scandal, in which Salomon Brothers Inc. made fraudulent bids to purchase larger-than-permitted stakes of government debt.

**Reports:** H Rept 102-722, Parts I & II; S Rept 102-126.

### KEY ACTION

**June 2** — The **House** Energy and Commerce Committee approved HR 3927.

**Aug. 6** — The **House** Banking Committee approved alternative version of HR 3927.

**Sept. 16** — The **House** rejected S 1699, 124-279.

---

given various regulators new authority to impose rules on the sales practices in the government bond market. *(1991 Almanac, p. 114)*

A second Senate bill (S 1699), which was passed in September of 1991 after the scandal surfaced, would have clarified that fraudulent bids on Treasury bonds and other false statements involving that market were violations of the Securities Exchange Act of 1934.

On the House side, Edward J. Markey, D-Mass., chairman of the Energy and Commerce Finance Subcommittee, introduced a more sweeping bill (HR 3927) in November 1991; he was joined by the subcommittee's ranking Republican, Matthew J. Rinaldo of New Jersey. Their bill closely tracked the views of the SEC that the largely unregulated Treasury market needed closer attention, similar to the sort that existed for other securities.

House Banking Committee Chairman Henry B. Gonzalez, D-Texas, and Monetary Policy Subcommittee Chairman Stephen L. Neal, D-N.C., drew up a draft bill to require Treasury to experiment with new bond auction methods that could both increase investor participation and reduce the government's borrowing cost.

A larger question involved preserving public confidence in the huge government securities market; a loss of confidence could raise the cost of financing the federal deficit. The government bond market did not operate under the same disclosure and trading rules that helped prevent fraud in the market for privately issued securities. There were fears that the government market could have been corrupted and that the government's ability to finance its operations would have been damaged, which would have raised the cost of government borrowing for the taxpayer.

The Treasury Department, with the Federal Reserve Board, the New York Fed and the SEC, proposed regulatory and legislative changes Jan. 22, 1992 — that were much less sweeping than the House effort — to combat the sort of fraud found in the Salomon case.

## HOUSE COMMITTEE ACTION

Action on the legislation in 1992 kicked off in the House Energy and Commerce Telecommunications and Finance Subcommittee on May 7. The panel approved HR 3927 by voice vote.

But the subcommittee's speedy approval belied remaining tensions. Treasury Department and Federal Reserve Board officials criticized the measure on the grounds that it would unduly burden the market in Treasury securities. They argued that the bill would raise costs to bond traders that ultimately would be passed on as higher interest costs to the government — and cause a bigger

federal deficit.

The bill contained a variety of provisions intended to prevent trading fraud and to make it easier for the SEC and other regulators to probe alleged violations.

Like S 1247, the bill would have renewed Treasury's general authority to regulate the capital of bond traders. And it would have allowed banking and other regulators to establish sales practice rules. It also would have allowed Treasury to require traders with large holdings of Treasury bonds to make periodic reports on their positions.

The bill would have given the SEC two new grants of authority. The agency would have been permitted to require that bond dealers keep records of their transactions and make them available upon request. The SEC also could have stepped in if it appeared that price information on Treasury bonds in the resale, or secondary, market was not widely distributed or incomplete.

The full committee approved HR 3927 on June 2; the committee acted without debate, amendment or any apparent disagreement and approved the measure by voice vote — all of which disguised the significant fight among three government agencies over the need for such dramatic change.

### Banking Committee

The House Banking Committee weighed in on Aug. 6, approving a version of HR 3927 that would have preserved the role of federal banking regulators in the tightened regulation of the government securities market.

Chairman Gonzalez said the Energy and Commerce Committee would have given the SEC too much authority to regulate dealings by banks, which conducted the majority of the transactions in government securities. That, he said, represented "nothing less than an effort to fatten the jurisdictional reach of the Energy and Commerce Committee," which oversaw the SEC.

Gonzalez offered an amendment that would have left it to banking regulators, such as the Federal Deposit Insurance Corporation (FDIC) and the Federal Reserve System, to enforce the new regulations in the bill. It was approved by voice vote.

The Gonzalez amendment also would have changed the procedures governing the auction of government securities. The changes would have required the creation of a fully automated system allowing remote participation for all qualified brokers. The aim was to broaden access beyond the small number of primary dealers that had a near-monopoly in the auctions.

## HOUSE FLOOR

With time running out in the 102nd Congress, Dingell asked the House leadership to bring the Senate bill directly to the floor, where Finance Subcommittee Chairman Markey inserted the text of a substitute House bill — cutting out the Banking Committee's contribution. The new version of S 1699 combined language from the Energy and Commerce and Ways and Means committees.

After an appeal to the House leadership to pull the measure from the suspension calendar failed, an angry Gonzalez took the floor to blast the bill as "nothing more than another insatiable grab for jurisdiction by this power-hungry, insatiable committee known as the Energy and Commerce Committee."

Markey said the attempt to pass the measure under suspension was an effort to get it approved quickly and get it to conference. But the move clearly rankled members who believed that the bill — and its controversial elements — did not belong on the suspension calendar.

The fight over the bill also pitted the Treasury Department and the Federal Reserve against the SEC. Gonzalez circulated a letter by Federal Reserve Chairman Alan Greenspan opposing the bill, saying that it would "open the door to unnecessary and costly regulation that would reduce the efficiency and liquidity of the government securities market and increase the burden on the taxpayer of financing the public debt."

SEC Chairman Richard C. Breeden weighed in with a letter to Dingell that said that the commission had jurisdiction when banks engaged in the trading of securities such as government bonds. Breeden also disputed the administration's contention that the bill would impose too great a regulatory burden on banks.

Gonzalez countered that the Salomon Brothers scandal involved a securities firm, not a bank, and that the Energy and Commerce bill "would abolish over 50 years of statutory precedent by displacing the primary banking regulator as the regulator of the government securities of banks."

Gonzalez prevailed, and the bill went down to a 124-279 defeat. *(Vote 395, p. 96-H)* ∎

# New Regulations Cleared for GSEs

A compromise bill to strengthen federal oversight of the nation's two largest government-sponsored enterprises (GSEs) weaved its way through Congress to become law, despite grumblings by some members that the legislation was not strong enough. The measure was tacked on to an unrelated bill (HR 5334 — H Rept 102-1017) reauthorizing federal housing programs that cleared Oct. 8. President Bush signed it into law on Oct. 28 (PL 102-550).

The legislation created a new regulator within the Department of Housing and Urban Development (HUD) to oversee the Federal National Mortgage Association and the Federal Home Loan Mortgage Corp., better known as Fannie Mae and Freddie Mac. The two GSEs — which had combined liabilities of more than $1 trillion — were required to meet new "risk-based" capital standards aimed at ensuring that they could withstand fluctuations in interest rates, recession and other factors that might threaten their financial soundness.

Late-breaking opposition from Fannie Mae almost killed the bill for the year, but after some bad publicity, the huge company changed course and cooperated with the legislative effort.

The final GSE provisions were a compromise between bills (HR 2900, S 2733) that the House and Senate had passed earlier. The Senate bill had been considered stricter, particularly on capital standards, which were designed to provide a buffer in the event of financial difficulties. The final version of the bill adopted the Senate's

capital requirements. It dropped a number of unrelated provisions that had been included in the Senate version of the bill.

## BACKGROUND

Government-sponsored enterprises were congressionally chartered private corporations that received major breaks from the government, including direct lines of credit with the Treasury Department and implicit government backing of their financial soundness.

The bill grew out of concerns in the wake of the savings and loan debacle that taxpayers were at considerable risk should the GSEs fall into financial troubles. In 1990, Congress agreed that committees with jurisdiction would report bills to tighten regulations of the corporations.

Fannie Mae and Freddie Mac were private corporations that were chartered by the federal government to provide a secondary market for home mortgages. They bought mortgages from banks and thrift institutions, which used the money to finance additional mortgages.

Investor belief that the government would bail out the GSEs if they got into financial trouble enabled them to issue bonds at relatively low interest rates.

The House passed its original Fannie and Freddie oversight bill (HR 2900 — H Rept 102-206) in 1991. The Senate Banking Committee was on the verge of marking up a companion measure in late 1991, but work was halted after Fannie Mae said the legislation prepared by committee staff was too tough. *(1991 Almanac, p. 115)*

## SENATE ACTION

The Senate Banking Committee resurrected the bill on April 8, 1992, approving the measure (S 2733 — S Rept 102-282) by voice vote.

The bill, which paralleled but went beyond the 1991 House-passed bill, had been the subject of months of negotiations. Most, but not all, of the provisions were broadly acceptable to all sides — the administration, mortgage lenders, consumer and housing advocates, and the two corporations themselves.

Banking Committee Chairman Donald W. Riegle Jr. praised the panel for seeking to regulate the financial health of the two corporations. And the Michigan Democrat singled out a requirement for increased low- and moderate-income housing loans as an effort to "improve longstanding but mostly ignored . . . regulations."

The committee took just 25 minutes to agree to a block of relatively minor amendments and to adopt the draft bill by voice vote. Only Phil Gramm, R-Texas, registered a vocal objection to the measure. Gramm complained that the bill "will not increase capital or enhance the market." And he worried that the housing goals ran counter to the mandate to insulate taxpayers. "This lending is more risky than the average lending they do and may very well impair them," Gramm said.

At Gramm's request, the Senate bill included language stating that Fannie Mae and Freddie Mac did not enjoy the direct or indirect backing of the government. "I never intend to vote a dollar of taxpayer money to bail out one of these GSEs — period," he said.

Under the bill, the new regulator was to be largely outside the control of the HUD secretary — or that of the Office of Management and Budget. The regulatory office was not to be subject to appropriations (instead financed solely by fees assessed on Fannie Mae and Freddie Mac), and it could issue regulations affecting the safety and soundness of Fannie Mae and Freddie Mac without agency clearance.

Senate sponsors hoped this level of independence would ensure strong regulation and direct congressional oversight. Consumer advocates and the two corporations also favored an independent regulator.

The capital standards in the Senate bill were similar to those in HR 2900 and were patterned after standards that Congress had set for banks and thrifts. The Senate bill required that Fannie Mae and Freddie Mac maintain equity capital equal to 2.5 percent of their balance-sheet assets and 0.45 percent of off-balance-sheet assets. The latter number was significant because both enterprises sold hundreds of billions of dollars worth of securities backed by mortgages that they had acquired. These securities (and the underlying mortgages) were not carried on their balance sheets, but they benefited from the implicit government guarantee.

The bill required Fannie Mae and Freddie Mac to develop capital restoration plans, should they fail to meet the minimumn requirement. The bill set a "critical capital level" roughly equal to half the minimum level. If either corporation fell below that level, it would have to be placed under government control unless the new regulator, with the concurrence of the Treasury secretary, determined that such a move would not be in the public interest.

The bill also required Fannie Mae and Freddie Mac to meet a risk-based capital standard to be devised by the regulator to ensure that they could survive large swings in interest rates or loan defaults.

If the corporations failed to comply with the capital requirements, they and their officers would be subject to cease-and-desist orders and civil fines. This was one area of concern for Fannie Mae and Freddie Mac when the bill was being drafted. The committee version tightened the standard for imposing fines and included a number of opportunities for hearings to challenge regulatory findings.

A key difference between the Senate and House bills was a new requirement in the Senate version that the GSEs make special efforts to finance low- and moderate-income housing and housing in central cities, urban areas and other underserved areas. The new regulator was to set the goals, but the bill required that 30 percent of the two GSEs' loans in the first two years after enactment be for houses occupied by owners or renters whose incomes were below the medians in their geographic area.

The two corporations also were required to invest a combined $3.5 billion in houses occupied by owners and renters with incomes below 80 percent of their area's median.

## SENATE FLOOR

The Senate on July 1 overwhelmingly passed S 2733 by a 77-19 vote. Work on the regulatory bill had been essentially completed June 24. But passage was delayed by efforts to attach language proposing a constitutional amendment to require a balanced federal budget. The bill was passed after the Senate rejected two attempts to cut off a filibuster by opponents of the balanced-budget amendment. With their efforts to get an up-or-down vote on the budget amendment stymied, sponsors withdrew the controversial measure and permitted a final vote on the underlying regulatory bill. *(Vote 137, p. 19-S)*

On the floor, the Senate added unrelated provisions on money laundering, interstate branching by savings and loan associations, the liability of banks and other lenders

under the "superfund" hazardous waste cleanup law, and the regulation of limited partnerships undergoing reorganizations. Those provisions complicated prospects for a House-Senate conference, because several House committees would have had to be involved, resulting in jurisdictional and scheduling problems.

The Senate completed work June 23-24 on the central elements of S 2733, which was itself relatively non-controversial. The terms of the bill had been crafted during months of negotiations among senators on all sides and affected parties, including the two housing corporations, low-income housing and consumer advocacy groups, mortgage lenders and the Bush administration. Most participants praised the resulting bill as an acceptable compromise.

The Senate approved five amendments to S 2733 and rejected several others before turning to the debate over the balanced-budget amendment. Most of the amendments had little or nothing to do with the underlying regulatory bill, and several were the subject of floor fights.

One comprehensive amendment, offered by Banking Committee Chairman Riegle, made relatively minor changes in the bill's regulatory provisions and added language from several unrelated measures that previously had passed the Senate. It also would have made several changes in a sweeping banking overhaul bill enacted in 1991 (PL 102-242). *(1991 Almanac, p. 75)*

Riegle's amendment was approved by voice vote June 24. Its central provisions included:

● **Money laundering.** New authority for federal regulators to revoke banking charters or deposit insurance in cases where banks, thrifts and credit unions were convicted of money laundering. Similar language was included in the Senate-passed version of the banking overhaul bill the previous year. *(Money laundering, p. 121)*

● **Lender liability.** New exemptions for banks and other lenders from financial liability under the "superfund" hazardous waste cleanup law, when they acquired hazardous waste sites as a consequence of loan foreclosure. Similar language also was included in the Senate-passed version of the 1991 banking overhaul bill.

A section of that amendment drew fire because it also would have exempted municipalities from being named in superfund liability lawsuits, except by the Environmental Protection Agency. John H. Chafee, R-R.I., and Hank Brown, R-Colo., attempted to strike and to delay the effective date of this amendment, but their amendments to do so were rejected on tabling motions by votes of 52-44 and 54-42. *(Votes 126, 129, p. 17-S, 18-S)*

● **Thrift statute of limitations.** A change in existing federal law to extend from three years to five the time the Resolution Trust Corporation had to bring civil damage cases against former thrift operators. The statute of limitations was about to run out on hundreds of failed thrifts.

● **Foreign bank deposits.** A clarification in the 1991 banking overhaul bill that U.S. branches of foreign banks might accept certain non-retail deposits of less than $100,000.

The Senate acted on two other substantive amendments. One, offered by Christopher J. Dodd, D-Conn., was the text of his widely backed bill (S 1423) to curb abuses that had occurred as limited partnerships were reorganized, or "rolled up." Frustrated by Gramm's parliamentary moves that had kept the Banking Committee from considering the roll-up bill, Dodd successfully offered it to S 2733. It was approved by voice vote after an effort to kill it on a tabling motion failed 10-87. *(Vote 127, p. 17-S; roll-ups p. 131)*

Another adopted amendment, offered by Wendell H.

Ford, D-Ky., imposed a 15-month moratorium on the ability of federally chartered savings and loan associations to open branch offices across state lines. The Office of Thrift Supervision had ruled in April that interstate branching by thrifts was generally not prohibited by federal law. Interstate branching continued to be a controversial issue in banking circles, and opponents widely denounced the ruling. Ford's amendment was adopted by voice vote, after an effort to kill it on a tabling motion failed 15-82. *(Vote 128, p. 17-S)*

## FINAL ACTION

Efforts to bring the bill to conference were stymied, in part by a move by Gramm, who objected to the usually routine step of calling up the House bill and inserting the Senate language.

Instead of going to conference, staff members of the Banking committees negotiated informally to iron out the details of the GSE bill and strip out the unrelated Senate provisions.

Staffers negotiating the compromise were authorized to discuss only the core GSE bill; non-germane material in the Senate bill was dropped. By the end of September, agreement had been reached.

But Fannie Mae objected on Sept. 25 to one version of the bill, saying that the language was too vague and would have given the new regulator too much discretion to set the risk-based standards. That objection killed plans to bring the compromise bill to the House floor on Sept. 29.

Fannie Mae denied that it was trying to kill the legislation, but the episode brought a lot of criticism — some members threatened to be tougher on the GSE in the 103rd Congress — and negotiations resumed.

A key sticking point in those negotiations was the design of a so-called stress test to be used by the regulator in determining how much risk-based capital Fannie Mae and Freddie Mac would have to keep in reserve.

The final bill essentially kept the somewhat stronger stress test included in S 2733. In opposing the earlier compromise on the stress test, Fannie Mae said that it would have given the regulator discretion to set unnecessarily high capital standards that would have led to a mortgage credit crunch. The final version of the bill was hardly different from the earlier versions that Fannie Mae had scotched.

The House passed the compromise as a stand-alone bill (HR 6094) by voice vote on Oct. 3. But in an effort to boost the bill's chances, the language was included in the conference report on the housing bill. The House passed the conference report by 377-37 on Oct. 5, and it was cleared by the Senate Oct. 8. *(Housing bill, p. 367)*

Supporters heralded the GSE measure as a significant step toward improving the safety and soundness of Fannie Mae and Freddie Mac. "HR 6094 should enable the secondary mortgage markets to continue in their work for housing and should ensure that the American taxpayer will not bear undue risk in the future," said Rep. Bruce F. Vento, D-Minn.

But the measure's critics admitted that what they called a modest bill was better than no bill at all.

"I deeply wish we could go further," said Rep. J. J. Pickle, D-Texas. "But in the face of this enormous pressure from the GSEs, I am not at all sure that we could do better at this time in this House."

"There is no doubt that the bill is a vast improvement over what passed the House earlier this Congress," said bill opponent Rep. Jim Leach, R-Iowa. ■

# No Accord on Financial Adviser Bills

After a four-year effort, legislation to beef up federal oversight of the booming financial planning industry passed both House and Senate, but the two chambers were unable to reconcile their differences.

Both versions of the legislation (HR 5726, S 2266) would have imposed annual fees on investment advisers, with the proceeds to be used to pay for additional Securities and Exchange Commission (SEC) inspectors. The SEC was unable to keep up with the booming financial planning industry and had only about 50 staff members to oversee 17,500 investment advisers.

But the House bill would have gone further, requiring advisers to disclose information to clients about their fees and financial expertise and to issue reports to them summarizing charges incurred in the handling of their accounts. It also would have required advisers to determine that each recommended investment was "suitable" after taking into account their clients' financial positions.

The Senate passed S 2266 by voice vote Aug. 12; the House passed its more sweeping bill Sept. 22, also by voice vote. Staff began informal negotiations to iron out the differences in the bills but were unable to reach agreement.

## BACKGROUND

Congressional action came on the heels of revelations that some financial advisers had systematically bilked investors.

In one high-profile case, a California-based adviser, Steven Wymer, was charged by the SEC with ripping off numerous municipalities and pension funds for more than $100 million. Publicity over the case contributed to the bill's movement through the legislative process.

Over the previous decade, the number of financial planners registered with the SEC had grown more than three-fold. Assets under their management had increased from $450 billion to more than $5 trillion. But that growth was not matched by increases in SEC staff, and problems such as theft, conflicts of interest and incompetence by financial planners frequently went undetected. Under existing SEC staff levels, most financial planners could have expected an inspection once every 25 years or so.

"The investment adviser industry is the most unregulated sector of the securities industry," said Edward J. Markey, D-Mass., chairman of the House Energy and Commerce Telecommunications and Finance Subcommittee. "Most investment advisers wouldn't know an SEC inspector if they fell over one."

Under existing law, investment advisers paid a one-time $150 fee when registering with the SEC. The bills would have imposed annual fees of $300 to $7,000, depending on the amount of assets under a financial planner's control.

Action on the measure capped a four-year effort by

---

### BOXSCORE

➡ **Oversight of Investment Advisers (HR 5726; S 2266).** The bills would have increased user fees on investment advisers, or financial planners, to pay for increased oversight by the Securities and Exchange Commission.

**Reports:** H Rept 102-883; S Rept 102-312.

#### KEY ACTION

Aug. 12 — The **Senate** passed S 2266 by voice vote.

Sept. 22 — The **House** passed HR 5726 by voice vote.

---

Rep. Rick Boucher, D-Va. To move the bill, Boucher agreed to drop a controversial provision that would have made it easier for investors to sue advisers. Under existing federal and state laws, however, investors already had the right to sue financial planners for fraud.

## SENATE ACTION

The Senate Banking Committee approved S 2266 on May 21 by an 18-2 vote. To expedite approval, the committee approved an amendment by bill opponent Phil Gramm, R-Texas, that deleted a section that would have required financial planners to take into account a client's financial situation and investment experience and offer advice accordingly.

But bill sponsor Christopher J. Dodd, D-Conn., expressed optimism that a similar "suitability" provision would be included if the bill went to conference. The SEC supported the bill, said Dodd.

Under the bill, advisers would have been charged an annual fee ranging from $300 to $7,000, with the money used to pay for a substantial increase in the number of SEC inspectors.

The Senate passed the bill (S 2266) on Aug. 12 by voice vote.

## HOUSE ACTION

The House Energy and Commerce Subcommittee on Telecommunications and Finance approved the bill July 30 by voice vote.

The core of the bill — the annual user fees of $300 to $7,000 — was identical to the Senate bill.

But the House bill also would have imposed stricter rules on financial planners, requiring them to reveal their education and business qualifications to clients, disclose their fees and issue periodic reports summarizing all charges incurred by a customer.

In addition, advisers would have had to take into account a client's financial position and investment needs when devising an investment program.

The bill was strongly backed by Democrat John D. Dingell of Michigan, chairman of the full Energy and Commerce Committee, who said on the House floor in June that "there will be no action on other matters of interest to the securities industry . . . until we have acted favorably on this matter."

Committee Republicans had also signed onto the bill, which gained easy voice vote approval from the full committee Aug. 4.

### House Floor

The bill came to the House floor Sept. 22 and was passed by voice vote. Because of a parliamentary misstep, the House re-passed the bill the next day and gave it the

Senate bill number (S 2266) — a necessary step to go to conference.

But with the clock running out on the 102nd Congress, staff members instead negotiated informally in an effort to work out a new compromise bill that could be passed in identical form by both chambers.

Staff aides on both sides said they thought the differences on the underlying investment adviser bill would not be too difficult to iron out.

But key senators were not keen on another measure (HR 4313 — H Rept 102-890) that the House tacked onto the bill. HR 4313 would have required corporate accountants to report to the SEC when they found fraud as they audited corporate financial reports. There was no companion Senate bill. HR 4313 essentially would have written into law self-imposed standards followed by most accountants, which required auditors to check the books of firms in a manner that "reasonably detected" fraud and report such illegal acts to the SEC if the company did not.

Senate Banking Committee members were angling to add another complication. Eager to move legislation (S 1699) to tighten regulations on the $2.6 billion market in government securities, they discussed adding the measure to the investment advisers bill.

These obstacles were not overcome before the end of the session, and the legislation died. ∎

# CFTC Bill Addresses Trading Scandals

Shortly before adjourning, Congress cleared a bill reauthorizing the Commodities Futures Trading Commission (CFTC) and imposing significant new restrictions on futures trading. Applauded by futures exchanges and CFTC administrators, the bill (HR 707 — H Rept 102-978) strengthened the hand of agency regulators and allowed futures exchanges to offer new financial instruments exempt from the traditional regulatory restrictions previously imposed on all futures products.

The long-delayed bill took nearly four years to develop and pass, despite early momentum growing out of federal indictments in late 1989 of several traders in the Chicago futures trading pits. The final bill addressed problems related to the scandal — such as brokers trading for a client and for personal accounts at the same time, and outdated auditing methods for transactions. In addition, it permitted the CFTC to exempt certain exotic financial products, dubbed "swaps" and "hybrids" from regulations applied to other futures products. Hybrids combined some of the traits of more traditional financial instruments, such as stocks or bonds; swaps were arrangements involving debt obligations and currency transactions, which were primarily traded over the counter and were not regulated like other futures products.

The CFTC was the sole regulator for the futures industry and oversaw the Chicago Board of Trade and other futures exchanges. The agency was also in charge of regulating the individual markets for financial products.

The compromise on swaps, the most significant sticking point in crafting the legislation, was worked out in the final weeks of the session and was considered an interim solution. Because two studies on the swaps industry, a fast-growing segment of the financial futures business, were due before the CFTC was to come up for reauthorization again in 1994, a more substantial regulatory framework for the new products was put off until that time.

Also approved in the final bill was a provision allowing the Federal Reserve to set margin limits on stock-index futures, a type of trading instrument that was closely tied to stock prices and was used by investors to bet on the direction of the market and hedge against declines in the value of other investments.

Among the provisions left out of the bill was a transaction tax, which the exchanges strongly opposed. The tax could have raised up to $68 million by fiscal 1997 to go toward CFTC enforcement expenses.

## BACKGROUND

The push to increase the oversight authority of the CFTC began in 1989, when a series of trading scandals were uncovered in the pits of a Chicago futures exchange. But the focus of debate on the legislation soon moved from preventing fraud in the pits to the stickier issue of who should have jurisdiction over stock-index futures.

Since the October 1987 market crash, stock-index futures had been at the center of a debate about whether the stock market was a safe place, particularly for small investors. Part of the problem, critics argued, was the low level set for futures margins, the money an investor paid upfront for stock or futures contracts. Stock margins were set at 50 percent of the purchase price of the stock; futures margins, considered as good-faith deposits, varied but were generally below 20 percent of the purchase price. The solution pressed by Treasury Secretary Nicholas F. Brady, who had studied the 1987 crash before assuming his Treasury job, was to transfer regulation of these instruments to the Securities and Exchange Commission (SEC), which oversaw stocks.

The Chicago-based futures markets and the CFTC strongly opposed such a change, and the dispute halted progress on a CFTC reauthorization measure in the 101st Congress. *(1990 Almanac, p. 194)*

---

**BOXSCORE**

➡ **Commodity Futures Trading Commission reauthorization (HR 707, S 207).** The bill reauthorized the Commodity Futures Trading Commission and made several other changes in securities law aimed at curbing abuses in the trading pits. The bill also made it legal for futures exchanges to offer derivative financial futures products even if they did not meet the traditional regulatory guidelines.

**Reports:** H Rept 102-6; S Rept 102-22; conference report H Rept 102-978

**KEY ACTION**

Oct. 2 — **House** adopted conference report.

Oct. 8 — **Senate** cleared conference report

Oct. 28 — President Bush signed HR 707 — PL 102-546.

## 1991 Action

Both chambers passed new CFTC reauthorization bills (S 207, HR 707) in 1991, but the dispute over regulating stock-index futures derailed the effort for a third straight year. The House-passed version was silent on stock-index futures, while the Senate bill contained a compromise leaving the CFTC with exclusive jurisdiction over these instruments but giving the Federal Reserve Board new authority to oversee margins.

The Senate bill also included provisions creating a formula to determine whether hybrids should be regulated by the SEC or CFTC and authorizing the CFTC to exempt certain swaps from the Commodity Exchange Act. The House bill had no such provisions.

Preliminary conference negotiations began on the bill, but there was little progress. *(1991 Almanac, p. 111)*

## LEGISLATIVE ACTION

Real work began July 23, when House and Senate conferees from the Agriculture committees met to hash out differences in the House and Senate versions. While conferees agreed on new rules regarding conflicts of interest and insider trading, they deferred discussion of the most controversial items.

Marginal progress was made at the next meeting, July 29, but the prospect of resolving the jurisdictional questions remained unlikely, and the legislation was not expected to clear Congress. During that session, Senate conferees reluctantly agreed not to impose service fees on the nation's futures exchanges and brokers to help pay for the cost of new regulatory enforcement.

The Senate provision would have raised as much as $21.7 million a year by 1997, and senators argued that giving the agency new regulatory responsibilities would be meaningless without providing money to pay for them. But House conferees argued that levying service fees would tempt the appropriations committees to eliminate direct appropriations for the CFTC.

Meeting again on Aug. 4, conferees agreed on new regulations to restrict the practice of dual trading, in which brokers executed trades for themselves and their clients on the same day. Negotiators also reached an accord on standards for mandatory computerized auditing of futures trades, which lawmakers hoped would help prevent fraud. The aim of these auditing systems was to prevent traders from fraudulently supplementing personal accounts on the basis of their knowledge of clients' trading plans.

Then, in the fifth conference session on Aug. 11, a breakthrough in the negotiations was revealed. Glenn English, D-Okla., chairman of the House Agriculture subcommittee that oversaw the CFTC, said that negotiators had agreed informally to allow the Federal Reserve Board to set margin requirements for stock-index futures.

On Sept. 24, conferees cleared away the last obstacles to the legislation. "By God, we have a bill," said Sen. Patrick J. Leahy, D-Vt., bringing applause to the packed hearing room.

Under the compromise approved Sept. 24, the CFTC could allow trading of swaps and hybrids on the futures exchanges on a case-by-case basis and could exempt them from regulations applied to other futures commodities under the Commodity Futures Act. The decision temporarily resolved ambiguity about the legality of swaps that were being traded over the counter outside CFTC regulation. Conferees made it clear that the compromise on swaps was intended to buy time while they learned more about the new product market and determined the appropriate level of statutory control. "This authority is encouraged to be used sparingly," English said.

CFTC Chairman Wendy L. Gramm expressed support for the final compromise and stressed that the new bill would give futures exchanges flexibility in product offerings and allow U.S. exchanges to compete in a tougher global market.

The House approved the conference report Oct. 2; the Senate cleared it Oct. 8. President Bush signed the measure Oct. 28 (PL 102-546). ∎

# Provisions of CFTC Reauthorization

*As passed, the legislation (HR 707 — PL 102-546) to reauthorize/ the Commodity Futures Trading Commission did the following:*

## Limitation on Trading Practices

● **Dual Trading.** Prohibited dual trading in any futures market unless the CFTC provided a specific exemption. Dual trading occurred when brokers traded for a client and for themselves or a fellow broker on the same day. Abuse of dual trading could enable a broker to capitalize on inside knowledge of a client's order.

The CFTC could exempt an exchange if any of the following conditions were met:

● The exchange had an electronic internal audit system set up to monitor the times and amounts of all trades on the trading floor.

● The CFTC found that banning dual trading would be harmful to the public interest.

● The contract market was small, with less than 7,000 contracts changing hands each day. The CFTC could adjust this threshold to account for market liquidity, price volatility and other considerations.

● **Broker associations.** Forbade brokers from knowingly executing customer orders with someone with whom they were affili-

ated through a broker association or an employment or other relationship. Brokers would have to disclose to the exchange and to the CFTC any knowledge of business or financial relationships between traders.

## Regulatory Enhancement

● **Audit trails.** Required that exchanges put into place electronic or computerized systems to monitor all floor trades, recording the parties and the exact time of the transaction. Within three years, the auditing methods would have to be sophisticated enough to provide data to the market on a continuous basis and to independently register the time of each transaction and check it against the time entered by the trader. For the most part, the technology to establish these audit trails existed and was being purchased and installed by several of the major futures exchanges. With accurate auditing of transactions, dual trading would be permissible because trading abuses could be identified. The CFTC would have broad authority to inspect and monitor the audit trail technology and to determine when it met the statutory standards.

● **Audit reporting.** Required the CFTC to report within two years of enactment on how the futures exchanges were complying with the audit requirements. The General Accounting Office was also to report on audit trail compliance.

● **Market auditing.** Required that each futures market in each exchange maintained and used an audit system that included inspectors for floor trading, electronic records of transactions as they were reported and appropriated discipline for infractions.

● **Deficiency orders.** Set mandatory inspection guidelines for the CFTC to audit exchange systems at least once every two years. Flaws in the system would have to be reported and improved. The exchanges would have certain appeal rights regarding the inspections and findings.

● **Telemarketing fraud.** Required that futures associations establish supervisory guidelines for telephone solicitation. They could require that a member not enter an order by a new customer until three days after the customer signed an agreement acknowledging the risk involved in the trade.

● **Undercover operations.** Directed the CFTC to cooperate with federal agencies in requesting and arranging undercover operations.

● **Disciplinary committees.** Provided guidelines to the exchanges for establishing review panels on disciplinary actions for traders found to break the rules.

● **Board memberships.** Outlined the requirements for members serving on the oversight boards for each contract market and required that the futures associations refuse membership to individuals found to violate trading rules.

● **Floor trader registration.** Required all individuals who traded in a contract market for their own accounts to register with the CFTC. The registration could be revoked if a trader violated CFTC regulations. All registered traders would have to attend periodic ethics training seminars.

● **Increased penalties.** Established a range of felony penalties for individuals who violated trading rules. The penalties would be determined in part by the gravity of the infractions, as well as the financial strength of the individuals found guilty. The penalty for embezzlement would be increased to $1 million for corporations and $500,000 for individuals. The bill also would set criteria for establishing the financial liability of brokers who violated trading rules. The broker's firm could be held liable for claims arising from rules violations, and in cases in which the firm willfully selected the broker to aid in the violation, the firm could face punitive damages. The CFTC would have authority to force individuals who violated trading rules to pay restitution to clients.

● **Insider trading.** Made it a felony to trade on the basis of material, non-public information.

● **Commissioner requirements.** Set guidelines for CFTC commissioners and outlined the conditions under which a member of a futures market governing board violated conflict of interest rules.

● **Study directives.** Directed the General Accounting Office to study a fee collection system that would help pay for enforcement of the new rules. The CFTC also would be required to study the competitiveness of the U.S. futures trading industry in relation to those of other countries.

● **Computerized trading.** Recommended that the CFTC assist in the development and use of computerized trading systems in addition to the traditional open outcry trading then used in futures pits.

● **Published rules.** Required the CFTC to publish and allow public review of all guidelines governing civil penalties.

## Assistance to Foreign Exchanges

● Allowed the CFTC to assist foreign futures authorities in investigating possible violations of futures trading laws, when the investigation was deemed to be in the "clear interest" of the United States. Information regarding such an investigation could be disclosed only to Congress or during a judicial inquiry. The provision exempted certain information related to foreign futures exchange investigation from the Freedom of Information Act when the release of such information would violate confidentiality laws in the foreign country.

## Miscellaneous Provisions

● Authorized appropriations in the amount of $53 million for fiscal 1993 and $60 million for fiscal 1994.

● Authorized the CFTC to suspend or alter the registration of any person charged with violations of the Commodity Exchange Act.

● Empowered the CFTC to adopt recordkeeping and reporting requirements for futures commission merchants.

## Intermarket Coordination

● **Futures margins.** Allowed the Board of Governors of the Federal Reserve System to set or change margin levels required on stock-index futures transactions, or options on stock-index futures. The authority could be delegated to the CFTC on a daily basis. Margins were the good-faith deposits on futures transactions that ensured that the contract could be fulfilled by both parties.

● **Swaps and hybrids.** Authorized the CFTC to exempt certain exotic financial instruments from the requirements of the Commodity Exchange Act. The conference report specified that the exemption was to be used "sparingly." The provision was written to apply solely to swaps and other derivative products known as hybrids, forwards, and deposits, which defied the traditional formulation of futures products.

● **Studies of derivatives.** Directed the CFTC to cooperate with the Securities and Exchange Commission and the Federal Reserve Board to conduct a comprehensive study of swaps and the off-exchange derivatives trading industry. The study was supposed to examine whether a single federal agency should regulate the markets for futures, securities, options, swaps and derivative products. ■

# Legislation Targets Fraud In Financial Reporting

Legislation to require corporate accountants to blow the whistle on fraud they uncovered in the course of routine audits gained committee approval and passed the House, but the Senate had no companion measure, and the bill died.

The bill (HR 4313 — H Rept 102-890) won voice vote approval from the House Energy and Commerce Committee on July 28. It would have codified and greatly expanded self-imposed standards of the auditing profession aimed at disclosing fraud.

On the House floor, the measure was tacked onto another bill that would have increased federal oversight of the booming financial planning industry. That bill (HR 5726) passed the House by voice vote on Sept. 22 but went no further. *(Investment advisers, p. 126)*

HR 4313 was an outgrowth of a spate of corporate failures that resulted from fraud, often involving savings and loan associations, that either went undetected or was disguised by accountants hired to certify public financial reports.

The ongoing, taxpayer-financed salvage of failed thrifts "could have been avoided if the front line of defense — the accountants — did not turn a blind eye to the fraudulent activities of the institutions that employed them," said Rep. Edward J. Markey, D-Mass., a principal cosponsor of the bill and chairman of the Finance Subcommittee, which approved the bill July 9.

He noted that banking regulators pursuing fraud in failed thrifts had settled 11 lawsuits against accounting companies for $40 million and that 19 other cases seeking $2 billion in damages were pending. But Markey said that fraud in financial reporting was widespread beyond the thrift industry and said Congress had to act "to correct the current imbalance in incentives that leads some auditors to shield their clients rather than to protect the public."

Like most financial measures that emerged from Energy and Commerce, the bill was the product of extensive negotiations and had bipartisan support. While accountants did not wholeheartedly embrace an enlarged police role, they did not oppose the bill, which would have given them some protection from lawsuits stemming from their public disclosures.

"The accounting profession has adopted a number of new accounting standards over the last few years to improve financial reporting. This bill will enhance those efforts," said Matthew J. Rinaldo of New Jersey, ranking Republican on Markey's subcommittee.

## Provisions

The bill would have imposed several new reporting requirements on accountants and would have given the Securities and Exchange Commission (SEC) authority to seek civil penalties where auditors failed to meet the standards. The major provisions of the bill would have:

● Required accountants to conduct audits so as to "reasonably assure" detection of illegal acts that would have had a material impact on corporate financial statements and determine whether audited corporations were likely to stay in business for the coming year.

● Required accountants to report any illegal act they uncovered to appropriate corporate officials. If the act was expected to have a material effect on financial statements, or if an accountant believed that it would not be remedied, he would have had to report directly to the board of directors. This provision would have essentially codify existing professional standards for accountants.

● Required corporations whose boards were notified of illegal acts by accountants to inform the SEC within one business day and to inform accountants immediately of any such report. If an accountant was not told that the SEC had been informed, he would have had to report his findings to the SEC, or resign and inform the SEC.

● Prevented private lawsuits against accountants for information contained in reports to the SEC or to corporate boards (although the SEC could have brought charges against accountants for false reports).

● Permitted the SEC to seek civil fines and cease-and-desist orders against accountants who failed to comply with the bill's provisions.

Versions of the bill were attached in 1990 to a House-passed crime bill (HR 5269) and in 1991 to the Energy and Commerce version of a sweeping banking overhaul bill (HR 6) but did not survive in either measure. *(1990 Almanac, p. 486; 1991 Almanac, p. 75)*

HR 4313 did not include several controversial provisions from the earlier bills. For example, accountants would not have had to report publicly on the ability of internal corporate controls to detect and prevent fraud. And the SEC would not have been given authority to devise auditing standards, which were essentially the province of review boards established by the accounting profession. ■

# Legislation Guarantees Farm Credit Paybacks

Legislation aimed at ensuring that the Farm Credit System paid back the $1.3 billion it borrowed from the federal government in 1987 became law in 1992.

The House passed the bill Oct. 4 by voice vote; the Senate cleared the bill (HR 6125) on Oct. 7, also by voice. President Bush signed it into law Oct. 28 (PL 102-552).

The centerpiece of the bill was a requirement to speed up farm credit bank payments into a fund that would repay the $3.1 billion in principal and interest that the banks were expected to owe the federal government by the time the debt was to come due in the early part of the following century.

The bill was aimed at fixing weaknesses in the 1987 law that did not make clear how and when the government would be repaid. *(1987 Almanac, p. 381)*

The Farm Credit System was one of five government-sponsored enterprises (GSEs) that received breaks from the government in exchange for boosting lending in different sectors of the economy. It had more than $50 billion in outstanding loans, which were implicitly backed by the federal government. That backing became explicit in 1987, when a recession in the nation's farm economy led to the government bailout.

The measure was part of an ongoing effort to tighten oversight of the GSEs, which Congress and the administration agreed were insufficiently regulated and might have ultimately become a risk to the taxpayer.

An effort to pass a farm credit bill (HR 3298) in 1991

failed after Appropriations Committee Chairman Jamie L. Whitten, D-Miss., objected to a provision that would have likely merged a Jackson, Miss., bank into the system's Texas region. Members voted 221-203 in favor of the bill, but that was well short of the two-thirds majority that was required because the bill was brought up on the suspension calendar. *(1991 Almanac, p. 115)*

**House Action**

On Sept. 23, the House took up HR 3298 for the second time, passing it by voice vote. On the issue of the Jackson, Miss., bank, the House adopted a compromise requiring a referendum of Jackson Bank borrowers, allowing them to choose to merge with the Texas bank or seek another system bank with which to merge.

The House also adopted an amendment by Bill Gradison of Ohio, ranking Republican on the Budget Committee, who objected in 1991 that the bill contained accounting loopholes that would have allowed banks to avoid repayments to the fund. Gradison's amendment accelerated the banks' repayment of debt to the Treasury and reduced the period during which banks could count their debt repayment as regulatory capital from 15 to 12 years.

In addition, the House attached five unrelated farm bills to HR 3298, including a measure to encourage people to get into farming by relaxing eligibility requirements for Farmers Home Administration (FmHA) loans. Other provisions would have revised general FmHA loan programs, refined the sugar cane allotment process, clarified bankruptcy rules for vegetable vendors and allowed electronic tracing of cotton stored in federal warehouses. Several of these provisions drew Senate objections. *(Beginning farmers, p. 216)*

On Oct. 4, the House approved a new version of the bill (HR 6125), which resulted from negotiations between the House and Senate Agriculture committees and left out the unrelated farm bills to be passed separately. The Senate cleared the measure by voice vote Oct. 7. ■

# Congress Clears Extension Of Defense Production Act

Congress cleared a bill (S 347 — PL 102-558) to extend and expand the Defense Production Act (DPA) giving the president the authority to redirect military goods for use during wartime.

The Korean War-era law granted the president broad authority to redirect domestic goods to military use during times of national emergency. It had expired and gone without renewal for extended periods several times in the recent past. It expired Oct. 20, 1990, and although Congress did most of the work on a reauthorization in 1990, it failed to clear the bill before the 101st Congress adjourned. As a result, President Bush had to rely on other laws and executive orders to maintain his emergency acquisition powers during the Persian Gulf War. *(1990 Almanac, p. 202)*

In 1991, Congress again failed to complete work on a multiyear reauthorization of the DPA. Both chambers passed DPA bills, but work to reconcile them did not get under way that year. Instead, lawmakers approved two short-term extensions in 1991. *(1991 Almanac, p. 109)*

Although there was no action on the DPA reauthorization for much of the year, a conference agreement (H Rept 102-1028) was reached at the end of the first session.

A key difference between the House and Senate bills approved in 1991 had been Senate language to enact the Fair Trade in Financial Services bill. That measure would have given the Treasury Department and bank regulators authority to deny applications by foreign banks and securities firms for licenses in the United States if their home countries did not grant equal market access to U.S. banks and securities firms. While some House conferees supported the fair trade language, most did not, and the provision was dropped.

The bill extended the DPA through September 1994. Provisions aimed at securing the U.S. defense industrial base required the president to undertake a review and take steps to ensure a reliable supply of critical materials. Supporters said the reauthorization was aimed at modernizing the act for the post-Cold War period. One provision promoted the development of "dual use" technologies that had both defense and non-defense applications.

Under the bill, the Pentagon could continue to make loans and purchase guarantees to U.S. companies that agreed to supply the government with militarily significant goods and services during an emergency.

The House adopted the conference report Oct. 5 by voice vote. The Senate cleared the bill Oct. 8 by voice vote. Bush signed the measure Oct. 28. ■

# Gramm Takes On, Blocks Regulation of 'Roll-Ups'

Congressional efforts to move a widely backed bill that would have curbed abuses when limited partnership ventures were reorganized, or "rolled up," were stymied by the vehement opposition of Republican Sen. Phil Gramm of Texas.

Gramm used parliamentary tactics to bottle up a roll-up bill in the Senate Banking Committee, and he prevented an unrelated bill to which the Senate roll-up bill had been attached from going to conference. The unrelated bill (S 2733) would have beefed up federal regulation of government-sponsored enterprises (GSEs).

"I intend to do everything I can do to prevent this [bill] from becoming the law of the land," Gramm said.

Congressional action came in the wake of a slew of horror stories from investors in limited partnerships who said they were ripped off when the partnerships were restructured.

Even as Congress worked to enact legislation to deal with the issue, the Securities and Exchange Commission (SEC) drew up new proxy rules and other measures aimed at stemming abusive roll-ups.

## BACKGROUND

Limited partnerships were designed as long-term, non-traded entities in which investors pooled their funds under the supervision of a general partner, who managed the investment. In a roll-up, several limited partnerships were reorganized into a single publicly traded company. The stocks issued by such companies, and provided to investors in lieu of their partnership interest, had generally fared

poorly in securities markets; losses to original investors were calculated at more than $1 billion.

Most limited partnerships were concentrated in the slumping real estate and oil and gas industries, and many performed below expectations. Roll-ups were pitched to investors as a means of shoring up such faltering partnerships while providing them with an option to liquidate their investment.

Critics charged, however, that the general partners had often ripped off investors by reaping excessive management fees and boosting their equity positions at the expense of the limited, or non-management, partners.

A roll-up reform bill (HR 1885) passed the House in 1991. *(1991 Almanac, p. 113)*

## SENATE ACTION

The Senate Banking Committee met May 21 to mark up S 1423. But Gramm invoked a Senate rule that prohibited committees from meeting when the chamber was in session. Two weeks later, on June 3, Gramm insisted that a quorum be present as the committee prepared to mark up the roll-up bill, and acting Chairman Christopher J. Dodd, D-Conn., was forced to adjourn the meeting.

The widely backed bill, which had 72 cosponsors, would have eased federal proxy rules to make it easier for investors to fight a roll-up, and would have required that limited partners who opposed a roll-up be given alternative compensation, or "dissenter's rights," to the new stock offering.

The Senate bill had a somewhat narrower scope than the House-passed measure, which would have required a "fairness opinion" prepared by an independent expert with no stake in the proposed roll-up to be distributed to investors.

At the core of Gramm's opposition was the dissenter's rights section. He said at the markup that the provision would have allowed a minority of the limited partners to kill a deal, giving them rights they did not have under the original partnership.

Dodd, chairman of the Securities Subcommittee and author of the bill, countered that it was roll-up transactions that changed the rules in the middle of the game.

The two also disagreed over whether the bill would harm the market for limited partnerships, which had generated about $130 billion in capital investment. Dodd said that widespread reports of roll-up abuses made limited partnerships a less attractive investment. Gramm replied that the bill would dilute the powers of general partners and thus would discourage them from organizing limited partnerships.

The Investment Program Association, the national trade group for the sponsors and sellers of limited partnerships, supported the bill.

The fight occurred as the practice of rolling up partnerships was declining. In 1990-1991, 52 roll-ups or similar transactions were registered at the SEC; only eight were pending at the time of the markup.

A House Energy and Commerce Committee aide said, however, "There are a lot of [roll-up] deals out there that people would like to do but they are holding off, depending on what Congress does."

Although the SEC and the Treasury Department recognized that there were roll-up abuses, they opposed the bill, saying that the SEC already had the necessary authority and was working on the problem.

Dodd said that the administration did not strongly oppose the bill. "Basically the opposition is: 'We don't disagree with you. We'd like to maybe do it in our own time and our own way, but we're not arguing whether or not what you're pressing for makes sense,'" he said.

### Riding the GSE Bill

Stymied in committee, Dodd looked to attach the roll-ups bill to a "must-pass" bill on the Senate floor. The GSE bill, strongly backed by the administration, presented one such opportunity.

Although Banking Committee Chairman Donald W. Riegle Jr., D-Mich., pleaded with his colleagues not to load up the GSE bill with controversial amendments, Dodd persisted, and on June 24, his roll-ups amendment made to it onto the bill after easily surviving a tabling motion on a 10-87 vote. *(Vote 127, p. 17-S; GSEs, p. 123)*

But Gramm persisted. After the Senate passed the GSE bill, he objected to the usually routine step of calling up the House bill and inserting the Senate language. That added another obstacle to the bill going to conference. In the end, a "clean" version of the GSE bill, minus roll-ups and other unrelated provisions, was passed as part of another measure.

Dodd also offered the roll-up bill as an amendment during floor consideration of a sweeping energy bill (S 2166), but withdrew the amendment. ∎

# Bush Vetoes First of Two Major Tax Bills

A drive for middle-class tax relief provided the focus for the first of two major tax bills cleared by Congress in 1992. Assembled quickly in February and March, the $77.5 billion measure included a two-year middle-class tax credit, a permanent tax credit for families with children, and restoration of individual retirement account (IRA) deductions for middle-class taxpayers. It also incorporated six of seven tax cut proposals made by President Bush in January, including a tax credit for home buyers and restoration of so-called passive-loss deductions for the real estate industry.

Under the budget rules, all tax cuts had to be paid for, and Democratic leaders tried to turn that to their advantage by offsetting their tax cuts with increased taxes on the rich — including a higher top income tax bracket and a surtax on millionaires. They hoped to force Bush to choose between denying the middle class a tax break or raising taxes on the well-to-do — something he vowed not to repeat after signing a tax increase in 1990.

But the strategy fizzled. Democratic leaders found themselves pressing the rank and file to vote for a tax bill that everyone agreed was certain to die on Bush's desk. Bush vetoed the bill before it even reached the White House, and Democatic leaders could not muster the votes to override him. Bush suffered little or no blacklash: The final impression was of a president vetoing a political document, not serious legislation.

## BACKGROUND

The stage for a tax bill had been set months before, when Democrats began raising the banner of tax relief for the middle class, presenting it as a question of fairness as well as a tonic to the slowly recovering economy. Increasingly, however, they concentrated on the fairness argument, perhaps in part because most economists were warning that a tax cut would boost the deficit, drive up interest rates and choke off economic recovery.

Bush had resisted, stressing instead his proposal for a capital gains tax cut to stimulate economic growth. But by late December 1991, with his poll ratings slipping and widespread public support for a tax cut, he joined the call for middle-class relief.

### Bush's Proposal

In his Jan. 28, 1992, State of the Union address, Bush called on Congress to act by March 20 on a set of economic growth measures that included a capital gains cut, an investment tax allowance, a $500 per child increase in the personal income tax exemption, and penalty-free IRA withdrawals

---

### BOXSCORE

➡ **Tax bill (HR 4210).** The $77.5 billion measure would have provided tax credits for middle-income taxpayers paid for by tax increases on the well-to-do, including a new top tax bracket and millionaires' surtax. It would have repealed luxury taxes, extended a series of expiring tax breaks, restored passive-loss deductions on rental property, allowed a write-off of intangible assets and reduced capital gains taxes.

**Reports:** H Rept 102-432; conference report H Rept 102-461

#### KEY ACTION

Feb. 27 — The **House** passed HR 4210, 221-209.

March 13 — The **Senate** passed, 50-47.

March 20 — Conference report filed; the **House** adopted, 211-189; the **Senate** cleared 50-44. President Bush vetoed.

March 25 — The **House** failed to override veto, 211-215.

---

for certain medical and education expenses and for first homes.

Details of these and a range of other White House tax proposals were sent to the Hill the following day as part of Bush's fiscal 1993 budget. *(Bush budget, p. 85)*

Bush also announced several steps that did not require congressional approval, including a reduction in the tax withheld from employees' paychecks. The administration said that would mean a $345 cash boost in 1992 for the average married worker and, presumably, more money pumped into the economy. But it also would mean little or no refund for those taxpayers in 1993, and it was expected to add as much as $15 billion to the fiscal 1992 deficit as the government collected less in tax revenues.

Democratic leaders embraced the March 20 deadline, saying they did so not because Bush had ordered it but because passing a tax bill by that date was the right thing to do. However, they were clearly concerned that missing the date would give Bush an opportunity to accuse them of failing to act on urgent economic problems.

## HOUSE COMMITTEE ACTION

Democrats wanted a chance to put their own tax agenda up against the overall tax package in Bush's budget, which included a number of often-rejected proposals such as extending the Medicare payroll tax to all state and local workers. House Ways and Means Committee Chairman Dan Rostenkowski, D-Ill., insisted that Bush's proposal be introduced in its entirety. "I do not intend to tolerate cherry-picking of items from the president's package," he said. But House Republicans rejected the idea, deciding instead to present a slimmed-down GOP tax bill crafted in cooperation with the White House. That set the stage for an unusual sequence of actions by Ways and Means.

In a closed-door committee markup on Feb. 12, the panel's Democrats voted unanimously to send Bush's full tax package to the floor. The bill (HR 4210) was introduced not by Republicans but by Democratic Majority Leader Richard A. Gephardt, D-Mo. Furious, committee Republicans voted against the bill, charging that Gephardt had altered some of Bush's provisions and left out his spending cuts so that the plan lost half a billion dollars over six years.

### GOP Seven-Point Plan

The committee then defeated the Republican seven-point plan (HR 4200) on a straight 13-22 party-line vote. Democrats derided the measure, particulary because it did not include the increase in the personal exemption, the

main middle-class tax cut proposal in Bush's budget. The GOP bill would have:

- **Capital gains.** Set new, lower tax rates on profits from the sale of stock, real estate and other assets: 15.4 percent for gains on assets held three years or longer; 19.6 percent for assets held two years; 23.8 percent for assets held one year or less. The bill would have exempted gains on real estate or family owned businesses from the 24 percent alternative minimum tax (AMT), a provision of the tax code aimed at ensuring that individuals with large deductions still paid some taxes. The proposal was seen as particularly beneficial to older people hoping to sell their houses or businesses to finance their retirement.
- **Home buyers' credit.** Provided a tax credit of 10 percent of the purchase price of a house, up to $5,000, effective from Feb. 1, 1992, to Jan. 1, 1993. The credit would have been available for buyers who had not owned a house in the previous three years.
- **IRA deductions.** Allowed penalty-free withdrawals of up to $10,000 from IRAs, if the money were used to buy a first home or pay for certain education and medical expenses.
- **Passive losses.** Allowed real estate developers to use so-called passive losses from real estate to offset other types of income for tax purposes.
- **Accelerated depreciation.** Allowed a first-year deduction of 15 percent of the cost of newly purchased business equipment bought between Feb. 1, 1992, and Jan. 1, 1993.
- **Alternative minimum tax.** Simplified and provided flexibility in calculating depreciation deductions for purposes of computing the corporate version of the alternative minimum tax, a provision designed to ensure that corporations paid at least some taxes. The effect would have been to reduce somewhat the tax owed by corporations investing in large amounts of new equipment.
- **Pension funds.** Enacted new rules allowing real estate investment by pension funds.

### Democrats' Alternative

Ways and Means Democrats then turned their attention to completing their own tax proposal (HR 4287), based on a draft prepared by Rostenkowski. The Democratic plan featured higher taxes on the well-to-do to pay for a two-year middle-class tax cut, and a fresh approach to cutting the capital gains tax.

Even with the higher taxes, the Democrats' plan would have added $30.2 billion to the federal deficit over three years. Enough revenue would have been recouped when the tax cuts expired, however, that the bill would have produced a net gain of $13.9 billion by the end of 1997.

- **Middle-class tax cut.** The centerpiece of the bill was a two-year refundable tax credit of 20 percent of an employee's payroll tax contribution, up to $400 per year for couples and $200 for individuals. The credit would have lost an estimated $45.9 billion in revenues over six years.

Committee member Thomas J. Downey, D-N.Y., failed in an attempt to substitute a scaled-down version of his plan for an $800 credit for each child in a family; the vote was 13-7.

- **Higher taxes on the wealthy.** To recoup the lost revenues, the plan would have raised the top income tax rate to 35 percent from 31 percent for individuals with taxable income above $85,000 and couples with incomes above $145,000. Millionaires would have had to pay a 10 percent surtax, raising their effective tax rate to roughly 38 percent.

In a jab at skyrocketing boardroom salaries, corporations would have been barred from writing off more than $1 million of an executive's pay.

- **Capital gains.** The Democrats surprised nearly everyone, including themselves and the White House, by adopting a change in the capital gains tax long advocated by Republicans.

The plan would have allowed taxpayers to subtract the portion of their gain that was attributable to inflation when calculating the taxes they owed on profits from selling assets such as stocks and real estate purchased after Feb. 1, 1991. The change, known as indexing, would not have cost the government revenue until 1994, but after that, losses would have mounted, doubling from $1.2 billion in 1996 to $2.4 billion in 1997.

Rostenkowski originally proposed a less generous version of Bush's capital gains rate cut, which would have applied only to stock in start-up businesses and been targeted to middle income taxpayers. But the provision did not go over well with a solid bloc of committee Democrats. Rostenkowski then quickly substituted indexing to keep the support of senior Democrats on the panel, including Ed Jenkins, Ga.; Robert T. Matsui, Calif.; Beryl Anthony Jr., Ark.; and Andrew Jacobs Jr., Ind.

Indexing allowed the Democrats to make a change that had the appearance of producing a reduction in taxes on capital gains, while not immediately benefiting the wealthy or widening the deficit.

The Democratic plan also would have allowed individuals to exclude from their taxes 50 percent of the gain on sales of certain small business stock held more than five years. That translated into a 16.8 percent effective tax rate.

- **Corporate taxes.** In an effort to stimulate the economy, Rostenkowski's original package would have lowered the top corporate tax rate from 34 percent to 33 percent, and it would have lowered the corporate alternative minimum tax from 20 percent to 19 percent.

But at a series of Democratic Caucus meetings during the week of Feb. 17, it became clear that liberals were unwilling to accept a permanent reduction in the corporate rate when the middle class would have gotten only a two-year tax cut from the bill. Democratic leaders tried to salvage the corporate cuts by making them temporary, but even that did not satisfy critics.

"This is not what we think the Democratic Party ought to stand for," said David R. Obey, D-Wis., a leading opponent of the rate cuts.

The leadership then eliminated the corporate tax cut, saving $17.1 billion in what would have been revenue. Some of that was plowed back into the bill in the form of more generous corporate depreciation allowances.

Ways and Means Democrats decided to allow small-business owners, many of whom paid taxes under the individual rates and thus could see their taxes increase under the plan, to write off as much as $25,000 of the cost of equipment in 1992. The existing limit was $10,000.

They also adopted Bush's proposal to give corporations an additional first-year depreciation allowance of 15 percent of the cost of business equipment bought in 1992 and put into use before July 1, 1993.

And they included a proposal by Jenkins to allow companies paying under the alternative minimum tax to write off more of the cost of their investments than under existing law. Jenkins' plan, which would have made changes to the adjusted current earnings component of the Alternative Minimum Tax, was virtually identical to Bush's budget.

Other highlights of the Democratic package included:

● **Passive losses.** Restoration of certain passive-loss deductions. The proposal by Michael A. Andrews, D-Texas, would have allowed real estate professionals (those who spent 50 percent of their time and 500 hours a year in real estate activities) to deduct 80 percent of their rental losses from their ordinary income in calculating their taxes. The change would have been available only for buildings in existence at the time of enactment; it would not have covered new construction. The cost was to be offset by lengthening the depreciation period for new commercial buildings from 31.5 years to 41 years. In addition, the depreciation period for new residential buildings was to be lengthened from 27.5 years to 31 years.

● **Extenders.** Permanent extension of several expiring tax breaks. The most popular item on the list was the 20 percent tax credit for research and development expenses. Others were a credit to encourage investment in low-income housing, authority for the use of tax-exempt mortgage revenue bonds and small-issue manufacturing bonds, an exclusion for employer-provided educational assistance and a credit for employers who hired hard-to-place workers.

A health insurance deduction for self-employed individuals would have been extended for six months.

● **Charitable contributions.** A permanent exemption from the alternative minimum tax for gifts of property, such as stock, artwork and manuscripts, that had appreciated in value.

● **IRAs.** Penalty-free IRA withdrawals for first homes, medical costs and educational expenses.

● **Luxury taxes.** Repeal of the excise taxes enacted in 1990 (PL 101-508) on a portion of the cost of luxury yachts, airplanes, jewelry and furs. The tax on expensive cars would have remained, but the $30,000 threshold above which the tax applied would have risen with inflation.

● **Intangibles.** A requirement for businesses to write off most intangible assets — such as subscription lists, recipes and goodwill — over 14 years. Exceptions were made for software, government licenses, movies and other items, which could have been written off over a shorter period.

● **Deductions.** A two-year extension, through 1997, of the limit on deductions and the phase-out of the personal exemption for high-income taxpayers. The provisions would have raised $11.6 billion.

## HOUSE FLOOR ACTION

The $93.5 billion Democratic tax bill narrowly escaped defeat on the House floor Feb. 27, when party members grudgingly complied with a direct plea from their leadership to support the measure even though many of them considered it deeply flawed.

The House approved the bill by a vote of 221-210 and sent it to the Senate. Only one Republican voted for the bill, while 46 Democrats voted against it. *(Vote 30, p. 8-H)*

"Put me down as dissatisfied, yeah. It's terrible," Bush told reporters after the vote. "The Senate — there's still some hope there," he added.

Finding themselves short of a majority just hours before the scheduled vote, Democratic leaders fell back on a hard-nosed political appeal, arguing that their party had made tax cuts for the middle class its rallying cry for the year and could not turn back. They warned that the House would be pilloried if it ignored Bush's call for quick action on a tax bill. The lobbying worked. But many members voted for the bill hoping that it would be drastically changed or bog

down completely in the Senate. "If this were a free vote, I think members would have said, 'What the heck, I'll vote against this bill,'" said Ways and Means Committee member Don J. Pease, D-Ohio. "But gradually they came to understand that this was a very high-stakes game."

On a party-line vote earlier in the day, the House easily rejected the Republican seven-point tax plan endorsed by Bush. The measure included little middle-class tax relief and was aimed almost entirely at spurring economic growth. The bill, sponsored by Minority Leader Robert H. Michel of Illinois and Bill Archer of Texas, won only 14 Democratic votes and was defeated, 166-264. *(Vote 28, p. 8-H)*

In addition to a cut in the capital gains tax, the seven-point GOP bill included the $5,000 credit for first-time home buyers, penalty-free withdrawals from IRAs to purchase first homes, passive-loss deductions for real estate, the additional 15 percent depreciation for business equipment purchases, expanded depreciation under the alternative minimum tax and new rules allowing real estate investment by pension funds.

In an empty gesture on Feb. 26, the House voted 1-427 against the Gephardt bill that incorporated the full list of tax proposals in Bush's budget. By bringing it to a vote, Democrats had hoped to show how little support Bush's full tax plan had on Capitol Hill. But Republicans refused to vote for the package on the grounds that it was a partisan ploy. The lone member to vote yes, Bill Orton, D-Utah, said he opposed the measure but wanted "to get the process moving." *(Vote 25, p. 6-H)*

In the end, the Republican role in the floor debate was to add to the general air of doom felt by Democrats as they mulled whether to vote for their bill to raise income taxes by $77.6 billion over six years.

"The president of the United States comes to this chamber in the State of the Union and asks for a tax-cutting, job-creating bill, and the Democratic leadership gives him a tax-increasing, job-killing bill," said GOP Whip Newt Gingrich, R-Ga.

House leaders seemed surprised at the struggle needed to pass their bill. Some Democrats complained that it would add $30 billion to the federal deficit over two years, others that it did not contain generous enough incentives for savings and investment. Most worrisome to many was the inclusion of a permanent increase in taxes on the wealthy, with only a temporary tax cut for the middle class.

In some cases, said a senior Democrat, the leadership warned members that their votes would be remembered when it came time to hand out choice committee seats, many of which would come open the following year. "It was personal phone calls from Gephardt and the Speaker to pick up the last 30 votes," said Pease.

## SENATE COMMITTEE ACTION

The Senate Finance Committee approved a $57 billion version of the tax bill by an 11-9 party-line vote on March 3. By then, it was clear that the bill was going nowhere. Democrats were determined to pay for the middle-class tax relief with higher taxes on the wealthy, while Bush had renounced his 1990 decision to raise taxes, saying it was a mistake that he would not repeat.

The consensus in both parties was that it would be best to finish the fight off quickly. "The bottom line is as long as there are tax increases in this bill, it's going to be vetoed, and the veto will be sustained," said Minority Leader Bob Dole, R-Kan., a member of the committee. "Let's get on

with it."

Democrats worked out the details of the massive bill in private before the public markup.

● **Middle-class tax cut.** The bill included a $300-a-child tax credit, available to families making less than $50,000 a year. Families making between $50,000 and $70,000 would have qualified for a proportionately smaller credit. The credit, available for children under age 16, was permanent and non-refundable, which meant families would only receive it if they paid taxes.

● **Higher taxes on the wealthy.** The measure would have created a new top tax bracket of 36 percent, 1 percentage point higher than the House measure. To avoid appearing to raise taxes on the middle class, Committee Chairman Lloyd Bentsen, D-Texas, made the new rate apply to taxable individual incomes over $150,000, compared with $85,000 in the House bill. The spread was narrower for couples: $175,000 in the Senate bill compared with $145,000 in the House measure.

The Senate bill included the 10 percent surtax on millionaires.

● **Capital gains.** Like the House measure, the Senate bill would have reduced the tax on profits from sales of stock, real estate and other assets — but only for future investments, a feature that the White House said would prevent any immediate economic stimulus.

The Senate bill contained a complex new progressive rate structure for taxing gains on assets held at least two years. The new rates were 5 percent, 19 percent, 23 percent and 28 percent. Taxpayers in the 15 percent income tax bracket would generally have paid a 5 percent tax on capital gains. Upper-income taxpayers subject to the new 36 percent income tax rate would have continued to pay the existing capital gains rate of 28 percent.

Like the House measure, the Senate bill would have cut the capital gains tax on the sale of stock newly issued by small companies and held at least five years.

● **IRAs.** The bill included a proposal championed by Bentsen to restore the deductibility of IRA contributions for all taxpayers. Bentsen wanted to keep the maximum annual deduction at $2,000 in 1992 but allow it to increase in $500 increments pegged to inflation. Under existing law, only taxpayers who were not covered by a pension plan or whose incomes were below $25,000 for individuals or $40,000 for joint filers were eligible. Under the bill, individuals also could have made non-deductible contributions to a new type of IRA and withdraw the funds tax-free after five years. To reduce the revenue loss, the IRA changes were not to take effect until the following year.

● **Passive losses.** The Finance Committee bill endorsed the idea of allowing real estate professionals to once again use passive losses on rental property to reduce their tax burden. But the provision was narrower than the House version. As in the House bill, a person would have been required to spend 500 hours a year in real estate to qualify. But the rental losses could be written off only against other real estate income, such as that from managing or constructing a building. The House bill would have allowed a broader writeoff. Like the House version, the Senate bill would have applied only to existing property.

The Senate measure also included lengthy health and education sections not in the House bill.

### Compromise in Committee

During committee markup, Bill Bradley, D-N.J., and John D. Rockefeller IV, D-W.Va., tried to make the tax credit refundable, allowing poor families not on the tax rolls to get a check from the government. But Bentsen argued that the tax relief in the bill ought to be targeted to the middle class, not the poor, who had received a tax cut in 1990. Moreover, making the credit refundable would have cost $22.6 billion, requiring lawmakers to eliminate billions of dollars in business tax breaks and probably killing the bill. Bradley attracted only one other vote for his amendment, that of Dave Durenberger, R-Minn.

Rockefeller — chairman of the National Children's Commission, which endorsed the idea of a refundable child credit in 1991 — nonetheless voted against Bradley's amendment in a show of support for Bentsen. Bentsen gave Rockefeller something he wanted more — an amendment replenishing trust funds that provided family medical benefits to 120,000 coal miners who worked for companies that had gone out of business or otherwise stopped contributing to the funds. The amendment, which would have forced much of the coal industry to pick up the cost of providing health care for these miners, was adopted by a vote of 10-5, with five senators voting present.

Bentsen also sought to mollify concern about the poor not receiving a tax cut by making the existing earned income tax credit (EITC) easier to claim and broader. The EITC provided low-income families with a refundable tax break of as much as $1,384 in 1992 and an additional $376 for families with young children. Bentsen's bill would have repealed the portion of the credit targeted to children under age 1, using the funds to make the remaining credit more generous.

Bentsen also peppered the bill with provisions for domestic automakers, oil and gas drillers, small businesses, investors with capital gains, and others.

Donald W. Riegle Jr., D-Mich., a strong supporter of the auto industry, was pleased with a provision to dramatically increase the tariff on imported light trucks and minivans, such as the Range Rover from Britain and the Toyota 4-Runner from Japan. The existing tariff of 2.5 percent was to rise to 25 percent, raising an estimated $1 billion in revenue over five years.

To attract the support of Louisiana Democrat John B. Breaux, the bill included a provision allowing independent oil and gas drillers who were subject to the alternative minimum tax to write off more of their drilling costs. The industry would have received several other tax breaks as well.

Breaux also won committee support for an amendment to give restaurant owners a credit for payroll taxes paid on employees' tips in excess of the minimum wage. The five-year, $1.5 billion cost of the amendment was to be paid for by barring corporations from deducting private-club dues. The amendment passed by voice vote.

**Bentsen intentionally included all seven items from Bush's economic package, although some were altered. In addition to a capital gains tax cut and passive-loss deductions, they were:**

● An additional first-year depreciation allowance of 10 percent for equipment put in service before July 1, 1993.

● Up to $5,000 in tax credits for first-time home buyers who purchased previously unoccupied residences.

● Penalty-free withdrawals from IRAs to purchase first homes and to pay certain medical and educational expenses.

● New rules allowing pension funds to invest in real estate.

● More generous depreciation for companies that paid

under the alternative minimum tax.

The bill included numerous other provisions designed to win support in committee and on the floor:

● An 18-month extension of a handful of expiring tax provisions, including the research and experimentation tax credit, the targeted jobs tax credit, the low-income housing credit, the alternative minimum tax exemption for certain appreciated property, mortgage revenue bond tax incentives and incentives for employer-provided transportation benefits.

● A $1 million cap on the deduction a company could take on an executive's pay.

● Repeal of the luxury tax on yachts, private planes, furs and jewelry. The 10 percent excise tax on automobiles remained, but the $30,000 threshold would have risen with inflation.

● A deduction or credit for student loan interest.

● A provision allowing self-employed individuals to deduct all of the cost of health insurance premiums in 1993 and 1994. In 1992, the bill would have continued the existing 25 percent deduction.

● An increase in taxes on securities firms proposed by the Bush administration.

Also tacked onto the bill was a controversial demonstration program to provide loans to students regardless of family income. Under the program, the federal government would have provided the money for the loans directly to a school to help pay for a student's tuition. Any student could have borrowed up to $5,000 a year as an undergraduate and $15,000 a year as a graduate student; a $30,000 cap would have been placed on a student's total borrowing. Students would have repaid their loans through the IRS, paying 3 percent, 5 percent or 7 percent of their adjusted gross income, depending on how much they owed. The interest owed on the loans was to be equal to the average of the interest rates on the 10-year and 30-year Treasury bonds.

The administration opposed the program, saying that the Department of Education was not competent to run it and that it would cost too much money.

## SENATE FLOOR ACTION

The Senate passed a $71 billion version of the tax bill on March 13 by a vote of 50-47, with four Democrats voting no. The bill included a $28 billion tax cut for the middle class and nearly $20.7 billion in tax breaks for business and investors. *(Vote 51, p. 8-S)*

The party-line vote masked deep unease among many Democrats, who did not relish voting for a controversial tax bill that had almost no chance of becoming law. Many senators appeared to agree with Warren B. Rudman, R-N.H., who denounced both the Democrats and the White House for pandering to the electorate by offering tax cuts that would add to the record deficit, while doing virtually nothing to help the economy.

"There can be no doubt that the blame for this lies with Congress and the president, with Democrats and Republicans alike, most all of whom have been unwilling to make the hard choices or to explain to the American people that there is no such thing as a free lunch," Rudman said.

Democrats said that by 1996 the tax cuts in the bill would be fully paid for through higher taxes and thus not add to the deficit. But their estimates showed the bill losing revenue in 1993 and 1994.

After vowing at the start of the four-day Senate debate

to oppose all amendments, Finance Chairman Bentsen was unable to stop the onrush of members who knew the bill was doomed but insisted on seeking tax breaks for senior citizens, American Indians, small-business owners and many others.

Facing unanimous Republican opposition, Senate Democratic leaders were forced to scale back slightly the number of families eligible for the $300-per-child tax credit. The threshold for eligibility was changed from $50,000 a year to $47,500, with families making $47,500 to $60,000 qualifying for a proportionately smaller credit.

Democrats modified the credit after learning that the Senate parliamentarian did not intend to accept the assertion that the bill, as approved by the Finance Committee, complied with budget rules that barred adding to the deficit. Ranking Budget Committee Republican Pete V. Domenici of New Mexico was set March 11 to object that the bill violated the budget rules. To proceed with a budget waiver, Democrats would have needed a 60-vote majority, which they did not have.

Before Domenici could call for a vote, however, Bentsen amended the bill to scale back the child credit, bringing the measure into compliance with the budget rules.

To save revenue, Bentsen also proposed to stretch over two years the benefits of a temporary 10 percent increase in equipment depreciation for businesses.

But the most serious threat to the bill came from the Democratic ranks. An amendment March 12 by Carl Levin, D-Mich., and Bob Graham, D-Fla., would have eliminated the $28 billion child credit and substituted language urging the Senate to apply the revenue to what sponsors said was better long-term medicine for the economy — reducing the deficit and spending more on federal job training and transportation programs.

Having made middle-class tax relief their party rallying cry, Democratic leaders could not afford to let the amendment carry. Republicans, seeing a chance to cut out the core of the bill, joined in opposing a leadership motion to table (or kill) the amendment. When it looked as if the motion would fail, a visibly angry Majority Leader George J. Mitchell, D-Maine, prolonged the 15-minute vote for nearly an hour while he twisted arms for votes. Finally, three Democrats — Robert C. Byrd, W.Va.; Charles S. Robb, Va.; and Herb Kohl, Wis. — changed their votes, saving the middle-class credit.

After the Democratic switches, many Republicans followed suit; the final vote was 57-38. *(Vote 40, p. 6-S)*

It was a bitter defeat for Republicans, who were still angry with Mitchell for blocking an up-or-down vote on Bush's tax plan the day before.

The GOP assault on the Democrats' tax bill began March 11 when Finance Committee ranking Republican Bob Packwood of Oregon offered a slightly altered version of Bush's tax program.

Packwood conceded that the White House plan would "not catapult the economy in the next six months." But he claimed that, unlike the Democrats' plan, it was "a nudge in that direction" and offered the best opportunity for compromise with Bush because it did not contain tax increases.

But the financing of the GOP plan gave Democrats an opportunity to defeat it on a procedural motion. To comply with budget rules, Republicans proposed an array of mandatory spending cuts, asset sales and user fees to offset the cost of their bill, which the administration said would be $9.2 billion over five years.

But the Joint Committee on Taxation, Congress' revenue estimator, said that the plan would add $24.4 billion to the deficit over five years. Thus the bill was subject to a procedural objection, which required 60 votes to overcome. By a vote of 37-60, the Senate rejected a request by Republican leaders to waive the budget rule, killing the GOP tax plan. *(Vote 39, p. 6-S)*

Republicans made a final stab at killing the bill on March 13 when John Seymour, Calif., moved to strike the tax increases on the wealthy. Because that would have added to the deficit, Bentsen was able to prevent an up-or-down vote by raising a parliamentary objection. Overcoming the objection required 60 votes; the tally was 43-55. *(Vote 50, 8-S)*

### Other Amendments

Amendments adopted by the Senate on March 12 and 13 would have:

● Permanently extended the deduction for health insurance costs available to self-employed taxpayers, allowing them to deduct 75 percent of such costs in 1992 and the full amount thereafter. The existing 25 percent deduction was set to expire on June 30, 1992. The amendment was adopted by voice vote.

● Barred states from taxing retirement income of individuals who were not residents of the state. The amendment, offered by Harry Reid, D-Nev., was adopted by voice vote. At the time, 13 states, including California and New York, claimed authority to tax pensions of former residents who had moved to other states.

● Allowed couples earning less than $100,000 and individuals earning less than $75,000 to make penalty-free withdrawals of up to $10,000 from IRAs and other pension funds for the purpose of purchasing new cars. The amendment, sponsored by Arlen Specter, R-Pa., passed by voice vote.

● Barred investors who purchased failed thrifts from the federal government from getting tax breaks in addition to tax-free payments — a so-called double dip — that would not ordinarily be available to buyers of other failed businesses. The 96 deals negotiated in 1988 provided tax-free payments to the new thrift owners to offset losses taken on assets owned by the failed thrifts. In some cases, investors were also permitted to deduct the losses from their taxes.

The amendment, sponsored by Howard M. Metzenbaum, D-Ohio, and adopted by voice vote, would have barred tax deductions not claimed by March 4, 1991. The same provision was in the House tax bill.

● Endorsed in non-binding language the "full disclosure" of checks drawn on the House bank for which there were insufficient funds. The amendment, sponsored by Jesse Helms, R-N.C., sprang from the House debate over whether to release the names of House members who kited House bank checks. The amendment was adopted 95-2. Byrd voted against the amendment along with Alan Cranston, D-Calif., saying that it violated the Senate's long-standing policy of not interfering in internal matters of the House. *(Vote 41, p. 7-S)*

● Cut aid to families with dependent children by 10 percent beginning in 1994 for states that failed to require able-bodied welfare recipients age 18 and above without dependents to participate in state workfare programs. Welfare recipients who moved to a new state would have been limited to the level of benefits they received in their former state. The amendments were proposed by Alfonse M. D'Amato, R-N.Y.

Republicans wrestled throughout the debate over whether to try to amend the bill or simply let it pass and give Bush a chance to veto a purely Democratic product. Bob Kasten, R-Wis., offered an amendment to eliminate the tax increases and pay for a long list of tax cuts using savings from a spending freeze. The amendment was defeated on a parliamentary maneuver because it did not comply with budget rules.

## FINAL ACTION

Racing to meet the White House deadline, Democratic leaders rammed the final version, a $77.5 billion tax bill, through Congress on March 20. Even before he had received the bill, Bush gave a speech March 20 to announce his veto, saying that Democrats "could not resist their natural impulse to raise taxes." He used the occasion to launch a broad attack against the Democratic-controlled Congress, saying "it is no longer accountable to individual American citizens and voters, and this must change."

After Democratic leaders had hammered out the final bill in a late-night negotiating session March 19, the bill passed the House on March 20 by a vote of 211-189 — far short of the two-thirds majority needed to override a veto. One Republican, Olympia J. Snowe of Maine, supported the measure. The vote was even closer in the Senate, which cleared the bill, 50-44, later in the day over unanimous Republican opposition. *(House vote 54, p. 14-H; Senate vote 54, p. 8-S)*

### Compromises

The bill's dim future helped speed along negotiations on the final provisions, which were conducted in a day's worth of closed meetings between Rostenkowski and Bentsen.

In order to include several expensive tax cuts without adding to the deficit, they had to scale back some items and eliminate others, notably the $5,000 credit for first-time home buyers that was in the Senate-passed bill and was proposed by the Bush administration.

Also dropped were provisions on health-care reforms, direct education loans, tariff treatment of imported light trucks and welfare work requirements that the Senate had included in its bill. Rockefeller's coal miners' health provision stayed in. The miners' benefits were later enacted as part of the energy bill. *(Energy bill, p. 231)*

As approved by conferees, the bill would have:

● **Middle-class tax cut.** Included a $42.4 billion tax cut over five years — more than twice what was in the Senate bill and slightly less than in the House-passed version. As cleared, the bill offered not one but two tax credits aimed at the middle class.

The first was similar to a provision in the House bill. In 1992 and 1993, workers would have qualified for a 20 percent credit, based on their Social Security taxes, worth up to $150 a year for individuals and $300 for married couples. Taxpayers with adjusted gross incomes of less than $50,000 for couples and $35,000 for individuals would have qualified for the full credit. Individuals making more than $50,000 and couples making more than $70,000 would have been eligible for a partial credit.

The credit was to be refundable for poor families with children who did not pay taxes.

In addition, starting in 1994, families with children under age 16 would have been eligible for a permanent $300-per-child tax credit, like that in the Senate bill. The

full credit was to be available to families making less than $50,000 a year; those making more than $70,000 would not have gotten the tax break. The child credit was not refundable.

● **Higher taxes on the wealthy.** Imposed $64 billion in new taxes on the wealthy over five years. The bill would have created a new top income tax bracket of 36 percent, applied to taxable income of $115,000 for individuals and $140,000 for married couples.

Wealthy individuals would have had to pay a 10 percent surtax on income above $1 million. High-income taxpayers would have continued to see their deductions limited through 1996; they would have lost the personal exemption permanently.

Other provisions in the final bill would have:

● **IRAs.** Restored the full deductibility of contributions of up to $2,000 and created the new type of IRA included in the Senate bill, with non-deductible contributions and tax-free withdrawals after five years. Taxpayers who already had IRAs could convert them to the new type of IRA through Jan. 1, 1994.

The bill included penalty-free IRA withdrawals for first-time home purchases, for medical and education expenses, and for those receiving unemployment compensation for longer than 12 weeks.

● **Capital gains.** Cut the capital gains tax rate by establishing the progressive rate structure from the Senate bill: Those in the 15 percent income tax bracket would have paid no capital gains tax; those in the 28 percent tax bracket would have paid 14 percent; those in the 31 percent bracket, 21 percent; and those in the new 36 percent bracket, 28 percent.

The new rates would have applied only to assets held two years but would have included assets held before enactment.

The bill also included a 50 percent exclusion for individual and corporate investors with profits on the sale of stock in qualified companies with less than $100 million in gross assets.

● **Passive losses.** Allowed real estate professionals, including real estate agents, to deduct losses on rental property against other income from real estate investments. The tax break applied only to existing properties.

● **Extenders.** Extended many expiring provisions through June 30, 1993, including the research and development tax credit, mortgage revenue bonds, the exclusion for employer-provided educational assistance, small-issue manufacturing bonds, orphan drug tax credit, business energy tax credit, group legal services tax break and the targeted jobs tax credit.

The low-income housing tax credit would have been made permanent.

The 25 percent deduction for insurance costs for self-employed workers would have been extended for one year. Lawmakers abandoned efforts to expand the credit to 100 percent and make it permanent.

● **Intangibles.** Allowed taxpayers to write off intangible assets over 14 years and to elect a 17-year writeoff period for existing assets.

● **Investment allowance.** Allowed businesses to depreciate an additional 10 percent of investments in property over the following two years. The bill would also have increased the tax writeoffs available to small businesses that bought new equipment from $10,000 to $20,000 for the following two years.

● **Luxury tax.** Repealed the luxury tax for yachts, air

## Bush's Veto Message

*Following is the official text of President Bush's March 20 veto message on HR 4210, the tax bill:*

I am returning herewith without my approval HR 4210, the "Tax Fairness and Economic Growth Acceleration Act of 1992." In my State of the Union Message, I proposed a responsible, balanced economic growth program. I challenged the Congress to pass incentives for growth by March 20. The Congress failed to meet that challenge. The Congress' response, HR 4210, is a formula for economic stagnation, not economic expansion.

My Administration's economic growth program would create jobs, generate long-term economic growth, and promote health, education, savings, and home ownership. My plan would encourage investment and enhance real estate values — without tax increases.

Tax increases would undermine the emerging recovery and act as a barrier to long-term growth. I call on the Congress to pass the seven commonsense measures that I asked for by this date, without tax increases, and to join me in pursuing a long-term agenda for growth.

I am disappointed that after 52 days the Congress has produced partisan, flawed legislation. Rather than work in a constructive manner to strengthen the economy and to create jobs, congressional leaders chose the path of partisanship. HR 4210 would jeopardize the recovery. It would not create jobs. It would not create incentives for long-term growth, it does not contain a tax credit for first-time homebuyers, and it contains wholly inappropriate special interest provisions.

HR 4210 would increase taxes by more than $100 billion. More than two-thirds of all taxpayers facing tax increases as a result of this bill would be owners of small businesses and entrepreneurs. Small businesses are the primary source of new job creation.

HR 4210 would raise income tax rates substantially for some individuals, in some cases increasing marginal rates by more than 30 percent. This is the wrong time to raise taxes, to increase the deficit, or to send a message of fiscal irresponsibility to financial markets.

I am therefore returning HR 4210, and I ask the Congress again to pass my economic growth program, without raising taxes.

planes, furs and jewelry, and indexed for inflation the $30,000 threshold above which automobiles were subject to the tax.

● **Alternative minimum tax.** Lowered the business portion of the alternative minimum tax.

● **EITC.** Repealed the portion of the earned income tax credit available for children under age 1, and used the revenue to expand the benefits available to working families with children.

### Veto Override Fails

When the House voted on Bush's veto March 25, the Democrats' bill failed even to draw a majority — much less the two-thirds support needed to override. The vote was 211-215. *(Vote 55, 14-H)*

This outcome was never in doubt.

Indeed, Democratic leaders did not even lobby party members to support the override, which may have explained some of the defections; 52 Democrats opposed the bill on the override vote. Republicans demanded the vote to expose how fragile Democratic support was for the controversial measure. ∎

# Bush Vetoes Year's Second Tax Bill

The second major tax bill of 1992 started as a response to riots that tore apart sections of Los Angeles in late April and early May. But what began as a bipartisan effort by the White House and the Democratic-controlled Congress to provide federal tax benefits to help revitalize inner cities ended without result when President Bush vetoed the $27 billion measure Nov. 4, the day after his re-election defeat.

Sponsors had won broad support for the bill in Congress by including many popular tax breaks unrelated to urban aid. However, they did not foresee how opposed Bush would become in the midst of an increasingly tough campaign to virtually anything resembling a tax increase.

The House passed a $17 billion tax bill in July, which included a version of a White House proposal to create urban enterprise zones eligible for special tax benefits and other federal assistance aimed at spurring investment and employment. Enterprise zones were the centerpiece of the administration's response to the Los Angeles riots.

The bill ballooned to a $37 billion measure in the Senate, where lawmakers attached numerous expensive provisions, including a restored middle-class tax break for contributions to individual retirement accounts (IRAs), that had to be offset with new revenue.

The final bill — the product of negotiations primarily between House Ways and Means Committee Chairman Dan Rostenkowski, D-Ill., and Senate Finance Committee Chairman Lloyd Bentsen, D-Texas — was a $27 billion compromise that would have created 50 enterprise zones at a cost of $2.6 billion over five years, restored and expanded IRA deductions for middle-class taxpayers, and extended a handful of expiring tax breaks.

In addition, the bill would have repealed luxury taxes on yachts, furs, jewelry and airplanes; partially restored the passive-loss write-off for losses on rental property; provided for a 14-year writeoff period for most intangible assets, including good will; allowed penalty-free IRA withdrawals for certain uses; authorized pension plans to invest in real estate; and provided tax relief for companies that paid the alternative minimum tax.

To offset the lost revenue, which was required under existing budget rules, the bill included $27 billion in revenue raisers. Most had been either proposed or supported by administration officials during the year. Two revenue raisers that had rankled the White House — making permanent the limit on itemized deductions and the phaseout of the personal exemption for upper-income taxpayers — were removed in conference.

---

## BOXSCORE

➡ **Urban Aid Tax bill (HR 11).** The $27 billion bill would have created 50 enterprise zones at a cost of $2.6 billion over five years, restored and expanded IRA deductions for middle-class taxpayers, extended a handful of expiring tax breaks, repealed luxury taxes on yachts, furs, jewelry and airplanes, partially restored the passive-loss writeoff for losses on rental property and provided for a 14-year writeoff period for most intangible assets, including good will.

**Reports:** H Rept 102-1034; H Rept 102-631.

### KEY ACTION

July 2 — The **House** passed HR 11, 356-55.

Sept. 29 — The **Senate** passed the bill, 70-29.

Oct. 5 — **House-Senate** conference completed.

Oct. 6 — The **House** adopted the conference report, 208-202.

Oct. 8 — The **Senate** cleared the measure, 67-22.

Nov. 4 — President Bush vetoed HR 11.

---

But the Bush campaign repeatedly had attacked the Democratic nominee for president, Gov. Bill Clinton, for signing what it said were 128 tax increases in Arkansas, and Bush could not afford to do the equivalent right before the election.

## BACKGROUND

The tax bill was the second that Bush had vetoed in 1992. The first (HR 4210) was a much more partisan measure that Democratic leaders had assembled as an election-year rallying cry against Bush. It had centered on middle-class tax breaks paid for by higher taxes on the wealthy, a formula they knew that Bush was sure to veto. But they saw it as a chance to demonstrate that the president was more interested in protecting the well-to-do than he was in helping the middle class. *(First tax bill, p. 133)*

That strategy fizzled, however. The bill passed by slim margins in both chambers, and Bush took little public heat when he rejected it on March 20.

The Democratic leadership found that there had been scant advantage to be gained by moving a politically inspired tax bill in the middle of an economic downturn.

"People condemn us both," said Rep. Robert T. Matsui, D-Calif. "But I think it was more harmful to the Congress in the end. The president got no heat when he vetoed that bill."

Majority Leader Richard A. Gephardt, D-Mo., had said work on a second tax bill, presumably one that Bush would sign, would begin "as soon as possible" after the veto. But weeks went by with no work at all; distracted by the House bank scandal, Democratic leaders indicated that they no longer planned a second tax bill.

Still, beyond the controversial core elements, the first bill had contained a number of provisions that had wide support in Congress and the White House.

On June 16, the Senate Finance Committee gave voice vote approval to a bill (HR 3040) that contained several of these items, including an 18-month extension for the expiring tax provisions, repeal of the luxury taxes and a writeoff for the cost of acquiring certain intangible assets.

By then, tax-cut fever was again beginning to spread on Capitol Hill. The impetus was the devastating riots that exploded in Los Angeles in late April, focusing national attention on the plight of the inner cities and giving rise to calls for a variety of tax breaks to assist blighted urban areas. *(Urban crisis, p. 339)*

The new tax legislation became a vehicle for enterprise zones, an urban renewal strategy to offer tax incentives to get businesses to locate in blighted sections. One longtime

backer in the House was Charles B. Rangel, a Democrat from Harlem. Another proponent, Housing and Urban Development Secretary Jack F. Kemp, wanted to create 300 zones. But in general, there was considerable disagreement between Congress and the White House over how many to create and whether they would work.

## HOUSE COMMITTEE ACTION

The House Ways and Means Committee on June 25 approved a $14 billion tax bill aimed at aiding blighted urban neighborhoods, but committee Democrats rejected a White House proposal to include a waiver on capital gains taxes for investors who put money into enterprise zones.

The legislation, approved by voice vote, provided for the creation of 50 zones in economically distressed communities. To attract businesses and revitalize the areas, it would have provided tax breaks and other federal aid, costing $2.5 billion over five years. It included a credit for hiring zone employees; a first-year deduction, up to $20,000, for equipment newly purchased by a zone business; an annual deduction of up to $25,000 for purchasing stock in a zone business; and liberalized rules governing issues of bonds to finance redevelopment in enterprise zones.

In addition, the committee approved a collection of revenue-losers, including a permanent extension of the low-income housing tax credit, restoration of a deduction for losses on rental properties and a writeoff for intangible assets, such as customer lists and franchise rights.

Despite agreement on the basic approach, however, the bill reopened a split between Democrats and the White House over cutting the tax rate on capital gains — the profits from the sale of stocks, real estate and other assets.

The measure included a limited proposal, which would have allowed investors in a zone to defer taxes on capital gains only as long as the profits were reinvested in the zone. Otherwise, the profits would have been subject to the full capital gains tax.

The key vote during the two days of markup came on a substitute offered by Bill Archer of Texas, the committee's top Republican. His amendment, which was supported by the Bush administration, would have eliminated capital gains taxes for investors who sold businesses or other assets in an enterprise zone — whether or not they were reinvested there. "If we're going to use the private sector capitalist incentives, you've got to convince an investor it's worth the risk," Archer said. "And if you tell him you can never remove your money, you are going to undermine" the attraction of enterprise zones.

Democrats unanimously rejected Archer's amendment on a 23-13 party-line vote.

Rostenkowski had included enterprise zones in the bill chiefly at the behest of Rangel, a senior member of the committee. Rostenkowski also wanted to go along with the administration, which had put the zones at the top of its urban agenda.

Few other Democrats liked the idea, however, and even among House Republicans, support for enterprise zones was concentrated among a handful of members. Not only did Rostenkowsi believe that simply forgiving capital gains taxes was a bad idea, but it also might have lost him the support of committee Democrats, whose votes were crucial to getting the tax package out of committee, an aide said.

To win backing from members from rural districts, Rostenkowski also agreed that only half of the 50 enter-

prise zones would be in cities. The rest would be in distressed rural communities of not more than 10,000 square miles and with populations of at least 1,000 people.

That compromise angered urban members, who pointed out that it was the unrest in the cities that provided the impetus for the tax incentives in the first place.

### Intangible Assets

Another controversial component of the bill was a 14-year write-off period during which businesses could deduct the cost of most intangible assets from their taxable income. The IRS had challenged many deductions for intangibles, which included such things as state-of-the-art software, unique recipes and even good will (the value to a company of loyal customers, skilled workers or a well-known brand name).

Rostenkowski's bill was an attempt to settle the controversy by establishing a uniform writeoff period and defining what kinds of intangible assets could be written off and for how long.

The committee adopted an amendment by Byron L. Dorgan, D-N.D., eliminating language that would have allowed companies to deduct intangible assets acquired before the bill was enacted. The 22-11 vote for Dorgan's amendment reflected concern by many members about giving a retroactive tax break to companies that acquired valuable intangible assets during the takeover spree in the 1980s.

### Other Key Provisions

Other provisions of the bill would have:

● **Passive losses.** Allowed real estate professionals, including agents, to deduct losses on rental property (so-called passive losses) against other income from real estate investments, a tax benefit that was eliminated in 1986.

An amendment offered by Michael A. Andrews, D-Texas, and agreed to by voice vote, specified that individuals qualified if more than half of their "personal services" during a year were performed in the real estate business and if they had at least a 5 percent interest as owner-employees in a real estate concern.

● **Low-income housing credit.** Extended permanently the low-income housing tax credit, which gave a 10-year tax break to investors in rental property for the poor, at a cost of $2.4 billion over six years.

● **Targeted jobs credit.** Extended permanently the targeted-jobs tax credit, which benefited businesses that hired certain disadvantaged workers; 24-year-olds would have qualified, raising the threshold by two years. The provision would have cost $2 billion over six years.

● **Mortgage revenue bonds.** Extended permanently the mortgage revenue bond and mortgage credit certificate programs, which allowed state and local governments to use tax-exempt financing for low-income housing, at a cost of $1 billion over six years.

● **Other extenders.** Extended for 18 months several expiring tax breaks, including the research and development tax credit, employer-provided educational assistance, a tax exception for gifts of appreciated property and employer-provided legal services.

The 25 percent deduction for health insurance costs of the self-employed would have been extended for six months.

Together these provisions would have cost $2.7 billion over six years.

● **Luxury taxes.** Repealed the luxury tax for furs,

yachts, personal airplanes and jewelry, while indexing for inflation the $30,000 threshold above which the tax applied to automobiles. The excise taxes were enacted as part of the 1990 budget agreement (PL 101-508), but lawmakers complained that they had devastated the affected industries.

● **AMT.** Lowered the alternative minimum tax for corporations, at a cost of $1.4 billion over six years. The alternative minimum tax ensured that businesses paid at least some tax.

● **Tax credit on tips.** Gave a tax credit to employers equal to the payroll tax paid on employees' tip income. The $1.5 billion cost was offset by denying the deductibility of club dues.

● **Moving expenses.** Raised revenues by imposing a $5,000 cap on the existing deduction for moving expenses ($3.5 billion); delaying until 1997 a scheduled decline in the top estate tax rates on the wealthiest estates ($1.4 billion); raising taxes on securities firm inventories ($2.7 billion); and denying tax benefits to purchasers of failed thrifts ($421 million).

## HOUSE FLOOR ACTION

House leaders and the White House wrapped up two months of negotiations on the bill July 2, compromising on a plan to provide a deep capital gains tax cut and other federal aid to businesses that located in inner-city enterprise zones.

The $17 billion bill passed the House by a vote of 356-55 — a surprisingly comfortable margin for a measure that had seemed in danger of falling apart just the day before. Even though many rank-and-file lawmakers considered the final aid package inadequate, they voted for it in droves after the leadership argued passionately that the bill was the best it could do and that the credibility of the Congress was riding on the vote. *(Vote 268, p. 66-H)*

"This country has been torn apart in its urban areas because people do not have work and people do not have hope," Gephardt said. Conceding that the bill did not meet all the needs of the cities, he closed the hourlong debate on the bill, saying, "It's only a first step, but we've got to take that first step."

It was the first time since 1990 that the White House and Democratic leaders had collaborated in getting a tax bill written. Both Bush and House leaders were desperate for a legislative triumph before the July Fourth holiday so they could take to the campaign trail with ammunition to rebut criticism that Washington was paralyzed and riven by partisanship.

To prevent amendments, the House leadership brought the bill to the floor under special procedures that required a two-thirds majority to pass. On the final tally, there were 81 votes to spare.

As passed by the House, the bill would have created 50 enterprise zones at a cost of $2.5 billion, plus $2.5 billion in additional federal aid to attract businesses and revitalize the areas.

The measure also contained $12 billion in unrelated tax breaks, including the permanent extension of the low-income housing tax credit, restoration of the deduction for losses on rental property and the writeoff for intangible assets.

There was little floor debate on these provisions, and critics suggested that a minuscule amount of urban aid was being used as cover to push through a much larger package of tax breaks, mostly benefiting businesses and investors.

### Capital Gains Compromise

Enterprise zones survived because of some late-night deal-cutting by administration officials and Gephardt, who forged the capital gains compromise that was the key to attracting Republican votes for the bill.

Led by Housing Secretary Kemp and House Minority Whip Newt Gingrich, R-Ga., a handful of House Republicans insisted that capital gains taxes be waived when a business or investment in an enterprise zone was sold. They also wanted assets in the area at the time the zone was created to be eligible for the capital gains cut. "Why should we discriminate against the Korean grocer who has been fighting the war and creating jobs" in ghettos before the enterprise zone was even created, said Gingrich.

But Rostenkowski balked, aruging that forgiving capital gains taxes would encourage investors to use the enterprise zone as a tax shelter and then abandon the inner city after making a quick profit. In addition, he insisted that any tax benefits apply only to future investments because, he said, the purpose was to attract new investment, not to reward existing businesses by waiving the tax.

"I just felt it was unfair," he said. "What about the community next door that's not in the enterprise zone? They don't get a tax break, either."

Late in the evening of July 1, Gephardt worked out a compromise with Gingrich and the administration: Profits made in an enterprise zone would be taxed at a maximum rate of 14 percent (half the existing top rate of 28 percent). To qualify, an investor would have to maintain his investment in the zone for a minimum of five years. In addition, zone investors would be exempt from the alternative minimum tax.

Republicans eventually backed down on their demand that existing assets qualify for the lower rate. Kemp issued a statement after the House action saying he hoped the Senate version of the bill would lift capital gains taxes completely for people who invested in an enterprise zone.

During the negotiations, Democrats secured White House approval for $2.5 billion in additional spending through fiscal year 1997 to pay for expanded job training, education, health, housing and law enforcement programs.

### Selling the Deal

With the terms of the deal agreed upon, the White House and House leaders turned their attention to rounding up the votes. Bush put in a pitch for enterprise zones in a Capitol Hill meeting with Republicans. In a floor speech urging support for the bill, Gingrich praised Gephardt and hailed the inclusion of the capital gains provisions.

Democratic leaders had to deal with a mini-revolt among lawmakers who tried to bring up an unrelated benefits grievance by "notch baby" Social Security recipients. To head off the amendment, which would have increased benefit levels for 12 million retirees born between 1917 and 1926, House leaders opted to bring the urban aid bill to the floor under a suspension of the rules, a procedure usually reserved for non-controversial legislation that barred any amendments.

Meanwhile, organized labor groups were upset about a provision permitting non-unionized airlines to offer their pilots more generous benefit packages than were available to other employees. Existing law allowed only unionized airlines to discriminate in favor of pilots, and unions wanted to preserve that. Union officials said the main

beneficiary of the provision would be Federal Express Corp., a Memphis-based, non-unionized, airline courier company. Labor lobbyists wanted an amendment offered on the floor to remove the exemption, but that became impossible after the leadership brought the bill up under suspension of the rules.

## SENATE COMMITTEE ACTION

The Senate Finance Committee on July 29 approved a $31 billion tax bill. Although the size of the measure had grown, it still offered just $2.5 billion in aid to rehabilitate inner-city slums. The bill was approved by voice vote.

The measure contained a wealth of tax breaks for investors, middle-class families and businesses, but it did not include the tax break Bush wanted most — the cut in the capital gains tax rate.

The White House, faced with a faltering economic recovery and a difficult re-election campaign, had signaled that it would drop its demand for the tax cut if congressional Democrats would deliver a bill that provided other generous tax incentives intended to stimulate the economy.

Finance Committee Chairman Bentsen did just that. To gain White House support for the bill, he included variations of the six other tax incentives that Bush had proposed in January to give the economy a quick jolt — among them the $2,500 tax credit for first-time home buyers and generous additional writeoffs for businesses that bought equipment in the coming months.

Like Bush, the Democrats decided to drop a longstanding priority — in their case, a tax cut for the middle class — to break the yearlong stalemate on tax legislation.

### Bentsen-Roth IRA Plan

One of the most expensive parts of the bill was a provision to restore and expand the tax deduction for IRA contributions. Under a 1986 law, only workers without pensions or those with incomes of up to $25,000 for an individual or $40,000 for a couple could make fully deductible IRA contributions.

The provisions, authored by Bentsen and William V. Roth Jr., R-Del., gave IRA holders the option of not claiming an immediate tax deduction for deposits in return for getting tax-free withdrawals after keeping their money in the account for five years.

In an effort to reduce the cost, Bentsen delayed until 1994 the date the expanded IRA would take effect. Still, the provision would have lost $5.8 billion from 1994 to 1997. The bill would have allowed penalty-free withdrawals from IRA accounts beginning immediately for first home purchases, education costs, medical bills and unemployment, which was one of Bush's tax proposals.

### Enterprise Zones

Bentsen's bill provided for 25 enterprise zones, 15 of them in urban areas, eight in rural areas and two on Indian reservations. Bentsen insisted that the number be kept small, and he balked at waiving capital gains taxes for zone investors. "Let's not create tax shelters for arm's-length capitalists. Let's reward shirt-sleeve entrepreneurs," he said during the committee drafting session.

The bill provided a tax credit for employers hiring zone residents and made them automatically eligible for the targeted jobs tax credit, which provided incentives for employers to hire disadvantaged workers. Other tax benefits for zone businesses included an increase from $10,000 to $75,000 in the first-year tax writeoff available when a business bought certain equipment and property used in the zone, including real estate. Businesses in enterprise zones could depreciate equipment costs over fewer years than other businesses. And individuals were allowed an annual 50 percent deduction, up to $25,000, for the amount paid in cash for stock in an enterprise zone business.

States could issue tax-exempt bonds to finance land, factory and equipment purchases within a zone, and only 50 percent of the bond volume would count against the cap for the state's private-activity bonds.

The capital gains issue was all but ignored in the bipartisan rush to get a bill to the Senate floor. Committee Republicans made no effort to get the administration's proposal into the bill, although Housing Secretary Kemp held a news conference the day before the Finance Committee met to make a pitch for a zero capital gains tax rate.

Later, Kemp broke with the administration and urged Bush to veto the Senate Finance Committee bill if it reached his desk in that form. Minority Leader Bob Dole, R-Kan., characterized the bill's enterprise zone provisions as "very anemic" and promised that Republicans would offer a floor amendment substituting the administration's proposal.

### Winning Support

Bentsen won support for the measure by including numerous tax incentives that committee members had long sought. The bill would have expanded the tax break for donations of artwork to universities and other charitable organizations to include all gifts of appreciated property, including stocks, bonds and real estate. David L. Boren, D-Okla., Daniel Patrick Moynihan, D-N.Y., and John C. Danforth, R-Mo., had long worked for the changes, which cost $700 million over five years.

Like the House bill, Bensten's measure sought to repeal luxury taxes on personal airplanes, jewelry, furs and yachts and tie the excise tax on expensive cars to inflation.

While administration officials said they were happy with most of the Senate bill, they were opposed to sections aimed at overhauling federal programs to care for abused and neglected children, including foster care and adoption. The key provision sought to create an entitlement program — vehemently opposed by the Bush administration — to help states pay for services designed to keep troubled families together. *(Child welfare, p. 462)*

The Finance Committee bill contained provisions making some modest changes to Social Security and welfare programs, including proposals to make it easier for financially strapped states to claim federal funds for Job Opportunities and Basic Skills Training Programs (JOBS), the welfare-to-work program. Like the House bill, the Finance measure sought to increase the federal matching rate for JOBS funds, which varied by state. Unlike the House bill, it also would have increased by $100 million the total amounts available for JOBS for fiscal 1993 and 1994, to $1.1 billion and $1.2 billion, respectively.

In addition to the first-time home buyer credit, the bill included versions of the following Bush administration economic-growth proposals:

- A 15 percent expansion of the first-year depreciation allowance for certain equipment acquired by businesses in 1992.
- Elimination of the current earnings depreciation adjustment, which caused many businesses to pay more taxes than otherwise required under the alternative minimum tax.
- Permission for pension plans to invest in real estate.

# Highlights of the Tax Bill

*Though the $27 billion, five-year tax bill (HR 11 — H Rept 102-1034) initially was presented as a measure to help blighted inner cities in the wake of the Los Angeles riots, it evolved into much more during its progress through the House and Senate. Lawmakers attached dozens of unrelated provisions, many of which survived in conference.*

*Among the highlights, the bill cleared by Congress would have:*

### Revenue-Losing Provisions

● **Enterprise zones.** Created 50 enterprise zones, 25 in urban areas and 25 in rural areas, that qualified for special tax incentives and other federal assistance to attract businesses and help revitalize the areas. Following the House language, lawmakers agreed to offer zone businesses a 15 percent credit on the first $20,000 in wages paid to employees, a deduction of up to $25,000 for purchases of stock in zone businesses, more rapid writeoffs for property and a 50 percent cut in the capital gains tax on zone investments that had been held for at least five years.

Altogether, the tax benefits provided for enterprise zones would have been worth $2.6 billion over five years. The bill also would have authorized new direct federal spending targeted to the enterprise zones.

Conferees also adopted a Senate provision that would have made Indian reservations eligible for an array of special tax breaks to stimulate economic development.

● **IRAs.** Restored to middle-income taxpayers the tax deduction for contributions of up to $2,000 to individual retirement accounts (IRAs) beginning in 1995. Individual taxpayers making up to $75,000 and married taxpayers earning up to $100,000 would have qualified. Beginning in 1994, the bill would have created a new type of IRA; the holder would not have received an upfront deduction but could have made tax-free withdrawals after five years.

Taxpayers who already held IRAs could have converted to the new IRA beginning in 1993 without paying a 10 percent withdrawal penalty. Military personnel who left the service would have been permitted to make tax-free contributions of up to $25,000 in severance pay into an IRA. The bill included penalty-free IRA withdrawals for first-time home purchases, education and medical expenses and income for unemployed workers. People whose houses had been destroyed during recent natural disasters, such as Hurricane Andrew, would have qualified for penalty-free IRA withdrawals.

The IRA provisions would have cost $2.6 billion.

● **Passive losses.** Permitted people in the real estate industry to deduct against ordinary income losses on rental property (the so-called passive loss deduction). Conferees rejected a narrower Senate provision allowing the deduction to be taken only against income from real estate. The provision was estimated to cost $2.1 billion over five years.

● **Other real estate benefits.** Given passive loss relief to owners of small timber lots, given tax relief to real estate investors who were deeply in debt and allowed homeowners who sold their houses at a loss to roll that loss over until they were able to deduct it against ordinary income.

● **Extenders.** Extended permanently several popular tax breaks that expired in June, including the low-income housing tax credit to encourage the building of rental housing for the poor, the targeted jobs tax credit for businesses that hired disadvantaged workers, and the tax exemption for mortgage revenue bonds and mortgage revenue certificates, which financed subsidized mortgages to encourage home ownership.

These provisions would have cost $5.4 billion over five years.

Lawmakers agreed to extend for 12 months several other expired tax breaks, including those for employer-provided educational assistance, research and development, and orphan drugs (developed to treat rare diseases). Conferees dropped a Senate provision to allow small businesses to deduct the cost of health insurance for their employees, substituting the existing 25 percent deduction and extending it for 12 months.

● **Excise tax repeal.** Repealed excise taxes enacted in 1990 on yachts, personal airplanes, jewelry and furs. The $30,000 threshold above which the tax applied to automobiles was to be increased based on inflation. These provisions would have cost $5.4 billion over five years. The bill also would have repealed an excise tax of up to $100 on recreational boats, losing $394 million over five years.

● **Charitable contributions.** Exempted from the alternative minimum tax all gifts of appreciated property, including artwork and real estate. The alternative minimum tax was a section of the tax code aimed at ensuring that taxpayers who claimed many deductions paid at least some income tax. The provision, which would have been permanent, would have lost $319 million in revenue over five years.

● **Payroll tax credit.** Given employers a tax credit equal to the amount of payroll tax they paid on employees' tip income, at a cost of $1.3 billion over five years.

● Restoration of the deduction for losses on rental property (so-called passive losses) for people who were active in the real estate industry.

In addition, the bill included an 18-month extension of several expiring tax breaks. The Finance Committee had approved these provisions separately (HR 3040) by voice vote on June 16. The extensions were for: the research and development tax credit; the low-income housing credit; the group legal services exclusion; the partial deduction for health insurance costs of the self-employed; the exclusion for employer-provided education benefits; the targeted jobs tax credit; exemptions for mortgage revenue and qualified small-issue bonds; and the orphan drug tax credit.

### Revenue Raisers

The $31 billion cost of the bill was offset by provisions raising roughly the same amount over five years. Offsetting any tax increase was a requirement of the pay-as-you go

## Revenue Raisers

● **Securities tax.** Taxed securities dealers on the full value of their inventories, raising $3.7 billion. The accounting change was to be phased in over four years.

● **Real estate depreciation.** Lengthened the period over which owners could write off the cost of commercial real estate from 31.5 years to 40 years. By decreasing the yearly tax break, the provision would have raised $3 billion over five years.

● **Moving expenses.** Capped the existing deduction for moving expenses at $10,000, barred writing off closing costs and other moving expenses, and increased to 60 miles the distance someone had to move to qualify for the deduction. That would have raised $3.2 billion.

● **Estate tax.** Extended through 1997 the 53 percent and 55 percent tax rates on taxable estates of $2.5 million and larger. The tax rates, which were applied at the time the estate owner died, were scheduled to fall after 1993. Extending them would have raised $1.4 billion over five years.

● **Quarterly estimated payments.** Raised nearly $10 billion by increasing the amount that individual and corporate taxpayers who made estimated tax payments had to pay in order to avoid a penalty for underpayment. Individuals would have had two options — pay 90 percent of what they were estimated to owe in the current year or 120 percent of what they owed the previous year. Corporations would have had to pay the same amount they owed the previous year.

● **Thrift purchasers.** Barred investors who purchased failed thrifts from the government, principally in 1988, from receiving double tax benefits after March 4, 1991. Under the 1988 thrift deals, some investors were promised tax-free payments for undervalued assets owned by the thrift as well as a tax deduction on losses by those assets. In outlawing such double-dipping, the bill would have raised $421 million over five years.

● **Miscellaneous revenue raisers.** Barred companies from claiming a deduction for club dues ($1.4 billion), denied taxpayers interest on refunds as long as the Treasury sent the refund within 45 days ($195 million), barred business travelers from deducting the cost of bringing their spouses ($120 million) and increased the withholding rate on bonuses to 28 percent ($155 million).

● **Intangibles.** Required most intangible assets — such as a company's work force, subscription lists or good will — acquired after enactment to be written off over a 14-year period. That would have shortened the writeoff period for some intangibles and lengthened it for others, raising $425 million over five years. The bill would have denied the writeoff for costs associated with mergers and acquisitions. It would have allowed shorter writeoff periods for software, movie rights and several other types of intangible assets. Conferees dropped a section of the Senate bill allowing companies to claim retroactive writeoffs for intangibles they already owned.

## Miscellaneous Provisions

● **Pilot pension plans.** Allowed non-unionized airlines to offer their pilots more generous pension plans than those given to other employees.

Under existing federal pension law, only unionized airlines were permitted to discriminate in favor of their pilots. The provision was controversial because it was sought by Federal Express, the Memphis-based courier company, which was trying to fend off attempts to organize its employees.

● **Footwear imports.** Reimposed duties on imports of footwear made entirely with U.S. materials from countries that were part of the Caribbean Basin Initiative (CBI). But the bill would have granted exceptions for footwear manufacturers who located in Caribbean countries because of the duty-free treatment such footwear had enjoyed under the CBI. Those manufacturers could have continued to export their existing volume of footwear or the output of any factories under construction to the United States duty-free.

● **Child welfare.** Included major portions of the Family Preservation Act (S 4, HR 3603), which was aimed at keeping dysfunctional families together, thus lessening the need for expensive foster care. It also would have increased funding for JOBS, the work-training-education programs created in the 1988 welfare overhaul, and established demonstrations of a new workfare program. Together, the child welfare provisions would have cost an estimated $2.8 billion over five years. *(Child welfare, p. 462)*

● **Medicare.** Included a series of mostly minor changes to coverage and reimbursement policies for Medicare, the federal health program for the elderly and disabled. Among them were provisions to cut down on fraud and reduce payment for "durable medical equipment," such as wheelchairs, and to restore separate payments for doctors who interpreted EKGs. The separate EKG payments were eliminated in 1990.

The provisions would have extended Medicare coverage of drugs to prevent rejection in organ transplant patients. Dropped was a small-group health insurance reform proposal included in the Senate bill, as well as all provisions regarding Medicaid, the joint federal-state health program for the poor.

● **Customs Service.** Included the text of HR 5643, which would have modernized U.S. customs operations and permitted companies to file electronically much of the information necessary to clear goods through ports of entry.

---

rules that resulted from the 1990 budget summit. The Senate bill contained no income tax increases of the sort that had caused Bush to veto the massive tax bill (HR 4210) sent to him earlier in the year. Administration officials said that as long as that remained the case, Bush was likely to accept whatever tax bill he received.

Yet the White House was unhappy with several provisions aimed at raising income taxes for wealthy taxpayers. The bill would have made permanent a limitation on itemized deductions among high-income taxpayers, raising $6.5 billion. It also would have extended a higher rate on estate taxes through 1997 and maintained a limitation on the personal exemption for high-income taxpayers, for a total of $2.6 billion.

It would have modified the deduction for moving expenses to exclude certain deductible costs associated with breaking a lease or buying a house, bringing in $1.9 billion. Increasing the withholding rate on gambling earnings to

28 percent would have raised $107 million.

## SENATE FLOOR ACTION

The Senate got to work on the tax bill Aug. 11-12, but the list of potential amendments was too long to allow senators to finish before Congress broke Aug. 12 for the Republican National Convention. Before the recess, Bentsen appeared confident that he had beaten back the chief floor challenges. But by the time the Senate resumed action on the bill in late September, the dynamic had changed considerably, with growing signs of opposition from the White House. Bush had apologized in his Houston acceptance speech for having agreed to raise taxes as part of the 1990 budget deal, and on the campaign trail he promised he would never do it again, "ever." The Senate finally voted to pass the tax bill Sept. 29 by a vote of 70-29. *(Vote 249, p. 33-S)*

### Pre-Convention Decisions

Shrewd maneuvering by Bentsen and some bipartisan cooperation along the way seemed to clear the way in August for passage of the tax bill. Bentsen pre-empted critics of the enterpise zone and IRA provisions by modifying the committee-reported version of the bill.

Before the first amendment was offered on the floor, Bentsen altered the enterprise zone provisions to counter one of two principal objections — that the 25 zones in the committee bill were too few. Housing Secretary Kemp wanted 300; Sen. Bob Kasten, R-Wis., was proposing 150. But Bentsen argued that the $2.5 billion in spending permitted by the bill would be spread too thin among so many zones.

As a compromise, Bentsen upped the ante to $5.3 billion and permitted 125 zones — 75 in urban areas (40 of them in cities of under 500,000 people), 40 in rural areas and 10 on Indian reservations.

The expansion of the enterpise zone plan seemed to neutralize efforts to add a capital gains tax break for zone investors. Kasten, the principal sponsor of the capital gains amendment, opted not to offer it after Bentsen's maneuver pulled away the key support of Joseph I. Lieberman, D-Conn.

Bentsen also fought off a plan by Connie Mack, R-Fla., to grant wholesale capital gains relief to individuals and corporations, regardless of whether their investments were in enterprise zones. Mack fell 23 votes short of the 60-vote majority that he needed to get his capital gains amendment adopted. He was defeated, 37-57, on a procedural motion. The amendment was hardly debated; and seven Republicans voted no. *(Vote 188, p. 25-S)*

To pay for the enterprise zone changes, Bentsen first planned to drop two administration-backed initiatives — the $2,500 credit for first-time home buyers and the increase in first-year depreciation allowances for businesses that invested in new equipment.

John R. Chafee, R-R.I., tried instead to strike Bentsen's IRA provisions. Chafee argued that giving millionaires and other wealthy taxpayers the same benefit as the middle class was unfair — and unnecessarily expensive — and that there was inconclusive evidence that IRAs had boosted the nation's savings rate when they were universally available prior to 1986.

With more than three-fourths of the Senate signed on as cosponsors to bills restoring tax-excluded IRAs for everyone, Bentsen had no trouble killing Chafee's amendment on a tabling motion, 72-25. *(Vote 187, p. 25-S)*

After further manuevering, Bentsen agreed to cap IRA eligibility at $80,000 for individuals and $120,000 for joint filers. The $1.5 billion savings was enough to pay for the home buyer credit, and the two amendments were adopted by voice vote.

The only other vote on the bill came on an amendment by Bill Bradley, D-N.J., and Paul Wellstone, D-Minn., that would have curtailed so-called passive loss deductions for real estate developers and dropped two other corporate tax breaks.

In return, they would have added $2.8 billion in aid for disadvantaged youths through the existing Job Corps program and created grants to pay for neighborhood police forces, training for workers in small business and repairs to neighborhood infrastructure. The amendment, which would have waived existing caps on domestic discretionary spending, needed a 60-vote majority for adoption. It failed on a 14-80 vote. *(Vote 189, p. 25-S)*

Bentsen was all smiles as work on the measure ended for the time being, and he made the rounds of the Senate chamber shaking hands with Democratic and Republican staff members — a clear sign that he believed he had the situation under control.

The only item that appeared to stand in the way of administration support for the bill was the permanent extension of the tax increases on wealthy persons. One phased out the personal exemption; the other limited itemized deductions. Enacted in 1990, they were due to expire in 1995 and 1996, respectively. The White House wanted the tax extensions dropped, and Minority Leader Dole promised to offer an amendment in September to change that section of the bill.

### Campaign Mire

With the presidential campaign in high gear, the Senate resumed debate on the tax bill Sept. 23-25. By then, Democrats were waging a cold war with the Bush administration over whether a measure jam-packed with popular tax breaks — and a few tax increases — had any future in the midst of a fractious election year.

In a 34-59 vote that jeopardized the bill's prospects, the Senate overwhelmingly rejected Dole's amendment to remove the revenue-raising provisions that the White House opposed as backdoor tax increases. "The president of the United States is not going to sign a tax increase 30 days before the election," Dole said. *(Vote 240, p. 31-S)*

Dole's big problem was finding a way to offset the $7.7 billion that would have been lost in 1996 and 1997 by eliminating the provisions. Dole would have scaled back the assistance in the bill for inner cities, removed provisions to restore tax breaks for IRAs, and shortened to 12 months the extension given to a dozen expiring tax breaks.

Dole hoped the amendment would attract Democrats worried about appearing to support a tax increase just weeks before the election. But Bentsen defended the revenue raisers as necessary to balance revenue-losers in the bill. "We're not talking about raising taxes. We're talking about continuing taxes that are already there," he said.

During the debate, the Senate adopted a few significant amendments, including some modest health-care reforms, but progress was slow, and many lawmakers remained skeptical.

"It has a life expectancy right now of a moth, but it still has a chance," said Hank Brown, R-Colo.

The Senate rejected an amendment incorporating a proposal Bush had made at the GOP convention to allow taxpayers to apply up to 10 percent of their income taxes

toward reducing the federal deficit. Under the amendment, Congress would have had to reduce federal spending by a corresponding amount or trigger automatic spending cuts. The amendment, offered by Robert C. Smith, R-N.H., was killed on a largely party-line vote of 36-58. Bush had barely mentioned the idea since his speech, and the administration made little apparent effort to persuade Democrats to vote for the amendment. Democrats denounced the automatic spending cuts in apocalyptic terms, saying they would gut the federal budget. *(Vote 238, p. 31-S)*

The lack of White House attention to the bill in general exasperated some GOP senators, who said they had received no clear signal about how Bush would pay for the tax breaks he supported. "I have talked to the White House on numerous occasions . . . and I said, 'Can you give me a rough idea of what the president might accept?' " said Bob Packwood, Ore., the ranking Republican on the Finance Committee.

Yet many Republicans supported the overall bill because of specific tax provisions. Dole himself favored provisions to strike excise taxes on personal aircraft — an important industry in his state — and other luxury items. The total cost would be $522 million over five years.

### Writing off Good Will

Indeed, senators showed little interest in scaling back the bill's generous tax benefits. Paul Simon, D-Ill., was defeated 75-19 on a proposal to eliminate the provision allowing companies to write off good will. *(Vote 237, p. 31-S)*

Simon argued that allowing companies to write off their purchases of good will and other types of intangible assets over 16 years would "foster a new round of merger mania" and cost the federal government billions of dollars in future lost revenue. Organized labor strongly backed Simon's amendment, arguing that a new wave of takeovers would cost jobs while lining the pockets of wealthy financiers.

But Bentsen argued that the provision would eliminate costly litigation, creating savings that would be passed on to consumers.

During the three-day debate, Bradley waged a one-man battle against the broad array of tax breaks and provisions for narrow interests. Citing help for ferry boat operators, gunsmiths and cotton warehouse owners, Bradley said, "The list of winners in this bill goes on and on, each group narrower than the last, each group reaping benefits" at other taxpayers' expense. He criticized bill sponsors for relying on accounting gimmicks, warning that the cost of IRAs and other tax breaks in the bill could "explode" after five years, adding greatly to the deficit.

Packwood failed to kill the provision to allow non-unionized airlines to offer more generous pension plans to pilots than to other employees. His amendment was defeated 41-56. *(Vote 231, p. 30-S)*

Also tacked onto the bill — but considered unlikely to survive in conference — was a health-care amendment by Bentsen and Dave Durenberger, R-Minn., that was a slightly rewritten version of a bill (S 1872) the two senators introduced in 1991.

The bipartisan-backed provisions, added by voice vote, would have overhauled the insurance market for small businesses, requiring insurers to make coverage more available and affordable by limiting rate variations and outlawing exclusions for certain "pre-existing conditions" that made many people uninsurable. Another popular feature would have allowed self-insured people to deduct from their taxable income 100 percent of the amount they paid for insurance. The existing limit was 25 percent.

### Other Amendments

The Senate also adopted amendments to:

● Bar companies from writing off lawyers' fees and other costs associated with business mergers and acquisitions, under provisions in the bill allowing amortization of intangible assets. The provision, sponsored by Mitch McConnell, R-Ky., only applied to future acquisitions and was accepted by voice vote.

● Allow military personnel who received a lump severance payment upon leaving the military to defer taxes on up to $25,000 if the payments were deposited in an IRA. The amendment, sponsored by Frank H. Murkowski, R-Alaska, passed by voice vote.

● Extend through Sept. 1, 1993, a tax credit to encourage production of natural gas from hard-to-drill wells, such as coal beds and tight sand formations. The credit, due to expire at the end of 1992, was created in 1980 to encourage production of natural gas. The amendment passed by voice vote after a motion to table it was defeated, 41-57. *(Vote 230, p. 30-S)*

The Senate rejected amendments that would have:

● Eliminated a provision requiring taxpayers who made more than $75,000 to pay 20 percent more in estimated quarterly taxes than they owed the previous year. The amendment would have created a $1.3 billion revenue hole and, under the budget rules, it would have required 60 votes to pass. It was defeated by a vote of 57-37. *(Vote 234, p. 31-S)*

● Given business a one-time tax credit for the cost of providing employee child-care facilities, up to a maximum of $150,000. The amendment, sponsored by Dennis DeConcini, D-Ariz., was tabled (killed) by a vote of 50-46. *(Vote 233, p. 31-S)*

● Reduced by 20 percent the deduction tobacco companies could claim for advertising expenses. Under existing law, cigarette manufacturers could write off the full cost of advertising in the year in which it occurred. The amendment was defeated on a tabling motion by a vote of 56-38. *(Vote 235, p. 31-S)*

● Required that an amendment to raise taxes receive 60 votes in the Senate in order to pass. The amendment, sponsored by John McCain, R-Ariz., was defeated on a tabling motion, 32-60. *(Vote 236, p. 31-S)*

### Last Round

Before giving final approval to the bill on Sept 29, the Senate considered a long list of amendments.

Late in the evening of Sept. 25, the Senate adopted by voice vote amendments to:

● Provide a capital gains tax cut for investors who purchased stock in small businesses with $5 million or less in paid-in capital if they held onto the stock for at least five years. Investors could have received a 50 percent tax cut on stock held five years and paid no taxes on stock held at least 10 years. The amendment, sponsored by Dale Bumpers, D-Ark., would have cost an estimated $340 million over five years, to be paid for by barring taxpayers from deducting more than $19,000 in moving expenses.

● Bar subsidiaries of U.S. companies from deducting expenses in connection with doing business in Cuba. The amendment was sponsored by Bob Graham, D-Fla.

● Authorize $500 million in fiscal 1993 federal assistance to be spent on enterprise zones created under the bill and

for aid to other urban areas. The amendment was sponsored by Donald W. Riegle Jr., D-Mich., and Edward M. Kennedy, D-Mass.

During debate on Sept. 26, the Senate adopted by voice vote amendments to:

● Allow penalty-free IRA withdrawals in 1992 and 1993 for the purchase of new automobiles made in the United States. The amendment was offered by Arlen Specter, R-Pa.

● Allow people whose homes were destroyed or substantially damaged by hurricanes Andrew or Iniki or Typhoon Omar to qualify for the first-time home buyer credit created under the bill. The amendment was offered by Florida's Mack.

● Require a thrift holding company to reimburse subsidiaries if the company filed a joint return and used tax benefits generated by the subsidiary to defray a portion of its overall taxes. The reimbursement would have been the amount the subsidiary thrift would have received had it filed a separate tax return. The amendment was offered by Howard M. Metzenbaum, D-Ohio.

● Toughen federal laws against armed auto theft in an effort to deter "carjacking." Armed carjackers would have been subject to prison terms of not more than 15 years, or in cases where serious injury occurred, of not more than 25 years. If a victim died, the carjacker could have received life in prison. The amendment was sponsored by Larry Pressler, R-S.D.

● Allow timber owners who worked less than 100 hours a year on managing their wood lots to qualify for passive loss write-offs on their investments. To qualify, a timber business would have to be closely held, meaning ownership was vested in no more than five people or one family. The amendment was sponsored by Packwood.

● Clarify that federal payments for foster-care assistance could not be counted as gross income and therefore could not be taxed. The amendment was offered by Carl Levin, D-Mich.

● Impose mandatory sanctions on imports of fish, fish products and sport fishing equipment from countries that did not stop drift net fishing by the end of the year. The amendment, sponsored by Packwood, also would have denied port privileges to vessels engaged in drift net fishing and restrict fishing in the central Bering Sea.

● Phase out a tax on recreational boats that was enacted as part of the 1990 budget agreement. To offset the lost revenue, the amendment, offered by John B. Breaux, D-La., would have established a fee for use of the Federal Maritime Commission's electronic tariff filing system.

● Make the countries that were previously part of the Soviet Union eligible for the Generalized System of Preferences (GSP), under which goods from developing countries entered the United States at special, low tariff rates. The amendment was offered by Bentsen. Actually granting GSP benefits to those countries would have required separate congressional action.

● Reimpose duties on imports of footwear from countries given special treatment under the Caribbean Basin Initiative (CBI). Under CBI, Caribbean countries could export duty-free to the United States footwear that was assembled from U.S. materials. The amendment was offered by Majority Leader George J. Mitchell, D-Maine.

● Toughen provisions of U.S. trade law designed to prevent foreign companies from evading so-called anti-dumping actions that imposed duties on foreign imports being sold at less than market value. The amendment, which applied only to typewriter imports, was designed to prevent foreign manufacturers from locating assembly plants in the United States to escape paying duties on dumped typewriters. It would have established authority to impose comparable duties on imported component parts.

The amendment was sought by Smith-Corona, a British-owned typewriter company based in New York, and opposed by its chief competitor, Brother Industries, a Japanese-owned company with a U.S. assembly plant. It was sponsored by Republican Alfonse M. D'Amato and Democrat Moynihan, both of New York.

● Replace a provision in the bill establishing 10 enterprise zones at American Indian reservations with other tax benefits available for all Indian tribes, including a 10 percent tax credit for businesses based on wages and health insurance costs paid to Indian employees. A 30 percent wage credit was to be available for reservation employers whose employees were at least 85 percent Indians. The amendment — sponsored by McCain and Daniel K. Inouye, D-Hawaii — also would have created a 15 percent tax credit for investing in construction projects and infrastructure on reservations where unemployment was at least 300 percent above the national average. A smaller credit was available on reservations where unemployment was between 150 percent and 300 percent above the national average.

## CONFERENCE ACTION

The House-Senate conference began on Oct. 1 with conciliatory words from Rostenkowski and Bentsen. Both said their goal was to send Bush a bill he would sign.

With the clock ticking toward final adjournment, the two top congressional tax-writers did most of the negotiating on the final bill, finishing their work the evening of Oct. 5. The $27 billion compromise would have created 50 enterprise zones at a cost of $2.6 billion over five years; special tax benefits included a 50 percent capital gains tax cut for investors who put their money into a zone for five years. The bill also included Bentsen's proposal to restore and expand tax breaks for contributions to IRAs, along with an extension of a handful of expiring tax breaks.

In an effort to make the measure acceptable to Bush, Bentsen and Rostenkowski dropped the two revenue provisions for upper-income taxpayers — the limit on itemized deductions and the phaseout of the personal exemption — that were in the Senate-passed bill and that White House officials repeatedly had said would have to be removed for Bush to sign the bill.

The measure contained four of seven proposals for stimulating the economy put forward by Bush in January, including the passive loss deduction for real estate, penalty-free IRA withdrawals for certain uses, authorization for pension plans to invest in real estate, and tax relief for companies that paid the alternative minimum tax.

Left out were White House proposals for a first-time home-buyer credit, a cut in the capital gains tax rate and an expanded depreciation allowance for businesses.

## FINAL ACTION

The House narrowly voted to approve the final bill 208-202 early in the morning of Oct. 6. Many House lawmakers who had supported the bill when it passed overwhelmingly in July opposed the final version, believing that a veto was certain. "The sense was that this was just a waste of time and a waste of effort," said Timothy J. Penny, D-Minn. *(Vote 482,*

# Citing 'Special Interest' Slant, Bush Vetoes Tax Bill

*Following is the text of President Bush's Nov. 4 veto of the tax bill:*

I am withholding my approval of HR 11, the "Revenue Act of 1992," because it includes numerous tax increases, violates fiscal discipline, and would destroy jobs and undermine small business. The urban aid provisions that were once the centerpiece of the bill have been submerged by billions of dollars in giveaways to special interests.

My administration's agenda for tax legislation has been clear from the outset: a focused measure to encourage economic growth, address the needs of economically deprived urban and rural areas, and make a limited number of significant and broadly supported changes in the tax law. While certain provisions in HR 11 meet these objectives, the bill as a whole does not. Its 647 pages contain more than 600 provisions, require more than 25 new studies or reports, set up 4 new commissions and advisory groups, and mandate numerous new demonstration and pilot projects. Most of these provisions are unrelated to the true needs of the economy and the American people.

The original focus of the bill — to help revitalize America's inner cities — has been lost in a blizzard of special interest pleadings. In fact, the enterprise zones provisions in HR 11 account for less than 10 percent of the revenue cost of the measure. While the enterprise zones provisions are a step in the right direction, more than 75 percent of all seriously distressed communities are left out in the cold. In addition, the capital incentives are far too limited. My proposal would grant eligibility to all areas that meet objective criteria. My proposal also would provide a complete exclusion from capital gains taxation for all investors in enterprise zone businesses, including gains from good will, the principal asset created by small business.

The bill's other major urban aid provision, which authorizes assistance to distressed communities, is also inadequate. My "Weed and Seed" proposal, currently being implemented on a pilot basis, coordinates federal assistance to drug- and crime-ridden neighborhoods and targets much of the assistance to enterprise zone communities. HR 11 falls short of my plan. The bill adopts a business-as-usual approach to dispensing federal assistance. It ignores the administration's bottom-up method of combining strong law enforcement with resources to assist residents and neighborhoods in attaining economic self-sufficiency. Finally, communities currently benefiting from the pilot program could be denied continued funding because they may not be located in enterprise zones. It is regrettable that the Congress has not included a "Weed and Seed" program in a bill that I can sign.

The revenue provisions of HR 11 include some of my proposals, but omit three major components of my economic growth agenda. These are my proposals to provide a credit for first-time home buyers, capital gains tax relief for start-up businesses and incentives for investment in capital equipment. On balance, the revenue provisions of HR 11 are unacceptable. They would:

● Raise $33 billion in new taxes over five years on a wide array of American families, workers and small businesses.

● Increase taxes on individuals, including middle-class taxpayers, in numerous ways. For example, the bill limits deductions for moving expenses and for losses resulting from theft, fires and natural disasters.

● Repeal the 100 percent estimated tax safe harbor for small businesses. This would throw a monkey wrench into the primary engine of job creation.

● Raise numerous taxes on large employers, which will slow the recovery and undermine our competitive position in world markets.

● Lose about $2.5 billion in revenue as a result of more than 50 special relief provisions for limited numbers of taxpayers that have no policy justification.

● Impose needless and costly paperwork and recordkeeping burdens on the private sector.

HR 11 goes 180 degrees in the wrong direction in its treatment of expiring provisions of tax law. It would make permanent those expiring measures that are very costly and have negligible long-term benefits according to a broad range of government and private sector analysts. In contrast, the bill fails to make permanent the research and development tax credit and the deduction for 25 percent of health insurance premiums paid by self-employed individuals. It also fails to raise the health insurance deduction to 100 percent, as I have proposed.

The bill's Medicare provisions move in the opposite direction from the consensus view that we need to contain rising health-care costs. They would increase Medicare costs by an estimated $3 billion over 5 years. For example, they invite a flood of costly lawsuits to challenge Medicare payments made as long as 6 years ago. These provisions would burden the courts and undermine consistent nationwide application of Medicare rules.

Another costly provision of HR 11 would permanently divert income taxes from the general fund of the Treasury to the Railroad Provision Pension Fund. According to the Railroad Retirement Board, by the year 2016 this taxpayer subsidy could add $13 billion to this single industry pension fund. The diversion would set a dangerous precedent for other industry pension plans that may seek federal taxpayer support in the future.

HR 11 abandons all pretense of fiscal discipline. It would increase the deficit in fiscal years 1994, 1995 and 1996. "Mandatory" spending would rise by more than $7 billion over 5 years — at a time of growing consensus that this portion of the budget must be brought under control.

The bill also arbitrarily increases statutory spending limits to allow roughly $600 million in increased payments to Medicare contractors for administrative costs. To benefit these companies, the Senate voted by the narrowest possible margin to waive its own rule requiring compliance with legal spending limits. These limits on discretionary spending were agreed to by bipartisan majorities of both houses of Congress. It is irresponsible to waive them to benefit one group of companies.

I regret that my disapproval of HR 11 will prevent the enactment this year of many provisions that have my full support. However, the bill's benefits are overwhelmed by provisions that would endanger economic growth. I am therefore compelled to withhold my approval.

p. 118-H)

Republicans voted against the measure in overwhelming numbers, but they were joined by 79 Democrats, many of whom feared voting for a bill that had become identified with tax increases a month before the election and that was unlikely to become law. Budget Committee Chairman Leon E. Panetta, D-Calif., voted against the bill, describing it as a "budget-buster." He said the tax breaks were not fully financed and would add to the federal deficit beyond the five-year period during which the budget rules required that legislation be paid for. The worst contributors to the deficit, Panetta said, were the IRA provisions, which would lose considerable revenue after five years.

In its last major act of the year, the Senate voted 67-22 on Oct. 8 to clear the measure and send it to Bush. While senators from both parties challenged Bush's assertion that revenue provisions in the bill qualified as tax increases, it had become clear that the president was unlikely to sign

the measure and invite an attack from Clinton for ostensibly breaking his promise not to raise taxes again.

"If I'm reading the White House correctly, the bottom line is that the president will not sign the bill," said Dole.

### D'Amato's Filibuster

Final consideration in the Senate was delayed by D'Amato, who waged an ultimately unsuccessful all-night filibuster beginning Oct. 5. He was objecting to Bentsen and Rostenkowski's decision to drop the provision from the final bill that would have helped Smith-Corona. D'Amato, who was up for re-election, held the floor for 15 hours and 15 minutes — the sixth longest one-man filibuster in the history of the Senate. Though occasionally given brief respites by Moynihan and John Seymour, R-Calif., D'Amato remained on his feet, fortified by doses of tea, giving a rambling discourse on the loss of the U.S. manufacturing base.

D'Amato's filibuster became pointless, however, after the House effectively adjourned midday Oct. 6, because no changes could be made to the bill with the House gone.

D'Amato surrendered the floor minutes later. He did win one small concession. Senate leaders agreed to pass a free-standing bill (HR 3837) containing the typewriter provision, which occurred by unanimous consent Oct. 7. But it died as well because the House had left.

Those backing the bill still held out hope that Bush could be convinced that it was politically beneficial to sign the measures, despite the revenue provisions. Lawmakers and lobbyists launched a furious, last-minute blitz, arguing that failing to renew a handful of tax breaks included in the bill would amount to a tax increase for some taxpayers.

### Bush's Veto

Democratic leaders delayed sending the final version of the bill to the White House so that Bush could wait until after the election to make his decision. (Bush had 10 days, excluding Sundays, to sign or veto the bill after receiving it; otherwise it would have been pocket-vetoed.) But that maneuver and furious lobbying by groups backing the bill proved fruitless.

Bush vetoed the bill Nov. 4, saying it "includes numerous tax increases" and "giveaways to special interests" and would "destroy jobs and undermine small business." *(Text, p. 149)*

The veto killed the bill; having adjourned, Congress had no opportunity to override the president.  ∎

# Special Interest Tax Bills Die in Senate

In addition to the two big tax bills, the House also passed a series of mostly non-controversial tax measures aimed at correcting perceived inequities or glitches in the tax code, often to the benefit of some small universe of taxpayers and occasionally to the detriment of others. Although 27 of the measures won House approval, they never came up for a vote in the Senate and died at the end of the Congress.

The series of special interest tax bills was a bipartisan effort initiated by the members of the Ways and Means Committee with the acquiescence — if not full support — of Chairman Dan Rostenkowski, D-Ill.

In several respects, the process was a throwback to the old days of tax law debates in the House. Before 1980, it was common for the Ways and Means Committee to send individual tax changes to the floor under suspension of the rules, a special procedure that prohibited amendments, limited debate and required a supermajority for passage. The measures had to rise or fall on their own merit — a two-thirds majority was seen as a fair barometer of whether some proposal was acceptable enough to warrant passage.

That was also a time when the budget effect of tax changes was less critical. With the advent of budget reconciliation in 1980 — when deficit reduction first became an important consideration — tax bills became omnibus measures, limiting opportunities for individual initiatives. And by 1985, it generally was agreed that tax bills not intended to reduce the deficit could not add to it, either. That broad philosophy was formalized with the 1990 budget agreement. *(1990 Almanac, p. 111)*

Because of that rule, most of the 1992 bills included some mechanism to cover the revenue loss.

The Ways and Means Committee got the ball rolling July 8-9, approving more than two dozen of the little tax bills. The House then passed 27 of the measures over a three-week period under suspension of the rules.

### Rostenkowski Bill Passes

A number of the proposals were combined into a single bill (HR 2735), which the House approved by voice vote July 21. Rostenkowski had assembled the bill as a favor to committee members, many of whom were retiring and had been pushing these provisions for years. Sponsors said the measure contained less than $100 million in tax benefits, which were to be paid for by several revenue-raising provisions. The Bush administration, however, said the bill would have lost $26 million in 1993, drawing a veto threat.

As passed by the House, HR 2735 would have:

● Barred employees or shareholders from benefiting — through excessive salaries, for example — from earnings made by a tax-exempt social welfare organization.

● Made several changes to rules governing small business corporations, increasing the maximum number of shareholders from 35 to 50, for example, and treating these corporations as partnerships for the purposes of taxing gains on subdivided property.

● Shortened the period over which the cost of purchasing tuxedos for rental could be written off from nine years to two.

● Expanded the tax deferral available to livestock producers who were forced to sell cattle due to drought or "other weather-related conditions."

● Exempted certain small fishing operations from having to pay Social Security and unemployment taxes for their workers.

● Permitted private foundations to form common investment funds for charitable purposes.

● Exempted commercially reloaded ammunition from excise taxes in cases when the purchaser supplied empty shells of a similar type.

● Made it easier for rural cooperatives to qualify for an exemption from income tax if at least 85 percent of their income was derived from members.

● Required taxes on rental income, even if the rental period was brief.

## More Bills Approved

On July 27, the House passed several more of the mini-bills by voice vote, including measures that would have:

● Allowed a homeowner who sold a principal residence at a profit to subtract losses on sales of previous homes before calculating his capital gain for tax purposes (HR 5638).

● Allowed old buildings that were moved and then renovated to qualify for the rehabilitation tax credit, overturning a Treasury Department regulation denying the credit to moved buildings (HR 5637).

● Extended from two to four years the period in which individuals could reinvest insurance proceeds before capital gains taxes were owed to rebuild a home damaged in a federally declared disaster (HR 5640).

● Permitted tax-exempt bonds to be issued to finance new office buildings for the United Nations in New York City. The German government had offered free office space in Bonn to several U.N. agencies; New York was trying to keep the agencies by building new offices. Under existing law, tax-exempt bonds could not be used to finance U.N. buildings (HR 5639).

On July 28, the House took a roll-call vote on a bill to allow organizers of college football bowl games to continue to qualify for a tax exemption on contributions from corporate sponsors. The bill (HR 5645) was approved 296-123. *(Vote 327, p. 80-H)*

The IRS had proposed new rules requiring colleges and other charitable organizations to pay taxes on the corporate contributions they received for such events as the Mobil Cotton Bowl and the 1996 Olympic Games in Atlanta. The IRS ruled that the contributions amounted to purchased advertising and should be taxed as unrelated business income. The bill's sponsor disagreed, arguing that taxing the income from corporate sponsorships could mean the end of some of the smaller bowl games and could jeopardize the revenue that the games brought to participating universities.

Finally, the House passed 16 additional bills by voice vote on Aug. 3-4. As passed by the House, the bills:

● Exempted charitable organizations, such as volunteer fire departments, from the unrelated business income tax on proceeds from casino-night fundraisers and other games of chance. The bill (HR 5660) raised the lost revenue by increasing the withholding tax on gambling winnings.

● Revised the income reporting standards for very small, rural property and casualty insurance companies that applied under the alternative minimum tax system (HR 5642).

● Granted special tax deductions to owners of certain freight shipping containers, and provided benefits to certain small property and casualty insurers (HR 5674).

● Revised the tax consequences of renegotiating corporate debts to prevent forced bankruptcies (HR 5655).

● Exempted students who worked as summer camp counselors from Social Security taxes and clarified that Indian tribes could establish tax-deferred savings plans that were otherwise available to charitable organizations (HR 5656).

● Adjusted the tax treatment of certain income by tax-exempt farmer cooperatives and of interest on reserves held by housing cooperatives (HR 5650).

● Granted Group Health of New York Inc., a nonprofit health insurer, the same tax treatment reserved for Blue Cross/Blue Shield insurance providers; corrected a problem that caught some employee stock ownership pension plans in the middle of transactions at the time of a 1989 tax law change; and closed the so-called debt-equity whipsaw that gave tax benefits to both sides in certain securities transactions. The last provision, which was expected to raise $69 million, helped pay for several

other tax bills that had revenue losses (HR 5641).

● Permitted the St. Paul, Minn., Port Authority to restructure several hundred bond issues that were in default while retaining their tax-exempt status (HR 5659).

● Permitted charitable organizations, in particular the Brown Foundation of Kentucky, to cover obligations under the "superfund" hazardous waste cleanup law without jeopardizing their tax-exempt status (HR 5644).

● Exempted international ferry service from a per-passenger tax established to control gambling on international passenger ships (HR 5661).

● Exempted charitable organizations from certain excise taxes on gambling activities (HR 5648).

● Revised accounting rules as they applied to certain cotton warehouses so that income tax assessments were deferred until the income was actually collected (HR 5643).

● Clarified that payments to individuals under the Alaska Native Claims Settlement Act were not taxable (HR 5658).

● Extended the time limit for rolling over gains on the sale of a principal residence in cases where taxpayers' money was frozen in accounts at a failed financial institution (HR 5652).

● Converted existing agreements made before 1982 by estates that limited their tax liability by choosing to value land at its use (for example, agricultural) value, rather than its development value. Prior to 1982, estates had to agree not to change the use or sell the property for 15 years; after 1982, a 10-year usage agreement was required. The bill cut the 15-year standard to 10 in prior agreements (HR 5647).

● Clarified that deposits (essentially premiums) paid to certain perpetual property insurance companies were not below-market loans to the companies that constituted taxable income (HR 5657).

## Two Bills Rejected

During the three weeks of action, the House rejected only two of the small tax measures that had been approved by Ways and Means. Both were defeated because of the provisions used to offset the revenue they would have lost.

The first measure (HR 5653) would have fully exempted bonds issued to finance high-speed intercity rail systems from state caps on tax-exempt bonds. Under existing law, 75 percent of the bonds' value was not counted against the cap. The bill was defeated 48-369 on July 28. *(Vote 328, p. 80-H)*

Many lawmakers opposed a provision that would have required state and local governments to tell taxpayers what portion of their property tax payments was deductible on their federal tax returns and what portion consisted of non-deductible user fees. The provision was expected to raise revenue by preventing taxpayers from erroneously deducting user fees. Some Texas lawmakers also opposed the bill because of controversy surrounding a proposal to put a high-speed rail system in their state.

Rostenkowski later criticized his committee for having reported the bill by unanimous consent when a majority of committee members voted against it on the floor.

The other bill that failed (HR 5649) would have repealed a century-old "occupational" tax on producers and retailers of alcoholic beverages. It was defeated 200-207 on Aug. 4, gaining not even a simple majority, much less the two-thirds majority that each of the bills needed. *(Vote 360, p. 88-H)*

To offset the cost, the bill would have changed the collection point for diesel fuel excise taxes, thereby promising to reduce tax evasion and increase revenues. Refiners, who would have had to pay the tax (and pass it along to wholesalers and retailers), objected strenuously. ∎

# Democrats Target Japan in Trade Bill

Defying a Bush administration veto threat, the House passed a trade bill (HR 5100) aimed largely at opening Japanese markets to U.S. automobiles, auto parts and rice. The bill included language specifying that cars produced by Japanese-owned U.S. plants should contain 70 percent U.S. parts by 1994.

However the Senate never took up the measure, and it died at the end of the Congress.

## BACKGROUND

Dan Rostenkowski, D-Ill., chairman of the Ways and Means Committee and chief sponsor of the bill, put the measure together at the behest of the Democratic leadership. The bill was above all a political document, designed to draw attention in the middle of an election year to the sponsors' claim that the Bush administration had ignored unfair trade practices by U.S. competitors, particularly Japan. Unveiling the measure May 7, House Majority Leader Richard A. Gephardt, D-Mo., said the bill represented the Democrats' blueprint for moving toward a more aggressive, retaliatory trade posture.

As introduced, the bill's most controversial provisions would have required the president to negotiate a voluntary restraint agreement with Japan capping sales of Japanese cars in the United States at existing levels, and forced the Bush administration to negotiate an agreement with Japan to buy more U.S. automobiles before the cap could be raised.

In addition, the bill would have required the U.S. trade representative (USTR) to begin negotiations to lift Japanese barriers to U.S. automobile and auto parts and to start separate talks with Japan, Korea and Taiwan on boosting U.S. rice exports.

In drafting the bill, Rostenkowski — a frequent critic of attempts to force the White House hand on trade policy — rejected proposals made the previous year by Gephardt aimed at forcing the president to retaliate against countries that maintained large trade deficits with the United States.

Instead, the bill would have reauthorized for five years the so-called Super 301 section of U.S. trade law. That provision required the USTR to identify countries with major barriers to U.S. goods and target them for negotiations and possible retaliation. However, it gave the USTR latitude about what countries to name and even more latitude about imposing sanctions.

The Super 301 provision, which was created in the 1988 trade bill, lapsed in 1990. The administration did not want it revived. *(1989 Almanac, p. 144)*

The Democratic bill also included an unprecedented requirement that the USTR initiate Super 301 investigations of Japan on cars and auto parts, and of Japan, Korea and Taiwan on barriers to U.S. rice imports.

Other provisions of the measure would have:

● Established new procedures for annual USTR reviews, upon request by private industry, of foreign compliance with trade agreements, except the U.S.-Canada and U.S.-Israel free trade agreements. The provision, by Robert T. Matsui, D-Calif., was intended to give the U.S. semiconductor industry a way to press Japan to comply with an agreement to buy more U.S. semiconductors.

● Made various changes in customs law, including allowing electronic processing of customs-related transactions.

● Required enforcement of quantitative limits on machine tool imports from Taiwan, under the terms of a lapsed bilateral agreement, until a new agreement could be negotiated.

● Made several changes designed to make it more difficult for foreign producers to evade U.S. anti-dumping laws by importing parts from third-world countries and assembling the product in the United States. Anti-dumping laws prohibited foreign companies from selling goods in the United States at less than their "fair value."

## TRADE SUBCOMMITTEE ACTION

The Ways and Means Trade Subcommittee approved the bill by voice vote June 9 after removing the language requiring the administration to cap sales of Japanese cars in the United States. But the change did not satisfy the Bush administration, which made clear its staunch opposition to the bill. "We think that it's the Trade Contraction Act of 1992," Gary Edson, general counsel with the USTR, said after the committee action. "And we fundamentally think it's not redeemable by any of the changes made today."

The cap on Japanese auto sales would have applied not only to exports from Japan but also to vehicles produced in U.S. plants owned by Japanese companies. Some Democrats on the subcommittee agreed with Republicans that the provision could have cost U.S. workers in foreign-owned plants their jobs and deterred overseas companies from opening new U.S. plants.

Rostenkowski appeared briefly at the subcommittee drafting session to request that the auto provision be deleted.

"Though well-intentioned, [it] could have the effect of chilling foreign investment in the United States," he said. But he added that it was possible that an alternative plan could be devised for limiting Japanese imports without hurting U.S. workers by the time the full Ways and Means Committee considered the bill.

The subcommittee agreed by voice vote to remove the auto provision.

### Amendments

The subcommittee adopted by voice vote an amendment by Byron L. Dorgan, D-N.D., to require importers of foreign-produced grain and oil seeds, such as soybeans, to specify what the commodities would be used for in the United States. Dorgan said the provision, which was sought by the National Association of Wheat Growers, was intended to prevent companies from importing wheat from

---

## BOXSCORE

➡ **Trade Expansion Act (HR 5100).** The bill would have reauthorized for five years the so-called Super 301 section of U.S. trade law; required negotiations with Japan over automobiles and auto parts and with Japan, South Korea and Taiwan over rice; and specified that cars produced by Japanese-owned U.S. plants should contain 70 percent U.S. parts by 1994.

**Report:** H Rept 102-607.

### KEY ACTION

July 8 — The **House** passed HR 5100, 280-145.

---

Canada, mixing it with domestic grain and re-exporting it, taking advantage of Agriculture Department subsidy programs to boost sales abroad.

Other amendments adopted by the subcommittee would have:

● Changed the Special 301 section of U.S. trade law to toughen protection of U.S. patents abroad by requiring the USTR each year to identify countries that delayed issuing patents for U.S. goods to give their own producers a chance to copy the product. Sanctions were to be imposed against such countries if negotiations to eliminate the problem failed. The amendment, offered by Dick Schulze, R-Pa., was adopted by voice vote.

● Revised procedures by which U.S. companies could obtain relief, such as higher tariffs, when their domestic sales were threatened by low-cost imports from former communist bloc countries. The law specified that relief was only available when the imports came from communist countries. The amendment, offered by Schulze, sought to change that to state-controlled economies, so that countries that were no longer communist but subsidized exports could not dump products in the United States.

## WAYS AND MEANS COMMITTEE ACTION

The House Ways and Means Committee approved the bill by voice vote June 16 after the chief defender of the troubled U.S. auto industry, Sander M. Levin, D-Mich., withdrew an amendment aimed at forcing the Bush administration to open negotiations on placing tighter limits on car imports from Japan.

In a blow to the auto unions, Levin dropped his amendment after it became clear that Rostenkowski and several committee Democrats opposed it, despite Levin's feverish efforts to craft a compromise. Inclusion of the Levin proposal could have resulted in the referral of the bill to the Energy and Commerce Committee, something Rostenkowski seemed determined to prevent.

Levin's amendment, which never came to a vote, would have required the USTR to open negotiations with Japan within 45 days after the bill was enacted. In unusually stringent language, it specified that the talks "shall lead" to an agreement requiring that vehicles assembled at Japanese-owned factories in the United States, known as transplants, contain 70 percent U.S.-made parts and only 30 percent parts from Japan.

Several Democrats and most Republicans criticized the language. "Transplants must not be singled out for special treatment if the effect of that treatment is to reduce U.S. jobs or to discriminate against foreign corporations located in the U.S.," said Matsui, who threatened to vote against the trade bill if it contained the Levin provision.

Amendments, all adopted by voice vote, would have:

● Required the International Trade Commission to consider, in deciding whether to impose anti-dumping duties, the "actual and potential" decline of a U.S. industry's backlog of orders when threatened by low-cost imports. Anti-dumping duties were imposed on imports sold at less than market value if the sales threatened a U.S. industry. The amendment was offered by Rostenkowski.

● Revised the U.S. negotiating objectives in talks on the General Agreement on Tariffs and Trade (GATT) to ensure "strong and effective limitations" on the ability of the GATT to overrule U.S. countervailing and anti-dumping duty actions. Countervailing duties were imposed on imports that had foreign subsidies. The amendment was offered by Rostenkowski.

● Required the USTR to impose sanctions on countries that ignored protections for U.S. intellectual property if efforts to correct the problem were not successful within a year after the country was identified. The amendment was offered by Andrew Jacobs Jr., D-Ind.

● Exempted imports of phosphoric acid from Israel from trade law provisions that counted such imports along with those from other countries in deciding whether to impose anti-dumping and countervailing duties. The amendment was offered by Thomas J. Downey, D-N.Y.

● Given the president authority to bar imports from foreign companies that assisted foreign governments in the building of nuclear weapons. The amendment was proposed by Pete Stark, D-Calif., and Jim Bunning, R-Ky.

● Struck a section of the bill calling on the president to negotiate with other countries on an international trade embargo on Cuba. The amendment was proposed by Charles B. Rangel, D-N.Y.

## HOUSE APPROVAL

The House approved the bill July 8. But the vote, 280-145, was not nearly enough to override a presidential veto and raised doubts that the measure would go much further. *(Vote 273, p. 66-H)*

Before members began debate on the bill, they turned down a parliamentary effort to allow a floor amendment requiring the president to begin negotiations with Japan on a free-trade agreement. David Dreier, R-Calif., sponsor of the amendment, had been turned down by the Rules Committee and hoped to use a rare procedure to change the rule governing floor debate. Drier was defeated on a 247-167 vote. *(Vote 270, p. 66-H)*

### Limiting Japanese Sales

Gephardt and Levin succeeded in adding an amendment on the floor that would have mandated negotiations with the Japanese government over trade in automobiles and auto parts. The goal was to put into trade agreement form the assurances President Bush had received on his trip to Japan in January that Japanese carmakers would buy more U.S. parts and that Japanese markets would be opened wider for U.S. cars. Members were also motivated by a recent agreement by Japanese auto producers to limit the number of cars exported to Europe. Levin and others said they feared that Japan would try to make up a drop in their European sales by boosting exports to the United States.

The Gephardt-Levin amendment drew fire in particular for its requirement that cars made at transplant factories consist of at least 70 percent U.S.-made parts by 1994. Levin argued that nearly three-fourths of the U.S. trade deficit with Japan was auto-related. He noted that cars produced by U.S. automakers had about 85 percent domestic content; 70 percent for transplants would be more than reasonable, he said. Levin denied that the provision would require a specific limit on Japanese auto imports — essentially writing into a trade agreement what was a voluntary restraint agreement (VRA). "This bill doesn't write into law a VRA or anything else. It says negotiate," Levin said.

The auto amendment was adopted by a 260-166 vote, a surprisingly comfortable margin considering that the earlier version had failed to win majority support in the Ways and Means Committee. Both Rostenkowski and Trade Subcommittee Chairman Sam M. Gibbons, D-Fla., voted against it. *(Vote 272, p. 66-H)* ∎

# Trade Pact Buffeted by Election-Year Forces

President Bush signed the North American Free Trade Agreement on Dec. 17, leaving for his successor, Bill Clinton, the challenge of getting the pact through Congress. The accord, known as NAFTA, was aimed at joining the United States, Mexico and Canada into a huge free-trade zone. It promised to eliminate tariffs, duties and other trade barriers among the three countries over 15 years, allowing goods produced anywhere in North America to move freely across a continent with more than 360 million people and a combined economic output of more than $6 trillion a year.

## BACKGROUND

Bush and Mexico's President Carlos Salinas de Gotari had agreed in June 1990 to negotiate a free-trade agreement. The plan was accelerated by a stalemate in global trade talks under the General Agreement on Tariffs and Trade (GATT) and by Salinas' decision in 1990 to focus on more open trade with the United States as the best route to economic development for his country.

Bush formally notified Congress of his intent to negotiate such a pact in September 1990. On Feb. 5, 1991, he announced that Canada, which already had a free-trade agreement with the United States, would join in.

As a critical precondition for negotiating an agreement, Bush in 1991 won congressional approval for a two-year extension of so-called fast tract procedures, which gave Congress 90 days to act once a trade agreement was submitted, and required an up or down vote without amendments. The purpose was to give U.S. negotiating partners confidence that the terms they worked out with the administration would not be picked apart by Congress.

The AFL-CIO, which opposed NAFTA, made defeat of the fast track its legislative priority for the year. But the Bush administration prevailed, in large part because it issued an "Action Plan" addressing critics' concerns about NAFTA. The administration pledged to reject any weakening of U.S. environmental laws, to provide for workers adjustment assistance and to provide long transition periods for some industries threatened by the free-trade pact. *(1991 Almanac, p. 118)*

## CONGRESSIONAL CRITICISM

As the Office of the U.S. Trade Representative (USTR) negotiated details of the pact with Mexico and Canada in 1992, congressional critics led by House Majority Leader Richard A. Gephardt, D-Mo., kept up pressure on the White House. In a speech July 27, Gephardt accused the administration of ignoring promises made in the Action Plan. "As the agreement moves toward completion," he said, "it is becoming increasingly apparent that environ-

---

## BOXSCORE

➡ **North American Free Trade Agreement.** The accord promised to create a free-trade bloc in North America, eliminating tariffs, duties and other trade barriers among the United States, Mexico and Canada over 15 years.

### KEY ACTION

Aug. 12 — President Bush announced that Mexico, Canada and the United States had reached preliminary agreement.

Oct. 7 — Negotiators from the three countries initialed a final text of the NAFTA pact.

Dec. 17 — Bush, Canadian Prime Minister Brian Mulroney and Mexican President Carlos Salinas de Gotari signed the agreement at separate ceremonies in the three countries.

---

mental controls, worker-adjustment policies, protections for American and Mexican workers, and incentives for American manufacturers to remain in the United States are being omitted from the draft."

Gephardt outlined a far-reaching series of protections that he said would have to be included in the text of the accord if it was to win congressional approval. He called for turning trade adjustment assistance into an entitlement program; all workers who lost their jobs as a result of "short-term disruptions or long-term decline" attributable to the trade agreement would qualify for payments regardless of the cost. And he called for a dedicated, cross-border transaction tax to pay for programs in worker training, infrastructure development and environmental protection.

On Aug. 6, the House voted unanimously to warn Bush that it would not tolerate any pact that would weaken U.S. health, safety, labor or environmental laws. The vote came on a non-binding, "sense of the Congress" resolution (H Con Res 246) sponsored by Gephardt and Henry A. Waxman, D-Calif. The measure was adopted 362-0, with Republican and Democratic supporters of the trade talks joining with opponents to back a measure that they called "redundant, but not objectionable." *(Vote 376, p. 92-H)*

The House had adopted a similar non-binding resolution (H Res 146) in 1991, and Bush indicated at the time that he had no intention of jeopardizing U.S. laws during the free-trade negotiations.

### Campaign Fodder

In a Rose Garden ceremony Aug. 12, Bush announced that the United States, Mexico and Canada had reached preliminary agreement on the details of the trade pact and proclaimed it a "historic agreement" that would spur "economic growth in all three countries." Trade officials had completed a feverish two-week round of negotiations in Washington just hours earlier. With Bush slumping in the polls, the White House badly wanted to make the announcement before the Republican National Convention in Houston, which began Aug. 17.

Though Bush had made free trade a cornerstone of his re-election, he portrayed NAFTA primarily as a domestic initiative that would boost U.S. jobs at a time when the economy was slumping, even though administration officials conceded the pact would have little immediate effect on the U.S. economy. "Open markets in Mexico and Canada mean more American jobs," Bush said.

Many Democrats also emphasized the domestic implications, but their focus was on the potential job loss in some sectors of the economy as tariffs and other trade barriers were gradually lowered. "This is a jobs program for Mexico," said Michigan Sen. Donald W. Riegle Jr. in a

# NAFTA Highlights

*The North American Free Trade Agreement (NAFTA) was intended to join the United States, Mexico and Canada into a single free-trade bloc. About 65 percent of U.S. industrial and agricultural exports to Mexico was made eligible for duty-free treatment immediately or within five years. Mexico's tariffs averaged 10 percent, 2½ times the average U.S. tariff. If approved as signed, NAFTA promised to:*

**Motor vehicles and parts.** Cut Mexican tariffs on vehicles and light trucks from 20 percent to 10 percent immediately and eliminate duties on 75 percent of U.S. parts exports to Mexico within five years. Mexico's rules requiring a balance in imports and exports of autos and auto parts were to be phased out over 10 years.

**Auto rule of origin.** Require that automobiles and light trucks qualifying for the tariff cuts must derive at least 62.5 percent of their value from North American parts and manufacturing. The level set in the U.S.-Canada Free Trade Agreement was 50 percent. The goal was to prevent companies in other countries from funneling their autos through Mexico to evade U.S. tariffs.

**Telecommunications.** Eliminate discriminatory restrictions on U.S. sales to and investment in the Mexican market for telecommunications equipment and services.

**Textiles and apparel.** Immediately eliminate barriers to $250 million (more than 20 percent) of U.S. exports to Mexico and eliminate restrictions on another $700 million within six years. All North American trade restrictions were to be eliminated within 10 years, with rules of origin provisions to ensure that the benefits went to North American companies.

**Financial services.** Allow U.S. banks and securities firms to establish wholly owned subsidiaries in Mexico. Transitional restrictions were to be phased out by Jan. 1, 2000.

**Agriculture.** Immediately eliminate Mexican import licenses, which covered about 25 percent of U.S. agricultural exports and phase out all Mexican tariffs, which generally ranged from 10 percent to 20 percent, within 15 years.

**Insurance.** Permit U.S. companies with existing joint ventures to obtain 100 percent ownership by 1996; new entrants to the market would be able to obtain a majority stake in Mexican firms by 1998. By the year 2000, all equity and market share restrictions were to be eliminated.

**Investment.** Eliminate Mexican domestic content rules stating how much of the value of a product must be attributed to local parts and labor, permitting additional use of U.S. parts. U.S. companies operating in Mexico were to receive the same treatment as Mexican-owned firms. Mexico agreed to drop export performance requirements, which forced companies to export as a condition of being allowed to invest.

**Land transportation.** Allow U.S. trucking companies to carry international cargo to the Mexican states contiguous to the United States by 1995 and have cross-border access to all of Mexico by the end of 1999.

**Intellectual property rights.** Guarantee U.S. producers of high-tech, entertainment and consumer goods greater protection for their patents, copyrights and trademarks. NAFTA included protection for computer programs, sound recordings and motion pictures.

**Environment.** Allow the United States to continue to block imports that did not meet U.S. standards, and allow states and cities to enact even tougher standards; the United States could continue to enforce its international treaty obligations, including limits on trade in products such as endangered species and ozone-depleting substances; the parties agreed not to lower health, safety or environmental standards to attract investment.

---

statement issued after Bush's announcement. "What we need is a jobs program for America."

Opposition was particularly intense in Midwestern states because of concern about job losses in manufacturing plants and in the auto industry. One of the last issues resolved in the negotiations between U.S. Trade Representative Carla A. Hills and her Mexican and Canadian counterparts concerned protecting North American automakers from outside imports. Gephardt reacted quickly to the announcement, describing the pact as "terribly deficient." He said that provision should be made for worker retraining, infrastructure and environmental cleanup along the U.S.-Mexico border, although he indicated that that could be done as part of the implementing legislation.

In testimony before the Senate Finance Committee Sept. 8, Hills responded that NAFTA was "the greenest trade agreement ever negotiated." Among the important environmental provisions, Hills said, was one that would allow U.S. states to maintain environmental laws that were tougher than those at the federal level. Environmental groups had demanded this protection to prevent Mexico or Canada from challenging stringent state laws, such as pesticide regulations in California, on the grounds that they

unfairly blocked imports of fruits and vegetables that did not meet residue standards.

### Jobs Program

And, fulfilling a commitment made to congressional leaders in 1991, Bush proposed a new federal program for retraining workers who lost their jobs in industries battered by stiffer international competition. The program would have phased out two programs for displaced workers and replaced them with a $2 billion-a-year program to provide such workers with grants of up to $3,000 redeemable at colleges or technical institutions. Up to $670 million would have been reserved annually for workers displaced by NAFTA.

The program included direct payments to laid-off workers who had exhausted unemployment benefits but had not completed their training — another feature that Democrats insisted upon.

Senate Finance Committee Chairman Lloyd Bentsen, D-Texas, said the Bush plan had "some curbside appeal" but said the administration had proposed no credible way to pay for it, except by cutting other benefits.

Concern in Congress over NAFTA was not confined to

Democrats. Many members, even Republicans, withheld their endorsements, concerned that pre-election support for NAFTA could hurt them among constituents worried about losing jobs. "Members are worried about being blindsided in their districts," said retiring Rep. Ed Jenkins, D-Ga.

## CLINTON'S STANCE

Democratic presidential nominee Clinton took a softer line than many congressional Democrats, though he left himself room to attack Bush in the future as details of NAFTA and the public's response became clearer. "I will support a free-trade agreement with Mexico so long as it provides adequate protection for workers, farmers and the environment on both sides of the border," Clinton said. But he added that he intended "to review the details of the agreement and follow closely the expected congressional hearings on the issue."

Bush repeatedly attacked Clinton for not endorsing the pact and accused him of waffling under pressure from organized labor.

In a clearly orchestrated effort, several key Democrats, who were generally free traders and who had been supportive of NAFTA, announced that they would withhold their endorsements until after a congressional review. They criticized Bush for making an issue of Clinton's stance, saying Bush was jeopardizing the prospects for ratification by politicizing the issue. Included in the group were Bentsen, Sen. Max Baucus, D-Mont., and House Ways and Means Committee Chairman Dan Rostenkowski, D-Ill.

"This agreement is enormously complex," Bentsen told Hills at the Sept. 8 hearing. "The draft you have finally provided us is 2,000 pages long. It covers everything from corn to computers. Gov. Clinton did not even have that text. Yet the president thought Gov. Clinton should sign on."

On Oct. 4, Clinton finally endorsed NAFTA, but he said that, if elected president, he would seek tougher protections than Bush has negotiated for U.S. jobs, the environment and health and safety standards. In a speech at North Carolina State University endorsing the agreement, Clinton said he was convinced that NAFTA "will generate jobs and growth on both sides of the border if and only if it's part of a broad-based strategy, and if and only if we address the issues still to be addressed."

Saying that "the shortcomings in the agreement are really a reflection ... of the shortcomings in the Bush economic policy," Clinton listed several steps he would take if elected, none of which required renegotiating the NAFTA text. He said he would spend more than Bush on retraining workers and undertake more environmental cleanup along the border.

To help farmers, Clinton said U.S. laws restricting imports of fruits and vegetables with intolerable levels of pesticide residue should be strictly enforced. He also called for giving the public the right to challenge "objectionable" environmental practices by Mexico or Canada. Provisions of the agreement allowing foreign workers to enter the United States must be "properly implemented" to ensure that they are not brought in as strike breakers, he said.

Clinton also echoed concern expressed by U.S. truckers. "I want to note that this agreement allows Mexican truckers to drive in the United States without having to satisfy all the U.S. safety and training standards. That troubles me," Clinton said.

Endorsing a proposal made by several House Democrats, Clinton said that before implementing NAFTA, he would negotiate a side agreement establishing a U.S.-Mexico environmental protection commission empowered to enforce environmental laws on both sides of the border. "Such a commission would have the power to provide remedies, including money damages and the legal power to stop pollution," Clinton said. He called a side agreement signed by the Bush administration in September to establish an environmental commission "too little, too late."

In a statement responding to Clinton's speech, the White House said, "In every case, the administration has either already done what he proposed, or his ideas, if implemented, would not achieve the intended results."

## AGREEMENT SIGNED

At a ceremony in San Antonio on Oct. 7, trade negotiators from the United States, Mexico and Canada initialed the final text of the trade pact. Bush proclaimed that "as more open markets stimulate growth, create new products at competitive prices for consumers, we'll create new jobs at good wages in all three countries."

At a ceremony Dec. 17 at the headquarters of the Organization of American States in Washington, Bush, flanked by Hills and other negotiators, signed the NAFTA agreement. Canadian Prime Minister Brian Mulroney and Mexican President Salinas signed the agreement in similar ceremonies in their own countries.

As the year ended, it was not clear whether Clinton would move quickly to submit the pact for congressional approval, or delay action until he had had a chance to win passage for his own legislative priorities in the early days of his administration. While delay might upset relations with Mexico and be difficult to explain to Canada, Clinton would be under no procedural pressure to submit the pact to Congress. Having signed NAFTA before May 31, 1993, Bush ensured that it would qualify for the fast-track procedures. ■

# Two Bills Limiting Trade with China Vetoed

Twice in 1992, President Bush vetoed bills aimed at punishing China for human rights abuses and other practices. In both cases, the Senate upheld his veto.

The first bill (HR 2212), which had begun making its way through Congress in 1991, would have restricted China's access to normal trade status with the United States in 1992 unless the Chinese government made improvements in human rights and other areas. The second measure (HR 5318) would have denied normal trade status in 1993 to goods produced by Chinese state-owned industries unless the president certified to Congress that the Chinese government was making progress in addressing human rights, trade and weapons proliferation concerns. Goods that could not be exported to the United States under normal trade status were subject to very high tariffs.

## BACKGROUND

China gained normalized trade — or most-favored-nation (MFN) — status with the United States as part of a trade agreement completed in 1980. Under the Jackson-Vanik amendment to the 1974 trade act, the president had to renew that status annually, after waiving a requirement that denied MFN to communist countries that prohibited the free emigration of their citizens. The renewal came due each July 3. Congress could vote to reject the extension, but such an action was also subject to presidential veto.

Despite its name, MFN did not offer preferential treatment; the United States granted MFN status to nearly all its trade partners, allowing their exports to enter this country at low tariff rates. (MFN was not, however, the lowest tariff status. More than 125 developing countries paid even lower U.S. rates under the Generalized System of Preferences.)

Since 1989, when the Chinese government cracked down on pro-democracy demonstrators in Beijing's Tiananmen Square, many in Congress had been trying unsuccessfully to put conditions on the renewal of China's MFN status.

In 1990, the House passed a bill only to see it die because the Senate did not act on a companion measure. *(1990 Almanac, p. 764)*

On July 10, 1991, the House voted 313-112 in favor of a bill (HR 2212) to restrict the president's ability to renew MFN status for China in 1992.

Supporters argued that the United States should use this critical lever to try to alter China's human rights

---

## BOXSCORE

➡ **Conditional MFN for China (HR 2212, HR 5318).** The first bill would have placed restriction on renewing most-favored-nation (MFN) status in 1992 for goods imported from China. The second measure would have set conditions for renewing MNF status in 1993 for imports from Chinese state-owned industries.

**Reports:** H Rept 102-392; H Rept 102-658.

### KEY ACTION

Feb. 25 — The **Senate** cleared conference report on HR 2212, 59-39.

March 2 — President Bush vetoed HR 2212.

March 11 — The **House** voted to override the veto, 357-61.

March 18 — The **Senate** failed to override Bush, 60-38.

July 21 — The **House** approved HR 5318, 339-62.

Sept. 14 — The **Senate** approved HR 5318 by voice vote.

Sept. 22 — The **House** cleared bill by voice vote.

Sept. 28 — Bush vetoed HR 5318.

Sept. 30 — The **House** voted to override veto, 345-74.

Oct. 1 — The **Senate** failed to override, 59-40.

---

practices. In addition, there was increasing concern over China's deepening trade surplus with the United States, its alleged export of missile technology and its reported use of prison labor to produce exports. The Bush administration countered that it was equally concerned about nurturing reforms in China, but argued that MFN status was the wrong weapon to use.

Cutting off MFN, Bush and others argued, would hurt those Chinese in the private sector whose businesses were tied to exports and who were most committed to a market economy and democratic reforms.

With the House positioned to override a promised veto, the White House concentrated its lobbying efforts on the Senate, where the vote was expected to be much closer. Senate Majority Leader George J. Mitchell, D-Maine, had taken on Bush over the issue, clearly seeking to wrest control of China policy from the White House. The highpoint came July 23, when the Senate approved its version of the bill (S 1367) by a vote of 55-44 — short of the two-thirds that would be needed for an override.

House and Senate conferees produced a compromise bill (HR 2212) in late November, and the House approved it by an overwhelming vote of 409-21 on Nov. 27. But with no indication that Mitchell could increase his margin of support, the Senate did not take up the conference report before adjourning for the year.

The measure would have barred the president from renewing MFN status in 1992 unless he reported that China had accounted for and released citizens held as a result of the Tiananmen Square protests. He also would have had to report that China had made "significant progress" in human rights, trade and weapons proliferation. China would not have been eligible if it transferred certain ballistic missiles, missile launchers or equipment for building nuclear weapons to Iran or Syria. *(1991 Almanac, p. 121)*

## THE FIRST BILL

Action occurred early in 1992 as the Senate voted 59-39 on Feb. 25 to adopt the conference report on HR 2212, clearing the measure for the president. *(Vote 31, p. 5-S)*

Senators voting for the bill expressed concern about news reports that China had sold advanced ballistic missile technology and launchers to Pakistan recently and to other countries in the past. China agreed Feb. 21 to abide by an international agreement barring certain missile technology sales.

# First Veto Message on China MFN Status

*President Bush on March 2 vetoed legislation that would have placed conditions on the renewal of most-favored-nation trade status with China. Following is the text of the president's veto message:*

I am returning herewith without my approval HR 2212, the United States-China Act of 1991, which places additional conditions on renewal of China's most-favored-nation (MFN) trade status.

The sponsors of HR 2212 believe they can promote broad economic and foreign policy objectives in China by placing conditions on the renewal of China's MFN status. They expect that the Chinese will improve respect for human rights, cooperate in arms control and drop barriers to trade, given a choice between losing MFN and addressing these concerns.

Let me state at the outset that my administration shares the goals and objectives of HR 2212. Upholding the sanctity of human rights, controlling the spread of weapons of mass destruction, and free and fair trade are issues of vital concern. My objection lies strictly with the methods proposed to achieve these aims.

There is no doubt in my mind that if we present China's leaders with an ultimatum on MFN, the result will be weakened ties to the West and further repression. The end result will not be progress on human rights, arms control or trade. Anyone familiar with recent Chinese history can attest that the most brutal and protracted periods of repression took place precisely when China turned inward, against the world.

Recent agreements by the Chinese to protect U.S. intellectual property rights, to abide by the Missile Technology Control Regime Guidelines, to accede to the Nuclear Non-Proliferation Treaty by April, and to discuss our human rights concerns — after years of stonewalling — are the clear achievements of my administration's policy of comprehensive engagement.

We have the policy tools at hand to deal with our concerns effectively and with realistic chances for success. The administration's comprehensive policy of engagement on several separate fronts invites China's leadership to act responsibly without leaving any doubts about the consequences of Chinese misdeeds.

Our approach is one of targeting specific areas of concern with the appropriate policy instruments to produce the required results. HR 2212 would severely handicap U.S. business in China, penalizing American workers and eliminating jobs in this country. Conditional MFN status would severely damage the Western-oriented, modernizing elements in China, weaken Hong Kong, and strengthen opposition to democracy and economic reform.

We are making a difference in China by remaining engaged. Because the Congress has attached conditions to China's MFN renewal that will jeopardize this policy, I am returning HR 2212 to the House of Representatives without my approval. Such action is needed to protect the economic and foreign policy interests of the United States.

---

Democrats Tom Harkin of Iowa and Bob Kerrey of Nebraska, who were absent campaigning for the Democratic presidential nomination, presumably would have boosted the yes vote to 61. Supporters of the bill cheered their gain from the 55 votes that an earlier, tougher version had garnered in 1991. But even 61 votes was well shy of the two-thirds margin needed to override a veto; 67 votes were needed if all senators were present and voting.

Several senators who opposed the bill in 1991 but supported it this time cited weapons proliferation as a primary concern. Jim Exon, D-Neb., who switched his vote, said, "This is the time we ought to send some kind of signal to the Chinese." Finance Committee Chairman Lloyd Bentsen, D-Texas, argued that Congress needed to "tell the Chinese that there's a price to pay for its policy of repression and indiscriminate arms sales." But Frank H. Murkowski, R-Alaska, who defended Bush's policy, said "conditional MFN is the same thing as denial of MFN. Isolation [of China] is not the way to achieve our aim."

The White House lobbied hard against the conference report, and Minority Leader Bob Dole, R-Kan., could be seen on the floor pressing three Republicans in particular.

He failed to sway one of them, Jake Garn of Utah, but he held the vote of William S. Cohen of Maine and won a switch from Alfonse M. D'Amato of New York, who supported the measure the previous July but voted against it this time. D'Amato said afterward that if China failed to make progress on human rights, he would probably vote again to put conditions on its trading status.

In all, nine Republicans deserted Bush. Five Democrats supported him including Max Baucus of Montana, chairman of the Finance Subcommittee on International Trade. "Unilateral cutoff of MFN would hurt the United States far more than it would hurt China, especially since no other country would follow our lead. We would be all alone," Baucus said.

But Mitchell disagreed: "Our trade relationship with China is important to us, but it's more important to China," Mitchell said. "Enforcing American laws on trade does not jeopardize relations."

## Bush Wins Veto Fight

Bush vetoed the bill, as expected, on March 2. Also as expected, the House easily mustered enough votes March 11 to override him, but it was obvious that that was as far as the bill would go. The House vote was 357-61, well in excess of the two-thirds majority required to override. *(Vote 43, p. 10-H)*

During the House debate, several Republicans used harsh terms to denounce the administration's trade policy toward China. John Miller, of Washington, complained that "the president has asked us to follow a trade policy with China that is divorced from morality." And Dick Schulze, of Pennsylvania, said the "policy of appeasement has failed." Yet a two-thirds majority of House Republicans voted against Bush.

On March 18, the Senate refused to follow the House lead, voting 60-38 for the override, well short of the necessary two-thirds majority. Congress had yet to override a bill that Bush had vetoed; this was his 26th. *(Vote 52, p. 8-S)*

The margin was virtually unchanged from Feb. 25, when senators adopted the conference report on the bill. Two senators switched their positions from the Feb. 25 vote, however: D'Amato, R-N.Y., voted yes, and Garn voted no. In a statement he had inserted into the record March 18, D'Amato suggested that reports of Chinese weapons shipments to Iran had caused him to change his mind again. Garn switched his vote to support Bush on the veto.

## THE SECOND BILL

Three months later, on June 2, Bush announced that he

# Second Veto Message on China MFN Status

*Following is the text of Bush's Sept. 28 veto of a bill to restrict most-favored-nation status for China:*

I am returning herewith without my approval HR 5318, the United States-China Act of 1992, which places additional conditions on renewal of China's most-favored-nation (MFN) trade status.

I share completely the goals of this legislation: to see greater Chinese adherence to international standards of human rights, free and fair trade practices, and international non-proliferation norms. However, adding broad conditions to China's MFN renewal would not lead to faster progress in advancing our goals. To those who advocate this approach, let me set the record straight.

Our policy of comprehensive engagement lets the Chinese know in no uncertain terms that "business as usual" is not possible until they take steps to resolve our differences. Through multiple, focused measures, we are eliciting the results we seek.

This year China joined global efforts to control the spread of nuclear weapons and ballistic missiles by declaring adherence to the Missile Technology Control Regime's (MTCR) guidelines and parameters and signing the Nuclear Proliferation Treaty (NPT). Chinese behavior remains MTCR-consistent, and we have begun a dialogue with the Chinese on their responsibilities under the NPT. We continue to monitor vigilantly China's weapons export practices. We have used the sanction authorities available successfully and remain prepared to do so again if necessary.

We have made progress on the resolution of outstanding trade issues with our agreements to protect Intellectual Property Rights and to ban prison labor exports. I will not allow, however, market access to remain a one-sided benefit in China's favor while our bilateral trade deficit grows. If China fails to reduce trade barriers, we are prepared to take trade action under the statutory guidelines of Section 301 of the Trade Act of 1974.

The limited steps China has taken on human rights are inadequate. But our human rights dialogue gives us an avenue to express our views directly to China's leaders. Significant improvement in China's human rights situation, including freedom for all those imprisoned solely for the peaceful expression of their beliefs, remains our objective. It is easy to be discouraged by the pace of progress in this area. But it would be a serious mistake to let our frustration lead us to gamble with policies that would undermine our goals.

Withdrawing MFN or conditioning it, such that it will be withdrawn at a later date, will not promote these goals. HR 5318 imposes unworkable constraints on our bilateral trade. Among the casualties of this bill would be the dynamic, market-oriented regions of southern China and Hong Kong, as well as those Chinese who support reform and rely on outside contact for support.

The impact of this bill would extend beyond the state enterprise system, harming independent industrial and agricultural entities that have sprung up in China since the advent of economic reform and its opening to the outside. These family-owned and operated entities are interlinked in the manufacturing process with large, state-controlled factories and marketing agencies. They would not be shielded from the effects of this bill.

Americans too would be affected. This year our exports to China will climb to about $8 billion. China's retaliation for the loss of MFN would cost us this growing market and thousands of American jobs. We would cede our market share to our foreign competitors who impose no restrictions on their trade with China, at a time when China is taking market-opening measures that our trade negotiators fought to obtain.

Our policy seeks to address issues of vital concern to us and looks to the future of our relations with a country that is home to almost one-quarter of the human race. MFN is a means to bring our influence to bear on China. Comprehensive engagement is the process we use to transform this influence into positive change. The relationship between these two key elements of our China policy is a powerful one, and the absence of one element diminishes the potency of the other. We continue to advance broad U.S. objectives without imposing economic hardship on Americans because both elements of our policy are in place.

Engagement through our democratic, economic, and educational institutions instead of confrontation offers the best hope for reform in China. MFN is the foundation we need to engage the Chinese. HR 5318 places conditions on MFN renewal for China that will jeopardize this policy and includes a requirement that infringes upon the President's exclusive authority to undertake diplomatic negotiations on behalf of the United States.

In order to protect the economic and foreign policy interests of the United States, I am returning HR 5318 to the House of Representatives without my approval.

had decided to continue trade benefits for China for another year.

The House Ways and Means Committee responded July 2 by giving voice vote approval to yet another bill (HR 5318) placing stiff conditions on the president's ability to extend China's MFN status. While earlier measures would have applied to all U.S. imports from China, the new bill would have targeted only goods made by Chinese government-owned enterprises.

The plan, sponsored by Reps. Don J. Pease, D-Ohio, and Nancy Pelosi, D-Calif., would have subjected these goods to very high tariffs unless the president certified to Congress that the Chinese government was making significant progress in addressing human rights, trade and weapons proliferation concerns. The conditions were to apply for one year, beginning July 3, 1993. Goods produced by companies that were joint Chinese-foreign ventures, or by Chinese factories that were collectively or privately owned, would automatically have received MFN treatment for the year.

Pease said the change was intended to appeal to members who had complained in the past that denying MFN status to China would harm U.S. business interests and hurt reform-minded forces in China. But some critics on the committee said the change did not eliminate their objections to using trade sanctions to force a political change. Robert T. Matsui, D-Calif., said he doubted that it would be possible to distinguish easily between state-owned enterprises and those not subject to the higher tariffs imposed by the bill. "It would be more intellectually honest if we just cut off trade with China and then resume when China does what we want," he said. Because much trade with China would probably continue under MFN status, "it appears we want to have it both ways," Matsui said.

He and others also said that some high-profile deals involving U.S. companies might be jeopardized if the bill were enacted. A State Department official told the committee that a recent $1 billion deal between China and the

McDonnell Douglas Co. was one such threatened transaction.

Ways and Means agreed by voice vote to ask the Rules Committee to bring HR 5318 and a second MFN bill (H J Res 502) to the floor one after the other. H J Res 502 would have flatly rejected Bush's waiver granting China MFN in 1992.

The Ways and Means Trade Subcommittee had approved HR 5318 by voice vote June 29 after adopting an en bloc amendment offered by Pease that made relatively minor changes. One such change was to clarify that only goods produced by joint ventures automatically would be granted MFN treatment; goods exported, but not produced, by joint ventures would not automatically receive the low tariffs granted by MFN.

One amendment, offered by Trade Subcommittee Chairman Sam M. Gibbons, D-Fla., was adopted by voice vote in the full committee. The amendment added to the list of human rights conditions cited in the bill a requirement that China account for any U.S. military personnel taken prisoner during the Korean or Vietnam wars and transferred to China.

### Major Provisions

As approved by the committee, HR 5318 would have:
● Forbidden the president to grant China a Jackson-Vanik waiver for the 12 months beginning July 3, 1993, if the Chinese government had not accounted for and released persons imprisoned or detained as a consequence of the 1989 pro-democracy demonstrations.
● Forbidden the president to grant a Jackson-Vanik waiver if the Chinese government had not made "overall significant progress" in achieving a list of human rights, trade and weapons proliferation reforms.
● Automatically granted MFN treatment to goods produced by joint ventures or by collectively owned or privately owned Chinese enterprises, if a Jackson-Vanik waiver was not in effect for the 12-month period covered by the bill.
● Required the Treasury secretary to maintain a list of state-owned enterprises that would have been ineligible for MFN status, absent a waiver.
● In setting human rights conditions, specified among other things that the Chinese government had to prevent exports of goods made by prison labor, end religious persecution and grant press freedom in China and Tibet, and stop intimidating Chinese citizens in the United States.
● In setting trade conditions, specified among other things that the Chinese government had to protect intellectual property rights and cease unfair trade practices that restricted U.S. commerce.
● In setting weapons proliferation conditions, specified among other things that the Chinese government had to cease activities inconsistent with international control standards on missile technology, and nuclear, chemical and biological weapons. The bill would have prohibited a finding that China was meeting the weapons proliferations standard if it shipped certain missile launchers or nuclear materials to Syria or Iran.

### House Floor Action

Despite stiff opposition from the Bush administration, House members of both parties voted overwhelmingly July 21 for the Pease-Pelosi bill. The vote — 339-62 — was higher than the previous year's tally, when 313 members voted to restrict normal trade with China. The high point of House support for restrictions had come in 1990, when 384 members voted yes. *(Vote 286, p. 70-H)*

To punctuate its opposition to the administration's China policy, the House also voted 258-135 in favor of the resolution (H J Res 502) withdrawing China's MFN status immediately. The vote was considered a symbolic gesture, however; the Senate never took up the measure. *(Vote 285, p. 70-H)*

### Senate Committee Action

The Senate Finance Committee voted 11-9 along party lines Aug. 4 to report a bill restricting trade with China after July 3, 1993, unless the Chinese government began addressing U.S. concerns about human rights, weapons proliferation and the growing trade imbalance between the two countries. The Senate language was virtually identical to the House version of the bill.

John H. Chafee, R-R.I., and Minority Leader Bob Dole, R-Kan., attacked the measure as a political gesture aimed more at embarrassing Bush than pressuring the Chinese government. "It's the opening of the China MFN hunting season in the United States . . . [taking] potshots at George Bush," Dole said. Noting that the Senate had failed in March to override Bush's veto of a similar bill, Chafee asked, "Why are we doing this once again? . . . We know it's not going to go anywhere."

Mitchell returned the GOP fire. "I would suggest this is the annual 'apologize to the Chinese' season," he said. Mitchell conceded, however, that his arguments would not change any votes in committee and, by implication, on the Senate floor.

Opposition to restricting trade with China had historically been stronger in the Senate than in the House, and the bill presumably would not even have made it out of the Finance Committee had Chairman Bentsen not moved to report it without recommendation, a rare procedure.

Trade Subcommittee Chairman Baucus, who opposed limiting trade with China, was not present for the deliberations, but his proxy was cast in favor of the motion to report the bill. Had he voted no, the bill would have died on a tie vote.

Baucus and nine Senate colleagues who had opposed MFN restrictions in the past sent a letter to Bush on July 30 noting that negotiations with the Chinese government appeared to be yielding results in the areas of human rights, weapons proliferation and trade. "At the same time, we must frankly recognize areas in which more can be done," the letter said. But there was no suggestion that the 10 signers, including three other Democrats and Dole, intended to support the latest Senate MFN bill.

### Senate Approves Bill

On Sept. 14, the Senate approved the bill by voice vote. The lack of a roll call left unclear precisely how many votes the measure would have gotten.

An amendment offered by John Kerry, D-Mass., and Robert C. Smith, R-N.H., would have required China to cooperate with the United States in accounting for POWs and MIAs from the Vietnam and Korean wars. It was adopted by voice vote.

Dole temporarily injected some uncertainty into the debate three days later when he announced that he might reverse his position and vote for the MFN restrictions unless Beijing agreed to resume buying U.S. wheat. China, one of the largest importers of U.S. wheat, had vowed to stop wheat purchases completely to retaliate for a decision

announced earlier in the month by Bush to allow the sale of F-16 fighters to Taiwan. Dole, whose home state of Kansas was the leading U.S. wheat producer, had consistently voted against attaching conditions to China's MFN status. But, in a speech to an agriculture trade group, he warned: "If [the Chinese] can't separate the two, maybe MFN isn't that important to them." He added: " And maybe some of us who have supported them the last two or three years will take a walk."

### Final Action

With adjournment approaching, the Senate sent the bill back to the House, which accepted the Senate version and cleared the bill for the president by voice vote on Sept. 22. The swift action was intended to get the measure to Bush in time to prevent him from killing it with a pocket veto.

Bush vetoed the measure on Sept. 28, saying in his veto message that the bill would have posed "unworkable constraints on our bilateral trade" and that the casualties would have included "the dynamic, market-oriented regions of southern China and Hong Kong, as well as those Chinese who support reform and rely on outside contact for support." *(Text, p. 159)*

The House voted 345-74 on Sept. 30 in favor of an override. But the Senate upheld Bush's veto the next day by a vote of 59-40, short of the two-thirds needed to override the president. Dole stuck with Bush and voted no, reportedly after receiving assurances from Chinese officials that their wheat purchases would continue. *(House vote 441, p. 108-H; Senate vote 255, p. 33-S)* ■

# MFN Status Reviewed for Former Soviet Nations

The most-favored-nation (MFN) trade status of several East European countries was also reviewed in 1992. The status allowed greatly reduced tariffs on a country's exports to the United States. Nearly all U.S. trading partners had MFN status, but the Jackson-Vanik amendment to the 1974 Trade Act barred it for communist countries that did not allow free emigration. Congress agreed to grant the trade status to Albania, cut it off with Yugoslavia, and considered but did not pass a bill providing MFN status to Romania.

● **Albania:** On June 16, President Bush sent Congress a trade agreement with Albania, which included MFN treatment.

The House Ways and Means Trade Subcommittee approved MFN for Albania by voice vote July 23. The full committee followed suit July 29. The bill passed the House, also by voice vote, Aug. 3.

The Senate Finance Committee approved an identical bill by voice vote Aug. 4. By voice vote and without debate, the Senate on Aug. 11 cleared the measure (H J Res 507 — H Rept 102-764, S Rept 102-362) for the president, who signed it (PL 102-363) Aug. 26. MFN status was not expected to have a large, immediate impact on trade with Albania since the country was very poor, had few goods that could be sold in this country and little money with which to buy U.S. goods.

● **Romania:** Bush sent a U.S.-Romania trade agreement to Congress on June 22. Romania had had MFN status with the United States until 1988, when the country's government renounced it. At the time, Congress was about to vote to withdraw Romania's MFN status because of charges of religious persecution and other human rights abuses in that country.

The House Ways and Means Trade Subcommittee approved the bill July 23, the same day it considered the Albania measure. Human rights organizations asked the subcommittee to delay action until after elections in Romania, which were scheduled for Sept. 27. But the lawmakers went ahead, saying they would monitor developments to make sure that old-line Communists did not return to power. "The important thing is to give reassurance to the people and to the reformers . . . that they've got support," said Philip M. Crane, R-Ill. The full Ways and Means

Committee approved the bill (H J Res 512 — H Rept 102-870) on July 29.

The Senate Finance Committee approved its version of the measure (S J Res 320 — S Rept 102-454) on Sept. 22 without debate.

The House debated the bill but agreed on Sept. 24 to put off a vote until after the Romanian elections. Ways and Means Chairman Dan Rostenkowsi, D-Ill., urged a prompt vote to make sure there was time to complete the bill before adjournment. He said the Senate would not vote on the measure before Sept. 27. But Tom Lantos, D-Calif., argued that House passage would be considered a "vote of confidence in a regime that still largely depends on the hated . . . secret police to stay in power." Finally, on Sept. 30, the House rejected the measure by a vote of 88-283. Incumbent Romanian President Ion Iliesco, a former high-ranking Communist Party official, had dominated the Sept. 27 election and was expected to win in a runoff. *(Vote 436, p. 106-H)*

● **Yugoslavia.** House Ways and Means gave quick voice vote approval Sept. 16 to a bill to suspend Yugoslavia's MFN status with the United States. Sam M. Gibbons, D-Fla., chairman of the Trade Subcommittee, said that Yugoslavia "doesn't exist anymore" and argued that removing its MFN status would send a signal to the two remaining republics of the former East Bloc country — Serbia and Montenegro — that their support of the Serbians in Bosnia must stop.

Various ethnic factions in the republic of Bosnia-Herzegovina had been fighting a bloody civil war for months. Reports of atrocities committed on both sides — especially by the Serbs — had outraged the international community and led to calls for action against Serbia by members of Congress. Both the House and Senate had passed non-binding resolutions caling on the president and the United Nations to work to end the bloodshed. *(Yugoslavia, p. 532)*

Michael Habib, director of Eastern European Affairs for the State Department, said that while his department believed that MFN "should not be used as a political instrument and MFN should not be withdrawn for political reasons," it did not oppose the bill because U.S. trade with Serbia was negligible.

The bill included a provision to re-establish MFN if the president certified that it would bolster Yugoslavia's compliance with European human rights accords and that Yugoslavia had ended armed conflict with former republics and was respecting their borders.

The committee rejected, 7-20, an attempt by Crane to lift MFN status for Croatia.

The House approved the bill by voice vote Sept. 22.

The Senate approved a nearly identical version of the bill Sept. 30, amending it to insist that to regain MFN status, Serbia or Montenegro must have ceased all support of Serbian forces inside Bosnia-Hercegovina. The House accepted the Senate changes and cleared the bill (HR 5258 — H Rept 102-880) on Oct. 6. Bush signed it (PL 102-420) on Oct. 16. ∎

# House Attempt To Revise Export Controls Fail

Last-minute delaying tactics doomed a three-year push to update U.S. export control laws. Supporters of a bill (HR 3489 — H Rept 102-267) to revise Cold War restrictions on the export of high-technology goods argued that the legislation would boost U.S. trade and allow officials to concentrate enforcement on the most sensitive high-tech exports with military uses.

But, on the last day of the session, three House Republicans objected to provisions to lessen the authority of the secretary of Defense to block exports of high-tech goods that potentially could be used in weapons systems or had other military applications.

The members forced the leadership to abandon its attempts to pass a conference report on the bill by threatening to force a series of time-consuming procedural votes that would have prevented action on other bills for at least three hours — an unacceptable delay given the pressure to finish legislation before adjournment.

## BACKGROUND

The Export Administration Act, whose origins went back to the 1940s, had been used to keep computers and other sophisticated technology with possible military applications out of the hands of the Soviet Union and other potential U.S. enemies. Congress had been struggling for some time to revise these export restrictions, but the leadership had failed repeatedly to get the legislation through Congress.

A bill (HR 4653) to revise export controls cleared Congress in 1990 but was pocket-vetoed by President Bush because of an amendment restricting foreign aid to countries that used chemical weapons or aided others in manufacturing them. Bush did not want his foreign policy authority undermined. *(1990 Almanac, p. 198)*

With no reauthorizing legislation, the export act expired Sept. 30, 1990, and had been administered since that time by Bush under emergency powers.

With the disintegration of the Soviet bloc, the 17-nation Coordinating Committee on Multilateral Export Controls (Cocom), which included most NATO countries plus Japan and Australia, had agreed to greatly relax controls on many exports to countries that had been part of the former communist bloc.

Under the legislation introduced in the 102nd Congress (HR 3489), exporters would no longer have had to get licenses to ship high-tech goods to Japan, Australia and Western Europe. The bill also would have relaxed many controls on exports to Eastern Europe and the countries that made up the former Soviet Union. It also would have allowed export of most telecommunications equipment and certain software to the countries of the former Soviet Union.

The bulk of the legislative work on the bill was completed in 1991, with House passage of HR 3489 by voice vote Nov. 30.

Earlier in the year, on Feb. 20, the Senate had passed by voice a measure (S 320) that was virtually identical to the conference report that Bush had rejected in 1990. There was no conference action on the two bills before the session ended. Instead, the House returned S 320 to the Senate stamped "unconstitutional." The culprit was the provision imposing higher tariffs on countries and companies that contributed to the spread of chemical and biological weapons and of ballistic missiles. The change would have raised revenue, and such provisions must originate in the House. In the end, the chemical weapons sanctions were passed separately as part of an unrelated trade bill (HR 1724 — PL 102-182), but time ran out before the Senate could take up the export control measure again. *(1991 Almanac, p. 128)*

## LEGISLATIVE ACTION

The Senate moved quickly in 1992 and approved HR 3489 by voice vote on Jan. 22 with an amendment and sent it to conference.

At that time, the administration was still opposed to the House version of the bill. The administration objected to provisions that would have made it easier to sell telecommunications equipment to the Soviet Union, lifted controls on certain mass-marketed software and required U.S. sanctions against countries and foreign companies that exported nuclear-related goods.

The Senate version won the support of the Bush administration after Senate Democrats removed the provisions requiring sanctions against countries and foreign companies that contributed to the spread of nuclear weapons. Provisions toughening sanctions against nuclear proliferation but allowing the president final discretion were left in the bill.

On June 3, the House named conferees, but the conference report was not filed until Oct. 5. The following day, the last day of the session, three House Republicans — Duncan Hunter of California, Jon Kyl of Arizona and John R. Kasich of Ohio — successfully blocked House passage of the conference report.

Hunter, Kyl and Kasich disliked provisions that would have given the Commerce Department more control over export licensing decisions, blaming the agency for Iraq's military buildup before the Gulf War. *(Iraq, p. 545)*

The Senate approved the conference report by voice vote Oct. 8, but the House was already gone.

The final bill would have provided for the removal of controls on all exports to and from Cocom member countries and set criteria for easing restrictions on exports to countries still subject to Cocom export controls. It would have required the United States to implement Cocom agreements reached in June 1992 on exports of telecommunications equipment for civil uses and urged further liberalization of such controls. The bill would have restricted the sale of dual-use equipment and technology to terrorist countries and provided stricter sanctions against nuclear proliferation while allowing the president final discretion. ∎

# Minivan Import Tariffs Remain Unchanged

A measure to raise the import tariffs on four-door minivans to 25 percent faltered in 1992. Although the measure — included in a wide-ranging tariff bill (HR 4318) — passed the House in July, an attempt in the Senate to add similar language to the urban aid tax bill (HR 11) was defeated.

Backers of the tariff hike said that classifying minivans as passenger vehicles allowed Japanese carmakers to export them to the United States and pay only a 2.5 percent tariff. Arguing that minivans had many of the characteristics of trucks and cargo vehicles, supporters had hoped to reclassify the multipurpose vehicles as trucks, which would have boosted the U.S. tariff to 25 percent.

## BACKGROUND

The conflict over the classification began in 1989, when the U.S. Customs Service ruled that minivans were properly considered trucks. Six months later the Treasury Department overturned the Customs decision and ruled that any multipurpose vehicle (MPV) with two doors could be considered a truck, but that four-door minivans and other MPVs were properly classified as passenger cars for tariff purposes.

Minivans and other MPVs made up a $9 billion market for automobile manufacturers in 1992, with U.S. manufacturers such as Chrysler, General Motors and Ford controlling 88 percent of that market. The minivans, which were treated as trucks by the Environmental Protection Agency and the Transportation Department, had to meet less stringent emissions and fuel economy standards than passenger cars. However, the minivans were widely used as passenger vehicles, serving as the station wagon of the 1990s and widely marketed to families.

The push for changing the Treasury Department decision and forcing four-door minivans to be treated as trucks for tariff purposes mainly came from the Michigan delegation. On the House side, Sander M. Levin, D-Mich., successfully amended a tariff bill to include the change, and in the Senate, Donald W. Riegle, D-Mich., argued for amending the urban tax bill with similar language.

Opponents characterized the measures as costly for consumers, estimating that the price of minivans would rise between $4,000 and $6,000 per vehicle.

## LEGISLATIVE ACTION

The provisions to raise the minivan tariff first popped up as an amendment to HR 4318, a bill sponsored by Rep. Sam M. Gibbons, D-Fla., to make nearly 400 modifications to the U.S. tariff schedule, including removing the tariffs on a number of items. Levin successfully pushed an amendment to reclassify minivans and other multipurpose vehicles as trucks. The additional revenue raised by the subsequent tariff increases was to be used to offset losses incurred under the new tariff structure proposed in the bill. Finding revenue increases to mitigate drops in tariff rates was necessary under the pay-as-you-go rules of the 1990 budget agreement. *(1990 Almanac, p. 161)*

The Gibbons tariff restructuring bill was approved by the House Ways and Means Committee on June 24. Levin told colleagues that the provision would eliminate an anomaly in U.S. law: The Customs Service classified minivans as passenger vehicles, making them eligible for the low 2.5 percent tariff applied to most imported passenger vehicles.

Critics of the amendment called the move protectionist, but members approved it by a vote of 24-12. Bill Thomas, R-Calif., denounced the provision as an attempt by the U.S. automobile manufacturers "to curb a rapidly growing market" in the United States for Japanese minivans.

Bush administration officials also protested the minivan provision, which they said could hurt consumers by allowing U.S. auto manufacturers to raise the prices of their minivans. The provision could also violate "the spirit" of U.S. obligations under the General Agreement on Tariffs and Trade (GATT), the multilateral accord governing world trade, officials said.

Saying he opposed the provision "with all the depth I have in me," Ways and Means Trade Subcommittee Chairman Gibbons dismissed Levin's suggestion that the higher tariff would raise revenue. "This amendment, by increasing the tariff to an outrageous level, will prohibit the importation of all these vehicles. So the Treasury will not get one cent."

The amendment language made exceptions for vehicles imported from countries that sold fewer than 10,000 units, a move to allow minivan imports from Britain and Germany to continue.

The committee action came on the same day that the International Trade Commission found that imported minivans sold by Toyota and Mazda did not harm Detroit's Big Three automakers. The commission's finding meant that Japanese minivans would not be slapped with anti-dumping duties that could have raised their price by more than $2,000.

On July 31, the House passed the bill by a vote of 273-112, with supporters characterizing the change as protecting U.S. workers' jobs. *(Vote 357, p. 88-H)*

But opponents said it would unfairly single out Japanese carmakers in violation of international trade agreements, and they argued that President Bush would certainly veto the bill. They also said that there was a danger that Japan would retaliate by increasing tariffs on U.S. exports to Japan.

### Defeated on Tax Bill

The only significant action on the Senate side came Sept. 26, when Riegle proposed a minivan amendment to HR 11 — the tax bill that Bush later vetoed. *(Urban aid tax bill, p. 140)*

Riegle's provisions were similar to the Levin amendment to HR 4318 but were expressed as a sense of the Senate resolution rather than a statutory change in the Customs Service rules. The Riegle Amendment was rejected 36-37. *(Vote 245, p. 32-S)* ∎

# House, Senate Unreconciled On Funding Trade Agencies

Although both chambers independently passed a bill (S 2880) to reauthorize various trade agencies, the two versions remained unreconciled at the end of the session, and the bill died. The agencies were the Office of the United States Trade Representative (USTR), the United States International Trade Commission (ITC) and the United States Customs Service.

As drawn up by the Senate, the bill was considered a straightforward, two-year reauthorization of the trade agencies. But on the House floor, an amendment was added that would have meant significant changes in the U.S. Customs Service.

### Senate Action

The Senate Finance Committee on June 11 gave voice vote approval to S 2880 (S Rept 102-302), which would have reauthorized the three federal agencies with responsibility for trade. The Senate passed the measure, also by voice vote, Sept. 9.

Under the measure, Congress would have authorized $1.5 billion for the Customs Service during fiscal 1993 and 1994. The amount represented an increase of more than 16 percent over what was appropriated for fiscal 1992.

The USTR would have been reauthorized through 1994. In fiscal 1993, the agency would have received a budget of $21.7 million, which was 6.4 percent more than it got in fiscal 1992. The ITC, which also would have been reauthorized for two more years, would have received $45.2 million in fiscal 1993, also a 6.4 percent increase.

### House Action

In the House, the Ways and Means Committee did not act on the bill. Committee Chairman Dan Rostenkowski, D-Ill., amended the bill with a substitute on the House floor.

The substitute was agreed to by voice vote. It contained the trade agency authorizations as well as an amendment to modernize the U.S. Customs Service.

The language to update the Customs Service previously passed the House as part of the conference report on a tax bill, HR 11. *(Urban aid tax bill, p. 140)*

The provisions were an attempt to improve customs operations by aiding the processing of imported merchandise, increasing penalties for non-compliance with customs laws and providing the trade community with greater certainty concerning customs rules and regulations.

The House passed its amended version of S 2880 by voice vote Oct. 6. No conference was called during the waning hours of the session, and the bill died with the October adjournment.

# Two Attempts To Update Customs Procedures Fail

Efforts to pass legislation modernizing U.S. customs operations and permitting companies to file electronically much of the information necessary to clear goods through ports of entry were unsuccessful in the 102nd Congress.

The customs provisions were included in a major tax bill (HR 11 — H Rept 102-1034), which passed the House on Oct. 6 and was cleared by the Senate on Oct. 8. But President Bush vetoed the legislation. The House also approved customs provisions as part of broader trade legislation (HR 5100 — H Rept 102-607), which was never taken up by the Senate and died at the end of the Congress. *(Urban aid tax bill, p. 140; trade expansion act, p. 152)*

After lobbying by the U.S. Customs Service and business groups, who were worried that the changes would die as a result of other trade and tax disputes, the Senate Finance Committee decided to mark up a stand-alone customs bill (HR 5643), which was approved by voice vote Sept. 22.

Electronic filing of customs information was controversial because smaller brokers who handled such duties for importers feared that it would require them to make costly investments in new equipment. Large importers and brokerage companies would be able to employ electronic filing more readily, critics said.

In response, Finance Committee Chairman Lloyd Bentsen, D-Texas, agreed to phase in the new service over seven years and to allow electronic filing only on documents

required for entry. Other required documents, such as filings to the Food and Drug Administration, still would have to be submitted by hand.

The bill sought to toughen penalties against importers who failed to submit accurate information, authorize the Customs Service to use private laboratories to test and analyze merchandise, and allow private collection agencies to recover money owed to the federal government under customs laws. The bill would have required customs officials to board a sufficient number of vessels to ensure compliance with U.S. laws.

With the sessions nearing an end, the bill was held up by the threat of pending amendments from several top Democrats.

Senate Majority Leader George J. Mitchell, D-Maine, hoped to offer an amendment reimposing duties on imports of footwear from countries given special treatment by the Caribbean Basin Initiative (CBI). And Max Baucus, D-Mont., said he might seek to attach a bill that would give industries the right to petition the U.S. Trade Representative (USTR) if they believed a foreign country was not abiding by the terms of a trade agreement with the United States.

Bentsen pleaded with his colleagues not to offer their amendments, saying they would add unrelated provisions and prompt other lawmakers to do the same.

"If we start putting on amendments that are not germane . . . then the word is out: 'We've got ourselves a trade bill,'" Bentsen said.

"My concern is that we're going to load this thing down and we'll have no bill at all."

Bentsen's fears were borne out, and the bill died. ∎

# President Signs Measure Reauthorizing OPIC

Congress cleared legislation (HR 4996) to reauthorize the Overseas Private Investment Corporation (OPIC), an agency that provided insurance, loans and loan guarantees to assist U.S. businesses investing abroad. President Bush signed HR 4996 on Oct. 28 (PL 102-549).

Although an earlier House-passed version would have provided a more ambitious revamp of the organization charter, during the last weeks of the session conferees decided to put off questions about overhauling the agency charter.

The final bill earmarked funds for additional export promotion and required companies receiving OPIC assistance to abide by child labor laws and occupational safety and health standards. The legislation also authorized spending for the U.S. Trade and Development Program, which promoted export programs to developing countries. In addition, under the new law, the administration was allowed to reduce certain loan repayments from countries involved in the Enterprise for the Americas Initiative.

## BACKGROUND

OPIC was a self-financed organization with expenses paid for through fees and insurance premiums.

Legislation was introduced in April, with an emphasis on the job-creation aspects of export enhancement. At a time when the U.S. unemployment rate stood at 7.5 percent, sponsors estimated that the bill would generate at least 120,000 jobs each year; they said that in 1991, OPIC helped to create 13,000 U.S. jobs.

The thrust of the bill was to update OPIC's original language and eliminate outdated programs, as well as provide funding for other export programs, including the Trade and Development Agency. The major sticking point was an argument over whether the reauthorization should be for three years or five years. The final bill reauthorized OPIC for only two years.

OPIC's authorization expired on Sept. 30, 1992.

The bill had support from business groups, who argued that export enhancement was the best way for them to compete abroad with Japan and Germany.

## LEGISLATIVE ACTION

The House Foreign Affairs Committee reported HR 4996 on June 5, and members began floor debate June 17. But consideration of amendments and the final vote on the bill were delayed until later in the summer. During the June 17 debate, the bill received bipartisan support, with Republican members praising the legislation for its goal of expanding markets abroad for U.S. goods and services.

The House approved the bill by voice vote Aug. 5.

Lawmakers rejected by voice vote an amendment by Robert E. Andrews, D-N.J., to abolish OPIC within six months, transferring its responsibilities to the Office of Management and Budget.

In the only roll call vote, members rejected, 184-230, an amendment that would have eliminated a provision recommending that the administration transfer additional money to the capital projects office in the Agency for International Development (AID). *(Vote 367, p. 90-H)*

Amendment sponsor John Miller, R-Wash., argued that

assistance for capital projects was the least effective form of foreign aid and that AID was incapable of managing the program efficiently. But Sam Gejdenson, D-Conn., chairman of the House Foreign Affairs Subcommittee on International Economic Policy and Trade and the bill's principal sponsor, stressed that the aid would be more effective if tied to projects that required recipients to buy U.S. exports wherever possible. Other defenders said the money would be better used in capital projects than in the three programs from which it was to be transferred — economic support funds, multilateral aid to the Philippines and the Support for East European Democracy program. They also argued that the United States was far behind international competitors such as Japan and Europe in the use of "tied aid," which linked U.S. aid to purchases of U.S. goods and services.

The Senate on Oct. 1 gave voice vote approval to its version of the bill after substituting language (S 3294) reauthorizing the agency through 1993 with no changes. The Senate bill also stripped out much of the House language expanding other export programs.

House aides were skeptical that conferees would have time during the rush of last minute business to hash out program changes outlined in HR 4996. But as the end of the session approached, House and Senate staff members completed work on the bill.

The final bill reauthorized OPIC for two years; a number of other export-promoting programs were expanded, with a two-year total of $120 million for these programs. Much of the original House bill dealing with export promotion was included in the conference report.

In response to news reports alleging that some AID export programs provided incentives for U.S. companies to move abroad, language was added to the bill to prohibit the use of the funds for programs that encouraged companies to move facilities overseas if U.S. workers would be displaced.

"This language will promote the export of U.S. commodities — not U.S. jobs," said Gejdenson.

The House passed the conference report Oct. 5 by unanimous consent; the Senate cleared it by voice vote at the

---

## BOXSCORE

➡ **Reauthorization of the Overseas Private Investment Corporation (HR 4996, S 3294).** The bill reauthorized OPIC for two years, putting some additional restrictions on companies applying for aid. The legislation also expanded a number of other export-promotion programs, including the Trade and Development Agency. It provided grants for capital projects operated through the Agency for International Development that used U.S. goods and services.

**Reports:** H Rept 102-551; conference report H Rept 102-1026.

### KEY ACTION

Aug. 5 — The **House** passed HR 4996 by voice vote.

Oct. 1 — The **Senate** passed HR 4996 by voice vote.

Oct. 5 — The **House** adopted conference report.

Oct. 8 — The **Senate** cleared conference report.

Oct. 28 — President Bush signed HR 4996 — PL 102-549.

end of the session on Oct. 8.

**Provisions**

The final two-year reauthorization did not alter OPIC's charter, but included most of the substantive provisions in the House bill. The bill required companies receiving OPIC assistance to abide by child labor and worker health and safety laws and dropped language that might have excluded the nations of the former Soviet Union from participating in the export programs.

The legislation also:

● Authorized $55 million for fiscal 1993 and $65 million for fiscal 1994 for the Trade and Development Agency to provide funds for feasibility studies of development programs.

● Allowed the Department of Commerce to develop Commercial Centers in the independent states of the former Soviet Union or in the developing countries of Asia, Latin America and Africa. The Commercial Centers were to provide information on U.S. exporters and to facilitate U.S. export expansion into these markets.

● Authorized the Enterprise for the Americas Initiative, which established the criteria which Latin American and Caribbean countries had to meet to qualify for debt reduction benefits. ■

# Ex-Im Bank Reauthorized For Five Years

Congress approved a five-year reauthorization for the Export-Import Bank — a federal agency that provided market-rate loans and loan guarantees to foreign countries buying U.S.-made goods and services. The legislation (HR 5739) included a three-year reauthorization of the Ex-Im Bank's so-called tied-aid war chest, which allowed the agency to provide low-interest credits on the condition that the money be used to buy U.S. products.

President Bush signed the bill Oct. 21 — PL 102-429.

Also included in the cleared legislation was language to increase the ceiling for total financing, increase assistance to small and medium-sized export companies and ease repayment conditions to countries involved in the Enterprise for the Americas Initiative.

## BACKGROUND

Authorization for the Ex-Im Bank, which helped finance overseas purchases of U.S.-made goods, expired on Sept. 30, 1992. The reauthorization extended operations through fiscal 1997.

The Ex-Im Bank facilitated about $4 billion in export credits a year and guaranteed another $5 billion in export credits.

The tied-aid war chest was created to combat the use of similar financing deals by other countries, in particular Japan and France. Under tied-aid agreements, the United States provided low-interest loans to developing countries on the condition that the money be used to buy U.S. products.

In February, the Organization for Economic Cooperation and Development (OECD) passed regulations restricting the use of tied aid. However, when debating the reauthorization, supporters of the war chest argued that continued funding would allow Ex-Im Bank authorities to monitor loopholes in the OECD restrictions.

## LEGISLATIVE ACTION

The Senate Banking Committee approved the reauthorization (S 2864) June 18.

Paul S. Sarbanes, D-Md., chairman of the panel's International Finance and Monetary Policy Subcommittee, expressed concern that the OECD agreement would prevent the Ex-Im Bank from countering tied-aid practices by U.S. competitors, so he included language in the measure that would allow the agency to offer tied-aid deals to countries if they were in the United States' economic interest.

On July 30, the International Development Subcommittee of the House Banking Committee gave voice-vote approval to a five-year extension of the Ex-Im Bank's charter. The House bill extended the bank's tied-aid war chest for five years at an authorization level of $500 million a year. The House subcommittee also agreed by voice vote to nine amendments, including one by Jim Leach, R-Iowa, authorizing forgiveness of some Ex-Im Bank loans to Latin American countries as part of the administration's Enterprise for the Americas Initiative.

The full House took up the bill Aug. 4 and approved it by voice vote. Supporters cited statistics that showed that between 1985 and 1991, the dollar value of U.S. export doubled from $219 billion to $412 billion. In 1991, they said, the value of the Ex-Im Bank-assisted exports rose by nearly 30 percent.

The Senate approved an amended version of HR 5739 by voice vote on Aug. 12. The Senate bill extended the Ex-Im Bank's tied-aid war chest for three years. Like the House version, the bill allowed the Ex-Im Bank to sell or reduce some loans to some Latin American countries as part of the Enterprise for the Americas Initiative.

The House adopted a conference report (HR 102-1010) drafted by staff members by a vote of 332-44 on Oct. 5; the Senate cleared the report by voice vote on Oct. 8. In the final version, members decided on a three-year extension of the tied-aid set aside. *(Vote 483, pg. 118-H)* ■

# Law Enacted To Help Ease Latin American Debt

Legislation (HR 4059 — H Rept 102-667) to ease the debt burden on Mexico and several other Latin American and Caribbean countries as part of President Bush's Enterprise for the Americas initiative passed the House by voice vote on Oct. 2 and cleared the Senate Oct. 7, also by voice vote.

Bush signed the measure on Oct. 27 — PL 102-532.

The Enterprise for the Americas was aimed at promoting economic growth and political stability in Latin America and the Caribbean.

In addition to debt reduction, the initiative sought to promote trade and investment.

HR 4059 allowed the countries involved in the initiative to reduce their debt burdens by buying back some of the debt they owed the Commodity Credit Corporation (CCC).

The countries could repurchase their debt on advantageous terms, but they had to commit 40 percent of the

money they saved for environmental restoration and development projects.

Bill sponsor and House Agriculture Committee Chairman E. "Kika" de la Garza, D-Texas, said the measure was a "win-win" situation for the United States and its Latin neighbors. The United States would divest itself of about $500 million out of $1.4 billion in risk-laden debt owed to the CCC. This would also free foreign exchange money to allow the Latin countries to purchase additional U.S. foodstuffs.

In addition to easing their debt burdens, the countries also were to benefit from the local projects.

One aim of the bill was to fund environmental cleanup projects along the Mexican border. An industrial and population boom in Mexico had led to an increase along the border in air pollution, hazardous waste and sewage. Mexico was to be allowed to restructure $350 million in debt, which was expected to translate into about $30 million to $40 million for the environment. The bill also established a U.S.-Mexico Environmental Board to determine what border projects were especially needed.

In separate legislation (HR 5739 — HR 102-1010), Congress allowed the Export-Import Bank to forgive, sell or reduce some Ex-Im Bank loans to Latin American countries. And, as part of a bill (HR 4996 — H Rept 102-1026) to reauthorize the Overseas Private Investment Corporation (OPIC), lawmakers provided debt relief for Latin American countries that had received certain concessional loans. (Export-Import bank, p. 166; OPIC, p. 165)

**Committee Action**

The House Agriculture Committee approved the bill by voice vote on June 30. The committee bill sought to expand existing debt-relief provisions of the Enterprise for the Americas Initiative.

Mexico and eight other Latin nations were to be permitted to buy back 40 percent of their export credits owed to the CCC as of Jan. 1, 1991, if they devoted an equivalent amount of their own currencies to environmental projects. Export credits owed to the United States typically were repaid in dollars, which were a scarce commodity for these countries.

According to sponsor de la Garza, the nine countries owed about $1.45 billion in agriculture credits to the United States; about $580 million of that could be eliminated through the program.

The remaining debt was to be paid off, with interest, under a renegotiated schedule. Money for the debt relief would be appropriated separately.

Although the CCC was to forgo payment on up to 40 percent of the principal amount of the debt, de la Garza said the United States still stood to benefit.

"This bill provides a way ... to get a portion of this debt repaid ahead of schedule.... This kind of debt-for-environment swap is a win-win for all involved," de la Garza said.

The House Foreign Affairs Committee weighed in on Aug. 5 and expanded the scope of the bill to make concessional loans from the State Department's Economic Support Fund and Developmental Assistance programs eligible for principal reduction, renegotiation or other debt relief.

A version of the latter provisions was enacted as part of the OPIC reauthorization bill. ■

# Clinton Economic Summit Held in Little Rock

President-elect Bill Clinton took an early stab at the nation's deficit-ridden and recessionary economy by holding an economic conference Dec. 14-15 in Little Rock with more than 300 economists and business and labor leaders.

The economic meeting sent a signal throughout the country that Clinton was serious about addressing the No. 1 domestic problem.

However, the real problems were not expected to surface until Clinton put on paper a specific plan to cut existing government programs or raise taxes to finance other spending.

Clinton said he would not decide on the size and makeup of his economic package until the very last minute, in part to determine whether early signs of an economic recovery continued.

If they did, a smaller stimulus package could be required, he said.

Unemployment and inflation went down the last few months of 1992, while output, productivity and consumer confidence finally took an upward turn.

Many economists wondered whether federal pump-priming was the answer. Indeed, some economists believed that the billions it would add to the federal deficit would do more serious harm than good to the apparent recovery.

During the two-day economic conference, experts differed over the relative need to stimulate the economy compared with the need to make progress reducing the deficit.

However, in an interview published in The Wall Street Journal on Dec. 18, Clinton appeared to be trying to ease concerns that he would not give deficit reduction as high a priority as his plans to boost investment and spur economic growth.

According to the Journal, Clinton said that if push came to shove, his "inclination would be to increase spending less" rather than scale back his proposal to reduce the federal deficit by half over the next four years.

While the extraordinary economic sessions in Little Rock yielded few new insights into Clinton's economic plans, they presented the picture of an engaged president-elect with an unusually detailed knowledge of the issues.

Clinton and Vice President-elect Al Gore chaired the roundtable discussion for nearly 20 hours, asking numerous detailed questions about the economy and taking calls from viewers and listeners from across the country.

"I think that what happened in the last two days at least demonstrated to the people who were here, and I hope to the rest of the American people, that while our administration doesn't have all the answers and maybe never will, we're working hard on the problems," Clinton said after the sessions ended.

# Chapter 3

# GOVERNMENT/ COMMERCE

# Hill Enacts Cable TV Law Over Veto

## End-of-session action yields the only veto override of Bush's four years in office

Before adjourning for the year, Congress handed President Bush his first veto override by enacting a bill to rein in cable television rates. The drama of the veto battle overshadowed the only large-scale reregulation of an industry in the Reagan-Bush era.

Since it was deregulated from local control by Congress in 1984, the cable industry had grown into a $20 billion communications monolith serving 56 million subscribers, or about 60 percent of all homes with television. Along with the boom in cable programming, however, came complaints of poor customer service, discriminatory business practices keeping competitors from purchasing cable programming at fair prices, and — most of all — subscriber price increases of 61 percent since 1987, or three times the inflation rate.

Would-be competitors to cable, such as the home satellite dish and microwave "wireless" cable industries, also complained that the cable industry charged them up to 500 percent more than cable operators paid for the same programs, on terms that effectively kept many cable programs out of competitors' reach.

The bill was a major setback for the cable industry, which agreed with Bush administration claims that the measure would make cable rates rise, not fall. But it was a boon for broadcasters, who would be able to earn revenues from cable operators who retransmitted over-the-air local television programs. Hollywood sided with the cable industry in opposing the bill. Film producers objected that the bill gave broadcasters, but not them, a slice of the new revenues from the cable industry.

The new cable law aimed to control further rate increases until more competition developed in the cable industry. It required that nearly all of the nation's 11,000 cable operators bow to the mandates of the Federal Communications Commission (FCC) in the pricing of basic cable viewing packages and equipment rentals. Those who produced and sold cable's popular programming, including MTV, Nickelodeon and ESPN, would be required to offer their programs to cable's competitors at fair prices, terms and conditions.

Broadcasters, who since 1965 had been required by the FCC to give their programs to local cable systems to retransmit for free, were permitted to charge cable operators

---

## BOXSCORE

➡ **Cable Reregulation (S12, HR 4850).** Legislation to impose new rate and service regulations on the cable television industry. It was the only bill to be enacted over a veto by President Bush.

**Reports:** H Rept 102-628; S Rept 102-92; conference report H Rept 102-862.

### KEY ACTION

Jan. 31 — The **Senate** passed S 12, 73-18.

July 23 — The **House** passed HR 4850, 340-73.

Sept. 17 — The **House** adopted the conference report, 280-128.

Sept. 22 — The **Senate** adopted the conference report, 74-25.

Oct. 3 — President Bush vetoed S 12.

Oct. 5 — The **Senate** overrode the veto, 74-25. The **House** enacted S 12 — PL 102-385 over the veto, 308-114.

---

for the use of their programs. But station owners who feared being dropped by the local cable company also could forfeit that right and instead force cable operators to transmit their signals for free.

Even after the bill became law, the cable industry did not stop fighting the legislation. Turner Broadcasting System and Daniels Cablevision Inc., two of the most prominent cable programmers and system operators, filed suit against it. Among other claims, the suits alleged that cable operators' First Amendment rights were being infringed upon by the law's requirement that they must carry broadcast programs. Other cable systems and programmers also challenged additional provisions regarding access to cable programs and rate regulation. The suits were pending in federal court at year's end.

### BACKGROUND

That the Democratic-controlled Congress denied Bush a perfect veto record — a rarity in modern times — took on heightened importance at a time when the president was struggling to gain ground against Democratic presidential challenger Bill Clinton. It was the White House, after all, that stressed loyalty to the president as the main reason why Republicans should switch their cable bill votes.

"On this particular bill [Bush] had very little to trade with, other than loyalty to the party and loyalty to him. And he didn't get it," said James A. Thurber, director of the Center for Congressional and Presidential Studies at American University.

For bill supporters, the victory was sweet. Not only did it cap four years of efforts to bring rate relief to consumers, it also vindicated a risky strategy of courting the support of the broadcasting industry to push the regulatory measure through Congress.

Sponsors learned in 1990 that consumer groups alone could not win a battle against the cable industry. In that year, cable lobbyists and the Bush administration allied to kill a bill to reregulate the industry.

As the 102nd Congress got under way, bill supporters knew they had to broaden the appeal of the measure. Their answer was to recruit the lobbying clout of the National Association of Broadcasters — which for years had worked in concert with the Reagan and Bush administrations to

deregulate the broadcast industry.

To win broadcasters' support, sponsors agreed to include the so-called retransmission consent provision that allowed local television stations to negotiate with cable operators for permission to retransmit over-the-air signals. Local television stations had long complained that the cable industry made its billions largely by transmitting its broadcast signals for free. They argued that cable's three revenue sources — subscriptions, advertising and pay-per-view events — siphoned programs and advertising from over-the-air broadcasting, a service that remained free to viewers.

But the provision appeared contrary to the bill's goal of lowering cable rates. It also drew fire from Hollywood, because film studios that created broadcast programs would get none of the revenues directly.

Even Gene Kimmelman, the legislative director of the Consumer Federation of America who helped recruit broadcasters' support, had fears early on that cable operators would pass any fees directly on to consumers in the form of higher cable rates.

Opponents of the cable bill said the sponsors "made a pact with the devil" to ensure support for the legislation. But Kimmelman defended the strategy on grounds that the bill likely would have stalled without the clout of local broadcasters.

"It was a deal with the devil that I think was not a bad deal," he said. "The only way you win on this kind of an issue is if you've got enough muscle on your side. We had the perfect combination of rural, urban, consumers and broadcasters. And it still wasn't easy."

Broadcasters also brought with them another potent lobbying force: labor unions. Because most local television stations were union-run, unlike most cable systems, labor helped to shore up Democratic votes while well-heeled broadcast station owners kept Republicans in line.

In the end, proponents of reregulation credited the power of the issue itself. Lawmakers realized that constituents felt much the same way about television as they did about roads, schools and parks.

Just as Norman F. Lent, R-N.Y., was trying to persuade House lawmakers during the override debate that cable television was not a crucial public utility, several of his colleagues were huddled around a television set in the men's lounge off the House floor, watching the Monday Night Football game — a broadcast program — over the chamber's private cable system.

"Sometimes 60 million people wielding clickers in their living rooms are more powerful than a president wielding a veto pen," said Edward J. Markey, D-Mass., sponsor of the House bill.

## 1991 Action

The Senate Commerce, Science and Transportation Committee on May 14, 1991, approved a cable reregulation bill by John C. Danforth, R-Mo.

As promised by Danforth, the measure came down harder on the cable industry than an earlier effort in 1990 that was killed at the end of the 101st Congress amid opposition from the cable lobby and the Bush administration. The bill was approved by a vote of 16-3. *(1991 Almanac, p. 158; 1990 Almanac, p. 370)*

Like the 1990 effort, it would allow local governments and the FCC to regulate rates for basic cable service in areas where cable operators lacked effective competition. But the threshold of what constituted effective competition

was raised: Rather than requiring a certain number of broadcast outlets to be available in any market area, the bill declared that competition would exist only if another multichannel provider, such as satellite or wireless cable, also was available. The bill also took steps to dissuade cable operators from shifting popular programs away from the regulated basic package.

Critics of the bill, during and after the markup, said the panel should delay moving the measure until the FCC completed its redefinition of which cable operators faced effective competition, and were thus exempt from federal regulation.

On June 13, the agency tightened its standard by declaring cable operators free from regulation if the local area received six over-the-air broadcast stations — the previous rule required only three stations be available. The move boosted the percentage of cable systems that faced regulation from 3 percent to 60 percent of the nation's 11,000 systems. But the ruling did little to slow the momentum of the bill.

Because of the bill's harsher regulatory regime, opposition from the cable lobby and the Bush administration was even more intense than in 1990.

Perhaps most vexing to the cable industry were provisions aimed at curbing the consolidation of cable operators and programmers and those that would ban cable programmers affiliated with operators from unreasonably refusing to deal with competitors.

Under the Senate bill, the FCC would limit the number of subscribers that a cable company could reach nationwide, and programmers would be prevented from discriminating in the price and terms of their programs to impede competition.

### Retransmission Consent Lures Broadcasters

But an amendment to the bill, offered by Communications Subcommittee Chairman Daniel K. Inouye, D-Hawaii, to assure the support of the powerful broadcast lobby, provided the best ammunition for cable industry opposition. Approved by the panel by a voice vote, Inouye's "retransmission consent" provision sought to give financial relief to television broadcasters who had been hurt by cable's burgeoning popularity.

The amendment sought to allow broadcasters to negotiate with cable operators for the rights to retransmit their broadcast signal for a fee, at the risk of being dropped by cable operators reluctant to pay. Compensation could be in the form of cash but also could be negotiated in other forms such as promotional or advertising rights. Broadcasters that lacked such bargaining power with the local cable operator, such as smaller UHF channels, could forfeit that option and simply force cable operators to carry their signal free of charge.

The FCC in 1965 required cable systems to carry local stations as a way to help the then-burgeoning cable industry gain in the marketplace. Broadcasters argued during the reregulation debate that the cable industry no longer deserved such a privilege and should be charged for use of over-the-air signals.

The compensation option was high on the more powerful broadcasters' wish lists. But the so-called "must carry" option also was demanded by smaller, independent stations.

Inouye's effort was an attempt to please both factions, though the must-carry requirements had been thrown out by two federal courts in 1985 and 1987 on grounds that

they violated cable programmers' First Amendment rights to carry only programs of their choice.

The cable industry threatened that any broadcasters' fees would be passed on to consumers through higher rates. And it questioned the legality of the must-carry option. Inouye's amendment also caused the Hollywood film industry to get involved opposing the legislation, on grounds that studios would not receive a cut of any new revenues gleaned for broadcasters who transmitted their programs.

It would be another year, however, before the retransmission consent battle would be joined in earnest in the House. In the meantime, the Senate Commerce Committee focused on getting its bill to the floor quickly and with little debate.

## SENATE FLOOR ACTION

The Senate moved quickly in 1992 and on Jan. 31 overwhelmingly passed its cable reregulation bill by a vote of 73-18, after rejecting a weaker substitute measure by a vote of 35-54. (Vote 14, p. 3-S)

The substitute, which was offered Jan. 30 by Bob Packwood, R-Ore.; Ted Stevens, R-Alaska; and John Kerry, D-Mass., attempted to weaken the regulatory provisions of the bill. It would have eliminated language aimed at giving cable competitors better access to cable programs and contained no limits on cable system ownership. (Vote 13, p. 3-S)

The cable industry's lobbying effort against the bill never quite caught its stride. A memo revealing the industry's lobbying strategy, written by National Cable Television Association President James P. Mooney, was leaked to the media. The memo indicated that the substitute was viewed by the trade group mainly as a way to steer votes away from the main cable bill, rather than as a legitimate compromise. The memo urged the group's members to lobby against even the Packwood substitute should it pass.

The disclosure allowed Danforth to attack the substitute as a lobbying ploy.

A Jan. 27 White House statement opposing the cable bill further weakened prospects for the substitute. It warned of a veto of the main cable bill but did not explicitly favor the substitute. The statement said the Bush administration opposed the reregulatory provisions of the cable bill and instead wanted telephone companies to be allowed to enter the cable TV business to spur competition.

Though the substitute was rejected, sponsors agreed to add two of its provisions to the main bill to encourage administration support. One would prohibit local governments from awarding exclusive cable franchises. A second would broaden an exemption to a 1984 ban on telephone company entry into the cable business by allowing rural phone companies in areas with populations of 10,000 or less to offer cable services. The latter provision would later be dropped from the bill in conference committee.

Other amendments included one by John B. Breaux, D-La., that would require the FCC to study home shopping broadcast channels, and, by voice vote, one by Patrick J. Leahy, D-Vt., that would ensure that cable systems were compatible with all TV sets and videocassette recorders. (Vote 10, p. 3-S)

An amendment by Jesse Helms, R-N.C., approved 95-0, would allow cable operators to ban pornographic programs and require operators to place such shows on one channel available upon subscriber request. (Vote 12, p. 3-S)

Another amendment, offered by Wyche Fowler Jr., D-Ga., and approved by voice vote, would allow cable operators to ban the use of any public educational channels for programs containing "obscene" material.

## HOUSE COMMITTEE ACTION

The House waited until mid 1992 to weigh in on the increasingly controversial cable debate. However, hearings had been held on the issues of regulation and the future of broadcasting — and the competing broadcast and cable industries used the time to prepare for major lobbying blitzes.

House Energy and Commerce Telecommunications and Finance Subcommittee Chairman Markey on March 25 unveiled his long-awaited bill to reregulate the cable television industry by vowing to "rein in the renegades" who charged exorbitant rates, provided poor service and hoarded programming.

"At its core, this is pro-consumer, pro-competition legislation," Markey said. "This bill restores to consumers the power to choose the cable services they want and to pay no more than they have to."

While most legislation crafted by the Telecommunications Subcommittee had wide bipartisan support, Markey's cable measure was the product of panel Democrats, backed by the lobbying support of consumer groups, labor unions and — most importantly — the National Association of Broadcasters.

No Republicans attended a March 25 briefing held to unveil the bill, and Republican lawmakers were still reviewing the legislation days after its release. "There was no collaboration at all," said a minority staff aide.

A Markey spokesman said the views of members from both parties were taken into account, but that even most panel Democrats were not directly involved in the bill's drafting.

Meanwhile, key panel Republicans met with White House Chief of Staff Samuel K. Skinner on March 25 to discuss strategies to defeat the bill. But House Republicans, who along with most House members faced an uncertain electorate, found themselves torn between supporting their president and opposing a measure that had been billed as pro-consumer.

While stronger than a similar bill passed by the House by voice vote in 1990, the Markey bill hewed closely to the Senate-passed measure.

Both versions sought new federal controls on the price of basic cable service — as well as other rates found to be "unreasonable" — and provide competitors better access to programs controlled by the cable industry.

But the House bill also offered a few new twists. It would require cable operators who carried distant broadcast "superstations" to offer them to customers as part of the regulated basic package and would allow customers to organize watchdog groups to monitor local cable companies (neither provision would make it into the final product).

Under both bills, rate regulation could be avoided only if fewer than 30 percent of households subscribed to cable or if at least two sources of multichannel video programming were offered to at least half of the households and 15 percent subscribed.

The House bill would require the FCC to set a new rate for basic cable service, which it defined as the lowest-priced tier that would include all local and public, educational and government channels and any distant broadcast signals carried. Operators would be free to include additional programs in the basic tier.

For other cable offerings, except premium subscription movie channels, the bill required the FCC to identify cable industry "renegades" who charged unreasonable rates. The FCC would be required to consider increases in general consumer prices, as well as the comparable rates of similarly situated cable systems, in determining unfair rate increases.

The committee draft refined the Senate attempt to deter cable operators from shifting popular programming away from its regulated basic tier. The House proposal would mandate that any distant broadcast signals carried by a cable operator — including such popular superstations as Chicago's WGN and Atlanta's WTBS — be offered on the lowest-priced basic tier.

In contrast, the Senate bill would mandate that the regulated basic rate apply to the first tier that attracted at least 30 percent of cable subscribers, even if that package was not the lowest-priced.

By including distant signals in the basic tier, House sponsors sought to keep it popular enough to maintain the interest of cable programmers and advertisers.

Unlike the Senate bill, which would allow any citizen to appeal to the FCC to lower rates considered unreasonable, the House bill would allow only franchising authorities and local governments to file complaints with the FCC.

The House bill also would allow consumers to form groups, to be certified by the franchising authority, to monitor local cable systems' behavior. Each group would be required to be made up of at least 5 percent of a system's subscribers but would have no power to file FCC complaints.

In another departure from the Senate version, the bill would ban cable operators from forcing consumers to subscribe to a more expensive tier of service when they wanted only individual premium channels such as HBO or Showtime.

The price of home equipment also would be regulated. The bill would require the FCC to set a maximum price for remote control devices, converter boxes, additional outlets and installation. And the agency would set minimum standards for customer service and consumer protection.

The bill included language, similar to that put into the Senate bill by Leahy that would require cable operators to ensure that cable technology was compatible with advanced features in television sets and videocassette recorders.

The bill's attempts to enhance competition focused on two issues: giving broadcasters compensation for use of their signals and helping other potential competitors gain better access to cable programs.

### Broadcasters and Hollywood

The issue of how to compensate broadcasters and Hollywood studios for cable operators' use of over-the-air signals dominated House action.

Mirroring the Inouye retransmission consent provision in the Senate bill, Markey and Dennis E. Eckart, D-Ohio, sought to give broadcasters the option of negotiating with cable operators for permission to retransmit their local signals for a fee, or simply requiring the cable operator to carry their signal for free.

The provision was crucial to the support of broadcasters, but House sponsors had to maneuver around jurisdictional land mines to keep it in the final bill.

Judiciary Committee Chairman Jack Brooks, D-Texas, and Intellectual Property Subcommittee Chairman William J. Hughes, D-N.J., opposed the retransmission con-

sent provision because they said it ignored the copyright claims of film producers in Hollywood. They had hoped to attach to the cable bill a repeal of the entire 1976 cable copyright law that allowed cable operators to carry local broadcast signals free of charge. In its place would be a new scheme, embodied in a bill by Hughes (HR 4511), that would repeal the copyright law and set up an interim flat fee for cable's use of local and distant signals, with revenues going to local broadcasters and Hollywood studios.

Brooks and Hughes were backed by Hollywood and professional sports leagues, who opposed the retransmission provision because it would not allow them to directly benefit from any local fees negotiated between broadcasters and cable operators.

Markey insisted that retransmission consent fell "fully within" the jurisdiction of his panel and was unrelated to copyright questions. "Divvying up the pie is another set of issues," he said.

Apart from the retransmission consent debate, much of the cable industry's concerns centered on other provisions that would restrict business deals struck between cable operators and those who provided cable programs.

The Senate bill and the Energy and Commerce Committee draft would ban cable-affiliated program distributors from unreasonably refusing to deal with cable competitors who sought programming. It also would ban discrimination in the price, terms and conditions of the sale or delivery of programming.

Both bills also would deny the cable industry a provision it sought during the 1990 cable reregulation battle — language explicitly allowing exclusive contracts between cable operators and programmers.

Instead, both bills would prohibit cable operators from coercing programmers to enter into exclusive contracts as a condition of carriage.

### Telecommunications Panel Action

Markey's Telecommunications and Finance Subcommittee had been scheduled to mark up his bill the week of March 30, but action never proceeded beyond opening statements. Markey delayed action until the following week when it became apparent that several Democrats were siding with Republicans to push for a weaker bill.

On April 8, Markey had to struggle to muster the votes to get his bill out of his subcommittee. The panel approved the draft by a vote of 17-7, after rejecting a weaker alternative by Lent, the full committee's ranking Republican, by a 12-14 vote.

The bill prevailed despite the defections of three panel Democrats, Thomas J. Manton and James H. Scheuer of New York and Bill Richardson of New Mexico, to Lent's camp. The three Democrats voted "present" on the final bill, while three Republicans switched to support the measure.

The unusually divisive subcommittee action centered on two of the bill's key provisions.

One would require the FCC to set rates for a broadly defined basic cable service that would include local and distant over-the-air signals and possibly even the most popular cable channels such as CNN and MTV. The Republican alternative, backed by the cable industry, accepted the notion of basic rate regulation but proposed limiting the definition of a basic program tier to only broadcast and public, educational and government channels.

The other provision most objectionable to opponents

would ban cable-affiliated programmers from unreasonably refusing to sell programming to cable competitors such as satellites and so-called wireless microwave cable systems. The Lent proposal would have softened that language by explicitly allowing programmers to enter into exclusive arrangements with cable operators.

There was much speculation about why Richardson, Manton and Scheuer so strongly supported the cable position by pushing for weaker regulations, particularly because none of them had overtly sided with cable in the past.

Consumer groups launched a media campaign to criticize the Democrats, with whom they had largely been allied on other issues.

For New Yorkers Manton and Scheuer, the hometown influence of Time-Warner Inc. played a role. The nation's second-largest cable operator, Time-Warner controlled systems in Manhattan, Brooklyn and Queens.

"Like all congressmen, we take into account the hometown industry," Manton said, adding that Time-Warner employed about 2,000 people in his district, while complaints about cable rates and service had been few. "But there wasn't any pressure. I keep my own counsel."

A Scheuer spokesman said any implication that his vote was tied to campaign contributions was "stretching it. His only motivating factor was to get a bill that could pass."

Richardson said he wanted to ensure that cable operators would not be banned from negotiating exclusive deals with program providers.

The cable industry was grateful for the help. "You gave it your best shot," Mooney told Manton after the markup.

Markey's only defeat of the day came with the subcommittee's rejection by voice vote of a provision that would establish local citizens' groups to monitor local cable operators and franchising authorities. The groups would have no authority to lodge complaints about cable abuses. The provision was pushed by consumer organizations, including Ralph Nader's Public Citizen group.

Michael G. Oxley, R-Ohio, said the provision would lead to local "MTV clubs" and "video vigilantes" that intruded on cable business decisions.

Ron Wyden, D-Ore., defended the provision. "It's a great bill for all the major industries," he said. "But there is precious little that provides for strong citizen input."

Another amendment that prevailed by voice vote, by Don Ritter, R-Pa., would exclude home-shopping broadcast stations from a provision that would force cable operators to carry local broadcast signals.

The amendment was aimed at Home Shopping Network, a Clearwater, Fla.-based satellite channel fed to 11 broadcast stations owned by the company as well as 1,454 cable systems. Ritter said the company's broadcast stations did not meet the same public service standards that typical stations must meet — and that cable operators should not be forced to carry the channel.

Opponents of the Ritter amendment said the FCC, not Congress, should decide whether Home Shopping Network should be considered as different from other television station licensees.

### Energy and Commerce Action

The Energy and Commerce Committee on June 17 approved a scaled-back cable reregulation measure, after stripping out two controversial provisions that Chairman John D. Dingell, D-Mich., said would cause the bill to get bogged down by opponents in the Judiciary Committee.

One of the excised provisions, the broadcasters' retrans-

mission consent proposal, was considered almost certain to be restored on the House floor. But a major floor fight loomed over whether to restore the other provision removed during the markup that attempted to bolster competition to cable by giving satellite distributors and other potential competitors lower-priced access to cable programming.

The committee approved the bill (HR 4850) 31-12 after rejecting, by a party-line vote of 15-27, a Lent substitute similar to that offered in subcommittee.

Four Republicans crossed party lines to support the final bill: Carlos J. Moorhead, Calif.; Matthew J. Rinaldo, N.J.; Michael Bilirakis, Fla.; and Fred Upton, Mich. Three Democrats who had sided with Republicans on a weaker bill during April 8 action in the Telecommunications and Finance Subcommittee — Manton and Scheuer of New York and Richardson of New Mexico — switched to back their party's bill.

W. J. "Billy" Tauzin, D-La., vowed to try to restore his so-called program access provision on the floor, arguing that the cable bill "suffers from malnutrition" until it helps competitors get cable programming at more equitable prices.

"It's so gentle it could be called 'cable friendly,'" Tauzin said. "Without real competition, this bill lacks heart and soul and real strength."

Having finally won one round — after Dingell dropped the two controversial provisions — opponents turned up the volume on their assertions that the bill punished the cable industry for its successes, interfered with private business dealings and likely would cause cable rates to rise instead of fall.

"There have been growing pains," Lent said, referring to complaints about service and rapid price increases since deregulation. "The question is one of balance. I'm concerned that we do not act with too heavy a hand."

And though sponsors managed to thwart the Judiciary Committee, that panel's shadow continued to loom over the bill, particularly on the issue of broadcast retransmission consent. The Judiciary Subcommittee on Intellectual Property on June 18 approved the Hughes bill (HR 4511) that would phase out a 1976 copyright law allowing cable operators to retransmit the signals of local broadcasters free of charge.

Hughes and Judiciary Committee Chairman Brooks said they would seek to offer the bill as an amendment to HR 4850 when it reached the House floor.

Still, at the Energy and Commerce Committee markup the cable bill was amended in some ways to be tougher on the industry.

One amendment by Jim Cooper, D-Tenn., approved by voice vote after little debate, would allow the FCC to order refunds to consumers for any rate increases collected by a cable company between the time that a complaint about rates was filed and the time that the agency determined price-gouging had occurred.

Another amendment, by Ralph M. Hall, D-Texas, would allow local broadcasters to expand the number of cable systems that would be forced to carry their signals under so-called must-carry requirements if they transmitted between two larger metropolitan areas. It too was approved by voice vote.

But attempts by Cooper to impose stricter controls on cable — including a provision to set up consumer watchdog groups that would monitor local cable activities — were rejected by voice vote.

Also rejected, 15-28, was a Bilirakis amendment to force

cable operators in the markets of the Home Shopping Network's 11 stations to carry the 24-hour advertising channels if they also carried the QVC Network, a cable industry shopping channel. Home Shopping Network was headquartered in Bilirakis' district. QVC was near the district of panel member Don Ritter, R-Pa., who earlier had won a subcommittee amendment to exclude Home Shopping Network from the types of broadcast stations that cable systems must carry.

Other amendments approved by the panel included those by:

● Tom McMillen, D-Md., that would require the FCC to study the migration of sports programming from free, over-the-air television to pay television such as subscription cable and pay-per-view television.

● Gerry Sikorski, D-Minn., that would allow cable franchise authorities to set local rates for pay-per-view events that involve any professional sports championship games featuring their hometown teams. The amendment passed by a vote of 13-11.

● Richardson, that would require broadcasters to comply with equal employment opportunity guidelines.

## HOUSE FLOOR ACTION

House passage July 23 of the cable bill marked the first significant defeat for the giant cable industry and set up an election-year veto confrontation between Congress and President Bush.

The House passed HR 4850, 340-73, after overwhelmingly backing an amendment by Tauzin to force cable program vendors to sell their shows at fair prices to competitors such as the backyard satellite dish industry. *(Vote 313, p. 76-H)*

The vote also marked a surprisingly solid victory for cable's opponents — broadcasters and consumer groups — which had been pushing for restraints on the cable industry ever since it was freed by Congress from local government control in 1984.

The voting margin, and an equally strong Senate vote of 73-18 on the companion legislation, set Congress at odds with Bush, threatening to crack his unbroken record of successful vetoes.

Ninety-eight Republicans joined 241 Democrats to pass the bill. Many of the Republican defectors hailed from rural areas where broadcast signals were weak and television viewers had to rely on cable or satellite television for reception.

The Bush administration suffered fewer defections on an administration-backed substitute amendment by Lent, but it still went down to defeat by a vote of 144-266. Lent's proposal was a milder version of the cable regulation bill the House passed by voice vote in 1990. *(Vote 312, p. 76-H)*

But the first real sign that Bush was on the losing side of the cable issue — and headed for his first override — came on a crucial amendment by Tauzin to replace the "program access" provision dropped from the bill by the Energy and Commerce Committee.

Tauzin wanted to bar cable-affiliated programmers from refusing to sell programs at fair prices and terms to the home satellite dish and so-called wireless cable industries. His amendment prevailed by a vote of 338-68. *(Vote 311, p. 76-H)*

Under the Tauzin amendment, programmers affiliated with the cable industry would be barred from discriminating in the price, terms and conditions of programs they sold

to cable's competitors. Programs could be sold at different prices under certain conditions, such as volume discounts.

Energy and Commerce panelist Manton offered a weaker alternative favored by the cable industry. He called the Tauzin amendment "far-reaching and radical," saying it would set a government-mandated price for programming and cause program creators to lose control over their product. Cable's competitors, he added, already have access to programming.

"They want more than a jump start," Manton said of the satellite industry. "They want a free ride."

Manton's amendment would not have gone as far as Tauzin's. It would have barred any programming vendor "controlled" by a cable operator, rather than "affiliated," from refusing to deal with cable competitors to restrain competition. It also did not address discrimination in the prices, terms or conditions of program contracts. The amendment also would have allowed programmers and operators to enter into exclusive contracts, while the Tauzin amendment would allow such contracts only if the FCC determined they were in the public interest.

Manton was backed by Energy and Commerce Committee Chairman Dingell, members of the House Democratic leadership and the powerful cable lobby. Still, after impassioned speeches by Tauzin and Manton, the Manton amendment failed by a vote of 162-247. *(Vote 310, p. 76-H)*

As the cable bill headed toward a House-Senate conference committee, sponsors predicted swift conference action because most major differences between the bills had been eliminated.

But the Bush administration continued voicing its opposition to regulating cable until competition arrived. The White House pointed to a July 16 FCC ruling that allowed phone companies to carry video programs over a "video dial tone."

But because the ban preventing phone companies from owning those programs continued, the ruling was considered unlikely to lead to any phone company involvement in video delivery for at least a decade.

Sponsors succeeded in keeping the telephone-cable issue, and the host of questions it raised, out of the cable regulation debate.

They also skirted a fight with the Judiciary Committee over how to compensate broadcasters who provided programs to cable operators. The Rules Committee declined to allow two competing amendments to the bill: One was the Eckart retransmission consent provision dropped at the committee markup. The other was Hughes' to overhaul the entire copyright royalty payment system while requiring the cable industry to pay broadcasters, program creators and sports leagues for use of broadcast programs.

Sponsors were confident the broadcaster retransmission consent provision contained in the Senate-passed bill would be folded into the final bill in conference. Judiciary Committee Chairman Brooks vowed to continue his fight against the provision through the conference committee stage, but he ultimately declined to show up at the conference after concluding he lacked the votes on the panel to prevail on the issue.

## FINAL ACTION

House-Senate negotiators approved the conference report to the cable bill (S 12) by voice vote Sept. 9, moving one step closer to a veto confrontation with President Bush over the measure. Meanwhile, the cable industry picked up

some crucial last-minute support from the film industry.

Hollywood joined the fray in earnest on Sept. 10, when Jack Valenti, president of the Motion Picture Association of America, vowed to join cable industry efforts to stop the legislation on the Senate floor.

Valenti weighed in publicly after conferees left intact the Senate provision that would give broadcasters the right to charge cable operators for use of over-the-air signals. Broadcasters would not be required to give any of those new revenues to the film industry that created the programs.

"The industry cannot allow its valuable copyrights to be so casually treated and will fight side by side with opponents of the bill," Valenti said.

Hollywood's help was welcomed by the cable industry, which had tried to rebound from its legislative defeats by launching a massive last-minute advertising blitz the week of Sept. 7. The effort included full-page newspaper ads and targeted mailings claiming that the regulation bill would boost, not lower, cable rates. The industry argued that any fees paid to broadcasters would have to be passed on to consumers in the form of cable price hikes.

Bill advocates denounced cable's campaign as misleading, saying the bill would take steps to ensure that costs were not passed on to customers.

In a rapid 2½-hour meeting, conferees settled the few remaining differences between the chambers' bills that had not been resolved by staff over the August recess.

But two politically charged House provisions addressing future trends in cable television — the migration of sports events from free television to pay television and the foreign ownership of cable systems — were left out of the final bill.

Issues settled even before the conference got under way included key provisions for rate-setting and granting cable competitors better access to cable-originated programming.

Conferees accepted the House bill's process for requiring the FCC to set a price for basic cable television service. The commission would have to set its price based on several factors, including the price of basic cable service in the few areas that did have competing cable or satellite systems. That could result in basic cable fees dropping by as much as 30 percent, sponsors said.

But Danforth's original Senate bill would have come down harder on cable. It would have required cable operators to keep at least 30 percent of their subscribers on a basic viewing package or face rate controls on higher program offerings. That provision was designed to prevent cable operators from shifting their most popular programs onto a higher-priced package.

The compromise bill also would return to local governments some of the power they once had over cable rates, by allowing them — or subscribers — to complain that prices for non-basic cable programs such as ESPN, CNN or MTV were unreasonable. If the FCC agreed, it could set a new rate and refund the difference to subscribers.

However, the House definition of "basic" cable was narrowed. Rather than including long-distance broadcast "superstations" in the basic package, as the House bill proposed, conferees included only local broadcast signals and government access channels.

The final bill would allow both subscribers and local cable franchising authorities to file complaints with the FCC alleging that rates for other non-basic cable services were unreasonable (excluding premium movie channels or pay-per-view events). A House provision that would allow the FCC to grant overcharged customer refunds also was

retained in the final bill.

And within 10 years, as opposed to five in the House bill, all cable operators would have to upgrade their systems with "addressable" converter boxes that would enable subscribers to order a premium movie channel without being forced to subscribe to an entire higher-priced tier of programming. The cable industry protested this provision on grounds that a five-year conversion was not technically feasible.

The home-dish satellite and wireless cable industries also would get a leg up in their effort to gain cheaper access to cable programming. The conferees accepted House language, similar to the Senate bill, that would bar cable operators who owned a financial interest in programming from improperly influencing decisions regarding the price, terms and conditions of program sales to non-cable competitors.

## Sports Talk and Other Debates

Sports talk also dominated the conference, but not as much as had been expected.

Energy and Commerce Committee Chairman Dingell, who also chaired the conference, was prepared to offer an amendment that would have prohibited superstations from showing baseball games in competing teams' hometowns if local broadcasters also carried the games.

The provision was sought by former Major League Baseball Commissioner Fay Vincent, who resigned on Sept. 7. Without Vincent's support for the measure, Dingell said, there was no impetus to offer the amendment.

But conferees sparred over whether to forestall the ongoing flight of sports programming from free television to the pay-per-view arena.

Many professional and collegiate sporting events, including hockey, baseball and basketball games, had been increasingly available only on a pay-per-view basis. Markey said the public should not be forced to pay to watch pro sports on television, particularly because the teams enjoyed public benefits such as exemption from antitrust laws and playing in taxpayer-financed stadiums. A House provision that would have allowed local governments to set the price for pay-per-view championship professional sporting events was rejected amid opposition from the Senate conferees and House Republicans. But negotiators agreed to allow the FCC to study the issue.

Another conference debate was waged over the Florida-based Home Shopping Network.

The House bill would have excluded home-shopping broadcast stations from rules that forced cable operators to carry local broadcast signals. The Senate bill would have had the FCC study whether such home-shopping stations served the public interest and deserved the same benefits accorded other broadcast stations.

In the end, conferees agreed to a Dingell compromise that would leave it up to the FCC to determine after nine months whether cable operators should be forced to carry home-shopping broadcast stations on their systems. In the meantime, cable operators would not be forced to carry the channels.

Conferees put down another skirmish over a House provision that would have restricted the foreign ownership or control of any cable system in the United States. The provision was based on similar limits imposed on the ownership of broadcast stations and telephone companies.

Senate negotiators, along with House Republican conferees, opposed the provision on grounds that it would

hinder efforts to lower trade barriers worldwide. Markey argued that the cable industry had an increasingly vital hold on the nation's "telecommunications nervous system" and that the restriction should be extended to cable for national security reasons.

Senate negotiators won their bid to remove the ownership restrictions, but in turn accepted a related Markey "anti-trafficking" provision that would require investors to wait three years after purchasing a cable system before selling the system.

### House Conference Action

Entangled in the year's fiercest lobbying war, House lawmakers on Sept. 17 decided firmly in favor of broadcasters and consumer groups by adopting the final version of the conference committee's cable bill.

But the high-stakes political skirmish was far from over. Robust opposition from the cable industry and Hollywood helped turn 58 House votes against the measure. Still, the strength of the final vote suggested the House still could muster the two-thirds vote needed to override a promised veto by President Bush. The House adopted the conference report by a vote of 280-128. *(Vote 398, p. 98-H)*

"We will win a veto override in the House, flat out, no question about it," said sponsor Markey after the vote.

Democratic Chief Deputy Whip Barbara B. Kennelly, D-Conn., was less sanguine. "It would be unusual" for the House to prevail on the issue, she said. "This was an unhappy choice. You saw a lot of people voting late."

Before the vote, Bush renewed his threat to veto the legislation. "My vision for the future of the communications industry is based on the principles of greater competition, entrepreneurship and less economic regulation," Bush said in a Sept. 17 letter to Republican leaders. "This legislation fails each of these tests and is illustrative of the congressional mandates and excessive regulations that drag our economy down."

Opposition by Hollywood also put Democrats in an uncomfortable position. Motion picture executives were generous donors to party campaign coffers, including presidential candidate Clinton and vice presidential candidate Gore.

The cable bill was voted on the day after a Sept. 16 Hollywood fundraiser for Clinton and the Democratic Party that featured singer and movie-maker Barbra Streisand and reportedly raised $1.5 million.

Possibly for that reason, and to avoid fanning partisan flames, the House Democratic leadership did not work to rally floor votes for the final bill. Rather, Democratic sponsors stressed the bipartisan nature of the measure, citing leading roles by Republicans Rinaldo, Senate sponsor Danforth, and the support of Minority Leader Robert H. Michel, Ill.

But the tough choice for some Democrats was evident in the vote. Eighteen of the 22 lawmakers who did not cast a vote on the bill were Democrats. Among them were three California Democrats, including Senate candidate Barbara Boxer, who would have had to choose between consumer interests and Hollywood.

Indeed, to view the bill only as a partisan issue belied the hometown pressures faced by lawmakers on both sides of the aisle. Of the five members who switched their original July 23 "nay" vote on the bill to a "yea" on the conference report, four were rural Republicans whose constituents relied most heavily on cable service to improve their television reception.

Lawmakers also showed allegiance to their committee interests. Nine who served on the Judiciary Committee switched their votes to "nay" following the lead of committee Chairman Jack Brooks, D-Texas, who defended Hollywood's copyright interests issue and opposed the bill.

But judging from the vote tally, the power of media conglomerates based in California and the New York-New Jersey area, such as the Walt Disney Co. and Time-Warner Inc., appeared to have had at least as much influence on vote switchers as any loyalty to Democrats, Bush or hometown constituents.

"Basically," said bill advocate Eckart, most vote switching was "out of respect for the Judiciary Committee chairman and out of a fear of Hollywood."

In an effort to win support from regulation-shy conservatives, sponsors argued that the final bill was weaker on regulation and stronger on stimulating competition to cable than were the original bills.

The cable industry concentrated its firepower on the retransmission consent issue, saying the goal of giving broadcasters a new revenue stream would ultimately boost cable rates.

Repeating figures first cited by CBS President Laurence A. Tisch, top Republican opponent Lent of New York said broadcasters stood to gain as much as $1 billion a year from the provision — money that would come out of the pockets of cable consumers, he said. Broadcasters called that figure exaggerated.

"I know it is an election year, and we are all hungry for votes," Lent told lawmakers. "But this is not the way, because voters are smart enough to recognize that this bill is going to raise, not lower, their rates."

That message was hammered home to lawmakers and cable TV viewers so often that sponsors held two news conferences to debunk the charge. They said the bill's rate regulations would offset any cost increases associated with the broadcasters' retransmission provision.

"Cable has attempted to hoodwink consumers into thinking S 12 is bad for them," Markey said. He cited an April FCC study that said consumers would save $5.3 billion a year — a figure that was hotly disputed by cable officials.

Cable's ad campaign, which included two television spots aired by more than a dozen cable channels nationwide, was combined with a direct-mail effort that included fliers mailed in the monthly cable bills of 35 million subscribers. The direct-mail campaign also pushed the claim that cable rates would rise dramatically if the bill were to become law.

Local cable operators also set up telephone conference calls, which cable officials monitored, for consumers to complain about the bill to lawmakers' aides, and formed what opponents called "consumer front groups" to espouse their position.

Broadcasters also were not immune to using their own media to get their message out.

A Sept. 3 memo by senior board members of the National Association of Broadcasters urged the news departments of member stations across the country to "tell it like it is" on the cable issue and "generate the news stories."

Tim Wirth, D-Colo., the cable industry's leading Senate Democratic advocate, cried foul.

"The NAB wants broadcasters to manipulate the content of their news programs, which viewers presume is fair, objective and impartial, to influence legislation that advances their own economic interest," he said. "The public

# Citing Special Interests, Bush Vetoes Cable TV Bill

*Following is the text of President Bush's Oct. 3 veto of S 12, the bill to reregulate the cable TV industry:*

I am returning herewith without my approval S 12, the Cable Television Consumer Protection and Competition Act of 1992. This bill illustrates good intentions gone wrong, fallen prey to special interests.

Contrary to the claims made by its proponents, this legislation will not reduce the price Americans pay for cable television service. Rather, the simple truth is that under this legislation, cable television rates will go up, not down. Competition will not increase, it will stagnate. In addition, this legislation will cost American jobs and discourage investment in telecommunications, one of our fastest-growing industries.

S 12 is clearly long on promises. Unfortunately, it is just as clearly short on relief to the American families who are quite rightly concerned about significant increases in their cable rates and poor cable service. Although the proponents of S 12 describe the bill as pro-competitive, it simply is not. Indeed, the only truly competitive provision, one that would have expanded the ability of telephone companies to compete with cable companies in rural areas, was dropped from the bill at the last minute.

S 12 tries to address legitimate consumer concerns, but it does so by requiring cable companies to bear the costs of meeting major new federally imposed regulatory requirements and by adopting costly special interest provisions. For example, the bill requires cable companies for the first time to pay broadcasting companies, who have free access to the airwaves, to carry the broadcasters' programs. The undeniable result: higher rates for cable viewers.

Beyond increasing consumer costs, the bill takes certain key business decisions away from cable operators and puts them in the hands of the Federal Government. One provision, which is unconstitutional, requires cable companies to carry certain television stations regardless of whether the viewing public wants to see these stations. Another special interest provision would put the Federal Government in the position of dictating to cable companies to whom and at what price they could sell their programs. These types of federally mandated outcomes will discourage continued investment in new programs to the detriment of cable subscribers who have come to expect a wide variety of programming and new services.

I believe that the American people deserve cable television legislation that, unlike S 12, will deliver what it promises: fair rates, good programming and sound service.

---

trust has been replaced instead by the desire to advance their own narrow economic interests."

Both sides of the issue were accused of playing loose with figures. But it was clear by the time of the House vote that the cable lobby had begun to successfully erode support by casting doubts about the regulatory cost of the bill.

Peter H. Kostmayer, D-Pa., who voted for the original bill in July, said he could not make up his mind on the conference report until the morning of the vote. He voted against it, staffers said, in response to concern registered by constituents that the retransmission consent provision would raise rates.

## Senate Conference Action

The Senate on Sept. 22 cleared the final version of the bill (S 12) by a vote of 74-25, providing more than the two-thirds majority needed to override a threatened veto. *(Vote 225, p. 30-S)*

Despite the wide voting margins in both chambers, the Bush administration showed no signs of backing down on its veto threat. But reversing votes so close to a rough-and-tumble election would be tough. After each chamber had cast two votes on the measure, many lawmakers would be averse to being painted as flip-flopping on a perceived consumer bill.

The increasingly partisan nature of the veto battle concerned sponsors and lobbyists for the bill, who had taken pains to emphasize its bipartisan support, including the sponsorship of Sen. Danforth.

But the partisan lines already had been drawn. Vice presidential candidate Gore, a chief cosponsor of the measure, showed up Sept. 22 to cast his vote, marking only his third vote since nomination in July.

"President Bush is threatening to veto this bill so he can protect the ability of the big cable monopolies to keep soaking their customers," Gore said after the vote.

Judging from the Senate outcome, the cable industry got the least amount of bang for its lobbying buck.

Opponents were able to persuade just four Republicans and one Democrat, Wyche Fowler Jr. of Georgia, to vote "nay" on Sept. 22, switching their original Jan. 31 vote on the bill's passage.

Two other Democrats, Alan Cranston of California and David L. Boren of Oklahoma, were not present for the earlier vote and voted against the final bill.

All told, opponents were able to win only seven more "nay" votes on Sept. 22 atop the 18 stacked against the bill in January. Assuming all senators had voted, it would have taken 34 senators to sustain any veto.

Most surprising in the Senate vote was the large number of Republicans who remained in favor of the bill. Among them were eight Republicans who were up for re-election in 1992, including Alfonse M. D'Amato of New York, Arlen Specter of Pennsylvania and John McCain of Arizona. Minority Whip Alan K. Simpson of Wyoming and Republican Conference Chairman Thad Cochran of Mississippi also voted "yea."

John Seymour of California and Don Nickles of Oklahoma were the only Republicans facing re-election who switched their vote to oppose the measure.

But any vote-switching also could be attributed to serious differences of opinion that had emerged through the year over exactly what the bill would do — and how much it actually would save or cost consumers.

Conrad Burns, R-Mont., and Wirth led the Senate charge against the bill.

Burns, a leading proponent of allowing the Bell telephone companies into the video programming business, said the cable industry had created some 70,000 jobs during the 1980s and provided new viewing options to consumers. He also blasted the regulatory costs of the bill, which he pegged at up to $60 million annually at the federal level and more than $250 million at the state and local level.

Wirth, perhaps cable's staunchest ally in Congress, claimed that the bill was simply an effort by cable competitors to gang up on the industry.

"This legislation has turned into a free-for-all involving
*Continued on p. 183*

# Cable Reregulation Law Provisions

*As enacted by Congress on Oct. 5, the cable reregulation law (S 12 — PL 102-385):*

## RATE AND SERVICE REGULATION

● **Basic rate regulation.** Required the Federal Communications Commission (FCC) to ensure that rates for basic cable service, including necessary rental equipment, were reasonable for all cable systems that did not face effective competition.

● **Definition of basic cable.** Defined basic cable service as the lowest-priced package, or tier, of cable programs. It included retransmission of local over-the-air broadcast signals as well as public, educational and governmental-access programs. Cable operators could add additional programs to their basic packages (such as distant broadcast "superstations"), but rates for those programs also would be subject to rate regulation.

● **Definition of effective competition.** Exempted cable operators from rate regulation when they were subject to "effective competition." Such competition was defined as franchise areas in which fewer than 30 percent of households subscribed to the cable service. Competition also was considered present in areas served by at least two unaffiliated cable operators or their competitors when either of which reached at least 50 percent of households. Finally, competition was deemed present where the number of households subscribing to a competing programmer exceeded 15 percent of the total households.

● **Reasonable rates.** Required the FCC by April 3, 1993 (180 days after the enactment date), to regulate rates. In doing so, the commission was required to strive to reduce the administrative costs of the regulations on subscribers, cable operators, franchise authorities and the commission.

Rather than setting a single maximum rate for basic cable service, the FCC may adopt formulas "or other mechanisms or procedures" to regulate rates.

● **Setting basic rates.** Required the FCC to take into account the following factors when setting a basic rate formula:

● the rates of cable systems that were subject to effective competition;

● the cost of obtaining, transmitting or providing signals carried as part of the basic viewing package;

● other companywide costs related to providing a basic package;

● advertising revenues received by a cable operator during programming carried on the basic package;

● any franchise fee, tax or charge imposed by state and local authorities;

● costs incurred to satisfy franchise requirements to support public, educational or governmental channels; and

● a "reasonable profit" as defined by the commission.

Also, a 5 percent annual rate increase for basic cable television, allowed by the 1984 Cable Act (PL 98-549), was repealed.

● **Franchising authority.** Allowed local cable franchising authorities to exercise regulatory jurisdiction over the cable law's rate provisions. Authorities had to certify in writing that they would adopt and administer regulations consistent with those written by the FCC, that they had the legal authority to carry out such regulations and that their procedures allowed for adequate participation by all interested parties. The FCC could deny or revoke any such authority.

● **Premium channels.** Banned a cable operator from requiring customers to subscribe to any package other than the basic one in order to receive so-called premium movie channels (such as HBO or Cinemax) or other per-channel or per-program services. This provision did not apply to cable systems that lacked the technological means to carry it out. It also would expire in 10 years. Also, the FCC could — upon a request by a cable operator — waive the requirement after finding that compliance with this provision would lead to higher rates.

● **Cost of other cable offerings.** Allowed cable subscribers to file a complaint with the FCC that a cable system with no effective competition had unreasonably raised rates for any other program offering outside the basic viewing package. If the FCC found such rates unreasonable, it could establish reasonable rates and require that subscribers be refunded the unreasonable portion of their fee from the time their complaint was filed.

● **Rate complaints.** Allowed subscribers and franchising authorities to complain about existing cable rates only during a 180-day period after the effective date of the FCC's new rules. After that period, rate complaints could be leveled only against future rate increases and had to be filed within a "reasonable period of time" following the increase.

● **Existing rate agreements.** Allowed existing agreements between franchise authorities and cable operators lacking effective competition (based on the FCC's pre-July 1, 1990, "three-broadcast-signal" standard) to stay in effect until they expired. Such operators would then be subject to the new rate regulations.

● **Preventing loopholes.** Required the FCC, by April 3, 1993, to set standards and guidelines to prevent cable operators from evading rate regulation by such methods as shifting more popular programs away from the basic tier.

● **Small cable systems.** Required the FCC to write rules in a way that reduced the administrative burdens and costs of compliance for cable systems that had 1,000 or fewer subscribers.

● **Price reports.** Required the FCC to report annually on the average rates for basic cable service and other programming, as well as for converter boxes, remote controls and other equipment. The rates would be compared with systems that faced competition and those that did not.

● **Price discrimination.** Allowed federal, state and local officials to set rules barring price discrimination among existing and potential cable customers, other than "reasonable" discounts for senior citizens or other economically disadvantaged groups.

## Cable Service Regulations

● **Service standards.** Required the FCC, by April 3, 1993, to establish customer service standards for cable operators. Standards would set guidelines for cable operators' office hours, telephone availability, installations, outages, service calls, billings and refunds. States and franchising authorities would be free to enact or enforce stronger consumer protection laws.

● **Customer equipment.** Required the FCC, by Oct. 5, 1993, to issue rules requiring cable operators to notify customers about the use of cable converter boxes.

Home use of a converter box often was required by cable operators to allow reception of all cable channels. Such boxes often disabled certain functions of televisions and videocassette recorders (VCRs). Among them were the ability to watch a program on one channel while recording a program on another, to use a VCR to tape two concurrent programs that appeared on different channels and to use special features of a television such as a "picture in a picture" feature.

If a cable operators' system required use of a converter box in all cases, the operator would be required to notify customers that they might be unable to benefit from the special functions of their television sets or VCRs. Cable operators also were required to the extent technically and economically feasible to offer subscribers the option of having all other channels delivered directly to the subscribers' television set or VCR without passing through the converter box.

The FCC also was required to promote the commercial availability of converter boxes and remote control devices. And cable operators were required to allow customers who did not wish to use

a converter box, and who had compatible television or VCR equipment, to opt to have their cable operator install or reinstall their service without the use of a converter box. The operator also was required to specify the types of remote control units that were compatible with the converter box supplied by the operator.

Cable operators were prohibited from preventing or disabling a converter box from operating with commercially available remote control units.

● **Compatibility.** Required the FCC by Oct. 5, 1993, to report to Congress on ways to assure compatibility among cable systems, televisions and VCRs. The FCC would have to consider ways to: minimize interference with or the elimination of special functions of subscribers' television receivers or VCRs, allow viewers to watch a program on one channel while recording on another, and use advanced television picture generation and display features. The agency also was required to examine whether manufacturers should be required to incorporate compatibility features in all television receivers, as well as the cost to cable operators.

Within 180 days of submitting the report, the FCC was required to write rules intended to boost such compatibility.

● **Scrambling local signals.** Required the FCC, by Oct. 5, 1993, to issue rules outlining how cable operators might scramble, or encrypt, a local broadcast signal to protect against signal theft.

● **Home wiring.** Required the FCC by Feb. 2, 1993, to establish rules to determine who owned wiring installed by a cable operator within a subscriber's home after service was terminated.

● **Itemized bills.** Allowed cable operators, beginning Dec. 4, 1993, to identify as a separate line on subscribers' bills the amount of the total bill that was assessed as a franchise fee and the identity of the franchising authority that levied the fee. The operator also would be allowed to identify the amount of the total bill that resulted from requirements imposed on the cable operator by a franchise agreement to support public, educational or government channels.

● **Services and equipment not requested.** Barred a cable operator, after April 3, 1993, from charging for any service or equipment not affirmatively and specifically requested by a subscriber. A subscribers' failure to refuse a cable operator's proposal to provide such service or equipment would not be deemed an affirmative request for that service or equipment.

● **Program changes.** Allowed franchising authorities, beginning on Dec. 4, 1992, to require cable operators to give subscribers 30-days' notice before changing any channel assignment or video programming service provided on any channel. Cable operators also would have to inform subscribers that a designated office of the franchising authority would be open for public comment on the changes.

● **Technical standards.** Required the FCC, by Oct. 5, 1993, to establish minimum technical standards to ensure adequate signal quality for all classes of programming provided over a cable system. The standards would be updated periodically. Franchising authorities could petition to set more stringent technical standards.

● **Emergency broadcast announcements.** Required all cable networks to participate in the Emergency Broadcast System, an FCC program that called on broadcast stations to stand ready to relay government communications in case of a national emergency.

## PROMOTION OF COMPETITION

### Broadcasters

● **Carriage options.** Required that commercial television stations, by Oct. 5, 1993, and every three years thereafter, choose between the right to negotiate with cable operators for consent to retransmit their broadcast signals and the right to force cable operators to carry their signals for free.

If a station opted for retransmission consent, the requirements of the "must carry" provision below would not apply, and vice versa. If there were more than one cable system that served the same area, a station's choice would apply to all cable systems serving an area.

● **Retransmission consent.** Prohibited local cable operators or other video program distributors, as of Oct. 5, 1993, from retransmitting a local broadcast station's originating programs without its express authority. Exceptions included non-commercial broadcast stations, signals retransmitted directly to a home satellite dish of a broadcast station not owned, operated by or affiliated with a network, and signals of so-called superstations that transmitted signals beyond their broadcast area via satellite.

The FCC by Nov. 19, 1992, was required to begin writing rules governing broadcasters' rights to grant retransmission consent. The commission would have to consider the impact of this provision on basic cable rates and ensure that those rates were reasonable.

● **Must-carry.** Required cable operators to reserve up to one-third of their channel capacity to carry local commercial broadcast stations. Cable systems with 12 or fewer usable activated channels would have to carry the signals of at least three local commercial television stations. Carrying additional signals would be at the discretion of the cable operator.

Cable operators would be required to carry commercial stations on all cable systems within the station's viewing area, regardless of audience size. The FCC would have to adopt additional requirements when it set standards for high-definition television, an upcoming form of television that required more channel capacity and offered superior picture and sound quality.

A cable system with 300 or fewer subscribers would not be subject to this section as long as it continued to carry any signal of a broadcast television station. Cable operators would not be required to carry the signal of a local commercial television station that substantially duplicated another carried on the system. Nor would cable operators be forced to carry the signals of more than one local commercial television station affiliated with a particular broadcast network.

The FCC was required to issue new rules regarding the must-carry provisions by April 3, 1993.

● **Must-carry channel positioning.** Required that each signal carried by a cable operator to fulfill the must-carry requirements be carried on the same cable system channel number on which the local commercial station already broadcast, effective Dec. 4, 1992. Alternatively, the signal would have to be carried on the same channel on which it was carried on July 19, 1985, or on any other channel number that was mutually agreed upon by the station and the cable operator. The FCC would be responsible for resolving channel-positioning disputes.

Cable operators would be required to provide written notice to a local commercial television station at least 30 days before either discontinuing or repositioning a station. Cable operators were prohibited from discontinuing or repositioning a broadcast station when major television ratings were measuring the size of local television station audiences.

● **Complaints.** Required that whenever a local commercial television station thought that a cable operator had failed to meet its obligations under this section, the station notify the cable operator in writing. The operator would have 30 days to respond. Further complaints would have to be filed with the FCC. The commission would have 120 days from that time to rule on the complaint.

● **Non-commercial educational television.** Required that each cable operator, by Dec. 4, 1992, carry any qualified local non-commercial education television stations that requested to be carried on the system. Cable operators with 12 or fewer usable channels would be required to carry the signal of only one educational station. Operators with channel capacities ranging from 13 to 35 channels would be required to carry one to three non-commercial educational stations. Those with more than 35 usable channels would be required to carry the signals of three educational stations.

● **Low-power television stations.** Required that cable systems with 35 or fewer channels carry one qualified low-power television station — typically non-professional stations that transmitted from local schools or colleges. Those with 36 or more

channels would have to carry up to, but not more than, two qualified low-power stations. The requirements applied only to communities in counties that had no full-power station licensed and that were outside the nation's top 160 metropolitan areas. To qualify for must-carry status, a low-powered station had to meet public-interest requirements.

● **Home shopping channels.** Allowed cable operators to choose not to carry any commercial television station or video programming service that was used predominantly for the transmission of sales presentations or program-length commercials, pending the outcome of an FCC study regarding the public interest value of such stations. The study was to be completed by July 2, 1993.

● **Compulsory license.** Declared that nothing in the retransmission consent provision modified the compulsory copyright license provision of the 1976 Copyright Act or affected existing or future video-programming licensing agreements between broadcasting stations and video programmers.

### Access to Cable Programs

● **Program discrimination.** Required the FCC, by April 3, 1993, to develop safeguards to prevent video program distributors, including satellite broadcast programmers as well as cable operators who had a financial interest in a cable network, from "unduly or improperly influencing" decisions regarding the price, terms or conditions of program sales to non-cable program distributors.

Programmers generally were prohibited from engaging in "unfair methods of competition or unfair or deceptive acts" that deterred or prevented any competitor from providing programs to consumers.

● **Exceptions.** Allowed video programmers to impose reasonable requirements on distributors for creditworthiness, financial stability and ability to offer programs. They also could take into account differences in the cost of creating, selling or transmitting programs, as well as economies of scale or other savings attributable to the number of subscribers served by a distributor.

But vendors would be barred from entering into exclusive contracts with cable operators, except where the FCC determines such a contract was in the public interest. The ban against exclusive contracts for satellite cable programs between a cable operator and a cable-affiliated program vendor would expire in 10 years, unless the FCC determined the ban was still needed to preserve diversity and competition.

Exclusive contracts entered into before June 1, 1990, would not be affected. But non-cable distributors in areas not served by a cable operator would be allowed access to programs otherwise off-limits because of exclusive contracts.

● **Remedies.** Allowed any multichannel video program distributor who was denied fair access to cable programs to complain to the commission. The FCC could order appropriate remedies including setting new prices, terms and conditions of programming sales to the distributor.

● **"Coercion" and carriage agreements.** Required the FCC by Oct. 5, 1993, to establish rules governing carriage agreements between cable operators and video program distributors. This was intended to prevent a cable operator or other program distributor from requiring a financial interest in a program service as a condition for carrying the program. The agreements also would prohibit cable operators or other video program distributors from coercing a video programmer to provide exclusive rights as a condition of carriage.

● **Emerging cable competitors' public service requirements.** Required the FCC, by April 3, 1993, to begin considering how to impose public interest or other requirements on any provider of direct-broadcast satellite service that was not regulated as a common carrier.

Direct broadcast satellite was an emerging form of video programming for which the FCC had set aside frequencies. The service offered a higher-powered signal than existing satellite dishes required, allowing signals to be received by dishes as small as 1-foot in diameter.

The FCC also would have to examine the national nature of the service and the phase-in time necessary to impose fair public-interest obligations that reflected the extent to which these services were effective competitors to cable systems.

The provision also required that any future direct broadcast satellite service reserve a portion of its channel capacity, equal to no less than 4 percent and no more than 7 percent, exclusively for non-duplicated, non-commercial, educational and informational programs. Such service providers would have to offer national educational program suppliers capacity on their system at reasonable prices, terms and conditions that considered the nonprofit nature of those suppliers. Such providers would exercise no editorial control over any public or educational programming.

### Local Franchising Authorities

● **Local authorities as competitors.** Required that nothing in the law prohibit a local or municipal cable franchising authority from operating as a multichannel video-program distributor within its jurisdiction. The provision took effect Dec. 4, 1992.

● **Awarding franchises.** Prohibited franchising authorities, as of Dec. 4, 1992, from granting exclusive franchises and unreasonably refusing to award an additional competitive franchise.

● **Franchise liability.** Limited the ability of cable operators to collect damages against franchising authorities in lawsuits that alleged First Amendment or other violations because the franchising authority had agreed to build a competing cable system. Damages would be limited to attorneys' fees and legal costs.

● **Franchise renewal.** Required franchising authorities to begin the renewal process for a cable franchise six months after the cable operator submitted a renewal request. The franchising authority would be required to consider whether the operator had substantially complied with the existing franchise contract. A franchise authority could turn down a renewal if it notified a cable operator of problems and had given the operator adequate time to solve them.

### Market Control and Cross-Ownership

● **Ownership limits.** Required the FCC, by Oct. 5, 1993, to set reasonable limits on the number of subscribers that cable system owners were authorized to reach. The FCC also would limit the number of channels that could be occupied by a video programmer financially affiliated with a cable operator. The FCC also was required to study whether rules were needed to limit cable program distributors from creating or producing programming.

● **Sales of cable systems.** Prohibited a cable operator, as of Dec. 4, 1992, from selling or transferring ownership in a cable system within a 36-month period after the acquisition or initial construction of the system. The FCC could waive the provision to permit appropriate transfers in cases of default, foreclosure or other financial distress.

● **Cross-ownership.** Barred cable systems from owning so-called "wireless" or microwave cable licenses or operating a satellite master antenna service within their cable service areas. Such ownership that existed before enactment of the provision was allowed, however, and the FCC could allow other exceptions to ensure that all households in a franchise area were able to obtain video programs.

### Obscene and Violent Programs

● **Notice to subscribers.** Required cable operators to give subscribers 30 days' notice if they planned to provide a premium channel to non-subscribing customers for free. Premium channels under this provision were defined as any pay service offered on a per-channel or per-program basis that offered movies rated X, NC-17 or R by the Motion Picture Association of America. Subscribers would be allowed to request that the channel be blocked.

● **Protecting children from "indecent" programs.** Required the FCC by Feb. 2, 1993, to adopt rules allowing a cable operator to enforce a stated policy of banning programs that the operator reasonably believed described or depicted sexual or excretory activi-

ties or organs in a patently offensive manner under contemporary community standards. The FCC would be required to write rules to limit the access of children to such programs. The FCC would require cable operators to put indecent programs on a single channel known to subscribers and to block such a channel unless the subscriber requested access in writing. Programmers would be required to inform cable operators of programs considered indecent under FCC rules.

● **Public channels.** Required the FCC, by April 3, 1993, to establish rules that enabled a cable operator to ban the use of any public, educational or governmental access channel for any program that contained obscene material, sexually explicit conduct or material soliciting or promoting unlawful conduct.

● **Indecent programs on leased-access channels.** Required the FCC to require cable operators to designate one leased-access channel for any "indecent" leased-access program that the operator did not choose to prohibit. The operator would have to block that channel unless a subscriber requested access in writing.

## MISCELLANEOUS

● **Equal employment opportunity.** Required that the FCC promote equal employment opportunities in each of 15 specified job categories (expanded from nine under previous law) in the cable television industry, with a policy goal of achieving diversity of views in the electronic media. Cable operators also were required, in their annual reports, to identify by race, gender and job title the number of employees within each category. For television broadcast stations, the existing FCC regulations governing the minority hiring requirements of holders of television station li-

censes would be incorporated into law. The provision also required the FCC, by July 2, 1993, to revise broadcast rules to require a midterm review of a station's hiring practices before a license renewal.

Penalties for violations of equal employment opportunity laws would be increased from $200 a day for each violation to $500 a day for each violation.

By Oct. 5, 1994, the FCC was required to submit a report to Congress on the effect and operation of the equal employment opportunity provisions.

● **Antitrust laws.** Required that nothing in the law could alter or restrict the applicability of any federal or state unfair competition laws.

● **Sports programming.** Required the FCC to conduct an ongoing study on local, regional and national sports programs by broadcast stations, cable programming networks and pay-per-view services. The study would analyze, on a sport-by-sport basis, trends in the migration of such programming from broadcast stations that were free to viewers to cable networks and pay-per-view systems. The study also would examine the economic causes and social consequences of such trends.

● **Theft.** Increased, beginning on Dec. 4, 1992, the punishment imposed on individuals convicted of stealing cable service for commercial advantage or private financial gain, to bring penalties and remedies in line with those imposed on theft of satellite signals. The new penalties, which made commercial theft of cable service a felony, would be $50,000 and two years imprisonment for the first offense, $100,000 and five years imprisonment for any subsequent offense. ∎

---

*Continued from p. 179*
several large and wealthy commercial interests," Wirth said, referring to the broadcast and satellite industries.

## VETO OVERRIDE

Bush vetoed the measure on Oct. 3, saying the burdens of new regulation would cause cable television rates to rise, not decrease as sponsors claimed. *(Veto message, p. 179)*

Bush, his Chief of Staff James A. Baker III and Senate Minority Leader Bob Dole of Kansas worked hard to persuade enough senators to abandon their support for the legislation.

In doing so, the White House cast the showdown vote on the cable bill as a critical test of presidential loyalty. But Congress resoundingly rejected the argument Oct. 5 in a bow to the American public's desire for inexpensive television viewing.

The political miscalculation — and shrewd maneuvering by bill sponsors — contributed to President Bush's landmark defeat when Congress voted to override his veto.

Both chambers easily surpassed the two-thirds majority needed to hand Bush his first override of 36 vetoes, despite intense pressure on Republican senators to side with the president just weeks before the Nov. 3 election.

Minority Whip Simpson, who supported the bill but offered to switch his vote in behalf of Bush, said the White House came close to winning the 34 senators needed to sustain the veto.

"We never could bump up past 33" votes, said Simpson, who ended up voting for the final bill. "If we had had two or three more votes, we'd have made it."

When it became apparent that the votes could not be mustered, senators who promised to switch were released from their commitments.

As a result, the Senate voted 74-25 on the override, with

no senators switching positions from when the Senate adopted the bill's conference report Sept. 22. *(Vote 264, p. 34-S)*

Hours later, the House followed suit, voting to override by 308-114 — a greater margin than the 280-128 vote by which the House had adopted the conference report on Sept. 17. No House lawmakers switched their votes to support Bush, while 14 switched from "nay" to support the legislation. *(Vote 477, p. 116-H)*

Dole set the tone on the Senate floor by saying Democrats wanted to use the vote to embarrass the president one month before the election.

"This is politics," Dole said. "The merits of this legislation went out the window two weeks ago. Sustain the president's veto. He hasn't asked for much."

Democrats too had begun to put a partisan spin on the issue.

Gore took potshots at Bush before and after the veto, saying the president was "owned lock, stock and barrel" by the cable industry and was ignoring the needs of consumers.

But Gore backed away from plans to make a floor statement prior to the vote and canceled a press briefing after the vote.

Such restraint all but evaporated when the House acted. When the vote reached the number needed to override the veto, those on the Democratic side of the aisle erupted in rancorous cheers and applause, many shouting "four more months."

Still, most lawmakers were more interested in casting a vote for a popular consumer issue than in supporting or thrashing the president. Nearly half the Republicans in Congress supported the bill, most notably sponsor Danforth.

"The fact that a president's veto is overridden is not a slap in the face," Danforth said. "It merely is a disagreement on an issue." ∎

# Stage Set To Curb Bell Companies in '93

Legislation to protect consumers and competitors as the seven regional Bell telephone companies prepared to enter new business ventures never appeared on the House floor in the 102nd Congress. But the year was considered a dress rehearsal for 1993, when it was to become more imperative that Congress consider restrictions on the Bells.

The positioning of the Bell companies to advance into new areas came in the wake of a July 1991 court ruling that allowed the regulated phone monopolies to begin providing information services such as electronic Yellow Pages. Other bans on manufacturing telecommunications equipment and providing long-distance service remained.

The companies promised their liberation would spawn a bonanza of new services, ranging from dial-up classified advertising, home shopping and medical data to devices that pinpoint stolen cars.

But the newspaper industry and other potential competitors viewed the regional Bells as predators eager to use their control over local phone lines to dominate the expanding information industry.

Two powerful House chairmen began competing in 1992 for the right to put the unfettered Bells back in their cage: Judiciary Committee Chairman Jack Brooks, D-Texas, and Energy and Commerce Committee Chairman John D. Dingell, D-Mich.

Brooks seized the initiative early in the year with a carefully crafted bill (HR 5096) to impose steep legal hurdles on the regional Bells, whose combined annual revenues in 1992 exceeded $80 billion. Brooks' legislation was written completely in the lexicon of antitrust law, not regulatory law, in a concerted attempt to insulate it from the regulatory scope of Dingell's panel.

Brooks' measure won the approval of his Judiciary panel on July 1 but then failed to advance to the floor before Congress adjourned.

The bill had faced a likely veto by President Bush. A May 28 letter from Commerce Secretary Barbara Hackman Franklin said Brooks' restraints on the Bells "would not serve the public interest."

Still, Judiciary Committee approval of Brooks' bill gave newspaper publishers a small victory that was expected to help their cause in the 103rd Congress.

The phone companies had scored their first major legislative victory in 1991 when the Senate passed a bill (S 173), 71-24, by Commerce, Science and Transportation Committee Chairman Ernest F. Hollings, D-S.C., to allow the Bells to manufacture telecommunications equipment while also imposing separate-subsidy require-

ments and forcing the Bells to sell equipment to non-affiliated manufacturers at the same prices and terms that they sold to their own divisions.

The Hollings bill also died in 1992 when the House declined to act on it or a companion measure.

Brooks' and Hollings' successes were expected to spur Dingell and Telecommunications and Finance Subcommittee Chairman Edward J. Markey, D-Mass., to move quickly on their own package of Bell restraints.

"This issue is being teed up for 1993," said BellSouth spokesman Bill McCloskey.

## BACKGROUND

The seven regional Bell companies — Ameritech, Bell Atlantic, BellSouth, NYNEX, Pacific Telesis, Southwestern Bell and U.S. West — were born out of the 1982 court-ordered breakup of American Telephone and Telegraph Co.

As AT&T ventured into the long-distance arena, the Bells continued to provide low-cost, local telephone service capable of reaching virtually every corner of the nation.

But as the Bells were born, a U.S. District Court slapped restraints on them. While they were allowed to provide cellular phone service and engage in activities ranging from real estate speculation to antique dealing, they were not permitted to make telecommunications equipment, compete in the long-distance phone market or offer information services — three areas in which it was thought they would have an unfair competitive advantage.

With a guaranteed stream of revenues and control over almost every local phone in the nation, the Bells had significant powers, which, many feared, could pose a threat to captive consumers and competitors.

The Bell companies, for example, could use revenues from their local phone businesses to subsidize other profit-making ventures or to discriminate against competitors who relied on local Bell phone lines to provide their services.

For eight years, the Bells sought legal and legislative help to free them from post-divestiture restrictions intended to stifle such potential abuse. Until 1991, the courts and Congress refused to grant their wishes.

Senate passage on June 5, 1991, of the Hollings bill, which lifted the manufacturing ban, gave the Bells their first victory. A month later, U.S. District Court Judge Harold H. Greene — on orders from an appellate court — allowed the Bells into the information services market.

---

## Baby Bells Chronology

**1982** — The Justice Department and American Telephone & Telegraph Co. reach a settlement in a 1974 antitrust suit that separates AT&T's 22 local telephone divisions from the rest of the company. In exchange, AT&T is allowed into some unregulated areas.

**1984** — AT&T's local phone companies are integrated into seven regional Bell companies. Under an agreement with the U.S. District Court for the District of Columbia, they are barred from manufacturing equipment or providing long-distance and information services.

**1987** — U.S. District Court Judge Harold H. Greene declines a Justice Department request to lift the manufacturing and information bans because of the Bells' "bottleneck" control over local telephone services.

**June 1991** — The Senate passes S 173, to allow the Bells to make telecommunications equipment.

**July 1991** — Greene, on orders from the D.C. Circuit Court of Appeals, reverses 1987 decision and allows Bells into information services market. The Supreme Court on Oct. 30 denies newspaper publishers' petition to block the Bells from providing news and information services.

**May 1992** — House Judiciary subcommittee approves bill by Chairman Jack Brooks, D-Texas, that would codify all Bell restrictions.

---

(1991 Almanac, p. 165)
Judge Greene, who had overseen and enforced the 1982 consent decree that led to the breakup of AT&T, clearly was not happy with his own decision on July 26 to release the Bell companies from the binds that narrowed their business restrictions.

He had upheld all three business restrictions in 1987, but in 1990, the U.S. Court of Appeals for the District of Columbia ordered that he reconsider his continued ban on information services, saying he failed to prove that letting the Bells into that industry would raise prices or stifle competition.

Despite his suspicions, Greene said he could not meet such a test and had no choice but to reverse his previous ruling. Greene held out little hope that the Bells could be adequately regulated on the federal or state level.

But Greene delayed his decision and ordered that it not take effect until appeals were exhausted.

The D.C. Appeals Court cleared the way for the phone monopolies to immediately offer information services on Oct. 7. The appeals court called Greene's delay "an abuse of discretion" not in the public interest.

The Supreme Court on Oct. 30 denied a petition, 8-0, by newspaper publishers to block the seven regional Bell companies from providing news and information services. This meant the Bells were free to own and transmit over their phone lines a range of services through data base texts and video signals.

The Bells remained barred from offering cable television service under a 1984 law that deregulated the cable industry from local price controls.

Legislation to impose new regulations on the cable industry enacted into law in 1992 over President Bush's veto did not alter that ban, though the FCC took steps to further allow telephone companies to act as common carriers for video signals and to invest more in cable companies.
(Cable TV reregulation, p. 171)
The regional phone companies spent millions of dollars to preserve their entrance into the information services market. Among the ranks of their coalition of supporters were telecommunications companies that wanted to form joint-manufacturing ventures with the regional Bells and small businesses that wanted to advertise over the phone lines as well as in newspapers.

Disabled advocates eager to have services such as electronic Yellow Pages, text-to-voice conversion and voice recognition applications made more accessible also had been attracted to the Bells' cause.

## THE BROOKS BILL

Much of the Bells' gains over the previous year were darkened by the sudden emergence of the Brooks bill. The Subcommittee on Economic and Commercial Law approved the measure May 28 by a largely partisan 10-6 vote.

The bill would force the Bells to wait three years before seeking entry into the information services market and seven years before pursuing the electronic publishing and long-distance markets. After five years, a Bell company could seek to manufacture telecommunications equipment under the bill.

The Justice Department would first have to certify that there was "no substantial possibility" the Bells could use their monopoly to impede competition in any of the new markets. The bill would allow competitors to intervene in federal court to prevent the Bells' request.

The Bell companies considered the Brooks bill unnecessarily harsh. They considered the legal hurdles it sought to erect — especially empowering competitors to intervene in the process — tantamount to blocking their entry into new businesses.

Brooks said such strong constraints were "consistent with the core principles" of the existing court decree that restricted the Bells.

"I, for one, will not condone an industry born in a 19th century monopoly to be reborn in a sleeker, 21st century version," he said.

In contrast, Dingell's panel approached the issue from a regulatory perspective. The Energy and Commerce Subcommittee on Telecommunications and Finance, chaired by Markey, was drafting a bill that never moved in 1992. But an earlier version would have allowed the Bells into any new venture as long as the Federal Communications Commission (FCC) deemed the market competitive and the Bells complied with strict safeguards intended to protect competitors and consumers.

Markey's draft bill required the FCC to ensure competitors' access to the local phone network. It also required the Bell companies to operate a new line of business through a separate subsidiary that had its own bookkeeping and advertising. The FCC also would guarantee that local phone revenues were not used to subsidize any new business costs.

### Newspaper Interest

Bell strategists said the real motivation behind the Brooks bill was to protect the newspaper industry, which viewed electronic classified advertising as its No. 1 threat.

Bell lobbyists said the newspaper industry was hardly a textbook model of competition. Only 11 cities had two or more independent newspapers. Many of the largest newspaper conglomerates also owned television and radio stations in the same markets.

The newspaper industry's lobbying war chest was estimated at $1 million to $3 million. But Bell lobbyists, armed with $20 million, said newspapers did not need as much money because they had the power of the written word.

"In an election year when the climate in district after district is very unsettled for incumbents, an appeal from a publisher for support on a bill doesn't need to carry with it even a veiled threat," said Ameritech spokesman Peter M. Lincoln. "It's very difficult to do battle with people who buy ink by the barrel."

Bell opponents countered that the newspaper industry was just the most visible of the businesses threatened by the reach of the regional Bells.

"If it was solely the newspapers' fight, the Brooks bill wouldn't have passed the subcommittee," said Brian Moir of the Washington law firm Fisher, Wayland, Cooper & Leader, which represented business telephone users.

Indeed, the coalition aligned against the Bells included not only newspaper publishers and Moir's clients but also the Consumer Federation of America, AT&T and other long-distance companies, equipment makers, information service providers, the burglar alarm industry and the American Association of Retired Persons.

The coalition rejected Bell claims that their participation in the information services industry would create 1.46 million jobs and would add $110 billion to the nation's gross domestic product by the year 2001.

Instead, Bell opponents pointed to Commerce Department estimates that the information services industry would grow by 20 percent annually over the next five years

without Bell involvement. They also cited a 1989 Labor Department estimate that as many as 27,000 domestic jobs would be lost in the central switching industry alone if the Bells entered the manufacturing sector.

Michael D. Baudhuin, corporate vice president for AT&T said the battle was a replay of the fight over the telephone company's monopoly power that had raged ever since the telephone network was founded at the turn of the century.

"The simple fact is, you can't mix a monopoly with a competitive marketplace," Baudhuin said. "The [Bell] people who are promising they will act in the public interest, that they won't cross-subsidize, believe it in the marrow of their being. The problem is in the structure of what they are managing. It's the nature of the beast."

### Full Committee Action

The bill to impose legal restrictions on the seven regional Bell companies won full Judiciary Committee approval July 1.

But the committee killed a key component of the bill that would have forced the Bells to wait three to seven years before entering the equipment manufacturing and information-services markets, amid concern that the provision was too restrictive on the local phone monopolies.

The committee approved HR 5096 by a vote of 24-9, giving a somewhat diluted victory to Judiciary Chairman Brooks, newspaper publishers and others who feared the Bells could use their monopoly power against consumers and competitors.

"We are disappointed that the waiting periods were eliminated," said Gene Kimmelman, legislative director of the Consumer Federation of America, who otherwise was pleased with the outcome. "The real policy goal here is to keep the Bells out until there is enough competitive activity in the local markets."

Bell officials characterized the vote as a major setback in their efforts to provide information services such as electronic classified advertising — a market a federal court allowed them to enter last July.

Brooks had drafted his bill around antitrust law set by the Sherman Act of 1890 and the Clayton Act of 1914, thus avoiding a referral to the Energy panel.

"The fundamental framework set out here, based on generic principles in the Sherman Act, has got to be preferable to the piecemeal, mega-deal special pleading that masquerades as policy-making in other forums," said Brooks.

Brooks' bill would largely codify the original Bell restrictions imposed in the wake of the AT&T breakup but would effectively reverse Greene's July decision to allow the Bells to move unimpeded into the information service arena.

But the bill would make a key change: While the Bells were required to go to Judge Greene to seek exceptions to the various restrictions, the Brooks bill would require the Bells to go to the U.S. attorney general instead.

Critics, including many of Brooks' Democratic colleagues, opposed that provision, noting that the Justice Department in recent years had argued strongly that the Bells be allowed into the manufacturing and information services markets.

Even Attorney General William P. Barr, in a June 30 letter reiterating the Bush administration's veto threat, said the bill would "place the Department of Justice in an inappropriate regulatory role."

The Energy and Commerce panel's draft measure would give the FCC sole authority over granting and monitoring

Bell entry into the new fields. But lawmakers were dubious about that approach as well.

"The FCC cannot do this job. The Energy and Commerce Committee has said time and time again that there is an inadequate and insufficient regulatory network," said Mike Synar, D-Okla., a member of both the Energy and Judiciary panels. "We have to jump-start the Energy Committee to weigh in and assist us in this process."

The Brooks bill would not give the attorney general final say over the Bells' future, however.

It would allow any Bell company or competitor to appeal the attorney general's decisions to federal district court. The court would be required to take a fresh look — regardless of the Justice Department's stance — to determine whether enough competition existed to allow the Bells to enter a new market.

The requirement, known as a de novo review, was used in many antitrust cases involving mergers. But it drew opposition from Hamilton Fish Jr., R-N.Y., ranking member of the Judiciary panel.

"The de novo standard is unusual," said Fish. "Normally courts give deference to agency decisions."

He offered an unsuccessful amendment to kill the court's fresh review power and effectively handed the attorney general far greater authority over whether to allow the Bells entry into new markets. It failed 13-20.

By far, Brooks' biggest setback came when the committee killed a key aspect of his bill that would have imposed a lengthy waiting period on the Bells before they could even petition the attorney general to enter a new market.

Bowing to pressure from the Bells and from colleagues who believed the waiting periods were too restrictive, Brooks sought a compromise and won a short-lived victory to reduce the time frame to two years for non-publishing information services, two years for manufacturing and five years for long-distance service and electronic publishing.

But another amendment by Fish to eliminate the entire waiting period was then approved 18-15, giving the Bells their only victory. Still, under the bill the Bells would face lengthy court challenges as major hurdles to expanding into new ventures quickly. "You've got to add five years on each [waiver application] for litigation," said Dan Glickman, D-Kan. "This is a lawyer's dream."

The committee also rejected an attempt by Fish to weaken the legal standard set by the bill to guide the federal courts. Fish had proposed allowing the courts to permit the regional Bells to enter new markets if the move would be in the public interest, regardless of the impact on competition.

Other amendments adopted included those by:

● Brooks, to allow the Bells to continue doing business in any information services ventures they engaged in from last October, when the ban was lifted, to 60 days before enactment of the bill. The amendment was adopted by voice vote.

● John Bryant, D-Texas, to restore the bill's five-year waiting period for the Bells to request entry into the long-distance services market and the portion of the information services market related to the burglar alarm industry. Some Bell companies hope to wire homes with burglar alarms through telephone lines.

The amendment, adopted by voice vote, was a surprise victory for the alarm industry, which has 13,000 businesses nationwide. By winning the waiting period restriction, the industry proved better able than the newspaper publishers to keep the Bells at bay. ∎

# Amid Controversy, Hill Reauthorizes CPB

After two years of debate over whether the nonprofit Corporation for Public Broadcasting (CPB) lived up to its mandate to provide balanced, taxpayer-subsidized programming, the 102nd Congress cleared Aug. 4 a bill (HR 2977) to reauthorize the corporation for three years.

The bill sparked a freewheeling election-year debate in Congress that boiled over in the Senate and in the nation's editorial pages about the degree of objectivity in public broadcasting.

Critics said the CPB was rife with partisanship. Defenders rallied to the side of public broadcasting, saying it delivered educational and cultural programming that commercial broadcasting had little incentive to provide.

Though conservative critics called for privatizing public broadcasting, the debate resulted only in an unsuccessful attempt in the Senate to cut funding for the corporation.

Critics won concessions from bill sponsors, however, to include provisions designed to make the CPB more accountable and objective. For instance, the final bill required the CPB to make publicly available details of each organization that received a grant from the corporation. Also, grants to independent producers were to be spread out across the country.

Action on public broadcasting in 1992 opened in the Senate, where the bill to reauthorize the CPB remained stalled over the longstanding complaint among conservatives that its programs often revealed a liberal bias.

Several Republican senators had placed anonymous "holds" in 1991 on the Senate bill to reauthorize the CPB for three years, blocking the measure (S 1504) for months from full Senate consideration. The House had easily passed a companion measure (HR 2977) by voice vote Nov. 25, 1991.

The Senate on June 3 settled the debate over the political slant of public broadcasting's programming in agreeing to include in its version several provisions designed to bolster CPB's statutory mandate to provide objective and balanced programming. The House on Aug. 4 endorsed those changes in clearing the bill.

The final bill required the CPB to keep a public file on every organization that received a CPB grant, including all programs that were produced with the grants. The Independent Television Service, a nonprofit entity created by Congress in 1988 to steer money toward independent film producers, also faced stricter reporting requirements and had to show that grants were spread throughout a broad geographic area.

The bill authorized the CPB at $310 million for fiscal 1994, $375 million for fiscal 1995 and $425 million for fiscal 1996. It also made changes to the CPB board of directors, reducing the number of members from 10 to nine to avoid tie votes.

## BACKGROUND

The CPB was created by Congress in 1967 to channel federal dollars toward public broadcasting through grants

---

### BOXSCORE

➡ **Public Broadcasting Reauthorization (HR 2977, S 1504).** The legislation reauthorized the nonprofit Corporation for Public Broadcasting for three years.

**Reports:** H Rept 102-363; S Rept 102-221.

#### KEY ACTION

March 3 — The **Senate** voted to end debate on S 1504, 87-7.

June 3 — The **Senate** passed HR 2977, 84-11.

Aug 4 — The **House** cleared HR 2977 by voice vote.

Aug. 26 — President Bush signed HR 2977 — PL 102-356.

---

for public radio and television stations. While lawmakers held CPB's purse strings, decisions on programming were mostly made by the Public Broadcasting System (PBS), which fed programs by satellite to 345 local public broadcasting stations. This organizational structure was intended to insulate the selection of programs from influence by lawmakers and the executive branch. But critics said the structure failed to safeguard against government meddling, lead to biased programming and created a lack of accountability for taxpayer dollars.

Keeping lawmakers at a distance was one of the goals incorporated in the 1967 Public Broadcasting Act, signed by President Lyndon B. Johnson.

The law expanded the former National Educational Television to include a variety of public-interest programs and made "high-minded" programming, as it has come to be known, the goal of the CPB and PBS boards.

Such programming was intended to be more diverse, cultural and intellectually challenging than commercial TV and free from interference by government or the marketplace.

To insulate CPB and PBS from government propaganda and political pressure, most programming decisions were left up to local public stations, which were free to reject or air programs of their choice.

In addition, PBS was set up as a nonprofit corporation to provide diverse educational and public-interest programming and was not expected to answer directly to Congress. That left CPB funding as the only legislative hold lawmakers had over public television.

Despite such safeguards, public TV was not immune to political attack.

Each year the CPB went to Congress for funding and was often forced to adhere to congressional mandates to get money. Also, the board of the CPB was chosen by the president and confirmed by the Senate.

During the 1988 authorization, for example, many Republicans criticized PBS for programs sympathetic to communist struggles in Central America. *(1988 Almanac, p. 582)*

In 1982, 34 members of Congress, and Vice President George Bush, sitting as president of the Senate, made calls and wrote letters to CPB administrators threatening to cut its appropriation unless it restored funds to "The Lawmakers," a weekly series that looked favorably upon members of Congress. The program aired for another year.

President Richard M. Nixon in 1970 ordered CPB board members to drop critical coverage of the Vietnam War and instead concentrate on educational and environmental programming.

Public television had evolved in ways that angered both conservatives and liberals.

To the dismay of critics on the right, the 10-member board of the CPB had seen its ability to influence programming diminished. Until 1980, the CPB directly controlled

grant money for programs. But the board, the majority of whose members were appointed during the Carter administration, moved that responsibility to PBS.

In 1990 the CPB board reached a new agreement with PBS, at Congress' request, and gave even more programming power to PBS. In 1992, CPB contracted through PBS for much of its national programming, while also continuing to give direct grants to PBS and local stations.

Conservatives said the new structure eroded accountability and inhibited balanced programming. Others complained that the reorganization centralized too much power at PBS.

Another concern focused on CPB's funding. The 1980s heralded dramatic cuts, forcing local public stations to rely more on corporate underwriting for their livelihood.

In 1992, the federal government provided 17 percent of funding to public broadcasting. Corporate donations stood at 17 percent, while state and local governments, colleges, and private donations made up the rest. In contrast, in 1980, 27 percent of public television's funding came from the federal government, 10 percent from corporate funding, while the rest was made up by state and local governments, colleges and private donations.

### Attacks from the Right and Left

Controversial films produced and aired on public TV in 1991 put CPB and PBS on the defensive from conservative and liberal critics alike.

Rep. Don Ritter, R-Pa., who led a one-man crusade against program selections on public TV during House consideration of its CPB bill in 1991, focused his complaints on PBS' 1991 refusal to purchase "The Greenhouse Conspiracy," a 55-minute documentary highlighting the scientific uncertainties of global warming. Some local public stations aired the show but were forced to buy it outright at higher costs.

Ritter said PBS had aired only documentaries embracing global warming theories, particularly a program called "After the Warming."

Conservatives also were incensed over the program "Tongues United," an examination of the lives of African-American gay men. The episode was partly funded by a $5,000 grant from the National Endowment for the Arts.

Though many stations aired the show, the Rev. Donald E. Wildmon's American Family Association claimed credit for persuading 201 of PBS's 345 stations to pull it.

In the wake of that controversy, PBS on Aug. 12, 1991, decided to pull another documentary, called "Stop the Church." PBS cited a "pervasive tone of ridicule" against the Roman Catholic Church in the show's depiction of a 1989 demonstration by AIDS activists at New York's St. Patrick's Cathedral. It was the first time PBS had acknowledged keeping a program off the air purely because of its content. Many television critics denounced the decision as censorship.

### 1991 Action

Solutions for resolving concerns about program balance proved difficult for the 102nd Congress to find. The House had easily passed a bill (HR 2977) in 1991 to reauthorize the CPB for three years. But concern about liberal bias in the network's programming snagged the effort in the Senate. *(1991 Almanac, p. 168)*

During a Senate Commerce Committee markup in November 1991, Sen. John McCain, R-Ariz., won language requiring the board of the CPB to detail in its annual report what kind of programs were funded by PBS through taxpayer dollars.

The House bill, passed by voice vote Nov. 25, contained a similar provision — as well as stronger reporting require-

ments for the new independent filmmakers' entity. The CPB board did not oppose the provisions.

Both bills also permanently reduced the number of CPB board members to nine and staggered their terms.

Other than that, no one came forward with a plan to restructure public broadcasting to ensure balance in its program selections. Analysts at the Heritage Foundation, a conservative think tank, argued for complete privatization of public broadcasting, particularly in light of new educational viewing choices offered by cable television. But that idea failed to attract much serious attention.

Complaints about liberal programming were standard fare in CPB authorization and appropriations bills. But rhetoric in 1992 appeared louder than ever.

Presidential politics added fuel to the fire. Early in 1992, President Bush was under attack by Republican challenger Patrick J. Buchanan for not being tough enough on taxpayer funding for controversial arts and television programming.

While opponents supported much of the public network's educational, cultural and entertainment programs, political attention on programming selections had an impact.

## SENATE ACTION

The controversial bill to reauthorize the CPB passed its first floor test March 3, when a vote to end debate on a motion to proceed to the bill (S 1504) passed, 87-7. *(Vote 36, p. 6-S)*

But the success was short-lived. The measure quickly stalled, derailed by public broadcasting critics who instead steered debate toward a Republican crime-fighting package.

The snag came after Minority Leader Bob Dole, R-Kan., indicated that a Republican alternative to the Democrats' crime bill was to be offered as an amendment to the public broadcasting bill. Majority Leader George J. Mitchell, D-Maine, responded by pulling the broadcasting bill and moving to the conference report on the Democrats' crime bill.

Three months later, proponents of public broadcasting were more successful. Tossing aside complaints that public radio and television programming was rife with "elitism, sweetheart deals and one-sided partisanship," the Senate on June 3 passed HR 2977 by a vote of 84-11 after inserting the text of S 1504. *(Vote 114, p. 16-S)*

The action followed months of delay by Republicans who complained that public broadcasting programs often had a liberal bias.

The Senate passed the bill after two days of deliberation that paled in comparison to a parallel debate over public television that raged on the airwaves and in the nation's editorial pages.

In the end, concern over the political slant and utility of public broadcasting raised by the public debate boiled down to a fight over money. The Senate easily rebuffed an attempt by Trent Lott, R-Miss., made on behalf of a hospitalized Jesse Helms, R-N.C., to keep funding for public broadcasting at fiscal 1992 levels.

The Senate rejected, 22-75, Lott's amendment to keep authorized levels for the CPB at $275 million a year. Instead, the measure authorized a 50 percent increase in funding for public broadcasting. *(Vote 112, p. 15-S)*

But while lawmakers handily rejected the move to freeze funding, a much sharper budget-cutting ax loomed as the annual appropriations process got under way. Public broadcasting had to vie for fiscal 1993 funds with other popular programs such as Head Start and student aid. The programs were all funded under the same appropriations measure for the departments of Labor, Health and Human

Services, Education and related agencies. *(Appropriations, p. 657)*

## Mired in Controversy

The public broadcasting bill was mired in controversy from the beginning and continued to spark debate outside Congress to the end.

The battle began when several Republican senators lodged complaints that public broadcasting dollars were not adequately accounted for and that tax-funded documentaries and public affairs shows often had a liberal bias. Added to that were concerns that public broadcasting catered to the rich and amounted to what Lott called "an upper-middle-class entitlement program."

But while critics outside Congress — including the Heritage Foundation and other conservative groups — continued to call for privatizing public broadcasting, Senate opponents began to work with sponsors to fashion a compromise intended to answer concerns about the objectivity and accountability of public televison.

Sen. Ted Stevens, Alaska, third-ranking Republican on the Commerce Subcommittee on Communications, played an unusual mediating role between fellow conservatives and Democratic supporters of public broadcasting. Alaska's rural population relied heavily on public broadcasting for news, education and telegraph-style message services over public radio stations.

The bill reauthorized the CPB at $310 million for fiscal 1994, $375 million for fiscal 1995 and $425 million for fiscal 1996. The authorization, set two years in advance to maintain program continuity, funded program and administrative expenses for television stations that belonged to the private, nonprofit Public Broadcasting Service as well as National Public Radio member stations.

The Bush administration opposed the bill's funding levels and expressed concern about accountability, objectivity and balance in publicly funded programs.

On the floor, Dole and Lott sought to shift debate away from concerns about the political bias of public television and instead cast the issue in terms of fiscal responsibility.

Helms, a longtime foe of public television, had intended to play a lead role in the debate, particularly on the issues of funding levels and "obscene" programming. But he was hospitalized for heart bypass surgery before floor action.

Dole laid out a litany of complaints with public broadcasting in a lengthy speech. He called the CPB a "confusing, clumsy and inefficient bureaucracy with no power at the top and too much funding flowing to a privileged few."

Dole said the bulk of CPB's $100 million program fund was spent on grants to a handful of PBS stations whose programs serve viewers with an "Eastern elite mentality."

Dole and Lott argued that cable television had diminished the need for public broadcasting. In 1992, cable reached 61 percent of all television households.

But Stevens and Daniel K. Inouye, D-Hawaii, chairman of the Commerce Subcommittee on Communications, said public television was needed more than ever by those who could not receive or afford cable.

The question of liberal bias received less floor attention than expected, though Dole called it "the most important issue of all" in the debate. But Dole backed away from an effort to slash funding for the Independent Television Service, a program criticized as a hotbed for liberal documentary filmmaking. Dole had set out to cut funds for the service, which was created to foster the production of documentaries by independent filmmakers.

After four hours of negotiations with Inouye, Dole agreed to simply require that future grants under the program be distributed over a wider geographic range than New York and California.

Critics of public broadcasting managed to win some changes to address concerns that CPB was meeting its mandate to ensure balanced programming.

By voice vote, the Senate agreed to require the board to gather public comment about the quality, balance and diversity of its programs to help it determine whether to award grants to shows with opposing views.

The Senate agreed by voice vote to a provision that required the board's annual report to list in greater detail all program grant award amounts, names of recipients and producers and descriptions of programs.

The Senate also accepted, 93-3, an amendment by Robert C. Byrd, D-W.Va., that extended until midnight a 6 a.m.-to-8 p.m. ban on "indecent" programs. Stations that go off the air at or before midnight had the ban extended only until 10 p.m. *(Vote 113, p. 16-S)*

In addition to providing funding for CPB program activities, the bill authorized $42 million for each of the three years for capital investments in public television and radio facilities.

It also made changes to the CPB board of directors, reducing the number of members from 10 to nine to avoid tie votes. And board members' terms were staggered so that three terms expire every three years.

Other amendments accepted by voice vote included those by:

● Inouye, to add provisions of the House-passed bill. One clarified that it is a goal of public broadcasting to reach more deaf, hearing-impaired, blind and visually impaired people.

● Inouye and Stevens, to require the CPB to give more detailed accounts of how grant money is used.

● Larry Pressler, R-S.D., to require the CPB to report on the most effective way to use public broadcasting facilities to bring televised classrooms to rural areas.

● Mitch McConnell, R-Ky., to require that television programs funded by the CPB include a statement that the corporation "is a private, nonprofit corporation created by Congress" or similar language.

● Jeff Bingaman, D-N.M., to require the CPB to report on the best way to establish a public television channel dedicated to educating children.

## HOUSE ACTION

The House on Aug. 4 cleared the CPB reauthorization bill with little of the controversy over the objectivity of public broadcasting that had stymied the measure in the Senate.

Lawmakers passed by voice vote the Senate-passed bill that amended the earlier House version. Despite concerns about funding levels, Bush signed the measure into law Aug. 26 (PL 102-356).

The House had passed the earlier version of the bill by voice vote on Nov. 25, 1991.

On the House floor, Energy and Commerce Chairman John D. Dingell, D-Mich., was critical of Byrd's successful amendment that extended to midnight a ban on "indecent" television programming on commercial and public stations. Citing a 1988 U.S. Court of Appeals ruling that found a 24-hour ban on such programming unconstitutional, Dingell said the provision promised to be a "preordained failure" likely to be shot down by the courts. ∎

# Bush Signs Law Regulating 900 Numbers

The Senate on Oct. 7 cleared for the president's signature a bill to clamp down on abuses in the 900-number pay-per-call industry.

The legislation (HR 6191 — PL 102-556) marked the first federal regulation of the burgeoning pay-per-call telephone industry, which offered callers information or products and charged them by the minute over long-distance phone lines.

As cleared, the bill sought to protect consumers from unscrupulous 900-number phone services by requiring that callers be warned of the cost and terms of such calls.

Such services ranged from stock quotations and horoscopes to contests and sex "chat" lines. To counter the negative image surrounding the 900-services industry, many providers of such services supported the legislation.

The bill required a "preamble" to precede each 900-number call to inform the caller of the price and nature of the service provided. It also allowed the caller to hang up early without incurring a charge. Also, services aimed at children under 12 were banned.

HR 6191 incorporated compromises over minor differences between an earlier House measure (HR 3490) and a companion Senate bill (S 1579).

## BACKGROUND

The pay-per-call telephone industry burgeoned quickly after the 1984 breakup of AT&T by offering entertainment aimed at adults and children as well as fundraising, corporate promotions and technical help services.

In an industry in which the simple act of placing a call incurred hefty long-distance charges, opportunities for consumer abuse were rampant, charged 900-line critics.

Problems arose because 900 services turned to long-distance and local phone companies to bill callers, leaving many customers confused about how to challenge unfair charges.

Lawmakers had been inundated with stories about 900-number schemes, ranging from a $29.95 call for a credit card application usually available free from any bank, to contests that urged callers to redial to win prizes.

The information services industry originally had fought the preamble requirement and other bill provisions but in 1992 accepted legislation as necessary to salvage the reputation of 900 services.

Negative publicity had stunted the rapid growth of pay-per-call businesses. The industry jumped from $60 million in retail billings in 1988 to $445 million in 1989. In 1990, revenues almost doubled from the previous year to $880 million, according to Strategic Telemedia, a market research firm. But by 1991 such dramatic boosts were stymied, and revenues increased 20 percent to $975 million.

Steven J. Metalitz, vice president of the Information Industry Association, blamed the slowdown in part on a

---

## BOXSCORE

➡ **900-Number Regulations (HR 6191, HR 3490, S 1597).** Legislation to regulate the pay-per-call telephone industry.

**Reports:** H Rept 102-430, S Rept 102-190.

### KEY ACTION

Feb. 25 — The **House** passed HR 3490, 381-31.

Oct. 5 — The **House** passed a revised measure (HR 6191) by voice vote.

Oct. 7 — The **Senate** cleared HR 6191 by voice vote.

Oct. 28 — President Bush signed HR 6191 — PL 102-556.

---

loss of consumer confidence. "There are bad actors in the industry that have discouraged people from using these services," Metalitz said. "We think the challenge now is to restore confidence. Uniform national rules can do that."

Long-distance carriers also had become wary of handling such calls. Two of the four long-distance phone companies that contracted with 900-number providers dropped the service in 1991. US Sprint canceled contracts with 90 percent of its 900-service providers. And Illinois-based Telesphere Communications Inc. was under bankruptcy protection and no longer offered such services.

Still, many said the industry's future was bright. More respectable players were offering 900 services, such as McDonalds Corp., nonprofit fundraisers and media companies, and consumer complaints dropped.

The Federal Communications Commission (FCC) regulated 900-number services. The legislation went beyond existing rules that the FCC adopted in September 1991 by codifying them. Those rules required 900-number providers and phone companies to include a preamble, permitted customers to block the service, allowed customers to disconnect without being charged and required parental consent.

But jurisdiction over advertisements for 900-number services belonged to the Federal Trade Commission. Many of the bill's provisions were directed toward the trade commission as well as the FCC.

### 1991 Action

Lawmakers began prescribing a dose of regulatory medicine for the 900-number industry early in the 102nd Congress. Two House Energy and Commerce subcommittees rushed to approve consumer protections from 900-number telephone services. The Senate Commerce Committee also advanced a bill to impose regulation on the pay-per-call industry. *(1991 Almanac, p. 160)*

On Oct. 8, the House Energy and Commerce Committee combined the measure approved earlier in the year — HR 2330 and HR 2829 — into a comprehensive measure (HR 3490) that was similar to the FCC regulations. It sought to strengthen the new rules by codifying them into law. But that measure never advanced to the floor

The full Senate passed a sweeping measure (S 1579) by voice vote on Oct. 29 that cracked down on unscrupulous services. The services had to include an introductory message that laid out the costs of the call. Callers could hang up during that time and not be charged.

### LEGISLATIVE ACTION

The House moved early in the year to pass HR 3490 by a vote of 381-31 and then adopt the Senate bill number, S 1597. Only minor differences existed between the two bills.

The House then approved a revised 900-number bill (HR 6191) on Oct. 5 after incorporating changes requested by the Senate. The Senate cleared the measure the next day.

### House Action

The House on Feb. 25 passed a bill (HR 3490) that would protect consumers from unscrupulous 900-number phone services by requiring that callers be warned of the cost and terms of the call.

Phone customers would not be the only beneficiaries. Legitimate 900-number providers hoped the legislation would weed out dishonest providers and instill consumer confidence in pay-per-call services.

The House passed the bill, 381-31, and sent it back to the Senate after adopting the bill number of a companion Senate measure (S 1597). *(Vote 17, p. 4-H)*

Supporters, led by Rep. Bart Gordon, D-Tenn., were inspired to write the bill amid complaints that consumers were unaware of the price and terms of 900-number calls and that children were being lured into dialing the numbers.

"Legitimate services are penalized by the actions of a few," said Edward J. Markey, D-Mass., chairman of the House Energy and Commerce Telecommunications Subcommittee. "We can punish the hucksters while allowing legitimate business people to move forward."

The administration argued that the bill was unnecessary because federal agencies already had taken many of the same steps through regulations. But no veto threat was issued.

Under the House bill, 900-service providers would have to include a "preamble" before each call. It would disclose the name of the company offering the service, the price and the nature of the service. Callers could then hang up without incurring any charges.

The bill also would impose new restrictions on phone companies. They would have to disclose on customer bills how disputes with 900-number providers can be resolved — a provision not in the Senate bill.

Phone companies would be prohibited from disconnecting a phone over failure to pay a 900-number charge.

Customers also would be able to block 900-number calls from their phones. The bill would direct 900-number service providers to warn children younger than 18 that they should get parental consent before calling. The Senate bill banned any 900 service from being geared toward children 12 or younger.

The House on Oct. 5 approved a compromise measure, incorporating changes requested by the industry and the Senate, and renumbered the bill as HR 6191. The changes included more explicit preemption of the patchwork of state regulatory requirements for 900 services, and excluded pay-per-call services involving data sent to facsimile machines from the bill's consumer protection requirements. The FCC was also to study consumer issues involving data-based 900 services.

The Senate cleared HR 6191 by voice vote on Oct. 7.

## TELEMARKETING FRAUD

A related Senate bill dealing with the 900-number industry (S 1392) died in the House after getting hung up on last-minute snags. The bill would have required the Federal Trade Commission to set up rules defining and prohibiting deceptive, fraudulent and abusive telemarketing practices.

The Senate passed an earlier version of the bill on Nov.

---

# No Progress on Caller ID Bills

Legislation to allow telephone users to block new technological devices that reveal a caller's telephone number stalled in the Senate after Republicans tried to attach a controversial anti-crime measure to it. A similar Caller ID bill never advanced to the House floor.

Under the bills (S 652, HR 1305), blocking was to be available only on a per-call basis. Customers would have been allowed to access the blocking service by dialing a code.

The Senate measure quickly bogged down May 6 when Sen. Phil Gramm, R-Texas, attempted to tack on the latest Republican anti-crime bill amid claims that federal curbs on Caller ID devices were unnecessary. The move sparked Democrats to shelve the telephone legislation and turn to their anti-crime bill. *(Crime bill, p. 311)*

In 1991, the House Energy and Commerce Committee had approved HR 1305 (H Rept 102-324) on July 30; the Senate Judiciary Committee on Oct. 31 had approved S 652 (S Rept 102-247). *(1991 Almanac, p. 164)*

Bill sponsor Rep. Herb Kohl, D-Wis., said blocking the use of the device was needed to protect the privacy of those who placed phone calls. Caller ID already was available in 23 states in 1992.

The most controversial aspect of the bill was that it would pre-empt state regulation of the devices. In Indiana, Mississippi, New Jersey and Virginia, for example, Caller ID devices could not be blocked.

Those states would have been forced to offer customers the option to block Caller ID devices. States that offered per-line blocking would have been allowed to continue use of the devices.

"This is not an issue that needs federal pre-emption of state authority," said Thad Cochran, R-Miss. He said the Federal Communications Commission was preparing new rules on the issue, as were several states.

The bill also would ensure that Caller ID devices did not violate federal wiretap laws.

The Pennsylvania State Supreme Court had ruled that Caller ID devices violated that state's wiretap statute.

Among the bill's other options to protect phone customers from unwanted calls was a requirement that telephone companies that offered Caller ID also offer "call trace" — a service that would allow a recipient of an unwanted call to forward the number of that caller to the local phone company for investigation.

---

27, 1991. In 1992, the House on Sept. 29 amended the bill with the text of an Energy and Commerce Committee-approved bill (HR 3203 — H Rept 102-688).

But senators added an amendment Oct. 7 and sent S 1392 back to the House, where it died without final action.

The bill aimed to enable states and consumer agencies to better target and prosecute people who perpetrate illegal marketing activities and travel across state lines.

It also called on the FTC to set up a central information clearinghouse to help consumers and law enforcement officials track past offenses by telemarketers. ■

# Door Opened for Home Digital Recording

The Senate on Oct. 7 cleared a bill (S 1623) to compensate the music industry for home taping with digital audio technology, paving the way for the wide-scale introduction of the high-quality recording tapes and equipment into the U.S. market.

Digital audio technology offered near-perfect sound quality attractive to consumers. But the music industry feared a wave of illicit copying of original recorded works and pushed to keep the technology out of the United States without legislative protections to offset expected financial losses.

The bill applied to digital tape recording technology — first widely available in the United States in the fall of 1992, after a long delay — as well as any future advances in recordable compact discs.

The legislation reflected a compromise reached in 1991 between makers of the digital equipment and music performers and publishers.

The Senate passed an early version of the bill June 17 (S 1623) and then cleared the final measure Oct. 7 after it had made its way through three House committees and the House floor. The House passed its version (HR 3204) Sept. 22 — after inserting its bill into the shell of S 1623 — before shipping it back to the Senate.

President Bush signed the bill into law Oct. 28 (PL 102-563).

The digital audio tape law added a 3 percent royalty fee to the price of blank digital tapes and a 2 percent fee to the price of new digital recording equipment. The additional fees were to be shared among musicians, recording companies and music publishers to cover financial losses from illegal copying.

Makers of digital audio equipment also were required to install an electronic device in all digital recording equipment sold in the United States to prevent consumers from making more than one copy of an original recording.

## BACKGROUND

The legislation grew out of a compromise reached in July 1991 among the digital audio tape industry, retailers and musicians. It allowed consumers to make home copies of digital tapes without fear of violating copyright laws as long as single copies were made for personal use.

The compromise first gained widespread support in October 1991 at a key hearing of the Senate Judiciary Patents, Copyrights and Trademarks Subcommittee, which was the first panel to examine the deal reached in July 1991. Chairman Dennis DeConcini, D-Ariz., said the "historic agreement" promised to end legal wrangling that had delayed introduction of digital technology in the United States.

The decade-long disagreement between the music industry and retailers had stalled any legislation to protect musicians and publishers from losing potential royalties because of digital taping.

Digital tape technology achieved master-quality sound

---

## BOXSCORE

➡ **Digital Audio Recording (S 1623, HR 3204, HR 4567).** Legislation to compensate the music industry for home taping with digital audio technology.

**Reports:** S Rept 102-294; H Rept 102-873, Parts I-II; H Rept 102-780.

### KEY ACTION

June 17 — The **Senate** passed S 1623 by voice vote.

Sept. 22 — The **House** passed HR 3204 by voice vote and then substituted it with S 1623.

Oct. 7 — The **Senate** cleared S 1623 by voice vote.

Oct. 28 — President Bush signed S 1623 — PL 102-563.

---

reproduction, which led performers and music publishers to fear the loss of sales and royalties if consumers were allowed to make multiple copies of recorded works.

Blank digital audio tapes were introduced in limited numbers in the United States more than a decade before the legislation. But their use was stymied after music industry groups sued Sony Corp., saying that the company's digital recorders and blank digital cassettes infringed on copyright protections of their works and threatened the profitable music industry.

Under the 1991 deal, a royalty fee was to be added to every blank digital tape and all digital audio recorders sold to compensate music publishers, recording companies and artists for copyright infringement. In addition, an electronic chip was to be inserted in digital recording equipement to prevent more than one copy of an original recording from being made.

Digital audio technology, which began to arrive in U.S. stores from Japan in the fall of 1992, allowed consumers to make near-perfect copies of recorded music. Home taping cost the music industry about $1.5 billion a year, or about one-third of the industry's annual revenues, said Rep. Carlos J. Moorhead, R-Calif.

## HOUSE ACTION

After three House committees weighed in, the House on Sept. 22 passed a bill (HR 3204) by voice vote to resolve the battle between the music and electronics industries over widespread sale of digital audio equipment in the United States.

The House Energy Subcommittee on Commerce, Consumer Protection and Competitiveness on May 12 acted first, approving by voice vote an early version of the bill that the 102nd Congress later cleared.

The bill (HR 4567), by Cardiss Collins, D-Ill., reflected the industry-backed 1991 compromise to resolve the stalemate between the music and electronics industries over how to glean royalties for home recordings made on digital audio tape units.

The measure called for adding a 3 percent royalty fee to the price of digital tapes and a 2 percent royalty fee on recording equipment to compensate music publishers, recording companies and artists. It also required all digital audio equipment sold in the United States to be modified to prevent consumers from making more than one recording of an original digital source. Conventional analog tapes were not affected.

The full Energy and Commerce Committee on June 2 easily approved the bill by voice vote, allowing the measure to clear the first of three committee hurdles it faced. The House Judiciary and Ways and Means committees still had to act.

Alex McMillan, R-N.C., said consumers had been "caught in the middle" of the debate between the entertainment industry and the digital technology industry. He said the bill promised to end that struggle.

Action by a House Judiciary subcommittee on a similar

---

bill (HR 3204) quickly followed. The panel on July 31 approved the measure also aimed at compensating music performers and publishers for home recordings made by using digital audio technology. The bill, approved by voice vote in the Judiciary Subcommittee on Intellectual Property, became the legislative vehicle for the issue in the House.

Just as the Energy and Commerce bill, the Judiciary panel's version called for adding a 3 percent royalty fee to the price of blank digital tapes and a 2 percent fee to the price of new digital recording equipment. The royalties were to go to musicians, recording companies and music publishers to cover expected financial losses from the copying of original recordings.

The U.S. Register of Copyrights was to divide royalty payments into two funds — two-thirds for recording artists and one-third for those who controlled the copyrighted works.

Subcommittee Chairman William J. Hughes, D-N.J., won the panel's voice vote approval of an amendment that allowed recording artists to file suit against manufacturers of tapes or equipment that violated the royalty agreement incorporated in the legislation.

The bill also required makers of digital recording equipment to install an electronic device in units sold in the United States to prevent consumers from making more than one copy of an original recording.

The bill applied to digital tape recording technology as well as any advances in recordable compact discs.

The full House Judiciary Committee approved the bill by voice vote Aug. 11.

A House Ways and Means subcommittee then approved its version of the bill by voice vote Sept. 10. The measure, approved by the Subcommittee on Trade, was virtually identical to the earlier versions approved by the Energy and Commerce and Judiciary committees.

It called for compensating performers and copyright holders for home duplication of digital recordings by tacking on the same royalty fees to the price of blank digital audio tapes and new digital recording equipment as the earlier versions mandated.

This bill also required manufacturers to install electronic devices to prohibit more than one copy from being made of a single original recorded work.

The subcommittee added a technical amendment to clarify the scope of copyright infringement lawsuits that might result from the legislation.

The full Ways and Means Committee approved the bill by voice vote Sept. 16 and sent it to the House floor.

The House passed the bill by voice vote Sept. 22. Lawmakers then sent the measure to the Senate using the bill number of its companion measure (S 1623) that the chamber had passed June 17.

## SENATE ACTION

Senate action got under way a full year earlier. The Senate Judiciary Committee approved its companion measure (S 1623) on Nov. 21, 1991.

The full Senate did not follow suit until June 17, when it passed the bill by voice vote.

The bill added a royalty fee to the price of digital audio tapes and recording equipment to compensate music publishers, recording companies and artists. It also required all digital audio equipment sold in the United States be modified to permit multiple copies to be made from an original tape.

Before floor action, the bill was amended to make several technical clarifications, including one that excluded spoken word recordings, such as books on tape and instructional materials, from the scope of the bill.

After the measure wound its way through three House committees and won House floor passage, the Senate cleared the final version of the bill Oct. 7. ∎

# Radio Spectrum Allocation

Congress failed in 1992 to complete legislation begun the previous year to transfer use of a large portion of government-held radio frequencies to the private sector to foster commercial communications technologies.

House and Senate bills (HR 531 — H Rept 102-113; S 218 — S Rept 102-93) that moved during the first session of the 102nd Congress would have transferred 200 megahertz of government radio spectrum to civilian use. But the Bush administration and some Senate Republicans opposed the bills because they proposed to give away frequencies through the traditional system of lotteries rather than auctioning them off to the highest bidder.

Except for routine filing fees, the airwaves had always been free to those who met application standards set by the Federal Communications Commission (FCC). But the increasingly commercial nature of the crowded radio spectrum — hemmed in by a burgeoning cellular telephone industry and a well-entrenched radio and television broadcast industry — had led the Reagan and Bush administration to push for auctioning FCC licenses.

Critics of auctions worried that only rich people would have access to the radio spectrum, while advocates said the deepest pockets already controlled the airwaves by buying up radio licenses in the private marketplace.

In 1991, the House had passed HR 531 on July 9 by voice vote. The Senate Commerce Committee approved its spectrum allocation bill on May 14 but never sent it to the floor. *(1991 Almanac, p. 157)*

Senate Commerce Communications Subcommittee Chairman Daniel K. Inouye, D-Hawaii, and Ted Stevens, R-Alaska, worked out a compromise on the auctions issue, but lawmakers ran out of time before action could be taken on it. A staff draft of the auction proposal, released in May, sought to mandate an experimental program to allow the FCC to auction up to 30 megahertz of radio frequencies to the highest bidders. Broadcasting services and local public safety radio users would be exempt.

On a related issue in 1992, Senate Commerce Committee Chairman Ernest F. Hollings, D-S.C., withdrew an attempt to protect railroads and utility companies from an FCC plan to reallocate their radio frequencies to entrepreneurs of high-tech pocket phones and other communications technologies. Hollings threatened to block the FCC plan by attaching a ban onto the fiscal 1993 spending bill for the departments of Commerce, Justice and State. But he backed down after winning a Sept. 17 agreement from the FCC to modify its plans. *(Appropriations, p. 646)*

Because the radio spectrum was expected to be used far more extensively for private-sector technologies, both parties were coming around to the notion that radio spectrum use should not continue to be free. Yet broadcasters argued that any change in the allocation of free radio frequencies — particularly through auctions — could throw into question whether they remained beholden to requirements in the 1934 Communications Act that they must serve local public interests. ∎

# Two Rural Phone Bills Clear Congress

Just before adjournment, Congress cleared two bills that sought to ease lending restrictions on rural telephone cooperatives and improve telecommunications links among schools and hospitals.

The first bill (HR 5237 — PL 102-428), cleared by the House on Oct. 6 and signed into law Oct. 21, amended the Rural Electrification Act of 1936 (REA) to make it easier for small telephone and electric service cooperatives to obtain federally backed loans.

HR 5237 allowed rural cooperatives to repay federal telephone loans ahead of schedule. House Agriculture Committee Chairman E. "Kika" de la Garza, D-Texas, said the measure promised to free needed capital to extend more loans to improve rural telephone service.

The second measure (HR 5954 — PL 102-551) had been cleared by the House the day before and was signed into law Oct. 28. It exempted the Rural Telephone Bank from some key provisions of a 1990 federal credit law.

HR 5954 also included grant provisions — that had been stripped from HR 5237 — to help rural medical and educational institutions purchase advanced communications equipment to quickly transmit medical test results, lab slides and educational material to urban hospitals and schools.

As cleared, HR 5954 authorized no set amount to implement the telecommunications provisions, but the measure did set a ceiling of $1.5 million for each communications equipment grant.

## House Committee Action

The proposal to extend grants to schools and hospitals to improve telecommunications links with their urban counterparts began a circuitous route through the 102nd Congress in a House Agriculture subcommittee.

The House Agriculture Conservation, Credit and Rural Development Subcommittee approved the issue by voice vote June 3. At that time, the grant program was embodied in a separate bill (HR 5238) to provide federal grants to rural medical and academic institutions in need of modern telecommunications equipment.

At the same markup, the subcommittee approved an early version of HR 5237 that called for increasing the borrowing flexibility of rural electric and telephone cooperatives.

HR 5238 authorized $30 million to improve health-care services and $20 million to improve educational services by beefing up their telecommunications links with urban facilities. The bill allowed rural providers to consult more easily with specialists at large urban hospitals through interactive telecommunications equipment.

By voice vote, the panel approved an amendment by Chairman Glenn English, D-Okla., to remove a proposed 1 percent discount on rural telephone loans to companies that assisted the program.

The grants, which were limited to $1.5 million each, were to go to rural schools and hospitals to help them purchase high-technology communications equipment to transmit material such as medical test results, lab slides and curriculum information.

The new systems promised to allow students at high schools in rural Texas, for example, to participate in an economics class at a Dallas school. A similar link-up between hospitals could allow a radiologist in a a city hospital to consult with a patient being examined by a rural doctor.

The measure specified, however, that the grants be made available to rural institutions only in states that published a plan for upgrading and modernizing rural telecommunications infrastructure and that committed to paying 20 percent of the cost of starting the program.

Lawmakers said that requiring states to come up with such plans promised to lead to significant improvements in the availability and use of telecommunications technology and in the quality of schools and hospitals in rural areas.

Later that month, the full Agriculture Committee linked the telecommunications provisions in HR 5238 and the loan provisions in HR 5237 by folding the two bills into one. HR 5237 was approved by voice vote June 25.

## House Floor Action

The House on Aug. 5 passed HR 5237 by a vote of 359-60 under special expedited procedures that required a two-thirds majority for passage. (Vote 368, p. 90-H)

The measure established a three-year, $50 million grant program to help states bring interactive telephone and computer technologies to rural health-care facilities and schools. Grants were limited to $1.5 million each.

The bill also revised rules that allowed rural electric cooperatives to pay off loans to the Rural Electrification Administration ahead of their due date.

Leading the opposition were Rick Santorum, R-Pa., and John Porter, R-Ill., who argued that the bill expanded wasteful spending on REA programs. The population size of cities and towns eligible for the agency's funds was increased under the bill from 1,500 to 10,000, increasing the population base from 5.6 million people served to 45.4 million.

## Senate Action

The Senate on Oct. 5 trimmed the scope of HR 5237 significantly before sending it back to the House.

Frank R. Lautenberg, D-N.J., acting for Patrick J. Leahy, D-Vt., won voice vote approval of an amendment to strip the communications provisions from HR 5237.

The House on Oct. 6 later passed the revised bill, clearing it for the president's signature.

But in a separate move, the Senate on Oct. 5 attached the communications provisions to a bill (HR 5954) intended to bring the Rural Telephone Bank in line with the 1990 federal credit law.

The Rural Telephone Bank was established by Congress in 1971 to improve telecommunications in rural areas and make low-interest loans to rural telephone companies to allow them to upgrade their equipment.

Before sending the overhauled measure back to the House, the Senate stripped all the Rural Telephone Bank provisions from HR 5954.

The revised measure was designed to improve rural telecommunications systems to enable rural health-care providers to consult more easily with specialists at large urban hospitals.

The bill authorized $30 million to help improve communications with rural health-care facilities and $20 million to improve them with rural educational institutions. The program was to be administered by the Rural Electrification Administration.

The House on Oct. 6 cleared the final version of HR 5954 by voice vote. ∎

# Corrections Made to 1991's Transportation Bill

One year after Congress cleared a sweeping $151 billion transportation bill, lawmakers pushed through "technical corrections." The language that finally cleared in the fiscal 1993 transportation spending bill was designed to correct technical glitches in the 1991 law, but it also broadened the scope of some projects.

The House on Aug. 10 passed by voice vote a bill (HR 5753) to make a number of small changes to the 1991 highway and mass transit project authorization law (PL 102-240). *(1991 Almanac, p. 137)*

The bill stalled in the Senate. But the Senate slipped its own, more limited "technical corrections" language into the $13.2 billion fiscal 1993 transportation appropriations bill (HR 5518). *(Appropriations, p. 669)*

Most of the Senate provisions were true to their billing, involving only minor technical changes intended to correct mistakes made in the 1991 transportation law.

But the Senate language did broaden the scope of some road and transit projects. For example, at the urging of Senate Majority Leader George J. Mitchell, D-Maine, it expanded a pilot program to repair timber bridges.

## House Action

Public Works and Transportation Committee member Mel Hancock, R-Mo., won a $7.6 million authorization to build a highway loop around Branson, Mo., an Ozark mountain town of 5,000, in the bill (HR 5753) making "technical corrections" to the 1991 highway and mass transit project authorization law.

Hancock's victory came in the Public Works and Transportation Committee, which approved the separate technical corrections bill (HR 5753 — H Rept 012-833) Aug. 6. The bill, including the Branson project, authorized $30.9 million for six new road projects.

The House passed the bill Aug. 10 by voice vote. But the Senate never acted on the measure.

House sponsors had claimed that no new projects were included in the bill, which was designed to correct errors made in the 1991 highway and mass transit act.

Indeed, most of the 150-page bill aimed to correct wording mistakes, describe projects in greater detail or make existing laws consistent with the sweeping changes brought by the 1991 law.

But, as the new Branson bypass illustrated, the bill was not entirely technical — and included new projects.

The Branson project was included after money was shifted from other Missouri road projects authorized in 1991. Five additional projects, totaling $23.3 million, were included in the bill because sponsors said they were wrongly omitted from the 1991 transporation bill due to clerical errors.

Three of the projects were in the home state of Bud Shuster, R-Pa., ranking minority member of the Public Works Surface Transportation Subcommittee. Pennsylvania came away with $934.8 million in road projects in the 1991 transportation law, the largest amount of any state.

The technical corrections bill also recast road policy. The bill allowed states to defer paying until Aug. 1, 1994, their 20 percent share to match federal grants for mass transit systems — a favor previously extended only to highway projects. And the bill launched a two-year pilot pro-

gram to use recycled glass and plastic in highway projects.

Public Works Chairman Robert A. Roe, D-N.J., used the measure to give New Jersey officials detailed instructions on how to spend some of that state's highway dollars. The bill directed that $26 million be used over two years to build sound barriers along interstate routes in his Paterson district.

## Senate Action

The bill languished in the Senate, where senators had drafted their own technical corrections language and in-

---

## Public Works Chair Roe Opts Out of Re-Election Bid

The announced departure of House Public Works Chairman Robert A. Roe marked a sea change for the panel that handed out road, bridge, transit, airport and water projects.

Roe, a Democrat from New Jersey, joined the growing list of lawmakers choosing not to seek re-election in 1992. In a March 30 statement, he cited a need to spend more "quality time" with family and friends.

Next in line to lead the full committee was California Democrat Norman Y. Mineta, chairman of the Surface Transportation Subcommittee. He ran unopposed for the post.

A member of the reform-minded Watergate-era class of 1974 and known to eschew pork barreling, Mineta's ascension visibly altered committee dynamics.

Roe's crowning achievement was the 1991 $151 billion highway and mass transit authorization bill, which he adorned with a record 539 special road projects and billions of dollars for new mass transit systems around the country. *(1991 Almanac, p. 137)*

By contrast, as past chairman of the Aviation Subcommittee, Mineta pushed through a five-year, $20 billion aviation authorization bill in 1987 that he proclaimed was free of pet projects. *(1987 Almanac, p. 339)*

Still, Mineta proved adept at the earmarking game when it involved California. In the 1991 transportation bill, he steered $335 million in road projects to his home state, plus another $569 million toward his district for an extension of San Francisco's Bay Area Rapid Transit (BART) system.

Mineta inadvertently paved Roe's way in 1990, when — frustrated by a lack of leadership — he initiated the drive to topple fellow California Democrat Glenn M. Anderson from the Public Works chair.

After Mineta secured Anderson's ouster, second-ranking Roe decided to forfeit his chairmanship of the Science, Space and Technology Committee to run for the Public Works chair.

He beat Mineta in a Democratic Caucus vote, 121-107, largely because of seniority but also because lawmakers felt more comfortable with Roe's almost religious fervor for helping fellow members win public works projects for back home. *(1990 Almanac, p. 11)*

serted it in the fiscal 1993 transportation appropriations bill.

The Senate language also was used to grant favors to powerful lawmakers — though not as extensive as those in the House version.

One Senate provision extended a timber bridge pilot program, won in the 1991 transportation appropriations bill by Mitchell, to all "public roads," whether they received other federal aid or not. The language allowed Maine to use federal money to repair timber bridges on even the smallest rural roads.

The House bill was not so generous. It limited such projects to rural federal highways not included in a proposed National Highway System.

The Senate on Oct. 1 cleared the $13.2 billion fiscal 1993 transportation spending bill after both chambers adopted the conference report to the measure Oct. 1 by voice vote. Bush signed the bill into law Oct. 6 (PL 102-388). ∎

# Moynihan Ties Courthouse Project to Highway Funds

The House on July 28 wrote a surprise ending to a complicated eight-month-long saga starring Sen. Daniel Patrick Moynihan, D-N.Y. Members cleared a bill to restore $369 million in fiscal 1992 highway funds cut from the sweeping 1991 highway and mass transit law (PL 102-240) to help pay to renovate a Brooklyn, N.Y., courthouse.

The measure (S 2641), passed by voice vote, effectively eliminated spending for the $457 million courthouse project and subjected it to the normal appropriations process. President Bush signed the bill into law (PL 102-334) Aug. 6.

The House action was unexpected because appropriators and tax panelists had thrice balked at restoring the money. The Senate had passed the measure April 30.

Moynihan, a chief author of the $151 billion highway and mass transit authorization law, sparked the funding snafu after he inserted language in the sweeping 1991 transportation law to authorize funds to upgrade an overcrowded Brooklyn courthouse. *(1991 Almanac, p. 137)*

The project was estimated to cost $457 million, with actual spending occurring toward the end of the six-year bill. But the White House Office of Management and Budget (OMB) opted to calculate the courthouse as if it were a highway project, with higher upfront costs than public buildings.

OMB ruled that $1 billion in fiscal 1992 budget authority was needed to account for the project. That put the highway bill over a spending ceiling set by the 1990 budget agreement. So, to offset the courthouse and other smaller cost overruns, OMB cut the bill's budget authority by $1.2 billion for fiscal 1992, leaving state highway official shortchanged and angry.

The highway law had stipulated that if budget caps were exceeded, cuts were to occur only within its scope.

The highway money was to have provided an estimated 50,000 road construction and repair jobs nationwide in 1992. Instead, $457 million was to go to the courthouse project and another $449 million was scooped up by Congress to pay for a February extension of unemployment benefits (PL 102-

244). *(Unemployment compensation, p. 346)*

Many viewed the whole episode as a test of wills between Moynihan and the Bush administration. Moynihan accused the White House of abandoning its support for the courthouse, while the administration tried to portray Moynihan's provision as an example of the evils of pork barreling.

Moynihan on March 24 introduced a bill (S 2398) to repeal the courthouse provision and restore the lost highway funds, but it was not until the waning days of the 102nd Congress that Congress cleared a similar measure (S 2641).

Moynihan contended that the administration shared the blame. The General Services Administration (GSA), which was responsible for courthouse projects, drafted the provision, and the OMB made matters worse when it ruled that the project required a cut of more than twice the courthouse's $457 million price tag, he said.

GSA officials said they never intended the provision to end up attached to a mandatory spending bill such as the highway legislation and instead requested only that the project be made subject to later appropriations.

The irony was not lost on Senate Republicans. "At a time our nation is striving to create jobs and spur economic growth, I am especially troubled by the fact that all state [highway] allocations have been reduced nearly 6 percent" because of the courthouse provision, Pete V. Domenici, R-N.M., wrote in a Feb. 3 letter to Moynihan.

## BACKGROUND

The saga began in late November 1991, when Moynihan attached the renovation project during House-Senate negotiations over the six-year, $151 billion surface transportation authorization measure.

Moynihan hoped to settle a longstanding dispute about what to do with the overburdened U.S. District Court building in Brooklyn, which in 1989 became the first federal courthouse to be declared a "space emergency" by the Judicial Conference of the United States, a board that oversaw the federal court system.

Twelve judges at the courthouse pushed a plan to relocate it to an old post office building across the street, and Moynihan pressed the GSA to move forward with the plan. The agency informed Moynihan that it needed congressional approval and drafted the provision.

Moynihan insisted that he intended only to authorize the project, subject to later appropriations. But by attaching it to the highway bill, he effectively skirted the appropriations process. Programs authorized for highway and mass transit programs were considered mandatory spending because they were paid for by dedicated gasoline taxes from the Highway Trust Fund.

After Bush signed the highway bill into law on Dec. 18, OMB ordered the cut.

## LEGISLATIVE ACTION

Moynihan came under immediate pressure from state transportation officials to correct the problem. But his effort became much more difficult when Congress on Feb. 4 used $449 million of the money made available by the OMB decision to help pay for the extension of unemployment benefits. The Senate on March 24 passed Moynihan's initial bill (S 2398) that repealed the courthouse provision, restored the $1 billion and cleared the way for states to receive an

immediate 6 percent boost in highway funds. But the House Ways and Means Committee buried the bill because the unemployment measure had already used much of the funds.

On April 30 the Senate passed the second (and eventually successful) Moynihan bill (S 2641) to restore only $369 million to highway programs, as well as to repeal the courthouse language. But the bill languished for months in the House Public Works Committee, where lawmakers used the measure as a bargaining chip for other transportation-related concessions they sought from the Senate.

On May 20 Moynihan tried again. He added S 2641 to the House-passed fiscal 1992 supplemental appropriations bill (PL 102-302). But the provision was dropped in conference June 4 because House negotiators were not eager to help Moynihan after he tried to push the courthouse project through Congress without their approval.

After three failed attempts to restore $1 billion diverted by the courthouse project, Moynihan announced that he had given up. "I have gotten the message," Moynihan said on the Senate floor June 18.

Then, in a surprise move, the House on July 28 cleared for Bush the second Moynihan bill (S 2641) to restore $369 million in fiscal 1992 highway funds cut from the 1991 highway measure.

With that money restored, all states were finally able to start more highway projects in 1992. House Public Works Surface Transportation Subcommittee Chairman Norman Y. Mineta, D-Calif., said his state was to receive $34 million more in fiscal 1992 funds. Arkansas, home of ranking Public Works member John Paul Hammerschmidt said his state was to get an additional $3.6 million. ∎

# New Rules for Airline Reservations Systems

The House on Aug. 12 passed a bill to inject more competition into the airline reservation business, but the measure stalled in the Senate.

Instead, the Senate on July 2 attached to an unrelated foreign aid bill (S 2532) a provision that required the Transportation Department to complete by Sept. 1 new rules intended to spur competition in airline computer reservation systems. The House cleared the more limited bill on Oct. 3 and Bush signed it into law (PL 102-511) later that month.

The Senate never considered the more sweeping House remedy (HR 5466) that had passed the latter chamber Aug. 12. The bill barred airlines that own computer reservation systems from discriminating against rivals.

Travel agents and airlines nationwide relied on four major computerized reservation systems. Two companies — owned primarily by American and United airlines — controlled about 70 percent of the market.

Smaller carriers had complained that they were featured less prominently on the systems and that the flight information was structured to encourage agents to favor the two major airlines that owned the systems.

The bill prohibited the air carriers that owned the systems from using "architectural bias," charging other airlines booking fees or using any other arrangements that discriminated against other air carriers and travel agents.

# Bush Names Andrew Card To Head Transportation

President Bush on Jan. 22 named White House Deputy Chief of Staff Andrew H. Card Jr. as Transportation secretary, tapping a longtime political ally to carry out major changes in the nation's transportation policy.

The Senate confirmed Card as Transportation secretary by voice vote on Feb. 21. The Commerce, Science and Transportation Committee had approved Card on Feb. 18, also by voice vote.

Card, 44, an engineer and a former Massachusetts legislator, replaced Samuel K. Skinner, who took over as White House chief of staff after John H. Sununu resigned in December 1991. Card was an unsuccessful Republican gubernatorial candidate in Massachusetts in 1982.

The significance of the nomination lay more in the realm of presidential politics than transportation policy. Card did not have extensive experience with transportation issues. Instead, the nomination was widely viewed as a reward for years of loyal service to Bush.

Card managed Bush's crucial New Hampshire primary victory in 1988 and was considered among Bush's most valued political advisers.

As head of the Transportation Department, Card was responsible for carrying out sweeping policy changes ushered in by Skinner. Among other duties, Card was empowered to award to states airport, highway and mass transit grants authorized under a 1990 aviation law and the 1991 $151 billion surface transportation package.

Donald R. Quartrel, a member of the Federal Maritime Commission who served as Bush's domestic policy adviser during the 1988 campaign, described Card as "loyal, self-effacing and competent" and dismissed any notions that Card planned to use the office to help Bush's re-election campaign.

Thomas J. Donahue, president of the American Trucking Associations, said the nomination was "welcome news to the trucking industry" and called Card "a champion of limited taxation and government intrusion in transportation matters."

In the White House, Card was in charge of directing daily operations and served as a link between Bush, Sununu and other top White House officials. He was widely liked among Bush loyalists, but Skinner had been planning a Cabinet staff shuffle and had assisted Card in an unsuccessful bid to head the American Association of Railroads.

In naming Card, Bush passed over Skinner's top choice for his replacement, acting Secretary James B. Busey. Another contender had been Customs Commissioner Carol B. Hallett.

A Massachusetts native, Card served in the state House of Representatives from 1974 to 1983. He helped with the state Bush campaign in 1980. When he was named to the White House staff in 1983, Card was vice president of the CMIS Corp., a computer software company in Vienna, Va. From 1971 to 1974 he worked as a design engineer.

United and American airlines said the legislation was not needed because they were working to eliminate any bias in the software architecture of their computer reservation systems.

## BACKGROUND

The domestic airline industry, which was deregulated in 1978, had dwindled to just eight major carriers. The recession, combined with rising fuel costs, travelers' fears of terrorism abroad and price wars, had led to a $6 billion loss in industry revenues since the beginning of 1991. *(1991 Almanac, p. 152)*

Many lawmakers, including James L. Oberstar, D-Minn., chairman of the Public Works and Transportation Aviation Subcommittee, said improving airline competition boiled down to making the computer reservation systems fairer to all airlines.

"It's the driving force in determining who competes, who makes money and who survives," said Oberstar.

The four existing computer reservation services provided flight schedules and rates. They were all owned by airlines, but American and United controlled the two main reservation systems and dominated the market.

The two smaller reservation services charged that American and United discriminated against carriers by diverting passengers to the companies' parent airlines.

But opponents said the bill effectively abolished 26,000 contracts between travel agents and reservation systems companies and unfairly punished United and American airlines for devising two successful reservation systems.

The Bush administration also opposed the bill, saying it interfered with the market and with ongoing Transportation Department efforts to address computer reservations.

## LEGISLATIVE ACTION

Legislative action began in the House Public Works and Transportation Aviation Subcommittee. The panel on June 25 took aim at the major airlines, approving, 26-13, HR 5466 to bar airplane reservation services from unfairly steering passengers to a particular airline.

The measure prohibited discrimination against other carriers by the reservation services. The bill amended the Federal Aviation Act of 1958 to enhance competition among air carriers by prohibiting a carrier that operated a computer reservation system from discriminating against rivals.

Proponents said reservation systems discriminated against competing carriers by steering passengers to their parent airlines.

To foster competition among the airlines, the measure shortened from five years to three years the maximum length of a contract between a travel agent and a reservation system.

It also grandfathered existing contracts of under five years, if the reservation service and ticket agency agreed. William O. Lipinski, D-Ill., contended that the provision prompted renegotiation of all contracts, but his amendment to drop the language was rejected 19-20.

The House bill also required the Federal Aviation Administration (FAA) to ensure that airlines serving small communities had takeoff and landing "slots" at major hub airports. And it directed the Transportation Department to consider reducing the frequency of random drug tests for airline employees.

The full House Public Works and Transportation Com-

mittee on July 1 approved HR 5466 (H Rept 102-724) to prohibit airline reservation services from steering customers to a particular airline.

The House on Aug. 12 passed the bill to encourage more competition into the airline reservation system. The bill, passed by a vote 230-160, barred airlines that owned computer reservation systems from discriminating against competitors. *(Vote 386, p. 94-H)*

The bill was referred to the Senate Committee on Commerce, Science and Transportation, which took no action on it.

Still, the Senate did not ignore the issue.

On July 2 the Senate had attached to a bill to provide aid to the former states of the Soviet Union (S 2532) a related provision that required the Transportation Department to complete by Sept. 1 rules intended to make the computer reservation systems and distribution of airport slots fairer. *(Freedom Support Act, p. 523)*

The House cleared S 2532 on Oct. 3. Bush signed it into law Oct. 24 (PL 102-511). ∎

# Airport Program Extended In FAA Reauthorization

The Senate on Oct. 8 cleared a three-year reauthorization of most Federal Aviation Administration (FAA) programs that included a pared back one-year extension of the nation's airport improvement program.

The House on Oct. 6 passed the bill (HR 6168) that renewed the airport improvement program for the portion of fiscal year 1993 ending before May 1, 1993.

A multiyear reauthorization of the program to upgrade and expand airport terminals and runways was left for the 103rd Congress. Still, the limited reauthorization cleared the way for federal funds to flow to projects that were in the works in fiscal 1993.

The airport expansion program became embroiled in a separate controversy over a proposal to provide supplementary compensation to victims, or the families of victims, of international airline accidents. Similar compensation requirements were included in the Montreal Protocols on carrier liability, an international accord that the Senate failed to ratify.

The compensation issue grew out of the 1988 terrorist bombing of Pan Am Flight 103 over Lockerbie, Scotland.

Many senators had wanted to make the compensation plan part of the nation's statutory law and the Senate added language to do so to the FAA reauthorization bill. But in the end, the issue was dropped from the final FAA reauthorization measure after aircraft and engine makers raised last-minute concerns.

In the end, the reauthorization incorporated some of the provisions of previous House bills (HR 6093, HR 4691) as well as elements of the companion Senate bill (S 2642).

The final measure authorized $2 billion for airport improvement grants for fiscal 1993 from the Airport and Airways Trust Fund, which was fed by a 10 percent tax on all airline tickets. It also authorized facilities and equipment programs at $8.5 billion over fiscal years 1993-95.

The bill allowed airport grants to be used to build new structures and purchase equipment to de-ice aircraft, an action partly in response to the March 22 crash of a USAir

carrier in New York.

It contained provisions of a separate bill (HR 5465) that allowed the Transportation secretary to provide insurance to air carriers through September 1997, allowing commercial aircrafts to be used in wartime activities. The war risk insurance program that was used to insure commercial aircrafts called up for military use in times of national emergency expired Sept. 30. The House Public Works and Transportation Committee had approved HR 5465 July 1 by voice vote.

The measure also established a research program to be carried out by the FAA and the National Aeronautics and Space Administration (NASA) to promote the development and use of a new generation of quieter planes.

## HOUSE ACTION

An early version of the bill (HR 4691) began its journey through the 102nd Congress, moving swifty through an April 1 markup in the House Public Works Subcommittee on Aviation.

The bill was a two-year reauthorization of the FAA that fine-tuned some of the substantial changes Congress made to airport-improvement financing, including new airline ticket fees of up to $3 per flight for airport improvements. It was approved by voice vote.

The measure authorized $2 billion in fiscal 1993 and $2.1 billion in fiscal 1994 for the airport improvement program and $4.6 billion in fiscal 1993 and $5 billion in fiscal 1994 for FAA operations. It also required the FAA administrator to hire additional air traffic controllers in an effort to end up with 18,128 controllers at the end of fiscal 1993.

One amendment by William O. Lipinski, D-Ill., approved by voice vote, raised the amount of funds available to large airports under the airport improvement program from $20 million to $22 million.

Subcommittee Chairman James L. Oberstar, D-Minn., ruled out of order an amendment by Peter A. DeFazio, D-Ore., that required the FAA to issue within 90 days a regulation requiring better access to emergency window exits in aircrafts with 20 or more passenger seats. Oberstar said the amendment was not germane because it dealt with airline safety, which was addressed in separate legislation.

The Public Works and Transportation Committee on April 8 approved HR 4691 to authorize $2 billion in fiscal 1993 and $2.1 billion in fiscal 1994 for the airport improvement program and $4.6 billion in fiscal 1993 and $5 billion in fiscal 1994 for FAA operations.

Panel members also agreed, by voice vote, to an amendment by Chairman Robert A. Roe, D-N.J., that established a national commission to investigate the financial condition of the airline industry.

Before the bill headed to the House floor, the Ways and Means Committee on April 29 approved a continuation of the 10 percent airline ticket tax to finance airport and runway improvements nationwide. The panel's action ap-

---

> ## BOXSCORE
>
> ➡ **FAA Reauthorization (HR 6168, formerly S 2642, HR 4691).** The legislation authorized $2 billion for airport improvement grants for fiscal 1993 from the Airport and Airways Trust Fund. It also authorized facilities and equipment programs at $8.5 billion over fiscal years 1993-95.
>
> **Reports:** H Rept 102-503, Parts 1 and 2; S Rept 102-424.
>
> ### KEY ACTION
>
> April 8 — The **House** Public Works and Transportation Committee approved HR 4691.
>
> May 19 — **House** passed HR 4691, 410-2.
>
> Aug. 11 — The **Senate** Commerce, Science and Transportation Committee approved S 2642.
>
> Oct. 6 — **House** passed a revised bill, HR 6168, by voice vote.
>
> Oct. 8 — **Senate** cleared HR 6168 by voice vote.
>
> Oct. 31 — President Bush signed HR 6168 — PL 102-581.

---

proved by voice vote the financing portion of HR 4691.

Under the 1990 budget agreement, the airline ticket tax, which fed the Airport and Airways Trust Fund, was increased from 8 percent to 10 percent. The new revenues were earmarked for deficit reduction until Dec. 31, 1992. The Ways and Means Committee agreed to correct a technical error in the budget agreement to ensure that the additional funds went toward offsetting the deficit.

But the committee authorized spending from the trust fund for airport improvements, grants, operations, facilities and other programs at $7.4 billion for fiscal 1993, $8 billion for fiscal 1994. It set fiscal 1992 spending at $6.7 billion.

The full House on May 19 passed the two-year, $19.3 billion authorization bill by a vote of 410-2. *(Vote 127, p. 32-H)*

Of the $19.3 billion, $14.5 billion came from the Airport and Airways Trust Fund, which was fed mostly by a tax on airline tickets and other user fees.

Public Works and Transportation Chairman Roe said the bill reduced the "outrageous and unacceptable" surplus in the trust fund to $1.1 billion over the two-year period. The trust fund had a $7.5 billion surplus.

The bill authorized $4.1 billion in fiscal 1993 and fiscal 1994 for the airport improvement program, $9.6 billion over two years for FAA operations and $5.6 billion for air-traffic control system modernization.

Sponsors sought to resolve a fight between the FAA and the Port Authority of New York and New Jersey over aircraft noise rules that went into effect as part of a package of sweeping aviation policy changes included in the 1990 budget agreement.

That law allowed airports, with FAA approval, to levy passenger fees of up to $3 on each one-way trip to finance facility improvements such as new terminals, runways or access roads. As of 1992, some $5.5 billion collected from passengers had been invested in airport improvements, said Public Works Aviation Subcommittee Chairman Oberstar.

But the FAA had withheld its approval of a request by the New York-area port authority, which operated the region's three major airports, to impose passenger fees because of the authority's plans to restrict the use of noisy "stage two" jet engines in the area.

The FAA, with support from Senate Commerce Aviation Subcommittee Chairman Wendell H. Ford, D-Ky., pointed to a provision in the 1990 law that made approval of a passenger fee contingent on a local airport's compliance with new national noise reduction guidelines. Those rules called only for a gradual phase-out of the noisy jets.

House bill sponsors contended that the law allowed local entities to impose stricter noise controls, and the reauthorization bill allowed the New York-area port authority to do so.

The bill also prohibited the Transportation secretary from approving requests for any passenger facility charges

## Aircraft De-Icing Considered

In response to the March 22 crash of a USAir carrier in New York, provisions regarding the de-icing of aircrafts were included in broader legislation (HR 6168 — PL 102-581) to extend Federal Aviation Administration (FAA) programs.

As cleared by Congress Oct. 8, the bill's provisions allowed airport grants to be used to build new structures and purchase equipment to de-ice aircrafts.

A freestanding research bill (HR 4557 — H Rept 102-511) first won approval from the House Science, Space and Technology Subcommittee on Technology and Competitiveness March 25.

The panel's version authorized a research and development program to examine de-icing techniques to be carried out jointly by the FAA and the National Aeronautics and Space Administration (NASA).

It also authorized engineering, research and development programs for the FAA. The panel recommended $297.3 million for fiscal 1993, a 29 percent increase over Bush's $230 million request.

At the behest of Dan Glickman, D-Kan., the subcommittee added the provision calling for new regulations and research on de-icing of airplanes. Failure to de-ice an airplane was cited as a possible cause of the March 22 USAir crash at New York's LaGuardia Airport that killed 27 people.

The bill encountered a little turbulence April 8 before the full Science, Space and Technology Committee, which approved it by voice vote.

Funding for those programs was set at a level of $297 million for fiscal 1993, a 29 percent increase over President Bush's $230 million request. But the panel rejected a Republican amendment, 8-11, that would have scaled back the funding to $260 million.

The measure never advanced to the floor.

until appropriators had provided full funding for general airport improvements and a program that provided subsidies to small rural airports, known as the Essential Air Service Program.

The Bush administration supported the overall bill, according to a statement, but the White House opposed both provisions regarding airport passenger fees.

The bill raised from 75 percent to 85 percent the amount of money the federal government had to contribute for airport construction projects in small communities.

## SENATE ACTION

The Senate advanced a $31.3 billion companion measure (S 2642) that was far more generous in its authorization levels and that covered fiscal years 1993-1995 — one year longer than the House bill.

The Senate Commerce, Science and Transportation Committee on Aug. 11 kicked off the Senate action, approving the three-year authorization bill for FAA programs, including the airport improvement program.

Budget constraints prompted lawmakers to prune the bill's originally higher funding levels after the committee approved by voice vote a substitute amendment by Aviation Subcommittee Chairman Ford.

The amended bill, approved by voice vote, authorized $2 billion for airport improvement grants in fiscal 1993, rising to $2.3 billion by fiscal 1995. FAA facilities and equipment received $2.7 billion in fiscal 1993, rising to $2.9 billion in fiscal 1995. Operations and research received $5 billion in fiscal 1993, to $5.9 billion in fiscal 1995.

The measure continued Ford's efforts to reduce noise at the nation's airports by setting aside 12.5 percent, up from 10 percent, of airport improvement funds for programs to reduce noise. The bill also set aside $75 million for research into cutting noise levels.

As approved by committee, the bill required the FAA by November 1992 to impose new rules for de-icing planes, a provision that came in response to the March 22 crash of a USAir plane at New York's LaGuardia Airport.

Another amendment by Ford, approved by voice vote, set up the supplementary fund to compensate victims, or their families, of international airline accidents in accord with a similar program included in the Montreal Protocols on carrier liability, the international accord that the Senate never ratified in the 102nd Congress.

The 1988 terrorist bombing of Pan Am Flight 103 over Lockerbie, Scotland, and the 1983 downing of Korean jetliner KAL 007 by the former Soviet Union had brought the carrier liability issue to the forefront and sparked the call for supplemental compensation for victims of air terrorism.

But the issue also stalled the FAA reauthorization bill, blocking it from Senate floor action.

The impasse also kept the full Senate from resolving whether frequent-flier passengers should be required to pay so-called passenger facility charges — an issue that had been expected to spark heated floor debate. The fees were levied by airports to pay for airport improvements and ranged from $1 to $3 per one-way ticket.

During the Commerce markup, Richard H. Bryan, D-Nev., withdrew an amendment that called for exempting such passengers from the charges. But Bryan said the 1990 legislation that established the charges did not intend for such passengers to pay the fees. A provision in the House fiscal 1993 transportation appropriations bill (HR 5518) also exempted such passengers from paying the fee. *(Appropriations, p. 669)*

Sens. Daniel K. Inouye, D-Hawaii, John C. Danforth, R-Mo., and Bob Packwood, R-Ore., objected to the exemption on grounds that airports with high frequent-flier activity stood to lose too much revenue. The issue had been expected to be fought out on the Senate floor.

## FINAL ACTION

While S 2642 languished in the Senate, the House on Oct. 6 passed by voice vote a new, trimmed down FAA reauthorization (HR 6168 — H Rept 102-503, Parts 1 and 2). It renewed most FAA programs for fiscal 1993 through 1995 but extended the airport improvement program for only one year to avoid the dispute over the compensation program for victims of air terrorism. The Senate cleared the bill Oct. 8 by voice vote.

The bill incorporated the provisions of the previous House bills (HR 6093, HR 4691) as well as elements of the Senate FAA reauthorization (S 2642).

It authorized $2 billion for airport improvement grants for fiscal 1993 from the Airport and Airways Trust Fund. It also authorized facilities and equipment programs at $8.5 billion over fiscal years 1993-95.

Bush signed the bill into law Oct. 31 (PL 102-581). ∎

# Two-Year Reauthorization For Amtrak Clears

The Senate on Oct. 7 cleared two-year reauthorization legislation for Amtrak, the national passenger railroad.

The final measure (HR 4250), passed by voice vote, authorized $381 million for fiscal years 1993 and 1994 for operating expenses, $250 million for each year for capital expenses and $470 million over the two years for the Northeast corridor connecting Boston to Washington.

President Bush signed the bill into law Oct. 27 — PL 102-533.

House sponsor Al Swift, D-Wash., called Amtrak "the most efficient passenger rail system in the world" because it covered 79 percent of its costs with its own revenues. Federal subsidies authorized in the bill accounted for the remainder.

The bill also set aside funds to encourage the establishment of new routes in rural areas.

## House Action

A House Energy and Commerce subcommittee on March 5 kicked off action on an early version of the bill to authorize capital grants and operating assistance for Amtrak.

As approved by the Transportation and Hazardous Materials Subcommittee, the bill authorized $572 million for fiscal 1993 and $590 million for fiscal 1994 for capital improvements. Much of the funds were to be used to develop high-speed train operations between New York and Boston. The measure also authorized $397 million in fiscal 1993 and $331 million for fiscal 1994 for Amtrak to maintain its existing routes.

The bill was a substitute measure that made largely technical changes, while emphasizing the need for Amtrak officials to plan for future congestion from increased passenger service in the Northeast corridor.

Swift said he planned to introduce separate legislation to set aside one-cent per gallon of gasoline tax revenues toward an Amtrak trust fund for long-term capital improvements.

Amtrak President W. Graham Claytor asked the Senate Commerce Committee on Feb. 26 for such an arrangement. It was intended to raise about $1 billion a year. Claytor said the penny could be taken from the 2.5 cents-a-gallon gas tax that was devoted to deficit reduction.

The full House Energy and Commerce Committee on April 7 easily approved the $1.9 billion Amtrak authorization bill.

Federal subsidies for Amtrak were the target of Republican attacks, but the 1992 legislation won bipartisan support and was approved by voice vote with no amendments and little debate.

Swift said the bill authorized assistance that was "critical to Amtrak's ability to maintain and improve the national intercity rail passenger system."

Almost $575 million was authorized for fiscal 1993; $590 million was authorized for fiscal 1994 for capital improvements, including the development of high-speed train operations between New York and Boston.

For maintenance of existing routes, the measure authorized $397 million for fiscal 1993 and $331 million for fiscal 1994. Total funding for fiscal 1993 was $11 million higher than fiscal 1992.

The full House on Aug. 11 passed the bill after an 8-3 headcount of those on the floor at the time.

## Senate Action

The Senate Commerce, Science and Transportation Committee on June 16 gave voice vote approval to its version of a bill (S 2608) that reauthorized Amtrak through fiscal 1995.

The Senate measure authorized $331 million each year for Amtrak's operating expenses and $300 million each year for capital expenditures.

The bill gave Amtrak more flexibility to adjust its routes if passenger usage declined and required Amtrak to channel its resources into developing plans for high-speed passenger train service in the Northeast.

On Aug. 12, a day after the House acted, the full Senate at the request of Majority Leader George J. Mitchell, D-Maine, stripped all but the title from HR 4250 and inserted the text of S 2608. The Senate then passed the revised bill by voice vote.

## Final Action

House and Senate negotiators crafted a compromise bill. The House approved the conference report by voice vote Oct. 4 (H Rept 102-990).

As cleared by the Senate, it authorized $381 million for each fiscal year for operating expenses, $250 million for each year for capital expenses and $470 million over two years for the Northeast corridor connecting Boston to Washington. ∎

# Rail Strike Ended

Congress on June 25 acted to end a two-day shutdown of the nation's rail system, giving labor unions, freight railroads and Amtrak 38 days to resolve their longstanding disputes over wages, work rules and job security.

The latest, most bitter chapter in the 4-year-old labor talks ended when President Bush signed a measure (H J Res 517) at 1 a.m. on June 26 that adopted a bargaining process often used by professional baseball players during salary negotiations. If the parties failed to reach agreement after a specified period, a mutually chosen mediator was to make a decision based on each side's last, best offer.

The Senate, by an 87-6 vote, sent the measure to Bush immediately after the House approved it, 248-140. An amendment by Sen. Paul Wellstone, D-Minn., to scrap the new mediation process and instead impose a 30-day cooling-off period was rejected 76-18. (Senate votes 130, 131, p. 18-S; House vote 236, p. 58-H)

House Energy and Commerce Committee Chairman John D. Dingell, D-Mich., conceded the action was a defeat for labor unions but said it was necessary for Congress to act to avert national economic disaster. He and other pro-labor lawmakers acknowledged the political difficulty of interfering with the unions' right to strike.

"Congress is very uncomfortable in the role of picking winners and losers in labor disputes," said Rep. Al Swift, D-Wash., whose Energy Subcommittee on Transportation and Hazardous Materials handled the measure. "We are legislators. We are not labor negotiators."

Swift, joined by Transportation Secretary Andrew H. Card Jr. and other lawmakers, said the episode pointed to a

need to rewrite the 1926 Railway Labor Act, which imposed a lengthy, cumbersome negotiating process typically resulting in stalemates that must then be resolved by Congress.

### Strike or Lockout?

Unlike in April 1991, when Congress acted in 15 hours to stop a nationwide rail strike, in 1992 only one union, the International Association of Machinists, went on strike against one carrier, CSX Transportation Inc., after negotiations ended at midnight June 23.

Other unions had either reached agreement or delayed strikes as talks continued.

But the entire freight rail system still shut down. In a display of management solidarity with CSX, all 40 of the nation's largest rail freight carriers locked out workers after the midnight deadline. Rail carried one-third of the nation's intercity freight.

Passenger rail service was stalled in most parts of the country except on the East Coast. General Motors Corp. slowed production at several plants because of parts shortages.

Chief railroad negotiator Charles Hopkins said the nationwide lockout was necessary to counter the unions' "divide and conquer" strategy of striking only CSX. "If one railroad can be brought to its knees, then the only question is who is next on the hit parade," he said.

Labor unions and Democrats in Congress criticized the railroads and the Bush administration for not stopping the lockout, which chief White House economist Michael J. Boskin said cost the country $1 billion a day in productivity.

"Tactic or not, you shut it down. And you're the ones peddling all the information about the terrible, terrible things that would be done to this economy," Swift told railroad representatives at a June 24 hearing in his subcommittee.

The railroads and the Bush administration also stressed that railroads were part of a linked network that could not operate if even one carrier were grounded. Card invoked images of crops rotting in fields and commuters stranded nationwide.

Unions and Democratic lawmakers countered that the railroads contrived the national emergency to force Congress to step in and rule in management's favor. And they argued that no such "seamless" system existed during contract negotiations.

### 12th Congressional Intervention

The action marked the 12th time Congress had intervened to stop a nationwide rail shutdown since 1963.

Since 1988, unions representing about 200,000 machinists, engineers, dispatchers and track maintenance workers had been embroiled in bitter contract talks with the nation's 40 major rail freight carriers and Amtrak.

To stop a nationwide rail strike, Congress in April 1991 passed legislation creating a board to resolve the remaining disputes. Unions complained that the board sided with railroad positions, which led to the 1992 strike and lockout. *(1991 Almanac, p. 154)*

In 1992, rather than setting up another presidential review board, lawmakers and the administration opted to force the parties into binding arbitration with only one mediator.

Under the new law, if no agreement was reached between the two parties within 25 days, the mediator had 10 days to choose between the last offer made by either party. The president then had three days to reject the result, which allowed workers to strike or management to impose a lockout.

"One of the things we don't want anymore is people negotiating with bureaucrats," said the measure's author, Rep. Dennis E. Eckart, D-Ohio. ∎

---

# Coast Guard Bill Sputters Over Sporting Boat Fees

The House passed legislation (HR 5055) that reauthorized the U.S. Coast Guard for a year and authorized $3.6 billion for its programs in fiscal 1993, but the bill bogged down in the Senate.

For a second year in a row, the measure became the battleground over efforts to repeal a user fee on owners of recreational boats. In 1991, Congress cleared a Coast Guard reauthorization bill (HR 1776 — PL 102-241) after a major battle to eliminate the user fees was defused. The final bill included a non-binding resolution urging the Bush administration to repeal the fee. *(1991 Almanac, p. 153)*

In 1992, the fight to eliminate the user fee was resolved on separate legislation that banned boats that used large-scale nets from U.S. ports. *(Boat tax, p. 204)*

### House Action

Action began on the Coast Guard reauthorization bill in the House Merchant Marine and Fisheries panel: On June 4 it approved the $3.6 billion bill (HR 5055) by voice vote.

The fiscal 1993 authorization was $202 million less than President Bush had requested and $20 million more than was appropriated in fiscal 1992.

The full House followed suit on June 22, passing the bill by a vote of 304-22. *(Vote 207, p. 50-H)*

The bill authorized Coast Guard operations at $2.6 billion, acquisition and construction at $419 million and environmental compliance activities at $30.5 million for fiscal 1993.

The bill also stiffened penalities on drunken recreational boat operators in an effort to boost boating safety.

The authorized amount was the same as that requested by Bush and represented a 6 percent increase over fiscal 1992 spending. But the administration opposed several provisions, including one that shifted $80 million over the next five years from a sports fishing restoration program to the Coast Guard's boat safety program. It also opposed a provision, added by the Merchant Marine and Fisheries Committee, that prohibited procurement of foreign-made buoy chains.

The bill authorized the establishment of two oil-spill management centers in Texas and Massachusetts.

### Senate Action

The Senate Commerce, Science and Transportation Committee on June 16 gave voice vote approval to a companion Coast Guard reauthorization bill (S 2702 — S Rept 102-346).

The Senate included in its reauthorization a phase out of the Coast Guard tax on owners of recreational boats that was imposed in the 1990 budget accord. Committee Chairman Ernest F. Hollings, D-S.C., said the tax was unfair to boat owners who operated their vessels in rivers and lakes not regularly patrolled by the Coast Guard.

The full Senate never took up the Coast Guard bill. ∎

# Coast Guard Inspections of Foreign Ships Authorized

Provisions allowing the Coast Guard to inspect certain foreign vessels while they were dry-docked cleared Congress as part of a larger legislative package (HR 5617 — PL 102-587) of maritime-related bills.

The Coast Guard was authorized to inspect ships upon their arrival in a U.S. port to ensure compliance with safety laws and regulations. The measure allowed the guard to also inspect foreign-flagged vessels overseas provided that shipowners agreed and paid the costs of inspection. This right already existed for U.S.-flagged vessels in foreign ports.

Supporters of the bill argued that ships that undergo reconstruction or repair overseas should be inspected at the dry dock, where it would be easier to identify problems and suggest modifications.

The original measure (HR 4485 — H Rept 102-502) won the approval of the House Merchant Marine and Fisheries Committee on April 8. It passed the House by voice vote May 5. During the debate before the House vote, W. J. "Billy" Tauzin, D-La., chairman of the Merchant Marine Subcommittee on the Coast Guard and Navigation, urged passage to "ensure the most thorough [vessel] inspections possible."

In the Senate, the bill was approved by the Commerce, Science and Transportation Committee on June 16.

But in the waning days of Congress, the language of the bill was added to a large package of non-controversial maritime legislation. That measure cleared Congress on Oct. 7 and was signed by President Bush on Nov. 4.

## Scrapping Barges

Added to the same package was a measure that would prohibit the abandonment of large barges.

The legislation made abandoning barges illegal and empowered the Coast Guard to dispose of the scrapped vessels.

Previously, owners of barges had been allowed to abandon them as long as they did not obstruct navigation or pose an immediate environmental hazard. But a General Accounting Office study found that the abandoned ships often fouled the coastline and became dumping grounds for hazardous materials.

The original bill (HR 5397 — H Rept 102-768) had won the approval of the House Merchant Marine Subcommittee on Coast Guard and Navigation on June 18. Full committee approval came soon after on July 1. The House passed the measure by voice vote Aug. 3. While the bill was referred to the Senate Commerce Committee, it was never taken up. ■

# Foreign Ship Subsidies

The House on May 13 passed a bill (HR 2056) that took aim at foreign shipbuilding subsidies in an effort to boost the flagging U.S. shipping industry. But lawmakers failed at several attempts to advance the legislation, and it died.

In the waning days of the 102nd Congress, House lawmakers attached the bill to a separate measure (HR 2152 — H Rept 102-262) that banned from U.S. ports boats that used large-scale fishing nets. But the Senate stripped the shipping subsidy language from the broader bill days before the House cleared it Oct. 4.

## BACKGROUND

Several lawmakers wanted to eliminate subsidies enjoyed by shipbuilders in many foreign countries by requiring owners of commercial vessels that entered U.S. ports to certify to the U.S. Customs Service that their ship had not benefited from any foreign subsidy. Ships that had the benefit of subsidies were to be required to pay back the subsidy before gaining entry into the United States.

"Every other American worker, every other American business, is protected against subsidies except shipyard workers and their shipyards," said sponsor Sam M. Gibbons, D-Fla., during House floor debate.

Otherwise a staunch free-trade advocate, Gibbons had hometown reasons for pushing a bill to deter foreign ship subsidies. In his Florida district, a Tampa ship repair facility that employed 500 had been hurt by foreign ship subsidies.

Other bill proponents said 40 shipyards had closed nationwide and 120,000 jobs had been lost in the past two decades.

Congress eliminated U.S. shipbuilding subsidies in 1981, and in 1989 the United States entered into international discussions to get other countries — primarily Germany, Italy and France — to do the same. But progress in those talks had been minimal.

The Bush administration threatened to veto the legislation, saying it would hurt future negotiations.

## LEGISLATIVE ACTION

The House Merchant Marine and Fisheries Committee on Feb. 27 approved by voice vote a compromise version of HR 2056 that took aim at foreign shipbuilding subsidies.

The bill required all ships involved in foreign trade to certify that they were not built or repaired with the aid of foreign subsidies. Ships without certificates were to be barred from transporting goods in or out of U.S. ports.

Shippers and shipowners had strongly objected to a previous version of the bill as reported by the House Ways and Means Committee in 1991 because it threatened to take effect retroactively in October 1991. On July 11, 1991, the Ways and Means Subcommittee on Trade had approved the early version of the bill.

The 1992 bill did not take effect until enactment. It represented another attempt to revive the dying domestic shipbuilding business, which had been unable to compete with foreign-subsidized ships.

The Bush administration opposed the bill and instead favored continued talks intended to reach a multilateral agreement among shipbuilding nations.

Under the bill, shipowners who had vessels built or repaired at subsidized foreign shipyards were not able to use such shipyards if they wanted to do business in the United States. The measure also subjected foreign-made vessels to countervailing duties and anti-dumping provisions.

The revised bill required the Commerce Department to publish a list of foreign shipyards that received government subsidies.

For the second year in a row, the committee also approved by voice vote an amendment that sought to gradu-

## House Efforts To Regulate Foreign Ships Stalled

Legislation (HR 1126 — H Rept 102-984, Part 1) that would have extended U.S. labor laws to cover foreign-flag ships in American waters stalled in the House, after winning the approval of the Education and Labor Committee.

The bill also had been referred to the House Merchant Marine and Fisheries Committee. But it languished there as a result of its late arrival and the poor health of committee Chairman Walter B. Jones, D-N.C.

A comparable Senate bill (S 3235), introduced on Sept. 15 at the end of the legislative year, fared no better. It saw no action during the closing days of the session.

The legislation would have applied U.S. labor laws to foreign-flag passenger ships that regularly transported people to and from U.S. ports. In addition, coverage would have been extended to U.S.-owned foreign-flag ships that transported liquid or dry goods and to offshore fish processing vessels that operated in U.S. territorial waters.

These ships would have been subject to the Fair Labor Standards Act, which guaranteed a minimum wage and overtime pay for workers and regulated child labor practices. They would have also been compelled to comply with the National Labor Relations Act, which governs collective bargaining.

### House Committee Action

The measure was taken up by the Labor Standards Subcommittee on Feb. 27, where it was approved by voice vote.

One amendment, offered by subcommittee Chairman Austin J. Murphy, D-Pa., that would have exempted cargo container ships from the requirements, also was approved by voice vote.

At the subsequent full committee markup June 10, Murphy argued that it was time to end the "unfair double standard" that applied the laws to ships under the U.S. flag but exempted ships flying foreign flags.

But Tom Petri, R-Wis., opposed the bill, saying that he was concerned that it might conflict with provisions of international law and that it might have an adverse effect on trade and cruise ships.

Nevertheless, HR 1126 won the voice vote approval of the committee.

The measure was then slated to be taken up by the Merchant Marine and Fisheries Committee. But there was little chance of committee approval — even if Jones had been healthy — given the bill's late arrival and the lack of a companion measure in the Senate.

ally repeal a 1990 user fee on recreational boat owners. The amendment, which was eventually enacted into law after it was attached to separate legislation, phased out the user fee beginning in fiscal 1993. *(Boat user fees, this page)*

The full House on May 13 took up the subsidy bill and voted to levy penalties on ships that were built or repaired using subsidies from foreign governments.

The House passed HR 2056, 339-78, after debate focused on how the penalties affected negotiations with other countries over shipbuilding subsidies. *(Vote 121, p. 30-H)*

Bill Archer, R-Texas, led an unsuccessful fight against the shipbuilding provision. He argued that it threatened to unfairly penalize shipowners and U.S. ports by encouraging subsidized ships to do business in other countries, such as Canada and Mexico.

Archer offered a motion to send the bill back to the Merchant Marine and the Ways and Means committees with instructions to strip the shipbuilding provisions. It was rejected, 179-237. *(Vote 120, p. 30-H)*

The bill provision to repeal the user fee on recreational boats attracted wide support on the floor, although the administration objected to it on budgetary grounds.

Boat owners had vigorously lobbied Congress to repeal the tax since the 1990 budget agreement called for a user fee to be levied on all recreational boats to defray the cost of U.S. Coast Guard services. On July 31, 1991, the Coast Guard began imposing the tax.

The Senate on Oct. 10 folded HR 2056 into a Senate version of the shipbuilding measure (S 3338), which was then introduced in the Senate. But the bill failed to advance.

House lawmakers also sought to inject some life into the foreign subsidy measure when they attached it Aug. 10 to a separate measure (HR 2152) to ban drift net fishing. *(Drift net sanction, p. 286)*

Two days later, the Senate stripped the foreign shipbuilding provisions before passing the drift net measure. ■

# Controversial Boat Tax To Be Phased Out

The 102nd Congress enacted legislation on an unrelated bill that included a timetable for phasing out a controversial tax on the owners of recreational boats, ending a year-long battle that was sparked after the tax was levied as part of the 1990 budget agreement.

Lawmakers tried several times to repeal the boat tax. But success came only after language to phase out the tax was attached to a separate measure (HR 2152 — H Rept 102-262) that sought to end the use of large-scale fishing nets. The House cleared the revised drift net legislation Oct. 4, and President Bush signed it into law Nov. 2 (PL 102-582). *(Drift net sanction, p. 286)*

In the waning days of the session, HR 2152 had bounced back and forth between the chambers. On its final round, the Senate on Aug. 12 altered House changes and returned the measure to that chamber. The Senate had kept intact the gradual repeal of the boat tax, and the House later accepted the change.

The language put in place a timetable for the phaseout of the Coast Guard user fee by Oct. 1, 1994. It called for making up the attendant budget shortfall by imposing a new fee on those who used a Federal Maritime Commission data base on tariff information.

The Coast Guard user fee was first levied on boaters as part of the 1990 congressional-White House budget agreement as a revenue-raising measure. The fee had raised only $47 million in the two years since its implementation — far short of the $262 million the White House's Office of Management and Budget had predicted.

In 1992, the House reiterated its opposition to the boat tax — after having gone on record against the tax in 1991. On May 13, the House passed, 339-78, a separate bill (HR 2056) regarding foreign shipbuilding subsidies that included a gradual repeal of the fee. *(1991 Almanac, p. 154; Vote 121, p. 30-H)*

### Boat Tax Levied in 1991

Finding a way around the boat tax had become a yearly exercise since its enactment. On July 31, 1991, the Coast Guard began imposing the tax, which ranged from $25 for boats between 16 and 20 feet long to $100 for boats 40 feet and longer.

Boat owners had vigorously lobbied Congress to repeal the tax since the 1990 budget agreement called for a user fee to be levied on all recreational boats to defray the cost of Coast Guard services.

Lawmakers argued that the tax was not a user fee because it applied to boat owners who operated their vessels on inland lakes and waterways not served by the Coast Guard. Opponents also argued that even boat owners who were able to benefit from Coast Guard services had seen the Coast Guard cut back its services to boaters.

William J. Hughes, D-N.J., called the fee "unjust," adding that "this fee has wasted scarce Coast Guard services, burdened millions of boat owners and generated a small percentage of the revenues it was projected to raise."

### Repeal Attached to Unrelated Bills

Action began in the House, where the Merchant Marine and Fisheries Committee on Feb. 27 approved by voice vote an amendment to a separate bill (HR 2056 — H Rept 102-284 — Part II) that took aim at foreign shipbuilding subsidies. The amendment sought to gradually repeal a 1990 user fee on recreational boat owners.

The full House on May 13 then passed HR 2056, 339-78, with the repeal of the user fee on recreational boats attracting wide support on the floor. The Bush administration objected to the gradual repeal on budgetary grounds. *(Vote 121, p. 30-H)*

The language phased out the fee beginning Oct. 1, 1992, and ending Oct. 1, 1994. The timetable called for repealing the user fee on boats 21 feet or shorter on Oct. 1, 1992; on boats 37 feet or shorter by Oct. 1, 1993, and all other recreational boats by Oct. 1, 1994.

To replace lost revenues, the bill assessed a new computer access charge on the shipping industry for use of the Federal Maritime Commission's data base of shippers' charges, or tariffs. Shippers had to file their rates — shipping prices on U.S. waterways — with the Federal Maritime Commission, and the bill charged a new fee to access the computer information.

On July 31, the Senate attached a provision similar to the boat tax repeal language in HR 2056 to its version of the drift net bill (HR 2152). The House on Aug. 10 accepted that change as well as adding other unrelated provisions.

On Aug. 12, the Senate rejected all but the boat tax repeal and passed the new version of HR 2152 by voice vote. The House accepted the Senate changes and cleared the bill Oct. 4. Bush on Nov. 2 signed the final drift net bill (PL 102-582). ∎

# A Variety of Transportation Bills Advance

Congress enacted, and the House and Senate advanced, several bills during the second session of the 102nd Congress regarding transportation. They included:

## AVIATION WORKER FINES AND APPEALS

The 102nd Congress enacted a bill aimed at protecting aviation employees who had been assessed civil fines by the Federal Aviation Administration (FAA).

The House on Aug. 3 passed the bill (HR 5481) by voice vote. It required the FAA to advise pilots, flight engineers, mechanics or repairmen of the nature and reason for potential civil fines before they were levied. The bill also required that aviation employees be given a chance to rebut the charges.

The bill allowed the FAA to levy civil penalties against aviation employees for violating such things as safety regulations, bans against civil aircraft flights over security zones and requirements that passengers be notified of the lack of security at certain airports. The Public Works and Transportation Subcommittee on Aviation approved the bill June 25. The full Public Works and Transportation Committee followed suit July 1 (H Rept 102-671).

As approved by committee, HR 5481 allowed pilots and flight engineers to appeal any FAA civil fines to the National Transportation Safety Board. It was amended during the full committee markup by a vote of 30-26 to include mechanics and repair personnel.

Before the legislation, aviation industry employees had been allowed to appeal civil fines only to the FAA administrator's office — which oversaw the officials who issued fines. Supporters of the bill said such an arrangement was a conflict of interest.

The Senate on Aug. 12 passed the bill by voice vote, clearing it for President Bush, who signed it into law (PL 102-345) on Aug. 25.

## CRUISES TO NOWHERE

In an effort to improve the competitiveness of the U.S. maritime industry, the House on Sept. 22 passed a bill that prevented foreign-owned ships from engaging in the domestic cruise business. The measure died in the Senate.

The bill (HR 5257 — H Rept 102-835), passed by voice vote, applied to foreign-owned, foreign-built ships that took advantage of a loophole in domestic shipping laws intended to reserve the domestic cruise industry for U.S. ships.

The Merchant Marine Subcommittee of the House Merchant Marine and Fisheries Committee approved the bill by voice vote June 18. The full committee followed suit July 1.

The measure brought so-called voyages to nowhere — which included dinner cruises, whale sightseeing trips and fishing expeditions — under merchant marine laws that required U.S.-flagged ships and U.S. crews.

In 1992, foreign-flagged vessels offering cruises that returned to the same port without having passengers disembark in a foreign country were able to skirt U.S. labor, safety and hiring laws. Under the bill, all ships departing U.S. ports to engage in such voyages were required to be built, owned and operated in the United States.

The bill phased out the involvement of foreign vessels in the trade, allowing some to continue their business for up to 20 years to recoup their investments before the ban took effect completely.

## CREW DOCUMENTS

The House on Sept. 9 passed a bill (HR 4394 — H Rept 102-669) that required all crew members of tugs, towboats and barges navigating inland waterways to obtain official documents as seamen. The measure snagged in the Senate.

The purpose of asking for the documents was to require the workers to submit to drug testing and background checks for a criminal record.

The House Merchant Marine and Fisheries Subcommittee on Coast Guard and Navigation had approved the bill on a 14-7 vote on June 25.

In 1992, seafarers aboard U.S. merchant vessels of at least 100 gross tons were required to hold merchant mariner documents. But the law exempted vessels operating only on inland rivers and lakes. More than 3,000 tugs and towboats operated on inland waterways, many carrying hazardous cargoes. HR 4394 sought to extend its requirements to all crew members.

The bill was referred to the Senate Commerce, Science and Transportation Committee, where it stalled.

## MODERNIZING THE NOAA FLEET

The Merchant Marine Committee on July 1 approved by voice vote a bill (HR 5324 — H Rept 102-896) that authorized $430 million over four years to replace and modernize the 22-vessel fleet of the National Oceanic and Atmospheric Administration. But the full House never considered the measure.

The panel rejected, 8-32, an amendment by Gene Taylor, D-Miss., that required all of that agency's vessels to be built or repaired in U.S. shipyards.

The Oceanography Subcommittee had approved the bill June 24.

## EXTENDING TERRITORIAL WATERS

The House Merchant Marine and Fisheries Committee approved a measure April 8 (HR 3842 — H Rept 102-843 — Part I) that clarified that the United States had sovereignty over waters 12 nautical miles from its coast. The full House never considered the measure.

The bill, approved by voice vote, codified a 1988 presidential order that extended the territorial zone from three nautical miles. The Justice Department dismissed questions about whether the president had the authority to extend the territorial zone by executive order.

The bill also revised several maritime and fisheries laws to make them conform to the 12-mile limit.

## TRUCKER-CUSTOMER QUARRELS

The Senate on Sept. 30 passed by voice vote a bill that attempted to resolve pricing disputes between bankrupt trucking companies and their former customers.

The measure failed to advance in the House where opposition from House lawmakers in behalf of the Teamsters made it impossible for the 102nd Congress to clear the bill.

The bill (S 1675 — S Rept 102-359) by Jim Exon, D-Neb., settled a controversy over huge discounts offered by truckers during the competitive years after industry deregulation in 1980.

Because many of those discounts were never filed with the Interstate Commerce Commission, estates of bankrupt trucking companies had been pressuring past clients to pay more for the shipments on the grounds that the shippers were undercharged.

The U.S. Supreme Court in 1990 ruled that the trustees sought such reimbursement. An Exon effort to reverse the ruling through legislation died in the 101st Congress.

The 1992 bill, rather than dismissing the trucking company estates' claims, allowed estates to choose between appealing to the Interstate Commerce Commission for a ruling or accepting an expedited settlement process for a percentage of the alleged undercharges.

The Senate passed the bill after Exon negotiated with several senators who sought to stall the measure in behalf of trucking companies and unions.

The Senate Commerce, Science and Transportation Committee had approved the bill June 16.

A companion measure (HR 3705) by Barney Frank, D-Mass., was not acted on by the House Public Works and Transportation Committee. Many lawmakers on that panel and within the House Democratic ranks opposed the bill, amid an intense lobbying push by the Teamsters union, which favored the Supreme Court ruling and opposed the measure.

## FAA MAPS FOR GENERAL AVIATORS

The House on July 30 passed by voice vote a bill that required the FAA to publish charts for general aviation pilots detailing safe routes through heavily congested air traffic control areas. But the bill failed to advance in the Senate.

The House Public Works Subcommittee on Aviation approved the bill June 25. And the full committee followed suit on July 1 (HR 3243 — H Rept 102-712).

The bill directed the FAA to publish charts showing clearly identifiable corridors through which general aviation pilots could better fly to and from congested airports without interfering with the flight patterns of commercial planes. Use of the charts was optional for pilots.

A companion bill in the Senate (S 1895) was referred to the Commerce Committee, where it stalled. ■

# Three Small-Business Programs Passed

In an effort to create jobs and pull the nation out of recession, the 102nd Congress cleared three bills intended to help small businesses get loans, attract venture capital and win more federal research money.

The Senate on Aug. 12 sent President Bush one bill (HR 4111) that boosted a federal small-business loan program intended to provide capital to small businesses. The measure increased the authorized funding level of the Small Business Administration's (SBA) guaranteed loan program from fiscal 1992-94.

The measure also incorporated the language of a separate bill (HR 5191) to revise a program to give a financial boost to companies that invested in fledgling small businesses.

The House on Oct. 5 cleared a third bill (S 2941) to promote commercialization by small businesses of the government's technical and scientific innovations. The final measure, which incorporated the language of an earlier House version (HR 4400), required key federal agencies to earmark a larger portion of their outside research budgets for small businesses. The bill expanded the small business innovation research program, which had been hailed as a success by Congress and federal agencies in generating some $1 billion in commercial spinoffs for small businesses.

## SMALL BUSINESS LOANS

The House Small Business Committee acted early on the bill (HR 4111 — H Rept 102-492) to increase funding for loans to small businesses, easily approving the legislation March 11. The action came as demand for small business loans was on the upswing.

With little debate and by voice vote, the panel approved the bill that increased the authorized funding level of the SBA's guaranteed loan program for so-called 7(a) business loans. The bill authorized $5 billion in fiscal 1992, $6 billion in fiscal 1993 and $7 billion in fiscal 1994.

Congress appropriated $3.5 billion for the loan program in fiscal 1992. The limit on guaranteed loans established in the fiscal 1992 Commerce-State-Justice appropriations bill (PL 102-140) was $3.5 billion. That required an appropriation of about $170 million to cover expected loan losses and subsidies. *(1991 Almanac, p. 531)*

Committee Chairman John J. LaFalce, D-N.Y., said program funding fell short by about $800 million in fiscal 1992 due to an unexpected onslaught of loan requests.

The Bush administration had asked Congress in February to pass a $1.2 billion supplemental spending bill — to be offset by spending cuts elsewhere — to replenish the loan fund in fiscal 1992. But committee members were reluctant to take that approach, saying it threatened to force deep reductions in other important programs.

In an effort to meet the growing demand for small-business loans, the House on May 14 passed the bill on a 399-2 vote. *(Vote 122, p. 30-H)*

LaFalce said the legislation allowed credit-worthy companies to borrow money, create jobs and get the recession-damaged economy moving. The measure stood to enable 60,000 small businesses to receive an average loan of $100,000, he said.

The Senate passed an amended version of the bill Aug. 6. The Senate then cleared HR 4111 on Aug. 12. Bush signed the bill into law Sept. 4 (PL 102-366).

## SMALL-BUSINESS CAPITAL

Before leaving for the August recess, the House on Aug. 12 folded the text of a separate bill (HR 5191) that substantially revised the government program aimed at providing venture capital to small businesses into HR 4111, the measure increasing funding for small business loans.

The House Small Business Committee on June 24 gave the venture capital bill its start, approving HR 5191, 39-0.

In 1992, the SBA funneled venture capital to small businesses through small-business investment companies (SBICs). But these investment companies were failing, said committee Chairman LaFalce.

The insolvencies were attributed to the faltering economy and the SBIC program structure. The program encouraged firms to borrow money through the SBA for long-term investments, which provided virtually no return to the businesses for a number of years.

The small-business investment company program was launched in 1958 to help small firms expand and acquire venture capital for start-up costs or research expenses. The program helped launch such firms as Apple Computer, Federal Express, Cray Research and Nike.

But with the recession and cases of mismanagement, the program had fallen on hard times. The bill represented an attempt to prevent further SBIC failures by allowing institutional investors to invest in the SBICs to improve cash flow. Under HR 5191, the federal government was allowed to pay some of the interest on the SBIC loans in return for a share of the profits at a later date.

The House passed HR 5191 on a 356-2 vote July 31. It allowed so-called small-business investment companies to delay interest payments on loans owed to the SBA. *(Vote 356, p. 86-H)*

The Senate Small Business Committee approved HR 5191 on Aug. 6. The bill, approved 17-0, differed slightly from its House-passed companion. But the differences were expected to be worked out informally.

Both chambers' measures allowed so-called small-business investment companies to delay interest payments on loans owed the SBA. The companies used SBA financing to make investments in small businesses.

Institutional investors such as pension funds also were encouraged to buy equity in small-business investment companies through a provision that suspended taxes on unrelated business income.

The Senate bill, unlike the House measure, allowed investments by state or municipal governments to be considered "private capital" when determining how much was to be borrowed from the SBA.

Those investments were not to exceed 33 percent of a company's private capital.

The full Senate passed HR 5191 on Aug. 10 by voice vote.

The House then rolled HR 5191 into HR 4111, the bill that boosted a federal small-business loan program. The Senate on Aug. 12 cleared the larger loan bill and Bush signed it into law Sept. 4 — PL 102-366.

## RESEARCH FUNDS

Another bill (S 2941) cleared by the 102nd Congress required federal agencies to earmark a larger portion of

their research and development budgets for small, high-technology business applications.

The House Small Business Subcommittee on Procurement, Tourism and Rural Development approved the early House version (HR 4400) on May 13. The full Small Business Committee followed suit May 20, approving the measure on a 39-0 vote.

The provisions of HR 4400 also were incorporated into the fiscal 1993 defense authorization bill (HR 5006), which the Senate eventually cleared Oct. 5 and Bush signed into law Oct. 23 (PL 102-484). *(Defense authorization, p. 483)*

The early version of the bill reauthorized a program known as the Small Business Innovation Program through fiscal 2000 and more than doubled, to 3 percent, the federal funds set aside by each federal agency for small businesses to use in developing commercial applications of new technologies.

Under the program, which was intended to promote commercialization of the government's technical and scientific innovations, federal agencies were required to set aside 1.25 percent of their research and development budgets for contracts to be awarded to small businesses.

During fiscal 1990, participating companies received $460 million out of a federal research budget of about $75 billion.

The original bill increased the research and development set-aside to 2.5 percent, but the full committee approved, by voice vote, an amendment by Andy Ireland, R-Fla., that increased the set aside to 3 percent by fiscal 1996 — a level that was eventually pared back to 2.5 percent.

The measure also was referred to the House Armed Services, Foreign Affairs and Science, Space and Technology committees.

The House Science panel's Technology and Competitiveness Subcommittee on June 24 approved the bill. The full Science Committee acted soon after, approving HR 4400 on July 1 on a 7-4 vote.

The Science panel settled on a more modest increase in the program than the level agreed to by the Small Business Committee. The Science panel agreed to increase the research set-aside to 2 percent by fiscal 1996, as compared with the 3 percent set-aside approved by the Small Business Committee for the same period.

The House on Aug. 11 passed HR 4400 (H Rept 102-554, Parts 1-3) to expand the program designed to help small businesses take part in federal research activities.

The bill, which was passed by voice vote, boosted the amount of money 11 major federal agencies spent on research performed by small businesses.

Before the bill, agencies with outside research and development budgets exceeding $100 million were required under the Small Business Innovation Research Program to set aside at least 1.25 percent of their budgets for research projects performed by small businesses.

In a compromise of the versions worked out by House committees, the House-passed bill called for gradually increasing that requirement, beginning in fiscal 1994, to 2.5 percent by fiscal 1998. In fiscal 1996, when the level was to be set at 2 percent, the bill allowed any agency to block further increases if it determined that the quality of research had declined and that continuing it threatened to harm research activities.

The 10-year-old small-business program, which had generated $1 billion in commercial spinoffs, was regarded as a success by federal agencies, the General Accounting Office (GAO) and Congress. A 1992 GAO study found that more than $1 billion in commercial spinoffs had been generated by the program, a figure that was expected to reach $3 billion by the end of 1993.

The bill had met resistance from colleges and universities, which generally opposed expanding the program. They were fearful that it threatened to cut into academic research budgets.

But Ireland, the ranking minority member of the House Small Business Committee, countered that only $460 million of the government's total $38 billion in research spending was directed toward the estimated 4,000 small businesses that participated in the program. The bill channeled about $950 million to small businesses.

HR 4400 also created a program to ease the way for small businesses to commercialize basic research developed in federal laboratories and universities.

Under that program, each agency whose total research and development budget topped $1 billion a year reserved 0.25 percent of it by 1996 to fund cooperative research projects between small businesses and a researcher from a federal laboratory, university or nonprofit research institution.

Meanwhile, the Senate had begun work on its version of the bill (S 2941), which incorporated the House language with minor changes. The House accepted those alterations and cleared the final bill Oct. 5 by voice vote.

Bush signed S 2941 into law Oct. 28 (PL 102-564). ■

# National Map Project Reaches Destination

The House on April 30 cleared a bill (HR 2763) to create a program to chart the nation's geological features, ending the legislation's two-year journey through Congress.

The bill moved quickly and early in the second session of the 102nd Congress, with action beginning in the Senate.

In 1992, less than 20 percent of the United States had been mapped for its geologic features — a shortcoming the Senate sought to address with passage March 31 of HR 2763 to create a national geologic mapping program.

The bill authorized the U.S. Geological Survey to lead the program with help from states and academia. The bill, passed by voice vote, authorized $37 million in fiscal 1993, rising to $56 million in 1996, according to the Congressional Budget Office.

Although large-scale topographical maps of the United States existed, maps tracing the nation's energy, mineral and water resources and geological features essential for the safe siting of such things as toxic and nuclear waste dumps had been completed only for Kentucky and Massachusetts. The U.S. Geologic Survey did not have a geologic mapping program until 1987.

The House had passed by voice vote its version (H Rept 102-333) of the bill by Nick J. Rahall II, D-W.Va., on Nov. 19, 1991. In 1991, the Senate version (S 1179) had moved smoothly through the Energy and Natural Resources Committee, with the support of sponsor and Chairman J. Bennett Johnston, D-La., after winning approval, 20-0, on Oct. 30, 1991.

In 1992, the Senate adopted the House version of the bill, with a few minor amendments, sending the measure back to the House.

The House accepted the Senate changes and cleared the bill April 30. President Bush signed the measure into law May 18 (PL 102-285). ■

# No New Product-Safety Legislation Passed

Legislation (HR 4706 — H Rept 102-649) to reauthorize the Consumer Product Safety Commission (CPSC) and mandate new regulations for children's toys and bicycle helmets moved rapidly through the House but was not taken up by the Senate before adjournment.

The Senate acted on two separate measures to promote the use of bicycle helmets by children (S 3096 — S Rept 102-406; S 2952). But the House failed to act on either of them.

Congress created CPSC in 1972 as an independent safety watchdog agency over potentially dangerous consumer products.

The agency quickly became a battleground between consumer advocates and a free-market, deregulation-minded series of Republican administrations.

It was a long-sought victory for consumer activists when Congress passed legislation in 1990 to reauthorize the troubled agency.

The two-year bill (PL 101-608) speeded up CPSC rulemaking and generally gave the agency more teeth to enforce its regulations. It was the first stand-alone reauthorization since 1981. *(1990 Almanac, p. 393)*

Because of the history of political controversies at CPSC, lawmakers had tried to assert control over the agency through the appropriations process. In 1985, for example, Congress cut funds for two commissioners, reducing the agency's membership to three. Ostensibly a budget-driven move, the provision also reduced the number of Reagan appointees.

By 1989, the commission's budget had dropped to $35 million, down from a high of $43 million in fiscal 1979, and staff had been cut almost in half. Even so, the agency still oversaw the safety of an estimated 15,000 consumer products.

## Expected Defeat

Consumer groups were not surprised when reauthorization legislation failed in 1992. The House passed HR 4706 by voice vote Sept. 10, which authorized $42.1 million and $43.2 million for CPSC in fiscal 1993 and fiscal 1994, respectively.

The bill contained a provision, based on a bill (HR 3809) authored by Rep. Cardiss Collins, D-Ill., that would have required manufacturers to label toys with small parts as potential choking hazards. In addition, the bill would have banned the sale of small balls to children under the age of three.

The legislation also would have mandated standards for bicycle helmets.

The House Energy and Commerce Subcommittee on Commerce, Consumer Protection and Competitiveness had approved HR 4706 by voice vote on April 2. As approved by that panel, funding was set at $45 million for fiscal 1993 and $48 million for fiscal 1994.

The toy safety provisions required the labeling of toys with small parts that might become dislodged in a toddler's mouth, and set minimum size requirements for balls intended for children under the age of three.

Members rejected, 8-9, an amendment by ranking panel member Alex J. McMillan, R-N.C., that would have reduced the authorization levels in the bill to $39 million for fiscal 1993 and the same amount adjusted for inflation for fiscal 1994.

The House Energy and Commerce Committee approved HR 4706 on June 18, after reducing authorized funding levels for consumer product safety programs.

The committee passed the measure (HR 4706), to reauthorize the agency through fiscal 1994, by a vote of 32-10.

In a compromise offered by Jim Slattery, D-Kan., the panel agreed, 26-17, to fund the agency at $42 million in fiscal 1993 and $45 million in fiscal 1994.

Even without an authorization bill, funding for the agency through the fiscal 1993 spending bill for the Veterans Administration, Housing and Urban Development and independent agencies (H Rept 5679 — PL 102-389) jumped to $48.4 million from $40.2 million the previous year. *(Appropriations, p. 639)*

A separate bill (S 3096 — S Rept 102-406) to promote the use of bicycle helmets by riders under the age of 16 got the nod from the Senate Commerce Committee Sept. 11. Approved by voice vote, the bill authorized states to receive federal grants to provide helmets to low-income families with children under the age of 16, beefed up enforcement of bicycle helmet laws and educated cyclists on the need to wear a helmet.

The Senate passed S 3096 by voice vote Sept. 25 and sent it to the House, which never acted on it.

A similar bill (S 2952) introduced by Sen. Howard M. Metzenbaum, D-Ohio, to establish a grant program under the National Highway Traffic Safety Administration for the purpose of promoting the use of bicycle helmets also died in the 102nd Congress. ∎

## Franklin Confirmed As New Commerce Secretary

Amid some concerns on her trade policies, Barbara Hackman Franklin was confirmed Feb. 27 as Commerce secretary. She replaced Robert A. Mosbacher, who joined President Bush's re-election team.

The Commerce, Science and Transportation Committee had approved the nomination of Franklin, 51, on Feb. 18.

John D. Rockefeller IV, D-W.Va., was the only panel member to cast a no vote on the Franklin nomination, saying that administration trade policies needed drastic changes.

Rockefeller said that Franklin would be only a "capable steward of the status quo."

Committee Chairman Ernest F. Hollings, D-S.C., also expressed concern that Franklin would not sufficiently challenge President Bush's free-trade policies.

"We're trying to educate this new secretary on competitiveness on reciprocal trade policies," Hollings said.

Franklin was head of her own management consulting firm, and she served as a member of the Consumer Product Safety Commission during the 1970s.

# Product Liability Bill Narrowly Defeated

The Senate came closer than it had in 12 years to passing a bill (S 640) that would have set national standards for personal injury lawsuits that resulted from faulty products. But the legislation was narrowly defeated, largely because of a lack of Senate floor time to debate the issue.

No action was taken on a companion House measure (HR 3030), sponsored by J. Roy Rowland, D-Ga. An attempt early in the year to attach the Senate measure to a voter registration bill (S 250) failed.

The Senate product liability bill, sponsored by Bob Kasten, R-Wis., was altered in 1992 to pick up Democratic support, most notably by John D. Rockefeller IV, D-W.Va. For instance, it no longer sought to cap damages.

Supporters were eventually able to persuade the leadership to allow a cloture vote on the product liability bill itself. But this too proved unsuccessful, when S 640 fell two votes shy of the 60 needed to close debate.

## BACKGROUND

Congress had been trying for more than a decade to restrict jury awards for injuries caused by faulty products. Advocates said juries often granted excessive awards, driving up business costs and deterring product innovation. Although some states already had passed product liability restrictions, proponents said a federal statute was needed to create national standards for such lawsuits. Trial lawyers and consumer groups had successfully joined forces to stop such bills, saying they would unfairly punish the victims of faulty merchandise.

In each Congress since the 97th, legislation introduced was perennially deadlocked in a conflict that pitted manufacturers, pharmaceutical companies and the insurance industry against consumer groups and trial lawyers. The conflict reached dramatic proportions in 1986 when Sen. Ernest F. Hollings, D-S.C., a former trial lawyer, briefly filibustered a bill (S 2760) that made it to the Senate floor. He contended that common law tradition and state law should govern lawsuits, rather than a federal standard. *(1986 Almanac, p. 287)*

In 1991, separate versions of product liability legislation were introduced in the House and Senate. In the Senate, S 640 was approved, 13-7, by the Commerce, Science and Transportation Committee on Oct 3. The House bill (HR 3030) was jointly referred to the Judiciary and the Energy and Commerce committees, where no action occurred. *(1991 Almanac, p. 177)*

The bills attempted to smooth the legal process in cases involving faulty products by instituting uniform national standards, such as a two-year statute of limitations on filing lawsuits. They would have limited each party's liability to pay non-economic damages in cases in which there was more than one defendant. The legislation would also have provided incentives to settle lawsuits early and set an alternative dispute resolution system.

In addition, the measures had set new tougher stan-

---

## BOXSCORE

➡ **Product Liability (S 640, HR 3030).** Legislation to set national standards for the filing of personal injury lawsuits and offer incentives for early settlement.

**Reports:** S Rept 102-215.

### KEY ACTION

Sept. 10 — An attempt to invoke cloture on S 640 failed, 58-38.

---

dards for the awarding of punitive damages and set caps on the amount that could be given to defendants. But in an effort to broaden its appeal and pick up more Democratic support, sponsors eliminated the caps.

The Senate bill, while winning Commerce Committee approval, had also been referred to the lawyer-dominated Judiciary Committee, where action was pending in early 1992.

While U.S. manufacturers and their advocates on Capitol Hill had long pushed for nationwide product liability standards, the tort reform issue gained new momentum in 1992 at the Republican National Convention in Houston.

Both President Bush and Vice President Dan Quayle used their convention addresses to blast the legal profession and the high cost of litigation in the country.

But critics had long claimed that the changes proposed in the House and Senate bills would have unfairly lowered damage awards and shifted more of the legal burden onto the victims of faulty products.

## LEGISLATIVE ACTION

Frustrated by slow movement on product liability bills in 1991, Senate supporters tried a number of maneuvers in 1992 to bring the legislation to a final vote. Kasten, sponsor of S 640, and other supporters had determined that more forceful tactics would be needed to counter the opposition of some Senate Democratic leaders, including Majority Leader George J. Mitchell, D-Maine.

To avoid the lawyer-dominated Judiciary Committee, where strong resistance was expected, Kasten successfully attached his tort reform legislation to the voter registration bill (S 250). *(Voter registration, p. 75)*

But on May 12, S 250 was pulled from the floor after Senate leaders failed, by a vote of 58-40, to muster the three-fifths majority (60) needed to invoke cloture and limit debate on the bill. *(Vote 87, 12-S)*

When Mitchell brought up the "motor voter" bill again two days later, he called for a vote on a motion to table, or kill, Kasten's amendment in the hope of separating the two issues. Mitchell won the gambit, 53-45, after five senators, who said they supported the intent of Kasten's legislation, voted against him. Included in this group was fellow cosponsor Rockefeller, who said that Kasten was employing "divisive partisan tactics" that diminished the merits of the product liability issue and stifled full debate. *(Vote 89, 13-S)*

The vote nonetheless bolstered product liability proponents, who said they would be within striking distance if the bill came to the floor on its own. This opportunity arrived after sponsors threatened to offer it as an amendment to any bill that came up, forcing Mitchell to give the issue a stand-alone cloture vote on Sept. 10.

Despite this victory, the attempt to invoke cloture ultimately failed. At one point during the vote supporters appeared to have the 60 votes needed to bring the bill up

for debate. But the prospect of a lengthy debate on the controversial issue proved too costly for Mitchell, who persuaded Bob Kerrey, D-Neb., to withdraw his "yea" vote and instead "pair" with an absent senator who wanted to vote "nay." That prompted a round of other vote-switching that ultimately left the bill sponsors two votes shy. The final cloture vote, 58-38, killed the measure for the year. *(Vote 199, 26-S)* ∎

# Vertical Price-Fixing Bill Dies in the House

Bowing to small-business groups, the House rejected a compromise bill aimed at punishing manufacturers who unfairly raised prices charged to discounters. The action effectively killed the measure for the 102nd Congress.

Opponents objected after a House-Senate conference committee removed a provision intended to help small businesses escape triple damages if they showed that they were "so small in the relevant market as to lack market power."

Supporters of the measure said that the practice — which involved collusion over product pricing between a manufacturer and favored retailers — was becoming increasingly common. They argued that vertical price-fixing was costing consumers up to $20 billion in higher prices annually.

But the measure faced tough opposition from small-business groups and the White House. These opponents feared that if the bill became law, retailers would be subjected to large numbers of lawsuits by competitors.

## BACKGROUND

Vertical price-fixing resulted when manufacturers, at the behest of retail customers, raised the prices they charged discount operations to stop them from undercutting smaller retailers.

Since a 1911 Supreme Court decision, vertical price fixing had been automatically, or "per se," illegal. But administration policy and two court decisions in the past decade had created ambiguity about what was enough evidence to warrant a jury trial. They also cast doubt on whether vertical price fixing would be punished in the courts.

Congress had been trying to alter price-fixing laws for several years. Bill supporters claimed that the practice was becoming prevalent as the result of the emergence of large-volume discount stores.

The two Supreme Court decisions raised questions about the quantity and type of evidence needed to prosecute a price-fixing complaint. Backers of legislation said that those court rulings made it practically impossible for discount retailers to bring their price-fixing cases to court.

The first was a 1984 ruling in *Monsanto Co. v. Spray-Rite Service Corp.* that a complaining discounter must provide direct evidence that a manufacturer and another retailer had intended to maintain resale price levels. The 1988 case, *Business Electronics Corp. v. Sharp Electronics Corp.*, held that there was no per se violation of antitrust laws unless the manufacturer and the retailer agreed to set a specific price.

In addition, bill supporters complained, the Justice Department under Presidents Ronald Reagan and Bush had given up the enforcement of the price-fixing laws. The department's last vertical price-fixing case had been heard in 1980.

A bittery fought antitrust bill to prevent manufacturers from fixing prices by their dealers died at the end of the 101st Congress. The House passed a measure (HR 1236) but a related bill (S 865) stalled in the Senate as it had when the House passed similar legislation in 1987. *(1990 Almanac, p. 539)*

The legislation would have clarified the case law by declaring price fixing to be illegal. It would have set new standards for juries deliberating price-fixing cases. More specifically, the measure would have allowed discount retailers to bring suit against a manufacturer and competing retailers without detailed proof that a price-fixing arrangement had been made.

In 1991, the House and Senate each passed different versions of the legislation. The key difference in the two versions revolved around a provision in the House bill (HR 1470) that would have offered some protection for small businesses that engaged in price fixing.

The provision, by Rep. Tom Campbell, R-Calif., would have allowed those businesses to escape the triple damages usually awarded to successful plaintiffs in price-fixing cases if they could show that they lacked market power. *(1991 Almanac, p. 291)*

## LEGISLATIVE ACTION

The Senate agreed to a conference on March 18, and the conferees filed a report June 22 on S 429.

Conferees removed Campbell's triple damages provision and essentially incorporated the Senate version of the two bills into the conference report. They argued that the Campbell amendment would lead to protracted litigation to determine which businesses were "small" as defined by the bill and thus entitled to the special protection afforded by the provision. They also said that large manufacturers would be able to use the amendment to avoid triple damages by claiming that they did not have a large share of the market.

The report was rejected by the House on June 30 by a vote of 175-225. *(Vote 251, p. 33-S)*

There was already a sizable opposition to the bill in the House, where many members worried about the impact on manufacturers and retailers. But without the Campbell provision, opponents in the House argued, the measure would have almost certainly hamstrung small businesses with staggering legal costs and in many cases driven them into bankruptcy.

The bill was strongly opposed by the National Federation of Independent Business, the largest small-business lobby. The White House also threatened a veto. President Bush and other Republican opponents contended that the bill would shackle small businesses with more lawsuits that benefited only lawyers. ∎

> ## BOXSCORE
>
> ➡ **Vertical Price Fixing (S 429, HR 1470).** The legislation sought to make it easier for discount retailers to bring and win vertical price-fixing suits against a manufacturer and a competing retailer.
>
> **Reports:** H Rept 102-237; S Rept 102-42; conference report H Rept 102-605.
>
> ### KEY ACTION
>
> June 30 — The **House** rejected the conference report to S 429, 175-225.

# Pesticide Rules Remain Unchanged

Efforts to rewrite the Federal Insecticide, Fungicide and Rodenticide Act (FIFRA), which governed the labeling and use of the nation's pesticides, failed to advance in the 102nd Congress, with lawmakers reluctant to take on the complex and politically charged issue in an election year.

Both environmentalists and representatives of the chemical industry had been lobbying for changes in the law since it was reauthorized in 1988.

Environmental and consumer protection groups wanted to make it easier to take pesticides off the market quickly if they proved dangerous. Pesticide producers and users wanted to amend the law to prevent local governments from regulating pesticide use. Most agriculture industry offices argued that local regulations made it too expensive to manufacture and market pesticides.

Caught between the two sides, lawmakers opted not to rewrite the law. Even a federal court decision issued in July that prohibited any pesticide residues from foods, was unable to break the legislative logjam. Though the Agriculture Subcommittee on Department Operations, Research and Foreign Agriculture did mark up a FIFRA revamp bill (HR 3742) on May 19, the measure died with no further action in the 102nd Congress.

## BACKGROUND

The last major change in pesticide laws came in 1988, when Congress rewrote FIFRA and accelerated the timetable for the Environmental Protection Agency (EPA) to review existing pesticide licenses based on new scientific standards and information. *(1988 Almanac, p. 139)*

Since the early 1970s, the EPA had been working on such a review but had made little headway. The 1988 legislation set a 1997 deadline to complete the review and increased fees charged to chemical producers to pay for it.

The mammoth task, known as "reregistration," was designed to review all pesticides in light of existing scientific standards. It required pesticide manufacturers to update laboratory tests to show whether chemicals or their components caused cancer, birth defects or a variety of other medical problems. About 400 pesticides were undergoing the lengthy review.

Because of the cost associated with the lengthy reregistration process, some chemical companies had decided not to market their pesticides and had taken them off the market. That caused problems for fruit and vegetable farmers dependent on those chemicals to grow their crops.

But sorting out all the difficulties became a highly charged issue for Congress as the 1992 election approached: Voters feared their health was being threatened, and farmers and pesticide makers feared their livelihood was at stake.

And finding consensus seemed likely to remain difficult. A compromise would have had to satisfy agricultural chemical manufacturers, farmers, environmentalists and consumers — interests with widely divergent views.

A compromise also had eluded Congress because food safety policy involved technical language and complex scientific ideas. In addition, the issue sparked turf battles because eight committees in Congress had jurisdiction over the issue and four federal agencies were involved in administering food safety laws.

In the Senate, committees with jurisdiction included: Agriculture; Foreign Relations; Labor and Human Resources; Environment and Public Works; and Commerce, Science and Transportation. And in the House, the Agriculture, Energy and Commerce, and Foreign Affairs committees had jurisdiction.

In the executive branch, the EPA and the Food and Drug Administration were the lead agencies. Supporting roles were played by the Agriculture and Commerce departments.

And debate over FIFRA, and its related law, the Federal Food, Drug and Cosmetic Act was complicated because of the wide range of different issues involved, from local regulation of pesticide use to what could be considered legal pesticide residue levels.

### Court Overturns EPA Rule

The U.S. Court of Appeals for the 9th Circuit ruled July 8 that pesticides known to cause cancer could not be used on some foods because traces of the chemicals remained on the foods even after processing.

The action effectively overturned the EPA rule that had allowed the use of pesticides known to cause cancer on some processed foods as long as the chemicals posed only a "negligible" hazard to human health.

The EPA had interpreted a provision of law — known as the Delaney clause — that allowed the use of some chemicals but specifically prohibited chemical residues in processed food when they had been shown to cause cancer.

The Delaney clause had been added to the Federal Food, Drug and Cosmetic Act in 1958 to reflect concerns about the increased risk of cancer from food additives including pesticides. Its rigid language was intended to safeguard against the tendency of some chemicals to concentrate in processed food, giving consumers a more intense dose.

However, scientific tests for pesticide residues had gotten more sensitive since that time. Because it became possible to detect minute levels of pesticides, federal regulators had contended that pesticide use would virtually have had to be banned to enforce Delaney to the letter of the law.

Enforcement procedures were further complicated by a different provision of the Federal Food, Drug and Cosmetic Act that stated that it was permissible to use carcinogenic chemicals on fresh foods if the benefit derived from having an adequate and low-cost food supply outweighed the public health risk.

Problems arose because EPA regulators could not easily track where the fresh produce went after harvest, which made it virtually impossible to carry out the letter of the law regarding processed foods. This had led EPA to permit pesticides linked with cancer to be used on all foods.

The Natural Resources Defense Council — plantiff in the lawsuit against the EPA — contended that EPA rules on processed foods were too lax and violated the law. The council had asked the court to order the EPA to halt the use of all pesticides on food that was to be processed when chemical residues had been shown to cause cancer, and the court agreed.

### Alar on Apples Scare

Another issue that provoked heated debate was how fast dangerous pesticides could be taken off the market.

The 1989 scare over Alar, a pesticide used on apples and which was found to leave carcinogenic residues on the apples, was illustrative of the problem.

After the National Resources Defense Council released an Alar study in 1989, sales of Washington state apples plummeted. Concern centered on the EPA, which had collected preliminary evidence of the potential cancer risks of Alar for more than 10 years but had not withdrawn the pesticide from use.

An outcry from political leaders from both parties, including President Bush, resurrected calls for an overhaul of food safety laws to streamline EPA rules to allow suspected carcinogens to be removed more quickly from the market.

But momentum for legislative action quickly dissipated after environmentalists and pesticide manufacturers refused to compromise on an overhaul of food safety laws.

Under existing rules, federal regulators could halt the use of pesticides by either initiating a lengthy administrative process or invoking an emergency measure. The administrative process could take up to a decade to complete, while immediate removal of a pesticide in an emergency could be done only if regulators showed that there was an immediate danger to public or environmental health.

Before emergency steps could be taken, the agency also was required to have enough evidence to go forward with a full administrative proceeding. Many experts had said EPA officials were reluctant to invoke emergency measures because they feared the action would prompt pesticide manufacturers to wage costly and time-consuming lawsuits.

## LEGISLATIVE ACTION

Legislation that would overhaul the nation's major pesticide law won quick voice vote approval from a House Agriculture subcommittee May 19, but saw no further action in the 102nd Congress.

The measure (HR 3742) would have revamped FIFRA, the major law regulating pesticide use in the United States.

The Agriculture Subcommittee on Department Operations, Research and Foreign Agriculture approved several controversial amendments, including one to allow chemical companies to sue the government for damages when their pesticide registrations were unfairly suspended.

The panel also approved an amendment to bar local restrictions on pesticide use and extended certain protections to farm workers who reported the misuse of pesticides.

Perhaps most notable were the three key issues the subcommittee left in its draft bill but did not debate: easing restrictions on the use of chemicals for fruits and vegetables and other "minor" crops, promoting the use of organic chemicals and limiting the level of pesticide residue on food.

There was still plenty for members to argue about.

The subcommittee bill included a mixture of provisions supported by consumer advocates and environmentalists, and others favored by the agricultural chemical lobby.

But chemical companies were the clear winners when the Agriculture subcommittee finished with the bill.

They easily won amendments to fend off major changes in how the government removed pesticides from the market in emergencies and to allow pesticide makers to seek legal damages when such action was unfairly taken.

Pat Roberts of Kansas, the ranking subcommittee Republican, won an amendment on a 13-7 vote to mandate that the EPA collect all relevant data about the potential benefits of using a particular pest killer when considering suspending the pesticide.

But the panel then quickly modified the amendment to place the burden of collecting such information on the chemical makers. The change came after Chairman Charlie Rose, D-N.C., won an amendment by voice vote to require pesticide manufacturers to provide such information to the EPA and update it regularly.

The subcommittee's original draft, sponsored by Rose, would have allowed the EPA to move more quickly to suspend a pesticide from use if it had been determined to pose an imminent threat to public health and safety.

Under existing law, the EPA was required to collect all relevant information about a pesticide's benefits before it could suspend its use. Collecting such information could be costly and take anywhere from three months to a year.

### How Much Home Rule?

The issue of federal pre-emption was another of the controversial items that was decided in favor of the chemical companies.

For years, chemical companies had argued that the nation's key law regulating the use of agricultural chemicals prohibited local governments from making such rules. But a 1991 Supreme Court decision opened the door to a proliferation of local ordinances, and sent chemical companies running to Congress for help. Chemical producers wanted Congress to specify that only state and federal governments could regulate the use of agricultural chemicals.

Rose, who did not support efforts to pre-empt local authority to regulate chemicals, had included a compromise provision in his bill that would have set up a system to pre-empt local authority, while still giving localities a voice in the process. Under the draft bill, states were required to devise plans under which local governments could appeal decisions or apply for waivers. The state plans would have been subject to final approval by the EPA.

Democrat Charles Hatcher, who chaired the Agriculture Subcommittee on Peanuts and Tobacco and whose southwestern Georgia district grew peanuts and pecans, said Rose's plan did not go far enough to prevent local regulation and that the existing system was "unduly burdensome" to chemical companies.

Hatcher had introduced a rival bill (HR 3850) that would have completely pre-empted all local authority. He argued that his plan was "clearer and cleaner." He offered his bill as an amendment to Rose's measure at the markup.

Panel member Steve Gunderson, R-Wis., also offered an amendment dealing with federal pre-emption. His plan would have established a twofold system under which federal and state governments would have exclusive control over the licensing and approval of pesticides — a process that required extensive scientific data and expertise. Local governments would have been allowed to regulate how pesticides are applied, to require notification of their use and even to ban aerial spraying.

The subcommittee approved Hatcher's amendment by voice vote, and rejected Gunderson's alternative, also by voice.

### Minor Crops

Lawmakers also dealt with a problem which confronted growers of so-called minor crops, which included everything from Belgian endive to oranges. Such farmers were concerned that pesticide makers were increasingly avoiding the high cost of EPA rules by taking key pesticides off the market.

The subcommittee incorporated a bill in the FIFRA overhaul measure that would have allowed the EPA to waive certain data requirements and potentially eliminate some of the costly tests for minor-use chemicals. The EPA administrator would have had to determine that a chemical would not pose an "unreasonable risk to human health."

The minor-use problem dated to 1988, when Congress sought to speed up a review of all agricultural chemicals registered under FIFRA. Pesticide makers had said that the costs of the review were so high that it no longer made economic sense to produce some chemicals for certain uses.

Predictions that even more pesticides would be taken off the market had led the American Farm Bureau Federation and other agricultural organizations to create the Minor Crop Farmer Alliance, a loosely configured group of about 110 organizations, that lobbied Congress to ease rules for pesticides used on minor crops.

In general, a minor crop was defined by what it was not: something other than wheat, corn, soybeans, cotton or rice — the five major crops whose prices were supported by the federal government. Fruits and vegetables were minor crops. But even the major crops could have been considered minor if they were grown in small amounts.

Lobbyists for the Minor Crop Farmer Alliance found a sympathetic audience in the House Agriculture Committee. Committee Chairman E. "Kika" de la Garza, D-Texas, introduced on April 8 a bill (HR 4764) that would have made minor-use pesticides more available to farmers. That bill was included in the measure drafted by the subcommittee.

### Other Amendments

In another victory for the chemical lobby, the subcommittee also approved by voice vote an amendment by Charles W. Stenholm, D-Texas, to give pesticide makers the right to sue the EPA for damages if the agency suspended marketing of one of the company's pesticides in a capricious fashion.

Under existing law, the federal government could reimburse pesticide manufacturers for losses incurred because of banned pesticides only if Congress appropriated money to cover the cost.

Stenholm argued that his provision would "protect all of the parties from arbitrary and frivolous proceedings." The panel approved the amendment over the EPA's objections.

Agricultural chemical producers also won an important battle over who could regulate pesticide use.

The subcommittee approved an amendment by Georgia's Hatcher to put a much stricter prohibition on local government pesticide regulation than the original draft bill contained.

Other amendments approved by the subcommittee included:

● An amendment by Jim Jontz, D-Ind., to protect farm workers who reported violations of federal pesticide laws from retaliation by their employers. It was approved by voice vote.

● An amendment by Bill Barrett, R-Neb., to give pesticide users who unintentionally violated federal pesticide restrictions a written warning rather than a fine for the first offense. It was approved 13-8.

● An amendment by Bill Sarpalius, D-Texas, to prohibit the EPA from collecting pesticide registration fees after Jan. 1, 1997. It was approved by voice vote. ∎

# Agriculture Escapes Staff Downsizing

Lawmakers talked about downsizing the huge bureaucracy of the Agriculture Department in 1992, but took no action to cut back on the agency's regional offices or staffs.

Perhaps the most compelling reason for change came from the Agriculture Department itself. In response to a congressional request, the department was unable to state how many people worked for it, what they did or where they were.

Even Agriculture Secretary Edward Madigan agreed that "some organizational and management improvements are needed at the U.S. Department of Agriculture."

A General Accounting Office (GAO) report dated September 1991 first prompted members of Congress to call for a leaner Agriculture Department, and, significantly, many of the appeals were from farm-state lawmakers.

Both Senate Agriculture Committee Chairman Patrick J. Leahy, D-Vt., and Rep. Dan Glickman, D-Kan., introduced bills (S 2752; HR 4784) that would have cut back on the number of Agriculture Department field offices. Though the efforts received substantial attention, neither bill saw even committee action in the 102nd Congress.

However, Madigan on Jan. 7, 1993, announced plans to begin closing and consolidating more than 1,000 U.S. Department of Agriculture field offices. And the new Agriculture secretary in the Clinton administration, Mike Espy, glided through his Senate confirmation hearing Jan. 14, promising to make restructuring the department a top priority.

## BACKGROUND

The Agriculture Department was the nation's third largest federal civilian agency in 1992, with more than 110,000 workers. Just four of its programs employed 63,000 people at more than 11,000 locations at an annual administrative cost of $2.4 billion.

The Agriculture Department's Agriculture Stabilization and Conservation Service, the Farmers Home Administration and the Soil Conservation Service accounted for many of the department's field offices. These programs dated back to President Franklin D. Roosevelt's New Deal in the 1930s and had not seen major restructuring since then.

The Agriculture Stabilization Service was created as part of the 1933 Agriculture Adjustment Act, which launched the federal crop price-support program. Douglas Bowers, an Agriculture Department historian, said the agency began setting up its field offices almost immediately.

The mission of the stabilization service was to help farmers who grew crops covered by the federal price-support program to obtain benefits. The service helped farmers complete paperwork, processed it and wrote benefit checks. At the outset, difficult travel conditions had required the service to locate offices in most of the nation's counties.

According to the GAO, in 1991 the service maintained

## Food Pyramid Redrawn to New USDA Guidelines

The Agriculture Department on April 28 unveiled a guide to healthy eating, but the $855,000 price tag to redo an accompanying graphic induced indigestion for some lawmakers.

A version of the graphic, which used a pyramid to display good eating habits, had been completed more than a year earlier, but Agriculture Secretary Edward Madigan called for additional studies that led to the 1992 revised graphic.

Some critics charged that the delay in issuing the guide was in response to meat industry opposition to the original graphic. And others complained that the revision was too similar to the original pyramid to justify its cost.

Senate Agriculture Committee Chairman Patrick J. Leahy, D-Vt., said, "It doesn't matter whether USDA picked a pyramid, a bowl or an upside-down ketchup bottle to show consumers what to eat. USDA's delay cost nearly $1 million, and the administration ended up right where they started."

Madigan said that the food guide was delayed to study how effective the pyramid would be in communicating its message.

The pyramid and an accompanying 30-page booklet downplayed the role of meat in the ideal diet, especially compared with the former "four basic food groups" that had been in place since the 1950s. For example, the guide said people should eat between six and 11 servings of grains and cereals a day and two to three servings of meat.

Along with the graphic, the department issued a 30-page color booklet that described the variety of nutrients necessary for a balanced diet and a list of the foods containing these nutrients.

offices in at least 85 percent of the nation's 3,150 counties. But the Agriculture Department considered only 16 percent of those counties farming communities.

The Farmers Home Administration (FmHA) was originally created as the Resettlement Administration in 1935. It was folded into the Agriculture Department in 1937 and got its name under a 1946 reorganization effort.

The mission of the FmHA extended well beyond farmers. It helped spur the development of rural America. In its early years, the agency concentrated on alleviating rural poverty by providing loans to bankrupt farmers to help them keep their land. It also extended loans to small towns and individuals to improve living conditions in rural areas.

The agency was the farmer's lender of last resort. For farmers who could not get money elsewhere, the FmHA either extended a direct loan or backed a private loan with a federal guarantee.

The Soil Conservation Service was originally called the Soil Erosion Service when founded in 1933 and located in the Interior Department. Two years later, it was shifted to the Agriculture Department, where it assumed its new name.

In keeping with its moniker, the agency's mission was to encourage farmers to promote soil conservation. It offered

technological advice and served all U.S. farmers.

These three agencies, with their widely divergent missions and distinct beneficiaries, had had no reason to work together.

### Problem Highlights

Mounting evidence of waste and mismanagement compiled by Senate Agriculture Chairman Leahy and others succeeded in highlighting some of the Agriculture Department's problems. Some examples:

● Clark County, Nev., which included urban Las Vegas, had 13 Agriculture Department employees for three separate agencies that provided services for 40 farmers.

● A section of South Carolina's coast, roughly 135 miles long and 75 miles wide, had more than 300 Agriculture Department employees in 38 separate offices that served 4,100 farms. According to Leahy, only half those farms were eligible for federal price-support payments in 1987. Many of the offices were less than 25 miles apart.

● A Wall Street Journal front-page article April 8 highlighted the efforts of the Agriculture Department's office in suburban Fairfield County, Conn., to use up its federal funds. At the time, no farmers in the county were enrolled in the federal price-support program.

Such stories of agency offices with no farmers to help prompted the first serious review of the Agriculture Department's sprawling field-office network in five decades.

## LEGISLATIVE ACTION

Sen. Richard G. Lugar, R-Ind., was the first out of the gate, calling on Secretary Madigan in February to close 53 county offices that had annually spent more in overhead than they handed out in federal benefits to farmers. Armed with updated data, Lugar increased that number and called for closing 92 offices.

Congress needed to "put [USDA's] managerial house in order before someone outside the agricultural family does it for us," Lugar, ranking member of the Senate Agriculture Committee, said.

And Glickman, chairman of the House Agriculture Wheat, Soybeans and Feed Grains Subcommittee, joined the battle the week of April 6, when he introduced legislation (HR 4784) to consolidate hundreds of Agriculture Department county offices. The bill also aimed to cut back on the amount of paperwork farmers had to contend with each year to qualify for federal subsidy payments.

Glickman's bill would have consolidated the three separate agencies into one office, called the Farm Services Administration. Local offices of the three agencies would have been consolidated into one district office.

"Voters are sending a new set of instructions to Congress lately," he said. Those instructions — to cut the deficit and make existing programs work better — are something that members of Congress ignore at their peril, he said.

Leahy emerged with a different proposal. He called for the establishment of a review group along the lines of the independent base closure commission that was used in 1991 to shut down unnecessary military bases. (1991 Almanac, p. 427)

But consolidation proposals encountered the usual congressional resistance to any plan that would take federal tax dollars out of the hands of home-state voters.

The organized farm lobby raised concerns about field office cutbacks. Keith Heard, executive vice president of

the National Association of Corn Growers, said that while "there's always room for efficiencies," the Agriculture Department needs to make sure that "the services stay out there for the farmers' use."

"We're seeing more and more regulations and policy requirements for the farming community at the same time that they're talking about consolidation," Heard said.

### Administration Response

Madigan said April 8 that he had hired 10 organizational experts to spawn better cross-agency cooperation and had directed the agencies to better share data.

And he announced May 11 that he had formed a "SWAT team" to investigate waste in the department's field offices.

Madigan's plan called on the Agriculture Department and the White House Office of Management and Budget to employ a team of experts to study the field office structure and recommend changes — shutdowns, mergers and reorganizations.

Madigan's recognition of the problem and his initiatives staved off any further congressional action for the 102nd Congress. The two key lawmakers — Glickman and Leahy — who had come forward with plans to revamp the Agriculture Department's field offices allowed the session to end without pushing their plans forward. ∎

# New Farmers To Get Guaranteed Loans

President Bush signed a bill Oct. 28 (HR 6129 — PL 102-554) that made it easier for young people to get loans to start farms. The bill also placed, for the first time, a limit on the number of years that farmers were eligible for government-backed loans from the Farmers Home Administration (FmHA), the lender of last resort for farmers.

The bill survived despite a last-minute glitch over how the FmHA authorized banks to grant loans to farmers. An earlier bill (HR 4906), similar to HR 6129 except for the loan provision, passed the House. The Senate passed it with an amendment. But because the House had adjourned prior to the Senate action, the House could not take up the amended version of HR 4906.

House leaders, prepared for this possibility, had approved another bill — HR 6129 — which contained a compromise bank loan provision. The Senate then was able to take up HR 6129 and clear it just prior to adjourning the 102nd Congress.

## BACKGROUND

According to a 1987 census of U.S. agricultural workers, the American farming population was aging rapidly, with fewer and fewer young people getting into the business. While the number of farmers 65 and older had increased by nearly 21 percent, the number of farmers aged 25 to 34 had decreased by 15 percent.

And banks, always reluctant to take on risky farming loans, were even more unwilling to give the money to young farmers who were trying to break into the business.

E. "Kika" de la Garza, D-Texas, chairman of the House Agriculture Committee, argued that "as our farming population ages and many farmers near retirement, younger people who want to farm are finding it increasingly difficult to obtain credit to buy into these farm operations."

And according to Daniel K. Akaka, D-Hawaii, the average American farmer was 52 years old. There were twice as many farmers in the United States over the age of 60 as there were under the age of 35. "Clearly we are not doing enough to attract rural youth to farming," Akaka said.

## HOUSE COMMITTEE ACTION

The bill got its start on May 14 when the House Agriculture Subcommittee on Conservation, Credit and Rural Development approved an earlier version of it (HR 4906) on a 19-0 vote.

But the bill, originally designed to make it easier for beginning farmers to get government-backed loans, became the vehicle for much larger changes to federal farm credit programs during the markup.

By the time the subcommittee approved the bill, members had adopted a host of substantive changes to FmHA loan programs, just as many of them had wanted to do in the 1990 farm bill. *(1990 Almanac, p. 323)*

The measure, sponsored by subcommittee Chairman Glenn English, D-Okla., also would have made changes to regulations for the Farm Credit System, including a provision that required examinations of member banks at least every three years. Existing law mandated the examinations annually.

The most contentious amendment, offered by Timothy J. Penny, D-Minn., limited the number of years farmers could qualify for subsidized operating loans through the FmHA, the lending arm of the Agriculture Department. The amendment made farmers ineligible for direct government loans after 10 years in the program and for guarantees of private loans after 15 years.

Jerry Huckaby, D-La., objected, saying the amendment would hurt struggling farmers trying to get by. "We're going to force them out of business, arbitrarily," he said.

But Penny argued that it was the intent of Congress to encourage farmers to "graduate" from the federally subsidized loan program, and said that the Treasury could not afford to give them an open-ended commitment. The subcommittee agreed, approving the amendment, 11-4.

### Full Committee Action

The House Agriculture Committee approved the bill on June 25.

The bill called on the new farmers to draw up detailed 10-year plans to be eligible for the credit. Though members of the full committee debated the measure for more than four hours, they made few changes to the bill.

The committee approved by voice vote an amendment by Jill L. Long, D-Ind., that included women in the bill's definition of "socially disadvantaged," which made loans more available to them.

### HOUSE FLOOR ACTION

The bill (HR 4906) passed the House on Aug. 4 by voice vote. Members spent much of the floor time defending a

bill provision which made farmers ineligible for either direct or government-backed loans after 15 years.

De la Garza said that cutting off loans after 15 years was necessary to bring the program in line with its original purpose of providing farmers with financial help in the face of reluctance from other lenders.

"[The] FmHA has been allowed to stray from its original purpose as a temporary lender of last resort to become a de facto permanent source of credit for far too many borrowers," he said.

In other significant changes, the bill allowed banks that provided government-backed loans to farmers to determine whether a farmer was eligible for a loan. Under existing law, the FmHA made that decision.

Proponents said giving banks more leeway would get the money to the farmers faster. The bill also reduced government liability for these loans from 90 percent to 80 percent of the total loan.

### Second time around

Members of the House approved a bill (HR 6129) almost identical to HR 4906 on Oct. 6. Both bills were designed to attract more young people into the farming profession by easing some of the restrictions for direct and guaranteed loans from the FmHA.

The second bill, pushed and largely crafted by Penny, also established a new down-payment loan program to help farmers buy the ranches or farmland. It authorized low-interest 10-year loans for up to 30 percent of the land's purchase price for those down payments.

The original bill nearly died because of a dispute over a new bank loan approval policy for the FmHA. When the bill passed the House on Aug. 4, it included a provision that would have made it easier for commercial lenders to give out loans backed by the FmHA.

HR 4906 would have given the FmHA 14 working days to act on a lender's loan-guarantee application. If the FmHA did not act, the loan would have been approved automatically. However, those loans would have received only an 80 percent guarantee from the government, in contrast to the 90 percent guarantee for regular FmHA-approved loans.

Some members of the Senate, especially Kent Conrad, D-N.D., objected to that setup. Conrad pushed for a provision that would have required an answer from the FmHA — either yes or no — within 14 days of the application. The Senate approved HR 4906 with his amendment on Oct. 7.

But the House, which had effectively adjourned Oct. 6, could not act on the Senate-amended version of HR 4906.

House sponsors anticipated a last-minute compromise with Conrad by pushing through HR 6129, a bill identical to HR 4906 except for a compromise bank loan provision. It established a two-tiered system for expedited loan approval. For banks that had a long, positive history of dealing with the FmHA, the automatic approval provision applied. For banks newer to the system, the Senate provision requiring a yes-or-no answer kicked in.

Conrad said that he still opposed lender provisions but that it was not worth killing a bill when the "ultimate product" is satisfactory. "Because there's one provision that you disagree with, does that take down the whole bill?" he asked.

The Senate approved HR 6129 by voice vote on Oct. 8, clearing the measure for the president. ∎

---

# Law Passed To Protect Animal Research Labs

On Aug. 26, President Bush signed into law a bill (S 544 — PL 102-346) that made it a federal crime to vandalize animal research laboratories or farms. An upsurge in the number of attacks on animal facilities by animal rights extremists in recent years galvanized efforts by some members to make such crimes subject to federal sanctions.

One such group broke into the offices and labs of researchers at Michigan State University in February 1992, setting records on fire and destroying more than 30 years of data.

Bush's signature marked the end of a three-year debate on Capitol Hill on how to deal with the problem. Members had fought over what kinds of animal facilities to include and what kinds of damage to punish. In the end, the bill covered most violent acts against most animal facilities.

### BACKGROUND

Legislation to clamp down on animal rights activists who resorted to illegal entry or violence to make a statement passed the Senate in 1989 but did not make it through the House before the 101st Congress adjourned.

The effort to federalize such crimes was being pushed by farmers and researchers but was opposed by animal rights groups, who denounced it as a mere public relations to brand them as terrorists and stifle whistleblowers who exposed cruelty to animals. *(1990 Almanac, p. 441)*

In 1991, the Senate again passed a bill making both vandalism and duplication of records at the labs a crime. The House responded in 1992 with a bill that dramatically increased the number and kind of animal facility covered by the bill. It included everything from rodeos to farms and state fairs.

The new legislation did not, however, make it a federal crime to duplicate material from animal research facilities, something that animal rights groups had said would have made it much harder to prove cases of animal abuse in the research labs.

### HOUSE COMMITTEE ACTION

The House Agriculture Committee on April 2 approved a bill (HR 2407) to make it a federal crime to vandalize animal research facilities or farms.

The bill was aimed at halting the activities of radical animal rights groups that crossed state lines to commit acts of violence. In such instances, the bill made it a federal crime, punishable by up to 20 years' imprisonment, to steal animals or property or damage anything at an animal research facility, including laboratories and farms.

This version of the bill attracted a wide group of supporters. Bill sponsor Charles W. Stenholm, D-Texas, said he had 261 cosponsors, including most members of the Agriculture Committee.

Stenholm said the bill was necessary because "current

federal laws are not discouraging acts of violence."

But Martha Glenn, a lobbyist for the Humane Society, argued that the crimes were "already covered under state and local law." Glenn hastened to add that the Humane Society opposed all acts of violence in the name of animal rights.

Rep. Charlie Rose, D-N.C., said in a statement that the committee needed to examine animal cruelty problems at research labs. "Many of you here will say that this is not the issue, but I very much disagree. Much of the violence occurs when individuals know that there is abuse going on, but the U.S. Department of Agriculture does absolutely nothing to stop it."

The increasing number of violent attacks against research labs pushed more members to support the bill. George E. Brown Jr., D-Calif., who had previously expressed reservations, said the "excesses" by some animal rights groups "have generated the need for this."

Stenholm's bill was narrower than the earlier, introduced version of the bill. He offered the new bill as a substitute amendment (approved by voice vote) after the original came under fire because animal rights groups were concerned that it was overly broad. Opponents had also expressed concern that the measure might have inhibited investigation into illegal activity by research labs.

The new bill made it clear that it would not invalidate current whistleblower protection laws at the state and local level.

The measure also made it a federal crime to deliberately release an animal from a farm or research facility, or to illegally enter a farm or research facility with intent to vandalize.

### Judiciary's Turn

The House Judiciary Subcommittee on Crime and Criminal Justice on July 8 narrowly approved its version of a bill (HR 2407) to make it a federal crime to bomb animal research facilities.

The panel's version was significantly different from the House Agriculture Committee's version.

The subcommittee approved, 7-6, a substitute measure offered by panel Chairman Charles E. Schumer, D-N.Y., that reduced the types of animal facilities protected under the bill.

Schumer's substitute would have applied only to those labs that engaged in animal research or were a part of a farm. Any damage to the facility would have to exceed $50,000 to be covered under the bill (the Agriculture-passed bill had a $5,000 threshold).

Schumer and others expressed skepticism about the need to make such acts federal crimes.

Schumer said his version was "more reasonable" and would provide an alternative to be considered on the floor.

Other lawmakers also questioned the need for the bill. "No one in local law enforcement is asking for help," said

---

## BOXSCORE

➡ **Animal Labs Protection (S 544, HR 2407).** The bill made it a federal crime to vandalize animal research laboratories, farms or other places for housing animals such as state fairs.

**Reports:** H Rept 102-489, Part I-II.

### KEY ACTION

**April 2** — The **House** Agriculture Committee approved HR 2407.

**July 22** — The **House** Judiciary Committee approved a narrower version of HR 2407, 18-16.

**Aug. 4** — The **House** passed S 544 by voice vote after it was amended to include the provisions of HR 2407.

**Aug. 7** — The **Senate** cleared the bill by voice vote.

**Aug. 26** — President Bush signed S 544 — PL 102-346.

---

Steven H. Schiff, R-N.M. And William J. Hughes, D-N.J., called the bill a "false promise" to the states because "we don't have the resources to prosecute" these cases.

But George W. Gekas, R-Pa., warned that the threat by "animal rights terrorists" still existed. He said the substitute did not go far enough and that it would gut the original bill.

Gekas was one of 14 House Judiciary Committee members who cosponsored the orginal, broader version of HR 2407.

Schumer welcomed amendments by panel members to broaden the bill's appeal. George E. Sangmeister, D-Ill., successfully offered one such amendment that included aquariums and zoos under the bill's protection.

Schumer and Peter Hoagland, D-Neb., agreed to consider an amendment in the full committee to lower the $50,000 damage limit to ensure that most assaults were covered.

The full House Judiciary Committee approved that version of the bill July 22, on an 18-16 vote. Members narrowly rejected, on a 17-17 vote, an attempt to make the Judiciary bill the same as the one passed earlier by the Agriculture Committee.

The Judiciary Committee bill would have made it a federal crime to deliberately cause damage to research laboratories, farms, zoos or aquariums. During the July 22 markup, the committee approved an amendment to drop the damage threshold from $50,000 to $25,000.

Craig T. James, R-Fla., said it was necessary to make such incidents federal crimes in order to better coordinate prosecution across state borders.

But Schumer said the Agriculture bill was too sweeping and would take "a very broad approach to what seemed a very narrow problem." He added, "You can deal with this problem without going hog wild."

To win support for his narrower bill, Schumer had to convert Judiciary Committee members who had already gone on record backing the Agriculture Committee version. The key moment came when Gekas failed to win his amendment to broaden Schumer's bill on a tie vote.

Two of the 14 cosponsors on the Judiciary Committee — Harley O. Staggers Jr., D-W.Va., and Peter Hoagland, D-Neb. — opposed Gekas. And two other Democrats — Mike Kopetski, Ore., and Rick Boucher, Va., both of whom backed the original bill — later switched sides to back Schumer's bill after Gekas' amendment failed.

Kopetski said he supported the Schumer bill in a show of support for the chairman. Boucher said he voted for the Schumer bill to send the issue to the full House, where he planned to back the broader version of the bill.

### HOUSE FLOOR ACTION

The House on Aug. 4 passed under expedited procedures a broad measure to make it a federal crime to destroy animal research facilities.

Lawmakers passed a companion Senate bill (S 544) by

voice vote after stripping out its language and folding in that of the House version (HR 2407).

During House floor debate, members called the measure a compromise between two competing versions that were approved by the House Judiciary Committee on July 22 and the House Agriculture Committee on April 2. But Agriculture panel members emerged as the clear winners on at least two major areas of contention.

As passed by the House, the measure applied to virtually all places where animals were held, including research labs, farms, state fairs and dog shows — a position taken by the original Agriculture bill. The Judiciary Committee had tried to limit the reach of the bill to research labs and farms.

The final bill made it a federal crime to cause $10,000 or more in damage to an animal research facility. The level was $5,000 more than the Agriculture panel had wanted but $15,000 less than the Judiciary Committee's version.

The bill increased the possible punishment with each increase in the severity of the crime. For example, a violator would have been fined and sentenced up to one year in jail for disrupting an animal research facility. But a criminal would have faced up to 10 years in jail if the action seriously hurt someone and would have gotten life imprisonment if the violation killed someone.

In a key difference with the Senate version, the House-passed bill did not make it a crime for intruders to duplicate papers in an animal research lab. The Senate-passed measure would have made such duplication criminal, something many animal rights defenders argued would hinder legitimate investigations into animal abuse.

## SENATE FLOOR ACTION

The Senate on Aug. 7 cleared for the president a bill (S 544) to make it a federal crime to vandalize animal research laboratories.

Frankie L. Trull, president of the National Association for Biomedical Research, applauded the bill's passage. "The nation's biomedical research enterprise is a life-giving treasure that deserves federal protection," he said in an Aug. 5 statement.

But Alex Pacheco, chairman of the animal rights group People for the Ethical Treatment of Animals, called the bill "unnecessary." If anything, he said it "will just clog the federal courts."

Pacheco argued that both the House and Senate bills, as originally drafted by Rep. Stenholm and Sen. Howell Heflin, D-Ala., were aimed at workers who leaked damaging documents about lab research and exposed cruel treatment of animals. The bills were "originally intended to silence whistleblowers," Pacheco said.

But the final version of the bill did not include provisions in the original versions that would have made it a crime to duplicate material at research laboratories or to receive copied documents. ∎

# Congress Puts a Limit on Sports-Based Lotteries

Concerned that state-sponsored gambling could undercut the integrity of professional sports, the leaders of the major sports leagues successfully pushed Congress to clear legislation (S 474 — PL 102-559) that prohibited additional states from sponsoring sports-based lotteries.

The measure did not affect betting on horse and dog racing, or the numbers games that were the most common type of lottery. Only betting on professional and collegiate sports such as basketball, football and baseball was prohibited. "Gambling and sports do not mix," said Arnold "Red" Auerbach, president of the Boston Celtics, representing the National Basketball Association, when he appeared before a House Judiciary subcommittee.

Neither the U.S. attorney general nor the sports organization whose games were at stake could seek a federal court injunction to halt any state-sponsored gambling activity based on sports ranging from major league baseball to college football games.

The bill permitted Oregon, Nevada, Delaware and Montana, which had laws on the books allowing sports-based lotteries or allowed casino gambling on sports, to continue their policies. It also exempted New Jersey, which allowed casino gambling in Atlantic City, to be exempt from the bill's prohibitions until January 1994.

President Bush signed the bill into law Oct. 28.

## BACKGROUND

The sports leagues feared that cash-starved states would want to emulate Oregon, which in 1989 began a state-sponsored betting operation for pro football and pro basketball games. The state lottery grossed $14.5 million in state receipts in 1989 and 1990 combined, netting $4.9 million in profits.

Nevada's sports-gambling law generated $1.8 billion in betting and earned the state $3 million in new revenues in 1990. "We do not want our games used as bait to sell gambling," said Paul Tagliabue, commissioner of the National Football League. "Sports gambling should not be used as a cure for the sagging fortunes of Atlantic City casinos or to boost public interest in state lotteries."

Thirty-two states and the District of Columbia sponsored general lotteries, and opponents of the measure were concerned that several of the states strapped for cash would expand them to include betting on sporting events.

"It threatens to undermine public confidence and the integrity of the games themselves," said House cosponsor Hamilton Fish Jr., R-N.Y. "Mere breaks of the game or strategy choices by coaches would become the source of suspicion and cynicism."

The final version was very similar to the bill considered by House and Senate panels in 1991. The House Judiciary Subcommittee on Economic and Commercial Law approved a bill (HR 74) on Sept. 17, 1991. The Senate Judiciary Committee approved its version, S 474, on Nov. 21, 1991. *(1991 Almanac, p. 178)*

## FLOOR ACTION

The Senate passed S 474 on a 88-5 vote on June 2 after a debate over whether certain states that already had sport-gambling laws should be exempted. *(Vote 111, p. 15-S)*

A supporter of the bill, Bill Bradley, D-N.J., a former professional basketball star, said that sports "would become the gambler's game and not the fan's game. And

athletes would become roulette chips."

Opponents of the measure said Congress should not block the states from tapping a potentially lucrative revenue source. States considering sports gambling included Massachusetts, Rhode Island, Florida and New Jersey.

The bill exempted from any new restrictions all existing sports-betting schemes in Delaware, Nevada, Oregon and Montana, as well as horse racing, dog racing and jai alai games in all 50 states and the District of Columbia.

Charles E. Grassley, R-Iowa, attacked the bill's exemption for the four states that allowed sports gambling. "Why does Congress have the right to restrict the source of revenue for 46 states but not 50 states?," he asked.

Grassley offered an amendment that would have delayed the effective date of the bill for two years, enabling states to enact sports gambling laws before the federal ban took effect. His amendment was rejected by voice vote.

House sponsors initially folded their version in an anticrime bill (HR 3371), but when it became apparent that bill was going nowehere they took up S 474.

When House members considered the bill Oct. 5, William J. Hughes, D-N.J., added a provision to exempt New Jersey from the prohibition through 1993, so a statewide referendum could be held. Hughes said that would give the state "a one-year opportunity to decide for themselves if they want to legalize sports betting in Atlantic City's casinos."

Hughes added that it would be unfair to exempt Nevada and not New Jersey, the two states that competed most heavily for the nation's legalized gambling trade.

On Oct. 7, the Senate agreed to exempt New Jersey, clearing the bill for the president. ∎

---

# Competitiveness Council Headed for Demise

Despite the heightened resentment, the 102nd Congress did nothing to rein in the White House's controversial Council on Competitiveness headed by Vice President Dan Quayle. It was the office in charge of ensuring that agency regulations were not too burdensome on businesses.

The issue became moot after the Nov. 3 election. President-elect Bill Clinton said he would disband the council and lift the moratorium on new regulations imposed by President Bush early in 1992.

True to his word, Clinton dismantled the council on Jan. 22, 1993 — his second day in office as the 42nd president.

Democrats had complained that the council, working in concert with powerful business interests, repeatedly had pressured various executive branch agencies to relax regulations meant to enforce laws approved by Congress.

Legislative attempts to slap down the council's activities came from two directions. Both authorizing panels on government business, the House Government Operations Committee and the Senate Governmental Affairs Committee, approved measures (HR 5702 — H Rept 102-965, S 1942 — S Rept 102-244) to require the council and the Office of Management and Budget (OMB) to open to the public their meetings with members of the private sector on pending regulations.

The fight that made it to the House floor, however,

occurred on the spending bill that funded White House activities (HR 5488 — PL 102-393). But in the rush to adjourn, Congress dropped almost all controversial provisions in appropriations bills, including the Treasury-Postal Service provision that would have denied funding to the council.

## BACKGROUND

Amid escalating charges that the Bush administration was undermining environmental and health protection laws, Democrats began considering legislation in 1991 that would allow closer scrutiny of the regulatory process. The flurry of hearings and press accounts primarily targeted the role of the Council on Competitiveness and its chief, Quayle.

Administration officials said the council simply issued advice designed to ensure that regulations were imposed with the minimum possible expense to business. But critics likened the panel to a sinister, secret tribunal that had boosted big business at the expense of the nation's safety and environmental laws.

The Senate Governmental Affairs Committee approved a "sunshine" bill (S 1942) on Nov. 22, 1991, on an 8-3 vote, to require the administration to document its review of agency-proposed rules and justify any changes made.

Bush incited additional wrath early in 1992 when he proposed a 90-day moratorium on new regulations and called for an intensive regulatory review in his Jan. 28 State of the Union address.

Bush on April 29 extended the moratorium on new regulations for four more months amid stark disagreement over the success and scope of the endeavor. And at the GOP convention in Houston on Aug. 17-20, he promised to continue the moratorium indefinitely.

## LEGISLATIVE ACTION

Ignoring veto threats, House and Senate Democrats on Aug. 6 continued swiping at Quayle's Council on Competitiveness. The House Government Operations Committee approved a bill (HR 5702) to open the administration's regulatory review apparatus to greater public scrutiny. Similar to the measure (S 1942) approved by the Senate Governmental Affairs Committee in 1991, the House bill was approved by a party-line vote of 23-15.

Meanwhile, Senate Governmental Affairs Chairman John Glenn, D-Ohio, announced that he would try to have the Quayle council's $86,000 budget stripped from the spending bill that funded the White House (HR 5488) when it reached the floor. However, he ultimately withdrew his amendment after a lengthy floor debate. *(Appropriations, p. 626)*

The House sunshine bill was sponsored by Government Operations Committee Chairman John Conyers Jr., D-Mich. It would require the council, the Office of Management and Budget and any other administration entity that reviewed regulations to disclose to the public all written and oral communications it received about them. Such entities would have to publicly justify all proposed changes in writing. There would also be a 90-day limit for reviewing proposed rules.

Committee Republicans offered two amendments to extend the bill's sunshine concept to Congress' inner workings, but they were killed on party-line votes. Ranking Republican Frank Horton of New York offered a substitute proposal, but it was rejected on a voice vote. ∎

# White House Spending Bill Stalls in House

Legislation (HR 5928, H Rept 102-985) that would have revamped the way the president and the executive branch accounted for their travel expenses was approved by the House Post Office and Civil Service Committee but saw no further action in the 102nd Congress.

Though the measure had wide-ranging support, it came up only at the tail end of the session, and neither House nor Senate leaders made it a priority. Consequently, the bill was never sent to the House floor.

The bill would have capped the spending allowance for the White House at $185 million — a huge increase over the existing level of $100,000. Bill supporters said that the president already spent more than $185 million annually but was not required to account for it.

## BACKGROUND

The Democratic-sponsored bill was one of several volleys in the election-year war of words over how much the executive branch spent on travel. Members of the House Post Office subcommittee on Human Resources held several high-profile hearings to highlight how difficult it was to determine just how much the Bush administration annually spent in travel for members of the White House staff.

The White House operated under an authorization written in 1978 (PL 95-570) that had not been amended. At the time, the bill was lauded by its sponsors as a needed and rational way of ending the confused, topsy-grown White House staffing procedures. It also allowed Congress some oversight ability for White House staffing for the first time.

Under that system, however, the White House directly paid for only a small portion of its travel expenses, with the other departments of the executive branch, such as Defense, picking up the difference. (1978 Almanac, p. 796)

For example, White House records stated that President Bush spent only $29,000 on travel in fiscal 1991. Yet for that same fiscal year, the Defense Department calculated that it cost $40,243 to operate Air Force One for one hour of flying time. The Pentagon budget absorbed costs not paid by the White House.

Under existing law, both the president and the vice president were allowed free travel on government aircraft so long as the trip was not political.

Paul E. Kanjorski, D-Pa., chairman of the Human Resources Subcommittee and author of the bill, said only about 30 percent of the White House budget could be found by reading the various parts of the president's annual budget request.

The remaining 70 percent, he argued, was "hidden by the budgets of other federal agencies. We never see these costs, however, and the White House has repeatedly refused to disclose how much other parts of government spend on behalf of presidential or White House activities."

## LEGISLATIVE ACTION

On a party-line 3-2 vote, the Post Office and Civil Service Subcommittee on Human Resources on Sept. 17 approved legislation (HR 5928) that would have increased both the amount of money the president could spend on travel and the rules for disclosing such expenditures.

And the full Post Office and Civil Service Committee quickly followed suit, approving the bill on Sept. 23 on a 20-3 vote, with a majority of panel Republicans voting for the bill along with all the committee Democrats .

In addition to the $185 million for travel money, the bill approved by committee authorized about $83.1 million for the general operation of the White House.

The bill authorized $7.7 million for upkeep expenses, such as air conditioning, heating and repairs to the White House, and $40.5 million for the salaries of the White House staff, from presidential spokesman Marlin Fitzwater to White House telephone operators.

Many of the GOP members joined with Democrats on the committee vote after the argument was made that the larger White House travel budget proposed in the legislation was what the president already spent on travel when he used planes and other modes of transportation provided by federal agencies but which the White House did not pay for.

The administration had made more than 800 pages of documentation available to the committee to answer its questions about the expenses of the White House. At the subcommittee markup, Kanjorski said he had received a letter from the White House asking that the salaries of White House staff, which were included in the 800 pages, not be made a part of the committee record.

But in an unusual display of bipartisanship, the panel decided that the salaries should be made public. Rep. James P. Moran Jr., D-Va., said public disclosure was "the only truly effective limitation" on spending.

### Provisions

The bill would have required that the president regularly make public how the money was spent, and it also would have forced the White House to pay the higher costs of public planes when traveling for political purposes.

It would have required that the president reimburse the Defense Department for his use of Air Force One.

That meant the increase in the travel authorization contained in the bill was not as drastic as it sounded. In essence, bill drafters were authorizing what they believed the president already spent annually on travel.

The measure also would have required White House personnel to reimburse federal agencies for the entire cost of airplane trips taken for political reasons. The White House paid the cost of a first-class plane ticket plus $1 for political trips, which did not come close to covering the full cost of flying on government aircraft.

The $185 million also would have been used to pay for personal trips like the ones taken by Vice President Dan Quayle. The General Accounting Office issued a report earlier in 1992 that documented Quayle's various personal trips, including several jaunts with then-Transportation Secretary Samuel K. Skinner to play golf.

In addition, the bill called for making the White House budget absorb the costs of salaries of staff who belonged to a federal agency but had been sent to work at the White House, effective after the staff had worked there for one month. Under existing law, staffers could work for the White House for up to six months while their agencies continued to pay them. ∎

# Veto Threat Stops Hatch Act Simplification

Congress ended the 102nd Congress without acting on legislation designed to revamp the rules governing the political participation of federal and postal employees. Though a majority of members of both the House and the Senate supported simplification of the 1939 Hatch Act, President Bush effectively blocked consideration of the bill with his veto threat.

Senate Majority Leader George J. Mitchell, D-Maine, unsure of getting the necessary 67 presidential veto override votes, never sent the bill (S 914) to the floor. The House bill (HR 20) saw no action because the Democratic leadership there had waited for the Senate to act first.

The legislation introduced in 1991 was an effort to rewrite the 1939 law to clarify the rules, which were confusing as well as constraining. While not giving them free political rein, the bills allowed government workers to become more politically active outside the workplace. *(1991 Almanac, p. 185)*

The Hatch Act had long been considered outdated. Sen. Carl A. Hatch (1933-49) advocated the strict limits after a Senate panel had found that political appointees in the Works Progress Administration had coerced workers into making political contributions to protect their jobs.

But efforts to revise the law were blocked repeatedly by Republican presidents. President Gerald R. Ford vetoed legislation in 1976 to ease restrictions on the federal work force. President Reagan prevented a bill from ever reaching his desk in 1988 by threatening a veto. When President Bush vetoed a bill in 1990, he said it would have destroyed the political neutrality of civil servants. *(1976 Almanac, p. 490; 1988 Almanac, p. 620; 1990 Almanac, p. 408)*

When the Senate attempted to override the 1990 veto, Bush was able to persuade two senators — Alfonse M. D'Amato, R-N.Y., and Trent Lott, R-Miss., to change their votes and support his veto of the bill. That tipped the balance in his favor and his veto was upheld on a 65-35 vote.

Bill supporters had been encouraged because the 1990 elections brought two new supporters of Hatch Act revision, Larry E. Craig, R-Idaho, and Paul Wellstone, D-Minn., to the Senate. While that gave supporters their 67 votes to block passage, Bush would have had to change the mind of only one senator to sustain a veto.

The original Hatch Act prohibited employees from any active participation in partisan campaigns. There were no restrictions on participation in nonpartisan elections, such as those for local school board or town council.

While federal employees were allowed to contribute money to candidates, they could not stuff envelopes or work on a get-out-the-vote effort for a particular candidate or party. Federal employees were allowed to sport buttons during work and have bumper stickers on their cars.

Supporters of Hatch Act revisions said that the nation's 3 million federal employees were confused, as well as unduly restrained, by the jumble of rules and restrictions which appplied to their political rights.

One obstacle to passage of a Hatch Act revision bill in the 102nd Congress was regulations to clarify the rules circulated by the Office of Personnel Management (OPM). Republicans were hopeful they would sway some senators not to support any legislative revision.

However, the draft regulations did not attempt to make wholesale changes in the Hatch Act. Instead, they sought to allow federal employees greater freedom, as long as their activities were not part of an organized effort sponsored by a political party.

Officials from federal unions, who had been fighting for years to change the law, called the regulations a political ploy by the Bush administration to deter legislation.

## SENATE COMMITTEE ACTION

The Senate Governmental Affairs Committee approved the bill (S 914; S Rept 102-278) March 17, with all panel Republicans except Ted Stevens of Alaska opposing it. However, William V. Roth Jr., Del., was the only Republican to vote in person against it; the others submitted proxies. The committee sent the bill to the Senate floor on a 7-1 vote.

The committee bill prohibited any partisan politics during working hours. In their spare time, however, federal employees would have been allowed to more actively participate in campaigns.

Supporters of the legislation argued that federal workers should not have to give up their constitutional right to be active in politics because of their employment. Opponents maintained that the bill would politicize federal workplaces and lead to workers being coerced by their supervisors into campaign work.

A federal employee who stepped over the line of allowed activities would have been subject to a $5,000 fine and up to three years in jail.

The panel easily dispatched a set of seven amendments offered by ranking Republican Roth, all by 4-8 votes. The amendments:

● Gutted the bill by inserting language mandating that the Office of Personnel Management issue rules to clarify what conduct the Hatch Act allowed.

● Deleted a bill provision allowing federal workers to hold an office in a political party.

● Increased restrictions on political participation by federal employees with sensitive jobs, such as members of the Secret Service or the National Security Agency. Under existing law, most federal employees were covered by the Hatch Act. Only presidential appointees who were confirmed by the Senate were exempt.

● Prohibited all federal employees from accepting or soliciting campaign contributions. Glenn's bill maintained existing law that prohibited these employees from soliciting contributions from the general public. But the bill allowed employees to lobby other federal employees who belonged to the same federal organization for campaign contributions.

● Required each federal agency to vote on whether changes to the Hatch Act applied to them. Roth said that according to several surveys, many federal employees did not want the act changed. Glenn countered that "the constitutional rights of citizens should not be put up for referendum."

● Changed the effective date of the bill to Jan. 1, 1993. He said he was "very concerned about the effect it could have on this year's elections." But Glenn noted that the effective date of the bill was 120 days after enactment, which likely would have put it beyond the Nov. 3 elections. There is "no need to put it off" any longer, Glenn said. ■

# D.C. Statehood Initiative Dies in Committee

A measure (HR 4718) to make the District of Columbia the 51st state died in the 102nd Congress without full House action. Statehood supporters were unwilling to take up House floor time to debate the measure because they knew that they could not override a threatened veto by President Bush.

Under the bill, only buildings in a "federal enclave" were to remain under the exclusive control of Congress. Capitol Hill, the White House, the Supreme Court and all federal buildings surrounding the mall area were to have been included in the enclave, an area of approximately 1,400 acres, called the National Capital Service Area.

## BACKGROUND

This was the second time that the House District of Columbia Committee had approved a statehood bill. The panel reported out a similar measure in 1987, but — as in 1992 — the measure to give the federal city more autonomy never saw any floor action.

The push for statehood had gained new momentum in 1990 when District residents elected Jesse Jackson to be a "shadow" senator to lobby members of Congress on the issue. Jackson had met with 53 members of the Senate, with mixed results.

According to Frank Watkins, national coordinator for the statehood campaign, 31 senators told Jackson that they planned to vote for statehood. That list included 30 Democrats and Arlen Specter, R-Pa.

But to gain support for their bill, backers had to address several important questions. Perhaps the most important dilemma for the District was whether statehood was constitutional under Article 1, Section 8, Clause 17 of the U.S. Constitution.

The clause says it is in the power of Congress "to exercise exclusive legislation in all cases whatsoever, over such District (not exceeding 10 miles square) as may, by cession of particular states, and the acceptance of Congress, become the Seat of Government of the United States."

The Bush administration contended that, absent a constitutional amendment, Congress could not give back control over the lands ceded to it by Maryland and Virginia more than 200 years ago.

And the D.C. panel's ranking Republican, Bill Lowery, Calif., concurred, saying, "The permanent seat of government was created by the Constitution, not by Congress."

Supporters of statehood argued that District residents had all the burdens of states with none of the benefits. "How can we demand that federal taxes be paid and that local people die in wars and then specifically deny them the right to express their position at the ballot box?" asked House D.C. Committee Chairman Ronald V. Dellums, D-Calif.

But other members contended that because of the annual federal payment, District residents were already treated differently than state citizens. Congress appropriated $630.5 million for fiscal 1992 (PL 102-111) for the District. The funds were intended to compensate the city for the costs of accommodating the federal government. (Appropriations, p. 681)

Republicans may have had another reason for being opposed to giving the District voting representation in Congress: District residents traditionally had voted for Democratic presidential candidates, and the three non-voting members of Congress from the District were all Democrats.

## LEGISLATIVE ACTION

Democratic supporters of creating the 51st state — New Columbia — received a boost March 26 when the House District of Columbia's Judiciary Subcommittee, on a party-line vote of 5-3, voted to grant statehood to the District of Columbia. The panel approved a bill (HR 2482) to give the District the same voting rights as other states, including the election of two senators and a voting House member. Under existing law, District residents were represented by a D.C. delegate, who could vote in committee but not on the floor, and two "shadow" senators, who had no voting privileges.

Bill sponsor and D.C. Democratic Del. Eleanor Holmes Norton said after the markup that no state in the history of the Union was admitted the first time it tried, and she would not be surprised if the bill failed this time.

Norton argued that "there is growing and outspoken impatience in every ward of the District with an inferior form of American citizenship unique to the residents of Washington, D.C."

If people were unhappy at not having congressional representation, "they can move to Maryland," countered Thomas J. Bliley Jr., Va., the committee's ranking Republican.

The panel adopted, 5-3, four amendments by Norton to provide for a two-year transition commission to help the District become a state, allow the new state to impose taxes on federal property if Congress permitted, prohibit the new state from changing existing height limitations on buildings without the consent of Congress and grant voting rights to residents who lived in the federal enclave.

### Full Committee Action

To sustained applause, the House District of Columbia Committee on April 2 approved legislation that called for creating a 51st state called New Columbia.

With statehood advocate Jackson and D.C. Mayor Sharon Pratt Kelly looking on from the front row of a crowded hearing room, the panel approved the bill (HR 4718) on a 7-4 party-line vote.

It was a proud moment for Norton, a freshman in the House. She got a standing ovation after giving a four-page closing statement in support of the measure, and Committee Chairman Dellums said in a choked voice that there was nothing he could add to her impassioned plea for statehood.

The committee considered two amendments during the markup, both dealing with the annual federal payment to the District.

Rep. Dana Rohrabacher, R-Calif., an ardent opponent of statehood, lost his bid to delete a provision for a federal payment to the new state on a 4-7 vote. He called it a "totally unjustified expenditure."

Norton countered with a successful provision to allow the new state to continue to get a federal payment under a process established by a law signed by President Bush in 1991. That law (PL 102-102) set the federal payment at 24 percent of locally raised revenue. Norton's amendment was approved, 7-4. (1991 Almanac, p. 190) ∎

# D.C. Health-Benefits Act Meets Defeat

The House District of Columbia Committee on June 10 shot down, on a 3-6 party-line vote, a resolution (H J Res 480) that would have overturned a D.C. City Council act expanding health-care benefits to non-traditional partners of city workers.

Congress failed to approve the resolution before June 11 in order to override the D.C. act. However, no money was appropriated to implement the act.

The Fiscal Affairs and Health Subcommittee on June 4 voted by voice vote to send the resolution to the full committee, without recommendation.

Under the act, members of non-traditional family groups, such as homosexual couples, unmarried couples and their children, would have been able to register with the D.C. government as domestic partners, thus qualifying them for family health-benefits coverage if one of the partners worked for the D.C. government. City employees would have assumed the total cost of the additional coverage for their partners.

Congress had 30 legislative days to review all D.C. Council acts under the 1973 Home Rule Act. If a disapproving resolution was not passed by both the House and the Senate and signed by the president, the council act became law.

Resolution sponsor Clyde C. Holloway, R-La., joined several religious leaders in speaking against the act, which Holloway said would undermine traditional family values.

He also said that legal experts questioned whether the proposal would be pre-empted by the 1974 Employee Retirement Income Security Act (ERISA), which regulated employee health benefits and superseded state laws. (ERISA, p. 362)

But committee Chairman Ronald V. Dellums, D-Calif., said that he was satisfied with a letter from the D.C. Corporation Counsel and the D.C. Council's general counsel that the health-benefits measure would not be affected by ERISA.

Holloway said after the markup that he was prepared to keep fighting the D.C. measure. "We're not satisfied that this is the end," he said. "This is much deeper than ERISA to me."

Holloway ended up trying to offer an amendment to the fiscal 1993 D.C. appropriations bill (HR 5517) when it was being considered by the House that would have prohibited any of the bill's funds from being used to implement the city law. But Holloway was denied the opportunity to offer his amendment on a procedural vote that blocked any more amendments to the bill. (Appropriations, p. 681)

But in the end, the city was prevented from spending any money to implement the act, as the Senate had included similar language in its version of the bill. The House on Sept. 24 voted 235-173 to instruct House conferees to keep the Senate language in the spending bill. (Vote 420, p. 102-H) ∎

# Administration Opposes Election Day Holiday

Legislation to render Election Day an unpaid federal holiday never made it to the House floor in the 102nd Congress, in part because it was opposed by administration officials who feared it could evolve into another costly day off for government workers.

Rep. Ron Wyden, D-Ore., sponsored the bill, hopeful that the extra attention to voting would involve more citizens in the election process. It passed through the Post Office and Civil Service Committee without opposition, but the bill then stalled. Ironically, voter turnout in the 1992 election was considerably higher than expected, due to the addition of a major third-party candidate in the presidential race and a record number of departures from Congress.

The legislation (HR 3681) was prompted by predictions of a record-low turnout for the 1992 elections. Bill supporters hoped that making the first Tuesday after the first Monday in November an unpaid federal holiday every two years would prompt public awareness of the civic responsibility of voting, including local debates, parent-student educational seminars and voter registration drives.

### Disturbing Voter Trends

As a legal holiday, "Democracy Day" would have been similar in status to Martin Luther King Day, Christmas and the Fourth of July. But, unlike those holidays, it would have been purely symbolic. Federal workers would not have been urged to take the day off and could not have been paid if they did.

Bill sponsors pointed to disturbing voting trends as evidence of the need to draw more attention to Election Day. In 1988, George Bush captured the presidency with the backing of just 26 percent of the possible electorate because barely 50 percent of eligible voters turned out.

The trend was repeated in the midterm congressional elections two years later. In 1990, voter turnout amounted to 36.4 percent of the voting-age population and 54.7 percent of registered voters — the lowest turnout for an off-year election since 1942.

The percentage of voters participating in elections for local, state and national offices also had been steadily declining since 1960.

### Committee Approval

The House Post Office and Civil Service Committee on March 11 approved HR 3681 (H Rept 102-510) by voice vote. In approving the bill, panel members said they hoped making Election Day a symbolic holiday would reverse recent voting trends.

"What we're trying to do is bring the greatest stature, the greatest prestige to this day.... We see this [bill] as a beginning, not an end," said Wyden.

Wyden said sponsors had been careful "not to overclaim, not to overstate" the effects of an unpaid holiday on voter turnout, and he stressed that diverse factors were behind the dip in voter participation.

Prior to the March 11 markup, both the Justice Department and the Office of Personnel Management (OPM) notified the committee of their opposition to the bill. The Justice Department warned that the bill would set a precedent and might evolve into a paid day off for federal workers.

OPM officials also raised concerns that the bill would pressure the private sector to add another holiday for employees and could complicate collective-bargaining agreements.

Addressing concerns about potential costs, OPM estimated that it cost more than $300 million in salaries alone to give federal workers a paid federal holiday.

Sponsors of a companion Senate bill (S 1901) — Tom Daschle, D-S.D., and Orrin G. Hatch, R-Utah — delayed any Senate action until the matter was resolved in the House.

∎

# Honoraria Ban Remains For Federal Workers

Congressional attempts to reverse the honoraria ban for rank and file federal employees stalled in 1992. At year's end, employees were still required to put any money earned from honoraria into a federal escrow account.

The only discernable action on the issue came from the federal courts, which ruled the prohibition to be unconstitutional. But the court then suspended its ruling pending final decision on a Justice Department appeal.

As a result of 1989 Ethics Reform Act (PL 101-194), federal workers were prohibited from accepting honoraria. The act, which went into effect in January 1991, prohibited the acceptance of money for writing and speaking, even if the subject matter was unrelated to an employee's official duties. *(1989 Almanac, p. 51)*

But, many in Congress did not realize that the tightened ethics rules also caught all federal workers in the net. The new honoraria code was primarily directed toward outside activities by House members and their staff. Lawmakers proposed a quick legislative fix to reverse the prohibition.

Consequently, a bill (HR 3341) to exempt many federal employees from the ban was passed by the House on Nov. 25, 1991. HR 3341 would have lifted the ban for all but highly paid federal workers and political appointees. *(1991 Almanac, p. 186)*

But a similar measure (S 242) — which the Senate Governmental Affairs Committee approved on Feb. 27, 1991 — stalled due to opposition from Sen. Robert Byrd, the powerful chairman of the Appropriations Committee. Byrd had objected to the measure because it would have allowed some higher level Senate staff to accept honoraria. This would have altered a deal that he had helped broker banning senators and their staff from accepting fees in exchange for a pay raise for members. Byrd did not want to amend the compromise (PL 102-90) — signed into law Aug. 14, 1991 — so soon after enactment. *(1991 Almanac, p. 22)*

### Ban Declared Unconstitutional

The ban was declared unconstitutional March 19 by U.S. District Court Judge Thomas Penfield Jackson. He threw out the portion of the ethics law that pertained to federal employees, but restrictions on members of Congress remained in effect.

Jackson said that the law violated employees' First Amendment right to free speech. But, he barred enforcement of the ruling to allow the Department of Justice to appeal the decision. The appeal was argued in November before the U.S. Court of Appeals, D.C. Circuit. A decision had not been handed down at the end of the year. ∎

# Maritime Administration

The House on Sept. 9 passed a bill (HR 4484) that reauthorized the activities of the Maritime Administration. But the bill and companion Senate legislation (S 2701) quickly ran aground and failed to advance in the 102nd Congress.

The Transportation Department agency administered shipping subsidies, implemented bilateral maritime agreements and maintained the nation's two cargo fleets used to transport troops and supplies in wartime — the National

Defense Reserve Fleet and the Ready Reserve Force. *(1991 Almanac, p. 540)*

The measure reauthorized $765 million for the agency in fiscal 1993. It was $228 million more than the Bush administration had requested.

The bulk of the funding increase was intended for the Ready Reserve fleet, which consisted of 97 ships for transporting wartime cargo. The Bush administration had requested $126 million for the fleet in fiscal 1993; the committee-approved bill authorized $315 million — a $189 million increase.

In related action, House and Senate committees also approved separate bills (HR 4156 — H Rept 102-495, S 2700) that authorized $19.1 million in fiscal 1993 for the Federal Maritime Commission, the independent agency that regulated international and domestic maritime trade. Both bills later stalled.

### Legislative Action

The House Merchant Marine Committee acted first, approving HR 4484 by voice vote June 4.

The full House on Sept. 9 passed HR 4484 (H Rept 102-570) by a vote of 331-48 to reauthorize the Maritime Administration and the maintenance of a fleet of cargo ships used to transport troops and supplies during wartime. *(Vote 387, 94-H)*

The bill authorized $765 million for the administration, which included $423 million for the 100-ship National Defense Reserve Fleet and $225 million for subsidies to help U.S. ship owners compete in foreign trade.

In the Senate, the Commerce, Science and Transportation Committee on June 16 approved by voice vote a companion bill (S 2701). The bill authorized $537 million for fiscal 1993. The full Senate failed to take up the measure. ∎

# Congress Acts on Various Federal Operations Bills

The committees charged with administering the federal government, Governmental Affairs, Government Operations and Post Office and Civil Service, acted on several measures in 1992 dealing with federal employees, federal-state relations, paperwork and fraud.

Some of the measures became law, others died at the end of the 102nd Congress.

## DEFENSE WORKERS

A bill (HR 4991) to aid defense workers who lost ther jobs due to defense spending cutbacks, failed to clear at the end of the 102nd Congress. But similar provisions were included in the fiscal 1993 defense authorization (PL 102-484). *(Defense authorization, p. 483)*

The prospect of hundreds of thousands of defense workers being laid off from their jobs prompted the legislation, which was intended to offer some relief. The bill, approved by the House Post Office and Civil Service Committee May 20, gave workers advance notice of their termination and special job-transition benefits.

Sponsored by William L. Clay, D-Mo., chairman of the Post Office and Civil Service Committee, the measure required the Defense Department to give 120 days' notice before laying off employees because of defense cutbacks

due to the dissolution of the Soviet Union and required the Pentagon to continue to pay its portion of health insurance for laid-off workers for up to 18 months.

The bill also required other federal agencies to give at least 60 days' notice of impending layoffs.

The measure authorized 6-month severance packages for eligible Defense Department civilian workers as an incentive for taking early retirement, as well as mandated the temporary continuation of existing health benefits for displaced workers.

Other provisions of the bill required the Office of Personnel Management to expand its job listings to include all vacant positions and to ensure that displaced employees were given full consideration for vacancies at other federal agencies before any candidate from outside the agency was hired.

## STATE AID DISBURSEMENT

The House on Oct. 3 cleared for the president legislation (HR 5377 — PL 102-589) that gave states more time to come up with plans for disbursement of federal aid. President Bush signed the bill Nov. 10.

The bill extended for one year the effective date of a law (PL 101-453) that gave the Treasury secretary the authority to negotiate with each state how its federal aid would be transferred.

The states pushed for the extension because the Treasury Department had not issued the regulations on how the law would work until the week of Sept. 28.

At issue was who got the interest on the billions of dollars transferred between the federal and state governments. Under the law, if a state withdrew the federal money before a project started, then the states had to pay interest to the federal government. If the federal government was late in sending the money to the state, the federal government was responsible for paying the interest. *(1990 Almanac, p. 414)*

The Senate approved HR 5377 by voice vote Oct. 2, after amending it to include the provisions of a related Senate bill (S 2970), sponsored by Jim Sasser, D-Tenn. The final version included language to offset the projected cost to the Treasury of extending the cash disbursement law, estimated by the White House budget office at $75 million.

To offset that, the bill as cleared did two things: It extended for four years a pilot project that allowed private lawyers to go after money owed to the federal government; and it codified an IRS policy called "matching," which checks people who are owed a tax refund against a list of those who owe the government money (for defaulted school loans, for example), thus allowing the government to withhold the refund.

## MORE FUNDS FOR GOVERNMENT ETHICS

The Senate on Oct. 7 cleared for the president a bill (S 1145 — PL 102-506) to lift the cap on how much the Office of Government Ethics could spend each year. President Bush signed the bill Oct. 26.

The House had passed the bill Aug. 4.

The Office of Government Ethics was created in 1978, as part of the post-Watergate government reform. It was charged with setting guidelines and issuing advisory opinions on conflict-of-interest matters, and it monitored each federal agency's ethics program.

Although the ethics office was limited by statute to a

yearly authorization of $5 million, about $6.3 million was appropriated for the agency for fiscal 1992. Congress appropriated about $8 million for the agency in the fiscal 1993 spending bill for the Treasury, U.S. Postal Service and general government activity (HR 5488 — PL 102-393). *(Appropriations, p. 626)*

## REWARDS FOR WASTE-BUSTERS

The House on Oct. 4 cleared for the president legislation (HR 2263 — PL 102-487) that permanently authorized a program to reward federal employees who disclosed information on fraud, waste and abuse that led to cost savings for the government. President Bush signed the bill Oct. 24.

The bill made government contract workers and former federal employees eligible for the awards, which could not exceed $20,000.

The Senate passed the bill Sept. 24, deleting from the measure provisions that would have increased the amount a federal agency could pay a worker for finding a better way to do his or her job. Many federal agencies rewarded their employees for doing their job more efficiently with cash bonuses or plaques.

The House accepted the Senate amendment by voice vote.

## NO ADDITIONAL PAY FOR VETS

Congress failed to clear a bill, (HR 3209) that would have authorized additional pay for federal and Postal Service employees who were called to active duty during the 1991 Persian Gulf War. The House passed the measure March 18, but it saw no action in the Senate.

The bill, approved 354-57, would have compensated these employees for the difference between their government salaries and their military pay while they were in the gulf from funds already appropriated to the agencies. *(Vote 51, p. 12-H)*

Gary L. Ackerman, D-N.Y., sponsor of the bill, said, "We owe these brave men and women a debt of gratitude."

Opponents of the legislation argued that it violated the pay-as-you-go provisions of the budget agreement and cited an Office of Management and Budget study that said the bill, if enacted, would cost $13 million. Ackerman countered that the Congressional Budget Office said the net effect of the salary increases would be zero.

The measure, which was approved by the House Post Office and Civil Service Committee on Nov. 13, 1991, also would have allowed the 17,000 federal and postal employees called to active duty to make up back contributions to the Thrift Savings Plan, a federal retirement program. HR 3209 also would have extended life and health insurance benefits during the service period. *(1991 Almanac, p. 189)*

## EEOC REVISIONS FAIL

Congress did not clear legislation (HR 3613) that was designed to make it easier and faster for federal workers to file discrimination or sexual harassment complaints.

The bill was approved by the House Post Office and Civil Service Committee on July 1, by a 17-0 vote. But the measure saw no further action.

A key provision of the bill would have changed the procedure for investigating discrimination complaints. Under existing law, the investigations were conducted by the

agency that employed the worker. Under the bill, alleged violations of equal employment opportunity laws would have been adjudicated by the Equal Employment Opportunity Commission.

The bill also would have required agencies to respond to complaints more quickly and simplify filing requirements.

## PAPERWORK REDUCTION FAILS

Congress was unable to send to the president a bill (HR 5851) that was designed to cut back on federal paperwork requirements.

The Senate on Oct. 5 passed the bill by voice vote. But senators amended the bill, attaching unrelated provisions, and it died without House action. The bill would have set up a new commission to study ways to reduce federal paperwork requirements.

The core provisions, passed by both the House and the Senate, would have created a 19-member commission on Information Technology and Paperwork, based on a similar panel created in 1974. Rep. Frank Horton, R-N.Y., sponsor of the original Paperwork Reduction Act and of HR 5851, said that despite the success of the original commission, paperwork requirements still needed to be pared.

The Senate added to this bill the provisions of S 260, sponsored by Carl Levin, D-Mich., whose language would have streamlined the federal acquisition process for commercial items and off-the-shelf purchases.

But the House did not act on the amended version before adjourning Oct. 9.

## BANKRUPTCY BILL FAILS

Congress came close to sending a measure to the president aimed at streamlining and speeding up the handling of bankruptcy proceedings. But the House failed to take final action on the measure before adjourning.

The Senate gave voice vote approval to the bill (S 1985 — S Rept 102-279) on Oct. 7.

During hasty negotiations to hammer out a compromise bill the week of adjournment, lawmakers agreed to a provision that would encourage individual debtors to file for bankruptcy under Chapter 13 rather than Chapter 7. Under Chapter 13, people facing bankruptcy received a specific time period, typically three to five years, in which to repay their debts through a payment plan. In a Chapter 7 bankruptcy, debtors' assets were liquidated immediately to pay creditors. The bill would have raised debt limits for Chapter 13 bankruptcy from $350,000 to $1 million.

Conferees accepted Senate provisions to create a nine-member national bankruptcy commission to review the cumbersome U.S. Bankruptcy Code and to require companies filing for Chapter 11 bankruptcy to continue paying retiree benefits during bankruptcy proceedings.

But they dropped a Senate provision that would have protected the Manville Corp. from asbestos-liability claims. Under its Chapter 11 reorganization, Manville formed a trust to protect itself from asbestos-liability suits. A bankruptcy court ordered claimants to seek payment from the

trust and not the company. The Senate language, vehemently opposed by labor and environmental groups, would have codified the bankruptcy court's authority to issue such a direction and set a precedent for companies to use trust arrangements to protect themselves from product and environmental liability suits.

The Senate measure, sponsored by Howell Heflin, D-Ala., and Charles E. Grassley, R-Iowa, the chairman and ranking Republican of the Subcommittee on Courts and Administrative Practice, won voice approval from the Judiciary Committee on March 19.

On June 17, S 1985 passed the Senate by a vote of 97-0. (Vote 123, p. 17-S)

The relatively non-controversial bill was waylaid for a while by an unrelated amendment offered by John C. Danforth, R-Mo., suggesting that candidates for office, including presidential candidates, hold substantive discussions on the federal budget deficit. The amendment was approved, 65-32, after some minor modifications by Senate Majority Leader George J. Mitchell, D-Maine. (Vote 122, 17-S)

A similar bill (HR 6020 — H Rept 102-996), introduced in the House by Jack Brooks, D-Texas, would have set stricter bankruptcy filing deadlines and authorized judges to hold regular status conferences with debtors and their creditors to expedite the proceedings.

The House Subcommittee on Economic and Commercial Law approved HR 6020 for full committee action on Sept. 25. The House Judiciary Committee gave voice vote approval to the measure Sept. 30. The House approved HR 6020 on Oct. 3, after agreeing by voice vote to substitute its language for S 1985.

Supporters of the bankruptcy law reform said that the record 940,000 bankruptcy filings in 1991 made it imperative for bankruptcy cases to be processed more quickly. There were 740,165 bankruptcy filings in the first three quarters of 1992.

## COPYRIGHT SYSTEM GETS OVERHAUL

Congress cleared and President Bush signed legislation (S 756 — PL 102-307) designed to improve the nation's copyright system.

Under the legislation, certain authors of works copyrighted before Jan. 1, 1978, no longer needed to formally seek a second 47-year term of copyright protection for their work. For works copyrighted in 1978 or later, the law already provided a copyright term of 50 years after the death of the author.

Also included in the legislation was a provision requiring the librarian of Congress to establish a National Film Registry to preserve significant U.S.-made motion pictures.

Both chambers had passed separate but similar measures (HR 2372 — H Rept 102-379, S 756 — S Rept 102-194) in 1991, but the bills were left for final consideration in 1992. (1991 Almanac, p. 297)

The House and Senate both cleared an amended version of the bill, incorporating the substance of the House bill in the final measure, by voice vote June 4.

The president signed the bill into law June 26. ∎

# ENERGY/ ENVIRONMENT/ SCIENCE

# Energy Bill Surges Toward Enactment

## *Sweeping legislation addresses foreign-oil needs, public utilities, nuclear power plant licensing*

The 102nd Congress opened with fierce debate over the Persian Gulf War and impassioned calls for a national energy policy to wean Americans from their addiction to Middle Eastern oil.

It ended with passage of a sprawling energy bill, the first major attempt to decrease U.S. oil dependence since the late 1970s. It took a nonstop work schedule maintained throughout the session to produce a 443-page conference report that cleared Congress Oct. 8, shortly before adjournment. On Oct. 24, President Bush signed the legislation (PL 102-486), which included pieces of his proposed energy strategy.

The legislation sought to make policy advances across the spectrum of energy industries and issues.

Electric utilities were expected to see the most dramatic change under a rewrite of the 1935 Public Utility Holding Company Act. The bill's so-called PUHCA reform allowed established utilities and independent producers to compete freely in the wholesale power market — a change that sought to increase competition and, with it, efficiency. Related provisions provided independent producers with greater access to utility-owned transmission lines.

There were tax incentives for conservation, for renewable energy and for cars that ran on non-gasoline fuels, as well as tax relief for independent oil and gas drillers.

The bill streamlined the licensing process for nuclear power plants and mandated greater energy efficiency for appliances, plumbing equipment and buildings.

Federal and state governments were required to start buying cars that ran on alternative fuels, with private companies to follow later. The bill also authorized billions of dollars for research and development projects within the Energy Department and restructured the department's

---

## BOXSCORE

➡ **National Energy Strategy (HR 776).** Major energy legislation to restructure the electricity industry, encourage conservation, renewable energy and alternative fuels and make it easier to build nuclear power plants.

**Reports:** H Rept 102-474, Parts 1-9; S Rept 102-72; conference report H Rept 102-1018.

### KEY ACTION

Feb. 4 — The **Senate** voted to begin work on S 2166, 90-5.

Feb. 19 — The **Senate** passed S 2166, 94-4.

March 11 — The House Energy and Commerce Committee approved HR 776, 42-1.

May 27 — The **House** passed HR 776, 381-37.

June 16 — The Senate Finance Committee approved a package of energy-related tax provisions.

July 23 — The **Senate** voted to proceed to HR 776, 58-33, two votes shy of the 60 votes needed to limit debate.

July 27 — The **Senate** successfully voted to limit debate on HR 776, 93-3.

July 30 — The **Senate** passed HR 776, as amended, 93-3.

Sept. 10 — House-Senate conference began.

Oct. 1 — Conferees approved the final report.

Oct 5 — The **House** adopted the conference report, 363-60.

Oct. 8 — The **Senate** cleared the legislation by voice vote.

Oct. 24 — President Bush signed HR 776 — PL 102-486.

---

uranium enrichment program into a government-owned corporation that eventually could be privatized.

Yet for all this, the bill failed to resolve some of the most heated energy controversies to emerge in the previous two decades: whether to drill for oil off the U.S. coasts and in Alaska's Arctic wildlife refuge, make cars and trucks more fuel-efficient or impose energy taxes to curb consumption. Taken as a whole, the final bill was expected to cap rather than significantly reduce growing dependence on foreign oil.

That disappointed some lawmakers and policy analysts who believed the gulf war presented a historic opportunity for a more dramatic rewrite of the nation's energy policy.

But it also appeared to reflect the limits of the possible where energy policy was concerned — at least in 1992.

For one thing, experts warned that clear, long-term goals were needed to reorient energy practices that went to the heart of the way the country lived and worked — a process some likened to turning a large supertanker.

"Great policy shifts come slowly," said Sen. J. Bennett Johnston, D-La., the key Senate author of the energy bill. "They're hard to do, and they're hard to undo."

## Political Limitations

Perhaps more daunting were the political limitations on crafting energy policy.

The developing legislation was continually tugged between the competing interests of producing states and consuming regions. Lawmakers struggled to bridge the gap between the demands of energy production and environmental protection.

The desire for greater energy independence had to compete with other goals, such as limiting the financial drains

on taxpayers and businesses. The public had little stomach, for example, for an energy tax that would encourage conservation.

And lawmakers were hesitant to lead where the voting public was unlikely to follow.

That left Congress with an energy bill that many believed offered a balanced foundation for cleaner and more secure energy supplies, but one that did not chart a decisive course away from current reliance on imported oil.

"It's a whole lot better than nothing," said Eric Uslaner, a political science professor at the University of Maryland who had written a book about the politics of energy policy.

Nevertheless, Uslaner thought the legislation could play a destructive role if policy-makers became complacent and assumed the bill was enough to guide energy policy well into the next century: "If we're lucky, it will get us through this one."

## BACKGROUND

Traditionally, it had taken a crisis of some sort to push new energy policies through Capitol Hill.

In late 1990 and early 1991, that spark was provided by the Persian Gulf crisis and resulting oil price surges. But public interest faded quickly as prices dropped and the war ended, and the war would not have been enough to propel such a sweeping policy bill.

The gulf war, however, coincided with an institutional ripening on energy policy.

In July 1989, President Bush announced plans to draft a comprehensive "national energy strategy." That massive document was going through final revisions in the winter of 1990-91, and ultimately was released in February 1991.

In Congress, lawmakers also had been sidling up to the notion of rewriting energy laws.

The remaking of the Clean Air Act in the 101st Congress had focused attention on the environmental consequences of fuel consumption. To some, the pursuit of clean air led inevitably to greater energy conservation, cleaner-burning fuels and, perhaps, nuclear power.

Meanwhile, domestic oil production was slipping and imports were rising, eventually accounting for close to half of all U.S. oil consumption, with no end in sight. That dependency presented not only a worrisome security risk but also an immediate drain on the nation's balance of payments.

The Persian Gulf crisis was the flame that made all these kernels explode into a flurry of legislation.

### 1991 Action

Johnston took the lead early in 1991, drafting a massive energy bill (S 1220, originally S 341) and guiding it through the Senate Energy and Natural Resources Committee, which he chaired.

But that legislation faced strong criticism from environmental groups and their allies and stalled over the summer.

In the House, Rep. Philip R. Sharp, D-Ind., began marking up a parallel bill (HR 776) in his Energy and Commerce Subcommittee on Energy and Power. The subcommittee reported that bill to the full committee in October 1991, but it moved no further that year.

Johnston made an end-of-session push on his bill, but on Nov. 1 failed to muster the 60 votes necessary to bring it to the floor.

Johnston had relied heavily on Republican support to help advance his energy package. He consulted closely with

the administration, and during committee markup Republican votes often provided the victory margin for key measures such as the Arctic drilling provision.

But that strategy got Johnston into trouble with Democrats on two fronts: On substance, especially the Arctic drilling, Johnston appeared to have strayed too far from mainstream thinking within his party. And he also irritated fellow Democratic committee chairmen by writing policy for issues in their jurisdiction, such as nuclear power and electric utility regulation.

Forty-four senators, including nine fellow committee chairmen, blocked his energy bill from coming to the Senate floor — largely because it would have allowed oil and gas drilling in the Arctic refuge. Johnston left the vote dispirited and unsure how to proceed. Although various Democrats pledged to return with revised energy legislation in 1992, the likely contours or prospects for such a bill remained in doubt. *(1991 Almanac, p. 195)*

## SENATE FLOOR ACTION

Congress revived the energy legislation quickly in the second year. A second, stripped-down version of the 1991 bill passed 94-4 on Feb. 19 after several days of floor debate and some significant amendments. The new bill did not include fuel efficiency mandates or allow for drilling in the Arctic refuge. *(Vote 28, p. 5-S)*

### Prelude

After the bill's November 1991 defeat, action in the new year shifted to the Democratic Caucus, and by the week of Jan. 27, Johnston had come to an agreement with his former critics. Johnston agreed to drop the Arctic drilling provision from his bill and keep it out. In exchange, the dissident Democrats agreed not to block the bill from the floor or try to append higher fuel efficiency mandates.

That was a minimal sacrifice for proponents of new mileage standards. With the automobile industry in serious economic trouble, lawmakers recognized the timing was not propitious to pass major new mileage requirements.

Johnston also worked to smooth out differences with rival chairmen while nonetheless holding on to Republican support.

Wyoming Sen. Malcolm Wallop, the ranking Republican on the Energy Committee and cosponsor of the original bill, agreed to cosponsor the new version. And the administration abandoned earlier threats to veto any energy bill that did not allow Arctic drilling to begin.

Johnston introduced the new, leaner energy bill (S 2166) on Jan. 29.

The bill retained the core of the earlier version (S 1220) but discarded its controversial proposals to open Alaska's Arctic National Wildlife Refuge to oil and gas drilling and to increase federal gas mileage standards. The revised measure sought to speed construction of nuclear power plants and natural gas pipelines, mandate the use of non-gasoline fuels and certain energy-efficiency technologies, and authorize energy-related research and development projects.

### To The Floor

Johnston cleared a key hurdle Feb. 4, when senators voted 90-5 to begin work on the bill. *(Vote 15, p. 3-S)*

In the opening week of debate, senators who had criticized the bill as harmful to the environment won some changes to their liking. Lawmakers agreed to strengthen conservation and energy-efficiency sections, and to restore

certain environmental protections relating to hydroelectric power plants and natural gas pipelines.

The Senate also overwhelmingly approved an amendment by Al Gore, D-Tenn., urging the administration to speed up the phaseout of ozone-depleting chemicals.

But environmentalists lost key battles to soften provisions aimed at boosting nuclear power and to provide more support for non-gasoline transportation fuels. Their proposals had drawn strong opposition from the administration and could have jeopardized Republican support for the bill.

### Nuclear Power

One of the most contentious fights came over the bill's provisions to streamline federal licensing of nuclear power plants. Senators narrowly rejected an effort to trim some of those changes, delivering an important victory to the administration and the nuclear power industry.

As written, the bill authorized the Nuclear Regulatory Commission to issue a single operating and construction license, rather than two licenses as had been customary. The commission already had established a combined license procedure, but parts of that plan had been challenged in court.

Advocates said the changes were critical if a new generation of nuclear plants were to be built. They insisted that nuclear critics had exploited the existing procedures, unfairly delaying plants with frivolous objections.

But Bob Graham, D-Fla., chairman of the Nuclear Regulation Subcommittee of the Environment and Public Works Committee, argued that the proposed changes went too far. Graham offered an amendment to allow the combined license but guarantee critics could have a full, second hearing before plant operation if they raised valid safety concerns or new information.

Wyche Fowler Jr., D-Ga., who cosponsored the amendment, said, "This body cannot allow even the perception that public participation is expendable, undesirable or unwelcome."

Johnston offered a rival amendment that added some guarantees for public participation but stopped short of the Graham proposal. Senators voted 52-43 on Feb. 6 to table the Graham amendment and then adopted Johnston's proposal by voice vote. (Vote 20, p. 4-S)

### Alternative Fuels

Senators also wrangled at length over an amendment by James M. Jeffords, R-Vt., to promote non-gasoline motor fuels. The Senate eventually voted 57-39 to kill the proposal with a tabling motion. (Vote 18, p. 4-S)

The amendment sought to ensure that, by the year 2001, 10 percent of motor fuel sold by refiners would be so-called alternative fuels, such as ethanol, methanol, natural gas or electricity. To meet that target, oil refiners would have to make alternative fuels at least 10 percent of their fuel production.

Jeffords had tried for years to win support for such a proposal, but the Senate Energy Committee the previous year refused to put it in the energy bill. In an effort to boost support, Jeffords modified the proposal to include oil from small wells, known as stripper wells, to count against the mandates.

Jeffords argued that his proposal was the only means to actually combat growing oil imports and give the nation more control over its energy supply.

But Don Nickles, R-Okla., said oil refiners in his state were in no position to produce alternative fuels. "That is like trying to mandate to the apple tree that you produce 10 percent oranges."

The administration had warned that the Jeffords amendment could draw a veto, and the proposal was also a prime target for oil lobbyists.

### Energy Efficiency

The Senate agreed to a series of amendments, all on voice vote, to strengthen the bill's energy-efficiency provisions. Among the most significant were proposals to set national energy-efficiency standards for most lamps and for electric motors. Senators also voted to direct federal agencies to implement all energy-efficiency improvements that would pay for themselves within 10 years.

Senators agreed to drop some other controversial items from the bill.

On hydroelectric power, the bill had proposed to eliminate federal licensing for projects 5 megawatts or less and limit federal environmental review. On a voice vote, the bulk of those changes were struck from the bill. Johnston agreed to the amendment but said the original language would have done more to promote new hydropower projects.

### PUHCA Reform

One of the biggest items in the bill was its provision to loosen federal regulation of the wholesale electric power market. The controversial PUHCA proposal sought to make it easier for small generators to sell power and for utilities to build plants outside their home bases.

The proposal became popular with the natural gas industry, which was expected to be the fuel of choice for many independent generating plants envisioned under the bill.

Renewable energy producers also could benefit, especially if the final version enhanced their ability to ship power to different wholesale customers.

But sponsors said the biggest beneficiaries would be consumers, who would reap the rewards of competition in lower electric rates.

Consumer and environmental groups initially showed more apprehension than interest, wary it would open the door to utility misconduct.

A coalition of utilities vigorously opposed the entire PUHCA proposal. This group, known as the "Just Say Nos," warned of unreliable players entering the market, jeopardizing supply and imposing higher rates.

The issue had been expected to spark huge debate, but Johnston successfully negotiated agreements with some of the biggest skeptics.

Sen. Donald W. Riegle Jr., D-Mich., chaired the Banking Committee, which had oversight of the utility law. Riegle was among those who argued that independent power producers be assured access to utility-owned transmission lines. This was also the position of environmental and consumer groups, who said that only such guarantees would prevent utilities from stifling competitors by denying them a way to get power to wholesale customers.

Utilities strongly opposed such mandates, and Johnston originally vowed to keep them off his bill. But on the Senate floor, he agreed to address the issue in conference with the House.

Johnston also moved to head off other concerns about the electricity proposal.

Opponents sensed the Senate tide was against them.

Several senators who had been expected to offer anti-PUHCA amendments settled for compromises or simply made floor statements.

All of the PUHCA-related amendments ultimately were approved by voice vote. Key changes included:

● **Self-dealing.** To avert a concern among consumer groups that PUHCA changes would open the door to the utility abuses that prompted the Depression-era law, Riegle and Johnston agreed on an amendment to protect consumers.

The amendment was designed to prevent so-called self-dealing, whereby a utility builds an independent power plant then sells power to itself, potentially at inflated rates. Under the amendment, utilities could buy power from an independent affiliate only if state regulators determined that the sale would benefit consumers.

● **State review.** State regulators would be allowed to give conditional approval of a utility's plan to buy power from an independent generator and recover costs from its customers. They could also revoke such approval down the road.

Johnston's bill originally had directed state regulators to make a binding decision up front about whether to approve such a plan. But Richard H. Bryan, D-Nev., and other critics said that proposal would tie regulators' hands and could force them to stick rate payers with unfair costs.

● **Debt.** A compromise amendment, approved by voice vote, would allow state regulators to examine the debt load of an independent generator and impose a specific debt-equity ratio if needed. The arcane but hotly contested issue arose from a fear that independent producers would have a financing edge over federally regulated utilities, which are required to maintain a prescribed equity-to-debt ratio.

### Coastal Drilling

Floor debate included large battles over two offshore oil and gas drilling amendments sponsored by Graham.

As drafted, the bill would have banned new drilling leases off the California and New Jersey coasts until the year 2000. On the Senate floor, lawmakers added similar moratoriums for the coastal areas of New England, Oregon and Washington.

Graham's first amendment sought to extend that protection to the Florida coast and directed the government to buy back some existing federal leases there.

Johnston countered with a temporary drilling moratorium and lease buyback for the South Florida coast, an area already declared off-limits until the year 2000 by President Bush. Unlike Graham's proposal, the moratorium would not affect the waters off the Florida Panhandle, which are believed to hold large oil and gas reserves.

While Graham argued of environmental risks to the state's delicate coastlines, Johnston said that oil tankers, not offshore rigs, accounted for virtually all oil spills. Johnston's substitute was accepted 53-45, and Graham's underlying amendment then passed by voice vote. *(Vote 24, p. 4-S)*

Graham's second amendment, even more worrisome to the oil industry, sought to rewrite leasing policy for all offshore areas. His proposal would have allowed the cancellation of leases seriously threatening the environment and given more weight to environmental concerns in granting leases. Johnston's motion to kill that amendment by tabling it passed 51-47. *(Vote 25, p. 5-S)*

Senators also severely cut back a proposed fund to encourage states to allow drilling off their shores. The bill would have set aside 37.5 percent of new offshore leasing revenues for coastal states and communities, much of it expected to go to Louisiana, Texas and California. Senators agreed by voice vote to trim that impact aid to 12.5 percent, cap it at $300 million annually, and restrict the money to environmental protection and restoration. Another 4 percent of revenues would go to a separate fund for all coastal states, not only those that allow offshore drilling.

### Losing Streak

Consumer and environmental groups lost a series of roll call votes on amendments the week of Feb. 17. Johnston fought the proposals with administration support. *(Votes 21-27, pp. 4-S, 5-S)*

Defeated were proposals to:

● Authorize the Federal Energy Regulatory Commission to order refunds to natural gas customers who had been overcharged. Rejected, 41-57.

● Create an independent board to investigate safety issues at nuclear power plants. Killed on tabling motion, 63-35.

● Restrict the ability of gas-pipeline owners to use federal eminent domain powers under the bill's expedited pipeline licensing. Killed on tabling motion, 60-35.

● Establish an industrial energy efficiency program that would ask companies to voluntarily report their energy use. Killed on tabling motion, 58-40.

● Direct the administration to ensure a transition to alternative motor fuels, to reach 30 percent by 2010. Killed on tabling motion, 64-34.

### Arctic Wildlife Refuge Redux

Although Johnston predicted that the Senate would not allow oil and gas exploration in the Arctic National Wildlife Refuge (ANWR) as part of his revised energy bill, that did nothing to slow the storm of speeches, rumors and parliamentary intrigues as the energy debate got under way.

ANWR was an emotional issue for advocates of drilling, who had thought the energy bill offered their best chance to open the refuge, and to opponents, who successfully rallied to block the proposal on the grounds that it would irreparably hurt the environment.

Passions ran especially high in the Alaska delegation, where Republican Sens. Frank H. Murkowski and Ted Stevens both reflected the state's official impatience to get at the petroleum deposits that might lie under the Arctic refuge.

Murkowski and Stevens cited national arguments for the drilling, saying oil from the refuge would help cut imports, create tens of thousands of jobs nationwide, and provide federal revenue for the various research and development programs in the energy bill. But the most immediate economic impact would be within Alaska, and the state's political leaders chafed at the notion that national politicians and environmental groups exercised control over their lands and livelihood.

But while the Alaska senators had reserved the right to offer an amendment to restore Arctic drilling, they ultimately decided not to press for the vote they realized they could not win.

"Politics have overtaken policy," Murkowski said, blaming Democrats for blocking the drilling measure in the interest of election-year politics.

His anger was seconded by Steve Symms, R-Idaho, who blasted colleagues concerned about unemployment but un-

willing to allow drilling to go forward.

"If we really care about jobs and economic recovery . . . we should develop our resources," said Symms. "The Senate likes to suck and blow in the same breath, and it does not work."

## Assessments

The final product overwhelmingly passed by the Senate Feb. 19 also won the endorsement of Energy Secretary James D. Watkins, despite its failure to provide drilling in the Arctic refuge.

Sponsors Johnston and Wallop said the strong vote boded well for final action in 1992. Johnston said the legislation would lay the foundation for a "made in America" energy policy.

But the 94-4 victory margin belied some tepid sentiments toward the bill. While senators cited worthy provisions, they also expressed dissatisfaction with it as a national energy policy.

Gore, who wanted to radically revisit energy policies in light of global climate change, called the bill "a well-intentioned anachronism."

"It's the last of the big production bills," said Gore, who nonetheless praised the effort and voted for the bill.

There also was disappointment on the other side of the political spectrum among senators who wanted to revitalize energy industries.

Republican Don Nickles of Oklahoma, who sat on the Energy Committee, was unhappy that the Senate did not include Arctic drilling and placed many coastal areas off-limits to drilling.

Only four senators felt strongly enough to vote against the bill: Dave Durenberger, R-Minn.; Paul Wellstone, D-Minn.; Bob Graham, D-Fla.; and Robert C. Smith, R-N.H.

Environmental lobbyists, who were instrumental in defeating the earlier version, said the bill was much improved but still highly flawed.

Natural gas and nuclear groups were pleased by proposals to help their industries, but the oil companies found little to like.

## HOUSE ACTION

The energy spotlight then shifted to the House, where the full Energy and Commerce Committee in March approved a parallel bill that had been passed out of its Energy and Power Subcommittee the previous fall.

The House bill was more to the liking of environmentalists and tilted still farther in that direction as eight other committees with rival jurisdiction marked up their pieces of an overall energy package.

But the administration and industry groups won back some ground in the Rules Committee and on the House floor. On May 27, the House voted 381-37 for a bill that had much in common with the Senate version. *(Vote 144, p. 19-S)*

Major provisions would ease licensing for natural gas pipelines and nuclear power plants, overhaul electric utility regulations, promote cars that run on non-gasoline fuels and mandate greater energy efficiency.

The bill also contained new restrictions on energy production, most notably extensive bans on offshore oil drilling.

## ENERGY AND COMMERCE COMMITTEE

The Energy and Commerce Subcommittee on Energy

and Power had approved a large energy bill in fall of 1991 (HR 776), but full committee Chairman John D. Dingell, D-Mich., had been awaiting the Senate outcome before moving forward.

On March 11, 1992, less than one month after passage of the Senate energy measure, the full Energy and Commerce panel gave swift and overwhelming approval to its own national energy policy. The vote was 42-1, with William E. Dannemeyer, R-Calif., casting the sole dissent.

The legislation (HR 776) sought to restructure the wholesale electricity industry, mandate greater energy efficiency and the use of non-gasoline fuels, promote "clean coal" and renewable energy, and make it easier to build natural gas pipelines. It also called on oil importers and refiners to send a small portion of their oil to the nation's Strategic Petroleum Reserve.

Members made few major changes to the 400-page bill, which Philip R. Sharp, D-Ind., drafted during nine days of markup in his Energy and Power Subcommittee the previous year. Members did agree, however, to provide some new protections for existing electric utilities under the proposed industry restructuring and to ensure utility payments toward cleaning up aging federal uranium enrichment facilities.

## PUHCA Reform

Like the Senate bill, the House measure proposed relaxing the 1935 Public Utility Holding Company Act (PUHCA) to free utilities and non-utilities alike to build wholesale power plants nationwide.

Unlike the Senate measure, however, Sharp's bill authorized the federal government to force utilities to ship a competitor's electricity on its transmission lines. Supporters of this so-called transmission access provision wanted to ensure that utilities would not suffocate competitors by denying them access to potential customers.

Proponents of so-called PUHCA reform, including the administration, said the change would boost electricity supply and lower rates by allowing new players into the market.

But some utilities and their allies argued that the changes would only disrupt a stable electricity system that has worked well for decades. They were particularly opposed to mandatory transmission access, which they said could hamstring utility operations and force them to subsidize competitors.

Tom McMillen, D-Md., and other committee members had been expected to offer contentious amendments to limit transmission access and other provisions that could disadvantage existing utilities.

But Sharp and full committee Chairman Dingell, working with the panel's ranking Republicans, headed off those challenges by drafting a take-it-or-leave-it deal on transmission.

That compromise laid out guidelines under which federal regulators could order a utility to ship another company's power and required that utilities receive just compensation for such services.

Opponents accepted the offer, although some voiced ongoing worries about the final product. Utilities had sought more extensive and specific guarantees for their interests.

"What some thought would erupt into enormous conflict has instead erupted into enormous consensus," Sharp told the reporters and lobbyists jamming the committee room.

# Rockefeller Outlasts Fierce Resistance . . .

One of the most controversial items in the energy bill had no direct bearing on energy production or consumption, but on the status of a health-care fund for retired coal miners and their families.

Sen. John D. Rockefeller IV, D-W.Va., had dedicated himself to rescuing a troubled union health fund of about 120,000 retired coal miners and their beneficiaries. Many of the unionized coal operators that agreed to provide the benefits had since gone out of business, and the remaining companies said they could not afford to keep up the fund.

When the Senate Finance Committee amended the tax provisions of the House energy bill in June 1992, Rockefeller insisted on adding a provision to bail out the miners' fund through a tax on all bituminous coal operators — union and non-union.

The proposal was identical to one Rockefeller added to an earlier tax bill (HR 4210) that was vetoed. But his proposed solution — to tax all bituminous coal operators — was unacceptable to the administration and some senators, particularly those from states with non-union coal companies. *(First tax bill, p. 133)*

During the Finance markup on June 16, Minority Leader Bob Dole, R-Kan., and other critics lashed out at the idea of holding companies liable for health benefits they never negotiated. The Bush administration sharply opposed the provision, and Steve Symms, R-Idaho, warned that its inclusion "might mean the failure of the entire energy package." But Rockefeller said the miners' benefits were in serious jeopardy and must be saved.

The 10-8 vote was largely partisan, with no Republicans voting for the measure. David L. Boren of Oklahoma was the only Democrat to vote against it. Two Republicans, Sens. Dave Durenberger of Minnesota and Orrin G. Hatch of Utah, voted present.

### Administration's Wrath

As the revised energy bill moved to the Senate floor, Rockefeller's proposal brought down the wrath of the administration and Malcolm Wallop, R-Wyo., who vowed to bring down the energy bill he helped write rather than let the tax on coal operators go through. But those opponents clearly were uncomfortable blocking an energy bill they had spent much of the year touting.

Wallop and Rockefeller held talks to try to reach a compromise. Another key player was Democratic Whip Wendell H. Ford of Kentucky, who was caught between the needs of union and non-union coal operators in his state.

By the week of July 20, the White House had jumped into the talks as well and appeared anxious to break the impasse. The administration at first denied the need for federal action for the coal miner retirees, but then officials began proposing non-tax alternatives to ensure the health fund.

The talks dismissed the notion of an industry-wide tax, and instead focused on tapping the mine workers' over-supplied pension fund to wipe out the existing deficit in the health fund. To keep up with the ongoing health costs of the retirees, the plan reportedly called for a system of assigning "orphan" miners to companies linked to their original employers.

On July 23, Rockefeller held an afternoon news conference with United Mine Workers President Richard L. Trumka to announce that the sides were "very close."

An hour and a half later, the key senators were closeted in the Capitol offices of West Virginia Democrat Robert C. Byrd, the Senate president pro tempore. After an hour, the cluster of lobbyists outside began speculating that a deal was at hand. But the door remained shut at the appointed time for the cloture vote to begin work on the energy bill — 7:20 p.m.

When the key players emerged, it was to cast opposing votes on the cloture petition.

White House and Energy Department lobbyists were on hand to urge a "no" vote. Only three Republicans, Don Nickles of Oklahoma, Charles E. Grassley of Iowa and Arlen Specter of Pennsylvania, broke ranks and voted to bring the bill to the floor.

It was an ironic reverse image of the previous Novem-

### Conflict and Consensus

The transmission access compromise was part of a 41-amendment package offered by Sharp and approved by voice vote.

The package included revisions in the bill's energy efficiency section that would extend efficiency standards to a broader range of commercial-size heating and cooling equipment, and modify the standards for electric motors and lights to conform with the Senate energy bill.

In a separate voice vote, members also agreed to establish voluntary efficiency targets for energy-intensive industries and a grant program to help them meet these targets. Some committee Republicans said the provision would impose new paperwork burdens on industry.

However, members refused to establish federal efficiency standards for faucets.

Sharp praised the bipartisan support for energy efficiency, recalling fierce Republican opposition to measures such as appliance standards in the 1980s. But old regional schisms were evident in debates on oil and gas issues.

The House bill sought to boost the Strategic Petroleum Reserve, a stockpile of oil held in salt caverns in Louisiana and Texas, to 1 billion barrels. To help meet that target, the bill would have required oil importers and refiners to set aside about 1 percent of their oil to send to the reserve.

During markup, Clyde C. Holloway, R-La., proposed limiting the set-aside requirement to oil importers, thereby giving domestic producers a small advantage.

W. J. "Billy" Tauzin, D-La., quickly added his impassioned support for the provision. Holding up a New Orleans newspaper with a story on oil drillers fleeing the United States, Tauzin warned of impending disaster in the domestic oil and gas industry. But members rejected the amendment, saying it would unfairly burden the Northeast and other areas that rely heavily on oil imports, and might violate free-trade pacts.

The administration had fiercely opposed the language, which supporters estimated would raise gas and heating oil prices about a half-cent per gallon.

# ...To Pass Bailout of Miners' Fund

ber, when Wallop and administration lobbyists criticized environmentalists and their allies for successfully filibustering an earlier version of the energy bill.

When the cloture vote failed, the administration sought to blame Rockefeller and the Democratic leadership. "The Rockefeller coal tax amendment should never have been able to delay or scuttle the energy bill," Energy Secretary James D. Watkins said in a prepared statement.

But Johnston, chief sponsor of the Senate energy bill, said those who supported the filibuster were potentially dooming the sweeping legislation. Democrats voted uniformly to invoke cloture.

And Rockefeller earlier in the day defended his determined stance. While he supported the energy bill, the West Virginian said, he could not abandon his fight to secure the threatened benefits.

"I will not yield. I will not yield," Rockefeller said. "The only power I have on this as a single senator is — I will not yield."

After the cloture vote, negotiators on the dispute continued to work through the night, and by the morning of July 24 reportedly had agreed to the principles of a settlement.

### Coal Accord Reached

By July 28 negotiators were confident that a deal was set.

Senate leaders had scheduled a second cloture vote to limit debate and allow a vote on the revised bill, but Wallop said that vote was simply a formality; Republicans who had voted against bringing the bill to the floor the previous week wanted an opportunity to show their support for the measure given that the coal dispute was supposedly resolved.

But even as senators began the successful cloture vote, the coal deal was unraveling.

It took until about 11 that night to resolve the snag, finally clearing the way for floor consideration of the energy bill the next day.

The compromise proposal abandoned the notion of a new coal tax and instead sought to bail out the anemic health fund with a package of measures.

The plan called for using a "reach back" formula that would trace as many retired miners as possible back to their previous employers or, if that company has gone out of business, a related company.

The plan would shift $210 million over three years from the union's overstocked pension fund into the health fund. And after 1995, it would also tap interest on the Abandoned Mine Lands fund for up to $70 million a year. The abandoned lands fund, which was filled by a fee on coal companies, was created to reclaim old mining lands.

The plan would also protect the health benefits of as many as 100,000 additional miners, covered under the old contracts, whose companies might go bankrupt. In exchange for these new guarantees for the fund, union lobbyists agreed to impose cost controls on the health fund.

Johnston, who had feared Rockefeller's proposal would bring down his energy bill, on the Senate floor tipped his hat to the West Virginian's ultimate success: "... He brought us to the brink of disaster and, at the last minute, scooped the baby off the tracks — and in the process saved the coal miners of West Virginia."

And the coal provisions proved solidly fused enough to survive yet another test: House Republican conferees and Democratic conferee J. J. Pickle, D-Texas, while negotiating the tax issues during conference action on the energy bill again threatened to remove the one Rockefeller had pushed.

Pickle eventually agreed to the coal provision in order to let the energy bill go forward, but said it was unfair to make companies with no current connection to the coal business pay for some of the miner benefits: "It is as if we are a street gang mugging an innocent passer-by, and justifying it by saying that our family and friends are hungry."

But Rockefeller and other proponents stood their ground and the language eventually passed as part of the overall energy bill.

### Uranium Enrichment

The most extensive scuffle of the markup came over the bill's complicated proposal to revive the Energy Department's flagging uranium enrichment operations. Enriched uranium was used in nuclear defense work and in civilian power plants.

To help make the enrichment operations more profitable, the bill authorized a new government corporation to move ahead on uranium enrichment.

The bill also sought to ensure that $500 million a year would go to clean up the existing enrichment facilities, with the money to come from corporation profits. But if profits were insufficient, the bill would mandate a backup fee on enrichment customers to make up the difference.

During full committee markup, Sharp offered an amendment to specify how the fee would be assessed on utilities that used enrichment services.

Peter H. Kostmayer, D-Pa., strongly objected to that proposal, saying that enrichment plants were first built for defense needs and civilian utilities should not be forced to bear a heavy share of the cleanup costs.

Kostmayer proposed capping the utilities' share of the cleanup costs at $2.8 billion.

But Sharp and others said the utilities were trying to get a free ride by shifting costs to the Defense Department and foreign customers.

Kostmayer eventually withdrew his amendment, and Sharp's revised proposal was approved, 13-3.

The vote delighted the National Taxpayers Union, which for years has crusaded to make utilities that bought enriched uranium pick up a larger share of the operation's expenses.

## OTHER COMMITTEE ACTION

After Energy and Commerce moved, there were related markups in eight additional committees. The most significant additions came in the Interior and Merchant Marine

panels, each of which added provisions sought by environmentalists such as offshore drilling bans, and in Ways and Means, which added an entire new section of energy-related tax provisions.

Five other committees — Public Works, Science, Foreign Affairs, Judiciary and Government Operations — made smaller additions or revisions. There was considerable confusion about how to reconcile the competing committee agendas prior to floor action. It took House Speaker Thomas S. Foley, D-Wash., and the Rules Committees to referee some of the disagreements and get one bill to the floor.

### Energy Taxes

When Ways and Means drafted a tax bill in February, it generally ignored pleas from both environmentalists and energy industry lobbyists to adopt tax measures that would help guide energy policy.

But the committee was in a different mood when it turned to the energy bill the week of April 27, adopting tax breaks from both sets of wish lists.

Environmental lobbyists won a "green" tax package designed to promote renewable energy, conservation and cars that ran on non-gasoline fuels.

Most controversial was a new tax credit for energy produced from wind or biomass — burning crops to produce energy. Robert T. Matsui, D-Calif., sponsored the proposal, which would provide a credit for such energy of 1.5 cents per kilowatt-hour. It was approved by voice vote.

Another California Democrat, Pete Stark, lost, 9-21, an attempt to limit the credit to biomass alone, saying wind energy already could compete without federal help.

Without debate, the committee also agreed to new tax incentives for cars and other vehicles that ran on so-called alternative fuels such as natural gas or alcohol-based fuel, as well as for refueling stations for those vehicles.

Members also agreed to extend an existing investment tax credit for solar and geothermal energy and to adjust tax treatment of employer-provided transit subsidies to put more emphasis on mass transit and less on commuting by car.

To pay for these tax breaks, members agreed to phase out tax deductions that encouraged development of certain minerals, such as lead and mercury, and to increase excise taxes on certain chemicals that deplete the ozone layer. However, individual members won exemptions for a small group of chlorofluorocarbons and some halons used as fire retardants.

Ways and Means also offered some solace to independent oil and gas drillers, who had made tax reform a top priority.

Many drillers fell under the so-called alternative minimum tax, a formula designed to ensure that corporations paid some taxes regardless of how many deductions were claimed. Drillers had complained that the minimum tax stifled production because they could not write off as much of their drilling and exploration costs as they once could under the regular tax code.

Bill Archer, R-Texas, ranking Republican on Ways and Means, on April 29 originally offered an amendment to allow all oil and gas companies to write off more of their expenses under the minimum tax, but was defeated 16-20.

The next day, Archer returned with a more modest version that would only apply to independent drillers, not the large integrated oil corporations. It was approved 19-16.

On several other issues where Ways and Means shared juridiction with Energy and Commerce, the tax-writing panel staked out a rival position.

On oil, the Energy-approved bill would have forced importers and refiners to send about 1 percent of their oil or a cash equivalent to the Strategic Petroleum Reserve unless the administration dramatically speeded up filling the reserve.

But Ways and Means approved, 23-12, an amendment by Michael A. Andrews, D-Texas, to strike the set-aside from the energy bill. Several members said the reserve benefits all taxpayers and should be filled through general appropriations, not a de-facto oil tax.

The two committes also clashed over Energy and Commerce's uranium enrichment proposal, which included a potential fee on nuclear utilities to help clean up the government's aging enrichment plants.

Energy and Commerce had rejected calls to cap the amount of such a fee. However, Ways and Means Chairman Dan Rostenkowski, D-Ill., included a $2.5 billion ceiling in his version of the bill, which the committee approved with little debate.

### Interior Committee

In the Interior and Insular Affairs Committee, Chairman George Miller, D-Calif., moved aggressively to place an environmental mark on the evolving House energy bill. Miller drafted a 16-title bill that was amended during a marathon markup session April 8, and approved the next day on a largely partisan 29-15 vote.

The Interior bill included many provisions on controversial nuclear issues, including plant licensing and radioactive waste. Other sections addressed offshore drilling, restructuring the government's uranium enrichment enterprise and energy production on federal lands.

Committee Republicans and a coalition of energy industry groups attacked Miller's proposals, saying they would greatly restrict additional nuclear and offshore energy production.

"Where is the energy in this energy bill?" Rep. Joel Hefley, R-Colo., complained of the package.

Only two Republicans, Barbara F. Vucanovich, Nev., and Guam Delegate Ben Blaz, voted to report the bill.

The Interior bill conflicted with Energy and Commerce's legislation in several areas where the two panels shared jurisdiction. And the Bush administration strongly opposed Miller's proposal, particularly its provisions regarding nuclear power.

But environmentalists warmly embraced the Miller plan, saying it would bring balance to an energy package that they said was dominated by industry interests.

During committee markup, most of the debate focused on the nuclear industry.

The parallel Senate energy bill contained language to streamline the licensing process for nuclear plants. Miller's bill also included an overhaul of the licensing process but guaranteed greater access for critics to raise safety issues.

Although some Republicans criticized the licensing provisions, they did not try to strike them. And during markup, members adopted two amendments placing further potential restrictions on licensing new nuclear plants.

Nuclear power advocates also were on the losing side of two votes involving a high-level nuclear waste dump and the government's uranium enrichment program.

At Vucanovich's urging, members defeated a provision in the Energy Committee bill that would have helped the

federal government build a nuclear waste dump at Yucca Mountain, Nev.

Administration officials thought Nevada would delay needed permits for the dump studies, and the Energy Committee bill would have allowed the federal government to pre-empt state environmental laws.

On uranium enrichment, the Interior bill would have restructured the current federal program and — like the Energy and Commerce-approved version — potentially levy a fee on nuclear utilities to help pay for cleaning up the aging enrichment plants.

Kostmayer unsuccessfully offered an amendment that would have capped the utilities' share of the cleanup at $2.5 billion. A similar amendment had been rejected in the Energy committee and failed again, 19-26, in Interior. However, the Ways and Means Committee — which shared jurisdiction on that aspect of the uranium enrichment proposal — had approved such a cap.

But the nuclear industry won one battle when the committee narrowly killed a provision that would have let states veto federal license renewals for existing plants. Several dozen nuclear plant licenses were to expire within the next 20 years, and the industry was eager to keep many of the plants in service. Rep. Calvin Dooley, D-Calif., who offered the amendment striking the provision, said such veto authority would unfairly open the relicensing process to political pressures.

Addressing numerous complex and controversial rules regarding radioactive waste, the bill would allow states to control the disposal of certain low-level radioactive waste if the federal government pursued plans to deregulate it. Members also voted, 10-6, to add language by Rep. Jim Jontz, D-Ind., allowing states to close their borders to low-level waste but not to exclude the transport of waste through their states.

## Coastal Drilling Ban

The Interior bill also included new restrictions on coastal drilling. It banned new drilling off the East and West coasts, in Alaska's Bristol Bay and off Florida until 2002.

Members agreed to devote 3 percent of federal revenues from offshore drilling to an environmental protection fund for coastal states. But they rejected amendments that would have placed a short-term moratorium on existing drilling off the Florida Panhandle and directed the administration to buy back 73 leases in the Florida Keys.

The Merchant Marine and Fisheries Committee shared jurisdiction on coastal drilling and on April 30 approved its own proposals for the energy bill.

The committee had earlier approved extensive coastal drilling bans in a freestanding bill (HR 4722) by Chairman Walter B. Jones, D-N.C. Members voted 28-16 to attach the Jones bill to the omnibus energy package. They subsequently reported the amended energy bill by voice vote.

In addition to placing most of the nation's coastal waters off limits until the year 2000 and restricting future leases, the committee's amendments would have tapped offshore drilling revenues to help coastal states finance environmental projects and aid developing countries in reducing greenhouse gases.

Merchant Marine's proposal set out a shorter drilling ban than the Interior bill, blocking new oil and gas leases until 2000 instead of 2002.

But other provisions were more restrictive. The committee voted, 32-12, to strengthen the bill's original drilling ban on portions of the Gulf of Mexico up to 30 miles off the Florida coast, extending it westward. The bill also would encourage the administration to buy back some existing leases.

However both sets of drilling proposals went beyond existing moratoriums announced by President Bush in June 1990. And both bills drew veto threats and a heavy counterattack from the energy industry.

Energy Secretary Watkins accused the committees of seeking to capsize energy legislation to damage the administration.

## Science, Space and Technology

The Science, Space and Technology Committee on April 1 approved, by voice vote, a five-year, $17.2 billion energy research and development bill and folded it into the larger energy package (HR 776). The committee also approved the narrower research bill (HR 4559).

The action came over the objections of Science Committee Republicans, who said the broad authorization levels in the research measure amounted to an invitation to House appropriators to make energy policy.

Ranking Science Committee member Robert S. Walker, R-Pa., said the Science Committee bill "is a $17 billion uncontrolled spending plan" that conceded all specifics and project decisions to appropriators. He said the committee was "throwing make-believe money at the problem."

Opposition from Republicans mounted after the committee defeated two GOP efforts to scale back the bill's authorization levels. A less costly Republican substitute that would have authorized spending for fiscal 1993 alone, rather than over five years, was turned back by a 10-12 show of hands; the committee also rejected, on a party-line 20-32 vote, an effort to cap the authorization level for fiscal 1993 at $2.4 billion, as Bush requested in his budget.

Overall, the bill sought to provide a modest increase for energy-related research and to tilt that spending away from coal and nuclear fission toward conservation, renewable energy, advanced oil recovery and nuclear fusion.

Although Science Committee members had made previous attempts to pass authorizing bills for energy programs, those efforts had consistently sputtered out. In the Senate, Sen. J. Bennett Johnston, D-La., chaired both the appropriations and authorizations panels in charge of Energy Department spending and had little incentive to tie his own hands.

The Science committee also approved, by voice vote, an amendment that would create a national research program to determine whether electromagnetic radiation from such sources as electric power lines and appliances caused health problems.

And it approved its own version of the proposal to restructure the government's troubled uranium enrichment program into a government-owned corporation.

Four other committees — Foreign Affairs, Government Operations, Judiciary and Public Works — made relatively minor changes to portions of the Energy and Commerce bill.

Most of the changes sought to clarify committee jurisdiction over parts of the bill or to bring its provisions into accord with other bills.

## Other Committee Input

The draft approved April 30 by the Government Operations Committee:

● Adjusted provisions affecting federal energy conserva-

tion and use of alternative fuels, including requiring agencies to list their energy costs as a separate line item and giving them until the year 2005 — five years longer than the Energy and Commerce bill — to install conservation measures that would pay for themselves within 10 years.

The draft approved April 30 by the Public Works Committee:

● Reworked sections of the bill aimed at streamlining federal rate-making for oil pipelines, and partly grandfathered in some existing pipeline rates.

● Removed some special privileges for drivers of vehicles that used non-gasoline fuels, such as natural gas or methanol.

The draft approved April 30 by the Judiciary Committee:

● Reworked a provision that would give the Federal Energy Regulatory Commission the increased authority to weigh anti-trust issues when deciding whether to mandate that utilities provide access to their transmission lines.

● Added language protecting the financial stake of certain investors in oil and gas resources that were entangled in bankruptcy proceedings.

The draft approved April 29 by the Foreign Affairs Committee:

● Fine-tuned provisions to promote the export of so-called clean coal and renewable energy technologies.

### Parliamentary Muddle

Energy Chairman Dingell initially resisted incorporating the other committees' amendments into his draft, but Speaker Foley held a meeting with the chairmen on May 12 and urged them to resolve as many disagreements as possible.

In the following days, committee staff did just that, and panels with relatively minor amendments were able to wrap up their negotiations quickly. But some major stumbling blocks remained on issues such as uranium enrichment, nuclear power and the Strategic Petroleum Reserve — issues that put Energy and Commerce at odds with the Interior and Ways and Means committees.

When the Rules Committee convened May 19, it faced sizable disputes between rival committee chairmen as well as proposed amendments from individual members. All told, members and chairmen requested more than 140 amendments. Some were hedges because members and even chairmen did not know the text of the final bill.

Negotiations continued off stage while the Rules Committee took more than five hours of testimony. By the time the panel was ready to draw up a framework for the bill, some disputes had disappeared.

Still, the Rules panel failed to wade through all of the disputes in time to meet the leadership's schedule and had to issue guidelines for floor consideration in two parts. The second half of the floor rule was not issued until after the House had debated the bill for a full day.

Panel Republicans went along with the procedure but first seized on the confusion as proof that the committee system was hopelessly diffuse and should be reformed.

## HOUSE FLOOR ACTION

The energy bill debated on the House floor was not expected to dramatically decrease the nation's dependence on foreign oil but it did signal a movement away from the laissez-faire energy policies that dominated the 1980s.

Some of the bill's most significant provisions were decided without floor votes. For example, the House Rules Committee decided to include sweeping bans on offshore oil and gas drilling that had been approved in the Interior and Merchant Marine committees. And Rules refused to allow a separate floor vote to strike or limit the bans, effectively sealing them in place in the overall House bill.

The bill also included a sweeping overhaul of the federal law governing electric utilities, tax incentives for renewable energy and cars that ran on non-gasoline fuels, and tax relief for independent oil and gas drillers — none of which were subject to amendments.

Four House committees had agreed on restructuring the government's uranium enrichment program, but disagreed about how to allocate costs for cleaning up the old enrichment plants. At issue was how much nuclear utilities that bought uranium from the plants should pay for the cleanup and how much the federal government should pay. The panels agreed to a compromise — approved by Rules — that would create a 15-year cleanup account, to be funded at $500 million a year. Utilities would pay about 30 percent of that, roughly $155 million the first year, but no more than $2.5 billion over 15 years.

### Nuclear Wins

The House voted to adopt expedited licensing procedures for new nuclear plants, handing an important victory for the nuclear power industry.

Concern about global warming and passage of the 1990 amendments to the Clean Air Act had generated renewed interest in nuclear power, which did not generate the damaging emissions created by coal or gas-fired power plants. But no one had been sure whether that interest would translate into floor votes for the industry.

The parallel Senate energy bill already contained licensing provisions favored by the nuclear industry, so the issue was poised to be debated in conference. At issue was what bargaining position, if any, the House would endorse.

The Energy and Commerce Committee remained silent on the issue. But the Interior panel had added a licensing proposal that the industry said would be used to block plant operations unfairly.

The bill sent to the House floor included Interior's licensing overhaul, but critics were also given the right to offer a substitute version that was advocated by the nuclear industry — the same language included in the Senate energy bill.

On the floor, Miller argued that public distrust, not regulatory tangles, had brought the nuclear industry to a standstill.

But supporters said licensing took far longer in this country than in Western Europe or Japan and characterized the vote as a referendum on whether the country would retain even the possibility of building new nuclear plants.

The final tally was not even close. The House adopted the pro-nuclear language in place of Interior's proposal 254-160, almost a 100-vote margin. *(Vote 134, p. 34-H)*

The licensing debate was largely an academic one because no utilities had ordered new nuclear plants or wereexpected to do so soon. But the vote was a significant symbolic win for an industry that had been on the defensive, and it was bolstered by a second pro-industry vote on high-level radioactive waste.

Over the strenuous objections of the Nevada delegation, members by voice vote agreed to allow the federal government to pre-empt state permitting laws as it studied whether to build a high-level waste dump at Yucca Mountain, Nevada. Energy and Commerce Chairman Dingell,

who had added the plan to his committee's bill only to have it stripped out in Interior, offered the amendment to restore it.

But Dingell did not try to reinsert a related proposal he had put into the bill during committee markup pertaining to plans for a temporary radioactive waste dump. The language would have effectively singled out Nevada as the host state for the temporary dump, as well as the odds-on favorite for the permanent repository.

## Pro-Rationing

The regional disputes that had dominated the energy policy debates of the 1970s and '80s re-emerged in the floor fight over new gas production restrictions that were being adopted or discussed in Oklahoma, Texas and Louisiana.

Gas states had retained for many years so-called pro-rationing policies limiting production to ensure proper management of wells and to protect the rights of multiple drillers drawing from the same gas reservoir.

But critics said the newer proposals went beyond such policies and were instead aimed at increasing gas prices by decreasing production.

Edward J. Markey, D-Mass., and James H. Scheuer, D-N.Y., sponsored an amendment to create federal oversight of such state production limits and prohibit such measures when they were aimed at increasing gas prices.

Markey said prices had jumped since states such as Oklahoma had begun adopting the new policies and warned that the trend could cost consumers $6 billion over the following year. He indicated that 38 states were net gas importers, while 12 were net exporters.

Gas-state members lashed out at the proposal as an assault on states' rights. They said the restrictions were not aimed at boosting prices and that gas producers were not the ones benefiting from the recent price surge.

But Markey won on a 238-169 vote that split heavily along regional lines. *(Vote 135, 18-S)*

## New Consensus

Sharp said the bill heralded an emerging consensus on federal energy policy, noting that there was little controversy over some of the bill's significant provisions to promote energy efficiency and alternative fuels and to overhaul federal utility regulations.

The utility provisions involved changing the 1935 Public Utility Holding Company Act (PUHCA) to make it easier for independent companies to produce and sell power on the wholesale market.

The so-called PUHCA reform was once thought to be a political tar baby that would muck up the entire energy bill. But the consensus version drafted in Energy and Commerce left critics outnumbered, and no one tried to offer an amendment to delete or change the provision.

However, there was one major floor fight on the bill's provisions to encourage the use of non-gasoline transportation fuels, such as ethanol, methanol, natural gas and electricity.

Jontz wanted to boost the use of ethanol, an alternative fuel derived from corn, by requiring that it be used to enhance the octane content of gasoline. The proposal sought to establish that gasoline contain 8 percent ethanol by 2006.

Jontz and his allies said the ethanol would help cut oil imports and would replace current octane enhancers that were environmentally damaging.

But the amendment fell prey to an array of critics and was defeated, 198-211. *(Vote 133, p. 18-S)*

Some objected to a mandate that they said would boost gas prices and give ethanol an unfair advantage over other alternative fuels. Others worried that ethanol, while less toxic than existing octane enhancers, would generate higher smog-causing emissions.

On energy efficiency, the House voted, 328-79, to adopt national efficiency standards for plumbing equipment. The vote strengthened the bill's overall measures to boost the energy efficiency of federal agencies, buildings, and electric appliances and motors *(Vote 132, p. 18-S)*

The House removed one key difference with the Senate — and the administration — during its final day of floor debate. On a 263-135 vote, members excised a proposal that would have forced oil importers and refiners to help fill the Strategic Petroleum Reserve, the nation's oil stockpile. *(Vote 140, p. 19-S)*

Ways and Means Chairman Dan Rostenkowski offered the floor amendment to remove the oil set-aside, and members voted almost 2-to-1 to delete the provision despite strong appeals to preserve it.

Congress has in the past refused to appropriate enough money to fill the reserve, and Gerry E. Studds, D-Mass., called it "hallucinatory" to think it would do so soon, with budgets tighter than ever. "I don't think hoping and praying and wishing and dreaming are sufficient grounds for public policy," Studds said.

## Radioactive Waste

Members agreed to a provision that could permit states to begin regulating radioactive materials in the absence of federal oversight.

The provision involved certain low-level radioactive materials known as "below regulatory concern" waste.

The Nuclear Regulatory Commission had proposed deregulating these materials and allowing them to be placed in regular landfills — prompting an outcry from environmental groups — but had not yet implemented the controversial plan.

The Interior Committee in October 1991 approved a bill (HR 645) to thwart the proposal and later added similar language to the energy measure. It specified that if the federal government went ahead with plans to deregulate the waste, the states would be empowered to start policing it.

Energy Committee Chairman Dingell initially fought to keep the measure out of the energy bill, but as the floor debate advanced he negotiated a compromise with the Interior Committee. The compromise retained conditional state power to regulate the disputed radioactive material but imposed more-stringent conditions on granting that state authority.

In exchange, Interior agreed to drop another controversial proposal to require the Environmental Protection Agency to issue cleanup standards for sites with radiation contamination. Dingell's compromise amendment was approved by voice vote.

In another vote, Sam Gejdenson, D-Conn., sought to add new restrictions on low-level waste disposal but was turned back on a 117-293 vote. *(Vote 141, p. 19-S)*

## Energy vs. Environment

The House also tussled over a series of proposals regarding energy development on public lands that were approved by the Interior Committee as part of its energy

package but opposed by Energy and Commerce.

The Interior Committee had endorsed proposals to restrict hydroelectric power development on public lands, including banning new dams and dam relicensing in national parks and allowing states to veto dams on rivers subject to state environmental protection.

On the floor, Interior Chairman Miller successfully added those restrictions to the overall energy bill on a 318-98 vote. *(Vote 143, p. 19-S)*

Miller and other supporters of the restrictions said the Federal Energy Regulatory Commission, which oversaw the licensing, could not be trusted to take into account the environmental threats posed by the dams, and they characterized the amendment as a boost for environmental and states' rights.

The administration fiercely opposed the proposal, saying it would run counter to its own efforts to streamline hydropower licensing.

Dingell tried to head off Miller and his supporters with a compromise offer: Dingell's amendment would have placed some new environmental restrictions on hydroelectric projects, but substantially fewer than the Miller proposal.

Members voted on Dingell's substitute first, splitting almost evenly. But in the final minutes of the vote, several members switched their votes to oppose Dingell, and the measure was defeated 195-221. Lawmakers then adopted Miller's language. *(Vote 142, p. 19-S)*

Dingell and Miller jockeyed over Interior's proposals on coal, and oil and gas leases on federal lands.

Interior had approved a series of provisions to encourage drawing coal from abandoned mines and to strengthen environmental protection for coal development.

In this case, Miller and other key members of Interior accepted a Dingell compromise version that included somewhat fewer environmental safeguards. Dingell's version was adopted by voice vote.

Rep. Craig Thomas, R-Wyo., tried to delete one part of the package — to extend an existing coal fee used to pay for mine reclamation. But members rebuffed Thomas on a voice vote and retained the provision to extend the fee an additional 15 years.

### Assessments

Few lawmakers or lobbyists were thrilled with the final product, which stopped well short of the environmental wish list on the one hand and the energy producers' desires on the other. But virtually all factions found something to like in the bill, or at least not too much to dislike.

Members from several gas-producing states were the exception. They were enraged by a provision limiting states' rights to regulate gas production. Of the 37 members who voted against the bill, 20 were from the gas-producing states of Oklahoma and Texas.

Although the Bush administration still had qualms about several of those provisions, Energy Secretary Watkins praised the package as a step toward the most "comprehensive and balanced energy legislation ... seen in 20 years."

Lawmakers from both parties generally praised it as an important step toward controlling, if not ending, oil dependency.

"[The bill] will take giant steps toward easing this nation's oil addiction and put us on a firm course toward a more secure energy future," said Sharp, the bill's chief architect.

## SENATE ACTION

Senators on July 30 voted 93-3 to attach energy-related tax proposals to an energy policy bill they had passed in February. Minutes later, they sent the revised package to conference with a parallel House measure (HR 776), which passed May 27. *(Vote 163, p. 22-S)*

Although the Senate had approved an energy bill earlier in the year, House passage of a parallel bill did not automatically clear the way for the two measures to go to conference.

Instead, Sen. J. Bennett Johnston, D-La., and other supporters of the Senate energy bill had to weave in new tax provisions, negotiate several filibuster threats and conduct a second round of floor debate before the two energy proposals could meet in a House-Senate conference.

### Taxes

The Senate energy bill (S 2166) approved in February contained no tax measures. But after the House added tax items to its parallel bill, Finance Chairman Lloyd Bentsen, D-Texas, insisted that his panel be given a chance to draft its own energy taxes before the two measures went to conference.

The Senate Finance Committee on June 16 approved a package of energy-related tax provisions, paralleling many of the tax items included in the House-passed energy bill (HR 776).

The package would provide tax incentives for renewable energy, conservation and cars that run on clean-burning fuels, and give tax relief to independent oil and gas drillers.

To pay for these items, the panel proposed closing a loophole that let taxpayers deduct some club dues and increasing the tax on some ozone-depleting chemicals.

However, senators made some adjustments to the House tax provisions and added a highly controversial coal tax to help pay for health benefits for retired miners. The coal provision, by John D. Rockefeller IV, D-W.Va., was approved 10-8. *(Miners' benefits, p. 236)*

Although the tax provisions technically were approved as amendments to the House energy bill, the plan was to add them to the overall Senate energy legislation.

### Drillers' Relief

The proposed relief for independent oil and gas drillers was the most expensive tax break in the package, estimated to cost about $1 billion over five years.

Like a similar provision in the House bill, the Senate proposal would let drillers write off some exploration costs even if they paid the so-called alternative minimum tax, a formula that ensured that all corporations paid some taxes and that denied those benefits.

The House provision was temporary, but the Senate proposal would make the tax change permanent.

Bill Bradley, D-N.J., made an unsuccessful attempt to strike the proposal, saying it could not be justified in tight fiscal times, given other unmet needs.

Bradley sought to put the tax in perspective by drawing a sharp comparison with Bush's proposed urban aid plan, which he said would cost about $2 billion. "This is a subsidy to oil and gas that is equal to half of what the president has proposed to do for all of urban America," Bradley said.

But Boren reminded colleagues that independent drillers were in dire straits, with the number of active onshore rigs at the lowest level on record: "This is not a

# High Noon at Yucca Mountain

In the final days of the session, the fate of the energy bill hung on a legislative face-off between Sen. J. Bennett Johnston, D-La., and Nevada's two Democratic senators, Harry Reid and Richard H. Bryan.

It was the latest battleground for a raging dispute over plans to put a nuclear waste dump at Yucca Mountain, Nev.: a battle that pitted Johnston's political strength as a powerful chairman against the institutional strength the Senate allotted every senator to defend his state's interests.

In late 1987 Johnston engineered a conference agreement naming Yucca Mountain as the sole site to be considered for a planned federal dump to store high-level nuclear waste. Reid held up that legislation with filibuster threats for several weeks, although the proposal eventually became law.

In 1992, chairing final House-Senate negotiations on a massive energy policy bill, Johnston insisted on adding new language to help the government open the proposed Yucca dump.

But no sooner had Johnston inserted the Yucca Mountain provision than Bryan began issuing filibuster threats anew. Those threats quickly blossomed into a formal campaign by Bryan and Reid against the energy bill, although one that would ultimately end in failure: The Senate on Oct. 8 voted 84-8 against the two and in favor of completing work on the energy bill. *(Vote 266, p. 35-S)*

"We face this every time there is an opportunity to screw Nevada — there is an appetite to do so," Bryan said.

## Showdown

Shortly after the conference committee approved the disputed provision, Johnston discounted the likelihood that Bryan would make good on his filibuster threats or that they would succeed.

"We can't let one man stop the whole energy bill," Johnston said.

But others familiar with Bryan and Reid on this issue had no doubts that they would try and try hard.

Bryan ousted Nevada's Republican Sen. Chic Hecht in the fall of 1988 largely on the basis of Hecht's belated opposition to the planned Yucca dump. And Hecht's malapropism — he once said he did not want the state to become "a nuclear suppository" — did little to persuade Nevadans of the seriousness with which he approached the issue.

With Bryan's election, the Nevada congressional delegation and Nevada Gov. Bob Miller were united in opposition to the dump — a position that reflected prevailing political sentiment in the state. And because individual senators wield far more power institutionally than House members, Reid and Bryan in particular had been expected to carry the battle against the dump even at the cost of an energy bill.

"There is no downside for the Nevada delegation in killing this bill," said Daniel Becker, a Sierra Club lobbyist.

## Reprise

Going into the fight, Reid and Bryan already had won one showdown with Johnston over the energy bill. In July, they forced Johnston to pledge to oppose a House-sponsored provision that would have let the federal government bypass state environmental permit requirements as it studied the proposed dump site.

Johnston honored that pledge, but in conference insisted on a different provision that critics said could lead to unsafe radiation exposure standards for the dump.

The House bill had directed the Environmental Protection Agency (EPA) to reinstate 1985 standards governing the disposal of nuclear waste to protect public health, except for portions that had been struck down by a federal court.

But Johnston instead wanted the agency to issue new standards specifically tailored to the Yucca Mountain site. Johnston, who was eager to move ahead with the proposed dump, said the old standards might require the government to make huge expenditures without providing any added health benefits for Nevada residents.

Under his proposal, later adopted by the conference committee, the new standards would be based on a study to be conducted by the National Academy of Sciences (NAS).

The Nevada delegation and several environmental groups protested that Johnston was trying to fix the regulatory process in favor of opening the Yucca dump and at the expense of Nevadans' health.

Johnston and some other lawmakers countered that such criticisms were overstated or off-base.

Report language accompanying the bill specified that the NAS study could look at issues not mentioned in the bill, including collective doses of radiation. And it stated that the EPA would not be strictly bound by the findings or parameters of the study when it made its final rule.

But critics were not assuaged, in part citing confusion over the legal implications of the provisions. And they noted that Johnston began by attempting to write specific disposal standards into the energy bill, settling for the milder language after House negotiators refused to go along.

When the House took up the final energy bill Oct. 5, Barbara F. Vucanovich, R-Nev., offered a motion designed to strip the Yucca Mountain language from the final energy bill. The House rebuffed the effort on a 102-323 vote. *(Vote 473, p. 116-H)*

That left the matter to the Senate, where only six senators joined Reid and Bryan to oppose cloture on the energy bill.

But the Nevadans were not expected to allow their crusade to die. Reid and Bryan both said they had done their best and would continue to fight the dump.

"People said this was a done deal three years ago. They're saying the same thing today. And they're wrong," Bryan said. "I remain confident there will be no nuclear dump at Yucca Mountain."

case of crying wolf."

And Dole stressed the importance of helping domestic producers by recalling the Persian Gulf War: "There are only three letters why we were in the gulf: they are O-I-L."

Bradley's amendment to strike the tax relief was defeated, 6-14.

Senators also approved a series of tax measures to promote non-conventional fuels and fuel conservation.

Tom Daschle, D-S.D., won support, 15-5, for broadening existing tax breaks for ethanol.

The amendment also broadened a tax credit that producers of ethanol-blended fuels could take as an alternative to the fuel-tax exemption. Daschle's amendment allowed the credit to be taken under the alternative minimum tax as well as the regular tax code.

Finance also approved tax breaks for buyers of cars that run on clean-burning fuels, such as natural gas or electricity.

The House bill included a similar provision, but Donald W. Riegle Jr., D-Mich., claimed that approach favored natural gas over other alternative fuels. He persuaded his colleagues to adopt a different version of the proposal.

Riegle's amendment gave car buyers a $2,000 deduction for cars that run solely on natural gas.

It provided a $1,200 deduction for owners of cars that used other alternative fuels and up to $2,000 if buyers could prove that they spent more than $1,200 to convert the car to run on an alternative fuel.

Staff members said there would also be a 25 percent tax credit for the cost of buying electric vehicles and larger tax breaks for alternative-fuel trucks, buses and refueling equipment.

The provision was approved by voice vote after senators defeated, 9-11, an earlier version of the amendment.

On another issue, John B. Breaux, D-La., won support for an amendment that would give regulated, integrated natural gas companies some of the same tax advantages then limited to independent producers.

Breaux said the companies needed flexibility to write off some of their exploration costs. He said the companies could not exploit the advantages enjoyed by independent producers because their gas systems were regulated by public service commissions. His amendment passed 13-7.

In other votes, the panel:

● Rejected, 8-12, a Bradley amendment to eliminate existing tax breaks for the production of lead, mercury, uranium and asbestos. Bradley's proposal tracked language in the House bill that also would eliminate those tax advantages.

● Rejected, 1-19, Delaware Republican William V. Roth Jr.'s proposal to give a $100 tax credit to people who turn in old, inefficient cars.

## The Road to Conference

The Finance markup represented one step forward toward getting the bill to conference and one step back: The Bush administration and many Senate Republicans fiercely opposed Rockefeller's coal tax, threatening progress of the overall energy bill. However, Rockefeller refused to back off the proposal.

The bill also faced determined opposition from Nevada senators who threatened a filibuster over a House provision to make it easier for the federal government to build a nuclear waste dump at Yucca Mountain, Nev.

Johnston, who routinely redefined parliamentary audacity, sprang into action, using his clout as chairman of both the Energy Committee and the Appropriations subcommittee responsible for the energy and water development bill.

When Johnston called a markup of the appropriations bill on July 21, he announced that he had attached both House and Senate versions of the omnibus energy bill as a backdoor way to get them into conference.

Johnston's Appropriations panel approved the spending bill by voice vote, with the energy bills attached.

But that strategy did not get far.

Byrd, who was chairman of the full Appropriations Committee and who shared Rockefeller's attentiveness to the coal miners in his state, promptly canceled a full committee markup scheduled for July 22.

Byrd marked up the spending measure later in the week but on the condition that the energy bills would be jettisoned or revisited before the bill was sent to the Senate floor.

## Yucca Mountain

Johnston's next step was to strike a deal with the Nevada senators.

The two sides had been negotiating over the Yucca Mountain issue for weeks. Although Johnston earlier had agreed to oppose the House pre-emption language, he would not rule out other provisions dealing with nuclear waste and warned that his offer came with a time limit.

That was not good enough for Democratic Sens. Harry Reid and Richard H. Bryan, who set about making good on threats to filibuster or otherwise delay the energy bill.

Bryan's office said it had prepared more than 100 amendments to offer should the bill come to the Senate floor.

In the end, Johnston went to the Senate floor on July 22 to publicly assure the Nevadans that he would work to keep Yucca Mountain out of the bill that emerged from conference.

Johnston also said he would fight any attempt to put a temporary nuclear waste dump in Nevada or to store waste at the Yucca Mountain site on a trial basis.

That left only the coal dispute in the way of taking up the energy bill.

Rockefeller's proposal brought down the wrath of the administration and of Malcolm Wallop, R-Wyo., who vowed to bring down the energy bill he helped write rather than let the tax go through.

Although both sides negotiated furiously to compromise, they did not succeed in time for a July 23 motion to limit debate. Senators voted 58-33 to proceed with the bill, two votes shy of the 60 votes needed to invoke cloture. (Vote 150, p. 20-S)

Only three Republicans, Don Nickles of Oklahoma, Charles E. Grassley of Iowa and Arlen Specter of Pennsylvania, broke ranks and voted to bring the bill to the floor.

It was an ironic reverse image of November 1991, when Wallop and administration lobbyists criticized environmentalists and their allies for successfully filibustering an earlier version of the energy bill.

When the cloture vote failed, the administration sought to blame Rockefeller and the Democratic leadership.

"The Rockefeller coal tax amendment should never have been able to delay or scuttle the energy bill," Energy Secretary Watkins said in a prepared statement.

But Johnston, chief sponsor of the Senate energy bill, said those who supported the filibuster were potentially dooming the sweeping legislation. Democrats voted uni-

formly to invoke cloture.

And Rockefeller earlier in the day defended his determined stance. While he supported the energy bill, the West Virginian said, he could not abandon his fight to secure the threatened benefits.

After the first cloture vote, however, negotiators pressed on until they reached a settlement. The compromise proposal abandoned the notion of a new coal tax and instead sought to bail out the anemic health fund with a package of measures.

Senate leaders scheduled a second July 27 cloture vote to limit debate and allow a vote on the revised bill, but Wallop said that vote was a formality; Republicans who had voted against bringing the bill to the floor the previous week wanted an opportunity to show their support for the measure given that the coal dispute was supposedly resolved.

But even as senators began the 93-3 cloture vote, the coal deal was unraveling. It took until about 11 that night to resolve the snag, finally clearing the way for floor consideration of the energy bill the next day. *(Vote 154, 21-S)*

## SENATE FLOOR DEBATE

The floor debate began July 28, once the coal tax settlement was in hand. Senators approved that compromise, which did not include an industrywide coal tax, on voice vote.

Although the full Senate had debated and passed a version of the major energy bill in February, it took three days of floor action to review the new tax provisions approved by the Finance Committee and to make final adjustments in the base bill.

Much of that time was devoted to unrelated disputes such as health care and financial partnerships, as senators scrambled to attach floundering bills to the more buoyant energy legislation.

### Aid to Drillers

Senators turned back an attempt to remove the bill's tax relief for independent oil and gas drillers.

The proposal, similar to a provision in the House-passed energy bill, would allow independent drillers to write off certain expenses under the so-called alternative minimum tax.

Bradley led the charge to remove the Finance Committee's proposed tax relief for drillers. The tax relief would cost about $1 billion over five years, and Bradley said that money could be better spent on unmet social needs.

Bob Packwood, Ore., the ranking Republican on the Finance Committee, said that many companies complained about the minimum tax and that it was unfair to single out one industry for special relief.

But those criticisms were overshadowed by senators' claims that the tax provision was necessary to reverse a severe slump in the drilling industry.

Senators from oil- and gas-producing states said the alternative tax formula took a particularly heavy toll on drillers, who were required to invest substantially in exploration without any guarantee of finding oil or gas.

Bentsen made the motion to table, or kill, Bradley's amendment to remove the producers' tax relief, and senators agreed 63-32. *(Vote 159, p. 21-S)*

### Byways

Senate rules did not require amendments to bear any

relation to the underlying bill, and Bradley's amendment was one of the few offered that truly addressed energy policy.

Wallop at one point pleaded with colleagues to stop "dabbling in the occult."

Specter of Pennsylvania sent the bill on one detour when he sought to attach an unrelated health-care proposal during floor debate.

But some senators questioned the merits of his proposal, while others said it was inappropriate to attach it to the energy bill.

Bentsen lodged a parliamentary objection, saying the bill would violate congressional budget rules. Specter asked senators to waive those rules, but his request was defeated, 35-60. *(Vote 160, p. 21-S)*

On the other side of the aisle, Christopher J. Dodd, D-Conn., tried to tack on an embattled bill dealing with the structure of financial partnerships. Dodd eventually backed down and withdrew his proposal.

Senators adopted an amendment by Democrat Bob Graham of Florida and Republican Steve Symms of Idaho to let states issue tax-exempt bonds for high-speed rail projects regardless of state-by-state limits on the amount of such bonds.

Under existing law, 25 percent of the bonds for high-speed rail counted against state bond caps. Symms said this put rail projects at a disadvantage for financing because there were no such limits on tax-exempt bonds for some other transportation projects, such as airports.

The proposal would offset the expected decrease in federal revenue by curtailing an existing tax deduction for moving expenses. Taxpayers in 1992 could deduct moving expenses if they relocated more than 35 miles from their homes. The amendment would change that distance restriction to allow deductions only for moves of more than 55 miles.

Johnston sought to kill the amendment with a tabling motion but failed, 40-55. The amendment subsequently was approved by voice vote. *(Vote 161, p. 22-S)*

## CONFERENCE ACTION

The next step, albeit a large one, was to send the two bills to conference. Although there were many parallels between the House- and Senate-passed energy bills, they also included key differences:

● **PUHCA reform and transmission.** Both bills contained proposals to overhaul the 1935 Public Utility Holding Company Act to make it easier for utilities and independent producers to compete to produce and sell electricity at the wholesale level but with substantial differences between the two proposals.

Most significant was the House insistence on so-called mandatory transmission access — empowering the Federal Energy Regulatory Commission to order utilities to transmit a competitor's power on its transmission lines so long as there is ample capacity and the utility is justly compensated. The Senate-passed bill was silent on transmission access, but Johnston had since offered a potential compromise on the issue.

● **Alternative-fuel fleets.** Both bills sought to promote the development of cars and other vehicles that run on non-gasoline fuels by mandating that federal fleets significantly convert to such vehicles. But the two chambers parted ways over whether to extend such mandates to a large number of private fleets. The Senate bill included

alternative-fuel mandates for many state, private and municipal fleets, while the House version limited such requirements to companies that produce so-called alternative fuels.

● **Natural gas production.** The House bill would block state authority to regulate natural gas production if it is aimed at boosting the price of natural gas. Key Senate negotiators strongly opposed this language as an unnecessary and undue infringement on state authority, and the Bush administration had said it would be cause to veto the bill.

● **Offshore drilling.** Both bills would ban temporarily oil and gas drilling off much of the nation's coastline and require the government to cancel and buy back some existing leases. Although the House provisions generally were more restrictive, the key conflict was with the administration, which opposed the language in both bills.

● **Uranium enrichment.** Both bills included proposals that would convert the Energy Department's troubled uranium enrichment program into a government-owned corporation. But the measures diverged, particularly on the issue of how to assess liability for the program's unrecovered costs and the expense of cleaning up the existing enrichment facilities.

### Coordinating the Negotiations

Coordinating who would negotiate which parts of the massive bills took some time and effort.

The Senate appointed 31 conferees. House Speaker Thomas Foley, D-Wash., chose 100 just before the August recess then, on Sept. 9, fine-tuned those assignments.

Energy Secretary Watkins, on the eve of the conference, weighed in with a 17-page list of concerns. In an accompanying letter, Watkins warned that a good number of those items could draw a presidential veto.

Among the objections were proposals to restrict offshore oil and gas drilling, limit state regulation of natural gas production, and curb licensing of new hydroelectric power plants.

Administration officials also opposed various provisions that they said would violate budget rules.

### Conference Begins

The opening conference session was held Sept. 10 in the huge Cannon caucus room, one of the few Hill locales large enough to accommodate all of the lawmakers required tosign off on all or part of the final bill.

Johnston and Dingell were the lead negotiators for all but the tax sections of the two energy bills. Those titles were to be handled by Bentsen and Ways and Means Chairman Rostenkowski in a separate conference.

House and Senate negotiators made some headway during the opening meeting, tentatively approving staff-drafted compromises on a host of energy efficiency programs.

Those programs included mandatory federal efficiency standards for certain lights, appliances and electric motors, and urging state utility regulators to develop rate policies that promoted efficiency.

On electric vehicles, negotiators agreed to numerous research, development and demonstration programs to promote cars and other vehicles that ran solely or in part on electricity. Two of those programs would be authorized at $90 million, collectively, over five to 10 years.

Those sections represented a significant portion of the two bills and some of the most important to environmental

groups and their allies.

But they were also among the easiest to resolve because both chambers had adopted similar language on most provisions. Conferees deferred action on some additional and more-controversial efficiency provisions.

Conferees also agreed to a provision in the House bill seeking to ensure that fuel sellers posted the correct octane level of gasoline.

There were some overtures on the complicated issue of overhauling utility regulations.

Johnston, the conference chairman, made the opening move on the issue during the Sept. 10 meeting, unveiling his proposal for guaranteeing transmission access.

While some advocates of transmission access criticized that proposal as too weak, they nonetheless viewed it as encouraging movement from Johnston, who earlier had pledged to block any proposal on mandatory transmission.

However Wallop, who had strongly opposed such guarantees, made it clear that Johnston was speaking only for himself and not on behalf of all Senate conferees.

### Week Two

While negotiations on the comprehensive energy measure continued the week of Sept. 14, they were more noteworthy for what they left unresolved than for what they settled.

At the Sept. 16 session, negotiators agreed to additional efficiency provisions.

Among the second-round agreements was a compromise version of their respective proposals to promote more energy-efficient buildings. The compromise would prod states to adopt commercial and residential building codes with minimum efficiency provisions and would require that homes meet such standards to qualify for federal mortgage assistance.

On other efficiency provisions, each chamber traded off in acceding to the other's wishes.

For example, Senate negotiators agreed to adopt a House proposal to set energy efficiency standards for a range of plumbing fixtures. The Senate bill had included such standards only for shower heads.

For their part, House conferees adopted a Senate proposal promoting energy efficiency standards for manufactured housing.

Negotiators also agreed to a compromise package of coal programs, primarily research and development of cleaner ways to burn coal. Both bills had similar proposals for coal research, although House negotiators prevailed in establishing environmental and efficiency criteria for many such programs.

Similarly, negotiators reconciled comparable proposals for a series of joint ventures to promote renewable energy.

The House abandoned its bid to create an incentive payment of up to 2.5 cents per kilowatt-hour of energy produced from renewable sources.

The provision was largely symbolic because appropriators were considered unlikely to provide money for such payments.

Negotiators also agreed to adopt, with some modifications, a House proposal to simplify the federal ratemaking process for interstate oil pipelines.

### Week Three

A third week of frenzied negotiations ended in a muddle, with lawmakers moving toward agreement on major issues such as electric utility restructuring but failing to

take definitive action on any major disputes.

There was ample frustration and pessimism throughout the week.

"This is like negotiating with the provinces of the former Soviet Union," said conference chairman Johnston, referring to the multiple House committees with conferees on the bill. Foley called a meeting with key chairmen on Sept. 25, citing concerns about the bill's slow progress. But several House lawmakers and staff said the delays were symptomatic of Johnston's own, eleventh-hour negotiating style.

Helping to propel the bill was what one lawmaker termed "the embarrassment quotient" — no one wanted to be responsible for capsizing a major energy bill that already had passed both chambers with strong support.

Democrats were mindful that Bush could use a failed bill against them politically, while the administration in turn did not want to stand in the way of passing energy legislation.

Most of the week's public negotiating sessions focused on issues solely in the jurisdiction of the Senate Energy and House Energy and Commerce committees, such as alternative fuels, electric utility restructuring, natural gas and the Strategic Petroleum Reserve.

On Sept. 25, House conferees from the Interior and Insular Affairs Committee joined in to consider some of the issues in their jurisdiction. They reached tentative accords on certain provisions regarding coal mining and federal onshore oil and gas leases.

There was also movement toward a compromise version of a House provision to establish a baseline for greenhouse gas emissions.

## Alternative Fuels

One of the most persistent disagreements came over the issue of alternative fuels.

Johnston and some other Senate negotiators had pressed hard for their provisions, saying only an ambitious fleet program would prod automakers and fuel providers to iron out glitches that had blocked previous efforts to move toward these fuels.

Dingell took a tough stance against such mandates, however, saying they would force automakers in his district to produce alternative-fuel cars before there was a proven market for them and before they had adjusted to produce the cleaner-burning cars mandated by the 1990 amendments to the Clean Air Act.

Although the week's negotiations provided some movement on the issue, great distance remained, and both sides accused the other of intransigence on the issue.

At one point late in the week, Johnston appeared ready to give up on including mandates for private fleets — citing Dingell's opposition. He translated Dingell's comments to mean: "Detroit don't want this program, and we ain't going to have it."

But other lawmakers urged both sides to keep working on the issue in hope of a compromise. Key Senate negotiators had long touted the alternative-fuel fleet program as one of their bill's most signficant provisions to reduce oil imports.

## PUHCA Reform

While no formal deals were struck, negotiators appeared to be moving closer together on the complicated matter of electric utility restructuring.

Senators on Sept. 23 moved away from an earlier hard-line stance against opening up access to utility transmission lines; they offered to include provisions allowing federal regulators to order transmission access in some circumstances, provided the House agreed to the specifics of the Senate bill on changing the PUHCA law.

That offer did not overwhelm the House, which wanted far stronger transmission provisions and would not abandon some of its provisions for adjusting the 1935 utility law.

Dingell warned that he had been a reluctant supporter of reworking the Depression-era law and that he must feel sure that changes would preserve that law's original intent to rein in the power of utility monopolies.

"We are all sons of mother Eden," Dingell said. "The people may have changed, but their dispositions really haven't, especially when you put them in charge of an electric utility."

Nevertheless, House negotiators were heartened to see some movement in their direction on the transmission issue. And the House submitted an offer on PUHCA reform, which showed a willingness to bend to the Senate will on several matters, such as giving utilities greater flexibility to operate power plants overseas.

## Natural Gas

Both bills sought to encourage the use of natural gas, a relatively clean-burning fuel that was in plentiful supply in the United States. To that end, both measures proposed new fast-track licensing procedures for natural gas pipelines, provided operators were prepared to assume greater financial risk.

After the bills were drafted, however, the Federal Energy Regulatory Commission had issued dramatic new rules designed to promote competition in the gas pipeline business. Those changes were expected to create substantial upheaval, with some larger customers in particular jumping to new suppliers.

That left some House lawmakers worried that those changes, coupled with those in the energy bills, would create too much instability and too much risk for residential customers.

As a result, House negotiators proposed abandoning the major provisions in both bills on pipeline licensing. In return, the House would agree to abandon language in its bill that would effectively undermine the new FERC pipeline rules.

Johnston suggested dropping the natural gas title.

But the House was unwilling to abandon its language ensuring the fair treatment of imported Canadian natural gas and, more important, limiting state powers to regulate the production of natural gas, known as pro-rationing.

The House bill, influenced by the clout of Northeastern and Midwestern lawmakers on the Energy and Commerce subcommittee that drafted it, also would broaden the president's authority to sell oil from the petroleum reserve to include economic conditions as well as physical supply disruptions. And it called for creating a reserve of refined petroleum in the Northeast.

However, Senate negotiators said there was no money to fund a new regional reserve, and it appeared likely that proposal would have to be downscaled or eliminated.

## Conference Completed

House and Senate negotiators approved the final legislation early Oct. 1, at the close of a grueling conference session that spread over 11 hours. Their agreement left only the tax-related portions of the bill to be resolved

before the entire package could go back to the House and Senate for final votes.

## PUHCA Reform

Although lawmakers had become increasingly united on the general thrust of PUHCA reform, negotiating the details had been one of the most difficult challenges of the conference.

The House generally placed more restrictions on what utilities could do under the new rules and included potent language intended to open utility transmission lines to independent producers. Senate conferees were particularly critical of that House transmission access proposal, arguing that it could place unfair burdens on existing utilities and their ratepayers.

Sharp and Johnston cleared the way for the deal by directing their key staff aides to draft a comprehensive proposal that could become the basis for a final settlement.

That proposal surfaced Sept. 28. And while it generated some howls of outrage from both ends of the spectrum, the draft defined a political center on the issue.

After some tinkering, House negotiators emerged with a transmission access proposal that they believed would be strong enough to work.

Environmental groups had been key supporters of those changes, believing competition would open up opportunities for renewable energy producers and prod established utilities to promote conservation.

In exchange, the House moved in the direction of the Senate on other provisions, such as letting utilities buy power from independent affiliates as long as state regulators approve the deals.

Conferees also agreed to a new provision — not in either original bill — that would potentially allow utility holding companies to build plants overseas, as long as they did not use assets from their domestic utility affiliates to do so.

That proposal upset Sen. Dale Bumpers, D-Ark., who called it a radical departure from established practice that could jeopardize domestic ratepayers. But Bumpers lost a bid to have it removed from the bill.

## Alternative Fuels

Negotiators had bitterly quarreled over how far to go in mandating that government and private companies switch over to vehicles than run on non-gasoline fuels.

Conferees eventually settled on a combination of the House and Senate requirements for fleets.

Federal and state fleets would have to begin purchasing alternative-fuel vehicles promptly, as would certain companies that sell non-gasoline fuels.

Private companies and municipalities could face similar fleet purchase mandates beginning in 1999, although the Energy secretary would have discretion to delay those requirements until 2002.

## Offshore Drilling Mandate

An issue that could not be resolved was offshore oil and gas drilling.

The Senate bill placed bans on new oil and gas leasing in many coastal waters, called for the government to cancel and buy back some existing leases off the Florida Keys and sought to increase states' share of coastal drilling revenues.

The House bill went further, imposing more and longer drilling bans and requiring additional lease buy-backs off the North Carolina coast and in Alaska's Bristol Bay.

In conference, Johnston urged the House to drop the

buy-back provisions for fear that they would violate the terms of the 1990 budget agreement and trigger a sequester. An official from the White House Office of Management and Budget confirmed that threat during the conference session.

House Interior Chairman George Miller, D-Calif, proposed substituting the buy-back language with five-year drilling moratoria for the three affected areas, but Johnston said that would still run afoul of the budget pact.

Several Democratic House conferees objected, suggesting politics had guided the administration's decision to deem the proposal in violation of the budget accord. The administration had opposed the drilling restrictions in the energy bills, although many of the areas in question already were protected by a leasing moratorium imposed by Bush. Eventually, Miller called for abandoning the section of the bill dealing with coastal drilling. Both he and Johnston agreed the controversial issue would have to be addressed in the next Congress.

## Yucca Mountain

In July, Nevada Sens. Bryan and Reid had threatened to filibuster over a provision in the House-passed bill that would have pre-empted their state's authority to issue environmental permits for federal studies needed to place a nuclear waste dump at Yucca Mountain.

Johnston dissolved that filibuster threat by pledging to fight in conference to remove the offending language — which negotiators subsequently did.

But the morning of Sept. 30, Johnston struck a deal with key House negotiators — Dingell, Sharp and Miller — to insert a different provision regarding the planned dump. *(Yucca mountain, p. 243)*

This one would require the National Academy of Sciences to conduct a study on the proper radiation disposal standards for the dump. The Environmental Protection Agency (EPA) then would be required to issue new radiation standards for Yucca Mountain consistent with the findings of that study.

The EPA issued disposal standards in 1985 but abandoned them after parts were struck down by a federal court.

Nevada opponents cried foul at the conference action, saying the same safety standards should be applied to Yucca Mountain as were applied to other nuclear waste facilities. Opponents also said the terms of the proposed study were slanted to produce a weak standard.

But Rep. Barbara F. Vucanovich, R-Nev., lost a vote among House conferees to delete the provision.

Reid and Bryan subsequently announced plans to filibuster the conference report, a potent threat given the short time remaining before an expected Oct. 6 adjournment.

Johnston defended his Yucca Mountain proposal as an effort to get reasonable standards for the planned dump for high-level defense and commercial nuclear waste and discounted the risk of a filibuster.

"We can't let one man stop the whole energy bill," Johnston said.

## Natural Gas

Although the bill contained many provisions to promote the use of natural gas, in the final hour negotiators dropped the title formally devoted to that fuel.

Both the House and Senate originally had voted to create new fast-track procedures for licensing natural gas

pipelines. But those provisions were called into question when the Federal Energy Regulatory Commission subsequently overhauled its natural gas pipeline rules in an effort to boost competition.

That new rule, which had fierce critics and supporters, proved too much and too controversial to reconcile with the natural gas section of the energy bill. Lawmakers eventually agreed to drop the natural gas pipeline proposals, as well as a provision that could have undermined implementation of the new FERC rule.

They also dropped an explosive item in the House bill that would have limited state power to "pro-ration," or control, gas production.

But bowing to concerns that pro-rationing could be misused to constrict supply and drive up gas prices, conferees included a more limited statement on the issue pledging commitment to free and fair gas markets. And Northeastern lawmakers won provisions to ensure the fair treatment of imported Canadian natural gas.

A provision to streamline the licensing process for nuclear power plants had been approved in identical form in both chambers and was included in the final bill.

Other key sections of the final bill sought to:

● **Strategic Petroleum Reserve.** Broaden the president's authority to sell oil from the reserve to include easing sharp price increases linked to supply disruptions.

● **Radioactive waste.** Give states some power to regulate certain low-level radioactive waste if the federal government moved to deregulate it.

● **Hydropower.** Maintain some House-passed limits on licensing new hydroelectric dams, such as for rivers in federal parks.

● **Coal and oil shale.** Promote recovery of coal bed methane and clarify the status of disputed oil shale claims in Colorado, Utah and Wyoming.

● **Global warming.** Establish a climate protection director within the Energy Department and include measures to help establish baseline data on greenhouse gas emissions.

● **Uranium enrichment.** Restructure the federal uranium enrichment program into a government-owned corporation with an eye toward converting it into private enterprise. Nuclear utilities that had bought fuel from the aging enrichment plants would have to help pay for their clean-up, as much as $150 million a year capped at $2.25 billion over 15 years, adjusted for inflation.

### Final Snags

Even after the main conferees finished their work, some potential legislative snags remained.

By Oct. 2, the final bill faced at least one filibuster threat from Nevada senators unhappy with the language regarding Yucca Mountain.

And tax provisions in the House- and Senate-passed energy bills, including incentives for renewable energy and tax relief for independent oil and gas drillers, remained entangled in complex negotiations over other tax legislation. Negotiations over those provisions were being handled by conferees from the Senate Finance and House Ways and Means panels.

Those tax negotiators worked through the weekend and agreed upon a final package Oct. 4, completing the last piece of the lengthy energy bill.

Once again, Rockefeller's language to ensure the health benefits of retired coal miners was a source of controversy and delay.

House Republican conferees and Democratic conferee

J. J. Pickle, D-Texas, balked at including the provision in the final bill — holding up final floor action.

Pickle eventually agreed to the coal provision in order to let the energy bill go forward, but warned his colleagues that they were setting a dangerous and potentially expensive precedent by bailing out the ailing health fund.

And he said it was unfair to make companies with no current connection to the coal business pay for some of the miner benefits: "It is as if we are a street gang mugging an innocent passer-by, and justifying it by saying that our family and friends are hungry."

But Rockefeller and other proponents said something must be done to honor the contracts of the retirees, many of whom faced serious mining-related illnesses and staggering health bills.

On the energy provisions more directly related to energy production and consumption, negotiators adopted a compromise of parallel House- and Senate-passed proposals.

Their handiwork included a so-called green tax package advocated by environmental groups, including incentives for mass transit, conservation, renewable energy and cars that run on non-gasoline fuels.

Independent oil and gas drillers also won one of their key goals: tax relief to the tune of an estimated $1 billion over five years.

To pay for these tax breaks, the bill increased taxes on some ozone-depleting chemicals and capped existing tax benefits for employer-provided parking. The bill also included a hodgepodge of small revenue raisers, such as increasing the withholding rate for gambling winnings.

## FINAL PASSAGE

The House approved the final bill (HR 776 — H Rept 102-1018) 363-60 on Oct. 5, and the Senate passed it by voice vote three days later after defeating a threatened filibuster. *(Vote 474, p. 116-H)*

With the tax portion of the bill finally in hand, House leaders moved quickly after conference to pass the entire energy bill amid the end-of-session press.

Barbara F. Vucanovich, R-Nev., offered a motion designed to strip the Yucca Mountain language from the final energy bill. The House rebuffed the effort on a 102-323 vote. *(Vote 473, p. 116-H)*

In the Senate, Nevada Democrats Bryan and Reid opposed the bill over the language regarding radiation standards for Yucca Mountain, which they said could make it easier to place a high-level nuclear dump in their state.

The two said the language represented the latest effort to force the nuclear dump on Nevada without regard to fairness or science.

As part of their campaign, they also played off rumors that the revenue offsets in the bill might prompt President Bush — who had recently pledged to never, "ever" raise taxes — to veto the entire energy package .

Bryan and Reid raised the point in an Oct. 6 letter to Bush, noting that "it would be difficult to reconcile your recent statements with opposition to increased tax burdens and the signing of this legislation into law."

But Republican House leaders already had indicated that Bush would sign the bill.

And Senate Minority Leader Bob Dole, R-Kan., brushed aside the suggestion that the energy bill constituted a significant violation of Bush's latest no-new-taxes pledge. With one exception, Dole said, the revenue raisers

were "compliance" matters. As for the tax increase on chlorofluorocarbons, or CFCs: "That's an environmental vote, and the president's the environmental president, so it fits right in."

In the end, the Nevadans found little support.

The Senate on Oct. 8 voted 84-8 against the two and in favor of completing work on the energy bill. *(Vote 266, p. 35-S).*

The bill then passed on a voice vote, capping a difficult journey that took virtually every day of the 102nd Congress.

## ASSESSMENTS

"The theme of this bill is energy made in America," Johnston said at a news conference following final passage. "We believe it is a signal accomplishment for the Congress."

Sharp called particular attention to the utility provisions, which were intended to revolutionize the electric industry to create greater competition and efficiency.

Energy Department officials also praised the final product, noting that it contained elements of a Bush administration energy plan submitted in early 1991.

The nuclear power industry fared well, as did natural gas. The electricity provisions were expected to promote small power plants fueled by natural gas, and natural gas also would be promoted as a motor fuel.

But large oil companies found little to promote domestic energy production, such as opening Alaska's Arctic National Wildlife Refuge to oil and gas drilling.

And environmental lobbyists, on the other hand, complained that the legislation was skewed in favor of nuclear power and ignored their chief prescription for decreasing oil dependence — forcing Detroit to build more fuel-efficient cars.

Once the conference moved to drop offshore drilling restrictions and add language on the nuclear waste dump, some environmental groups announced strong opposition to the bill.

However, some lawmakers said the bill did represent a major step toward reconciling energy policy and environmental considerations.

"It is a wonderful shift from where we have been going ever since the dawn of the fossil fuel revolution," said Sen. Tim Wirth, D-Colo. "We have for the first time the beginning of a balance between environmental and energy policy."

And the legislation did have the support of many renewable energy producers and some efficiency advocates.

"This energy bill gives Americans the good, the bad and the ugly," said Scott Denman, executive director of the Safe Energy Communication Council. "The renewable energy and efficiency provisions are a good start; the lack of automobile fuel efficiency standards is very bad; and the nuclear power and waste provisions are downright ugly."

Observers said that it would take years before the effects of some of the legislation's provisions were felt and that results could vary depending on energy markets and how vigorously the federal government carried out the legislation.

The Energy Department projected that the bill could reduce oil imports by about 4.7 million barrels a day by 2010. When the bill passed, U.S. consumption stood at about 17 million barrels per day and was expected to rise.

There were no claims that the legislation would achieve or even approach "energy independence," the policy goal of earlier energy debates.

"Neither the President, nor the Congress, nor the public is willing to support the massive energy tax increases, subsidies, regulations or changes in lifestyle that would be necessary to dramatically reduce our dependence on foreign oil," Sharp said.

However, the energy bill was one of the few major pieces of legislation to move through the 102nd Congress, which was often stymied by partisan squabbling.

"We have beaten gridlock," Sharp proclaimed as the House prepared to vote on the final bill Oct. 5.

"It is nothing short of miraculous, the number of interests that have come together in this," agreed Wallop, who helped write the Senate bill. ∎

# Provisions of Energy Policy Act

*President Bush on Oct. 24 signed the Energy Policy Act of 1992, the first major legislative attempt to curb U.S. oil dependence in more than a decade.*

*The new law (PL 102-486) was a huge document, touching on virtually every sector of the energy industry. Its passage marked the culmination of the fierce energy policy debates that accompanied the Persian Gulf War, and it combined elements of the Bush administration's energy strategy and dozens of legislative proposals.*

*Key provisions of the law sought to restructure the electric*

### ENERGY GOALS

#### Global warming

● **Greenhouse gases.** Required, within two years, an administration study on the methods and costs of curbing greenhouse gas emissions. The study was to assess the feasibility of stabilizing such emissions by 2005, or of reducing them. The study also was to examine the potential to cut carbon dioxide emissions 20 percent below 1988 levels by 2005.

*utility industry to promote more competition, provide tax relief to independent oil and gas drillers, encourage energy conservation and efficiency, promote renewable energy and cars that run on non-gasoline fuels, make it easier to build nuclear power plants, and authorize billions of dollars in energy-related research and development. But the end product was a political and policy compromise that was expected to cap rather than significantly reduce U.S. dependence on foreign oil.*

*As enacted, key provisions of the energy legislation:*

Within 18 months the Energy secretary was required to submit another study assessing specific policies to cut greenhouse emissions, including caps on emissions and federal efficiency standards for automobile fuel economy and industrial processes.

● **Energy strategy.** Required the Energy secretary to develop a least-cost national energy strategy that promoted energy efficiency and sought to limit the emission of carbon dioxide and other greenhouse gases. The plan was to take into account the economic, energy, environmental and social costs of various energy technologies. It was to seek to attain a 30 percent increase in efficiency by

2010 and a 75 percent increase in the use of renewable energy by 2005, both based on 1988 levels. The law also set a goal of decreasing oil consumption, from 40 percent of total energy use to 35 percent, by the year 2005.

The least-cost strategy was required as part of the Energy Department's next biennial energy plan as of February 1993.

● **Voluntary emissions reductions.** Created a national accounting system to track voluntary cuts in greenhouse gas emissions, potentially to be credited against any future mandated reductions. The Energy Department was charged with estimating baseline emissions for 1987 through 1990 and beyond, as well as issuing guidelines for a voluntary system for recording baseline emissions and subsequent reductions by individual companies or other entities that produce greenhouse gases, including coal bed methane.

● **International initiatives.** Established a technology transfer program to promote the export of domestic energy technologies to cut greenhouse gas emissions through such means as financial aid to projects. The Energy Department was to administer the program working with the Agency for International Development. The law authorized $100 million for the program in each of fiscal years 1993-98.

The legislation also created a fund to aid global efforts to fight greenhouse warming, authorized at $50 million in fiscal 1994 and unspecified amounts in the next two years. It specified that no money could be put into the fund until the United States ratified the U.N. Framework Convention on Climate Change, which committed nations to rolling back their emissions of greenhouse gases. However, the Senate ratified that treaty Oct. 7.

### Fleets and fuels

● **Alternative-fuel fleets.** Mandated that certain government entities and private businesses with fleets of automobiles or light trucks phase in vehicles that run on non-gasoline or alternative fuels.

● **Eligible fuels.** Designated as eligible alternative fuels: methanol, ethanol and other alcohols; mixtures of at least 85 percent alcohol with gasoline or other fuels; natural gas; liquefied petroleum gas; hydrogen; coal-derived liquid fuels; electricity, including that derived from solar energy; and any other fuels that are primarily non-petroleum.

An alternative-fuel vehicle could be one that ran solely on these fuels or a so-called dual-fueled vehicle that ran on both conventional and alternative fuels. However, the bill generally directed fleet operators to run the vehicles purchased under these mandates solely on alternative fuels unless they were not available. That requirement did not apply to fleets owned by private businesses and municipalities to protect them against potential price gouging.

● **Eligible fleets.** Applied purchase mandates to fleets of 20 or more vehicles that were centrally garaged and operated in a major metropolitan area, provided that the parent companies, government agencies or other entities owned 50 or more vehicles nationwide. In the case of federal fleets, however, individual agencies or federal entities operating 20 or more vehicles in an urban area qualified for the purchase mandates regardless of whether they owned 50 vehicles.

● **Federal requirements.** Expanded programs directing the government to buy cars and light trucks that run on non-gasoline fuels. The legislation directed the federal government to buy at least 5,000 alternative-fuel vehicles in 1993, at least 7,500 in 1994 and at least 10,000 in 1995. In addition, individual federal fleets were required to phase in alternative-fuel vehicles — at least 25 percent of new vehicle purchases in fiscal 1996, rising to 75 percent by fiscal 1999 and each year thereafter.

The mandates also generally applied to Congress, the White House and the U.S. Postal Service.

● **Alternative fuel providers.** Required that producers of alternative fuels begin phasing in alternative-fuel vehicles for their own fleets, beginning with 30 percent of those purchased in model year 1996 and rising to 90 percent by model year 1999.

The mandate applied to companies whose primary business was producing, processing or distributing alternative fuels for use as an end product — such as ethanol refiners or electric utilities. If a company had affiliates, only those divisions that were significantly engaged in the alternative-fuels business were affected.

The requirement was not to kick in until 1998 for electric utilities that committed to buying electric vehicles.

● **State fleets.** Required, pursuant to a federal rule-making, that states begin phasing in alternative-fuel vehicles for their government fleets at the following rate: 10 percent of new vehicles in the 1996 model year, rising annually to 75 percent in model year 2000 and thereafter.

States could opt out of these purchase mandates if they submitted a plan, to be approved by the Energy secretary, that would result in an equal or greater number of alternative-fuel vehicles by such means as converting conventional-fuel vehicles.

● **Private and municipal fleets.** Set a two-stage timetable for forcing private companies and municipalities to phase in alternative-fuel vehicles.

The bill set purchase targets for these fleets of 20 percent in model year 1999, rising to 70 percent in 2006 and thereafter. The bill called on the Energy secretary to issue a rule to achieve those targets. The secretary was to have broad discretion to modify or drop the mandates altogether if the program proves unfeasible.

If the early rule-making did not result in a fleet purchase program, the legislation mandated a second, later rule-making to be completed by the year 2000 and mandating alternative-fuel vehicle purchases beginning at 20 percent in 2002 and rising to 70 percent in 2005.

● **Exemptions.** Exempted from alternative-fuel mandates a number of large fleets, such as rental cars, car dealers' stock, law enforcement or emergency vehicles, certain military vehicles and non-road vehicles, such as farm and construction vehicles. The mandates also were limited to light-duty vehicles weighing less than 8,500 pounds, although there was some discretion to include urban buses.

● **Credits.** Allowed eligible fleets to earn credits for exceeding the purchase mandates. Those credits could be applied toward another year or transferred to another fleet covered under the law's alternative-fuel vehicle purchase requirements.

● **Penalties.** Established civil penalties of up to $10,000 per violation for private businesses that disobeyed the law's alternative fuel purchase and reporting mandates.

● **States.** Issued federal guidelines for state programs to promote the use of alternative-fuel vehicles and authorized $10 million a year for five years to aid such state efforts. Incentives could include tax breaks, special parking for alternative-fuel vehicles and public education campaigns.

● **Mass transit and school buses.** Authorized $30 million in each of fiscal years 1993-95 to help establish urban and school bus fleets that ran on alternative fuels.

● **Natural gas.** Removed certain existing legal restrictions on the sale or transport of natural gas for use in motor vehicles.

● **Labeling.** Directed the Federal Trade Commission (FTC) to develop uniform labeling requirements for alternative fuels and alternative-fuel vehicles.

● **Loans.** Established a low-interest loan program to help small businesses convert their fleets to alternative-fuel vehicles. The bill authorized $25 million for this program in each of fiscal years 1993-95.

### Electric Vehicles

● **Demonstration projects.** Created a program to demonstrate the viability of vehicles that run solely or in part on electricity. The bill authorized up to 10 joint demonstration projects, with at least half of the funding to come from non-federal sources. The program was to include subsidizing the cost differential between electric vehicles and conventionally fueled ones, although the federal share of such subsidies was to be capped at $10,000 per vehicle. The program was authorized at $50 million over 10 years.

The federal government also was authorized to help states develop an infrastructure for electric vehicles, and the legislation called for up to 10 cost-shared joint ventures, each capped at $4 million, to promote technologies, facilities and regulations to support electric vehicles. This infrastructure program was authorized at $40 million over five years.

● **Research and development.** Required the Energy secretary to create a five-year research and development program for electric vehicles, in consultation with other agencies, utilities and automakers. It also authorized joint research and development programs with industry in areas such as advanced batteries for electric vehicles, high-efficiency electric power trains and hybrid power trains that drew on electricity and conventional liquid fuels. Project costs were to be split at least equally with the private sector or other non-federal sources, except in the case of a specific effort to develop fuel cell technology.

This program was authorized at $60 million in fiscal 1993, rising yearly to $100 million in fiscal 1998.

### Alternative fuels

● **Goal.** Directed the Energy secretary to develop a plan to promote alternative fuels and so-called replacement fuels, motor fuels that could be mixed with conventional gasoline or diesel fuel. The plan was to evaluate a goal of replacing 30 percent of projected petroleum-based motor fuel by the year 2010. At least half of these replacement fuels were to be from domestic suppliers.

● **Supply plan.** Directed the Energy secretary to analyze the supply and demand for alternative fuels and obtain voluntary commitments from suppliers to provide these fuels.

## RENEWABLE ENERGY

### Promotion

● **Demonstration programs.** Expanded and adjusted an existing program to promote the commercial development of various renewable energy and energy efficiency technologies, authorizing $50 million in fiscal 1994 for a series of joint ventures. The projects could promote a range of renewable technologies, including: high- and low-temperature geothermal energy; solar thermal energy including solar water heating; photovoltaic and wind energy systems; biomass; and fuel cells. The projects were to include at least one for-profit business, and federal funds generally were to account for no more than half the costs of each joint venture. They would be selected on a competitive basis and could include measures such as subsidizing loans for renewable energy projects.

The demonstration projects were in addition to a broader Energy Department research program on renewable energy, authorized at $209 million for fiscal 1993 and $275 million for fiscal 1994. Within that authorization, $22 million in fiscal 1993 was allotted to research into superconducting technologies to improve the efficiency and capacity of electric power equipment.

● **Export councils.** Expanded the duties of a federal working group to promote renewable energy and establish a parallel group for energy efficiency. The groups, which were to be chaired by the Energy secretary, were to seek to promote exports that advanced renewable energy and energy efficiency, particularly to lesser-developed countries. The law authorized the two groups to station an outreach officer, knowledgeable in efficiency and renewable energy technologies, in both the Caribbean Basin and the Pacific Rim.

● **Data bank.** Directed the Commerce Department to keep a data bank on the demand for energy technologies in developing countries as well as the availability of U.S. services to meet those needs, particularly with regard to renewable energy and energy efficiency.

● **Technology transfer.** Created a technology transfer program to help export U.S. renewable energy technologies, particularly to developing countries. The program was to be run by the Energy Department, working with federal working groups on renewable energy and the Agency for International Development, and was authorized at $100 million in each of fiscal 1993 through 1998.

The legislation also authorized $6 million in each of fiscal 1994, 1995 and 1996 to train people from developing countries to operate and maintain renewable energy equipment.

● **Production incentive.** Authorized the Energy secretary to grant incentive payments of up to 1.5 cents per kilowatt hour of energy produced from certain renewable energy sources. The incentive was available for a maximum of 10 years, for facilities that first began producing renewable energy within 10 years of the law's enactment.

The payments were to be made out of available appropriations, casting doubt on the likelihood that they would be implemented.

● **Award.** Authorized cash awards to individuals or organizations that established breakthroughs in the development of renewable energy technologies. The legislation authorized up to $50,000 a year in fiscal 1994-96 for this program.

### Hydroelectric power

● **Licensing.** Allowed third-party contractors to prepare some environmental documents and reviews for proposed hydroelectric power projects, potentially speeding the licensing process for these proposals.

However, the legislation also stiffened existing licensing requirements in several respects.

It barred licensing new hydroelectric dams within areas managed by the National Park Service if they would have an adverse impact on the lands.

The law also strengthened the role of several federal agencies vis-à-vis the Federal Energy Regulatory Commission (FERC) in determining federal hydropower licenses. For example, it clarified that a FERC license did not automatically grant the licensee the right to build roads, pipeline or transmission lines to the project over federal lands. Instead, the Bureau of Land Management and Forest Service must have approved rights of way and could potentially set conditions for them.

● **Federal dams.** Called for a study, within two years, on the potential for boosting hydropower production at existing federal facilities. Another study was to examine the potential for selling more federal hydropower by cutting back on water for reclamation or by boosting conservation, as well as analyzing possibilities for enhancing fish and wildlife through these measures.

● **Federal oversight.** Study the possibility of removing federal licensing jurisdiction for hydroelectric projects on fresh waters in Hawaii and establish expedited licensing procedures for three projects in Alaska. The law allowed the self-financing Bonneville Power Authority to spend money directly for certain hydropower improvements without further appropriation.

### Standards

● **Federal building standards.** Required the Energy secretary to set minimum efficiency standards for federal buildings within two years of passage, to take effect one year after that. All new federal buildings would have to meet those standards, which would be developed in consultation with industry groups and relevant federal agencies.

New public housing and new homes receiving federal mortgages through agencies such as the Federal Housing Administration and the Department of Veterans Affairs also were to have to meet the federal standards.

● **Non-federal building standards.** Required states within two years to update their commercial building codes to meet or exceed model industry standards designed to enhance energy efficiency. The states also were encouraged, but not required, to update their residential building codes to boost energy efficiency. The bill directed the Energy secretary to create a technical assistance program to help local officials and others involved with building codes update and enforce their provisions.

● **Homes.** Directed the Energy secretary to issue voluntary guidelines to help states and localities rate the energy efficiency of residential buildings and authorize technical assistance to develop

these rating systems.

The law also authorized a mortgage pilot program to promote the sale of energy-efficient homes and the installation of energy-saving improvements in existing homes. The bill directed the secretary of Housing and Urban Development (HUD) to establish the pilot program in five states within six months of passage. Within two years of beginning projects in those states, the program was to be expanded nationwide.

● **Manufactured housing.** Required the HUD secretary to recommend ways to make manufactured housing more energy efficient and to test the energy performance of such housing.

The bill gave states the power to set their own insulation and efficiency standards for manufactured housing if HUD failed to set new federal standards within one year of enactment. States were exempted from setting these standards.

● **Industrial efficiency.** Authorized grants of up to $250,000 to industry associations to promote energy efficiency in their field. The law directed the Energy secretary to report on the benefits of establishing mandatory efficiency reporting and voluntary efficiency targets for industries that were major energy consumers.

The legislation also authorized another grant program to help states promote energy-efficient technologies in the food, lumber, wood, petroleum, coal and other manufacturing industries.

It directed the Energy secretary to establish voluntary guidelines for industrial plant insulation and energy-efficiency audits and offered technical assistance to promote those guidelines.

● **Electric motors.** Established new federal efficiency standards for commercial and industrial electric motors, ranging from 1 horsepower to 200 horsepower. The law also authorized the Energy secretary to establish testing requirements and then efficiency standards for small electric motors — those under 1 horsepower — when feasible and economically justifiable.

● **Lights.** Set minimum efficiency standards for certain fluorescent and incandescent reflector lamps. The bill also authorized the Energy secretary to set standards for some high-intensity discharge lamps. And it mandated that the FTC establish labeling standards for a wide range of lamps.

● **Plumbing fixtures.** Established federal minimum efficiency standards for showerheads and other plumbing equipment, such as faucets, toilets and urinals. Restricting the water flow of such equipment in turn curbs the amount of energy required to heat or pump the water.

● **Commercial and industrial equipment.** Established efficiency standards for commercial heating systems and air conditioners and authorized the Energy secretary to create efficiency standards for utility distribution transformers.

The bill directed the Energy secretary to help create a voluntary efficiency labeling system for office equipment. Failing that, the bill authorized the FTC to develop a mandatory system.

● **Efficiency labels.** Authorized the federal government to help industry develop a voluntary efficiency labeling program for windows and fluorescent light fixtures, known as luminaires, and to establish a mandatory program if the private sector failed to establish a voluntary one within several years.

● **Regional centers.** Authorized federal grants to set up 10 demonstration centers across the nation to showcase the most efficient lighting, heating, cooling and building technologies. It authorized $10 million in each of fiscal 1994-96 for this program. At least half the money for these centers was to be from non-federal sources.

● **Appliances.** Commissioned an administration study on the merits of helping manufacturers develop high-efficiency appliances and equipment that went beyond minimum government standards, as well as a second report on programs aimed at phasing out older, less-efficient appliances.

● **Federal energy use.** Established a range of measures to prompt federal agencies to pay more attention to energy efficiency in running their building management and procurement policies.

The law set a January 2005 deadline for federal agencies to install energy and water efficiency improvements that would pay for themselves within 10 years, and it established a federal fund to help pay for such energy-saving projects. That fund was authorized at $10 million in fiscal 1994, $50 million in fiscal 1995 and open-ended amounts thereafter. The law authorized a separate demonstration program to install new efficiency technologies in federal buildings; with funding levels of up to $5 million annually in fiscal 1993-95.

It mandated that the president's budget include specific agency-by-agency information on energy costs and the expense of meeting federal energy efficiency goals.

And the legislation allowed agencies that made energy savings to keep half of that money for additional efficiency improvements and related expenditures. This provision did not include the Defense Department and was subject to appropriations.

● **Bonuses.** Authorized $250,000 a year in fiscal 1993-95 for government bonuses of up to $2,500 apiece for managers of federal facilities who save energy.

● **Utilities.** Directed state electric utility regulators to consider adopting policies that promote energy efficiency and conservation by electric utilities, rather than the building of new power plants. Regulators also were to have to consider these directives for natural gas utilities.

The law also established a grant program to encourage this so-called least-cost planning. The grant program was authorized at $5 million a year in fiscal 1994, 1995 and 1996, and each grant was limited to $250,000.

The bill also included language to promote such efficiency planning by the Tennessee Valley Authority and by customers of the Western Area Power Administration.

● **States.** Amended the existing state energy conservation program to allow the Energy secretary to provide states with up to $1 million to help establish state revolving funds to finance energy-efficiency improvements in state and local government buildings. It also permitted states to use the grants for a range of programs, including training building designers and contractors and adopting retrofit standards for buildings to increase efficiency.

The law specified that, in order to receive federal aid under the conservation program, states must allow vehicles to turn left on a red light after stopping provided they were turning from a one-way street onto a one-way street.

## NUCLEAR POWER

### Licensing

● **One-step licensing.** Adopted the Nuclear Regulatory Commission's proposal, currently under review by the federal courts, to issue a combined construction and operation license for nuclear power plants instead of the traditional process of granting two licenses. The commission would have to certify that the terms of the license had been met.

The change eliminated a second public hearing then required before a plant could begin to operate, unless critics could show that the plant had failed to follow the specifications of the combined license in a way that could endanger public health or safety.

If the Nuclear Regulatory Commission (NRC) opted for a second hearing, it was to be allowed to permit the reactor to begin operating in the interim so long as it would not jeopardize public health or safety. The bill clarified that the commission's final decision to allow or prohibit plant operation under a combined license was subject to judicial review.

### Advanced reactors

● **Research.** Authorized a research and development program to commercialize advanced reactor technologies that were meant to be safer and more efficient than existing designs, allotting $213 million for the effort in fiscal 1993.

Within 180 days of the bill's enactment, the Energy secretary was to submit a five-year plan for commercializing these reactor designs. The law set October 1996 as the target date for approving a standardized design for an advanced light-water reactor. The En-

ergy Department was to provide technical and financial assistance for companies seeking to develop such reactor designs and could help pay for some of the required research and engineering. The bill also set 1996 as the target date for researching other advanced technologies, such as high-temperature, gas-cooled reactors and liquid-intake reactors, to determine whether the government should select in 1996 one of those technologies for a demonstration project. This portion of the advanced reactor commercialization effort was authorized at $100 million over fiscal 1993-97.

● **Demonstration project.** Directed the Energy secretary to solicit preliminary engineering proposals for an advanced reactor demonstration project and to report to Congress by October 1998 whether the government should build a full-scale prototype reactor. That report was to include cost estimates, based on a requirement that at least half the money come from the private sector.

## URANIUM ENRICHMENT

### Government corporation

● **Enrichment corporation.** Set a July 1, 1993, deadline to restructure the Energy Department's uranium enrichment program into a government corporation aimed at processing uranium ore more efficiently and staving off foreign competition, potentially to be sold to private investors. The corporation was to enrich uranium and sell it to the Energy Department and other domestic and foreign customers, such as nuclear power plants. It was to be run by a five-member board of directors, to be appointed by the president with the advice and consent of the Senate.

The new corporation was directed to lease two existing Energy Department enrichment plants, at Paducah, Ky., and Piketon, Ohio, for at least six years. After that, the corporation was to have exclusive rights to lease the facilities for longer periods.

The corporation was directed to charge fees that would generate a profit. It was also authorized to handle the marketing of highly enriched or weapons-grade uranium from former Soviet republics, to be converted into lower-grade uranium for civilian use. The Bush administration in 1992 agreed to purchase weapons-grade uranium from Russia.

The law gave the corporation exclusive rights to develop a promising enrichment technology, known as Atomic Vapor Laser Isotope Separation (AVLIS), although it was to pay the federal government royalties for the privilege. The corporation could take preliminary steps toward moving ahead with AVLIS but would have to set up a private, for-profit business to build a plant using the new technology. The enrichment corporation could make grants of up to $364 million to this private enterprise for work leading up to construction of an AVLIS plant.

● **Privatization.** Directed the corporation to draw up a plan for privatizing the enrichment enterprise, potentially through a stock offering or merger. The corporation then would be authorized to implement the plan subject to presidential approval and a period of congressional review.

● **Debt.** Sought to recover some of the federal government's past investment in the enrichment operation. There was strong disagreement over the extent of unrecovered costs: Some claimed that the government incurred no such costs, while other critics estimated them as high as $11 billion.

The law did not set a specific debt that must be repaid but sought to recapture money for the federal Treasury in several ways. The government was to hold stock in the corporation equal to at least $3 billion and receive corporation net profits in the form of dividends. In addition, the Treasury would glean the proceeds from a stock sale if the enterprise is privatized.

● **Price-Anderson Act.** Clarified that the existing uranium enrichment plants were to continue to qualify for financial protections under the Price Anderson Act, which limits industry liability in the case of a nuclear accident. However, the law stated that a new AVLIS plant would not qualify for such federal liability protection.

● **Overfeed program.** Encouraged the new corporation to create a voluntary "overfeed" program, which would add extra uranium to the enrichment process to drive down power costs and pass the savings on to customers in the form of lower prices.

● **Cleanup.** Made the federal government and nuclear utilities share the cost of cleaning up the Energy Department's aging enrichment plants. The cleanup and decommissioning work was expected to cost about $20 billion.

The law established a $480-million-a-year fund to clean up the aging enrichment plants, with authorizations indexed for inflation. Nuclear utilities were to pay about 31 percent of this (the percentage of enriched uranium that was produced for their use) over 15 years, up to $150 million a year but no more than $2.25 billion total, or a similar sum indexed for inflation. Individual utilities were to pay in proportion to the amount of enriched uranium they had purchased from the program. The federal share was to come from congressional appropriations.

● **Uranium and thorium milling.** Authorized $270 million to help clean up uranium mill sites that were used to supply government programs and $40 million for thorium mill site cleanup.

● **Uranium reserve.** Established a strategic uranium reserve for defense and government research purposes consisting of the amount of U.S. defense-related uranium stockpiles at the time of passage. This provision sought to aid domestic producers by stabilizing the uranium market.

The law also directed the government to study the technological and economic factors involved with converting highly enriched uranium into lower grade uranium suitable for commercial use.

● **Imports.** Required U.S. nuclear power plant owners who imported raw or enriched uranium to report annually on the seller and country of origin of the uranium or enrichment services.

## NATURAL GAS

### Regulation and review

● **Imports.** Loosened existing restrictions on Canadian natural gas, blocking the need for special import approvals and specifying that neither federal nor state regulators could treat it differently than domestic natural gas once it was in this country.

● **Pro-rationing.** Declared congressional support for competitive natural gas markets. This language was a much-watered down version of a controversial provision in the House energy bill regarding state regulation of natural gas. That bill would have barred states from imposing gas production restrictions aimed at boosting prices. States would still have been allowed to impose traditional "pro-rationing" regulations to protect the respective claims of multiple drillers tapping a common reservoir or to prevent waste.

Conferees' report language accompanying the energy legislation stated that the Supreme Court already had established limits on state powers to regulate natural gas production that should effectively preclude efforts to boost prices through unnatural supply controls.

## STRATEGIC PETROLEUM RESERVE

### Stockpile

● **Expansion.** Directed the administration to expand the Strategic Petroleum Reserve to 1 billion barrels as soon as possible. The law authorized a series of measures to achieve this goal, including transferring oil from the Naval Petroleum Reserve. If the president found that domestic oil production had declined to a level that jeopardized national security, the president could direct the Energy secretary to buy oil from stripper wells, defined as wells producing 15 or fewer barrels a day on average.

● **Drawdown.** Broadened the conditions under which the president was authorized to sell oil from the reserve to include economic factors, such as a sharp increase in the price of oil, rather than solely in the event of physical shortages or supply disruptions.

● **Insular areas.** Authorized a study on the oil vulnerability of insular areas.

## TAX PROVISIONS

### Energy Taxes

● **Transportation benefits.** Restructured the tax treatment of employer-provided transportation benefits to encourage more mass transit and carpooling.

The bill allowed employers to provide tax-free mass transit and carpooling subsidies of up to $60 a month, up from $21 a month. At the same time, it capped tax-free parking benefits, which were unlimited, at $155 per month. The new rules applied to transit benefits provided as of Jan. 1, 1993.

● **Conservation subsidies.** Did not tax the rebates utilities provide residential customers for buying or installing conservation measures, beginning in 1993. When utilities provided such conservation rebates to non-residential customers, they would continue to be fully taxed through 1994. In 1995, 40 percent of those rebates would be tax free, rising to 50 percent in 1996 and 65 percent in 1997.

● **Alternative-fuel vehicles.** Provided tax deductions for buying (or converting) vehicles that ran on alternative fuels and for related refueling equipment.

The bill allowed a deduction of up to $2,000 for cars that ran on non-gasoline fuels. In the case of cars able to run on alternative and conventional fuels, the deduction only applied to the marginal expense of creating the alternative-fuel capability.

The deductions were to be at $5,000 for trucks or vans weighing between 10,000 pounds and 26,000 pounds, and $50,000 for heavier trucks and vans or for buses that seat at least 20 adults.

These deductions were to reduced by 25 percent as of 2002, 50 percent in 2003, 75 percent in 2004 and be removed in 2005.

The bill also provided a deduction for the cost of fueling equipment for alternative-fuel vehicles, to be capped at $100,000.

Fuels that qualified for these provisions were natural gas, liquefied natural gas, liquefied petroleum gas, hydrogen, electricity or any other fuel that was at least 85 percent methanol, ethanol or another alcohol, or ether. But the deduction would not be applied to electric vehicles that qualify for a new tax credit described below.

● **Electric vehicle credit.** Provided a 10 percent tax credit for the cost of buying an electric vehicle. The credit would be capped at $4,000 per vehicle and be phased out after 2001, ending entirely in 2005.

● **Renewable energy.** Created a production credit for energy generated by wind or "closed-loop biomass," crops grown exclusively to produce electricity. Producers were to earn a 1.5-cent credit for every kilowatt hour of electricity produced from these sources, but the credit was to be phased out if the price of electricity from these sources rose above a certain threshold. The credit was to be available for 10 years after a renewable energy facility had been put into service.

The bill also permanently extended an existing business energy tax credit for investments in solar and geothermal energy.

● **Oil and gas drillers.** Provided tax relief for independent oil and gas drillers under the so-called Alternative Minimum Tax. The changes, which were to be permanent, are estimated to cost about $1 billion over five years.

● **Nuclear decommissioning.** Sought to encourage nuclear utilities to put more money into decommissioning funds for eventual cleanup. The bill was to loosen certain investment restrictions on money placed in a decommissioning fund. The law also was to lower the tax rate on earnings in a decommissioning fund to 22 percent beginning in 1994 and 20 percent as of 1996.

● **Ethanol blending.** Broadened existing tax breaks for ethanol-blended gasoline.

● **State financing.** Made it easier to build environmental improvements at hydroelectric dams by excluding financing for such projects from federal limits on how many tax-exempt bonds each state can issue.

● **Non-conventional fuels.** Enabled facilities that produce gas from biomass or synthetic fuels from coal to qualify for an existing tax credit prior to 1996.

### Offsets

● **Chemical tax.** Increased the excise tax on certain ozone-depleting chemicals, such as chlorofluorocarbons. The increase was not to affect halons and other ozone-depleters used in foam insulation. The increases were expected to raise about $1 billion over five years.

● **Offsets.** Included a range of tax measures unrelated to energy policy to pay for some of the energy-related tax breaks in the law. These provisions included:

—**Seller-financed mortgages.** Required reporting the tax identification numbers of all parties to a seller-financed mortgage transaction.

—**Backup withholding.** Increased from 20 percent to 31 percent the amount of tax withheld from certain payments to taxpayers who failed to provide taxpayer identification numbers or supplied obviously incorrect information.

—**Gambling winnings.** Increased the withholding rate on gambling winnings from 20 percent to 28 percent, as of 1993. However the law raised the threshhold amount for withholding from $1,000 to $5,000.

—**Travel expenses.** Denied a tax deduction for travel expenses related to out-of-town employment that lasts more than a year, effective as of 1993.

## RADIOACTIVE WASTE

### Nuclear

● **Nuclear negotiator.** Extended the term of the federal nuclear waste negotiator two years to January 1995. The negotiator position was created by the 1982 Nuclear Waste Policy Act (PL 97-425) to help the government identify host sites for nuclear waste repositories.

The energy bill also was to modify the waste policy law to exclude U.S. territories and freely associated states from consideration as possible volunteer hosts for a temporary nuclear waste facility.

● **Yucca Mountain dump.** Required the Environmental Protection Agency (EPA) to issue new public health and safety standards for a proposed high-level nuclear waste dump at Yucca Mountain, Nev., after completion of a National Academy of Sciences study of the issue.

EPA issued regulations for radioactive waste disposal in 1985, but portions were struck down by a federal appeals court in 1987.

The House bill had directed the EPA to reinstate the 1985 standards, save the provisions that had been rejected by the court. But conferees instead directed the EPA to issue new standards specific to the Yucca Mountain site.

The new standards were to be based on a study to be conducted by the National Academy of Sciences, to be completed no later than the end of 1993. According to the legislation, the EPA standards should prescribe a maximum radiation exposure level for individuals — a departure from the previous standard, which dictated exposure levels for the population as a whole.

The law also directed the NRC to modify its licensing criteria for the repository based on the assumption that the Energy Department was to continue to oversee the facility indefinitely after it has been closed in order to guard against intrusion. Previously, the NRC had been directed to assume that active monitoring would continue for only 100 years after closure.

Report language accompanying the bill specified that the National Academy of Sciences study could look at issues not mentioned in the bill, including collective doses of radiation. And it stated that the EPA was not strictly bound by the findings or parameters of the study when it made its final rule.

● **Waste report.** Directed the Energy Department to prepare a report on whether existing nuclear waste programs were sufficient to

handle any waste that would be generated by newly licensed nuclear plants. The report was to be prepared in collaboration with the NRC and the EPA and was due within one year of the bill's enactment.

- **State regulation.** Revoked a controversial NRC proposal, then on hold, to deregulate aspects of low-level radioactive waste and allow it to be buried in ordinary landfills.

The legislation empowered states to regulate aspects of low-level radioactive waste if the federal government went ahead with plans to deregulate it. States could regulate the disposal or off-site incineration of such wastes.

## PUHCA

### Electric utilities

- **Wholesale generators.** Created a category of wholesale power producers that are exempt from the 1935 Public Utility Holding Company Act (PUHCA). The change was to allow utilities to operate independent wholesale plants outside their service territories and encourage independent producers to operate generating plants. Many of the independent plants were expected to be small- to medium-sized facilities, fueled by natural gas or renewable energy.

Power producers would have to apply to the Federal Energy Regulatory Commission for this designation on a case-by-case basis. The commission was to have 60 days to make the determination, and applicants were to attain the status on a good-faith basis while the decision was being made. The exemption would apply only to producers that generate and sell electricity wholesale, although that restriction would not apply to a company engaged in retail power sales overseas.

Utilities cannot win this exempt status for plants that have already been built and their costs all or partially included in a utility's rate base unless all affected state utility commissions determined that it would benefit consumers to do so.

- **Safeguards.** Banned utilities from buying power from an independent affiliate unless state regulators determined that the sale would benefit consumers. The ban was an attempt to prevent so-called self-dealing, whereby a utility builds an independent power plant then sells power to itself at inflated rates.

The law allowed "hybrid" power plants, pieces of which are owned by a utility and included in its rate base and other pieces of which are exempted from PUHCA rules under the new classification. However, a utility could not own both the exempt and non-exempt portions of such a hybrid plant, eliminating some risks of ratepayer abuse.

The legislation set clearer restrictions on rate setting when a utility leased an independent power plant.

- **State review.** Allowed state regulators to examine the debt load of an independent generator and impose a specific debt-to-equity ratio if needed. Some utility advocates feared that independent producers would have a financing edge over federally regulated utilities, which were required to maintain a prescribed debt-to-equity ratio.

The law granted state regulators access to the relevant financial records of wholesale power generators that were exempt from the PUHCA law, as well as any affiliated utility. This access applied to all affected state utility commissions.

- **Foreign investment.** Changed existing law to allow registered utility holding companies covered under the PUHCA law to build or invest in power plants or distribution facilities in foreign countries. The Securities and Exchange Commission would be responsible for regulating those investments to protect the utility's ratepayers. State regulators could offer recommendations for or against such investments, but would not be required to approve such a deal.

However, state regulators would oversee foreign electricity investments by utilities that were not owned by registered holding companies and could block them if they determined that the investments would jeopardize ratepayers.

- **Transmission access.** Allowed wholesale electricity generators to request that the Federal Energy Regulatory Commission order a utility to transmit their power. FERC is authorized to issue this order whenever the transaction is in the public interest.

Wholesale producers would have to pay for this transmission, and those charges would have to cover the utility's transmission costs plus a reasonable return on investment. Mandatory transmission orders would not be allowed when they jeopardized the reliability of established electric systems.

The law banned FERC from issuing a transmission order that would result in a wholesale power producer selling directly to consumers or in "sham transactions" whereby a third party buys electricity wholesale and resells it to disguise what is basically a retail transaction.

The transmission language did not fully apply to the Bonneville Power Administration and the Tennessee Valley Authority.

### Octane-Level Posting

- **Enforcement.** Strengthened state authority to enforce octane posting requirements and extend such posting to non-traditional automotive fuels such as diesel fuel, some reformulated gasoline and gasohol. The provisions were meant to deter octane mislabeling, whereby suppliers overrepresent the octane level of gas.

## RESEARCH AND DEVELOPMENT

### Energy Research

- **Goals.** Outlined goals for federal energy research including reducing reliance on imported oil, minimizing the health and environmental hazards of energy production and use — including the generation of greenhouse gases — and enhancing U.S. competitiveness.
- **Management.** Required the Energy secretary to prepare a management plan for energy-related research and commercialization programs, consistent with the goals above, and submit the first plan to Congress within a year of enactment. The plan would subsequently have to be updated every other year. The law created an advisory board to help the Energy secretary prepare this and other reports required by the legislation.

The legislation included other general guidelines and requirements for Energy Department research and development programs. For example, the secretary would have to send Congress a management plan for any major construction project involving $100 million or more and could not spend money on such a project until Congress had had 30 working days to review that report.

Another provision restricted financial aid under the Energy Department's research and development programs to companies that substantially contributed to the U.S. economy, effectively tightening the terms under which foreign-owned companies would qualify.

The law also laid out cost-sharing requirements for most of the energy-related research and development programs: non-federal sources would have to account for 20 percent of the funding for research programs, and at least 50 percent of demonstration or commercial application projects. However, the Energy secretary has discretion to reduce or, in the case of basic research, waive those requirements.

And the legislation directed the Energy secretary to account for so-called uncosted obligations, money that had been obligated for programs but not spent.

- **Programs.** Authorized an array of research and development programs to reduce consumption of imported oil. The Energy Department had been operating without an annual authorization bill to guide its spending priorities. The authorization provisions, which were pushed by House negotiators, sought to redirect the agency in certain ways such as increasing the department's emphasis on efficiency and renewable energy. The House bill had included specific, five-year authorizations, but in conference those were generally shrunk to two years or eliminated in favor of open-

ended authorizations.

Some of the specific programs included:

—**Advanced oil recovery.** Promoting techniques to get more oil out of wells, particularly existing wells that would otherwise be abandoned. The bill allotted $57.25 million for the program in fiscal 1993 and $70 million in fiscal 1994. An additional program promoted gleaning oil from Eastern and Western shale beds, authorized at $5.25 million in fiscal 1993 and $6 million in fiscal 1994.

—**Natural gas.** Enhancing conventional gas production and helping discover ways to extract natural gas from unconventional sources, such as tight sands and Devonian shales, surface gasification of coal and methane recovery from biofuels. The law also called for a program to promote natural gas use through improved emissions controls and storage facilities, and permitted the Energy secretary to create a research center specifically dedicated to tapping the petroleum in the Midcontinent region.

These programs were authorized at just under $30 million in fiscal 1993 and $45 million in fiscal 1994.

—**Transportation energy.** Promoting techniques to reduce oil consumption in the transportation sector through increased efficiency and substitute or alternative fuels. Many of these programs were to take the form of cooperative research agreements or demonstration projects, with costs being shared by the private sector. The law specifically called for research and development on technologies to increase the efficiency of conventional gasoline-burning cars, to improve the capability of vehicles that run on non-gasoline fuels, to promote hydrogen-fueled cars and to reduce dangerous emissions from diesel engines. These programs were authorized at $120 million for fiscal 1993 and $160 million for fiscal 1994.

—**Efficiency.** Authorizing a large research and development program to promote energy efficiency and the use of renewable energy in the building, industrial and utility sectors. The bill allotted $178 million for these efforts in fiscal 1993 and $275 million in fiscal 1994.

The specific programs within this effort included: natural gas and electric heating and cooling technologies, improving the energy efficiency and reducing the adverse environmental impact of pulp and papermaking industries, creating more efficient heat engines and better construction designs.

—**Fusion energy.** Authorizing $340 million for fusion research in fiscal 1993 and $380 million in fiscal 1994, with an emphasis on U.S. participation in an international nuclear fusion research program.

—**Nuclear waste.** Authorizing the Energy secretary to design and implement a five-year research and development plan aimed at developing technologies to reduce the hazards of nuclear waste from civilian reactors. The program was authorized at $4.7 million for fiscal 1993 and had an open-ended authorization for fiscal 1994.

—**Fuel cells.** Authorizing a five-year program to promote fuel cells, which use an electrochemical process to transform a fuel's chemical energy into electrical energy without combustion — a cleaner and more efficient way to produce power. The program was authorized at $52 million in fiscal 1993 and $56 million in fiscal 1994, within the Energy Department's overall energy research and development authorization.

—**Fast Flux test reactor.** Authorizing $70 million from the Energy Department's fiscal 1993 cleanup budget to keep the Fast Flux reactor operational. The reactor is at the Hanford reservation in Washington state, part of the department's nuclear weapons complex. The department had wanted to shut down the reactor, but area lawmakers had objected, fearing layoffs and saying the facility could be used for ongoing nuclear programs.

—**Economic growth.** Establishing several research programs designed to foster the development of advanced materials and manufacturing techniques related to increased energy efficiency.

—**Electromagnetic fields.** Increasing and coordinating federal research on the potential health hazards of electromagnetic fields, which were generated by utility transmission lines, comput-

ers and other electrical appliances. The legislation authorized $65 million for the program over fiscal 1993-97, and the program authorization expired as of January 1998.

—**Basic energy science.** Authorizing $967 million in fiscal 1993 for basic research on chemistry, geology and other areas related to energy production and consumption.

—**Education.** Providing post-secondary programs to promote math and science education for low-income and first-generation college students.

## COAL

### Clean Coal Promotion

● **Advanced technologies.** Authorized $278 million in fiscal 1993 and such sums as needed in fiscal 1994-97 for federal research and development projects designed to promote advanced coal technologies, including efforts to burn coal with fewer acid emissions and to convert coal for use as a transportation fuel. The program would seek to speed development of these technologies for commercial use by 2010 or sooner. Specific program areas included:

— The non-fuel use of coal; for instance, as a component of chemical production.

— Coal-refining technologies to help reduce emissions and facilitate the production of coal-based transportation fuels to displace imported oil.

— Underground coal gasification, to convert coal on site to a cleaner-burning and more easily transported fuel. The program in this field could have included one or more demonstration projects.

— Burning coal in connection with various solid wastes, such as used tires, to produce energy.

— Magnetohydrodynamics, a high-temperature coal-burning process that uses a magnetic field to create electricity.

The legislation was to allow but not mandate continuation of the Energy Department's ongoing Clean Coal Technology program, which helped fund industry projects to demonstrate innovative coal technologies.

● **Technology transfer.** Created a technology transfer program to export "clean coal" energy technologies to other nations. The program was to be developed by the Energy Department, working with the Agency for International Development and a newly created interagency "clean coal" subgroup of the Trade Promotion Coordinating Committee.

The law authorized federal support for at least one demonstration project. The financial assistance could take the form of subsidizing the incremental cost between a customary coal-burning facility and one that employed a cleaner-burning technique. The program was authorized at $100 million a year in fiscal 1993-98. The legislation gave preference to projects that would decrease harmful emissions from coal use or increase the efficiency or cost-effectiveness of coal use.

The administration also would have some leeway to promote the export of conventional coal-burning technologies, in addition to the "clean coal" techniques.

● **Exports.** Required within 180 days of passage the development of an interagency plan to boost U.S. coal exports. The plan must address trade barriers to U.S. coal and recommendations for alleviating these barriers, as well as an assessment of the environmental implications of coal exports.

● **Small coal operators.** Expanded an existing program to help pay the permitting costs of coal operators who produce less than 300,000 tons annually.

● **Retiree health benefits.** Created a program to ensure the health benefits of about 120,000 retired union coal miners and their dependents who worked for companies that had gone out of business or were no longer paying into the miners' health fund. The law was to bail out the anemic health fund by letting the union shift $210 million over three years from its overstocked pension fund. It was to force many of the original companies, or a

related business, to pay for its retirees. The legislation extended the Abandoned Mines Land fund, a reclamation fund gleaned from a fee on coal companies, until 2004 and tapped interest on the fund to help pay for the health benefits. In exchange, the miners' union agreed to certain health-care cost containment measures.

The law also established a second fund to protect the health benefits of thousands of additional coal miners whose benefits might have been jeopardized in the future.

● **Coal-bed methane.** Sought to promote the recovery of methane gas, found in coal seams, for use as a fuel. The gas was viewed as a hazard and it was usually released into the atmosphere, but advocates believed it needed to be recovered to limit greenhouse gas emissions and to utilize its energy potential.

The legislation sought to break the logjam over conflicting ownership rights that could complicate methane recovery. States that did not yet have a mechanism for resolving such conflicts and promoting methane recovery would have up to three years to develop one. If they failed to do so, the Interior secretary would be required to implement a program to let methane recovery take place in those areas. Interior could establish "pooling" arrangements under which a designated developer would extract the methane gas and the subsequent profits would be held in escrow until conflicting ownership claims were resolved.

However, states could block such federal intervention through a governor's petition or by action of the state legislature. Methane drillers would have to get permission from owners of adjacent coal mines, and those coal operators still would be free to vent the methane gas for safety reasons.

The provision applied immediately to West Virginia, Pennsylvania, Kentucky, Ohio, Tennessee, Indiana and Illinois, although that list was subject to revision by the Interior secretary. It specifically would not affect Colorado, Montana, New Mexico, Wyoming, Utah, Virginia, Washington, Mississippi, Louisiana and Alabama.

● **Remining.** Adjusted current regulation to encourage remining, or drawing additional coal from abandoned mines or refuse piles.

● **Subsidence.** Held mine operators accountable for some property damage created by subsidence, a sinking or shifting in the land caused by underground mining. Compensation would include restoring or replacing damaged homes, non-commercial buildings or contaminated water supplies.

● **Mining rights.** Temporarily blocked any administrative policy changes on coal mining rights on certain federal lands. At issue was determining who held rights (referred to as "valid existing rights") to mine coal on federal lands, including parks and other sensitive areas, that were later put off-limits to drilling under the 1977 Surface Mining Control and Reclamation Act (PL 95-87). The Bush administration reportedly had considered issuing a new policy that would have allowed strip mining on some of these lands. However, the legislation banned any change in the policy for one year, effectively deferring to state law on the matter.

● **Indian grants.** Authorized federal grants to the Navajo, Hopi, Northern Cheyenne and Crow Indians to help them develop regulations governing surface coal mining and reclamation on their lands.

## OIL PIPELINES

### Rates

● **Streamlining.** Directed the Federal Energy Regulatory Commission to simplify its method for setting "just and reasonable" rates for interstate oil pipelines. However, the law allowed rates that were approved at least one year before enactment and that were not subject to challenge to remain in effect. It also directed the commission to streamline consideration of rate changes.

## FEDERAL ONSHORE LEASES

### Oil, Gas Leases

● **Leasing bids.** Specified that all federal oil and gas leases run

for 10-year primary terms, regardless of whether they were issued on a competitive or non-competitive basis. Before, non-competitive leases ran for 10 years while competitive leases lasted only five — a situation some critics said discouraged drillers from bidding competitively for federal leases.

● **Oil shale claims.** Designated a settlement for disputed, pre-1920 oil shale claims to about 250,000 acres in Colorado, Utah and Wyoming that were under federal control. The bill specified that claimholders who already had won initial certification of plans to develop oil shale on their holdings could go ahead and buy the federally controlled land for $2.50 an acre. However, other claimholders could only buy rights to the oil shale, not other minerals or the surface property, or pay fees to maintain their claims.

● **Allegheny National Forest.** Increased environmental safeguards on oil and gas development in the Allegheny National Forest.

● **Stripper wells.** Allowed certain small oil and gas wells, known as stripper wells, to continue operating on federal lands even after the mineral rights reverted to the federal government.

## INDIAN ENERGY AND INSULAR AREAS

### Indian Energy Resources

● **Commission.** Established an Indian Energy Resource Commission to promote the development of energy resources on land belonging to American Indians through measures such as tax incentives. The commission was charged with developing a report within one year. The commissionn was to be disbanded 30 days after the report was submitted to Congress.

● **Federal aid.** Authorized a federal program of financial aid and technical assistance to promote energy independence for American Indians. The aid was to include grants and low-interest loans for projects that, among other things, would create vertically integrated energy industries within tribal reservations. These programs were authorized at $30 million a year in fiscal 1994 through 1997.

The law also authorized an additional $10 million in each of fiscal 1994 through 1997 to advance tribal regulatory policies that would enhance energy development.

● **Insular areas.** Authorized up to $2 million annually for federal grants to help insular areas decrease their energy dependence.

● **PCB cleanup.** Allowed the Marshall Islands and Federated States of Micronesia to be eligible for "superfund" money to clean up contamination by polychlorinated biphenyls (PCBs) that occurred during U.S. trusteeship of the islands.

## MISCELLANEOUS

● **Plutonium shipments.** Required a presidential study on the safety of shipping plutonium by sea, including the safety of the storage casks and the potential risks and demands on individual states. The report was due within 60 days of enactment, to be followed within three months by a presidential plan, in consultation with the NRC, to implement its recomendations. This provision was aimed at Japan, which had begun shipping plutonium from France to use as fuel in nuclear power reactors.

● **Whistleblower protection.** Increased legal protections for employees of nuclear facilities — including those run by the Energy Department and its contractors — who reported possible health and safety violations.

● **Fuel prices.** Authorized a study and pilot program to examine using the futures and options markets to purchase fuel in an effort to protect government entities that purchased fuel — such as the Low Income Housing Energy Assistance Program, which helped the poor pay home heating and cooling bills — from price surges.

● **Set-asides.** Directed agency heads to try to funnel at least 10 percent of the contracts authorized in the bill to small businesses owned by women or minorities, to historically black colleges and universities, or to universities with student bodies that were at least 20 percent Hispanic or Native American. ∎

# Nuclear Waste Dump Gets Cautious Nod

In the final hours of the 102nd Congress, the Senate cleared legislation that ended a lengthy battle and paved the way for the Energy Department to begin storing certain defense-related nuclear waste at the Waste Isolation Pilot Plant (WIPP), a $1 billion facility near Carlsbad, N.M.

The House approved the conference report Oct. 6 by voice vote; the Senate followed suit two days later. President Bush signed the bill Oct. 30 — PL 102-579.

Built in the salt caverns 2,000 feet below the New Mexico desert, the site was designed to store plutonium-tainted waste from the nation's nuclear weapons factories. The dump had been ready, but the Energy Department lacked the necessary congressional approval to begin storing waste there.

The legislation transferred the New Mexico dump site to the Energy Department and set certain restrictions to be met before testing could begin. Those conditions included oversight by the Environmental Protection Agency (EPA). For example, before the site could be used, the agency was to issue public safety standards to ensure that the waste be safely disposed of. It also authorized federal aid to the state of New Mexico, to the tune of $20 million a year for 15 years.

The final terms were more restrictive than the Bush administration wanted but represented the minimum some lawmakers wanted to consider to let the project to go forward.

The compromise was drafted by the Senate Energy and Natural Resources Committee and three House panels — Armed Services, Energy and Commerce and Interior. It had the support of most of the New Mexico delegation. Energy Secretary James D. Watkins had threatened to begin laying off workers at the site if there was no movement toward opening the facility.

## BACKGROUND

Congress authorized the Energy Department to begin construction of the WIPP project in 1979. It was designed and built as a permanent repository for transuranic nuclear waste, considered low in radiation but high in toxic plutonium.

The Energy Department first intended to open the site in 1988, but in 1987 a federal court struck down the EPA disposal standards for transuranic waste because they violated other EPA standards for drinking water. In addition, congressional investigators had doubts about the safety and stability of the facility. A key problem was the stability of the rock within WIPP's caverns that could have endangered workers and the integrity of waste containers during the test phase.

Other problems developed in opening the WIPP site once it was complete. Before the repository could be made available for a series of tests to determine its suitability it

---

### BOXSCORE

➡ **Waste Isolation Pilot Plant (S 1671, HR 2637).** The legislation paved the way for the opening of the Energy Department's underground nuclear waste-storage facility, located near Carlsbad, N.M., but also set oversight conditions.

**Reports:** H Rept 102-241, Parts 1-3; S Rept 102-196; conference report H Rept 102-1037.

### KEY ACTION

Oct. 6 — The **House** adopted the conference report on S 1671 by voice vote.

Oct. 8 — The **Senate** cleared the legislation by voice vote.

Oct. 30 — President Bush signed the bill Oct. 30 — PL 102-579.

---

had to be transferred from the Interior Department's Bureau of Land Management to the Energy Department. Such a "land withdrawal" was to be done either administratively or legislatively, though only a legislative withdrawal would have been permanent.

Frustrated by congressional inaction, the Energy Department on Oct. 3, 1991, attempted to obtain control of the site through the less preferable administrative transfer route. But the state of New Mexico filed suit and prevailed in a decision issued nearly two months later on Nov. 26. *(1991 Almanac, p. 224)*

The attempt to seize the WIPP site by executive fiat prodded Congress into moving legislation. A legislative solution promised to assure greater environmental oversight as well as financial compensation for New Mexico.

The Senate passed a bill (S 1671) Nov. 5, 1991, to let waste storage begin in exchange for certain payments to state and local governments and the department's pledge to abide by certain environmental standards. In the House, the three committees with jurisdiction over the issue approved competing versions of a waste dump bill (HR 2637) that generally would have imposed stiffer environmental conditions than the Senate version.

Prodded by the threat that the administration would act unilaterally, the House moved to reconcile the draft bills. With the court ruling, however, Bill Richardson, D-N.M., said the pressure was on the Energy Department to negotiate a deal more to the House's liking. "If they don't, we'll sit on them," Richardson said.

## COMPROMISE REACHED

Before Congress could make a move in 1992, a U.S. District Court judge called a firmer halt to the Energy Department's efforts to open the nuclear waste dump in New Mexico. U.S. District Judge John Garrett Penn, who had previously issued a temporary injunction on the waste shipments, ruled Feb. 3 that the administration could not proceed without congressional authorization.

This gave lawmakers more time to craft a bill to everyone's liking.

The congressional impasse finally broke in mid-June, when chairmen of the three rival committees — Interior, Energy and Commerce, and Armed Services — agreed on a compromise version of the bill.

For years, controversy had stalled the Energy Department's efforts to open a low-level nuclear dump in New Mexico to store the waste of the nation's atomic bomb factories. Even as the House seemed poised to pass a bill (HR 2637) allowing trial storage at the dump, the project remained enmeshed in conflict. New doubts about the merits of the tests had emerged, and lawmakers were considering imposing conditions opposed by the Bush administration.

Both the Senate and House bills would set restrictions on the land withdrawal and the proposed testing. While the Bush administration could live with the terms of the Senate bill passed in November 1991, it was unhappy with the stricter environmental requirements in the House proposal.

The House version would give the EPA a stronger role in overseeing tests at the dump and allow much less waste to be buried at the facility during the test phase.

Even those terms were not strong enough for Richardson of New Mexico, a longtime critic of the facility.

Richardson threatened to offer an amendment to block any test storage at the site until EPA certified that the dump would meet the agency's standards for radiological disposal — standards that had yet to be written.

His position was strengthened considerably by a June study by the National Academy of Sciences that questioned the wisdom of the administration's planned tests at the site.

The report's overall scientific recommendations did not necessarily jibe with Richardson's views; for example, the panel was generally supportive of the project and backed some underground testing at the dump.

But the political benefits flowed to Richardson. First, the report suggested that the specific tests the administration was planning were ill-conceived and wasteful.

Second, the Energy Department launched a damage-control effort that ultimately backfired on Capitol Hill.

A top Energy Department official complained to the academy's president that the study was being distorted by the news media and urged him to clarify the panel's position to key legislators. But that letter became public, and several staff aides said the final result was to weaken the department's standing.

Nevertheless, Richardson was considered unlikely to prevail. He was the only member of the New Mexico delegation backing that restriction, which would significantly delay any testing at the site.

"I've been hanging alone for years on this," Richardson said.

Arrayed against him were members from states with Energy Department nuclear facilities, where waste that would ultimately be sent to the dump had been piling up.

And the three chairmen who drew up the compromise bill pledged to oppose any amendments on the House floor.

Some aides who worked on the compromise believed that the draft contained ample protections against unwarranted tests.

Under its terms, the EPA had to certify that proposed tests at the dump site were necessary. If the criticisms raised in the National Academy of Sciences study were valid, they said, that standard should effectively block the planned tests.

That language was not in the Senate bill, and Richardson and other WIPP critics hoped that one effect of the study would be to strengthen the House's position in an eventual conference on the bill.

The administration defended its planning and said the tests would yield important information about the safety of storing waste in the salt caverns.

Another eventual point of contention was money. While the Senate bill included about $600 million in impact aid for New Mexico, the House draft bill included only $40 million already authorized.

### Fine-Tuning Continues

House and Senate negotiators were still working the week of Sept. 28 to reach a deal on a bill (S 1671) that would allow the Energy Department to begin testing the new storage site in New Mexico to house defense-related nuclear waste.

The latest House proposal gave significant ground on the issue of EPA safety standards. House members wanted the EPA to issue final standards on the disposal of radioactive waste before the Energy Department could begin to use the WIPP site in the salt caverns below the desert.

The existing House offer would continue to require EPA safety standards to be in place before defense-related waste could be stored at the New Mexico site. But it would not require those standards to apply to a separate repository planned for Yucca Mountain, Nev., to house high-level nuclear waste from commercial nuclear power plants.

Yet action on the bill was stalled the week of Sept. 28, with many of the conference participants distracted by other business, especially the completion of work on the huge energy bill (HR 776).

The New Mexico repository bill also got entangled in a controversial water projects bill (HR 429) that would have revamped the operation of California's Central Valley Project. Interior Committee Chairman George Miller, D-Calif., reportedly had agreed to the Yucca Mountain exemption, in exchange for help in retaining the California water project reforms. But until the water bill moved, Miller was unwilling to give up his leverage to allow the New Mexico dump bill to advance. *(Yucca mountain, p. 243; energy bill, p. 231; omnibus Western water projects, p. 264)*

## FINAL ACTION

Final approval of the measure was nearly derailed by Sen. Richard H. Bryan, D-Nev. He and other members of the Nevada delegation were angry about provisions in the conference agreement that could have indirectly allowed the Energy Department to use weaker safety standards on a proposed Nevada site for storage of high-level nuclear waste.

But, according to Bryan's staff, he finally gave in and allowed the bill to move in the final hours of the Senate session, after receiving assurances from New Mexico's senators — Pete V. Domenici, R, and Jeff Bingaman, D — that they would revisit the safety standards issue in the 103rd Congress.

The final agreement gave the House negotiators much of the safety standards they had sought, but sped up the timetable for federal action, which pleased Senate conferees.

It called on the EPA to issue new safety standards for the dump within six months of enactment. And EPA approval of the Energy Department's testing plan for the site had to be approved within 10 months of enactment.

The agreement specifically stated that the new EPA safety standards would apply only to the New Mexico site and not to another proposed facility for high-level radioactive waste at Yucca Mountain, Nev. That was what angered Bryan and other Nevadans.

James Bilbray, D-Nev., took to the House floor Oct. 6 to denounce the agreement, which he blamed on Senate Energy and Natural Resources Chairman J. Bennett Johnston, D-La.

"He stuck it to us in the energy bill, he stuck it to us in the WIPP bill, and that is why I have risen in opposition," Bilbray said.

The compromise measure also included an annual $20 million payment for 15 years to the state of New Mexico for

costs associated with locating the site there. That was about half the $600 million the Senate bill would have authorized, but was significantly more than the one-time, $40 million payment contained in the original House measure.

House Energy and Commerce Chairman John D. Dingell, D-Mich., defended the agreement, saying, "This is a good resolution of a very difficult series of questions, and a very, very large number of conflicting interests and concerns."

After years of controversy, the WIPP project was given the congressional nod of approval to start without a roll call vote. The House adopted the conference report by voice vote Oct. 6; the Senate cleared it the same way on Oct. 8. ■

# Federal Agencies Liable For Waste Violations

After years of effort, Congress cleared and President Bush signed into law a bill that explicitly removed sovereign immunity claimed by federal agencies as a shield against prosecution and fines for violating federal solid and hazardous waste laws.

According to lawmakers such as Senate Majority Leader George J. Mitchell, D-Maine, the federal government had long been among the country's worst polluters, with the prime offenders being the Energy and Defense departments' nuclear weapons and energy complexes.

The principal shield federal polluters used to protect themselves from punishment under the nation's pollution laws was stripped away in the bill Congress cleared Sept. 23.

By an overwhelming margin of 403-3, the House voted to approve the conference report for the measure (HR 2194 — H Rept 102-886). Within hours, the Senate followed suit, passing the measure by voice vote. *(Vote 409, p. 100-H)*

President Bush signed the bill Oct. 6 — PL 102-386. Though the administration originally opposed the bill, the final product addressed many of its earlier concerns.

The bill had a straightforward purpose, said Mitchell: "The federal government should not be above the law." Mitchell authored the earlier Senate version of the bill (S 596).

## BACKGROUND

In states such as Ohio, Maine and Washington, hazardous and nuclear wastes had been dumped, had escaped into the air and had contaminated groundwater supplies.

While the Environmental Protection Agency (EPA) and various state legal authorities had attempted to rein in federal pollution through fines and lawsuits, the facilities had claimed sovereign immunity. In effect, they said that while they were bound by U.S. and state environmental laws, they could not be punished if they violated them.

One of the more notorious examples of this was in Fernald, Ohio, where an Energy Department plant had spewed at least 393,000 pounds of uranium into the surrounding environment over the previous three decades. When the EPA slapped the department with a $372,000 fine, the department refused to pay, saying the EPA lacked jurisdiction.

That view was disputed by Congress, which said the solid-waste Resource Conservation and Recovery Act (PL 94-580) waived sovereign immunity for federal polluters. That view had not been unanimously supported by the federal courts: In a ruling (*U.S. Department of Energy v. Ohio*) in 1992, the Supreme Court said Congress had not explicitly exempted federal facilities.

In the House, the bill was written by Ohio Democrat Dennis E. Eckart, who promptly garnered 140 original co-sponsors. The bill passed easily by voice vote June 24, 1991. *(1991 Almanac, p. 222)*

"There is a horrible double standard in America, in which the federal government has been saying 'Don't do as I do, do as I tell you,' " Eckart said. "We've now resolved that in favor of safe and full enforcement of our federal environmental laws."

The Senate bill had a rockier path — at one point it attracted an amendment dealing with documents leaked during Supreme Court Justice Clarence Thomas' confirmation — but nonetheless passed by an overwhelming 94-3 on Oct. 24, 1991. *(1991 Almanac, p. 274)*

After that, the bill's progress slowed as House and Senate negotiators sought to work out differences between the two bills and deal with a flurry of objections from the Bush administration.

## REACHING AGREEMENT

The administration especially objected to provisions that involved mixed hazardous and nuclear waste, shipboard hazardous waste, and how to treat old munitions and emissions from federally owned sewage treatment plants.

Federal agencies, especially the Energy Department, complained that the bill would require them to dispose of dangerous mixed hazardous and nuclear wastes even though safe disposal technology had not been invented. Conferees agreed to give federal facilities with mixed waste a three-year grace period to come up with such technologies.

The administration also said that under the bill, ships that carried hazardous materials in their holds would be considered hazardous waste sites and thus subject to greatly increased record-keeping and inspection responsibilities.

Negotiators began resolving the problems in 1992 by changing the bill to say any hazardous waste generated on a ship would not be subject to the bill's hazardous waste rules unless the material was kept on board for more than 90 days (to stop ships from becoming floating waste dumps).

Another obstacle to enactment that lawmakers faced was what to do with the myriad munitions — both conventional and chemical — that littered military installations. The final bill required the EPA to write regulations specifying when munitions should be treated as hazardous waste.

The bill also classified federally owned wastewater treatment plants as less-regulated solid waste facilities and exempted them from the hazardous waste strictures of the bill. Administration officials had worried that because some hazardous waste occasionally could taint wastewater at federal facilities, all the wastewater was to be treated as hazardous waste.

The bill also authorized federal agencies to pay the legal costs of employees sued for violating the bill, when they did so in the scope of their job. ■

# Rocky Mountain Arsenal To Be Wildlife Refuge

The Army's huge Rocky Mountain arsenal in Colorado was to be transformed into a de facto wildlife refuge under a bill cleared by Congress on Sept. 25 — even though parts of the proposed refuge had become so contaminated that they were on the nation's list of its worst hazardous waste sites.

The House accepted several Senate amendments that aimed to ensure the cleanup of the refuge and, by voice vote, approved the amended bill (HR 1435 — H Rept 102-463). The Senate passed the bill by voice vote Sept. 18.

President Bush signed the measure Oct. 9 — PL 102-402.

Contamination from years of chemical weapons work at the arsenal by the Army and its prime contractor, Shell Oil Co., was concentrated on about 20 percent of the arsenal. The Army, which had managed the arsenal since 1942, had left the unused portion of the facility in its natural state.

Though just about nine miles north of Denver, an untainted part of the arsenal had become a haven for wildlife, with large populations of bald eagles, falcons, prairie dogs and deer. The arsenal had attracted about 50,000 visitors over the previous two years. Tranforming the arsenal into a refuge had long been a goal of Rep. Patricia Schroeder, D-Colo., the bill's sponsor.

The Army and Shell Oil were to be responsible for cleanup of the arsenal under the bill, but the Interior Department was charged with operating the refuge. The arsenal was not to become an official wildlife refuge until the cleanup was completed, a process that was expected to take up to 20 years. But it was to be managed as if it were a refuge in the interim.

The House Merchant Marine Committee Fisheries and Wildlife Subcommittee on June 25 had approved the bill (HR 1435) by voice vote, and the full committee followed suit July 1, also by voice vote.

"The diversity of wildlife there — so close to an urban center — is truly unique," said subcommittee Chairman Gerry E. Studds, D-Mass. More than 130 fish and wildlife species exist on or near the arsenal. ∎

# Additional Bills Address Other Energy Issues

A year of rigorous work on a wide spectrum of energy issues, from mining to fuel standards, culminated in a law (PL 102-486) viewed as the first major attempt to decrease U.S. oil dependence since the late 1970s. But a handful of other energy-related measures also got lawmakers' attention during the second session. Those included:

## SERVICE STATION COMPETITION

A slew of bills moved in 1992 in response to charges that oil companies were using unfair tactics to squeeze out competition with their retail stations. But none of the measures advanced to the floor.

The House Energy and Commerce Committee approved a bill (HR 5000 — H Rept 102-1029) by voice vote June 2

to prohibit oil companies from setting unduly stringent franchise terms that would effectively force independent station owners out of business.

Some operators had complained of companies demanding that they stay open around the clock or keep more than one mechanic on duty. Critics said companies were setting such demands to squeeze out independent franchisers and convert their stations to company-owned outlets.

The Senate Energy and Natural Resources Committee on July 1 approved a companion bill (S 2656 — S Rept 102-325) to HR 5000 to strengthen the hand of service station operators in their franchise negotiations with oil companies.

The bill, approved 20-0, would bar oil companies from placing unduly stringent contract terms on franchisees.

But while those bills lingered, four additional bills aimed at protecting independent gasoline marketers and station operators from big oil companies moved through House and Senate committees the week of Aug. 10.

The Senate Judiciary Committee on Aug. 12 approved a bill (S 790 — S Rept 102-450) that would bar oil producers and refiners from owning their own gas stations. At the same markup, the panel also approved two related bills (S 2041 — S Rept 102-423 and S 2043 — S Rept 102-458) that would limit how much refiners could charge for gas they sold wholesale to service stations. Neither of those measures advanced to the Senate floor.

The House Energy and Commerce Subcommittee on Energy and Power on Aug. 11 approved another bill (HR 2966), which also would restrict refiners' wholesale gas prices.

The House bill sought to address so-called price inversions, when refiners charged their wholesale customers more than they charged retail customers at gas stations they owned.

Mike Synar, D-Okla., the bill's sponsor, said there was no legitimate justification for wholesale prices being higher than retail pump prices. His bill specified that refiners could not charge wholesale customers more than 94 percent of the retail price at their own station.

Carlos J. Moorhead, Calif., the ranking Republican on the Energy and Power Subcommittee, said a refiner might have legitimate reasons for dropping retail prices, such as to compete in a localized price war.

And he warned that the legislation could backfire, causing some refiners to abandon their wholesale operations and thus limit supply for independent marketers.

Subcommittee Chairman Philip R. Sharp, D-Ind., agreed that it would be better for the industry to correct the problem on its own, but he said approving the bill in subcommittee could help accomplish that: "We hope to give them a wake-up call by moving." Synar's bill was approved by voice vote. The full committee did not act on the bill.

Two of the three bills approved by Senate Judiciary also addressed price inversions by limiting how much refiners could charge their wholesale customers. One of these (S 2041) was sponsored by Charles E. Grassley, R-Iowa, the other (S 2043) by Paul Simon, D-Ill.

The third Senate bill, sponsored by Dennis DeConcini, D-Ariz., took a different approach by barring refiners from operating gas stations.

DeConcini said large oil companies were charging artificially low prices at their stations to force independent station owners out of the market.

But industry critics said DeConcini's proposal threat-

ened to reduce competition at the retail level, possibly raising prices and reducing convenience for customers.

Hank Brown, R-Colo., tried unsuccessfully to go further and also block independent gas marketers from owning retail stations. Panel members said those marketers were not affecting competition, and Brown's amendment was rejected on a voice vote.

## PIPELINE SAFETY

The House on Oct. 6 cleared a bill that aimed to curb environmental damage from natural gas and hazardous liquid pipelines. The Senate had passed the bill by voice vote Oct. 5.

The bill (S 1583 — S Rept 102-152) reauthorized pipeline safety laws and required the Transportation Department to consider potential harm to the environment when setting safety requirements for pipelines. Existing rules emphasized the protection of life and property.

The bill also required the department to study the use of safety valves to shut off the flow of natural gas whenever a leak occurred.

The Senate first passed the bill Oct. 7, 1991. The House took up the bill Sept. 15, 1992, substituting provisions from a House pipeline safety bill (HR 1489 — H Rept 247, Parts 1-3). Those provisions put more emphasis on environmental concerns than did the Senate bill.

Senators agreed to the House amendment Oct. 6 and added an amendment of their own, concerning the completion of the Page Avenue Extension project in Missouri, which would connect St. Louis County to St. Charles County. The House concurred in the Senate amendment later the same day, clearing the measure for the president.

President Bush signed the bill Oct. 24 (PL 102-508).

## COLORADO'S OIL SHALE RESERVES

Legislation (HR 3168 — H Rept 102-610, Parts 1, 2, 3) to promote natural gas drilling within Colorado's federal naval oil shale reserves got the nod from three House committees but never advanced to the floor.

The Interior and Insular Affairs Committee on June 3 approved HR 3168 by voice vote. Proponents said the federal government must drill the gas or lose it to private interests that were drawing down the reservoir from outside the boundaries of the naval reserve.

The Energy Department conducted some gas drilling in the reserve area, but only under limited conditions. The bill sought to provide far greater access, authorizing the Interior secretary to issue gas leases for certain portions of the reserves in Colorado's Garfield County.

The government would take 12.5 percent royalties from any drilling revenues, to be split evenly between Colorado and the federal Treasury. The drilling was not expected to affect the oil shale deposits.

But the bill quickly faced opposition on jurisdictional and fiscal grounds.

The Armed Services Committee contended that it had jurisdiction over the oil shale reserve, created to provide the Navy with a ready supply of oil. And there were disputes over whether the proposal ultimately would save or cost the federal Treasury money.

The House Energy and Commerce Committee on July 9 also approved, by voice vote, the bill to open two Navy oil shale reserves in Colorado to oil and gas exploration.

The reserves were established early in the century to give the Navy access to oil that could be obtained from the oil shale deposits.

## EASTERN vs. WESTERN COAL INTERESTS

The House Interior Subcommittee on Mining and Natural Resources approved March 10 a controversial bill (HR 693) to protect Eastern coal mining operations from Western competitors who extracted low-sulfur coal from public lands.

Action halted on the measure after the Interior and Insular Affairs Committee on June 3 postponed markup of the bill that pitted Eastern and Western coal interests against each other.

Sponsored by subcommittee Chairman Nick J. Rahall II, D-W.Va., the measure sought to prohibit the Interior Department's Bureau of Land Management (BLM) from leasing its property for coal mining operations whose activities would compete with privately owned coal mining companies.

"BLM [has] refused to even consider the effects development of a proposed federal lease might have on coal markets — any coal markets — not just coal markets that have traditionally been met by coal produced in the Appalachian and Midwestern states. This flat-out refusal reflects an inequitable approach to the management of public resources," Rahall said.

Despite opposition by two Westerners — Barbara F. Vucanovich, R-Nev., and Craig Thomas, R-Wyo. — the subcommittee approved the bill.

"This creates an unwarranted opportunity for government interference in the market for coal," Vucanovich said. Thomas called it a thinly veiled attempt at "regional protectionism."

## ENERGY LABS

The Senate attempted to gently nudge the Department of Energy's high-technology laboratories into the existing post-Cold War, business-dominated era through passage of a bill (S 2566) July 1. However, the bill died in the House.

The labs' longstanding task — top-secret nuclear weapons development — fell to a 30-year low in activity in 1991, according to the trade publication Aviation Week and Space Technology.

The labs, including facilities at Los Alamos and Sandia in New Mexico and at Lawrence Livermore in California, were scrambling for new missions. Lawmakers believed their high-technology facilities and professional expertise made them ideal for research work in emerging technologies such as superconductivity, fuel cells and environmental cleanup.

"Clearly we need more cooperation" between industry and the government labs, said Sen. Pete V. Domenici, R-N.M., who cosponsored the proposal with J. Bennett Johnston, D-La.

The bill was also supported by Jeff Bingaman, D-N.M. As approved, it would authorize and encourage the labs to form partnerships with businesses, universities (including historically black colleges) and other federal agencies.

The bill also sought to allow Energy Department laboratory workers to do government work outside the labs without losing their ability to return, as was the case under existing post-federal employment statutes.

The Senate Energy and Natural Resources Committee had approved the bill (S Rept 102-287) by voice vote May 13. ∎

# West Is Focus of New Water Policy

Despite the ardent opposition of California lawmakers with ties to agribusiness, Congress cleared a 40-title omnibus bill that promised to have a wide-ranging effect on the West's most valuable natural resource: water.

The move was part of a reappraisal of traditional notions of how Western water should be used. For much of the West's history, a river's water was considered wasted unless its bounty was spread over farmland or sent crashing through power-generating turbines.

One prime example of traditional Western water policy was California's Central Valley Project (CVP), the largest federal irrigation and power project. It controlled about one-fifth of the state's usable water supply — enough for every household in the state. But the project, instead, was devoted to agriculture, sending more than 85 percent of its supply in 1992 to 23,000 farming operations located up and down the 500-mile-long Central Valley.

Critics of the project and others like it said federal water policy had been slow to recognize the urbanization of the West. Urban interests — both from the East and West — not only were demanding more water but were increasingly aware of the environmental costs imposed by traditional water uses. The drought that continued to parch the West for a sixth year only intensified the reappraisal — given the fact that water-intensive farming enterprises often were given first call on increasingly scarce water.

As a result, the political dynamic in Congress in 1992 was ripe for a sea change in water policy.

In the House, George Miller, D-Calif., rose in 1991 to become chairman of the Interior and Insular Affairs Committee. As a representative of the urban East Bay area near San Francisco, Miller long had been determined to put an end to special breaks for Western agricultural interests and to divert more water to the valley's decimated wetlands and refuges, as well as to urban families.

In the Senate, Democrat Bill Bradley of New Jersey was chairman of the Energy and Natural Resources Subcommittee on Water and Power. He had been a longtime champion of revamping federal water policy and was in a position to exert his opinions.

Over the protests of rural Western interests, they managed to insert provisions into a traditional water projects bill that aimed to significantly change water use West-wide to reflect urban and environmental values.

In its most significant provisions, the omnibus water

---

## BOXSCORE

➡ **Omnibus Water Bill (HR 429, HR 5099).** The wide-ranging legislation sought to revamp the operations of the Bureau of Reclamation's sprawling Central Valley Project in California, protect the shores of the Grand Canyon from damaging water releases from the Glen Canyon Dam and authorized $924 million to complete the massive Central Utah Project.

**Reports:** H Rept 102-114, Part 1; S Rept 102-267; conference report H Rept 102-1016.

### KEY ACTION

March 19 — The **Senate** Energy and Natural Resources Committee approved HR 429.

April 10 — The **Senate** passed HR 429 by voice vote.

May 28 — The **House** Interior and Insular Affairs Committee approved HR 5099.

June 20 — The **House** passed HR 5099 by voice vote; it was immediately attached to the main water bill, HR 429, which also passed by voice vote.

Sept. 15 — **House-Senate** conferees met.

Oct. 3 — Conferees signed off on compromise measure.

Oct. 6 — The **House** adopted the conference report by voice vote.

Oct. 8 — The **Senate** cleared the measure, 83-8.

Oct. 30 — Bush signed the bill into law — PL 102-575.

---

bill (HR 429 — PL 102-575) signed by President Bush on Oct. 30 completed and revamped huge water projects all across the West:

• It significantly modified the operations of the Central Valley Project by reassigning water away from valley farmers for environmental and wildlife uses. It also spread the water around the state's urban centers by allowing water contractors to sell their water to willing buyers outside the valley.

• It protected the shores of the Grand Canyon by mandating changes in the operation of the Colorado River Storage Project's huge Glen Canyon Dam. Though the dam's hydroelectric facility provided power to users throughout the Southwest, its fluctuating water released through its power-generating turbines had begun to significantly erode the beaches and shoreline of the Colorado River in the Grand Canyon.

• It authorized $924 million to complete the Central Utah Project, a series of massive water diversion tunnels and pipelines that would bring more Colorado River water to rapidly growing cities in the center of the state. It also mandated environmental protections that once would have been unheard of in a Western water project of this size.

• It authorized completion of the Buffalo Bill Dam in Wyoming, as well as many other smaller projects.

That is not to say traditional users did not have their day: Despite environmental protections, most of the water projects in the bill were for the traditional purposes of irrigation and power provision. Irrigation farmers did not get large-scale increases in the cost of their water. And there were provisions to settle water rights disputes with Indian tribes.

But it was the Central Valley Project title that crystallized the debate over water policy, and because it was California, attracted the most attention.

Environmentally minded lawmakers hailed the Central Valley title as an important step in protecting the ecology of the Sacramento/San Joaquin Delta and in breaking the monopoly that valley farmers long had held over the project water.

Valley farmers had warned that changes in their decades-old system of receiving inexpensive water could bankrupt California's breadbasket.

But environmental and urban concerns, linked with the sheer momentum given the bill by Western lawmakers interested in the bill's three dozen other titles, carried the

Central Valley Project reform past the desperate opposition of California lawmakers such as Republican Sen. John Seymour and of the Bush administration.

President Bush was caught between the need to bow to the concerns of California farmers, a potent force in a critical electoral state, and the equally crucial need to carry the rest of the West, where the bill's package of water projects proved a powerful lure. Bush signed the bill Oct. 30 despite calls from Interior Secretary Manuel Lujan Jr. and Agriculture Secretary Edward Madigan that he veto it.

Bush acknowledged as much in his bill-signing statement: "Several of the provisions that substantially reform the operation of the Central Valley Project in California are less flexible and more intrusive on the rights of the state of California and current project beneficiaries than I would have preferred," he said.

## BACKGROUND

The 1992 omnibus water bill continued a tradition of federal activism in water policy that dated back to 1902, when the first irrigation and reclamation laws were passed to encourage the development of the West.

When the 102nd Congress convened for its second session in January, it was poised to finish off a legislative struggle that had raged throughout 1991 — sparked, to some extent, by the ascension of Miller to the chairmanship of the House Interior and Insular Affairs Committee.

Miller was part of a group of lawmakers who helped push through the last major revision of national reclamation law, in 1982 (PL 97-293). That bill was intended to end a long-simmering dispute over who should get subsidized federal water, which originally was meant solely for small family farms of 160 acres or less.

The 1982 law ended up allowing not-so-small farm operations — up to 960 acres — to get the low-cost resource. Many large agribusinesses continued to get subsidized water by splitting their operations — on paper — into 960-acre pieces. Moreover, some farming operations were "double dipping" by using subsidized water to grow surplus crops whose prices were guaranteed by the government. Miller unsuccessfully attempted to push reform of the reclamation law in 1987. (1982 Almanac, p. 353)

In 1990 a similar bill passed in the House but died in the Senate. (1990 Almanac, p. 356)

In 1992, though, the focus began to turn toward the Central Valley Project, partly because of the continuing California drought. Because of the drought, less project water was making its way past the farms of the valley and into the vital marshes and wildlife refuges used by the state's salmon and wildfowl.

Lower water levels led to greater contamination of what marsh water remained. The result was the widely publicized selenium poisoning of the Kesterson Wildlife Refuge near Gustine, Calif., in 1991, and the deaths of thousands of wildfowl.

Moreover, urban users who were being asked to cut their water usage were thirstily eyeing the project. At a time of scarcity, project water still was being sold to farmers at rates so inexpensive that many could grow water-intensive crops like rice, alfalfa and cotton in what was, for all intents and purposes, a desert.

Moreover, many of the valley's farmers were in the process of signing new 40-year water contracts with the Bureau of Reclamation, which would lock out other California users until well into the next century.

### 1991 Action

Miller, who rose to the chairmanship of the Interior Committee in 1991, had already tried unsuccessfully to change the project's operations through a rider on a bill (HR 355) to provide drought relief to California.

The omnibus water bill (HR 429), was originally introduced by Craig Thomas, R-Wyo., in January 1991 to authorize funds for the Buffalo Bill Dam in his state. As the bill began to wend its way through Congress, Miller and Bradley seized on it as a vehicle for change — as well as for dozens of good old-fashioned popular water spending projects. (1991 Almanac, p. 218)

By the time the bill was approved by the Interior and Insular Affairs Committee on May 1, the committee had bundled into the original HR 429 some 21 other titles for projects across the West.

But bundled with those popular projects were some of the reforms Miller had been seeking for years, and which were not so politically attractive.

Most significant, Miller revived the 1982 Reclamation Reform Act in HR 429, which imposed strict limits on which farm operations could receive subsidized water. There was also a title to eliminate double dipping by farmers. There were as yet no reforms of the Central Valley Project in the bill.

The newly expanded HR 429 first passed the House in June. But a 29-title version of the bill stalled in the Senate and did not get beyond the hearing stage in that chamber. The bill would change significantly in 1992.

## SENATE COMMITTEE ACTION

Action on the bill in 1992 began in the Senate Energy and Natural Resources Committee, where Water and Power Subcommittee Chairman Bradley had crafted a wide-ranging version of HR 429 for the Senate's consideration. The committee approved the bill by voice vote March 19.

After having listened to dozens of hours of testimony for more than a year preceding the creation of the bill, and after some last-minute horse-trading, Bradley submitted his version of HR 429 at a markup March 19.

Unlike the House version of the bill, Bradley's version was aiming not so much at West-wide water subsidies but at the West's largest reclamation project, the Central Valley Project, with its 23,000 farms, its network of massive dams and its huge (1,845-megawatt) power generating capacity.

Bradley said it was time for the Central Valley Project to enter the late 20th century, a time when agriculture was dwarfed by other sectors of the state's economy. He said it no longer made sense to operate a project that parceled out 85 percent of project water to farmers and only 15 percent to cities and wildlife.

To make the bill more palatable to rural lawmakers, Bradley removed the controversial sections dealing with water subsidies.

But CVP farmers would see real changes in the way project water was used and distributed: Contracts were shortened, water sales outside the project were permitted, and water was to be reserved for wildlife.

The provisions were supported by retiring Sen. Alan Cranston, D-Calif. But they were furiously opposed by the state's junior senator, Seymour. Like his mentor, California Gov. Pete Wilson, Seymour was closely allied with Central Valley agricultural interests, whose representatives com-

# Bradley Survives Deep Water Plunge

New Jersey Democrat Bill Bradley proved that he had not gotten in over his head when he decided to wade into California's water problems.

As chairman of the Senate Energy and Natural Resources Subcommittee on Water and Power, Bradley decided to take the lead role in shepherding through the chamber his version of a bill (HR 429) that would rework the way the Central Valley Project water was shared among California farmers, industries and cities.

The measure also took a stab at longstanding Western water practices by emphasizing the need for new projects to use federally subsidized water not just for irrigation and power, but to protect wildlife and wetlands.

"Sen. Bradley has learned more about Western water than a senator from New Jersey ever had thought he had need for," said Malcolm Wallop., Wyo., ranking Republican on the full committee.

Bradley's aggressive stance on the Central Valley Project embodied several recurring themes of his Senate tenure: concern for the environment, opposition to agricultural subsidies, a willingness to tackle arcane subjects and, not least, tenacity in the face of apparent setbacks.

But on March 19, the full Energy and Natural Resources Committee rejected Bradley's painstakingly crafted solution for the project — and adopted, wholecloth, one hastily written by the California agriculture industry and sponsored by California Republican John Seymour. The Seymour bill did not go as far as Bradley's in its environmental protection. Seymour's bill for example, substituted specific set-asides for environmental purposes for more vaguely worded goals, and a number of stopgap construction measures designed to help fish migration and stem mortality.

But Bradley — joined by Energy Chairman J. Bennett Johnston of Louisiana — did nothing to stop the move. They knew Seymour could bottle up a bill he didn't like in the committee. Bradley and Johnston wanted to keep the bill moving — a committee markup was only the beginning of a long evolutionary process.

Seymour recognized that himself: He did very little gloating March 19, careful not to antagonize Bradley. Seymour noted that even though Bradley's proposal went far beyond his in its environmental protections, the New Jersey senator had not relegated the first-term Republican to the sidelines.

Bradley, Seymour said, "went out of his way [to] work very closely with us in the state."

Bradley relied on timing and did not make a countermove until after the full Senate approved its version of HR 429, replete with Seymour's pro-agribusiness Central Valley Project provision, April 10.

When the bill went to conference several months later, Bradley's Central Valley provisions underwent a miraculous rebirth. Miller and Bradley hammered out a conference deal that was very much like Bradley's original proposal in spirit — including specific amounts of water set aside for fish and wildlife, as well as a fund for environmental restoration — and that final version was approved by the Senate on Oct. 8.

Seymour's Central Valley provisions were stripped out of the bill, and died as a separate measure (HR 3365) with the 102nd Congress.

plained that such massive changes would bankrupt the valley's farmers.

Seymour's opposition threatened to derail the bill. After days of intense, closed-door bargaining, Bradley grudgingly capitulated to Seymour's demands.

Bradley's Central Valley title was stripped out of the bill before the entire package was formally considered by the committee, and an agriculture-oriented package (S 2016) sponsored by Seymour was inserted in its stead. It did not change the project's existing allocation and contracting system, as Bradley sought, nor did it guarantee extra water for the region's wildlife at the expense of farmers. But it did propose spending about $300 million in wildlife mitigation construction projects.

In the end, Energy and Natural Resources Committee Chairman J. Bennett Johnston, D-La., who had indicated support for Bradley's original proposal, remarked, "The action we propose today is not an endorsement of the Seymour provision. But it is a desire to move the bill."

Johnston said he hoped to fight for a more environmentally oriented provision when the Senate and House met in conference later in the year.

Bradley went along with Johnston's strategy even though he thought the provisions passed by the committee "sacrifice[d] the environment for subsidized crops."

Seymour was careful not to gloat, but said his provision's emphasis on agriculture more faithfully reflected the needs of his state.

The bill also contained a number of new titles not in the House bill — most notably one written by Sen. Mark O. Hatfield, R.-Ore., that mandated a wide-ranging study of Western water policy.

"Everything in the Western United States, from agriculture to energy and industrial production to transportation and recreation, is dependent on water," Hatfield said. "Every one of those things is threatened by the absence of a national water policy."

## SENATE FLOOR ACTION

The Senate passed HR 429 by voice vote and with no debate April 10, moments before Congress adjourned for a two-week recess.

But the bill's quick passage belied remarks inserted in the record by Johnston and Bradley; both made it clear that the bill, as passed, would never become law.

Johnston said the Central Valley Project title "was deeply flawed.... Let me be clear that I would find it very difficult to support an agreement in conference that does not ensure meaningful reform of the Central Valley Project or that broadens the opportunities for abuse of the reclamation program's subsidy limitations."

Bradley's remarks were just as blunt: "All members need to be aware that enactment of the legislation in its present form would represent a severe and unwarranted setback for the state of California."

The California water battle was not the first time Bradley had tackled issues whose complexity and lack of relevance to New Jersey packed little in the way of political payoff in his home state. Bradley devoted years, for example, to the 1986 effort to simplify the tax code and, later, to reform the system of Third World debt.

But sometimes that national outlook got him in trouble with those voters he most needed to court: In the 1990 election he squeaked by with only 50 percent of the New Jersey vote.

Bradley had also shown no sympathy for the country's system of "grandfathered" water rights that did not take into account new needs for urban uses and the environment — or for subsidies for farmers. In his own region, Bradley had supported efforts to allow longtime water rights holders on the Delaware River to be charged for riverway improvements. And Bradley aroused agricultural interests' ire when he tried in the 1990 farm bill to cut the 18-cent-per-pound sugar price support by 2 cents.

The combination of Bradley's celebrity past (he was a Rhodes scholar and, later, a basketball star with the New York Knicks) and his recent attention to global issues had renewed his national popularity: In California, political insiders were still in awe of a glittery 1989 Hollywood fundraiser that netted him $600,000 in one night.

His interest in California water issues dated to 1987 when he assumed the helm of the Water and Power Subcommittee, which had jurisdiction over the Interior Department's Bureau of Reclamation projects.

Bradley often joked that he tried to get the bureau to build a couple of big water projects in New Jersey, only to discover that its projects were all west of the Mississippi.

But unlike other chairmen of the committee, who had tended to be Westerners, he took an activist role toward Western resource issues that had previously been left to fester when a given state's senators failed to reach consensus.

The Central Valley Project was a case in point. Despite congressional studies questioning its cost — both fiscal and environmental — California's senators had never been able to swim in sync on a solution. Seymour advocated a pro-agriculture approach, and Alan Cranston, a Democrat, took a more urban and environmental tilt. The result was gridlock, exacerbated by six years of drought.

Bradley initiated an August 1991 General Accounting Office report that documented how selenium-heavy runoff from the project was draining into the Kesterson Wildlife Refuge, a wetlands retreat for migrating waterfowl, and how low-cost water was being used to grow surplus crops. Bradley held several hearings in California on the problem, listening to 75 witnesses.

His efforts did not meet with complete approval, though.

"He's not being hung in effigy, but he and [House Interior Committee Chairman Rep. George] Miller are not the most popular people in the valley," said Rep. Calvin Dooley, D-Calif., a member of the House Interior Committee. Miller, another California Democrat, wrote the original omnibus water bill that passed the House last year.

The story of the Western water bill showed that an Eastern lawmaker did not necessarily have to steer clear of explosive Western issues.

"On the contrary," Bradley said back during the committee's first markup March 19. "This shows if you're serious and if you do your homework, you can move something forward."

---

By that time the bill had grown to some 40 titles between the House and Senate versions. That gave Bradley, Johnston and Miller a good deal of political leverage. By the time the conferees would meet, almost every Western senator, no matter how sympathetic to Seymour, would have a politically popular water project tucked away somewhere in the massive 390-page bill.

## HOUSE COMMITTEE ACTION

In order to get the Central Valley Project provisions favored by Bradley and Miller into the already passed House bill, Miller introduced a new measure (HR 5099) that dealt solely with the project. The House Interior and Insular Affairs Committee approved the measure on a voice vote May 28.

The Central Valley Project Reform Act aimed to revamp the way the project's water was distributed by amending the project's original charter. The bill placed the water needs of fish and wildlife on nearly equal footing with those of agriculture and hydropower.

Miller's new bill followed Johnston's model but included several concessions to agricultural interests to attract the support.

Miller dropped a controversial proposal that had been sought by Johnston in the Senate to set aside a minimum of 1.5 million acre-feet of water for fish and wildlife purposes — about a fifth of the project's water supply.

Miller agreed to add a provision to allow local irrigation districts to veto outside water transfers if the transfers exceeded 20 percent of a district's water supply.

He also agreed not to press for water-pricing reform, which would have linked water prices to the amount of water consumed, charging the top prices for the highest consumption.

The bill established a novel system to allow Central Valley farmers who received low-cost federal water to turn around and sell it at open-market prices to cities or to other non-project users.

Long-term water contracts would now be drawn up for no longer than 20 years, half the existing term. The bill also directed the Interior Department to take whatever steps were necessary to double the region's population of anadromous fish — salmon and other species that journey from salt water to fresh to breed — by 2002 and restore stream and shoreline habitat. The provisions were to be paid for by a fee on water transfers and increases in water and power rates.

Until then, no new long-term contracts were to be approved until fish and wildlife conditions improved.

But all the compromises added up to a bill that Miller said would still protect the region's environment and free up water for cities and business, while addressing enough farm concerns that rural lawmakers like Rep. Richard Lehman, D-Calif., could announce their qualified support for the deal.

## HOUSE FLOOR ACTION

The House passed HR 5099 on June 20 by voice vote. The bill was immediately attached to the main water bill, HR 429, which also passed on a voice vote that same day.

As HR 429 came up for debate on the floor, opponents of the bill began to weigh in. The administration issued a statement that said it supported some of the concepts in the omnibus bill, but nonetheless threatened to veto it because of the Central Valley provisions. California Gov. Wilson, a Republican, also did what he could to slow down the progress of the bill, telling his representatives in Washington that he did not support the deal.

Spurred by the governor's opposition, valley lawmakers such as Democratic Rep. Calvin Dooley who had originally been part of the Interior Committee deal withdrew their support.

"As it stands now, the bill ... is unacceptable to the agricultural communities of the Central Valley," Dooley said on the floor.

But the wide support that the bill enjoyed was underlined by the fact that neither Dooley nor his allies felt confident enough to call for a roll call vote.

Miller used his floor time as the bill's manager to pound home criticisms about the large-scale water subsidies — about $400 million a year — he said were enjoyed by a relative handful of Central Valley farmers and to express concern for environmental needs.

Republicans such as Rep. James V. Hansen, R-Utah, said on the floor that they supported the bill. Not incidental, of course, was the fact that the bill included a $924 million authorization for the Central Utah Project.

The bill originally contained no water price increases, even though valley farmers were getting their water for as little as $3.50 an acre-foot (326,000 gallons). Urban users throughout California were paid more than $100 an acre-foot.

But Sam Gejdenson, D-Conn., noting that the rural lawmakers had withdrawn from the deal that had gotten the bill out of committee, offered an amendment to institute a three-tier pricing system: The first 60 percent of a farmer's water allotment would be at the low subsidized price; the next fifth would be at a price halfway between the subsidized price and the full-cost price; and the final fifth of the farmer's allotment would be at full cost.

The amendment was approved by voice vote.

## CONFERENCE ACTION

The House's approval of the bill set the stage for a massive conference committee markup of the two differing versions of HR 429. After months of behind-the-scenes negotiating, conferees finally met Sept. 15, nearly three months after the bill had been passed by the House.

As was to be expected, California politics lent drama to the meeting. Miller presented a conference compromise that left environmentalists and urban water users applauding and Republicans and farm-region Democrats fuming that their allies would be "devastated."

Though Miller presented the offer, it was clear that Sen. Bradley, had a strong hand in crafting the proposal. At some point, Bradley's name was hurriedly blacked out from the cover of the 40-page proposal.

The offer once again attempted to make fish and wildlife preservation a central goal of the water project. It mandated that 1 million acre-feet — about a seventh of the project's supply in a good year — be set aside for environmental and wildlife uses annually. Water users were to be charged an extra $50 million a year for an environmental restoration fund. In many respects the offer resurrected many provisions that Miller, in the House, and Bradley and Johnston, in the Senate, had dropped from their original bills in order to gain passage out of committee.

The proposal also limited contracts to 20 years and required that environmental impact statements be completed before any such renewal. It kept the tiered pricing system and shunted the first $50 million in extra revenues into a fish and wildlife restoration fund.

California Republicans and Farm Belt Democrats scathingly criticized the proposed deal. In a last-ditch move, Gov. Wilson announced that his state government had reached a "tentative" agreement with the Bush administration to transfer the entire project to state control. But no timetable or price tags were mentioned, and the budget crisis in which California found itself in mid-1992 made it unlikely that the state could find money to buy the multi-billion-dollar project.

The meeting adjourned without a vote. It would be the conference's first and only formal meeting.

Intense negotiations continued in private throughout September. On Oct. 3, a draft compromise written by Sens. Johnston and Bradley began circulating for conferees' signatures. It would eventually garner an unofficial majority and was soon headed for the House floor.

The final compromise kept the goal of doubling fish populations by 2002. After that goal was met, water contracts could be renewed for 25-year periods — the 40-year contract would be no more. A compromise 800,000 acre-feet of CVP water would be set aside for fish and wildlife purposes. And water contractors were now able to sell their water outside the valley to any buyer at market prices. But local water districts could veto any sales in excess of 20 percent of a local district's supply.

## FINAL ACTION

The House scheduled floor debate for Oct. 5 and in the early hours of Oct. 6 approved the conference report by voice vote. Despite hours of bitter debate by many California Republicans and farm-region Democrats, the bill's outcome was clear.

A resigned Lehman talked of a common response as he lobbied other lawmakers against the bill: "Time and time again over that period of time, I have been told, 'You're right, Rick, we would like to help you, Rick, but we got a little project in the bill....'"

Also weighing in in favor of the bill were important California interests such as Southern California's Metropolitan Water District, the California Business Roundtable, the Sierra Club and Trout Unlimited.

The bill's fate was assured when California Republican Bill Thomas moved to shunt the bill back to committee and strip out all of the Central Valley provisions. The motion failed 159-244. *(Vote 480, p. 118-H)*

The House then approved the conference report by voice vote.

### Senate Clears Bill

The Senate cleared the bill (HR 429 — H Rept 102-1016) on an 83-8 vote Oct. 8 and sent it to President Bush for his signature. *(Vote 267, p. 35-S)*

Seymour fought bitterly against the bill in its final

*Continued on p. 272*

# Provisions of Water Projects Bill

*The 1992 omnibus water projects law had something in it for almost every interest group that depended on federally reclaimed water, the lifeblood of the West. There were provisions for cities, wildlife preservationists, and irrigation and power users.*

*The 40-title law, signed Oct. 30, combined provisions to complete, alter and repair popular water projects such as the $924 million Central Utah Project with bitterly contested mandates such as the overhaul of the Bureau of Reclamation's massive Central Valley Project in California.*

*The Central Valley provisions were hailed as an important step in protecting the ecology of the Sacramento/San Joaquin Delta and in breaking the monopoly Central Valley farmers long had held over the project, which controlled a fifth of the water supply of the nation's most populous state. Valley farmers, however, warned that changes in their decades-old system of receiving inexpensive water might bankrupt California's breadbasket. But the sheer momentum of the other long-sought-after provisions carried the bill past the desperate opposition of California lawmakers, such as the soon-to-be defeated Republican Sen. John Seymour and the Bush administration.*

*President Bush was caught between the need to bow to the concerns of California farmers, a potent force in an election year, and the electoral need to carry all of the West, where the bill's package of water projects proved a powerful lure. Bush signed the bill despite calls from Interior Secretary Manuel Lujan Jr. and Agriculture Secretary Edward Madigan to veto the bill.*

*In addition to the Central Valley Project provisions, the bill (HR 429, H Rept 102-1016, PL 102-575) also provided protections for the Grand Canyon, the completion of the Buffalo Bill Dam in Wyoming, restored water rights to numerous American Indians and launched a study of the nation's water use — an increasingly important issue. Following are provisions of the bill, as enacted:*

## CENTRAL VALLEY PROJECT

### Shifting Water From Farms to Wilderness

● **Purposes.** Made wildlife and environmental protection, mitigation and restoration official purposes of the Central Valley Project, along with irrigation, flood control and power. It mandated that the Interior Department's Bureau of Reclamation seek to restore natural streambanks and channels in the Central Valley.

● **Impact.** Required the Interior Department to complete an environmental impact statement analyzing the effects of the bill within three years.

● **Environmental goals.** Prohibited the Bureau of Reclamation from entering into new water contracts with Central Valley Project users until the following conditions were met:

    ● A program was developed to double population levels of salmon, steelhead, striped bass, sturgeon, American shad and other anadromous fish over the average level attained from 1967 through 1991.

    ● A program was developed to reduce damage to the environment caused by the operation of the Central Valley Project's vast array of pumping plants, dams and canals.

    ● A minimum of 800,000 acre-feet of Central Valley Project water was set aside for fish, wildlife and environmental restoration, including wetlands. An acre-foot is approximately 326,000 gallons of water, enough to cover an acre of land with a foot of water. The U.S. Fish and Wildlife Service continued to have authority to determine how that water would be managed.

    ● Adoption of changes by the project to reduce the number of migratory fish killed. Among such changes were the installation of a device at Shasta Dam to reduce high water temperatures linked to the deaths of migratory fish and modification of the fish trap at Keswick Dam to reduce the number of fish killed as they passed through the spillway.

    ● Development of a fish and wildlife restoration plan by the Interior Department for the San Joaquin and Stanislaus rivers by Sept. 30, 1996.

    ● Allowed for three-year contracts to be drafted in the interim while the environmental impact statement was being completed.

● **Exceptions.** Allowed the Bureau of Reclamation to temporarily reduce water reserves for wildlife and the environment by up to 25 percent if natural conditions such as droughts mandated such a change. Any unneeded water could be used for agricultural purposes.

● **Environmental studies.** Directed Interior to complete numerous studies within five years, including studies on water conservation, alternative water supplies, temperature control, hatchery operations, salmon migration and water supplies. Within two years, a report on the project's effects on migratory fish and the groups economically dependent upon them was to have been completed.

● **Restoration fund.** Established a restoration fund of up to $50 million a year to carry out the law's environmental and wildlife mandates. The account would be funded through surcharges on Central Valley water users. For example, agricultural water users were to be levied a charge of up to $6 for each acre-foot of water used, and municipal and industrial water users were each to be assessed a maximum of $12 for each acre-foot. Any state or agency that had not previously been a project customer faced a fee of up to $25 per acre-foot. And to encourage water users to renew their contracts quickly, those who did not do so would face additional surcharges equal to 150 percent of the fee. The bill set a series of additional surcharges for Friant Division water users until Sept. 30, 1999, after which time they were subject to a $7 per acre-foot surcharge.

Any revenues from the sale of project water to those outside the project would be deposited in the restoration fund. Any revenues from a new tiered-pricing system would also be put in the fund. The bill allowed Interior to aid state governments, Indian tribes and nonprofit groups that were assisting in efforts to follow the bill's mandates.

● **Land program.** Authorized the Interior Department to preserve project water by buying irrigated farmland to improve water conservation and quality in any given water district or if the land was no longer suitable for sustained agricultural production.

● **Water capacity.** Required the Interior Department to develop within three years a least-cost plan to increase, over a 15-year period, the project's water production by the same amount that was to be diverted to fish and wildlife purposes.

● **Water sales.** Allowed Central Valley Project users to sell their water allotments at market prices as long as the sales posed no adverse environmental or groundwater effects. Project contractors had to pay full cost for water later sold to agricultural users and higher rates for water sold to municipal and industrial users. The bill allowed conventional Central Valley Project users the right to bid on outside water sales first, as long as they agreed to pay the same price charged outsiders. Any water transfers or sales that would shift more than 20 percent of a water district's water allotment would be subject to review by the Interior Department or the affected water district.

● **Contract renewals.** Authorized renewal of existing long-term water contracts for a 25-year period; successive renewals also could be for up to 25 years. Before the bill passed, contracts were renewed for 40 years. Contracts renewed after Jan. 1, 1988, were subject to new charges mandated for the restoration fund.

● **Water prices.** Created a tiered-pricing system to encourage water conservation. Longstanding subsidized water rates applied to the first tier, which covered the first 80 percent of the total amount of water allocated in any contract. The subsidized rate was as low as $3.50 an acre-foot but could be higher depending on the district. A second tier applied to the next 10 percent of the water used and the price for that water was halfway between the longstanding contract rate and the government's full cost of delivering the water, which was $15 to $50 an acre-foot, depending on the

district and the distance it was from a Central Valley Project storage or pumping facility. The final 10 percent of water allocated under any contract would be subject to a price equal to the full cost of supplying the water.

Any water used to produce a crop that could provide breeding grounds for wildfowl was exempted from the tiered pricing system.

## CENTRAL UTAH PROJECT

• **Authorization.** Authorized over five years $924.2 million for the completion of the Central Utah Project, the last major section of the Colorado River Storage Project. It is a system of reservoirs, pipelines and aqueducts to divert water from the Uintah Basin, a part of the Colorado River Basin east of Salt Lake City, over the Wasatch Mountains to the Bonneville Basin in western Utah. The authorization gave the Central Utah Water Conservancy District the option to use the Bureau of Reclamation as the main contractor to complete construction of the project or to use a private group.

• **Bonneville Unit.** Authorized $242.5 million for the construction of the Bonneville Unit of the Central Utah Project. The bill required local water users to pay 35 percent of the project's construction costs and half the cost of conducting feasibility studies.

The Bonneville section authorized $150 million for a major pipeline that would deliver 116,300 acre-feet of water to more than 175,000 acres of farmland in rural western-central Utah, $69 million to complete the Diamond Fork System, $10 million for a study of ways to better manage and recharge groundwater supplies, $10 million for construction of water-management demonstration facilities in Wasatch County in northeastern Utah and $1 million to study ways to reduce the salinity of Utah Lake, a prime water resource for central Utah. Another $1 million was authorized to study the impact on the Provo River's salinity levels when the river was diverted to the Central Utah Project.

• **Strawberry and Duchesne rivers.** Authorized $30.5 million to construct three reservoirs, rehabilitate the Farnsworth and build permanent water diversion facilities on the Strawberry and Duchesne rivers in northeastern Utah. The project was intended to stem any harm to fish and wildlife breeding areas in those streams that could occur when water was diverted for irrigation.

• **Uintah Indians.** Set provisions to maintain the operation of the Uintah Indian Irrigation Project, a water delivery system that irrigated farmland on the Uintah and Ouray Indian reservations.

• **Rebates.** Allowed certain counties, two years after the bill was enacted, to decline project water and have any ad valorem taxes paid in advance for project water rebated. The bill set up a $40 million program to extend cost-shared development grants to Utah's counties, with the exception of Salt Lake and Utah counties.

• **Water conservation.** Required the Central Utah Water Conservancy District to complete a water conservation plan by Jan. 1, 1995, with the goal of cutting projected water consumption by at least 30,000 acre-feet a year. The bill authorized a study of water-pricing policies to encourage conservation. It also created a conservation advisory board to set minimum conservation targets.

• **Surplus crops.** Levied a surcharge on project water used to produce government-subsidized surplus crops (wheat, feed grains, cotton, rice). The fee equaled 10 percent of the full cost to the government of delivering the water.

• **Fish, wildlife and recreation protection.** Provided for the conservation and restoration of fish, wildlife and recreation resources affected by past and future Central Utah Project facilities. To carry out these mandates, the bill established a five-member commission appointed by the president. It authorized up to $1 million a year to pay for the commission's expenses and created a $13.75 million trust fund to pay for ongoing conservation activities after the project's completion.

The bill provided $15 million to buy 25,000 acre-feet of water to augment stream levels for fish and wildlife. It also provided funds to lease water necessary to sustain fish and wildlife in the upper Strawberry River, the Uintah Basin and the Diamond Fork River. The measure also authorized $1.3 million to buy big-game winter

rangelands, $14 million to preserve wetlands around the Great Salt Lake and $16.7 million to establish a Utah Lakes Wetlands Preserve. It provided protection for the southern half of Provo Bay from commercial development and provided $22 million for various habitat and streambed restoration projects. The measure also authorized $5 million to restore lakes in the Uintah Mountains for fisheries and recreation and $22.8 million to improve existing fish hatcheries and build new ones.

• **Ute Indians:** Set forth a water rights agreement reached among the Ute Indians, the state of Utah and the Central Utah Water Conservancy District in which the Indians were guaranteed $2 million a year for the next 50 years for Indian water diverted by the Bonneville Unit. The bill ratified the 1990 Ute Indian compact, regarding tribal water rights and use of the Central Utah Project water. It authorized $45 million to help the tribe improve farming operations and $125 million over three years for an economic development fund.

## THE GRAND CANYON

### Protecting the Nation's Crown Jewel

• **Glen Canyon Dam.** Directed the Interior Department to operate Glen Canyon Dam, which empties into the Colorado River north of the Grand Canyon, in such a way as to minimize damaging environmental effects on Grand Canyon National Park and the Glen Canyon National Recreation Area.

• **Environmental impact statement.** Required the department, within two years after enactment, to complete a final environmental impact statement on the operation of Glen Canyon Dam.

• **Audit.** Required Interior's comptroller general, within two years after enactment, to complete an audit of the costs and benefits of the dam not only to water and power users, but to natural, recreational and cultural resource users.

• **Fees.** Required local power users to shoulder the full cost of preparing the environmental impact statement. The bill set aside proceeds from electric power sales to pay for the study and credited those revenues against power users' repayment obligations.

• **Power levels.** Directed the Energy Department to find economically and technically feasible ways to replace any power lost due to the bill's environmental regulations. The measure directed the Energy Department to study changes in the operation of Hoover Dam to replace lost power or to study adjusting the system's power transmission lines for the same purpose.

## OTHER RECLAMATION PROJECTS

• **Leadville Mine drainage tunnel.** Authorized $10.7 million for the construction of a plant to treat contaminated water flowing from the World War II-era Leadville Mine drainage tunnel in Colorado into the East Fork of the Arkansas River. The bill also authorized new concrete linings for the tunnel and provided for restoration of fish and wildlife resources in the Arkansas River Basin.

• **East Texas' Lake Meredith salinity control.** Authorized construction and testing of a series of wells to intercept salt water leaching into Lake Meredith, a Bureau of Reclamation storage reservoir in East Texas. The brine was to be disposed of by deep-well injection. The federal government was to pay no more than 33 percent of the project's cost.

• **Mid-Dakota Rural Water System.** Authorized the Interior Department to make $100 million in grants and loans to the Mid-Dakota Rural Water System Inc., a nonprofit corporation, to build a water system providing safe and reliable water to central South Dakota users. The bill also alloted a $100,000 annual grant to restore regional wetlands known as "Prairie Potholes." It also required local water users to put in place a water conservation program.

• **Central Arizona Project.** Provided for the repair or replacement of four siphons along the Hayden-Rhodes Aqueduct at the Salt River, the New River, the Hassayampa River and the Aqua Fria River as well as Jackrabbit Wash and Centennial Wash — all part of the Central Arizona Project.

## RESEARCH PROJECTS

● **Wastewater and groundwater studies.** Directed the Interior secretary to enter into cost-shared studies on ways to reuse agricultural, domestic, municipal and industrial waste water in five feasibility studies and four demonstration projects in California, Arizona and Colorado.

● **South Dakota study.** Authorized a five-year demonstration program to determine whether the soils of the Lake Andes-Wagner area had unsafe levels of selenium, a pollutant that leaches from irrigated farmland and contaminates water supplies. The bill required the Interior Department to certify that any new water project complied with federal water-quality standards and would not produce selenium contamination.

Pending completion of the demonstration project, the bill authorized $175 million to complete the Lake Andes-Wagner Unit, which was to irrigate 45,000 acres of dry-farmed land using water from the North Bay arm of Lake Francis Case. An additional $24 million was allocated for the Marty II Unit, a 3,000-acre irrigation project designed to serve the Yankton Sioux Reservation. The project diverted Missouri River water to the reservation.

● **High Plains groundwater program.** Raised the authorization ceiling for the High Plains groundwater program. The bill alloted $31 million for the program, up from $20 million. The project was designed to investigate and build projects to show the potential for artificially recharging aquifers and recharging groundwater supplies.

● **Western water policy review.** Directed the president to review Western water resource problems and issues, including programs administered by the U.S. Geological Survey and the Bureau of Reclamation, and to report findings within three years of enactment. The bill authorized $10 million to create an 18-member advisory commission to study expected Western water resource and storage problems, federal water policy and water resource problems faced by rural communities. The commission also was to review the water-allocation system, flood control and interstate compacts in the West.

● **San Francisco demonstration project.** Authorized the Interior Department to work with the city and county of San Francisco to examine the feasibility of "greenhouse-based" water reclamation technologies, especially those that used densely populated marsh and pond ecosystems to purify polluted water for reuse. The bill mandated that the cost of the project would be shared equally by the federal and local governments.

## ENVIRONMENTAL, RECREATION PROJECTS

● **South Dakota's biological diversity trust.** Authorized a federal trust fund of up to $12 million for projects to protect or restore the best examples of South Dakota's biological diversity, its rare species and ecosystems. The bill authorized up to $7 million over the next five years to establish a wetlands foundation to be operated by the South Dakota Game Fish and Parks Foundation to buy and preserve the state's outstanding wetlands.

● **California's Sonoma Baylands.** Authorized a $15 million wetlands demonstration project in the San Francisco Bay-Sacramento/San Joaquin Delta to use dredged materials to restore and expand the area's Sonoma Baylands by July 1, 1994. The project was to have been been carried out by the U.S. Army Corps of Engineers.

## INDIAN WATER RIGHTS

● **Standing Rock Indian Reservation.** Made additional water available to the Standing Rock Sioux Indians in South Dakota for irrigation. The provision altered the Garrison Diversion Unit Reformulation Act of 1986. A related section required that the Three Affiliated Tribes of the Fort Berthold Reservation and the Standing Rock Sioux Indians be compensated for the taking of reservation lands when the Garrison Dam and reservoir and the Oahe Dam and reservoir were built. The payment was not to exceed $149.2 million for the Three Affiliated Tribes and $90.6 million for the Standing Rock Sioux Indians.

● **San Carlos Apache Indians.** Provided Arizona's San Carlos Apache Indians 152,435 acre-feet of water annually and $38.4 million to start a fund to develop water resources in exchange for the federal government's use of 292,406 acre-feet of the Indian tribe's water.

## MISCELLANEOUS

● **Renaming Salt-Gila Aqueduct.** Renamed this section of the Central Arizona Project after former Arizona Gov.. and Republican Sen. Paul Fannin and former Democratic Sen. Ernest McFarland.

● **New Mexico's Vermejo project.** Transferred Lake 13 in New Mexico from the federal government to New Mexico's Vermejo Conservancy District but allowed the U.S. Fish and Wildlife Service to continue to manage the lake as part of the Maxwell National Wildlife Refuge.

● **New Mexico's Rio Grande floodway.** Modified the Rio Grande Floodway Project, a series of flood control levees along a 55-mile stretch of the Rio Grande River, to reduce New Mexico's contribution to the project. The move came after it was determined that federal projects, such as the Bosque del Apache National Wildlife Refuge, were the main beneficiaries of the $50 million project.

● **Washington's Sunnyside Valley.** Conveyed a small parcel of improved, but no longer used, property in the town of Sunnyside, Wash., to the Sunnyside Valley Irrigation District. The district planned to sell the land and use the proceeds to build a district office building.

● **Colorado's Plataro Reservoir and Dam.** Directed the Interior secretary to accept a one-time payment of $450,000 from Colorado's Conejos Water Conservancy District in exchange for transferring the operation and maintenance of the Plataro Dam and Reservoir to the district. The federal government, however, was to retain authority over the recreational and environmental uses of the dam and reservoir.

● **California's Redwood Valley.** Authorized the Interior Department to sell or accept prepayment of two loans totaling $7.3 million made to the Redwood Valley County Water District, in Mendocino County, to build water-pumping facilities to divert water from Lake Mendocino to Redwood Valley. The terms of the prepayment plan were still to be negotiated at time of passage.

● **California's United Water Conservation District.** Authorized the Interior Department to sell or accept prepayment of an $18.7 million loan made to this Ventura County water conservation district. The loan was extended to make improvements to the Freeman Diversion Dam on the Santa Clara River to increase water supplies to the Oxnard Plain for irrigation and domestic purposes and to recharge the ground water. The terms of the prepayment plan were yet to be negotiated at time of passage.

● **Montana irrigation project.** Directed the Energy Department to sell low-cost Pick-Sloan Missouri River Basin Project power to the Haidle Irrigation Project, in Prairie County, Mont., and to the Hammond Irrigation District in Rosebud County, Mont.

● **California's San Juan Suburban Water District.** Required the Interior Department to credit the San Juan water district for the $300,000 cost of two water pumps purchased by the district for use at the Bureau of Reclamation's Folsom Dam.

● **Oklahoma's Mountain Park.** Authorized the Interior Department to sell or accept prepayment on the Tom Steed Reservoir from the Mountain Park Master Conservancy District in Oklahoma. The reservoir provided a supplemental municipal and industrial water supply to the Oklahoma cities of Altus, Snyder and Frederick.

● **New Mexico's Elephant Butte Irrigation District.** Transferred title to certain easements, ditches, laterals, canals, drains and rights of way from the Interior Department to the Elephant Butte Irrigation District and El Paso County Water Improvement District No. 1. The respective districts had provided the facilities to the federal government for the project.

● **National Historic Preservation Act.** Amended the 1966 National Historic Preservation Act to clarify and streamline the act to help facilitate the preservation of historical resources. ■

*Continued from p. 268*
legislative round. He willingly participated in a crippling 15-hour filibuster that Sen. Alfonse M. D'Amato, R-N.Y., waged against the 1992 tax bill (HR 11) to protest the deletion of a provision that promised to save the jobs of 875 Smith-Corona typewriter factory workers in upstate New York. *(Urban aid tax bill, p. 140)*

When D'Amato finally gave up and the Senate turned to HR 429, Seymour insisted that the entire 396-page bill be read in its entirety, tying up that chamber for most of the day.

Seymour said, "I put people and jobs first, animals and plants second, and try to find a balance that will accommodate those two principles. Unfortunately, Miller's principles and philosophies have been exactly the reverse."

But the portents were not good for Seymour. On Oct. 6, a delegation of stalwart Western Republicans, including Malcolm Wallop of Wyoming, Jake Garn of Utah and John McCain of Arizona, met with White House Chief of Staff James A. Baker III to lobby for Bush's signature. They were looking not at Seymour's lonely stance, but at the big projects benefiting their states and their political prospects.

"We tried to tell Seymour that it was in his interest to see the glass as half full," said a staff aide to Garn. "The provisions worked out in the bill are less onerous by far than what the enviros had wanted."

They argued that the projects they had in the bill were significant to their states — the completion of the Central Utah Project, the Buffalo Bill Dam in Wyoming and protection for the Grand Canyon — and that they should not be threatened by the opposition of a lone California senator.

On Oct. 8 Seymour had to admit defeat. Facing a vow by Senate Majority Leader George J. Mitchell, D-Maine, to keep the Senate in session until the water bill was disposed of, Seymour acquiesced. He agreed to a deal under which the Senate considered a separate Central Valley Project bill (S 3365) that was more modest in its environmental protection measures and that was backed by the valley's farm interests. But since the House had already wrapped up its work for the session, action on that bill was simply a symbolic gesture. That helped Seymour save some face while he was running an ultimately unsuccessful Senate re-election campaign. ∎

# Solid Waste Problem Remains Insoluble

A two-year effort by Rep. Al Swift, D-Wash., to reauthorize the Resource Conservation and Recovery Act — the nation's main solid and hazardous waste law — stalled in the 102nd Congress when a slimmed-down compromise bill (S 2877) came under attack by industry representatives and environmentalists.

The Resource Conservation and Recovery Act (RCRA) was the nation's main solid waste law. Yet the increasing tide of garbage the nation generated, combined with the dwindling number of landfills in which to place it, generated bitter conflicts — clashes Congress had hoped to address through a comprehensive rewrite of the law.

But the task proved as difficult as finding a home for New York's infamous garbage barge: Midwestern states complained of being dumping grounds for Eastern garbage; environmentalists were opposed to new increases in incineration; and the Bush administration opposed the effort to rewrite the law as unnecessary.

The result: In the House, the Energy and Commerce Committee came up with a slimmed-down reauthorization bill (HR 3865) that sidestepped regulation of industrial, and oil and gas wastes to concentrate on municipal and household garbage. The Senate Environment and Public Works Committee drafted a somewhat broader bill (S 976). Neither bill advanced.

Instead, faced with opposition from the Bush administration, the full Senate passed a much narrower bill (S

---

### BOXSCORE

➡ **Solid Waste Law (HR 3865, S 976, S 2877).** Legislation to reauthorize the Resource Conservation and Recovery Act, the nation's main solid waste law, and regulate the growing problem of out-of-state waste.

**Reports:** H Rept 102-839; S Rept 102-301.

#### KEY ACTION

May 20 — The **Senate** Environment and Public Works Committee approved S 976, 12-5.

July 2 — The **House** Energy and Commerce Committee approved HR 3865, 28-15.

July 23 — The **Senate** passed S 2877, 89-2.

---

2877). That measure, by Sen. Daniel R. Coats, R-Ind., dealt only with the issue of interstate garbage. The bill allowed state governors to ban or limit garbage imports, subject to a request by local authorities. But the bill allowed landfills that already received out-of-state garbage to continue to do so under a grandfather clause.

### BACKGROUND

The Resource Conservation and Recovery Act (PL 94-580) was the nation's main law governing the disposal of hazardous, industrial and municipal wastes. Its authorization expired in 1988, but it was not until Nov. 22, 1991, that Swift, chairman of the Transportation and Hazardous Materials Subcommittee, introduced legislation to renew it. The reauthorization measure focused on the smallest — but most politically charged — element of the solid waste universe: municipal trash.

Swift had planned eventually to add provisions dealing with industrial and mining waste and recycling used oil and hazardous materials — problems that collectively dwarfed those posed by municipal solid waste. But faced with opposition from industry and the administration, such provisions never got into the bill.

Though the task of rewriting the nation's main solid waste law began early in the first session of the 102nd Congress, action did not get under way in earnest until 1992. And despite the increasingly precarious state of the nation's landfills and garbage incinerators, the administra-

tion showed few signs of easing its pro-business opposition to reauthorizing the law.

In the Senate, Max Baucus, D-Mont., had pledged to move his bill (S 976), which was pending before the Environment and Public Works Committee in early 1992, to the Senate floor for a vote by April 30. Baucus did so to placate Coats, who unsuccessfully tried in 1990 to get Congress to approve a measure that allowed his state and others to ban the import of garbage.

Coats had not given up his battle and had similar legislation ready in 1992. But he had agreed not to push a bill if Baucus kept his pledge to complete action on S 976 by April.

Baucus' bill allowed states to ban garbage imports, but only if they had an environmentally sound waste management plan in place. It also set an ambitious goal of recycling 50 percent of all municipal waste by the year 2000.

Though Baucus did not view the bill as controversial, the Environment and Public Works subcommittee he chaired was caught off guard in September 1991 when Environmental Protection Agency (EPA) administrator William K. Reilly testified that revamping the solid waste law was "unnecessary" and threatened to add unneeded layers of regulation. Vice President Dan Quayle's Council on Competitiveness also opposed the effort. The administration's opposition delayed development of some of the bill's more technical aspects, and the White House never softened its opposition to the rewrite.

On the House side, Swift in 1991 introduced half of the Resource Conservation and Recovery Act rewrite (HR 3865), which dealt with municipal solid waste. Swift took a consensus approach to the bill, crafting it after holding numerous informal meetings with committee members and inviting comments from hundreds of interested parties.

The House bill allowed states to charge fees on out-of-state garbage, but only if the states had a garbage management plan. The bill also encouraged recycling and federal procurement of recycled goods. *(1991 Almanac, p. 228)*

## SWIFT DEVELOPS HIS PROPOSAL

After getting a head start during the first session, House action began early in 1992. Yet, signs of trouble were evident from the start.

Even as a House panel was slated to mark up the wide-ranging rewrite of the nation's main solid waste law the week of March 23 key issues such as recycling, out-of-state garbage imports and the future of trash incineration had yet to take shape.

Nonetheless, Swift, the sponsor of the markup vehicle (HR 3865), was confident that he had the votes to move a version of the bill out of his Energy and Commerce Subcommittee on Transportation and Hazardous Materials and through the full committee.

Swift expected the bill to be passed in the House in 1992 for two reasons: first, there was a critical need to reduce the growing mountain of trash headed for the nation's dwindling number of landfills. Second, the Energy and Commerce Committee hoped to get RCRA out of the way before the beginning of the 103rd Congress, when the committee was slated to turn to the reauthorization of the "superfund" toxic waste law (PL 96-510).

Swift's bill hewed to a moderate line. The measure:

• Allowed states that had EPA solid-waste management plans to levy a 1,000 percent surcharge on garbage coming from states that did not have such plans in place.

• Declined to designate municipal incinerator ash —

which often had high concentrations of heavy metals and toxic chemicals — as a hazardous waste. It banned the ash from regular landfills if it was found to have the potential for contaminating ground water. It also encouraged incineration operations to divert as much recyclable or noncombustible material as possible.

• Encouraged more recycling by giving manufacturers the option of designing packaging that was either made from recycled material, easily recycled or reusable at least five times. The bill required industry to recycle 40 percent of paper, glass and steel by 1995.

Opposition to the bill came from both industry and conservationists. Environmentalists preferred a greater emphasis on recycling and waste reduction as the last, best hope of reducing the solid-waste stream. But businesses worried that markets had not developed for many recyclable items.

It also was clear from the start that any RCRA rewrite was bound to face a raft of amendments. Lawmakers lined up early to offer amendments to give the bill more power in mandating recycling, scaling back incineration and giving local communities the right to determine whether they want out-of-state trash imports.

Among them:

• Pennsylvania Democrat Peter H. Kostmayer proposed to sharply rein in the construction or expansion of municipal waste incinerators and treat their ash as strictly regulated hazardous waste. Kostmayer's plan placed so many restrictions on incineration that it effectively banned the process by the year 2000.

• Rick Boucher, D-Va., proposed to allow cities and counties to decide whether they wanted to build a modern landfill able to accept out-of-state waste. Boucher's proposal pleased both environmentalists and waste management company executives who wanted garbage to go to large, regional state-of-the-art landfills.

• Rep. Edward J. Markey, D-Mass., proposed a national bottle bill provision to require that all bottles and containers be given a specified refund value to create a market for recyclables.

## HOUSE SUBCOMMITTEE ACTION

The Energy and Commerce Subcommittee on Transportation and Hazardous Materials approved an early version of the House bill (HR 3865) on March 26. A key provision in the bill gave local agencies control over whether to accept imported waste. The provision did not apply to landfills accepting out-of-state waste before Nov. 26, 1991.

But under the bill, localities stood to lose such veto power 42 months after enactment if their state had not put into place an EPA-approved solid-waste management plan.

Boucher offered and won his amendment backed by the waste management industry and some environmentalists regarding the transport of solid waste across state lines. It replaced a more restrictive provision included in the subcommittee draft.

The amendment allowed only a local jurisdiction with zoning authority over an importing landfill — not state authorities — to ban garbage imports. It required any local jurisdiction that decided to accept imported waste to meet the latest design standards for landfills. An effort by Bill Richardson, D-N.M., to allow states to regulate out-of-state trash, instead of localities, failed.

Richardson also failed to win two controversial amendments strongly supported by environmentalists that called for tightening the regulation of incinerator ash. He withdrew one amendment that redefined ash produced by municipal

solid-waste incinerators as hazardous waste, requiring it to be strictly regulated and disposed of in a single-purpose landfill. The other amendment, which failed, 4-13, imposed a moratorium on the construction of such incinerators until the year 2000 and greatly restricted them thereafter.

Another amendment by Gerry Sikorski, D-Minn., that banned the burning of non-combustible items and all batteries, also failed by voice vote.

The subcommittee approved an amendment by Cardiss Collins, D-Ill., that rewarded individual companies for meeting new recycling targets. Such companies were exempt from industrywide sanctions.

A successful amendment by Don Ritter, R-Pa., encouraged the recyclying of polycarbonate resin plastic. The amendment required such plastic products weighing more than 0.1 kilograms to be stamped with their own recycling code number — '8.' The code was intended to make the plastic easily identifiable as recycling material.

Another successful amendment by W. J. "Billy" Tauzin, D-La., and Dennis E. Eckart, D-Ohio, generally exempted from recycled-content requirements packaging for some food products, such as fresh meats and dairy products. Packaging for such products had to meet recycled-content standards only if the Food and Drug Administration determined such packaging was safe.

An amendment by Swift banned the composting or the incineration of lead acid, mercuric oxide or rechargeable dry cell batteries in municipal incinerators six months after passage. After Jan. 1, 1993 the amendment also prohibited the sale of any alkaline manganese, zinc-carbon and consumer mercuric-oxide batteries with a mercury content of more than 0.025 percent. The amendment also required that battery recycling programs be put in place. Small consumer penlight-type batteries were exempt, pending further study by the EPA.

## HOUSE COMMITTEE ACTION

The full Energy and Commerce Committee spread the drafting of HR 3865 over three weeks. And even while it looked doubtful that Congress had time to pass a rewrite of the nation's solid-waste law, the full committee did move in late June to resolve the most vexing issue sparked by the debate — the states' desire to control out-of-state garbage flowing into landfills.

On June 23, the Energy and Commerce Committee gave voice vote approval to language that granted states some control over such waste.

The interstate garbage amendment became significant as Baucus, the author of a companion Senate garbage bill, on June 18 threw his support behind the Senate's stand-alone bill (S 2877) that gave states even more power. A narrowly focused measure had a better chance of passage, he said, than the much broader RCRA reauthorization.

As the number of landfills nationwide continued to diminish, there had been an increase in the interstate commerce in garbage. States with plenty of landfill space, such as Pennsylvania, Indiana and New Mexico, complained that they were becoming the dumping ground for waste generated in such space-short states as New Jersey and New York.

But there was little that states could do to stop the dumping because the U.S. Constitution prevented them from passing any law interfering with interstate commerce. That fact was brought home by two Supreme Court rulings June 1 that struck down two states' out-of-state trash laws.

In *Chemical Waste Management v. Hunt* and *Fort*

*Gratiot Sanitary Landfill v. Michigan Department of Natural Resources*, the Supreme Court ruled that Alabama and Michigan violated the interstate commerce clause of the Constitution, which declared that the free flow of commerce can be regulated only by Congress.

The House RCRA reauthorization originally sought to resolve the issue of state control over out-of-state waste by giving communities and not states the sole power to limit out-of-state wastes being brought into their boundaries.

That set off howls of protests from state governments. Ron Wyden, D-Ore., reflected their views when he argued at the June 23 markup that the provision gave a "superminority" of towns the power to decide an entire state's waste policies.

Boucher then offered an amendment that allowed governors to stop a local dump from taking waste imports — if the out-of-state wastes took up landfill capacity intended for local garbage. The amendment was approved by voice vote.

But that was as far as the committee was willing to go, preferring to keep most of the power in the hands of communities. As bill sponsor Swift said, "all garbage is local."

So it was no surprise that the committee then turned down, on a voice vote, an effort by Richardson — a strong proponent of state control over out-of-state garbage imports — to force communities to notify state governments if they choose to accept out-of-state waste. Members also rejected an amendment by Don Ritter, R-Pa., that weakened local communities' control in the case of landfills near state boundaries. Ritter sought to exempt from local control out-of-state waste that came from less than 50 miles away.

### Incinerator Issues

The second key fight came over incineration, one of the three major options for waste disposal, along with recycling and using landfills. The committee dropped language that regulated the disposal of incinerator ash. Environmentalists had sought to have incinerator ash classified as hazardous waste, but the bill was silent on the issue and left incinerators unbound by tougher rules.

Some members argued not only that incineration was environmentally harmful but that incinerators' need for a constant supply of material to burn discouraged recycling.

Kostmayer unsuccessfully proposed his amendment that placed a moratorium on new incinerator construction until the year 2000.

Tauzin appeared to sway the committee against the proposal when he argued that Congress should not take away a disposal option as basic as incineration. The committee rejected Kostmayer's amendment, 7-17.

Consideration of the bill collided with a two-day national rail shutdown, which required the full Energy Committee's attention. When the committee resumed the markup June 29, lawmakers faced dozens of amendments. (Rail strike, p. 201)

Among them was one unsuccessfully offered by Henry A. Waxman, D-Calif., on June 30 to tackle the 7.6 billion-ton problem of industrial waste, which the draft bill ignored. By comparison, the total amount of municipal solid waste was estimated at 180 million to 200 million tons. Waxman's amendment mandated that the EPA issue standards for industrial waste, the disposal of which, he said, was largely left unregulated. Industrial waste included scrap metal, paper and plastics, medical wastes and scrap tires.

But committee members feared a costly onslaught of new regulations and rejected the amendment. Instead, the committee agreed, 26-16, to have EPA study the problem.

## Recycling Pushed

Markey on June 30 unsuccessfully offered his amendment to put in place a national bottle-deposit system that mandated the recycling of glass, plastic and metal beverage containers.

Markey defended the proposal as mainstream, noting that 10 states had bottle-deposit laws. But opponents said such a provision undermined existing state recycling programs. The amendment was defeated when the committee met the next day, 16-27.

Instead, the committee adopted by voice vote a "multiple option" recycling strategy pushed by Swift, which applied only to bottles, jars and cans. The provision gave industries that used such containers a choice among meeting industrywide recycling rates by 1995 (65 percent for aluminum, 40 percent for glass, 40 percent for steel and 25 percent for plastic), making containers reusable or reducing package bulk by at least 15 percent by July 1, 1996.

Energy Committee Chairman John D. Dingell, D-Mich., won an amendment that required newspapers with circulations of at least 200,000 to use 35 percent recycled newsprint by 1995 or face a fee of $25 for every ton of newsprint not made with recycled materials.

Though some members, such as Ritter, said the provision flew in the face of the bill's flexible philosophy, the amendment was approved 32-10.

On another topic, the committee agreed to strike language from the bill that forced greater disclosure of the solid waste rule-making activities of Vice President Quayle's Council on Competitiveness — a key to attracting Republican support for the bill. The move, in an amendment by Ritter, released the council from disclosure requirements that had been mandated by the bill draft. Instead, the amendment required the EPA to post all proposed solid-waste rules.

Surprisingly, Swift — who had often expressed hostility toward the council — supported Ritter's amendment, which passed 25-18.

## Committee Approval

The Energy and Commerce Committee on July 2 finally approved HR 3865 on a vote of 28-15. The final version that one lawmaker wryly said was "championed by no one" emerged as a slimmed-down municipal garbage and recycling measure and managed to attract support from both parties.

It set new standards governing recycling, state waste-management plans and the interstate transportation of solid waste.

By the time the bill finished its long journey out of committee, it was missing any regulations over the much larger universe of industrial and hazardous waste and the recycling of bottles nationwide.

The absence of such provisions caused disappointed environmentalists to team up with anti-regulation conservative Republicans in calling for the bill's defeat.

Approval ended a markup session that stretched over three weeks and that was marked by impassioned rhetoric, delaying tactics by conservative Republicans and protests by environmental groups.

Yet when all the votes were cast, 10 Republicans found enough to like in the bill to vote for its approval, giving the measure its comfortable 13-vote margin.

At the time, the bipartisan support was thought to improve the bill's chances on the House floor, where there was more support for environmentally oriented measures than in the Energy and Commerce Committee.

Still, a dozen leading environmental groups opposed the bill, calling it a "toothless" measure that did little to solve the nation's waste problems. Environmentally sensitive lawmakers such as Waxman, Sikorski and Kostmayer voted against the bill. Waxman vowed to add tougher recycling and disposal provisions to it on the House floor — but the measure never made it that far.

## SENATE ACTION

The Senate also pushed to rewrite RCRA in 1992. After weeks of work, the Environment and Public Works Committee approved Baucus' rewrite bill (S 976) on May 20 on a 12-5 vote. The full Senate, however, passed a more limited bill (S 2877) on July 23, and it too died at adjournment.

### Work Begins on S 976

The Environment and Public Works Committee began its markup of S 976 on May 13. At that meeting, lawmakers rejected, 6-10, a plan to force states to recycle bottles and cans. Also during the markup, the committee approved a compromise that allowed states to block some shipments of out-of-state waste.

James M. Jeffords, R-Vt., offered the unsuccessful amendment to create a nationwide bottle bill. The proposal called for establishing a 10-cent deposit for metal, glass and plastic beverage containers holding up to 1 gallon.

The markup's second major vote came on the volatile issue of interstate waste shipments.

Some states feared becoming dumping grounds for out-of-state garbage and wanted power to block trash shipments. But those proposals set off an alarm in states that relied on landfills and incinerators outside their borders.

Baucus and ranking member John H. Chafee, R-R.I., negotiated furiously with other senators on this issue and presented a compromise proposal at the markup.

Their proposal allowed governors to keep imported waste out of state landfills and incinerators, provided that affected local communities and solid-waste councils requested such action and that it did not breach existing disposal contracts. Governors were not allowed to block such waste from environmentally sound landfills and incinerators that accepted out-of-state waste in 1991.

However, the bill removed the governors' authority to stop out-of-state waste after 1994 if their state landfills violated new federal environmental standards.

Governors from states that accepted a large amount of out-of-state waste — more than 1 million tons during 1991 — were allowed to freeze imports at that level. And at the request of the local government and waste-planning council, the governor was permitted to cap the amount of out-of-state waste at a particular landfill at 30 percent. The provision was expected to apply to Pennsylvania, Ohio, Virginia and Indiana — major trash importing states.

The amendment passed by voice vote after members added language by Harris Wofford, D-Pa., giving his state extra power to limit the percentage of out-of-state trash it accepted. Pennsylvania imported an unusually large amount of trash.

Harry Reid, D-Nev., had tried to win greater state veto power over out-of-state waste, proposing to let governors block such waste without a request from the local community where it was to be shipped.

But Frank R. Lautenberg, D-N.J., said such a plan threatened to balkanize waste planning and Reid's amendment was rejected by voice vote.

Among a series of smaller amendments, Dave Duren-

berger, R-Minn., persuaded members to adjust some of the bill's recycling targets for packaging. His amendment to increase the target for glass packaging and decrease it for steel — setting both at 40 percent — passed 12-0.

### Environment and Public Works Approves S 976

At a final markup session, the Senate Environment and Public Works Committee on May 20 approved S 976 on a vote of 12-5 but only after several members sought relief for steel mills and a neighborhood near an incinerator.

Republicans Alan K. Simpson of Wyoming, Robert C. Smith of New Hampshire, Steve Symms of Idaho, Durenberger and Jeffords voted against the bill.

In the three-hour markup, the panel approved only one controversial amendment, which dealt with halting the Ohio waste incinerator's operation.

The amendment by Howard M. Metzenbaum, D-Ohio, was approved 10-7. It prevented the operation of a hazardous-waste incinerator in East Liverpool, Ohio, until various legal challenges were resolved. Metzenbaum said there were irregularities in the way the Waste Technologies Industries plant was granted its operating permit from the EPA; it was only 1,100 feet from an elementary school.

The committee turned back, 8-16, an attempt by Durenberger to allow companies that used scrap paper to continue to use the recycling symbol — the triangle of chasing arrows. The bill allowed only companies that used "post consumer" waste or recycled waste to use the symbol.

Durenberger said that companies that recycle overruns, scrap and other wastepaper should get credit, too.

But Democratic senators argued that "recycled" means a product is made up of material that had been used and discarded, not scrap material that gathered up on the shop floor and reworked.

Durenberger also pushed an unsuccessful amendment that sought to give financially pressed steel companies a break from cleaning up waste on their property. Durenberger withdrew the amendment when members noted that other industries clamored for exemptions.

The committee passed on voice vote a Durenberger amendment that prohibited industries from discharging hazardous wastes into sewers, which he said was one of the law's biggest loopholes.

Beyond the amendments, the bill:

● Allowed ash from municipal incinerators to be treated as regular solid waste, thus allowing easier disposal.

● Prohibited putting lead acid batteries in landfills or incinerators and required battery retailers, wholesalers and manufacturers to take back old batteries for safe disposal.

## SENATE PASSES NEW BILL

As the summer drew on opposition to S 976 mounted. By July, Senate sponsors had abandoned hope of passing a major rewrite of the nation's main solid-waste law in 1992.

Instead, the Senate the week of July 20 turned to the more limited but politically palatable issue of giving states the power to control out-of-state garbage imports.

After spending most of the week locked in nettlesome debate and negotiations over the issue, the Senate on July 23 passed 89-2 the slimmed down bill (S 2877) that gave governors limited power to block imports of out-of-state trash. *(Vote 151, p. 20-S)*

But to win over senators from garbage-exporting states, sponsors were forced to craft significant relief for such states as New York and New Jersey. Among the entice-

ments was a key provision that barred most governors from interfering with existing interstate waste shipment contracts.

The issue was a crusade for Indiana Republican Coats, whose state received 1.45 million tons of imported waste in 1991. He said the large amount of waste coming into Indiana was beginning to cause significant landfill problems.

In 1990, Coats got an even more sweeping garbage ban attached to the fiscal 1991 District of Columbia appropriations bill on a 68-31 vote. But the provision was later stripped from the spending bill in conference. *(1990 Almanac, p. 891)*

From that time on, Coats was poised to offer a similar amendment but held off while the Environment and Public Works Committee drafted S 976.

But when the controversial RCRA bill stalled Coats was prepared to attach his proposal to must-pass spending bills. That prompted Baucus to agree to strip the politically popular language of S 976 and move it as a separate bill (S 2877).

Prospects for S 2877 were far from certain, given that Congress had only about eight weeks remaining to get its work done before adjournment.

The narrower interstate-waste bill allowed governors to ban or limit garbage imports, subjected to a request by local authorities. Landfills that received out-of-state garbage, however, were allowed to continue under a grandfather clause.

The measure gave the governors of Indiana, Ohio, Pennsylvania and Virginia — states that received the most out-of-state trash — additional power to stem garbage imports. Governors of those four states were able to bar imports without first receiving a request from local authorities and were allowed to freeze trash imports at 1991 or 1992 levels, whichever was less.

In addition, the four governors were able to limit out-of-state garbage imports to the largest landfills in their states to 30 percent of 1991 levels.

The bill stated that no governors were to force landfill operators to turn away waste if they were bound by an existing contract to accept it. However, the exception for Indiana, Ohio, Pennsylvania and Virginia effectively meant that starting in 1999 the governors of those states were able to force contracts to be broken to meet waste limit targets.

For two days, Senate floor action on S 2877 was tied up with the amendment by Coats to give Indiana, Ohio, Pennsylvania and Virginia governors the power to break contracts between landfill operators and out-of-state municipalities searching for a dump. Frank R. Lautenberg, D-N.J., said changing the bill's original mandate — that no governors could force landfill operators to turn away waste if bound by an existing contract to accept it — unfairly harmed his state, which faced a severe landfill shortage.

After two days of negotiations, Coats and Lautenberg settled on a compromise that, starting in 1999, allowed the four governors to force large landfill operators to limit garbage imports to meet waste limit targets even if the action violated an existing contract.

Western senators tried to amend the bill to make any governor eligible for the expanded powers. But the amendment failed on a 60-31 tabling motion after sponsors said its passage threatened to kill the bill. Lautenberg had threatened to filibuster the measure if the amendment had been adopted. *(Vote 149, p. 20-S)*

To the end, the bill drew broad criticism from Western lawmakers who said that while it protected certain states, others were to be forced to accept garbage from waste-management companies looking for new places to ship waste. ■

# No Consensus Reached on Forest Protection

The standoff between the timber industry and those who wanted to preserve the last stands of Pacific Northwest old-growth forests was made all the more bitter by the economy and the election year. But Congress failed, for the third straight year, to achieve any consensus on a plan to manage the forests, home of the threatened northern spotted owl.

Scientists said the old-growth forests were the backbone of a unique ecosystem. The forests' streams were the spawning grounds for the Northwest's salmon runs. The trees helped keep the water clear and were home to many species of wildlife.

But the towering stands of Douglas fir and spruce were also prime sources of timber — a vital part of the region's economy, which sputtered even as the urban parts of the Pacific Northwest boomed. Nevertheless, logging in the region had come to a virtual standstill, as federal courts had agreed with environmentalists that the Agriculture Department's Forest Service and the Interior Department's Bureau of Land Management had violated federal forest management laws and, in some cases, the Endangered Species Act (PL 93-205).

As many as 60,000 jobs hung in the balance, according to a report written by respected forest scientists for the House Agriculture, Interior and Insular Affairs, and Merchant Marine and Fisheries committees. The report, "Alternatives for Management of Late-Successional Forests of the Pacific Northwest," became the backbone for HR 4899, a forest protection and endangered species bill. The Agriculture Committee approved a version of the bill that would have placed 6.8 million acres of old-growth forests off-limits to logging to stem the decline of the spotted owl. But it came at a price: Scientists said it could cost 22,000 to 27,000 timber-related jobs.

A more stringent bill by the House Interior Committee, which would have protected 9 million acres, never made it out of the panel after disgruntled regional lawmakers called on House Speaker Thomas S. Foley, D-Wash., to intervene for a better deal.

Finally, Oregon Republican Sens. Bob Packwood and Mark O. Hatfield introduced a bill (S 1156) that was much more to the timber industry's liking. It would have provided guaranteed timber sales and worker retraining programs and restricted citizen appeals of controversial timber sales. But the bill stalled in the Energy and Natural Resources Committee.

## BACKGROUND

At issue was a battle that pitted timber companies eager to harvest the remaining stands of old-growth forests against conservationists eager to protect them.

Environmentalists had sought to preserve the forests by using the protection that the Endangered Species Act provided forest inhabitants, most notably the northern spotted owl. The owl was declared threatened in 1990.

But such efforts had been countered by timber-dependent communities and the forest industry in the Northwest. They argued that placing the forests off-limits would cost jobs and destroy the economic backbone of an entire region.

An impasse over the fate of the northern spotted owl and timber jobs was unbroken when the 101st Congress adjourned because the authorizing committees were unable to referee the fight between timber interests and environmentalists. House Agriculture Committee and Interior Committee subcommittees staged futile last-minute attempts to move legislation to regulate federal timber sales in the Northwest.

The Bush administration waited until mid-September 1990 to weigh in with a proposal that asked Congress to exempt timber sales in the region from environmental laws. But the plan was seen as unrealistic. *(1990 Almanac, p. 296)*

By the end of 1991, lawmakers still had not devised a legislative solution to the controversy. Instead, Interior Secretary Manuel Lujan Jr. announced his decision to convene the high-level Endangered Species Committee, known as the "God squad" — the only committee empowered to grant exemptions to the Endangered Species Act. The panel was asked to weigh the economic dislocation facing the logging industry against protecting the owl.

Lujan's decision came at the request of the Bureau of Land Management, which targeted about 750 million board feet of timber to be cut down for sale in 1991. But in June, the Fish and Wildlife Service issued an opinion that 52 of the sales would jeopardize the spotted owl. The bureau modified eight of those sales to meet the objections, but the remaining 44, on a small fraction of Oregon federal forestland, had been in limbo.

The disputed sales involved 4,400 acres that were expected to yield 219 million board feet of wood, valued at $69 million.

Members of Oregon's congressional delegation were pleased with Lujan's decision but cautioned that it would not be a panacea for the region's problems. They believed a legislative solution was still needed.

"In requesting a 'God squad' review, the secretary of the Interior has hardly solved the Northwest timber crisis. But, he has put a lie to the contention that there is no place in the Endangered Species Act for people," said Rep. Les AuCoin, D-Ore.

Several bills, including a compromise measure (HR 3263) from Washington, Oregon and California lawmakers, were attempting to find a way of managing timber harvests and protecting the owl. However, nothing was approved by committee during the first session of the 102nd Congress. *(1991 Almanac, p. 210)*

## HOUSE ACTION

With no resolution in sight early in 1992 on how best to manage the Pacific Northwest's ancient forests, House Interior and Insular Affairs Committee Chairman George Miller, D-Calif., began drafting a legislative proposal that he planned to move swiftly.

"It is my intention, working with all the relevant chairmen, to move an ancient forest bill this year," Miller said at a timber policy oversight hearing March 24.

Miller's staff had nearly finished drafting the measure with the help of the Agriculture and Merchant Marine committees.

The bill, which was being labeled a compromise, was expected to hew closely to the strictures of the Endangered Species Act and allow smaller timber harvests in old-growth forests than those sought by industry.

The bill also was expected to seek forestwide protections for the owl's habitat and the area's watershed, and to

give timber-dependent communities a steady, if diminished, harvest level.

The proposal joined a list of at least a dozen other bills that sought to resolve the timber crisis. None of the measures had moved past the hearing stage.

### Panels Approve Bills

The week of May 4, subcommittees of the Interior and Insular Affairs Committee and the Agriculture Committee approved separate versions of the ancient-forest protection bill (HR 4899).

On May 7, the Interior Subcommittee on National Parks and Public Lands narrowly approved what was considered the most restrictive option other than a logging ban. Its version of HR 4899 attempted to restore owl, salmon and other species populations by setting about 9 million acres in old-growth reserves off-limits to logging. It would allow about 1.6 billion board feet of timber harvests annually, compared with 4.2 billion annual levels in the 1980s. The decline in logging was predicted to cost 28,000 to 35,000 jobs.

The Agriculture panel met the next day to mark up its version of HR 4899. Members were sympathetic to the timber workers during the Agriculture markup.

"There are many people out there without any jobs, with communities hurting," said Forest, Family Farms and Energy Subcommittee Chairman Harold F. Volkmer, D-Mo.

The Agriculture Committee version would allow annual timber harvests of about 2.1 billion board feet in its first three years. Job losses were estimated at 22,000 to 27,000. The plan would give the spotted owl a 50-50 chance of recovery, scientists had said.

The committee also approved an amendment to study California's Sierra range for additional protection.

And it turned down a substitute by Bob Smith, R-Ore., that was the legislative embodiment of "owl preservation plan" the Bush administration released in May.

The following week, the Agriculture Forests Subcommittee on May 13 rejected, 3-6, a different bill (HR 3414) to prohibit most below-cost timber sales after opponents said the measure would reduce timber cutting and cost jobs.

Below-cost timber sales cost more to administer than they generated in revenues for the Treasury. Pre-sale tasks performed by the Forest Service included building roads to timber sites, determining sale boundaries and administrative work.

As originally introduced, HR 3414 would have established a new accounting system for calculating timber sale costs and would have required a sale-by-sale analysis of cost and revenue.

But in responding to Forest Service objections, bill sponsor Jim Olin, D-Va., drafted a substitute that would have allowed the Forest Service to analyze the profitability of the timber sales on a forest-by-forest basis rather than requiring an analysis of individual sales.

Still, opponents said the bill would pose too sweeping a burden on timber-dependent communities, particularly those in the Pacific Northwest already threatened by efforts to preserve the northern spotted owl.

## 'GOD SQUAD' MEETS

The Bush administration's trio of steps May 14 to balance timber jobs in the Pacific Northwest against the fate of the threatened owl threw the controversial issue back in Congress' lap.

To avoid lengthy legal disputes, Congress had to end a longstanding deadlock over how best to protect the owl in federal old-growth forests.

The administration's action also was certain to add to the debate over the reach of the Endangered Species Act, which faced reauthorization in 1992. (Endangered Species Act, p. 280)

Lawmakers had set aside legislative proposals to protect the old-growth forests until a Cabinet-level panel ruled on the 44 timber sales in Oregon.

The seven-member Endangered Species Committee, known as the "God squad," voted May 14 to suspend the act and allow logging on 13 of the 44 disputed tracts of federal timberland that were home to the owl.

On the "God squad" panel were Lujan, Agriculture Secretary Edward Madigan, Environmental Protection Agency Administrator William K. Reilly, Army Secretary Michael P. W. Stone, Council of Economic Advisers Chairman Michael J. Boskin, Undersecretary of Commerce for Oceans and Atmosphere John A. Knauss and Oregon state representative Tom Walsh, who was Portland's public transit director.

The committee voted 5-2 to allow logging on only 13 tracts. The law required five votes for the Endangered Species Act to be sidestepped. Lujan said the 13 were of significant size, had no alternatives and would not impinge on the owl's "critical habitat."

The panel also called on the BLM to come up with a plan to return the owl population to healthy levels.

Reilly and Walsh cast the two votes against the plan.

Lujan's alternative would set aside some 2.8 million acres of timberland and 1.5 million acres of parks and wilderness as spotted owl conservation areas. The patchwork of areas could support an estimated 1,340 pairs of owls — less than half the 3,000 pairs that were known to exist.

By contrast, the legally mandated recovery plan would set aside 5.4 million acres of forestland and 2.1 million acres of wilderness and national parks — levels that were projected to help restore the owl's population to a level that would take it off the list of threatened species. It was scheduled to take effect within 60 days if Congress or the courts did not move to halt it.

It was only the second time the committee had voted to override the nation's species protection law. But the sales still could not go forward unless two federal court injunctions were lifted.

Interior Secretary Lujan also released his own "preservation" plan for the owl immediately after the vote. It called for limited protection for the owl to save regional timber jobs.

The rival plan required congressional approval, and such action appeared unlikely. Interior Department officials said the plan could lead to the owl's extinction by writing off much of its coastal range habitat to logging — yet would still cost between 15,000 to 17,000 timber jobs.

Lujan simultaneously released the government's official recovery plan for the owl, required under the Endangered Species Act. It sought to revive the owl's population to levels high enough to allow it to be removed from the list of threatened species. The plan would cost up to 32,000 jobs, which Lujan called unacceptable.

Packwood, the Oregon Republican who in 1991 supported the administration's plan to convene the "God

squad," was so dismayed that he declined to introduce Lujan's alternative recovery plan in the Senate.

"The preservation plan is kind of a halfway plan," Packwood said.

### Congress Reacts

Reaction from Congress was swift.

Environmentally minded lawmakers branded the administration steps shortsighted and said they would fail to protect the owl.

Congressional allies of the region's troubled timber industry said Lujan's rival plan would cost far too many jobs in an industry already hard hit by automation, the export of raw logs and migration to the South.

Pacific Northwest lawmakers said the action threatened to further polarize the longstanding debate over the owl, the ancient forests and jobs.

"What the administration did was contradictory and confusing," said Rep. Peter A. DeFazio, an Oregon Democrat whose district was home to many of the affected timber workers. "It was not helpful at all."

Rep. Sid Morrison, a Washington state Republican who had tried to mediate the dispute between the timber industry and environmentalists, said, "This does not do what the delegation feels we have to do to prevent future listings [of other forest species]."

Still, Sen. Slade Gorton, R-Wash., said he would introduce Lujan's rival preservation plan in the Senate, and Rep. Bob Smith, R-Ore., said he would follow suit in the House.

But neither lawmaker held out much hope for its passage. "I don't think it has a chance," said Smith. "It surely didn't meet my expectations as far as jobs losses go."

## FOLEY DERAILS INTERIOR PLAN

Foley might have been Speaker of the House, but he was also a card-carrying member of the Pacific Northwest delegation that remained tied in knots by plans to save the northern spotted owl that could hurt the region's economy.

The week of June 15, Foley used his political muscle as Speaker to achieve a regional goal: derailing the Interior Committee plan (HR 4899) to manage the region's ancient forests and that nearly every member of the delegation opposed. Environmentalists favored it, and the plan seemed to be moving swiftly toward passage.

The Interior Committee abruptly short-circuited its June 17 markup after last-minute arm-twisting by Foley eroded support for the bill. That inaction had the side effect of suddenly raising the profile of a less stringent version of the same bill in the Agriculture Committee. After a grueling June 18 markup, Agriculture approved its version of HR 4899 on a 27-15 vote.

The Agriculture Committee plan would put about 6.8 million acres of old-growth forests into reserves that were off-limits to logging, compared with 9 million acres under the Interior bill. While it offered less protection to the threatened owl, it sought to preserve 6,000 to 8,000 jobs, compared with the Interior proposal. Foley and many members of the delegation found this version more acceptable.

The Agriculture Committee action marked the first time an authorizing committee had approved a legislative solution to the forest issue.

Since HR 4899 was referred to both committees, the Interior Committee was required to take some action for the bill to make it to the House floor.

After the vote, Agriculture Committee Chairman E. "Kika" de la Garza, D-Texas, predicted that the House would approve an old-growth forest bill in 1992.

But then a planned markup by the Interior Committee was scheduled, canceled and then rescheduled for June 17. And when the committee turned to the ancient forest bill that morning after breaking for a vote on the House floor, Chairman Miller abruptly canceled the markup.

"I had the votes this morning," Miller said. "I didn't have the votes later this morning, I assume because the Speaker made some phone calls."

A Foley aide, who did not want to be identified, confirmed that the Speaker had lobbied some wavering members against the bill. That apparently turned the tide.

DeFazio said Foley attended a meeting of a delegation dominated by members from Oregon, Washington and Idaho on the night before the markup. With the exception of Jim McDermott, D-Wash., the members were united in opposing the Interior version being pushed by Miller and subcommittee Chairman Bruce F. Vento, D-Minn.

For weeks, DeFazio — whose district might have borne the brunt of the job losses — had taken the delegation's lead in pushing for a less restrictive measure. He was unsuccessful in selling it to Miller. "[Miller's] staff had been spending more time negotiating with the Ancient Forest Alliance [an environmental group] than they have with us," DeFazio complained.

The Foley aide said the Speaker's intervention was meant to spur Miller and his staff into negotiations with DeFazio and the rest of the delegation.

Miller and Foley met the afternoon after the canceled markup. Miller only said it was a "good" meeting. The committee never resumed action on the bill.

## SENATE ACTION

A Pacific Northwest old-growth forest proposal (S 1156) favored by the timber industry was effectively killed after its fate was linked with an unrelated environmental measure (HR 2929) to protect millions of acres of California desert by creating two national parks and 73 wilderness areas.

The meshing of the two highly politicized bills occurred during a rancorous Aug. 5 markup by the Energy and Natural Resources Committee.

Both John Seymour, R-Calif., and Packwood used the bills to showcase a conflict between jobs and the environment, trumpeting their support for the former over the latter.

Fellow Oregon Republican Hatfield had long sought to have the committee consider the timber bill, which Packwood introduced in May 1991. Both said the bill would protect the forests and the owls while preserving the timber industry and the towns that had become economically dependent on it.

Committee Democrats such as Tim Wirth, D-Colo., also pushed to move a House-passed measure that would protect millions of acres of the California desert. The bill had attracted wide support, gaining the backing of most of the state's newspapers and many of its cities and counties. Outgoing Sen. Alan Cranston, D-Calif., who had pushed similar proposals for years, had made passage a priority and pushed to get the Energy and Natural Resources Committee to consider it Aug. 5. *(California desert, p. 282)*

But as the committee turned to the timber bill, Wirth and Paul Wellstone, D-Minn., quizzed Seymour, an opponent of the desert protections, on whether he would try to

block a vote on the California bill.

When Seymour indicated he would oppose the bill, Wirth moved to fold the desert proposal into the timber bill: He wanted to ensure that if the desert bill were blocked, so would be the Republican's timber proposal.

Seymour immediately tried to quash the move, but his tabling motion failed on an 9-11 vote. Seymour then moved to end any further consideration of either bill, invoking a special Senate rule that allowed him to object to the continuation of the markup.

The session ended with Wirth's proposal to link the two bills left up in the air.

Timber industry lobbyists were furious at Wirth for holding up their pet bill, while environmentalists lambasted Seymour for putting his opposition to the California desert protection bill ahead of the needs of timber workers.

The timber bill was expected to solidify Packwood's support in Oregon's timber-dependent communities. While purporting to preserve the Northwest's forests, it would limit judicial appeals of timber sales in federal forests, mandate that the economic health of timber communities be taken into account in forest planning and set up various funds and commissions to aid displaced timber towns.

Logging in old-growth forest preserves would even be permitted if it would enhance the forest's resistance to insects, or for other "ecosystem values."

As Hatfield said, "We're trying to keep a little hope alive in the hearts and minds of the people of our area."

But environmentalists had attacked the bill as limiting citizen rights to appeal timber decisions. They also said the legislation would not sufficiently protect owls and other endangered species and would allow logging in old-growth forests. ∎

# Endangered Species Act Remained in Limbo

Not surprisingly, a bill (HR 4045) to reauthorize the Endangered Species Act went nowhere.

The law was conceived in 1973 as a fire wall to keep politics and money from deciding the fate of America's threatened animal and plant species. But when the act faced renewal in 1992, its reauthorization became embroiled in politics and money: the politics of an election year and the economic imponderables of a recession.

Sponsor Gerry E. Studds, D-Mass., said that, with the nation still feeling the effects of the poor economy, "the emotional climate might not be right."

The Endangered Species Act (PL 93-205) was among the most popular and well-known laws ever passed by Congress. The recovery of the bald eagle, a symbol of America, and the stabilization of the grizzly bear population were just two examples of protection given species under the act.

But, fueled by the dirth of jobs, an anti-environmental backlash had made the act a highly divisive issue in several states, most notably Oregon, California and Washington.

Moreover, environmentalists had long known that as the economy slid, so did concerns about the environment.

In timber-dependent communities in Oregon, interest was intense in 44 planned timber sales on federal land that were halted because of the act's protection of the northern

spotted owl. Timber industry lobbyists contended that 5,000 jobs were hanging in the balance. Legislative efforts to co-manage the timber lands and timber jobs also failed in 1992. *(Old growth forest protection, p. 277)*

In California, builders and landowners were nervously awaiting the outcome of a petition to list the California gnatcatcher — a small bird that nested in prime developable coastal areas — as a threatened species. California builders said up to 200,000 jobs in the region could be affected.

And in Washington state, attempts to save several species of endangered salmon threatened to raise the state's electric rates by $200 million.

## Tough Reauthorization Proposed

By congressional intent, the law did not consider economic factors in deciding whether to list a species as endangered. Section 4 of the act states that listing decisions should be made "solely on the basis of the best scientific and commercial data available."

The ramifications for jobs and businesses could only be considered later, by the Cabinet-level Endangered Species Committee — known as the God Squad. The committee convened in 1992 at the request of the Bureau of Land Management, which wanted to go ahead with the 44 Oregon timber sales held up by the act's protection of the spotted owl.

Conservationists had welcomed the introduction Nov. 26, 1991, of a tough reauthorization bill by Studds, chairman of the Merchant Marine subcommittee with Endangered Species Act jurisdiction. *(1991 Almanac, p. 209)*

Studds' bill sought authorization of $517 million over five years for the Interior and Commerce departments to carry out the act, more than twice what was authorized for 1988 through 1992.

Previously, the Interior Department's Fish and Wildlife Service had attracted environmentalists' ire for not developing species recovery plans quickly enough. Studds' proposed reauthorization required that such plans be developed by Dec. 31, 1996, for all 601 species awaiting protection. It also gave the service a two-year deadline to come up with a recovery plan for any species listed after 1993.

On the other hand, a key complaint of business interests is the act's emphasis on saving species on an inefficient, individual basis. This had sometimes forced projects to be halted by the discovery of a small population of endangered or threatened species, even if they were being protected elsewhere.

Studds' bill directed Fish and Wildlife — and the National Marine Fisheries Service, which ran recovery programs for endangered marine animals — to emphasize "integrated multi-species recovery plans" that would maintain and restore discrete habitats.

Under such an approach, businesses, local government and federal agencies could call for a promising habitat or watershed to be set aside as the breeding area for an array of species, allowing several species to be saved while also permitting development nearby.

The bill gave federal agencies 60 days to respond to violations without fear of lawsuits but allowed citizen legal action within that period for emergencies that posed "a significant risk to the well-being of any listed species."

A new feature in the bill was a $20 million revolving Habitat Conservation Fund to allow states, local businesses and advocacy groups to work together to study species conservation. ∎

# Tree Bark OK'd for Use in Cancer Drug

Congress cleared legislation (HR 3836) on July 23 to provide a constant supply of a cancer-fighting substance called taxol, derived from the bark of the Pacific yew tree. The chemical compound had shown significant promise in treating ovarian cancer and had the potential to treat other forms of cancer.

The law required that yews be harvested before an area of public land was opened to commercial logging, unless the action threatened loggers' safety. Under the law, trees had to be harvested in such a way as to promote new growth; and new trees had to be planted.

The law called for a halt to further harvesting of the trees if a synthetic substitute for taxol was found.

## BACKGROUND

Known as the Taxus brevifolia, the slow-growing Pacific yew grew in the underbrush of the ancient forests in the Pacific Northwest. It was considered almost worthless and was destroyed during logging operations or sold by the Agriculture Department's Forest Service for use as fence posts and lumber.

But in 1990, the National Cancer Institute reported that a substance, taxol, in the yew's bark was effective in treating ovarian cancer and possibly breast cancer. More than 12,000 women a year died from ovarian cancer. Taxol, the drug based on the chemical, was being manufactured by Bristol-Myers Squibb Co.

Under congressional pressure, the Forest Service announced March 4 that it was adopting a new policy to limit wasteful destruction of the Pacific yew.

Before a joint hearing of three House subcommittees, George M. Leonard, associate chief of the Forest Service, said that yew trees on public lands would be sold, with a few exceptions, only to further the production of taxol.

The U.S. Forest Service and the Interior Department's Bureau of Land Management had agreed to supply Bristol-Myers with 750,000 pounds of yew bark annually for five years.

Despite the administration's pronouncement, lawmakers, urged on by medical groups, decided to push through legislation requiring federal land agencies to ensure that yew bark was not wasted.

## HOUSE COMMITTEE ACTION

Legislation to ensure the harvest of the yew had to make its way through three House committees — Agriculture, Interior and Merchant Marine.

On May 12, the Fisheries and Wildlife Conservation Subcommittee of the Merchant Marine Committee ap-

---

### BOXSCORE

➡ **Pacific Yew (HR 3836, S 2851).** The bill provided for the management of federal lands containing the Pacific yew to ensure a sufficient supply of taxol, a cancer-treating drug made from the tree's bark.

**Reports:** H Rept 102-552, Parts 1,2,3; S Rept 102-323.

### KEY ACTION

July 7 — The **House** passed HR 3836 by voice vote.

July 23 — The **Senate** passed HR 3836 by voice vote.

Aug. 7 — President Bush signed HR 3836 — PL 102-335.

---

proved a bill, sponsored by its chairman, Gerry E. Studds, D-Mass., that sought to guarantee that yews were harvested for the manufacture of taxol. The legislation directed the government to inventory the trees in federal forests to make sure that they were cut before an area was opened for logging.

The next day, Agriculture's Forests Subcommittee approved a leaner substitute version of Studds' bill by Chairman Harold L. Volkmer, D-Mo., to ensure that harvest levels and methods guaranteed that the trees would grow back.

On May 14, the House Merchant Marine and Fisheries Committee approved Studds' version of the bill. Both the Merchant Marine and the Agriculture versions of the bill halted federal management of the trees if a synthetic substitute for taxol was found.

The House Interior Subcommittee on National Parks and Public Lands approved the legislation June 4. The bill resembled the Merchant Marine and Agriculture bills, with some technical modifications.

Continuing its advance through the House, the legislation won approval from the Interior Committee on June 10 and the Agriculture Committee on June 18.

## HOUSE FLOOR ACTION

The House passed the bill July 7. The legislation directed the government to inventory yew trees growing in the underbrush of forests in the Pacific Northwest. Once their location was known, the trees were to be harvested before any other logging activity, unless the action threatened the safety of loggers.

The bill also required that the trees be cut in such a way as to encourage them to sprout new growth and that saplings be planted to maintain supplies of taxol — the cancer-fighting agent found in the tree's bark.

The measure authorized research on alternatives to taxol. If a synthetic substitute for the substance was found, loggers would not be required to harvest the yew before cutting commercial timber.

## SENATE ACTION

On July 1, the Senate Energy and Natural Resources Committee approved, 20-0, a measure (S 2851) similar to the bill moving through the House to ensure that the yew was harvested for the manufacture of the anti-cancer drug taxol.

The Senate on July 23 cleared the House bill for the president's signature. ∎

# Desert Protection Bill Is Blocked in Senate

California Republican Sen. John Seymour ultimately blocked a Democratic bill (HR 2929) to protect vast swaths of desert in Southern California in 1992. The House had passed the measure overwhelmingly in November 1991.

The California desert — which included the East Mojave and Death Valley — was considered a priceless natural resource, the domain of a panoply of wildlife.

But off-road enthusiasts also prized it for its trackless spaces. Miners said there was a fortune in minerals below its shifting sands. The California desert also was home to major military bases.

The House passed its California desert bill (HR 2929 — H Rept 102-283, Part 1) on a 297-136 vote on Nov. 26, 1991. *(1991 Almanac, p. 228)*

The measure was a longtime goal of retiring Sens. Alan Cranston, D-Calif., and Tim Wirth, D-Colo. The bill sought to protect almost 7 million acres of the desert by dividing it into 73 wilderness areas and two national parks — the 3.3 million-acre Death Valley and the 800,000-acre Joshua Tree national monuments. It also designated 1.5 million acres of the East Mojave Desert as a protected national monument.

The measure placed much of the areas off-limits to miners and off-road vehicle users. However, in a compromise, bill sponsor Rep. Mel Levine, D-Calif., altered the measure to reserve at least 114 miles of routes and trails for continued off-road vehicle use and allowed current mining and ranching claims to remain valid for years.

Nonetheless, the bill was unanimously opposed by California lawmakers who represented the region and its miners, ranchers and off-road vehicle users. In the Senate, they were joined by Seymour.

The Bush administration also opposed the legislation, saying it threatened to cost jobs and put the desert off-limits to all but backpackers.

The Senate Energy and Natural Resources Committee scheduled a markup of the bill Aug. 5, but Seymour blocked it on a procedural motion, and the session ended before the panel could begin anew.

## SENATE ACTION

The Energy and Natural Resources Committee effectively linked the fate of the panel's two most politicized bills at an Aug. 5 markup: a Pacific Northwest old-growth forest proposal (S 1156), favored by the timber industry, and the California desert protection bill (HR 2929). *(Old growth forest protection, p. 277)*

In the end, the action spelled defeat for the California desert bill as well as the old-growth forest measure. But the move was driven more by the 1992 political season than any intent to kill the desert measure.

The political reverberations were particularly intense because both issues had become entwined in two hard-fought Senate campaigns waged by Bob Packwood, R-Ore., and Seymour in 1992.

Packwood, who ultimately won re-election, was locked in a tight race with well-known Democratic Rep. Les AuCoin. Seymour, appointed to his seat in 1991, also faced an uphill battle, which he ultimately lost, against his Democratic challenger, former San Francisco Mayor Dianne Feinstein.

Both Seymour and Packwood were using the bills to showcase a conflict between jobs and the environment, trumpeting their support for the former over the latter.

Fellow Oregon Republican Mark O. Hatfield had long sought to have the committee consider the timber bill, which Packwood introduced in May 1991.

Hatfield had won assurances that the timber bill was to be marked up at the Aug. 5 committee meeting. But committee Democrats including Wirth also pushed to move the California desert bill at the same meeting.

The desert bill had attracted wide support, gaining the backing of most of California's newspapers and many of its cities and counties. Outgoing California Democrat Cranston, who had pushed similar proposals for years, had made passage a priority and also pushed to get the Energy and Natural Resources Committee to consider it at the Aug. 5 meeting.

Cranston had made the desert bill a personal crusade, backing similar legislation since 1974 to protect the fragile desert area.

But his plan had been frustrated for a decade by the other California senator.

Former Republican Sen. Pete Wilson and then his replacement, Seymour, who led the battle against the bill, argued that it displaced too many people and threatened to cost 20,000 jobs and $3 billion in income.

The administration said the bill threatened to hamper operations at various military bases in Southern California.

But as the committee turned to the timber bill, Wirth and Paul Wellstone, D-Minn., quizzed Seymour on whether he would try to block a vote on the California bill.

When Seymour indicated that he planned to oppose the bill, Wirth moved to fold the desert proposal into the timber bill: He wanted to ensure that blocking the desert bill also blocked the Republican's timber proposal.

Seymour immediately tried to quash the move to link the two measures, but his tabling motion failed on the 9-11 vote. Faced with defeat, Seymour then invoked a special Senate rule that allowed him to object to the continuation of the markup, and that effectively ended it. The markup ended with Wirth's proposal to link the two bills still up in the air.

Any hope of revisiting the issue late in the second session of the 102nd Congress disappeared the week of Sept. 21. The Senate Energy and Natural Resources Committee closed up shop that week without acting on the California desert bill. ∎

# Mining Law Overhaul Is Stymied Again

Congress came closer than it had in years, but ultimately failed to pass a comprehensive rewrite of the nation's 120-year-old mining law. The 102nd did, however, fold a modest mining law change into the fiscal 1993 spending bill for the Interior Department and related agencies.

Action began with House lawmakers pushing a bill (HR 918) by Nick J. Rahall II, D-W.Va., that aimed to change the 1872 Mining Law to conform to 20th century realities. Proponents said the original law, passed when the settlement of the West was a national priority, was partly re-

sponsible for a litany of ills.

Problems included a continued hemorrhage of federal land to private use for as little as $2.50 an acre; improper use of mining claims for real estate development; a legacy of abandoned mines left to scar the landscape and pollute water supplies; and the practice of mining companies (often foreign-owned) extracting billions of dollars in minerals without paying royalties to the federal Treasury.

The House took up the bill during the last-minute crush of business Oct. 4 and voted on several amendments — most notably rejecting an amendment by Peter A. DeFazio, D-Ore., to impose a royalty fee of up to 12.5 percent of gross receipts derived from mining public lands. But the House never finished debating the bill, and it died when Congress adjourned.

A companion Senate bill (S 433) by Dale Bumpers, D-Ark., never made it out of the Energy and Natural Resources Committee. But Senate appropriators sought their own reforms and inserted them into the fiscal 1993 appropriations bill (HR 5503 — conference report H Rept 102-901) for the Interior Department and related agencies. The Senate voted Aug. 5 to fold in the provisions and passed a version of the spending bill the same day.

In conference, however, all but minor changes in the mining law were stripped from the Interior appropriations bill. The surviving provision imposed a new annual $100 fee on miners to keep their mining claims active. The change did away with a longstanding requirement that miners perform $100 worth of mining-related work each year to keep a claim active — a mandate that environmentalists said led to the unnecessary scarring of public lands. The House adopted the conference report to the fiscal 1993 Interior Department appropriations bill Sept. 30 by voice vote. The Senate cleared the final Interior spending bill Sept. 30 by voice vote. President Bush signed the appropriations bill Oct. 5 (PL 102-381). *(Appropriations, p. 686)*

## BACKGROUND

Efforts to reform the 1872 law were nearly as old as the law itself. As early as 1879, a federally appointed public land commission recommended that it be rewritten.

But it was not until 1987 that efforts to overhaul the law began. The Interior Subcommittee on Mining and Natural Resources, chaired by bill sponsor Rahall, reviewed the law, and the effort produced in 1989 a widely read report by the General Accounting Office (GAO) that documented abuses and revealed conflicts with federal land-management policies.

For 120 years, the 1872 Mining Law had made mining one of the most favored uses of Western federal land. Mining superseded anything else the land might be used for, such as grazing, logging or recreation, unless the government specifically withdrew the land from mining purposes.

In 19 states, mostly in the West, the law guaranteed "free and open access to certain public lands to prospect" for minerals, according to the Interior Department's Bureau of Land Management (BLM). The GAO noted that the law gave mining advantages over other uses that ran "counter to other national natural resource policies and legislation." There were 1.2 million active claims in the country; 160,000 new claims were filed in 1988, a 1990 GAO report said.

The law was enacted to promote the development and settlement of the West, and in that it was successful — hard-rock mining was a $9 billion industry that employed about 47,000 people, according to the Congressional Research Service. Many small towns in the West were dependent on mining income.

But critics said the law had turned into a massive giveaway to large, often foreign-owned corporations. Corporations and individuals used the law's provisions to patent or take title to 3.2 million acres of federal land for hard-rock mining for as little as $2.50 an acre. Miners were able to extract minerals such as gold, silver and platinum without paying royalties to the Treasury — unlike oil and gas operations. The scarred landscapes often left behind were expected to cost $11 billion to restore.

The law also was used by speculators to buy land inexpensively and turn it into developments, resorts and vacation homes. A 1990 GAO study said that of 59 mining claim sites it visited, "33 had unauthorized residences ranging from small, run-down shacks to permanent, more expensive, year-round dwellings.... All these claim holders live rent-free on public land."

### How the Mining Law Worked

Under the law, a miner was able to patent a claim by following these steps:

● A prospector "located" or staked a claim for hard-rock minerals (gold, silver, lead, zinc, copper) that the prospector believed were held in a patch of public land. The miner filed a claim with the BLM. Cost: $10.

● To maintain the claim, the miner had to do $100 worth of "work" each year on the claim. Though the miner still did not own the land, he or she could live on the claimed property while prospecting.

● If minerals were shown to be under the ground, the claim holder was able to buy or "patent" the claim — obtain clear title to the surface and the minerals underneath — for $2.50 to $5 an acre. After 1990, miners were required to post bonds to ensure that there was money to restore the land once mining was finished. Of the 1.2 million active mining claims, about 550 claims a year were patented, the BLM said.

## HOUSE SUBCOMMITTEE

After decades of digging, those who wanted to revamp the 1872 Mining Law finally struck gold June 24. The House Interior and Insular Affairs Committee approved HR 918 on a vote of 26-19.

The bill called for miners to pay more to extract hard-rock minerals from federal land and imposed stricter rules to restore the environment afterward.

The bill sought to give the government a fair return for the minerals extracted from public lands. It ended the system of land patenting, which allowed miners and mining companies to take ownership of mineral-rich federal land for as little as $2.50 an acre.

The measure proposed to impose an annual rent of as much as $25 an acre on mining claims and strengthened rules to ensure that the environment was restored after mining.

Also for the first time, an 8 percent royalty on hard-rock mineral receipts was to be imposed under an amendment that Oregon Democrat DeFazio succeeded in adding to the bill. According to the GAO, the royalty stood to raise more than $289 million a year. The amendment was approved by voice vote.

The measure also stood to alter land-use policy by making mining compete equally with all other public land

uses. To that end, the bill required land-management agencies to survey their property to determine which, if any, areas were not suitable for mining because of environmental, cultural or recreational attributes. Such lands were to be withdrawn from mining. Mining claims had precedence over any other use unless the land was specifically withdrawn from mining under the 1976 Federal Land Policy and Management Act.

Last, the bill established an abandoned mine reclamation fund to begin cleaning up abandoned mines — a chore that was estimated to cost about $11 billion.

Western lawmakers vigorously opposed the bill. They had long blocked similar legislation.

Indeed, action on the bill came only after West Virginia Democrat Rahall moved June 24 to jump-start the process by discharging the bill directly to the full committee. The full committee approved the move on a close 24-20 vote amid strong complaints by Western Republicans.

Rahall acted after failing to muster the votes needed to get the six-member mining subcommittee he chaired to approve the bill. The bill had been pending since he introduced it Feb. 6, 1991. *(1991 Almanac, p. 217)*

The discharge motion prompted Don Young, R-Alaska, to protest bitterly. "This committee is becoming a committee that is socializing the nation's natural resources," he said. "You can get a land claim, you can get a mining claim easier in Russia than you can in the United States."

Rahall and other bill supporters dismissed the "gloom-and-doom predictions" of Young and other opponents. They said similar moves requiring the coal mining industry to pay royalties and restore the environment allowed the industry to prosper.

The bill also was referred to the House Agriculture and Merchant Marine committees, the latter of which moved the bill along without changes Sept. 16.

The House Agriculture Committee took little time Sept. 10 to approve the bill. The panel had only limited jurisdiction over report requirements in the bill for the Forest Service, a branch of the Agriculture Department.

The committee approved a set of amendments that allowed the Forest Service to conduct studies necessary to determine whether mining should be allowed at the same time the Forest Service was drafting long-term plans for managing the federal forests. No mining study was required to be done separately (H Rept 102-711 — Pt. II).

## HOUSE ACTION

The full House on Oct. 4 began a landmark debate over overhauling the 120-year-old mining law (HR 918 — H Rept 102-711). But facing the press of end-of-the-session business and the hostility of Western representatives, lawmakers adjourned without completing consideration of the bill.

Bill author Rahall vowed to work in the 103rd Congress for what he called necessary reforms of the 1872 Mining Law. But mining-state lawmakers hailed the downfall of what they said was a "disastrous" bill.

Barbara F. Vucanovich, R-Nev., had proposed 150 amendments to the bill to slow its passage. But it was the House's hectic adjournment schedule that kept the bill from resurfacing after debate was suspended Oct. 4. The measure threatened to take up valuable time, especially since the companion Senate bill (S 433) had not advanced. Members also noted that the Bush administration vowed to veto the bill.

Bill opponents said the legislation threatened to devastate the mining industry and cost thousands of jobs.

On the House floor, Oregon Democrat DeFazio lost a bid to raise the bill's royalty level to 12.5 percent of gross receipts. The amendment failed 161-237. *(Vote 467, p. 114-H)*

On the other side of the issue, Vucanovich lost an effort, 136-254, to strike the royalty provision from the bill. *(Vote 469, p. 114-H)*

The House wrapped up work on the bill Oct. 4 but never got back to it before adjourning.

## INTERIOR APPROPRIATIONS ACTION

Senate appropriators took a modest step toward revising the 1872 Mining Law in the fiscal 1993 Interior appropriations bill (HR 5503 — conference report H Rept 102-901).

The part of the law singled out by critics was the provision that claim holders conduct at least $100 worth of mining-related "work" each year. Critics contended that the work requirement only encouraged claim holders to scar the environment unnecessarily.

Urged on by the Bush administration, Senate appropriators joined their House counterparts by including a provision to turn the annual work requirement into an annual $100 fee to keep claims active. The fee could earn the government $41.3 million in revenues annually, according to the Congressional Budget Office.

The provision was supported by the Bush administration.

On the floor, Bumpers on Aug. 5 called for a one-year ban on all new mining patent claims to preserve public lands while the Senate considered its separate, more sweeping mining reform measure (S 433).

Bumpers attempted a similar maneuver on the fiscal 1992 appropriations bill, but was stymied by Western senators such as Nevada Democrat Harry Reid.

Reid, however, promised Bumpers that Western senators would not block the consideration of Bumpers' mining law legislation by the Energy and Natural Resources Committee.

But Bumpers' S 433 had not gone anywhere. So, in an effort to discharge his promise of 1991 and to make an end run around any further legislation, Reid sponsored an amendment that, in his words, imposed "more reform . . . than in the history of the whole act."

Indeed, the amendment made several substantive changes to the mining law. Under the Reid amendment, miners stood to pay fair market value to take claim to the land.

In an effort to stop land speculators who had been using the law to grab land for real estate development, the amendment also required that land revert to the federal government if a claim holder stopped mining it. And it ensured that miners meet all federal environmental standards for restoring land to its original state when mining operations were completed.

Bumpers scoffed at the changes, calling them "diversionary tactics." He criticized Reid's amendment for failing to mandate royalty payments and tougher environmental restoration standards.

But Bumper's move Aug. 5 to table (kill) Reid's amendment failed 44-52. And Reid's amendment was then adopted on a voice vote. *(Vote 172, p. 23-S)*

In conference Reid's changes were rejected. Rep. Sidney R. Yates, D-Ill., chairman of the Interior Appropriations Subcommittee, said the Senate mining reforms were "cos-

metic" and could derail comprehensive overhaul. Senate conferee Bumpers agreed, saying most of the real value of these lands was in the subsurface, which miners could still exploit for free.

Yates engineered a deal in which Senate appropriators agreed to drop the Senate mining package in return for the House's dropping an increase in grazing fees, which was included in its version of the Interior spending bill. It was the third year in a row that grazing fee increases voted on by the House had been traded away in conference. ∎

# Congress Pressures Bush To Attend Rio Summit

After months of indecision, President Bush announced May 12 that he would attend the U.N. Conference on Environment and Development in Rio de Janeiro, Brazil, in June, largely defusing a congressional effort to prod his attendance.

The House and Senate had passed varying versions of a non-binding resolution (H Con Res 292) by Rep. Dante B. Fascell, D-Fla., the Foreign Affairs Committee chairman, urging Bush to attend the meeting and show "leadership" there.

Similar resolutions were introduced by Sens. John Kerry, D-Mass. (S Con Res 89), and Al Gore, D-Tenn. (S Con Res 87), and by Reps. Gus Yatron, D-Pa. (H Con Res 266), and Robert G. Torricelli, D-N.J. (H Con Res 263). None of those resolutions advanced beyond the committee level, and some did not make it that far.

The House was scheduled May 12 to consider a final reconciled version of the House- and Senate-passed resolution, but action was sidetracked when Fascell was unavailable to manage the bill.

Such resolutions, which expressed the sense of the Congress on a particular issue, required passage in the same form by both chambers but did not require the president's signature.

Still, the resolutions sent a clear election-year message to the administration that Congress disapproved of Bush's initial resistance to commit to attend the conference. For his part, Bush at first was reluctant to attend only to be forced into signing binding treaties to limit the United States' and other nations' emissions of "greenhouse" gases, such as carbon dioxide. Carbon dioxide was a principal cause of the greenhouse effect that many scientists said produced global warming.

When the administration's negotiators succeeded in softening treaty language so that it contained no specific commitments, Bush pledged to go, saying "environmental problems are global, and every nation must help in solving them."

## BACKGROUND

The summit was billed as one of the largest international gatherings of nations in the post-World War II era, with more than 140 nations slated to attend. Its goal was the creation and signing of international treaties to arrest the changes in the global climate caused by pollution and to protect the Earth's forests and the diverse species within them.

Another hoped-for outcome was the signing of an "Earth Charter," an international statement linking environmental protection with economic development.

The Bush administration had been a cautious, conservative presence at the international negotiating forums leading up to the Earth summit.

The negotiations, which moved along several tracks for two years, were working toward agreements on climate change, biological diversity and the Earth Charter and were being readied for signature by the time of the summit.

Industrial superpowers Germany and Japan, as well as the entire European Community, had agreed to limit their carbon dioxide emissions to 1990 levels through the end of the century. The United States, which accounted for 20 percent of the world's carbon dioxide emissions, opposed such caps.

Instead, the administration maintained that U.S. initiatives already in place, such as a ban on other greenhouse gases (like chlorofluorocarbons) and its program to plant a billion trees were enough to stabilize emissions.

The U.S. delegation argued that each country should decide how to go about cutting greenhouse emissions.

Also attracting controversy was developing countries' demand that industrialized nations transfer money and technology to them to help spur development without harming the environment. U.S. negotiators resisted committing such financial resources as part of the summit.

The United States was committed to using market mechanisms, rather than aid, to guide countries into making environmentally sound decisions, according to the U.S. State Department's U.N. Conference Coordination Center.

The isolation of the United States was underscored the week of Feb. 3, when Rep. Gerry Sikorski, D-Minn., and Gore chaired an international meeting of legislators in Washington, where those attending contrasted their governments' environmental commitments with the United States' cautious approach.

## HOUSE ACTION

The House Foreign Affairs Subcommittee on Western Hemisphere Affairs took the lead in pressing for a commitment from the administration. On Feb. 4, the subcommittee approved a resolution (H Con Res 263) urging the president to participate in the summit.

The committee resolution, approved by voice vote, asked the administration to take the initiative on financing the conference's proposed action plan and to support any new institutions the conference might create. The resolution then stalled.

The House Foreign Affairs Subcommittee on Human Rights and International Organizations approved another non-binding resolution (H Con Res 266) by voice vote Feb. 20. The resolution called on Bush to join other heads of state committed to attend the June conference. But this resolution also failed to advance.

The full House on March 17 passed another version of Fascell's resolution (H Con Res 292) under special expedited procedures. Approved by voice vote, it was stronger in tone than a companion Senate version. It stated that the United States should place a "high priority" on the summit's success through "the personal participation of the president of the United States."

The House resolution encompassed several similar resolutions (H Con Res 263 and H Con Res 266) that two Foreign Affairs subcommittees had considered.

## SENATE ACTION

The Senate Foreign Relations Committee on March 4

approved by voice vote yet another non-binding resolution (S Con Res 89) by Massachusetts Democrat Kerry, which called on Bush to participate in the U.N. conference on the global environment.

Unlike the similar House resolution (H Con Res 263), the Senate measure urged merely the president's participation, not his attendance.

Sen. Mitch McConnell, R-Ky., raised concerns about the potential impact of the conference on American jobs and successfully offered an amendment to the resolution to discourage Bush from committing to any action that threatened to reduce U.S. jobs.

The full Senate on April 7 approved its version of the non-binding resolution calling on Bush to take a leadership role in the international conference.

The resolution (H Con Res 292), passed 87-11, was similar to the one the House passed. The Senate measure urged Bush to support international environmental cooperation and take a "strong and active role" at the conference in Brazil. *(Vote 67, p. 10-S)*

Despite that bipartisan tone, all the opponents to the Senate resolution on the floor were Republican.

Sen. Malcolm Wallop, R-Wyo., said, "If global warming is occurring and if it is harmful, the [U.N. conference] solution will do nothing to solve this potential problem."

Wallop successfully offered amendments that called for any additional financial contributions from the United States to be voluntary and added language stating that global warming is only a "potential" threat.

The Senate then added its resolution (S Con Res 89) to the shell of the House-passed resolution and sent it back to the House for final approval — action that did not come before the end of the session. ∎

# Dolphin Protection Bills Target Tuna Fishing

Congress cleared separate bills that imposed sanctions on nations using dolphin-killing drift nets in their fishing fleets and allowed the administration to implement an international agreement to place a global ban on other tuna-fishing practices that killed dolphins.

One measure, HR 2152 (H Rept 102-262, Parts 1-2), was cleared by the House on Oct. 4 by voice vote and signed into law Nov. 2 (PL 102-582). It sought to enhance the effectiveness of U.N. Resolution 46-215 in an effort to end large-scale drift net fishing on the high seas. The miles-long nets snared everything in their paths — including dolphins, tortoises and sea birds — though they were used mainly for tuna fishing.

HR 2152 bounced back and forth between the chambers. On one round, the Senate amended the bill to put in place a timetable for the repeal of controversial Coast Guard user fees by Oct. 1, 1994 — a change eventually accepted by the House.

The bill discouraged the fishing practice by broadening import sanctions applicable under U.S. law to countries whose ships continued to use dolphin-killing drift nets after Dec. 31, 1992. It banned from U.S. ports boats that used the nets and halted imports of fish and sports fishing equipment from countries that still used drift nets.

The other measure, HR 5419 (H Rept 102-749, Parts 1-

2), was cleared by the Senate on Oct. 8 by voice vote and signed by President Bush on Oct. 26 (PL 102-523). It authorized the administration to implement an international agreement to establish a global moratorium on tuna-fishing practices using purse seine nets, which also trapped and killed dolphins.

Sponsored by Gerry E. Studds, D-Mass., the bill was supported by the administration. Both Mexico and Venezuela, which had increased their use of purse seine nets, had indicated that they would abide by the law. Under the bill, if a nation did not adhere to the moratorium, the United States could ban all tuna imports from that country; if the violation continued, it could ban 40 percent of the value of all its seafood products.

## BACKGROUND

A growing threat to the world's marine life prodded members of the 102nd Congress to begin considering legislation that would impose sanctions against nations that employed fishing practices that threatened dolphins, turtles, sea birds and threatened species of fish.

Japan, possessor of the world's largest drift net fishing fleet, had announced Nov. 26, 1991, that it would phase out all drift net fishing by the end of 1992. But Japan was not the only offender. Signs of the practice had been detected in the Northeast Atlantic and other areas.

The bill (HR 2152) introduced by Studds won voice vote approval from the Merchant Marine panel's Subcommittee on Fisheries and Wildlife on Sept. 27, 1991. It was improved in full committee Oct. 3 and referred to the Ways and Means Committee, which failed to mark up the bill before the first session ended.

The committee-approved bill allowed the president to ban imports from any nation that permitted drift net fishing and required the imposition of sanctions on any country not heeding the United Nation's call for a ban on drift nets by June 30, 1992. *(1991 Almanac, p. 231)*

## LEGISLATIVE ACTION

The House voted unanimously Feb. 25 to strengthen a U.N. policy against large-scale drift net fishing by imposing U.S. sanctions on countries that continued the practice.

The House passed HR 2152, 412-0. The bill would prevent fishing vessels from a country that practiced drift net fishing from docking at any U.S. port. *(Vote 19, p. 6-H)*

But the future of the bill was unclear. The Senate had not scheduled any action on the measure, and Bush opposed the legislation.

The bill would support two U.N. resolutions (44-225; 46-215) that called for an end to drift net fishing by the end of 1992. Most countries had indicated that they would abide by the ban.

Drift nets, usually made of plastic and up to 30 miles long, were used to catch fish just below the water's surface. But they often trap birds and marine life, which fishing fleets then discarded. The nets had caused extensive damage to fish and mammal populations.

Under the bill, the president would be required to impose import sanctions on countries that continued to use drift nets.

Imports of shellfish, fish, fish products or sport fishing equipment from such countries would be banned.

Bush said the bill would not give the administration enough flexibility and would encroach on the foreign policy

prerogatives of the executive branch.

### Ways and Means Approves HR 5419

The House Ways and Means Committee on July 29 approved by voice vote a bill calling for a worldwide ban on tuna-catching practices that killed dolphins.

The measure (HR 5419) would grant the administration authority to lift a ban on the import of tuna from Mexico and Venezuela if those countries pledged to cease fishing practices that killed dolphins.

### Senate Amends HR 2152

Meanwhile, the Senate on July 31 passed by voice vote an amended version HR 2152. The Senate amended the bill by voice vote to attach a partial repeal of a tax on recreational boat owners.

Boat owners since fiscal 1991 had been required to buy decals for their vessels to pay for services rendered by the Coast Guard. They ranged from a $25 decal for boats 16 to 20 feet long to a $100 decal for boats 40 feet or longer. The fees were set to expire after fiscal 1995.

The Senate measure would continue the fees only until the end of fiscal 1994. It would exempt boats shorter than 20 feet and reduce the fee for boats between 21 and 27 feet from $50 to $35, while exempting boats under 37 feet after fiscal 1993.

### Senate Approves Stripped Down HR 2152

The Senate approved the drift net bill (HR 2152) Aug. 12 after stripping two unrelated provisions included in the House version. They would have restricted operations of foreign-subsidized ships in the United States and subsidized the construction of stations at which U.S. pleasure boats could discharge wastes. The bill was sent back to the House.

The House version had included three provisions of interest to the maritime community, two of which were removed by the Senate. One provision added by Sam M. Gibbons, D-Fla., would have required ships entering the United States to certify that they were built or repaired without foreign subsidy or face financial penalties.

Another provision sought to stop boats from discharging their wastes into the water by funding a cooperative program with states to build a network of boat pump-out stations along the coasts. The federal government would pay up to 75 percent of the cost.

Another provision, which the Senate left intact, would repeal a Coast Guard user fee on small vessels that had irked pleasure boaters since it was put into place in 1990.

After the Senate's action, some lawmakers derided the back-and-forth of the bill: "This process is silly," said Rep. Don Young, R-Alaska.

### House Passes HR 5419

The House on Sept. 24 passed, 389-15, a bill to authorize a five-year global moratorium on dolphin-killing drift net fishing. *(Vote 421, p. 102-H)*

For reasons not fully understood, schools of dolphins and yellowfin tuna often swam together in the Eastern Pacific. Fishermen used purse seine nets around dolphin schools to catch tuna, killing tens of thousands of dolphins in the process. New fishing methods, however, had reduced the mortality rate, and the bill's purpose was to make dolphin-safe fishing mandatory.

The dolphin conservation measure (HR 5419) also would establish a dolphin-safe tuna market in the United States.

It would provide $3 million annually for research into tuna-fishing methods that did not threaten dolphins, and it would reauthorize a treaty that ensured access for U.S. vessels to productive tuna-fishing grounds in the Western Pacific, where dolphins are not likely to be trapped by nets.

"We have the opportunity to finally put a halt to this intentional killing of federally protected marine mammals," said Studds, the bill's sponsor.

Opponents, such as Randy "Duke" Cunningham, R-Calif., argued that the bill would cost some tuna fishermen their livelihoods.

### Final Action

Bills designed to end the use of drift nets cleared Congress in the closing week of the session. In the process, members also repealed a controversial tax on recreational boat users.

The Senate on Oct. 8 cleared HR 5419 by voice vote.

Earlier, the House on Oct. 4 cleared another measure to ban from U.S. ports boats that used large-scale nets. HR 2152 had bounced back and forth between the chambers. On its most recent round, the Senate on Aug. 12 altered House changes and returned it to that chamber.

The Senate had originally, on July 31, inserted into the bill the repeal of the Coast Guard user fee that had been levied on boaters as part of the 1990 budget agreement. The fee, according to Studds, has raised only $47 million in the two years since its implementation — far short of the $262 million the Office of Management and Budget predicted. (The House repealed the fee May 13, 339-78, on a vote on a separate bill, HR 2056, but the Senate took no action on that measure.)

On Oct. 4, the House accepted the Senate changes and sent it to Bush, who signed it Nov. 2. ∎

# Corps of Engineers Bill Cuts Some Big Projects

Congress sent to President Bush a biennial reauthorization of U.S. Army Corps of Engineers water projects. The $2.1 billion bill (HR 6167) authorized, over five years, a raft of projects for harbors, dredging of waterways and flood control.

The final measure was a scaled-back version of an earlier House bill (HR 5754) that would have authorized about $1 billion more for water projects. But lawmakers trimmed the measure after administration officials said Bush would veto the bill because it was too costly.

House Public Works Committee Chairman Robert A. Roe, D-N.J., hailed the bill as providing not only "environmental benefits but economic benefits as well."

The bill included a $195.8 million project to deepen the Delaware River Channel that runs through Delaware, New Jersey and Pennsylvania and a $144 million flood-control project in Las Vegas. In all, new projects were authorized in 17 states and Puerto Rico. State and local government contributions came to roughly $600 million.

The final version did not include some of the most costly projects proposed by lawmakers. The House rejected a $698 million project that would have built the country's fifth-highest dam, ostensibly to protect 300,000 residents of

the Sacramento area from 200-year floods.

The president signed the bill on Oct. 31 (PL 102-6167).

## BACKGROUND

Work on a water projects bill became a biennial exercise for Congress after a 1986 agreement broke a stalemate over cost-sharing by states and local communities. A long debate over whether local users and beneficiaries of projects should bear a greater share of the costs had kept Congress from approving a water projects bill since 1976. *(1986 Almanac, p. 127)*

The 1986 bill developed a formula under which local governments were forced to fund 20 percent to 30 percent of the projects' costs. A local share of 5 percent or 10 percent had been typical before 1986.

Most of the projects included in HR 6167 had been pushed for years by lawmakers but received the support of the Army Corps of Engineers only in the previous two years. Corps officials studied the costs and benefits of the projects as well as their environmental impact.

The fact that the measure usually passed with overwhelming support was indicative of the popularity of corps projects in river and harbor locales nationwide. The money, which was used to dredge harbors and channels and provide flood control, pumped federal dollars into local areas.

## HOUSE ACTION

Work on the water projects bill started with HR 5754, which was considered by the Public Works and Transportation Subcommittee on Water Resources on Aug. 5 and by the full committee one day later.

Backroom negotiations led to relatively easy voice vote approval of a measure that would authorize 23 new water projects at a $3 billion cost to the federal government.

In all, new projects were to be authorized in 17 states and Puerto Rico. State and local government contributions were to be roughly $600 million.

The panel members sidestepped a dispute over the most costly item, a $698 million flood-control project known as the American River Watershed in California. The project would have built new levees, raised existing ones around Sacramento and constructed a concrete detention dam near Auburn. The federal share of the project would have been $456.2 million.

The dam, a perennial California issue, had been championed for six years by California Democrats Vic Fazio and Robert T. Matsui. Lawmakers agreed to fold the dam, originally a separate measure (HR 5414), into the bill in July.

With the California delegation split about whether or what kind of dam should be built, the panel did not act on the project in the hope that the delegation could reach a compromise.

But the lawmakers could not. When the measure was brought upon the House floor Sept. 23, California members

---

### BOXSCORE

➡ **Water Projects Authorization (HR 6167, formerly HR 5754).** The bill authorized $2.1 billion in federal funds for water projects proposed by the U.S. Army Corps of Engineers.

**Reports:** HR 5754, H Rept 102-842.

#### KEY ACTION

Aug. 6 — The **House** Public Works and Transportation Committee approved HR 5754.

Sept. 23 — The **House** passed HR 5754, 326-87.

Oct. 5 — The **House** passed HR 6167 by voice vote.

Oct. 8 — The **Senate** cleared HR 6167 by voice vote.

Oct. 31 — President Bush signed HR 6167 — PL 102-6167.

---

engaged in a protracted debate over whether the watershed project was worthwhile.

Environmental and economic concerns led to its defeat. Opponents such as Tom Petri, R-Wis., said the dam would destroy the last remaining free-flowing section of the river, used by an estimated 500,000 people a year for recreation, all in an effort to protect as-yet undeveloped land in the flood plain.

Another opponent, George Miller, D-Calif., said there were less expensive measures, such as levee replacement and the reformulation of the nearby Folsom Dam for flood control, that should be investigated before building such a huge dam.

Conservatives such as John T. Doolittle, R-Calif., also opposed the dam because they wanted an even bigger, multipurpose structure built. And most major environmental groups opposed the dam as well because it would flood 34 miles of the pristine American River canyon.

With all those disparate forces going against the dam, the House adopted a Petri amendment to strike its authorization, 273-140. *(Vote 415, p. 102-H)*

The vote came despite a personal appeal from Fazio. "I am deeply disappointed," he said. "More than 300,000 residents and $28 billion in property are still at risk in Sacramento."

Before passing the bill, 326-87, the House rejected attempts by Republican Dan Burton of Indiana to reduce the measure's authorization level. *(Vote 418, p. 102-H)*

Members rejected, 125-282, an amendment to cut three visitor centers in Mount Morris, N.Y., Vicksburg, Miss., and Alton, Ill. Lawmakers also turned back another Burton amendment that would have trimmed the bill's authorization level by $300 million by limiting its construction account. *(Vote 417, p. 102-H)*

With time running out in the session, lawmakers approved a compromise measure, HR 6167, on Oct. 5. It scaled back some projects and eliminated others, such as the $400 million Kentucky Lock Program.

## SENATE ACTION

The Senate was primarily a bystander in the debate over the water projects bill. Lawmakers never took up its version of the measure, which the Environment and Public Works Committee reported straight to the Senate with no markup May 15.

The bill included authorization for 22 new projects at a $2.4 billion cost to the federal government and a $800 million share for local entities. It included $467 million for the California flood control project and $468 million for the Kentucky Lock Addition, both of which were removed from the House bill.

When differences over the California project prevented the measure from being brought up on the floor, the Senate instead decided to pass HR 6167, clearing it for the president's signature. ∎

# Chambers Can't Agree on Montana Wilderness Bill

Legislation that would have demarcated Montana's federally protected wilderness traveled a long legislative path but ultimately died in the 102nd Congress, leaving Montana as one of only two Western states — along with Idaho — without a statewide federal wilderness plan.

The House and Senate passed significantly different versions of the bill (S 1696), but last-minute pressures in the waning days of the second session prevented sponsors from holding a formal conference, and a final attempt to push a compromise proposal through the Senate got sidetracked.

The original Senate version of the bill (S 1696 — S Rept 102-255) was a hard-fought compromise between Montana Sens. Max Baucus, D, and Conrad Burns, R. *(1991 Almanac, p. 232)*

Backers of the bill said the measure would help the state balance its development needs while conserving its pristine wilderness.

But opponents said the bill would block needed development, drive business away and give the U.S. Forest Service the power to make lasting land management decisions that would not be subject to judicial review.

The Senate-passed version would have placed 2.2 million acres in various categories of protected wilderness. The bill also would have created thousands of acres of special land management and environmental study areas in Montana. The Senate passed the bill on March 26 on a 75-22 vote. *(Vote 55, p. 8-S)*

The bill was jointly referred to the House Interior and Insular Affairs Committee and the Agriculture Committee.

The Interior Committee approved the measure 26-19 on Sept. 17; the Agriculture Committee followed suit, approving the measure by voice vote Sept. 24. The House committees added more than 300,000 acres of protected land to the original Senate version (H Rept 102-958).

The full House passed the bill Oct. 2 on a 282-123 vote. The House first rejected the Senate-passed version of the bill by voice vote the same day. *(Vote 455, p 112-H)*

As passed by the House, the bill would have protected 2.57 million acres and shifted many wilderness area boundaries to protect more headwaters and areas such as elk calving grounds.

House members rejected, by voice vote, an amendment by Peter H. Kostmayer, D-Pa., that would have significantly expanded the protected areas covered by the bill, closing off virtually all remaining roadless areas in Montana to logging — some 3.4 million acres.

With pressure building to finish work quickly, Baucus met with the Montana delegation after the House vote to craft a compromise proposal and avoid having to go through a formal, time-consuming House-Senate conference.

### Baucus' Compromise

Baucus' compromise proposal would have protected 2.39 million acres and would have strengthened the state's claim on water rights in wilderness areas.

But Burns preferred the original Senate bill much more than the House version or the follow-up compromise proposal. And as a result of Burns' objections, a number of senators placed a hold on the compromise, and Baucus was

prevented from bringing it up for consideration before adjournment.

The Montana wilderness debate also defined the reelection campaigns of Rep. Pat Williams, D-Mont., who fought to increase the state's environmental wilderness areas, and Rep. Ron Marlenee, R-Mont., who promoted managed development of the state's natural resources. Both lawmakers were forced to run against each other because of the reapportionment following the 1990 census that eliminated one of Montana's two House seats. Williams prevailed over Marlenee in the general election. ■

# Hill Takes Up Wide Range Of Environmental Issues

Environmental bills met with mixed success in the second session of the 102nd Congress. Some of the smaller bills got caught up in the legislative rush at the end of the year. Environmental lobbies were successful in stopping congressional proposals to open up parts of an Arctic wildlife refuge to oil exploration.

## UDALL FOUNDATION

An effort to honor the 30-year congressional career of retired Rep. Morris K. Udall, D-Ariz., with a foundation devoted to fostering environmental awareness was realized early in 1992.

The Senate, by voice vote, passed the bill (S 2184 — PL 102-259) on Feb. 4 that established the Morris K. Udall Scholarship and Education Foundation in Tucson to expand awareness of environmental issues and to award scholarships, fellowships and research in environmental studies.

The House on March 3 cleared S 2184 on voice vote.

The measure authorized $40 million for the creation of the foundation and established a trust fund to receive private donations.

Three months prior to the final House action President Bush announced he would pocket veto — not sign into law — a similar bill (S 1176). Bush challenged on constitutional grounds a provision in S 1176 that would have given Congress the power to appoint a majority of the 10-member board that would oversee the foundation. *(1991 Almanac, p. 235)*

Rather than pressing for a showdown on whether the pocket veto was properly applied by the president, bill supporters chose to introduce and act on a clean bill, and language was included that gave the president more room to appoint members to the foundation board.

President Bush signed the bill into law on March 19.

But despite the achievement in its authorization, sponsors of the Udall bill were unable to get funds approved for the center in the final Interior appropriations bill (HR 5503). The Udall center was among a slew of projects that were not included in the conference report to the appropriations bill as conferees worked to reduce the overall funding level of the bill. Sponsors said they would attempt to find start-up funding for the Udall center in 1993.

## STEAMTOWN MUSEUM

A controversial museum that was designed to memorialize the age of steam-powered locomotion received $13 mil-

lion in federal funds for fiscal 1993, despite charges by some that it was one of the most crass examples of pork barrel politics.

The House Interior Subcommittee on National Parks and Public Lands on Nov. 26, 1991, gave voice vote approval to HR 3519, which would have capped the authorization for the unfinished project at $53 million, only $1 million more than had already been appropriated.

But as the full committee was marking up the bill (H Rept 102-434) on Feb. 5, Rep. Bruce F. Vento, D-Minn., offered an amendment that raised the overall cap to $66 million.

Vento, the chairman of the Parks subcommittee, offered the amendment after negotiating with Joseph R. McDade, the ranking member of the Appropriations Committee. Steamtown was located in McDade's district.

The House Interior and Insular Affairs Committee approved the bill with the $66 million cap by voice vote on Feb. 5. As introduced by McDade, the bill would have authorized $73 million.

Colorado Republican Joel Hefley echoed much of the minority view on Steamtown, saying it was of dubious historical value and on "nobody's priority list" except the Pennsylvania congressional delegation.

The project, designed to bring visitors back to the age of the steam locomotive, was under construction in Scranton, Pa.

Steamtown, which was designed to offer steam-powered excursions and a collection of 19th century locomotives and rail cars, was originally authorized in a 1986 omnibus spending bill and had come under attack ever since as a pork barrel project with limited historical significance.

Conferees on the Interior Appropriations bill (HR 5503 — PL 102-381), at the urging of Rep. John P. Murtha, D-Pa., included $13 million for Steamtown. Murtha argued that the funds were needed for economic development in Scranton. (Appropriations, p. 686)

## ARCTIC WILDLIFE REFUGE

Despite strong lobbying by the oil industry, lawmakers failed to pass legislation to permit oil and gas drilling in Alaska's Arctic National Wildlife Refuge.

The issue created an intense struggle between environmentalists who said the refuge was one of the last unspoiled ecosystems in the country and lobbyists for oil interests who claimed the area was rich in oil and gas resources and should be developed.

But the anti-drilling forces held the upper hand in the 102nd Congress. They forced sponsors of the Senate version of a massive energy bill (S 1220) to abandon a provision for Arctic drilling before the overall bill could move. (1991 Almanac, p. 208)

The Senate passed a revised energy bill (S 2166) on Feb. 19, but without any provision on drilling in the refuge. (Energy bill, p. 231)

A House bill (HR 1320) to allow Arctic drilling was never acted on by the Merchant Marine and Fisheries Committee.

## UNDERSEA RESEARCH

Legislation that would have written into law an undersea research program administered by the National Oceanic and Atmospheric Administration made it through the House, but it died at the end of the 102nd Congress with no action taken on it by the Senate.

The program, which was started in 1980 and which had never been formally authorized, channeled funding to new research projects — in such fields as offshore dumping of sewage and dredging — through five centers.

As approved by the House Merchant Marine and Fisheries Committee on Jan. 29, the bill (HR 3247 — H Rept 102-469) would have set the program's authorization level at $20 million for fiscal 1992, rising by $5 million each year through fiscal 1996.

The committee approved an amendment by ranking committee Republican Robert W. Davis, Mich., to require that a new center be located at a university on one of the Great Lakes. Members also added language from Committee Chairman Walter B. Jones, D-N.C., to streamline the review of research proposals and ensure that grant money would not be diverted to administrative costs.

On May 6, the House failed to pass the bill under suspension of the rules. The vote was 255-133, which was short of the amount needed to pass a bill when the rules were suspended. (Vote 97, p. 24-H)

Then on June 29, the House did pass the bill, 265-86. (Vote 240, p. 58-H)

By a 245-86 vote, the House rejected a proposal the same day to freeze funding at the fiscal 1992 level of $17.2 million. (Vote 239, p. 58-H)

Members voted, 245-86, to agree to an amendment that authorized $23 million for fiscal 1993 and an increase of $2.1 million for each of the fiscal years 1994-96. (Vote 238, p. 58-H)

The measure was referred to the Senate Commerce Committee, which did not act on the matter.

## OCEAN DUMPING

Legislation that would have reauthorized an Environmental Protection Agency program that regulated ocean dumping overcame some hurdles in the House but ultimately died in a Senate Committee.

The House Merchant Marine Committee on Jan. 29 approved the bill (HR 3749 — H Rept 102-423) by voice vote. The measure would have authorized $14 million each year through fiscal 1995 for the EPA program.

The measure would have reauthorized a 1972 ocean dumping law and stiffened laws against illegal dumping.

Under the program, the EPA designated the dumping sites and decided who could use them. Materials that could endanger marine or human life could not be dumped. Violators of the law could lose their vessels, which could then be sold by the federal government.

The measure would have allowed New York City to continue to dump sewage sludge through 1992.

The House on Feb. 4 passed the legislation by voice vote.

Following House passage, the bill was referred to the Senate Environment and Pubic Works Committee, which did not act on it.

## SCENIC TRAIL

A bill (HR 6184 — PL 102-461) that directed the National Park Service and the U.S. Forest Service to study the feasibility of creating a national, coast-to-coast scenic trail became law in 1992.

The trail was to link wilderness areas and historic trails and use existing paths whenever possible, according to bill

sponsor Rep. Beverly B. Byron, D-Md. The trail was intended to follow the route taken by three hikers in 1990 and 1991.

The House Interior Subcommittee on National Parks and Public Lands approved an earlier version of the bill (HR 3011) by voice vote on Feb. 6. And the full Interior Committee approved HR 3011 (H Rept 102-466) on Feb. 19 by voice vote.

The House approved the bill on March 24 by voice vote under suspension of the rules.

With little discussion, the Senate Energy and Natural Resources Committee on Sept. 23 approved the bill (S Rept 102-463) by voice vote after adding minor changes.

The full Senate passed the bill by voice vote on Oct. 7.

Late in the session, House sponsors introduced nearly identical legislation (HR 6184) that incorporated changes to HR 3011 made in the Senate. The House passed HR 6184 on Oct. 6, and the Senate cleared the measure on Oct. 8. President Bush signed the bill on Oct. 23.

## RADON ABATEMENT

Legislation to renew programs established by the 1988 Indoor Radon Abatement Act passed both chambers in 1992. But there was not enough time to reconcile the differences between the two versions.

The 1988 law set up regional radon centers to help inform the public of the dangers of radon gas. When concentrated, radon gas was considered a factor in lung cancer. *(1988 Almanac, p. 151)*

The Senate on March 10 passed a measure (S 792), 82-6, that would have reauthorized federal programs aimed at reducing radon contamination. *(Vote 37, p. 6-S)*

In addition to renewing radon programs through 1994, the legislation would have required certification of contractors who tested for radon and testing of the devices they use mandated that schools regularly check for radon, extended a grant program that provides funds to state governments to reduce radon in public buildings, and set up a presidential commission to educate the public on the dangers of the gas.

The House Energy and Commerce Committee on Sept. 17 gave voice vote approval to a companion bill (HR 3258 — H Rept 102-922). The Subcommittee on Transportation and Hazardous Materials approved the bill by voice vote earlier the same day.

The House passed S 792 on Sept 29 after incorporating language from HR 3258.

The House measure was similar to the one passed by the Senate. But the House language would not have required radon testing in federally owned housing.

The Senate did not act further on the measure as amended by the House, and it died awaiting further action.

## OZONE DEPLETION

Acting just days after reports that the protective ozone layer in the atmosphere faced possible destruction, the Senate on Feb. 6 approved, 96-0, an amendment to the energy bill (S 2166, later HR 776) by Sen. Al Gore, D-Tenn., that urged the administration to speed up the phaseout of ozone depleting chemicals known as chlorofluorocarbons (CFCs). *(Vote 19, p. 4-S)*

When the energy bill was being debated in October 1991, the administration was opposed to a similar proposal. But after reports in early February warned of the possible destruction of the ozone layer, the White House signaled that it would support the ozone amendment offered by Gore. *(Energy bill, p. 231)*

Ozone protects humans from cancer-causing ultraviolet solar radiation. In early February, NASA scientists disclosed that there were unusually high CFC levels over the Northern Hemisphere, as far south as New England.

The United States was a signatory to the Montreal Protocol, a 1987 international treaty that commits nations to phasing out CFCs. The 1990 amendments to the Clean Air Act also mandated that production of CFCs be phased out. *(1990 Almanac, p. 229)*

The final energy bill signed into law (PL 102-486) increased the base rate for the excise tax on ozone depleting chemicals to $3.35 per pound in fiscal 1993, rising to $5.35 per pound in fiscal 1995 and increasing 45 cents per pound each year thereafter.

But the measure reduced the scheduled tax rate for some of the minor ozone depleting chemicals, including ones used for foam insulation and medical sterilants.

## NATIONAL PARKS PROJECTS

Provisions of a bill aimed at stemming the tide of pork barrel projects funded with National Park Service money became law late in the second session.

On March 19, the House Interior Subcommittee on National Parks and Public Lands approved a bill (HR 4276) by voice vote that was designed to prohibit funding or spending of appropriated money on National Park Service historic projects that had not gone through the authorization process.

The bill was intended to deter spending on unauthorized projects such as the roundly criticized Lawrence Welk birthplace in North Dakota. *(1991 Almanac, p. 677)*

Subcommittee Chairman Bruce F. Vento, D-Minn., said the bill would free up funds for more urgent projects, such as repairing the Lincoln and Jefferson memorials in Washington.

The House Interior Committee on March 25 approved the bill (H Rept 102-480) by voice vote.

The full House on April 7 passed the bill, 381-0. *(Vote 72, p. 18-H)*

On Sept. 22, the Senate Energy Committee approved the measure (S Rept 102-461) by voice vote with minor amendments.

The major provisions of the bill were folded into a large water reclamation bill that was signed by the president on Oct. 30 (HR 429 — PL 102-575). *(Omnibus Western water projects, p. 264)*

## NEW ENGLAND GROUND FISH

The House passed a revised bill (HR 5557) by voice vote Sept. 22 to soften a proposed 50 percent cut in the allowable harvest of New England ground fish, such as cod and haddock. But the Senate never completed action on the measure and it died at the end of the 102nd Congress.

The House-passed bill was introduced by Rep. Gerry E. Studds, D-Mass., late in the session in an effort to win passage before Congress wrapped up its work in 1992. It represented a compromise version of two previous bills (HR 2919, S 2849) that had been working their way through the House and Senate.

The House Merchant Marine and Fisheries Subcommittee on Fisheries and Wildlife Conservation kicked

off action on a similar bill May 12. The panel approved HR 2919 to give New England fishermen a slight reprieve from stringent fish harvesting rules imposed to reverse the harvesting of Atlantic cod, haddock and hake to the point of extinction.

Under a secret September 1991 consent agreement with the Boston-based Conservation Law Foundation, the Commerce Department's National Marine Fisheries Service agreed to direct the New England Fishery Management Council to ensure that ground fish stocks doubled in five years.

The agreement required the allowable harvest of ground fish stocks to be cut in half immediately. The region's fishing industry said the cut was draconian. Studds' bill sought to override that agreement and phase in the harvest cutback over seven years. The bill also encouraged the federal government to seek new markets for underused fish, such as mackerel and dogfish.

In the Senate, a similar measure (S 2849 — S Rept 102-412) had been advancing in the Commerce, Science and Transportation Committee, which approved the bill by voice vote on June 16. The bill sought to establish a plan to replenish major stocks of commercial ground fish — especially cod, haddock and flounder — that sponsor John Kerry, D-Mass., said were seriously depleted in New England. The bill went to the Senate floor where it languished.

The full House Merchant Marine Committee approved its version (HR 2919 — H Rept 102-885 — Part I) July 1. The next day Studds sought to avoid a conference and introduced a compromise version (HR 5557) that incorporated provisions from the House and Senate bills.

The House passed HR 5557 by voice vote on Sept. 22. It was placed on the Senate calendar two days later, but never advanced.

## EXOTIC BIRDS

The House on Oct. 5 cleared a bill (HR 5013) that banned the importation of endangered exotic wild birds. The United States was the world's largest importer of such birds, and much of the international pet trade existed to feed U.S. demand.

President Bush signed the bill Oct. 23 — PL 102-440.

HR 5013 also reauthorized the African Elephant Conservation Act and established a national biological resources center.

Bill proponents said the United States, as the world's largest importer of rare birds, had a responsibility to ensure that would-be pet owners were not participating in the extinction of tropical bird species.

The bill banned the importation of 11 species of wild birds and encouraged the purchase of captive-bred exotic birds, rather than wild exotic birds.

The bill also established a national center for biological resources to inventory the nation's animal and plant species.

The House Merchant Marine Fisheries and Wildlife Subcommittee began action on HR 5013, approving the measure June 25. The full House Merchant Marine followed suit July 1.

The House Ways and Means Subcommittee on Trade, which had jurisdiction over the trade provisions in the bill, also approved the bill July 23. The full Ways and Means Committee gave its approval July 29.

The full House passed the measure Aug. 11 by voice

vote under expedited procedures. It was sent to the Senate Environment and Public Works Committee the next day, which moved it to the floor without changes Sept. 30.

The full Senate passed an amended version of the bill by voice vote Sept. 30. And the House agreed to those changes Oct. 5, clearing the bill for the president.

## PROTECTING 'OLD FAITHFUL'

After a two-year effort, the 102nd Congress failed to give additional protection to the unique geothermal resources of Yellowstone National Park — home of the famous "Old Faithful" geyser.

A bill (HR 3359) that the House had passed a year earlier, on Nov. 25, failed to advance in the Senate. The measure by Rep. Pat Williams, D-Mont., prohibited wells from being drilled to tap the geothermal power of Corwin Springs, which runs under the park. *(1991 Almanac, p. 232)*

In 1992, the Senate Energy and Natural Resources Committee on July 1 unanimously approved, 20-0, a modified version of HR 3359 (S Rept 102-363). But the bill advanced no further.

Increased development around the park, and the plans of a neighboring property owner, the Church Universal and Triumphant, to tap the geothermal power of Corwin Springs, which runs under Yellowstone, sparked concerns about the park's famous hot springs and geysers.

The amended version of the bill imposed a four-year moratorium on geothermal development within a 15-mile radius of the park until a National Park Service study was complete. It placed a permanent moratorium on geothermal leasing on federal lands within 15 miles around the park.

Still, the measure attempted to protect the property rights of nearby owners by allowing them to sue in federal district court if their property rights were violated.

## COLORADO WILDERNESS

After more than a decade's worth of work, the House on Sept. 14 moved closer to protecting Colorado's wilderness — and the water that nourished it — passing by voice vote a bill (S 1029 — H Rept 102-810) to reserve nearly 700,000 acres of high country land.

But time ran out in the 102nd Congress before the House could take final action. The Senate on Oct. 10 had amended the bill and shipped it back to the House, where it died.

The sticking point was over House language that reserved an explicit federal water right to feed areas protected by the bill. The issue became a major point of disagreement between the version approved by the Senate in 1991 and the one crafted by the House Interior Committee and passed by the House in 1992.

The original Senate version (S Rept 102-129) included no such explicit rights. *(1991 Almanac, p. 231)*

The legislation sought to protect an area larger than the size of Rhode Island: 670,960 acres in 21 wilderness units and an additional 110,000 acres of special management areas that had somewhat looser levels of protection.

The House Interior and Insular Affairs Committee had approved a version on July 8 by voice vote that sidestepped the contentious water rights issue.

The Colorado delegation and committee leaders, especially National Parks and Public Lands Subcommittee

Chairman Bruce F. Vento, D-Minn., agreed to resolve the issue on the House floor.

Water usage was serious business in the West, and landowners upstream from federally protected wilderness areas were concerned that they could lose access to water if a reserved federal water right was claimed to sustain wilderness areas.

Only a small portion of the areas to be protected by the bill stood to be affected by any water rights language. Still, the issue threatened to set a precedent for future wilderness bills, both in Colorado and elsewhere.

In most wilderness areas, the headwaters of the streams originated on federal lands. But of the 21 Colorado areas proposed for wilderness designation in the bill, one received its water from a stream that began outside the area.

In a bow to state rights, the Senate-passed version explicitly denied any federal water rights in that case. The Interior Committee-approved language was silent on the issue despite calls from environmentalists to ensure water rights for wilderness areas.

But by the time the bill reached the House floor compromise language was included to explicity protect federal water rights — a claim that vexed state officials throughout the West.

The bill went back to the Senate on Oct. 8, where Wendell H. Ford, D-Ky., won an amendment backed by Colorado's senators, Democrat Tim Wirth and Republican Hank Brown, that prohibited the construction of new or expanded water projects in areas to be protected by the bill.

But the Senate version explicitly disclaimed any federal water right. House lawmakers never acted on the revised version.

## WILDERNESS MANAGEMENT

The House Interior and Insular Affairs Committee on Aug. 12 approved legislation designed to improve the management of the nation's wilderness areas. But the bills failed to advance.

The committee by voice vote approved en bloc three separate bills dealing with the way the Agriculture Department's Forest Service (HR 4325) and the Interior Department's Fish and Wildlife Service (HR 4327), Bureau of Land Management and National Park Service (HR 4326) manage wilderness areas.

Opponents said the bills threatened to add another unnecessary layer of bureaucracy to already bloated and overtaxed agencies.

Even though Congress had increased spending for the nation's 94.9 million acres of wilderness in recent years, the money was not earmarked in agency budgets, and no agency officials were specifically charged with managing the acreage, said Rep. Bruce F. Vento, D-Minn.

For example, Congress had increased spending for the management of Forest Service wilderness by 80 percent since 1987. But a General Accounting Office study found that 37 percent of the appropriated funds were spent on other programs.

Proponents said the funding problem resulted in wilderness areas falling into disrepair nationwide. Such areas lacked sufficient signs to direct visitors, and their recreational facilities were dilapidated and offered few services to help visitors view the sites, Vento said.

The bills required each agency to place one person in charge of wilderness management and dedicated funds for

wilderness in each agency's budget. The bills also set up a nationwide monitoring system, created a national academy to train professional managers and set up an institute for wilderness research.

The Forest Service bill also attempted to consolidate the management of the 2.3 million-acre Frank Church River of No Return Wilderness in central Idaho. The area was subdivided into two regions, four national forests and six ranger districts.

The bills drew opposition from Republicans: Robert J. Lagomarsino, Calif., branded the bills "congressional micromanagement."

## MINING RESTRICTIONS

Legislation that sought to protect federal rangelands from being mined without ranchers' approval died at the close of the 102nd Congress after a two-year journey through Congress.

The Senate on Oct. 7 passed an amended version of the bill (S 1187 — S Rept 102-218) to require that miners seek ranchers' approval before prospecting on federal land, but the House took no final action. The Senate passed its first version of the bill Nov. 26, 1991.

Seeking a middle ground between the competing rights of Western ranchers and miners, the House had previously passed a version of S 1187 on Sept. 15 by voice vote.

As passed, the bill required miners to restore the land to its original condition — something that miners argued was far too expensive.

The House passed S 1187 after inserting the provisions of a companion House measure (HR 450). The House on July 28 had rejected HR 450 after Westerners warned that it threatened to give the government undue power to restrict mining. HR 450 failed 248-168 under special rules that required a two-thirds vote for passage. (Vote 329, p. 80-H)

Opponents of the measure said it placed undue hardship on miners who were seeking to extract gold, silver, lead or zinc from federal lands. At issue was a 76-year-old law that allowed both ranchers and miners to use the same federal land.

The 1916 Stock Raising Homestead Act allowed miners to explore federal lands for minerals without first gaining the permission of ranchers. Only after a miner had decided to extract minerals did he have to give ranchers 30 days' notice. The law covered about 70 million acres of land in the West.

Ranchers said that prospectors had disrupted ranching operations and damaged the grazing lands.

The bill required miners to give 30 days' notice to ranchers who owned surface property before prospecting the land. The bill also required miners to try to get ranchers' consent before starting to dig and to restore mined land to its previous condition.

The House Interior Committee had approved HR 450 by voice vote on June 17.

## MARINE DIE-OFF

The House on Aug. 3 passed by voice vote a bill to set up a coordinated federal response to the occasional, mysterious mass coastal strandings and deaths of marine mammals such as dolphins and whales. The measure failed to advance in the Senate.

The bill (HR 3486 — H Rept 102-758), sponsored by

Thomas R. Carper, D-Del., proposed to create a bank to preserve tissue samples of healthy marine mammals so that when such die-offs occurred, scientists could use the normal tissue to determine the reasons for the unusual events.

The bill came in response to the 1987-88 die-off of bottlenose dolphins off the Atlantic Coast. Before officials could respond, nearly half the bottlenose population had died. *(1988 Almanac, p. 168)*

As passed, the bill authorized $500,000 a year in fiscal 1993 and 1994 to run the program.

The House also passed, on voice vote, legislation (HR 5350) to authorize $500,000 over two years to set up a similar bank to store tissue samples of Great Lakes fish. The measure also died of inaction in the Senate.

## ANTARCTICA

The House Merchant Marine and Fisheries Committee on Aug. 6 approved legislation by voice vote to implement an unratified treaty banning mining and oil drilling in Antarctica for 50 years. But the bill stalled.

The bill (HR 5459) stood to implement the Protocol on Environmental Protection to the Antarctic Treaty (Treaty Doc. 102-22) — a pact that established Antarctica as a natural reserve devoted to peace and science.

The measure also prohibited U.S. vessels from discharging oil into Antarctic waters and imposed strict waste disposal requirements at U.S. outposts on the continent. It also expressed the sense of Congress that the minerals development ban imposed by the treaty should be left in place indefinitely.

## BEACH POLLUTION

The House on Sept. 22 passed a bill (HR 12) by voice vote to require states to monitor their beaches and coastal waters for pollution. But the measure died of inaction in the Senate.

The proposal, sponsored by New Jersey Reps. William J. Hughes, a Democrat, and H. James Saxton, a Republican, was a revised version of a similar measure that failed in the closing week of the 101st Congress.

The goal of the revised bill was to have uniform testing of coastal waters to warn beach-goers if the waters were unsafe — something New Jersey already did. *(1990 Almanac, p. 290)*

In the late 1980s, however, New Jersey's beaches were buffeted with waves of pollution and bad publicity. Its lawmakers said the state was being penalized for monitoring its beaches, while nearby non-testing states benefited from their ignorance.

The bill directed the Environmental Protection Agency to set uniform standards for beach water quality and required states within three years to test with that standard in mind. It also required the states to post signs on beaches notifying the public of potential health risks during periods when the water quality does not comply with state coastal recreation water standards.

Unlike the 1990 legislation, however, the bill did not require states to shut down beaches that failed to meet EPA standards.

## BLM REAUTHORIZATION

The Senate Energy and Natural Resources Committee approved a bill (HR 1096) that reauthorized the activities of the Interior Department's Bureau of Land Management (BLM) through fiscal 1995. The full Senate never took up the legislation.

Members approved the bill Sept. 22 on a 11-9 vote after agreeing to strip from it virtually all the controversial provisions of the companion measure that had passed the House in 1991. *(1991 Almanac, p. 216)*

As approved, the Senate version would merely authorize the activities of the BLM for the next three fiscal years.

The version that passed the House on July 23, 1991, stood to change the way the agency administered public lands and increase the fees ranchers paid to graze cattle on public lands in the West.

Western lawmakers opposed the grazing increases, which required ranchers to pay a maximum fee of $2.62 per animal unit — the amount of forage needed to feed one mature cow or five sheep for a month. The legislation also required the BLM to give greater attention to environmental concerns in its administrative plans for the 270 million acres of public lands that it managed.

## AVIATION PARK

The House on Oct. 4 cleared a bill (HR 2321 — H Rept 102-449) by voice vote that created a new national park in Dayton, Ohio, to honor the founding brothers of flight — Orville and Wilbur Wright.

Among the different areas important to the history of aviation that were included in the national park was the Wright Cycle Co., the bicycle shop that the Wright brothers owned and operated while they were doing their airplane experiments.

The bill was intended to honor the hometown of the Wright brothers and their friend and business partner African-American poet Laurence Dunbar.

The Wright brothers built and flew the world's first airplane and established an aviation school in Dayton. The bill proposed to add four sites to the national park system, each with existing national historic landmarks associated with the Wright brothers. Dunbar's home was to be included.

The House on March 4 narrowly mustered the two-thirds majority needed to pass the bill. The bill passed, 278-133, under suspension of the rules, despite significant opposition from Republicans who stood with the White House against the measure. *(Vote 35, p. 8-H)*

The Senate passed its version of the measure Oct. 1, after adding several technical amendments. The House on Oct. 4 agreed to the amendments through an enrolling resolution (H Res 596) that cleared the bill.

The Bush administration had originally opposed the bill as too costly and unnecessary because many of the sites were already historic landmarks. Bill opponent Dan Burton, R-Ind., said it stood to cost as much as $10 million over five years, compared with an earlier version estimated to cost $1.25 million.

But Bush on Oct. 16 signed the final version into law (PL 102-419).

The Congressional Budget Office estimated that it would to cost between $3.3 million and $5.5 million to restore and develop the sites for the park and up to $1 million annually to manage them.

## HISTORIC PRESERVATION

The House on June 2 passed by voice vote two bills (HR 4801 and HR 3905) that reauthorized the Historic Pres-

ervation Fund and the Advisory Council on Historic Preservation. But the bills died in the Senate.

The Historic Preservation Fund was funded through royalties paid to the government from offshore oil and gas leases; it collected up to $150 million annually. It provided matching funds for the National Trust for Historic Preservation, as well as for state preservation programs. HR 4801 continued to require oil and gas royalties to be diverted to historic preservation through fiscal 1997.

The second bill (HR 3905) reauthorized the advisory council, which provided Congress and the public with expertise on whether buildings or sites deserved to be protected, and advised agencies that were trying to comply with various historic preservation statutes. The reauthorization gave the council $5 million a year, through the end of fiscal 1996.

"The council has played a unique role in terms of arbitrating differences as to the preservation of historic fabric and appropriate action by a developer to modify historic property," said Bruce F. Vento, D-Minn., the bill's floor manager. ∎

# Science Education Grants

The House cleared legislation (S 1146 — PL 102-476) Oct. 3 that authorized $70 million over two years for National Science Foundation (NSF) grants to technical or two-year colleges for science and math programs.

The Senate bill was virtually identical to an earlier version of the bill originally passed by the House Aug. 10 (HR 2936).

Sponsors of the legislation said that it was important to strengthen the associate degree college system. In 1992, 43 percent of all undergraduate students were at two year colleges; 30 percent of those students were likely to transfer to 4 year colleges.

The House Science Subcommittee on Science, Space and Technology on March 18 gave voice vote approval to HR 2936. The Technology and Competitiveness Subcommittee had approved an earlier version of the bill in October 1991 *(1991 Almanac p. 246)*.

The bill earmarked $35 million in grants for both fiscal 1992 and 1993, although the money would have to have been earmarked from funds already authorized for the National Science Foundation.

The grants were intended to strengthen science and math programs at junior or community colleges to provide students the skills needed in high-technology manufacturing and related fields, especially for "non-traditional" students and high school dropouts. Grants also assisted two-year schools in forming partnerships with four-year schools.

The full House Science and Technology Committee followed suit on April 2 and approved the bill by voice vote.

The House on Aug. 10 passed the bill by voice vote.

The House passed bill required that community college grant recipients make matching contributions toward the education programs to be eligible for the NSF grants.

The bill also incorporated language from legislation (HR 3606) sponsored by Peter Hoagland, D-Neb., that established a national technology education program for two-year colleges.

The Senate on Oct. 2 approved by voice vote its version of the science and math grant legislation (S 1146), after amending the bill with the provisions of HR 2936. ∎

# NASA Funding Includes Space Station

A one-year $14.9 billion NASA re-authorization bill (HR 6135) cleared Congress on Oct. 7, one day after President Bush signed into law a spending bill that carved out a different set of priorities for the space agency and appropriated $14.3 billion for programs in fiscal 1993. Both measures provided $2.1 billion for the controversial space station *Freedom*.

As in past years, the House started early on an ambitious multi-year measure to authorize spending for the National Aeronautics and Space Administration. And as in the past, hopes dissolved of finishing work before the appropriators when the Senate failed to act swiftly.

The Senate on Oct. 7 cleared, by voice vote, a revised bill (HR 6135) to authorize appropriations to NASA. The House passed HR 6135 by voice vote Oct. 6. The new bill incorporated a deal between two previously passed versions of HR 4364. That bill passed the House on May 5 but was never brought to the Senate floor.

President Bush signed HR 6135 on Nov. 4 — PL 102-588.

The final authorization figure represented a reduction of $347.4 million from the House-passed version of HR 4364 and $101 million from the president's request for fiscal 1993. The bill provided an authorization for all NASA programs under a single title in contrast to the two-tiered approach initially taken by the House. Under the plan conceived by House authorizers, space programs would have been categorized as either basic or discretionary. Appropriators were to order from the discretionary menu only after basic needs were fully funded.

Although it was debated at length, authorizers and appropriators found it impossible to provide full funding for space station *Freedom*, a multi-billion dollar program to maintain the U.S. position at the front of manned space exploration. The $2.1 billion was considered sufficient to honor the commitments made to the U.S. partners in the space station program.

Full funding was provided for the Landsat program, a critical element of the U.S. global change research program known as Mission to Planet Earth.

The final bill also incorporated language to enhance the nation's commercial space competitiveness. Many of those provisions had been contained in another bill (HR 3848) to spur the development of commercial space activities.

"There is no question that we are living in challenging times for the nation's space and aeronautics program. Yet, it is also a time of rare opportunity. The end of the Cold War has led us to revisit many of the assumptions that have guided our program for the last 35 years. . . . HR 6135

---

## BOXSCORE

➡ **NASA Reauthorization (HR 6135, formerly HR 4364).** The bill authorized $14.9 billion for space programs in fiscal 1993.

**Report:** H Rept 102-500.

### KEY ACTION

April 1 — The **House** Science, Space and Technology Subcommittee on Space approved HR 4364.

April 8 — The **House** Science, Space and Technology Committee approved HR 4364.

April 29 — The **House** rejected an amendment to HR 4364 that would have eliminated $2.3 billion for the space station, 159-254.

May 5 — The **House** passed HR 4364 by voice vote.

June 16 — The **Senate** Commerce, Science and Transportation Committee approved HR 4364.

Oct. 6 — The **House** passed HR 6135 by voice vote.

Oct. 7 — The **Senate** cleared HR 6135 by voice vote.

Nov. 4 — President Bush signed HR 6135 — PL 102-588.

---

takes account of these opportunities while maintaining a healthy and productive space and aeronautics program in the midst of our constrained fiscal environment," said House Science, Space and Technology Committee Chairman George E. Brown Jr., D-Calif.

## BACKGROUND

In an era defined more by fears of a deepening recession than by dreams of flights to the galaxies, NASA saw its once-unwavering support in Congress fade. Even Brown, a key defender of the space station and other ambitious space endeavors, said his support was weakened in the face of continuing cost overruns, technical problems and concerns that the station's cost might reduce money for other science projects.

Internal management squabbles also chipped away at the agency. Adm. Richard H. Truly was forced to resign as administrator Feb. 12 after a long-standing power struggle with Vice President Dan Quayle's National Space Council. His ouster troubled some of NASA's champions in Congress, and there was wariness when President Bush chose a relatively unknown person to take over. Daniel S. Goldin became the ninth head of NASA on April 1 and proved to be a fierce defender of space programs. *(Goldin, p. 299)*

Even so, Brown's House Science Committee was fighting an uphill battle to wrest control of setting space policy from the Appropriations Committee. In 1991, the House authorizing panel helped set the tone for the new Congress by proposing early in the session to reduce the president's budget request by nearly $500 million — the first time in several years that lawmakers had attempted to curb the space agency's funding authority. But by the time the multi-year NASA reauthorization bill (HR 1988 — PL 102-195) was cleared for Bush on Nov. 22, it was largely symbolic because Congress already had approved the fiscal 1992 spending bill. *(1991 Almanac, p. 236)*

The House authorizers, no matter how early they started, had a strong force to contend with in the Senate. In that chamber, Commerce, Science and Transportation Committee Chairman Ernest F. Hollings, D-S.C., exerted additional influence as a top member of the Appropriations Committee.

NASA programs were funded annually through the Veterans Affairs (VA), Housing and Urban Development and Independent Agencies spending bill, which pitted costly space projects against crucial assisted housing programs. *(Appropriations, p. 639)*

As 1992 opened, the $2 billion space station was poised

to remain the key battle in both the authorization and appropriation bills. Since 1984, the government had spent $5 billion on the Bush administration priority although construction had not begun. But space station advocates had a strong argument, even as the program was criticized for cost overruns and questionable scientific value. They touted how many jobs were at stake in NASA contracts and subcontracts throughout the country.

## HOUSE SUBCOMMITTEE ACTION

The administration requested slightly less than $15 billion for NASA in fiscal 1993, a 4.5 percent increase over fiscal 1992. Lawmakers promptly complained that the agency needed more to pursue all of the projects on its plate.

Charging that Bush administration officials also had failed to set priorities for the nation's space program, the House Science Subcommittee on Space on April 1 approved a three-year authorization bill (HR 4364) that laid out two budget menus for the space program: basic and discretionary.

Under the bill, NASA's basic spending plan totaled $14.4 billion for fiscal 1993 and included spending for ongoing science and technology programs, the space shuttle and the controversial space station *Freedom*.

Appropriators were to order from the discretionary menu only after basic needs were fully funded. The discretionary menu included a massive program to study global climate and a new solid-rocket program. The bill authorized $15.3 billion for fiscal 1993 for basic and discretionary programs combined.

Ranking minority member James F. Sensenbrenner Jr., R-Wis., called the bill "a true bipartisan effort to put some sense into the NASA budget" — sense, he said, that was lacking in the administration's request.

It was also an attempt to challenge appropriators' penchant for funding pet projects at the expense of other vital space agency programs.

Panel authorizers included a jab at Quayle's space council, requiring that the council's executive director be confirmed by the Senate.

Overall, the bill signaled the opening shot in a critical budget season for NASA. It was approved the same day that Goldin was sworn in as the agency's new administrator.

### First-Tier Budget

The House space panel's bill tried to protect agency programs that it considered critical by putting them in its first-tier budget. That section of the bill authorized about $600 million less than the administration requested. It included:

● $2.25 billion for the space station in fiscal 1993, the same amount requested by the administration.

● $389 million for construction, $70 million more than the administration budget.

● $22 million to test equipment in preparation for a future experiment on relativity, which had been cut by the administration.

Like the administration proposal, the committee bill eliminated a planned comet and asteroid fly-by mission. And it went further to cut most of the $125 million NASA had sought to develop a new launch system with the Defense Department. The panel bill included $40 million to study the planned project to lift heavier loads

into space.

But panel members hoped that appropriators would come up with enough money to go beyond their bare-bones agenda to fund items on the second-tier list. Within that category, authorizers approved $371 million for the Earth Observing System, a massive satellite and data system designed to relay information about the atmosphere.

The bills also authorized other second-tier projects, including $32 million in fiscal 1993 for two robotic missions to the moon and a related study requested by the administration.

The committee bill initially had set an especially high hurdle for an advanced solid-rocket motor project, being built in the district of Appropriations Chairman Jamie L. Whitten, D-Miss.

President Bush excluded the program from his budget request. The subcommittee bill originally authorized $440 million for the rocket motor program, but only if appropriators provided $15.3 billion in fiscal 1993 for all NASA programs.

The language stood to set up a staredown with Whitten, but Bud Cramer, D-Ala., urged the committee to blink. Cramer offered an amendment that authorized $260 million for the rocket motor project even if appropriators provided less than the $15.3 billion target.

Sensenbrenner opposed the amendment, saying it undermined the bill's attempt to move away from spreading agency funding over too many programs. But panel Chairman Ralph M. Hall, D-Texas, warned that an all-or-nothing approach was too risky, and members adopted Cramer's compromise 16-10.

When asked later whether Whitten would find the money to keep the rocket motor project going, Hall said, "I predict he'll be his usual successful self."

### Council Confirmation

Ron Packard, R-Calif., tried to strike the requirement that the Senate confirm the space council's executive director, saying it stood to further politicize space policy.

But Hall and Sensenbrenner objected, saying the proposal was aimed at ensuring that the executive director testify before congressional committees. Some lawmakers feared the council was exerting too much influence over space policy.

The panel rejected Packard's amendment 4-7. But Rep. John J. Rhodes III, R-Ariz., warned that the confirmation requirement risked snagging the entire bill.

## HOUSE COMMITTEE ACTION

House Science Committee members challenged appropriators the week of April 6 to preserve funding for the nation's key space programs.

The authorization panel gave voice vote approval to a three-year bill (HR 4364) for NASA that directed appropriators to continue the controversial space station *Freedom* and the space shuttle.

Actual spending for NASA was set in the annual appropriations bill for Veterans Affairs, Housing and Urban Development and independent agencies, but the bill did not move through Congress until later in the year. The authorization bill was intended to chart priorities for that spending.

Panel Chairman Brown called on the committee April 8 to approve a measure "that can remain productive and resilient even during periods of budgetary stagnation." But

he acknowledged that preserving NASA's budget promised to be difficult in a tight fiscal climate.

Under the NASA authorization bill, core and discretionary programs were separated to set priorities and to minimize funding of pet projects by appropriators.

The $15.3 billion bill for fiscal 1993 authorized $14.3 billion for ongoing science and technology programs that made up the core of NASA's space program and $952.1 million for discretionary spending.

But debate at the markup over funding priorities signaled that the effort by Science Committee authorizers to maintain strong NASA funding levels was not going to be easy.

Tim Roemer, D-Ind., revived the previous year's dispute over the space station by unsuccessfully proposing to delete from the bill all authorizations for the project. In 1991, appropriators also sought to kill the space station, only to have it later restored on the House floor. *(1991 Almanac, p. 239)*

Other panel members countered that freeing up the $2.25 billion fiscal 1993 space station authorization only invited appropriators to set space policy by spending the money on their favorite projects. The amendment was defeated, 8-17, leaving the fight over the space station for the House floor.

### Setting Priorities

The NASA bill came at a critical stage in many ongoing space agency programs. Estimated costs of key space projects had increased sharply as they moved from the planning to the building stage, forcing lawmakers to choose between allocating more money than planned or killing a project already under way.

By writing a multi-year authorization, the Science panel sought to set funding priorities for programs that spilled over a period of years. Such an approach gave authorizers some leverage to ensure that funding for long-term programs was not sidetracked by appropriators.

Such leverage was not as crucial in the Senate, where the chairman of the Commerce, Science and Transportation Committee — Hollings — also sat on the Appropriations Committee. The Senate Commerce panel resisted multi-year authorizations until 1988.

A multi-year authorization bill (PL 102-195) was passed by the House and Senate in 1991, but it did not authorize specific funding levels for fiscal years 1993-94. The 1992 authorization specified detailed funding levels for fiscal 1993 and set more general targets for fiscal 1994 and 1995.

The $15.3 billion fiscal 1993 authorization was slightly higher than Bush's request. Its core programs included:

● $2.25 billion for the space station in fiscal 1993, the same amount requested by the administration.

● $286.9 million for construction of facilities, $32.3 million less than the administration requested.

● $22 million to test equipment in preparation for an experiment on relativity, which had been cut by the administration.

But panel members were bracing for a battle with appropriators over providing enough spending for items on authorizers' discretionary list. Included in that category was $371 million for the Earth Observing System, a massive satellite and data system designed to relay atmospheric information.

Another point of friction developing was over the advanced solid rocket motor project, being built in Whitten's district.

The Science Subcommittee bill placed the project in the discretionary account. The full Science Committee also voted to shift $80 million for a related facility to the discretionary category.

The Science panel also faced pressure from another direction — the Bush administration — over the controversial provision to require the executive director of the National Space Council to be confirmed by the Senate.

Though the provision survived a challenge in subcommittee, ranking minority member Robert S. Walker, R-Pa., offered a successful amendment in full committee to strike it from the bill.

## HOUSE FLOOR ACTION

The space station *Freedom* survived its first major challenge of the year, when the House on April 29 rebuffed efforts to scuttle funding for the program. But even bigger tests of survival loomed for the beleaguered low-orbit research facility.

Lawmakers rejected, 159-254, an amendment that called for eliminating $2.3 billion for the space station for fiscal 1992 from the authorization bill. *(Vote 90, p. 22-H)*

"It's not just a jobs program. It's not just a scientific experiment. It is an independent step if man is to learn how to survive in space," Brown said in defending the space station.

The venue for the space station debate quickly shifted to the Appropriations committees, where lawmakers were hard pressed to find $7 billion in domestic spending cuts required to meet the 1990 budget agreement. NASA spending was in direct competition with other domestic programs because it was part of a broader appropriations bill that funded the VA, HUD and independent agencies.

The amendment by freshman Roemer of Indiana proposed to shift $1.1 billion in fiscal 1993 space station funds toward other NASA programs. It also proposed moving $1.2 billion toward deficit reduction and veterans health care and housing.

But because the vote did not involve making spending decisions, there was less pressure on lawmakers to choose between the space station and other programs.

At the appropriations stage, lawmakers who wanted to scuttle the space station were confident that the voting margin would change in their favor — a hope that was never realized.

"An appropriations vote [for the space station] could be characterized as a vote to cut HUD. This vote couldn't," said space station opponent Dick Zimmer, R-N.J.

In 1991, the House Appropriations Subcommittee on VA, HUD and Independent Agencies voted to eliminate all space station funding. But the project was restored on the House floor after an intense lobbying effort by the White House and congressional supporters.

Overall the three-year authorization proposed to boost total NASA funding by 6.3 percent over fiscal 1992.

The space station was proposed by President Ronald Reagan in 1984 as an $8 billion manned research facility to be in operation by 1994. But delays and cost overruns plagued the program, which in 1992 was estimated to cost as much as $40 billion.

In an attempt to scale back the project, NASA trimmed the proposed crew size from eight to four and limited the scope of research. That, in turn, threw the station's scientific merits into question.

NASA planned to launch the first phase of the project

# Goldin Takes Over as NASA Chief

Daniel S. Goldin was sworn in April 1 as the ninth head of the National Aeronautics and Space Administration, one day after winning swift Senate confirmation.

Goldin replaced Adm. Richard H. Truly, who resigned after a longstanding power struggle with Vice President Dan Quayle's National Space Council. The administration had only praise for Truly when it announced his resignation Feb. 12. But Truly said he was asked to step down, and lawmakers said he was forced out.

Truly's ouster troubled some lawmakers, and concern was expressed when President Bush chose a relatively unknown person to take over. Sen. Al Gore, D-Tenn., initially worried that Goldin could become a political pawn of the space council.

But Goldin apparently eased those concerns in private sessions with key lawmakers and in public testimony before the Commerce Committee. He assured the panel that, if nominated, "I will be in charge of NASA."

Goldin, 51, was a NASA engineer before becoming a top executive at TRW, a private aerospace corporation. As manager of TRW's space and technology division since 1987, Goldin oversaw the construction of many spacecraft. He also worked on the Pentagon's Brilliant Eyes and Brilliant Pebbles projects, part of the Strategic Defense Initiative, known as star wars.

Even without Truly's departure, NASA faced a tough budget year. With it, congressional allies said they would have to combat charges that the agency was adrift.

## Truly's Difficult Times

Truly took over NASA after the explosion of the space shuttle *Challenger*, helping guide the agency through the attacks and demoralization that followed.

But during his tenure he also had to struggle with ongoing program defects, such as the flawed Hubble Telescope, and criticism that the agency had not adapted to changing times.

And Truly ran afoul of the space council, a board of space-related agency heads and other Bush administration officials that Quayle led.

While NASA officials continued to envision a strong role for the space shuttle, the council wanted to move toward smaller, less expensive launch systems.

The two bodies also clashed over plans for the massive Earth Observing System, a project to study the global climate. Observers said the space council also considered Truly too lax in pushing for its priority — manned expeditions to the moon and Mars.

Truly reportedly disagreed with the council's judgments on these issues, as well as its efforts to direct space policy. Besides the council, Truly was confronted with a number of studies and reports directing changes in agency management and policies.

Congress had its own criticisms of Truly and NASA. While Truly was generally respected, he was not considered indispensable. Nevertheless, many lawmakers and staff were dismayed by the timing, leaving the agency without a spokesman on the eve of a new budget season.

"This resignation could not have come at a worse time for NASA," said Rep. Jim Bacchus, D, whose district included Florida's so-called Space Coast.

## Goldin Breezes In

Goldin breezed through the Commerce hearing March 27 on his nomination, and four days later the Senate sent his name to the floor without waiting for the committee to vote. The Senate confirmed the nomination on voice vote.

Yet when Bush nominated Goldin in March to become the new administrator of NASA, few people had heard of him.

Some suspected he was chosen so he could become a shill for Quayle and his space council, pushing their plans for the space agency and bypassing Congress.

Five months later, Goldin had won high marks from lawmakers and others who had observed him lobbying strenuously for Congress to continue funding the controversial space station *Freedom*. And NASA was an agency that was on the rebound from its share of troubles.

"My personal hope is he could stay on, even if we have a Democratic president," said George E. Brown Jr., D-Calif., chairman of the House Science, Space and Technology Committee.

In the battle for *Freedom*, Goldin had been far more visible on Capitol Hill than Truly was at the same time the previous year. Besides speaking with reporters and editorial boards to sway public opinion, Goldin met with most members of Congress individually and with their state delegations. "He has made a good impression on the Hill," Brown said.

After being sworn in as administrator in early April, Goldin repeatedly said that NASA must do a better job setting clear goals and justifying its budget to Congress and the public. But he also invoked the sweeping themes of spaceflight and exploration to rally support for the agency.

Following the vote on the House floor July 29 to save the space station, Goldin called Bush with the news.

Then he walked outside to speak with reporters: "This is a victory for America's future," he said. "In difficult economic times, Congress stood up and did what's right for the country."

in November 1995, with the complete assembly to be launched in late 1999.

Most lawmakers who spoke in favor of the space station represented districts or states with lucrative space station contracts. The project had cost $7 billion by 1992 and had spawned an estimated 75,000 jobs in 39 states, with most in California, Alabama and Texas.

"Can you deprive your state and your constituents of this important source of jobs and revenue?" asked Tom DeLay, R-Texas.

But David R. Obey, D-Wis., whose state was not a major beneficiary, countered, "There is no bigger pork item in the domestic budget than this item. We don't have any room in the budget for this turkey."

Other key lawmakers and NASA officials stressed the project's long-term value for manned-space research.

NASA administrator Goldin echoed administration support for the project in an April 28 speech at the Ameri-

can Institute for Aeronautics and Astronautics. "The primary purpose of space station *Freedom* is to be the premier outpost in humankind's effort to learn how to live and work in space," he said.

### Passage

The House on May 5 passed the bill to guide the government's beleaguered space program through fiscal 1995, one which fully backed the space station. Members passed the three-year authorization bill (HR 4364) by voice vote after beating back an effort to strip money for the space station during the previous week's debate on the bill.

With the space station debate temporarily resolved, most of the remaining floor debate on the authorization bill came over whether to build the new rocket motor.

The project, known as the Advanced Solid Rocket Motor, was expected to cost about $3 billion. It was being built in the district of Appropriations Chairman Whitten and had enjoyed the strong support of House appropriators.

But critics said the new rocket motor was not really needed, especially if it would not be ready in time to help build the space station.

President Bush left the project out of his fiscal 1993 budget request. On the House floor, Wayne Owens, D-Utah, urged Congress to follow suit.

Owens said the existing redesigned rocket motor, which was made in Utah, could handle NASA's needs. He said the new program was behind schedule and over budget.

"Let's cut our losses before they multiply," Owens said.

But other members objected, saying it stood to cost as much or more to cancel the project. Owens eventually withdrew his amendment.

Instead, lawmakers approved an amendment by Rep. James V. Hansen, R-Utah, that cancelled the project if it was not ready in time to help build the space station — specifically by the sixth of a series of shuttle flights designed to lift components of the space station into orbit for assembly. Those flights were scheduled to begin in late 1995.

The bill authorized $260 million to research and develop the project in fiscal 1993, considerably less than the $440 million needed to press ahead as fast as possible. It authorized the additional $180 million only if appropriators gave NASA an overall budget of $15.3 billion or more in fiscal 1993.

## SENATE COMMITTEE ACTION

The Senate Commerce, Science and Transportation Committee on June 16 approved a $14.7 billion authorization bill for NASA for fiscal 1993 that proposed to trim most space programs to keep big-ticket projects such as the space station on track.

The committee used the shell of the House bill (HR 4364) and inserted its own language, authorizing $2 billion for the space station *Freedom* and $288 million for the Earth Observing System, the massive unmanned satellite and data system intended to relay atmospheric information.

The bill also authorized almost $400 million for the controversial new rocket motor for the space shuttle, which the White House zeroed out in its budget plan.

Unlike the House-passed version, which reauthorized the space agency for three years, the Senate draft authorized the agency for one year only. Proponents of a one-year authorization said it allowed Congress to exercise more oversight.

The committee-approved authorization had a smaller price tag for fiscal 1993 than the $15.3 billion House-passed version. Senators reduced the bottom line after chipping funding from virtually every space program, including $200 million from the space station, $50 million from space shuttle operations and $95 million from a proposed new launch system to lift heavier loads into space.

The bill was a clear response to the House-passed version, which called for setting up a two-tiered system of funding to authorize $14.3 billion for NASA's "core programs," including the space station and space shuttle, and $952 million for discretionary ones such as the new rocket motor.

The Senate bill sought to salvage the pet projects of senators that the House bill placed in its discretionary pot.

For example, the House bill directed appropriators to reserve $288 million for the Earth Observing System only after all basic NASA programs are funded.

It was the centerpiece of a large-scale, multisatellite project to track global change, known as the Mission to Planet Earth. The satellite also was a favorite of Al Gore, D-Tenn., chairman of the Science, Technology and Space Subcommittee and author of the Senate bill.

NASA planned to launch the Earth Observing System in 1998 to rapidly collect data on everything from rain to wind to temperature changes. Gore and other supporters hoped the data would help policy-makers reverse environmental damage.

By making cuts in most space programs, the Senate bill preserved the $288 million for the Earth Observing System in fiscal 1993.

The Senate bill also authorized funds for the Advance Solid Rocket Motor project built in the home district of Appropriations Committee Chairman Whitten. The project — whose cost was roughly $3 billion — proposed to build a more powerful rocket motor for use on the space shuttle.

Critics had charged that the project was behind schedule and might not be done in time to make a more powerful shuttle to help build the space station. While the House put the rocket's authorization in its discretionary account, the Senate bill fully funded it.

Almost half of the Senate bill's authorization — $7.1 billion — was to go to the space agency's research and development programs. Included was nearly $3 billion for space science projects.

Only one item attracted opposition from panel members: Richard H. Bryan, D-Nev., successfully offered an amendment to delete $13.5 million for a project to search for extraterrestrial life. Bryan said the program already had consumed $32 million and was unnecessary.

Even Gore found it difficult to defend the program. While he said it had "many, many useful features," he agreed that other more pressing projects made it dispensable.

But Ted Stevens, R-Alaska, tried to save the Star Trek-like program. "This nation is the only nation left on Earth that can be looking" for other life, Stevens said.

Countered John McCain, R-Ariz., "Perhaps we're the only nation on Earth foolish enough to spend this kind of money."

The committee voted 11-6 to delete the program. Three Democrats — Daniel K. Inouye of Hawaii, John D. Rockefeller IV of West Virginia and Charles S. Robb of Virginia — joined three Republicans — Stevens, Bob Kasten of Wisconsin and Slade Gorton of Washington — voting to continue funding.

The bill also reflected changes in the world since the Soviet Union was dismantled last year. A provision by Jim Exon, D-Neb., formerly a hard-line opponent of the Soviets, directed NASA to study the Russian space program for ways to use Russian space assets in the U.S. space program.

## FINAL ACTION

With two widely divergent bills to reconcile, action on the NASA authorization bill halted for nearly four months. Congress during that time shifted its full attention to the 13 must-pass spending bills for fiscal 1993.

Space station supporters won another major victory when the VA-HUD spending bill (HR 5679) cleared Congress on Sept. 25 with funding for the controversial project in tact. The House on July 29 had rejected, 181-237, a vigilant attempt to abandon the manned-exploration venture. It was the third vote in 13 months to preserve the space station. *(Appropriations, p. 639)*

The authorizers did not turn back to their bill until the end of the second session. A compromise bill (HR 6135) was developed with provisions agreed on by both chambers. The first House-passed bill (HR 4364) had never advanced to the Senate floor. The House acted on the compromise NASA authorization bill Oct. 6, giving it voice vote approval.

Given another opportunity, the Senate moved quickly Oct. 7 to clear HR 6135, also by voice vote.

As cleared, HR 6135 authorized:

● $2.1 billion for the space station *Freedom*.

● $1.3 million for space shuttle production, of which $315 million was authorized for the Advanced Solid Rocket Motor program. The rocket motor, which was to be built in Whitten's district, received $360 million in the appropriations bill for fiscal 1993.

● $838.5 million for earth sciences and applications. Landsat remained fully authorized. ∎

---

# NOAA Programs Funded

The Senate cleared legislation (HR 2130 — H Rept 102-500, S Rept 102-364) Oct. 7 to renew National Oceanic and Atmospheric Administration (NOAA) weather and coastal research programs. Funding was authorized for updating weather satellites and radar systems, as well as modernizing NOAA research fleets that monitored marine and coastal areas.

The House had passed the legislation Oct. 6.

President Bush signed the bill Oct. 29 (PL 102-567).

The House passed its initial version of the bill (H Rept 102-133, Parts I-II) in November 1991. But a companion measure never made it to the Senate floor during the first session. *(1991 Almanac, p. 236)*

The Senate on Aug. 12, 1992, amended and passed the House bill to authorize the agency at $1.5 billion in fiscal 1992 and $1.7 billion in fiscal 1993.

The bill also aimed to slow the pace of closures of national weather stations. The National Weather Service wanted to modernize and consolidate the stations, reducing the number from 250 to 115 uniform offices.

The measure banned the closing of weather stations nationwide until 1996 and imposed stricter criteria for closing stations to ensure that levels of service remained acceptably high. ∎

---

# Super Collider Survives Opposition in House

The controversial superconducting super collider, a massive underground atom smasher being built in Waxahachie, Texas, survived another year of funding battles, but not before nearly capsizing amid midsummer opposition.

Advocates said the device would be a huge high-speed particle collider designed to help scientists discover the fundamental secrets of matter. The Bush administration, which staunchly backed the $8 billion-plus atom smasher, recommended $650 million for the project in fiscal 1993.

House appropriators on the Energy and Water Development spending bill (HR 5373 — PL 102-377) trimmed that to $484 million, citing tight budget constraints but ongoing support for the project. *(Appropriations, p. 659)*

However, on the House floor, critics led a charge to kill the project altogether. These opponents won a 232-181 vote to end the program after arguing that it was of dubious scientific merit and ever-escalating costs. *(Vote 201, p. 50-H)*

But the administration and other supporters waged an effective counteroffensive in the Senate, where appropriators included $550 million for the project and were able to stave off a floor vote to kill it. In conference, appropriators approved $517 million for the project in fiscal 1993.

Ironically, the last hurdle was the administration. Because the energy and water appropriations bill also included nuclear testing restrictions opposed by President Bush, there was a risk that he would not sign the bill. However, Bush agreed to stomach those restrictions in order to save the super collider and signed the bill into law Oct. 2. ∎

---

# Partisan Feuding Scuttles Competitiveness Bills

Fearful that the United States was slipping behind in the fight for world markets, some lawmakers advocated programs seeking to enhance the nation's technological and manufacturing prowess. The American Technology Pre-Eminence Act of 1991 cleared early in 1992, but Congress failed to pass additional legislation aimed at boosting the nation's competitive stance.

Bills (S 1330 — H Rept 102-841, S Rept 102-226; HR 5231 — H Rept 102-685) were approved in both chambers that sought to reauthorize and expand programs within the Commerce Department to help U.S. industries develop and implement advanced technologies. Those programs included creating more outreach centers to teach advanced manufacturing techniques and government-backed loans for critical technologies.

However, the bills fell prey to partisan squabbling over the proper government role in technology development. Congress failed to approve a final version before adjournment.

## HOUSE SUBCOMMITTEE ACTION

Amid widespread laments about the nation's economic prospects, the House Science Subcommittee on Technology and Competitiveness approved a new bill (HR 5231) by voice vote June 24 to boost U.S. competitiveness.

# High-Tech Research Gets a Boost

After several years of failed attempts, Congress on Jan. 28 cleared a bill to help American high-technology industries compete around the globe.

The House voted 392-1 to agree to Senate amendments to the competitiveness bill (HR 1989 — S Rept 102-157), known as the American Technology Pre-Eminence Act of 1991. The Senate had approved the same version in the final hours of the 1991 session, but the action came too late for the House to endorse the compromise before adjourning. *(Vote 3, 2-H; 1991 Almanac, p. 234)*

President Bush signed the bill Feb. 14 — PL 102-245.

The bill reauthorized key technology-related programs within the Commerce Department, including the National Institute of Standards and Technology. The institute was a top government laboratory that helped industry develop cutting-edge technologies.

Passage came as economic troubles were intensifying congressional debate over the nation's competitiveness and how actively the government should intervene to promote American industry.

The measure authorized $348 million for fiscal 1992 and $359 million for fiscal 1993 for Commerce's technology programs. Most of the funding was to go to the institute. In each year, $100 million was earmarked for the institute's advanced technology program to provide grants to businesses and joint ventures to research and develop new technologies.

In fiscal 1993, the bill authorized another $35 million to upgrade and renovate institute facilities. The bill directed the Commerce Department to survey the status of technologies critical to the U.S. economy and develop a plan to support those industries.

To win White House support, Democratic legislators had to drop a provision for a $10 million loan program to help companies research commercial applications for new technologies. The Bush administration maintained that the loan program would have amounted to an industrial policy allowing bureaucrats to direct technology development and choose marketplace winners and losers. The loan program had been added in the House at the urging of Rep. Norman Y. Mineta, D-Calif.

The compromise also dropped a requirement that companies repay grants that led to successful commercial ventures.

As approved, the bill sought to coordinate and expand federal efforts to improve the international competitiveness of U.S. enterprises. It authorized $1.4 billion in fiscal 1994-97 for grants to promote advanced technologies, create a network of outreach centers to help manufacturers adopt modern production techniques, and expand the capital available to develop critical technologies.

Several Republicans on the panel said they preferred their own competitiveness package (HR 5229), drafted by Robert S. Walker, R-Pa., ranking member on the full Science Committee.

But Tim Valentine, D-N.C., who chaired the subcommittee and sponsored HR 5231, said the Republican version encompassed tax and antitrust policies far beyond the Science Committee's jurisdiction.

Valentine acknowledged that his bill, which the panel revised slightly, was narrower. But he said it would spur U.S. competitiveness on the matters within the panel's jurisdiction.

Tom Lewis, R-Fla., the subcommittee's ranking member, also complained that the competitiveness bill would cost too much. Lewis offered an amendment to cut the bill's authorization levels but was rebuffed on a voice vote.

## HOUSE COMMITTEE ACTION

The House Science, Space and Technology Committee on July 1 approved the legislation to enhance U.S. competitiveness, but it remained threatened by partisan squabbling over how best to cure the nation's ailing economy.

Members voted 8-2 in support of HR 5231 after lengthy and often heated debate between Democrats and Republicans.

The bill sought to coordinate and expand federal efforts to help U.S. businesses compete, such as establishing a network of outreach centers to help manufacturers adopt modern production techniques.

Other provisions would let the federal government provide loans to develop critical technologies, authorize $1.4 billion in fiscal 1994-97 for grants for advanced technologies and allow greater access to federal information of potential commercial value.

The Commerce Department had already threatened to recommend a veto, saying the bill called for unnecessary and duplicative federal programs.

Walker, the panel's ranking member, attacked the measure as ideologically misguided and absurdly narrow: "It has nothing to do with the fundamental competitiveness problems that face this nation."

Walker again tried unsuccessfully to replace it with his own competitiveness bill (HR 5229), which sought to give tax and legal relief to businesses and force down the federal debt.

But Chairman George E. Brown Jr., D-Calif, said the bulk of Walker's proposals fell outside the panel's jurisdiction, and the committee eventually rejected his substitute by voice vote.

Committee members acknowledged that the bill they endorsed represented only a small part of the problem but said it was nonetheless an important step forward.

Valentine, who chaired the Technology and Competitiveness Subcommittee, which drafted the competitiveness bill, said the measure attempted to bridge the divide and present a bipartisan plan of action.

While some committee Republicans backed the bill or parts of it, Walker complained that it ignored fundamental barriers to U.S. economic growth, such as the massive federal debt.

Walker argued that members should ignore traditional jurisdictional limits and approve his broad bill.

Most of the debate focused on the first portion of Walker's bill, which called for allowing taxpayers to voluntarily devote up to 10 percent of their taxes for debt reduction, a proposal touted by President Bush during the presidential race.

By doing so, taxpayers would simultaneously authorize dollar-for-dollar spending cuts. The cuts would be in the form of across-the-board reductions in all domestic programs save Social Security, the Federal Deposit Insurance Fund and interest payments on the debt.

Walker said the huge federal debt was the key obstacle for U.S. businesses because it drove up the cost of capital. He said his plan could eliminate the deficit by 1997 and reduce the debt by two-thirds within 12 years.

But Democrats said the blanket cuts were a crude way to reduce spending and could cripple programs that also aided U.S. competitiveness. And they said proposed tax breaks within Walker's bill, estimated to cost $100 billion, flew in the face of his stated dedication to deficit reduction.

After defeating Walker's substitute bill, members also rejected his amendment to cut the authorization levels in the committee bill.

After the markup, Valentine issued a statement criticizing the Commerce Department's veto threat: "I am extremely disappointed that some administration officials have decided to play political football with the economic future of this nation."

## SENATE ACTION

The Senate passed its bill (S 1330), designed to promote the nation's manufacturing sector, by voice vote late June 30. Like the House bill, the measure sought to expand existing Commerce Department efforts to improve and disseminate advanced manufacturing technologies. It proposed creation of a national quality laboratory to help train industry workers.

The bill authorized $55 million in fiscal 1993, jumping to $145 million in fiscal 1994 and $125 million in fiscal 1995.

## HOUSE ACTION

The bill burst through the partisan logjam in the House but too late to become law in 1992.

House members passed the bill (HR 5231) on Sept. 23, 287-122, after wading through a stack of unfriendly amendments by Walker. *(Vote 412, p. 100-H)*

They next inserted the text of that bill into the companion Senate measure (S 1330) and sent it back to that chamber, where it died.

During House floor debate, members rejected numerous Walker amendments to delete or weaken portions of the bill. *(Votes 406, 407, 408, 410, 411, pp. 98-H, 100-H)*

The measure had the support of many Democrats, some Republicans and a number of industry groups.

But Walker and other critics said the bill called for unneeded spending and exemplified a wrongheaded approach to competitiveness.

Walker wanted the House to debate his competitiveness bill (HR 5229), which called for a host of sweeping changes such as revising product liability laws and cutting the capital gains tax.

The divisions intensified with the election cycle, as President Bush began championing Walker's proposal to let citizens dedicate some of their taxes to debt reduction, and Democratic presidential nominee Bill Clinton began touting some provisions in the Democratic-led bill.

Partisan dickering slowed the bill's progress in committee and on the House floor, dashing sponsors' hopes of passage. ∎

# States Denied Immunity From Patent Penalties

Congress considered several measures in 1992 to revise the patent and copyright system. Those included:

## PATENT AND TRADEMARK INFRINGEMENT

The House cleared two bills Oct. 3 that imposed legal penalties on state governments for infringing on patent and trademark protections. The Senate had quickly passed the measures on June 12 by voice vote.

One measure (S 758) stripped state governments of their claim of "sovereign immunity" from legal penalties for infringing on a patent. It specifically amended the 1970 Plant Variety Protection Act, which protected breeders of new varieties of plants, to allow an inventor who believed his patent had been violated by a state government or state-sponsored university to sue the offending institution for damages.

The other bill (S 759) held state governments similarly liable for trademark infringements.

President Bush signed S 758 on Oct. 28 — PL 102-560; S 759 on Oct. 27 — PL 102-542.

The legislation came in response to a series of federal court decisions that said states and state-run universities were immune from federal penalties for patent and trademark infringements unless Congress specifically removed that immunity. States were shielded from such penalties under the Constitution's sovereign immunity clause in the 11th Amendment.

In 1990, President Bush signed similar legislation (HR 3045 — PL 101-553) making state governments liable for legal penalties for copyright infringement. *(1990 Almanac, p. 541)*

Dennis DeConcini, D-Ariz., who authored the bills, said they were intended to "protect the constitutionally enshrined incentive to invent."

The Senate Judiciary Committee approved the two measures (S Rept 102-280) on Feb. 6 by voice vote. The committee rejected, 4-9, an amendment by Charles E. Grassley, R-Iowa, that would have exempted state and local governments from treble damages in patent and copyright infringement suits. Defendants in such cases could be subjected to such damages under existing law.

A Senate Judiciary subcommittee on July 17 had approved the two measures (S 758, S 759). As approved, they allowed private individuals and organizations to sue states and state officials for patent and trademark infringements. The Subcommittee on Patents, Copyrights and Trademarks voted 5-0 to approve the two bills.

"Permitting states to infringe patent rights with impunity leads to the anomalous result of state universities being permitted to infringe private universities' copyrights and patents but not vice versa," said DeConcini.

## PATENT EXTENSIONS

Patent owners might have found it much harder to win special extensions from Congress under legislation that passed the House on Aug. 4. But the legislation died after failing to advance in the Senate. Critics said the measure would have made patent extensions to three food and drug manufacturers that probably would have faced barriers to such extensions under the broad new terms of the bill.

Members voted 278-131 in favor of the measure (HR 5475), only five votes more than the two-thirds majority needed to pass the bill under expedited procedures that limited debate and disallowed amendments. *(Vote 361, p. 88-H)*

The House Judiciary Committee had approved HR 5475 on July 22.

Under the bill, an individual would have had to prove governmental misconduct that resulted in substantial harm to the patent holder. Delays in approval of allowing a drug or other product onto the market would no longer have been enough reason to extend the patent.

Congress last set out rules for consideration of patent extensions in 1984. Under that law, to be eligibile for patent extensions, an individual had to prove that government action or inaction had resulted in material harm to the patent holder.

Critics maintained that the three companies granted extensions by the bill — including Procter & Gamble Co., maker of the fat substitute Olestra — should have had to meet the tough new conditions. Instead, they would continue to have exclusive manufacturing and marketing rights for the remainder of the new patent terms.

The Olestra extension "is contrary to the interests of consumers [and is] unfair to other companies that have relied on the expiration of the [Procter & Gamble] patents in accordance with current law," said Terry L. Bruce, D-Ill.

Also granted patent extensions would have been two anti-inflammatory drugs — Ansaid and Lodine — produced by the Upjohn and American Home Products companies, respectively. Both patents would have been extended for two years.

William J. Hughes, D-N.J., chairman of the House Judiciary Subcommittee on Intellectual Property, acknowledged that the separate extensions incorporated in the bill probably would not qualify under the new, stricter standards. But he argued that "fairness dictates that these petitions be judged by pre-existing standards, not by ones we formulated" later.

As passed by the House, the bill established statutory standards for the consideration of future patent extension bills. The central requirement of the new standards was that the patentee who was seeking an extension show that any material harm caused by government action or inaction — for example, by an unjustified delay in the regulatory approval process — was the result of governmental misconduct, such as dishonest or deceitful behavior or negligence on the part of federal officials.

## PATENT MAINTENANCE FEES

The Senate on Oct. 7 cleared a bill (HR 5328 — H Rept 102-993) to give patent holders more time to pay their maintenance fees, the cost of filing and keeping current records on patents. It passed by voice vote. The House passed the measure by voice vote Oct. 3.

President Bush signed HR 5328 on Oct. 23 — PL 102-444.

Under existing law, people holding patents had up to six months to pay their maintenance fees before their patents expired. A patent holder had to convince the head of the Patent Office that any delay was unavoidable in order to get a patent reinstated.

The bill gave patent owners an additional 24 months to pay if they could prove that their failure to pay, while perhaps avoidable, was unintentional.

## PATENT OFFICE REAUTHORIZATION

The Senate passed a measure (S 3325) on Oct. 5 to reauthorize the Commerce Department's Patent and Trademark Office for fiscal 1993. It died in the House without action.

The measure would have authorized the use of $99 million collected from user fees to offset the agency's costs. That was $12.3 million more than the appropriation bill for the Commerce Department (HR 5678 — PL 102-395) provided for fiscal 1993. *(Appropriations, p. 646)* ∎

# Bills Seek Support for U.S. Technology

As the United States faced increasing global competition in the high technology fields, Congress considered a number of measures aimed at strengthening the nation's technology base. Those included:

## LANDSAT

Management of the Landsat Remote-Sensing Satellite Program was shifted to the National Aeronautics and Space Administration (NASA) and the Defense Department under legislation (HR 6133) cleared by the Senate by voice vote Oct. 7, a day after the House passed it.

President Bush signed HR 6133 on Oct. 28 (PL 102-555).

The program had been managed by the Commerce Department's National Oceanic and Atmospheric Administration.

The Landsat program, developed by the NASA in 1972, took pictures of Earth that were used for environmental planning, oil and gas development, and military surveillance.

But the program floundered during the 1980s after an effort to transfer it to the private sector. The resulting problems and insecure funding had jeopardized development of the program's newest remote-sensing satellite, the Landsat 7.

HR 6133 was a compromise version of previous House and Senate bills (HR 3614 — H Rept 102-539; S 2297 — 102-445), which had minor differences between them.

The compromise bill watered down a Senate provision to require that federal agencies and affiliated users be able to get images from the existing satellite program at cost, and that pictures from a planned new satellite be available to all users on that basis. The final language would "encourage" one fee.

The Senate Commerce, Science and Transportation Committee approved its bill (S 2297) on Aug. 11 to restructure the Landsat satellite photography program.

The legislation directed NASA and the Defense Department to jointly manage the satellite program. The bill mandated that federal agencies and affiliated users be able

to get images from the current satellite program at cost, and that pictures from a planned new satellite be available to all users on that basis.

The House on June 9 passed by voice vote its bill to restructure the Landsat satellite program and promote development of a new-generation satellite.

In keeping with a Bush administration directive issued in February, the House bill (HR 3614) would have transferred management of the program from the Commerce Department jointly to NASA and the Defense Department, and would have authorized them to spend federal funds for developing Landsat 7. Specific federal authorizations for Landsat were included in the NASA and Defense authorization bills. *(NASA reauthorization, p. 296; defense authorization, p. 483)*

In exchange for this federal support, the bill stipulated that government agencies should have access to Landsat images generated by existing satellites at cost rather than at the higher fees that were charged to private users. The administration was expected to establish a uniform, at-cost price policy for pictures generated by the new satellite.

The legislation also set up an advisory council for the satellite program that included representatives from a range of groups that used the images. And it called for a technology demonstration program to help promote a private land remote-sensing industry.

## HIGH-SPEED COMPUTER NETWORK

The House passed a bill June 29 to promote a high-speed national computer network, but the measure died in the Senate.

The computer bill (HR 5344 — H Rept 102-567) would loosen current law and allow the National Science Foundation (NSF) to carry a broader array of information on its computer network, known as NSFnet.

The network was used by scientists, schools and research laboratories.

The bill would allow the network to carry more commercial information, a move advocates said would lower costs for education and commercial users alike.

NSFnet ultimately would serve as the backbone for an ambitious high-speed network for education and research groups.

The House Science, Space and Technology Subcommittee on Science on June 4 approved by voice vote a bill (unnumbered) that would allow greater access by individuals and corporations to the NSF's national computer network. It would allow the network to carry computer traffic that was not necessarily associated with research and education purposes.

Users of the network said that by opening up the network to other services, its capacity to support research and education would be augmented.

On June 10, the full committee approved HR 5344, legislation to promote development of a high-speed computer network for education and research groups. Under the bill, the NSF's existing computer network would be broadened to provide the new computer capability.

## DEBT FOR SCIENCE

The House on Aug. 10 passed a bill (HR 3215 — H Rept 102-654, Part I) to promote scientific cooperation between the United States and Latin America. The measure died after the Senate amended and passed it Oct. 7, leaving no time for the House to act on the changes.

Among the programs it encouraged were so-called debt-for-science swaps, whereby the federal government would pay off part of a nation's foreign debt in exchange for its participation in research and education work.

The administration opposed the bill, saying there already were enough federal programs to enhance scientific collaboration with Latin America.

The House Science, Space and Technology Subcommittee on Science had approved HR 3215 on May 19. As approved, the bill sought to establish an inter-American scientific cooperation program at the National Science Foundation (NSF) to provide the United States' share of funding for joint research, education exchanges and information transfer.

The bill would authorize $10 million to be spent annually by NSF for fiscal 1992 and 1993.

Members approved by voice vote an amendment by Democrat Rick Boucher of Virginia, chairman of the subcommittee, to clarify that the NSF could not put any constraints on countries as a condition for funding a debt-for-science exchange.

Ranking subcommittee Republican Ron Packard of California also won voice vote approval for his amendment to ensure that the NSF would not spend more than 25 percent of its budget for international cooperative scientific activities on programs under the measure.

## WATER DESALINATION

The Senate on Oct. 7 cleared legislation (HR 3673 — H Rept 102-556) to advance research on new water desalination techniques. Advocates hoped that the technology would provide a cheaper way to desalinate large volumes of water.

The House on June 29 passed the bill to expand and coordinate federal research on removing salt or pollutants from water with membrane filters to produce drinkable water. It also authorized the National Science Foundation (NSF) to establish a research program on membrane technology and recommended $2.5 million for the program in fiscal 1993.

President Bush signed HR 3673 on Oct. 24 (PL 102-490).

The Bush administration initially opposed the bill, saying a new program was unnecessary because the Interior Department already funded desalinization research.

But Ron Packard, R-Calif., one of the bill's key sponsors, said the membrane research program was of critical importance to drought-stricken regions and the nation as a whole: "It has become apparent to those in California and the Southwest that conservation, by itself, will not provide the ultimate solution to the desperate situation that exists in that part of the country."

## FIRE SAFETY

Legislation requiring the installation of fire safety equipment in federal office buildings and housing passed the House by voice vote Aug. 10. But the Senate never acted on the measure.

Under existing law, federally owned buildings were exempt from local fire codes. Advocates said the new bill (HR 3360 — H Rept 102-509) was needed because many federal

buildings were old and had been neglected.

The bill called for most newly constructed and leased federal office buildings for more than 25 employees to be equipped with sprinklers.

The bill also would have required that federally subsidized housing units have smoke detectors. In some cases, sprinklers would also have been installed, depending on the size of the building.

The bill got the nod from the House Public Works Committee on July 1. The House Science Committee on April 2 had also given voice vote approval to HR 3360.

## METRIC PACKAGING

American shoppers were spared the worry about liters and kilograms under legislation (HR 5343 — H Rept 102-581) cleared by the Senate on July 21. It had passed the House on June 29. The speedy passage clarified that Congress did not expect food packagers to convert to the metric system.

President Bush signed HR 5343 on Aug. 3 (PL 102-329).

At issue was a prior law, the American Technology Pre-Eminence Act (PL 102-245), that sought to promote metric labeling on some products to make them easier to export. But some packagers worried that those provisions could be interpreted as requiring them to redesign existing containers and sell in metric units. (National technology pre-eminence act, p. 302)

The new legislation amended the labeling provisions to clarify that packagers did not need to convert to metric-sized packaging. The United States was virtually alone in using the avoirdupois measurement system, based on pounds and ounces.

## COMMERCIAL SPACE

The House on Aug. 6 passed by voice vote a bill (HR 3848) designed to promote the commercial space industry. Although the Senate never acted it, some of the provisions became law in the reauthorization bill (HR 6135 — PL 102-588) for the National Aeronautics and Space Administration. (NASA reauthorization, p. 296)

The bill, sponsored by Ralph M. Hall, D-Texas, and approved July 1 by the Science, Space and Technology Committee, sought to encourage the federal government to use private sector equipment for space launches.

Sponsors agreed to an Armed Services Committee request to delete a section that would have placed restrictions on using decommissioned missiles for space launches. Armed Services wanted more time to review those provisions.

## BIOTECH RULES

Manufacturers of genetically altered plants, bacteria and animals had an easier time getting them to market after President Bush outlined new guidelines the week of Feb. 24.

The new policy sought to closely regulate only products that appeared to carry special risk, such as pharmaceuticals, rather than all new biotechnologies.

The Bush administration did not release new rules, but the president's policy statement served as a guide for agencies to assess old rules or write new ones.

## JOINT VENTURES

Prodded by worries about the nation's flagging competitiveness, the Senate voted to make it easier for companies to conduct joint manufacturing ventures. However, the measure died in the 102nd Congress when the House failed to act on the Senate bill (S 479 — S Rept 102-146) or a House companion (HR 1604 — H Rept 102-972).

The Senate on Feb. 27 passed, 96-1, its bill to loosen antitrust restrictions on such joint manufacturing after senators toned down a section that would have largely restricted protections to U.S.-based manufacturing. The Bush administration had attacked the section as protectionist. (Vote 34, p. 6-S)

The proposal encompassed industries across the spectrum but was expected to be most useful in high-technology fields that often required extensive capital investment.

Democrat Patrick J. Leahy of Vermont, the bill's chief sponsor, cited the semiconductor industry, where the high cost of new plants discouraged American companies from producing the popular memory chips on their own. "We invented it," Leahy said of the semiconductor chip, "and it has been turned into an engine for Japanese jobs and growth."

Congress had already eased antitrust restrictions on cooperative research and development efforts through the 1984 National Cooperative Research Extension Act. The new bill sought to extend that legal umbrella to joint manufacturing as well. (1984 Almanac, p. 258)

As passed by the House, the bill gave companies relief from antitrust laws in two areas as long as they notified the Justice Department of plans to form a cooperative manufacturing venture.

First, the bill required critics seeking to sue the joint venture as anticompetitive to meet a higher standard of proof than had been required. Second, companies found guilty under that higher standard would be subject only to actual damages rather than three times that amount, as the existing law provided.

Supporters said the bill would encourage companies to enter into joint ventures without fearing penalties under the antitrust statutes and would thus create more jobs.

Howard M. Metzenbaum, D-Ohio, offered the sole dissent, saying current antitrust laws did not deter cooperative production accords. He cited a joint venture by IBM and Apple Computer. Instead, Metzenbaum said, antitrust laws heightened competition and in turn spur advances in American competitiveness.

Sponsors did face some obstacles. The first, and most time-consuming, was an attempt by John McCain, R-Ariz., to offer an amendment that would have provided the president with a line-item veto on spending bills. McCain was eventually rebuffed but not before he spoke in its behalf and Appropriations Committee Chairman Robert C. Byrd, D-W.Va., delivered a marathon opposition address. (Enhanced rescissions, p. 114)

The more germane stumbling block was a controversial provision that Joseph R. Biden Jr., D-Del., added to the bill during committee markup in July 1991. It stated that the antitrust exemption would apply only if the joint manufacturing operations were principally located within the United States and the companies had each made a "substantial commitment" to the U.S. economy.

The provision drew protests from the European Community and the Bush administration, which threatened a veto. Administration officials said the provision would undermine U.S. efforts to open overseas markets. The conflict forced sponsors to hold a cloture vote to begin consideration of the bill.

But soon after senators voted 98-0 to shut off debate on

the motion to proceed, they closed in on compromise language that was adopted the next day. *(Vote 32, p. 5-S)*

As revised, the bill would apply the antitrust benefits to joint ventures that would bring "substantial" benefit to the U.S. economy and that were located either in the United States or in countries that granted reciprocal legal privileges to U.S. companies.

Hank Brown, R-Colo., who helped write the compromise, hailed the emphasis on reciprocity as a model for other trade legislation.

The debate came just days after Attorney General William P. Barr blasted the discriminatory impact of Japanese business arrangements and pledged to challenge them with U.S. antitrust laws.

The administration said it could accept the Senate bill as amended.

The parallel House bill (HR 1604) set a 30 percent cap on foreign participation in joint ventures that would be eligible for the special antitrust treatment. That bill passed the Judiciary Committee in June 1991. ∎

Chapter 5

# LAW & JUDICIARY

# No Compromise Forged on Crime Bill

*Both chambers remained divided along party lines
over death penalty, inmates' rights, gun control*

After a year of fits and starts, Congress failed to clear anti-crime legislation to expand the federal death penalty to more crimes and require a waiting period for the purchase of handguns. Neither Democrats nor Republicans wanted the sweeping anti-crime bill badly enough to hammer out a compromise in a presidential election year in which crime fell behind the economy and health-insurance reform as an issue that could mobilize voters.

The conference report for the omnibus anti-crime measure (HR 3371) would have extended the federal death penalty to more than 50 crimes, restricted death row inmates' ability to challenge their sentences and imposed new gun-crime penalties. The bill authorized more than $3 billion for prisons and law enforcement.

The conference report had been narrowly approved in the House at the end of 1991. It languished in the Senate throughout 1992, appearing briefly on the floor in March and October. Republicans blocked it both times. The same issues continued to divide the two parties: Democrats did not want tough Republican restrictions on the ability of death row inmates to ask for federal review of their sentences under habeas corpus provisions. And Republicans objected to handgun control provisions.

The crime bill (HR 3371) included the text of another bill (S 3282) that required a five-day waiting period for potential handgun purchases, allowing time to check a buyer's background.

This provision, known as the Brady bill, was named for James S. Brady, former press secretary to President Ronald Reagan, who was wounded in a 1981 assassination attempt on the president. Brady and his wife, Sarah, lobbied hard for the provision.

Early in the year, Republicans unsuccessfully pushed their own crime bill (S 2302), which did not include handgun control.

After the crime bill died for the year, the Brady bill failed to pass as a separate measure when Senate Republicans blocked efforts to bring it to the floor. That bill included a seven-day waiting period for handgun purchases.

## BACKGROUND

For 10 years, anti-crime proposals had generated a lot of heat but little action until the waning days of each

---

## BOXSCORE

➡ **Omnibus Anti-Crime bill and Brady bill (HR 3371; S 3282).** The crime bill would have extended the federal death penalty to more than 50 crimes and restricted death row inmates' ability to challenge their sentences. It included a provision, known as the Brady bill, to require a waiting period for the purchase of handguns.

**Report:** Conference report H Rept 102-405.

### KEY ACTION

**March 19 — Senate** cloture vote on HR 3371 failed, 54-43.

**Oct. 2** — Second **Senate** cloture vote failed, 55-43.

**Oct. 5 — Senate** Republicans blocked S 3282 from consideration.

---

biennial Congress, as Election Day approached. *(1989 Almanac, p. 259; 1988 Almanac, p. 85; 1986 Almanac, p. 92; 1984 Almanac, p. 215; 1982 Almanac, p. 419)*

But in 1991, President Bush threw down the gauntlet early in the session by challenging Congress to enact a crime bill within 100 days. Much of what the president wanted had been on the table in 1990, only to get swept away in House-Senate bargaining at the end of the 101st Congress. The 1990 crime bill was gutted by a conference committee on the eve of adjournment. Stripped out were an assault-weapons ban, death penalty provisions and limits on death row appeals, among other provisions. Left in the measure that eventually passed (PL 101-647) were non-controversial items such as new sanctions against thrift fraud and more funding for local law enforcement. *(1991 Almanac, p. 262)*

Picking up where they left off in 1990, the Bush administration and congressional Democrats vied throughout 1991 to see who could appear toughest on crime. The Bush administration's 1991 crime proposal (HR 1400, S 635) sought to apply the federal death penalty to about 40 crimes, most of which involved murder. The proposals also limited the ability of death row inmates to challenge the constitutionality of their sentences through so-called habeas corpus petitions. The bills proposed a "good faith" exception to the exclusionary rule, which barred prosecutors from using illegally obtained evidence against a defendant. And the measures stiffened penalties for firearms offenses.

Senate Democrats countered with S 618, to authorize capital punishment for 44 federal offenses, restrict habeas corpus petitions, loosen the exclusionary rule, ban assault weapons and authorize $1 billion in aid to state and local law enforcement agencies. The measure also included racial-justice safeguards and required that death row prisoners have adequate counsel as a condition to limits on habeas corpus.

For the second time in a row, however, the quarrel ended in stalemate. The House narrowly approved a compromise version of the bill (HR 3371), but, with Bush insisting that it did not go far enough in restricting appeals by convicted criminals or relaxing evidentiary rules, Senate Republicans blocked it.

Nonetheless, the bill was a landmark of sorts: It marked the first time both chambers had approved a waiting period for handgun purchases. A second gun-control provision, to

ban sales and possession of at least nine types of U.S.-made semiautomatic assault weapons, was dropped from the final bill.

### 1991 Action

Because the Senate crime bill contained proposals that had been thoroughly debated in 1990, Senate leaders decided to skip the usual public hearings and Judiciary Committee action and bring the legislation directly to the Senate floor. The Senate passed the bill 71-26 on July 11.

By voice vote, the House Judiciary Committee on Sept. 26 passed HR 3371, which took a less stringent approach to fighting crime than Bush and the Senate wanted. The bill allowed prisoners to challenge their sentences as having been racially motivated, prohibited use of coerced confessions at trial and extended other protections to defendants.

The House began work on HR 3371 on Oct. 16 and passed it 305-118 on Oct. 22. The bill narrowly rejected an amendment that would have greatly restricted appeals by inmates on death row. Bush, who disliked the bill approved by the Judiciary Committee, warned that "the American people will not accept a crime bill that is tougher on law enforcement than it is on criminals."

Death row inmates routinely sought writs of habeas corpus in federal courts, after their regular appeals failed, in an effort to overturn their convictions and delay execution. Often such proceedings postponed executions for years, to the frustration of state prosecutors and victims' families.

Although Congress had weighed numerous proposals for habeas corpus revision over the preceeding two years, most of the movement on the subject was taking place in the Supreme Court. As Presidents Ronald Reagan and Bush transformed the makeup of the high court, the justices took an increasingly tough line on the rights of criminal defendants. *(1991 Almanac, p. 264)*

House and Senate conferees began work on HR 3371 after Nov. 21, when GOP senators dropped their objections to naming conferees. Meeting in a rare Sunday session, conferees reached agreement on a final version of HR 3371 on Nov. 24. But Republicans complained they were "steamrolled" on a series of votes that led to the adoption of weaker provisions on habeas corpus, the exclusionary rule and the death penalty for state gun crimes.

On Nov. 27, the House barely eked out a 205-203 win for the conference report. But the Senate failed 49-38 to invoke cloture, 11 votes short of the 60 needed to shut off a filibuster threat by Republicans, who called it a "pro-criminal" bill.

That suspended the political argument until the 1992 election season and left the legislation in limbo.

## SENATE ACTION

After the crime bill squeaked past the House on a close vote in 1991, the action in 1992 centered on the Senate.

In some election-year gamesmanship, Senate Republicans and Democrats fought for control of crime-related issues the week of March 2 and scheduled a political "showdown" for March 10. The eventual outcome, however, left both sides where they started — at an impasse.

The gauntlet was thrown down March 3, this time by GOP leader Bob Dole of Kansas, Phil Gramm of Texas and other Republicans, who in a news conference vowed to bring to the Senate floor a crime measure backed by Bush. Gramm said he would find a way to raise the issue every week until it passed.

Democrats complained that it was Republicans who had blocked action in 1991 on the sweeping anti-crime measure, HR 3371, approved in a House-Senate conference.

On March 4, Gramm appeared ready to amend an unrelated bill, the reauthorization of the Corporation for Public Broadcasting (S 1504), with the Bush crime bill (S 2305). *(CPB, p. 187)*

But Majority Leader George J. Mitchell, D-Maine, made a pre-emptive strike, calling the conference report on HR 3371 back to the floor. It had been idling on the Senate calendar since a similar cloture effort failed in November 1991.

Republicans objected to that move, and senators proceeded to debate the issue for the next two days until Mitchell on March 5 filed another motion to invoke cloture. The two sides agreed to vote on the question March 10, but Democrats remained doubtful that they could muster the 60 votes needed to shut off debate.

The two sides disagreed mainly over how much to restrict death row inmates' petitions to federal courts under the process known as habeas corpus.

Thrown into the confusion was legislation (S 2305), drafted by Strom Thurmond, R-S.C., ranking member of the Judiciary Committee, and backed by Bush, that allowed federal judges to deny a habeas petition if they decided the prisoner had received a "full and fair" hearing in state courts.

The Republican measure also excluded the so-called Brady bill — language imposing a waiting period for the purchase of handguns. The Brady bill had been approved in similar forms by both chambers in 1991.

### First Cloture Vote

Slim chances for enactment of anti-crime legislation in 1992 dwindled to almost nothing March 19 when Senate Democrats failed to stop a Republican filibuster of the Democratic-backed bill.

The Senate voted 54-43 to invoke cloture, six short of the votes needed to shut off debate on a motion to proceed to a House-Senate conference agreement on the bill, HR 3371. *(Vote 53, p. 8-S)*

The vote appeared to be a deciding blow in a fight that had begun March 3 when the Senate Republicans said they would not abandon their efforts to push their own version of crime legislation (S 2305). Texan Gramm called the conference agreement a "sham crime bill" and reiterated his plan to bring up S 2305 regularly for the rest of the year.

"We should do it once a week, until either the president signs a bill or until this Congress ends," he said.

Judiciary Committee Chairman Joseph R. Biden Jr., D-Del., said chances for passage of the Thurmond bill were no better than for HR 3371.

Biden blamed Republicans and the National Rifle Association (NRA), which opposed the Brady language, for the demise of the bill.

It was supported by several police organizations, including the Fraternal Order of Police, which also favored the bill's extra funding for local law enforcement.

### Second Cloture Vote

Despite an intense lobbying effort by gun control activists for anti-crime legislation, the Senate could not muster the votes to cut off a threatened Republican filibuster on the crime bill. The vote on Oct. 2 effectively killed the measure for 1992.

The loss was no surprise to senators and others familiar with the longtime fight over the bill. Democrats and Republicans had been at an impasse since November 1991. In the end, neither party wanted the bill badly enough to work out their differences.

In a replay of the previous year's Senate battle over crime, Democratic senators led by Judiciary Committee Chairman Biden failed to win enough votes to cut off an expected Republican filibuster on the bill. The 55-43 cloture vote fell five votes short of the 60 needed to stop debate and move to consideration of the bill. For the second year, Democratic senators from Alabama and Louisiana voted against the cloture motion. *(Vote 262, p. 34-S)*

The crime bill would have imposed new gun-crime penalties, extended the federal death penalty to more than 50 crimes and restricted death row inmates' ability to challenge their sentences — but not enough for Republicans' liking. The measure included the legislation known as the Brady bill that established a five-day waiting period for handgun purchases to allow for a police background check.

Republicans did not support the handgun control provisions and Democrats did not want tough Republican restrictions on the ability of death row inmates to ask for federal review of their sentences under habeas corpus provisions.

Bush said he would accept the Brady language if it were part of a crime package that included the tougher habeas corpus restrictions.

Gun control proponents led by Biden and Brady's wife, Sarah, blamed the bill's troubles on the gun lobby: "It's about the NRA," Biden said of Republicans' opposition.

But Thurmond, ranking Republican on Judiciary, said the bill was not tough enough. Passing it, Thurmond said, would be "tantamount to handing the jailhouse keys to thousands of convicted felons."

The Senate floor was the scene of a high-stakes political gambit in which both sides were bluffing, as Biden and Thurmond threw out compromise agreements only to have them summarily rejected by the other side.

Biden held a news conference Oct. 1 with the nation's top police groups, including the Fraternal Order of Police and the National Association of Police Organizations. He offered to strike all habeas corpus provisions from the bill to neutralize that issue. Biden, whose staff had been negotiating for weeks with Attorney General William P. Barr on the bill, also offered to negotiate throughout the night with Barr and his staff. The heads of the police organizations, led by FOP President Dewey R. Stokes, offered to mediate.

Biden said Oct. 2 that the talks ended at 2:30 a.m. with no resolution.

Stokes, who did help mediate, said the two sides disagreed over several small issues. No matter what was tried, he said, the sides never fully compromised.

Then on the Senate floor, Biden again made his offer to Thurmond to take out habeas corpus provisions. He also offered to throw out provisions that would bar the use of coerced confessions at trial, reversing a Supreme Court decision in *Arizona v. Fulminante.* The provisions had been strongly opposed by Republicans.

But Thurmond continued to denounce the measure. He finally refused Biden's offer, saying that habeas corpus must be addressed in the bill.

Biden then argued that Thurmond's refusal to agree proved his assertion that Republicans were still holding out over the Brady provisions.

Thurmond then offered to introduce a new measure including the Brady bill, as well as the habeas corpus provisions that Bush wanted. Biden refused.

"There you go," Thurmond said.

During the vote, Sarah Brady said she would continue lobbying until adjournment for passage of the Brady provisions by themselves.

She dismissed Thurmond's proposal to Biden and said she understood Biden's refusal to accept it. "That was not a serious proposal," she said.

## Brady Bill Dies

With the crime bill declared dead, an equally futile effort was made to resurrect the Brady bill as a separate measure. Congress firmly rejected handgun control on Oct. 5 when supporters in the House and Senate were unsuccessful in their push for consideration of S 3282 by itself.

The Senate began the week by putting Bush on the spot. Majority Leader Mitchell attempted to bring up the Brady bill, which required a seven-day waiting period before purchase of a handgun to allow for police background checks. Republican senators objected, and the measure was never considered.

The measure differed from the gun control compromise provisions included in the failed anti-crime legislation. The compromise provisions in the crime bill required a five-day waiting period.

Mitchell appealed to Bush to call off the Republican opponents and throw his support behind the Brady bill.

"It is up to you, Mr. President," Mitchell said. "I hope that for the American people you will say yes."

Sen. Howard M. Metzenbaum, D-Ohio, also implored Bush to support the bill.

"The reason we do not have a Brady bill or a crime bill is that the president has not put his shoulder to the wheel," Metzenbaum said. "It is his responsibility. It is on his doorstep. He can get the few extra votes needed to cut off a filibuster."

Bush had said he would support the gun control provisions if they were part of a sweeping anti-crime package that included tough provisions that he wanted to further restrict death row inmates' ability to challenge their sentences under habeas corpus rules.

However, Republicans, led by Sen. Larry E. Craig of Idaho, argued that Mitchell was attempting to sell a bill that the House and Senate had never voted on. He said S 3282 never made it to either floor because it had less support than the broader HR 3371.

Moreover, argued Craig, a longtime gun control foe, the bill would threaten Americans' civil rights. He said police should be held liable when guns were sold to convicted felons or other people who could not legally own firearms. But under the bill, police would not be held liable. Likewise police would not be held legally responsible if they denied gun ownership to someone who could lawfully own one.

Craig compared the provision to the Los Angeles case of Rodney King, who was beaten by police earlier in 1992 after being stopped for a traffic violation. "I can understand why the law enforcement community does not want to be held liable," Craig said. "They really did not want to be held liable in the issue of Rodney King. But the American citizens said we must hold them responsible for their acts."

The next day, Oct. 6, House Judiciary Committee Chairman Jack Brooks, D-Texas, attempted to revive some provisions of the anti-crime legislation but also was thwarted by Republicans. ■

# Stiff Penalties Instituted for Carjackers

Congress cleared a bill Oct. 8 establishing stiff penalties for "carjacking," the armed robbery of a vehicle while the driver was present. The bill, HR 4542, made carjacking a federal crime with a maximum penalty of life in prison when the theft resulted in death. The bill also required that major car parts be marked with identification numbers to be registered in an FBI parts registry.

The final version included a compromise on the ID numbers between Charles E. Schumer, D-N.Y., chairman of the Judiciary Subcommittee on Crime and Criminal Justice, and Energy and Commerce Committee Chairman John D. Dingell, D-Mich. Dingell argued that such labeling had not proved effective but would cost automakers millions of dollars.

The compromise phased in the labeling of car parts over five years.

The bill was prompted by a rash of carjackings throughout the United States — particularly in large cities such as New York and Detroit — including some that resulted in the death of the driver.

## COMMITTEE ACTION

The House Judiciary Subcommittee on Crime and Criminal Justice gave voice vote approval May 21 to legislation (HR 4542) creating a new federal offense for armed carjacking. The bill stipulated that the offender must have moved the stolen car across state lines.

The maximum penalty for the crime was 15 years. In addition, the bill raised the maximum penalty for importing or exporting stolen cars from five to 10 years.

The bill also directed the secretary of Transportation to push a theft prevention plan requiring that major car parts — frames, engines, transmissions and windows — be stamped with the vehicle's identification numbers.

The full House Judiciary Committee approved HR 4542 by voice vote July 28.

The bill made carjacking a federal crime and required the dozen or so most sought-after auto parts in each car and truck sold in the United States to be marked with identifying numbers. The numbers would be put into an FBI computer data base, which could be used by police to trace stolen parts.

The measure also directed the Customs Service to spot-check cars being shipped abroad to determine if they were stolen.

### Turf Wars

Spurred by a rash of carjackings across the country, members of Congress continued to move on a measure designed to make it easier for law enforcement authorities to track down stolen automobile parts.

The House Energy and Commerce panel gave voice vote

---

## BOXSCORE

➡ **Carjacking (HR 4542).** The bill made carjacking a federal crime with a maximum penalty of life in prison when the theft resulted in death.

**Report:** H Rept 102-851.

### KEY ACTION

July 28 — The **House** Judiciary Committee approved HR 4542.

Sept. 17 — The **House** Energy and Commerce Committee approved HR 4542.

Sept. 22 — The **House** Ways and Means Committee approved HR 4542.

Oct. 6 — The **House** passed HR 4542 by voice vote.

Oct. 8 — The **Senate** cleared HR 4542 by voice vote.

Oct. 25 — President Bush signed HR 4542 — PL 102-519.

---

approval Sept. 17 to its version of HR 4542, making carjacking a federal crime.

But a dispute between the Energy and Commerce and Judiciary committees threatened to bog down HR 4542.

"The recent wave of carjackings must be halted," said Cardiss Collins, D-Ill. "Auto theft is not just an economic tragedy, it is a human tragedy."

Losses from car thefts cost consumers $8 billion annually, Collins said.

The legislation also tried to cut into the chop shop business — where stolen cars were received and dismantled and the parts sold — by expanding an FBI data base of identification numbers for parts from autos that were popular with thieves.

The bill required that the 14 most desired parts in every vehicle — the frames, engines, transmission and windows — be marked and that those numbers be put into an FBI computer to enable authorities to trace stolen parts.

At the time, only parts for certain cars — those most popular with car thieves — were marked by manufacturers and cataloged by the FBI.

The dispute over the bill arose over whether to require car manufacturers to place identification numbers on major parts in car lines. The Judiciary Committee voted in July to require that all parts of all car models be marked. That was estimated to cost the automobile industry about $48 million a year.

At the urging of the automobile industry, Energy Committee Chairman Dingell proposed a substitute amendment striking the parts identification requirement for all cars. The panel also agreed to drop the parts-marking requirement on the most often stolen cars when manufacturers had installed an anti-theft device in that car line.

Schumer, sponsor of the original bill, criticized the Energy panel for removing the parts-marking requirement for all car lines, saying the Dingell bill created "a loophole big enough to drive a stolen Mack truck through."

But Energy panel members said there was no evidence that marking parts in all car lines would deter car thefts. "It does not cover all vehicles because a large number of vehicles are simply not candidates for theft," Dingell said.

"The end result," added Michael G. Oxley, R-Ohio, "would be to make auto manufacturers and dealers of used auto parts jump through regulatory hoops at great expense to themselves for a program that has not even proved effective."

### Ways and Means

The legislation aimed at decreasing the number of carjackings nationwide moved closer to the House floor Sept. 22 when the Ways and Means Committee gave voice vote approval to HR 4542, making such theft a federal

crime carrying a penalty of 15 years in prison.

The bill also contained U.S. Customs provisions under the jurisdiction of Ways and Means, which left unresolved a dispute between the Judiciary Committee and Energy and Commerce Committee over provisions that would require automakers to label expensive car parts with identification numbers to be on file at the FBI.

Ways and Means approved language requiring the U.S. Customs Service to spot-check used cars being shipped abroad to crack down on the export of stolen vehicles and parts.

Sam M. Gibbons, D-Fla., successfully offered an amendment providing Customs with flexibility in determining how to conduct the checks.

Customs officials said that at the time they checked about 1 percent of the 450,000 cars exported each year.

Bill Thomas, R-Calif., said used-car dealers were concerned that the bill could be a burden for them because it would require them to check ID numbers on car parts before selling them.

"If it becomes excessively burdensome on the average person, I think we ought to put an end to it, but I think we

should go ahead with it for now," Gibbons said.

## FINAL ACTION

During the week of Oct. 5, Congress took opposite stands on crime measures, firmly rejecting handgun control while soundly passing the bill that addressed a new national crime fear — carjacking. The bill (HR 4542) sailed through both chambers by voice vote. *(Crime bill, p. 311)*

HR 4542 made carjacking a federal crime with a maximum penalty of life in prison when the theft resulted in death. The bill also required that major car parts be marked with ID numbers that would be registered in an FBI parts registry.

The final version included a compromise on labeling between Schumer, chairman of the Judiciary Subcommittee on Crime and Criminal Justice, and Energy and Commerce Chairman Dingell. The compromise phased in the labeling over five years, gradually increasing the number of vehicles for which marking was required. The bill allowed the attorney general to determine whether the marking program was effective and exempted from the system certain car lines with auto theft devices. ■

# Independent Counsel Law Expires

Congress failed to reauthorize the Watergate-era law establishing procedures for appointing an independent counsel to prosecute alleged wrongdoing by federal officials. The law expired Dec. 15, 1992.

Both the House and Senate bills attempted to reauthorize the law for five years.

Enacted 14 years earlier on the heels of the Watergate scandal, the law gave the U.S. attorney general the authority to request an independent counsel to investigate allegations of wrongdoing by high-ranking executive branch officials.

The independent counsel was appointed by a special three-judge panel and was independent of the Justice Department.

Both bills were clouded by the costly Iran-contra affair, as well as the House bank and Post Office scandals. Republicans felt singled out by the counsel, and Congress' own scandals left the bill without strong leadership backing. A key controversy centered on how Congress should be included under the law.

House and Senate panels approved legislation the week of Sept. 14 to extend the Independent Counsel Act, leaving supporters hoping that despite waning odds, the embattled law might be reauthorized.

But vociferous Republican objections to renewal of the law killed last-minute efforts to reauthorize the measure in the 102nd Congress.

Republicans, furious about Iran-contra, were especially angry about the 1992 indictment of former Defense Secretary Caspar W. Weinberger for allegedly withholding in-

**BOXSCORE**

➡ **Independent Counsel (S 3131, HR 5840).** Legislation to reauthorize the Independent Counsel Law for five years. The law gave the attorney general the authority to request an independent counsel to investigate allegations of wrongdoing by high-ranking executive branch officials.

**Report:** S Rept 102-417.

**KEY ACTION**

Sept. 16 — The **Senate** Governmental Affairs Committee approved S 3131.

Sept. 29 — **Senate** consideration of the bill was blocked.

formation from Congress.

## BACKGROUND

When Congress first passed the independent counsel law in 1978, the Watergate scandal was still fresh.

President Richard M. Nixon had tried to fire special prosecutor Archibald Cox, who had demanded secret Oval Office tapes. The attorney general and his assistant resigned rather than fire Cox. Finally, the third-ranking person at the Justice Department, Solicitor General Robert H. Bork, got rid of Cox.

That Oct. 20, 1973, episode, known as the "Saturday Night Massacre," made clear the conflict in an administration trying to control an investigation of itself. Five years later, the incident became a rallying cry, leading to legislation requiring appointment of an independent counsel to pursue wrongdoing by high-ranking executive branch officials. *(1978 Almanac, p. 835)*

In the wake of the Iran-contra scandal, President Ronald Reagan grudgingly signed a reauthorization law in 1987 following overwhelmingly favorable votes in both houses of Congress. The Iran-contra investigation, led by independent counsel Lawrence E. Walsh, looked into allegations that members of Reagan's administration diverted funds from the sale of weapons to Iran to support the contras in Nicaragua. It took six years and cost taxpayers an estimated $32 million. *(1987 Almanac, p. 363)*

At that time, the law was subject to a court challenge. The Reagan administration argued that the act unconstitu-

tionally denied the president important executive power because it allowed a special three-judge court to appoint the independent counsel and determine the scope of the investigation. The panel appointed the counsel at the request of the U.S. attorney general after he had found that "reasonable grounds" existed to believe that criminal activity had occurred.

But in 1988 the Supreme Court by a 7-1 vote upheld the law's constitutionality. Its ruling in *Morrison v. Olson* said that for certain kinds of criminal investigations involving potential conflicts of interest, Congress may set the rules for handling the inquiries without infringing on the president's constitutional authority to enforce the law. *(1988 Almanac, p. 123)*

By 1992, the independent counsel law had survived three presidents and relentless opposition from the Justice Department. It had led to 11 independent investigations, three of them resulting in standing convictions.

## SETTING THE STAGE

And yet, on the eve of the law's expiration on Dec. 15, 1992, the Independent Counsel Act appeared headed for extinction. Why? Its deadline came amid the longest and costliest independent counsel investigation ever — the Iran-contra affair — and in a year marked by allegations of congressional wrongdoing.

"The Democratic leadership's willingness to let this statute die is rooted in their problems with managing the scandal-ridden House," said Rep. George W. Gekas, R-Pa.

Democratic leaders denied Gekas' charge. But in 1992, scandal was indeed in the air again. And this time the focus was on Congress, particularly the House of Representatives.

Since October 1991, House members had been under investigation for routinely overdrawing their accounts at the since-closed House bank. In early 1992, a separate scandal at the House Post Office emerged.

Key Democrats had been implicated in a scheme in which members reportedly used expense vouchers or campaign checks to obtain cash in transactions disguised as stamp purchases. And individual House and Senate members also had been under investigation in 1992. *(House bank scandal, p. 23; House post office investigation, p. 47)*

The atmosphere made it difficult for the Democratic leadership to take a strong hand in reauthorizing the reform-era law. And although Congress arguably fell under the jurisdiction of the law as much as possible, House Democrats had been wary of the debate over how Congress should be included.

House leaders acknowledged that the political scandal might have been a factor early in 1992 in sidestepping the independent counsel controversy, but they denied any overt effort to hold up reauthorization legislation. Members in both chambers introduced bills (S 3131, HR 5840) in August.

Rep. Don Edwards, D-Calif., said the reauthorization legislation was "too important" to be delayed by politics. "I just think it would be terrible to allow it to die," said Edwards, a member of the House Judiciary subcommittee. "There is no other way that we can handle cases in which the administration is involved in criminal conduct."

The Democrats were mobilized in 1992 by Attorney General William P. Barr's refusal to appoint an independent counsel to investigate possible crimes surrounding U.S. assistance to Iraq before Iraq invaded Kuwait in Au-

gust 1990. The House Judiciary Committee had asked for the counsel. A special counsel reviewing possible administrative wrongdoing in $5.5 billion in bank loans to Iraq announced Dec. 9 that there was no need to appoint an independent counsel in the case. *(Iraq, p. 545)*

It was apparent early in the year that the odds were against passage of reauthorization legislation. Beyond Congress' own embarrassments were concerns raised by the six-year-old Iran-contra investigation by independent counsel Walsh.

It had cost about $32 million, according to Walsh, who announced Sept. 17 that he was closing the investigation. It had resulted in 10 convictions. But the most publicized convictions, those of former national security adviser John M. Poindexter and his deputy, Oliver L. North, had been overturned on appeal, largely for reasons having nothing to do with Walsh's prosecution. Walsh had been accused, mostly by the GOP, of recklessly using his prosecution power and unlimited budget.

The Bush administration opposed the reauthorization bills, as did many Republicans, who said the Justice Department had the career staff to handle such investigations. And the department, which had opposed the legislation since its 1978 inception, complained that independent counsels were neither held accountable nor subject to the department review required of other government prosecutors.

Republicans had been more inclined to oppose the law because it targeted executive branch wrongdoing, and Republicans had been in the White House for 12 of the 14 years of the counsel post's existence.

Still, groups off the Hill had been vigilant in pressing for reauthorization. "If we don't have a credible way of addressing the situation . . . in the highest levels of government," said Fred Wertheimer, president of the public interest group Common Cause, "you leave a huge gap in the system of justice."

## LEGISLATIVE ACTION

Although a House subcommittee and a Senate committee approved independent counsel bills in September, the legislation died later that month when Senate Minority Leader Bob Dole, R-Kan., blocked the Senate bill from coming to the floor.

House and Senate panels approved legislation the week of Sept. 14 to extend the 1978 Independent Counsel Act, leaving supporters in Congress hoping that despite waning odds, the embattled law might be reauthorized. It was set to expire in December.

Both the Senate Governmental Affairs Committee and the House Judiciary Subcommittee on Administrative Law and Governmental Relations approved their chamber's version of the bill by voice vote.

Members were working under a tight deadline: To pass the bill in both chambers, backers had to work out vast differences with Republicans in the few weeks before adjournment.

### Lawmakers Show Ambivalence

Bill proponents argued that an independent counsel law was needed because the executive branch could not be allowed to investigate itself. But the Justice Department argued that the law usurped its prosecutorial authority.

Many lawmakers, even those who overwhelmingly approved the measure twice before, were ambivalent in 1992.

William S. Cohen, R-Maine, one of the Senate's most steadfast defenders of the act, advised his colleagues not to be swayed by the Iran-contra investigation.

"The real issue . . . is the notion that somehow this has been directed toward Republicans," Cohen said, warning that Republicans should not be so quick to bury the act. "We may well rue the day that we presided over the final rites of this legislation should there be a Democratic president."

House and Senate proponents were trying to amend their bills to appease Republicans, but the issue of congressional coverage dogged both chambers.

The Senate Governmental Affairs Committee gave voice vote approval to the Senate version Sept. 16, despite concerns raised by ranking Republican William V. Roth Jr. of Delaware that the bill did not go far enough in applying the law to Congress.

Roth argued that neither existing law nor the Senate bill sponsored by Carl Levin, D-Mich., and Cohen adequately covered congressional wrongdoing.

Levin disagreed.

The Senate bill, which renewed the act for five years, would allow the attorney general to either seek appointment of an independent counsel to investigate members of Congress or prosecute members himself. "Our bill makes it clear that members of Congress are covered," Levin said.

In response to the cost of the Iran-contra investigation, the bill made independent counsels more accountable for expenses. The counsel would have to submit an annual report justifying expenses and comply with Justice Department spending policies.

On Sept. 17, the House Judiciary Subcommittee on Administrative Law and Governmental Relations also approved the bill by voice vote, adding several amendments aimed at pleasing Republicans and voters.

Subcommittee Chairman Barney Frank, D-Mass., successfully offered an amendment identical to the Senate's on accountability.

The House also followed the Senate's lead in amending the bill to limit the counsel's per diem rates and travel expenses for work done in Washington.

Steven H. Schiff, R-N.M., argued that the independent counsel operated without controls. "If we don't do something," Schiff said, "Congress will soon be considering the Independent Counsel Oversight Act."

### Final Blockage

Vociferous Republican objections to the renewal of the Independent Counsel law killed last-minute efforts to reauthorize the measure in the 102nd Congress.

Dole, noting that he had received a letter of opposition to the bill from 28 senators, blocked Senate consideration late Sept. 29 of legislation (S 3131) that would have reauthorized the law for five years.

Dole said there was not enough time before the planned adjournment in early October to debate such controversial legislation. "There comes a time when we have to decide we are going to stop legislating," he said.

Although bill sponsors said they had enough votes to overcome a Republican filibuster, Senate Democrats conceded that it could take two to six days to force a vote on the bill.

Levin said that Republicans were "killing the most important single Watergate reform on the books." ∎

---

# Legal Services Corporation Legislation Stalls

Once again, a number of controversial issues stood in the way of the passage of legislation to reauthorize the Legal Services Corporation (LSC).

The corporation, which provided legal services to the poor, had long been the subject of ideological wrangling. In 1992, battles centered on whether the program's lawyers could work on redistricting cases or be involved in abortion-related activities.

LSC was run by an 11-member board of directors. Clients were represented by local, nonprofit Legal Services programs funded primarily by the federal corporation in Washington.

Authorizing legislation was passed by the House in May. But a related bill never reached the Senate floor. President Bush had promised to veto the bill unless it contained provisions prohibiting LSC attorneys from taking abortion cases.

The Senate measure (S 2870) authorized the corporation for six years, one year longer than its companion in the House. In addition, both bills would have expanded restrictions on the cases LSC lawyers could have handled, including lobbying.

Existing law dictated that attorneys could lobby if they were not doing so with federal funds. Both bills would have incorporated this existing law and barred grass roots lobbying, addressing the concern of some members that program lawyers would help organize and push local efforts on political issues.

Other provisions of the bills would have:

● Prevented program lawyers from involvement in any local, state or federal redistricting cases.

● Prohibited representation of convicted drug dealers in public housing eviction cases.

● Restricted the use of funds for representation of undocumented aliens on matters not related to wages and other employment rights, housing or transportation. At the same time, the Senate bill expanded the categories of aliens who could be represented to include those in foster care and those with federal work authorization permits.

● Continued the ban on involvement in class action suits against local, state and federal governments.

## BACKGROUND

Members of Congress had long been at odds over the role of legal aid lawyers and what restrictions should be placed on those who provided assistance to the poor — often as adversaries of the federal government.

Democrats and legal services' advocates had long argued that the poor should receive the same range of legal assistance through the Legal Services Corporation that were available to those who could afford to hire counsel.

However, Republicans wanted LSC lawyers kept out of controversial political issues. They had argued that the corporation was not established to deal with such matters.

The Reagan administration opposed funding Legal Services, resulting in sizable cutbacks in fiscal 1982. It took

nine years for spending to again reach 1981 levels. However, in 1989 and the years that followed, Congress again solidly supported the program. *(1989 Almanac, p. 721)*

The Bush administration did not seek to abolish LSC or significantly cut its funding. But Bush did support more restrictions than those imposed by Congress

Over the years, Congress had sought to appease critics by adding more and more restrictions on the type of work open to LSC lawyers.

Because of almost yearly battles over the scope of these restrictions, Congress had not cleared an authorization bill since 1977. That measure (PL 93-222) expired in 1980. The House had last passed a reauthorization bill in 1981, but it died after the Senate did not take it up. *(1981 Almanac, p. 408)*

The task of funding and shaping the program had been left in the hands of appropriators, who kept the program afloat in the annual appropriations bill for the Departments of Commerce, State and Justice and the Judiciary. For fiscal 1993, the corporation received $357 million, up slightly from $350 million the year before. *(Appropriations, p. 646)*

Legislation to reauthorize the LSC advanced no further than the House Judiciary Committee in 1991. The committee on July 16 approved HR 2039 by a vote of 25-7. The measure offered a five-year reauthorization to the quasi-independent corporation. No funding limits were set. *(1991 Almanac, p. 295)*

## HOUSE ACTION

The measure (HR 2039) was brought to the House floor on two separate occasions in 1992 before finally being passed on May 12.

The sponsor of the House bill, Barney Frank, D-Mass., had introduced it largely at the request of Neal Smith, D-Iowa, chairman of the House Appropriations Subcommittee on Commerce, Justice, State and the Judiciary. Smith, whose subcommittee appropriated money for the LSC, pushed for House passage to give him added clout in the appropriations conference.

Smith had asked his colleagues to pass an authorization measure, even if there was little chance of final enactment. He claimed that the lack of an authorizing bill from the House had put him at an increasing disadvantage during negotiations with his counterparts in the Senate.

He pointed to the 1991 appropriation, which was $5 million less than the Bush administration recommendation but identical to the Senate recommendation. Smith claimed that the lack of an authorizing measure left him little leverage to ask for more funds. *(1991 Almanac, p. 542)*

First, HR 2039 came to the House floor briefly on April 2 but was postponed without a vote.

Then, on May 6, the chamber debated the measure and voted on a number of amendments without taking a final vote on the bill itself.

One of those amendments, offered by Bill McCollum, R-Fla., would have banned the use of any public or non-federal funds for a broad range of activities prohibited at the time for privately raised funds: lobbying, redistricting cases and cases involving abortion. It was rejected, 156-257. *(Vote 106, p. 26-H)*

Finally on May 12, the measure was considered and passed by a vote of 253-154. *(Vote 118, p. 30-H)*

During floor debate members adopted two amendments expanding program restrictions.

The first, offered by Charles W. Stenholm, D-Texas, and adopted on a 286-123 vote, would have barred program lawyers from working on any case involving federal or state redistricting or census-related activities. *(Vote 116, p. 28-H)*

Another amendment, offered by Lamar Smith, R-Texas, and adopted by voice vote, would have prevented LSC lawyers from representing undocumented aliens on matters not related to wages and other employment rights, housing or transportation. The ban would have applied to deportation proceedings stemming from criminal activity as well as to pending immigration cases.

And in a vote that surprised and pleased abortion-rights lobbyists, the House rejected, 188-216, an amendment by George W. Gekas, R-Pa., that would have prohibited Legal Services lawyers from getting involved with any case involving abortion, or any lobbying activity pertaining to abortion legislation. *(Vote 115, p. 28-H)*

Christopher H. Smith, R-N.J., a leading House opponent of abortion, argued that loopholes in existing law — and reinstated in the bill — allowed Legal Services lawyers to participate in some abortion cases, taking away funding needed to represent the poor on legal matters that affected them more often, such as landlord-tenant disputes.

But others claimed that Gekas' amendment was unfair to the poor because it would have limited access to legal representation that was available to anyone with enough money to pay for it.

"We all know that the rich will have access to lawyers," said John F. Reed, D-R.I.

Gekas tried to cast his amendment outside Congress' bitter abortion debate, saying it would make the program neutral on the issue because program lawyers would not be allowed to participate on either side of the question.

But that tactic might have cost him some traditional anti-abortion votes, too. "We picked up people who were supporters of Legal Services who normally don't vote with us," said a lobbyist for Planned Parenthood.

## SENATE ACTION

On July 1, the Labor and Human Resources Committee approved, by voice vote, a measure (S 2870) similar to HR 2039.

Approval came without debate, but some committee Republicans argued the bill did not go far enough in limiting the types of cases Legal Services attorneys might take. They also wanted stricter accountability standards for the program.

Labor Committee Chairman Edward M. Kennedy, D-Mass., said he hoped senators could work out their differences over program restrictions and find "common ground."

Kennedy co-sponsored the bill with Republican Warren B. Rudman of New Hampshire, ranking member of the Appropriations Subcommittee on Commerce, Justice, State and Judiciary. Rudman, who retired in 1992, was a long-time advocate of the program.

But the measure was never taken up in the Senate because of members' desire to avoid votes on controversial issues, namely abortion.

In addition, senators were not pressed by their colleagues on the Appropriations Committee — as were their counterparts in the House — to pass an authorization bill to increase their leverage as conferees. ∎

# Racial Justice at Issue in Carnes Hearings

In a decisive victory for President Bush, the Senate voted 62-36 on Sept. 9 to confirm Bush's nomination of Edward Earl Carnes Jr. to the 11th U.S. Circuit Court of Appeals, over strong objections from key Democrats and the nation's leading civil rights groups.

The vote brought to a close months of haggling over Carnes, an Alabama assistant attorney general who had headed that state's capital punishment litigation division since 1981. Carnes' supporters and opponents asked senators to choose between two views of the nominee: Some, including a handful of black politicians and lawyers and one prominent Alabama civil rights lawyer, said Carnes had fought for racial fairness. But civil rights groups said Carnes perpetuated racial discrimination in Alabama's criminal justice system.

Although Carnes' role as a national advocate for the death penalty was a deciding factor for a few senators, the vote was far from a referendum on the death penalty. For most senators the decision was instead a statement on crime and race in a tense election year in which no one could afford to appear soft on crime and candidates were steering clear of racial justice issues.

Most senators who voted against Carnes, primarily liberal Democrats, said they were concerned about his statements before the Senate Judiciary Committee on April 1 about race and capital punishment.

"I do not believe that capital punishment is applied in a racially discriminatory manner in Alabama or in the nation," Carnes had said.

Opponents argued that confirmation would send the wrong message to minorities in the wake of the verdict in the police beating of black motorist Rodney King and ensuing violence in Los Angeles in April. Edward M. Kennedy, D-Mass., contended that statistics, including a study by the General Accounting Office, backed up discrimination charges.

"Death penalty justice in America is separate and unequal," Kennedy said, ". . . and the Senate should not confirm a nominee who cannot see it."

Carnes was to replace Judge Frank M. Johnson, who retired in October 1991. Johnson was credited with furthering desegregation and racial justice in the South. The 11th Circuit continued to hear the majority of the nation's civil rights cases.

One Republican, Arlen Specter of Pennsylvania, voted against confirmation. Specter, who voted to confirm Carnes in a Judiciary Committee vote May 7, was locked in a tough Senate race against Democrat Lynn Yeakel. Philadelphia, where Specter had some black support, was important to him. In a July 31 letter to the senator, Yeakel expressed her opposition to Carnes and asked Specter to change his vote. Specter said his vote had nothing to do with politics or Yeakel: He opposed Carnes because of concerns about the nominee's record on racial discrimination. Specter defeated Yeakel in November.

## BOXSCORE

➡ **Nomination of Edward Earl Carnes Jr. to 11th U.S. Circuit Court of Appeals.** The controversial nomination was approved over objections from key Democrats and some leading civil rights groups. Other civil rights groups supported Carnes.

### KEY ACTION

Jan. 27 — President Bush nominated Alabama's assistant attorney general, Edward Earl Carnes Jr., to the 11th Circuit Court of Appeals.

April 1 — Hearing on the nomination before the **Senate** Judiciary Committee.

May 7 — The **Senate** Judiciary Committee approved nomination, 10-4.

Sept. 9 — The **Senate** voted 66-30 to cut off debate, then confirmed the nomination 62-36.

Vermont Sen. Patrick J. Leahy, a Democrat, also voted for Carnes in committee and against him in the full Senate. Leahy said he was concerned about how Carnes' role as a death penalty advocate might affect his decisions as a judge. "I was not able to convince myself that Carnes could be an impartial arbiter in death penalty cases," Leahy said.

Confirmation of Carnes and his tough anti-crime, pro-death penalty stance had appeared certain early on, but in the final four months, civil rights groups seemed to be gaining momentum with some senators, such as moderate Sam Nunn, D-Ga.

Charges from the civil rights community did cost Carnes some votes, but those criticisms were dulled by support from some blacks and a civil rights lawyer who said Carnes had fought racism in the courts. In the end, most moderates, including Nunn, voted for Carnes. Nunn said he favored Carnes' stance on the death penalty and had found no evidence of racism in his record.

"He's been very sensitive to racial justice issues, probably more so than most judges that have come through here," Nunn said.

As for the objections of civil rights supporters, Nunn said, "They're also against the death penalty, and I don't agree . . . a large part of the civil rights community is for him."

After the vote, Howell Heflin, D-Ala., Carnes' primary backer on the committee and in the Senate, said Carnes' history showed "that he had a record of fighting for civil rights and racial justice at a time when it was unpopular to mention the words."

## BACKGROUND

On Jan. 27, Bush nominated Carnes, 41, for a lifetime appointment to the 11th Circuit, which included Alabama, Florida and Georgia. Although he had never been a judge, Carnes, Alabama's assistant attorney general, had made a name for himself nationally as an advocate of the death penalty. He crafted Alabama's capital punishment law.

Carnes was also well-known to some members of the 102nd Congress. During the drafting of anti-crime legislation, he pushed to limit the number of times death row defendants could ask for federal review of their cases.

Carnes had headed Alabama's capital punishment division since 1981. He got mixed reviews from members of the civil rights community, some of whom contended that he was insensitive to racial discrimination in the criminal justice system. Yet others said Carnes was void of racial prejudice and had fought against racial discrimination.

The Carnes nomination came in the wake of a fight over Kenneth L. Ryskamp, the Miami trial judge whose nomination failed in committee in 1991. Ryskamp, also nomi-

nated to the 11th Circuit, had been criticized for controversial statements from the bench and insensitivity to civil rights issues. *(1991 Almananc, p. 289)*

The NAACP was Carnes' primary opponent in the civil rights community.

"He has been a part of a system that has excluded blacks from the jury," said Edward A Hailes Jr., a lobbyist with the NAACP's Washington office. Hailes said Carnes' defense of Alabama's capital punishment system was inappropriate because it executed blacks convicted of killing whites in disproportionate numbers.

Carnes also had lobbied against federal "racial justice" legislation that would have let a prisoner challenge his death sentence based on statistics showing that the sentences were meted out disproportionately to people of his race.

Although the NAACP opposed him, Carnes received support from Morris S. Dees Jr., a prominent civil rights attorney and executive director of the Southern Poverty Law Center, a nonprofit organization specializing in class action suits and discrimination cases. Dees' support convinced some senators that Carnes could be fair on civil rights issues.

## CONFIRMATION HEARING

Sen. Heflin chaired the April 1 committee confirmation hearing on Carnes. No Democrats cross-examined Carnes, and Howard M. Metzenbaum, D-Ohio, did not attend because of a conflict with another hearing.

However, a spokesman for Chairman Joseph R. Biden, D-Del., said the process was one of the lengthiest ever given to a circuit court nominee, second in duration only to the confirmation procedure the previous year for Ryskamp.

Although Biden did not attend Carnes' hearing, he read the testimony and was briefed on the proceeding.

In his testimony, civil rights lawyer Dees said that while he did not support the death penalty, he believed Carnes was fair and void of racial prejudice.

"He goes to an integrated church," Dees said. "He has never belonged to a country club." (Membership in a country club with a history of discrimination against blacks and Jews contributed to Ryskamp's defeat.)

The Leadership Conference on Civil Rights, which lobbied on behalf of about 180 civil rights organizations, stopped short of opposing Carnes' nomination but asked the committee to take a closer look at his record. "We feel very strongly that there should not be a rush to judgment," said Ralph G. Neas, executive director of the conference.

"I do not believe that capital punishment is applied in a racially discriminatory manner in Alabama or in the nation," Carnes told the committee. "If I thought that, I would not support it, much less have spent the time I have spent working in the area."

Carnes said, however, that he was troubled that the numbers of minorities jailed for homicides, put on death row and executed were higher than those for whites. He related those figures to "economic disparity and hardship and also the deterioration of the family unit."

## COMMITTEE VOTE

With the Rodney King verdict on their minds, the Senate Judiciary Committee on May 7 voted 10-4 to recommend Senate confirmation of Carnes to the 11th Circuit Court of Appeals.

As the Judiciary Committee prepared to vote May 7, members had wondered whether they should view Carnes as some civil rights groups did — a "prince of death" who overzealously supported capital punishment — or consider him a tough-on-crime nominee needed on the bench.

President Bush harshly criticized the committee for moving too slowly on the nomination, while Metzenbaum and some civil rights leaders complained that Carnes' nomination had been rushed through the process.

Metzenbaum, who sat on the committee, had placed a "hold" on the nomination April 8. He believed the committee expedited Carnes' nomination ahead of other circuit court nominees selected before him. He wanted members to scrutinize Carnes more thoroughly before voting.

The NAACP complained that committee Chairman Biden rushed Carnes through the committee without adequately considering his record on racial discrimination or his lack of judicial experience. But because Carnes had gotten mixed reviews from a civil rights community usually united on such matters, senators who might ordinarily have come down heavily on the side of civil rights had remained silent. It was the Democratic allies of civil rights groups who were largely absent from the process.

Carnes' opponents were particularly critical of his lack of judicial experience and his stated view that death sentences were never based on race.

"Last week's events in Los Angeles underscore the importance of ensuring the public confidence in fairness and impartiality of the criminal justice system," said Metzenbaum, one of four Democrats who voted against Carnes.

The acquittal of officers charged in the beating of black motorist Rodney King had sparked riots in Los Angeles at the end of April. *(Urban crisis, p. 339)*

Committee Chairman Biden also voted against Carnes, saying the choice represented "the closest decision on how to vote on a nominee that I've had." However, Biden said, "I can think of no worse time for a nominee with [this] record ... than in the aftermath of what I believe is a tragedy that occurred in part because of the nature of the jury selection process in Los Angeles."

Edward M. Kennedy of Massachusetts and Paul Simon of Illinois were the other "nay" votes.

### Heflin's Support

But most senators voted with Heflin, Carnes' main supporter on the committee. Heflin was the only Democrat who spoke in support of Carnes and said that when he looked into Carnes' background, he was "surprised to learn of his strong support from the civil rights community in Alabama."

The split among Democrats reflected divisions in the civil rights community as well. Hailes, a lobbyist for the NAACP's Washington office, said Carnes was insensitive to racial discrimination in the courts and had upheld the practice in many instances. Hailes said that to the NAACP the vote represented Congress' first test after the King verdict on the issue of racial justice in the courts. "It's a real slap in the face to African Americans," he said.

But that view was countered by the testimony of Dees, a prominent civil rights lawyer. Dees, well-known for his many cases against members of the Ku Klux Klan, said Carnes was not racially prejudiced and had often publicly fought discrimination.

Although Kennedy and Metzenbaum said they respected Dees, Carnes' record on capital punishment and his refusal to agree with them that racial discrimination existed in the courts outweighed his testimony.

## Opposition Mobilizes

Before the committee vote, no member of the House or Senate openly opposed Carnes. Although the NAACP had lobbied against him, there was no concerted campaign among civil rights groups or even a news conference after Bush announced the nomination in January. The nomination received scant mention in the national media.

Moreover, opposition that did emerge focused mainly on Carnes' strong, open advocacy of the death penalty. He wrote Alabama's death penalty statute, one of the nation's toughest. He also lobbied Congress on the issue.

But no senator would oppose Carnes solely on the capital punishment issue. Judiciary Committee Chairman Biden, one of the four who voted against Carnes, took pains after the vote to show that his opposition stemmed from other concerns. Biden supported capital punishment.

Meanwhile, support for Carnes had been formidable. Heflin, a senior member of the Senate Judiciary Committee and a former chief justice of the Alabama Supreme Court, dismissed opposition as largely based on Carnes' advocacy of the death penalty.

But after the May 7 vote, civil rights groups including the NAACP, the Southern Christian Leadership Conference and the Congressional Black Caucus suddenly stepped up efforts against Carnes, maintaining that he had helped to perpetuate racism in the jury selection process.

On May 14, the Congressional Black Caucus joined with the NAACP, the Alliance for Justice, the National Bar Association (made up of black attorneys) and the Leadership Conference on Civil Rights in a news conference denouncing the Judiciary Committee's vote.

On May 20, civil rights leaders including Coretta Scott King and Joseph E. Lowery, president of the Southern Christian Leadership Conference, sent a letter to senators asking that they consider Carnes' record on civil rights issues before voting.

And on June 11, Rep. John Lewis, D-Ga., a prominent activist in the 1960s, met with Senate Majority Leader George J. Mitchell, D-Maine, to ask him to put off the confirmation vote. Lewis was joined by John Conyers Jr., D-Mich., of the black caucus and Wade Henderson, director of the NAACP's Washington bureau.

In a tense meeting July 29 with Mitchell, black caucus members said the expected confirmation of Carnes could hurt Democratic presidential candidate Bill Clinton's standing with black voters.

"We are deeply concerned that your decision to bring the Carnes nomination before the full Senate will make it difficult for the Congressional Black Caucus to mobilize the black vote, especially in the South," Conyers and Ronald V. Dellums, D-Calif., said in a July 27 letter to Mitchell.

Also, Sens. Kennedy, Metzenbaum, Bill Bradley, D-N.J.; Alan Cranston, D-Calif.; Tim Wirth, D-Colo.; and Frank R. Lautenberg, D-N.J., sent a letter to colleagues June 24 urging them to vote against Carnes.

Carl Levin, D-Mich., also said he opposed Carnes because of his testimony before the Judiciary Committee that racism did not exist in the criminal justice system. "Race is a real issue in America, and we have to be sensitive on the issue of race," he said.

But the belated push put Senate Democrats on the spot. Only four of the eight Judiciary Committee Democrats had voted against the nomination. In addition, Dees had testified before the Judiciary Committee on April 1 in support of Carnes, convincing some senators that the civil rights community was not in accord on the nominee.

Dees, who headed the Southern Poverty Law Center in Montgomery, Ala., opposed the death penalty but praised Carnes for his fairness and lack of racial bias. In fact, said Dees, Carnes worked to secure sanctions against judges who he believed were racially biased.

Civil rights lobbyists then said senators missed the point. It was not Carnes' advocacy of the death penalty that warranted opposition, they said, but indications that he had defended death sentences imposed on blacks by all-white juries even when prosecutors intentionally excluded black jurors.

A handful of senators delayed full floor action on the nomination while the civil rights groups tried to generate more public opposition.

Hailes said the groups hoped a June 12 letter from Biden to senators explaining why he voted against Carnes would help their cause. Biden said he was concerned about Carnes' "failure to see, or at least to acknowledge, the fundamental unfairness of race-based jury selection. . . ."

Mixed signals from the civil rights community generally made it difficult for Senate Democrats to oppose a presidential nomination. In Carnes' case, one of the most active civil rights lobbying groups, the Leadership Conference on Civil Rights, was conspicuously noncommittal during the hearing process. As an umbrella group that lobbied on behalf of 180 organizatons, the conference had been in the forefront of debates on civil rights issues in Congress.

Ralph G. Neas, executive director of the conference, said that the conference's stance on Carnes was not unusual because the group rarely took a position on judicial nominations.

## VOTE DELAY

The Senate on Aug. 7 effectively put off until September a vote on the Carnes nomination.

The move came after a plea to Majority Leader Mitchell from the Congressional Black Caucus to delay the vote until after the presidential election. A cloture vote to shut off an expected filibuster was scheduled for the week of Sept. 7.

The temporary delay came Aug. 7 when the Senate voted 91-0 for a motion by Carnes' supporters to bring the nomination to the floor. The vote put into effect an earlier agreement among Senate leaders to schedule the actual confirmation vote for a later date to avoid bogging down other Senate action.

Judiciary Committee Chairman Biden said the deal was likely to clear as many as 18 stalled judicial nominations and allow senators "ample" time to review Carnes' record.

Although some senators questioned Carnes' lack of judicial experience and his sensitivity to racial discrimination in the criminal justice system, a majority voted with their colleague, Heflin, who said Carnes had strong support in Alabama's civil rights community. Carnes had called for sanctions against Alabama judges whose behavior he considered racist.

But most civil rights groups, including the NAACP and the Leadership Conference on Civil Rights, opposed Carnes. And senators including Biden said they voted against Carnes partly because the nominee said he believed the criminal justice system was free of discrimination.

On the floor Aug. 7, Heflin defended Carnes and said his critics were driven mainly by their opposition to the death penalty. Carnes headed Alabama's capital litigation division, and in that role he wrote Alabama's death penalty law — one of the nation's toughest.

## FINAL ACTION

In a victory for the president, the Senate voted 62-36 on Sept. 9 to confirm Carnes to the 11th U.S. Circuit Court of

## Senate Confirms Terwilliger
## As Deputy Attorney General

Voting late the night of April 9, the Senate summarily confirmed George J. Terwilliger III for deputy attorney general despite a sexual harassment allegation.

In this instance, the Senate Judiciary Committee drew on painful lessons learned during the wrenching confirmation process for Supreme Court nominee Clarence Thomas in October 1991. *(1991 Almanac, p. 274)*

Before voting to send the nomination of Terwilliger to the floor, Chairman Joseph R. Biden Jr., D-Del., and the all-male committee were careful to give a full hearing to suggestions of harassment from a woman formerly employed by Terwilliger.

After President Bush nominated Terwilliger, former U.S. attorney in Vermont, an FBI investigation uncovered a conflict between him and Sandra Strempel, a former deputy, in which Terwilliger allegedly made offensive comments to Strempel at a staff meeting.

Strempel and others said that when she arrived at the meeting and announced she had some information to share, Terwilliger jokingly asked if she were pregnant.

Later in private practice, Strempel was contacted by the FBI and subsequently phoned by Biden. She agreed to testify at confirmation hearings April 2.

At the hearing, Biden carefully explained the process that had brought Strempel before the committee. Had she not decided to testify, he said, "I would have subpoenaed you," a veiled reference to the fact that Thomas' accuser, Anita F. Hill, had been an unwilling witness who was finally asked to testify after leaks to the press.

None of the committee's Republicans, meanwhile, showed up to question Strempel.

Both Democrats and Republicans were highly criticized in 1991 for being insensitive to women for their handling of the Thomas nomination. Before the harassment complaint was made public, many senators knew that it was being investigated yet still voted to send Thomas' name to the floor with a favorable recommendation.

That put Biden on the defensive, yet on April 7 the chairman insisted that the committee handled the Terwilliger nomination no differently than the procedure for Thomas. Besides, he said, the situations were "significantly different," because Strempel had agreed to testify.

However, South Carolina's Strom Thurmond, the committee's ranking Republican, was not so sure. The Thomas-Hill experience, he said, "probably had something to do with it."

Terwilliger, questioned by Biden on April 2, said he did not remember the exchange in question, but added: "If I said this, I failed as a manager."

The committee ultimately approved the nomination, voting 12-1 late in the afternoon of April 9. Paul Simon, D-Ill., cast the lone "no" vote. Biden said that he was concerned about the claims against Terwilliger, but he believed the nominee had "matured."

Appeals, over strong objections from key Democrats and the nation's leading civil rights groups.

The vote brought months of haggling to a close. *(Vote 193, p. 26-S)*

And despite the list of senators who spoke against the nominee, the cloture vote to end debate and proceed to the vote was 66-30, six more than needed. *(Vote 192, p. 25-S)*

In confirming Carnes, the Senate provided a needed political feather for Bush, who was pushing his election year agenda and filling more federal court vacancies with conservative judges. The appointment left 18 vacancies in the federal appeals courts.

The confirmation was also a big win for Heflin, who, as a powerful senior senator and a former chief justice of the Alabama Supreme Court, was able to secure the votes for a Republican.

The vote was a defeat for Democratic leaders, including Mitchell and Biden, who both voted against the nominee. However, the greatest blow was to the battered civil rights community, which was handed a defeat that called into question the groups' clout with Congress. The groups said they were not only dismayed that a Democratic Senate confirmed Carnes but also concerned that the Senate might no longer view them as the voice of black Americans on civil rights issues.

Carnes was confirmed over the objections of old guard civil rights leaders including Benjamin Hooks, executive director of the NAACP and Coretta Scott King, widow of Martin Luther King Jr. The Congressional Black Caucus also lobbied against Carnes.

Some Carnes supporters, including Alan K. Simpson, D-Wyo., said civil rights groups waited too long — until after the Judiciary Committee had voted — to begin a major campaign against Carnes. But civil rights leaders said senators ignored their objections.

NAACP officials said they attempted during the August recess to apply political pressure in the 11th Circuit, made up of Alabama, Georgia and Florida. But only one senator from the region, Wyche Fowler Jr., D-Ga., voted against Carnes.

The groups were thwarted primarily by the support of civil rights lawyer Morris Dees and by black politicians and lawyers who sent letters to senators supporting Carnes.

The vote was not an easy call for some senators, because they received conflicting information about the nominee.

Carnes, for example, did not carry the political baggage of some previous conservative nominees. He never belonged to an all-white country club; he attended an integrated church.

Carnes sought sanctions against judges whose statements or actions he found to be racially insensitive and discriminatory. He also had openly opposed racial discrimination in jury selection.

"I do not contend that Mr. Carnes is a racist," Biden said.

Carnes' opponents said they objected to the way Carnes had handled appeals in cases in which lawyers had obtained convictions after improperly striking blacks from juries.

Supporters argued that Carnes had not participated in those jury strikes, and had ordered those who worked for him not to do so.

"My position was not to judge whether or not that was good practice," Carnes had testified. "My position in the lawsuit was to advocate the position of the state of Alabama."

Although Carnes said he did not condone the practice, Biden argued, his toleration of it should have kept him off the federal bench.

∎

# Democrats Ready To Mold Federal Bench

Judges did not get the campaign airtime accorded the budget deficit, health care or even marijuana, but the election of Bill Clinton to the presidency was expected to be a watershed in the evolution of the federal judiciary. Clinton gained control of the judicial appointment process at a time of near-record vacancies, giving him the opportunity to counter a 12-year effort by Republicans to fashion the federal bench to their liking.

During his four-year presidency, George Bush kept faith with the politics of his predecessor, Ronald Reagan, and appointed conservative jurists.

Bush also made an effort to appoint more female judges, finishing with a record level of female appointees to the federal district courts. But he named a smaller percentage of blacks and Hispanics than did President Jimmy Carter.

Had Bush been re-elected, he would have had the chance to appoint more than 100 additional judges.

Instead, Clinton was to fill those slots and create a significant judicial legacy — potentially naming 250 judges, or close to one-third of the federal bench, in his four-year term. Clinton was also likely to face one or two Supreme Court openings, giving Democrats their first chance to name a justice since Lyndon B. Johnson chose Thurgood Marshall in 1967.

Clinton was expected to stress diversity more heavily in his selections, boosting the percentage of women and minorities on the bench.

And there would be more opportunities for judges whose views departed from the "strict constructionist" conservative mold, particularly on the issue of abortion rights.

Clinton touched on both points in response to an American Bar Association questionnaire in the fall of 1992.

"I believe that public confidence in our federal judiciary is furthered by the presence of more women lawyers and minority lawyers on the bench, and the judicial system and the country benefit from having judges who are excellent lawyers with diverse perspectives," he wrote.

Clinton, a lawyer, said he would look for people with a demonstrated commitment to individual rights, including the right to privacy — the controversial legal principle that had been used to assert women's constitutional right to abortion.

That was expected to prompt some role-switching among liberal and conservative interest groups.

Liberal groups that fought such Bush nominees as Supreme Court Justice Clarence Thomas looked ahead with anticipation rather than dread for the first time since the Carter administration.

Meanwhile, conservatives braced for a watchdog role, forming a new group to monitor Clinton's nominations and lobby for candidates with conservative views.

## Bush Legacy

During his term, Bush appointed 185 district and circuit court judges, close to one-fourth of the federal bench. The number of judgeships had grown to 825 in regular district and appeals courts.

Conservatives were happy with his choices. Mark Bredemeier, general counsel for the conservative Landmark Legal Foundation, said Reagan began a deliberate and successful campaign to stock the bench with adherents of "judicial self-restraint."

"If there's one thing from a conservative standpoint that George Bush did do a good job of, it was continuing that same course in the judiciary," Bredemeier said. *(Supreme court review, p. 326)*

Like Reagan, Bush said he wanted judicial conservatives who would not "legislate from the bench." That translated into judges with a comparatively restrictive view of individual rights. These conservative or constructionist judges believed in a relatively narrow reading of the Constitution and federal law, asserting that it is the role of legislators, not the courts, to establish new individual rights and broad social remedies. In certain contexts, their perspective tended to favor the rights of government over those of the individual.

By contrast, "liberal" judges were inclined to construe constitutional and other legal texts more broadly — finding protections for criminal defendants and women seeking abortions, for example, that were not explicit in the Constitution.

Many of Bush's selections for the circuit, or appeals, courts were in fact promotions for Reagan appointees to district courts.

For the district courts, Bush often turned to nominees with experience as state judges or federal magistrates.

Sheldon Goldman, a political science professor at the University of Massachusetts at Amherst who specialized in analyzing judicial appointments, said such promotions bolstered the professionalism of the federal judiciary.

Several Democrats said the overall quality of Bush's appointments was higher than Reagan's. But others offered strong criticisms.

George Kassouf, director of a project at the liberal Alliance for Justice to monitor and lobby on judicial nominees, said the caliber of Bush's appointees was erratic — some were distinguished and others had marginal credentials.

And Kassouf was highly critical of Bush's record on reaching out to women and minorities.

Joseph R. Biden Jr., D-Del., chairman of the Senate Judiciary Committee, also faulted Bush's choices on ideology and demographics: "There wasn't any diversity of any consequence."

Goldman disagreed, at least on women.

Bush selected 36 female judges during his term, 19.5 percent of all his appointments. That included 29 female appointees to the district bench, a record 19.6 percent. Bush also appointed seven women — or 18.9 percent of his choices — to federal appeals courts.

Carter, who appointed more judges than did Bush, named a greater number of women — but a smaller percentage.

But Kassouf said Bush should have appointed more women than Carter because Bush encountered a larger pool of qualified female candidates.

And Bush's record for minority appointments dropped well below Carter's, although it was somewhat higher than that of the Reagan administration.

Bush appointed 12 black judges to the district and appeals courts, including Thomas, who was later elevated to the Supreme Court. Bush named eight Hispanic judges,

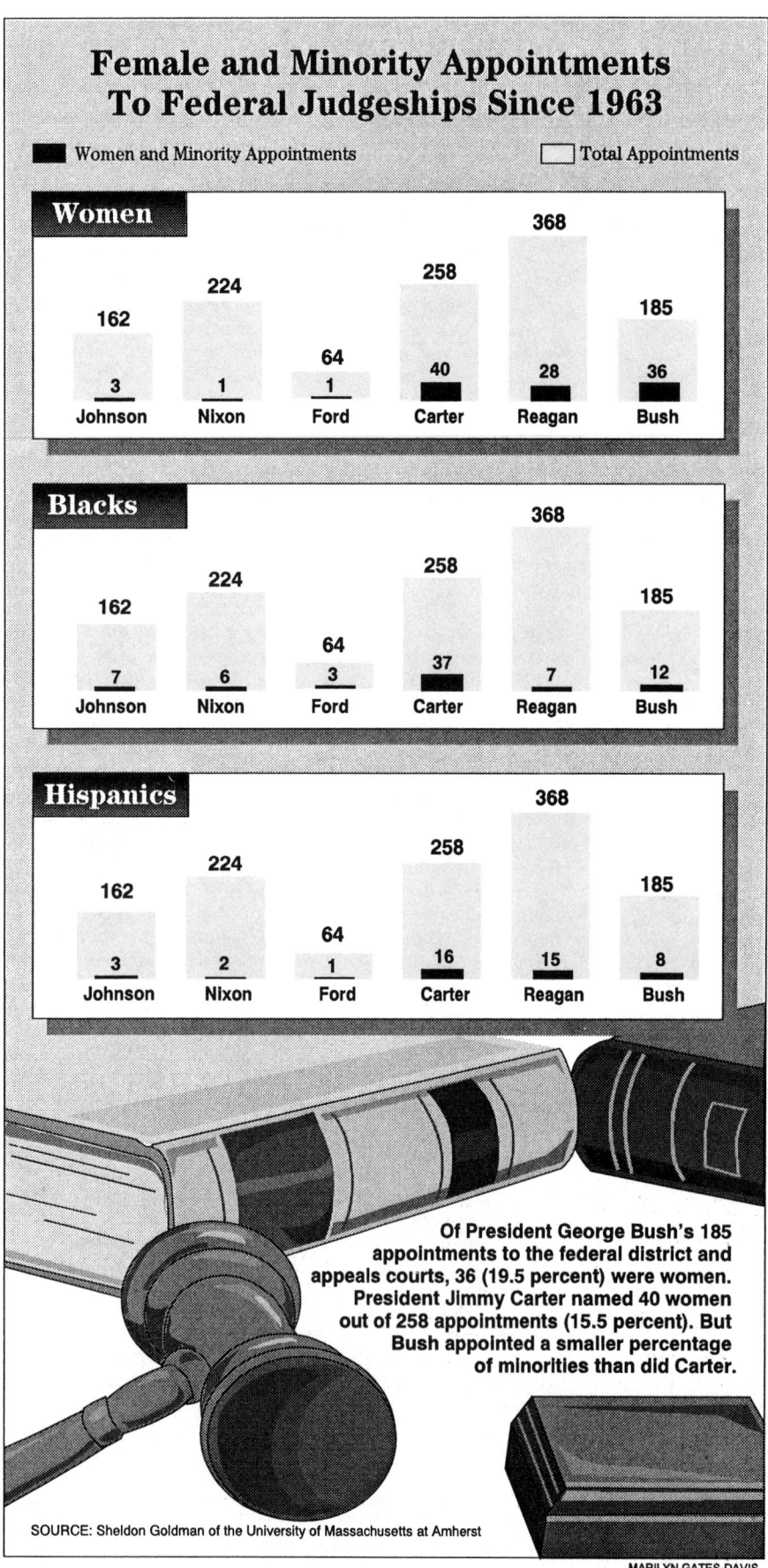

## Female and Minority Appointments To Federal Judgeships Since 1963

■ Women and Minority Appointments    ☐ Total Appointments

### Women

| | Johnson | Nixon | Ford | Carter | Reagan | Bush |
|---|---|---|---|---|---|---|
| Total | 162 | 224 | 64 | 258 | 368 | 185 |
| Appointments | 3 | 1 | 1 | 40 | 28 | 36 |

### Blacks

| | Johnson | Nixon | Ford | Carter | Reagan | Bush |
|---|---|---|---|---|---|---|
| Total | 162 | 224 | 64 | 258 | 368 | 185 |
| Appointments | 7 | 6 | 3 | 37 | 7 | 12 |

### Hispanics

| | Johnson | Nixon | Ford | Carter | Reagan | Bush |
|---|---|---|---|---|---|---|
| Total | 162 | 224 | 64 | 258 | 368 | 185 |
| Appointments | 3 | 2 | 1 | 16 | 15 | 8 |

Of President George Bush's 185 appointments to the federal district and appeals courts, 36 (19.5 percent) were women. President Jimmy Carter named 40 women out of 258 appointments (15.5 percent). But Bush appointed a smaller percentage of minorities than did Carter.

SOURCE: Sheldon Goldman of the University of Massachusetts at Amherst

MARILYN GATES-DAVIS

six to district courts and two to circuit courts. By contrast, Carter appointed 37 black judges and 16 Hispanics.

Several observers said Bush officials may have had a hard time finding women and minorities who shared the conservative judicial philosophy or political affiliations Bush sought to promote.

"We have to keep in mind that the Bush administration was not actively seeking liberal Democrats," said Goldman. To the extent that women and minorities were overrepresented among Democratic ranks, he said, they were underrepresented in Bush judicial appointments.

Republican senators also bore some responsibility for the percentage of female and minority appointments. It had been customary for senators of the president's party to suggest names for federal district court openings in their states.

But Kassouf said those senators generally offered the names of white men.

In November 1990, Bush wrote to Senate Minority Leader Bob Dole, R-Kan., urging GOP senators to suggest more women and minorities.

Momentum subsequently quickened, with the bulk of such appointments coming in the second half of Bush's term.

As time went on, Goldman said, Bush was more willing to soften his ideological criteria and reach out to some political moderates and Democrats to place more women on the bench.

Kassouf and others also speculated that political considerations may have pressured Bush and Republican senators to approve more female judges before the 1992 election.

### Room at the Top

As striking as the nature of Bush's appointees was the number of appointments he could have made, but did not.

Bush got off to a slow start on nominations and never caught up, especially after a 1990 law added 85 seats to the bench.

Appointments slowed further amid Thomas' tumultuous Supreme Court confirmation hearings and while the administration and the Senate Judiciary Committee squabbled in late 1991 over how to control access to FBI background checks on nominees.

At the close of the 102nd Congress, Bush officials had failed to nominate candidates for 46 judicial vacancies.

And the Judiciary Committee had failed to vote on another 53 pending nominations — effectively canceling those selections.

Those 99 vacancies had strained the court system, particularly in regions with many openings.

Democrats and Republicans alike criticized the administration's slowness in naming nominees and pushing them through the confirmation process. Several said White House and Justice Department officials had overly rigid screening criteria.

"There was a saliva test of purity that was rather unattractive," said Alan K. Simpson, R-Wyo., a senior member of the Judiciary Committee. "While they were waiting for the 100 percenter to show up, they lost the 90 percenter."

Some Republicans had quietly urged the White House to move faster. But they said the administration did not seem to see the pending election as a pressing deadline.

"I guess no one really expects to lose," said one Republican committee staff aide.

Orrin G. Hatch, R-Utah, ranking member of the Judiciary Committee, said Bush made "a big mistake" in leaving so many spots unfilled. "I think Democrats plan to take full advantage of all the vacancies — unlike the Republicans."

However, Hatch also faulted some Senate Democrats. He said Biden was sincere about trying to process candidates, but other Democrats sought to stall nominations in the hopes of saving the spots for a Democratic president.

Bush also criticized the Senate pace. "Unfortunately the Senate has failed to match previous efforts to fill vacancies following enactment of a judgeship bill and also has failed to match previous efforts in confirming judges in a presidential election year," Bush wrote in late August in response to the bar association questionnaire.

But Biden's staff aides noted that the committee approved a robust 124 nominations during the 102nd Congress, 66 of those in 1992 — more than were approved in recent presidential election years.

Biden conceded that election-year politics may have contributed to blocking some particularly controversial nominees in favor of candidates who could generate broader backing. But he said the committee could not have processed more.

As a result, Clinton inherited those 99 vacancies — the highest end-of-the-year tally in the 14 years for which such records were available. And that was before attrition began to free additional seats during the transition. By Feb. 1, the number of district and appeals court vacancies had grown to 113.

Goldman estimated that in four years Clinton might appoint one-third of the federal judiciary — more than 250 judges.

Clinton had said he wanted to appoint more women and minorities, and because Clinton was open to more liberal judicial philosophies than was Bush, he was expected to have a large supply of acceptable female and minority candidates from which to draw.

Arkansas state judges were elected rather than appointed, but as governor, Clinton had the power to fill several dozen unexpected judicial vacancies. Clinton often turned to women and blacks for those temporary openings, although he also rewarded some political allies.

Clinton also pledged to select judicial nominees with a strong regard for individual rights, who would promote equal opportunity and safeguard access to abortion.

However, Bredemeier said it was premature to assume that Clinton would choose strong liberal or activist judges. He noted that Clinton's Cabinet included both liberals and moderates.

Clinton and the Senate Judiciary Committee would be challenged to find an efficient way to fill the many vacancies.

Biden said he had urged Clinton to streamline the handling of nominations, with one official shepherding nominees through confirmation proceedings.

Under Bush, Biden said, it was unclear who in the White House or Justice Department was in charge. "Nobody really knew who had the keys to the gate," he said.

Regardless of Clinton's pace, however, observers noted that Reagan and Bush judges would be heavily represented on the bench at least through the first decade of the 21st century.

## Role Reversal

The new political dynamic made for some attitude adjustments in the Senate and among interest groups that tracked appointments.

Senate Democrats had been stockpiling names of people they wanted to see become federal judges and at last had a chance to advance their candidates.

Meanwhile, Hatch and other Republicans were expected to look closely at nominees who were no longer presifted through a conservative sieve.

Yet when nominees had strong senatorial backing, senators were sometimes loath to fight a colleague's choice.

During Bush's term, the Democrat-led Judiciary Committee openly fought only a handful of nominees.

Of the 66 judges confirmed in 1992, for example, only Edward Earl Carnes Jr. triggered a serious battle. Some civil rights groups accused Carnes, an Alabama assistant attorney general, of racial insensitivity. He was confirmed 62-36 after heated debate in committee and on the Senate floor. *(Judicial nominations, p. 319)*

As members of the minority party, Senate Republicans were put in an even weaker position to fight nominations. Hatch said Clinton and the Democrats generally had a right to their nominees, as long as they were qualified: "They won the election."

He said most openings were for district courts, where judges were more constrained by precedent than at the appeals level, and where political ideology played a lesser role.

Whatever posture Republican lawmakers adopted, Clinton was expected to proceed under critical scrutiny.

In the fall of 1992, the conservative Free Congress Foundation started a Judicial Selection Monitoring Project to build a grass-roots network to spread information on judicial appointments and to lobby for conservative nominees. Robert H. Bork, the conservative former judge who lost a bruising Supreme Court confirmation battle in 1987, was on the project's advisory board and wrote the initial fund-raising letter.

Marianne E. Lombardi, deputy director for the foundation's center for law and democracy, said conservatives feared that liberal activists would dominate the selection process and prod Clinton to fill the courts with activist judges.

Lombardi noted that liberals had insisted that Bush apply no litmus test — such as opposition to abortion — to his judicial nominees.

"We're going to hold them to their own standards," Lombardi said. ∎

# Centrist Base Emerges on Court

A Supreme Court dominated by Reagan-Bush appointees surprised nearly everyone during its 1991-92 term by reaffirming the core holdings of a more liberal era on church-state questions and on the emotional issue of abortion.

Indeed, the court charted a surprisingly moderate course in a number of areas, displaying an unexpected respect for precedent and a concern for institutional credibility.

The justices had been expected to dismantle old rules for strict separation of religion and government and to scrap the 1973 *Roe v. Wade* decision giving women a right to abortion. By 5-4 votes, they did neither.

The key development of the term was the emergence of a centrist trio on the court: Justices Sandra Day O'Connor, Anthony M. Kennedy and David H. Souter. O'Connor and Kennedy were Ronald Reagan appointees; Souter was named to the court by George Bush.

An analysis by *The New York Times* found that when the three voted together, they were never on the losing side. Kennedy and Souter were seldom on the losing side, period. Each dissented in only eight of the 107 cases decided with a full opinion. Souter, especially, proved to be a swing vote: He was with the majority in 13 of the 14 cases decided by a 5-4 vote.

The three centrists joined liberals Harry A. Blackmun and John Paul Stevens to preserve existing standards for separation of church and state and to protect what O'Connor described as the "essential holding" of *Roe*: that up to the point of fetal viability, a woman has a right to end her pregnancy through abortion "without undue interference from the state."

Aligned against them were Chief Justice William H. Rehnquist and Justices Byron R. White, Antonin Scalia and Clarence Thomas.

The election Nov. 3 of Democrat Bill Clinton as the 42nd president appeared to signal that a decade-long shift to the right on the high court was drawing to a close. At least on the abortion question, it was apparent that the anti-*Roe* tide had turned. *(Abortion, p. 387)*

Overall, the court proved itself reluctant to embark on new voyages in constitutional law. O'Connor and Kennedy, in particular, showed a preference for caution and a penchant for picking carefully through the complexities of a case.

## School Prayer

The court's school prayer decision was a defeat for President Bush, whose Justice Department had urged the court to use the case to throw out past rulings and give religion a larger role in public life.

The court instead reaffirmed longstanding precedents June 24 when it ruled, 5-4, that official prayer at a public-school graduation violated the constitutional separation of church and state.

Bush said he was disappointed in the decision. "The court has unnecessarily cast away the venerable and proper American tradition of non-sectarian prayer at public celebrations," Bush said.

The case, *Lee v. Weisman*, was brought by a Rhode Island man who objected to the invocation and benediction delivered by a rabbi at his daughter's middle-school graduation ceremony.

Writing for the majority, Kennedy agreed that the prayers were unconstitutional because "the state, in a school setting, in effect required participation in a religious exercise."

Kennedy took note of the fact that the court, in other rulings, had allowed prayer at the beginning of sessions of Congress and state legislatures. But he said that was an entirely different matter.

"The atmosphere at the opening of a session of a state legislature where adults are free to enter and leave with little comment and for any number of reasons cannot compare with the constraining potential of the one school event most important for the student to attend," Kennedy wrote.

The Justice Department had urged the court to discard a 1971 precedent that set a three-part test for determining whether a government action amounts to the establishment of religion.

That 1971 decision, in *Lemon v. Kurtzman,* required the state to show that the disputed activity had a secular purpose, that its primary effect neither advanced nor inhibited religion and that it did not foster excessive church-state entanglement.

The Justice Department urged a more lenient standard that would allow prayer and other religious elements in public life so long as they did not "coerce participation" or establish an official religion.

But Kennedy said the court did not need to reconsider the *Lemon* principles because the Rhode Island prayer incident so clearly violated the constitution's ban on the establishment of religion.

Scalia wrote a dissenting opinion — joined by Rehnquist, White and Thomas — complaining that the majority opinion "lays waste a tradition that is as old as public-school graduation ceremonies."

Scalia argued that prayer has been an "important unifying mechanism" at such occasions and that "it is a shame to deprive our public culture of the opportunity, and indeed the encouragement, for people to do it voluntarily." Non-believers, he said, would face only the "minimal inconvenience of standing or even sitting in respectful non-participation."

## Hate Crimes

In another major decision, the justices June 22 struck down a St. Paul, Minn., "hate crimes" law, saying it violated free-speech rights by singling out certain kinds of offensive expression for punishment.

The ruling cast doubt on laws and university speech codes throughout the country that had been adopted to punish acts and remarks motivated by prejudice.

But the decision did not affect a 1990 federal law requiring the Justice Department to gather and publish statistics on hate crimes. *(1990 Almanac, p. 506)*

A key question was whether the court was prepared to strike down not just laws that banned specific acts as hate crimes but also less direct measures — such as laws that required stiffer penalties for crimes if there was evidence that they were motivated by racial bias or other prejudice.

Legislation (HR 4797, S 2522) along those lines was introduced in Congress by Rep. Charles E. Schumer, D-N.Y., and Sen. Paul Simon, D-Ill., and was passed by the

House on Oct. 3. But the bill died when the Senate failed to act on it. The measure would have directed the U.S. Sentencing Commission to set guidelines to increase the penalty for any federal crime motivated by prejudice based on the victim's race, gender, religion or sexual orientation. *(Hate crimes, p. 333)*

The court did not directly address such measures, but the justices accepted a Wisconsin case for the 1992-93 term that challenged such "enhanced penalty" laws.

The Minnesota hate-crime case, *R.A.V. v. City of St. Paul,* was the most important dispute involving controversial political expression since the court ruled in 1989 and 1990 that statutes barring flag-burning were unconstitutional violations of the First Amendment. *(1989 Almanac, p. 307; 1990 Almanac, p. 524)*

The St. Paul ordinance prohibited the use of symbols, including burning crosses and swastikas, likely to create "anger, alarm or resentment" on the basis of race, color, creed, religion or gender.

The ordinance was challenged by a white teenager who was charged under the law after allegedly burning a cross on a black family's lawn. The Minnesota Supreme Court upheld the law, saying it outlawed only "fighting words" — conduct that inflicts injury or incites violence.

The U.S. Supreme Court had ruled in the past that "fighting words" were among the few categories of speech — like obscenity — not protected by the First Amendment.

The court was unanimous in striking down the law, but it split 5-4 on the reasoning. "The First Amendment does not permit St. Paul to impose special prohibitions on those speakers who express views on disfavored subjects," said Scalia, writing for the majority of the court's justices.

Scalia said that the St. Paul ordinance was unconstitutional because it barred only specified categories of "fighting words," based on the content of speech.

"Those who wish to use 'fighting words' in connection with other ideas — to express hostility, for example, on the basis of political affiliation, union membership or homosexuality — are not covered," Scalia wrote in an opinion joined by Chief Justice Rehnquist and Kennedy, Souter and Thomas. "Selectivity of this sort creates the possibility that the city is seeking to handicap the expression of particular ideas."

Scalia said that cross-burning and other bias-inspired acts were "reprehensible" but could be prosecuted as other kinds of crime, such as arson. "St. Paul has sufficient means at its disposal to prevent such behavior without adding the First Amendment to the fire," Scalia wrote.

Four other justices — Blackmun, O'Connor, Stevens and White — agreed that the law was unconstitutional, but for different reasons than those the majority gave.

Writing for the four, White argued that the law was unconstitutional because it was too broad, outlawing not just "fighting words" but also "expressive conduct that causes only hurt feelings, offense or resentment and is protected by the First Amendment."

White warned that the majority opinion "casts aside long established First Amendment doctrine" and was wrong to argue that the government cannot legitimately distinguish among categories of "fighting words."

"This selective regulation reflects the city's judgment that harms based on race, color, creed, religion or gender are more pressing public concerns than the harms caused by other fighting words," White said. "In light of our nation's long and painful experience with discrimination, this determination is plainly reasonable."

## Smoking Lawsuits

In another important case, the court ruled June 24 that a federal cigarette labeling law does not protect tobacco companies against all personal-injury suits under state law.

The court ruled 7-2 in the most important part of the decision, which cleared the way for smokers to sue the tobacco industry for allegedly misleading the public about the hazards of cigarette smoking. It fractured on the question of how far the right to sue extended.

The case had been watched closely because of its implications not only for health and tobacco interests but also for the question of how explicit Congress must be for federal statutes to pre-empt state law.

The case, *Cipollone v. Liggett Group,* involved the family of a woman who died from lung cancer in 1984 after smoking for 42 years. At issue was a federal law, enacted in 1965 and revised in 1969, that required tobacco companies to put health warning labels on cigarette packages. The law specifically barred states from requiring tobacco companies to provide additional warnings.

The 1969 version also said that states could not prohibit or restrict tobacco advertising or promotion as long as packages were labeled in accordance with federal law.

Tobacco companies argued that Congress had intended to pre-empt all health-related damage claims under state law, saying that the purpose of the statute was to impose uniform federal standards on cigarette manufacturers.

The court took a narrower view, saying that Congress would have to be more explicit if federal law was to supersede state law so broadly.

"Congress' enactment of a provision defining the preemptive reach of a statute implies that matters beyond that reach are not pre-empted," Stevens wrote, in a passage that some analysts viewed as an important departure from past decisions that had taken a broader view of pre-emption.

Although the court ruled 7-2 in rejecting the industry's position that it should be shielded from all claims, the majority split on the question of whether any claims were barred.

Writing for a plurality of four, Stevens argued that the federal law did pre-empt some claims — principally those asserting that smokers had not been adequately warned about health hazards after 1969. But Stevens said that tobacco companies could be sued for damages on other grounds, including allegations that they conspired to withhold information and intentionally misrepresented the health hazards of smoking.

"Congress offered no sign that it wished to insulate cigarette manufacturers from longstanding rules governing fraud," Stevens wrote.

In a concurring opinion for himself and two others, Blackmun said the majority opinion should not have disallowed any claims. He said the federal law at issue did not provide enough "unambiguous evidence of congressional intent" to justify any pre-emption of state damage suits.

In a dissent on the other end of the spectrum, Scalia and Thomas agreed with the industry's argument that tobacco companies should have been shielded from all such suits.

Although the court's decision was fractured, anti-smoking activists hailed it as a milestone.

"It's a compromise — but a compromise that vastly favors the plaintiffs and disadvantages the tobacco industry," said Alan B. Morrison, director of the Public Citizen Litigation Group, who filed a brief in behalf of several health groups supporting the Cipollone family.

But Phillip Morris Inc., one of the cigarette companies involved in the case, contended that the decision would have "little practical effect" on litigation. The company called the decision a "significant victory" because it barred suits based on claims that smokers were not warned of health hazards after 1969.

### Mail-Order Sales Tax

The court dealt a blow to revenue-hungry states in a May 26 decision denying them the power to force out-of-state mail-order companies to collect state sales tax. But the court invited Congress to make the final call about whether the 25-year-old prohibition on such taxation ought to be lifted.

Congress showed no great interest in acting on the issue. When legislation requiring mail-order companies to collect taxes on out-of-state sales came up in 1987, it quickly died in committee because of intense lobbying by retailers and disagreement between state and local governments about how they would share the revenue.

Facing the same impediments, the bill's sponsor, House Judiciary Committee Chairman Jack Brooks, D-Texas, did not reintroduce the bill in 1992.

In the case before the court, *Quill Corp. v. North Dakota,* the justices by 8-1 reversed a 1991 ruling of the North Dakota Supreme Court that permitted the state to collect a tax (called a use tax) on sales made by out-of-state mail-order companies.

Many states contended that out-of-state mail order businesses enjoyed an unfair advantage over local retailers because they did not collect sales taxes on the merchandise they sold. More than 30 states had laws on the books requiring some remittance of state taxes on such sales, but those laws were unenforceable. State officials said they were losing $3.3 billion a year in uncollectable taxes.

In 1967, the Supreme Court said that a company had to have a physical presence in a state to be subject to its taxes. The court ruled that, without such a presence, state taxation violated the constitutional protection of due process and also placed a burden on interstate commerce.

The North Dakota court declared that the 1967 decision (*National Bellas Hess Inc. v. Department of Revenue of the State of Illinois*) had become obsolete in light of the growth of the mail-order industry and subsequent Supreme Court rulings on taxation by the states. But the Supreme Court disagreed.

However, the decision gave the states reason to fight on.

In a unanimous portion of the ruling, the justices overturned the due process part of the 1967 decision. Noting that "our due process jurisprudence has evolved significantly" in 25 years, Stevens wrote that regardless of where a company was located, "the continuous and widespread solicitation of business within a state" made it acceptable for states to tax resulting sales.

In other words, while separate constitutional concerns still prevented states from taxing sales by businesses that did not have a physical presence in the state, the due process clause of the Constitution no longer applied.

Then, in an unusual move, the ruling all but encouraged Congress to resolve the dispute between states and mail-order companies.

Noting that the Constitution gives Congress the authority to regulate interstate commerce, Stevens wrote that "the underlying issue is not only one that Congress may be better qualified to resolve, but also one that Congress has the ultimate power to resolve."

What killed past attempts to do so was the opposition of segments of the mail-order business, which key members of Congress supported. Several large retailers in the industry were from Chicago, home of Ways and Means Committee Chairman Dan Rostenkowski, D-Ill. And the mail-order industry counted on the support of Senate Majority Leader George J. Mitchell, D-Maine, whose state was home to mail order giant L. L. Bean.

Brooks' bill also had been crippled by infighting among state and local governments, which could not agree on a formula for sharing revenue from the taxes. Brooks said he would reconsider the issue if state and local governments could "come to a meeting of the minds" on how to apportion the revenue.

Negotiations also were under way between state tax administrators and the mail-order industry. According to Dan Bucks, director of the Multistate Tax Commission, a group of tax administrators from 33 states, the Supreme Court decision "is likely to accelerate, rather than derail, progress toward a negotiated settlement between states and direct-marketers."

### Massachusetts House Seats

The high court June 26 overturned Massachusetts' challenge to congressional reapportionment following the 1990 census, ending the state's quest to retain 11 House seats.

The unanimous decision forced Massachusetts to adopt a new, 10-seat map. The ruling also assured Washington state of nine House seats, an addition of one.

Massachusetts had contended that the federal government improperly included federal personnel overseas when reapportioning House seats. A three-judge federal panel agreed, ruling Feb. 20 that overseas personnel were included in an "arbitrary and capricious way." Exclusion of the overseas personnel would have given Massachusetts an additional seat at Washington's expense.

But the Supreme Court reversed the lower court's decision, sparking three different opinions on the grounds for its ruling. O'Connor, writing for the majority, said it was permissible for the Commerce secretary to include overseas personnel in the census count. In any case, she wrote, the action was not subject to judicial review.

Stevens, though concurring with the judgment, agreed with three other justices that the Commerce secretary's action was reviewable. And Scalia argued that Massachusetts lacked proper standing to challenge the constitutionality of census allocations.

### Write-In Votes

The court ruled June 8 that states may prohibit write-in voting, rejecting arguments that such laws violate citizens' rights to free speech and political association. The justices, in a 6-3 decision *(Burdick v. Takushi)*, upheld a Hawaii ban on write-ins, saying it imposed only a "very limited burden" on voters' rights.

In Hawaii, the Democratic Party was the predominant political force, and its nominees often ran unopposed. It was one such uncontested race for state Legislature that spawned the case before the Supreme Court.

Alan B. Burdick, a Honolulu voter who did not want to vote for the only candidate on the ballot, challenged the Hawaii law that banned write-ins.

The Supreme Court, upholding an appeals court decision, concluded that the write-in ban was not unconstitutional because it was "part of an electoral scheme that

# Major Supreme Court Decisions of 1991-92

The Supreme Court ended its 1991-92 term June 29, capping the year with its landmark decision in a Pennsylvania abortion case.

Earlier, the court postponed a decision on the other major abortion-related case on its docket. It ordered a new round of arguments in *Bray v. Alexandria Women's Health Clinic*, a case raising questions about whether protesters could be sued under a federal civil rights law for blocking abortion clinics.

Following are some of the most important rulings of the Supreme Court's 1991-92 term, listed in the chronological order in which they were issued. Dissenting justices are identified in parentheses:

*Simon & Schuster v. Members of the New York State Crime Victims Board*, 8-0, Dec. 10. A state "Son of Sam" law, prohibiting publishers from paying criminals for their stories, violates First Amendment guarantees of free speech and free press.

*Freeman v. Pitts*, 8-0, March 31. A school district under a desegregation order can be freed of court control gradually as it achieves racial equality in specific aspects of its operations.

*Quill Corp. v. North Dakota*, 8-1, May 26. States may not tax the sales of out-of-state mail-order companies, although Congress could pass a law allowing them to do so. (White)

*Burson v. Freeman*, 5-3, May 26. States have the power to prohibit electioneering near a polling place. (O'Connor, Souter, Stevens)

*Burdick v. Takushi*, 6-3, June 8. States may prohibit write-in voting so long as there are other ways for candidates to get on the ballot. (Blackmun, Kennedy, Stevens)

*United States v. Alvarez-Machain*, 6-3, June 15. The United States government can kidnap a suspected criminal abroad to bring him to trial — even if the foreign country objects and has an extradition treaty with the U.S. (Blackmun, O'Connor, Stevens)

*Georgia v. McCollum*, 7-2, June 18. Criminal defendants cannot exclude people from juries on the basis of race. (O'Connor, Scalia)

*New York v. United States*, 6-3, June 19. Congress cannot order states to assume legal liability for low-level nuclear waste generated within their borders. (Blackmun, Stevens, White)

*R.A.V. v. City of St. Paul*, 9-0, June 22. A local government's "hate crime" ordinance — which includes a ban on cross-burning and the display of swastikas — violates the First Amendment's free-speech guarantee.

*Cipollone v. Liggett Group*, 7-2, June 24. A federal cigarette labeling law does not protect tobacco companies against all personal-injury suits under state law. The only claims barred are those expressly pre-empted by the language of the federal law. (Scalia, Thomas)

*Lee v. Weisman*, 5-4, June 24. Inviting a member of the clergy to offer a prayer at a public-school graduation violates the Constitution's prohibition against the establishment of religion. (Rehnquist, Scalia, Thomas, White)

*U.S. v. Fordice, Ayers v. Fordice*, 8-1, June 26. A state has not fulfilled its constitutional obligation to desegregate a public university system if its policies continue to foster racial discrimination — even if they are apparently race-neutral. (Scalia)

*Lucas v. South Carolina Coastal Council*, 6-3, June 29. Property owners may be entitled to compensation when government regulation deprives their property of all economic value. (Blackmun, Souter, Stevens)

*Planned Parenthood of Southeastern Pennsylvania v. Casey*, 5-4, June 29. Women have a right to have an abortion in the early stages of pregnancy, but states may regulate abortion so long as they do not impose an "undue burden" on a woman's ability to terminate her pregnancy. (Rehnquist, Scalia, Thomas, White)

provides constitutionally sufficient ballot access." Hawaii election law allowed candidates outside the established parties to get on a nonpartisan primary ballot.

The court said the state had a legitimate interest in avoiding "unrestrained factionalism" in its elections and averting "sore-loser candidacies."

White wrote the majority opinion, which was supported by Chief Justice Rehnquist and Justices O'Connor, Scalia, Souter and Thomas.

A dissenting opinion by Kennedy, Blackmun and Stevens noted that large numbers of voters cast blank ballots in uncontested races in Hawaii, concluding that "many Hawaii voters are dissatisfied with the choices available to them.

"The write-in ban thus prevents these voters from participating in Hawaii elections in a meaningful manner," Kennedy wrote in his opinion for the three dissenters.

## Voting Rights

In a setback for civil rights activists, the Supreme Court on Jan. 27 narrowly interpreted the 1965 Voting Rights Act and rejected arguments that eliminating an elected official's authority constituted a voting rights violation.

The case was brought in Alabama by minority officials who had been elected to two counties' commissions in federally mandated black-majority districts.

Historically, each county commissioner could determine expenditure of funds allocated to his road district. But by the time the black county commissioners took office, the white majorities on the commissions had stripped the offices of this power.

The Bush administration sided with the black officials and argued that such changes in local law should be covered under Section 5 of the Voting Rights Act. That section required officials in 16 states to have election law changes examined for possible discriminatory effects and "precleared" by the federal government.

But the court, in a 6-3 vote, said the Voting Rights Act required preclearance only for laws affecting "voting qualification or prerequisite to voting, or standard, practice or procedure with respect to voting."

∎

# Bill Extends Assistance to Bilingual Voters

Congress cleared legislation (HR 4312 — PL 102-344) Aug. 7 that extended and expanded the bilingual assistance provisions of the Voting Rights Act of 1965.

The provisions required election officials to provide bilingual services in jurisdictions with significant numbers of non-English speaking voters. Supporters of the bill used the renewal of the voting act provisions as an opportunity to expand mandated bilingual assistance into areas not previously covered by the law.

Paul Simon, D-Ill., a cosponsor of the Senate version of the bill (S 2236) told his colleagues during floor debate that not passing the measure would "jeopardize the means by which hundreds of thousands of limited-English-speaking U.S. citizens would exercise their right to vote."

The bill extended the bilingual assistance provisions for 15 years, to the year 2007. In addition, it expanded the scope of these provisions to encompass a greater number of non-English speaking voters.

The legislation required that bilingual services be provided in jurisdictions with 10,000 or more non-English speakers, even if these people did not make up 5 percent of the total population.

House and Senate supporters of the bill justified this new requirement by arguing that the old law excluded a number of heavily populated counties with large numbers of non-English speaking citizens such as Los Angeles, San Fransisco, Chicago and Philadelphia.

## BACKGROUND

Congress last renewed provisions of the 1965 Voting Rights Act (PL 89-110) in 1982 to extend the enforcement provisions of the law for 25 years and make it easier to prove certain voting rights violations.

President Ronald Reagan, in signing the extension measure (PL 97-205), called the right to vote "the crowning jewel of American liberties" and said the legislation "proves our unbending commitment to voting rights." (1982 Almanac, p. 373)

One section of the bill extended until 1992 provisions requiring certain areas of the country to provide bilingual election materials.

In 1992, bilingual ballots were printed in counties in which at least 5 percent of the population did not speak English. Sixty-eight jurisdictions had met this requirement.

## HOUSE ACTION

The House Judiciary Subcommittee on Civil and Constitutional Rights approved HR 4312 by voice vote May 7.

---

## BOXSCORE

➡ **Bilingual Ballots (HR 4312, S 2236).** The measure extended, for 15 years, provisions of the Voting Rights Act of 1965 that required bilingual election assistance to be rendered in jurisdictions with large numbers of non-English speaking voters. The bill also increased the number of jurisdictions covered under the act.

**Reports:** H Rept 102-655; S Rept 102-315.

### KEY ACTION

June 4 — The **House** Judiciary Committee approved HR 4312.

June 18 — The **Senate** Judiciary Committee approved S 2236, 12-2.

July 24 — The **House** passed HR 4312, 237-125.

August 7 — The **Senate** passed HR 4312, 75-20.

August 26 — President Bush signed HR 4312 — PL 102-344.

---

The measure won the voice vote approval of the full committee on June 4.

The committee defeated by voice vote an amendment offered by Henry J. Hyde, R-Ill., that would have raised to 50,000 or more the number of non-English speakers necessary in a jurisdiction for the services to be required.

Panel members also defeated, 9-25, an amendment by Bill McCollum, R-Fla., that would have required a disclaimer on voting ballots stating that the official version of the ballot was the English version. McCollum said that because errors might occur when translating ballot information, such a disclaimer would be necessary. But William J. Hughes, D-N.J., argued that the simple solution would be to make sure there were no translating errors.

### House Passage

After fighting off opposition from Judiciary Committee Republicans, Democratic proponents of the legislation were easily able to shore up enough support to pass the bill on the floor. The measure was passed in the House by a vote of 237-125 on July 24. (Vote 319, p. 78-H)

McCollum offered a substitute to the bill that would have extended the bilingual assistance for only five years and would have excluded additional cities and counties from qualifying. The amendment was defeated 142-233. (Vote 314, p. 76-H)

Republicans who opposed the bill argued that Congress was continuing to force struggling states to spend money on federal mandates.

However, it was Gary Condit, D-Calif., who offered a Republican-backed amendment that almost proved fatal to the bill. The amendment would have required the federal government to fund federally mandated local efforts to provide bilingual voting assistance. The U.S. attorney general would have been responsible for directing dollars to the states. The amendment was defeated 184-186. (Vote 315, p. 76-H)

Condit said the bill's mandates would double the cost of elections in one county in his district.

Democrats argued that if the amendment were adopted, localities would no longer be required to comply with bilingual voting assistance laws. "The obligation will disappear for local governments to deal with language minorities," said Howard L. Berman, D-Calif.

Finally, in an attempt to force a vote on the provision, McCollum put forth the Condit amendment again in the form of a motion to send the bill back to committee. Again the House was divided.

Craig Washington, D-Texas, argued that the amendment would stand in the way of a citizen's right to vote. "We delegate responsibility to the attorney general to decide under what circumstances and where the Voting Rights Act will be enforced," Washington said.

The motion was rejected 172-195. *(Vote 318, p. 76-H)*

## SENATE ACTION

On June 18, the Senate Judiciary Committee voted 12-2 to approve S 2236. Only Republicans Alan K. Simpson of Wyoming and Strom Thurmond of South Carolina voted against it.

Simpson, who spoke for nearly two hours in opposition and offered five unsuccessful amendments in committee argued that the bill would encourage divisiveness among the nation's racial and ethnic groups. "I think we have to be very careful when we treat certain people special," Simpson said. The bill could encourage minorities not to learn English, he added.

Simon, who cosponsored the bill with Orrin Hatch, R-Utah, argued that minorities wanted to learn English but they did not have the opportunity to do so. As an example, he cited people in Los Angeles who were on waiting lists for English language lessons.

Simpson asked senators to extend the provision for one year rather than 15 so that they could collect additional statistics from the U.S. Census Bureau to determine whether bilingual ballots had increased voter participation among the targeted minority groups. This amendment was defeated, 4-10.

### Senate Passage

The full Senate took up the related House bill (HR 4312) — which had won that chamber's approval two weeks earlier — on the morning of Aug. 7. The measure passed by a vote of 75-20. *(Vote 180, 24-S)*

On the floor, Simpson once again tried to alter the bill. He offered an amendment that would have extended the provisions for five years, as opposed to the 15 years stipulated in the bill. This amendment, a more generous version of the one defeated in the Judiciary Committee, was rejected by a vote of 32-63. *(Vote 178, 24-S)*

Simpson also offered an amendment that would have required the federal government to pay for the mandated bilingual ballots and other voter assistance. In support of this provision, Simpson argued that it was unrealistic to impose the cost of these new requirements on cash strapped jurisdictions. He called on supporters of the bill to have the "courage to fund it."

But Sen. Edward M. Kennedy, D-Mass., countered that requiring the federal government to fund what is a constitutional requirement of the states, would set a "terrible precedent." The amendment was defeated by a vote of 35-60. *(Vote 179, 24-S)*

Finally, Simpson agreed to withdraw another planned amendment that would have required a study on the effectiveness of bilingual voting measures. He did so after Simon promised to support efforts to enact these provisions in 1993. ∎

# Pornography Victims' Compensation Act

After repeated attempts, legislation that would have allowed rape victims and their families to sue hard-core pornographers won the approval of the Senate Judiciary Committee before getting snagged in controversy and strong opposition.

While the bill's goal of providing more legal recourse to victims of sex crimes was a popular political topic in an election year, First Amendment concerns continued to dog the measure, making it difficult for backers to muster support for it. In addition, no companion measure was introduced in the House.

The bill aimed to make those who produced or distributed hard-core pornography liable if victims could prove the material incited the offender to commit the crime. Senators were pushing the bill in response to heinous crimes in which attackers said they were influenced by violent pornography.

The fight over the bill, crafted by Mitch McConnell, R-Ky., created alliances between conservative Republicans and some feminists, splitting women's groups on the issue. Meanwhile, opponents argued that enactment of the bill would result in censorship and would take responsibility for the crime away from the attacker.

"The greatest danger is establishing the precedent that producers and distributors of constitutionally protected material can be held liable for the criminal acts of others," said Chris Finan, executive director of The Media Coalition Inc., which represented groups such as the American Booksellers Association.

### Senate Action

The Senate Judiciary Committee met to consider S 1521 on two occasions without taking a final vote on the measure.

At the first attempt, on April 8, the panel lost its quorum before members could vote on the bill or the amendments that had been offered.

The committee took up the measure again on June 11, approving two amendments that had been offered by Sens. Arlen Specter, R-Pa., and Howell Heflin, D-Ala. These had been agreed to by Charles E. Grassley, R-Iowa, a cosponsor and key backer of the bill on the committee.

Specter's amendment would have required the defendant in the civil suit to be convicted of the production, distribution or sale of hard-core or child pornography before the victim could bring a court action.

Heflin's change would have permitted such suits only after the perpetrator of the violent crime had been convicted of the act.

But before a final vote could be taken, the compromise brokered between Grassley and other members of the committee collapsed over a new amendment offered by Chairman Joseph R. Biden Jr., D-Del.

Biden's amendment would have required proof that the pornographer or distributor knew the material was obscene before it was produced or distributed.

In a heated exchange, Grassley accused the chairman of adding an un-

---

**BOXSCORE**

➡ **Pornography Victims' Compensation Act (S 1521).** The bill would have given legal recourse to victims of violent sex crimes and the families of those murdered by allowing them to sue the producers and distributors of hard core pornography.

**Report:** S Rept 102-372.

**KEY ACTION**

June 25 — The **Senate** Judiciary Committee approved S 1521, 7-6.

welcome element to a deal previously worked out. An irritated Grassley, who had already agreed to the changes by Heflin and Specter, rejected Biden's proposal, and asked that consideration again be delayed.

Finally, on June 25, the committee voted 7-6 to approve the legislation.

Members approved S 1521 only after the committee narrowly rejected the Biden amendment that had been the point of contention just two weeks before.

Biden argued that the bill would be unconstitutional without the amendment and could punish people who might sell hundreds of films or books without knowing the content of every one.

Ranking Republican Strom Thurmond of South Carolina disagreed. "This amendment says to porn peddlers that they will not be held civilly liable for their criminal acts unless they are foolish enough to commit the identical criminal act twice," he said.

Moreover, Thurmond said, the amendment would gut the bill. "This amendment, stated simply, is a pro-criminal amendment," he said. "It creates a giant loophole. Voting for this amendment will be selling out the victims of violent crime."

The amendment was defeated 7-7 on a mostly party-line vote. Democrats Heflin and Dennis DeConcini, Ariz., voted against Biden; Republican Specter voted for the amendment.

In the vote on the measure itself, Biden opposed it along with a majority of Democrats. Only Heflin of Alabama and DeConcini voted for it. Republicans supported the legislation with the exception of Specter, who was absent during the vote. ■

# Abortion Issue Eclipses Religious Freedom Bill

Legislation to provide stronger protection for the free exercise of religion barely advanced in the 102nd Congress after it became embroiled in the far reaching abortion debate.

The bills would have reversed a 1990 Supreme Court decision allowing states broad latitude in infringing upon religious practices.

House Republicans opposed the bill because they said it would have allowed some women to obtain abortions on religious grounds, giving them a loophole if abortion rights were to be restricted in the future. Republicans also argued that it was the job of the Supreme Court, not Congress, to interpret the Constitution.

In the House, the measure (HR 2797) stalled after winning approval in the House Judiciary Committee. A related bill (S 2969) in the Senate was never taken up by the Judiciary Committee.

The Supreme Court held in *Employment Division v. Smith* that states could impose laws that infringed on religious practices as long as the laws were reasonable and not aimed at a particular religious practice.

In the *Smith* case, two American Indian men were fired from their jobs at a private substance-abuse rehabilitation center for ingesting peyote, a hallucinogenic drug, as a religious sacrament during church ceremonies while off duty.

The men were denied unemployment benefits by the state of Oregon, whose officials argued that the compelling interest of the state in enforcing laws on illegal drugs outweighed that of the two men in continuing their reli-

gious activities. The men argued that the state's interest was not compelling enough to warrant infringement on their religious practices. The Supreme Court, in effect, took away the compelling interest test when it ruled that a state did not have to prove it had a compelling interest if it enforced a law that infringed on religious practices. The bills would have restored the test.

Various groups supported the legislation, including several Jewish organizations, the Mormon Church and many Protestant groups.

Religious groups lobbying for the bill argued that since the Supreme Court decision, the rights of individuals to practice their religion were repeatedly violated. In one case, a Jewish woman in Michigan sued the county of Clinton because the medical examiner did not notify her before ordering an autopsy for her son, who had been killed in a car crash. She claimed that according to her religious beliefs, the body should not have been defiled. Based on the Supreme Court ruling, a U.S. District Court ruled that the family's rights had not been violated.

In 1990, Rep. Stephen J. Solarz, D-N.Y., and Sen. Joseph R. Biden Jr., D-Del., introduced bills that would have reversed the court's decision. But the legislation died at the end of the 101st Congress after some supporters dropped out over the abortion issue.

**House Committee Action**

Despite claims from supporters that the bill was "absolutely neutral" as far abortion was concerned, the issue once again generated strong, primarily Republican, opposition in 1992.

The House Judiciary Subcommittee on Civil and Constitutional Rights approved HR 2797 on June 24.

The bill, once again introduced by Solarz, was approved 5-3, on a party-line vote.

During the subcommittee's consideration of the bill, Henry Hyde offered five amendments, all of which were rejected by voice vote.

One amendment would have spelled out that the bill did not provide access to "abortion services or funding." Subcommittee Chairman Don Edwards, D-Calif., warned that abortion language would make the bill "politically unfeasible."

At full committee the measure was approved by voice vote on Oct. 1.

At a separate markup the day before, Hyde once again offered his amendment concerning abortion. And, as at subcommittee, it was defeated. ■

# Other Judiciary Measures Considered in 1992

The year saw congressional action on a myriad of judicial issues ranging from legislation aimed at fighting hate crimes to proposals for dealing with police brutality.

While many Judiciary Committee proposals were transformed into law, others were left to languish or be considered by the 103rd Congress.

## JUDICIAL ADMINISTRATION

A measure (S 1569 — PL 102-572) that aimed to improve the operations of the federal court system cleared Congress on Oct. 7 and was signed by President Bush on

Oct. 29.

The bill, which implemented some of the findings of the Federal Courts Study Committee, provided for improvements in the judicial financial administration and revised the judicial survivors' annuity system.

The committee was created by a 1988 law to look at ways to improve the federal court system. Many of the recommendations of the committee, which had finished its work two years earlier, were incorporated in the Judicial Improvements Act of 1990. *(1990 Almanac, p. 520)*

The bill won voice vote passage in the House on Oct. 3 and in the Senate four days later.

The measure also incorporated the language of a separate bill (HR 5933 — H Rept 102-1006) that reauthorized the State Justice Institute.

The institute funded studies on improving the operations of state courts and sponsored meetings of judges from different states to discuss issues of common interest.

The legislation authorized $20 million for the institute for fiscal 1993-94 and $25 million for fiscal 1995-96.

A similar bill (HR 6185) was pocket vetoed because of the White House's objection to language concerning the federal claims court jurisdiction.

## COPYRIGHTS

Legislation (HR 4412 — PL 102-492) that allowed writers, scholars and others to use parts of unpublished copyrighted works cleared Congress and was signed by President Bush on Oct. 24.

The bill upheld the "fair use" principle, which allowed the use of copyrighted works without permission of the author or his estate.

Fair use helped journalists, academics and others who wanted to reproduce parts of a work to comment on it or critique it. The legislation applied the principle to unpublished works, allowing courts to find their use acceptable if fair.

The measure, which passed the House on Aug. 11 and the Senate on Oct. 7, was drafted in response to federal court decisions that supporters claimed were having a chilling effect on the work of journalists and others.

## TORTURE VICTIMS

Congress cleared and the president signed a bill (HR 2092 — PL 102-256) allowing U.S. citizens to file civil lawsuits against foreigners living in the United States who, in an official capacity, engaged in torture or extra-judicial execution outside of the United States.

The bill required lawsuits to be filed within 10 years of the alleged abuse.

In addition, the victim had to have exhausted all legal remedies in the country where the torture took place before bringing suit in the United States.

The measure passed the House by voice vote on Nov. 25, 1991. The Senate passed the bill on March 3, 1992 and it was signed by the president on March 12. *(1991 Almanac, p. 297)*

## INSLAW

Partisan wrangling continued in Congress over allegations that the Department of Justice stole software from INSLAW Inc., a federal contractor.

In 1982, the Justice Department awarded the company a three-year, $10 million contract to implement a case management software system at 94 department offices.

Shortly afterward, according to Democratic congressional investigators, high-level department officials ignored the company's property rights and used the software at locations not covered by the contract.

On Sept. 10, House Judiciary Committee members asked Attorney General William P. Barr to seek an independent counsel to investigate whether there was a conspiracy to steal software.

But Barr refused to seek a counsel, claiming that his appointment in November 1991 of Judge Nicholas Bua to investigate the case was adequate.

The committee's request, approved by a party-line vote of 21-13, came after the release of an investigative report in August that concluded that high-level department officials might have conspired to steal the software and later blocked inquiries into the matter.

Republicans argued that the investigation, handled by Democrats, had made accusations without evidence. Democrats were "allowing personal reputations to be harmed on the basis of hearsay," said Carlos J. Moorhead, R-Calif. "This case is really about a contract dispute. This committee has become the special-prosecutor-of-the-month club."

## HATE CRIMES

Legislation to strengthen mandatory sentencing guidelines for federal offenses that involved "hate crimes" passed the House. But the measure died after the Senate failed to act on it in the closing days of the session.

The bill (HR 4797 — H Rept 102-981) would have defined a hate crime as one that was motivated by hatred, bias or prejudice based on race, religion, ethnicity, color, gender or sexual orientation. Under the measure, if a federal crime of any sort were motivated by such hatred or prejudice, the judge would have had to have sentenced the felon to additional time in prison. Prison terms would have been extended by roughly one-third.

The measure won the voice vote approval of the House Judiciary Subcommittee on Crime and Criminal Justice on Aug. 5, and the full committee on Sept. 30. The House passed the bill by voice vote Oct. 3.

## MILITARY MEDICAL MALPRACTICE

Legislation (HR 3407 — H Rept 102-1043) that would have allowed members of the U.S. military to sue the government for medical malpractice won the approval of the House Judiciary Committee.

Under the Federal Tort Claims Act of 1946, members of the Armed Forces were prohibited from suing the government in cases of negligence at military medical facilities.

HR 3407 would have allowed malpractice suits only in cases involving non-combat-related injuries and when treatment occurred in the United States, at permanent medical facilities. Plaintiffs would have been able to collect only compensatory damages. No punitive damages could have been awarded.

The House Judiciary Subcommittee on Administrative Law gave voice vote approval to the bill on June 24. The full committee followed suit on Aug. 11.

House Republicans and the administration opposed the bill and argued that given the government's disability payments to veterans, enacting HR 3407 would result in a "double remedy at the expense of the taxpayer."

## DNA TESTING

Legislation (HR 3088) that would have promoted DNA technology in solving crimes passed the House in the waning days of Congress, but was never taken up in the Senate.

DNA carries a unique genetic code of each individual and had been used to identify violent criminals.

The bill, which passed the House on Oct. 5, would have authorized $10 million for four years for state and local governments to establish DNA crime labs. It also would have established privacy and quality control guidelines for the labs.

## JUVENILES AND GANGS

Legislation (HR 5194 — PL 102-586) that aimed at stemming juvenile violence cleared Congress and was signed by President Bush on Nov. 4.

The bill, which won voice vote passage in the House on Oct. 2 and the Senate on Oct. 7, reauthorized for four years the Justice Department's Office of Juvenile Justice and Delinquency Prevention. The measure authorized up to $150 million for fiscal 1993 for the office, which was charged with finding ways to prevent children from becoming juvenile delinquents and devising alternatives to detention for juveniles already incarcerated.

Included in the authorization were funding increases for state grants to help deter juvenile violence and financial incentives to encourage states to try alternatives to imprisonment for teens convicted of non-violent offenses.

## CHILD ABUSE

Congress cleared a measure (HR 1253 — PL 102-528) that authorized $600,000 for the State Justice Institute to develop judicial training courses on child custody law to aid courts in identifying those homes at high risk for the abuse of parents or children.

The measure, which passed the House on Oct. 3 and the Senate on Oct. 7, was signed by president on Oct. 27.

## POLICE BRUTALITY

In the wake of the Rodney King beating trial verdict in California, Congress began considering ways to give the federal government greater latitude in fighting police misconduct.

In urging Congress to act, Rep. John Conyers Jr., D-Mich., blamed the riots in Los Angeles that followed the King verdict on "the anger of citizens with nowhere to turn for protection against an out-of-control police department." *(Urban crisis, p. 339)*

On Oct. 22, 1991, the House passed, as part of the crime bill (HR 3371), provisions of another measure (HR 2972) that would have given the attorney general additional authority to sue a police department to halt patterns and practices of police misconduct that violate the Constitution. But the crime bill was stalled throughout the entire year and neither chamber took up HR 2972 as a free standing bill. *(1991 Almanac, p. 262; Crime bill, p. 311)*

The bill would have given the Justice Department — which has the authority to prosecute individual officers — much greater latitude in the war against police brutality. It would have also required the Justice Department to collect and publish statistical information on the use of excessive force by the police.

## NOMINATIONS PROCESS

The tumultuous Senate Judiciary Committee confirmation hearings for Clarence Thomas in 1991 moved the Senate in 1992 to re-examine the judicial nominating process. But there were ultimately few changes, as Senate Democrats focused on shifting the blame for the controversy by stressing the need for the president to consult with them before choosing a candidate.

Thomas' nomination to the Supreme Court embarrassed Senate Judiciary Committee Chairman Joseph R. Biden, Jr. and other panel members after it was revealed that charges of sexual harassment brought forth against the nominee by former colleague Anita Hill had not been adequately investigated. The charges became public only after being leaked to the media. *(1991 Almanac, p. 274)*

Calls for changes in the judicial nomination process came from both ends of Pennsylvania Avenue. This led Senate Majority Leader George J. Mitchell, D-Maine, to appoint a task force to look for ways to improve the process. The group, composed entirely of Democratic committee chairmen, recommended no major changes in the Senate's procedures. Instead, its key proposals focused on the administration and the selection process.

"We do not expect the president to shrink the scope or exercise of his constitutional powers," Mitchell said on Feb. 4, outlining the recommendations of the task force. But, he added, the Senate must also exercise its powers — which entail giving its "advice and consent" on the nomination. Mitchell stressed that under the Constitution, the president and Senate are to act jointly on nominations.

Not surprisingly, President Bush refused all requests for consultation, arguing that the choice of the candidate is the president's prerogative.

The task force, which made its recommendations to the full Senate, also criticized Bush's post-Thomas policy of restricting Senate Judiciary Committee access to FBI background reports on nominees.

But on Feb. 7, the administration and members of the Judiciary Committee reached a deal giving senators and key staff access to the background reports under tighter security. And later in the year, on June 25, Biden promised all senators access to the FBI files and warned the president that he would oppose any nominee if the Senate was not consulted beforehand.

## CUSTOMS' DAMAGES

Legislation that would have held the U.S. Customs Service liable for damages negligently inflicted to private property during searches and seizures passed the House but was never taken up in the Senate.

The bill was inspired by complaints from a Florida man who incurred $9,000 worth of damages when Customs agents searched his boat. The law on the books allowed the man to sue for no more than $1,000 and prohibited the service from offering any kind of settlement, even if the agents were negligent.

The measure would have allowed the Customs Service to be sued to compensate for damages, although punitive damages would still have been prohibited. Additionally, the government would have been allowed to settle claims, with a cap of $50,000.

The bill (HR 2731 — H Rept 102-776) won the voice vote approval of the House Judiciary Subcommittee on Administrative Law on March 11. The full committee followed suit on April 30, approving an amendment making

the service liable for damages only to property inspected, not all items passing through Customs. Finally, it was passed by the House on Aug. 11.

But President Bush threatened a veto of the bill, arguing that it would have exposed the government to too many liability claims. It was never taken up by the Senate.

## SEX DISCRIMINATION

To assuage women's groups angered by a 1991 civil rights compromise, several senators tried unsuccessfully to move legislation that would have eliminated caps on damages allowed for victims of sex and other types of discrimination.

But after a swift and early victory in the Senate Labor and Human Resources Committee, where the bill was approved by voice vote on March 11, the measure stalled because of opposition from the Bush administration and senators concerned about its impact on small businesses.

The Civil Rights Act of 1991 (PL 102-166) gave victims of intentional discrimination based on gender, religion or disability the right to bring suit for monetary damages. But as part of a compromise with the Bush administration, supporters of the bill agreed to impose caps on these damage awards, from $50,000 to $300,000, depending on the size of the company involved. *(1991 Almanac, p. 251)*

S 2062 (S Rept 102-286) and a companion measure in the House (HR 3975) would have eliminated these caps for women, members of religious minorities and the disabled. Victims of racial discrimination could already win unlimited damages under a Reconstruction-era law.

## GUN CONTROL

Legislation (HR 5633) that would have required gun dealers to report the names of people who bought more than one firearm within a 30-day period won the approval of the House Judiciary Subcommittee on Crime and Criminal Justice. But while the panel approved the bill by a vote of 7-5, it stalled because of opposition from the Bush administration and House Republicans.

HR 5633 would have broadened the existing requirement, in which people who purchased more than one firearm in a five-day period were listed with the Bureau of Alcohol, Tobacco and Firearms.

In introducing the bill, Crime Subcommittee Chairman Charles E. Schumer, D-N.Y., said that the "ever-widening" black market for guns made keeping records of multiple purchases important.

On the same day, the panel also approved, by voice vote, a measure (HR 5634), that would have prohibited anyone convicted of a violent crime or drug felony from ever purchasing a firearm. But this bill also advanced no further.

## BATTERED WOMEN

Legislation (HR 1252 — PL 102-286) that promoted the use of expert witnesses in cases in which battered women assaulted or killed their abusers was cleared by Congress and signed into law on Oct. 27.

The bill, which passed the House on Oct. 3 and the Senate on Oct. 7, authorized $600,000 to the State Justice Institute to provide grants to organizations to collect information on expert testimony about the psychological state of battered women and to help women find expert defense witnesses. ∎

# 102nd Congress Advanced Several Immigration Bills

The passage of the Immigration Act of 1990 (PL 101-649) effectively removed the broader issue of immigration reform from the national agenda. But, in the ensuing two years, Congress remained involved in fashioning immigration policy. Several proposals became law in 1992. The thorny issue of Haitian refugees, however, remained unresolved. *(1990 Almanac, p. 474)*

## CHINESE NATIONALS

Congress cleared and the president signed a measure that provided thousands of Chinese refugees permanent residency in the United States.

The measure (S 1216 — PL 102-404) allowed about 80,000 Chinese residents who were in the United States during the June 1989 Tiananmen Square massacre of democracy demonstrators to apply for residency starting July 1, 1993.

The Chinese nationals were already protected, by an executive order, from deportation through Jan. 1, 1994. But lawmakers said the bill was designed to provide permanent protection that would ease concerns in the Chinese community.

The bill passed the Senate on May 21 and the House on Aug. 10. It was signed by President Bush on Oct. 9.

## SOVIET SCIENTISTS

Legislation aimed at encouraging unemployed Soviet scientists to bring their knowledge to America cleared Congress and was signed by the president on Oct. 24.

The bill (S 2201 — PL 102-509) allowed 750 nuclear scientists and their families to emigrate from the former Soviet Union to work in America.

After the collapse of the Soviet Union in 1991, some scientists — particularly those involved with weapons development — were offered substantial sums of money to work for developing nations bent on creating weapons of mass destruction.

Supporters of the measure argued that it would help deter an exodus of Soviet scientific talent to countries such as Iran or Iraq.

Introduced Feb. 6 by Hank Brown, R-Colo., the bill did not increase the 140,000 visa slots available to immigrants with "special skills." But it did amend existing law to allow the scientists to live and work in America over the next four years.

In addition, it required the attorney general to designate a class of scientists in nuclear or other high-tech defense-related fields as having exceptional scientific skills, allowing them to work in America.

The measure was approved by the Senate Judiciary Committee on April 8 and by the Senate on May 20. It won the approval of the House Judiciary Committee on Aug. 6 and passed the House by voice vote on Sept. 21.

## JAPANESE-AMERICANS

A federal fund created to compensate Japanese-Americans interned during World War II was expanded under legislation that cleared Congress on Sept. 16 and was

signed by the president Sept. 27.

The Civil Liberties Act of 1988 (PL 100-383) had authorized $1.25 billion for the fund to pay each internee $20,000. However the original estimate of 60,000 claimants was about 20,000 too low, prompting members to revisit the issue. *(1988 Almanac, p. 80)*

The bill (HR 4551 — PL 102-371) increased the fund's authorization by $400 million, to a total of $1.65 billion, to provide enough funding to compensate all 78,000 estimated claimants.

The measure, sponsored by Richard A. Gephardt, D-Mo., also made non-Japanese spouses and parents who were interned along with a Japanese spouse or child eligible for compensation.

The bill passed the House on Sept. 14 and the Senate two days later.

## VISA EXEMPTIONS

The House passed legislation by voice vote Sept. 29 aimed at speeding the entry of foreign visitors into the United States. The bill went no further.

The measure (HR 5555 — H Rept 102-910) would have made permanent a pilot program, set to expire in fiscal 1994, allowing nationals of selected countries to enter the United States without a visa as long as they stayed no longer than 90 days. The 21 nations exempt from the visa requirements at the time were those whose nationals generally did not stay longer than their allotted time.

In addition, the Immigration and Naturalization Service would be required to set up six pre-inspection stations no later than Nov. 1, 1996, at foreign airports to help process people with U.S. entry visas as they left the country of departure.

The legislation, aimed at speeding up the inspection process for foreigners and decreasing the number of undocumented aliens, won voice vote approval from the House Judiciary Committee on Aug. 11.

The bill, introduced by Charles E. Schumer, D-N.Y., was approved by voice vote by the Subcommittee on International Law, Immigration and Refugees on July 23.

The measure directed the attorney general to determine which six foreign airports were the points of departure for the largest number of passengers to the United States. Pre-inspection stations would be established in at least three foreign airports. Three more stations would be set up in foreign airports that allowed the largest numbers of undocumented aliens to enter the country. ■

# LABOR/ HOUSING/ VETERANS

# Cities Seek Help From Congress

*Washington's response to urban crisis was stymied*
*by fiscal and political anxiety*

Three days of violence erupted in Los Angeles in late April after four white police officers were acquitted on all but one charge in the March 3, 1991, beating of black motorist Rodney King. As the riots focused the country on the poverty, crime and unemployment of a major urban center, all eyes turned toward Washington for a federal response to end the crisis and help the cities.

Congress negotiated with the Bush administration on a quick-fix emergency urban aid bill (HR 5132 — PL 102-577) to benefit Los Angeles and Chicago, whose downtown had sustained water damage from flooding in April. The package gave $1.1 billion in disaster loans and grants, including $500 million for summer jobs for young people across the country.

Then Congress promised to work out a long-term, far-reaching initiative to help all cities. It never materialized. What emerged was a small demonstration proposal to try out enterprise zones, which gave tax breaks to businesses willing to locate in blighted urban areas. That proposal was tacked on to a controversial tax bill (HR 11) that President Bush eventually vetoed.

States and cities had operated enterprise zones for years, but the idea ran into trouble on the federal level because of differences between Democrats and Republicans over the use of capital gains tax breaks to stimulate the economy. Republicans were for a capital gains tax break. Democrats were wary that allowing it in the cities would lead to cutting the tax rate — 28 percent at the time — for everyone, which they said would benefit only the wealthy.

Despite differences over how the enterprise zones should be structured and how many there should be, the House and Senate agreed to create 50 zones, with 25 in rural areas and 25 in cities. Investors who put their money into a zone for five years would receive a 15 percent credit on the first $20,000 for purchases of stock in zone businesses along with more rapid tax write-offs for property.

Springtime in Los Angeles: Vermont Avenue after three days of violence.

REUTERS

Tax benefits for enterprise zones would be worth $2.6 billion over five years.

Another idea, to authorize $3 billion to help cities cope with the recession, died in the 102nd Congress. The bill (HR 5798) was pushed by John Conyers Jr., D-Mich., chairman of the House Government Operations Committee, but the full House never acted on it.

## BACKGROUND

It often takes a tragedy to drive bold policy initiatives. But in the wake of the Los Angeles riots in April — by most accounts the worst civil disturbance in generations — the ensuing silence from Capitol Hill the week of May 4 was deafening.

Just about all of political Washington, from Bush on down, lost little time condemning the violence, expressing concern about the jury verdict in the King police-beating trial that touched it off and generally lamenting the poor state of American race relations.

But, boxed in by a combination of political risks, budget

constraints and lack of a clear consensus on how to address the ills plaguing America's cities, neither Bush nor congressional Democrats were rushing forward with radical new agendas.

Lawmakers said the policy fallout of all the unrest would be paltry. Congress was likely to pass a supplemental appropriations bill to provide $1 billion in emergency assistance and small-business loans not only to riot-torn Los Angeles but also to flood-ravaged downtown Chicago. *(Appropriations, p. 579)*

Members also were likely to stick an "urban relief" label on a raft of proposals already in the pipeline and well on their way to enactment anyway, including a reauthorization of the Job Training Partnership Act and another bill to extend unemployment benefits. *(JTPA, p. 358; unemployment, p. 346)*

Members also could focus on legislation that did not entail federal dollars. But even some of those proposals — most notably the omnibus crime bill that Senate Republicans had been blocking for months — had problems. *(Crime bill, p. 311)*

In the end, members privately agreed, the Los Angeles riots of 1992 were not likely to be remembered as a catalyst for change.

"I'm skeptical that people will be transformed by this," said Rep. Barney Frank, D-Mass.

### Touching a Partisan Nerve

Much of the early response to the unrest was marked by partisan bickering over which party was at fault.

On May 4, Bush spokesman Marlin Fitzwater touched a nerve by suggesting that the failure of President Lyndon B. Johnson's Great Society anti-poverty programs of the 1960s was responsible for "many of the root problems that have resulted in inner-city difficulties."

That brought an outcry from those programs' supporters.

House Speaker Thomas S. Foley, D-Wash., among others, called the statement "totally absurd." Said Foley: "There hasn't been a single program identified in this general sweeping criticism of the legislation of the '60s." Citing Medicare, aid to education, food stamps, Head Start and college loan programs, he said: "We can go through a long list that has made a very positive contribution to the fairness and justice of our society."

In the face of widespread condemnation, Bush backed off somewhat, with administration officials scurrying to point out that spending for many popular Great Society social programs had increased — with the president's support — during his tenure.

But Bush also refused to say Fitzwater was wrong.

"In the past decade, spending is up, a number of programs are up," the president told newspaper editors in a May 6 conference call. "And yet, let's face it, that has not solved many of the fundamental problems that plague our cities."

The administration's indecision on the issue, including on-again, off-again plans for a legislative package and a California trip with an ever-changing agenda, played right into the hands of Democrats, who renewed old charges that Bush could not or would not lead on domestic policy.

Said Rep. Henry A. Waxman, D-Calif., whose Los Angeles district was among those affected by the riots: "If the initial reaction of political leaders is to try to figure out who else to blame, it doesn't give you much hope for the future."

### Political Danger Zones

Both Bush and congressional Democrats found themselves boxed in by diverse circumstances when trying to respond to the newly rediscovered urban crisis.

For Bush, the considerations were mostly political.

The June 2 California primary was technically a formality, because the president had wrapped up more than enough delegates to ensure his re-nomination. But challenger Patrick J. Buchanan remained a force from the right. He, too, traveled to Southern California after the riots, to praise the King verdict and chide Bush for not being more law-and-order oriented.

"This orgy of violence and lynching cannot be used to shake down the American taxpayer for another Great Society," Buchanan said.

Bush needed not only to hold on to his right wing but also to prove to doubters that he did have a domestic agenda. That set up a danger zone as well.

If he embraced too broad a social agenda, even a conservative one, Bush ran the risk of getting into a "me too" fight with the prospective Democratic nominee, Arkansas Gov. Bill Clinton. "And he can't outbid Clinton," warned Dave Mason, an analyst with the Heritage Foundation, a conservative think tank based in Washington.

Democrats had a different but equally serious political problem in trying to address the ills of the urban poor just as the party was taking pains to embrace the middle class.

"I think people are nervous because they don't know how this will affect them politically," said Thomas J. Downey, D-N.Y., acting chairman of the House Ways and Means subcommittee that oversaw unemployment and welfare issues.

Agreed the Heritage Foundation's Mason: "If the Democrats sign up for nothing more than more Great Society programs, they run the risk of exacerbating their old image."

Downey said one way to bridge the gap was for the Democrats to embrace "universalist" solutions that helped both the poor and the middle class. Examples, he said, included reforming the health-care system and improving efforts to make absent parents pay child support.

Other Democrats said the key was to persuade middle-class Americans that helping the poor was in their own economic interest. "Everybody's livelihood depends on our ability to bring the cities back into the mainstream of society," said Sen. John Kerry, D-Mass.

But congressional Democrats had larger obstacles: the federal deficit and a president dead set against tax increases.

Speaker Foley told reporters May 6 that the Democrat-passed tax bill (HR 4210) and the so-called walls bills (HR 3732, S 2399) to allow funding transfers from defense to domestic programs would go a long way toward addressing urban problems. But Congress sustained Bush's veto of the tax bill, and neither chamber could muster a majority to break down the budget walls. *(First tax bill, p. 133; walls bill, p. 104)*

"We ain't got the money," conceded Sen. Dale Bumpers, D-Ark., at a May 5 press conference to release a study documenting the effectiveness of the Supplemental Feeding Program for Women, Infants and Children, known as WIC. He had been asked why he was not pushing faster for the program to be fully funded.

And members were loath to offer broad programs and then not be able to pay for them. Said Downey: "The worst thing would be to offer an effort and have it fail."

Democrats also did not want a repeat of what House Budget Committee Chairman Leon E. Panetta, D-Calif., referred to as "the tax bill fiasco." Rather than reaping political hay by making Bush veto a tax bill that included benefits for the middle class and a tax hike for the rich, Democrats ended up hurting themselves as well. The tax bill's demise highlighted how little was getting done in Washington.

"The American people are tired of that. They don't want to get messages," Panetta said. "They want the Congress and the president to work together."

But beyond parochial budget and political concerns, both Republicans and Democrats said a major reason for the dearth of sweeping proposals was that members truly did not know what to do.

"We may not know much, but one thing we're sure of is [that] nobody has a magic bullet," said Rep. Bill Gradison, R-Ohio, a former mayor of Cincinnati.

Agreed Rep. Julian C. Dixon, D-Calif., "Let's face it. We're short of money, and just reaching in our pockets and asking how much is not going to do the job. We need to find new answers."

And some predicted that things would get worse before they got better.

"I think we're going to see a lot of rhetoric, but the hard, cold reality is we're heading for the kinds of major disinvestment ... that led to events in L.A. in the first place," said Robert Greenstein, who headed the Washington-based Center on Budget and Policy Priorities, a liberal think tank. A pending constitutional amendment forcing the federal government to balance its budget would prompt severe federal spending cuts, Greenstein predicted. Cities would be doubly hurt by the resulting cost-shifting from federal to state to local governments. *(Balanced-budget amendment, p. 108)*

"And the cuts will be disproportionately focused on programs that serve the weakest constituencies, which are the poor and minorities," Greenstein said.

None of that meant politicians would stop trying to fashion some solutions.

In a May 8 speech to a Los Angeles youth organization, Bush called on Congress to enact several old administration proposals. His list included enterprise zones, his America 2000 education initiative, and Housing and Urban Development Secretary Jack F. Kemp's Home Ownership and Opportunity for People Everywhere (HOPE) plan to allow public housing tenants to own their homes.

In the House, the most immediate vehicle, aside from the supplemental appropriations bill providing emergency relief, was the unemployment bill approved by Downey's Ways and Means subcommittee May 6.

In cooperation with Clinton, Downey and House Majority Leader Richard A. Gephardt, D-Mo., wanted to add several initiatives to the bill, including an overhaul of the federal child welfare bureaucracy. They wanted to showcase the difference between the Democrats' agenda and Bush's. *(Child welfare, p. 462)*

The Congressional Black Caucus, in cooperation with the House Democratic leadership, also was hoping to fashion a package. It would be based, according to caucus Chairman Edolphus Towns, D-N.Y., on the group's budget plan, which would cut defense spending authority by nearly $50 billion in fiscal 1993 and plow it back into domestic spending.

Although the budget plan garnered a mere 77 votes when the House voted on it in March, Towns, like Downey,

said the events in Los Angeles could have prompted some reconsideration. "As a result of what occurred, people are beginning to focus on the fact that there are some serious problems we need to address," Towns said May 7.

Things were more fluid in the Senate, where members proposed no sweeping packages but rather put forth some individual initiatives

Kerry, for example, said he hoped to strip out of the stalled crime package a provision to help inner-city youth enter law enforcement, as well as push his "Youthbuild" bill (S 1100), which would put disadvantaged youth to work rehabilitating housing.

And on May 6 Sen. Edward M. Kennedy, D-Mass., called for a supplemental appropriations bill that would provide $5 billion for anti-poverty programs. Kennedy said the amount should be added to the deficit by declaring a budget "emergency," but Bush officials already had declined emergency status for the less sweeping House bill.

## DEVELOPING AN APPROACH

Bush and congressional Democrats struck a fragile truce the week of May 11, with cordial words about working together to aid the inner cities of America.

Following the three days of rioting in Los Angeles the week of April 27, Bush and the Democrats gingerly stepped forward with proposals to aid blighted urban areas with new jobs and social programs. They met at the White House May 12 to exchange preliminary ideas.

The catalyst appeared to be the desires of both parties and the president to do something positive and to avoid the appearance of political gridlock — something the polls said citizens viewed with growing disgust.

"Both need evidence that they can act when problems arise," said Norman J. Ornstein, a political analyst at the American Enterprise Institute, a think tank based in Washington, D.C. "If they don't act when one of the largest cities in the country burns down, they're going to have trouble arguing they should be re-elected."

That meant that rather than goading each other with poison pill proposals, such as a cut in the capital gains tax, both sides tried to offer suggestions that could receive bipartisan approval.

House Speaker Foley, for example, suggested putting together two urban initiatives. The first would include ideas that Democrats and the administration agreed on. Next, Democrats would propose legislation that they knew Bush would be unlikely to sign but that would give Democrats a chance to distinguish themselves from Republicans.

"I have a little less confidence that we could agree on a total long-range program for the cities," Foley said. "But I am not willing personally to say that what we can agree to will be the end of our efforts in the future."

During the White House meeting Bush proposed a six-point plan, including some ideas he had pushed vigorously in the past, such as providing subsidies to parents who wished to send their children to private schools, and some he had not pushed as hard, such as enterprise zones. Such zones would provide incentives for businesses to locate in urban areas.

Bush also announced May 13 that the Federal Home Loan Bank Board would provide $600 million in low-interest loans to people and businesses hurt by the L.A. riots. "It's one way we can underscore the fact that we are serious about helping Los Angeles recover," Bush said. Those loans would come on top of aid from the Small Business Admin-

istration (SBA) and the Federal Emergency Management Agency (FEMA). With Bush's blessing, the House passed the emergency supplemental appropriations bill May 14 to provide disaster relief for riot-damaged sections of Los Angeles and to Chicago for repairs following massive flooding. The bill appropriated $495 million for FEMA to provide $300 million in disaster assistance and for the SBA to subsidize $500 million in disaster loans.

### Compromise: Election Liability?

But as Congress and the president moved forward on an urban package, both faced a host of political risks during an election year.

For Bush, the risk was that he would not be able to deliver an aid package that he had promised for the domestic front — his well-known weak spot. Congress could push him too far by sending a bill that he found too expensive, that raised taxes or that added to the federal deficit, any of which might prompt him to veto the measure.

For Democrats, the risk was that if they did get a bill enacted, Bush would take all the credit, scoring a huge domestic policy coup. And the Democrats could lose their main calling card in the presidential election — the charge that Bush was incapable of doing anything about the country's economic and social problems.

"Their whole campaign is based on the fact that he doesn't have a clue," said Thomas E. Mann, director of governmental studies at the Brookings Institution, a Washington think tank.

Moreover, while Bush and the Democrats said they wanted to work together and they wanted an urban relief package, the path to enactment was littered with policy differences and budget roadblocks.

"There's every incentive to work together and every reason to see how it will break down in the end," Mann said.

For example, most Democrats said Bush's school choice proposal was a non-starter. "What would school choice do for the Los Angeles riots?" asked House Education and Labor Chairman William D. Ford, D-Mich. (School choice, p. 455)

And while both Democrats and Republicans appeared to be in favor of creating federal enterprise zones, they differed on one related hot-button issue — capital gains. A capital gains tax of 28 percent of net profit was due the government upon the sale of assets such as stocks, homes or businesses. (Enterprise zones, p. 345)

Republicans wanted to promise business owners there would be no capital gains tax if they sold a business that had been located in an enterprise zone for at least two years.

Democrats viewed that as a foot in the door to lowering the capital gains rate in general, which they felt would favor the rich. They did not want to waive the tax.

Also, there was little love among the Democrats for HOPE, the prized program of Housing Secretary Kemp. HOPE helped public housing tenants buy their units from the government. Appropriators said they were concerned that congressional leaders might promise more money for the program at the expense of other housing and environmental and space programs, which were all funded out of the same appropriations pot. (Appropriations, p. 639)

"We're in a very tight bind," said Bill Green, R-N.Y., the ranking minority member of the House Appropriations Subcommittee on VA, HUD and Independent Agencies. He noted, too, that the states were more interested in having

Congress fund the HOME Investment Partnerships program, a Democratic initiative that sent block grant money to the states and cities to build and renovate low-income housing. (Housing bill, p. 367)

"My fear is that the [Democratic] leaders are not knowledgeable about housing and will cut a bad deal," said subcommittee Chairman Bob Traxler, D-Mich. "They'll do the deal for the sake of the politics."

Neither side, however, was on the verge of negotiating any deals. Democratic leaders spent the week trying to figure out what sort of process to use in approaching the urban aid issue. To avoid complaints from members about being left out, House leaders met with mayors, committee chairmen, members of the black caucus and Hispanic representatives to discuss possible proposals and strategy.

"Everything is being talked about," said Rep. Maxine Waters, D-Calif., whose district was engulfed by the riots.

Senate Finance Committee Chairman Lloyd Bentsen, D-Texas, wanted urban initiatives attached to the fast-moving unemployment bill because he was worried that the more he had to shepherd measures through the Senate floor, the more they would be exposed to unfriendly add-ons.

But as the week wore on, it became clear that Bush was willing to sign both an urban bill and an unemployment measure. Foley said the measures would go through separately, as would a bill to extend several expiring tax breaks.

### The Main Issue — Money

In the end, most lawmakers agreed that neither policy differences nor strategy would be the most difficult problem to iron out of the urban agenda. How to pay for it would be.

Under the rules of the 1990 budget agreement, all new spending had to be offset either by cuts in programs or an increase in revenues, such as taxes. Republicans were adamant that they would not pay for an urban initiative with taxes or by declaring an emergency and adding to the deficit.

"This isn't going to be a tax-increase bill," said Richard G. Darman, director of the Office of Management and Budget (OMB). "That's not going to be productive."

House Armed Services Committee Chairman Les Aspin, D-Wis., had called for knocking down the budget wall between domestic and defense spending to free about $6 billion to pay for an urban bill. "The tragic events in Los Angeles have demonstrated that urban relief is necessary," Aspin said May 15.

But Republicans were opposed to changing the budget walls, too. Under the 1990 budget agreement, cuts in defense spending had to be used to lower the federal deficit.

That left one option — for Congress to cut existing programs — which was never an easy proposition.

So with the usual budget constraints, both sides may have been weaving little more than a political cover — and a thin one, at that. Disagreement within the parties was apparent.

New York Mayor David N. Dinkins, a Democrat, called the administration's proposals "a pittance" and "woefully inadequate." He said the nation's mayors, unlike Bush, did not only recently realize that the cities needed help. "We know what we need, and we've known it all along," said Dinkins.

But Dinkins, along with other big-city mayors, was pushing for a $35 billion urban aid package — something the Democrats would not give them either.

"It's not a Republican problem that we face," Baltimore Mayor Kurt Schmoke told The Baltimore Sun. "I met with the Democratic leadership of the House, and these people just don't get it."

Foley, Senate Majority Leader George J. Mitchell, D-Maine, and House Majority Leader Gephardt sent Bush a letter May 11, outlining the Democratic priorities for an urban aid package.

It included: a crime control bill that was hung up in the Senate because of Republican opposition; enterprise zones; the extension of several expiring tax breaks, such as the low-income housing tax credit; an extension of federal unemployment benefits; and a speedup of about $3.6 billion in funds available to states for the Surface Transportation Act of 1991 to provide jobs.

Administration officials had not yet tallied the total amount Bush was requesting in aid for his proposals, which already included: $500 million for a "weed and seed" program to "weed out" criminals in bad neighborhoods and "seed" the neighborhood with money for Head Start, community health centers, drug treatment and housing assistance; $1 billion in fiscal 1993 for HOPE; welfare reform, such as allowing states and cities to waive certain welfare rules; and a youth job training program.

"The dollar amounts are not enormous by Washington standards, although they are substantial," acknowledged Darman, after meeting in May with the House Republican Conference to talk strategy for urban aid.

Kemp, on the other hand, was hoping that the budget would not stand in his way. He had been pushing for enterprise zones and HOPE for years, and he did not want them to lose momentum.

"We've got to decide whether we're for people or budgets," Kemp said. "I'm for the budget constraints, but there's an urgent unmet need to create wealth and opportunity in the inner city."

## PROGRESS BY THE INCH

With the first brief summit meeting on urban issues, Congress and the Bush administration took more baby steps the week of May 18 toward putting together a package of urban programs in response to the Los Angeles riots.

White House Chief of Staff Samuel K. Skinner, budget director Darman and White House lobbyist Nicholas E. Calio went to Capitol Hill on May 20 to meet with Democratic and Republican leaders from the House and Senate. But the conversation stuck mostly to the logistics of negotiations without moving toward substance.

Both sides continued to say they wanted to reach an agreement. But Democrats and Republicans alike had to restrain themselves from upping the partisan ante by offering proposals repugnant to the other side.

Foley said that Democrats might have to wait for the election of a new president to get the types of programs and funding they really wanted.

"We don't feel that the administration's commitment to urban America and renewal is anywhere near strong enough to represent real, serious, long-term answers to the problem," Foley said. "I think that is very, very clear."

Republicans, however, said the Democrats had no clear vision of what they wanted for the cities, besides pouring in more money.

"Their basic approach is hopeless and self-destructive," said House Minority Whip Newt Gingrich, R-Ga.

### Movement Elsewhere

But while an urban aid package trudged along, Congress proceeded on several fronts with legislation bearing the "urban" imprint:

● **Emergency Aid.** The Senate, for example, passed a $1.9 billion "dire emergency" supplemental appropriations bill May 21.

● **Unemployment.** The House acted on legislation to extend federal unemployment benefits.

● **Housing.** The House Banking Committee approved legislation reauthorizing low-income housing programs following subcommittee action May 20.

● **Crime.** And the House Education and Labor Committee approved legislation May 20 that would expand federal programs to keep juveniles away from violent gangs and criminal activities. *(Juvenile justice, p. 334)*

As far as formulating more extensive legislation, House Democratic leaders had been cautious not to exclude any member — or mayor for that matter — who wanted a voice in the process. They set up an urban task force, including black caucus members, Hispanic members and committee chairmen, to direct the course of negotiations with the administration.

And they decided to rotate members in and out of the negotiations, with House Majority Leader Gephardt taking the lead role. Foley and Mitchell would get involved in the talks only if Bush were present.

### Too Many Chefs?

But with so many members involved, the Democrats faced struggling with "too many chefs." The problem, one Democrat said, was that there was no Jesse Jackson in Congress — one person alone with the standing to speak for the inner cities.

And Democrats did not appear to know exactly what to ask for in the negotiations.

"It's early, and we're still trying to identify a package and what will be in that package," said Waters, whose district bore the brunt of the riots.

Republicans, however, stuck to their announced reform agenda. Gingrich spoke repeatedly about the need for enterprise zones, which would use tax incentives to lure businesses into inner cities; for helping low-income families buy their own homes to give them a stake in their communities; and for "Weed and Seed," President Bush's proposal to weed out criminals from bad neighborhoods and then seed those neighborhoods with money for social programs.

Republicans named Rep. Vin Weber, R-Minn., to represent them in the negotiations. Weber was closely aligned with Gingrich and with HUD Secretary Kemp. Weber had announced he would not seek re-election in November.

## DEMOCRATIC PLAN

Following the Los Angeles riots, House Democrats developed the makings of a $9 billion plan to assist urban areas.

A House Democratic task force working on urban aid legislation came up with a preliminary list of ideas the week of May 25, not yet shown to Senate Democrats, to pump more money into many popular programs, such as Head Start for disadvantaged children and the Job Training Partnership Act to train the needy.

House and Senate Democrats had to agree quickly on a set of proposals if they were serious about hammering out an urban aid package with the Bush administration. Bush

already had proposed a six-point plan of proposals he had been unsuccessfully pushing throughout his term, such as tax incentives for businesses that moved into enterprise zones and more money to help low-income people become homeowners.

Members of Congress and the Bush administration frequently said that they had about one month to enact legislation before partisan politics and presidential electioneering began in the summer of 1992.

The $9 billion proposal came from a task force list divided into four sections: job training, education and children, economic investment and community development. Ideas included:

● Expanding the job training act at a cost of $500 million by providing 65,000 people with six-month public service jobs that paid $7 an hour. The work included renovating school buildings. Another possibility was to extend or make permanent the targeted jobs tax credit, which went to employers who hired hard-to-place workers. And a new demonstration project had been proposed to train and employ 20,000 jobless adults, ages 21 to 30, who lived in high poverty areas.

● Enlarging several popular programs such as childhood immunization; WIC; Head Start and the Chapter 1 compensatory education program for disadvantaged children.

● Combining an enterprise zone program with Bush's "Weed and Seed" program.

Other Democratic possibilities included more money for the administration's HOPE and HOME Investment Partnerships, the Democrats' housing block grant program.

## ENTERPRISE ZONES FOCUS DEBATE

Giving tax breaks to businesses that located in enterprise zones — blighted inner-city neighborhoods in need of economic resuscitation — emerged as the centerpiece of urban aid negotiations between Congress and the White House the week of June 1.

But the talks dragged on without resolution of any portion of an urban aid package.

Participants had not discussed details of how enterprise zones would work or what tax breaks would be used — a topic that could blow up into a partisan brawl. Nor had they broached what the bill would cost and how they would pay for it — the touchiest subject of all.

And congressional negotiators on an emergency spending bill forced a confrontation with the White House on June 5 by ignoring a request to pare the bill and support enterprise zones in return for presidential approval of summer jobs money.

At the White House on June 2, President Bush suggested to Democratic leaders that they concentrate on moving enterprise zones alone, rather than combined with other elements of his six-point proposal, which included more money for low-income home ownership and "Weed and Seed" funding.

The next day, House Majority Leader Gephardt countered with a House Democratic proposal, put together the week of May 25, to boost existing programs, such as Head Start and job training for needy adults, by $10.8 billion in one year.

Lawmakers informally set a July 4 deadline to wrap up an urban bill. In July and August, Democrats and Republicans would be attending their political conventions and would have little incentive to avoid partisan attacks.

### A Patina of Hesitancy

But the slow pace of the talks made that date appear increasingly unrealistic. Charles O. Jones, political science professor at the University of Wisconsin at Madison, said "a patina of hesitancy" pervaded the urban aid discussions.

Part of the problem was that once Congress and Bush decided what they wanted to do, they would have to pay for it. "If you're going to open up this can of worms, then you're talking about big bucks and they're not there," Jones said.

And Republicans, he said, were reluctant to deliver any extra money to Democratic mayors. Jones' contention was borne out June 3, when the House Government Operations Committee rejected, 20-20, legislation to inject $5.4 billion into nearly 40,000 municipalities nationwide. Six Democrats joined 14 Republicans in voting against the bill.

But if Congress failed to put together a package, the consequences could be even more severe. "God knows if there's another kind of riot, everybody's going to get blamed," Jones said.

Ornstein, of the American Enterprise Institute, concurred: "If nothing happens in Congress and another riot occurs, it will only reinforce the feeling among Americans that Congress is doing nothing."

Although Congress had not acted yet, talk continued. Bentsen convened the Senate Finance Committee June 3 to examine the enterprise zone concept, which was previously included in the tax bill (HR 4210) that Bush vetoed.

Committee Democrats made it clear that they would not support tax breaks for enterprise zones alone. Instead, they had to be combined with job training and education programs to help the residents of those areas.

"If other things are not done," warned Donald W. Riegle Jr., D-Mich., "it won't be enough."

At the same time, Senate Minority Leader Bob Dole, R-Kan., said he was not sure how enterprise zones would work and how they would be paid for.

Bentsen agreed: "I just don't want to bust the budget to do this."

Kemp had no answers on financing. "I put growth and opportunity ahead of the budget," he said.

And Kemp still would have to persuade members of his own party that spending money on urban areas was good for society at large.

Bill Gradison of Ohio, the ranking Republican on the House Budget Committee and a member of the Ways and Means Committee, represented the city of Cincinnati. He was one of the few Republican members speaking against enterprise zones.

"I think enterprise zones simply move investments around and that they don't create new jobs," he said, adding that voters resented rewarding the rioters of Los Angeles. "It's not part of the road to re-election in southwestern Ohio . . . and I'm not some suburban congressman talking about us and them."

## STILL HUNG UP

Nearly two months after the riots had rocked Los Angeles, Congress was still hung up over how to structure an aid package to help blighted urban areas across the country.

House Majority Leader Gephardt, who had run the urban aid negotiations, said he would give the talks a C-plus, adding that the two sides had an even chance of coming together or falling apart.

At that point, Congress and the White House had agreed to enact the $1.1 billion supplemental spending bill (PL 102-302) with money for loans and grants to rebuild Los Angeles and to provide 360,000 summer jobs for young people around the country.

# Interest Renewed in Enterprise Zones

The riots in Los Angeles left more than 50 people dead and destroyed hundreds of businesses. They also — briefly — breathed new life into an old idea to help blighted inner cities: enterprise zones.

Yet the flurry of activity to renew efforts to enact legislation that would give federal tax incentives to businesses that opened or relocated in impoverished areas of the nation's cities produced no tangible results in 1992.

An emergency urban aid supplemental (HR 5132 — PL 102-302) that cleared Congress June 18 was intended as part of a broader urban aid initiative, but in the end it contained the only money that Congress would provide to inner cities in 1992 as a response to the L.A. riots. No money was earmarked for enterprise zones. *(Urban aid supplemental, p. 579)*

The other big urban aid proposal that grew out of the riots, which incorporated the negotiated plan to set up dozens of enterprise zones, was the large tax bill (HR 11) Congress cleared just before adjournment. President Bush vetoed that bill Nov. 4. *(Urban aid tax bill, p. 140)*

In HR 11, the House and Senate agreed to create 50 zones, with 25 in rural areas and 25 in cities. Investors who put their money into a zone for five years were to receive a 50 percent capital gains tax cut — a provision the administration said was imperative. Zone businesses would receive a 15 percent credit on the first $20,000 in wages paid to employees, a deduction of up to $25,000 for purchases of stock in zone businesses and more rapid tax write-offs for property.

Just before the riots, Congress had passed enterprise zone legislation in another tax bill, HR 4210, that was vetoed by Bush on March 20. It had included a $700 million demonstration plan to create 10 urban and rural enterprise zones. *(First tax bill, p. 133)*

While Congress bickered for years about enterprise zones, cities and states took the lead, testing the idea with state and local tax incentives. Enterprise zones were spread throughout 36 states and the District of Columbia. Twenty-two of those states said they had created 258,395 jobs, and 18 states reported capital investments in their zones totaling $28 billion as of June 1991.

The term "enterprise zone" was coined in England in 1978 to describe a plan to redevelop large industrial areas in the East End of London.

A year later, Stuart M. Butler, director of domestic policy studies for the Heritage Foundation, a conservative think tank based in Washington, imported the idea to the United States. He modified it to apply to neighborhoods and small businesses, rather than to large industrial areas.

Butler believed that the existing examples had been moderately successful despite the absence of federal tax breaks. "You really see a very limited version of what is possible," he said.

In Congress, some members worried that tax breaks for businesses in enterprise zones might become an excuse not to spend money on other social programs.

And the House Ways and Means Committee had approved a massive tax bill that included urban and rural enterprise zones, which would provide tax breaks for businesses that located in certain impoverished areas. *(Urban aid tax bill, p. 140)*

Yet, whether a consensus on urban aid could be found would depend not on members of the tax-writing committee but on the highest levels of the administration and on top Democratic leaders.

Rep. Charles B. Rangel, D-N.Y., said he was pessimistic that the administration as a whole would stand behind an urban package that included enterprise zones as well as job training and education provisions.

HUD Secretary Kemp had tried to rally the administration to aid the cities.

"Jack Kemp is out there by himself," Rangel said.

Democratic leadership aides said the Rules Committee could add education and job training provisions to the tax bill before it was sent to the House floor.

Rangel said that without those additions, "the enterprise zones would be a farce."

Gephardt pledged on the floor that members would be given an opportunity to debate enterprise zones before the Fourth of July. But he said the legislation could reflect the Democrats' proposals if a compromise could not be reached with Republicans.

Weber, who had represented Republicans in the urban aid negotiations, shared Rangel's pessimism. But he added: "It's not dead till it's dead."

Although enterprise zones were the centerpiece of

Bush's urban aid proposal, the Ways and Means Committee approved a plan crafted by Chairman Dan Rostenkowski, D-Ill., that met strong opposition from Republicans.

Members were split primarily over Rostenkowski's elimination of a cherished Republican provision — a waiver of the capital gains tax payable when a business was sold.

Most Republicans maintained that the lure of profit without the tax was what would draw businesses to impoverished urban areas.

Rostenkowski instead included a provision that would allow deferral of capital gains taxes from enterprise zone businesses provided that the money was reinvested in another enterprise zone business.

Some Democrats were skeptical that enterprise zones could solve the ills of poverty.

"I think it would be more cost-effective to dump the money out of an airplane over the ghettos," said Downey, a member of Ways and Means who had championed federal benefits for the long-term unemployed.

In the Senate, Finance Committee Chairman Bentsen said he would move a bill with enterprise zones in it after the House sent one over, most likely in late July.

## Postscript

Bush eventually vetoed the $27 billion tax bill (HR 11) including urban aid because it contained three dozen revenue-raising provisions that he said were tax increases. It was the second time that Bush killed a tax bill in 1992. He vetoed the first one in March over tax increases on the rich that were to be used to pay for a middle-class tax cut. ■

# Unemployment Bills Extend Benefits

After temporarily extending unemployment benefits three times in less than a year, Congress and President Bush thought they had put the unemployment issue to rest by making permanent changes to the system. A measure (HR 5260 — PL 102-318) signed into law July 3 was designed to allow benefits to kick in more easily during periods of high jobless rates.

During his first address to a joint session of Congress on Feb. 17, 1993, President Clinton told the nation he was prepared to extend unemployment benefits yet again, this time for seven months.

Unemployed workers usually qualified for 26 weeks of state unemployment benefits.

Before Congress jumped in in 1991 and passed an emergency benefits program, a federal-state program called "extended benefits" was in place to provide an extra 13 weeks of compensation.

Frustrated with the difficulty workers faced in getting those extra benefits, Congress temporarily overrode that program and gave states an extra 13 or 20 weeks of benefits, depending on the number of unemployed people in the state.

Then, with 600,000 workers poised to exhaust those benefits in mid-February 1992, Congress cleared another extension on Feb. 4, which Bush also signed (HR 4095 — PL 102-244). That gave workers an extra 13 weeks of benefits after exhausting both state benefits and the first federal emergency benefits. Altogether, unemployed workers became eligible for either 52 or 59 weeks of benefits through July 4.

Congress cleared its second unemployment bill of the year July 2, and Bush signed it July 3.

The final measure (HR 5260) included a permanent change to the unemployment system — something Bush had vowed he would not accept. It was to cost $5.5 billion over six years, giving unemployed workers in 15 states 26 extra weeks of benefits and in all other states and the District of Columbia 20 extra weeks until March 6, 1993.

## BACKGROUND

Twice in 1991, Bush blocked bills to provide additional compensation on top of state benefits to unemployed work-

---

## BOXSCORE

➡ **Unemployment Compensation (HR 4095, HR 5260).** Legislation cleared early in the year offered an additional 13 weeks of compensation for the unemployed who exhausted their 26 weeks of state benefits and then exhausted the 13 to 20 weeks of extended federal benefits enacted in 1991. The second bill of the year also extended emergency unemployment benefits. To avoid further extensions, it included permanent changes to the system designed to allow non-emergency extended benefits to kick in more easily during periods of high unemployment.

**Reports:** H Rept 102-543; conference report H Rept 102-650.

### KEY ACTION

**Jan. 28** — The **House** Ways and Means Committee gave voice vote approval to HR 4095.

**Jan 30** — The **Senate** Finance Committee approved its version of HR 4095, also by voice vote.

**Feb. 4** — The **House** passed HR 4095, 404-8; the **Senate** followed suit, 94-2.

**Feb. 7** — President Bush signed HR 4095 — PL 102-244.

**May 20** — The **House** Ways and Means Committee gave voice vote approval to HR 4727.

**May 27** — The **House** Ways and Means Committee gave voice vote approval to a revised bill, HR 5260.

**June 9** — The **House** passed HR 5260, 261-150.

**June 11** — The **Senate** Finance Committee approved its version of HR 5260 by voice vote.

**June 19** — The **Senate** passed HR 5260 by voice vote.

**July 2** — The House adopted the conference report on HR 5260, 396-23; the Senate cleared it 93-3.

**July 3** — President Bush signed HR 5260 — PL 102-318.

---

ers. Then, as Thanksgiving approached and the economy worsened, the administration relented, although Bush continued to insist that the measure be paid for under the pay-as-you-go rules of the 1990 budget agreement.

The ultimate compromise (HR 3575 — PL 102-164), cleared by Congress on Nov. 15 and signed by Bush the same day, provided for a temporary extension of benefits at a cost of $5.3 billion, which was paid for by tightening a loophole on those paying quarterly taxes. A second bill, enacted Dec. 4 (PL 102-182), completed a second step of the compromise by boosting the benefits all states would receive at a cost of $380 million. That was paid for by shortening the applicable period of the extension program, from July 4 to June 13. *(1991 Almanac, p. 301)*

The recession, however, continued to take its toll on the American work force. The Labor Department reported that since July 1990, when the recession began, the seasonally adjusted number of unemployed people had increased by 2.1 million and stood at 8.9 million in December 1991. The civilian unemployment rate in December was 7.1 percent, up from 6.2 percent at the beginning of 1991.

House Ways and Means Chairman Dan Rostenkowski, D-Ill., was particularly upset that his home state's unemployment rate shot up to 9.3 percent in December. "There's real pain in my neighborhood, in my city, in my state and across America," Rostenkowski said. "If this is not an emergency, then tell me what is."

### How The System Worked

The insured employment rate was based on the number of jobless still collecting benefits. It did not include those who had exhausted benefits but remained unemployed.

Many states also devised rules limiting the number of people who qualified for any unemployment compensation. That kept the insured unemployment rate low, which reduced the states' costs. But many lawmakers complained that the result was an insured rate that did not reflect a state's true unemployment.

Rep. Thomas J. Downey, D-N.Y., and other Democrats

had long wanted to change the extended benefits trigger from the insured unemployment rate to the total unemployment rate. But it was not until a compromise was struck in 1991 to provide six, 13 or 20 weeks of extra benefits that Senate Republicans also began to dislike the existing system.

## FIRST ROUND: HR 4095

Congress cleared a measure (HR 4095 — PL 102-244) Feb. 4 that offered an additional 13 weeks of compensation for the unemployed who exhausted their 26 weeks of state benefits and then exhausted the 13 to 20 weeks of extended federal benefits enacted in 1991. Altogether, jobless workers were to receive either 52 or 59 weeks of benefits, depending upon the severity of the unemployment in their state.

The Labor Department estimated that 1.5 million of the 3.1 million people receiving the 1991 extended benefits would remain unemployed long enough to receive the latest 13 weeks of benefits. The bill also made the extended benefits available through July 4, three weeks longer than allowed in existing law.

### 'Emergency' Extension Proposed

Barely two months after winning passage of the 1991 bill to give the unemployed extended benefits, congressional Democrats decided to confront Bush again with an "emergency" extension.

The White House was not initially forthcoming on whether it would oppose a new unemployment bill. Campaigning in New Hampshire on Jan. 15, Bush responded ambiguously to a question about his stance: "If a frog had wings, he wouldn't hit his tail on the ground. Too hypothetical."

Rostenkowski proposed giving workers 26 or 33 extra weeks of benefits rather than 13 or 20 weeks as the new law (PL 102-182) allowed. That would be on top of the 26 weeks of unemployment compensation provided by the states.

Rostenkowski also proposed extending the expiration date for eligibility from June 13 to Oct. 3.

House Republican leader Robert H. Michel of Illinois showed similar concern about the high unemployment numbers. In separate meetings Jan. 9 with White House Chief of Staff Samuel K. Skinner and budget director Richard G. Darman, Michel said Congress would have to extend the benefits further if the unemployment situation did not turn around.

When Congress and the White House did reach a consensus on the need for another law extending federal unemployment benefits, the snag was how to pay for them.

The White House wrote up a proposal to provide additional weeks of unemployment compensation to American workers who had still not found work after collecting the 26 weeks of state benefits and the 13 to 20 weeks of extended benefits that Congress authorized late the previous year.

Michel said he was all for moving another extension of jobless benefits, but he insisted that Congress find a way to offset the estimated $4.5 billion cost.

But that outstanding question was not stopping House and Senate Democrats, who moved with lightning speed to enact a new bill (HR 4095).

The new extension, as proposed by Rostenkowski, would cost $3.5 billion in fiscal 1992 and $1 billion in fiscal 1993. The 1990 budget law allowed such new spending programs only if they were offset by spending cuts or tax increases, or if Congress and the president jointly declared an emergency.

Rostenkowski scheduled a markup of HR 4095 for Jan. 28. "We will crank this thing out of here next week," said

Downey, acting chairman of the Ways and Means Subcommittee on Human Resources and instigator of the 1991 extension.

Senate Finance Committee Chairman Lloyd Bentsen, D-Texas, also planned to introduce a bill, though he did not say whether he favored declaring an emergency to pay for it.

### Committee Action

The House Ways and Means Committee on Jan. 28 gave voice vote approval to a compromise version of HR 4095 crafted by Rostenkowski and Michel. It cut the cost of Rostenkowski's original proposal to $2.7 billion, mainly by changing the deadline for eligibility from Oct. 3 to July 4.

The cost would be offset by $2.2 billion left over from the 1991 bills and $500 million in accelerated collection of estimated taxes from large corporations.

The Senate Finance Committee approved its version of the bill Jan. 30, also by voice vote. Chairman Bentsen noted that the original extension would run out in mid-February for more than 600,000 workers. The latest extension, he said, "represents a sorely needed helping hand as the economy continues to flounder."

### First Bill Clears

With overwhelming votes in the House and Senate, Congress on Feb. 4 cleared for the president's signature the bill to further extend benefits for the long-term unemployed.

The action also set a new deadline of July 4 for the next time Congress had to confront the unemployment issue, although leaders of both parties hoped to come up with a more lasting solution before then.

The House voted 404-8 to pass HR 4095, the second extension of jobless benefits in three months. The Senate followed suit the same day on a 94-2 vote. The only "nay" votes in both chambers were cast by conservative Republicans. *(House vote 4, p. 2-H; Senate vote 17, p. 4-S)*

Bush signed the bill into law Feb. 7 — PL 102-244. "We are delighted Congress acted so quickly," White House spokeswoman Judy Smith said after final passage. "We are anxious to get the bill so we can get the benefits to those in need."

As both the House and Senate debated the bill, few Republicans stood up to voice support for the measure. Instead, each chamber's floor was commanded mostly by Democrats, who decried the tough economic times that required the legislation and jabbing the president for resisting similar measures the previous year.

"I wish this meant the president has seen the light. I am afraid it is just that he has felt the heat," said House Majority Whip David E. Bonior, D-Mich. "Let us get this bill on the president's desk before he changes his mind."

House Minority Leader Michel, who brokered the compromise on behalf of Bush, said the bill's passage "shows that Congress and the administration can work together in a timely fashion to respond to the problems of this nation."

The funding issue was the key to the compromise, yet it became a point of dispute during Senate floor debate. Sen. Hank Brown, R-Colo., cited Congressional Budget Office (CBO) estimates that showed the new bill would cost money and thus add to the deficit.

The congressional agency disputed much of the White House estimate on the $2.2 billion pay-as-you-go surplus. A Jan. 13 Office of Management and Budget (OMB) report said Congress raised a surplus of $1.1 billion in fiscal 1992 and would raise an extra $1.1 billion in fiscal 1993 as a result of legislation enacted in 1991.

Brown raised a point of order against the new jobless benefits bill, citing the CBO estimates and the budget law's pay-as-you-go requirements. But both Democrats and Republicans rallied against him, with GOP senators declining to make an issue of deficit spending and Democrats benignly adopting the White House budget estimate even though they previously had stood by the CBO.

A motion by Tom Daschle, D-S.D., to waive the budget act prevailed on an 88-8 vote, far more than the 60-vote supermajority needed. (Vote 16, p. 3-S)

### Provisions

Besides providing an extra 13 weeks of benefits, HR 4095:

• Speeded up the estimated tax payment rules for corporations with $1 million or more in taxable income.

• Provided railroad workers, who were covered by a separate unemployment program, the same benefits as other workers.

• Extended from Jan. 31 to June 30 the deadline for Michigan to repay a $181 million installment on a loan from the federal government.

Michigan owed $417 million from loans from the federal government from 1980 to 1985, when the state ran out of money to pay its state unemployment benefits.

## SEARCH FOR A PERMANENT FIX

Once they had provided a quick infusion of money to the unemployed, key members of Congress wanted to find ways to permanently fix the system — mainly by making it easier for the jobless to receive extended benefits.

Downey had been pushing for permanent changes for more than two years. In 1992, he finally won the support of leaders of both parties.

"I think that should be done," said House Speaker Thomas S. Foley, D-Wash., on the day the new extension passed the House.

Permanent law allowed jobless workers to collect extended benefits only when the total number of people collecting benefits in the state reached a certain trigger. Due to disparities between those who were collecting benefits (the "insured" unemployment rate) and those who had exhausted benefits and remained unemployed, some states had to reach total unemployment rates as high as 15 percent for their workers to receive federal compensation.

Without the 1991 emergency legislation to provide extra benefits, only two states would have qualified in 1992 for the federal extended benefits program. Some members wanted to use the total unemployment rate, or a combination of an insured and a total rate, as the trigger for extended benefits.

"If we have learned anything from the current recession, it is that the unemployment insurance safety net is filled with holes and jobless Americans have paid a heavy price for this delay," Downey said.

Rep. Nancy L. Johnson of Connecticut, a Republican on Downey's subcommittee, said she wanted to encourage states to allow their unemployed workers to receive partial benefits when they found part-time work.

Other Ways and Means Republicans, including E. Clay Shaw Jr. of Florida, the ranking minority member of the subcommittee, and Fred Grandy of Iowa, pushed to take the unemployment trust fund "off-budget." That would have allowed taxes collected from employers for unemployment benefits to remain dedicated to that purpose. At the time, the trust fund was little more than an accounting device

used to track revenues and payments for state and federal benefits. Any surplus in the federal program went into the Treasury's general fund.

## ROUND TWO: HR 5260

Congress cleared its second bill of the year on July 2, just prior to the July 4 deadline, when workers who had used up their 26 weeks of state benefits would no longer have been eligible for federal emergency benefits.

The final measure (HR 5260 — PL 102-318) included a permanent change to the unemployment system — something Bush had vowed he would not accept — that allowed non-emergency extended benefits to kick in more easily during periods of high unemployment. It was to cost $5.5 billion over six years, providing unemployed workers in 15 states with 26 extra weeks of benefits and workers in all other states and the District of Columbia with 20 extra weeks until March 6, 1993. Workers who had already exhausted their federal emergency benefits were not eligible for more.

### Democrats Clash with Administration

With federal emergency unemployment benefits set to expire July 4, congressional Democrats clashed with the administration twice the week of April 27 over what to do next to help the nation's 9.2 million unemployed workers. As of March, the national unemployment rate remained at 7.3 percent, unchanged from the month before.

Although Democrats zeroed in on Secretary of Labor Lynn Martin's unwillingness to present the administration's ideas at two congressional hearings, it was clear that neither Congress in general nor Democrats in particular were sure about how to proceed.

Democrats and Republicans seemed to agree that they should extend emergency benefits beyond July. Martin suggested extending them until the end of the year. Many Democrats would continue them into 1993.

Moreover, House Democrats wanted to overhaul the entire unemployment compensation system. The administration was opposed to that. Senate Democrats were interested in permanent changes but fearful of fierce Republican opposition.

And on top of policy disagreements, lawmakers disagreed about financing. House Democratic proposals to pay for an unemployment bill were already under attack. But neither the Senate nor the administration had made any suggestions.

In testimony before the Senate Finance Committee on April 29 and the House Ways and Means Subcommittee on Human Resources the next day, Martin repeatedly frustrated lawmakers by offering to negotiate an unemployment bill behind closed doors rather than describing the administration's position in public.

Martin would not say how many weeks of benefits the administration wanted to provide workers. She did not say how much she was willing to spend. And she would not say how the administration proposed to pay for the program, except to say that tax increases were unacceptable.

Still, her testimony was significant. Congress had been grappling with how to help the long-term jobless for more than a year, but this was the first time the secretary of Labor testified on the subject. And she expressed support for extended benefits. Republicans were given something to support, even though they opposed Democrats' more far-reaching ideas.

## Rostenkowski-Downey Proposal

But despite the two-day clash with the administration, the only tangible proposal on the table belonged to Rostenkowski and Downey.

They proposed a sweeping $7 billion bill (HR 4727) to overhaul the system and eliminate the need for Congress to step in periodically to pass emergency benefits.

The bill would extend the emergency benefits program, providing 13 or 20 weeks of benefits through the end of the year or until the month after the national unemployment rate's three-month average fell below 6.5 percent.

Downey said his top priority was to permanently change the "trigger" that released extended unemployment benefits. Downey wanted to base eligibility on the total unemployment rate — which included people who quit their jobs — to release the benefits more easily. He would also increase the federal share of benefits from 50 percent to 75 percent.

The administration and most Ways and Means Republicans opposed Downey's attempt to change the trigger, saying it would release too many benefits costing too much money.

Downey also had problems paying for his bill. The bill would cost $7 billion and raise $8.8 billion over five years, according to a preliminary estimate by the Congressional Budget Office and the Joint Committee on Taxation. But the bill would not be paid for year by year, as required by budget rules.

On the Senate side, Bentsen had not introduced legislation. He had said he wanted to extend benefits, though he was concerned about the administration's idea to do so only through the end of the year.

## Ways and Means Subcommittee Approval

In the week after the Los Angeles riots, House Democratic leaders moved to turn pending legislation to extend unemployment benefits into a showcase for challenging Bush on what they said was his lack of domestic policies.

The Ways and Means Subcommittee on Human Resources on May 6 gave voice vote approval to the new, $5.9 billion unemployment compensation bill (HR 4727).

The Bush administration already opposed the Democrats' unemployment provisions, which would permanently change the way the system worked by making it easier for workers to receive extra benefits.

But threatening the prospects for enacting additional unemployment legislation was a new plan by Downey to attach another domestic initiative — a Downey-sponsored overhaul of federal child welfare programs (HR 2571) — to the jobless bill. That would add at least $3.5 billion to the five-year cost of the measure. *(Child welfare, p. 462)*

Meanwhile, House Majority Leader Gephardt also wanted to use the unemployment bill as a vehicle to speed up federal dollars to cities and states for "infrastructure" projects such as road and bridge building. Other possible riders, Downey said, included authority to create "enterprise zones" in inner cities and an extension of temporary tax laws such as the low-income housing tax credit.

Grandy, a member of the Human Resources Subcommittee, said the legislation "sounds like it's becoming politically radioactive."

In the Senate, Finance Committee Chairman Bentsen was worried that he would not be able to move unemployment legislation through his chamber if members thought they could tack any pet program onto the bill. "I want to enact foster-care reform, but that would be very difficult to do with all the competing interest groups wanting to add

their own provisions," Bentsen said.

As approved by Downey's subcommittee, the unemployment bill would give workers up to 20 or 26 weeks of extra federal benefits if they had exhausted their state compensation and not yet returned to work — 26 weeks if the state's total unemployment rate averaged at least 9 percent over six months, 20 weeks for all others.

The new bill would make federal benefits available at least through Jan. 1, 1993, or until the month after the national unemployment rate's three-month average fell below 6.5 percent. As of March, the national unemployment rate remained at 7.3 percent, unchanged from the month before.

Downey had originally proposed giving workers an extra 13 or 20 weeks of benefits, but he was able to increase the number by dropping a proposed change in the way states calculated whether workers were eligible for benefits. Existing law required workers to have a long-term employment history to qualify for benefits.

Grandy offered an amendment on behalf of the administration to temporarily extend emergency unemployment benefits. This was the first specific indication of what the administration would support.

The Grandy amendment would extend benefits by 13 or 20 weeks through Oct. 3; then by seven or 13 weeks through Jan. 2, 1993; then by four or seven weeks through Feb. 13, 1993. The panel rejected it by voice vote.

In another key change to permanent law, Downey's bill would declare the unemployment program "off-budget," an attempt to make the federal unemployment taxes collected from employers solely dedicated to that purpose.

Republicans Shaw and Grandy supported the off-budget provision, saying that it was important for unemployment taxes to be directly tied to benefits. The administration opposed it, however.

To pay for his bill, Downey would extend a highly controversial tax provision that many Republicans and Democrats — including Downey's state governor, Mario M. Cuomo — opposed.

The provision, enacted in the 1990 White House-congressional budget agreement and named for Rep. Don J. Pease, D-Ohio, essentially raised taxes on higher-income taxpayers by limiting their allowable itemized deductions. Joint filers with adjusted gross incomes of $100,000 or more had to reduce their claim by 3 percent of their income over $100,000. If the adjusted gross income was $150,000, the itemized deductions would be reduced by multiplying $50,000 by 3 percent: $1,500.

The Pease provision was due to expire at the end of 1995; Downey would extend it through 1997 to raise $7.2 billion over five years.

Critics said that the provision hurt taxpayers' ability to deduct state and local taxes — a sensitive issue in states such as New York with high state income taxes. The American Federation of State, County and Municipal Employees opposed the provision, as did Cuomo, out of fear that taxpayers would pressure state and local governments to keep their taxes down.

Downey said he was not enthusiastic about extending the Pease provision but that he needed a way to pay for his bill. "If someone has a better financing mechanism, I'll entertain it," he said.

A second financing mechanism, known as "PEP," the personal exemption phaseouts, would raise $4.5 billion over five years. For every $2,500 increment over $157,900 (joint filers) and $105,250 (individual) in adjusted gross income, each personal exemption would be reduced by 2 percent: $43.

Altogether, the unemployment bill would spend $5.9 billion over five years and would raise a net increase of $8.8 billion in revenue. Downey hoped to use the $2.9 billion left over to pay for his overhaul of child welfare programs.

## WAYS AND MEANS ACTION

Expecting trouble with its expensive unemployment bill, the House Ways and Means Committee agreed by voice vote May 20 to approve a scaled-back measure to give long-term unemployed workers up to 26 weeks in extra benefits.

Chairman Rostenkowski put in a less costly substitute to HR 4727 to win enough support for a favorable committee vote. The substitute would cost $6 billion, down from $8.8 billion, and would raise $6.3 billion in revenues, down from $11.7 billion.

Before committee action, Rostenkowski tried to negotiate a compromise with top Bush administration officials by lowering the cost of his bill. He said he floated possible compromise language to the administration, the Democratic leadership and the minority members.

The administration, Rostenkowski reported, said, " 'No, we can't be for this,' and 'No, we can't be for that.' "

The main sticking point between Democrats and the administration was the Democratic bill's permanent changes to the unemployment system. House Democrats, in particular, were committed to making permanent changes so that extended benefits would kick in automatically during high periods of unemployment. The changed procedures would end the need for Congress to continually vote on temporary infusions of funds.

The administration said those changes would cost too much money.

House Democrats, however, believed they had the upper hand with Bush. If Congress could get an unemployment bill with permanent changes to the president's desk, they argued that he would be hard pressed to veto it. A veto, they believed, would hurt him in an election year. "Maybe he vetoes it; let him explain it to people," said Downey.

Senate Finance Committee Chairman Bentsen also said he wanted to make permanent changes to the unemployment system, but he was not certain whether he could get a bill with such provisions through his chamber. In the Senate, minority members wielded far more power than in the House and could make it difficult for Bentsen to move an unemployment bill that the administration opposed.

House Democrats had initially discussed loading the unemployment legislation with non-germane items addressing concerns raised by the Los Angeles riots.

Ultimately, however, they decided to negotiate with the administration on a separate urban package and to leave the unemployment bill to move by itself. This way, Democrats could press the president to accept permanent changes to the unemployment system without slowing down an urban aid package. *(Urban crisis, p. 339)*

### Provisions

The substitute bill that cleared the committee would provide unemployed workers with either 20 or 26 weeks of federal emergency benefits, depending upon the unemployment rate in their state. Those would be available for people who had exhausted their 26 weeks of state benefits.

The extra benefits would be phased out over a three-month period, providing 10 or 13 weeks of benefits during that time to people who had run out of state benefits. Those would begin on Jan. 1, 1993, or on the month after the three-

month average national unemployment rate fell below 6.5 percent, whichever came earlier.

The most recent national unemployment rate had been 7.2 percent in April, or 9.2 million people. That was down from 7.3 percent the previous two months.

After the emergency benefits expired, the unemployment system was to revert back to providing workers with the possibility of receiving an extra 13 weeks of joint federal and state benefits after their first 26 weeks ran out. But the bill also would have permanently changed the trigger that released those 13 weeks of benefits. The trigger would change from a state's insured unemployment rate to its total unemployment rate. The insured rate was the percentage of unemployed workers who qualified for jobless benefits, a measure that had been slow to release benefits.

The total rate included all unemployed people, even those who had never held jobs before and those who had voluntarily quit jobs and were therefore ineligible — according to many states' rules — to receive benefits. Republicans complained that the total rate would allow too many states to qualify for extended benefits and thus cost too much.

The substitute bill eliminated two controversial proposals — one to pay for benefits and one that would help cover costs in the future.

Rostenkowski dropped language that would have taken the unemployment trust fund "off-budget," so that federal unemployment taxes would no longer go into the general Treasury. Members of the House Budget Committee had objected to doing that.

To pay for the original bill, Downey and Rostenkowski included a controversial tax provision that essentially raised taxes on higher-income taxpayers by limiting their allowable itemized deductions.

The substitute dropped that funding mechanism, the Pease provision. In place of the Pease provision, the full committee called for paying for the bill with three methods:

First, the bill would change the tax rules for people who paid estimated taxes quarterly. Under the bill's second financing provision, businesses would not be allowed to take tax deductions for executive compensation packages — salary and other compensation, such as stock options — over $1 million. And finally, the substitute retained the "PEP" provision, or personal exemption phaseouts, from the original subcommittee bill. This was to raise $4 billion over five years.

### Ways and Means Approves Revised Bill

After discovering that legislation to extend unemployment benefits would add $140 million to the federal deficit over five years, the House Ways and Means Committee rewrote the financing mechanisms so the measure would instead reduce the deficit by an estimated $249 million. The committee approved the new $5.8 billion bill (HR 5260) by voice vote May 27.

The measure would provide 20 to 26 weeks of emergency federal benefits to workers whose 26 weeks of state benefits had run out. The new bill included three changes in revenue-raising provisions. It would:

● Change the date for prohibiting businesses from taking tax deductions for executive compensation packages worth more than $1 million.

● Delete the estimated income tax provision for self-employed people who paid on a quarterly basis.

● Delay for one year the rate decrease in the federal unemployment payroll tax that employers paid.

With these provisions, the bill would be paid for over a six-year period. But the revenues would not come in during

the same year as the outlays. The bill would still require a House waiver of the budget law because it violated the pay-as-you-go requirements of the 1990 budget agreement between Congress and the White House.

## House Passage

The House voted 261-150 on June 9 to pass the $5.8 billion bill (HR 5260). *(Vote 179, p. 44-H)*

The emergency program would be phased out over three months, giving eligible workers 10 or 13 weeks of benefits starting either Jan. 1, 1993, or the month after the national unemployment rate's three-month average fell below 6.5 percent, whichever came first.

Bush had threatened to veto that bill, complaining about its cost, the type of taxes used to pay for it and the permanent structural changes that would be made to the system. "If the administration vetoes this bill, it has to do with building Bush's conservative base by taking us on," Downey said.

Republicans had tried to defeat a parliamentary vote enabling the House to proceed with its work on the unemployment bill. But it was approved 232-182. *(Vote 176, p. 44-H)*

Republicans also tried to vote down the rule governing debate of the unemployment bill but failed again, 225-182. *(Vote 177, p. 44-H)*

And Republicans failed on a motion by Bill Archer, R-Texas, to send the bill back to the Ways and Means Committee, by a vote of 191-219. *(Vote 178, p. 44-H)*

Besides opposition to the substance of the House unemployment bill, the administration and many Republicans did not like the way it was financed. The bill included a waiver of the 1990 budget agreement's pay-as-you-go rules, requiring that any money spent in one year be fully offset by cuts or tax increases in that same year.

Athough the House bill would raise an extra $249 million over six years, it did not cover its costs in each year — something to which OMB objected.

The bill would be paid for by prohibiting businesses from taking tax deductions for executive compensation packages worth more than $1 million; extending the personal exemption phaseout for high-income taxpayers — thereby reducing their deductions — for two years through fiscal 1997; and adjusting the federal unemployment tax rate paid by employers.

## Senate Finance Committee Action

Despite House passage of an unemployment bill that Bush had threatened to veto, the Senate attempted to avert a showdown over how far the federal government should go to help the long-term unemployed.

Senate Finance Committee Chairman Bentsen wrote a bill that was far more conciliatory toward the White House, making fewer permanent changes to the unemployment compensation system than the House bill would. The Senate Finance Committee approved Bentsen's $5.4 billion bill (HR 5260) by voice vote June 11.

Minority Leader Dole refrained from criticizing Bentsen's bill and did not mention his own unemployment plan, which the administration supported. Furthermore, Senate Finance ranking Republican Bob Packwood, Ore., announced that he would support the Bentsen bill, abandoning the proposal he had pushed with Dole.

## Provisions

Bentsen's bill was more generous than the House measure in extending the emergency benefits program. It continued to provide 26 or 33 weeks of benefits through March 6, 1993, as long as the national unemployment rate remained at least 7 percent.

If the national rate fell below 7 percent for two consecutive months, benefits would drop to 10 and 15 weeks. And if the rate fell below 6.8 percent for two months, benefits would drop to seven and 13 weeks.

The administration supported a more modest extension, at a cost of $2.8 billion, according to a CBO estimate. Under the Bush proposal, workers who exhausted their state benefits by Jan. 2, 1993, would qualify for either 13 or 20 weeks of federal benefits. Those who used up state benefits by March 6 would qualify for seven or 10 weeks.

While the House bill would eliminate the existing trigger, which was based on the "insured unemployment rate," in the Senate, Bentsen took a more conservative approach to changing the extended benefits trigger. He would give states a choice of which trigger to use — the existing insured unemployment rate or a total unemployment rate.

Using the former would cost the states less because states had to match federal funds. Under the latter, benefits would be triggered if a state's jobless rate hit 6.5 percent for three months, assuming that figure was 10 percent higher than the jobless rate in the same quarter in either of the previous two years.

The Senate bill, unlike the House bill, would cost $5.4 billion between 1992 and 1997 and would raise an extra $458 million over that five-year period. Like the House bill, it would not be paid for in each individual year.

The Senate measure would be financed by tax provisions included in the tax bill (HR 4210) that Bush vetoed March 20. *(First tax bill, p. 133)*

Those provisions included:

● Allowing any amount from a pension or annuity plan or a tax-sheltered annuity to be rolled over tax-free to an individual retirement account. Remaining money would be taxed at a rate of 20 percent;

● Modifying estimated tax payment rules for large corporations; and

● Requiring most securities dealers to pay tax on their inventories.

## Senate Floor Action

With only scant opposition from Republicans, the Senate passed by voice vote June 19 a $5.4 billion extension of unemployment benefits for long-term jobless workers, sending the two chambers off to conference.

Dole said the Democrats' bill was headed for a veto and suggested that Democrats, Republicans and administration officials get together and negotiate one large tax package to take care of unemployment, expiring tax breaks and other items on the urban agenda.

Bush had threatened to veto the $5.8 billion House measure, which would permanently change the structure of the unemployment compensation system. However, the administration was relatively silent regarding the Senate bill, which did not have the same far-reaching changes but provided more generous short-term benefits.

## Dole's Substitute Rejected

Senate Republicans, acknowledging that they did not have the votes to defeat Bentsen's bill, agreed ahead of time not to demand any roll call votes so senators could go to their home states for the weekend.

Dole offered an $11 billion substitute, which he said the administration supported, to extend unemployment benefits and to, among other things, create federal enterprise zones, extend some expiring tax breaks and repeal the tax

on yachts, furs and other luxury goods.

The Dole amendment was rejected by voice vote. Bentsen said the Senate would consider enterprise zones and other tax matters in the near future.

Dole said administration officials would be willing to accept some of Bentsen's permanent changes to the unemployment system as part of a larger package.

The Senate also agreed June 18, by 84-3, to an amendment by Bob Graham, D-Fla., that would continue to exclude the wages of temporary foreign agricultural workers from the unemployment tax. Sens. Wendell H. Ford, D-Ky., Harry Reid, D-Nev., and Paul Simon, D-Ill., voted against it. *(Vote 124, p. 17-S)*

## FINAL ACTION

Following the news that the national unemployment rate had leaped three-tenths of a percent in June, lawmakers cleared for the president's signature what they hoped would be the last bill extending benefits for the long-term jobless.

The July 2 action came just prior to the July 4 deadline, when workers who had used up their 26 weeks of state benefits would no longer have been eligible for federal emergency benefits.

In a morning meeting with reporters, Bush said that the unemployment rate was "not good news" but that he might veto the unemployment bill if it cost too much.

By the end of the day, though, Bush called the measure "an important safeguard for workers who still can't find jobs as the economy continues to grow." He promised to sign the bill and did so July 3.

The conference agreement between the House and Senate cost $5.5 billion over six years, providing unemployed workers in 15 states with 26 extra weeks of benefits and workers in all other states and the District of Columbia with 20 extra weeks until March 6, 1993. Workers who had already exhausted their federal emergency benefits were not eligible for more.

The House voted 396-23 to adopt the conference report on HR 5260. The Senate approved it 93-3. Three Republican senators voted no: Hank Brown of Colorado and Larry E. Craig and Steve Symms of Idaho. Four senators were absent: Jesse Helms, R-N.C., William V. Roth Jr., R-Del., Terry Sanford, D-N.C., and John W. Warner, R-Va. *(House vote 267, p. 64-H; Senate vote 145, p. 20-S)*

### Permanent Changes

The cleared bill gave members of Congress the peace of mind that they might no longer have to vote for emergency benefits or scrimp for money to pay for them.

The conference report included a permanent change to the unemployment system, which allowed non-emergency extended benefits to kick in more easily during periods of high unemployment. The change was to begin March 7, 1993, the day after the emergency program was set to expire.

The conference report included the Senate "trigger" provision, giving states the choice of sticking with the existing system or switching to an easier way of releasing funds. The existing system released extended benefits when the insured unemployment rate, which was the percent of people receiving unemployment benefits, reached a certain level.

The optional trigger allowed states to release funds according to the total unemployment rate, which was based on all people who were unemployed and looking for work, regardless of whether they qualified for benefits. Generally,

a state's insured unemployment rate was far lower than its total rate, making it difficult for benefits to kick in. The House bill would have required that states switch to the total unemployment rate.

Because the extended benefits program was paid for equally by states and the federal government, it would cost the states more money if they chose to use the easier trigger. Bush and other Republicans had opposed this because it would also cost the federal government more money.

If a state triggered the extended benefits program, workers would receive 13 extra weeks of compensation after using up their state money. The state would have to have a total unemployment rate of 6.5 percent for the most recent three months and the rate had to be at least 10 percent higher than during the same period in either of the two previous years.

In states where the total unemployment rate was at least 8 percent, workers would receive an additional seven weeks, for a total of 20.

But before the extended benefits program took over, workers would be relying on the emergency program.

In states where the total unemployment rate was at least 9 percent, jobless workers would receive 26 extra weeks of benefits. People in all other states would get 20 extra weeks. As long as the national unemployment rate remained at 7 percent or higher, the number of weeks available would remain at 20 or 26.

If, however, the national unemployment rate dropped below 7 percent for two consecutive months, benefits would fall to 10 or 15 weeks. And if the rate fell below 6.8 percent for two months, benefits would fall to seven or 13 weeks.

### Three Financing Provisions

Essentially, the conference report favored the more conservative Senate bill in a bid to win Bush's signature. Several provisions from the House bill were dropped, including the mandatory change to the extended benefits trigger, an increase in the percent of money the federal government paid for extended benefits, and an increase in the workers' wage base on which employers paid unemployment taxes.

To pay for the measure, three financing provisions were included. The first changed the rules for large corporations that estimated their tax payments on a quarterly basis. Beginning June 30, 1992, corporations were to base their tax payments on 97 percent of what they owed. After 1996, the payments were to be based on 91 percent.

The existing law called for corporations to make those payments based on 93 percent of what they owed. Between 1993 and 1996, the existing law would raise that to 95 percent and drop it to 90 percent in 1997.

This change would bring in $800 million, according to the Joint Committee on Taxation.

The conference report also adopted the House's "PEP" provision, which raised taxes for high-income earners. Under PEP, or personal exemption phaseouts, personal exemptions were to be reduced by 2 percent, or $43, for every $2,500 in adjusted gross income over $157,900 for joint filers and $105,250 for individuals. It would expire at the end of 1996.

According to the Joint Committee on Taxation, the provision would raise $2.7 billion.

And finally, the bill made a change to distributions from retirement plans, giving people the option of rolling over money directly to an Individual Retirement Account. If the money was not rolled into an IRA, it was to be taxed at 20 percent. This would raise $2.1 billion, according to the Joint Committee. ∎

# Family Leave Waits for Clinton

Congress failed late in 1992 to override President Bush's veto of legislation requiring unpaid leave of up to 12 weeks to workers for the birth or adoption of a child or the illness of a close family member. It was an expected denouement to an old debate. What emerged on the eve of the presidential election was a clear-cut social policy difference between Bush and Democratic nominee Bill Clinton.

Family leave was one of Clinton's top campaign issues. His running mate, Sen. Al Gore, D-Tenn., spoke frequently of how fortunate he was to take time off from work when his young son lay critically ill in the hospital after a car hit him. Clinton won the election, and the 103rd Congress quickly shipped the Family and Medical Leave Act to the new president, who promptly signed the bill on Feb. 5, 1993, putting an end to almost eight years of attempts to turn the legislation into law.

The House passed the bill (HR 1) on Feb. 3 by 265-163. The next day the Senate approved its version (S 5), 71-27, and sent it back to the House as HR 1. The House cleared the measure by agreeing to the Senate version, 247-152. Bush had vetoed the measure in 1990 and 1992, saying he refused to place another government mandate on business. Previous family leave measures, beginning in 1985, never passed. Some early versions would have applied to companies with as few as 15 employees who had worked only three months. But the first bill to make it to the White House raised the minimum number of workers to 50 and attracted key support from Republicans such as Rep. Marge Roukema of New Jersey.

At the start of the 102nd Congress, two senators brokered a compromise that earned strong bipartisan support in the Senate. Christopher J. Dodd, D-Conn., and Christopher S. Bond, R-Mo., made several changes to the legislation — such as exempting key employees — to appease business interests. Conservatives, including Daniel R. Coats, R-Ind., who had felt uncomfortable opposing "pro-family" legislation but did not want to hurt businesses, then signed on.

Nevertheless, without Bush's support, the bill still could not become law. Only the Senate had the votes to override a veto, 68-31, on Sept. 24. The House sustained Bush's veto 258-169 on Sept. 30.

When the new Congress convened in January 1993, family and medical leave became the top legislative priority for the new White House. HR 1 was nearly identical to the bill Bush vetoed. The measure:

● Allowed workers to take up to 12 weeks of unpaid leave during any 12-month period because of the birth or adoption of a child; the need to care for a child, spouse or parent with a serious health condition; or the worker's own serious illness;

● Applied to employees who had worked for the same employer for at least one year and for at least 1,250 hours that year;

● Exempted businesses that employed fewer than 50 people;

● Allowed employers to deny leave to a worker who fell among the highest paid 10 percent of workers if that person was considered a key employee whose leave would result in "substantial and grievous economic injury" to the business.

The new law (PL 103-3) was to become effective in six months, after final regulations were published in the Federal Register. Because the law applied only to businesses with 50 or more workers, about 95 percent of all employers would be exempt. But the 5 percent subject to the law employed about 60 percent of all workers.

## BACKGROUND

Advocates of family leave legislation had argued since 1985 that the United States was all but alone among industrialized nations in failing to guarantee parents job-protected leave to care for newborns. But the Reagan and Bush administrations, backed by the small-business community, insisted that mandated leave would disrupt companies and undermine their competitiveness.

The 1986 version of the Family and Medical Leave Act, which won only the approval of the House Education and Labor Committee, was a much stronger bill than the one that eventually became law seven years later. As approved by the panel, the bill required public and private employees with 15 or more workers to grant up to 18 weeks of unpaid leave to employees to care for newborn, newly adopted or seriously ill children or parents. The legislation also required employers to grant up to 26 weeks of unpaid disability leave to employees with serious medical conditions. Health insurance benefits were to continue while the employee was on leave. The employee had the right at the end of the leave period to reclaim his or her old job, or a comparable one, with full benefits and seniority. (1986 Almanac, p. 584)

A family leave measure got the nod from the House Education and Labor Committee again in 1987, only to languish thereafter. The Senate Labor and Human Resources Committee did not advance the proposal beyond hearings until 1988.

Election-year politics was a key factor in the squelching of the family leave bill that finally advanced to the Senate

## BOXSCORE

➡ **Family and Medical Leave (S 5).** The legislation required that businesses give all but their top employees up to 12 weeks of unpaid leave to take care of a new baby or an ill family member.

**Reports:** H Rept 102-135; S Rept 102-68; conference report H Rept 102-816.

### KEY ACTION

**Aug. 5** — **House-Senate** conferees worked out a compromise bill.

**Aug. 11** — The **Senate** adopted the conference report to S 5 by voice vote.

**Sept. 10** — The **House** cleared S 5, 241-161.

**Sept. 22** — President Bush vetoed S 5.

**Sept. 24** — The **Senate** refused to sustain the veto, voting 68 to 31 — two votes more than the two-thirds necessary.

**Sept. 25** — The **House** voted 239-39 to postpone the veto-override vote on S 5 until Sept. 30.

**Sept. 30** — The **House** voted to sustain the veto, 258-169, 27 short of the two-thirds needed.

floor in 1988. Accusing Republicans of obstructionism, Majority Leader Robert C. Byrd, D-W.Va., pulled the measure (S 2488) from the floor after an attempt to invoke cloture failed. The cloture vote split largely along party lines, adding fuel to the Democrats' campaign-season arguments that Republicans were anti-family. *(1988 Almanac, p. 261)*

In 1989, family leave legislation was approved by three House committees and a Senate committee early in the year but failed to reach the floor in either chamber. *(1989 Almanac, p. 359)*

Intense lobbying began anew in 1990, another election year. The House on May 10 became the first chamber to pass the family leave bill. The Senate cleared it the next month, by voice vote. Bush vetoed the bill June 19; the House easily sustained the veto July 25, rendering a Senate vote unnecessary. *(1990 Almanac, p. 359)*

### 1991 Action

Both chambers approved family leave bills (S 5, HR 2) in 1991. The legislation was one of the Democrats' top priorities early in the year. But after it became clear that for a second year in a row, Democrats could not muster the votes to override a veto, the measure lost its momentum. *(1991 Almanac, p. 311)*

Early in the year, the chances for passage of the legislation seemed good. Lynn Martin, who voted for the legislation in 1990 as a Republican House member from Illinois, was Bush's new Labor secretary. Also, the powerful American Association of Retired Persons was putting its muscle behind the bill.

But business groups argued that the bill would be too costly, and they had an ally in the president, who remained dug in against federal mandates on businesses.

The House Education and Labor Committee had started the bill on a fast track by approving HR 2 on March 20. The Senate Labor and Human Resources Committee approved S 5 on April 24.

The Senate acted first, approving its version Oct. 2 by voice vote. A roll call vote of 65-32 followed on a substitute offered by Bond.

The House passed HR 2 on a vote of 253-177 on Nov. 13. Subsequently, the House passed S 5 after substituting the text for HR 2.

As sent to conference, the Family and Medical Leave Act mandated that businesses give up to 12 weeks of unpaid leave to employees at the birth or adoption of children or when employees or their children, spouses or parents were seriously ill.

## CONFERENCE ACTION

Sponsors of long-dormant legislation to require businesses to grant unpaid leave to workers with new babies or family or medical emergencies trotted their bill back out just in time to hang it around President Bush's neck on the eve of the Republican National Convention.

**More than eight months after the bill passed the House and Senate in nearly identical forms, conferees on the measure (S 5) finally met Aug. 5, 1992, and swiftly approved a compromise that made only minor changes.**

As agreed to by conferees, the measure would require that businesses with more than 50 workers give all but their top employees up to 12 weeks of unpaid leave for the birth or adoption of a child, or for the serious illness of the worker or an immediate family member.

But while the bill enjoyed broad bipartisan support in both chambers, it seemed highly unlikely that sponsors could muster the supermajority needed to override Bush's promised veto.

Knowing early that the measure stood little chance of becoming law in 1992, sponsors figured they could still use it to make a political statement.

"This bill would provide modest, humane protections for employees who have family or medical emergencies," said Rep. William L. Clay, D-Mo., chairman of the conference and sponsor of family leave legislation dating back to 1986. "This is what family values are all about."

Agreed Roukema of New Jersey, one of the earliest Republican backers of family leave legislation: "This is not just symbolism. This is health care. This is job security."

Sponsors pointed out that a key difference between the 1992 bill and the 1990 version was the strong bipartisan support in the Senate, where a compromise was forged between S 5 sponsors Dodd and Bond.

The Senate never took a roll call vote on the 1990 bill, but the 1992 version, which included many provisions to soften the impact on employers, earned 65 votes when it passed in October 1991. The three absent senators on record in support, noted Dodd, would produce the needed override margin.

Among changes in the 1992 bill were provisions that allowed employers to exempt the highest-paid 10 percent of their work force and that restricted eligibility for leave to employees who had worked at least 25 hours per week for the previous 12 months.

Because it would apply only to those businesses with more than 50 workers, the measure already exempted more than 95 percent of employers.

The only changes made by conferees concerned provisions extending leave rights to congressional employees. The new language included enforcement and grievance provisions that paralleled those in the 1991 civil rights bill (PL 102-166). *(1991 Almanac, p. 251)*

The bill extended leave rights to federal civil service employees.

## SENATE ACTION

On the eve of the Republican National Convention, the Senate approved the legislation to require businesses to give unpaid leave to workers with new babies or family medical emergencies.

The Senate adopted the conference report to S 5 by voice vote Aug. 11.

Dodd had sought a roll call vote, but Republican leaders told him they would block it, preventing the bill from leaving the chamber before the August recess, which began Aug. 13.

Despite the concessions made in the conference agreement, the administration continued to oppose the bill.

"They were not willing to deal," Bond said of the administration. "I think the president is just plain wrong on this."

Dodd said he delayed bringing up the bill in the Senate in the hope that Bush's switch from John H. Sununu to Samuel K. Skinner as White House chief of staff in 1991 would mean that the administration would become more amenable to family leave. That did not happen.

Bond said Bush's refusal to support family leave was a missed opportunity to underscore his concern for family values. "I think the failure to support it is a failure to reinforce what is a very important part of his platform,"

Bond said.

Senate Minority Leader Bob Dole, R-Kan., said the issue was not whether family leave was good, because everyone agreed it was a good thing. Instead, Dole said, "what we are really trying to decide is whether the government knows best how to spend everyone's benefit dollars."

If the government imposed the family leave benefit, Dole said, businesses would cut back on other benefits.

## HOUSE ACTION

Family values and politics got big play in a lengthy debate on an emergency leave bill Sept. 10. But at least for the 1992 election year, it appeared that neither words nor votes would translate into policy.

The conference agreement on a measure (S 5 — H Rept 102-816) designed to protect employees who chose to stay home with a new child or sick relative was cleared by the House on Sept. 10 by a 241-161 vote. But lacking the margin to override an expected presidential veto, the bill had little chance of survival. (Vote 390, p. 96-H)

Predicting a similar veto scenario to 1991, Republicans described the bill as an election-year ploy to embarrass Bush, who pushed the issue of family values to center stage during the August GOP convention in Houston.

Democratic presidential nominee Bill Clinton had voiced strong support for the bill, promising to sign a family leave measure if elected.

But the verbal sparring over "family values" on the campaign trail translated into only a handful of bills, such as family leave, that were caught in the partisan crossfire. That was because Democrats and Republicans were rushing to the aid of families in distress from different angles: Democrats were looking at costly programs to help meet basic social needs, while Republicans would strengthen the "moral fabric" through such legislation as restricting abortion and regulating what could be shown on public television. Because each side held its "values" dearly, compromise was difficult.

On the House floor, many Republicans argued that the family leave measure would hurt small businesses and that employee leave policies should not be mandated. "The House can't even run its own business. How dare we put ourselves in the place of workers and employers who might want to reach different agreements?" said Minority Leader Robert H. Michel, R-Ill.

But advocates, mostly Democrats, said it was time to put politics aside and put America's families first. "If family values are important, and they are, there is no more important piece of legislation than family leave," said House Speaker Thomas S. Foley, D-Wash. "This is not a generous bill," Foley added. It would not require "even one day of paid leave."

The Senate appeared to have enough support to override the expected veto with a two-thirds majority. But the outlook was glummer in the House, where support for the conference agreement waned from the 253-177 vote on a nearly identical bill on Nov. 13, 1991. However, 18 Democrats and two Republicans who voted for the bill in 1991 were absent during the 1992 round. Several, such as Gerry E. Studds, D-Mass., and Mike Synar, D-Okla., faced crucial primary elections.

Three Democrats and three Republicans who voted no in 1991 switched in 1992. The Republicans were Tom Coleman of Missouri, C. W. Bill Young of Florida and H. James Saxton of New Jersey.

### Lengthy Debate

Family leave opponents repeatedly defined the bill as yet another Democratic effort to regulate industry, increase the bureaucracy and set the stage for costly litigation. "This Congress has already done enough to hurt the economy," said George F. Allen, R-Va., a member of the Small Business Committee. "Stop meddling."

Several members, including Majority Leader Richard A. Gephardt, D-Mo., recounted stories of taking off work to care for a sick child. "We were lucky . . . we had employers who understood," he said. No one, he added, "should have to choose between job or family."

The 3½-hour debate even included mention of such legendary figures as jazz musician Louis Armstrong.

Republican Henry J. Hyde of Illinois, one of 37 GOP supporters of the measure, lamented what he viewed as a general misunderstanding of family values. He recounted Armstrong's response when asked to describe jazz: "If you have to ask, you don't really know."

The inability of bill sponsors to muster enough votes to guarantee a showdown with the president illuminated a key point: It could be difficult to turn campaign rhetoric into policy — no matter who won.

"Talk is a lot cheaper than action," said Democrat Thomas J. Downey of New York. "It is no surprise to me that we have no major legislation."

Downey, who supported family leave, had put forward several proposals in 1992 geared toward meeting the basic needs of poor families. Only one, known as the Family Preservation Act (HR 3603), had even a slight chance for passage. (Child welfare, p. 462)

"Nothing has radically changed on the Hill because of the family values debate," agreed Ellen Nissenbaum, legislative director of the liberal Center on Budget and Policy Priorities.

Roukema, a highly vocal GOP supporter of the family leave bill, was not as pessimistic. Many of the so-called family values issues, which she broadened to include improved economics for poor families, better health care and more opportunities for home ownership, would be "top of the agenda" for the next year, she said.

Gary Bauer, president of the conservative Family Research Council, was concerned about how the campaign talk on strengthening family morality might ultimately play out in policy. He said legitimate debate was to be found in pursuing "values" as Republicans defined them. "But a real agenda must include family economics, educational choice and how we provide opportunities in the child-care area," he said. Legislation pending late in the session was not as crucial as issues raised in the campaign, he said.

Even Downey admitted that little could be done in the final days of Congress.

"We're a very bad Greek chorus to an otherwise interesting Greek drama. The sooner we exit, the happier the whole world will be."

## BUSH'S ALTERNATIVE PLAN

Although both the House and Senate already had passed family and medical leave bills and approved a conference report on the final bill, President Bush announced Sept. 16 an alternative to the mandate for big businesses to provide unpaid leave to their workers.

Bush vetoed the bill Sept. 22, calling instead for Congress to adopt a family leave tax credit for businesses that

# President Bush's Veto Message

*Following is the text of President Bush's Sept. 22 veto of the Family and Medical Leave bill:*

I am returning herewith without my approval S 5, the "Family and Medical Leave Act of 1992." This bill would mandate that public and private employers with 50 or more employees provide their employees with leave under certain circumstances.

I want to strongly reiterate that I have always supported employer policies to give time off for a child's birth or adoption or for family illness and believe it is important that employers offer these benefits. I object, however, to the federal government mandating leave policies for America's employers and work force. S 5 would do just that.

America faces its stiffest economic competition in history. If our nation is to succeed in an increasingly complex and competitive global marketplace, we must have the flexibility in our workplace to meet this challenge. We must ensure that federal policies do not stifle the creation of new jobs or result in the elimination of existing jobs. The administration is committed to policies that create and preserve jobs throughout the economy — serving the most fundamental need of working families.

My administration is also strongly committed to policies that foster a complementary relationship between work and family and encourage the development of a strong employer-employee partnership. If these policies are to meet the diverse needs of our nation, they must be carefully, flexibly, and sensitively crafted at the workplace by employers and employees, and not in Washington, D.C., through Government mandates imposed by legislation such as S 5.

Therefore, I have transmitted to the Congress legislation to establish an alternative flexible family leave plan that will encourage small and medium-sized businesses to provide family leave for their employees.

My flexible family leave plan is based on a refundable tax credit for businesses that establish non-discriminatory family leave policies for all their employees. A refundable tax credit of 20 percent of compensation (for a credit of up to $100 a week — to a maximum total credit of $1,200) would be available for all businesses with fewer than 500 employees, for a period of family leave up to 12 weeks in length. Family leave would include the birth or adoption of a child or the care of a seriously ill child, parent or spouse. It also would cover a serious health condition that prevents the employee from performing his or her job. This approach will cover almost all workplaces — smaller companies that S 5 does not cover that are less likely to provide leave to their employees. My plan covers about 15 million more workers than would be eligible under S 5 and 20 times the number of workplaces. Those not affected by my plan work for large businesses, which generally have established family leave policies.

I want to emphasize again that my bill will help where the concern is most acute — with small and medium-sized businesses and the workers in those businesses. S 5 misses these key workplaces by excluding businesses with fewer than 50 employees. We know that these hard-pressed small companies usually offer fewer benefits than large firms, that they generate most of our new jobs — in fact, they provide the majority of people with their first job — and that they are more likely to employ women and reentrants to the labor force.

Under my proposal, many more of the millions of men and women employed by smaller businesses would be able to take advantage of family leave.

The tax credit approach to the family leave issue will provide the flexibility workers and employers need to enable them to establish the optimal package of benefits that meets their particular needs. This way the parties can decide which package of benefits is best suited to them. In addition, because a tax credit is not a mandate, it does not put struggling firms at an economic disadvantage in the global marketplace. It maintains the competitiveness of American business while providing the benefits American workers need. It provides positive incentives, not mandates with veiled costs that impede growth.

Both the House and Senate passed family leave legislation almost one year ago, but they have kept it in the filing cabinet until now. That is nearly an entire year with no action or any willingness to depart from a federally mandated approach, only an interest in politicizing the issue.

I have proposed a truly flexible family leave program. I am willing to work with the Congress to get it passed and signed into law immediately.

There appears to be a pattern here. Three years ago, my administration had a fundamental disagreement with these same congressional committees on child care policy. It took the Democratic-controlled Congress more than a year to get the point — I would not buy a government-controlled and -mandated child care program. When they got serious, we rapidly hammered out flexible child care legislation patterned after my proposal that allowed *individuals* to choose their benefits.

The same holds true for family leave. If the Congress is serious about encouraging family leave, I ask those members of Congress who have joined me in the past in opposing government mandates to work with me again. The Congress should pass a family leave bill quickly that provides positive incentives for family leave and is responsive to the needs of workers and employers. ∎

---

voluntarily adopted leave policies. The president said he objected to mandating how businesses should conduct themselves. *(Veto text, above)*

Bush wanted to offer businesses tax credits of up to $1,200 per worker if they gave employees time off for family emergencies. The plan, to be offered to businesses with fewer than 500 employees, would cost about $500 million, according to the White House.

Bush's timing, however, ensured that his plan could not become law in 1992. The day after his announcement, Congress sent its bill to the White House for Bush's promised veto.

Roukema, a longtime supporter of the legislation, called Bush's idea "an interesting supplement to the basic bill. But it is no substitute."

"To use the tax incentives does not give you the job guarantee," she said.

Roukema said she was extremely disappointed that Bush did not try to compromise on the family leave legislation while it was going through the legislative process.

"I think his advisers have painted him into a very unfortunate corner," she said. The proposal, she said, was obviously an attempt to give Bush a reason for vetoing the legislation.

"I don't know of anybody who doubts that at all," agreed Sen. Dodd. "This is not a sincere offer at all."

Rep. Dick Armey, R-Texas, who opposed the family leave legislation, said the timing of Bush's proposal was

"unfortunate," but added that he and the administration were busy fighting the S 5 mandate earlier.

"To the extent the president's proposal is political, it's in response to the timing of the Democrats," Armey said. "They thought this is a great time to embarrass the president" by sending him a family leave bill so close to the election.

## SENATE OVERRIDES VETO

After four years and 32 vetoes from President Bush, the Senate finally had the votes needed to override his objections to a bill.

Voting 68 to 31 — two votes more than the two-thirds necessary — the Senate on Sept. 24 refused to sustain the president's veto of the Family and Medical Leave Act. But while the Senate hurdled Bush's formidable veto barrier, the House was not expected to do the same. House members voted 239-39 on Sept. 25 to postpone the veto-override vote on S 5 until Sept. 30.

In a presidential campaign in which family values had been discussed as frequently as foreign policy and the economy, the family leave legislation took on added significance. Democratic vice presidential candidate Al Gore, D-Tenn., returned to the Senate to speak and vote for the bill.

"When it comes to family leave, President Bush says, 'Read my lip service' to family values," Gore said. But he quickly added that the issue was not one of Democrats vs. Republicans: "This is not a partisan issue. The president is isolated on this."

Nevertheless, Republican opponents accused the Democrats of sitting on the bill for most of the year so they could bring it up just before the election and embarrass Bush. And they sought to portray Bush as supporting family leave — just not in its existing shape.

"All of us, Democrat or Republican, are for some form of parental family leave," said Larry E. Craig, R-Idaho, who was promoting Bush's tax credit plan for businesses that voluntarily offered leave.

But the president's most recent proposal came too late to be incorporated into the pending legislation or to be enacted in the 102nd Congress.

The 1992 override vote included two switches and an appearance by three previous absentees. Ted Stevens, R-Alaska, voted to sustain the veto; he had previously supported the bill. David L. Boren, D-Okla., voted to override the veto; he had previously opposed the bill.

And three senators who were absent for the first vote voted to override: Tom Harkin, D-Iowa; Bob Kerrey, D-Neb.; and David Pryor, D-Ark.

## HOUSE SUSTAINS VETO

The House voted Sept. 30 to sustain the president's long string of unbroken vetoes in a 258-169 vote that failed to override his objections to the Family and Medical Leave Act. It was 27 votes short of the two-thirds needed. (Vote 443, p. 108-H)

The failure to override meant the bill was dead for the 102nd Congress, bringing to a close another chapter in the saga of family leave. The bill would have given 12 weeks of unpaid leave to workers during family emergencies.

House Education and Labor Committee Chairman William D. Ford, D-Mich., said that after seven years of working on the issue, he had watered down the bill considerably to appease business groups.

But he warned members that this was their last chance to vote for a weak bill. "I promise you I'll put a good bill on President Clinton's desk, and he'll sign it," Ford said.

Earlier in the day, however, House Speaker Foley said he did not see "any need to change" the bill for Clinton.

Bill opponents battled the perception that they were simply against the concept of family leave. Instead, they portrayed themselves as having a better idea: tax credits for businesses to induce them to provide leave to employees.

House Minority Whip Newt Gingrich, R-Ga., pleaded with Democratic leaders on the floor. But Democrats derided Bush and the Republicans for having introduced the idea after pending legislation had been wrapped up.

Rep. Steve Gunderson, R-Wis., said that if Democrats had been willing to reduce the number of weeks of unpaid leave, they would have gotten a law.

The override vote in the House was the third family leave vote in that chamber in the preceding year. And the outcome was not surprising, given the large number of Democrats who had previously voted against the bill.

On Nov. 13, 1991, the House voted 253-177 to pass the bill. At that time 287 votes would have been needed for an override; 48 Democrats voted against the measure.

On Sept. 10, members voted 241-161 to approve the conference report. They needed 268 votes to reach two-thirds, but 42 Democrats voted against it.

On the override vote, the same number of Democrats — 42 — voted to sustain the president's position. ■

# Congress Overhauls 1982 Job Training Act

An overhaul of the nation's largest job training program, which cleared Congress on Aug. 11, might have fallen short of being a panacea for the growing number of unemployed workers, but it did attempt to fix flaws in the system and target limited funds to the needy.

President Bush's signing of the package of amendments (HR 3033 — PL 102-367) to the 1982 Job Training Partnership Act (JTPA) on Sept. 7 culminated nearly four years of work to craft a bill that could both steer clear of changing the formula for sending federal funds to the states and make the locally run programs more accountable to Washington officials.

At the crux of this refurbished JTPA was a basic faith in the underlying design of the program: That a partnership between government and industry to train the disadvantaged worked better than depending on public service employment — in the manner of JTPA's predecessor, the Comprehensive Employment and Training Act (CETA).

The amendments to the 1982 law separated youth and adult programs, directed more aid to those facing steep barriers to employment — such as high school dropouts — and provided for stricter Labor Department oversight of state-run programs.

The final push for passage came from two directions: the troubles in Los Angeles the week of April 26, which heightened Washington's awareness of the need for jobs and other urban relief, and the desire of both parties and the president to have a major job training initiative to parade out before the Nov. 3 elections.

Orrin G. Hatch of Utah, the ranking minority member of the Senate Labor Committee, referred to the bill as one of the few concrete things Congress did to aid America's ailing cities in the wake of the Los Angeles riots. *(Urban crisis, p. 339)*

But just how concrete was a matter of debate. The fiscal 1993 spending bill for the Labor Department (HR 5677 — PL 102-394) called for about $3 billion in training grants to the states and $1 billion for Job Corps. That was slightly less than the program had received the previous year; JTPA was estimated to reach only 5 percent of those eligible. *(Appropriations, p. 651)*

Yet the JTPA amendments had all the right political elements to be popular. They offered job opportunities for the poor, money to localities and the mechanism to leverage the contribution of private industry. The legislation tightened the loopholes that allowed fraud and abuse to seep into the old JTPA system and plugged in new programs to target high poverty communities.

"It is a competitive world out there, and for those who need a second chance, JTPA offers choice, chance and opportunity," said Labor Secretary Lynn Martin.

The bill had passed the House in 1991 and the Senate in

---

## BOXSCORE

➡ **Job Training Partnership Act amendments (HR 3033, S 2055).** The legislation amended the 1982 job training act to fix flaws and target the truly needy.

**Reports:** H Rept 102-240; S Rept 102-264; conference report H Rept 102-811

### KEY ACTION

**Oct. 9, 1991** — The **House** passed HR 3033, 420-6.

**April 9** — The **Senate** passed S 2055 by voice vote.

**July 29** — Approved by **House-Senate** conference as HR 3033.

**Aug 7** — The **Senate** adopted conference report.

**Aug 11** — The **House** cleared legislation.

**Sept 7** — President Bush signed HR 3033 — PL 102-367.

---

April, by large margins in both chambers and in only slightly varying forms. Conferees ratified the nearly 300 changes made by staff members in both chambers on July 29. The conference report was adopted by voice vote in the Senate on Aug. 7 and in the House four days later.

### BACKGROUND

For the past three decades the federal government had undertaken a series of job-training programs, mainly to increase the earnings of participants and reduce their dependence on welfare programs, such as food stamps and Aid to Families with Dependent Children.

The first post-World War II program in the early 1960s focused on adults facing potential displacement as a result of automation. By the mid-1960s, that emphasis shifted to minorities and youth.

In 1973, Congress folded a variety of employment and training services — including the War on Poverty's Job Corps — into the Comprehensive Employment and Training Act. CETA empowered local governments to operate training programs for the unemployed and to offer them public service jobs. Riddled with problems, CETA was amended and reauthorized several times in its nine-year history. But after attempting several fixes to that abuse-ridden program, lawmakers let it expire in 1982 and began anew.

JTPA is the phoenix that rose from the ashes of that far different approach to federal job training. Sen. Edward M. Kennedy, D-Mass., coauthored JTPA with Vice President Dan Quayle, then a GOP senator from Indiana. The private sector was brought in as a full partner, and funds were cut back considerably — from a high of nearly $9 billion in 1978 to slightly more than $3 billion four years later.

But soon after JTPA's inception, some of the criticism began anew. Lawmakers were compelled as early as the 100th Congress in 1988 to consider fundamental changes to JTPA, as government oversight reports zeroed in on inadequate oversight and subsequent overcharges by private contractors.

### Funding Formula Dispute

But a proposed rejiggering of funding formulas and the potential loss of revenue to some states killed efforts in 1990 to make the program more accountable. *(1990 Almanac, p. 365)*

JTPA funds were distributed to the states by a three-part, equally weighted formula with two-thirds based on unemployment rates and one-third on the number of economically disadvantaged people in the area. Major disagreements arose from efforts to alter the formula to emphasize poverty rates rather than unemployment rates.

The bill (HR 2039) that passed the House in 1990 would have changed the government's formula for figuring the

federal funding that each state received for summer youth programs, while leaving intact the formula for determining funding for adult programs. The measure (S 543) introduced in the Senate would have altered the funding formula for all JTPA programs. Lawmakers argued that some states — including Texas, Louisiana, Michigan and Indiana — would lose money. The result was a stalemate.

By the time new legislation was crafted in the 102nd Congress, only the administration expressed preference for a formula that would give greater weight to poverty rates.

### More Problems Emerge

Meanwhile, as Congress took longer than expected to legislate fixes to the 1982 law, more vulnerabilities in the national job training program emerged. Lawmakers questioned whether the program targeted those most in need, such as dropouts and displaced homemakers. Although JTPA was considered more successful than the previous programs in placing participants in jobs, evidence grew that applicants already most likely to succeed were being selected. The General Accounting Office issued a report in 1989 that said the program boosted its success rate by spending fewer dollars serving the "less job-ready enrollees" than those more groomed for being hired.

The inspector general at the Department of Labor zeroed in on specific contracts. A report released on March 26, 1992, found that the state of Kentucky offered $6.9 million in JTPA money to attract the Toyota Motor Corp. and another firm to locate there. Toyota made no commitment to train JTPA participants and, in fact, "recruited and hired only the most skilled and experienced individuals available."

JTPA proponents argued that those reports had unfairly tainted the program. Despite the "few bad apples in the system," JTPA has aided "those in need of a second chance, those that the education system has failed," said Rep. Bill Goodling of Pennsylvania, ranking minority member of the House Education and Labor Committee.

Some state and local organizations with much to gain from the JTPA amendments pushed for the bill to clear before the fiscal 1993 spending bill was taken up. The Appropriations committees had said that funds for job training might be curtailed if the program's problems were not addressed.

### Other Job Training Approaches

The signing of the JTPA legislation in September did not put the lid on the jobs issue, as the election-year economy waned and the unemployment problem rose.

JTPA sponsor Sen. Paul Simon, D-Ill., touted the passage of the amendments as a major legislative achievement at the same time that he pushed with Sen. David L. Boren, D-Okla., to include $400 million in the urban aid tax bill (HR 11) for a modern-day version of the Works Progress Administration and the Civilian Conservation Corps — jobs programs of the 1930s that built bridges and other infrastructure projects (WPA) and sent inner-city youth into the country to plant trees (CCC). HR 11 was vetoed by President Bush. *(Tax bill, p. 133)*

Boren also pushed to get a $50 million provision in the Defense authorization bill (HR 5006 — PL 102-484) that sought to revive the 1930s programs as 10 demonstrations of the Youth Civilian Community Corps, a program to provide skills training in exchange for community service.

Meanwhile, President Bush came out with a plan on Aug. 24 that included a $2 billion-a-year package of new and retooled job training programs. Bush promised this at a campaign stop in Ansonia, Conn., 71 days before the presidential election. He said the $10 billion cost over five years would be paid for by cutting spending for other, unspecified federal programs.

### How the Program Worked

Under JTPA, governors divided their states into service delivery areas, known as SDAs, which received funds and delivered services. SDAs typically were political jurisdictions (cities, counties) — or a consortium of smaller jurisdictions.

Federal money flowed to the service area, which turned it over to a locally appointed Private Industry Council, referred to as a PIC. Each PIC consisted primarily of business people, with other members drawn from economic development, education and rehabilitation agencies, organized labor, community-based organizations and public employment services. These people decided what services would be provided, planned job training programs and contracted with job training providers.

More than 600 SDAs operated throughout the country in 1992. New York state had 32; Rhode Island had three.

Applicants were occasionally recruited from other social welfare offices. Because there were more income-eligible people than funds to help them, the councils had devised point systems based on other barriers to employment. A teenage mother without a car, for example, was considered a more likely candidate than a less encumbered but equally unskilled person.

Once chosen, the applicant was assessed to determine appropriate training. Among JTPA activities were: occupational classroom training to teach technical skills, basic education to earn a high school equivalency degree, on-the-job training in a specific occupation and job search assistance.

## LEGISLATIVE ACTION

Once lawmakers backed off the divisive attempt to change the formula for distributing federal job training funds to the states, the amendments to the 1982 law were largely non-controversial.

In 1991, members were eager to help the jobless as the recession deepened. Committees focused on trying to make the training programs more effective and efficient; a bill (HR 3033) overwhelmingly passed the House on Oct. 9 by a 420-6 vote. A similar job training measure (S 2055) was introduced in the Senate on Nov. 26 by Simon, chairman of the Labor Subcommittee on Employment and Productivity, but time ran out in 1991 before it could be considered. *(1991 Almanac, p. 315)*

The legislation moved quickly in the second session, and S 2055 passed the Senate on April 9. The major task in 1992 was thrown to the House-Senate conferees, who had to reconcile nearly 300 differences — many of them minor — between the two bills. Once accomplished, a highly praised and popular conference report was then adopted by both chambers in August.

### Senate Action

The Senate Labor and Human Resources Committee on March 11 gave S 2055 voice vote approval. As crafted in committee, the measure required that 65 percent of adults and 70 percent of youths served by the program be economically disadvantaged — living at or below the poverty line — and face other barriers to employment such as homelessness and a lack of basic skills.

S 2055 passed the full Senate, also by voice vote, on April 9.

The JTPA amendments faced few obstacles at that point. The political battle over tampering with state funding had been fought and discarded.

### Conferees' Task

The conferees, mostly at a staff level, spent about four months working through the differences between the House and Senate versions. Although most differences were minor, some issues required careful, lengthy negotiations.

The House bill required the Labor secretary to prescribe uniform procurement standards based on Office of Management and Budget rules, such as those requiring competitive bidding. Those standards applied to other federal grant programs. The Senate version gave the states more flexibility by putting the onus on each state governor to establish the standards to improve accountability.

The establishment of State Human Resource Investment Councils was a major unresolved issue because the council provision had been omitted from the final Senate bill with the understanding that it would be addressed in conference. The House bill gave the states the option of combining existing advisory groups into a single council to create better coordination between the JTPA program and other service programs, such as vocational and adult education and a key component of the 1988 Welfare Reform Act (PL 100-485) — the Job Opportunities and Basic Skills Program (JOBS) — aimed at putting welfare recipients to work.

The administration strongly supported the councils. But several interest groups to be represented on the council were concerned that their individual needs might be lost in the coordination effort.

Bret Lovejoy of the American Vocational Association, for example, said mixing education with JTPA in the voluntary councils was not a good idea. "To mix those two systems, however laudable it might sound, would put students on the short end of the stick," he said.

The existing law provided no percentage breakdown of in-school versus out-of-school participation in the job training program. Dropouts were considered the most difficult to reach and serve. Consequently, the House bill required that at least 60 percent of the youths served in the program be out of school; the Senate bill called for at least 50 percent. The House version also allowed the governor to lower the targeting requirement to a minimum of 40 percent if the dropout rate in that area was less than 10 percent.

The Senate bill proposed a lower set-aside for older people who were not economically disadvantaged.

While both bills limited on-the-job training to six months, only the House bill barred from the program employers who had exhibited any pattern of failing to provide participants with continued long-term employment or failing to give them the same wages and benefits as similar employees.

### Conferees Sign Off

It was meant to be a celebration. But on July 29, after four years of wrangling over how to tighten the 1982 Job Training Partnership Act, House and Senate conferees fell two issues short of a quick sign-off to nearly 300 negotiated changes.

Even so, champagne corks popped as the nearly completed conference agreement was hailed as a major accomplishment by both Kennedy, chairman of the Senate Labor and Human Resources Committee, and William D. Ford, D-Mich., chairman of the House Education and Labor Committee.

With the major points settled, conference staff members then reached tentative agreement on the two remaining issues: grievance procedures for workers laid off by a company that relocated and subsequently qualified for JTPA funds to train new workers; and the establishment of a $1 million set-aside to ensure that all states had enough administrative funds to run a JTPA program.

Among the broader issues settled by conferees were:

● **Procurement**: The House version, which prevailed, required the Labor secretary to prescribe uniform procurement standards, including competitive bidding on buying training services. But state governors were permitted some flexibility in establishing the standards to improve accountability, as the Senate bill required.

● **State Human Resource Investment Councils**: The Senate agreed to the House proposal that gave states the option of combining advisory groups into a single council to create better coordination of federal services. State governors were given a voice on who was appointed to the councils.

● **Jobs for Employable Dependent Individuals**: The Senate pushed for and won a slight revision to this program, a Kennedy priority. It gave bonuses to states for providing job training to welfare recipients. Added incentives were given for including absent parents in the program.

● **Out-of-school youths**: The House receded to the Senate version, which called for at least half of the youths in the program to be out of school. The initial legislation provided no such guidelines. Dropouts, however, were considered the most difficult to reach, and the new JTPA aimed to reach such needy people.

● **Older workers**: The Senate version prevailed. It retained a state set-aside of 3 percent of the funds for participation by people older than 55. The House had pushed for a larger set-aside after JTPA was criticized for being primarily a youth program.

● **On-the-job training**: The initial law provided a subsidy to the employer equal to 50 percent of the wages paid to the trainee. That provision was often cited as an area for potential abuse. The negotiated agreement limited training to six months and included some of the House language that barred employers who had shown signs of abusing the program.

## FINAL ACTION

The conference agreement was adopted by the Senate by voice vote on Aug. 7, and by the House four days later. There was mostly praise for the final legislation, which attempted to strengthen the nation's chief job training program at a time when the lack of employment opportunities was one of the nation's biggest headaches.

But the jobs problem had escalated to such a degree by the time the measure cleared that even a key sponsor of JTPA noted the programs' shortfalls on the House floor. Ford said some JTPA administrators had turned federal funds into "pure subsidies to local businesses, paying half the wages for a constant stream of new employees who train on the job as carwashers, dishwashers or broom pushers for six months until the subsidy runs out, their training ends, and a new trainee replaces them."

Ford said that the new law would be a test of the concept of private-public partnership. "I believe that if the legislative changes we are making today do not put an end to the abuses and too-frequent failures of the system, the system itself will have to be changed."

But local and state governments eager to move forward on the new job training program rules greeted the overhaul with enthusiasm. "I think what this will do is allow us to be creative," said Joan Crigger of the U.S. Conference of Mayors. ■

# Labor Can't Save Striker Replacement Bill

Legislation that sought to close a loophole in the law and protect the jobs of striking workers died in the Senate, despite a heavy lobbying effort to save it by the nation's principal labor lobby, the AFL-CIO.

Stiff opposition from Senate Republicans, who said the bill would have encouraged more strikes, could not be successfully countered by the bill's sponsors, and Democrats were forced to abandon the measure.

Existing law barred companies from firing workers solely for going on strike. But House and Senate supporters of the striker replacement legislation said companies in the 1980s had begun applying a little noticed 1938 Supreme Court decision that allowed employers to temporarily or permanently replace striking workers unless the employees were protesting unfair or unsafe labor practices.

The bill sought to close this loophole by nullifying the 1938 decision.

"For working families, there is no difference between being permanently replaced and being fired," said House Majority Leader Richard A. Gephardt, D-Mo.

But Republican opponents, including the administration, said the measure would encourage more strikes and damage the economy, which was already well into a recession.

In the end, opponents were successful in blocking work on the bill, forcing Senate Democratic backers to pull the measure from the Senate calendar.

## BACKGROUND

The striker replacement bill was a particularly difficult test for organized labor, which already was facing declining union membership and waning clout on Capitol Hill.

But the issue of protecting strikers gained momentum as a bitter strike at the New York Daily News and also at coal mines in West Virginia in 1991 drew national attention.

As a result, the striker replacement bill was considered a top priority of the labor community in 1992.

"There may not be a more critical measure that's considered by this Congress," said Ernie DuBester, a lobbyist for the AFL-CIO, which then represented about 15 million unionized workers, when the House was considering a companion bill (HR 5) in 1991.

Bill backers argued that every year as many as 10,000 workers were being permanently replaced for participating in lawful strikes.

Rep. William L. Clay, D-Mo., estimated that almost 300,000 people had been permanently replaced in the previous 10 years.

The House passed its version of the bill (HR 5) on July 17, 1991, by a roll call vote of 247-182, which was 39 short of the number needed to override a promised veto. *(1991 Almanac, p. 313)*

---

## BOXSCORE

➡ **Striker Replacement (HR 5, S 55).** Considered one of the highest priorities of the labor lobby in 1992, the bill sought to nullify a 1938 Supreme Court decision that allowed companies to hire permanent replacements for striking employees.

**Reports:** H Rept 102-57, Parts 1-3; S Rept 102-111.

### KEY ACTION

June 11 — The **Senate** cloture vote on S 55 fails, 55-41.

June 16 — Second **Senate** cloture vote on S 55 fails, 57-42.

---

Labor lobbies, led by the AFL-CIO, had argued strongly for enactment of either the House or Senate version of the bill, saying some companies were using the 1938 court decision to replace striking union workers with lower-paid, non-union workers.

Rep. Charles A. Hayes, D-Ill., a former labor organizer in the meat-packing industry, said enactment of the bill would have prevented manipulation of employees by "greedy employers whose sole purpose is to increase profits at the expense of workers."

Proponents also said that using permanent replacement workers, or even threatening to use them, undermined the fairness of the collective bargaining process, which guided the contract renewal process between management and organized labor.

But opposition was strong and steady in the Republican ranks, especially in the Senate, where opponents could wield more power and employ more delaying tactics than their counterparts in the House.

President Bush and Labor Secretary Lynn Martin were strongly opposed to the bill, saying it would encourage strikes and tip the balance toward labor's side in contract negotiations.

## SENATE FLOOR

To halt work on the measure, Republican opponents to the striker replacement bill used legitimate delaying tactics and Senate procedures that required sponsors to come up with a supermajority to cut off debate by invoking cloture and limit debilitating amendments.

The first attempt on June 11 by sponsors to invoke cloture failed to get the 60-vote minimum needed. That vote was 55-41. *(Vote 120, p. 16-S)*

During floor debate before the vote, Howard M. Metzenbaum, D-Ohio, argued that workers' main protection and leverage in collective bargaining had been "gutted" in recent years by companies all too willing to replace anyone who went on strike. He cited Caterpillar Inc.'s threat in April 1992 to replace 12,600 striking members of the United Auto Workers union at its plants.

But opponents said the government should not dictate how businesses deal with labor and added that the bill would have given an unfair advantage to labor negotiators.

On June 9, Labor Secretary Martin renewed the threat of a veto, saying the bill would "create an environment ripe for confrontation, intransigence and an increase in work stoppages."

After the first failed cloture vote, Bob Packwood, R-Ore., inserted substitute language aimed at pulling over more support from the GOP side.

The Packwood compromise version would have allowed employers and unions to submit unresolved contract disputes to a federally appointed fact-finding panel.

Under the proposal, if the employer agreed with the

panel's recommendations and the union rejected them, the employer could hire permanent replacement workers for the strikers. If, however, the strikers assented to the mediator's proposals, the employer would be barred from hiring permanent replacements.

Robert McGlotten, AFL-CIO director of legislative affairs, said the Packwood substitute drew a reasonable balance between both camps. "It's a hell of a lot fairer when both employers and labor have to be honest with a third-party mediator who can come in and say: 'Look, let's lay out all the facts.' "

But Orrin G. Hatch, R-Utah, the ranking member of the Labor and Human Resources Committee, attacked the compromise plan, saying Packwood's fix was worse than the original version and would create an intrusive role for the federal government in the private business sector.

He said the bill would "overturn 54 years of federal labor law" to "please one interest group." Hatch said the bill would have given the AFL-CIO a "new weapon" to launch strikes.

The language Packwood inserted into the bill failed to attract any GOP votes.

On June 16, members again failed to invoke cloture, 57-42. Only Al Gore, D-Tenn., and Tim Wirth, D-Colo., added their names to the list of those who wanted to end debate and proceed to the bill. Gore and Wirth had missed the first vote while they were attending the Earth Summit in Brazil. (Vote 121, p. 17-S)

After the second attempt at cloture failed, Senate Majority Leader George J. Mitchell, D-Maine, withdrew the bill from the calendar.

Some thought the bill's collapse, which followed rejection of the family and medical leave bill (S 5), raised questions about the labor lobby's effectiveness and clout on Capitol Hill. (Family leave, p. 353)

Remarking on the defeat of both bills, one AFL-CIO official said the 1988 plant-closing notification bill (PL 100-370), which required 60 days' notice to workers before a factory closing, had been the lobby's last major legislative success. (1988 Almanac, p 213) ■

# ERISA Reform Falls to Veto Threats

Despite a determined effort by members of the House Education and Labor Committee, two bills designed to make major changes to the Employee Retirement Income Security Act (ERISA), the 1974 law that governed most private pensions and other employee benefits, died in the 102nd Congress.

One bill (HR 2782) would have given states more latitude to set employee benefit standards for those people working under contract for the state. Another measure (HR 1602) would have amended ERISA to clarify how insurance companies and other health care providers should respond to claims from health insurance policy holders.

The full House approved HR 2782 and the House Education and Labor Committee approved HR 1602, but the Bush administration put members on notice that the president would veto both measures, quashing the drive to move them forward for the remainder of the Congress.

There was no action in the Senate on either bill.

## ERISA PRE-EMPTION

Bill supporters and opponents agreed on one thing: both bills would have made drastic changes to a central provision of ERISA — the pre-emption clause.

The sweeping 1974 law was designed as a wide-ranging solution to the many systemic problems then plaguing the nation's pension laws.

But some members said that the law's reach had gone far beyond its drafters' intentions.

One clause in the huge law had led to court decisions that the bill's drafters "never contemplated," said Rep. William D. Ford, D-Mich. That clause read: "The provisions of this title . . . shall supersede any and all State laws insofar as they may now or hereafter relate to any employee benefit plan."

Federal courts, including the Supreme Court, had interpreted that clause to mean that states could not get involved in most aspects of employer-employee relationships, including sensitive subjects like health care. And many

employees had argued that without state regulation, they had no recourse when insurance companies denied their claims.

ERISA was primarily designed as a pension protection plan. The law set out a detailed, complex system for ensuring that workers' retirement income would indeed come to them upon retirement. A new agency was developed to police pension system operators, and the federal government began guaranteeing payment of pensions in the event of business failure. (1974 Almanac, p. 244)

Prior to ERISA, pensions were not protected. If a company went out of business without enough funds to cover pensions, workers lost out.

The pension law was silent on the operation of health-care plans and other "employee welfare" benefits — with one exception. That exception pre-empted the states from regulating all benefit plans covered by ERISA.

### An Aching Back Begins It All

Until 1987, many lawmakers had assumed that people denied benefits unfairly could sue in state court to get their claims paid under provisions for breach of contract. But that year, the Supreme Court ruled in *Pilot Life Insurance Co. v. Dedeaux* that such cases were covered under ERISA and could be decided only by using ERISA as the applicable law. (1987 Almanac, p. 14A)

The case involved Everate W. Dedeaux of Gulfport, Miss., who hurt his back in 1975 while working for Entex Inc. Entex had a long-term disability policy with Pilot Life Insurance Co. For three years, Pilot Life kept readjusting Dedeaux's claim: giving him his benefits for a period, then denying his claim, then paying again.

Dedeaux took the company to court in 1980, arguing that Pilot Life had violated state common law by acting in bad faith and breaching the contract. He lost in the U.S. District Court for the Southern District of Mississippi, which ruled that ERISA pre-empted his claim. In other words, his only option was to sue under ERISA, because the law pre-empted all state laws dealing with employee

benefits. But under ERISA, Dedeaux would have been able to recover only the exact disability funds the company owed to him; no punitive damages or other awards were allowed. He then won on appeal to the Court of Appeals for the Fifth Circuit.

But the Supreme Court unanimously ruled on April 6, 1987, that Dedeaux could not sue based on state common law, because his disability plan was covered under ERISA, thus pre-empting all state law.

Lawmakers said that after that decision they were deluged with complaints from people denied some form of their employee benefits. "I have received letters from policyholders around the country who feel that they have no recourse against their insurance companies for unfair terminations or denials," said Howard L. Berman, D-Calif., author of both HR 1602 and HR 2782.

## HEALTH-CARE CLAIMS

The legislation was approved by a bitterly divided House Education and Labor Committee on July 30. Supporters said it would have made it easier for people to collect on their health-care claims. But opponents argued that HR 1602 would drastically increase the cost of health insurance. The panel approved the bill on a 25-15 party-line vote.

The acrimonious two-day session was marked by short tempers and sharp exchanges between Dick Armey, R-Texas, and Chairman William D. Ford, D-Mich. Armey used every procedural tactic at hand — including repeated requests for roll call votes and a move to adjourn the meeting — in an unsuccessful attempt to prevent the panel from reporting the bill to the full House.

But the committee easily defeated six GOP amendments in lopsided votes.

The bill, known as the Health Insurance Claims Fairness Act, would have helped people who were seeking payment of health-care benefits from their insurance provider. It would have amended ERISA to mandate a maximum 30-day period for approval or denial of claims. In cases of a life-threatening illness, the approval time would have been limited to three days.

To resolve disputes over claims, the bill set out a three-part system. People at odds with their insurance company could have chosen to settle the matter through binding arbitration or mediation, or they could have gone to court. People who were successful in court would have been awarded attorney's fees.

In cases of fraud on the part of the insurance provider, the bill would have allowed judges to award punitive damages.

Armey called the bill an "irresistible incentive for a whole new kind of medical litigation." And in Labor Secretary Lynn Martin's July 28 letter to the Education Committee, she said the "legislation would only exacerbate health-care costs and reduce access to affordable heath care." Martin said she would have recommended that President Bush veto the bill.

But Pat Williams, D-Mont., chairman of the Labor-Management Relations Subcommittee, said the purpose of the legislation was to ensure that "valid health-care claims are paid." The goal was "simply to protect consumers from some insurance company misbehavior," he said.

ERISA allowed no punitive damages and provided only for lawyers' fees in some cases, thus making it difficult for people to sue.

## STATE CONTRACTS

The House Education and Labor Committee on June 10 approved by voice vote a bill (HR 2782) that would have given the states more power to set standards for the employee benefit programs of local contractors.

Supporters said that the bill would have clarified the original intent of ERISA. Although it explicitly pre-empted all state laws that dealt with "any employee benefit programs," some state laws "clearly were not within the original intent of ERISA pre-emption," according to Ford.

Ford and bill sponsor Berman proposed three kinds of state laws that would be permitted under the bill:

● **Prevailing wages.** The bill would have allowed states to require employers to pay their workers the prevailing level of employee benefits in the state when working on state contracts. (The Davis-Bacon federal wage law would prevail if the contracts involved federal funds.)

● **Apprenticeship programs.** The bill would have allowed states to establish minimum requirements and certification standards for apprenticeship programs or other training programs.

● **Unpaid pensions.** For plans that covered several employers (generally union contracts), the bill would have allowed states to provide additional means by which the pensions could be collected if a business did not properly contribute. For example, under some state laws, a pension plan operator could put a lien on a building under construction if the contractor had not fulfilled his obligation.

Such exceptions, though highly sought after by states and employee advocacy groups, would "carve the heart out of ERISA's pre-emption clause," said Harris W. Fawell, R-Ill. The bill generated intense opposition from business groups, who feared that it would open the door to 50 new and differing sets of mandated employee benefits.

Before the markup, the administration had circulated a letter, signed by Martin and Health and Human Services Secretary Louis W. Sullivan, warning that the bill would "resurrect the threat of conflicting and inconsistent state regulations" and saying President Bush would likely veto it.

But committee Democrats contended that the bill was necessary to restore longstanding state laws that federal court decisions had wiped out. Ford said "cleaning up" ERISA was needed so that states would no longer be deprived of their rights to determine how to treat their contract employees .

In 1989, the 2nd U.S. Circuit Court of Appeals, in *General Electric Co. v. New York State Department of Labor*, struck down a century-old New York state law that required employers to pay their workers the prevailing level of employee benefits when working on state public works projects. That law dated back to 1894, according to the AFL-CIO, but the court ruled that ERISA pre-empted it.

In 1990, the 9th U.S. Circuit Court of Appeals in California, in *Hydrostorage Inc. v. Northern California Boilermakers Local Joint Apprenticeship Committee*, reversed a state administrative order that established minimum standards for apprenticeship programs. The court ruled that such programs were exclusively under federal jurisdiction because of ERISA pre-emption.

The courts were split over whether ERISA pre-empted state laws letting pension plans collect unpaid contributions.

### How Broad?

The three exemptions were at the heart of the debate over ERISA: Just how broad did Congress intend the pre-emption clause to be?

It was mainly Republicans who advocated a very broad pre-emption interpretation and Democrats who made a states' rights argument. When ERISA was enacted in the 1970s, it was just the opposite.

In those days, Democrats said they were fighting entrenched state governments that were largely sympathetic to the business community. But in 1992, employee advocates, such as the Pension Rights Center of Washington, were finding it easier to get their proposals through state legislatures than through Congress.

Ford acknowledged the irony June 10 when he said he could recite "chapter and verse" the states' rights arguments that Republicans had used against the original law.

But, he said, the courts had gone too far in killing state laws that in any way dealt with employee benefits, so Congress had to step in and "restore the integrity of the original purpose of the act."

Ford and Patsy Mink, D-Hawaii, both members of Education and Labor in 1974, said the only purpose of the pre-emption clause was to protect pension plan uniformity.

But Republicans argued that the assault on pre-emption could mean trouble for businesses. Fawell said employers would more likely offer their employees higher benefits if regulations were uniform across the country. If that changed, he said, employers would just stop offering the benefits. "It's that simple," he said.

## HOUSE ACTION

On Aug. 4, the House passed HR 2782, which would have allowed states to mandate wage levels for workers on state contracts.

Bill supporters argued that recent court cases had gone too far in upholding the ERISA pre-emption of state laws. "The purpose of this legislation is simply to correct what many of us believe is a misreading of ERISA by the courts," said Pat Williams, D-Mont., chairman of the Labor-Management Relations Subcommittee of the House Education and Labor Committee. "We are trying with this legislation to restore state laws."

But opponents said any new exemptions would drive employers away from offering benefits. "I am strongly opposed to this attempt to open the cornerstone of ERISA, the state pre-emption provision, which has contributed significantly to the development of employee benefit programs," said Fred Grandy, R-Iowa.

An amendment by Paul B. Henry, R-Mich., allowed some Republicans to back the measure. It said prevailing state wage laws would apply only to state-funded public works projects. "This was the issue of greatest concern to many in the business community," he said. "The amendment is intended to prevent ... broad, mandated benefits laws."

Henry's amendment also would have allowed state contractors to apply the prevailing wage law in their own way, as long as they offered employees the same dollar value as state-mandated benefits. For example, contractors could have given employees additional wages instead of a health-care plan.

Finally, the amendment spelled out what kind of legal remedies states could have used to help unions collect benefits. Unions would have been permitted, for example, to put a lien on a building to force contractors to pay employee benefits. The original bill did not place any restrictions on states.

The House rejected, 140-266, an attempt by Fawell to delete a section that would allow states to set minimum standards for apprenticeship programs. (Vote 359, p. 88-H) ■

# GOP Kills OSHA Overhaul

In 1992, the House Education and Labor Committee wrote an overhaul of the 1970 Occupational Safety and Health Act, but Democrats were unable to win the support of Republicans, who were concerned about new burdens on business. The bill (HR 3160) died without further action.

Labor Secretary Lynn Martin said she would have recommended that President Bush veto the legislation.

The bill, crafted by committee Chairman William D. Ford, D-Mich., would have been the first big change to the Occupational Safety and Health Act (PL 91-596) in more than 20 years. The act gave the secretary of Labor the authority to set safety and health standards for the protection of workers and required employers to provide a workplace free from hazards likely to cause death or serious injury to employees.

When the law was written, the Bureau of Labor Statistics reported that of the nation's 80 million workers, 14,500 were killed each year and 2.2 million were injured.

As of 1990, the bureau reported that of 92 million workers, 6.4 million were injured each year. It also said that at least 2,900 — and probably more — were killed. The National Safety Council, a nonprofit group in Chicago, said that as of 1991, the number of workers killed annually was closer to 10,200.

Such high numbers, plus a deadly fire in September 1991 that cost 25 lives at a Hamlet, N.C., poultry-processing plant, spurred committee action.

## HOUSE COMMITTEE ACTION

The Education and Labor Committee gave voice vote approval May 28 to HR 3160. The bill would have increased criminal penalties — from the six-month maximum to a 10-year maximum — for workplace safety violations that resulted in a worker's death. The bill also would have applied the penalties to supervisors. Under existing law, only employers could have been held liable.

The bill would have required businesses to establish workplace safety and health programs. The programs would have offered education and training to employees to reduce hazards and prevent injuries and illnesses.

In addition, businesses would have been required to establish joint committees for employers and employees to work together to improve job site conditions in companies with 11 or more full-time workers. The committees would have been authorized to review the employer's safety and health program, conduct inspections and make recommendations.

Republicans had been generally reluctant to overhaul OSHA legislation. They argued that workplace safety problems had to do with poor agency enforcement, and they maintained that new rules would have been too costly to small businesses and generally burdensome.

"This bill will not make our workplace safer; it will bury us in paperwork," said Dick Armey, R-Texas.

Democrats said the legislation needed to be brought up to date. And they said their changes would actually have saved employers money by reducing injuries and thereby cutting claims for workers' compensation.

Paul B. Henry, R-Mich., and ranking Republican Bill Goodling, Pa., offered a less far-reaching substitute that would have required the government to consider a rule's cost-effectiveness and its possible effect on employment when setting health and safety standards. The committee

rejected the amendment, 14-25, splitting down party lines. The substitute also would have required employers to consult an "employee participation committee" on health and safety issues — but only for businesses with 50 or more workers.

Although Ford failed to reach a compromise with Henry, the chairman still made changes to appease Republicans and business interests.

Originally, the requirement of a joint health and safety committee would have applied to all employers with 11 or more workers; he changed that to 11 full-time employees. In companies with unions, employee committee members would have been chosen by the union; he struck a provision that non-union companies would chose the members by secret ballot, a section businesses objected to. Instead, OSHA would have approved alternatives to selecting workers. Ford also added language stressing that the committees were to be non-adversarial in addressing health and safety issues.

He dropped a provision requiring OSHA to issue 20 separate standards governing various workplace problems that the agency had previously pledged to provide. For example, OSHA had said the previous year that it would issue "confined space entry" standards. These would have regulated workers who had to go into chemical tanks, vats or manholes, where they could have been overcome by toxic chemicals or lack of oxygen.

However, Ford kept the requirement that OSHA issue a standard within two years to control ergonomic — or environmental — hazards such as the repetitive strain injury that could come from using a computer or video display terminal. OSHA would have been required to write regulations outlining how businesses should respond to the problem.

The committee agreed by voice vote to two amendments, one by Cass Ballenger, R-N.C., and one by Robert E. Andrews, D-N.J. The Ballenger amendment would have allowed OSHA citations issued to employers to be dropped if the violations were caused by employees who violated company work rules.

The Andrews amendment would have required OSHA to target inspections of worksites to those with a high potential for death, serious injury or exposure to toxic materials. ■

# Labor Measures Address Careers for Women

The Labor committees in both chambers considered a number of workplace-related measures throughout 1992. Those included:

## WOMEN'S OCCUPATIONS

The Senate cleared legislation (HR 3475 — PL 102-530) by voice vote Oct. 7 to help businesses provide women with apprenticeships in non-traditional occupations. The bill was originally introduced by Rep. Constance A. Morella, R-Md. It won House approval by voice vote Sept. 29, and President Bush signed it Oct. 27.

The bill directed the Department of Labor to give community-based organizations competitive grants for providing technical assistance to a number of employers and labor unions in preparing the workplace to employ women. The bill also required the Labor Department to make labor unions and employers aware that grants would be available.

"This legislation is important because it would help to increase the retention of women in non-traditional occupations — jobs which pay women 30 percent more than conventional occupations in which women are employed," said Sen. Nancy Landon Kassebaum, R-Kan. "Jobs in the skilled trades and technical positions provide low-income women and welfare recipients with a true path to economic self-sufficiency."

## WOMEN SCIENTISTS

The House passed legislation (HR 3476) by voice vote Sept. 29 that would have established a 17-member Commission on the Advancement of Women in the Science and Engineering Work Forces. But the measure went no further.

The commission would have studied barriers in industry, government and academia for women scientists, reporting on its findings in 18 months.

The bill, introduced by Constance A. Morella, R-Md., was approved by the Education and Labor Committee on Sept. 24.

"Women are underrepresented, underemployed and underpaid in the fields of science and engineering," said Patsy T. Mink, D-Hawaii. "The bill represents a first step toward raising the awareness of Americans about barriers facing women in these fields and toward suggesting some possible solutions."

## BLACK LUNG BENEFITS

The House passed a black lung benefits bill (HR 1637 — H Rept 102-882) on Oct. 1 to make it easier for coal miners and their survivors to collect benefits from the Black Lung Disability Trust Fund administered by the Labor Department. But the legislation went no further in the 102nd Congress.

The bill, passed by voice vote, would have authorized $65 million over five years, beginning in fiscal 1993.

The bill allowed survivors or widows of miners who were receiving black lung benefits to automatically receive survivor benefits without having to prove that the death was a result of black lung. And survivors of miners who were not receiving benefits at death only had to prove that the miner was disabled by black lung at death, without having to prove that the death resulted from black lung.

The House Education and Labor Committee approved the bill July 29.

The bill would have greatly restricted the amount of medical evidence a mine owner could produce to refute a miner's claim. Bill supporters contended that owners typically produced reams of medical information that miners could not afford to counter.

The bill would also award "reasonable" fees to attorneys representing coal miners, even if the miners lost their case.

Republicans attacked the bill as too expensive. Bill Goodling of Pennsylvania, the committee's ranking GOP member, said the bill would make the black lung program "simply another form of Social Security, or a full employment for attorneys program."

But bill sponsor Austin J. Murphy, D-Pa., said it was

time to "begin the long process of repairing the black lung program."

## DAVIS-BACON REVISION

Legislation to revise the 1931 Davis-Bacon Act won voice vote approval Sept. 23 from the House Education and Labor Committee. But the legislation never advanced to the floor.

The Davis-Bacon Act required contractors for federal and public works projects to pay workers the prevailing local wage rate, usually union wages. The act was intended to prevent construction companies offering substandard wages from underbidding local companies.

The legislation (HR 1987 — Rept 102-956) aimed to relieve small construction companies, many of them minority-owned, from Davis-Bacon requirements. It raised the size of contracts covered by the act from the existing $2,000 minimum. New construction contracts valued at $100,000 or more and alteration contracts of $15,000 or more would have to comply with Davis-Bacon. Smaller contracts would be exempt.

Backers of the change said the existing threshold excluded small and minority-owned construction companies from federal contracts because they could not afford to pay union wages.

Many Republicans opposed the Davis-Bacon Act, saying it hurt businesses and artificially inflated the cost of government contracts. Short of repealing the act, some Republican members wanted to see an even higher threshold.

But bill sponsor Austin J. Murphy, D-Pa., insisted that the new threshold would be reasonable. "We did not forget the needs of business," he said.

The bill was approved 5-1 by the Labor Standards Subcommittee on Aug. 4.

## CHILD LABOR

A sharply divided Senate Labor Committee on March 11 approved legislation to toughen child labor laws after Democratic sponsors tried to mollify Bush administration concerns about imposing stricter criminal sanctions on violators. The Senate never took up the measure.

The panel approved the bill (S 600 — S Rept 102-380) on a 10-7 party-line vote. The bill would have removed the existing requirement that an employer could not face criminal penalties until the second conviction. As crafted by Howard M. Metzenbaum, D-Ohio, Christopher J. Dodd, D-Conn., and Labor Chairman Edward M. Kennedy, D-

Mass., it also prohibited employers who had been convicted from receiving federal grants, loans or contracts for three years. And the Labor Department would be required to compile and make available to school districts the names of employers who had violated child labor laws.

Democrats originally wanted employers convicted of willfully violating child labor laws to face up to five years in prison for the injury of a child and up to 10 years in prison for the death of a child. A second conviction would have doubled those penalties.

But during committee consideration Democrats dropped that provision and retained existing law, which included criminal penalties of up to six months in prison.

The Bush administration argued that because Congress had recently raised civil penalties from $1,000 to $10,000, members should wait to see if that worked as a deterrent before increasing the criminal penalties.

In a letter to Kennedy on the day of the markup, Labor Secretary Lynn Martin threatened that President Bush would veto the bill because it would destroy jobs for teenagers and create too much paperwork for her department.

Committee Republicans echoed her sentiments. "Employers are saying they will not hire young people if the stings and strings of S 600 become law," said ranking Republican Orrin G. Hatch of Utah. Hatch called the measure "a young adult anti-employment bill."

But Metzenbaum said he thought it would be politically untenable for Bush to try to kill the bill. "I can't believe that under any circumstances in a political year that he would seek to veto legislation protecting children," Metzenbaum said.

The Fair Labor Standards Act of 1938, which governed wages and working conditions for children, set the minimum work age at 14; limited the hours and types of work for 14- and 15-year-olds; and restricted employment of children under 18 in dangerous jobs, such as mining, manufacturing and meat-slicing.

Fourteen- and 15-year-olds could work no more than three hours a day before or after school hours and 18 hours during a school week. When school was out, they could work eight hours a day and 40 hours a week.

As approved in committee, the bill also:
- Required certificates of employment for minors under the age of 18 who did not have a high school diploma.
- Added to the list of hazardous occupations for 16- and 17-year-olds: poultry processing, fish and seafood processing and pesticide handling.
- Prohibited employment of children under age 14 as agricultural workers, except for children who worked on their family's farm. ∎

# Housing Bill Cleared at Session's End

A $66.5 billion two-year reauthorization of housing programs was among the last major bills to clear the 102nd Congress. Although strongly opposed by Housing and Urban Development (HUD) Secretary Jack F. Kemp, who said that it abandoned 2-year-old reforms directed at reducing the number of defaults on the government mortgage fund, President Bush signed the bill Oct. 28.

The legislation started out early in 1992 chiefly as a vehicle to fine-tune programs created by the 1990 omnibus housing bill (PL 101-625) that were aimed at giving more Americans the chance to own homes. Those programs included the administration's Homeownership and Opportunity for People Everywhere (HOPE) — a program designed to sell public housing to tenants — and the Democrats' HOME Investment Partnerships Act, which provided federal funds to state and local governments on a matching formula.

As momentum for aiding cities increased, pumped up by the riots that shook Los Angeles in April, the legislation grew into an 1,100-page bill that included initiatives aimed at community revitalization and ways to renovate older public housing units. The final measure also contained a new title that gave uniform marching orders to several federal agencies to gradually eliminate lead-based paint from public and private housing.

Yet what grabbed the ardent support of many lawmakers were not the provisions to streamline housing programs. It was the problem of "mixed housing." Numerous districts experienced outbreaks of violence in public and subsidized housing as an influx of younger disabled residents moved into complexes that once housed only the elderly. Many of them were mentally disabled or drug abusers who qualified for public housing under the broadened definition of disability. The bill struck a compromise that provided safety to the elderly while protecting the rights of the disabled.

But forging a bipartisan legislative package that both chambers could accept proved a rugged task. Substantially different legislation was approved by the Senate and House Banking committees the week of June 15. While the Senate worked with the administration to craft a bill that included some of the ideas generated by Kemp for getting the federal government out of the business of subsidized housing, the House version defied Kemp's requests.

In particular, the bill that headed to the House floor lifted some of the Federal Housing Administration (FHA) reforms imposed in the 1990 bill — a move that immediately triggered a veto threat. The Senate version left intact the 2-year-old attempt to shore up the financially troubled

FHA mortgage insurance fund. The government's single-family-home insurance program was intended to spur home ownership by encouraging banks to make loans to families lacking the money for a 10 percent to 20 percent down payment. But warnings sounded during negotiations on the 1990 bill indicated that the FHA was losing money and could become insolvent without the reforms — including a 57 percent cap on the financing of closing costs for home buyers.

Kemp also strongly opposed the House bill because he said it gave short shrift to his initiatives. The Senate version included some of his requests, such as a small set-aside for a demonstration of his "Choice in Management" program, designed to test the effectiveness of giving residents of troubled public housing authorities the ability to choose alternative management.

The partisan split on the House side was mended after considerable negotiations and a series of compromises that drew GOP backing. Consequently, prospects for a housing bill increased Aug. 5 when the House voted, 369-54, in favor of the measure.

"We've gone a distance," said Marge Roukema, R-N.J., ranking member of the House Banking Subcommittee on Housing and Community Development. She was confident that the administration would support the measure, despite the existing veto threat.

But the outlook darkened briefly when the Senate failed to pass S 3031 before the August recess. An unidentified Republican put a hold on the bill Aug. 12, and even a plea by Senate Majority Leader George J. Mitchell could not force a release. On the second go-around Sept. 10, the measure was passed and sent to a conference with the House.

Because of the Senate delay, there was precious little time as conferees and staff sat down the week of Sept. 21 to begin resolving hundreds of House-Senate differences, both major and minor. However, staff worked around the clock to produce the bulk of a conference document that members could ratify. It was reconciling the final differences between the two bills — and attempting to meet the demands of Kemp — that proved an arduous undertaking. Even so, conferees completed work Oct. 2 with strong Republican backing after three days of negotiations and despite the continued disapproval of Kemp.

The compromise bill resolved the difficult issue of mixing the elderly and the disabled in a shrinking supply of public and subsidized housing by allowing landlords to give the elderly preference in some units but requiring them to set aside at least 10 percent for the disabled. The final

measure also broadened the new set of rules to clarify and strengthen the federal role in eliminating lead-based paint from homes; streamlined several existing housing programs; and established new initiatives, including one to provide new construction job training skills to youth.

The final measure (HR 5334) was cleared by the Senate on Oct. 8 after surviving a series of convoluted strangleholds on all Banking committee bills. The House on Oct. 5 gave it a resounding vote of 377-37.

Giving it further momentum as it headed to the White House, the housing bill was yoked with a largely unrelated measure high on the list of Treasury Department priorities that would put stricter controls on the nation's two largest government-sponsored enterprises: the Federal National Mortgage Association, known as Fannie Mae, and the Federal Home Loan Mortgage Corp., known as Freddie Mac.

All of this contributed to the president's decision to sign the measure over the objections of his Cabinet secretary. Kemp, a popular member of the Republican party who made known his aspirations for the 1996 presidential race, often differed with Bush.

Kemp's primary peeve on the housing bill was over the removal of safeguards on the FHA. However, by the time the authorization bill headed to conference, the appropriators already had lifted the 57 percent limit on the financing of FHA closing costs.

Kemp admitted that his opposition to the authorization bill was mostly symbolic. "I'm sending a signal that I'm not going to be the HUD secretary that stood by while the FHA was pillaged," Kemp said.

## BACKGROUND

Contradictory forces tugged on the 1992 housing bill from the start. Some lawmakers and housing groups touted the drafting of the measure as an important piece of urban legislation. But other members viewed the reauthorizing legislation as not enough of a radical departure from the basic thrust of a 1990 omnibus housing bill (PL 101-625) to warrant priority treatment.

Two years earlier Congress had overhauled federal programs with the aim of increasing the stock of affordable housing and helping public housing tenants buy their units. The Cranston-Gonzalez National Affordable Housing Act was the first major revision of federal housing policy since 1974. (1990 Almanac, p. 631)

The conceptualization of the 1990 bill sprung from congressional dissatisfaction with the Reagan administration's gutting of federal housing programs. Lawmakers had a purpose in plunging forward on a bipartisan measure that could begin reversing some of that damage and providing more Americans with shelter. By contrast, the 1992 endeavor was geared simply as a fix-it bill.

Both chambers agreed that implementation of the two centerpiece programs of the 1990 bill, HOME and HOPE, should be made easier. By 1992, both the Democratic-backed HOME Investment Partnerships program and the administration's Homeownership and Opportunity for People Everywhere (HOPE) were hampered by design flaws and a shortage of funds.

Alan Cranston, D-Calif., chairman of the Senate Banking Subcommittee on Housing and Urban Affairs, called passage of a bill in 1992 critical to ensure that HOME and HOPE "work in practice as well as in theory." It was also the last housing bill that Cranston would shepherd through Congress. He did not seek re-election in 1992 because of ill health.

Reggie Todd, head of the National Community Development Association, an organization of administrators of community and housing programs, said municipalities were having trouble implementing HOME because of confusion over federal regulations — especially in the area of funding.

Congress provided no funds for either the HOME or HOPE programs in the fiscal 1991 spending bill. During negotiations on the fiscal 1992 appropriations bill (HR 2519 — PL 102-139) for Veterans Affairs (VA), HUD and independent agencies, lawmakers and the administration disagreed over how much money to give the two new programs. Congress cleared a measure that reordered the administration's priorities: The HOME partnerships received $1.5 billion while the HOPE program received only $136 million. (1991 Almanac, pp. 334, 516)

But the HOME program faced other problems. The 1990 bill had laid out a three-tiered system of matching payments from states and local government before the federal government would provide grants. Appropriators waived that system in fiscal 1992 after local officials said it created fiscal problems. A major undertaking in 1992 was to reinstate a workable matching system that could maximize the federal dollars without placing too heavy a burden on the localities.

The tempo of bill negotiations quickened after the violence in Los Angeles in late April. The burning and looting were a reaction to the jury verdict in the Rodney King police-beating trial. But what became evident in Washington was a lack of a clear consensus on how to address the ills plaguing America's cities. Bill sponsors viewed the riots as a cry for better housing. (Urban crisis, p. 339)

House Banking Committee Chairman Henry B. Gonzalez, D-Texas, called the version his committee crafted "a modest response to the rising needs of the nation's distressed cities."

But the increasingly outspoken secretary of HUD, Kemp, already had made his housing policy imprint in the 1990 bill. He used the Los Angeles events to promote interest in another administration concept: enterprise zones, which were designed to give tax breaks to businesses willing to locate in the most blighted parts of town. (Urban aid tax bill, p. 140)

Although Kemp began in 1992 by working with the Senate to fine-tune and enhance the existing housing law, he began dragging his feet when he feared that some of his hard-won signature work from two years earlier might be reversed, particularly on the mortgage loan reforms.

**Warnings of a possible replay of the national savings and loan debacle with the Federal Housing Administration mortgage insurance fund alarmed both the administration and lawmakers, persuading them to significantly tighten rules for home buyers in the 1990 law. The new requirements were expected to weed out people more likely to default on the mortgages.** (1990 Almanac, p. 657)

Members of the real estate industry fought successfully in 1992 to reverse those FHA rules, claiming that the stricter regulations could prevent as many as 60,000 families each year from purchasing a house.

"The administration regulations have caused the FHA to atrophy," agreed House Banking Chairman Gonzalez.

## HOUSE SUBCOMMITTEE ACTION

The housing bill had a rough start in the House. The partisan fault lines appeared daunting on May 20 as the House Banking Subcommittee on Housing and Community

# Fine Points of the Housing Bill

*House-Senate conferees on the two-year housing reauthorization bill met Sept. 30 and Oct. 2 to hammer out an agreement that both chambers could endorse. They also worked with administration officials to incorporate changes based on objections raised by Housing and Urban Development Secretary Jack F. Kemp.*

*As cleared by the Senate on Oct. 8 and signed by President Bush on Oct. 28, the bill included the following highlights:*

● **Authorization levels.** Federal housing and community development programs — including rural housing — were authorized at $32.5 billion for fiscal 1993 and $34 billion for fiscal 1994.

● **Mixed housing for the elderly and disabled.** A compromise to settle a dispute between the elderly and younger disabled people over who should be given priority for a shrinking supply of federal housing was considered one of the most important provisions. It allowed public housing authorities to designate separate housing based on age or disability, subject to the approval of the Department of Housing and Urban Development (HUD).

It also allowed owners of federally subsidized housing designed for the elderly to give preference to the elderly if they set aside 10 percent of the units for the disabled.

Additional funding was to be authorized for service coordinators in public and subsidized housing to deal with the difficulties — including outbreaks of violence — the two groups encounter living side-by-side.

● **Lead-Based Paint Hazard Reduction Act.** Considered groundbreaking, the lead section of the bill created rules to reduce and eliminate lead-based paint poisoning hazards in private and federal housing. Home buyers had the chance to test for lead paint before purchase. Federal grants were to go to states and localities to reduce hazards in all low-income housing. Requirements for evaluating and reducing paint hazards in federally subsidized housing were to be phased in.

The bill standardized directives for the Environmental Protection Agency (EPA) and the Occupational Safety and Health Administration (OSHA). It strengthened protection for workers facing lead hazards through OSHA and directed the EPA to establish or approve state certification programs for lead inspections. Training and certification requirements were imposed on all lead contractors.

● **HOME Investment Partnerships Act.** The 1990 program created by Democratic senators, which required local governments to match federal housing contributions, had lacked a workable formula that balanced the goals of partnership with the difficulty communities had generating the necessary funds. The bill established a two-tiered system that asked localities to match 25 percent for substantial and moderate rehabilitation and 30 percent for new construction. Publicly issued debt could be used for up to 25 percent of the total match. The bill also offered a reduced match for communities with extremely high poverty rates.

The bill eliminated restrictions on new construction

and allowed up to 10 percent of HOME funds to be used for administrative costs.

● **Federal Housing Administration (FHA).** The bill raised the FHA single-family home loan limits to whichever was less: 95 percent of an area's median home price or 75 percent of the 1992 loan limit set by the Federal Home Loan Mortgage Corp., which was $151,725. It did not address the 57 percent cap on the financing of FHA closing costs. That 1990 restriction was lifted in the spending bill for HUD (HR 5679 — PL 102-389).

● **Administration initiatives.** The $855 million authorization for Kemp's pet project to sell public housing to tenants, Homeownership and Opportunity for People Everywhere (HOPE), included up to $40 million for a Youthbuild program. Youthbuild provided construction job skills to disadvantaged youths through their involvement in building low-income housing.

The bill also established pilot projects for several other Kemp concepts, including Choice in Management, designed to allow residents of troubled public housing units to choose alternative management, and Moving to Opportunity, to help families with children move out of high poverty areas.

● **Preservation of federally assisted housing.** The bill reauthorized the 1990 preservation provisions with modifications. Faced with the potential loss of many subsidized housing units and the displacement of low-income and elderly tenants, Congress enacted strong laws to preserve subsidized housing, including strict limits on paying off 40-year mortgages after 20 years, thus ending low-income use of the housing.

Changes to the 1990 rules included elimination of the so-called windfall profits test under which HUD had attempted to exempt property owners in many areas from the housing preservation provisions.

The bill also established a 40-year loan term for owners and purchasers to qualify for FHA insured financing on equity loans.

● **New Towns Demonstration Program.** Assistance was targeted to two areas in or near Los Angeles that were affected by the riots in April. The program also called for comprehensive community revitalization.

● **Homeless assistance.** Programs under the Stewart B. McKinney Homeless Assistance Act were reauthorized with small changes. A demonstration program known as Safe Havens for the Homeless was created to provide shelter and support for people living on the street.

● **GSE and banking provisions.** A major unrelated measure attached to the final conference bill aimed to overhaul the structure for regulating government-sponsored enterprises (GSEs) such as the Federal National Mortgage Association (Fannie Mae).

Also attached was the Annunzio-Wylie Anti-Money-Laundering Act, a House priority measure that strengthened anti-money-laundering requirements on non-bank financial institutions.

The Senate, in exchange, was allowed to attach a series of non-controversial technical fixes to bank laws.

Development approved a $35.4 billion reauthorization bill.

The 22-13 vote on the fiscal 1993 housing bill divided along party lines, with Republicans opposing the measure's funding levels, a provision to remove limits on FHA financing and the lack of support for administration initiatives.

The panel spent two days wrangling over nearly 60 amendments and deferred several of those issues until full committee, including the problem of how to integrate the elderly population in a limited supply of federally assisted housing with younger disabled people.

The Senate Banking Subcommittee on Housing and Urban Affairs postponed its plans to mark up a housing reauthorization bill the same week. Panel Republicans asked for the delay, saying they wanted to work with Democrats to craft a bipartisan bill that would also include several new initiatives from Housing Secretary Kemp. But they said they could not move forward without administration guidance, which had not been forthcoming.

The House subcommittee's draft measure would reauthorize housing programs for only one year, evidence of the growing philosophical gap between House Banking Chairman Gonzalez and the equally outspoken Kemp. Gonzalez wanted to maintain his flexibility on the chance that he could gain more of what he wanted in 1993 — on the chance that there might be a Democratic administration.

Both Gonzalez and Kemp viewed the Los Angeles riots as a cry for better housing. The chairman said his bill would "provide an economic stimulus for the nation's sagging economy" through generous block grants to states and localities.

Republican lawmakers used the urban unrest to bring new attention to the centerpiece of the administration's housing strategy: Homeownership and Opportunity for People Everywhere (HOPE), a program designed to sell public housing to tenants. Democrats pushed the HOME program, which provided federal funds to state and local governments on a matching formula.

The strategies collided when ranking subcommittee member Roukema unsuccessfully proposed to raise the local matching funds requirement under the HOME program from the 10 percent called for in the subcommittee draft bill to 25 percent.

"While I appreciate the financial difficulties of the states and localities, the federal budget is not trouble-free," Roukema said.

Barney Frank, D-Mass., called it the "to-hell-with-Los-Angeles amendment."

Roukema, revealing early her willingness to depart from the GOP ranks, was successful in her bid to increase the bill's authorized funding for the HOME program from $1.5 billion to $2.1 billion. The administration had requested $700 million.

Bruce F. Vento, D-Minn., argued that as a new program, pushed more by the Senate than the House, it did not have the track record to warrant the higher funding.

But the panel voted, 19-16, in favor of the increase for HOME.

Another amendment by Roukema, to reduce the measure's funding levels across the board by approximately $5.3 billion, was defeated, 16-19. Immediately after, Sam Johnson, R-Texas, proposed that funding for the administration's HOPE program be increased by $1 billion over the $290 million in the bill, an amendment that was rejected, 11-24.

It became obvious that even the Republicans were divided on some issues after the panel defeated, 10-25, an amendment offered by Roukema and Stephen L. Neal, D-N.C., to retain the existing 57 percent limit on the amount of closing costs that could be financed in single-family mortgages insured by the FHA. The draft bill contained a provision that prohibited the HUD secretary from using his discretionary authority to establish any limit on the amount of closing costs that could be FHA-financed.

The panel agreed, by voice vote, to an amendment by Gerald D. Kleczka, D-Wis., to begin exploring a new approach to mixing populations of the elderly and the mentally disabled in public housing. There was growing concern among elderly tenants that younger disabled people had brought drugs and other societal problems into the units.

"This is one of the most anguishing issues," Frank said of the effort to weigh the fears of the older population against the needs of the disabled.

Kleczka's compromise amendment would designate floors and units in public housing for the elderly but would not evict anyone already in residence. But members felt that more fine-tuning needed to be done to protect the rights of the disabled.

The longest and most heated debate was triggered by an amendment that was rejected by voice vote. Frank Riggs, R-Calif., offered a 72-page radical restructuring of the public housing system, dubbed "perestroika" by its supporters in the administration. It called for a greater choice in management and ownership of units, with the goal of providing tenants with greater flexibility to buy their apartments.

Charles E. Schumer, D-N.Y., said the administration "doesn't have the foggiest idea what goes on in public housing."

Among the amendments the panel approved by voice vote were:

● A package offered en bloc that included technical changes to the FHA, incentives for solar energy and the administration's "safe havens" program to provide small residential facilities for seriously mentally ill homeless people.

● By Maxine Waters, D-Calif., to increase by $50 million several programs aimed at providing housing to families at risk of losing children to foster care.

● By Roukema, to allow certificates and vouchers in the Section 8 housing subsidy program to be used for buying a home and making mortgage payments. It was approved on the condition that it be modified by the full committee.

● By Frank, to require a jurisdiction to include an anti-poverty plan within its comprehensive housing affordability strategy. State and local governments must submit such a strategy evaluating regulatory barriers that increase housing costs.

● By Ben Erdreich, D-Ala., to allow mobile-home owners to qualify for federal aid as first-time home buyers.

● By Bill Orton, D-Utah, to set aside $375 million of the $1 billion authorized for the National Homeownership Trust for use in connection with mortgage revenue bonds.

● By Floyd H. Flake, D-N.Y., a technical fix to ensure that public housing that did not require public financing was nonetheless eligible for the HOPE II multifamily homeownership program.

## HOUSE COMMITTEE ACTION

The House Committee on Banking, Finance and Urban Affairs approved by voice vote a bill (HR 5334) on June 16

to authorize $29.7 billion for fiscal 1993. The panel rebuked nearly all of Kemp's new ideas and cut by more than half the administration's funding request for HOPE, the focal point of the administration's 1990 housing strategy, which aimed to give public housing tenants a chance to purchase the federal units.

Kemp told Chairman Gonzalez in a June 15 letter that the House version violated "the spirit of bipartisanship that made the 1990 National Affordable Housing Act possible."

As approved by committee, the bill authorized $2.1 billion for the Democratic-backed HOME program; the president had requested only $700 million for the housing block grants to state and local governments.

But the major administration concern was over the new requirements for obtaining matching funds from the localities.

Although the House panel approved a largely Democratic bill, Republicans scored one major victory when an amendment to scale back funding by nearly $7 billion offered by Roukema was approved on a 27-22 vote. Eight of the 31 Democrats on the panel voted for the lower budget figures.

Roukema, ranking minority member of the Housing and Community Development Subcommittee, argued that unrealistically high authorization figures would be a "red flag," signaling to Kemp that there could not be a bipartisan agreement in 1992.

Before the markup, the full Banking Committee had resolved a number of thorny issues deferred by the subcommittee, including the problem of how to integrate the elderly population in federally assisted housing with younger disabled people. Older tenants argued that the younger residents brought drugs and other societal problems into the units.

The compromise worked out by Frank and Kleczka — and agreed to by voice vote — would give owners of buildings originally designed for the elderly the option of maintaining a preference for older people as long as a set number of units were reserved for other groups, such as nonelderly handicapped.

Frank was defeated in his bid to force removal of certain regulatory barriers to affordable housing. His amendment, offered with Riggs, would have given HUD the authority to say whether a state or local government was in violation of using zoning or "artificial environmental concerns" to increase housing costs and limit the supply of lower-income housing.

This issue had become a major crusade for Frank.

But several members compared giving the federal housing agency the power to enforce this amendment over local laws to "throwing Br'er Rabbit in the brier patch."

"It is too much for us to trust HUD," said Mary Rose Oakar, D-Ohio, who at the same time echoed other members' difficulty in opposing the well-respected Frank.

"I'll take a lot less respect and a little more support," Frank said.

A compromise amendment offered by Doug Bereuter, R-Neb., to delete the section in Frank's amendment that would have allowed HUD to withhold HOME funds or Community Development Block Grants from errant local governments was defeated, 11-37.

Immediately after, the panel rejected Frank's amendment by voice vote.

The panel voted, 31-19, to approve another Frank amendment that would push HUD to implement rules for provisions of the 1990 bill not yet acted on.

## HOUSE FLOOR ACTION

Prospects for the housing bill increased considerably Aug. 5 when the House voted overwhelmingly in favor of a $28.8 billion reauthorization measure.

With the backing of most Republicans, the House voted 369-54 to pass the bill (HR 5334), which sent a strong signal to the Bush administration that members of both parties were willing to negotiate on the most controversial issues. (Vote 366, p. 90-H)

Those issues included a House provision to make it easier for home buyers to finance the cost of a mortgage from the Federal Housing Administration and a revision of existing rules to make it easier for state and local governments to obtain matching federal grants for low-income housing initiatives.

For Roukema and other bill sponsors, including Frank and Banking Committee Chairman Gonzalez, the bipartisan floor vote was a long way from the sharply divided subcommittee vote on May 20, which split 22-13 along party lines. The floor action set up a much less contentious House-Senate conference, because the Senate version of the bill (S 3031) had bipartisan backing.

The actual revisions to the House bill as it proceeded to the floor and gained Republican backers were more conciliatory than substantive. The funding level was scaled back from the initial $35.4 billion proposed for fiscal 1993. But that was mainly symbolic because the separate fiscal 1993 spending bill for HUD, which preceded the authorization bill to the House floor by a week, called for $25.4 billion for housing programs. (Appropriations, p. 639)

On the floor, a group of amendments accepted en bloc by voice vote did move toward some of the Republican goals. The compromise offered a 4 percent across-the-board cut in funding and increased from 10 percent to 20 percent the flat local matching requirement for the Democratic block grant program called HOME.

This still fell far short of what the administration wanted: the more rigid three-tiered system of matching payments that was contained in the 1990 bill. Appropriators waived that system in fiscal 1992 after local officials said it created budgeting problems.

The floor amendments also included some of the administration initiatives, such as a program that would allow poorly managed public housing units to be transferred to another management entity.

Republicans did not get all they wanted, however. Just before final passage the House defeated, 147-277, a GOP motion to recommit the bill to committee and require more funding for HOPE. (Vote 365, p. 90-H)

### Mixed Housing

Those who worked the hardest on ensuring floor passage, including Frank and Republican Chalmers P. Wylie of Ohio, said that a key reason for the bill's overwhelming support was a carefully worded provision that sought to resolve the unsettling problem of how to integrate the disabled — including the mentally ill — with elderly residents in public and subsidized housing units.

What seemed a relatively minor provision was in fact a major one. The House compromise to provide an equitable way of mixing the two disparate populations in federal housing won some of the strongest bipartisan praise and gave the bill the push it needed for passage.

"This was one of the most popular parts of the bill," said Frank. The bill's programs for the poor, he said, were not as important for most members as were its provisions for the elderly.

Problems were mounting in many public housing districts, where younger disabled people moved into public and assisted housing that once included only older people. Many newcomers were mentally disabled people who no longer were being hospitalized and who qualified for public housing under the broadened definition of disability. Some of the newcomers also were alcohol and drug users.

Several members recounted incidents of violence in their districts. Rosa DeLauro, a Democrat who represented New Haven, Conn., spoke on the floor about an elderly public housing resident who was killed in her apartment by a non-elderly resident.

"This painful tragedy created a reaction of fear and resentment among the elderly population not only in Crawford Manor, where this incident took place, but throughout the city," she said.

Local public housing officials had been urging Congress for nearly five years to resolve the growing crisis. Yet advocacy groups for the disabled feared that any changes in existing housing policy would unfairly deny housing to those in need.

The House Banking Committee had received testimony suggesting a wide range of options, from complete segregation of the two populations to complete integration, which some believed was the only way to avoid violating fair housing laws. Some middle-range solutions were also offered, including the costly proposal to provide special services and hire service coordinators to help ease the lifestyle differences between the two groups.

What the committee finally accepted was a provision crafted primarily by Kleczka of Wisconsin. It allowed housing authorities to designate different housing projects for separate or mixed populations "as long as the needs of all eligible populations are addressed to the extent practicable in an allocation plan."

As incentives, the proposal permitted a person denied a unit in an elderly-only building to seek additional rental assistance subsidies. Further, it required that at least 5 percent of the housing money allocated for reconstruction of obsolete housing projects be used to reconfigure public housing as an alternative for single people who were not elderly.

The committee compromise also included strict wording to prevent the housing authorities from evicting tenants to create elderly-only buildings. The committee report warned that "such evictions may be tempting." On the other hand, the bill did not preclude incentives for moving tenants.

### Housing Industry Support

Many key housing industry groups were satisfied with the House bill. Steve Driesler, senior vice president for government affairs for the National Association of Realtors, said that he was "very pleased" with the vote.

The Realtors, who had a strong influence over Republican votes, pushed hardest for the elimination of FHA rules. Yet the veto threat loomed over the House bill mainly because it would eliminate a rule that allowed FHA borrowers to use their loans to finance only up to 57 percent of closing costs associated with taking out a mortgage. This would reverse efforts pushed by the administration in the 1990 bill aimed at bolstering FHA solvency. But Realtors

and other housing lobbyists had argued that the 1990 rules — if not reversed — threatened to block 60,000 families who could otherwise afford home ownership.

An effort to remove the FHA provision failed in subcommittee on a 10-25 vote, with seven Republicans voting against the administration position to retain the rules.

Although the Senate version did not attempt to alter the existing FHA restrictions, Driesler of the National Association of Realtors was confident that the rules would be eliminated in 1992. The appropriations bill for housing included a similar lifting of the 2-year-old regulation.

The administration also had raised objections to the House proposal to substantially increase the limit on FHA single-family home loans — from its current limit of $124,875 to about $151,725. Administration officials maintained that this provision would move the federal mortgage agency away from its traditional role as a resource for the lower-income, first-time home buyers. The industry insisted that it would increase the opportunity of home ownership for more families.

## SENATE COMMITTEE ACTION

After weeks of tense negotiations within Congress and with Kemp, the Senate Banking, Housing and Urban Affairs Committee on June 18 unanimously approved by voice vote a bill to authorize $22 billion for fiscal 1993 and $22.8 billion for fiscal 1994. Unlike the House bill, the Senate version endorsed the administration's push toward getting the federal government out of the business of subsidized housing. It also sought to refine and expand the Democrats' partnership concept of giving more money to state and local governments to meet housing needs.

"What we have here is a marriage of different philosophies," said Committee Chairman Donald W. Riegle Jr., D-Mich.

As it did two years earlier, the Senate Banking Committee worked with the administration to craft a bipartisan bill. Two of the remaining contentious points — matching funds for the HOME program and the mixing of the elderly and the disabled in public housing — were expected to be worked out before it was sent to the floor.

Yet floor action hardly seemed likely on the eve of the committee vote after 96 amendments were filed to the draft bill and talks between the members appeared to have broken down. Some members, including Christopher S. Bond, R-Mo., worked through the night to develop a compromise that could be approved by the full committee. The entire markup took less than two hours.

As approved by committee, the Senate version included six key components: additional support for community-based efforts through HOME, empowerment to low-income youth through the new Youthbuild program to provide construction training jobs, a strengthening of fair housing enforcement efforts, steps to prevent lead poisoning of children, expansion of affordable housing by providing more credit to the Federal Housing Authority and a modified version of Kemp's new agenda.

Although substantially rewritten from what the Housing secretary initially had proposed, the Senate version included a demonstration of his "Choice in Management Program" — which sought to give tenants of troubled public housing units the opportunity to switch management — and pieces of another new program called "Take the Boards Off," a proposal to allow public housing that was at least 50 percent vacant to be transferred to nonprofit organizations for renovation.

The measure also included a small authorization for a new program that would provide interest-free second mortgages for up to $15,000 on any home built or renovated in a state or federal enterprise zone.

## SENATE FLOOR ACTION

It took two takes to get the housing bill through the full Senate by unanimous consent. The process required the mutual cooperation of all senators; often, it meant a number of deals or tradeoffs.

On Aug. 12, as the countdown to recess pressured senators to move quickly on the measure so that conference action could begin, it appeared that the deals were sealed for a smooth passage. But an unidentified Republican had put a hold on S 3031. And even a plea by Senate Majority Leader George J. Mitchell of Maine, urging immediate passage, could not push the bill over that one last hurdle.

Housing Subcommittee Chairman Cranston and others who had worked hard through the week to appease their colleagues were frustrated. "I am particularly dismayed by the manner in which one Republican senator chose to derail the bill, since I believe the legislation has wide bipartisan support," Cranston said.

There was only speculation on why the bill was derailed so late in the process. One possibility was that the opposition was rooted in the growing Republican dislike for Housing Secretary Kemp. The secretary's initiatives for selling public housing would be advanced through the bill, giving him something tangible to tout at the upcoming Republican convention in Houston.

The bill poised for Senate action would have gone further than the House version on new initiatives. A negotiated bipartisan amendment that was to have been offered on the Senate floor would have given Kemp several programs geared primarily toward getting the federal government out of subsidized housing and giving tenants of troubled public housing units more options to choose their managers. The amendment also would have slightly scaled back a new program designed to prevent lead poisoning of children.

What loomed between the bipartisan compromise and Senate floor passage was the threat of unwanted amendments. A possibility on the housing bill was that John Kerry, D-Mass., would bring up an amendment to overhaul the National Flood Insurance Program by reducing premiums for communities that refrained from building in coastal hazard areas. By late afternoon on Aug. 12, however, Kerry agreed not to jeopardize the larger measure with an amendment.

Then the remaining obstacles were overcome: Alfonse M. D'Amato, R-N.Y., said he would not put a hold on the bill if the flood insurance issue were dropped. Republicans Connie Mack of Florida and Malcolm Wallop of Wyoming said they would not introduce technical fixes to the 1991 bank overhaul bill (PL 102-242). Democrat Terry Sanford of North Carolina also agreed not to attempt similar fixes to the banking measure. *(1991 Almanac, p. 75)*

### The Second Go Round

On the second go round Sept. 10, Majority Leader Mitchell brought up the housing bill, and, unlike the scenario Aug. 12, this time all the deals held.

After a week of intense conversation between senators and the administration, no one spoke as the Senate passed the $22.7 billion measure with some negotiated changes, and sent it to a conference with the House.

Only hours earlier, the measure appeared doomed. HUD Secretary Kemp had raised objections to several minor provisions in the bill. But unlike the series of events that led to a stranglehold on the bill in August, this time GOP senators decided the differences could be worked out in conference.

Republican Phil Gramm of Texas, who had been asked to put a hold on the measure, instead offered a colloquy for the record stating that the "time frame we are operating under does not allow us to resolve these differences tonight."

## CONFERENCE ACTION

Under the pressure of near-adjournment, conferees and staff jumped in quickly to resolve House-Senate differences on the housing measures during the week of Sept. 21. Relief for inner cities and poverty-stricken communities was considered more crucial than partisan bickering as conferees plowed through a 547-page side-by-side bill comparison.

"I think we are going to get a bill. But both sides have to approach this conference with the understanding that we're not both going to get what we want," said Frank, a House conferee.

But in the chaos of an election year, there was concern that even the most well-intentioned bill could get caught in the political mire. The White House budget office had issued a series of policy statements on both the House and Senate bills criticizing specific sections in each. While the Senate had worked with the administration to smooth out objectionable provisions, the House resisted bowing to White House demands. Most notably, the House bill continued to eliminate several reforms begun two years earlier to shore up the FHA single-family mortgage insurance program.

Some staff people speculated that the easier legislative vehicle for administration priorities, especially increased funding for HOPE, would be the appropriations bill (HR 5679) for housing programs.

The major housing industry groups had shifted their lobbying efforts to the appropriations measure. But their key demand — the lifting of the 1990 FHA reforms — was at odds with the administration position of keeping the rules intact. The 1990 reform imposed a limitation of 57 percent on the amount of closing costs that home buyers could finance, instead of paying up front. Peter Morgan of the National Association of Realtors said the provision to remove the rule would be more secure in the spending bill, which included funding for a top administration priority, the $40 billion space station *Freedom.*

### Making HOME Work

With the big industry associations out of the picture, it was the low-income housing and community development groups that had to work the hardest for passage of the 1992 housing bill.

"It is a workaday kind of bill," said Barry Zigas, president of the Washington-based National Low Income Housing Coalition. "But it does very important things." Most significantly for his members, it would put the HOME program on track in many areas of the country that suffered from lack of affordable housing.

Congress had radically changed federal housing policy two years earlier by replacing a series of narrow block

grants to communities with an intricate partnership concept to leverage local money. It required local governments to match federal contributions at a certain percentage, depending on the project.

But as dollars grew more scarce, the HOME program became tougher for many municipalities to put into action. Conferees struggled with nearly a dozen fixes to make HOME work. At the outset, plan creators envisioned a flurry of activity among private and public interests to create more affordable housing options for lower-income families.

"I'm not sure how long we can keep the enthusiasm up without the necessary changes," said Jim Park of the National Community Development Association, an organization of community and housing program administrators.

Consensus existed on several points: that the HOME program should be easier for community-based housing organizations to use, state and local governments should share the financial responsibility, and the more burdensome regulations — such as restrictions on new construction and local-federal matching requirements — should be loosened to get the program moving.

The technical issues were resolved quickly. Other differences had to be weighed more carefully — particularly how federal HOME dollars should be matched locally.

The Senate asked for a modified tiered match of 35 percent from the localities for new construction and substantial rehabilitation and 25 percent on moderate rehabilitation and tenant assistance. The House version was more lenient: It would establish a flat matching requirement of 20 percent. Further, House members felt that the participating communities should be allowed to consider publicly issued or borrowed debt as part of the local contribution. The Senate was more specific in limiting the use of debt.

The 1990 bill required a three-tiered match, ranging from 25 percent for rental assistance and housing rehabilitation to 50 percent for construction. However, appropriators threw a curve ball to authorizers by eliminating the local matching provision for fiscal 1992, saying that many localities faced financial difficulties.

Administration officials and Congress generally agreed that a new matching formula was the only way to make the partnership concept work. Without it, cities and states would have little stake in the housing program, and dwindling resources would be put elsewhere.

"For housing advocates, the bottom line is how much money is going into housing," said Zigas.

But Park, who represented the cities and communities involved in local housing initiatives, argued that too large a matching requirement would result in less participation in the program.

"It's a tough choice. There needs to be a match, but it can't be an obstacle."

## Trouble Spots

As conference action proceeded, a few trouble spots threatened to bog down the process. For one, only the House version contained a set of regulations that would permit housing to be designated for elderly-only, with certain limitations. Outbreaks of violence against the elderly by younger disabled tenants — including the mentally disabled and drug abusers — had pushed lawmakers to do something for older tenants. With the Senate being asked to weigh in on a solution to the "mixed housing" problem, there was concern that Democrat Tom Harkin of Iowa, an outspoken advocate for the disabled, might attempt to

sway conferees to change the carefully worded compromise.

A new title created in the Senate bill — but not in the House version — that sought to eliminate lead-based paint hazards delayed the naming of House conferees. House Energy and Commerce Committee Chairman John D. Dingell, D-Mich., had asked for a conference on one section of that lead title. The House Education and Labor Committee also wanted some oversight of the lead abatement provisions because it involved worker safety.

There was concern that Rep. Henry A. Waxman, D-Calif., a vocal advocate for reducing environmental lead hazards, might try to change the Senate language, a long-negotiated compromise struck with Kemp and the White House.

### Conferees Sign Off

Conferees completed work Oct. 2 with strong Republican backing after nearly three days of negotiations and despite a veto threat from the administration.

The compromise bill resolved the difficult issue of mixing the elderly and the disabled in a shrinking supply of public and subsidized housing by allowing landlords to give the elderly preference in some units but requiring them to set aside at least 10 percent for the disabled.

The bill also included a major new set of rules to clarify and strengthen the federal role in eliminating lead-based paint from homes; streamlined several existing housing programs; and established new initiatives, including one to provide construction job training skills to youth.

House Banking Committee Chairman Gonzalez said as conferees sat down for their final meeting that he had made considerable concessions to meet the demands of the administration, especially on Kemp's pet project, HOPE. The Senate version already was closer to the authorization level the administration had requested for the program to help low-income people buy their own housing units.

But Kemp said in an Oct. 2 letter to Gonzalez that the conference agreement fell short on a number of issues, especially on his objective of retaining the 2-year-old limits on FHA closing costs. Conferees wanted to strike that law and let borrowers finance up to 100 percent of their closing costs so that home buyers did not have to pay so much money up front.

But, in fact, conferees had little power to effect any changes in the FHA rules. Congress lifted the rule in the fiscal 1993 spending bill for HUD (HR 5679), which the Senate cleared on Sept. 25 and which was expected to be quickly signed by President Bush because it contained the funding for the $40 billion space station *Freedom*.

Yet Kemp remained adamant that something should be done by the authorizers to protect the FHA loan guarantee fund from possible fiscal collapse.

"This is a little insane," said House conferee Frank. "We're sitting here with a veto threat for not overturning a bill that Bush has probably already turned into law."

### Conference Give-and-Take

Much of the conference give-and-take occurred over the fine-tuning of existing programs. Kemp used his leverage on several key points, including funding levels for HOPE: Conferees raised HOPE's authorization to $855 million for fiscal 1993. However, this had little real effect because it exceeded the fiscal 1993 appropriation by $504 million.

"Symbolism is important here," insisted Wylie, ranking member of the House Banking Committee. "It gives HOPE some backing."

The administration gained something more tangible when negotiations turned to the HOME program, an intricate partnership concept designed to leverage local money. Conferees devised a new formula for requiring state and local governments to match the federal contribution: 25 percent for tenant assistance and rehabilitation, and 30 percent for new construction. Administration officials still objected because they felt more extensive rehabilitation should also be in the 30 percent category.

What Kemp gained, however, was an agreement to reduce the amount of public debt that state and local governments could use as part of their share. Under the conference agreement, borrowings could make up only 25 percent of the local share, rather than 50 percent as stipulated in a staff recommendation.

On other issues, conferees agreed to a number of non-controversial initiatives aimed at easing regulatory burdens on the nation's banks and thrifts. An unresolved issue was whether to attach to the conference agreement a separate, newly drafted measure (HR 6094) to strengthen regulations on two government-sponsored enterprises (GSE's).

That decision was left to the discretion of Gonzalez, with the understanding that the House would first attempt to move the GSE bill as a free-standing measure.

### Getting the Lead Out

The new lead-based paint abatement provisions nearly boiled down to a take-it-or-leave-it deal. The House was expected to accept the new title in the Senate housing bill to establish a $250 million annual grant program for eliminating lead-based paint hazards from homes, or face a Senate threat to strip the entire section from the conference agreement.

But to the conferees' surprise, they negotiated a middle course that sought to broaden the scope of the lead provisions to give more specific direction to the Environmental Protection Agency (EPA) and the Occupational Safety and Health Administration (OSHA). As such, House conferees accepted the Senate title by voice vote.

"We've now proven that we're lead-free," said Gonzalez.

At one point, the lead issue appeared headed for a turf battle. Energy and Commerce Chairman Dingell secured a seat at the conference table on lead provisions. Waxman, a leading advocate of reducing environmental lead hazards, also became a conferee. The Education and Labor Committee won jurisdiction on those items addressing certified contractors and inspectors — the areas in which the functions of the Department of Housing and Urban Development (HUD) overlap with the EPA and OSHA.

But numerous provisions of another House bill (HR 5730) that also called for significant lead reduction were incorporated into the Senate lead title and then fine-tuned to meet each of the House committees' concerns.

"This is a rare triumph for a comprehensive bill that gives complementary marching orders to both HUD and EPA," said Don Ryan, executive director of the Alliance to End Childhood Lead Poisoning, a national nonprofit public interest organization.

The Senate Banking Committee had gathered significant data: Low-level lead poisoning afflicted as many as 3 million children under age 6 and caused reading and other learning disabilities; more than 3 million tons of lead in the form of lead-based paint remained in American homes, and despite the enactment of laws in the early 1970s requiring the federal government to eliminate lead-based paint in federally owned, assisted and insured housing, the federal response to the "national crisis" remained slight.

According to Ryan, local government officials and landlords were confused about how to deal with lead-paint hazards. Thousands of lawsuits were pending nationwide, filed on behalf of children who already had shown the lead-poisoning symptoms. The new rules took a preventive approach. "It would start putting in place procedures on how to protect the most children," he said.

As approved by the conferees, the bill increased HUD's competitive grant program to state and local governments for lead-based paint hazard reduction in private, low-income housing. It also authorized a program to evaluate and reduce the problem in federally owned and subsidized pre-1978 low-income housing. Provisions outlined how the "lead-hazard reduction" activities would be performed by certified contractors, including certification rules and penalties for non-compliance.

## FINAL ACTION

Many lawmakers, public housing officials and low-income housing and health advocates were relieved when the housing bill finally cleared Congress in the final hours before adjournment. The conference agreement had received a resounding vote of 377-37 in the House on Oct. 5. But it was three days before the Senate sent it to the White House by voice vote. *(Vote 476, p. 116-H)*

There was a remaining hurdle: Kemp wrote to White House budget director Richard G. Darman requesting a veto. However, President Bush ignored Kemp's request and signed HR 5334 — PL 102-550 on Oct. 28.

"Kemp would have been well-advised to tell Bush to sign it," said Wylie, ranking member of the House Banking Committee. Wylie, a friend and former House colleague of the president, wrote a letter to Bush asking for his signature.

All in all, most members found little to oppose in the bill. Even with Kemp's vocal opposition, only 35 House Republicans voted against the conference measure.

"The House vote was a definitive statement," said Roukema.

For reasons including the sentimental fact that it was Cranston's last housing bill, the measure became a priority for Senate Majority Leader Mitchell. According to observers, Mitchell tugged it from the clutches of Republican Phil Gramm of Texas, who had put a hold on the bill at Kemp's request. Mitchell forced Gramm to release his hold by slapping a hold on a bill near and dear to Gramm: the Commodity Futures Trading Commission reauthorization (HR 707). Gramm's wife, Wendy L. Gramm, was chairman of the agency that oversaw futures exchanges. *(CFTC reauthorization, p. 127)*

Cranston said the bill would tackle a major national problem: the dwindling supply of affordable housing.

"We still have a very long way to go, but this is a very good bill," Cranston said. "Our mission is clear . . . our options straightforward." ∎

# Urban Aid Measures Fail Despite Riots' Impetus

A slew of bills intended to aid thousands of U.S. cities struggling with a national recession were introduced in the 102nd Congress with the high hopes of their sponsors. But none advanced to the floor of either chamber.

Many Democrats said an emergency cash infusion to city governments in fiscal 1992 could help boost regional economies and create jobs, especially on public works projects that local governments had shelved because of the poor economy. The matter was considered particularly urgent after an unpopular jury verdict led to violence and rioting in Los Angeles at the end of April. *(Urban crisis, p. 339)*

But most Republicans and some Democrats opposed the bills, saying that no money existed to fund them and that the recession would end before the projects began.

## COMMITTEE ACTION

One city aid bill approved in committee was HR 4073 (H Rept 102-524), sponsored by Banking, Finance and Urban Affairs Committee Chairman Henry B. Gonzalez, D-Texas.

The Housing and Community Development Subcommittee on March 4 gave voice vote approval to the legislation, which would have authorized $15 billion in fiscal 1992 for state and local governments for such jobs programs as construction and rehabilitation of public buildings and other public facilities.

Gonzalez estimated that the emergency aid would create more than 600,000 jobs. But GOP opponents said the bill would have increased the federal budget deficit and violated the pay-as-you-go rules of the 1990 budget agreement.

By voice vote, members approved an amendment by ranking member Chalmers P. Wylie, R-Ohio, to prohibit the use of a tax increase to pay for the bill.

The full Banking Committee approved the bill March 9 in a party-line voice vote.

At the markup, John W. Cox. Jr., D-Ill., said the possibility that the bill would increase the deficit had bothered him, but he said he voted for the bill anyway to "get it out in the open" in case money could be found.

No action occurred on the bill after it was reported to the full House on May 14.

### Other City Aid Bills

Government Operations Committee Chairman John Conyers Jr., D-Mich., authored several city aid bills, all of which saw some action but no success. The first bill (HR 3601) would have authorized $2 billion in fiscal 1993, with the funding increasing by $3 billion each year until reaching $14 billion in fiscal 1997.

The Subcommittee on Human Resources and Intergovernmental Relations approved the bill in a party line 6-3 vote Feb. 27.

Aid would have been distributed under a complex formula that considered unemployment rates and per capita incomes in urban and semi-urban areas.

Conyers wanted to designate the spending in HR 3601 as "emergency" so it would not have to be offset by cuts in other programs.

But committee opponents said they could not support a bill that increased the deficit, so Conyers delayed work on it.

Conyers also waited to see if money might be found in a budget bill (S 2399) that would have torn down the "firewalls" in the 1990 budget deal that blocked the transfer of funds from defense to domestic accounts. But when the House rejected that bill, 187-238, March 31, Conyers abandoned the idea. *(Budget walls, p. 104)*

He then drafted a city aid bill that turned into HR 5259, which sought to authorize $5.4 billion in aid in fiscal 1992 and fiscal 1993. But after a series of delays, HR 5259 was rejected, 20-20, by the panel June 3.

Conyers' final attempt at a city aid bill in 1992 was HR 5798, a whittled-down version of HR 5259. It fared a little better than its predecessors but ultimately died at the end of the session.

Approved, 31-10, by the Government Operations Committee on Aug. 11, HR 5798 (H Rept 102-872) sought to authorize $3 billion for 18,500 cities and localities in fiscal 1992 and fiscal 1993.

Unlike other versions of Conyers' bills, HR 5798 would have required appropriators to offset costs with program cuts elsewhere. This provision helped Conyers garner critical GOP voters, who earlier had opposed his city aid proposals, saying they would have increased the deficit.

Members agreed by voice vote to an amendment by Cardiss Collins, D-Ill., to require 10 percent of any aid under the bill to be set aside for work by small businesses run by women or minorities.

But despite the bill's gain in committee, the House never considered it.

Conyers said the bill was intended to give appropriators an option to help cities. "If they find themselves putting their hands into the hat for cities this year, they will have our bill there," he said.

But other panel members said the bill was merely symbolic, because appropriators would not have been able to find money to fund it. Gerald D. Kleczka, D-Wis., said the bill "throws a sop to our mayors .... They may remember us in November. But they won't see the money in December." ∎

# Veterans' Job Training

The House Veterans' Affairs Committee approved a bill (HR 5254) on May 28 that authorized on-the-job training for Persian Gulf and certain other veterans, aiming to provide them with stable jobs. Under the bill, employers had to certify in writing that they planned to employ veterans in positions for which they were trained. As an employer incentive, the federal government would subsidize half the employees' wages.

Although HR 5254 never advanced to the floor, similar provisions were included June 4 in HR 5006 (PL 102-484), the Defense Department's authorization bill. *(Defense authorization, p. 483)*

A House Veterans' Affairs subcommittee had given voice vote approval May 20 to draft legislation, later numbered HR 5254, to give job training and opportunities to veterans who had been recently discharged because of defense cutbacks.

The bill, approved by the Education, Training and Employment Subcommittee, authorized $75 million per year for fiscal 1993 through 1995.

The federal government would subsidize half the wages — up to $12,000 for disabled veterans and $10,000 for others — for veterans discharged after Aug. 2, 1990. Training would be funded for no longer than 15 months for each veteran. An employer would provide on-the-job training and promise to then hire the veteran permanently.

The bill, introduced by subcommittee Chairman Timothy J. Penny, D-Minn., also stipulated that the hiring of veterans would not displace workers already on the job.

### Vietnam Veterans' Job Training

Congress cleared legislation Oct. 7 that included provisions to expand job assistance programs for Vietnam-era veterans. The original bill (HR 4342) expanded eligibility for the veterans readjustment appointment program and other federal employment opportunities. It also extended the Vietnam-era veterans employment and training program.

The Veterans Subcommittee on Education, Training and Employment passed the bill March 12, and the full committee passed it May 28. The House passed it June 9. Provisions of HR 4342 were later incorporated into HR 5008 (PL 102-568), which revised the federal system of compensation for veterans' survivors. (*Veterans compensation, p. 378*) ∎

# More Aid Funded for Homeless Vets

Homeless veterans earned additional benefits under legislation (HR 5400 — PL 102-590) cleared by the Senate Oct. 7. The measure was designed to enhance existing services provided by the Labor Department and the Department of Veterans Affairs (VA).

The legislation reflected increased concern about the plight of homeless veterans. House Veterans' Affairs Committee Chairman G. V. "Sonny" Montgomery, D-Miss., said some reports estimated that 30 percent of the homeless were veterans.

The measure aimed to send veterans benefits counselors to 83 VA-run facilities providing readjustment counseling, shelter for homeless veterans and assistance for the mentally ill.

Under the bill, the VA could also establish grants for new assistance programs for homeless veterans. Before passage of the bill, there was no provision for the VA to make such grants.

The legislation also authorized the VA to lease or donate 10 percent of VA properties repossessed because of loan defaults to nonprofit groups and state agencies to provide housing for homeless veterans.

The measure authorized $48 million each year for fiscal 1993 through 1995. It also expanded the authorization for certain homeless employment programs from $2.2 million for fiscal 1993 to $10 million for fiscal 1993, $12 million for fiscal 1994 and $14 million for fiscal 1995.

## LEGISLATIVE ACTION

Harley O. Staggers Jr., D-W.V., chairman of the House Veterans' Affairs Housing and Memorial Affairs Subcommittee, introduced HR 5400 on June 16.

The measure moved quickly. The Housing Subcommittee approved it June 18, followed by full committee approval July 23. The comprehensive bill then passed the House by voice vote under fast-track procedures July 27.

On the Senate side, the Senate Veterans' Affairs Committee approved a version by Chairman Alan Cranston, D-

---

### BOXSCORE

➡ **Homeless Veterans Act (HR 4500; S 2512).** The bill established comprehensive services for homeless veterans, including housing assistance.

**Reports:** H Rept 102-721; S Rept 102-361.

### KEY ACTION

July 27 — The **House** passed HR 5400 by voice vote.

Sept. 8 — The **Senate** inserted the text of S 2512 into HR 5400 and approved HR 5400 by voice vote.

Oct. 3 — The **House** agreed to the Senate amendment to HR 5400 by voice vote.

Oct. 7 — The **Senate** cleared HR 5400 by agreeing to the **House** amendment by voice vote.

Nov. 10 — President Bush signed HR 5400 — PL 102-590.

---

Calif., (S 2512) on June 24. The Senate then inserted its version of the bill and passed HR 5400 by voice vote Sept. 8.

Following Senate approval, Montgomery on Oct. 3 called for the House to agree with the Senate amendment.

On Oct. 7, the Senate cleared the measure by agreeing to a compromise version that incorporated provisions from both the House and Senate bills. The president signed HR 5400 (PL 102-590) on Nov. 10.

### Provisions

One provision from the House bill established a three-year pilot program to create up to four VA service centers for homeless veterans. The centers would provide counseling and vocational and other services.

Under a Senate provision, the bill authorized the VA to sell properties at a discount to nonprofit organizations and government agencies that would use them to shelter or house homeless veterans. This authorized the VA to make loans directly to nonprofit organizations and state agencies for shelters.

Senate Committee Chairman Cranston said a previous program required an organization to finance a purchase through its cash reserves or a conventional mortgage. According to Cranston, those options were unsuitable for nonprofit organizations, which seldom had large amounts of cash on hand.

Another Senate provision extended a program run by the Labor Department to reintegrate homeless veterans into the labor force. The program, which would have expired in October 1993, received increased funding authorization from $2.2 million for fiscal 1993 to $10 million for fiscal 1993, $12 million for fiscal 1994 and $14 million for fiscal 1995.

Robin Higgins, deputy assistant secretary of labor for veterans employment and training, testified at a hearing April 9 that in fiscal 1990, the agency contacted 11,493 homeless veterans through the program's outreach efforts; 5,204 of them enrolled in the program and 2,309 of those were placed in jobs. ∎

# Benefits Increased for Veterans, Survivors

Congress cleared two bills to increase compensation or expand benefits for veterans and their survivors. These included a cost of living adjustment (COLA) and a revision of the system for providing compensation to spouses and children. The adjustment in benefits took effect Dec. 1.

## COLA ADJUSTMENTS

Congress approved a COLA to veterans with service-connected disabilities and to survivors of veterans who died of service-related causes.

The rates increased on Dec. 1, 1992, by the same percentage as Social Security and veterans pension benefits. These increased rates affected 2.2 million veterans and 350,000 survivors.

Congress cleared the bill (S 2322) on Sept. 30, and President Bush signed it Oct. 24 (PL 102-510).

### Background

Veterans' COLA raises had previously been marked by conflict. In 1990, Congress had failed to pass a veterans COLA even though it granted a COLA to Social Security recipients.

Members had tried to attach provisions to that year's COLA bill ensuring compensation to some veterans suffering from cancer after exposure to Agent Orange, a chemical defoliant. The bill stalled when opponents called the measure too costly and questioned the link between cancer and Agent Orange.

In January 1991, when national attention turned to U.S. military forces in the Persian Gulf, Congress overwhelmingly approved a 5.4 percent cost of living increase for disabled veterans for 1991.

Later in 1991, Congress also approved a less controversial 3.7 percent increase that reflected inflation as measured by the consumer price index. *(1991 Almanac, p. 325)*

### Legislative Action

The House Veterans' Affairs Committee approved the original House measure (HR 4244) on July 23. The measure would have authorized a 3.2 percent COLA. At that rate,

---

## BOXSCORE

➡ **Veterans' COLA Increases (S 2322, HR 4244).** The bill provided a cost of living adjustment in compensation (COLA) paid to veterans with service-connected disabilities and to survivors of veterans who died of service-related causes.

**Reports:** H Rept 102-752; S Rept 102-322.

### KEY ACTION

July 28 — The **Senate** passed S 2322 by voice vote.

Aug. 4 — The **House** passed HR 4244 by voice vote, then inserted text into **Senate** version and passed S 2322 by voice vote.

Sept. 22 — The **Senate** agreed to **House** amendments by voice vote.

Sept. 30 — The **House** cleared **Senate** amendments to **House** amendment by voice vote.

Oct. 24 — President Bush signed S 2322 — PL 102-510.

---

➡ **Dependency and Indemnity Compensation Reform Act of 1992 (HR 5008, formerly S 2323).** The bill reformed the payment of dependency and indemnity compensation to survivors of veterans who died from service-connected causes.

**Reports:** H Rept 102-753, Parts I and II; S Rept 102-376.

### KEY ACTION

Aug. 10 — HR 5008 passed the **House** by voice vote.

Sept. 22 — The **Senate** inserted S 2323 into the text of HR 5008 and approved it by voice vote.

Oct. 3 — The **House** agreed by voice vote to the **Senate** amendments with a new amendment to HR 5008.

Oct. 7 — The **Senate** agreed to **House** amendment by voice vote.

Oct. 29 — The president signed HR 5008 — PL 102-568.

---

basic compensation for a totally disabled veteran would increase $54 a month, from $1,680 to $1,734.

Meanwhile, the Senate passed its version (S 2322) on July 28, tying the COLA adjustment to the increase in Social Security and VA pension benefits.

The House on Aug. 4 incorporated its language into the text of S 2322 and passed it with a specified 3.2 percent increase. At that time Douglas Applegate, D-Ohio, chairman of the House Veterans' Affairs Subcommittee on Compensation, Pension and Insurance, said the percentage increase could be adjusted to reflect the actual change in the consumer price index.

On Sept. 22 the Senate approved House changes to the bill, but with no fixed percentage for the COLA increase.

The House cleared the measure Sept. 30 by agreeing to the Senate arrangement. It would tie the COLA to the consumer price index or rate of inflation, which also determined the rate of increase for Social Security benefits.

Bush signed the measure Oct. 24.

## DEPENDENTS' BENEFITS

Congress in 1992 finished work on a measure (HR 5008 — PL 102-568) that increased benefits to veterans' survivors and dependents. The bill was funded by reducing benefits for veterans who, based on Internal Revenue Service information, did not need them.

The bill extended coverage to widows of veterans who died before Oct. 1, 1992.

### Background

As of 1992 the Department of Veterans Affairs (VA) paid benefits to survivors of service members or veterans who died from a disease or injury related to military service. Benefits paid to widows were based on the veteran's rank and ranged from $616 to $1,580. Survivors included spouses, unmarried children under 18, children between 18 and 23 who were in school and children over 18 who required special medical care.

The VA paid benefits to nearly 276,000 surviving spouses and 37,628 children, according to Alan Cranston, D-Calif., chairman of the Senate Veterans' Affairs Committee.

### House Committee Action

On July 8, the House Veterans' Affairs Compensation, Pension and Insurance Subcommittee approved HR 5008 by voice vote.

The measure, introduced by subcommittee Chairman Applegate, authorized increased benefits for survivors of veterans who died of combat-related injuries.

The bill revised the formula determining the funding so all surviving spouses would receive at least $750 per month. The previous 1992 rate of $636 a month had been set in December 1991.

The measure also increased the added amount paid for dependents from $71 per month per child to $100 a month per child in fiscal 1993, $150 per month in fiscal 1994 and $200 per month in fiscal 1995.

The full House Veterans' Affairs Committee then gave voice vote approval to the legislation July 23.

As approved, the minimum monthly payment to survivors went up $114. The payment would be increased by an additional $50 a month if the veteran died in the line of duty or was totally disabled as a result of a service injury.

Members approved, by voice vote, an amendment that increased the education benefits available to veterans and extended through fiscal 1996 the $2 fee on prescription drugs for veterans with non-service-related disabilities.

### House Floor Action

House Veterans' Affairs Committee Chairman G. V. "Sonny" Montgomery, D-Miss., was vindicated when the full House passed HR 5008 by voice vote Aug. 10.

Montgomery managed to secure a commitment from House Ways and Means Committee Chairman Dan Rostenkowski, D-Ill., that savings from veterans programs would be used for other veterans, not for an omnibus energy bill (HR 776).

In 1990, the House Veterans' Affairs Committee successfully recommended legislation requiring the secretary of Veterans Affairs to reduce or withhold benefits from veterans who did not need them, based on income information from the Internal Revenue Service. The law had been set to expire Sept. 30, 1992.

On April 30, 1992, Ways and Means tacked a provision to the energy bill extending the savings measures for five years and authorizing use of the money for tax incentives for the oil and gas industry and energy conservation.

However, on Aug. 5, when Ways and Means reviewed HR 5008 to increase benefits to widows, members approved provisions allowing the Veterans' Affairs Committee to pay for the bill with the savings.

The Congressional Budget Office (CBO) estimated that the bill would cost $172 million in fiscal 1993 and $1.3 billion through fiscal 1997.

### Senate Action

The Senate Veterans' Affairs Committee approved a companion measure (S 2323) by voice vote June 24, setting basic monthly compensation for surviving spouses at $725.

The full Senate then approved HR 5008 by voice vote after replacing its text with the similar Senate bill.

HR 5008 then headed back to the House. Because members wanted to push the bill through both houses before adjournment, House and Senate aides sought a compromise.

Besides the $725 under the Senate bill, surviving spouses would have also received increases based on the length of the veteran's military service. For example, for 30 or more years of service, a surviving spouse would receive an additional $100 per month; for five to 10 years, $20 a month.

The House version provided the same rate of compensation for widows regardless of their spouse's rank. The bill set the base monthly rate of compensation at $750 effective Jan. 1, 1993. The payment increased an additional $50 a month if the veteran died in the line of duty or was disabled as a result of a service-related injury.

The Senate bill also required the VA to conduct a study to determine whether benefits were adequate to support survivors of veterans.

### Final Action

The House passed a compromise version of HR 5008 by voice vote Oct. 3. The Senate cleared the measure soon afterward on Oct. 7.

Under the compromise, basic monthly compensation for surviving spouses was raised to the House-proposed level of $750. Surviving spouses received additional compensation of $165 per month if the veteran was totally disabled for at least eight years from a service-connected injury or illness.

The president signed the legislation Oct. 29 (PL 102-568). ■

# Reserve Forces Personnel Get Loan Guarantees

In the closing days of the 102nd Congress, members cleared a bill (HR 939) that expanded eligibility for the VA Home Loan Guaranty Program to members of the National Guard and Reserve who had served at least six years. The president signed the bill on Oct. 28 (PL 102-547).

## LEGISLATIVE ACTION

The measure (H Rept 102-292, Part 1) won voice vote approval from the House Veterans' Affairs Subcommittee on Housing and Memorial Affairs on July 18, 1991, and the full committee on July 23, 1991.

The House Ways and Means Committee next gave voice vote approval to one provision under its jurisdiction on Feb. 12, 1992. Members amended the bill (H Rept 102-292, Part 2) to clarify for tax purposes the determination of veterans' gross income relating to indebtedness for VA home loans. The full House then passed the bill by voice vote on March 3, 1992.

On the Senate side, the Veterans' Affairs Committee approved its version (S 3108 — S Rept 102-405) by voice vote Aug. 8. S 3108 would have established a pilot program from fiscal 1993 through fiscal 1997 for VA-guaranteed home loans with adjustable-rate mortgages. The measure won Senate approval by voice vote Oct. 1.

The House then agreed to a compromise version by voice vote Oct. 5, and the Senate cleared the bill by voice vote Oct. 7.

### Provisions

The measure extended to certain members of the re-

serve forces eligibility to receive home, farm and business loans through a veterans home loan guarantee program.

Reservists who had served at least six years were thus eligible for the program, which had previously been open only to active-duty veterans.

As a compromise between House and Senate language, the bill provided for a demonstration project on adjustable-rate mortgages during fiscal 1993 and 1994 for regional VA offices.

The measure also allowed veterans to negotiate interest rates directly with lenders for fiscal 1993 and 1994. Previously, the VA secretary determined the permissible interest rates for the home loan program.

In addition, the measure included provisions from another bill (S 2528) regarding home loans to American Indians and Alaska natives. It provided for a five-year pilot program for direct loans up to $80,000 to Indian veterans on trust lands. ∎

# Comprehensive Health Bill Lowers VA's Drug Costs

Congress cleared an omnibus health bill (HR 5193 — PL 102-585) that included provisions for psychological counseling for women who were sexually harassed during military service and a health registry for Persian Gulf veterans.

Members also resolved a longstanding controversy over discounted drug prices for federal agencies.

Traditionally, hospitals, nursing homes and health maintenance organizations had been able to negotiate cut rates for popular drugs. Some of the deepest discounts, however, had been enjoyed for years by the Department of Veterans Affairs. (VA).

But while the VA represented about 1 percent of all prescription drug sales, Medicaid accounted for closer to 15 percent of the market. And faced with the new requirements, many drugmakers chose to raise prices for the VA rather than to lower them for Medicaid. As a result, the VA estimated that it would spend an additional $117 million on drugs in fiscal 1991. *(1991 Almanac, p. 521)*

It took more than a year of negotiations to iron out how to solve the VA's problem without hurting Medicaid, but the new legislation ensured that prices would be lowered for the Department of Veterans Affairs (VA). *(Medicaid drug prices, p. 426)*

## HOUSE ACTION

On May 28 the House Veterans' Affairs Committee voted 30-0 to expand veterans' health-care benefits and services by approving HR 5192. The bill clarified that the VA had the authority to collect on Medicare supplemental insurance policies, known as "medigap" policies, for care provided beginning April 7, 1986, for non-service-connected disabilities. Medicare would have had to reimburse the VA for services to Medicare-eligible veterans receiving "non-mandatory" care.

By voice vote, the committee also approved HR 5193, which expanded cost-sharing agreements between the VA and the Department of Defense (DOD). The measure al-

lowed the VA to provide medical services in areas where DOD health facilities were scheduled to close. Provisions from HR 5192 were later written into HR 5193.

As passed by the House on Aug. 4, the bill authorized the VA to provide medical services to beneficiaries of the Civilian Health and Medical Program of the Uniformed Services (CHAMPUS), dependents of DOD personnel and military retirees. Beneficiaries of the VA's health program for dependents could be treated at DOD facilities. The bill required the VA to consult with veterans organizations about the agreements and show that veterans' health care was not adversely affected.

## SENATE COMMITTEE ACTION

The Senate Veterans' Affairs Committee on June 24 approved by voice vote a measure to improve veterans health programs. But the panel, after approving several amendments to the Senate version of an omnibus veterans health bill (S 2575), delayed final action on that measure because of disagreements over drug pricing.

The committee approved legislation (S 2973) by voice vote that would improve treatment programs for women veterans who had experienced physical or psychological trauma as a result of sexual assault, harassment or rape. Approval followed Senate hearings in which women veterans testified that they had been sexually assaulted by fellow officers. The measure covered only incidents that occurred during active duty.

Under the bill, women veterans would have to be treated following diagnosis by a VA doctor. The VA secretary could contract with other health facilities for the care. The measure would also establish a toll-free telephone number to provide assistance and referrals. It was later incorporated into HR 5193.

The committee then approved the health measure (S 2575) on Aug. 7 by voice vote after further negotiations on the drug discount question.

## FINAL ACTION

The Senate added its amendments to HR 5193 by voice vote Oct 1. The House then passed another version of HR 5193 by voice vote Oct. 5.

Just before the Senate was scheduled to take up the bill

### BOXSCORE

➡ **Veterans' Health-Care Improvements (HR 5193, formerly S 2575).** The bill improved health-care services to veterans. It included provisions for lowered drug prices for the Department of Veterans Affairs and psychological counseling for women veterans who were sexually harassed during military service.

**Reports:** H Rept 102-714, Part I; S Rept 102-401.

### KEY ACTION

Aug. 4 — The **House** passed HR 5193 by voice vote.

Oct. 1 — The **Senate** inserted the text of S 2575 and approved HR 5193 by voice vote.

Oct. 5 — The **House** approved changes to HR 5193 by voice vote.

Oct. 8 — The **Senate** cleared HR 5193.

Nov. 4 — President Bush signed HR 5193 — PL 102-585.

# VA Facilities Smoking Ban Reversed

Veterans who smoked won a long-awaited showdown with VA Secretary Edward J. Derwinski when Congress rolled into an omnibus health bill a controversial provision reversing a VA smoking ban. Before his resignation Sept. 26, Derwinski had fought hard against allowing smoking in veterans hospitals.

The issue heated up in August 1991 when Derwinski announced that VA hospitals would no longer sell tobacco products after Oct. 1, 1991. Under Derwinski, the department also issued a directive in 1992 requiring that VA health facilities be smoke-free by Dec. 31, 1993.

Many veterans groups and members of Congress deplored the secretary's actions and added a provision to the health bill that reversed the smoking ban.

### Fight on the Floor

On May 29, the House Veterans' Affairs Committee approved, by voice vote, an amendment to HR 5192 by Harley O. Staggers Jr., D-W.Va., that would allow VA hospitals and facilities to provide an indoor smoking area and would require VA commissaries to sell tobacco products. Staggers said the no-smoking policy in VA hospitals was unfair to those veterans who chose to smoke. When the health bill finally reached the floor, members were prepared for a showdown. Some members presented impassioned pleas for the provision, maintaining that veterans were being psychologically damaged because they had lost the right to smoke. "How can we restrict their freedom, when they fought so hard for ours?" said Susan Molinari, R-N.Y.

Others added that the government had encouraged veterans to smoke as young men by supplying them with cigarettes.

Opponents of the provision contended that smoking contributed to other health problems and pointed out that private hospitals did not allow smoking. Richard J. Durbin, D-Ill., and Timothy J. Penny, D-Minn., who said that the tobacco lobby was behind the opposition, sponsored an amendment to strike the smoking provision.

In a compromise, Rep. Bob Wise, D-W.Va., offered an amendment to the Durbin-Penny amendment that struck the provision requiring that cigarettes be sold at VA health-care facilities but kept the language mandating the smoking areas. Members adopted the amendment 338-71 on Oct. 1. *(Vote 450, p. 110-H)*

The Penny-Durbin amendment as amended then won voice vote approval from the House.

### Stalling in the Senate

Although House Veterans' Affairs Committee Chairman G. V. "Sonny" Montgomery, D-Miss., supported the measure, Senate Veterans' Committee Chairman Alan Cranston, D-Calif., vowed to fight it.

Just before the Senate was scheduled Oct. 7 to take up the omnibus health bill (HR 5193), which included sections of HR 5192, several senators blocked consideration of the measure. They opposed the smoking amendment as well as provisions to lower VA drug prices. But bill supporters won over the dissenting senators, and the bill passed by voice vote.

Although the Bush administration opposed reversal of the anti-smoking provisions, the president did not threaten to veto the bill. He signed HR 5193 (PL 102-585) on Nov. 4. ■

Oct. 7, however, several senators blocked consideration of the measure by placing a "hold" on it.

They opposed the drug-pricing legislation and a provision from HR 5192 that would reverse a VA decision to ban smoking in VA hospitals.

The drug-pricing provisions inspired an intense lobbying effort by pharmaceutical companies and a last-minute fight.

Ultimately, a compromise was worked out that included the agreed-upon language — similar to the provisions of HR 2890, which sought limits on drug prices procured by the VA — in HR 5193, the House companion to S 2575.

To push through other initiatives in a short time, the House had also amended HR 5193 to include the text of HR 5192, which included the controversial provision reversing a VA decision to ban smoking in VA medical facilities by requiring the VA to establish designated smoking rooms in department hospitals. VA Secretary Edward J. Derwinski had fought hard against the smoking provision before his resignation Sept. 26 *(Derwinski resignation, p. 383)*

The Bush administration, while opposing the anti-smoking provisions that had been part of HR 5192, did not threaten to veto the bill. *(Smoking ban, above)*

"Today I believe we will cast a vote for veterans and for stretching the federal government's health-care dollar further," Sen. John D. Rockefeller IV, D-W.Va., said on the floor Oct. 8 as the Senate cleared the measure by voice vote. Rockefeller, a member of both the Veterans' Affairs

and Finance committees, helped broker the final deal.

The president signed the measure Nov. 4 (PL 102-585).

### Provisions

HR 5193 sought to lower drug prices for the VA. The measure also:

● Reversed a VA ban on smoking in veterans' health-care facilities and required the VA to designate smoking rooms for veterans.

● Established a health registry for Persian Gulf War veterans to monitor them for health effects of exposure to burning oil fires and other adverse environmental conditions. The registry also kept track of general health trends.

● Expanded cost-sharing agreements between the VA and Defense Department medical facilities.

● Provided psychological counseling to women veterans who were sexually harassed or abused during military service.

● Authorized the VA to provide medical services to beneficiaries of CHAMPUS. Beneficiaries are dependents of Defense Department personnel and other military retirees. Under the cost-sharing agreement, beneficiaries of the VA's version of CHAMPUS, which covered some veterans' dependents, were served at Defense health-care facilities.

● Clarified that the VA had the authority to collect on Medicare supplemental insurance policies, known as "medigap" policies, for care starting April 7, 1986, for disabilities not connected to a veteran's service. ■

# Congress Broadens Scope Of Veterans' Programs

Congress addressed several other bills related to veterans programs and compensation. These measures included:

## RADIATION COMPENSATION

Congress cleared a measure (S 775) to expand compensation to veterans exposed to certain kinds of radiation during wartime. The president signed the legislation Oct. 30 (PL 102-578).

The measure expanded the list of 13 types of cancer-related diseases eligible for compensation under the Radiation-Exposed Veterans Compensation Act of 1988 (PL 100-321) to include cancers of the salivary gland and urinary tract.

The bill, a compromise with the House measure (HR 3236), also removed an eligibility requirement that said that diseases had to appear within 40 years of exposure for the veteran to receive compensation.

Republican Rep. John Paul Hammerschmidt of Arkansas said the federal government owed compensation to veterans who suffered from cancer because of wartime radiation exposure.

The measure had originally been part of a wider bill that carried the 1991 cost of living adjustments (COLA), but because of controversy about the radiation provisions, the COLA bill passed separately. *(1991 Almanac, p. 325)*

S 775 was approved by the Senate Veterans' Affairs Committee on June 26, 1991, (S Rept 102-139) and by the Senate by voice vote Nov. 21, 1991. The House gave voice vote approval to the measure on Sept. 30, 1992, and the Senate cleared it by voice vote Oct. 7.

## POST-TRAUMATIC STRESS DISORDERS

The Senate cleared comprehensive veterans health-care legislation (S 2344) on Sept. 25. The bill expanded treatment of post-traumatic stress disorder, a combat-related psychological problem.

The president signed the bill Oct. 9 (PL 102-405).

The measure improved services to homeless veterans and authorized the Department of Veterans Affairs (VA) to provide marriage and family counseling to Persian Gulf veterans and their families.

It also aimed to rein in appropriators with a provision to ban appropriations for any major veterans medical projects that had not first been authorized.

The Senate had passed a similar bill (S 869) on Nov. 20, 1991, substituting the text for a House measure (HR 2280). The House amended the bill on Nov. 25, 1991, adding the language requiring the House and Senate Veterans' Affairs committees to approve any move by appropriators or the VA secretary to fund construction of VA medical facilities. But Senate appropriators blocked the bill when it came back to that chamber. *(1991 Almanac, p. 331)*

In 1992, the Senate on March 11 passed by voice vote S 2344, a slightly different version of the Senate legislation that stalled at the end of 1991.

The House approved the measure by voice vote May 12. As approved, it required authorization for medical projects of $300,000 or more. It was aimed at appropriators who funded pork-barrel projects for their districts.

House members insisted on a conference with the Senate. Conferees eventually agreed to the appropriations provision (H Rept 102-871). The House approved the conference report on Sept. 24, and the Senate approved it Sept. 25, both by voice vote.

Also among the provisions was a requirement that the VA secretary assess the department's ability to provide treatment for post-traumatic stress disorder.

The new bill allowed thousands of Vietnam War veterans to get treatment without having to prove that the disorder was war-related. A diagnosis by a medical professional was still required, however.

Under previous law, veterans who believed they suffered from the ailment had to get approval from the VA before they could receive treatment.

Another provision made Persian Gulf veterans and their spouses, children and parents eligible for marriage and family counseling. It authorized $10 million a year in fiscal 1993-94 for the counseling program.

## VOCATIONAL AND EDUCATIONAL AID

The Senate on Sept. 25 passed legislation to improve vocational rehabilitation programs for veterans with disabilities connected to their service. By voice vote, the text of S 2647 was inserted into the House version (HR 5087). But the House and Senate did not resolve their differences, and the bill died.

The measure would have also increased educational benefits for veterans.

The House Veterans' Affairs Subcommittee on Education, Training and Employment approved the bill by voice vote July 9. The full House Veterans' Affairs Committee then approved the bill July 23 (H Rept 102-751). It passed the House by voice vote Aug. 10.

Under one provision, a veteran who was on active duty on Aug. 2, 1990, and who completed General Equivalency Diploma (GED) requirements within a year of the bill's enactment was eligible for education benefits whether still on active duty or not. Previously, military personnel had been eligible only if they had completed GED requirements before leaving active duty.

The measure was timely because some people had neared completion of diploma requirements before being sent to the Persian Gulf War and then were discharged before completing the requirements. These veterans were ineligible for the education benefits.

The measure also would have made several changes to the veterans educational assistance program, extending eligibility for benefits to certain veterans who left the service and then re-entered.

The Congressional Budget Office estimated that the bill would have cost $5 million in fiscal 1993 and $27 million through fiscal 1997. The measure would have been paid for by savings that veterans had almost lost to an omnibus energy bill (HR 776) *(Veterans compensation bill, p. 378; energy bill, p. 231)*.

## EMPLOYMENT DISCRIMINATION

On Oct. 6, the House passed, by voice vote, legislation (HR 1578) that would have barred employment discrimination against members of the armed services. The Senate did not agree to the final version, thus killing the bill for the 102nd Congress.

The measure would have barred denial of employment, benefits or promotions to people who were applicants or

members of the armed forces or who had an obligation to serve.

The measure also would have required employers to re-employ veterans after service and make an effort to accommodate disabled veterans.

Specifically, the bill would have clarified that a veteran's military involvement could not have been a "motivating factor" in a hiring decision. The measure had aimed to give Persian Gulf War veterans a better understanding of their legal rights upon returning to work. Existing language on veterans' employment rights was too complex to understand, bill supporters said.

The measure was approved 33-0 by the House Veterans' Affairs Committee on April 11, 1991 (H Rept 102-56). The House then passed the bill by voice vote on May 14, 1991.

The Senate passed HR 1578 by voice vote Oct. 1, 1992, after inserting its version, S 1095. The House approved changes to the bill on Oct. 5 by voice vote. The measure went back to the Senate, which took no further action. ■

# Secretary Derwinski Quits After Troubled VA Tenure

After weathering months of criticism from veterans groups, Veterans Affairs (VA) Department Secretary Edward J. Derwinski resigned Sept. 26. His resignation did not surprise followers of veterans issues. Derwinski had been under fire for controversial decisions during his tenure, such as wanting to allow non-veterans to use veterans health facilities. He appeared to be jeopardizing campaign support from veterans for President Bush's November 1992 re-election effort.

After Derwinski announced his resignation, Bush gave him a job as deputy chairman for ethnic coalitions on the Bush/Quayle campaign. Because Derwinski remained popular among many Polish voters, Bush had hoped that Derwinski could mobilize support from ethnic voters — particularly working-class Democrats.

Following Derwinski's resignation, Deputy VA Secretary Anthony J. Principi became acting secretary of the department. Prior to serving in the VA, Principi was a minority counsel for the Senate Veterans' Affairs Committee.

### Term in Office

Derwinski, a Republican congressman from Illinois from 1959 to 1983, became the nation's first secretary of Veterans Affairs in 1989.

His tenure began as it ended — under a cloud. Derwinski's confirmation was delayed by allegations that 12 years earlier he had tipped off South Korea about a prominent South Korean who was about to defect to the United States.

Derwinski conceded that in 1977, at the height of the investigation into "Koreagate" — an alleged conspiracy by that nation to influence U.S. legislation by bribing members of Congress — he inadvertently told a South Korean embassy official that a South Korean intelligence officer was about to defect to the United States. As ranking member on the then-House International Relations Subcommittee on International Organizations, Derwinski had learned that the panel was going to harbor the defector.

Derwinski nevertheless gained confirmation. He had

previously been twice confirmed by the Senate, in 1983 to be a counselor at the State Department and in 1987 when he became the department's under secretary for security assistance, science and technology.

Derwinski had some early successes as VA secretary. Under his tenure, funding for VA health care rose $1 billion each year — from $30 billion in outlays in fiscal 1989 to $34 billion in fiscal 1992 — even in the face of budget-cut threats.

His decision to compensate Vietnam War veterans suffering from illnesses that some linked to exposure to the chemical defoliant Agent Orange was also well received by veterans groups.

Derwinski announced in March 1990 that the VA would compensate veterans who suffered from a rare form of cancer — non-Hodgkins lymphoma. He followed up in May 1990 by announcing that the VA would begin compensating veterans for a group of cancers known as soft-tissue sarcomas.

Previous claims to the link between Agent Orange and cancer had been dismissed by the Reagan administration. A report issued by the Centers for Disease Control also said there was no evidence to suggest a link with exposure to Agent Orange.

VA support for Agent Orange compensation, despite doubt by federal agencies, was seen as a vote of loyalty to the veterans. Veterans had been concerned that some members of Congress, such as House Veterans' Affairs Committee Chairman G. V. "Sonny" Montgomery, D-Miss., were skeptical of Agent Orange compensation.

### Signs of Trouble

Throughout his term in office, Derwinski had a series of small run-ins with various veterans organizations, such as when he agreed to a request from administration POW-MIA negotiators to give Vietnam $250,000 in obsolete VA medical equipment to encourage cooperation. Many veterans still viewed Hanoi as the enemy, and their outrage led Derwinski to rescind the proposal. But a few major policy problems with veterans organizations ultimately sealed Derwinski's fate.

Derwinski and Health and Human Services Secretary Louis W. Sullivan proposed in 1991 that VA hospitals in Southern rural communities accept poor non-veteran patients with no other local access to health care. The move would have furthered Derwinski's plan to expand funding sources for VA health care by pulling in Medicare dollars.

Veterans groups opposed the plan because they believed the VA should take care of veterans first and maintain health-care facilities for that purpose. Many argued that empty beds in the VA hospitals were a result of restrictive eligibility for veterans, not a lack of demand. Derwinski ultimately dropped the plan.

He also angered many veterans in August 1991 by announcing that VA hospitals would no longer sell tobacco products after October 1991. He issued a directive for VA health facilities to be smoke-free by the end of 1993.

A storm of protest ensued from veterans groups and some members of Congress. Later, Congress voted to include a provision blocking the smoking ban in an omnibus veterans health bill.

The Veterans of Foreign Wars called for Derwinski's resignation in August 1992 and in September withheld a much-needed endorsement for Bush's re-election. The group had endorsed Bush in 1988 and Ronald Reagan twice before. Derwinski's problems as a political liability for the president's re-election campaign were seen as a major factor in his resignation. ■

# HEALTH/ EDUCATION/ HUMAN SERVICES

# Bush Rejects Abortion Rights Bills

## *President again uses veto to continue anti-abortion policies established during the Reagan years*

Congress and the White House remained at a standoff over the abortion issue in 1992, as President Bush used his veto power to hold off legislation that would have loosened federal restrictions on abortion. The result was a continuation of every anti-abortion policy imposed since Ronald Reagan became president in 1981.

However, 1992 was likely to be the last year those policies were in force. Democratic Gov. Bill Clinton of Arkansas, who was elected president on Nov. 3, was a supporter of abortion rights who vowed during the campaign to reverse most of the Reagan-Bush restrictions.

The key development in the year's legislative battle was the Supreme Court's June 29 decision in *Planned Parenthood of Southeastern Pennsylvania v. Casey*. Both supporters and foes of abortion rights had expected the court to strike down *Roe v. Wade*, the landmark 1973 decision that legalized abortion nationwide. Abortion rights supporters hoped that such a decision would spark a backlash strong enough to win passage of legislation writing abortion rights into federal law.

But the court surprised nearly everyone by issuing a split decision. While it upheld several restrictions in the contested Pennsylvania law, including a requirement that women seeking abortions wait 24 hours, a 5-4 majority reaffirmed *Roe's* core holding of a woman's right to end her pregnancy. The court's new test, enunciated by Justice Sandra Day O'Connor, was whether a particular restriction imposed an "undue burden" on that right.

The decision clearly narrowed the abortion right as laid out in *Roe*, but its mixed effect left abortion-rights leaders without a rallying point. Poll after poll showed strong

---

## Legislative Roundup

As in previous years, Congress in 1992 fought the abortion battle on a variety of legislative fronts. Following are the major bills that included abortion-related provisions and the particular issue in dispute:

- **Freedom of Choice Act** (HR 25, S 25) sought to codify a woman's fundamental right to end her pregnancy prior to fetal viability, as spelled out in the 1973 Supreme Court ruling, *Roe v. Wade*.
- **Family Planning Reauthorization** (HR 3090, S 323) would have overturned the so-called gag rule prohibiting abortion counseling or referral at federally funded family planning clinics.
- **Fiscal 1993 Labor-HHS Appropriations** (HR 5677) included language to suspend the gag rule in family planning clinics and allow federal funding of abortions in certain cases of rape or incest.
- **Fiscal 1992 Supplemental Appropriations** (HR 5620) included suspension of the gag rule.
- **National Institutes of Health Reauthorization** (HR 2507, S 2899) included language to drop an administration ban on funding of transplantation research using fetal tissue from elective abortions.
- **Abortions in Military Hospitals** (S 3144) sought to overturn a ban on abortions paid for by the woman herself in overseas military medical facilities.
- **Fiscal 1993 Defense Authorization** (HR 5006) included provisions to permit self-paid abortions in overseas military medical facilities.
- **Fiscal 1993 Defense Appropriations** (HR 5504) included provisions to permit self-paid abortions in overseas military medical facilities.
- **Fiscal 1993 Foreign Operations Appropriations** (HR 5368) included funds for the United Nations Population Fund and would have overturned the so-called Mexico City policy that barred U.S. aid to organizations that performed or "actively promoted" abortion.
- **Fiscal 1993 D.C. Appropriations** (HR 5517) would have allowed the District of Columbia to use locally raised tax funds to pay for abortions.

*See also the Supreme Court's 1992 ruling on* Planned Parenthood of Southeastern Pennsylvania v. Casey, *p. 398.*

---

support for a woman's right to terminate a pregnancy but even stronger support for the sorts of restrictions upheld in the Pennsylvania law.

As a result, congressional leaders decided not to force a floor fight over the so-called Freedom of Choice Act (HR 25, S 25), which would have codified a woman's right to an abortion. They feared the bill would become the target of amendments imposing the kind of restrictions upheld in *Casey*, amendments unacceptable to many abortion-rights advocates.

Members did, however, vote on a variety of other abortion-related issues, including the so-called gag rule prohibiting abortion counseling in federally funded family-planning clinics, proposals to allow U.S. servicewomen and military dependents to obtain abortions in overseas military medical facilities if they paid for the procedure themselves, and efforts to lift an administration ban on research using fetal tissue from elective abortions.

In every case, both the House and Senate voted to relax the restrictions but failed to muster the two-thirds majorities needed to override actual or threatened Bush vetoes. Altogether, Bush in 1992 vetoed four bills because of abortion language; abortion-related language was dropped from the final versions of three other measures to avert threatened vetoes.

## BACKGROUND

For more than a decade after *Roe v. Wade*, the House was a stronghold for abortion opponents. In the late 1970s and most of the 1980s, House members took the lead in imposing a series of abortion-related restrictions, mostly on funding matters. Often, they acted despite Senate objections, secure in the knowledge that Presidents Reagan and

Bush would back them up.

The Supreme Court's 1989 decision in *Webster v. Reproductive Health Services*, which gave states new latitude to restrict abortion access, changed all that. Just as *Roe v. Wade* had galvanized anti-abortion forces 16 years earlier, so the 5-4 ruling in *Webster* rejuvenated abortion-rights activists.

For the first time since 1973, a woman's fundamental right to abortion appeared to be in jeopardy.

In the House, the decision prompted a swing of 50 votes toward the abortion-rights cause, although the total remained far short of the two-thirds needed to relax abortion restrictions over Bush's objections. *(1989 Almanac, p. 296)*

In 1991, after the first post-*Webster* congressional elections, both the House and Senate voted to ease a variety of restrictions that had been imposed in the years since abortion opponents had burrowed into various nooks and crannies of federal agencies.

Gains for abortion-rights forces were particularly notable in the House.

However, Congress never mustered the two-thirds majority in both houses needed to override Bush's veto. The president was unshakable in his anti-abortion stance, drawing praise from groups opposing abortion even as moderates in his own party warned his position could hurt him at the polls in 1992. *(1991 Almanac, p. 339)*

The warning was ignored. Anti-abortion Republicans, backed by the White House, remained firmly in control during August platform debates at the GOP's national convention in Houston. Abortion-rights backers failed to win enough support among delegates to force a floor debate on the portion of the platform that called for a constitutional amendment to ban abortion outright. Many Republican moderates, especially women, were repelled by the absolutist tone of the platform.

In the end, however, it probably did not matter. Although Bush undoubtedly lost some votes because of his anti-abortion stance, economic concerns dominated the presidential election all year.

And in congressional races, abortion proved once again to be an issue that cut both ways. As in each of the elections since the Supreme Court thrust the matter back into the national limelight in 1989, abortion-rights backers and abortion foes both won victories and suffered defeats at the polls. And both sides claimed — with some justification — to represent the mainstream opinion on the issue.

## FREEDOM OF CHOICE ACT

Abortion-rights advocates began 1992, a pivotal election year, determined to press the Freedom of Choice legislation. But Bush was ready for them.

Bush used a March 3 speech to a Chicago meeting of the Assocation of Evangelicals to decry the legislation (HR 25, S 25). The bill, he said, "would impose on all 50 states an unprecedented regime of abortion on demand, going well beyond even *Roe v. Wade*. This is not right, and it will not become law as long as I am president of the United States of America."

Backers of the measure, who maintained that it would merely codify the state of the law under *Roe*, assailed the president's remarks.

"His politically motivated scare tactics and distortions about the Freedom of Choice Act are unsupported by any facts," said Kate Michelman, president of the National Abortion Rights Action League (NARAL). Bush's veto threat, Michelman said, "demonstrates that the president is much more interested in kowtowing to the anti-choice minority than in safeguarding the health and lives of American women."

Abortion foes outlined their position at a March 4 hearing before the House Judiciary Subcommittee on Civil and Constitutional Rights.

"The humanity of the pre-born has become the great 13th floor of society — we all know it's there but we pretend it isn't," said Rep. Henry J. Hyde, Ill., the subcommittee's ranking Republican and one of Congress' leading anti-abortion voices.

Attorney General William P. Barr did not testify, but he did send along with Acting Assistant Attorney General Timothy E. Flanigan a three-page letter threatening a veto and questioning whether Congress had the constitutional authority to pass the bill.

"... [I]n our view congressional legislation in this area would usurp a field of legislation traditionally reserved to the states," Barr's letter said.

That view was disputed by Harvard constitutional law Professor Laurence H. Tribe, a leading abortion-rights advocate.

"Proposals to guarantee the reproductive freedom of women fit squarely within Congress's commerce power," Tribe testified, adding that an additional case could be made for Congress's power under the 14th Amendment.

"Most of what is said about this law" by opponents, Tribe added, "is political rhetoric and not legal analysis."

### House Subcommittee Action

The House Judiciary Subcommittee on Civil and Constitutional Rights got a jump on the Supreme Court's *Casey* ruling, marking up its version of HR 25 on June 18. The 5-3 vote broke along straight party lines, with Democrats voting for and Republicans against the measure.

It was actually the second time the subcommittee had approved the bill. The first was in 1990, just over a year after the court handed down its decision in *Webster v. Reproductive Health Services*. But the 101st Congress adjourned before the full Judiciary Committee could take up the bill that year. *(1990 Almanac, p. 528)*

In 1992, House and Senate sponsors coordinated their strategy in an effort to keep the bills compatible.

They planned to amend the legislation at some point to clarify that it was not intended to overrule certain post-*Roe* Supreme Court decisions, such as those allowing states to require parental involvement in a minor's abortion decision and those upholding bans on public funding of abortions.

But the goal at subcommittee was to keep the bill clean. That was met, after Democrats voted together to fend off a series of amendments offered by Hyde.

Among the Hyde changes rejected on voice votes were proposals to: permit states to restrict abortions after the first trimester of pregnancy; allow states to require "informed consent" and waiting periods for women seeking abortions; and allow laws providing for notification to husbands of women having abortions. The panel also defeated Hyde amendments to explicitly allow states to bar public funding for abortions and impose parental consent laws. Democrats said they were unnecessary.

The only close call came on a Hyde amendment to allow states to bar doctors "from holding themselves out as providing abortions that are solely based on the sex of the fetus."

That amendment ultimately failed on a 4-4 tie, with

Craig Washington, D-Texas, voting with the Republicans. "I didn't see anything wrong with the amendment," said Washington. "I certainly wouldn't want to see an ad like that in the Yellow Pages."

### Forcing the Issue

Less than two weeks after the subcommittee acted, the court issued its *Casey* decision. Congressional leaders said the ruling did not obviate the need for action on the Freedom of Choice bills.

"The [*Casey*] decision demands a legislative response," said Senate Majority Leader George J. Mitchell, D-Maine. "The Congress must act to ensure that the fundamental right of American women to choose for themselves is not lost, as states respond to this decision's invitation to enact restrictions."

Backers also wanted to force members to say once and for all whether they supported a woman's right to have an abortion. Neither chamber had ever voted directly on that issue, although the Senate in 1983 rejected, 49-50, a proposed constitutional amendment to void *Roe v. Wade* and return the question of abortion regulation to the states. *(1983 Almanac, p. 306)*

Putting to a vote the ultimate question on abortion was just fine with abortion opponents, who said the Freedom of Choice bill went further than most Americans wanted.

"The mandatory abortion on demand absolutism of this bill is dramatically out of touch with the more considered judgment of the American people," said Sen. Orrin G. Hatch, R-Utah.

"The more the issue is debated . . . the more Americans will be educated, sensitized and mobilized" against abortion, said Rep. Christopher H. Smith, R-N.J., co-chairman of the House Pro-Life Caucus.

### Committee Action

The House Judiciary Committee approved HR 25 by 20-13 on June 30, the day after the *Casey* decision. On July 1, the Senate Committee on Labor and Human Resources approved S 25 by 12-5. Both bills were amended before they were approved.

Sponsors contended that the original legislation sought to freeze in place the state of abortion law up to, but not including, the 1989 *Webster* decision. They said restrictions the court had upheld after *Roe* but before *Webster* would still be allowed.

The most important of these were requirements for parental notice or consent before a minor could obtain an abortion, and state and federal laws prohibiting public funding of abortion, which the court upheld in a 1980 case, *Harris v. McRae*.

Opponents of the bill hotly disputed that analysis. They said the Freedom of Choice legislation would strike down not only the restrictions approved in *Webster* and *Casey* but also public funding prohibitions and requirements for parental involvement. The American Civil Liberties Union, which backed the bill, agreed that it would bar parental involvement laws.

Sponsors insisted such claims were not true but to allay doubts they agreed to several changes to "clarify the intent" of what had been a one-page measure.

As amended, both bills explicitly said that states would not be prevented "from requiring a minor to involve a parent, guardian, or other responsible adult before terminating a pregnancy."

Abortion rights groups opposed notification and con-

sent laws, but polls showed overwhelming support for them.

"I don't believe we can create good family relationships by legislating them," said HR 25 sponsor Don Edwards, D-Calif., who offered the language as an amendment at the Judiciary markup. "But by adopting *Roe* as our standard, we also are adopting decisions" made by the court under *Roe*'s framework that permitted parental involvement laws.

Both bills also stipulated that states could protect "unwilling individuals from having to participate in the performance of abortions to which they are conscientiously opposed."

Sponsors had maintained that language was unnecessary too, because the federal Public Health Service Act had included such a "conscience clause" for nearly two decades.

The Senate version underwent even more changes, partly because its sponsors needed 60 votes to overcome a likely filibuster from abortion foes, and partly because Mitchell had expressed doubts about the constitutionality of the original bill.

Among other things, the Senate version explicitly allowed states to decline to use public funds to pay for abortions.

Also added to the Senate measure were "findings" that "Congress has the affirmative power" under the Constitution's Commerce Clause and the 14th Amendment "to prohibit state interference with interstate commerce, liberty or equal protection of the laws."

The section also stipulated, at the insistence of Mitchell, a former federal judge, that the purpose of the bill was to establish a statutory, as opposed to a constitutional right.

### Opponents Fight Back

The changes did little to mollify abortion opponents. Indeed, their strategy at both the House and Senate markups was to offer amendments they knew would be voted down in order "to illustrate the extreme nature of this bill," in the words of Hyde.

One amendment, which Hyde withdrew before it came to a House Judiciary Committee vote, would have permitted states to bar most abortions after the first trimester of pregnancy.

Hyde said that more than 150,000 such abortions were performed each year.

Edwards, however, pointed out that such a ban would not have survived even the *Casey* test.

Another Hyde amendment, to specifically permit states to bar public funding of abortions, was defeated by a vote of 14-19 after bill sponsors insisted it was not necessary.

The committee similarly rejected a Hyde amendment that would have permitted "informed consent" laws like the Pennsylvania provision upheld in *Casey*. The vote was 10-23.

The most heated debate came over the "conscience clause" provision. An amendment offered by F. James Sensenbrenner Jr., R-Wis., would have allowed states to shield entire institutions, such as Catholic hospitals, from having to perform abortions.

But bill sponsors said that was unnecessary, because the bill could not be read to require private institutions to provide abortions.

Said Patricia Schroeder, D-Colo., "Hospitals don't perform abortions, people do."

By 17-16, members instead adopted a substitute offered by Mike Kopetski, D-Ore., shielding only individuals with moral objections to abortion from having to participate in the procedure.

The Senate Labor Committee markup the next day covered much of the same ground.

As in the House committee, Senate opponents were suspicious of the parental "involvement" language added to the bill, arguing that it could be construed to allow laws requiring parental notification but not consent.

"If you want to allow a state to require consent, you should use the word consent," said Hatch.

Bill backers insisted that consent laws would be allowed, but by a vote of 13-4 tabled a Hatch amendment that would have spelled that out.

By an identical vote members also tabled another Hatch amendment that would have permitted 24-hour waiting periods like the one upheld by the court in *Casey*.

And by the same margin again, they tabled an amendment offered by Daniel R. Coats, R-Ind., that would have forbidden abortion providers from "holding themselves out" as providing abortions for sex selection.

Several members who ultimately voted against the proposal said they were sympathetic to Coats' amendment and found such abortions repugnant.

"I just don't know what 'holding out' means," said Paul Wellstone, D-Minn.

### Subsequent Action

As of July 31, it appeared that the Senate would try to take up S 25 beginning Aug. 4. But it was not clear that sponsors could round up the 60 votes needed to cut off debate on the motion to proceed to the bill.

Some Republican cosponsors of the measure said they would not vote for cloture because they thought Democrats were trying to use the bill for political gain.

"I feel strongly about the bill, but this is just sheer politics and I have no desire to play games," said Sen. Nancy Landon Kassebaum, R-Kan.

Like their House counterparts, Senate backers also worried about their ability to hold off unwanted amendments. Sen. Warren B. Rudman, R-N.H., planned to offer one proposal that was giving sponsors fits: an amendment to codify the "undue burden" standard set forth by the court in the *Casey* decision.

That was a far less stringent standard than the court set out in *Roe v. Wade*, the 1973 ruling whose principles the Freedom of Choice Act sought to codify. Under *Roe*, most state restrictions were not allowed.

"I'm firmly pro-choice," Rudman told reporters July 30, "but I happen to think [the *Casey* standard] is the right mix. We could put this issue behind us once and for all."

Still uncertain about votes, by early August House and Senate leaders threw in the towel. While vote-counters in both chambers said they could produce margins for passage, they were less certain about being able to fend off amendments opposed by the abortion-rights groups who were the measure's principal backers.

Mitchell said that during an Aug. 3 meeting, House and Senate sponsors and representatives of abortion-rights groups "recommended that action in the Senate be deferred until after the House of Representatives passes the bill. . . . After giving the matter careful consideration, I have decided to accept this recommendation, unanimously made, and not to try to pursue this matter during this legislative period."

But Speaker of the House Thomas S. Foley, D-Wash., on Aug. 6 said that his chamber was not ready to proceed, either. "We just do not at this point either have the time to bring it up nor do I think we are ready to resolve some of the problems on the procedure before" the recess for the Republican convention, he told reporters.

Although both leaders said they hoped to bring the bill up after Congress returned in September, they made no effort to do so. The legislation died with the end of the Congress in October.

## ABORTION COUNSELING

An administration regulation prohibiting abortion counseling or referrals in federal funded family planning clinics was the subject of both legislative and court battles in 1992.

In the end, legislative attempts to overturn the rule were thwarted by Bush's veto but a federal court blocked its implementation on technical grounds.

The court's ruling involved a March 20 administrative directive to regional administrators of the family planning program from William R. Archer III, deputy assistant secretary of Health and Human Services (HHS). The directive said that doctors in federally funded clinics — but not nurses or other health professionals — could discuss abortion with patients in limited circumstances.

The directive also said that the Department of Health and Human Services would begin enforcing the so-called gag rule for the first time since it was issued by the Reagan administration on Feb. 2, 1988. The rule, which applied to all family planning clinics funded under Title X of the Public Health Service Act, had been in abeyance for years while family planning groups challenged its legality. Even after the Supreme Court upheld it May 23, 1991, the regulation remained in limbo. Opponents of the the gag rule said the real purpose of the March 20 directive was to stifle opposition to the counseling ban from physician groups and thus mute some of the criticism in Congress.

But if that was the administration's objective, it did not succeed. Among those not satisfied was the American College of Obstetricians and Gynecologists. "We do not believe the recently issued Title X regulations have significantly, if at all, loosened the gag rule for physicians," said a statement issued by the group March 24. "And this ambiguous, at best, concession does little for the majority of poor women who receive health care from nurses, counselors and social workers."

The American Medical Association (AMA) was only slightly mollified. A statement from Executive Vice President James S. Todd called the guidelines "a step in the right direction" but added that the AMA "continues to support legislation that would completely repeal the 'gag rule.'"

The directive said that the rules did not "prevent a woman from receiving complete medical information about her condition from a physician."

But that distinction between physicians and other staff had nursing organizations up in arms.

"We are very offended by this," said Barbara K. Redman, executive director of the American Nurses Association. "Nurses have more training on counseling and teaching of patients than doctors do, and they're fully capable of providing these services."

Some critics also questioned the legality of the Archer directive.

"If they wanted to change the regulation, they should

have changed it," rather than simply issuing a memo, said Henry A. Waxman, D-Calif., chairman of the House Energy and Commerce Health Subcommittee and sponsor of the Title X reauthorization bill.

Groups opposed to the counseling ban sued on just that basis, contending that any significant change made by the memorandum was a violation of the Administrative Procedures Act, which required a public notice and comment period.

### The Family Planning Bill

In November 1991, the House failed by 12 votes to override Bush's veto of the fiscal 1992 spending bill for the Departments of Labor, Health and Human Services (HHS), and Education. The veto was provoked in large part by language blocking enforcement of the gag rule for a year. The provision was subsequently dropped.

In 1992, the House tried a more direct approach. On April 30, it passed HR 3090, which would have overturned the gag rule and written into law guidelines in effect from 1981 to 1988. Those called upon clinics to give women with unintended pregnancies "nondirective" counseling about all options, including abortion. The bill also would have reauthorized the family planning program for five years at $180 million in fiscal 1993, rising to $219 million in fiscal 1997. The program, Title X of the Public Health Service Act, served about 4 million teenagers and low-income women in about 4,000 clinics nationwide.

Passage came by a vote of 268-150, well short of the two-thirds needed to override Bush's threatened veto. But the margin showed how far abortion rights forces had come. (Vote 95, p. 24-H)

It was the first time the House had passed a family planning bill since 1984. On its last attempt, in 1985, the legislation garnered only 214 votes — less than a majority and considerably less than the two-thirds required for passage under the fast-track suspension of the rules procedure used. (1985 Almanac, p. 301)

The major impediment to a family planning reauthorization bill had long been the question of whether girls under 18 should have to notify a parent before they could obtain an abortion. Backers of abortion rights who opposed such parental notification requirements knew that a majority of the American public, and, they presumed, a majority of House members, favored such a requirement.

But abortion foes opted at the last minute not to offer a parental-notification provision on the floor. They said they were hindered by procedural difficulties that would have prevented a straight up-or-down vote on a strict notification proposal. Opponents, however, said the real reason was that abortion foes lacked the votes to prevail.

Indeed, abortion opponents did not even seek to eliminate from the bill the language overturning the abortion counseling ban. "We're not convinced we had 218 votes to strike it," said Smith.

Still, anti-abortion groups hailed the House's failure to muster an override majority.

"President Bush's veto will ensure that tax funds don't go to agencies that promote abortion as a method of birth control," said Douglas Johnson, legislative director for the National Right to Life Committee, the leading proponent of the rules.

Groups opposed to the rules said they would not give up. "I believe we can override a veto, and we're going to pull out all the stops," said David J. Andrews, acting president of the Planned Parenthood Federation of America.

Andrews said the organization's 170 affiliates would give up the $34 million they received through the Title X program in 1991 before they would abide by the counseling ban.

### House Floor Debate

Most of the House debate on April 30 centered on the counseling ban.

"This is about government interference in the doctor-patient relationship," said J. Roy Rowland, D-Ga., one of the two physicians who served in the House in the 102nd Congress.

But backers of the rules insisted they were needed.

"The question is, should taxpayers subsidize the promotion and facilitation of abortion?" said Republican Vin Weber of Minnesota.

Those urging repeal of the gag rule included not only members who generally supported abortion rights but also some who opposed abortion.

"If we are opposed to abortion, we must support family planning to reduce the incidence of abortion," said Timothy J. Penny, D-Minn., one of about 80 House Democrats who were consistent anti-abortion votes.

Members seeking a middle ground included Ralph Regula, R-Ohio, and Richard J. Durbin, D-Ill., each of whom offered amendments to clarify the counseling requirements.

Regula's amendment, adopted by voice vote, reiterated that abortion counseling would be provided only if the patient requested it.

Durbin's amendment, also approved by voice, would have expanded the "conscience clause" already included in the Public Health Service Act. It would have allowed a counselor or clinic to decline to provide abortion information, as long as a patient seeking it could be referred to a nearby clinic that would provide the counseling.

Durbin likened his amendment to the way Catholic hospitals handled methods of family planning they did not condone.

Catholic health facilities could receive Title X funds for providing natural family planning services, as long as they referred clients who wanted to use the pill or other birth control methods to other clinics.

Abortion opponents insisted that neither amendment improved the bill.

Hyde said the problem with Durbin's amendment "is that it's all wind-up and no pitch." Hyde said requiring reluctant counselors to refer patients to others who would do abortion counseling was "forced complicity."

### Parental Notification

By far the biggest surprise was the absence of a floor fight over parental notification.

Rep. Thomas J. Bliley Jr., R-Va., originally planned to offer an amendment he tried unsuccessfully to append to the bill during 1991 consideration by the Energy and Commerce Committee. The amendment would have required notification of at least one parent 48 hours before a girl under 18 could obtain an abortion from an entity that received Title X funds. From its inception in 1970, Title X had forbidden the use of program funds for abortions, but many recipients were hospitals or other facilities that also performed abortions.

The committee defeated the amendment by 20-23, largely because it lacked enough exceptions. Critics, including several who said they supported parental-notification laws, complained that the amendment would have allowed

# Abortion Language Prompts Veto of Family Planning Bill

*Following is the text of President Bush's Sept. 25 veto message of S 323, a bill that would have amended the Family Planning Act:*

I am returning herewith without my approval S 323, the Family Planning Amendments Act of 1992. This legislation would extend and amend the federal family planning program under Title X of the Public Health Service Act.

If the scope of S 323 were limited to family planning, I would approve it. My Administration has an excellent record in support of family planning. About this there can be no question. Our approach to reauthorizing Title X was embodied in a bill transmitted to the Congress on February 25, 1991. We need a family planning program to deliver preventive, pre-pregnancy services.

Unfortunately, S 323 is unacceptable because it would override current regulations that are designed to maintain the Title X program's integrity as a pre-pregnancy family planning program. The bill would require projects supported by Title X family planning funds to counsel pregnant women on, and refer them for, abortions. Such a requirement is totally alien to the purpose of the Title X program. Title X is a quality health-care program that provides pre-pregnancy family planning information and services and refers pregnant women to health-care providers who can ensure continuity of care.

Under current regulations, upheld by the U.S. Supreme Court, pregnant women who seek services from clinics funded by Title X would be referred to qualified providers for prenatal care and other social services, including counseling. Moreover, nothing in these regulations prevents a woman from receiving complete medical information about her condition from a physician. The Supreme Court specifically found that the regulations regarding the Title X program in no way violated free speech rights.

In a memorandum to Department of Health and Human Services Secretary Louis H. Sullivan on November 5, 1991, I reiterated my commitment to preserving the confidentiality of the doctor/patient relationship. In that memorandum, I also repeated my commitment to ensuring that the operation of the Title X family planning program is compatible with free speech and the highest standards of medical care. My memorandum makes clear that there is no "gag rule" to interfere with the doctor/patient relationship. There can be no doubt that my Administration is committed to the protection of free speech.

I have repeatedly informed the Congress that I would disapprove any legislation that would transform this program into a vehicle for the promotion of abortion. Unfortunately, the Congress has seen fit to entangle this family planning program in the politics of abortion.

I believe that the Title X family planning program should be reauthorized. I now urge the Congress to adopt a bill that promotes true family planning rather than requiring Federal tax dollars to be used in a manner that promotes abortion as a method of birth control.

---

the rule to be waived if a pregnancy was caused by a father's incest, but not by incestuous relations with a brother or uncle.

The amendment also would have allowed the notice to be waived for medical emergencies if the girl's life was in danger from the pregnancy, but not if the pregnancy merely presented a serious health threat.

The amendment also lacked — for technical reasons, said Bliley aides — a "judicial bypass" provision that would have allowed a girl to seek permission for an abortion from a judge if she feared telling her parents. The Supreme Court had repeatedly required such bypass provisions in state parental notification laws.

Bliley withdrew his amendment late April 28, just hours before the House Rules Committee was scheduled to decide whether to allow it to be offered on the floor.

"The problem was parliamentary," Bliley explained later. Bliley said bill sponsor Waxman was going to try to offer an amendment to the amendment "that would in effect gut my amendment," and it probably would have won.

Thus, he said, he decided not to offer his. "I would offer it in a heartbeat if I thought I could get a clean vote on it," he said.

Waxman, however, said Bliley decided not to offer the amendment because his side thought the proposal lacked the votes. "That's the only conclusion I can reach."

After House passage, HR 3090 was sent to conference with S 323, a bill passed by the Senate in July 1991 that would have overturned the counseling ban but not reauthorized the underlying family planning program. Title X had been operating on emergency funding since its last authorization expired in 1985.

### Conference, Final Action

On Aug. 6, the House voted for the fifth time since 1991 to block or overturn the gag rule when it approved the conference report on S 323 (H Rept 102-767).

The compromise bill, ironed out in a brief conference the week of July 27, contained the text of HR 3090 as passed by the House in April, including the language to reauthorize the Title X program. But the vote, 251-144, was once again short of an override margin. *(Vote 375, p. 92-H)*

The Senate followed suit on Sept. 14, approving the conference report by voice vote.

Bush vetoed the measure Sept. 25. "I have repeatedly informed the Congress that I would disapprove any legislation that would transform this program into a vehicle for the promotion of abortion," Bush said in his veto message. "Unfortunately, the Congress has seen fit to entangle this family planning program in the politics of abortion." *(Veto message, above)*

That set up a veto override confrontation that bill sponsors knew they would lose. The Senate acted first, voting 73-26 on Oct. 1 to override the veto. *(Vote 254, p. 33-S)*

It was only the second time in the Bush presidency that the Senate mustered the two-thirds needed to enact a bill over the president's objections. The first came a week earlier when members voted to override a veto on legislation to guarantee workers unpaid leave for family and medical emergencies. *(Family leave bill, p. 353)*

But, as expected, the House on Oct. 2 sustained the veto of the bill to repeal the gag rule. Its 266-148 vote fell 10 short of the two-thirds majority needed. *(Vote 452, p. 110-H)*

### Appropriations Action

House members in July let pass another chance to try to block the counseling ban. Although the annual Labor-HHS-Education appropriations bill had been the focus of 1991 efforts to reverse the gag rule, House backers let the

1992 bill (HR 5677) go forward without such language.

John Porter, R-Ill., who wrote previous year's language, said another effort would be "futile. The votes are not going to change."

Another prominent abortion rights backer on the Appropriations panel, Vic Fazio, D-Calif., agreed. "There's a lot of sentiment that this should be resolved, one way or the other, on the Waxman bill [HR 3090]," he said.

Another major reason no attempt was made to attach the language to the funding bill was that Labor-HHS Subcommittee Chairman William H. Natcher, D-Ky., had asked members not to. "This bill should not be used for this purpose, and I will object," Natcher said.

In previous years, tensions had escalated between Natcher, a longtime abortion opponent, and abortion rights backers on the committee and in the House Democratic Caucus. But members were loath to cross the powerful subcommittee chairman, who in 1992 was appointed acting chairman of the full committee due to the ill health of Chairman Jamie L. Whitten, D-Miss.

Matters were different in the Senate. On Sept. 10, the Senate Appropriations Committee set the stage for two separate fights over the gag rule, adding language on the issue to both the fiscal 1993 spending bill for Labor-HHS (HR 5677) and to a supplemental fiscal 1992 appropriations bill providing funds for hurricane victims in Florida and Guam (HR 5620). *(Appropriations, p. 651)*

The Labor-HHS action was not a surprise. Subcommittee Chairman Tom Harkin, D-Iowa, had announced months earlier that he intended to add a provision to block enforcement of the gag rule as well as language allowing federal funding of abortions in certain cases of rape or incest.

Identical abortion-counseling language prompted Bush to veto the fiscal 1992 version of the Labor-HHS bill, and similar rape-incest language drew a veto of the fiscal 1990 bill. In both cases the language was dropped after the House failed to muster enough votes for an override. *(1991 Almanac, p. 339; 1989 Almanac, p. 707)*

The move to attach the gag-rule suspension to the supplemental appropriations measure was less expected. The draft committee report on the bill said the provision needed to go into the fast-track emergency relief measure because the Bush administration planned to begin enforcing the counseling ban at the nation's 4,000 family planning clinics on Sept. 23. (Administration officials later moved the date back to Oct. 1).

Unlike the language in the Labor-HHS bill, the provision in HR 5620 would have blocked enforcement of the rules only until the conclusion of a federal court case brought in April by the National Family Planning and Reproductive Health Association and a group representing nurse-practitioners, who delivered most of the care in the clinics. The suit charged that the administration violated procedural rules in implementing the ban.

The gag-rule provisions in both bills were dropped Sept. 14, however, as part of a deal that prevented a Senate filibuster on S 323, the family planning reauthorization, which also would have overturned the counseling ban. The rape-incest provisions were dropped during the House-Senate conference on the Labor-HHS bill Sept. 30.

### The Court Ruling

On Nov. 3, a three-judge panel in Washington barred implementation of the gag rule on grounds that the March 20 administrative directive altering the rule had substantively changed the original 1988 regulation. The court said the change — which would have permitted doctors but not other health professionals to counsel clinic patients about abortion — should have been the subject of a formal rule-making process.

The 1988 rules, which had been upheld by the Supreme Court in 1991 but had never actually taken effect, were more restrictive, barring abortion counseling or referral by virtually all clinic personnel under almost all circumstances.

The administrative document softening the gag rule "is substantially amending and even repudiating part of its original regulation" wrote U.S. Circuit Judge Patricia Wald. Such action, she said, required a formal "notice and comment" period that had not been provided. Thus the court reinstated a stay on implementation that had been imposed in May by a district court judge but lifted July 1. The administration had put the gag rule into effect Oct. 1, but the court's decision effectively blocked that attempt for the year.

The ruling was likely to mark the end of the effort to bar abortion counseling at family planning clinics. Clinton promised during the campaign that he would lift the ban once he became president.

## FETAL RESEARCH

The Senate Labor and Human Resources Committee on Feb. 5 kicked off the first round in Congress' 1992 abortion debate, approving a bill that sought to overturn an administration ban on research using fetal tissue from elective abortions.

At issue was a funding moratorium first imposed in 1988 by Reagan administration health officials. Preliminary results from privately funded research indicated that transplanted fetal tissue showed promise treating a wide variety of serious diseases, including diabetes, Parkinson's disease and Alzheimer's disease.

The moratorium was imposed pending a special advisory committee's review of potential ethical concerns. Both the special committee and NIH's permanent advisory panel recommended that funding for the research be allowed if safeguards were instituted to separate a woman's decision to have an abortion from her decision to donate the fetal tissue for research.

But Bush administration officials rejected the advisory groups' recommendations, and in late 1989 they announced that the funding ban would be continued indefinitely.

The fetal tissue provisions were a part of omnibus legislation (HR 2507) to reauthorize portions of the National Institutes of Health (NIH). The House had passed its version, with similar provisions to overturn the fetal tissue funding ban, in July 1991. But its 274-144 vote was short of the two-thirds margin needed to override a threatened presidential veto. *(1991 Almanac, p. 343)*

### Senate Committee Action

While the bill included major policy provisions regarding research on women's health problems and the inclusion of women and minorities in clinical trials, virtually all of the debate at the Senate committee markup centered on the fetal tissue provisions. The panel approved the bill by 13-4.

The strength of the final vote was significant, because as recently as mid-1991, committee Chairman Edward M. Kennedy, D-Mass., thought the fetal tissue provisions so

controversial he did not include them in his version of the NIH reauthorization (S 1523). The fetal tissue provisions approved by the committee were drawn from another bill (S 1902), sponsored by committee member Brock Adams, D-Wash., and cosponsored by Kennedy.

Republicans Nancy Landon Kassebaum, Kan., James M. Jeffords, Vt., and Strom Thurmond, S.C., joined all of the committee's Democrats in voting for the bill. During debate, Thurmond made a point of mentioning that his daughter Julie suffered from diabetes, one of the diseases that research involving fetal tissue had shown early promise in treating.

During the Senate committee markup, ranking Republican Orrin G. Hatch, Utah, raised the possibility that the bill could be subject to a filibuster on the Senate floor.

Ignoring the threats, members rejected, 4-13, a substitute provision offered by Hatch. His amendment called for a study of the feasibility of conducting transplant research using fetal tissue obtained from miscarriages and ectopic pregnancies, in which the fetus becomes implanted in a woman's fallopian tube instead of her uterus. Such pregnancies, if not terminated, can be fatal to the woman.

By voice vote, the committee also rejected an amendment offered by Thurmond that would have permitted federal funding of fetal tissue transplantation research but would have restricted researchers to use of tissue from abortions performed because of rape or incest, or to save the woman's life.

For its part, the Bush administration made it clear it would oppose any attempts to overturn the ban. "We do not object to fetal tissue transplantation research where the tissue is derived from a source other than an induced abortion, such as from the treatment for an ectopic pregnancy," Health and Human Services Secretary Louis W. Sullivan said in a Feb. 4 letter to committee members. However, Sullivan said, research using tissue from induced abortions "has the potential of providing an incentive to abortion. It could also create a demand cycle, dependent upon maintaining the legality of induced abortions."

Opponents of the ban argued that it was wrong to simply throw away aborted tissue. "We can't just discard this tissue. We ought to use it," said Paul Simon, D-Ill.

Ban opponents also disputed claims that such research, if successful, would encourage women to have abortions.

Organs for transplants were often obtained after deaths from automobile accidents or gun-related crimes, said Adams, but "no one wants to encourage more car crashes or shooting deaths."

Backers of the ban, however, held firm.

If the research eventually resulted in significant new treatments or cures, said Daniel R. Coats, R-Ind., "the amount of fetal tissue that's going to be needed will far exceed" even the amount that could by provided by the estimated 1.4 million elective abortions performed annually.

Hatch, while acknowledging that the research had potential benefits, argued that the bill in its existing form could not be passed. NIH, he said, should not be "needlessly embroiled in matters in which the larger community holds polarized views."

His amendment to study the use of tissue from miscarriages and ectopic pregnancies, said Hatch, "would facilitate research using fetal tissue without getting us into the abortion debate."

But opponents of the amendment cited letters from scientists who said that such tissue had already been stud-

ied and rejected for scientific use, because it was often abnormal or diseased.

## Senate Floor Action

The Senate passed the NIH bill April 2 by a vote of 87-10, with members making it clear they wanted the research funding ban eliminated. *(Vote 66, p. 10-S)*

The key vote came March 31, when the Senate rejected, 23-77, an amendment offered by Hatch that would have slightly modified the ban but retained its principal elements. *(Vote 61, p. 9-S)*

Senators were clearly swayed by the pleas of members who opposed abortion but rejected contentions by the Bush administration and anti-abortion groups that transplant research involving aborted fetal tissue would, if successful, encourage abortions.

"I do not believe that this bill would, in any way, encourage abortions. I would not support it if this was the case," said Thurmond.

"I believe that for the sake of [his daughter] Julie and those individuals who suffer from diabetes and other serious diseases, we cannot afford to lose this opportunity to develop a cure," he said.

Mark O. Hatfield, R-Ore., another ardent abortion foe, agreed. "I strongly believe that allowing fetal tissue research is a pro-life position," he said. In fact, Hatfield added, such research could lead to a reduction in abortions.

"If fetal tissue transplants are proven through research to be successful, parents who learn that their baby has a genetic defect may have an option other than abortion," he said.

Hatfield and others paid tribute to former Rep. Morris K. Udall, D-Ariz., whose Parkinson's disease had forced his resignation in 1991, and to his daughter, Ann Udall, who was watching from the gallery after lobbying many senators to lift the ban.

"After watching what Mo and his family have gone through, I have to ask the question again: Can we deny this opportunity of hope to the millions of others who suffer from debilitating diseases?" Hatfield said.

Even senators who urged that the ban be kept said they supported research using fetal tissue, provided it did not come from elective abortions.

"I want fetal tissue research. I want it to continue," said Hatch, whose amendment would have permitted funding of research involving tissue obtained as a result of miscarriages or abortions to end ectopic pregnancies.

But Kennedy, sponsor of the bill, noted that scientists said that fetal tissue from miscarriages and ectopic pregnancies was rarely suitable for transplants.

## Conference, Final Action

Bush made the next move, issuing an executive order on May 19 to establish "fetal tissue banks" to collect tissue for research from miscarriages and ectopic pregnancies.

"I think this is a pro-research president who is making tissue available so that we don't have to go to ethically questionable sources," said James O. Mason, HHS assistant secretary for health.

The executive order apparently had its desired effect. The House on May 28 adopted the conference report on HR 2507 (H Rept 102-525), but the margin of victory was smaller than when members voted on the original bill in 1991. The final tally was 260-148. Two-thirds would have been 272. *(Vote 147, p. 36-H)*

There was furious lobbying on both sides. Fourteen

# Fetal Tissue Research at Issue in Veto of NIH Bill

*Following is the text of President Bush's June 23 veto message on HR 2507, a bill that would have reauthorized the National Institutes of Health. The House tried but failed to override the veto on June 24.*

I am returning herewith without my approval HR 2507, the "National Institutes of Health Revitalization Amendments of 1992," which would extend and amend biomedical research authorities of the National Institutes of Health (NIH).

Before discussing the flaws of HR 2507, I must clarify two misperceptions. First, HR 2507 is not necessary to assure that federal spending continue for biomedical research or for research related to any disease, disorder or condition. Second, HR 2507 is not necessary to increase support for research targeted at women's health needs. Great progress is being made in the area of women's health under the valued leadership of the first female director of the NIH [Bernadine P. Healy].

HR 2507 is unacceptable to me on almost every ground: ethical, fiscal, administrative, philosophical and legal. I repeatedly warned the Congress of this at each stage of the legislative process. The bill's provisions permitting the use of tissue from induced abortions for federally funded transplantation research involving human subjects are inconsistent with our nation's deeply held beliefs.

Moreover, it is clear that this legislation would be counterproductive to the attainment of our nation's health research objectives.

HR 2507 is objectionable because it would lift the current moratorium on the use of federal funds for fetal tissue transplantation research where the tissue is obtained from induced abortions. Let it be clear: This is not a moratorium on research. It is only a moratorium on the use of one source of tissue for that research. I believe this moratorium is important in order to prevent taxpayer funds from being used for research that many Americans find morally repugnant and because of its potential for promoting and legitimatizing abortion.

My administration is strongly committed to pursuing research to find cures and treatments for such disorders as Parkinson's disease, diabetes and Alzheimer's disease that have been held out as areas where fetal tissue research might be pursued. Fetal tissue transplantation research relating to these disorders can proceed without relying on tissue from induced abortions. Medical experts at the Department of Health and Human Services have assured me that ectopic pregnancies and spontaneous abortions provide sufficient and suitable tissue to meet anticipated research needs. Therefore, on May 19, 1992, I issued an executive order establishing a fetal tissue bank that will collect tissue from these sources so as to meet the needs of the research community. The bank will provide tissue directly to scientists for their research. This approach truly represents the pro-research and ethical alternative that will allow this research to go forward without relying on a source of tissue that many find to be morally objectionable.

HR 2507 also contains fiscally irresponsible authorization levels. The total cost of the provisions in this legislation could exceed the FY 1993 budget I presented to the Congress by $3.2 billion. It is exceedingly unlikely, if not impossible, that the Congress can fund the programs contained in HR 2507 while complying with the requirements of the [1990] Budget Enforcement Act.

That being the case, the expectations that this bill will create are unreasonable. Those who suffer from the many diseases and disorders that are the subject of this unrealistic legislation will be sadly disappointed.

HR 2507 is also objectionable because its provisions regarding the appointment of "Ethics Advisory Boards" are inconsistent with the Appointments Clause of the Constitution. HR 2507 would effectively give these boards unilateral authority to make decisions concerning major research initiatives. As a policy matter, these decisions should be made by the president's chief officer on health issues: the secretary of Health and Human Services. More fundamentally, however, the Appointments Clause requires that officers vested with this type of power be appointed by the president by and with the advice and consent of the Senate.

Instead, HR 2507 provides that they are to be appointed by the secretary of Health and Human Services and then purports to circumscribe the discretion of the appointment authority by imposing various requirements concerning the boards' composition. HR 2507's provisions regarding the Scientific and Technical Board on Biomedical and Behavioral Research Facilities and the Office of Research on Women's Health likewise raise Appointments Clause problems.

In addition, HR 2507 contains reporting requirements that impair the separation of powers.

For example, the bill would require the director of the National Cancer Institute to submit to specified committees of the Congress the original plan, and any revisions to that plan, regarding certain cancer research. This requirement to submit to the Congress what is in essence a draft plan without the prior review and approval of the executive branch clearly interferes with the deliberative process of the executive branch. The internal workings of the executive branch should be just that — internal. To require the executive branch to display each step in its deliberative process to the Congress would destroy my ability to speak as the single voice of a unitary executive.

I am also troubled by the increasingly frequent imposition of reporting requirements. HR 2507 imposes a significant number of new reporting requirements on an executive branch that already suffers under the burden of literally thousands of such requirements. Last October, I noted that "taken together such reports put a heavy burden on the reporting agencies at a time of scarce resources." Thus, I called for "an effort to minimize reporting requirements, both in terms of the number and frequency of reports that must be submitted, as well as the level of detail required." Bills such as HR 2507 move us in the opposite direction.

For these reasons, I am returning HR 2507 without my approval, and I ask the Congress to adopt a simple extension of those appropriations authorizations for the National Institutes of Health that need to be extended.

members who voted against the bill in July 1991 voted for it May 28. But 16 members switched their votes the other way.

Bill supporters said they planned to press ahead anyway, if only to force Bush to cast an unpopular veto.

"He's got to make the decision to tell people with Alzheimer's disease, with Parkinson's disease, with diabetes and with genetic diseases that the research will be stopped that will hold promise for them," said Waxman, the bill's House sponsor.

Supporters of the ban said they were confident they would prevail. "This was the toughest vote for us," said Smith, co-chairman of the House Pro-Life Caucus. On an actual override vote, when party loyalty was more important, he said, "we have more than enough votes to sustain the veto."

The final tally would have been a little closer had some of the bill's strongest backers not missed the vote by a

fluke. When the bells rang to signal the roll call, Vic Fazio, D-Calif., was meeting in a small room on the third floor of the Capitol with a group of congresswomen, including Patricia Schroeder, D-Colo., Patsy Mink, D-Hawaii, and Nancy Pelosi, D-Calif. The bells in that room malfunctioned, and the four members missed the roll call. Their votes would not have changed the outcome.

Abortion foes declared victory after the vote. "The pro-abortion movement is desperately seeking to legitimize the harvesting of aborted fetuses, to further weave legal abortion into the fabric of society," said the National Right to Life Committee's Johnson. "Thanks to President Bush, we believe they will fail."

Much of the debate centered on the fetal tissue funding ban and, specifically, Bush's May 19 executive order.

Opponents said the order was a politically motivated ploy. "I can tell you from experience, it just won't work," declared Rowland, a physician. Rowland said tissue from miscarriages is often diseased; ectopic pregnancies, in which the fetus is implanted outside the woman's uterus, are medical emergencies that do not allow time to assemble the medical team needed to recover fetal tissue for research.

Ban opponents also cited a statement newly issued by Otis R. Bowen, who had been HHS secretary under Reagan when the funding ban was first imposed in 1988. Tissue from miscarriages and ectopic pregnancies, said Bowen, "has always been unaffected by the ban, but the problems of quality and availability are so unsurmountable that research has come to a halt. This political compromise will not work."

But supporters of the ban said the bank should be given a chance.

"What the president has wisely done is to provide an ethical, rational and effective means by which fetal tissue research can be conducted," Smith said.

They cited their own experts, including them NIH Director Dr. Bernadine Healy, who personally supported research using aborted fetuses. "I believe that such a bank with an established and NIH-funded tissue procurement effort will provide a means to continue the transplantion research effort," Healy wrote.

The Senate cleared the NIH bill June 4, approving the conference report HR 2507 by a vote of 85-12. Three members who supported the bill in April voted against the conference report. All three, Alfonse M. D'Amato, R-N.Y., Don Nickles, R-Okla., and Daniel R. Coats, R-Ind., were outspoken abortion opponents. Coats said he supported NIH's work and had hoped the provision overturning the fetal tissue ban would be removed in conference. (Vote 115, p. 16-S)

Bush vetoed the bill June 23, and a day later, won the seventh straight abortion-related veto fight of his presidency as the House came up 14 votes short of the two-thirds majority needed to override. The House vote was 271-156. (Vote 222, p. 54-H)

Bush said in his veto message that allow research using aborted tissue was "inconsistent with our nation's deeply held beliefs" and could serve to promote and legitimize abortion. (Veto message, p. 395)

No sooner had the veto been sustained than sponsors of the measure announced a new "compromise" version of the bill, which they vowed to put on Bush's desk before the Republican convention in August.

Waxman, sponsor of HR 2507, described the new bills as a "good-faith effort to meet the president halfway."

They dealt not only with the tissue research ban, but also with some monetary provisions Bush had found objectionable.

The new bills (HR 5495, S 2899) eliminated provisions of the NIH bill authorizing funds for NIH land purchases and for renovating research facilities, and changed most of the specific authorization levels to "such sums as may be necessary," leaving actual funding levels to the discretion of appropriators. Sponsors hoped the concessions would at least remove the budgetary and "pork" objections raised by some Republicans and by Bush.

On the fetal research question, the new bills required that researchers first attempt to use the fetal tissue "bank" that Bush ordered created in May. If the bank was unable to provide adequate tissue, researchers could pursue other sources, including remains from elective abortions.

"If the bank works as the president has promised, then no tissue from abortion will ever be used," said Waxman. "But if the bank doesn't work, then we still have the responsibility to help these people. Americans with Parkinson's and diabetes should not be held hostage to the politics of abortion."

Abortion opponents were quick to blast the new plan. Rep. Smith of New Jersey called the proposal "absolutely unacceptable. This is nothing more than a redo of the fight we just had."

### Senate Committee Action, S 2899

The Senate Labor and Human Resources Committee July 29 approved the new bill, S 2899, by voice vote.

"This is major legislation that should never have been vetoed in the first place," Kennedy said. "With these good faith revisions, it deserves to be enacted."

But Hatch, the panel's ranking Republican, said the new measure did not represent much of an improvement.

"Anyone who thinks this bill is not politically motivated is not operating on all cylinders," Hatch said. "We're just spinning our wheels for nothing but politics' sake."

That opinion was shared by the Bush administration. "This measure does not represent a compromise, but rather another attempt to promote federally funded abortion-dependent research," Sullivan wrote in a July 28 letter to Kennedy. "It is merely a political construction."

### Senate Floor Action, S 2899

The Senate voted 85-12 on Oct. 2 to take up S 2899. That vote was needed to avert a threatened Hatch filibuster. (Vote 263, p. 34-S)

Over the weekend of Oct. 3 and 4, Hatch and Kennedy reported that they neared a compromise under which the tissue banks would have been given a somewhat longer lead time to become established. Hatch asked for two years; Kennedy was said to have offered 18 months.

But any deal was ultimately scuttled by those at both poles of the debate. Hardline abortion foes — who were prepared to continue the filibuster without Hatch — did not want the ban lifted under any circumstances. On the other side, opponents of the ban did not want the tissue banks written into statute when a President Bill Clinton could make the entire matter go away with the stroke of a pen on Jan. 20, 1993. The Arkansas governor had promised to take such action to overturn the funding ban if he was elected.

In the end, with the Senate eager to finish work for the year, Senate Majority Leader Mitchell pulled the bill from the floor. But in declaring that the fight was over for 1992,

Mitchell announced that he would make the NIH bill S 1 in the 103rd Congress, and that the Senate would pass it during its first week of legislative business in 1993.

"Only in the last few days of a session can 85 senators vote one way . . . 12 senators vote another . . . and the 'No's' prevail," Mitchell said. In 1993, he said, "The Senate will stay in session as long as is needed in order to get this bill passed the first week the Senate is in session."

## ABORTIONS IN THE MILITARY

For the first time since abortion-rights advocates began pushing the issue in 1990, legislation (S 3144) to overturn an administration ban on abortions in overseas military medical facilities made it to the president's desk. But Bush pocket vetoed the measure Oct. 31, three weeks after Congress had adjourned for the year.

The House June 4 voted for the second consecutive year to add language to the annual defense authorization bill (HR 5006) that would allow servicewomen and military dependents to obtain abortions in overseas military medical facilities if they paid for the procedure themselves. The amendment was identical to one adopted in 1991 but dropped during a House-Senate conference.

The amendment was adopted by a slightly bigger margin than the year before. The 1992 tally was 216-193; in 1991 the amendment was approved by 220-208. *(Vote 163, p. 40-H)*

Six House members who voted against the amendment in 1991 switched sides. They were Bill Dickinson, R-Ala.; Bernard J. Dwyer, D-N.J.; Marilyn Lloyd, D-Tenn.; Al McCandless, R-Calif.; Dan Rostenkowski, D-Ill.; and Robin Tallon, R-S.C.

By far the most dramatic change was Lloyd's. In a speech that drew applause from abortion rights advocates, the longtime abortion foe said her bout with breast cancer caused her to rethink her position.

"I value the right to make my own decision about my health care and about my treatment options," Lloyd said. "I'm convinced all women should have access to the best reproductive health care services available when they're faced with their own difficult and very trying decisions."

House abortion-rights backers opened a second front June 29, as the House Appropriations Committee added similar language to the fiscal 1993 spending bill for the Defense Department (HR 5504).

In 1991, abortion language approved by the Appropriations Committee was dropped on the House floor because it violated House rules against authorizing on appropriations measures. The 1992 version merely barred the Pentagon from spending funds to enforce its ban on self-paid abortions. Such "funding limitation" amendments were permitted. The House passed the defense spending bill, including the abortion language, July 2.

Despite veto threats from Bush, the language was retained in the Senate versions of both the authorization and appropriations bills. But as Congress rushed to adjourn, sponsors of those measures pressured abortion-rights supporters to allow the provisions to be dropped.

They worked out a deal stripping the provisions from the defense bills but sending them to Bush separately in a bill introduced in August by Senate Armed Services Chairman Sam Nunn, D-Ga.

That bill (S 3144) originally contained provisions relating to CHAMPUS, the health program for military dependents. But as the Senate was wrapping up action on the

defense authorization bill Sept. 18, Nunn substituted the abortion language for the other provisions in the bill and got it passed by unanimous consent. Nunn acted so quietly that neither the supporters nor foes of abortion rights knew the bill had been passed.

After the abortion language was stripped from the defense bills the week of Sept. 28, all that remained was for the House to pass S 3144. It did so Oct. 3, by a vote of 220-186, but not before one final, angry debate between partisans on both sides. *(Vote 458, p. 112-H)*

Abortion opponents charged that the provision would allow women to seek abortions at any time in their pregnancy for any reason.

"It permits and authorizes abortion on demand without any restriction, and it uses taxpayer facilities to do it," said Hyde.

But Schroeder, who managed the bill for proponents, disputed that assertion.

"I do not think that anybody in this body thinks that military hospitals were running abortion mills before 1988," when the current ban went into effect, Schroeder said.

## OVERSEAS FAMILY PLANNING

Abortion-rights forces hoped to use the annual foreign aid spending bill (HR 5368) to overturn two administration policies they said interfered with overseas family planning efforts. But leaders ultimately dropped from the bill language certain to prompt a Bush veto.

As passed by the House June 25, the measure included $20 million for the United Nations Population Fund (UNFPA). Abortion foes opposed the funding, charging that the organization had funded population control programs in China, whose government had been accused of coercing abortions.

The Senate, however, not only kept the UNFPA money, but in committee Sept. 23 added language to the bill that would have overturned the so-called Mexico City policy that barred U.S. aid to organizations that performed or "actively promoted" abortion.

However, with Congress eager to adjourn for the year, conferees dropped both provisions from the final version of the measure in order to avert a veto.

## DISTRICT OF COLUMBIA

In the strange atmosphere of end-of-session legislating, Congress moved quickly the week of Sept. 21 to clear the fiscal 1993 spending bill for the District of Columbia so the president could veto it.

The bill (HR 5517), approved by both the House and Senate by voice vote Sept. 24, prohibited the use of federal funds for abortions except to save the woman's life. It was silent, however, about the District using locally raised tax funds to pay for abortions, an omission that prompted Bush vetoes in 1991 and 1989.

1992 was no different. Bush carried out his promise and vetoed the measure Sept. 30. Appropriators knew the veto was coming and did not even bother to try an override.

"The votes are not there," said Rep. Julian Dixon, D-Calif., chairman of the appropriations subcommittee that oversaw the measure. "We know that from past years."

Rather, both the House and Senate later Sept. 30 passed a new bill (HR 6056) with the abortion prohibition added back. That measure became law Oct. 5 (PL 102-382). ∎

# Divided Court Reaffirms Right to Abortion

While political activists framed election-year debate about abortion in black-and-white terms, the Supreme Court's 1992 ruling on the issue was cast in legal gray.

In a June 29 decision upholding most of a Pennsylvania law regulating access to abortion, the court groped for a middle ground on the divisive social issue.

In a 5-4 ruling, the court reaffirmed what it called the "essential holding" of *Roe v. Wade*, its 1973 decision establishing a woman's right to have an abortion in the early phases of pregnancy.

But the court said states could regulate abortion, provided they did not impose an "undue burden" on the woman's basic right to decide.

The four dissenting justices made clear that they would overturn *Roe v. Wade* if and when they got one more sympathetic justice on the court.

That fact was viewed with alarm by Justice Harry A. Blackmun — the author of the 1973 decision and the oldest member of the court.

"I am 83 years old," Blackmun wrote in a separate opinion. "I cannot remain on this court forever, and when I do step down, the confirmation process for my successor well may focus on the issue before us today."

Blackmun's fears were allayed to some degree when Democrat Bill Clinton was elected president on Nov. 3. Clinton, during the campaign, vowed to appoint abortion-rights supporters to the court if he had an opportunity to name one or more justices.

Many legal analysts had expected the court's decision in the 1992 case, *Planned Parenthood of Southeastern Pennsylvania v. Casey*, to weaken abortion rights without directly addressing the status of *Roe*. So it was a surprise when the conservative-dominated court made a point of reaffirming a woman's right to end a pregnancy in its early stages — and made it clear that a total ban on abortion would be found unconstitutional.

The five-member majority was formed by two justices who had always supported *Roe* — Blackmun and John Paul Stevens — and a centrist trio made up of Justices Sandra Day O'Connor, Anthony M. Kennedy and David H. Souter. O'Connor and Kennedy were appointed to the court by President Ronald Reagan. Souter was one of

## Is *Roe v. Wade* Dead?

That was the question constitutional scholars and court watchers were asking after the Supreme Court's June 29 decision in *Planned Parenthood of Southeastern Pennsylvania v. Casey*. At issue was the relationship of the new decision to *Roe*, the landmark 1973 decision that legalized abortion nationwide.

A major difficulty in making that interpretation was that *Roe* itself meant different things to different people. As a result, some thought the *Casey* decision left *Roe* fundamentally unaltered, while others said it overturned *Roe* — in practice if not in actual words.

Here were some of the key questions:

### What did *Roe v. Wade* say?

The 1973 ruling, written by Justice Harry A. Blackmun, declared that the guarantee of liberty in the 14th Amendment to the Constitution extends a right of privacy "broad enough to encompass a woman's decision whether or not to terminate her pregnancy."

But *Roe* also recognized that states have a legitimate interest in protecting both the pregnant woman's health and the potential life represented by the fetus. Said the decision:

"[A]ppellant and some [friends of the court] argue that the woman's right is absolute and that she is entitled to terminate her pregnancy at whatever time, in whatever way, and for whatever reasons she alone chooses. With this we do not agree.... The court's decisions recognizing a right of privacy also acknowledge that some state regulation in areas protected by that right is appropriate.... We, therefore, conclude that the right of personal privacy includes the abortion decision, but that this right is not unqualified and must be considered against important state interests in regulation."

The heart of the decision was the so-called trimester framework — dividing the nine-month pregnancy into three equal parts — which Blackmun described as follows:

"For the stage prior to approximately the end of the first trimester, the abortion decision and its effectuation must be left to the medical judgment of the pregnant woman's attending physician.

"For the stage subsequent to approximately the end of the first trimester the State, in promoting its interest in the health of the mother, may, if it chooses, regulate the abortion procedure in ways that are reasonably related to maternal health.

"For the stage subsequent to viability, the State in promoting its interest in the potentiality of human life may, if it chooses, regulate, and even proscribe, abortion except where it is necessary, in appropriate medical judgment, for the preservation of the life or health of the mother."

In the companion case *Doe v. Bolton*, handed down the same day as *Roe*, the court made clear that it took a liberal view of what "health" meant: "[T]he medical judgment may be exercised in the light of all factors — physical, emotional, psychological, familial, and the woman's age — relevant to the well-being of the patient. All these factors relate to health."

### How was *Roe* interpreted?

A literal reading of *Roe* seemed to allow states considerable leeway to regulate abortion. But under *Roe's* original holding, a woman had a "fundamental right" to terminate a pregnancy before fetal viability, and any state efforts to regulate that choice had to survive "strict scrutiny" and demonstrate a "compelling state interest."

Under that rubric, the court in subsequent cases struck down a wide array of abortion restrictions including 24-hour waiting periods, requirements that all abortions be performed in hospitals, and so-called informed consent laws requiring women seeking abortions to be given information about fetal development and abortion alternatives.

Until the 1989 *Webster* case, the only major restrictions allowed by the court were parental notification and consent laws, as long as minors could seek permission from a judge if they feared involving their parents (*Bellotti v. Baird*, 1979; *Hodgson v. Minnesota*, 1990, among others), and state and federal

Bush's two appointees.

Although the three-justice plurality significantly reduced the scope of abortion rights, their opinion was praised by Blackmun as an "act of personal courage and constitutional principle."

Blackmun noted that earlier court opinions had given little reason to expect the court would so strongly reaffirm abortion rights. "But now, just when so many expected the darkness to fall, the flame has grown bright," Blackmun wrote.

## The Pennsylvania Law

At issue was a Pennsylvania law that did not outlaw abortion but imposed several restrictions on a woman's ability to end a pregnancy. Under the law:

● Doctors were required to inform women of the risks of and alternatives to abortion and then wait 24 hours before performing the abortion.

● Women under 18 were required to have the consent of one of their parents or a judge.

● Married women were required to notify their husbands of their intent to have an abortion.

● Doctors were required to report to the state information on abortions, including who referred the patient and whether the fetus was viable.

● An exemption was provided for medical emergencies — situations in which the woman faced the risk of death or substantial impairment.

The U.S. Court of Appeals for the Third Circuit in 1991 upheld all parts of the law except the spousal-notification requirement. The appeals court said the standards set by *Roe* had been discarded by the Supreme Court in its 1989 decision, *Webster v. Reproductive Health Services*, upholding a Missouri abortion law. *(Webster decision, 1989 Almanac, p. 296)*

Under *Roe*, women had a "fundamental right" to choose abortion, which could be restricted only to serve a "compelling" state interest. That subjected abortion regulations to the most stringent form of court review — "strict scrutiny" — under which most restrictions in the first six months of pregnancy were deemed unconstitutional.

Using that standard, the Supreme Court in 1983 and 1986 struck down restrictions very similar to those in the Pennsylvania law. In *Webster,* however, a changing court opened the door to much broader state regulation of abortion.

## A New Standard: 'Undue Burden'

Amid the confusion generated by *Webster,* the Pennsylvania case gave the court an opportunity to re-examine

---

laws barring public funding for abortions not needed to save the woman's life (*Harris v. McRae*, 1980, upholding the so-called Hyde amendment barring federal funding for abortions except in life-threatening situations).

### How did *Webster* change that?

In the 1989 case *Webster v. Reproductive Health Services*, the court signaled — but did not expressly say — that it no longer considered abortion a fundamental right. Thus, both sides agreed, it essentially invited states to pass their own laws limiting abortion.

The *Webster* decision, a 5-4 ruling, upheld several provisions of Missouri's law, including those requiring doctors to perform tests for viability on fetuses of more than 20 weeks gestation before performing an abortion and barring the use of public employees or facilities to perform abortions not needed to save the woman's life.

*Webster*, like *Casey*, was a split ruling, with justices writing seven opinions and with no single opinion joined by more than three justices. Chief Justice William H. Rehnquist and Justices Byron R. White, Antonin Scalia and Anthony M. Kennedy directly attacked *Roe*. Justice Sandra Day O'Connor refused to go that far, although she provided the fifth vote to uphold the Missouri restrictions.

### How did *Casey* change *Webster?*

In upholding most of the contested provisions of Pennsylvania's restrictive abortion law, *Casey* in many ways was simply *Webster*, part two.

Specifically, the court upheld provisions requiring a 24-hour waiting period and mandating that women seeking an abortion be given state-sponsored material about fetal development and abortion alternatives.

But unlike *Webster*, the plurality opinion in *Casey* did address the fundamental question of a woman's right to abortion. And, much to the surprise of those on both sides, it affirmed it.

But the opinion written by Justice Sandra Day O'Connor made clear that the right she was embracing was not nearly as unlimited as the one for which *Roe* became known. The trimes-

ter framework, said the opinion, "undervalues the State's interest in potential life, as recognized in *Roe.*" Thus, the decision discarded the trimester system, and in its place substituted a rule under which only state regulations that impose "an undue burden" on a woman's choice would be invalidated.

Using that new standard, the justices proceeded to overturn a provision of the Pennsylvania law that would have required a married woman to notify her husband before obtaining an abortion.

### If *Casey* upheld a woman's right to abortion, what's the difference between it and *Roe?*

Everything, according to abortion rights advocates.

"The difference between undue burden and fundamental right is itself fundamental" said Delegate Eleanor Holmes Norton, D-D.C., a former law professor.

They noted that in upholding the Pennsylvania provisions, the court expressly overturned two previous cases — *Thornburgh v. American College of Obstetricians and Gynecologists*, 1986, and *Akron v. Akron Center for Reproductive Health*, 1983 — that had used the *Roe* framework to strike down restrictions virtually identical to Pennsylvania's. *Thornburgh* struck down an informed consent provision, and *Akron* struck down a 24-hour waiting period. "In upholding the Pennsylvania law, there is no doubt that the court has gutted the core holding of *Roe,*" said Carol Tracy of the Women's Law Project, the Philadelphia group that served as co-counsel for Planned Parenthood in the Pennsylvania case. "The real *Roe v. Wade* prohibits laws like Pennsylvania's that encumber the abortion choice with delay, administrative hurdles and expense."

But opponents said that analysis put too fine a point on things.

"The court reaffirmed the core holding of *Roe v. Wade*, that the states may not place significant barriers, much less prohibitions, on abortion, not just in the first three months, but in the fourth and the fifth and the sixth month up to viability, and even after that must allow abortion for health," said Douglas Johnson, the National Right to Life Committee's federal legislative director.

*Roe*. The result was a splintered court and five opinions totaling 156 pages that were filled with bitter disagreements, anguished reasoning, personal asides and broad disquisitions on the role of the court in society.

Only two justices — Blackmun and John Paul Stevens — continued to hold that abortion was a fundamental right.

Four justices — Chief Justice William H. Rehnquist, Byron R. White, Antonin Scalia and Clarence Thomas — said outright they wanted to overturn *Roe*.

The three remaining justices held the balance of power. In an opinion they wrote jointly, O'Connor, Kennedy and Souter reaffirmed what they called the "essential holding" of *Roe*: that a woman has a right to have an abortion before a fetus is viable.

It was a surprising conclusion because both Kennedy and O'Connor had been critical of *Roe* in the past. Indeed, Kennedy signed an opinion in *Webster* that would have effectively overturned *Roe*. This was Souter's first abortion case since joining the court in 1990.

While all expressed doubts about the wisdom of *Roe*, the three justices made a sweeping argument about a woman's right to control her reproductive life.

"The mother who carries a child to full term is subject to anxieties, to physical constraints, to pain that only she must bear," the justices said. "Her suffering is too intimate and personal for the state to insist, without more, upon its own vision of the woman's role."

In declining to overturn *Roe*, the three justices said that nothing less was at stake than the life plans of a generation of women and the integrity of the Supreme Court itself.

"For two decades of economic and social developments, people have organized intimate relationships and made choices that define their views of themselves and their places in society, in reliance on the availability of abortion," the justices said.

Invoking the principle of stare decisis — that the court should not overturn precedents lightly — the three said they should avoid seeming to surrender to political pressure.

"A decision to overrule *Roe*'s essential holding under the existing circumstances would address error, if error there was, at the cost of both profound and unnecessary damage to the court's legitimacy," they argued.

While upholding a woman's right to end a pregnancy in its early stages, the three justices backed away from a crucial element of *Roe*: the view that abortion was a fundamental right, regulation of which would have to withstand strict scrutiny.

The three also discarded Roe's trimester framework for determining whether and how abortions could be regulated. Under that scheme, abortions were largely unrestricted for the first three months of a pregnancy, could be regulated to protect a woman's health in the second trimester and could be barred in the third trimester unless the woman's health was at risk.

In place of the trimester framework and the standard of strict scrutiny, the three justices established a new standard for assessing the constitutionality of abortion rules.

Regulations could be upheld, the justices argued, if they did not impose an "undue burden" on a woman seeking an abortion by placing "substantial obstacles" in her path.

Applying that new standard, the court concluded that all elements of the Pennsylvania law were constitutional except the spousal notification requirement. Under that requirement, the court said, women who feared physical harm from their husbands "are likely to be deterred from procuring an abortion as surely as if [Pennsylvania] had outlawed abortion in all cases."

But the court concluded the law's "informed consent" provisions and 24-hour waiting period were not "substantial obstacles" and overruled past decisions that found similar provisions unconstitutional.

Although only three justices endorsed the "undue burden" test, they controlled the outcome of the case. They were joined by Stevens and Blackmun in striking down the spousal-notice requirement. The four dissenters agreed with the central bloc of three that the rest of the law should be upheld, so the vote on those parts of the statute was 7-2.

### The Dissenters

Abortion rights advocates outside the court argued that the "undue burden" standard gutted *Roe*. The court's four dissenters, in an opinion written by Rehnquist, agreed.

"*Roe* continues to exist, but only in the way a storefront on a Western movie set exists: a mere facade to give the illusion of reality," Rehnquist wrote.

In an unequivocal repudiation of *Roe*, Rehnquist wrote, "We believe that *Roe* was wrongly decided, and that it can and should be overruled."

The dissenters argued that restrictions on abortion should be subject to the lowest level of legal scrutiny and should be upheld if they were merely "rationally related to a legitimate state interest."

The dissenters argued that the "undue burden" standard was so vague that it was not clear what regulations would stand or fall.

"The inherently standardless nature of this inquiry invites the district judge to give effect to his personal preferences about abortion," said Scalia in another opinion for the four dissenters.

### Guam, Mississippi Cases Rejected

Although *Casey* was by no means a consensus decision, the court made it clear for the rest of 1992 that it had no wish to revisit the thorny subject of abortion.

On Nov. 30, the court declined to hear an appeal of a lower court ruling invalidating Guam's restrictive abortion law.

Three justices voted to hear the case, *Ada v. Guam Society of Obstetricians and Gynecologists*, one short of the four required to put it on the court's docket for the 1992-1993 session. The decision effectively killed the law, which was struck down by a federal district court in August 1990. A federal appeals court agreed with the district court's decision in April 1992. The Guam law, which was passed in March 1990 but never enforced, would have outlawed virtually all abortions in the U.S. island territory in the Pacific.

Although the decision was seen as a setback for abortion opponents, the court evened things out a week later when it declined to hear another case brought by abortion-rights advocates. The case, *Barnes v. Moore*, a case challenged a 1991 Mississippi law requiring women seeking abortions to wait 24 hours before undergoing the procedure. The high court's action left the law in effect.

Although the *Casey* decision upheld a 24-hour waiting period similar to Mississippi's, lawyers opposing the law in the *Barnes* cases argued that since the poor, mostly rural state had only three abortion providers, the waiting period constituted an "undue burden" that *Casey* said made a state's restriction impermissible. ■

# Despite Numerous Plans, No Health Reform

After nearly a year of frenzied and often partisan jousting over the health care issue, the 102nd Congress adjourned with almost nothing to show on what had become a top tier electoral issue. No proposed solution could muster more than a few dozen supporters although nearly everyone agreed that the existing system cost too much and left too many people with no or inadequate insurance coverage.

Both House and Senate Democrats — whose leaders early in the year boldly predicted floor action on major bills — were embarrassed by their inability to coalesce around any single plan. About all Democrats managed to agree on was that the various plans put forth separately by House and Senate Republicans and by President Bush were inadequate to either bring down costs or broadly expand insurance coverage.

The Senate did twice pass — as part of two failed tax bills (HR 4210, HR 11) — a bipartisan "incremental" proposal aimed at making insurance both more available and more affordable for small businesses. In HR 4210, lead sponsor and Senate Finance Committee Chairman Lloyd Bentsen, D-Texas, wanted to force President Bush to veto health insurance changes included in the President's own proposal. (Bush vetoed the overall bill because it would also have raised taxes on the wealthy). Bentsen included the same package of changes in HR 11, but only because if he had not, Senate Republicans were prepared to offer their own, similar plan as a floor amendment, potentially embarrassing Democrats on an issue on which they had otherwise enjoyed the upper hand politically. But both times House negotiators forced the package out of the final bills.

## THE VARIOUS PLANS

## BACKGROUND

Already an issue of growing political importance, health care reform was firmly placed on the national agenda with the surprise victory of Democrat Harris Wofford over former Bush Attorney General Dick Thornburgh in Pennsylvania's special Senate election in November, 1991. But while Wofford rode the health issue to victory by keeping his promises general, translating such promises into specifics proved difficult for members from both parties.

Congress took no action in 1991 to overhaul the health-care system, pushing into 1992 a very loud cry for reform from both political parties. More than three dozen health-care proposals circulated during the first session of the 102nd Congress and it became increasingly difficult to boil them down into an approach with strong consensus backing. *(1991 Almanac, p. 350)*

Democrats found themselves divided into roughly four camps. For those favoring full-scale reform of the system, about equal numbers seemed to back fullscale national health insurance similar to Canada's, a "play or pay" plan under which businesses would have the choice of either providing workers with insurance or else paying a tax to have the government do it for them, and a "market based" care system that would rely on better managing the way health was delivered. At the same time, some Democrats, led by Bentsen, preferred an "incre-

mental" bill that would make only minimal changes both parties could agree on, leaving the larger decisions for a later date.

The GOP was more united on the issue, but not much more. Republicans in both the Senate and House introduced comprehensive reform proposals (S 1936, HR 5325) during the 102nd Congress; the Senate in November, 1991, and the House in June 1992. Both the House and Senate packages had many elements in common with each other, with the plan President Bush unveiled in February, and with the "incremental" package being pushed by some Democrats. Key among the common elements were "insurance reforms" designed to make private insurance more available and affordable by outlawing exclusions based on pre-existing medical conditions and narrowing the range of premiums insurers could charge different customers, particularly those in small groups.

But Republicans also disagreed about key issues, including whether or not to limit the tax deduction for employers who provided their workers with health insurance and the exclusion from taxes for the workers who received such benefits. The tax issue was so controversial, in fact, that the Bush administration never sent to Congress a bill for the tax-credit proposal that was the centerpiece of the Bush plan.

By mid-1992, House Democrats tried to rally behind a bill (HR 5502) whose primary emphasis was controlling costs by imposing a national health budget. It was approved by a House subcommittee, but went no further. In the Senate, most of the action took place behind closed doors, as Democrats embarked on a "consensus building" process that culminated in the compromise ultimately embraced on the campaign trail by Democratic presidential nominee Bill Clinton — combining a strict cost-control approach with major private-sector reforms.

## "PLAY OR PAY"

The first legislative volley was fired in January by the Senate Labor and Human Resources Committee, which approved a bill that embraced the "play or pay" approach, which was to require employers to either provide insurance to workers and their dependents or else pay a tax to fund a broad new government plan.

By a party-line vote of 10-7 the panel approved a revised version of so-called HealthAmerica legislation (S 1227) introduced in June, 1991 by Senate Majority Leader George J. Mitchell, D-Maine. *(Highlights, p. 402)*

The sweeping committee bill (unnumbered), in addition to imposing a play-or-pay system, also sought to slow spiraling health care costs with the creation of a Federal Reserve-like health expenditures board that was to be charged with setting rates for medical care.

"The American people face a crisis in health care, and the country needs action," said Sen. Edward M. Kennedy, D-Mass., Labor Committee chairman and a lead cosponsor of the Mitchell bill.

House Democrats also appeared to be moving in that direction. "For the immediate future, some version of [play or pay] is probably the avenue to health care reform,"

# Senate Bill Highlights

*Draft health-care overhaul legislation approved Jan. 22 by the Senate Labor and Human Resources Committee was a somewhat revised version of a bill (S 1227) introduced in June 1991 by Senate Majority Leader George J. Mitchell, D-Maine.*

*Some of the changes were made to get around the fact that S 1227 was referred not to Labor but to the Finance Committee. Other changes, particularly those relating to cost-containment, were made by Labor Chairman Edward M. Kennedy, D-Mass., to secure Democratic votes in committee.*

*Here are the highlights of the bill as approved in committee.*

## PLAY OR PAY

The centerpiece of the bill would create a so-called play-or-pay system, which would require employers either to provide workers and their dependents with a minimum package of health insurance benefits or pay a tax to help fund a new public insurance program.

The new public plan, called AmeriCare, would provide insurance to people not covered by employers, including most of those currently covered by Medicaid, the joint federal-state health program for the poor. Employees and those covered by AmeriCare would generally be required to pay 20 percent of their premium costs, as well as certain deductibles and copayments, with costs for low-income individuals and families subsidized by the government.

The tax would be set at a level high enough to encourage most employers to provide coverage themselves but not so high as to impose an "excessive burden" on employers.

## COST CONTAINMENT

The bill included more than a dozen separate provisions aimed at slowing the rise of health-care costs. Some of the more significant include:

● **Federal Health Expenditure Board.** The bill would create an independent entity, similar to the Federal Reserve, to set national expenditure goals and convene annual rate negotiations between those who pay for health care and those who provide it. If negotiations succeeded, the rates would be binding; if negotiations reached an impasse, the board would issue its own binding rates.

● **Standardized claim forms.** The expenditure board would also be required to develop a single, standardized insurance claim form to reduce administrative costs imposed by the multiplicity of forms from various insurers.

● **Outcomes research.** The bill would increase by $50 million the budget for the Agency for Health Care Policy and Research, charged with measuring the effectiveness of various medical treatments. The Pepper Commission, a bipartisan study group, estimated that unnecessary or ineffective health care adds as much as $18 billion a year to the nation's health tab.

## MALPRACTICE

The bill would establish a grant program for states to experiment with alternatives to the current court-based system used to adjudicate malpractice cases. Maine, for example, has a law shielding some specialists from lawsuits if they meet certain standards of care. Virginia and Florida had laws providing for no-fault programs for some birth-related injury claims. Under such plans, families could collect compensation even if a physician was not found to have acted improperly.

## INSURANCE REFORM

The bill would set federal standards for private health insurance sold to small businesses in an effort to make such insurance more available as well as more affordable.

Among other things, insurance companies would no longer be allowed to deny coverage to businesses based on workers' pre-existing health conditions and would be limited in the amount they could raise premiums for businesses with higher-than-average claims.

## COMMUNITY HEALTH CARE

The bill would authorize an additional $1.3 billion over five years for new community health centers, which would provide primary health care in medically underserved rural and inner-city areas.

## STATE FLEXIBILITY

The bill would give states increased ability to design their own health-care systems.

States would be allowed, for example, to establish their own "single payer" systems, under which the state would act as the primary insurer. States could pool funds from employer premiums and taxes as well as from Medicare, the federal health insurance program for the elderly and disabled.

States opting for the single-payer approach would have to provide the same level of coverage guaranteed under the basic bill, and their cost-containment programs would have to meet the targets established by the health expenditure board.

In addition, up to five states would be allowed to set up their own programs that are neither "single payer" nor play-or-pay. Again, the programs would have to meet the bill's basic requirements for coverage and cost containment.

House Speaker Thomas S. Foley, D-Wash., said Jan. 23.

But even as supporters hailed play or pay, it was still not clear whether it had a constituency beyond Capitol Hill. The momentum behind it remained an almost exclusively "inside the Beltway" phenomenon with little national public support.

Indeed, House Democrats who held town hall meetings on the health-care issue in January reported considerable voter interest in a "single-payer" plan, under which the government would finance all health care — similar to what was being done in Canada.

"Play or pay is the in-town compromise with interest groups," said Robert Blendon, a Harvard University researcher who specialized in public opinion about health care. "It has mild support [from the public] but no passion. The passion is to get rid of the insurance industry."

The attraction of play or pay for lawmakers, Blendon said, was that it was less unacceptable to the health industry than a single-payer national health insurance plan. Play or pay's chief advantage was that it "will not get the $4 million media campaign against it" from insurance and medical groups who ardently opposed national health insurance, Blendon said.

But with that lack of opposition came a lack of support that threatened any play-or-pay proposal.

The lack of passion for play or pay was evident at the Senate Labor Committee markup, where in opening statements, three Democrats and Republican James M. Jeffords of Vermont said they wished the legislation went even further.

"I would prefer a national single-payer system" said Paul Wellstone, D-Minn., who was preparing his own legislation to that effect. Nevertheless, he added, "I think this bill is an important step forward."

Democrats Howard M. Metzenbaum of Ohio and Paul Simon of Illinois said they supported play or pay as a first step toward a single-payer system.

One who did not apologize for the limited scope of the bill was Committee Chairman Kennedy, who had been crusading for national health insurance for more than two decades.

"There will be universality in this program," Kennedy said. "Everyone will be covered."

Approval of the measure marked the third time in the past four years the panel approved legislation aimed at making health insurance universally available. Kennedy bills requiring employers to provide workers insurance were approved in 1988 and 1989 but died without reaching the Senate floor. *(1989 Almanac, p. 171)*

Kennedy made a point of noting that Majority Leader Mitchell promised that this time the full Senate would get a chance to vote.

In a statement released after the markup, Mitchell repeated his vow: "It is my intention to make every effort to see that comprehensive health care reform is passed in this Congress."

Labor Committee Republicans (with Jeffords the notable exception), attacked the Democratic bill as too government-intrusive.

"The method of putting it all in the hands of the federal government is not the way to go," said conservative Orrin G. Hatch of Utah, the ranking minority member.

"I have never heard of any product or service, which, if regulated by government, you get a better choice, quality and supply," he said.

Moderate Dave Durenberger of Minnesota also doubted

the voter appeal of play or pay. "Government plans and government solutions are not what people are looking for," he said.

One of the changes Kennedy made to Mitchell's bill — in order to win support from some panel Democrats — was to beef up the powers of the health expenditure board.

In the original bill, the board was to convene rate negotiations between purchasers and providers of health care. In the new version, if the negotiations were unsuccessful, the board would set rates itself.

But members rejected, by voice vote, an even stronger cost-containment amendment offered by Jeff Bingaman, D-N.M. Describing his proposal as "the big stick," Bingaman wanted statutory language that would impose national caps for health spending, tying them to annual increases in the gross national product.

Kennedy said the caps "put us into a kind of straitjacket . . . when it comes to health-care costs."

Hatch agreed: The amendment "puts an albatross on an already sinking ship."

### Bush Opposes Play or Pay

The Bush administration also registered strong opposition. In separate letters to panel members, both Health and Human Services Secretary Louis W. Sullivan and Labor Secretary Lynn Martin said they would recommend Bush veto the bill if it reached his desk.

Martin wrote that the bill "would create a massive dislocation of workers and their dependents from their current coverage, create a public plan of an enormous scale and impose unacceptably high costs on employers and the public."

Sullivan and Martin based their complaints on the results of a study conducted by the Washington-based Urban Institute analyzing the effects on the economy of a play or pay plan.

The key finding of the study, commissioned by the Labor Department, was that many more employers than originally expected would opt to put their workers in the public plan, and that taxpayer costs would rise by as much as $36 billion annually.

"This study shows that play-or-pay proposals would result in lost jobs, higher employer costs, higher taxes and a huge new government-run health program," said Sullivan. "The fact is, play-or-pay is the wrong medicine, and we shouldn't take it."

But Democratic backers of the plan disputed those findings. Sen. John D. Rockefeller IV, D-W.Va., who as chairman of the bipartisan Pepper Commission drafted one of the first major play-or-pay plans, said the study "distorts and ignores the fact that under our current health system, families are being shifted from private coverage to *no* coverage whatsoever."

## THE BUSH PLAN

Bush planned to unveil his health reform proposals in his State of the Union address Jan. 28, and in his proposed fiscal 1983 budget to be sent to Congress the next day.

But an unexpected uprising by House Republicans forced the administration into at least a temporary retreat.

When administration officials came to Capitol Hill on Jan. 23 to brief Republicans on it the lawmakers cried foul. They did not want to endorse a plan that reflected little of their thinking and none of their input on substance or strategy.

# The Bush Health-Care Plan . . .

*President Bush traveled to Cleveland on Feb. 6 to unveil his long-awaited plan to overhaul the nation's health-care system. The 94-page administration "white paper" was full of assurances that the estimated 36 million Americans who lacked health insurance would be able to get it, and that a system projected to cost more than $800 billion in 1992 year would soon come under control.*

*Here are the highlights of the president's plan:*

## INCREASING ACCESS

### Tax Credits, Tax Deductions

● Low- and moderate-income families would be eligible for a transferable health insurance credit or a tax deduction to cover health insurance costs up to:

$1,250 for individuals with incomes up to $50,000;

$2,500 for married couples with incomes up to $65,000;

and $3,750 for families of three or more with incomes up to $80,000.

The credits and deductions would be phased in over five years.

● Individuals could take either a tax credit (reducing taxes owed) or a tax deduction (reducing taxable income), whichever is most advantageous.

● Low-income families who do not earn enough to pay taxes could collect their credit in a voucher that they could use to purchase insurance. States would be responsible for administering the voucher program.

● **Eligibility.** All who do not receive assistance from other federal programs (Medicare, Medicaid, etc.) would be eligible.

● **Transfers.** Vouchers could be transferred only to a private insurer for the purchase of health insurance.

● **Phaseout of credit and deduction.** The maximum credit would be available to individuals and families with incomes up to approximately 100 percent of the federal poverty level ($11,140 for a family of three).

The credit would phase down to a minimum at 150 percent of the poverty level ($16,710 for a family of three). The minimum credit would be 10 percent of the maximum, or:

$125 for individuals

$250 for couples

$375 for families of three or more.

Individuals with incomes up to the top of the income range could choose instead to deduct the cost of health insurance, up to the maximum (either $1,250, $2,500 or $3,750). Employer contributions to a health plan would be deducted from the allowable deduction, which would also phase down for those with incomes within $10,000 of the maximum.

● **Inflation adjustment.** Both the credit and deduction amounts, as well as the maximum income thresholds, would be adjusted annually for inflation.

● **Self-employed.** Individuals would be able to deduct 100 percent of the cost of their health insurance premiums or receive the applicable credit, whichever is greater. (Current law is 25 percent.)

## THE INSURANCE MARKET

### Basic Benefits

● States would work with private insurers to develop basic health insurance benefit packages that matched the price levels of the tax credit.

● Health insurers would be required to insure all groups that want to buy health insurance. Coverage would be guaranteed and renewable.

● Pre-existing conditions clauses that limit coverage during the first months with a new employer would no longer be allowed.

### Health Insurance Networks

● The plan would establish networks of small business groups to reduce costs of administering health insurance policies. It would exempt insurance sold through networks from state premium taxes, coverage mandates and laws restricting managed care arrangements. This would enable small companies to purchase less expensive health insurance than is currently available.

### Mandated Benefits

● The plan would prohibit states from passing laws requiring health insurance to include specified benefits or

"We are beyond just supporting things by word of mouth because we're in it too deep," said Nancy L. Johnson, R-Conn., a member of the Ways and Means Subcommittee on Health and a longtime player on health issues.

As a result, the White House made an abrupt about-face. Portions of the president's address were hastily rewritten. The budget, which had been moved up from its regular Feb. 4 release date to help Bush present a double assault on domestic policy, was nearly delayed as government presses came to a halt.

Copies already printed were called back and the health provisions excised. The new book contained only a few paragraphs of generalities on health-care reform.

The White House also rescheduled the unveiling of "the

president's comprehensive health plan" for a speech in Cleveland Feb. 6.

The 94-page administration "white paper" ultimately unveiled was full of assurances that the estimated 36 million Americans who lacked health insurance would be able to get it, and that a system projected to cost more than $800 billion in 1992 would soon come under control. *(Highlights, this page)*

The president's plan also promised that no new taxes would be needed to pay for the potential new cost to the Treasury, which White House budget officials estimated to be $100 billion over the next five years.

And the plan made clear Bush's oft-stated predilection for building on the existing system, which he called "the best in the entire world," rather than overhauling it or

# ... Highlights and Proposals

coverage provisions that "unduly limit flexibility for health plans."

## Insurance Affordability

● Premiums that insurers charge for similar policies sold to companies in a single block of business could vary by no more than 50 percent.

● The plan would phase in a health-risk adjustment across insurers, removing premium disparities and allowing for plan flexibility.

## CONTAINING COSTS

### Malpractice

● The plan would "encourage" states to revise malpractice laws by eliminating joint and several liability for punitive damages; capping punitive damages; eliminating rules that permit double recovery; and promoting pretrial alternatives to going to court.

● It would promote alternative dispute resolution and discourage litigation. A party that refused to participate in mediation or another alternative and subsequently lost in court would have to pay the other party's attorney fees.

### Administrative Costs

● The plan would standardize claims procedures by encouraging use of a single, universal insurance claim form and electronic billing systems.

● It would streamline medical review of claims, focusing on patterns of inappropriate use of medical resources.

### Coordinated Care Incentives

● It would encourage more coordinated care options in Medicare and Medicaid by having individuals obtain care through health maintenance organizations or other forms of managed care.

● It would exempt certain health plans from state laws restricting coordinated care in the private sector.

### Patient Responsibilities

● The president would increase spending for federal primary and preventive care services, such as community and migrant health centers, which provide primary care,

and the National Health Service Corps, which places health professionals in medically underserved rural and inner-city areas.

● It would encourage people to use safety belts, stop smoking, maintain healthier diets and get more exercise to lower the rate of preventable illness and injury.

● It would improve consumer information with new federal guidebooks on insurance options.

## HOW TO PAY

### Governmental Cost

● The White House estimates that the tax credits and deductions would cost the federal government $100 billion over the next five years and $35 billion in 1997, when they would be fully phased in. Bush officials have declined to break down costs by year before 1997.

### Suggested Offsets

● The plan proposes no specific sources to offset the costs, although the administration claims that savings from the above cost-containment provisions and from Medicare and Medicaid changes, detailed below, "will yield public-sector savings that would be sufficient to offset" the credit and deduction costs.

● **Medicare.** It would eliminate "disproportionate share" payments to hospitals serving high numbers of patients with no insurance coverage. The plan says such payments, projected to total $2.3 billion in fiscal 1992, would be less necessary with more coverage available. Bush also proposed phasing down special payments to teaching hospitals (estimated to cost $3.2 billion in fiscal 1992). Congress has repeatedly rejected the latter proposal.

● **Medicaid.** The most dramatic proposal in the package would eliminate the open-ended entitlement status for most of the acute-care portions of Medicaid, the joint federal-state health program for the poor.

Medicaid coverage for institutional care for the elderly and disabled and for elderly recipients who are also eligible for Medicare would not be affected.

The remainder of the program would be converted to a lump sum, based on each state's total per capita costs in 1992 and adjusted after that for inflation.

---

turning to some form of government-run system, as most Democrats supported.

The central feature of Bush's plan would expand low-income individuals' and families' access to private health insurance by means of a new voucher system based on tax credits, which reduced taxes owed. Middle-income earners who paid their own premiums would also receive relief through new tax deductions, which lowered taxable income.

The vouchers would be used to buy health insurance or offset the cost of insurance plans. Those with incomes too low to pay taxes would receive vouchers equal to the maximum tax credit: $1,250 for individuals, $2,500 for married couples and $3,750 for families of three or more.

"My plan puts the emphasis on expanding access while

preserving choice people now have over the type of health-care coverage and health care they receive," Bush said in his speech before the Cleveland Chamber of Commerce.

But if the Bush plan was long on ambition and scope, it was short on details that would prove controversial to any one of the many interest groups that had a stake in the current system. That included health-care providers, insurance companies and businesses as well as patients.

The lengthy document left key questions unanswered about what sorts of insurance plans would be available and how the system would be administered.

And in the most telling acknowledgment of the obstacles before it, the Bush plan also finessed the touchy issue of financing. It talked fuzzily about streamlining the insurance market and reducing government red tape to lower

the cost of health care. But it avoided specifying how to offset the $100 billion in revenues that would be given up in the next five years by the tax credits and deductions, offering only vague suggestions about reducing the cost of Medicare and Medicaid, the federal health-care programs for the elderly and the poor.

### Democrats Blast Bush's Plan

Democrats immediately blasted Bush's plan, arguing that unlike his previous, successful efforts on clean air and child-care legislation, the president had no intention of trying to pass a comprehensive health bill.

"This is not a proposal to deal with the problem of health care," said Senate Majority Leader Mitchell. "This is a proposal to deal with the perception that the president doesn't care about health care."

Even some Republicans doubted how much the plan could reduce health costs. Asked what the plan did to control costs, Sen. Bob Packwood, Ore., said it would do "relatively little."

Despite the partisan politicking, the Bush plan included a long list of features common to most of the Democratic plans. Such features included overhauling the private insurance market, emphasizing preventive care, allowing states to design innovative health delivery systems, and addressing the way malpractice cases were handled.

"Here we have a real chance to make tremendous progress," said Sen. John H. Chafee, R-R.I., sponsor of the main Senate Republican bill (S 1936) introduced in November, 1991.

Conspicuously absent from the plan was a proposal from early drafts that would have helped finance the plan's new tax credits and deductions by taxing high-income workers on a portion of employer-provided health insurance.

### Benefits Tax Ousted

Although it would have raised significant sums towards offsetting the total costs of the plan, the proposal to tax health insurance was put in the round file after howls from Republican House members.

Bush probably saved himself a headache by leaving the proposal out. Although it had the potential to reap considerable savings from well-off taxpayers — the exclusion from taxes of health insurance premiums was projected to cost the federal government $37.7 billion in fiscal 1992 — taxing fringe benefits had long been one of Congress' hottest hot-button issues.

The benefits tax was anathema both to organized labor, whose members had long given up wage increases in favor of rich benefit packages, as well as employers, who also reaped tax savings from providing health insurance to their workforces.

The last time Congress tinkered with the taxability of health insurance was in the case of the infamous Section 89, a provision of the 1986 tax bill that sought to prevent companies from giving higher-paid workers richer fringe benefits. Workers with "discriminatory benefits" were required to pay income taxes on the value of such perks. But the test to determine if companies were discriminating was so complicated that business groups revolted, and Congress repealed the provision in 1989. *(1989 Almanac, p. 341)*

In 1987, Reps. Pete Stark, D-Calif., and Bill Gradison, R-Ohio, chairman and ranking Republican, respectively, of the House Ways and Means Subcommittee on Health, tried to finance an early version of the Medicare Cata-

strophic Coverage Act by taxing the value of the portion of Medicare that the federal government subsidized. They were forced to abandon the proposal after complaints from both Democrats and Republicans. *(1987 Almanac, p. 493)*

Ironically, the abandoned Bush proposal was nearly identical to a plan put forth by the Treasury Department in 1984, when Congress was beginning the deliberations leading up to the 1986 tax reform bill.

After protests from Packwood, among others, the proposal was altered in the plan President Reagan brought to Congress in 1985.

"If taxation of employee benefits is in the bill, that in itself will make the entire bill unacceptable to me," said Packwood, then chairman of the Finance Committee.

Ultimately, like the Bush plan, the benefits tax was dropped altogether.

In the end, Bush may have accomplished his political mission by finally putting his name on a government-led proposal for change. Yet by declining to put the weight of his office behind a detailed legislative package, the president probably assured that the conflict in Congress would continue right to Election Day in November. His proposal did not alter the political dynamic as much as perpetuate it.

"Health-care reform really is a no-win issue for a politician," said James S. Todd of the American Medical Association. "Because to make it come out right, you either have to reduce benefits or raise taxes, neither of which is going to win you votes."

## BENTSEN'S INCREMENTAL MEASURE

The Senate Finance Committee was the next to act, approving as part of a hotly contested tax bill the most sweeping health-care proposal put forward since its ill-fated Medicare Catastrophic Coverage bill in 1987. *(Highlights, p. 402)*

The core of the proposal sought to reshape — through federal regulation — the private insurance market for small businesses. It would have limited the cost of health insurance policies for businesses with 50 employees or less and prohibited insurers from denying coverage to employees or their dependents.

The proposal also would have allowed self-employed individuals to deduct 100 percent of the costs of their health insurance instead of the existing 25 percent — a provision that would cost the Treasury an estimated $3.6 billion over two years.

Offered by Finance Chairman Bentsen, as part of the committee's 1992 tax bill, the health-care provisions were a slightly revised version of a bill (S 1872) he introduced in 1991. While the proposal did not go nearly as far as many of the other Democratic bills under consideration, Bentsen's "incremental" measure still would have represented a significant assertion of federal control into the private marketplace.

Yet the health-care proposal received scant attention amid the election-year melee in Congress over tax relief for the middle-class. The Finance Committee on March 3 approved the tax bill on a party-line vote of 11-9. No one on the committee raised an objection or sought to amend the health provisions. *(First tax bill, p. 133)*

Bentsen said he was surprised but not unhappy that the health provisions slipped through essentially unnoticed. "That's all right with me, as long as I get the bill through," he said.

# Health Provisions in Tax Bill

*Following are the major health provisions of the tax bill approved by the Senate Finance Committee on March 3:*

Beginning on Jan. 1, 1994, for most states, the bill would establish minimum federal requirements for state laws governing the sale of health insurance to businesses with two to 50 employees. (States whose legislatures meet only every two years would be given extra time.) The requirements would be developed by the National Association of Insurance Commissioners. Among them:

● Insurers could not exclude individuals in a group from coverage and could not cancel policies due to claims experience or health status.

● Insurers would be prohibited in most cases from denying coverage due to pre-existing health conditions.

● Annual increases in premiums for small-employer health plans would be limited to no more than 5 percent over the underlying increase in health-care costs.

● New requirements would limit the amount by which insurers could vary premiums for different groups. Generally, the bill would prohibit "medical underwriting," the process by which insurers assess risk according to the current health status of members of a group, their occupation and claims filed in the past.

● Premiums could only vary within specific price bands, although insurers could still vary premiums according to age, sex and geographic region.

● The General Accounting Office (GAO) would be required to report on the impact of the rating restrictions on the price and availability of insurance for small businesses.

● Insurers violating standards would be subject to a federal excise tax equal to 25 percent of premiums received on policies sold to small businesses.

● Insurers offering coverage to small employers would have to offer at least two insurance packages, which would otherwise be exempt from state mandates that certain services be covered.

The more generous "standard benefit" package is defined in the legislation. It includes physician, hospital, mental health and preventive services, and dental, podiatrist and optometrist care.

States would be allowed to define their own "basic benefit" package, which could be less generous and require larger deductibles and copayments, although it would have to include some limit on out-of-pocket spending.

## SELF-EMPLOYED HEALTH INSURANCE PREMIUMS

The bill would allow self-employed individuals to deduct 100 percent (up from 25 percent) of the cost of health insurance premiums for federal income tax purposes, beginning Jan. 1, 1993.

Companies may now deduct 100 percent of health insurance premiums.

The provision would expire at the end of 1994; the 25 percent deduction in current law expires in June 1992.

## OUTCOMES RESEARCH

The bill would significantly increase authorized funding for the Agency for Health Care Policy and Research, created in 1990 legislation to study the effectiveness of various forms of medical care. The bill would authorize $225 million in fiscal 1993, $275 million in fiscal 1994 and $300 million in fiscal 1995, up from originally authorized amounts of $148 million and $185 million in fiscal 1993 and 1994, respectively.

The agency would be required to emphasize producing practice guidelines for clinical treatments and conditions that significantly affect national health costs.

## COST COMMISSION

The bill would establish an 11-member Health-Care Cost Commission, which would collect and report data associated with public and private health costs in the United States and internationally, and make recommendations for health-care cost containment.

## MEDICARE PREVENTIVE SERVICE BENEFITS

The bill would expand Medicare, the federal health insurance program for the elderly and disabled, to cover annual flu shots and vaccinations for tetanus and diphtheria every 10 years.

The bill would also allow Medicare coverage for routine medical checkups of the 300 or so children currently covered by Medicare because they suffer from serious kidney disease.

Unlike most private insurance plans, Medicare is almost exclusively an acute-care program and pays for only very limited preventive services.

As introduced, the measure would have covered tests for early detection of colorectal and breast cancer, but the provisions were dropped from the bill for cost reasons.

The bill would authorize demonstration projects to test the feasibility and desirability of providing other preventive services through Medicare, including screening for glaucoma, high cholesterol levels, osteoporosis, and a one-time physical assessment for all Medicare beneficiaries between ages 65 and 75.

## MANAGED CARE

The bill would establish a program of voluntary federal certification of managed-care plans — entities that oversee both the financing and provision of health services to members — and of utilization review programs that oversee the appropriateness of treatment decisions that are made by doctors and other health professionals.

States would be barred from passing laws restricting the activities of federally certified plans.

In fact, there was little to argue about, since both Republicans and Democrats agreed on the broad outlines of efforts to reshape the insurance market for small business, as well as most of the bill's other provisions.

Indeed, in a year when debate over health care grew increasingly partisan, S 1872 was Congress's only major bipartisan proposal. Its lead cosponsor was Sen. Dave Durenberger of Minnesota, ranking Republican on the panel's Medicare subcommittee and a leading health expert in the Senate. Nine of its 24 cosponsors were Republicans. And President Bush's own health overhaul plan included several provisions lifted almost verbatim from the measure.

In fact, there was considerably more dissent on the Democratic side, with some members uncertain about the wisdom of proceeding with Bentsen's incremental approach to health reform.

The bill "is a very, very small step," said Wellstone, who unveiled his own sweeping health overhaul bill on March 5.

Bentsen opted to proceed anyway. "I do not look on it as a substitute for total health-care reform. I do not look on it as an obstacle to total health-care reform," he said at a National Press Club luncheon March 4. But, he added, because "I know that we're not going to have comprehensive health-care reform this year . . . we tried to do what we could in the Finance Committee."

There was virtually no disagreement about most of the bill's health-care provisions, including the most costly one: to put the self-employed on the same footing as employers in the tax treatment of health insurance premiums.

Similarly, no disagreement surfaced over provisions to expand preventive care services offered under Medicare, the federal health insurance program for the elderly and disabled, or to beef up the role of the federal agency charged with assessing the cost-effectiveness of medical treatments and services.

And, in a fairly dramatic turn of events, both Democrats and Republicans signed on to the concept of federal regulation of insurance — traditionally a state role. The federal government first tiptoed into the waters of health insurance regulation with 1988 and 1990 bills to tighten what had been voluntary federal standards for "Medigap" policies designed to supplement Medicare coverage. *(1990 Almanac, p. 572)*

The insurance industry opposed the Medigap bills as an unwarranted federal intrusion, but its support of efforts at federal intervention in the small-group area was an indication of how far the debate moved in only two years.

Insurers "know the alternative is [for Congress] to go to Canada or some other approach on more sweeping health reform, said Durenberger. Under the Canadian system, the federal government paid all the nation's health bills, leaving no role for private insurance.

But experts expressed doubts that S 1872 or any other of the various small-group insurance proposals would be able to make health insurance at once more available and more affordable.

Consumer groups wanted to require so-called "community rating," under which insurers would charge everyone the same price.

The limits on price variation in Bentsen's proposal, which allowed differences for age and sex, "leave small employers with significant financial incentives to avoid hiring women, older workers and disabled people," according to Judith Waxman, director of government affairs for Families USA, a Washington consumer advocacy group.

Furthermore, said Waxman, under the leeway in the bill, insurance companies would still have been able to entice lower-risk groups with low premiums but then "raise rates when the group is no longer young and healthy."

The insurance industry believed the opposite was true: that the Bentsen price limitations were too stringent. The requirement that insurers accept all comers while limiting how much premiums could vary would drive up costs for those who could currently afford insurance, they maintained.

"Community rating is Robin Hood in reverse — taxing the younger employee groups getting started to pay the costs for well-established firms with mature workers," said Bruce Butler, representing The Travelers insurance group.

And even if Congress did find a midpoint at which coverage would be available to all at a price many could afford, studies suggested that small employers might still opt not to offer workers plans.

A study in the Feb. 19 Journal of the American Medical Association of the first year of a New York State program that subsidized half the insurance costs for small businesses found that insurance coverage rose by only 3.5 percent. Even if all businesses were made aware of the program, said the study's authors, the proportion of firms offering insurance would be unlikely to rise by more than 16.5 percent.

The Senate passed the tax bill with the Bentsen health plan in it, but the proposals were dropped in House-Senate conference when House members objected.

## OTHER PROPOSALS

In the meantime, other major proposals were being added to the pile of those under serious consideration.

### Wellstone's 'Single Payer' Bill

The same week the Finance Committee was marking up Bentsen's bill, Wellstone unveiled a version of a Canada-like "single payer" bill (S 2320) as a companion to a House bill (HR 1300) introduced in 1991 by Rep. Marty Russo, D-Ill.

"A national health insurance program is the simplest, most efficient, most equitable way to reform our health-care system," said Wellstone. "There is no more effective approach than single-payer."

The single-payer plans would effectively have eliminated the private insurance industry, making the federal goverment responsible for paying all medical bills. They would have covered virtually all medical services, including long-term care, with no required premiums, deductibles or copayments. Cost control would have come via strict annual budgets and fee schedules for medical services negotiated between government agencies and health-care providers.

The plan was to be financed by a series of tax hikes, including increases in personal and corporate income taxes and taxes on Social Security benefits. But sponsors maintained that even with the tax increases, most people would have seen a net decrease in their out-of-pocket health costs.

### Managed Competition System

At the other end of the spectrum, the Conservative Democratic Forum, a group of 60 conservative and moderate Democrats, on April 8 unveiled its approach to health-care reform.

The group's proposal — which was not translated into bill form until September — sought to create a "managed competition" system in which consumers could shop for health services on the basis of price and quality. Medicaid, the joint federal-state health program for the poor, would have been expanded to cover everyone with incomes at or below the

# Highlights of House GOP Bill

*Legislation introduced June 4 by House Republicans (HR 5325) closely resembled both the plan put forward by President Bush in February and the one Senate Finance Committee Chairman Lloyd Bentsen, D-Texas, was promoting. Bentsen's plan was approved by the Finance Committee as part of the tax bill vetoed in March. Here are the major provisions of the House Republican plan:*

## SMALL-EMPLOYER INSURANCE

Like the Bush and Bentsen plans, the bill would set federal requirements for health insurers aimed at making plans both more available and affordable to those who work for small companies. It would limit coverage exclusions for people with pre-existing health problems and for small groups with a history of high medical bills. The bill would also limit annual premium increases and premium differences among small groups. Insurers would have to offer at least two plans, one providing only "essential medical and preventive benefits" and the other a more generous package. But plans would otherwise be exempt from state mandates that certain services be covered.

## SELF-EMPLOYED
## HEALTH INSURANCE PREMIUMS

Like the Bush and Bentsen plans, HR 5325 would allow self-employed people who purchase their own insurance to deduct 100 percent of their premium costs from their taxable income. At the time, corporations could deduct all premium costs for employees, but the self-employed could take only a 25 percent deduction, and even that was scheduled to expire June 30.

## COMMUNITY AND RURAL HEALTH

The bill would authorize an additional $300 million annually over the next five years for the expansion of the federal community health center program. Such clinics provide basic primary care for medically underserved populations, primarily those with low incomes, but also those who live in rural or remote areas. The program received a $527 million appropriation in fiscal 1992. The bill would also provide community health center professionals with malpractice coverage under the Federal Tort Claims Act. That would reduce costs for malpractice insurance, freeing funds for patient care.

In provisions aimed at improving rural health care, the bill authorized a series of grants to train emergency medical personnel, develop air transport systems to move patients to medical facilities, and to improve telecommunication links between rural and urban hospitals. The bill would also reauthorize a program providing extra Medicare payments to rural hospitals to offset higher costs for serving a larger proportion of Medicare patients than urban and suburban facilities.

## MALPRACTICE

The bill went even further than the Bush proposal to reduce health costs arising from doctors practicing "defensive" medicine and to control rising malpractice premiums. (The Bentsen bill included no malpractice section.) The most sweeping provision would require all medical liability disputes to be handled first through a dispute resolution process (such as arbitration or mediation) before plaintiffs could go to court. It would limit attorney fees, cap damages for pain and suffering, and require that any punitive damages be paid to the state, with funds going to programs to reduce malpractice incidents. Like both the Bush and Bentsen plans, the bill would also increase funding for the Agency for Health Care Policy and Research, which studied medical care effectiveness.

## "MEDISAVE" ACCOUNTS

Unlike the Bush plan, the House Republican bill did not include sweeping new tax credits to enable low-income people to purchase insurance. But it would authorize individual "Medisave" accounts — an attempt to include consumers in health-cost containment. Under the program, employers could make tax-deductible contributions to employee accounts. Workers could then use the money to purchase insurance and pay other medical costs. The incentive to contain costs was that leftover funds, if any, would accrue to the employee as regular taxable income.

## STANDARDIZED CLAIMS PROCESSING

The bill, like the Bush plan, sought to reduce administrative costs for health care by mandating standardized forms and increasing the use of electronic billing systems. It would also require the use of Social Security numbers for all medical claims and require hospitals, physicians and insurance companies to use uniform reporting standards.

## PHYSICIAN REFERRALS

The bill picks up on an initiative first pushed in 1989 by Rep. Pete Stark, D-Calif., that would prohibit, in most cases, patient referrals to health facilities in which referring physicians have an ownership or investment interest. Studies had found repeated instances of increased use of laboratories, medical imaging and physical therapy clinics and other facilities owned by referring doctors. *(Background, 1989 Almanac, p. 167)*

poverty line.

"We agreed that improvements needed to be made in the affordability and accessibility of health insurance for Americans," said the group's chairman, Charles W. Stenholm, D-Texas. "But we were not convinced that it is necessary to destroy our private enterprise system of insurance and health delivery, nor is it necessary to put thousands of Americans out of work by burdening their small-business employers to the point where they were forced out of business."

Members did endorse one financing option others had shied away from. The proposal included a plan to eliminate employers' tax deductions for the cost of health insurance over an amount deemed sufficient to provide a "basic" package of services.

Since the definition of "basic" was not yet set, no estimate was available for how much the proposal would raise. But Rep. Michael A. Andrews, D-Texas, one of the plan's authors, said it was safe to assume it would account for "several billion dollars."

### Michel's Bill

On June 4, House Minority Leader Robert H. Michel, R-Ill., introduced a bill (HR 5325) that 82 of the party's 166 representatives signed onto as cosponsors. The bill also had the blessing of the Bush administration.

Like the Bush and Bentsen plans, the bill would have set federal requirements for health insurers aimed at making plans more affordable and available to those who worked for small companies. It would limit coverage exclusions for people with pre-existing health conditions and for small groups with a history of high medical bills. And it would limit annual premium increases and premium differences among small groups.

Other areas addressed by the measure included malpractice insurance and increased access to community health facilities.

"We are absolutely convinced that this package can be enacted now," said Bill Gradison, Ohio, ranking Republican on the Ways and Means Subcommittee on Health and the party's leading health expert. *(Highlights, p. 409)*

### Dingell-Waxman Bill

On June 30, two more health policy heavyweights joined the fray. That day, Reps. John D. Dingell, D-Mich., and Henry A. Waxman, D-Calif., who chair, respectively, the House Energy and Commerce Committee and its Subcommittee on Health and the Environment, introduced HR 5514.

The Dingell-Waxman bill envisioned full-fledged national health insurance. It would have combined a single payer, the federal government, with a delivery system heavily dependent on managed care, an approach favored by many conservatives. It would have been financed primarily through a new value added tax (VAT), the equivalent of a national sales tax, on most goods and services.

## WAYS AND MEANS ACTION

The only formal action of the year in the House on health reform came June 30, when the Ways and Means Subcommittee on Health by voice vote approved HR 5502, a "first step" bill backed by the leadership that would have imposed national limits on health spending and expanded access to health insurance for pregnant women, children and those who worked for small businesses. *(Highlights, p. 411)*

The heart of the Ways and Means subcommittee bill was its cost-containment section, which called for Congress

to set national limits on health spending that would gradually have reduced health-care inflation to the growth rate of the overall economy.

The key element of the plan would have set maximum payment levels for doctors, hospitals and all other health-care providers, services and products.

House leaders, particularly Majority Leader Richard A. Gephardt, D-Mo., said they hoped that the focus on cost control would unite Democrats who disagreed on how to reshape the health-care delivery system, while at the same time differentiating them from the Republicans.

The best thing about the bill, Stark said, was that "it is designed to prejudice no major proposal." Rather, he said, it was a first step that could lead to a full-blown national health insurance system, an employer-based system or some hybrid.

Democratic leaders also hoped the bill would resonate with voters, who told pollsters all year of their deep concern about the problems of the health-care system but showed only a very limited understanding of complex legislative proposals.

"It's not hard at all to explain," Gephardt said of the Ways and Means bill. "All you have to do is pull out these charts that show how fast costs are going up. Everybody understands that."

But the bill had political drawbacks, too.

A key one, noted Stark, was that in proposing national spending limits, "we've absolutely solidified our opposition. The doctors don't like it. The hospitals don't like it. The drug companies don't like it, and the insurance companies don't like it."

Republicans didn't like it either. "Trying to let the government run our health-care system would be an absolute nightmare," Bush said.

On the other hand, liberals who did not mind taking on some of Congress' most powerful special interests did object to the fact that the bill would not have guaranteed all Americans access to health insurance coverage.

Even the upbeat Gephardt acknowledged that omission. "Sometime, I hope soon, we'll be able to guarantee every American access to high-quality, affordable health care," he said. "In the meantime we intend to get started."

But there was one serious problem: Few Democrats seemed willing to vote for the bill. The first time the 23 Ways and Means Democrats discussed the measure June 3, said Stark, only about seven said they would support it.

The trouble, he acknowledged, is that members were loath to vote for a bill that would surely incur the wrath of the powerful community of medical providers but at the same time do little to expand access to health insurance for those who lacked it.

Said Ways and Means Democrat Thomas J. Downey, D-N.Y., "It's not a bad idea, but normally when you have a lot of bad things, you have good things, too. In this case, you just have things against you."

In the end, the doubters won out. The full Ways and Means Committee never marked up the measure and it died with the end of the Congress.

## SECOND TAX BILL ACTION

Senators made one final and unsuccessful attempt to tackle the health issue during the September consideration of the year's second tax bill, HR 11. *(Urban aid tax bill, p. 140)*

The amendment, offered by Bentsen and Durenberger, was virtually identical to language included in the Senate

# Ways and Means Bill Highlights

*According to House Majority Leader Richard A. Gephardt, D-Mo., the rationale behind HR 5502, the Health Care Cost Containment and Reform Act, was that it represented a "first step" toward addressing the nation's health-care problems. Most Democrats could support it, Gephardt said, because it did not preclude future action on the more comprehensive proposals Democrats had yet to agree on.*

*The bill shared key elements with "incremental" plans like the one approved by the Senate Finance Committee in March and those advanced by President Bush and House Republicans (HR 5325). But unlike those plans, it also included strict cost controls that were anathema to most Republicans and some Democrats as well.*

*These are some of the key provisions of the bill approved July 1 by the Ways and Means Subcommittee on Health:*

## COST CONTAINMENT

The bill would establish national health budgets to control health-cost inflation. Spending would be controlled by three mechanisms: creating optional hospital and physician cost-containment programs that states could design themselves, allowing qualified health maintenance organizations to negotiate rates directly with health-care providers, and establishing maximum payment levels for all providers.

The maximum rates would apply not only to doctors and hospitals but also to nursing homes and to makers of medical equipment and prescription drugs. Annual increases would be gradually limited until 1998, after which annual health spending could grow no faster than the economy as a whole. According to the Congressional Budget Office, the cost-containment provisions would save $114 billion a year by 2002.

## HEALTH INSURANCE REFORM

Like the plans advanced by the Finance Committee, Bush and House Republicans, the bill would establish federal standards to ensure the availability and affordability of insurance for small-business owners and their workers.

The bill would ban blanket denial of coverage to an individual or group because of an existing health condition, and would limit the duration of temporary exclusions for "pre-existing conditions" when people change jobs.

## PREMIUMS FOR THE SELF-EMPLOYED

As in virtually all health overhaul plans, the bill would allow the self-employed to deduct 100 percent of their health insurance premiums from federal taxes. The existing 25 percent deduction limit expired June 30, along with the other tax "extenders."

## ADMINISTRATIVE SIMPLIFICATION

Also like the Finance, Bush and House Republican plans, the bill seeks to lower administrative costs by streamlining and standardizing the health-care insurance claims process.

The bill would mandate creation of a uniform electronic billing system, and would call for patients to be given special cards that would allow immediate verification of eligibility and benefits.

## FRAUD CONTROLS

As in the House Republican bill, the bill includes a proposal (originally pushed by bill author and subcommittee Chairman Pete Stark, D-Calif.) to bar doctors from referring patients to ancillary health facilities, such as laboratories or medical imaging clinics, in which they have a financial interest.

The bill would also establish a national program to detect cases of medical fraud, particularly the filing of false insurance claims.

## BENEFIT EXPANSIONS

The bill would expand coverage under Medicare, the federal health insurance program for the elderly and the disabled, to include outpatient prescription drugs and certain preventive benefits that are not currently covered.

Beginning in 1998, the bill would also expand Medicaid, the joint federal-state health program for the poor, to cover all pregnant women and children up to age 6 in families with incomes up to double the federal poverty level, which is currently $13,950 a year for a family of four.

By 1999, Medicaid would be extended to all children under age 19 in families with incomes up to double the poverty level, and by 2002, to all people under age 65 with incomes up to 133 percent of the poverty level.

Unlike the existing program, which required states to pay between 20 percent and 50 percent of Medicaid costs, the new benefits would be fully federally financed, using savings from the cost-containment provisions.

Finally, the bill would establish a new federal program, with hospital and outpatient benefits similar to Medicare's, for children up to age 19 from families who have no insurance yet are too wealthy to qualify for Medicaid. Families of the children would pay a monthly premium based on the yet-to-be determined cost of the program.

version of HR 4210, the tax bill Bush vetoed in March.

A slightly rewritten version of S 1872, a bill introduced by Bentsen and Durenberger in 1991, sought to make several "incremental" changes in the nation's health care system.

The most significant of the bipartisan-backed provisions would have overhauled the insurance market for small businesses by requiring insurers to make coverage both more available and affordable by limiting rate variations and outlawing exclusions for certain "preexisting conditions" that made many people uninsurable.

Another popular feature would have allowed self-insured individuals to deduct from their taxable income 100 percent of the amount they paid for insurance. The limit was 25 percent.

Bush never got a chance to veto the health provisions of the earlier tax bill because the House opposed them, and Bentsen was forced to strip them out. The version included in HR 11 met the same fate.

"I didn't think it was a good bill when he introduced it and I don't know what he's done to make it any better," said Stark, chairman of the Ways and Means Subcommittee on Health.

Stark said he and other House health policymakers had reached the conclusion that overhauling the small group insurance market in the absence of other changes would have been "counterproductive," because it would have raised rates for more businesses than it would have lowered them for.

Bentsen, however, didn't have much choice about whether or not to include the provisions in HR 11. Republicans had made it clear if Bentsen didn't put in his own plan, they were prepared to offer their own.

"We were determined to go forward," with or without Bentsen's help, said Chafee, sponsor of a Republican consensus bill, S 1936, that included many provisions similar to those in S 1872. ∎

# Oregon Health-Care Plan Rejected by Bush

For more than a year, Oregon state officials had been lobbying for federal permission to start up what was widely recognized as an innovative solution to the problem of those lacking health insurance.

Ballyhooing of the experimental plan came to naught Aug. 3, when the Bush administration denied the state's request for a waiver of federal requirements needed to allow the Oregon law to take effect.

While the plan's designers maintained that it was not intended as a model for a national health system overhaul, they hoped the experiment could help clarify issues in the broader debate — particularly the difficulty of controlling costs while broadening coverage.

Under the Oregon Health Plan, passed by the legislature in 1989 and completed in 1991, more than 120,000 low-income Oregonians without health insurance would have gained coverage under Medicaid, the joint federal-state health program for the poor.

In exchange, the services Medicaid covered would have been cut back for new enrollees and those currently served. Decisions on what to offer — and what to exclude — would

have been made based on an elaborately designed priorities list that ranked the costs and benefits of 709 ailments and their treatments (such as surgery for appendicitis).

It was the latter provision that touched off one of the hottest controversies in health circles. Proponents argued that it was better to give a lot of people some care than to give a few people everything.

Critics charged that the Oregon plan amounted to rationing — with those losing out possibly facing death sentences.

The state legislature in 1991 proposed funding the first 587 of the 709 items on the list during the program's first year. Among the maladies that did not make the cut was treatment for extremely low-birthweight infants.

The debate forged some unlikely alliances. Firmly backing the plan was the entire Oregon congressional delegation, including Republican Sen. Bob Packwood and Democratic Rep. Les AuCoin, who faced in a bitter November election for Packwood's seat.

Leading the charge against the plan were Rep. Henry A. Waxman, D-Calif., chairman of the House Energy and Commerce Subcommittee that oversaw Medicaid and Sen. Al Gore, D-Tenn., a former member of Waxman's subcommittee and the Democrats' successful 1992 vice presidential candidate. They objected because the plan would have cut services to Medicaid recipients. Among the organizations opposed to the plan was the National Right to Life Committee, which rarely found common ground with Waxman or Gore.

## Conflict with Disabilities Act

The Bush administration was caught squarely in the middle.

On one hand, Bush officials lauded the plan repeatedly as an embodiment of their desire for states to act as laboratories for new policies. The plan, noted the administration's fiscal 1992 budget, "clearly breaks new ground in seeking to deal with a major problem." It also received favorable comments in Bush's fiscal 1991 and fiscal 1993 budgets.

Officials also wanted to boost Packwood's re-election efforts in his race against AuCoin (which Packwood narrowly won). While both supported the plan, it was Packwood, along with Democratic Rep. Ron Wyden of Oregon, who spearheaded efforts to obtain the waiver of Medicaid laws.

But the plan had negatives, too.

One was its projected cost: more than $100 million in new federal funds, a big problem for an administration trying to trim spending on entitlement programs such as Medicaid.

The biggest problem turned out to be a potential conflict with another Bush-backed initiative, the landmark 1990 Americans with Disabilities Act (PL 101-336), which prohibited discrimination on the basis of health condition. *(1990 Almanac, p. 447)*

"While there are some desirable features to the Oregon Medicaid waiver application . . . we are very troubled by the prioritization process which legitimates the withholding of medically effective treatments" for disabled people, or those who after treatment would be left with a disability, wrote the Consortium for Citizens with Disabilities in a July 24 letter to Bush. The consortium, which included groups such as the Spina Bifida Association of America and the AIDS Action Council, led efforts to enact the antidiscrimination law.

While the disability groups had been trying to make their case since late 1991, a likely turning point was a March 2, 1992, meeting with Bush attended by Robert Powell, a vice president of the National Right to Life Committee. The committee's opposition was based on its stance against euthanasia. Powell, a cancer survivor, told Bush that if the Oregon plan had been in effect when he was sick as a child, he would have died.

The administration based its denial on that conflict. "The record regarding the manner in which the list of condition-treatment pairs was compiled contains considerable evidence that it was based in substantial part on the premise that the value of the life of a person with a disability is less than the value of the life of a person without a disability," said a legal analysis accompanying the official denial letter from Health and Human Services Secretary Louis W. Sullivan to Oregon Democratic Gov. Barbara Roberts.

Oregon officials were upset by the denial, which they had not anticipated.

"If the administration is truly concerned about health-care reform, they could work with the state to resolve these issues," Packwood said.

"I can only conclude that the administration is not sincere about either health-care reform or state experimentation."

And Wyden conceded that efforts to enact the waiver through legislation were unlikely at least for the remainder of the 102nd Congress.

"The administration's objections really go right to the heart of the program," Wyden said. "We may have to go back to the drawing board." ■

# NIH Bills Fall to Fetal Tissue Controversy

Abortion-related controversies prevented Congress from completing work on legislation to reauthorize expiring portions of the National Institutes of Health and make other significant changes to NIH, the nation's pre-eminent biomedical research establishment.

The primary purpose of both HR 2507 (vetoed by President Bush in June) and S 2899 was to reauthorize the National Cancer Institute and National Heart, Lung and Blood Institute, the two largest of NIH's 16 research branches.

Both bills bogged down in controversy because of proposals to increase NIH-funded research of diseases primarily affecting women and to require that women and minorities be included as subjects in NIH-funded clinical trials.

Most controversial were provisions to lift a four-year-old ban on funding research using fetal tissue from elective abortions. The abortion language helped prompt the June 23 veto that the House failed to override.

The Senate took up a slightly pared-down bill (S 2899) on Oct. 2 that would have allowed researchers to try to obtain tissue from special "banks" that would collect samples from miscarriages and ectopic (tubal) pregnancies but not from elective abortions. Members voted 85-12 to limit debate on the motion to take up the measure. But it was ultimately pulled in the face of a continued filibuster threat by anti-abortion senators.

The abortion fight changed course quickly in 1993. True to his campaign pledges, President Clinton issued a Jan. 22 memorandum to remove a 1988 Reagan administration moratorium on research using fetal tissue from elective abortions.

Freed from the politics of the abortion debate, the NIH bill was approved by a Senate panel Jan. 26 with none of the Republican dissent that had stalled the measure in previous years.

The bill (S 1), approved 16-0 by the Labor and Human Resources Committee, would reauthorize through fiscal 1996 the expiring programs within the 16 institutes of NIH. "This is a different political climate," said Orrin G. Hatch of Utah, the Senate panel's ranking Republican and chief opponent of lifting the fetal tissue ban. "My most significant concern ... is now largely moot."

Researchers considered fetal tissue critical in finding treatments or even cures for such illnesses as diabetes, Parkinson's disease and Alzheimer's disease. Those who opposed such research, however, said it would encourage women to have abortions.

The bill sought to codify Clinton's action but also require the secretary of Health and Human Services to set up safeguards governing the conduct of such research. For example, the purchase or sale of human fetal tissue would be prohibited, as would the direct donation of such tissue.

The 1993 Senate bill was very similar to the one cleared by Congress before the Bush veto in 1992. One difference was a new provision to improve the coordination of AIDS research activities among NIH institutes.

## BACKGROUND

Disputes over whether Congress or the executive branch should call the shots for NIH dated back to 1971, when President Richard M. Nixon declared war on cancer. The issue was whether to marshal research resources through NIH's existing National Cancer Institute or to create an agency whose top administrator would report directly to the president. The compromise that emerged in legislation (PL 92-218) kept activities centered at the existing institute but gave its director authority to take annual budget requests directly to the president. (Congress and the Nation, Vol. III, p. 566)

In 1974, Congress made its first foray into the fetal research fray. As part of a reauthorization of NIH training programs (PL 93-348), Congress placed a moratorium on research on "the living human fetus, before or after abortion," unless the purpose was to assure the fetus' survival. The law also created a two-year National Commission on the Protection of Human Subjects of Biomedical and Behavioral Research, which was to recommend whether or how such research was to proceed. (1974 Almanac, p. 379)

The commission concluded that fetal research could be ethically acceptable if safeguards were imposed. The 1975 regulations stemming from commission findings, still technically in effect in 1992, stipulated that research on live fetuses that would pose more than a "minimal risk" to the woman or fetus was permitted only if it was performed to meet the health needs of that specific fetus or pregnant woman. Research on aborted fetuses was allowed, but it could not require any changes in either the timing or method of the abortion.

Starting in 1980, some members wanted to require periodic reauthorization of all of NIH's 11 (there were 16 by the end of 1992) institutes. At the time, only the two largest — the cancer institute and the National Heart, Lung and Blood Institute — required renewal.

Reauthorization plan backers, led by Henry A. Waxman, D-Calif., chairman of the House Energy and Commerce subcommittee that oversaw the agency, said the change would make NIH more accountable to Congress. But opponents, including most of the biomedical research establishment, argued that the plan would make research priorities too vulnerable to pork barrel politics. The plan was ultimately shelved.

Oversight battles came to a head in 1984 and 1985, when President Ronald Reagan vetoed two NIH reauthorizations. Reagan said the 1984 bill included too many "overly specific requirements for the management of research that place undue constraints on executive branch authorities and functions." Bush officials used that same argument to criticize HR 2507. The 1985 bill, said Reagan, included too many "objectionable provisions that seriously undermine and threaten the ability of NIH to manage itself" and would "exert undue political control" over NIH. Bush officials repeated those arguments.

While Congress did not have a chance to respond to Reagan's 1984 veto because it came after members adjourned for the year, lawmakers took charge a year later, overriding Reagan's veto by huge margins — 380-32 in the House and 89-7 in the Senate. *(1985 Almanac, p. 287)*

The issue during Bush's four years in office centered on a funding moratorium imposed in 1988 by Reagan administration health officials on fetal tissue transplantation research using tissue derived from elective abortions. Preliminary results of privately funded fetal tissue research had shown promise for treating a wide variety of thus-far incurable maladies, including not only diabetes but also Parkinson's disease and Alzheimer's disease.

The moratorium was imposed pending a special advisory committee's review of potential ethical concerns. Both the special committee and NIH's permanent advisory panel recommended that funding for the research be allowed if safeguards were instituted to separate a woman's decision to have an abortion from her decision to donate the fetal tissue for research.

But Bush administration officials rejected the advisory groups' recommendations, and in late 1989 they announced that the funding ban would be continued indefinitely.

Opponents of the ban argued that it was wrong to ignore the promise held out by research using aborted tissue. *(Abortion, p. 387)*

---

## BOXSCORE

➡ **NIH Reauthorization (HR 2507, S 2899).** The primary purpose of the legislation was to reauthorize the National Cancer Institute and National Heart, Lung and Blood Institute, the two largest of NIH's 16 research branches. But the bills carried controversial provisions, such as language to increase NIH-funded research of diseases primarily affecting women. Most controversial were provisions to lift a four-year-old ban on funding research using fetal tissue from elective abortions.

**Reports:** H Rept 102-136; S Rept 102-263; conference report H Rept 102-525.

### KEY ACTION

Feb. 5 — The **Senate** Labor and Human Resources Committee approved HR 2507, 13-4.

April 2 — The **Senate** passed HR 2507, 87-10.

May 28 — The **House** adopted the conference report, 260-148.

June 4 — The **Senate** cleared HR 2507, 85-12.

June 23 — President Bush vetoed HR 2507.

June 24 — The **House** sustained the veto, 271-156.

Oct. 2 — The **Senate** voted to limit debate on S 2899, 85-12.

---

"We can't just discard this tissue. We ought to use it," said Paul Simon, D-Ill.

### 1991 Action

Legislation (HR 2507) to reauthorize the two largest of the then-13 NIH branches, lift a Bush administration ban on fetal tissue research and mandate the inclusion of women and minorities in most clinical tests of new treatments or drugs was passed by the House in July but did not advance in the Senate. *(1991 Almanac, p. 346)*

A veto threat was first made when the House Energy and Commerce Committee on June 4 approved the bill on a straight party-line vote of 27-16.

The administration and panel Republicans said their primary problem was that the legislation allowed Congress to micromanage the nation's premier biomedical research establishment.

The struggle with the administration continued July 25 as the House approved HR 2507. The vote was 274-144, a strong showing but short of the two-thirds margin needed to override the promised veto. Many women members were infuriated by the administration's objections to provisions that required NIH to devote more resources to women's health and mandated the inclusion of women and minorities in more of NIH's clinical tests.

### SENATE ACTION

The Senate Labor and Human Resources Committee on Feb. 5 approved the House-passed HR 2507. Although by far the most controversial, the fetal tissue provisions were only a small part of omnibus legislation to reauthorize portions of the National Institutes of Health.

Members approved the bill by a vote of 13-4.

Republicans Nancy Landon Kassebaum, Kan., James M. Jeffords, Vt., and Strom Thurmond, S.C., joined all of the committee's Democrats in voting for the bill. Ignoring the threats, members rejected, 4-13, a substitute fetal research provision offered by Hatch. His amendment called for a study of the feasibility of conducting the research using tissue obtained from miscarriages and ectopic pregnancies, in which the fetus becomes implanted in a woman's fallopian tube instead of her uterus. Such pregnancies, if not terminated, can be fatal to the woman.

Similarly, the committee by voice vote rejected a Thurmond amendment that would have permitted federal funding of fetal tissue transplantation research but would have restricted researchers to use of tissue from abortions performed because of rape or incest, or to save the woman's life.

#### Funding Levels, Women's Health

Although the fetal tissue debate took center stage, the primary purpose of the bill was to renew the portions of

NIH requiring periodic reauthorization. While most of the agency was permanently authorized, the two largest components — the National Cancer Institute and the National Heart, Lung and Blood Institute — were not.

The bill reauthorized both through fiscal 1997, with fiscal 1993 funding set at $2.37 billion for the cancer institute and $1.5 billion for the heart, lung and blood institute. Bush in his fiscal 1993 budget asked for $2 billion and $1.2 billion, respectively.

The bill also tracked the House legislation in providing statutory authority for an Office of Research on Women's Health, which NIH created in 1990 after considerable congressional pressure. The office was to oversee the study of ailments primarily afflicting women. Both the Senate and House bills also mandated the inclusion of women and minorities as subjects in clinical research conducted or funded by NIH.

## SENATE FLOOR ACTION

The research promise of fetal tissue produced two overwhelming Senate votes against the funding ban during consideration of HR 2507.

The key vote came March 31, when the Senate rejected, 23-77, an amendment offered by Hatch that would have slightly modified the ban but retained its principal elements. *(Vote 61, p. 9-S)*

Two days later, on April 2, members approved the NIH bill, including the provision to overturn the funding ban, by 87-10. *(Vote 66, p. 10-S)*

It was uncertain at that point whether the strong Senate vote would lead to the first successful override of a Bush veto. Hatch said the vote on his amendment was, in effect, a free one for senators "because they know the House will sustain the veto."

But Rep. Henry A. Waxman, D-Calif., sponsor of the House bill, said all-out lobbying by groups representing medical researchers and disease sufferers had changed many minds. He predicted the final NIH bill would pass the House by a bigger vote than before.

The only issue other than fetal tissue research to provoke much debate was two proposed surveys of Americans' sexual behavior: one focused on teenagers and the other on adults.

As it had done in the past on sensitive issues, the Senate fudged. It approved one amendment that would allow the studies and another that would bar them. In July 1991, members approved contradictory provisions on parental notification before teenagers could obtain abortions.

The sex surveys, which the Department of Health and Human Services (HHS) had declined to fund even though they were approved through the scientific peer-review process, had been at issue for more than a year. During House consideration of HR 2507, members rejected proposals to forbid funding of the surveys. But two months later, during consideration of the fiscal 1992 Labor-HHS appropriations bill, the Senate adopted a funding ban offered by Jesse Helms, R-N.C., after a motion to kill the proposal failed by a vote of 34-66. *(1991 Almanac, p. 501)*

Because the appropriations measure halted funding for only a year, Helms was back, hoping to permanently bar funding for the two surveys. Helms charged that "the sexual liberation crowd" was backing them in an effort "to cook the scientific facts to legitimize homosexuality and other sexually promiscuous lifestyles." Backers of the surveys said they were needed to help develop effective ways to prevent and combat sexually transmitted diseases, including AIDS.

"There are lives at stake here," said Simon, who offered the amendment to allow survey funding. "We are not going to protect ourselves through ignorance."

Edward M. Kennedy, chairman of the Labor and Human Resources Committee, said Helms' amendment "would politicize the scientific process and undermine our ability to deal with urgent health and social problems."

As so often happened when Helms, the committee's ranking member, and Kennedy faced off, the debate occasionally turned ugly. At one point, after Kennedy refused to read aloud some of the more explicit questions proposed for inclusion in the survey, Helms made a snide reference to his colleague's personal troubles involving charges against his nephew for an alleged rape at the family's estate in Palm Beach. (He was later acquitted.) Said Helms, "These questions may be all right for a nightclub in Miami or Palm Beach at 2 o'clock in the morning on Saturday night, but they are not fit for young children."

The Senate ultimately approved Simon's amendment to allow the surveys by 57-40; it then voted 51-46 to approve Helms' ban as well. Ten senators voted for both amendments. *(Votes 64, 65; pp. 9-S, 10-S)*

### Other Amendments

The Senate adopted a package of amendments to improve NIH's ability to perform in-house research. The package, adopted by voice vote, included amendments by:

● Barbara A. Mikulski, D-Md., to authorize unspecified sums for the "renovation or replacement" of the Warren G. Magnuson Clinical Center in Bethesda, Md., an NIH hospital. It would also authorize NIH to purchase up to 300 acres elsewhere in Maryland for a satellite campus.

● By Mikulski, to order studies of NIH's ability to recruit and retain support personnel such as nurses and technicians, and of ways to streamline the procurement process.

● By Mikulski, to authorize the establishment of a child-care center for NIH employees.

● By Bob Dole, R-Kan., to authorize $72 million for fiscal 1993 and unspecified sums for fiscal 1994 through 1997 to expand and intensify NIH-funded research on prostate cancer. Dole underwent treatment for the disease in December 1991, joining Ted Stevens, R-Alaska, Helms and Alan Cranston, D-Calif., as senators who had publicly acknowledged such treatment. The amendment would authorize an additional $20 million in fiscal 1992 and unspecified sums thereafter for grants to state and local health departments for prostate cancer prevention and screening programs.

● By Bill Bradley, D-N.J., to authorize $15 million in fiscal 1993, rising to $30 million in fiscal 1996, for studies to improve and develop vaccines to protect against major childhood diseases.

● By Patrick J. Leahy, D-Vt., to authorize $30 million annually in fiscal 1993 through 1999 for grants to develop and operate state cancer registries to collect data on cancer cases. A separate $1 million would be authorized for a study of why certain states had high death rates for breast cancer.

● By Don Nickles, R-Okla., to require HHS to produce an annual report on the 20 illnesses that represented the leading causes of death in the United States and the amount the department spent on research into, prevention of and education about those illnesses.

● By James M. Jeffords, R-Vt., to establish a task force to study the potential for contamination of the homes and family members of workers who were exposed to hazardous substances on the job.

● By Dennis DeConcini, D-Ariz., to increase from five to 10 years the maximum jail term for those found to have violated the bill's ban on the sale or misuse of fetal tissue.

# NIH — The Big Picture

*Most of the debate over the NIH reauthorization bill (HR 2507) centered on its provision overturning the Bush administration's ban on tissue transplant research using the remains of aborted fetuses. But that was only a small piece of a voluminous bill. As agreed to by House and Senate conferees, HR 2507 sought to:*

## Authorizations

• **National Cancer Institute.** Authorize $2.2 billion for fiscal 1993 and unspecified amounts for fiscal 1994-96.

• **National Heart, Lung and Blood Institute.** Authorize $1.4 billion for fiscal 1993 and unspecified amounts for fiscal 1994-96.

• **National Institute on Aging.** Authorize $500 million for fiscal 1993 and unspecified amounts for the subsequent three years. This was the first specific authorization for the aging institute. Previously, only the two largest institutes — for cancer and for heart, lung and blood — required periodic legislative renewal.

## Women's Health

• **Inclusion of women and minorities in research.** Require that women and minorities be included (unless their inclusion was specifically deemed inappropriate) as subjects in all research funded by NIH.

• **Office of Women's Health.** Provide statutory authority for the Office of Research on Women's Health within NIH to ensure that women's health needs were addressed in research activities conducted or supported by NIH.

## Science Fraud

• **Office of Scientific Integrity.** Provide statutory authority for an independent Office of Scientific Integrity to address allegations of scientific misconduct.

• **Whistleblower Protection.** Require regulations to provide protections for those who reported or cooperated in investigations concerning scientific misconduct.

## Protection of Health Facilities

• **New federal crime.** Make it a crime to enter a federally funded health facility to alter or destroy records, release or injure laboratory animals, or damage property.

## Other

• **Contraceptive and infertility research.** Authorize $20 million in fiscal 1993 and unspecified amounts for the following three years to establish and operate research centers to study contraceptives and infertility.

• **Research facility construction.** Authorize $100 million in fiscal 1993 and unspecified amounts for the following three years for the construction, expansion or renovation of public and nonprofit private research facilities.

• **Senior Biomedical Research Service.** Expand from 350 to 750 the number of people who could serve at any one time in the Senior Biomedical Research Service. The service permitted senior clinical or biomedical research scientists to earn salaries higher than otherwise allowed under federal rules.

---

Earlier, on March 31, members by voice vote adopted a Hatch amendment to authorize $7.6 million over three years for NIH to develop a plan for involving pregnant women, infants and children in clinical studies of vaccines to prevent HIV, the AIDS virus.

## CONFERENCE ACTION

The 1992 battle was not the first clash between Congress and the executive branch over which branch should be the dominant force in setting research policy. But rarely had the stakes been so high. On the line was not only Bush's unbroken streak of 16 vetoes that Congress tried and failed to override but also his standing with the anti-abortion community. Both sides agreed that the conference report would be approved easily; the question was whether sponsors could muster the two-thirds majority to signal Congress' ability to override the promised veto.

The administration pulled out all the stops, with President Bush making personal phone calls to wavering members and James O. Mason, the Department of Health and Human Services' assistant secretary for health, making rounds on Capitol Hill.

On May 19, Bush tried to reassure members who supported the research by issuing an executive order to establish a "human fetal tissue bank" to collect tissue for research from miscarriages and ectopic pregnancies, in which the fetus implants itself outside the mother's uterus, threatening both the woman and the fetus.

Many researchers were quick to criticize the "bank" as unworkable, mainly on grounds that tissue in it would be unusable because of genetic flaws or other problems. Other researchers, however, said they felt the bank would aid those studying transplantation.

Also, the "bank" had already been rejected. The order was identical to an amendment rejected by a 23-77 margin when the Senate had considered the NIH bill in April.

### House Remains Anti-Abortion

The House proved once again May 28 that it remained a stronghold for anti-abortion forces. Members failed to provide the two-thirds majority needed to override an expected veto on a bill to lift the administration ban on research using tissue from aborted fetuses.

Although the House adopted the conference report (H Rept 102-525), the margin of victory was smaller than when members voted on the original bill in 1991. The final tally was 260-148. Two-thirds would have been 272. *(Vote 147, p. 36-H)*

Furious lobbying was effective — but for both sides. Fourteen members who voted against the bill in 1991 voted for it May 28. But 16 members switched their votes the other way.

Bill supporters, acknowledging that their chances for an override appeared slim, said they planned to press ahead anyway, if only to force Bush to make an unpopular veto. "He's got to make the decision to tell people with Alzheimer's disease, with Parkinson's disease, with diabetes and with genetic diseases that the research will be stopped that will hold promise for them," said Waxman, the bill's sponsor.

While both sides knew the fetal research provisions would determine the vote, each camp tried to use other aspects of the measure to muster support or opposition.

Backers of the bill stressed its provisions emphasizing

increased research on the health needs of women. "This bill represents the federal government's long overdue realization that women's lives and health really do matter," said Olympia J. Snowe, R-Maine, co-chair of the Congressional Caucus for Women's Issues, which helped write the provisions.

Opponents argued that it was a budget-buster because it would authorize more spending than Bush had sought.

"This is no time to promise the American people more than we can afford," said Jim Ramstad, R-Minn.

But the emphasis was on the fetal tissue funding ban and, specifically, Bush's May 19 executive order to establish the fetal tissue "banks."

Opponents said the order was a politically motivated ploy that could not work in practice. "I can tell you from experience, it just won't work," declared J. Roy Rowland, D-Ga., a physician. Rowland said tissue from miscarriages was often diseased; ectopic pregnancies, in which the fetus was implanted outside the woman's uterus, were medical emergencies that did not allow time to assemble the medical team needed to recover fetal tissue for research.

But ban supporters said the bank should be given a chance. They cited experts, among them NIH Director Bernadine Healy, who supported research using aborted fetuses. "I believe that such a bank with an established and NIH-funded tissue procurement effort will provide a means to continue the transplantation research effort," Healy had written.

### Senate Clears Bill

The Senate cleared the bill June 4, approving the conference report by a vote of 85-12. *(Vote 115, p. 16-S)*

## VETO SUSTAINED

Bush won his seventh straight abortion-related veto fight June 24 as the House came up 14 votes short of the two-thirds majority needed to pass the bill to reauthorize government-funded health research programs and allow researchers to use tissue from aborted fetuses.

Voting 271-156, the House failed to override the June 23 veto of HR 2507. Among his objections, Bush cited a provision that would reverse an administration ban on research that used fetal tissue from elective abortions. *(Vote 222, p. 54-H; veto message, p. 395)*

But both the veto and the ensuing House debate touched on a variety of other issues. Bush and bill opponents called the measure a budget-buster because of its authorization levels, and dubbed as "pork barrel" sections of the bill that would have authorized funds for rehabilitation of research facilities and allowed NIH to purchase land for a new satellite campus in Maryland.

Meanwhile, 26 of the 28 female members in the House supported the bill, and many of them sought to highlight other provisions relating to women's health: requirements to increase NIH-funded research into diseases primarily affecting women and inclusion of women and minorities as subjects in NIH-funded clinical trials.

Many female House members who had been working for gender equity in health research took Bush's veto personally. "I'm very angry today," said Louise M. Slaughter, D-N.Y. "I hope this is the last time we see this demeaning and awful thing of saying to the women in this country, 'You just don't count.'"

At a news conference following the vote, several female members said they were particularly outraged by the floor statement of House Minority Whip Newt Gingrich, R-Ga., whose presentation showed how the bill's requirements for

including women and minorities in clinical trials would dramatically increase the costs of research.

"It's always been cheaper to keep women out of research because we're more chemically complex," said Patricia Schroeder, D-Colo., co-chair of the women's caucus.

"But women are paying for this research, and historically, they have been kept out of it."

## ROUND 2: S 2899

No sooner had House members sustained the veto than sponsors of the measure were announcing a new "compromise" version of the bill, which they vowed to put on Bush's desk before the Republican convention in August.

Waxman, sponsor of HR 2507, described the new bills as a "good-faith effort to meet the president halfway."

The bills (HR 5495, S 2899) would eliminate the provisions authorizing the purchase of land for NIH and the renovation of research facilities, and change most of the specific authorization levels to "such sums as may be necessary," leaving actual funding levels to the discretion of appropriators. Sponsors hoped these concessions would at least remove the budgetary and "pork" objections to the bill.

On the fetal research question, the new bills would require that researchers first attempt to use a fetal tissue "bank" that Bush, in an executive order issued in May, created to mollify some fetal research advocates. The bank would collect tissue from miscarriages and ectopic pregnancies but not from elective abortions.

The wild cards in the debate were the provisions dealing with women's health. They were the product of several years' work by the Congressional Caucus on Women's Issues. Among its findings were that federal research officials had devoted fewer dollars to diseases that primarily afflicted women and that women had been excluded from many studies of ailments that afflicted men and women equally.

Sponsors underscored the importance of the provisions by leaving them funded in the new bills with specific dollar authorizations: $325 million in fiscal 1993 for breast cancer research and an additional $75 million for research into cancers of the female reproductive system.

At the Labor Committee markup on the new bill July 29, Chairman Kennedy said he hoped it would satisfy the administration's concerns, not only on fetal tissue but also on other provisions of the bill.

"This is major legislation that should never have been vetoed in the first place," Kennedy said. "With these good faith revisions, it deserves to be enacted."

But Hatch, the panel's ranking Republican, said the new measure was not much of an improvement.

"Anyone who thinks this bill is not politically motivated is not operating on all cylinders," Hatch said. "We're just spinning our wheels for nothing but politics' sake."

The Bush administration shared that opinion.

"This measure does not represent a compromise but rather another attempt to promote federally funded abortion-dependent research," wrote Health and Human Services Secretary Louis W. Sullivan in a July 28 letter to Kennedy. "It is merely a political construction."

The Senate waited until Oct. 2 to vote on the new measure. The 85-12 vote was sufficient to limit debate on the motion to consider the bill. The cloture vote was needed to avert a threatened filibuster by Hatch. *(Vote 263, p. 34-S)*

However, controversy continued to embroil the measure, and it went no further.  ∎

# Drug Makers To Pay Fees for FDA Reviews

Although an unrelated last-minute snag nearly defeated the bill, Congress approved a groundbreaking measure Oct. 7 requiring manufacturers of most prescription drugs to help underwrite the costs of federal safety and efficacy reviews. President Bush signed the legislation Oct. 29.

Under the measure, makers of prescription drugs and "biologicals," products such as vaccines and blood products, were required to pay both annual "facilities" fees and fees every time they submitted a drug for approval to the Food and Drug Administration (FDA). The facilities fees began at $60,000 and rose to $138,000 in the fifth year. The application fees started at $100,000 and rose to $233,000 in five years. Drugmakers also had to pay a separate fee for each drug marketed, starting at $5,000 and rising to $14,000. Small and start-up companies were allowed to pay reduced or no fees. The FDA promised to use the fees — estimated to raise more than $300 million over five years — to speed up the drug review process.

"The current federal budget situation offers little prospect that adequate resources will be available to the FDA to do the job it should be doing in the years ahead," said Edward M. Kennedy, D-Mass., chairman of the Senate Labor and Human Resources Committee and a lead sponsor of the bill. "Without the additional funds that user fees will provide, the FDA faces the prospect of being unable to keep up with scientific advances, and needed new drugs will be delayed in reaching the public."

## Spat Over Vitamins

The final product, painstakingly negotiated among administration officials, lawmakers and representatives of the affected drug companies, was nearly derailed by a spat between Orrin G. Hatch, Utah, ranking Republican on the Labor Committee, and his former aide, David A. Kessler, head of the FDA and the key mover behind the bill.

Hatch wanted Kessler to back off proposed regulations to implement a 1990 law overhauling food labels and controlling claims that food manufacturers could make for their products. Specifically, Hatch was concerned about the impact of the regulations on makers of vitamins and dietary supplements. The compromise that sprung the user-fee bill called for studies on how such products should best be regulated and included a moratorium until Dec. 15, 1993, on the regulations as they applied to the dietary supplement and vitamin industries.

## BACKGROUND

In moving forward on legislation to require drug companies to help underwrite the costs of federal approval of products, Congress laid to rest a longtime standoff pitting two presidential administrations against Congress and pharma-

---

### BOXSCORE

➡ **Prescription Drug User Fees (HR 6181, formerly HR 5952).** The precedent-setting legislation required prescription drug manufacturers to pay "user fees" to help offset the cost of federal safety and efficacy reviews.

**Reports:** H Rept 102-895.

#### KEY ACTION

**Sept. 17** — The **House** Energy and Commerce Committee approved HR 5952 by voice vote.

**Sept. 22** — The **House** passed HR 5952 by voice vote.

**Oct. 6** — The **House** introduced a compromise bill, HR 6181, and passed it by voice vote.

**Oct. 7** — The **Senate** cleared HR 6181 by voice vote.

**Oct. 29** — President Bush signed HR 6181 — PL 102-571.

---

ceutical manufacturers.

The administrations of Presidents Ronald Reagan and Bush had been pushing since the mid-1980s for drug company "user fees" to help offset the federal Food and Drug Administration's (FDA) costs for approving prescription drugs.

But the matter stalled until key lawmakers — most notably Kennedy, chairman of the Senate Labor and Human Resources Committee, and John D. Dingell, D-Mich., and Henry A. Waxman, D-Calif., chairmen, respectively, of the House Energy and Commerce Committee and its Subcommittee on Health and the Environment — signed on in the summer of 1992.

Until then, pharmaceutical companies and leading congressional Democrats had steadfastly opposed the fees because at least some of the funds would have gone into the Treasury, not back to the FDA.

Previous administration proposals "would have amounted to a tax on innovation" to reduce the federal budget deficit, according to Gerald J. Mossinghoff, president of the Pharmaceutical Manufacturers Association (PMA), the industry's Washington-based trade group.

That was not the case with HR 5952. As approved by the House, the bill imposed fees that would go directly back to the FDA to reduce the time it took the agency to review approval applications.

## LEGISLATIVE ACTION

The bill (HR 5952) moved rapidly from House subcommittee to House passage during one week in mid-September, but Sen. Hatch almost derailed the measure over labeling standards for vitamins, an unrelated issue.

The Senate never acted on HR 5952. As the House prepared to adjourn, members ultimately approved a new bill, HR 6181, a compromise version that addressed Hatch's concerns and made it easier for smaller or start-up companies to have some fees reduced or waived. The Senate cleared HR 6181 in a wrap-up session immediately before adjournment.

## HOUSE ACTION

Moving uncharacteristically fast, the House passed HR 5952 by voice vote Sept. 22, less than one week after it was formally introduced by Energy and Commerce Committee Chairman Dingell.

The House Energy and Commerce Subcommittee on Health and the Environment had approved HR 5952 by voice vote Sept. 15, and the full committee approved the bill two days later with the blessing of the drug industry.

The bill imposed fees that would go directly back to the

FDA to speed up the agency's application review and approval time.

The $327 million that the measure was expected to raise over five years could enable the agency to hire an additional 600 employees, said Waxman, chairman of the health subcommittee. According to FDA estimates, the new workers could help reduce approval time from 20 months to 12 months. "Breakthrough" drugs reviewed under a fast-track procedure could be acted on in as few as six months.

While the proposal was considerably less sweeping than the one put forth in the president's fiscal 1993 budget, it was tentatively endorsed by the administration. A committee aide said administration officials had participated in the negotiations to craft the measure and had given oral assurances of their approval.

A Sept. 14 letter sent jointly to Energy and Commerce Committee Chairman Dingell and ranking Republican Norman F. Lent, N.Y., by FDA Commissioner Kessler, detailed a series of speed-up goals the agency would try to meet using the additional funds.

While preferring its own broader plan, the administration would nevertheless "look favorably upon legislation that moves toward our goal. The committee's proposal under consideration appears to do just that," Kessler had told Waxman's subcommittee in August.

### Tight Budget Prompts Compromise

Drugmakers compromised when they realized that given tight budgets, the FDA was unlikely to gain major new government funding any time soon. The agency's workload, however, was exploding, and the resulting bottleneck in getting drugs approved was hurting the pharmaceutical industry.

Drugmakers had a limited time in which they were the exclusive purveyors of products before generic copies could be marketed. Since patent life for drugs began to run before the FDA approved the product for sale, every delay at FDA reduced a drug's sales window and cost companies potential profits.

One reason for FDA delays was the growing number of new drug applications. In 1980, companies filed 66 applications to begin clinical trials on potential new drugs. By 1991, that had grown to 504 applications.

Similarly, filings for drug approvals (which included data on safety and effectiveness) had ballooned in volume and complexity.

"The average weight of a new drug application in the mid-1960s was approximately three to six ounces," Irwin Lerner, president and CEO of New Jersey-based Hoffman-LaRoche, told the health subcommittee hearing in August. "In contrast, the estimated weight of recent new drug applications — when filed in triplicate — are well over 5,000 pounds. With each new drug application weighing almost three tons, it is no wonder that the FDA is buried in a sea of paper."

But pharmaceutical makers, through the PMA, agreed to the fees only with certain conditions.

First, said the PMA's board, the fees must add to existing FDA appropriations rather than replace existing funds. They must be both "reasonable" in amount and totally dedicated to improving the approval process. Finally, said PMA officials, they must be based on a long-term commitment by the federal government to make specific improvements to the approval process.

As approved by the full committee, the legislation met PMA's test. It also met with bipartisan support from subcommittee members.

"User fees, it appears, are going to be the only way we're going to be able to speed up this process," said Thomas J. Bliley Jr., R-Va.

Agreed Waxman: "We've been struggling for years to find a way to speed up the approval of breakthrough drugs. . . . This bill, if it is enacted, will get lifesaving drugs to people faster."

## SENATE HEARING

But the fast-moving bill ran into a snag in the Senate — threatening hopes for enactment in the waning days of the 102nd Congress.

While Congress and industry representatives had resisted the imposition of such fees for years, both had concluded in the previous few months that fees were the only way to feed more resources to the FDA, whose workload was growing much faster than its funding.

But dissent disrupted what had been a broad consensus because of objections raised by Hatch, ranking Republican on the Senate Labor and Human Resources Committee and a key player in making FDA policy.

At a Sept. 22 hearing, Hatch — a longtime supporter of the user fee concept — said that the process could be moving too fast and that he still had serious reservations.

"We shouldn't move too hastily before we lock ourselves into user fees as a method of increasing FDA funding," Hatch said.

### The FDA Pipeline

At the hearing, FDA Commissioner Kessler — a former Hatch staff member — made an impassioned plea to the committee and particularly to his former boss to pass the user fee bill.

The new fees, Kessler told the committee, were "essential if the FDA is to fulfill its responsibility to ensure that drugs are safe and effective and reach the people who need them. New drugs and biologics that are coming to the FDA for review show potential for the treatment of afflictions for which there currently are no cures. The FDA must be prepared to ensure that those products are safe and effective and to get them approved for use in patients as rapidly as possible."

It took the FDA an average of 20 months to approve applications for new drugs, Kessler testified, and an average of 40 months to approve new biotechnology products. And things were only going to get worse, he said.

"What makes me lose sleep at night is what's in the pipeline," Kessler said, noting that drugs and biotech products already in testing had the potential to increase the agency's workload eight- to tenfold over the next several years.

But Hatch told his former aide that he remained unconvinced of the need for immediate action.

Among the concerns he cited were the potential for fees to be increased by unreasonable amounts by future Congresses or administrations and the lack of assurances in the legislation that the funds actually would speed up the approval process as FDA had promised.

Hatch also expressed concern about the possibility that fees to be paid by each drug manufacturing plant (in addition to fees that would be paid each time a company submitted a drug for FDA approval) amounted to more of a tax than a user fee.

At the hearing, Hatch raised with Kessler an unrelated FDA issue that Hatch had pursued the previous week during consideration of the fiscal 1993 spending bill for the

# Prescription Drug Fees Provisions

*Congress cleared a measure (HR 6181 — PL 102-571) Oct. 7 requiring manufacturers of most prescription drugs to pay "user fees" to help underwrite the costs of federal safety and efficacy reviews.*

*As signed by the president Oct. 29, the law:*

## Title I: Prescription Drug User Fees

● **Authority to assess and use drug fees:** Authorized the secretary of Health and Human Services (HHS) to assess and collect fees from makers of prescription drugs, beginning in fiscal 1993. Fees were to be credited to the Food and Drug Administration's (FDA) appropriations account for salaries and expenses. Exempted from the definition of prescription drugs were blood and most blood products, "crude" allergy extracts (such as those used in allergy shots) and biologic products used to test other biologic products, such as blood. Also exempt were certain products used to speed blood clotting during surgery, "large volume parenterals" such as caloric supplements and electrolyte replacements, and generic copies of previously approved prescription drugs.

● **Human drug application and supplement fee.** Required fees to accompany the submission of applications to the FDA for approval of new drugs. Half the fee was payable when the application was filed; the other half was due 30 days after the agency acted on the application or 30 days after the application was withdrawn. Application fees were as follows: $100,000 in fiscal 1993, $150,000 in fiscal 1994, $208,000 in fiscal 1995, $217,000 in fiscal 1996 and $233,000 in fiscal 1997. Lower fees were imposed for applications for which clinical data on safety and effectiveness were not required or for supplements to existing applications that included clinical data. Those fees were as follows: $50,000 in fiscal 1993, $75,000 in fiscal 1994, $104,000 in fiscal 1995, $108,000 in fiscal 1996 and $116,000 in fiscal 1997.

● **Prescription drug establishment fees.** Required annual fees to be paid by makers of those prescription drugs for which no generic copies were yet available. Only makers who had new drug applications or supplements pending after Sept. 1, 1992, would be assessed. Fees were due by Jan. 31 of each year, beginning in 1993. They were as follows: $60,000 in fiscal 1993, $88,000 in fiscal 1994, $126,000 in fiscal 1995, $131,000 in fiscal 1996 and $138,000 in fiscal 1997.

● **Prescription drug product fees.** Required makers of drugs who had new drug applications or supplements pending after Sept. 1, 1992, to pay an annual fee for each approved drug for which no generic copies were yet on the market. Fees were as follows: $6,000 in fiscal 1993, $9,000 in fiscal 1994, $12,500 in fiscal 1995, $13,000 in fiscal 1996 and $14,000 in fiscal 1997.

● **Small-business exceptions.** Stipulated that prescription drug manufacturers with fewer than 500 employees who did not already have a drug on the market were required to pay only half the application fee. To aid start-up companies, such manufacturers also were permitted to defer fee payment until one year after the application was submitted.

● **Fee waivers and reductions.** Authorized the HHS secretary to waive or reduce fees when such action was "necessary to protect the public health" or when the fees would "present a significant barrier to innovation because of limited resources" available to the drugmaker. This provision was intended to protect the makers of "orphan" drugs, medications for rare diseases. Without government incentives, the cost of developing such drugs typically exceeded profits. The secretary also could reduce fees in cases in which the fee would exceed the cost of FDA review.

● **Limits on fee assessments pending appropriations.** Beginning in fiscal 1994, forbade HHS from assessing fees unless appropriations for FDA salaries and expenses were greater than the amount appropriated in fiscal 1992, adjusted for inflation.

● **Annual reports.** Within 60 days after the end of each fiscal year in which fees were collected, required HHS to submit to the House Energy and Commerce and the Senate Labor and Human Resources committees an annual report identifying progress made toward reducing the time FDA took to process drug applications. Within 120 days of the end of the fiscal year, required a second report detailing how the fees were used by FDA.

● **Sunset.** Provided that authority to assess and collect fees expired Oct. 1, 1997, the first day of fiscal 1998.

● **Animal drug user fee study.** Required a study by HHS, in consultation with manufacturers of animal drug products and other interested people, of whether, and under what conditions, to impose user fees to improve the process of reviewing applications for new animal drugs. The study was to be completed and forwarded to the House Energy and Commerce and Senate Labor and Human Resources committees by Jan. 4, 1994.

## Title II: Dietary Supplements

● **Moratorium.** Prohibited HHS from enforcing provisions of the 1990 Nutrition Labeling and Education Act (PL 101-535) pertaining to dietary supplements and vitamins, minerals, herbs and similar nutritional substances until Dec. 15, 1993.

● **New regulations.** Amended the nutrition labeling act to require promulgation of new regulations regarding dietary supplements, vitamins and other such products by June 15, 1993. Required the regulations to be made final by Dec. 31, 1993.

● **Health claims.** Stipulated that while the moratorium was in effect, the HHS secretary could approve labeling involving health claims with which a significant portion of the scientific community agreed.

● **Recommended daily allowances.** Prohibited until Nov. 8, 1993, implementation of regulations that would alter food labeling standards for vitamins and minerals. The FDA had proposed eliminating the existing requirements for "recommended daily allowances" and replacing them with new standards of "reference daily intakes." The RDI's, as they were called, reflected more recent scientific data showing that people could maintain good health by consuming lower quantities of vitamins and minerals than was previously thought and previously recommended under the RDA's.

● **Reports and studies.** Required HHS, within 30 days of enactment, to submit to the House Energy and Commerce and Senate Labor and Human Resources committees a report detailing the FDA's "enforcement priorities and practices" with respect to dietary supplements, vitamins and other such substances. Required the General Accounting Office to conduct a study, due one year after enactment (with an interim report due six months after enactment), analyzing how FDA used its resources to regulate dietary supplements to prevent deception and risk to the public health. Required the Office of Technology Assessment to conduct a study, due within six months of enactment, of the relationship between the regulation of dietary supplements, vitamins and such substances and health outcomes, with an emphasis on how other countries regulated such products.

departments of Labor, Health and Human Services, and Education. *(Appropriations, p. 651)*

By a vote of 94-1, members added to HR 5677 Hatch's amendment to place a one-year moratorium on implementation of nutrition labeling regulations as they applied to food supplements such as vitamins and herbs. *(Vote 218, p. 29-S)*

Kessler, noting that he was speaking for himself and not for the administration, said he might be amenable to such a moratorium.

The admission was something of a surprise, because the FDA chief had gained national acclaim — and managed to outrage both the food and drug industries — with his unrelenting attacks on questionable health claims.

Hatch agreed later that he might look more favorably on the user fee bill if he got his nutrition labeling moratorium, but a staffer stressed that his concerns about user fees still needed to be addressed. The moratorium, said the aide, "is necessary, but not sufficient."

## FINAL ACTION

After resolving the unrelated dispute over labeling standards for vitamins and other food supplements, Congress cleared a user fee bill Oct. 7.

In a procedure already complicated by the vitamin labeling dispute and the departure of House members during a Senate filibuster Oct. 6, members ultimately approved a new compromise bill, HR 6181. It was introduced in the House before dawn Oct. 6 and passed hours later. The Senate cleared HR 6181 by voice vote Oct. 7.

### Hatch's Vitamin Regimen

Senate approval was held up until the last minute by Hatch, ranking Republican on the Senate Labor and Human Resources Committee.

Hatch, a longtime backer of the user fee concept, used the measure to accomplish another legislative objective — getting the FDA to back off plans to limit health claims that could be made by makers of vitamins and other dietary supplements.

Hatch's interest in the matter was both personal and parochial. Vitamins were an important industry in Utah, and Hatch was an avid user, sometimes offering visitors to his office what one source described as "glasses of green goop."

The amendment Hatch had successfully attached to the Labor-HHS appropriations measure (HR 5677 — PL 102-974) on the Senate floor was dropped in conference. The appended language would have blocked for one year implementation of final regulations for a 1990 nutrition labeling law (PL 101-535) as they applied to vitamins and supplements.

Hatch made it clear that he would not allow the user fee bill through until the vitamin labeling moratorium was addressed — although he stressed that he also had substantive problems with portions of the user fee bill.

In the end, however, changes to the user fee portion of the bill were minimal.

As in the original House bill, manufacturers of prescription drugs and "biologicals," such as vaccines, would be required to pay both annual "facilities" fees, general payments for the use of FDA services, as well as fees every time they submitted a drug to FDA for approval.

Under the bill, all fees — worth about $337 million over five years — would have to be plowed back into the FDA. Commissioner Kessler had promised to use the funds to hire more staff to speed up the time FDA took to review applications. FDA's goals were to cut from 12 months to six the

---

## User Friendly Food Labeling

Victory for consumers was declared at the outcome of a food labeling skirmish raging among several federal agencies. The outgoing Bush administration announced Dec. 2 that most processed foods must include uniform labels that not only showed how much fat each portion contained but also told consumers how that should figure into their diets. The new regulations were required to be in place by the summer of 1994.

"The Tower of Babel in food labels has come down," declared Louis W. Sullivan, secretary of the Department of Health and Human Services (HHS).

Sullivan, along with Food and Drug Administration (FDA) Commissioner David A. Kessler, was a winner in the administration food label war. They had been fighting Agriculture Secretary Edward Madigan about whether the labels should include recommended daily diet information.

The new back panel of labels was to use a format much closer to the FDA's proposal than to the Agriculture Department's idea. While the FDA wanted to include information showing consumers how fat and other food components figured into their diets, the Agriculture Department argued that the FDA's plan was too complicated.

The new regulations were the result of the Nutrition Labeling and Education Act of 1990 (PL 101-535). The bill required HHS to establish definitions for natural, light and low-fat foods. It also said that food processors could not post health claims (such as low-sodium content) on a package unless the label also listed other important nutritional information, such as the amount of cholesterol or fat. *(1990 Almanac, p. 575)*

---

average review time for "breakthrough" drugs, and from 20 months to 12 the time it took to review all other drugs.

The main substantive change in the new bill was to make it easier for smaller or start-up companies to have the facility fee reduced or waived. Several House members and senators had expressed concern that the user fees could block the growth of biotechnology companies, which were at the cutting edge of medical research.

### Another Look at Vitamins Likely

The vitamin compromise delayed the pending regulations until Dec. 15, 1993, similar to Hatch's amendment on the Labor-HHS bill. But it also included more language that would, in the words of one Senate staff member, "put in place a structure to look at this whole thing comprehensively."

The bill, for example, ordered studies into how other countries regulated health claims made for non-drug items and the potential health risks of deceptive claims made for vitamins and dietary supplements.

The measure also continued to allow the FDA to approve certain claims under an existing law, although the agency would be temporarily barred from disapproving claims.

Industry groups had been incensed by FDA's plans to regulate claims they could make for their products, arguing that the regulations would effectively reclassify all of their products as drugs. ∎

# Drug, Mental Health Programs Revamped

A measure to overhaul federal substance abuse and mental health programs — including block grants to states — finally cleared Congress on July 1, after three years of partisan and regional strife.

The legislation reorganized the Alcohol, Drug Abuse and Mental Health Administration (ADAMHA) by essentially disbanding it.

Under the structure signed into law July 10, the agency's three research branches, the National Institute of Mental Health, National Institute on Drug Abuse, and National Institute on Alcohol Abuse and Alcoholism, were folded into the National Institutes of Health, becoming NIH's 14th through 16th institutes. Both ADAMHA and NIH were under the auspices of the Cabinet-level department of Health and Human Services (HHS). Senate sponsors and the Bush administration had pushed for the reconfiguration to bring researchers closer together.

ADAMHA's remaining programs, which administered funds to states to provide treatment and prevention services, were reconstituted as the Substance Abuse and Mental Health Services Administration (SAMSA).

In another major policy change, the existing Alcohol, Drug Abuse and Mental Health block grant program, to be administered by SAMSA, was split into two programs, one for substance abuse and another for mental health. House sponsors, led by Henry A. Waxman, D-Calif., chairman of the House Energy and Commerce Subcommittee on Health and the Environment, had been trying since 1988 to break up the block grant to make states more accountable to the federal government about how the money was spent.

"This has been an extraordinarily difficult, painstaking effort," Edward M. Kennedy, D-Mass., chairman of the Senate Labor and Human Resources Committee and sponsor of the Senate version of the bill, said when conferees came to agreement. Issues that had held up legislation since 1988 included how much flexibility to give states in spending federal mental health and substance abuse dollars and whether to continue to favor states with large cities.

Members also sparred over the issue of tobacco use. They ultimately approved language requiring states to enforce laws prohibiting the sale of tobacco to anyone under

---

## BOXSCORE

➡ **Alcohol, Drug Abuse and Mental Health Reorganization (S 1306, HR 3698).** The bill reorganized the way the federal government underwrote mental health and substance abuse research and services. It disbanded the Alcohol, Drug Abuse and Mental Health Administration (ADAMHA), folding its research branches into the National Institutes of Health and reconstituting remaining programs as the Substance Abuse and Mental Health Services Administration (SAMSA).

**Reports:** H Rept 102-522; S Rept 102-131; conference report H Rept 102-546.

### KEY ACTION

**March 4** — The **House** Energy and Commerce Committee passed HR 3698 by voice vote.

**March 24** — The **House** passed the measure by voice vote.

**May 12** — **House-Senate** conferees approved conference report on S 1306.

**May 19** — The **House** failed 264-148 to muster supermajority needed to approve S 1306 under fast-track procedures.

**May 28** — The **House** voted 214-157 to recommit S 1306 to a House-Senate conference.

**June 3** — New conference report (H Rept 102-546) filed.

**June 4** — Bob Graham, D-Fla., blocked the **Senate** from taking up conference report.

**June 9** — The **Senate** adopted conference report, 86-8.

**July 1** — The **House** cleared measure, 358-60.

**July 10** — President Bush signed S 1306 — PL 102-321.

---

age 18. States that failed to meet the requirements could lose up to 40 percent of their federal alcohol and drug abuse treatment funds. *(Tobacco sales, p. 424)*

The final measure also contained language banning the use of federal funds for "needle exchange" programs to help prevent the spread of AIDS by providing drug addicts with sanitized needles. The House had twice defeated earlier versions of the conference report because they did not include that ban.

The bill authorized $1.5 billion in fiscal 1993 and an unspecified amount in fiscal 1994 for the new Substance Abuse Block Grant. The new Mental Health Block Grant program was authorized at $450 million in fiscal 1993 and unspecified sums the following year. Congress had appropriated $1.36 billion for the combined block grant program for fiscal 1992. States could use block grant funds to support prevention, treatment and rehabilitation services; they could also make grants to community mental health centers serving low-income and other needy people.

## BACKGROUND

Final approval of the measure marked the end of a prolonged battle.

The story began in 1981 when President Ronald Reagan sought to replace many categorical grants with block grants. GOP lawmakers had been pushing block grants since the 1960s as a way of moving decision-making authority back to state and local governments. Some lawmakers, including Waxman, continued to support categorical grants as the best means of ensuring that federal money was spent the way Congress intended. But Congress passed legislation (PL 97-35) that created a number of block grants, including one that combined 10 substance abuse and mental health programs. The Alcohol, Drug Abuse and Mental Health Block Grant was to treat those who suffered from alcoholism, drug addiction or mental illness. *(1981 Almanac, p. 463)*

Members fought for years to control the grant's funding formula to benefit their own states and constituencies, while Waxman and the House fought to split up the block grant.

The House first passed a bill to split the block grant in 1988, as part of an omnibus anti-drug bill. The final mea-

sure (PL 100-690) ultimately reauthorized ADAMHA through fiscal 1991, but the House's block grant proposal was dropped in conference. The funding formula, however, was changed to channel more money to urban areas. *(1988 Almanac, p. 85)*

The House tried again in a 1989 drug bill (HR 3630) to split grant programs, but that bill never made it out of conference. *(1989 Almanac, p. 252)*

For the Senate, in which nearly all members represented rural areas, the priority was to remove the urban bias. In 1990, the Labor panel approved a bill (S 2649) that would have altered the formula. But it died without reaching the Senate floor.

The fight heated up again during the 1991 recession when so many states found their budgets in the red.

### 1991 Action

The two chambers pushed separate legislation in 1991 to reauthorize the big block grant financing treatment of substance abuse and mental illness. While a House subcommittee sought to divide the block grant in two, the Senate wanted to keep it together but alter the formula for distributing money. *(1991 Almanac, p. 348)*

By voice vote, the Senate on Aug. 2 passed a $1.5 billion bill (S 1306) that left the grant intact but revised the funding formula to accommodate members from rural states. Those members argued that abuse of drugs other than cocaine was severe in rural areas and that treatment was needed. The existing formula had been derived from studies that showed more people at risk for drug abuse in urban areas than in rural communities.

A bill (HR 3698) pending before the House Energy and Commerce Committee at the end of 1991 proposed splitting the block grant, establishing one grant for mental health and another for substance abuse. Waxman, chairman of the Health and Environment Subcommittee, said states should be more accountable to Congress for how the money was spent. Republicans argued that states needed more flexibility, rather than less. The subcommittee approved the bill 6-4 on Nov. 6. The bill retained the existing funding formula for substance abuse programs, leaving the urban bias untouched. But Waxman made changes in the formula for mental health grants, based on the number of people at risk. New treatment programs pushed the bill's total above $2 billion.

## LEGISLATIVE ACTION

The House moved early in 1992 to approve legislation splitting up the largest single federal treatment program for substance abuse and mental illness and giving states more specific instructions on how federal money should be spent. Waxman had long opposed the block grant concept, arguing that separating the grants would make states more accountable to Congress.

Although the measure sailed through the House, it ran counter to the preferences of the Bush administration and the Senate. A Senate-passed measure changed the formula under which funds were allocated but otherwise left the block grant intact.

Members declared a truce in a 3-year-old battle the week of May 11, as House and Senate conferees approved an ADAMHA overhaul measure that split the block grant to please the House and changed the funding formula to please the Senate, while accommodating the House. Further objections — mostly from states that stood to lose money under the new funding formula — delayed passage for two months.

## HOUSE ACTION

After compromising on Democratic efforts to force states to outlaw smoking by minors, the House Energy and Commerce Committee on March 4 approved a bill to revise and extend a $1.4 billion block grant program for state alcohol, drug abuse and mental health programs.

The bill (HR 3698), approved by voice vote, sought to split up the federal treatment program for substance abuse and mental health and give more specific instructions to states on how to spend the money.

Sponsored by Waxman, HR 3698 reversed the policy initiated a decade earlier, when the Reagan administration merged funds for programs administered by the Alcohol, Drug Abuse and Mental Health Administration. The goal was to redirect money and power to states and local governments.

The bill established separate grants: $1.1 billion for alcohol and drug abuse programs and $303 million for a Mental Health Services Block Grant.

### Tobacco Interests Prevail

During subcommittee consideration, members hotly debated another Waxman provision to force states to deny cigarettes to minors under 18.

The original bill would have required states to enact laws setting the legal age for buying cigarettes at 18. Missouri, Montana and New Mexico had no law on minors and smoking.

Waxman also wanted to direct the HHS secretary to cut off grants to states that did not enact laws by 1994 and to withhold funding from those that did not enforce the laws.

Republicans won the fight, however, when the panel adopted 11-10 a gutting amendment by Thomas J. Bliley Jr., R-Va., a strong defender of tobacco interests. It barred the secretary from withholding funding from states on the basis of the smoking restrictions.

In full committee, Waxman and Mike Synar, D-Okla., another anti-smoking activist, offered a greatly watered down amendment. It required states to submit a plan to the HHS secretary by fiscal year 1994 showing how they intended to enforce their laws against selling tobacco products to those under 18.

Failure to submit the plans would result in partial loss of federal substance abuse block grant funds — 10 percent in fiscal 1994, 20 percent in fiscal 1995, 30 percent in fiscal 1996 and 40 percent in fiscal 1997.

### House Floor

The full House approved the legislation by voice vote March 24.

The bill (HR 3698) revised and extended the $1.4 billion block grant program for state alcohol, drug abuse and mental health programs through fiscal 1994. Although the measure sailed through the House, it ran counter to the preferences of the Bush administration and the Senate, which in 1991 passed a $1.5 billion measure (S 1306) to change the formula under which funds were allocated but otherwise left the block grant whole.

Waxman opposed the block grant concept because he wanted to make states more accountable to Congress. He said federal substance abuse prevention and treatment programs were inadequate. "The block grant no longer pro-

# Enforcement Required on Tobacco Sales Bans

States were required to enforce legislation barring the sale of tobacco products to minors under legislation signed by President Bush July 10 (S 1306 — PL 102-321) to reauthorize federal mental health, drug and alcohol abuse programs.

All but a handful of states already had laws prohibiting those under a certain age from purchasing cigarettes, chewing tobacco or other tobacco products. But few states made any attempt to enforce those laws, said anti-smoking advocates.

"States have not placed tobacco use in the same category as they've placed use of illegal drugs and even alcohol by minors," said Clifford E. Douglas, associate director of government relations for the American Lung Association.

The legislation, the main purpose of which was to overhaul the agency that oversaw mental health, alcohol and drug abuse research and treatment, also included the first major anti-tobacco provision to emerge from Congress since it banned smoking on domestic airline flights in 1989. (1989 Almanac, p. 749)

But it was also the last such provision to emerge from the 102nd Congress. In exchange for leaving the provision in the final bill, Senate sponsor Edward M. Kennedy, D-Mass., promised lawmakers from tobacco states that he would shelve his other anti-smoking legislation. That meant that Kennedy, who headed the Senate Labor and Human Resources Committee, would not press for floor action on S 1088, a measure to authorize $110 million for public education about the health risks of using tobacco. The panel approved the measure by voice vote June 19, 1991.

In the House, Henry A. Waxman, D-Calif., who chaired the House Energy and Commerce Subcommittee on Health and the Environment, had been an outspoken tobacco opponent. But anti-smoking legislation had not been a top issue for the panel in 1992. The lead on anti-tobacco issues had fallen to Mike Synar, D-Okla., a subcommittee member who wrote the tobacco language in the mental health and substance abuse bill.

The language, crafted as a compromise between Synar and Subcommittee Republican Thomas J. Bliley Jr., Va., whose Richmond district included the country's largest cigarette processing plant, was hammered out before the bill left the House in March.

While the provision was not as strong as Synar originally wanted, it promised to put some teeth into existing laws regarding the sale of tobacco products to minors.

First, every state was required to ban the sale or distribution of tobacco products to anyone under age 18. That was to affect six states, according to the lung association. New Mexico, Missouri and Montana had no minimum age requirement for the purchase of cigarettes (although New Mexico did have a minimum age for the purchase of smokeless tobacco). In addition, Kentucky, Georgia and Delaware had minimum ages under 18 years old.

The bill also required that states enforce their laws "in a manner that can reasonably be expected to reduce the extent to which tobacco products are available to underage youths."

States were to report annually about their efforts, which were required to include "random, unannounced inspections" of locations where tobacco products were sold. States determined not to be enforcing their laws could lose up to 40 percent of their federal substance abuse funds.

vides an effective means of meeting the public health crisis which drug and alcohol abuse represent," he said.

The Bush administration did not aggressively oppose the House measure, but it did register objections to separating the grants. According to a statement from the White House Office of Management and Budget, administration officials hoped to fashion a compromise during the pending conference with the Senate.

During House floor debate, Bliley, the Health Subcommittee's second-ranking Republican, said that Republicans still opposed breaking up the block grant system even while agreeing to some compromises with Waxman.

"This shifting of money from the block grant to set-asides and categorical grant programs significantly reduces the flexibility of states to address the critical needs of their populations," Bliley said.

Bliley and other Republicans had argued that the funding levels for other provisions in the bill were too high, and Waxman agreed to some cuts.

The bill provided $1.1 billion for alcohol and drug abuse programs in fiscal 1992 and $303 million for mental health programs.

Another compromise with Bliley considerably softened a tobacco provision that would have required states to enact laws setting the minimum legal age for buying cigarettes at 18 and to enforce them rigorously.

The compromise still required states to enact laws prohibiting cigarette sales to those under 18 (only Missouri, Montana and New Mexico had no such law).

But instead of the strict enforcement requirements favored by Waxman and anti-smoking activist Synar, the bill directed states to enforce the laws in a manner that could "reasonably" be expected to reduce the availability of tobacco products to minors.

## Bill Highlights

As passed by the House, the bill:

● Reauthorized existing categorical grants for a number of programs, including substance abuse prevention for high-risk youth and pregnant and postpartum women.

● Created a financial assistance program to help community trauma centers affected by drug-related violence. The program was to assist those communities where costs had risen because of the high incidence of violence. The bill authorized up to $50 million for fiscal 1992, increasing to $100 million in fiscal 1994.

● Established an Office of Rural Mental Health under the National Institute of Mental Health to improve the availability of mental health services in rural areas. Authorization levels for the office and for mental health research were set at no less than $5 million for fiscal 1992, $8 million for fiscal 1993 and $10 million for fiscal 1994.

- Required states to submit treatment plans for drug- and alcohol-abuse programs with the goal of increasing accountability.
- Revised the formula for allocating funds to states under the mental health services block grant. The formula would be based on the number of people at risk for mental illness in each state. At the time, mental health dollars were allocated to the states under the same formula used to figure funding for state substance abuse programs, which tended to favor urban areas. Waxman argued that because mental health was a separate issue not always driven by the same factors as substance abuse, it should have a different formula.
- Required states to include strategies for reducing the use of tobacco products by minors in their substance abuse prevention programs.

## CONFERENCE ACTION

Members declared a truce in a 3-year-old battle over federal mental health and substance abuse programs the week of May 11, as House and Senate conferees approved an overhaul of the agency that oversaw them.

After years of strife, it took only minutes May 12 for conferees to approve a compromise version of S 1306, legislation to reauthorize for two years the Alcohol, Drug Abuse and Mental Health Administration.

Issues that had held up legislation since 1988 included how much flexibility to give states in spending federal mental health and substance abuse dollars and whether to continue to favor states with large cities.

Members also sparred over the issue of tobacco use. They ultimately approved language requiring states to enforce laws prohibiting the sale of tobacco to anyone under age 18. States that failed to meet the requirements could lose up to 40 percent of their federal alcohol and drug abuse treatment funds.

### What the Bill Did

Actually, rather than reauthorizing the drug abuse and mental health agency, the bill dismantled it. Under the new structure, the agency's three research branches, the National Institute of Mental Health, National Institute on Drug Abuse and National Institute on Alcohol Abuse and Alcoholism, were transferred to the National Institutes of Health.

The remaining programs, which administered funds to provide mental health and addiction services, made up a new agency called the Substance Abuse and Mental Health Services Administration (SAMSA). That agency had three components: the Center for Mental Health Services, the Center for Substance Abuse Prevention and the Center for Substance Abuse Treatment.

In another major policy change, the existing Alcohol, Drug Abuse and Mental Health block grant program, to be administered by SAMSA, was split into two programs, one for substance abuse and another for mental health.

The bill authorized $1.5 billion in fiscal 1993 and an unspecified amount in fiscal 1994 for the new Substance Abuse Block Grant. The new Mental Health Block Grant program was authorized at $450 million in fiscal 1993 and unspecified sums the following year.

### Classic Compromise

The final bill was a classic compromise, with each side swallowing something it did not like in exchange for getting something it really wanted.

What the Bush administration and Senate forces wanted was the reorganization of the agency.

Putting the three research entities into NIH benefitted both sets of researchers, said HHS Secretary Louis W. Sullivan, by providing for "greater exchange of information and the sharing of expertise in neuroscience and behavioral research."

In addition, said Orrin G. Hatch, Utah, the Senate Labor Committee's ranking Republican, moving the mental health institute to NIH would help "de-stigmatize" mental illnesses and ensure they were treated as legitimate diseases.

But House sponsors, particularly Waxman, had resisted the move. They feared that without the cachet of the research institutes, Republican administrations would find an excuse to cut funding for the remaining services' programs.

On the other hand, House conferees did reach their goal of splitting the mental health and substance abuse block grants.

A key problem, said Waxman, was that states were neglecting mental health services in favor of addiction programs. At a 1991 hearing, Waxman pointed out that states were devoting an average of only 20 percent of their block grant funds to mental health.

"The structure and administration of the Alcohol, Drug Abuse and Mental Health Services Block Grant has not served the needs of the mental health field," Waxman said.

Opponents, however, including House Republicans, urged the continuation of the existing combined grant to allow states flexibility.

On the ever-sensitive issue of funding formulas, conferees essentially split the difference between the Senate and House versions.

The problem, noted Senate Labor and Human Resources Committee Chairman Kennedy at the May 12 conference, was that "once you begin tinkering with the formula, you get winners and losers."

Under existing law at the time, the formula for determining how much money each state received was weighted toward states with urban areas, on the theory that their populations were at the highest risk for substance abuse.

In the Senate, whose composition gave rural interests considerably more clout than in the House, members wanted the formula weighted toward rural states. The House bill's formula, by contrast, would have provided more rural funding than existing law, but less than the Senate measure.

In the end, members created a formula that gave rural states a larger share while cushioning the blow for some urban states that would have lost considerable funding under the original Senate plan.

## FINAL ACTION

Legislation to reorganize federal efforts to fight mental illness and substance abuse suffered several setbacks before clearing on July 1.

The first was in the House on May 19, as members failed to muster the supermajority needed to approve the measure under the chamber's fast-track procedure.

The House voted 264-148 to approve the conference report on S 1306 (H Rept 102-522), legislation to reauthorize and overhaul ADAMHA. But that was well short of the two-thirds margin required for passage under the House's "suspension" calendar. The suspension procedure, which limits debate and allows no amendments, is intended for non-controversial bills. *(Vote 128, p. 32-H)*

Backers of the bill knew it would face opposition from members whose states stood to lose funding under a new formula for distributing substance abuse and mental health funds. But they did not count on a last-minute statement

criticizing the conference report from Bush drug czar Bob Martinez, particularly given that the administration formally supported the bill. Martinez, director of the White House Office of National Drug Control Policy, was unhappy that the measure would lift a ban on federal funding of programs that allowed the distribution of clean hypodermic needles to drug addicts to prevent the spread of AIDS and other blood-borne diseases.

"If they had a problem, they should have let us know earlier," said Democrat Waxman, sponsor of the House version of the measure.

Waxman said that sponsors would bring the conference report back to the House floor under regular procedures.

It was the funding formula change that prompted the bill's temporary demise. Legislators of both parties from states that stood to lose money voted against the measure.

The Florida delegation was the most vocal, voting 19-0 against the conference report. A letter from the Florida Department of Health and Rehabilitative Services estimated that the state would lose $16.5 million in block grant funds for fiscal 1992 under the new formula, which reduced funding to certain states with large urban areas. Because fiscal 1992 was nearly over, Florida would have to give money back to the government.

"A reduction of ADAMHA funds eight months into this fiscal year would be a devastating blow to our ability to maintain the current marginal levels of critically needed alcohol, drug abuse and mental health services," said Democrat Jim Bacchus, one of a half-dozen Florida members who spoke against the new formula.

The Texas delegation was less vocal but nearly as devastating to the final tally. Only two of 27 members, Democrats Albert G. Bustamante and Henry B. Gonzalez, voted in favor of the conference report.

At the same time, several Republican votes were lost after the complaints from Martinez, a former governor of Florida. Although administration officials had said earlier that the president would sign the measure, a May 18 statement from Martinez's office criticized the bill for its failure to bar needle exchange programs.

### Second Failure

The House failed again May 28 to approve compromise legislation to reorganize the nation's substance abuse and mental health programs.

By a vote of 214-157, members recommitted S 1306 to a House-Senate conference. *(Vote 150, p. 38-H)*

The motion adopted by the House instructed conferees to restore Senate-passed language barring federal funding for the needle exchange programs.

### Senate Snag

After the House voted to recommit the bill to conference, members restored the ban on needle exchanges and a new conference report (H Rept 102-546) was filed June 3.

But members from states that stood to lose money under a new formula for distributing substance abuse and mental health prevention funds were still unhappy. When the Senate tried to take up the conference report June 4, Bob Graham, D-Fla., objected. The Senate was scheduled to vote June 9 on Graham's motion to recommit the bill to conference yet again.

But on June 9, the Senate approved the conference report. The 86-8 vote followed unsuccessful efforts to sink the bill by Graham, whose home state was one of nine that stood to lose funding under the new formula by which federal grants would be distributed to states. *(Vote 119, p. 16-S)*

Graham did succeed in delaying the vote by several days, forcing, among other things, the entire conference report to be read aloud. It took about two hours. Members ultimately voted to break his threatened filibuster by a vote of 84-9. *(Vote 117, p. 16-S)*

### Cleared at Last

S 1306 finally cleared Congress on July 1 when the House approved the conference report.

The measure included language banning the use of federal funds for needle exchange programs that would help prevent the spread of AIDS by providing drug addicts with sanitized needles.

The House first voted, 266-138, to waive all points of order against the conference report; then, following some debate on the funding formula, approved the report on a 358-60 vote. *(Votes 252-253, p. 62-H)*

Most of the opposition came from the states that stood to lose money under a new formula for distributing funds. Said Tom Lewis, R-Fla.: "Florida, a microcosm of the nation's drug problems and anti-drug successes, will lose $16.5 million in critically needed substance abuse and mental health funding unless implementation of this bill is delayed." ∎

# Discount Drug Prices for Medicaid Relaxed

Pummeled by complaints, Congress backed away somewhat from an ambitious 1990 plan to require drugmakers to provide discounts to Medicaid, the joint federal-state health program for the poor.

As part of the 1990 budget reconciliation bill (PL 101-508), Congress had required that drugmakers sell their products to state Medicaid programs at the lowest price they offered to other bulk purchasers. Traditionally, hospitals, nursing homes and health maintenance organizations had been able to negotiate cut rates for popular drugs.

Some of the deepest discounts, however, had been enjoyed for years by the Department of Veterans Affairs (VA). The discounts, drug industry officials said, had been

inspired by both patriotic and public relations impulses.

But while the VA represented about 1 percent of all prescription drug sales, Medicaid accounted for close to 15 percent of the market. And faced with the new requirements, many drugmakers chose to raise prices across the board rather than lower them for Medicaid.

VA officials, already complaining about a lack of funds, cried foul to partisans in Congress, who moved quickly to cut the department out of the new program. To prevent Medicaid's windfall from coming at the expense of the VA, HR 5193 exempted the VA from the program, allowing drugmakers to resume deep discounts for veterans hospitals without having to offer them to Medicaid.

To ensure that the VA was given preferential treatment, the legislation required discounts of at least 24 percent. The bill also required discounts for certain other federally funded health facilities, such as community health centers and public hospitals serving large numbers of indigent patients.

But it took more than a year to iron out how to solve the VA's problem without hurting Medicaid. The final compromise, which let the VA out of the program while at the same time raising slightly the minimum discounts companies would have to provide Medicaid, was folded into an otherwise unrelated veterans health bill, HR 5193.

## BACKGROUND

In 1990, Congress moved to force drug manufacturers to give bulk-purchase discounts to Medicaid, the joint federal-state health-care program for the poor. Included in the fiscal 1991 budget-reconciliation bill (HR 5835 — PL 101-508) was a provision requiring pharmaceutical companies to offer state Medicaid programs the same discounts they provided to other bulk purchasers, such as the Department of Veterans Affairs. The requirement was expected to save $1.9 billion over five years. *(1990 Almanac, p. 570)*

The staff for the Senate's Special Aging Committee, in studying prescription drug prices, had discovered that the VA, groups of hospitals and health maintenance organizations often negotiated deep discounts on bulk purchases of drugs, but Medicaid programs did not.

"We simply cannot . . . cut Medicaid drug benefits, while drug manufacturers continue to profit from an unreasonable pricing scheme," Sen. David Pryor, D-Ark., chairman of the Special Committee on Aging, testified at the time.

At $3.3 billion in 1988, drugs represented a major Medicaid expense. According to the Aging panel, Medicaid drug outlays for states that offered benefits rose 224 percent from 1980 to 1988, largely because of increased prescription drug prices. At the same time, Medicaid purchases accounted for a significant 15 percent to 20 percent of overall prescription drug sales.

Congress passed the provision over the objections of the Pharmaceutical Manufacturers Association, which argued initially that the plan would not save money because drug therapy was usually more cost-effective than other forms of medical treatment. The industry also said its rapid price increases had been necessary to cover the rising cost of bringing drugs to market.

However, the law did not work as intended. After it took effect in January 1991, VA officials said drug companies had eliminated longstanding discounts to the VA to avoid having to sell to Medicaid at such low prices. It was costing the VA millions of dollars.

---

## BOXSCORE

➡ **Medicaid Prescription Drug Prices (HR 5193, formerly HR 2890, S 1729).** The legislation significantly altered a landmark 1990 law that required drugmakers to provide discounts on products sold to Medicaid.

**Reports:** H Rept 102-714, Part 1; H Rept 102-384, Parts I and II; S Rept 102-259.

### KEY ACTION

Feb. 5 — The **Senate** Labor and Human Resources Committee approved S 1729, 17-0.

Aug. 11 — The **Senate** Veterans' Affairs Committee approved S 2575, which included a provision addressing VA drug prices.

Sept. 17 — The **House** Energy and Commerce Committee approved HR 2890.

Sept. 22 — The **House** passed HR 2890 by voice vote.

Oct. 6 — The **House** passed HR 5193, incorporating a revised HR 2890, by voice vote.

Oct. 8 — The **Senate** cleared HR 5193 by voice vote.

Nov. 4 — President Bush signed HR 5193 — PL 102-585.

---

The fiscal 1992 spending bill (PL 102-139) for the VA and Department of Housing and Urban Development exempted the VA from the budget law's provision, in the apparent hope that the drugmakers would return to the old prices. The exemption would expire June 30, 1992, or when other legislation was passed to address VA-Medicaid drug pricing.

Meanwhile, the House Veterans' Affairs Committee in November 1991 passed HR 2890, to permanently exempt the VA from Medicaid drug pricing calculations.

## LEGISLATIVE ACTION

The House committees that oversaw the VA and Medicaid reached a compromise with passage of a bill (HR 2890) that raised the minimum discount for Medicaid, exempted the VA from the "best price" rule for Medicaid and required drugmakers to reinstitute discounts of at least 24 percent to veterans. It also extended the right to discounts to other federal health facilities.

It took the Senate, however, somewhat longer to sort out the drug discount mess. At one point, the VA problem was addressed as part of S 2575, an otherwise unrelated veterans health bill.

Then the Finance Committee inserted provisions similar to those in the House bill into its version of the urban aid tax bill, HR 11. House negotiators, however, refused to discuss the matter as part of the tax bill.

A compromise was worked out that included the agreed-upon language — similar to the provisions of HR 2890 — in an omnibus veterans health bill (HR 5193), the House companion to S 2575.

As cleared by Congress Oct. 8, HR 5193 lowered drug prices for the VA, reversed a VA ban on smoking in veterans' health-care facilities and included provisions for psychological counseling for women who were sexually harassed during military service. *(Veterans health care, p. 380)*

## SENATE ACTION

The Senate addressed the fallout from the Medicaid law in ways similar to the House, although in two different bills.

### Labor and Human Resources

In February, the Senate Labor and Human Resources Committee unanimously approved a measure (S 1729) requiring drugmakers to provide discounts to Public Health Service clinics at the larger of either a set discount or the discount provided to the VA.

On a 17-0 vote, the panel approved a compromise version of S 1729, introduced by Chairman Edward M. Kennedy, D-Mass. It was one of several prompted by the 1990

law requiring drug companies to provide the same discounts on drugs sold to Medicaid that they were already providing to other bulk purchasers.

As approved by the committee, the bill required that Public Health Service entities — including family planning clinics, community and migrant health centers, black lung clinics, drug treatment clinics and community mental health clinics — be able to purchase drugs at a set discount rate or the price negotiated by the VA, whichever was lower.

Drug companies were not required to roll back prices to levels in effect before the passage of the 1990 Medicaid law. But the secretary of Health and Human Services was to work with clinics to negotiate for better prices that were available before Oct. 1, 1990, at discounts of 90 percent or more. That action mainly affected the cost of birth control pills in family planning clinics.

### Veterans Affairs

As part of an unrelated veterans health bill (S 2575), the Senate on Aug. 7 approved by voice vote an amendment requiring drug companies to enter into a "master agreement" to offer discounts to all federal buyers.

After a long night of negotiating, the Senate Veterans' Affairs Committee announced a compromise on legislation Aug. 7 to ensure that the VA received drug discounts from pharmaceutical companies.

Under the compromise, pharmaceutical companies were to enter into a "master" agreement with the federal government to sell drugs at discounted prices to federal agencies, including the VA, Department of Defense and the Public Health Service. If companies did not agree to the plan, they would not be allowed to sell drugs to any federal agencies, nor could they receive payment for drugs under Medicaid.

The agreement was worked out between committee Chairman Alan Cranston, D-Calif., and John D. Rockefeller IV, D-W.Va., and Republicans Alan K. Simpson of Wyoming and Frank H. Murkowski of Alaska.

"The point of this is not to get pharmaceuticals," Rockefeller said, but to save the VA money so it could then assist more veterans. The agreement would give the VA more clout in demanding lower prices from drug companies, he said.

"VA is 1 percent of pharmaceutical purchases," Rockefeller said, "so VA doesn't really have the driving power. So this is a very firm enforcement mechanism."

## HOUSE ACTION

After months of negotiations and heated lobbying by health groups, legislation finally began moving in the House to rewrite the 1990 Medicaid drug-pricing law that ended up causing some drug prices to rise instead of fall.

The House Energy and Commerce Committee approved by voice vote Sept. 17 its version of HR 2890, a bill approved by the House Veterans' Affairs Committee in November 1991. The Energy Committee's Subcommittee on Health and the Environment had approved the bill by voice vote Sept. 15.

The bill was intended to close a loophole in the 1990 law requiring drugmakers to offer state Medicaid programs the same discounts given to other bulk-drug purchasers. But rather than lowering their prices for drugs sold to Medicaid, many drugmakers responded to the new law by raising prices for other purchasers, particularly the VA, which for years had enjoyed some of the deepest drug discounts.

The Veterans' Affairs Committee had acted quickly in 1991 to stem the damage to the VA: As approved by the committee, HR 2890 exempted the VA from the requirement that Medicaid receive the "best price" offered to other customers such as VA. This meant that the VA could continue to receive a deeper discount than Medicaid.

The measure also required drugmakers to roll prices back to their Oct. 1, 1990, levels, plus an increment for inflation.

But when the measure was taken up by the Energy and Commerce Committee in 1992, which had jurisdiction over Medicaid, members worried that simply exempting the VA would jeopardize the size of Medicaid's discounts, thus trading one problem for another.

Energy and Commerce Committee members were also concerned about the effect rising drug prices were having on Public Health Service entities under their jurisdiction, including family planning clinics and community and migrant health centers.

Individual committee members, along with interest groups representing both buyers and sellers of prescription drugs, offered a huge array of options. But in the end, with time running out, members could find consensus only for the slimmest fix.

As approved by the full committee, the bill still exempted the VA from the best price calculation. It also exempted certain public hospitals that served a disproportionate share of low-income patients, community and migrant health centers, family planning clinics, maternal and child health clinics, health-care centers for the homeless and federally funded AIDS prevention and treatment centers.

To protect Medicaid's interests, the bill increased slightly the minimum discount the 1990 law imposed as an alternative to the best price requirement. Bulk purchasers at the time got either the best price or the minimum discount, whichever was lower. Under the law, the required minimum discount in 1992 was 12.5 percent, rising to 15 percent in 1993 and thereafter. The bill raised the discount for the remainder of 1992 and all of 1993 to 15.7 percent.

With the consent of Veterans' Committee Chairman G. V. "Sonny" Montgomery, D-Miss., and ranking Republican Bob Stump, R-Ariz., the bill eliminated that panel's requirement for the price rollback to 1990 levels. The rollback was heatedly opposed by the prescription drug industry.

Instead, the bill required that the VA receive a discount of at least 24 percent off the average price charged to nonfederal buyers. Committee aides said the 24 percent discount would offset the amount VA prices had risen since the Medicaid law took effect.

"For this year, politics is the art of the possible, and we ought to do what we can," said Henry A. Waxman, D-Calif., chairman of the Energy Committee's Subcommittee on Health and the Environment, who had wanted to make more sweeping changes.

But Thomas J. Bliley Jr., R-Va., who offered the compromise that was ultimately adopted, said he was not yet convinced of the need to overhaul the entire law.

"We simply do not have enough data today to change the system that was put in place less than two years ago," he said.

### House Floor

The House approved HR 2890 on Sept. 22. It was designed to restore deep discounts on prescription drugs sold

to the VA and certain other federal and nonprofit health-care providers.

The measure, jointly referred to the veterans panel and the Energy and Commerce Committee, exempted the VA, certain other federal buyers and some public hospitals from the 1990 law's requirement that Medicaid receive the "best price" at which a drug was offered for sale. Thus, drug companies could resume giving deep discounts to VA and other exempt purchasers without having to offer the same discount to Medicaid.

The bill did not require that companies roll back prices to their 1990 levels for the VA, as required by the version approved by the veterans committee in 1991. Instead, it required that the VA receive a discount of at least 24 percent on the average price for which a drug was sold to non-federal buyers.

Medicaid still would be entitled to the biggest discounts offered to non-exempt bulk purchasers, such as hospitals and health maintenance organizations. The bill also would increase slightly the minimum discounts Medicaid must receive.

Backers of the measure warned that the bill did not solve the entire problem posed by the Medicaid law.

"We should make no mistake about it, the drug companies are consistently trying a divide-and-conquer strategy," said Ron Wyden, D-Ore., one of the authors of the original 1990 law. "As soon as the ink is dry on this legislation, they

are going to be looking for cracks and holes and opportunities to foist huge price hikes on other buyers."

Michael Bilirakis, R-Fla., a member of both the veterans and energy committees, agreed.

"I imagine we will have to revisit this issue again next year," he said.

## FINAL ACTION

It took more than a year to iron out how to solve the VA's problem without hurting Medicaid.

After the House committees reached their compromise, the Senate Finance Committee (which oversaw Medicaid in the Senate) inserted provisions similar to those in HR 2890 into its version of the tax bill, HR 11. House negotiators, however, refused to discuss the matter as part of the tax bill. *(Urban aid tax bill, p. 140)*

A compromise was worked out to include the agreed-upon language — similar to the provisions of HR 2890 — in HR 5193, the House companion to S 2575.

"Today I believe we will cast a vote for veterans and for stretching the federal government's health-care dollar further," Rockefeller said on the floor Oct. 8. Rockefeller, a member of both the Veterans' Affairs and Finance committees, helped broker the final deal.

The House passed HR 5193 by voice vote Oct. 6, and the Senate cleared the measure by voice vote Oct. 8. ■

# Attempts To Revise Orphan Drug Law Stall

Congress renewed a fight in 1992 that pitted the powerful pharmaceutical industry against patients suffering from rare diseases.

At issue was whether to alter the 1983 Orphan Drug Act (PL 97-414), which sought to spur development of medicines for ailments that afflicted fewer than 200,000 people. Drug sales for such a limited market did not usually recoup the costs of development, so the law provided incentives for drug companies to "adopt" and bring to market promising drugs. Incentives included tax credits and seven years of "market exclusivity" during which no other company could sell that drug.

A bill (S 2060) to revise the orphan drug law moved through the Senate Labor and Human Resources Committee but went no further.

But Congress recognized orphan drug manufacturers in the provision of another drug-related bill. The so-called user fee bill (HR 6181 — PL 102-571), which required manufacturers of most prescription drugs to help underwrite the costs of federal safety and efficacy reviews, included provisions to waive fees for manufacturers of orphan drugs.

## BACKGROUND

The introduction of orphan drug legislation in the 102nd Congress was a revival of legislation that President Bush had vetoed.

The 1990 orphan drug bill would have limited the reach of the 1983 law granting drug companies economic incentives to develop and market medications to treat rare diseases. Although a compromise measure was approved by voice votes in both chambers in 1990, Bush pocket-vetoed

the bill, saying that the changes were unnecessary. *(1990 Almanac, p. 577)*

At the beginning of the 102nd Congress, members brought back the fight over the orphan drug law. However, Health and Human Services Secretary Louis W. Sullivan vowed in 1992 to recommend another veto if Congress passed a bill similar to the one vetoed in 1990.

### The 1983 Orphan Drug Law

The 1983 orphan drug law had granted drug companies several incentives, including tax credits and seven years of exclusive marketing rights, to develop treatments for rare diseases. Both drugmakers and groups representing rare-disease patients agreed that the law had been a success. In the decade before the law was passed, the federal Food and Drug Administration (FDA) approved only 10 new drugs for "orphan" diseases. In the nine years up until 1992, more than 60 new medicines had been brought to market and more than 350 others were in development.

But some critics thought that in a few cases the law had worked too well, with drug manufacturers reaping windfall profits either by using their government-granted monopolies to charge excessive prices or because an orphan drug turned out to benefit more patients than was originally thought.

Ceredase, for example, approved in 1991 to treat Gaucher's Disease, a rare enzyme-deficiency disorder, could cost $350,000 per year per patient. And sales of human growth hormone, at costs of $10,000 to $30,000 annually, rose rapidly as doctors used the drug to treat disorders other than the rare form of dwarfism for which it was originally approved.

Nevertheless, the drug industry vehemently opposed

any changes to the law. Industry officials said weakening the act's incentives would undermine companies' desire to develop new orphan drugs. They also said it was unfair to change the rules in the middle of the game.

"The last thing pharmaceutical companies need is more uncertainty," testified Gerald Mossinghoff, president of the Pharmaceutical Manufacturers Association, at a March 3, 1992, hearing on proposals to alter the law. Mossinghoff said that pharmaceutical research and development was already highly risky, uncertain and expensive.

FDA Commissioner David Kessler also testified that the bill would discourage development of orphan drugs and place too large an administrative burden on the federal government, which would have to collect sales data from manufacturers and determine when to end a drug company's monopoly.

### SENATE ACTION

Sens. Nancy Landon Kassebaum, R-Kan., and Howard M. Metzenbaum, D-Ohio, proposed changes to the law to spur more price competition by reducing or eliminating some of the incentives.

They introduced a bill (S 2060) in November 1991 that would have ended the seven-year exclusive marketing rights allowed for highly profitable drugs under the orphan drug law, terminating a company's protected monopoly on a product if sales reached $200 million. Other companies could then seek FDA approval to market the drug. With a few exceptions for drugs already on the market or in development, drugs whose sales exceeded the cap would lose their market exclusivity, thus allowing competition.

But the bill was also designed to be more palatable to drug companies. For example, it would have lengthened from seven to nine years the period of market exclusivity for orphan drugs.

In the face of veto threats and the presence of scores of

---

> **BOXSCORE**
>
> ➡ **Orphan Drug Amendments (S 2060).** The bill aimed to revise the orphan drug provisions of the Federal Food, Drug and Cosmetic Act, the Public Health Service Act, and the Orphan Drug Act.
>
> **Report:** S Rept 102-358.
>
> **KEY ACTION**
>
> July 1 — The **Senate** Labor and Human Resources Committee passed S 2060 by voice vote.

---

drug-industry lobbyists, the Senate Labor and Human Resources Committee on June 17 took up the Kassebaum-Metzenbaum bill. But the measure proved unacceptable to some committee members.

Orrin G. Hatch of Utah, ranking Republican on the Labor Committee, said the probable effect of the measure would be fewer drugs produced and fewer people benefiting from potential breakthrough discoveries.

Others complained that the $200 million sales cap was unfair and arbitrary. "It doesn't take into account the firm that invests $150 million in development compared to the firm that invests $10 million," said Dave Durenberger, R-Minn.

And opponents argued that the measure dealt with the symptoms of a problem rather than its cause. "The real problem area is our failure to come up with a comprehensive way to control health-care prices," said Christopher J. Dodd, D-Conn.

Sponsors, however, said opponents were being cowed by the intense drug-industry lobbying. "It's shameful," said Metzenbaum. "If the same amount of money spent on lobbying [against the bill] was spent providing free drugs, the world would be a much better place."

The panel debated but did not formally approve the measure. Following the debate, the Senate Labor and Human Resources Committee on July 1 approved S 2060 by voice vote. The Senate did not take further action on the orphan drug legislation.

Orphan drug manufacturers were recognized later in the session, however, when Congress approved and the president on Oct. 29 signed HR 6181 (PL 102-571), the so-called user fee bill. One provision, aimed at orphan drug manufacturers, allowed the HHS secretary to waive or reduce user fees when such action was "necessary to protect the public health" or when the fees would "present a significant barrier to innovation because of limited resources" available to the drugmaker. *(FDA user fees, p. 418)* ∎

---

# Generic-Drug Approval Process Tightened

Congress finally responded to widespread industry abuses in the approval process for generic copies of brand-name drugs by passing legislation (HR 2454) that increased the authority of the Food and Drug Administration (FDA) to oversee the industry.

Under the measure, the FDA could punish those found to have defrauded or otherwise abused the abbreviated approval process for marketing generic copies of brand-name drugs.

### BACKGROUND

Abuses of the generic drug-approval process grew out of 1984 legislation (PL 98-417) that sought to spur drug-price competition by making it easier to bring to market generic copies of already approved drugs.

Under the 1984 law, makers of generic drugs no longer

had to prove that their products were safe and effective. Instead, using an abbreviated process, they could simply demonstrate that their drug was a "bioequivalent," meaning that it had the same therapeutic action as a brand-name product whose safety and efficacy had previously been shown. *(1984 Almanac, p. 451)*

What Congress failed to anticipate, however, was the tremendous financial advantage for the first generic copy to make it to market after the expiration of a brand-name drug's original patent. Because that first copy often ended up with as much as half the generic market, some manufacturers took illegal means to ensure that their drug was first.

The competition led to a variety of abuses, including the bribing of FDA officials and even the substituting of samples of actual brand-name drugs for generic copies to assure passage of bioequivalence tests.

The scandal became public in 1989, primarily as the result of inquiries by House Energy and Commerce's Oversight Subcommittee.

That and subsequent investigations by the FDA and federal prosecutors led to criminal guilty pleas or convictions of industry officials and FDA employees. As of April 28, 1992, eight companies and 27 individuals had been convicted of abusing the fast-track process by which generic drugs were brought to market.

The industry-wide scandal also resulted in convictions of five former FDA employees for accepting bribes, and fines totaling nearly $15 million for companies found to have abused the fast-track approval process. In addition, more than 100 products whose approval was found to have been improperly handled were taken off the market.

In one case, a federal court in Baltimore on April 13, 1992 fined Vitarine Pharmaceuticals $2 million for fraud involved in bringing a copy of a blood pressure drug to market. Among other things, the company substituted the brand-name drug it was purporting to copy in tests to determine if the copy was "bioequivalent" to the original.

John D. Dingell, D-Mich., chairman of both the Oversight Subcommittee and the full committee, sponsored legislation (HR 2454) to address the committee's findings. The bill gave the Department of Health and Human Services (HHS) powerful new tools to police the industry, including authority to refuse to accept, review or approve generic drug applications from people or companies found to have defrauded or otherwise abused the process, and to withhold drug approvals from companies or individuals under criminal investigation in connection with drug approvals.

The legislation was crafted by a bipartisan group that included, in addition to Dingell, Oversight Subcommittee ranking Republican Thomas J. Bliley Jr., Va., and Sens. Edward M. Kennedy, D-Mass., and Orrin G. Hatch, Utah, chairman and ranking Republican, respectively, of the Labor and Human Resources Committee.

## 1991 House Action

Congress took its first steps to combat the abuses on July 29, 1991, when a House subcommittee approved a bill granting new enforcement authority to the Department of Health and Human Services. *(1991 Almanac, p. 362)*

More than a year of backroom bargaining led to the voice vote approval of HR 2454 by the Energy and Commerce Subcommittee on Health and the Environment. The measure, sponsored by committee Chairman Dingell, had a good chance to make it through Congress quickly: cosponsors included every member of the committee from both parties.

Dingell called the bill a "very fine and responsible answer" to "major and massive criminal misbehavior" by some generic drugmakers.

Capitol Hill must act, added Bliley, because "the ge-

---

**BOXSCORE**

➡ **Generic-Drug Enforcement (HR 2454, formerly S 1164).** The bill prescribed new federal penalties for anyone found to have abused the process by which generic copies of brand-name prescription drugs were approved, including barring individuals and companies from future dealings with the Food and Drug Administration.

**Report:** H Rept 102-272.

### KEY ACTION

Oct. 31, 1991 — The **House** passed HR 2454, 413-0.

April 10 — The **Senate** passed HR 2454 by voice vote.

April 28 — The **House** cleared HR 2454 by concurring with **Senate** amendments by voice vote.

May 13 — President Bush signed HR 2454 — PL 102-282.

---

neric drug industry, unique among the industries regulated by FDA, is a creature of the Congress."

The House Energy and Commerce Committee next gave voice vote approval to the measure on Sept. 25, 1991. Finally, the House overwhelmingly approved HR 2454 on Oct. 31, 1991. The measure passed by a vote of 413-0.

## SENATE ACTION

Senators gave voice vote approval April 10 to a substitute version of HR 2454 offered by Kennedy, chairman of the Labor and Human Resources Committee.

"As the price of brand-name prescription products continues to soar, it becomes increasingly urgent that we re-establish generic drugs as credible market competitors," said Kennedy, who wrote the Senate bill with Hatch of Utah, the ranking Republican on the Labor Committee, and John McCain, R-Ariz. "Crucial to this effort is an FDA that can refuse to deal with bad actors who have abused the system for drug approval and regulation."

The bill then went back to the House, which had passed a slightly different version .

A controversial feature of both bills was that they would bar affected companies from further dealings with the FDA for at least a year and up to 10 years in certain cases.

"Some have suggested that no sanction at all should be imposed on companies since individuals are, in the end, responsible for criminal acts," said Hatch, primary Senate sponsor of the 1984 law. "But the generic drug scandal has revealed so many instances of fraud and pervasive criminality, as well as the utter selfish manipulation of the generic approval process, that we have been forced to reject that approach."

Following Senate approval, the House cleared the Senate version on April 28. The resident signed the legislation May 13, 1992 (PL 102-282).

### Provisions

The bill imposed civil penalties for those found to have defrauded the generic-drug approval process. Its core provisions allowed — and in some cases required — the FDA to bar individuals or companies convicted of offenses related to the drug approval process from future dealings with the agency.

As cleared for the president, HR 2454 provided for:

● **Mandatory debarment.** Required the secretary of Health and Human Services to forbid any corporation convicted of a felony in connection with the generic-drug approval process after the date of enactment from submitting or assisting in the submission of any application for generic drugs for at least one year and up to 10 years. A second offense within the 10 years following a first ban resulted in mandatory permanent debarment.

The secretary was required to permanently debar individuals convicted of any felony relating to the development or approval of any new drug, generic or brand name. Indi-

viduals were barred from providing any services to anyone involved in the FDA drug-approval process.

● **Permissive debarment.** Authorized the secretary to bar from further dealings with the drug-approval process both individuals and companies in certain cases. Examples included those convicted of felonies related to the drug-approval process before the date of enactment, those convicted of misdemeanors related to the drug-approval process and anyone convicted of conduct that the HHS secretary determined "undermines the process for the regulation of drugs." Also subject to debarment would be

"high managerial agents" of a company who had actual knowledge of crimes related to the drug-approval process and failed to report them.

● **Withdrawal of drug approval.** Required the HHS secretary to withdraw approval for drugs in cases in which the approval was "obtained, expedited or otherwise facilitated" through illegal means. The secretary was also authorized to suspend distribution of other drugs made by a company found to have abused the process.

● **Penalties.** Provided civil penalties of up to $250,000 for individuals and $1 million for companies.  ■

# Congress Acts To Oversee Infertility Clinics

Prompted by a growing number of complaints from couples disappointed in expensive artificial insemination procedures, Congress cleared a bill Oct. 8 that established new regulations governing infertility clinics.

The bill (HR 4773 — PL 102-493) required clinics to report their success rates to the Department of Health and Human Services (HHS). The government was then required to publish the information for use by couples seeking providers of such care.

## BACKGROUND

Since 1978, when Louise Brown became the first test-tube baby, the in vitro fertilization method and a newer procedure called gamete intrafallopian transfer grew in popularity among infertile American couples. However, countless couples had their hopes dashed, sometimes after spending many thousands of dollars. An estimated 2.4 million couples in the United States were infertile in 1992. Couples seeking fertility assistance spent nearly $1 billion in 1991.

The push for government regulation of the procedures grew out of complaints that couples were being exploited by greedy, relatively uncontrolled clinics. Experts in the field charged that to maximize clientele, infertility clinics specializing in fertilization procedures often exaggerated pregnancy success rates, giving couples false hopes.

While clinics boasted of success rates of between 30 and 50 percent, a 1989 congressional survey of 146 clinics found that only about 9 percent of the women who had in vitro fertilization gave birth to live babies. Additionally, a minority of the clinics was responsible for most of the successful births.

## LEGISLATIVE ACTION

The House Energy and Commerce Subcommittee on Health and the Environment first heard testimony on the legislation (HR 3940) in February 1992. After a markup by members of that subpanel on March 26, Ron Wyden, D-Ore., a sponsor of HR 3940 and long a booster of additional regulations for the clinics, introduced a clean bill (HR

---

## BOXSCORE

➡ **Infertility Clinic Regulation (HR 4773, formerly HR 3940).** The legislation required stricter oversight of infertility clinics, including the annual publication of a consumer booklet comparing the rates, services and successes of different clinics.

**Reports:** H Rept 102-624, S Rept 102-452

### KEY ACTION

June 29 — The **House** passed HR 4773 by voice vote.

Oct. 8 — The **Senate** cleared HR 4773 by voice vote.

Oct. 24 — President Bush signed HR 4773 — PL 102-493.

---

4773) that included changes recommended by witnesses at the February hearing.

Under the bill, sponsored by Wyden and Norman F. Lent, R-N.Y., fertility clinics were required to report their pregnancy success rates to HHS. The HHS secretary, in conjunction with the Centers for Disease Control, would determine the definition of success rate.

The bill also mandated that HHS issue each year a consumer guide booklet reporting the clinic information. The booklet would note which clinics failed to report their success rates. The booklet was also to include the names of the embryo laboratories each clinic used.

In addition, the HHS secretary was directed to establish a model program for inspecting and certifying embryo labs. Information about the model was to be made available to states. Although the states were not required to adopt the model, their failure to do so was to be reported in the guide.

On April 7, HR 4773 was approved by a bipartisan mix of members on the House Energy and Commerce Committee. Committee members said the consumer guide would give couples vital information about a clinic before they underwent the process, which could cost as much as $10,000 a month. Fertility clinics that did not provide information on success rates would be identified, and the embryo laboratories that each clinic used would also be listed.

However, the bill contained no sanctions for submission of false data.

"Couples, for the first time, would have the tools to be informed consumers" and would be able to avoid clinics that promise more than they actually deliver, said Wyden.

The House took up the non-controversial measure on June 29, passing it by voice vote under fast-track procedures.

On the Senate side, the Labor Committee approved the bill by voice vote Sept. 16, without amendment. The legislation cleared Congress after the Senate passed it by voice vote on Oct. 8.  ■

# Lead Poisoning Rules Enacted Into Law

Controversial lead legislation was enacted into law as part of a measure to reauthorize housing programs. It culminated two years of difficult negotiations on new rules to help prevent lead poisoning, especially among children, without overburdening cash-poor cities and industries.

The lead provisions of the housing bill (HR 5334 — PL 102-550) were considered costly and difficult to push through Congress because of intense lobbying by the real estate industry and others who argued that they would slow home-buying.

The health community and environmentalists backed the measure, however, and conferees worked out a bipartisan compromise that included key provisions of HR 5730, a stand-alone lead bill crafted by Al Swift, D-Wash., and Henry A. Waxman, D-Calif.

Lead is a toxic metal found to cause developmental disabilities in children.

The final measure implemented key recommendations of a strategic plan released in 1991 by the federal Centers for Disease Control. The bill:

● Required disclosure of the risks of lead poisoning before the sale or rental of older homes.

● Required the certification of contractors who provided lead abatement and inspection services. States that implemented the program were to receive new federal grants, while those that did not would risk losing building grants. Certification was also required for building renovators and remodelers, with standards to be set by the Environmental Protection Agency (EPA).

● Required inspection and abatement of lead hazards in low-income housing, for which $375 million would be authorized.

● Directed the EPA and the Occupational Safety and Health Administration (OSHA) to establish training and certification requirements for contractors who used lead products.

## 1991 Action

The debate opened in 1991 in both House and Senate panels on legislation aimed at protecting children from exposure to lead and the associated health risks.

The Senate Environment Committee approved its bill (S 391) on Aug. 1. The bill required the EPA to restrict the use of lead in a variety of products that were most likely to result in lead entering the environment and the food chain.

The House Energy and Commerce Subcommittee on Health and the Environment approved a more sweeping bill (HR 2840) on Nov. 4. That measure sought to tighten the federal standard on how much lead in drinking water was considered safe.

The bill also required replacement of lead-contaminated water lines, installation of new equipment by water companies and inspection of apartments for lead.

But significant opposition to the House bill held up consideration by the full committee. Concerns about provisions that required cities to undergo costly inspections for lead in public housing complexes led several members to say they would oppose the measure.

## HOUSE SUBCOMMITTEE ACTION

Discussion in 1992 first began on the more narrow approach to reducing the amount of lead in the environment.

The House Energy and Commerce Subcommittee on Transportation and Hazardous Materials on April 2 approved a bill (HR 3554) by voice vote that sought to ban the import or manufacture of products, including most lead-laden paints and inks, that contained any but the smallest amount of lead.

Subcommittee Chairman Swift got language folded into the bill that would relax some restrictions on construction materials and plastic additives containing lead.

But there were stricter mandates for lower lead levels in brick mortar and zinc-enriched industrial paints commonly used on large structures such as bridges and water towers.

The bill exempted lead used for medical purposes, radiation shielding, mining analysis and military purposes. But it required products containing lead to be clearly labeled.

## HOUSE COMMITTEE ACTION

The House Energy and Commerce Committee approved compromise legislation Aug. 5 to ban some lead uses and require labeling of lead products. The vote was 39-4.

The bill (HR 5730), introduced by Swift, was a combination of HR 3554 and HR 2840, a more comprehensive and expensive bill introduced in 1991 by Waxman, chairman of the Subcommittee on Health and the Environment.

The new Swift bill included much of Waxman's measure but removed more troublesome provisions that would have required financially struggling cities such as New York and Chicago to reduce human exposure to lead in drinking water by replacing lead pipes.

Also absent were provisions to require real estate agents to disclose evidence of lead contamination to potential home buyers and require landlords to test for lead in apartment buildings and disclose lead content to rental applicants. Both were opposed by the National Association of Realtors, which argued that the proposals would drive up housing prices.

Cities remained concerned about the cost. The bill authorized $60 million, a relatively small amount, to carry out its mandates.

Under HR 5730, the EPA was required to inspect schools and day-care centers for lead hazards, and notify parents and school officials. The bill authorized $30 million to help schools with lead abatement costs if they found hazards. Another provision strengthened existing law requiring water testing in schools and day-care centers.

Thomas J. Bliley Jr., R-Va., argued that $30 million would not be enough to remove lead from thousands of schools and centers.

Bliley offered an amendment that would have allowed the poorest schools to receive grants to pay for lead removal and would not have required federal inspection. Poor urban areas tended to have the most serious lead problems.

Bliley's amendment was rejected 19-24.

Under the measure, businesses were required to label lead-based products and discontinue manufacturing others.

Labeling provisions sought to:

● Ban the import, manufacture or processing of ink and brick mortar, effective one year after enactment of the bill. Lead-based paints, mirror coatings, vehicle window

coatings and architectural glass would be banned three years after enactment.

• Exempt some products from the ban, including those used for medical purposes, radiation protection and fire testing in the mining industry.

• Restrict lead use in food packaging, processed food and ceramics and crystal.

• Establish a program to license lead-based paint abatement contractors.

## HOUSING BILL CONFEREES SIGN OFF

It became obvious in October that the housing bill was the only moving vehicle for the lead provisions.

The Senate-passed version contained very carefully negotiated language to reduce lead-based paint poisoning hazards in private and federal housing.

As the measure was sent to conference, it looked as if the House conferees would not have much room to make changes.

Much to everyone's surprise, House-Senate conferees on the housing bill agreed to broaden the scope of the lead provisions to incorporate numerous provisions of Waxman's HR 5730.

At one point, the lead issue appeared headed for a turf battle. Energy and Commerce Chairman John D. Dingell, D-Mich., secured a seat at the conference table on lead provisions. Waxman also became a conferee. The Education and Labor Committee won jurisdiction on those items addressing certified contractors and inspectors — the areas in which the functions of the Department of Housing and Urban Development (HUD) overlapped with those of the EPA and OSHA.

"This is a rare triumph for a comprehensive bill that gives complementary marching orders to both HUD and EPA," said Don Ryan, executive director of the Alliance to End Childhood Lead Poisoning, a national nonprofit public interest organization.

The House adopted the conference agreement on Oct. 5 by a vote of 377-37. The Senate cleared it by voice vote three days later. President Bush signed it Oct. 28. *(Housing bill, p. 367)* ∎

# Lawmakers Focus on Health-Care Issues

While overhauling the nation's health-care system was much discussed during the 102nd Congress, there was far more movement on legislation that dealt with more manageable health-care concerns.

Among the smaller bills that became law were measures reauthorizing programs for the disabled, malpractice limitations for actions against doctors helping the poor and legislation to widen federal financing opportunities for students studying in the health-care fields.

## MEDICAL DEVICES

Compliance with a 1990 law that stiffened federal oversight of medical equipment was delayed six months under legislation enacted in June.

The Senate passed the bill, S 2783, by voice vote on May 21. The legislation extended until Nov. 28 the deadline for the federal Food and Drug Administration to issue final regulations for implementing sections of the law (PL 101-629), which sought to streamline the marketing approval process for new devices, improve the oversight of equipment already on the market and make it easier to recall defective products. *(1990 Almanac, p. 579)*

The extension delayed the requirement for manufacturers to devise tracking systems for certain implanted devices, such as heart pacemakers, and equipment used in patients' homes, such as oxygen tanks.

The House approved the bill by voice vote May 28. President Bush signed it June 16 — PL 102-300.

## LONG-TERM CARE

Sellers of insurance to protect consumers from the cost of long-term health care would have been subject to new federal regulations under a bill approved by the Senate Labor and Human Resources Committee on July 1. The bill went no further.

The panel approved the bill, S 2141, as a follow-up to legislation approved by Congress in 1990 that regulated "Medigap" plans providing supplemental coverage above the amount provided by Medicare, the federal health insurance program for the elderly and disabled. *(1990 Almanac, p. 572)*

S 2141 would have established federal standards for coverage, prohibited high-pressure sales tactics and revised the way insurance agents were paid to change their incentive to sell people more policies than necessary.

To gain Republican support, bill sponsor and committee Chairman Edward M. Kennedy, D-Mass., dropped a provision that would have required all policies to include inflation-protection clauses. Many policies, purchased years in advance of the time they were used, wound up providing insufficient coverage.

Although similar bills were introduced in the House, no action was taken on them.

## AIDS

A House Ways and Means subcommittee approved a bill to make it easier for women with AIDS-related disorders to qualify for federal disability benefits. But the full committee never marked it up.

The Ways and Means Subcommittee on Social Security approved the measure, HR 5792, by voice vote Aug. 12.

Sponsors said the bill was needed because the Social Security Administration's proposals to streamline the eligibility process for AIDS patients were incomplete.

Under 1992 rules, people whom doctors certified to be suffering from certain HIV-related disorders, such as pneumocystis carinii pneumonia, were assumed to have AIDS and to be disabled, which qualified them for benefits. HIV is the AIDS virus. Those with other HIV-related ailments, however, still had to prove that they were too disabled to work.

In December 1991, the Social Security Administration (SSA) expanded its definition of HIV-related disabilities to

make it easier for women and children to qualify. Women manifest different symptoms than do homosexual men, for whom early AIDS definitions were drafted.

But sponsors said the new rules did not go far enough.

"Under SSA's current regulations, HIV-infected women must go to unfair lengths to prove their disability, unnecessarily delaying treatment and shortening their lives," said bill sponsor and subcommittee member Robert T. Matsui, D-Calif.

Under the bill, certain ailments often seen in women with HIV, including some forms of cervical cancer and pelvic inflammatory disease, would have automatically qualified for a disability determination.

But subcommittee Republicans contended that the bill would have unnecessarily micromanaged eligibility for the two main federal disability programs, Supplemental Security Income and Social Security Disability Insurance.

The former was available to low-income elderly, blind or disabled people; recipients automatically also qualified for Medicaid, the health program for the poor. Social Security Disability Insurance was for people who had worked long enough to qualify for regular Social Security coverage; after two years, they qualified for medical benefits under Medicare.

"I fear this sets a poor precedent," said subcommittee ranking Republican Jim Bunning, Ky. By qualifying more women for benefits, the measure would have cost the federal government more money — although how much more was unclear. Under budget rules, members would have to come up with a way to offset any new spending.

## REHABILITATION ACT

Congress passed legislation (HR 5482) revising the Rehabilitation Act of 1973. The House adopted the conference report Oct. 2, and the Senate cleared the legislation Oct. 5.

The president signed the bill Oct. 29 — PL 102-569.

Last reauthorized in 1986, the Rehabilitation Act served primarily to authorize grants to states to maximize employment opportunities for the disabled so that they could lead more independent lives.

HR 5482 reauthorized federal rehabilitation programs through fiscal 1997, provided for funds toward independent living centers, rehabilitative training centers, and employment, transportation and technical assistance programs. The total authorization for fiscal 1993 was $2.6 billion.

Early leadership on the bill had come from Sen. Tom Harkin, D-Iowa. Harkin's Senate Committee on Labor and Human Resources approved its version of the bill (S 3065) by voice vote July 29.

Although the act was best known for its provisions barring discrimination in federally funded activities against those with disabilities, its primary purpose was to provide grants to states to help fund programs aimed at helping the disabled lead independent lives. It was last reauthorized in 1986. *(1986 Almanac, p. 272)*

The changes to the act made by HR 5482 were considered more evolutionary than revolutionary. Among the provisions were ones to make it easier for those with disabilities to qualify for rehabilitation services and to give them more choices of available services. The bill also eliminated all references to "handicaps," a word that had fallen out of favor with advocates for the disabled.

The House Committee on Education and Labor approved HR 5482 by voice vote July 8. It passed the full

House by voice vote Aug. 8. The Senate passed its version, S 3065, on Aug. 11, shortly before the summer recess.

Conferees quickly ironed out technical differences between the House and Senate versions, and the conference version was adopted by both chambers.

## MALPRACTICE SUIT IMMUNITY

Legislation (HR 6183) that provided federal malpractice protection for doctors and other health professionals who worked in federally backed community health centers was cleared by Congress on Oct. 8. The president signed the bill Oct. 24 — PL 102-501.

The Senate cleared the measure by voice vote after the House passed it Oct. 6. The bill was a slightly revised version of HR 3591, which the House had approved Sept. 15.

Federally funded community and migrant health clinics, which served mostly low-income patients in areas with few or no other health-care providers, spent roughly $58 million a year to purchase private malpractice insurance. The bill covered clinic workers under the Federal Tort Claims Act and made the federal government the defendant in any malpractice actions. Sponsors estimated that the savings could be used to extend services to an additional half million low-income people a year.

## MEDICARE PAYMENT RULES

Congress had hoped to reform some of Medicare's administrative procedures, as well as address areas of waste and fraud in the program, the federal health system for the elderly and disabled. But the language designed to do that was quashed after it was attached to the tax bill (HR 11), which President Bush vetoed. *(Urban aid tax bill, p. 140)*

Introduced as HR 3837 by Rep. J. J. Pickle, D-Texas, the measure grew out of an investigation conducted by the House Ways and Means Oversight Subcommittee, chaired by Pickle.

Among the bill's provisions was one that would have stopped the payment of benefits to dead people.

"Federal agencies ... have been sending millions of dollars each month in benefit checks, Social Security and others, to deceased individuals, some of whom have been dead for up to six years," Pickle told his colleagues Aug. 3.

The bill aimed to crack down on unscrupulous sellers of medical equipment by barring Medicare payments for certain items sold by telephone. It would have tightened rules requiring private insurance plans to pay benefits for people who were also covered by Medicare.

The bill also would have changed the system for paying overtime to U.S. Customs Service inspectors, which Pickle said was vulnerable to abuse.

Ways and Means ordered the bill reported April 1. The Energy and Commerce Committee, which shared jurisdiction over Medicare, approved the measure July 28.

On Oct. 7, during debate on the tax bill (HR 11), HR 3837 was amended. All Medicare provisions were eliminated and replaced by language designed to prevent U.S. companies from moving out of the country. The provisions were a sop to New York Sens. Alfonse M. D'Amato, R, and Daniel Patrick Moynihan, D, who were conducting a filibuster because the tax bill did not include a measure to keep a Smith-Corona typewriter factory from moving out of their state.

Many of the original HR 3837 provisions on Medicare

changes were attached to the tax bill, which finally cleared Congress. However, President Bush vetoed the legislation Nov. 4.

## RESEARCH ON DES

Congress cleared legislation Sept. 30 that authorized research and public education programs on the health effects of DES (diethylstilbestrol), an anti-miscarriage drug found to cause severe health problems in the children of women who took it. The president signed the bill (HR 4178 — PL 102-409) on Oct. 13.

HR 4178 authorized unspecified amounts through fiscal 1996 for the programs, to be operated by the National Institutes of Health.

The House bill, sponsored by Louise M. Slaughter, D-N.Y., passed Aug. 10. The Senate Labor and Human Resources Committee approved a companion measure (S 2837) by Tom Harkin, D-Iowa, on Sept. 16, and the Senate cleared the legislation Sept. 30.

DES, a synthetic estrogen, was prescribed to an estimated 5 million pregnant women between 1938 and 1971. The drug had been linked to a rare form of vaginal cancer in daughters of those women. Other studies suggested links to other health problems in the women themselves and in some of their sons.

## MAMMOGRAPHY REGULATIONS

Under a bill cleared by Congress on Oct. 7 and signed by the president Oct. 27, breast cancer screening facilities had to meet minimum federal standards.

The measure (HR 6182 — PL 102-539) required federal certification for equipment and personnel performing mammography, a special X-ray technique used to detect breast cancer in its early stages.

HR 6182 was a new, compromise version of HR 5938 and S 1777. The Senate Labor and Human Resources Committee approved S 1777 on Sept. 16. The House had passed HR 5938 on Sept. 24 by a vote of 390-18. *(Vote 424, p. 104-H)*

The new bill was introduced Oct. 5 and passed by voice vote in the House on Oct. 6. The Senate cleared it by voice vote Oct. 7.

## PREVENTIVE HEALTH

An array of programs aimed at preventing disease and injury were reauthorized through fiscal 1996 under legislation cleared by Congress on Oct. 7 and signed by the president Oct. 27.

As it emerged from a year's worth of negotiations in a House-Senate conference, the measure (HR 3635 — PL 102-531) renewed existing programs and created new ones designed to improve Americans' health. The House passed the conference report (H Rept 102-1019) by voice vote Oct. 6; the Senate cleared the bill by voice vote Oct. 7.

"I believe that the most fundamental flaw in our health-care system today is its preoccupation with patching and mending and its virtual neglect of prevention and health promotion," said Sen. Tom Harkin, D-Iowa, who led the charge in the Senate for an increased emphasis on prevention programs. "As a result of this flaw in our national health policy, not only are health costs increased, but the quality and length of the lives of many Americans are needlessly reduced."

The compromise bill boosted to $205 million the authorization for the Preventive Health Services Block Grant. The block grant provided money for states to use for such purposes as rodent control and rape crisis counseling. Appropriators gave the block grant $148.8 million for fiscal 1993.

Initiatives included programs to screen and prevent lead poisoning in children, to screen and prevent infertility arising from sexually transmitted diseases and to establish a nonprofit foundation to help fund research on disease prevention and health promotion. *(1991 Almanac, p. 363)*

## ALZHEIMER'S DISEASE

Programs designed to increase research into Alzheimer's disease and help families cope with it were reauthorized under legislation cleared by Congress on Oct. 7 and signed by the president Oct. 24.

The bill (S 1577 — PL 102-507) reauthorized at unspecified amounts a series of Alzheimer's related programs, including a council that coordinated programs and information-sharing among the federal agencies that studied the ailment.

The House on Oct. 6 approved by voice vote an amended version of S 1577, which the Senate originally passed in 1991. *(1991 Almanac, p. 364)*

The 1992 bill combined elements of the Senate bill with provisions included in HR 3082, which the House had passed June 29. The Senate cleared the measure by voice vote Oct. 7.

## CANCER REGISTRIES

States were encouraged to set up registries that kept track of cancer cases under legislation cleared by Congress on Oct. 7 and signed by the president Oct. 24.

The measure (S 3312 — PL 102-515) authorized the Department of Health and Human Services (HHS) to use up to $30 million to make grants to states to operate registries that kept track of cancer cases. The aim was to facilitate research on different forms of the disease. Separately, the bill ordered the National Cancer Institute to study why breast cancer was more common in some states than in others.

Both provisions were originally part of an omnibus bill to reauthorize portions of the National Institutes of Health (NIH) that President Bush vetoed in June. *(NIH reauthorization, p. 413)*

The Senate originally passed S 3312 on Oct. 2; the House passed it with minor changes Oct. 6, and the Senate cleared it Oct. 7, all by voice vote.

## FDA ENFORCEMENT

Despite approval by the House Energy and Commerce Committee, legislation (HR 3642) to increase and standardize the enforcement powers of the federal Food and Drug Administration (FDA) never made it to the House floor.

Energy Committee members approved the bill July 9 by a straight party-line vote of 27-16. The vote represented a major increase in support since an earlier version of the measure, HR 2597, was approved by the panel's Subcommittee on Health and the Environment in October 1991.

The bill's plain language belied the intensity of the

opposition it engendered among industries regulated by the FDA, including food producers and makers of drugs, medical devices and cosmetics. The FDA regulated products that accounted for 25 cents of every U.S. dollar spent.

Sponsors pointed out that the FDA already had most of the powers the bill would have conferred, including authority to: embargo products suspected of violating safety and other standards of the Food, Drug and Cosmetic Act; issue subpoenas; assess civil penalties; inspect plant records; and detain illegally imported foods and order them destroyed if they posed a danger to public health.

The legislation was needed, sponsors said, because the Food and Drug Act had not been overhauled since it was passed in 1938. Instead, FDA authority had been added in bits and pieces as Congress had addressed individual problems in regulated industries. The bill would have standardized enforcement powers across the agency and granted subpoena power the FDA did not have.

But industry representatives saw the measure as a threat — and as a license for federal regulators to go on fishing expeditions, looking for problems in their facilities.

The administration officially opposed the bill, and after the committee markup, House members never brought it up on the floor.

## HEALTH-CARE FRAUD

The Senate on Oct. 3 passed by voice vote a bill (S 2652) designed to increase penalties for health-care fraud. But the bill went no further.

The measure would have made health-care fraud by either patients or providers — such as hospitals and doctors — a federal crime.

Under the legislation, convictions could have led to a maximum sentence of 10 years. If bodily harm occurred as a result of the fraud, the maximum sentence would double.

The bill would have authorized $20 million to hire 200 additional FBI agents to investigate medical fraud, $5 million for 50 U.S. attorneys to prosecute cases under the act and another $5 million for inspectors at the Department of Health and Human Services to investigate health-care fraud.

Defendants convicted of medical fraud could have received a maximum of 10 years in prison and a fine as high as $250,000. Fraud that resulted in bodily harm could have resulted in a maximum of 20 years in prison.

## DRUG LICENSING DEADLINE

Under a bill (S 3163 — PL 102-353) signed by President Bush on Aug. 26, states had an additional two years to meet licensing deadlines imposed under a 1988 law intended to stop the resale of prescription drugs.

The Senate passed S 3163 by voice vote Aug. 11. It had been introduced Aug. 10 by Labor and Human Resources Committee Chairman Edward M. Kennedy, D-Mass., and Orrin G. Hatch, Utah, the panel's ranking Republican. The House cleared the bill by voice vote Aug. 12.

Among other things, the 1988 Prescription Drug Marketing Act (PL 100-293) required wholesale distributors of prescription drugs to be licensed in the state in which they conducted business.

Twenty-three states had not yet set up such licensing mechanisms, although the requirement had been scheduled to take effect Sept. 14, 1992. Among the areas that would almost certainly not have been in compliance on that date were New Jersey, Pennsylvania and Puerto Rico, home to a significant number of drug manufacturing facilities. *(1988 Almanac, p. 322)*

Sponsors said the bill was needed to prevent potential disruptions in drug distribution. The measure created a two-year program during which distributors in states that had not instituted licensing programs could register instead with the Food and Drug Administration.

## AGENCY FOR HEALTH-CARE POLICY

The Senate cleared legislation (HR 5673) by voice vote Sept. 30 that reauthorized the Agency for Health Care Policy and Research.

The president signed the bill Oct. 13 — PL 102-410.

The federal agency was charged with measuring the quality and cost-effectiveness of medical procedures. The agency, created in the 1989 budget-reconciliation law (PL 101-239), was the federal government's outpost for "outcomes" research — studies of which medical procedures worked best and which provided the best value. Most policy-makers agreed that outcomes research was an essential element of health-care cost containment.

The agency also published "practice guidelines" for physicians faced with ailments for which myriad treatments were available, such as lower back pain.

The House had approved the bill Sept. 24 by a vote of 397-8. *(Vote 425, p. 104-H)*

The bill renewed the agency through fiscal 1995 at unspecified amounts.

## MEDICAL TRAINING

The House cleared legislation (HR 3508) Sept. 29 that overhauled federal funding options for students who trained for employment in the health professions. The Senate had passed HR 3508 by voice vote Sept. 25.

The president signed the bill Oct. 13 — PL 102-408.

House and Senate conferees reached agreement Sept. 24 on the bill, which updated and renewed the programs that helped fund the training of doctors, nurses and other health professionals.

The conference agreement authorized slightly more than $1 billion over four years for the programs. The final product, the culmination of months of staff-level negotiations, rewrote the aid programs so that they focused more specifically on the training of professionals who delivered primary care services (pediatrics, family practice) and those who planned to practice in rural, inner-city and other medically underserved areas.

Both the House and Senate had passed different versions of the legislation in November 1991. *(1991 Almanac, p. 362)*

HR 3508 reauthorized Titles VII and VIII of the Public Health Service Act, which provided aid to students and to institutions that trained doctors, nurses and other professional health workers.

Aid to students was provided through direct loans, loan guarantees and scholarships, while funds for institutions were awarded through grants and contracts.

The bill also extended for four years the Health Education Assistance Loan program, known as HEAL, which provided federal backing for loans made to students in training for health professions. It included provisions aimed at reducing the rate of student defaults on such loans. ▪

# Congress Expands College Loan Eligibility

With all eyes focused squarely on the beleaguered middle class, Congress cleared legislation July 8 that allowed any student, regardless of income, to obtain a federally guaranteed loan to finance a college or trade school education.

The student loan provisions, incorporated into a wide-ranging bill (S 1150) to revise the Higher Education Act of 1965 (PL 89-329), marked a dramatic reversal of education policy as carried out since 1981, when a budget-cutting campaign inspired by the Ronald Reagan administration spurred Congress to restrict loans to those in families earning less than about $30,000 a year.

The Higher Education Act governed federally guaranteed loans and outright grants for education after high school, providing $11.7 billion in student aid in 1992.

The bill signed by President Bush on July 23 focused on the middle class in three ways: It raised the loan limits for regular subsidized loans — the best-known were Robert T. Stafford loans — so that more families could qualify for more money. The new law created an unsubsidized Stafford loan program for which any student could qualify. And it removed a family's home or farm equity from calculations of how much aid — in loans or grants — a student qualified for to attend school. The bill also allowed interest rates on Stafford loans to adjust to market rates, capping at 9 percent.

In 1992, 6 million students received a total of $21.5 billion in federal, state and private student aid, in the form of both guaranteed loans and Pell grants, named for Sen. Claiborne Pell, D-R.I., chairman of the Education, Arts and Humanities Subcommittee of the Labor and Human Resources Committee. The federal guaranteed loan program paid the interest while students were in school and then guaranteed loan repayment if students defaulted. Under the new unsubsidized loan program, students were required to begin paying the interest on their loans as soon as they received them.

Legislation was approved by the Senate Labor and Human Resources Committee and the House Education and Labor Committee in 1991, but the bills did not reach the floor before the end of the first session. Although both measures aimed to make student aid more available to middle-income families, the Senate bill was more modest in scope.

The conference measure that eventually cleared both chambers in 1992 encompassed student financial assistance, aid to historically black colleges and universities, grants to academic libraries, and programs to recruit and

---

## BOXSCORE

➡ **Higher Education (S 1150, HR 3553).** Educational aid programs were opened to more middle-class students through the creation of an unsubsidized loan program for all students, regardless of income, and by the removal of a family's home or farm equity from calculations of how much financial aid a student needed to attend school. The law also included a demonstration program eliminating banks as middlemen for issuing loans to students.

**Reports:** H Rept 102-447; S Rept 102-204; conference report H Rept 102-630.

### KEY ACTION

Feb. 21 — The **Senate** passed S 1150, 93-1.

March 26 — The **House** passed HR 3553, 365-3.

June 16 — Conferees approved S 1150 by voice vote.

June 30 — The **Senate** adopted the conference report by voice vote.

July 8 — The **House** cleared the conference report, 419-7.

July 23 — President Bush signed S 1150 — PL 102-325.

---

train teachers for elementary and secondary schools. It also aimed to address a litany of horror stories about shaky loans and rising defaults through so-called integrity provisions. And it allowed students to apply for federal financial aid using a free federal form.

The new law included a controversial "direct loan" demonstration program that cut out the role of banks in issuing subsidized loans. Instead, the government was to provide loans directly to students through their schools. The demonstration included students from schools with $500 million in loan volume, with 35 percent of the institutions required to allow students to repay their loans according to the amount of money they earned after graduation. The other students would repay their loans according to the regular fixed rate.

But while middle-income families generally benefited from the expected boon in student aid from the legislation, poor students had no real gains.

Both the House and Senate had tried — but failed — to turn the Pell grant program, a popular college scholarship program providing basic tuition and living stipends to lower-income students, into an "entitlement" — a mandatory spending program that would guarantee that all eligible students received the maximum amount of money authorized by law. If authorizers set the maximum level at $3,500, for example, any student who qualified for the maximum amount would get $3,500.

Under rules in force at the time, the size and extent of Pell grants was left in the hands of congressional appropriators. They had the discretion, but rarely the money, to fund the program at the fully authorized level.

But both House and Senate lawmakers were forced to drop the Pell grant "entitlement" from their bills before bringing the legislation to the House and Senate floors. The reason: the high cost, estimated by the Congressional Budget Office (CBO) at about $62.7 billion over five years.

"When the Pell grant entitlement didn't survive from the committees to the floors, that dashed a lot of high hopes," said Selena Dong, legislative director for the U.S. Student Association, which lobbied on behalf of students. "It's hard to be enthusiastic."

When Pell grants were created in 1972 as Basic Educational Opportunity Grants, they were supposed to be the foundation of all student aid. But by the 1990s, loans were the real foundation, accounting for more than two-and-a-half times the amount of grants in 1990-91. And while Pell grants bought 50 percent of the average cost of higher education in 1980, by 1991 they covered only 25 percent.

One goal that lawmakers set for themselves at the start of the reauthorization process in 1991 was to shift what they viewed as an imbalance between grants and loans. College officials and students testified that too many people were taking out too many loans, going deeply into debt and not receiving enough offsetting grant money.

Without the Pell entitlement, however, lawmakers did not achieve that goal.

## BACKGROUND

The stated goal of the 1965 Higher Education Act was to give every American the opportunity to go to college. It created scholarships for students with "exceptional financial need" and guaranteed bank loans to students from both lower- and middle-income families. Indeed, federal student aid programs enabled millions of young people to pursue careers that were beyond their parents' reach. The program was also a boon to institutions of higher learning. *(1965 Almanac, p. 294)*

But after more than 25 years, the programs, last reauthorized in 1986, were in trouble. Middle-income, working-class students found it harder and harder to borrow money as eligibility rules tightened. Poor students received fewer direct grants and took on more and more loans. The act's reputation suffered further damage from shaky loans, rising defaults and the collapse of the nation's largest student loan guarantee association. The system, said Richard F. Rosser, president of the National Association of Independent Colleges and Universities, "has become a nightmare for most people."

That nightmare was only partially addressed by the 102nd Congress. Lawmakers labored for two years to overhaul the Higher Education Act, but in the end, said House Education and Labor Committee Chairman William D. Ford, D-Mich., they produced "a jump forward, but a smaller jump than it could have been."

### First Session Action

In 1991, committees in both chambers produced bills that did not reach the floor before adjournment. *(1991 Almanac, p. 365)*

The five-year House bill (HR 3553) was the more dramatic of the two: It sought to replace the existing student loan program with a system of direct loans disbursed by a student's college, university or trade school. That provision, designed to save money by cutting out the banks as middlemen, survived as a demonstration project only. The bill also sought to transform Pell grants, the principal stipend for low-income students, into an entitlement program — guaranteeing that every student who qualified would receive a grant. That provision did not survive either.

The more modest, seven-year Senate bill made Pell grants an entitlement in the late 1990s, after the budget constraints imposed by the 1990 budget law would have been lifted.

The House Education and Labor Subcommittee on Postsecondary Education approved a $100 billion draft reauthorization bill on Oct. 8, 1991, including bipartisan proposals to increase both loans and grants to middle-class students. That put it at odds with the Bush administration, which wanted to target money to the neediest students and cut back on spending for other students.

Controversial provisions included the Pell entitlement and a proposal to replace the guaranteed student loan system with direct government loans to students, cutting 13,000 private lenders out of the process. Republicans and the administration opposed both proposals as costly and cumbersome.

But turning Pell grants into an entitlement was a top priority for several higher education groups. The federal government spent about $5.4 billion annually on Pell grants to 3.4 million students, mostly from low-income families. One proposal sought to raise the family income threshold for Pell grants to $50,000 a year, from $30,000. The House subcommittee bill sought to increase the maximum Pell grant from $3,100 to $4,500. Under the existing law, appropriators set an overall total for Pell grants and divided the money among all eligible students. Although students in theory could qualify for $3,100, they did not receive the full amount if enough money was not available. In 1991-92, they received $2,400, and in 1992-93, $2,300. Although appropriators were spending twice as much money on Pell grants than a decade earlier, dissatisfaction prevailed; college tuition had risen faster than inflation and, while the number of students receiving grants had gone up, the amounts they received fell short of their need for aid.

Committee freshman Robert E. Andrews, D-N.J., took the lead in the direct loan debate, estimating that direct lending could save $1.4 billion a year by eliminating federal interest subsidies for lenders. All students could borrow money under the proposed program, but only lower-income students would receive interest subsidies from the government while they attended school.

The House Education and Labor Committee approved HR 3553 by 26-14 on Oct. 23. Ranking Republican Tom Coleman of Missouri tried but failed to strip out the measure's two most controversial components — one to provide open-ended funding for Pell grants, the other to institute a direct loan program. The House committee ignored 1990 budget law constraints and voted to make Pell grants an entitlement immediately.

The next day, Oct. 24, the Senate Labor and Human Resources Subcommittee on Education approved its higher education bill (S 1150) by 14-0. The measure continued all existing student aid programs at higher funding levels, but created no new ones. Like the House bill, the legislation sought to loosen eligibility standards for grants and loans so more middle-class students could get them. But it was slightly less generous than the House bill. Basically, the House committee chose to disregard the 1990 budget agreement, which placed limits on spending and called for pay-as-you-go funding of all new entitlements; the Senate panel tried to obey it.

The Senate Labor and Human Resources Committee approved S 1150 unanimously on Oct. 30. However, the 17-0 vote masked sharp partisan divisions over the provision to gradually transform Pell grants into an entitlement. Opponents feared that more entitlements would drive up the already burgeoning federal deficit. "A lot of us would like to get out of the entitlements," said Utah's Orrin G. Hatch, the committee's ranking Republican. "The deficit is running out of control."

## LEGISLATIVE ACTION

Senate Democrats dropped plans to mandate spending for Pell grants on Feb. 21 and promptly passed a massive bill expanding student financial aid. The House followed suit March 26, overwhelmingly approving legislation that virtually assured that Congress would send President Bush

a bill geared to the middle-class desire for more access to guaranteed student loans and federal grants. The strong bipartisan House vote set up a relatively easy conference with the Senate because the most controversial issues, including Pell grants, had been resolved.

House and Senate conferees quickly came to agreement the week of June 15 on a bill to allow any student, regardless of income, to obtain federally guaranteed loans. In approving the bill by voice vote June 16, conferees agreed to include a "direct loan" demonstration program that would cut out the role of banks in issuing loans subsidized and guaranteed by the government. Instead, the government would provide direct loans to students through their schools. The demonstration would include students from 500 schools. After the formal conference, however, but before the conference report was adopted, members agreed to a compromise changing the 500 schools to schools with $500 million in loan volume. There was some concern that 500 schools could have resulted in more than $700 million in loans.

The Senate adopted the conference report June 30 and the House cleared it July 8.

Education Secretary Lamar Alexander said he would recommend that President Bush veto the legislation because of the direct loan provision. But in the end, under pressure from committee Republicans, Bush signed the bill July 23.

## SENATE ACTION

Sidestepping a partisan and likely losing battle, Senate Democrats dropped plans to mandate spending for Pell grants and whisked a massive bill expanding all federal student financial aid programs to passage on Feb. 21.

By 93-1, the Senate approved S 1150, a seven-year extension of the Higher Education Act of 1965. Jesse Helms, R-N.C., cast the lone "nay." *(Vote 30, p. 5-S)*

Members of the Labor and Human Resources Committee viewed the bill as a potent political salve for middle-class voters, who were struggling to pay soaring college costs.

The measure increased the size of loans and grants and expanded the number of students eligible to receive them. But the White House criticized the bill, saying it neglected poor students and gave too much money to those from high-income families.

The bill authorized $17.4 billion in fiscal 1993, the bulk of it for financial aid programs. Congress appropriated $11.7 billion for student aid in fiscal 1992 and $828 million for all other higher education programs.

### The Entitlement Issue

For higher education lobbyists, the centerpiece of the bill had been a committee-approved provision to transform the Pell grant program, which provided scholarships for low-income students, into an entitlement. The grants were subject to annual appropriations. Although Congress had authorized a maximum grant of $3,100 per student, that amount had never been funded. The most a student received in 1991-92 was $2,400.

Tired of raising authorization levels with no discernible effect, Senate Democrats decided to mandate full funding of the program beginning in fiscal 1997. The entitlement was delayed until then to avoid the 1990 budget law's pay-as-you-go requirement, set to expire in fiscal 1995.

Advocates said bigger Pell grants were crucial to avoid loading students with excessive debts and risking loan defaults down the line.

But Sen. Nancy Landon Kassebaum, R-Kan., ranking minority member of the Education Subcommittee, planned to offer an amendment to strip the Pell entitlement from the bill. She had argued that the federal deficit was too high to permit the creation of another uncontrollable spending program. Working with Kassebaum was Sen. Sam Nunn, D-Ga., who had held widely publicized hearings in 1990 on fraud and abuse in the student loan program. And the White House threatened to veto the bill if the provision stayed.

Only one Republican, Sen. James M. Jeffords of Vermont, promised to vote for the entitlement.

But before the two sides could come to a showdown on the floor, Pell himself took out the spending requirement. He said he would reserve the right to offer an amendment later to restore it.

Pell refused to say why he backed off from a fight, but committee sources said he feared that the entire bill could be killed if someone lodged a point of order against it. Under Senate rules, an objection could be raised to a bill committed to spending money in a future year without a budget resolution.

Although only 51 votes, a simple majority, were needed to overcome a point of order, the entire bill would have been lost if entitlement supporters fell short. If Pell instead offered the plan as an amendment to the bill, only the amendment would be at risk.

In the end, Pell decided not to offer the amendment because he was afraid he would lose. That would have made it harder for him to accept the House entitlement position in conference.

Even without the entitlement clause, the bill increased the maximum Pell grant to $3,600 in 1993-94, subject to appropriations.

The bill also boosted the average annual income ceilings for a family to qualify for a Pell grant from about $30,000 to about $40,000, adding 600,000 students to the program.

Furthermore, the bill excluded the value of a family's home or farm from the calculation of family income if the income was $50,000 or less.

### Direct Loans and the IRS

In the weeks leading up to the vote, three senators — Paul Simon, D-Ill., Dave Durenberger, R-Minn., and Bill Bradley, D-N.J. — created a groundswell of interest in adding a direct student loan program to the government's portfolio, to be funded by the U.S. Treasury with the Internal Revenue Service (IRS) collecting the repayments. A version of this eventually became the direct loan demonstration program.

But many members were leery of creating a loan entitlement after shying away from a grant entitlement.

The sponsors later added their proposal to the pending tax bill, HR 4210, but it was dropped in conference. Bush vetoed the tax bill March 20. *(First tax bill, p. 133)*

The education bill awaiting House action contained a direct loan program.

Under the existing guaranteed student loan system, students borrowed money from banks and the federal government paid the interest on the loan while the student was in school; the student repaid the loan after graduation. If the student defaulted, a guarantee agency reimbursed the bank, and the government reimbursed the guarantee agency if it could not collect from the student.

According to a study commissioned by the Department of Education, student loans were a lucrative business for banks, ranking third in profitability after credit cards and commercial and industrial loans. The direct loan proposal had thoroughly riled bankers, who argued strenuously to Congress and the media that they could run the program better than the government.

Simon, Durenberger and Bradley enlisted college presidents to make their case; they also waged a public relations campaign calling for a stop to the subsidizing of banks at the expense of students. They estimated that they could save taxpayers $2.7 billion a year by eliminating the government's interest-subsidy payments to banks. Instead, they would have the U.S. Treasury issue bonds, sending the money raised directly to post-secondary schools for the students' tuition.

The government, under the senators' proposal, would charge students an interest rate equal to that of the 52-week Treasury bill plus 2 percent.

Under existing programs, the unsubsidized Supplemental Loans to Students and the Parent Loans for Undergraduate Students, known as PLUS, were capped at the 52-week Treasury bill rate plus 3.25 percent, not to exceed 12 percent. The subsidized Robert T. Stafford loan, the most popular program, cost students 8 percent interest for the first four years of repayment and 10 percent for the remaining years.

Unlike Stafford loans, the Simon-Durenberger-Bradley loan proposal would be available to anyone, regardless of income. Stafford loans were generally limited to families earning less than $60,000 a year. But the direct loan would have been expensive for students, because the government would not pay interest on the loans while the students were in school.

Upon graduation, students would be required to pay back their direct loans with a flat percentage of their income — 3 percent, 5 percent or 7 percent, depending on the size of the loan. People would make payments until the interest and principal was paid off or for 25 years. After 25 years, the loan would be forgiven, even if it was not completely repaid.

Loan repayments would be made with income tax payments, overseen by the IRS. Simon, Durenberger and Bradley said that the IRS would ensure that defaults were minimal.

The administration, which first floated the concept of a direct loan program and then tried to quash it, threatened to veto the bill over this issue, too.

But the Office of Management and Budget (OMB) raised no objection to having loans repaid through the IRS.

### Loan Problems

As Senate Labor Committee members had crafted their bill in 1991, they were acutely aware of problems in the guaranteed student loan program. Many for-profit trade schools had abused the system, signing up students for loans but not teaching them skills needed to win jobs and pay back the debt. In fiscal 1991, defaults cost the government a whopping $3.6 billion, up from about $200 million 10 years earlier.

The committee responded by making it easier to kick schools out of the loan program. Existing law allowed a school's graduates to default at a rate of up to 35 percent before stopping aid to all students at the school. In fiscal 1993, the rate was set to drop to 30 percent. The Senate bill

cut schools out if their default rate reached 25 percent in fiscal 1995.

Members also decided to require each state to create or choose an agency to oversee the finances and management of every post-secondary school receiving federal student aid. The provision sparked an outcry among lobbyists for colleges and universities, who said that the requirement would add an extra layer of bureaucracy to their dealings with state licensing agencies and accreditation groups.

The American Council on Education, an umbrella group for colleges and universities, led the lobbying campaign against the provision.

Sen. Terry Sanford, D-N.C., a former president of Duke University, offered an amendment to differentiate between schools that needed oversight and those that did not, essentially separating colleges from trade schools. The amendment, adopted by voice vote, called upon states to help pinpoint schools that were abusing the loan program. It left enforcement to the Department of Education.

## HOUSE ACTION

The House on March 26 overwhelmingly approved legislation to provide financial aid to college and trade school students, virtually assuring that Congress would send Bush a bill geared to the middle-class desire for more access to guaranteed student loans and federal grants.

The 365-3 vote to pass a five-year reauthorization (HR 3553) of the Higher Education Act set up a relatively noncontroversial conference with the Senate. *(Vote 62, p. 16-H)*

Both measures sought to open federal post-secondary loan and grant programs to more students from middle-income families. The two bills did that by raising the income limits for families eligible for Pell grants and Stafford loans.

Under the House bill, a family could earn up to about $78,500 a year for its student to qualify for a subsidized Stafford loan, up from the existing limit of about $67,600. CBO estimated that the House bill would add another 1.1 million borrowers to the Stafford loan program, with 900,000 of those coming from families with incomes above $35,000. At the time, about 3.7 million students received loans each year.

The bill also raised the maximum income level for Pell grant eligibility from about $30,000 to about $49,000. (The final bill raised the income threshold to $42,000, if the maximum $3,700 grant were funded.) That allowed an additional 1.4 million students to qualify for the grants, which went to 3.8 million students a year.

One provision in particular helped more students qualify for these programs: The bill eliminated a family's home, farm or small business from the formula used to determine a student's financial need.

### Pell Forestalls Veto

Both Democrats and Republicans spoke of "hard-pressed middle-income families" and how Congress was about to help them.

"The heart and soul of this bill is what it does for middle-income working families and their sons and daughters who want to go off to higher education," said Pat Williams, D-Mont., a senior member of the House Education Subcommittee on Postsecondary Education.

Tom Petri, R-Wis., echoed the theme: "College and trade school tuitions keep rising, and the middle class, in particular, is increasingly hard pressed to foot these bills."

What the measure did not do, however, was make full funding for Pell grants a "mandatory" budget item, as the House Education and Labor Committee planned when it approved the original House bill (HR 3553) on Oct. 23, 1991. Panel Chairman Ford had to drop that provision because he could not get the support of the Democratic leadership to waive the 1990 budget agreement, which required new "entitlement" spending to be offset with tax increases or spending cuts.

The committee bill involved a $60 billion entitlement over five years. Ford's substitute, incorporated into the bill as it came to the floor, changed the Pell grant program back to the "discretionary" budget category, subject to annual appropriations.

As a result, there was no guarantee that students would receive more grant money the following year.

Ford said his bill still represented a step forward, but he acknowledged: "I had really hoped to come to the floor with a bill that would give us a giant leap forward."

Yet his concession enabled the bill to move forward without controversy, and it appeared to have partly mollified the Bush administration, which had threatened a veto. Education Department spokeswoman Etta Fielek said the administration still had some concerns about the bill's "middle-class" focus and some of its provisions, but that officials believed they could resolve those issues in conference.

### Why Ford Shifted Position

For six months, Michigan's Ford had been trying to persuade fellow House Democrats to support a plan that would ensure that every eligible student in the country could receive a grant from the federal government to attend college or trade school.

Despite his pleading, the Education and Labor Committee chairman went to the House floor the week of March 23 with a version of HR 3553 that not only had no entitlement for the Pell grant program but also required students to pay for the privilege of receiving student loans.

And in the process of pushing a bill to the floor, Ford alienated key committee Republicans who had traditionally worked with Democrats to move education legislation.

For the most part, however, Ford found himself rebuffed by fellow Democrats, mainly because his bill would have shifted $62.7 billion into Congress' mandatory spending category over the next five years. Under budget-reconciliation rules, new entitlements had to be offset by cuts or revenue increases to prevent increasing the federal deficit. Ford's plan did neither.

"I'm frustrated," Ford said. "The Congress went along and got in the box of the budget agreement of 1990 and stands here writhing while the country goes to hell."

But other Democrats said it was nearly impossible to support a plan that would add to the deficit.

"I do not feel creating an entitlement is the best way to proceed," said House Speaker Thomas S. Foley, D-Wash.

Added Majority Whip David E. Bonior, D-Mich.: "There are a good number of people who would have problems with an entitlement in the House and the Senate."

Indeed, the Senate on Feb. 20 had dumped a similar Pell grant entitlement when it became clear that the provision was likely to scuttle the entire bill. Pell, the program's namesake, said he hoped that the House would bring an entitlement provision to the House-Senate conference so that he could restore it.

When Ford also was forced to drop the entitlement, Pell said: "I understand, since I was not able to get it into my bill."

An aide to one top House Democratic leader said it did not seem worth forcing such a painful vote when the Senate did not have the votes to enact a Pell grant entitlement over Bush's threatened veto.

But higher education lobbyists were bitter that the House leadership would not support a floor vote on the Pell grant entitlement. "The administration and Congress part company on education when it comes to funding, but the leadership appears reluctant to push those differences and put some money into education," said one higher education lobbyist.

### Middle-Class Needs

From the start, Ford told his committee members to write a bill according to what they thought should be done, rather than what they thought would pass. Over the objections of Republicans, Democrats wrote in an entitlement for Pell grants and created a new direct loan program to replace the existing guaranteed loan system. A direct loan system would cut out all the banks and middlemen, with the federal government issuing loans directly to students through their schools.

Members from both parties agreed on the need to aid more middle-class students. For example, the committee bill would create an unsubsidized student loan program to allow any student, regardless of income, to borrow money for tuition.

Education members also agreed to change the federal aid formula, which determined who received how much aid, by eliminating a family's home, farm or small business from being calculated as a part of the family's assets.

The result of this and other "need analysis" changes, according to CBO, would be 1.1 million new borrowers in the guaranteed student loan program, with 900,000 of those expected to come from families with incomes of more than $35,000. The bill would also draw in 1.4 million new Pell grant recipients, with the number of students from families earning more than $40,000 a year jumping from 70,000 to 350,000.

Without the entitlement provision, however, Pell grant students would continue to be at the mercy of appropriators, who usually provided less money for the program than authorized.

### Funding Headaches

After moving his bill through committee in October 1991, Ford was unable to bring it to the floor in early 1992 because of funding difficulties. Budget Committee Chairman Leon E. Panetta, D-Calif., objected that Ford had made no effort to pay for it.

Ford had hoped to wait out the budget agreement, assuming that it would soon crumble and that he would not have to play by its rules.

As the months went by, however, Democratic leaders instructed Ford and Panetta to work out their differences. Staff members got together, but both sides were intractable.

In early March, Speaker Foley called in Panetta and Ford once again. The two chairmen debated the Pell entitlement and pay-as-you-go rule before members of the leadership. This time, according to several sources, Foley told Ford and Panetta to find a way to pay for the bill.

Ford took the first ax to the bill himself. On March 16, he introduced a substitute bill (HR 4471) that eliminated

the Pell grant entitlement and put the program back in the hands of appropriators. CBO estimated that the change would save $60 billion of the $62 billion in new mandatory costs.

Ford also cut the "special allowance" that the government paid to banks when student loan interest rates did not match the market rates. Trimming the federal contribution from 3 percent to 2.85 percent saved $180 million over five years.

But even with these and other changes, Ford came up $1.2 billion short of paying for his substitute bill.

Ford asked Tom Coleman of Missouri, the ranking Republican of the Subcommittee on Postsecondary Education, and Bill Goodling of Pennsylvania, ranking GOP member of the full committee, to cosponsor the new bill.

Coleman said Ford assured him that the bill was paid for. A few days later, he found out it was not. "I would be very reluctant to support anything that adds to the deficit," Coleman said.

The bipartisan harmony that normally accompanied an education bill to the House floor was coming unraveled. Ford aides said that the chairman had told Coleman that he was still trying to find ways to pay for the bill. Panetta was looking, too.

Finally, Panetta suggested the week of March 16 that Ford raise the money by imposing 5 percent loan origination fees on two loan programs — Supplemental Loans for Students and Parent Loans for Undergraduate Students — and by maintaining existing origination fees on the Stafford loan program.

Origination fees were subtracted from a loan when it was issued, although the student had to pay back the full amount. Congress added the fee to the student loan program in 1981 as part of a deficit-reduction bill; Ford had planned to phase those out in 1992.

At first, Ford appeared willing to accept Panetta's loan origination fee plan. But college students and their lobbyists had pushed hard against it.

"What a crazy way to pay for something," said the U.S. Student Association's Dong. "All it is going to do is just force students to take out more loans."

Overnight, Ford balked. Just before the Rules Committee convened March 19 to consider debate guidelines for the higher education bill, Ford let it be known that he would ask to make his substitute in order, even though it fell short of the pay-as-you-go mark by more than a billion dollars.

That morning, the Speaker called Ford and Panetta to his office. Ford made his case again. Again the Democratic leaders rejected it. Later that day, the Rules Committee issued a rule governing floor debate; it included a provision making Panetta's origination fees part of the bill.

### Riled Republicans

Ford then seemed to have cleared the hurdles within his own party, but he still faced a veto threat from the Bush administration, which objected to the direct loan program and charged that the bill would provide too much aid to middle-income students.

Ford also risked losing the trust of Coleman and Goodling, who remained disturbed about other deals that they said Ford made but never delivered on.

Coleman said he agreed to cosponsor Ford's substitute bill only if Ford turned the direct loan program into a demonstration project. Coleman said that he also insisted that the program be capped at $500 million a year, as opposed to creating a full-fledged program as originally

approved by the committee.

But Ford's substitute bill did not include a cap on direct loans. Instead, it said the Education secretary had to pick a group of schools with a combined loan volume of $500 million under the current system. The students at those schools would have a contractual right to receive direct loans — in other words, the program would be an open-ended entitlement for those schools.

Coleman and Goodling confronted Ford about the change before the Rules Committee convened. But Ford said he would not revise the language.

"There never was discussion of a cap," Ford insisted. "That wasn't even an idea in Tom Coleman's head until OMB put it into his head this morning."

Coleman, however, insisted that he had been wronged. "I think we better consider [taking] my name off the substitute," he told members of the Rules Committee.

Republicans complained that this was the second time that Ford had broken a deal that year. In February, Ford scrapped an elementary and secondary school improvement bill that contained a provision on school choice that he didn't favor. *(School choice, p. 455)*

### Targeting Trade Schools

Besides its focus on expanding student aid for the middle class, the wide-ranging bill also sought to put the brakes on the rising rate of student loan defaults. Responding to reports that shady trade schools had been signing up the homeless or illiterate for courses that would not give them the training they needed to get a job, the Education Committee approved language to: prohibit schools from using commissioned salesmen and recruiters; require pro rata tuition refunds for students who found the training inadequate; and give increased authority to states to oversee schools with high default rates.

During floor debate, Marge Roukema, R-N.J., Maxine Waters, D-Calif., and Bart Gordon, D-Tenn., banded together on several amendments to further protect the federal Treasury and students against suspect trade schools.

They appeared to have the votes on their side, so Ford did not fight them. Among amendments approved on voice votes were:

● A Roukema amendment to eliminate schools from the guaranteed student loan program if their students had a default rate of 25 percent for three years in a row. The bill had a similar provision but set the cutoff rate at 30 percent.

● A Gordon amendment to cut schools from the Pell grant program if they had been kicked out of the guaranteed student loan program for high defaults.

● A Waters amendment to disallow Supplemental Loans for Students to those participants enrolled in a course of study that was less than two years long and did not lead to an associate degree.

● A Waters amendment to prohibit schools from having more than 85 percent of their students receiving federal student financial aid or institutional scholarships.

### Sallie Mae Debate

The only other point of major controversy involved an unsuccessful amendment by Bill Gradison, R-Ohio, and J. J. Pickle, D-Texas, to tighten oversight of the Student Loan Marketing Association (Sallie Mae), the federally chartered corporation that operated the secondary market for student loans.

Gradison and Pickle wanted to put Sallie Mae under the regulatory oversight of the Treasury secretary rather

than the Education secretary.

While a for-profit, shareholder-owned corporation, Sallie Mae also carried the definition of government-sponsored enterprise, meaning that its bonds carried an implicit federal guarantee in the marketplace, much like other secondary market enterprises for home loans and farm loans. Many lawmakers were worried that these government firms could put the federal Treasury at risk should they suddenly collapse like the savings and loan industry. So Congress had been stepping up its regulatory control. (GSE, p. 123)

"The private markets believe that if Sallie Mae ever reneges on its debt, we will spend taxpayer dollars to make its creditors whole," Gradison said. "It is only prudent to put into place a firm regulatory structure to prevent this situation from arising."

But members of the Education and Labor Committee maintained that Sallie Mae did not need the same oversight as other government-sponsored enterprises because its assets — guaranteed student loans — were already backed by the federal government. The House rejected the Gradison-Pickle amendment 181-232. (Vote 57, p. 14-H)

### Other Amendments

In other action, the House:

● Rejected, 28-385, an amendment by Paul B. Henry, R-Mich., to require all students to have either a high school degree or a general equivalency diploma before they could qualify for federal student aid. Opponents argued that the requirement would hurt middle-aged blue-collar workers who needed to return to school for job retraining. (Vote 56, p. 14-H)

● Rejected, 85-314, an amendment by Edolphus Towns, D-N.Y., to allow some Pell grants to go to some prisoners. (Vote 58, p. 14-H)

● Subsequently agreed, 351-39, to a Coleman and Gordon amendment to prohibit Pell grants from going to prisoners in federal and state prisons. (Vote 59, p. 14-H)

## CONFERENCE ACTION

As the House and Senate bills went to conference, they looked remarkably similar. However, conferees had to resolve the varying authorization levels for Pell grants and the loan limits for Stafford loans.

The House maintained the existing limits on the amount of money a student could borrow: $2,625 for the first two undergraduate years, $4,000 for the remainder of the undergraduate education and $7,500 for graduate or professional students.

The Senate, on the other hand, boosted the loan limits to $3,000 for the first year, $3,500 for the second year, $5,500 for the remainder of the undergraduate program and $9,000 for graduate or professional students.

The House bill also included a demonstration program for direct government loans, which would cut out the banks and provide money directly to schools. The Senate bill did not have such a provision, although the Senate had included a direct loan demonstration program on the 1992 tax bill (HR 4210) that President Bush had vetoed in March.

The House bill also created an unsubsidized student loan program, using the same terms as the Stafford program but making loans available to all students regardless of income.

The Senate bill did not create a new program, but it proposed to open up the Supplemental Loans for Students

program to dependent undergraduate students who could show the ability to repay the loan.

### Direct Loan Agreement

House and Senate conferees quickly came to agreement the week of June 15 on a bill to allow any student, regardless of income, to obtain federally guaranteed loans to finance a college or trade school education.

The student loan provisions marked a dramatic reversal of education policy as carried out since 1981, when a budget-cutting campaign inspired by the Ronald Reagan administration spurred Congress to restrict loans to those in families earning less than about $30,000 a year.

Conferees, in approving the bill by voice vote June 16, agreed to include a "direct loan" demonstration program that would cut out the role of banks in issuing loans subsidized and guaranteed by the government. Instead, the government would provide direct loans to students through their schools. The demonstration would include students from 500 schools, with 35 percent of the institutions required to allow students to repay their loans according to the amount of money they earned after graduation.

Education Secretary Alexander said he would recommend that Bush veto the legislation because of the direct loan provision.

"It's a shame that at the last minute the conferees took a bill that was shaping up to be a help to college students and destroyed it by adding a loan entitlement program that will create billions of dollars of new unlimited government debt," Alexander said.

Proponents said the direct loan program could save the federal government billions of dollars a year if it completely replaced the existing guaranteed student loan system and its many middlemen. In September 1991, the General Accounting Office (GAO) estimated that the savings could reach $1.5 billion a year. In a follow-up study, the GAO estimated that the federal government could save about $4.5 billion over five years by switching to direct loans.

The administration and officials from the student loan industry, including banks, securities markets and guarantee agencies, said the federal government would be taking on too much debt by issuing the loans directly rather than backing them indirectly. Administration officials had initially said they would accept a pilot project to test the idea but balked at the size proposed.

Republican Sen. Durenberger, who pushed the direct loan concept with Democratic Sen. Simon and Rep. Andrews called the veto threat "dumb," particularly because the administration had previously said it would support a $100 million demonstration.

Durenberger had argued for a $500 million trial, although with 500 schools allowed in the program, the cost could be far more than $500 million.

And Pennsylvania's Goodling, ranking Republican on the House Education and Labor Committee, said that while he did not like the size of the demonstration, "I don't think my advice to the president would be to veto the bill."

On the other hand, Goodling said, he believed that Democrats wanted Bush to veto the bill to embarrass him in an election year.

"I think they intentionally tried to put him in this spot, and I wouldn't fall for that," he said.

House Education and Labor Chairman Ford denied that allegation, but nevertheless tweaked Bush for his opposition to direct loans. "The only people upset about

saving that money are the bankers who are losing a profit," he said. "The president can choose the bankers or the student."

## Broadening Loan Access

Although the direct loan program captivated the conferees, it was a relatively small part of the bill. Both House and Senate members attempted to rewrite the law that governed all federal financial aid programs with the intention of bringing in more middle-class students and boosting aid for low-income students.

At the time, 6 million students received a total of $21.5 billion in federal, state and private student aid, in the form of both guaranteed loans and direct grants. The federal guaranteed loan program paid the interest while students were in school and then guaranteed loan repayments if students defaulted.

To broaden access to guaranteed loans, the conference agreement included a new, unsubsidized student loan program designed by the House that would be available to all students, regardless of how much money their families earned. Students would be able to borrow money from banks, but the students — rather than the government — would pay the interest on their loans while they were in school.

CBO said about 800,000 students were expected to benefit in 1993 under this program.

And a key change in determining how much financial aid a student needed to attend school would add 900,000 new borrowers to the Robert T. Stafford loan program, the most popular of the subsidized, guaranteed loans. The bill removed a family's home or farm equity from calculations of how much aid a student needed.

The size of Stafford loans, too, would be increased from their existing levels.

And interest rates would be allowed to adjust to market rates, capping at 9 percent. Formerly, students paid a flat 8 percent interest rate during the first four years of repayment and 10 percent thereafter. In 1992, with interest rates so low, many students were paying more than the market called for.

## No Parity for Poor Students

But while middle-income families would generally benefit from the expected boon in student aid, poor students had no real gains to point to.

Both the House and Senate had tried to turn the Pell grant program into a mandatory spending program guaranteeing all eligible students access to federal aid.

Under existing rules, the size and extent of Pell grants was left to congressional appropriators who had the discretion, but rarely the money, to fund the program at the fully authorized level.

Both House and Senate lawmakers were forced to drop the Pell grant entitlement from their bills before bringing the legislation to the House and Senate floors. The reason: the high cost, estimated by CBO at about $62.7 billion over the next five years.

As approved in conference, the bill increased the authorized maximum grant to $3,700 in the 1993 academic year, up from the existing $3,100.

The bill also raised the income ceiling that determined eligibility; for a family of four, the cap jumped from $30,000 a year to about $42,000.

However, appropriators at the time allowed no more than a $2,400 maximum grant. And that amount was dropped to $2,300 in fiscal 1993.

The Education Department had already reported a $1.5 billion shortfall in the program from the previous year.

Members of the higher education community had difficulty mustering enthusiasm for the bill because they feared that some of its "need analysis" provisions might have unintended consequences.

Need analysis was the examination of a family's income, expenses and other variables affecting how much the family could afford to pay to send a child to postsecondary school.

For example, conferees no longer required that a family's home or farm equity be counted as part of assets available to pay tuition.

The American Council on Education, an umbrella organization for many higher education associations, estimated that 461,000 students would lose their Pell grant awards (under the new rules, they would not appear to be needy) and 900,000 would receive smaller grants if appropriators continued to fund the grants at a $2,400 maximum.

At the same time, 150,000 students who did not receive grants would qualify under the bill's new need analysis formula, and 1.3 million students would qualify for an increase of at least $100.

But lawmakers said their estimates from CBO did not support those figures. "This formula is not going to cut anybody out," Ford said.

According to CBO, if the $3,700 authorized Pell maximum were funded by appropriators, 1 million new students would receive grants. That was because the rules of need analysis depended on the amount of funding: The higher the funding level, the more students qualified for grants. But if the grants remained at $2,400, about 100,000 fewer students would receive grants. Most of them would be single independent students. Conferees changed the rules to exclude independent students under 24 years old who had $4,000 in annual income and had not been listed on their parents' tax returns for two years.

## Grants for Prisoners

Conferees did, however, agree to allow prisoners to receive Pell grants, a switch from the House position. The House had voted 351-39 to drop prisoners from the program.

Members also voted against a compromise amendment — 314-58 — similar to the Senate's language that would have provided Pell grants to prisoners except those on death row.

Missouri's Coleman, the ranking minority member on the House Education Subcommittee on Postsecondary Education, argued that Congress should not allow prisoners, who had no income at all, to be first in line for a limited pot of student aid.

"How can we be rewarding prisoners first?" Coleman asked.

But House and Senate Democrats argued that educating prisoners could help reduce the recidivism rate, saving society more money in the long run.

"Certainly we ought to give these people a chance," said Rep. Charles A. Hayes, D-Ill.

House members voted 17-9 to accept the Senate language, which prohibited Pell grants for prisoners serving a life sentence without parole or awaiting the death penalty. Goodling voted with the Democrats in favor of the Senate language, while Democrat Tim Roemer of Indiana voted

*Continued on p. 454*

# Higher Education Act Provisions

*In reauthorizing the Higher Education Act of 1965, Congress sought to open federal student financial aid programs to more middle-class families. The act governed federal loans and grants for students to attend college and trade schools, and the reauthorization allowed all students, regardless of income, to borrow money to pay for their education.*

*The $100 billion higher education law (S 1150, H Rept 102-630, PL 102-325) also governed aid to historically black colleges and universities, grants to academic libraries, and programs to recruit and train teachers for elementary and secondary schools. As signed by the president July 23, the law:*

## Federal Pell Grant Program

●**Name change.** Changed the name of the program, which provided grants to undergraduate students to help pay for tuition and expenses, to the "Federal Pell Grant" program. House Education and Labor Committee members wanted to make sure that students and their families knew that the grants came from the federal government and not from the states or schools. The grants were named for Sen. Claiborne Pell, D-R.I., the program's original sponsor. In fiscal 1992, about 3.8 million students received $5.6 billion in Pell grants, which were directed toward the neediest students.

●**Maximum award.** Authorized appropriators to increase the maximum Pell grant to $3,700 for academic year 1993-94, up from $3,100. Grants were to be authorized to increase by $200 a year to $4,500 by 1997-98. Despite the increase in authorization levels, appropriators were forced to cut the maximum Pell grant awarded to students in fiscal 1993, from the standard $2,400 per student down to $2,300 per student.

●**Award rules.** Authorized that, in any academic year in which appropriators provide a maximum basic grant above $2,400, the amount of a student's grant is to equal $2,400 plus one-half of the amount by which the maximum grant exceeds $2,400. Also added to the grant was the smaller of the following: the remaining one-half of the excess amount above $2,400; or the sum of the student's tuition and the student's allowance (or expenses) determined by the bill.

●**Minimum award.** Changed the minimum grant to $400 per student, up from $200.

●**Incarcerated students.** Allowed Pell grants to cover the cost of tuition, fees, books and supplies for incarcerated students, but specified that no grants could go to students under a death sentence or serving a life sentence without possibility of parole.

●**Insufficient appropriations.** Required the secretary of Education to tell Congress if, for any fiscal year, the amount of money appropriated for Pell grants was not enough to pay for eligible students.

●**Period of eligibility.** Allowed students to receive Pell grants during the time it took them to complete an undergraduate degree without any time limits.

●**Drug-free workplace.** Eliminated the provision that said Pell grant recipients were considered "individual grantees" under a 1988 anti-drug law (PL 100-690), which requires people receiving grants from the government, including Pell grant recipients, to maintain a drug-free workplace. Members felt the law was not applicable to students.

●**Need analysis.** Repealed the existing formula and used a single need-analysis formula for all programs.

## Federal Trio Programs

●**Authorization.** Required the secretary of Education to continue funding programs to prepare students from disadvantaged backgrounds for postsecondary education and to provide support services for students attending postsecondary schools. Those programs included Talent Search, Upward Bound, Student Support Services, Educational Opportunity Centers and Staff Development Activities. The law authorized $650 million in fiscal 1993. Of that amount, the law required that $11 million be used for the Ronald E. McNair Postbaccalaureate Achievement Program, to provide disadvantaged college students with help preparing for doctoral study.

## National Early Intervention Scholarship and Partnership Program

●**Activities authorized.** Authorized the secretary of Education to create a program that encouraged states to provide a guarantee to eligible low-income students who obtained a high school diploma that they would receive the financial assistance needed to attend postsecondary school. The program offered incentives to states to provide counseling, mentoring, academic support and other services to elementary, middle and secondary school students who were at risk of dropping out. The program also provided information to students and their parents about financing a college education and the advantages of obtaining a postsecondary education.

●**State plan.** Required each state seeking federal grant money to submit a plan to the secretary of Education for carrying out the program. The plan had to outline a scholarship component and an early intervention plan. States were required to provide matching funds — from state, local and private resources — of no less than 50 percent.

●**Grant amounts.** Required that the maximum amount of the scholarship grant received by any eligible student be established by the individual state. But the minimum grant was not to be less than the smaller of these two amounts: the maximum Pell grant funded for that fiscal year, or 75 percent of the average cost of attendance for an in-state student in a four-year program at a public institution of higher education.

●**Eligible students.** Defined an eligible student as someone who: participated in the early intervention program; was under 22 years old at the time of the first grant award; received a high school diploma or a certificate of high school equivalence on or after Jan. 1, 1993; was enrolled or accepted for enrollment at an institution of higher education within the state's boundaries, although the state was allowed to offer grants to students who attended school outside the state.

●**Distribution of funds.** Required the secretary of Education to award grants on a competitive basis to states if the amount appropriated was less than $50 million. If it was more than $50 million, the secretary was required to allocate funds to states based on the Elementary and Secondary Education Act (PL 100-297) formula. That law provided funds to help educate disadvantaged students and generally guided the funds to the poorest school districts.

●**Authorization.** Authorized $200 million in fiscal 1993 to fund this program.

## Presidential Access Scholarships

●**Scholarships.** Created a scholarship program of awards to students who were eligible for Pell grants. They must have demonstrated academic achievement and participated in a preparatory program for postsecondary education. Authorized $200 million in fiscal 1993.

●**Amount.** Equaled $400, or 25 percent of the Pell grant the student was awarded that year, whichever was greater. If Congress did not appropriate enough money in an academic year, the amount paid to each student was reduced proportionately. Students could receive the scholarships for four academic years, or for five academic years for a five-year undergraduate program.

●**Eligibility.** Required students to be enrolled or accepted for enrollment in a minimum two-year degree or certificate program.

Students must have demonstrated academic achievement and preparation for postsecondary education by taking classes in the following areas while in high school: four years of English; three years of science; three years of mathematics; either three years of history or two years of history and one year of social studies; and either two years of a foreign language or one year of computer science and one year of a foreign language. Students must have earned a grade point average of at least 2.5 on a 4.0 scale in the final two years of high school. Students must either have participated in an early intervention program or have ranked in the top 10 percent of their high school graduating class. Each student who wanted a scholarship must have submitted an application to the secretary of Education.

## Model Program Community Partnership and Counseling Grants

● **Authorization.** Required the secretary of Education to award grants to develop model programs to counsel students about college opportunities, pre-college requirements, admissions, financial aid and student support services; and to develop programs that stimulate community partnerships with schools by providing tutoring, mentoring, work experiences and other services that make a postsecondary education a realistic goal for students. Authorized $35 million in fiscal 1993.

## Public Information

● **Authorization.** Required the secretary of Education to award a contract to create a computerized data base of all public and private financial assistance programs, to be accessible to schools and libraries through either computer modems or toll-free telephone lines; and to offer a toll-free information line to provide financial assistance information to parents, students and others. The law also authorized the secretary to enter into contracts with public agencies, nonprofit private organizations and institutions of higher education to conduct an information program designed to encourage economically disadvantaged, minority or at-risk students to continue their education after high school. Authorized $20 million in fiscal 1993.

## National Student Savings Demonstration Program

● **Authorization.** Created a demonstration program to test the idea of establishing a national student savings program to encourage families to save for their children's college education and reduce the loan indebtedness of college students. The law authorized the secretary of Education to award a demonstration grant to no more than five states. States must apply to the secretary to receive the grant, describing how the savings program would work and how many children would be served. The federal contribution to start each child's account was not to exceed $50. Authorized $10 million in fiscal 1993.

## Pre-Eligibility Form

● **Authorization.** Authorized the secretary of Education to develop a common federal financial aid form, distribute and process the form on a year-round basis free of charge to students and parents; and issue, based on the student's information, the amount of money the student might expect to receive in federal aid and the amount the family could expect to contribute.

## Technical Assistance for Teachers and Counselors

● **Authorization.** Required the secretary of Education to award grants to local educational agencies to use for special training for guidance counselors, teachers and principals to counsel students about college opportunities, pre-college requirements, college admissions and financial aid. The law required the secretary to give priority to school districts in which the proportion of students who continued on to higher education was significantly below the national average and in which the proportion of students who were educationally disadvantaged was above the national average. Authorized $40 million in fiscal 1993.

## Federal Supplemental Educational Opportunity Grants (SEOG)

● **Name change.** Changed the name of the program, which provided matching funds to schools to distribute as grants to their neediest students, to "Federal Supplemental Educational Opportunity Grants." The program generally was used to supplement Pell grants, and that preference was to continue. The average award was $715 per student. In fiscal 1992, appropriators provided $577 million, with grants going to 907,000 students. The law authorized $675 million in fiscal 1993. The law dropped the federal share of the program from 85 percent to 75 percent, requiring schools to increase their match from 15 percent to 25 percent.

## State Student Incentive Grants (SSIG)

● **Authorization.** Increased the maximum grant to $5,000 a year from the existing $2,500. The law authorized $105 million in fiscal 1993 in grants to states to help them provide grants to students attending postsecondary schools and grants to students performing campus-based community service work. In fiscal 1992, Congress appropriated $72 million for the SSIG program (which states are required to match dollar for dollar), giving 240,000 students an average of $600 each. President Bush proposed eliminating the program in his fiscal 1993 budget, arguing that the program was established as an incentive for states to provide student aid and that federal incentives were no longer needed.

## Students From Migrant and Seasonal Farmworker Families

● **Authorization.** Expanded from three to five years the grants made by the secretary of Education for two programs for students from migrant families. The law authorized $15 million in fiscal 1993 for a high school equivalency program for migrant students who were at least 16 years old. It also authorized $5 million for the college assistance migrant program, to help students with counseling, tutoring, health and other services.

## Robert C. Byrd Honors Scholarship Program

● **Authorization.** Increased the authorization to $10 million in fiscal 1993, from $8 million, for the program that provides $1,500 scholarships to outstanding students for their first year at a college or university. The law required states to spread the scholarships across the state, rather than awarding them according to congressional districts. It eliminated the awards ceremony and allocated scholarships among states based on the ratio of children between the ages of 5 and 17 within the state compared with all states.

## Assistance to Institutions of Higher Education

● **Need lead in.** Repealed the program providing payments to institutions of higher education, which was based on the number of students receiving Pell grants. The law also repealed the Veterans Education Outreach Program, which provided tutoring and counseling for veterans at postsecondary schools. It received a $2.7 million appropriation in fiscal 1992.

The bill reauthorized the Special Child-Care Services for Disadvantaged College Students at $20 million in fiscal 1993, the same as before. This program was used for grants to colleges and universities to provide child care to disadvantaged students.

## Guaranteed Student Loans

● **Name change.** Changed the name of the federal government's most popular student loan program from the Robert T. Stafford Student Loan Program to the Federal Robert T. Stafford Student Loan Program to make recipients aware of the funding source. Extended the program, which allowed students to borrow money from private banks, through Oct. 1, 1998. Under the program, the federal government paid the interest on the loan while the student was in school and guaranteed repayment of the principal should the student default.

In fiscal 1992, 3.7 million students received Stafford loans worth $10.3 billion. Congress appropriated $4.8 billion to pay the

interest on loans and to cover about $3.4 billion in defaults.

● **Guarantee authority.** Required that the government stop guaranteeing new loans after June 30, 1994, if the secretary of Education had not issued final regulations putting these Higher Education Act amendments into place by then. The Education Department had yet to issue regulations for changes to the loan program made in the 1986 reauthorization of the Higher Education Act. Final student loan regulations for the 1980 reauthorization were not put into place until one month after the 1986 reauthorization was signed into law.

● **Stafford annual loan limits.** Capped loans for undergraduate students who had not successfully completed the first year of school at the current $2,625 for full-time students. Loans for undergraduate students who had successfully completed the first year of a program were set at $3,500, up from $2,625.

Loans for undergraduate students who had successfully completed two years were set at $5,500, up from $4,000.

The annual loan limit for graduate and professional students was raised to $8,500, up from $7,500.

Changes in undergraduate loan amounts were scheduled to take effect July 1, 1993. Changes in loans for graduate students took effect Oct. 1, 1993.

● **Stafford interest rates.** Changed the interest rate for students to a variable rate made up of the 91-day Treasury bill rate plus 3.1 percent, with a cap of 9 percent, effective Oct. 1, 1992. Previously, the interest rate was 8 percent during the first four years of repayment and 10 percent for the remainder of repayment.

● **Federal Supplemental Loans for Students (SLS).** Maintained the loan limits for first- and second-year independent students at $4,000 and raised it for students who had completed their second year of school to $5,000. Graduate and professional students were allowed to borrow $10,000, up from $4,000. Conferees rejected the Senate provision to open this program to dependent students; instead, they created an unsubsidized Stafford loan program for all students.

● **SLS interest rates.** Lowered the cap on SLS interest rates to 11 percent, down from 12 percent, for any loan made on or after Oct. 1, 1993. Interest was to be calculated based upon the 52-week Treasury bill rate plus 3.1 percent, down from the current 3.25 percent. The law instituted an origination fee of 5 percent on all SLS loans.

● **Parent Loans for Undergraduate Students (PLUS).** Increased the annual loan limits from $4,000 to the cost of education minus other financial aid, effective July 1, 1993. This loan program became limited to parents who did not have an adverse credit history. Previously, no credit history was required.

● **PLUS interest rates.** Lowered the cap on PLUS interest rates from 12 percent to 10 percent for any loan made on or after Oct. 1, 1993. Interest was to be calculated based upon the 52-week Treasury bill rate plus 3.1 percent, down from the existing 3.25 percent. The law instituted an origination fee of 5 percent on all PLUS loans.

● **Windfall on interest rates.** Instituted a windfall provision on loans with an 8 percent interest rate, when the Treasury bill rate plus 3.1 percent was less than 8 percent. The Education Department was allowed to determine whether this provision should be applied to existing loans; it would, however, apply to loans made after July 23, 1992. The rationale was to keep interest payments on student loans in line with market interest rates, so that banks did not collect huge interest payments from students and the government when market rates were lower. If the government was paying 8 percent interest on a student's loan, the difference between the T-bill rate plus 3.1 percent and the 8 percent rate was credited to the government. When the borrower was making the 8 percent interest payments, the difference was credited to the borrower. The lender could reduce the borrower's final payments on the loan using the windfall provision.

● **Consolidation loans.** Allowed married borrowers, in addition to individuals, to consolidate their student loans. If the loans

totaled at least $7,500 but less than $10,000, the consolidation loans were to be repaid in 12 years; loans of $10,000 up to $20,000 were to be repaid in 15 years; loans of $20,000 up to $40,000 were to be repaid in 20 years; and loans of $40,000 up to $60,000 were to be repaid in 30 years.

● **Income sensitive repayment.** Required lenders to offer students the option of repaying their loans according to an income-sensitive repayment schedule. For Stafford and SLS loans, the lender was required to offer the student that option six months before the student's first payment was due. The repayment schedule was to be established by the lender according to guidelines set by the secretary. The repayment was to be in installments spread over five to 10 years. This covered loans made to new borrowers on or after July 1, 1993.

● **Deferments.** Reduced from 13 to three the types of situations in which a student could defer repayment of a loan. Students could apply for deferment if they were in school, unemployed or suffering from economic hardship. During deferments, the secretary of Education paid the interest on the loans. This applied to new borrowers, effective July 1, 1993.

● **Lender of last resort.** Required guarantee agencies to develop rules and operating procedures for lender-of-last-resort programs so that information about loans was made available to schools and students were counseled about their loan obligations. This was for guarantee agencies to provide loans when no other lender could be found. A guarantee agency or lender was not required to make loans to students at a school when past students from that school had a default rate that exceeded 25 percent for the most recent year calculated by the secretary of Education; at a school that had not been eligible for and had not participated in the loan program during the most recent 18 months; or to a school that was currently subject to a limitation, suspension or termination proceeding by any guarantee agency or by the secretary.

● **Default reduction programs.** Required each guarantee agency to allow a borrower who defaulted on a loan to renew eligibility for student financial aid when the borrower had made six consecutive monthly payments. The law said the agency could only require the borrower to make monthly payments that were reasonable and affordable based on the borrower's financial circumstances.

● **Unsubsidized Stafford loans.** Created a program to provide unsubsidized Stafford loans to students who did not qualify for federally subsidized Stafford loans. This program was nearly identical to the Stafford program, except that students were to pay interest on their loans while they were in school or while the loans were in deferment. The interest could be paid quarterly or monthly, or it could be capitalized and paid off with the principal after the student left school. Students were required to pay an origination and insurance fee of 6.5 percent on all unsubsidized loans.

● **Exceptional performance.** Required the secretary of Education to designate lenders, servicers and guarantee agencies as exceptional performers when they had loan collections that equaled or exceeded 97 percent. Servicers handled the loan paperwork for a bank. Guarantee agencies were required to pay each lender or servicer 100 percent of the unpaid principal and interest on all loans that were submitted for payment when the lender or servicer made the exceptional category. The law required the comptroller general to conduct a study of this provision within three years and send it to Congress. The secretary could end the program if it were in the best interest of the Treasury.

● **Loan forgiveness.** Authorized the secretary of Education to conduct a demonstration program in which the Education Department assumed Stafford student loans for people who entered the teaching and nursing professions and for people who performed national community service. The program would be authorized at $10 million in fiscal 1993 and would be effective for any new borrower after Oct. 1, 1992.

The borrower was required to: be employed full time as a nurse in a public hospital, a rural health clinic, a migrant health center,

the Indian Health Service, an Indian health center, a Native Hawaiian health center or an acute care or long-term care facility; be employed as a full-time teacher in certain schools that had trouble attracting faculty, teaching mathematics, science, foreign languages, special education, bilingual education or any other field beset by a shortage of qualified teachers; or agree in writing to volunteer for service under the Peace Corps Act or under the Domestic Volunteer Service Act of 1973, or perform comparable service as a full-time employee of a tax-exempt organization. The borrower could not receive compensation that was greater than either the minimum wage or an amount equal to 100 percent of poverty-line income for a family of two, whichever was greater.

The law required the secretary to assume repayment of 15 percent of the total amount of Stafford loans borrowed by the student for the first or second academic year; 20 percent for the third or fourth academic year; and 30 percent for the fifth academic year.

● **Default rates.** Required the secretary of Education to annually publish a list with the default rates of each lender, loan holder, guarantee agency and all schools of higher education.

● **Standardized forms.** Required the secretary of Education to work with guarantee agencies, lenders, institutions of higher education, secondary markets, students, third-party servicers and other organizations involved in providing student loans to prescribe standardized and simplified forms and procedures for: origination of loans, electronic funds transfer, guarantee of loans, deferments, servicing and other loan issues. This included providing a common application form for all student loans.

● **Default reduction management.** Authorized the secretary of Education to spend $25 million in fiscal 1993 to reduce defaults on student loans. Activities would include program reviews, audits, debt management programs and training activities. Defaults should be reduced by 5 percent compared with the previous fiscal year.

● **Closed schools.** Required the secretary of Education to repay the amount owed on a student's loan if the student was unable to complete the course of study because the school closed or if the school falsely certified the student's eligibility to borrow money. The secretary would then pursue any claim against the school and its principals.

● **Debt management options.** Authorized the secretary of Education to buy the notes of borrowers who were considered to be at high risk of default and who submitted a request to the secretary for an alternative method of repayment. The secretary could offer these borrowers one or more options, including graduated or extended repayment and income-contingent repayment. The secretary had to set up schedules for repayment, to last no more than 25 years. No more than $200 million could be used to buy loans for this program.

● **Special allowances.** Reduced the special allowance the federal government paid to lenders to the 91-day Treasury bill rate plus 3.1 percent, down from 3.25 percent. The special allowance was the interest subsidy the government paid to lenders when a student was in school or the student had received a deferment on repaying the loan. A lender also received the special allowance when the Treasury bill rate plus 3.1 percent exceeded the flat interest rate paid by the student.

● **Sallie Mae.** Required the Student Loan Marketing Association (Sallie Mae) to maintain a 2 percent capital ratio of shareholder equity to total assets or submit a business plan to the secretary of the Treasury describing how it would increase its capital ratio.

Sallie Mae was a so-called government-sponsored enterprise — created by the federal government but privately owned and operated — that bought student loans from lenders and then sold bonds backed by the loans. The bonds had the implicit backing of the federal government. Sallie Mae's assets at the end of 1991 were $45.3 billion, and its net income was $345.1 million.

● **Default rate trigger.** Reduced the default rate used to determine whether a school was eligible to participate in the student loan program from 30 percent over three consecutive years to 25 percent. The 30 percent mark would be used in fiscal 1993, and the 25 percent would kick in the following year.

● **Guarantee agency termination.** Authorized the secretary of Education to terminate a guarantee agency if the agency failed to submit a management plan that was acceptable to the secretary; if the secretary decided that the guarantee agency had failed to improve substantially in its administrative operations or financial condition; and if the secretary determined that the guarantee agency was in danger of financial collapse. The secretary would then assume responsibility for all functions of the guarantee agency and its loan insurance program.

## Federal Work-Study Programs

● **Authorization.** Authorized $800 million in fiscal 1993 to help support the cost of paying students who worked part time, usually in on-campus jobs. In fiscal 1992, Congress appropriated $615 million for the work-study program, which provided a total of $808 million in aid to 812,000 students.

● **Community service.** Required all schools, beginning in fiscal 1994, to use at least 5 percent of their work-study funds for community service work-study programs, unless the secretary waived the requirement because it would cause student hardship. Community service was defined as service to improve the quality of life for community residents, particularly low-income people, in such areas as health care, child care, literacy training and education.

● **Allocation of funds.** Authorized the secretary, when appropriations for college work-study exceeded $700 million, to allocate 10 percent of the excess money to schools in which at least 50 percent of Pell grant recipients graduated or transferred to four-year higher education institutions.

● **Institutional match.** Dropped the school portion of federal-school matching funds to 25 percent, from 30 percent.

● **Work colleges.** Authorized $5 million in fiscal 1993 to create a program within the college work-study program to encourage the use of comprehensive work-learning programs as part of a student's financial aid package, to reduce reliance on grants and loans. Schools had to apply to the secretary to be designated as a work college and had to match federal funds dollar-for-dollar. To be eligible, schools had to: be a public or private nonprofit institution with a commitment to community service; have operated a comprehensive work-learning program for at least two years; and require all students who lived on campus to participate in a comprehensive work-learning program.

## Federal Direct Loan Demonstration Program

● **Authorization.** Required the secretary of Education to conduct a direct loan demonstration program between July 1, 1994, and June 30, 1998. The program was an entitlement, with students at participating schools being given a contractual right to receive payments.

The secretary was to choose the schools, giving preference to those that had filled out an application. The secretary was to choose schools with an aggregate loan volume of $500 million for Stafford loans, SLS and PLUS loans. The schools should represent a cross section of all institutions of higher education participating in the federal student loan program. Students at schools participating in the direct loan program would not be eligible to receive federal Stafford loans, SLS or PLUS loans.

The federal direct loans were to have the same terms and conditions as the Stafford loan program. Both subsidized and unsubsidized loans would be available.

Within the demonstration, 35 percent of the schools were to offer repayment options to borrowers based on their incomes — if the secretary found that the department had found a way to collect the money and that the government would not lose any money over the long run.

The secretary was to award contracts to loan servicers and collection agencies, on a competitive basis, to collect the principal

and interest on loans; to collect defaulted loans; to establish and operate a central data system to maintain records on all direct loans; and to provide programs on default prevention.

The law required the comptroller general to submit a final report to Congress no later than May 1, 1998, evaluating the program, particularly the administrative costs per loan.

The law authorized unspecified amounts in fiscal 1993 to conduct the program. Administrative and servicing funds were capped at a total of $189 million for the entire demonstration program.

### Federal Perkins Loans

● **Authorization.** Authorized $250 million in fiscal 1993. This was a campus-administered program using a revolving loan fund to provide low-interest loans to students. About 3,300 schools participated at the time.

● **Loan limits.** Allowed all undergraduate students to borrow $3,000 per year and graduate or professional students to borrow $5,000 per year.

● **Campus match.** Increased the campus match to federal funds from 10 percent to 15 percent in fiscal 1993 and to 25 percent in the years thereafter. Schools with default rates of 7.5 percent or less could increase their campus match to at least 50 percent, which would give them more money to distribute. They could offer annual limits of $4,000 for undergraduates and $6,000 for graduate students.

● **Minimum monthly repayment.** Increased from $30 a month to $50 a month.

● **Interest rates.** Maintained the existing rate of 5 percent.

### Need Analysis

● **Amount of need.** Changed the definition of student need. Previously, the law defined need as the cost of school attendance minus the expected family contribution, based on financial means. Under the new system, need was defined as the cost of school attendance minus the expected family contribution for the student, minus the estimated financial assistance received in non-federal scholarships. The new need analysis provisions applied to all aid beginning July 1, 1993.

● **Cost of attendance.** Included tuition and fees; an allowance for books, supplies and transportation; and an allowance for room and board.

● **Family contribution.** Defined family contribution as the amount that the student and the student's family could be reasonably expected to contribute toward the student's postsecondary education for a specific academic year.

● **Data elements to determine expected family contribution.** Included the available income of the student and the student's spouse or the student and the student's parents; the number of dependents in the student's family; the number of dependents in the student's family who were enrolled, at least half-time, in a degree or other credential program at a postsecondary school; the net assets of the student and the student's spouse, or the student and the student's parents; the student's marital status; the age of the older parent; and the work-related expenses incurred when a dependent student's parents were employed or when the family was headed by a single parent who was employed, or when the student was married and the student's spouse was employed.

● **Expected family contribution for dependent students.** Equaled the sum of the parents' contribution from adjusted available income; the student's contribution from available income; and the student's contribution from assets.

● **Parental net worth.** Calculated the family's net worth by adding the existing balances of checking and savings accounts and cash on hand; the net value of investments and real estate, excluding the principal residence; and the adjusted net worth of a business or farm. Assets did not include the net value of a family's principal place of residence or a family farm on which the family lived.

● **Simplified needs test.** Required the secretary of Education to develop a simplified application section for financial aid for families who were not required to file an income tax return and who had a total adjusted gross income of less than $50,000. This applied to dependent and independent students. The elements to be used for the simplified needs analysis were: adjusted gross income; federal taxes paid; untaxed income and benefits; the number of family members; the number of family members in postsecondary education; and state and other taxes.

● **Zero expected family contribution.** Required the secretary of Education to consider a financial aid applicant to have an expected family contribution equal to zero if: the student's parents were not required to file a 1040 income tax form and the sum of the adjusted gross income of the parents was less than the maximum federal earned income credit — about $11,300.

### General Provisions

● **Correspondence schools.** Removed schools that enrolled more than 50 percent of their students in correspondence courses from eligibility for federal student financial aid programs. Students were not eligible for a grant, loan or work-study aid for a correspondence course unless the course led to an associate, bachelor's or graduate degree.

● **Bankruptcy and fraud.** Prohibited a school from qualifying for federal student aid programs if it had filed for bankruptcy or if the school, its owner or its chief executive officer had been convicted of a crime involving funds from financial aid programs.

● **Student aid application forms.** Required all students applying for federal student aid to use a federal application form produced by the Department of Education. No parent or student using the common form could be charged a fee for the collection, processing or delivery of financial aid. The secretary of Education could include no more than eight non-financial data questions chosen in consultation with the states to assist states in awarding state financial aid. States typically asked for additional information when awarding state aid, but the federal government was trying to keep the form simple. Postsecondary schools and states were to receive the data collected by the secretary free of charge. To foster competition and competitive bidding, the secretary was required to enter into no fewer than five contracts with states, institutions of higher education or private organizations to collect the financial aid information and process the form. The secretary also was required to include in these contracts a requirement that any charges by the contractor to the student or parent for additional data items required by a state or school be reasonable and not exceed the "marginal cost" of collecting, processing and delivering each item. Within 240 days of enactment, the secretary was required to develop a streamlined re-application form and process, including an electronic re-application process.

● **Toll-free information.** Required the secretary of Education to contract for and publicize a toll-free telephone service to provide timely and accurate information to the public about applying for financial aid. The service also had to include telecommunications devices for the deaf (TDDs).

● **Ability to benefit.** Stipulated that to receive financial aid, students without high school diplomas had to take an examination and receive a score demonstrating an ability to benefit from postsecondary education; or, the secretary of Education could approve an alternative to testing, run by the states.

● **Selective Service.** Required the secretary of Education to conduct data base matches with the Selective Service to confirm that students had fulfilled their requirement to register with the service.

● **Exit counseling.** Required each school to provide counseling to borrowers, either individually or in groups, about repaying their loans after they left school.

● **Campus security.** Required schools to collect statistics concerning the occurrence on campus of murder, sex offenses, robbery, aggravated assault, burglary and car theft. Schools also were required to develop and distribute a policy statement regarding campus sexual assault programs and the procedures followed once a sex offense occurred.

● **Program participation agreements.** Required schools to provide information regarding their administrative capability and financial responsibility to the secretary of Education, the appropriate state review agency, the appropriate guarantee agency and the appropriate accrediting agency or association.

● **Revenue from athletics.** Required schools that offered athletically related student aid to compile annually the total revenues and expenses from intercollegiate football, men's and women's basketball, all other men's sports and all other women's sports. The bill also required reporting the school's total revenues and operating expenses. The reports would be available to the secretary of Education and the public.

● **Delayed disbursement.** Prohibited schools from imposing any penalty, late fee or denial of access to classes, libraries or other school facilities because of the delayed disbursement of the proceeds of a student loan.

● **Commissions, bonuses and student recruitment.** Prohibited any commission, bonus or incentive based on enrollment to any person or business involved in student recruitment, admissions or financial aid awards. This was aimed at proprietary trade schools, to discourage them from improperly recruiting students who may not benefit from the education.

● **Criminal penalties.** Required that anyone who embezzled or misapplied funds from federal student aid programs be subject to a $20,000 fine and five years in prison. For stealing $200 or less, the fine would be up to $5,000, with one year in prison.

The same penalties would apply to attempted crimes. Fines were doubled from existing law, which did not cover attempted crimes.

## Program Integrity

● **State postsecondary review program.** Authorized the secretary of Education to designate one state postsecondary review agency in each state to review institutions of higher education to determine their eligibility to participate in federal financial aid programs. The law authorized $75 million in fiscal 1993 for the secretary to reimburse state agencies.

Criteria for the initial review of a school included: a default rate of at least 25 percent; a default rate of at least 20 percent when either more than two-thirds of the school's undergraduates were enrolled on at least a half-time basis and were receiving federal assistance or two-thirds or more of the school's expenditures came from student financial aid money; or a limitation, suspension or termination action by the secretary against the school during the preceding five years, among other items. Schools meeting one or more of the criteria were to be be reviewed.

The review was required to determine: the availability to students of catalogs, admission requirements, tuition and fee schedules; assurance that the institution maintained academic standards; and school compliance with safety and health standards, among other things.

If the state agency found that the school did not meet one or more of the standards, the agency was to notify the secretary.

● **Accrediting agency approval.** Established that no accrediting agency or association could be considered to be a reliable authority on the quality of education or training offered, unless the agency met standards established by the secretary of Education. Those standards were to include an appropriate measure of student achievement.

● **Eligibility and certification procedures.** Required the secretary of Education to determine a postsecondary school's legal authority to operate within a state, the accreditation status, and its administrative capability and financial responsibility for the school to qualify to participate in federal financial aid programs.

● **Financial guarantees from owners.** Authorized the secretary of Education to require financial guarantees from an institution participating or seeking to participate in any federal financial aid program. The secretary could require the assumption of personal liability by one or more people who exercised substantial control over the school.

## Partnerships for Educational Excellence

● **School, college and university partnerships.** Authorized the secretary of Education to make grants between $250,000 and $1 million to partnerships between institutions of higher education or state higher education agencies and secondary schools serving low-income and disadvantaged students. The partnerships would create programs to improve the retention and graduation rates at secondary schools; improve the academic skills of public and private nonprofit secondary school students; increase those students' opportunities to continue their education after secondary school; and improve the students' prospects for employment after secondary school. Grants could be awarded for up to five years and were to be well distributed geographically. The law authorized Congress to fund the program at $20 million in fiscal 1993.

● **Articulation agreements.** Required the secretary of Education to make grants to states to make awards to two- and four-year higher education institutions. The states could distribute the funds on a competitive basis or by their own formula for the schools to develop "articulation agreements," to ease the transition for students from two-year to four-year schools. The money could be used for faculty training, counseling services and outreach to students, among other things. The law authorized Congress to spend up to $25 million in fiscal 1993.

● **Telecommunications.** Authorized the secretary of Education to make grants to partnerships between public broadcasting and higher education groups, and public broadcasting, higher education groups and state and local governments or nonprofit groups, to acquire equipment for schools and campuses; to develop satellite, fiber-optic and other systems for local broadcasts; to provide training for elementary and secondary school teachers using videoconferencing, and to create a loan service of captioned films for people with hearing disabilities. The federal share could not exceed 50 percent. Authorized $10 million in fiscal 1993.

## Academic Libraries and Information Services

● **Grants.** Authorized grant programs to libraries to acquire technological equipment; to train people in library and information science; to help the nation's major research libraries strengthen their collections; and to help historically black colleges and universities and other institutions serving minorities with programs in library and information sciences to train and educate African-Americans. The law included $20 million in fiscal 1993 for college library technology and cooperation grants; $10 million in fiscal 1993 for library education, research and development; $20 million in fiscal 1993 for improving access to research library resources, and $15 million in fiscal 1993 for strengthening library and information science programs and libraries in historically black colleges and universities and other institutions serving minorities.

## Institutional Aid

● **Strengthening institutions.** Authorized $135 million in fiscal 1993 in grants to institutions with severe financial difficulties. Funds could be used to develop faculty, run student services and support libraries and laboratories.

The reauthorization created a category, authorizing $45 million in fiscal 1993, to support institutions serving Hispanics. Those schools had to have an enrollment of undergraduate full-time students that was at least 25 percent Hispanic. No fewer than 50 percent of the Hispanic students had to be low-income, first-generation college students; an additonal 25 percent of Hispanic students had to be either low-income or first-generation college students.

● **Historically black colleges and universities.** Authorized $135 million in fiscal 1993 in grants to help schools raise money from alumni and other sources, to establish or improve teacher education programs to prepare students to teach in elementary or secondary public schools in their state; and to create community outreach programs to encourage elementary and secondary students to develop their academic skills and interest in higher educa-

tion. The bill would raise the minimum grant from $350,000 to $500,000.

The bill authorized $20 million in fiscal 1993 to provide grants to 16 institutions to attract minority students to graduate study. But it stipulated that the five schools that were currently receiving money would be the only ones funded if no more than the current $12 million in appropriations was provided. In fact, appropriators only provided $11.5 million for fiscal 1993, so the additional schools were not to receive funding.

The new schools were:

> Florida A&M University School of Pharmaceutical Sciences, Tallahassee, Fla.
>
> Xavier University of Louisiana College of Pharmacy, New Orleans.
>
> North Carolina Central University School of Law, Durham, N.C.
>
> Southern University School of Law, Baton Rouge, La.
>
> Texas Southern University School of Law or School of Pharmacy, Houston.
>
> Morgan State Graduate School, Baltimore.
>
> Hampton University Graduate School, Hampton, Va.
>
> Alabama A&M Graduate School, Normal, Ala.
>
> North Carolina A&T State University Graduate School, Greensboro, N.C.
>
> University of Maryland Eastern Shore Graduate School, Princess Anne, Md.
>
> Jackson State Graduate School, Jackson, Miss.

The schools receiving grants in 1992 were:

> Morehouse School of Medicine, Atlanta.
>
> Meharry Medical School, Nashville, Tenn.
>
> Charles R. Drew Postgraduate Medical School, Los Angeles.
>
> Atlanta University, Atlanta.
>
> Tuskegee University School of Veterinary Medicine, Tuskegee, Ala.

## Educator Recruitment, Retention and Development

● **State and local programs for teacher excellence.** Authorized $350 million in fiscal 1993 to provide funds to state and local educational agencies and institutions of higher education to improve the skills of classroom teachers, to establish state academies for teachers and school leaders and to provide a comprehensive review of state requirements for teacher certification.

The secretary of Education was to distribute half the money according to the number of people in the state ages 5 to 17 compared with other states, and half the money based on the amount of money a state received under Chapter 1, the compensatory education program geared to disadvantaged children.

Local education agencies that received state funds would use the money for teacher training and recruitment, to form business partnerships and to attract military veterans into teaching.

State education agencies that received funds would use them to conduct a study of state teacher education programs and to establish state academies for teachers and school leaders. The academies for teachers would aim to improve elementary and secondary school teachers' knowledge and teaching skills in key academic subjects. Academies for school leaders would aim to improve the training and performance of school principals and other leaders and to increase the number of people who were highly trained to be principals and school leaders.

Institutions of higher education could apply for state grants to assist local education agencies in providing teacher training.

● **National teacher academies.** Authorized $35 million in fiscal 1993 for the secretary of Education to award grants to establish up to three national teacher academies for English, mathematics, science, history, geography, civics and government and foreign languages. Grants were to be awarded competitively to institutions of higher education and private nonprofit educational organizations. Funds were to be used to provide training programs for teachers and administrators to improve their knowledge in a particular subject area; to provide techniques for teaching that knowledge to students; and to offer the most recent applied research findings regarding education and the classroom.

● **Teacher corps.** Authorized state education agencies to designate "teacher corps" schools, public elementary or secondary schools that had the highest levels of poverty and the lowest levels of student achievement in the state. The state education agency also was to choose people to become members of the teacher corps. They would be people who intended to teach students with disabilities, students with limited English and preschool children. Corps members also should have been members of minority groups that were underrepresented in the teaching profession or in the subject area in which they wished to teach or people who intended to teach science or math. Teacher corps members were to receive $5,000 scholarships for no more than three years while pursuing an undergraduate or graduate degree. Each recipient had to promise to work as a teacher for three years in a teacher corps school. Authorized $25 million in fiscal 1993.

● **National Board for Professional Teaching Standards.** Authorized $20 million between Oct. 1, 1992, and Sept. 30, 1997, for the national board, which was created in 1987 with funding from the Carnegie Corp. of New York and other foundations to draw up guidelines for voluntary certification of teachers nationwide. The federal funds could only be used for research and development directly related to teacher assessment and certification procedures for elementary and secondary school teachers. The federal share was 50 percent of the cost.

● **Alternative routes to teacher certification and licensing.** Authorized $15 million in fiscal 1993 for grants to states to develop alternative teacher certification or licensing requirements. The programs were to emphasize the participation of people from minority groups.

● **Class size demonstration grant.** Authorized $3 million in fiscal 1993 to provide grants to local education agencies to test the benefits of reducing class size on the educational performance of students and on classroom management and organization. The federal share of the program was 50 percent. The secretary of Education was required to give priority to demonstration projects that involved at-risk students, including educationally or economically disadvantaged students, students with disabilities, students with limited knowledge of English and primary grade students.

● **Middle school teaching demonstration programs.** Authorized $5 million in fiscal 1993 for competitive grants to institutions of higher education to develop model programs with a specialized focus on teaching grades 6 through 9.

● **Minority teacher recruitment.** Authorized $30 million in fiscal 1993 for grants to states to help school support workers or school paraprofessionals, such as teachers' aides, who were minorities to become certified or licensed teachers. Within 10 years of completing postsecondary course work, the person had to go to work within that school district and repay the student financial aid received, plus interest.

● **Programs to encourage minority students to become teachers.** Authorized $15 million in fiscal 1993 for grants to partnerships of one or more institutions of higher education; one or more local educational agencies; state educational agencies, and community-based organizations. Grants were to be used to improve recruitment and training in education for minority students, to increase the number of minority teachers, and to identify and encourage minority students in grades 7 through 12 to prepare for careers in elementary and secondary school teaching.

● **National mini-corps program.** Authorized $10 million in fiscal 1992 to provide grants to institutions of higher education to help first-generation college students, low-income students and

children of migrant workers enroll in postsecondary school and to provide them with the support they need to stay in school.

### International Education

• **Authorizations.** Authorized $80 million in fiscal 1993 to continue funding undergraduate and graduate language centers and area centers, such as centers for European or African studies; language resource centers; undergraduate international studies and foreign language programs; and intensive summer language institutes.

The bill authorized a program of competitive grants to consortia of American universities, colleges, museums and research societies operating overseas to help American scholars conducting research. The bill also authorized $5 million in fiscal 1993 for grants to institutions of higher education and public or nonprofit private libraries to acquire periodicals and other research materials published outside the United States.

• **Business and international education programs.** Authorized $11 million in fiscal 1993 for grants to institutions of higher education to pay the 50 percent federal share of the cost of planning, establishing and operating centers for international business education.

The centers were supposed to be national resources for the teaching of improved business techniques and strategies that emphasized the international context in which business was transacted. They also were to provide instruction in foreign languages and in the cultures and customs of U.S. trading partners.

• **Institute for International Public Policy.** Authorized $10 million in fiscal 1993 for the secretary of Education to award a competitive grant for a group to establish an Institute for International Public Policy.

The institute was to conduct a program to increase the number of African-Americans and other underrepresented minorities in the international service, including private international voluntary organizations and the U.S. foreign service. The institute was to conduct a junior year abroad program open to students from historically black colleges and universities, tribally controlled Indian community colleges and other schools of higher education with significant minority populations. The institute also was supposed to offer a master's degree in international relations.

### Construction, Reconstruction and Renovation of Academic Facilities

• **Improvement of academic and library facilities.** Authorized $350 million in fiscal 1993 for federal grants to states to be given out by formula, with half the funds to be distributed based on population and half by the number of students attending colleges and universities.

States were to match the federal funds with 25 percent of the money received. States then were to distribute grants to colleges and universities with priority to schools that served large numbers or percentages of minority or disadvantaged students.

Schools were to provide matching funds equal to 50 percent of the grant received. If the school had received a direct, non-competitive award of federal funds (an "earmark" in an appropriations bill) within the two preceding fiscal years for facilities construction, renovation or improvement, then the school was ineligible to receive any money under this program.

Grants could be used for improving, renovating or repairing any academic facility; improving and renovating any library building; improving and renovating broadcast, cable and satellite equipment for postsecondary educational television and radio programming; and building academic and library facilities.

• **Historically black college and university capital financing.** Authorized the secretary of Education to insure up to $375 million in bonds, with proceeds to be lent to historically black colleges and universities to finance capital projects.

Of that, no more than $250 million was to be used for loans to private historically black colleges and universities and no more than $125 million was to be used for loans to historically black public colleges and universities.

### Cooperative Education

• **Authorization.** Authorized $30 million in fiscal 1993 for grants to institutions of higher education to offer work experiences to students to help them in future careers and to help them financially while in school.

### Graduate Programs

• **Grants to encourage women and minority participation in graduate education.** Authorized $25 million in fiscal 1993 for grants to institutions of higher education and consortia of those schools to help them identify talented undergraduates who demonstrated financial need and who were from minority groups underrepresented in graduate education or were women underrepresented in fields of study in graduate education such as math and science. Grants also were to be used to provide those students with a chance to participate in a program of research and scholarly activities to prepare them for graduate study.

• **Patricia Roberts Harris Fellowship Program.** Authorized $60 million in fiscal 1993 for grants to minorities and women who were underrepresented in master's, professional and doctoral education programs.

• **Jacob K. Javits Fellowship Program.** Authorized $30 million in fiscal 1993 for the secretary of Education to award fellowships for graduate study in the arts, humanities and social sciences to students selected for their achievement and promise.

• **Assistance for training in the legal profession.** Authorized $7 million in fiscal 1993 for the secretary of Education to carry out a program to assist minority, low-income or educationally disadvantaged college graduates in pursuing a law degree through an annual grant or contract with the Council on Legal Education Opportunity. A legal training project could provide: assistance and counseling in gaining admission to accredited law schools; a six-week intensive summer program designed to prepare minority, low-income or educationally disadvantaged people for the successful completion of legal studies; or an academic-year program of tutorial services, academic advice and counseling to help students successfully complete their legal training.

### Postsecondary Improvement Programs

• **Fund for the improvement of postsecondary education.** Authorized $20 million in fiscal 1993 for the secretary of Education to make grants to, or enter into contracts with, institutions of higher education and other public and private nonprofit institutions and agencies, to enable them to improve postsecondary education by: encouraging reform; making structural changes in postsecondary schools; introducing cost-effective methods of instruction and operation; and introducing reforms in graduate education, in the structure of academic professions and in recruiting and retaining faculty. No grant could exceed $20,000.

• **Women and minorities science and engineering outreach demonstration.** Authorized $10 million in fiscal 1993 for the secretary of Education to make grants to schools to help them run a program to identify and encourage women and minority elementary and secondary school students to pursue higher education in preparation for careers in science and engineering.

### Community Service Programs

• **Urban community service.** Authorized $20 million in fiscal 1993 for the secretary of Education to make grants to urban postsecondary schools to support planning, research, training and other activities that would help develop programs that would help urban communities address such pressing problems as work force preparation, poverty, health care and underperforming school systems.

• **Innovative projects for community service.** Authorized $15 million in fiscal 1993 to institutions of higher education to promote the development of literacy and mentoring programs to be operated by schools in their own communities. ∎

*Continued from p. 445*
with Republicans against it.

### Conferees Ratify Agreements

Higher education conferees ratifed close to 1,400 staff recommendations June 11, narrowing considerably the differences between the House and Senate reauthorizations of the Higher Education Act of 1965.

Included among the recommendations the conferees approved were:

• An increase in the maximum Pell grant authorization from $3,100 to $3,700 a year.

• An increase in the limits for the annual Robert T. Stafford guaranteed student loan from $2,625 to $3,500 for full-time, second-year students; from $4,000 to $5,500 for full-time undergraduates who had completed two years of school; and from $7,500 to $8,500 for full-time graduate students.

• And the creation of an unsubsidized guaranteed student loan program for all students, regardless of income. Students — rather than the government — would be required to pay the interest while they were in school.

### Direct Loans

Lawmakers were intrigued a year earlier by an idea to bypass neighborhood banks and provide student loans directly from the government to students through their schools.

Because the federal government subsidized the banks for making the student loans, the thinking was that the government could eliminate that cost by making the loans itself. But the administration, which debated the idea for months, came out against it. OMB Director Richard G. Darman said the risk to the Treasury was too great and that the loans would add to the federal deficit until they were paid back years later.

Still, the idea caught fire in Congress. In the Senate, Simon and Durenberger expanded the plan to require that loans be repaid according to income. That proposal, though, was never attached to the Senate's higher education bill (S 1150).

The House, led by freshman Andrews, initially wanted to replace the guaranteed student loan program with a direct loan program. Facing Republican opposition, members agreed to try the idea on a limited basis as a demonstration.

In conference, however, the issue was how large that demonstration program should be. The House bill called for the Education secretary to choose a group of schools with a combined loan volume of $500 million under the existing system. Students at those schools would have a contractual right — or entitlement — to receive direct loans. Students could receive more than $500 million in loans as the years went on.

But Coleman said Chairman Ford had reneged on a deal to cap the program at $500 million a year, rather than allowing it to be open-ended. In conference, the administration and Republican conferees tried to cut back the size of the demonstration and put a cap on it.

But Andrews said he would fight in conference to increase the size of the demonstration program so that it would serve 500 schools. At $500 million, it would probably only serve 300.

Andrews said he questioned why Bush would want "to give welfare checks to banks" rather than loans to middle-class students.

"This is the corporate analogy of Ronald Reagan's wel-

fare queen, who collected three checks a month and drove a Cadillac," he added.

Andrews also wanted to persuade conferees to lower the "special allowance" subsidy paid to banks when a student was in school. At the time, the federal government paid banks interest on the loans, calculated at 3.25 percentage points plus the 91-day Treasury bill rate — then 3.66 percent.

The House recommended lowering the special allowance subsidy to 2.85 percent plus the 91-day Treasury bill rate. House and Senate staffers compromised at 3.1 percent.

Banks said the change would cost them big money. "We have indisputable evidence that lenders are abandoning loans to students enrolled in short-term programs as a result of unprofitability of short-term loans," said John E. Dean, a lawyer representing the Consumer Bankers Association.

Dean cited the Bank of America, which had recently announced that it would no longer make short-term loans to trade school students in California. "We can only assume that Congressman Andrews is indifferent to the needs of those students."

## FINAL ACTION

The Senate adopted by voice vote June 30, and the House cleared on July 8, the conference report to a five-year, $100 billion student aid bill (S 1150) to reauthorize the Higher Education Act of 1965. The act governed loans and grants for students to attend college and trade schools, and the reauthorization allowed all students, regardless of income, to borrow money to pay for their education. The bill passed the House 419-7. *(Vote 274, p. 66-H)*

The bill opened aid programs to more middle-class students by removing a family's home or farm equity from calculations of how much aid a student needed to attend school.

Bush had threatened to veto the bill because it included a demonstration program allowing the government to make direct loans to students, cutting out the middleman role of banks.

Education Secretary Alexander said the program "destroyed" the bill and would create billions of dollars of new government debt.

But Republican lawmakers who helped write the bill went to the White House on June 25 and talked to Bush for about 20 minutes.

"We told him frankly that we thought we had fought the fight and the bill was overwhelmingly good," said Coleman. "We told him it would be hard to explain why he was vetoing this bill that helps middle-income families."

After the meeting, W. Henson Moore, Bush's deputy chief of staff, called Ford, asking for a compromise.

According to the lawmakers' aides, Moore suggested that Ford and Senate Labor Committee Chairman Edward M. Kennedy, D-Mass., drop the provision specifying that 500 schools be included and change it to schools with a combined loan volume of $500 million — as in the original House bill, which the administration had previously opposed. With 500 schools, the government would have had to provide about $700 million to $1 billion in loans. The final provision was aimed at schools with $500 million in loan volume.

Bush dropped his veto threat the week of June 29 and signed the bill July 23. ∎

# Scorned School Bill Dies in Senate

In a repeat of the 101st Congress, Senate Republicans again blocked Congress from passing legislation (S 2) that sought to improve public schools. Few members liked the Neighborhood Schools Improvement Act, which would have provided $800 million in block grants to states and schools, leaving specific reforms up to local education officials.

Democrats moved the bill along because they did not want to appear as if they were obstructing President Bush from working on education. But Bush's advisers threatened a veto because the bill that emerged contained no mention of the administration's America 2000 education proposals, such as national student testing or giving parents more choice in whether to send their children to public or private school. Additionally, the bill provided no funding to create Bush's "break the mold" New American Schools. The administration also had wanted to institute widespread flexibility waivers to test the idea of eliminating state and federal regulations and red tape. The bill, however, allowed for flexibility waivers in only 750 schools and only for programs for disadvantaged students.

Neither Democrats nor Republicans expressed much support for the conference report (H Rept 102-916). Republicans disliked it because it lacked Bush's initiatives. Democrats disliked it because it did not go far enough and did not authorize enough money.

"This is the first time in 18 years that we've brought an education bill to the House floor without enthusiasm from both sides," said Rep. Bill Goodling, Pa., the ranking Republican on the Education and Labor Committee.

Nevertheless, the House approved the bill; a cloture vote in the Senate failed by one vote.

## School Choice

Of Bush's proposals, school choice was the most politically volatile. Bush spoke frequently on the campaign trail of the need to help poor students go to the schools that rich students attended. He wanted to conduct a $500 million school choice demonstration program to make matching grants of up to $500 per middle- and low-income child. The money was to go to states and localities, which would be given certificates of up to $1,000 per child to be used at any public or private school.

School choice advocates said the plan would spur competition, forcing bad schools to improve to retain and attract students.

Detractors feared that sending public money to private

---

## BOXSCORE

➡ **Elementary and Secondary School Improvements (S 2, HR 4323, HR 3320).** Legislation to provide block grants to states to improve education. Although President Bush pushed hard for a school choice provision that would have given parents federal support in choosing a public or private school for their children, both chambers rejected it. The final measure failed on a cloture vote.

**Reports:** H Rept 102-691; S Rept 102-43; conference report S Rept 102-916.

### KEY ACTION

Jan. 28 — The **Senate** passed S 2, 92-6.

May 20 — The **House** Education and Labor Committee passed HR 4323, 23-12.

Aug. 12 — The **House** approved HR 4323, 279-124.

Sept. 25 — **House-Senate** conferees agreed on a conference report by voice vote.

Sept. 30 — The **House** adopted the conference report to S 2 by voice vote.

Oct. 2 — The **Senate** voted 59-40 to cut off debate, one vote short of invoking cloture.

---

schools would erode public education. They questioned how schools that lost both students and government funding could ever improve under a choice program. Senate Democrats agreed to allow the block grant money for public school choice only, but House Democrats refused to go along with either public or private school choice.

Goodling attributed the unusual education partisanship to the vagaries of the election year and the Democrats' fear of letting Bush be known as the education president.

After listening to Republican complaints on the House floor, Dale E. Kildee, D-Mich., chairman of the Subcommittee on Elementary, Secondary and Vocational Education, conceded that the bill was not perfect. "The only perfect law I'm aware of was written on Mount Sinai," he said. "This is Capitol Hill."

## BACKGROUND

Bush pledged in 1988 to be the education president, but Democrats insisted that his goals were meaningless without more money. In the first three years of Bush's presidency, the Democrat-controlled Congress bottled up his proposals or linked them to large money increases that the administration was unwilling to accept.

Still, Bush could be credited with starting a national dialogue about what needed to be done to improve students' education and what role the federal government should play. Bush convened a meeting of the nation's governors in 1989 in Charlottesville, Va., where they developed national education goals. Those goals included increasing high school graduation rates and making American students No. 1 in math and science by the year 2000.

In January 1991, Bush, stung by charges that he had no domestic agenda, fired Education Secretary Lauro F. Cavazos and replaced him with Lamar Alexander, an aggressive former governor of Tennessee. Alexander crafted a $690 million plan that Bush unveiled April 18, 1991. It would overhaul the nation's troubled education system at the state and local levels using a limited amount of federal money to fund model programs and offer incentives for change. Included in the "America 2000" program were voluntary national testing for fourth-, eighth- and 12th-graders, merit pay for teachers, creation of non-traditional schools, and a proposal to give parents a choice of whether to send their children to public or private schools with federal support. School choice was an administration priority — and the most controversial of Bush's education proposals. Many lawmakers feared that sending public funds

to private schools could encroach on the separation of church and state when religious schools were involved. *(1991 Almanac, p. 377)*

But America 2000 became Bush's rallying cry, and he and Alexander barnstormed the country in an effort to enlist cities and states to join. The 102nd Congress, meanwhile, had not been scheduled to take up elementary and secondary education programs, which had been reauthorized for five years in 1988 (PL 100-297). Instead, Education committees worked on reauthorizing the Higher Education Act. *(Higher education, p. 438)*

But because of Bush's insistence on talking about the dire state of public education, Democrats grudgingly responded with elementary and secondary education bills that essentially allowed local school districts to try some of his ideas, albeit under different names.

Initially, House Democrats went along with a modified version of Bush's private school choice plan. Education Committee Democrats, while generally opposed to the choice concept, worked out a compromise in 1991 with then-White House Chief of Staff John H. Sununu and the panel's ranking Republican, Goodling of Pennsylvania. It was to allow local school districts to use some of the federal money for public and private school choice plans — but only if the state constitution allowed it and the school district wanted it.

Given those restrictions, only two states would have qualified — Vermont and Wisconsin — and neither allowed money to go to religious schools.

### 1991 Action

The $700 million measure (HR 3320) approved 26-12 by the House Education and Labor Committee on Oct. 17, 1991, included Bush's school choice proposal, but differed from Bush in other areas. It essentially left it up to the local school districts to decide what reforms to make. States could apply for five-year grants to be approved by the Education secretary, and they needed to set up panels to devise plans that included specific goals. States would make funds available to school districts, which could use the money for many activities, including choice and non-traditional schools.

School-choice opponents waged a two-day battle to limit choice to public schools, but the committee defeated a public-school choice amendment, 17-23. Bush supported the House measure.

Senate Democrats did not compromise on choice.

The Senate Labor and Human Resources Committee approved its bill by voice vote Nov. 13. It authorized $850 million in fiscal 1992 for block grants to states for education improvement and unspecified amounts for the next four years. This bill, too, was much less specific than the Bush plan on how the states should spend the funds. But unlike the House committee bill, the Senate committee bill allowed choice only among public schools.

In the waning days of the 1991 legislative session, Majority Leader George J. Mitchell, D-Maine, tried to have the Senate take up S 2, but Republicans blocked it.

State officials and educators generally favored block grants and typically were nonplused by the congressional debate's partisan tone. Brown University education Professor Theodore Sizer, who headed the Coalition of Essential Schools, said the Senate's block grants were not necessarily "business as usual," as Bush and Alexander contended. "In some states it will be; in some states it won't be," Sizer said. Yet Sizer also said he did not mind if Bush wanted to put his stamp on the bill: "As an educator, I don't care, as long as something gets done."

## LEGISLATIVE ACTION

The Senate overwhelmingly passed legislation to help fund education improvement programs for elementary and secondary schools, five days after decisively rejecting a public-private school choice demonstration program.

House Education and Labor Committee Chairman William D. Ford, D-Mich., then dumped HR 3320 and replaced it with HR 4323, which included no reference to school choice. That bill won House approval just in time to prevent Bush from seizing the spotlight at the Republican National Convention to denounce Democrats for holding up an education bill.

The House adopted a conference report near the end of the 102nd Congress, but a cloture vote in the Senate failed by one vote to cut off debate. That killed the bill for the year.

## SENATE ACTION

Legislation to help fund education improvement programs for elementary and secondary schools passed the Senate on Jan. 28. The measure won qualified praise from the Bush administration despite the Senate's rejection of a "school choice" provision, the president's proposal to spawn competition among public and private schools.

### School Choice Rejected

Following a generally partisan debate over the basic philosophy of public education, the Senate on Jan. 23 rejected the Bush administration's "school choice" proposal to send public funds to some private schools.

The 36-57 vote came on a sharply scaled-back amendment to set up six demonstration projects in which federal school aid could be used to allow low-income students to attend the schools of their parents' choice. *(Vote 5, p. 2-S)*

Offered by Orrin G. Hatch, R-Utah, the amendment to a Democratic school improvement bill (S 2) proposed spending $30 million on the program, far less than the nationwide choice plan outlined in President Bush's "America 2000" plan for elementary and secondary education.

Choice proponents had hoped that by limiting the amendment to a small demonstration program, Democratic senators might be willing to try it.

But Senate Democrats said from the outset that they would not allow the administration to get a foot in the "choice" door. "We are not about to privatize every school district in America as some would do," said Edward M. Kennedy, D-Mass., chairman of the Labor and Human Resources Committee and the chief sponsor of S 2.

Only three Democrats voted for Hatch's amendment: Bill Bradley, N.J., John B. Breaux, La., and Joseph I. Lieberman, Conn.

Meanwhile, five of the Senate's 43 Republicans voted against it, including John H. Chafee, R.I., who said the proposal would prove what the Senate already knew: "It will show public school children sent to private schools do better than those at public schools."

Education Secretary Alexander expressed dismay after the vote.

"It is astonishing to me that the Senate could not bring itself to support even a demonstration project to determine what might happen if poor families are given more of the

same choices of all schools that wealthy families already have," he said.

### Model Compromise

The Senate bill authorized $850 million in fiscal 1992 to be distributed among the states in block grants. Individual schools were to compete for the money by proposing education improvement plans. The states would also be allowed to keep some of the money for statewide efforts, such as teacher training, public school choice and new model schools.

The bill bogged down when Jesse Helms, R-N.C., offered a non-binding "sense of the Senate" resolution urging the Supreme Court to allow prayer in schools. Senators were at first reluctant to vote on the amendment but ultimately rejected it, 38-55. *(Vote 4, p. 2-S)*

Senators also cut the guts out of Bush's New American Schools plan, approving a compromise that excluded private schools from receiving money.

The Senate voted 96-0 to approve the compromise, as worked out between Democrats and Thad Cochran, R-Miss., to give more money to states that wanted to try to create model schools. Cochran had proposed spending $100 million in fiscal 1992 to allow Alexander to choose who could create public and private "break the mold" schools. *(Vote 2, p. 2-S)*

But Democrats strenuously objected to letting Alexander decide where all the money would go. The compromise allowed states to set aside 25 percent of their block grant — up from 10 percent in the original bill — for new schools. Only public schools would qualify, and chief state school officers would oversee the proposals.

The Senate also approved 95-0 an amendment by Mark O. Hatfield, R-Ore., to allow 300 school districts in six states to petition Alexander for a waiver of federal regulations. *(Vote 3, p. 2-S)*

### Kennedy's Outrage

Although Congress traditionally had worked on a bipartisan basis to pass education legislation, S 2 became a political battleground in election year 1992, with Bush trying to assert his "education president" label and Democrats striving to prove otherwise.

The school choice issue was the main point of real friction. Bush and Alexander argued that all children should be able to vote with their feet, leaving bad schools for better schools, which would in turn spur schools to improve through the competition for students.

Not all Democrats were unsympathetic. Sen. Herb Kohl, D-Wis., said he would have voted for the Hatch amendment if it had excluded religious schools so that Milwaukee, which had a small choice program, could receive federal aid. But after talking to Alexander, Kohl said the administration refused to rewrite the amendment.

Kennedy, in a voice that grew hoarse and cracked, railed against the Hatch amendment and the administration's entire education thrust. "What have we heard on the floor these last three days? New schools, new schools, new schools," Kennedy shouted, pounding on his lectern. "What are we hearing tonight? Private schools, private schools, private schools."

Hatch, repeating an administration theme that Democrats were unwilling to try new education ideas, said that "what we have just witnessed is a terrific argument for business as usual."

### Final Senate Action

The 92-6 vote came just hours before President Bush gave his State of the Union address, as Democrats and Republicans sought to distinguish themselves on a hot election-year topic. *(Vote 9, p. 3-S)*

Alexander said the bill (S 2) included important parts of Bush's America 2000 education plan: more flexibility for schools using federal money and some federal money for his New American Schools program.

"These are real steps forward," Alexander said. "Still, these steps do not go far enough, fast enough, and the president will keep fighting for more radical change in the American system."

Alexander said the administration would continue to seek provisions to give middle- and low-income families more of the same choices to send their children to private schools that wealthy families already had.

Democrats, however, criticized Bush for not trying to go far enough with his education proposals. "So far, the president has been content with endorsing goals rather than laying out comprehensive proposals for reform," said Kennedy, chief sponsor of S 2.

The bill authorized $850 million in fiscal 1992 to be distributed among the states in block grants. Individual schools would compete for the money by proposing education improvement plans, with 75 percent of all funds going to schools with the lowest levels of academic achievement or the highest levels of poverty.

In a compromise with the administration, the bill allowed states to spend 25 percent of the money — up from 10 percent in the original bill — on creating New American Schools, but the money could go only to public schools. Other permissible statewide reform efforts included teacher training and public school choice.

The grants were to be provided over five years if schools showed progress in student achievement. In anticipation of the authorization measure, congressional appropriators in 1991 had committed $100 million for fiscal 1992, if legislation were enacted by April 1.

But the money was never spent because the bill never passed.

Before final passage, the Senate voted 55-43 on a tabling motion to kill an amendment by Don Nickles, R-Okla., to allow states to require welfare recipients to make their children attend school. *(Vote 7, p. 2-S)*

The Senate also rejected a non-binding motion by Tim Wirth, D-Colo., to override the 1990 budget agreement between the White House and Congress to allow money from defense cuts to go to domestic programs such as education. The vote was 45-53. *(Vote 8, p. 2-S)*

## HOUSE ACTION

After the Senate rejected school choice, Education and Labor Committee Chairman Ford dumped the 1991 House education bill (HR 3320) and replaced it with HR 4323, which made no mention of choice. The new bill was approved unenthusiastically in committee and on the House floor.

### Ford Scraps Compromise

In February, at the urging of the national teachers' unions, Ford dumped HR 3320 and replaced it with HR 4323, which included no reference to school choice. Committee Democrats also bowed to pressure from the National School Boards Association and rewrote the language so that local school boards would retain total authority over the bill's provisions for designing "reform" plans for public school education.

At the time, Ford said he was angry that the Bush administration characterized the committee's original bill as allowing choice, when Ford believed the language was so restrictive that it would virtually prevent public money from going to private and church-related schools. He said the first attempt to spend federal dollars on religious schools would result in a lawsuit, tying up the program.

Ford also said that the comfortable Senate vote rejecting school choice led him to believe there was no need to try to compromise with the administration.

Ford's about-face was sure to spark a fight with the administration, particularly because Bush was trying to portray Democrats as conducting "business as usual" on education.

Goodling, who helped craft the original bill, was not an advocate of choice but had played a key mediation role between conservatives in the White House and liberal Democrats. Yet he found out about Ford's new bill only a few days before it was introduced, when a Democratic committee member casually mentioned it during a conversation about higher education.

"All of a sudden I was surprised to learn I was no longer a player," Goodling said.

He said he did not understand why Democrats changed their minds about allowing some states to use federal dollars for school choice. "All we were doing was giving them the choice of making the choice," Goodling said.

But House Democrats said the 1991 compromise with Sununu, allowing restricted school choice, had been simply a strategic decision designed to fend off a more far-reaching choice amendment that they feared they might lose on the House floor. Ford said the language would have protected members from being forced to go on the record in a floor vote.

### Committee Vote

A peevish House Education and Labor Committee voted 23-12 on May 20 to approve a school reform bill that neither Democrats nor Republicans cared for and that neither party believed would radically improve elementary and secondary education.

The vote split along party lines with just one Democrat, Patsy T. Mink of Hawaii, voting against passage. Four Republicans did not vote — Tom Petri of Wisconsin, Marge Roukema of New Jersey, Susan Molinari of New York and Mickey Edwards of Oklahoma.

The reform bill (HR 4323), a response to President Bush's America 2000 plan, was to authorize $700 million in the first year for block grants to states and unspecified sums for the next nine years. The grants could be used for teacher training or other programs to improve education. Democrats would have preferred to boost authorization levels for existing programs rather than introduce a new initiative, but they felt compelled to match Bush's proposals to prevent the president from taking center stage on education issues.

Republicans, however, were angry that the bill did not include Bush's top education priority — school choice. The controversial choice plan involved providing government subsidies to allow parents to choose whether to send their children to public or private school. It was being tried in several states. Milwaukee, for example, had a plan that allowed parents to send their children to public or private school, but not to religious school. And Minnesota had a public school choice plan that did not include private or religious schools.

Alexander said Bush would veto the new bill, calling it a "business-as-usual" approach to education.

During committee consideration, two Republicans attempted to reinsert school choice. Both failed.

Rep. Dick Armey, R-Texas, offered an amendment requiring that at least 25 percent of the bill's funds be spent to establish or expand state choice programs for public, private or religious schools. It was rejected 7-31.

Goodling also offered a substitute that was nearly identical to the bill Ford spiked. It included the school choice compromise. Goodling's amendment was rejected by a vote of 13-27.

### Local Input

The new bill also scaled back language promoting community involvement in improving local schools.

Under both House bills, state educational agencies were to apply to the secretary of Education for a portion of the appropriated money. Meanwhile, a local committee in each school district was to write a plan for improving its schools. Each 25-member committee was envisioned to include local political, education and business leaders as well as parents, teachers, counselors and students.

The committee was to set goals and develop an improvement plan. Activities authorized by the bill included: developing New American Schools, which could mean revamping a school to operate in a new way; naming as "merit schools" schools that had improved their performance on tests and other curricular measures; allowing site-based school management; coordinating health and social services with education; and improving the use of technology in schools.

Under the old bill, the local school board would have had to approve the committee's plan before sending it to the state education agency to compete for funds. But the school board would have needed the committee's approval to make changes.

School board members angrily objected to that requirement, saying it would undercut their authority as elected officials. "Just because it's called a reform plan doesn't mean school boards should step aside," said Edward R. Kealy, director of federal programs for the National School Boards Association, which represented more than 15,000 school boards with 97,000 members.

At their annual Washington legislative conference in February, 700 school board members from across the country visited members of Congress to complain about the provision. They wore buttons with a slash through the bill number, HR 3320.

Goodling, a former teacher, principal and school board president, said school boards could have changed the nation's education system long ago, if they were up to it. "Why pass legislation if they are totally in charge?" Goodling asked.

But in response to the board members' criticism, the revised education bill allowed school boards to approve the committee plan with or without modification; disapprove the plan; or return the plan to committee for more work.

"We kept warning that it would be very embarrassing to Congress to go forward with a big education initiative and people at the grass-roots level would walk away from it," Kealy said.

## HOUSE FLOOR ACTION

In an unusual show of partisanship on the education front, the House passed a school reform bill that the ad-

ministration denounced and Democrats only weakly supported. Not so surprising, however, was the defeat of two Republican amendments that would have allowed the federal government to subsidize the cost of private school tuition.

The House voted 279-124 on Aug. 12 to pass the Neighborhood Schools Improvement Act (HR 4323), just in time to prevent President Bush from seizing the spotlight at the Republican National Convention to blame Democrats for holding up an education bill. *(Vote 385, p. 94-H)*

The legislation was the Democratic response to Bush's America 2000 plan, which aimed, in part, to foster competition among schools by giving parents some choice in where to send their children. HR 4323 was to authorize $800 million in fiscal 1993 for block grants to states. The grants could be used for teacher training, school construction or whatever else local school officials believed would improve education.

Alexander called the bill "even worse than worse than awful," and said he would recommend a presidential veto.

Chairman Ford had pressed ahead with HR 4323, saying he was moving Bush's legislation. But he also had called the measure "clichés and show business," maintaining it was "not going to revolutionize anything."

Those words were thrown back at him on the floor of the House, as he and other Democrats weakly supported the measure. Many committee Democrats said they would prefer to increase funding for existing programs, which were targeted to disadvantaged students.

The House promptly named conferees to meet with the Senate.

"Don't hold me responsible if it doesn't get to the president's desk," Ford said in an interview, adding that it was possible that Republican senators would hold up the bill in that chamber. That was the case on the last day of the 101st Congress, when Senate Republicans blocked the chamber from clearing an education bill. *(1990 Almanac, p. 610)*

Still, Republicans were not accustomed to voting against education bills.

Steve Gunderson, R-Wis., a member of the House committee and co-chief deputy whip for the GOP, was one of 32 Republicans to break with the administration and vote in favor of the bill.

Gunderson supported a Goodling amendment to replace the bill with what was essentially the original committee measure. That substitute was rejected 140-267. *(Vote 384, p. 94-H)*

But Gunderson said he believed the Goodling substitute and the bill were not too different, and he ultimately voted for final passage. "When adults play politics with education, it is unfortunately the children who get trampled," he said.

The House also defeated an amendment by Dick Armey, R-Texas, that would have required that 25 percent of a school district's grant be used for school choice programs, including private schools.

Armey argued that "competition would only make public schools better." His amendment was rejected 80-328. *(Vote 383, p. 94-H)*

## CONFERENCE ACTION

In the Senate, Majority Leader George J. Mitchell, D-Maine, was forced to call for a cloture vote to cut off anonymous Republican objections and choose conferees to work on the bill (S 2 — S Rept 102-43). The vote, taken Sept. 15, passed 85-6. *(Vote 203, p. 27-S)*

Both the House and Senate bills authorized block grants for programs to improve education through teacher training, school construction or whatever local school officials believed would help. The Senate authorized $850 million in fiscal 1992, and the House authorized $800 million in fiscal 1993.

Administration officials said they disliked the House bill on several grounds: It no longer contained school choice language, its standards and testing provisions were more cautious than the Senate's, and it had no separate authorization for Bush's New American Schools plan to create "break the mold" schools.

They also disliked language allowing money to be spent on "coordinated health services," which could be interpreted to mean school-based health clinics. Many Republicans opposed those clinics because they feared they would be used to pass out condoms.

The Senate bill did not allow public money to pay for private and parochial school tuition, either. And a compromise worked out on the Senate floor in January essentially cut the guts out of the New American Schools idea. Alexander wanted to spend $200 million handing out grants to states to create public and private schools that approached education in new and inventive ways.

But Democrats strenuously objected to letting Alexander decide where all the money would go. Under a compromise, the Senate bill allowed states to set aside 25 percent of their block grant for innovative schools. Only public schools could qualify, and chief state school officers were to oversee the proposals.

Even if Congress had managed to clear a bill and even if Bush had signed it, it was unlikely to receive a significant amount of money. Serious budget constraints had prompted appropriators to limit new money for education.

### Adoption of Conference Report

By voice vote, members approved the conference report to an $800 million school reform bill on Sept. 25. The bill authorized block grants to states and local education agencies to improve elementary and secondary education. Twenty percent of the block grant money would go to states, and 80 percent would go to local education agencies, with 90 percent of that money going to individual schools.

President Bush mulled over whether to veto the bill, although it was clear that the bill might never reach him because of Senate rules allowing any one member to hold up legislation.

Hatch's inability to persuade the Democrats to agree to any administration proposals was a serious blow to Bush's hopes of signing an education bill.

Still, although Alexander had called the House education bill "worse than worse than awful," and had grudgingly refrained from threatening a veto on the Senate version, White House and Education Department lobbyists were eager to find something to make the legislation acceptable.

"I think it would be awful if we don't come up with a bill here," said Hatch, who was not pleased with the legislation.

The final bill House and Senate Democrats worked out contained no mention of such initiatives as national testing or public school choice and no funding to create "break the mold" schools.

Hatch, the ranking Republican on the Senate Labor

and Human Resources Committee, wanted to increase the ratio of state money to 35 percent, the Senate's original position.

He wanted that money to be used for "break the mold" New American Schools and for public school choice, also in the Senate bill.

The administration originally hoped to spend $200 million on New American Schools and to use block grants to give vouchers to families to help pay for private and parochial school education.

Hatch was particularly upset that the Democrats included "school delivery standards" in the final bill. The bill would encourage states to evaluate whether their schools had good equipment, supplies, teachers and facilities.

Democrats were worried that children would be blamed for failing to get a good education when it could be the school that was at fault.

"We have to determine whether the child is failing or the school is failing," said Kildee, chairman of the Education and Labor Subcommittee on Elementary, Secondary and Vocational Education.

But Hatch said he feared that if standards were set for the schools, parents could sue the states if a school did not meet those standards. And courts might force the states to spend money to bring schools up to speed.

House Education Committee Chairman Ford told Hatch that he would not budge on any of the issues. "I don't want you to feel I'm playing games with you," Ford said. "I don't have any bargaining room on these items."

## FINAL ACTION

For the second time in four years, legislation intended to reform public schools was spiked.

Alexander had recommended that President Bush veto S 2, an $800 million block grant to states and schools that contained few of Bush's reform proposals.

But the Senate killed the bill before it reached the president.

Both Democrats and Republicans disliked the bill, the latter because it lacked Bush's initiatives and the former because it lacked money and didn't go far enough. The bill presented to each chamber contained no mention of Bush proposals such as national testing or school choice, and no funding to create "break the mold" schools. The bill essentially left reforms up to local education officials.

In a letter to congressional leaders, Alexander called the bill "a monument to business-as-usual thinking" and accused Democrats of "cynical end-of-the-session high jinks." He said the bill "evidences the cozy relationship between the majority members of the Education committees and the entrenched education special interests that are most responsible for the current state of American schools and who have a vested interest in preventing any real and legitimate change."

The House adopted the conference report, but a cloture vote in the Senate failed by one vote, 59-40, on Oct. 2. Forty Republicans voted to block further action on the bill. Dave Durenberger, R-Minn., did not vote. *(Vote 261, p. 34-S)* ∎

# Head Start Expanded

The Senate cleared a bill (HR 5630, H Rept 102-763) on Sept. 24 which sought to increase participation and institute cost-saving measures in the Head Start program for disadvantaged preschool children. President Bush signed the measure Oct. 7 — PL 102-401.

The bill's key sponsor, Rep. Matthew G. Martinez, D-Calif., said the changes would add few costs to the program, make better use of existing dollars and allow more children to receive better Head Start services.

The bill required Head Start schools to provide literacy and child development training for parents of children enrolled in classes. It also allowed local Head Start associations to buy the buildings they used. Prior to the new law, Head Start grant money could only be used for renovations of existing property, not for purchases.

Bill supporters argued that the power to buy was necessary because rental facilities were often temporary. Also, suitable rental properties did not exist in communities like south-central Los Angeles, and renovations were often more expensive than purchasing new space.

The measure also made it easier for a community to win waivers of the requirement that it provide 20 percent matching funds to qualify for grants. The administration was able to take into account five elements, including whether the community was located in an area recently hit by a major disaster, when reviewing the community's ability to get the funds.

## War on Poverty Legacy

Begun in 1965 as part of President Lyndon B. Johnson's War on Poverty, Head Start offered a panoply of educa-

tional and social services intended to put economically disadvantaged preschool children on a comparable footing with their more affluent peers. Although the law defined eligible children only as those below the age for compulsory school attendance (age 7 in most states), Head Start regulations said that children served should be at least 3 years old and that 90 percent of enrollees had to be from families with incomes below the federal poverty line.

Head Start was one of the federal government's popular social service programs that received a funding boost — despite tight budget restrictions — for fiscal 1993. The spending bill for the departments of Labor, Health and Human Services, and Education (HR 5677 — PL 102-394) allocated $2.8 billion for the nutrition and health program for preschoolers, up from $577 million in fiscal 1992. *(Appropriations, p. 651)*

Full funding for the Head Start program had been considered in 1990 as part of an omnibus reauthorization of human services programs (HR 4151 — PL 102-501). The measure did authorize $5.92 billion for fiscal 1993. Budget contraints, however, made that impossible. *(1990 Almanac, p. 552)*

### Legislative Action

The House Education and Labor Subcommittee on Human Resources approved HR 5630 on July 23. Panel chairman and bill sponsor Martinez said the program was serving less than one-third of eligible children in 1992. He said it "should be the cornerstone of our social policy."

The House Education and Labor Committee on July 30 quickly approved HR 5630 to make the key changes in the popular program for disadvantaged preschool children.

The House passed the measure Aug. 3 by voice vote and sent it over to the Senate, where it was cleared for the president's signature nearly two months later. ∎

# Congress Advances Various Education Bills

With education moving to the forefront of the domestic agenda, Congress considered other education-related measures in 1992. Those included:

## VIDEO PROGRAMS

The Senate cleared legislation Oct. 7 aimed at helping preschool and elementary school students through video programs focused on school readiness.

The bill (S 3134 — PL 102-545), which passed the House on Oct. 6 by voice vote, directed the Education secretary to award grants to develop and distribute video programs for children and for parents, child-care providers and educators. One of the six national education goals outlined by President Bush and the nation's governors in 1989 was to make sure children entered school "ready to learn." The bill, known as the Ready to Learn Act, also established a "ready to learn" satellite channel to distribute the programming.

The measure, signed by Bush on Oct. 27, authorized $50 million in fiscal 1993. It was initially approved by voice vote Sept. 16 by the Senate Labor and Human Resources Committee and by the full Senate on Oct. 1. The House amended the bill before sending it back to the Senate to be cleared.

## EDUCATION RESEARCH

The House passed legislation by voice vote Sept. 22 to reauthorize and restructure the Office of Educational Research and Improvement (OERI), the research branch of the Department of Education. The bill went no further.

The restructuring aimed to improve education by promoting research, development and dissemination of information. The bill (HR 4014) would have created an 18-member board of governors to oversee the office and develop research priorities. The board would consist of education researchers, teachers, parents, school administrators and others to be appointed by the secretary of Education.

The bill was approved by the Education and Labor Committee on May 20. It sought to restructure the Education Department's research and information programs, establishing an Educational Research Policy and Priorities Board to set a research agenda. The Senate Labor Subcommittee on Education, Arts and Humanities approved a companion bill by voice vote March 12.

The Senate subcommittee's bill (S 1275), sponsored by subcommittee Chairman Claiborne Pell, D-R.I., was a seven-year, $300 million measure to extend OERI's authority. The bill restructured the office along the lines of the National Science Foundation (NSF), creating a board of governors to advise the director on educational research. The nine members would be appointed by the president based on their use of research in education. The office's existing advisory council would be eliminated.

The bill also authorized $70 million in fiscal 1993 to create five national directorates on education to split research into different areas. The NSF also divided its work that way. The new directorates would be: curriculum, instruction and assessment; early childhood learning, families and community; educational achievement of historically underserved populations; school organization, structure and finance; and post-secondary and adult education.

At the time, the office supported educational research in 26 centers across the country. Grants to those centers would continue under the bill, although the directorates might conduct some research of their own.

In anticipation that the office might someday oversee a testing system for elementary and secondary students, members added a National Education Standards and Assessment Council, which would be responsible for developing educational standards.

## EDUCATION OF THE DEAF

The House cleared legislation (HR 5483 — PL 102-421) by voice vote Oct. 6 reauthorizing Gallaudet University, the National Technical Institute for the Deaf and other programs for people with hearing programs through fiscal 1997. President Bush signed the bill Oct. 16.

Gallaudet, in Washington, and the technical institute, in Rochester, N.Y., received most of their funding from the federal government.

The House Education and Labor Committee approved the bill 35-0 on July 8, and the House approved it by voice vote Aug. 10. The Senate passed it Oct. 5 by voice vote. ∎

# Child Welfare Bill Victim of Tax Veto

Major portions of a costly child welfare overhaul program wound up in a $27 billion urban aid tax measure that became one of the last bills President Bush acted on: He vetoed it.

The prospects had been bleak for the free-standing legislation, which aimed to help abused and neglected children without consigning them to the overburdened foster home system. The $7 billion measure (HR 3603) that passed the House Aug. 6 on a 256-163 vote would have imposed a millionaires' surtax to pay for the creation of a capped entitlement program to help states pay for services designed to keep troubled families together. The administration was vehemently opposed to both the surtax and the new entitlement.

The child welfare legislation became linked with the tax bill after Senate Finance Committee Chairman Lloyd Bentsen, D-Texas, attached the Senate version (S 4) of the child welfare bill to the tax measure (HR 11) during committee action July 29. *(Urban aid tax bill, p. 140)*

The House sponsor of HR 3603, Democrat Thomas J. Downey of New York, was encouraged by the inclusion of the child welfare provisions in the much broader tax measure. HR 11 began as a bipartisan effort by the White House and Congress to help revitalize inner cities and won broad support among lawmakers because it was sprinkled with popular tax breaks. But while both Republicans and Democrats stongly embraced the "family values" intrinsic in the child welfare initiative, the parties were at odds on its costs and funding mechanism.

Many members who supported the basic thrust of the provisions designed to preserve families and streamline the foster care system still voted against the urban aid tax bill (HR 11). Normally considered a fiscal conservative, Timothy J. Penny, D-Minn., said that "even though the deficit is our No. 1 priority, children deserve our attention." Yet Penny did not vote for the urban aid package.

The House bill also included an anti-hunger component sponsored by House Budget Committee Chairman Leon E. Panetta, D-Calif., that would have increased food stamps to families with children, especially those on the brink of homelessness.

However, those provisions were not included in the conference report on HR 11.

## BACKGROUND

A battle with the Bush administration began early in the 102nd Congress over how to straighten out the federal foster-care system, which was considered backwards.

---

### BOXSCORE

➡ **Child Welfare Overhaul (HR 3603, S 4 — provisions incorporated into HR 11).** Bills to expand and revamp federal programs for abused and neglected children; and to increase support for family services so that foster care would not be needed as often. The House version included an anti-hunger component aimed at increasing food stamps for families with children.

**Reports:** H Rept 102-684; conference report on HR 11, H 102-1034.

#### KEY ACTION

Sept. 24, 1991 — The **House** Ways and Means Subcommittee on Human Resources approved HR 2571, on voice vote.

July 2 — The **House** Ways and Means Committee approved HR 3603, 24-12.

July 29 — The **Senate** Finance Committee incorporated S 4 into HR 11.

Aug. 6 — The **House** passed HR 3603, 256-163.

Nov. 4 — President Bush vetoed HR 11.

---

Both Democrats and Republicans in Congress made it one of their top legislative priorities because they felt that taxpayers were paying for pounds of cure for a problem that ounces of prevention might have solved.

"The foster-care system is collapsing under the enormous strain," said Rep. Nancy L. Johnson, R-Conn. "The numbers are skyrocketing, and they're very difficult cases."

Yet while nearly everyone agreed that more resources should have been available for services to prevent child abuse and neglect, lawmakers differed on how to refocus federal spending.

The House Ways and Means Subcommittee on Human Resources did approve a bill (HR 2571) on Sept. 24, 1991 that would have increased funding for programs in the child-welfare sections of the Social Security Act that paid for efforts to keep families together. Under the system as it existed, federal funding for foster care for children who would otherwise qualify for welfare was unlimited, but funding for services that could prevent children from needing expensive foster care was restricted.

Witnesses before the subcommittee had testified that spending money to keep families together could save federal funds. In general, the costs of keeping a family together were about one-third the cost of keeping a child in foster care. Federal spending for foster care was not limited, but funds to keep families together had been squeezed by budgetary requirements.

But for the second year in a row, action on child-welfare legislation stalled in the House after winning subcommittee approval. The Senate took no action on its companion measure, S 4. *(1990 Almanac, p. 556; 1991 Almanac, p. 385)*

### New Demands

Congress had last addressed the child-welfare issue in 1980, when the most pressing problem was children "drifting" from foster family to foster family. *(1980 Almanac, p. 417)*

For a time, the law Congress passed to address the problem (PL 96-272) seemed to be working. Foster-care caseloads declined as more children were either reunited with their parents or legally freed for adoption into a permanent home.

But since the mid-1980s, AIDS, homelessness, teen pregnancy, alcohol abuse and the widespread crack cocaine epidemic had combined to overwhelm the system.

Reports of child abuse and neglect more than doubled over the previous decade. At the same time, foster-care caseloads had been rising while the number of available

foster families had declined. And in a new social phenomenon, "boarder babies" of drug-addicted or AIDS-afflicted mothers were being abandoned in hospitals.

The skewed nature of the incentives in the child-welfare system was a key problem, experts said. Because federal money for foster care for poor children was guaranteed in the form of an "entitlement" program, states were encouraged to remove children from their families.

At the same time, federal assistance for programs that paid for less expensive preventive or support services — aimed at keeping children with their parents — had to be approved by Congress from year to year. That money had not been keeping up with the need, the experts suggested.

According to the Children's Defense Fund, costs for the federal foster-care program — an entitlement — rose by 122 percent between fiscal 1981 and fiscal 1990. At the same time, funds for the child-welfare services program — subject to the annual appropriations process — grew by 54 percent. That, the group said, represented a growth in real dollars of only 6 percent, even without taking into account the larger number of children who needed services.

The bulk of funding came from programs under Title IV of the Social Security Act, which were overseen by the tax-writing Ways and Means and Finance panels. These programs included the Child Welfare Services Program (Title IV-B) and the Foster Care and Adoption Assistance programs (under Title IV-E). States also funded child-welfare services with a portion of the amount they received each year under the Social Services Block Grant, Title XX of the Social Security Act.

## LEGISLATIVE ACTION

The bill (HR 2571) to overhaul the child welfare system that was approved by the House Ways and Means Subcommittee on Human Resources on Sept. 24, 1991, lacked a financing mechanism. In 1992, the House Ways and Means Committee on July 2 approved a new version of the bill (HR 3603) after deciding where to get $7 billion to pay for its programs: from millionaires. Despite strong administration objections, HR 3603 — known as the Family Preservation Act — passed the House on Aug. 6.

S 4 was introduced early in 1991 and given a priority number. Nonetheless, it languished in the Senate until the following year when it was attached to a massive urban aid tax bill (HR 11) during Senate Finance Committee action on July 29.

The child welfare provisions became a major component of the final conference agreement that emerged on HR 11 and were expanded to include more "family" issues.

### House Ways and Means Committee

Advancing a long-term effort to improve child welfare services, the House Ways and Means Committee voted 24-12 on July 2 to approve HR 3603, with only Johnson defecting from Republican ranks to support the bill.

The bill also sought to raise funds for a measure to get more food to children, especially those in families on the brink of homelessness. That legislation was named after Rep. Mickey Leland, D-Texas, the founding chairman of the Select Committee on Hunger who died in a 1989 airplane crash during a hunger relief mission to Ethiopia.

Although the measure embraced family values dear to both political parties, Republicans deserted the effort over the financing mechanism, which would have imposed a surtax on millionaires.

"We've talked a lot about children in this Congress. But this is the first time that we are doing something," said Downey, a principal author of the bill.

But Wade F. Horn, commissioner of the Department of Health and Human Services' Administration for Children, Youth and Families, told the panel during the markup that the administration strongly opposed the measure. "We do not have a quarrel with the need to do something for children," he said. But he said President Bush had indicated he would veto any bill with a tax increase such as the millionaire's surtax. The administration also had problems, he said, with elements of the bill such as requirements imposed on the states to expedite clearing the backlog of child welfare cases.

The bill would have imposed a 10 percent surtax on people with incomes above $1 million as of Jan. 1, 1993. The committee estimated that the plan would raise $8.2 billion over five years. Of that, $3.5 billion would go for child welfare services, $3.5 billion for child nutrition programs and $1.2 billion for deficit reduction.

Republican Fred Grandy of Iowa attempted to strike the financing language from the bill, but he was defeated on a 14-23 vote.

Johnson failed in two attempts to amend the bill. She first tried to cap federal funding for state administrative costs of running the foster-care and adoption programs. That was rejected on a 13-23 vote. She then attempted to eliminate the procedures for establishing a new child welfare review system, which fell on a voice vote.

As approved by committee, the key element of the bill created a permanent capped entitlement program under the existing Social Security Child Welfare Services Program. The bill also established a five-year grant program for state court systems to streamline the handling of child welfare cases. Growing social problems, such as high poverty rates and increasing family breakup, had placed high demands on state and local systems for handling these cases.

### Leland Bill

The anti-hunger component known as the Leland bill was a scaled-back version of bills (HR 1202, S 757) approved by the House and Senate Agriculture committees in 1991. Those initiatives would have cost about $5.6 billion over five years in expanded food stamp benefits. *(1991 Almanac, p. 389)*

The modified version of the anti-hunger bill, which was added to HR 3603 at the Rules Committee before House floor consideration, aimed to give families with children the benefit of regulations that applied to elderly and disabled people. It allowed them to deduct a larger portion of their housing costs when calculating their income for stamp applications.

### House Floor Action

The $7 billion measure to impose a new tax on millionaires to pay for expanded welfare services and nutrition assistance for children passed the House on Aug. 6 with enough support to solidly position it for conference consideration with the urban aid tax bill that was moving through Congress.

"We found the right horse to ride into conference," said Panetta, sponsor of the anti-hunger component of the Family Preservation Act and chairman of the Budget Committee. "The key thing here is that we have latched onto the debate on family values."

Both Republicans and Democrats strongly embraced the "family values" intrinsic in the initiative, but the parties were vehemently at odds on its cost and funding mechanism. The 256-163 vote on the bill, with 19 Republicans voting yea, illuminated those fault lines. *(Vote 372, p. 90-H)*

Even more indicative of GOP sentiment was the 191-230 vote on a motion to recommit the bill to committee to substitute a Republican alternative that would have struck the millionaires' surtax, eliminated the hunger relief provisions and made changes in the child welfare system that would not have increased federal spending. *(Vote 371, p. 90-H)*

"We're not having a debate here. This is a eulogy: The Family Preservation Act is dead," Grandy said during floor action. "My condolences."

Downey, principal author of the child welfare portion of the bill, felt that the only potential for passage would be as part of the tax bill. He was encouraged by the language added to the $31 billion tax bill (HR 11) by Senate Finance Committee Chairman Bentsen during committee action July 29. The provision added to HR 11 by Bentsen would create a similar capped entitlement program to bolster the child welfare system. That bill, which also faced a veto threat, passed the House on July 2 and was headed to the Senate floor. However, HR 11 did not include anti-hunger provisions.

Panetta had hoped that the childhood hunger relief programs in the Family Preservation Act would also be brought into any conference action on HR 11. The millionaires' surtax, on record as being supported by the House, might have also been considered as an additional funding mechanism for the large tax bill, which offered tax breaks to the wealthy as well as aid to rehabilitate inner cities.

The only Republican to speak in behalf of HR 3603 was Marge Roukema of New Jersey. "I support it in the memory of Mickey Leland," she said.

Otherwise, the GOP opposition to the bill was targeted at what Republicans referred to as the Democrats' insistence on "tax and spend."

But many Democrats pointed to the beleaguered support system for children and said that too many children were suffering. "To say that no more money is needed is to look reality in the face and not understand what is happening," Downey said.

## FINAL ACTION

House and Senate conferees finished their work the evening of Oct. 5 on what became a $27 million tax bill to establish 50 enterprise zones to attract investment, restore and expand tax deductions for individual retirement accounts, extend a number of expiring tax provisions along with a host of other alterations to existing tax law. The House adopted the conference report Oct. 6; the Senate cleared it Oct. 8.

Buried within the massive legislation were fairly significant child welfare provisions. The anti-hunger component of the House bill did not survive in the conference proceedings.

The bill sent to the president amended Title IV of the Social Security Act to provide entitlement matching funds to the states for family preservation and family support services, subtance abuse prevention and treatment and respite care services. The entitlement ceiling was set at $135 million in fiscal 1993. By fiscal 1997, the ceiling was to be $595 million.

Under the conference agreement, the funds could be used for such family preservation and support services as programs designed to help children at risk of foster-care placement to remain with their families, more follow-up care to families in which a child had been returned and services to strengthen the functioning of a family — including parenting skills. ∎

# Supplemental Food Program Improved

Congress cleared two bills in 1992 geared toward improving a popular federal program, the Special Supplemental Food Program for Women, Infants and Children, better known since 1972 as WIC.

Considered one of the few government welfare programs that worked, WIC provided nutritional advice and supplementary food to low-income women and children up to age 5. Participants exchanged special vouchers for infant formula and other specified foods, such as eggs and cereal, at retail stores. But because of limited funding, only about 5.3 million people were served — about half of those who met the federal eligibility guidelines in 1992.

### FARMERS' MARKETS

Legislation (HR 3711 — H Rept 102-540) expanding and reauthorizing a pilot project that promoted the use of fresh fruits and vegetables in the WIC program passed the House, amended, June 22 and was cleared by the Senate the next day. President Bush signed HR 3711 on July 2 — PL 102-314.

The bill increased authorized funding from $3 million annually to $6.5 million, allowing additional states to participate.

The bill received voice vote approval from the House Agriculture Committee on June 4 after it was amended to emphasize the committee's role in overseeing the program.

The bill (HR 3711) had been approved May 20 by the House Education and Labor Committee — the panel with jurisdiction over the WIC program. Agriculture asked for oversight because language in the measure involved the use of fresh commodities.

A companion measure (S 2761) passed the Senate by voice vote on May 20.

The $3 million farmers' market project was originally authorized for three years in the 1988 Hunger Prevention Act (PL 100-435).

### PRICE FIXING

Legislation (S 2875) that imposed civil penalties on infant-formula manufacturers who cheated the popular WIC program was cleared by the House on Oct. 6, four months after the Federal Trade Commission (FTC) charged the three largest manufacturers for anti-competitive practices.

President Bush signed the bill Oct. 24 — PL 102-512.

"Let our message today be loud and clear: Hungry children and their mothers are more important than corporate profits," said Sen. Patrick J. Leahy, D-Vt., the bill's sponsor. The Senate had passed the bill Oct. 5.

The FTC concluded on June 11 after a two-year investi-

gation that the three big manufacturers of infant formula had driven up costs to the program through the alleged price-fixing. Negotiated settlements were reached with Mead Johnson & Co. and American Home Products Corp., but no settlement was reached with the third firm, Abbott Laboratories.

The bill mandated civil penalties of up to $100 million per year on companies that fixed prices or engaged in related anti-competitive activities that hurt the WIC program. It also barred those manufacturers found guilty from participation in the WIC market for up to two years. ∎

# Welfare-Related Bills

Congress considered a number of welfare-related measures in 1992. Those included:

## WELFARE-TO-WORK

The House Ways and Means Committee on June 24 and 25 turned months of rhetoric about welfare reform into some concrete proposals. But those provisions became part of an omnibus tax bill, HR 11, that President Bush vetoed at the close of the 102nd Congress. *(Urban aid tax bill, p. 140)*

At a closed-door markup, members approved the package of provisions that covered both ends of the ideological spectrum, including some ideas submitted by the Bush administration in its fiscal 1993 budget.

The largest item in the package sought to make it easier for states to fund the welfare-to-work programs Congress required as part of its most recent major welfare overhaul, the 1988 Family Support Act (PL 100-485). *(1988 Almanac, p. 349)*

Under that law, states were required to set up education, training and work programs called JOBS (Job Opportunities and Basic Skills), aimed at helping welfare recipients leave the public rolls. The federal government guaranteed about $1 billion per year, but states had to match the funds at varying rates. Because of the recession, however, many states had not claimed their full allotments for JOBS programs.

The proposal approved by the committee, by Thomas J. Downey, D-N.Y., acting chairman of the Human Resources Subcommittee, and full committee Chairman Dan Rostenkowski, D-Ill., was aimed at making more funds available both to states that had drawn down their full share of JOBS funds and those that had not. The complicated formula would have allowed states to use unclaimed federal matching funds and, in some cases, would have increased the federal match rate to 90 percent. The provision was estimated to cost an estimated $390 million over five years.

The package also included some welfare-reform proposals the Bush administration sought in its fiscal 1993 budget, including one allowing welfare recipients to save up to $10,000 in their effort to become self-sufficient through work, training or education without losing their welfare benefits.

Finally, the package included the text of HR 3450, legislation calling for a demonstration of "micro-enterprise" programs that enabled welfare recipients to start small businesses. The bill was a bipartisan effort spearheaded by Ways and Means member Fred Grandy, R-Iowa, Tony P. Hall, D-Ohio, and Bill Emerson, R-Mo. Hall and

Emerson were chairman and ranking Republican, respectively, of the Select Committee on Hunger. Also spearheading the effort was Mike Espy, D-Miss., who headed that panel's domestic task force.

Two Ways and Means subcommittees on June 18 had approved the proposals to alter rules for social programs they oversaw. Both the Human Resources and Social Security subcommittees marked up and sent on to the full committee packages for inclusion in a larger bill.

## WELFARE TRACKING

Legislation designed to identify factors that led to welfare dependency and develop strategies for reducing it won voice vote approval in the Senate on Jan. 29. The bill was referred to three House committees, none of which acted on the measure.

The bill (S 1256), introduced by Sen. Daniel Patrick Moynihan, D-N.Y., would have required the secretary of Health and Human Services (HHS) to collect and analyze information about who received welfare, for what reasons and for how long.

The secretary was to determine which statistics would be most useful in tracking and predicting welfare dependency. The information was then to be reported annually to Congress using those new statistical measures.

The bill had been approved by the Senate Labor and Human Resources Committee on Oct. 30, 1991.

In the House, the bill was jointly referred to Ways and Means, Agriculture and Education and Labor.

## CHILD ABUSE

Federal programs created to assist the estimated 2.5 million children who suffered from abuse or neglect were reauthorized through fiscal 1995 under a bill (S 838) cleared by the Senate on April 9. President Bush signed the bill on May 28 — PL 102-295.

The measure, which the House passed April 7, was the result of a deal negotiated by members of the House Education and Senate Labor committees. Both chambers in 1991 passed legislation (HR 2720, S 838) to reauthorize the programs but remained apart on funding levels and some new initiatives. *(1991 Almanac, p. 387)*

The compromise authorized $321.7 million for fiscal 1992 for programs under the 1974 Child Abuse Prevention and Treatment Act. Funding levels for fiscal 1993-95 were not specified.

## NUTRITION PROGRAMS FOR CHILDREN

Congress cleared legislation (S 2759 — S Rept 102-645) to authorize $650,000 in fiscal 1993 and $800,000 in 1994 to reimburse homeless shelters for providing meals to children under the age of six.

Acting on voice votes, the Senate on May 20 passed S 2759 and another bill (S 2760) introduced by Agriculture Chairman Patrick J. Leahy, D-Vt., both aimed at enhancing nutritional programs for children.

The House passed S 2759 on July 28 with amendments, and the Senate cleared it July 30. President Bush signed the bill Aug. 5 — PL 102-342.

The other measure, S 2760, to authorize child nutrition programs and establish a breast-feeding promotion program to foster wider public acceptance, died in the House. ∎

# Service Programs for the Elderly Renewed

A straightforward four-year re-authorization of the 1965 Older Americans Act — minus a provision on the so-called Social Security earnings test — was cleared by the House on Sept. 22, assuring the continuation of important nutrition and service programs for the elderly but not necessarily assuring more money.

President Bush signed the bill Sept. 30 (PL 102-375), exactly one year after the programs had expired, resulting in frozen spending levels for fiscal 1992. Because of the effort by appropriators to keep domestic spending down in fiscal 1993, the funding outlook for existing programs for older Americans — as well as some new initiatives in the cleared legislation — did not improve in 1992.

Even so, considerable maneuvering was done in the 102nd Congress to assure reauthorization. The Older Americans Act had to be separated from the explosive and costly issue of raising the amount of money an older worker might earn before losing Social Security benefits. Much to the dismay of advocates for the elderly, the Older Americans Act had been taken hostage to the Social Security earnings test at the end of 1991.

The House had overwhelmingly passed a bill in 1991 (HR 2967) to reauthorize the 1965 law that provided for transportation and employment programs and federal meals for the elderly poor, including Meals on Wheels. The Senate moved quickly on passing a similar bill (S 243). But action halted for the year after Sen. John McCain, R-Ariz., added an amendment to repeal the earnings test.

Rather than holding a House-Senate conference to reconcile the differences between the two bills, the House passed another bill April 9, 1992 that would have significantly liberalized rather than repealed the amount of money older people could earn before losing Social Security benefits. That bill, calculated to add $3.8 billion to the deficit over five years, sat in the Senate for months while Senate Finance Committee Chairman Lloyd Bentsen, D-Texas, attempted to free the Older Americans Act by pushing through committee on June 11 a free-standing bill (S 2038) that dealt solely with the earnings test.

Liberation did not occur until Sept. 10, when the Senate defeated a similar Social Security earnings test proposal offered by McCain during action on the fiscal 1993 spending bill (HR 5488 — PL 102-919) on the Treasury Department and Postal Service. The Senate moved quickly Sept. 15 to pass a clean version of the Older Americans Act (S 3008) and then substituted that language for HR 2967. The House cleared it seven days later.

House Education and Labor Chairman William D. Ford, D-Mich., said that the elderly had turned to the programs in the Older Americans Act for more than 25 years. "I am proud that we have been able to keep their safety net intact. They deserve our support — it is as simple as that," he said.

---

## BOXSCORE

➡ **Older Americans Act (HR 2967).** The legislation reauthorized for four years numerous service and nutrition programs — including the popular Meals on Wheels — that had served the nation's elderly since the original law passed in 1965.

**Report:** H Rept 102-199

### KEY ACTION

**April 9** — The **House** passed HR 2967, with an amendment, 340-68.

**Sept. 15** — The **Senate** passed S 3008 by voice vote and then substituted the language for HR 2967.

**Sept. 22** — The **House** cleared HR 2967 by voice vote.

**Sept. 30** — President Bush signed — PL 102-375.

---

But in 1992, that safety net was shrinking.

The bill sent to the White House authorized $1.7 billion in fiscal 1993 for preventive health care, increased services to the poor and minority elderly and training and counseling for family members caring for older relatives at home. Nearly 70 percent of the funds were used for grants to states.

However, the fiscal 1993 spending bill (HR 5677 — PL 102-974) for the Department of Health and Human Services provided less than $1 billion for programs for the aging.

## BACKGROUND

President John F. Kennedy in 1963 sent Congress the first presidential message dealing exclusively with programs for the aged. In it, he proposed legislation authorizing federal funds to develop services for the elderly, train personnel and build recreation centers.

Responding to this and to a subsequent Senate report, Congress enacted the Older Americans Act in 1965 to improve and expand federal and state programs for the aging. The law created an Administration on Aging in the Department of Health, Education and Welfare (reorganized in 1980 as the Department of Health and Human Services). It also authorized appropriations of $5 million for fiscal 1966 for grants to states for community planning and coordination of programs for the elderly.

The Senate special Committee on Aging had issued a report March 16, 1965 concluding that the problem of income for the elderly was becoming more serious because of "a trend toward a smaller percentage of the over-65 population in the nation's work force and a longer life expectancy for this age group." One of the recommendations aimed at increasing employment for the aged suggested that earning limitations on old-age assistance recipients be liberalized. *(1965 Almanac, p. 356)*

Sen. McCain echoed this proposal throughout his quest in the 102nd Congress to link the reauthorization of the Older Americans Act to a repeal of a separate law dictating the amount of money a Social Security recipient could earn before losing some benefits. He argued that the removal or liberalization of the earnings limits on older workers receiving Social Security checks would put more of the seniors back in the work force. However, he failed to convince his colleagues of the connection. *(Earnings test, p. 469)*

Over the years, the Older Americans Act had been reauthorized a dozen times to strengthen the Administration on Aging and to create new programs. Congress last reauthorized for four years the popular nutrition and support services for the elderly in 1987. The legislation (PL 100-175) defined "older Americans" as people 60 or older, except in community work programs, where it meant people 55 or older. It created programs aimed at preventing

abuse, neglect and exploitation of the elderly. It also authorized for the first time funding to provide non-medical home care for the frail elderly. *(1987 Almanac, p. 511)*

The central goal of the Older Americans Act never faltered from the original, which was to foster independence for older people by providing a broad network of social and community services to those in the greatest economic and social need. Those included in-home services to help older frail and disabled individuals remain in their homes as long as possible, senior center programs to support group activities for social, physical, educational, recreational and cultural purposes, nutrition programs, legal assistance and advocacy. The basic philosophy was to keep the elderly at home and avoid unnecessary or premature institutionalization.

### First Session Action

Programs under the Older Americans Act had expired Sept. 30, 1991, despite considerable progress during the first session to reauthorize and expand the law. Funding for the act, which included grants to states, was continued through the fiscal 1992 appropriations measure. *(1991 Almanac, p. 382)*

The House Education and Labor Committee gave voice-vote approval July 30, 1991 to HR 2967, a bill to reauthorize programs that served the elderly for four years. A minor section of the bill that included a provision requiring the administration to hold a National Conference on Aging in 1993 evoked a veto threat on the grounds that the conference mandate impinged on executive branch prerogatives. The measure changed the name from the White House Conference on Aging and gave Congress more authority to set the agenda and policies of the conference.

The conference on aging dispute was resolved by the time the House passed HR 2967, 385-0, on Sept. 12. House Democrat Matthew G. Martinez, Calif., chairman of the House Education Subcommittee on Human Resources, broke the impasse by successfully offering amendments on the floor that still set the 1993 date but changed the name back to the White House Conference on Aging. The administration also was given slightly more leverage in choosing the number of policy committee members for the event.

A different — and less easily reconciled — controversy then plagued similar legislation moving through the Senate. The Senate Labor and Human Resources Committee passed S 243, 13-3, on July 17. It was when the bill moved to the floor on Nov. 12 that senators revived a prickly issue: the limit on the amount of money older Americans could earn while continuing to collect Social Security benefits. Before passing the bill, the Senate adopted by voice vote an amendment by McCain that sought to repeal the Social Security earnings test.

Considered a hot potato, the earnings test was then passed off to House-Senate conferees to resolve in 1992. But a conference was never held during the second session. Instead, the House revised its version of the Older Americans Act to include a different approach to easing the earnings limit on the elderly.

## HOUSE ACTION

The House voted overwhelmingly April 9 on a new version of the Older Americans Act that included an amendment to double the amount of money older people could earn before Social Security benefits would be curtailed. People between the ages of 65 and 69 would be able to earn up to $20,000 a year in a measure that was calculated to add $3.8 billion to the deficit over five years.

Another $3.5 billion in provisions included one to boost benefits for widows and widowers over age 80 who began receiving benefits before turning 65.

Under pay-as-you-go budget regulations required by the 1990 White House-congressional budget agreement, Congress could not raise the cost of entitlements such as Social Security without also raising taxes or cutting costs elsewhere.

But House leaders put the bill under a special fast-track procedure that called on members to suspend the rules. Members adopted that procedure in a 269-139 vote. And that prevented anyone from objecting to the measure on budgetary grounds or from adding amendments to it. *(Vote 86, p. 22-H)*

Then the House voted 340-68 to pass the amended version of HR 2967, reauthorizing important service and nutrition programs for the elderly. *(Vote 87, p. 22-H)*

The bill included $2.1 billion in reauthorizations for four years through 1995. The usually non-controversial measure included preventive health care for older people; a boost in services to low-income and minority elderly, such as the popular Meals on Wheels program; and training for those who wished to provide in-home care for family members.

The House had passed the measure 385-0 on Sept. 12, 1991 without the Social Security amendment. But the Senate agreed by voice vote Nov. 12 to an amendment from McCain to repeal the earnings cap completely — at a cost of about $28 billion over five years.

The Senate bill, as passed in 1991, allowed people between 65 and 69 to receive Social Security benefits regardless of how much money they earned. Under existing law, people who earned more than $10,200 a year lost $1 in benefits for every $3 they earned. People 70 and older were not subject to limits.

The House bill received bipartisan support from members eager to help their older constituents.

And it was the usually tightfisted Republicans who wanted to go beyond the House bill and adopt the Senate's plan to repeal the earnings test completely. Dennis Hastert, R-Ill., for example, said that a repeal would induce older people to stay in the work force, benefiting the economy and the U.S. Treasury. In the end, Hastert supported the less expensive House version.

### Rostenkowski Strikes a Deal

Instead of agreeing to the Senate's $28 billion provision on the repeal of the Social Security earnings test, House Ways and Means Chairman Dan Rostenkowski, D-Ill., had worked with Minority Leader Robert H. Michel, R-Ill., to prevent the House from adopting the Senate language. The two House leaders struck a deal. Rostenkowski, who usually insisted on abiding by the budget rule, said he backed down after members refused to pay for the change with a payroll tax.

The compromise bill would raise the amount of money that people could earn from $10,200 to $20,000 in five years. The earnings limit would rise to $12,000 in 1993, and then by $2,000 a year until 1997.

It was unclear the day before the vote whether the Rostenkowski-Michel agreement would hold. GOP members, including Ways and Means ranking Republican Bill Archer of Texas, vigorously opposed what they considered a measure that would go only halfway.

However, Rostenkowski and Michel had the administration on their side. Rostenkowski spoke to White House Chief of Staff Samuel K. Skinner and budget director Richard G. Darman on April 8, and they said President Bush would support the $7 billion bill.

But on April 10, Bush criticized the House bill during a

White House news conference and said that he wanted to avoid a massive increase in the deficit. "The matter is not settled yet," said Bush, noting that he favored easing the earnings limit.

But a few members disliked both the House and Senate versions, and urged Congress to abide by the budget rules, including House Budget Committee Chairman Leon E. Panetta, D-Calif., who said that although the Social Security trust fund had a surplus, the point of the budget agreement was to prevent Congress from raiding it. "What we're doing here is helping seniors now and hurting seniors later," Panetta said.

But the American Association of Retired Persons (AARP) supported the compromise. "It's a responsible effort to make it easier for older people to work without losing benefits," said John Rother, legislative director.

Still, Bill Gradison, R-Ohio, a member of the Ways and Means Committee, also opposed the bill even though he supported easing the earnings test. Gradison and Panetta joined Sen. Bentsen in opposing any change to Social Security without paying for it. The Senate on April 7 approved a Bentsen amendment to the fiscal 1993 budget resolution that essentially upheld the 60-vote requirement for legislative changes to Social Security benefits that didn't have offsetting cuts or revenues. *(Budget resolution, p. 98)*

## SENATE ACTION

The Senate passed by voice vote Sept. 15 a clean version (S 3008) of the measure to amend the 1965 Older Americans Act, substituting that language for the House version (HR 2967).

After HR 2967 had passed the House in April with an amendment to the Senate's Social Security measure, it was sent back to the Senate. At that point, four options existed: The Senate could agree to the House changes and send the bill to the president, further changes could be made to the bill, a conference could be requested with the House, or the bill could linger indefinitely.

When it appeared that the last course was being taken, sponsors of the Older Americans Act considered how to push through a clean version of the bill that did not include the controversial Social Security earnings test.

The programs for the elderly finally were liberated from the Social Security issue Sept. 10 when the Senate defeated a similar proposal offered by McCain of Arizona during action on the fiscal 1993 spending bill (HR 5488 — PL 102-393) for the Treasury Department and Postal Service. *(Appropriations, p. 626)*

Until then, sponsors of the Older Americans Act were reluctant to bring forth the bill for fear of McCain. He had attached an outright repeal of the earnings test on Nov. 12, 1991, virtually killing the measure for the year.

The removal of a highly charged provision of the so-called Social Security earnings test did successfully jump-start the $1.7 billion reauthorization of popular programs that had provided the elderly with transportation, employment and meals for more than 25 years.

"This is one of the most important legislative tools we have to assure that older Americans have proper nourishment, are protected against abuse, and have new opportunities to live a full and useful life," said Sen. Brock Adams, D-Wash., chairman of the Labor and Human Resources Subcommittee on Aging and a sponsor of the bill.

Besides reauthorizing programs to assist the elderly, including Meals on Wheels, the measure contained changes to target older people most in need, especially low-income minorities. The bill strengthened provisions related to

abuse prevention. It also sought to resolve a dispute between Congress and the administration on a White House Conference on Aging, an opportunity for older Americans to voice their concerns in Washington. Under the bill's provisions, the conference would be held no later than Dec. 31, 1994, and congressional appointees would be included on the policy committee.

Several powerful lobbying groups for the elderly had urged lawmakers to push forward on the Older Americans Act, which had expired in September 1991. Advocates for the elderly also hoped passage of a reauthorization bill would bolster their case to retain existing funding levels on such key programs as in-home services and home-delivered meals. Because 1992 was one of the tightest budget years for the spending bill (HR 5677) for Health and Human Services, the federal agency with jurisdiction over programs for the aged, some of those services faced the possibility of deep cuts in fiscal 1993. *(Appropriations, p. 651)*

### Other Hurdles

The earnings test was not the only hurdle the bill faced in the rush to pass it before adjournment. Sen. Connie Mack, R-Fla., also threatened to block the measure if it did not include a provision that would clarify that the Administration on Aging — which oversaw implementation of the act — would use annually updated data from the Census Bureau in allotting funds to the states.

"My home state of Florida has one of the nation's fastest, if not the fastest, growing older populations. When we speak of the graying of America, we are truly speaking of Florida," Mack said. Adams assured Mack that the amendments contained such language.

## FINAL ACTION

The four-year reauthorization of the 1965 Older Americans Act was cleared by the House Sept. 22 by voice vote. It did not include a provision to either repeal or liberalize the amount of earnings a Social Security recipient could earn before losing some benefits.

As signed by President Bush Sept. 30, the bill:

● Consolidated and strengthened provisions relating to elder abuse prevention. The new Elder Rights title also expanded outreach and public benefit and insurance counseling programs.

● Increased low-income minority participation by requiring state and local agencies on aging to set the goal of reaching more of those in need with supportive and nutrition services. The law also required intrastate funding formulas to take into account the number of individuals in greatest economic and social need.

● Authorized a White House Conference on Aging to be conducted no later than Dec. 31, 1994. It also provided for the first time an expanded congressional role in the conference by including congressional appointees with the president's appointees to the conference policy committee.

● Authorized a new program to provide counseling and training to family care-givers of frail people.

● Authorized several research and demonstration programs, including pension counseling and ombudsmen for older tenants in publicly assisted housing.

● Reauthorized the Administration for Native Americans Act. The 1974 law provided financial assistance to Native American organizations.

● Authorized meals for the elderly in public schools to promote joint activities with troubled students. ∎

# Efforts To Repeal Earnings Test Fail

There was no shortage of attempts throughout the 102nd Congress to repeal or ease the existing limits on how much older workers could earn before Social Security benefits were curtailed.

Nothing succeeded, however, as each of those proposals collided with the realities of what such changes to the Social Security trust fund would cost.

In his fiscal 1992 budget request, President Bush proposed increasing the earnings limit by $1,000 over the following two years. Republican Sen. John McCain of Arizona argued that a simple liberalization was inadequate.

In 1992, retirees ages 65 to 69 could earn up to $10,200 annually and collect full Social Security benefits. If they earned more, their benefits were reduced by $1 for every $3 they earned over that amount. In 1991 the figure had been $9,720. Those ages 62-64 could earn up to $7,440 and collect full benefits, but if they earned more, their benefits were reduced by $1 for every $2 they earned. In 1991, the figure was $7,080. *(Chart, p. 470)*

McCain, who counted older Americans as a large bloc of his constituency, wanted the federal government to stop cutting the Social Security benefits of retirees under age 70. He was not the first member of Congress to tackle the so-called Social Security earnings test, but in 1992 he was the toughest fighter. While many lawmakers were willing to consider a liberalization of the existing rules, McCain stood his ground — until the very end of the session — on an out-and-out repeal of the law.

McCain's chief vehicle for his crusade to repeal the earnings test became the otherwise non-controversial reauthorization of the 1965 Older Americans Act (HR 2967). The law had provided elderly people with important nutrition and service programs for 25 years. After McCain's Social Security earnings test amendment was attached to HR 2967 at the end of 1991, action stalled on the bill for nearly a year.

Looking for a middle ground, House Ways and Means Chairman Dan Rostenkowski, D-Ill., and his Senate counterpart, Finance Committee Chairman Lloyd Bentsen, D-Texas, had introduced proposals in 1991 that would have been more generous to working retirees than the administration plan but less radical than McCain's. Both plans called for paying the tab by increasing taxes. The two chairmen were determined to abide by the 1990 White House-congressional budget agreement, which required any loss of revenue to the federal government to be offset by an increase in taxes or cuts in other spending.

Under Rostenkowski's bill (HR 2838), the earnings test for those from age 65 to 69 would increase by $1,200 in 1992 and by $3,000 in 1993. To pay for it, the plan called for phasing in by 1996 a $3,000 increase in the Social Security wage base.

Under Bentsen's legislation (S 2038), the earnings limit was to increase gradually to $11,100 in 1993 and to $89,700 by 2001. The taxable wage base under his proposal would have risen to $58,200 in 1993 and to $89,700 by 2001.

However, the Ways and Means committee never marked up Rostenkowski's bill. Instead, the House amended the Older Americans Act in early 1992 to include a more generous version of Rostenkowski's proposal — minus the tax increase — and sent it back to the Senate, where it sat for several months.

Bentsen, in an effort to free the Older Americans Act from the earnings test, did successfully move S 2038 through the Finance Committee on June 11. But the stalemate continued: Neither the free-standing earnings test bill nor the Older Americans Act advanced to the Senate floor.

Meanwhile, McCain latched onto two fast-moving fiscal 1993 appropriations measures with additional bids to remove the earning limits on older workers.

The spending bill for agriculture (HR 5487 — PL 102-341) got bogged down on the Senate floor July 28 over a heated debate about the earnings test for Social Security recipients. In the end, the Senate agreed by voice vote to an amendment by McCain that expressed the sense of the Senate that the earnings test should be repealed or changed.

The watershed event occurred on the spending bill (HR 5488 — Pl 102-393) for the Treasury Department and Postal Service on Sept. 10. As the hour grew late, senators voted against McCain's amendment to allow senior citizens to earn higher wages without sacrificing Social Security benefits.

McCain, torn between his crusade to repeal or raise the Social Security earnings cap and his support of the Older Americans Act, finally agreed to release his hold on the Older Americans Act. But he told his colleagues that "the matter of the earnings test itself, however, has not been resolved and will continue to be an issue to be addressed, certainly in the next Congress."

## BACKGROUND

Since the Social Security earnings test was created in 1939, Congress had raised it more than a dozen times, most recently in the Social Security Act Amendments of 1983 (PL 98-21). The earnings test only measured income from work and disregarded income from pensions and investments. The amount of earnings affected changed each year at the rate that average wages in the overall work force fluctuated. *(1983 Almanac, p. 219)*

Almost immediately after the 1983 boost, Congress resumed trying to tinker with the earnings limit.

Each year, members sponsored repeal legislation. Because fears about the cost of a repeal had kept such measures from getting off the ground, support for them had been politically risk-free.

Not far behind the scenes, defining the political debate were thousands of older Americans. Retirees argued that they could not survive on Social Security alone but were penalized for working to supplement their income.

McCain and other members pushing for repeal of the earnings test were primarily championing the position of the approximately 5 million members of the National Committee to Preserve Social Security and Medicare.

By contrast, the American Association of Retired Persons, with 33 million members, was the largest advocate for the elderly. The organization long had supported an increase in the earnings limit and contended that repeal of the limit should be considered only if Congress refused to liberalize it.

Many Democratic leaders also contended that the repeal plan was too costly and primarily would benefit the wealthy.

Social Security Administration Commissioner Gwendolyn S. King said the administration supported a small increase in the earnings test but opposed repeal because of its estimated $28 billion price tag.

"We really do need to rethink this policy, but in the rethinking we need to be fiscally responsible," King said.

Repeal efforts also stirred bitter complaints along generational lines. Repeal would mean that the wages of younger Americans — who were often likely to be less well off than their parents or grandparents — would be placed in the pockets of older people, said Paul S. Hewitt, vice president for research for the National Taxpayers Union Foundation, a nonpartisan economic think tank "dedicated to fiscal responsibility." The foundation opposed repeal.

Older doctors, lawyers and business owners, more likely to work because their careers were so lucrative, would reap a windfall, Hewitt maintained.

### Cost as a Stumbling Block

A major stumbling block was how to pay for repeal.

The Social Security Administration estimated that 10 percent of the cost of paying out additional benefits would be offset by tax revenues. The remainder would come from the Social Security trust fund.

As eager as many members were to please the elderly, they were loath to touch the trust fund, which was politically sacrosanct. It amounted to a rainy day fund for future beneficiaries: The money tucked away was expected to help pay the cost of benefits for thousands of baby boomers who would begin receiving payments about the year 2010.

At the end of calendar year 1991, the trust fund held an accrued surplus of $282 billion after paying out $273.4 billion in benefits and collecting $330 billion. In calendar 1992, the agency expected to increase that surplus by $62.3 billion unless the economy stalled further and reduced tax revenues.

While the fund was expected to build up to $1.2 trillion by the year 2000, the agency estimated that it would be paying out $460 billion a year in benefits at that time. In an economic downturn, the fund would have only enough money to pay out benefits for two years.

According to the Office of Management and Budget, repeal would cost the Social Security trust fund $28 billion over five years. The estimate by the Congressional Budget Office was slightly lower at $26.2 billion.

Some proponents of repeal argued that the move would bring many older Americans back into the work force, increasing federal tax revenues.

The nonpartisan National Center for Policy Analysis supported repeal of the test, arguing that costs would be offset by taxes paid by the newly employed elderly. The center estimated that 700,000 older Americans would enter the work force if the limit were lifted, paying about $4.5 billion in taxes over five years. McCain set the figure at $3 billion.

Opponents pointed to studies by the Social Security Administration that found that boosts in the earnings limit had triggered only negligible increases in the number of working seniors.

### 1991 Action

Yet large numbers of older Americans favored repeal, and several factors combined in 1991 to give the issue steam.

For the first time, Rostenkowski introduced legislation

---

## How the Earnings Test Worked

Under the retirement test, Social Security benefits were reduced when non-disabled elderly workers earned income above a certain amount.

Retirees from ages 62 to 64 could earn up to $7,440 in 1992 without facing a cut in benefits. Those from 65-69 had up to $10,200 annually in "exempt income." And when benefits were cut, the reduction was less for the older retirees.

The test did not apply to workers over 70. Neither did it apply to pensions, rents, dividends, interest, and other types of "unearned" income. These forms of income were exempted to encourage savings for retirement.

The earnings limits were raised slightly over 1991 amounts. Following are examples of how the retirement test worked in 1991:

John — age 63, with $4,000 in annual benefits before the retirement test is applied:

| | |
|---|---|
| Earnings in 1991 | $8,080 |
| Exempt amount for under age 65 | 7,080 |
| Excess over exempt amount | 1,000 |
| Benefit reduction — 50% of excess | 500 |
| Benefits John received in 1991 | 3,500 |

Ida — age 67, with $4,000 in annual benefits before the retirement test is applied:

| | |
|---|---|
| Earnings in 1991 | $10,320 |
| Exempt amount for 65 and older | 9,720 |
| Excess over exempt amount | 600 |
| Benefit reduction — 33% of excess | 200 |
| Benefits Ida received in 1991 | 3,800 |

SOURCE: House Ways and Means Committee

---

in the Ways and Means Committee to ease the earnings test. He said at the time that he was proposing initiatives to help shape the Democratic agenda. While all were worthwhile, he said, not all could be funded, and House members would have to choose.

Although members of his committee did not support funding a liberalization of the earnings test, Rostenkowski's move put the issue before Congress.

Campaign-year considerations also helped revive the issue. Members not known for supporting repeal became slower to condemn the plan for fear of alienating older voters.

Even Pete V. Domenici, N.M., who as ranking Republican on the Senate Budget Committee was a vehement budget watchdog, declined to oppose the repeal when McCain's amendment to repeal the Social Security earnings test was offered Nov. 12 during Senate floor consideration of the Older Americans Act (HR 2967). Faced with choosing between the interests of a popular constituency and holding the line on federal spending, senators skipped a floor fight and adopted the amendment by voice vote. Many senators believed it would be taken out in conference with the House. (1991 Almanac, p. 384)

The ball then fell into the House's court, where repeal legislation enjoyed widespread support.

Caught up in the jockeying was the reauthorization bill, which included such popular programs as Meals on Wheels.

While this was not "must pass" legislation — the older Americans program was continued through the appropriations process — the measure called for needed expansions. *(Older Americans Act, p. 466)*

Democrats attempted to work out a compromise: raising the earnings limit without abolishing it. But time ran out in the session, setting the stage for Capitol Hill to revisit the issue in 1992.

## SENATE COMMITTEE ACTION

Setting up a potential confrontation with President Bush over tax increases, Senate Finance Chairman Bentsen signaled the week of June 8 that he was ready to deal again on a proposal to raise the amount of money an older worker could earn before losing Social Security benefits.

The Finance Committee on June 11 gave voice vote approval to a free-standing bill (S 2038) that gradually would raise the amount of money an older worker could earn before benefits were reduced. The measure also sought to increase Social Security payroll taxes on higher wage earners.

The committee's action was an attempt to ply off the controversial earnings test issue from a bill (HR 2967) to reauthorize the Older Americans Act, which Bentsen had blocked from Senate floor action. His new proposal was similar to a plan put forward by Rostenkowski, who subsequently backed down after other Ways and Means members refused to pay for the earnings test change with a payroll tax.

Because the House must initiate all revenue measures, Bentsen's action effectively asked Rostenkowski to move his earnings-test bill again.

A Bentsen-Rostenkowski union could have put President Bush and Republicans on the spot over the issue of payroll taxes.

Bush also had proposed an increase in the earnings test — and several Republicans had pushed for an outright repeal of the earnings limit on Social Security recipients. But Republicans had steadfastly opposed any change in the tax system.

Repeal advocates, led by McCain, were considered the main obstacles to Bentsen and Rostenkowski's desire to raise the earnings-test ceiling. McCain did not want to split the earnings test from the Older Americans Act.

Under Bentsen's proposal, the earnings limit would rise to $11,100 in 1993, $21,000 by 1997 and $51,000 by 2001. To pay for the increase, Bentsen proposed raising Social Security taxes on higher-income workers.

Existing law required both the employer and employee to pay a tax equal to 6.2 percent of the first $53,400 of earnings.

The "wage base" subject to this payroll tax rose automatically each year; it was projected to reach $57,900 in 1993, $69,300 in 1997 and $84,600 by 2001.

The Bentsen bill called for raising the taxable wage base to $58,200 in 1993, $71,100 by 1997 and $89,700 by 2001.

Rostenkowski's bill, on the other hand, would have used a slightly different formula to phase in a $3,000 increase in the Social Security wage base by 1996.

Bentsen and Rostenkowski said the proposed tax increase merely reflected Congress' intent, in a 1977 overhaul of Social Security, that 90 percent of every individual's taxable wage be subject to the payroll tax.

That proportion went down in the 1980s as the wages of higher earners grew faster than the average — as "the rich got richer," according to Rostenkowski.

## AGRICULTURE APPROPRIATIONS

McCain, anxious to keep alive the debate on doing away completely with the Social Security earnings test, attempted to attach an amendment to the spending bill for the Agriculture Department (HR 5487) during Senate floor action July 28. After a lengthy and heated debate, the Senate finally agreed by voice vote to a revised amendment by McCain that expressed the sense of the Senate that the earnings test should be repealed or changed. *(Appropriations, p. 676)*

McCain, who faced re-election in a state with a vocal elderly population, said, "It is clear that this is an issue of fairness. We need the skill and experience of older Americans. The earnings test is outdated, unjust and clearly discriminatory."

Supporters of the earnings test contended that eliminating it would primarily benefit wealthy, elderly Americans.

"I have seen some giveaways come to this floor in 16 years, but none so blatant and irresponsible as this," said Daniel Patrick Moynihan, D-N.Y.

## TREASURY-POSTAL APPROPRIATIONS

The persistent Social Security issue sought out another "must-pass" fiscal 1993 spending bill on Sept. 10. This time, the earnings test was effectively killed for the year when it failed to muster the necessary votes as an amendment to the Treasury Department and Postal Service appropriations measure (HR 5488). *(Appropriations, p. 626)*

McCain had brought to the floor a new proposal to raise the amount of money an older worker may could before losing Social Security benefits. McCain, suspending his effort to repeal the earnings test, instead offered an amendment to increase the cap on the test to $50,000 over five years.

But he ran into a problem: Because it would effectively increase spending from the Social Security trust fund, it needed a 60-vote waiver from the 1990 budget law. The 51-42 vote to waive the law was nine votes short. *(Vote 201, p. 27-S)*

McCain and other bill proponents said that raising the earnings test would put more seniors into the work force, broadening the taxable wage base and helping the economy.

"Tragically, so many seniors in America today have to return to work because of rising health-care costs, food costs and other things," McCain said.

Most senators agreed that the earnings limit should be liberalized in some fashion — even Finance Chairman Bentsen and Bush had indicated their support. But there was no consensus on how to pay for the change.

Bentsen's Finance Committee in June had approved a free-standing bill (S 2038) to increase Social Security payroll taxes on higher wage earners to pay for a liberalization of the earnings test. But like most efforts to raise taxes, it had gone nowhere under the fervent opposition of Bush and Republicans.

Bentsen objected to McCain's proposal because it provided no offset. It "threatens the financial integrity of the Social Security trust fund," Bentsen said. "Make no mistake about it. It threatens the fund's safety." ■

# Social Security Remains Division of HHS

For the third time in a decade, the House voted overwhelmingly to give the Social Security Administration independence from the Cabinet-level Department of Health and Human Services (HHS). Twice before, the measure had died in the Senate; in 1992, the fate was the same.

The House passed a bill (HR 5429) on June 29 to establish an independent three-member board to run a free-standing Social Security agency.

The Senate Finance Committee approved a different measure (S 33) on June 11 that called for an independent Social Security agency governed by a single commissioner appointed by the president and advised by a seven-member board. Neither bill advanced to the Senate floor before Congress adjourned, and the effort died.

Proponents of the legislation had believed there was a chance of passage in the Senate because of growing concern about the financial health of the Social Security-administered disability fund. Trustees of the disability fund sounded the alarm early in 1992, warning that the coffers could be empty as early as 1995 in a worst-case scenario and by 1997 under an "intermediate" outlook.

As a potential solution, lawmakers considered an overhaul of the Social Security system that administered the fund.

The Social Security trust fund — which included the disability fund — had a strong overseer in Sen. Daniel Patrick Moynihan, D-N.Y., chairman of the Senate Finance Social Security Subcommittee, who disliked that the White House had so much control over agency dollars and used the trust fund annually to help offset the federal deficit.

He had been saying for years that separating Social Security from HHS would give the agency far more autonomy to direct and protect the fund.

Proponents of giving the Social Security agency independence argued that the agency had a contract with the American worker, who paid into the trust fund for use upon retirement or disability. More than 100 interest groups, including the powerful American Association of Retired Persons (AARP), had supported the independence plan.

But the administration had repeatedly countered that it opposed any effort to separate Social Security from HHS. The agency was run in 1992 by a commissioner, Gwendolyn S. King, who reported to HHS Secretary Louis W. Sullivan.

However, Moynihan remained confident that one day the agency would be independent. "Sometimes it takes 20 years to do something," he said. "I've been at this for 10."

## BACKGROUND

Created in 1935, during the height of the Great Depression, Social Security provided financial security for Americans after thousands lost their savings in bankrupt institutions. It was established as an independent entity and run by a three-member bipartisan board.

However, four years later the board was co-opted by a federal agency and had remained under other agencies' control since then.

The movement to return the agency to independent status began in the early 1970s, soon after the federal budget was "unified" in fiscal 1969 to reflect all federal spending, including the Social Security trust fund.

But the real push to create a separate Social Security did not come until the 1980s, after the Reagan administration wreaked havoc by cutting the agency's staff 21 percent and eliminating 265,000 recipients of disability benefits from the rolls. Many beneficiaries were later reinstated.

"When so many people were kicked off the disability rolls, it seemed high time to insulate Social Security from political pressure," said John C. Rother, legislative director of AARP.

Legislation to make Social Security independent first began to move in 1986, when the House passed HR 5050. The measure died in the Senate. (1986 Almanac, p. 594)

The legislation reached the House floor again in 1989, that time as part of the Omnibus Budget Reconciliation Act. The Senate refused to go along, and the effort died. (1989 Almanac, p. 221)

## LEGISLATIVE ACTION

The outlook was not much better for the legislation in the 102nd Congress. Aside from the administration's objections, there was a gulf between the House and Senate versions of the plan. The key difference between the two versions was that the House bill sought to establish an independent three-member board to run the agency; under the Senate draft, the agency was to be governed by a single commissioner appointed by the president and advised by a seven-member board.

The House passed HR 5429 (H Rept 102-621) by a 350-8 vote on June 29.

"I see this vote as an opportunity to do something tangible this year to strengthen the Social Security system," said Dan Rostenkowski, D-Ill., the bill's sponsor and chairman of the House Ways and Means Committee. (Vote 242, p. 58-H)

Rostenkowski's committee had given voice vote approval to the bill June 24.

The Senate Finance Committee approved a companion measure (S 33 — S Rept 102-304) June 11. Long advocated by Moynihan, the measure sought to give the agency far more autonomy to direct and protect the Social Security trust fund.

The measure still had few Republican supporters in the Senate. Among them was Mark O. Hatfield of Oregon.

But against the bill was the ranking member of the Subcommittee on Social Security, Minority Leader Bob Dole of Kansas.

The administration argued that Moynihan's bill would remove a vital service from a department that oversaw companion programs for the elderly.

Sen. John H. Chafee, R-R.I., made the argument: "If it ain't broke, don't fix it."

# Notch-Baby Problem Still Insoluble

Lawmakers in both chambers again pondered the Social Security "notch" dilemma but to no avail. By year's end, nothing was done to settle a discrepancy in retirement benefits that put retirees born after 1917 at the short end of the stick.

The notch-baby problem arose nearly 10 years earlier, when people born in 1917 turned 65 and began retiring.

Several million retirees born between 1917 and 1921 were caught between a pair of fixes made to the Social Security benefit system in the 1970s.

A change in 1972 turned out to be overly generous and threatened to bankrupt the program. In 1977, the earlier change was rolled back, reducing benefits for retirees born after 1921. However, recipients born through 1916, some of whom were already retiring, were allowed to continue receiving benefits under the 1972 formula.

Those born in between — in the notch — were given a choice of the less-generous post-1977 benefit schedule or a phased-down version of the 1972 formula.

The upshot: Retirees in the notch generally got lower benefits than those born before, but higher benefits than those born after.

Congress was told in 1989 that little could be done to solve the problem. The Senate Finance Committee's Social Security Subcommittee released a study that year by the National Academy of Social Insurance that concluded no action should be taken to correct the inequity. *(1989 Almanac, p. 223)*

The first dust-up in 1992 over the notch issue occurred in June when Rep. Barney Frank, D-Mass., led a group of House notch-baby supporters in an unsuccessful attempt to attach a fix to the pending tax and urban aid bill (HR 11).

In the Senate, a proposed fix to the notch-baby problem came to a vote in the Senate on the fiscal 1993 spending bill (HR 5488 — PL 102-393) for the Treasury Department and Postal Service. Once defeated as part of that measure, the issue became moot during the brief remainder of the session.

## Tax Bill Manuever

The House got a shock the week of June 29 when a handful of members tried to force a floor vote to increase Social Security benefits for notch-baby retirees. The result was a near clash of budget, generational and election-year politics that had members running for cover and left two Democrats — Peter A. DeFazio of Oregon and Frank — battered and bruised.

Supporters, who wanted to extend the notch fix to 1926 babies, said the change would cost $48 billion over 10 years, money that the trust funds held in surplus and that could be readily spent.

Critics said the cost could reach $300 billion by 2010 and grow indefinitely. That was because the Social Security trust funds would lose huge amounts of interest that accrued on the surplus, which was accumulating to help pay benefits to post-World War II baby boomers when they retired.

Frank decided to try to attach a notch-baby fix to the pending tax and urban aid bill (HR 11). He and DeFazio threatened to use a parliamentary maneuver, requiring 218 votes, to force a floor vote on the notch question. With about 287 cosponsors for one notch bill (HR 917), it seemed likely that they would win. *(Urban aid tax bill, p. 140)*

Frank then attempted to cut a deal with Ways and Means Committee Chairman Dan Rostenkowski, D-Ill., and the Democratic leadership to bring a free-standing notch bill to the floor by August — a bill that would pay for itself, at least in part.

But when Frank took the idea to DeFazio and Mary Rose Oakar, D-Ohio, they rebelled, partly because they did not like Frank's proposal to pay for the benefit increase.

But DeFazio said he didn't trust the Ways and Means Committee to report an acceptable bill and feared that he would not be allowed to offer an alternative.

It was clear at a July 1 caucus of House Democrats that members were angry over being put in a box by Frank and DeFazio. Voting against the notch fix was seen as potential political suicide. On the other hand, of the 280 House members who had voted just three weeks earlier in favor of a balanced-budget amendment to the U.S. Constitution, 175 were also notch-fix cosponsors. *(Balanced budget, p. 108)*

In the end, the House Democratic leadership avoided the pain of a notch vote by bringing the tax bill to the floor under a procedure that prevented DeFazio's parliamentary gambit.

## Treasury-Postal Rider

During Senate consideration of the Treasury-Postal spending bill on Sept. 10, it again became obvious that when it came to mollifying elderly voters, even some of the most fiscally conservative senators could turn into allies.

The notch-baby question was a case in point. It revealed a sharp but virtually even division in the Senate on whether to give extra benefits to the several million retirees born after 1916 who got stuck between the pair of fixes to the Social Security benefit system made in the 1970s.

But when it came time to waive the budget act to fix the notch-baby problem with extra benefits for those born after 1916, the Senate voted 49-49 on a motion that required 60 votes for adoption. Such deficit fighters as Kent Conrad, D-N.D., and Bob Graham, D-Fla., voted in favor of the proposal, estimated to cost $22 billion in the first five years. *(Vote 200, p. 26-S)*

Democrat Terry Sanford of North Carolina, who was fighting a tough re-election campaign, offered the amendment as "simply an issue of fairness."

Sanford argued that there would be enough money in the Social Security trust fund to pay for the influx of new benefits, which he estimated at less than $3.5 billion in 1992.

"The money is there," Sanford said. "If it is not paid to these people who are entitled, it will be spent on something else.... If we were in a private corporation and spending retirement funds in this manner, all the corporate officials would go to jail for misusing pension funds."

Opponents, headed by Finance Committee Chairman Lloyd Bentsen, D-Texas, argued that the proposal would "recklessly endanger the Social Security program."

Bentsen estimated that the costs would result in $300 billion in benefit costs and revenue losses to the Social Security trust fund by the year 2020. He also pointed out that there would be no funding mechanism to offset those costs. ∎

# Hill Gets Tougher With Deadbeat Parents

Congress considered several measures in 1992 to impose stricter penalties on non-custodial parents who failed to uphold their child-support obligations.

Courts annually ordered parents to pay about $11 billion in child support, but less than half was ever paid at all, let alone paid on time, according to the Commerce Department.

The so-called "deadbeat dad" or "deadbeat parents" situation angered many lawmakers who viewed the delinquency as both willful neglect and, in many cases, another drain on the nation's beleaguered welfare system.

## OUT-OF-STATE ENFORCEMENT

Congress cleared legislation (S 1002 — PL 102-521) that made it a federal crime for parents who lived in another state to avoid paying child support. It was signed by the president on Oct. 25.

The measure, which passed the House on Oct. 3 and the Senate on Oct. 7, limited criminal liability to those who willfully avoided payments. Those who could not afford child-support payments were not covered by the bill.

Persons who intentionally avoided payments for six months and owed at least $2,500 could face up to six months in jail and a fine of up to $5,000. Repeat offenders could be sentenced to up to two years in prison and fined as much as $250,000.

A related measure (HR 5304) aimed at improving the administration of child support payments passed the House on Oct. 3 but was never taken up by the Senate. HR 5304 would have prohibited a state court from modifying a child support payment order issued from a court in another jurisdiction.

### House Action

Failure to pay child support would be punishable by as much as six months in jail and a $5,000 fine under a bill (HR 1241 — H Rept 102-771) that won voice vote approval April 9 by the House Judiciary Subcommittee on Crime. For a second conviction, the penalty would increase to two years in prison and a $250,000 fine.

Sponsor Henry J. Hyde, R-Ill., and other supporters of the measure said states had passed few laws to punish parents, mostly men, who refused to pay up.

Hyde said, "Denying a little kid food and clothes is stealing; it's child abuse."

William J. Hughes, D-N.J., opposed it, saying that lawmakers were confusing state and federal responsibilities. "We don't handle family domestic matters at the federal level. That's up to the state," he said.

But Chairman Charles E. Schumer, D-N.Y., responded, "No one has come up with a better way. We ought to give this one a shot."

Hyde said the bill had already had a positive effect: State welfare officials reported that support payments increased after congressional hearings discussed the possibility of punishing delinquent parents.

The House Judiciary Committee approved HR 1241 on July 1. Bill supporters said making a federal crime out of failure to pay child support was necessary because few states had passed laws to punish parents — mostly fathers — for not paying and because by the time a case was

developed under state law, the offender often had left the state.

The House passed the legislation on Aug. 4 by voice vote.

### Senate Action

Legislation similar to HR 1241 won voice vote approval from the Senate Judiciary Committee on Sept. 17.

Under the Senate version, S 1002, those who fled their state after not paying child support for at least six months and were at least $2,500 in arrears could get up to six months in prison and be fined up to $5,000.

Repeat offenders could be sentenced to two years in prison and fined a maximum of $250,000.

The panel approved, by voice vote, an amendment by Herb Kohl, D-Wis., to limit criminal liability to those who willfully avoided payments. Those who could not afford child-support payments would not be covered by the bill.

After the markup, bill sponsor Richard C. Shelby, D-Ala., promised to push for full Senate consideration of the measure as soon as possible.

### Final Action

The Senate cleared the legislation (S 1002) on Oct. 7 to make it a federal crime for parents who lived in another state to avoid paying child support. The House had passed the bill Oct. 3.

But the so-called "deadbeat parents" bill had been amended since its introduction to protect parents who could not afford to pay. The bill, a compromise between HR 1241 and S 1002, required the federal government to prove willful failure to pay child support.

The measure also authorized funding for states to enforce criminal laws on interstate child support.

Sen. Kohl, a principal author of the bill, said the measure was a popular one in Congress.

"All of us are speaking with the same voice when we say it's time to stop letting non-custodial parents who deliberately ignore their children's financial needs get away with neglect," Kohl said.

## CREDIT REPORTING BILL CLEARS

The Senate cleared legislation (HR 6022 — PL 102-537) on Oct. 5 that would require consumer credit agencies to include in credit reports information regarding a consumer's failure to meet court-ordered child support payments. The president signed it Oct. 27.

The measure, sponsored by Rep. Larry LaRocco, D-Idaho, was named after Rep. Ted Weiss, D-N.Y., who died Sept. 14. (Obituaries, p. 73)

"Ted Weiss devoted his career to helping people, and it is only appropriate that legislation designed to help children from broken homes is named after him," Sen. Richard H. Bryan, D-Nev., said of the Ted Weiss Child Support Enforcement Act, which was an amendment to the Fair Credit Reporting Act.

"There are 12 million children in this country who get less than they deserve because their parents are not paying court-ordered child support," Bryan said.

Under the bill, credit bureaus were to record delinquencies of $1,000 or more.

"Delinquent child support debt should be considered by credit granters, just as they consider delinquent mortgage payments or the failure to make car loan payments," Bryan said.

## PAYMENT ADMINISTRATION BILL FAILS

The House passed a bill Oct. 3 aimed at improving the administration of child support payments, but the measure died in the Senate.

The bill (HR 5304 — H Rept 102-982) would have prohibited a state court from modifying an order of another state court that would affect child support payments.

The House Judiciary Subcommittee on Administrative Law and Governmental Relations had approved HR 5304 on Sept. 17.

As sponsored by panel Chairman Barney Frank, D-Mass., and approved by voice vote, HR 5304 provided an exception only if the person receiving the child support payments resided in the state where the modification was sought, or agreed to seek the modification in another state court.

The House Judiciary Committee had approved HR 5304 on Sept. 30. ∎

# Indian Health Services Reauthorized

Congress cleared legislation (S 2481 — PL 102-573) on Oct. 7 to reauthorize until the year 2000 health services for American Indians. The president signed the bill Oct. 29.

The legislation set goals for Indian health care by improving services and targeting new beneficiaries. It also reflected members' increased concern about drug and alcohol abuse in Indian communities and diseases associated with Fetal Alcohol Syndrome (FAS).

## BACKGROUND

Historically, Indians had suffered from certain health traumas at a higher rate than other Americans. According to the Indian Health Service (IHS), Indian mortality rates were double those of the rest of the U.S. population, largely because of tuberculosis, alcoholism and diabetes. American Indian men and women died of alcohol-related causes in disproportionate numbers.

A main goal of the 1992 reauthorization was to raise Indian health standards by the turn of the century. The House and Senate bills laid out 61 health goals to reduce the incidence of such problems as cancer, infant mortality and alcoholism.

During debate, some members expressed concern that existing programs had either proved inadequate or had not been implemented.

They cited a report submitted in 1991 by the inspector general for the Department of Health and Human Services (HHS), questioning the effectiveness of several youth, alcohol and substance abuse treatment programs run by IHS.

In response, many new programs were aimed at afflictions primarily affecting Indian women and adolescents. In particular, the measure established a plan to study and treat infant mortality-related illnesses, such as Fetal Alcohol Syndrome. An Indian child was roughly three times as likely as a non-Indian child to be born with FAS, a condi-

---

### BOXSCORE

➡ **Indian Health-Care Amendments (S 2481, HR 3724).** The bill amended the Indian Health Care Improvement Act and authorized appropriations for Indian health-care programs.

**Reports:** H Rept 102-643, Parts 1 and 2; S Rept 102-392.

#### KEY ACTION

Sept. 15 — The **House** passed HR 3724, 330-36.

Sept. 18 — The **Senate** passed S 2481 by voice vote.

Oct. 3 — The **House** amended S 2481 and approved it, 335-74.

Oct. 7 — The **Senate** agreed by voice vote to **House** changes to S 2481.

Oct. 29 — President signed S 2481 — PL 102-573.

---

tion describing birth defects in children whose mothers drank alcohol during pregnancy.

## HOUSE ACTION

The House Energy and Commerce Committee approved the House measure (HR 3724) by voice vote April 7. The bill focused on federal programs that would reauthorize and provide health-care and other social services to about 1.2 million American Indians.

Members approved amendments by voice vote expanding treatment for FAS and adding family therapists to mental health services available to Indians.

The House Interior and Insular Affairs Committee approved a similar version of the bill by voice vote April 29. The Interior Committee's version included substance abuse provisions and specific provisions to deal with FAS.

Members reached a compromise on the two committee versions before they reached the floor. A new bill was introduced as HR 5752, which members inserted into the text of HR 3724. On Sept. 15, the House approved HR 3724 by a vote of 330-36. As approved, the measure did not specify yearly funding but included the substance abuse prevention provisions. *(Vote 392, p. 96-H)*

During floor consideration, members disagreed over a provision of HR 3724 that exempted tribes that ran their own health-care programs from reimbursing the government for medical services. At the time, only the Navajo tribe operated its own health-care program. The exemption was written into the bill to avoid straining the tribe's limited resources and violating its sovereignty, according to Bill Richardson, D-N.M.

But William E. Dannemeyer, R-Calif., offered an amendment that would allow the Indian Health Service to collect payments from a tribe's insurance plan. Dannemeyer said the exemption would reduce the amount of benefits available to all Indians. The amendment was defeated 165-199. *(Vote 391, p. 96-H)*

The House approved by voice vote an amendment by Byron L. Dorgan, D-N.D., to develop a model substance abuse program at the Standing Rock Indian Reservation in North and South Dakota.

## SENATE ACTION

A companion Indian health bill (S 2481) moved through the Senate Indian Affairs Committee on June 16, but only after senators agreed to rewrite core provisions on alcohol and drug abuse.

Ranking Republican John McCain, Ariz., offered an amendment that would have effectively repealed portions of two anti-drug laws (PL 99-570 and PL 100-690) that fell under the jurisdiction of the IHS. *(1988 Almanac, p. 85 )*

McCain called for further consideration of the alcohol and substance abuse provisions of the bill.

After voice vote approval of McCain's amendment, Chairman Daniel K. Inouye, D-Hawaii, pledged to schedule hearings to discuss McCain's concerns so that a new version of the bill could be prepared before the bill went to the floor.

Programs removed under McCain's plan included detoxification and rehabilitation for youths who were alcohol or substance abusers and a treatment program for families of youth substance abusers. According to a committee staff member, McCain wanted to review the effectiveness of the programs in light of the concerns outlined in the inspector general's report. Since the report dealt with concerns about adolescents, McCain also wanted to bring attention to similar programs aimed at adults.

In response to McCain's concerns, the committee held another hearing July 30 to address the alcohol and substance abuse provisions.

Another McCain amendment made the director of Indian health a presidential appointee subject to Senate confirmation, for a term of up to four years. The director had previously been appointed by the secretary of HHS. According to McCain, the office needed greater accountability to Congress. From the Nixon administration until 1992, there had been only two Indian health directors.

Inouye said McCain's amendment would likely politicize the office. Nevertheless, the amendment was accepted.

Other changes in the bill included a third amendment by McCain to lower, from 40 percent to 20 percent, the tribal contribution to a new tribal health scholarship assistance program. It would permit the HHS secretary to tailor the health objectives described in the surgeon general's Healthy People 2000 report for the health needs of American Indians.

Tom Daschle, D-S.D., citing a severe shortage of health personnel in rural South Dakota, Montana and Alaska, offered an amendment to increase recruitment of professionals from the areas with the greatest demand.

"Evidence indicates that if you recruit individuals from the area in which you are seeking to fill positions, the odds are much greater that you will succeed in retaining them," Daschle said. The amendment was approved by voice vote.

The panel also approved an amendment by Frank H. Murkowski, R-Alaska, to provide funding for patient travel both to and from medical treatment in those remote regions of Alaska where costly commercial air travel was the only means of transportation. Funds were previously provided for the trip to receive medical services but not for the return.

## FINAL ACTION

On Sept. 18, the Senate passed S 2481 without the drug and alcohol provisions that had been removed by McCain's earlier amendment.

Members from both houses and their staff met informally to work out differences between the two bills.

In response to administration concerns, members agreed to remove certain provisions from the Senate bill. One provision removed would have expanded medical coverage and medical provider options for low-income older and disabled Indians by authorizing IHS to pay Medicare Part B premiums for certain Medicare-eligible Indians.

Another provision removed would have required IHS to contract to administer health programs in tribes and tribal organizations that owned health facilities. Inouye had argued that the disparate treatment was contrary to Indian self-determination policy and promised continued investigations into the policy in the 103rd Congress.

Members also deleted one final provision during House-Senate negotiations that would have amended the Social Security Act. The amendment would have permitted tribal health-care providers to collect Medicare payments for outpatient services offered in tribal clinics.

The House, after reinserting the drug and alcohol provisions, overwhelmingly approved S 2481 by a vote of 335-74 on Oct. 3. Senators agreed to the changes and cleared the measure by voice vote Oct. 7. *(Vote 460, p. 112-H)*

## PROVISIONS

The legislation reauthorized the Indian Health Care Improvement Act of 1976 (PL 94-437) and the Indian Alcohol and Substance Abuse Prevention and Treatment Act, which was included in the 1986 omnibus anti-drug bill (PL 99-570).

As approved, it authorized roughly $940 million for fiscal 1993, committee aides said. The total 1991 appropriation for the Indian Health Service (IHS), which administered programs first authorized in the 1976 Indian Health Care Improvement Act, was $1.6 billion.

The bill established 61 goals aimed at reducing the incidence of such ailments as diabetes, cirrhosis and cancer by the year 2000. The Indian population suffered disproportionately from those afflictions.

The bill set more stringent standards by which to measure progress toward the goal of raising the health status of Indians.

It enhanced professional programs to draw more Native Americans into the Indian Health Service. It also provided for comprehensive school health education programs and established an Office of Indian Women's programs.

Members then included provisions to provide financial assistance to tribal governments for safe water and sanitary waste disposal facilities. The bill also exempted payments received by an Indian Health Service facility from consideration in determining appropriations for services to Indians.

The drug and alcohol provisions included a specific amendment to require the Indian Health Service to address inhalant abuse in the context of substance abuse. Aside from continuing previously existing drug and alcohol abuse provisions, it authorized several substance abuse and demonstration projects specific to certain tribes.

Under the bill, the IHS director, then appointed by the secretary of Health and Human Services, would be subject to confirmation by the Senate. Sponsors hoped the change would make the agency, which provided health-care services to 1.2 million American Indians and Alaska natives, more accountable to the Indian population and give the director more clout with the administration. ∎

# Grants to Tribal Courts Held Over for 103rd

The Senate and House passed different versions of legislation (HR 4004) designed to help Indian tribes retain their sovereignty by shoring up their tribal justice systems. But members did not work out their differences, and the measure never cleared.

Under federal law, Indian tribes were accorded authority over any tribal governance that was not specifically divested to Congress. A 1968 Indian civil rights law ensured that Indian tribes had the right to exercise legal jurisdiction over their affairs. Tribal courts, however, had long suffered from a lack of funding and organization.

## House-Senate Differences

The bill would have authorized grants for fiscal 1993-1997 for tribes to bolster tribal court systems.

The main difference between the House and Senate bills was that the Senate version provided a mechanism for a Tribal Judicial Conference that would help establish a formula for funding tribal courts and intertribal appellate courts.

The House version would have set up an Office of Tribal Justice Support within the Bureau of Indian Affairs that would have the grant-making authority. The office would provide funds, technical assistance and information to Indian tribes to develop, improve or maintain native tribal justice systems.

## LEGISLATIVE ACTION

House and Senate committees approved similar bills the week of June 15 to aid tribal justice and court systems.

The Senate Indian Affairs Committee on June 16 gave voice vote approval to a bill (S 1752) mandating the creation of a nationally based tribal judicial conference, which would establish formulas for the distribution of federally funded grants to Indian tribal courts.

The House Interior Committee on June 17 approved by voice vote a similar bill (HR 4004) that would establish an Office of Tribal Justice Support within the Bureau of Indian Affairs to provide money for tribal justice systems and logistical support, training and technical assistance to tribal court systems.

On July 27 the House passed HR 4004 by voice vote. The Senate then inserted its version into the House bill on Aug. 6. Slade Gorton, R-Wash., added an amendment on the Senate floor providing for a study of the impact on federal and tribal courts of federal court review of tribal courts' final orders.

The remaining difference between Senate and House versions was the question of whether to give more authority to the Bureau of Indian Affairs or the tribal conference. Members said they would revisit the issue in the 103rd Congress. ∎

---

# Bill Seeks Improvement of Indian Lands Management

A measure aimed at improving the administration of government programs on Indian reservations won approval in the Senate but did not make any progress in the House. The measure (S 2977) would have created programs within the Bureau of Indian Affairs to improve the management of Indian farmlands and ranches that had suffered from a lack of federal investment.

## BACKGROUND

According to committee aides, Indian agriculture programs had not been a priority of the Bush or Reagan administrations.

The bill was the third major legislative effort since 1986 aimed at improving farming and ranching opportunities on Indian lands.

Bill sponsor Tom Daschle, D-S.D., said the United States had assumed a trust responsibility to the tribes and to the individual land owners for protection of property. But he said that the United States needed to pay more attention to administration of land management programs, citing a Bureau of Indian Affairs report that showed that more than 1.1 million acres of Indian trust land remained idle nationwide.

Daschle also said that in the 20 years prior to 1992, actual dollar levels for the Indian agriculture program had remained static, and, because of inflation, funding for the programs had been cut to half of their original levels. Over that period, the number of Bureau of Indian Affairs personnel involved in agriculture or natural resources management had also decreased dramatically.

## SENATE ACTION

The Senate Select Indian Affairs Committee and the House Interior and Insular Affairs Committee held a joint hearing on S 2977 on Sept. 22. The Department of the Interior met with staff following the hearing to work out bill changes regarding the administration's management role.

The Senate Indian Affairs committee approved S 2977 by voice vote Sept. 25.

The bill would have required the Bureau of Indian Affairs to develop programs in conjunction with Indian tribes to improve productivity and management. It also would have allowed tribes to gain more control over tribal farmlands and provide at least 20 scholarships to Indian students to study land management.

Following committee approval, the full Senate took up the legislation Oct. 2.

John McCain, R-Ariz., added an amendment to respond to the remaining concern of the Interior Department: that the Secretary of the Interior would be given new responsibility in managing lands.

McCain said the bill's purpose was to streamline the administration of the programs and to empower the Indian tribes to assure a greater role in program management.

His amendment clarified that the secretary would not have had to take on any additional land management responsibilities other than those specified in existing law. The Senate then approved the legislation by voice vote.

In the rush to adjourn, however, the House failed to act on S 2977. ∎

# Several Indian-Related Measures Pass

Congress addressed a number of other bills dealing with Indian and Native Hawaiian programs during the session. They included:

## HAWAIIAN HEALTH CARE

Legislation to reauthorize federal Native Hawaiian health-care programs through fiscal year 2000 was signed into law as part of the defense appropriations bill (HR 5504, PL 102-396). Both the House and Senate approved the defense spending bill by voice vote Oct. 5. *(Defense appropriations, p. 592)*

The Hawaiian health-care legislation reauthorized the 1988 Native Hawaiian Health Care Act, designed to promote disease prevention and primary health care among Native Hawaiians. No funding levels were set in the bill.

The bill aimed to improve the health of Native Hawaiians and set 40 goals for better health to be achieved by the year 2000, including reductions in infant mortality and breast cancer. The bill funded health centers for Native Hawaiians, as well as medical scholarships for Native Hawaiian students.

The measure also expanded and diversified the role of Papa Ola Lokahi, the Native Hawaiian health board, which coordinated health-care services provided to Native Hawaiians. Native Hawaiians, who made up 20 percent of the state's population, had a high mortality rate compared with the rest of the country.

The Senate Select Committee on Indian Affairs approved Chairman Daniel K. Inouye's, D-Hawaii, version of the Hawaiian health-care bill (S 2681) by voice vote on May 13.

On Aug. 5, the House Energy and Commerce Committee took up a similar bill (HR 5346) sponsored by Hawaii Democrats Patsy T. Mink and Neil Abercrombie. After some debate, the committee approved the measure on a party-line vote of 28-15.

Opposition to the House bill came from Republicans led by William E. Dannemeyer of California, ranking member of the Energy Subcommittee on Health and the Environment. Dannemeyer had argued that the program was unnecessary because health care for Native Hawaiians was already being provided by other federal health programs.

The Senate passed S 2681 on Aug. 7 by voice vote. But the House delivered a setback Sept. 30 when a motion to pass the bill under fast-track procedures, which required a two-thirds vote (282 votes in this case), failed 228-194.

Opponents maintained that the legislation was unnecessary because poor Native Hawaiians were eligible for health care under the Community Rural and Migrant Health Center Programs.

Both chambers later cleared the defense spending bill with the Hawaiian health-care provisions included by voice vote Oct. 5

## JOB TRAINING PROGRAMS

The Senate cleared legislation by voice vote Oct. 7 to simplify the way Indians received federal job training assistance. President Bush signed the measure Oct. 23 — PL 102-477.

The bill (S 1530) allowed tribal governments to submit plans to the secretary of the Interior to consolidate all job training programs under one administrator.

Tribal governments had previously been overwhelmed by the paperwork required by each of the four government agencies — Labor, Education, Interior and Health — that administered Indian job training programs, said Sen. Paul Simon, D-Ill., the bill's sponsor. The bill created a demonstration project within the Interior Department to review plans to combine programs.

The Senate Indian Affairs Committee had first approved the bill by voice vote Aug. 2, 1991 (S Rept 102-188). The full Senate approved the measure by voice vote Oct. 30, 1991.

The House Interior and Insular Affairs Committee next gave voice vote approval to its version of the bill on May 20, 1992 (H Rept 102-905). The House approved the measure by voice vote Sept. 29 and sent it back to the Senate for final approval.

## PRESERVING LANGUAGES

Legislation that sponsors hoped would preserve the remaining American Indian languages was cleared the week of Oct. 5. The president signed the measure Oct. 26 (PL 102-524).

The House passed S 2044 on Oct. 2, and the Senate followed suit Oct. 5. The bill authorized grants and programs to assist Indians and assure the survival of their native languages. The grants were intended to support community language programs, to train Indians to teach languages and to produce teaching materials.

The measure established a program within the administration for Indians to make grants to Indian groups working to sustain Indian languages. The bill authorized $2 million in fiscal 1993 and unspecified amounts through fiscal 1997.

The Senate Select Indian Affairs Committee had passed the measure on July 2 (S Rept 102-343). On Aug. 5, the full Senate passed S 2044 by voice vote.

## UNACKNOWLEDGED TRIBES

The House cleared legislation (HR 2144) by voice vote Oct. 3 to create a panel to study the problems facing unacknowledged Indian tribes and the financial difficulties of recognized tribes in California. The president signed the bill on Oct. 14 — PL 102-416.

Many Indian tribes lost their lands when the government revoked their federal recognition as part of the 1958 Rancheria Termination Act. These tribes included the United Auburn Indian Community, a 125-member group residing 35 miles from Sacramento, and about 40 other California tribes. Federally recognized tribes had more access to economic aid and other public assistance.

The measure authorized $700,000 to establish the California Indian Policy Council, which would study unacknowledged tribes and the financial problems of recognized tribes.

The House had approved an earlier version of the measure by voice vote Aug. 12. The Senate Select Indian Affairs Committee then approved a version Sept. 25 (S Rept 102-441) by voice vote. The full Senate also approved the bill by voice vote Oct. 2.

## INDIAN DEVELOPMENT ACT

The Senate passed by voice vote Aug. 12 a measure (S 3118) to revise the Buy Indian Act, which gave preferential treatment to Indian-owned businesses seeking work with the Bureau of Indian Affairs and the Indian Health Service. But the House did not act on the measure.

An earlier attempt at reforming the act (S 321) had been vetoed by President Bush on Nov. 16, 1990, over language that would have required formal certification that companies were owned by Indians. *(1990 Almanac, p. 423)*

The new version represented a compromise that would have required spot checks to confirm the eligibility of Indian businesses for preferential contracts.

The measure also would have set aside for small businesses all Buy Indian contracts below $1 million.

The Senate also had approved by voice vote an amendment offered by Sen. Daniel K. Inouye, D-Hawaii, to reduce the civil penalties for non-compliance from $50,000 to $1,000.

The measure had received Senate Indian Affairs Committee approval Aug. 6 by voice vote (S Rept 102-368).

## INDIAN RESEARCH

In the rush to adjourn, the House failed to act on S 3155, which would have established a nonpartisan National Indian Policy Research Institute at George Washington University in Washington, D.C.

It would have authorized $1 million in fiscal 1994 and unspecified sums through fiscal 1996.

The Senate Select Committee on Indian Affairs had approved the bill by voice vote on Sept. 29 (S Rept 102-443). The Senate then passed the bill by voice vote Oct. 2.

## MIMBRES INDIAN TRIBE

On Sept. 30, the House rejected, 179-243, a bill (S 1528) that would have established a national monument in honor of the Mimbres Indian tribe of New Mexico. The bill, sponsored by Sen. Jeff Bingaman, D-N.M., also would have established an archeological protection system for Mimbres historical sites. *(Vote 447, p. 110-H)*

Critics of the measure objected to provisions that would allow the government to buy land from unwilling landowners to create the monument. They argued that Mimbres culture could be adequately protected by expanding existing federal parks.

The bill passed the Senate on Nov. 26, 1991. The Senate Energy Committee had approved the bill (S Rept 102-222) 20-0 on Oct. 30, 1991. The House Interior and Insular Affairs Committee approved the bill (H Rept 102-949) by voice vote Sept. 23, 1992.

## INDIAN VETERANS MEMORIAL

The House also failed to act on S 3157, which would have authorized the creation of a memorial to Indian veterans who died in combat. The Senate Select Indian Affairs Committee approved the measure (S Rept 102-440) by voice vote Sept. 18. The Senate approved it by voice vote Oct. 2.

The bill would have authorized the federal government to donate a site for the monument but would not have authorized any other federal spending.

## INDIAN RIGHT TO FILE SUIT

The House passed three bills by voice vote the week of Aug. 3 that would have given Indian tribes the right to sue the government over the past seizure or use of tribal lands. They also would have clarified the terms of a 1971 settlement. The Senate did not act on the measures.

The House passed HR 5658 on Aug. 3. It would have guaranteed that dividends paid to Alaska natives from certain land sales authorized by the Alaska Native Claims Settlement Act of 1971 would not have been subject to federal, state or local taxes. Members of the corporations in charge of the sales were afraid that the original act was too vague.

The House Ways and Means Committee had reported the measure (H Rept 102-750) on July 29.

On Aug. 4, the House passed HR 1206, which would have allowed the Pueblo of Isleta tribe of New Mexico to file a claim under the Indian Claims Commission Act of 1946 for lands taken by the U.S. government — even though the statute of limitations for such actions had run out.

Bill supporters said that as a result of poor legal advice from the Bureau of Indian Affairs, the tribe might not have been adequately compensated for land acquired by the government. The legislation would have authorized a U.S. Claims Court to hear the case but would not have granted the tribe any damages.

The bill (H Rept 102-777) was approved by the House Judiciary Committee on July 28.

On Aug. 4, the House also passed HR 4209, which would have allowed the Cherokee, Choctaw and Chickasaw Indian tribes to sue the U.S. government for having constructed a waterway without their consent. The waterway was built during the 1940s on a part of the Arkansas River owned by the tribes. The bill would have given U.S. courts jurisdiction over the case.

The measure (H Rept 102-773) had passed both the Administrative Law and Governmental Relations Subcommittee and the full House Judiciary Committee by voice vote on April 1 and July 1 respectively. ■

# DEFENSE

# Pentagon Gets Most of Its Wish List

*Demands for cuts in military spending give way to election-year pressure to save defense-related jobs*

In shaping the fiscal 1993 defense authorization bill, Congress made few dramatic cuts in the Pentagon's budget request. Congressional demands to cut defense spending generally gave way to election-year concerns that such cuts would cost defense jobs during a recession.

However, several provisions in the $274 billion bill (HR 5006) laid the groundwork for potential cuts in manpower and hardware spending by the mid-1990s going far beyond the long-term reductions that President Bush had outlined for the post-Soviet world.

In addition to authorizing funds for military programs of the Department of Defense, the defense bill authorized $11.9 billion of the $12.1 billion requested for defense-related programs of the Energy Department, most of which involved the development and manufacture of nuclear weapons and nuclear power plants for Navy ships.

In their versions of the bill, the Senate and House each recommended significant cuts in several major weapons programs. But with the economy in disarray and defense industries already squeezed by Bush's cutbacks, the conferees could agree on only a few major reductions. The bill:

● Authorized $4.05 billion — about three-quarters of the amount Bush requested — to continue the anti-missile defense program known as the Strategic Defense Initiative (SDI). Sentiment in the Senate for deeper cuts endangered the overall bill and stalled floor action for more than a month until a compromise was reached.

The companion defense appropriations bill (HR 5504 — PL 102-396) funded SDI at the $3.8 billion anticipated in the Senate compromise.

● Included the $2.7 billion sought by the administration to buy four final B-2 bombers, bringing the fleet of radar-evading planes to 20. But before more B-2s could be built, Congress required that the Pentagon report back on the plane's cost and capability and that members then cast a vote to proceed.

● Sliced about a fourth from the amounts Bush requested for F/A-18 combat jets and C-17 long-range cargo planes. But more typically, conferees who shaped the final version of the bill backed whichever chamber approved the larger

---

## THE MAJOR ISSUES

*See also the following stories on major issues that dominated debate on the Defense bill.*

➤ **B-2 bombers.** Congress agreed to complete a fleet of 20 of the radar-evading planes . . . . p. 496

➤ **Strategic Defense Initiative.** The anti-missile defense program received $3.8 billion of the $5.4 billion requested . . . . . . . p. 498

➤ **Seawolf-class submarine.** The administration sought to cancel the submarine, but Congress appropriated funds for at least one more . . . . . . . . . . . . . p. 502

➤ **V-22 Osprey.** The Pentagon softened its resistance to building the hybrid airplane/ helicopter . . . . . . . . . . . . . p. 505

➤ **Combat aircraft.** Lawmakers approved continued work on a new generation of tactical aircraft but ordered the Pentagon to sort out "roles and missions." p. 506

➤ **Defense conversion spending.** Congress included $1.5 billion to help military personnel, defense contractors and communities adjust to defense cuts . . . p. 509

---

amount for new fighter planes. They did restrict some spending until the Pentagon presented a long-term plan to consolidate and pay for a new generation of fighters.

● Cushioned the impact of defense cutbacks on military personnel, defense companies and local economies by authorizing $1.5 billion for "economic conversion" programs. This included $694 million for technology programs aimed at helping the defense industry adapt to the commercial marketplace, $132 million to help communities adjust to defense-related changes and $686 million for transition assistance to personnel leaving the services.

● Adopted the administration's request to cut the number of active-duty military personnel to 1,766,500, a reduction of 100,400 from the cap in fiscal 1992. The measure also set a ceiling of 1,095,080 on membership in National Guard and reserve units — a reduction of 40,000 rather than the 116,000-member cutback sought by the administration. The bill also ordered additional cutbacks on U.S. deployments in Europe by the end of fiscal 1996.

The House passed its version of the bill (HR 5006), 198-168, on June 5. The Senate passed its version (S 3114) by voice vote on Sept. 19.

The conference committee completed its work on Oct 1. The House adopted the conference report (H Rept 102-966), 304-100, on Oct. 3. The Senate voted to adopt the report by voice vote the same day, but paperwork delays held up formal action to clear the bill for the president until Oct. 5

President Bush signed the bill (PL 102-484) on Oct. 23.

## THE PRESIDENT'S PROPOSAL

When President Bush presented his fiscal 1993 budget on Jan. 29, he offered what he portrayed as a $50 billion defense cut. More precisely, he proposed cutting $50 billion over five years from the $1.7 trillion, six-year defense plan that he had proposed a year earlier for the same period.

"By 1997," he said, "we will have cut defense by 30 percent since I took office."

But the immediate savings would be less dramatic. Bush proposed $291 billion in defense-related outlays for

the Pentagon and other agencies in fiscal 1993, a $16.3 billion reduction from estimated spending for fiscal 1992.

Excluding the budgetary aftereffects of the Persian Gulf War, the Defense Department estimated the administration's request at $281 billion in budget authority — $10 billion less than the level Bush had projected a year earlier.

But the Pentagon calculated that this would lead to actual outlays of $286 billion in fiscal 1993 — a reduction of only $6 billion from the prior year's projection.

Bush's approach to defense budget-cutting produced a gap between long-range reductions and immediate savings.

The president offered no significant cuts in the budget for the military payroll — beyond the five-year, 25 percent reduction that was already under way — or for operations and maintenance.

Cutting uniformed manpower more rapidly would have required involuntary discharges on a large scale, which Pentagon officials contended would shatter the morale of personnel. And they argued that the projected budget for operations and maintenance was essential so that the smaller force that was being shaped could retain its fighting edge.

Instead, Bush accelerated his previously planned cutbacks by cutting more deeply into weapons procurement and development. But money for such military hardware was doled out to contractors in installments over several years. Thus, cuts in budget authority for procurement and research yielded much smaller cuts in immediate outlays.

Of the $281 billion in requested budget authority, $268 billion would be earmarked for military programs of the Defense Department (excluding the public works budget of the Army's Corps of Engineers).

Defense-related programs conducted by the Energy Department accounted for $12.1 billion. They included $4.8 billion to develop and manufacture nuclear warheads and $4.6 billion to clean up radioactive and other hazardous waste at defense-related Energy Department installations.

The remaining $1.2 billion was for miscellaneous defense-related programs of other agencies.

Bush linked his hardware-heavy defense cuts to the demise of the Soviet Union in two ways:

● Because Russian President Boris N. Yeltsin and leaders of the other former Soviet republics had agreed to radical reductions in nuclear weaponry, Bush proposed a sharp cutback in the production of strategic arms, including: ending production of the B-2 stealth bomber after 20 planes and canceling outright production of long-range, bomber-launched cruise missiles and of powerful nuclear warheads for Trident II submarine-launched missiles.

● On the assumption that Pentagon planners no longer needed to anticipate a massive Soviet weapons program aimed at nullifying the technical superiority of U.S. conventional arms, the budget request embodied a fundamental shift in the Pentagon's weapons procurement strategy.

## BOXSCORE

➡ **Fiscal 1993 defense authorization (HR 5006, S 3114).** The bill authorized $274 billion in defense spending. It also laid the groundwork for cuts in military personnel and weapons production.

**Reports:** H Rept 102-527; S Rept 102-352; conference report H Rept 102-966.

### KEY ACTION

June 5 — The **House** passed HR 5006, 198-168.

Sept. 19 — The **Senate** passed S 3114 by voice vote.

Oct. 1 — **House-Senate** conferees completed their work.

Oct. 3 — The **House** adopted the conference report, 304-100. The **Senate** cleared the report by voice vote.

Oct. 23 — President Bush signed HR 5006 — PL 102-484.

Under the new approach, Defense Secretary Dick Cheney announced, the Pentagon would continue to fund the development of new prototypes intended to push back the frontiers of weapons technology. But not all of those new weapons would be rushed to the assembly line.

The new plan's most immediate results would be cancellation of production plans for the *Seawolf*-class nuclear submarine and for the Army's Comanche helicopter. On the other hand, Bush's budget would continue planned production of other high-tech weapons, including Aegis destroyers for the Navy and the Air Force's C-17 cargo plane. Moreover, development of the Air Force's new F-22 fighter would continue, with the expectation of full-scale production beginning in 1996.

Bush's request for $77.1 billion in budget authority for military personnel costs in fiscal 1993 assumed that the number of active-duty service members would decline from 2 million at the end of fiscal 1991 to 1.86 million at the end of fiscal 1992 and 1.77 million by the end of fiscal 1993.

Similarly, the budget request would slice the number of National Guard and reserve personnel to slightly more than 1 million, a reduction of 131,000 from the number on the rolls at the end of fiscal 1991.

The budget would fund a 3.3 percent pay raise for both uniformed personnel and civilian employees.

For the array of anti-missile defense research programs that made up SDI, Bush requested a total of $5.3 billion in budget authority, including $1 billion earmarked for defenses against short-range (or "tactical") missiles.

To bring the total fleet of operational B-2 bombers to 20, the budget requested almost $2.7 billion in budget authority for four more planes in fiscal 1993 and congressional approval to spend $1 billion that was appropriated for an additional plane in fiscal 1992 but which could not be spent without express congressional action.

The Navy's procurement request included $3.4 billion in budget authority for four additional destroyers equipped with the Aegis anti-aircraft system. And it included $832 million for a nuclear power plant and other components that would be used in an aircraft carrier slated for inclusion in the fiscal 1995 budget.

Major budget requests for aircraft programs included:
● $2.7 billion for eight additional C-17 cargo planes;
● $1.8 billion for 48 F/A-18 fighters plus $1.1 billion to develop a larger version of that plane;
● $2.2 billion to continue development of the F-22 fighter; and
● $443 million to continue development of the Comanche "scout" helicopter.

### Initial Reaction

When Bush challenged Congress to cut defense spending by $50 billion over six years "and no deeper," he said, "To do less would be insensible to progress, but to do more

would be ignorant of history."

To do anything else also seemed politically impossible as members of Congress faced the reality of cutting defense jobs in an economy already stunned by recession.

Despite demands from some members for a post-Cold War "peace dividend" several times as large, the impact of specific defense cuts hampered the search for greater reductions.

At a hearing on Jan. 31, Senate Armed Services Committee Chairman Sam Nunn, D-Ga., cited what he called "very sobering" estimates that 2 million military and civilian workers could lose their jobs even under the Bush plan.

Ranking House Budget Committee Republican Bill Gradison, Ohio, said some lawmakers were already in a "state of shock" over what proposed cuts in major weapons systems would do to their districts. "I don't see the defense budget entering into free fall because, quite apart from national defense, it means jobs," he said.

While some in Congress had pushed for bigger cuts in manpower as a way to save money, administration officials insisted that reducing personnel faster than the 25 percent cut already under way would severely damage morale and endanger future security.

Such reductions "would end up destroying the finest military force this nation has ever fielded," Defense Secretary Cheney told Nunn's committee on Jan. 31 as he defended the Bush plan. "If we try to reduce the force too quickly, we can break it."

But Senate Budget Committee Chairman Jim Sasser, D-Tenn., on Jan. 29 called Bush's proposed defense cuts "token at best." He added, "Now I ask you: Where's the peace dividend in that defense cut? I think failing to reduce defense spending more over the next five years is going to cost us very, very dearly in desperately needed investment right here in the United States."

While withholding judgment on the specifics of the Bush plan, the chairmen of the two Armed Services committees faulted the administration for not providing a more rigorous rationale for its budget proposals.

"We need an analysis from the ground up of the real threats Americans face in this new world," said House Armed Services Chairman Les Aspin, D-Wis. "I don't think you'll get the right number and I'm sure you won't get the right composition" by just trimming the Cold War budget.

### House Budget Committee

The first real skirmish in the year's defense budget battle came on Feb. 27, when the House Budget Committee sought to cut less than 3 percent from Bush's defense request as part of its annual budget resolution.

The committee's action sounded like a more decisive break with Bush's budget: It was widely described as twice as large a cut from the previously projected budget as the Pentagon reductions that Bush proposed in January.

However, what mattered ultimately was how deeply the defense budget was cut, not the ratio between two proposals to cut it. Measured in real terms, Bush's proposed defense budget for fiscal 1993 was $281 billion, which the House committee trimmed to $273.4 billion — a relatively modest reduction of $7.6 billion, or 2.7 percent.

The panel acted after it was briefed by Aspin on several options he had developed for a long-term structuring of military forces. The Budget Committee's action was in keeping with Aspin's preferred strategy, which called for cutting from $4.6 billion to $7.6 billion from Bush's January request.

Aspin's plan envisioned U.S. forces in the late 1990s that would be significantly reduced from Cold War levels but still large enough to conduct simultaneously a massive ground war in the Middle East, an aerial defense of South Korea against a North Korean attack and a minor intervention on the scale of the 1989 occupation of Panama.

Liberal Pentagon critics, including Reps. Barney Frank, D-Mass., and Ronald V. Dellums, D-Calif., had hoped that the disintegration of the Soviet Union and growing support for domestic spending to counter the economic slump would create powerful leverage for deeper cuts. "This is a historic moment we should seize," Dellums said. Referring to meeting domestic needs, he said, "You can't get there from here with that modest a cut."

Even some relatively conservative members, while opposing a more rapid drawdown of U.S. forces overseas in the immediate future, criticized the Pentagon's plan to keep 150,000 U.S. troops in Europe after 1995. "I can't conceive of us getting involved in a war in Europe anytime soon," said House Defense Appropriations Subcommittee Chairman John P. Murtha, D-Pa.

Nunn and Aspin indicated that they contemplated eventual reductions to as few as 75,000 troops in Europe.

On March 24, Nunn broke with Aspin and warned against any reductions in Bush's fiscal 1993 defense request. "In order to make [even Bush's] reductions," Nunn said, "by 1996, 1 million jobs will be lost in the Defense Department and an additional 1 million jobs in the defense industry."

## HOUSE COMMITTEE ACTION

On May 13, the House Armed Services Committee approved, 47-8, a defense authorization bill (HR 5006) for fiscal 1993 that would trim Bush's $281 billion budget request to $274 billion, the amount earmarked for defense by the House-passed version of the annual budget resolution. The Senate had passed a budget resolution allowing $6 billion more for defense.

The House Armed Services bill included $1 billion for a yet-to-be drafted program to cushion the economic impact of a long-term cutback in defense spending. Most of the cuts the Armed Services panel made in Bush's request came from certain supply, maintenance and overhead funds. The panel insisted that these funds could be pared without affecting the safety or combat readiness of U.S. forces.

The committee's bill included most of the money Bush requested for major weapons, including the B-2 stealth bomber and the Strategic Defense Initiative (SDI).

After Aspin proposed the $7 billion defense cut in February, he was enraged when Defense Secretary Cheney warned that such a reduction would force massive military layoffs and put U.S. forces at risk. "All of the dire predictions . . . didn't happen," Aspin said.

The $2.7 billion recommended by the panel for B-2 bombers was the amount Bush requested for four more planes to fill out the scaled-down fleet of 20 B-2s the Pentagon was seeking. That small force, intended to carry non-nuclear precision-guided "smart" bombs, was similar to what Aspin and other congressional leaders had been calling for. Earlier Air Force plans had envisioned many more B-2s and put more emphasis on their ability to carry nuclear weapons.

But the committee, which for several years had opposed building more B-2s, was not yet convinced that the big bat-

winged plane would be as difficult for radars to detect as specifications require or that the Air Force had driven a hard enough bargain to buy out the contract at the lowest price. So the panel specified that money could not be spent until the Pentagon reported on the plane's capabilities and cost and Congress voted explicitly to allow expenditure of the $2.7 billion.

The committee bill approved the bulk of Bush's SDI budget — $4.3 billion of the $5.4 billion requested. Bush's request mirrored the policy enacted by Congress in 1991: that the program's top priority should be deployment over several years of a ground-based missile defense that complied with the 1972 U.S.-Soviet treaty limiting anti-ballistic missile (ABM) defenses.

But the committee denied the entire $576 million requested to develop Brilliant Pebbles. Many Republicans favored these space-based anti-missile interceptors, which would be barred by the ABM Treaty.

Continuing a three-year feud between Congress and Cheney, the committee added to the bill $755 million to continue development of the V-22 Osprey, a hybrid airplane/helicopter sought by the Marine Corps as a troop carrier.

Asserting that the Osprey would be too expensive, Cheney had tried to kill it. But it enjoyed strong support in the large congressional delegations from Texas and Pennsylvania, home to the Osprey's prime contractors.

The committee also added a provision to cut the office budget of the Pentagon comptroller 5 percent for each month the department refused to spend $790 million that Congress appropriated in fiscal 1992 for the V-22. In July, Cheney reversed his long-held position and agreed to a compromise that included moving ahead with the Osprey's development.

### Revamping Procurement

The panel approved a plan crafted by Aspin and senior committee Republican Bill Dickinson of Alabama to significantly reorder the Pentagon's plans for a new generation of tactical combat aircraft.

Under the committee's approach, the top priority would be fielding the AX, a new carrier-based bomber to replace the Navy's venerable A-6E. The panel's bill would increase the $165 million requested for the AX to $740 million. Partly to pay for the AX, the committee slashed to $545 million the $1.1 billion requested to develop enlarged E and F models of the F/A-18 carrier-based plane, which was used as both a fighter and a bomber.

The panel also sliced $200 million from the $2.2 billion requested to develop the Air Force's new F-22 fighter.

The committee's tactical aircraft package reflected a new approach to weapons procurement in a period when the Soviet threat had evaporated and Pentagon budgets were headed downward. The committee called for extensive testing of prototypes to wring out problems before signing up for full production of a a complex new weapon.

"The practice of the past has been to develop and buy successive new generations of weapons, each fast on the heels of the preceding one," the committee said. "This no longer makes sense in the post-Soviet world."

In another example of increased caution in moving toward full production, the House committee approved $2.19 billion to build six wide-body C-17 cargo planes rather than the $2.9 billion the Air Force requested for eight planes. The committee complained of production delays, some related to chronic fuel leaks in the test model.

A second theme of the House Armed Services' procurement approach was the importance it placed on spending to upgrade some weapons and to buy others at a slow rate to keep key contractors in the defense business at a time of cutbacks. The committee ordered the Pentagon to spend $225 million that was appropriated in fiscal 1992 to upgrade early model M-1 tanks with the larger cannon and night-vision equipment of later versions.

The panel also added to Bush's request:

● $89 million to equip early model Bradley troop carriers with better protection against enemy fire;

● $250 million to equip 36 "scout" helicopters with AHIP target-finding electronics; and

● $363 million, in addition to the $235 million requested, to buy MLRS artillery rockets and launchers. Under the administration's plan, production of the rockets would stop in 1993 but resume in 1994.

The committee also ordered the Air Force to plan on buying more F-16 Air Force fighters in fiscal 1994, instead of ending production with the 24 planes authorized in the bill for fiscal 1993 ($649 million). The $68 million the Pentagon requested to shut down the line would be used instead to buy components needed for the additional planes.

The committee's approach was intended to keep the F-16 production line going as a hedge, in case the F-22 program went sour. It also held open the option of developing an improved F-16 as a lower-cost complement to the F-22. And the promise of continued employment at General Dynamics' F-16 plant in Fort Worth, Texas, didn't hurt the political prospects for Aspin's bill in the third-largest state delegation in the House.

In a May 14 speech, Cheney objected to the committee's efforts to keep defense production lines humming. "If we spend too much time. . . keeping old production lines open, then what we will have invested our money in is outmoded manufacturing technology," he said.

### Personnel Plans

The committee sought to retain slightly more National Guard and reserve members than the "Base Force" that Cheney wanted to arrive at by 1997.

This was in part an acknowledgment of the political clout of Guard and reserve units scattered across most congressional districts. But Aspin also insisted that National Guard ground combat divisions were a good buy, costing a fourth as much to operate as units staffed by full-time Army personnel.

For fiscal 1993, the House committee's bill would cut the 1.13 million-member Guard and reserves by 67,000, rather than 116,000 as requested by Cheney. In particular, the bill would cut the Army Guard by 11,200 rather than the 48,000 assumed in the budget request.

Over five years, Cheney wanted to reduce the Army National Guard from 431,200 to 338,000, a reduction of 21.7 percent. But Aspin wanted to trim about half as many members, leaving the Army Guard close to 380,000.

However, the committee coupled its promise of a more prominent role for the Guard with provisions intended to sharpen its edge by:

● Requiring that by 1997, 65 percent of the personnel taken into the Guard as officers and 50 percent of those taken in as enlisted personnel have at least two years of experience in the active-duty military;

● Requiring that each Guard combat unit be associated with an active-duty Army unit that would review the

Guard unit's training and readiness and comment on all promotions to the rank of captain or higher;
- Mandating stricter physical fitness standards; and
- Increasing by 2,000 the number of active-duty personnel assigned as advisers to Guard and reserve units.

### Urban Concern

Two days after the Armed Services Committee approved the $7 billion cut from Bush's request, Aspin urged that those savings be used to pay for an urban aid program.

"The major issue right now is, where are we going to get the money for an urban package?" Aspin said May 15. "I have a suggestion."

Responding to the pleas for urban assistance that followed riots in Los Angeles, Aspin urged Senate and House budget negotiators to stick with the lower, House-passed defense ceiling. His committee's bill "demonstrated that the Pentagon's level of defense spending is not necessary," he said. "The tragic events in Los Angeles have demonstrated that urban relief is necessary." *(Urban crisis, p. 339)*

Dickinson, the committee's ranking Republican, quickly responded that he was "adamantly opposed" to Aspin's urban aid plan, and it faded from debate over the defense bill.

## HOUSE FLOOR ACTION

Reacting to the end of the Cold War and the budget crunch at home, the House broke significant new ground with the $270 billion defense authorization bill for fiscal 1993 that it passed June 5.

The measure (HR 5006) was approved, 198-168. *(Vote 172, p. 42-H)*

The House added to the bill a moratorium on nuclear weapons tests, a move that had long been vigorously opposed by Republican administrations. And the House earmarked $1 billion of Pentagon funding to help defense contractors, their employees and their communities adjust to the long-term defense spending retrenchment.

But the House debate also highlighted an important change in the politics of defense budgeting in the solidly Democratic House. As had become usual in recent years, the bill bore the strong imprint of Armed Services Committee Chairman Aspin. This time, however, on two of the bill's most contentious issues, Aspin prevailed over a majority of fellow Democrats by linking centrist Democrats with a nearly solid Republican bloc.

The bipartisan alliance protected Aspin's proposals, embodied in the committee bill, to authorize:
- $4.3 billion for an SDI program aimed at deploying ground-based interceptors within several years.

Aspin's center-right coalition defeated an amendment by Richard J. Durbin, D-Ill., that would have slowed work on the anti-missile program.

Durbin's amendment to cut $938 million from the SDI funding recommending by Armed Services was rejected 161-211, but it was heavily supported by voting Democrats (149-77) and by Independent Bernard Sanders, Vt. Republicans overwhelmingly opposed the amendment (11-134). *(Vote 169, p. 42-H)*

The House also rejected outright, 117-248, an amendment by California Democrats Ronald V. Dellums and Barbara Boxer that would have slashed the total for anti-missile development to $2.3 billion, with $1.1 billion earmarked for theater defense work and $1.2 billion for de-

fenses against strategic missiles. *(Vote 168, p. 42-H)*
- $2.7 billion to buy four more B-2 bombers, fielding a fleet of 20, provided the Pentagon could convince Congress that the stealth plane could deliver acceptably, even if imperfectly, on its promised invisibility to radar. To hold this position, Aspin beat back an amendment by Thomas H. Andrews, D-Maine.

The 162-212 vote by which the House rejected Andrews' amendment to bar procurement of additional B-2 bombers reflected the same underlying pattern of liberal Democrats being overpowered by a coalition of Republicans with more conservative Democrats. *(Vote 170, p. 42-H)*

Democrats supported Andrews' amendment, 139-89, and Republicans opposed it, 22-123. Sanders supported the amendment.

Aspin and his aides touted the nuclear test ban and economic conversion provisions as new issues for a post-Cold War era in which old left-right labels had lost their meaning.

Liberals opposing his B-2 and SDI proposals were stuck on "the old agenda ... last year's fights," Aspin argued. The Bush administration had adapted those programs to new, post-Soviet missions in response to congressional demands, he said.

But many of Aspin's Democratic opponents contended that he was at fault for ignoring new realities, shoring up political support for costly weapons at a time when the deficit was climbing and domestic needs went unmet.

Said B-2 opponent Andrews: "Democrats can either rise above the pack or try in vain to rationalize yet another bum decision — buying weapons we don't need with money we don't have to confront an enemy we no longer face."

The night before the SDI and B-2 fights, several liberal Democrats who opposed Aspin's positions flew south — literally — to attend the Earth Summit in Rio de Janeiro, Brazil, reducing the potential opposition votes.

Before taking the bill to the House floor, Aspin had to defend the committee's version of the bill against pressures to spend more on defense. The House-Senate conference committee on the annual budget resolution had settled on $277 billion for defense, splitting the difference between Bush's $281 billion request and the $274 billion mark that the House had previously approved. But Aspin made it clear he would resist spending more.

The relatively close vote to pass the defense bill obscured the strength of the center-right alliance on SDI and the B-2 because most Democrats supported final passage (167-56), while Republicans voted heavily against it (30-112).

Republican opposition may have been fueled in part by adoption of two amendments:
- By Les AuCoin, D-Ore., to allow service members stationed abroad and their dependents to obtain privately funded abortions in U.S. military hospitals. The amendment was adopted, 216-193. *(Vote 163, p. 40-H; Abortion, p. 387)*
- By Frank, slicing $3.5 billion from the amount authorized for overseas base costs. This was one of several so-called burden-sharing amendments the House adopted that were aimed at reducing the cost of Pentagon operations overseas. Frank's amendment was adopted, 220-185. *(Vote 155, p. 38-H)*

"Does America's victory in the Cold War have no fiscal dividend?" Frank asked in arguing for his proposal. "Has America not earned the right after 45 years in defense of freedom, at the expense of the American people, to begin to

enjoy a little savings?"

### Burden-Sharing Debate

Frank's amendment and the other proposals to slash U.S. defense spending abroad reflected a smoldering congressional sentiment that U.S. deployments abroad effectively subsidized allies who were also commercial rivals, permitting them to invest in their economies money that they would otherwise have to spend on defense.

"We no longer can bankroll the world," argued Budget Committee Chairman Leon E. Panetta, D-Calif. Fred Grandy, Iowa, urged fellow Republicans to back the $3.5 billion reduction sponsored by Frank as "a prologue to the realities of living under a balanced budget amendment."

And Majority Leader Richard A. Gephardt, D-Mo., called for a U.S. retrenchment in the name of "post-Gorbachev realism."

But Herbert H. Bateman, R-Va., blasted one of the amendments as a retreat from the realities of a still dangerous world: "There is more opposition to our being a superpower in this Congress than there is in any [other] responsible legislative body ... including our former enemies'."

Frank's amendment was the only one of four that would cut the fiscal 1993 budget and the only one opposed by Aspin. Nevertheless, it carried by 35 votes.

The amendment stipulated that U.S. troops could remain but only if allied governments offset the cut in U.S. funding. Democrats backed the proposal 180-68, and Republicans opposed it 39-117. Independent Sanders voted "aye."

On June 5, opponents attempted to overturn the Frank amendment, but it was reaffirmed, 202-164. *(Vote 171, p. 42-H)*

The other overseas cost-cutting amendments adopted by the House were:

● By Patricia Schroeder, D-Colo., barring the deployment in Europe of more than 100,000 U.S. military personnel after fiscal 1995. The cap on troops in Europe was 235,000; about 210,000 were deployed there. The Bush administration wanted to retain about 150,000 troops.

In the 241-162 vote for Schroeder's amendment, Republican support was nearly as strong as it was for Frank's amendment: Republicans voted 34-120 on the proposal; Democrats backed it 206-42. Sanders voted aye. *(Vote 156, p. 38-H)*

● By Gephardt, requiring that the number of U.S. personnel stationed abroad be reduced by the end of fiscal 1995 to no more than 60 percent of the number deployed at the end of fiscal 1992. The requirement would be waived in case of war, an armed attack on any U.S. ally or a presidential declaration of emergency.

According to Gephardt, the amendment would reduce by about 160,000 members the number of U.S. personnel deployed overseas, which at the time numbered nearly 400,000. The amendment was approved 225-177. *(Vote 157, p. 40-H)*

● By John R. Kasich, R-Ohio, and Panetta, requiring the president to negotiate agreements with South Korea and NATO countries. Under the agreements, by the end of fiscal 1994, those countries would absorb almost all costs incurred on their turf by U.S. forces, other than the salaries of U.S. nationals.

The agreements, modeled on one signed in 1991 by Japan, would have to relieve U.S. forces of all taxes and all costs for utilities and services, leases, salaries and benefits of non-U.S. employees; construction and maintenance of

facilities; and environmental restoration. If such arrangements were not concluded, 5 percent of the fiscal 1993 budget for operations and maintenance of overseas bases and 10 percent of the corresponding budget for fiscal 1994 would be transferred to be used at domestic bases.

Panetta said the amendment could save $1 billion over two years. It was adopted 396-9. *(Vote 154, p. 38-H)*

### Nuclear Weapons Cutbacks

The nuclear test ban amendment, adopted 237-167, would bar nuclear weapons test explosions during fiscal 1993 unless the president certified to Congress that a former Soviet republic had conducted a nuclear test. *(Vote 164, p. 40-H)*

The amendment was a forerunner of a test ban that was eventually forced on a reluctant Bush administration as part of the annual energy and water appropriations bill, (HR 5373 — PL 102-377). *(Underground testing ban, p. 517; appropriations, p. 659)*

All former Soviet states except Russia had renounced nuclear weapons, and Russia announced its own test moratorium in 1991.

The House also adopted these amendments relating to nuclear weapons:

● By Aspin and Foreign Affairs Committee Chairman Dante B. Fascell, D-Fla., increasing by $250 million the amount earmarked to help dismantle the former Soviet nuclear arsenal. The amendment also earmarked for antiproliferation projects $100 million of the amount authorized by the bill. Adopted 356-54. *(Vote 160, p. 40-H)*

● By Nicholas Mavroules, D-Mass., a non-binding declaration that it was a goal of U.S. policy to negotiate an agreement among countries armed with nuclear weapons that would limit U.S. and Russian forces to no more than 2,000 weapons and would hold other countries to a lower limit.

The amendment also called for a global agreement to end by 1995 the production of plutonium and high-powered uranium used in nuclear weapons and to place existing stocks of such material under international control. Adopted 278-135. *(Vote 162, p. 40-H)*

Unexpectedly, the House rejected, 83-318, an amendment by Lane Evans, D-Ill., that would have required the Energy and Defense departments to issue annually a public report on the number and type of weapons and the amount of fissile material in the U.S. nuclear stockpile. *(Vote 158, p. 40-H)*

The amendment would have allowed the Energy secretary to waive the reporting requirement on grounds of national security. But it would have required a detailed public explanation of the policy and the technical reasons for invoking the waiver.

Evans insisted that such an explanation was necessary to prevent the agencies from using vague language to justify a blanket waiver. However, Energy Secretary James D. Watkins warned that the detailed explanation would, in itself, give away secret information. Initially Aspin and John M. Spratt Jr., D-S.C., who headed the Armed Services Committee's panel on nuclear weapons production, had supported Evans. But they accepted Watkins' argument and voted against the amendment.

### Economic Conversion

The congressional budget resolution had earmarked $1 billion of the fiscal 1993 defense budget to help laid-off defense workers and military personnel, weapons contrac-

tors and communities adjust to the rapid drop in defense spending brought on by the Soviet collapse.

House Democrats assembled a 188-page amendment to parcel out the money among several existing programs, which they argued would not only cushion the shock of cutbacks but would channel industrial and human resources into new areas that would generate economic growth.

The Democratic package, offered as an amendment by Martin Frost, Texas, was adopted 275-105. *(Vote 166, p. 40-H)*

The Democratic package would require defense contractors to give hiring preference to displaced military personnel and defense workers. The House rejected, 147-235, a Republican amendment offered by Larry J. Hopkins, Ky., that would have given the Pentagon discretion over whether to apply that requirement and would have deleted various other provisions. *(Vote 165, p. 40-H)*

### Other Amendments

The House rejected, 90-283, an amendment by Dellums and Maxine Waters, D-Calif., that would have reduced the amount authorized in the defense bill by 10 percent, or $27.4 billion. *(Vote 167, p. 42-H)*

"Our national security is under attack now by huge deficits, crumbling infrastructure ... and the cities [are] ready to explode," Dellums said. Waters, whose Los Angeles district was the scene of rioting, asked, "Which wars do we want to fight?"

Also rejected, by voice vote, were amendments:

● By Wayne Owens, D-Utah, requiring a study of the cost of terminating the C-17 cargo plane program and resuming production of C-5 long-range cargo planes.

The Rules Committee did not allow Owens to offer amendments he had drafted that would have deleted from the bill half the $2 billion the committee recommended to develop the F-22 fighter and the entire $832 million the committee approved, as requested, to begin work on a nuclear-powered aircraft carrier.

● By Dana Rohrabacher, R-Calif., to delete from the bill a provision that would bar the Navy from sending ships based in San Diego to shipyards in Long Beach and San Pedro, Calif., for short-term repair work. The committee provision was backed by Armed Services Republicans Duncan Hunter and Randy "Duke" Cunningham, both of whom represented the San Diego area.

The House adopted by voice vote an amendment by Democrat David E. Skaggs of Colorado requiring the Energy Department to establish a medical screening program for employees of the agency's nuclear weapons production facilities who were subject to significant health risks as a result of their exposure to hazardous or radioactive materials.

Also adopted by voice vote was an omnibus amendment, offered by Aspin, that incorporated dozens of noncontroversial amendments including, for example, proposals:

● By Gene Taylor, D-Miss., earmarking $70 million to begin work on a large helicopter carrier to transport 2,000 Marines. The ship would be built at a Litton Industries shipyard in Pascagoula, Miss.

● By Schroeder, authorizing the Pentagon to grant or lend supplies or equipment to U.N. peacekeeping forces.

● By Aspin, earmarking $4.3 million for facilities at an Air National Guard base in Madison, Wis.

● By Howard L. Berman, D-Calif., barring any federal subsidy to companies participating in military trade shows or conventions overseas.

## SENATE COMMITTEE ACTION

The Senate Armed Services Committee approved a defense authorization bill July 24 after debate on issues including the B-2 stealth bomber and the Strategic Defense Initiative (SDI).

As drafted by the panel, the fiscal 1993 authorization bill would result in an overall defense budget of $274.5 billion, $7 billion less than Bush requested but $3.5 billion more than the counterpart measure (HR 5006) passed in June by the House.

This would be $2.9 billion lower than the defense ceiling set by the final version of the congressional budget resolution.

The Senate committee bill, which was approved 17-3, would authorize:

● $4.3 billion of the $5.4 billion requested for the SDI anti-missile program, the same amount approved by the House.

● $2.7 billion, as requested, to buy four additional B-2s, which would bring to 20 the number approved by Congress.

As happened a year earlier, the fate of these two controversial programs became linked in the end-game bargaining within the committee:

To pressure Chairman Nunn and other centrist Democrats to boost the SDI authorization in the bill, Republicans threatened to block additional procurement of the B-2, a bomber Nunn strongly supported.

At first, Nunn proposed $4 billion for SDI, including $200 million for the space-based interceptor missiles — known as Brilliant Pebbles — that most Republicans viewed as the key to eventual expansion beyond an initial ground-based deployment that would have only limited capability.

On July 23, three amendments that would have increased the SDI total — and Brilliant Pebbles' share of the total — were rejected by narrow margins, with the committee splitting essentially along party lines.

Then the committee approved, 11-9, an amendment by Carl Levin, D-Mich., to drop from the bill funding for the additional B-2s. Six Republicans supported the proposal.

The final deal was struck the next day, with the committee approving 14-6 an amendment by Richard C. Shelby, D-Ala., that boosted the SDI authorization to $4.3 billion, including $350 million earmarked for Brilliant Pebbles. The committee then reconsidered Levin's B-2 amendment, voting 11-9 to reinstate funding for the four B-2s.

When the dust had settled, the essential politics of the committee's SDI position seemed unchanged from 1991: Once again, a tenuous alliance of right and center had lined up behind an SDI program aimed at deploying a limited, ground-based system while deferring until the next decade any deployment of space-based anti-missile weapons. *(1991 Almanac, p. 407)*

But SDI opponents planned to try, as they did in 1991, to break the pro-deployment coalition when the bill reached the Senate floor.

Opponents of the B-2 also planned another effort to block funding with the help of an important convert: Levin, who had confounded fellow liberals by backing the B-2 in prior years. Levin said that he had decided that four additional planes "don't add $2.5 billion worth of military capability."

### Other Provisions

The Senate committee's bill included the $2.2 billion requested to develop the Air Force's new F-22 fighter. But it ordered the Pentagon to pick and choose among several other proposed new combat planes to eliminate duplication.

The panel approved $944 million of the $1.1 billion requested to develop larger versions of the Navy's F/A-18 fighter. But the panel also ordered the Air Force to buy these "E" and "F" models of the F/A-18 as less expensive complements to the F-22. The Air Force had planned to develop a new plane.

The committee also eliminated from the bill $683 million requested to buy the final 24 F-16 fighters that the Air Force had planned to purchase. The House bill not only authorized funding for those planes but ordered the Air Force to continue F-16 purchases for the next few years.

To make it easier to reduce the size of the military by encouraging more military and civilian personnel to retire voluntarily, the committee bill included provisions:

● Allowing military personnel to apply for retirement after 15 years of service, instead of the 20 years usually required.

● Authorizing civilian Pentagon employees in job specialties that were over strength to receive a bonus of up to $20,000 if they retired early.

## SENATE FLOOR ACTION

The Senate passed its $274 billion version of the defense authorization bill (S 3114) by voice vote in the early hours of Sept. 19 at the end of a marathon session in which it considered more than 60 amendments.

Approval of the bill had been delayed for more than a month after the vote on a floor amendment indicated sentiment in the Senate to slash $2 billion from Bush's $5.3 billion request for SDI. With Bush's threat of a veto to back them up, SDI backers vowed to block final action on any bill that would cut the anti-missile defense program that deeply.

Eventually, Armed Services Chairman Nunn and his allies engineered a compromise authorizing $3.8 billion for SDI research.

The Senate bill also included the $2.69 billion the administration sought to build four final B-2 bombers. But it provided for a ban on nuclear testing that the administration opposed.

### SDI Showdown

The Senate, opening debate on the defense authorization bill, signaled its readiness Aug. 7 to outdo the House in cutting funding for the Strategic Defense Initiative.

It was a novel twist in the continuing dickering between the chambers over funding for SDI. For several years, the Senate had backed higher funding than the House did for the administration's controversial anti-missile defense program.

The Senate refused to kill an amendment by Budget Committee Chairman Sasser to cut authorized funding for SDI to $3.3 billion, $1 billion less than the amount approved in June by the House.

A move by to table (kill) the SDI-cutting amendment failed, 43-49. The tabling amendment was offered by John W. Warner of Virginia, the ranking Republican on Armed Services. *(Vote 182, p. 24-S)*

Malcolm Wallop, R-Wyo., the Senate's leading advocate

of the administration's SDI program, refused to let the Senate proceed to a final vote on Sasser's SDI-cutting amendment. The defense measure was pulled from the floor, and Nunn warned that the bill could die.

If that happened, Nunn said, there would be a stopgap appropriations bill that would gut key programs and prohibit most of the post-Cold War "defense conversion" initiatives contained in the authorization bill.

Before the SDI dispute bogged down the defense bill, the Senate on Aug. 7 had adopted, 91-2, a purely symbolic amendment putting members on the record in favor of provisions that the Armed Services Committee already had included in the bill to cushion the impact of the defense cutback on weapons manufacturers and their communities. The programs were priced at nearly $1.7 billion in fiscal 1993 alone. *(Vote 181, p. 24-S)*

To reinforce the case for moving on with the authorization bill, Nunn, Defense Appropriations Chairman Daniel K. Inouye, D-Hawaii, and full Senate Appropriations Chairman Robert C. Byrd, D-W.Va., warned on Aug. 12 of alarming consequences if, because of an impasse over SDI, the Pentagon was funded by a stopgap spending bill after the new fiscal year began Oct. 1.

Under the usual rules governing such a "continuing resolution," Inouye said, no new projects could be started, nor would programs be funded that Congress had added to the administration's budget request.

As an example, Inouye pointed to the Mississippi-built helicopter carrier in Nunn's bill, "sought by Sens. [Trent] Lott and [Thad] Cochran," uncharacteristically identifying the two GOP senators from that state who requested the ships.

"You're talking about tens of thousands of jobs here," Nunn said. "I don't believe [Wallop and his potential allies] realize how close to the cliff we are."

### Breaking the Impasse

Yielding by a narrow margin to threats of a veto, the Senate backed down Sept. 17 from the effort to slash $2 billion from Bush's $5.3 billion request for SDI.

After rejecting Sasser's amendment 48-50, the Senate adopted, 52-46, a $3.8 billion SDI alternative crafted by Nunn. *(Votes 214, 215, p. 28-S)*

That move fit into an emerging pattern on Capitol Hill of Democratic efforts to avert showdowns with Bush that would delay adjournment, interfere with members' re-election campaigning and muddy the duel between Bush and Democratic presidential nominee Bill Clinton.

But another vote on the defense bill lay the groundwork for a major confrontation with Bush on nuclear testing. By a 55-40 vote, the Senate on Sept. 18 approved an amendment by Mark O. Hatfield, R-Ore., to impose a nine-month halt to nuclear tests. It would be followed by a permanent ban on tests after the end of fiscal 1996 unless another country was still conducting tests. *(Vote 217, p. 29-S)*

Hatfield's amendment was adopted instead of an amendment by William S. Cohen, R-Maine, that would have imposed a shorter initial moratorium followed by a permanent ban at the end of fiscal 1998. Cohen's proposal also would have allowed the president to waive the test ban for one year to gain leverage to negotiate a comprehensive test ban.

But many members realized that the issue was likely to be determined — as it ultimately was — on the separate energy and water appropriations bill. Each chamber had included provisions to limit nuclear testing in its version of

that bill. The administration had threatened to veto the defense bill if it included a testing ban.

The Senate also defied a veto threat by leaving in the bill a provision that would allow U.S. military personnel and their dependents stationed abroad to obtain abortions in overseas U.S. military hospitals, provided they paid for the procedure.

By a vote of 36-55, the Senate rejected an amendment by Daniel R. Coats, R-Ind., that would have eliminated the abortion provision. *(Vote 220, p. 29-S)*

The Senate also rejected, 45-53, an amendment by Patrick J. Leahy, D-Vt., to drop from the defense bill $2.69 billion for four additional B-2 stealth bombers. *(Vote 216, p. 28-S)*

## Other Amendments

Among the non-controversial provisions the Senate adopted by voice vote were two by Nunn to:

● Increase by $250 million, to $650 million, the amount the Pentagon could spend to help dismantle the former Soviet arsenal.

● Bar the stationing in Europe of more than 100,000 U.S. personnel after fiscal 1996. The Bush administration wanted to stabilize the U.S. deployment to Europe at about 150,000.

An amendment co-sponsored by Florida Sens. Bob Graham, D, and Connie Mack, R, to tighten the U.S. trade embargo against Cuba, was adopted by voice vote. The amendment embodied the "Cuba Democracy Act," (HR 5323) passed Sept. 24 by the House. *(Cuba, p. 557)*

An amendment by Byrd, adopted by voice vote, would require the president to investigate more thoroughly and report to Congress on most efforts by a foreign company to buy a U.S. defense contractor.

Byrd said the Bush administration had taken too lax an approach toward reviewing potential sales: "We have established a pattern where only the most blatantly risky cases receive scrutiny and, even then, they are likely to get the go-ahead."

The Senate adopted by voice vote a number of amendments aimed at aiding the conversion of communities, defense workers and industries to a civilian economy.

The most far-reaching of these, by Edward M. Kennedy, D-Mass., would require early notification to defense contractor employees of possible layoffs because of canceled contracts. Employees would become eligible for retraining services under the Job Training Partnership Act six months before a scheduled layoff.

The Senate also adopted defense conversion amendments:

● By Claiborne Pell, D-R.I., directing the secretary of Defense to encourage defense contractors to branch out through such actions as accepting diversification costs as allowable under Pentagon contracts.

● By Pell, requiring the Pentagon to report to Congress on the cost and impact of requiring defense contractors to provide transitional health insurance to employees who lost their jobs because a Pentagon contract was canceled.

● By Joseph I. Lieberman, D-Conn., requiring the Pentagon to encourage its many research laboratories to expand the scope of their joint projects with private industry. The amendment was intended to give private companies more access to the labs' advanced technolgy.

● By Harry Reid, D-Nev., requiring the Energy Department to prepare a work force transition plan for any facility slated to lose 10 percent of its employees in one year, including the nuclear weapons test site in Nevada.

● By Richard H. Bryan, D-Nev., requiring the Energy Department to study the feasibility of converting the Nevada test site to a commercial facility for solar energy reserch.

● By Charles S. Robb, D-Va., authorizing the Pentagon's Office of Economic Assistance — which dispensed grants to help communities adjust to the loss of defense-related jobs — to also award grants to help communities with many such jobs to plan for prospective cutbacks.

● By David L. Boren, D-Okla., to establish a pilot program of "civilian community corps" camps, modeled on the Civilian Conservation Corps of the 1930s.

Other amendments that the Senate adopted by voice vote included:

● By Levin, authorizing the use of Pentagon funds to assist international peacekeeping operations. For fiscal 1993, the amendment would allow up to $300 million to be spent but only if the Office of Management and Budget counted such expenditures against the defense category of the 1990 budget law limiting discretionary spending.

● By Jeff Bingaman, D-N.M., adding to the bill $96 million to fight the proliferation of nuclear, chemical and biological weapons. This included $56 million for research on non-proliferation, $20 million to support U.N. non-proliferation operations in Iraq and $20 million for other international non-proliferation activities.

● By John Glenn, D-Ohio, imposing mandatory sanctions on companies that promoted the proliferation of nuclear weapons. Among other things, the amendment would bar such companies from doing any business with the federal government.

● By John McCain, R-Ariz., imposing mandatory sanctions on governments and private parties that transferred to Iraq or Iran equipment or technical know-how that would help those countries develop advanced weapons, such as cruise missiles, "smart bombs" and stealth aircraft.

● By Leahy, banning for one year the sale or export of anti-personnel land mines and calling on the president to negotiate an international ban on the transfer of such weapons.

● By Kennedy, requiring a report to Congress on the desirability of Pentagon assistance to mine-clearing operations in countries such as Afghanistan, Cambodia and Angola, where the presence of millions of anti-personnel mines impeded refugee resettlement efforts.

● By Joseph R. Biden Jr., D-Del., requiring U.S. companies to lease from the Defense Department at a fair market rate any Pentagon equipment being displayed by the company at an overseas trade show. The requirement could be waived by the secretary of the Army, Navy or Air Force.

● By David Pryor, D-Ark., barring any expeditures for a radar-jammer designated ASPJ, intended for Navy fighter planes. Funds could be spent only to cover the cost of canceling the program. Under development since the mid-1970s, the ASPJ repeatedly failed to perform up to specification in tests.

● By Pryor, limiting to $100 million the amount the SDI program could spend on consultants in fiscal 1993. Pryor said this measure would cut about $65 million from planned consultant fees.

● By Alan J. Dixon, D-Ill., increasing by $4 million the authorization to develop a high-tech shell for tank cannons.

● By Nunn and Warner, increasing by $20 million the amount authorized for military-funded research on AIDS.

● By McCain, providing that local governments and pri-

vate companies that acquire abandoned military bases would be indemnified by the Defense Department against any lawsuits or legal penalties resulting from hazardous waste left at the site by its Pentagon tenants.

● By Howard M. Metzenbaum, D-Ohio, limiting the degree to which the Pentagon would protect against legal liability any contractor cleaning up toxic or hazardous waste at a current or former base. The amendment barred such protection against a liability resulting from a contractor's gross negligence or intentional misconduct.

● By Pete V. Domenici, R-N.M., providing that, if a service member was dishonorably discharged by a military court because of abusing a spouse or child, the spouse retained a right to some portion of the pension or other benefits that would otherwise have been provided.

By a vote of 73-12, the Senate tabled (and thus killed) an amendment by Christopher J. Dodd, D-Conn., authorizing the president to guarantee export loans up to a total value of $1 billion, to promote the export to allied countries of U.S.-manufactured defense equipment. Dodd had tried unsuccessfully to attach a similar provision to several bills in 1991. *(Vote 221, p. 29-S)*

## FINAL ACTION

The final, $274.3 billion version of the defense authorization bill (HR 5006) was crafted by a conference committee that completed its work on Oct. 1.

The House approved the conference report (H Rept 102-966), 304-100, in a rare Saturday session on Oct. 3. *(Vote 461, p. 112-H)*

In a procedural shuffle in the rush toward adjournment, the Senate agreed the same day by voice vote that the chamber would automatically "deem" the conference report to be approved whenever it received the official paperwork confirming the House action. The paperwork finally caught up with legislative reality on Oct. 5, the day on which the Senate officially adopted the report, clearing the defense bill for Bush's signature.

The Senate-House conferees had found it easier to cut personnel and to cushion the economic impact of cutbacks than to cancel costly weapons.

Conferees embraced House initiatives to shake up the politically influential National Guard and to slice the number of U.S. personnel overseas by 40 percent. And they adopted Senate proposals for a wide-ranging review of the division of labor among the armed services and to allow unneeded military personnel to retire after 15 years of service, rather than the 20 years that had been required.

When it came to cutting back on major weapons, however, the conferees agreed on long-range policies but not on specific, immediate reductions. In most cases, they opted for the more generous of the Senate and House alternatives as far as fiscal 1993 funding was concerned.

For example, they rejected a House effort to cut more than $500 million from the effort to develop a new version of the Navy's F/A-18 fighter plane, a Senate effort to terminate production of the Air Force's F-16 fighter and a Senate effort to slow preliminary work on a nuclear-powered aircraft carrier.

And they acceded to the House proposal for $225 million to continue upgrading the Army's AHIP scout helicopters and the Senate's decision to add $1.2 billion for a large helicopter carrier.

In each case, proponents of the chosen option cited a post-Cold War need for the particular weapon. Taken col-

lectively, however, the decisions suggested that — in an election year with the economy in trouble and the defense industry contracting rapidly even under Bush's program — it was easier for the conferees to agree on ways to give out money than on ways to cut off money.

The conference report's authorization of $274.3 billion for defense-related programs of the Pentagon and Energy Department was $7.2 billion less than Bush had requested. The final bill authorized $200 million less than the Senate approved in September, but $3.2 billion more than was approved early in June by the House.

Reflecting the Pentagon budget's transition away from the Soviet-oriented programs of the past, the battles over conventional weapons overshadowed disputes over strategic arms that had dominated congressional defense debates through the 1980s.

The conference report authorized:

● $4.05 billion for the anti-missile Strategic Defense Initiative, compared with Bush's request for $5.4 billon. Conferees split the difference between the $4.3 billion agreed to by the House and the $3.8 billion that the Senate approved by a narrow margin after a slender majority of senators had indicated their support for authorizing only $3.3 billion.

The conference total included $300 million of the $575 million requested to develop space-based anti-missile rockets, including Brilliant Pebbles, which Republicans viewed as essential to SDI's long-term mission.

Conferees accepted a House provision stipulating that the initial, ground-based defense system should be designed to be consistent with the current form of the 1972 treaty limiting anti-ballistic missile systems. SDI planners had assumed that Russia would agree to revisions in the pact that would ease some of its restrictions.

● $2.69 billion for four additional B-2 stealth bombers to complete the scaled-back force of 20 that the Air Force sought.

Neither these four nor a fifth B-2, which was authorized in fiscal 1992, could be built unless Congress voted in 1993 to allow their completion after receiving reports from the Pentagon on the plane's cost and on its ability to evade radar detection. Prior to that vote, no more than $900 million of the $2.69 billion could be spent.

The House had favored allowing only $600 million to be spent before the follow-up vote, while the Senate favored allowing $1.2 billion.

Conferees also dropped from the defense bill two controversial provisions that had been included in other legislation:

● A ban on nuclear testing, which was incorporated into the energy and water appropriations bill (HR 5373). Despite administration opposition to the testing ban, Bush on Oct. 2 signed the energy spending bill, which also included $517 million for the superconducting super collider, a politically appealing atom smasher in Texas.

● Authorization for military personnel and their dependents stationed abroad to obtain privately funded abortions in U.S. military hospitals. The provision was passed in a separate bill (S 3144), with members fully aware that Bush would veto that measure.

Congress' reluctance to mandate immediate procurement cuts was vividly illustrated by the conferees' efforts to reshape plans for Navy and Air Force combat aircraft.

The administration's budget request included funds to buy a final group of 24 F-16s ($683 million) and 48 "C" and "D" model F/A-18s ($1.66 billion). It also included nearly

*Continued on p. 495*

# Fiscal 1993 Defense Authorization Provisions

*HR 5006 (PL 102-484) authorized $274 billion in defense spending for fiscal 1993. Following are the bill's major provisions, including comparisons with President Bush's budget request and with the versions of the bill enacted by the House and Senate. As enacted, the legislation:*

## Strategic Weapons

● Authorized, as requested, $1.26 billion to continue development of the B-2 stealth bomber and $2.69 billion to buy four additional B-2s so as to complete the scaled-down force of 20 planes sought by the Air Force.

Both chambers had approved the B-2 funds. But House-Senate conferees who crafted the final version of the bill specified that only $900 million of that amount could be spent unless Congress voted in 1993 to allow completion of those four planes plus a fifth that was funded in the fiscal 1992 budget. That vote was to come after the Pentagon reported to Congress on the B-2's cost and its ability to evade radar detection.

To make the 20-plane force fully operational, the Air Force said it planned to request from Congress a total of $5.7 billion more in fiscal 1994-96.

● Approved $409 million of the $446 million requested to modernize B-1 and B-52 bombers that were already in service. Taking a cue from the Senate bill, the conference report also required the Pentagon to conduct realistic tests of B-1s and B-52s in conventional bombing missions against simulated air defenses. The Senate Armed Services Committee had indicated that it would support upgrades for only a portion of the more than 270 B-1s and B-52s.

● Authorized $148 million to wrap up production of a long-range, stealthy cruise missile (designated ACM). After the budget request was submitted in January, the Air Force concluded that it would need the additional funds. Even as they approved the funds, the conferees chastised the Air Force in uncharacteristically blunt terms for seeking a congressional "bailout" from its management "fiasco."

● Approved $440 million to modify C-135s, with most of the funds earmarked to continue a 10-year-old program of equipping the tanker planes with more powerful jet engines. Both chambers had approved the $527 million requested to upgrade the hundreds of Boeing C-135s — similar to 707 jetliners — that were in use by the Air Force, mostly as midair refueling tankers.

● Incorporated a House provision ordering the Air Force to put new engines on some tankers operated by National Guard and reserve units. But conferees also ordered the Pentagon to analyze in detail whether a reduction in the tanker fleet would obviate the need to upgrade more than 150 other planes in Guard and reserve units.

● Approved the request for 21 Trident II submarine-launched missiles ($764 million) and $223 million for components to be used in additional missiles that were slated for inclusion in the fiscal 1994 request.

## Strategic Defense and Space

● Approved $4.05 billion for the Strategic Defense Initiative (SDI), splitting the difference between the $4.3 billion agreed to by the House and the $3.8 billion narrowly approved by the Senate. Compared with Bush's $5.4 billion request, both chambers had placed more emphasis on the part of the program aimed at deploying relatively quickly a ground-based defense of U.S. territory against attack by a relatively small number of missiles.

The conference total included only $300 million of the $576 million Bush requested for space-based anti-missile rockets, including those known as Brilliant Pebbles, which Republicans viewed as essential to eventually expanding SDI's scope.

The conferees repealed the goal set in the fiscal 1992 defense bill of deploying a limited, ground-based defense by 1996. In their report, they endorsed a new Pentagon plan that envisioned deployment by 2002.

They also approved a House-passed provision stipulating that the initial, ground-based defense comply with the 1972 treaty limiting anti-ballistic missile (ABM) systems. SDI planners had assumed that Russia would agree to ease some of the restrictions in that pact.

The conferees set a $135 million limit on consultants for the SDI program. The Senate version of the bill included a provision, sponsored by Arkansas Democrat David Pryor, to limit consultant fees to $100 million. According to Pryor, SDI spent $165 million for consultants in fiscal 1992.

● Approved the $287 million requested to buy satellites to detect the launch of long-range missiles. In addition, the conferees approved $412 million to develop more sophisticated devices for detecting a missile attack and assessing its target.

● Approved $25 million to develop an anti-satellite weapon, a project the House had rejected. But they dropped from the bill $15 million to develop a target-finding system for anti-satellite missions.

● Ordered a study to review alternative budgets for the Pentagon's program of space satellites and launchers to trim as much as 15 percent from projected requests.

Because of new developments in satellite and launcher technology, the conferees argued, the Pentagon might be able to make do with fewer satellites in orbit, more reliance on commercial satellites, and more reliance on less expensive, non-satellite communication systems.

● Authorized the requested amounts for the rockets already being used to loft military satellites into orbit: $525 million for Titan IVs and $269 million for the smaller Atlas-Centaurs.

● Trimmed the amounts requested for two projects that conferees said would pick Pentagon pockets to develop space vehicles intended largely for civilian missions: They approved $150 million of the $175 million requested for the so-called National Aerospace Plane, intended to take off from a runway and soar into orbit. Arguing that the effort to develop a prototype craft was premature, the conferees approved funding to wrap up that phase of the program while continuing basic research. In future years, they specified, the amount spent in the defense budget for the project could be no more than twice NASA's share.

They approved $85 million of the $125 million requested for a "national launch system" — a family of launch rockets, including one intended to carry much heavier satellites than any already in service. Not more than half the amount authorized could be spent until the Pentagon sent Congress a plan detailing how the Defense Department and NASA would fit this joint program into their long-term budget plans and how the Pentagon would save money by using the new launchers instead of the rockets already in service.

## Ground Combat

● Approved $148 million to keep intact the production lines for M-1 tanks.

The president's budget requested $25 million to modify M-1s. But during the summer, the administration agreed to a much more ambitious, congressionally supported program to modernize the tank fleet with electronic gear for driving and fighting at night. The conferees ordered the Army to start by upgrading the oldest M-1s, installing not only the new electronics but also the larger guns and heavier armor already installed in the most recent models.

● Added $85 million to buy 60 additional Bradley armed troop carriers and $40 million to begin upgrading existing vehicles. The president's budget had included no funds for additional Bradley production, requesting only $104 million to wrap up an existing contract.

After the war with Iraq, Bradley crews complained that they lacked a laser rangefinder for the vehicle's 25mm cannon. The conferees added $5 million to the bill to develop such an improvement.

● Allowed the Pentagon to pay for those tank upgrade programs with proceeds from the sale to other countries of older tanks and

troop carriers.

● Approved the Army's $5 million request to begin buying lightweight tanks to equip its rapid-reaction divisions, intended for aerial deployment. The conferees added to the bill $15 million to revive a canceled program to put a tank cannon on a version of the Marine Corps' LAV armored cars.

● Approved $17 million to continue work on potential cannon improvements. Contending that the collapse of the Soviet threat eliminated the need for a new tank more powerful than the M-1, however, neither chamber had approved the $42 million requested to develop a larger tank cannon.

● Approved the $145 million requested to upgrade self-propelled artillery so they could fire more quickly and accurately. Conferees added to the bill $13 million to develop for the Army and Marine Corps large-caliber cannon light enough to be carried by small helicopters.

● Authorized the $188 million requested to continue production of ATACMS artillery rockets, plus a total of $338 million to buy 73 launchers for smaller MLRS artillery rockets and 30,000 of the rockets.

The administration had sought $197 million for 44 mobile launchers for the MLRS rockets and $2 million for miscellaneous related costs but no funds to buy additional rockets.

● Approved the $443 million requested to continue developing the Army's Comanche "scout" helicopter, which the Senate had dropped from the bill.

However, the conferees endorsed the Senate's objections to the Pentagon's plan to build three prototypes and then shelve the program. So they added a provision to fence half the funds until the Pentagon certified that its long-term budget plans included funds to gear up for eventual production of the Comanche.

● Added $225 million to the administration's budget to upgrade 36 older scout helicopters with missiles and target-finding electronics. The proposal followed the lead of the House.

● Granted the administration's request for $49 million for miscellaneous improvements to the Apache anti-tank helicopter and $282 million to develop a "Longbow" modification with more powerful engines and more sophisticated target-finding electronics. In addition, the conferees authorized $117 million for interim Apache upgrades.

● Approved the $176 million requested to equip 170 pickup trucks with batteries of Stinger anti-aircraft missiles and to buy components for additional systems intended for future budgets.

● Added $9 million to develop an antiaircraft version of the LAV armored car.

● Authorized $512 million to buy two planes equipped with JSTARS radar, designed to find ground targets far behind enemy lines. The conferees adopted a Senate initiative.

The president's budget requested $311 million for one plane.

### Tactical Air Combat

● Required the Defense Department to send Congress two detailed studies, a process that was intended to impose budgetary discipline on the services' plans for new combat airplanes:

One was an analysis by the chairman of the Joint Chiefs of Staff of the division of labor among the services, known in Pentagon jargon as a "roles and missions" study. Mandated every three years by the 1986 defense reorganization act, such a report was already due by the end of 1992. The conferees ordered that the analysis be a "thorough, everything-on-the-table review," focusing on combat aircraft.

In particular, they asked whether one service could take over certain specialized missions — such as radar jamming — that require expensive airplanes. And they asked whether a single type of aircraft could be used by all services to perform similar combat missions.

The second study required by the conference report was an analysis by the secretary of Defense of how much of their planned combat airplane programs the Air Force and Navy could afford over the next 20 years.

In conducting this study, conferees said, department officials were to consider not only the declining defense budgets that were in prospect but also the portion of its total budget that each branch typically allocated to aircraft procurement. They insisted that the study assume tighter budgets would allow fewer planes to be built overall — and fewer to be built in any one year — than the services planned.

● Approved $683 million, as requested, for 24 Air Force F-16s. But the bill barred any spending to buy additional F-16s pending completion of the two studies.

● Authorized $1.15 billion for 36 of the Navy's F/A-18s, a reduction of 12 planes ($513 million) from the request.

● Specified that, for the following three aircraft development programs, no more than 65 percent of the total authorized could be spent until the two studies were submitted:

— The Air Force's F-22 fighter. The conferees authorized $2.2 billion, as requested.

— Larger "E" and "F" versions of the F/A 18. The conferees authorized $944 million, about 80 percent of the amount requested.

— A stealthy, carrier-based bomber designated AX. The conferees authorized the $166 million that was requested.

The conferees also required the Navy to rely more on prototypes than it had planned in the AX and the F/A-18 "E" and "F" projects.

● Provided that the Pentagon must choose between Air Force C-135s and Navy P-3s for electronic eavesdropping missions. Both services had requested funds to modernize their electronic intelligence planes. The conferees approved $57 million, the total requested. But, as proposed by the Senate, they ordered that the Defense secretary pick which of the planes would be used by both services and earmark all the money to upgrade that fleet.

● Approved both the $530 million requested for upgrades of the Navy's Prowler and the $68 million requested for work on the Air Force's Ravens.

Responding to the Senate's efforts to try to force the Pentagon to settle on one of those two types of radar jamming planes, the conferees included a provision barring use of more than 65 percent of the Raven money until the Pentagon sent Congress the roles and missions study and the Air Force guaranteed that its long-term budget plans included the Raven.

● Added $24 million for 30 additional copies of a 50-mile-range, Israeli-designed missile to be carried by B-52 bombers.

● Approved only $105 million of the $218 million requested to buy HARM anti-radar missiles. Instead of buying the 846 new missiles requested, the conferees told the Pentagon to upgrade the same number of early model HARMs.

### Naval Forces

● Authorized the full $832 million requested for the nuclear power plant and other components of a new aircraft carrier. The Navy said it planned to request the bulk of the ship's cost — probably about $4 billion — in the fiscal 1995 budget. In an effort to delay the major request until fiscal 1996, the Senate had approved only $350 million of the fiscal 1993 request for "long lead-time" items.

● Approved $3.30 billion, all but $50 million of the amount requested, for four Burke-class destroyers and the $246 million requested for two minesweepers.

● Effectively canceled $442 million in shipbuilding projects from the 1992 defense appropriations bill that had not been authorized.

It was a routine skirmish in a continuing turf war between the Armed Services and Appropriations committees. The authorization conferees — who were members of the two chambers' Armed Services panels — added to their bill a provision using those funds instead to cover part of the cost of the fiscal 1993 shipbuilding program.

● Authorized the $404 million requested for 200 Tomahawk cruise missiles.

The Senate had approved $229 million for 100 long-range Tomahawks — half the number requested — arguing that a slower production rate would keep the assembly line open longer, thus preserving the option of buying more weapons than planned.

● Backed $133 million of the $155 million requested to develop a new nuclear-powered submarine designated Centurion, intended to be less expensive than the two Seawolf-class ships that were

already being built.

• Approved the $195 million requested to develop two new types of sub-hunting sonars.

The House had approved only $52 million of the $195 million requested to develop two new types of sub-hunting sonars. In granting the full request, the conferees attached conditions echoing the reasoning behind the House reduction: With Soviet nuclear subs in midocean no longer a major threat, they said, the Navy should reorient its anti-sub investments toward technologies that could be deployed quickly to hunt for small submarines in remote, shallow seas.

• Authorized $27 million, a $9 million increase over the amount requested, to continue development of a helicopter-borne laser called Magic Lantern, intended to detect underwater mines.

## Air and Sea Transport

• Approved $1.81 billion for six C-17 cargo jets, a reduction of two planes ($703 million) from the request for the long-range, wide-body planes. For components to be used in C-17s slated for the fiscal 1994 budget, the conferees approved $251 million instead of the $206 million requested.

With production of the planes lagging, the conferees added to the bill provisions linking the release of new procurement funds to the pace of the assembly line producing previously funded C-17s. They also included a House-passed provision requiring that major components of the C-17 be tested for their resilience to anti-aircraft fire.

• Approved the $300 million requested for eight Hercules cargo planes, and the conferees added $328 million for 12 additional planes earmarked for National Guard and reserve units.

• Adopted a Senate initiative to add $1.20 billion for a large helicopter carrier able to carry 2,000 Marines.

• Included the $755 million that both chambers had added to the bill to continue work on the V-22 Osprey tilt-rotor aircraft, intended as a Marine Corps troop carrier.

But the conferees accepted a Senate provision allowing only half that amount to be spent until the Marines reported to Congress on the crash in July of an Osprey prototype.

• Approved $613 million of the $1.2 billion requested to begin buying additional high-speed cargo ships to haul abroad the combat gear of U.S.-based Army units.

The Navy planned to use the money, together with $1.88 billion previously appropriated, to obtain 20 new ships by some combination of building new vessels and modifying existing commercial ships. No more than five foreign-built ships could be purchased for conversion.

## Military Personnel

• Approved the request to cut the number of active-duty personnel to 1,766,500, a reduction of 100,400 from the fiscal 1992 cap.

• Added to the bill a provision allowing the Defense secretary to exceed the active-duty ceiling if necessary to avoid forcing military careerists out of uniform before they completed the 20 years of service needed to qualify for retirement pay.

• Authorized a ceiling of 1,095,080 on membership in National

Guard and reserve units. This was a reduction of nearly 40,000, rather than the 116,000-member cutback the administration proposed.

• Included several elements from a House-passed package intended to make the Army National Guard more combat-ready.

One such provision required the Guard to draw a larger proportion of its new members from former active-duty personnel. Another required an active-duty Army unit to oversee the training of each Guard unit.

Also approved was a provision requiring the Army to assign 3,000 experienced active-duty members to support Guard and reserve units. But the conferees dropped from the House package a requirement for semi-annual physical fitness evaluations and for dismissal or retirement of any Guard member who could not pass screenings within nine months.

• Added, as usual, funds for equipment earmarked for Guard and reserve units.

In this bill, the additions totaled $696 million, more than half for Hercules cargo planes and smaller aircraft.

## Operations, Maintenance

• Approved a Senate provision barring the deployment in Europe of more than 100,000 U.S. troops after fiscal 1996. A House provision had set a 1995 deadline for reaching that ceiling. The Bush administration planned to keep 150,000 troops in Europe.

• Included a House provision mandating a reduction of 40 percent in the total number of U.S. military personnel stationed overseas. But the conferees set a 1996 deadline, rather than the 1995 date approved by the House.

• Reduced $500 million from the amount earmarked for operating costs at overseas bases in the hope of making allied governments pay a larger share of the cost of stationing U.S. troops on their soil. It was a modest gesture compared to the House version of the bill, which would have sliced $3.5 billion on the same rationale.

The conferees also added to the bill a non-binding declaration that the budget for overseas base costs should decline significantly in fiscal 1994-96.

• Cut $1.07 billion from the amount requested to purchase additional supplies in an effort to force the Pentagon to draw down its inventories of spare parts and supplies.

• Cut from the budget request $3.11 billion to make various changes in the "defense business operating fund," a revolving fund the Pentagon used to finance operations such as routine overhauls and spare parts purchases.

## Other Provisions

• Included a provision barring the purchase by a foreign government or foreign-owned company of any of the 36 largest U.S. defense contractors or any contractors supplying the Pentagon with secret technology.

• Authorized $168 million to combat the proliferation of nuclear, chemical and biological weapons.

• Increased to $800 million the amount that could be drawn from Pentagon funds to help former Soviet republics dismantle some of their arsenals. ∎

*Continued from p. 492*

$3.5 billion as the down payment on a new generation of combat planes: $2.2 billion to develop the Air Force's new F-22 fighter; $1.1 billion to develop larger "E" and "F" models of the F/A-18; and $165 million to begin developing a small stealth bomber, designated AX, to fly from aircraft carriers.

The last issue settled in the conference was whether to authorize long-lead-time funds to guarantee continued F-16 production in fiscal 1994. After the dispute had delayed conclusion of the conference for nearly a day, the two sides basically took a dive:

They approved $683 million, the amount requested, to buy 24 more F-16s and to begin shutting down the assem-

bly line. The conferees did not mandate its termination, but they barred any expenditure to continue F-16 production beyond fiscal 1993 until the Pentagon submitted two studies to Congress.

One was to examine military "roles and missions," with particular emphasis on rationalizing future combat aircraft programs. The other was to attempt to fit into planned future budgets whatever aircraft programs the first study called for.

The conferees authorized nearly the amounts requested for the new generation of development projects, including:

• $2.2 billion for the F-22, as requested;

• $944 million for the F/A-18 E and F, more than 80 percent of the request; and

● $165 million for the AX, as requested.

But while they could not agree on cuts in particular programs, the conferees did lay the groundwork for subjecting the Navy and Air Force programs to a single set of policy and budget decisions. The conference report provided that:

● No more than 65 percent of the amount authorized for any of the three new programs could be spent until after submission of the reports on roles and missions and long-term funding.

● Both the AX and the F/A-18 E and F programs were required to rely more heavily on prototypes than the Navy had planned. In addition, the enlarged F/A-18 could not cost more than 125 percent of the cost of the current C and D model F/A-18s.

### Other Provisions

Other highlights of the conference report included:

● A ceiling of 1,095,080 on membership in National Guard and reserve units, a reduction of nearly 40,000 from the fiscal 1992 ceiling. The administration had proposed a reduction of nearly 116,000.

● A package of House-passed provisions that imposed on the National Guard higher standards of physical condition, training and experience.

● A $3 billion cut from the amount requested for spare parts and supplies, linked to various new rules intended to tighten the Pentagon's inventory control.

● $1.51 billion for "economic conversion," including $686 million for transition assistance to personnel leaving the services, $132 million to help communities adjust to defense-related changes in the local economy and $694 million for technology programs aimed at helping the defense industry adapt to the commercial marketplace.

Bush signed the defense bill (PL 102-484) on Oct. 23. ■

# Funds Approved for Last B-2 Bombers

Congress approved President Bush's request in 1992 for $2.7 billion to build a final set of four B-2 bombers. But lawmakers provided that funds for those planes and for a fifth, which was previously appropriated, could not be spent until passage of follow-up legislation.

The subsequent approval was to be based on reports that Congress demanded from the Pentagon on the stealth plane's cost and its effectiveness in evading radar detection.

The provisions were incorporated in the fiscal 1993 bills on defense authorization (HR 5006 — PL 102-484) and defense appropriations (HR 5504 — PL 102-396). *(Defense authorization, p. 483; appropriations, p. 592)*

Supporters of the B-2 boasted of their success in keeping the program alive; opponents declared victory in that construction of the costly aircraft was coming to a close.

## BACKGROUND

President Jimmy Carter's administration first made public in 1980 what had been a top-secret effort to develop the stealth bomber. By 1991, the Pentagon had spent $31 billion to develop the B-2 and build the first 15.

The B-2 had long been controversial because of its high cost, a result of the exotic design and materials that were intended to make it difficult to detect. In 1990, Bush reduced the number of B-2s planned from 132 to 75.

Support for the plane was further endangered by the collapse in 1991 of the Soviet military threat that the plane was chiefly designed to counter. The Pentagon shifted its emphasis to promoting the B-2 as a super-weapon for conventional bombing missions in the post-Cold War world.

In 1991, Bush requested $4.8 billion for four additional B-2s. As had happened for several years, the House voted to end B-2 production while the Senate supported Bush's request. Conferees on the fiscal 1992 defense authorization bill (PL 102-190) forged a compromise: The final version of the bill authorized $1.6 billion for continued research and development of the B-2. It also authorized $1.8 billion to build additional parts and components while barring construction of additional planes beyond the 15 previously authorized. And it provided for an additional $1 billion

that could be used for a 16th plane, but only if Congress subsequently approved it by law. *(1991 Almanac, p. 403)*

The B-2's appeal was further damaged by reports that in July 1991 it had failed a Pentagon test of its ability to slip past radar.

## BUSH'S PROPOSAL

Bush reduced the goal for the B-2 once again as he presented his fiscal 1993 budget proposal, calling for an end to production after the completion of 20 planes. In addition to the 15 planes already authorized, Bush sought permission to spend the $1 billion appropriated the previous year for a 16th plane, plus $2.7 billion in additional funding for four more.

In reducing its ambitions for the size of the B-2 fleet, the administration was driven by efforts to cut Pentagon spending and by the new round of weapons cutbacks promised by Bush and Russian President Boris N. Yeltsin.

Even before Bush's announcement at the end of January, some of the B-2's defenders protested reports that a cutback was planned. In a Jan. 8 letter, Sen. John Seymour, R-Calif., urged Bush to carefully consider any cuts in the Northrop Corp.'s B-2 production, which, he noted, contributed $1.2 billion a year to his state's "troubled economy." Rep. Robert K. Dornan, R-Calif., warned against cutting weapons programs to meet "arbitrary budget targets" and argued that "during a time of decreasing defense dollars, the B-2 is just the type of aircraft we need."

## HOUSE ACTION

Backing away from its total opposition for several years to building more B-2s, the House accepted Bush's proposal to complete a 20-plane fleet but attached the condition that Congress would have to vote again to release the funds after receiving reports from the Pentagon on the B-2's cost and stealthiness. An amendment to cut off all further B-2 production was rejected on the House floor.

At a hearing of the House Armed Services Committee on Feb. 20, Chairman Les Aspin, D-Wis., gave a first indi-

cation that his panel might be willing to accept the administration's plan.

Aspin told Air Force Secretary Donald Rice that if he had a good case for the additional planes "we'd be interested in hearing it because we might be interested in adopting your position."

At a hearing of an Armed Forces subcommittee on May 1, Air Force officials said they were testing three methods of fixing the problem discovered the previous July, when a flight test revealed that one type of radar could detect the B-2 more easily than permitted by its design specifications.

Air Force Gen. John M. Loh said some combination of those approaches would make the B-2 sufficiently stealthy. "I don't believe it has to [meet the initial specification] to be an operationally effective bomber," Loh said.

Aspin suggested that could be enough to satisfy him. "I suspect it will take a very long time and a very large amount of money" to meet the technical standards set nearly a decade earlier, he said. "I'm not sure that achieving that standard is worth it." This contrasted with the attitude taken by Senate Armed Services Committee member Carl Levin, D-Mich. Previously one of the few Senate liberals to support B-2 production, Levin had begun insisting that the Air Force hold the plane strictly to the initial standards.

Republican Rep. John R. Kasich, Ohio, a leader of the anti-B-2 coalition, dismissed the debate over whether to buy 15 planes or 20. "We're going to focus on the money," he told reporters.

Loh said it would cost $7 billion more to make fully operational the 15 B-2s already purchased. By comparison, enlarging the force to 20 bombers would cost an additional $2.6 billion, he told the House panel.

But Kasich complained that the B-2 contracts already in force might require the government to pay large penalties. "We face the potential of huge close-out costs," he said. "I don't want to pay those."

To give Pentagon officials an incentive to drive hard bargains with B-2 contractors, Kasich argued, Congress should appropriate a lump sum: The lower the amount sucked up by termination costs, the more bombers the Air Force could buy, up to a ceiling of 20.

On May 13, the House Armed Services Committee approved, 47-8, its version of the defense authorization bill. It included Bush's request for $2.7 billion to complete a fleet of 20 B-2s, plus the $1.26 billion that he sought for continued development. But the committee was not convinced that the big, bat-winged plane would be as stealthy as promised nor that the Pentagon was driving a hard enough bargain to buy out the contract at the lowest price. Thus, the panel's version of the authorization bill specified that the money on B-2s could not be spent until:

- The Pentagon reported on efforts to improve the plane's "stealthiness;"
- The Pentagon reported on the cost of fielding a force of 20 bombers;
- The General Accounting Office reviewed those two reports; and
- Congress voted to allow expenditure of the $2.7 billion.

The committee's bill also prohibited use of funds to buy more than 20 B-2s. And it urged the Air Force to press contractors to shave several hundred million dollars from the Air Force's projected total cost of $44.4 billion for a complete B-2 fleet.

"The B-2 fight is over, and we're declaring victory," Aspin said.

The B-2 provisions remained intact when the full House passed the defense authorization bill, 198-168, on June 5.

Aspin beat back an amendment by Thomas H. Andrews, D-Maine, seeking to bar procurement of additional B-2 bombers.

The 162-212 vote by which the House rejected Andrews' amendment found liberal Democrats overpowered by a coalition of Republicans with more conservative Democrats. *(Vote 170, p. 42-H)*

Democrats supported Andrews' amendment, 139-89, and Republicans opposed it, 22-123. Independent Beranrd Sanders, Vt., supported the amendment. The minority of Democrats who support the B-2 included several liberals from California, where the B-2 was built.

Noting that Aspin had backed an end to B-2 production in 1991 and that the Soviet Union had since disintegrated, Andrews argued, "Nothing has happened that would compel us" to build more.

His ally, Bart Gordon, D-Tenn., cited members' support for a balanced-budget amendment as an argument to stop building B-2s. "The budget is balanced by tough choices," he said. "I urge my colleagues to put their votes where their mouth is."

But Aspin countered that the additional planes would provide a hefty boost in firepower for a relatively modest additional investment. And he underscored that Congress would decide whether the additional funds would be spent after reviewing Pentagon efforts to make the B-2 live up to its billing as a radar-evader.

Democratic leaders gave Aspin a king-of-the-hill rule that would have helped him protect the committee's recommendation to buy four more B-2s, had a majority voted for Andrews' amendment. Aspin did not need to offer his alternative.

On July 2, during consideration of the companion defense appropriations bill (HR 5504), the House rejected, 173-248, a similar amendment to cut off B-2 funding. The defeat of the amendment by Timothy J. Penny, D-Minn., demonstrated that B-2 opponents had lost ground since consideration of the authorization bill. Seven members who had voted against the cut in June supported Penny, but 14 went the other way. *(Vote 265, p. 64-H)*

## SENATE ACTION

The Senate, which had repeatedly supported administration requests for B-2 funding, did so once again. As in the House, an amendment to cut off further funding was rejected on the Senate floor.

The $2.7 billion that the administration requested for four B-2s was included in the version of the defense authorization bill that was approved by the Senate Armed Services Committee, 17-3, on July 24.

But signs of growing resistance to the B-2 were planted in the committee, where opponents gained an important convert in Levin, who had in previous years confounded fellow liberals by backing the B-2. This time, he said, he decided that four additional planes "don't add up to $2.5 billion worth of military capability." He also contended that the Air Fore had circumvented a provision he added to a previous defense funding bill that was designed to make the B-2's contractor use its profits to make good any performance shortfalls in the plane.

On Sept. 18, during floor debate on the defense authorization bill, the Senate rejected, 45-53, an amendment by Patrick J. Leahy, D-Vt., to drop the $2.7 billion for addi-

tional B-2s. *(Vote 216, p. 28-S)*

Leahy had campaigned to halt production of the B-2 bomber since 1989, when the Air Force was planning a fleet of 132 of the costly planes.

By September 1991, with the Soviet threat evaporating, the Air Force had reduced its planned fleet to 75 B-2s and was emphasizing the plane's value in carrying non-nuclear "smart" bombs against regional military powers such as Iraq. Leahy's effort to kill the program in the fiscal 1992 defense appropriations bill failed, 48-51.

Offering his amendment Sept. 18, Leahy dismissed the contention that a 20-plane fleet of B-2s was still needed for non-nuclear missions. "With the breakup of the Soviet Union, it is an aircraft without a mission justifying its price tag," he said.

But Democrat Sam Nunn of Georgia, chairman of the Senate Armed Services Committee, cited Air Force testimony that two B-2s, each carrying a two-man crew and flying from bases in the United States, could carry out a conventional mission against a heavily defended target that otherwise would require dozens of conventional planes and more than 3,000 U.S. personnel, most of them stationed overseas.

"We get a whole lot of leverage and we reduce the risk many-fold to American men and women," Nunn said.

Compared with his effort a year earlier, Leahy picked up the support of Levin and Republicans Hank Brown, Colo., and Arlen Specter, Pa. But five senators who supported Leahy in 1991 voted against his amendment a year later: Democrats John B. Breaux and J. Bennett Johnston of Louisiana, Kent Conrad, N.D., and Terry Sanford, N.C., and Republican John McCain, Ariz.

Quentin N. Burdick, D-N.D., who died Sept. 8, voted in 1991 to end B-2 production. But his widow, Jocelyn Birch Burdick, sworn in Sept. 16 to fill the seat, voted against Leahy's amendment.

## FINAL ACTION

The final version of the defense authorization bill (HR 5006) included funding for a final order of B-2s but barred spending much of the money for them until a follow-up vote by Congress.

The measure provided $1.26 billion to continue development of the B-2 and $2.69 billion for four additional B-2 stealth bombers, completing the scaled-back force of 20 that the Air Force planned to buy.

But neither these four nor a fifth B-2, which was authorized in fiscal 1992, could be completed unless Congress voted to allow their completion after receiving reports from the Pentagon on the plane's cost and on its ability to evade radar detection. Prior to that vote, no more than $900 million of the $2.69 billion could be spent.

The House had favored allowing only $600 million to be spent before the follow-up vote, while the Senate favored allowing $1.2 billion.

Nor was that to be the end of all spending on the B-2s. To make the 20-plane force fully operational, the Air Force planned to request from Congress a total of $5.7 billion more in fiscal 1994-96.

The B-2 compromise was also included in the final version of the defense appropriations bill (HR 5504).

Bush signed the appropriations bill on Oct. 6 and the authorization bill on Oct. 23. ∎

# Scaled-Down SDI Survives Its Critics

Congress approved $3.8 billion of the $5.4 billion that President Bush requested for fiscal 1993 for the Strategic Defense Initiative (SDI).

As significant as the funding amount was the survival of the fragile consensus negotiated in 1991: to press ahead with the controversial anti-missile defense program but on a less ambitious scale than originally envisioned.

Rather than a global umbrella of defenses against intercontinental missiles, as initially advocated by President Ronald Reagan, the scaled-down SDI placed greater emphasis on early deployment of a ground-based defense system within the limits of the Anti-Ballistic Missile (ABM) Treaty of 1972.

In 1992, the House, where opposition to SDI had been strongest, rejected efforts on the floor to cut the $4.3 billion proposed for the program by the House Armed Services Committee in the fiscal 1993 defense authorization bill (HR 5006). But the House measure would have denied any funds for work on Brilliant Pebbles — small, space-based interceptors that many conservatives considered the most important part of developing a long-term anti-missile defense. Bush had sought $576 million for Brilliant Pebbles as part of the SDI total.

Sharp divisions over SDI surfaced during Senate debate over the authorization bill. In a procedural skirmish Aug. 7, the Senate signaled support for an amendment that would have cut Bush's $5.4 billion request to $3.3 billion. Sup-

porters of SDI, determined to block such deep cuts, stalled action on the defense bill for more than a month until agreement was reached on $3.8 billion.

The final version of the defense authorization bill called for $4.05 billion for SDI, including $300 million to develop space-based interceptors. But the final version of the companion defense appropriations bill (HR 5504) limited SDI funding to the $3.8 billion anticipated in the Senate compromise.

## BACKGROUND

Reagan launched SDI in 1983 with sweeping rhetoric, describing it as a method of rendering nuclear missiles "impotent and obsolete." But his vision of an impenetrable shield against Soviet attack faced opposition because of its huge cost, disputed technical feasibility and inevitable clash with the U.S.-Soviet ABM Treaty, which limited anti-missile defenses to a single ground-based site.

In 1991, Bush redefined SDI's emphasis with a program called GPALS, an acronym for "global protection against limited strikes." It was envisioned as a combination of space-based Brilliant Pebbles and ground-based missiles. Its goal was to protect U.S. territory, allies or overseas forces against relatively small attacks such as might be launched by a Third World country with short-range (or "tactical") missiles or by a renegade military unit.

The change troubled some of SDI's staunchest conservative backers but mollified some of the program's critics.

Among the sticking points, however, was that Bush's modified SDI program still would require renegotiation or repudiation of the ABM Treaty.

As part of the fiscal 1992 defense authorization bill (PL 102-190), Congress negotiated its own compromise between SDI supporters and critics. The congressional agreement excluded Brilliant Pebbles from the initial anti-missile deployment. Instead, it directed the president to deploy by 1996 a ground-based anti-missile system at a single site near Grand Forks, N.D., which would be consistent with the ABM Treaty. But the deal also called on the president to negotiate with the Soviet Union changes in the treaty to allow more extensive tests and deployments. *(1991 Almanac, p. 407)*

## BUSH PROPOSAL

At the start of 1992, Bush proposed $5.4 billion for SDI in fiscal 1993. That total included $1.06 billion for defenses against short-range missiles. The remaining $4.36 billion, for defense against long-range weapons, consisted of:

● $2.13 billion for work on a network of ground-based weapons intended to protect U.S. territory against attack by up to 200 missile warheads;

● $576 million for research on the Brilliant Pebbles space-based interceptor missiles;

● $850 million for work on more exotic defenses, such as anti-missile lasers, intended for deployment in the next century; and

● $755 million for basic research and support.

### Congressional Reaction

By the spring of 1992, the fragility of the prior year's compromise on SDI was underscored in congressional hearings. Senate Armed Services Committee Chairman Sam Nunn, D-Ga., accused the Pentagon of seeking too much money for space-based weapons while slowing deployment of the ground-based missile defense that Congress had made the program's first priority.

At an Armed Services subcommittee hearing on April 9, Nunn charged that the administration milked hundreds of millions of dollars from key elements of the ground-based system and used the funds instead for space-based programs that would not contribute to the quickly deployed defense mandated by Congress.

As a result, he said, the ground-based deployment would be unduly delayed and would be ineffective without elements barred by the ABM Treaty.

"You stuck to your old program, and we tried to lay out a congressional consensus for a new program," Nunn said to Henry Cooper, director of the SDI program. "You're betting Congress is going to come around."

Cooper responded that he had substantially reshaped his program to match the priority Congress placed on ground-based defenses.

The $576 million that the administration sought for space-based weapons in fiscal 1993 was 11 percent of the total SDI request, he pointed out, the same percentage Congress had earmarked for space weapons in the fiscal 1992 SDI appropriation.

For the longer term, Cooper said, he had boosted by $4 billion his planned funding for the initial, ground-based deployment, including $1.7 billion taken from projected spending for Brilliant Pebbles. "I'm spending $6 on [ground-based and theater defenses] for every $1 I'm spending on Brilliant Pebbles," he said.

Cooper invoked a provision of the 1991 defense bill that deferred deployment of the Republican-supported Brilliant Pebbles but provided for "robust research."

When Cooper invoked that provision, Nunn shot back, "It's more than robust. It's dominant."

Cooper estimated that it would cost $20 billion to complete development of a ground-based, limited defense system and to deploy it at one site. An additional $5 billion would be needed to beef up that system later with "Brilliant Eyes," satellites designed to detect attacking missiles and guide interceptors toward them.

Expanding the system to include five to seven ground sites, as contemplated by Bush's program, would cost an additional $10 billion.

A particularly sore point with Nunn was Cooper's decision to de-emphasize funding for the ground-based surveillance and tracking system (GSTS). This missile-borne heat sensor would be launched when attacking missiles were detected in order to guide interceptors.

Without GSTS, Nunn argued, ground-based defenses at a single site could protect only a portion of U.S. territory for years to come. "I don't think I can sell that," he said.

Cooper replied that budget limits had killed GSTS deployment but not development. He contended that there were less expensive alternatives.

In another development with an effect on SDI, the Army on April 7 scaled back its claims for success of the Patriot missile against Iraqi Scuds launched during the Persian Gulf War.

During and immediately after the war, Bush and others had claimed that Patriots — anti-aircraft weapons modified to intercept short-range missiles — had destroyed or knocked off course the vast majority of Scuds.

Those claims, coupled with dramatic televised footage of Patriots appearing to strike incoming Scuds, gave SDI a strong political boost in 1991.

But critics contended that the Army presented no data to support the claimed success rate. On April 7, 1992, Army officials told the House Government Affairs Committee that Patriots successfully engaged 70 percent of the Scuds they were fired at over Saudi Arabia (rather than the 80 percent initially claimed) and 40 percent of the Scuds fired at over Israel (rather than 50 percent).

Officials of the General Accounting Office and the Congressional Research Service testified that there were large gaps in the data the Army had used to substantiate its earlier claims.

At a hearing of the full Armed Services Committee on May 20, Nunn repeated his criticism of the administration's SDI priorities. Nunn blasted Cooper for allowing the earliest deployment date for the initial, ground-based defense to slip to 1997.

But committee Republicans, led by SDI proponent Malcolm Wallop, Wyo., defended Cooper's priorities. They emphasized that the inclusion in the fiscal 1992 defense bill of the language calling for "robust funding" of Brilliant Pebbles.

Wallop and other Republicans contended that the initial deployment should be expanded to include several ground-based sites and Brilliant Pebbles, whether or not Russia agreed to modify the ABM Treaty.

To the extent that he favored deployment of any anti-missile defense, Nunn had little alternative but to strike a deal with the GOP because most Democrats doubted such a system was urgently needed. Nunn insisted that there was a limit to how far he would go to accommodate Republicans.

"There's a common impression around here that it's my job to hold any coalition together," he said in an interview. "There's a point at which I'm ready to disengage."

## HOUSE ACTION

The House version of the defense authorization bill (HR 5006) called for $4.3 billion for SDI but would have banned any funding for Brilliant Pebbles and would have deleted the 1996 target date for deploying a ground-based system.

That funding level was set in the version of the bill that was approved, 47-8, on May 19 by the House Armed Services Committee. The full House fended off amendments to cut SDI before approving its version of the defense bill on June 5.

The Armed Services Committee also had attached to the bill an amendment by SDI skeptic Charles E. Bennett, D-Fla., identifying compliance with the ABM Treaty as a national goal.

Bennett's amendment acknowledged that the treaty could be amended. And House Armed Services Chairman Les Aspin, D-Wis., who cosponsored Bennett's amendment, repeated his view that anti-missile defenses would be essential as more countries acquired the ability to field small numbers of nuclear armed missiles. "Unless you've got defenses, you're leaving yourself open to blackmail," he said.

### Floor Debate

On the House floor, Aspin's center-right alliance defeated an amendment by Richard J. Durbin, D-Ill., that would have sliced $938 million from the committee's $4.3 billion for SDI.

Before the debate, Aspin had asked the Rules Committee to disallow consideration of Durbin's proposal. Democratic leaders refused to go that far, but they did give Aspin a tremendous advantage: The panel ruled that all potential amendments dealing with anti-missile funding would be considered under a "king-of-the-hill" procedure in which the House would vote on as many as four amendments but the only one to be adopted would be the last one to collect more "yeas" than "nays."

That gave Aspin the option of offering as the last in a series of SDI amendments one that would have reaffirmed the committee's $4.3 billion program. As the last amendment voted on, Aspin's position would have prevailed, assuming it was approved, even if Durbin's amendment had gotten a larger majority.

There was irony for Democratic liberals who found themselves on the disadvantageous end of the king-of-the-hill procedure:

It had been used by Democrats during the Reagan administration to guarantee that defense amendments that they backed prevailed even when Republicans offered alternative amendments on the same subject that were politically attractive. Members could vote for both the Republican and Democratic alternatives on a given subject, confident the latter would prevail because it held the clean-up position in the sequence of votes.

During the debate on his amendment, Durbin and his allies hammered at dissipation of the threat of a Soviet missile attack. And they discounted the immediacy of any long-range missile threat to the United States from hostile smaller countries.

"Few if any of these nations are even remotely likely to produce a long-range [missile] in the next 10 to 15 years,"

argued Timothy J. Penny, D-Minn. "There is no urgency at this time."

But proponents insisted that the United States had to start down the road to deployment.

"It's going to be 10 years before anybody gets a missile threat," Aspin told a reporter. "But it's going to be 10 years before we have [an anti-missile] system."

Durbin's amendment was rejected 161-211, but it was heavily supported by voting Democrats (149-77) and by Independent Bernard Sanders, Vt. Republicans overwhelmingly opposed the amendment (11-134). *(Vote 169, p. 42-H)*

Once the House rejected Durbin's amendment, Aspin did not offer his offsetting amendment. The bill as passed incorporated the Armed Services panel's SDI position, authorizing $4.3 billion for anti-missile defense work. This included $3.2 billion for defenses against long-range (or "strategic") missiles and $1.1 billion, the amount Bush requested, for work on defenses against short-range (or "theater") missiles. The bill sought to deny all funds requested for Brilliant Pebbles space-based missile interceptors.

The House also rejected outright, 117-248, an amendment by California Democrats Ronald V. Dellums and Barbara Boxer that would have slashed the total for anti-missile development to $2.3 billion, with $1.1 billion earmarked for theater defense work and $1.2 billion for defenses against strategic missiles. *(Vote 168, p. 42-H)*

The Dellums-Boxer amendment also would have abolished the SDI organization and repealed the legislation enacted in 1991 declaring it a national goal to deploy relatively quickly a limited, ground-based anti-missile defense that would comply with restrictions in the ABM Treaty.

## SENATE ACTION

The Senate reached a compromise of $3.8 billion in funding for SDI before passing its version of the fiscal 1993 defense authorization bill by voice vote on Sept. 19. But agreement was reached only after the bill was blocked for more than a month by SDI supporters outraged at indications the Senate was inclined to approve an amendment forcing even deeper cuts on the anti-missile program.

The Senate Armed Services Committee had approved its version of the defense authorization bill, 17-3, on July 24 after contentious debate on issues including SDI. The committee bill would have authorized $4.3 billion of the $5.4 billion requested for the program, the same amount approved by the House.

The panel also approved $2.7 billion, as requested, to buy four final B-2 bombers. *(B-2, p. 496)*

As happened in 1991, the fate of these two controversial programs became linked in the endgame bargaining within the committee:

To pressure Chairman Nunn and other centrist Democrats to boost the SDI authorization in the bill, Republicans threatened to block additional procurement of the B-2, a bomber Nunn strongly supported.

At first, Nunn proposed $4 billion for SDI, including $200 million for the space-based Brilliant Pebbles.

On July 23, three amendments that would have increased the SDI total — and Brilliant Pebbles' share of the total — were rejected by narrow margins, with the committee splitting essentially along party lines.

Then the committee approved, 11-9, an amendment by Carl Levin, D-Mich., to drop from the bill funding for the additional B-2s. Six Republicans supported the proposal.

The final deal was struck the next day, with the committee approving 14-6 an amendment by Richard C. Shelby, D-Ala., that boosted the SDI authorization to $4.3 billion, including $350 million earmarked for Brilliant Pebbles. The committee then reconsidered Levin's B-2 amendment, voting 11-9 to reinstate funding for the four B-2s.

When the dust had settled, the essential politics of the committee's SDI position seemed unchanged from 1991: Once again, a tenuous alliance of right and center had lined up behind an SDI program aimed at deploying a limited, ground-based system while deferring until the next decade any deployment of space-based anti-missile weapons.

## Floor Debate

Debate on the fiscal 1993 defense authorization bill began on Aug. 7 and then quickly came to a halt when the Senate signaled its readiness to outdo the House in cutting funding for SDI.

It was a novel twist in the conflict between the chambers over funding for SDI. For several years, the Senate had backed higher funding than the House did for the administration's controversial anti-missile defense program.

The Senate refused to kill an amendment by Budget Committee Chairman Jim Sasser, D-Tenn., to cut authorized funding for SDI to $3.3 billion, $1 billion less than the amount approved in June by the House.

Sasser's amendment would have cut funding for the initial limited, ground-based defense to $1.5 billion, compared with the $2.13 billion requested and the $2.09 billion included in the Senate Armed Services Committee's version of the bill.

A motion by John W. Warner, R-Va., to table (kill) Sasser's SDI-cutting amendment failed, 43-49. *(Vote 182, p. 24-S)*

Proponents contended that the rationale for SDI had collapsed with the demise of the Soviet Union.

Sasser denounced SDI's promise of a defense against missile attack as a "scam" akin to "meteor insurance" for a private home. "We bought it in a moment of Cold War panic," he said. "We're stuck paying the premium."

But he insisted that the amendment was not an effort to kill SDI. "We've lost that battle," he said. "What I'm trying to do is impose some budgetary sense on the SDI program."

Wallop, the Senate's leading backer of a large-scale SDI defense, attacked the amendment as a veiled effort to kill the program by stretching it out and driving up the cost. "The amendment would effectively deny Americans even a limited defense," he said.

Nunn told the Senate, "If we're serious" about deploying a limited defense anytime soon, "we must fund the program at the level recommended."

## Measure Stalls

During the week of Aug. 10, Wallop threw up a procedural roadblock to resumed debate on the defense authorization bill, vowing to prevent the Senate from proceeding to a vote on Sasser's amendment to cut SDI funding.

Wallop, who had little vocal support from other Republicans, remained unapologetic about his dilatory tactics. "This is not a debate that needs to be ended because we have a summer recess," he said Aug. 10. "This is a debate that ought to be carried on in full in front of the American people."

Sasser refused to let the Senate dispose of other amendments on the bill until his was resolved. Hence the impasse.

The defense bill was pulled from the floor with a warning from Armed Services Chairman Nunn that there might not be time to finish it when Congress reconvened in September. If that happened, Nunn said, there would be a stopgap appropriations bill that would gut key programs and prohibit most of the post-Cold War "defense conversion" initiatives contained in the authorization bill. *(Conversion, p. 509)*

"This may be the year we all go over the cliff," Nunn said Aug. 12.

To reinforce the case for moving on with the authorization bill, Nunn, Defense Appropriations Subcommittee Chairman Daniel K. Inouye, D-Hawaii, and full Senate Appropriations Chairman Robert C. Byrd, D-W.Va., warned on Aug. 12 of alarming consequences if, because of an impasse over SDI, the Pentagon was funded by a stopgap spending bill after the new fiscal year began Oct. 1.

Under the usual rules governing such a "continuing resolution," Inouye said, no new projects could be started, nor would programs be funded that Congress had added to the administration's budget request.

As an example, Inouye pointed to the Mississippi-built helicopter carrier in Nunn's bill, "sought by Sens. [Trent] Lott and [Thad] Cochran," uncharacteristically identifying the two GOP senators from that state who requested the ships.

"You're talking about tens of thousands of jobs here," Nunn said. "I don't believe [Wallop and his potential allies] realize how close to the cliff we are."

## Finding a Compromise

Yielding by a narrow margin to threats of a veto, the Senate backed down Sept. 17 from the effort to slash SDI funding.

The action came as the Senate returned to the fiscal 1993 defense authorization bill that had been in limbo for more than a month.

With SDI backers blocking final action on any bill cutting the anti-missile program as much as Sasser's amendment — and the administration backing them up with a veto threat — Nunn and his allies engineered a compromise to authorize $3.8 billion for SDI research.

After rejecting Sasser's amendment 48-50, the Senate adopted Nunn's alternative by a vote of 52-46. *(Votes 214, 215, p. 28-S)*

The key to the compromise was the leverage that Nunn and Warner got from the companion defense appropriations measure.

Defense Appropriations Subcommittee Chairman Inouye and senior subcommittee Republican Ted Stevens, Alaska, told Nunn and Warner that they could line up a majority of the Appropriations panel behind a compromise SDI research figure of $3.8 billion. And the White House indicated that it could live with that amount.

The scenario began to play out the morning of Sept. 17, when the Appropriations Committee approved a defense bill (HR 5504) including $3.8 billion for SDI research. *(Appropriations, p. 592)*

But the panel nearly bogged down in the same quagmire that had stalled Senate action on the authorization bill.

The Appropriations Committee's $3.8 billion budget for SDI was recommended by Inouye, who said that $3.8 billion was "a more fiscally acceptable level" than Bush's request.

In a bid to mollify Republican SDI backers, Inouye and Stevens made the appropriation a lump sum, giving the

administration free rein to allocate reductions among parts of the program.

But Sasser once again offered an amendment to reduce SDI to $3.3 billion. Besides noting the support for that position in the Senate, Sasser cited a report the previous day by the General Accounting Office (GAO) alleging that SDI officials had exaggerated the success of several tests.

Stevens countered with a warning that the appropriations bill would be deadlocked, like the authorization measure, if it did not provide at least $3.8 billion for SDI.

A motion to table Sasser's amendment was rejected 14-14. But the amendment then failed by the same vote. The committee went on to approve the appropriations bill, 26-0.

That night, the Senate returned to the long-stalled authorization bill. Nunn cited the Appropriations action as "a rather significant change in the atmosphere."

Sasser dismissed the Appropriations action as a dead heat. He and his ally, Dale Bumpers, D-Ark., insisted that their case was buttressed by the GAO report. "The failures of tests of SDI have either been hidden or misrepresented," Sasser declared. "Perhaps that $3.3 billion ... is too generous."

Characterizing SDI expenditures thus far as "$30 billion down a rat hole," J. Bennett Johnston, D-La., urged his colleagues not to be cowed by Bush's threat to veto any defense bill providing less than $3.8 billion for SDI research. "If it takes a veto and staying here in October [to achieve a larger SDI cut], we ought to do it," Johnston declared.

For their part, backers of the higher amount virtually sat out the debate, although Nunn pointedly reminded his colleagues of a long list of politically attractive programs in the defense bill that he said were at risk if the measure perished. He said these included initiatives aimed at softening the impact of defense cutbacks on communities and individuals as well as "the large number of military construction projects affecting virtually every state in the union."

Nunn and Warner had agreed that success for their $3.8 billion compromise hinged on assembling a switch list of Democrats and Republicans who had initially supported the deeper SDI cut sought by Sasser. And they agreed that the Sasser amendment would have to be rejected by a wide enough margin that no single senator would have to weather the wrath of SDI foes.

For the sake of breaking the impasse on the authorization bill, Democrats Bob Graham, Fla., and David L. Boren, Okla., and Kansas Republican Nancy Landon Kassebaum — all Sasser allies in August — had agreed to follow Nunn and Warner this time.

But the carefully choreographed strategy nearly came apart when Larry Pressler, R-S.D., who had opposed Sasser in August, switched the other way, voting for the $3.3 billion amendment. Pressler said he had been swayed by the GAO's criticism of SDI officials.

Taking account of absent senators, that set the stage for a 49-49 tie vote — which would have killed Sasser's amendment, but increased the potential political heat on Kassebaum and the others.

Nunn turned to Charles S. Robb, D-Va. Though he had opposed previous efforts to cut SDI funding, Robb supported Sasser's amendment in August on the grounds that the program was moving too quickly toward deployment of anti-missile weapons. But before floor debate resumed in September, he had assured Nunn that he would vote for a higher funding level if needed to get the defense bill passed.

Side by side in front of the Senate dais, Robb and Kassebaum briefly conferred and then both voted against Sasser's amendment, which thus was rejected 48-50.

The Senate passed the defense authorization bill by voice vote on Sept. 19.

## FINAL ACTION

The final version of the defense authorization bill (HR 5006) that was hammered out by a House-Senate conference committee called for $4.05 billion in funding for SDI, compared with Bush's request for $5.4 billion.

The conferees split the difference between the $4.3 billion agreed to by the House and the $3.8 billion that was so painfully negotiated in the Senate.

The House approved the conference report, 304-100, on Oct. 3. *(Vote 461, p. 112-H)*

The Senate gave its approval by voice vote the same day, although the end-of-session paperwork jam delayed the official approval until Oct. 5.

Despite the $4.05 billion in the authorization bill, the Senate compromise on $3.8 billion for SDI ultimately prevailed because that amount was included in the final version of the companion appropriations measure (HR 5006).

In presenting the conference report on that bill, Inouye told the Senate, "$3.8 billion is the amount we pledged, and it is the amount we delivered."

The House adopted the conference report on the appropriations bill by voice vote Oct. 5, and the Senate followed suit the same day.

Bush signed the appropriations bill (PL 102-396) on Oct. 6 and the authorization bill (PL 102-484) on Oct. 23. ∎

# Congress Funds *Seawolf* Development

The fall and rise of the *Seawolf* submarine vividly demonstrated the concerns — both global and hometown — that protected most major defense programs from deep cuts in 1992.

In the administration's fiscal 1993 budget, President Bush proposed canceling all but the first of this projected class of ships.

But Congress insisted that at least one more of the nuclear-powered subs be built. That position drew political strength from members whose constituents worked in the Connecticut shipyard where the sub was built, and it gained a military rationale from concern that the United States would lose the "industrial base" needed to make underwater vessels to combat some future threat.

Bush's effort to rescind previously appropriated *Seawolf* funding was revised to permit a second *Seawolf* to be built, and Congress included $150 million for the submarine's continued development in the fiscal 1993 defense appropriations bill (HR 5006). *(Appropriations, p. 592)*

The *Seawolf* (SSN-21) was proposed by the Navy in 1982 as a highly sophisticated replacement for the *Los Angeles*-class submarine (SSN-688), which was scheduled

to be phased out by 1997.

The *Seawolf* was designed to be quieter and faster than the *Los Angeles* and to carry twice as many weapons. But the *Seawolf*, with a price tag estimated as high as $2 billion per sub, was criticized as superfluous with the demise of the Soviet threat that it was intended to combat.

As part of the administration's defense cutback in 1991, the Navy already had scaled back its initial plan to buy three *Seawolfs* a year. Instead, the plan had been to purchase one *Seawolf* a year through fiscal 1995, and then six more through fiscal 1999. The Navy also wanted to introduce a newer, less expensive submarine, known as the *Centurion*, by fiscal 1998.

### Pre-Emptive Lobbying

In January, 1992, word that Bush was about to go after the *Seawolf* in his proposed budget sparked an energetic lobbying campaign by the congressional delegations from Connecticut and neighboring Rhode Island.

The submarine was built in Groton, Conn., by the Electric Boat division of General Dynamics. The company, which was the largest employer in Rhode Island and the second largest in Connecticut, said it needed to build one new *Seawolf* a year to stay in operation. Even then, the company planned to let go half of its 21,500 workers by 1997.

In a Jan. 8 letter to Defense Secretary Dick Cheney, Sen. Christopher J. Dodd, D, and five other members of the Connecticut congressional delegation said that terminating the *Seawolf* program would do "incalculable damage" to the nation's ability to design and build submarines. "The eventual cost of this hasty termination would far outweigh any potential, short-term dollar savings," they wrote.

Besides costing jobs, advocates for the sub argued, canceling the *Seawolf* would undermine the national defense by forcing the shutdown of one of only two U.S. shipyards that built nuclear-powered submarines.

"If you're going to be able to produce these submarines, you've got to have a steady flow and a predicted flow," said Sen. John H. Chafee, R-R.I., a former secretary of the Navy. "It's not a matter of turning on or off the faucet."

But John McCain, R-Ariz., who led an unsuccessful attack against the submarine in the Senate in 1991, said he was confident that "lack of administration support would end the program." *(1991 Almanac, p. 635)*

Critics emphasized flaws in the *Seawolf* program. Welding problems discovered during construction of the first *Seawolf* threatened to delay its completion as much as a year past the 1995 target. With about $6 billion approved by 1992 for procurement of the *Seawolf*, and only one partially constructed, opponents said it was difficult to justify the additional expense.

"It's a little quieter, a little faster, can go a little deeper and carries more weapons. But when you put it all together, it is not worth the cost," said Norman Polmar, a naval author and outspoken critic of the sub.

He and many others argued that the Navy should keep open the production line for the lower-cost *Los Angeles* instead until the next-generation sub could be built.

But the Navy and the *Seawolf's* supporters argued that the older SSN-688 had no more capacity for improvements to meet any expanded military threat.

"They're kidding themselves," said naval analyst Norman Friedman. "Any attempt to make a cheaper submarine will result in a crummier submarine that will cost as much."

### Bush's Proposal

The budget that Bush proposed anticipated $2.2 billion, enough to complete the single *Seawolf* that won initial funding in 1989. He proposed rescinding $3.4 billion in funds that were appropriated in fiscal 1991 and 1992 for two additional ships.

By March, even the most ardent backers of the *Seawolf* set their sights on salvaging contracts for, at most, two more vessels beyond the one already under construction. Some said that it would be an uphill fight to save just one more.

With their expectations downsized, proponents of the submarine said several developments bolstered their case:

● A federal appeals court March 17 upheld the Navy's decision in 1991 to award the contract for the second *Seawolf* to General Dynamics' Electric Boat Division in Groton, Conn., where the first of the subs was under construction. Newport News Shipbuilding and Dry Dock Co., a division of Tenneco Inc. and the only other U.S. shipyard capable of building nuclear-powered submarines, had filed suit over the contract. The Virginia shipbuilder argued that the Navy had not given enough consideration to the economic impact that loss of the contract would have on Newport News.

● An internal Navy document, written by Adm. Bruce DeMars, director of the naval nuclear propulsion program, strongly endorsed the need for the United States to maintain its nuclear shipbuilding capacity and called Electric Boat "the world's premier resource for submarine design and construction technology."

DeMars said the next-best option to the *Seawolf* would be to resume building the improved *Los Angeles*-class submarine to bridge the gap until production of a next-generation submarine could begin, probably by the end of the decade. "With an extended hiatus in submarine construction, it is difficult to see how nuclear-powered submarine design and construction skills could survive," DeMars wrote.

● The chairmen of the House and Senate Defense Appropriations subcommittees, which were to consider Bush's proposal to rescind funding for the second and third *Seawolfs*, also indicated support.

John P. Murtha, D-Pa., chairman of the House subcommittee, told Electric Boat backers from Connecticut and Rhode Island on March 12 that if they could show that the costs of canceling the submarine "are excessive," his committee "would be very willing to take that into consideration and, I'm sure, would support an additional production, if it's cost-effective."

Daniel K. Inouye, D-Hawaii, chairman of the Senate subcommittee, said in an interview on March 18 that he was "going to do what I can to fight the rescission." He said he would try to get funding for at least one more *Seawolf*.

"Frankly, I think we're in a stronger position than we were a few weeks ago," said Rep. Sam Gejdenson, D-Conn.

One other bright sign for *Seawolf* supporters: Paul Tsongas announced March 19 that he was dropping his presidential bid, guaranteeing Bill Clinton the Democratic nomination. Clinton had said he favored building one or two more *Seawolfs*, a position Tsongas criticized as "pandering" to Connecticut voters.

### The Rescissions

In March, Bush sent Congress a list of 68 rescissions totaling $3.6 billion. The White House portrayed the cuts in previously approved spending as a broad assault on pork

barrel spending by lawmakers. But the bulk of the cuts — $2.77 billion — were to come from cancellation of the second and third vessels of the *Seawolf*-class, which in past years had the administration's full support. *(Enhanced rescissions, p. 114)*

The White House list of rescissions grew to $5.7 billion by April, when the House Appropriations Committee countered by drafting its own package of $5.8 billion in proposed cuts.

The House appropriators insisted on preserving funding for one of the two *Seawolfs* that Bush had asked Congress to kill. The Defense Appropriations subcommittee opted to preserve $1 billion for that submarine while cutting $1.9 billion that had been appropriated for another.

The House Appropriations Committee formally approved its counter-proposal of $5.8 billion in rescissions by voice vote on April 29. The panel made up for the $1 billion in *Seawolf* spending by proposing $1.7 billion in cuts in defense research, development, testing and evaluation.

On April 30, the Senate Appropriations Committee voted, 19-9, to approve an $8.3 billion package of spending cuts. Unlike the House committee's version, the bill also responded to a final installment of rescissions proposed by Bush, which brought his rescissions package to a total of $7.9 billion.

The Senate committee voted to preserve not just one but both of the *Seawolf* submarines that Bush sought to cancel.

The strong lobbying by New England members of Congress to save jobs in their region was not mentioned by the appropriators, whose members cited instead the arcane economics of defense contracting.

House Defense Appropriations Subcommittee Chairman Murtha said the money already spent on the second *Seawolf,* plus what it would cost to terminate that contract, made it wasteful not to go ahead and build the sub. He argued, though, that building a third sub would not make sense.

His Senate counterpart, Inouye, said that all the costs of terminating the *Seawolf* contracts and ending construction could reach $4.4 billion — much more than the nearly $3 billion required to keep building the subs.

But some senators protested the trade-offs, such as proposed cuts in spending for the Strategic Defense Initiative, that the committee came up with to permit the *Seawolf* program to continue.

The rescission packages went to the floors of both chambers the week of May 4. Democrats kept tight control of the debate and the outcome:

● By a 61-38 vote on May 6, the Senate approved an $8.3 billion rescission package (S 2403) that left in place nearly $3 billion for programs that Bush sought to cut — including funding for two *Seawolf* submarines. Instead, the bill substituted cuts in the Strategic Defense Initiative, the B-2 bomber program and other defense projects backed by the administration. *(Vote 85, p. 12-S)*

● By a 412-2 vote on May 7, the House approved a $5.8 billion rescission package (HR 4990) that protected funding for one *Seawolf,* substituting cuts in research, development, testing and evaluation, and various weapons programs.

The vote on final passage was not a true test of House sentiment, however. An earlier vote on whether to substitute Bush's rescissions for those approved by the House Appropriations Committee split largely along party lines, 150-266. *(Votes 112, 113, p. 28-H)*

The House and Senate totals differed because the House considered only three of the four rescission packages Bush sent to Congress, deferring action on a fourth until a House-Senate conference.

The administration issued stern warnings that the Senate bill would be veto bait if left unchanged. While it objected to the House bill, the administration issued no veto threat against it, and House Appropriations' ranking Republican Joseph M. McDade, R-Pa., said he thought Bush would sign the measure if it were presented to him in that form.

The Senate's vote on *Seawolf* funding was decisive but not overwhelming. After heavy lobbying by Connecticut and Rhode Island senators, the Senate rejected, by a 46-52 vote, an amendment by McCain that would have restored Bush's proposal to cut nearly $3 billion to build two more of the subs. *(Vote 83, p. 12-S)*

"We literally cannot afford to live in the past," said McCain, arguing that the *Seawolf* was designed to counter a Russian nuclear submarine threat that no longer existed. Instead, he said, the submarines' enormous costs would rob resources and jobs from other, more vital areas of defense production.

But Senate Defense Appropriations Chairman Inouye argued that the combined costs of equipment already purchased, charges for canceling the construction contracts and federal expenses for shutting down the shipyards could run from $3.4 billion to $4.4 billion, exceeding the amount that Bush proposed to save. "There is no savings whatsoever," Inouye said.

Even if McCain had won, it apparently wouldn't have mattered. Appropriations Chairman Robert C. Byrd, D-W.Va., already had guaranteed an unamended final bill when he used a parliamentary maneuver to ensure that any amendment that passed would have been wiped out by later passage of his own substitute.

**Final Action**

In the end, Congress opted to save one of the two *Seawolf* submarines that Bush had proposed to cut.

Congress' $8.2 billion package of proposals to rescind previously approved spending (HR 4990), most of it in defense, exceeded the $7.9 billion in rescissions that Bush asked for, but it changed many of the targets of the budget ax.

House-Senate conferees compromised between the House position calling for money to build one more of the subs and the Senate effort to protect funds for two more.

The final legislation cut $1.3 billion. That left roughly $1.7 billion, more than enough to finish building the second submarine.

Conferees agreed to set aside $550 million of that on the condition that the secretary of Defense use it to start building a third *Seawolf,* restart production of *Los Angeles*-class submarines, or otherwise protect the industrial base for submarine construction.

Approval of the conference report reconciling House and Senate rescission bills (H Rept 102-530) came May 21 in votes of 404-11 in the House and 90-9 in the Senate. *(House vote 137, p. 34-H; Senate vote 108, p. 15-S)*

President Bush signed the rescissions bill (PL 102-298) on June 4.

Confirming Congress' determination to keep the *Seawolf* project alive, lawmakers included in the fiscal 1993 defense appropriations bill (HR 5006 — PL 102-396) $150 million for continued development of the submarine. ■

# Cheney's Bargain With Hill Keeps Osprey Production

Prospects for the V-22 Osprey may not have appeared good in 1992, at least at first glance. The hybrid craft — designed to take off and land like a helicopter but fly like a conventional airplane — had been opposed since 1989 by Defense Secretary Dick Cheney.

Therefore, the proposed Marine transport plane would have seemed an obvious target in a year of defense budget-cutting. Nor were its prospects enhanced by the untimely crash of a prototype in the Potomac River near Washington on July 20, killing four Marines and three civilians. The accident received prominent play on the local television newscasts watched by members of Congress.

But politically, at least, the Osprey proved unsinkable because of its strong base of support in Pennsylvania and Texas, where its prime contractors were located. With President Bush campaigning for re-election, Cheney switched gears on July 2, weeks before the prototype's crash. The Defense secretary offered to proceed with development of the V-22 — without committing to eventual production. In return, he asked Congress to approve $10 million to begin designing a conventional helicopter as an alternative. And Bush's Democratic opponent, Bill Clinton, endorsed development of the Osprey, describing it as valuable for the types of missions the military would undertake in the aftermath of the Cold War.

Congress funded Cheney's bargain, including $755 million for the Osprey and $10 million for the alternative helicopter in the fiscal 1993 defense appropriations bill (HR 5504 — PL 102-396). The House version of that bill had included the $755 million for the V-22 but not the $10 million for development of an alternative. The Senate, anticipating the compromise that emerged in the House-Senate conference committee, provided for the opposite: Its version had omitted the $755 million for the Osprey but included the $10 million for the alternative.

The V-22 was also authorized in the companion fiscal 1993 defense authorization bill (HR 5006 — PL 102-484), although the final version of that measure adopted Senate-passed language prohibiting the Pentagon from spending more than half of the $755 million until the Marines reported to Congress on the July crash of the prototype.

## BACKGROUND

The Osprey was a "tilt-rotor" craft, shaped much like a conventional airplane, except that at each wingtip a large engine drove a huge propeller. At takeoff, the engines were positioned vertically so that the spinning propellers acted as helicopter rotors, pulling the plane aloft.

Once the craft was in the air, the engines swiveled to a horizontal position, the props pulled the craft forward and the wings kept it airborne in conventional flight. The engines pivoted once again to a vertical position for a helicopter-style landing.

For a decade, the Marines' procurement priority had been been replacing its CH-46 troop carriers from Vietnam War era. The Marine brass eagerly sought Ospreys that could fly nearly twice as fast — 300 mph — while carrying 24 fully equipped infantrymen ashore from transport ships.

Despite the Marines' enthusiasm, however, Cheney con-

cluded soon after taking office that the $30 billion price tag to develop the Osprey and to buy more than 500 was too steep. But Congress forced him to keep the program going by authorizing and appropriating funds in the annual defense bills.

Some members of Congress argued that the tilt-rotor technology deserved federal support because it held great promise for civil aviation. For many, the appeal was in the jobs the project produced, particularly in Pennsylvania and Texas, two states with large and influential congressional delegations.

The district of House Armed Services Committee member Curt Weldon, R-Pa., southwest of Philadelphia, was the home of Boeing Corp.'s Vertol division, one of the Osprey's two main contractors. The second was Textron's Bell Helicopter division in Fort Worth.

## CHENEY'S COMPROMISE

Congress geared up for another year of conflict with Cheney over funding for the Osprey. In its version of the annual defense authorization bill, the House Armed Services Committee not only included $755 million for three Ospreys, it also ordered Cheney to spend $790 million for three that had been authorized in fiscal 1992 — and proposed reducing the staff of the Pentagon controller by 5 percent for each month that Cheney did not obligate the money.

But Cheney sought a truce. On July 2, he offered to build more Ospreys and to lay the groundwork for eventual production — without committing to it — if Congress would give him more flexibility in spending the $790 million previously appropriated for the program and if it would let him solicit bids on helicopters that might be used for the troop-lift job.

Weldon dismissed the allocation of funds to design an alternative helicopter as "nothing more than a face-saver for the Pentagon." But at least one company had been grooming a horse for that race.

The Connecticut-based Sikorsky Helicopter division of United Technologies had proposed combining a large fuselage with the proven power plant of its H-60 helicopter, which served as the Army's Blackhawk troop carrier and the Navy's LAMPS sub-hunter.

This new S-92 helicopter would be slower and have a shorter range than the Osprey. But the Pentagon also reduced the speed and range specifications that were to be used to evaluate aircraft competing for the Marine troop-lift mission.

However, Weldon heatedly warned that Osprey backers on Capitol Hill would fight any effort to move the goal posts. "We're not going to let [the Pentagon] back off on performance requirements the Marines established 10 years ago," he said.

## AFTER THE CRASH

One of the five Osprey prototypes had been destroyed in a June 1991 crash that caused no fatalities. In the more serious 1992 crash, the Osprey crashed into the Potomac River while preparing to land at the Marine air base at Quantico, Va.

Pentagon spokesman Pete Williams told reporters July 21 that the crash "raises serious questions about the V-22 program." But he also said that Cheney was sticking with the compromise he proposed to Congress July 2.

While lamenting the deaths, Osprey backers contended that such accidents were the price of developing a revolutionary aircraft such as the V-22.

"I'm not reading any negative impact among the members," Weldon said July 22.

"Tough as it is, these things happen," said House Defense Appropriations Subcommittee Chairman John P. Murtha, D-Pa. "Unless they find some fundamental fault [in the aircraft's design], I don't think it'll change many minds in Congress."

But one influential backer, House Armed Services Committee Chairman Les Aspin, D-Wis., spoke of buying about 50 of the craft — only a tenth of the production originally contemplated — to use in special missions. Aspin's opinion seemed even weightier when he was named secretary of Defense by President Clinton in 1993. ■

# Pentagon Told To Rethink Aircraft Roles

Congress approved $5.1 billion of the $6 billion that President Bush requested for combat aircraft in fiscal 1993. But lawmakers signaled their concern that the Pentagon was committing too much money to develop too many tactical planes in an effort to fulfill the wish lists of each service.

Congress approved $683 million for a last batch of 24 F-16 fighters that Bush sought for the Air Force. It also approved $1.3 billion for 36 F/A-18s, which the Navy used as both fighter and ground attack planes, compared with the $1.8 billion that Bush requested for 48 of the planes.

For new planes in development, Bush requested $2.2 billion for the Air Force's new F-22 fighter, $1.1 billion for a larger version of the F/A-18 and $166 million for a stealthy, carrier-borne bomber designated AX that was intended for use by both the Navy and Air Force. In the fiscal 1993 defense appropriations bill (HR 5504 — PL 102-396), Congress ultimately provided $2 billion for the F-22, $944 million for the enlarged F/A-18 and $166 million for the AX.

But after the House and Senate came up with conflicting lists of which planes to fund fully and which to cut, conferees crafting the final version of the fiscal 1993 defense authorization bill (HR 5006 — PL 102-484) settled instead for a demand that the Pentagon justify its plans.

The measure held back some of the funds for development of the new aircraft until the Pentagon submitted to Congress an analysis of the future "roles and missions" of the armed services and of the long-term cost of the aircraft programs. The Pentagon had plans under way to spend $350 billion over two decades on the new generation of combat aircraft.

## BACKGROUND

As the House Armed Services Committee prepared to draft the annual defense authorization bill in the spring, Committee Chairman Les Aspin, D-Wis., sent the Pentagon an early warning signal: He hinted that he might trim the spending request for the Air Force's new F-22 fighter.

Other critics had been questioning the Navy's plan to develop a larger version of the F/A-18 already in service. At the same time, Aspin and others wanted the Navy to move with more urgency in developing the AX, a new long-range, ground-attack plane for carriers.

The F-22 and the modified F/A-18 (designated the "E" and "F" models) were the largest conventional arms programs in the Air Force and Navy research and development requests for fiscal 1993.

Aspin did not emphasize it in the Armed Services Committee's April 29 hearing on tactical aircraft modernization plans, but the key assumption underlying his critique of the plan was that all of the Pentagon's tactical aircraft programs — Navy and Air Force — should be viewed as part of a package.

One politically explosive implication of that viewpoint was that if Congress deemed the Navy's AX budget too stingy, it could fatten it by drawing funds — either in fiscal 1993 or over the long run — not only from the Navy's F/A-18E/F but also from the Air Force's F-22. Congress rarely had attempted that kind of explicit, interservice funding transfer on a significant scale involving major weapons.

At the April 29 hearing, Navy and Air Force leaders summarized their plans to replace over 20 years their melange of tactical aircraft, a category that included combat planes other than long-range bombers such as the B-1 and B-2. They were planning two new types for each service:

● The F-22, successor to the F-15 as the Air Force's premier air-to-air fighter. The F-22 program suffered a damaging and embarrassing setback when the only flying prototype crashed and burned during testing at Edwards Air Force Base in California on April 25.

● The "multirole fighter," a less expensive plane, not yet selected, that would replace the smaller F-16 in Air Force service.

● The F/A-18E and F/A-18F, substantially enlarged versions of F/A-18 models used by the Navy and Marine Corps as both fighters and ground-attack planes.

● The AX, intended to carry up to six tons of bombs for several hundreds of miles and to find ground targets at night or in bad weather.

Aspin singled out the AX as the most urgently needed. The A-6Es of 1960s vintage that served as the Navy's long-range bombers were aging, and the search for a replacement was set back by nearly a decade when the A-12 bomber was canceled in 1991 because of cost increases and technical flaws. (1991 Almanac, p. 431)

Under the Pentagon timetable, the first of the new generation of combat planes to enter service were to be the F-22 and the F/A-18E/F, both slated for production starting in 1996. By contrast, AX production was not to start until 2002 at the earliest, when the average A-6E would be more than 30 years old.

At the hearing, Aspin challenged those priorities, contending that the political transformation of the nations of the former Soviet Union eliminated the possibility of Russia's aircraft industry quickly spawning sophisticated new fighter designs that could outstrip the F-15 and F-16.

Accordingly, he contended, the most pressing need was to retool the Navy's creaking bomber force. "Although we had a lot of fighters and enough deep-strike aircraft overall to do the job" in the Persian Gulf War, he said, "the

number and age of the Navy's attack aircraft could limit some operations in the future."

In an April 28 speech to a defense industry association, Aspin cited the F-22 as a potential "silver bullet," an extremely capable weapon that could be purchased in small numbers for use in operations in which its unique — and costly — high-tech qualities would give U.S. forces critical leverage.

Aspin did not elaborate, but the implication was that he might favor far fewer than the 648 F-22s that the Air Force planned to buy for a total of $75 billion.

But in the April 29 House hearing, Air Force Chief of Staff Gen. Merrill A. McPeak, a career fighter pilot who still flew F-15s to stay in practice, defended his service's plan to field the F-22 by the end of the 1990s.

McPeak told the House panel that Soviet-built Su-27s and MiG-29s already matched the F-15 for sheer aerodynamic virtuosity, although superior electronic gear and pilot training gave U.S. forces a big edge.

In addition, he argued, the F-22's radar-evading stealthiness and its ability to cruise at supersonic speed without using fuel-hungry afterburners were needed to let the Air Force take the battle to the enemy. "Our idea of air superiority . . . is that we fight in the other guy's airspace," he said. "We're not going to be able to take the F-15 into hostile airspace in 2010. We didn't take it to Baghdad."

The $5 billion effort to develop the larger E and F versions of the F/A-18 also faced criticism.

When the A-12 program collapsed and budget pressures stifled the Navy's plan to develop its own version of the new Air Force fighter (ultimately, the F-22), the Navy was left with no plan to replace the fighters and ground attack planes that would wear out before the AX was ready for service.

The enlarged F/A-18 was intended both to fend off any shortfall in carrier-based combat jets and, for the longer haul, to complement the AX as a versatile strike fighter, able to take on targets on the ground or in the air. Compared with the models already in service, the new F/A-18s would have a fuselage about 4 feet longer, wings about 4 feet wider and more powerful engines intended to let the plane carry a larger weapons payload farther.

On April 29, Armed Services member George J. Hochbrueckner, D-N.Y., scoffed that the ostensibly modified design was "essentially . . . a new airplane. . . . That's why it's going to take four to five years to develop."

By contrast, he insisted, the F-14s built near his Long Island district by Grumman Corp. and already in service, could easily be adapted to the strike fighter role with no costly redesign.

Adm. Jerome L. Johnson, vice chief of naval operations, dismissed this suggestion with the same argument that Pentagon brass had used against Hochbrueckner's several previous proposals to either continue F-14 production or to upgrade existing planes with more powerful engines and electronics: Navy leaders deemed the F-14 too expensive to operate compared with the more modern F/A-18.

Besides faulting the Pentagon's aircraft-modernization plan for its priorities, Aspin also complained April 29 that the projected total cost of $350 billion over 20 years was far more than could be borne by the relatively stringent defense budgets in prospect.

McPeak and Johnson each argued that the cost each year of his branch's aircraft-modernization program would not exceed the amount that had been spent annually for tactical aircraft procurement in recent decades.

But Aspin insisted that the end of the Cold War rendered irrelevant any comparisons with the budgets of the past few decades. "The defense budget is going to be a lot lower than it was during any time you guys are looking at," he warned. "We're not going to have the average [airplane budget] for 1980-93."

## HOUSE ACTION

Aspin's proposal to speed development of the AX and hold back work on other new combat planes was reflected in the defense authorization bill (HR 5006) that was approved by the House Armed Services Committee, 47-8, on May 13 and passed by the full House, 198-168, on June 5.

Making the point that traditional ways of thinking about the defense budget would have to be challenged, the measure incorporated a plan crafted by Aspin and senior committee Republican Bill Dickinson of Alabama.

Under the approach in the House bill, the top priority would be fielding the AX to replace the Navy's venerable A-6E. The Persian Gulf War "put in sharp relief the Navy's need for a longer-range, capable new attack plane," the Armed Services Committee said.

The House sought to increase the $166 million requested for the AX to $741 million. Partly to pay for the AX, the measure would have slashed to $599 million the $1.1 billion requested to develop enlarged E and F models of the F/A-18.

The House also trimmed $200 million from the $2.2 billion requested to develop the Air Force's new F-22 fighter. This was largely to dramatize the argument that similar weapons should compete for funds, regardless of which branch of the armed services sponsors them.

The House bill called for $615 million for 24 F-16 fighters, as requested. But the committee earmarked $68 million for components to be used in additional F-16s in fiscal 1994, spurning the administration's request to use that amount to close down F-16 production. The panel ordered the Air Force to continue buying small lots of the plane, partly as a hedge against problems with the F-22.

Pentagon spokesman Pete Williams said May 14 that the committee's effort to accelerate the AX was risky. "There's no need to rush it," he said, because the Navy planned to use F/A-18s as an interim replacement for A-6Es. But the House panel took a dim view of that plan because the F/A-18 had no stealth qualities and had a relatively short range when carrying a full bombload.

Furthermore, Navy officials contended that fatter budgets could not speed AX development. But the committee disagreed: With the Soviet threat gone, the panel argued, the AX could be designed by using stealth principles already in hand. By contrast, the A-12 carrier bomber, which was canceled early in 1991 because of cost and design problems, was to have been much stealthier than the B-2 or other existing aircraft. One practical effect of the committee's position was that, of five designs entered in the AX competition, one based on the F-22 and another based on the A-12 could have a leg up.

The House's tactical aircraft package reflected a new approach to weapons procurement in a period when the Soviet threat evaporated and Pentagon budgets were headed downward. The Armed Services Committee called for extensive testing of prototypes to wring out problems before signing up for full production of a complex new weapon.

"The practice of the past has been to develop and buy

successive new generations of weapons, each fast on the heels of the preceding one," the committee said. "This no longer makes sense in the post-Soviet world."

The committee ordered the Navy to test prototypes before moving to production of either the AX or the new F/A-18 models.

Arguing that the F/A-18E and F would be "fairly minor" modifications of the existing models, the Pentagon's Williams objected to the panel's insistence on prototype testing. "It's not like we're starting over again," he said. "There's nothing fundamentally new in the design."

That view was echoed by many members from Missouri and Massachusetts, where the F/A-18's airframe and engines, respectively, were built.

But the priorities set by Aspin were not universally approved. The House Defense Appropriations subcommittee marked up a version of the annual defense appropriations bill on June 18 that approved the Navy's requests for F/A-18 and AX funding. The panel also added $225 million to the bill to upgrade existing F-14 Navy fighters. The administration contended that it could not afford that project, but it was avidly backed by the Grumman Corp. and by members of the New York congressional delegation.

The appropriations bill, which the House passed 328-94 on July 2, adopted the same funding levels for the Air Force's F-22 and F-16 as did the companion authorization bill.

## SENATE ACTION

The Senate version of the defense authorization bill, as crafted by Armed Services Committee Chairman Sam Nunn, D-Ga., also attempted to force the Pentagon to narrow its menu of new combat planes.

The measure was approved by the Armed Services Committee, 17-3, on July 24 and passed by the full Senate by voice vote on Sept. 19.

"The department's current plans are unaffordable, reflect inadequate coordination of parallel service requirements and do not reflect a thorough assessment of roles and missions," Nunn's committee wrote.

But the Senate chose different priorities for a scaled-back tactical aircraft program. In particular, its version did not reflect the House's enthusiasm for shifting resources in order to encourage rapid development of the AX.

The Senate approved only $50 million of the $166 million requested to develop that new, long-range stealthy bomber.

On the other hand, the Senate approved $944 million of the $1.1 billion requested to develop the larger versions of the Navy's F/A-18, compared with the House effort to cut the request by half

But the Senate Armed Services panel also ordered the Air Force to buy these "E" and "F" models of the F/A-18 as less expensive complements to the F-22. The Air Force had planned to develop a new plane.

The Senate bill recommended that production of the F/A-18 be slowed to 24 planes annually, instead of the planned rate of 48 planes.

The Senate bill included the $2.2 billion requested to develop the Air Force's new F-22 fighter. But it ordered the Air Force to make plans to build that plane efficiently at much slower rates than the 48-per-year pace that was planned.

Taking yet another position opposite that of the House, which had ordered the Air Force to continue building F-16 fighters for several years, the Senate bill rejected even the

$683 million requested to buy a final installment of 24 F-16s.

Because both carrier-based AXs and the Air Force's long-range bombers were being touted as capable of stealthy, precision strikes against targets almost anywhere in the world, the Senate committee ordered the Pentagon to conduct a comprehensive analysis of the cost and effectiveness of alternative mixes of each type of plane. "The question is not whether we need one or the other, but how much of each," the committee said.

Concurring with the other congressional committees dealing with the defense budget, Senate Appropriations contended that the services could not afford all of the new combat aircraft programs on the drawing board. Lumping all of them into a single account, the committee recommended $3.49 billion in its version of the fiscal 1993 defense appropriations bill (HR 5504). The measure was approved by the committee, 26-0, on Sept. 17 and passed by the full House, 86-10, on Sept. 23. *(Appropriations, p. 592)*

The Senate bill said the Pentagon could allocate the money as it wished but had to certify to Congress that long-range budget plans included adequate funding to complete whatever programs were begun.

Like the authorization measure, the Senate version of the appropriations bill denied the request for 24 additional F-16 fighters. And like the companion bill, the appropriations measure called for building only 24 of the 48 requested F/A-18s.

## FINAL ACTION

Confronted with conflicting House and Senate views on which combat aircraft to cut back, the conferees who wrote the final version of the authorization bill (HR 5006) took the path of least political resistance — generally approving the higher of the funding amounts proposed for each plane for fiscal 1993.

For example, they rejected a House effort to cut more than $500 million from the effort to develop a new version of the Navy's F/A-18 fighter plane and a Senate effort to terminate production of the Air Force's F-16 fighter.

Nonetheless, Nunn said Oct. 1, "Everybody looking at the [tactical] air package knows that you can't buy them all."

The conferees authorized nearly the amounts requested for the new generation of development projects, including:
- $2.2 billion for the F-22, as requested;
- $944 million for the F/A-18 E and F, more than 80 percent of the request; and
- $166 million for the AX, as requested.

But while they could not agree on cuts in particular programs, the conferees did lay the groundwork for subjecting the Navy and Air Force programs to a single set of policy and budget decisions. The conference report provided that:
- Both the AX and the F/A-18 E and F programs would be required to rely more heavily on prototypes than the Navy had planned. In addition, the enlarged F/A-18 could not cost more than 125 percent of the cost of the existing C and D model F/A-18s.
- No more than 65 percent of the amount authorized for any of the three new programs could be spent until after the Pentagon submitted to Congress two reports:

One was to be an analysis by the Joint Chiefs of Staff chairman of the division of labor among the services, known in Pentagon jargon as a "roles and missions" study. Mandated every three years by the 1986 defense reorganization act, such a report was due at the end of 1992. The

conferees ordered that the analysis be a "thorough, every-thing-on-the-table review," focusing on combat aircraft.

In particular, they asked whether one service could take over certain specialized missions — such as radar jamming — that required expensive airplanes. And they asked whether a single type of aircraft could be used by all services to perform similar combat missions.

The roles and missions report had not been made public by early in 1993, but press reports indicated that Gen. Colin L. Powell Jr., chairman of the Joint Chiefs, had proposed only marginal changes in any military programs.

The second study required by the conference report was an analysis by the secretary of Defense of how much of their planned combat airplane programs the Air Force and Navy could afford over the next 20 years.

In conducting this study, conferees said, department officials were to consider not only the declining defense budgets in prospect for years to come but also the portion of its total budget that each branch typically allocated to aircraft procurement. Conferees insisted that the study assume that tighter budgets would allow fewer planes to be built overall — and fewer to be built in any one year — than the services planned.

The last issue settled in the conference was whether to authorize long-lead-time funds to guarantee continued F-16 production in fiscal 1994. After the dispute had delayed conclusion of the conference for nearly a day, the two sides basically took a dive.

They approved $683 million, the amount requested, to buy 24 more F-16s and to begin shutting down the assembly line. The conferees did not mandate its termination, but they barred any expenditure to continue F-16 production beyond fiscal 1993 until the Pentagon submitted to Congress the two studies on roles and missions and aircraft costs.

The House approved the conference report on the defense authorization bill, 304-100, on Oct. 3. The Senate agreed by voice vote to approve the report the same day, although the measure was formally cleared for the president's signature on Oct 5. Bush signed the measure (PL 102-484) on Oct. 23.

The final version of the companion defense appropriations bill (HR 5504) included not only $615 million for 24 Air Force F-16s but also $68 million for components to be used in additional F-16s that would be included in the fiscal 1994 budget.

On most other programs to buy or develop tactical airplanes, the bill conformed to the authorization measure, providing:

- $1.2 billion for 36 Navy F/A-18s.
- $2 billion to continue development of the Air Force's F-22 fighter;
- $944 million to develop enlarged versions of the F/A-18; and
- $166 million to develop the new AX bomber to fly from aircraft carriers.

The bill also added to the request $200 million for a long-term program to refurbish the Navy's F-14 long-range fighter planes.

The House adopted the conference report on the appropriations bill by voice vote on Oct. 5, and the Senate did the same later that day, clearing the bill for the president. Bush signed the measure (PL 102-396) on Oct. 6. ■

# Congress Ups Defense Conversion Spending

Congress added more than $1.5 billion in defense funds to President Bush's budget request in fiscal 1993 to help military personnel, defense contractors and local communities adjust to the downturn in defense spending.

The efforts, many of them expanding programs that already existed, were authorized in the annual defense authorization bill (HR 5006) and funded in the companion defense appropriations bill (HR 5504.)

Philosophically opposed to such federal spending programs, the Bush administration had contended that the most effective ways to help those displaced by the military's downsizing was to improve the overall state of the economy.

But large, bipartisan majorities in Congress favored federal expenditures, drawn from the defense budget, to cushion the impact of the defense spending reductions that followed the end of the Cold War.

## BACKGROUND

With hundreds of thousands of defense-related jobs, hundreds of businesses and numerous communities in jeopardy, lawmakers groped for ways to relieve the pain of a shrinking defense budget.

But the solutions were so diverse and the problems so complex that Congress soon seemed too entangled in its own partisan battles to do much for the veterans of the Cold War.

"Defense conversion" once meant turning missile plants into factories that made farm equipment. In 1992, it took on a much broader meaning that encompassed an overall plan for the economy and the structure of the nation's defense.

The proposals ranged from broad spending packages targeted at creating jobs and assisting hard-hit communities and workers, to trimming taxes and resisting calls for deeper Pentagon cuts.

"What you're seeing is the beginning of a debate that will be going on for the next decade: What do we do with all the money we used to spend on defense?" said Sen. Phil Gramm, R-Texas.

The House's fiscal 1993 budget resolution, approved March 5, assumed as much as $6.6 billion in spending for so-called conversion projects. These included community development, worker retraining and research aid, as well as increased spending on transportation and housing. (Budget resolution, p. 98)

At the same time, Senate Republicans used a report by the Congressional Budget Office on the potential disruptions for defense-related workers and industries to warn against cutting defense by more than Bush had proposed.

"If we cut a lot more, it will be devastating," said Sen. Trent Lott, R-Miss., whose state was home to Ingalls Shipbuilding, a major defense contractor. "But if we keep on a planned, controlled, steady decline, we can cope with it.... The best thing I can do for my constituents is to keep those

# Defense Conversion Highlights

The following are highlights of the defense conversion programs that were included in the fiscal 1993 defense authorization bill (HR 5006 — PL 102-484) and the companion defense appropriations bill (HR 5504 — PL 102-396):

## Retirement Pay

In an initiative championed by Senate Armed Services Committee Chairman Sam Nunn, D-Ga., $254 million went to pay pensions to military personnel who took the option of retiring after 15 years of service instead of the 20 years previously required.

Nunn contended that the early retirement option obviated the need to dismiss service personnel before they were eligible for pensions. The option was to be available only through fiscal 1995 and only to service members in ranks and job specialties deemed overstaffed by Pentagon managers.

Early retirees would receive reduced annuities. But they could increase their military pensions after retirement, collecting credit — up to 20 years' service — by taking a job in some approved category of public service, such as education, law enforcement or health care.

In addition, nearly $200 million was approved for programs intended to tide over displaced military and civilian employees of the Pentagon until they were established in new lines of work. This included:

● $40 million for programs to encourage early retirement by members of reserve forces and the National Guard. Some retiring members could receive lump-sum severance payments, and some could continue receiving education benefits under the so-called Reserve GI Bill.

● $72 million for severance payments of up to $25,000 to civilian Pentagon employees who chose early retirement before fiscal 1997.

● $76 million to continue for up to 18 months health-care insurance payments for former service members and former Pentagon civilians.

## Worker Retraining

More than $200 million was provided to train former Pentagon and defense industry employees for new jobs.

Of this amount, $84 million was for worker relocation and training programs conducted by the Labor Department under the Job Training Partnership Act (JTPA). A provision of the fiscal 1991 defense authorization bill (PL 101-510), passed in 1990, transferred $150 million in

Pentagon funds to JTPA retraining and employment-assistance programs specifically aimed at displaced defense workers.

Besides transferring an additional $75 million for the program, the fiscal 1993 authorization bill amended JTPA to increase the number of defense workers who were eligible for its programs because of "substantial" layoffs by their employers. It reduced from 100 to 50 the number of jobs lost for a layoff to qualify as "substantial."

Among the retraining initiatives in the bills were:

● $75 million to reimburse companies that hired former military personnel for part of the cost of retraining them.

● $65 million to help former military personnel, civilian Pentagon employees and defense industry workers become teachers. Participants in this program — another of Nunn's initiatives — could receive up to $5,000 to cover the cost of preparing for certification as teachers. And for their first two years as teachers, their salaries could be underwritten by the Defense Department up to a total of $50,000.

● $20 million to establish college training programs in environmental restoration and hazardous waste management and to award fellowships in those programs to displaced defense workers.

## Community Assistance

The package also provided programs intended to help communities plan for economic development and diversification in the wake of layoffs at local military bases or defense companies. This total included:

● $80 million for grants administered by the Commerce Department's Economic Development Administration.

● $80 million for grants administered by the Defense Department's Office of Economic Adjustment. The authorization bill expanded the scope of this program to assist planning efforts by communities that had not yet been hit by the defense downturn but that wanted to avert a future crunch by reducing their dependence on defense dollars.

● $50 million for "impact assistance" to school districts that suffered a sudden drop in enrollment because a military base closed or a defense plant shut down.

## Defense Industries

The package included $549 million appropriated — out of $665 million authorized — to help defense contractors become more competitive in the civilian market-

ships coming."

Between these positions were numerous more-targeted proposals to help defense workers and companies adjust to a post Cold-War budget:

Former military personnel could become teachers. Resources used for building weapons could be diverted to cleaning up the environment. Federal incentives could be provided for joint military-commercial research projects or the development of crucial technologies. Loans could be provided for small defense contractors to find other work.

But just pumping funds into such proposals could prove

futile, some warned, without a more comprehensive plan to improve the economy so that new jobs and business opportunities for defense workers and defense-related companies would be available.

"This isn't a defense problem. This is an economic problem," said Gordon Adams, director of the Defense Budget Project, a private group that generally supported a leaner military program. "The wrong approach is to say, 'How do we manacle a defense worker to a training desk and make him into a hamburger flipper or a computer specialist?' If there aren't jobs being created out there,

place while retaining the capacity to produce military hardware.

Among those efforts were the following:

● **"Dual-use critical technologies."** $97 million for the government's contribution to consortia created to develop and foster applications of innovations that had both military and civilian uses.

By law, these partnerships had to include two or more commercial companies and, insofar as "practicable," the federal contribution could cover no more than 50 percent of a consortium's total budget. The Pentagon was to select projects for funding through open competition, based on criteria that included the technical excellence of the proposal and the qualifications of the participants.

This program was created in fiscal 1991 and had already funded projects such as high-speed communications and computer data storage.

● **"Commercial-military integration partnerships."** $48.5 million for a new program that was to be modeled on established "critical technologies" consortia. But it was intended to promote technologies that were more commercially viable and less militarily essential, although still applicable to potential Pentagon needs. Fuel cells and water purification systems were cited as types of technology that might be funded.

These partnerships did not have to include more than a single private company. But they were limited to five years' duration, and the federal contribution could not cover more than 50 percent of the costs in the first year, decreasing to 40 percent in the second year and 30 percent annually thereafter.

Criteria for the competitive selection of these projects included not only the technical excellence of the proposal and the qualifications of the participants but also the likelihood that the partnership could survive without federal funding after five years.

● **Extension programs.** $97 million to support centers sponsored by the federal government, by state or local governments or by private organizations to help defense-dependent companies enter the commercial marketplace with dual-use products.

California and New York already sponsored such outreach programs, which were intended to help corporate managers steeped in the Pentagon's procurement practices learn how to find markets, advertise, keep their books and deal with commercial suppliers.

Federal funding could last for no more than five years, starting at a 50 percent cost share and declining to no more than 30 percent in the third year and beyond.

● **"Regional technology alliances."** $97 million for closely situated federal labs, universities and high-tech companies that jointly developed and commercialized critical dual-use technologies.

This program was authorized in fiscal 1992, but no funds were appropriated for it. The fiscal 1993 authorization bill boosted from 30 percent to 50 percent the federal government's allowable share of funding for such a regional alliance.

● **Manufacturing.** $179 million for four programs aimed at developing and disseminating more efficient processes that could be applied to either new or existing technologies. The largest of the four components ($97 million) was earmarked for extension programs in manufacturing to be managed by state governments and regional public agencies.

An additional $29 million was provided for an existing process through which the federal government and participating universities jointly funded programs in manufacturing engineering. Another $29 million was earmarked to disseminate to small- and medium-sized contractors techniques of "agile" manufacturing, which would allow a company to shift more easily from one product to another. And $24 million was to fund government-industry partnerships to develop manufacturing processes that reduced health, safety and environmental hazards.

● **Synthetic materials.** $29 million for government-industry partnerships to develop new methods to synthesize materials and products.

In addition to approving funds for those programs, the defense authorization bill also doubled a decade-old program that set aside a small percentage of the Pentagon's annual research and development budget to fund research proposals from small businesses. Over the five years, the bill gradually increased, from 1.25 percent to 2.5 percent, the share of the defense research budget earmarked for this so-called small-business innovative research (SBIR) program. It also included in the baseline from which the set-aside was calculated more than $11 billion worth of programs that were previously excluded.

The combination of those changes provided the Pentagon's SBIR program with about $426 million in fiscal 1993, compared with the $225 million requested.

Subsequently, the SBIR provisions of the defense bill were incorporated into a broader bill (S 2941) that was cleared for the president Oct. 6 and signed into law on Oct. 28 (PL 102-564).

This measure boosted the SBIR set-aside formula in stages to 2.5 percent for all federal agencies. By one estimate, this was expected to increase the SBIR total from $484 million in fiscal 1991 to $1.2 billion by fiscal 1997.

there aren't jobs for people to be trained for."

Jobs quickly became the issue when Bush proposed his six-year, $50 billion defense cut, which many on Capitol Hill said they hoped to enlarge.

The congressional Office of Technology Assessment (OTA) estimated that between 1 million and 1.4 million defense-related jobs, including those in the military, could be lost by 1995 because of budget cuts. While the losses would be relatively small when compared with the overall economy, said OTA, certain defense-related industries and communities could be devastated.

Others raised concerns that the elimination of jobs would mean the loss of skills and facilities that were crucial for the long-term defense of the nation.

"We are proceeding in an unorganized, unplanned and ad hoc fashion with little or no thought to what capabilities the country might need in the future," said Rep. Dave McCurdy, D-Okla., chairman of the Armed Services Committee's Defense Industrial Base panel.

The administration's position that the free market would take care of dislocated defense workers and businesses was echoed by many Republicans in Congress. "I

want to give [defense savings] back to the American taxpayer," Gramm said. "The Democrats want to expand the size of government."

Administration officials noted that the overall reduction in defense was relatively small compared with cutbacks after World War II and the Korean and Vietnam wars.

"Since the economy successfully adapted to more rapid reductions following World War II and the Korean War, there is little reason to think that the present changes will be troublesome," the president's Council of Economic Advisers wrote in the 1991 annual economic report.

But critics argued that the economy was not nearly as robust as it was during previous downsizings.

"In several ways, in fact, important conditions that smoothed earlier transitions do not exist today," an OTA report said. "Unlike the situation after World War II ... many defense companies and divisions of companies have no civilian business to go back to, and no real abilities or interest in converting to civilian production."

Job losses that could be absorbed in a prospering economy "are not so easily swallowed when growth is flat, still less during a recession," said OTA.

By May, Democratic leaders in both chambers were assembling packages of defense conversion programs in the $1 billion-to-$2 billion range.

In the Senate, a 21-member Democratic task force May 21 announced a long list of recommendations. The measures, which would cost an estimated $1.2 billion, included economic adjustment assistance for hard-hit communities, retraining for workers and programs to help defense industries shift to civilian work.

"The president has no plan, no program and no plan to have a program," Senate Majority Leader George J. Mitchell, D-Maine, told reporters May 21, noting that the administration was pledging millions of dollars to demilitarize the former Soviet Union.

"It should be unacceptable to Americans ... that their government has a plan to help convert the economy of the Soviet Union from defense production to civilian production and has no comparable plan in our own country," Mitchell said.

In the House, Armed Services Committee Chairman Les Aspin, D-Wis., was compiling a $1.4 billion "reinvestment" package as an amendment to the $274 billion defense authorization bill (HR 5006).

Sponsors said that both plans relied primarily on the expansion of existing programs and did not call for pouring federal funds into high-tech public works projects, such as high-speed rail systems, which some had proposed.

"They use proven, successful programs that do not create big new bureaucracies," said David Pryor, D-Ark., chairman of the Senate task force.

## HOUSE ACTION

The House included $1 billion for defense conversion programs in the fiscal 1993 defense authorization measure (HR 5006), which it passed, 198-168, on June 5. (*Defense authorization, p. 483*)

House Democrats assembled a 188-page amendment to parcel out the money among several existing programs, which they argued would not only cushion the shock of cutbacks but would channel industrial and human resources into new areas that would generate economic growth.

The Democratic package, offered as an amendment on the House floor by Martin Frost, Texas, was adopted 275-105. (*Vote 166, p. 40-H*)

Among its major components were:

● $180 million to help those leaving the military and displaced defense workers become math and science teachers in needy communities. The provision would provide each beneficiary with a $5,000 stipend while securing state teacher's credentials and would subsidize each recipient's teaching salary for as much as $50,000 over two years. It would prohibit schools from cutting their regular teaching staffs and substituting the subsidized teachers.

● $150 million for public-private sector consortiums to develop critical technologies with both military and civilian applications. The consortiums also would be allowed to use the resources of Pentagon laboratories.

● $50 million for investment in companies to enable them to develop critical technologies.

● $200 million to provide job training for former service personnel and for certain civilian federal employees and defense contractor employees displaced as a result of defense cuts.

● $100 million for grants to help state and local governments plan for economic diversification and industrial changes to adjust to reduced defense spending.

The Democratic package would require defense contractors to give hiring preference to displaced military personnel and defense workers. The House rejected, 147-235, a Republican amendment offered by Larry J. Hopkins, Ky., that would have given the Pentagon discretion over whether to apply that requirement and would have deleted various other provisions. (*Vote 165, p. 40-H*)

The House version of the fiscal 1993 defense appropriations bill (HR 5504) included $1 billion for such defense conversion programs. The House approved that bill, 328-94, on July 2.

## SENATE ACTION

The Senate included $1.7 billion for defense conversion programs in its version of the fiscal 1993 defense authorization bill (HR 5006), which it approved by voice vote on Sept. 19.

The Senate kicked off its debate on the defense bill by adopting, 91-2, a purely symbolic amendment that reprised provisions that the Armed Services Committee already had included in the bill to cushion the impact of the defense cutback on weapons manufacturers and their communities. (*Vote 181, p. 24-S*)

Committee member Jeff Bingaman, D-N.M., said a recorded vote would give Senate conferees leverage to protect the Senate's economic conversion provisions in negotiations with the House over the final version of the bill.

But the most obvious and immediate payoff of the amendment was political: As several members rose on the Senate floor to laud the conversion package, several Democrats held a news conference nearby to lambaste the Bush administration's own conversion program as inadequate.

Describing the Senate package, Armed Services Chairman Sam Nunn, D-Ga., said, "Some hardship is inevitable. "We're trying to minimize that."

To encourage relatively senior personnel to leave the services voluntarily, and thus reduce the need for involuntary layoffs, the bill temporarily would allow military personnel to retire after 15 years of service rather than after the 20 years usually required to qualify for a pension.

Because military pensions were based on the number of years of service, early retirees would receive a smaller annuity than those who served 20 years.

Military personnel who retired with fewer than 20 years of service could earn credit for up to five additional years — boosting their eventual retirement pay — by taking public service jobs in education, law enforcement and health care.

To cover the projected increase in retirement pay, the measure would authorize $463 million. But the Armed Services Committee predicted that the early retirement provision would save $1.1 billion over five years.

Another provision would authorize personnel whose job specialties were not transferable to the civilian sector — notably, service members in the combat arms — to apply for up to one year of paid leave to obtain training in civilian skills.

For civilian Pentagon employees in overstaffed job specialties and those employed at military bases slated for closure, the bill would offer incentive payments of up to $20,000 if they resigned or retired.

The measure would authorize $298 million to help defense industry workers find new jobs and to help communities dependent on defense bases and contractors to diversify their economies.

Insisting that targeted spending was needed to preserve key elements of the defense industrial base and to channel the fruits of earlier defense investment into the civilian economy, Armed Services added provisions that would authorize $607 million for various economic-conversion programs. For instance, this included:

● $200 million to assist defense contractors in developing "dual-use" technologies, applicable to civilian and military production.

● $100 million to develop commercial products that capitalized on the concentration of particular skills in a region.

● $100 million to stimulate private investment in critical technologies.

The Senate's version of the companion defense appropriations bill (HR 5504) for fiscal 1993 included $2 billion for such defense conversion programs. The bill won Senate passage, 86-10, on Sept. 23 but only after a floor amendment to pin down how the conversion money would be

given out. (Appropriations, p. 592)

The Senate Appropriations Committee had funded the $2 billion as a lump sum, in part by eliminating from the bill hundreds of millions of dollars that the administration had requested for various research projects that, the committee argued, were intended to help defense contractors re-tool for commercial business.

As drafted by the committee, the bill would have given the Defense Department discretion to allocate the $2 billion among conversion-related projects, including those projects for which specific requests had been denied.

But the Senate's version of the companion defense authorization bill had parceled out money to dozens of specific conversion-related projects. And senators who had hammered out that package were unwilling to see their carefully brokered deal unraveled.

By voice vote, the Senate adopted an amendment by David Pryor, D-Ark., that earmarked more than half of the appropriations bill's conversion fund for projects that were specified in the authorization measure. For instance, Pryor's amendment added $470 million from the conversion fund to the $130 million that was already in the bill for transition grants to workers and communities hit by defense cutbacks. And the amendment doled out $675 million among 10 of the conversion projects specifically covered by the authorization bill.

## FINAL ACTION

The final version of the defense authorization bill (HR 5006) included $1.5 billion for defense conversion programs. (Highlights, p. 510)

The House approved the conference report on the bill, 304-100, on Oct. 3. The Senate, which voted to approve the report by voice vote the same day, formally cleared it Oct. 5. President Bush signed the measure (PL 102-484) on Oct. 23.

The final version of the companion defense appropriations bill (HR 5504) provided the actual funds for those conversion programs. The House adopted the conference report on the appropriations bill by voice vote Oct. 5, and the Senate did the same later that day, clearing the bill for the president. President Bush signed the measure (PL 102-396) on Oct. 6. ∎

# START Ratified Despite Soviet Collapse

The Senate on Oct. 1 approved ratification of the Strategic Arms Reduction Treaty (START), which provided for a reduction of about one-third in the arsenals of long-range missiles and bombers of the United States and the former Soviet Union.

In exercising its usual constitutional responsibility to provide advice and consent on treaties, the Senate faced the unusual circumstance in this case of considering a far-reaching arms control pact with a country that no longer existed.

Signed July 31, 1991, by President Bush and Soviet President Mikhail S. Gorbachev, the START treaty provided for a reduction in the U.S. inventory of intercontinental nuclear bombs and missile warheads from more than 12,000 to fewer than 9,000. It provided for reducing the Soviet stock of such weapons from about 11,000 to

6,000. (1991 Almanac, p. 419)

But the Soviet Union disintegrated at the end of 1991. In a treaty amendment (or "protocol") signed May 23, 1992, the four republics that assumed control of the former Soviet nuclear arsenal agreed to take on the obligations the treaty would have imposed on the Soviet government.

The START treaty had taken nine years to complete, with large bureaucracies on each side hashing out details.

## SENATE COMMITTEE ACTION

On Feb. 19, the Foreign Relations Committee began preliminary hearings on the START Treaty. Once praised as a landmark agreement cutting the nuclear arsenals of the United States and the Soviet Union, it had become in some ways a Cold War anachronism.

Foreign Relations Chairman Claiborne Pell, D-R.I., urged the administration to offer amendments to the treaty, allowing for lower weapons levels and new signatories from among the former Soviet republics.

Sam Nunn, D-Ga., chairman of the Armed Services Committee, said, "There has to be further clarification" on a number of issues, including legal questions created by the changed circumstances in the former Soviet Union, before the Senate took final action. But he said he was "not for holding up the treaty indefinitely."

Secretary of State James A. Baker III urged the Senate to ratify the treaty. He told the Foreign Relations Committee on Feb. 5 that the verification procedures in the pact were significant and should be locked into place.

Baker was the lead witness in another Foreign Relations Committee hearing on the treaty June 23. He called START "critical to the end of the nuclear arms competition."

"For the first time since the dawn of the nuclear age," he said, "we've agreed to real reductions in [long-range] nuclear weapons levels rather than simply setting limits on their rate of increase."

But before the Foreign Relations Committee sent the Senate a resolution approving the treaty, members debated adding a provision intended to pressure three former Soviet republics to follow through on a pledge they made to give up all nuclear weapons within seven years.

The START cuts fell particularly heavily on land-based intercontinental ballistic missiles (ICBMs), which were the backbone of the former Soviet force. U.S. officials had contended for more than two decades that such weapons posed an especially ominous threat to peace, particularly when they were equipped with multiple warheads.

A few conservative critics, such as Frank J. Gaffney Jr., who was a Pentagon official during the Reagan administration, warned that START would allow Russia to field a large number of particularly dangerous weapons, including as many as 1,000 ICBMs in mobile launchers. Gaffney also questioned whether Russian President Boris N. Yeltsin had a strong enough whip hand over the former Soviet military to follow through on the much deeper cuts that he and Bush had pledged to incorporate in a START II treaty.

But Defense Secretary Dick Cheney and the Joint Chiefs of Staff strongly endorsed START in a June 26 hearing. Joint Chiefs Chairman Gen. Colin L. Powell Jr. dismissed Gaffney's objections as "tortured reasons" and said that the country should "take a good deal that's before us now."

Baker strongly opposed any delay in ratification. "While it serves as a framework for . . . deeper reductions, [START] also ensures that significant reductions will begin and begin now," he said. "We need to put START in place right now."

In his June testimony, Baker argued that START marked an important step toward heading off the emergence of new nuclear-armed states from the debris of the Soviet Union. The key, Baker said, was a protocol to the treaty signed in May by the four republics in which former Soviet nuclear weapons were deployed. It provided that all four countries would sign START, but that only Russia would deploy the weapons the treaty would have allowed the Soviet Union to maintain.

The agreement bound the other republics — Ukraine, Belarus and Kazakhstan — to forswear all nuclear weapons by signing the 1968 nuclear non-proliferation treaty. Each also promised in a letter to dispose of all deployed strategic weapons within seven years. Baker said the letters were legally binding on the republics. But Democrats Joseph R. Biden Jr., Del., and Paul S. Sarbanes, Md., suggested that the Senate should formalize the link between START and the republics' commitments to give up nuclear arms.

"That commitment is not in the treaty or the protocol," Sarbanes said. "That's in the separate letters, which are not being submitted for approval in the same manner."

Contributing to congressional unease over the matter, some leaders in Ukraine and Kazakhstan had argued that those republics should retain some nuclear arms as a counterweight to the large nuclear forces of neighboring Russia.

### Committee approval

The Senate Foreign Relations Committee on July 2 approved, 17-0, a resolution to ratify the START treaty.

The committee added to the resolution of approval several conditions intended to lend greater legal formality to a series of agreements by which Russia and three other former Soviet republics had assumed obligations that the treaty originally ascribed to a Soviet Union that no longer existed.

One of the conditions stipulated that the United States regarded the protocol signed in Lisbon, Portugal, on May 23 as tantamount to an integral part of the treaty. In the protocol, Russia, Belarus, Ukraine and Kazakhstan agreed to assume the Soviet obligations.

Other conditions similarly stipulated that U.S. ratification of START was based on compliance by Belarus, Ukraine and Kazakhstan with various commitments that they would dispose of former Soviet strategic weapons and would forswear deployment of any nuclear weapons by signing the 1968 nuclear non-proliferation treaty.

Over the objection of Foreign Relations Republicans, the committee also adopted a condition by Biden that directed the president to seek, as part of any future treaty reducing strategic nuclear arms, an agreement for the parties to monitor each others' nuclear stockpiles and nuclear weapons production plants. U.S. officials had resisted foreign inspection of the nation's nuclear stockpile and plants.

The Biden condition bound U.S. negotiators trying to wrap up a follow-on treaty that would implement the much deeper strategic arms cuts, known as START II, agreed to June 17 by Bush and Yeltsin. *(START II, p. 516)*

## SENATE ACTION

The Senate on Oct. 1 easily approved ratification of the Strategic Arms Reduction Treaty (START), a product of nine years of often difficult negotiations between the United States and the former Soviet Union to reduce significantly their strategic nuclear arsenals.

The somewhat cursory debate and minimal dissent on the Senate floor, however, reflected the changed status of the historic treaty in the wake of the Soviet Union's demise.

After blocking attempts by a few conservatives to amend the treaty (Treaty Doc 102-20), the Senate approved ratification by a vote of 93-6, far more than the two-thirds vote required. *(Vote 253, p. 33-S)*

Treaty backers said that despite ongoing negotiations on details of the Bush-Yeltsin plan, the START reductions were needed to set the stage for the additional arms cuts and as a hedge against the possible re-emergence of unfriendly governments in the former Soviet Union.

"No one can or should argue that START is a panacea,"

# Major START Treaty Provisions

Following are the key provisions of the Strategic Arms Reduction Treaty (START) between the United States and the former Soviet Union:

**Overall ceilings.** During the seven years after ratification, each side had to reduce its strategic arsenal to no more than 6,000 aerial bombs and missile warheads (subject to special "counting rules"). These could be carried by no more than 1,600 long-range ballistic missiles and heavy bombers.

Of the 6,000 bombs and warheads, no more than 4,900 could be carried by ICBMs (intercontinental ballistic missiles) or submarine-launched missiles.

Neither country's remaining missile force could have a total throw-weight greater than 54 percent the size of the Soviet force in 1991. Throw-weight was an indicator of the number and size of nuclear warheads a missile could carry.

**Missile counting rules.** Each type of missile was to be counted as having an agreed number of warheads — 10 apiece for the American MX and the Soviet SS-18, for example. No existing missile could be tested with more than its assigned number of warheads. And no new missile could be tested with more than 10 warheads.

To allow each country to disperse its warheads over a larger number of missiles, up to 1,250 warheads could be "down-loaded" from existing missiles, with that number subtracted from the number attributed to those missiles under the treaty.

**Bomber and cruise missiles rules.** To encourage a shift from missiles to bombers, certain bomber-launched weapons were not counted against the 6,000-weapon ceiling. That was the major reason that START did not cut arsenals as deeply as the 50 percent reduction described by some of its supporters.

Non-nuclear cruise missiles and nuclear missiles with ranges of less than 600 kilometers were not covered.

Unless it was equipped to carry long-range nuclear cruise missiles, a bomber was counted as one delivery vehicle (against the ceiling of 1,600) carrying one warhead (against the ceiling of 6,000), no matter how many gravity bombs and short-range missiles it carried.

Long-range cruise missiles were counted against the 6,000-weapon ceiling under formulas that, in effect, exempted from the limit as many as several hundred missiles for each country.

**'Heavy' ICBMs.** Neither side could deploy more than 154 ICBMs larger than the Soviet SS-19 and the United States' MX. And such heavy missiles could carry no more than 10 warheads apiece. This cut the SS-18 force by 50 percent.

New heavy missiles were barred, and the SS-18 could not be modified to increase its throw-weight.

**Mobile ICBMs.** No more than 1,100 warheads could be deployed on mobile ICBMs. To aid in verification, there were several restrictions on how mobile missiles could be based and how they could operate when away from their bases.

**Third-party weapons.** Neither country was permitted to circumvent START by transferring treaty-limited weapons to a third party, except for "existing patterns of cooperation" — a phrase intended to cover the U.S. sale to Britain of Trident II sub-launched missiles.

**Sea-launched cruise missiles.** To accommodate Soviet demands for limits on the U.S. Navy's Tomahawk sea-launched cruise missile (SLCM), which was built in both nuclear and conventional versions, each country was required to announce annually its plans for deploying over the following five years any nuclear-armed SLCMs with a range of more than 600 kilometers.

No more than 880 such weapons could be deployed.

The U.S. Navy had planned to deploy 637 nuclear Tomahawks. But as part of his nuclear arms reduction initiative in January, President Bush announced that the 350 nuclear Tomahawks then deployed would be moth-balled.

**Backfire bomber.** The Soviet Union promised to deploy no more than 500 Backfire bombers. For 20 years, U.S. negotiators had insisted that this plane was an intercontinental bomber, while Soviet negotiators denied it.

**Post-Soviet republics.** Under an annex (or protocol) to the treaty signed at Lisbon in May, and made a part of the treaty, the former Soviet republics of Russia, Ukraine, Belarus and Kazakhstan — where all former Soviet strategic weapons were located — accepted the obligations imposed by START on the Soviet government.

Ukraine, Belarus and Kazakhstan agreed to bar nuclear weapons from their territory by signing the 1968 Nuclear Non-Proliferation Treaty as "non-nuclear weapon states."

In separate letters, those three governments pledged to eliminate all nuclear weapons within seven years.

---

said Majority Leader George J. Mitchell, D-Maine. "Even as we move toward ratification of START, we look forward to receiving another, more far-reaching strategic arms accord. But each agreement is a step forward."

He noted that the treaty was the first ever to reduce strategic, or long-range, nuclear weapons.

Richard G. Lugar, R-Ind., added that while many hoped democratic reforms in the former Soviet Union continued, "we cannot be certain that democracy will succeed. If new, unfriendly regimes come to power, we want those regimes to be legally obligated to observe START limits and verification provisions."

START critics, led by Malcolm Wallop, R-Wyo., argued that the initial treaty did not go far enough and should be delayed. Wallop called for combining START with the Bush-Yeltsin pact.

"We are in fact considering a treaty that is outdated," Wallop said. He dismissed arguments that ratification of the treaty was needed for subsequent arms reductions, saying that if the nuclear powers were "on the threshold of a new world . . . this treaty is irrelevant, and if we are not on the threshold of a new world, this treaty is inadequate."

Wallop also complained that the historic pact was being rushed through in the final hours of the session, without being

given adequate consideration by the Senate. But after he threatened to filibuster, the Senate on Sept. 29 voted 87-6 to limit debate on the measure. *(Vote 246, p. 32-S)*

Subsequently, Wallop was defeated in attempts to amend the treaty so that it would not have gone into effect until the president certified that all multiple-warhead ICBMs would be eliminated (16-83), that most non-deployed missiles and launchers would be eliminated (11-88), and that mobile ICBMs and launchers for mobile ICBMs would be eliminated (10-86). *(Votes 247, 248, 250, pp. 32-S, 33-S)*

The Senate's resolution of ratification already included a number of conditions and declarations to hold the republics' feet to the fire to comply with the treaty and provisions of the May 23, 1992, protocol. It also sought to enforce promises by Belarus, Ukraine and Kazakhstan to eliminate nuclear weapons from their territory within seven years.

The Senate agreed Sept. 30 by voice vote to an amendment by John W. Warner, R-Va., strengthening one condition, which would have delayed the treaty from going into effect if the four republics had not reached agreement among themselves on how to implement their side of the arms-reduction deal.

Warner noted that since the protocol had been signed, some republic officials had indicated that the agreement could be more difficult than originally thought.

The Senate also directed the president in negotiating subsequent pacts to seek agreement on monitoring each others' nuclear stockpiles and production plants, something U.S. officials had resisted in the past. ∎

# START II Arms Reductions Easier Signed Than Done

An arms reduction treaty that President Bush and Russian President Boris N. Yeltsin crafted in 1992 called for slashing the number of U.S. and Russian nuclear warheads to no more than 6,500. The treaty thus provided for the removal from service of more than two-thirds of the nearly 24,000 warheads deployed as of 1990 by the United States and the Soviet Union.

The second Strategic Arms Reduction Treaty — START II — was agreed upon in broad terms by Bush and Yeltsin in June, then signed on Jan. 3, 1993. It was sent to the U.S. and Soviet legislatures for approval of ratification.

The treaty called for eliminating from service all weapons carried by multiple-warhead, land-based (MIRVed) missiles, which U.S. officials long had regarded as the most threatening type in the former Soviet arsenal. And the agreement envisioned the reductions being achieved as early as the year 2000, provided the United States helped Russia bear the cost of demobilizing its large nuclear force.

But signing the treaty, which fleshed out the broad agreement reached by the two presidents in June, might have been the easiest part of achieving those sweeping reductions.

This second treaty presumed compliance with the first START treaty, signed in July 1991 but approved by the Senate only on Oct. 1, 1992. *(START I, p. 513)*

START I, negotiated between the United States and the Soviet Union, reduced the strategic warhead inventories by about one-third. But after the Soviet Union disin-

## Warhead Allotments

| | 1990 | Start I | Start II |
|---|---|---|---|
| **Total warheads** | | | |
| United States | 12,646 | 8,556 | 3,500 |
| Soviet Union | 11,012 | 6,163 | 3,000 |
| **Total warheads on land-based missiles** | | | |
| United States | 2,450 | 1,400 | 500 |
| Russia | 6,612 | 3,153 | 504 |
| **Total warheads on multiple-warhead, land-based missiles** | | | |
| United States | 2,000 | 1,100 | 0 |
| Russia | 5,958 | 2,460 | 0 |

tegrated, that pact had to be recast by a series of negotiated appendices to bind the four former Soviet republics that controlled parts of the former Soviet nuclear force.

The agreement on START II was announced by Bush on Dec. 30, after three final issues were resolved in a series of phone conversations between Bush and Yeltsin and in face-to-face negotiations between U.S. Secretary of State Lawrence S. Eagleburger and Russian Foreign Minister Andrei V. Kozyrev. Those endgame agreements:

● Allowed Russia, which was required by START I to scrap 154 of its giant, 10-warhead SS-18 missiles, to retain some of the armored launch silos. The remaining silos would have to be partly filled with concrete, so that they no longer could contain SS-18s.

● Allowed Russia, to avoid the cost of developing a new, single-warhead missile, to keep a certain number of its multiwarhead SS-19s, from which it removed all but one warhead.

● Allowed the United States to exempt from treaty limits some of its bombers by assigning them solely to conventional missions. However, the United States would retain the right to reassign those planes to a nuclear role, as older, nuclear-armed B-52s were retired. ∎

# Reconnaissance Pact OKs Mutual Overflights

An "Open Skies" treaty binding the United States, Russia and other European countries to allow reciprocal reconnaissance overflights was once considered a radical arms control proposal. But it seemed so unremarkable in the post-Cold War world that its signature March 24 drew scant notice in the United States.

The Senate failed to take final action on the pact. And only the Foreign Relations Committee held hearings on the subject in 1992.

### BACKGROUND

President Dwight D. Eisenhower proposed a similar agreement in 1955 that would have relied on state-of-the-art aerial photography to deter sudden changes in military deployments that might have ignited crises. Soviet officials spiked that plan as a crude effort to legitimize U.S. spying.

With the collapse of the Soviet Union and changes in military technology, the treaty signed in 1992 was more symbolic than Ike's plan would have been in its day: U.S. and Russian reconnaissance satellites could have ferreted out much more detail about military forces than could the relatively pedestrian equipment slated for the original Open Skies inspection planes.

But U.S. negotiator John Hawes contended that this treaty could provide the reassurances Eisenhower intended for his plan: "The tangible value of this thing is . . . 'confidence building,'" Hawes said.

President Bush resuscitated Eisenhower's Open Skies idea in May 1989, extending the proposed inspections beyond the territory of the United States and the former Soviet Union to cover their allies and former allies. The Open Skies Treaty that resulted was signed in Helsinki, Finland, by the United States, the 15 other NATO members, the five surviving members of the Warsaw Pact and four former Soviet republics: Russia, Belarus, Ukraine and Georgia.

The inspection regime was not designed to verify compliance with specific arms limitations but was intended to moderate international tensions by making countries' military deployments more "transparent." Accordingly, negotiators agreed that the planes should carry equipment that was able to distinguish between a truck and a tank.

For more than two years after Bush first floated the agreement, Open Skies negotiations stalled.

U.S. negotiators insisted that flights be permitted over any part of a signatory's territory, allowing a country to temporarily block a flight only for safety reasons — if, for instance, the proposed itinerary would take the observation plane dangerously near a scheduled missile test.

Soviet officials rejected such wide-open access and also insisted that overflight rights cover signatories' bases in countries not party to the treaty, such as U.S. bases in South Korea and Japan.

The deadlock appeared to have been broken in late 1990, when Soviet Foreign Minister Eduard A. Shevardnadze dropped the demand for third-country overflights and offered to allow total territorial access, provided the United States would let the Soviet Union supply the planes to overfly Soviet territory.

However, Moscow repudiated a tentative agreement on those terms after Shevardnadze resigned in December 1990, warning of the threat of a right-wing coup. Such a putsch came in August 1991, led by Defense Minister Dmitri T. Yazov and other hard-liners. The coup's failure led to the Soviet Union's collapse.

Open Skies negotiations resumed late that year, and the deal finally struck was along the lines Shevardnadze had proposed.

### Provisions

Besides conventional cameras, the treaty provided that the inspection planes could carry infrared viewing equipment to permit night operations and radar that could detect ground objects covered by clouds.

But the radar authorized for use in the treaty could not actually make truck-from-tank distinctions. To thwart commercial espionage of the detection equipment, the treaty allowed use only of gear already on the commercial market.

The pact assigned each of the 25 countries an annual quota of reconnaissance flights that it must allow other signatories over any part of its territory on 72 hours' notice.

The most overflights assigned to any country was 42, the number accepted by the United States and by Russia and Belarus, which shared a quota.

The treaty required Ukraine and several large NATO members to accept 12 overflights annually and assigned fewer flights to smaller European countries, with Portugal having the lowest quota, two flights.

For the first three years after the treaty was ratified, however, each country's quota was to be reduced by 25 percent. Each signatory was allowed to conduct the same number of overflights of any other country that it received from that country.

The treaty did not guarantee that other countries would avail themselves of the overflight opportunities. The largest number of inspection flights was expected to be flown over the states of the former Soviet Union and Eastern Europe. "Everybody wants to fly over Russia and Belarus," said Hawes. "Nobody wants to fly over us." ∎

# Collapse of Soviet Union Speeds Nuclear Test Ban

After many attempts in previous years, Congress acted in 1992 to ban all nuclear test explosions after Sept. 30, 1996.

Test ban opponents first appended test limitation provisions to the House and Senate versions of the defense authorization bill (HR 5006 — PL 102-396). But the provisions were dropped from that bill because the energy and water appropriations bill included the test ban in a package that was too politically appealing for a reluctant Bush administration to veto.

The final version of the $22 billion energy and water appropriations bill (HR 5373 — PL 102-377) incorporated the provision, initially adopted in the Senate, that banned underground nuclear weapons tests for nine months. Existing treaties banned testing in the air and at sea.

After the nine months, the bill allowed a limited number of tests through 1996 to test safety-related improvements to weapons already deployed. It banned all underground explosive tests after Sept. 30, 1996, unless another country conducted such tests.

Despite President Bush's vigorous opposition to the test ban, he accepted the bill, in large part because it included funding for the superconducting super collider, a huge atom smasher to be built in Texas.

## BACKGROUND

For four decades, a test ban was largely a distant dream of liberal activists. Every president from Dwight D. Eisenhower to Ronald Reagan proclaimed an end to testing as a national goal, but only Jimmy Carter accorded the goal more than lip service.

In fiscal 1986 through 1988, the House annually had approved an amendment to the defense authorization bill that would have barred tests of nuclear weapons with an explosive punch greater than 1,000 tons of TNT. But those votes were largely symbolic, taken on the assumption the Senate would reject any significant nuclear test limitations.

And, indeed, so long as the Soviet nuclear threat was intact, a majority of senators seemed to accept the contention of Pentagon and Energy Department nuclear weapons

specialists: that continuous testing was required to check on the safety and reliability of weapons already in the U.S. stockpile.

But with the disintegration of the Soviet Union — and with Russian President Boris N. Yeltsin observing a self-imposed nuclear test moratorium — test ban proponents in 1992 stepped up their efforts to terminate the U.S. testing program.

For the first time, they were supported by Senate Armed Services Committee Chairman Sam Nunn, D-Ga., who echoed what had long been one of the liberals' arguments: That a halt to testing might give Washington more diplomatic leverage to dissuade other countries from trying to develop nuclear weapons.

## HOUSE ACTION

Reacting to the end of the Cold War and the budget crunch at home, the House broke significant new ground with the $270 billion defense authorization bill for fiscal 1993 that it passed June 5. *(Defense authorization, p. 483)*

In particular, the House added to the bill (HR 5006) a one-year moratorium on nuclear weapons tests, a move that had long been vigorously opposed by Republican administrations.

The nuclear test ban amendment, adopted 237-167, barred nuclear weapons test explosions during fiscal 1993 unless the president certified to Congress that a former Soviet republic had conducted a nuclear test. *(Vote 164, p. 42-H)*

All former Soviet states except Russia had renounced nuclear weapons, and Russia announced its own test moratorium in 1991.

Reportedly, the United States conducted six tests annually, which defense officials said were necessary to test the reliability of weapons already in the stockpile and to design warheads with safety features that would make them less likely to explode in case of an accident and harder for a terrorist to detonate.

Test-ban sponsor Mike Kopetski, D-Ore., and his allies contended that computer simulations and other non-explosive experiments could be used instead of test explosions. They also argued that a test ban would give the United States more diplomatic leverage to prevent additional countries from developing nuclear weapons.

But critics of a test ban, such as Jon Kyl, R-Ariz., scoffed at that argument. "The rogue nations of the world are going to continue developing nuclear weapons whether we stop testing or not," he said.

## SENATE ACTION

While the Bush administration tried to head off the test ban, it faced an uphill battle. By early summer, more than half the Senate was already on record as endorsing the ban.

Appearing before the Senate Foreign Relations Committee on July 23, Richard A. Claytor, the Energy Department's assistant secretary for defense programs, called the proposed moratorium "very harmful." He said the moratorium would not stop "rogue nations like Iraq, Iran and North Korea from developing their own nuclear weapons," as some advocates had said, and could in fact encourage proliferation by making the U.S. arsenal less secure.

He said a new administration policy would limit tests to those essential for safety and reliability but not for mod-

ernization. The administration announced its new policy July 10 and said that it expected to conduct no more than six tests per year over the next five years, with no more than three tests per year exceeding 35 kilotons, equal to 35,000 tons of TNT.

Claytor acknowledged that the administration already had planned to limit tests in 1992 to six but said that those planned were being reviewed to determine whether they were required for safety reasons.

But a panel of experts disagreed. They told the Foreign Relations Committee July 23-24 that testing was unnecessary, either for safety reasons or as a deterrent to other nations considering developing nuclear weapons.

Retired Rear Adm. Eugene J. Carroll, deputy director of the Center for Defense Information, said the U.S. nuclear arsenal was not as vulnerable to accidents as the administration had implied. "We've done everything wrong that's possible to do wrong with those weapons, and they haven't exploded yet," he said, citing examples of weapons caught in fires and "crunched" by machinery.

The witnesses also argued that, contrary to the administration's contention, the moratorium would encourage other nations to cease testing and would be an important step toward achieving nuclear non-proliferation. "We have to lead by example, not by telling people they can't test," Carroll said.

### Energy and Water Bill

On Aug. 3, the Senate approved 68-26 an amendment by Mark O. Hatfield, R-Ore., to the fiscal 1993 energy and water appropriations bill (HR 5373) to impose a nine-month testing halt followed in 1996 by a permanent ban. *(Vote 167, p. 22-S)*

But that vote overstated Senate support for the proposal because several opponents voted for the amendment for tactical reasons. *(Appropriations, p. 659)*

### Defense Authorization

Armed Services Committee Chairman Nunn had offered a compromise testing proposal during his committee's markup of the defense authorization bill July 23-24. Nunn's plan would have allowed no more than three tests a year for safety reasons and phased out all testing by 1998. The committee did not agree to the plan.

Proponents of the ban then took their case to the Senate floor.

The proposal faced its toughest challenge on Sept. 18, when Senators voted 55-40 to impose a nine-month moratorium on nuclear testing. The provision, which was an amendment offered by Hatfield to the Senate's version of the defense authorization bill (HR 5006), also would have permanently banned all nuclear testing after fiscal 1996, unless another country was still conducting tests. *(Vote 217, 29-S)*.

Senators rejected an attempt by William S. Cohen, R-Maine, that would have imposed a shorter initial moratorium followed by a permanent ban at the end of fiscal 1998. Cohen's proposal also would have allowed the president to waive the test ban for one year to gain leverage to negotiate a comprehensive test ban.

After Bush signed the Energy and Water bill (PL 102-377), which contained the same provisions as the defense bill, on Oct. 2, conferees on the defense bill stripped their bill of the test ban language. ∎

# Commission Calls for Women on Warships

Debate over the role of women in the military continued in 1992. A 15-member panel recommended to President Bush that women be allowed onto warships but kept out of other direct combat roles, including Air Force pilot positions.

Congress also reacted angrily to a tale of military sexual harassment that gained national attention. At least 26 women told of being assaulted during a convention in the summer of 1991 of the Tailhook Association, a private club of naval aviators.

In response, Congress barred the organization, which had been closely associated with the Navy, from receiving federal funds.

## WOMEN IN COMBAT

In a Nov. 15 report to Bush, a commission created by congressional mandate recommended that the ban on assigning women to warships be repealed but that women not be assigned to ground combat units. The commission also recommended, 8-7, that the ban on assigning women to combat aircraft be reinstated in law.

Women were barred by law only from serving on warships, though they served as crew members on supply and repair vessels. They were barred from serving in ground combat units by Pentagon policy.

As part of the fiscal 1992 defense authorization bill (PL 102-190), Congress repealed the statutory ban on assigning women to fly combat planes in the Navy and Air Force. The bill also established the presidential commission that made its recommendations in November. *(1991 Almanac, p. 414)*

Rather than managing to reach a consensus on the role of women in combat, the commission's debates had a fractious tone, with members on each side of the issue contending that their opponents viewed the evidence through ideological blinders.

In the panel's report, five commissioners argued that permitting women in combat "will have a devastating impact on combat readiness, unit cohesion and military effectiveness." They contended that some advocates of wider roles for military women assumed "that the military must pay any price and bear any burden to promote equal opportunities and career progression for an ambitious few."

But the minority case for assigning women to combat cockpits was argued by seven commissioners, including retired Air Force Gen. Robert T. Herres, the former vice chairman of the Joint Chiefs of Staff who chaired the panel. "Laws and policies based on paternalistic notions do not demonstrate the value society places on women," the commissioners said. "They demean women's intelligence and abilities, deny them the respect that they deserve as equal members of society and deny the armed forces the use of the best-qualified individuals."

### Debate in Congress

Even before the panel made its recommendations, debate over the role of women in the military continued in Congress.

While many leaders of the Armed Forces objected to allowing women in combat roles, retired Adm. Elmo R. Zumwalt disagreed. Zumwalt, the Navy chief who broke the back of the Navy's race problem through aggressive actions in the early 1970s, insisted during an House Armed Services hearing July 29 that the combat ban helped skew the overall attitude of male service members toward women.

Testifying alongside Zumwalt, retired Maj. Gen. Jeanne M. Holm, who in 1971 became the Air Force's first female general, made a similar argument. "The exclusion of women from the full range of shipboard assignments hurts Navy women's careers, morale and acceptance within the sea service," she said.

Summing up this theme, House Armed Services Chairman Les Aspin, D-Wis., said, "The combat arms are the essence of each service. The whole promotion system and prestige in the service is oriented to the combat arms."

The following day, Air Force Chief of Staff Gen. Merrill A. McPeak and Marine Corps Commandant Gen. Carl E. Mundy Jr. acknowledged that women's service careers were handicapped by their exclusion from assignment to front-line combat units. Nevertheless, each reiterated opposition to putting women in combat roles.

"Combat is about killing people," McPeak said. "Even though logic tells us that women can do that as well as men, I have a very traditional attitude about wives and mothers and daughters being ordered to kill people."

Chief of Naval Operations Adm. Frank B. Kelso II took a more flexible stance, noting that younger Navy members agreed that combat exclusion was part of the service's problem in gender relations. While he insisted that other factors also should be considered in deciding the issue, Kelso told the panel, "You have to look at . . . the combat exclusion law."

The Armed Services Committee's three senior women lambasted the services for being slow off the mark to deal with the mistreatment of women.

Personnel Subcommittee Chairwoman Beverly B. Byron, D-Md., noted that there were no women among the senior aides seated behind the service chiefs. Each of the four pointed out women in his entourage, few of whom held high rank.

"Men must accept women as human beings, not as sex objects," Marilyn Lloyd, Tenn., angrily told the service chiefs. Like Byron, Lloyd was a relatively conservative Democrat who typically backed the Pentagon.

Patricia Schroeder, D-Colo., long one of the Pentagon's most outspoken liberal critics, made no reference to two incidents in which she had been the object of obscene comments by Navy and Marine Corps personnel. But when Air Force chief McPeak said he opposed assigning women to combat roles even though he could not articulate a logical reason, Schroeder audibly sighed.

"Where do women go?" she asked. "There just doesn't seem to be the respect, even among the top leaders."

Several Republicans insisted that assigning women to direct combat would be a problem in their part of the country.

"Speaking from a Southern exposure, I tell you it would not be popular at all to mandate that women be in combat roles, particularly . . . in infantry or special forces combat," said Bill Dickinson, Ala., the panel's senior Republican.

Randy "Duke" Cunningham, R-Calif., a retired Navy pilot, insisted that it would be especially intolerable to assign women to warships. "You cannot confine men and

women in a close space . . . for months at a time, and not have something happen," said Cunningham, who added that he saw no objection to assigning women to fly Air Force B-2 bombers operated from land bases.

But a different view was expressed by Arthur Ravenel Jr., an independent-minded but relatively conservative Republican whose South Carolina district included the Charleston Navy Yard and the Parris Island Marine Corps base.

Ravenel said an end to the combat-exclusion rule was inevitable. He invoked an old-fashioned Southern metaphor to make his point that allowing qualified women in combat billets was a good idea that the public would support. "It's not the size of the dog in the fight," he said. "It's the size of the fight in the dog."

## TAILHOOK

Sexual harassment of women in the military also became a hot issue in 1992, as women told a tale of assault at the annual naval association convention.

The assaults occurred in 1991 in Las Vegas during the convention of the Tailhook Association, a private club of naval aviators that had worked closely with the Navy hierarchy over the years. During one evening, at least 26 women, half of them Navy officers, were manhandled or had clothing removed as they passed through a group of male Navy and Marine officers in a crowded hallway of the convention hotel.

Navy Secretary H. Lawrence Garrett III, Chief of Naval Operations Kelso and dozens of other top brass attended the convention but said they witnessed no improper behavior.

Lt. Paula Coughlin, a helicopter pilot who was one of the victims, filed a formal complaint, triggering an internal Navy investigation that dragged on for months, reportedly slowed by widespread stonewalling. On June 18, Garrett asked the Defense Department's inspector general to take over the inquiry.

But during the week of June 22, Coughlin took her case to the public in lengthy interviews with The Washington Post and ABC News. On June 26, Garrett resigned, reportedly at the lightly veiled suggestion of higher-ranking administration officials.

Defense Appropriations Subcommittee Chairman John P. Murtha, D-Pa., brushed aside the Navy's investigation as "clearly a cover-up" and added: "We intend to pursue it until the people who were responsible are punished and discharged from the service."

The Senate Armed Services Committee also had pressured the Navy to unearth the truth about the Tailhook episode by refusing to send to the Senate the promotions of 4,500 Navy and Marine Corps officers.

On July 1, the committee approved 1,126 of the delayed promotions after Pentagon officials cleared those officers of any involvement in the Tailhook meeting.

In a provision of the fiscal 1993 defense appropriations bill (HR 5504 — PL 102-396), Congress barred the Tailhook organization from receiving any federal funds. *(Appropriations, p. 592)* ∎

# FOREIGN POLICY

# Bush Signs Freedom Support Act

*Law backs president's commitment to help ex-Soviets build democracy, shed decades of communist rule*

Aid for the former republics of the Soviet Union, one of President Bush's top foreign policy initiatives, won congressional passage as the Freedom Support Act (S 2532).

The measure was most of all a statement of policy and of political commitment to helping Russia and the other 11 ex-Soviet republics as they struggled to build democracy and shed 75 years of communist rule.

It authorized $410 million in bilateral assistance to the republics. It also authorized a $12.3 billion increase in the U.S. contribution to the International Monetary Fund (IMF), which the administration had sought even before it became one of the lead agencies coordinating support for Russia and its neighbors.

The legislation expanded U.S. efforts to help dismantle the former Soviet nuclear arsenal and to assist the military establishment in converting to civilian activities. It endorsed U.S. participation, with up to $3 billion in previously appropriated funds, in currency stabilization funds for the republics. And it revised a number of Cold War-era laws to reflect the collapse of communism.

Early in 1992, leading members of Congress and foreign affairs experts faulted the Bush administration for moving too slowly to formulate a package of U.S. aid to assist and encourage the consolidation of democracy and free markets in the former republics. President Bush announced his proposals on April 1, just before the leading Democratic candidate for president, Arkansas Gov. Bill Clinton, was scheduled to give a major foreign policy speech.

Congressional leaders welcomed Bush's initiative, although there was resistance over the weeks that followed, especially among House Democrats, to approving the authorization measure before the administration acted on various domestic spending programs.

The Senate Foreign Relations Committee approved its version of the aid authorization measure (S 2532), 14-4, on May 13. The Senate passed the bill, 76-20, on July 2.

In the House, the Foreign Affairs Committee approved its version (HR 4547) by voice vote June 10. The measure passed the House, 255-164, on Aug. 6.

---

## BOXSCORE

➡ **Freedom Support Act (S 2532, HR 4547).** Authorized $410 million in bilaterial assistance to Russia and the other 11 ex-Soviet republics as they began to build a democracy after 75 years of communist rule. The measure also authorized a $12.3 billion increase in the U.S. contribution to the International Monetary Fund.

**Reports:** S Rept 102-292; H Rept 102-569; conference report H Rept 102-964.

### KEY ACTION

April 1 — President Bush announced his proposal for an initiative aimed at stabilizing Russia's economy.

May 13 — The **Senate** Foreign Relations Committee approved S 2532, 14-4.

June 10 — The **House** Foreign Affairs Committee approved HR 4547 by voice vote.

July 2 — The **Senate** passed S 2532, 76-20.

Aug. 6 — The **House** passed HR 4547, 255-164.

Oct. 1 — The **Senate** adopted the conference report on S 2522 by voice vote.

Oct. 3 — The **House** cleared the legislation, 232-164.

Oct. 24 — President Bush signed S 2532 — PL 102-511.

---

The measure that moved through Congress included all of the essential elements of Bush's proposal, although lawmakers imposed some conditions on aid and gave the administration less discretion than it had sought over how much to spend.

Conferees on the measure agreed to soften a Senate provision that would have cut off aid unless the president determined that Russia was withdrawing its troops from the Baltic States within 12 months of enactment. The final version said Russia would be ineligible for aid if it failed to make significant progress in withdrawing troops, but the measure permitted the president to waive the provision on grounds of national interest. *(Highlights, p. 526)*

A more restrictive condition concerning Russian troop withdrawal from the Baltics was imposed in the fiscal 1993 foreign operations appropriations measure (HR 5368), which provided funding for the $12.3 billion IMF increase and for $417 million in economic and technical assistance to the former Soviet republics.

The Senate approved the conference report on the ex-Soviet aid authorization bill (S 2532 — H Rept 102-964) by voice vote on Oct. 1. The House cleared the measure for the president, 232-164, on Oct. 3

The president signed the measure (PL 102-511) on Oct. 24.

### BACKGROUND

Even before the Soviet Union crumbled at the end of 1991, leading members of Congress and many foreign policy experts faulted Bush for failing to commit substantial U.S. aid to bolster the evolutionary changes sought by Soviet President Mikhail S. Gorbachev. But the administration and its allies argued that money would be wasted, and perhaps even be used to prop up the existing system, if aid were provided before reforms were irrevocably in place. *(1991 Almanac, p. 463)*

In early 1992, after the fall of communist rule in Moscow, demands built for the Bush administration and Congress to take more aggressive action in providing U.S. assistance to the former Soviet republics.

In a confluence of pleas from across the political spectrum, leading lawmakers from both parties, former Presi-

dent Richard M. Nixon and U.S. Ambassador to Russia Robert S. Strauss, all warned during the week of March 9 that such aid would be crucial if the republics' moves toward democracy were to succeed.

Those calling for action appeared united in their attempt to reverse what they saw as a potentially dangerous trend toward isolationism in an election year dominated by domestic concerns.

They said failure to provide aid would be far more costly to the United States, both in terms of national security and lost economic opportunity, than the price of any immediate assistance.

"We've all made a mistake, and we've let this get presented as an aid program or as an assistance program or as charity," Strauss told the Senate Foreign Relations Committee on March 11. "We have lost sight of the fact that, if we do it right, that we have a tremendous self-interest."

Strauss — a longtime Democratic Party leader and former U.S. trade negotiator who was appointed to the Moscow post by the Republican president — said he found it "shocking" upon his return to the United States to discover that the issue was not even being discussed in the presidential primary campaign. "This ain't beanbag we're playing.... These are big-time issues; this is life and death," he said.

Four leading senators, who had just returned from Russia and Ukraine, also called the same day for more U.S. action. The bipartisan group, led by Armed Services Committee Chairman Sam Nunn, D-Ga., and Richard G. Lugar, R-Ind., recommended a series of steps to encourage more private U.S. investment in the republics and to help convert the former Soviet defense industry to civilian production.

"The place in history of President Bush will be judged by what happens in our own government in treating this as a priority over the next several months," Nunn said. He added that the administration needed to be more "engaged" than it was the previous year when lawmakers enacted a $500 million aid package without active White House support.

Only hours later, Bush, who had said little recently about foreign aid, spoke in unusually strong terms about the link between international and domestic policies.

"Turning our back on the world is simply no answer. I don't care how difficult our economic problems are at home," he told a convocation of foreign policy specialists sponsored by Nixon's presidential library. "We invested so much to win the Cold War, we must invest what is necessary to win the peace."

The audience had heard earlier in the day from Nixon, who had set the theme for the conference in a widely circulated memorandum that lambasted U.S. policy toward the republics as "pathetically inadequate." Nixon told the group that if the Russian experiment with freedom failed, "dictatorship, rather than democracy, will be the wave of the future."

But Deputy Secretary of State Lawrence S. Eagleburger told a House subcommittee, also on March 11, that "simply throwing money" at the problem could be counterproductive and that efforts should be directed at strengthening private-sector activity.

"Indeed, money indiscriminately pumped into the region could hinder reform and promote the very dependencies that have for too long existed in these countries," he said.

For fiscal 1992 and 1993, the administration requested $620 million in technical and humanitarian assistance for the republics, he said. This would be in addition to $860 million already available and $3.5 billion in loan guarantees that had been provided since January 1991 for the purchase of U.S. agricultural goods.

While the administration had also asked for a $12 billion increase in the U.S. contribution to the IMF, the request became mired in partisan conflict over foreign aid.

Democratic members of the Foreign Relations Committee told Strauss that their party would support the increased contribution if the administration actively lobbied Republicans to vote for it. In an unusual move, Patrick J. Leahy, D-Vt., chairman of the Appropriations subcommittee with jurisdiction over the IMF, appeared during the hearing to make a similar pledge in person. But, he said, "I cannot pass the administration's package by myself." Previously, Leahy had said the request was dead.

## BUSH PROPOSAL

On April 1, Bush announced that the United States would participate in a $24 billion multilateral assistance initiative aimed at stabilizing Russia's economy and would provide additional U.S. assistance, including increased food credits, to Russia and the other former Soviet republics.

Lawmakers generally welcomed President Bush's proposal. But those promoting the assistance predicted that enactment would require strong guidance from Bush and congressional leaders to avoid potentially disruptive election-year turbulence.

"It will take the best skills of enlightened leadership," said Rep. Henry J. Hyde, R-Ill. "Some people are sure to look at this as money going to St. Petersburg, Russia, rather than St. Petersburg, Florida."

As senior members of Congress had encouraged him to do for months in urging such a package, Bush presented the assistance as insurance for the United States against the re-emergence of an unfriendly regime rather than as a handout to the former Soviet people.

"The stakes are as high for us now as any that we have faced in this century," Bush said at a televised White House news conference. "If this democratic revolution is defeated, it could plunge us into a world more dangerous in some respects than the dark years of the Cold War." *(Text, p. 14-E)*

While emphasizing that the United States must lead, Bush made clear that the financial effort would be international. While emphasizing the depth of assistance required, he and White House officials downplayed the cost to American taxpayers.

"It's not a tremendous amount of money," Bush said. "Our commitment is very, very substantial."

Much of the president's package required no legislative action. However the administration viewed congressional endorsement as crucial, both to provide some of the bilateral aid and to put a bipartisan imprimatur on the overall effort.

Lawmakers repeated their pledge to support the administration's effort — if Bush invested political capital in pushing through the proposals. "We do have to stop the politics on this one," said House Majority Leader Richard A. Gephardt, D-Mo. "It's got to be bipartisan."

The administration appeared ready to take Congress up on the offer. Secretary of State James A. Baker III said on April 1 that he was "ready to go up there tomorrow and start fighting for this legislation."

In a letter to Congress on April 3, Bush wrote, "This is an issue that transcends any election.... I urge all members of Congress to set aside partisan and parochial interests."

But there were also early signs of potential resistance. House Majority Whip David E. Bonior, D-Mich., threatened to organize a move against assistance to Russia until the administration supported legislation to extend unemployment benefits and to create jobs.

"No way should the president get a dime — and I mean not a single dime — until he's signed off on help for Americans," Bonior said April 2.

And even the talk of bipartisanship had enough partisan overtones to make lawmakers wary of predicting success for the plan. Democrats applauded Bush for his aid initiatives and then went on to criticize him for offering them too late.

Within minutes of Bush's announcement, Clinton, campaigning for the Democratic presidential nomination, gave a foreign policy speech in New York that largely mirrored the president's proposals for helping the former Soviet empire. But he too criticized the president for delay.

"The present administration has been overly cautious on the issue of aid to Russia, not for policy considerations, but out of political calculation," Clinton said. "Now, prodded by Democrats in Congress, rebuked by Nixon and realizing that I have been raising this issue in the campaign since December, the president is finally, even now as we meet here, putting forward a plan of assistance to Russia and the other new republics.... I'd really like it if I could have as much influence on his domestic policy."

In an effort to explain his timing, Bush said that the administration had been pulling together the components of a package for months and had just been able to work out the details with allies. Administration officials also noted that the Russian government of President Boris N. Yeltsin had only recently implemented credible economic reforms on which the administration had conditioned U.S. assistance.

"This isn't any Johnny-come-lately thing, and this isn't driven by election-year pressures," Bush said. "It's what's right for the United States."

### Short on Details

Leahy, who headed the Foreign Operations Appropriations Subcommittee, was also critical of the administration's vagueness about the price tag for the aid. Honesty about the cost would be "the real test of leadership," he said.

Administration officials said it was difficult to pinpoint the exact amount because much of the proposed assistance was already in the pipeline or in the form of guarantees or loans that would not involve direct U.S. outlays. And the amounts needed to be appropriated were, for the most part, requested earlier by the administration — including $470 million for humanitarian, technical and other assistance in fiscal 1993 and a $12.3 billion increase in U.S. backing for the International Monetary Fund.

Bush's package included three parts: the multilateral initiative of seven industrialized nations, the extension of additional food credits and a legislative package to provide authorization for several additional assistance proposals.

The multilateral initiative called for $24 billion in aid in 1992, much of it as loans and guarantees, rather than direct assistance. Of that amount, $18 billion was to be in bilateral and multilateral assistance aimed at bolstering Rus-

sia's balance of payments. The package also included a multilateral fund to stabilize the Russian currency.

Bush also announced that he would increase by $1.1 billion the export credits available for purchase of U.S. agricultural goods by the former republics. Of this amount, $600 million was to be targeted for Russia (and counted as part of the U.S. contribution to the $18 billion portion of the multilateral initiative). The remaining $500 million was to be available for the other former Soviet republics.

The third component was the legislative package, which was sought to provide congressional endorsement for the president's proposals and allow waivers of Cold War-era laws that limited U.S. assistance for, and private business activities in, the former republics.

## SENATE ACTION

The administration sought passage of the legislation first in the Senate, where support for the aid appeared greatest. Baker went to Capitol Hill on April 8-9 to press for quick action.

He told the Foreign Relations Committee on April 9 that President Bush hoped to have the legislation in hand by mid-June, in time for a scheduled summit meeting in Washington with Yeltsin.

Calling U.S. support for reforms in the former Soviet states the most "pressing national security imperative," Baker said that congressional action would send "a very powerful signal of our willingness to help."

Members of the committee, many of whom had been advocating such aid since 1991, indicated a willingness to aim for the June deadline. "I, and I suspect everyone else here, intend to work energetically with you to enact this program," Joseph R. Biden Jr., D-Del., told Baker.

However, several Democrats chided Baker for attaching an urgency to assisting the former Soviets that the administration lacked when it came to addressing domestic problems.

"I'll guarantee you that there'd be no rush to deal with legislation by July or August to try to provide some assistance and encourage economic development in the Bridgeports or Hartfords or Detroits or San Franciscos or wherever else in this country," said Christopher J. Dodd, D-Conn.

Baker countered that the aid would serve U.S. interests. The failure of reforms could mean the re-emergence of an enemy that would eat up "a whale of a lot of money" in future defense costs, he said, while success could mean more defense savings to help the domestic economy.

Baker found an unusually strong ally in Alan Cranston, D-Calif., who called on Senate leaders to discourage "nit-picking" on the bill and avoid linking it to domestic issues: "If we let it get bogged down in that way, we will have a total disaster, and we will fail to move this legislation on any kind of a sensible schedule."

By May, however, House leaders had escalated their demands for action first on domestic legislation, and senators became increasingly vocal in demanding more details from the administration. The administration's goal of winning enactment before Yeltsin's June visit appeared to be slipping out of reach.

"This is a mess.... It's a political mess, but it's also a budgeting mess," Sen. Bob Kasten, R-Wis., told administration witnesses at a hearing on May 6.

Numerous amendments, including several to impose what sponsors saw as harmful restrictions on the assis-

# Freedom Support Act Highlights

*The Freedom Support Act (S 2532 — PL 102-511), the legislation authorizing aid to the former Soviet republics, included provisions that:*

● Authorized $410 million in bilateral assistance to Russia and 11 other republics. The money was made available in fiscal 1993 for a wide range of purposes including humanitarian needs, health care, democratic reforms, the promotion of private enterprise, trade, education, environmental protection, transportation, telecommunications, drug education, refugee assistance, energy efficiency and nuclear reactor safety.

The legislation mostly left it to the administration to decide how funds should be spent. However, the programs were supposed to promote a free-market system in the republics as well as provide opportunities for U.S. businesses.

● Placed several conditions on the aid: Assistance was to be terminated if the president determined that a republic was guilty of gross violations of human rights or international law, or if it failed to meet certain arms control obligations.

In the case of Russia, assistance had to be cut off if the president determined that the country had failed to make "significant progress" in removing its troops from the Baltic States of Estonia, Latvia and Lithuania. However, a more stringent requirement concerning Russian troops in the Baltics was contained in the foreign operations spending bill, which appropriated the aid money.

Most of the conditions in the Freedom Support Act could be waived if the president determined that was in the U.S. interest. However, this did not apply to a prohibition in the bill against any aid to the government of Azerbaijan until the president determined that it was taking "demonstrable steps to cease all blockades and other offensive uses of force against Armenia and Nagorno-Karabakh."

● Authorized a $12.3 billion increase in the U.S. contribution to the International Monetary Fund (IMF). The increase did not involve any U.S. outlays but was needed by the IMF to build up its reserves so that it could carry out lending programs for many nations, including the former Soviet republics. The increase, in fact, was negotiated long before the collapse of the Soviet Union, but it failed to win congressional approval earlier because of lawmakers' reluctance to approve any foreign aid.

● Expressed congressional support for U.S. participation, with sums of up to $3 billion in previously approved funds, in multilateral currency stabilization funds for Russia and the other republics. About half the money was to go toward the U.S. share of a $6 billion fund planned by leading industrial nations to help stabilize the Russian ruble.

● Authorized the use of $800 million from the Pentagon budget to help the former Soviet republics dismantle nuclear and other weapons of mass destruction. The funds, half of which were approved in fiscal 1992, could also be used to assist the former Soviet military establishment to convert to civilian activities and to prevent out-of-work Soviet scientists from selling their knowl-edge about nuclear weapons to potentially dangerous nations.

The United States had already committed about $190 million of the funds to transport nuclear weapons from other republics to Russia, to build a new storage facility there for radioactive waste from dismantled weapons, and to build science centers in Russia and Ukraine to employ weapons experts.

● Allowed the president to use $100 million in security assistance funds to help dismantle and halt the proliferation of nuclear, biological and chemical weapons worldwide. It allowed another $40 million in defense funds to be used to support international non-proliferation efforts, such as those carried out by the International Atomic Energy Agency and the U.N. Special Commission on Iraq.

● Authorized $12 million for the establishment of American business centers to help U.S. businesses and state development offices pursue joint ventures and other business activities in the republics.

These were to include centers specifically devoted to promoting agribusiness and environmental business opportunities.

It also encouraged the administration to use existing funds to promote U.S. exports to the republics.

● Allowed the president to establish a Democracy Corps of private U.S. citizens to provide technical and other assistance in setting up local democratic institutions and civic organizations in the republics.

It authorized up to $15 million for the program in fiscal 1993.

● Promoted space trade and cooperation between the United States and the republics by expediting approval of U.S. purchases of former Soviet space hardware, technology and services, and by promoting trade missions for the U.S. aerospace industry.

● Made the republics eligible for agricultural credit assistance under the Food for Progress program, which was designed to promote free enterprise in emerging democracies. It also authorized technical assistance for the republics to improve food production and distribution systems.

● Authorized $25 million for the Department of State and the U.S. Information Agency to set up diplomatic posts and other offices in the republics.

● Authorized $71 million for student, business, agricultural and other exchange programs between the United States and the former Soviet republics. Of this amount, $20 million was set aside for short-term visits by secondary school students from the republics to the United States.

● Extended the Support for East European Democracy (SEED) program, already applied in Poland and Hungary, to the rest of Eastern Europe. SEED aid was designed to boost private enterprise in these countries.

● Changed several Cold War-era laws to reflect the collapse of communism.

For example, the bill removed the names of the former Soviet republics from the list of communist nations ineligible for aid under the 1961 Foreign Assistance Act.

tance, surfaced during informal drafting of a package (S 2532) by the Foreign Relations Committee. The markup, originally scheduled for May 7, was delayed for a week as members wrestled with details and as domestic issues moved to the top of the agenda.

When President Bush held a treaty-signing ceremony at the White House with Ukrainian President Leonid Kravchuk on May 6, reporters' questions focused almost exclusively on Bush's response to urban unrest. *(Urban crisis, p. 339)*

"It stands in some jeopardy of falling off the tracks at almost every stage," Lugar, a leading proponent of assistance, warned administration officials the same day at a hearing held jointly by the Agriculture Committee and the Foreign Operations Appropriations Subcommittee.

Senators told the witnesses that it would be virtually impossible for them to vote for the bill if they could not explain to constituents how much the aid program would cost and exactly what the legislation would do.

They complained that the administration was trying to have it both ways by announcing a $5 billion U.S. contribution to a $24 billion international aid package for Russia, while claiming that no new appropriations would be required of Congress. At the same time, they said, the vaguely worded proposal — which Secretary of State Baker acknowledged was more a policy statement than a piece of legislation — left far too much unsaid.

"If I went back home to a community forum and was asked to report on what we're doing . . . I tell you honestly, I wouldn't have the slightest idea what to tell my people back home," said Kent Conrad, D-N.D.

Leahy, chairman of the Agriculture Committee and the Foreign Operations Subcommittee, said provisions giving the administration maximum flexibility were unacceptable.

"It writes Congress really out of the act, except to provide the money, and I suppose if it turns out there are mistakes or problems, Congress will quickly be back in so it can share the blame," he told Richard L. Armitage, the State Department official coordinating the aid program.

Ultimately, lawmakers jettisoned some of the open-ended provisions proposed by the administration, including authority for the president to spend "such sums as may be necessary" to carry out exchange and technical aid programs and to waive all other laws in order to provide the aid.

### Committee Action

The Senate Foreign Relations Committee approved the aid legislation (S 2532) with limited revisions by a vote of 14-4 on May 13.

Minutes after the first touchy amendment was offered, Secretary of State Baker was on the phone, trying to sell its sponsor Jesse Helms, R-N.C., on a compromise.

Helms pressed ahead, but lost, 3-15, on his amendment to require collateral for multinational loans to the republics.

More important, Baker's quick call to the committee signaled that the administration was giving the aid package the priority that lawmakers said was needed.

Although the committee redrafted the proposal, its version generally gave the administration what it requested, including approval of the $12.3 billion increase in the U.S. contribution to the International Monetary Fund.

Most of all, said Chairman Claiborne Pell, D-R.I., the measure provided a "statutory expression of commitment" by Congress to work with the administration on its assis-

tance effort.

Voting against the legislation were Helms; Larry Pressler, R-S.D.; Hank Brown, R-Colo.; and Dodd.

Dodd, who was up for re-election in an economically strapped state, was the most openly critical of the bill, lashing out against provisions giving the administration wide discretion to carry out aid programs. "We're virtually abdicating our role," he said. But Dodd offered no amendments.

The question for backers of the legislation was whether tampering with the bill at the margins might open the floodgates for more damaging amendments on the Senate floor, where support was less solid.

While Helms' amendment was blocked, two others of concern to the administration were approved.

The first, offered by John Kerry, D-Mass., would prohibit the administration from providing any assistance to Azerbaijan until the president certified to Congress that it had stopped its blockade and use of force against Armenia. The two republics were locked in battle over control of the Nagorno-Karabakh region.

Richard L. Armitage, coordinator of the U.S. aid program in the former Soviet republics, told the committee that the administration opposed the amendment because it would put the United States on one side of a complicated ethnic dispute.

Lugar said the amendment might be the first of many "editorial statements" that could ultimately bring down the bill.

But Kerry, who said the conflict was too explosive to ignore, prevailed on a 14-4 vote.

The committee also approved, 19-0, an amendment by Biden that would block U.S. assistance to any republic that transferred missile technology or material, equipment or technology that might allow another country to manufacture weapons of mass destruction. Armitage said the administration agreed "in principle" with the amendment but preferred to have as clean a bill as possible.

As approved by Foreign Relations, the legislation included language submitted by the Senate Armed Services Committee to broaden the allowable uses of $400 million approved in 1991 to help dismantle the Soviet nuclear arsenal. Under the bill, the funds could be used to assist with the conversion of military industries and equipment to civilian purposes and to help with the withdrawal and relocation of former Soviet military forces.

### Yeltsin's Visit

The administration did not win passage of the aid package in time for Yeltsin's visit to Washington the week of June 15. But the burly, silver-haired Russian president was greeted as a hero and a world-class celebrity.

He signed an unprecedented arms control agreement with President Bush and talked about mutually beneficial trade, then made sweeping, unqualified promises to cooperate with U.S. officials on such touchstone issues as Vietnam prisoners of war. *(Arms proliferation, p. 555; POW/MIA probe, p. 560)*

When he came to Capitol Hill on June 17 and entered the House chamber, members of Congress greeted him with chants of "Bo-ris, Bo-ris" and hailed him with numerous standing ovations.

Yeltsin did not disappoint, clearly winning over those lawmakers who had been skeptical of his commitment to democratic reforms and his willingness to become an American ally.

"The idol of communism, which spread everywhere social strife, animosity and unparalleled brutality, which instilled fear in humanity, has collapsed," he said to thundering applause from a packed chamber. "It has collapsed never to rise again. I am here to assure you we will not let it rise again in our land."

Members were not immediately certain whether Yeltsin's personal popularity would translate into the long-term economic and political support he sought.

"I like what he said. I appreciate it," said Rep. John P. Murtha, D-Pa., after Yeltsin's speech before a joint meeting of Congress — the first of any Russian or Soviet leader. "But I'm not anxious, without a real plan, to support more aid."

Rep. Stephen L. Neal, D-N.C., said members would still get their directions from constituents and "if you ask the average person back home, they'd say we need the money here."

As recently as June 16, the Senate Democratic Caucus had been deeply split over the wisdom of bringing the president's aid proposal to the floor. But Senate Majority Leader George J. Mitchell, D-Maine, told reporters after a leadership luncheon with Yeltsin on June 17 that many members felt that the Russian president had made a "strong and persuasive" case.

"It's not so much that Yeltsin won them all over," said one Senate Democratic aide, "as much as his appearance improved the climate in which a vote will be taken. . . . It's easier now for people to vote for it politically."

### Floor Action

Putting aside election-year anxiety over foreign aid, the Senate on July 2 overwhelmingly approved the Bush administration's comprehensive aid initiative for Russia and it neighbors.

The Senate passed the legislation (S 2532), termed the Freedom Support Act, 76-20. Democrats supported the measure, 43-13; Republicans backed it, 33-7. Eleven of the 20 senators who opposed the measure were facing election in November. (Vote 148, p. 20-S)

Lugar, who managed the bill for the Republicans, called the aid program "an investment in political, economic and social reform in these new states that will pay dividends many times over in new American exports and the savings generated in our defense budget."

But opponents complained during a sometimes rancorous debate that Bush was unwilling to devote similar resources to domestic problems. At one point, Donald W. Riegle Jr., D-Mich., described the president as "drunk on foreign policy."

Because the measure authorized a combination of new and existing proposals — some of which required no outlays of funds — cost estimates varied widely. The legislation only authorized the assistance, and Congress had yet to appropriate new funding called for in the bill.

The Congressional Budget Office (CBO) estimated the cost of the measure's provisions authorizing aid for the former Soviet republics and Eastern Europe at nearly $1 billion in fiscal 1993, but that figure did not include funds required to back billions of dollars in already approved or proposed agricultural and export credits.

"The political statement provided by passage of this bill is probably more important than the dollar amounts contained in it," Lugar said.

The three-day debate on the measure was dominated by expressions of concern over the sagging U.S. economy. In the mountain of amendments to the measure was a pro-

posal, offered July 2 by Riegle, to require the president to match about $1 billion in economic aid included in the bill with a similar level of support for domestic programs.

Riegle's amendment was tabled (killed), 64-32. (Vote 146, p. 20-S)

The only Republicans who supported Riegle's amendment — Bob Kasten, Wis.; Daniel R. Coats, Ind.; John Seymour, Calif.; and Arlen Specter, Pa. — were up for election.

Perhaps the most serious threat to the aid package came from an amendment that would have barred most U.S. aid for Moscow unless the president certified that Russia was making "significant progress" toward removing its troops still based in the Baltic states.

Dennis DeConcini, D-Ariz., who offered the amendment July 1 with Larry Pressler, R-S.D., argued that the fledgling nations "cannot be completely free as long as they are still being occupied by the very same army which humiliated and terrorized the Baltic people for five long decades."

Lugar countered that the effect of the amendment would be to "nullify" the Freedom Support Act because the president could not make such a certification. There were still more than 100,000 troops from Russia and the Commonwealth of Independent States based in the newly independent Baltic states of Estonia, Latvia and Lithuania.

Foreign Relations Committee Chairman Pell, who managed the bill on behalf of the Democrats, then proposed to modify the amendment by delaying the certification requirement for a year.

Despite Pressler's complaint that the amendment amounted to a "sellout" of the Baltic people, his motion to table (kill) the Pell amendment fell short, 35-60. (Vote 139, p. 19-S)

Demonstrating their support for the Baltic states, senators subsequently voted 96-0 in favor of an amendment by Robert C. Byrd, D-W.Va., to authorize the president to provide shipments of non-lethal military equipment to the Baltics. (Vote 143, p. 19-S)

There were several other efforts to attach policy conditions to the aid initiative. But the administration had signaled at the outset that the inclusion of such conditions would kill the bill. Lugar and Pell led efforts to successfully block most of the policy amendments.

Specter proposed language that could have required U.S. representatives to multilateral banks to oppose loans to the former republics unless they were secured by royalties from commodity exports. The amendment, similar to a proposal that had been defeated by the Senate Foreign Relations Committee, was tabled (killed), 75-21. (Vote 147, p. 20-S)

Another Republican, Hank Brown of Colorado, took a different tack, proposing tough restrictions on the $12.3 billion increase in the U.S. contribution to the IMF.

Brown, a persistent critic of the fund, sought to limit the contribution to the U.S. share of IMF money actually provided to the former republics. His amendment was also tabled (killed), 77-20. (Vote 142, p. 19-S)

In something of a surprise, the administration did not contest an amendment offered by Alfonse M. D'Amato, R-N.Y., to bar the use of U.S. aid and credits to repay debts owed by the former republics to international financial institutions. D'Amato said that, without such a restriction, U.S. aid could "redeem banks that poured money down a black hole." D'Amato's amendment was approved by voice vote.

In an effort to ease congressional anxieties over embark-

ing on a potentially costly aid initiative, the administration and the bill's supporters sought to downplay the amount of funding provided in the measure.

Pete V. Domenici, N.M., the ranking Republican on the Senate Budget Committee, said that the cost of the legislation's assistance to the former Soviet Union would be $620 million — the administration's $470 million aid request for the former republics in fiscal 1993, plus $150 million in fiscal 1992 assistance already appropriated by Congress.

But the CBO cautioned that assessing the cost of the measure was difficult, in part because "the administration does not have budget-quality estimates of its program."

The CBO said that the administration had announced plans to finance $2.9 billion of exports of agricultural commodities for the former Soviet Union in 1992. Although Congress was required to set aside appropriated funds for such programs — the CBO said that a subsidy of $558 million would be needed to back the $2.9 billion worth of credits — the bill did not include those costs.

Pell and Lugar crafted an amendment to strike the open-ended grant of budget authority sought by the administration, setting specific funding amounts for many of the categories of direct assistance. The amendment was approved by voice vote.

Bill Bradley, D-N.J., bucked the budget-cutting mood in Congress and proposed an amendment that would have supported a dramatically expanded program of educational exchanges with the former republics.

But several senators, notably Appropriations Committee Chairman Byrd, were opposed to the program's cost, which Bradley said would exceed $1 billion over five years.

After Byrd hinted that he would lead a filibuster against the amendment, Bradley scaled back the proposal to a one-year program costing about $76 million. He said the amendment, approved by voice vote, would fund exchanges involving 17,000 students, including 13,000 high school students.

In other action, the Senate:

● Approved, 93-4, a strongly worded sense of the Senate amendment by Byrd opposing the proposed sale of the LTV Corp., a U.S. missile manufacturer, to a buyer backed by the French government. The deal later fell through. (Vote 141, p. 19-S)

● Approved amendments aimed at supporting home-state interests, including a proposal by Byrd to authorize $35 million to promote clean coal technologies in the former republics.

● Approved a sense of the Senate amendment, offered by D'Amato, supporting aid to help Israel absorb an influx of immigrants from the former Soviet Union. D'Amato had hinted that he might try to amend the bill with a portion of Israel's controversial request for U.S. loan guarantees. (Israeli loan guarantees, p. 539)

## HOUSE ACTION

From the beginning, House leaders had made it clear that their backing for the measure to aid Russia and its neighbors would come with a price in domestic policy funding.

House leaders grew increasingly annoyed that the administration was bashing Congress over management problems and opposing Democratic domestic initiatives even as it sought bipartisan backing for the aid plan.

"In that context, it's an illusion for them to think they will pass an aid package for Russia," said a House leadership aide. "The votes just won't be there."

Majority Leader Gephardt upped the ante in the struggle for House backing when he told a Ways and Means subcommittee on April 9 that passage of the aid bill was tied to the fate of a Democratic plan to make permanent changes in jobless benefits. Gephardt's comments took on added significance because he had been one of the strongest congressional advocates for helping the former Soviet states.

Gephardt warned that if Bush resisted the Democrats' initiative, "the reverberations will be felt from the unemployment lines in America to the bread lines in Moscow. He must persuade Americans that he cares as much about their livelihoods and aspirations as he does about those of the people of the Commonwealth of Independent States."

House Democrats also were particularly wary of the package's $12.3 billion IMF funding increase, saying they would insist that the administration round up a majority of Republican votes for the IMF increase before they went along.

Banking Committee Chairman Henry B. Gonzalez, D-Texas, said May 14 that he had agreed to a request by International Development Subcommittee Chairwoman Mary Rose Oakar, D-Ohio, to delay action on the measure until after her primary for re-election June 2. Gonzalez said he thought it would be difficult for the committee to act before then, in any event, because details remained to be worked out with the administration.

### Committee Action

The House Foreign Affairs Committee easily approved its version of the aid package (HR 4547) by voice vote on June 10.

But Democratic leaders said they would not schedule floor debate in either chamber until agreement was reached on several domestic issues, including urban aid and unemployment insurance. They argued that, for practical political reasons, members who were up for re-election would be hard pressed to justify a vote for foreign aid before some action was taken to resolve problems at home.

Before marking up their version of the bill, Foreign Affairs leaders made a pitch for bipartisanship that proved successful in committee but was unlikely to have much impact on the broader debate. Committee Chairman Dante B. Fascell, D-Fla., who was retiring at the end of the year, told members that despite the prevailing political winds, they had a responsibility to act on the aid package.

"It would be easy to kill this legislation," he said. "It's either a full moon or a monsoon or it's an election season. ... There is no good time to act."

Ranking Republican William S. Broomfield, Mich., also set to retire, added: "The stakes for future generations are simply too great to be lost in the politics of the moment."

The House committee bill was similar to the measure passed by Senate Foreign Relations in May.

In addition to authorizing the IMF increase, the House bill included authorization for approximately $610 million in assistance for fiscal 1992 and 1993.

However, HR 4547 tightened conditions on aid and put limits on the amount of money to be spent, provisions that were not included in the Senate version.

The House bill said that aid could be provided only if the republics were making "significant progress" in democratic and economic reforms, were exhibiting respect for internationally recognized human rights and were adhering to existing arms control agreements.

The committee agreed to a proposal by Stephen J.

Solarz, D-N.Y., to delete language in the draft bill requiring that the republics need only to be taking steps toward these goals in order to get the aid. Solarz argued that the tougher language might prevent more stringent, and possibly lethal, conditions from being attached on the House floor.

Members also agreed by voice vote to an amendment by Wayne Owens, D-Utah, to prohibit any of the aid from going to Azerbaijan until the president certified that the republic was "taking measurable steps" to end its blockade and use of force against Armenia and the autonomous region of Nagorno-Karabakh. The Senate bill contained a similar but slightly tougher prohibition.

The House bill would authorize $584.7 million for fiscal 1992 and 1993 to the republics for humanitarian and food aid, to assist with democratic and economic reforms, to encourage U.S. private investment and trade, to help convert the former Soviet military establishment to civilian uses and to promote energy efficiency and environmental protection.

The committee also agreed by voice vote to allow up to $15 million of the funds to be used to establish a "democracy corps" of U.S. citizens who would go to the republics for two-year stints to help set up democratic institutions outside the capital cities.

An additional $25 million would be provided to the State Department and the U.S. Information Agency to help set up offices and embassies in the republics.

An amendment by Jim Leach, R-Iowa, to use $150 million of the funds to enable thousands of former Soviet students and business managers to study and work in the United States was rejected by voice vote.

The bill endorsed U.S. participation, involving up to $3 billion in previously approved money, in a fund to help stabilize the currencies of the former republics.

The legislation called for expanding the uses and amount of funding available from the defense budget to help dismantle the former Soviet nuclear arsenal. The bill would also allow the money to be used to establish science and technology centers to provide jobs for scientists and others formerly engaged in weapons production. The money could also be used to assist with conversion of defense industries to civilian purposes.

### Floor Action

Setting aside fears that recession-weary constituents would retaliate in November, House members voted overwhelmingly on Aug. 6 for the legislation to send financial and other assistance to the former states of the Soviet Union.

All efforts to amend the measure were blocked by an unusually united leadership, and the measure (HR 4547) was approved 255-164. *(Vote 374, p. 92-H)*

Republican and Democratic leaders and the White House rallied behind the aid bill, making passage possible at a time when many politicians were far more concerned about the loss of jobs and urban strife at home than the plight of a former enemy.

Sponsors argued that the bill, which included the $12.3 billion increase in the U.S. commitment to the International Monetary Fund, was vital to U.S. self-interest. They warned that failure to support emerging democracies in Russia and 11 other republics could prove far more costly in the long run.

"We cannot live safe and prosperous and free if there is turmoil and upheaval in a vast land that possesses some 30,000 nuclear warheads," said Lee H. Hamilton, D-Ind., chairman of the Foreign Affairs Committee's Subcommittee on Europe and the Middle East. "If their reforms fail or are derailed, all of us are worse off."

But many lawmakers complained bitterly about the need to spend more at home. "I do not know how we can do this for Russia or anybody else and continue to ignore our cities," said Maxine Waters, D-Calif., whose Los Angeles district was struggling to recover from the devastating riots of April.

For months, House Democratic leaders had said they would not schedule a floor vote on aid for the former Soviet republics until the administration agreed to a number of domestic spending initiatives.

The path to House passage was cleared Aug. 5, when administration officials tentatively agreed in a meeting with House leaders to accelerate about $370 million in spending on public works programs and to make new loan guarantees available to local communities, possibly as much as $2 billion.

Majority Leader Gephardt and Majority Whip Bonior said they were encouraged by the ongoing negotiations with budget director Richard G. Darman and Transportation Secretary Andrew H. Card Jr. Still, they warned that they would hold up the bill when a conference agreement came before the House for final approval if the tentative deal fell through.

"So help me God, if there's a reneging . . . there will be hell to pay for sure," Bonior told the Rules Committee on Aug. 5.

The agreement to spend more on domestic programs did not alone ensure passage of the bill. A remarkable coalition of current and former public officials, business groups and peace activists also lobbied heavily for the aid legislation.

In an Aug. 3 letter, designed as much to provide political cover for members worried about constituent reaction as to persuade, Bush told members that failure to help the struggling republics "would be a tragic mistake for which history will surely judge us harshly."

Former Presidents Ronald Reagan, Jimmy Carter, Gerald R. Ford and Richard M. Nixon also wrote that the vote could be the most important one members would cast.

"The stakes could not be higher," they said, in a letter read by Gephardt on the House floor. "If we fail to seize this historic opportunity now, authoritarianism could return to Moscow and elsewhere, the anticipated peace dividend could evaporate, future markets and jobs for Americans could be lost, and nuclear weapons may again threaten the lives of our children."

Conservatives who were frequently critical of foreign aid spending joined in the plea for action in this case.

"If you vote no today, be sure in your hearts that you understand the burden that you are taking," said Minority Whip Newt Gingrich, R-Ga., "because you are willing to risk the collapse of democracy in Russia and stand to one side and do nothing about it."

One potential stumbling block was strong opposition to a rule providing for floor debate but prohibiting amendments. Sponsors of the bill had argued that the aid could be derailed if it was burdened by conditions or by amendments on extraneous domestic issues.

"I think it's critically important that we keep this simple and precise," said Hamilton, who noted growing opposition in Russia to Yeltsin's reforms. "Time is really of the essence. . . . Yeltsin is on the bubble. He really is on the precipice."

Those seeking amendments — including one by Waters to make $10 billion in loan guarantees available to U.S. communities — were not swayed. They vowed to fight the rule on the floor and predicted a close vote.

But in a remarkable miscalculation, Waters, members of the Congressional Black Caucus and others opposed to the rule decided to hold a news conference just as debate on the rule was drawing to a close. When they returned to the House floor, they discovered that the rule already had been approved by voice vote because no one in the chamber had requested a recorded vote.

"They just screwed up," said one pleasantly surprised Democratic supporter of the bill who had been trying to round up votes in favor of the rule.

Waters, who was in her first term, said she would just "chalk this one up. I thought the floor was covered."

But Paul E. Kanjorski, D-Pa., another opponent of the closed rule, was outraged. He said he had left the floor to attend a caucus meeting with representatives of Clinton's presidential campaign only to return and find that the rule had passed.

"I was at a meeting to support the party's nominee. You'd think the leadership would have protected us," he said.

## FINAL ACTION

House and Senate conferees on Sept. 24 quickly resolved their differences over the legislation (S 2532) to authorize $410 million in bilateral assistance and make a host of changes in existing law to encourage private investment in the former Soviet republics.

The Freedom Support Act also would authorize a $12.3 billion increase in the U.S. contribution to the IMF, which was undertaking a broad program to help bolster the Russian economy.

House conferees agreed to drop a provision in their version of the bill that would have appropriated — as well as authorized — the funds. Senate Appropriations Committee Chairman Byrd, who carefully guarded his turf, had objected.

Instead, the Senate included the IMF appropriation in its version of the fiscal 1993 foreign operations appropriations bill (HR 5368).

Still included in S 2532 were conditions on U.S. aid to the republics that the administration had hoped to avoid.

However, conferees agreed to soften a Senate provision that would have cut off aid unless the president determined that Russia was withdrawing its troops from the Baltics within 12 months of enactment.

The conference report (H Rept 102-964) said Russia would be ineligible for aid if it failed to make significant progress in removing troops, but it allowed the president a national interest waiver of the provision.

Larry Pressler, R-S.D., who sponsored the original Senate amendment, said that "as a practical matter, the State Department has our message. I know Congress will conduct regular oversight on this important issue."

About 100,000 former Soviet troops remained in the independent Baltic states of Estonia, Latvia and Lithuania. Russian President Yeltsin maintained that they could not be withdrawn quickly because his government did not have enough housing or jobs for returning soldiers.

Administration officials lobbied strongly against any legislative conditions, arguing that the assistance was largely in U.S. — not Russian — interests. Richard L. Armitage, the coordinator of the U.S. assistance effort, said

after the conference that the administration would have preferred no conditions, "but all in all we're pleased."

Conferees agreed to leave to the president's discretion the creation of a Democracy Corps, intended to help the former Soviets establish democratic institutions at the local level. The Senate and administration officials had opposed the House-passed plan as duplicating existing programs.

Aid for the former republics of the Soviet Union was given final approval by the Senate on Oct. 1.

The Senate approved the conference report by voice vote and with no debate.

But there was more debate and dissent in the House, which cleared the measure for the president on Oct. 3 on a vote of 232-164. *(Vote 462, p. 112-H)*

Several lawmakers complained that the United States was providing the assistance too quickly without imposing conditions, which they said might ultimately protect U.S. security.

They noted that the Russians were in the process of selling two, and possibly three, diesel-powered submarines to Iran, making that country the first on the Persian Gulf to have a submarine force.

"This does not make any sense," said John R. Kasich, R-Ohio. "It is critical that we do something to let democracy flourish, but I mean, my goodness, we cannot do it this way. The world cannot sit back and let the Russians today sell submarines."

But sponsors of the aid package argued that failure of the United States and other nations to help the republics build free-market economies would only increase their need to sell weapons abroad to earn much-needed cash. They noted that the legislation included about $1.4 billion in humanitarian, economic, technical and other assistance to help dismantle the former Soviet nuclear arsenal, as well as to boost private enterprise and democracy in the republics.

"The historic democratic and free-market reforms of Russian President Boris Yeltsin hang in the balance," said Foreign Affairs Committee Chairman Fascell. "Failure of the Congress to adopt this legislation would be a severe blow."

In the final House deliberations on the measure, sponsors had to fight deep-seated antagonism and distrust of the former Soviet Union.

"There is not enough money in the world to bail them out of their current economic conditions," said Jon Kyl, R-Ariz. "In terms of doing something to help them feel good, it is totally appropriate that we attach certain kinds of conditions which would help to modify the behavior of the hard-liners."

But House Minority Leader Robert H. Michel, R-Ill., said such conditions might have the ultimate effect of forcing Yeltsin out and leaving power in the hands of those opposed to democratic reform. "We are talking about them against us, and Yeltsin is with us," Michel said.

Fascell predicted "tens of thousands of new jobs for Americans in the export business, 12 new markets in which to sell U.S. goods and services, access to 250 million new consumers who are anxious to purchase American-made products, access to greater petroleum reserves and other natural resources."

### Appropriators' Conditions

The aid authorized in S 2532 depended on appropriations in the foreign operations appropriations measure (HR 5368), which funded $417 million in bilateral aid and appropriated the $12.3 billion for the IMF. *(Appropriations,*

*p. 612)*

But the conference committee on that bill became embroiled in debate over proposals to place stiff conditions on Russian aid, which had been attached to the Senate version of the bill by Appropriations Committee Chairman Byrd.

His amendment would have prohibited aid to Russia until Moscow either withdrew its military forces from Estonia, Latvia and Lithuania, or agreed to a timetable for withdrawal. Byrd exempted humanitarian aid from his amendment.

The administration strongly opposed the provision but decided to defer an all-out battle in order to expedite Senate passage of the measure. In an Oct. 2 letter to lawmakers, the White House warned that the amendment "would result in a cutoff of U.S. assistance" and said that the problem was addressed by conditions in S 2532, the authorization bill.

But Byrd was unyielding. "We have a time bomb ticking on our hands," he told the conferees, arguing that Russia's continued military presence in the Baltics could spur civil unrest.

Under a complicated compromise that was written into the final version of the appropriations bill, only half of the assistance could be provided unless the president certified by June, 1993 that there has been "substantial progress" toward establishing a timetable for withdrawal of Russian troops.

If Russia still had not removed its forces by the end of September, 1993 — or had not set up a timetable to do so

— further assistance would be cut off.

The conditions may not have been as strict as they appeared because the definition of "substantial progress" was open to broad interpretation.

The White House letter noted that Russia had reached an agreement with Lithuania on withdrawal, and said there has been "considerable progress" in removing forces from the Baltic nations.

With far less controversy, the conference committee on the foreign aid appropriations bill eliminated a second Senate amendment aimed at restricting aid to Russia. The amendment by Helms would have barred all but humanitarian aid to Moscow until the president certified that Russia had ceased selling arms to Iran.

The appropriations conferees also earmarked a substantial amount of the $417 million for specific purposes, some of which could benefit domestic interests. The legislation required that $50 million in U.S. agricultural commodities be provided to the former republics.

The conference committee also earmarked $50 million for scholarships and other educational exchange programs.

### President's Approval

President Bush signed the Freedom Support Act (S 2532 — PL 102-511), authorizing aid to the former Soviet republics, on Oct. 24.

He signed the fiscal 1993 foreign operations appropriations bill (HR 5368 — PL 102-391), which provided new funding required for portions of the aid package, on Oct. 6. ∎

# Hill Supports Use of Force To Aid Bosnia

Fighting that raged in the former republics of Yugoslavia during 1992 underlined the uncertainty surrounding the role of the United States in a world no longer dominated by the U.S.-Soviet superpower standoff.

After the fall of communism, Yugoslavia broke into feuding republics riven by ancient ethnic rivalries. What remained of Yugoslavia was controlled by Serbia, which fought for territory and dominance with neighboring Croatia and Bosnia-Herzegovina.

While the initial U.S. response was to distance itself from the conflict, calls for action in Congress increased with the rising death toll and with grim stories of "ethnic cleansing" and detention camps run by the Serbian forces that were attacking the Muslim-dominated breakaway state of Bosnia-Herzegovina. But the pleas for U.S. involvement were countered by warnings from Pentagon officials that the United States must proceed cautiously lest it find itself mired in an intractable fight that would prove costly in terms of both money and lives.

Nonetheless, the administration decided in August to seek U.N. authorization of military force, if necessary, to ensure the delivery of humanitarian relief to Bosnia-Herzegovina. Both the House and Senate approved resolutions (S Res 330, H Res 554) strongly endorsing the effort, which was intended to send a signal to the warring factions that the international community was willing to act.

Two months later, lawmakers went further, earmarking $35 million in the fiscal 1993 foreign operations appropriations bill (HR 5368) in refugee assistance for Bosnia, Croatia and Slovenia, and $20 million in fuel and construction

materials for Bosnia, Croatia and Kosovo. And in a move that put the United States more squarely on one side of the conflict, Congress authorized the president to provide up to $50 million in military equipment to Bosnia. But no U.S. arms or intervention followed during the Bush administration.

## BACKGROUND

Open warfare erupted after Bosnia-Herzegovina declared its independence from the Serbian-dominated Yugoslav federation. In April and May alone, more than 5,700 people were killed and 22,000 wounded.

Ethnic Serbs, Muslims and Croats were intermingled throughout Bosnia, which the United States recognized as an independent state. Serbian forces, including militia units of Bosnian Serbs as well as units of the Serbian-dominated former Yugoslav military establishment, seized control of about two-thirds of Bosnia-Herzegovina's territory.

To the outside world, the carnage became most visible in Sarajevo, the capital of Bosnia, where Serbian forces cut off food and medical supplies from the city's more than 300,000 residents.

Bosnian President Alija Izetbegovic appealed publicly for U.S. warplanes to attack Serbian artillery that were bombarding the city from the hills above Sarajevo with up to 10 shells per minute.

### Congress Calls for Action

The congressional calls for action began on June 4,

when Senate Foreign Relations Committee Chairman Claiborne Pell, D-R.I., urged Bush to consider military means to enforce U.N. economic sanctions on the Belgrade regime and to suppress Serbian forces.

Expressing reluctance to get involved militarily, Bush told reporters the same day, "I think prudence and caution prevents military actions ... At this juncture, I want to stay with these sanctions."

On June 10, Foreign Relations member Richard G. Lugar, R-Ind., urged Bush to ask the United Nations Security Council to set a deadline for Serbian forces to honor a cease-fire already ordered by the council. "The killing must stop," Lugar said. "And we should generate the diplomatic momentum — and military will — necessary to provide a credible ultimatum."

The next day, the Foreign Relations Committee approved unanimously a non-binding resolution by Carl Levin, D-Mich., calling on Bush to urge U.N. Secretary General Boutros Boutros-Ghali to draw up a plan and a budget for "such intervention as may be necessary" to enforce its cease-fire demand. The resolution (S Res 306), backed by leaders of both parties, won Senate approval by voice vote on June 12. This proved to be only a prelude to more significant congressional resolutions in August.

On June 11, Bush reiterated the U.S. commitment to cooperate in U.N. relief efforts but appeared to discount the possibility of U.S. intervention to pacify the conflict. "We're not the world's policeman," he told reporters. "It's a very complicated situation."

Lugar and others insisted that the immediate crisis in Bosnia-Herzegovina underscored the importance of formulating U.S. policy to deal with deeply rooted nationalist, regional and ethnic tensions that had been suppressed throughout the Cold War by U.S. and Soviet hegemony. "The world has to establish the fact that these things can only be worked out in diplomacy," Lugar said.

But members of Congress were ambivalent about the effectiveness of military intervention. Even those who called for action emphasized that they did not want the United States to act alone. "If there is any [military] action, it must be collective, and it must involve the French and the Germans," Foreign Relations member Joseph R. Biden Jr., D-Del, said June 11.

During the week of June 29, the United Nations began an airlift of relief supplies into Sarajevo. The Bush administration sent C-130 transport planes loaded with humanitarian supplies and expressed willingness to provide air support but not combat troops.

"The United States is not going to inject itself into every single crisis, no matter how heart-rending, around the world," President Bush told reporters July 2. "I am not interested in seeing one single United States soldier pinned down in some kind of a guerrilla environment."

---

## BOXSCORE

➡ **War in former Yugoslavia republics (S Res 330, H Res 554, HR 5368).** The House and Senate approved resolutions urging the United Nations to authorize military force, if necessary, to ensure relief shipments to beseiged Bosnia-Herzegovina, formerly part of Yugoslavia. The fiscal 1993 foreign operations approprations bill authorized the president to provide up to $50 million in U.S. military equipment to Bosnia if a U.N. arms embargo was lifted.

**Reports:** H Rept 102-1011, S Rept 102-419

### KEY ACTION

**Aug. 11** — The **Senate** approved its resolution, S Res 300, 74-22; the **House** approved its version, H Res 554, by voice vote.

**Oct 1** — The **Senate** approved the foreign operations appropriations bill, HR 5368, 87-12.

**Oct. 5** — The **House** adopted the conference report on HR 5368, 312-105; the **Senate** cleared the measure by voice vote.

**Oct. 6** — President Bush signed HR 5368 — PL 102-391.

---

U.S. involvement was endorsed by some on Capitol Hill. "Should any actions by Serbian forces threaten the success of this operation or the security of U.N. personnel, it would be in order to take steps as needed to deal with that threat," Sen. Al Gore, D-Tenn., said on July 1.

But other members expressed concern that U.S. troops could become ensnared in combat without Congress' assent. Sen. Robert C. Byrd, D-W.Va., protested that the administration had entered into "adventures in ethnic policing" without seeking approval before Congress left town for the Fourth of July recess. "I hope that we are not going to be treated to a recess war," Byrd said.

Although Bush had sought Congress' support before the Persian Gulf War in 1991, he denied that he was required to do so. In campaigning for re-election, the president had become increasingly blunt in rejecting Congress' assertion of constitutional authority to approve the commitment of U.S. forces to likely combat. *(1991 Almanac, p. 437)*

"Some people say, 'Why can't you bring the same kind of purpose and success to the domestic scene as you did in Desert Shield and Desert Storm?'" Bush told a Texas Republican convention in Dallas on June 20. "And the answer is I didn't have to get permission from some old goat in the United States Congress to kick Saddam Hussein out of Kuwait!"

## COMMITTEE ACTION

The Senate Foreign Relations Committee approved a resolution Aug. 6 calling on the president to work within the United Nations to use "all necessary means, including the use of military force" to protect humanitarian relief shipments to Bosnia-Herzegovina.

In addition, the resolution included language authorizing the use of force "to place heavy weapons belonging to all factions in Bosnia-Herzegovina" under the supervision of the United Nations. The panel approved the resolution, 12-4.

Just hours after the Foreign Relations Committee voted, Bush vowed to step up efforts to gain approval for a U.N. resolution authorizing force to protect aid shipments, saying that food and medicine should be provided to Bosnia-Herzegovina "no matter what it takes."

The resolution — sponsored by several senators, including Majority Leader George J. Mitchell, D-Maine, and Minority Leader Bob Dole, R-Kan. — was a hastily crafted response to mounting evidence of Serbian atrocities, including reports of Nazi-style concentration camps.

Several senators said televised images of brutality evoked memories of the Jewish Holocaust during World War II. Citing atrocities attributed to the Serbian forces, Sen. Joseph I. Lieberman, D-Conn., told reporters Aug. 5

that "we hear in them echoes of conflicts in Europe little more than 50 years ago."

But that sense of outrage was matched by fears that U.S. troops — even as part of a multinational force — might become bogged down.

"This could be a quagmire and then some," said Rep. John P. Murtha, D-Pa., chairman of the House Appropriations Defense Subcommittee, who had visited Sarajevo. "It's the perfect example of something you couldn't solve with minor military action."

Some leading Democrats, including Arkansas Gov. Bill Clinton, the party's presidential nominee, argued that the United States was under a moral obligation to try to stop the violence despite the risks. "History has shown us that you can't allow the mass extermination of people and just sit by and watch it happen," Clinton said.

Clinton and a number of senators went further than Bush did in making specific calls for military action. "I would begin with air power against the Serbs to try to restore the basic conditions of humanity," Clinton said Aug. 5.

On Aug. 7, Bush told reporters that "pictures of the prisoners rounded up by the Serbian forces and being held in these detention camps are stark evidence of the need to deal with this problem effectively." But, he said, "I do not want to see the United States bogged down in any way into some guerrilla warfare."

During closed briefings, military officials told senators that tens of thousands of troops would be needed just to secure the Sarajevo airport and establish a safe corridor for aid.

Lieberman and other senators argued that the resolution would not commit the United States to deploy ground forces. "This is not Operation Balkan Storm," he said.

After a debate in which moral considerations were weighed against military realities, the Foreign Relations Committee dropped draft language that would have authorized military force to ensure access to the Serbian-run prison camps.

Even with that provision removed, however, four Republicans voted against the resolution.

## FLOOR ACTION

On Aug. 11, the House and Senate passed resolutions supporting a U.N. declaration of willingness to use military force if that proved to be what was needed to deliver humanitarian relief to war-ravaged Bosnia-Herzegovina.

But even as Congress voted to threaten international intervention, some lawmakers still expressed apprehension that the United States could be rushing into an intractable ethnic conflict that would lead to the loss of American lives.

"The injection of ground forces will be putting those forces into an absolute quagmire such as Lebanon or Northern Ireland," said Sen. John H. Chafee, R-R.I. "I hope those who are boldly proposing humanitarian aid realize that this effort will come with serious obligations."

Supporters of the non-binding resolutions argued that a strong message needed to be sent to the Serbs that the world community would respond to widespread reports of torture, murder and starvation of Bosnia's Croats and Muslims. They said they hoped that just the threat of multilateral intervention would lead to a lessening of violence.

"We are not sure what will stop them," said Lieberman, a cosponsor of the Senate resolution (S Res 330). "But one thing I know, the possible fear of allied military force against them holds a better hope than anything else we

have tried up until now."

The alternative, he said, "is to stand by, read the stories I have read today — another 300,000 Muslims trapped, starving, babies malnourished — and simply say there is nothing we can do."

The non-binding Senate resolution, adopted 74-22, called on the president to seek U.N. authorization to use "all necessary means" to ensure the provision of humanitarian relief in Bosnia-Herzegovina and to gain access for U.N. and International Red Cross personnel to refugee and prisoner of war camps throughout the former Yugoslavia. (Vote 186, p. 25-S)

The resolution also called on the Security Council to review the impact of an arms embargo on Bosnia-Herzegovina.

Support for the resolution was largely bipartisan. It was sponsored by the bipartisan Senate leadership; 51 Democrats and 23 Republicans voted for the measure.

The House, by voice vote, adopted a similar resolution (H Res 554) Aug. 11 that largely endorsed the administration's efforts to seek a U.N. resolution on the use of force. On Aug. 13, the U.N. Security Council approved the U.S.-backed resolution calling for the use of "all measures necessary" to facilitate the delivery of humanitarian relief in Bosnia-Herzegovina.

## APPROPRIATIONS AMENDMENT

A provision authorizing arms for the Bosnians was added to the fiscal 1993 foreign operations appropriations bill (HR 5368) when it reached the Senate floor.

The amendment, offered by Biden, authorized the president to provide up to $50 million in U.S. defense equipment for Bosnia if the United Nations lifted its embargo against arms shipments to any of the warring elements of the former Yugoslavia. The amendment left it up to the president to decide whether to provide the authorized equipment.

The Senate approved the amendment by voice vote, but only after it sparked spirited debate.

For many in the Senate, the issue was one of fairness. The ban on arms shipments, Biden argued, left Bosnians almost defenseless against attacks by well-armed Serbians.

He cited eyewitness accounts of Serbian massacres of thousands of Bosnian civilians. "Are we truly to adjourn, having done nothing?" Biden asked.

But John W. Warner, R-Va., who had supported the administration's cautious approach toward the crisis in the former Yugoslavia, said that providing such aid would only deepen the involvement of the United States in a region where all sides had engaged in brutality.

Although Acting Secretary of State Lawrence S. Eagleburger signaled his opposition to the amendment, Warner said the administration would not object if the Senate approved it by voice vote. With strong bipartisan support for the amendment, the administration wanted to avoid an embarrassing defeat on a recorded vote.

The Senate also approved $35 million in refugee assistance for Bosnia, Croatia and Slovenia, and $20 million in fuel and construction materials for Bosnia, Croatia and Kosovo.

The Senate approved the foreign operations bill, 87-12, Oct. 1. With minimal debate, the House on Oct. 5 adopted the conference report on the $26.3 billion spending measure, 312-105. The Senate approved the legislation by voice vote later that day.

President Bush signed the measure (PL 102-391) Oct. 6. But no arms shipments or military intervention followed in 1992. ∎

# Bush Sends U.S. Troops to Somalia

In one of the final major decisions of his presidency, George Bush sent almost 28,000 U.S. soldiers to the African country of Somalia to aid workers in their distribution of food to the starving populace.

The problem in Somalia had been growing throughout 1992. Relief efforts were at a standstill because of pandemic theft and extortion by gangs of heavily armed gunmen in areas where political structures had disintegrated.

By early December, with the nightly news and daily papers recounting the suffering of the Somali people, Bush decided that action in conjunction with the United Nations was necessary.

Congress had already adjourned for the year when Bush first announced the deployment Dec. 4. Although most individual members in both chambers were supportive of the intervention, it was not until Feb. 4, 1993, that the Senate approved a resolution approving the Bush action (S J Res 45).

## BACKGROUND

For 22 years after Mohammed Siad Barre seized control of Somalia in 1969, he parlayed Somalia's propinquity to the oil-rich Arabian peninsula into a cornucopia of superpower arms and aid drawn first from Moscow, and then, beginning in 1978, from Washington. But his repressive regime spawned insurgent movements that drove him from power in January 1991.

By the end of that year, the country had disintegrated into warring factions, loosely organized along clan lines and armed to the teeth with the rifles, grenade launchers and larger weapons stockpiled by the Barre regime.

The civil war, coupled with a prolonged drought, triggered famine as food-distribution networks collapsed and hundreds of thousands of refugees assembled in camps.

With an estimated 30 percent of the Somali population facing starvation, the United Nations Security Council approved an emergency airlift of relief supplies in July.

### Congressional Concern

With international relief officials warning that a generation of children in Somalia were at risk from war and famine, a senior Republican member of the Senate Foreign Relations Committee called in midyear for a U.N. security force to protect food shipments to the East African country.

Testifying July 22 before the House Select Committee on Hunger, Nancy Landon Kassebaum of Kansas urged the establishment of a U.N. force "to ensure that food gets to those in need." She testified shortly after returning from the region.

Kassebaum was at odds with the Bush administration, which said it would be premature to deploy U.N. peacekeepers until there was a cease-fire in Somalia.

But Kassebaum said the "situation has reached the point where the U.N. should go forward with the security force" even if there is no cease-fire.

"This is not without substantial risk and cost," she said. "But I believe it is a risk worth taking. Every day hundreds of relief workers in Somalia put their lives at risk. Every day hundreds of children die."

Several members of the Hunger panel, including Chairman Tony P. Hall, D-Ohio, already had gone on record in favor of a proposed 500-member U.N. force to protect food shipments.

Some lawmakers said the Somalia crisis could become more devastating than the 1984 famine in Ethiopia, which killed about 1 million people. Relief agency officials had said up to 2 million Somalians were in immediate danger of starvation.

Testifying for the administration, Assistant Secretary of State for International Organization Affairs John R. Bolton said the United States was the largest single contributor of relief aid for Somalia, providing more than $60 million in emergency assistance since early 1991.

But Bolton said that because of the violent instability in the country, the administration was wary about using U.N. peacekeepers. He said one of the country's warlords had boasted that the U.N. observers "would be killed for the boots and berets."

But the Senate on Aug. 3 approved by voice vote a resolution urging President Bush to seek action by the United Nations.

The resolution (S Con Res 132) said Bush should urge the U.N. "to deploy a sufficient number of security guards" to protect emergency food shipments to the war-torn country.

On the same day the Senate acted, a Bush administration official reported that up to one-quarter of the children in Somalia under 5 had died because of war and famine, while 1.5 million Somalis faced starvation.

James Kunder, director of the Agency for International Development's Office of Foreign Disaster Assistance, who had visited Somalia a short time before, voiced support for the immediate deployment of a United Nations' security force.

State Department officials previously had said that it would be premature to deploy the force until warring factions agreed to the presence of U.N. troops.

The House approved the resolution one week later on Aug. 10.

## ADMINISTRATION RESPONSE

Bush authorized a U.S. relief airlift Aug. 14. Between August and December, the United States, in conjunction with relief agencies, delivered 17,000 tons of supplies.

A 3,500-member multinational military force had been slated for dispatch under U.N. auspices to act as peacekeepers. But only 500 of the U.N.-sponsored troops were allowed in the country by the feuding warlords, and the rules governing their deployment rendered them virtually helpless to stop raids on relief convoys and warehouses by heavily armed and undisciplined gangs of young men and boys.

With the death toll rising from war and famine in Somalia, the Bush administration positioned four ships with 2,100 Marines in the waters near the East African nation.

But Assistant Secretary of State Herman J. Cohen told the House Foreign Affairs Subcommittee on Africa on Sept. 16 that the Marines were limited to providing support for an airlift of U.N. peacekeeping forces. "We have no intention of landing a Marine expeditionary force in Somalia," Cohen said.

Rep. Amo Houghton, R-N.Y., criticized the administration's response to the deepening crisis and described a U.S.-backed plan to deploy 500 U.N. peacekeeping forces to the country as insufficient.

### The Deployment

On Nov. 25, with no public notice, Bush offered U.N. Secretary-General Boutros Boutros-Ghali the use of a large U.S. force to pacify Somalia to the point where the stalled relief efforts could resume.

Boutros-Ghali recommended to the Security Council on Nov. 30 that such a U.N.-sponsored force be deployed and that — in contrast to the stringent limitations traditionally placed on U.N. peacekeeping forces — these "peacemaking" forces be authorized to use whatever force was needed to allow the relief effort to resume.

The authorizing resolution adopted Dec. 3 by a unanimous vote of the 15-member council was carefully negotiated to accommodate two sets of demands: The Bush administration insisted that U.S. troops, which would make up the largest share of the force, be under U.S. command. However, several states from Africa and other parts of the developing world insisted that the United Nations not simply give the United States free rein to conduct the operation, as had been the case in the 1991 war against Iraq.

The resolution endorsed, indirectly, Boutros-Ghali's acknowledgement that, as a practical matter, the force would have to be under U.S. command.

But it specified that the secretary-general would have a hand in designing the command structure for the force. It also gave the Security Council a voice in when to end the operation.

The resolution also established a fund through which wealthy U.N. members could subsidize the participation in the Somali operation of military forces from poorer states.

On Dec. 4, Bush announced that he would deploy as many as 28,000 U.S. troops to Somalia to aid in distribution of food to the starving population as the backbone of the multilateral force approved by the Security Council.

"Only the United States has the global reach to place a large security force on the ground in such a distant place, quickly and efficiently, and thus save thousands of innocents from death," Bush said in a brief televised address Dec. 4.

He insisted that the force would have a limited objective. "We will create a secure environment in the hardest-hit parts of Somalia, so that food can move from ships overland to the people in the countryside now devastated by starvation," he said. "Once we have created that secure environment, we will withdraw our troops, handing the security mission back to a regular U.N. peacekeeping force."

President-elect Bill Clinton hailed the Security Council decision as a "historic and welcome step." And he lauded Bush for proposing the U.S. role: "I commend President Bush for taking the lead in this important humanitarian effort."

Most congressional leaders also backed the deployment, citing the enormity of the Somali tragedy that had been driven home daily to Americans by news accounts picturing starving children.

"The president has acted wisely, and in a circumstance where he had very little choice without grave humanitarian consequences resulting," said House Speaker Thomas S. Foley, D-Wash., emerging from a meeting Dec. 4 during which Bush briefed congressional leaders.

Spearheading the U.S. contingent were 1,800 Marines in an amphibious task force just off the Somali coast, equipped with some helicopters armed for ground attack and others designed as troop carriers. They were backed up by the aircraft carrier *Ranger*.

That initial wave was reinforced by up to 16,000 Marines from Camp Pendleton, Calif., and up to 10,000 Army troops, most of them from the 10th Mountain Division, stationed at Fort Drum, N.Y.

## CONGRESSIONAL REACTION

Even as they endorsed the Somalia deployment, many congressional leaders touched on some of the issues that would be ripe for debate when future military missions were weighed.

Indiana Democrat Lee H. Hamilton, the prospective chairman of the House Foreign Affairs Committee, insisted that his support for the Somalia deployment was conditioned on a clear delineation of its scope. "The mission has to be sharply defined so that you know what they are in there to do and what they are not in there to do," he said. "When they accomplish what they are supposed to do, they come out."

A few congressional heavyweights struck a more cautious tone even toward the Somalia deployment.

Georgia Democrat Sam Nunn, the influential chairman of the Senate Armed Services Committee, asked whether this decision paved the way for similar deployments to other countries where thousands were threatened by widespread communal violence. "Is this a precedent for going into Liberia?" he asked. "How do we rationalize this with what's going on in Bosnia?"

House Defense Appropriations Subcommittee Chairman John P. Murtha, D-Pa., opposed the involvement in Somalia. "When I see the pictures [of starving children], I have the same concern," Murtha said Dec. 2, "but I just don't see the national interest."

So large a deployment would soak up funds from an already shrinking defense budget, Murtha said, thus eroding the Pentagon's readiness to protect more vital U.S. interests, such as might be threatened by a new crisis in the Middle East or by the rise of right-wing forces in the former Soviet republics.

And, like Nunn, Murtha worried that this decision would open the door to additional costly commitments where no vital national interest was at stake. "You've got people starving in a lot of different places, and we can only afford so much," Murtha said. "This could set a precedent that destroys our ability to respond [to mortal threats] down the road."

Bush had hoped to end the U.S. involvement in Somalia before Clinton was inaugurated Jan. 20, but was unable to do so.

In a Dec. 10 letter to congressional leaders, Bush said U.S. troops would remain in Somalia "only as long as necessary to establish a secure environment for humanitarian relief operations."

The U.S. force was "necessary to address a major humanitarian calamity, avert related threats to international peace and security and protect the safety of Americans and others engaged in relief operations," Bush said.

In the letter, Bush maintained that "we do not intend that U.S. armed forces deployed to Somalia become involved in hostilities" but that they will "have the support of any additional armed forces necessary to ensure their

safety and the accomplishment of their mission."

The letter provided Congress all the information the president was required to provide under the War Powers Resolution when U.S. forces were deployed overseas in a situation entailing a significant risk of combat.

But like every other president since the war powers measure was enacted in 1973, Bush contended that it was an unconstitutional infringement on his powers as commander in chief of the armed forces. To avoid appearing to concede the act's validity while also avoiding a showdown on the issue, Bush followed the longstanding practice of providing Congress with the information required by the act but stipulating that the letter was "consistent with" the War Powers act, rather than being pursuant to the disputed legislation.

On Dec. 11, the two predominant Somali warlords in the Mogadishu area, Mohammed Farah Aidid and Mohammed Ali Mahdi, agreed in a meeting sponsored by U.S. diplomatic troubleshooter Robert Oakley to withdraw their armed units from the capital.

### Concern About Outcome

Some lawmakers became concerned that as the Marines achieved success in alleviating the misery in Somalia, hard questions about the mercy mission and its long-term implications were being swept aside.

At the first congressional hearing on the Somalia operation Dec. 17, members of the House Foreign Affairs Committee grilled Bush administration officials about the mission, called Operation Restore Hope. But mostly they wanted to know, as Rep. James L. Oberstar, D-Minn., put it, "How do we get out?"

Deputy Assistant Secretary of Defense James L. Woods said U.S. forces were to remain in the country until they established a "secure environment" for private relief groups to deliver assistance.

Reiterating a statement by Gen. Colin L. Powell Jr., chairman of the Joint Chiefs of Staff, Woods said that "we're looking at an operation that will take two or three months." At that point, a smaller U.N. peacekeeping force was expected to provide protection for aid deliveries.

Yet Woods and Assistant Secretary of State Herman J. Cohen seemed to have no illusions about the difficulty of maintaining a secure environment without U.S. muscle in a country where anarchy had reigned for months.

Cohen revealed that the United States was actively lobbying within the United Nations for a first-of-its-kind peacekeeping force — one that would "be heavily armed, with very robust rules of engagement." Cohen said he hoped that the U.N. force, whose size had not yet been determined, could be in place within two to three months.

Rep. Toby Roth, R-Wis., said that the problem with Cohen's scenario was that "we can't really go by hope here. . . . That comes under the heading of wishful thinking, and that's gotten us into some big problems. And that's why I'm concerned about the U.S. getting bogged down in Somalia."

When Roth asked Cohen and Woods whether they could guarantee that no U.S. troops would be in the country in a year, Cohen would only say "that is the current intention of the administration."

Reflecting the sensitivity within the administration to such questions, the Joint Chiefs declined to send a representative to testify.

A joint contingent of Marines and French legionnaires arrived Dec. 16 in the hard-hit inland town of Baidoa,

paving the way for the first food deliveries under protection of U.S. forces.

U.S. forces also largely restored order to Mogadishu, permitting aircraft and ships to deliver humanitarian aid to the Somali capital.

Most members at the hastily called Foreign Affairs hearing echoed the view of Rep. Robert E. Andrews, D-N.J., who praised Bush for making a "good, proper, short-term decision" in acting to "liberate the people of Somalia from death and disease."

But Andrews said that Clinton would have to deal with the consequences of Bush's bold step. In an interview, Andrews said that "if Bush had won the election, there would have been a lot more thought given to the long-term consequences" of the operation.

Among such consequences, said Hamilton, the new chairman of the Foreign Affairs Committee, was the precedent that Operation Restore Hope could set.

"We've got a lot of problems around the world," Hamilton said. "Not all the suffering takes place in Somalia." He asked Cohen whether the United States was prepared to deploy military forces in such troubled countries as Haiti and Bosnia-Herzegovina. *(Haiti, p. 558; Yugoslavia, p. 532)*

Cohen responded that the operation "doesn't necessarily set a precedent" because of the unique situation in Somalia, including the absence of any government there. Only the U.S. military possessed the capability to overcome the enormous logistical difficulties in the war-torn country, he said.

Hamilton and other members closely questioned the administration's decision not to have U.S. forces forcibly disarm the warring gangs, who had made it nearly impossible for relief organizations to operate. Cohen said that "coalition forces do not have time to go house to house looking for arms — they have to protect food convoys."

That triggered sharp criticism from Donald M. Payne, D-N.J. The United States helped arm Somalia during the Cold War, he said. "For us to simply allow arms in abundance" and then withdraw from the country, he said, "to me is a flawed policy."

### Questions About Costs

Despite the widespread support among members of Congress for the U.S. intervention to aid the starving people of Somalia, questions surfaced early in 1993 about how much the effort would cost the deficit-burdened U.S. Treasury.

A Defense Department calculation put the cost at roughly $583 million for a three-month deployment, nearly doubling earlier estimates. In one of his last acts as president, Bush took a parting shot at congressional pork barrel spending on Jan. 15 by submitting a list of defense cuts to pay the costs of Operation Restore Hope.

Members of Congress were under no obligation to accept cuts in their favored programs that were urged upon them by a president who soon after departed the White House. But Bush's list of proposed rescissions underscored the need to find funds somewhere for the Somalia mobilization, a problem that the Clinton administration inherited in 1993.

In his proposal, Bush took aim at the research grants, earmarked for particular universities and colleges throughout the country, that Congress included in the fiscal 1993 defense appropriation bill (PL 102-396). The money was to be transferred from the targeted items to pay for additional expenses incurred because of the Somali operation, includ-

# U.N. Somalia Resolution

The resolution on Somalia that the U.N. Security Council adopted unanimously on Dec. 3 attempted to balance U.S. insistence on retaining command of its troops with concerns of other nations that the world organization have a say in the military operation it authorized.

The language was cloaked in diplomatic niceties. The United States was referred to simply as a "member state" that had offered its assistance. Secretary-General Boutros Boutros-Ghali and "the member states concerned" were instructed "to make the necessary arrangements for the unified command and control of the forces involved" and "to establish appropriate mechanisms for coordination."

In other key points, the resolution:

● Recognized "the unique character" of the "human tragedy" in Somalia and said that it required an immediate and exceptional response."

● Welcomed the U.S. offer as well as "offers by other member states to participate in that operation."

● Authorized the U.N. secretary general "and member states cooperating to implement the offer referred to ... above to use all necessary means to establish as soon as possible a secure environment for humanitarian relief operations in Somalia."

● Urged U.N. members to "provide military forces and to make additional contributions, in cash or in kind."

● Asked the secretary general "and, as appropriate, the states concerned, to report to the council on a regular basis, the first such report to be made no later than 15 days after the adoption of this resolution, on the implementation of this resolution and the attainment of the objective of establishing a secure environment so as to enable the Council to make the necessary decision for a prompt transition to continued peacekeeping operations."

---

ing hazard pay for members of the military and full-time pay for reservists called up.

The grants had been a subject of debate within Congress. Nunn had objected that the grants were earmarked for favored colleges of influential members rather than being awarded competitively with peer review to test their worthiness.

But Senate Defense Appropriations Subcommittee Chairman Daniel K. Inouye, D-Hawaii, contended that without such earmarks, smaller schools would be frozen out of big-dollar government research contracts that tended to go to prestigious Ivy League institutions.

In addition to the grants, Bush proposed transferring to the Somali operation $248 million that had been slated to buy eight C-130 cargo planes for a National Guard base in the home state of Rep. W. G. "Bill" Hefner, D-N.C.

And he sought to rechannel $40 million that Congress inserted in the bill at Inouye's behest for cultural preserva-

tion on military lands and $1 million that Inouye had won to help keep brown tree snakes out of Hawaii.

## MARINES RETURN

On Jan. 20, 1993, while President Clinton was taking the oath of office, 850 Marines were beginning their journey home from Somalia.

Those Marines were the first forces to return to the United States from Operation Restore Hope. They left behind nearly 24,000 U.S. troops who were still trying to make the country safe for food distribution.

The United States brought part of its troops home in the hope of prodding the United Nations to begin taking over the relief effort. Under an agreement adopted unanimously by the U.N. Security Council on Dec. 3, the United Nations had pledged to make the Somali relief effort an international undertaking after an initial, U.S.-led deployment.

And some lawmakers seemed determined to make sure that other nations equally shouldered the financial costs of the Somali rescue effort, as well as the risks to their troops.

During Defense Secretary Les Aspin's confirmation hearing Jan. 7. Senate Appropriations Committee Chairman Robert C. Byrd, D-W.Va., recalled that during the Persian Gulf War, "I insisted that other countries pay for that operation."

Allies paid all but about $7 billion of the $61 billion cost of the war against Iraq.

Regarding Somalia, Byrd said, "I'm worried that any expansion of the mission or extension of the deployment would have serious budgetary consequences."

Aspin agreed that the Clinton administration needed to find a way to subsidize such U.S.-led international operations.

"If we're going to do more Somalias — and presumably when you look around the world there's an awful lot more places that the same thing could happen," Aspin said, "how are we going to establish a funding mechanism so that the American taxpayer is not stuck with the bill or not stuck with the whole bill?"

## SENATE RESOLUTION

The Senate on Feb. 4, 1993, approved by voice vote a measure (S J Res 45) authorizing the use of force in support of the U.N.-sponsored operation to establish a "secure environment" for delivery of relief supplies to the war-torn country.

With no fixed date set for the withdrawal of the estimated 20,000 troops in Somalia, some senators stepped up calls for the United Nations to take over leadership of the operation. Thad Cochran, R-Miss., released a statement saying, "Time is running out on our willingness to do this job by ourselves."

The resolution urged Clinton to consult with Boutros-Ghali with the goal of transferring the mission to a U.N.-led force "at the earliest possible date."

The measure skirted thorny questions over the War Powers Resolution by stating that the resolution is "consistent with" the 1973 law, which required that a president seek congressional approval when troops face "imminent involvement in hostilities." ■

# Israeli Loans Guaranteed in Spending Bill

In August, President Bush and Israeli Prime Minister Yitzhak Rabin agreed on terms for a five-year package of loan guarantees, which Jerusalem had been seeking for more than a year to help the small country absorb hundreds of thousands of Jewish immigrants from the former Soviet Union. The deal easily gained the backing of Congress, long a wellspring of support for Israel. The U.S. guarantees for $10 billion in loans were intended to help Israel obtain favorable rates on commercial loans.

The guarantees were attached to the fiscal 1993 foreign operations appropriations bill (HR 5368). The Senate cleared the foreign aid bill on Oct. 5, and Bush signed it the next day (PL 102-391).

Until the agreement in August, Bush had blocked action on the loan guarantees because Rabin's predecessor, Yitzhak Shamir, insisted on aggressively expanding Jewish settlements in territories that Israel had occupied since the Six-Day War in 1967.

Complications on aid to Israel had erupted the previous year. In September 1991, Bush asked for a 120-day delay in action on the loan guarantees. Many members lambasted the president — and then quietly agreed to delay the contentious matter. Bush wanted to put off the matter to avoid undermining Middle East peace talks, which began in Madrid in October 1991.

Publicly, U.S. officials referred to the settlements as "obstacles to peace." Privately, Bush was said to view Shamir's hard-line resistance to curtailing new settlement construction as a personal affront.

Pro-Israel members of Congress vowed to spurn Bush's call for delay. But when it became obvious that they lacked the votes to override a veto, they reluctantly went along with the postponement.

With the loan guarantees stalled, Congress failed to enact the fiscal 1992 foreign aid appropriations bill that was to have been the vehicle for the Israel assistance. Instead, foreign aid was funded through a continuing resolution (PL 102-145) that expired in March and was then followed by a second stopgap funding measure (PL 102-266).

The outlook was equally bleak early in 1992. Two members of the Senate Appropriations Committee — Foreign Operations Subcommittee Chairman Patrick J. Leahy, D-Vt., and ranking Republican Bob Kasten, Wis. — led an unsuccessful effort in March to forge a compromise on the loan guarantees.

The stalemate ended after Rabin's Labor Party swept to victory in Israel's parliamentary elections in June. The more conciliatory Rabin pledged to restrain the growth of most settlements. In agreeing to the loan guarantees, Bush

---

## BOXSCORE

➡ **Israel loan guarantees (HR 5368).** U.S. guarantees for $10 billion in commercial loans to Israel over five years were included in the fiscal 1993 foreign operations appropriations bill. Congress approved the assistance after a new government in Israel resolved differences with the Bush administration that had blocked action on the guarantees for nearly a year.

**Reports:** S Rept 102-18; conference report H Rept 102-1011.

### KEY ACTION

Oct. 1 — The **Senate** passed HR 5368 (which had been amended in the Senate Foreign Operations Appropriations Subcommittee to include the loan guarantees) , 87-12.

Oct. 5 — The **House** approved the conference report on HR 5368, 312-105; the **Senate** cleared it by voice vote later that day.

Oct. 6 — President Bush signed HR 5368 — PL 102-391.

---

also sought to repair relations with the American Jewish community, which had become frayed over the issue.

Under the terms of the agreement, Israel agreed to pay all costs associated with the program. After the first year's installment of $2 billion, subsequent installments of guarantees were to be reduced by any amount that Israel spent on settlements in its occupied territories. The president could suspend the program, but Congress would be able to reverse that decision with a two-thirds vote by each chamber.

The United States did not provide loans to Israel; it backed loans negotiated by Israel with private commercial lenders. But funds had to be set aside to cover any potential losses, with the amount depending on the estimated risk that Israel would default on the loans and the United States would have to bear the costs. Administration budget experts fixed the required set-aside of funds for the first-year installment of $2 billion in guarantees at 4.5 percent, although congressional budget experts argued for a greater "subsidy."

## BACKGROUND

Israel sought the $10 billion in guarantees over five years to help absorb a hugh influx of immigrants, most coming from what was the Soviet Union. U.S. Jewish leaders had said that prospects for increasing instability in the former republics of the Soviet Union could lead to the rise of anti-Semitism and a boost in the numbers of Jews wanting to leave.

The Bush administration supported such aid in principle but was strongly opposed to Israel's expansion of settlements on occupied land.

During the Six-Day War with Arab states in 1967, Israel captured the Golan Heights, the Gaza Strip and the West Bank as well as East Jerusalem. The Bush administration considered the settlements — especially those on the West Bank — an obstacle to regional peace and a violation of international law. Early in 1992, reports grew that the administration might explicitly link the request for guarantees to a settlement freeze in the territories. Critics of Israel's policies insisted that such a connection was logical, that Soviet immigrants would be forced to settle in the occupied territories because that was where much of Israel's new housing was being built.

Israel's request threatened to present Congress with stark and unpalatable alternatives. Politically, it appeared to offer a grim choice in an election year: Alienate Jewish supporters of Israel or fuel the anger of recession-pinched voters who were fed up with foreign aid spending.

As a foreign policy question, the choice appeared

# The History of U.S. Aid to Israel

Aid for Israel had taken on aspects of an international entitlement program, seemingly as automatic as Social Security benefits. Year in and year out, usually with no debate, Congress earmarked about one-fifth of the $15 billion foreign aid budget for Israel.

When Egypt was included, the annual level of aid earmarked by Congress for the two countries rose to more than $5 billion by 1992, one-third of all U.S. foreign assistance spending.

A series of extraordinary events, including Iraq's missile attacks on Israel during the Persian Gulf War, pushed grant assistance for Israel to the highest total ever in fiscal 1991, with estimates exceeding $4 billion. This included $650 million in war-related economic assistance that Congress approved in March 1991.

Because Israel received grants and loans from a variety of sources — with aid often provided under defense bills as well as the foreign aid bill — it was difficult to ascertain how much all types of assistance cost the United States.

High levels of aid for Israel did not begin until the 1970s. From 1948 through 1970, the United States provided Israel a total of about $1.6 billion in military and economic aid — most of it in the form of loans.

The first huge increase in assistance came after the Yom Kippur War of 1973. Aid again rose dramatically — in tandem with assistance for Egypt — after those two countries made peace in 1979.

But during Israel's first tenuous years in the early 1950s, the United States provided very little help to the Jewish state.

In 1948, shortly after Israel's declaration of independence, President Harry S. Truman took the important step of recognizing the new nation. But Truman included Israel in the arms embargo he imposed on the Middle East.

In an effort to stem the spread of communism in the region, the Eisenhower administration attempted to forge close relationships with Arab states, sometimes at Israel's expense. Throughout the 1950s, the United States never provided Israel with more than $86.4 million in annual aid, and the bulk of the assistance was in the form of loans under the Food for Peace program.

The policy of limiting transfers of military equipment to Israel continued through most of the 1960s, according to William B. Quandt, a Middle East expert who served on the National Security Council staff during the Carter administration. Quandt, who became a senior fellow with the Brookings Institution, said Israel did not rely heavily on U.S. weaponry in the 1967 Six-Day War.

In 1968, under congressional pressure, the Johnson administration expanded shipments of advanced arms to Israel, approving the sale of 50 Phantom fighter-bombers. But it was not until the Nixon administration that annual aid for Israel moved to the billion-dollar range.

In October 1973, following the surprise attack by Egypt and Syria that began the Yom Kippur War, President Richard M. Nixon ordered a massive airlift of U.S. military equipment to Israel. Congress then overwhelmingly approved Nixon's request for $2.2 billion in emergency military assistance for the country.

Israel had received strong congressional backing since its creation. But during the 1970s, lawmakers became increasingly assertive in their efforts to help the Jewish state. Congress began earmarking specific amounts of assistance for Israel in 1971.

I. L. "Si" Kenen, former chairman of the American Israel Public Affairs Committee (AIPAC), the leading pro-Israel lobbying group, said in an interview in 1973 that he was so confident of congressional backing for AIPAC causes that he rarely ventured to Capitol Hill. "There is so much support for Israel that I don't have to," he said.

## Camp David Accords

The second major boost in the aid program came after the conclusion of the Camp David Accords in 1979. President Jimmy Carter requested a special $4.8 billion package of loans and grants to be shared by Israel and Egypt; the supplemental appropriation was in addition to the regular aid program of nearly $2 billion for Israel and nearly $1 billion for Egypt. *(1979 Almanac, p. 137)*

Quandt said the aid was not offered as "an explicit quid pro quo" for the two countries agreeing to peace terms. But the assistance was an important inducement for continued cooperation from both sides. In the years that followed, Egypt began insisting on similar treatment from the United States to the aid provided to Israel.

Assistance for the two countries was closely tied through the mid-1980s. In the early 1990s, however, the programs became "delinked." The Bush administration forgave $6.7 billion in Egyptian military debt in 1990. Though Israel was not granted a similar concession, U.S. aid was dramatically increased during the Persian Gulf War.

In the 1980s, members of Congress were successful in securing favorable terms for assistance to Israel, in addition to boosting aid levels.

Before the mid-1970s, most aid for Israel was provided in the form of loans. In fiscal 1981, economic aid became an all-grant program; military aid had been in the form of grants since fiscal 1985.

Also beginning in fiscal 1985, lawmakers had included language in foreign operations bills stating that it was the "policy and intention" of the United States that aid provided under the Economic Support Fund (ESF) be at least equal to Israel's debt repayments to the U.S. government. Israel used most of the $1.2 billion it received annually under the ESF program to pay military debts.

That was one of several unique benefits accorded Israel. It was the only country that received ESF aid in a lump sum at the beginning of the fiscal year, rather than in quarterly installments. The same terms applied to most of the $1.8 billion in Foreign Military Financing aid provided to Israel in fiscal 1991. Investing in U.S. government securities, Israel was able to reap interest income from the military and economic aid.

equally unsettling: Side with Israel if it demanded assistance with no strings attached, or support President Bush if he demanded a halt to new Israeli settlements in occupied territories as the price for new U.S. assistance. And either choice could have affected the course, and perhaps even the survival, of the fragile Middle East peace talks.

But all sides had it in their interests to avoid a showdown that would mean a wrenching public debate over U.S. aid to the Jewish state.

As 1992 began, the starting point in the search for compromise was a proposal offered the previous year by Leahy. Under Leahy's plan, Congress would act in 1992 on only the first $2 billion installment of the five-year package that Israel requested. Addressing the administration's opposition to Israel's settlements policy, the United States would also deduct from the guarantees the amount that Israel spent developing settlements in the occupied territories. *(1991 Almanac, p. 460)*

In an interview on Jan. 17, 1992, Zalman Shoval, Israel's ambassador to the United States, said there were "some positive and also some negative aspects" to Leahy's plan. Adding that Israel never expected to receive the guarantees without some "terms and provisions" attached, Shoval said, "Nobody is expecting a blank check or, in this case, blank guarantees."

Although U.S. Jewish leaders were unwavering in their support for Israel and reluctant to express criticism publicly, there were indications that they had reservations about the hard-line policies of the Shamir government.

A poll conducted in November 1991 of 205 leaders of major Jewish organizations, sponsored by the Wilstein Institute of Jewish Policy Studies, showed that the leaders were far more willing than Shamir to seek compromises.

A large majority of those surveyed, 78 percent, said they would freeze the growth of settlements in the West Bank if necessary to secure receipt of the guarantees.

Even more of the Jewish leaders — 88 percent of those surveyed — would support Israel offering territorial compromise in the occupied territories in return for "credible guarantees of peace" from Arabs.

While taking a tough line toward Shamir's government, Bush attempted to repair badly frayed relations with U.S. Jewish leaders. When the controversy over loan guarantees first erupted, Bush had portrayed himself as an underdog who was "up against some powerful political forces." Referring to a massive fly-in of leaders of Jewish organizations, who were lobbying Congress that day in behalf of the loan guarantees, Bush said at a news conference on Sept. 12, 1991 that he was being confronted by "1,000 lobbyists on the Hill working the other side of the question."

Pro-Israel lawmakers and leaders of the Jewish groups, whose lobbying trip had been scheduled long before the president's request for a delay, were outraged. They saw Bush's remarks as a subtle attempt to encourage the notion that Jewish organizations represent a conspiratorial "force" secretly manipulating the U.S. political system for the benefit of Israel.

For many Jewish leaders, the frictions were smoothed over when Bush offered an apology.

In a Sept. 17, 1991, letter to Shoshana S. Cardin, chairman of the Conference of Presidents of Major American Jewish Organizations, Bush said his comments "were never meant to be pejorative in any sense."

Months later, however, the anger still had not subsided for some. "It was one of the most disgusting things I have ever heard come out of a president's mouth," Rep. Howard

L. Berman, D-Calif., said in a December 1991 interview. "He tried to make it [the lobbying] look ugly and parochial."

Despite Israel's strong support in Congress, senior members expected President Bush to win if it came to a showdown.

"It is my guess that the president's position on the loan guarantees will prevail in 1992," said Lee H. Hamilton, D-Ind., chairman of the House Foreign Affairs Subcommittee on Europe and the Middle East.

## COMMITTEE DEBATE

By February, Secretary of State James A. Baker III was negotiating privately with Israel's Ambassador Shoval in search of a compromise on the loan guarantees.

During congressional testimony Feb. 5 and 6, Baker's few blunt comments about Israel spoke volumes about the Bush administration's increasingly hard-line view of the request.

"What we say is if you want us to come forward here with significant additional assistance for Israel — over and above the very substantial amounts of $3 [billion] to $4 billion dollars that we grant every year anyway — if you want additional aid, then please don't do it under circumstances that would contravene the long-established policy of the United States of America," Baker told the House Foreign Affairs Committee on Feb. 6.

There was no doubt about the policy to which he was referring: Since 1967, U.S. administrations had regarded Israel's policy of building settlements in its occupied territories as an obstacle to peace in the Middle East.

Beyond restating U.S. policy in his congressional testimony, Baker seemed to question Israel's credit-worthiness, a crucial factor in determining the amount of funding that would have to be set aside to back loan guarantees.

Rep. Benjamin A. Gilman, R-N.Y., told Baker that Israel had an excellent record of repaying past loans. Baker retorted that this was accurate, but only "because we appropriate the money up here with which to repay ourselves."

Baker was referring to a provision that had been included in foreign aid legislation since fiscal 1985 stating that it is the "policy and intention" of the United States that economic aid for Israel be at least equal to the amount of debt repaid.

While Baker was challenging Israel's economic reliability, Leahy was also offering some tough talk on the loan guarantees. Leahy, whose Appropriations Subcommittee on Foreign Operations had jurisdiction over the request, told reporters Feb. 6 that he took "the same position this country has for 25 years — there should not be settlements."

If supporters of Israel were thinking of attempting to end-run the administration by persuading Congress to approve the guarantees with minimal conditions, they faced a significant obstacle in Leahy. "Now everybody accepts that you have to have at the very least — to get any bill through — a Leahy dollar-for-dollar reduction" in loan guarantees to reflect Israel's expenditures on settlement expansion, Leahy said.

With stopgap foreign aid funding expiring in March, the overdue fiscal 1992 foreign operations appropriations bill remained the likely vehicle for any congressional action on loan guarantees. But Leahy warned that he would adjourn the markup on the appropriations bill if any of his

subcommittee colleagues attempted to begin a "bidding war" on guarantees. *(1991 Almanac, p. 646)*

On Feb 21, Rep. David R. Obey, D-Wis., chairman of the House Appropriations Subcommittee on Foreign Operations, opened the first congressional hearing focusing exclusively on the loan guarantees by warning Israel and its U.S. supporters that "American taxpayers — given their understanding of what this proposition is — would be, to a very large extent, opposed to the provision of these guarantees."

Like his Senate counterpart Leahy, Obey echoed the Bush administration's hard line against new settlements. "I agree with that policy," he said, "and I think it's the responsibility of Congress to uphold that policy."

In an apparent slap at Shamir's hard line, Obey said he did not "feel any particular obligation" to back "the agenda of any set of Israeli politicians within their own country."

Senate Appropriations Committee Chairman Robert C. Byrd, D-W.Va., also challenged the Shamir government's policy in the territories. In a statement Feb. 19, Byrd said that without a change in that policy, any promise by Israel that it would not use U.S. funds on settlements "is an exercise in building a paper dam."

Byrd released a study by the General Accounting Office, which showed that $400 million in loan guarantees approved in 1990 by Congress — on the condition that they not be used for settlement construction — enabled Israel to use other money for that purpose.

Although supporters of Israel said that 73 senators had endorsed granting Israel the guarantees with no strings attached, what mattered most was the increasingly hard line being taken by those — such as Leahy, Byrd and Obey — who controlled legislation on the issue.

Offering a glimpse of the congressional debate on the issue, pro-Israel members of Obey's subcommittee strongly backed providing the guarantees. Rep. Lawrence J. Smith, D-Fla., accused the Bush administration and journalists of subjecting the Israeli request to unfair scrutiny.

### Baker's Ultimatum

The week of Feb. 24 began with Baker offering an ultimatum in two days of testimony before the House and Senate Foreign Operations subcommittees. He outlined two alternatives for providing Israel with loan guarantees. Each required significant concessions from Shamir's government. Baker said:

● The administration "will support loan guarantees of up to $2 billion for five years" — Israel's full request — if there is "a halt or an end to settlement activity" in occupied territories. He conceded that "the current government of Israel has a problem with that."

● Or the United States would provide loan guarantees "of some lesser amount, if there was a halt or end to new construction activity." The amount being considered was $1 billion in loan guarantees for a single year, according to lawmakers.

Baker said that, under this option, Israel would be allowed to complete housing that was under construction by a certain date: "Let's say Jan. 1, 1992." The cost of completing the housing would be deducted from the guarantees.

If Israel were to violate the terms of the agreement by building new settlements, Baker said the United States would reserve the right to "end any provision for absorption assistance [guarantees] at that point."

Baker repeatedly said that Israel had to choose whether to continue to expand settlements or receive the guarantees. "The choice is Israel's," he said. "She can determine whether . . . she wants to take action which would permit the strong support of both the legislative and executive branches for these loan guarantees or not."

Some lawmakers described Baker's testimony as a "take it or leave it" approach to Israel.

Many members of the Appropriations subcommittees — many of whom had strongly backed Israel's requests for aid in the past — criticized Baker for issuing an ultimatum to the Jewish state.

Kasten compared the plight of Jews in the former Soviet Union, which had seen a rise in anti-Semitism, to the situation in Nazi Germany. "For millions of families, help came too late," he said. "We do not want history to repeat itself."

But Obey indicated that he might be comfortable funding foreign aid with a continuing resolution for the remainder of the fiscal year, leaving the loan guarantee request in limbo. "There is nothing in that bill that I have to have," he told reporters.

On Feb. 27, Leahy offered a compromise plan to provide up to $2 billion a year in loan guarantees for five years — the full request sought by Shamir.

But he also proposed giving Bush much of the authority that the administration demanded to slow or stop the aid if Israel persisted in its expansion of settlements.

"I'm pushing a plan that has elements that are going to make the administration unhappy and a number of senators unhappy," Leahy, the chairman of the Senate Appropriations Subcommittee on Foreign Operations, said in an interview. "So it's probably not all that bad a plan."

Leahy's plan provided that:

● A five-year program of loan guarantees of up to $2 billion a year be established, with the president determining the amount to be made available each year. During the first year, the amount of guarantees provided would be reduced by the amount Israel spent to complete housing and infrastructure already under construction.

● If Israel engaged in new settlement activity, the president had the authority to suspend further provision of guarantees. Congress could move to continue the guarantees by voting a resolution of disapproval within 30 days of the suspension. But Bush could veto the resolution.

Leahy's plan gave the president the authority — but also the politically unappetizing responsibility — to decide whether Israel violated the terms of the agreement. Congress might then vote on the matter, with uncertain consequences.

"If the administration has made a reasonable decision in cutting off [the guarantees], he wins. If he's made an unreasonable decision, then he loses," Leahy said in arguing that Congress should have a role in the process.

The senator said he was "increasingly optimistic" that the compromise would be accepted by his Republican counterpart on the subcommittee, Kasten, and other congressional supporters of Israel. Daniel K. Inouye, D-Hawaii, a longtime backer of aid to the Jewish state, said Feb. 27 that there was a "good possibility" of agreement on the proposal.

"If we don't have an agreement, my recommendation would be that we forget a foreign aid bill this year," Leahy said.

In an effort to jar loose the stuck negotiations over Israel's request, the Senate Appropriations Subcommittee on Foreign Operations set March 17 to begin considering

the delayed fiscal 1992 foreign aid appropriations bill (HR 2621), amended to include yet another compromise proposal to provide Israel with at least a portion of its requested $10 billion in loan guarantees. *(Appropriations, p. 609)*

After weeks of inconclusive discussions between the administration and Israeli officials, Subcommittee Chairman Leahy had reached agreement on the matter with Kasten. Speaking with reporters March 10, Leahy called the plan "a realistic compromise," similar to the series of proposals he previously had floated.

Although Leahy declined to provide details, congressional sources and others familiar with the compromise said it would have ensured Israel a portion of the guarantees it was seeking in fiscal 1992 — reportedly about $850 million. In return, the government of Prime Minister Shamir would agree to finish only those houses in its occupied territories that were already under construction.

Bush then would have had wide discretion in disbursing or withholding the rest of the $10 billion package through fiscal 1996.

In forging his compromise with Kasten, Leahy made at least a symbolic break with the administration.

In scheduling the markup — despite the host of unresolved questions — Leahy appeared to be prodding the administration to choose among clear alternatives: accept the compromise, offer a counterproposal or forget about the fiscal 1992 foreign aid bill.

## Compromise Crumbles

The long-running efforts to seek a compromise on loan guarantees collapsed during the week of March 16, doomed by the Bush administration's unbending opposition to Jewish settlements in occupied lands and by election-year political pressures in the United States and Israel.

The administration and lawmakers turned to political damage control in assigning blame for the outcome.

On March 17, Bush rejected the final congressional compromise attempt. He indicated that the proposal contained unacceptable loopholes that would have allowed Israel to continue to expand settlements in the territories it had occupied since the 1967 war with Arab states.

"We are in a position right now where we are unable to bridge the gap," State Department spokeswoman Margaret D. Tutwiler said March 19.

When the administration spurned his final offer, Leahy questioned whether the White House negotiated in good faith.

"What was asked of us was not compromise but capitulation," he said in a floor speech.

The Vermont Democrat said March 18 that the president "made clear he would veto the Kasten-Leahy compromise." He said Bush offered a counterproposal that amounted to a "take it or leave it proposition." Leahy said the White House plan stood little chance of winning Senate approval.

The administration portrayed its stance in a far more conciliatory light. Tutwiler insisted that the administration's counterproposal was "fair and balanced and meets U.S. policy."

At a State Department news briefing March 18, Tutwiler appeared to minimize the differences between the administration's proposal and the one offered by the two senators.

Both proposals would have authorized the full $10 billion in guarantees, and both would have given the president

discretion over the long run to suspend the guarantees if Israel persisted in settlement activity.

But the plan by Leahy and Kasten would have guaranteed that Israel would receive an initial installment of approximately $800 million in loan guarantees within 30 days of enactment of the legislation.

Under the administration's proposal, Israel reportedly had to negotiate a broad "loan agreement" — including methods to verify a halt to settlement expansion — before receiving a first installment of $300 million in guarantees.

"Congress has asked the administration to issue loan guarantees first, then ask questions later, and that is simply not acceptable," Tutwiler said.

While pro-Israel lawmakers had long been pessimistic over prospects for an agreement, the president's rejection of the Kasten-Leahy proposal was a bitter pill.

Many saw it as merely the most recent demonstration of a deep animus toward Israel.

At a hearing of the House Foreign Affairs Subcommittee on Europe and the Middle East on March 17, Mel Levine, D-Calif., a stalwart supporter of Israel, said that the administration had sabotaged the traditionally strong ties between the two countries.

"At the highest level of this government, there's an effort to undermine the relationship between the United States and Israel and undermine public confidence in that relationship," Levine said. "And it's a tragedy, and it shouldn't be occurring."

Some pro-Israel lawmakers accused the administration of denying the Shamir government help in absorbing Jewish immigrants in order to affect the outcome of Israel's election in June. Shamir's Likud Party was being opposed by the Labor Party, led by Rabin, who was viewed by Middle East analysts as more conciliatory on settlements and regional peace issues.

Before a showdown meeting with Leahy and Kasten, Bush presented the administration's opposition to settlements in moderate terms.

"We have close historic relations with Israel, and they will always be that way," Bush said.

"But we have a difference now, it appears, in terms of these settlements, but I have said over and over again that we want to help. We want to help in a humanitarian way, but we simply are not going to shift and change the foreign policy of this country," he said.

That tone was adopted by Tutwiler in her attempts to foster the impression that differences between the Leahy-Kasten plan and the administration's counteroffer were minor.

At one point during the State Department news briefing on March 18, Tutwiler said that it was her understanding that the first installment of loan guarantees would be provided "up front, no questions asked; it's done. No conditions; it's yours, $300 million."

If that statement were accurate, there would be only a difference of about $500 million in the crucial initial phase of the proposals devised by the administration and Congress. That immediately raised questions as to why Kasten and Leahy rejected a plan that apparently was so close to their own.

At other points in the briefing, however, Tutwiler said it was her understanding that the $300 million would be released only after terms for the entire package were agreed upon.

Congressional sources familiar with the administration's plan insisted that Israel would have had to agree to

several provisions before any guarantees would be provided.

There were other differences in the two plans: The administration generally authorized up to $10 billion in guarantees over six years, while the senators' plan established a more formal five-year loan guarantee program "not to exceed $2 billion a year," Leahy said.

The administration plan also provided the president with a freer hand in setting annual levels of guarantees.

## AGREEMENT WITH ISRAEL

Ultimately, it was political change in Israel, not the United States, that reopened consideration of the loan guarantees.

The opposition Labor Party won a clear victory in the Israeli national elections June 23, catapulting Yitzhak Rabin into the prime minister's seat and ousting hard-liner Yitzhak Shamir.

Bush administration officials and members of Congress began to view the request for guarantees in a new light, although the administration was initially cautious in displaying its enthusiasm for a change of administration in Israel.

In testimony given June 24 before the House Foreign Affairs Subcommittee on Europe and the Middle East, Assistant Secretary of State Edward P. Djerejian said that the Labor Party's support of a freeze on the construction of at least some settlements was closer to the U.S. position than Likud's outright rejection of restrictions on settlements.

Once Rabin took office, he promised to curtail some settlement construction, although he had said those deemed integral to Israeli security would be expanded.

On Aug. 11, Prime Minister Rabin and Bush announced agreement on "basic principles" for a package of $10 billion in loan guarantees.

The announcement made at Bush's vacation home in Kennebunkport, Maine, was a unity tableau intended to erase several years of U.S.-Israeli tensions.

Bush took pains to express his admiration for Israel and its prime minister. The president said it had been a "true pleasure" to host Rabin and his wife. The United States and Israel, he said, had "a special relationship — it is one that is built to endure."

Settlement of the dispute was greeted with enthusiasm by many members of Congress.

But some expressed strong reservations over indications that U.S. Treasury funds might have to be set aside to back the loan guarantees, which were to be issued in $2 billion annual installments over the following five years.

Initial estimates put that cost at about $140 million a year.

The loan guarantee set-aside was required by the 1990 Budget Enforcement Act, but the law left it up to the administration's Office of Management and Budget (OMB) to calculate the exact percentage, depending on the anticipated risk.

OMB reportedly calculated initially that a subsidy of at least 7 percent would be needed to back the guarantees. The agreement provided for Israel to bear only 3.5 percent of those costs, however. That would have required Congress to come up with at least $70 million a year to pay for the program.

Obey said Israeli officials had assured him that their government would pay all the associated costs. Noting that

he had not seen the terms of the agreement, Obey said: "I expect that commitment to be kept."

Merging re-election campaigning with Middle East policy-making, Bush told an appreciative audience of B'nai B'rith members in Washington on Sept. 8 that he was about to send Congress the loan guarantees.

Then, on Sept. 11, he announced that the administration had agreed to let Saudi Arabia spend up to $9 billion buying F-15 fighters.

He made that announcement to another appreciative audience, this time of workers who built the planes in St. Louis.

On the loan guarantees, the final deal worked out between Israel and the administration required Israel to pay the full subsidy to back the loans, quieting the congressional concern that the United States might have to shell out at least $70 million a year.

OMB reduced the subsidy it required from the reported initial estimate of 7 percent to the 4.5 percent — or $90 million — that was required for the first-year installment of $2 billion in loan guarantees.

"As long as there's no cost to the U.S. taxpayer, there will be no problem," said Leahy.

## FINAL ACTION

After long debating the sensitive issue, lawmakers took their first substantive action on Israel loan guarantees on Sept. 18, when the Senate Foreign Operations Appropriations Subcommittee approved the fiscal 1993 foreign operations appropriations bill (HR 5368) by voice vote. The subcommittee's version of the bill included the $10 billion, five-year program of U.S. guarantees for commercial loans to Israel.

Because Israel had agreed to pay the $90 million subsidy required by OMB's "scoring" of the risk involved in the first-year guarantees, the administration was able to avoid making a request for an appropriation to cover the guarantees.

But the Congressional Budget Office (CBO), which made independent budget estimates for Congress, reportedly scored the subsidy at about 13 percent.

In effect, CBO and OMB differed over the prospects for an Israeli default.

Some lawmakers believed that such distinctions were meaningless because it was impossible to accurately assess the risk involved.

"You're trying to quantify the unquantifiable," said Obey.

But the CBO estimate of the loan guarantee subsidy, along with its scoring of other programs, forced Leahy and Kasten to find reductions elsewhere in the foreign operations bill.

And because outlays — actual spending during the fiscal year — translated into higher levels of budget authority, they trimmed $283 million in budget authority.

The foreign operations appropriations bill, including the Israel loan guarantees, was approved by the Senate Appropriations Committee, 25-1, on Sept. 23. The Senate passed the bill, 87-12, on Oct 1. *(Vote 256, p. 33-S)*

With minimal debate, the House adopted the conference report on the measure (H Rept 102-1011), 312-105, on Oct. 5. The Senate cleared the measure by voice vote later that day. *(Vote 470, p. 114-H)*

President Bush signed the measure (PL 102-391) on Oct. 6. ∎

# Prewar Policy With Iraq Under Scrutiny

A simmering bank scandal, some revealing secret documents and a tenacious committee chairman gave new life during 1992 to lingering Democratic charges that the Bush administration coddled Iraq until virtually the eve of its 1990 invasion of Kuwait.

On July 9, 20 of the 21 Democrats on the House Judiciary Committee formally asked Attorney General William P. Barr to seek an independent counsel to investigate possible criminal violations in the administration's prewar policy toward Iraq. That set in motion procedures under a law that was enacted in 1978, in response to the Watergate scandal, providing for the appointment of such special prosecutors to investigate allegations of wrongdoing by senior government officials.

On Aug. 10, Barr rejected the request for an independent counsel, dismissing "vague and conclusory" allegations of wrongdoing against the administration in which he served.

But in October, a majority of Democrats on the House and Senate Judiciary committees made a new request to Barr based on the administration's handling of a bank fraud case involving billions of dollars in illicit loans to Iraq.

This time, Barr attempted to defuse the controversy by naming a special prosecutor reporting directly to him. On Dec. 9, Barr's counsel, retired federal judge Frederick B. Lacey, released a 190-page report staunchly defending the administration's handling of criminal charges in the case involving the Atlanta branch of the Italian-owned Banca Nazionale del Lavoro (BNL). Barr endorsed Lacey's conclusion that there were "no reasonable grounds" to warrant further investigation.

Democrats denounced that decision and urged President-elect Bill Clinton to pursue the case. Clinton promised that his attorney general would look into the matter in 1993.

## BACKGROUND

For months, Democrats had demanded an independent counsel to investigate possible criminality and coverup. "Certain aspects of this affair bear the marks of a major scandal involving, at best, improper conduct, and at worst, criminal activity by U.S. government officials," Charles E. Schumer, D-N.Y., said at a hearing of the House Banking Committee on May 21.

President Bush repeatedly insisted that "there wasn't anything illegal" involved in what he characterized as efforts to bring Iraq's Saddam Hussein into the family of nations. He said his administration simply attempted to work with the Iraqi ruler "on grain credits and things of this nature to avoid aggressive action," as the president put it at a news conference on June 4. "And it failed. It failed."

But the uproar tarnished the U.S.-led military triumph in the Persian Gulf War of 1991, as did Saddam's defiant survival after the war. (1991 Almanac, p. 437; post-war Iraq, p. 552)

### Gonzalez's Crusade

The confrontation over prewar Iraq was instigated by the House Banking Committee's chairman, Henry B. Gonzalez, D-Texas.

The combative 76-year-old chairman — who had previously staged investigative hearings into scandals in the savings and loan industry — said he became interested in the issue following a 1989 raid by federal agents on the Atlanta branch of BNL, the bank owned by the Italian government. The raid uncovered evidence that the bank had made billions of dollars in unauthorized loans to Iraq, including about $1.25 billion in loans guaranteed by the Agriculture Department's Commodity Credit Corporation (CCC).

Since 1983, Iraq had been a leading recipient of CCC guarantees, which backed private bank loans for sales of U.S. agricultural commodities. Shortly after the raid, Baghdad sought $1 billion in new loan guarantees for fiscal 1990. (Chronology, p. 550)

Beginning in February 1991, Gonzalez delivered a series of "special order" speeches — usually to an empty House chamber — in which he provided chapter and verse on the BNL case and U.S. assistance for Iraq during the 1980s.

Asked why it took so long for Gonzalez's crusade to generate interest, Banking Committee member Barney Frank, D-Mass., said, "You guys in the media and my guys up here don't pay enough attention to Henry B."

But that changed when Gonzalez began providing evidence to support his allegations in the form of hundreds of documents painstakingly subpoenaed by the Banking Committee from several government agencies.

Gonzalez and other Democrats said the documents revealed that in November 1989 the State and Agriculture departments overrode the objections of other agencies in gaining administration approval of Iraq's request for $1 billion in guarantees.

Gonzalez cited an internal State Department memo expressing concerns that the burgeoning scandal "could blow the roof off the CCC." The Oct. 13, 1989, memo raised the possibility that CCC-guaranteed loans "may have been diverted from Iraq to third countries in exchange for military hardware."

Gonzalez's penchant for bolstering his case with classified documents, which he entered into the Congressional Record, also proved controversial. Attorney General Barr charged May 15 that release of the documents jeopardized national security. In a letter to Gonzalez, he said the administration would not provide additional documents unless the chairman agreed to protect them from "unauthorized disclosure."

Democrats insisted that the administration was seeking to prevent release of the documents merely because they contained embarrassing material. But Deputy Secretary of State Lawrence S. Eagleburger argued that "chaos" would result if other members of Congress followed Gonzalez's lead and revealed classified material.

Gonzalez was undaunted. "The committee will not be steamrolled by the White House," he said, "and, if necessary, I will seek subpoena authority in order to obtain the information and the persons I am seeking."

## BANKING COMMITTEE HEARING

The situation was first fully joined at a Banking Committee hearing on May 21, where the election-year implications of the explosive issue were never far beneath the surface.

Several Democrats predicted the allegations could damage Bush's re-election bid. "Bush's one remaining strength is foreign policy," Frank said in an interview. "This goes right to the heart of that."

Republicans accused the Democrats of election-year efforts to tarnish Bush's triumph in the Persian Gulf War. "The administration is being mugged today," said Toby Roth, Wis. "This smacks of a kangaroo court."

And senior administration officials fought back, vigorously denying any wrongdoing and arguing that the administration was motivated by strategic interests in pursuing close ties with Saddam.

Providing loan guarantees for Iraq "was one of the few tools we thought we had to moderate his conduct," said Eagleburger. But near the end of the hearing, he wearily conceded, "I have said 15 times today that it didn't work."

Eagleburger said the "selective disclosure" of documents by Gonzalez had "led, knowingly or otherwise, to distortions of the record, half-truths and outright falsehoods, all combined into spurious conspiracy theories and charges of a cover-up," he said.

Eagleburger, Under Secretary of Agriculture Richard T. Crowder and Deputy Secretary of Treasury John E. Robson testified they had no proof that Iraq diverted CCC-guaranteed loans to buy arms.

Eagleburger cited congressional support for continuing assistance to Iraq as a factor in the administration's decision to approve additional CCC guarantees. "I might note as well at this time members of Congress, along with various agricultural trade interests, were urging the administration to provide the full amount of credit guarantees requested by Iraq," he said.

But because of concerns that the pending BNL investigation could turn up fraud in the program, the administration divided the $1 billion in guarantees into two $500 million installments. Iraq received only the first installment. The program was suspended in April 1990 after Department of Agriculture investigators found that Iraq had violated rules of the CCC program.

When Iraq invaded Kuwait four months later, the administration cut off all trade with Baghdad and no further guarantees were provided. From fiscal 1983 until the termination of the program, the United States authorized $4.5 billion in CCC loan guarantees for Iraq.

Eagleburger said that in August 1990, Iraq "held approximately $1.9 billion in outstanding credit guarantees." He added, "The administration intends to assert claims against Iraq for debts owed to the United States."

Committee Democrats repeatedly charged that the Bush administration, and the Reagan administration before it, were partly responsible for creating the "monster" of Saddam Hussein.

Schumer termed the Iraqi leader a "Frankenstein." Frank said, "He's more like Dracula, because he's so difficult to kill."

Schumer, who also chaired the Judicary Subcommittee on Crime and Criminal Justice, said that he was "particularly interested in the conduct of the Department of Justice in the BNL investigation and whether other agencies attempted to influence or impede the investigation."

Documents released by Gonzalez revealed that some U.S. officials believed that indictments in the case were imminent in the fall of 1989. But the indictments were not handed up until Feb. 28, 1991 — the day after Bush announced the cease-fire in the Persian Gulf War.

During a special order speech, Gonzalez released a 1990

## 30 Days: What the CIA Didn't Say

**Sept. 14** — Sentencing hearing begins for Christopher P. Drogoul, former manager of the Atlanta branch of Banca Nazionale del Lavoro (BNL). The government accuses him of making more than $4 billion in unauthorized loans to Iraq. In a statement on the House floor, Henry B. Gonzalez, D-Texas, cites a CIA report that casts doubt on a central tenet of the government's case: that BNL officials in Rome were not aware of Drogoul's activities.

**Sept. 17** — In a letter to the attorney prosecuting the case, the CIA indicates only that it had "publicly available information" that BNL-Rome was aware of the illegal activities undertaken by the Atlanta branch of the bank.

**Oct. 5** — Judge Marvin H. Shoob agrees to a request from prosecutors that he recuse himself from the case. In his order, he says that senior government officials apparently tried to "shape this case" and that key information might have been withheld from prosecutors in Atlanta.

**Oct. 6** — The CIA acknowledges that it misled the court by not saying it had classified reports on the matter. But the concession comes only after Gonzalez and the chairman and ranking Republican on the Senate Intelligence Committee raise concerns about the agency's Sept. 17 statement.

**Oct. 8** — The Intelligence Committee steps up its investigation of the government's handling of the case, but officials from the Justice Department and CIA disagree over who is to blame for allowing incomplete information to be provided to the court.

**Oct. 14** — Intelligence Chairman David L. Boren, D-Okla., writes Attorney General William P. Barr, asking him to seek appointment of an independent counsel to investigate whether crimes were committed in the government's handling of the BNL case. Barr had turned down a similar request in August from Democrats on the House Judiciary Committee.

internal memo from the Federal Reserve Board that indicated that the U.S. Attorney's office in Atlanta had encountered difficulties in investigating BNL. The memo said that "these difficulties have been compounded by what is perceived as interference from the Justice Department in Washington."

### Directive 26

Excerpts from a 1989 document fueled new debate May 29 over the Bush administration's prewar efforts to court Iraq's Saddam

At another hearing of the House Banking Committee, Sam Gejdenson, D-Conn., released excerpts of National Security Directive 26 — a statement of U.S. policy toward the Persian Gulf region that Bush signed on Oct. 2, 1989. The administration declassified the document at Gejdenson's request but deleted many sections.

Democrats seized on the document as evidence that Bush was personally responsible for "shameless prewar coddling of Saddam Hussein," as Gejdenson put it.

The directive, drawn up more than a year after Iraq had won its eight-year war against Iran, stated that "the United States government should propose economic and political incentives for Iraq to moderate its behavior and to increase our influence with Iraq." The administration subsequently approved the $1 billion in agricultural loan guarantees for Iraq.

But the policy statement also appeared to bolster the

administration's claims that it used a stick as well as the carrot of loan gurantees in its dealings with Iraq. It said any use of chemical or biological weapons by Iraq or progress toward developing nuclear weapons would trigger U.S. economic sanctions.

Gejdenson, who chaired the House Foreign Affairs Subcommittee on International Economic Policy and Trade, charged that "the administration has at every turn tried to block, delay, obscure and interfere with" his panel's investigation of the prewar Iraq policy.

The charge was echoed by Rep. Charlie Rose, D-N.C., chairman of the Agriculture Subcommittee on Department Operations, and in testimony submitted by John D. Dingell, D-Mich, chairman of the Committee on Energy and Commerce, and Doug Barnard Jr., D-Ga., who chaired a Government Operations Subcommittee.

But Jeanne S. Archibald, general counsel of the Treasury Department, responded that no one in the administration ever suggested "explicitly or implicitly that we should cover up embarrassing or elicit activities."

Republicans complained that Democrats were merely sensationalizing differences over foreign policy for political gain in an election year. Rep. Chalmers P. Wylie, R-Ohio, said the cover-up allegations look "a little bit like politics as usual."

The most serious allegations were lodged by Rose, who asserted that the Bush and Reagan administrations had long been aware of evidence that the U.S. agricultural loan guarantee program may actually have been used to underwrite weapons purchases by Iraq. "This is a lot bigger scandal than Iran-contra," said Rose.

## THE ATLANTA PROSECUTION

Bolstered by the pointed remarks of a federal judge, Democrats on the House Judiciary Committee indicated they were increasingly inclined to request formally that Barr name an independent counsel to investigate the Bush administration's prewar dealings with Iraq.

Under the independent counsel law (PL 100-191), which was enacted in 1978 but permitted to lapse in December 1992, such a request by a majority of members of either party on the House or Senate Judiciary Committee required Barr to respond within 30 days. He was required to indicate whether he had decided to pursue a preliminary inquiry into the allegations and, if not, to explain why not. *(Independent counsel, p. 315)*

The Judiciary Committee's direct involvement in the case began with a bitterly partisan committee hearing June 2.

"The burden of proof has now shifted to the administration," said Schumer. "Given this, they must convince Congress as to why there should not be an independent counsel."

While the Judiciary Committee was debating the issue, a U.S. district judge in Atlanta sharply criticized the administration's handling of the criminal case that had spurred the Democratic calls for an independent counsel.

Christopher P. Drogoul, the former manager of the Atlanta branch of BNL bank, pleaded guilty June 2 to illegally authorizing more than $5.5 billion in loans to Iraq — about a quarter of which had been guaranteed by the Department of Agriculture.

But Drogoul angered Judge Marvin H. Shoob by not delivering on an earlier pledge to provide a detailed account of what role higher-ups of the bank and U.S. officials

might have had in the bank fraud. Shoob, who was appointed to the federal bench by President Jimmy Carter in 1979, then issued his own call for an outside investigation of the matter.

"This case ought to have a special prosecutor because I'm not getting the information from Mr. Drogoul," Shoob said, according to media accounts of the court session.

Drogoul's plea arrangement heightened suspicions among many lawmakers that something was amiss in the Justice Department's BNL probe. In return for his cooperation with the continuing investigation of BNL, the government dropped all but 60 of 347 counts of fraud against Drogoul.

Schumer said Drogoul's plea "asks more questions than it answers. Why was the indictment that led to this plea delayed 15 months? Was Christopher Drogoul free-lancing or was he working with officials of the Iraqi government or the United States government?"

Judiciary Committee Chairman Jack Brooks, D-Texas, who provided periodic updates on developments in Atlanta during his committee's hearing, said pointedly that criminal activity need not be proved in order to make the request for an independent counsel.

"The question before this committee is simply whether there is a need for further investigation by an independent counsel of possible federal criminal law violations and conflicts of interest by executive branch officials," he said.

Republicans argued that the issue had been manufactured by Democrats seeking an election-year political advantage. Jim Ramstad, R-Minn., asked, "Would we be holding this hearing if the presidential election were not five months away?"

Henry J. Hyde, R-Ill., surprised Brooks and Rose by reading from letters that showed they had urged the administration to pursue expanded business opportunities in Iraq.

Hyde, who declined to disclose his source of the letters, said they showed that "this notion of cozying up to the Iraqis wasn't exclusively the province of the executive branch."

A letter from the under secretary of Agriculture to Brooks, dated just three months before Iraq's invasion of Kuwait, thanked him for his "interest in the continued participation of Iraq" in the loan guarantee program.

Hyde also read from a 1989 letter to Deputy Secretary of State Eagleburger — signed by Rose and other North Carolina lawmakers — urging the State Department to press for a joint manufacturing venture with Iraq.

Clearly taken aback, Rose fumed to Hyde, "How did you get that letter?" Rose said his staff had signed the letter without his consent.

At a news conference June 4, Bush scoffed that the clamor for an independent counsel was instigated by "a lot of people that opposed what happened in the war," a reference to Democrats who opposed authorizing force against Iraq.

"Let them look at it," he said. "It's no problem to me.

"But I think at some point somebody ought to say where is all this money going that goes to pay for these special prosecutors, rummaging through files and proving nothing."

### An Early Warning

On June 23, a soft-spoken economist emerged from the State Department bureaucracy to recount his effort in 1989 to warn the Bush administration about the dangers of

# Hill Calls for Investigation Of Altered Documents

Even some Republicans who denounced Democratic efforts to investigate the Bush administration's prewar policy toward Iraq acknowledged that they were troubled by the case of the doctored documents.

"That by itself justifies a full investigation," said George W. Gekas, R-Pa., at a House Judiciary Committee hearing June 2.

Commerce Department officials conceded that documents detailing the sales of defense-related items to Iraq were altered before they were provided in 1990 to the House Government Operations Subcommittee on Commerce, Consumer and Monetary Affairs.

Many lawmakers were equally disturbed by the contention of subcommittee Chairman Doug Barnard Jr., D-Ga., that the Justice Department had not adequately investigated the matter. Barnard told the Judiciary Committee that information his panel provided to Justice about the documents issue "has been repeatedly ignored."

Barnard's subcommittee subpoenaed the information shortly after Iraq's August 1990 invasion of Kuwait. It sought the department's list of "dual use" exports to Iraq — civilian goods that can have military applications and therefore require export licenses.

Between 1985 and 1990, the Reagan and Bush administrations approved licenses for $1.5 billion in dual use exports to Iraq. During that period, more than two-thirds of all license applications for dual use sales to that country were approved.

Barnard told the Judiciary Committee that in October 1990, shortly after the Commerce Department began providing the requested information, "the subcommittee received an anonymous telephone call informing us that the caller had been instructed to make certain alterations" in the documents.

After learning of the incident, the Commerce Department's inspector general conducted an internal investigation. In a report released in June 1991, Inspector General Frank DeGeorge found that changes had been made on 68 of 771 export licenses provided to the subcommittee.

DeGeorge discovered that personnel from the department's Bureau of Export Administration altered records on some licenses for exports of trucks "to eliminate a reference to a design for military use."

The report did not identify who ordered the alterations. But Wendell L. Willkie II, general counsel of the department, told the House Banking Committee on May 29 that Dennis E. Kloske, former under secretary for export administration, "authorized those changes." Willkie called the alterations "certainly unjustified and inappropriate."

Several Democrats expressed doubt that Kloske — who testified in April 1991 that he had urged the administration to tighten controls on sales to Iraq — undertook the action on his own. "I'm not suspicious at all that Dennis Kloske did it," Barnard said.

Barnard said that while he had no evidence of who else might have ordered changes in the records or why, he was aware that members of the National Security Council staff — including Brent Scowcroft, assistant to the president

for national security affairs — took a strong interest in the subcommittee's request for information.

During fall 1990, when his panel was negotiating with Commerce for the records, Barnard said Kloske told the subcommittee: "Look, it's out of my hands; it's up to the White House." Kloske, who resigned from the department in 1991, shortly after his congressional testimony, was unavailable for comment.

After the inspector general's report failed to identify who might have been responsible for the alterations, Barnard wrote to then-Attorney General Dick Thornburgh asking the Justice Department to investigate.

But the investigation proceeded fitfully, Barnard said. In August 1991, he said, two "junior attorneys" from the department interviewed the subcommittee staff. He added that "inquiries disclosed that the Justice Department had not followed up on staff suggestions."

The Justice Department subsequently wrote Barnard that an investigation was continuing.

In June of 1992, the Judiciary panel received new information on the altered documents.

Commerce Department officials consistently had testified that the alterations were made by a small group of officials in the Bureau of Export Administration, acting on their own, under the direction of former Under Secretary Kloske.

But documents released by the Judiciary Committee revealed that other agencies had expressed interest in the release of the export licenses: Iain S. Baird, director of export licensing at Commerce, told department auditors that "State [the State Department] said trucks classified as military vehicles should be re-classified as cargo trucks."

Baird said that "he thought Commerce had been set up, as a conscious effort to distance Bush and Baker from Iraq beforehand," according to a March 1991 interview with the auditors. The statement included no elaboration, and the auditors apparently did not ask him what he meant.

After a lengthy period out of public view, Kloske surfaced with a statement to the Judiciary Committee. In an unsworn interview with a committee attorney, Kloske said that at the time that the disputed documents were supplied he was under "daily supervision" from aides to then-Commerce Secretary Robert A. Mosbacher about what data was being provided to Congress.

Rep. Charles E. Schumer, D-N.Y., whose staff aide conducted the interview with Kloske, charged that Commerce Department auditors were aware that Kloske "was not making the decisions and people higher up were."

On July 9, 20 of the 21 Democrats on the House Judiciary Committee asked Attorney General William P. Barr to seek an independent counsel to investigate the administration's dealings with Iraq, including the circumstances surrounding the alteration of export licenses.

Barr turned down the request. But the prosecutor he appointed to examine the Iraq issue, retired federal judge Frederick B. Lacey, urged the Justice Department to pursue questions about the altered documents.

dealing with Saddam Hussein.

The House Judiciary Committee heard testimony from Frank M. Lemay, a midlevel State Department official who wrote an explosive memo raising the possibility that U.S. agricultural loan guarantees might have been misused to underwrite Iraqi purchases of military equipment.

Lemay told the panel that he felt at the time that if the allegations in his memo turned out to be true "then the administration has an even bigger foreign policy problem on its hands that will have to be dealt with."

But the memo's distribution was tightly restricted, Lemay testified. And while Secretary of State James A. Baker III apparently was informed of Lemay's concerns, the administration authorized $1 billion in additional loan guarantees to Iraq in late 1989.

"A steady theme that emerges is that, at the very least, the administration did an incompetent job," Romano L. Mazzoli, D-Ky., a member of the Judiciary Committee, said in an interview. "At the worst, you have an active cover-up."

Some lawmakers expressed concern that Lemay could become a scapegoat for a failed prewar policy toward Iraq.

"I'm too junior to be set up on this thing," he said. Lemay told the committee he was merely trying to do his job.

His startling memo, dated Oct. 13, 1989, was a summary of a meeting with Agriculture Department officials who had reviewed alleged improprieties in the loan guarantee program with Iraq.

The officials recently had returned from Atlanta, where they interviewed Justice Department attorneys investigating the BNL bank branch there.

In his memo, Lemay said Larry T. McElvain, director of Agriculture's Commodity Credit Corporation operations division, expressed concern that commodities purchased with U.S. loan guarantees "were bartered in Jordan and Turkey for military hardware."

The memo also said that Kevin Brosch, an Agriculture Department attorney, noted that the U.S. attorney for Atlanta had said "there was some indication that diverted funds (and possibly direct bank-lent funds) were used to procure nuclear-related equipment. Noted in particular were a 'nuclear fuel compounder' and a 'nose cone burr.' "

Urging that the State Department "proceed with caution" in authorizing new loan guarantees, Lemay wrote that "if smoke indicates fire, we may be facing a four-alarm blaze in the near future."

In the weeks before Lemay's testimony, Brosch and McElvain disputed his account of their 1989 conversation. At a House Banking Committee hearing May 21, Brosch called Lemay's memo "totally misleading" and portrayed him as ill-informed about the loan guarantee program.

But Lemay stuck to his story, saying that "I was quite taken aback when I read the testimony of my Agriculture Department colleagues."

He told the panel that "I had never heard of a nuclear nose cone burr or a nuclear fuel compounder before that meeting."

Lemay said that only his immediate supervisor at the bureau of Economic and Agricultural Affairs, Sam Hoskinson, discussed the memo with him at length.

Lemay added that someone outside that bureau categorized the memo as "not for the system" — a procedural designation that he said "would have severely restricted the distribution of the memo."

Lemay said that the former under secretary for economic and agricultural affairs, Richard T. McCormack, told him that he subsequently provided a less-detailed account of his assertions to Baker. But several weeks after Lemay's original memo, State Department officials led the move to provide new loan guarantees to Iraq.

## PROSECUTOR REQUESTED

On July 9, Democrats on the House Judiciary Committee presented Barr with an election-year dilemma by formally asking him to seek appointment of an independent counsel to probe possible criminal misconduct associated with the Bush administration's prewar policy toward Iraq.

Twenty of the committee's 21 Democrats signed a letter to the attorney general requesting the independent counsel to investigate allegations that current and former administration officials illegally assisted Saddam Hussein's regime before its 1990 invasion of Kuwait, and sought to "conceal information about potential criminal activity from Congress."

Committee Chairman Brooks said the request for an independent counsel was not an attempt to challenge the administration's policy of "tilting" toward Iraq before the Persian Gulf War. "The stupidity of that policy speaks for itself," he said.

"What we are concerned about is the possibility that high administration officials, in their zeal to carry out this policy and then to keep it from being exposed, may have broken the law," he said.

Among the committee's Democrats, only Rick Boucher of Virginia opposed the request. Boucher said he believed a "traditional criminal investigation" of the allegations by the Justice Department would be sufficient.

Under the independent counsel law, the Judiciary Committee members asked the attorney general to apply to a special three-judge panel for the appointment of an independent counsel.

Barr had 30 days to decide whether to seek a preliminary inquiry. If he decided to do so, he would then have another 90 days to decide whether to request the appointment of an independent counsel. At the end of 90 days, he could ask for a 60-day extension from the three-judge panel.

In their letter, Judiciary Committee Democrats focused on allegations that the White House sought to delay or influence the Justice Department's criminal investigation of BNL's Atlanta branch.

They also requested that the independent counsel investigate the circumstances surrounding the deliberate alteration of U.S. export licenses for Iraq, which had been provided by the Commerce Department to the House Government Operations Committee in 1990. *(Box, p. 546)*

Committee Democrats relied on new information on the BNL investigation released July 7 by Gonzalez, the Banking Committee chairman.

In a floor speech, Gonzalez cited notes made by a Treasury Department official that he said demonstrated extraordinary White House interest in the BNL case.

The notes referred to a 1989 conversation between Gail McKenzie, an assistant U.S. attorney in Atlanta who was leading the BNL prosecution, and an unidentified White House official. According to the notes, McKenzie was left with the impression that the White House was concerned about the "embarrassment level" of the case.

Gonzalez also alleged that the CIA warned the administration in 1989 — just days before it approved $1 billion in

# Tilting Toward Iraq: A Chronology

*Rep. Henry B. Gonzalez, D-Texas, and other critics cited the following chain of events as evidence of extraordinary efforts by the Reagan and Bush administrations to help Iraq until it invaded Kuwait:*

**Sept. 4, 1980** — Iraq asserted that Iranian artillery units attacked the Iraqi border town of Khanaqin, the first significant military action in the eight-year war between the two nations. The United States adopted a neutral stance.

**Feb. 26, 1982** — In a policy shift, the State Department dropped Iraq from its list of terrorist nations, paving the way for an expansion of U.S. exports to Iraq. Many in Congress objected to the action, particularly after Abu Nidal, whose group had claimed responsibility for terrorist attacks around the world, returned to Baghdad in September of that year. The Carter administration had first placed Iraq on the terrorist list in 1979.

**Dec. 15, 1982** — The Agriculture Department announced that the United States would provide $210 million in Commodity Credit Corporation (CCC) loan guarantees to finance food sales to Iraq. By the end of fiscal 1983, the department had authorized guarantees for $364.5 million in sales.

**Nov. 26, 1984** — The Reagan administration's gradual tilt toward Iraq in the Iran-Iraq war culminated in its decision to restore full diplomatic relations with Baghdad. Iraq had severed ties during the 1967 Arab-Israeli war. During 1984, the president also authorized the CIA to share "limited intelligence" with Iraq, according to the Senate Intelligence Committee. Documents released by Gonzalez show that the intelligence-sharing continued until 1990.

**Aug. 20, 1988** — Iran and Iraq agreed to a U.N.-brokered cease-fire. Later in 1988, Iraq became the subject of international denunciations for using chemical weapons in its war against Kurdish rebels. But agricultural trade between the United States and Iraq continued to expand. The United States provided more than $1 billion in CCC loan guarantees for Iraq in both fiscal 1988 and fiscal 1989.

**Aug. 4, 1989** — Federal agents raided the Atlanta branch of Banca Nazionale del Lavoro (BNL), an Italian bank that was a key source of U.S. loans for Iraq, including about $1.25 billion guaranteed by the CCC. The agents uncovered evidence that the bank had lent billions of dollars to Iraq without reporting the transactions to U.S. banking regulators.

**October 1989** — Documents released by Gonzalez refer to a national security directive — reportedly signed by President Bush in this month — directing agencies to expand economic ties with Iraq. The following month, after an intense debate within the administration, the United States approved $1 billion in CCC guarantees for Iraq.

**April 2, 1990** — An internal Department of Agriculture memo released by Gonzalez indicated that officials believed that indictments were imminent in the BNL case. But the indictments were not handed up for nearly a year. Later in April, the Agriculture Department suspended CCC guarantees for Iraq, citing financial irregularities in the program. From fiscal 1983 through fiscal 1990, the United States provided about $4.5 billion in agricultural guarantees, according to the Agriculture Department.

**July 31, 1990** — As tensions rose along the border between Iraq and Kuwait, Assistant Secretary of State John H. Kelly reiterated the administration's opposition to legislation — then gaining support in Congress — that would have imposed tough economic sanctions on Iraq.

**Aug. 2, 1990** — Iraq invaded Kuwait and within hours occupied the entire country. President Bush issued an executive order prohibiting all trade with Iraq.

**Jan. 16, 1991** — Allied forces began their aerial bombardment of Iraq. Six weeks later, on Feb. 23, the United States and its allies launched the successful ground operation to eject Iraqi forces from Kuwait.

**Feb. 28, 1991** — On the day after President Bush announced a cease-fire in the war with Iraq, Attorney General Dick Thornburgh announced indictments in the BNL scandal.

fiscal 1990 agricultural loan guarantees for Iraq — that BNL loans had been used by Iraq to buy weapons.

A secret CIA report indicated "that several of the BNL-financed front companies in the network were secretly procuring technology for Iraq's missile programs and nuclear, biological and chemical weapons programs," Gonzalez said.

## Barr Denies the Request

In an Aug. 10 letter to the House Judiciary Committee, Barr rejected the request for an independent prosecutor.

He said the panel's Democrats had relied on "vague and conclusory" allegations of wrongdoing in seeking a counsel to investigate possible criminal activity arising from administration support for Iraq before the Persian Gulf War.

Committee Democrats bitterly denounced the decision as politically motivated. Chairman Brooks accused the administration of "stonewalling, plain and simple."

Brooks told reporters Aug. 10 that "it leaves all of us as American citizens with one overriding question: What is the administration trying to hide in the record of its assistance to Saddam Hussein?"

But Barr concluded that there was no "specific and credible information" that high-ranking administration officials had committed any crimes.

In his letter, Barr rejected criticisms of his department and called the handling of the BNL bank investigation "entirely proper."

He said any alleged delays resulted from a desire for a thorough investigation, adding that a review of the case by Justice Department officials in Washington was "in no way politically motivated."

The attorney general's conclusion was challenged publicly by the judge in the BNL case.

In an interview with The Washington Post, published Aug. 12, Judge Shoob also raised concerns over possible White House interference in the case. Shoob previously had called for an independent counsel.

## The One-Man Theory

In September, new revelations in the prosecution of the BNL bank revived the Iraq controversy and brought it to the forefront in the super-charged atmosphere of the approaching presidential election.

The most controversial aspect of the BNL prosecution was the government's contention that the scheme to provide billions of dollars in unsecured loans to Iraq was engineered by Atlanta branch manager Drogoul, acting alone and defrauding his employer.

But that central tenet of the government's case came

under fire as soon as Drogoul's sentencing hearing began Sept. 14. Under a plea agreement, Drogoul had pleaded guilty to 60 counts of fraud and tax evasion in return for cooperating with prosecutors.

House Banking Committee Chairman Gonzalez gave a floor speech that day raising the first serious questions about the government's "rogue operation" theory.

Gonzalez cited a CIA report showing that as the funding that Drogoul's bank branch provided to Iraq grew larger, Iraqi officials began demanding that senior BNL officials in Rome sign off on the loans.

Reading from the CIA report, Gonzalez said, "BNL agreed to this request, and the loans were then signed by bank officials in Rome."

The revelation reverberated from Washington to Atlanta. If Drogoul's attorneys could show that the former bank manager was authorized to make the loans, the charge that he defrauded the Rome headquarters of BNL might be proved groundless.

Prosecutors, worried how the judge would react, sought and received a classified CIA letter concerning what it knew about BNL's activities.

The Sept. 17 letter, signed by acting general counsel David P. Holmes, said the CIA "has publicly available information, acquired in the December, 1989-January, 1990 time frame, that BNL-Rome was aware of the illegal activities engaged in by BNL-Atlanta."

It turned out that the CIA possessed a number of intelligence reports — not just publicly available information.

But when the Senate Intelligence Committee tried to determine how and why such a mistake could have occurred — with the integrity of a major criminal case at stake — it received sharply divergent answers from CIA and Justice Department officials.

In closed committee sessions Oct. 8 and 9, CIA representatives maintained that they were following the "strong advice" of Justice in releasing the misleading letter, according to Intelligence Committee Chairman David L. Boren D-Okla. Justice Department officials countered that they had left the decision up to the CIA.

On Oct. 1, Shoob granted Drogoul's motion for a new trial.

As the handling of the BNL prosecution emerged as a key issue, some Democrats turned to foreign policy considerations in imputing a possible motive for administration actions.

Gonzalez, citing State Department cables and assorted other documents, suggested that the administration acceded to a request by Italian officials for "damage control" by limiting the scope of the BNL prosecution.

The bank was virtually an agency of the Italian government, and its top officials were political appointees. Any effort to prosecute those officials could have harmed relations between Rome and Washington.

Sen. Howard M. Metzenbaum, D-Ohio, cited allegations that a "CIA front organization was involved with loans to Iraq."

If such allegations were true, he said, the United States might be involved "in arms sales to Iraq, as well as a possible cover-up."

The CIA launched an internal investigation, and the Justice Department ordered an FBI probe of the incident.

### Renewing the Request

On Oct. 14, Senate Intelligence Committee Chairman Boren said that the newly released information "compels"

Barr to reconsider his refusal to seek an independent counsel.

Noting Barr's rejection in August of the initial request for an investigation, Boren argued that at that time most of the events relating to the misleading CIA letter "had not yet even occurred."

Boren's call for "a truly independent investigation" of the BNL case was echoed the next day by Brooks, chairman of the House Judiciary Committee, and Joseph R. Biden Jr., D-Del., chairman of the Senate Judiciary Committee.

The Democratic majority on Brooks' committee renewed the previously rejected formal request for an independent counsel, this time joined by a majority of Democrats on Biden's committee.

Barr responded to the mounting criticism on Oct. 16 by appointing Lacey to review the Justice Department's "entire handling of the BNL matter."

But that did little to satisfy Democrats. Boren dismissed the selection of Lacey — in essence, a hand-picked investigator who reported to Barr — as "not a satisfactory substitute" for an independent counsel chosen by a special three-judge panel.

Although Barr expressed confidence that Justice Department officials "have done nothing wrong," he said that Lacey's investigation did not preclude the appointment later of a full-fledged independent counsel.

The law governing independent counsels was not reauthorized by Congress and was due to expire on Dec. 15. But investigations begun by then could go ahead.

Sen. Al Gore of Tennessee, the Democratic vice presidential nominee, charged Oct. 15 that Bush was "presiding over a cover-up that is significantly larger than the Watergate cover-up."

The political ramifications were not lost on Republicans. John H. Chafee, R.-R.I., a member of the Senate Intelligence Committee, complained that Boren held a news conference just days after the committee began looking into the matter. "It can't take any more of a political turn," he said in an interview.

Boren indicated that if Barr refused to request an independent counsel, the Intelligence Committee — which had begun taking sworn depositions from administration officials — would hold hearings on BNL.

That aggressive posture marked something of a departure for Boren, who conceded that he was sometimes criticized as "too bipartisan."

During his six-year tenure as chairman, which ended in January 1993, Boren was supportive of the intelligence community. He played a decisive role in shepherding CIA Director Robert M. Gates through Senate confirmation hearings in 1991 that focused on charges of politicization at the agency and on Gates' role in the Iran-contra affair. *(1991 Almanac, p. 486)*

Thus, the agency's new problems were also a test of Boren's decision to put his faith in Gates as intelligence director.

Boren pulled no punches in criticizing the administration for its handling of BNL. He quoted Atlanta Judge Shoob, who had recently recused himself from the case at the prosecution's request, as saying "that decisions were made at the top levels of the United States government and within the intelligence community to shape this case."

While chiding the CIA for failing to provide "extremely relevant documents" to prosecutors in the BNL case, Boren emphasized that the FBI had received substantial

intelligence information from the CIA.

"These documents should have given rise to an intensive questioning of Italian officials and questioning of CIA officals" about the quality of the data, he said.

### Barr Responds, Again

On Nov. 16, Barr wrote members of Congress that he had acquiesced in a "preliminary investigation" under terms of the independent counsel statute. He promised to decide before the statute's mid-December expiration whether to seek an independent counsel in the Iraq affair.

Barr added that Lacey, his counsel on the matter, had said he was "far from concluding that there has been any violation of any Federal statutes." Nonetheless, Barr said, Lacey had informed him that the assertions in Boren's letter seeking a probe had "met the statutory criteria for commencing a preliminary investigation: i.e., they constituted specific information from a credible source sufficient to constitute grounds to investigate whether a law may have been violated."

Barr said that he had therefore asked Lacey to proceed with a preliminary investigation "of matters related to the production of CIA documents and information concerning the BNL loans to or on behalf of Iraq, to the Department of Justice, the United States Attorney's office in Atlanta, the United States District Court in Atlanta and the United States Congress."

Although Barr took the step of ordering a preliminary investigation in late October, Democrats noted that he did not make that decision public until mid-November, after the presidential election.

On Dec. 9, Barr rejected the renewed request from Democrats to seek an independent counsel in the Iraq case. He based his decision on Lacey's conclusion that there were "no reasonable grounds" to warrant further investigation.

Although Lacey sharply criticized Justice and CIA officials for the "fiasco" surrounding the submission of the misleading statement to the court in the Atlanta trial, he said he had found "little fault" with the administration's overall conduct in the BNL prosecution.

Citing his own expertise as a former prosecutor, the retired federal judge said: "Had there been any corruption here in the Justice Department in this case, I would have smelled it and I would have found it."

At a stormy two-hour news conference, Lacey, a Republican, bitterly denounced the "unbridled attacks of a legislator," a reference to Gonzalez. Lacey said that "many decent people have had their careers tarnished and their reputations stained" by "baseless charges."

"You've been taken in by them," said Lacey, scolding journalists. "Or if you haven't been taken in by them, you've been writing about them, which I think is even worse."

Lacey examined the circumstances surrounding the CIA's misleading letter to the Atlanta prosecutors in a classified section of his report, which was not publicly released, although it was provided to several congressional committees. He acknowledged that the CIA letter was "absurd — everybody who read it should have gone into paroxysms of laughter."

Lacey said that, partly because of what he termed "a societal clash" between Justice and the CIA, there were inadequate procedures in place for handling classified cables. "We were unable to determine who at Justice saw what and when, and that is part of my criticism," he said.

He said he discerned no "corrupt intent" on the part of CIA or Justice Department officials, although some potentially important classified cables were not provided to Justice until a few months before Lacey issued his report, more than three years after the outset of the BNL investigation.

Lacey's report said that senior administration officials — including then-Secretary of State James A. Baker III — took a strong interest in the BNL prosecution in 1989, when the administration was considering $1 billion in agricultural guarantees for Iraq.

The Atlanta attorneys handling the BNL case were told by Agriculture Department officials that Baker considered the program "very important" to U.S. foreign policy. But Lacey's report concluded that "the prosecutors did not buckle, and foreign policy considerations did not move them."

Democrats, who professed not to be surprised by Lacey's report or by Barr's decision, attacked both with relish. "To all those who are concerned about the propriety of the Justice Department investigating itself in this highly charged case, Judge Lacey says, 'not to worry — trust us,'" said House Judiciary Committee Chairman Brooks.

Brooks and other Democrats urged President-elect Clinton to aggressively pursue charges of criminal activity associated with the BNL case. They also vowed to push in 1993 for enactment of a new independent counsel statute to replace the one that Congress had permitted to expire on Dec. 15.

Clinton told a news conference Dec. 10 that he would back reviving the independent counsel statute. He stopped short of calling for such a counsel in the Iraq case but said as president he would ask his attorney general to make recommendations concerning the affair. "I certainly think we need to know more about it than we now know," Clinton added.

Some senators floated the idea of creating a special Senate committee to investigate the matter. Boren, who was departing as chairman of the Intelligence Committee, said his panel's investigation into the BNL case would continue in 1993. ∎

# Saddam's Staying Power

As 1992 began, President Bush predicted that Saddam Hussein's luck would soon run out. As the year ended, however, Bush had been humiliated in his quest for re-election while Saddam remained in power, mockingly rejoicing in the political defeat of his military adversary.

In early 1993, Bush responded to provocations from Saddam by launching air strikes that dominated the final days of the U.S. president's term.

In a television interview that aired Jan. 3, 1992, Bush had described Iraq's ruler as "increasingly isolated" and vulnerable to overthrow.

"It is my understanding that the people are getting more and more discontented with this brutal dictator as each day goes by," Bush said. "History will show a tyrant of that nature simply cannot last forever by brutalizing his own people."

But others proved more prophetic. Rep. Stephen J. Solarz of New York, who had been a leading Democratic supporter of the administration's decision to use force after Iraq's invasion of Kuwait, pleaded for the United States to help arm and train Iraqi opposition groups.

"If the administration doesn't move in that direction, it may find in a year from now that Bush will be out of power and Saddam Hussein will still be in," said Solarz, who later lost his own bid for re-election. "That would be an incredible denouement to the Persian Gulf War."

Throughout the year, Saddam continued what White House spokesman Marlin Fitzwater called a "cheat and retreat" response to United Nations requirements that Iraq disarm and turn over all of its capabilities to develop nuclear, chemical and biological weapons. Saddam failed to carry out promises for political reforms, and he refused to sell Iraqi oil that was badly needed to enable him to feed his people because he detested U.N. requirements concerning how the funds could be used.

## A Series of Showdowns

In March, reports that Bush was considering the use of military force to destroy Iraq's weapons sites and facilities refocused Capitol Hill's attention on Saddam's continued defiance in the face of an international economic embargo.

"Iraq must comply" with the U.N. mandate, Gen. Colin L. Powell Jr., chairman of the Joint Chiefs of Staff, told the Senate Armed Services Committee on March 20.

Asked about a report in The Washington Post that he had opposed proposals for a military strike against Iraq, Powell said, "We have a variety of tools available to us to make sure that Iraq does comply — diplomatic tools, economic tools, political tools, and yes, the armed forces of the United States. And I can assure this committee that if we are called upon to be a part of this solution, we will perform our role in an absolutely professional way with desired results."

The same day, Saddam averted another in a series of showdowns with U.N. inspectors.

U.N. officials announced that Saddam had disclosed new information about his arsenal and had agreed to destroy equipment used to make Scud missiles.

But some members of Congress urged the administration to move more aggressively to put a stop to Iraq's off-and-on compliance.

On March 18, Sen. Al Gore, D-Tenn., called the administration's reportedly renewed determination to unseat the Iraqi leader "better late than never."

Calling for "clear and decisive action," House Armed Services Committee Chairman Les Aspin, D-Wis., said on March 20 that Saddam should be told that he would face military action unless he fully cooperated with the U.N.

"Should the Iraqis prevent the U.N. experts from completing their mission, a swift and decisive coalition airstrike on the facilities in question should be the response," he said.

Chiding Bush for a "threat-and-forget strategy" toward Saddam, Aspin said, "Iraq stalls and refuses to comply, and we still can't get our act together."

## The Human Toll

For all of the anger and frustration at Saddam's survival, there was also concern in Congress over the human toll of continuing international economic sanctions against Iraq.

There were reports of widespread malnutrition and disease as well as human rights abuses in Iraq — especially against Kurds in the north and the Shiite population in the south.

On March 18, Majority Whip David E. Bonior, D-Mich., appeared before the House Select Hunger Committee to appeal to the administration to release "at least some of the $600 million in frozen Iraqi assets" in the United States to provide humanitarian assistance to the Iraqi people.

"The president should take whatever action necessary to see that food and medicine are made available to the Iraqi people," Bonior said.

But Deputy Assistant Secretary of State Melinda Kimble blamed Saddam, not U.S. policy, for the suffering in Iraq. She noted his refusal to cooperate with a U.N. plan to permit Iraq to sell oil and use much of the revenue to buy food and medicine.

She said that, while there was some malnutrition in Iraq, it was not "generally a problem."

"U.N. officials have assured us that there are adequate stocks of food in Iraq," she said.

This assessment was disputed by other witnesses, including Charles LaMuniere, who directed emergency programs for UNICEF, the U.N. children's relief agency. "The majority of Iraqi women and children suffer food shortages and a lack of proper sanitation," he said.

The following day, human rights advocates told the Senate Foreign Relations Committee that Kurds had been slaughtered in mass executions and could face another wave of killings.

Andrew Whitley, executive director of the human rights group Middle East Watch, compared the Iraqi campaign against the Kurds in the late 1980s with Nazi Germany's systematic extermination of millions of European Jews and others during World War II.

Whitley said evidence — some it gleaned from detailed records found in secret police buildings overrun by Kurdish guerrillas — documented the use of torture, mass execution, forced relocation and poison gas on Kurdish civilians.

In addition, Whitley described the "disappearance" of up to 300,000 relocated Kurds who he said may have been transported to "death camps."

After a failed Kurdish uprising that followed the gulf war, the United States and allies established a safe zone for Kurds in northern Iraq. But in the early months of 1992, Iraq blockaded the zone, stopping most food and fuel shipments.

On June 2, the House called for a continuation of the United Nations' presence in northern Iraq to protect the Kurdish minority from attack by Saddam. The non-binding resolution (H Con Res 299) was approved by voice vote.

## The Parking Lot Compromise

A three-week standoff between Iraq and the United Nations was resolved peacefully July 26 after Baghdad allowed U.N. inspectors to enter an agricultural ministry building that had become a focal point of their efforts to uncover details of Saddam's weapons program.

Bush, who raised the U.S. military profile in the region in a show of force, said Saddam had "caved in" by agreeing to the inspection.

But the compromise — painstakingly negotiated by Rolf Ekeus, head of the U.N. special commission on Iraq's weaponry, and Iraqi envoy Abdul Amir al-Anbari — barred from the agriculture building representatives from the United States and its allies in the gulf war coalition.

At a July 29 hearing of the House Foreign Affairs Subcommittee on Europe and the Middle East, Democrats charged that the administration had acquiesced in a bad deal with Saddam to resolve the inspection standoff.

"This is a humiliating spectacle," said Tom Lantos, D-Calif., who argued that the administration repeatedly had

been mocked by Saddam's behavior.

Delays in proceeding with the inspection may have enabled Iraqi officials to remove incriminating material. When a reconstituted U.N. team finally went through the installation July 29, they found no evidence of the weapons program.

On July 29, Secretary of State James A. Baker III held talks with Iraqi Shiite and Kurdish opposition leaders — the highest-level contact the administration had conducted with the opposition.

Most lawmakers said they would back a military strike against Iraq as long as the United States was part of a multilateral coalition, similar to the one that defeated Iraq in the gulf war.

Following a July 28 briefing for members by the president and his senior advisers, David L. Boren, chairman of the Senate Intelligence Committee, characterized support for such an action as "unusually bipartisan."

A small group of members from both parties went further, urging the administration to consider going it alone if, as some feared, the gulf war allies proved reluctant to participate in renewed military action.

The administration should first seek the endorsement of the United Nations, said Sen. Richard G. Lugar, R-Ind. But barring that, he said, unilateral U.S. action should be considered as "the last possibility."

Lawmakers maintained that election-year politics had no role in their reaction to the crisis with Iraq. Democrats fell in line behind their presidential nominee, Arkansas Gov. Bill Clinton, who issued a tough statement backing Bush before the standoff at the Agricultural Ministry had been resolved.

"Let there be no mistake," he said July 23. "If the United Nations decides to use force to ensure Iraqi compliance with the cease-fire agreements, I will support American participation in such action."

But it was perhaps inevitable during a political year that foreign policy would quickly become embroiled in presidential campaigning.

Democrats tried to refute the conventional wisdom that renewed hostilities with Iraq would play to Bush's strength in foreign policy.

Dave McCurdy, Okla., chairman of the House Intelligence Committee, called the developing crisis a "lose-lose" situation for the president because voters would only be reminded that Saddam remained in power after the allied victory in the gulf.

Gore, the Democratic vice presidential nominee, picked up the same theme in responding to administration gibes that the Democratic ticket lacked foreign policy experience.

If Bush and Vice President Dan Quayle are "such whizzes," asked the Tennessee senator, "why is it that Saddam Hussein is thumbing his nose at the entire world?"

## Final Skirmishes

The final days of the Bush administration brought a final round of skirmishes with its archenemy Saddam.

On Jan. 13, 1993, 110 U.S., British and French planes attacked installations in Iraq. They destroyed or damaged some of the four radar and communications sites targeted but only one of four targeted clusters of anti-aircraft missile launchers, according to Pentagon officials.

Iraqi forces disbanded two of the other missile sites, they said. One errant bomb struck a building, described as an apartment house by the Iraqi government.

Despite those mixed military results, Bush and other U.S. officials contended that the raid achieved its two purposes:

- Disrupting an air defense network that threatened allied planes patrolling the southern part of Iraq to enforce a ban on Iraqi flights in that "no-fly zone."
- Signaling to Saddam that the allied governments insisted on Baghdad's compliance with all the restrictions imposed on Iraq in the wake of the 1991 war to eject its forces from Kuwait.

The attack followed several Iraqi military moves, including two efforts to intercept U.S. planes over the no-fly zone that was established to protect Iraq's Shiite minority. A U.S. F-16 shot down an Iraqi MiG-25 on Dec. 27, shortly after the first of those incidents.

Bush also announced that an armored batallion with more than 1,100 soldiers, armed with M-1 tanks and Bradley fighting vehicles, would be dispatched to Kuwait, where they would reinforce 300 U.S. special forces personnel in the country for a training exercise.

President-elect Clinton and Secretary of State-designate Warren M. Christopher emphasized that the incoming administration stood "shoulder to shoulder" with Bush, as Christopher put it, in their insistence that Iraq fully comply with all U.N. Security Council resolutions.

In an interview with The New York Times published Jan. 14, Clinton said he could imagine a "new start" in U.S. relations with Iraq if Saddam's government began complying with all U.N. demands. "I'm not obsessed with the man," Clinton said, "but I'm obsessed with the standards of conduct embodied in those United Nations' accords."

Clinton appeared to be attempting to eliminate the element of a personal confrontation from U.S.-Iraq relations, reducing the standing Saddam seemed to seek from a one-on-one grudge match with a U.S. president.

After news accounts of the interview emphasized Clinton's reference to a possible "new start," however, he vigorously denied any intention of easing up on Iraq. "There is no difference between my policy and the policy of the present administration," he said Jan. 14. Based on Saddam's conduct, Clinton said, "I cannot imagine" circumstances under which he would normalize relations with Iraq.

There were no ambiguities in the congressional response to the attack on Iraq. "The message . . . should be clear," House Majority Leader Richard A. Gephardt, D-Mo., said the day of the attack. "Democrats and Republicans — the Bush administration and the Clinton administration — will not tolerate violations of the U.N. resolutions."

And some members of Congress called for more far-reaching steps. Senate Foreign Relations Committee member Richard G. Lugar, R-Ind., warned of "tenacious probing" by Iraq's leader "to find the day, month or year in which the United States and its allies tire . . . and allow Saddam to proceed with dangerous foreign policy aims."

Anticipating that future Iraqi actions also would elicit allied attacks, Lugar said he hoped "the next military strikes will be substantially more comprehensive and that additional United Nations debate will include discussion of the termination of Saddam's leadership."

However, some Arab governments that had played key roles in the coalition that ejected Iraq from Kuwait, including Syria, issued disapproving statements after the new U.S.-led attack.

Some Arab leaders complained that the United States

was applying a double standard to the enforcement of Security Council resolutions, attacking Iraq for disregarding some while using a kid-gloves approach to Israel, which was defying a U.N. demand that it readmit 400 deported Palestinians.

The skirmishes with Iraq continued with incidents on the following dates:

● Jan. 17: U.S. Navy ships fired 45 Tomahawk cruise missiles at a factory where Iraq was suspected of developing nuclear weapons. The Pentagon said that the factory southeast of Baghdad was heavily damaged but that one missile shot down by Iraqi anti-aircraft fire landed near a hotel in Baghdad. Iraqi officials said the explosion killed two people. A U.S. jet also downed an Iraqi fighter in the northern no-fly zone.

● Jan. 18: Allied aircraft attacked several anti-aircraft sites in the southern and northern parts of the country. A senior Pentagon official said the raid in the south "neutralized" the Iraqi air defense capability there. Iraq said the attacks killed 21 people.

● Jan. 19: A Pentagon spokesman said that in response to continued Iraqi incursions into the northern no-fly zone, U.S. aircraft attacked a radar installation and an anti-aircraft artillery site.

### Clinton v. Saddam

The presidential succession seemed to produce something that repeated allied air strikes against Iraq could not — a kinder, gentler Saddam Hussein, in tone if not in deeds.

A day before Bill Clinton was sworn in as the nation's 42nd president on Jan. 20, 1993, the Iraqi government offered him an olive branch in the form of a unilateral cease-fire. The Iraqi government said it hoped to "start a constructive dialogue" with Clinton.

In a further concession, Baghdad announced that it would no longer place conditions on flights of U.N. weapons inspectors entering the country.

But Clinton told CBS News on Jan. 19 that it would be "almost inconceivable" that his administration would have good relations with Iraq as long as Saddam remained in power.

And skirmishes on Clinton's first full days in office, Jan. 21 and 22, fed the skepticism in Washington that Saddam intended to abandon his resistance to the no-fly zones that the United States and its allies had imposed on the northern and southern sections of Iraq.

In both cases, U.S. fighter jets fired at Iraqi ground installations in the northern no-fly zone after a radar's search beam was aimed at allied planes, according to the new administration.

The new administration sought to underscore the continuity in the U.S. response to Saddam. "It is the American policy," Clinton told reporters after the Jan. 21 skirmish, "and that's what we're going to stay with."

Christopher, who was confirmed as secretary of State on Jan. 20, added, "I think what happened today is a reflection of the determination that the Clinton administration will have in that area.... When their radar illuminates our pilots, we're going to protect our pilots." ∎

# Arms Proliferation Bill Dies in Final Hours

Though legislation (S 1128) that would have imposed sanctions on countries that trafficked in technology used for the manufacture of nuclear weapons passed both the House and the Senate, it did not become law in 1992.

In its final phase, the bill was attached during conference action to another measure (HR 3489) that would have reauthorized the 1979 Export Administration Act. But that bill died in the final hours of the 102nd Congress when the House was unable to clear the conference report. *(Export controls, p. 162)*

## SENATE ACTION

The Senate approved the measure by voice vote on April 9.

The bill's sponsor, John Glenn, D-Ohio, called it the most significant such legislation since passage of the Nuclear Non-Proliferation Act of 1978.

The measure would have prevented domestic and foreign companies that were involved in nuclear proliferation from obtaining U.S. government contracts for at least a year. Foreign governments found to be involved in the nuclear trade would have been barred from receiving assistance and purchasing weapons from the United States.

Financial institutions, such as international banks, that had "materially and with requisite knowledge" contributed to nuclear proliferation would have been barred from operating in the United States.

The measure would have given the president authority to determine whether transfers of weapons technology had occurred. In a concession to administration objections, the bill was modified so the president could have waived penalties on governments found to be transferring certain design information or components if he certified that sanctions "would have a serious adverse effect on vital U.S. interests."

But the president could not have waived sanctions on a foreign government that provided an actual nuclear weapon or components necessary to complete such a device.

Sen. Claiborne Pell, D-R.I., the chairman of the Foreign Relations Committee, said the waiver "allows the president limited leeway but requires that a very tough standard be met."

Pell, whose panel unanimously approved the Glenn bill in November 1991, said the penalties mirrored those included in the broad chemical and biological weapons sanctions bill passed in 1991 (HR 1724 — PL 102-182). *(1991 Almanac, p. 493)*

The Bush administration came under attack several times in 1992 for proposing sales of military equipment to foreign nations, including Saudi Arabia and Pakistan. But despite strong talk from members of Congress, the sales went through without any major problems.

### Pakistan

The administration's decision to allow commercial military sales to Pakistan was attacked July 30 by Senate

sponsors of a law that they say clearly banned such transactions.

Three lawmakers said in a letter to Secretary of State James A. Baker III that a 1985 law cutting off all U.S. aid and military sales to the Asian nation, if it was found to possess a nuclear weapon, was unambiguous.

"We cannot comprehend how our simple and direct language could conceivably be interpreted as permitting commercial sales," said Sens. Larry Pressler, R-S.D., John Glenn, D-Ohio, and Alan Cranston, D-Calif.

They wrote that if the administration did not like the restriction, known as the Pressler amendment, it should "seek a revision of the law, not . . . find some totally baseless legal rationale for evading it."

All U.S. military and economic aid, as well as government-to-government arms sales, were stopped in October 1990 when President Bush was unable to certify that Pakistan did not possess a nuclear device.

However, Baker told the Senate Foreign Relations Committee earlier in 1992 that limited commercial sales of military spare parts were being allowed to continue.

Michael J. Matheson, a State Department legal adviser, testified before Foreign Relations on July 30 that the administration interpreted the ban in the 1985 Foreign Assistance Act (PL 99-83) to apply only to government activities because the provision was included in a bill governing foreign assistance and because commercial sales were not specifically banned.

He said the administration had nonetheless decided to prohibit sales that would allow Pakistan to acquire new military capabilities or to upgrade existing systems. "Commercial arms exports have been significantly restricted — above and beyond what we believe is required by law," Matheson said.

Deputy Assistant Secretary of State John R. Malott said the limited sales give the United States leverage over Pakistan that could be useful in promoting U.S. non-proliferation policies in South Asia.

"By continuing the commercial sales we're leaving the door open slightly with Pakistan to engage in a kind of dialogue with us that we think is necessary," Malott said.

He said that if Pakistan felt it had been weakened by the U.S. sanctions, it could "turn to other nations for military assistance . . . and further pursue its nuclear program."

Pakistan, once among the top recipients of U.S. aid, had complained that it was being unfairly penalized for a nuclear program that was pursued in response to a similar program in neighboring India.

But Glenn, who was not a member of Foreign Relations, testified that the administration's policy was reminiscent of U.S. strategy toward Iraq before that country's invasion of Kuwait, when the administration hoped that continued trade would lead to U.S. influence over Saddam Hussein.

"There are a lot better ways to redress our balance of trade than by peddling arms or dual-use goods to countries with lousy non-proliferation credentials," Glenn said. "This policy did not work with Iraq. It is a continuing failure with respect to China. And it surely never worked with Pakistan."

He said that $4 billion in U.S. aid to Pakistan during the 1980s did little to slow that nation's nuclear program and that "there is considerable evidence that America's aid and high technology probably contributed to Pakistan's nuclear and missile capabilities."

In 1992, Pakistan's foreign secretary said his country had a nuclear capability in 1989.

## Saudi Arabia & Israel

Merging re-election campaigning with Middle East policy-making, President Bush in September agreed to let Saudi Arabia spend up to $9 billion to buy F-15 fighters.

On Sept. 11, Bush announced the F-15 sales to an appreciative audience of workers who built the airplanes.

Bush made the quick stop in St. Louis during a campaign swing through Missouri, a pivotal electoral state, to announce that he had approved Saudi Arabia's request to buy 72 additional F-15 fighter jets, built in that city by the economically troubled McDonnell Douglas Corp.

The U.S. Air Force had ordered its final batch of F-15s, so the Saudi sales would prolong for a few more years 7,000 jobs at McDonnell Douglas plants and more than 30,000 jobs at subcontractors.

Bush's approval of the sales mirrored his announcement on a campaign stop a week earlier that he was reversing a decade-old policy by approving the sale to Taiwan of F-16 fighters built by General Dynamics Corp. in Fort Worth, Texas.

Congress could have blocked the arms deal, but legislators allowed it to go forward in part because Israel did not appear inclined to seek a confrontation over the sales.

Saudi Arabia already had "C" and "D" model F-15s, designed to attack other aircraft. No foreign sales had been allowed of the F-15E, the version of the plane equipped with sophisticated electronic gear for precision attacks on ground targets. The 72 planes in the new package, designated F-15XPs, reportedly were to have some ground attack capability, but less than the "E" model.

Democratic presidential nominee Bill Clinton had said that he would support the sales only if they did not include an offensive version of the F-15. Clinton told B'nai B'rith on Sept. 9 that he favored the sale as long as it did not "undermine our commitment to Israel's qualitative edge."

With little hope of blocking the sale to Saudi Arabia, House opponents attacked the sale with sharp rhetoric.

At a hearing of two House Foreign Affairs subcommittees on Sept. 23, administration officials defended the $9 billion deal, saying that it would promote U.S. security interests in the Middle East by buttressing Saudi Arabia against possible aggression from Iraq and Iran.

But many lawmakers, particularly strong supporters of Israel, disagreed. Rep. Howard L. Berman, D-Calif., said the sale "would be a major escalation of the Middle East arms race and yet again affirm our role as premier arms peddler to the world."

With Bush and key Democrats in favor of the deal, however, Berman conceded that he would be unable to get the needed two-thirds vote in the House and Senate for his resolution disapproving the sale (H J Res 548).

Rep. Charles E. Schumer, D-N.Y., took a different tack than Berman, offering a resolution (H J Res 549) that would condition the sale upon Saudi Arabia's renouncing the Arab boycott of Israel. But the administration opposed attaching any conditions.

Deputy Assistant Secretary of Defense Carl W. Ford Jr. and Under Secretary of State Frank Wisner tried to assure lawmakers that the sale would not erode Israel's qualitative edge in weaponry in the Middle East.

Ford told the panels that the 72 F-15XP fighters in the proposed deal will not be equipped with the state-of-the-art avionics of the more advanced F-15Es. ∎

# U.S. Expands Economic Embargo of Cuba

Language designed to tighten the screws on the U.S. economic embargo of Cuba became law with President Bush's signature Oct. 6. The provisions were enacted as part of the fiscal 1993 defense authorization bill (HR 5006 — PL 102-396).

Ever since Fidel Castro seized power in Cuba in 1959, the U.S. government fought, both overtly and covertly, to topple the avowed communist from power. One tool in that fight was a U.S. embargo, which prohibited U.S. companies from trading with Cuba and prevented Cuban goods from entering the United States. Travel between the two countries was also restricted.

## COMMITTEE ACTION

The House Foreign Affairs Committee on May 21 began, but did not finish, work on legislation to toughen economic sanctions against Cuba. Two proposed amendments caused a sharp split in the panel, with supporters of the measure arguing that the amendments would weaken the embargo that supporters had hoped to strengthen.

Chairman Dante B. Fascell, D-Fla., ended the markup when the panel split sharply over proposals that would have allowed the sale of food and medicine to Cuba.

The bill, which supporters said was designed to build pressure for a transition to democracy in Cuba, sought to impose civil and criminal penalties on U.S. corporate subsidiaries in other countries that did business with Cuba. Companies that had existing contracts with the Cubans could fulfill them.

In addition, the measure called for barring from U.S. ports for six months any vessel that transported goods or passengers to or from Cuba. It also opened normal phone and mail links to the island nation in the hope that increased communication with the United States would encourage Cubans to change their system of government.

Finally, the bill would have allowed the president to impose economic sanctions against nations that provided assistance to Cuba.

The collapse of communism in the Soviet Union and Eastern Europe had deprived Castro of his political and economic patrons. Cuba's centrally planned economy was in a tailspin, leading some foreign policy experts to predict the collapse of the Castro government. Many Cuban-American groups had lobbied vigorously for new tough sanctions that they argued would help topple the weakened regime.

The Bush administration had opposed an earlier version (HR 4168) of the measure that would have mandated sanctions against other nations. The White House had also opposed the penalties on corporate subsidiaries, arguing that they would have imposed an undue burden on U.S. companies operating abroad.

But the administration came out in favor of the bill after working out a compromise to give the president discretion to impose the sanctions.

More important, when bill supporters agreed to the provision exempting existing contracts, the White House reversed a longstanding policy of opposing penalties against U.S. corporate subsidiaries in third countries.

The legislation had broad bipartisan support and was expected to win easy approval. But the panel divided over two linked amendments that would have eased restrictions on humanitarian assistance.

The committee approved, 11-10, an amendment offered by Ted Weiss, D-N.Y., that would have allowed the sale of medicine and medical supplies to the Cuban government. The final version of the bill allowed only donations of medical supplies to organizations not affiliated with the government.

Weiss offered another amendment to allow the sale or donation of food and agricultural products to the Cuban government for humanitarian purposes.

Fascell and bill sponsor Robert G. Torricelli, D-N.J. argued that the Weiss amendments would water down the bill and promised to work to defeat them. Torricelli said they would "subsidize the Castro regime."

Ileana Ros-Lehtinen, R-Fla., the only Cuban-American in Congress, also opposed the amendments.

"If Mr. Castro was a member of this committee, I'm sure he'd be a cosponsor of the bill with these amendments," Ros-Lehtinen said.

On June 4, during its second markup, the panel rejected the Weiss amendment that would have allowed U.S. companies to sell food to the Cuban government for humanitarian purposes. The measure allowed the donation of food and medical supplies only to non-governmental organizations.

The other Weiss amendment, already approved by the panel, was weakened by another amendment offered by Torricelli.

The Weiss amendment would have allowed the sale of medicine and medical equipment to the Cuban government. But the committee gave voice vote approval to Torricelli's amendment that sanctioned such sales only if the U.S. government could verify, through on-site inspections, that the supplies would not be re-exported or misused for purposes of torture.

Torricelli labeled it a compromise between the limits in the bill and the previously approved Weiss amendment. But Weiss accused him of effectively killing his proposal by setting impossible conditions, adding that U.S. on-site inspections in Cuba "can't happen and won't happen."

Robert S. Gelbard, principal deputy assistant secretary of State for Inter-American Affairs, told the committee that on-site inspections might be possible in some circumstances.

"It depends on the commodity," he said.

On June 5, the committee approved by voice vote a reintroduced version of the bill (HR 5323) that incorporated the changes made at the markup the day before.

## FLOOR ACTION

The House passed the Cuba Democracy Act (HR 5323 — H Rept 102-615, Part I) by a 276-135 vote on Sept. 24. The Senate had approved identical language Sept. 18 by voice vote as an amendment to the fiscal 1993 defense authorization bill (HR 5006).

The Senate amendment was proposed by Bob Graham, D-Fla. Two attempts by Christopher J. Dodd, D-Conn., to weaken or kill the embargo amendment were defeated by the Senate by votes of 73-12 and 24-61. *(Votes 221, 222, p. 29-S)*

Fascell, chairman of the House Foreign Affairs Commit-

tee who had long pressed for tougher sanctions against Cuba, said the bill "seeks to hasten the day when Castro's grip is lifted from the neck of the Cuban people."

The bill prohibited foreign subsidiaries of U.S. companies from engaging in new trade with Cuba, a thriving business that provided an estimated $700 million in annual sales.

It also allowed the Treasury Department to apply civil fines of up to $50,000 — in addition to criminal penalties — against U.S. citizens who violated the Trading With the Enemy Act by traveling to Cuba.

While punishing Castro's regime, the bill attempted to support the Cuban people by letting private U.S. groups deliver food and medicine to Cuba. It also permitted the president to establish telecommunications links with Cuba.

The legislation, championed by the influential Cuban American National Foundation, won the support of both President Bush and Arkansas Gov. Bill Clinton, his Democratic opponent in the campaign for president.

Bush backed the bill in spite of concerns previously raised by the State Department about similar legislation. The State Department had indicated that some U.S. trading partners had opposed the ban on sales to Cuba by U.S. foreign subsidiaries.

Opponents of the measure argued that it would do little to loosen Castro's grip on power and that it would harm U.S. companies operating overseas.

Lawmakers from Connecticut were the most vocal opponents. Among the corporations that would be hardest hit by the ban on indirect trade was Hartford-based United Technologies, whose subsidiaries did an estimated $10 million in business annually with Cuba. Dodd argued that Cuba would make up for any shortfall of imported goods by buying more from Europe and Asia.

"They will have the business the day after this amendment carries or is signed into law," said Dodd, who failed in several attempts to block the amendment to the defense bill.

The House took up the bill after Torricelli dropped tax provisions that would have put the measure under the jurisdiction of the Ways and Means Committee.

Conferees on the fiscal 1993 defense authorization bill (HR 5006) left the Cuba provision in their final bill, thus when the president signed the defense authorization on Oct. 6, the Cuba bill became law. *(Defense authorization, p. 483)*

The political impact of the sanctions was underscored by the locale of the signing: Bush saved the ceremony for a campaign appearance in Miami, where Cuban-American groups had lobbied for the bill. ∎

# Bush Stance Unyielding on Haitian Refugees

The House and its committees took several actions during 1992 to protest the Bush administration's policy of returning Haitian refugees. But none of those measures became law, and the policy was inherited and retained by the Clinton administration in early 1993.

The issue stemmed from a coup in Haiti on Sept. 30, 1991, in which the military ousted Jean-Bertrand Aristide, the island nation's first democratically elected president. Aristide came to the United States, and U.S. policy became a demand for negotiations to bring him back to power, despite qualms among some U.S. officials concerning his militant leftist politics.

Aristide's ouster and the crackdown on dissent that followed produced a flood of Haitians fleeing to the United States on rickety boats. By February 1992, about 15,000 had attempted the trip, and thousands of them were filling a tent city created at the United States' Guantanamo Naval Base in Cuba.

The Bush administration maintained that the Haitians were fleeing bad economic times in their homeland, not the political repression that would qualify them for asylum, and sent many back after hearings at the Guantanamo base.

"In our view, there is not one single documented case of a repatriated Haitian being persecuted or targeted after his return," Secretary of State James A. Baker III told the Senate Foreign Relations Committee on Feb. 6.

But human-rights organizations and some members of Congress insisted that the Haitians were fleeing political oppression.

"The specter of our country turning back those who have fled an anti-democratic government is wrong," Charles E. Schumer, D-N.Y., said during a House Judiciary Committee hearing on Feb. 20.

Returning from a one-day trip to Haiti on Feb. 19, Rep. Charles B. Rangel, D-N.Y., said the State Department had made no serious effort to find out what happened to repatriated Haitians.

"What the State Department is really saying is that they just don't know what is happening to these poor people, but they're just not honest enough to admit it," he said.

## BUSH'S DIRECTIVE

The dispute escalated after Bush issued a directive on May 24 that Haitian refugees rescued at sea should be summarily returned — without being taken to the overfilled Guantanamo center and without hearings first to air their claims of political persecution.

Rangel and others protested that the administration was violating international law requiring that refugees be given an opportunity to make their case for asylum.

"It's an election year, and people don't want poor black folks coming here," Rangel said in a televised interview. "If these people came from a country that had oil or if they had some wealth, there would be adjustments made."

But Bush defended his decision in an appearance May 27 at a school in Atlanta. He reiterated that most of those fleeing Haiti were economic, not political, refugees who would not qualify for asylum. He said that the Guantanamo base was almost filled to its 12,500-person capacity and that Haitians could apply for asylum to U.S. embassy personnel in Haiti.

"We're trying not to be mean about it," Bush said, "but we're trying to say, 'Listen, we've got to live by the laws of this land.' "

Many Republicans in Congress echoed Bush's warning

about a deluge of refugees if such restrictions were abandoned.

## CLINTON'S TURNABOUT

During and just after the 1992 presidential campaign, Bill Clinton pledged to give Haitians a hearing before sending them back. But as president-elect, Clinton came under pressure to revisit that pledge in late 1992 upon reports that thousands of Haitians were preparing to set sail for the United States on homemade boats as soon as he took office.

In a Voice of America radio address broadcast to Haitians on Jan. 14, 1993, Clinton announced that he was retaining Bush's policy. The president-elect warned that Haitians would continue to be intercepted and returned by the Coast Guard once he became president.

The next day, Coast Guard Adm. J. William Kime announced a stepped-up effort to intercept boats filled with Haitians, deploying as many as 22 Coast Guard and Navy ships off Haiti's shores.

Clinton told reporters that he still believed that summary repatriation was wrong but had come to see the practice as necessary in the short term to help political negotiations advance and to protect the Haitians.

"I will end the practice . . . when I am fully confident I can do so in a way that does not contribute to a humanitarian tragedy," said Clinton, who promised in the meantime to improve the processing of claims for U.S. asylum that were filed in Haiti.

The announcement came amid a flurry of unprecedented diplomatic activity concerning Haiti, involving Bush and Clinton administration officials, deposed Haitian President Aristide, the Organization of American States and the United Nations.

As a result of those negotiations, Aristide on Jan. 11, 1993, made a radio address urging Haitians not to flee the country. And Aristide later rescinded a statement calling on Clinton to halt forced repatriations.

Refugee advocacy groups sharply criticized Clinton's reversal, saying the policy of forced repatriation violated international and U.S. refugee law.

However, Rangel toned down his past criticism of the repatriation policy and praised the new drive by the outgoing and incoming administrations to restore democracy to Haiti.

Noting that Haiti's deposed president had endorsed Clinton's approach, Rangel said, "I'm not going to be more Haitian than Aristide."

## LEGISLATIVE ACTION

During 1992, the House and its committees took the following actions concerning Haiti:

● The House passed legislation (HR 3844) on Feb. 27 that would have suspended the return of Haitian refugees for six months. The bill, which was approved 217-165, also would have required a study of Haitians who had been returned to their homeland. (Vote 34, p. 8-H)

The bill's sponsor, Romano L. Mazzoli, D-Ky., said it was narrowly drawn so that only those Haitians already at Guantanamo would be protected from being returned. But that made it effectively moot because most of those "boat people" already would have been returned before its passage.

And three days earlier, the Supreme Court had ruled,

8-1, that the Bush administration could complete the return of the Haitians.

The House adopted, 241-144, an amendment by E. Clay Shaw Jr., R-Fla., that would have authorized the federal government to reimburse state and local governments for the increased costs of caring for Haitians. (Vote 33, p. 8-H)

The measure had won initial approval, 5-3, in the Judiciary Subcommittee on International Law, Immigration and Refugees on Feb. 5

The Judiciary Committee had approved the measure, 21-12, on Feb. 20.

The full committee by voice vote added an amendment by John Conyers Jr., D-Mich., that would have directed the State Department to deny visas to any Haitian who provided financial or other support to the military coup. It also would have denied visas to anyone involved in terrorist acts against the Haitian people after the coup.

● After Bush's directive in May to summarily return Haitians who were intercepted at sea, Stephen J. Solarz, D-N.Y., and other lawmakers introduced legislation (HR 5360) that would have prevented U.S. officials from returning refugees from any country without determining whether they would face persecution in their native lands.

A similar bill (S 2826) was introduced in the Senate by Edward M. Kennedy, D-Mass., and Mark O. Hatfield, R-Ore.

At a hearing June 11 of the House Foreign Affairs Subcommittee on International Operations, Solarz likened the rejection of Haitian refugees to the United States' refusal before World War II to admit German Jews fleeing Nazi persecution.

"The new U.S. policy announced last month sends a strong signal around the world that a nation need not observe basic humanitarian standards when it is inconvenient to do so," Solarz said, reading from his prepared testimony.

● The House Foreign Affairs Committee on June 18 approved by voice vote a bill to tighten U.S. economic sanctions against Haiti's military government.

The legislation (HR 4761) sought to freeze U.S. assets of Haitians who assisted in the military coup in September 1991 that overthrew Aristide.

The panel approved by voice vote an amendment by Robert G. Torricelli, D-N.J., to bar ships that used Haitian ports from entering U.S. ports for 180 days.

● The House Foreign Affairs Committee on Sept. 30 gave voice vote approval to legislation (HR 5360) that would have required the federal government to screen refugees to determine if they should be permitted to enter the United States.

The bill would have required the United States to adhere to the 1951 U.N. Refugee Convention and Protocol, which set guidelines for determining if a person was a refugee.

The protocol, which the United States signed in 1968, required signatory nations to determine whether each potential applicant met the criteria for refugee status. A refugee was defined as someone who feared persecution in his own country as a result of his political beliefs, religion or ethnic background.

The administration claimed that passage of the bill would have led to an uncontrollable exodus of Haitians to the United States. But bill supporters argued that a dramatic increase in the number of refugees fleeing Haiti since Aristide's overthrow was evidence that many feared persecution.

■

# No Evidence Found of POWs in Vietnam

A select Senate Committee that spent more than 15 months investigating the fates of thousands of servicemen listed as prisoners of war (POW) or missing in action (MIA) concluded its investigation in January 1993 saying that it found no "compelling evidence" to suggest that American prisoners were alive in Southeast Asia almost 20 years after the Vietnam War ended.

But in a final report issued Jan. 13, 1993, the Senate Select Committee on POW-MIA Affairs held out the possibility that some U.S. soldiers had languished in enemy hands for at least a period of time after the hostilities ended.

The 1,000-page report capped a $1.9 million investigation that focused primarily on the missing from the Vietnam War but also covered missing military personnel from World War II, the Korean War and the Cold War.

During its short life span, the select committee held 22 days of public hearings, with testimony from 144 witnesses, including former secretaries of Defense and State, former North Vietnamese military officials and members of POW families and activist groups.

Committee members also made numerous trips to Vietnam, Laos and Cambodia, the Soviet Union and Korea in attempts to track down prisoners or any artifacts that could help determine their fate.

Committee Chairman John Kerry, D-Mass., and other panel members cited the declassification of an immense volume of POW records held by the Defense Department as a singular accomplishment that they said would distinguish the committee's record in congressional history annals.

"The result of the committee's efforts has been the most rapid and comprehensive declassification of materials on a single subject in American history," the report said.

More than 1 million documents relating to POW and MIA cases were declassified and made available to the public at the National Archives.

## BACKGROUND

The committee was created by the Senate on Aug. 2, 1991, after a renewed national interest in the subject of U.S. POWs and MIAs. Some of the interest was prompted by a stream of media reports about photographs purporting to show live American prisoners from the Vietnam War. *(1991 Almanac, p. 491)*

Vietnam War activists had maintained that American prisoners might still have been alive and urged Congress to launch a full investigation and to give the issue a full airing.

A dozen or so congressional inquiries into the matter had already been conducted since the end of the war, all of varying degrees of length, sophistication and clout. But one common characteristic they shared were their many inconclusive results concerning what truly happened to thousands of men who vanished in wartime.

The lack of concrete, uncontestable findings led some Vietnam War activist groups to charge that the government was hiding information from the public on unaccounted-for military personnel.

Kerry said the main mission of the select committee was to investigate the matter in public view, so that families of the missing would be able to know as much about a particular POW or MIA file as did the committee, its staff or Pentagon officials who were called to testify.

## APRIL TRIP

Members of the committee returned from a mission to Southeast Asia on April 27 saying they were granted unprecedented access to Vietnamese prison camps and foreign intelligence data.

From April 17-27, the five-member Senate delegation met with U.S. POW-MIA field experts and Thai intelligence officers in Bangkok, Thailand; with Vietnamese defense ministers and MIA archivists in Hanoi; toured prison camps in Vietnam; and traveled inside Laos and Cambodia.

"We are no longer knocking on the door; that door is open," said Kerry, who was a Navy officer in Vietnam's Mekong Delta in 1968-69. "And the question is whether we're going to be allowed now to walk through room to room, basement and attic, and be able to find the answers to our questions."

Kerry and other members said at a Washington news conference on April 28, however, that they found no solid evidence to suggest that any of the 2,266 Americans who were unaccounted for from the Vietnam War were being held against their will nearly two decades after the fighting ended.

Panel member Hank Brown, R-Colo., who served in Vietnam in 1965-66 in the Navy, said the panel's investigation would be stronger and more credible as a result of the trip, despite the lack of evidence.

But Sen. Charles S. Robb, D-Va., a highly decorated veteran who commanded an infantry company in combat in Vietnam, said he had mixed feelings about the trip.

Robb said that "on balance" he came away feeling the trip was worthwhile. But he said he was distressed over the Laotian government's failure to produce detailed information. "We pushed it in a lot of different ways, and the records simply don't exist," Robb said. "The Vietnamese keep very good records. The Cambodians have some records. The Lao have very, very few records of any kind."

Members said continued assistance from Vietnam would help determine more about the fates of the missing.

Increased Vietnamese cooperation on the POW-MIA issue was rewarded by the Bush administration on April 29. The State Department announced that it was granting an exception to the economic embargo of Vietnam to permit sales of food, medicine and other items "to meet basic human needs."

The department also lifted restrictions on projects in Vietnam by non-governmental and nonprofit organizations.

"The decision to take these two steps is in response to Vietnam's strengthened commitments to take positive actions on POW/MIA issues and its support of the United Nations' political settlement process in Cambodia," said State Department spokeswoman Margaret D. Tutwiler. "It is in keeping with the established U.S. policy of a step-by-step process for normalizing relations with Vietnam."

## RUSSIAN CONNECTION

Russian President Boris N. Yeltsin, in a June 15 interview with NBC News, raised the possibility that U.S. mili-

tary personnel missing since the Vietnam War might have been kept alive as late as 1992 in the former Soviet Union.

"We don't have complete data and can only surmise that some of them may still be alive," Yeltsin said through an interpreter. "That is why our investigations are continuing. Some of them may have ended up in psychiatric asylums."

But U.S. Defense Department officials, while vowing that the government would fully investigate Yeltsin's statement, reportedly were skeptical of his claim.

And Kerry also reacted cautiously to Yeltsin's statements, indicating that the Russian president had only mentioned the possibility that Americans could be alive, not that they were alive or had ever even been held.

On June 23, the committee released the names of more than 100 American POWs who Yeltsin said were interrogated by the Soviet Union and possibly sent to China after the Korean conflict.

The administration dispatched officials to Moscow to investigate the claim. But nothing was said to have panned out. And the final committee report gave no support to the claim.

## WHAT THE PENTAGON KNEW

In a series of hearings during the week of June 22, panel leaders Kerry and Robert C. Smith, R-N.H., charged that the Pentagon knew that scores of U.S. soldiers had most likely been left behind in enemy hands after the Vietnam War.

In questioning witnesses from the Nixon administration, senators repeatedly turned to President Richard M. Nixon's assurance to the nation in March 1973 that "all of our American POWs are on their way home."

Kerry said the committee's review of Defense Department documents showed that 244 Americans who were not returned at the end of the war "should have been recorded 'in captivity' " after Operation Homecoming — the official repatriation of prisoners in April 1973 that became the symbol of the war's end.

Kerry said 111 Americans from the list of 244 were later found to have died, which left 133 soldiers who were either POW or MIA.

"The information available to the committee does constitute evidence that some Americans remained alive in Indochina after Operation Homecoming," Kerry said. "This is enough in my mind to contradict official statements made then and repeated for almost two decades."

Smith went further:

"Speaking for myself, I interpret the [committee's] evidence as saying that POWs and MIAs have been alive, or were alive, up through 1989," Smith said on June 23. "I stand on that. I don't ask others to."

Kerry disagreed with Smith at a hearing June 25, saying that Smith's position on soldiers' being held as late as 1989 "is not my view."

A number of former high-level Pentagon officials, appearing before the committee during the week of June 25, denied charges of a POW/MIA cover-up by the military and the Nixon administration.

"At the termination of Homecoming we had no current, hard evidence that Americans were still held prisoner in Southeast Asia," Roger E. Shields, the deputy assistant secretary for international economic and POW/MIA affairs from 1971 to 1977, told the committee.

But under questioning from Kerry, Shields said the

Defense Department was aware of "a list" of military personnel believed to be POWs who were not returned in Operation Homecoming.

Charles Trowbridge, deputy director of the Defense Intelligence Agency's Special Office for POW/MIA Affairs, concurred with Shields' testimony.

"We had no information, no current information, where we could go and put our hands on some individual that was alive at the time," Trowbridge said.

Pentagon spokesman Pete Williams on June 25 told reporters that while the "public line" of the Defense Department had been that all POWs were returned, the Defense Intelligence Agency was "continuing to gather information and intelligence on people still unaccounted for.... So the actions of the government were at odds with whatever the policy statement may have been in 1973."

## DECLASSIFYING DOCUMENTS

The Senate, in a resolution (S Res 324) passed 96-0 on July 2, urged the administration to act "expeditiously" to declassify and make available to the public all files of military personnel listed as POW or MIA. Files could remain classified if they were considered sensitive to national security. *(Vote 144, p. 19-S)*

Earlier in the day the select committee approved the resolution, 12-0.

The committee was prepared to release most of the classified files it had obtained from the government if the administration had not acted soon afterward to do so. Under Senate rules, the committee had to first request that the president declassify the files before it could take action to release what it already had accumulated from government agencies.

Release of thousands of files occurred on July 23, the same day the committee met to assess the administration's progress in declassifying the files.

The release came a day after President Bush signed an executive order requiring all federal agencies to release files and other information relating to POW/MIA cases.

Pentagon spokesman Williams on July 23 said that 30,000 pages of files were declassified, and he said he expected that nearly 1.5 million pages of formerly secret files would ultimately be made public after being reviewed.

## PEROT: MEN WERE LEFT

In a series of hearings in August, the committee returned to the question of how much the government knew about men who might have been left behind. Much of the focus centered on men who were thought to be left in Laos, which did not sign the Paris Peace Accords that provided for the repatriation of prisoners.

Ross Perot, a billionaire Texas businessman and independent presidential candidate in 1992, testified before the committee on Aug. 11 that there was sufficient evidence to believe the government left U.S. military personnel in Southeast Asia after the Vietnam War ended.

"There is no question in my mind that we left people in Laos, and I think I can prove it to any rational person," Perot said.

Perot said he had worked for more than 20 years, spending over $3 million of his own money, in trying to win release of any prisoners who might have been left in Indochina.

Perot had been scheduled to appear before the select

committee on June 30 but declined because of his fears of a "media circus."

Following Perot on Aug. 12 was former Assistant Secretary of Defense Richard Armitage, who said it was possible that some men were left behind. But he discounted theories that they had been held for years and years against their will.

"There are Americans in Indochina," he said. "I don't know the circumstances; they may be living freely."

Two former Defense secretaries — Melvin R. Laird (1969-73) and James R. Schlesinger (1973-75) — told the committee on Sept. 21 that the Nixon administration had every reason to believe that Americans were left behind in enemy hands as U.S. troops were withdrawn from Vietnam in 1973.

But on Sept. 22, Nixon's secretary of State, Henry A. Kissinger, denounced as a "flat-out lie" any suggestion that Nixon advisers knew of Americans left behind in Vietnam or neighboring Laos.

"We did not know of confirmed prisoners, and had we known it, we would have taken the most drastic steps," said Kissinger, defending his reputation as the architect of the accord with North Vietnam that ended the Vietnam War and secured him the Nobel Peace Prize.

Asked about the White House assertion in 1973 that all the POWs were on their way home, Schlesinger said, "I was somewhat surprised that we could assert all were out."

Asked directly by Charles E. Grassley, R-Iowa, if soldiers were left behind, Schlesinger said, "I can come to no other conclusion."

He said Pentagon officials reacted with "anger and shock" after Operation Homecoming when they realized that "so few were coming home from Laos," where a number of pilots were known to have survived crashes during the war.

"It is evident that the Laotians gave no true accounting of the Americans who had been taken in Laos," Schlesinger said.

Schlesinger speculated that some may have been summarily executed. And Kerry said that others may have been killed in combat on the ground or simply died of exposure in the jungle.

But Kissinger said neither Schlesinger or Laird ever suggested when they were in office that Americans were left behind in Southeast Asia.

In other testimony that seemed to undercut Kissinger's assertions, Winston Lord, a senior aide to Kissinger in 1970-73, said on Sept. 21 that Nixon had made a "very tough decision" in proceeding with the withdrawal.

"American society would have blown apart" if Nixon had resumed bombing and halted the withdrawal to force the release of any POWs that were still being held, Lord said.

## SATELLITE IMAGES

The committee held an extraordinary set of hearings on Oct. 15-16 to discuss and analyze in a public forum intelligence data gathered by Defense satellites.

The images appeared to show distress signals from downed pilots.

Intelligence officials testified that most cases of suspected symbols in reconnaissance photos turned out to be shadows or optical illusions.

Duane P. Andrews, assistant secretary of Defense for command, control, communications and intelligence, urged caution about the images, saying a healthy sense of skepticism was in order while analyzing them. But Andrews' sense of caution was not well-received by some members of the panel, who charged that the Defense Department had long focused more on dismissing or "debunking" evidence of distress signals and live-sighting reports than in following them up.

"You don't need absolute proof to render a judgment. . . . This may be the only evidence that we find that points to specific men," said Grassley.

Grassley accused Andrews and Defense Intelligence Agency analysts of following up on live-sighting reports with the same energy and enthusiasm as they might give a "UFO sighting."

But Andrews, defending the work of his office, said Defense officials "have been indicted" by "incomplete, selectively leaked intelligence" that was tendentious in nature.

Andrews also was critical of the Senate hearings being held in open session, even though all of the testimony and evidence was carefully prepared to exclude any references that might harm national security.

On Nov. 10 and Nov. 11, Veterans Day, the panel turned its attention from Vietnam to the missing from World War II, Korea and the Cold War.

At the outset, Kerry cautioned that the "passage of time and the uncertainty of war makes it highly unlikely we will learn everything" about POWs or MIAs from previous wars.

Smith, R-N.H., said records retrieved by the committee from the U.S. government "show in explicit detail that North Korea did not return a large number of U.S. servicemen at the end of the [Korean War] and that some of the men left behind were sent to communist China and the Soviet Union."

Smith said the documents revealed that officials in Washington believed men were still alive in captivity at the end of the Korean War.

Just as they did after the Vietnam War, Smith asserted, officials covered up that likelihood through a "pattern of denial, misleading statements and outright lies."

The Defense Department listed 8,177 men as unaccounted for from the Korean War, in which 54,246 troops were killed. This compared with the 2,264 POWs and MIAs from the Vietnam War, in which 58,151 service members died.

Alan Ptak, deputy assistant secretary of Defense for POW/MIA Affairs, said a Pentagon review of Russian archives had resulted in "no evidence" that U.S. POWs from the Vietnam War or the Korean War were interrogated by the Soviet Union or transferred there.

But retired Gen. Dmitri Volkogonov, who was the senior military adviser to Yeltsin, testified that the Soviet Union held six Americans as prisoners on spy charges during the Korean War and helped nine Americans desert during the Vietnam War.

Volkogonov, who also served as the Russian chairman of a U.S.-Russian commission investigating Soviet involvement with American prisoners, said as many as 49 prisoners held by North Korea may have been interrogated by the Soviets.

Speaking through a translator, Volkogonov said it would be logical to assume that Soviet advisers also interrogated American prisoners during the Vietnam War.

The general also told the committee there was reason to believe some U.S. servicemen from World War II were

executed under orders of Soviet dictator Josef Stalin in the 1940s.

In a Nov. 5 letter to the Senate committee, Yeltsin said Russian officials found evidence that U.S. soldiers had been held in camps and prisons of the former Soviet Union and discovered "shocking facts of some of them being summarily executed by the Stalin regime and, in a number of cases, being forced to renounce their U.S. citizenship."

Yeltsin added that "a number of former U.S. citizens have stayed in Russia voluntarily after World War II and still reside here."

After World War II, Volkogonov said, 119 Americans were held as Soviet prisoners when Soviet troops liberated more than 22,000 Americans from German POW camps.

At the end of the hearings on wars other than Vietnam, family members of the missing argued that the committee should have sought to have its authorization extended to provide more time to investigate other POW and MIA cases.

## RETURN TRIP

On Nov. 12-22, panel members Kerry, Tom Daschle, D-S.D., and Hank Brown, R-Colo., went on a 10-day investigative tour through Hanoi and Ho Chi Minh City as well as Laos.

During the trip, the senators and staff traveled to prison camps, pored over Vietnamese military records and war relics.

After returning, Kerry said on Nov. 23 that Vietnam might not be willing to assist the committee if nothing was done to reward its course of cooperation. He urged President Bush to take action in his final weeks in office to ease the trade embargo on Vietnam.

"We could lose the opportunity at hand," Kerry said. "You can't have this be a one-way street forever."

Brown also said some sort of diplomatic gesture by Bush would be appropriate. But he cautioned against giving trade incentives to Vietnam, saying the trade embargo was the "one trump card" that needed to be retained.

At a Veterans Day ceremony in Little Rock, Ark., President-elect Bill Clinton said, "I have sent a clear message that there will be no normalization of relations with any nation that is at all suspected of withholding any information" on missing U.S. soldiers.

On Dec. 14, Bush took a step in the effort to reward Vietnam without abandoning pressure for still greater cooperation on the POW/MIA issue. He permitted U.S. companies to sign contracts immediately with Hanoi for commercial dealings that would not go into effect until such time as the longstanding economic embargo was lifted.

White House press secretary Marlin Fitzwater said a new "liberal licensing policy" would allow activities including "opening offices in Vietnam, hiring staff, writing and designing plans, and carrying out feasibility studies and engineering and technical surveys."

## STOCKDALE, FAMILIES

One of the highlights of the committee's closing hearings the week of Nov. 30 was testimony from retired Adm. James B. Stockdale, the former running mate of independent presidential candidate Perot.

Stockdale said he fully believed that no living Americans had been left behind in Vietnam after the war.

"I would not have come back if they were," said Stockdale, who became a leader of POWs while he was held and tortured in Vietnam after his plane was shot down in September 1965.

He said he was not as sure if prisoners were returned from Laos.

Stockdale said the government would have better handled the POW issue if it had conducted thorough debriefings of returned prisoners, many of whom would have been able to give details at the time about people listed as MIA or POW that may be lost now.

In testimony on Dec. 3, family members of POWs criticized the Senate probe and urged that negotiators be much more demanding of the Vietnamese.

"The Vietnamese are slowly and methodically out-negotiating our negotiators and once again are ignoring that my husband is one of these forsaken," said Carol Hrdlicka, the wife of Capt. David L. Hrdlicka, who was shot down over Laos on May 18, 1965. "They know where my husband is. I know this," she said. "It is embarrassing as an American citizen to see my country manipulated again and again by this tiny country."

Also at its Dec. 2 session, the panel looked into the somewhat unorthodox practices of direct mail companies that had raised funds for alleged POW search and rescue efforts and the distribution by some groups of doctored photographs purporting to show live POWs in Southeast Asia.

Panel member John McCain, R-Ariz., a former POW in Vietnam, characterized as a "cruel fraud" the faking of photographs.

Kerry said committee information on such practices would be turned over to the Justice Department for possible criminal investigation.

"The hopes of families have been unfairly torn and tattered as a consequence of those actions," Kerry said. "That is a predatory action. It is disgraceful. Grotesque."

Kerry said retired Air Force Col. Jack Bailey, founder of a POW-search effort called Operation Rescue, had been involved in distributing such photographs and fund raising and declined to testify to the committee. While not accusing Bailey and others of crimes, Kerry said: "Their unwillingness to be here under oath speaks volumes."

Committee documents indicated that Bailey had raised $2.3 million using direct mail solicitations from 1985 to 1990, some with appeals such as: "Those of us here have only until December [1987] to get them out. After that, no telling what the savage communists might do."

Another quotation read: "If I can't raise $13,671.77 by Oct. 31, vital intelligence gathering cannot continue. And American servicemen will die in the jungles of Vietnam."

## FINDINGS

In the final report, titled Report of the U.S. Senate Select Committee on POW/MIA Affairs, the committee criticized top U.S. government officials for dismissing the possibility that men might have been left behind but rejected charges that they possessed any "certain knowledge" that prisoners were abandoned.

The report, which was signed by all 12 members of the committee — six Democrats and six Republicans — said, "There is, at this time, no compelling evidence that proves that any American remains alive in captivity in Southeast Asia."

But it also said, "We acknowledge that there is no proof that U.S. POWs survived, but neither is there proof that all

of those who did not return had died. There is evidence, moreover, that indicates the possibility of survival, at least for a small number, after Operation Homecoming."

The report rejected outright theories held by some Vietnam POW activists that the government covered up knowledge of prisoners being held against their will.

"The isolated bits of information out of which some have constructed whole labyrinths of intrigue and deception have not withstood the test of objective investigation, and the vast archives of secret U.S. documents that some felt contained incriminating evidence have been thoroughly examined by the committee, only to find that the conspiracy cupboard is bare."

The Defense Department listed 2,264 Americans as unaccounted for from the Vietnam War, but the committee said the number of Americans whose fate is "truly unknown is far smaller."

Kerry said that through investigation with the cooperation of the Defense Department, the committee determined that 135 "discrepancy cases" remained in which there was reason to believe that governments in Southeast Asia may have known the fate of the individual.

For the remainder of the 2,264, the committee said the government determined that, in most cases, death was considered almost certain but that it could not be proved because bodies were unrecoverable from crash sites, especially ones at sea or in areas of heavy combat where ground had been lost to the enemy.

After the report was released, Kerry said that more cooperation from Vietnam, Laos and Cambodia was essential to obtaining the fullest possible accounting for missing Americans.

"This report does not close the issue," he said. "It is not meant to. This report provides the reality base from which we can now make real judgments about probabilities and possibilities."

Vice Chairman Smith said, "There's evidence that some POWs may have survived to the present, and some information still remains to be investigated. However, at this time, there's no compelling evidence that proves that. And that's a fact, and we all agree to that."

Smith had been one of the more aggressive proponents of the possibility that POWs remained alive.

In 1991, he said that, while he could not speak for others on the panel, he believed there was strong evidence to suggest U.S. prisoners had been held in Southeast Asia well into the 1980s.

In a footnote in the committee's report, Smith and Grassley dissented from a majority view that neither "live-sighting" reports nor other sources of intelligence provided any grounds for encouragement that POWs may still be alive. They wrote that they believe there is "evidence that POWs may have survived to the present."

The committee officially dissolved after release of the report.

In late January 1993, Kerry and Smith said they had asked to meet with Clinton to discuss the report and to suggest ways in which the administration could pick up where the committee left off.

Smith suggested that a high-level official in the National Security Council be designated the official administration point person for POW/MIA affairs.

Both Kerry and Smith said the permanent standing committees of the Senate would be able to continue the investigation if events warranted.

Kerry said he would be able to hold follow-up hearings if he needed to in the Foreign Relations Subcommittee on Terrorism, Narcotics and International Operations, which he chaired.

Smith said he would be able to conduct similar follow-up work in the Armed Services Committee, of which he was a member. ■

# Intelligence Agencies Feel Budget Ax

Congress trimmed President Bush's budget request by almost 6 percent in passing a fiscal 1993 intelligence bill (HR 5095) that authorized a secret budget that was believed to be slightly more than $19 billion. The Senate cleared the bill Oct. 2 by voice vote.

Subsequently, however, the Senate cleared a defense appropriations bill that cut intelligence spending even further — to an estimated $17.5 billion.

The defense spending bill (HR 5504 — PL 102-396) was believed to include a separate budget of $11 billion for tactical intelligence activities of the armed services. Thus, the nation's intelligence spending reportedly totaled $28.5 billion.

The annual authorization measure encompassed activities of the Central Intelligence Agency (CIA), the National Security Agency and other activities of what is known as the National Foreign Intelligence Program (NFIP).

With the Cold War over and demands growing for the government to do more to address domestic needs, the fiscal 1993 budget was ripe for attack.

Leaders of the House and Senate Intelligence committees recognized these pressures early on and started the year with enthusiastic plans to reorganize the nation's web of intelligence programs. *(Intelligence reorganization, p. 567)*

Though the plans for a dramatic overhaul did not become law, members did respond to pressure by cutting the secret agencies' budgets by nearly 6 percent, turning back calls in the Senate to cut even more.

## HOUSE ACTION

The House Intelligence Committee approved legislation May 12 that would have cut 5 percent from the Bush administration's budget request for intelligence activities in fiscal 1993, according to Chairman Dave McCurdy, D-Okla.

The nation's overall intelligence budget was classified, but it was widely reported to be about $30 billion a year. McCurdy said the committee had reduced spending below the level authorized in fiscal 1992.

"This is a significant cut, far exceeding the percentage by which it now appears the defense budget will be reduced," he said.

But the intelligence authorization bill (HR 5095), approved by the committee in closed session, did not include McCurdy's proposal to reorganize intelligence agencies.

And some committee members reportedly had fought to make even deeper cuts in the intelligence budget.

McCurdy said the committee specified that about $400 million in savings resulting from the budget cuts be used to aid in converting defense industries to other purposes.

With little debate, the House on June 25 agreed to the committee bill, with its 5 percent cut from Bush's budget request.

The intelligence budget, which funded activities of the CIA, the Defense Intelligence Agency, the National Security Agency and other intelligence activities throughout the federal government, was believed to be about $30 billion a year.

The fiscal 1993 authorization measure (HR 5095; H Rept 102-544, Part 1) was approved by voice vote.

McCurdy said the legislation did not include proposals to restructure the nation's multiagency intelligence apparatus because of extensive efforts by new CIA Director Robert M. Gates to reorganize his agency and other intelligence operations administratively.

"Given Mr. Gates' willingness to work with us, I believe it is important to give his changes a chance to work," McCurdy said in a statement. He said the committee would monitor the changes and make other recommendations if necessary.

In House floor debate, members cited the end of the Cold War and the changing global threat both to defend and oppose the spending cuts called for in the authorization bill.

McCurdy said the legislation recognized the political reality that a reduced threat from the Soviet Union, the main target of U.S. intelligence efforts for more than 40 years, would require spending cuts.

But he said further reductions might seriously harm intelligence efforts as the U.S. military presence around the world was being reduced and intelligence operations were becoming more crucial.

Committee leaders cited growing concerns over nuclear weapons proliferation among Third World nations, increased foreign espionage against U.S. businesses and arms control monitoring as reasons for not trimming further.

"Indeed, people speak of a new world order when it more accurately could be called a new world disorder.... It is indeed a dangerous world," said Bud Shuster, Pa., the ranking Republican on Intelligence.

In a statement June 18, the White House said it strongly opposed the bill because the cuts would "seriously impede" its ability to conduct intelligence business. It complained of substantial cuts in funding and personnel, a 34 percent reduction in the FBI's foreign counterintelligence budget, cancellation of important technical collection systems and elimination of certain key analytic centers.

Despite all that, however, the administration did not threaten a veto.

An amendment was offered to the intelligence authorization by Norm Dicks, D-Wash., to allow use of funds in the bill for an advanced airborne reconnaissance system.

The secret reconnaissance program was under review; the authorization presumably would allow for a new airborne reconnaissance system to modernize the program. Boeing Co., one of the nation's premier aircraft manufacturers, was based near Dicks' district.

## SENATE ACTION

The Senate Intelligence Committee approved legislation July 1 to put into law many of the organizational changes for the intelligence community that CIA director Gates had announced in April.

The fiscal 1993 intelligence authorization bill, approved by the panel in closed session, allowed Gates to shuffle appropriated funds among several intelligence agencies, subject to Congress' agreement.

The intelligence bill approved by the House had not included Gates' restructuring plan or the more sweeping proposals devised by the chairmen of the House and Senate Intelligence committees in February.

David L. Boren, D-Okla., chairman of the Senate committee, said his panel's bill cut about 5 percent from the administration's request for intelligence activities in 1993, approximately the same reduction as that of the House bill.

### Senate Floor Action

Two days after rejecting an even larger cut as a threat to national security, the Senate on Sept. 23 agreed to reduce the U.S. intelligence budget by 5 percent, or about $1 billion from the White House request.

The cut, similar to one the House had approved, was included in the fiscal 1993 intelligence authorization bill (S 2991), which was approved by voice vote.

Senate debate all but confirmed that the NFIP component of the supposedly secret intelligence budget was about $20 billion.

The discussion on the fiscal 1993 intelligence measure underlined the difficulty lawmakers had in defending a secret budget when pressure was growing to divert intelligence spending to domestic programs or to deficit reduction.

In 1991, a veto threat forced Congress to drop from the annual authorization bill a provision that would have required the overall intelligence budget figure to be made public, but calls to do so re-emerged during the 1992 Senate debate. *(1991 Almanac, p. 482)*

"How are we ever to get a handle on this massive bureaucracy if we cannot discuss publicly even how much money is being spent?" said Budget Committee Chairman Jim Sasser, D-Tenn.

Dale Bumpers, D-Ark., offered an amendment to reduce the intelligence budget by an extra $1 billion, arguing that global changes had lessened the need for spending that had grown to counter a communist threat that had disappeared.

"The Soviet Union does not exist. The rationale for this massive intelligence budget does not exist," Bumpers said.

He argued that lawmakers were reluctant to reduce spending even as they complained at home about the inability of Congress to reduce the deficit.

"I know what they say: 'I am for a constitutional amendment to balance the budget,' " Bumpers said. " 'I am for line-item veto. I am for anything except facing the music.' "

But Intelligence Committee members countered that they already had reduced the administration's budget request for national intelligence programs by more than $1 billion and that tactical military intelligence programs had also been cut by about half that amount.

Earlier, the committee had announced that the president's budget had been reduced by 5 percent, which Bumpers said allowed anyone who "finished third-grade arithmetic" to calculate the size of the intelligence budget at $20 billion.

Committee members also said deeper cuts in the budget could impede intelligence efforts even as more complex threats, including arms proliferation in the Third World,

were emerging in the wake of communism's collapse.

"The Cold War is over, yes, but it is still a very dangerous, unstable, volatile world, and we need to have not less intelligence but more intelligence," said William S. Cohen, R-Maine.

Boren also argued that a strong intelligence program was making it possible for the United States to cut its defense budget.

Bumpers' amendment was rejected by a vote of 35-57. *(Vote 223, p. 29-S)*

The White House disliked the bill for reasons that went beyond the budget cutback.

In a statement Sept. 22, the administration objected that some of the bill's provisions would "unwisely restrict the president's flexibility to organize the conduct of U.S. foreign intelligence activities."

One objection was to a provision that required the director of central intelligence to provide "objective national intelligence, independent of political considerations."

The administration said that writing this provision into law "threatens to transform policy disagreements into arguments about whether the law has been broken."

The administration said it also opposed a provision coordinating military intelligence activities under a new Department of Defense Tactical Intelligence Program.

It said such a move toward centralization might make these intelligence operations less responsive to the military missions they were supposed to support.

## FINAL ACTION

The House on Oct. 2 approved by voice vote a conference report on the fiscal 1993 intelligence authorization bill (HR 5095) that cut the administration's request by nearly 6 percent, or more than $1 billion.

The Senate cleared the measure for the president' signature by voice vote Oct. 2.

The measure also included plans to streamline U.S. intelligence operations, largely reflecting changes already made by CIA Director Gates.

One of the major changes was the creation of a central imagery authority within the Department of Defense to coordinate the collection and dissemination of intelligence gathered through satellite and aerial reconnaissance. The Pentagon had created a similar office in May in response to congressional proposals earlier in the year for a separate National Imagery Agency to oversee the activities, which had been spread throughout the sprawling Defense Department.

Boren said the new office was a victory for taxpayers because it would mean greater accountability and less duplication in one of the costliest intelligence-gathering programs.

Conferees also agreed to create a more independent National Intelligence Council, made up of senior intelligence analysts and outside experts, to produce national intelligence estimates. These analyses were used by top government officials in making foreign and defense policy decisions.

During Gates' confirmation hearings in 1991, numerous witnesses testified that the estimates had lost much of their value because of political disputes within the agency and the failure of analysts to provide the kind of information policy-makers needed. *(1991 Almanac, p. 486)*

The legislation also attempted to make it easier for the

intelligence director to manage intelligence operations in other agencies by writing into law the budgeting and other powers that the director had under executive orders issued over the years, but that in practice were often ignored by agency heads.

House Intelligence Committee Chairman McCurdy said the spending reduction set by House-Senate conferees, which was larger than the 5 percent cut called for in the House and Senate versions of the bill, was necessitated by global changes and pressing domestic budget demands.

He said the collapse of the Soviet Union had left the intelligence community "at a critical juncture . . . without a clear focus for their activities."

McCurdy added that the conferees, who resolved their differences at a meeting Sept. 29, had tried to target outdated and redundant programs without harming the ability of the intelligence community to monitor and respond to continued threats to U.S. security. The bill also reflected plans to reduce intelligence personnel levels by 18 percent by 1997, he said.

Earlier, Senate Intelligence Committee Chairman Boren said the cut "puts us on a glidepath toward restructuring the community without endangering its effectiveness."

The legislation expressed the "sense of Congress" that the annual intelligence budget total should be made public, but it did not force the issue.

Steven Aftergood, director of a project on government secrecy for the Federation of American Scientists, called the secret budget amount, as well as other provisions in the bill, a "perpetuation of the Cold War mind-set. . . . It's foolish, and it's anachronistic."

HR 5095 referred for the first time to the Pentagon's National Reconnaissance Office (NRO), a program that was previously so secret that its very existence was classified, although its operations were widely known. The office was responsible for the building and operation of spy satellites.

However, the legislation included a provision that exempted disclosure of the total number of NRO employees, their names, titles and salaries from Freedom Of Information Act requests.

Similar exemptions existed for the CIA and the National Security Agency.

Aftergood called the restriction another layer of secrecy designed "to keep you from figuring out what essentially we have already figured out" — the size of the NRO budget. By looking at other line items in the Pentagon budget, such as "other procurement, Air Force," Aftergood and others had estimated that NRO spent about $5 billion a year.

However, Boren said that while details about the reconnaissance office staff would mean little to the public, they "could disclose significant information about the nature of NRO's classified activities."

One continuing threat addressed by the legislation was the unlawful disclosure of classified information by former employees.

The bill allowed the Defense secretary to provide financial and other help to unemployed former employees of the Defense Intelligence Agency if he determined that the aid was needed "to maintain the judgment and emotional stability" of such employees and to stop them from releasing government secrets.

Despite frequently voiced misgivings about the bill's spending reduction and other provisions, Bush signed the measure (PL 101-496) on Oct. 24. ∎

# Congress OKs Limited Intelligence Fixes

While some members began the 102nd Congress with high hopes for reorganizing the nation's intelligence community, in the end they settled for more moderate changes drawn up by the Bush administration.

CIA Director Robert M. Gates offered a plan that he said would make intelligence operations more efficient and refocus them on possible post-Soviet threats from Third World nations and other sources.

The Intelligence Committee chairmen, Sen. David L. Boren, D-Okla., and Rep. Dave McCurdy, D-Okla., set aside more sweeping overhaul legislation and incorporated provisions in the fiscal 1993 intelligence authorization bill that largely reflected the changes Gates had made. These included a new central imagery office in the Pentagon to oversee intelligence gathered through satellite and aerial reconnaissance and the use of outside experts in preparing certain intelligence analyses.

## Boren-McCurdy Plans

Citing the end of the Cold War and pressures to reduce defense-related spending, Sen. Boren and Rep. McCurdy introduced almost identical bills (HR 4165, S 2198) on Feb. 5 to reorganize and refocus the nation's intelligence apparatus.

Acknowledging that the administration already had launched a similar internal review, Boren said he and McCurdy hoped their plans would encourage "bolder action.... Nibbling around at the edges or putting a Band-Aid on here and there is not what is needed for a time in which the world is totally changed."

The Intelligence chairmen said their proposals were intended as starting points for discussions with the administration, colleagues and experts in the field, not as a final product.

But they said that sweeping changes in the way the United States collected, analyzed and dispersed intelligence were inevitable, especially in light of pressures to cut the nation's intelligence budget, estimated to be about $30 billion a year.

As with any organizational restructuring, the proposals were expected to get stiff opposition from those who had the most to lose — including the many agencies throughout the government, such as the Department of Defense, whose intelligence operations would be consolidated under one national intelligence chief.

The CIA, whose operations would have been trimmed substantially, issued a statement citing efforts under way by Gates to revamp U.S. intelligence operations.

The two ranking Republicans on the Intelligence committees expressed reservations about the congressional initiative.

"I think it's very premature," said Rep. Bud Shuster, Pa. "I believe we should give Bob Gates the opportunity to get his feet on the ground.... And we should then be working in concert with him."

Boren said he had talked to Gates for "about five minutes" about his proposal but indicated that the CIA director and other officials would be consulted extensively as the legislation worked its way through Congress.

Shuster, who declined an offer to cosponsor the House bill, said he also had serious concerns that the new national

intelligence chief called for in the bills would have unprecedented authority over domestic counterintelligence operations. Boren and McCurdy denied that.

Frank H. Murkowski, Alaska, the ranking Republican on Senate Intelligence, said he shared the concern about the pervasive influence of this new intelligence "czar" but added that he would continue to review the legislation.

Murkowski, who along with Boren was entering his final year on the committee, had been working closely with the chairman on drafting the reorganization legislation, which both said was a priority. But Murkowski said he decided not to sign on to the package when some last-minute changes, including those concerning the powers of the new intelligence chief, were made to forge a McCurdy-Boren proposal.

"However, I don't want people to read too much into the fact that I am not cosponsoring the bill at this time," he said in a statement.

Boren and McCurdy said their bills would have simplified and consolidated the many intelligence activities that were spread throughout the federal government.

They would have created a director of national intelligence (DNI), a job likely to be filled by Gates. The intelligence chief would have had authority over the budget and operations of all U.S. intelligence activities except tactical intelligence gathered for military operations, which would have been consolidated under Pentagon control.

McCurdy said that, unlike other "czars" appointed to oversee government activities such as anti-drug operations, the intelligence chief would be "a czar with teeth. He's going to be a czar with muscle; he's going to be a czar with troops and forces and budget."

The CIA director nominally oversaw the U.S. intelligence community but did not have final say over the budget or allocation of resources.

The bills would have assigned two deputies to assist the director in a new National Intelligence Center. A deputy director for estimates and analysis would have coordinated intelligence analysis that at the time was conducted by the CIA and analysts throughout the government. The purpose would have been to pull together those operations and eliminate duplication, the sponsors said.

"Our plan would create in one place a world-class think tank to inform our policy-makers and help attract the best and brightest in the country to the analytical field," Boren said.

A second deputy director would have been appointed to oversee and coordinate intelligence-collection activities conducted by civilian and military agencies, such as the Defense Intelligence Agency and the National Security Agency. Under this jurisdiction, a new National Imagery Agency would have coordinated intelligence-gathering with satellites.

Either this deputy director or the director of national intelligence would have had to be a high-ranking military officer, a provision designed to improve coordination of military and civilian intelligence efforts.

The CIA would continue as a separate agency but would have its activities limited to clandestine operations and the collection of intelligence by its agents stationed throughout the world.

However, both sponsors sought to downplay any dimin-

ishment of the CIA's role. They said such human intelligence-gathering operations had become more critical than ever in a world in which the threat to U.S. security was less apparent than it was during the Cold War.

McCurdy said that the new structure would have given the director of national intelligence more flexibility to respond to world events by allowing him to shift resources between different intelligence agencies and to rotate employees in and out of the National Intelligence Center.

In addition, the legislation would have separated the intelligence budget, which was largely under the Department of Defense, and put it under the control of the DNI. The overall dollar amount would also have been made public for the first time, although the details would have remained classified.

The legislation also would have created a new Committee on Foreign Intelligence made up of the DNI; the national security adviser; the Secretaries of State, Defense and Commerce; and other officials who would set goals for the intelligence community.

### Reaction to the Plan

Advocates of streamlining the nation's intelligence community were warned Feb. 20 that a seemingly more efficient system might not be the best.

Former CIA Director James R. Schlesinger told the Senate Intelligence Committee that competition and duplication were sometimes useful in the world of intelligence and their elimination could mean the loss of "potentially fruitful differences of view."

"The last thing we need in intelligence is a monolith that establishes an official line," Schlesinger said at a hearing, the first in a series on the reorganization legislation.

The centerpiece of Boren's and McCurdy's plans was the creation of a director of national intelligence and a National Intelligence Center, changes intended to consolidate many of the overlapping intelligence activities then conducted throughout the federal government.

Boren and McCurdy had said they were not wedded to their similar proposals, but they argued that the end of the Cold War and tight budgets required a rethinking of how the United States collected and used intelligence to protect its national security.

"Just like many companies in the private sector which are undergoing restructuring, our goal must be a better product at lower cost," Boren said.

It was clear from the kickoff hearing, however, that there was not yet a consensus among committee members that massive reorganization legislation was needed.

Murkowksi said Senate Intelligence should, at the least, give Gates a chance to make his own reorganization proposals. Murkowski said it was possible that many changes could be made through executive orders and that very little would have to be done legislatively.

Gates had begun an intensive review of intelligence activities shortly after assuming his post late in 1991. Gates said in his confirmation hearings that he recognized that the intelligence community, which for years had been focused primarily on the Soviet threat, would have to change if it was to continue to receive public support.

Schlesinger said that proposals in the bills to consolidate intelligence-gathering activities, especially those using expensive high-tech equipment such as spy satellites, could have produced large savings.

But he said that putting the analysis of such information under one roof could be counterproductive. Schle-

singer noted that there were thousands of users of intelligence throughout the government with many different needs. If they found that they were not getting the analysis they required, he said, they would look for other ways to get it.

"The single-minded pursuit of efficiency will not have the sought-after effect," Schlesinger told the committee. "Rather, it will result in the accepted, winked-at or under-the-table diversion of resources to intelligence activities that will inflate the actual, if not the nominal, bill for intelligence."

Retired Gen. William E. Odom, former director of the National Security Agency, said he generally supported the reorganization plans but was troubled by proposals to centralize intelligence analysis. He said that military leaders and Cabinet secretaries needed in-house analysts who would understand the questions that had to be answered. "Otherwise, I do not see how any policy-maker will get the analysis he wants," Odom said.

He added that there was a "popular misconception" that the White House, and to a lesser degree the secretaries of State and Defense, depended heavily on the CIA for intelligence analysis.

In fact, he said, the CIA submitted studies that were often "watered down through editing and approval processes, too late and usually answering questions no one asked."

Odom suggested a scaled-down central analysis unit that would "look for gaps, for issues that are ignored by all other intelligence analysis staffs."

Odom also said that the Boren-McCurdy proposal to give the new director of national intelligence control over a separate intelligence budget would probably not work when it came to the activities of other agencies and could be unwise in the long run. He said that the secretary of Defense, whose budget included most intelligence funding, was more successful than an intelligence chief at winning appropriations on Capitol Hill.

But Boren noted that the CIA director, while responsible for supervising the intelligence community, was often powerless to do so. In intelligence collection, the director of central intelligence had "no explicit authority over collection agencies other than the CIA itself," Boren said. "He can beg and he can plead, but he cannot direct and he cannot coordinate."

Odom and Schlesinger emphasized that it was often the personalities of policy-makers and those holding intelligence jobs — not the bureaucratic structure — that determined whether the system worked well.

"I know no way to organize that will compensate for lack of wisdom, curiosity and insight," Odom said.

Hearings on the House side also were inconclusive on the proposed legislation.

At a March 4 hearing before the House Intelligence Committee, former intelligence officials urged caution and sought time for the administration to implement its restructuring plan. Some committee members agreed, but others questioned whether the entrenched intelligence bureaucracy voluntarily could make changes of the magnitude envisioned by Congress.

"The mere fact of introducing the legislation has been helpful," said Bobby R. Inman, former director of the National Security Agency (NSA). "There is an enormous amount of resistance within the bureaucracy.... The legislation has sent a very loud and clear signal."

Intelligence experts and panel Republicans preached

caution. "A massive reorganization is something we're going to have to be very, very careful about," said Larry Combest of Texas. He said it might have been better to let the changes evolve from within the intelligence community.

Retired intelligence experts urged the committee to work with the administration to try to ease opposition from the agencies.

"If you ram it down their throats, there's going to be some resistance, obviously, and some foot-dragging," said former CIA Director William E. Colby. He also said that merely drawing a new organizational chart — no matter how well thought out — would not necessarily lead to a better system. Any improvements, he said, would have to be the product of "cooperation and leadership" by intelligence agency heads.

Some committee members disagreed. "Frankly, I'm not confident the intelligence community can make the changes on their own," Barbara B. Kennelly, D-Conn., said.

Added to the congressional misgivings was Defense Secretary Dick Cheney's statement March 16 dismissing the bills to reorganize sprawling U.S. intelligence operations as "so severely flawed that selective amendments would not make either of them acceptable."

In a March 17 letter to House Armed Services Committee Chairman Les Aspin, D-Wis., Cheney also argued that the bills were unnecessary because the administration was moving on its own to restructure intelligence.

Cheney, whose department had authority over most intelligence activity and funding, said that taking control from the Pentagon could cut the effectiveness of intelligence support for military action.

## Gates Responds

Rejecting congressional proposals for legislation to reorganize U.S. intelligence agencies, CIA director Gates announced April 1 a series of administrative changes in the gathering, analysis and coordination of intelligence operations.

Testifying before the first hearing ever held jointly by the Senate and House Intelligence committees, Gates warned against locking into law any new structure for the intelligence community in an effort to take account of the collapse of the Soviet Union and the end of the Cold War.

"In a world as fast-changing as what we have seen in the last three or four years," he said, "our ability quickly to adjust structurally, as well as reallocate resources, must be preserved and even enhanced."

The organizational changes Gates summarized for the two panels were the product of 14 task forces that he established in November 1991 to recommend improvements in the management and organization of the CIA and the intelligence community. He had pledged a sweeping reorganization during his 1991 Senate confirmation hearings as director of intelligence. *(1991 Almanac, p. 486)*

Gates accepted the recommendations of all but one task force, ordering changes such as a stronger management staff to help him weed out duplication among intelligence agencies and revisions in the production of intelligence estimates to alert policy-makers to a wider range of possible interpretations of often ambiguous intelligence data.

Boren and McCurdy lauded the scope and speed of Gates' reforms. But they insisted that legislation was needed to give Gates the authority to root out duplication among intelligence agencies.

In particular, the two chairmen challenged Gates' decision not to create an agency in charge of all satellite and aerial reconnaissance, most of which currently was controlled by the Defense Department.

One of Gates' task forces had recommended creating an agency in charge of all such intelligence collection by "imagery." But senior Pentagon officials vigorously opposed the idea, and Gates decided to move much more cautiously. As a first step, he and Defense Secretary Cheney agreed that the Pentagon would create a small organization to coordinate the design of tactical photo reconnaissance equipment intended for military use and "national" equipment, such as satellites.

Boren criticized Gates' decision as "a glaring gap . . . in an area where many, many of our dollars are going."

McCurdy saw the problem as a turf fight over the very expensive business of designing and operating satellites. "Congress will have to take action to enable you to overcome the bureaucratic and turf problems that will arise," he told Gates.

McCurdy later described the issue more pointedly to a reporter: "The Department of Defense has the money, and they don't want to give it up."

As part of its fiscal 1993 budget request, the administration requested legislation to allow the intelligence director to reprogram appropriated funds among the several agencies that made up the intelligence community, subject to the usual procedures by which Congress oversaw such moves.

Gates described several of his organizational changes as similarly intended to beef up the director's ability to manage the community efficiently.

The Intelligence Community Staff, which backstopped the director in his role as central coordinator, would be replaced by a new staff charged with establishing a division of labor among agencies and reducing unneeded duplication.

As the new staff's first executive director, Gates chose Richard Haver, who was Cheney's assistant for intelligence policy.

Several of Gates' other moves were intended to insulate from bureaucratic pressures the "national intelligence estimates" that the intelligence community produced for top national decision-makers. To underscore its independence from any single agency, the National Intelligence Council, which oversaw drafting of the estimates, would be moved out of the CIA headquarters complex. The council would be given two newly appointed vice chairmen:

● One routinely would perform post-mortems on previously written estimates to assess their accuracy.

● The other would supervise the drafting of estimates, ensuring that they took account of dissenting views among agencies and that they told officials not only what the intelligence experts deemed most likely to happen but also what might occur instead if that "best estimate" turned out to be mistaken.

"We need to be straightforward about what we know, what we're estimating and what our confidence level is," Gates told the committees.

This vice chairman for estimates would promote the use of the "red team/blue team" technique, using separate teams of analysts to write competing drafts of an estimate. This was intended to reduce the risk that important perspectives would be overlooked. Gates told the committees that he would increase the number of academics and other specialists from outside government on the National Intelligence Council and that the vice chairman for estimates would come from the private sector.

Aside from the thorny issue of who would control imaging systems, with their massive budgets, Gates endorsed as a general principle coordinating the use by different agencies of each type of intelligence-gathering technique. This was similar to the central management that the National Security Agency provided for electronic eavesdropping (referred to as "signals intelligence").

The CIA director had created an office in the agency to allocate assignments among intelligence agents — referred to as HUMINT, for "human intelligence" — so that each job would go to the agency "that has the best chance of acquiring the information at the least cost and least risk."

Recognizing the extent to which intelligence agencies relied on publicly available data in media reports and technical journals, Gates also planned to name an official on the community management staff responsible for cataloging the "open source" holdings of each agency.

In the effort to ensure that the CIA placed a higher priority on supporting the military, particularly during crises, Gates created an office of military affairs headed by Army Maj. Gen. Roland Lajoie. Lajoie was the first chief of the Pentagon's On-Site Inspection Agency, set up to verify Soviet compliance with the 1988 treaty scrapping intermediate-range nuclear force missiles.

Beyond his steps to reorganize the intelligence community, Gates also announced several changes in the operation of the CIA, including:

● Managers' performance evaluations would take account of any complaints that they politicized subordinates' work, an effort to reduce the risk that analysts would feel pressured to shade their products to back up policies favored by their superiors. Also, an ombudsman was appointed to advise analysts with complaints about such pressure.

● CIA personnel would be trained about their legal obligation to report possible criminal activity they discovered in the course of their work. In addition, each department in the agency would designate an official to funnel such information to the appropriate law enforcement agencies. The agency had come under fire for not passing along information it came across relating to possible criminal activity relating to the Bank of Credit and Commerce International.

● As part of Gates' pledge to be more forthcoming with the public, the agency created an office to review secret documents for possible declassification. The office would review all national intelligence estimates on the former Soviet Union that were 10 years old or older and all documents more than 30 years old, beginning with those relating to President John F. Kennedy and the CIA-sponsored invasion of Cuba at the Bay of Pigs in 1961. ■

# Byrd's Plan for CIA Facility Put on Hold

A plan to move part of the CIA to West Virginia was put off indefinitely after some lawmakers challenged the decision, arguing that the only reason that location had been chosen was the influence of Senate Appropriations Committee Chairman Robert C. Byrd, D-W.Va.

Budgetary constraints gave CIA Director Robert M. Gates a diplomatic way out of a corner March 31, as he put on hold a fiercely disputed plan to relocate 6,000 agency employees to sites in West Virginia and in Virginia's Prince William County.

"In the current budgetary environment," Gates said in a letter to lawmakers involved in the issue, "higher-priority intelligence requirements must take precedence."

According to Gates, the move's estimated cost had increased from $1.2 billion to $1.4 billion.

Byrd and Virginia Republican Sen. John W. Warner, who also had supported the move, bowed to Gates' decision. "In light of the tough budgetary constraints that continue to face us," said Byrd, "it is only realistic to postpone this effort."

When Gates appeared before a joint meeting of the House and Senate Intelligence committees on April 1, Warner pressed him to resuscitate the personnel shift as soon as possible. But Gates replied that the move would require "a more predictable budgetary environment."

## BACKGROUND

In 1991, the intelligence agency proposed relocating CIA workers in two new facilities in West Virginia and Prince William County, Va., at a cost of $1.2 billion. After that decision was disclosed, critics inserted language in the fiscal 1992 intelligence authorization bill requiring a new, public site-selection process and evidence that the consoli-

dation would save money. *(1991 Almanac, p. 482)*

Members of Congress also asked the CIA inspector general to look into the selection process. His Feb. 20 report found no violation of laws or regulations. But it concluded that key members of Congress were given inaccurate information or intentionally kept in the dark during the site selection in 1991 and that the overall process was poorly managed.

"It confirmed my worst concerns," said House Intelligence Committee Chairman Dave McCurdy, D-Okla., one of the most outspoken critics of the West Virginia move. "Not only were we not kept informed, but we were deliberately not kept informed."

McCurdy said his committee would closely monitor the CIA as it proceeded with plans to consolidate workers scattered in 21 offices throughout the Washington area.

"I think proponents of this are going to have a very difficult time sustaining their case," McCurdy said.

In a statement released by his office Feb. 27, Byrd did not address specific findings of the inspector general's report but called it "balanced, thorough, and credible." He said he expected the CIA "to expeditiously implement the IG's recommendations for improvement of the CIA's procedures."

According to the report, selection of the West Virginia site was based to a large extent on political considerations. Its detailed account portrayed an agency conscious of its dependence on congressional funding — and well aware of Byrd's relentless quest to obtain more federal facilities for his economically depressed state.

It quoted an internal CIA document, distributed in February 1991, as saying that "political realities appear to indicate that our best chance of obtaining congressional approval for a second consolidated compound would be to

locate that compound in West Virginia."

The inspector general said that impression arose during a meeting between CIA officials and Byrd on Oct. 16, 1990. The report found "no evidence Sen. Byrd made any statement that might be construed as pressuring the agency."

During the meeting, however, Byrd "noted that he had been helpful in providing the funds to locate an FBI fingerprinting facility in West Virginia" and that, pending receipt of an agency report on consolidation the following February, "he might also be able to identify funds for CIA's plans."

Byrd also proposed that the agency let his staff know what funds were needed for the report, and the agency subsequently suggested $2 million. The money was later provided in a fiscal 1991 appropriations bill.

The report said that CIA personnel who attended a February meeting with committee staff "came away with the clear impression that the chairman's support would be forthcoming if the site selected was in West Virginia."

Over the next several months, the agency continued to look at sites in both West Virginia and Virginia, and lawmakers representing Virginia — including Warner and Republican Rep. Frank R. Wolf — expressed increased interest in the decision. House Intelligence also began to question the selection process.

The report found that subsequently both Wolf and House Intelligence were misled into thinking that the selection process was much less further along than it actually was. For example, in May, Wolf was told by the CIA that no decision had been made on the West Virginia site when in fact an internal CIA group had done so four days before then.

Earlier that month, the report said, agency officials reportedly were encouraged by a Senate Appropriations Committee aide to go with a plan to relocate at sites in West Virginia and in Virginia. Although accounts differed, the report stated that one agency official "recalled it being suggested that this approach would be more palatable to Congress, and that Sens. Byrd and Warner had come to agreement on the issue."

On June 19, CIA Director William Webster met with Byrd and told him that he had decided on the two-site option. According to the report, Byrd asked Webster not to discuss his decision with any other lawmakers until meeting with Senate Intelligence Committee leaders the following day. Webster left his session with Byrd for a previously scheduled meeting with McCurdy, where he made no mention of the decision. McCurdy found out the following day when Byrd's and Warner's offices issued news releases announcing the relocation plan.

In one strange twist, the report said agency officials became worried in early 1991 when they heard the West Virginia tract referred to as "the Byrd Property." An investigation revealed that the land had once been owned by H. F. Byrd Inc.

Agency personnel called the Senate Appropriations Committee staff to determine whether the chairman had ever had any personal connection to the property. They were assured that there was no conflict of interest.

Former Sen. Harry F. Byrd Jr., I-Va., (1965-83), who was not related to the current senator, told Congressional Quarterly that the property was owned by his father's company but was sold in the early 1970s. ∎

# Indictments, Pardons Revive Iran-Contra

President Bush's Christmas Eve pardons of former Defense Secretary Caspar W. Weinberger and five other Republicans involved in the politically charged Iran-contra scandal stood as a powerful closing emblem of 12 years of divided government.

The surprise reprieve brought swift condemnations from several key Democrats in Congress and equally forceful applause from some Republicans. However, the criticism was softer than might have been expected had Bush taken such unilateral action only a few weeks earlier.

Political fallout from the pardons was expected to surface in hearings in 1993 to reauthorize the recently expired independent counsel law, under which special prosecutor Lawrence E. Walsh had been investigating Weinberger and others in connection with Iran-contra.

Earlier in 1992, a federal grand jury indictment of Weinberger spurred renewed interest in Walsh's investigation, which began in late 1986.

Weinberger was indicted June 16 on charges of perjury and making false statements to Iran-contra investigators. The indictment alleged that he concealed the existence of 1,700 pages of personal notes that detailed the Reagan administration's decision to approve arms sales to Iran in 1985 and 1986 in return for the release of American hostages in Lebanon.

Weinberger, who pleaded not guilty to all of the charges on June 19, called the indictment a "grotesque distortion of prosecutorial power and a moral and legal outrage."

Both Democrats and Republicans came to Weinberger's defense, pointing out that he had a record of opposition to the arms-for-hostages sale. Some Republican lawmakers charged that Walsh's investigation was politically inspired, had run out of control and should be cut off. Angered by the Weinberger case and rumors that former President Ronald Reagan himself could face indictment, GOP members called for abolishing the independent counsel law, which expired Dec. 15.

A new stir was caused by a second indictment of Weinberger that was announced just days before the presidential election. It was explosive because of a passage in the indictment that suggested that Bush knew more about the Iran-contra affair than he had previously let on. Senate Republicans claimed the timing was politically motivated and requested the Justice Department to name an independent counsel to investigate whether Bill Clinton's campaign had a hand in it. Attorney General William P. Barr denied the request.

## BACKGROUND

The Iran-contra operation involved the sale of weapons to Iran — at least in part in an effort to negotiate the release of U.S. hostages in the Middle East — and the diversion of some of the arms sale profits to aid the contra rebels in Nicaragua despite a congressional ban on U.S. assistance. The elaborate policy was conducted in secret by

the Reagan White House in 1985 and 1986.

The November 1986 announcement of the operation and the subsequent political fallout were the darkest days of Reagan's presidency. A presidential commission chaired by former Sen. John Tower, R-Texas, issued a report in February 1987 sharply critical of Reagan's handling of his staff, which it said mismanaged the Iran-contra policies. Chief of Staff Donald T. Regan was replaced shortly afterward by former Sen. Howard H. Baker Jr., R-Tenn. *(1987 Almanac, p. 61)*

A special House-Senate committee held public hearings on the scandal in the summer of 1987, but the probe failed to uncover whether Reagan or then-Vice President George Bush knew beforehand about the diversion of funds to the contras.

The controversy continued to live on in federal courts and the political arena after Reagan's presidency ended. Two key Reagan administration officials involved in the affair, former national security adviser John M. Poindexter and his deputy, Oliver L. North, were found guilty of lying to Congress, but the convictions were overturned on appeal.

During Bush's presidential campaign in 1988, the spotlight focused on his involvement. Bush maintained that he was "out of the loop" when Reagan aides decided to divert funds to the contras. The 1987 congressional Iran-contra report said: "The vice president attended several meetings on the Iran initiative, but none of the participants could recall his views."

## WEINBERGER INDICTED

After nearly six years of work and more than $30 million of federal money spent, Walsh's investigation of the Iran-contra scandal came up with its biggest fish in June: Weinberger, the former Defense secretary.

Among the charges against Weinberger were that he lied under oath to the congressional Iran-contra committees by denying that he had advance knowledge of a 1985 Israeli shipment of U.S.-made missiles to Iran and by testifying that he was unaware of contributions by Saudi Arabia to the Nicaraguan contras. It was Weinberger's own notes that led to the indictment. Investigators found 1,700 pages of Weinberger notes at the National Archives.

In his testimony before the Iran-contra committees, Weinberger repeatedly denied that he kept detailed notes. In a 1987 deposition taken by the House select committee that investigated Iran-contra, Weinberger said he understood that former Secretary of State Henry A. Kissinger wrote memos on every meeting he attended.

"I wish I had done that with Day One of this administration," Weinberger said. He gave Congress notes from only one White House meeting, according to Walsh's office.

Weinberger angrily denied the allegations.

Prosecutors acknowledged that the former Defense secretary objected to the arms-for-hostages scheme. The indictment said that Weinberger's notes document that, after the November 1985 missile transfer, he "informed President Reagan that such arms shipments were illegal."

Democratic and Republican lawmakers rallied to Weinberger's defense. In an April letter to Weinberger's attorney, the leaders of the Senate Iran-contra committee, Warren B. Rudman, R-N.H., and Daniel K. Inouye, D-Hawaii, said that Weinberger's recollection of specific events was less important than the "adamant position that the secretary consistently took with the president in opposing sales

to Iran, on which the testimony was incontrovertible."

Rep. Lee H. Hamilton, D-Ind., who chaired the House committee, said on June 17 that he had "high regard for Secretary Weinberger" but added that he had not reviewed the evidence against him.

New charges were brought against Weinberger on Oct. 30, but a judge dismissed them because they were brought past the five-year statute of limitations.

## CLAIR GEORGE CONVICTED

While Weinberger's case was just beginning, another Iran-contra trial ended. Clair E. George, a former top CIA official, was convicted on Dec. 9 of lying to Congress. Although George was acquitted on five other counts, the jury found that he gave misleading answers in 1986 to congressional committees looking into the scandal.

"This marks the first time that a senior CIA official was convicted of felony offenses for crimes committed while he was in his position at the CIA," said prosecutor Craig Gillen. It was George's second trial; the first one ended in a mistrial in August when the jury was deadlocked.

## CHRISTMAS EVE PARDONS

On Christmas Eve, Bush brought his strongest weapon to the match: the presidential pardon. In addition to Weinberger and George, Bush pardoned:

● Robert C. McFarlane, former national security adviser, who pleaded guilty on March 11, 1988, to withholding information from Congress. He was sentenced to two years' probation and 200 hours of community service and fined $20,000.

● Duane R. Clarridge, a former senior CIA official who was scheduled to go on trial in March 1993 on eight counts of perjury, all involving allegedly false statements he made about the secret missile shipment to Iran.

● Elliott Abrams, former assistant secretary of State for inter-American affairs, who pleaded guilty on Oct. 7, 1991, to four misdemeanor charges of withholding information from Congress. He was sentenced to two years' probation and 100 hours of community service.

● Alan D. Fiers Jr., former head of the CIA Central American Task Force under George, who pleaded guilty on July 9, 1991, to two misdemeanor charges of withholding information from Congress. He was sentenced to one year of probation and 100 hours of community service.

The pardons came six years into Walsh's investigation of how the Reagan administration came to make secret arms-for-hostage sales to Iran and divert the profits to aid the Nicaraguan contras.

Bush explained the pardons by saying the men were all "patriots" who had given the country years of public service and had not profited from their involvement in the scandal.

And Bush said the prosecutions of the six men represented not law enforcement, but "the criminalization of policy differences."

"These differences should be addressed in the political arena, without the Damocles sword of criminality hanging over the heads of some of the combatants," Bush said. *(Text, p. 48-E)*

Walsh said Bush's action improperly set some former administration officials above the law and constituted a "cover-up" of misdeeds. And Walsh said the pardons were particularly troubling in light of the fact that Bush appar-

ently had withheld notes requested by the independent counsel's office. Bush had become a "subject" of his ongoing investigation, Walsh said.

Senate Majority Leader George J. Mitchell, D-Maine, and House Majority Leader Richard A. Gephardt, D-Mo., were among those criticizing the pardons.

"The pardon maintains the appearance of an Iran-contra cover-up, suggests presidential approval of violations of law, and condones ill-founded foreign policy decisions that never would have been made in the light of day," Gephardt said in a release.

But those condemnations were somewhat muted by reports that House Speaker Thomas S. Foley, D-Wash., and Armed Services Committee Chairman Les Aspin, D-Wis., Clinton's nominee for Defense secretary, had been contacted by the White House in advance of the announcement and had given tacit approval to a Weinberger pardon.

Several days later, aides to both lawmakers clarified those reports.

An aide to Foley said the Speaker had indicated only that he would not criticize a Weinberger pardon and was "shocked" when Bush pardoned the other five men as well. Similarly, Aspin's aide said Aspin had discussed only Weinberger's case and disagreed with Bush's characterization of the offenses as only possible misdeeds or policy differences.

Meanwhile, Senate Minority Leader Bob Dole, R-Kan., called the pardons a "Christmas Eve act of courage and compassion" and reiterated prior criticisms of Walsh. Dole had challenged Walsh's indictment of Weinberger, just prior to the election, as politically motivated.

Sen. Orrin G. Hatch, R-Utah, who was on the congressional committee that investigated Iran-contra, said he would have liked to see even broader pardons for those implicated in the independent counsel's investigation.

"Lawrence Walsh is a perfect example of an independent counsel gone wrong," said Hatch, who was slated to become ranking member of the Judiciary panel. "The conspiracy and cover-up only existed in the head of Judge Walsh."

Congress had no authority to rescind or alter the six Iran-contra pardons.

The presidential power to pardon is an absolute one granted by the Constitution. A pardon wipes out guilt and punishment, as if the offense had never been committed.

Carl Levin, D-Mich., chairman of the Senate Government Operations subcommittee that oversaw the independent counsel law, raised the possibility of investigative hearings concerning the pardon in 1993 as part of Congress' debate over renewing the lapsed independent counsel law. *(Independent counsel, p. 315)*

Levin said that could include letting Weinberger air his accusations that Walsh had improperly persecuted him, and allowing Walsh to testify in response. As such, the hearings could touch on Weinberger's notes and other issues that would have come up in a trial.

In the House, Don Edwards, D-Calif., a senior member on the Judiciary Committee, was among those who viewed the pardons as a major assault on Congress. "It strikes at the heart of the most important job that Congress has, which is the oversight of the executive department," he said. ■

# Task Force Says No Secret Hostage Deal

In a final twist to the long-running saga of the "October surprise" allegations, a House task force recommended early in 1993 that the Justice Department consider bringing perjury charges against several people who claimed to have information buttressing the story.

The special task force said Jan. 13 that it had debunked 12-year-old allegations that operatives for the Reagan-Bush presidential campaign had conspired to delay release of American hostages held by Iran.

For years, proponents of the October surprise theory alleged that in the waning days of the 1980 presidential campaign, aides to Ronald Reagan tried to prevent President Jimmy Carter's administration from securing a dramatic hostage release. The prospect of such a political coup became known as the October surprise.

According to the thesis, Reagan campaign manager William J. Casey and other officials negotiated a secret arms deal with Iranian officials to induce Tehran to delay the release of the 52 American hostages until after Election Day.

The report of the 13-member task force unconditionally rejected the allegations, concluding: "There is no credible evidence supporting any attempt by the Reagan presidential campaign — or persons associated with the campaign — to delay the release of the American hostages in Iran."

The report stated that there was "wholly insufficient evidence" that anyone associated with the Reagan-Bush campaign communicated with representatives of the Ira-

nian government.

Lee H. Hamilton, D-Ind., who chaired the task force, praised the 10-month, $1.3 million investigation as a model of bipartisanship. But Republicans bitterly criticized the entire exercise as a Democrat-inspired boondoggle, even as they claimed vindication in the report's exoneration of Reagan and Bush.

A separate Senate subcommittee investigation had released its report on Nov. 23, 1992, stating that it could find no conclusive evidence that officials from the 1980 Reagan-Bush campaign negotiated a secret agreement.

## BACKGROUND

Allegations of a secret deal to stall the hostages' release had circulated for years. But the scenario gained new attention in April 1991, when a former Carter administration National Security Council aide, Gary Sick, wrote an article discussing possible contacts between the Reagan campaign and the Iranian government.

The hostage crisis, which dragged on from Nov. 4, 1979, to Jan. 20, 1981, consumed Carter's presidency and played a significant role in his defeat for a second term. After negotiations with Iran to secure the hostages' release stalled, Carter ordered a rescue attempt in April 1980, but it failed, and eight soldiers were killed in an accident. *(1980 Almanac, p. 352)*

As talks carried on into the fall of 1980, Reagan cam-

paign officials warned that Carter might try to engineer an "October surprise" to boost his re-election chances. Sick alleged that the Reagan campaign may have short-circuited such a deal. Former Iranian President Abol Hassan Bani-Sadr told The New York Times that a meeting between Republicans and Iranians was held in Paris in October 1980.

Richard V. Allen and two other top Reagan-Bush campaign officials acknowledged that they met in Washington with an Iranian emissary in September or October, but said they rejected an offer to deliver the hostages in a way advantageous to Reagan.

The charges were explosive because of the suggestion that vice presidential candidate George Bush may have traveled to Europe in the fall of 1980 to negotiate the deal. Bush denied that he was part of any such negotiations and said his travel at the time was well documented.

The secretive Casey, a World War II spymaster who was Reagan's CIA director from 1981 until his death in 1987, was at the center of speculation about a secret agreement. News reports suggested that Casey was in Europe at the time the negotiations supposedly took place. The Senate subcommittee probe concluded that Casey conducted "potentially dangerous" efforts to collect intelligence on the Carter administration's efforts to gain the release of the hostages.

## HOUSE PROBE

With the 1992 election just nine months away and President Bush a subject of scrutiny, the House conducted a politically charged debate Feb. 5 on whether to authorize a special October surprise task force.

Approved by a 217-192 vote, H Res 258 established a task force of eight Democrats and five Republicans to look into the allegations. *(Vote 13, p. 4-H)*

Its chairman, Hamilton, said that while the seriousness of the charges compelled Congress to undertake the investigation, "I genuinely hope that these allegations can be disproved conclusively."

Republicans lashed out at the investigation, charging that Democrats were listening to "wackos and weirdos."

"Who's going to be your chief investigator, Geraldo Rivera?" asked Toby Roth, R-Wis. Republicans sought to expand the probe to look into matters potentially damaging to Democrats. Minority Leader Robert H. Michel, R-Ill., offered an amendment to require the task force to look into any attempts by the Carter administration to negotiate the release of the hostages prior to the election. Michel's amendment was defeated on a straight-line party vote, 158-249. *(Vote 12, p. 4-H)*

In an effort to quell criticism that the investigation was designed to damage Bush before the election, Hamilton announced on July 1 that preliminary information indicated that Bush probably did not travel to Europe during the time period alleged by Sick and others.

"All credible evidence leads to the conclusion that President Bush was in the United States continuously during the Oct. 18-22, 1980, time frame and that he was not attending secret meetings in Paris," said Hamilton.

"We are glad that Congress, in a bipartisan report, concluded today what we knew all along, that President Bush had no involvement with any alleged meetings in Paris in October 1980 and, in fact, he never left the country at that time," said a White House statement.

### Task Force Conclusions

The House task force released its findings Jan. 13, 1993, rejecting the 12-year-old allegations.

The 968-page report was likely to be Congress' final word on the longstanding charges, which had been a thorn in the side of two Republican presidents. It went even further than an earlier Senate report, released in November, in spiking the allegations.

Hamilton said the task force found that nearly all of the sources for the October surprise turned out to be "wholesale fabricators or were impeached by documentary evidence." Attorneys for the panel said it had informed the Justice Department of people who might have lied to Congress.

Despite its extensive investigation, the task force was unable to obtain Casey's passport.

The report became fodder for the Republicans. Rep. Henry J. Hyde, Ill., the ranking Republican on the task force, tried to turn the tables on Democrats who had supported the investigation. He accused the Carter administration of trying to negotiate its own arms-for-hostages swap. He charged that in 1980, Carter administration officials offered to provide Iran with $230 million worth of weapons — part of $12 billion in Iranian assets frozen by Carter after the Americans were seized — if Tehran freed the hostages.

Sen. Jesse Helms, R-N.C., raised the issue during the confirmation hearings for Warren M. Christopher, President-elect Bill Clinton's nominee for secretary of State.

Hamilton insisted that the offer by Carter's administration was not comparable to the Reagan administration's arms-for-hostages dealings with Iran during the mid-1980s. Carter offered only to unfreeze the assets after the hostages were released, Hamilton said.

## SENATE PROBE

The investigation by the Senate Foreign Relations Subcommittee on Near Eastern and South Asian Affairs found no "sufficient credible evidence" to support allegations that the Reagan-Bush campaign tried to delay the hostages' release.

Unlike the House inquiry, the subcommittee never received the approval of the full chamber for its probe. After Democrats were unable in 1991 to get the 60 votes needed to cut off debate on a resolution (S Res 198) authorizing the probe, Democrats tapped Reid Weingarten to act as special counsel. *(1991 Almanac, p. 490)*

In his report, released Nov. 23, Weingarten said that although the Reagan administration "privately acquiesced in some limited Israeli shipments of American-made weapons to Iran and slightly relaxed" a policy of limiting shipment of weapons to Iran, there was no credible evidence that actions were taken as "a reward to the Khomeini regime in exchange for an agreement relating to hostages."

Weingarten said the failure to obtain Casey's passport and other important documents impeded the investigation. He concluded that Casey conducted "informal, clandestine and potentially dangerous" efforts to collect intelligence on Carter administration negotiations with Iran. ∎

# Chapter 10

# APPROPRIATIONS

# Appropriators Work Quickly in '92

*Budget rules survive early attacks, clearing way for
swift disposition of all 13 spending bills*

A year that looked to be impossible for congressional appropriators turned out to be one of the most efficient, as lawmakers managed to clear all 13 regular appropriations bills by Oct. 5, just days after the Oct. 1 start of fiscal 1993 and one of the earliest dates they had gotten all the bills done in two decades.

Few would have predicted such an orderly finish nine months earlier, when Congress began the year amid concerns that election-year politics, tightened spending caps, the shaky state of the 1990 budget deal and a shorter-than-usual work year would all combine to make it impossible to finish work on every spending bill.

Some legislators predicted they would end the year by wrapping most or all of the bills into a massive continuing resolution. That worried Democrats, however, who feared that such a "CR" would hand President Bush an opportunity to bash the Democratic-led Congress right before the elections for failing to do its most fundamental job.

But after early attacks left the 1990 budget agreement and its strict spending caps unscathed, ending the uncertainty over whether appropriators might somehow find more money for their bills, Congress settled down to an orderly process of churning out the 13 measures.

Bush and the appropriators clashed repeatedly over priorities, particularly when Bush sent a lengthy list of proposals to Capitol Hill to rescind previously appropriated spending.

But the two sides found a way to compromise most of their differences, and Congress was on track for an early finish when lawmakers ran into one final roadblock: Bush threatened to veto any bill that failed to meet a "freeze" test he had outlined in the budget he proposed in January but had barely mentioned since then.

While some Democrats talked of confronting the president, leaders reasoned that they could not win a veto fight with the president, and appropriators made last-minute trims in all their bills to meet Bush's cap.

## A Slow Start

Despite the fact that presidential primary elections and the need to go home and campaign made 1992 a shorter year than most, the appropriations process got off to a slow start.

It wasn't until Democrats failed in late March to knock down the budget "walls" between defense and domestic spending to get more money for domestic programs that the Appropriations committees knew how much money they had to spend. Then appropriators were distracted by a time-consuming battle with President Bush over whether to cancel billions in spending they had been approved the year before. *(Budget walls, p. 104)*

Money worries continually slowed the process. After two years of increases for domestic appropriations, the strict spending caps approved as part of the 1990 budget agreement were beginning to bite hard, forcing a cut in some spending below prior-year levels. House appropriators lost valuable time explaining that to their colleagues. They also had to wait while House leaders worked to persuade ailing House Appropriations Chairman Jamie L. Whitten, D-Miss., to turn over day-to-day committee operations to ranking Democrat William H. Natcher of Kentucky.

When House Appropriations subcommittee chairmen finally sat down to divide the roughly $506 billion discretionary spending pie among their panels on June 3, they found themselves $7 billion short of what the Congressional Budget Office (CBO) said they needed in outlays (actual spending) to keep the domestic spending even with inflation. That allocations process marked the formal beginning of the appropriations season.

## Pace Quickens by August Recess

After their slow start, appropriators moved quickly during the summer months. By the August recess, the House had finished all 13 bills and the Senate seven. Only one had been sent to the White House, however: the agriculture appropriations bill. Bush signed the measure Aug. 14.

With less than a month to clear the other 12 bills between the end of the recess and the beginning of the new fiscal year, Democratic leaders had to wrestle with an election-year challenge. Should they knuckle under to the demand Bush had made during the Republican National Convention that they freeze domestic appropriations at the previous year's level or should they defy him, arguing that they had already spent substantially less than allowed under the 1990 budget rules? In the end, they calculated that voters would not grasp the distinction and that Bush would win both the veto fight and the political battle. Members were clamoring to wrap up Congress' business so they could go home to campaign, and the appropriators' last-minute trims in several spending bills allowed them to do that.

Congress passed only a single short-term continuing resolution (HJ Res 553 — PL 102-376), good through Oct. 5, to allow time to finish work on the bills. President Bush signed the last five bills on Oct. 6, finishing with foreign operations.

Thanks to the cuts needed to meet Bush's limit, plus additional cuts in defense and foreign aid, total discretionary spending in the 13 bills was $16.2 billion below the spending caps and about $6.9 billion below what Congress approved for fiscal 1992.

Congress also cleared two supplemental appropriations bills that provided additional fiscal 1992 funding:

● **Urban aid.** The first supplemental provided $1.1 billion to help rebuild riot-torn Los Angeles, repair Chicago's flooded downtown and fund nationwide summer youth jobs and school programs.

● **Disaster/defense.** A second supplemental provided $11.1 billion in aid for storm-stricken Florida, Hawaii and Guam, plus $4.1 billion in unrelated defense spending and $500,000 in urban aid. ∎

# Status of Appropriations
## 102nd Congress — Second Session

| Bill | House | Senate | Final | Story |
|---|---|---|---|---|
| **Agriculture and related agencies**<br>(HR 5487 — H Rept 102-815) | Passed<br>6/30/92 | Passed<br>7/28/92 | Signed 8/14/92<br>PL 102-341 | p. 676 |
| **Commerce, Justice, State, Judiciary**<br>(HR 5678 — H Rept 102-918) | Passed<br>7/30/92 | Passed<br>8/3/92 | Signed 10/6/92<br>PL 102-395 | p. 646 |
| **Defense**<br>(HR 5504 — H Rept 102-1015) | Passed<br>7/2/92 | Passed<br>9/23/92 | Signed 10/6/92<br>PL 102-396 | p. 592 |
| **District of Columbia**<br>(HR 6056 — H Rept 102-899) | Passed<br>9/30/92 | Passed<br>9/30/92 | Signed 10/5/92<br>PL 102-382 | p. 681 |
| **Energy and Water Development**<br>(HR 5373 — H Rept 102-866) | Passed<br>6/17/92 | Passed<br>8/3/92 | Signed 10/2/92<br>PL 102-377 | p. 659 |
| **Foreign Operations**<br>(HR 5368 — H Rept 102-1011) | Passed<br>6/25/92 | Passed<br>10/1/92 | Signed 10/6/92<br>PL 102-391 | p. 612 |
| **Interior and related agencies**<br>(HR 5503 — H Rept 102-901) | Passed<br>7/23/92 | Passed<br>8/6/92 | Signed 10/5/92<br>PL 102-381 | p. 686 |
| **Labor, Health and Human Services, Education**<br>(HR 5677 — H Rept 102-974) | Passed<br>7/28/92 | Passed<br>9/18/92 | Signed 10/6/92<br>PL 102-394 | p. 651 |
| **Legislative Branch**<br>(HR 5427 — H Rept 102-1007) | Passed<br>6/24/92 | Passed<br>10/1/92 | Signed 10/6/92<br>PL 102-392 | p. 633 |
| **Military Construction**<br>(HR 5428 — H Rept 102-888) | Passed<br>6/23/92 | Passed<br>8/5/92 | Signed 10/5/92<br>PL 102-380 | p. 623 |
| **Transportation and related agencies**<br>(HR 5518 — H Rept 102-924) | Passed<br>7/9/92 | Passed<br>8/5/92 | Signed 10/6/92<br>PL 102-388 | p. 669 |
| **Treasury, Postal Service, General Government**<br>(HR 5488 — H Rept 102-919) | Passed<br>7/1/92 | Passed<br>9/10/92 | Signed 10/6/92<br>PL 102-393 | p. 626 |
| **VA, Housing and Urban Development, Independent Agencies**<br>(HR 5679 — H Rept 102-902) | Passed<br>7/29/92 | Passed<br>9/9/92 | Signed 10/6/92<br>PL 102-389 | p. 639 |
| **Disaster/Defense Supplemental**<br>(HR 5620 — H Rept 102-672) | Passed<br>9/18/92 | Passed<br>9/15/92 | Signed 9/23/92<br>PL 102-368 | p. 583 |
| **Urban Aid Supplemental**<br>(HR 5132 — H Rept 102-577) | Passed<br>5/14/92 | Passed<br>5/21/92 | Signed 6/22/92<br>PL 102-302 | p. 579 |

# Emergency Aid for Cities Tops $1 Billion

Congress' first concrete response to the devastating April riots in Los Angeles came when the House passed a $494.7 million supplemental appropriations bill May 14. The measure was designed to direct small-business loans and emergency grants to L.A. and to Chicago, where the recent collapse of a tunnel beneath the Chicago River had flooded the city's downtown.

The House bill turned out to be just the opening bid, however. One week later, the Senate quadrupled the size of the measure to nearly $2 billion by adding money for a nationwide program of urban aid. The extra money was to go for summer youth jobs, a Head Start summer program for preschool children, a summer-school program for disadvantaged neighborhoods and the administration-backed "Weed and Seed" program, which aimed to "weed" drug dealers and and other criminals out of inner-city neighborhoods and "seed" the areas with social programs.

Senate backers, including some Republicans, fought off attempts to strip out the nearly $1.5 billion they added to the House bill and defeated a move to force Congress to cut other spending to pay for the programs. Virtually all of the money was to be provided on an "emergency" basis, exempt from spending caps set in the 1990 budget agreement.

Despite a White House veto threat over the size of the bill, House-Senate conferees June 5 decided to keep all the Senate add-ons and leave the bill's price tag at $2 billion. Participants in negotiations between the White House and key members of Congress said last-minute insistence on the full amount by Senate Majority Leader George J. Mitchell, D-Maine, blocked a compromise on a smaller amount, but Mitchell flatly denied the account.

In the end, it wasn't the veto threat from President Bush that forced the bill to slim down, it was strong GOP opposition and intransigence among rank-and-file Democrats in the House.

Some Democratic leaders wanted to send Bush the $2 billion conference report and force him to issue what they assumed would be a politically embarrassing veto. But when House vote-counters ran a whip check, they found that too many members objected to the size of the bill, either because it would have added $2 billion to the deficit or because rural and suburban members thought it would send too much money to the inner cities.

Bowing to reality, leaders accepted a White House compromise that cut the bill to $1.1 billion. The conference report was adopted by the House on June 18, seven weeks after the riots, by a vote of 249-168.

## BOXSCORE

➡ **Fiscal 1992 Urban Aid Supplemental (HR 5132, formerly HR 5069).** The bill provided funds to help rebuild riot-torn Los Angeles and Chicago's flooded downtown. The measure also provided funding for summer youth jobs and school programs in U.S. cities.

**Reports:** H Rept 102-518; conference report H Rept 102-577.

### KEY ACTION

**May 12** — The **House** Appropriations Committee passed HR 5069 by voice vote.

**May 14** — The **House** passed HR 5069, 244-162.

**May 19** — The **Senate** Appropriations Committee passed measure as HR 5132, 16-1.

**May 21** — The **Senate** passed HR 5132, 61-36.

**June 5** — **House-Senate** conferees approved HR 5132.

**June 18** — The **House** adopted conference report on HR 5132, 249-168; the **Senate** cleared the measure by voice vote.

**June 22** — President Bush signed HR 5132 — PL 102-302.

The Senate cleared the measure by voice vote later the same day.

While the supplemental was intended as part of a broader urban aid initiative, in the end it contained the only money that Congress would provide to inner cities in 1992 as a response to the L.A. riots. The other big urban aid proposal that grew out of the riots — a plan to set up dozens of "enterprise zones" where investors and businesses would get special tax breaks and other federal assistance — was finally incorporated in the tax bill (HR 11) Congress cleared just before adjournment. Bush vetoed that bill on Nov. 4. *(Urban aid tax bill, p. 140; urban crisis, p. 339)*

## HOUSE COMMITTEE ACTION

In response to two urban disasters — riots in Los Angeles and a serious flood in Chicago's downtown — House Appropriations Committee Chairman Jamie L. Whitten, D-Miss., introduced a $494.7 million supplemental appropriations bill (HR 5069) May 6 to provide emergency assistance and small-business loans. The House Appropriations Committee passed the bill by voice vote on May 12 in an expedited markup session.

The fiscal 1992 measure contained $300 million to enable the Federal Emergency Management Agency (FEMA) to provide disaster relief payments, primarily for damage in Chicago that occurred when a tunnel beneath the Chicago River collapsed and flooded numerous buildings in the city's downtown.

The measure also provided an increase in the limit on FEMA's direct loans by $22 million, bringing the cap to $28 million.

The bill also provided up to $169.7 million in disaster loan subsidies for the Small Business Administration, enough to subsidize $500 million in loans. The committee agreed to an administration-requested amendment to make $150 million of the $500 million in SBA loans contingent on a future presidential declaration of need.

The committee rejected by voice vote an amendment by Commerce, Justice, State Appropriations Subcommittee Chairman Neal Smith, D-Iowa, that would have authorized an additional $1.45 billion for SBA's general small-business loan guarantee program.

Harold Rogers, R-Ky., objected that the money required to leverage the loan guarantees Smith wanted would draw a presidential veto or trigger an automatic spending cut in domestic appropriations bills.

The bill also included $25 million in administrative expenses for carrying out the disaster loan program. The

loans were to be aimed primarily at businesses damaged or destroyed in Los Angeles.

The bill was to be considered emergency spending, exempt from the spending caps agreed to in the 1990 budget agreement.

## HOUSE FLOOR ACTION

The House passed the supplemental May 14 on a narrower-than-expected vote of 244-162, with strong opposition from members who felt that Chicago's city government could have prevented much of the flood damage there had it been quicker to respond to early indications of trouble in the tunnel that later collapsed and caused the disaster. *(Vote 125, p. 32-H)*

As passed, the measure would have made available a total of $822 million in grants and loans from FEMA and the SBA.

Republicans opposed the bill by more than a 2-to-1 margin, despite strong support for it from the Bush administration.

"Chicago was a big factor in people voting no," said GOP whip Newt Gingrich of Georgia. "We were more sympathetic to Los Angeles."

Gingrich also warned that Republican defections on the emergency aid bill could spell trouble for Democratic urban assistance initiatives that went beyond proposals outlined by President Bush. "I told the Democrats that [Republicans] would vote for a real reform package," Gingrich said. "There's no sentiment in rural and suburban America in sending more money to inner city mayors."

F. James Sensenbrenner Jr., R-Wis., and others made several attempts to amend the measure to block aid to Chicago. He called the measure "indemnification of the gross negligence of municipal employees of Chicago," arguing that the flood resulted from incompetence on the part of city officials — some of whom had since been fired — for failing to heed warnings that a bulkhead between the tunnel and river was leaking.

Sidney R. Yates, D-Ill., fired back at Sensenbrenner, complaining that "there was some [bureaucratic failure] in Los Angeles, too."

The bill came to the floor under a rule that prohibited amendments. Sensenbrenner attempted a parliamentary move to alter the rule but lost on a procedural vote, 262-139. *(Vote 123, p. 30-H)*

The emergency aid was not specifically earmarked for Los Angeles and Chicago. Rather, the measure was intended to supplement general disaster relief programs operated by FEMA and the SBA. Both programs were triggered by presidential disaster declarations, a point that Joseph M. McDade of Pennsylvania, ranking Republican on the Appropriations Committee, used to counter arguments against sending aid to Chicago.

He noted that Bush had declared the Chicago flood a disaster, making affected businesses eligible for FEMA and SBA assistance. "The president is the person under the law to make a disaster declaration. Once those declarations are made, the funding requests follow," McDade said.

As passed, the bill was designed to:

● **FEMA grants and loans.** Provide an additional $300 million for fiscal 1992 in emergency disaster aid and allow FEMA to make an extra $22 million in direct loans. The latter were used by state and local governments to meet federal cost-sharing requirements.

● **SBA loans.** Provide an increase of $169.7 million to cover the costs of $500 million in SBA disaster loans.

Under credit reform provisions enacted in 1990, appropriations for loan programs were made to account for the subsidy involved, in this case chiefly the amount that was not expected to be repaid.

Only $118.8 million was to be available immediately, financing $350 million in loans. The remaining $50.9 million (financing an additional $150 million in loans) was to become available following a presidential declaration of need to cover additional emergencies.

The bill also increased the SBA's appropriation for administrative expenses by $25 million.

● **Gang violence.** Earmark $5 million in previously appropriated money for the FBI to finance a task force on gang violence in Los Angeles.

The Bush administration had agreed to declare the full $494.7 million as an emergency expense. Under the terms of the 1990 budget agreement, that obviated the need to provide offsetting spending cuts.

## SENATE COMMITTEE ACTION

After quadrupling the size of the bill to some $1.94 billion by adding $1.45 billion for nationwide increases for summer youth and school programs and other urban aid, the Senate Appropriations Committee voted 16-1 to approve the bill in a short markup session May 19.

The additions to the bill had bipartisan support, not just from Chairman Robert C. Byrd, D-W.Va., and ranking Republican Mark O. Hatfield of Oregon, but also from two influential non-committee members: Edward M. Kennedy, D-Mass., Orrin G. Hatch, R-Utah, chairman and ranking member, respectively, of the Senate Labor Committee, which had jurisdiction over many of the programs the appropriators were seeking to bolster.

The extra money was to go for a nationwide effort to fund summer youth jobs, a Head Start summer program for preschool children, a Chapter I summer program for elementary and secondary schools and the administration-backed Weed and Seed program for high crime areas.

The major add-ons were:

● Summer Youth Employment summer jobs program — $700 million.

● Head Start Summer Program — $250 million.

● Chapter I Summer School program — $250 million.

● "Weed and Seed" neighborhood crime reduction program — $250 million.

Despite the bipartisan support, the add-ons broke the fragile truce between Congress and the White House over designating the measure as emergency spending. The extra money was to be available only if Bush declared it emergency funds under the budget rules. Some Republicans charged that was an attempt to "set up" the president. The White House warned that it had "serious concerns" about the dollar amounts.

## SENATE FLOOR ACTION

The Senate approved the $1.94 billion bill May 21 on a 61-36 vote, short of the margin backers needed to be certain they could override any veto by President Bush. Supporters of the measure fought off attempts to strip out the $1.45 billion that they added to the House bill, and they defeated an attempt to force Congress to pay for the programs rather than fund the bill through deficit spending under the budget rules' exemption for emergencies. The White House did not indicate exactly where it stood on the

bill, but the administration agreed during the debate to support a compromise formula for distributing the bill's summer youth jobs money, and that was taken a sign that Bush would likely agree to at least part of the extra funding. *(Vote 109, p. 15-S)*

The plan to make the money available only if Bush agreed to call it emergency funding and thereby exempt it from the spending caps set by the 1990 budget agreement drew criticism from some Republicans.

"We're creating a political ambush for the president," said Thad Cochran, R-Miss. "The beneficiaries of those programs are going to be told that the Congress believes you need these additional funds, but the president doesn't."

Trent Lott, R-Miss., offered an amendment to strike the extra spending, arguing that it made the bill "a political *Titanic* that's beginning to sink."

That touched off a familiar dispute, with Byrd retorting that the administration could find emergency spending for allies such as Egypt and Israel, but balked when it came time to spend money on emergencies at home.

But in a deviation from the usual debate, Republican Hatch strongly defended the extra spending.

"It isn't very often that I stand up and argue that we should spend more money in certain areas," Hatch said, insisting that the programs he sought to fund were worthwhile.

Of Head Start, he said, "It works, it's efficient, it helps the most vulnerable at a time when they are the most vulnerable."

The Senate voted 37-62 to reject Lott's attempt to strike the $1.45 billion. *(Vote 106, p. 15-S)*

Earlier, the Senate had voted 45-52 to reject a proposal by Bob Graham, D-Fla., to pay for the extra spending in the bill with cuts in other programs, instead of financing it by adding to the deficit. *(Vote 102, p. 14-S)*

Graham argued that the cost of the bill should not be passed on to the next generation. But Byrd and Hatfield opposed the amendment on the grounds that it would enable Bush to veto the urban aid measure indirectly by refusing to approve a separate package of spending cuts (the so-called rescission bill — HR 4990) that Graham envisioned using to offset the supplemental. *(Rescissions, p. 587)*

In a move that was expected to trigger strong White House opposition, the Senate voted 59-40 to approve an amendment by Frank R. Lautenberg, D-N.J., to waive the usual state or local matching requirement in order to accelerate federally funded highway and transit construction projects. *(Vote 101, p. 14-S)*

The White House indicated some willingness to be flexible on the bill when it helped broker a behind-the-scenes compromise on the formula for distributing the $675 million (reduced by $25 million from the committee-passed amount) that would go to fund summer jobs for young people.

The compromise was designed to steer money toward smaller urban areas, because many senators worried that cities in their states would get short shrift under an original formula seen as tilting toward big cities.

Under the new formula, the first $100 million would go to the nation's 75 largest cities, and the second $100 million would go to the states to be distributed at the governors' discretion. The balance would be distributed according to the original formula, based on poverty rates and unemployment.

## CONFERENCE ACTION

By the time House-Senate conferees convened to work out a compromise, they had an explicit White House veto threat to contend with over the size of the bill. On June 5 they ignored the threat, however, agreeing to a $2 billion bill.

Despite House Republican pleas for restraint, House Democrats and the bipartisan Senate conference delegation essentially stuck with the higher of Senate- and House-passed numbers for key appropriations accounts. The administration had requested that most of the Senate money be dropped.

Ranking House Appropriations Republican McDade insisted that the result would be no bill. He cited a June 5 letter from Richard G. Darman, director of the Office of Management and Budget (OMB), saying the president's senior advisers would recommend a veto.

"The cities will suffer, the people will suffer," McDade said. "It's a tragedy."

Senate Appropriations Chairman Robert C. Byrd, D-W.Va., said he hoped there would be no veto. "I still have faith that the president is his own man and is not in the control of his handlers," Byrd said.

Most Senate Republican conferees seemed to support the final measure, though Pete V. Domenici of New Mexico said he would oppose it on the floor. House Republican conferees broadly opposed it.

In addition to keeping virtually all of the major aid money added by the Senate, conferees also resolved a difference over SBA loan funding by giving both sides what they wanted.

The Senate had shifted some of the House-passed SBA disaster loan money and administrative spending to business loan subsidies.

The conferees restored the disaster loan money and the administrative expenses and increased the amount the Senate had put toward business subsidies.

Conferees and the administration differed sharply over four major add-ons: the $675 million for youth summer jobs and the $250 million each to begin a summer Head Start program, to expand summer school activities for the disadvantaged financed through Chapter 1 and to expand the Weed and Seed program.

Administration officials had urged Congress to add only $500 million for youth summer jobs and leave the other matters to separate, broader negotiations over urban aid. That appeal went nowhere, however.

In agreeing to accept the Senate's Head Start, Chapter 1 and summer jobs aid, House conferees insisted on dropping proposed formula changes that would have targeted most of the money to urban areas. Instead, existing law formulas, which would be more beneficial than the Senate proposal to rural areas, were to govern distribution of the money.

Conferees met for about three hours June 4 and concluded their deliberations in only 30 minutes the following day.

Much of the second day was spent discussing changes to Senate-passed language that would have barred federal assistance to individuals indicted or otherwise charged with crimes stemming from the Los Angeles riots.

Sen. Arlen Specter, R-Pa., objected that the provision was too open-ended and violated constitutional due process protections. He proposed limiting the aid deferral to 90 days, the California constitution's deadline for speedy tri-

als. Rogers complained that his constituents did not want their tax dollars aiding rioters. Specter proposed that where judges agreed to allow prosecutors 180 days to bring a case to trial, an application for federal aid also could be held for 180 days. That was agreed to by conferees.

## FINAL ACTION

After stalling for two nearly weeks to see whether they had the votes to insist on the larger version of the bill, the House and Senate approved a stripped-down $1.1 billion supplemental on June 18. Before the final vote, congressional leaders modified the conference report without formally reconvening the conference itself.

The House approved the compromise conference report on a 249-168 vote. The Senate passed it by voice vote later the same day, clearing it for Bush, who had earlier sent word that he would sign the measure. Passage came seven weeks after the Los Angeles riots that prompted the bill. *(Vote 206, p. 50-H)*

The bill was roughly half the $2 billion measure House and Senate conferees had approved June 5, after Democratic leaders were said to have nixed a White House compromise offer nearly identical to the measure that ultimately passed.

After racing through the House, the Senate and a House-Senate conference, the supplemental had stalled the week of June 8, stopped dead by a test of wills between congressional appropriators and the Bush administration.

OMB director Darman and White House chief of staff Samuel K. Skinner confirmed June 9 that Bush would veto the bill if it was not put on a diet. "We will go through the veto thing if we have to," said Darman.

Democratic strategists conceded a veto would almost certainly be sustained, but some believed that vetoing urban aid in the wake of the riots would make Bush look insensitive in an election year. It would be "a very petty veto," said one senior House aide.

But this struck some Democrats as a bad time and a bad issue on which to fight the White House. While Congress and the administration dickered, the cities were going without the aid that both sides said was important. Mindful of the embarrassing loss Democratic leaders had suffered in March when they failed to win rank-and-file support for a bill to allow the use of defense savings for domestic programs, some Democrats were advising compromise.

"This is one where it's better to work out a compromise with the administration," said House Budget Committee Chairman Leon E. Panetta, D-Calif.

Before the conference report could even get far enough to be vetoed, Panetta said, it would have difficulty passing the House, where only 44 Republicans had voted for the much smaller House bill May 14.

The decision to defy the administration was out of character for the appropriators, who had compromised with OMB on recent supplemental spending bills to avoid just such a showdown.

Indeed, parties to the pre-conference negotiations said they were holding talks with OMB and were on the verge of confecting a deal when they got signals from House and Senate leaders to insist on the big bill. Some who were involved in the negotiations said Senate Majority Leader Mitchell orchestrated the hard-line strategy, but Mitchell strongly denied it.

"What you're saying is a complete fabrication," said Mitchell when asked about that version of events. "There's never been a deal." Mitchell noted that the Senate bill had strong support from Senate Republicans. "In order for this to be true, it would assume that I somehow control Republican senators," Mitchell said.

Nonetheless, a senior House member insisted privately that Mitchell was "the driving force" behind the decision to confront the Bush administration with the Senate bill and invite a veto.

"We were a millimeter away from an agreement," said the member. The deal would have adopted the House version of the bill, plus $500 million of the $675 million the Senate had added for summer youth jobs. Negotiators would have had to drop at least $750 million for summer school programs and the Weed and Seed initiative; they also would have had to agree to take up an urban enterprise zones initiative backed by the White House to employ tax breaks to attract jobs to inner-city areas.

Resistance to the compromise crumbled after House vote-counters discovered they could not pass the $2 billion bill in the House, which had originally approved only a $494.7 million aid package. Faced with that fact, leaders accepted the White House compromise. "That's pretty much the explanation," House Speaker Thomas S. Foley, D-Wash, told reporters.

As they had on other fiscal issues earlier in the year, rank-and-file Democrats seemed more fiscally conservative than their leaders, bridling at the prospect of an urban aid bill that would have added $2 billion to the deficit.

The downsizing of the bill was not an unalloyed partisan victory, since many Senate Republicans had strongly supported the larger bill.

As part of the bargain, House Majority Leader Richard A. Gephardt, D-Mo., pledged the House leadership's intention to bring legislation to the floor before the July Fourth recess to create the urban enterprise zones.

Rep. Vin Weber, R-Minn., called that pledge excessively vague, saying Republicans should have held out for a more specific commitment. "I think we've given away our best leverage," he said of the GOP agreement to pass the urban aid bill. "This is a political win for the Democrats."

Negotiators approved the stripped-down $1.1 billion version behind the scenes and then brought it straight to the floors of both the House and the Senate. That avoided having to reconvene the conference.

As cleared, key provisions in the urban relief bill provided:

● **SBA disaster loans.** $169.7 million in emergency spending to subsidize up to $500 million in direct loans. Of this money, $50.9 million in spending and $150 million in loans was to be held in reserve, available only on further request by the president.

● **SBA business loans.** $70.3 million for SBA's regular business loan program, which would leverage $1.45 billion in loans. The non-emergency money was to be offset by money Congress had rescinded from other programs earlier in the year.

● **FEMA disaster relief.** $300 million in emergency spending for FEMA.

● **Summer jobs.** $500 million for summer jobs for young people. Of the total, $100 million was earmarked for the nation's 75 largest cities. The other $400 million was to be distributed according to the existing formula for summer youth jobs.

Acting House Appropriations Committee Chairman William H. Natcher, D-Ky., said the money would provide an additional 360,000 jobs for youth during the summer. ■

# Funds Swiftly Committed to Disaster Relief

Just 10 days after President Bush asked for the money and less than a month after Hurricane Andrew flattened parts of Florida and Louisiana, Congress cleared an $11.1 billion aid package for victims of that storm and two others in Hawaii and Guam.

The bill also included an additional $4.1 billion for unrelated defense programs and $500 million in urban aid, with most of the defense money going for wrap-up costs of Operation Desert Shield/Desert Storm. The bill returned to the Treasury most of a special $15 billion account that Congress had provided to pay war-related costs not met by U.S. allies.

The supplemental originally had begun as a catchall, $7.5 billion defense-spending measure that was passed by the House on July 28.

But when killer storms hit three states and the island territory of Guam after the House passed the original bill but before the Senate could take it up, the measure changed dramatically.

Hurricane Andrew raged through parts of Florida and Louisiana in late August, while halfway around the world, Typhoon Omar wreaked havoc on Guam. Bush asked for a package of aid for storm victims on Sept. 8, and a House measure was introduced Sept. 9. But without waiting for House Appropriations to act, the Senate Appropriations Committee grafted its own $7.5 billion aid measure onto the House-passed defense supplemental Sept. 10.

The very next day, Hurricane Iniki roared across Hawaii's "Garden Isle" of Kauai. Four days after that, on Sept. 15, the full Senate took up the committee-passed disaster/defense bill and added $3 billion in direct assistance, loans and loan guarantees, more than $1.2 billion of it for Hawaii.

The House never passed its own separate disaster supplemental. Instead, appropriators from both chambers went straight to conference.

Two potentially crippling controversies — whether to rebuild hurricane-devastated Homestead Air Force Base in South Florida and whether to retain bill language blocking enforcement of disputed labor regulations on the use of "helpers" on federally funded construction projects — were resolved before final passage of the conference report.

Democrats agreed to drop the labor regulations provision, which had provoked a veto threat. A compromise on Homestead provided just enough money to clean up the base and restore the airfield to working order, while leaving a decision on rebuilding to the Base Closure and Realignment Commission in 1993.

Conferees worked behind closed doors Sept. 17 and 18 before producing the final compromise, which was agreed to by the House the same day on a voice vote and cleared

## BOXSCORE

➡ **Fiscal 1992 Disaster/Defense Supplemental (HR 5620).** The bill provided $11.1 billion in aid for storm-stricken Florida, Hawaii and Guam, plus $4.1 billion in unrelated defense spending and $500,000 in urban aid.

### KEY ACTION

July 21 — The **House** Appropriations Committee passed HR 5620 by voice vote.

July 28 — The **House** passed HR 5620, 297-124.

Sept. 10 — The **Senate** Appropriations Committee passed HR 5620, 26-0.

Sept. 15 — The **Senate** passed HR 5620, 84-10.

Sept. 18 — **House-Senate** conferees agreed to a conference report; **House** adopted by voice vote; **Senate** cleared, also by voice vote.

Sept. 23 — President Bush signed HR 5620 — PL 102-368.

later that day by the Senate, also on a voice vote.

The impending congressional and presidential elections and the broad willingness to extend aid to storm victims in so many different areas helped propel the bill much more quickly than the year's other supplemental. That measure (HR 5132) to provide disaster relief to riot-torn Los Angeles and flood-damaged Chicago and urban aid to other cities took six weeks to move to the president's desk, dogged by fights over urban aid and a veto showdown over the size of the bill.

## HOUSE COMMITTEE ACTION

The House Appropriations Committee approved the original, $7.5 billion supplemental spending bill (HR 5620) on July 21 to close out the account for the war in the Persian Gulf and provide billions in new funding for military pay, equipment refurbishment and other war-related items.

The bill, passed by voice vote, returned to the Treasury $12.5 billion that Congress had put in a special fund to pay the U.S. share of the cost of Operation Desert Shield/Desert Storm. A total of $15 billion was appropriated to the fund in March 1991. With the fund closed out, the net cost of the war to U.S. taxpayers — beyond what would have otherwise been spent on U.S. military forces — was calculated at $7.4 billion, including money from the fund plus other U.S. money shifted to war costs in the early stages of the effort to free Kuwait. *(1991 Almanac, p. 680)*

According to committee figures, U.S. allies paid for the vast majority of the war's costs. Allied contributions amounted to $48.1 billion in cash and $5.7 billion in in-kind assistance. Appropriators put the total cost of the conflict at $61.1 billion (the figures do not add because they are rounded).

In addition to covering war-related costs, the bill was designed to provide additional fiscal 1992 appropriations for a variety of military and non-military purposes, including environmental restoration of defense installations, the cost of defender services in federal trials and a U.S. contribution for international peacekeeping forces.

Taken together, the bill was a complicated and confusing hodgepodge of new, transferred and canceled spending that moved more than $20 billion around the fiscal landscape to achieve net new spending of about $7.5 billion.

Most of the spending was requested by the Bush administration, much of it as part of the ordinary fiscal housekeeping process in which the government provided new money or reshuffled previous appropriations to meet costs that were larger than expected or were not anticipated at

all when the fiscal year began Oct. 1, 1991.

This bill departed from the pattern set by most recent supplemental spending bills in that it required almost no emergency spending exempt from the caps set by the 1990 budget agreement. The only emergency money was $30 million proposed for drought relief in California and other Western states, money that could be spent only if the president agreed to designate it as emergency funds.

The bill also included $737 million in mandatory spending for unemployment insurance and a cost-of-living increase for veterans. Under 1990 budget rules, mandatory spending that met existing program requirements fell outside the appropriations caps and did not require an emergency exemption.

The major reason appropriators did not need emergency designation for the bulk of the bill was that they had a huge pot of money outside the normal budget process to draw from — the remains of the $15 billion in U.S. funds appropriated for the war and what was left of billions more contributed by allies.

Before closing out both the U.S.-funded Persian Gulf Regional Defense Fund and the allies' Defense Cooperation Account, appropriators took out $5.2 billion to pay for lingering costs of the gulf war. Of that money, roughly $2.9 billion came from the allies and $2.2 billion from the United States.

Appropriators used the money to pay for a variety of expenses they said stemmed from the war. The largest item was $3.2 billion in maintenance costs, primarily to repair and refurbish equipment worn or damaged during the conflict. Another $1.6 billion was to go for war-related regular pay and separation pay for military personnel.

Other military costs unrelated to the war were to be paid for by tapping unused 1992 defense money. These items included a little more than $1 billion for environmental restoration of defense facilities, $80.1 million for replacement of the Pentagon heating and cooling plant and $3.4 million to expedite the investigation of sexual harassment at the Navy's infamous Tailhook convention. *(Women in the military, p. 519)*

## FLOOR ACTION

The House approved the $7.5 billion supplemental July 28, but only after narrowly defeating a Republican-led effort to force a vote on giving the president a line-item veto. Passage of the spending bill came on a 297-124 vote.

Earlier, the Democratic leadership prevailed, 207-199, on a procedural vote that barred Republicans from changing the rules for debate in a way that would have allowed them to offer the line-item veto amendment. The close vote was a sign of heightened election-year jitters over congressional spending. Members went on to approve the rule itself on a 230-174 vote. *(Votes 326, 323, 324, pp. 78-H, 80-H)*

A second fight flared briefly over a provision in the supplemental that would have prevented the Labor Department from enforcing controversial regulations permitting the use of low-paid "helpers" on federally funded construction projects. Efforts to strike the language failed, and its inclusion drew a veto threat from the White House.

Acting Appropriations Committee Chairman William H. Natcher, D-Ky., stressed that the bill fell entirely within spending guidelines agreed to in the 1990 budget summit, largely because budget negotiators had agreed to put the costs of the war in the Persian Gulf outside the budget caps.

Critics of the measure charged that appropriators were actually using part of the $12.5 billion in U.S. war funds that they said were going back to the Treasury to offset the bill's non-war-related defense spending. But Natcher denied that, insisting the entire $12.5 billion would be returned to the Treasury untouched and that the non-war-related defense costs fell within normal 1992 spending caps.

In early skirmishing over the rule governing floor debate, Rules Committee ranking Republican Gerald B. H. Solomon of New York urged members to change the rule so they could vote squarely on the line-item veto. Proponents argued that the president could save significant amounts of money if he were able to veto individual line items in appropriations bills, rather than having to veto an entire bill to get at a few items.

Solomon's proposal would have permitted the president to line out funds in any 1993 appropriations bill. Congress could then vote by simple majority to disapprove that act, but if the president then vetoed the disapproval, it would have taken a two-thirds vote by the House and the Senate to restore the funds. Critics argued that that would constitute a radical shift of spending power from Congress to the president.

In later debate, Texas Democrat Charles W. Stenholm sought to drop the bill's provision on helpers on federally funded construction projects subject to the Davis-Bacon Act.

Stenholm objected to deciding such an important issue as an afterthought to a spending bill, but he went on to argue that the use of low-paid helpers eventually would save $600 million a year in federal construction costs.

House Education and Labor Committee Chairman William D. Ford, D-Mich., said the helper rule would subvert the intent of Davis-Bacon — which required federal contractors to pay the locally prevailing wage, usually interpreted to mean union scale — by undercutting local construction wages and promoting "more sub-wage jobs for untrained people."

Stenholm's motion to strike the provision failed on a 172-242 roll call vote. *(Vote 325, p. 80-H)*

## SENATE COMMITTEE ACTION

Congress left for its August recess after the House passed the defense supplemental. By the time it got back, matters had changed radically. In late August, parts of Florida and Louisiana were devastated by Hurricane Andrew, while halfway around the world, Typhoon Omar rampaged across Guam.

Bush called for a $7.7 billion relief package on Sept. 8. Then House Appropriations Committee Chairman Jamie L. Whitten, D-Miss., introduced an $8.8 billion package on Sept. 9.

Traditionally, House Appropriations initiated action on spending bills, but Senate appropriators did not stand on ceremony. On Sept. 10, the Senate Appropriations Committee took up the House-passed defense supplemental, added its own $7.5 billion relief package for storm victims and passed the measure on a vote of 26-0.

All three relief proposals were similar combinations of immediate assistance for storm victims and longer-term help for rebuilding storm-damaged areas. Speedy agreement on a consensus measure seemed likely, but Senate Appropriations signalled trouble when members voted 12-8 before passing the relief proposal Sept. 10 to reject a criti-

cal portion of the package — a proposal by Bush to rebuild Homestead Air Force Base, which was badly damaged by Hurricane Andrew.

Backers of the reconstruction argued that Homestead was critical to the economy of hurricane-devastated South Florida, and that it filled an important role as a base for drug-interdiction efforts and for monitoring the hostile regime in Cuba.

But opponents of the plan to devote more than $480 million in emergency funds as a partial payment for the reconstruction tab argued that Homestead was high on the list of bases likely to be recommended for shutdown by the Base Closure and Realignment Commission in 1993, and as such represented a bad investment.

"This crowd's got to sober up," said committee member Ernest F. Hollings, D-S.C. "You can't be throwing around a half a billion dollars because you feel sorry for Florida ... let's use the money for other things."

Nine committee Democrats joined three Republicans in agreeing to an amendment by Harry Reid, D-Nev., that removed all but $26 million of the Homestead money, leaving just enough for demolition, cleanup and preparation of a master plan for the possible rebuilding of the base.

Jim Sasser, D-Tenn., chairman of the Military Construction Appropriations Subcommittee and an opponent of the Reid amendment, warned after the vote that Bush likely would veto the measure if it cleared Congress without the Homestead reconstruction funds.

The measure also carried two other poison pills that made it certain veto bait.

One was the House-passed provision to permanently prohibit the Department of Labor from enforcing new "helper" regulations on federally funded construction projects covered by the Davis-Bacon Act. The other was a provision that would have put a moratorium on enforcement of Bush administration regulations barring abortion counseling in federally funded family planning clinics.

Save for those provisions and the deletion of the Homestead money, however, the $7.5 billion Senate aid bill closely paralleled the $7.7 billion proposal the administration unveiled Sept. 8. Each earmarked roughly two-thirds of its appropriated spending for grants and other direct assistance and about one-third for loans and loan guarantees. Each also devoted the lion's share of the money to Florida, which was hardest hit by Hurricane Andrew.

Each devoted the largest single chunk of money — about $1.9 billion — to the Federal Emergency Management Agency (FEMA), with smaller but significant amounts for various Defense Department activities, Department of Agriculture crop loss relief and Small Business Administration efforts to get businesses back on their feet.

The Senate Appropriations Committee sliced some $454 million out of the amount originally proposed for Homestead, but added back more than $350 million in other areas. J. Bennett Johnston, D-La., won passage of an amendment that added $100 million for aquaculture crop loss relief — including aid to farmers of crawfish, catfish and oysters in Louisiana.

Daniel K. Inouye, D-Hawaii, added $198 million in military construction funds for damaged military facilities on Guam. Johnston also added $55 million for the Economic Development Administration. None of that extra money was included in Bush's request.

The $8.8 billion package introduced by House Appropriations Chairman Whitten included most of the spending categories outlined in the Bush and Senate Appropriations

proposals but would have added more money to several of them. FEMA, for instance, would have gotten $2.5 billion instead of the $1.9 billion in the White House and Senate proposals. The House measure would have boosted crop loss relief administered by the Commodity Credit Corporation to $520 million, instead of the $320 million in the other two packages. The House bill also contained $400 million for food stamps, money not included in either of the other two packages.

Whatever the final shape of the relief package, it looked as if Congress and the White House would be able to avoid the usual fight over how to pay for it. Technically, the bill's domestic spending proposals would exceed spending caps and trigger a punitive, across-the-board spending cut known as a sequester.

But in a rare show of unanimity, all sides agreed that the best way to pay the bill would be to designate the spending as an emergency, exempt from the rules, thereby borrowing most of the money and adding it to the deficit.

"It's a classic example of an emergency," said House Speaker Thomas S. Foley, D-Wash.

"Some of it unquestionably will be over the budget," said Bush. "It's a large financial burden. But the personal and human need is even more staggering."

In related action at its Sept. 10 markup, the Senate Appropriations Committee made numerous changes in the underlying defense supplemental previously passed by the House. One of the largest was a decision to turn back to the Treasury $14.7 billion of the $15 billion originally appropriated for the U.S. share of Operation Desert Shield/Desert Storm. The House had voted to return $12.5 billion of the money.

Senate appropriators also added an urban aid title to the combined supplemental bill, voting to pull $500 million in direct spending from a House-passed tax bill (HR 11) and put it instead in the supplemental. The money was to go to a variety of agencies, with the largest single chunk, $300 million, going to the Interagency Council as a block grant for eligible programs.

## SENATE FLOOR ACTION

The day after the Senate Appropriations Committee met, Hurricane Iniki rampaged across Hawaii's "Garden Isle" of Kauai. Four days after that, on Sept. 15, the full Senate took up the committee-passed disaster/defense supplemental and added $3 billion in direct assistance, loans and loan guarantees, more than $1.2 billion of it for Hawaii, with most of the rest going for the re-estimated needs of the victims of Hurricane Andrew in Florida and Louisiana and Typhoon Omar on Guam. The Senate approved the measure by a vote of 84-10. (Vote 206, p. 27-S)

During debate on the measure, the Senate added $1 million impact assistance grant to a Nevada county that Sen. Reid said was left "holding the bag" for a $1 million school bond when the F-117 stealth fighter was moved to New Mexico and defense-related jobs went with it. The Senate also approved economic development assistance for Kansas electric cooperatives damaged during severe storms in June and July.

The Senate rejected an amendment by Sen. Larry E. Craig, R-Idaho, that would have stricken a provision from the bill that barred the use of low-wage "helpers" on federally funded construction projects covered by the Davis-Bacon Act. Craig wanted to allow the Department of Labor to enforce controversial regulations permitting the use of

helpers, and he argued that the practice would save the federal government billions in construction costs. But pro-labor Democrats argued that use of helpers would undermine the apprenticeship program among skilled construction workers and lead to shoddy construction. The Senate voted 37-58 to reject the amendment. *(Vote 205, p. 27-S)*

## FINAL ACTION

With an election looming and sympathy strong for victims of the killer storms, Congress acted quickly to finish up the disaster relief measure bill and its companion defense provisions.

Just 10 days after Bush asked for the money and less than a month after the onslaught of Hurricanes Andrew and Iniki and Typhoon Omar, Congress cleared an $11.1 billion aid package for the storms' victims.

Final approval of the disaster relief bill, which carried with it $4.1 billion for unrelated defense programs and $500 million for urban aid, came on Sept. 18. The House passed the measure by voice vote, and the Senate cleared the legislation for the president later the same day, also by voice vote. Bush signed the bill five days later, on Sept. 23.

The final compromise was worked out in an informal, closed-door conference between Senate, House and administration participants Sept. 17 and 18.

Clearing the two sticking points in the bill paved the way for final passage:

● Although appropriators feared Bush would veto the bill if it did not include the full $480.6 million he wanted as a down payment on the cost of rebuilding South Florida's Homestead Air Force Base, the veto threat did not materialize. Bush wanted the base rebuilt to help the shattered South Florida economy recover, but critics said the base was high on the list of military installations likely to be recommended for shutdown by the Base Closure and Realignment Commission in 1993. The $92 million provided in the compromise bill was enough to demolish damaged buildings, clean up the base, restore the airfield to working order and draw up a preliminary plan for possible reconstruction.

● The White House did issue an unequivocal veto threat against the provision in the measure that would have blocked the Department of Labor from enforcing controversial "helper" regulations. The regulations allowed contractors to pay non-skilled helpers less than the prevailing wage on federally funded construction projects subject to the Davis-Bacon Act. Numerous pro-labor Democrats wanted the language in the bill, but House leaders concluded that Bush would carry through with a veto if it were retained. Although Democrats changed the permanent ban to a temporary one in an attempt at compromise, the White House's Office of Management and Budget (OMB) did not drop the veto threat, and House Democrats agreed to back off when the disaster package came to the floor.

John P. Murtha, D-Pa., chairman of the House Defense Appropriations Subcommittee and a foe of the helper regulations, said a decision to avoid veto conflicts with OMB on the regular 1993 spending bills put Democrats at a disadvantage. "This idea that we're going to agree to everything gives OMB and secretary general [OMB Director Richard G.] Darman all the power in the world," he complained.

The bill moved with unusual speed through a process that had snared other measures. The last time Congress produced an emergency aid package — a measure (HR 5132 — PL 102-302) in the spring to help rebuild riot-torn Los Angeles and flood-damaged Chicago — it took six weeks and a veto standoff to get the money approved. *(Urban aid supplemental, p. 579)*

According to the House Appropriations Committee, the final disaster package included $6.3 billion in grants for disaster victims, rebuilding funds and other spending, plus $4.8 billion in various loans and loan guarantees. The lion's share of the money was to go Florida, with smaller amounts for Hawaii, Louisiana and Guam.

Florida's Democratic Gov. Lawton Chiles, who spent considerable time on Capitol Hill lobbying his former Senate colleagues for more aid, pronounced himself reasonably satisfied with the legislation, but he said the state needed still more money to recover. "There will be other supplementals," he said. "Maybe some of those other bills will clean it up."

Major items in the package included nearly $3 billion for FEMA, $400 million for food stamps, $482 million for crop losses and $432 million for the Small Business Administration's disaster loan program. The bill also contained a host of smaller items for agencies ranging from the FBI to the U.S. Travel and Tourism Administration, some of it to replace federal property damaged by the storms, and other funds to help rebuild local economies.

The final bill was a complex hybrid measure built on the defense supplemental originally passed by the House almost a month before any of the storms struck. Those provisions, as modified in the House-Senate compromise on the bill, included $4.1 billion in wrapup spending for the costs of Operation Desert Shield/Desert Storm, almost all of it from funds provided by U.S. allies. The bill would returned to the Treasury nearly $14.7 billion of the $15 billion originally appropriated to cover the U.S. share of the costs of the Persian Gulf War.  ∎

# Bush Calls for Cuts in 'Pork-Barrel' Spending

In a tough, partisan speech on March 20, President Bush sharply criticized Congress' "pork-barrel" spending practices and unveiled a plan to force repeated votes on his proposals to rescind previously appropriated fiscal 1992 spending.

In the speech, Bush singled out for ridicule several projects from an initial list of 68 that he challenged Congress to kill. Included were funds for local parking garages and research on asparagus-yield declines, meat and prickly pears. Nearly $3 billion of Bush's $3.6 billion in proposed fiscal 1992 cutbacks were to come from canceling construction of two *Seawolf* submarines, a proposal Bush did not mention.

"The examples would be funny if the effect weren't so serious," Bush said. "Americans have every right to be outraged and disgusted. It's their money."

Bush and congressional "porkbusters" wanted to force individual, politically embarrassing votes on each of the rescission proposals, and they planned to keep peppering congressional Democrats with new rescission proposals every week to keep the issue alive.

But bipartisan anger among congressional appropriators eventually squelched that plan. Bush ultimately sent four separate groups of rescissions worth about $7.9 billion to Capitol Hill, but the White House backed away from its plan to keep sending a package a week. Although Bush highlighted domestic projects when he made his spending-cut proposals, the vast majority of his cuts — $7.1 billion of the $7.9 billion total — was to come from defense programs.

Congressional Republicans kept the pressure on the appropriators by threatening to invoke an obscure rule that permitted a minority in the House and Senate to force the rescissions out of the Appropriations committees if the panels had not acted within 25 days of continuous session. Allowing for various recesses, that gave the committees until early May to act.

House and Senate appropriators assembled two different rescission packages, accepting some of Bush's proposals, but rejecting many of the items he wanted to cut and adding others the president wanted to protect.

The key controversy came over funds Bush wanted to cut for the *Seawolf* nuclear submarine, which critics said was conceived to meet a Soviet submarine threat that no longer existed. Bush wanted to cut nearly $3 billion for construction of the second and third subs, but House Appropriations voted to preserve money for one and Senate Appropriations voted to keep the money for both. Democrats and Republicans alike rallied to protect submarine-building jobs in Connecticut and Rhode Island.

Both committees were careful to produce spending cuts

---

## BOXSCORE

➡ **Fiscal 1992 Rescissions (HR 4990, S 2403).** The legislation authorized the cutting of $8.2 billion in previously appropriated spending. President Bush's proposal was to rescind $8 billion.
**Reports:** H Rept 102-505; conference report H Rept 102-530.

### KEY ACTION

May 6 — The **Senate** passed S 2403, 61-38.

May 7 — The **House** passed HR 4990, 412-2.

May 12 — The **Senate** amended HR 4990 with the text of S 2403 and then passed HR 4990 by voice vote.

May 20 — Approved by **House-Senate** conference as HR 4990.

May 21 — Conference report adopted by the **House**, 404-11; the **Senate** cleared the conference report, 90-9.

June 4 — President Bush signed HR 4990 — PL 102-298.

---

that exceeded those requested by Bush. The House panel, which began assembling a bill before Bush had sent all his proposals to the Hill, produced a $5.8 billion package on April 29 that exceeded the $5.7 billion total of Bush's first three rescission packages. Senate Appropriations approved an $8.3 billion bill on April 30 that topped the $7.9 billion total of all four of Bush's proposals.

After the Senate passed its bill May 6 and the House approved its measure May 7, both sides convened a contentious House-Senate conference to produce a compromise package. Negotiators reached quick agreement on most of the small items but stalled over the big-ticket defense programs.

The hangup concerned how many *Seawolf* submarines to cut, and whether and how much to cut administration-backed funding for the Strategic Defense Initiative (SDI) and the B-2 bomber.

In the end, the conferees opted to save one of the *Seawolf* subs that Bush wanted to cut, insisted on a cutback in SDI and rejected trims in dozens of the domestic projects that Bush ridiculed in his March 20 speech. The $8.2 billion package exceeded Bush's $7.9 billion in rescission requests, and it gave Democrats a chance to cut what they called "executive-branch pork," more than $2 million worth of projects that included a study of sexual aggression in Nicaraguan fish.

House and Senate passage of the conference report on May 21 came by big margins that masked GOP disappointment that the cut-by-cut voting strategy had been abandoned. But Republicans claimed victory nonetheless.

Rep. Gerald B. Solomon, R-N.Y., said that any time Congress got into a bidding war with the White House over cutting rather than increasing spending, that had to be considered a win, even if Bush did not get exactly what he wanted.

## BACKGROUND

Presidential proposals to rescind previously appropriated spending were nothing new. From the time the so-called rescission process was put in place by the 1974 Budget Act through the day before Bush's first 1992 rescission package came to Capitol Hill on March 10, presidents had sent Congress $61.4 billion in spending-cut proposals. Congress approved only $19.3 billion of those, but together with another $43.8 billion of its own rescissions, Congress enacted cuts worth $63.1 billion — nearly $2 billion more than the White House had proposed.

What was new about the plan by Bush and the mostly Republican congressional "pork-busters" was the aim to make a highly partisan issue out of the cuts by sending

Congress scores of rescission proposals and then attempting to force a series of politically embarrassing votes on each of the cuts between then and the fall elections.

A president's authority to rescind spending was quite weak. He might propose rescissions and freeze the relevant funds, but if Congress ignored the proposals, they expired after 45 days and the money had to be spent.

In practice, Congress had usually felt politically compelled to respond to presidential rescission proposals. This time was essentially no different but for GOP plans to raise the political stakes. Republicans threatened to make use of an obscure rule that allowed one-fifth of either the House or the Senate to move to discharge the Appropriations committees from considering rescission proposals if the panels had not sent the proposals to the floor within 25 days of continuous session. With a timeout for the Easter recess in mid-April, floor battles over the spending cuts were set to begin in May.

Bush picked his rescission proposals from a list of 1,391 potential cuts identified by the White House's Office of Management and Budget (OMB).

Congressional Republicans initially said OMB would pick and choose from the $1.2 billion worth of projects on the list and send up a new batch every week or so. But sharp, bipartisan criticism from congressional appropriators and bitter warnings from Senate Appropriations Chairman Robert C. Byrd, D-W.Va., that the game would hurt both sides apparently caused the White House to reassess those plans.

In the end, Bush sent up four groups of cuts worth $7.9 billion, and there was a broad, bipartisan agreement that Congress should match or exceed that total.

The spending cuts that drew the most attention were the ones Bush proposed on March 20, and although the president characterized the projects on his list as congressional pork, the vast majority of the $3.6 billion in that package of rescission proposals — nearly $3 billion of the total — would have come from canceling construction of the second and third *Seawolf* submarines, a project originally requested by the White House.

Another $547.7 million was to be taken out of public housing construction, funding that was approved by Congress with bipartisan support but over which Congress and the Bush administration had deep philosophical differences.

The remaining $86 million in savings was to come from 65 spending cuts that ranged in size from $20 million to $39,000. The White House list tilted toward projects sponsored by Democrats, but not exclusively. According to an analysis assembled by congressional aides, the targeted projects were connected in some way — such as personal request or location — to 45 individual members and four state delegations, including 17 Republicans.

Among the Republicans were some heavyweights: Senate Minority Leader Bob Dole of Kansas was to lose funding for a University of Kansas study grant; and Pete V. Domenici of New Mexico, ranking Republican on the Senate Budget Committee, was to lose funding for a municipal center in Bloomfield, N.M., and for a research project on jojoba oil.

The list of affected Democrats was almost twice as long, with 28 targeted to lose at least one project. Senate Appropriations Chairman Byrd was to lose $800,000 in funding for a project to conduct economic and market analysis and some product development for Appalachian hardwoods. House VA-HUD Appropriations Subcommittee Chair-

man Bob Traxler, D-Mich., led the list of targeted Democrats, with seven projects proposed for cuts, ranging from a $20 million Environmental Protection Agency research and training facility in Bay City, Mich., to a $39,000 project to develop fusarium wilt-resistant celery germplasm at East Lansing, Mich.

## HOUSE COMMITTEE ACTION

When the House Appropriations Committee's Democratic subcommittee chairmen began putting together their own rescissions package in early April, Bush had sent Congress three groups of proposals that totaled $5.7 billion, with most of the cuts coming in a March 10 defense package and the higher-profile March 20 package Bush unveiled in his speech.

The House appropriators were determined to top that total by about $100 million, and some Democrats warned that while they would be happy to more than match the president dollar for dollar, they might cut some programs the administration would not want to see trimmed.

House appropriators were working against a procedural deadline that was expected to fall on May 6, when just one-fifth of the House's members could vote to discharge from the Appropriations Committee any or all of Bush's scores of rescission proposals.

Eleven of the 13 House Appropriations subcommittees met April 8-9 to put together spending-cut proposals that would meet or exceed the subcommittee-by-subcommittee dollar totals in Bush's proposals.

Just as the subcommittees were completing work April 9, the White House sent up another package of 28 rescission proposals totaling $2.2 billion, all of them defense cuts. The committee wound up deferring consideration of that package until the House-Senate conference met in May.

House committee staff assembled the subcommittee recommendations into a bill and a report over the Easter recess, and the full committee took up the measure April 29, voting by voice to approve the $5.8 billion package of cuts.

With the vast bulk of Bush's proposed cuts coming from defense programs, it was no surprise that the biggest difference between the Bush administration and the appropriators turned on what to do about the two enormously expensive *Seawolf* nuclear submarines, which were designed before the collapse of the Soviet Union to counter a submarine fleet that was no longer considered a threat.

Bush wanted to kill nearly $3 billion for construction of the second and third *Seawolf* subs, but House Appropriations voted to preserve money for one of the craft.

The fight over the *Seawolf* symbolized the political difficulties of cutting defense to suit the new, post-Soviet world order.

After years of agitating for defense cuts, some congressional Democrats found themselves fighting to save multi-billion-dollar weapons systems, at least in part to protect jobs at hometown defense plants. Some of the strongest support for the *Seawolf* came from liberal Democrats in Connecticut, where the subs were built.

Jobs were barely mentioned during the public Appropriations deliberations, however. Instead, the decisions to continue building the subs appeared to turn on the arcane economics of defense contracting.

House Defense Appropriations Subcommittee Chairman John P. Murtha, D-Pa., said the money already spent on the second *Seawolf*, plus what it would cost to terminate

that contract, made it uneconomical not to go ahead and build the sub. He added, though, that building a third sub would not make sense.

To keep money for one of the submarines, the House panel opted to substitute $1.7 billion in cuts in research, development, testing and evaluation.

Despite the tense partisanship that surrounded the exercise, the House Appropriations markup saw comparatively little party bickering. John T. Myers of Indiana, who was filling in as ranking Republican due to the temporary absence of Joseph M. McDade of Pennsylvania, urged his colleagues to support the committee bill. "This is something that's absolutely necessary," he said. "I think we have little choice."

About the only partisan flare-up came during committee debate on an amendment by Jerry Lewis, R-Calif., that would have stricken $41.7 million in "excess funds" that Lewis argued amounted to a "Speaker's slush fund" controlled by House Speaker Thomas S. Foley, D-Wash.

Lewis said language adopted by the committee in a prior year allowed unspent money under the jurisdiction of the Legislative Branch Subcommittee to accumulate and become available for purposes other than what it was appropriated for.

But Legislative Branch Subcommittee Chairman Vic Fazio, D-Calif., disagreed. "There's no slush fund here," he said. "That's an old canard that's been kicking around for years." Fazio said that under mutually agreed upon procedures, the money could be spent for other purposes only if the target program had been authorized and both he and Lewis agreed to the reprogramming.

The committee defeated Lewis' amendment on a voice vote, and Lewis declined to ask for a show of hands or a roll call.

Not so Norm Dicks, D-Wash., who insisted on a show of hands in his attempt to restore $1.4 million for a park in the Calumet Historic District in Michigan. Dicks argued that the park was supported by the National Park Service and the governor of Michigan, but Interior Appropriations Subcommittee Chairman Sidney R. Yates, D-Ill., said the project had not been authorized and that its total cost was as much as $30 million to $40 million. Dicks lost, 6-30.

### Subcommittee Cuts

Cuts made by the committee's subcommittees included the following:

● **Commerce, Justice, State:** Bush proposed $21.4 million in cuts from programs under the jurisdiction of this panel — $14 million for a U.S. broadcast relay station in Israel and $7.4 million for public telecommunications facilities grants for the Commerce Department.

● **Defense:** At $4.8 billion, the Defense Subcommittee had the highest rescission target, nearly $3 billion of which was to come from canceling construction of the second and third *Seawolf* submarines. The subcommittee opted instead to preserve $1 billion in funding for one submarine while cutting $1.9 billion for another.

● **Foreign Operations:** The subcommittee had no rescission target under the Bush proposals but decided to propose about $100 million in cuts anyway. Some of the cuts were said to come out of aid to Peru that the administration suspended the week of April 6 in the wake of President Alberto Fujimori's decision to dissolve the Peruvian Congress. A member of the subcommittee said the panel's cuts "won't have an impact on foreign policy, but they will save the taxpayers' money."

● **Interior:** The panel went beyond its $24.1 million target, proposing $28.7 million in rescissions.

The subcommittee ignored Bush's request for cuts of $5.9 million in an Indian business grant program and $2 million in a native Hawaiian Cultural and Arts Program.

The bulk of the panel's cuts, $16.3 million, came from rescissions proposed by Bush for Indian reservation road sealing (which staffers said would come from national highway funds) and for renovation projects in Perth Amboy, Trenton and Paterson, N.J.

Additional cuts came from the Calumet Historic District project in Michigan and historic trails projects in Iowa, Nebraska and Utah.

● **Labor-HHS:** In the jurisdiction of the Labor-HHS Subcommittee, Bush proposed to trim $25 million from health professions programs, which provided funds to medical and other specialty schools to help train doctors, nurses and other health workers. Both the Reagan and Bush administrations had been trying to eliminate many of these items for years.

The subcommittee's response, drawn up by panel chairman William H. Natcher, D-Ky., and ranking Republican Carl D. Pursell, Mich., was to save $19 million by trimming 1 percent off the roughly $2 billion in "delayed obligations" that were not supposed to become available until Sept. 30.

The remaining $6 million reduction was to come from trimming the number of full-time employees the Public Health Service may hire.

● **Legislative Branch:** The Legislative Branch Subcommittee had no rescission proposals on the Bush list, but the panel opted to cut about $20 million from their franking privileges, which allowed free mailing to constituents.

● **Transportation:** The Transportation Subcommittee needed to find $9.9 million to meet its target. Bush had proposed to cut local rail-freight assistance, an $11.5 million federal program established in 1973 to allow continuation of local freight service on lines abandoned by national shippers. The administration typically recommended zeroing out the program, but appropriators routinely rescued it.

The subcommittee took only $5 million from the program, with the remainder coming from unused funds from a program that until 1978 reimbursed states for money that they had spent to build roads over federal dam projects.

● **VA-HUD:** The subcommittee exceeded its $623.8 million target. It rejected Bush's proposed $547.7 million cut in funds for construction of new public housing, substituting a 4 percent, across-the-board cut in assisted housing, including cuts in public housing, Section 8 vouchers and certificates, the HOME Investment Partnerships program, the Home Ownership and Opportunity for People Everywhere program, known as HOPE, and flexible subsidies for financially troubled Section 8 projects.

The subcommittee also cut EPA construction grants by 1 percent for each grant, which cut $24 million from the $2.4 billion in EPA's waste-water construction grants program. The $13 million 1992 appropriation for NASA's Search for Extraterrestrial Intelligence program would be cut by $4 million.

## SENATE COMMITTEE ACTION

Senate Appropriations acted virtually simultaneously with its House counterpart, voting 19-9 on April 30 — one day after House Appropriations voted on its bill — to approve an $8.3 billion package of spending cuts (S 2403).

While the House bill covered only three of Bush's rescission packages, the Senate measure covered all four, which totaled $7.9 billion.

Senate Appropriations Chairman Byrd had promised to give the president's suggestions full consideration, but he warned that the Senate would "look elsewhere as well" for ways to cut spending, and he said he would work to block any efforts to tie up the Senate with individual votes on every one of the president's proposed cuts.

"That would be chaos, when one considers the time that would be involved in that sort of foolishness and frivolity," he said.

"They're not going to get a separate vote on items over here," he said, warning that appropriators would "wean the White House" of any notion of doing that by reminding the administration that "this is a two-way street," and that the White House could suffer from the process as well.

"This started out as a Congress-bashing exercise," Byrd said, adding that whether it ended in spending-cut compromises or mutually destructive political warfare "depends on how much hardball they [the White House] want to play."

During committee markup action, Senate appropriators were much more aggressive than their House counterparts in warning the White House that this was a fight both sides could lose. The committee proposed to slash funding for such administration-backed projects as the B-2 bomber and SDI. In an especially personal touch, the committee voted to cut $400,000 in funding for renovation of the vice presidential mansion.

"I hope they'll see ... that Congress, while it doesn't want to play this game, can play this game," said Byrd. "It might be the better part of wisdom not to push this thing."

The Senate panel ended up rejecting Bush's proposal to kill funding for the two *Seawolf* subs. Senate Defense Appropriations Subcommittee Chairman Daniel K. Inouye, D-Hawaii, argued that all the costs of terminating the *Seawolf* contracts and ending construction could reach as high as $4.4 billion — much more than the nearly $3 billion required to keep building the subs.

To make up for the Seawolf money, the Senate panel substituted several cuts in big-ticket defense programs, many of them strongly backed by the White House. Included in the proposed rescissions were:

● $1.3 billion for SDI.
● $1 billion for one B-2 bomber.
● $564.9 million for various *Seawolf* components, some of which were for a sixth submarine.
● $528.5 million for the advanced cruise missile and the Peacekeeper (MX) missile.
● $207 million for M1-A2 tank production and related costs.
● $131 million for the national aerospace plane technology program.

The tradeoffs angered some Republican senators. Jake Garn of Utah said he wanted to protect funds for the Seawolf, but not at the expense of star wars. Ted Stevens of Alaska, ranking Republican on the Defense Appropriations Subcommittee, said he opposed building the submarine and could not support a bill that would "bring to a halt" the work on star wars.

Domenici said he and some other committee Republicans would probably recommend that the president veto the bill if it emerged from Congress as approved by the committee. Domenici, Garn and Stevens joined six other committee Republicans to vote against the measure.

But ranking Republican Mark O. Hatfield of Oregon and three other panel Republicans (Alfonse M. D'Amato of New York, Don Nickles of Oklahoma and Warren B. Rudman of New Hampshire) joined Democrats in voting for the bill, signaling that the president would not have solid GOP support in opposing the cuts.

In fact, even some of the Republicans who voted against the measure displayed annoyance with Bush for reopening the previous year's spending decisions and doing it in such a partisan way. "I think it's regrettable that we're in this situation," said Garn. "What the administration is doing is playing a political game .... I hate to see us legislate in that way."

If politics was the game, committee Chairman Byrd was determined to show that he and the Democrats could one-up the president.

During the March 20 speech, Bush alluded to projects such as research on asparagus-yield decline and the prickly pear in explaining why "Americans have every right to be outraged and disgusted" with congressional spenders.

In the April 30 markup session, Byrd shot back with proposals to strip funding for 31 "unnecessary and wasteful" National Science Foundation grants, including money for studies of the sexual aggression of Nicaraguan fish, the importance of lawyers to the middle class and the mating behavior of swordfish.

Likewise, he said the committee would recommend cutting money for National Institutes of Health grants to study such things as why people fear dentists.

"These items were not congressional earmarks; they are not congressional pork," Byrd said. "Rather, they are grants made by ... the executive branch."

"The president opened up a Pandora's box," Byrd added. "The farther down the road it gets, the meaner it's going to get. And it's not going to do the president any good, and it's not going to do this institution any good."

## SENATE FLOOR ACTION

Display of the sort of parliamentary legerdemain for which he was renowned in the Senate, Byrd controlled the floor process so thoroughly that Republicans had virtually no meaningful chances to amend the committee-approved rescission bill.

By a 61-38 vote on May 6, the Senate approved the $8.3 billion rescission package (S 2403) that left in place nearly $3 billion in funding Bush sought to cut for two *Seawolf* submarines, substituting cuts in SDI, the B-2 bomber and other defense projects backed by the administration. *(Vote 85, p. 12-S)*

The administration issued stern warnings that the Senate bill would be veto bait if left unchanged. The administration's veto threat singled out the Senate's cuts in SDI and the B-2, additionally raising strong objections to Senate cuts in the National Aerospace Plane, the National Launch System and some unidentified classified projects.

The Senate's vote on the *Seawolf* funding was decisive but not overwhelming. After heavy lobbying by Connecticut and Rhode Island senators — whose states were home to the shipyards that built the submarines — the Senate rejected, by a 46-52 vote, an amendment by John McCain, R-Ariz., that would have restored Bush's proposal to cut nearly $3 billion to build two of the subs. *(Vote 83, p. 12-S)*

"We literally cannot afford to live in the past," said McCain, arguing that the *Seawolf* was designed to counter a Russian nuclear submarine threat that no longer existed.

Instead, he said, the submarines' enormous costs would rob resources and jobs from other, more vital areas of defense production.

But Senate Defense Appropriations Subcommittee Chairman Inouye argued that the combined costs of equipment already purchased, charges for canceling the construction contracts and federal expenses for shutting down the shipyards could run as much as $3.4 billion to $4.4 billion, exceeding the amount that Bush proposed to save. "There is no savings whatsoever," Inouye said.

Even if McCain had won, it apparently wouldn't have mattered. Byrd had already guaranteed an unamended final bill when he used a parliamentary maneuver to ensure that any amendment that passed would have been wiped out by later passage of his own substitute.

In a grudging compliment to Byrd, Domenici said, "That does not bother the senator from New Mexico.... The rule is, if you do not know the rules, you get stuck by them. If you know the rules, you play by them."

After the House later passed its version of the rescission bill (HR 4990), the Senate took up the House measure on May 12, stripped out the House's numbers and inserted its own bill (S 2403), passed HR 4990 by voice vote and asked to go to conference with the House.

## HOUSE FLOOR ACTION

While Byrd had to resort to parliamentary maneuvering in the Senate, House Democrats used their overwhelming numerical superiority to limit GOP opportunities to change the committee-passed rescissions bill in the House.

Control was so tight that in one case, Democrats even ordered TV cameras turned off in the House Rules Committee to deprive angry Republicans of the opportunity to make their case to a C-SPAN cable TV audience.

By a 412-2 vote on May 7, the House approved a $5.8 billion rescission package (HR 4990) that protected funding for one *Seawolf*, substituting cuts in research, development, test and evaluation and various weapons programs. The vote on final passage was not a true test of House sentiment, however. An earlier vote on whether to substitute Bush's rescissions for those approved by the House Appropriations Committee split almost purely along party lines, 150-266. *(Votes 112, 113, p. 28-H)*

The House bill was smaller than the Senate's because the House considered only three of the four rescission packages Bush sent to Congress, deferring action on the fourth until the House-Senate conference. The $5.8 billion House bill exceeded the $5.7 billion total of Bush's first three spending-cut packages, while the Senate's $8.3 billion bill exceeded the $7.9 billion total of all four Bush proposals.

While the administration warned that the Senate bill was veto bait, it objected to but did not threaten to veto the House bill. House Appropriations ranking Republican McDade said he thought Bush would sign the measure if it were presented to him as the House had passed it.

The key fight was over Bush's proposal to kill funding for two *Seawolf* submarines. While the House had gone halfway by killing money for one, the Senate had insisted on building both subs.

House Defense Appropriations Subcommittee Chairman Murtha said he thought the conference would likely compromise by dropping the Senate's insistence on money for both *Seawolf* submarines, settling for only one. That would free up enough money to restore most of the Sen-

ate's $1.3 billion cut in SDI and the $1 billion cut in the B-2 bomber program, if conferees were so inclined.

During floor consideration, House Democrats controlled events by writing a rule for floor debate that blocked all Republican attempts to amend the bill except one that was virtually guaranteed to lose: the single, either-or vote that would have substituted Bush's original three rescission packages, which added up to fewer dollars in cuts than the committee bill.

Republicans could also have offered a motion to recommit the bill to committee but without instructions as to how to change it.

Rules Committee ranking Republican Solomon challenged the restrictive rule in the committee and on the floor but was outvoted along party lines. He even lost his chance to showcase the Rules Committee debate on C-Span when Martin Frost, D-Texas, objected to the TV cameras and asked that they be turned off. Frost said the hearing was "highly technical" and that the presence of cameras would just prolong debate. Solomon said the move was "outrageous" and moved to have the cameras stay, but he lost on a 2-6 party-line vote.

## CONFERENCE ACTION

House-Senate conferees quickly agreed on most of the small items but stalled over how to cut big-ticket defense programs during conference sessions the week of May 11.

"We're at an impasse," said Murtha, explaining that the House and Senate remained split over how many *Seawolf* submarines to fund and whether to cut spending for SDI and the B-2 bomber.

Republicans suggested that Bush would accept the House's decision to save one *Seawolf*, and the White House had issued a veto threat against the Senate's decision to save both. It was widely believed that the key to a compromise acceptable to Bush was a package that would save one submarine and restore some or all of the funding for SDI and the B-2.

Murtha said there was "reason to believe" the White House would agree to funding for the second of three *Seawolf* subs, but defense conferees could not agree on the necessary trade-offs.

In three meetings May 13 and 14, conferees agreed on a series of cuts in domestic and foreign aid programs that would save $432 million, barely 5 percent of the $8.3 billion overall package. Included were rescissions from eight Appropriations subcommittees: : Commerce-Justice-State, Energy-Water, Foreign Operations, Interior, Labor-HHS, Legislative Branch, Military Construction and Transportation.

Conferees finally compromised on May 20 by agreeing to save only one of the two *Seawolf* submarines Bush proposed to cut, insisting on a cutback in SDI and rejecting trims in dozens of domestic projects that Bush ridiculed when he took Congress to task March 20 for what he said was pork-barrel spending.

The $8.2 billion package made the overwhelming majority of its cuts in defense and exceeded by about $300 million the $7.9 billion in rescissions Bush asked for. In retaliation for Bush's campaign to target congressional pork, appropriators lashed out at what they called "executive-branch pork," proposing more than $2 million in cuts for projects that included a study of sexual aggression in Nicaraguan fish.

Although most of the rhetorical warfare between Bush

and congressional Democrats dealt with domestic spending projects, the largest and most controversial cuts came in defense. Conferees resolved their differences as follows:

● **Seawolf submarines.** In the largest single cut in his $7.9 billion package, Bush proposed to rescind nearly $3 billion for construction of the second and third *Seawolf* subs. The House originally voted to protect money for one of the subs, while the Senate opted to continue funding for both. The conferees compromised by cutting $1.3 billion, which left roughly $1.7 billion, more than enough to finish building the second submarine.

Conferees agreed to set aside $550 million of that on the condition that the secretary of Defense use it to start building a third *Seawolf,* restart production of *Los Angeles*-class submarines, or otherwise protect the industrial base for submarine construction.

● **Strategic Defense Initiative.** In looking for substitute rescissions when it opted to continue funding for the two *Seawolf* subs, the Senate slashed funding for SDI by $1.3 billion, provoking a veto threat. In the end, conferees said they found the Pentagon had already spent $800 million of that money, leaving only $500 million to cut. Conferees opted to rescind $200 million of that.

● **B-2 bomber.** The Senate originally proposed to slash $1 billion for construction of a single B-2 bomber. The conferees cut that in half, agreeing to a rescission of $500 million.

Together, defense cuts accounted for $7.2 billion of the $8.2 billion worth of rescissions in the bill.

Most of the other $1 billion came from domestic spending ($164 million was in foreign aid). The bulk — $597 million — was in cutbacks in Department of Housing and Urban Development money that appropriators said HUD would not need for assisted-housing programs in 1992.

The appropriators rejected Bush's proposed $547.7 million cut in HUD's new public housing construction account, reasoning in part that it would cost 7,600 construction and related jobs.

Most of the remaining cuts came in much smaller items, some as small as a $39,000 project for celery research in Michigan. But Bush ran into a buzz saw of opposition over projects such as these, primarily from Byrd, who repeatedly displayed his anger at Bush's lampooning of congressional spending practices.

Byrd willingly sacrificed one of his own items among the targeted projects — a $750,000 grant for research into Appalachian hardwoods in West Virginia — but led the charge to protect most of the rest, and he organized the campaign to shoot back at Bush by going after executive-branch research projects.

Byrd led appropriators in insisting on cutting $2 million from the National Science Foundation, money he suggested be taken from research on such things as the mating behavior of swordfish and the sexual mimicry of swallowtail butterflies. "We had no intention of looking at them until the president made his political pitch," Byrd said of studies, which he emphasized had not been proposed by Congress.

Bush's initial salvos in March were accompanied by warnings from congressional Republicans and GOP aides that the president intended to send a new package of spending cuts to Capitol Hill every week until the fall elections, forcing votes on each of the individual cuts.

But the fury of the congressional reaction apparently convinced the White House to back off, and Byrd pronounced the plan to force cut-by-cut votes a bust. "The president to that extent failed," Byrd said. "I don't think the people have been served by politicizing the process . . . and I don't think [Bush] would be well-advised to pursue that course any further."

## FINAL ACTION

Approval of the conference report reconciling House and Senate rescission bills came May 21 in votes of 404-11 in the House and 90-9 in the Senate. *(House vote 137, p. 34-H; Senate vote 108, p. 15-S)*

The overwhelming margins masked unhappiness among some Republicans, who applauded appropriators for exceeding Bush's dollar target but criticized Democratic leaders for blocking individual votes on all of Bush's proposed cuts. Ultimately, however, Republicans claimed victory.

Solomon said that any time Congress got into a bidding war with the president over cutting rather than increasing spending, that had to be considered a win, even if Bush did not get exactly what he wanted. ∎

# $254 Billion Defense Bill Clears

The $254 billion fiscal 1993 defense appropriations bill cleared by Congress on Oct. 5 included two Senate initiatives that carried high political voltage. The spending bill (HR 5504) provided only $3.8 billion of the $5.4 billion that President Bush requested for the Strategic Defense Initiative (SDI), and it included $210 million for breast cancer research to be conducted by the Army.

The House adopted the conference report on the bill by voice vote Oct. 5, and the Senate followed suit the same day, clearing the bill for the president.

During Senate action on the companion defense authorization bill, a majority of senators had demonstrated support for trimming funding for SDI, the anti-missile defense program, to $3.3 billion. But a narrow majority eventually voted for a $3.8 billion SDI allowance after leaders of the Defense Appropriations Subcommittee as-

sured some senators that they would hold the line at that amount in conference with the House, which had approved $4.3 billion. *(SDI, p. 498)*

Subcommittee Chairman Daniel K. Inouye, D-Hawaii, told the Senate on Oct. 5 that "$3.8 billion is the amount we pledged, and it is the amount we delivered."

The breast cancer initiative, sponsored by Tom Harkin, D-Iowa, started out as a renewed effort to whittle down SDI after critics lost the battle over the $3.8 billion appropriation. As adopted by the Senate, Harkin's amendment to the appropriations bill would have reduced SDI by enough to add $185 million to the $25 million previously approved by the House for Army-financed research on breast cancer.

Immediately after the amendment was approved, however, it was retroactively modified to simply increase can-

cer research funding, without an offsetting reduction in SDI.

The administration's Office of Management and Budget planned to count the cancer research funds as domestic rather than defense spending under limits set by the 1990 budget law, according to spokesman Tom Bruce. But he said that would not force a compensating reduction in other programs because domestic discretionary appropriations would still be less than the maximum allowed.

The defense spending bill provided $253.8 billion, $7.3 billion less than Bush requested, for Pentagon programs other than the separately funded military construction budget. *(Military construction, p. 623)*

According to Inouye, the bill provided $16.3 billion less than was appropriated for fiscal 1992 and $34 billion less than was appropriated for fiscal 1991.

As was typical of defense appropriations bills, HR 5504 conformed to the companion defense authorization bill (HR 5006) so far as most major weapons programs were concerned. *(Defense authorization, p. 483)*

SDI was one of a few significant instances of the bill earmarking less than was authorized for a major program. The final version of the authorization bill called for $4.05 billion.

In a few other prominent cases, the appropriations bill earmarked funds for projects that were not authorized, such as $300 million for an amphibious landing ship. The bill also added to the budget request $1.57 billion for National Guard and reserve equipment. This was more than either chamber had approved in its respective versions of the bill and $872 million more than was authorized.

In political terms, what distinguished the defense appropriations most clearly from the authorization bill was the more widespread — or at least more forthright — earmarking of Pentagon funds for projects that were backed by congressional clout.

In some cases, HR 5504 transferred funds from the Pentagon to other departments, in effect circumventing budget limits on Appropriations subcommittees that draft the funding bills for those agencies. For instance, $303 million was earmarked for the Coast Guard — a part of the Transportation Department — and $126 million was shifted to the Energy Department to buy oil for its Strategic Petroleum Reserve.

In other cases, members of the Senate and House Appropriations committees used the bill to direct the Pentagon to fund projects of interest to constituents. In HR 5504, such add-ons to Bush's budget request ranged from $50 million to cushion the impact on local communities of the scheduled shutdown of the Philadelphia Naval Shipyard to $1 million to eradicate brown tree snakes that had infested Guam and threatened Hawaii by stowing away in civil and military ships and planes.

**Major Weapons**

The bill included basically the amounts requested and authorized for most major weapons programs, including

---

**BOXSCORE**

➡ **Fiscal 1993 appropriations for the Defense Department (HR 5504).** The $254 billion spending bill provided funds for the Pentagon.

**Reports:** H Rept 102-627; S Rept 102-408; conference report H Rept 102-1015.

**KEY ACTION**

July 2 — The **House** passed HR 5504, 328-94.

Sept. 23 — The **Senate** passed HR 5504, 86-10.

Oct. 5 — The **House** adopted the conference report by voice vote; **Senate** cleared conference report by voice vote.

Oct. 6 — President Bush signed HR 5504 — PL 102-396.

---

four B-2 stealth bombers ($2.7 billion), four Navy destroyers ($3.3 billion) and an $832 million down payment on a nuclear-powered aircraft carrier.

Tracking the authorization bill, it approved less than Bush requested for several major projects. For instance, the bill appropriated $2 billion to develop the Air Force's new F-22 fighter (instead of the $2.2 billion requested) and $1.8 billion for six C-17 cargo planes (instead of the $2.5 billion requested for eight planes).

By the same token, HR 5504 paralleled the authorization measures in adding to Bush's request funds for several projects that the administration opposed — or had come to accept under congressional pressure. One example was the inclusion of $755 million to continue developing the V-22 Osprey, a tilt-rotor aircraft intended as a Marine Corps troop carrier. Similarly, the bill added to the budget funds to upgrade existing M-1 tanks and Bradley troop carriers, partly to keep alive the production lines for those weapons.

In addition to SDI, there were other cases in which the bill appropriated substantially less than was authorized:

● For a $1.2 billion helicopter carrier to be built in Mississippi, the bill provided only an initial $305 million.

That marked a rare departure from the Appropriations committees' longstanding opposition to such "incremental" funding of a major purchase. With few exceptions, the panels insisted that weapons purchases be fully funded in a single bill so that they could weigh a project's total cost.

In this case, the conferees said, they were suspending the "full funding" rule so that the Navy could sign a contract, thus locking in the price and delivery schedule guaranteed by a contract option due to expire at the end of 1992.

● The conferees approved only $10 million for termination costs, instead of the $125 million requested to continue developing a satellite launch rocket that was intended to carry much heavier satellites than any currently in use.

The conferees objected that NASA was not paying a fair share of the cost of this ostensibly joint project, so that the Pentagon was bearing most of the cost of a project for which it had no need. Conferees on the authorization bill had expressed the same complaint but authorized $85 million and ordered the administration to make NASA pay more.

**Earmarking**

As usual, Pennsylvania came off well in the conferees' allocation of congressionally mandated spending. The Keystone State was home to House Defense Appropriations Subcommittee Chairman John P. Murtha, D, to the panel's senior Republican, Joseph M. McDade, and to Senate Defense Subcommittee member Arlen Specter, R.

The bill's economic conversion package, which provided more than $1.5 billion to fund various projects to help military personnel, defense industries and localities adjust to the reduction in defense spending, included several

# Funding for Major Weapons

Following is a comparison of President Bush's request for major weapons programs in fiscal 1993, the amounts approved by the Senate and House, and the amounts provided in the final version of the defense appropriations bill (HR 5504 — PL 102-396). Some amounts include money for spare parts or for components to be included in weapons that will be funded in future budgets. All amounts are for procurement, except those lines labeled R&D, which indicate funds exclusively for research and development. *(Amounts in millions of dollars)*

| PROGRAM | BUSH REQUEST Number | Amount | HOUSE BILL Number | Amount | SENATE BILL Number | Amount | FINAL PASSAGE Number | Amount |
|---|---|---|---|---|---|---|---|---|
| **Strategic weapons** | | | | | | | | |
| B-2 bomber | 4 | $ 2,687 | 4 | $ 2,687 | 4 | $ 2,687 | 4 | $2,687 |
| Advanced cruise missile | | 0 | | 0 | | 127 | | 127 |
| Trident II missile | 21 | 764 | 17 | 664 | 21 | 764 | 21 | 764 |
| Strategic Defense Initiative R&D | | 5,388 | | 4,312 | | 3,800 | | 3,800 |
| Brilliant Pebbles (Part of SDI) R&D | | 576 | | 0 | | 350 | | 300 |
| **Ground combat** | | | | | | | | |
| M-1 tank upgrade | | 0 | | 0 | | 122 | | 161 |
| Bradley troop carrier production and upgrade | | 0 | | 200 | | 150 | | 125 |
| MLRS artillery rockets and launchers | | 199 | | 449 | | 257 | | 405 |
| ATACMS long-range conventional missile | 340 | 163 | 351 | 167 | 351 | 167 | 351 | 167 |
| Comanche scout helicopter R&D | | 443 | | 443 | | 0 | | 418 |
| AHIP scout helicopter | | 0 | 36 | 225 | | 0 | 36 | 225 |
| Longbow attack helicopter upgrade R&D | | 282 | | 307 | | 0 | | 307 |
| JSTARS radar plane | 1 | 311 | 1 | 311 | 2 | 512 | 2 | 512 |
| **Transportation** | | | | | | | | |
| C-17 cargo plane | 8 | 2,514 | 6 | 1,906 | 6 | 1,856 | 6 | 1,810 |
| Osprey tilt-rotor aircraft R&D | | 0 [1] | | 755 | | 0 | | 755 |
| LHD helicopter carrier | | 0 | 1 | 1,205 | 1 | 1,050 | 1 | 305 [2] |
| LSD-41 amphibious ship | | 0 | 1 | 300 | | 0 | 1 | 300 |
| Fast cargo ships | | 1,201 | | 801 | | 1,201 | | 613 |
| **Naval warfare** | | | | | | | | |
| Aircraft carrier components | | 832 | | 832 | | 350 | | 832 |
| Aegis destroyer | 4 | 3,347 | 3 | 682 [3] | 4 | 3,254 | 4 | 3,254 |
| Tomahawk cruise missiles | 200 | 404 | 200 | 404 | 100 | 229 | 200 | 404 |
| *Seawolf*-class sub R&D | | 0 | | 150 | | 150 | | 150 |
| **Tactical air combat** | | | | | | | | |
| F-16 Air Force fighter | 24 | 683 | 24 | 615 | | 0 | 24 | 615 |
| F/A-18 Navy fighter | 48 | 1,658 | 48 | 1,571 | 24 | 1,078 | 36 | 1,200 |
| F/A-18 "E" and "F" model R&D | | 1,134 | | 1,137 | | 54 | | 944 |
| F-22 fighter R&D | | 2,224 | | 2,024 | | 0 | | 2,024 |
| AX ground-attack plane | | 166 | | 166 | | 0 | | 166 |

[1] *Administration subsequently accepted program.*

[2] *Partial funding*

[3] *Plus $1.9 billion transferred from available Pentagon funds*

Pennsylvania projects in addition to the $50 million to cushion the impact of closing the Philadelphia Navy yard. *(Defense conversion, p. 509)*

Another Pennsylvania touch in the bill was $2 million to start a nurse-training pilot project at a community college in Murtha's district. He had tried unsuccessfully to fund the program in the fiscal 1992 defense bill.

The bill also included $176 million earmarked for research projects at 28 colleges. In the Senate, Armed Services Committee Chairman Sam Nunn, D-Ga., and others had long objected to such earmarks because they bypassed competitive bidding in which schools seeking research funds were subjected to "peer review" by scholars.

The conference report called for competitive review of the seven academic projects that were requested by senators. But the remaining 21, sponsored by House members, were to be funded with no competition.

## BACKGROUND

Of all the Appropriations subcommittees, only the two covering defense and the two that drafted the military construction measure had to coexist with authorizing committees that were so solidly established as arbiters of policy. Moreover, unlike most legislative committees, the two Armed Services panels shepherded to enactment an annual authorization bill that included detailed funding limits.

Most legislative committees authorized the programs they oversaw in relatively general terms, thus leaving the counterpart Appropriations panels considerable leeway in drafting the bills that actually provided funding. Although the House Foreign Affairs and Senate Foreign Relations committees drafted a detailed authorization bill, the measure routinely bogged down short of enactment.

Strictly speaking, both the authorization and appropriations bills for defense dealt with the Pentagon budget in large chunks: Army operations, Navy aircraft procurement, and Air force research and development, for example. But in their accompanying reports, the Armed Services and Appropriations committees further allocated those funds among hundreds of specific programs, and the Pentagon generally went along. The fiscal 1992 spending bill provided $270 billion, which was 95 percent of the total amount provided for defense-related activities in that fiscal year. *(1991 Almanac, p. 621)*

Since the late 1960s, the two Armed Services panels had expanded the scope of their annual authorization bill, which in 1992 covered the entire Pentagon budget except for military pay and benefits. Since the mid-1980s, dealings between Senate Armed Services and Senate Defense Appropriations occasionally had become contentious.

When the Senate took up the fiscal 1992 defense appropriations conference report, that chronic tension over turf erupted in a rare public clash between the two powerful committees. The Appropriations panel easily prevailed as the bill was cleared by a vote of 66-29, perhaps because the procedural situation — an up-or-down vote on the bill's conference report — prevented Armed Services members from targeting the specific projects in dispute. But the verbal skirmishing was fierce considering the small percentage of the defense budget at stake.

On major issues, however, the two panels in each chamber seemed to have worked out a modus vivendi, facilitated by the fact that all four shared an essentially hawkish viewpoint. In general, the Armed Services panels tried to anticipate issues of special interest to Appropriations members, and the Appropriations subcommittees usually respected the funding ceilings set by the authorizers on major procurement and research programs.

The Appropriations panels insisted on their right to treat authorization levels as a ceiling that they could go below, rather than as floors they must reach. Senate Appropriations Committee Chairman Robert C. Byrd, D-W.Va., had insisted on this point with particular vigor, routinely objecting to provisions in any authorization bill — defense or otherwise — that bound the Appropriations panels to provide no less than some specified amount for a particular program.

## HOUSE COMMITTEE ACTION

The $253 billion Pentagon funding bill approved June 18 by the House Defense Appropriations Subcommittee set the stage for high-stakes battles over the Navy's long-term plans for building warships and developing a new generation of combat airplanes.

The bill was marked up and approved by the subcommittee in private, but sources said it essentially conformed to House action on the companion defense authorization bill (HR 5006), passed June 5, which sliced $10 billion from Bush's Pentagon budget request for fiscal 1993.

And the Appropriations panel approved the amounts authorized in HR 5006 for two of the most controversial weapons programs: $2.7 billion to build four additional B-2 stealth bombers and $4.3 billion for SDI.

### Combat Aircraft

The Defense Subcommittee essentially approved the Navy's request for $1.1 billion to develop an enlarged version of the F/A-18 combat jet and $165 million to begin work on a long-range "stealthy" bomber, designated the AX, intended to fly from aircraft carriers.

The panel also added $250 million to the bill to upgrade existing F-14 Navy fighters. The administration contended that it could not afford this project, but it was avidly promoted by the Long Island-based Grumman Corp., which built the F-14s, and by members of the New York congressional delegation.

That put subcommittee Chairman Murtha on a collision course with House Armed Services Committee Chairman Les Aspin, D-Wis., whose panel essentially reversed the priority of the F/A-18 and AX projects.

As drafted by Aspin's committee and passed by the House, the authorization bill nearly halved funding to develop the new "E" and "F" models of the F/A-18 — to $599 million. Contending that the new, enlarged versions amounted to a substantially new design, the committee ordered the Navy to test prototypes of the F/A-18 "E" and "F" before trying to start production.

On the other hand, Armed Services told the Navy to speed up development of the AX, approving in the authorization measure more than four times the amount requested — $741 million, rather than $166 million.

The authorization bill added no funds to the small amount the administration requested for F-14 modifications. *(Combat aircraft, p. 506)*

### Dealing Destroyers

The Appropriations subcommittee also funded only three of the four *Burke*-class destroyers requested by the

Navy. Previous budgets had funded 22 of these ships, which were being built at a shipyard in Bath, Maine, and another in Pascagoula, Miss.

The subcommittee earmarked the funds that had been sought for the fourth destroyer to build instead a large aircraft carrier to haul 2,000 Marines and the helicopters to carry them ashore.

The administration planned to request funds for the carrier in the fiscal 1996 budget. But funding for that ship was the Marine Corps' second-highest priority in 1992. And Murtha, a decorated Marine veteran who saw combat in Vietnam, demonstrated anew that there was no such thing as an ex-Marine.

The destroyer cutback also could have been intended by some members as a jab at Maine Democrat Thomas H. Andrews, in whose district some of the destroyers were being built. Against the strong opposition of Murtha and Defense Subcommittee member Norm Dicks, D-Wash., Andrews led an unsuccessful effort to kill the B-2 bomber program during House debate on HR 5006.

## HOUSE FLOOR ACTION

Amid much talk about the need to crack down on the deficit, the House cut nearly $800 million from the defense appropriations bill before passing it July 2. However, as with most of the other funding bills passed since the House rejected the balanced-budget constitutional amendment June 11, the reduction amounted to a fraction of the amount appropriated in the bill, and the specific cuts approved were largely symbolic.

The $251 billion version of HR 5504 passed, 328-94. *(Vote 265, p. 64-H)*

Confounding widespread predictions that members would try to vindicate their votes against the constitutional amendment by voting to kill many big-ticket programs, the House rejected proposals to slash two of the most costly and controversial programs in the bill: the B-2 stealth bomber and the Strategic Defense Initiative.

Critics came much closer to slicing SDI funds than they had come a month earlier, when they tried to make a larger cut in the companion defense authorization bill: Illinois Democrat Richard J. Durbin's effort to cut $700 million from the $4.3 billion included in the appropriations bill for SDI lost by only 16 votes; his effort on June 5 to cut SDI by $1 billion had fallen short by 50 votes.

On the other hand, opponents of the B-2 actually lost ground between the two defense debates, even though in that interval both chambers of Congress debated the balanced-budget amendment, and President Bush and Russian President Boris N. Yeltsin agreed to slash their long-range nuclear arsenals. *(Balanced-budget amendment, p. 108)*

Before reporting the bill to the House, the Appropriations Committee had cut $8.6 billion from Bush's $261 billion budget request. The amendments adopted on the House floor brought the total reduction to $9.4 billion. However, that net reduction reflected nearly $3 billion that the committee added to the bill for several major weapons the administration did not request — and in most cases vigorously opposed — but which commanded strong congressional backing.

These congressional initiatives included: construction of two large amphibious landing ships; additional production of Stinger anti-aircraft missiles; continued upgrades of the Army's Bradley troop carrier and the Navy's F-14 fighter jet; and continued development of the V-22 Osprey aircraft. Taken individually, each of those five programs arguably filled a clear military requirement. But taken together, they underscored the depth of congressional resistance to cutting defense-related jobs in economically tight times.

In the case of the V-22, Congress dug in its heels so deeply over three years that Cheney on July 2 announced a partial capitulation, offering to continue developing the aircraft without promising to eventually buy it.

The bill included $1 billion for an "economic conversion" package — also part of the the authorization bill — to help laid-off defense workers, military personnel, weapons contractors and communities adjust to the rapid drop in defense spending brought on by the Soviet Union's collapse.

Also included was a provision increasing from $400 million to $650 million the total the president could draw from the Pentagon's appropriations for fiscal 1992 and 1993 to help dismantle the former Soviet nuclear arsenal. The bill provided $25 million, added by the Appropriations Committee, to fund joint research programs intended to wean former Soviet scientists from the weapons industry.

HR 5504 funded all military activities of the Defense Department except the facilities construction program, which was separately funded in the military construction spending bill (HR 5428). Combined with defense-related programs carried out by the Energy Department, House action on the two Defense Department appropriations bills brought the total defense-related appropriation for fiscal 1993 to $273 billion, compared with Bush's request for $281 billion.

### Large but Soft

Of the $762 million cut from the bill on the House floor, $700 million came from two amendments by Byron L. Dorgan, D-N.D.

By any standard, they sliced hefty amounts from the bill. But both were aimed at the kind of political softballs that might have been slammed over the fence even in a year when there was less agitation for budget cuts. The amendments cut:

• $500 million by reducing the armed services' inventory of spare parts and equipment, including medical supplies, clothing and fuel. These inventories had mushroomed during the Reagan administration's defense buildup, and the General Accounting Office had recommended a cut of $5 billion from fiscal 1992 levels.

• $200 million to force a reduction in the use of private consultants, a perennial target of congressional budgeters.

In each case, Subcommittee Chairman Murtha agreed to the amendment without complaint, and Dorgan refrained from demanding a roll call vote, which he could have won overwhelmingly.

### Saving Strategic Arms

Noting that SDI was conceived by President Ronald Reagan as a defense against Soviet attack, Durbin cited the Bush-Yeltsin arms agreement as a reason for members who had opposed his proposed SDI cut in June to back the smaller $700 million cut he offered to HR 5504. "We are spending literally billons of dollars to defend against a threat that no longer exists," he said.

But he also tried to ride the wave of budget-cutting rhetoric, taunting members who had tried to kill a $15 million appropriation for a parking garage in Newark, N.J., just a day earlier. "Take your budget-balancing fervor away

from parking garages and put it where it counts," Durbin said.

Noting that the House had debated SDI at some length during consideration of the defense authorization measure, Murtha discouraged SDI backers from rehearsing their arguments against a further reduction, and the debate ended in less than 15 minutes.

"We've got 45 Newark parking garages in this one amendment," Durbin called out as he buttonholed members coming on the floor to vote.

He picked up support from 26 who had voted against his SDI amendment in June. Among them were several members who had been prominent in the budget-balancing debate, including Illinois Republican Harris W. Fawell and Pennsylvania Republican Rick Santorum. But those converts were partly offset by 11 members, all but one of them Democrats, who switched in the opposite direction.

The amendment to cut SDI was rejected 201-217. *(Vote 263, p. 64-H)*

Timothy J. Penny, D-Minn., offered the amendment to delete from the bill $2.7 billion to buy four additional B-2 bombers.

But compared with an almost identical amendment offered to the authorization bill June 2, Penny lost more than he gained from switchers: Seven members who voted against the cut in June supported Penny, but 14 went the other way. Penny's amendment was rejected 173-248, a margin of 75 votes. *(Vote 265, p. 64-H)*

The anti-bomber amendment in June had lost by only 50 votes, 162-212.

By voice vote, the House also rejected a Penny amendment that would have deleted from the bill $786.8 million earmarked to buy 17 Trident II submarine-launched strategic missiles, plus components for additional Trident IIs slated for inclusion in future budgets. That amount represented a reduction of four missiles and $200 million from Bush's request.

### '11,000 Workers . . .'

The House also shouted down an amendment by Andy Ireland, R-Fla., that, in effect, would have cut from the bill $1.9 billion that the Appropriations Committee had used to help pay for three destroyers.

The committee had approved three of the four *Arleigh Burke*-class destroyers requested, but it included only $682 million in the bill. To fund the balance of the ships' cost, it included a provision stipulating that $1.9 billion be transferred to the shipbuilding account from the so-called Defense Business Operating Fund (DBOF).

DBOF was a revolving fund through which the Pentagon financed the sale to operating units of supplies, parts and maintenance services.

The transfer was possible, the committee argued, because the fund was selling goods and services for significantly more than they cost and had accumulated an unnecessarily large cash surplus.

Though the committee did not link the two actions, this backdoor funding for the destroyers allowed it to earmark $1.5 billion for two amphibious landing ships designed to land Marine combat units on hostile shores. Neither was requested by the administration. They were built in Mississippi and in Louisiana.

"That isn't what [the DBOF money] was appropriated for," complained Ireland, a longtime critic of what he called shenanigans by Pentagon bookkeepers.

But members of the Appropriations panel maintained that the funding transfer was routine and that the additional ships were essential to preserve the country's amphibious shipbuilding capacity: "11,000 people would be immediately unemployed" if Ireland's amendment prevailed, Democratic committee member Dicks said.

The amendment was rejected by voice vote.

### Bits and Pieces

The House gestured toward fiscal responsibility with three other amendments involving much smaller sums of money.

Deficit reduction took on a personal edge when the House adopted, 218-200, an amendment to delete from the bill $10 million earmarked for the Edward R. Roybal Foundation to underwrite research on aging. Roybal, 76, a Democrat from California, was retiring from the House at the end of the second session. *(Vote 264, p. 64-H)*

Branding the appropriation "one of the most bloated pork barrel projects that we've seen," Indiana Republican Dan Burton called for its removal.

As the House prepared to vote on the amendment, Roybal, who was chairman of the Treasury and Post Office Appropriations Subcommittee, patrolled the floor, urging colleagues to oppose it.

But in the final minutes of the 15-minute tally, as the "yeas" climbed to within striking distance of victory, several members switched their votes from "nay" to "yea," including Roybal's fellow California Democrat Barbara Boxer, who was running for the Senate.

By voice votes, the House also adopted amendments:

● By John R. Kasich, R-Ohio, deleting $52 million earmarked for severance pay to local citizens employed at U.S. bases in the Philippines, which were being closed at the insistence of the Philippine government.

● By Penny, to rescind $25 million appropriated in fiscal 1992 to buy a supercomputer for the University of Alaska. Noting that the Cray computer would have been built in a district adjacent to Penny's, Alaska Republican Don Young sardonically commended Penny for "cutting jobs from his people."

Following are the major provisions of HR 5504 as passed by the House:

### Strategic Weapons

In addition to approving $2.69 billion, as requested, to buy four more B-2s, the House approved the $91 million requested to improve the fleet of 97 B-1 bombers, built in the mid-1980s.

Despite expenditures totaling $3 billion, the B-1's "defensive avionics" — the network of black boxes intended to locate enemy defenses and confuse them with electronic jamming — never had worked as intended. In its report on the bill, the Appropriations Committee told the Air Force to conduct an open competition to select a defensive system for the plane.

The committee said the bill's cut in Trident II production from 21 missiles to 17 was justified, partly by the Bush-Yeltsin agreement to slash strategic forces and partly because the success of Trident II tests meant fewer test missiles would be needed.

To develop an unmanned launch rocket for very heavy satellites, the bill included double the $125 million requested. The $250 million earmarked by the Appropriations panel for the "national launch system" included $46 million from an Air Force effort to develop a smaller launcher and $36 million from SDI.

## Ground Combat

In its report, the committee reiterated previous demands that the Pentagon spend $225 million that Congress added to the defense budget in 1991 to upgrade older M-1 tanks. The bill required that, as a part of any upgrade program, the 105mm cannon on older tanks be replaced with the 120mm gun carried by later M-1s.

The Army requested no funds to buy additional Bradley armored troop carriers. But the House bill included $200 million to keep the production line warm through a combination of building more Bradleys and upgrading existing ones. The House also added $32 million to the bill to develop a laser range-finder and satellite navigation system for the Bradley.

The House also added funds for two heavy-duty vehicles used by combat engineers to clear the way for tanks and troop carriers, adding:
- $71 million for 100 high-speed armored bulldozers for the Army and National Guard. That brought the appropriation to $99 million for 141 bulldozers.
- $6.2 million to develop a portable bridge carried on an M-1 tank chassis.

The bill boosted by $25 million — to $307 million — the amount to develop the Longbow target-finding radar for the Apache missile-armed, anti-tank helicopter. It provided the 12 smaller Cobra anti-tank copters requested for the Marines ($124 million) and added 10 more for the Marine Corps Reserve ($126 million).

It included the $443 million requested to develop the Comanche armed scout helicopter. However, like the authorization bill, it added $225 million to the budget request to modernize 36 existing scouts.

For two of the Pentagon's most widely deployed anti-tank missiles, the bill included the amounts requested:
- $154 million for nearly 3,200 laser-guided Hellfires;
- $183 million for more than 9,000 optically guided TOWs.

The bill also included an additional $10 million to equip older TOWs with a more powerful warhead. And it boosted by $10 million more than the request — to $120 million — the amount earmarked to continue development and to prepare for production of the Javelin anti-tank missile, small enough to be carried by one soldier.

It would provide the $123 million requested to develop a vehicle designated LOSAT that would carry ultrahigh-speed rockets intended to punch through tank armor. In its report, the committee objected to a decision by the Army to slow the project.

Like the authorization measure, the appropriations bill more than doubled the $197 million requested for the MLRS artillery rocket system. The request would have paid for 44 launchers for the Army. HR 5504 boosted that total to $124 million for nearly 30,000 rockets and $355 million for 115 launchers, distributed between the Army and Marine Corps.

For 351 of the longer-range ATACMS artillery rockets, the bill included $167 million, an increase of 11 missiles (and $4 million) from the request.

It included all but $13 million of the $717 million requested to continue developing and building JSTARS radar planes, intended to find ground targets for ATACMS far behind enemy lines.

The $127 million requested for 170 pickup trucks armed with batteries of Stinger anti-aircraft missiles was included. But the bill also added $50 million to the budget to buy 600 Stingers in individual, one-person launchers. The committee said this was intended to keep the production line open so that the Pentagon could decide in 1993 whether to buy more Stingers.

## Tactical Air Combat

With only minor modifications, the bill funded the Navy's plans for carrier-based combat planes, providing:
- $1.6 billion for 48 "D" model F/A-18s, used as both fighters and bombers;
- $1.1 billion to develop by 1996 larger "E" and "F" models of the F/A-18; and
- $166 million to develop, by early in the next decade the stealthy A-X ground-attack plane.

In drafting the authorization bill, the House Armed Services Committee had shifted more than half a billion dollars from the new F/A-18 model to speed A-X development.

The appropriations bill also added to the budget request $225 million to begin modernizing the electronics in F-14 carrier-based fighters and to modify the planes for ground-attack missions.

The F-14 upgrade was fervently supported by F-14 pilots. Equally important, it was supported by members of Congress from New York who represented the Long Island area, where the planes' manufacturer was located. But the program was just as strongly opposed by Navy brass, on the grounds that the older F-14s cost more to operate than F/A-18s.

But the appropriations bill conformed with the authorization measure in dealing with the Air Force's modernization plans. It provided $2 billion of the $2.2 billion requested to develop the F-22 fighter and $615 million, as requested, for 48 F-16 fighters. The $68 million budgeted to shut down the F-16 production line was earmarked instead to buy components that would be used in F-16s to be purchased in fiscal 1994.

The bill provided the $869 million requested for nearly 1,200 AMRAAM air-to-air missiles and the $76 million requested for 102 one-ton "smart" bombs to be carried by long-range fighters. But it also added to the budget:
- $24 million for 30 Have Nap missiles, which also had a one-ton warhead but which were larger and would be carried by B-52 bombers, and
- $100 million for 100 smaller SLAM missiles, with 500-pound warheads.

## Naval Combat

As requested, the bill included $832 million to buy the nuclear power plant and other components for an aircraft carrier slated for inclusion in the fiscal 1995 budget request.

In addition to denying funds for one of the four destroyers, the committee warned the Navy that it should slow the production rate of the destroyers so that shipyards would have a continuous stream of business until a subsequent class of warships was ready for production.

The bill provided the $404 million requested for 200 long-range Tomahawk cruise missiles and the $257 million requested for 330 Standard anti-aircraft missiles. But it boosted by $33 million — to $193 million — the amount to develop a secret system to better protect ships against cruise missile attacks.

Bush had proposed canceling two of the three Connecticut-built submarines of the *Seawolf*-class, which had been funded since 1989. But after a strenuous campaign by members from New England, Congress insisted on building

two of the three. HR 5504 added $150 million to the budget to continue development of the new design.

The bill included the $432 million requested for 320 anti-submarine homing torpedoes and the $38 million requested for the ASROC missile, designed to hurl a small anti-sub torpedo more than 10 miles. But it also added $10 million to the budget to prevent a one-year break in ASROC production.

For 24 of the SH-60 anti-sub helicopters, which were carried by most of the Navy surface warships, the bill provided $406 million, dropping from the budget request $32 million for training equipment that previously had not been included in Navy plans. The bill boosted by $127 million — to $162 million — the amount to develop new engines and electronics for an improved version of the P-3 long-range anti-sub patrol plane.

As requested, the bill included $246 million for two minesweepers. But the committee strongly indicated that it would disregard recent decisions to buy fewer of the ships than had been planned. The bill also added $27 million to the budget to develop Magic Lantern, a helicopter-borne laser for detecting mines.

The bill added $300 million to the budget to restore funds rescinded earlier in 1992 from the appropriation to build a large, high-speed supply ship to accompany combat fleets. An additional $200 million previously appropriated for the ship had not been affected.

### Air and Sea Transport

Like the authorization bill, HR 5504 provided six of the eight C-17 cargo planes requested, appropriating $2.1 billion of the $2.7 billion requested for C-17 production.

Instead of the $300 million requested for eight C-130 cargo planes for the Air Force, the bill included $420 million to buy 16 C-130s for reserve and Air National Guard units.

To continue developing the V-22 Osprey, a hybrid airplane-helicopter that the Marine Corps wanted for a troop carrier, the bill added $755 million to the budget. The bill also denied the $10 million requested to develop a new helicopter as an alternative replacement for the Marines' fleet of Vietnam-era helicopters.

Cheney had tried since 1989 to cancel the Osprey on the grounds that the Pentagon could not afford the $30 billion cost of developing and building the several hundred that would be needed by the Marines. But Congress had rebuffed Cheney because of strenuous efforts by members from Pennsylvania and Texas, home of Osprey contractors.

On July 2, Cheney offered to continue developing the Osprey if Congress allowed him also to begin developing a conventional helicopter, thus postponing the final decision on which aircraft the Marines would buy.

"We have gotten everything we asked for," said Rep. Curt Weldon, R-Pa. "We will build new Ospreys and move this revolutionary program forward."

The bill included $453 million, instead of the $464 million requested, for 20 large CH-53E helicopters, used by the Navy and Marine Corps as cargo haulers and minesweepers.

---

# Defense Appropriations

*(HR 5504 — PL 102-396, as signed by the president, in millions of dollars):*

| | Bush Request | House Bill | Senate Bill | Final Bill |
|---|---|---|---|---|
| Military personnel | $ 76,982.0 | $ 76,896.2 | $ 76,368.6 | $ 76,275.0 |
| Operations and maintenance | 74,813.5 | 71,710.2 | 70,281.8 | 69,406.0 |
| Procurement | 55,610.0 | 53,743.3 | 52,103.2 | 55,375.9 |
| Research and development | 39,075.7 | 38,770.1 | 36,066.8 | 38,234.8 |
| Revolving and management funds | 1,123.8 | 16.6 | 2,325.2 | 1,737.2 |
| Medical and other defense programs | 12,616.9 | 11,278.4 | 11,172.8 | 11,027.8 |
| Other agencies | 199.6 | 168.9 | 213.4 | 246.6 |
| Economic conversion | 0 | 0 | 2,000.0 | 472.0 |
| Miscellaneous provisions and scorekeeping adjustments | 612.0 | −717.0 | 153.8 | 1,011.3 |
| **Total** | **$ 261,133.5** | **$ 251,866.7** | **$ 250,685.6** | **$ 253,786.6** |

SOURCE: House, Senate Appropriations committees

---

It included $801 million of the $1.2 billion requested to expand the fleet of fast cargo ships designed to carry U.S.-based Army units to distant trouble spots. An additional $1.9 billion previously appropriated for this purpose had not yet been spent.

### Personnel Issues

The bill included $67.5 billion for pay and benefits of active-duty military personnel, a reduction of $424 million from the budget request. That would support an active-duty force of 1.75 million members, a reduction of nearly 119,000 from the fiscal 1992 budget.

Compared with the request, the bill would slice 10,000 members apiece from the Army and Navy. And the committee ordered the two services to make the cuts in headquarters staffs. The Navy cut was motivated, in part, by congressional unhappiness over the Navy's slow progress toward cleaning up the Tailhook scandal.

For National Guard and reserve personnel, the bill included $9.4 billion, $240 million more than was requested. That would support a Guard and reserve force of 1.07 million members, 66,150 more than the administration recommended.

The bill added $1.13 billion to the budget for equipment for National Guard and reserve units. It also added $50 million to beef up training of the National Guard and Army Reserve.

The bill added $3 million to the budget to establish a pilot program of youth camps for high-school dropouts, to be run by the National Guard.

### Operations and Maintenance

For day-to-day costs of training and maintenance, the bill included $71.7 billion, a $3.1 billion reduction from the request. As part of the ongoing congressional campaign to make allied governments bear more of the cost of stationing U.S. forces abroad, the bill included none of the $1.55 billion requested for salaries of foreign nationals employed at U.S. bases.

And it included none of the $801 million requested for maintenance of overseas facilities.

## SENATE COMMITTEE ACTION

The Senate Appropriations Committee approved a $250 billion spending bill for the Pentagon on Sept. 17, after nearly bogging down in the same quagmire that had stalled Senate action on the companion defense authorization bill.

As approved 26-0 by the panel, HR 5504 included $3.8 billion for anti-missile defense research under SDI.

Republican backers of SDI had halted action on the Senate version of the authorization measure (S 3114) early in August after a procedural vote indicated that the Senate would approve a floor amendment by Jim Sasser, D-Tenn., cutting the authorization for SDI research to $3.3 billion — $1 billion less than the Senate Armed Services Committee had recommended and $2 billion less than President Bush requested.

Moreover, Sasser's amendment would have placed most of the burden of reductions on the more ambitious projects that SDI proponents prized.

The Appropriations Committee's $3.8 billion budget for SDI was recommended by Defense Appropriations Subcommittee Chairman Inouye. Inouye said $3.8 billion was "a more fiscally acceptable level" than Bush's request.

In a bid to mollify Republican SDI backers, Inouye and senior subcommittee Republican Ted Stevens, Alaska, made the appropriation a lump sum, which gave the administration free rein to allocate reductions among parts of the program.

When the Appropriations Committee took up the defense spending bill Sept. 17, however, Sasser offered an amendment to reduce SDI to $3.3 billion. Besides noting the support for that position in the Senate, Sasser cited a report the previous day by the General Accounting Office alleging that SDI officials had exaggerated the success of several tests.

Stevens countered with a warning that the appropriations bill would be deadlocked, like the authorization measure, if it did not provide at least $3.8 billion for SDI.

A motion to table Sasser's amendment was rejected 14-14. But the amendment then failed by the same vote. That night, the Senate returned to the long-stalled authorization bill, adopting the $3.8 billion compromise for SDI.

The $250.4 billion approved by the Appropriations Committee was $10 billion less than the administration asked for. It was $20 billion less than appropriated for fiscal 1992 and $34 billion less than appropriated for fiscal 1991.

### Bill Highlights

As the administration requested, the Senate committee's bill would cut nearly 99,000 personnel from the active-duty military payroll. However, like the Senate Armed Services Committee, the Appropriations panel recommended a reduction of slightly more than 12,000 in the membership of National Guard and reserve units. The administration wanted a reduction of nearly 113,000 in Guard and reserve membership.

In an attempt to pressure allies to pick up more of the cost of stationing U.S. forces in Europe, the panel cut $175 million from the amount requested to operate overseas bases. It also added $25 million to extend the leave time given service members being transferred from Europe to look for housing near their new posts in the United States.

The panel deleted $3 billion from the budget request in an effort to force the Pentagon to use up some of its stockpiled spare parts and supplies.

But the committee added more than $2 billion for various programs intended to cushion the impact of the defense budget downturn on local areas, defense contractors and their employees. Included in this total was $600 million to help defense contractor workers make the transition to new lines of work.

The panel also added $60 million for disaster relief operations by the military, such as the large deployments of personnel to Florida and Hawaii after recent hurricanes.

As requested, the bill included funds to buy:

- Four additional B-2 stealth bombers, which would complete the fleet of 20 planned by the Air Force; and
- 21 Trident II submarine-launched nuclear missiles.

The committee dropped the $175 million the administration sought for the Pentagon's share of developing a so-called national aerospace plane that would take off from a runway like an airplane and soar into orbit.

The panel added funds to keep several ground combat system production lines in business, including:

- $122 million to upgrade early-model M-1 tanks to the "A2" model, with a larger cannon, heavier armor and night-vision equipment;
- $150 million to buy Bradley armored troop carriers and to upgrade existing ones; and
- $58 million to buy 30,000 more MLRS artillery rockets.

### Combat Aircraft

Like Senate Armed Services, the Appropriations Committee denied the request for 24 additional F-16 fighters, noting that the Air Force had more than 1,300 of the planes. Moreover, Inouye said, President Bush's decision to allow Taiwan to buy 150 F-16s would provide enough work to keep that production line intact for years.

The committee approved only 24 of the 48 requested F/A-18s, which the Navy and Marine Corps used as fighters and ground attack planes.

Concurring with the other congressional committees dealing with the defense budget, Senate Appropriations contended that the services could not afford all five of the new combat aircraft programs on the drawing board. In all, the services had asked for $4.19 billion to develop:

- The Air Force's F-22 fighter;
- The Navy's AX carrier-based, long-range bomber;
- Enlarged "E" and "F" models of the F/A-18;
- The Army's Comanche scout helicopter; and
- A new Longbow version of the Apache attack helicopter.

Lumping all five into a single account, the committee recommended $3.49 billion. The committee said the Pentagon could allocate the money as it wished, but it must certify to Congress that long-range budget plans included adequate funding to complete whatever programs were started.

Like Senate Armed Services, the Appropriations panel approved only $350 million of the $832 million sought as a down payment on a new nuclear-powered aircraft carrier. But the appropriators encouraged the Navy to stay with its plan to ask for the remaining $4 billion in the fiscal 1995 budget. Armed Services ordered a one-year delay.

The bill would fund four *Burke*-class destroyers, as requested. And it would approve 12 of the requested 24 SH-60-type anti-sub helicopters.

The committee added $1.1 billion for a helicopter carrier to be built in Pascagoula, Miss., by Litton Industries. And it approved six of the eight C-17 wide-body cargo jets the administration wanted.

It added no funds for the controversial V-22 Osprey tilt-

# Pentagon as Cancer-Fighter?

The electoral dynamics of 1992 as the "Year of the Woman" were vividly highlighted Sept. 22, when the Senate voted 89-4 to cut $200 million from the Strategic Defense Initiative (SDI).

The proposal by Tom Harkin, D-Iowa, had the politically irresistible feature of earmarking most of the money for research on breast cancer. *(Vote 228, p. 30-S)*

But GOP supporters of SDI had warned that they would tie up indefinitely any defense funding bill that did not promise SDI at least $3.8 billion, the amount in the appropriations measure before Harkin's amendment.

So in an equally stark display of members' determination to quickly wrap up the session and get home to campaign, the Senate immediately voted to restore to SDI the $200 million that Harkin had ostensibly cut.

Republican Alfonse M. D'Amato of New York had laid part of the groundwork for the Senate's double flip Sept. 17, when he offered an amendment to the labor appropriations bill (HR 5677) that would have transferred $214 million from Pentagon budget accounts to fund research on breast cancer. The amendment was rejected 43-53, but that large a "yea" vote demonstrated the issue's political potency. *(Labor appropriations, p. 651)*

The same day, the Senate rejected 48-50 an amendment by Jim Sasser, D-Tenn., to the defense authorization bill (S 3114) that would have cut SDI funds to $3.3 billion.

When the Senate took up the companion defense appropriations measure, Harkin, whose sisters both died of breast cancer, offered his amendment. Ridiculing SDI as "star wars," he asked, "Do we want to spend $200 million on star wars against a non-existent enemy, or do we want to spend that money on breast cancer research to fight a very real enemy that is going to kill 46,000 American women this year?"

Among Republicans who had opposed Sasser's earlier efforts to cut SDI — and who were up for re-election — the answer to Harkin's rhetorical question evidently was clear. D'Amato, who had voted against Sasser's proposed SDI cut, co-sponsored Harkin's. Other campaigning Republicans who voted for Harkin's amendments were Don Nickles of Oklahoma, Bob Kasten of Wisconsin, Christopher S. Bond of Missouri and Arlen Specter of Pennsylvania. Bond and Specter faced women opponents.

Eventually, senators who had voted against Harkin began changing their votes to "yea," including John McCain, R-Ariz., whose Democratic opponent in November was a woman. With Harkin's victory becoming a rout, his opponents decided to throw the match. By one unofficial tally, 29 members switched their votes from "nay" to "yea."

As soon as the amendment was approved, it was retroactively amended to restore the bill's SDI allowance to $3.8 billion, while still adding to the bill $200 million for Army-financed breast cancer research. That motion, by Alaska's Ted Stevens, the senior Republican on the Defense Appropriations Subcommittee, was adopted without dissent. Stevens later told a reporter that Harkin went along after being warned that, if SDI were cut below $3.8 billion, "we won't have the votes to pass the bill."

---

rotor plane, which the administration had opposed until 1992. But appropriators approved report language strongly endorsing the program, thus indicating that the omission of money was intended as a bargaining ploy for use in conference negotiations with the House.

## SENATE FLOOR ACTION

The Senate passed the annual defense appropriations bill Sept. 23 after two days of debate dominated, as usual, by amendments that reflected their sponsors' constituents.

The $251 billion version of HR 5504 was approved, 86-10. *(Vote 229, p. 30-S)*

Characteristically, the defense spending bill appropriated essentially the same amounts that had been authorized in the companion bill for major weapons programs: $2.69 billion for B-2 bombers, for instance, and $3.25 billion for four Navy destroyers.

Of three dozen amendments to the bill voted on by the Senate on Sept. 21-22, only one would have significantly changed the amount recommended by the Senate Appropriations Committee for a major program: An amendment by Tom Harkin, D-Iowa, adopted 89-4, would have shifted $200 million from SDI to breast cancer research. It was immediately revised to provide the cancer research funds without reducing SDI. *(Box, above)*

More customary constituent interests were prominent among most of the other amendments, most of which were adopted by voice vote on Sept. 22. Among them:

● By Georgia Democrats Sam Nunn and Wyche Fowler Jr., adding $20 million to buy the Marine Corps Reserve an executive jet built by Savannah-based Gulfstream Aerospace.

● By John W. Warner, R-Va., adding $40 million to buy the Army Reserve and the National Guard the type of night vision equipment used extensively by U.S. forces during the Persian Gulf War. A division of International Telephone and Telegraph Corp. in Roanoke, Va., was a major supplier of such devices.

● By Minority Leader Bob Dole, R-Kan., adding $56 million for four Blackhawk troop-carrying helicopters, earmarked for the Kansas National Guard.

The bill even provided a vehicle for enterprising senators to fund programs in other agencies: An amendment by Louisiana Democrats J. Bennett Johnston and John B. Breaux, also adopted by voice vote, appropriated to the Commerce Department $100 million for disaster assistance to commercial fishermen who had uninsured losses as a result of hurricanes Andrew or Iniki in the summer of 1992 or Hurricane Hugo in 1989.

The bill included a $2 billion "defense conversion" fund to cushion the impact of Pentagon budget cutbacks on defense contractors, their employees and their communities.

The Appropriations Committee had funded this lump sum, in part, by eliminating from the bill hundreds of millions of dollars that the administration had requested for various research projects that, the committee argued,

were intended to help defense contractors retool for commercial business.

As drafted by the committee, the bill would have given the Defense Department discretion to allocate the $2 billion among conversion-related projects, including those projects for which specific requests had been denied. But the Senate's version of the companion defense authorization bill parceled out money to dozens of specific conversion-related projects. And senators who had hammered out that package were unwilling to see that carefully brokered deal unraveled.

By voice vote, the Senate adopted an amendment by David Pryor, D-Ark., that earmarked more than half the appropriations bill's conversion fund for projects specified in the authorization measure. Pryor's amendment added $470 million from the conversion fund to the $130 million that was already in the bill for transition grants to workers and communities hit by defense cutbacks. And the amendment doled out $675 million among 10 of the conversion projects specifically covered by the authorization bill.

### University Research

The Senate also adopted by voice vote a Nunn amendment requiring the secretary of Defense to allocate funds among 12 university research projects on the basis of a "merit-based selection process" with "peer review" of the projects by qualified academic experts.

For years, Nunn and his allies had battled efforts by Appropriations Committee members to earmark funds in the defense spending bill for research projects at favored schools, thus bypassing the peer-review process that governs the award of most federal research funds. The appropriators countered that the review process was dominated by an "old boys" network of research-oriented schools that allocated most of the federal funds to each other.

"These grants are a way for the non-establishment schools to compete with the Harvards, Stanfords and MITs which have made it a big business to obtain federal grants," Defense Appropriations Subcommittee Chairman Inouye told the Senate on Sept. 22.

In drafting the defense bill, Inouye's panel tried to skirt the annual showdown with Nunn by earmarking a total of $96 million for 12 schools but also giving the Defense secretary discretion to award "such amounts as he deems appropriate."

But Nunn objected that the panel's approach still did not ensure that other schools could compete for the funds. His amendment required that money be awarded only after an open competition judged by peer review. However, the peer review panels set up under his amendment could be drawn exclusively from less prominent schools.

### Other Amendments

An amendment by Dale Bumpers, D-Ark., that would have cut from the bill $1 billion earmarked for intelligence programs was rejected 35-57 on Sept. 21. (Vote 223, p. 29-S)

On Sept. 22, by a vote of 49-49, the Senate rejected an amendment by Jesse Helms, R-N.C., that would have barred from participation in the annual federal employee charity drive any organization attempting to force the Boy Scouts or any other youth group to accept homosexuals or atheists as members or leaders. Helms had offered the same amendment to the annual labor appropriations bill (HR 5677) on Sept. 18, when it was adopted by voice vote. (Vote 227, p. 30-S; Labor/HHS/Education, p. 651)

The Senate adopted several other amendments by voice vote on Sept. 22, including those:

• By Nunn, increasing by $400 million the amount that could be drawn from Pentagon accounts to help former republics of the Soviet Union reduce their arsenals and convert their defense industries to peaceful uses.

• By Bumpers, requiring the Pentagon to commission an independent analysis of the future of the Trident II submarine-launched missile.

The following are the major provisions of HR 5504 as passed by the Senate:

### Strategic Programs

The $2.69 billion requested for four additional B-2 stealth bombers would complete the fleet of 20 planes the Air Force planned to buy. But to modify the 97 B-1 bombers built in the mid-1980s, the bill included only $120 million, about one-third of the amount requested.

In its report accompanying the bill, the Appropriations Committee questioned plans to spend $3 billion to upgrade the B-1s, with much of that money earmarked to help the planes penetrate enemy air defenses. The panel ordered the Air Force to commission an independent study of the value of converting half the B-1s to carry conventionally armed cruise missiles, which the planes could launch from beyond the reach of enemy defenses.

The bill included $148 million — $66 million more than requested — to wrap up loose ends of the stealth cruise missile program, truncated by the president as part of his nuclear weapons reduction plan announced in January 1992.

To continue buying various rockets used to boost satellites into orbit, the bill included all but $33.4 million of the $793.6 million requested:

• $482 million for Titan IVs, used to launch the largest satellites; and

• $278 million for smaller Delta and Atlas rockets.

But the bill included none of the $300 million requested to develop two new space launchers, which the Appropriations Committee dismissed as too costly and superfluous. These were the National Launch System, intended to launch very heavy satellites, and the National Aerospace Plane, intended to take off from a runway and soar into orbit.

### Ground Combat

To modernize early model M-1 tanks with the larger 120mm cannon and heavier armor carried by later versions, the bill added $122 million to the budget. It also included a provision to let the Army spend on this project $237 million paid by other countries to buy older, surplus U.S. tanks. Under existing law, proceeds from foreign arms sales went to the Treasury.

Congress started the M-1 modernization program over the objections of the Bush administration. But in August, as Bush doled out budgetary largesse on the campaign trail, the administration dropped its opposition.

The bill included $27 million of the $42 million requested to develop an even larger tank cannon but earmarked the funds for other cannon research. The demise of the Soviet threat eliminated the need for a bigger gun, the committee said.

To keep the production line for Bradley armored troop carriers going, the bill included $150 million to be spent to build new Bradleys and modernize older ones. But the Appropriations Committee warned that this was the last time it would support Bradley funding that was not included in the administration's request.

The bill added $15 million to add ceramic armor tiles to

the thin metal roofs of LAV armored cars used by the Marine Corps. It also added $25 million to develop and buy versions of the LAV modified to carry anti-aircraft missiles.

As requested, the bill included $124 million for 12 Marine Corps Cobra helicopters, armed with anti-tank missiles. It also included $92 million to modify the Army's more heavily armed Apache anti-tank copters, a $43 million increase over the budget request intended to accelerate improvements based on lessons learned from the Persian Gulf War.

The budget requested more than $700 million to develop more modern armed helicopters: $282 million for the so-called Longbow version of the Apache and $443 million for the smaller Comanche "scout" aircraft.

Lumping the two together with programs to develop three combat airplanes, the Appropriations Committee provided $3.49 billion of the $4.19 billion requested for all five and ordered the Pentagon to sort out which of the projects it could afford in an era of declining defense budgets.

While leaving it to the Pentagon to decide how each program would fare, however, the Senate panel strongly suggested that it would not support continued funding for the Comanche unless the Pentagon leadership made a commitment to put it into production.

Unlike the House, the Senate did not add $225 million to the bill to continue modernizing the existing fleet of scout helicopters.

To gear up for production of the Javelin, a one-man anti-tank missile, the bill included $119 million, $10 million more than was requested.

The budget requested $197 million for 44 launchers for the MLRS artillery rocket but included no funds for additional rockets. To take advantage of the existing MLRS production contract, the Senate bill included $257 million in new funds for MLRS, to which it added $48 million left over from prior-year budgets for a total buy of 44 launchers plus 30,000 rockets.

The Senate also added to the budget $27 million to accelerate development of a version that could fly farther than the 20-mile-range MLRS.

The bill also included $167 million for 351 of the much larger ATACMS artillery rockets, an increase above the request of $4 million and 11 rockets.

For two JSTARS radar planes, designed to find ground targets far behind enemy lines, the bill included $512 million, plus $79 million to buy components that could be used in two additional planes to be funded in fiscal 1994. The budget requested only $201 million for one JSTARS, plus advance funding of $28 million for a single plane in fiscal 1994.

The bill also added $35 million to speed development of a small terminal, to be mounted in the jeeplike trucks called "humm-vees," through which front-line commanders could receive JSTARS data.

As requested, the bill included $168 million for 129 humm-vees armed with batteries of Stinger anti-aircraft missiles. It also added $11 million to the budget to test armored anti-aircraft vehicles that could better protect front-line ground troops, a role the Appropriations panel said might be filled by Stinger-armed Bradleys.

### Tactical Air Combat

The bill included no funds for F-16 fighters, although the budget requested $683 million for 24 planes. Like Senate Armed Services, the Appropriations panel insisted that foreign sales would keep the General Dynamics plant in Fort Worth busy for a few years, preserving the option of future U.S. purchases. As requested, the bill included $211 million to develop modifications that would adapt the F-16 to attacking battlefield targets.

The bill also included $1.08 billion for 24 F/A-18 jets, used by the Navy and Marines as both fighters and ground attack planes. The budget requested $1.66 billion for 48 planes.

Like the House-passed bill, the Senate measure added $175 million to the budget to upgrade the Navy's F-14s.

It denied the $56 million requested for the ASPJ radar-jammer which, the Appropriations panel said, had failed key tests and was near cancellation.

The budget requested $2.22 billion to develop the Air Force's F-22 fighter, $166 million to develop a carrier-based stealth bomber designated AX and $1.08 billion to develop a larger version of the F/A-18.

Along with the Army's new attack helicopters, these three programs were lumped into a single account for which the measure appropriated $3.49 billion, about 83 percent of the budget request.

The committee complained that both the F-22 program and the effort to develop "E" and "F" models of the F/A-18 were proceeding too quickly.

The bill included $1.06 billion for 756 AMRAAM air-to-air missiles, a reduction of $115 million (and 112 missiles) from the budget request. Noting that the missile was just coming into service, the Appropriations Committee dropped from the bill $28 million requested to develop an advanced version of AMRAAM.

As requested, the bill included $76 million for 102 1-ton "smart" bombs with a range of up to 40 miles and small enough to be carried by long-range fighter planes.

But the Senate also added to the budget:

● $24 million for Israeli-designed Have Nap missiles; and

● $90 million for 90 smaller SLAM missiles, with 500-pound warheads and a range of 50 miles.

### Naval Warfare

The bill included $350 million of the $832 million requested for components to be used in an aircraft carrier the administration planned to request in the fiscal 1995 budget. The Senate Armed Services Committee made that cut in the companion authorization bill, telling the Navy to delay the ship by one year. The Appropriations panel said the ship still should be requested in fiscal 1995.

For four *Burke*-class destroyers, the bill included $3.25 billion, reducing the request by $93 million in light of lower-than-anticipated prices in contracts let in 1992 on similar ships.

To buy 100 long-range Tomahawk cruise missiles — half the number requested — the bill included $229 million, a $175 million reduction. But it included the $257 million requested for 330 Standard long-range, ship-based anti-aircraft missiles.

The bill included $207 million — $47 million more than requested — to develop a secret system to better protect ships against cruise missiles.

As a result of budgetary limits, no more than three — and maybe only two — *Seawolf*-class submarines were to be built. Even so, the committee argued, the development program for the class had to be completed, so it added $150 million to the bill.

As requested, the bill included $432 million for 320 anti-submarine homing torpedoes and $38 million for

ASROC missiles.

However, the committee put in the bill only $16 million of the $30 million requested to develop an improved model of the big Mark 48 torpedoes carried by submarines.

The disappearance of the huge Soviet submarine fleet that had long dominated Navy planning was cited by the Appropriations Committee as justification for several such cuts. The bill also:

● Trimmed to $133 million — $22 million less than was requested — the appropriation to develop future submarines.

● Included none of the $21 million requested as the down payment on a $300 million project to develop a torpedo-sized underwater robot, intended to be launched from submarines to find enemy mines.

● Provided $238 million for 12 of the SH-60 sub-hunting helicopters carried by most surface ships. The budget had requested $492 million to continue the annual production rate of 24 helicopters that had been in effect for years.

● Included only $8 million of the $35 million requested to develop an improved version of the P-3C long-range, land-based, anti-sub patrol plane. The House had appropriated $162 million.

For two minesweepers, the bill included $222 million, a $24 million cut from the budget request that was based on savings achieved in the fiscal 1992 minesweeper contract. It also boosted by $4 million, to $15 million, the amount earmarked to develop Magic Lantern, a helicopter-borne mine-detecting laser.

### Air and Sea Transport

Following the lead of the Armed Services Committee, the Appropriations panel included in the appropriations bill $1.86 billion for six C-17 wide-body, long-range cargo planes, a reduction of two planes ($658 million) from the request.

The bill also funded only enough components to build eight planes in fiscal 1994 rather than the 12 requested. But though the number of such long-lead-time components funded thus decreased, the appropriation increased by $45 million to $251 million because the slower production rate boosted overhead costs.

Instead of the eight Hercules medium-range cargo planes requested at $300 million, the bill included $740 million for 21 planes.

Unlike the House-passed version, the Senate bill did not add to the budget request $755 million to continue work on the Osprey. But Senate appropriators made it clear that the aircraft would fare well in the Senate-House conference on the bill.

However, the bill included the $10 million that Defense Secretary Cheney requested to begin developing a conventional helicopter that eventually could compete with the Osprey.

For 20 large CH-53E cargo helicopters, the bill included $453 million, $12 million less than was requested.

Like the House, the Senate added to the bill $1.1 billion for a large helicopter carrier designed to haul 2,000 Marines and their choppers.

The bill also included the $1.2 billion requested to expand the fleet of high-speed cargo ships to haul the tanks and other heavy equipment of U.S.-based Army divisions to trouble spots.

### Personnel

As requested, the bill funded an active-duty military payroll of 1.77 million personnel, down nearly 99,000 members from the fiscal 1992 active-duty force ceiling.

But the Appropriations Committee reduced Bush's request for personnel funding by $449 million to take account of the fact that the fiscal 1992 force was smaller than its legal ceiling allowed.

Like the other congressional defense committees, Senate Appropriations rejected Bush's proposal to cut nearly 113,000 members from National Guard and reserve units.

Accordingly, the bill added to the budget request $358 million to cover the cost of a Guard and reserve roster of 1,107,255 — 100,555 members more than Bush requested. Compared with the fiscal 1992 Guard and reserve ceiling, the bill reduced the number of personnel by only 12,292.

In addition, it added to the budget $630 million for equipment for Guard and reserve units, most of it for aircraft. The bill also added:

● $25 million to give service members returning from European assignments 10 days of paid leave, rather than four, to look for housing near their new posts.

● $6.4 million to force the Navy to maintain its reserve fleet of fishing boats and other small craft modified to serve as minesweepers.

● $1 million to continue operating an Air Force Reserve squadron of 10 weather reconnaissance planes based at Keesler Air Force Base, near Biloxi, Miss. For years, the Air Force had tried to make some other agency absorb the cost of this "hurricane hunter" unit.

But no other agency was willing to, so congressional delegations from Southeastern states routinely forced the Air Force to foot the bill.

● $14 million to fund a pilot project of up to eight youth camps, operated by the National Guard, to help young, unemployed high school dropouts develop job skills.

In a related move, the bill established new junior ROTC, or Reserve Officers' Training Corps, programs in 450 high schools.

The Appropriations Committee said, "Such programs in our inner cities could offer an alternative . . . serving as a productive outlet for the need for group identity and group activity."

### Operations and Maintenance

The most notable single initiative in the bill's $70.3 billion appropriation for daily operations and maintenance was a $3 billion reduction linked to a variety of changes in the way the Pentagon managed its $88 billion inventory of spare parts and supplies.

"During the 1980s, [Pentagon] managers overbought items to negate the 'hollow forces' problems encountered during the 1970s," the Appropriations Committee said. "The cultural mind-set . . . changed from meeting minimum essential needs to maximizing the availability of parts and supplies."

One of the ways the measure tried to combat this mind-set, for instance, was by slicing $1 billion from the operating budget requests of the armed services.

That was intended to encourage the units to root out of their warehouses unneeded parts and supplies, the value of which would be credited to their operating accounts when the supplies were returned to the Pentagon's central supply agency.

The bill also cut $300 million from the amount requested to cover the cost of operations in Europe.

Of that reduction, $175 million was intended to give the Pentagon an incentive to bargain with allied governments

to cover a larger share of the cost of stationing U.S. forces on their territory.

The remaining $125 million was in anticipation that U.S. negotiators would persuade allied governments to increase the amount they would pay to cover the residual value of U.S.-built military facilities from which U.S. forces were being withdrawn.

The bill added $60 million to the budget request to beef up Pentagon planning and training to cope with natural disasters.

Characteristically, the Appropriations Committee had cut hundreds of millions of dollars, which it insisted would have no impact on Pentagon operations.

For example, the bill cut $455 million from the budget request because the panel wanted to change the way units were charged for services and spare parts.

Other such reductions included:
- $60 million from the amount requested for consultants.
- $88 million because inflation was less than was assumed when the administration's budget was drawn up.
- $44 million because delays in concluding arms control treaties meant that certain verification activities would not begin as scheduled.
- $41 million to reduce travel costs.

## FINAL ACTION

As crafted by conferees, the $254 billion defense appropriations bill for fiscal 1993 accelerated the decline in Pentagon spending. As the post-Soviet drawdown gained momentum, HR 5504 took an ax to operating costs as well as weapons procurement, although hardware programs continued to have the greatest reduction.

Bush requested $261 billion for programs in the bill, which funded essentially the entire defense budget except for military construction programs and defense-related nuclear projects conducted by the Department of Energy and funded in the energy and water spending bill. That was $9 billion less than Congress appropriated in the corresponding bill for fiscal 1992. Pentagon purchasing power had declined annually for several years, when adjusted for inflation, but the 1992 budget request was the first since the mid-1970s to decline significantly in absolute terms.

In the final version of HR 5504, Congress sliced more than $7 billion from Bush's request, providing $16 billion less than it had appropriated a year earlier.

Of the major accounts in the Defense Department budget, the bill made the smallest year-to-year change in the military personnel account, which covered pay and fringe benefits for members of the armed services: For fiscal 1992, Congress appropriated $78 billion. Bush requested $77 billion for fiscal 1993, and the bill trimmed $707 million from his proposal.

As requested, the bill reduced the number of active-duty military personnel to 1.77 million, a reduction of nearly 99,000 from the fiscal 1992 ceiling. But the resulting savings were partly offset by congressional add-ons to ease the transition of active-duty members to civilian life and to restore large cuts that Bush proposed in National Guard and reserve units.

Compared with the previous bill, the biggest slash was in the procurement accounts: Compared with the $64 billion appropriated for fiscal 1992, Bush requested less than $56 billion in fiscal 1993 — a 14 percent reduction. Counting nearly $300 million to buy medical equipment, which was included in a separate part of the bill with all other medical costs, HR 5504 appropriated about $240 million less for procurement than Bush requested.

Reflecting a general consensus at the Pentagon and on Capitol Hill in support of a robust defense research and development program, the fiscal 1993 request of $39 billion was only slightly less than the previous appropriation. HR 5504 trimmed less than $1 billion from that request.

Counting $9 billion earmarked for medical programs, Bush requested nearly $84 billion for operations and maintenance, slightly more than Congress appropriated for fiscal 1992. For nearly two decades, "O & M" funding had been politically sacrosanct because it had been treated as the part of the Pentagon budget most directly related to combat readiness.

But for the first time in this era of defense cuts, Congress made significant reductions in the O & M request, including only $78 billion for those costs (including the medical funds).

Denying any intention of cutting the tempo of military operations, the House-Senate conference committee that negotiated the final version of the defense appropriations bill targeted most of that $6 billion reduction so that the Pentagon would be forced to use some of its massive inventory of spare parts and supplies.

An additional $340 million of the O & M cut was aimed at pressuring U.S. allies overseas to pay a larger share of the cost of stationing U.S. forces abroad. But the conferees did not go as far as the House, which had deducted from its version of the bill the entire $1.5 billion requested to pay the salaries of foreign nationals employed on U.S. overseas bases.

### Science Projects

Appropriators also inserted $95 million in unauthorized, science-related university building projects into HR 5504 just 2½ weeks after Rep. George E. Brown Jr., D-Calif., had successfully stripped the same items from the energy spending bill.

At issue were 10 building projects that lawmakers had at first inserted into the energy and water appropriations bill (HR 5373) during conference, most of them in the home states of appropriators. (Energy and water, p. 659)

It was traditional for appropriators to put such projects in the bill, but in 1992 Brown, chairman of the Science, Space and Technology Committee, cried foul. When the energy and water conference report came to the House floor Sept. 17, Brown proposed that the funding be deleted unless the projects were duly authorized after a competitive selection process. To the surprise of many, including himself, he won, 250-104.

But that was not the end of it.

First, supporters unsuccessfully floated the idea of authorizing the 10 disputed projects in the energy policy bill (HR 776). (Energy bill, p. 231)

Then, conferees inserted them into the defense spending bill.

Brown, who had been on alert for the 10 projects to resurface, said he discovered them by perusing the only available copy of the defense appropriators' lengthy conference report. "It was just lucky that I found it," he said. "I think they deliberately did their best to conceal what they were doing."

Brown led a floor fight Oct. 5 to defeat the rule for the defense spending bill so that he could have the projects removed, but this time the rule was upheld, 250-171. (Vote 472, p. 116-H)

Brown attributed the turnaround to aggressive lobbying by the lawmakers with projects at stake — "from the Speaker on down." One of the grants was $8 million for Washington State University in the district of House Speaker Thomas S. Foley, D.

Defense Subcommittee Chairman Murtha was unapologetic about including the disputed building projects. Murtha noted that conferees had also included money for breast cancer research and impact aid to communities near military bases. "We always try to help as many members as we can," he said.

Murtha said that Inouye, his Senate counterpart, — whose state was to get a $10 million project — had requested that the House include them and that the House had acquiesced in the give-and-take of the conference committee.

## FINAL PROVISIONS

The $254 billion defense appropriations bill for fiscal 1993, signed Oct. 6 by President Bush, accelerated the decline in Pentagon spending. As the post-Soviet drawdown gained momentum, HR 5504 aimed a budgetary ax at operating costs as well as weapons procurement, although hardware programs continued to bear the brunt of the reduction.

Bush requested $261 billion for programs in the bill, which funded essentially the entire defense budget except for military construction programs and defense-related nuclear projects conducted by the Department of Energy. That was $9 billion less than Congress appropriated in the corresponding bill for fiscal 1992. Pentagon purchasing power had declined annually for several years, when adjusted for inflation, but the fiscal 1993 budget request was the first since the mid-1970s to decline significantly in absolute terms.

The major provisions of HR 5504 follow:

### Conversion Package

The bill provided more than $1.5 billion to help military personnel, defense contractors and local communities adapt to the downturn in defense spending. This included:
- $575 million for research and development (R & D) programs expressly designed to help defense-oriented companies retool to produce commercially viable products.
- $306 million for other R & D programs to develop technologies with civilian and military applications.
- $254 million to fund a provision of the companion defense authorization act (HR 5006) that temporarily allowed military personnel to retire and begin collecting pensions after 15 years of service, instead of the 20 years normally required.
- $632 million for other programs, including community planning assistance and job training and transition health insurance for service personnel and defense contractor employees.

### Military Personnel

To pay the active-duty force of 1,766,500 requested by Bush, the conferees approved $1.3 billion less than he proposed. Of that reduction, $843 million was attributed by the conferees to unspecified "fact of life" changes in personnel costs. The additional reduction of $449 million was possible, they said, because the services had fewer members than the number allowed for in the budget.

The administration's request would have reduced the number of National Guard and reserve personnel by nearly 113,000 to 1,006,700 — a 10 percent cut in one year. As it did in 1991, Congress refused to consider so rapid a reduction. The bill permitted a cut slightly more than one-third as large as Bush proposed, setting a ceiling for fiscal 1993 at 1,079,930 members.

To pay and operate the larger-than-planned force, the bill added $384 million to the budget request.

It also added $1.57 billion for equipment earmarked for Guard and reserve units. Two-thirds of that amount was earmarked for cargo planes, small executive-transport planes and helicopters.

### Strategic Weapons

The bill included the $2.69 billion requested for four B-2 stealth bombers. These would complete the scaled-back force of 20 planes planned by the Air Force. Under terms of the companion defense authorization bill, however, most of the funds for these planes could be spent only if Congress voted in 1993 to complete their construction.

Despite reservations that had been expressed by the Senate Appropriations Committee, the bill included $300 million of the $356 million requested to continue upgrading the fleet of B-1 bombers built in the mid-1980s. But the conferees ordered the Air Force to provide information the Senate panel had requested about the program, which was projected to cost $3 billion.

The bill also included $148 million to close out production of a long-range, stealthy, cruise missile intended to be launched from bombers. This was $66 million more than was requested for the project in January but covered the estimated cost of a funding plan unveiled by the Air Force later in the year.

As requested and approved by the Senate, the bill provided $764 million for 21 Trident II submarine-launched missiles. Citing the collapse of the Soviet threat, the House had funded only 17 missiles ($664 million).

The conference report included $150 million of the $175 million requested for the Pentagon's share of a joint civil-military project to develop a national aerospace plane intended to take off from a runway and fly into orbit.

But the bill included only $10 million of the $125 million requested for the Defense Department's share of another jointly funded space project — the national launch system. This program was intended to produce rockets that could boost into orbit much heavier payloads than any already in use.

Congress routinely had slashed funding requested by NASA for its share of the program. The House version of HR 5504 included $250 million — double the request — so the Pentagon could take over the project. But the conferees accepted the Senate's view that the Pentagon could not afford the program and that it should be canceled.

### Ground Combat

To upgrade early model M-1 tanks with the larger cannon, heavier armor and night-fighting electronics of the newest A2 models, the bill earmarked $161 million in new funds plus $197 million in proceeds from the sale of older tanks to other countries.

The administration had requested no funds for this project. But all four congressional defense committees — appropriators and authorizers — added the program to the fiscal 1993 budget, partly as a way of keeping intact M-1 assembly facilities in Ohio and Michigan. Campaigning for re-election in Michigan, Vice President Dan Quayle had announced that the upgrade would proceed.

The bill also added to the budget request $125 million to keep the production line for Bradley armored troop carriers "warm" by building new Bradleys and updating older ones with the heavier armor and more sophisticated electronics built into the newer versions.

It also included $16 million — half the amount the House added to the budget request — to develop Bradley improvements, including a laser range-finder.

Two House initiatives adding funds for specialized vehicles to support M-1 and Bradley operations were largely incorporated in the bill:

● $40 million for 118 ultra-heavy-duty tractor-trailer rigs, intended to quickly move 70-ton M-1 tanks long distances, and

● $89 million for 126 high-speed armored bulldozers, able to keep pace with the M-1s and dig tank-sized foxholes.

To modify the Apache anti-tank helicopter, including putting a target-finding radar on the Longbow version, the bill included $307 million, as approved by the House — $25 million more than was requested.

For less sophisticated, near-term improvements in the Apache fleet, it included $92 million, nearly double the amount requested.

It included the $124 million requested to buy a dozen smaller Cobra attack helicopters for the Marine Corps. But it also added to the request $126 million to buy an additional 10 Cobras for Marine reserve units.

To continue developing the smaller Comanche armed scout helicopter, the bill included $418 million of the $443 million requested. However, following the lead of the House, the bill also added to the budget $225 million to install new target-finding electronics on 36 existing scout helicopters.

For decades, the overriding challenge to U.S. ground-combat planners was the Soviet Union's hordes of tanks and the rapid pace at which it developed new tanks that were more heavily armed and armored. The Soviet collapse greatly moderated that threat, but the war with Iraq underscored another one: the proliferation in dozens of Third World countries of relatively modern tanks, mostly of Soviet, British or U.S. origin.

So, despite the end of the Soviet threat, the bill included generally the amounts requested for several anti-tank weapons programs:

● $134 million, instead of the $154 million requested, for nearly 3,200 Hellfire missiles, carried by Apache helicopters.

● $183 million, as requested, for more than 9,000 TOW missiles, launched from several types of helicopters and ground vehicles.

● $120 million, an increase of $10 million over the request, to gear up for production of the Javelin anti-tank missile, small enough to be carried by one person; and

● $123 million, as requested, to continue developing LOSAT, an armored tank hunter carrying extremely fast rockets intended to punch through the armor of any tank.

As requested, the bill included $125 million to continue upgrading the Army's self-propelled 155mm artillery so they could fire more rapidly and more accurately. And it included $48 million to buy towed 105mm cannon for use by "light" Army units that relied for transport on airplanes and helicopters that could not carry the larger cannon.

Following the Senate's lead, it added to the request $13 million for the Army and Marine Corps to test towed 155mm cannon that were light enough to be carried by helicopter.

The budget requested $197 million for 44 MLRS artillery rocket launchers for the Army but no funds to buy additional rockets. Taking advantage of an existing contract, the conference report included a total of $405 million for 30,000 rockets and 97 launchers distributed among the Army, the Marines and the National Guard.

Both chambers had included $167 million in the bill for 351 larger, longer-range ATACMs artillery rockets.

The budget requested, and the House approved, $311 million to buy one JSTARS airborne radar plane, designed to detect ground targets far behind enemy lines. Like the Senate's version, however, the final version of the bill included $512 million for two of the planes.

It also added to the budget $35 million to develop a ground terminal mounted in a "humvee"-type pickup truck so combat commanders close to the front lines could receive JSTARS data.

As requested, the bill included $127 million to buy 170 humvees equipped with batteries of Stinger short-range anti-aircraft missiles. But the bill also added funds for armored anti-aircraft vehicles that would fare better near the front lines than would pickup trucks:

● $19 million for a version of the Marines' LAV armored car equipped with an anti-aircraft gun and Stingers, and

● $16 million to test the feasibility of mounting anti-aircraft missiles on a Bradley troop carrier and to test the value of arming anti-aircraft vehicles with missiles other than Stingers.

### Air Combat

As requested, the bill included $615 million for 24 Air Force F-16s. But it also included $68 million for components to be used in additional F-16s that would be included in the fiscal 1994 budget. The Bush administration had planned to buy no additional F-16s after fiscal 1993.

On most other programs to buy or develop tactical airplanes, the bill conformed to the authorization measure, providing:

● $1.2 billion for 36 Navy F/A-18s. The budget requested $1.6 billion for 48 planes.

● $2 billion, of the $2.2 billion requested, to continue development of the Air Force's F-22 fighter.

● $944 million of the $1.1 billion requested to develop an enlarged version of the F/A-18; and

● $166 million, as requested, to develop a new, stealthy bomber, designated AX, to fly from aircraft carriers.

The bill also added to the request $200 million for a long-term program to refurbish the Navy's F-14 long-range fighter planes.

For the radar-guided AMRAAM, the only air-to-air missile in production for U.S. forces, the final bill conformed to the Senate's version, providing $756 million to buy 1,040. The budget requested and the House approved $869 million for 1,155 AMRAAMs.

Yet another legacy of the war with Iraq that surfaced in the bill was the high political standing of "smart" bombs, which TV viewers saw blast targets with seemingly unerring accuracy. The bill included the $76 million requested for 102 bombs of one type, which had a one-ton warhead and could be carried by large fighter planes. But it also added to the budget:

● $24 million for larger, Israeli-designed Popeye missiles, to be carried by B-52 bombers, and

● $90 million for smaller SLAM missiles.

### Naval Warfare

To buy the nuclear power plant and other "long lead-

time" components of an aircraft carrier slated for inclusion in the fiscal 1995 budget request, the bill included the $832 million requested.

It also included $3.25 billion of the $3.35 billion requested for four Aegis destroyers, as approved by the Senate. The House had approved only $682 million in new funds but also would have transferred from other Pentagon accounts enough to cover the cost of three destroyers.

As requested, the bill included:

- $404 million for 200 Tomahawk long-range cruise missiles, which could be carried by many surface ships and submarines, and
- $257 million for 330 Standard anti-aircraft missiles.

To develop a network of defenses and decoys to protect ships against cruise missiles, the bill included $222 million, $62 million more than was requested.

As the Soviet army's tanks dominated U.S. planning for ground combat, so the number and quality of the Soviet navy's submarines had long made anti-submarine warfare the U.S. Navy's priority.

Conferees on HR 5504 cited the demise of the Soviet sub threat as one reason for two cuts they made in the budget request. The bill included:

- $361 million for 21 ship-borne, sub-hunting versions of the Army's Blackhawk helicopter. The budget requested $438 million for 24 of the craft, and
- $14 million of the $35 million requested for the fiscal 1993 increment of an effort to develop a new sub-hunting computer and software for the fleet of Orion long-range, land-based patrol planes. On Oct. 14, the Navy announced that it was canceling the $1.5 billion program, on which it had spent about $400 million.

On the other hand, the bill included $150 million to continue developing the *Seawolf*-class submarine. Bush tried to cancel construction of all but the first of this projected class of ships, which was designed with the Soviet threat in mind. But Congress had insisted that at least two be built.

And even with the Soviet sub threat gone, the Navy warned of the many countries equipped with small diesel subs, which were hard to detect because they were so quiet. Perhaps for that reason, the bill included basically the amounts requested for other anti-sub programs, including:

- $135 million, of the $155 million requested, to develop a nuclear-powered sub, dubbed *Centurion*, intended to be less expensive than the *Seawolf*; and
- $432 million, as requested, for 320 anti-sub homing torpedoes.

The bill added to the request $10 million to contine production of a ship-launched anti-sub missile designated ASROC.

For two minesweepers, the bill included $236 million, a reduction of $10 million from the budget request. It added $14 million to the request to continue developing a helicopter-borne, mine-hunting laser called Magic Lantern.

## Air and Sea Transport

All four defense funding committees agreed that the Air Force was trying to accelerate too quickly production of the C-17 wide-body cargo plane. The final version of HR 5504 included $1.81 billion for six of the long-range jets instead of the $2.51 billion requested for eight planes.

But as a hedge against problems with the C-17, the bill also added to the budget request $26 million to develop the option of refurbishing for longer use some of the Air Force's Vietnam War-era C-141 cargo planes.

The bill included $965 million for 28 Hercules medium-range cargo planes, rather than the $300 million requested for eight. Most of the added planes were earmarked for Guard and reserve units.

Both chambers had added to the budget request $755 million to continue preparing for production of V-22 Osprey tilt-rotor planes, designed for the Marines to use as troop carriers. Though Defense Secretary Dick Cheney had tried to squelch this program since 1989, he had been stymied by broad congressional support, anchored in Texas and Pennsylvania, where the program's two main contractors were based.

In July, a few weeks before an Osprey prototype crashed near Washington, D.C., Cheney offered to proceed with development of the plane but also asked Congress to approve $10 million requested to begin designing a conventional helicopter that the Marines could use instead of the Osprey.

The bill included the $10 million.

To expand the Navy's fleet of relatively fast cargo ships, designed to quickly load and unload the tanks and other combat gear of U.S.-based Army units, the bill included $613 million, instead of the $1.2 billion requested. Along with $1.9 billion appropriated for sealift in previous years, the new funds were to be deposited in a national defense sealift fund, which could be used to build new ships or to buy and modify existing commercial ships.

Like the House version, the final bill added $300 million to the request for an amphibious landing ship. Both chambers had included in the bill more than $1 billion for a large helicopter carrier designed to carry 2,000 Marines and up to 40 big troop-carrying helicopters. But in an effort to squeeze additional programs into this bill, the conferees agreed to include only $305 million — enough to get the ship under contract, thus locking in a price and delivery schedule guaranteed by an option due to expire at the end of 1992.

The balance of the ship's cost would have to be included in future funding bills, making this a rare departure from the Appropriations committees' vigorous opposition to such "incremental funding" of a major program.

In general, the committees insisted on "full funding" in a single bill of any major program so members could judge it in light of its full cost.

## Other Provisions

The bill added $176 million earmarked for research programs at specific colleges to the budget request. And it included $95 million for construction projects at 10 universities, earmarks that the House had thrown out of the annual energy and water appropriations bill.

It included a Senate initiative adding $210 million to the budget request for Army research on breast cancer.

The bill also included funds for various other agencies, including:

- $303 million to be transferred to the Coast Guard.
- $65 million for emergency assistance to commercial fishermen who suffered uninsured losses in recent hurricanes; and
- $126 million for the Energy Department's Strategic Petroleum Reserve.

The bill also included a provision authorizing payment of an undetermined amount to Turkey as a gesture of regret for the accidental launch from the U.S. aircraft carrier *Saratoga* of a missile that severely damaged an escorting Turkish destroyer and killed several of that ship's crew. ■

# Foreign Aid Funded for Six Months

Congress gave final approval April 1 to a $14.6 billion stopgap foreign aid bill that included $270 million in increased funding for U.N. peacekeeping operations and permitted expanded efforts to aid the former Soviet Union.

The same day, President Bush signed the bill (H J Res 456 — PL 102-266), which funded international aid programs for the nearly six months that remained in fiscal 1992. The measure filled the vacuum created by the failure of Congress in 1991 to approve a full-year appropriations measure for fiscal 1992. The full-year spending bill became entangled in the administration's dispute with Israel over loan guarantees.

The continuing resolution (CR) provided most of the $350 million increase in international peacekeeping funds that the administration sought for fiscal 1992. The funding was for assessed contributions to the United Nations and supported U.N. operations aimed at forging or preserving fragile peace agreements in Cambodia, El Salvador, Yugoslavia and other nations.

While attention was focused on the administration's broad new legislative proposal for the former Soviet republics, the continuing resolution also permitted the administration to provide $150 million in technical and humanitarian assistance in fiscal 1992. (Freedom Support Act, p. 523)

Although the measure appropriated no new aid, it made it easier for the administration to shift aid previously allocated for other countries to the former republics. The continuing resolution also repealed a pair of Cold War-era laws that prevented most Export-Import Bank lending to the Soviet Union.

## BACKGROUND

Congressional support for foreign assistance was so weak in 1992 that some key lawmakers expected most U.S. aid programs to shut down March 31, with the expiration of the continuing resolution enacted in 1991 that funded such programs.

As the week of March 23 ended, the House and its Appropriations Committee had failed to take any action on a new stopgap measure that members had crafted to fund foreign aid for the remainder of the fiscal year.

Rep. David R. Obey, D-Wis., the chairman of the House Appropriations Subcommittee on Foreign Operations, said March 25, "The most likely outcome is that come Tuesday night [March 31], our aid missions will close, and Peace Corps volunteers will not be paid."

Sen. Bob Kasten, R-Wis., said he anticipated that the deadline would be missed, adding, "The question is what we do after that." Kasten — a tireless supporter of Israel — was considering an amendment to any continuing resolution that would have provided loan guarantees sought by the Jewish state, a move that could have further muddied the situation.

Bush already had pledged to veto any legislation that would have provided loan guarantees without requiring Israel to restrict settlement construction in the territories it occupied. (Israeli loan guarantees, p. 539)

A funding suspension of more than a few days could have disrupted a host of U.S. aid programs, from refugee relief to emergency disaster assistance.

Administration officials said that previously approved aid was available to fund programs in the event of a cutoff. But there would be no one to manage the programs because salaries for employees of the Agency for International Development (AID) — the lead agency in providing U.S. assistance abroad — would be halted.

The House approved a fiscal 1992 foreign aid appropriations bill (HR 2621) in June 1991. But the bill got caught up in the controversy over loan guarantees for Israel, forcing Congress to resort to a five-month continuing resolution in October (PL 102-145). (1991 Almanac, p. 646)

The need for a second stopgap measure arose after the administration failed to reach a compromise on Israel's request with Kasten and Patrick J. Leahy, D-Vt., chairman of the Senate Appropriations Subcommittee on Foreign Operations.

While foreign aid was typically political poison for lawmakers in an election year, an unusual set of circumstances had made the continuing resolution an even tougher sell.

House members, tarred by the widening scandal over kited checks, were particularly reluctant to vote to send resources overseas. "Everyone is gun-shy now," said Rep. Henry J. Hyde, R-Ill. (House bank scandal, p. 23)

Obey blamed the administration's failure to address the nation's domestic needs for the decline in support for foreign aid. "We are paying the price for that domestic policy vacuum," he said.

House leaders had been seeking to have the unpopular continuing resolution approved quickly and quietly, without a recorded vote. But that strategy met resistance from Republicans, who seemed eager to voice their opposition to the continuing resolution.

"No way we can do a foreign aid CR on a voice vote right now," Rep. Steve Gunderson of Wisconsin, a deputy Republican whip, said March 26.

Some lawmakers said a strong pitch from the president for the continuing resolution would provide political cover for Democrats as well as Republicans.

Obey was more concerned about the possibility that Senate supporters of Israel would try to revive the loan guarantees on the must-pass stopgap bill. During a March 25 interview, he could not contain his anger at senators he described as "so damned greedy" that they would risk Israel's established aid program by continuing to press for the guarantees.

In recent years, Congress had required the administration to provide Israel's entire allocation of military and economic aid shortly after the start of the fiscal year. But under the continuing resolution, the administration provided only half of the aid.

Clearly enraged by the tactics deployed by Israel's backers, Obey asked, "When are people going to realize that enough is enough, even for Israel?"

## MEETING THE DEADLINE

The rush to pass the continuing resolution began hours before the expiration of the 1991 continuing resolution on March 31. The House approved the $14.6 billion measure, 275-131. (Vote 63, p. 16-H)

When the March 31 deadline passed without Senate action, the Office of Management and Budget prepared an order that would have required AID effectively to shut

# Foreign Operations Appropriations

*(In thousands of dollars)*

| | Fiscal 1991 Appropriation | President's Request | House Bill | Continuing Resolution |
|---|---|---|---|---|
| **Multilateral Aid** | | | | |
| World Bank | | | | |
| Paid-in capital | $ 110,592 | $ 70,126 | $ 70,126 | $ 70,126 |
| *Limitation on callable capital* | *(2,899,610)* | *(2,267,418)* | *(2,267,418)* | *(2,267,418)* |
| Global Environmental Facility | — | — | 50,000 | — |
| International Development Association | 1,064,150 | 1,060,000 | 1,060,000 | 1,060,000 |
| International Finance Corporation | 40,331 | 50,000 | 40,331 | 40,331 |
| Inter-American Development Bank | 91,299 | 90,389 | 90,389 | 90,389 |
| *Limitation on callable capital* | *(2,235,077)* | *(2,235,077)* | *(2,235,077)* | *(2,235,077)* |
| Enterprise for the Americas investment fund | — | 100,000 | 100,000 | — |
| Asian Development Bank | — | 25,526 | 25,526 | — |
| Asian Development Fund | 126,854 | 174,955 | 158,793 | 126,854 |
| African Development Bank | 10,136 | 8,987 | 8,987 | 8,987 |
| African Development Fund | 105,452 | 135,000 | 135,000 | 105,452 |
| European Development Bank | 70,021 | 70,021 | 70,021 | 70,021 |
| International Monetary Fund (U.S. quota increase) | — | 12,158,000 | · — | — |
| State Department international programs | 284,730 | 250,212 | 300,612 | 284,730 |
| Other | 10,601 | 50,001 | 3,001 | — |
| **TOTAL, Multilateral Aid** | **$ 1,914,166** | **$ 14,243,217** | **$ 2,112,786** | **$ 1,856,890** |
| **Bilateral Aid** | | | | |
| Agency for International Development (AID) | | | | |
| Development assistance | 1,313,683 | 1,277,000 | 1,376,635 | 1,313,683 |
| Sub-Saharan Africa, development aid | 800,000 | 800,000 | 1,000,000 | 800,000 |
| Operating expenses | 474,884 | 521,039 | 519,039 | 519,039 |
| Enterprise for the Americas: debt reduction | — | 304,340 | 65,000 | — |
| Economic Support Fund | 3,991,000 | 3,228,000 | 3,216,624 | 3,216,624 |
| Multilateral Assistance for Philippines | 100,000 | 160,000 | 160,000 | 100,000 |
| Assistance for Eastern Europe | 369,675 | 400,000 | 400,000 | 369,675 |
| Other | 214,341 | 170,218 | 337,218 | 237,420 |
| **Subtotal, AID** | **$ 7,263,583** | **$ 6,860,597** | **$ 7,074,516** | **$ 6,556,441** |
| State Department | | | | |
| International narcotics control | 150,000 | 171,500 | 150,000 | 150,000 |
| Migration and refugee aid | 520,648 | 510,557 | 680,000 | 680,000 |
| Anti-terrorism assistance | 12,026 | 15,000 | 15,000 | 12,026 |
| **Subtotal, State Department** | **$ 682,674** | **$ 697,057** | **$ 845,000** | **$ 842,026** |
| Peace Corps | 186,000 | 200,000 | 200,000 | 200,000 |
| Overseas Private Investment Corp. *(loan levels)* | *(290,000)* | *(400,000)* | *(400,000)* | *(400,000)* |
| Other | 38,000 | 74,393 | 53,143 | 55,330 |
| **TOTAL, bilateral aid** | **$ 8,170,257** | **$ 7,832,047** | **$ 8,172,659** | **$ 7,653,797** |
| **Bilateral Military Aid** (appropriated to the president) | | | | |
| Foreign military financing | 4,663,420 | 4,640,000 | 4,150,900 | 4,150,900 |
| *Estimated loan program* | — | *(313,961)* | *(404,000)* | *(404,000)* |
| International military education and training | 47,196 | 52,500 | 47,196 | 47,196 |
| Special defense acquisition *(limitation on obligations)* | *(350,000)* | *(275,000)* | *(275,000)* | *(275,000)* |
| Other | 664,862 | 48,000 | 38,000 | 38,000 |
| **TOTAL, military aid** | **$ 5,375,478** | **$4,740,500** | **$ 4,236,096** | **$ 4,236,096** |
| **Export Assistance** | | | | |
| Export-Import Bank | 750,000 | 555,778 | 650,613 | 650,613 |
| Export assistance *(loan levels)* | — | *(9,525,000)* | *(11,000,000)* | *(11,000,000)* |
| Trade and development | 35,000 | 35,000 | 40,000 | 35,000 |
| International peacekeeping | — | 350,000 | — | 270,000 |
| Small-business emergency loans | — | — | — | 107,025 |
| **GRAND TOTAL** | **$ 16,245,401** [1] | **$ 28,026,542** [2] | **$ 15,196,946** [3] | **$ 14,596,721** [4] |

[1] *Fiscal 1991 total included $500,000 in other assistance for Eastern Europe.*
[2] *Administration request included $270 million to refinance already concluded foreign military sales.*
[3] *House bill included a 1 percent cut in most categories and $135 million for deficit reduction.*
[4] *Continuing resolution applies a 1.48 percent cut, totaling $212.7 million, to all categories except earmarked aid.*

SOURCE: House Appropriations Committee

down. The order would have forced more than 2,000 furloughs at AID. The Senate approved the measure, 84-16, on April 1, just before the order was to be executed. *(Vote 62, p. 9-S)*

The House then cleared the measure, accepting without objection an unrelated amendment attached by the Senate that provided $107 million in additional funding for the Small Business Administration's disaster loan program.

The brief hangup in the Senate was caused largely by the continuing dispute over Israel's request for $10 billion in U.S. loan guarantees. Dennis DeConcini, D-Ariz., and other supporters of Israel said they intended to amend the measure with loan guarantees despite Bush's pledge to veto any legislation that did not also require Israel to freeze the construction of settlements in its occupied territories.

The regular foreign aid bill for fiscal 1992 had been scuttled after the administration and members of the Senate failed in 1991 to reach agreement on the loan guarantees, which Israel was seeking to absorb a wave of Jewish immigration from the former Soviet Union. Angered by the administration's tough stance, some supporters of Israel were eager to challenge the president, although there appeared to be no prospect to override a veto.

But officials from American Jewish organizations feared another showdown with the White House and persuaded the senators not to attach the loan guarantees to the continuing resolution, according to congressional sources.

In an arrangement negotiated by Senate leaders, the lawmakers settled instead for a vaguely worded, nonbinding resolution (S Res 277) that expressed support for "appropriate loan guarantees" for Israel.

The resolution, originally sponsored by Frank R. Lautenberg, D-N.J., was approved 99-1, with only Sen. Robert C. Byrd, D-W.Va., casting a nay vote. *(Vote 63, p. 9-S)*

But the vote provided little indication of how the Senate would approach a substantive loan guarantee proposal. Many of those who agreed with the administration's position, such as Minority Leader Bob Dole, R-Kan., also voted for the resolution.

### Modest Funding

Although the stopgap spending bill reduced aid more than $1 billion below the level enacted in fiscal 1991, lawmakers approached it with a distinct lack of enthusiasm.

"I'm quite surprised at the strong vote, but I don't think it indicates support for foreign aid," Rep. William S. Broomfield, R-Mich., said after the House vote.

The debate in both chambers was brief and perfunctory, as few members spoke in support of the bill.

But faced with a suspension of nearly all aid programs as well as the impending layoff of thousands of employees at AID, the Peace Corps and other agencies, most lawmakers felt they had little choice but to approve the continuing resolution.

Recognizing the anti-foreign aid mood that had gripped Congress, Obey, who managed the bill, emphasized the relatively modest level of spending that would be provided.

Foreign aid funding in the bill was $700 million below the fiscal 1992 legislation, which the House had approved the previous June. It was also $13.1 billion below the administration's budget request for fiscal 1992, primarily because the continuing resolution did not include the requested $12.2 billion increase in U.S. financial backing for the International Monetary Fund (IMF).

Obey said that Treasury Secretary Nicholas F. Brady urged lawmakers to approve the IMF funding request, the

centerpiece of the administration's aid package for the former republics. But, Obey said, "the IMF request cannot pass unless the president engages in a major national campaign" and made "a personal effort to round up votes for it."

The bill generally retained the spending formula from the stopgap bill that expired at the end of March. It funded programs at the level enacted in fiscal 1991 or the level in the House-passed bill for fiscal 1992, whichever was lower.

A number of important programs were exempted from the formula, including aid for refugees around the world and operating expenses for the Peace Corps and AID. Without the waiver for operating expenses, AID would have had to furlough an estimated 4,000 employees about one day a week for the remainder of the fiscal year, according to agency officials.

The legislation also retained earmarks from the House-passed bill for a host of popular humanitarian programs, including $250 million for AID's child survival programs and $10 million for the United Nations Children's Fund.

In order to provide additional peacekeeping support, however, Obey reduced all assistance programs — except those going to a few countries for which Congress had usually earmarked aid, such as Israel and Egypt — by an additional 1.48 percent, which saved more than $200 million.

Obey also tweaked his Senate counterparts by eliminating 16 earmarks from the fiscal 1991 bill, many of which were included by senators.

For example, the legislation ended earmarks for military aid for Morocco and for a host of international environmental programs that had been backed strongly by Sen. Kasten, Obey's Wisconsin colleague.

The Senate, which typically set more funding requirements than the House, was in a weak position to challenge the action. Administration officials worked with Obey and other House members in crafting the measure and would have opposed efforts by senators to reattach the earmarks.

Aid for the Philippines was also cut. Under the Multilateral Assistance Initiative, the Philippines was due to receive $160 million in fiscal 1992, but the continuing resolution cut that to $100 million.

### El Salvador Compromise

The bill included a compromise on military aid for El Salvador, an issue that had divided Congress and the executive branch for more than a decade.

The measure allowed the administration to spend for non-lethal supplies $21.3 million in previously approved assistance to the Salvadoran military. But the legislation transferred the remainder of the administration's request for fiscal 1992, $63.8 million, to a fund to rebuild the country and retrain combatants.

The government of El Salvador and left-wing guerrillas had signed a peace agreement in January 1992, ending the country's long-running civil conflict.

The continuing resolution placed tighter restrictions on the administration than a draft authorization bill that was approved by the House Foreign Affairs Committee in March but went nowhere. The committee had briefly attempted to revive and retool an authorization bill that had failed in 1991. *(1991 Almanac, p. 470)*

Unlike the draft authorization bill, the stopgap spending bill required that the administration seek the approval of key congressional committees before spending the remaining aid for fiscal 1992.

Joe Moakley, D-Mass., chairman of a House task force on El Salvador, expressed disappointment that the measure provided any aid for the country's military forces. "While it's not the agreement we'd like," he conceded, "it's the best one we can get."

### Middle East Concerns

Most of the discussion in the Senate concerned what was not included in the bill — the loan guarantees and restrictions on aid to Jordan.

Sen. Hank Brown, R-Colo., had intended to offer an amendment requiring the administration to certify that Jordan was observing the U.N. embargo on Iraq before giving the kingdom any assistance. Numerous news reports alleged that Jordan was helping Iraq circumvent the embargo.

But Brown dropped his amendment after Secretary of State James A. Baker III personally provided assurances that he would ensure that Jordan abided by the U.N. resolutions.

That outraged Sen. Alfonse M. D'Amato, R-N.Y., who called it an "absolutely contemptible act" to provide aid for Jordan without requiring presidential certification. D'Amato was one of 16 senators to oppose the continuing resolution.

After approving the stopgap bill, which did not mention Israel's request for loan guarantees, the Senate conducted the first extended congressional debate on the request when it took up the nonbinding resolution.

Lautenberg attempted to cast the symbolic resolution in positive terms. "It simply puts the United States Senate on record in support of loan guarantees for Israel," he said.

But Dole and others said the measure was so ambiguous that it could be interpreted to mean almost anything, including support for the administration's Middle East policies.

Kasten vowed to include loan guarantees on future legislation, possibly the administration's aid plan for the former Soviet republics. "This is only the beginning" of congressional efforts to enact the guarantees, Kasten said.

# Bill Reflects New Foreign Aid Interests

Congress approved $12.3 billion in new financing for the International Monetary Fund (IMF) and $10 billion in loan guarantees for Israel when it sent President Bush the first foreign aid appropriations bill in nearly two years.

With minimal debate, the House on Oct. 5 adopted the conference report on the $26.3 billion spending measure (HR 5368); the Senate approved it by voice vote later that day.

The bill cut about $1.1 billion from the administration's request for fiscal 1993. The final version of the legislation provided $12.5 billion more than the House-passed bill, which did not include the IMF appropriation, and $162 million less than the Senate bill.

In a number of areas, the bill marked a significant departure from foreign aid legislation enacted during the Cold War: A House-Senate conference committee on Oct. 2 moderated tough restrictions imposed by the Senate on aid to Russia — a program that did not exist the last time such a conference convened.

New controversies, reflecting the evolution of congressional foreign policy interests, replaced old ideological struggles. Over administration objections, the conferees authorized up to $50 million in U.S. military equipment for the besieged republic of Bosnia.

That represented the strongest congressional action favoring one side in the former Yugoslavia, although it did not compel Bush to provide the aid.

But the changing ideas about foreign assistance did not extend to the Middle East, where most U.S. military and economic aid continued to flow. The bill provided $3 billion

> ### BOXSCORE
>
> ➡ **Fiscal 1993 Foreign Operations appropriations (HR 5368).** The $26.3 billion spending bill provided funding for foreign operations.
>
> **Reports:** H Rept 102-585; S Rept 102-419; conference report filed in the House, H Rept 102-1011.
>
> #### KEY ACTION
>
> June 25 — The **House** passed HR 5368 by a vote of 297-124.
>
> Oct. 1 — The **Senate** passed HR 5368 by a vote of 87-12.
>
> Oct. 5 — The **House** agreed to conference report by a vote of 312-105; the **Senate** agreed to conference report by voice vote.
>
> Oct. 6 — President Bush signed HR 5368 — PL 102-391.

in aid for Israel and $2.1 billion for Egypt, the same levels as in recent years.

Congress had long been a wellspring of support for Israel, and the authorization of the five-year program of loan guarantees for Jerusalem — on top of the $3 billion in direct aid — made the bill more palatable for many members.

Excluding the one-time appropriation for the IMF, the measure provided $1.4 billion less than the fiscal 1991 aid bill, which was the last one to clear Congress.

That sharp reduction in spending helped ease anxiety among lawmakers about casting an election-year vote for foreign aid.

"It's a very tight bill, and we gave people some arguments to take home and defend," said Rep. David R. Obey, D-Wis., chairman of the House Appropriations Subcommittee on Foreign Operations.

Passage of the legislation also represented a qualified success for the Bush administration. The loan guarantees and the IMF appropriation — an essential component of the administration's aid initiative for the former Soviet republics — were regarded as legislative priorities by the White House.

In addition, the measure included $417 million in economic and technical assistance for the former Soviet republics and $50 million to restructure debts owed by Latin American governments.

But the administration was forced to swallow major reductions in military aid and in Economic Support Funds (ESF), a key category of economic assistance.

The conference committee agreed to convert military assistance grants for three NATO allies — Turkey, Greece and Portugal — into low-interest loans. The bill provided $3.5 billion in military aid, a $596 million reduction from the fiscal 1992 level.

Funding for ESF, a program of cash transfers and other assistance for key U.S. allies, was cut by $498 million from fiscal 1992 to $2.7 billion.

## BACKGROUND

In 1991, Congress did not enact a full-year foreign operations measure on a normal schedule. Instead, it funded foreign operations through a continuing resolution that provided funding through March 31, 1992, because a fiscal 1992 bill was not enacted before then. *(1991 Almanac, p. 646)*

Congress on April 1 then approved a $14.6 billion stopgap foreign aid spending bill (H J Res 456), which funded international aid programs for the six months that remained in fiscal 1992. *(Stopgap foreign aid, p. 609)*

Like a full-year foreign aid bill, the two successive stopgap spending bills paid for foreign aid and U.S. participation in a variety of international military and economic efforts.

More than three-quarters of the money in the bills went toward bilateral military and economic assistance programs. They also funded U.S. quotas in multilateral banks and development institutions as well as export assistance programs.

Also, most activities of the Agency for International Development (AID), the primary provider of U.S. foreign aid, were funded by the spending bills.

Congress scrapped the fiscal 1992 bill as part of an agreement with the Bush administration to defer consideration of Israel's request for $10 billion in loan guarantees.

Israel was seeking the guarantees to back $10 billion in commercial loans, which were to be used to help absorb the expected influx of Jewish immigrants from the Soviet Union and Eastern Europe in the next five years. With the guarantees in hand, the Israeli government was able to negotiate lower rates for the loans.

The two men with the most to say about the foreign operations bill were an unlikely pair of liberals from rural states: Obey from Wisconsin and Sen. Patrick J. Leahy, D-Vt., the chairmen of the House and Senate Foreign Operations subcommittees.

While other lawmakers had earned more recognition for their foreign policy expertise, none had as much direct influence on U.S. foreign policy.

Congress had been unable to clear a foreign aid authorization measure — which was supposed to set broad guidelines for providing U.S. foreign assistance — since 1985. In that void, the House and Senate Foreign Operations subcommittees effectively took on the role of authorizers as well as appropriators.

The two chairmen clashed, sometimes bitterly, over turf and specific provisions in the bill. But they shared the same overall objective regarding U.S. foreign aid spending: Both supported shifting funds from military aid programs to development and humanitarian assistance.

Obey, in particular, made a strong personal imprint on the bill. He assumed the chairmanship of the House subcommittee in 1985, when the top priority of the Reagan administration's foreign assistance program was to bolster key allies as bulwarks against communism.

Helped immeasurably by the demise of communism and with a more pragmatic occupant in the White House, Obey reduced the percentage of military aid provided in the bill. During fiscal 1987, military assistance accounted for 37 percent of the funding in the bill. In the fiscal 1992 House bill, military aid made up 28 percent of the funding.

Instead, Obey funneled more money to a range of health and development programs that were specifically geared toward improving the lot of the world's poor, especially poor children.

## HOUSE COMMITTEE ACTION

A House subcommittee on June 12 cut $1.2 billion from the Bush administration's foreign assistance request for fiscal 1993.

The bare-bones, $13.9 billion foreign aid budget approved by voice vote by the House Appropriations Subcommittee on Foreign Operations was $249 million below the continuing resolution (PL 102-266) that was funding foreign aid in fiscal 1992. And that measure had provided the lowest level of foreign aid since 1983.

Subcommittee Chairman Obey said he felt obliged to seek deep reductions in foreign assistance because of the funding shortfall for domestic programs, which was forcing other Appropriations subcommittees to make draconian cuts.

"I think people are going to be in agony because of the reductions the [Appropriations] committee has made," he said. "Certainly that will be the case with this bill."

Even with the cuts, Obey was dubious that the bill would be approved by a Congress increasingly opposed to overseas spending. "The question is whether any foreign aid bill can pass the House this year," he said.

Obey added that he planned to offer an amendment on the House floor to cut an additional $400 million from the bill in the name of deficit reduction.

The panel gave an important boost to the administration's massive aid proposal for the former republics of the Soviet Union, approving $417 million in assistance.

The subcommittee did not consider the administration's request for $12 billion in additional financing for the IMF, the centerpiece of its aid request for the former republics.

But Obey said he would not object if the authorization bill for the former republics also included language appropriating the administration's request. Obey had long been critical of the request, arguing that the administration had failed to demonstrate sufficient support for the proposal.

### Where Cuts Fell

The panel achieved much of its savings in foreign aid by making significant changes in the military assistance program.

The subcommittee reduced military assistance by $688 million from existing levels by eliminating grants to Turkey and other U.S. allies in Europe that hosted NATO bases. The panel approved replacing the grants with market-based loans.

Under the subcommittee's action, the administration's $543 million request for military aid for Turkey in fiscal 1993 — $500 million of it in grants — would have been provided entirely in the form of loans.

The fiscal 1993 military aid levels already were well below the level requested by the administration, according to country-by-country allocations for fiscal 1992 aid re-

# Foreign Aid Spending

*(HR 5368, as cleared for the president, in thousands of dollars)*

| | Fiscal 1992 Appropriation | Fiscal 1993 Bush Request | House Bill | Senate Bill | Final Bill |
|---|---|---|---|---|---|
| **Multilateral Aid** | | | | | |
| World Bank | | | | | |
| Paid-in capital | $ 69,089 | $ 70,126 | $ 62,180 | $ 62,180 | $ 62,180 |
| *Limitation on callable capital* | *(2,233,903)* | *(2,267,418)* | *(2,010,513)* | *(2,010,513)* | *(2,010,513)* |
| International Development Association | 1,044,332 | 1,060,000 | 1,024,332 | 1,024,332 | 1,024,332 |
| Global Environment Facility | — | — | — | 30,000 | 30,000 |
| International Finance Corp. | 39,735 | 50,000 | 35,762 | 35,762 | 35,762 |
| Inter-American Development Bank | 85,053 | 77,889 | 76,738 | 76,738 | 76,738 |
| *Limit on callable capital* | *(2,202,040)* | *(2,235,077)* | *(2,202,040)* | *(2,202,040)* | *(2,202,040)* |
| Enterprise for the Americas investment fund | — | 100,000 | 75,000 | 100,000 | 90,000 |
| Asian Development Bank | — | 51,041 | 25,514 | 25,514 | 38,014 |
| Asian Development Fund | 124,979 | 144,474 | 75,000 | 75,000 | 62,500 |
| African Development Bank | 8,854 | — | — | — | — |
| African Development Fund | 103,893 | 135,000 | 103,893 | 103,893 | 103,893 |
| European Development Bank | 68,986 | 70,021 | 68,986 | — | 60,000 |
| U.S. Quota, International Monetary Fund | — | 12,313,857 | — | 12,313,857 | 12,313,857 |
| State Department International programs | 280,522 | 256,650 | 310,000 | 312,500 | 310,000 |
| **TOTAL, multilateral aid** | **$ 1,825,443** | **$ 14,329,058** | **$ 1,857,405** | **$ 14,040,802** [1] | **$ 14,207,276** |
| **Bilateral Aid** | | | | | |
| Agency for International Development (AID) | | | | | |
| Development assistance | 1,287,945 | 1,265,500 | 1,343,480 | 1,387,480 | 1,387,480 |
| Sub-Saharan Africa development/disaster aid | 788,175 | 775,600 | 880,000 | 900,000 | 900,000 |
| AID operating expenses | 511,303 | 572,456 | 549,181 | 552,256 | 551,316 |
| Enterprise for the Americas: debt reduction | — | 202,119 | — | 100,000 | 50,000 |
| Economic Support Fund | 3,167,979 | 3,112,000 | 2,739,000 | 2,526,086 | 2,670,000 |
| Multilateral aid for Philippines | 78,522 | 80,000 | 40,000 | 40,000 | 40,000 |
| Assistance for Eastern Europe | 364,211 | 450,000 | 400,000 | 400,000 | 400,000 |
| Assistance for ex-Soviet nations | — | 350,000 | 417,000 | 417,000 | 417,000 |
| Other | 235,230 | 275,696 | 187,224 | 148,596 | 172,064 |
| **Subtotal, AID** | **$ 6,433,365** | **$ 7,083,371** | **$ 6,555,885** | **$ 6,471,418** | **$ 6,587,860** |
| State Department | | | | | |
| International narcotics control | 147,783 | 173,000 | 147,783 | 147,783 | 147,783 |
| Migration and refugee aid | 669,949 | 570,000 | 669,949 | 669,949 | 669,949 |
| Anti-terrorism assistance | 11,848 | 15.555 | 15,555 | 11,848 | 15,555 |
| **Subtotal, State Department** | **$ 829,580** | **$ 758,555** | **$ 833,287** | **$ 829,580** | **$ 833,287** |
| Peace Corps | 197,044 | 218,146 | 218,146 | 218,146 | 218,146 |
| Overseas Private Investment Corp. *(loan levels)* | *(400,000)* | *(535,000)* | *(—)* | *(655,000)* | *(650,000)* |
| Other | 54,511 | 68,303 | 64,938 | 67,598 | 65,793 |
| **TOTAL, bilateral aid** | **$ 7,514,500** | **$ 8,128,375** | **$ 7,672,256** | **$ 7,586,742** | **$ 7,705,086** |
| **Bilateral Military Aid** | | | | | |
| (appropriated to the president) | | | | | |
| Foreign military financing (grants) | 3,992,298 | 4,089,225 | 3,300,000 | 3,840,000 | 3,300,000 |
| *Estimated loan program* | *(404,000)* | *(360,000)* | *(855,000)* | *(315,000)* | *(855,000)* |
| International military education and training | 44,573 | 47,500 | 42,500 | 42,500 | 42,500 |
| Special defense acquisition fund | | | | | |
| *(limitation on obligations)* | *(230,935)* | *(280,930)* | *(150,000)* | *(250,000)* | *(225,000)* |
| Other | 77,734 | 110,498 | 81,596 | 82,806 | 176,366 |
| **TOTAL, military aid** | **$ 4,114,605** | **$ 4,247,223** | **$ 3,424,096** | **$ 3,965,306** | **$ 3,518,866** |
| **Export Assistance** | | | | | |
| Export-Import Bank | 640,996 | 682,000 | 778,509 | 786,150 | 786,150 |
| Export assistance *(loan levels)* | *(11,000,000)* | *(11,385,000)* | *(—)* | *(13,000,000)* | *(15,500,000)* |
| Trade and development | 34,483 | 40,000 | 40,000 | 40,000 | 40,000 |
| **GRAND TOTAL** | **$ 14,130,027** | **$ 27,426,656** | **$ 13,772,266** | **$ 26,419,000** | **$ 26,257,378** |

NOTE: The Senate Appropriations Committee approved an across-the-board cut of $118,974,000 for international financial institutions. The Enterprise for the Americas investment fund was excluded from the reduction.

SOURCE: House Appropriations Committee

leased by the State Department.

There were other aspects of the bill that the administration was expected to oppose. Rep. Mickey Edwards, Okla., the subcommittee's ranking Republican, said the inclusion of $20 million in assistance for the U.N. population fund probably would cause the legislation to be vetoed because of the administration's position that the program supported abortions. Edwards' amendment to strip the provision from the bill was defeated by voice vote.

The panel focused heavily on the administration's request for about $202 million to restructure the debts of several Latin American countries.

Obey had not included the funding, part of the administration's Enterprise for the Americas initiative, in the chairman's markup of the legislation. He said the proposal was similar to an administration proposal in 1990 to forgive $6.7 billion in Egypt's military debt, which was strongly opposed in the House.

"We got a lesson two years ago about what happens when you put debt relief in a bill," he said.

Rep. Robert L. Livingston, R-La., offered an amendment that would have fully funded the administration's request, arguing that the proposal could stimulate increased trade with Latin America.

In one of its few roll call votes, the subcommittee defeated Livingston's proposal, 6-7. But Obey subsequently said he would be receptive to an alternative plan under which the United States would sell to private investors its loans to Latin American countries.

Edwards indicated that the Treasury Department also might back such a proposal.

The subcommittee resolved the issue of military assistance to El Salvador with far less partisan squabbling than in the past. The panel approved, 7-5, Obey's amendment to provide $11 million in non-lethal aid to the Salvadoran military, which signed a peace agreement with the country's left-wing rebels in January.

The panel rejected, 2-10, a second Livingston amendment that would have cut off all U.S. military assistance to Jordan. Several members said that Secretary of State James A. Baker III had personally lobbied against the amendment.

But the subcommittee signaled its displeasure with Jordan's dealings with Iraq. It approved by voice vote an amendment by Edwards that would require the president to certify that Jordan was abiding by the U.N. embargo of Iraq as a condition of future military aid.

In other action, the subcommittee:

● Provided increased funding for disaster aid and African drought relief. The panel approved $69 million in international disaster assistance, $29 million more than the administration request. The subcommittee also approved $80 million in emergency drought relief for Africa.

● Earmarked the full administration request for $3 billion in military and economic aid for Israel and $2.1 billion for Egypt, the two largest recipients of U.S. assistance.

## Full Committee Action

The House Appropriations Committee on June 18 slashed the Bush administration's foreign aid budget for fiscal 1993 by $1.3 billion, approving deep cuts in military assistance to longtime U.S. allies such as Turkey and Portugal.

With no Republican opposition, the committee, by voice vote, approved $13.8 billion in foreign aid for fiscal 1993, a reduction of nearly $300 million from the continu-

ing resolution that funded foreign aid in fiscal 1992.

The panel left largely untouched the bill (HR 5368) passed by the Appropriations Subcommittee on Foreign Operations. Subcommittee Chairman Obey said members had expressed strong support for cutting foreign aid.

Subcommittee ranking Republican Edwards said that, as a percentage of the gross domestic product, "This is the smallest foreign aid bill we've had in our history."

While lawmakers endorsed the reductions, some expressed concern about Obey's announced plan to cut $400 million from the bill when it moved to the House floor.

That cut would be the first installment in Obey's five-year plan to reduce the budget deficit. He said there would be "no exceptions from the across-the-board reductions — none."

Congressional backers of Israel were worried about the potential impact of the amendment on the Jewish state. The amendment could force supporters of Israel to publicly defend foreign aid at a time when it was widely unpopular.

The across-the-board cut "could cost Israel $100 million, and it would hurt Egypt as well," said Lawrence J. Smith, D-Fla., a member of the Foreign Operations Subcommittee and an ardent supporter of Israel. The Appropriations Committee earmarked $3 billion in aid for Israel and $2.1 billion in aid for Egypt — the same amount as in recent years.

## Cuts for Turkey, Portugal, Greece

The legislation would fundamentally alter the military assistance program for Turkey, Portugal and Greece — countries that have received billions of dollars in U.S. aid largely because they were home to NATO bases.

It would require that aid for the so-called base rights countries be provided in the form of market-based loans instead of grants and low-interest loans. The panel also reduced the overall amount of military aid provided for the three countries.

In the report accompanying the bill, the committee said "given the end of the Cold War and given the state of the budget deficit" the countries should be "graduated" to a less costly program of loans.

For Turkey, the change would be especially significant. The administration had requested $543 million — $500 million in grants — for Turkey. The bill would place a ceiling of $450 million in market-based loans for Ankara.

The administration, which relied heavily on Turkey's air bases to provide assistance for Kurds in northern Iraq, sharply criticized the action.

"It's a disaster," said one State Department official. But administration officials conceded that because of the mood in Congress, it would be next to impossible to add more money to the bill.

The bill also set a ceiling of $315 million in loans for Greece, eliminating $30 million in grants from the administration's request. It cut $10 million in military aid from the administration's request of $100 million for Portugal, again requiring that it be provided entirely in loans.

Overall, the bill reduced the administration's military aid request by $823 million. Administration officials said the reductions would leave less than $200 million to meet military aid requests for every country except for Israel and Egypt.

The legislation also cut $373 million from the administration's request for $3.1 billion in economic support fund aid. Such aid was provided largely in the form of cash transfers to key U.S. allies.

### Aid for Ex-Soviets

While the administration's comprehensive proposal to help the former republics of the Soviet Union had faced delays, economic aid for them sailed through the Appropriations Committee. *(Freedom Support Act, p. 523)*

The bill included $417 million in aid for the former republics, the full administration request. There was no attempt in either the subcommittee or the full committee to reduce the amount in the aid package. The measure earmarked $50 million in scholarship programs for visiting students from the former republics.

But panel Republicans said Bush would almost certainly veto the bill because it included $20 million in aid for the U.N. Population Fund. The administration had long opposed funding for the U.N. agency because it operated in China, which had been condemned for its policy of coerced abortions.

Obey revived his proposal from 1991 that linked aid for the population fund with the president's extension of favorable trade treatment for China. The bill would authorize funding for the U.N. agency, which Bush opposed, only if Congress approved most-favored-nation status for China, which Bush sought. Edwards predicted that the administration would spurn that approach. *(1991 Almanac, p. 657)*

### Obey's Imprint

Obey's imprint was evident not only in the deep cuts in military assistance but also in substantial funding increases for several development and humanitarian-aid programs.

The bill provided $330 million in aid for international family planning programs, about $84 million more than the administration request. In addition, the measure provided $670 million for the State Department's migration and refugee aid programs, a $100 million increase over the funding sought by the administration.

The measure included $779 million in funding — $97 million more than the administration request — for the Export-Import Bank, which financed foreign purchases of U.S. goods through loans and loan guarantees. There was growing support in Congress for programs that promoted U.S. exports.

But the bill provided no money for AID's proposal to increase assistance for large-scale projects, such as dams and telecommunications systems, in less-developed countries. The administration had requested $100 million for capital projects, and a group of key senators had advocated a massive increase in spending for the program.

The spending bill also would have:

● Prohibited almost all military assistance for Guatemala, whose security forces repeatedly had been criticized for human rights abuses.

● Provided $11 million in non-lethal military assistance to El Salvador, a substantial cut from the administration's request of $40 million. The remainder of the aid was to be transferred to a fund for demobilizing combatants from the country's civil war, which ended in January.

● Imposed tough conditions on military aid for Indonesia, partly in response to the massacre by Indonesian security forces of unarmed civilians in East Timor. The bill required the administration to notify Congress before providing military aid, and the report accompanying the bill said "the committee does not believe that Indonesia should receive any United States military assistance" in fiscal 1993.

● Provided no funding for the administration's $202 million request to restructure the debts of several Latin American countries. Obey criticized the request as "a political fig leaf" that would do little to ease the region's debt burden.

## HOUSE FLOOR ACTION

The House overwhelmingly endorsed a deep cut in the nation's foreign assistance program June 25, approving a $13.8 billion version of HR 5368 that sliced about $1.3 billion from the Bush administration's request for fiscal 1993.

The bill was approved 297-124. Democrats supported the measure, 205-51. Republicans backed it, 92-72, although several party members voiced support for even greater reductions. *(Vote 235, p. 58-H)*

The administration protested that the appropriations bill provided an "inadequate" level of aid funding. Although encouraging the House to pass the bill so that it would "move forward through the legislative process," the administration also threatened to veto it over a provision to aid the U.N. Population Fund.

In perhaps its most significant action, the House approved a reduction of $24 million in development assistance, the amount the administration had requested in such aid, for India.

Dan Burton, R-Ind., who sponsored the amendment, said it was intended to punish India for its harsh military crackdown in the Punjab and Kashmir regions. But Burton and other members said the amendment also was supported because of a widespread desire to cut funding from the bill.

The amendment, opposed by the administration, was approved 219-200. *(Vote 233, p. 56-H)*

The House also approved about $36 million in reductions to the U.S. contribution to multilateral development banks and the operating expenses of the Agency for International Development (AID). It also barred the use of U.S. funds for training Indonesian military officers.

But the bill crafted by the Appropriations Subcommittee for Foreign Operations remained largely intact through floor action. Obey said he took "great pride" in the fact that the measure, expressed as a percentage of the gross domestic product, "is the tightest foreign aid bill in the history of the country."

Obey and Edwards warned lawmakers that if the bill was defeated, the administration would try to gain passage of a stopgap spending bill with higher funding levels. "That could cost $500 million more," Edwards said.

### Unhappy Administration

The legislation fully funded the administration's request for $417 million in aid for the former republics of the Soviet Union. But there was a great deal that the administration opposed in the bill.

The administration said that the elimination of military assistance grants to U.S. allies in NATO — Greece, Turkey and Portugal — "could diminish our military readiness in the Persian Gulf, the Mediterranean and the Balkans."

But Republican members did not challenge Obey's call to end "the welfare program for less-wealthy NATO allies." Largely as a result of the change from grants to market-based loans for those countries, military aid funding in the bill was $823 million below the administration's request.

The bill included $400 million in aid to Eastern Europe — a $50 million cut from the administration request — and imposed new guidelines on how the assistance program should be managed.

It provided no funding to forgive the official debt of Latin American countries under the Enterprise for the Americas initiative, which had been a top legislative priority of the Treasury Department.

Obey opposed the $202 million request for debt relief on the basis that it would do little to address the region's massive debt. But the bill provided $75 million — $25 million less than the administration request — for a regional investment fund that was part of the Latin American initiative.

The administration statement on the bill said Bush would veto the measure because it included $20 million in aid for the U.N. Population Fund. The White House opposed funding for the agency on the grounds that it "supports a program of coercive abortion or involuntary sterilization" in China.

### Rules Fight

Many lawmakers said funding in the bill would have been decimated if the rule governing consideration of the measure had been less restrictive. As approved, the bill cut more than $300 million in foreign aid from the levels in the continuing resolution that funded foreign aid in fiscal 1992.

The restrictive rule "ended up being good for the administration" because it protected the bill's funding from attack, said Doug Bereuter, R-Neb. But Bereuter said the rule "was bad for individual members" whose proposals were not considered.

Other Republicans were far more harsh in their comments. Robert S. Walker, Pa., accused the Democrats of deploying "Bolshevik" tactics by regularly limiting the number of amendments to appropriations bills. But Obey said that Republican arguments in favor of allowing more budget-cutting amendments were made hollow by the administration's call for higher aid levels. He said House Republicans had been "panicked" by recent polls showing Bush's support to be slipping.

"There is nothing more pitiful than the sight of politicians in full flight," Obey said.

The resolution providing for consideration of the bill (H Res 501) was approved 246-177, with the vote largely divided along partisan lines. *(Vote 231, p. 56-H)*

Obey decided not to offer his planned amendment to force an additional 1 percent reduction in all foreign assistance programs. That amendment already had been scaled back from the $400 million cut he had proposed during his subcommittee's consideration of the bill.

Obey said he had been asked by the administration to drop the proposal. Pro-Israel groups also lobbied intensively against the amendment, which would have forced a rare reduction in aid to Israel.

It turned out to be a good week for U.S. supporters of Israel. Despite the budget-cutting mood in Congress, the foreign aid bill approved by the House earmarked $3 billion in Israel and $2.1 billion for Egypt — the same amount as in recent years.

### Targeting India

Several members complained that Burton's amendment, although ostensibly targeted at India, would end up harming other recipients of U.S. development assistance. Chester G. Atkins, D-Mass., called the proposal a "bizarre hostage-taking," which could cut aid to "victims of drought and famine in Africa."

But the amendment was boosted by anti-foreign aid sentiment and supported by "a number of people reacting

to the Sikh populations in their districts," Obey said.

Burton agreed that his proposal was important to members with constituents of Sikh descent because Sikhs had been victimized by Indian security forces in the Punjab.

An amendment offered by Reps. Ronald K. Machtley, R-R.I, and Tony P. Hall, D-Ohio, would prohibit the administration from using International Military and Education Training assistance funds for Indonesia. The administration had proposed spending $2.3 million to train Indonesian officers in fiscal 1993.

Hall said the amendment, approved by voice vote, was intended to protest human rights abuses by the Indonesian army in East Timor.

The House also approved a proposal to trim U.S. financing for the World Bank and AID's budget. Obey and other Democrats successfully watered down the motion, offered by John T. Myers, R-Ind., which was approved 392-28. *(Vote 234, p. 56-H)*

## SENATE COMMITTEE ACTION

More than a year after Israel requested U.S. loan guarantees to help pay for absorbing Soviet immigrants, a Senate subcommittee provided the first congressional approval for the package Sept. 18.

In marking up the fiscal 1993 foreign aid appropriations bill, the Senate Appropriations Subcommittee on Foreign Operations included the Bush administration's proposal for $10 billion in loan guarantees to be given Israel in $2 billion installments over the next five fiscal years.

The subcommittee approved by voice vote the $13.8 billion aid bill, which cut $1.3 billion from the administration's request.

The subcommittee's bill closely tracked the aid measure approved by the House in June. Like that measure, it slashed about $800 million from the administration's request for military aid. Most of the savings would come from converting military assistance grants for a trio of U.S. NATO allies — Turkey, Greece and Portugal — to market-based loans.

The bill provided $417 million for the former republics of the Soviet Union, the full administration request. It also included $100 million in new aid for African famine victims and $25 million for refugees from the war-torn republics of the former Yugoslavia.

But the centerpiece of the Senate bill was the $10 billion loan guarantee package, which Israel had sought to help it take in hundreds of thousands of Soviet Jewish immigrants. Bush and Israel's new prime minister, Yitzhak Rabin, reached agreement on the aid in August, ending a bitter dispute between Washington and Jerusalem over Israel's expansion of settlements in occupied territories.

A new controversy immediately arose because of concern among lawmakers over suggestions that Israel would pay only half of the funding needed to cover the risk of a default on the loans. Since making its request in 1991, Israel had consistently said that U.S. taxpayers would not be asked to foot the bill for the program.

The Office of Management and Budget (OMB) had originally estimated those costs at about 7 percent a year.

To assuage those concerns, Jerusalem renewed its pledge to pay the full amount of the required subsidy for the program. The administration reportedly scaled back the requirement to 4.5 percent, although officials had declined to make the figure public.

But Leahy, chairman of the Foreign Operations Sub-

committee, said the issue could remain a problem because the Congressional Budget Office (CBO) was apparently at odds with OMB over the "scoring," the estimate of the funding needed to back the program. "OMB scored one way, and CBO scored another," he said.

Although CBO had not issued a final estimate, its preliminary assessment of the subsidy was believed to be significantly higher than the 4.5 percent reportedly calculated by OMB. Opponents of the program could seize on that discrepancy to charge that the administration was underestimating the risk of an Israeli default.

Yet Leahy predicted that the issue would not derail the program. "An Israeli loan guarantee package will go through in the legislation," he told reporters before his panel marked up the bill.

### Potential Obstacles

The subcommittee approved the foreign aid spending bill in routine fashion, as Leahy urged senators to defer controversial matters to quickly move the bill to the floor.

But the subcommittee's action did not foreclose further efforts to restore military grants for Turkey and the other NATO allies. The chairman of the Appropriations Committee, Robert C. Byrd, D-W.Va., had been a tireless supporter of aid for Turkey.

Like the House version, the subcommittee's bill provided $20 million for the U.N. Population Fund, which was nearly certain to subject the bill to a veto threat.

The panel also eliminated all military aid for El Salvador, a reflection of Leahy's desire to send what he called a "clear signal we're not going to prop up" the Salvadoran military forces.

The ranking Republican member of the subcommittee, Bob Kasten of Wisconsin, suggested that the provision also could trigger a veto. The House had included $11 million in non-lethal aid for El Salvador.

The administration had signaled notably strong opposition to a provision that would require the president to certify that Indonesia was making progress in improving its human rights performance before providing military training funds to the country. The amount of assistance involved was small — only $2.3 million — but the administration was interested in retaining ties with the Indonesian military.

The subcommittee's measure would provide $100 million to help Latin American countries restructure their debts. That was about half of the White House's fiscal 1993 request for $202 million for Latin American debt relief under its Enterprise for the Americas program.

The House version of the bill included no funding for the debt relief.

### Full Committee Action

Belying the ingrained congressional opposition to foreign aid, the Senate Appropriations Committee on Sept. 23 approved a $26.4 billion aid bill that included loan guarantees for Israel and $12.3 billion in new financing for the IMF.

As reported from the committee on a 25-1 vote, HR 5368 was about $1 billion less than the Bush administration's foreign aid request for fiscal 1993. It was $12.6 billion more than the House-passed bill, which did not include IMF funding.

Excluding the IMF appropriation, which entailed no budgetary outlays, the bill provided $14.1 billion in foreign aid — nearly $500 million less than the level enacted in

fiscal 1992.

The panel handed the administration several victories, most notably the appropriation for increased funding for the IMF. That had emerged as the centerpiece of the Freedom Support Act (S 2532), the administration's comprehensive aid initiative for the former republics of the Soviet Union.

In a series of closely contested votes, the committee restored cuts in the administration's request for military aid for El Salvador, Indonesia and NATO allies that had been approved by the Subcommittee on Foreign Operations. That added more than $550 million to the bill.

The measure authorized the administration's request to guarantee up to $10 billion in loans for Israel — a five-year program to help that country absorb hundreds of thousands of Jewish immigrants from the former Soviet Union.

Although the loan guarantees had attracted broad congressional support, the committee confronted a lingering question over how much funding needed to be set aside to ensure against the risk of an Israeli default.

The estimate by CBO of the money that had to be set aside — known as a subsidy — helped to push outlays in the bill over the ceiling established for foreign aid by the Appropriations Committee.

The CBO estimate, which had not been made public, had been downplayed by lawmakers as a bookkeeping matter. But Leahy and Kasten were forced to offer an amendment cutting more than $100 million in outlays from other sections of the bill.

The amendment, approved by voice vote, eliminated the U.S. contribution to the European Bank for Reconstruction and Development and shaved other funding.

Although the administration supported most of the amendments approved by the committee, the foreign aid bill was under a veto threat because of two abortion-related provisions.

The legislation would repeal restrictions on aid for international family planning organizations that promote the use of abortion and would provide $20 million for the U.N. Population Fund.

In addition, the administration opposed an amendment sponsored by Appropriations Chairman Byrd that barred U.S. assistance to Russia, except for humanitarian aid, until Moscow agreed to withdraw its forces from the three Baltic nations. The panel approved the amendment by voice vote.

The administration was concerned about the impact of Byrd's amendment on the aid program. The appropriations bill included $417 million in aid for the former republics, but it had not been decided how much of that assistance would be allocated to Russia.

### Aid to Indonesia, El Salvador

Leahy had hoped to move his panel's bill to the floor relatively unscathed. Those hopes were dashed almost as soon as the full committee began marking up the measure.

Daniel K. Inouye, D-Hawaii, and Ted Stevens, R-Alaska, moved to ease tough conditions that Leahy had placed on $2.3 million in military training assistance for Indonesia. Leahy attached the restrictions because of the massacre in 1991 by the Indonesian military of as many as 100 unarmed civilians on the island of East Timor.

The subcommittee's bill would have required the president to certify that Indonesia had asked an impartial international organization to resolve the fate of those still unaccounted for from the East Timor massacre. Without such a

certification, the training program could not go forward.

Inouye argued that continuing the program "is the best way for the U.S. military to help Indonesia learn human rights."

After a lengthy debate that highlighted Indonesia's growing strategic and commercial importance to the United States, the committee approved, 15-12, the milder conditions proposed by Inouye and Stevens. Their amendment required the secretary of State to report on steps taken by the Indonesian government to educate its armed forces on human rights issues.

The House-passed bill cut off all military training assistance for Jakarta.

A similar battle was fought over a familiar controversy — military aid for El Salvador. The subcommittee's bill would have cut the entire $11 million in non-lethal military aid that had been approved by the House.

Under the subcommittee's bill, the $11 million would have been transferred to a fund that had been set up to help the country recover from its 12-year civil war. Leahy said that there was $30 million in previously approved U.S. military aid that had yet to be delivered to the armed forces.

But Kasten countered that the aid cutoff would send the wrong signal to the government of President Alfredo Cristiani at a crucial time. Kasten said that the Cristiani government "is putting itself at risk" by trying to purge the armed forces of officers guilty of human rights abuses.

With only a handful of members present, the vote on Kasten's amendment to restore the $11 million was decided by proxies. Kasten had his votes lined up and won a 14-12 victory.

Leahy appeared angry because some senators who previously had expressed support for an aid cutoff either failed to vote or changed positions. Leahy thought he had the proxy of Wyche Fowler Jr., only to be informed by Byrd that the Georgia Democrat supported Kasten's amendment.

### NATO Grants; IMF Support

While the committee spent most of its time considering amendments involving a few million dollars, it approved several big-ticket items with minimal debate.

In an action that put the Senate squarely at odds with the House, the committee approved, 15-9, an amendment by Thad Cochran, R-Miss., to restore $540 million in military grants and low-interest loans for a trio of NATO allies — Turkey, Greece and Portugal.

Leahy's subcommittee had endorsed a House proposal to eliminate such grants, converting them to market-based loans, and Leahy pointedly reminded his colleagues that accepting Cochran's amendment would add "more than half a billion dollars" to the bill.

But the amendment drew strong backing from Byrd, a longtime supporter of aid to Turkey. "Just look at the map," he said. "One will see the strategic importance and the geopolitical importance of Turkey."

Byrd also gave his assent to an amendment from Pete V. Domenici, R-N.M., funding the administration's request for the IMF. The amendment was approved by voice vote.

The chairman had objected to the House including the $12.3 billion appropriation on the measure authorizing aid to the former Soviet republics, called the Freedom Support Act. But with the IMF financing provided on what he viewed as a proper vehicle — an appropriations bill — he dropped his opposition.

The approval of Domenici's amendment removed an obstacle that had delayed a House-Senate conference committee considering the Freedom Support Act. In approving the measure Sept. 24, the conference committee eliminated the IMF appropriation from that legislation.

### Israel Guarantees

No foreign aid bill was enacted in 1991 because of an impasse that developed over the administration's refusal to support loan guarantees for Israel so long as that country continued to expand settlements in occupied territories. The two sides reached an agreement in August after the new government of Israel's Prime Minister Yitzhak Rabin pledged to curb the settlement expansion.

Israel was seeking U.S. guarantees to back $10 billion in commercial financing. With the guarantees in hand, Jerusalem would be able to negotiate more favorable terms on 30-year loans.

By law, the Office of Management and Budget (OMB) was required to estimate the size of the subsidy needed to back loan guarantee programs, a process called "scoring." In scoring the first installment of $2 billion, the OMB estimated the subsidy cost at 4.5 percent of the program.

Israel already had agreed to pay that cost — about $90 million — enabling the administration to avoid making a separate request for an appropriation to cover the guarantees. But CBO, which made independent estimates for Congress, reportedly had scored the subsidy at about 13 percent.

In effect, CBO and OMB differed over the prospects for an Israeli default. Yet some lawmakers believed that such distinctions were meaningless because it was impossible to accurately assess the risk of a default.

"You're trying to quantify the unquantifiable," said Obey, chairman of the House Appropriations Subcommittee on Foreign Operations.

But the CBO estimate of the loan guarantee subsidy, along with its scoring of other programs, sent Leahy and Kasten scrambling to find reductions elsewhere. And because outlays — actual spending during the fiscal year — translated into higher levels of budget authority, they trimmed $283 million in budget authority.

Their amendment eliminated $70 million in budget authority for the European Bank for Reconstruction and Development, which provided loans to the former Soviet Union and Eastern Europe, and $213 million in economic aid.

The bill approved by the committee also would have:

● Earmarked $72 million in economic and military aid for Morocco, a country that consistently had won strong Senate support. The House bill included no earmark for Morocco.

● Provided $100 million for debt restructuring for Latin American countries under the administration's Enterprise for the Americas initiative. The House bill provided no funding for debt relief.

● Permitted deliveries of food and some humanitarian aid to Pakistan. Its U.S. aid was cut off in 1990 because of its nuclear weapons program.

## SENATE FLOOR ACTION

The Senate endorsed tough actions to counter Serbian aggression against Bosnia-Herzegovina and to restrict Russian arms sales to Iran as it handily approved HR 5368.

The Senate passed the $26.5 billion appropriations measure, 87-12, on Oct. 1, sending it to House-Senate conferees. *(Vote 256, p. 33-S)*

The Senate bill granted Israel's request for the United States to guarantee $10 billion in loans over five years, a proposal that was backed by the Bush administration and enjoyed broad support in Congress.

In addition, it appropriated $12.3 billion in new financing for the IMF, which the administration had been seeking as a key component of its aid initiative for the former republics of the Soviet Union

The funding in the Senate version of the bill was about $800 million less than the president's aid request for fiscal 1993. It was about $12.8 billion more than the House-passed version, which did not include the IMF funding.

The Bosnia amendment, offered by Joseph R. Biden Jr., D-Del., allowed the president to provide up to $50 million in U.S. defense equipment for Bosnia if the United Nations lifted its arms embargo against that country.

The Senate approved the amendment by voice vote, but only after it sparked spirited debate.

For many in the Senate, which earlier in 1992 passed a resolution authorizing the deployment of multilateral military force in Bosnia, the issue was one of fairness. The ban on arms shipments to all the republics of the former Yugoslavia, Biden argued, had left Bosnians almost defenseless against attacks by well-armed Serbians.

He cited eyewitness accounts of Serbian massacres of thousands of Bosnian civilians as evidence that the West needed to take stronger action to help Bosnia. "Are we truly to adjourn, having done nothing?" Biden asked.

The amendment authorized the aid, but it would be up to the president to decide to provide the equipment.

But John W. Warner, R-Va., who had supported the administration's cautious approach toward the crisis in the former Yugoslavia, said that providing such aid would only deepen the involvement of the United States in a region where all sides had engaged in brutality.

Although acting Secretary of State Lawrence S. Eagleburger signaled his opposition to the amendment, Warner said the administration would not object if the Senate approved it by voice vote. With strong bipartisan support for the amendment, the administration wanted to avoid an embarrassing defeat on a recorded vote.

The administration also had adamantly opposed conditions on aid for the former republics of the Soviet Union. But it made no effort to block approval by voice vote of an amendment by Jesse Helms, R-N.C., that conditioned most aid to Russia on a presidential certification that Moscow was not supplying weapons to Iran.

Helms, whose amendment exempted shipments of U.S. humanitarian aid, said he was responding to recent reports that Moscow was planning to sell submarines to Iran. The Senate bill included $417 million for a range of technical and humanitarian aid for the former republics.

On both amendments, the administration indicated a clear willingness to take its chances with the House-Senate conference committee. Neither provision was included on the House-passed bill.

### Few Reductions

Despite the chronic unpopularity of foreign aid, there were only a few attempts to eliminate funding in the bill. Some senators, such as Hank Brown, R-Colo. — a longtime opponent of IMF funding — were content to express their views in sense of the Senate resolutions.

Helms launched the only frontal assault on foreign aid, offering an amendment to cut funding in the bill by 10 percent. The savings would have been used to reduce the federal budget deficit. Popular earmarked accounts, such as aid to Israel and Egypt, would have been exempt from the cut, meaning that other programs would have had to be reduced by more than 10 percent.

The amendment was defeated, 38-58. As might have been expected, several senators facing tough re-election battles supported the Helms amendment. But the proposal also found backing among some Democratic foreign policy leaders, such as Sam Nunn, Ga., and David L. Boren, Okla. *(Vote 252, p. 33-S)*

The Senate approved by voice vote an amendment by Nancy Landon Kassebaum, R-Kan., that limited aid to Morocco. Kassebaum's amendment placed a ceiling of $52 million on military and economic aid unless the president certified that the kingdom was cooperating with a U.N. peace plan to end conflict in the Western Sahara.

Kasten argued in favor of maintaining an earmark of $72 million in aid for Morocco. But his amendment substituting a sense of the Senate resolution for Kassebaum's tougher conditions failed, 40-56. *(Vote 251, p. 33-S)*

The Senate by voice vote approved an amendment — cosponsored by a number of senators — that prevented the Agency for International Development (AID) from providing incentives for U.S. companies to relocate overseas. The senators were responding to a recent report on the CBS News program "60 Minutes" showing AID officials trying to induce U.S. businesses to move to Central America.

Appropriations Committee Chairman Byrd said the "craziness" of trying to create jobs abroad instead of in this country "is so obvious and so fundamentally unsound that I can only shake my head in wonder."

AID officials denied that the agency had intended to lure U.S. companies overseas.

Senators also approved by voice vote an amendment freezing salaries at AID headquarters.

### Limiting Conflicts

The Senate began debate on the measure Sept. 30, after lawmakers agreed by unanimous consent to limit the number of amendments. The initial list of about 50 amendments included proposals on issues as diverse as dual-use technology and a dog sled trip to Antarctica. But many of the amendments were never offered, and Senate consideration of the measure became something less than the exercise in global policy-making it often turned into.

The bill approved by the Senate contained significant differences with the House-passed bill, however. The House legislation required the administration to convert about $800 million in military grants and low-interest loans for Turkey, Greece and Portugal to market-based loans.

But the Senate restored $540 million in funding for grants to the three NATO allies. It also approved by voice vote an amendment by Sen. Alfonse M. D'Amato, R-N.Y., aimed at ensuring that Greece received $7 in military aid for each $10 provided to Turkey.

The so-called 7:10 ratio, which Congress annually guaranteed, was an important issue for Greek-American voters in D'Amato's home state.

The Senate bill eliminated $69 million in funding that the House had included for the European Bank for Reconstruction and Development, which provided loans to the former Soviet republics and Eastern Europe.

It also included $100 million to restructure some debt owed by Latin American governments, a Treasury Department proposal that had attracted strong House opposition.

The Senate legislation also authorized up to $15 million

in funding to support efforts to resolve the fate of U.S. military personnel missing in Southeast Asia since the Vietnam War. The provision would allow the Pentagon to provide defense equipment to Laos and Cambodia for operations to find missing U.S. military personnel.

### Aiding Pakistan

A largely overlooked provision in the Senate measure lifted restrictions on shipments of food and some humanitarian aid to countries barred from receiving such assistance.

As it was originally drafted, the amendment — attached by Mark O. Hatfield, R-Ore., during the Appropriations Committee's consideration of the bill — would have allowed such assistance to flow even to countries designated by the State Department as supporting international terrorism.

Hatfield modified his amendment on the floor to close that possible loophole. But the measure would still enable the administration to provide limited assistance to Pakistan. Aid to Islamabad had been barred since 1990 because of its nuclear weapons program.

The Senate approved by voice vote an amendment, offered by Domenici, eliminating a House requirement to shift most U.S. aid for Eastern Europe and the Baltic States — now largely provided for regional programs — into direct bilateral assistance.

The administration opposed the House language on the grounds that it limited executive branch flexibility in making foreign policy.

The Senate also approved by voice vote amendments:
● By Tom Harkin, D-Iowa, that required U.S. representatives to international financial institutions to oppose loans to countries whose military expenditures exceeded their combined expenditures on health and education programs. The president could waive the provision, however, if he determined that it would harm U.S. national interests.
● By Minority Leader Bob Dole, a longtime backer of Armenia, earmarking $5 million to help refugees in that former Soviet republic.
● By Joseph I. Lieberman, D-Conn., earmarking $20 million for "an urgent program of humanitarian assistance" for Kurds in northern Iraq.
● By Mitch McConnell, R-Ky., to bar the Pentagon from transferring aircraft to the Drug Enforcement Administration to carry out counternarcotics operations in Guatemala.

## FINAL ACTION

In the final version of HR 5368 that was sent to Bush, Congress approved $12.3 billion in new financing for the IMF and $10 billion in loan guarantees for Israel.

The House on Oct. 5 adopted the conference report on the $26.3 billion spending measure, 312-105. The Senate approved the legislation by voice vote later that day. *(Vote 470, p. 114-H)*

The bill cut about $1.1 billion from the administration's request for fiscal 1993. The final version of the legislation provided $12.5 billion more than the House-passed bill, which did not include the IMF appropriation, and $162 million less than the Senate bill.

In a significant change from foreign aid spending bills enacted during the Cold War, the House-Senate conference committee on Oct. 2 moderated tough restrictions imposed by the Senate on aid to Russia — a program that did not exist the last time such a conference convened.

Over administration objections, the conferees authorized up to $50 million in U.S. military equipment for the

republic of Bosnia. That represented the strongest congressional action favoring one side in the former Yugoslavia, although it did not compel Bush to provide the aid.

The changing ideas about foreign assistance did not extend to the Middle East, where most U.S. military and economic aid continued to go. The bill provided $3 billion in aid for Israel and $2.1 billion for Egypt, the same levels as in recent years.

Congress had long been a wellspring of support for Israel, and the authorization of the five-year program of loan guarantees for Jerusalem — on top of the $3 billion in direct aid — made the bill more acceptable to many members.

Excluding the one-time appropriation for the IMF, the measure provided $1.4 billion less than the fiscal 1991 aid bill, which was the last one to clear Congress.

"It's a very tight bill, and we gave people some arguments to take home and defend," said Obey.

Passage of the legislation also represented a qualified success for the Bush administration. The loan guarantees and the IMF appropriation — an essential component of the administration's aid initiative for the former Soviet republics — were regarded as legislative priorities by the White House.

In addition, the measure included $417 million in economic and technical assistance for the former Soviet republics and $50 million to restructure debts owed by Latin American governments.

But the administration was forced to swallow major reductions in military aid and in Economic Support Funds (ESF), a key category of economic assistance.

The conference committee agreed to convert military assistance grants for three NATO allies — Turkey, Greece and Portugal — into low-interest loans. The bill provided $3.5 billion in military aid, a $596 million reduction from the fiscal 1992 level.

Funding for ESF, a program of cash transfers and other assistance for key U.S. allies, was cut by $498 million from fiscal 1992 to $2.7 billion.

### A Russian Compromise

The conference committee faced conflicts over issues including military aid for the NATO allies, debt forgiveness and abortion.

Yet no issue took more time or effort to resolve than the stiff conditions on aid for Russia that had been attached to the Senate bill by Byrd, chairman of that chamber's Appropriations Committee. The amendment would have prohibited aid to Russia until Moscow either withdrew its military forces from Estonia, Latvia and Lithuania, or agreed to a timetable for withdrawal. Byrd exempted humanitarian aid from his amendment.

The administration strongly opposed the provision, but decided to defer an all-out battle in order to expedite Senate passage of the measure. In an Oct. 2 letter to lawmakers, the White House warned that the amendment "would result in a cutoff of U.S. assistance" and said that the problem was addressed by conditions in legislation (S 2532) authorizing aid to the former Soviet republics. *(Freedom Support Act, p. 523)*

But Byrd was unyielding. "We have a time bomb ticking on our hands," he told the conferees, arguing that Russia's continued military presence in the Baltics could spur civil unrest.

With the proceedings dragging on — and Byrd raising the possibility of a filibuster if his amendment were stripped — Byrd, Obey and Leahy left the conference for a private meeting.

While the lawmakers were sequestered, Robert S. Strauss, the U.S. ambassador to Russia, called from Moscow to try to break the deadlock. But the dramatic gesture — Strauss telephoned about 5 a.m. Moscow time — went ignored as Byrd declined to leave the meeting to take the call.

Nonetheless, the three men emerged a short time later with a complicated agreement in hand. Under the compromise, only half the assistance could be provided unless the president certified by the following June that there had been "substantial progress" toward establishing a timetable for withdrawal.

If Russia still had not removed its forces by the end of the next September — or had not set up a timetable to do so — further assistance would be cut off.

It was not clear how much, if any, of the $417 million in the bill for the former republics would be affected by this provision. The administration had not yet allocated the assistance among the newly independent states.

But the conditions could be less onerous than they appeared because the definition of "substantial progress" was open to broad interpretation. The White House letter noted that Russia had reached an agreement with Lithuania on withdrawal, and said there had been "considerable progress" in removing forces from the Baltic nations.

With far less controversy, the conference committee eliminated a second Senate amendment aimed at restricting aid to Russia. The amendment by Helms would have barred all but humanitarian aid to Moscow until the president certified that Russia had ceased selling arms to Iran.

As the conference agreed to remove Helms' provision, Leahy declared that he "didn't have a dog in this fight."

The conferees also earmarked a substantial amount of the $417 million for specific purposes, some of which could benefit domestic interests. The legislation required that $50 million in U.S. agricultural commodities be provided to the former republics.

The conference committee also earmarked $50 million for scholarships and other educational exchange programs.

### Cutting Military Aid

Byrd also was at the center of the dispute over military aid for Turkey and the two other countries that host NATO bases. The Appropriations chairman had been a tireless supporter of aid for Turkey.

The House and Senate were far apart on the issue. The House cut all military assistance grants for the three NATO allies — replacing them with market-based loans — but the Senate restored $540 million in grants and low-interest loans.

Byrd was the leading proponent of the Senate's position, but it seemed untenable at a time when foreign aid was so unpopular. Even if he had succeeded in conference, there would have been intense House opposition to increasing the funding in the bill by $540 million.

The conference committee essentially split the difference between the two chambers. It eliminated military grants but approved $450 million in low-interest loans for Turkey, $315 million for Greece and $90 million for Portugal. The annual interest rate on such loans is about 5 percent.

The panel attempted to assuage Turkey, an important ally in the Persian Gulf region, by providing $125 million in economic aid. Neither the House nor the Senate had included the earmark in its bill.

Despite an intense lobbying campaign by the administration and U.S. corporations, the conferees also cut $2.3 million in military training assistance that the administra-

tion requested for Indonesia.

Supporters of the aid cutoff, which was originally included in the House version of the bill, said the action was warranted because of the massacre of as many as 100 civilians in 1991 by Indonesian forces on the island of East Timor.

But U.S. corporations operating in Indonesia feared a backlash from President Suharto's government if the provision became law. Obey, who defended the House stance, said "a number of business people have contacted various conferees with concerns about this amendment."

Opposition to the cutoff was led by Sens. Inouye and Stevens, who proposed mild conditions in place of scrapping the aid. When it became clear that the conference would — at a minimum — impose tougher restrictions on the program, they gave up their fight.

The conference committee dropped abortion-related provisions that had triggered a veto threat. Both chambers had approved $20 million in aid for the U.N. Population Fund. The administration opposed such aid because the agency operated in China, which had been condemned for its coercive abortion policy.

The conferees easily reached an agreement on $50 million in funding for Latin American debt forgiveness under the administration's Enterprise for the Americas program. The House had provided no funding for debt restructuring, while the Senate had appropriated $100 million.

### Middle East Dominance

Because of the cuts in the two main categories of bilateral assistance — Foreign Military Financing (FMF) and ESF — the dominant position of Israel and Egypt among aid recipients had become even more pronounced.

Congress earmarked $3.1 billion in FMF for the two allies, leaving only about $350 million for all other recipients of that assistance. Lawmakers earmarked $2 billion in ESF for Israel and Egypt, leaving only $670 million for other countries.

As in past years, the bill also contained a host of other provisions that provided unique benefits for Israel. It was the only country that was entitled to receive its entire military and economic aid within the first 30 days of the fiscal year, enabling Jerusalem to collect interest on the assistance.

The conferees approved the guarantees that Israel had been seeking for favorable interest rates on $10 billion in commercial loans to help it absorb hundreds of thousands of Jewish immigrants. The action was needed because the House had completed its bill before Bush and Rabin agreed on terms of the package.

Jerusalem had agreed to pay costs associated with the program, which for the first installment of $2 billion were expected to amount to $90 million.

Also for the Middle East, the conference committee earmarked $20 million in economic aid and $40 million in military aid for Morocco, which typically had a strong lobbying presence on Capitol Hill.

But the conferees approved a Senate amendment offered by Kassebaum that limited Morocco to $52 million in aid unless the president certified the kingdom was cooperating with the U.N. peace process in the Western Sahara.

### Multilateral Aid

While slashing available funds for bilateral assistance, Congress increased funding for worldwide programs that supported refugees, efforts to protect the environment and family planning.

The bill provided about $670 million to aid refugees, an

increase of more than $200 million since fiscal 1990. It earmarked $35 million to help refugees in Bosnia, Croatia and Slovenia. It also included $350 million for international population planning programs, a $130 million increase since fiscal 1990.

The conferees approved $650 million for a number of environmental initiatives, reflecting the heightened concern in Congress over problems such as global warming.

They also approved an amendment from the Senate bill to appropriate $30 million for the World Bank's Global Environmental Facility, which backed efforts to preserve biodiversity and other environmental programs.

The legislation provided funding for several regional aid initiatives, which had emerged as alternatives to traditional bilateral assistance programs.

The bill included $400 million to promote private-sector development and provide technical assistance for Eastern Europe and the Baltic States, $50 million less than the administration sought. It also provided $800 million in economic development aid for sub-Saharan Africa, along with $100 million specifically allocated for emergency disaster relief in the region. The legislation earmarked $25 million in aid for war-torn Somalia, where an estimated 1.5 million people were at risk from famine.

## AID and Trade

Although members from both parties expressed frustration with continuing management problems at AID, there was a consensus that little could be done to fix the troubled agency until after the presidential election. With an annual budget of more than $6 billion, AID administered most bilateral and multilateral assistance programs.

The latest embarrassment for AID occurred when the television news program "60 Minutes" broadcast a story showing AID officials attempting to induce U.S. companies to relocate in Central America.

That produced a wave of outrage on Capitol Hill. The conference committee responded by combining House and Senate language aimed at barring AID from providing any incentives to lure companies abroad.

The legislation also sought to address persistent complaints that foreign aid was a "giveaway" program by increasing funds for export promotion activities.

The conference committee approved $757 million to back $15.5 billion in loans and financing extended by the Export Import Bank. The administration had requested $633 million for the program.

The conferees also adopted a Senate amendment requiring the administration to increase the amount of economic aid it provided in support of large-scale infrastructure projects. Under the amendment, about 10 percent of the aid provided to the former Soviet republics, Eastern Europe and other regions had to be made available for so-called capital projects.

Supporters of the proposal, such as Boren, had long believed that U.S. companies would benefit if more aid were tied to the development of projects such as airports and telecommunications networks.

The conferees also:

● Reduced the administration's request for military assistance to El Salvador from $40 million to $11 million, as both chambers had done. With a peace agreement in place, only non-lethal aid could be provided to the Salvadoran armed forces. The remaining $29 million was transferred to a fund established to assist the country in recovering from its 12-year civil war.

● Retained prohibitions on military assistance for Peru. The Senate bill would have allowed the president to provide the aid if President Fujimori made good on a pledge to restore constitutional democracy in the country.

● Approved an amendment, originally offered by Hatfield, that allowed the president to provide some food aid and humanitarian supplies to Pakistan. Such aid had been barred since 1990 because of Islamabad's nuclear weapons program. But the conference report stipulated that Congress must agree to the aid shipments.

● Endorsed a Senate proposal authorizing the president to provide up to $15 million in U.S. military equipment for Cambodia and Laos to support their efforts to find missing American service personnel from the war in Southeast Asia.

President Bush signed the foreign aid bill (PL 102-391) on Oct. 6. ∎

# Construction Bill Steps Up Base Closures

The fiscal 1993 military construction budget represented a big shift in Pentagon priorities: less money for new base construction and improvements and more money to implement two previous rounds of base closures.

The $8.39 billion bill (HR 5428) was about $170 million less than the fiscal 1992 appropriation but provided $1.28 billion more for base closures. The additional money came out of the military construction account.

The Defense Department estimated that base shutdowns approved by Congress in 1989 and 1990 were to cost $8 billion. Lawmakers were expected to target more bases in 1993.

Before many of the bases could have been turned over to state and local governments or to private developers, significant environmental hazards needed to be cleaned up.

As members of Congress drew up the bill, traditionally the least controversial of the 13 appropriations bills, they discussed repeatedly the difficulty of crafting the fiscal 1993 bill.

## HOUSE ACTION

Action on the bill began on June 11, as the House Appropriations Military Construction Subcommittee marked up an $8.6 billion draft version of the measure.

As approved by the subcommittee, the bill's total spending would have matched President Bush's request. Bush requested a $290 million cut over fiscal the 1992 bill.

As usual, the panel rewrote the administration's request for base construction projects, adding $500 million to the president's $1.9 billion request. Following the lead of the defense authorization bill, the subcommittee pared $100 million from the president's $221 million request for NATO's so-called infrastructure fund. (Defense authorization bill, p. 483)

The panel approved a 168 percent increase in funding over fiscal 1992 for domestic base closures, to be paid for through cuts in base construction and in NATO assistance.

The subcommittee bill would have provided $2 billion for base closings; 1992 funding was $758 million.

The big shift in the bill's priorities came on the heels of Congress' effort in 1991 to close 25 military bases. That followed a 1989 effort, in which Congress approved 86 bases for complete or partial closure.

Many of the bases to be closed had severe pollution problems and were to require much time and money to clean up. Saying that the Defense Department was dragging its feet, lawmakers earmarked $444 million for such environmental cleanup; the previous year's earmark was $220 million.

### Full Committee

The full committee approved HR 5428 on June 18 by voice vote with no significant amendments.

To speed up base shutdowns, the bill gave the Pentagon much more flexibility in deciding where to spend the money than it had with other accounts.

While appropriators significantly cut the amount available for base construction, compared with the previous year, it was $500 million more than the administration requested. As approved by the committee, about three-fifths of such unrequested money was to land in states represented by members of the Military Construction Subcommittee. The panel had 13 members; their states would have received $293.4 million for 61 unrequested base construction projects.

The largest chunk of unrequested base construction money, $80.2 million, was slated for Texas, represented on the subcommittee by Republican Tom DeLay. Other Texas beneficiaries included former subcommittee member Ronald D. Coleman, D, whose district was to receive $25 million, and Armed Services Committee Democrat Solomon P. Ortiz, whose district was in line for $30.2 million.

California, with two panel members — ranking Republican Bill Lowery and Democrat Vic Fazio — was alloted $42.4 million in unrequested projects.

Subcommittee Chairman W. G. "Bill" Hefner, D-N.C., added $15.7 million for his district to the bill.

Full committee Chairman Jamie L. Whitten, D-Miss., was not left out. Mississippi was slated to receive $26 million in unrequested projects, including $19 million for an access road for Camp McCain, near the border of Whitten's and fellow Democrat Mike Espy's districts.

### House Floor

The bill emerged relatively unscathed June 23 from a restive House. Members passed the measure, 390-33, but only after an afternoon filled with unusual procedural votes demanded by Republicans who were upset by the House leadership's intention to restrict amendments to another spending bill, the politically charged legislative appropriations measure (HR 5427). *(Vote 217, p. 52-H)*

The sole amendment to the military construction bill was a 1 percent across-the-board cut, adopted 266-156. The cut was approved over the protests of bill sponsors, who said the measure already was bare-bones. The bill's total was reduced to $8.5 billion. *(Vote 214, p. 52-H)*

---

**BOXSCORE**

➡ **Military Construction Appropriations (HR 5428).**

**Reports:** H Rept 102-580; S Rept 102-355; H Rept 102-888 (Conference Report)

**KEY ACTION**

June 23 — The **House** passed HR 5428, 390-33.

August 5 — The **Senate** passed HR 5428 by voice vote.

Sept. 24 — The **House** adopted conference report; **Senate** cleared it.

Oct. 5 — President Bush signed HR 5428 — PL 102-380.

---

"You are talking about a bill that has already been cut and is below last year's spending . . . even in light of the fact that we have tremendous backlogs and needs to provide decent housing for our military personnel," DeLay said.

Timothy J. Penny, D-Minn., an advocate of the cut, said, "I cannot think of a single project in this bill that could not shoulder a 1 percent cut." But Penny added in an interview that "there wasn't much pork this year" in the military construction bill.

But there was some special projects funding. The bill contained about $500 million for 170 construction projects not requested by the Defense Department, many of them in the districts of Appropriations Committee members.

An attempt to remove one high-profile project was easily defeated as members rejected, 143-276, an amendment by Dan Burton, R-Ind., to strip a $19 million appropriation for the access road for Camp McCain in Mississippi. The road was not requested by the Pentagon, which gave a low priority to spending so much on Camp McCain, a 440-troop National Guard base used for tank training. *(Vote 213, p. 52-H)*

"This is pure pork," Burton said. "It's pure pork, and we know it."

Military Construction Subcommittee members said the measure was the best they could produce, given budget constraints, but that funding was inadequate, especially for family housing. One problem was finding housing for personnel returning home because of big troop cuts in Europe.

The bill probably was the least controversial of the 13 annual appropriations measures, but it was temporarily held hostage by Robert S. Walker, R-Pa., who forced a series of unusual procedural votes to express Republican anger at the Democrats' intention to move the legislative appropriations bill under a restricted rule.

In one instance, members were forced to file past Walker and Democratic floor manager Lindsay Thomas, D-Ga., in an archaic "teller" count on a re-vote of the across-the-board amendment.

## SENATE ACTION

Strapped Senate appropriators on July 31 approved an $8.2 billion version of the bill that pared about $250 million from the House-passed version.

The Appropriations Committee approved HR 5428 by voice vote. The committee added $150 million to the House appropriation to implement two rounds of military base closings, fully funding President Bush's $2.2 billion request.

The Senate Committee took a hard line on new military construction, cutting almost $700 million from the House bill. The House measure included $2.5 billion for military construction, the Senate version $1.8 billion.

But Senate appropriators were more generous with the family housing accounts, approving $4.2 billion, $200 million more than the House allowed.

Military Construction Subcommittee Chairman Jim Sasser, D-Tenn., said that the bill represented "painful cutting" and that as a result, the committee declined, in all but a few

# Military Construction Spending

*(HR 5428 — H Rept 102-888, as approved by House-Senate conferees on Sept. 22, in thousands of dollars):*

| | Fiscal 1992 Appropriation | '93 Bush Request | House [1] Bill | Senate Bill | Conference Agreement |
|---|---|---|---|---|---|
| **Military Construction** | | | | | |
| Army | $ 841,820 | $ 409,750 | $ 534,520 | $ 366,260 | $ 425,270 |
| Navy | 827,467 | 347,722 | 396,059 | 336,829 | 368,887 |
| Air Force | 911,554 | 672,450 | 698,599 | 704,690 | 717,280 |
| Defense agencies | 724,740 | 311,526 | 308,176 | 194,516 | 262,116 |
| NATO infrastructure | 225,000 | 221,200 | 121,200 | — | 60,000 |
| National Guard and reserves | 628,672 | 187,150 | 443,404 | 481,681 | 554,748 |
| **Subtotal** | **$ 4,159,253** | **$ 2,149,798** | **$ 2,501,958** | **$ 2,083,976** | **$ 2,418,301** |
| **Family Housing** | | | | | |
| Army | 1,557,120 | 1,555,990 | 1,572,079 | 1,507,857 | 1,523,819 |
| Navy | 902,140 | 1,073,947 | 1,029,495 | 1,055,587 | 1,039,680 |
| Air Force | 1,075,283 | 1,264,398 | 1,260,895 | 1,204,074 | 1,211,727 |
| Defense agencies | 26,200 | 28,400 | 28,400 | 28,400 | 28,400 |
| Homeowners Assistance Fund | 84,000 | 133,000 | 133,000 | 133,000 | 133,000 |
| **Subtotal** | **$ 3,644,743** | **$ 4,055,735** | **$ 4,023,869** | **$ 3,928,918** | **$ 3,936,626** |
| Base realignment and closure | 758,600 | 2,184,300 | 2,034,300 | 2,184,300 | 2,034,300 |
| **GRAND TOTAL** | **$ 8,562,596** | **$ 8,389,833** | **$ 8,560,127** [1] | **$ 8,197,194** | **$ 8,389,227** |

[1] *Figures do not include a 1 percent across-the-board cut the House imposed.*

SOURCES: House and Senate Appropriations committees

instances, to sign on to any of the new projects in the House bill, concentrating instead on its own new projects.

The committee zeroed out Bush's request for overseas construction. Appropriators said the tight military construction budget should be directed solely to domestic bases.

The big winner in the bill was Hawaii, home of Daniel K. Inouye, D, chairman of the Defense Appropriations Subcommittee. Hawaii would have received $200 million in unrequested funds to build about 1,000 family housing units.

Alaska, home of the ranking Republican on the Defense Appropriations Subcommittee, Ted Stevens, was slated to get about $100 million more than it received in the House bill.

Although Phil Gramm of Texas was ranking Republican on the Military Construction Subcommittee, the Senate bill cut about $75 million in projects for his state from the House version of the bill.

Apparently anticipating that powerful Senate Appropriations Committee Chairman Robert C. Byrd, D-W.Va., would take care of his state, the House did not include any money for it in its version of the bill. However, Byrd secured $30 million in the final version, mostly for "reserve centers."

Although the Senate bill would have fully funded the administration's request to implement two rounds of military base closures, Senate appropriators complained that the Pentagon had underestimated how much it would cost to close the bases and clean up a host of environmental problems on the sites.

While both the House and Senate gave the Pentagon a relatively free hand in implementing the base closures, the Senate bill directed the General Accounting Office to re-

view the base-closing effort before the fiscal 1994 military construction bill was marked up.

At the last minute, Sasser found room for about $12 million for five projects not authorized in defense bills. The money came, he said, from family housing maintenance. "I know how strongly senators feel" about home state projects, Sasser said.

The bill went to the floor Aug. 5 and passed by voice vote.

"We were being asked to fit a size 13 foot into a size 9 shoe," Sasser said. "There was no way to draft a bill without inflicting a great deal of pain and making some very difficult choices."

## CONFERENCE

In a brief meeting to sign off on a conference agreement that was ironed out beforehand, House and Senate appropriators gave voice vote approval Sept. 22 to a compromise $8.39 billion version of the bill.

The Senate cleared the bill by voice vote two days later, hours after the House adopted the conference report (H Rept 102-888), also by voice vote.

Negotiators dodged some controversy, as members had to grapple with an administration edict that the measure would be vetoed if it exceeded the president's $8.39 billion request. The House passed an $8.56 billion measure, compared with the Senate's $8.20 billion version.

Sasser complained that Bush's threat to veto any spending bill exceeding his request tied the hands of military construction appropriators. He said Defense Appropriations Subcommittee Chairman Inouye — whose state was a big winner in the bill — had indicated that he was willing to shift some monies from the separate defense appropriations measure to the specialized bill that funded military construction. *(Defense, p. 592)*

"It appears now that the defense [appropriations] conferees will leave a substantial amount of budget authority on the table," Sasser said. "In normal years we would be able to reallocate those funds from the Defense Subcommittee to the Military Construction Subcommittee. But we can't do that this year" because of the veto threat.

A Senate committee staff aide said the transfer could have been several hundred million dollars.

"To comply with the White House targets, we've had to make some very difficult decisions indeed," Sasser said.

Conferees also agreed to pare $150 million from Bush's $2.18 billion request to implement base closures. The Senate bill had fully funded the request.

The conference agreement dropped Bush's $105 million request to build a chemical weapons disposal facility at the Anniston, Ala., Army Depot. The project was a Pentagon priority and was expected to be funded in future years.

For family housing, members agreed on $3.94 billion. But to make room for new housing projects, conferees slashed almost $200 million from Bush's request to improve existing housing. ■

# Treasury/Postal Bill Survives Battles

With looming political battles squelched by conferees, a $22.56 billion spending measure (HR 5488) for the Treasury, Postal Service and general government breezed through the House and Senate on Oct. 1 with little opposition.

Democratic appropriators took a verbal slap at Vice President Dan Quayle's Council on Competitiveness but otherwise left untouched the funding level needed to run the controversial White House regulatory review panel.

House and Senate conferees also scaled back a Senate provision to prohibit political activities by the White House "drug czar."

The fiscal 1993 spending measure funded many day-to-day government functions such as tax collection and customs inspections, dictated personnel policy for a nationwide federal work force and set the limits on executive branch spending — including all White House functions. And in the 1992 election year, members of Congress targeted some of the presidential activities that usually got only routine scrutiny.

The tension began to build in the spring when David E. Skaggs, D-Colo., a member of the House Appropriations Treasury-Postal Subcommittee, won committee and full House approval for a provision to cut $86,000 from White House operations. That was the amount that had been requested for the salaries of two staff members on the White House Council on Competitiveness.

The council was a regulatory review panel, chaired by Quayle, that had come under Democratic attack for delaying or reversing regulations issued by Cabinet departments and other agencies. Democrats maintained that the council was effectively circumventing the will of Congress, often through secret actions.

The Senate restored funding for the council in its version of the bill, but then took a swipe at another White House function: the Office of National Drug Control Policy. The office had been run by two very public and partisan figures — William J. Bennett and Bob Martinez. Paul Simon, D-Ill., won an amendment on the Senate floor to prohibit involvement by the so-called drug czar in partisan politics.

During conference negotiations Sept. 25, Senate subcommittee Chairman Dennis DeConcini, D-Ariz., after consulting with Simon, offered to reword the final language to ban the director from participating only in "public appearances for political campaigns." Conferees accepted it quickly.

By contrast, Skaggs argued into the night for his wording on the Competitiveness Council. But Republican con-

---

## BOXSCORE

➡ **Fiscal 1993 appropriations for Treasury Department, U.S. Postal Service and general government (HR 5488).** The $22.56 billion bill provided funding for agencies under the Treasury Department, including the Internal Revenue Service, General Services Administration and U.S. Customs Service. It also funded the U.S. Postal Service and the executive branch.

**Reports:** H Rept 102-618; S Rept 102-353; conference report H Rept 102-919.

### KEY ACTION

July 1 — The **House** passed HR 5488, 237-166.

Sept. 10 — The **Senate** passed HR 5488, 82-12.

Sept. 25 — HR 5488 approved by **House-Senate** conference.

Oct. 1 — The **House** adopted conference report, 291-126; the **Senate** cleared the bill by voice vote.

Oct. 6 — President Bush signed HR 5488 — PL 102-393.

---

ferees refused to budge. Skaggs finally agreed to a "managers' statement," which had no statutory effect, that included extensive language requesting that all council activities "be made available for public review."

Conferees also shaved off nearly $200 million during lengthy negotiations to stay within the strict funding guidelines set by the White House and grudgingly agreed to by congressional appropriators. Conferees easily trimmed about $100 million from the $1.3 billion account to update the computer systems of the Internal Revenue Service.

More difficult was a move that threatened to result in higher postal rates for everyone. The committee cut $78 million from an already reduced annual subsidy to the Postal Service to cover the cost of giving nonprofit groups lower mailing rates.

The bill did not cut into the large salaries and expense accounts as much as previously expected, thus averting major layoffs of federal employees — especially at the Treasury Department and U.S. Customs Service.

### BACKGROUND

The fiscal 1993 funding cycle on the Treasury-Postal Service bill marked the last for the joint stewardship of Rep. Edward R. Roybal, D-Calif., and Sen. DeConcini, known for their vastly different styles and approaches. Roybal, who retired from Congress at the end of 1992, was replaced as chairman of the Treasury-Postal Service Subcommittee by Steny H. Hoyer, D-Md.

Even when they had very similar goals, DeConcini, a smooth but aggressive former prosecutor and negotiator, and Roybal, a low-key former social worker and educator, had very different ideas about how to achieve them.

DeConcini was conservative and well-known for his partiality to law enforcement causes. In 1989, he turned down an offer from President Bush to become the nation's first drug czar.

Roybal was more liberal and frequently sought to move funds toward the disadvantaged.

Of the 13 spending measures, the Treasury-Postal bill delved deepest into the nuts-and-bolts of government operations, which allowed both men to help their causes. The bill covered the costs of operations, from tax collection to printing money, as well as subsidized mail delivery and the government procurement activities and construction projects of the General Services Administration.

The issue of postal rate subsidies often put Roybal and DeConcini on opposite sides of the negotiations. Although the U.S. Postal Service, a quasi-public agency, funded most of its own activities, the federal government provided mil-

# Treasury, Postal Service Spending

*(HR 5488, as cleared for the president, in thousands of dollars)*

| | Fiscal 1992 Appropriation | Fiscal '93 Bush Request | House Bill | Senate Bill | Final Bill |
|---|---|---|---|---|---|
| **Treasury Department** | | | | | |
| U.S. Customs Service | | | | | |
| Salaries and expenses | $ 1,266,305 | $ 1,324,070 | $ 1,331,070 | $ 1,326,417 | $ 1,315,917 |
| Operations, air interdiction | 175,932 | 138,983 | 136,783 | 132,416 | 132,416 |
| Air facilities construction | 12,100 | — | — | 4,600 | 4,600 |
| Other | 17,981 | 16,500 | 16,500 | 16,500 | 16,500 |
| **Subtotal, Customs** | **$ 1,472,318** | **$ 1,479,553** | **$ 1,484,353** | **$ 1,479,933** | **$ 1,469,433** |
| Internal Revenue Service | | | | | |
| Administration and management | 141,372 | 160,948 | 157,368 | 150,728 | 157,368 |
| Processing tax returns, assistance | 1,657,944 | 1,648,960 | 1,648,960 | 1,634,298 | 1,634,298 |
| Tax law enforcement | 3,579,879 | 3,852,588 | 3,835,192 | 3,835,501 | 3,835,347 |
| Information systems | 1,294,713 | 1,580,865 | 1,566,909 | 1,480,341 | 1,480,341 |
| **Subtotal, IRS** | **$ 6,673,908** | **$ 7,243,361** | **$ 7,208,429** | **$ 7,100,868** | **$ 7,107,354** |
| Bureau of Alcohol, Tobacco and Firearms | 336,040 | 357,419 | 355,419 | 371,324 | 366,372 |
| U.S. Secret Service | 475,423 | 470,372 | 470,372 | 467,938 | 469,155 |
| Bureau of the Public Debt | 189,000 | 201,233 | 189,000 | 194,643 | 194,643 |
| Financial Management Service | 231,500 | 219,146 | 214,146 | 214,069 | 214,069 |
| Other | 244,857 | 268,971 | 256,681 | 259,797 | 265,059 |
| **TOTAL, Treasury Department** | **$ 9,623,046** | **$ 10,240,055** | **$ 10,178,400** | **$ 10,088,572** | **$ 10,086,085** |
| **Postal Service** | | | | | |
| Postal subsidies | 470,000 | 121,912 | 200,000 | 200,000 | 121,912 |
| Non-funded liabilities | 40,575 | 38,614 | 38,614 | 38,614 | 38,614 |
| **TOTAL, Postal Service** | **$ 510,575** | **$ 160,526** | **$ 238,614** | **$ 238,614** | **$ 160,526** |
| **Executive Office of the President** | | | | | |
| President's compensation | 250 | 250 | 250 | 250 | 250 |
| White House Office and residence | 43,247 | 44,245 | 39,969 | 42,763 | 42,983 |
| Vice president's residence | 324 | 337 | 306 | 324 | 324 |
| Council of Economic Advisers | 3,345 | 3,508 | 3,154 | 3,345 | 3,428 |
| National Security Council | 6,145 | 6,218 | 5,631 | 6,118 | 6,118 |
| Office of Management and Budget | 51,934 | 54,479 | 48,974 | 51,934 | 52,981 |
| Office of National Drug Control Policy | 177,622 | 135,749 | 119,382 | 185,790 | 178,990 |
| Other | 35,436 | 36,005 | 32,834 | 35,376 | 35,653 |
| **TOTAL, Executive Office** | **$ 318,303** | **$ 280,791** | **$ 250,500** | **$ 325,900** | **$ 320,727** |
| **Independent Agencies** | | | | | |
| General Services Administration | | | | | |
| Federal Buildings Fund | 271,000 | 336,159 | 402,040 | 353,516 | 330,501 |
| Other | 196,124 | 196,360 | 188,876 | 188,424 | 192,436 |
| *Limitation on use of revenues* | *(4,152,613)* | *(4,754,332)* | *(4,820,209)* | *(4,703,808)* | *(4,717,251)* |
| **Subtotal, GSA** | **$ 467,124** | **$ 532,519** | **$ 590,916** | **$ 541,940** | **$ 522,937** |
| Office of Personnel Management | | | | | |
| Annuitants, health benefits | 2,503,535 | 4,044,245 | 4,149,245 | 4,149,245 | 4,149,245 |
| Annuitants, life insurance | 14,249 | 12,433 | 12,433 | 12,433 | 12,433 |
| Civil Service retirement and disability | 6,078,686 | 6,690,000 | 6,900,000 | 6,900,000 | 6,900,000 |
| Salaries and expenses | 120,611 | 124,797 | 122,121 | 120,820 | 123,227 |
| **Subtotal, OPM** | **$ 8,717,081** | **$ 10,871,475** | **$ 11,183,799** | **$ 11,182,498** | **$ 11,184,905** |
| Federal Election Commission | 18,808 | 21,031 | 20,531 | 21,031 | 21,031 |
| National Archives | 152,143 | 165,045 | 163,045 | 167,045 | 165,045 |
| U.S. Tax Court | 32,050 | 34,500 | 32,435 | 33,500 | 32,435 |
| Other agencies | 63,225 | 68,539 | 68,809 | 67,942 | 68,351 |
| **TOTAL, Independent agencies** | **$ 9,450,431** | **$ 11,693,109** | **$ 12,059,535** | **$ 12,013,956** | **$ 11,994,704** |
| **GRAND TOTAL** | **$ 19,902,355** | **$ 22,374,481** | **$ 22,727,049** | **$ 22,667,042** | **$ 22,562,042** |

SOURCE: House Appropriations Committee

lions of dollars each year for lower mail rates for nonprofit groups and associations. For fiscal 1993, as in 1992, Bush had asked for substantially less than the Postal Service request, hoping to force Congress to pass reform measures on the issue.

Roybal said it was up to the authorizing committees to reform the subsidies. DeConcini argued that not enough money was available to fund the full Postal Service request.

In 1991, Roybal had said that the most difficult issue for appropriators to resolve was how much to provide for the postal agency. The Bush administration had requested $182.8 million. However, the final $19.9 billion fiscal 1992 bill (HR 2622 — PL 102-141) included $470 million for the subsidies. The higher subsidies pushed the final bill's cost above a previous calculation of $19.7 billion. *(1991 Almanac, p. 591)*

In 1992, despite the concerns of postal officials, Congress adhered to Bush's request of $121.9 million for the postal subsidies.

## HOUSE COMMITTEE ACTION

Early in the year, it looked as if the fiscal 1993 spending bill for the Treasury, Postal Service and general government could become a pivotal battleground in the war between Congress and the White House over federal regulatory policy.

An amendment to the $22.7 billion draft bill, withdrawn in a June 10 subcommittee markup but still an option for full committee consideration or floor action, would eliminate funding for Quayle's Council on Competitiveness.

Many Democrats would have liked to take on Bush's regulatory policies in general, and Quayle's council in particular, for playing such a strong role in reviewing — and sometimes relaxing — agency regulations. *(Council on Competitiveness, p. 220)*

"I feel strongly that the council violates the standards and proper rules that apply anywhere else in contacts with the [federal] agencies," said amendment sponsor Skaggs.

Skaggs' amendment generated a vigorous debate in the closed-door markup, sources said. In the end, the subcommittee agreed to include language critical of the council because many were concerned that slashing the appropriation itself would provoke a veto of the entire spending bill.

The draft bill included $11.2 billion for the Office of Personnel Management (OPM), which set policies for the government work force and administered its health benefits, life insurance and annuities to retirees.

Hoyer inserted language into the subcommittee draft that would prohibit OPM from making any changes to federal retirees' health benefits.

The agency created a major stir in April when officials asked insurers participating in the government's health insurance program to cut costs in several ways, including a requirement that Medicare-eligible federal retirees pay the difference between Medicare-approved fees and fees charged by doctors that did not accept Medicare.

### Full Committee Action

Lawmakers critical of the administration's "improper" regulatory activities scored an initial victory June 25 when the House Appropriations Committee approved a fiscal 1993 spending bill for the Treasury, Postal Service and general government that eliminated funding for the Council on Competitiveness. The committee voted 30-18 to cut $86,000 from White House operations funded by the bill.

That was the amount the council's chairman, Quayle, requested for the salaries of two staff members on the council.

Skaggs called council activities "at best improper and probably illegal." He pointed to efforts to delay regulations on Clean Air Act amendments and on those protecting workers exposed to formaldehyde.

Among the defenders of the council were Republicans Tom DeLay of Texas and John T. Myers of Indiana. "Partisanship is unworthy of this committee," said DeLay. Myers argued that the council played a key role in trying to make industry more competitive. Other members said the council had effectively handled regulatory issues. For example, they said, in July 1991 the council helped revise rules that loosened the definition of wetlands while maintaining protection for ecologically important areas.

Frank R. Wolf, R-Va., also stirred the committee when he waved a large bottle of Crazy Horse Malt Liquor and called it an insult to American Indians. He offered an amendment to give the Bureau of Alcohol, Tobacco and Firearms the authority to prohibit such use of prominent people's names on alcoholic beverage labels. Crazy Horse was a Sioux hero and spiritual leader.

After considerable debate and some questions — which remained unanswered — about whether the Appropriations Committee had jurisdiction over this issue, the amendment was approved, 29-11, on a show-of-hands vote.

As approved by the committee on a voice vote, the bill provided:

● $200 million for the U.S. Postal Service, a reduction of $270 million from the fiscal 1992 level. Most affected would be subsidies to charitable, educational and other nonprofit groups that received reduced postage rates.

● $1.3 billion for the U.S. Customs Service, $64.8 million more than the previous year, with a recommendation to hire more inspectors, especially along the Southwest border.

● $1.6 billion for new computer systems at the IRS. The committee said in the report that the IRS should fully fund the Tax Systems Modernization Effort — an extensive streamlining of the agency's computer network.

## HOUSE ACTION

The House threw a hefty punch at the executive branch July 1, knocking out the administration's regulatory council and some overhead costs, before passing a $22.7 billion spending bill.

Democrats scored a victory in preserving provisions in the bill to cut off funding for the Council on Competitiveness. An amendment by Joseph M. McDade, R-Pa., to restore the funding fell on a 183-236 vote. *(Vote 256, p. 62-H)*

After nearly 10 hours of debate on a number of fiscal matters, the measure passed on a largely party-line vote of 237-166. *(Vote 262, p. 64-H)*

Besides reducing the budget line item for the council, the Skaggs language included in the committee bill said that no part of any appropriation made in the bill may be used to fund the council "or any successor organization."

The bill would not necessarily put the council out of business, because its employees were detailed from other agencies, but it would send a message to the administration, according to critics.

"On one level it is [only] a symbolic vote; [but] it also sends a message to the White House that this kind of

behavior will not be tolerated," said Gary Bass of OMB Watch, a nonprofit group that monitors the White House budget office.

Bush threatened to veto the appropriations bill if it cut funding for the council. "This is intervening in the executive branch, and this is purely a political move," Bush told reporters July 2.

Democrats also took a wider fiscal swipe and voted 330-87 for an amendment offered by Bob Wise, D-W.Va., to cut $15.1 million across the board from the Office of the President, which includes the Office of Management and Budget, special assistants to the president and some of the expenses involved in running both the White House and the residence of the vice president. *(Vote 258, p. 62-H)*

A less targeted belt-tightening amendment offered by Democrats Timothy J. Penny of Minnesota and Byron L. Dorgan of North Dakota was agreed to on a 388-27 vote. It would shave $26 million off the bill by freezing 14 administrative accounts at fiscal 1992 levels. Those included the Treasury Department headquarters, the U.S. Mint and the Bureau of Public Debt, which processes savings bonds. *(Vote 255, p. 62-H)*

Still, the bill contained some spending increases for fiscal 1993: The U.S. Customs Service received funding for more inspectors along the Southwest border; there was financing for several federal building projects; and there was money for a costly streamlining of electronic systems at the IRS.

## Council on Competitiveness

The central struggle that took shape on the fiscal 1993 Treasury, Postal spending bill — which covered the government operations most closely aligned with revenue and debt — actually had very little to do with money.

It had a lot to do with who controlled regulatory policy.

Skaggs and other Competitive Council critics, which included the AFL-CIO as well as consumer and environmental organizations, charged that the council staff had gutted Clean Air Act regulations and delayed regulations protecting workers from formaldehyde. Congressional critics were also angry that the council had refused to send representatives to congressional hearings or provide documents to committees.

Council advocates, including the American Medical Association, the National Association of Manufacturers and the U.S. Chamber of Commerce, countered that the group had acted responsibly in pushing along the often bogged-down federal regulatory process. For example, Wolf read from numerous letters on the House floor that cited the importance of the White House regulatory group in prodding the Food and Drug Administration (FDA) to get life-saving medications on the market. "Those with cystic fibrosis thank the council."

Henry A. Waxman, D-Calif., who oversaw a health panel with jurisdiction over the FDA, said that Wolf's comments were "off the point. We do not need a Competitiveness Council to figure out how to move the regulatory process at FDA along."

Republican Whip Newt Gingrich of Georgia warned Democrats of political consequences if they cut council funding. "Do not go back home and tell small business you are sorry about red tape if you vote against the McDade amendment.... Joe McDade has the only amendment on this floor to re-establish the only branch of federal government which is fighting against bureaucracy and red tape."

Skaggs produced a letter from Arkansas Gov. Bill Clinton, the presumptive Democratic presidential nominee, saying that while he agreed that the regulatory burden on manufacturers "is often heavy and at times unbearable" and that some form of regulatory review was needed, he objected to the fact that the Council on Competitiveness conducted all its work in secret.

## Post Office Snafu

Meanwhile, a White House plan to require the quasi-private U.S. Postal Service to pay $315 million into the federal Treasury died a quiet death on the floor.

The plan, as incorporated in the president's fiscal 1993 budget, would have imposed additional fees on the Postal Service to cover the cost of paying pension and health benefits to employees who retired after the 1971 reorganization of the service.

Although the plan had Roybal's backing, it ran into intense opposition from postal officials and union letter carriers. William L. Clay, D-Mo., chairman of the House Post Office and Civil Service Committee, struck the provision from the fiscal 1993 spending bill on a point of order.

As a result, however, the spending bill passed by the House was $315 million over budget.

The White House Office of Management and Budget had asked for the $315 million because officials said the Postal Service had not yet covered the cost the government incurred in paying benefits to postal employees retiring after the 1971 postal reorganization.

But the Postal Service and postal employee unions, which launched a massive lobbying campaign not to be held responsible for the money, argued that the debt had been settled two years earlier when the service paid a lump sum of $2.1 billion to cover its employees' share of the government's health benefits program. The agency estimated that it would have reimbursed the Treasury more than $9 billion by 1995 under a series of bills passed between 1985 and 1990.

George B. Gould, legislative and political director of the National Association of Letter Carriers, said the payment from the fiscally strapped Postal Service would have resulted in a postal rate increase and possible layoffs for union employees. "It is an indirect tax that the administration would not have to take blame for," he said.

Clay's move to strike the payment provision — it was deemed legislation on an appropriations bill — had been sanctified by the Rules Committee two days earlier when Roybal and Wolf had sought a rule for floor debate that would have waived points of order on that section of the bill.

But the Rules Committee refused to offer such protection as even Republicans declined to go along with the administration plan.

"I did not support what the administration was doing, although I normally do," said Gerald B. H. Solomon of New York, the ranking Republican on Rules.

Postal officials said the separation agreement hammered out by Congress in 1970 established only vague terms on what would be owed the government for benefits paid to those employees who retired after the reorganization.

Most retired postal employees, as well as those departing in 1992, had spent a large portion of their career paying into both the civil service retirement system and the federal health benefits program. Calculating the independent Postal Service share of those costs had been an accounting nightmare.

An attempt to settle the dispute was made in the 1990 deficit-reduction law (PL 101-508), when a number of key supporters of the Postal Service, including Sen. Ted Stevens, R-Alaska, helped forge the deal to finally "discharge" the liabilities of the Postal Service.

But early in 1992, the White House reopened the issue by requesting an "interest" payment on the 1990 obligation totaling $945 million over three years, saying the money received so far "would not be adequate" to cover the actual cost of benefits.

Bill Bergen, a legislative representative at the Postal Service, said: "We've given at the office and given at the office on this thing. It is very discouraging to see it come up again."

### Postal Service Still Takes a Hit

But the Postal Service still took a hit from the House, as members declined to alter the Appropriations Committee's decision to make major cuts in postal subsidies to nonprofit groups. The bill provided $200 million for the Postal Service, a reduction of $270 million from the fiscal 1992 level.

The Postal Service funded most of its own activities but received an annual appropriation, primarily to compensate for the amount lost each year because charitable, nonprofit groups received free or lower rates of mail. Both Congress and the administration had been encouraging an overhaul of this subsidy system to reduce the federal contribution.

But when the Senate threatened a much smaller cut in postal subsidies in 1992, to $383 million, it sent nonprofit groups scurrying to lobby members. A compromise was reached that added $87 million to the $383 million with the understanding that the postage rate on magazine-sized material would increase. At the same time, the nonprofits were guaranteed no rate increases until after fiscal 1993.

Jo Merrill of the March of Dimes said her group was concerned about the reduction in postal subsidies and viewed the promise of keeping existing rates through fiscal 1993 as only "a temporary fix." She said her group was working hard on the Senate side to develop a more permanent solution.

Neal Denton, director of the Alliance of Nonprofit Mailers, which was made up of about 120 groups, also said that unless there was a permanent legislative solution, "nonprofits are in very serious jeopardy."

### Other Amendments

Other action taken on the Treasury, Postal bill included:

● Andrew Jacobs Jr., D-Ind., tried, but failed, to sharply reduce the budget for former presidents. His amendment to cut $1.6 million for the office allowances for former presidents was rejected by a 202-205 vote. The amendment would not have affected the pensions for the four former presidents or Mrs. Lyndon B. Johnson. (*Vote 259, p. 62-H*)

● Dan Burton, R-Ind., tried, but also failed, to eliminate $15 million in funding for a nine-level garage to serve a new federal courthouse in Newark, N.J. Burton called the project "pork, pure and simple." The project fell in the district of Democrat Donald M. Payne, but that faced the possibility of change under a new redistricting plan. The amendment was rejected, 89-313. (*Vote 260, p. 64-H*)

## SENATE COMMITTEE ACTION

Every person sending a letter through the mail was expected to feel the impact of Congress' attempt to cut domestic spending.

The $22.7 billion version of HR 5488 approved by the Senate Appropriations Committee on July 31 and the Treasury-Postal Subcommittee the day before continued to target the quasi-private postal agency for reduced funding, while increasing funds for such administration priority areas as law enforcement and drug interdiction.

The Senate recommendation for postal subsidies matched the House version of the bill, passed July 1, which meant the reduction would almost certainly become law unless a way was found to reverse the decision on the Senate floor.

In addition, both House and Senate bills included language that would restrict the Postal Service from making up for the loss in appropriations by increasing the nonprofits' mailing rates.

The result of the spending cut, said Senate appropriators and Postal Service officials, was that all postage rates — including the basic 29-cent stamp — could well go up sooner rather than later. "All postal users will have to pay for this with increased rates," said Pete V. Domenici of New Mexico, the ranking Republican on the Senate Treasury-Postal Subcommittee.

The new postmaster general, Marvin Runyon, already had projected a $2 billion deficit for the agency in fiscal 1993.

The president's budget had requested only $122 million in fiscal 1993 for the nonprofit mailing subsidies. The administration also asked for legislation to overhaul the postal subsidy system so that only the charitable groups would receive the low rates. But no such legislation was under way.

Meanwhile, in other Senate action on HR 5488, the partisan House battle to eliminate funding for the White House Council on Competitiveness did not catch fire among Senate appropriators.

The Senate committee bill restored $86,000 requested in the president's budget for council staff salaries.

## SENATE FLOOR ACTION

The vaunted political clout of organized senior voters was not enough to overcome the Senate's fear of busting the budget or its desire to finish its must-do business for the year.

Two time-weary but persistent Social Security issues — each in search of a moving vehicle — sought out the fiscal 1993 spending bill for the Treasury Department and Postal Service on Sept. 10. But as the hour grew late, senators once again resisted appeals to provide more benefits for a group of retirees known as "notch babies" and to allow senior citizens to earn higher wages without sacrificing Social Security benefits.

Once those amendments were dispensed with, the Senate quickly passed the $22.66 billion bill, 82-12, and sent it to conference with the nearly identical $22.73 billion House version. (*Vote 202, p. 27-S*)

Both bills were slightly more than the $22.37 billion Bush requested.

Although it had nothing to do with Social Security, the bill provided a convenient target for senators who had been frustrated in their attempts to move pet amendments to the floor. And when it came to mollifying elderly voters, even some of the most fiscally conservative senators could turn into allies.

The notch-baby question was a case in point. It revealed a sharp but virtually even division in the Senate on whether to give extra benefits to several million retirees, born after 1916, who got stuck between two fixes to the Social Security benefit system made in the 1970s. The result had been a group of retirees who generally got lower benefits than those born before 1917. (*Notch babies, p. 473*)

But when it came time to waive the budget act to fix the notch-baby problem, the Senate voted 49-49 on a motion that required 60 votes for adoption. Such deficit fighters as Kent Conrad, D-N.D., and Bob Graham, D-Fla., voted in favor of the proposal, estimated to cost $22 billion in the first five years. (*Vote 200, p. 26-S*)

Democrat Terry Sanford of North Carolina, who was fighting a tough re-election campaign, offered the amendment as "simply an issue of fairness." He argued that there would be enough money in the Social Security trust fund to pay for the influx of new benefits, which he estimated at less than $3.5 billion this year.

"The money is there," Sanford said. "If it is not paid to these people who are entitled, it will be spent on something else. . . . If we were in a private corporation and spending retirement funds in this manner, all the corporate officials would go to jail for misusing pension funds."

Opponents, headed by Finance Committee Chairman Lloyd Bentsen, D-Texas, argued that the proposal would "recklessly endanger the Social Security program." He estimated that the costs would result in $300 billion in benefit costs and revenue losses to the Social Security trust fund by the year 2020. He also pointed out that there would be no funding mechanism to offset those costs.

### Bid To Change Earnings Test Fails

John McCain, R-Ariz., subsequently brought to the floor a new proposal to raise the amount of money an older worker may earn before losing Social Security benefits. McCain, who previously had sought an outright repeal of the so-called earnings test, offered an amendment to increase the cap on the earnings test to $50,000 over five years. (*Earnings test, p. 469*)

Under existing law, people ages 65 to 69 who earned more than $10,200 in 1992 would lose $1 in benefits for every $3 they earned.

McCain and other bill proponents said that raising the earnings test would put more seniors into the work force, broadening the taxable wage base and helping the economy. "Tragically, so many seniors in America today have to return to work because of rising health-care costs, food costs and other things," McCain said.

But McCain ran into the same problem as the notch-babies amendment: Because it would effectively increase spending from the Social Security trust fund, it needed a 60-vote waiver from the budget law. The 51-42 vote to waive the law was nine votes short. (*Vote 201, p. 27-S*)

### Controversies Continue

In other action on the Treasury-Postal spending bill, senators approved, by voice vote, an amendment by Simon to prohibit the White House "drug czar" from participating in partisan politics after Jan. 1, 1993. Simon said that the many political activities done by the two men who had held the office since its creation in 1988 led him to propose the amendment.

Simon called the Office of National Drug Control Policy a "dumping ground" for political appointees — 49 of the 109 staff members were political appointees.

In heading to a House-Senate conference, the two versions of the bill differed on funding for the Council on Competitiveness. The House bill sought to eliminate funding for the council's two-member staff, while the Senate provided the $86,000 that Bush had earmarked for the office.

However, the House provision already had triggered a veto threat and was expected to be removed to avoid confrontation with the White House over the issue.

John Glenn, D-Ohio, offered a similar amendment to strike the council's funding, but he lacked the support of both DeConcini and Domenici, chairman and ranking member, respectively, of the Treasury-Postal Appropriations Subcommittee. Glenn ultimately withdrew it after lengthy discussion.

DeConcini said he was prepared to oppose the amendment although he did not "condone what the council has done under the vice president." He added later that going after the funding for the council was the wrong approach. "If the dispute is how the council operates, then the solution should be to change the way the executive branch reviews regulations."

## CONFERENCE ACTION

It had all the makings of a good year-end showdown: Bush would have been forced to veto the bill that paid for his room and board and all of his advisers. But with Congress eager to leave town, appropriations conferees hastily retreated from a prolonged political battle.

As a result, a $22 billion version of HR 5488 appeared, after two days of meetings Sept. 24-25, to be well within the parameters of what the administration indicated the president would accept. Conferees worked late Sept. 25 on a host of other details but anticipated no major controversies.

Bush said he would veto any appropriations measure that exceeded limits for discretionary spending. He had requested slightly more than $11 billion in discretionary spending for the Treasury-Postal bill: Going into conference, the House version would have exceeded that by $433 million; the Senate, by more than $355 million.

However, just hours before the conference began, the full Appropriations Committee raised the final Treasury-Postal allocation to nearly $11.3 billion, which simplified the conferees' task. The $200 million cut was found even before they entered the crowded conference room, coming at the expense of the IRS and the Postal Service.

A more difficult chore — not accomplished until the very end of the conference negotiations — was to soften some of the accompanying report language that the administration vehemently opposed. House conferees ultimately caved in, leaving the Council on Competitiveness' budget unscathed.

That left one more veto-bait issue: a Senate-floor amendment by Simon to prohibit the White House "drug czar" from participating in partisan politics.

Although the drug czar provisions, like the Quayle council, sparked considerable debate, the final agreement was carefully worded to avoid triggering the threatened veto.

### IRS Takes a Hit

The easiest target for budget cutting was the roughly $1.5 billion that the administration had requested — and both chambers initially agreed to — to modernize the

sorely inefficient computer systems for handling tax returns at the IRS.

In fact, the president's budget had proposed delaying the release of $97 million for the tax modernization plan until the last day of the fiscal year, essentially shifting the money into fiscal 1994. Conferees on Sept. 24 agreed to delete that amount from the total and urge the IRS to instead request the funds in 1993. Conferees found another $3.5 million in IRS savings from a variety of miscellaneous functions.

A far more difficult, large-scale reduction proposal did not come up for discussion until the second day of negotiations. Conferees eventually agreed to reduce, by $78 million, the $200 million subsidy recommended in both bills for the Postal Service. That left the agency with only $122 million to subsidize special mailing rates for nonprofit groups.

It was severe but delicate surgery that seemed to satisfy postal groups. "If it had been a $100 million cut, it would have started to make me nervous," said Gould of the National Association of Letter Carriers.

The general belief among the lawmakers, with which Gould concurred, was that the cut ultimately would result in a rate increase to all postal users.

### War on Drug Spending

Some of the major deal-making occurred Sept. 25 over a $75.7 million fund in the Office of National Drug Control Policy that was annually transferred to other agencies that participated in the ongoing war against drugs. Although each of the conferees — including Hoyer and Domenici — said it was not good practice to allocate the special drug funds for other agencies, that did not stop any of them from claiming a share of the pot for their special concerns.

Hoyer supported Wolf in his request for shifting nearly $3 million to the U.S. Marshals Service, a unit of the Justice Department, for additional patrolling of the Wash-

ington area. Wolf raised the highly charged "carjacking" problem as one rationale for the additional funds. Senate conferees finally cut a deal: Wolf got $2.5 million for the Marshals Service and the Senate got about $7 million for U.S. Border Patrol air interdiction in Southwest states, a pet program of Domenici and DeConcini.

## FINAL ACTION

The Senate late on Oct. 1 cleared the conference report by voice vote. The House had earlier approved the conference report on a 291-126 vote. *(Vote 449, p. 110-H)*

Bush signed the $22.56 billion bill five days later. It fell well within the funding parameters he set for the measure, and the final version contained no political swipes at either the White House's Council on Competitiveness or Office of National Drug Control Policy.

Even so, there were still some dollars earmarked for the lawmakers' favorite hometown programs. Two House Democrats from California — Nancy Pelosi and Roybal — fought for and won a $2.5 million earmark from a special "drug war" account. The money was to go to the San Francisco Department of Health for its fight against the drug-related AIDS epidemic.

On the Senate side, Republican Arlen Specter of Pennsylvania made a special appearance at the conference to secure $37 million for a federal building to be constructed in the heart of downtown Philadelphia.

And Hoyer and Wolf cut a deal for "family values" when they obtained a $5 million earmark from the General Services Administration's new construction funds. The money would go toward establishing three "flexiplace" telecommuting centers — two in the Maryland suburbs of Washington and one in Virginia — allowing federal employees who commute as much as four hours each day to report to the same job far closer to home. ∎

# Congress Looks At Its Own Bottom Line

Congress kept its own fiscal 1993 spending bill under the level set in fiscal 1992, but it did so with accounting finesse rather than a budget ax.

On the bottom line, the $2.275 billion legislative branch appropriations bill (HR 5427) trimmed budget authority from the fiscal 1992 bill by $28.7 million. The fiscal 1992 bill had provided $2.304 billion for Congress and its related agencies.

Congress cleared the bill Oct 5; President Bush signed the measure (PL 102-392) the following day, despite his harsh criticism of Congress during the 1992 presidential campaign.

The bill made it through Congress and past the president in part because it was $53 million below the level allowed for it by the budget resolution. Also, the Congressional Budget Office (CBO) estimated that actual expenditures during fiscal 1993 — measured as outlays — were to be 6.5 percent below the fiscal 1992 level.

All of this, Democrats contended, amounted to a fiscal austerity not reflected in the executive branch.

"Between 1979's and 1993's legislative budgets, we have held the legislative branch to virtually zero growth in constant dollars. . . . The executive branch has grown by 34 percent," said Vic Fazio, D-Calif., chairman of the House Legislative Appropriations Subcommittee.

But the decline in the fiscal 1993 bill came from bookkeeping shifts and from holding the line on associated agencies, not from cuts in congressional operations.

The Senate appropriated $2 million more than fiscal 1992 levels for its operations. While the House total appeared to fall nearly $23 million below the 1992 level, the decline was the result of a scorekeeping procedure that credited the 1993 House tally for returning to the Treasury almost $28 million that was appropriated but not spent in past years.

Without that credit, the 1993 funding level for the House was $5 million higher than the previous funding level, and the bill came in less than $1 million below the 1992 level.

## BACKGROUND

Even in the midst of scandal, Congress financed its own operations with a bill built more on tradition than logic. And that longstanding tradition was likened to obfuscation: It required sleuth work to detect how much Congress spent on travel, committees and staff. Even members' salaries and fringe benefits were not easily identified line items in the budget.

The fiscal 1992 spending bill for the legislative branch included a $23,200-a-year raise for senators. Though the well-publicized raise was the central feature of the

---

## BOXSCORE

➡ **Fiscal 1993 Legislative Branch Appropriations Bill (HR 5427).** The spending bill provided $2.275 billion for the fiscal 1993 operations of the House and Senate and related agencies.

**Reports:** H Rept 102-579; S Rept 102-418; conference report H Rept 102-1007.

### KEY ACTION

June 24 — The **House** passed HR 5427, 279-143.

Oct. 1 — The **Senate** passed HR 5427, 75-23.

Oct. 3 — HR 5427 approved by **House-Senate** conference.

Oct. 4 — The **House** adopted conference report, 253-143.

Oct. 5 — The **Senate** cleared the measure, 68-30.

Oct. 6 — President Bush signed HR 5427 — PL 102-392.

---

$2.3 billion spending bill that cleared Congress Aug. 2, 1991, the bill language read more like secret code than an outright appropriation of federal funds. *(1991 Almanac, p. 544)*

When the uproar over House members' check-kiting habits and use of the post office turned into full-blown investigations in 1992, the public wanted to know more about congressional perks. Yet the spending bill gave no easy clues as to how much was spent on members' barber shops, dining rooms, parking spaces and other privileges of power. *(House bank scandal, p. 23; post office investigation, p. 47)*

## HOUSE COMMITTEE ACTION

The House Legislative Appropriations Subcommittee on June 10 approved a $1.8 billion spending bill to fund Congress' own operations.

According to the House subcommittee, the bill represented a 5.7 percent reduction in outlays from fiscal 1992. It also fell 1.1 percent below fiscal 1992 budget authority, which was frozen for fiscal 1993 by the full House Appropriations Committee on June 11.

Sensitive to the anti-Washington mood in the electorate, House appropriators proposed a tight bill that reduced the number of legislative branch positions.

Because the subcommittee approved a 3.7 percent cost of living pay raise for employees and renewed a commitment to improve the Library of Congress, the bill required eliminating more than 1,800 positions in the House and nearly 500 positions in joint House-Senate staffs and other agencies. But these positions, while authorized, were not filled.

Subcommittee leaders feared the cuts were not stringent enough for their colleagues, and they took pains to warn against more drastic reductions. "To cut gratuitously across the board below this level is really just to make a political statement," said Fazio.

"There's a tendency for self-flagellation when this bill comes to the House," said Jerry Lewis, Calif., the subcommittee's ranking Republican. "But in the final analysis we have to fund our operations."

### Less for Mailings

The proposed cuts fell well short of those demanded by 114 House Republicans who signed a letter to President Bush pledging to support a veto of any bill that did not halve congressional spending.

Lewis, who faced a challenge to his chairmanship of the Republican Conference and was caught off-guard by the letter's circulation in April, said he would encourage its author, C. Christopher Cox, R-Calif., and others to target cuts in specific programs, such as the Joint Economic Committee, rather than seek a deep across-the-board reduction.

Democrats, meanwhile, harbored no doubts that the bill would become a target for criticism, as it often was in the past.

"The little leaguers around here," said David R. Obey, D-Wis., "will always demagogue" this bill.

"We'll forever be the place for freshman Republicans to cut their teeth," added Fazio, referring to annual free-lance attempts to chop funds from the bill on the House floor.

Hoping to quell criticism, the subcommittee took several belt-tightening acts. For House mail, the subcommittee approved $53 million in funding. That represented a one-third reduction from the $80 million that was initially approved for fiscal 1992, but the cut was not as painful as it sounded. New rules required mailing costs to be itemized by each member, which made franked mail less attractive in an election year. Congress was able to cancel $20 million in fiscal 1992 funding for House mail and another $20 million in Senate mail costs in a rescissions package (HR 4990 — PL 102-298) signed by Bush on June 4. *(Enhanced rescissions, p. 114)*

The subcommittee also approved language to prohibit House members from sending franked mass mailings outside their districts, a controversial, though common, practice in the past two years as redistricting held out the prospect of changing district boundaries. Congress approved a similar ban in the campaign finance bill (S 3) that was vetoed May 9. *(Campaign finance, p. 63)*

The ban, however, would not affect the 1992 elections. It was not to take effect until the start of the 1993 fiscal year, and members were not permitted to send any mass mailings within 60 days of an election. A similar ban was later imposed by administrative order in time to halt summer mailings. *(Franking ban, p. 61)*

Panel members also went out of their way to squelch talk of a "congressional slush fund." In the past, Congress retained for future use any funds that were appropriated but not spent. At the markup, Fazio made a point of publicly signing a "reprogramming" order that permitted $8.1 million appropriated in fiscal 1991 to be spent to prevent furloughs for 829 employees. Lewis also signed the order. "We want to use up the backlog and do it publicly," said Fazio.

The panel also put an end to the "no year" funding that had allowed Congress to build up these reserves.

Further, Democrats highlighted language in the spending bill that directed the House clerk to track down employees who were delinquent on student loans — a subject of White House brickbats — and to begin collecting.

### Feeling the Freeze

The fiscal 1993 appropriation for House salaries and expenses, which included committees and personal staffs, was set at $704.4 million, compared with $713.5 million in fiscal 1992.

The appropriation for the attending physician's office was frozen at its 1992 level, $1.5 million, while the Capitol police were dealt a modest cut from $64.1 million to $62.9 million. More efficient scheduling was expected to allow the force to retain all but five of the existing 1,357 jobs.

The nearly $500,000 reduction at the General Accounting Office brought its appropriation to $442.2 million. The reduction required the elimination of 162 jobs.

Budget authority for the Office of Technology Assessment and the Congressional Budget Office was essentially frozen at $21.0 million and $22.5 million respectively. Funds for the Congressional Research Service were frozen at $56.6 million, and a loss of 38 jobs was predicted there.

The rare increase went to the Library of Congress, which saw its $248.3 million fiscal 1992 appropriation go up by $1.2 million. The library was in the middle of a massive computer cataloging program.

### Full Committee

House appropriators spent just 15 minutes discussing HR 5427 before giving it their unanimous approval June 18.

Appropriations Democrats depicted the funding bill as fiscally tightfisted, repeatedly pointing to a 5.7 percent reduction in outlays from fiscal 1992 and a 1.1 percent reduction in budget authority.

But committee leaders were concerned enough about the measure's potential for use as a battering ram against Congress that they planned to request an unusual rule to restrict cost-cutting amendments when the full House considered the bill.

"Without it, we'll be on the floor for a week," said Fazio. He added, "This is the tightest bill we've ever offered."

Fazio repeatedly pointed out that the bill reduced the number of positions permitted in the legislative bureaucracy by more than 2,300. But those cuts largely existed on paper. The bill reduced the number of positions permitted for members' personal staffs by 1,847 to 7,833 — precisely the number of people who were working in this category April 30.

Some infuriated Republicans said the committee's claims of parsimony were based on sleight of hand, and they hoped to offer a score of amendments to cut congressional funds in many areas.

Freshman Republican Rick Santorum, Pa., said he planned to propose an amendment to cut the House mail budget by roughly $20 million to bring the funding level to the amount spent in fiscal 1991.

The General Accounting Office (GAO) was also near the top of the Republican hit list. "The GAO has demonstrated itself, in more than one instance, to be in the employment of the Democratic majority," said Lewis, the subcommittee's ranking Republican.

The bill reduced GAO funding by $19 million, 1 percent of the fiscal 1992 appropriation. Minority Leader Robert H. Michel, R-Ill., and others were considering an amendment to cut the budget by 30 percent.

Lewis, who supported the bill in committee and praised Democrats for giving the GOP more of a voice than usual, threatened to offer an amendment to cut the budget for the Joint Economic Committee by one third.

## HOUSE FLOOR ACTION

Following two days of partisan rancor, House Democrats on June 24 successfully pushed through a fiscal 1993 budget for the chamber that Republicans complained did not do enough to curb spending, perks or the power of the majority party.

HR 5427 was approved 279-143, with an overwhelming majority of Democrats opposing an overwhelming majority of Republicans. The bill's $1.8 billion total for the operations of the House and various congressional agencies represented a cut of less than 2 percent from fiscal 1992. *(Vote 230, p. 30-S)*

Always a favorite target for Republicans seeking to embarrass the Democrats, the bill attracted more GOP fire than usual as the minority party attempted to fan the anti-Congress fervor sparked by the House bank and Post Office scandals.

Though Republicans praised the bill as unusually lean,

they attempted to trim it further with a slew of amendments that many members could have had a hard time voting against in an election year. But almost all the GOP efforts were foiled by the Democrats, who used their numerical advantage and parliamentary moves to block most of the amendments from coming to a vote. Republicans could do little more than carp at the Democrats with blistering rhetoric and parliamentary hand grenades of their own.

The changes that were approved were largely symbolic. One amendment halted the century-old tradition of allowing members to pocket an average of nearly $500 each in taxpayer funds for one round-trip journey from home to the Capitol each year.

Seeking to position themselves as hawks against the nation's whopping budget deficit, members approved another amendment to rescind $6.8 million in leftover money from 1991 — an action that took almost an hour of debate, during which the national debt (currently $3.9 trillion) grew by about $40 million.

The bill, most of which funded personnel costs for the legislative branch's 38,000-employee bureaucracy, included enough funds for roughly the same number of House workers as in 1991, about 12,300. But the cuts could force the House to scale back its work force through attrition as members and other supervisors struggled to fund raises for their staff, House officials said. In what appeared to be a symbolic gesture of sacrifice, leaders from both parties allowed their own office budgets to be pared by 4 percent, more than most offices.

In other agencies, the Appropriations Committee said the bill would cut more than 300 jobs from the GAO and the Library of Congress, which had about 10,000 employees between them.

## Process as Substance

The biggest fight over the bill came on the Democrat-crafted rule governing floor debate.

In past years, Democratic leaders allowed the Republicans open access to try to change the bill on the floor, relying on their majority status to vote down amendments they did not like. But in 1992, the Democrats insisted on using a restrictive rule limiting floor amendments to protect members from tough votes.

The Republicans recoiled June 23, the day before the bill hit the floor. As the Rules Committee crafted the measure that would govern the bill, GOP firebrand Robert S. Walker, Pa., slowed House business to a crawl. He repeatedly objected to Democratic members' requests for unanimous consent to make one-minute speeches and demanded vote after vote on routine matters, insisting at one point on a rare teller vote, a time-consuming procedure during which members filed down the aisles to record their yeas and nays.

The tactic accomplished little, though it may have em-

### Legislative Spending
*(HR 5427 — PL 102-392 — in thousands of dollars)*

| Agency | Fiscal 1992 Appropriations | House Bill | Senate Bill | Final Bill |
|---|---|---|---|---|
| **Congressional Operations** | | | | |
| Senate | $ 449,568 | — | $ 451,451 | $ 451,451 |
| House of Representatives | 693,970 | 692,333 | 692,333 | 671,333 |
| Joint Items | 80,716 | 79,496 | 81,737 | 80,476 |
| Office of Technology Assessment | 21,025 | 21,025 | 21,025 | 21,025 |
| Congressional Budget Office | 22,542 | 22,542 | 22,542 | 22,542 |
| Architect of the Capitol | 151,633 | 101,632 | 152,098 | 149,613 |
| Congressional Research Service | 56,583 | 56,583 | 58,000 | 57,291 |
| Government Printing Office (congressional printing) | 91,591 | 89,591 | 89,591 | 89,591 |
| **Subtotal** | **1,567,628** | **1,063,202** | **1,568,777** | **1,543,322** |
| **Related Agencies** | | | | |
| Botanic Garden | 2,862 | 2,906 | 10,131 | 4,906 |
| Library of Congress | 248,308 | 249,530 | 256,086 | 252,808 |
| Architect of the Capitol (library buildings) | 15,187 | 9,733 | 9,733 | 9,733 |
| Copyright Royalty Tribunal | 130 | 130 | 130 | 130 |
| Government Printing Office (non-congressional) | 27,082 | 29,082 | 29,082 | 29,082 |
| General Accounting Office | 442,647 | 442,167 | 440,167 | 435,167 |
| **Subtotal** | **736,216** | **733,548** | **745,329** | **731,826** |
| **Grand Total** | **$ 2,303,844** | **$ 1,796,750** | **$ 2,314,106** | **$ 2,275,148** |

SOURCE: House Appropriations Committee

boldened the Democrats. Repeatedly interrupted by floor votes, the Rules Committee listened to members seeking to offer floor amendments into the early evening. But the panel's Democrats had already made up their minds.

A total of 32 amendments had been proposed, all but four by Republicans. Sponsors of five withdrew their amendments. Of the 27 that remained, the committee decided to allow only 10 Republican and two Democratic amendments to be offered on the floor.

Or so the Rules Committee Republicans thought. When they read the fine print later, they discovered that five of the GOP amendments were not protected from points of order on the floor — effectively meaning they could be offered but not actually considered. "We were tricked," ranking Republican Gerald B. H. Solomon of New York announced on the floor June 24 as the House began debating the rule. "This rule is an insult."

Even Michel, the usually reserved Republican leader, fumed, his face red with anger as he scolded the Democrats. "I think it is outrageous," he said.

Walker again infuriated the Democrats with his speech against the rule when he compared the plight of House Republicans to that of slaves in the pre-Civil War South and Jews in Nazi Germany. "That is the kind of petty despotism which is represented in this rule," he said.

The Republicans attempted to paint the rules vote as one of substance and not of process. "This is a put-up vote; this is one that counts," said Rick Santorum, R-Pa.

Butler Derrick, D-S.C., the Rules Committee's vice chairman, defended the Democrats' action: "Obviously, anyone knows we cannot consider 32 amendments on this

bill. We would be here for a month."

The rule was approved 244-179. *(Vote 224, p. 54-H)*

The 15 blocked amendments included proposals to slash committee funding; to cut the CBO's budget and require it to start charging fees for its publications, which Republicans claimed were biased in favor of Democratic views; to block members from buying computerized voter registration lists for taxpayer-funded mass mailings; to cut off former Speakers' office budgets after three years; and to cut the House Postmaster's budget in half. Two others would have mandated across-the-board cuts.

As the Republicans predicted, Fazio raised points of order against each of the five amendments that were not protected by the rule.

Fazio's point was based on a House rule that prohibited changing existing laws on an appropriations bill. That happened frequently on every spending bill, including this one, but such provisions could survive only if no one objected or if they were protected by the rule.

Among the amendments killed by Fazio were:

● Two by Santorum to authorize $100,000 for "space audits" of House-controlled rooms in the Capitol complex. Republicans complained that the Democrats hogged most of the prime space in the Capitol.

● A proposal by George F. Allen, R-Va., to phase out the jobs of the 11 low-level employees who ran the House's automatic elevators, which Allen said would save $154,000 a year. "It is ludicrous to pay operators to run automatic elevators," Allen said. "As a member of this body, I know members of Congress are capable of pushing the buttons themselves."

Democrats made a joke out of the proposal. Craig Washington, D-Texas, warned Allen against putting down elevator operators because "I worked my way through college operating an elevator in a one-story building."

● A proposal by George W. Gekas, R-Pa., to prohibit senior retiring House members from converting campaign funds to personal use after they retired.

Under a compromise enacted in 1989, after 1992 senior members (those elected before 1980) were no longer allowed to convert their campaign funds to personal use once they left office. Gekas wanted to prevent 1992's bumper crop of retirees from doing so. Forty members who were leaving the House after 1992 were elected before 1980, but only one, Walter B. Jones, D-N.C., said he would convert the money to personal use.

Jones came to the floor, apparently ready to fight, but Fazio prevented the matter from coming to a vote. "It is important that we keep faith with the Ethics Reform Act," Fazio said, referring to the law that included the compromise to end the so-called grandfather clause. *(1989 Almanac, p. 51)*

"This is my first foray into this thing; I'm not going to give up," Gekas said afterward. "We're mounting pressure."

### End of Mileage Payments

On the other amendments, Democrats overwhelmingly killed the ones they did not like, while the ones they accepted passed nearly unanimously.

Most popular was one rescinding $6.8 million in money appropriated for 1991 but unspent. A dozen members spoke in favor of the bill, by Dick Swett, D-N.H., and Scott L. Klug, R-Wis., and it passed 426-0. Lewis called it an attempt to show that "this year there will be a major effort to cut back spending and thereby impact the national debt." *(Vote 225, p. 54-H)*

Not so popular was an amendment by Pat Roberts, R-Kan., to end the 20-cents-per-mile payments to members for one trip from home and back each session, first authorized in 1866. Roberts' amendment, approved by voice vote, eliminated the $210,000 appropriation for mileage payments, and he predicted that they would not return.

"I am not a very popular person right now," Roberts said in an interview. "I had some good-natured and some not-so-good-natured comments about what represents good government."

It is unknown how many House members collected the payments. Various House officials said they either knew little about the payments or refused to release details. The payments, which members applied for by certifying that the money was for a trip that was not paid for from other official travel allowances, could range from just a few dollars to several thousand for Guam's non-voting member. In some cases, the payment exceeded the price of an airline ticket, allowing some members what Roberts called a windfall.

The Senate separately appropriated $60,000 each year for the payments. Records show that all 100 senators and the vice president received their mileage payment from the fiscal 1992 spending bill, ranging from $2,076 each for Hawaii's two senators to $4 for Virginia's Charles S. Robb, D.

The House also:

● By voice vote rejected a Roberts amendment to bar spending on so-called legislative service organizations — issue-oriented confederations of like-minded members such as the Congressional Black Caucus. Roberts said the organizations could be abusing official funds, but members from both parties defended the groups.

● By 417-2, agreed to prohibit members from sending franked mass mail outside their districts as soon as the bill was signed into law, instead of by Oct. 1, 1992, as originally proposed by the Appropriations Committee. The sponsor, Bill Thomas, R-Calif., had been trying to cut off such mailings before the election year heated up. On June 25, he offered a resolution in the House Administration Committee to cut off mailings postmarked after July 15, but it failed 10-12. The mailings were eventually cut off July 30. *(Franking ban, p. 61; vote 227, p. 56-H)*

● By 376-45, agreed to an amendment by Jim Ross Lightfoot, R-Iowa, to cut the franking budget by 10 percent, to $47.7 million. *(Vote 229, p. 56-H)*

● By 134-292, rejected an amendment by Cox to slash the GAO's budget by 25 percent. Republicans had long complained that the GAO was biased in favor of Democrats. *(Vote 226, 56-H)*

## SENATE COMMITTEE ACTION

Gambling that voters would ignore a demand by Bush for big cuts in the congressional bureaucracy, Capitol Hill appropriators recommended just a slight nick in their own funding.

With not a word of debate and no open drafting sessions, the Senate Appropriations panel approved a $2.3 billion legislative funding bill on a 26-0 vote Sept. 23. The funding in the Senate version of HR 5427 represented a 1.25 percent cut in funds appropriated for House, Senate and various congressional agency operations from the fiscal 1992 bill.

Committee Republicans did not join in the president's Congress-bashing. "This is an extremely responsible bill," said Slade Gorton of Washington, the ranking Republican on the Legislative Branch Subcommittee.

In a Sept. 10 campaign speech before the Detroit Economic Club, Bush called for "right-sizing" the federal government and offered to cut the White House budget by

one-third if Congress did the same. He also proposed a 5 percent cut in the pay of federal employees making more than $75,000.

The panel disregarded those recommendations, and even the cuts it did approve were subject to immediate scrutiny. The White House Office of Management and Budget estimated that the bill represented a $2.3 million reduction in actual outlays; the Congressional Budget Office estimated a $119.3 million decrease.

The bill did come in $356.3 million below the president's budget request, but that was based on congressional requests, and some House Republicans urged a veto as a way of highlighting congressional profligacy.

### Merger With Other Bills

Chairman Robert C. Byrd, D-W.Va., opened the five-minute Appropriations markup by urging senators not to offer any controversial amendments that would have to be revisited on the floor.

While the panel heeded his request, the potential for partisan bickering and political grandstanding had already led Byrd to delay consideration until the last moment. The panel sent the bill to the Senate just eight days before the 1992 fiscal year ended Oct. 1 and less than two weeks before Congress was scheduled to adjourn.

Although the committee bill did not differ dramatically from the one approved by the House June 24, the outlook was for a short continuing resolution to keep Congress operating into the 1993 fiscal year. Several Appropriations Committee aides said the measure ultimately could get folded into an omnibus spending bill that also would cover defense and foreign aid. One aim of such a bill was to save legislative branch funding from a veto showdown.

Like the House, the Senate Appropriations Committee trimmed or froze funds for nearly all its operations. Most of the differences in joint items, such as the higher Senate funding for the Library of Congress and the Botanic Garden, were not expected to cause a conflict between the two chambers.

Language on the General Accounting Office (GAO), however, was expected to cause trouble on the floor and with the House. The committee appropriated $2 million for an independent audit and peer review of GAO. It was included at the request of Senate Republicans, who like their colleagues in the House contended that the GAO had become an arm of Democratic committee chairmen.

Legislative Branch Subcommittee Chairman Harry Reid, D-Nev., said the language should "clear the air." But while the action greased Appropriations Committee approval, it also amounted to legislating on an appropriations bill — which could have raised procedural problems with the Senate Governmental Affairs Committee or the House Government Operations panel.

Moreover, the Appropriations Committee added language requiring committees to reimburse GAO for employees detailed to their offices, a proposal affecting heavy users of GAO staff, particularly House Energy and Commerce Chairman John D. Dingell, D-Mich.

## SENATE FLOOR ACTION

By promising to ratchet down congressional funding by 15 percent over the next three years, senators cleared the way for the last appropriations bill — one providing $2.2 billion for Congress' own operations — to pass the Senate on Oct. 1.

The Senate approved HR 5427 by a vote of 75-23. A continuing resolution allowed funding to continue past the Oct. 1 beginning of the 1993 fiscal year. (Vote 259, p. 34-S)

"If we had scheduled this a week ago, it would have taken a week," said Gorton. "This was actually a lower level of rhetoric than I expected."

After days filled with rumor that Republicans planned to offer a number of amendments to dramatically cut congressional staff and salaries, only one cost-cutting amendment was offered. And it was scaled back enough that even Reid joined 84 other senators in supporting the amendment. Thirteen voted against it, including Gorton. (Vote 257, p. 34-S)

The amendment was offered by John Seymour, R-Calif., who was running an uphill race to hang on to his seat. It ordered a decline in spending of 5 percent a year for each of three fiscal years, although Gorton said he doubted that the amendment could bind future Congresses. The amendment also ordered an independent audit of congressional staff needs and an end to the practice of sliding funds unspent in one year forward into the next.

Despite the big vote for his amendment, Seymour openly wondered how many of his colleagues wanted to see it survive a conference with the House.

"Listening to the side conversations on the floor, they're counting on conferees to do the dirty work for them," he said.

The next day, the House voted 402-1 to instruct its conferees to support the amendment. (Vote 453, p. 110-H)

House appropriators had been more frugal than their Senate counterparts, cutting the appropriation by 4 percent from the fiscal 1992 bill. The Senate measure fell just 1.25 percent below it before the Seymour reduction.

### Ending Senators' Liability

The Senate approved two other get-tough amendments by voice vote. With voters griping about congressional perquisites, the Senate approved an amendment by Charles E. Grassley, R-Iowa, to require additional disclosure about the cost and purpose of overseas congressional travel.

The Senate also reacted to criticism for exempting itself from most federal labor laws by directing a bipartisan task to review the extent to which the Senate should be covered by laws such as the Occupational Safety and Health Act or the Fair Labor Standards Act.

But on one law Congress extended to itself, the 1991 civil rights measure (PL 102-166), the Senate quietly reversed itself to remove its members' personal liability for violations. Whether to do so had been one of the hottest issues on the Senate floor in 1991. An amendment shifting liability to the government was offered by Reid, with backing from Majority Leader George J. Mitchell, Maine, and Minority Leader Bob Dole, Kan. It was accepted without a word of explanation. (1991 Almanac, p. 251)

The Senate rejected 11-87 an amendment by Republican Sen. John C. Danforth, Mo., to establish a $1 million fund for nominees for presidential appointments to hire attorneys for confirmation hearings. Danforth did not mention Clarence Thomas, but in 1991 he was publicly outraged by the lengthy process his former aide had been put through in order to win his seat on the Supreme Court. (Vote 258, p. 34-S; 1991 Almanac, p. 274)

Reid pointedly asked if the amendment was retroactive — it was not — and suggested that it was an idea worth study but not ripe for adoption.

## FINAL ACTION

When House and Senate conferees on HR 5427 met on

Saturday, Oct. 3, they accepted each chamber's recommendation for its own funding, and then basically split the difference on the related agencies. Across the board, the House had been more tightfisted — the Senate said unrealistically so — with funding for the other entities funded by the bill.

The House approved the bill's conference report on a 253-143 vote Oct. 4; the Senate cleared it the next day on a 68-30 vote. *(House vote 463, p. 114-H; Senate vote 265, p. 35-S)*

As cleared, the $2.275 billion fiscal 1993 legislative branch appropriations bill trimmed budget authority from fiscal 1992 by $28.7 million.

The bill was $53 million below the level allowed for it by the budget resolution. Also, the Congressional Budget Office estimated that actual expenditures during fiscal 1993 — measured as outlays — were to be 6.5 percent below the fiscal 1992 level.

The CBO estimate on the reduced outlays allowed conferees to drop the Senate amendment by Seymour that called for a 15 percent reduction in obligations over three years. Conferees noted that one Congress cannot bind its successors on such matters.

The General Accounting Office was the bill's big loser, and both the Botanic Garden and the Library of Congress were denied new funds for projects that in another year might have been easily approved.

For instance, the House rejected a Senate amendment that would have allowed the start of construction of a new glass roof for the Botanic Garden Conservatory just south of the Capitol. The 1933 grand dome had been torn down the previous spring when it was deemed structurally unsafe. The bill included $2 million to have the design and construction documents prepared.

(Under rules changes issued in March 1992, House members no longer received free plants and flowers from the Botanic Garden, although they were permitted to keep plants they already had. Senators were still permitted two free plants that were tended by Botanic Garden personnel.)

The GAO budget was clipped by $7.5 million partly in response to harsh Republican criticism that the congressional research arm had become a Democratic leadership appendage.

But in exchange for approving that cut, conferees scrapped a Senate amendment that ordered an independent audit and peer review of the agency's work. Conferees also rejected a Senate amendment that would have required committees to reimburse the GAO for staff members detailed to them.

While Republicans were angered by the elimination of the Senate amendments, Democrats did bow to GOP pressure on another matter: They ordered the GAO to provide accounting standards and guidelines for legislative service organizations (LSOs).

Republicans had long criticized the organizations for collecting dues from congressional offices and then using them for expenses barred under House rules. According to a USA Today survey, the 30 LSOs collected $4.1 million from House offices in the previous year.

## Mail Costs Decline

The House and Senate were able to hold the line on their budgets in large part because congressional mail had dropped off dramatically. Two factors contributed to the decline in mail expenses: voter anger and member accountability.

Amid voter complaints about congressional perquisites and Republican criticism of incumbent-protection practices, the appeal of franked mass mail waned. Moreover, since 1991, House and Senate members had been required to disclose how much each spent on mail. This combination resulted in the lowest election-year expenditure on mail in more than a decade for the House — $57.5 million — according to a Congressional Research Service estimate.

The Senate had $20 million to spend on mail in fiscal 1993, compared with the $11.7 million it actually spent in 1991, the last non-election year.

House members had $47.7 million at their disposal for franked mail, compared with $31.3 million spent in 1991. (The House total appeared as $26.7 million in the conference report because the $21 million rescission was scored as a credit.)

## Supreme Court Decision

Conferees approved a Senate amendment to permit senators to transfer up to $100,000 from their mail accounts to their office accounts. The House had no similar provision.

The conference dropped a Senate amendment added by Grassley, designed to increase accountability for congressional travel. Conferees said the amendment was unnecessary because of the existing practices.

In response to Republican criticism, the House eliminated the practice of carrying over unspent funds. Republicans complained that the account was a slush fund for the Speaker, a charge Democrats vehemently denied. The House rescinded to the Treasury a $6.8 million balance from past years.

Conferees left in place a Senate amendment eliminating senators' personal liability in discrimination cases brought under the 1991 Civil Rights Act. The bill included $825,000 to fund a Senate Office of Fair Employment Practices to help senators comply with the law — one of the first worker-protection laws to apply to Congress. (The House established its fair employment office in 1988.)

As often happened with must-pass legislation on the eve of adjournment, HR 5427 became the vehicle for an unrelated and undebated piece of legislation.

An amendment approved by conferees at the behest of Fazio provided a nine-month moratorium on implementation of a 1990 Supreme Court decision, *Adams Fruit Co. Inc. v. Barrett.* The decision allowed workers injured on the job to sue their employers under the federal Migrant and Seasonal Agricultural Worker Protection Act even after they had collected state worker's compensation.

Talks to negotiate a law to limit growers' liability and provide added workplace protection for migrant workers broke down in the weeks just before Congress adjourned. With California Democratic Reps. Leon E. Panetta negotiating on behalf of growers and Howard L. Berman on behalf of workers, Fazio nudged both sides back to the table by offering the legislative branch appropriations bill as a vehicle for a deal.

The provision imposed a nine-month moratorium so that the matter could be revisited by the 103rd Congress.

While the amendment was cleared with growers, workers and the White House, the only mention of the unlikely amendment in either chamber was by New York Republican Rep. Gerald B. H. Solomon, the ranking member on the Rules Committee. He said the amendment had his approval and was important to apple growers in his district. ∎

# VA, HUD, Agencies' Plates Filled With Pork

Congress cleared the fiscal 1993 Veterans Affairs (VA), Housing and Urban Development (HUD) and Independent Agencies spending bill Sept. 25 after loading up the annual appropriations measure with twice the amount for "special purpose" pork barrel projects as in 1991 and almost quadruple the amount from 1990.

The $86.9 billion bill (HR 5679) funded veterans' benefits, low-income housing programs, the National Aeronautics and Space Administration (NASA), the Environmental Protection Agency (EPA) and other independent agencies.

Unlike past years, when a few lawmakers complained loudly about earmarks for projects in certain other members' districts, the 1992 bill brought barely a peep about the increased funding allocated for those projects. Even Jack F. Kemp, HUD secretary, kept quiet and refrained from writing to committee members.

A prime location for member projects was in the "special purpose grants" section of the HUD account. In fiscal 1991, Congress funded $73 million for those grants over Kemp's vehement objections. Kemp contended that projects should be chosen through a competitive process within HUD to avoid the appearance of preferential treatment or improprieties.

In fiscal 1992, the amount for special purpose grants doubled to $150 million. "They went too far," said Kemp — but that is about all he said. And appropriators knew President Bush would sign the bill even if Kemp objected because they had included funding for the space station *Freedom*, a priority for the president.

In fiscal 1993, the VA-HUD bill included $260 million for special purpose grants. As in past years, the House initially refrained from including earmarks in its bill. But the Senate had included $126 million in projects. So in conference, the House added a similar amount, boosting the total beyond anything ever seen.

Conferees also included $2.1 billion for the space station, down slightly from the $2.25 billion Bush requested for fiscal 1993. The space station funds were criticized by some because the federal budget was so tight and the federal deficit was so high. Supporters, however, pointed to the number of jobs hinging upon the construction and operation of the space station to cement their victory.

## BACKGROUND

The appropriations bill for the VA, HUD and independent agencies, including EPA and NASA, was a catchall measure originally intended to cover all non-Cabinet level agencies. But Congress elevated the VA to the Cabinet in 1989; HUD had been transformed in 1965 under President

---

## BOXSCORE

➡ **Fiscal 1993 VA-HUD appropriations bill (HR 5679).** The bill provided $86.9 billion in fiscal 1993 appropriations for the Departments of Veterans Affairs (VA), Housing and Urban Development (HUD), and certain independent agencies, including the National Aeronautics and Space Administration and the Environmental Protection Agency.

**Reports:** H Rept 102-710; S Rept 102-356; conference report H Rept 102-902.

### KEY ACTION

**July 29** — The **House** passed HR 5679, 314-92.

**Sept. 9** — The **Senate** passed HR 5679, 92-3.

**Sept. 25** — The **House** agreed to the conference report, 286-97; the **Senate** agreed to conference report by voice vote.

**Oct. 6** — President Bush signed HR 5679 — PL 102-389.

---

Lyndon B. Johnson, and bills had been introduced in Congress to raise the EPA to Cabinet level as well. Altogether the annual measure funded 25 separate departments, agencies and commissions.

While the agencies had grown, their requests for funds had grown far faster than the funds available. Appropriators also had to weigh the needs of NASA against the needs of the homeless, of low-income families unable to pay their rent, and of veterans seeking medical care.

In the spring of 1991, House Appropriations VA-HUD Subcommittee Chairman Bob Traxler, D-Mich., realized he did not have enough money for all the bill's programs. So Traxler proposed killing NASA's big-ticket space station *Freedom* to pay for his other domestic accounts.

It was a dramatic proposal, as the space station was the centerpiece of U.S. space policy and a personal priority for President Bush. *(1991 Almanac, p. 516)*

Since 1984, the government had spent $5 billion on the space station, although construction had not begun. Originally, it was expected to cost about $8 billion and to be finished by 1992.

But by 1992, some cost estimates exceeded $40 billion, and the station was not slated for completion until the end of the century.

Traxler's first stab at cutting the space station set off a lobbying scramble that lasted throughout the fiscal 1992 appropriations process.

A diverse coalition of veterans, environmentalists, housing advocates and academic institutions joined forces to keep the space station funding from being revived. They feared that funding *Freedom* would mean taking money from their programs.

But those on the side of the space station were able to drive home to lawmakers how much money and how many jobs were sent home in space station contracts and subcontracts. With jobs at stake in a shaky economy, the space station's advocates ended up holding more sway. *Freedom* was ultimately given $2.03 billion.

Another struggle over *Freedom* took place during consideration of the fiscal 1993 spending bill, with similar results.

## HOUSE COMMITTEE ACTION

Meeting behind closed doors for nearly three hours, the House Appropriations VA-HUD Subcommittee on June 25 approved a VA-HUD spending bill, which included $1.73 billion for the piloted space station. *Freedom* was to be used to conduct scientific experiments in a weightless environment.

# VA, HUD, Independent Agencies Spending

*(HR 5679, as cleared for the president, in thousands of dollars)*

| | Fiscal 1992 | '93 Bush Request | House Bill | Senate Bill | Final Bill |
|---|---|---|---|---|---|
| **Veterans Affairs** | | | | | |
| Compensation and pensions | $ 15,841,620 | $ 16,494,239 | $ 16,494,239 | $ 16,494,239 | $ 16,494,239 |
| Readjustment benefits | 635,400 | 729,000 | 729,000 | 814,010 | 814,010 |
| Insurance and indemnities | 25,740 | 22,730 | 22,730 | 22,730 | 22,730 |
| Loan funds | 771,192 | 787,790 | 779,083 | 788,214 | 784,083 |
| Medical care | 13,599,920 | 14,631,920 | 14,631,920 | 14,666,920 | 14,642,723 |
| Medical research | 227,000 | 242,000 | 242,000 | 232,000 | 232,000 |
| Construction projects | 714,255 | 651,391 | 779,696 | 490,396 | 688,620 |
| Other | 947,096 | 983,819 | 960,467 | 993,465 | 1,001,336 |
| **TOTAL, Veterans Affairs** | **$ 32,762,223** | **$ 34,542,839** | **$ 34,639,135** | **$ 34,501,974** | **$ 34,679,741** |
| **Housing and Urban Development** | | | | | |
| HOPE grants | 136,000 | 1,010,246 | 361,000 | 786,000 | 661,000 |
| HOME program | 1,500,000 | 700,000 | 600,000 | 1,500,000 | 1,000,000 |
| Assisted housing | 7,236,201 | 7,936,764 | 10,024,934 | 3,581,934 | 8,961,665 |
| Expiring Section 8 subsidies | 8,205,128 | 6,832,632 | 6,796,135 | 6,796,135 | 6,796,135 |
| Low-income housing projects | 2,450,000 | 2,282,436 | 2,282,436 | 6,000,000 | 2,282,436 |
| Federal Housing Administration | 243,911 | 370,652 | 323,525 | 283,649 | 243,149 |
| *(Limitation on guaranteed loans)* | *(60,000,000)* | *(57,146,000)* | *(57,146,000)* | *(57,146,000)* | *(57,146,000)* |
| Drug elimination grants | 165,000 | 165,000 | 165,000 | 175,000 | 175,000 |
| Ginnie Mae (receipts) | −279,700 | −322,500 | −322,500 | −322,500 | −322,500 |
| *(Limitation on guaranteed loans)* | *(74,769,293)* | *(77,700,000)* | *(77,700,000)* | *(77,700,000)* | *(77,700,000)* |
| Homeless assistance | 449,960 | 537,278 | 537,278 | 589,000 | 571,550 |
| Community development grants | 3,400,000 | 2,900,000 | 4,000,000 | 4,100,000 | 4,000,000 |
| Other HUD accounts | 575,543 | 1,254,476 | 893,460 | 1,761,626 | 338,685 |
| (Rescissions) | −940,497 | −333,000 | −333,000 | −333,000 | −333,000 |
| **TOTAL, HUD** | **$ 23,141,546** | **$ 23,333,984** | **$ 25,328,268** | **24,917,844** | **24,696,620** |
| **NASA** | | | | | |
| Research and development | 6,409,750 | 7,731,400 | 6,670,650 | 7,102,800 | 7,075,000 |
| Space station | (2,030,000) | (2,250,000) | (1,725,000) | (2,100,000) | (2,100,000) |
| Space flight | 5,124,400 | 5,266,500 | 4,961,500 | 5,086,000 | 5,086,000 |
| Construction of facilities | 525,000 | 319,200 | 525,000 | 319,200 | 525,000 |
| Administration | 2,256,900 | 1,675,927 | 1,613,952 | 1,645,200 | 1,630,076 |
| **TOTAL, NASA** | **$ 14,316,050** | **$ 14,993,027** | **$ 13,771,102** | **$14,153,200** | **14,316,076** |
| **Environmental Protection Agency** | | | | | |
| Research and development | 320,900 | 338,500 | 338,500 | 323,000 | 323,000 |
| Abatement, control and compliance | 1,127,825 | 1,091,860 | 1,362,280 | 1,149,085 | 1,350,690 |
| Superfund | 1,600,128 | 1,750,000 | 1,416,228 | 1,616,228 | 1,573,528 |
| Construction grants | 2,400,000 | 2,500,000 | 2,400,000 | 2,650,000 | 2,550,000 |
| Salaries, other | 1,196,000 | 1,342,862 | 1,118,188 | 1,242,698 | 1,095,706 |
| **TOTAL, EPA** | **$ 6,644,853** | **$ 7,023,222** | **$ 6,635,196** | **$ 6,981,011** | **$ 6,892,924** |
| **Other Independent Agencies** | | | | | |
| Federal Emergency Management Agency | 1,873,084 | 1,017,886 | 805,544 | 1,036,638 | 827,270 |
| Disaster relief | (1,285,000) | (492,095) | (292,095) | (492,095) | (292,095) |
| *(Limitation on direct loans)* | *(6,000,000)* | *(8,000,000)* | *(40,000,000)* | *(40,000,000)* | *(40,000,000)* |
| Planning and assistance | (285,827) | (259,043) | (255,543) | (257,743) | (253,243) |
| Food and shelter program | (134,000) | (100,000) | (109,000) | (134,000) | (129,000) |
| National Science Foundation | 2,570,500 | 3,027,000 | 2,723,485 | 2,732,750 | 2,733,548 |
| Research, facilities | (1,993,000) | (2,407,500) | (2,138,360) | (2,052,000) | (2,130,360) |
| Education | (465,000) | (479,500) | (465,000) | (510,000) | (487,500) |
| Other independent agencies | 236,681 | 242,965 | 198,164 | 266,509 | 242,284 |
| FSLIC resolution fund | 30,328 [1] | 6,815,054 | 2,666,510 | 2,659,328 | 2,661,510 |
| **GRAND TOTAL** | **$ 82,425,265 [1]** | **$ 90,566,977** | **$ 85,870,832 [2]** | **$ 86,849,254** | **$ 86,919,973** |

[1] *Fiscal 1992 total does not include $15.87 billion obligated for the savings and loan bailout fund.*
[2] *House grand total includes a 1 percent cut in discretionary spending (except veterans' medical care) of $517.7 million, not reflected in individual line-items.*

SOURCE: House Appropriations Committee

Subcommittee Chairman Traxler said he presented members with two options: a bill with the space station, and a bill without it. He said the committee voted 6-5 in favor of the space station.

Traxler said he would support an amendment on the House floor to stop funding the space station — similar to the one that on June 17 axed the superconducting super collider, a giant atom smasher. *(Superconducting super collider, p. 301; energy/water, p. 659)*

And he promised committee members who favored the space station that he would only support an amendment that allowed a straight up or down vote on the project, rather than one that would transfer the money to other programs.

"The point of the matter is, we don't have enough money," Traxler said. "Programs are under great stress and strain, and it's only going to get worse."

Ranking Republican Bill Green, N.Y., also opposed the project, saying the cost was taking money away from other space programs.

"I think the space station is a black hole for NASA," he said.

The space station was designed to be a steppingstone for planetary exploration by allowing scientists to study how human beings reacted to long periods in the weightless environment of outer space. But it came under fire from some scientists for not being well thought out.

In 1991, Traxler touched off a furious round of lobbying by groups funded under his bill when his subcommittee voted 6-3 to take out the space station and use the $2 billion for other programs, such as housing and veterans' health care.

However, Traxler's move to strike the space station was repudiated on the House floor by a 240-173 vote. The Senate voted 35-64 against killing NASA's top project.

Because the subcommittee meeting was closed, it was not clear who changed votes in 1992 to keep the space station in the bill.

Including the space station, NASA was to receive $14.04 billion in fiscal 1993, compared with the $14.99 billion recommended by Bush. In fiscal 1992, NASA received $14.32 billion.

### Full Committee Action

The House Appropriations Committee sidestepped a fight over NASA's space station *Freedom* on July 23 when it approved HR 5679 by voice vote.

But Traxler vowed to offer an amendment to strike the controversial space project when HR 5679 reached the House floor.

Traxler said that if the House did not adopt his amendment, he would offer a second amendment to cut all spending except veterans' medical care by 2 percent. He said that would be necessary because G. V. "Sonny" Montgomery, D-Miss., chairman of the Committee on Veterans' Affairs, planned to strip the bill of two revenue-raising provisions, leaving it more than $300 million higher than the committee's budget ceiling.

At the request of Appropriations Committee member Richard J. Durbin, D-Ill., the Congressional Budget Office (CBO) looked at what would happen to other VA-HUD programs in future years if the space station were fully funded. CBO found that because of the cap on discretionary spending, programs including veterans health care and housing would have to be cut.

Durbin said that if the amendment to strike the space

station was successful, he would try to give $349 million to the Labor, Health and Human Services Subcommittee for health research.

The VA-HUD bill was a tight one, with most programs receiving either the fiscal 1992 funding or the amount requested by Bush for fiscal 1993. Traxler said the committee generally chose to go with the lower figure.

Under the committee bill, the Department of Veterans Affairs received $34.3 billion in fiscal 1993, compared with $34.5 billion requested by Bush and $32.7 billion appropriated in fiscal 1992.

HUD received $24.5 billion in fiscal 1993, $2 billion more than Bush requested. But the administration's home ownership program for public housing tenants and low-income renters received $361 million, the same as in fiscal 1992 and far less than the $1 billion Bush requested.

Another housing program, HOME Investment Partnerships, received $600 million in fiscal 1993. HOME was a block grant to the states to allow construction, renovation and rental assistance. Bush had requested $700 million.

The panel also voted 16-23 by a show of hands to leave in a $500,000 earmark for the National Academy of Sciences to study what constitutes a wetland.

## HOUSE FLOOR ACTION

The romantic lure of space exploration and the jobs created by such an endeavor secured the future of the space station *Freedom* from the shears of Congress' naysayers and deficit cutters.

The House on July 29 rejected an attempt by Traxler to abandon the manned-exploration venture. The vote was 181-237. *(Vote 334, p. 82-H)*

The House had voted three times in the previous 13 months to preserve the controversial space station, expected to cost between $30 billion and $40 billion by the year 2000.

"I think that this is it," said NASA chief Daniel S. Goldin. "I'm confident that we now have this thing settled down."

The vote to keep the space station also signaled the beginning of a revival of NASA's image. Congress' support for the space agency had faded in recent years following reports of cost overruns and technical failures such as the Hubble telescope's malfunctioning mirror in 1990.

"The space station *Freedom* represents the future for our country, not only in our ability to compete in global technology, but in the quality of our lives in the 21st century and beyond," said Frank R. Wolf, R-Va.

The $85.8 billion version of HR 5679 provided $1.73 billion for the space station.

Although funding for the space station survived, the program took heat from politicians and lobbying groups for siphoning money from other domestic programs, such as housing for the homeless and veterans' medical care.

Calling it an "orbiting tin can," Marcy Kaptur, D-Ohio, said the country could not afford a $120 billion, 30-year mortgage on the future.

On the flip side, some members argued that Congress could not afford to give up the space station because of its potential for enabling scientific discoveries that could cure cancer, AIDS and other diseases.

### Why *Freedom* Survived

On June 17, House members, struck by deficit-reduction fever, voted to kill funding for another big science

project, the superconducting super collider. (Funding was later restored.)

That vote came on the heels of an emotional and bitter fight over a constitutional amendment to balance the federal budget. Although the balanced-budget amendment lost, talk of taming the deficit sounded the death knell in the House for funding the giant $8 billion atom smasher under construction in Waxahachie, Texas.

The dramatic vote, which cut $450 million proposed for the project in fiscal 1993, struck fear through the ranks of space station proponents. But one month later, the fever appeared to have subsided for the space station, which was far more expensive than the super collider.

"The month gave the opposition a grand opportunity to organize," acknowledged Traxler.

Other factors also played a part in why the super collider rather than the space station was axed. For one thing, the concept of a particle accelerator propelling beams of protons in opposite directions to produce high-speed collisions was less likely to fire the imagination than the simple thought of cruising through the heavens.

And although both the space station and the atom smasher spread contract dollars around the states, the super collider was most closely identified with just one state — Texas. The space station, however, did not have one home.

Finally, the United States was building the space station in partnership with Canada, Japan and nine of the countries in the European Space Agency — a commitment that would have been embarrassing to break. The super collider was almost exclusively an American project.

### Goldin's Crucial Role

NASA administrator Goldin played a crucial role in whipping up support for *Freedom* by meeting with lawmakers, newspaper editorial boards and reporters to convince them of its value.

"Name a member we haven't met with," said one senior NASA official.

During the floor debate, Goldin sat next to the chamber in the office of Minority Whip Newt Gingrich, R-Ga., phoning and meeting with members who still had doubts.

In April, the House had also voted in favor of *Freedom* on an authorization bill. Members voted 159-254, rejecting an amendment that would have eliminated funding for the space station. (NASA reauthorization, p. 296)

On the vote on HR 5679, Democrats split 142-110 in favor of killing the station by striking $1.2 billion from its budget in fiscal 1993, leaving $525 million to cover the cost of ending the program. On the Republican side, 38 voted to end the funding and 127 voted to preserve it. The lone independent, Bernard Sanders of Vermont, voted to kill the space station.

While some members were swayed by the romance of space exploration alone, many others supported the space station for the jobs it provided.

"A vote against this amendment is a vote for jobs right here on Earth right now," said Rep. Bill Lowery, R-Calif., a longtime space station supporter.

NASA officials played that angle hard. They passed out maps of the United States highlighting 37 states and the District of Columbia — homes to about 75,000 jobs supported by space station contracts. Further breakdowns showed the number of dollars and jobs flowing into congressional districts.

Traxler argued, however, that if Congress wanted to enact a jobs program, it should create one that cost less than $50,000 or $75,000 per employee.

"Let us do a building-the-infrastructure program," he proposed. "Fix the potholes! Make the bridges safe! Run some water lines to people that have grossly polluted water."

Indeed, many space station opponents were not interested in killing the project to reduce the deficit. Instead, they wanted to kill the space station to pay for other things.

### The Final Budget Frontier?

Space station advocates said they doubted that the project would be subjected in the future to such a thorough going-over.

"We think this will put the issue behind us," said Science Committee Chairman George E. Brown Jr., D-Calif.

Brown said that in 1993 there would be two key differences. First, the budget walls separating domestic and defense spending were to come down, lessening the pinch felt by domestic programs.

Second, Traxler retired from Congress in 1992 and would not be back to lead the fight against the space station. "Mr. Traxler's departure will remove a major element," Brown said.

Although both House Speaker Thomas S. Foley, D-Wash., and Majority Leader Richard A. Gephardt, D-Mo., supported the space station, Traxler had waged a personal campaign against it, receiving support from the influential Budget Committee chairman, Leon E. Panetta, D-Calif.

Traxler's successor on the VA-HUD Subcommittee was expected to be Louis Stokes, D-Ohio, who voted against the space station. But his opposition appeared to be far less entrenched than Traxler's, and he was expected to go along with the consensus of his colleagues. Ohio had benefited greatly from the space station, receiving $101 million in contracts and 253 jobs.

During floor debate, Stokes said he had mixed emotions about the space station. Cleveland was home to the Lewis Research Center, which did all the space station's electrical work. It was next door to his district.

At the same time, Cleveland suffered from the same problems that plagued other urban areas.

"Cleveland, like Los Angeles, California, has all the ingredients to go up in smoke, any given day, at any given hour, on the slightest provocation," Stokes said.

With the VA-HUD bill lacking money for public housing and other programs to help cities, Stokes said his vote against the space station was a vote of conscience.

He also said it was a vote against an agency run "as though it were a white male, old boys' country club." NASA has few minorities anywhere in the agency, he said.

Brown said he supported Stokes' concerns about the lack of minority contracts issued by NASA and the low number of minorities employed there.

Goldin, too, said that he hoped to improve minority participation in the program and that he had already spoken to contractors about the importance of diversity in their workplaces.

Although the space station emerged unscathed, another NASA offshoot was virtually wiped out on the House floor.

The project, the Advanced Solid Rocket Motor, under construction in the home district of Appropriations Chairman Jamie L. Whitten, D-Miss., was expected to cost about $3 billion. Critics said the new rocket motor was not needed, particularly because it was not likely to be ready in

time to help build the space station. Wayne Owens, D-Utah, complained that the rocket motor was being built solely because it was located in Whitten's district.

"The argument needs to be made out loud," Owens said. "Should our affection, our respect and our gratitude for the gentleman from Mississippi, Chairman Whitten, lead us to build a useless, unnecessary and costly $3 billion rocket?"

Whitten, who had temporarily yielded his powerful post because of illness, protested that the rocket motor was developed after the space shuttle *Challenger* exploded in 1986; it was designed to improve shuttle safety and increase the amount of weight a shuttle could carry. "The location came after all these decisions had been made," Whitten said.

Owens' amendment, to cut the rocket motor by $380 million of the $480 million allotted for fiscal 1993, was approved 249-159. *(Vote 340, p. 82-H)*

Despite the rocket motor cut in the House bill, HR 5679 had exceeded its budget limit by the end of floor debate July 29. The House then agreed by voice vote to an amendment by Dan Burton, R-Ind., to cut the bill across the board by 1 percent, excluding funds for veterans' medical care.

Members subsequently passed HR 5679 by a vote of 314-92. *(Vote 344, p. 84-H)*

## SENATE COMMITTEE ACTION

In the Senate, members of the Appropriations Committee approved a version of HR 5679 on July 31 that provided $2.1 billion for the space station. NASA officials said the project needed at least $1.9 billion to keep the program going.

Jake Garn, R-Utah, an avid space supporter, said the space station had enough votes to survive a promised attack on the Senate floor by Dale Bumpers, D-Ark.

Although the space station emerged unscathed, the Advanced Solid Rocket Motor project was given only $50 million by the Senate panel.

Ernest F. Hollings, D-S.C., called the rocket motor "a matter of safety" and promised to fight for it on the Senate floor. "If we have another explosion, we're not only going to lose astronauts, we're going to lose the space program."

## SENATE FLOOR ACTION

Rallying for "jobs today and jobs tomorrow," the Senate firmly turned back a second attempt in 14 months to kill the space station *Freedom* during consideration of HR 5679.

The Senate voted 34-63 on Sept. 9 against an amendment by Dale Bumpers, D-Ark., that would have slashed the $2.1 billion designated for the space station in fiscal 1993. *(Vote 194, p. 26-S)*

"Humans are going to leave planet Earth," said NASA chief Goldin. "We're going to travel in space."

Following the Senate vote, Goldin stood outside the chamber writing a note to Appropriations VA-HUD Subcommittee Chairwoman Barbara A. Mikulski, D-Md., and Garn thanking them for their work shepherding the project. "Future generations will look back on your leadership," Goldin wrote.

### Bumpers vs. Jobs: Bumpers Loses

Bumpers had crusaded to cut the estimated $333.5 billion federal deficit by eliminating funding for big-science,

high-technology projects, such as the space station, the superconducting super collider and the Strategic Defense Initiative (SDI) anti-missile program.

His only success to date had been in efforts to trim $1 billion from SDI on the defense authorization bill. *(Defense authorization, p. 639)*

For the most part, senators had repeatedly rebuffed Bumpers, preferring to save jobs in the aerospace and science industry.

"I truly believe that in space station *Freedom*, we are going to generate jobs today and jobs tomorrow — jobs today in terms of the actual manufacturing of space station *Freedom*, but jobs tomorrow because of what we will learn," said Mikulski.

The Goddard Space Flight Center was in Mikulski's home state of Maryland, and space station contracts with such companies as McDonnell Douglas Corp. and Falcon Microsystem were worth close to $18 million to the state, NASA estimated.

The space station was expected to generate about 75,000 jobs in nearly 40 states, according to NASA documents.

The Arkansas senator's failure ensured that Congress would fund the space station in fiscal 1993 and appeared to signal a permanent end to the funding debate.

The Senate's $86.8 billion version of HR 5679 included $2.1 billion for the space station. Bumpers' amendment would have cut that figure by $1.6 billion, leaving $500 million to close out the station's contracts.

From that $1.6 billion cut, Bumpers wanted to designate $262 million for veterans medical care and research and use the rest to reduce the deficit.

### The *Freedom* Controversy

The space station had been a lightning rod for criticism because of its huge cost, estimated to cost between be $30 and $40 billion.

That was money critics said was sorely needed for such domestic programs as housing for the homeless and veterans medical care. And it was money that could be used to shave the deficit.

Paul Simon, D-Ill., said Congress' inability to cut spending — particularly for the space station — underscored the need for a constitutional amendment requiring a balanced budget.

"When we stand on this floor and argue day after day about the size of the budget deficit and then agree to fund programs of this magnitude," said William S. Cohen, R-Maine, "then I say there is no hope we will ever bring our budget deficit under control."

Besides attacking the space station's cost, Bumpers ridiculed the project as scientifically worthless. Numerous science groups opposed it, including the American Physical Society, the American Society of Cell Biology, and the American Geophysical Union. They argued that besides having little scientific merit, the station's cost threatened other space and science projects.

In addition, several medical groups dismissed claims by space station proponents that research conducted aboard *Freedom* could lead to cures for cancer, AIDS and other diseases.

"The American public, policy-makers and cancer victims should not be misled by unsupported claims that answers to the cancer problem lie within the realm of space exploration," wrote Lee W. Wattenberg, president of the American Association for Cancer Research, in a letter to Bumpers.

Mikulski, however, savaged the critics, accusing them of lacking the vision necessary to foster new inventions and medical breakthroughs.

When the Wright brothers were inventing the airplane, Mikulski said, people asked: "What are you doing that for? We have enough problems on the ground. Why are you trying to go up there?" Concluding her look backward, she asked, "Do we want to just be sitting with all of our great dreams at a Smithsonian Institution behind us, looking at what once were dreams turned into technological reality?"

Her answer, she said, was no.

### Switching Votes

Although the debate was a lackluster replay of 1991's, with a 34-63 tally in 1992 and a 35-64 tally in 1991, a number of senators switched their positions.

Robert C. Byrd, D-W.Va., Wendell H. Ford, D-Ky., Harry Reid, D-Nev., and John W. Warner, R-Va., voted to fund the space station in 1991. In 1992, they voted to kill it.

Warner said he decided to vote against the project because of its cost, even though NASA said that 1,096 jobs in Virginia were dependent on the space station and that Virginia contracts were worth more than $1 billion.

For Virginians, Warner said, the space station would cost about $3 billion over 30 years. "I am sure the taxpayers of Virginia can use this amount of money for various domestic and infrastructure programs that are lacking in funding at the present time," he said.

Another four senators who voted to kill the station in 1991 voted to save it in 1992. They were: John B. Breaux, D-La., J. Bennett Johnston, D-La., Daniel Patrick Moynihan, D-N.Y., and Claiborne Pell, D-R.I.

Johnston, a principal backer of the superconducting super collider, said he met with Goldin last month and was impressed with his progress in streamlining the agency's budget.

A spokesman for Pell said the vote was a close call for the senator. "On balance, he thought this is not the time to pull back on a valuable project . . . or give up on the vision of international cooperative leadership in space," said William F. Bryant.

### Testing the Water

In other major action on the spending bill, the Senate voted 78-10 to extend a liability statute of limitations from three to five years to allow the Resolution Trust Corporation (RTC) to recoup money from directors or officers of failed thrifts who fraudulently took money from their institutions. *(Vote 190, p. 25-S)*

Tim Wirth, D-Colo., said the extension was needed because the RTC had been slow to go after people. Garn, the ranking member of the Banking Committee, said he was afraid the amendment would discourage people in rural areas from serving on the boards of their local savings association.

The Senate also rejected a motion to kill an amendment by John H. Chafee, R-R.I., to delay new water standards for one year and require the Environmental Protection Agency (EPA) to study the health risk of radon in drinking water. The vote was 43-53. *(Vote 195, p. 26-S)*

By agreeing to Chafee's amendment, the Senate killed an amendment by Pete V. Domenici, R-N.M., that would have frozen the EPA program that tests water for new contaminants. That would have meant that tests would be conducted for only 36 contaminants — one-third of the total that were part of a phased-in testing program. Some

contaminants that Domenici's amendment would have excluded from testing were mercury, chlordane, dioxane, asbestos, PCB and cyanide.

The Senate subsequently voted 92-3 to pass the fiscal 1993 VA-HUD spending bill at $87.76 billion, $3.7 billion below the president's request. *(Vote 196, p. 26-S)*

## FINAL ACTION

A House-Senate conference committee approved the VA-HUD spending bill Sept. 22.

The report included $14.36 billion for NASA, with $2.1 billion going to *Freedom*.

The space station dominated discussions of the bill in both the House and the Senate for two years. The report also included $360 million for the Advanced Solid Rocket Motor, which was supposed to help in the construction of the space station.

The House had included $1.73 billion for the space station, down from $2 billion in fiscal 1992 and from the $2.25 billion Bush requested for fiscal 1993. Conferees adopted the Senate's $2.1 billion figure.

### Advanced Solid Rocket Motor

The conference also found money for the Advanced Solid Rocket Motor. It received $360 million in fiscal 1993. The House had voted 249-159 in July 1992 to cut $380 million out of the $480 million appropriators had allotted. The Senate followed suit, leaving only $50 million to shut down the project.

But at the start of the conference, Whitten, who temporarily had stepped aside as Appropriations Committee chairman because of illness, walked in and stood leaning on his cane for 10 to 15 minutes until Mikulski, the Senate Appropriations subcommittee chairman, arrived. She walked up to him and said, "We're working hard for you." He then left.

Despite objections to the project by Garn, the ranking Republican on the Senate VA-HUD Subcommittee, conferees funded it above what the House and Senate originally had recommended.

Garn said he was disappointed, particularly because the project — estimated to cost $3 billion — was unlikely to be ready until much of the space station construction was well under way.

To pay for the solid rocket motor and the space station, appropriators said they were forced to reduce funding within NASA and to kill some programs altogether. The National Aerospace Plane, which would be capable of taking off and flying into a low-level orbit, no longer received funding. Neither did the Space Exploration Initiative to send people to the moon and Mars, nor the Climsat Earth probe.

### Compromise on HOPE Program

Conferees also adopted a Senate provision to shift the burden of paying for foreclosures on VA mortgages from the federal government to the lenders. That would save $405 million in fiscal 1993, committee staff estimated. The Mortgage Bankers Association opposed the provision, saying lenders would be less likely to offer those loans.

Conferees provided $25 billion to HUD. Included in that figure was $661 million for Homeownership and Opportunity for People Everywhere (HOPE), the pet program of HUD Secretary Kemp. HOPE was designed to help low-income people and public housing tenants buy

single-family homes and units in public housing projects.

HOPE had received $136 million in fiscal 1992. The House had recommended freezing that level; the Senate had concurred with the administration's request for $1 billion.

The Democratic housing initiative, called HOME Investment Partnerships, a block grant to cities and states to improve low-income housing, received $1 billion in fiscal 1993, down from $1.5 billion in 1992. Bush had requested $700 million for the program, the House had suggested $600 million and the Senate had recommended $1.2 billion.

The conference concluded with a disagreement over one item. House conferees had refused to accept a Senate provision that would loosen requirements for putting in place the EPA program that tested water for contaminants. The House insisted on its position, leaving the Senate to either back down or return the report to the House.

### Bill Clears With Special Projects

Congress on Sept. 25 cleared HR 5679 after loading up the annual appropriations measure with "special purpose" pork barrel projects.

The Senate approved the conference report on the $86.9 billion bill by voice vote Sept. 25 following the House vote of 286-97 passing the report earlier that day. *(Vote 432, p. 106-H)*

Unlike past years, when a few lawmakers complained loudly about earmarks in other members' districts, 1991 brought barely a peep about the increased funding allocated for those projects.

A prime location for member projects was in the "special purpose grants" section of the HUD account. Kemp had contended that projects should be chosen through a competitive process within HUD to avoid the appearance of preferential treatment or improprieties. His complaining so annoyed appropriators that the Senate subcommittee cut his first-class travel privileges and zeroed out his public affairs staff for fiscal 1991. Conferees restored the items before sending the bill to the president.

Few complaints were heard on the House and Senate floors in part because so many projects were spread across the country, benefiting so many lawmakers. Senate subcommittee Chairwoman Mikulski received 1,100 requests for $44 million worth of earmarks in 1992.

Mikulski and other appropriators defended the practice of earmarking funds for specific projects by citing the poor economy.

"The demand is clearly linked to one of the worst recessions in modern times, if not the worst since the Great Depression," said one Senate Appropriations Committee aide.

HUD officials seem resigned to the earmarks and hoped for a day when the president would have a line-item veto, leaving the art of doling out grants to the executive branch.

"We obey the law; we obeyed it last year, and we'll obey it this year," said HUD Deputy Secretary Alfred A. DelliBovi. "If they're trying to help local communities, the best thing they could do is to cut the taxes and let the people spend the money before it's collected."

The special purpose grants were similar to projects local communities conduct using federal Community Development Block Grants (CDBG). They included funding for "infrastructure" to rebuild streets, sewers and bridges; money for low-income housing and public housing authorities; and money to build or operate senior centers, health clinics and other social service programs.

Frequently, earmarks were directed toward the states and districts of influential appropriators. Two members who were notorious for bringing home the bacon were Senate Appropriations Chairman Byrd and Traxler, House Appropriations Subcommittee chairman.

West Virginia received $19.25 million from 13 projects. Of those, the Senate put eight in the bill, and the House put in five.

A few of the West Virginia projects included:
● $3.2 million to continue renovating an abandoned building to convert it into an economic development and training center in Elkins.
● $700,000 to build a child development center in Buckhannon.
● $100,000 for an addition to the local fire and emergency rescue building in McDowell County.
● And $1.8 million to finish building the Mid-Atlantic Aviation and Training Center near Clarksburg.

Michigan received $18.38 million from 10 projects, including $8.6 million for two projects in Bay City and Bay County — Traxler's district. Some of those projects included:
● $5.9 million to the Bay County Building Authority to build a conference center.
● $2.7 million to the Bay Area Foundation in Bay City for "municipal infrastructure, economic development and other municipal purposes."
● And $1.9 million to the City of Mackinac Island to restore historic buildings and for other purposes. ∎

# Conferees Drop Controversy, Hold Spending

The House and Senate on Oct. 1 quickly passed the conference report for a $23 billion fiscal 1993 spending bill for the departments of Commerce, Justice and State after conferees dropped all provisions that had drawn a veto threat from the White House.

The spending bill (HR 5678) also was well below the president's budget request of $23.9 billion. Most programs received only slight increases over fiscal 1992.

The bill included $10 billion for the Department of Justice and related agencies, about the same as in fiscal 1992. That final figure represented one of dozens of House-Senate compromises. The Senate had proposed $10.3 billion, while the House had proposed $9.5 billion. The bill included increases in funding particularly for law enforcement organizations such as the Drug Enforcement Administration and the FBI. The bill also provided $13.2 million in law enforcement funds for "Weed and Seed," a pilot program established by the Justice Department aimed at pushing out drug dealers and revitalizing drug-ravaged communities.

To speed up the 1992 appropriations process, the Senate moved early on its own version of the bill. Traditionally, the House hammered out its bill first, and the Senate used that as a vehicle.

But Ernest F. Hollings, D-S.C., chairman of the Senate Appropriations Commerce, Justice, State Subcommittee, said he wanted to move quickly, because Congress had little time to clear the bill before its targeted adjournment date of Oct. 2. Hollings, therefore, moved ahead with his own bill (S 3026) before the House had completed work on its measure.

## BACKGROUND

The appropriations bill for the departments of Commerce, Justice and State had traditionally been driven by the numbers — numbers such as annual drug arrests, federal prosecutions and prison beds.

In 1990, the Justice Department found that one in four of the nation's households was affected by crime. Weapons and firearms cases rose in federal courts by 24 percent. The federal prison system, with an estimated 62,000 inmates, suffered from overcapacity and its population was expected to grow at least 10 percent in 1991.

Such statistics — and the political pressure they produced on Congress — fueled five anti-crime and -drug bills and the near-quadrupling of the Justice Department's budget over the preceding decade.

But overall funding for the sweeping bill, which covered everything from FBI agents to U.S. embassies abroad to weather satellites, had little more than doubled. The result

---

## BOXSCORE

➡ **Fiscal 1993 Commerce, Justice, State and federal judiciary appropriations (HR 5678, S 3026).** The bill provided $23 billion for programs under the departments of Commerce, Justice, State, the federal judiciary and related agencies.

**Reports:** H Rept 102-709; S Rept 102-331; conference report H Rept 102-918.

### KEY ACTION

July 30 — The **House** passed HR 5678, 242-153.

Aug. 3 — The **Senate** passed HR 5678 by voice vote.

Sept. 25 — **House-Senate** conferees approved HR 5678.

Oct. 1 — The **House** adopted conference report, 302-117; the **Senate** cleared conference report, 82-16.

Oct. 6 — President Bush signed HR 5678 — PL 102-395.

---

was that with the Justice Department getting a bigger piece of the pie, the Commerce Department, which competed with Justice for domestic spending in the bill, was held back.

The Justice Department and the judiciary dominated the bill. In the $22 billion fiscal 1992 bill, they received 78 percent of the domestic spending. Ten years earlier, Justice and the federal bench composed about 40 percent of domestic spending. (1991 Almanac, p. 531)

Meanwhile, Commerce Department money went from 36 percent of domestic spending 10 years earlier to a projected 19 percent in fiscal 1992.

In fiscal 1992, however, Commerce received more attention. Because of some first-time and emergency expenses in the department to repair the National Oceanic and Atmospheric Administration fleet and to put extra money toward weather satellites, the department's percentage increase — about 12 percent — was actually higher than Justice's 10 percent.

The skirmishes on the Commerce, Justice, State appropriations bill rarely involved large amounts of money because most members agreed with the anti-crime priority.

Instead, floor fights usually broke down into annual philosophical battles: over the National Endowment for Democracy's approaches in promoting democratic reforms overseas; accusations that the Legal Services Corporation was biased; and debates about whether TV Marti broadcasting to Cuba was necessary in an era of declining communism.

## COMMITTEE ACTION

Federal law enforcement agencies, long immune from serious budget concerns, were dealt a double blow July 23 when House and Senate Appropriations Committees each approved separate fiscal 1993 spending bills that cut funding for such agencies as the FBI and the Drug Enforcement Administration (DEA).

The committees approved substantially different versions of a spending measure. Appropriators eventually had to reconcile a difference of more than $1 billion between the House bill, approved at $22.3 billion, and the Senate bill of $23.6 billion.

To stay within each bill's spending allocations, many appropriations were at or below President Bush's fiscal 1993 budget request of $24 billion.

Both bills were approved by voice vote July 23. The Senate Commerce, Justice, State Subcommittee had approved the measure by voice vote a day earlier, and the House subcommittee approved its bill June 30.

"This is a tough, lean bill," said Harold Rogers of Kentucky, ranking Republican on the House subcommittee.

# Commerce, Justice, State Spending

Here are the totals from the fiscal 1993 spending bill (HR 5678 — H Rept 102-918) for the departments of Commerce, Justice and State, the federal judiciary and related agencies, as cleared for the president Oct. 1.

*(in thousands of dollars)*

| | Fiscal 1992 Appropriation | Fiscal 1993 Bush Request | House Bill | Senate Bill | Final Bill |
|---|---|---|---|---|---|
| **Department of Justice** | | | | | |
| Office of Justice Programs | $ 696,611 | $ 618,520 | $ 654,928 | $ 697,742 | $ 693,312 |
| Legal activities | 2,493,880 | 2,438,358 | 2,217,973 | 2,338,881 | 2,340,586 |
| Organized crime drug enforcement | 363,374 | 399,126 | 378,954 | 369,514 | 385,248 |
| Federal Bureau of Investigation | 1,927,231 | 2,119,683 | 1,910,777 | 2,071,435 | 1,975,423 |
| Drug Enforcement Administration | 717,104 | 771,468 | 702,933 | 750,668 | 718,684 |
| Immigration and Naturalization Service | 937,841 | 1,042,117 | 940,019 | 990,694 | 965,000 |
| Federal prison system | 2,087,790 | 2,197,671 | 1,806,714 | 2,118,130 | 1,982,937 |
| Other | 152,275 | 378,535 | 333,073 | 373,249 | 350,682 |
| **TOTAL, Justice Department** | **$ 9,376,106** | **$ 9,965,478** | **$ 8,945,371** | **$ 9,710,313** | **$ 9,411,872** |
| **Related Agencies** | | | | | |
| Equal Employment Opportunity Commission | 211,271 | 245,341 | 218,682 | 212,982 | 222,000 |
| Federal Communications Commission | 126,309 | 153,336 | 68,536 | 126,309 | 128,500 |
| Federal Trade Commission | 69,200 | 74,050 | 69,200 | 69,650 | 69,650 |
| Securities and Exchange Commission | 157,485 | 158,761 | 157,485 | 119,923 | 127,235 |
| Other related agencies | 38,309 | 49,268 | 38,958 | 35,194 | 39,626 |
| **The Judiciary** | | | | | |
| Supreme Court | 24,588 | 25,897 | 23,890 | 25,473 | 25,606 |
| Courts of Appeals, District Courts and Other Judicial Services | 2,250,319 | 2,695,391 | 2,331,641 | 2,322,630 | 2,346,269 |
| Administrative Office of the United States Courts | 44,681 | 53,639 | 45,927 | 44,951 | 45,100 |
| Other | 53,502 | 63,207 | 57,065 | 56,450 | 57,362 |
| **TOTAL, Judiciary** | **$ 2,373,090** | **$ 2,838,134** | **$ 2,458,523** | **$ 2,449,504** | **$ 2,474,337** |
| **Department of Commerce** | | | | | |
| National Institute of Standards and Technology | 246,713 | 310,677 | 250,869 | 596,978 | 384,007 |
| National Oceanic and Atmospheric Administration | 1,688,247 | 1,673,017 | 1,541,455 | 1,647,798 | 1,649,282 |
| Bureau of the Census | 290,290 | 338,398 | 306,814 | 287,784 | 297,255 |
| International Trade Administration | 209,160 | 202,158 | 194,149 | 215,292 | 213,851 |
| Patent and Trademark Office | 88,441 | 99,000 | 89,129 | 86,672 | 86,672 |
| Economic Development Administration | 328,882 | 14,000 | 262,199 | 257,500 | 244,118 |
| Other | 235,355 | 247,668 | 228,544 | 235,458 | 231,052 |
| **TOTAL, Commerce Department** | **$ 3,087,088** | **$ 2,884,918** | **$ 2,873,159** | **$ 3,327,482** | **$ 3,106,237** |
| **Related Agencies** | | | | | |
| Maritime Administration | 307,161 | 312,419 | 480,370 | 264,886 | 564,236 |
| Legal Services Corporation | 350,000 | 525,034 | 364,000 | 350,000 | 357,000 |
| Small Business Administration | 1,652,125 | 563,467 | 859,069 | 817,821 | 835,277 |
| Other related agencies | 27,303 | 28,234 | 24,368 | 25,005 | 24,655 |
| **Department of State** | | | | | |
| Administration of Foreign Affairs | 2,733,189 | 2,915,922 | 2,861,743 | 2,789,965 | 2,927,411 |
| International Organizations and Conferences | 1,035,113 | 1,608,551 | 1,376,406 | 1,379,129 | 1,379,129 |
| Other | 65,711 | 77,025 | 69,108 | 71,860 | 70,877 |
| **TOTAL, State Department** | **$ 3,834,013** | **$ 4,601,498** | **$ 4,307,257** | **$ 4,240,954** | **$ 4,377,417** |
| **Related Agencies** | | | | | |
| Arms Control and Disarmament Agency | 44,527 | 47,585 | 45,863 | 47,000 | 46,500 |
| Board for International Broadcasting | 207,491 | 220,000 | 220,000 | 232,000 | 220,000 |
| United States Information Agency | 1,087,094 | 1,144,039 | 1,126,702 | 1,198,879 | 1,164,083 |
| Other related agencies | 43,884 | 46,602 | 46,602 | 45,602 | 46,302 |
| **GRAND TOTAL** | **$ 22,992,456** | **$ 23,858,164** | **$ 22,304,145** | **$ 23,273,504** | **$ 23,214,927** |

SOURCE: House Appropriations Committee

"This is not one of our prouder moments."

Rogers blamed the funding cuts on the subcommittee spending allocation handed down by the full Appropriations Committee.

The Senate's spending allocation was higher than the House's, but cuts still had to be made. Subcommittee Chairman Hollings said he had to turn down $8.5 billion in senators' requests for projects for their states.

"We've got to sober some of these folks up around here," he said.

Upcoming negotiations between House and Senate appropriators were expected to be complicated because House and Senate Appropriations Committees provided different spending levels for the two subcommittees. The House allocation was set at about $22.7 billion and the Senate number at $23 billion.

### Nothing Was Sacred

For budget-cutting appropriators, even departments long afforded priority status were not safe from the knife. The Justice Department, always a congressional favorite because it included law and drug enforcement agencies, received $374 million less than appropriators provided for fiscal 1992 under the House bill, which allocated $8.9 billion. The Senate bill was proposing $9.5 billion, a slight increase over the 1992 figure of $9.3 billion. The president requested $10 billion.

Meanwhile, the Commerce Department received $3.3 billion under the Senate bill, an increase of $340 million over fiscal 1992. The House provided $2.9 billion, a decrease of $116 million.

The State Department fared well under both bills. Under the House version, the department received $4.3 billion, up $578 million over fiscal 1992. The Senate also provided $4.3 billion. Both appropriations included $140 million for construction of a new embassy building in Moscow.

The Judiciary also received increases under both bills, although less than the president requested. Both bills provided $2.5 billion, compared with $2.3 billion in fiscal 1992.

House Subcommittee Chairman Neal Smith, D-Iowa, said the subcommittee funded Justice Department programs at 93 percent of existing services levels, plus 25 percent of increases requested by Bush.

However, the House subcommittee funded some justice programs — organized-crime drug enforcement, federal prison salaries and expenses, FBI and DEA — above the formula amount. Even so, the FBI's salaries and expenses were $15.3 million less than fiscal 1992 levels, while DEA was $13.7 million less under the House bill. FBI funding for salaries and expenses was $209 million less than the president requested and DEA was $68.5 million less.

No money was included in the House bill for new prison construction.

The Senate and House also took a tack that angered FBI and DEA officials. The bills eliminated categories of overtime paid to special agents for both agencies. FBI overtime was cut by $47 million. DEA overtime was cut $16 million. An aide to Hollings said some of the cuts were proposed after the subcommittee learned that the agents at both agencies were allowed to collect three hours of overtime a week for time spent on physical exercise.

However, the total appropriations for both agencies increased slightly under the Senate bill. The FBI received $2 billion, up from $1.9 billion in fiscal 1992, and DEA received $750.7 million, up from $716.7 million. The bill provided full funding of the FBI's request for anti-crime programs, including an initiative targeting Asian organized-crime operations. DEA received 93 new agents under the Senate bill.

### Veto Threat

Besides expected fights over dollars, appropriators also had to ward off a veto threat aimed at the House bill. In a letter to Rogers, Richard G. Darman, director of the White House Office of Management and Budget, said Bush would veto the bill over concerns about the activities of the Legal Services Corporation, the embattled program that provided legal aid to the poor.

Smith, who insisted that money for programs under his jurisdiction be authorized, pushed for House passage of legislation (HR 2039) reauthorizing funding for the corporation. Because its cases sometimes placed it at odds with federal policies, Legal Services had been the subject of many battles between Congress and the White House. (Legal services reauthorization, p. 317)

The administration had threatened to veto HR 2039, arguing that the bill allowed Legal Services lawyers to work on abortion-related cases and to lobby in some cases.

Rogers offered an amendment to the House bill that would have provided that the appropriations bill fund only activities permitted under existing law, not in the authorization bill. The amendment was defeated 16-25.

## FLOOR ACTION

Caught up in election-year budget cutting, the House and Senate pushed aside appropriators the week of July 27 and sliced millions of dollars in administrative costs from the 1993 spending bills for the departments of Commerce, Justice and State and the judiciary.

The House passed its $22.3 billion version of HR 5678 on July 30 on a largely party-line vote of 242-153. The Senate completed consideration of S 3026 on July 28 but held its bill at the desk pending House action. Congressional custom dictated that spending bills be passed first in the House, so after House passage, the Senate amended HR 5678 with the language of S 3026 and requested a conference. (House vote 354, p. 86-H)

The Senate bill cost $23.6 billion, partly because the Senate Appropriations Subcommittee on Commerce, Justice, State and Judiciary received a larger allocation for discretionary spending. While both bills included appropriators' cost-cutting initiatives, some members wanted to cut even more.

In the Senate, Bob Graham, D-Fla., successfully offered an amendment to cut departmental administrative costs, effectively freezing spending at fiscal 1992 levels.

The amendment was a defeat for an angry Hollings who, along with ranking Republican Warren B. Rudman of New Hampshire, had worked since January to draft the bill.

Hollings' efforts to drum up votes to defeat the amendment were no match for Graham's talk of deficit reduction. Graham also invoked the name of Democratic presidential candidate Bill Clinton and likened the proposal to Clinton's plan to cut the federal payroll.

Hollings, arguing that the subcommittee bill was already substantially below President Bush's request, accused Graham of grandstanding.

"It is a game," Hollings said. "Everyone within the hearing of our voice knows that."

Graham offered three amendments to the spending bill. The first cut $1.4 million from the $32.7 million for Commerce Department operations. After the Senate adopted that amendment 50-42, two other Graham amendments were

adopted by voice vote. The second shaved $8.1 million from the $118.2 million in administrative costs for the Justice Department. The third cut about $85 million from $2.1 billion in State Department overhead. *(Vote 153, p. 21-S)*

Rudman argued that the bill's funding for the Justice Department did not provide enough for it to enforce the Americans with Disabilities Act, which went into effect July 26. "Even under the committee recommendation, it will be impossible," he said.

An aide to Hollings said that because the cuts were politically popular, appropriators were not likely to succeed in taking out the Graham amendments in conference.

After Graham's success in the Senate, House appropriators did not put up a fight July 30 when Byron L. Dorgan, D-N.D., offered an amendment that froze spending for the State Department, cutting $19 million from the bill. The amendment was adopted by voice vote.

### Economic Aid

Advancing a congressional theme of cutting government spending while helping the economy, both bills included provisions designed to boost employment.

The Senate bill included $229 million in defense conversion funding to assist communities hard hit by the closing of military bases. The House bill included none.

However, the House did include funding for the Economic Development Administration (EDA), which proponents said would help the economy. Supporters had to fight off attempts to eliminate the program.

The House rejected an amendment offered by Dan Burton, R-Ind., to cut $235 million in assistance programs for the EDA, a Commerce Department agency that provided grants for community projects and job creation. The administration had requested no assistance funds; the Senate provided $150 million.

Burton accused members of using the EDA to fund pork barrel projects for their home states. Joseph D. Early, D-Mass., shot back that the deficit was caused by Republican administrations. Burton fired back that spending originated in the Democrat-dominated House. His amendment was defeated 76-339. *(Vote 350, p. 86-H)*

### TV Marti Stays on the Air

The House voted to continue $12.7 million in funding for TV Marti, the United States Information Agency television station that broadcast to Cuba, just hours after voting to scrap it.

Members first voted 206-194 to approve an amendment to cancel funding for the station after Bill Alexander, D-Ark., and other members said the programs were not reaching Cubans. Alexander called the station "a wasteful, ineffective Cold War relic." *(Vote 352, p. 86-H)*

But Florida members, who strongly supported TV Marti, said its programming provided an important service to many Cubans. "It is having a direct impact; people are seeing it," said Democrat Dante B. Fascell. "If they are not seeing it, then they want to see it." In a procedural move, members asked for a second vote on Alexander's amendment, which was then rejected 181-215. *(Vote 353, p. 86-H)*

### Administration Objections

Both bills prompted veto threats from Bush. The president opposed a provision written by Hollings in the Senate bill to protect railroad and utility companies. The provision blocked a Federal Communications Commission (FCC) proposal to move railroad and utility companies from pre-

mium low-frequency radio bands sought by producers of high-tech pocket phones and other rapidly developing telecommunications technologies.

Hollings argued that the FCC plan harmed the operations of railroads, electric power companies and rural electric cooperatives using the frequencies.

The administration contended that the Senate was pushing a policy that could hurt economic growth by attempting to impinge on the commission's discretion to award radio spectrum licenses.

"The committee's action would impede the ability of the FCC to accommodate these developments," said an administration statement.

The provision had drawn fire from small manufacturers of emerging technologies, including computer companies.

Bush had threatened to veto both the House and Senate bills over concerns about the Legal Services Corporation.

House subcommittee Chairman Smith insisted that money for programs under his jurisdiction be authorized before funding was appropriated. He had pushed for House passage of legislation, HR 2039, approved May 12, reauthorizing funding for the corporation. But the administration had threatened to veto the bill, arguing that the bill would allow Legal Services lawyers to work on abortion-related cases.

The Senate authorization bill, S 2870, approved in committee July 1, also allowed Legal Services lawyers to work on abortion-related cases.

House appropriators did not allow Bill McCollum, R-Fla., to amend the bill to include a provision to clarify that corporation funding would be spent according to existing law, which disallowed Legal Services work on cases involving abortion.

## FINAL ACTION

In a rush to complete action on the Commerce, Justice, State spending bill, House and Senate conferees Sept. 25 stripped the bill of the controversial provisions that had drawn a veto threat from President Bush. Members compromised on nearly 200 areas of contention.

Hollings said the Senate cut its bill by about $117 million to bring it more in line with the House.

Under the bill, Hollings said, overall law enforcement dollars increased by about $500 million. An aide to Hollings said the Justice Department received a 5 percent increase over the fiscal 1992 level of $9.3 billion. The Judiciary also received a 5 percent hike over its fiscal 1992 spending level of $2.3 billion.

The measure no longer included a provision that the administration said would allow Legal Service Corporation lawyers to work on abortion-related cases.

Legal Services received $357 million, slightly more than Bush requested.

Also dropped was a controversial Senate provision, crafted by Hollings, designed to protect railroad and utility companies. The provision would have blocked a proposal by the FCC to move utilities off the premium low-frequency radio bands sought by producers of high-tech pocket phones and other telecommunications technologies.

### Hollings' Victory

Despite smooth sailing through a hasty conference, the bill had been battered by a storm of controversy for months.

Since July, key members of the House, led by Energy

and Commerce Committee Chairman John D. Dingell, D-Mich., had been locked in a battle with Hollings over who should control the nation's airwaves — Congress or the executive branch.

As an appropriations subcommittee chairman, Hollings wanted Congress to supersede the FCC's rule-making authority because he believed one of its proposed rules could adversely affect utilities and consumers. He included in the Senate's version of the appropriations bill a provision that would block a proposed FCC regulation to allocate prime low-frequency airwave space for companies to use for development of emerging technologies such as wireless laptop computers. Hollings' provision would have delayed the allocation for eight years. *(Radio spectrum, p. 193)*

The move angered House members, activated a tough lobbying effort by the companies pushing emerging technologies and prompted a veto threat from Bush.

Hollings was the winner, however, after his artful political prodding persuaded the FCC to back down, making the issue moot. The subcommittee chairman exerted some control over the FCC's budget, and, as chairman of the Committee on Commerce, Science and Transportation, Hollings oversaw some of its operations as well.

In including the provision, Hollings also invited a turf battle with Dingell, whose Energy and Commerce Committee had jurisdiction over the issue. Dingell argued that by pushing the provision, Hollings was violating congressional rules that prohibited legislating on an appropriations bill.

In an Aug. 5 letter to House Speaker Thomas S. Foley, D-Wash., Dingell asked Foley to intervene by appointing members of the Energy and Commerce Committee as conferees on the appropriations bill.

The FCC's proposed regulation would have forced existing larger low-frequency users — including Amtrak and many utility companies — to share the radio spectrum with companies providing communications devices including wireless laptop computers and other high-technology inventions.

Hollings argued that while he supported emerging technologies, he also wanted to watch out for companies that provided essential services now using the airwaves; they would not be adequately protected under the FCC's plan, he maintained.

A Hollings aide said Amtrak used low-frequency microwave systems to control switches on train tracks and by utilities to provide power to consumers' homes.

Under the proposed rule, the aide said, these companies could face being relegated to less reliable frequencies on the spectrum. If that happened, "power goes off in people's homes and trains crash," the aide said.

### New Technologies

In response to Hollings' provision, which he added to the appropriations bill during the subcommittee's markup on June 30, computer companies entered the fray.

Led by California-based Apple Computer Inc., they argued that the FCC's proposed regulation could make the United States more competitive with Japan and other countries, while creating new manufacturing jobs for the many Americans who were out of work.

FCC Chairman Alfred C. Sikes and the companies' House allies backed their argument.

In testimony before the Senate Commerce Subcommittee on Communications, Sikes said that the emerging technologies would generate more than 100,000 new jobs and $30 billion in investment opportunities.

Hollings' provision would have prohibited the commis-

sion from using its funding to "develop, issue, implement or enforce" regulations to allocate space to the computer companies, he said.

The issue was solved when the FCC announced Sept. 17 that it would drop much of its proposal and ensure that the existing users were protected.

Hollings in turn dropped his provision, saying in a statement that he was satisfied that the FCC had recognized the "legitimate concerns of existing users."

Said Hollings' aide: "They're right to be moving forward with new technologies, but you can't do that by running roughshod over the existing users."

### Law Enforcement Increases

As approved by conferees, the bill included $10 billion for the Department of Justice and related agencies, about the same as in fiscal 1992. The final figure represented one of dozens of House-Senate compromises. The Senate had proposed $10.3 billion, while the House had proposed $9.5 billion.

The bill included increases in funding particularly for law enforcement organizations such as the DEA and the FBI. The bill also provided $13.2 million in law enforcement funds for "Weed and Seed," a pilot program established by the Justice Department aimed at pushing out drug dealers and revitalizing drug-ravaged communities.

### Good News for NIST, NOAA

The Commerce Department received $3.1 billion, about the same as in fiscal 1992. Under the conference report, several agency budgets were cut, and two received hefty increases: the National Institute of Standards and Technology (NIST) and a section of the National Oceanic and Atmospheric Administration (NOAA).

NIST received $384 million under the bill, up from $246.7 million in fiscal 1992. The increase reflected the interest of Hollings in furthering scientific advances. The Senate had wanted to provide $597 million and the House $250.9 million.

The conference agreement also provided $1.65 billion for NOAA, down from $1.69 billion in fiscal 1992. However, construction projects under the agency increased sharply from $34.9 million to $94.5 million.

The increase drew criticism in the House from Burton, who fought an annual battle against pork barrel projects in appropriations bills.

Burton charged that members added the construction projects "in the dead of night," in conference, without a vote by the full House and Senate. The projects were spread across the country.

Meanwhile, funding for the department's Economic Development Administration fell from $328.9 million to $244.1 million, below both the House and Senate proposals. The House would have provided $262.2 million, and the Senate $257.5 million. Funding for the Minority Business Development Agency also dropped from $42.5 million to $37.9 million.

The State Department received $4.4 billion, up from $3.8 billion.

Finally, the federal judiciary received $2.5 billion under the bill, up from $2.4 billion in fiscal 1992.

Once the controversial provisions affecting the Legal Services Corporation and the nation's airwaves were dropped, the conference report on HR 5678 sailed through the House and Senate on Oct. 1.

The Senate cleared the bill 82-16 after the House passed the measure 302-117 earlier in the day. *(House vote 448, p. 110-H; Senate vote 260, p. 34-S)* ∎

# Labor-HHS Funding Quietly Approved

Shorn of any semblance of controversy, the $246 billion spending bill for the departments of Labor, Health and Human Services (HHS), and Education and related agencies was quietly cleared by Congress on Oct. 3.

The subdued final step was in marked contrast to what had been a turbulent trip for the measure (HR 5677), which funded many of the federal government's most popular social programs, including Head Start for preschoolers, Meals on Wheels for the elderly, and the Job Corps, a residential training program for young people in need of job skills.

To avert a threatened veto, conferees had to cut eight-tenths of 1 percent from each program over which they had direct control. Those discretionary programs were worth roughly $62 billion. (Much of the measure's total was for mandatory entitlement programs such as Medicaid, whose spending was determined by other committees.) President Bush had threatened to veto the measure unless its discretionary total was under the $61.97 billion he sought in his fiscal 1993 budget.

Conferees also dropped a veto-bait provision that would have allowed federal funding of abortions in certain cases of rape or incest. During Senate floor consideration members dropped still another abortion-related provision that would have blocked enforcement of the so-called gag rule, which prohibited abortion counseling in federally funded family planning clinics. Those contested regulations took effect Oct. 1, 1992, but subsequently were stayed by a federal appeals court Nov. 3.

## BACKGROUND

The Labor-HHS spending bill had become an example of the tension in Congress between lawmakers' penchant for creating new social programs and their increasing inability to provide funds for them.

The bill often got caught in an institutional tug of war between the authorizing committees, which set overarching policy by creating, revising and extending federal programs, and the Appropriations committees, which decided exactly how much money those programs would get.

Even in the best budget years, Labor-HHS appropriators could not hope to fully fund the more than 500 programs that came under their purview. The measure provided funds to three Cabinet departments and 18 related agencies — more money than any other spending bill except defense — but most of the money went to entitlement programs for which funding levels were determined by eligibility formulas and other criteria set by law.

Despite increasingly tight budgets, the authorizing com-

---

## BOXSCORE

➡ **Fiscal 1993 appropriations for the departments of Labor, Health and Human Services, and Education (HR 5677).** The $246 billion spending bill provided funding for most federal social programs.

**Reports:** H Rept 102-708; S Rept 102-397; conference report H Rept 102-974.

### KEY ACTION

July 28 — The **House** passed HR 5677, 345-54.

Sept. 18 — The **Senate** passed HR 5677, 82-13.

Sept. 30 — A **House-Senate** conference approved HR 5677.

Oct. 3 — The **House** approved the conference report, 363-47. The **Senate** approved the conference report by voice vote.

Oct. 6 — President Bush signed HR 5677 — PL 102-394.

---

mittees often made it more difficult on the appropriators to satisfy the many claims in the bill.

In 1991, although the spending cap for the Labor-HHS bill increased by more than $2 billion, it was not enough to maintain service levels of existing programs. That was partly because in 1991 the authorizing committees created several new social spending programs.

For example, Congress authorized $880 million to help cities and other areas cope with the burgeoning costs of the AIDS epidemic. Appropriators provided $280 million for fiscal 1992. *(1991 Almanac, p. 501)*

Appropriators in 1991 also put an added burden on themselves for the next fiscal year. In an effort to skirt the budget ceilings set in the 1990 budget agreement, the Bush administration and House and Senate conferees agreed in 1991 to promise in advance more than $4 billion in "delayed obligations." That made the fiscal 1992 totals look larger, even though most of the money was not available until Sept. 30, the last day of the fiscal year. Because the money from the fiscal 1992 bill was not spent until fiscal 1993, it came out of the 1993 total, giving appropriators a smaller pot to work from.

With the money having come due in 1992, the committee said it would not spend itself any deeper into debt. Members not only denied the administration's request for an additional $2.9 billion in delayed spending, but also excoriated the practice as an "accounting gimmick" that "deceives the American public by giving the appearance that funds are available in one year when in fact they will not be available until the following budget cycle."

Indeed, House Appropriations Committee members cheered Acting Chairman William H. Natcher when he announced that the bill included "not one dollar" in delayed obligations.

## HOUSE COMMITTEE ACTION

Working behind closed doors, members of the House Appropriations Subcommittee on Labor, Health and Human Services, and Education completed work on their fiscal 1993 spending bill July 2.

It took the subcommittee two days to finish marking up the $244 billion measure, in what members described as one of the most difficult sessions ever. The subcommittee, which provided funding for some of the federal government's most popular health, social service and education programs, was hindered because the approximately $1 billion increase in budget authority it received in the annual allocation process was more than consumed by the $3 billion in 1993 spending that members put in the fiscal 1992 bill. Thus, the amount available for fiscal 1993 was reduced by roughly $2 billion.

# Labor, HHS, Education Spending

*(HR 5677, H Rept 102-974, as cleared for the president Oct. 3, in thousands of dollars):*

| | Fiscal 1992 Appropriation | Fiscal 1993 Bush Request | House Bill | Senate Bill | Final Bill |
|---|---|---|---|---|---|
| **Labor Department** | | | | | |
| Training grants to states | $ 3,033,382 | $ 3,031,448 | $ 3,003,048 | $ 3,104,952 | $ 2,979,023 |
| Job Corps | 955,101 | 909,503 | 989,010 | 958,722 | 966,075 |
| Trade adjustment, allowances | 226,250 | 211,250 | 211,250 | 211,250 | 211,250 |
| Unemployment insurance (advance) | 236,990 | 665,000 | 665,000 | 665,000 | 665,000 |
| *Trust fund* | *(2,248,885)* | *(2,315,913)* | *(2,332,354)* | *(2,284,153)* | *(2,265,792)* |
| Black lung disability | 917,948 | 943,783 | 944,783 | 944,783 | 944,783 |
| Occupational Safety & Health | 279,786 | 293,925 | 287,100 | 294,690 | 288,567 |
| Other | 1,868,592 | 1,944,705 | 1,984,064 | 2,000,527 | 1,986,716 |
| **Total, Labor Department** | **$ 7,518,049** | **$ 7,999,614** | **$ 8,084,255** | **$ 8,179,924** | **$ 8,041,414** |
| **Health and Human Services** | | | | | |
| Public Health | | | | | |
| Community Health Centers | 532,835 | 615,754 | 527,507 | 543,492 | 558,984 |
| AIDS programs | 312,303 | 338,924 | 362,308 | 391,081 | 385,560 |
| Centers for Disease Control | 1,488,538 | 1,600,685 | 1,619,167 | 1,658,612 | 1,671,131 |
| National Institutes of Health | 10,071,567 | 10,579,684 | 10,368,551 | 10,387,721 | 10,362,802 |
| Alcohol/Drug Abuse/Mental Health | 1,932,102 | 2,037,928 | 1,942,417 | 2,049,609 | 2,007,334 |
| Health Care Financing/Social Security | | | | | |
| Medicaid grants to states | 76,102,738 | 91,901,234 | 91,911,234 | 90,105,650 | 89,898,850 |
| Medicare and other Medicaid | 39,421,485 | 43,963,192 | 43,963,192 | 45,962,862 | 45,962,862 |
| Supplemental Security Income | 20,566,516 | 23,153,657 | 23,144,773 | 23,133,164 | 23,090,550 |
| Black lung benefits | 824,638 | 797,313 | 797,313 | 797,313 | 795,745 |
| Public Welfare | | | | | |
| Family support payments (AFDC) | 15,901,046 | 15,441,950 | 15,441,950 | 15,695,072 | 15,663,072 |
| Workfare programs | 1,000,000 | 1,000,000 | 1,000,000 | 1,000,000 | 1,000,000 |
| Low-Income Home Energy Assistance | 1,500,000 | 1,065,000 | 891,000 | 2,805,905 | 2,783,458 |
| Community Services Block Grant | 437,418 | 5,000 | 394,710 | 457,642 | 440,895 |
| Child-care grants | 825,000 | 850,000 | 841,500 | 975,000 | 892,800 |
| Social Services Block Grant (Title XX) | 2,800,000 | 2,800,000 | 2,800,000 | 2,800,000 | 2,800,000 |
| Head Start | 2,201,800 | 2,801,800 | 2,720,322 | 2,801,800 | 2,779,386 |
| Programs for the aging | 846,472 | 850,693 | 838,228 | 850,693 | 839,198 |
| Foster care, adoption assistance | 2,614,005 | 2,988,668 | 2,988,668 | 2,924,014 | 2,924,014 |
| Other | 3,536,147 | 3,328,788 | 3,470,758 | 3,409,106 | 3,536,934 |
| **Total, HHS** | **$ 182,914,610** | **$ 206,120,270** | **$ 206,023,598** | **$ 208,748,736** | **$ 208,393,575** |
| **Education Department** | | | | | |
| Elementary and Secondary Education | | | | | |
| Compensatory education (Chapter 1) | 6,695,679 | 6,817,632 | 6,749,455 | 6,760,368 | 6,699,452 |
| Impact aid | 771,698 | 532,130 | 763,981 | 757,756 | 750,155 |
| State block grants (Chapter 2) | 474,600 | 465,220 | 466,191 | 463,320 | 458,413 |
| Drug-free schools | 623,963 | 653,963 | 612,472 | 608,659 | 598,367 |
| America 2000, School Choice | 99,115 | 767,500 | — | — | — |
| Bilingual, immigrant education | 225,407 | 233,645 | 231,308 | 224,191 | 225,927 |
| Special education | 2,854,895 | 2,943,400 | 2,920,103 | 3,045,773 | 2,965,891 |
| Higher Education | | | | | |
| Pell grants | 5,472,350 | 6,637,637 | 6,586,470 | 5,956,928 | 5,997,690 |
| Guaranteed student loans | 2,639,812 | 2,930,158 | 2,930,158 | 2,930,158 | 2,930,158 |
| *Liquidation and shortfalls* | *(6,356,289)* | *(3,050,930)* | *(3,050,930)* | *(3,050,930)* | *(3,050,930)* |
| Higher education grants | 827,903 | 853,481 | 831,408 | 851,245 | 837,930 |
| Vocational, adult education | 1,428,460 | 1,447,260 | 1,509,016 | 1,492,836 | 1,474,540 |
| Rehabilitation services | 2,077,158 | 2,138,263 | 2,125,385 | 2,199,107 | 2,168,480 |
| Libraries | 147,247 | 35,000 | 145,774 | 147,247 | 146,069 |
| Other | 2,937,147 | 2,785,928 | 3,059,976 | 3,015,582 | 2,999,862 |
| **Total, Education Department** | **$ 27,275,434** | **$ 29,241,217** | **$ 28,931,697** | **$ 28,453,170** | **$ 28,252,934** |
| Action | 198,592 | 205,137 | 201,502 | 204,875 | 201,526 |
| Corporation for Public Broadcasting | 275,000 | 275,000 | 272,250 | 310,000 | 292,640 |
| Other related agencies | 583,667 | 578,053 | 565,227 | 571,250 | 567,979 |
| **GRAND TOTAL** | **$ 218,765,352** | **$ 244,419,291** | **$ 244,078,529** | **$ 246,454,455** | **$ 245,736,568** |

SOURCE: House Appropriations Committee

## Full Committee

The stark reality of the spending ceilings in the 1990 budget agreement hit the House Appropriations Committee on July 23, as members by voice vote approved a bare-bones fiscal 1993 Labor-HHS spending bill.

The committee slashed funding for dozens of popular social programs and held most others to increases too small to keep up with inflation.

For the first time in years, subcommittee Chairman Natcher departed from his annual sermon about the many virtues of the subcommittee-approved measure.

"This bill doesn't suit any of us," said an unusually somber Natcher. "It's not the best bill we could have presented, but it's the best we could do with the money that was available."

The bill's grand total — $244 billion — belied the budget squeeze members faced.

That was because $179 billion, nearly three-fourths of the bill's total, was for entitlement programs whose funding appropriators could not control. Those programs included parts of Medicare, the federal health insurance program for the elderly and disabled; Medicaid, the joint federal-state health program for the poor; and Aid to Families with Dependent Children, the principal federal-state welfare program.

Appropriators controlled the remaining $61.7 billion, up $943 million from the prior year.

But that, noted the report, represented an increase in budget authority of only 1.5 percent, less than half the inflation rate.

## Debts Come Due

Because the committee had to absorb the delayed obligations from fiscal 1992, the bill looked considerably less generous than President Bush's fiscal 1993 budget request.

Many popular programs that received increases under the measure nevertheless got less than Bush requested.

They included Head Start, the popular health, nutrition and social service program for preschoolers ($2.7 billion: up $518 million from fiscal 1992 but $81 million less than Bush sought); the National Institutes of Health ($9.2 billion, $279 million more than fiscal 1992 but $165 million less than Bush requested); and the Chapter 1 remedial education program for the disadvantaged ($6.7 billion, $54 million more than in fiscal 1992 but $68 million less than Bush wanted).

The biggest single hit was to LIHEAP, the low-income energy assistance program that helped the poor pay utility bills. It received $891 million, down from $1.4 billion available in fiscal 1992.

Also facing cuts were block grant programs that provided money for states to provide services to pregnant women and infants ($639 million, down $6.5 million from fiscal 1992); to provide mental health and substance abuse prevention and treatment ($1.3 billion, down $13.6 million from fiscal 1992), and to deliver preventive health services ($133 million, down $1.3 million from the previous year).

As usual, members barely tampered with the bill at the full committee level. The only semblance of discord came over an amendment offered by Republican Robert L. Livingston of Louisiana that sought to prevent the Occupational Safety and Health Administration from enforcing rules pertaining to requirements for use of seat belts and motorcycle helmets. The amendment was defeated by a 15-20 show of hands.

## Abortion Fight Avoided

In deference to Natcher's new status as acting chairman of the full Appropriations Committee, members declined to seek to add language to the bill to block implementation of the so-called gag rule, which prohibited abortion counseling in federally funded family planning clinics.

Such language in the fiscal 1992 bill drew a veto from Bush, and a subsequent override attempt fell a dozen votes short of the necessary two-thirds margin. *(1991 Almanac, p. 339)*

Members involved in the 1991 fight provided a variety of explanations. John Porter, R-Ill., who wrote the fiscal 1992 bill's language, said another effort would be "futile. We've gone through this exercise twice, and the votes are not going to change."

Agreed another prominent abortion rights backer on the panel, Vic Fazio, D-Calif., "There's a lot of sentiment that this should be resolved, one way or another, on the Waxman bill." That bill, HR 3090, to reauthorize the family planning program and overturn the counseling ban, passed the House on April 30. Its sponsor was Henry A. Waxman, D-Calif. *(Abortion, p. 387)*

But a major reason no attempt was made to attach the language to the bill was that Natcher had asked members not to. "This bill should not be used for this purpose, and I will object," Natcher said.

In recent years tensions had escalated between Natcher, a longtime abortion opponent, and abortion rights backers both on the committee and in the House Democratic Caucus.

But in this case Natcher's concern was to prevent the bill from being vetoed. Indeed, Natcher voted in April in favor of the family planning reauthorization bill that included language to overturn the counseling ban.

And with the always-feared Natcher also at the helm of the full committee, members seemed more loath than ever to cross him.

## HOUSE FLOOR ACTION

Before passing HR 5677 on July 28 by a vote of 345-54, House members bucked their recent trend of trimming appropriations bills on the floor and trounced an amendment to cut each line item in the measure by a minuscule 1.05 percent. The amendment, offered by Dan Burton, R-Ind., failed by a convincing 95-290. *(Votes 322, 320, p. 78-H)*

The bill was so tight that the Bush administration's official position statement complained that the $244 billion bill "reduced many programs, including high-priority programs of proven value," below the level requested by Bush in his fiscal 1993 budget.

In fact, HR 5677 was so tight that Natcher threw away his annual speech extolling the virtues of the programs the measure would fund. Instead, he echoed the complaints of the subcommittee chairmen whose bills preceded Labor-HHS on the House floor. "I can only repeat what my colleagues have said — this is the most difficult year I can remember since I have been on the Labor-HHS Subcommittee," said Natcher, who had served on the panel since 1967.

## Entitlements Eat Up the Bill

Indeed, during the brief floor debate July 28, Republicans and Democrats complained far more about what the

bill would fail to fund than about excessive spending.

Members from Frost Belt states were particularly upset about proposed cuts to LIHEAP, which helped the poor pay utility bills. The bill cut the program by nearly 40 percent, from roughly $1.4 billion in fiscal 1992 to $891 million.

"At the proposed fiscal 1993 level, it is estimated that over 21 million eligible families would not get any assistance," said William F. Clinger, R-Pa.

Others pointed out that the $9.2 billion the measure would provide for the National Institutes of Health, a bipartisan darling, was $165.3 million less than the amount that Bush requested.

Deficit-sensitive members complained about increases the measure included for entitlement programs such as Medicaid, the joint federal-state health program for the poor, and parts of Medicare, the federal health insurance program for the elderly and disabled. Spending for entitlement programs, which provided benefits automatically to all who qualified, was set to rise from $164.6 billion to $188.2 billion.

"I believe this Congress must address the problem of entitlements," Burton said. "If we limited entitlements in this bill to no more than a 2 percent growth, we would save — get this — $20 billion in this one bill."

Such mandatory programs accounted for just under 75 percent of the bill's total, but appropriators had only limited authority to alter the laws governing those totals.

Indeed, while the bill approved by the House Appropriations Committee included several provisions that would have altered some entitlement programs, all were struck on the floor by members of the committees with jurisdiction over the programs. Under House rules, appropriations measures could not include "legislative" language.

The net result of losing the language deemed "out of order" was that appropriators found themselves with a hole in the bill of nearly $500 million.

The stricken language would have altered some provisions of Medicare, Medicaid, student loans and Supplemental Security Income, the federal welfare program for the aged, blind and disabled.

For example, among the provisions struck was one that would have required nursing homes that participated in Medicaid to pay a user fee to cover the costs incurred in ensuring that they met federal health and safety standards. With the user fee gone, no money was left to cover Medicaid survey and certification activities for nursing homes. Thus, appropriators had to go back and cut something else to find the money.

### Amendments Up and Down

As usual, members attempted few changes to the bill, partially because the programs it funded were so popular, but mostly because of the respect — and fear — most members had for Chairman Natcher.

With Natcher's assent, members did adopt by voice vote an amendment offered by Livingston that failed during committee consideration the previous week.

The amendment blocked a rule proposed by the Occupational Safety and Health Administration regarding on-the-job use of seat belts and motorcycle helmets and requiring employers to provide driver safety programs.

A letter to members from the National Federation of Independent Business, a leading small-business lobby pushing the amendment, said: "This sweeping regulation will negatively affect every small business in America

whose employees are required to drive on the job. The last thing your small-business owners need is to become driver education teachers."

Members also approved an amendment by Lamar Smith, R-Texas, that reduced by $5.7 million funding to be used for travel by employees of agencies funded under the bill. The amendment did not reduce any funding totals, rather it limited amounts that could be used for travel.

Finally, members approved an amendment offered by House Education and Labor Committee Chairman William D. Ford, D-Mich., to set at $2,300 the maximum amount college students could receive under the Pell grant program. That was a reduction of $100 from fiscal 1992. As reported by the Appropriations Committee, the bill would have permitted the secretary of Education to reduce the maximum grant even further if demand for grants exceeded available funding.

Besides defeating the Burton amendment to cut the bill across-the-board, members also defeated by voice vote an amendment by Philip M. Crane, R-Ill., to delete funding for the Corporation for Public Broadcasting. CPB, which was funded two years in advance in an effort to separate programming decisions from politics, received $272 million in fiscal 1995, down from the fiscal 1994 level of $275 million approved in 1991. *(Public broadcasting, p. 187)*

## SENATE COMMITTEE ACTION

During the Sept. 10 subcommittee and full committee markup of HR 5677, Labor-HHS Subcommittee Chairman Tom Harkin, D-Iowa, complained that the budget caps resulting from the 1990 budget agreement left his increase for discretionary programs too small to keep up with inflation.

Harkin's discretionary total — the amount allowed for the programs over which appropriators had direct control — was $61.67 billion, up just 2 percent over the previous year.

And Harkin vowed to offer on the floor an amendment to move funds, just over $4 billion, from the defense side of the ledger to the domestic side. Harkin wanted to use the extra money to increase funding for popular health, education, and social service programs in the spending bill, including Head Start, the childhood immunization program, and the residential Job Corps.

In 1991, a similar Harkin amendment garnered only 28 votes, including just three Republicans. But in 1992, two committee Republicans announced that not only would they support Harkin's efforts, but also that if Harkin failed, they would offer their own amendments to move money from defense to the Labor-HHS bill.

"I believe this is an insufficient allocation for this subcommittee," said Arlen Specter, Pa., the panel's ranking Republican. Specter, who supported Harkin's amendment in 1991, announced that he was prepared to offer his own amendment, which would, at least, add funding to the Pell grant program for college students. Both the House and Senate versions of the spending bill reduced the maximum annual grant under the program from $2,400 to $2,300.

"I believe that the subcommittee ought to have a larger share of the federal budget than is currently being allocated," Specter said on the Senate floor in August, when he first announced that he would seek to redirect defense funds.

More surprising was an announcement by Alfonse M. D'Amato, R-N.Y., that he was prepared to offer an amendment to increase funding for breast cancer research.

D'Amato voted against Harkin's amendment in 1991, as well as against legislation in March that would have removed the budget "walls" between defense and domestic spending. Both Harkin and Specter voted to take down the walls. *(Budget walls, p. 104)*

"I think there certainly will be additional support" for efforts to increase spending for the Labor-HHS bill compared with 1991, D'Amato said after the markup. But he stopped short of predicting a win either for Harkin or for himself.

### Spreading It Thin

The budget squeeze that appropriators felt was evident by how they parceled out their discretionary funds.

For example:

● As it had in each of the last several years, the program that provided heating and cooling funds for low-income households took a hit. The $1.36 billion the bill appropriated (of which just over half would not become available until the last day of the fiscal year) was more than the administration sought ($1.07 billion) and more than the House provided ($891 million), but down from the $1.5 billion appropriated in fiscal 1992.

● The $10.37 billion the bill appropriated for the National Institutes of Health was an increase of more than $300 million over 1991, but $205 million less than the amount Bush sought.

● Similarly, the $6.76 billion for the Chapter 1 remedial education program was an increase of $65 million over fiscal 1992, but $57 million less than Bush requested.

● Impact Aid, which provided funds to school districts to offset the costs of serving children of federal workers, decreased nearly $20 million from fiscal 1992, to $752 million. Bush wanted it reduced even further, to $532 million. The House appropriated $764 million.

### A Few Winners

But the news was not all bad for program beneficiaries. Thanks in part to $265 million the subcommittee received as a result of the urban aid supplemental appropriation that Congress passed in June, the bill gave generous increases to some programs. *(Urban aid supplemental, p. 579)*

Among the winners were:

● The program to help parents obtain and pay for child care, which received $975 million in fiscal 1993, up from $825 million in fiscal 1992, and $125 million and $134 million more, respectively, than the amounts sought by Bush and approved by the House in July.

● Head Start, the popular health, nutrition and social service program for preschoolers, which received a $600 million increase over fiscal 1992 to $2.8 billion; the same as Bush requested and $81 million more than the House total.

● The Ryan White AIDS programs, named for the late Indiana teenager, which provided funds for the care of people with AIDS and HIV, the AIDS virus. The programs received $351 million — an increase of $75 million over fiscal 1992, $49 million more than Bush sought and $25 million higher than the House total.

● Women's health research. The bill earmarked $220 million for breast cancer research, $87 million more than in fiscal 1992. Another $69 million was set aside for research on cervical and ovarian cancer.

### Pell Grant Problems

But even when appropriators did manage to increase funding, they often fell short of the promises made by Congress in its authorizing bills.

In the 1992 funding cycle, no program better illustrated Congress' inability to live up to its own promises than the Pell grant program, which provided aid to low-income students attending college or trade school. *(Higher education, p. 438)*

In the higher education reauthorization (S 1150 — PL 102-325) passed with much fanfare in July, Congress underscored its desire to raise the maximum grant award by upping the authorization from $3,100 to $3,700 annually, even though in practice individual grants were capped at $2,400.

But House and Senate appropriators were caught in such a squeeze that not only did they not increase the maximum grant, they actually lowered it by $100. Appropriators were strapped by an infusion of new students receiving Pell grants, along with a $1.5 billion miscalculation by the administration on the amount of money needed for the program during the last two years.

The $5.956 billion set for Pell grants in the Senate bill in fiscal 1993 was actually a 9 percent increase over fiscal 1992. But a good deal of that money went toward covering the fiscal 1991 and 1992 shortfalls.

Specter said he found it "simply unacceptable" for Congress to authorize an increase in Pell grants while reducing the maximum grant in the appropriations bill.

## SENATE FLOOR ACTION

Senate consideration of HR 5677 was a battle of competing wants. During floor action the week of Sept. 14, senators' desire to avoid a presidential veto so they could leave town overcame the lure of adding money to some of the nation's most popular social programs.

Before the Senate completed action on the measure on Sept. 18, following three days of debate, members handily defeated three amendments that would have increased the bill's $240.9 billion total by moving money from the defense budget. President Bush had expressly promised to veto any bill that breached the so-called walls separating defense and domestic spending.

Members also dropped from the Appropriations Committee version of the bill two other provisions that a Sept. 16 Bush administration policy statement said would prompt a veto. One would have blocked proposed Labor Department regulations imposing new accounting requirements on labor unions. The other would have blocked enforcement of Bush administration regulations barring abortion counseling in federally funded family planning clinics. The latter provision was dropped as part of a deal that brought to the Senate floor free-standing legislation that would overturn the contested rules.

But even with the removal of these two provisions, the administration said that both the House and Senate versions of the measure exceeded the amount Bush requested in his fiscal 1993 budget for the domestic discretionary programs, over which appropriators had direct control. The White House Office of Management and Budget (OMB) said the House bill was $234 million over Bush's domestic discretionary total of $61.7 billion, while the Senate version was $1.8 billion over.

Appropriators and the Congressional Budget Office disputed the way OMB "scored" some of the bill's provisions and said both bills were lower than Bush's request. But under the 1990 budget agreement, OMB's estimates gov-

erned, leaving Congress to either cut the bills or risk a veto of the second-largest of the 13 regular spending bills.

And even if the scoring disputes were settled, the Senate version still contained a veto-bait provision that would allow federal funding of abortions in certain cases of rape or incest. Similar language included in the fiscal 1990 bill drew one of Bush's first abortion-related vetoes. *(1989 Almanac, p. 707)*

### Dozens of Amendments

As usual, the dozens of floor amendments offered fell into three categories: those addressing spending totals, those addressing sensitive social policy issues such as AIDS and drug abuse and those with little to do with the measure but whose sponsors saw the must-pass spending bill as a good vehicle for pet proposals that would otherwise die as Congress rushed to adjourn.

Of the spending amendments, by far the most controversial were the three that sought to transfer defense funds to the Labor-HHS bill.

For the second consecutive year, Harkin sought unsuccessfully to augment his bill by transferring money from unobligated Defense Department funds.

"This amendment does not really make a dent in these amounts on the [defense] side of the ledger, but for millions of American kids it can mean the difference between life and death," Harkin said of his proposal to take $4.1 billion in defense money and apportion it to health, social service and education programs, most of them aimed at children.

But defense budget guardians did not take kindly to Harkin's plan.

"Some people have the mistaken impression that unobligated balances really amount to money just simply lying around waiting for someone to come along and pluck it," said Sam Nunn, D-Ga., chairman of the Armed Services Committee. "It has not been obligated, but that does not mean it will not be obligated."

Others suggested that adopting the amendment would be making a promise Congress could not keep.

"We are only fooling ourselves if we think that this amendment will solve any of our problems," said Appropriations Committee Chairman Robert C. Byrd, D-W.Va. "Even if the House were to agree to this amendment ... the president is going to veto this bill, and we cannot override his veto."

Under Senate rules, Harkin's amendment needed 60 votes to pass because it required waiving congressional budget rules. It got 36, up from the 28 Harkin got in 1991, but still a long way from 60. *(Vote 208, p. 27-S)*

Two smaller amendments to add to the bill by taking defense money, both offered by Republicans, fared no better than Harkin's.

By a 30-67 vote, members defeated an amendment by Specter to move $2.9 billion in defense funds to the Pell grant college scholarship program, enough to fund the maximum grants at $2,800 per year. Under the bill, the amount of the maximum grant would drop from $2,400 in fiscal 1992 to $2,300 in fiscal 1993. *(Vote 209, p. 28-S)*

And by 43-53, members defeated a proposal by D'Amato to commandeer $214 million from defense research for research on breast cancer. *(Vote 211, p. 28-S)*

### Smoking Ban To Protect Kids

Among the non-spending amendments, the most sweeping was one offered by Frank R. Lautenberg, D-N.J., that required a ban on smoking in facilities that received federal funds for programs serving children under age 5. It was adopted by voice vote.

"This amendment will do for our youngest children what the airline smoking ban did for flight attendants and air passengers, and that is to protect them from deadly secondhand smoke, which the Environmental Protection Agency has confirmed to be a class A carcinogen," said Lautenberg, a longtime smoking foe.

Members also adopted two amendments offered by Jesse Helms, R-N.C., for whom the Labor-HHS bill had become a favorite target.

One Helms amendment, adopted by voice vote, barred from participation in the annual federal employee charity drive any organization that sought to compel the Boy Scouts of America to accept as members or leaders homosexuals or individuals "who reject the Boy Scout's oath of allegiance to God and country." Helms cited specifically the United Ways of San Francisco and Chicago, which he said had threatened to cut off funding for the scouts unless they accepted homosexuals and atheists.

The other amendment barred the use of anti-drug funds "to pay for homosexual educational, counseling or support services ... or to promote ... intravenous drug abuse or homosexual, bisexual or heterosexual activity, whether premarital or extramarital, in elementary or secondary schools."

But Helms was unsuccessful in pushing two other amendments.

One would have effectively barred any "needle exchange" programs using public money, by forbidding federal funds to states or localities that operated such programs, intended to reduce the spread of AIDS and other blood-borne diseases.

Members adopted instead, by a vote of 69-29, a substitute amendment offered by Edward M. Kennedy, D-Mass., and Orrin G. Hatch, R-Utah, reiterating a modified ban on the use of federal funds for such programs. *(Vote 212, p. 28-S)*

The ban was originally enacted as part of the reauthorization of the Alcohol, Drug Abuse and Mental Health Administration (PL 102-321) signed by Bush in July. *(ADAMHA, p. 422)*

Also defeated was a Helms amendment, similar to one included in the House bill, to block a rule proposed by the Occupational Safety and Health Administration regarding on-the-job use of seat belts and motorcycle helmets and requiring employers to provide driver safety programs.

The amendment was defeated by voice vote after members killed, by a vote of 43-55, a virtually identical substitute offered by Trent Lott, R-Miss. *(Vote 213, p. 28-S)*

Among the amendments unrelated to the bill was one offered by John McCain, R-Ariz., to give the president a limited line-item budget veto by making it easier for him to rescind individual provisions of appropriations bills without vetoing entire bills.

"We have to begin deficit reduction by eliminating government waste," said McCain.

But Appropriations Committee Chairman Byrd led the successful charge against the plan by reminding his colleagues of the importance of maintaining the separation of powers among the branches of government.

"Once we ever give that power to the president," said Byrd, "we will never get that power over the purse back."

McCain's amendment, which needed 60 votes to pass because it amended the budget rules, fell on a 40-56 vote. *(Vote 210, p. 28-S)*

## Other Amendments

Among the dozens of other amendments adopted, all by voice vote, were the following:

● By Ernest F. Hollings, D-S.C., to increase by $40 million funding for community health centers, boosting that program's total to $583 million. The amendment reduced by a comparable amount funding for Public Health Service evaluations.

● By Pete V. Domenici, R-N.M., to increase by $21 million, to $596 million, funding for the National Institute of Mental Health. The amendment reduced by a similar amount funding for HHS' Health Resources and Services Administration.

● By Domenici, to increase by $6 million funding for health care for the homeless. The amendment cut $6 million from the National Institute of General Medical Sciences.

● By Dennis DeConcini, D-Ariz., to increase by $7 million, to $12 million, funding for the National Youth Sports program. The amendment paid for itself by reducing by 4.1 percent the amount agencies covered under the bill may spend for consultants.

● By Don Nickles, R-Okla., to boost by $6.4 million funding for programs under the Older Americans Act, raising that total to $844.3 million. The amendment increased by a similar amount, from $100.4 million to $106.7 million, salary reductions ordered for HHS.

● By Paul Wellstone, D-Minn., to strike from the bill a provision prohibiting part-time students from receiving Pell grants.

● By David Pryor, D-Ark., to require agencies covered by the bill to account separately for consultant expenses.

Members also approved, 94-1, a Hatch amendment to delay for one year regulations regarding nutrition labeling on diet supplements, such as vitamins. Howard M. Metzenbaum, D-Ohio, author of the 1990 law the rules would implement, said he opposed the amendment, but voted for it on the theory that it would be dropped in conference. *(Vote 218, p. 29-S)*

## FINAL ACTION

Like a group of schoolchildren facing a meal of boiled spinach, grim-faced House and Senate conferees sat down Sept. 30 to divvy up the small amount of money they were allotted among the popular social programs funded in HR 5677.

In marked contrast to 1991, when negotiators took three weeks to iron out a final bill, the conference on the 1992 version was completed in just under eight hours.

With Congress eager to adjourn, and leaders pressing appropriators to produce bills that would pass muster with President Bush, many of the most difficult decisions had been made before the conference convened.

Virtually every controversial policy provision included in either version of the bill was jettisoned, most notably Senate language that would have permitted federal funding of abortion in certain cases of rape or incest.

Instead, the 1993 fiscal bill continued to carry the so-called Hyde amendment, included in every version of the bill since 1981. Named after Rep. Henry J. Hyde, R-Ill., it prohibited funding for abortions except in cases in which "the life of the mother would be endangered if the fetus were carried to term."

Conferees also capitulated to Bush administration demands to keep the bill's "domestic discretionary" total under the $61.97 billion the president requested in his fiscal 1993 budget. To meet that requirement — and avert a threatened veto — members lopped just under 1 percent off the amounts approved for each of the programs over which they had direct funding control.

## Few Funding Fights

Conferees engaged in fewer than their usual number of fights over funding levels for individual programs — a marked contrast to 1991's marathon negotiations.

"There was a recognition by everyone that there just wasn't money to play with," said Harkin.

Also unlike in 1991, conferees resisted the urge — and several Bush requests — to use "delayed obligations."

As it emerged from conference, the only program that received delayed funding was the low-income home energy assistance program, known as LIHEAP.

The popular program, whose funding had been cut repeatedly in preceding years because it was such a large target, received $663.8 million in regular funding and an additional $682 million on Sept. 30, 1993.

The $1.35 billion total was higher than the $1.1 billion that Bush requested but lower than its total fiscal 1992 funding of $1.5 billion.

Members deviated only rarely from the agreement worked out in advance by the House and Senate staffs, because they knew that every time they added funds to a pet program, they were increasing the amount by which every other program would have to be trimmed to stay under the discretionary total.

## Public Broadcasting Corporation

There were, however, some fairly pitched battles, including one over funding for the Corporation for Public Broadcasting (CPB), one of the related agencies included in the bill. *(Public broadcasting, p. 187)*

Sen. Ted Stevens, R-Alaska, objected to the staff proposal to fund the corporation at $291 million in fiscal 1995, up from the $275 million for fiscal 1994 provided in the 1991 bill. CPB was traditionally funded two years in advance so public radio and television stations knew how much they could budget to purchase programming.

Without at least $300 million, Stevens complained, rural and other small stations would have to cut back on their programming. In many areas of his state, Stevens said, people "don't get any news at all unless they get it from that public radio station."

But House subcommittee Chairman Natcher responded that the 12 percent increase approved in the Senate bill — up to $310 million — as well as the 6 percent hike he was willing to accept were both much larger than the increases for other programs he considered a higher priority.

"We don't have that anywhere else in this bill," said Natcher, pointing out that the National Cancer Institute was getting a boost of only 3 percent, and feeding programs for the elderly were rising by only 1 percent.

Stevens, however, refused to back down, insisting that unless CPB got at least $300 million, he not only would refuse to sign the conference report but would stall action on the bill when it came back to the Senate floor.

Stevens ultimately was mollified into accepting $295 million (later reduced to $293 million), after which he joked that he would sign the conference agreement after all, but only with his first name.

Another perennial funding fight was over State Legal-

ization Impact Assistance Grants to help states offset the costs for immigrants newly legalized under the 1986 Immigration Act.

Originally, the program was to provide states with $1 billion each year from fiscal 1987 through 1990, after which it would end. But many states were slow to begin claiming their funds, and for the previous several years appropriators had been deferring larger and larger portions until subsequent years, using the excess to provide more funding for other programs.

Legislators from California, however, which had been using its share, had been fighting a losing battle against the funding deferrals. And 1992 was little different.

"We've been involved with this for three years, and the answer has always been, 'We'll take care of it next year,'" said House conferee Edward R. Roybal, D-Calif. "But next year never seems to come."

Harkin responded that under the provision as written, California would get all of its money in 1993.

"That's what you said last year," Roybal shot back.

The final compromise provided $308 million for the grants in fiscal 1993, with an additional $812 million deferred to fiscal 1994.

### Dropping Policy Provisions

Conferees also disposed of touchy policy provisions that had been added to both bills. Some were dropped to satisfy Natcher, who prided himself on disallowing funding earmarks and policy matters that violated House and Senate rules — widely ignored on most other bills — governing what was permitted in spending bills.

Others were dropped because they proved too controversial.

Without discussion, members dropped a series of contested policy provisions, including an amendment offered on the Senate floor by Helms to bar any organization that sought to compel the Boy Scouts of America to accept homosexuals or atheists from participation in the annual federal employee charity drive.

Conferees similarly dropped provisions added by Hatch that would have stayed implementation of regulations regarding health claims made by makers of vitamins and other nutritional supplements, and by Sen. Lautenberg that would have required that smoking be banned in facilities that received federal funds for programs that served children under age 5.

After some debate, members also dropped a provision added on the House floor to block a rule proposed by the Occupational Safety and Health Administration regarding on-the-job use of seat belts and motorcycle helmets and requiring employers to provide driver safety programs.

Although he opposed it, Natcher initially resisted dropping the OSHA provision, noting that its sponsor, Rep. Livingston, "beat us pretty good on the House floor" when the provision was initially added.

By far the most-watched policy provision was the abortion language inserted by Harkin himself. And through much of the conference, it appeared that the issue would remain unresolved, thus forcing more votes on the matter in both chambers.

But Harkin ultimately relented. "Sometimes we have to take a stand for what we believe in and what we think is right," he said, adding that he found it "the height of hypocrisy" for Bush to suggest that it might be acceptable for a family member to have an abortion in a case of rape or incest but to deny to pay for the procedure for poor women in the same situation.

Nevertheless, Harkin conceded in agreeing to drop the language, "I can't jeopardize the whole bill over this. There's too much in there."

House conferees who supported the language said they agreed with Harkin's decision.

Said Steny H. Hoyer, D-Md., "There is a majority in both the House and the Senate" for the rape and incest exceptions, "but obviously not enough to override."

The conference report was approved by the House on Oct. 3, after only brief debate, by a 363-47 vote. Hours later, the Senate approved the measure by voice vote, clearing it for President Bush, who signed it Oct. 6. *(Vote 457, p. 112-H)* ∎

# Energy Bill Includes Nuclear Test Cutoff

Congress in 1992 greeted the end of the Cold War by passing historic restrictions on nuclear weapons testing, including an immediate nine-month moratorium and a total testing cutoff in late 1996 unless another nation was still conducting tests.

The House approved the testing restrictions, 224-151, on Sept. 24 as an amendment to the conference report on the $22 billion energy and water appropriations bill (HR 5373). The Senate, which already had endorsed similar language in its version of the bill, approved the final bill by voice vote later that night, clearing the way for the president's signature.

The votes presented a direct challenge to the Bush administration, which maintained that it needed to continue at least some safety-related testing as long as the country had nuclear weapons.

But President Bush did not veto the energy spending bill, which included $517 million to keep building the superconducting super collider, a highly favored White House project. The House in June had voted to kill the $8 billion-plus atom smasher, which was being built in Texas, but appropriators agreed in conference to keep funding the project.

Bush had always been a strong supporter of the project, but it held a particular political potency in 1992 because Texas held so many electoral votes in the presidential election.

The congressional action marked a dramatic victory for test ban proponents, who began 1992 unsure they could win any testing restrictions.

But the vote came over the angry protests of several House Republicans, particularly John T. Myers, Ind., the ranking member of the Appropriations subcommittee that oversaw the energy spending bill.

Myers charged that Democrats were ramming through testing restrictions that would endanger the safety of the nuclear arsenal.

The nuclear testing debate initially focused on a one-year moratorium that had substantial support in both chambers. The ban was intended to be a response to unilateral testing moratoriums imposed by Russia and France, encouraging them to continue their bans and to work toward a comprehensive test ban agreement for all nations.

In the House, lawmakers attached the one-year ban to both the defense authorization bill and the energy spending bill.

But as the issue moved to the Senate, some lawmakers began pressing for a more complex provision. Some senators sought to ensure ongoing tests for issues such as safety and reliability, while others pressed for not only an initial testing pause but also some commitment toward a permanent ban.

## BOXSCORE

➡ **Fiscal 1993 energy and water development appropriations bill (HR 5373).** The bill provided $22 billion for energy and water development projects.

**Reports:** H Rept 102-555; S Rept 102-344; conference report filed in the House, H Rept 102-866.

### KEY ACTION

June 17 — The **House** passed HR 5373, 365-51.

Aug. 3 — The **Senate** passed HR 5373 by voice vote.

Sept. 15 — **House-Senate** conference agreed to the bill.

Sept. 17 — The **House** adopted the conference report, 245-143.

Sept. 24 — The **Senate** cleared the conference report by voice vote.

Oct. 2 — President Bush signed HR 5373 — PL 102-377.

The Senate ultimately voted for the nine-month test ban, limited testing thereafter for safety issues, and provided for a total testing cutoff after late 1996 if the Russians did not conduct nuclear tests.

Those provisions were put forward by Sen. Mark O. Hatfield, R-Ore., Majority Leader George J. Mitchell, D-Maine, and Jim Exon, D-Neb. They were adopted first on the appropriations bill, then, in slightly modified form, on the defense authorization bill Sept. 18.

Those votes put the issue back in the House, where members struggled over the policy and politics of the issue.

Certain test ban advocates, including Mike Kopetski, D-Ore., sought to add the strongest testing restrictions possible to the energy appropriations bill — using the super collider as leverage against a possible veto.

But other test ban proponents were more amenable to fashioning a compromise with the administration, while Tom Bevill, D-Ala., chairman of the House Appropriations subcommittee that crafted the bill, fought to protect the spending bill from potentially lethal nuclear testing language.

An alternative was to craft testing language on the authorization bill being negotiated in conference committee, but lawmakers concluded that that legislation would be more easily vetoed.

The decision went to Speaker Thomas S. Foley, D-Wash., who met with Bevill, Majority Leader Richard A. Gephardt, D-Mo., Armed Services Chairman Les Aspin, D-Wis., John M. Spratt Jr., D-S.C., and Kopetski on Sept. 24. The group decided to press ahead with the Senate-passed restrictions on Bevill's energy appropriations bill.

## BACKGROUND

Both Bevill and his Senate counterpart, J. Bennett Johnston, D-La., were known for the speed with which they steered the annual energy and water appropriations bill through Congress. Usually the first spending bill to be marked up, it was also usually the first to be signed into law. It was not to be so in 1992, however, as the nuclear testing restrictions delayed the bill's progress.

The two Southern Democrats were well-matched to each other and the bills they oversaw. Both were pragmatic rather than ideological and adept at crafting a politically tenable distribution of the water-project money in the bill. And because the two did not always have to share power with authorizers, they enjoyed greater latitude in shaping energy and water policy.

Also, appropriators had not traditionally made significant changes in the bill's nuclear defense programs, which

# Energy, Water Development Spending

*(HR 5373, as approved in House-Senate conference, in thousands of dollars)*

| | Fiscal 1992 | Fiscal 1993 Bush Request | House Bill | Senate Bill | Final Bill |
|---|---|---|---|---|---|
| **Army Corps of Engineers** | | | | | |
| General construction | $ 1,284,142 | $ 1,230,488 | $ 1,325,502 | $ 1,363,937 | $ 1,360,503 |
| Operation and maintenance | 1,535,229 | 1,524,534 | 1,551,905 | 1,522,961 | 1,541,668 |
| Other | 790,864 | 781,749 | 786,263 | 745,632 | 764,962 |
| **TOTAL, Corps of Engineers** | **$ 3,610,235** | **$ 3,536,771** | **$ 3,663,670** | **$3,632,530** | **$ 3,667,133** |
| **Bureau of Reclamation (Interior)** | | | | | |
| Construction | 564,209 | 460,634 | 470,568 | 466,334 | 470,568 |
| Operation and maintenance | 258,685 | 274,760 | 284,010 | 269,760 | 274,760 |
| Other | 77,089 | 71,530 | 71,247 | 71,237 | 71,387 |
| **TOTAL, Interior** | **$ 899,983** | **$ 806,924** | **$ 825,825** | **$ 807,331** | **$ 816,715** |
| **Energy Department** | | | | | |
| Energy supply R&D | | | | | |
| Solar energy | 175,503 | 181,425 | 181,425 | 186,425 | 187,425 |
| Nuclear energy | 336,658 | 310,294 | 304,294 | 296,454 | 311,454 |
| Environment R&D | 353,310 | 384,700 | 356,700 | 363,700 | 356,700 |
| Fusion energy | 337,100 | 359,710 | 339,710 | 335,000 | 339,710 |
| Research and technical analysis | 867,158 | 971,608 | 871,608 | 901,608 | 966,408 |
| Environmental cleanup (non-defense) | 602,495 | 706,974 | 709,694 | 709,694 | 709,694 |
| Other | 289,679 | 273,742 | 184,202 | 176,702 | 144,402 |
| **Subtotal, R&D** | **$2,961,903** | **$3,188,453** | **$2,947,633** | **$2,969,583** | **$3,015,793** |
| Uranium supply and enrichment | 1,337,600 | 1,391,320 | 1,286,320 | 1,371,320 | 1,286,320 |
| Revenues | −1,547,000 | −1,462,000 | −1,462,000 | −1,462,000 | −1,462,000 |
| General science | | | | | |
| High-energy physics | 627,999 | 630,884 | 613,384 | 623,384 | 613,384 |
| Nuclear physics | 354,390 | 363,500 | 363,500 | 309,100 | 309,100 |
| Superconducting super collider | 483,700 | 650,000 | 33,700 | 550,000 | 517,000 |
| Other spending and prior-year carryovers | 6,400 | 8,300 | −11,700 | −21,700 | −21,700 |
| **Subtotal, general science** | **$1,472,489** | **$1,652,684** | **$ 998,884** | **$1,460,784** | **$1,417,784** |
| Nuclear waste disposal (civilian) | 275,071 | 391,976 | 275,071 | 275,071 | 275,071 |
| Atomic energy defense | | | | | |
| Research, development, testing | 1,943,950 | 1,938,100 | 1,905,410 | 1,934,910 | 1,955,410 |
| Production and surveillance | 2,515,478 | 2,415,700 | 2,415,700 | 2,353,630 | 2,343,630 |
| New production reactors | 515,500 | 4,028* | 171,800 | 170,028 | 34,028 |
| Environmental cleanup (defense) | 3,690,190 | 4,805,492 | 4,603,009 | 4,802,047 | 4,831,547 |
| Materials production | 1,876,900 | 1,681,725 | 1,665,643 | 1,649,043 | 1,604,043 |
| National security programs | 403,600 | 605,318* | 425,858 | 479,858 | 520,858 |
| Naval reactors | 818,000 | 807,000 | 807,000 | 807,000 | 807,000 |
| Nuclear waste disposal (defense) | — | — | — | 100,000 | 100,000 |
| **Subtotal, atomic energy** | **$11,977,518** | **$12,118,629** | **$11,874,459** | **$12,118,625** | **$12,118,625** |
| Departmental administration | 121,624 | 130,640 | 87,275 | 87,275 | 87,275 |
| Power Marketing Administration | 362,029 | 397,270 | 384,529 | 394,529 | 384,529 |
| Federal Energy Regulatory Commission | 141,071 | 163,639 | 142,801 | 158,639 | 158,639 |
| Revenues | −141,071 | −163,639 | −142,801 | −158,639 | −158,639 |
| Other Energy Department | 72,084 | 349,158 | 183,753 | 169,753 | 134,753 |
| **TOTAL, Energy Department** | **$16,967,647** | **$17,836,834** | **$16,476,533** | **$17,202,549** | **$17,158,759** |
| **Independent Agencies** | | | | | |
| Appalachian Regional Commission | 190,000 | 100,000 | 185,000 | 190,000 | 190,000 |
| Nuclear Regulatory Commission | 508,810 | 545,415 | 535,415 | 535,415 | 535,415 |
| Revenues | −488,848 | −524,315 | −514,315 | −514,315 | −514,315 |
| Tennessee Valley Authority | 135,000 | 100,723 | 135,000 | 135,000 | 135,000 |
| Other | 16,673 | 16,936 | 16,936 | 16,936 | 16,936 |
| **GRAND TOTAL** | **$21,839,500** | **$22,419,288** | **$21,324,064** | **$22,005,446** | **$22,005,643** |

*\* The administration amended its request after House and Senate passage.*

SOURCE: House Appropriations Committee

accounted for about half of its spending.

But Bevill and Johnston had failed to smooth over controversy about the Energy Department's superconducting super collider. Although the giant atom smasher represented a fraction of the department's research budget, it became a bull's eye for budget critics. (*Superconducting super collider, p. 301*)

Opponents ridiculed the $8 billion-plus project as costly scientific busywork. Their cause was bolstered by the project's cost overruns and the administration's failure to secure promised foreign investors.

But scientists hoped that studying particle collisions would give them clues into the origins of matter, as well as potentially lucrative scientific spinoffs.

A pet project of Bush's, the collider also provided political cover for some of the bill's water projects. Bush could not be too quick to veto the bill over water projects he considered wasteful without jeopardizing funding for the politically tenuous atom smasher.

While debate on the collider usually dominated debate on the energy and water spending bill, the political heart of the bill continued to be the water projects carried out by the Army Corps of Engineers and the Bureau of Reclamation.

Every state saw a piece of the water projects budget. The projects opened new shipping routes, brought irrigation water to parched farmland and safeguarded communities against floods. But many also came under attack as environmentally treacherous boondoggles.

The Energy Department's nuclear weapons program originally accounted for a modest fraction of the energy and water appropriations bill, but under the Reagan administration it came to represent about half the spending in the bill. Despite the growing prominence of the nuclear weapons spending account, however, the appropriations bill had not typically been an arena for shaping defense policy.

However, in recent years the Energy Department's nuclear weapons program had come under fierce criticism for environmental and safety problems and for slipshod management.

In the House, Bevill and his subcommittee had dramatically boosted spending for cleaning up nuclear weapons facilities. That account has risen from $1 billion in fiscal 1989 to $4.8 billion in the fiscal 1993 bill. It was the fastest growing portion of the nuclear defense program and was expected to cost tens of billions more before it was completed.

## HOUSE COMMITTEE ACTION

House appropriators began to fill in the outlines of a bleak budget picture, drafting an energy and water spending bill that included no new building projects, cut funding for some programs and slashed $166 million from Bush's request for a massive super collider.

The Appropriations Subcommittee on Energy and Water approved the $21.8 billion package for fiscal 1993 in closed session June 4.

The bill — the first of 13 annual spending bills to move through subcommittee — funded water projects, civilian energy research and nuclear weapons programs.

The parameters of the bill were set June 3, when the chairmen of all 13 appropriations subcommittees divided the overall pot of available money between their respective bills. That agreement allocated $9.9 billion in budget au-

thority for civilian energy and water programs, slightly less than the fiscal 1992 appropriation and significantly below the administration's request. A separate $11.9 billion was set aside for the nuclear defense programs in the bill. (*Fiscal 1992 bill, 1991 Almanac, p. 569*)

Subcommittee Chairman Bevill said the allocation left his panel with the task of spreading the pain around fairly. "The goal was to make sure everyone was a little unhappy — and we did that," Bevill said.

Among the disappointed was Jim Chapman of Texas, the fourth-ranking Democrat on the subcommittee and a strong proponent of the super collider. The bill held funding for the superconducting super collider even at $484 million. The administration had requested $650 million for the giant atom smasher, which was expected to cost more than $8 billion.

Chapman said the subcommittee's level funding threatened to delay the project 18 months and increased its costs by $300 million.

Many lawmakers considered the super collider a massive boondoggle, and these critics were expected to take a run at the project in the full committee, on the House floor, or both.

On other Energy Department research, the panel approved Bush's $181 million request for solar and renewable energy programs, about 3 percent above the fiscal 1992 appropriation. But the panel approved no new water projects.

For the defense portion of the bill, appropriators generally hewed to the recommendations laid out by the Armed Services Committee in its authorization bill (HR 5006). The money paid for the network of Energy Department laboratories, plants and test facilities that constructed the nation's nuclear bombs.

Appropriators cut roughly $200 million from Bush's original budget request, but the administration had volunteered most of those reductions anyway.

However, the panel did put restrictions on the Energy Department's controversial plans to consolidate hundreds of production jobs for the weapons complex at its plant in Kansas City, Mo. Those jobs were spread among Missouri, Ohio, Florida and Colorado.

David E. Skaggs, D-Colo., persuaded lawmakers to block the proposed consolidation until the Energy Department could prove the move would save money.

### Full Committee

The House Appropriations Committee sent HR 5373 to the floor after voting 24-21 to add a controversial one-year ban on nuclear testing.

The panel approved the $21.8 billion energy and water spending measure by voice vote June 11.

There was little to argue about beyond the nuclear testing provision; given slightly less money to spend than in fiscal 1992, the Energy and Water Appropriations Subcommittee adopted a straight-laced budget geared toward sustaining existing programs.

Bevill said the measure included no new water projects or engineering studies and no major new Energy Department construction efforts.

It also held funding for the superconducting super collider level at $484 million for fiscal 1993 — $166 million shy of what Bush had sought. Even that amount was expected to come under fierce attack on the House floor, however, particularly following the defeat of the balanced-budget amendment. (*Balanced-budget amendment, p. 108*)

The only program to get a large increase was the effort to clean up the nation's nuclear weapons plants. That program was slated to grow from $3.7 billion in fiscal 1992 to a recommended $4.6 billion for fiscal 1993.

Under the terms of a three-year budget pact, that money was to come out of a separate defense allocation and not compete directly with civilian programs funded in the bill.

### Test Ban's 2nd Appearance

Vic Fazio, D-Calif., offered the amendment to bar nuclear tests for one year unless the president could show that any of the former Soviet republics had tested nuclear weapons during that period.

The full House had already voted for a testing moratorium, approving it 237-167 as part of the defense authorization bill. On that vote, Appropriations panel members backed the ban by a roughly 3-2 ratio. (Defense authorization, p. 483)

Nevertheless, advocates were expecting a close vote on Fazio's amendment — mindful that some members might object to adding policy language to an appropriations bill.

Joseph M. McDade, R-Pa., called the defense bill "trash" that Bush would veto in its existing form.

Proponents hoped Bush would be more reluctant to reject a spending bill, but McDade warned that the proposed ban could capsize both bills.

McDade and other opponents insisted that some ongoing nuclear tests were needed to ensure the safety and effectiveness of the existing nuclear stockpile. The administration opposed the ban when it appeared on the defense authorization bill.

But advocates said there was no urgent need for tests in the coming year. And they said the United States could not hope to halt nuclear proliferation abroad if it did not set a strong example against testing.

Committee members ultimately voted narrowly for the amendment.

Afterward, Bevill said the test ban proposal did not belong in an appropriations bill: "I'd hate to get vetoed on something I shouldn't be dealing with in the first place."

But he was optimistic that the language would be removed or revised so that Bush would sign the final bill.

### Collider Trust Fund Draws Fire

The super collider was typically the most controversial item in the energy and water bill. Scientists hoped the collider would help them discover the origins of matter.

Bush had requested $650 million for the project in fiscal 1993 to begin major construction work. Subcommittee members said they supported the project but could not afford more than fiscal 1992's $484 million. And in full committee, no one tried to raise or lower that amount.

But collider critic Richard J. Durbin, D-Ill., objected to the creation of a trust fund for the program.

The appropriations bill would set up a trust fund for non-federal contributions to the collider and direct the Treasury to pay interest on money that sat unused. Because the administration had yet to drum up significant foreign contributions, the provision applied chiefly to Texas, which had been paying installments on its overall $1 billion pledge for the program.

Durbin fumed at the notion of Texas or foreign governments earning interest on their contributions and tried unsuccessfully to remove that portion of the trust fund provision.

But Bevill said it was only fair to give interest to whoever had put in the principal, and Durbin's amendment was defeated 13-24.

### Nuclear Waste Dumps

The energy and water bill included money to study where to build both a temporary and a permanent nuclear waste dump. Appropriators approved $275 million for those programs, $117 million less than the administration had sought. The money was to come out of fees levied on nuclear-waste producers.

Joe Skeen, R-N.M., attacked the temporary dump program, which had given money to the Mescalero Apache tribe in his state — among others — to consider hosting the dump.

Skeen offered an unsuccessful amendment that would have barred any additional payments to the tribe. He said the money would be wasted because state officials vehemently objected to the proposed dump.

But Bevill said Congress must stick with the process it put in place to find nuclear dump sites or risk unraveling the entire program. Skeen's amendment was defeated 20-28.

The studies for a high-level nuclear waste dump were centered on only one site, Yucca Mountain, Nev. (Yucca Mountain, p. 243)

In subcommittee, appropriators specified that $9 million of the nuclear waste money could go for state and local impact aid and oversight work. At the urging of Barbara F. Vucanovich, R-Nev., the full committee agreed to increase that sum to $12 million.

### Energy Research

The appropriations for energy research reflected a growing emphasis on renewable sources over nuclear power, although nuclear programs still received far more dollars overall.

Solar and renewable energy programs received a small increase, while nuclear research was cut in fiscal 1993.

The committee-approved bill also:
● Rejected an administration proposal to levy a millage fee on nuclear utilities to help pay for cleaning up uranium enrichment facilities.
● Rejected an administration proposal to raise the rates charged by power marketing authorities.

## HOUSE FLOOR ACTION

After watering the roots of the superconducting super collider project with hundreds of millions of research and construction dollars, the House on June 17 swung the budget ax and voted to kill the giant science project.

Members voted 232-181 to cut virtually all of fiscal 1993 funding for the atom smasher. It was a crippling and potentially fatal blow to a program that had been one of Bush's top science priorities. (Vote 201, p. 50-H)

The surprise vote emerged from a powerful confluence of discontents, some unique to the project and others foreshadowing a season of unprecedented budget austerity.

Indeed, money dominated the debate, and the outcome signaled a new-found resolve to slash away at the towering budget deficit at a time of perhaps unparalleled voter dissatisfaction.

There was also pent-up conflict and resentment over spending priorities. Members who had fought unsuccessfully to transfer defense spending to domestic needs and

win greater urban aid lashed out at what many saw as an esoteric science project chiefly benefiting fiscal conservatives in Texas.

Even some members eager to spend money on science balked, fearful the growing costs of the massive super collider project would devour other federal research efforts.

But the most potent element was the timing of the vote, just one week after a draining and divisive fight over a proposed constitutional amendment to balance the federal budget. With budget-cutting speeches — including their own — still ringing in their ears, many lawmakers found themselves unable to endorse the merits of the costly super collider.

"Timing is so much in life, and timing was with us," said Sherwood Boehlert, R-N.Y., a longtime critic of the super collider, after the vote.

Project managers had erected a political network for the super collider by seeding almost every state with research and procurement contracts. In 1991, members quashed a similar effort to kill the project by almost a 90-vote margin.

Members of the Texas delegation and other project supporters pledged to continue to fight for funding in 1992. But they were clearly shaken by the stunning outcome — a vote many had expected to go in their favor, albeit narrowly.

Even as Chapman, D-Texas, spoke of winning back members who had formerly supported the super collider, he saw little encouragement for a project with growing annual costs in a time of ever-tightening budgets.

"When do you get them back?" Chapman said. "Next year's even tougher than this year."

Ironically, the super collider vote came on consideration of an energy and water spending bill that was less than the fiscal 1992 level and the president's request, and was generally praised as a model of fiscal responsibility.

The $21.3 billion package (HR 5373) passed easily, 365-51, following the super collider vote. *(Vote 203, p. 50-H)*

### First at Bat

Even before the balanced-budget debate, super collider supporters knew they would have their work cut out for them. The project was moving into high gear and costs were shooting up just as budget caps were pressing down hard on domestic spending.

Bush requested $650 million for the super collider, $166 million more than the fiscal 1992 appropriation. Appropriators voted to hold the project's funding level at $484 million but knew even that much would draw fierce criticism.

Then came the June 11 floor vote on whether to adopt a constitutional amendment to balance the budget and hours of superheated speechifying on the deficit. After the House narrowly defeated the proposal, lawmakers vowed to show new budget-cutting zeal in upcoming votes on the annual appropriations bills.

Bevill detected trouble. Although he typically prided himself on being the first to get his bill through the House, he asked for a later slot.

But when no other panel was ready to move first, Bevill agreed to press ahead. As a result, many members said the super collider ran afoul of a restive mood gripping Congress that could have toppled any large project.

In the case of the super collider, however, additional factors were at work.

Although project directors had taken care to spread the super collider's research and procurement contracts over

an array of states, many of its most direct and immediate benefits went to Texas.

Some members believed Texas' powerful delegation had already laid claim to a disproportionate share of federal dollars and resented seeing the super collider built there as well. In 1992, that irritation was compounded by the fact that the Texas delegation included some of the staunchest supporters of a balanced-budget amendment.

Joe L. Barton, R-Texas, who sponsored one of the balanced-budget proposals, represented the district where the super collider was being built and was the leading House advocate for the project. Another Texan, Democrat Charles W. Stenholm, sponsored the lead balanced-budget amendment.

Lawrence J. Smith, D-Fla., one of 79 members who switched positions from 1991 to oppose the project, accused Barton of trying to have it both ways.

"The gentleman from Texas is obviously a contortionist, being on two sides of fiscal policy at the same time," Smith said.

Barton said he felt it was sufficient fiscal sacrifice to hold the super collider at the 1991 funding level.

Opponents of the super collider also helped spread the word that the Texans had mostly opposed an urban aid package, encouraging members concerned about cities to oppose the super collider.

Some lawmakers were also concerned that the super collider would steal money from high-energy physics projects in their states, notably at Fermilab in Illinois and the Linear Accelerator Center in Stanford, Calif.

Barton acknowledged these factors were at work, bolstered by the general political unrest and fear of voter anger. But he lamented that colleagues focused their fear and anger on the super collider project, which he claimed was progressing on schedule, on budget and with great promise.

"The best scientific brainpower in the world is working on this, and we just kicked them in the rear," Barton said.

### Cracks in the Shell

Budget concerns did appear to have provided the margin of victory to kill the super collider. But not everyone shared Barton's positive assessment of the project, and it was weakened by rising costs, vague scientific promise and alleged mismanagement.

Supporters conceded that cost estimates had almost doubled, but they were confident they could hold the existing $8.3 billion baseline if it was fully funded.

Even so, critics countered that the latest estimates excluded some construction costs and operating expenses. They said the super collider would end up costing closer to $11 billion.

Lawmakers also disputed what the country would get for that money.

Science Committee Chairman George E. Brown Jr., D-Calif., said the project had unmatched potential and was of great scientific importance. "Its termination would amount to a monumental decision to abandon pursuit of the next frontier in high-energy physics," said Brown.

But the science community qualified its support, in part because of fears it would crowd out spending for other research.

Even Dick Armey, a Texas Republican who voted for the program, said he was troubled that the super collider had not won a ringing endorsement from scientists: "You always want objective scientific information to validate

your politically mandatory position."

Proponents said the super collider would produce valuable spinoffs to enhance U.S. competitiveness and chip away at the budget deficit, but critics insisted that such claims were highly overstated.

### Rebellion

While both sides were expecting a close vote, super collider proponents generally believed they had the upper hand.

Martin Frost, D-Texas, a Rules Committee member, had helped set debate terms that favored the project: allowing supporters to offer a qualifying amendment but limiting opponents to an all-or-nothing proposal to strike funding.

Super collider opponents grumbled but did not try to block the rule, and the House approved it 377-44. *(Vote 195, p. 48-H)*

The amendment offered by Brown and other super collider supporters sought to address criticisms that the Bush administration could not produce the promised $1.7 billion in foreign contributions for the project.

Those concerns had escalated since Bush pressed the issue when he visited Japan in 1992 but came back empty-handed.

The administration insisted those and other negotiations were likely to bear fruit, but even some super collider supporters were impatient, and its critics were derisive.

Project foe Dennis E. Eckart, D-Ohio, likened the Energy Department's promises to secure foreign contributions to "Ross Perot's plan to balance the budget and Richard Nixon's plan to end the war."

Brown's amendment was intended to placate wavering lawmakers. It specified that the administration could not spend money on the super collider after May 1993 until it certified at least $650 million in foreign contributions for fiscal years 1993-95.

Super collider opponents called the amendment a fig leaf that would let members vote for the project while appearing fiscally responsible.

They complained that some of the foreign contributions would come in the form of overseas contracts for super collider parts and research. They said the Energy Department planned to use cheap foreign labor and credit the resulting savings as foreign contributions.

But the anti-collider group did not try to block Brown's amendment, and it passed on a voice vote.

The real battle came over another amendment, led by Eckart, to cut virtually all funding for the super collider in fiscal 1993.

That amendment called for cutting $450 million of the proposed $484 million, leaving $34 million to shut down the project. Members haggled about the super collider's alleged merits, deficiencies and price tag for more than two hours.

When the vote finally came well into the evening of the 17th, White House and Energy Department lobbyists were stationed at the doors to the House chamber to urge a "no" vote. While nervous, they were still predicting a narrow win.

The vote started out neck and neck, but soon the "yeas" crept ahead and stayed there, leaving many supporters dazed and groping to make sense of the vote.

Brown said that Democrats had defied their Appropriations leaders while Republicans repudiated their president: "It was a desire to rebel against almost everything."

Troubled by some members' comments that scientific

research was not essential, Brown said the vote boded ill for another big-money science project: the space station.

The super collider lost backing in both parties, but supporters were most surprised by the number of Republican defections. They had expected at least 100 minority members to vote for the project, but Republicans split evenly, 79-79.

While his choice was not a surprise by the time of the vote, Jerry Lewis of California was one of the Republicans who switched from his vote in 1991 and opposed the super collider. Some members said his and several other Republicans' kill votes reflected a leadership struggle between Lewis and Armey. Armey was challenging Lewis for head of the House Republican Conference.

But Lewis denied such a struggle was at work in the super collider vote and said he simply had trouble justifying the project's large expense.

### Reversal of Fortune?

No one was declaring the super collider dead yet.

The appropriations bill moved on to the Senate, which had typically given stronger support to the project. Johnston, who chaired the Energy-Water Appropriations panel, was among the super collider's key champions.

But while Johnston pledged to try to restore super collider funding in the Senate, he said it would be an "uphill battle" given the House vote.

Johnston said he had been ready to mark up the energy and water bill but would now hold off until he could convince senators of the merits of the super collider. He planned to hold a hearing to showcase support for the project in the scientific community.

In 1991, Dale Bumpers, D-Ark., tried to kill the super collider in the Senate but was rebuffed, 62-37. *(1991 Almanac, p. 579)*

Part of the political difficulty in restoring the money was the healthy margin of the House vote.

But Bevill and other advocates said some tentative supporters of the super collider voted against it at the last minute, when they saw that it was going down. Barton likened the vote to a drunken spree that some members could come to regret.

Meanwhile, the Energy Department had no immediate plans to alter ongoing work on the project.

### The Rest of the Story

The overall energy and water bill was generally well received.

Lawmakers praised the subcommittee for producing a bill that was $44 million under the fiscal 1992 total even before the vote to cut funds for the super collider. And it was more than $600 million less than Bush's budget request.

More than half of the bill, about $11.9 billion, funded nuclear defense programs run by the Energy Department, including a massive cleanup effort throughout the weapons complex.

There were no major amendments to this section, but Vucanovich complained about its controversial language to ban nuclear weapons testing for one year. The administration also opposed the proposed ban. *(Underground testing ban, p. 517)*

Members did adjust non-defense spending, voting 404-12 to trim about $21.5 million from the Energy Department's administrative expenses. But they rejected proposals by Howard Wolpe, D-Mich., to delete research

programs for new nuclear power technology and a space power system. *(Votes 199, 200, p. 48-H)*

Members also turned away three attempts by Dan Burton, R-Ind., to excise specific water projects in the bill. *(Votes 197, p. 48-H)*

## SENATE COMMITTEE ACTION

The sagging fortunes of the superconducting super collider rebounded the week of July 20, as Senate appropriators voted to continue funding the embattled science project.

The House in June voted to kill the massive atom smasher. But Senate appropriators disregarded that judgment and approved $550 million for the project in fiscal 1993.

The money was included in a $22 billion version of HR 5373 that the Senate Appropriations Committee approved July 23.

However, the super collider was not out of trouble yet. Bumpers was expected to lead a close fight on the Senate floor to cancel the project.

The appropriations panel also watered down a nuclear testing moratorium that was approved as part of the House energy and water spending bill.

Senate appropriators finished work on the spending bill but held it in committee because of ongoing controversy surrounding energy policy legislation.

Subcommittee Chairman Johnston was also the lead Senate sponsor of a massive energy policy bill that had passed both chambers but became deadlocked over several controversial provisions. *(Energy bill, p. 231)*

In an effort to get that legislation to conference, Johnston attached the texts of the companion House and Senate energy bills — without the tax provisions — to the energy and water spending bill during subcommittee markup on July 21.

But that tactic ran afoul of Appropriations Chairman Robert C. Byrd, D-W.Va., who then postponed full committee markup. When the full committee did consider the legislation two days later, Johnston said an agreement on the energy bill appeared close at hand. But because the energy controversy still was not settled, members agreed to hold the spending bill in committee until the panel could agree to abandon the energy policy provisions or revisit them.

### Super Collider

Supporters of the super collider were caught off guard by the House vote to kill it. After that, they had worked hard to put the project in the best possible light.

Johnston convened a posse of Nobel laureates to testify to the project's scientific merits, while the Bush administration stepped up its public relations campaign. In a guest op-ed piece in the July 21 Washington Post, Energy Secretary James D. Watkins compared the mission of the giant atom smasher to Columbus' journey to discover the New World.

Those steps set the stage for Johnston to move the energy and water bill with $550 million for the super collider. The proposed appropriation was not challenged in either the subcommittee or full Appropriations panel.

Bush had requested $650 million for the super collider in fiscal 1993. Johnston said budget pressures forced his panel to trim that but said his figure should be enough to keep the project on schedule and on budget.

### Nuclear Defense

More than half of the spending bill, $12.1 billion, was for nuclear weapons programs run by the Energy Department.

The House-passed moratorium imposed a one-year ban on nuclear testing so long as the former Soviet republics did not test. A parallel Senate measure (S 2064) had 52 cosponsors.

Johnston's panel added a substantial exception, allowing the administration to conduct nuclear tests if it first certified that they were needed to improve the safety of the weapons stockpile. The administration had recently said that all of its planned tests were for safety and reliability.

Johnston said it was critical to upgrade the safety of the nuclear arsenal, citing several near-accidents involving nuclear weapons.

Oregon Republican Hatfield, the ranking Republican on the Appropriations Committee and a key Senate sponsor of the more stringent test ban, criticized the weaker version included in the Senate appropriations bill.

Senate appropriators were given about $250 million more to spend for nuclear defense programs than their House counterparts. According to Johnston, they increased funding for technology transfer programs at the three national weapons laboratories and for technologies to clean up nuclear contamination in the weapons complex.

For cleaning up the nation's nuclear weapons facilities, Senate appropriators approved $4.8 billion, almost $200 million more than the House bill. The daunting cleanup was expected to cost at least $100 billion and was fast becoming the dominant part of the nuclear weapons program.

A politically sensitive aspect of the program was deciding whether former weapons contractors and workers should be used to run the cleanup program.

During full committee markup, Brock Adams, D-Wash., and Slade Gorton, R-Wash., sought to delay the Energy Department from finalizing a cleanup contract for the Hanford nuclear reservation in their state. Given the complex labor situation at the site, Adams said, it was premature to set terms for a comprehensive contract.

Johnston said he already had included language in the bill report along those lines but was unwilling to mandate it. The amendment was rejected, 9-14.

The Senate bill also allotted $375 million to study whether to build a high-level nuclear waste dump at Yucca Mountain, Nev., with $100 million of that to come from money for nuclear defense.

Harry Reid, D-Nev., who opposed the planned dump, objected to the defense contribution. He said the studies should continue to be funded solely out of fees paid by nuclear utilities.

But Johnston said the Defense Department was obligated to eventually contribute $850 million for the nuclear dump, which was to store defense and civilian wastes. Reid's amendment to strike the $100 million payment was defeated by voice vote.

### Water Projects

The Senate bill also included $3.6 billion for water projects by the Army Corps of Engineers and $807 million for the Western-based Bureau of Reclamation.

House appropriators did not approve any new water projects, citing tight budgets. By contrast, Johnston said his panel included 16 new projects, 11 of which were proposed by the administration.

Overall, however, Senate appropriators approved about $50 million less for water projects than their House counterparts.

## SENATE FLOOR ACTION

The Senate on Aug. 3 opened a new chapter in the arms control debate, voting for the first time to stop testing U.S. nuclear weapons and setting up a likely showdown between Congress and the White House on the issue.

The historic vote flew in the face of the Bush administration's insistence that it must continue testing the safety and reliability of aging warheads, even after the Soviet Union's demise.

Voting 68-26, the senators approved an immediate nine-month testing moratorium as well as an absolute ban after September 1996. The administration would be allowed to conduct more than a dozen tests in the interim to improve the safety of the nuclear arsenal. *(Vote 167, p. 22-S)*

The testing vote came on an amendment to the $22 billion energy and water spending bill for fiscal 1993, which the Senate later passed by voice vote.

On the same bill, senators also voted strongly in favor of continuing the $8 billion-plus superconducting super collider.

The House already had approved a one-year testing ban. But the administration opposed both a short-term testing moratorium and a total cutoff, and had warned that the testing restrictions would draw a veto.

The Aug. 3 vote was not expected to be the Senate's final word on the issue. Many senators apparently backed the testing restrictions on the assumption that the proposal would be refined — and possibly diluted — as part of the defense authorization bill (S 3114), which senators began debating Aug. 7.

Nevertheless, it was an unprecedented Senate endorsement of testing limits, and advocates delighted at the move in their direction.

Dr. Robert K. Musil, a longtime arms control advocate, had grown accustomed to Congress' dismissing the idea of ending nuclear tests. Now, he said, "people are quibbling about the details of the death."

Even some critics agreed that it no longer appeared to be a question of whether Congress would adopt testing restrictions in 1992 — but about which ones it would adopt.

### Test Ban

The congressional test ban drive began in the House, where lawmakers attached a one-year testing moratorium to both the defense authorization bill and the energy and water spending bill.

When the spending bill got to the Senate, appropriators added a significant loophole — allowing the administration to conduct nuclear tests that were needed to improve the safety of the weapons stockpile. The administration had said most of its planned tests were for safety purposes.

That did not wash with Sen. Hatfield and Majority Leader Mitchell, the chief Senate sponsors of a one-year ban.

Hatfield originally planned to offer the one-year ban — which had attracted 52 cosponsors — as an amendment during floor debate.

But he reworked the proposal over the weekend before the Aug. 3 vote in an effort to attract broader support.

As rewritten, the proposal banned testing for nine months rather than a year and allowed up to 15 tests over the following three years. Within that cap, most of the tests would have to be related to safety improvements. But one per year could be designated to improve weapons reliability, and the British government — which used the Nevada test site — could conduct one test a year.

The terms represented a concession for some arms control advocates, who wanted fewer or no new tests.

But sponsors also added something the anti-nuclear community had not hoped to win in 1992 — a call for a complete end to underground nuclear testing after September 1996.

Proponents said an immediate testing pause was necessary to respond to self-imposed testing limits by Russia and France, and to encourage them not to renew testing.

They said Russian President Boris N. Yeltsin had taken a political risk by halting testing. Several senators urged support of the nine-month ban to bolster Yeltsin's standing and the cause of democracy in the former Soviet republic.

But arms control advocates said the United States also had to commit itself to an absolute end to testing if it was to have any moral force behind its efforts to halt nuclear proliferation worldwide.

In theory, the United States already had pledged to end nuclear testing as part of the Nuclear Nonproliferation Treaty, which was up for renewal in 1995.

If the country was not clearly on a path toward such a ban by then, senators argued during floor debate, it could lose the controls already agreed to under that treaty.

"The time has come for the United States to stop dragging its heels toward a non-nuclear world," said Mitchell.

The administration said it already had restricted underground testing for verifying safety and reliability, rather than for developing new weapons technology. But Bush officials and other proponents said the continuation of that safety-related testing was critical.

Johnston made the case for safety-related testing during floor debate, citing numerous near-misses with nuclear warheads.

While the Senate proposal would allow up to 15 tests for these matters, a key Energy Department official for nuclear weapons programs said it would probably take at least 25 tests to prepare for those safety improvements.

Richard Claytor, the Energy official, said it would be wasteful to delay those tests with a nine-month or one-year moratorium because thousands of employees at the test site would be idled.

The administration also objected to a permanent testing cutoff in 1996.

The administration did not renounce the country's formal commitment to the idea of a comprehensive global test ban but had nonetheless stated that it would need to conduct tests for weapons safety and reliability as long as it maintained a nuclear deterrent.

While the administration's opposition to both a testing pause and a permanent ban was unequivocal, the Senate's disposition was less clear; Hatfield's revised amendment blurred the lines that had been established on the simpler, one-year moratorium.

The shift was enough to draw in Exon, the chairman of the Armed Services subcommittee on nuclear weapons, who had opposed the one-year ban.

But Armed Services Chairman Sam Nunn, D-Ga., was uneasy with the formulation.

Nunn said if the administration took an immediate

testing pause — an idea he seemed ready to support — it would need more than three years to finish needed safety tests before a complete testing ban.

Amid the confusion, Johnston eventually urged senators to support the proposal. He said he would take it to conference "with some skepticism but with good faith" while authorizers tried to hammer out more final language.

Seventeen Republican senators defied the administration to support the amendment — including several who were locked in close re-election fights in 1992.

Conversely, only three Democrats opposed the testing restrictions — the two Nevadans and Ernest F. Hollings of South Carolina.

Nunn, however, was expected to unveil a revised testing proposal when the issue came up during floor debate on the defense authorization bill.

In general, lobbyists said support was firmer for an immediate testing pause than for more long-term restrictions.

### Super Collider

In a recapitulation of the 1991 floor debate, Bumpers led an unsuccessful charge to kill the super collider.

Bumpers acknowledged at the outset that he did not have the votes to kill the project, but forged ahead to outline its deficiencies.

He predicted the true costs of the super collider would rise to about $20 billion, a price tag he said could not be justified by the project's limited scientific promise.

"We need to be on the cutting edge of science," Bumpers said, "but, Mr. President, this nation is on the cutting edge of bankruptcy."

But other senators defended the project as a wise investment. Johnston, who restored funding for the collider when the energy and water spending bill reached his Appropriations subcommittee, said the collider represented a small fraction of the government's research budget. He said federal entitlement programs, not research, were driving the growing budget deficit.

The collider's supporters had worried that the project could be bruised by anti-Texas sentiment, especially given the lead role of Texas Sen. Phil Gramm, R, in urging fiscal restraint in the form of a constitutional amendment to balance the federal budget.

But Lloyd Bentsen, D-Texas, threw off charges that the project was merely a public works boon for his state.

Just as Texas and other states invested in high-energy physics laboratories in other states, Bentsen said national investment in the super collider would reap national benefits.

In the end, Bumpers actually lost ground from the 1991 vote when 36 senators joined him — five more than in 1992. The 1992 vote was 62-32 to table, or kill, his proposal to shut down the super collider. *(Vote 166, p. 22-S)*

Bumpers criticized the Energy Department for distributing contracts for the super collider across 43 states. "Those state were chosen for political reasons," he said, "and it works."

Senators also defeated a second Bumpers amendment to require the administration to secure at least $650 million in foreign contributions for the project. The vote was 62-31 to table the amendment. *(Vote 168, p. 22-S)*

## FINAL ACTION

House and Senate appropriators on Sept. 15 approved a $22 billion compromise version of HR 5373, which allotted money for water projects, energy-related research and nu-

clear weapons programs in fiscal 1993. They agreed to spend $517 million for the super collider despite an earlier House vote to cancel the controversial project.

Critics of the super collider challenged that decision when the spending bill went to the House floor Sept. 17, but members voted 245-143 to adopt the compromise measure. *(Vote 399, p. 98-H)*

That vote was a victory for the Bush administration, which had strongly backed the $8 billion-plus device.

But the House had not yet voted on hotly contested nuclear testing restrictions in the bill, which could have set the chamber on a collision course with the administration.

Both the House and Senate-passed bills included restrictions on nuclear testing, and during the conference negotiators inserted a new version of testing restrictions that had tentative administration backing, according to Johnston.

But lawmakers made it clear that there were still significant differences on the issue — between members and with the administration — and that the testing issue would have to be debated on the House and Senate floors.

House leaders and test ban advocates agreed to postpone floor debate on nuclear testing in hopes of clarifying the administration and Senate positions on the issue.

But the Senate subsequently voted for more restrictive testing limitations than appropriators included in the conference bill, raising the odds that the House would follow suit.

The overall spending bill could not move to the Senate until House members voted on the testing issue.

The Bush administration had originally opposed the test ban language in both versions of the bill. But later the White House indicated that it could go along with some testing restrictions.

### The Debate Begins

Many lawmakers and anti-nuclear activists wanted to impose strong testing restrictions to respond to unilateral bans by the French and Russians, and to set a course toward a comprehensive test ban.

But the administration had argued that it needed ongoing tests to improve the safety and reliability of nuclear weapons.

The nuclear testing debate began in the House, where members voted to attach a one-year testing ban to both the energy spending bill and the defense authorization bill.

In the Senate, appropriators significantly softened that language to continue to allow safety-related tests.

But when the spending bill got to the Senate floor, it was changed again.

Senate Majority Leader Mitchell, Hatfield and Exon offered a new proposal to ban testing for nine months, allow limited testing over the next several years and cut off all testing after September 1996.

That language was adopted 68-26 on Aug. 3, but amid some confusion and with the expectation that it would probably be revised when senators turned to a defense authorization bill several days later. However, the authorization bill snagged on other issues, leaving the energy spending bill as the prime vehicle for the nuclear testing restrictions.

When House and Senate appropriators met to craft a final version of that bill, Johnston tried again to adjust the testing language — this time with a proposal he said he had negotiated with the administration.

Johnston's proposal called for imposing a five-month test ban and allowing roughly the same limited testing as the Hatfield-Mitchell-Exon version through September 1996. Af-

ter that date, certain testing could continue if the president certified that it was in the urgent national interest.

The president would have to submit that certification to Congress at the beginning of the budget cycle, giving lawmakers time to review the matter and potentially vote to block it.

Appropriations bill conferees included the Johnston language in the energy-water conference report, but with the knowledge that both chambers would have to debate the proposal and would have opportunities to change it.

The conference agreement went first to the House, where nuclear test ban advocates, including Kopetski and John M. Spratt Jr., D-S.C., wrestled with how to proceed.

Some in the group disliked Johnston's proposal because it shortened the initial testing moratorium and did not include a firm testing cutoff as of 1996 — in their view diluting the potency of testing restrictions toward promoting global non-proliferation.

They had some leverage to strengthen the proposal because the energy spending bill included funding for the super collider, one of Bush's priorities.

At the same time, test ban proponents did not want to overplay their hand and draw a veto they could not expect to override. Ultimately, they agreed to go along with plans to postpone the debate until the week of Sept. 21.

Spratt, a member of the Armed Services Committee, said some of the House test-ban advocates drew up a new formulation as a possible compromise.

That proposal, according to Spratt, would call for a six-month testing pause and give the administration some additional testing flexibility in the ensuing few years. But it would call for a testing cutoff as of October 1996 unless Congress voted to allow more testing.

Spratt said his group had forwarded its proposal to Hatfield, Exon and Mitchell, the key test ban advocates in the Senate. He was unsure if test ban proponents could reach an agreement with the administration, but said if that were to happen, it would likely occur in the Senate.

"It may be that all of a sudden someone finds a center of gravity," Spratt said on the night of Sept. 17.

However, when senators voted on the matter Sept. 18 on the defense authorization bill, they reiterated their support for stringent testing restrictions advocated by Hatfield and others — albeit by a slimmer margin than before, 55-40.

### Collider Restored

House and Senate negotiators agreed to provide $517 million for the super collider in fiscal 1993, far less than the administration's $650 million request but a significant victory in light of the House floor vote in June to eliminate the program.

That agreement galled opponents of the super collider, who said House negotiators had sold out the House position.

Not only did the conferees agree to restore funding for the super collider, but they agreed to $33 million more than House appropriators had approved for the project before the full House voted to kill it.

Some of those critics led a charge to reject the conference agreement on the overall spending bill and put the super collider back on the chopping block.

"How many times do we have to say no before this boondoggle goes away?" protested Joel Hefley, R-Colo.

But the conference bill was adopted by a 102-vote margin.

The conferees' agreement to keep funding the super collider was a welcome victory for its supporters and was expected to survive additional debate on the energy spending

bill. But if project supporters had dodged a bullet, they were still near the firing line.

For one thing, the $517 million allocation was significantly less than project managers had sought and could add to the time and cost of building the collider. That, in turn, could increase its vulnerability to political attacks.

And backers would be challenged to reverse a trend of eroding support for the project.

House Science Committee Chairman Brown was at the heart of the 1992 fight to keep the project alive and believed it would be funded through fiscal 1993.

But he predicted that the project's status would be precarious for some time. And Brown said that unless the Japanese agreed to make a substantial financial contribution to the project or the budget climate for domestic programs changed, he could be forced to rethink his support for the program in 1993.

### Avoiding Budget Problems

While Bush had complained of spendthrift appropriators, the energy spending bill was about $400 million less than Bush recommended.

The administration did propose some last-minute cuts in its own budget request.

Taking advantage of the changing international political climate, the administration decided to postpone plans to build an expensive new reactor to produce tritium gas for nuclear bombs.

The administration reduced its $170 million request for the reactor program to $4 million in fiscal 1993; conferees provided $34 million.

But rather than eliminating the funding altogether, the administration proposed redirecting $166 million to develop non-proliferation technologies at the national laboratories.

For their part, appropriators refrained from weighting the bill with extensive new water projects but did earmark $95 million for 10 university building projects.

As usual, the projects were largely clustered in appropriators' home states.

However, Brown challenged the projects on the House floor and said university building funds should be awarded through the appropriate authorizing committees.

Such earmarks were usually untouchable, because members were wary of crossing the appropriators they routinely solicited for help. And appropriators defended their choices as a legitimate balance to customary selection procedures, which they said favor administration prerogatives and a few elite schools.

But Brown's criticisms struck a responsive chord.

Members first rejected, 157-203, a motion to shut off debate on the issue. Next, they voted 250-104 in support of Brown's amendment to make the $95 million available only for authorized university projects that were selected on a competitive basis. *(Votes 400, 401, p. 98-H)*

### Testing Restrictions Remain

On Sept. 24, the House finally approved, 224-151, the testing restrictions, including an immediate nine-month moratorium and a total testing cutoff in late 1996 unless another nation was still doing tests. *(Vote 429, p. 104-H)*

The Senate, which already had endorsed similar language in its version of the bill, approved the final bill by voice vote later that night.

Although some lawmakers had worried that Bush would veto the spending bill over the testing restrictions, the president signed the bill Oct. 2. ■

# Fiscal Crunch Trims Transportation Bill

With little debate, the House and Senate sent to President Bush a $13.2 billion fiscal 1993 transportation spending bill that met the 1992 strict budget targets, but fell far short of providing the funding called for in the 1991 major highway and transit authorization law.

The spending bill (HR 5518) was cleared by the Senate after both chambers adopted the conference report to the measure on Oct. 1 by voice vote.

The year's spending pressures, including a threat by Bush to veto any appropriations bill that exceeded his budget request, resulted in lawmakers' appropriating $1.2 billion less for highway, mass transit, aviation, Coast Guard and rail programs than in fiscal 1992.

"This is the best and most fiscally responsible bill of any that has come before this Congress this year," said Tom DeLay, R-Texas, a member of the House Appropriations Subcommittee on Transportation.

But the measure ignored the promises of major funding increases made in the $151 billion Intermodal Surface Transportation and Efficiency Act (PL 102-240) enacted in 1991.

That six-year authorization — touted by Bush and Democrats alike as a job-creating boost for the nation's infrastructure — called for a fiscal 1993 mass transit spending level of $5.2 billion. HR 5518, however, called for a $3.8 billion transit program, about the same as in fiscal 1992.

Highway programs fared best in the bill. But while highway spending would be slightly higher than the fiscal 1992 appropriation, including $283.4 million for ongoing highway demonstration projects, the bill's overall highway spending was below the $18.3 billion authorization called for in the fiscal 1992 bill.

The spending limit from the Highway Trust Fund, which was fed by a 14-cents-per-gallon federal gasoline tax, was $15.4 billion, down from $16.1 billion in fiscal 1992. Added to that was another $2.7 billion for other highway programs that lawmakers agreed would be exempt from trust fund spending limits, including demonstration projects mandated in the 1991 authorization bill and a "minimum allocation" program to states that otherwise got shortchanged by highway funding formulas.

Lawmakers from so-called donor states — which contributed more in taxes to the Highway Trust Fund than they received in highway money — won their demand to make the minimum allocation program exempt from spending limits, thus allowing more money to be spent on the program.

The Federal Aviation Administration (FAA) took a $14.2 million funding cut from the 1991 level. The bill provided $8.9 billion in new budget authority for airport

## BOXSCORE

➡ **Fiscal 1993 appropriations for the Department of Transportation and related agencies (HR 5518).** The $13.2 billion spending bill provided funding for highway and mass transit programs.

**Reports:** H Rept 102-639; S Rept 102-351; conference report H Rept 102-924.

### KEY ACTION

July 9 — The **House** passed HR 5518, 306-74.

Aug. 5 — The **Senate** passed HR 5518, 74-22.

Sept. 24 — HR 5518 approved by **House-Senate** conference.

Oct. 1 — **House** adopted conference report by voice vote; **Senate** cleared conference report by voice vote.

Oct. 6 — President Bush signed HR 5518 — PL 102-388.

and aviation programs, including a $1.8 billion cap on spending from the Airport and Airways Trust Fund, which was fed by a 10 percent airline ticket tax.

Despite the austere program levels, members of the House and Senate appropriations panels retained ample funding for several programs that the Bush administration sought to eliminate, including $204 million for the Amtrak Northeast corridor improvement program, $8 million for local railroad assistance, $802 million to help urban mass transit systems with operating expenses and $13 million to research magnetic levitation train technology.

Appropriators also provided the full Bush request of $143 million for so-called intelligent vehicle highway systems, which sought high-tech solutions to traffic congestion and route management problems. Of that, $113 million would be steered mostly toward the states of lawmakers on the appropriations panels for on-site testing of such systems. New Jersey, home of Senate Transportation Appropriations Chairman Frank R. Lautenberg, received a share of $34 million.

The Coast Guard received $3.6 billion, $17.5 million more than in fiscal 1992. The amount included $303 million to be transferred from the Defense Department.

Amtrak, the federally subsidized passenger rail corporation, received $642 million, a $9 million cut from fiscal 1992.

### Veto Threats

The bill passed swiftly, primarily because appropriators decided to drop several controversial provisions that had drawn veto threats from Bush. Most controversial was a House provision that would have shifted $400 million in actual fiscal 1993 spending from foreign aid programs to transportation accounts — a maneuver that the Bush administration said would have breached the 1990 budget agreement's ban on using foreign aid funds for domestic purposes.

Other provisions rejected to avoid a veto included one that would have protected the jobs of airline employees affected by the sale of international routes. Another would have limited the working hours of airline flight attendants.

Policy initiatives that survived in the final bill included a measure to require U.S. automakers to carry labels, beginning Oct. 1, 1994, identifying the location of each vehicle's assembly and the content of foreign-made parts. Another provision exempted air passengers using frequent-flier coupons from paying "passenger facility charges," which were private fees levied on airline tickets by airports for improvements.

### BACKGROUND

The transportation spending bill was Congress' annual bid toward rebuilding the nation's crumbling roads and

# Transportation Spending

*(HR 5518, as cleared for the president, in thousands of dollars):*

| | Fiscal 1992 | Fiscal 1993 Bush Request | House Bill | Senate Bill | Final Bill |
|---|---|---|---|---|---|
| **Transportation Department** | | | | | |
| Office of the Secretary | $ 183,306 | $ 228,437 | $ 183,100 | $ 202,125 | $ 200,334 |
| Rural airline subsidies (trust fund) | *(38,600)* | *(38,600)* | *(38,600)* | *(38,600)* | *(38,600)* |
| Coast Guard | | | | | |
| Operating expenses | 2,340,272 | 2,460,900 | 2,397,139 | 2,223,500 | 2,205,000 |
| Acquisition, construction | 411,500 | 414,000 | 384,600 | 325,000 | 340,000 |
| Other | 609,450 | 639,730 | 634,230 | 1,039,800 | 737,365 |
| **Subtotal, Coast Guard** | **$ 3,361,222** | **$ 3,514,630** | **$ 3,415,969** | **$ 3,588,300** | **$ 3,282,365** |
| Federal Aviation Administration | | | | | |
| Operations | 4,360,000 | 4,606,000 | 4,538,000 | 4,545,000 | 4,538,000 |
| Facilities and equipment | 2,434,000 | 2,700,000 | 2,459,860 | 2,429,500 | 2,350,000 |
| Research, engineering, development | 218,135 | 230,000 | 236,856 | 229,500 | 230,000 |
| Other | 73 | — | — | — | — |
| **Subtotal, FAA** | **$ 7,032,208** | **$ 7,536,000** | **$ 7,234,716** | **$ 7,204,000** | **$ 7,118,000** |
| *Airport Trust Fund limit* | *(1,900,000)* | *(1,900,000)* | *(1,850,000)* | *(1,800,000)* | *(1,800,000)* |
| Federal Highway Administration | | | | | |
| Ongoing demonstration projects | 343,678 | — | 162,420 | 286,800 | 283,356 |
| New demonstration projects | 249,146 | — | — | — | — |
| Other | 433,283 | 15,000 | 56,080 | 3,000 | 68,120 |
| **Subtotal, FHwA** | **$ 682,429** | **$ 15,000** | **$ 218,500** | **$ 289,800** | **$ 351,476** |
| *Highway Trust Fund limit* | *(16,055,364)* | *(18,898,000)* | *(16,690,000)* | *(18,006,250)* | *(15,326,750)* |
| *Obligations exempt from limit* | *(1,299,797)* | *(300,000)* | *(2,677,000)* | *(480,000)* | *(2,677,000)* |
| National Highway Traffic Safety | 122,700 | 133,233 | 120,140 | 127,840 | 128,250 |
| *Highway Trust Fund limit* | *(138,000)* | *(173,000)* | *(138,000)* | *(146,500)* | *(141,650)* |
| Federal Railroad Administration | | | | | |
| Local Rail Freight assistance | 11,500 | — | — | 8,000 | 8,000 |
| Amtrak | 651,000 | 343,000 | 551,000 | 642,000 | 642,000 |
| Northeast Corridor improvement | 205,000 | — | — | 204,100 | 204,100 |
| Other | 93,579 | 85,530 | 85,119 | 123,983 | 96,261 |
| **Subtotal, railroads** | **$ 961,079** | **$ 428,530** | **$ 636,119** | **$ 978,083** | **$ 950,361** |
| Federal Transit Administration | | | | | |
| Formula grants | 1,520,000 | 541,299 | 755,125 | 650,975 | 650,975 |
| *Highway Trust Fund* | — | *(1,060,274)* | *(1,064,875)* | *(1,031,025)* | *(1,049,025)* |
| Discretionary grants | — | — | 132,000 | — | — |
| *Highway Trust Fund* | *(1,900,000)* | *(1,000,000)* | *(1,725,000)* | *(1,725,000)* | *(1,725,000)* |
| Washington Metro | 124,000 | 182,000 | 165,000 | 182,000 | 170,000 |
| Other | 228,000 | 126,701 | 119,425 | 128,025 | 119,425 |
| **Subtotal, Transit** | **$ 1,872,000** | **$ 850,000** | **$ 1,171,550** | **$ 961,000** | **$ 940,400** |
| *Highway Trust Fund limit* | *(1,900,000)* | *(2,150,000)* | *(2,875,000)* | *(2,845,000)* | *(2,859,150)* |
| Other Transportation Department | 204,274 | 230,551 | 200,885 | 169,465 | 211,879 |
| **TOTAL Transportation Department** | **$ 14,296,518** | **$ 12,803,148** | **$ 13,060,839** | **$ 13,392,773** | **$ 13,054,815** |
| **Related Agencies** | | | | | |
| Architectural and Transportation Barriers Compliance Board | 2,940 | 3,500 | 3,200 | 3,400 | 3,300 |
| National Transportation Safety Board | 34,676 | 36,413 | 36,000 | 36,000 | 36,000 |
| Interstate Commerce Commission | 40,923 | 45,030 | 43,930 | 43,930 | 43,930 |
| Panama Canal Commission *(limitation on expenses)* | *(509,500)* | — | *(530,000)* | *(530,000)* | *(530,000)* |
| St. Lawrence Seaway Toll Rebate | 10,250 | 11,608 | 10,400 | 10,250 | 10,250 |
| **GRAND TOTAL** | **$ 14,436,970** | **$ 12,951,363** | **$ 13,206,033** | **$ 13,538,016** | **$ 13,199,958** |
| *(Trust fund limitations)* | *($ 20,106,776)* | *($ 23,256,075)* | *($ 21,672,075)* | *($ 22,973,125)* | *($ 20,256,925)* |

SOURCES: House Appropriations Committee

bridges, relieving congested highways and helping the nation's mass transit systems get out of the red.

The measure was best known — and liked, among lawmakers — for providing federal matching dollars for state and local road and transit construction projects.

But it also shaped federal transportation policy, kept airports humming with the latest traffic-control equipment and bought tugboats, London Fog raincoats and oil-spill equipment for the Coast Guard.

Despite the belt tightening mandated in the 1990 budget agreement, 1991 proved to be a banner year for transportation. Congress boosted spending by 10 percent, and transportation was among the few items recommended for an increase in Bush's fiscal 1992 budget. Appropriators provided $14.3 billion for transportation projects in fiscal 1992. *(Spending bill, 1991 Almanac, p. 603)*

The increase in transportation spending was due in large part to a fortuitous coincidence: In 1991 a multi-year authorization for federal highway and transit programs also moved through Congress. *(Authorization bill, 1991 Almanac, p. 137)*

The authorization effort put the spotlight on the nation's corroding infrastructure. As it traveled its own bumpy road through Capitol Hill, the appropriations' measure benefited from lawmakers' generous mood toward the nations' roads, bridges and transit systems. In a rare spirit of cooperation, authorizers and appropriators were allied in the same goal: building support for their bills by providing members with money for local road projects.

At the start of the 102nd Congress, New Jersey Democrat Robert A. Roe assumed the helm of the House Public Works and Transportation Committee, which was responsible for shepherding the authorization bill. Roe's affinity for "demonstration projects," a classic form of road-project pork barreling, was a main reason his colleagues picked him.

With Roe, House Transportation Appropriations Chairman William Lehman, D-Fla., ran into none of the turf-warring opposition that had threatened Lehman's power in the past. There was only one caveat: Lehman had to make sure that New Jersey's needs were met — which he did.

But in 1992, budget realities hit home for both committees. The fiscal 1993 spending bill provided only $13.2 billion, returning the bill close to fiscal 1991 levels. HR 5518 met the 1992 budget targets, but fell far short of providing the funding called for in the 1991 surface transportation bill.

## HOUSE COMMITTEE ACTION

Highway programs faced major spending cuts and mass transit received a slight increase under a $13 billion fiscal 1993 spending bill the House Appropriations Subcommittee on Transportation approved by voice vote June 11.

But the states of lawmakers who reeled in large numbers of special road projects in 1991 felt the least pain from the spending cuts.

After subtracting $206 million that would come from the Defense Department for Coast Guard military expenses, the bill still fell about $1 billion below fiscal 1992 appropriations.

Key lawmakers who managed to get the lion's share of special road projects into the 1991 authorization bill were the primary beneficiaries of the appropriations bill. Spending for most of those projects was considered mandatory and exempt from limits Congress put on spending from the

Highway Trust Fund. The account jumped to slightly more than $1 billion in fiscal 1993 from $239 million in fiscal 1992. The bill also funded an additional $167 million for 50 ongoing special road projects.

States not slated to receive large numbers of special road projects had to build and improve their highways from a smaller pot of Highway Trust Fund dollars. Appropriators agreed to limit such spending to $14.3 billion, down from $16.8 billion appropriated in fiscal 1992.

The impact of the spending cuts on highway programs, however, was greater than it first appeared. The Federal Highway Administration had already reduced the $16.8 billion cap on spending from the trust fund to $15.6 billion to offset excess spending mandated in the 1991 highway and mass transit law — mostly due to a courthouse renovation project added at the insistence of Sen. Daniel Patrick Moynihan, D-N.Y. *(Brooklyn courthouse project, p. 196)*

### Provisions

Transit programs received $3.8 billion, compared with $3.7 billion in fiscal 1992. Formula grants for transit projects decreased from $1.9 billion to $1.7 billion in fiscal 1993. And operating assistance was cut to $720 million. But spending on specific transit projects increased from $1.3 billion to $1.6 billion.

New and ongoing rail projects in 25 cities received $640 million. They included Los Angeles, which was to receive $110 million; St. Louis, $51 million; and Dallas, $50 million.

The controversial Houston mass transit system, which had not been started, received an additional $40 million to add to its $147 million pot for the project.

The Federal Aviation Administration was the only major agency slated to receive a spending increase, up to $7.2 billion in fiscal 1993 from roughly $7 billion in fiscal 1992.

Amtrak funding took a $100 million cut, down to $550 million, which included grants to the passenger train corporation.

### Full Committee

The $13 billion fiscal 1993 transportation spending bill approved by the House Appropriations Committee on July 1 confirmed that lawmakers had to backpedal on promises made in 1991 when they passed a sweeping road and transit law.

Overall budget authority for highway, mass transit, Coast Guard and aviation programs decreased by 9 percent under HR 5518, which was approved by voice vote. In the fiscal 1992 spending measure, Congress boosted those programs 10 percent; the fiscal 1993 bill effectively returned spending to fiscal 1991 levels.

Spending on road programs from the Highway Trust Fund, which was fed by gasoline taxes, shrank from a fiscal 1992 level of $15.8 billion to $14.5 billion. The 1991 authorization bill had recommended $18.3 billion for fiscal 1993.

Funding for special highway programs, which included individual road projects and payments to states that contributed more in gasoline taxes than they got back in federal highway funds, increased from $1.3 billion in fiscal 1992 to $2.7 billion. Spending for those programs was considered mandatory and was exempt from trust fund limits.

The committee froze mass transit funding at the fiscal 1992 level of $3.8 billion, with most of that money coming from the transit account of the Highway Trust Fund. But money to help urban-area transit systems operate was cut 10 percent to $720 million.

The FAA received a slight boost, from $7 billion in fiscal 1992 to $7.2 billion in fiscal 1993. The increase went toward more personnel for operation and maintenance of the nation's air traffic control system.

Coast Guard spending was frozen at the 1992 level of $3.4 billion. The Defense Department provided $206 million more to help pay for the Coast Guard's military role.

Transportation appropriators blamed the spending cuts on the House's failure to alter the 1990 budget agreement, which prohibited transferring defense money for domestic purposes.

The committee defeated, on a 15-16 show of hands, an amendment offered by Dean A. Gallo, R-N.J., that would have frozen any increase in pay for the director and staff of the FAA's noise pollution office. Gallo said he had been trying for five years to get the FAA to issue an environmental impact statement on allowable noise levels at major airports in New York and New Jersey.

The committee also defeated by voice vote an amendment by Robert J. Mrazek, D-N.Y., that would have restored funding for development of a prototype magnetic levitation train, which would ride on an electromagnetic field rather than on rails. The 1991 surface transportation bill authorized $700 million for the project over six years; under the tight 1993 appropriations bill, money for the maglev train was erased.

## HOUSE FLOOR ACTION

Forced to choose between creating highway jobs and helping U.S. allies, House lawmakers on July 9 voted their hometown interests by agreeing to alter the 1990 budget agreement's ban on shifting foreign aid funds to domestic programs.

Despite cries of outrage from Republicans loyal to the budget pact, the House voted 213-190 to transfer $400 million from foreign aid coffers to highway, mass transit and aviation accounts. The House then passed HR 5518, the $13 billion fiscal 1993 transportation spending bill, by a vote of 306-74. *(Votes 282, 284; pp. 68-H, 70-H)*

The vote to transfer funds marked the first successful attempt by the House to change the five-year deficit-reduction deal between lawmakers and President Bush that erected budget walls between domestic spending, foreign aid and defense.

The amendment's sponsors, David R. Obey, D-Wis., Majority Leader Richard A. Gephardt, D-Mo., and leaders of the Public Works and Transportation Committee, said the funding shift was necessary to create about 150,000 jobs to recharge the flagging economy.

"The government itself has an obligation to get off its collective duff ... and recognize that the economy is in trouble," said Obey, chairman of the Appropriations Subcommittee on Foreign Operations. "We need to find a way to deal with the unemployment losses that we have seen all across the country."

Armed with charts showing the potential spending increases in road and transit projects for each state, Public Works Chairman Roe, Surface Transportation Subcommittee Chairman Norman Y. Mineta, D-Calif., and ranking subcommittee Republican Bud Shuster, R-Pa., mounted a full-court lobbying press to argue that the money was needed more urgently at home than abroad.

"It is time to say to the people overseas, 'Pay your own damned bills and let us spend our tax dollars with our people,'" Roe said.

But Republican opponents complained that the shift would open the floodgates for future raids on defense and foreign aid spending. Some Democrats also complained it would limit the nation's flexibility to respond to foreign aid crises ranging from the civil war among former Yugoslavian states to loan guarantees for Israel.

"This is not the way to handle foreign relations," said Howard L. Berman, D-Calif. "There is $7 billion of totally unused defense cuts ... from which this money could come."

### Highway, Transit Needs Prevail

Lawmakers voted to put hometown traffic jams and potholes ahead of foreign aid after seeing the promise of hundreds of road and transit projects in the 1991 sweeping surface transportation authorization law fade. Appropriators had been hamstrung by budget constraints to do little more than freeze programs at fiscal 1992 levels.

More than half the $400 million was to come from savings the House achieved June 25, when it passed a foreign operations bill (HR 5368) whose overall price tag was less than the spending target set for such programs by the fiscal 1993 budget resolution. *(Foreign operations, p. 612)*

The remainder was likely to come from foreign aid savings expected in the fiscal 1993 Commerce, Justice, State and Judiciary appropriations bill and domestic accounts in other domestic spending measures. *(Commerce/Justice/State, p. 646)*

In addition to providing $400 million in actual fiscal 1993 spending to states, the Obey amendment raised the level of future highway program obligations from the Highway Trust Fund from $14.4 billion to $16.7 billion. The 1991 authorization called for an $18.3 billion cap on the trust fund; President Bush's budget request was for $18.9 billion.

The Obey amendment also provided an additional $257 million for mass transit discretionary grants, $50 million for airport improvement grants and $38 million for Coast Guard operations.

The extra highway dollars would not go to any specific projects but instead would be added to lump-sum payments made to states. Still, Public Works panel leaders reminded those who opposed shifting the funds that they had the power to slash funding for pet road projects.

"Don't come to our committee and ask for help for your problems if the money isn't there," Shuster warned.

Public Works was slated to move soon on a measure making technical corrections to the 1991 surface transportation authorization law. At that time, the committee had the power to shift funds among projects, as long as the totals did not exceed authorized levels, Shuster said.

Unlike most authorizing committees, the Public Works panel wielded nearly as much power over spending as its counterpart Transportation Subcommittee on Appropriations. That was because the Public Works Committee granted contract authority, which amounted to promises of federal spending to states in the form of either block grants or specific projects.

Ironically, Shuster, Roe, Mineta and other key transportation lawmakers would have been least hurt by the appropriations bill's original lower spending levels. In the 1991 authorization law, those lawmakers won for their states the better part of 539 special road "demonstration projects," which were considered mandatory spending and thus were exempt from any limits on Highway Trust Fund

spending. Fiscal 1993 spending for such projects, which was set at slightly more than $1 billion, was up from only $239 million in fiscal 1992.

Appropriators were unable to alter any of those mandatory projects that came from the 1991 authorization bill but were able to add $164 million for 53 of their own new and ongoing projects in the spending bill.

Transportation Appropriations Subcommittee Chairman Lehman sided with Public Works leaders on the Obey amendment. But Lawrence Coughlin, R-Pa., the ranking member of the Transportation Appropriations Subcommittee who rarely strayed from Lehman on issues, opposed it.

Though the Obey amendment allowed states to begin moving on $2.25 billion worth of new highway projects in fiscal 1993, it was unclear whether most states would be able to spend the money.

Mineta said nearly 40 states still used less than 50 percent of their eligible highway funds in fiscal 1992.

Most were having trouble finding matching funds, which could be as high as 20 percent of a project's cost, needed to get all of their projects started.

States were allowed to defer payments on the state and local share until the end of fiscal 1993. But a Mineta amendment that would have extended that deadline until March 30, 1995, and included mass transit projects was rejected, 184-229. (Vote 279, p. 68-H)

### DOT Funding

In addition to trust fund spending, the bill provided $13 billion in new budget authority for the Transportation Department and related agencies, $1.26 billion less than the fiscal 1992 level.

The FAA received $4.5 billion for operations, an increase of $178 million over fiscal 1992 levels. The agency also received $2.5 billion for facilities and equipment, $1.9 billion for airport development and planning grants and $237 million for research, engineering and development activities.

The House also accepted, by voice vote, a Mineta amendment that required the FAA to issue limits on the hours that flight attendants must work, and set minimum rest periods.

The Federal Transit Administration received $1.8 billion for its formula grants program, which included a 10 percent cut in operating aid to urban transit systems to $720 million. Discretionary grants to specific transit systems totaled $1.9 billion, including $320 million for bus facilities, $640 million to upgrade rail systems and $640 million for new mass transit systems.

Amtrak, the federally subsidized national passenger rail corporation, received $405 million in grants, $101 million less than in fiscal 1992.

## SENATE COMMITTEE ACTION

The Senate Appropriations Committee on July 30 approved a $13.5 billion fiscal 1993 transportation spending bill, sidestepping whether to shift foreign aid funds toward domestic transportation programs.

Still, an unrelated fight loomed on the Senate floor over whether highway funds were distributed fairly to states.

Unlike its House companion bill, the Senate version of HR 5518, approved by a vote of 27-0, did not breach the so-called walls erected by the 1990 budget agreement that prevented transferring money among separate accounts for foreign, defense and domestic programs.

House lawmakers had voted to increase budget authority for the Highway Trust Fund from $14.4 billion to $16.7 billion by shifting $400 million in actual spending, or outlays, from foreign aid.

Senate appropriators were under less pressure to boost road and transit spending because the Senate's budget resolution allowed for higher overall transportation levels than the House's.

The Senate spending bill called for slightly less in outlays — $55 million — than the House version, according to Senate Transportation Appropriations Subcommittee Chairman Lautenberg.

For highway programs, the Senate bill allowed states to grant no more than $18 billion worth of contracts in fiscal 1993, compared with the House's limit of $16.7 billion and a fiscal 1992 limit of $15.7 billion. The money came out of the Highway Trust Fund, which was fed by a 14-cent federal tax on gasoline.

The House measure, however, spent another $2.7 billion from the trust fund on programs deemed exempt from the spending limits, including $1.1 billion for road demonstration projects mandated in the 1991 surface transportation law and $1.1 billion for a "minimum allocation" program intended to compensate states that paid more into the trust fund than they received in highway grants.

The Senate bill subjected those programs to the trust fund spending limits, putting only $300 million outside the ceiling for emergency relief programs.

As a result, the Senate bill reduced spending to $600 million for the mandatory special road projects and only $900 million for the minimum allocation program.

The Senate bill's $200 million lower spending level for the minimum allocation program had senators from so-called donor states seeing red.

Christopher S. Bond, R-Mo., protested that the Senate bill violated agreements in the 1991 highway bill to treat donor states more equitably. Missouri would have received at least $9 million less under the Senate bill.

"I have to address this on the floor," Bond told Appropriations Chairman Robert C. Byrd, D-W.Va.

### No New Projects Added

Lautenberg said he received 765 requests for new road projects from 85 senators. But, as with the House, Senate appropriators had no leeway to add new projects to the bill.

The Senate bill earmarked $279 million for ongoing special road projects apart from those mandated in the 1991 authorization bill. House appropriators had their own $164 million list of ongoing projects. Conferees typically accept projects in both bills after reducing them by 10 percent to 15 percent.

Other funding categories hewed closely to fiscal 1992 spending levels.

Mass transit received $3.8 billion, compared with $4 billion in the House bill. New rail systems were funded at $690 million, compared with $897 million in the House bill.

The FAA was funded at $9 billion, roughly the same as the House bill and slightly higher than fiscal 1992 levels.

The Senate bill differed from the House measure in several key areas:
- Lautenberg included $45 million for work on a prototype magnetic levitation train. The project was authorized in the 1991 surface transportation bill, but the House spending bill and the Bush administration budget request included no spending for it.
- The Senate bill provided $204 million to continue up-

grading the Northeast Amtrak corridor between Washington and Boston. The House included no funding for the project. The Senate also would spend $496 million on grants to the Amtrak passenger rail corporation, compared with $405 million in the House bill.

• Both the House and Senate provided $143 million for research and testing of "intelligent vehicle-highway systems," which applied high-tech solutions to congestion and traffic routing problems.

But the Senate bill spread the money around differently, adding $42 million for five projects in New Jersey and $10 million for a New York project.

• The Senate bill deleted House language to prohibit airports from levying passenger facility charges — new ticket taxes ranging from $1 to $3 to finance airport improvements — on travelers using frequent-flier certificates.

## SENATE FLOOR ACTION

The Senate on Aug. 5 passed a $13.5 billion version of HR 5518, after rejecting an effort to steer more dollars toward states that routinely got shortchanged when federal highway funds were doled out.

The Senate passed the bill by a vote of 74-22. *(Vote 171, p. 23-S)*

Bill sponsors did not address an ongoing fight between House leaders and the Bush administration over whether to shift defense or foreign aid funds to job-creating domestic programs such as highway and mass transit construction and repair projects. But Transportation Appropriations Subcommittee Chairman Lautenberg complained that budget constraints kept the bill from achieving levels of investment called for in the 1991 $151 billion, six-year surface transportation reauthorization.

"I wish that this bill could do more, much more," Lautenberg said. "The nation has consistently under-invested in our physical infrastructure."

Facing the largest cuts were the Coast Guard, mass transit and Amtrak. The Coast Guard received $33.6 million less than what would be provided under a House companion bill for acquiring ships, helicopters and other equipment.

But the Senate measure provided funding for programs slated to get no money under the House bill and the Bush administration request. Among them, an experimental magnetic levitation train project received $45 million and a program to encourage freight rail carriers to continue operating along unprofitable rural lines would get $8 million.

Spending on road projects from the Highway Trust Fund was capped at $18 billion, compared with $16.8 billion in the House measure. However, the House bill also included $2.7 billion for highway programs outside of the trust fund limit.

The Senate spent $600 million on special demonstration projects mandated by the 1991 authorization, while the House bill spent $1 billion. There were no new road projects in either bill, though the Senate spent $279 million, compared with $164 million in the House measure, on additional ongoing projects that had been authorized before the sweeping transportation law was enacted.

The bill also contained $3.8 billion for the Federal Transit Administration, below the House-passed level of $4 billion. Of that amount, $690 million went toward new transit systems in 27 cities, compared with $897 million for 26 cities provided by the House bill. The Senate bill included $110 million for Los Angeles, $90 million for Hono

lulu, $80 million for Portland, Ore., and $71.7 million for the Newark, N.J., area.

An additional $690 million went toward modernizing older transit systems, compared with $640 million provided by the House bill. And $345 million was earmarked for discretionary bus programs, compared with $320 million in the House measure.

Aviation programs received a slight increase to $9 billion from the fiscal 1992 level of $8.8 billion. Grants for airports were increased from $1.5 billion to $2 billion.

The Senate bill, unlike its counterpart in the House, would spend only the money allocated to transportation programs in the chamber's fiscal 1993 budget resolution. The House-passed bill would transfer some foreign aid funds to domestic transportation programs.

The Bush administration threatened to veto the House bill because of the Obey amendment. But Majority Leader Gephardt and Majority Whip David E. Bonior of Michigan on Aug. 5 met with White House budget director Richard G. Darman, Transportation Secretary Andrew H. Card Jr. and House Republican leaders to discuss other ways to increase transportation spending by as much as $400 million.

Among other options, Bonior suggested reclassifying some defense accounts within the Coast Guard as domestic spending and putting those funds toward road or transit projects. Another funding source was $369 million in fiscal 1992 highway dollars that was to be available once Bush signed Congress' repeal of a Brooklyn, N.Y., courthouse project.

House Speaker Thomas S. Foley, D-Wash., on Aug. 6 said the administration was "inclined favorably" toward adding as much as $400 million to transportation programs. He said the money was likely to come from "reprogramming," not from shifting funds as Obey suggested.

### Senate Sticks to Parochial Battles

The Senate renewed what had become an annual war between the states over how to fairly allocate highway money.

After a lengthy fight during consideration of the 1991 surface transportation authorization, Congress devised new formulas intended to steer more money to donor states that routinely paid more in gasoline taxes into the Highway Trust Fund than they got back in highway dollars.

A so-called minimum allocation formula, devised in 1982, was broadened to assure such states a 90 percent return on their gasoline tax dollar, up from 85 percent. The 1991 law also stipulated that the money would not be subject to annual limits on trust fund spending.

In 1992, the House adhered to those agreements and funded the expanded minimum allocation program at $1.1 billion without counting that money against the trust fund spending ceiling.

But Senate appropriators, in a budget-cutting effort, made all highway programs subject to the trust fund's spending constraints — resulting in only $900 million for the minimum allocation program.

Bond lost his bid to get the Senate to adopt the House's position on the issue on a vote of 39-57. *(Vote 170, p. 23-S)*

Other amendments accepted by the Senate, by voice vote, included those by:

• Bond and Bob Graham, D-Fla., as amended by John C. Danforth, R-Mo., to help find jobs for workers affected by the transfer of a foreign route from one air carrier to another.

- Graham, to freeze the Transportation Department's administrative funding at its fiscal 1992 level.
- Barbara A. Mikulski, D-Md., to require automakers to disclose on new cars where each vehicle was built and its percentage of domestic parts, starting in the 1993 model year..

The overall Senate spending bill also included "technical corrections" to the 1991 transportation law. Most of the provisions involved minor changes, though the scope of some road and transit projects were to be broadened.

## FINAL ACTION

House-Senate conferees, bowing to end-of-session veto threats by President Bush, finished work on HR 5518 by paring it to $13.2 billion and removing two airline labor provisions opposed by the White House.

Negotiators from the House and Senate Transportation Appropriations subcommittees, who adopted the conference report by voice vote Sept. 24, were forced to scale back the measure after Bush threatened to veto any spending bill that exceeded his budget request.

The House transportation bill was $903 million in budget authority over the Bush request, while the Senate measure was $501 million over.

Appropriators easily met the goal by rejecting a provision in the House-passed bill, added as an amendment by Obey, that would have shifted $2.6 billion in budget authority from foreign aid to transportation programs. Other savings were won through a routine transfer of funds from the Defense Department budget to the Coast Guard and by making small cuts in other areas.

The bill capped spending from the Highway Trust Fund at roughly $15 billion. That was less than the fiscal 1992 level of $16.8 billion but did not include $2.7 billion for highway programs that were exempt from the spending limit. Mass transit programs received $3.8 billion, roughly the same as in fiscal 1992, and the FAA received $7.1 billion.

### Airline Labor Protection

Meeting Bush's fiscal demands seemed to cause less grief for appropriators than ceding to the president's veto threats on two provisions aimed at helping flight attendants and displaced airline employees.

One, in the House bill, would have limited the working hours of flight attendants to 14 hours for domestic and international flights and 16 hours for short-range flights within the continent. Sponsors called it a safety issue, but a Bush statement said the provision would not add to the public safety and would interfere with existing bargaining agreements.

The other provision would have required the Transportation secretary to determine, before agreeing to transfer international routes from a failed airline to a new carrier, that the new airline has given priority hiring status to employees of the failed carrier.

The issue was of crucial importance to 17,000 former pilots and employees of Pan American World Airways Inc.,

which went bankrupt in December 1991 and sold its international routes to United and Delta airlines. A "first right of hire" law that would have forced United and Delta to give the employees priority status that expired in 1988.

"A statutory mandate for such unneeded labor protection is highly objectionable," said a Sept. 22 letter to appropriators from Darman.

Lawmakers from both parties harshly denounced the veto threats.

"I say if they want to veto it, let them veto it," said Sen. Alfonse M. D'Amato, R-N.Y., whose state was home to 7,000 unemployed former Pan Am workers.

But other conferees said House leaders sent word to give in on such veto threats or risk returning for a lame-duck session to complete vetoed spending bills.

"Nothing pains me more than to cave in on this issue," said Lautenberg. "I really think it's outrageous that we have to be subjected to these kinds of pressures."

A House leadership aide denied there was undue pressure, saying leaders only asked appropriators to expedite their bills' passage.

### No Givebacks

Intramural skirmishes between House and Senate lawmakers made up the rest of the unusually rancorous conference. In one, senators reluctantly dropped a proposal they said was aimed at putting more highway funds to work more quickly.

Lautenberg argued that states often do not use all of the money set aside for highway "demonstration" projects and a "minimum allocation" program that compensated states that got shortchanged by routine funding formulas.

The Senate proposed allowing states to volunteer to send back into the Highway Trust Fund any money allocated for those programs in fiscal 1993 that would not be spent during the year. The funds then could be steered toward projects that needed the money during fiscal 1993.

Lautenberg stressed that states doing so still would be able to reclaim the money in later years. But many lawmakers — particularly those from donor states that benefited from minimum allocation funds — feared their states would get shortchanged.

Senate conferees relented and also agreed to a House plan to exempt special highway projects and the minimum allocation program from Highway Trust Fund spending limits — another key demand of donor-state lawmakers. But Lautenberg won his bid to fund a project to improve the Amtrak northeast corridor at $204 million.

In other conference action:
- A program to develop a prototype magnetic levitation train was dropped, but conferees agreed to boost research for the program to $13 million.
- Automakers, beginning in model year 1995, were required to list on price stickers where each vehicle was built and its percentage of domestic parts.
- Air passengers who used frequent-flier tickets were exempted from passenger facility charges — private fees of up to $3 per one-way trip levied by airports to pay for improvements. ■

# Agriculture Funded at $60.5 Billion

Despite the labyrinth of programs it contained, the spending bill for the Agriculture Department and related agencies was the first of the 13 regular appropriations bills through the gate and onto the president's desk in 1992. The Senate cleared a $60.5 billion agriculture appropriations bill Aug. 11 without any major dispute.

The bill provided $13.5 billion for traditional agriculture programs, $2.7 billion for soil and other conservation initiatives and $2.9 billion for rural programs such as the Rural Electrification Administration in fiscal 1993.

But the bulk of the bill's funds — more than $38 billion — was for domestic food programs. The food stamps program got $28 billion for fiscal 1993, a $5 billion increase from fiscal 1992 levels. The Appropriations Committee had virtually no control over spending for the food stamps program because it was an entitlement — the cost of the program was determined by how many people were eligible to receive benefits.

The popular Women, Infants and Children (WIC) supplemental feeding program also received a substantial increase. It got $2.86 billion — $260 million more than in fiscal 1992. Matthew F. McHugh, D-N.Y., said that while the increase was substantial, "I wish we could have done better."

Most of the debate on the Agriculture spending bill centered on two programs — the market promotion program, which gave matching grants to companies to sell American goods overseas, and the wetlands reserve program, part of the 1990 farm bill that was designed to take 1 million acres of farmland out of production and let them revert to wetlands.

In the end, the marketing program got $150 million — $50 million less than in fiscal 1992, but twice as much as the House had wanted to provide. The wetlands did not fair as well, getting no funding for fiscal 1993.

## BACKGROUND

The appropriations bill for agriculture was considered Rep. Jamie L. Whitten's annual work of art. Virtually all of the measure's provisions bore the signature of the Mississippi Democrat, a member of Congress for 50 years and chairman of both the House Appropriations Committee and its Agriculture subcommittee. Farm-state lawmakers often said that Whitten put the bill together line by line and dollar for dollar.

Those dynamics started to change in 1992. Whitten, who had been recovering from what close associates had said was a stroke earlier in the year, temporarily handed over the reins of the full Appropriations Committee to William H. Natcher, D-Ky., on June 9. *(Obituaries, p. 73)*

---

### BOXSCORE

➡ **Fiscal 1993 Agriculture Appropriations (HR 5487).** The bill provided $60.5 billion in fiscal 1993 for farm and nutrition programs.

**Reports:** H Rept 102-617; S Rept 102-334; conference report H Rept 102-815.

#### KEY ACTION

June 30 — The **House** passed HR 5487, 312-99.

July 28 — The **Senate** passed HR 5487, 88-9.

Aug. 6 — **House-Senate** conferees reached agreement on HR 5487.

Aug. 11 — The **House** adopted conference agreement, 299-100; the **Senate** cleared it by voice vote.

Aug. 14 — President Bush signed HR 5487 — PL 102-341.

---

The stewardship of the annual agricultural spending bill changed in the Senate, too. Dale Bumpers, D-Ark., guided the bill through the process as acting chairman of the Senate Agriculture, Rural Development and Related Agencies Appropriations Subcommittee while Chairman Quentin N. Burdick, D-N.D., was ill. Burdick died Sept. 8.

Whitten and Burdick, both of whom entered politics during the Depression, remained loyal to agriculture policies framed by the New Deal, when farm programs had much in common with public works projects. The Soil Conservation Service, for instance, spent much of its money building terraces and drains. The Rural Electrification Administration was almost single-handedly responsible for wiring rural America with electricity and telephone service.

The two men's loyalty to this earlier era had meant fewer dollars for new programs and only small changes in the focus of the Agriculture Department.

Whitten, in particular, held the philosophy that agriculture was one of the cornerstones of the American economy and that the government had an almost moral duty to be partner to farmers, both by bolstering raw commodity prices and encouraging unlimited production.

Yet most of the government's policies on farm subsidies, agricultural credit and food stamp programs remained under the purview of the House and Senate agriculture committees, which generated multi-year farm authorization bills.

Whitten's subcommittee had direct control over about $12 billion in discretionary spending for the Agriculture Department, which ran research and conservation programs in every state and in some cases in every county, and for related agencies such as the Food and Drug Administration. Generally, every state got its share of the research dollars, construction projects and rural development programs.

For fiscal 1993, 133 special research projects were inserted by farm-state lawmakers into the bill at a cost of $73.4 million. Among the projects was a $25,000 grant to Virginia Polytechnic Institute and State University to study the destructive powers of procerum root disease in killing trees and a $9 million grant to fund research on water quality nationwide.

### HOUSE COMMITTEE ACTION

Tight budget constraints made for tough choices for the House Appropriations Committee on June 25 when it approved a $59 billion spending bill (HR 5487) for the Agriculture Department and related agencies for fiscal 1993.

# Agriculture Spending

*(HR 5487, as cleared for the president, in thousands of dollars)*

| | Fiscal 1992 | Fiscal 1993 Bush Request | House Bill | Senate Bill | Final Bill |
|---|---|---|---|---|---|
| **Agriculture Programs** | | | | | |
| Agricultural Research Service | $ 711,443 | $ 713,978 | $ 695,393 | $ 684,089 | $ 695,393 |
| Cooperative State Research | 505,981 | 416,023 | 446,006 | 469,027 | 482,244 |
| Extension Service | 419,325 | 417,320 | 417,928 | 422,944 | 424,928 |
| Animal and plant inspection | 452,335 | 429,229 | 441,339 | 443,300 | 443,300 |
| Food safety and inspection | 473,512 | 450,967 | 489,867 | 489,867 | 489,867 |
| Crop Insurance | 583,370 | 621,171 | 589,690 | 595,742 | 595,742 |
| Commodity Credit Corporation | 7,250,000 | 9,200,000 | 9,200,000 | 9,200,000 | 9,200,000 |
| Other | 1,224,545 | 1,229,772 | 1,202,659 | 1,184,319 | 1,204,427 |
| **Subtotal** | **$ 11,620,511** | **$ 13,478,460** | **$ 13,482,882** | **$ 13,489,288** | **$ 13,535,901** |
| **Conservation Programs** | | | | | |
| Soil Conservation Service | 849,978 | 790,828 | 862,388 | 895,388 | 885,388 |
| Conservation Reserve Program | 1,611,277 | 1,606,540 | 1,578,517 | 1,578,517 | 1,578,517 |
| Wetlands Reserve Program | 46,357 | 160,893 | — | 54,900 | — |
| Other conservation | 246,847 | 164,222 | 243,847 | 236,197 | 242,847 |
| **Subtotal** | **$ 2,754,459** | **$ 2,722,483** | **$ 2,684,752** | **$ 2,765,002** | **$ 2,706,752** |
| **Rural Development Programs** | | | | | |
| Farmers Home Administration | | | | | |
| Rural Housing Fund | | | | | |
| New budget authority | 1,333,836 | 1,124,557 | 1,452,202 | 1,432,826 | 1,420,967 |
| *(Loan authorization)* | *(2,476,630)* | *(1,718,350)* | *(2,352,730)* | *(2,284,130)* | *(2,413,630)* |
| Agricultural Credit | | | | | |
| New budget authority | 557,626 | 437,335 | 491,605 | 465,726 | 478,700 |
| *(Loan authorization)* | *(4,200,240)* | *(2,877,000)* | *(3,393,206)* | *(3,268,169)* | *(3,331,206)* |
| Rural Development | | | | | |
| New budget authority | 161,185 | 160,331 | 159,418 | 159,418 | 159,418 |
| *(Loan authorization)* | *(860,000)* | *(900,000)* | *(935,000)* | *(935,000)* | *(935,000)* |
| Rural water and waste disposal grants | 350,000 | 300,000 | 400,000 | 381,000 | 390,000 |
| Other Farmers Home | 155,028 | 248,028 | 126,734 | 154,240 | 152,190 |
| Rural Electrification Administration | | | | | |
| New budget authority | 220,974 | 228,792 | 286,583 | 245,542 | 243,153 |
| *(Loan authorization)* | *(2,288,075)* | *(1,779,456)* | *(2,043,435)* | *(1,797,360)* | *(1,797,360)* |
| Other rural development | 572 | 15,437 | 15,359 | 15,359 | 15,359 |
| **Subtotal** | **$ 2,766,190** | **$ 2,514,480** | **$ 2,931,901** | **$ 2,854,111** | **$ 2,859,787** |
| **Domestic Food Programs** | | | | | |
| Food stamps program | 23,362,975 | 29,051,000 | 26,719,691 | 29,051,000 | 28,115,357 |
| Child nutrition programs | 6,068,315 | 6,480,285 | 6,674,521 | 6,767,484 | 6,826,553 |
| Transfer from Customs receipts | (4,675,092) | (4,272,138) | (4,290,455) | (4,290,455) | (4,290,455) |
| Women, Infants and Children | 2,600,000 | 2,840,000 | 2,860,000 | 2,860,000 | 2,860,000 |
| Other food programs | 658,313 | 648,836 | 645,776 | 645,776 | 645,776 |
| **Subtotal** | **$ 32,689,603** | **$ 39,020,121** | **$ 36,899,988** | **$ 39,324,260** | **$ 38,447,686** |
| **International Programs** | | | | | |
| PL 480 (Food for Peace) | 1,486,000 | 1,408,897 | 1,538,767 | 1,574,000 | 1,573,380 |
| *(Program level)* | *(1,607,485)* | *(1,478,599)* | *(1,661,240)* | *(1,735,628)* | *(1,698,870)* |
| CCC export loan subsidy | 155,524 | 388,170 | 388,170 | 388,170 | 388,170 |
| *(loan authorization)* | *(5,700,000)* | *(5,700,000)* | *(5,700,000)* | *(5,700,000)* | *(5,700,000)* |
| Other | 121,090 | 120,163 | 120,590 | 120,590 | 120,590 |
| **Subtotal** | **$ 1,762,614** | **$ 1,917,230** | **$ 2,047,527** | **$ 2,082,760** | **$ 2,082,140** |
| **Related Agencies** | | | | | |
| Food and Drug Administration | 759,924 | 591,000 | 778,097 | 779,997 | 779,997 |
| Other | 159,906 | 137,448 | 131,914 | 131,914 | 131,914 |
| **GRAND TOTAL** | | | | | |
| New budget authority | **$ 52,526,238** | **$ 60,381,222** | **$ 58,907,757*** | **$ 61,427,332** | **$ 60,547,821** |
| *Loan authorization* | *(15,567,945)* | *(13,019,806)* | *(14,453,258)* | *(14,062,659)* | *(14,250,196)* |

*\* House bill total included a $49.3 million reduction of appropriations.*

SOURCE: Senate Appropriations Committee

Appropriators cut $125 million from a program to market U.S. goods abroad, $189 million from Agriculture Department wetlands and conservation programs, and roughly $9 million from domestic food donation programs.

The cuts allowed for spending increases in the popular WIC food program and the Food and Drug Administration (FDA). As approved by the appropriations committee, WIC was slated to get $2.86 billion in fiscal 1993, $260 million more than the fiscal 1992 appropriation; FDA would get $778 million, $18 million more than fiscal 1992.

Most of the spending in the bill was for mandatory programs over which appropriators had little control. Included in the mandatory account was $26.7 billion for the food stamp program and $9.2 billion for crop subsidies.

Agriculture programs would get $13.5 billion in fiscal 1993, and rural development programs were slated for $2.9 billion.

The committee approved $2.1 billion for foreign assistance programs, including agriculture export subsidies and the Food for Peace program, under which surplus crops were distributed to less-developed or famine-stricken regions of the world.

Even before the bill was approved, Agriculture Secretary Edward Madigan had denounced a proposed cut in the market promotion program, which promoted U.S. products abroad.

The controversial program provided matching funds to companies to help them sell products abroad. Program defenders said it helped establish markets for U.S. goods and increased sales; detractors branded it a subsidy for wealthy companies.

After published reports highlighted some of the fiscal 1992 payments, including $4 million to the Dole Food Co. and $9 million to Sunkist Growers, members were unable to justify spending another $200 million on the program and cut it to $75 million.

The panel also declined to fund a wetlands reserve program, for which President Bush had requested $161 million in fiscal 1993. The program, mandated by the 1990 farm bill, paid farmers for setting aside their wetlands. The program was designed to protect wetlands without financial hardship to farmers.

Appropriators said they would await the results of a nine-state pilot wetlands program then under way before allocating more funds.

## HOUSE FLOOR ACTION

The House on June 30 ignored calls to reorganize the Agriculture Department, and passed a $59 billion agriculture appropriations bill for fiscal 1993 that made no major changes in bedrock farm programs or the agencies that supported them.

After more than nine hours of debate, the House passed the bill (HR 5487), on a 312-99 vote, which trimmed spending for administrative costs and a popular but controversial international food loan program and eliminated federal overseas promotion of U.S. tobacco products. *(Vote 250, p. 60-H)*

But the major priorities of the bill remained the same as those approved by the Appropriations Committee. As approved by the House, agriculture programs would receive $13.5 billion, conservation programs would get $2.7 billion and rural development programs were slated to receive $2.9 billion.

Two longstanding farm programs escaped heavy cuts:

the Soil Conservation Service, one of the earliest New Deal farm programs, which tied a farmer's eligibility for subsidies to his farm conservation practices; and the Agriculture Department's Extension Service, which conducted outreach programs on farming and nutrition and had offices in each of the nation's 3,150 counties.

To stay within caps placed on domestic discretionary spending, the bill would have frozen most programs, including all salary and administrative expenses — except for those at the FDA — at their fiscal 1992 levels. The resulting bill had a price tag that was $1.4 billion less than Bush requested.

But even pressing budget constraints did not lead lawmakers to eliminate $57.7 million for special research projects, many of which were slated for the home districts of appropriators. These special projects included $260,000 to study cranberry and blueberry diseases in New Jersey and $120,000 to research animal-waste disposal in Michigan.

The House, however, did turn back repeated efforts to provide funding for environmentally sensitive farm programs mandated by the 1990 farm bill (PL 101-624) in favor of existing farm programs.

Overall, the biggest loser was the market promotion program. It was a longtime target of Appropriations Committee Chairman Whitten.

The committee had cut the program from $200 million to $75 million. The House went further, and approved by a 331-82 vote an amendment by Wayne Owens, D-Utah, to stop any of the program's funds from being used to promote tobacco products overseas. *(Vote 249, p. 60-H)*

On the House floor, the ailing Whitten allowed Matthew F. McHugh, D-N.Y., to control action on the agriculture bill June 30.

But many members took to the floor to pay tribute to the 82-year-old man who had controlled the agriculture spending bill almost continuously since 1949. Natcher called Whitten "the best friend the American farmer has had in the last 50 years."

And Bob Traxler, D-Mich., praised Whitten's tenure in the House, saying, "Someday someone might serve here for a longer period of time, but no one will ever serve any better."

The strength of support for Whitten provided some insight into the easy defeat of amendments that would have funded several new farm programs at the expense of programs he supported.

Jim Jontz, D-Ind., found it rough going when he unsuccessfully offered several amendments to fund the programs, created under the 1990 farm bill. *(1990 Almanac, p. 323)*

Among them was the wetlands reserve program. The wetlands program had received $46 million in fiscal 1992, enough money to protect roughly 50,000 acres, according to Jontz. But the bill would have provided no money for the program in fiscal 1993 and would have prohibited the Agriculture Department from expanding the program until a status report on the program was completed.

Jontz's effort to shift $46 million from flood prevention programs to the wetlands program was defeated 109-308. *(Vote 244, p. 60-H)*

"I thought the farm bill did a good job of avoiding a collision between environmentalists and farmers," Jontz said. "But these programs will not work if they're not funded."

Jontz cited a letter from the Bush administration that

bemoaned scant funding for wetlands as one of the major flaws in the bill.

But McHugh countered that there was not enough money to go around and that results should be studied before spending more money.

Jontz also lost a fight to provide $120,000 for an independent board to set standards for organic foods, and was defeated in his attempt to cut 10 percent — roughly $5.7 million — from members' earmarked research programs and divert the money to organic farming research. Both defeats came on voice votes.

Also rejected was Jontz's attempt to increase to $30 million a water-quality project that encouraged farmers to use less chemicals in farming, thus producing less chemical-tainted runoff. The bill provided $6.75 million for the program. That amendment failed 18-396. *(Vote 245, p. 60-H)*

And despite impassioned pleas for fiscal restraint, Harris W. Fawell, R-Ill., and Timothy J. Penny, D-Minn., also lost their joint effort to delete $57.7 million in research money for special projects. The House crushed the amendment on a 126-295 vote. *(Vote 243, p. 58-H)*

Fawell said such projects were the "purest form of pork-barrel spending" and had never undergone the scrutiny of public hearings and markups.

But David Price, D-N.C., countered that "agriculture research is important, it is vital, it is an investment in our future."

One spending cut adopted during the marathon session was a roughly $50 million slice from the overhead accounts of all agencies covered under the bill except the FDA.

Also cut was $25 million from the $1.6 billion program that distributed U.S. food to less-developed or famine-stricken countries.

## SENATE COMMITTEE ACTION

The Senate Appropriations Committee on July 23 approved by voice vote a $61.4 billion spending bill for fiscal 1993 for the Agriculture Department and related agencies.

The measure reflected a tremendous surge in the number of Americans eligible for supplemental food assistance. Almost half the bill's funds — $29 billion — were for the food stamps program in fiscal 1993, up $6 billion from fiscal 1992.

The amount revealed a trend in the agriculture appropriations bill toward more spending for domestic food programs and less for typical farm programs. Arkansas' Bumpers said July 22 that the bill was "more an urban bill than a rural bill."

Thad Cochran, R-Miss., concurred: "What once was an agriculture appropriations bill has now become a nutrition bill."

Bumpers called the Women, Infants and Children special supplemental feeding program a "top priority" for the panel, which approved a 10 percent increase in the program's funding to $2.86 billion, the same as the House-passed bill.

As approved by the committee, agriculture programs would get $13.5 billion, conservation programs $2.7 billion and rural development $2.9 billion in fiscal 1993, also in line with the House-passed numbers.

Like the House-passed bill, the Senate measure would have frozen most personnel and overhead accounts at their fiscal 1992 spending levels. But increases in child nutrition programs, the food stamps program and a controversial

international marketing assistance program put the Senate bill's funding total at nearly $2.5 billion more than the House version.

The market promotion program won a reprieve from the Senate panel. The Bush administration had requested $200 million for the program, but the House cut the spending to $75 million. The Senate bill restored the bulk of the funds, giving the program $174.5 million for fiscal 1993.

Bumpers conceded that "perhaps there have been excesses" in the program but said that it provided a much-needed boost to American goods. He also said the huge House cut would have sent a message to program administrators that Congress would oversee the program carefully.

Both the House and Senate bills prohibited the Agriculture Department from continuing its pilot program to streamline inspections at slaughterhouses after April 1, 1993. The bills provided an additional $39 million to hire more inspectors and prevent employee furloughs.

The Senate bill also did not fund the wetlands reserve program. Cochran commended both the wetlands and another conservation program as "excellent environmental programs" and said he was unhappy that the committee did not have the $161 million the Bush administration had requested for the programs.

Bumpers said he, too, wished that there had been enough funds to go around. But he signaled that, until the Agriculture Department included Arkansas in the states eligible for the wetlands program, funding would not be forthcoming.

The states eligible to participate in the pilot program were California, Iowa, Louisiana, Minnesota, Mississippi, Missouri, New York, North Carolina and Wisconsin.

Despite tight fiscal constraints, senators managed to find $61.6 million for special research projects requested by members, commonly called pork barrel spending.

These projects included $1.4 million for alternative pest control in Arkansas, $2 million for a biotechnology consortium in Iowa and $250,000 to research alternative uses for potatoes in North Dakota.

## SENATE FLOOR ACTION

Despite concerns about federal spending, the Senate on July 28 turned back several attempts to slice funds from the $61.4 billion fiscal 1993 spending bill for the Agriculture Department and related agencies.

The Senate passed the bill (HR 5487) on a vote of 88-9 after shunning three cost-cutting amendments that would have eliminated a federal subsidy program for honey, slashed about $100 million from a controversial market promotion program and frozen spending for the Rural Electrification Administration at fiscal 1992 levels. *(Vote 158, p. 21-S)*

The Senate, by voice vote, diverted $54.9 million from farm program administrative expenses to the wetlands reserve program. And at least two senators — Paul Simon, D-Ill., and David L. Boren, D-Okla. — got approval from their peers to earmark funds for special, hometown projects they had sought. But when it came to cutting programs to reduce federal deficit spending, the Senate declined.

On a tabling motion that passed 56-41, the Senate killed an amendment by Hank Brown, R-Colo., that would have eliminated funding for a program that supported domestic honey prices. *(Vote 157, p. 21-S)*

Brown said that the program was unnecessary and that its elimination would have shaved $23 million off the bill's

overall price tag.

Domestic beekeepers were eligible for government loans equal to a minimum of 53.8 cents for each pound of honey produced. The loans essentially set a floor for domestic honey prices because the government agreed to buy the honey that beekeepers were unable to sell at that price.

Proponents said the program ensured crop pollination and argued that eliminating the program would offer minimal savings.

"This is a brave assault on the federal deficit here tonight," Kent Conrad, D-N.D., said sarcastically. "Let's get serious. This isn't even worth talking about."

But opponent John H. Chafee, R-R.I., said only 1 percent of the nation's 212,000 beekeepers were enrolled in the program — many of them from North Dakota and South Dakota. He added that the program had cost an average of $56 million a year over the past five years.

Chafee also reminded the program's predominantly Democratic supporters that Democratic presidential nominee Arkansas Gov. Bill Clinton had called for its elimination.

"The only way we are going to solve this budget deficit is that each step counts," said Chafee. "There is no silver bullet."

In another cost-cutting effort, Richard H. Bryan, D-Nev., was able to get only 23 senators to agree to his amendment to slash $100 million from the market promotion program that provides grants to private companies to promote U.S. products overseas. (Vote 156, p. 21-S)

About $200 million a year was spent on the program to help companies cover the cost of advertising domestically grown goods overseas by granting them a subsidy. But news reports drew attention to the fact that program recipients included highly profitable American companies, such as Pillsbury Co. and Welch Foods Inc.

Bryan said the program was "simply out of control" and amounted to "corporate welfare."

But Bumpers mounted a successful, passionate defense.

He argued that the program was necessary to help U.S. companies compete in the world market. Bumpers also circulated a letter showing how much each state benefited from the program.

Brown countered that American products "sell because of their attributes and because they are competitive," not because the government underwrites their promotion overseas.

The only major change to the bill came when members agreed to fund the wetlands reserve program at $54.9 million in fiscal 1993. The amount was more than $100 million less than Bush requested. The House-passed bill included no funding for the program.

To get the money, the Senate cut $28.2 million from computer purchases by the federal crop insurance program and the Agricultural Stabilization and Conservation Service, which administered farm programs and had offices in almost every county in the nation. An additional $26.7 million was transferred from the Commodity Credit Corporation, which essentially served as the Agriculture Department's bank.

Patrick J. Leahy, D-Vt., chairman of the Agriculture Committee and sponsor of the amendment, called the wetlands program the "heart of an historic compromise" between farmers and environmentalists in the 1990 farm bill.

Leahy used the amendment to criticize Agriculture Secretary Madigan for not moving more quickly to streamline the department's thousands of field offices. Leahy and

Richard G. Lugar, R-Ind., had been pushing Madigan to close unnecessary farm program field offices. (Downsizing USDA, p. 214)

"It makes no sense to modernize four computer systems if the four farm service agencies were to be consolidated," Leahy said.

The bill also bogged down over a heated debate about the so-called earnings test for Social Security recipients. In the end, the Senate agreed by voice vote to an amendment by John McCain, R-Ariz., that would express the sense of the Senate that the earnings test should be repealed or changed.

Under existing law, working Social Security recipients got fewer benefits if they earned more than $10,200 in 1992. The earnings limit was indexed to inflation and changed yearly. McCain, who faced re-election in a state with a vocal elderly population, wanted the test repealed. (Earnings test, p. 469)

"It is clear that this is an issue of fairness. We need the skill and experience of older Americans. The earnings test is outdated, unjust and clearly discriminatory," McCain said.

Supporters of the earnings test contended that eliminating it would predominantly benefit wealthy, elderly Americans.

"I have seen some giveaways come to this floor in 16 years, but none so blatant and irresponsible as this," said Daniel Patrick Moynihan, D-N.Y.

In the last amendment of the lengthy session, Tom Harkin, D-Iowa, was forced to abandon an effort to restrict the pre-election travel of Bush administration political appointees. The amendment would have limited such trips from Oct. 1 through Nov. 4 to no more than the number traveled during the same period in 1991.

But Minority Leader Bob Dole, R-Kan., denounced the move as "pure petty politics" and warned Democrats that he would block any further time agreements if the amendment succeeded — a threat that would have brought Senate action to a halt. Harkin withdrew his amendment.

## CONFERENCE ACTION

House and Senate negotiators Aug. 6 crafted a $60.5 billion compromise fiscal 1993 spending measure for the Agriculture Department and related agencies that salvaged a controversial marketing program but provided no spending for a wetlands reserve initiative.

The price tag of the final agreement reached by conferees was midway between the Senate-passed $61.4 billion measure and the $59 billion bill passed by the House on June 30.

Negotiators made a clear trade-off on the two major items in disagreement between the two chambers' spending bills: House conferees agreed to double their appropriation to $150 million for the marketing program and Senate negotiators agreed to go along with a House proposal to provide no funds for the wetlands reserve program.

Lawmakers also agreed on a compromise figure of $40 million for a debt relief program for the nations of Latin America — which was a top priority for the Bush administration. The agreement represented a middle ground between the $69.5 million that the House bill would have provided at Bush's request and the $13 million the Senate bill would have allocated.

Bush and the State Department had put on a full-court press to get funding for the program, known as the Enter-

prise for the Americas Initiative.

But negotiators spent most of their time during the nine-hour session tussling over special projects requested by members. A $2.7 million proposal for a regional research center at the University of Maine to discover different uses for wood, which the Senate included in its bill at the behest of Majority Leader George J. Mitchell, D-Maine, held up a final conference agreement for hours.

Conferees eventually agreed to provide nearly $4.2 million for wood utilization research and included language supporting both the Maine project and another in North Carolina.

The wetlands program also prompted controversy. Bumpers, acting chairman of the Senate Agriculture Appropriations Subcommittee, first said he was unwilling to eliminate all spending for the wetlands program because "the Senate has very strong feelings about this program."

But House negotiators prevailed, arguing that no funding for the program should be provided until the Agriculture Department completes its evaluation of it. "We don't have enough information" to judge how it is working, said Matthew F. McHugh, D-N.Y.

In the end, Bumpers agreed to take the $54.9 million out of the bill. Negotiators agreed to include language in the conference report that required the Agriculture Department to disclose to Congress how the program was doing within 90 days after the bill becames law.

Conferees also restored in the compromise bill much of the $54.9 million that the Senate version would have cut for

Agriculture's computer systems. The Senate bill had redirected that money to the wetlands program.

After giving ground on the wetlands program, Senate negotiators showed little willingness to slash funding for the market promotion program.

Sen. Bob Kerrey, D-Neb., said the market promotion program was necessary to help U.S. goods and companies sell abroad. And Bumpers cited Agriculture Department statistics showing that the program created 38,000 U.S. jobs.

Senate negotiators dug in their heels in support of the initiative and conferees finally agreed to provide the $150 million for the beleaguered program. But in a bow to House concerns, conferees included "tough" report language intended to correct some of the past abuses.

Richard J. Durbin, D-Ill., arguing unsuccessfully for the House position, said that while he "believed in the [program's] concept," he had deep concerns that it had not been "managed well." He said that approving $150 million for the program would send the wrong signal to the Agriculture Department that it was "business as usual."

### Final Action

The Senate Aug. 11 cleared for the president a $60.5 billion agriculture appropriations bill by voice vote (HR 5487 — PL 102-341). The House had adopted the conference report on a 299-100 vote earlier the same day. (Vote 379, p. 92-H)

President Bush signed the bill Aug. 14.  ∎

# D.C. Appropriations Tied to Social Issues

Congress cleared a spending bill for the District of Columbia government in time for the city's Oct. 1 start of the 1993 fiscal year but not before imposing its will on city policy.

Lawmakers sent President Bush two versions of the spending bill because Bush vetoed the first one (HR 5517) complaining that the bill failed to prohibit the city from using local funds for abortions, although the bill had banned the use of federal funds for the procedure.

Congress then cleared a new bill (HR 6056) on Sept. 30, which included a ban on both local and federal funds for abortions except when the procedure could save the woman's life.

The House on Sept. 30 passed HR 6056, 230-160. The Senate then cleared the new bill later the same day by voice vote.

Although expected, the veto still angered House Appropriations D.C. Subcommittee Chairman Julian C. Dixon, D-Calif., and many city officials, including D.C. Mayor Sharon Pratt Kelly. Dixon said that even though the Supreme Court ruled in June 1992 that states cannot outlaw all abortions, "the law of the land makes no difference to President Bush."

Dixon said he did not push for a veto override because "the votes are not there."

As cleared, HR 6056 provided the city with a federal payment of $624.9 million to compensate for being home to the federal government.

And it included $5.6 million to help city hospitals cope with the cost of uncompensated care at hospital trauma

centers.

The measure also provided $52 million for federal contributions to city employees' retirement funds and $5.5 million to pay for expenses associated with the 1993 presidential inaugural.

But these dollar figures were down substantially from the $714 million the House had originally planned to give the District government, which had included $30 million for an anti-crime initiative proposed by Mayor Kelly. But congressional leaders heeded Bush's threat that he would veto any spending bill that came in over his budget request and brought all the spending bills in line with the president's wishes. The bill's total was then reduced to $688 million.

The measure also allowed the city to raise $4 billion of its own funds through taxes and the city lottery.

When providing the District of Columbia with federal funds, Congress and the Bush administration often took the opportunity to influence city policy as well.

In addition to the restriction on using local funds for abortions, the measure also ordered a citywide referendum on instituting the death penalty and prohibited the city from spending any funds to implement a new law allowing unmarried couples to register as domestic partners in order to qualify for certain health benefits.

The death penalty initiative, placed on the Nov. 3 ballot, was soundly rejected by 67 percent of the District's voters.

The provision ordering the death penalty vote was added in the Senate by Richard C. Shelby, D-Ala., whose

former legislative aide, Thomas Barnes, was murdered on Capitol Hill.

## BACKGROUND

Because the District was the federal city its spending bill was never immune from political symbolism and personal politicking. Abortion activists, for example, had used the bill since 1989 to roll back a ban on the use of federal funds for abortion in the District unless the woman's life was in danger. Consequently, the District spending bill was also vetoed in 1989 and 1991 over the abortion language. *(1989 Almanac, p. 757; 1991 Almanac, p. 616)*

The annual federal payment to the District was supposed to cover the costs and lost tax revenues that resulted from the federal presence in the city. The federal government owned 43.2 percent of the land area in the District of Columbia but paid no real estate taxes. The federal government also demanded numerous services from the city.

Over the years, there had been considerable debate as to how to set the federal payment. The 1973 home rule bill had authorized the federal payment at certain levels, fixing it at $425 million for 1985 and beyond. But when the relationship between Congress and then-Mayor Marion S. Barry Jr. soured in the late 1980s, the federal payment froze as city expenditures grew.

The 1990 election of Sharon Pratt Kelly as mayor, with her "clean sweep" campaign pledge, broke the impasse with Congress temporarily. A law (PL 102-102) was passed in 1991 that established a formula for determining the annual federal payment to the city. *(1990 Almanac, p. 190)*.

However, the brief honeymoon between the new District mayor and Congress faded throughout 1992, as evidenced by the renewed push for statehood, a proposal to give the District more autonomy from the demands of Congress as well as voting representatives on Capitol Hill. *(D.C. statehood initiative, p. 223)*

## HOUSE COMMITTEE ACTION

Under the spending bill approved June 23 by the House District of Columbia Appropriations Subcommittee, the city received $30.8 million in federal funds to help combat crime.

Approved by voice vote, the bill gave the city $624.9 million in federal funds, which was provided to compensate for costs and lost tax revenues that resulted from hosting the federal government. That amount was about $6 million less than the $630.5 million the city received in fiscal 1992.

But with the $30.8 million to fight crime added in, the city would have received a total of $655.6 million in federal funds — the amount requested by Mayor Kelly.

Reaching that amount was important to city officials

---

## BOXSCORE

➡ **Fiscal 1993 appropriations for the District of Columbia (HR 6056, HR 5517).** The $4.7 billion spending bill provided a $624.8 million federal payment to the District and allowed the city to raise $4 billion in local revenue. HR 5517 was vetoed by President Bush over abortion-related language.

**Reports:** HR 5517: H Rept 102-638; S Rept 102-333; conference report HR 102-899; recommitted conference report HR 102-906.

### KEY ACTION

**July 8** — The **House** passed HR 5517 by voice vote.

**July 30** — The **Senate** passed HR 5517 by voice vote.

**Sept. 23** — HR 5517 approved by **House-Senate** conference.

**Sept. 24** — The **House** adopted conference report by voice vote.

**Sept. 24** — The **Senate** cleared conference report by voice vote.

**Sept. 30** — President Bush vetoed HR 5517.

**Sept. 30** — The **House** passed HR 6056, 230-160; The **Senate** passed HR 6056 by voice vote.

---

because of the legislation enacted in 1991 authorizing a federal payment equal to 24 percent of local tax revenue, beginning in fiscal 1993. Under that formula, city officials estimated that they should receive $655 million.

As in past years, the D.C. spending bill was a focal point for debate over funding for abortions. As he did last year, D.C. Subcommittee Chairman Dixon included language stating that no federal funds in the bill could be used to perform an abortion except to save the woman's life.

The subcommittee bill made no mention, however, of whether the city's locally raised funds could be used to pay for abortions.

The D.C. spending bill received quick voice vote approval from the House Appropriations Committee on July 1, but bill sponsors expected a fight when the measure reached the House.

HR 5517 provided $624.9 million in federal payments to reimburse the city for the cost of housing the federal government. It also included a one-time federal contribution of $30.8 million to help fight the city's high crime rate.

## HOUSE FLOOR ACTION

A law enacted in the District of Columbia that would have benefited domestic partners sparked emotional debate in the House on July 8 before lawmakers passed HR 5517, a spending measure that provided $714 million in federal funds for the city.

Under the city's policy, unmarried partners, homosexual couples and the children of such "non-traditional" families were allowed to register with the city. In turn, the law permitted partners of District government employees, and their children, to be eligible for the group health insurance offered to city employees.

Rep. Clyde C. Holloway, R-La., objected strongly to the new policy and sought to offer an amendment prohibiting any of the bill's funds from being used to implement the domestic partners law.

Holloway said he was disturbed by the policy because he believed its original intent "was to make it legal to have same-sex marriages in this country."

He argued that while the domestic partners policy was portrayed as a "harmless way to extend health-care benefits," in practice it "would undermine the institution of marriage and will send shock waves through society."

But Dixon said the real issue behind the amendment was whether the District of Columbia had a right "to promulgate rules and regulations governing benefits for its citizens."

Dixon's view was supported by fellow California Democrat Ronald V. Dellums, chairman of the House District of Columbia Committee, who urged his colleagues to move beyond this "absurd and ridiculous debate."

## District of Columbia Spending

*(in thousands of dollars)*

| | Fiscal 1992 Appropriation | President Bush's 1993 Request | House Bill | Senate Bill | Final Bill |
|---|---|---|---|---|---|
| **Appropriations to D.C.** | | | | | |
| Federal payment | $630,500 | $630,500 | $624,854 | $624,854 | $624,854 |
| Contributions to retirement fund | 52,070 | 52,070 | 52,070 | 26,035 | 52,070 |
| Advance appropriation, fiscal year 1994 | 0 | 0 | 0 | 28,027 | 0 |
| Federal contribution to crime and youth initiative | 0 | 0 | 30,799 | 30,799 | 0 |
| Inaugural expenses | 0 | 5,514 | 5,514 | 0 | 5,514 |
| Other | 13,280 | 0 | 483 | 2,519 | 5,562 |
| Subtotal | 695,850 | 688,084 | 713,720 | 712,234 | 688,000 |
| **Other Appropriations** | | | | | |
| D.C. Institute for Mental Health | 1,000 | 0 | 140 | 1,000 | 0 |
| Children's National Medical Center | 3,000 | 0 | 140 | 2,000 | 0 |
| George Washington University Medical Center | 0 | 0 | 0 | 250 | 0 |
| Advance appropriation, fiscal 1994 | 0 | 0 | 0 | 24,875 | 0 |
| Advance appropriation, fiscal 1995 | 0 | 0 | 0 | 24,875 | 0 |
| International Very Special Arts | 0 | 0 | 0 | 500 | 0 |
| **Total, Federal Funds** | 699,850 | 688,084 | 714,000 | 765,734 | 688,000 |
| Appropriations, fiscal 1993 | 0 | (688,084) | (714,000) | (687,957) | (688,000) |
| District-raised funds | $3,895,772 | 4,013,658 | 3,954,141 | 4,026,177 | 3,988,421 |
| **Total D.C. budget** | $4,595,622 | $4,701,742 | $4,668,141 | $4,791,911 | $4,676,421 |

SOURCE: House Appropriations Committee

Dellums asked, "What makes us think we are more intelligent, more moral and more ethical than people in the District of Columbia who have these rights and prerogatives?"

Holloway was denied the opportunity to offer his amendment on a procedural vote that effectively blocked any more amendments. After the House voted 231-181 in favor of that move, the bill was passed by a voice vote. *(Vote 275, p. 66-H)*

### Funds To Curb Crime

The appropriations bill also included a one-time federal contribution of $30.8 million to boost the city's anti-crime effort. The funds were to be directed to Mayor Kelly's youth and crime initiative.

Dixon told the House that "our committee is greatly concerned about the serious problems of crime and violence in the District."

District of Columbia Delegate Eleanor Holmes Norton, a Democrat, told Dixon she appreciated the fact that the committee did not try to tell the District how to solve the crime crisis.

The bill required, however, that the mayor and the city council submit to Congress a joint report detailing the objectives and funding requirements of the anti-crime program.

The city's crime rate also motivated an unsuccessful amendment drafted by Bob McEwen, R-Ohio. The amendment would have prohibited use of the bill's funds to enforce a current restriction on the possession or use of Mace in the District.

McEwen said city residents, particularly women, who wanted to use Mace for protection should be allowed to carry it.

But Dixon said the issue should be left to the city council to resolve, adding that city council Chairman John A. Wilson had said he would move on emergency legislation to legalize the use of Mace in the city. McEwen then agreed to withdraw his amendment.

### Abortion Language Reappears

As approved by the House, the legislation stated that no federal funds in the bill could be used for an abortion except to save the woman's life. But the measure placed no restrictions on the use of District funds to pay for abortions.

Similar language in the 1991 bill resulted in a veto by President Bush, and a prohibition on the use of District funds for abortions was eventually added.

In 1992, House abortion opponents also relied on a presidential veto to prevent the use of local funds for abortions.

Christopher H. Smith, R-N.J., co-chairman of the Pro-Life Caucus, said that because the bill's abortion language reversed existing law, the president would veto it. Smith dismissed as a diversionary tactic the argument that restricting the use of local funds denied District residents the right to home rule.

"I would suggest that respect for home rule is not absolute and certainly does not take precedence over respect for human life," Smith said.

D.C. Delegate Norton reminded Smith that the Supreme Court, "dominated by members of his own party," ruled recently that there should be "at the very least, local options on the troublesome question of abortion, and so what we have in the United States is a local option for everyone, every one of the 50 states and all of the territories — except for the District of Columbia."

## Bush Veto Message

*Following is the text of Bush's Sept. 30 veto of HR 5517, the fiscal 1993 appropriations for the District of Columbia.*

I am returning herewith without my approval HR 5517, a bill providing appropriations for fiscal year 1993 for the District of Columbia.

Although I do not object to the funding provided by the bill, its language concerning the use of funds for abortion is unacceptable. I have stated my intention to veto any bill that does not contain language that prohibits the use of all congressionally appropriated funds to pay for abortions except when the life of the mother would be endangered if the fetus were carried to term. The limitation I propose is identical to the one included in the District of Columbia Appropriations Acts for FY 1989, FY 1990, FY 1991, and FY 1992.

HR 5517 would place such a limitation on the use of Federal funds to pay for abortion. However, the bill would permit congressionally appropriated local funds to be used for abortions on demand. As a matter of law, the use of local funds in the District of Columbia must be approved by Congress and the President through enactment of an appropriations act. Under these circumstances, the failure of HR 5517 to prohibit the use of all funds appropriated by the bill to pay for abortions, except in the limited circumstances mentioned above, is unacceptable.

From the outset of my Administration, I have repeatedly stated my deep personal concern about the tragedy in America of abortion on demand. As a Nation, we must protect the unborn. HR 5517 does not provide such protection. I am therefore returning HR 5517 without my approval.

## SENATE COMMITTEE ACTION

In approving HR 5517 on July 23, the Senate Appropriations Committee found a way to give the city the funds it needed to operate but did so only by deferring half of the annual federal contribution to the city employee retirement fund.

District of Columbia Subcommittee Chairman Brock Adams, D-Wash., said the action, which reduced the retirement fund contribution from $52 million to $26 million for fiscal 1993, was "bad policy and bad government" but necessary to give the city the funds it needed.

The shortfall was expected to be made up in fiscal 1994, and Adams emphasized that the funds were only deferred, not cut. The full committee approved the bill by voice vote, a day after the subcommittee gave it similar approval.

The subcommittee's ranking Republican, Christopher S. Bond, Mo., agreed that cutting the retirement fund was a bad move because of the precedent it might set.

Senate appropriators faced a difficult task in 1992 because their allocation for federal funding for the District of Columbia totaled $688 million, about $26 million less than the $714 million provided by the House.

Both the Senate and House bills provided $624.9 million to cover the costs of housing the federal government and $30.8 million in a one-time contribution to help the city fight crime.

But the spending bills differed in other funding categories. The House bill earmarked $5.5 million for the 1993 presidential inauguration and $400,000 for the Metropolitan Police Department. The Senate bill set aside no funds for either program.

And the bill approved by the Senate Appropriations Committee provided $250,000 for the renovation of George Washington University Hospital, while the House version included no such funds.

Senate appropriators allotted $2 million to the Children's National Medical Center trauma and research center, while the House bill provided $140,000.

The measure also authorized the city to spend about $4 billion of its own locally raised revenue, a figure similar to the House-approved bill.

### Sewage Fees

The only disagreement over the bill during the Senate Appropriations Committee and earlier subcommittee action occurred over a regional dispute involving the assessment of sewage treatment fees.

In its fiscal 1993 budget, the District government had called for levying a fee on users of the city's Blue Plains Wastewater Treatment Plant, which served suburban residents in Maryland and Virginia. The assessment was to bring about $12 million into the city coffers. About $3 million of that amount was to come from residents in Maryland and Virginia.

But the Maryland and Virginia congressional delegations vigorously opposed the proposed fee and argued that the 1973 Home Rule charter forbade the District from levying taxes on its neighbors.

Rep. Steny H. Hoyer, D-Md., was successful in getting language added to the House bill that prohibited the city from assessing the sewer fee. He claimed that the fee was simply "a backdoor commuter tax."

But when the Senate subcommittee considered the bill, Adams stripped Hoyer's language and added a provision to allow the District to charge the fee for one year, starting Jan. 1, 1993, and required that the local jurisdictions undertake negotiations to resolve the issue. Adams said that the matter was a regional problem and should be settled on the local level.

But Hoyer, who stood in the back of the room throughout the subcommittee markup, had an ally in Maryland Sen. Barbara A. Mikulski, D, a member of the full Appropriations Committee.

When the full committee met the next day, Mikulski successfully offered an amendment removing Adams' provision and restoring the House sewer tax prohibition. Mikulski's amendment was approved by voice vote, with Adams casting the only "no" vote.

Like the House bill, the Senate bill stated that no federal funds could be used for abortions except to save a woman's life, but it placed no restrictions on the use of local funds for abortions.

## SENATE FLOOR ACTION

Concerns about crime and violence in the nation's capital dominated Senate debate July 30 on the D.C. spending bill.

And while senators ultimately agreed to provide $766 million in federal funds to the District government over fiscal years 1993 and 1994, they also voted to attach some strings to the federal payment.

As passed on a voice vote, the Senate version of the bill required District voters to choose whether to allow the death penalty for first-degree murder convictions. That was a compromise from an earlier amendment that would have made murder convictions in the District a capital offense.

The push to attach a capital punishment provision came from Alabama Democratic Sen. Shelby, whose former legislative aide, Thomas Barnes, was shot to death on Capitol Hill in January. Shelby introduced his amendment by reading off the names and ages of the 248 murder victims that were killed so far in 1992.

Carl Levin, D-Mich., threatened to filibuster the Shelby amendment, prompting Adams to seek a compromise. Adams' first proposal would have allowed the city to hold a citywide referendum on the death penalty in the next election.

But Shelby objected, saying the plebiscite might not come before 1994. The Senate, voting 50-45, killed Adams' proposal on a tabling motion. *(Vote 164, p. 22-S)*

Adams then offered a modified version of his compromise, which required the District to hold the referendum within 90 days of enactment. Senators approved that language by voice vote.

Senators did not challenge the funding in the bill but sought to assert their will over the District's policies. Citing the biblical cities of Sodom and Gomorrah, Trent Lott, R-Miss., sought to prohibit the District government from implementing a new domestic partnership ordinance, which extended health and other benefits to unmarried couples, including homosexuals.

Adams' effort to table Lott's amendment failed, 41-51, and the language subsequently was approved by voice vote. *(Vote 165, p. 22-S)*

## FINAL ACTION

In the strange atmosphere of end-of-the-session legislating, Congress moved quickly the week of Sept. 21 to clear the District spending bill so the president could veto it.

House and Senate negotiators on HR 5517 averted one threatened veto Sept. 23 by cutting the bill to bring it into compliance with President Bush's request for $688 million in federal funds for the city.

But members expected the District spending measure to be vetoed anyway because it failed to include the abortion restrictions Bush wanted.

The bill prohibited using federal funds for abortions except to save the woman's life.

It said nothing, however, about the District using its own money to pay for abortions, an omission that caused Bush to veto it.

Both chambers approved the conference report by voice vote Sept. 24.

Before the House completed work on the conference agreement, it made its opinion known by voting on a couple of controversial local issues, blocking a city law allowing unmarried couples to register as domestic partners and ordering the city to hold a referendum on instituting the death penalty.

### Local Issues

When the conference report reached the House early Sept. 24, House members voted, 235-173, to send the bill back to conference with instructions to keep Senate language prohibiting any funds in the bill from being used to implement the city's domestic partnership law. *(Vote 420, p. 102-H)*

House opponents of the city's domestic partners policy said it legalized same-sex marriages.

Tom DeLay, R-Texas, who offered the motion, said the

nation's capital was a symbol to the nation and should recognize only "an intact family."

District supporters argued futilely that Congress should not overturn laws that the city government approved. House D.C. Subcommittee Chairman Dixon said the House action was "an affront to home rule." But Dixon also said he was not surprised by the vote because in an election year homosexuality was "too volatile" an issue for members to support.

After the House vote, negotiators met quickly later in the day and agreed to accept the Senate language.

In a personal reaction to the vote, Barney Frank, D-Mass., who in 1987 became the second member of Congress to acknowledge that he was gay, wondered how the action helped traditional families.

"I find it hard not to take this personally.... How does it help family values to inflict pain on other people?" Frank said.

The House also voted, 264-129, to accept Senate language requiring the city to hold a referendum on whether to allow the death penalty for first-degree murder convictions. *(Vote 428, p. 104-H)*

D.C. Delegate Norton pleaded with her colleagues not to force the District to have the referendum, saying that the District government was moving on its own toward such a vote. She asked them to "respect the democratic process" and "to let us do what you want us to do ourselves."

### The Dollar Amounts

To meet Bush's fiscal 1993 request, appropriators were faced with cutting $26 million from the House-passed bill and $5 million in fiscal 1993 funds from the Senate's version.

The program hit hardest was D.C. Mayor Kelly's crime and youth initiative, a comprehensive effort to curb the city's crime rate, which was provided with $30.8 million under both the House and Senate bills.

Conferees cut the funds. Senate D.C. Subcommittee Chairman Adams said all the bill's funding levels "went out the window" as a result of the veto threat.

HR 5517 gave the District government a federal payment of $624.9 million.

The bill also included $52 million for the federal contribution for city employee retirement funds. The Senate had halved this figure to provide funds for the mayor's crime initiative and other projects, but Senate conferees agreed to restore the full amount.

Negotiators agreed to provide $5.5 million for city expenses for the 1993 presidential inauguration and about $5.6 million to partially reimburse city hospitals for the cost of uncompensated care at hospital trauma centers.

### Veto and New Bill

As expected, Bush vetoed HR 5517 on Sept. 30 because the spending measure failed to prohibit the city from using local funds for abortions.

Once HR 5517 was returned to Congress, Dixon quickly brought up HR 6056, which included a ban on the use of local and federal funds for abortions except when the procedure could save the life of a woman, and the House on Sept. 30 passed it 230-160.

The Senate then cleared the new bill later the same day by voice vote. *(Vote 437, p. 106-H)*

The president signed HR 6056 (PL 102-382) on Oct. 5. ■

# Scaled-Back Interior Funding Zips Through

Congress cleared a fiscal 1993 appropriations bill for the Interior Department and related agencies that was filled with politically popular home-state projects, though overall spending levels were slimmed down from previous years.

The $12.15 billion spending measure (HR 5503) funded not only the Interior Department but the Agriculture Department's National Forest Service, the Energy Department's fuel research program, and a host of cultural and educational programs such as the Smithsonian Institution and the National Endowment for the Arts.

The conference report for the bill was approved by the House on a voice vote the morning of Sept. 30, and by the Senate a few hours later.

Rep. Ralph Regula, R-Ohio, noted that the bill was $74 million below President Bush's budget request, and $373 million below the fiscal 1992 allocation.

Sidney R. Yates, D-Ill., House Interior Appropriations Subcommittee chairman, said the bill would underfund the nation's natural resources. But Yates, like other appropriators, accepted the realities of a tight budget and a president threatening to veto any bills that came in over his request. Thus, a bill that in prior years had taken days to approve passed each chamber in a matter of minutes.

The lack of controversy was due in part to the bill's reduced nature; members, for example, were unable to win funding for new recreation visitor centers at national parks. It also reflected the fact that the perennial controversial items either were not in the bill or had been politically resolved.

For the previous several years, for example, attempts had been made to increase the fees ranchers paid to graze their cattle on public lands and increase the states' share of the cost of collecting royalties from oil and gas wells operating on federal land. Both moves were hotly opposed by Western lawmakers. Though the House approved both initiatives in 1992, negotiators dropped both. Conferees did retain a new annual fee to charge miners $100 to keep their mining claims active.

The National Endowment for the Arts, under attack during the past three years by critics who said it supported obscene art, had a new, politically conservative director — Anne-Imelda Radice — who strived in 1992 to limit the endowment's funding of art that could be considered sexually explicit or obscene.

That allowed the endowment to settle back into much-welcomed anonymity. Though the endowment garnered $175.9 million, the same amount as in fiscal 1992, it won a new funding category for an international arts program.

Still, even though the bill provided less spending than fiscal 1992's $12.5 billion allocation, appropriators found

---

## BOXSCORE

➤ **Fiscal 1993 appropriations for the Interior Department and related agencies (HR 5503).** The $12.15 billion measure provided funding for programs under the Interior Department and related agencies such as the Smithsonian Institution, National Endowment for the Humanities and National Endowment for the Arts.

**Reports:** H Rept 102-626; S Rept 102-345; conference report H Rept 102-901.

### KEY ACTION

July 23 — The **House** passed HR 5503, 329-94.

Aug. 6 — The **Senate** passed HR 5503 by voice vote.

Sept. 23 — A **House-Senate** conference approved report on HR 5503.

Sept. 30 — The **House** adopted conference report by voice vote; the **Senate** cleared conference report by voice vote.

Oct. 5 — President Bush signed HR 5503 — PL 102-381.

---

room for a slew of home-state projects.

For example, House appropriator Norm Dicks, D-Wash., fought hard for construction funds for a project known simply as "A Walk on the Mountain." The project called for building a covered skywalk in downtown Tacoma, Wash., which one Park Service officer noted was "well removed from any national park service area."

On a clear day, however, "A Walk on a Mountain" promised at least to provide a view of a park — Mount Rainier National Park — and to provide information about the peak.

Though Sen. Don Nickles, R-Okla., grumbled that the project looked like it "ought to be funded by the Chamber of Commerce, not the National Park Service," Dicks got $2 million in construction funding for it in the bill.

Negotiators also funded the Steamtown Railroad Museum in Pennsylvania, providing $13 million for the project, though it received much unfavorable publicity as an example of congressional pork barrel politics. Pennsylvania members pushing for the project were Republican Joseph M. McDade and Democrat John P. Murtha.

And in the National Forest recreation fund, appropriators directed that some $400,000 in recreation management and cultural resources be funneled to Wayne National Forest in eastern Ohio. The provision was pushed by ranking member Regula.

In the Forest Service budget, appropriators avoided the controversial issue of setting timber harvest targets for the Pacific Northwest, citing the "tremendous uncertainty facing the timber sales program at this time" — a reference to courtroom battles over the Endangered Species Act and the National Forest Management Act.

The bill also included an array of unusual provisions. One, pushed by Rep. James A. Traficant Jr., D-Ohio, mandated that all entities covered under the bill buy American-made goods and equipment.

Another amendment added in the Senate by Pete V. Domenici, R-N.M., singled out Hollywood for opprobrium, stating that Congress "believes that corporate America ... weaken[s] the moral fiber of the nation by hiding behind the faceless masks of such corporations and institutions in a relentless search for profits, sales and publicity without regard to the moral content of their products or services." The amendment pleaded for a return to personal and corporate responsibility.

## BACKGROUND

Perhaps more than any other appropriations bill, the Interior measure reflected the rapidly changing attitudes

# Interior Spending

*(HR 5503, as cleared for the president, in thousands of dollars)*

| | Fiscal 1992 | Fiscal 1993 Bush Request | House Bill | Senate Bill | Final Bill |
|---|---|---|---|---|---|
| **Interior Department** | | | | | |
| **Bureau of Land Management** | | | | | |
| Management of lands | $ 532,149 | $ 546,247 | $ 531,967 | $ 545,665 | $ 544,877 |
| Firefighting | 120,473 | 119,560 | 119,560 | 119,310 | 119,310 |
| Payments in lieu of taxes | 103,677 | 105,000 | 105,000 | 105,000 | 105,000 |
| Other | 253,747 | 279,707 | 262,054 | 267,162 | 267,733 |
| Subtotal | $ 1,010,046 | $ 1,050,514 | $ 1,018,581 | $ 1,037,137 | $ 1,036,920 |
| **Fish and Wildlife Service** | | | | | |
| Resource management | 512,870 | 544,075 | 530,211 | 531,177 | 535,085 |
| Construction, anadromous fish | 113,447 | 49,410 | 47,513 | 90,351 | 82,085 |
| Land acquisition | 97,891 | 79,509 | 67,397 | 78,615 | 76,192 |
| Other | 23,971 | 40,980 | 32,171 | 36,151 | 33,606 |
| Subtotal | $ 748,179 | $ 713,974 | $ 677,292 | $ 736,294 | $ 726,968 |
| **National Park Service** | | | | | |
| Operations | 953,498 | 1,031,813 | 992,059 | 989,282 | 992,431 |
| Construction | 272,326 | 137,686 | 237,806 | 206,570 | 231,801 |
| Land acquisition, state aid | 105,227 | 144,404 | 106,500 | 119,271 | 118,911 |
| Other | 56,117 | 55,478 | 43,452 | 51,778 | 51,752 |
| Subtotal | $ 1,387,168 | $ 1,369,381 | $ 1,379,817 | $ 1,366,901 | $ 1,394,895 |
| **Bureau of Indian Affairs** | | | | | |
| Indian programs | 1,274,322 | 1,256,483 | 1,354,151 | 1,335,944 | 1,353,899 |
| Construction | 149,658 | 81,591 | 152,446 | 141,746 | 150,896 |
| Other | 105,974 | 44,466 | 57,366 | 53,366 | 56,866 |
| Subtotal | $ 1,529,954 | $ 1,382,540 | $ 1,563,963 | $ 1,531,056 | $ 1,561,661 |
| Geological Survey | 582,619 | 540,267 | 587,668 | 570,821 | 581,692 |
| Minerals Management Service | 204,461 | 203,189 | 202,891 | 199,391 | 202,391 |
| Bureau of Mines | 174,464 | 141,364 | 173,056 | 176,513 | 175,729 |
| Office of Surface Mining | 111,181 | 113,482 | 113,874 | 113,874 | 113,874 |
| Territorial affairs | 141,629 | 95,833 | 128,404 | 120,097 | 125,357 |
| Department offices | 126,758 | 136,564 | 123,696 | 122,907 | 123,482 |
| **TOTAL, Interior** | $ 6,204,262 | $ 5,903,259 | $ 6,157,283 | $ 6,166,032 | $ 6,232,510 |
| **Forest Service (Agriculture Department)** | | | | | |
| National forest system | 1,342,529 | 1,367,727 | 1,312,937 | 1,306,077 | 1,318,481 |
| Forest research | 180,509 | 170,099 | 186,657 | 178,723 | 184,281 |
| Firefighting | 187,411 | 197,785 | 192,785 | 188,785 | 190,785 |
| Emergency firefighting fund | 110,589 | 187,000 | 187,000 | 187,000 | 187,000 |
| Construction | 271,711 | 310,525 | 241,449 | 258,570 | 257,447 |
| Timber receipts (to Treasury) | (−72,748) | (−75,366) | (−75,366) | (−75,366) | (−75,366) |
| Other | 277,890 | 305,780 | 205,805 | 229,635 | 227,317 |
| **TOTAL, Forest Service** | $ 2,370,639 | $ 2,538,916 | $ 2,326,633 | $ 2,348,790 | $ 2,365,311 |
| **Energy Department** | | | | | |
| Clean coal (delayed advance appropriation) | −50,000 | −25,000 | 0 | 0 | −525,000 |
| Fossil energy research | 444,332 | 311,325 | 412,597 | 422,669 | 421,939 |
| Naval Petroleum Reserve | 232,335 | 238,094 | 238,094 | 238,094 | 238,094 |
| Energy conservation | 536,322 | 521,430 | 591,859 | 571,288 | 583,866 |
| Strategic Petroleum Reserve | 77,287 | 50,975 | 50,975 | 50,975 | 50,975 |
| Other | 90,676 | 53,192 | 55,739 | 49,939 | 49,939 |
| **TOTAL, Energy Department** | $ 1,330,952 | $ 1,150,016 | $ 1,349,264 | $ 1,332,965 | $ 819,813 |
| **Other Related Agencies** | | | | | |
| Indian health | 1,705,954 | 1,651,452 | 1,898,211 | 1,847,632 | 1,874,351 |
| Indian education | 76,570 | 81,205 | 81,274 | 81,205 | 81,274 |
| Smithsonian Institution | 331,837 | 364,700 | 348,286 | 341,545 | 347,224 |
| National Endowment for the Arts | 175,955 | 175,955 | 175,955 | 174,745 | 175,955 |
| National Endowment for the Humanities | 175,955 | 187,059 | 178,934 | 178,678 | 178,934 |
| Other agencies | 151,276 | 171,984 | 181,328 | 172,607 | 180,103 |
| **GRAND TOTAL** | $ 12,523,400 | $ 12,224,546 | $ 12,649,152 | $ 12,643,449 | $ 12,150,492 [1] |

[1] *House grand total includes a 0.85 percent cut in discretionary spending of $104.98 million, not reflected in individual line items.*

SOURCE: House Appropriations Committee

and demographics of America in the 1990s.

The bill charted the nation's vacillation between one view, rooted in the settling of the West, that public lands were places of economic opportunity; and another, nourished in a region increasingly urban, that the lands were a natural endowment to be preserved for future generations.

Such wavering was seen in battles sparked by the bill's natural resource and land management programs at the Park Service, Bureau of Land Management, Fish and Wildlife Service and the Forest Service. It also resonated through the bill's perennial wild card — the National Endowment for the Arts (NEA).

Fault lines on the spending bill split along regional, not partisan, boundaries. Since the bulk of the nation's public lands were in the West, it was there that the battles were being fought.

Thus the Interior's Department once low-profile Bureau of Land Management became an arena for warring resource users, pitting those who valued the bureau's 269.5 million acres for grazing, logging and mining, against those who valued it for recreational and environmental purposes.

In the Forest Service, a similar struggle was under way as timber interests fought against a public that made little distinction between national parks, which were conserved, and national forests, which permitted logging. National forests were increasingly seen as valuable for endangered species and for recreation, uses often incompatible with logging.

Interior's Fish and Wildlife Service also was caught in the middle as the main implementer of the 1973 Endangered Species Act — a law that had become a lightning rod of competing priorities. The service's efforts to protect threatened salmon, for example, collided with the task of the Interior's Bureau of Reclamation, which managed the generation of cheap hydroelectric power in the West.

Not all the fights on the bill involved environmental politics. The NEA, one of the independent agencies funded under the bill, had provoked hours of debate in 1991 over whether federal arts funding should be extended without strings or whether funds should be restricted to art that met some specified moral standard. *(1991 Almanac, p. 555)*

The 1992 bill marked the first time in recent years that the NEA was quietly given its funding.

## HOUSE COMMITTEE ACTION

House appropriators on June 16 approved a $13.2 billion spending bill for the Interior Department and related agencies that included a 7 percent boost in budget authority for fiscal 1993 over fiscal 1992, but a host of prior-year commitments already had consumed much of the new spending.

The House Appropriations Subcommittee on the Interior also jumped into long-simmering controversies, proposing to raise both grazing fees for ranchers and fees that mining patent claim holders had to pay to keep claims active.

The Interior spending bill funded the agencies that managed the nation's vast natural resources, from mining to forests to national parks to wilderness areas. It also funded a panoply of cultural and artistic organizations such as the National Endowment for the Arts.

Even though the $13.2 billion in budget authority was 7 percent higher than fiscal 1992, the committee was allocated just $12.6 billion in outlays — money that appropri-

ators actually could spend. Of that, Chairman Yates estimated there would only be about $8.5 billion left over for fiscal 1993, once spending was set aside for previous commitments.

For example, in 1991, appropriators agreed to dramatically increase the fund to fight forest fires on land maintained by Interior's Bureau of Land Management and the Agriculture Department's Forest Service. But to do so, said Yates, appropriators put off paying about $328 million for the program until fiscal 1993.

The tough decisions needed to meet the looming spending restraints were what prompted Rep. Murtha to move to close the appropriations meeting. The subcommittee voted 8-2 to do so, with only Yates and Tom Bevill, D-Ala., voting to keep it open.

When members emerged from the two-hour markup, the subcommittee had crafted a bill that in its broad outlines was similar to the fiscal 1992 plan. There were no major changes in spending priorities, and the bill continued several past attempts to overhaul land-use policy — including increasing fees for mining patents and grazing, and continuing a moratorium on offshore oil exploration.

A number of agencies received modest increases under the bill: for example, the Forest Service received about $2.5 billion, compared with $2.26 billion for fiscal 1992; and the Bureau of Land Management, $1 billion, compared with $910.4 million in fiscal 1992.

The Bureau of Indian Affairs received $1.56 billion, about a $30 million increase over the $1.53 billion appropriated in fiscal 1992. The big winner, though, was a related program — the Indian Health Service, to which the subcommittee allotted $1.89 billion, about $184 million more than in fiscal 1992.

Yates said the Bush administration's request would have drastically underfunded the programs that provided health and medical services to about 1 million American Indians and Native Alaskans. He said it was the only area under which appropriators added substantial amounts of money to Bush's budget request.

Among the cultural agencies, the National Endowment for the Arts and the National Endowment for the Humanities each received slight increases to $178.9 million for fiscal 1993, compared with $175.9 million provided each agency in fiscal 1992. The Smithsonian Institution received a $16 million boost, to $348 million for fiscal 1993.

But several agencies were funded at levels below those of 1992, mainly because of deep cuts in their construction budgets: the Interior Department's National Park Service received $1.38 billion, compared with $1.39 billion for fiscal 1992; and the Fish and Wildlife Service received $677 million, compared with $748.2 million for fiscal 1992.

Once again, panel appropriators tackled a key controversy that bedeviled the bill in 1991, approving language that would increase grazing fees 33 percent. At the time, ranchers paid $1.97 a month per animal to graze on public lands. The provision increased that fee to $2.62 a month.

On another controversial issue, the bill set no new targets for timber harvests in the Pacific Northwest, home of the threatened northern spotted owl, nor did it limit judicial review of any proposed timber sales.

The bill included language urging the Forest Service to emphasize ecological considerations in managing forests and to minimize clear-cutting.

Panel member Dicks of Washington declined in 1992 to add any amendments setting aside money for retraining displaced timber workers in the Northwest, in the hope

that a comprehensive Pacific Northwest forest bill pending before the Interior and Agriculture committees would advance. No final action was taken in 1992 to balance forest protection with potential job loss. *(Old-growth forest protection, p. 277)*

The spending bill set aside up to $232 million for the Forest Service's timber sales program, which exceeded what was needed given the number of court injunctions now restricting such sales in the region. The bill, however, included language that would allow any excess money to be diverted to other areas.

Panel appropriators also sought to overhaul the nation's mining patent law by approving language that required claim holders to pay a $100 annual holding fee or lose their claim. In 1992, mining patent claim holders were only required to do $100 worth of "work" over the life of their claims to keep them active.

### Full Committee

A chaotic skirmish over a small timber-subsidy program stalled the $12.7 billion Interior appropriations bill just as House consideration was getting under way.

The controversy was over a program that called for $3.5 million in emergency payments to timber-dependent counties in the Pacific Northwest. Though the region's appropriators favored the program, a rule governing the bill's floor consideration — which was later overturned — allowed opponents to seek to strike the timber payments from the bill.

The battle represented the tip of a deeper, perennial fight between congressional authorizers and appropriators over who set policy.

Both sides sought to use HR 5503 as the battleground over control of public lands policy.

When the House Appropriations Committee approved the bill by voice vote June 29, they included spending for programs that the authorizing committees, which were supposed to write policy, had not approved.

The timber payments program was a case in point. Appropriators called for continuing for a third year "emergency" payments to Pacific Northwest counties where the timber industry had been hamstrung by a dispute over the threatened northern spotted owl.

Another section of the committee-approved bill overhauled the policy governing cattle-grazing on federal land and boosted grazing fees. Appropriators also prescribed policy for such small items as a proposed set of jetties at Oregon Inlet in North Carolina.

The actions agitated two authorizers who had been asserting their power on the Interior and Insular Affairs Committee, Chairman George Miller, D-Calif., and National Parks and Public Lands Subcommittee Chairman Bruce F. Vento, D-Minn. They complained that appropriators were encroaching on their turf by writing legislation in what should be a policy-neutral spending bill.

In a June 30 letter to Rules Committee Chairman Joe Moakley, D-Mass., Vento and Miller cited 31 policy provisions in HR 5503 that they said were under the jurisdiction of their panels.

"What they were doing was cherry-picking, taking all the plums and leaving us to serve vinegar," Vento said on July 1.

The Rules Committee, which had an unstated policy of deferring to authorizing committee chairmen when turf disputes were raised, agreed.

After Vento brought his complaints before Rules late in

the evening June 30, the panel cast a rule that allowed opponents to seek to strike 15 of the 31 disputed provisions on the floor. As a result, the timber payments program, among others, was left unprotected.

News about the action did not start trickling out until the next morning, July 1, just as the House was scheduled to take up the bill.

"It caught everyone flat-footed," said Les AuCoin, D-Ore., an appropriator who along with Dicks had written the timber-county payments provision in the spending bill. "To take this from Oregon counties would have hit them like a bolt out of the blue," AuCoin said.

He hustled over to the House floor after hearing about the rule. And with the help of a fellow Pacific Northwest lawmaker, Speaker Foley, AuCoin managed to have the bill pulled from the floor as members were giving opening statements. Foley required that the bill be sent back to the Rules Committee for a revised rule.

Foley called Moakley and argued, apparently persuasively, that the committee had blocked efforts to attack the timber program in previous years.

Within hours, the Rules Committee met a second time and agreed to block opponents from seeking to strike the timber-county payments from the bill.

The committee also agreed to allow E. "Kika" de la Garza, D-Texas, to offer an amendment on the floor to strike a bill provision that raised grazing fees by 33 percent. But the rule allowed opponents to seek to strike most of the other disputed provisions.

The panel also agreed to make 11 other items subject to approval only if they were formally authorized. Included was funding for the Bureau of Land Management, which needed to be reauthorized in 1992.

The rule was at least a partial victory for Vento and Miller. Both had been trying — so far unsuccessfully — to move a separate bill (HR 5099) to protect huge swaths of the ancient forests of the Pacific Northwest to save the northern spotted owl. The bill also included a provision to provide economic support to hard-hit timber communities in the Pacific Northwest. Miller and Vento viewed the provision as a politically necessary component to attract support for their broader measure.

"This will provide a good incentive for members to move on the broader issue" of forest policy, Vento said.

## HOUSE FLOOR ACTION

After heated debate over federal grazing fees and Northwest timber sales, the House on July 23 passed a $12.7 billion version of HR 5503.

The spending bill, which passed 329-94, provided $481 million more than the Bush administration requested. *(Vote 306, p. 74-H)*

The bill had been delayed for weeks while the rules governing debate were revised to clear the way for lawmakers to offer amendments striking unauthorized items.

But the Rules Committee, at the urging of Northwest appropriators and Speaker Foley, did not allow any amendment that killed the "emergency" payments to Northwest logging communities.

When the bill came to the floor July 22, Subcommittee Chairman Yates conceded that 11 other items had not been authorized and removed them from the bill.

As in past years, efforts to raise fees on ranchers who grazed cattle on federal lands prompted much of the controversy surrounding the bill. Lawmakers rejected by a

vote of 164-245 an effort by Charles W. Stenholm, D-Texas, to remove a proposed increase in grazing fees. *(Vote 300, p. 72-H)*

The existing fee was $1.97 per animal unit month — the amount of forage it took to feed a mature cow for a month. Proponents of raising the fee said the amount was a fraction of what ranchers paid to graze cattle on private land. The bill raised the fee by 30 percent to $2.56.

The grazing fee increase was similar to one proposed in a bill to reauthorize the Bureau of Land Management (HR 1096).

Proponents of raising the fees argued that large corporations that own herds and graze them on federal land should pay their fair share. Mike Synar, D-Okla., called the officials of oil and insurance companies that own large cattle herds "welfare cowboys" and said they benefit from an unwarranted grazing subsidy.

But Western lawmakers critical of raising grazing fees countered that smaller ranchers would be driven out of business by higher fees.

### Timber Sales

Lawmakers also sparred over timber sales in the Pacific Northwest, as well as the future of the 1973 Endangered Species Act.

Jim Jontz, D-Ind., sought to cut the amount of timber the National Forest Service allowed to be sold when such sales did not result in a profit to the Treasury. By reducing so-called below-cost timber sales, the amendment would have cut the bill's $1.3 billion appropriation for the service by $16.8 million, or 10 percent of the amount set aside for the preparation of timber harvests.

But in an effort to protect hometown logging jobs that depended upon such timber sales, Dicks and AuCoin successfully softened the effect of Jontz's amendment. They offered substitute language, which was narrowly approved, 212-206, to trim the Forest Service's administrative costs and achieve similar cost savings without limiting timber sales. The House then approved the altered Jontz amendment by voice vote. *(Vote 302, p. 74-H)*

Lawmakers earlier tangled over the trade-off between protecting the environment and preserving timber jobs. Rod Chandler, R-Wash., sought to highlight potential job losses by offering, but later withdrawing, an amendment that would have cut $8.5 million from the account to list endangered and threatened species.

Bill sponsors also averted another perennial battle to eliminate funding for the National Endowment for the Arts. An amendment by Philip M. Crane, R-Ill., to strike the $179 million for the endowment failed 85-329. *(Vote 298, p. 72-H)*

The House did, however, reduce endowment spending to fiscal 1992 levels when an amendment by Cliff Stearns, R-Fla., to cut $3 million from the agency's budget was approved 251-171. *(Vote 304, p. 74-H)*

Lawmakers also voted to lift a ban on deer hunting in the Mason Neck National Wildlife Refuge in Virginia, adopting an amendment by Bill Brewster, D-Okla., by a vote of 255-160. The spending bill had called for banning hunting in the area to respond to the safety concerns of nearby residents and protect the population of nesting eagles that used the area. *(Vote 299, p. 72-H)*

Lawmakers also approved:

● An amendment by Byron L. Dorgan, D-N.D., Lamar Smith, R-Texas, and Timothy J. Penny, D-Minn., that cut $48 million from administrative overhead costs of various agencies. The amendment was approved 257-162. *(Vote 296, p. 72-H)*

● An amendment by Joan Kelly Horn, D-Mo., to cut $224,000 from the office of the Interior secretary.

The House rejected an amendment by Barbara F. Vucanovich, R-Nev., that would have made the bill's ban on mining claim patents apply only to new patent applications filed after the bill became law. The amendment was rejected by voice vote.

## SENATE COMMITTEE ACTION

The $12.6 billion version of HR 5503 approved, 27-0, July 29 by the Senate Appropriations Committee had no hint of the 1991 controversy over "pornographic" art that bedeviled the bill's account for the National Endowment for the Arts.

Instead, Appropriations Committee Chairman Robert C. Byrd, D-W.Va., warned fellow appropriators that some senators might very well take a "meat ax" to the project-laden bill on the Senate floor in the name of fighting pork barrel projects.

Because most of the spending in the bill was discretionary, it attracted nearly 3,000 requests for local projects from 98 senators. Among them were recreation areas, research projects and land acquisition for parks.

But Byrd counseled caution when some senators pushed for pet projects, warning that too many special projects could threaten the bill.

"The Senate cannot and should not be accused of pork barrel spending," Byrd said July 28, as the Interior Appropriations Subcommittee marked up the bill. The next day, chairing the full committee, Byrd, who was well known for winning projects for West Virginia, rallied his colleagues to "withstand the meat-ax assaults to the bill on the floor."

The Interior spending bill, Byrd said, was crafted to avoid the 1991 policy controversies. The measure included no provisions to raise the fees ranchers paid to graze their cattle on public land. There was no moratorium on new mining patent claims and no attempt to make states pay more of the cost of collecting royalties from oil and gas wells on public lands. All of those provisions were in the House version that passed July 23.

Nonetheless, Senate floor debate was expected to get entangled in efforts to revamp the 1872 Mining Law, to halt money-losing timber sales and to prevent the Bush administration from limiting the rights of residents to mount legal challenges against logging in national forests.

The spending bill funded the management of about 460 million acres of publicly owned land, including the nation's parks, wildernesses and forests.

Many agencies were slated for cuts from spending levels approved in fiscal 1992: the Park Service was down by $20.9 million, the entire Interior Department by $37.7 million and the Forest Service by $23.6 million. The Indian Health Service was perhaps the only big winner; after years of cuts, it received a $141.7 million boost, to $1.85 billion in fiscal 1993.

But as was often the case, controversy revolved not around funding levels in the spending bill but around its policy prescriptions.

### Grazing Fees Sidestepped

The committee sidestepped one of the bill's perennial bones of contention: setting the price ranchers should pay the federal government to graze their cattle on public land.

In 1992, the fee was $1.92 per cow (or sheep) a month — a slight decrease from the 1991 level, and a price that was generally much lower than what private pastures charged.

The House-passed bill raised the fee 33.3 percent to $2.56 a month. Interior Department Secretary Manuel Lujan Jr. had said he would support changes in the fee structure.

But the Senate Appropriations Committee turned aside the issue; instead, it directed Interior to complete a new study on "new grazing fee concepts" by March 1, 1993.

### Mining Reform

Senate appropriators agreed to a modest step toward revising the 1872 Mining Law, which had long aroused the ire of environmentalists and fiscal conservatives.

In previous years, the Interior Appropriations Subcommittee, which had been dominated by Westerners, had refused any attempts to revamp the law, which made federal land available for mining at prices as low as $2.50 an acre. Critics said it had been abused by land speculators and allowed mining conglomerates to exploit the public's land while paying no royalties on the minerals they extracted.

One part of the law singled out by critics was the provision that claim holders conduct at least $100 worth of mining-related "work" each year. Critics contended that the work requirement only encouraged claim holders to scar the environment unnecessarily.

Urged on by the Bush administration, Senate appropriators joined their House counterparts by including a provision to turn the annual work requirement into an annual $100 fee to keep claims active. The fee could earn the government $41.3 million in revenues annually, according to the Congressional Budget Office.

But unlike the House, Senate appropriators declined to place a moratorium on new mining claims until separate legislation to overhaul the 1872 Mining Law moved through Congress. The House Interior and Insular Affairs Committee on June 24 approved a bill (HR 918) to temporarily halt future mining claims; another measure (S 433) was pending in the Senate. *(Mining law overhaul, p. 282)*

In a related matter, Senate appropriators refused to increase the states' share of the cost of collecting royalties from oil and gas operations on federal land.

In 1992, the federal government charged states 25 percent of its collection costs. The House bill increased that to a 50-50 split, saving the federal government about $40 million.

But Western senators, led by Malcolm Wallop, R-Wyo., opposed any increase, saying that the federal government was inefficient and that the states could collect the royalties less expensively.

### Timber Harvest Unspecified

Senate appropriators also treaded lightly around the divisive battle over the management of the old-growth forests of the Pacific Northwest. Logging on federal forests in the region was slowing to almost a standstill because federal courts ruled that the administration's forestry practices violated national forest management laws and the Endangered Species Act. *(Endangered Species Act, p. 280)*

Because of the court-imposed restrictions, the bill did not set a recommended timber harvest level, as it had in past years. However, in the report accompanying the bill, appropriators called for $227.9 million in timber sales.

Such a level would allow a national harvest of 7.2 billion board feet of timber, including 2.3 billion board feet in the Pacific Northwest. That level was a sharp decrease from the region's historic timber harvest levels of 4 billion to 5 billion board feet.

But while timber cutting had decreased, the bill encouraged harvesting of naturally felled trees by continuing a $115 million program to encourage timber salvage operations.

Slade Gorton, R-Wash., told the committee that he would seek an amendment on the floor to allow salvage operations even in protected Pacific Northwest forests that were home to the threatened northern spotted owl.

## SENATE FLOOR ACTION

The 1872 Mining Law was the main target in HR 5503 during the annual shootout over the management of the nation's public lands. The Senate passed the measure by voice vote Aug. 6.

During three days of heated debate, the Senate turned back efforts to end the practice of below-cost timber sales on federal land and to raise the fees charged to large ranches that grazed their herds on public rangeland predominantly in the West.

As in previous years, those who wanted to revamp the country's land and forest management laws to reflect new environmental and fiscal realities tried to use the $12.6 billion bill to advance their agendas. Their effort came amid ongoing resistance among the authorizing committees to address such issues.

Senators from resource-dependent Western states mounted a furious counterattack with emotional speeches about the way of life in the West and pre-emptive amendments designed to give a little ground to the reformers.

So it was that Harry Reid, D-Nev., found himself offering a successful amendment to require miners to pay more to patent federal lands and to clean up an area afterward. Reid pushed his amendment to hold off a call by Dale Bumpers, D-Ark., to impose a complete moratorium on all new mining claims until the mining law was radically overhauled.

Likewise Larry E. Craig, R-Idaho, an ardent supporter of the timber industry, also found himself successfully offering an amendment to "streamline" people's appeals of timber sales. Craig's amendment sidetracked an amendment offered by Wyche Fowler Jr., D-Ga., to broaden the appeals process.

Although it was among the smallest of the 13 annual appropriations measures, the Interior bill invariably attracted a raft of amendments that often required lengthy debate in the Senate.

The bill's 1992 consideration was no different despite the increasingly irritated pleadings of Appropriations Committee Chairman Byrd and Senate Majority Leader George J. Mitchell, D-Maine, who warned that the bill's lengthy consideration was pushing the Senate toward a Saturday session.

Noticeably absent was any controversy over "obscene" art, which had plagued funding for the National Endowment for the Arts in past years. Conservative lawmakers apparently were satisfied with Anne Imelda Radice, installed at the helm of the arts endowment.

### Mining Law Reform

But the lack of debate over arts funding left more time for the bill's more traditional land-management battles.

Bumpers renewed his years-long crusade to revamp the general mining law: "Every year," he said, "billions of dollars' worth of hard-rock minerals are being taken off the

federal land ... [and] we do not get 1 cent and are quite often called on to clean up."

The bill as passed by the full committee July 29 contained one reform measure. To keep claims active, miners had to perform $100 worth of "work" each year — something environmentalists said leads to needless scarring of the land. The Senate spending bill, like the House-passed version, dropped the work requirement and instead required miners to pay a flat $100 annual fee to keep their claims active. The provision was supported by the Bush administration.

On the floor, Bumpers called for a one-year ban on all new mining patent claims to preserve public lands while the Senate considered a separate, more-sweeping mining reform measure (S 433).

Bumpers attempted a similar maneuver on the fiscal 1992 appropriations bill, but was stymied by Western senators such as Reid. Reid, however, promised Bumpers that Western senators would not block the consideration of Bumpers' mining law legislation by the Energy and Natural Resources Committee.

But Bumpers' S 433 had not gone anywhere, though a House mining overhaul proposal (HR 918) was approved by the Interior and Insular Affairs Committee on June 24.

In an effort to discharge his promise of 1991 and to make an end run around any further legislation, Reid sponsored an amendment that, in his words, imposed "more reform ... than in the history of the whole act."

Indeed, the amendment made several substantive changes to the mining law. In 1992, miners paid the federal government $2.50 to $5 an acre to patent a claim. Under the Reid amendment, they had to pay fair market value to take claim to the land.

In an effort to stop land speculators who had been using the law to grab land for real-estate development, the amendment required that land revert back to the federal government if a claim holder stopped mining it. Finally, it ensured that miners meet all federal environmental standards for restoring land to its original state when mining operations were completed.

Bumpers scoffed at the changes, calling them "diversionary tactics." He criticized Reid's amendment for failing to mandate royalty payments and tougher environmental restoration standards.

But Bumper's move to table (kill) Reid's amendment failed 44-52. And Reid's amendment was then adopted on a voice vote. (Vote 172, p. 23-S)

### Going After the Forest Service

The battle over the mining law marked just the beginning of the assault on Western land management policies. Fowler unsuccessfully offered an amendment to cut funding for the Forest Service's road-building program and reduced the number of timber sales that result in losses to the Forest Service.

But opponents such as Craig argued that Fowler's amendment increased the price of an average home greatly and cost thousands of timber jobs. Craig moved to quash the amendment, and on a tabling motion, it fell on a 50-44 vote. (Vote 173, p. 23-S)

Fowler also lost a bid to ensure that residents have a right to appeal Forest Service timber sale decisions — something the Bush administration had tried to restrict.

The Senate rebuffed the effort and instead approved an amendment by Craig that would, while allowing appeals, tighten the time period for filing them and force appellants to travel to the "vicinity" of the forest to make their case.

Conrad Burns, R-Mont., who supported Craig's amendment, said if a critic wanted to appeal a Forest Service timber sale but did not want to make the effort to visit the site, "then it should be thrown out as frivolous."

Gorton of Washington also unsuccessfully pushed an amendment that would have allowed logging companies to remove dead trees from old-growth forests in the Pacific Northwest — a move derided by opponents as an end run around the Endangered Species Act. It was killed on a tabling motion on a vote of 60-35. (Vote 176, p. 23-S)

### Grazing Fee Increase Fails

James M. Jeffords, R-Vt., pushed the last major overhaul measure, but the Senate shunned his bid to raise grazing fees by 25 percent. The amendment would have raised grazing fees to $2.40. The House-passed spending bill called for boosting fees to $2.56.

The 1992 debate was not nearly as spirited as in 1991. But when Byrd quickly moved to table the amendment, the issue drew a surprisingly close 50-44 vote. (Vote 177, p. 24-S)

Ranchers paid $1.92 monthly to graze each cow — substantially lower than what private pastures charged. While failing, Jeffords attracted six more votes to his side than he did in 1991 by calling for limiting the grazing fee increase only to large ranches with more than 500 head of cattle.

But opponents used the same arguments they had in the past, saying it would hurt "the family rancher" and defending the low fees as justified because of the poor quality of federal rangeland.

In other action, the Senate spending bill froze administrative overhead costs at the Interior Department. The freeze was part of an amendment pushed by Bob Graham, R-Fla.

## FINAL ACTION

The slow drumbeat of defeat for those who profited from the public lands of the West continued the week of Sept. 21 as lawmakers slapped on a new annual fee for holding mining claims while refusing to restrict opponents of timbering in public forests of the Pacific Northwest.

The actions came as House and Senate conferees met to write a $12.15 billion final version of HR 5503, which they approved by voice vote Sept. 23.

The conferees also stripped out a set of modest mining law revisions that Westerners had hoped would derail calls for major reform. Western members were able to salvage some partial victories:

● In return for adding the mining fee, conferees left intact the existing system of collecting royalties from oil- and gas-drilling operations on public land. In 1992, states paid one-fourth of the collection costs and the federal government paid the rest. The House-passed bill would have split the costs between state and federal governments.

● As part of the deal to strip out the mining reform package, conferees dropped a House-passed plan to raise by 33 percent the fees charged to ranchers who grazed their cattle on public land.

### No Showdown on Elk Hills

When conferees, led by House Interior Appropriations Subcommittee Chairman Yates, planned to meet, it appeared that they were heading toward a showdown with the Bush administration over spending totals. According to the

Office of Management and Budget, the relatively small Interior bill was over the president's request, topping it by $1.7 billion — an amount that would have been extremely difficult to excise from the bill's discretionary spending.

But $1.2 billion of that overage came from a perennial dispute about what to do with the government's valuable Elk Hills Naval Petroleum Reserve in California. The administration wanted to turn its operation over to private oil companies and said leasing fees would bring $1.2 billion. Senate Appropriations Chairman Byrd said it was bad policy to turn over a strategic asset to private companies and vowed to fight.

But by the time the conference convened, the administration had dropped the Elk Hills demand. That left $443 million to cut from the House version of the bill and $502 million from the Senate's. Conferees took care of most of that by nicking all the bill's programs by 0.85 percent.

That meant that a bill that usually was a smorgasbord of popular home-state projects for parks, recreation and wilderness was relatively lean. For the second year in a row, the bill funded no new visitor centers in the nation's parks. And conferees turned down a project that would have been a lock in most years — an environmental educational center honoring former Interior Committee Chairman Morris K. Udall, D-Ariz.

But the conferees agreed, at the urging of Rep. Murtha to keep $13 million for the "Steamtown" railroad museum and park outside Scranton, Pa. The project had been widely criticized as pork-barrel politics, but Murtha argued that it was necessary for economic development.

Conferees soon found themselves facing the tough land-use issues that always bedeviled the bill.

● **Timber.** Conferees agreed to compromise on changes in the process by which opponents of logging could appeal Forest Service approvals. Under the new procedure, appellants were limited to people who had "standing" — those who had participated in the Forest Service's decision-making process over whether to log a certain parcel of land. They had 45 days to appeal, and the Forest Service had 15 days afterward to respond.

Both environmentalists and industry liked the compromise: industry because it gave more certainty to a process that had been interrupted by late appeals and environmentalists because it negated a growing movement to strip away the appeals process.

The bill also allowed "salvage" timber sales in the Pacific Northwest as long as endangered-species habitat was not degraded. Because of drought and insect infestation, there were thousands of acres of dying trees that loggers argued should be taken out rather than wasted.

● **Mining.** Western senators, hoping to hold off a mining law bill gathering momentum in both chambers, added a set of modest changes, including a provision that would make miners pay market value to patent a mining claim, rather than the current $2.50 to $5 an acre.

But Yates said the changes were merely "cosmetic." Bumpers, another proponent of mining reform, said most of the real value of these lands was in the subsurface, which miners could still use for free.

Yates engineered a deal in which the Senate dropped the reform package in return for the House dropping its increase in grazing fees. It was the third year in a row that grazing fee increases voted upon by the House had been traded away in conference.

Western senators seemed resigned to playing off groups of Western resource users against each other. "We've been pitting miners against ranchers since I've been in the Senate," said Reid, who had authored the mining package.

The House and Senate agreed to the conference report Sept. 30, sending the bill to Bush. ∎

# POLITICAL REPORT

# Democrats Reclaim Electoral College

## *Clinton was favored by the youngest and oldest, the best and least educated, the suburbs and cities*

Arkansas Gov. Bill Clinton portrayed himself during the campaign as a different kind of Democrat. On Nov. 3, there was a different kind of result, with Clinton shredding the Republican-oriented electoral map that had been in place for most of the past quarter-century.

Clinton carried 32 states plus the District of Columbia, won 370 of the 538 electoral votes and outscored President Bush, 43.0 percent to 37.4 percent. It was the most sweeping triumph for any Democrat since President Lyndon B. Johnson in 1964 and the best showing for any Democratic challenger since Franklin D. Roosevelt ousted Republican Herbert Hoover from the White House in 1932.

Clinton benefited from a favorable backdrop, with voter attention focused on the struggling economy and the widespread perception that Bush was doing little about it.

Polling throughout the year found that nearly 80 percent of the nation believed the country was on the wrong track. Exit polls found the vast majority of voters favoring a change in government. And Clinton, who had advertised himself as an agent of change throughout the campaign, rode that sentiment to the White House.

The tide of discontent also lifted another apostle of change, independent candidate Ross Perot, who achieved the largest vote total for an independent in presidential election history as well as the biggest vote share — 18.9 percent — since 1912.

Yet the election was not only a "no" vote for Bush. Clinton projected himself as a fiscally conscious Democrat articulating the spirit of the vote-rich baby boom generation. He also had roots and appeal in the South, which had been a regional killing field for Democratic presidential candidates in recent elections.

He won in large part because he held the edge in swing groups that are key to victory. Clinton won a plurality among independents — the first time they had broken

**Bill Clinton on election night.**

### For the Record

● Clinton was the first Democrat to be elected president without carrying Texas since Texas joined the Union.

● Clinton was the first candidate since 1952 to be elected without having won the New Hampshire primary.

● Clinton was the first president-elect from the baby boom generation born after World War II.

● Clinton was the first president-elect who had not served in military uniform since Franklin D. Roosevelt.

● Clinton-Gore was the first successful all-Southern ticket since 1828.

for a Democrat since 1964 — according to Voter Research and Surveys (VRS), which did Election Day exit polling for the television networks. VRS also found Clinton with a clear lead among self-described moderates.

And he ran virtually even with Bush among white voters (again the best showing by a Democrat since 1964) while building a large advantage among blacks and Hispanics.

Clinton also enjoyed a huge edge among those who viewed their family's financial situation as getting worse — one-third of the electorate, according to the survey. That outweighed the hefty pro-Bush edge among those who felt their family's financial situation was getting better, a group that made up one-fourth of the voters.

Feelings of economic anxiety helped Clinton reclaim such traditional Democratic territory as Waterbury, Conn., and Etowah County (Gadsden), Ala., where blue-collar voters had trended Republican in recent elections.

The same dynamic helped Clinton nail down the biggest electoral prize of all, California, where the economy was at a half-century low and where the Bush forces conceded early. California, with 54 electoral votes, led a list of nine states voting Democratic for president for the first time since 1964.

The gender gap appeared in the exit polling, although both sexes backed Clinton (women by 9 percentage points, men by 3 points). A bigger gulf was evident between voters who were married and those who were single. Singles preferred Clinton by 16 percentage points in the VRS sample; married voters broke evenly between Clinton and Bush.

And there were signs that Democrats benefited from what Clinton strategist James Carville called the "May-December coalition." Clinton ran best not among fellow baby boomers, but among the youngest and oldest of voters.

He had a 10-point advantage among voters under 30, many in the "MTV generation" that was cultivated by Clinton and his running mate, Tennessee Sen. Al Gore. But

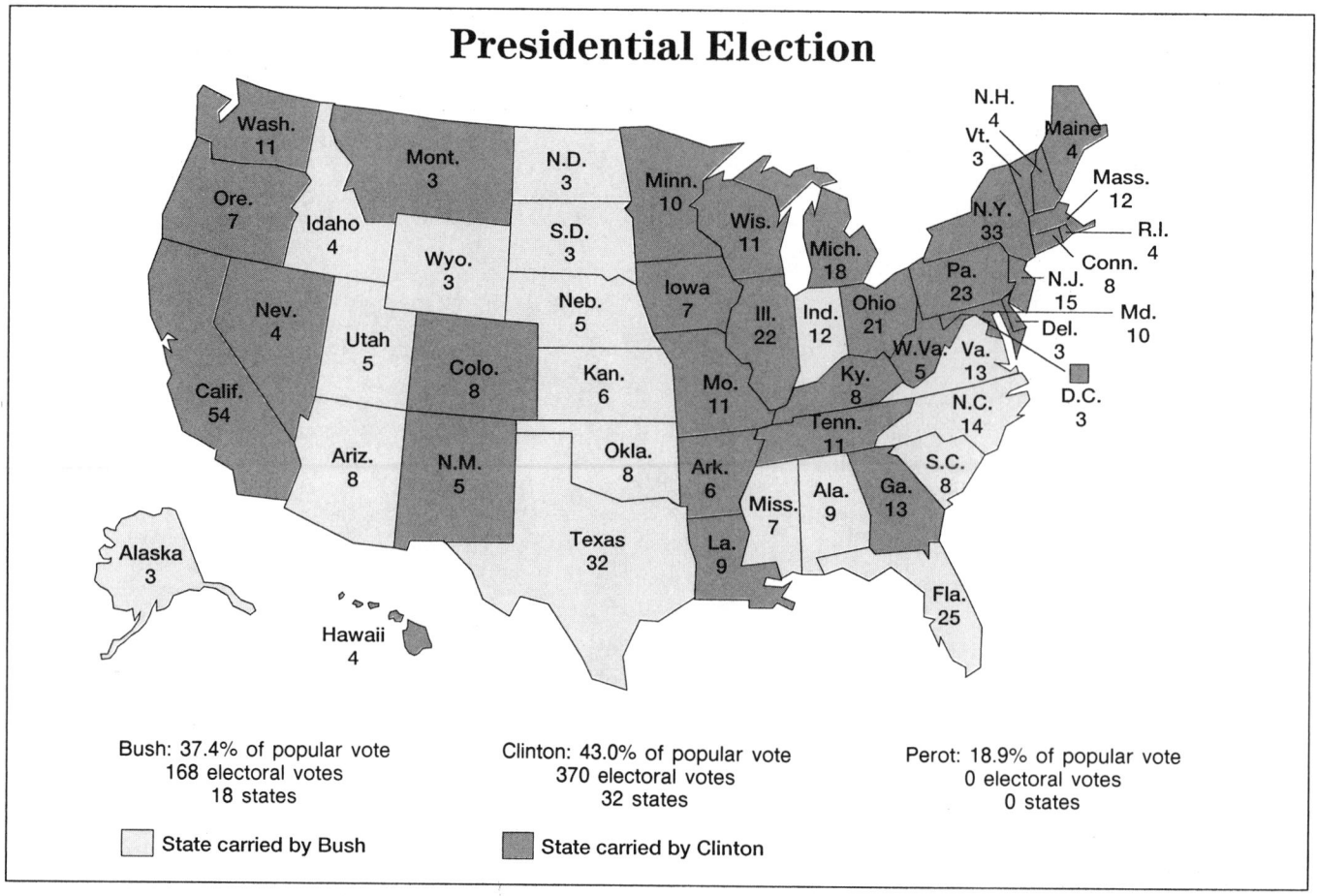

# Presidential Election

Bush: 37.4% of popular vote
168 electoral votes
18 states

Clinton: 43.0% of popular vote
370 electoral votes
32 states

Perot: 18.9% of popular vote
0 electoral votes
0 states

☐ State carried by Bush　　■ State carried by Clinton

he had an even healthier lead (12 percentage points) among voters age 60 and over, many of whom began voting during the New Deal years and have remained loyal to the Democrats ever since.

Clinton carried voters between 30 and 59, but his edge among them was in the low single digits.

Similarly, the VRS survey suggested a pro-Clinton coalition that bridged the best-educated and the least. In that category, his largest leads were among voters with less than a high school education (27 points ahead) and those with postgraduate schooling (13 points ahead).

## Chewing Up the 'L'

Clinton's victory did not come out of the blue. The Democrats in defeat had been quietly positioning themselves.

In 1984, Democratic nominee Walter F. Mondale carried just one state and the District of Columbia. Shortly thereafter, shell-shocked Democrats from Southern and Western states formed the Democratic Leadership Council (DLC) in an effort to reorient the party. From its inception, the DLC strived to position the party more in the mainstream of American politics, emphasizing pro-growth, pro-defense and anti-crime themes.

The DLC was not able to wrest the presidential nomination from party liberals in 1988, however, and Democratic nominee Michael S. Dukakis carried just 10 states. But while Dukakis disappointed those who sensed a chance for victory after two terms of Ronald Reagan, the 1988 results included signs of recovery.

Iowa and Oregon voted Democratic in 1988 for the first

time since 1964; Washington for the first time since 1968. And Dukakis came within 5 points of capturing a half-dozen other states, including California, Illinois, Pennsylvania, Maryland and Missouri.

In 1992, the DLC's approach came into its own with the ascendance of Clinton, a former chairman of the group. Clinton was also able to mesh the mainstream group with the machinery of the Democratic National Committee (DNC). Under Ronald H. Brown, who became DNC chairman in 1989, the national party apparatus became far more pragmatic and campaign oriented.

The emblem of these changes was the 1992 Democratic National Convention in New York, which showcased not only the Clinton-Gore ticket but the party's new posture. Even Perot paid tribute to the demonstration by saying the Democratic Party had "revitalized itself."

So, with the national mood remaining favorable through the fall, Clinton was able to win the Dukakis beachheads and more — including the nine states that had not voted for a Democrat for president since 1964.

The nine were an impressively disparate group — New Hampshire and Vermont in upper New England; New Jersey and Illinois in the industrial Frost Belt; Colorado, Montana, Nevada and New Mexico in the Rockies; and California on the Pacific coast.

In the process, Democrats chewed up the Republican "L," the part of the country that had been the linchpin of the so-called Republican lock. The "L" started at the Canadian border, moved south through the Rocky Mountain and Plains states to the Mexican border, then turned east across the South to the Atlantic Ocean. Adding Alaska, which had

# A Regional Breakdown

Clinton swept all of the states in the East (plus the District of Columbia), most of those in the Midwest and West, and enough of those in the South to keep President Bush from being competitive in the electoral vote. The popular vote percentages shown below are based on official returns. Candidate percentages do not total 100 percent due to rounding.

| | Popular Vote | | | Electoral Votes | |
| --- | --- | --- | --- | --- | --- |
| | Clinton | Bush | Perot | Clinton | Bush |
| East | 47% | 35% | 18% | 127 | 0 |
| Midwest | 42 | 37 | 20 | 100 | 29 |
| South | 41 | 43 | 16 | 47 | 116 |
| West | 43 | 34 | 22 | 96 | 23 |
| **Total** | **43%** | **37%** | **19%** | **370** | **168** |

REUTERS

**Bush concedes on election night.**

also voted Republican in recent years, the "L" encompassed 26 states that offered 223 electoral votes in 1992.

When Ronald Reagan first won the White House in 1980, he swept every state in the "L" except for Jimmy Carter's home state of Georgia. In 1984, Reagan won them all. So did Bush in 1988, sweeping every one of the 26 states by a margin of at least 5 percentage points.

In 1992, though, Clinton punched holes in the "L" and even cut large swaths through it. And Bush was not in a position to make up the losses elsewhere. Lagging in the polls in California, Illinois and New York, he gave up on them early in the campaign. And he then lost all the battleground states of the industrial Frost Belt where he chose to make his last stand.

Ohio and New Jersey were close; Bush's deficit was 1 point in Ohio, 2 points in New Jersey. He lost Wisconsin by

4 points in spite of an all-day train ride through the state on the Saturday before the election. And he lost Michigan by 7 points, a state hard hit by the loss in recent years of hundreds of thousands of jobs in the automobile industry.

Bush, though, could find some solace in Michigan. He narrowly carried Macomb County in the Detroit suburbs. In recent years, the county had been one of the most closely watched barometers of the sentiments of working-class Reagan Democrats.

## An Altered Equation

In winning five of the last six presidential elections, Republicans succeeded by executing a simple formula: Concede the cities to the Democrats, but win the suburbs and the rural areas. In most states over the last quarter-century, that had been a winning formula.

In 1992, Democrats changed the equation by making deep inroads into the suburban vote. In California, for instance, Bush won Orange County, but lost Riverside, San Bernardino and Ventura counties, none of which had voted for a Democratic presidential candidate since 1964.

In Missouri, suburban St. Louis County broke from its Republican presidential voting pattern to back Clinton. So did Bucks, Delaware and Montgomery counties outside Philadelphia, which all supported the Democratic presidential candidate for the first time since LBJ's landslide.

Altogether, there were 28 predominantly suburban counties across the country with a population of at least 500,000. Dukakis carried only six of them in 1988; Clinton won three times as many.

The key question, and one that was impossible to answer, was whether the 1992 election was the start of a new Democratic era in presidential politics as 1968 was for the Republicans, or whether it was an aberration — much as Carter's victory in 1976 proved to be.

That question would have to wait until 1996, but in the meantime, the Democrats' electoral outlook was immeasurably brightened. Not long before 1992, many observers and many within the party itself suggested that Democrats might be locked out of the White House for the rest of the century. In 1992, at least one means of entry was found.

"We didn't find the key to the electoral lock here, we just picked it," said Clinton campaign adviser Carville the day after the election.

And with the leadership of both the White House and

## The Final Polls

Conflicting polls generated confusion and doubt in the final week of the campaign, much as they had at other times in the campaign year. But after the final pre-election weekend, nearly all polling organizations projected a winning margin for Clinton.

| | Clinton | Bush | Perot | Undecided or Other |
| --- | --- | --- | --- | --- |
| **Actual Popular Vote** | **43%** | **38%** | **19%** | |
| Gallup/ CNN/USA Today | 44 | 37 | 14 | 5 |
| Lou Harris | 44 | 38 | 17 | 1 |
| CBS News/ New York Times | 45 | 37 | 15 | 3 |
| Washington Post | 43 | 35 | 16 | 6 |
| ABC News | 44 | 37 | 16 | 3 |
| NBC News/ Wall Street Journal | 44 | 36 | 15 | 5 |
| Battleground Poll | 40 | 36 | 19 | 5 |

Congress, Democrats controlled their destiny.

## The Look of a Mandate

Soon after the result was clear, Senate GOP leader Bob Dole of Kansas weighed in, saying Clinton did not get much of a mandate because he did not win a majority of the popular vote. In truth, Clinton's vote percentage was the fourth-lowest of anyone elected president.

Yet two of those who won with a lower percentage than Clinton were Abraham Lincoln and Woodrow Wilson, regarded as two of the strongest executives in the nation's history. Lincoln and Wilson showed that a president does not need a majority of the popular vote to be effective — just a clear-cut margin of victory, a willingness to use the power of the office, and plenty of friendly faces to work with on Capitol Hill. Both Lincoln and Wilson were re-elected.

Clinton's 43 percent and his wins in 32 states matched the numbers posted in 1968 by Richard M. Nixon, who began the recent era of Republican domination. Nixon was able to work successfully with a Congress dominated by Democrats in both the House and Senate, and he won 49 states when re-elected in 1972.

Despite his modest popular vote, Clinton scored a more sweeping triumph than the last Democrat to have won the White House: Carter. When he won in 1976, Carter carried just 23 states, only two of them in the western half of the country (Texas and Hawaii).

Clinton's triumph was far broader geographically. He won states in every region, beginning with a sweep of the East. He won the Midwest except for Vice President Dan Quayle's home state of Indiana and the deep-dyed GOP Plains states of Kansas, Nebraska, and North and South Dakota. Even more surprising, Clinton won the West — except for Alaska and the traditionally Republican Rocky Mountain states of Arizona, Idaho, Utah and Wyoming. Even in Arizona, which stayed in the GOP presidential column for the 11th straight election, Bush's margin was just 2 percentage points.

That reduced Bush's base essentially to the South, where he won more than two-thirds of his electoral votes (116 out of 168). Yet even there, Clinton picked off five states (Arkansas, Georgia, Kentucky, Louisiana and Tennessee). By seriously contesting other parts of Dixie, Clinton tied Bush down during the fall campaign.

Florida, which Bush won by nearly 1 million votes in 1988, went for the president in 1992 by a margin of just over 100,000. Texas, which Bush had won four years earlier by almost 700,000 votes, backed him by about 214,000 in 1992.

And North Carolina, which was comfortably in the Bush column in 1988, remained there by less than 20,000 votes in 1992.

Bush had an easier time in much of the Deep South. His three best states according to percentages were Mississippi (50 percent), Alabama (48 percent) and South Carolina (48 percent). All three had a large number of white fundamentalist Christians, who once again proved to be among the party's most loyal constituencies — as they had since 1980. According to the VRS survey, they gave the president more than 60 percent of their votes.

## Turnout and Perot

Conventional wisdom had held that higher turnout would benefit the Democrats, because the additional voters would be apt to be change-oriented and more supportive of Clinton or Perot than Bush.

That seemed to happen. Turnout was up to 104.4

---

# Perot Fares Well

Independent Ross Perot failed to carry a state Nov. 3, but his 18.9 percent share of the popular vote was the highest that any independent or third-party candidate had garnered since former President Theodore Roosevelt ran as the candidate of the Progressive Party in 1912. Following is a list of third-party and independent candidates who received more than 10 percent of the popular vote. The name of the third party is indicated in parentheses, where applicable.

| Candidate | Year | % of Vote |
|---|---|---|
| Theodore Roosevelt (Progressive) | 1912 | 27.4 |
| Millard Fillmore (Whig-American) | 1856 | 21.5 |
| **Ross Perot (independent)** | **1992** | **18.9** |
| John C. Breckinridge (Southern Democrat) | 1860 | 18.1 |
| Robert M. La Follette (Progressive) | 1924 | 16.6 |
| George C. Wallace (American Independent) | 1968 | 13.5 |
| John Bell (Constitutional Union) | 1860 | 12.6 |
| Martin Van Buren (Free Soil) | 1848 | 10.1 |

---

million, the first time an American election had exceeded 100 million votes. The bump up from the 1988 figure (91.6 million) was the largest increase in turnout in 40 years.

First-time voters, according to the VRS survey, cast 11 percent of the ballots and went heavily Democratic, with 48 percent backing Clinton, 30 percent Bush, and 22 percent Perot.

But the big turnout probably benefited Perot even more than Clinton. VRS found that about 15 percent of Perot's voters would have stayed home if Perot had not been on the ballot. Anger with the system was as central an issue for Perot as his frequent calls for deficit reduction.

Perot, with 19.7 million votes, showed impressive strength across the nation. He fell below 10 percent of the vote only in Mississippi and the District of Columbia, while reaching at least 20 percent of the vote in 30 states (including all of New England, Florida, Ohio and Texas, and every state in the western half of the country with the exception of New Mexico and Hawaii). Perot even finished second ahead of Clinton in Utah and second ahead of Bush in Maine.

Perot's weakest region was the South. In part, it was because he drew only 7 percent of the black vote (compared with 11 percent for Bush and 82 percent for Clinton, according to the VRS survey) and only 15 percent of the votes of white fundamentalist Christians, both major constituencies.

Perot ran best among self-described independents, men under 30, and voters who viewed their family's financial situation as getting worse. But he was still unable to carry a single state and was shut out in the electoral vote.

In the end, the most remarkable fact of the election may have been that Bush, the hero of Desert Storm whose approval ratings set records in 1991, plummeted to the second-worst finish of any incumbent president ever to seek re-election.

Only William Howard Taft, in 1912, did worse (with 23 percent). Like Taft, Bush was beset by a reinvigorated Democratic Party on one hand and by a tenacious, charismatic third candidate on the other.

In both elections, 80 years apart, most voted for change. And most of those who voted for change opted for the change offered by the Democrats. ■

# Official 1992 Presidential Election Results

*(Based on reports from the secretaries of state for the 50 states and the District of Columbia)*

| State | Total Vote | Bill Clinton (Democrat) Votes | % | George Bush (Republican) Votes | % | Ross Perot (Independent) Votes | % | Other Votes | % | Plurality (D/R) |
|---|---|---|---|---|---|---|---|---|---|---|
| Alabama | 1,688,060 | 690,080 | 40.9 | 804,283 | 47.6 | 183,109 | 10.8 | 10,588 | 0.6 | 114,203 R |
| Alaska | 258,506 | 78,294 | 30.3 | 102,000 | 39.5 | 73,481 | 28.4 | 4,731 | 1.8 | 23,706 R |
| Arizona | 1,486,975 | 543,050 | 36.5 | 572,086 | 38.5 | 353,741 | 23.8 | 18,098 | 1.2 | 29,036 R |
| Arkansas | 950,653 | 505,823 | 53.2 | 337,324 | 35.5 | 99,132 | 10.4 | 8,374 | 0.9 | 168,499 D |
| California | 11,131,722 | 5,121,325 | 46.0 | 3,630,575 | 32.6 | 2,296,006 | 20.6 | 83,816 | 0.8 | 1,490,750 D |
| Colorado | 1,569,180 | 629,681 | 40.1 | 562,850 | 35.9 | 366,010 | 23.3 | 10,639 | 0.7 | 66,831 D |
| Connecticut | 1,616,332 | 682,318 | 42.2 | 578,313 | 35.8 | 348,771 | 21.6 | 6,930 | 0.4 | 104,005 D |
| D.C. | 227,572 | 192,619 | 84.6 | 20,698 | 9.1 | 9,681 | 4.3 | 4,574 | 2.0 | 171,921 D |
| Delaware | 289,735 | 126,054 | 43.5 | 102,313 | 35.3 | 59,213 | 20.4 | 2,155 | 0.7 | 23,741 D |
| Florida | 5,311,219 | 2,071,651 | 39.0 | 2,171,781 | 40.9 | 1,052,481 | 19.8 | 15,306 | 0.3 | 100,130 R |
| Georgia | 2,321,125 | 1,008,966 | 43.5 | 995,252 | 42.9 | 309,657 | 13.3 | 7,250 | 0.3 | 13,714 D |
| Hawaii | 372,842 | 179,310 | 48.1 | 136,822 | 36.7 | 53,003 | 14.2 | 3,707 | 1.0 | 42,488 D |
| Idaho | 482,142 | 137,013 | 28.4 | 202,645 | 42.0 | 130,395 | 27.0 | 12,089 | 2.5 | 65,632 R |
| Illinois | 5,050,157 | 2,453,350 | 48.6 | 1,734,096 | 34.3 | 840,515 | 16.6 | 22,196 | 0.4 | 719,254 D |
| Indiana | 2,305,871 | 848,420 | 36.8 | 989,375 | 42.9 | 455,934 | 19.8 | 12,142 | 0.5 | 140,955 R |
| Iowa | 1,354,607 | 586,353 | 43.3 | 504,891 | 37.3 | 253,468 | 18.7 | 9,895 | 0.7 | 81,462 D |
| Kansas | 1,157,236 | 390,434 | 33.7 | 449,951 | 38.9 | 312,358 | 27.0 | 4,493 | 0.4 | 59,517 R |
| Kentucky | 1,492,900 | 665,104 | 44.6 | 617,178 | 41.3 | 203,944 | 13.7 | 6,674 | 0.4 | 47,926 D |
| Louisiana | 1,790,017 | 815,971 | 45.6 | 733,386 | 41.0 | 211,478 | 11.8 | 29,182 | 1.6 | 82,585 D |
| Maine | 679,499 | 263,420 | 38.8 | 206,504 | 30.4 | 206,820 | 30.4 | 2,755 | 0.4 | 56,600 D |
| Maryland | 1,984,878 | 988,571 | 49.8 | 707,094 | 35.6 | 281,414 | 14.2 | 7,799 | 0.4 | 281,477 D |
| Massachusetts | 2,773,664 | 1,318,639 | 47.5 | 805,039 | 29.0 | 630,731 | 22.7 | 19,255 | 0.7 | 513,600 D |
| Michigan | 4,274,673 | 1,871,182 | 43.8 | 1,554,940 | 36.4 | 824,813 | 19.3 | 23,738 | 0.6 | 316,242 D |
| Minnesota | 2,347,947 | 1,020,997 | 43.5 | 747,841 | 31.9 | 562,506 | 24.0 | 16,603 | 0.7 | 273,156 D |
| Mississippi | 981,793 | 400,258 | 40.8 | 487,793 | 49.7 | 85,626 | 8.7 | 8,116 | 0.8 | 87,535 R |
| Missouri | 2,391,565 | 1,053,873 | 44.1 | 811,159 | 33.9 | 518,741 | 21.7 | 7,792 | 0.3 | 242,714 D |
| Montana | 410,611 | 154,507 | 37.6 | 144,207 | 35.1 | 107,225 | 26.1 | 4,672 | 1.1 | 10,300 D |
| Nebraska | 737,546 | 216,864 | 29.4 | 343,678 | 46.6 | 174,104 | 23.6 | 2,900 | 0.4 | 126,814 R |
| Nevada | 506,318 | 189,148 | 37.4 | 175,828 | 34.7 | 132,580 | 26.2 | 8,762 | 1.7 | 13,320 D |
| New Hampshire | 537,943 | 209,040 | 38.9 | 202,484 | 37.6 | 121,337 | 22.6 | 5,082 | 0.9 | 6,556 D |
| New Jersey | 3,343,594 | 1,436,206 | 43.0 | 1,356,865 | 40.6 | 521,829 | 15.6 | 28,694 | 0.9 | 79,341 D |
| New Mexico | 569,986 | 261,617 | 45.9 | 212,824 | 37.3 | 91,895 | 16.1 | 3,650 | 0.6 | 48,793 D |
| New York | 6,926,560 | 3,444,450 | 49.7 | 2,346,649 | 33.9 | 1,090,721 | 15.7 | 44,740 | 0.6 | 1,097,801 D |
| North Carolina | 2,611,850 | 1,114,042 | 42.7 | 1,134,661 | 43.4 | 357,864 | 13.7 | 5,283 | 0.2 | 20,619 R |
| North Dakota | 308,133 | 99,168 | 32.2 | 136,244 | 44.2 | 71,084 | 23.1 | 1,637 | 0.5 | 37,076 R |
| Ohio | 4,939,859 | 1,984,919 | 40.2 | 1,894,248 | 38.3 | 1,036,403 | 21.0 | 24,289 | 0.5 | 90,671 D |
| Oklahoma | 1,390,359 | 473,066 | 34.0 | 592,929 | 42.6 | 319,878 | 23.0 | 4,486 | 0.3 | 119,863 R |
| Oregon | 1,462,643 | 621,314 | 42.5 | 475,757 | 32.5 | 354,091 | 24.2 | 11,481 | 0.8 | 145,557 D |
| Pennsylvania | 4,959,810 | 2,239,164 | 45.1 | 1,791,841 | 36.1 | 902,667 | 18.2 | 26,138 | 0.5 | 447,323 D |
| Rhode Island | 453,365 | 213,299 | 47.0 | 131,601 | 29.0 | 105,045 | 23.2 | 3,420 | 0.8 | 81,698 D |
| South Carolina | 1,202,527 | 479,514 | 39.9 | 577,507 | 48.0 | 138,872 | 11.5 | 6,634 | 0.6 | 97,993 R |
| South Dakota | 336,254 | 124,888 | 37.1 | 136,718 | 40.7 | 73,295 | 21.8 | 1,353 | 0.4 | 11,830 R |
| Tennessee | 1,982,638 | 933,521 | 47.1 | 841,300 | 42.4 | 199,968 | 10.1 | 7,849 | 0.4 | 92,221 D |
| Texas | 6,154,018 | 2,281,815 | 37.1 | 2,496,071 | 40.6 | 1,354,781 | 22.0 | 21,351 | 0.3 | 214,256 R |
| Utah | 743,999 | 183,429 | 24.7 | 322,632 | 43.4 | 203,400 | 27.3 | 34,538 | 4.6 | 119,232 R |
| Vermont | 289,701 | 133,592 | 46.1 | 88,122 | 30.4 | 65,991 | 22.8 | 1,996 | 0.7 | 45,470 D |
| Virginia | 2,558,665 | 1,038,650 | 40.6 | 1,150,517 | 45.0 | 348,639 | 13.6 | 20,859 | 0.8 | 111,867 R |
| Washington | 2,288,230 | 993,037 | 43.4 | 731,234 | 32.0 | 541,780 | 23.7 | 22,179 | 1.0 | 261,803 D |
| West Virginia | 683,677 | 331,001 | 48.4 | 241,974 | 35.4 | 108,829 | 15.9 | 1,873 | 0.3 | 89,027 D |
| Wisconsin | 2,531,114 | 1,041,066 | 41.1 | 930,855 | 36.8 | 544,479 | 21.5 | 14,714 | 0.6 | 110,211 D |
| Wyoming | 200,617 | 68,160 | 34.0 | 79,347 | 39.6 | 51,263 | 25.6 | 1,847 | 0.9 | 11,187 R |
| | 104,420,887 | 44,908,233 | 43.0 | 39,102,282 | 37.4 | 19,741,048 | 18.9 | 669,324 | 0.6 | 5,805,951 D |

# Women, Minorities Join Senate

The 1992 elections ushered in the most diverse freshman class in Senate history, including record numbers of women and minorities. An institution viewed as an almost exclusive enclave of white males was made more representative of the country.

When the new Senate convened in January 1993, the six women among its 100 members included the first black woman senator, Democrat Carol Moseley-Braun of Illinois, and the first pair of women to represent a state, Democrats Dianne Feinstein and Barbara Boxer of California.

It also included the first American Indian senator in more than 60 years, Democrat Ben Nighthorse Campbell of Colorado.

But for all the drama of the historic elections, the Senate as a whole barely shifted in terms of partisanship or ideology.

And for all the talk of a seething, anti-incumbent electorate, voters ousted only four of the 26 incumbents on the Nov. 3 ballot — Republicans Bob Kasten of Wisconsin and John Seymour of California and Democrat Terry Sanford of North Carolina.

A fourth incumbent, Democrat Wyche Fowler Jr., lost a Nov. 24 runoff to Republican challenger Paul Coverdell. A victory by Democrat Kent Conrad in the Dec. 4 North Dakota special election gave Democrats a 57-43 edge in the 103rd Congress — the same as in the 102nd.

Election Day was the end of a roller-coaster ride of political expectations.

Just a month earlier, Democrats were dreaming of a 60-seat majority that could thwart GOP-led filibusters. They fell short of that goal, despite recapturing the White House.

President Clinton's victory appeared to have a minimal impact on Senate races. However, the presence of two moderate Southerners at the top of the ticket enabled Democratic Senate candidates to run with their presidential ticket instead of away from it.

If Senate Democrats did not meet the soaring expectations of the months immediately preceding the election, they defied the predictions of disaster they faced a few years ago.

"The conventional political wisdom was the Republicans would gain [seats] in the Senate in 1990 and then regain control of the Senate in 1992," said Majority Leader George J. Mitchell, D-Maine. "The conventional political wisdom is usually wrong, but rarely has it been so wrong."

The 1990 contest was a wash, and Democrats picked up a seat in Pennsylvania's special election in 1991.

At that point, Senate Democrats faced considerably longer odds than their Republican counterparts. They had more seats to defend (21 vs. 15), they faced a party led by a popular incumbent president and many had to explain why they voted against authorizing the use of military force in the Persian Gulf.

The Democrats caught a break when some of their most vulnerable incumbents either retired or lost in the prima-

| U.S. Senate | |
|---|---|
| **103rd Congress*** | **102nd Congress** |
| Democrats 57 | Democrats 57 |
| Republicans 43 | Republicans 43 |
| **Democrats** | |
| Freshmen | 9 * |
| Incumbents re-elected | 13 |
| Incumbent defeated | 2 |
| **Republicans** | |
| Freshmen | 5 |
| Incumbents re-elected | 10 |
| Incumbents defeated | 2 |

*The number of Democratic freshmen increased to nine when Sen. Bob Krueger was appointed to replace Treasury Secretary Lloyd Bentsen and Harlan Mathews was named to replace Vice President Al Gore.*

ries. Others heeded the warning signs and ran aggressive campaigns, in some cases launching pre-emptive negative attacks on their challengers.

The Republicans also had their share of tenacious, well-funded incumbents who went on the offensive early and never let up. Most notable were three who were initially considered ripe for defeat — Arlen Specter of Pennsylvania, Bob Packwood of Oregon and Alfonse M. D'Amato of New York.

"If anybody told me the president would get 38 percent of the vote and we were going to be in a runoff in one Senate race and have 42 in hand, I would have thought that was a very unlikely scenario," said Texas Sen. Phil Gramm, chairman of the National Republican Senatorial Committee. "Given we were swimming against the electoral tide, I think we did well."

The results demonstrated anew that Senate races are often determined by local factors and the personality of the candidates rather than national trends.

Clinton's stunning win in rock-ribbed Republican New Hampshire could not pull along Democrats vying for the Senate and governor's seats. The savings and loan scandal of the Keating Five was not enough to unseat Democratic Sen. John Glenn of Ohio or Republican Sen. John McCain of Arizona.

## Women's Surge

In an election season dubbed the "Year of the Woman," five of the 11 women nominated won Senate races, setting a record.

But like their male predecessors, female challengers learned that the experience, money and the name recognition associated with incumbency remain enormous hurdles. The six women who ran against elected incumbents all lost.

The October 1991 confirmation hearings of Supreme Court Justice Clarence Thomas provided the initial impetus for the unprecedented gains by women Senate candidates. *(1991 Almanac, p. 274)*

For many women and some male viewers, the televised image of the all-white, all-male Senate Judiciary panel grilling Professor Anita F. Hill about her harassment charges against Thomas was "the picture worth a thousand words," said Ruth Mandel, director of the Center for the American Woman and Politics at Rutgers University.

The highly publicized rape trials of William Kennedy Smith and boxing champion Mike Tyson, the reported mistreatment of women at the Tailhook convention of naval aviators in 1991 and allegations that Democratic Sen. Brock Adams of Washington sexually harassed staff members further fueled interest in female candidates; many of those candidates argued that they would be more sensitive to women's issues.

And those women had the appeal of being candidates who were outside the normal scope of power in Washington.

But sustaining voter interest and winning voter confi-

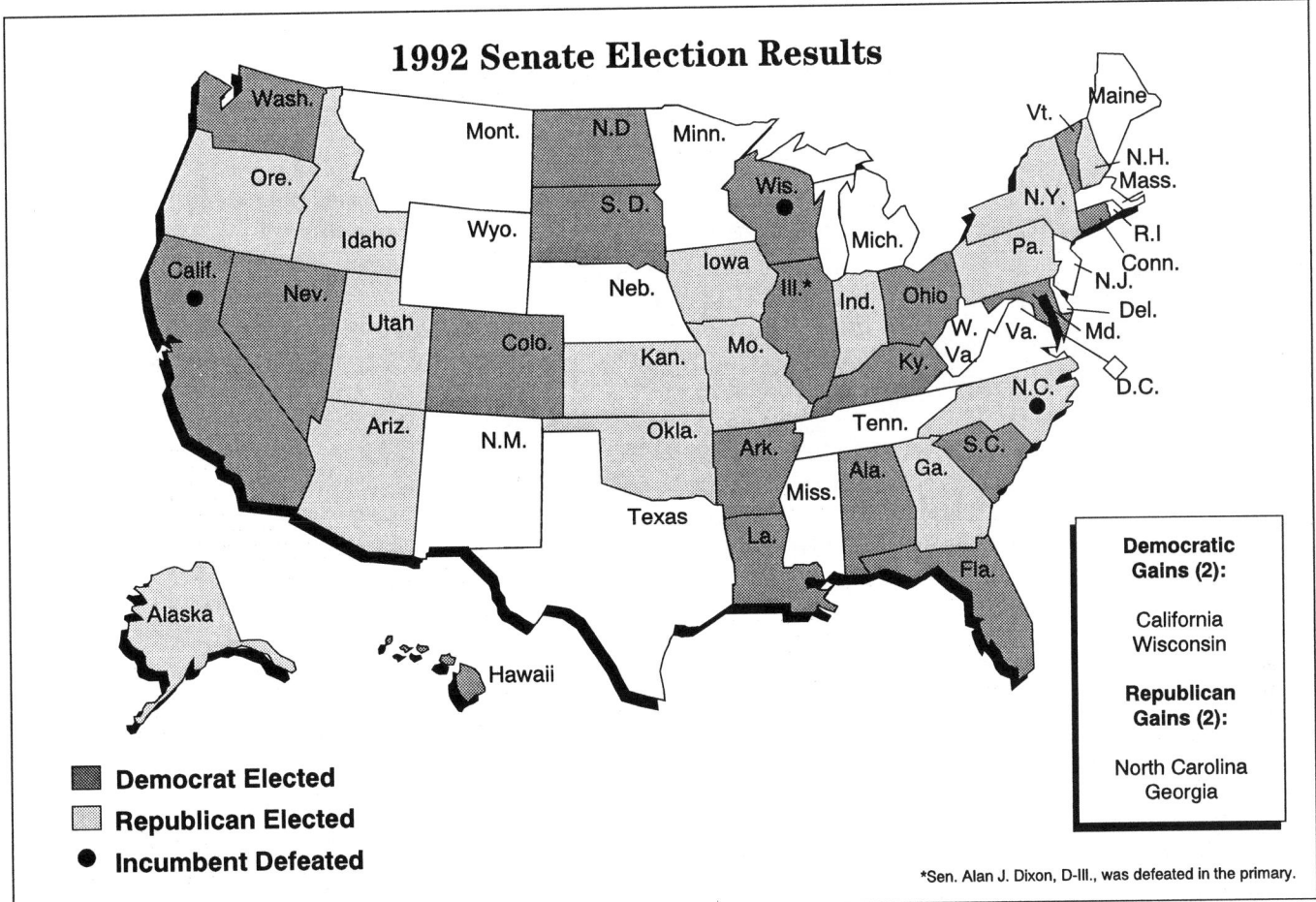

## 1992 Senate Election Results

Democratic Gains (2):

California
Wisconsin

Republican Gains (2):

North Carolina
Georgia

■ Democrat Elected
□ Republican Elected
● Incumbent Defeated

*Sen. Alan J. Dixon, D-Ill., was defeated in the primary.

dence also required political seasoning. Every victorious female Senate candidate was a veteran Democratic politician.

In California, former San Francisco Mayor Feinstein and Rep. Boxer were well-known political pros who knew how to dodge negative assaults.

Both also benefited from an uncharacteristically strong effort by their state party. California Democrats "were well organized; they did a good job of registering new voters in the last few months, and they were able to do this in part because they were united at the top of the ticket," said Gary C. Jacobson, a political scientist at the University of California at San Diego.

Boxer — whose huge lead narrowed when she was attacked as an insider with 143 overdrawn checks at the House bank — saved her money for a crucial late advertising blitz. Pitted against conservative Republican TV commentator Bruce Herschensohn, Boxer was also aided by Clinton's commanding California victory.

Feinstein's task seemed simpler. Her popularity and large treasury easily overwhelmed the little-known Seymour, who had been appointed by Republican Gov. Pete Wilson to fill the remainder of his Senate term. She won with more than a 1.7 million-vote margin.

Remarkably, Feinstein was able to win outright or hold Seymour to razor-thin margins in Southern California's white, affluent suburbs, such as Orange and San Bernardino counties. In virtually every major county south and east of Los Angeles she improved upon her numbers against Wilson in the 1990 governor's race.

Boxer relied on huge margins in liberal Northern California to cover losses in the GOP-dominated south. Losing many more areas of Southern California than Feinstein did, Boxer won with a narrower 529,000-vote margin.

Both Moseley-Braun and winner Patty Murray, D, in Washington state stumbled near the end, but their political experience and the euphoria that followed their unexpected primary victories helped them weather the late storms.

Moseley-Braun's underfunded bid was boosted in the Democratic primary when Sen. Alan J. Dixon was dragged down by an expensive mudslinging campaign with attorney Al Hofeld.

Moseley-Braun, the Cook County recorder of deeds and a former state legislator, picked up enormous good will in her path-breaking quest. Her Republican opponent was Chicago lawyer Rich Williamson, a former appointee from the Reagan and Bush administrations who had little following in the state.

Williamson attacked Moseley-Braun for being too liberal, and he tried to link her to other black politicians who were less popular with whites. Nothing seemed to throw Moseley-Braun off stride until the disclosures that her family divided a $28,750 check to her mother from the sale of timber rights on family property. The money should have been reported to state officials who might have ordered it used to pay for the care of Moseley-Braun's mother, a nursing home patient whose expenses were covered by taxpayers. The candidate said she would pay the state $15,000 to settle the dispute.

The controversy made October a rough month for

# Senate Term Expiration Years

## — 1994 —

### (34 Senators: 21 Democrats, 12 Republicans, 1 undetermined)

Akaka, Daniel K., D-Hawaii
Bingaman, Jeff, D-N.M.
Bryan, Richard H., D-Nev.
Conrad, Kent, D-N.D.
Burns, Conrad, R-Mont.
Byrd, Robert C., D-W.Va.
Chafee, John H., R-R.I.
Danforth, John C., R-Mo.
DeConcini, Dennis, D-Ariz.
Durenberger, Dave, R-Minn.
Feinstein, Dianne, D-Calif.
Gorton, Slade, R-Wash.

Hatch, Orrin G., R-Utah
Jeffords, James M., R-Vt.
Kennedy, Edward M., D-Mass.
Kerrey, Bob, D-Neb.
Kohl, Herb, D-Wis.
Lautenberg, Frank R., D-N.J.
Lieberman, Joseph I., D-Conn.
Lott, Trent, R-Miss.
Lugar, Richard G., R-Ind.
Mack, Connie, R-Fla.
Mathews, Harlan, D-Tenn. [2]

Metzenbaum, Howard M., D-Ohio
Mitchell, George J., D-Maine
Moynihan, Daniel Patrick, D-N.Y.
Riegle, Donald W. Jr., D-Mich.
Robb, Charles S., D-Va.
Roth, William V. Jr., R-Del.
Sarbanes, Paul S., D-Md.
Sasser, Jim, D-Tenn.
Wallop, Malcolm, R-Wyo.
Wofford, Harris, D-Pa.
Texas seat [1]

## — 1996 —

### (33 Senators: 16 Democrats, 16 Republicans, 1 undetermined)

Baucus, Max, D-Mont.
Biden, Joseph R. Jr., D-Del.
Boren, David L., D-Okla.
Bradley, Bill, D-N.J.
Brown, Hank, R-Colo.
Cochran, Thad, R-Miss.
Cohen, William S., R-Maine
Craig, Larry E., R-Idaho
Domenici, Pete V., R-N.M.
Exon, Jim, D-Neb.
Gramm, Phil, R-Texas

Harkin, Tom, D-Iowa
Hatfield, Mark O., R-Ore.
Heflin, Howell, D-Ala.
Helms, Jesse, R-N.C.
Johnston, J. Bennett, D-La.
Kassebaum, Nancy Landon, R-Kan.
Kerry, John, D-Mass.
Levin, Carl, D-Mich.
McConnell, Mitch, R-Ky.
Nunn, Sam, D-Ga.
Pell, Claiborne, D-R.I.

Pressler, Larry, R-S.D.
Pryor, David, D-Ark.
Rockefeller, John D. IV, D-W.Va.
Simon, Paul, D-Ill.
Simpson, Alan K., R-Wyo.
Smith, Robert C., R-N.H.
Stevens, Ted, R-Alaska
Thurmond, Strom, R-S.C.
Warner, John W., R-Va.
Wellstone, Paul, D-Minn.
Tennessee seat [2]

## — 1998 —

### (34 Senators: 19 Democrats, 15 Republicans)

Bennett, Robert F., R-Utah
Bond, Christopher S., R-Mo.
Boxer, Barbara, D-Calif.
Breaux, John B., D-La.
Bumpers, Dale, D-Ark.
Campbell, Ben Nighthorse, D-Colo.
Coats, Daniel R., R-Ind.
Coverdell, Paul, R-Ga.
D'Amato, Alfonse M., R-N.Y.
Daschle, Tom, D-S.D.
Dodd, Christopher J., D-Conn.
Dole, Bob, R-Kan.

Dorgan, Byron L., D-N.D.
Faircloth, Lauch, R-N.C.
Feingold, Russell D., D-Wis.
Ford, Wendell H., D-Ky.
Glenn, John, D-Ohio
Graham, Bob, D-Fla.
Grassley, Charles E., R-Iowa
Gregg, Judd, R-N.H.
Hollings, Ernest F., D-S.C.
Inouye, Daniel K., D-Hawaii
Kempthorne, Dirk, R-Idaho
Leahy, Patrick J., D-Vt.

McCain, John, R-Ariz.
Mikulski, Barbara A., D-Md.
Moseley-Braun, Carol, D-Ill.
Murkowski, Frank H., R-Alaska
Murray, Patty, D-Wash.
Nickles, Don, R-Okla.
Packwood, Bob, R-Ore.
Reid, Harry, D-Nev.
Shelby, Richard C., D-Ala.
Specter, Arlen, R-Pa.

[1] *A special election in Texas was set for May 1, 1993, to fill the seat vacated by the resignation of Treasury Secretary Lloyd Bentsen. Former Rep. Robert Krueger was named to fill the seat in the interim.*

[2] *Mathews was appointed to take the seat of Vice President Al Gore, who resigned Jan. 2, 1993. An election was to be held in 1994 to fill the last two years of Gore's term. Mathews said he would not be a candidate in 1994.*

Moseley-Braun, but Williamson lacked the stature to take advantage of the opening. And Bush practically conceded the state to Clinton, further complicating Williamson's task.

For Murray, the self-styled "mom in tennis shoes," attacks on her slim résumé and liberal views diminished her large post-primary lead. She responded with ads depicting GOP Rep. Rod Chandler's Capitol Hill tenure as a liability. Some of Chandler's odd, condescending comments late in the race only served to reinforce what Murray had been saying.

In Maryland, Democratic Sen. Barbara A. Mikulski coasted to a second term.

A lack of experience contributed to the defeat of the remaining six women candidates.

Nowhere was that handicap more evident than in Pennsylvania. Capitalizing on the ill will that Specter generated as Hill's chief interrogator during the Thomas hearings, Democrat Lynn Yeakel staged a stunning primary win in her first political campaign. But as the race shifted into the general election, Yeakel's "amateur night at the follies" was no match for Specter's "textbook campaign," said Terry Madonna, a political scientist at Millersville University in Pennsylvania.

Specter and some disenchanted Democrats said Yeakel had overemphasized the Thomas hearings, devoting too little attention to such problems as the federal deficit. She made a series of gaffes, including incorrectly blaming Specter and Republican presidents for a local store closing that occurred while Democrat Jimmy Carter was president. And she could not match Specter's $8 million-plus treasury, enabling him to air six weeks of unanswered early television advertising.

Portraying himself as an independent-minded, sometimes ornery scrapper, Specter convinced voters to return him to Capitol Hill because his seniority was invaluable. He adeptly cut into Yeakel's base early, capturing support from such traditional Democratic constituencies as union members, minorities and women.

Like Yeakel, Missouri Democrat Geri Rothman-Serot had limited exposure as a member of the St. Louis County Council. She had trouble raising money and put forth a less than energetic campaign. It was a missed opportunity: GOP Sen. Christopher S. Bond still only received 52 percent.

Rothman-Serot and the four other women — three Democrats and one Republican — had always been considered long shots. "What happened to them is what has happened to any Senate challengers who face well-financed, well-entrenched, popular incumbents," Mandel of Rutgers said. "It was nothing untypical."

## Outsiders Stay There

There was also much talk throughout election year of the presumed appeal of "outsider" credentials. The notion generally had less currency in Senate races than in House contests, perhaps in part because of the scandals at the House Post Office and bank.

The more successful "outsider" candidates still found political experience to be invaluable.

"Voters wanted outsiders, but they still want to believe people they vote for are up to the job, that they have the credentials," political scientist Jacobson said.

The combination of an outsider's image and an insider's résumé worked to the advantage of two Democratic Senate candidates — Russell D. Feingold, who defeated Kasten in Wisconsin, and Rep. Campbell, who defeated former GOP

state Sen. Terry Considine in Colorado.

Feingold slipped through Wisconsin's Democratic primary in much the same fashion that Moseley-Braun won in Illinois: He watched from the sidelines as his two well-funded Democratic opponents destroyed each other with negative campaigning. Feingold received an astounding 70 percent in the Sept. 8 primary, lifting him far above Kasten in post-primary polls.

Feingold stole a page from the 1990 playbook of Democratic Sen. Paul Wellstone of Minnesota, airing offbeat and often humorous ads. One touted an imagined endorsement from Elvis.

Notwithstanding his outsider image, however, Feingold also drew upon his 10 years in the state Senate. John Bibby, a political science professor at the University of Wisconsin at Milwaukee, described Feingold as an "insider in Democratic politics and a well-established, skilled campaigner who, like many candidates in Wisconsin, was seeking a role as an independent, maverick person."

Kasten, who had never topped 51 percent in his two previous Senate campaigns, attacked Feingold as liberal on taxes and spending and soft on crime. Feingold's lead shrunk.

On Election Day, Feingold compiled large margins in Milwaukee County and in his home base, Dane County (Madison), while minimizing Kasten's margin in the strongly Republican Milwaukee suburbs of Waukesha County.

Like Feingold, Campbell's outsider image belied his lengthy political résumé. Considine tried in vain to paint Campbell as another Capitol Hill pol who took advantage of congressional perks. One Considine spot criticized Campbell for accepting a free trip to Alaska paid for by an oil company. But voters had a hard time seeing the pony-tailed member of the Northern Cheyenne Council of 44 Chiefs as a Washington insider.

During the Colorado campaign, both men were caught distorting their military records. Also, Campbell had to defend his Alaska trip and his low House committee attendance record, while Considine was tainted by his ties to the failed Silverado Savings and Loan.

Campbell's constituents from the 3rd District stuck with him in the Senate campaign, providing the base for large additions in major counties elsewhere, such as Boulder, Adams, Denver and Arapahoe.

## The Southern Flank

Much of the Democrats' Southern flank in the Senate seemed exposed and potentially vulnerable going into 1992. Democrats defended seats in eight Southern and border states. Five of these incumbents were freshmen seeking their first re-election, and several had barely won in 1986.

Voter disenchantment with the national Democratic Party and with votes against the Persian Gulf War seemed especially problematic for the Southern Democrats. But both issues were mitigated as the campaign progressed — the Democrats nominated a moderate Southerner for president, and concern over the wobbly economy eclipsed the impact of the war vote.

In the end, five of the Southern Democrats were never seriously threatened. Bob Graham of Florida, Richard C. Shelby of Alabama, Wendell H. Ford of Kentucky and Dale Bumpers of Arkansas each won with at least 60 percent of the vote. John B. Breaux of Louisiana was elected with 73 percent of the vote in that state's all-party primary Oct. 3.

The GOP might regret not having given South Carolina

Bennett

Boxer

Campbell

Coverdell
Dorgan

Faircloth

Feingold

# New Faces in the Senate

| State | 102nd | 103rd | Freshman | Defeated | Incumbent |
|---|---|---|---|---|---|
| California | R | D | Dianne Feinstein | John Seymour | Seymour |
| California | D | D | Barbara Boxer | Bruce Herschensohn | Alan Cranston * |
| Colorado | D | D | Ben Nighthorse Campbell | Terry Considine | Tim Wirth * |
| Georgia | R | D | Paul Coverdell | Wyche Fowler Jr. | Fowler |
| Idaho | R | R | Dirk Kempthorne | Richard Stallings | Steve Symms * |
| Illinois | D | D | Carol Moseley-Braun | Richard S. Williamson | Alan J. Dixon [1] |
| New Hampshire | R | R | Judd Gregg | John Rauh | Warren B. Rudman * |
| North Carolina | D | R | Lauch Faircloth | Terry Sanford | Sanford |
| North Dakota | D | D | Byron L. Dorgan | Steve Sydness | Kent Conrad [2] |
| Utah | R | R | Robert F. Bennett | Wayne Owens | Jake Garn * |
| Tennessee | D | D | Harlan Mathews | | Al Gore Jr. [3] |
| Texas | D | D | Bob Krueger | | Lloyd Bentsen [4] |
| Washington | D | D | Patty Murray | Rod Chandler | Brock Adams * |
| Wisconsin | R | D | Russell D. Feingold | Bob Kasten | Kasten |

* Retired    [1] Defeated in primary    [2] Elected to North Dakota's other seat in a special election
[3] Resigned Jan. 2, 1993    [4] Resigned Jan. 20, 1993

Feinstein

Gregg

Kempthorne

Krueger

Mathews

Moseley-Braun

Murray

Sen. Ernest F. Hollings a stiffer test. If Republican Gov. Carroll A. Campbell Jr. had chosen to run, he "would have given Hollings a tougher race," said Emory University political scientist Merle Black. As it was, Hollings emerged with only 50.07 percent, his smallest percentage since first being elected to the Senate in 1966.

Republican nominee Tommy Hartnett, a former three-term House member and unsuccessful 1986 candidate for lieutenant governor, called Hollings arrogant and out of touch. Hollings occasionally seemed to act the part, saying Hartnett was "full of prunes" and making an offhand remark uncomplimentary to popular GOP Sen. Strom Thurmond. Hartnett also benefited from a strong statewide GOP effort that gave Bush his second-highest percentage vote in the country.

But in a year when voters were in no mood for politics as usual, Hollings was well-served by his iconoclastic and bombastic nature.

Sanford had no such luck in North Carolina. Like Hollings, he had voted against the war with Iraq. He seemed to compound his difficulties by doing little in the way of

campaigning and fundraising throughout much of his term.

The GOP nominee, businessman Lauch Faircloth, was a former Democrat and a former close friend of Sanford. Faircloth, who had the support of the Congressional Club, a conservative organization closely aligned with GOP Sen. Jesse Helms, was dubbed the "stealth candidate" because of his lack of personal campaigning. Sanford belatedly stumped throughout the state by election year.

The race's turning point was Oct. 9, when the 75-year-old Sanford underwent heart surgery and was sidelined for two weeks. Momentum shifted to Faircloth. The challenger scored with hard-hitting ads portraying Sanford as a liberal on welfare and spending issues. Faircloth ran well in the mountain west and held down Sanford's strength in the east.

Democrat Fowler of Georgia was also seen as vulnerable because of his slim 1986 victory margin and a voting record that was more liberal than that of a typical Southern senator.

Coverdell, a former Peace Corps director, had difficulty matching Fowler in fundraising but hammered him on the

stump. He said Fowler's voting record was comparable to that of Massachusetts Sen. Edward M. Kennedy, and he emphasized the incumbent's support for the 1990 budget agreement that increased taxes.

On Nov. 3, Fowler led Coverdell, 49 percent to 48 percent, with the Libertarian candidate drawing 3 percent. But Georgia election law calls for a general election runoff if no candidate wins a majority of the vote on Election Day.

In the low-turnout Nov. 24 runoff, Coverdell came back to edge Fowler with 51 percent of the vote, a winning margin of about 17,000 votes.

In another post-Election Day contest, the Dec. 4 special election to fill the remaining two years of the late Quentin N. Burdick's term, Democratic Sen. Kent Conrad won easily.

Conrad had announced in April he was retiring, but changed his mind after the death of Burdick. His opponent, Republican state Rep. Jack Dalrymple, ran an aggressive campaign but never came close.

## Unsinkable Incumbents

Some incumbents won re-election despite earlier indications that their political futures were in doubt. Several of them had to overcome charges of unethical behavior.

McCain quickly shook off the Keating Five scandal and was never pressed by his opponents, Democratic Party activist Claire Sargent and former GOP Gov. Evan Mecham, who ran as an independent.

Glenn's re-election bid was more troubled. After looking into Glenn's dealings with S&L operator Charles H. Keating Jr., the Senate Ethics Committee in 1991 found that Glenn, like McCain, had done nothing improper or illegal. But the investigation took some luster off of Glenn's heroic image as a former astronaut, as did the $3 million debt that lingered from his failed 1984 presidential campaign.

Glenn's Republican challenger, Lt. Gov. Mike DeWine, zeroed in on the Keating affair and Glenn's presidential debt. Glenn bitterly objected to the negative tenure of DeWine's campaign, but he criticized DeWine, a former House member, for having floated checks at the House bank.

Polls throughout the campaign indicated that Glenn held a slim lead. Just as Democratic Sen. Howard M. Metzenbaum did in 1986, Glenn racked up pluralities of nearly 200,000 votes in Cuyahoga County (Cleveland), held a small margin in Hamilton County (Cincinnati), and won by more than 2-to-1 in Lucas County (Toledo), finishing with 51 percent statewide to DeWine's 42 percent.

In New York, D'Amato had to contend with a stream of ethics allegations by the media and his political opponents. They said D'Amato used his influence to steer federal housing contracts to campaign contributors and family members. He had never been indicted or censured.

Whatever problems D'Amato had during the general election were dwarfed by those of state Attorney General Robert Abrams. Abrams won the Democratic primary over a high-powered field that included 1984 vice presidential nominee Geraldine A. Ferraro, but his victory was tarnished by that campaign's bruising nature.

With no time to waste after the Sept. 15 primary, Abrams was forced to spend valuable days refilling his depleted campaign treasury instead of trolling for votes.

The two candidates engaged in one of the year's most vicious campaigns. Perhaps the low point for Abrams was when he called D'Amato a fascist. Abrams quickly retracted the statement, although D'Amato rushed onto the airwaves commercials protraying the remark as an ethnic slur against Italian-Americans.

D'Amato was also well-served by his fervent devotion to state concerns, which had earned him the nickname, "Senator Pothole." Abrams compiled the usual huge Democratic margin in Manhattan, but D'Amato held down Abrams' edge in New York City's other boroughs, enabling him to make up the difference in the suburbs and upstate.

Although their ethics were not questioned, Republicans Packwood and Frank H. Murkowski of Alaska were also jeopardized this year. With a history of slim margins and little personal popularity, the two once again made the Democrats' top target lists.

But their Democratic challengers — Rep. Les AuCoin of Oregon and former Commerce Commissioner Tony Smith of Alaska — still faced uphill battles.

AuCoin and Smith also had trouble recovering from brutal primaries that drained their campaign treasuries and alienated some voters. Broke and bloodied, they had trouble finding a compelling issue.

In Oregon, Packwood and AuCoin both supported abortion rights and offered only slim differences on the critical question of timber rights. Packwood, who entered the final two weeks of the campaign with nearly $2 million, buried AuCoin in negative ads.

In Alaska, both contenders agreed that the Arctic National Wildlife Refuge should be opened for drilling.

Despite their financial advantages, Packwood got 52 percent of the vote; Murkowski got 53 percent.

## Party Prevails

Democrats faced steep odds in Utah, New Hampshire and Idaho. Relying on a rich tradition of party dominance, the GOP captured open seats in all three states, despite the presence of three credible Democrats.

Boise Mayor Dirk Kempthorne led perhaps the most innovative race of this group, running commercials that questioned the use of Capitol elevator operators and promised to use his sneakers instead of the Senate's subway trains.

As expected, Kempthorne dominated in Boise and neighboring communities. More important, he won comfortably in Bonneville County, which had been represented in the House by his Democratic opponent, Richard Stallings.

Boosted by Clinton's state victory, New Hampshire Democrat John Rauh won handily in liberal-leaning communities such as Concord, Hanover and Portsmouth, while remaining competitive in the larger cities of Manchester and Nashua. But GOP Gov. Judd Gregg carried many more of the tiny conservative towns, giving him a 14,600-vote edge.

For Utah Democratic Rep. Wayne Owens, the uphill battle was steep at the start and insurmountable by the finish. Utah — which has not elected a Democratic senator since 1970 — showed little inclination to change its ways. Owens won just three of 29 counties. Republican businessman Robert Bennett helped propel himself to his first elective office by contributing about $3 million to his campaign.

Several incumbents, and North Dakota Rep. Byron L. Dorgan, faced little threat throughout 1992 and coasted to victory Election Day. The remaining Democratic winners included Christopher J. Dodd of Connecticut, Harry Reid of Nevada, Patrick J. Leahy of Vermont, Tom Daschle of South Dakota and Daniel K. Inouye of Hawaii.

A few Republican senators demonstrated similar strength from start to finish: Don Nickles of Oklahoma, Daniel R. Coats of Indiana, Charles E. Grassley of Iowa and Bob Dole of Kansas. ∎

# Senate Membership — 103rd Congress

**Democrats** 57

**Republicans** 43

**Freshmen** 14

The 1992 election and the subsequent appointment of Texas' Lloyd Bentsen to be Treasury Secretary produced a freshman class in the Senate of 14. But the overall partisan makeup of the chamber did not change. Democrats opened the 103rd Congress with the same 57-43 edge they held in the 102nd Congress. Two seats switched from Democratic to Republican, while two seats went from the GOP to the Democrats.

In the chart below, freshmen are designated with a #, seats that switched parties with a † and 1992 winners (but not appointees) are in italics.

**Alabama**
Howell Heflin (D)
*Richard C. Shelby (D)*

**Alaska**
*Frank H. Murkowski (R)*
Ted Stevens (R)

**Arizona**
Dennis DeConcini (D)
*John McCain (R)*

**Arkansas**
*Dale Bumpers (D)*
David Pryor (D)

**California**
*Barbara Boxer (D) #*
*Dianne Feinstein (D) # †*

**Colorado**
Hank Brown (R)
*Ben Nighthorse
Campbell (D) #*

**Connecticut**
*Christopher J. Dodd (D)*
Joseph I. Lieberman (D)

**Delaware**
Joseph R. Biden Jr. (D)
William V. Roth Jr. (R)

**Florida**
*Bob Graham (D)*
Connie Mack (R)

**Georgia**
Sam Nunn (D)
*Paul Coverdell (R) # †*

**Hawaii**
Daniel K. Akaka (D)
*Daniel K. Inouye (D)*

**Idaho**
Larry E. Craig (R)
*Dirk Kempthorne (R) #*

**Illinois**
*Carol Moseley-Braun (D) #*
Paul Simon (D)

**Indiana**
*Daniel R. Coats (R)*
Richard G. Lugar (R)

**Iowa**
*Charles E. Grassley (R)*
Tom Harkin (D)

**Kansas**
*Bob Dole (R)*
Nancy Landon
Kassebaum (R)

**Kentucky**
*Wendell H. Ford (D)*
Mitch McConnell (R)

**Louisiana**
*John B. Breaux (D)*
J. Bennett Johnston (D)

**Maine**
William S. Cohen (R)
George J. Mitchell (D)

**Maryland**
*Barbara A. Mikulski (D)*
Paul S. Sarbanes (D)

**Massachusetts**
Edward M. Kennedy (D)
John Kerry (D)

**Michigan**
Carl Levin (D)
Donald W. Riegle Jr. (D)

**Minnesota**
Dave Durenberger (R)
Paul Wellstone (D)

**Mississippi**
Thad Cochran (R)
Trent Lott (R)

**Missouri**
*Christopher S. Bond (R)*
John C. Danforth (R)

**Montana**
Max Baucus (D)
Conrad Burns (R)

**Nebraska**
Jim Exon (D)
Bob Kerrey (D)

**Nevada**
Richard H. Bryan (D)
*Harry Reid (D)*

**New Hampshire**
*Judd Gregg (R) #*
Robert C. Smith (R)

**New Jersey**
Bill Bradley (D)
Frank R. Lautenberg (D)

**New Mexico**
Jeff Bingaman (D)
Pete V. Domenici (R)

**New York**
*Alfonse M. D'Amato (R)*
Daniel Patrick Moynihan (D)

**North Carolina**
*Lauch Faircloth (R) # †*
Jesse Helms (R)

**North Dakota**
*Byron L. Dorgan (D) #*
Kent Conrad (D)

**Ohio**
*John Glenn (D)*
Howard M.
Metzenbaum (D)

**Oklahoma**
David L. Boren (D)
*Don Nickles (R)*

**Oregon**
Mark O. Hatfield (R)
*Bob Packwood (R)*

**Pennsylvania**
*Arlen Specter (R)*
Harris Wofford (D)

**Rhode Island**
John H. Chafee (R)
Claiborne Pell (D)

**South Carolina**
*Ernest F. Hollings (D)*
Strom Thurmond (R)

**South Dakota**
*Tom Daschle (D)*
Larry Pressler (R)

**Tennessee**
Jim Sasser (D)
Harlan Mathews (D) *

**Texas**
Phil Gramm (R)
Bob Krueger (D) **

**Utah**
*Robert F. Bennett (R) #*
Orrin G. Hatch (R)

**Vermont**
James M. Jeffords (R)
*Patrick J. Leahy (D)*

**Virginia**
Charles S. Robb (D)
John W. Warner (R)

**Washington**
Slade Gorton (R)
*Patty Murray (D) #*

**West Virginia**
Robert C. Byrd (D)
John D. Rockefeller IV (D)

**Wisconsin**
*Russell D. Feingold (D) # †*
Herb Kohl (D)

**Wyoming**
Alan K. Simpson (R)
Malcolm Wallop (R)

*\* Mathews was named to replace Vice President Al Gore Jr.*
*\*\* Krueger was named to replace Treasury Secretary Lloyd Bentsen until a special election could be held in May 1993.*

# Wave of Diversity Spared Many Incumbents

A weak economy, overdrafted checks, "outsider" candidates and twisted new district lines: These were the factors setting the tone of 1992's House campaigns. Voter discontent and redistricting did take a toll on members who sought re-election, but the much-discussed possibility of an Election Day cyclone of anti-incumbent sentiment failed to materialize Nov. 3: Only 24 incumbents were defeated.

Republicans, who began the 1992 campaign cycle with high hopes for substantially eroding the Democratic majority in the House, had to settle for a very modest 10-seat gain.

Rarely has one party gained House seats while the other party captured the White House, but that was small comfort for the GOP, which a year earlier had expected a solid presidential victory and a significant number of House pickups.

While voters changed the partisan makeup of the House only slightly, the 1992 elections did dramatically change the demographics of the chamber. A record number of women and minorities was elected. But despite all the hoopla that 1992 would be the "Year of the Outsider," only 31 of the 110 House freshmen elected had never held elective office. And several of those had worked in government or party politics.

## Drag at the Top

In their most optimistic moments some 18 months before the election, GOP strategists mused that in 1992 they might end the Democrats' 38-year run as the House's majority party. With post-census reapportionment moving House seats from Democratic regions to the more Republican Sun Belt, and with a ticket topped by President Bush — buoyed in public opinion polls by the Persian Gulf War — the GOP seemed poised to challenge Democratic control of the House. Democratic members would be at risk, Republican incumbents secure and GOP chances enhanced in open-seat races brought on by retirements or redistricting.

Instead, a sour economy and Bush's evaporated popularity threatened to deprive the GOP of even a modest gain in House seats.

"On one level, we're pretty pleased," said Thomas J. Cole, executive director of the National Republican Congressional Committee. "An incumbent president has never lost and seen his party gain seats in the House, at least not in this century."

In fact, the only other time that took place was in 1892. That year, President Benjamin Harrison lost to Democrat Grover Cleveland while Harrison's GOP registered big gains in the House.

According to Cole, Republican House candidates outpolled Bush by more than 3 million votes. It was the first time since 1964 that down-ticket Republicans fared

## U.S. House

### 102nd Congress

| | |
|---|---|
| Democrats | 268 * |
| Republicans | 166 |
| Independent | 1 |

### 103rd Congress

| | |
|---|---|
| Democrats | 258 |
| Republicans | 176 |
| Independent | 1 |

### Democrats

| | |
|---|---|
| Net loss | 10 |
| Freshmen | 63 |
| Incumbents re-elected | 195 |
| Incumbents defeated | 16 |

### Republicans

| | |
|---|---|
| Net gain | 10 |
| Freshmen | 47 |
| Incumbents re-elected | 129 |
| Incumbents defeated | 8 |

*Includes two vacant seats.*

better than their party's presidential candidate.

But Cole acknowledged that many Republican House candidates were unable to counteract the drag from the top of the ticket, particularly in the 91 seats where no incumbents were running. Of those, Democrats won 57 (63 percent); Republicans captured 34.

"Unquestionably, it hurt us the most [in open seats] — unquestionably," he said.

Cole pointed to Democratic gains in three GOP-leaning districts where a strong showing by Democratic presidential nominee Bill Clinton affected the outcome: Pennsylvania's 13th, where Marjorie Margolies-Mezvinsky won the seat of retiring Republican Rep. Lawrence Coughlin; Washington's 4th, where Jay Inslee captured the seat of unsuccessful GOP gubernatorial candidate Sid Morrison; and Minnesota's rural 2nd, where David Minge was a surprise winner to succeed retiring conservative GOP Rep. Vin Weber.

## Democrats Crow; GOP Looks to '94

Democrats gloated over their election-year escape from predictions of a "triple witching hour" catastrophe — a year in which congressional and presidential elections coincide with redistricting. "Anything less than a 20- to 25-seat pickup for [the GOP] is a disaster," Vic Fazio of California, chairman of the Democratic Congressional Campaign Committee, said at a Nov. 5 news conference. "They had a major failure."

Out of the returns, however, Cole found a glimmer of promise for 1994, pointing to a number of races in which Democrats were lifted by a strong showing by Clinton — or in which Republican candidates were weakened by a commensurately poor performance by Bush.

Fazio agreed that for the rest of the 1990s, more seats would be competitive. "Some of the reapportionments . . . create more marginal seats," he said. "In addition, the electorate is increasingly disinclined to straight party voting."

## Scandals, Maps and Upsets

By far the most common symptom afflicting the 24 incumbents who lost Nov. 3 was unfavorable publicity over ethically questionable behavior.

Eight members with sizable numbers of overdrawn checks at the House bank lost; two of those eight — Democrats Joseph D. Early of Massachusetts and Mary Rose Oakar of Ohio — were cited by the House ethics committee as having abused their privileges at the bank. Overdrafts also contributed to the downfall of Democrats Jerry Huckaby of Louisiana, Gerry Sikorski of Minnesota, Thomas J. Downey of New York, Peter H. Kostmayer of Pennsylvania and Albert G. Bustamante of Texas, as well as Ohio Repub-

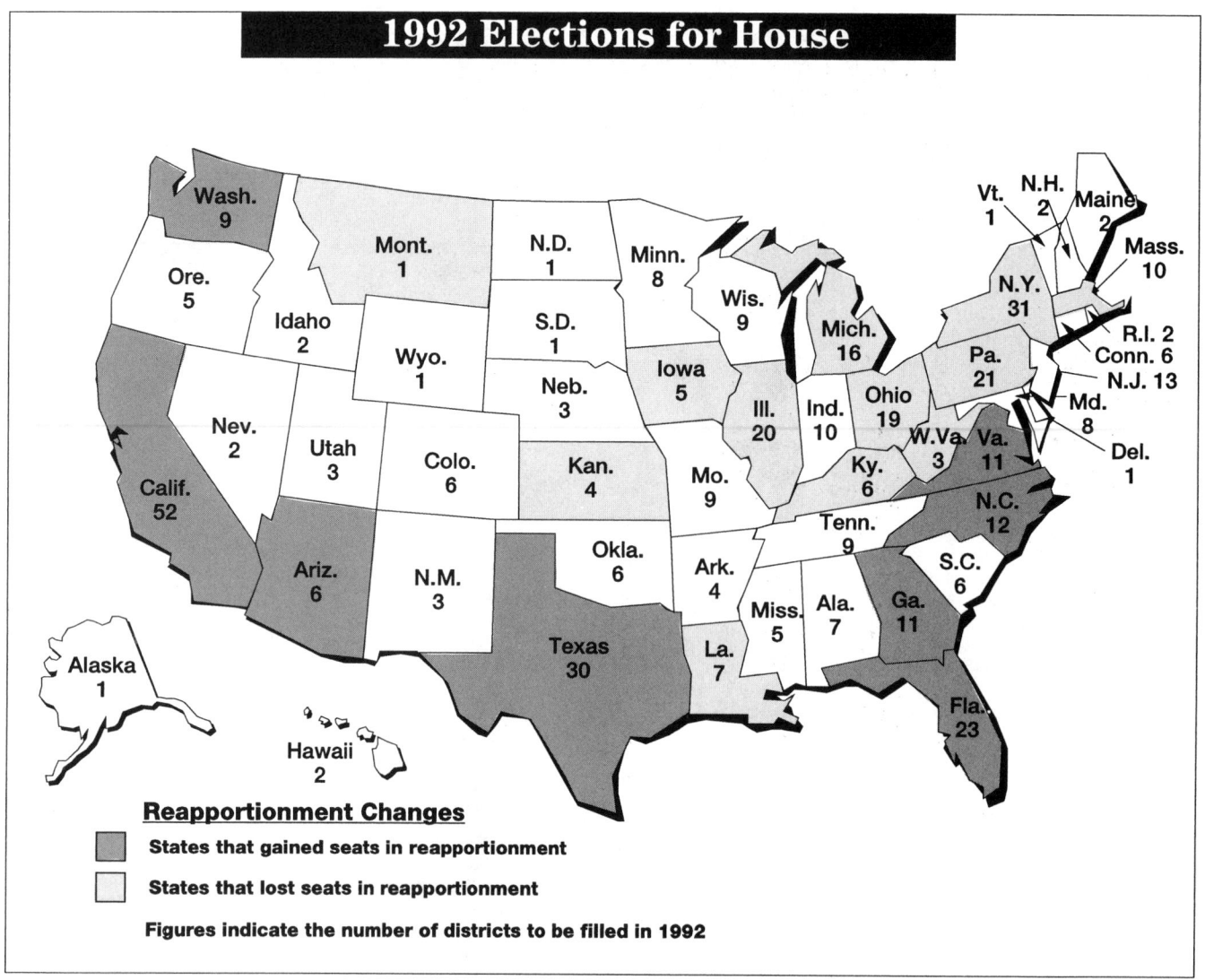

# 1992 Elections for House

Wash. 9

Ore. 5

Mont. 1

Idaho 2

N.D. 1

Minn. 8

Wis. 9

Vt. 1

N.H. 2

Maine 2

Mass. 10

N.Y. 31

S.D. 1

Wyo. 1

Neb. 3

Iowa 5

Mich. 16

Pa. 21

R.I. 2

Conn. 6

N.J. 13

Nev. 2

Utah 3

Colo. 6

Kan. 4

Ill. 20

Ind. 10

Ohio 19

W.Va. 3

Va. 11

Md. 8

Del. 1

Calif. 52

Ky. 6

N.C. 12

Ariz. 6

N.M. 3

Okla. 6

Mo. 9

Ark. 4

Tenn. 9

S.C. 6

Alaska 1

Texas 30

La. 7

Miss. 5

Ala. 7

Ga. 11

Hawaii 2

Fla. 23

## Reapportionment Changes

■ States that gained seats in reapportionment

□ States that lost seats in reapportionment

**Figures indicate the number of districts to be filled in 1992**

lican Bob McEwen. *(Box, p. 17-A)*

Bustamante, Oakar and Nicholas Mavroules, D-Mass., also faced allegations of impropriety for their behavior on matters beyond the House bank. Mavroules had only one overdraft, but he was hit in August with a 17-count indictment charging him with racketeering, bribery and tax evasion.

After scandal, redistricting was the leading cause of incumbent defeat. Democrats Dave Nagle of Iowa and Tom McMillen of Maryland and Republicans Clyde C. Holloway of Louisiana and Ron Marlenee of Montana lost after redistricting matched them against another incumbent. (Huckaby also lost in an incumbent-incumbent contest.)

In addition, Alabama Democrat Ben Erdreich and Georgia Democrat Richard Ray lost in districts that were redrawn to be considerably more Republican. Missouri Democrat Joan Kelly Horn, a winner by 54 votes in 1990, was given a less Democratic district in which to run. She lost to a well-organized GOP opponent.

The most surprising Democratic defeats were those of third-term Reps. Jim Jontz of Indiana and Liz J. Patterson of South Carolina. Though both occupied GOP-dominated districts, they had won re-election in 1988 despite a big Bush presidential vote; this time, with Bush losing the White House, they were ousted by underdog Republican

challengers. Another Democrat who lost in a traditionally Republican district was freshman Rep. John W. Cox Jr. of Illinois.

And a weak primary performance foreshadowed a poor general-election showing by Rep. John J. Rhodes III, R-Ariz.

### A Boost From Clinton

For the first time since 1976, Democratic House candidates — challengers and incumbents alike — enjoyed a luxury long afforded to GOP candidates in presidential-election years: The top of the ticket helped boost their vote. That was particularly noticeable in open-seat contests. But Clinton coattails also helped Democratic challengers oust four of the eight Republican incumbents who lost: Frank Riggs of California, Tom Coleman of Missouri, Bill Green of New York and Don Ritter of Pennsylvania.

Clinton's candidacy was a special blessing for many Southern Democratic incumbents, who in recent presidential-election years have seen hordes of voters shun their party's White House nominees.

In North Carolina, for instance, Clinton helped Democrats re-elect their four most vulnerable incumbents — Stephen L. Neal, H. Martin Lancaster, Tim Valentine and W. G. "Bill" Hefner. All four of those white incumbents

# 100 or More Overdrafts

The House ethics committee in April revealed the overdraft totals of 325 current and former House members to calm public furor over the taxpayer-subsidized bank. Overall, the numbers show that overdrafts were a significant factor in 1992 — especially when primary defeats and retirements are taken into account. *(Story, p. 23)*

Of the 269 sitting members with overdrafts, more than one in four (77) retired or were defeated in primary or general election bids for the House or other offices. Of those with clean House bank records, about one in six (28 of 166) had political careers cut short.

The more overdrafts members had, the more likely they were to be defeated or to retire.

Only six of 17 current members accused of having "abused their banking privileges" by the House ethics committee were back in 1993. Of the 46 members with 100 or more overdrafts, 25 (54 percent) retired or were defeated. Of the 389 with fewer than 100 overdrafts or none at all, 80 (21 percent) retired or were defeated.

| Incumbents | Number of Overdrafts | Status of Re-election |
|---|---|---|
| Robert J. Mrazek, D-N.Y. | 920 | Retired |
| Robert W. Davis, R-Mich. | 878 | Retired |
| Ronald V. Dellums, D-Calif. | 851 | Won |
| Charles Hatcher, D-Ga. | 819 | Defeated in primary |
| Stephen J. Solarz, D-N.Y. | 743 | Defeated in primary |
| Charles A. Hayes, D-Ill. | 716 | Defeated in primary |
| Gerry Sikorski, D-Minn. | 697 | Lost |
| Ronald Coleman, D-Texas | 673 | Won |
| Louis Stokes, D-Ohio | 551 | Won |
| Dennis M. Hertel, D-Mich. | 547 | Retired |
| Chalmers P. Wylie, R-Ohio | 515 | Retired |
| Carl C. Perkins, D-Ky. | 514 | Retired |
| Bill Alexander, D-Ark. | 487 | Defeated in primary |
| Henry A. Waxman, D-Calif. | 434 | Won |
| Bill Goodling, R-Pa. | 430 | Won |
| Edolphus Towns, D-N.Y. | 408 | Won |
| Duncan Hunter, R-Calif. | 399 | Won |
| Edward F. Feighan, D-Ohio | 397 | Retired |
| Harold E. Ford, D-Tenn. | 388 | Won |
| Mickey Edwards, R-Okla. | 386 | Defeated in primary |
| William L. Clay, D-Mo. | 328 | Won |
| Bill Lowery, R-Calif. | 300 | Retired |
| E. "Kika" de la Garza, D-Texas | 284 | Won |
| John Conyers Jr., D-Mich. | 273 | Won |
| J. P. Hammerschmidt, R-Ark. | 224 | Retired |
| Mary Rose Oakar, D-Ohio | 213 | Lost |
| Bob Traxler, D-Mich. | 201 | Retired |
| Mike Espy, D-Miss. | 191 | Won |
| Bob McEwen, R-Ohio | 166 | Lost |
| Lawrence J. Smith, D-Fla. | 161 | Retired |
| Carroll Hubbard Jr., D-Ky. | 152 | Defeated in primary |
| Thomas J. Downey, D-N.Y. | 151 | Lost |
| Barbara Boxer, D-Calif. | 143 | Won election to Senate |
| Joseph D. Early, D-Mass. | 140 | Lost |
| James H. Scheuer, D-N.Y. | 133 | Retired |
| Chester G. Atkins, D-Mass. | 127 | Defeated in primary |
| John Lewis, D-Ga. | 125 | Won |
| Vin Weber, R-Minn. | 125 | Retired |
| Michael Andrews, D-Texas | 121 | Won |
| Philip R. Sharp, D-Ind. | 120 | Won |
| Bill Thomas, R-Calif. | 119 | Won |
| Gary L. Ackerman, D-N.Y. | 111 | Won |
| Beryl Anthony Jr., D-Ark. | 109 | Defeated in primary |
| Dan Glickman, D-Kan. | 105 | Won |
| Jim Ross Lightfoot, R-Iowa | 105 | Won |
| Dale E. Kildee, D-Mich. | 100 | Won |

had been weakened by redistricting, which transferred loyally Democratic black voters from their districts into one of two new black-majority districts.

Particularly for Hefner, Clinton's presence was a boon. In 1984 and 1988, overwhelming Republican presidential margins in his district almost dragged him under. This year, Hefner defeated a competitive Republican opponent with 61 percent; it was his second-highest total since he was elected in 1974.

Positive top-of-the-ticket reverberations for Democratic House candidates were especially felt along the West Coast, where the Clinton-Gore ticket won decisively. Republicans, who had made optimistic projections of House gains in California, Washington and Oregon, faltered in those states.

In California, where the GOP-controlled state Supreme Court redrew House district lines to incorporate a seven-seat gain in reapportionment, Democrats entered the election with a 26-19 majority in the House delegation. Republicans thought the new map gave them a shot at winning a majority in the state's expanded 52-member delegation. But the GOP lost one of its own incumbents, failed to oust any Democratic incumbent and fell short of expectations in new and open districts. In the 103rd Congress, Democrats would hold 30 of California's 52 House seats.

In Oregon, Republicans remain outnumbered 4-to-1 in the state's House delegation, having failed to capture a GOP-leaning seat that was vacated by Democratic Rep. Les AuCoin, who ran for the Senate.

In Washington, Bush's anemic 32 percent tally was a poor backdrop for GOP House candidates. Of the four open-seat House races in Washington, Democrats took three. The state's nine-member delegation in the 103rd Congress would have just one Republican, 8th District open-seat victor Jennifer Dunn — down from three in the 102nd Congress.

Dunn was one of just three female Republican challengers — along with Tillie Fowler of Florida and Deborah Pryce of Ohio — to win election to the 103rd Congress, compared with

*Continued on p. 21-A*

# New Members in the House . . .

| State | District | Winner | Loser |
|-------|----------|--------|-------|
| Alabama | 2 | Terry Everett (R) | George C. Wallace Jr. (D) |
| | 6 | Spencer Bachus (R) | Ben Erdreich (D) # |
| | 7 | Earl F. Hilliard (D) | Kervin Jones (R) |
| Arizona | 1 | Sam Coppersmith (D) | John J. Rhodes III (R) # |
| | 6 | Karan English (D) | Doug Wead (R) |
| Arkansas | 1 | Blanche Lambert (D) | Terry Hayes (R) |
| | 3 | Tim Hutchinson (R) | John VanWinkle (D) |
| | 4 | Jay Dickey (R) | Bill McCuen (D) |
| California | 1 | Dan Hamburg (D) | Frank Riggs (R) # |
| | 6 | Lynn Woolsey (D) | Bill Filante (R) |
| | 10 | Bill Baker (R) | Wendell H. Williams (D) |
| | 11 | Richard W. Pombo (R) * | Patricia Garamendi (D) |
| | 14 | Anna G. Eshoo (D) | Tom Huening (R) |
| | 22 | Michael Huffington (R) | Gloria Ochoa (D) |
| | 25 | Howard P. ''Buck'' McKeon (R) | James H. ''Gil'' Gilmartin (D) |
| | 30 | Xavier Becerra (D) | Morry Waksberg (R) |
| | 33 | Lucille Roybal-Allard (D) | Robert Guzman (R) |
| | 36 | Jane Harman (D) | Joan Milke Flores (R) |
| | 37 | Walter R. Tucker (D) | No Republican candidate |
| | 38 | Steve Horn (R) | Evan Anderson Braude (D) |
| | 39 | Ed Royce (R) | Molly McClanahan (D) |
| | 41 | Jay C. Kim (R) | Bob Baker (D) |
| | 43 | Ken Calvert (R) | Mark A. Takano (D) |
| | 49 | Lynn Schenk (D) | Judy Jarvis (R) |
| | 50 | Bob Filner (D) | Tony Valencia (R) |
| Colorado | 3 | Scott McInnis (R) | Mike Callihan (D) |
| Delaware | — | Michael N. Castle (R) | S.B. Woo (D) |
| Florida | 3 | Corrine Brown (D) | Don Weidner (R) |
| | 4 | Tillie Fowler (R) | Mattox Hair (D) |
| | 5 | Karen L. Thurman (D) | Tom Hogan (R) |
| | 7 | John L. Mica (R) | Dan Webster (D) |
| | 12 | Charles T. Canady (R) | Tom Mims (D) |
| | 13 | Dan Miller (R) | Rand Snell (D) |
| | 17 | Carrie Meek (D) | No Republican candidate |
| | 20 | Peter Deutsch (D) | Beverly Kennedy (R) |
| | 21 | Lincoln Diaz-Balart (R) | No Democratic candidate |
| | 23 | Alcee L. Hastings (D) | Ed Fielding (R) |
| Georgia | 1 | Jack Kingston (R) | Barbara Christmas (D) |
| | 2 | Sanford Bishop (D) | Jim Dudley (R) |
| | 3 | Mac Collins (R) | Richard Ray (D) # |
| | 4 | John Linder (R) | Cathey Steinberg (D) |
| | 9 | Nathan Deal (D) | Daniel Becker (R) |
| | 10 | Don Johnson (D) | Ralph Hudgens (R) |
| | 11 | Cynthia McKinney (D) | Woodrow Lovett (R) |
| Idaho | 2 | Michael D. Crapo (R) | J.D. Williams (D) |
| Illinois | 1 | Bobby L. Rush (D) | Jay Walker (R) |
| | 2 | Mel Reynolds (D) | Ron Blackstone (R) |
| | 4 | Luis V. Gutierrez (D) | Hildegarde Rodriguez-Schieman (R) |
| | 16 | Donald Manzullo (R) | John W. Cox Jr. (D) # |
| Indiana | 5 | Steve Buyer (R) | Jim Jontz (D) # |
| Kentucky | 1 | Tom Barlow (D) | Steve Hamrick (R) |
| | 6 | Scotty Baesler (D) | Charles W. Ellinger (R) |
| Louisiana | 4 | Cleo Fields (D) | Charles Jones (D) |
| Massachusetts | 3 | Peter I. Blute (R) | Joseph D. Early (D) # |
| | 5 | Martin T. Meehan (D) | Paul W. Cronin (R) |
| | 6 | Peter G. Torkildsen (R) | Nicholas Mavroules (D) # |

# Incumbent

# . . . By State, Party and District

| State | District | Winner | Loser |
|---|---|---|---|
| Maryland | 4 | Albert R. Wynn (D) | Michele Dyson (R) |
| | 6 | Roscoe G. Bartlett (R) | Thomas H. Hattery (D) |
| Michigan | 1 | Bart Stupak (D) | Philip E. Ruppe (R) |
| | 2 | Peter Hoekstra (R) | John H. Miltner (D) |
| | 5 | James A. Barcia (D) | Keith Muxlow (R) |
| | 7 | Nick Smith (R) | No Democratic candidate |
| | 11 | Joe Knollenberg (R) | Walter Briggs (D) |
| Minnesota | 2 | David Minge (D) | Cal R. Ludeman (R) |
| | 6 | Rod Grams (R) | Gerry Sikorski (D) # |
| Missouri | 2 | James M. Talent (R) | Joan Kelly Horn (D) # |
| | 6 | Pat Danner (D) | Tom Coleman (R) # |
| New Jersey | 7 | Bob Franks (R) | Leonard R. Sendelsky (D) |
| | 8 | Herbert C. Klein (D) | Joseph L. Bubba (R) |
| | 13 | Robert Menendez (D) | Fred J. Theemling Jr. (R) |
| New York | 2 | Rick A. Lazio (R) | Thomas J. Downey (D) # |
| | 3 | Peter T. King (R) | Steve A. Orlins (D) |
| | 4 | David A. Levy (R) | Philip Schiliro (D) |
| | 8 | Jerrold Nadler (D) | David L. Askren (R) |
| | 12 | Nydia M. Velázquez (D) | Angel Diaz (R) |
| | 14 | Carolyn B. Maloney (D) | Bill Green (R) # |
| | 24 | John M. McHugh (R) | Margaret M. Ravenscroft (D) |
| | 26 | Maurice D. Hinchey (D) | Bob Moppert (R) |
| | 30 | Jack Quinn (R) | Dennis Gorski (D) |
| North Carolina | 1 | Eva Clayton (D) | Ted Tyler (R) |
| | 12 | Melvin Watt (D) | Barbara Gore Washington (R) |
| North Dakota | — | Earl Pomeroy (D) | John T. Korsmo (R) |
| Ohio | 1 | David Mann (D) | Steve Grote (I) |
| | 6 | Ted Strickland (D) | Bob McEwen (R) # |
| | 10 | Martin R. Hoke (R) | Mary Rose Oakar (D) # |
| | 13 | Sherrod Brown (D) | Margaret R. Mueller (R) |
| | 15 | Deborah Pryce (R) | Richard Cordray (D) |
| | 19 | Eric D. Fingerhut (D) | Robert A. Gardner (R) |
| Oklahoma | 5 | Ernest Istook Jr. (R) | Laurie Williams (D) |
| Oregon | 1 | Elizabeth Furse (D) | Tony Meeker (R) |
| Pennsylvania | 4 | Ron Klink (D) | Gordon R. Johnston (R) |
| | 6 | Tim Holden (D) | John E. Jones (R) |
| | 8 | Jim Greenwood (R) | Peter H. Kostmayer (D) # |
| | 13 | Marjorie Margolies-Mezvinsky (D) | Jon D. Fox (R) |
| | 15 | Paul McHale (D) | Don Ritter (R) # |
| South Carolina | 4 | Bob Inglis (R) | Liz J. Patterson (D) # |
| | 6 | James E. Clyburn (D) | John Chase (R) |
| Texas | 23 | Henry Bonilla (R) | Albert G. Bustamante (D) # |
| | 28 | Frank Tejeda (D) | No Republican candidate |
| | 29 | Gene Green (D) | Clark Kent Ervin (R) |
| | 30 | Eddie Bernice Johnson (D) | Lucy Cain (R) |
| Utah | 2 | Karen Shepherd (D) | Enid Greene (R) |
| Virginia | 3 | Robert C. Scott (D) | Daniel Jenkins (R) |
| | 6 | Robert W. Goodlatte (R) | Stephen Alan Musselwhite (D) |
| | 11 | Leslie L. Byrne (D) | Henry N. Butler (R) |
| Washington | 1 | Maria Cantwell (D) | Gary Nelson (R) |
| | 4 | Jay Inslee (D) | Richard ''Doc'' Hastings (R) |
| | 8 | Jennifer Dunn (R) | George O. Tamblyn (D) |
| | 9 | Mike Kreidler (D) | Pete von Reichbauer (R) |
| Wisconsin | 5 | Thomas M. Barrett (D) | Donalda Ann Hammersmith (R) |

# Incumbent

# Departing House Members

## Defeated in General Election

| Name, Party, State, District | Began | Defeated By |
|---|---|---|
| Albert G. Bustamante, D-Texas (23) | 1985 | Henry Bonilla, R |
| Tom Coleman, R-Mo. (6) | 1976 | Pat Danner, D |
| John W. Cox Jr., D-Ill. (16) | 1991 | Donald Manzullo, R |
| Thomas J. Downey, D-N.Y. (2) | 1975 | Rick A. Lazio, R |
| Joseph D. Early, D-Mass. (3) | 1975 | Peter I. Blute, R |
| Ben Erdreich, D-Ala. (6) | 1983 | Spencer Bachus, R |
| Bill Green, R-N.Y. (15) | 1978 | Carolyn B. Maloney, D |
| Clyde C. Holloway, R-La. (8) | 1987 | Richard H. Baker, R |
| Joan Kelly Horn, D-Mo. (2) | 1991 | James M. Talent, R |
| Jerry Huckaby, D-La. (5) | 1977 | Jim McCrery, R |
| Jim Jontz, D-Ind. (5) | 1987 | Steve Buyer, R |
| Peter H. Kostmayer, D-Pa. (8) | 1983 * | Jim Greenwood, R |
| Ron Marlenee, R-Mont. (2) | 1977 | Pat Williams, D |
| Nicholas Mavroules, D-Mass. (6) | 1979 | Peter G. Torkildsen, R |
| Bob McEwen, R-Ohio (6) | 1981 | Ted Strickland, D |
| Tom McMillen, D-Md. (4) | 1987 | Wayne T. Gilchrest, R |
| Dave Nagle, D-Iowa (3) | 1987 | Jim Nussle, R |
| Mary Rose Oakar, D-Ohio (20) | 1977 | Martin R. Hoke, R |
| Liz J. Patterson, D-S.C. (4) | 1987 | Bob Inglis, R |
| Richard Ray, D-Ga. (3) | 1983 | Mac Collins, R |
| Frank Riggs, R-Calif. (1) | 1991 | Dan Hamburg, D |
| John J. Rhodes III, R-Ariz. (1) | 1987 | Sam Coppersmith, D |
| Don Ritter, R-Pa. (15) | 1979 | Paul McHale, D |
| Gerry Sikorski, D-Minn. (6) | 1983 | Rod Grams, R |

*Kostmayer also served in 1977-81*

## Defeated in Primary

| Name, Party, State, District | Began | Defeated By |
|---|---|---|
| Bill Alexander, D-Ark. (1) | 1969 | Blanche Lambert |
| Beryl Anthony Jr., D-Ark. (4) | 1979 | Bill McCuen |
| Chester G. Atkins, D-Mass. (5) | 1985 | Martin T. Meehan |
| Terry L. Bruce, D-Ill. (19) | 1985 | Glenn Poshard |
| Beverly B. Byron, D-Md. (6) | 1979 | Thomas H. Hattery |
| Mickey Edwards, R-Okla. (5) | 1977 | Ernest J. Istook Jr. |
| Charles Hatcher, D-Ga. (2) | 1981 | Sanford Bishop |
| Charles A. Hayes, D-Ill. (1) | 1983 | Bobby L. Rush |
| Carroll Hubbard Jr., D-Ky. (1) | 1975 | Tom Barlow |
| Ben Jones, D-Ga. (4) | 1989 | Don Johnson |
| Joe Kolter, D-Pa. (4) | 1983 | Ron Klink |
| Robert J. Lagomarsino, R-Calif. (19) | 1974 | Michael Huffington |
| Clarence E. Miller, R-Ohio (10) | 1967 | Bob McEwen |
| Dick Nichols, R-Kan. (5) | 1991 | Eric R. Yost |
| Marty Russo, D-Ill. (3) | 1975 | William O. Lipinski |
| Gus Savage, D-Ill. (2) | 1981 | Mel Reynolds |
| Stephen J. Solarz, D-N.Y. (13) | 1975 | Nydia M. Velázquez |
| Harley O. Staggers, D-W.Va. (2) | 1983 | Alan B. Mollohan |
| Guy Vander Jagt, R-Mich. (9) | 1966 | Peter Hoekstra |

## Sought Other Office

| Name, Party, State, District | Began | Sought |
|---|---|---|
| Les AuCoin, D-Ore. (1) | 1975 | Senate [2] |
| Barbara Boxer, D-Calif. (6) | 1983 | Senate [3] |
| Ben Nighthorse Campbell, D-Colo. (3) | 1987 | Senate [3] |
| Tom Campbell, R-Calif. (12) | 1989 | Senate [1] |
| Thomas R. Carper, D-Del. (AL) | 1983 | Governor [3] |
| Rod Chandler, R-Wash. (8) | 1983 | Senate [2] |
| William E. Dannemeyer, R-Calif. (39) | 1979 | Senate [1] |
| Byron L. Dorgan, D-N.D. (AL) | 1981 | Senate [3] |
| Mel Levine, D-Calif. (27) | 1983 | Senate [1] |
| Jim Moody, D-Wis. (5) | 1983 | Senate [1] |
| Sid Morrison, R-Wash. (4) | 1981 | Governor [1] |
| Wayne Owens, D-Utah (2) | 1987 † | Senate [2] |
| Richard Stallings, D-Idaho (2) | 1985 | Senate [1] |

| [1] Lost in primary | [3] Won in general election |
|---|---|
| [2] Lost in general election | † Owens also served in 1973-75 |

## Retirements

| Name, Party, State, District | Began | Age |
|---|---|---|
| George F. Allen, R-Va. (7) | 1991 | 40 |
| Glenn M. Anderson, D-Calif. (32) | 1969 | 79 |
| Frank Annunzio, D-Ill. (11) | 1965 | 77 |
| Doug Barnard Jr., D-Ga. (10) | 1977 | 70 |
| Charles E. Bennett, D-Fla. (3) | 1949 | 81 |
| William S. Broomfield, R-Mich. (18) | 1957 | 70 |
| Lawrence Coughlin, R-Pa. (13) | 1969 | 63 |
| Robert W. Davis, R-Mich. (11) | 1979 | 60 |
| Bill Dickinson, R-Ala. (2) | 1965 | 67 |
| Brian Donnelly, D-Mass. (11) | 1979 | 46 |
| Bernard J. Dwyer, D-N.J. (6) | 1981 | 71 |
| Mervyn M. Dymally, D-Calif. (31) | 1981 | 66 |
| Dennis E. Eckart, D-Ohio (11) | 1981 | 42 |
| Dante B. Fascell, D-Fla. (19) | 1955 | 75 |
| Edward F. Feighan, D-Ohio (19) | 1983 | 45 |
| Joseph M. Gaydos, D-Pa. (20) | 1968 | 66 |
| Frank J. Guarini, D-N.J. (14) | 1979 | 68 |
| John Paul Hammerschmidt, R-Ark. (3) | 1967 | 70 |
| Claude Harris, D-Ala. (7) | 1987 | 52 |
| Dennis M. Hertel, D-Mich. (14) | 1981 | 43 |
| Larry J. Hopkins, R-Ky. (6) | 1979 | 59 |
| Frank Horton, R-N.Y. (29) | 1963 | 72 |
| Andy Ireland, R-Fla. (10) | 1977 | 62 |
| Craig T. James, R-Fla. (4) | 1989 | 51 |
| Ed Jenkins, D-Ga. (9) | 1977 | 59 |
| William Lehman, D-Fla. (17) | 1973 | 79 |
| Norman F. Lent, R-N.Y. (4) | 1971 | 61 |
| Bill Lowery, R-Calif. (41) | 1981 | 45 |
| Charles Luken, D-Ohio (1) | 1991 | 41 |
| David O'B. Martin, R-N.Y. (26) | 1981 | 48 |
| Raymond J. McGrath, R-N.Y. (5) | 1981 | 50 |
| Matthew F. McHugh, D-N.Y. (28) | 1975 | 53 |
| John Miller, R-Wash. (1) | 1985 | 54 |
| Robert J. Mrazek, D-N.Y. (3) | 1983 | 47 |
| Henry J. Nowak, D-N.Y. (33) | 1975 | 57 |
| Jim Olin, D-Va. (6) | 1983 | 72 |
| Don J. Pease, D-Ohio (13) | 1977 | 61 |
| Carl C. Perkins, D-Ky. (7) | 1985 | 38 |
| Carl D. Pursell, R-Mich. (2) | 1977 | 59 |
| Matthew J. Rinaldo, R-N.J. (7) | 1973 | 61 |
| Robert A. Roe, D-N.J. (8) | 1969 | 68 |
| Edward R. Roybal, D-Calif. (25) | 1963 | 76 |
| James H. Scheuer, D-N.Y. (8) | 1965 * | 72 |
| Dick Schulze, R-Pa. (5) | 1975 | 63 |
| Lawrence J. Smith, D-Fla. (16) | 1983 | 51 |
| Robin Tallon, D-S.C. (6) | 1983 | 46 |
| Lindsay Thomas, D-Ga. (1) | 1983 | 48 |
| Bob Traxler, D-Mich. (8) | 1974 | 61 |
| Vin Weber, R-Minn. (2) | 1981 | 40 |
| Howard Wolpe, D-Mich. (3) | 1979 | 53 |
| Chalmers P. Wylie, R-Ohio (15) | 1967 | 71 |
| Gus Yatron, D-Pa. (6) | 1969 | 65 |

*Scheuer did not serve in 1973-75*

## Died in Office

| Name, Party, State, District | Began | Age |
|---|---|---|
| Walter B. Jones (1) | 1966 | 79 |
| Ted Weiss, D-N.Y. (17) | 1977 | 64 |

# House Makeup, Party Gains and Losses

| | Seats | 102nd Congress Dem. | Rep. | 103rd Congress Dem. | Rep. | Gain/ Loss | | Seats | 102nd Congress Dem. | Rep. | 103rd Congress Dem. | Rep. | Gain/ Loss |
|---|---|---|---|---|---|---|---|---|---|---|---|---|---|
| Ala. | 7 | 5 | 2 | 4 | 3 | −1D/+1R | Neb. | 3 | 1 | 2 | 1 | 2 | |
| Alaska | 1 | 0 | 1 | 0 | 1 | | Nev. | 2 | 1 | 1 | 1 | 1 | |
| Ariz. | 6 † | 1 | 4 | 3 | 3 | +2D/−1R | N.H. | 2 | 1 | 1 | 1 | 1 | |
| Ark. | 4 | 3 | 1 | 2 | 2 | −1D/+1R | N.J. | 13 † | 8 | 6 | 7 | 6 | −1D |
| Calif. | 52 † | 26 | 19 | 31 | 21 | +4D/+3R | N.M. | 3 | 1 | 2 | 1 | 2 | |
| Colo. | 6 | 3 | 3 | 2 | 4 | −1D/+1R | N.Y. | 31 † | 21 | 13 | 18 | 13 | −3D |
| Conn. | 6 | 3 | 3 | 3 | 3 | | N.C. | 12 † | 7 | 4 | 8 | 4 | +1D |
| Del. | 1 | 1 | 0 | 0 | 1 | −1D/+1R | N.D. | 1 | 1 | 0 | 1 | 0 | |
| Fla. | 23 † | 9 | 10 | 10 | 13 | +1D/+3R | Ohio | 19 † | 11 | 10 | 10 | 9 | −1D/−1R |
| Ga. | 11 † | 9 | 1 | 7 | 4 | −2D/+3R | Okla. | 6 | 4 | 2 | 4 | 2 | |
| Hawaii | 2 | 2 | 0 | 2 | 0 | | Ore. | 5 | 4 | 1 | 4 | 1 | |
| Idaho | 2 | 2 | 0 | 1 | 1 | −1D/+1R | Pa. | 21 † | 11 | 12 | 11 | 10 | −2R |
| Ill. | 20 † | 15 | 7 | 12 | 8 | −3D/+1R | R.I. | 2 | 1 | 1 | 1 | 1 | |
| Ind. | 10 | 8 | 2 | 7 | 3 | −1D/+1R | S.C. | 6 | 4 | 2 | 3 | 3 | −1D/+1R |
| Iowa | 5 † | 2 | 4 | 1 | 4 | −1D | S.D. | 1 | 1 | 0 | 1 | 0 | |
| Kan. | 4 † | 2 | 3 | 2 | 2 | −1R | Tenn. | 9 | 6 | 3 | 6 | 3 | |
| Ky. | 6 † | 4 | 3 | 4 | 2 | −1R | Texas | 30 † | 19 | 8 | 21 | 9 | +2D/+1R |
| La. | 7 † | 4 | 4 | 4 | 3 | −1R | Utah | 3 | 2 | 1 | 2 | 1 | |
| Maine | 2 | 1 | 1 | 1 | 1 | | Vt.‡ | 1 | 0 | 0 | 0 | 0 | |
| Md. | 8 | 5 | 3 | 4 | 4 | −1D/+1R | Va. | 11 † | 6 | 4 | 7 | 4 | +1D |
| Mass. | 10 † | 11 | 0 | 8 | 2 | −3D/+2R | Wash. | 9 † | 5 | 3 | 8 | 1 | +3D/−2R |
| Mich. | 16 † | 11 | 7 | 10 | 6 | −1D/−1R | W.Va. | 3 † | 4 | 0 | 3 | 0 | −1D |
| Minn. | 8 | 6 | 2 | 6 | 2 | | Wis. | 9 | 4 | 5 | 4 | 5 | |
| Miss. | 5 | 5 | 0 | 5 | 0 | | Wyo. | 1 | 0 | 1 | 0 | 1 | |
| Mo. | 9 | 6 | 3 | 6 | 3 | | | | | | | | |
| Mont. | 1 † | 1 | 1 | 1 | 0 | −1R | **TOTALS** | 435 ‡ | 268 | 166 | 259 | 175 | −10D/+10R |

† Changed due to reapportionment.
‡ Vermont's Bernard Sanders is an independent.

Continued from p. 17-A
the 21 Democratic newcomers who are women.

## Republicans Stumble in Frost Belt

A concerted effort by the Bush-Quayle campaign to target states such as New Jersey and Michigan did little to help Republican House candidates. Clinton carried both states, and all Democratic incumbents won re-election.

Republicans mounted competitive House challenges to four Democratic incumbents in New Jersey — Robert E. Andrews, William J. Hughes, Frank Pallone Jr. and Robert G. Torricelli — but came up empty. Of three open-seat races, Democrats captured two, including the 8th District of retiring Democrat Robert A. Roe. Earlier in the campaign, the 8th was considered a prime GOP pickup opportunity.

Republicans hit the same wall in Michigan. Despite repeated visits from Bush an Quayle, Clinton carried the state, and Republicans made little progress in House elections. Spirited GOP challengers failed to dislodge the state's four most endangered Democratic incumbents — Bob Carr, Dale E. Kildee, David E. Bonior and William D. Ford.

Republicans won three of the state's five open seats, but the GOP failed to hang onto the open 1st District; that Upper Peninsula-based seat has been in GOP hands for much of the century, and the party's nominee, former Rep. Philip Ruppe, was considered likely to win back his former

seat. But he ran a lackluster campaign and lost to the Democratic nominee, former state Rep. Bart Stupak.

Ruppe was one of five former members — all Republicans — seeking to return to Congress. All lost. Voters dashed the comeback hopes of Joseph J. DioGuardi of New York, Charles Dougherty of Pennsylvania, Paul W. Cronin of Massachusetts and Beau Boulter of Texas.

## GOP Pickups

If Bush was no boost for GOP House candidates, he at least ran well enough in a number of states — particularly in the South — that many Republican House candidates were able to stay competitive.

Bright spots for the GOP included Georgia, where the GOP improved its standing in the delegation from 1-9 before the election to 4-7. Democratic Rep. Ray lost, two other Democratic incumbents got less than 60 percent, two open seats went Republican and House Minority Whip Newt Gingrich won re-election.

Ticket-splitting was heavy in districts in Kentucky, North Carolina and Clinton's home state of Arkansas. There Republicans circled the wagons to retain the open 3rd District, and also managed an upset victory in the open 4th.

Kentucky's 5th District was carried by Clinton, but GOP Rep. Harold Rogers ran ahead of the Democratic nominee and won with 54 percent. The politically
Continued on p. 24-A

# House Membership in 103rd Congress

## Alabama

1 Sonny Callahan (R)
2 Terry Everett (R) #
3 Glen Browder (D)
4 Tom Bevill (D)
5 Bud Cramer (D)
6 Spencer Bachus (R) #
7 Earl F. Hilliard (D) #

## Alaska

AL Don Young (R)

## Arizona

1 Sam Coppersmith (D) #
2 Ed Pastor (D)
3 Bob Stump (R)
4 Jon Kyl (R)
5 Jim Kolbe (R)
6 Karan English (D) #

## Arkansas

1 Blanche Lambert (D) #
2 Ray Thornton (D)
3 Tim Hutchinson (R) #
4 Jay Dickey (R) #

## California

1 Dan Hamburg (D) #
2 Wally Herger (R)
3 Vic Fazio (D)
4 John T. Doolittle (R)
5 Robert T. Matsui (D)
6 Lynn Woolsey (D) #
7 George Miller (D)
8 Nancy Pelosi (D)
9 Ronald V. Dellums (D)
10 Bill Baker (R) #
11 Richard W. Pombo (R) #
12 Tom Lantos (D)
13 Pete Stark (D)
14 Anna G. Eshoo (D) #
15 Norman Y. Mineta (D)
16 Don Edwards (D)
17 Leon E. Panetta (D)
18 Gary Condit (D)
19 Richard H. Lehman (D)
20 Calvin Dooley (D)
21 Bill Thomas (R)
22 Michael Huffington (R) #
23 Elton Gallegly (R)
24 Anthony C. Beilenson (D)
25 Howard P. "Buck" McKeon (R) #
26 Howard L. Berman (D)
27 Carlos J. Moorhead (R)
28 David Dreier (R)
29 Henry A. Waxman (D)
30 Xavier Becerra (D) #
31 Matthew G. Martinez (D)
32 Julian C. Dixon (D)
33 Lucille Roybal-Allard (D) #
34 Esteban E. Torres (D)
35 Maxine Waters (D)
36 Jane Harman (D) #
37 Walter R. Tucker (D) #
38 Steve Horn (R) #
39 Ed Royce (R) #
40 Jerry Lewis (R)
41 Jay C. Kim (R) #
42 George E. Brown Jr. (D)
43 Ken Calvert # (R)
44 Al McCandless (R)
45 Dana Rohrabacher (R)
46 Robert K. Dornan (R)
47 C. Christopher Cox (R)
48 Ron Packard (R)
49 Lynn Schenk (D) #
50 Bob Filner (D) #
51 Randy "Duke" Cunningham (R)
52 Duncan Hunter (R)

## Colorado

1 Patricia Schroeder (D)
2 David E. Skaggs (D)
3 Scott McInnis (R) #
4 Wayne Allard (R)
5 Joel Hefley (R)
6 Dan Schaefer (R)

## Connecticut

1 Barbara B. Kennelly (D)
2 Sam Gejdenson (D)
3 Rosa DeLauro (D)
4 Christopher Shays (R)
5 Gary Franks (R)
6 Nancy L. Johnson (R)

## Delaware

AL Michael N. Castle (R) #

## Florida

1 Earl Hutto (D)
2 Pete Peterson (D)
3 Corrine Brown (D) #
4 Tillie Fowler (R) #
5 Karen L. Thurman (D) #
6 Cliff Stearns (R)
7 John L. Mica (R) #
8 Bill McCollum (R)
9 Michael Bilirakis (R)
10 C. W. Bill Young (R)
11 Sam M. Gibbons (D)
12 Charles T. Canady (R) #
13 Dan Miller (R) #
14 Porter J. Goss (R)
15 Jim Bacchus (D)
16 Tom Lewis (R)
17 Carrie Meek (D) #
18 Ileana Ros-Lehtinen (R)
19 Harry A. Johnston (D)
20 Peter Deutsch (D) #
21 Lincoln Diaz-Balart (R) #
22 E. Clay Shaw Jr. (R)
23 Alcee L. Hastings (D) #

## Lineup

**Democrats** **258** *(Freshmen 63)*

**Republicans** **176** *(Freshmen 47)*

**Independent** **1**

*NOTE: # Freshman representative*

## Georgia

1 Jack Kingston (R) #
2 Sanford Bishop (D) #
3 Mac Collins (R) #
4 John Linder (R) #
5 John Lewis (D)
6 Newt Gingrich (R)
7 George "Buddy" Darden (D)
8 J. Roy Rowland (D)
9 Nathan Deal (D) #
10 Don Johnson (D) #
11 Cynthia McKinney (D) #

## Hawaii

1 Neil Abercrombie (D)
2 Patsy T. Mink (D)

## Idaho

1 Larry LaRocco (D)
2 Michael D. Crapo (R) #

## Illinois

1 Bobby L. Rush (D) #
2 Mel Reynolds (D) #
3 William O. Lipinski (D)
4 Luis V. Gutierrez (D) #
5 Dan Rostenkowski (D)
6 Henry J. Hyde (R)
7 Cardiss Collins (D)
8 Philip M. Crane (R)
9 Sidney R. Yates (D)
10 John Porter (R)
11 George E. Sangmeister (D)
12 Jerry F. Costello (D)
13 Harris W. Fawell (R)
14 Dennis Hastert (R)
15 Thomas W. Ewing (R)
16 Donald Manzullo (R) #
17 Lane Evans (D)
18 Robert H. Michel (R)
19 Glenn Poshard (D)
20 Richard J. Durbin (D)

## Indiana

1 Peter J. Visclosky (D)
2 Philip R. Sharp (D)
3 Tim Roemer (D)
4 Jill L. Long (D)
5 Steve Buyer (R) #
6 Dan Burton (R)
7 John T. Myers (R)
8 Frank McCloskey (D)
9 Lee H. Hamilton (D)
10 Andrew Jacobs Jr. (D)

## Iowa

1 Jim Leach (R)
2 Jim Nussle (R)
3 Jim Ross Lightfoot (R)
4 Neal Smith (D)
5 Fred Grandy (R)

## Kansas

1 Pat Roberts (R)
2 Jim Slattery (D)
3 Jan Meyers (R)
4 Dan Glickman (D)

## Kentucky

1 Tom Barlow (D) #
2 William H. Natcher (D)
3 Romano L. Mazzoli (D)
4 Jim Bunning (R)
5 Harold Rogers (R)
6 Scotty Baesler (D) #

## Louisiana

1 Robert L. Livingston (R)
2 William J. Jefferson (D)
3 W. J. "Billy" Tauzin (D)
4 Cleo Fields (D)
5 Jim McCrery (R)
6 Richard H. Baker (R)
7 Jimmy Hayes (D)

## Maine

1 Thomas H. Andrews (D)
2 Olympia J. Snowe (R)

## Maryland

1 Wayne T. Gilchrest (R)
2 Helen Delich Bentley (R)
3 Benjamin L. Cardin (D)
4 Albert R. Wynn (D) #
5 Steny H. Hoyer (D)
6 Roscoe G. Bartlett (R) #
7 Kweisi Mfume (D)
8 Constance A. Morella (R)

## Massachusetts

1 John W. Olver (D)
2 Richard E. Neal (D)
3 Peter I. Blute (R) #
4 Barney Frank (D)
5 Martin T. Meehan (D) #
6 Peter G. Torkildsen (R) #
7 Edward J. Markey (D)
8 Joseph P. Kennedy II (D)
9 Joe Moakley (D)
10 Gerry E. Studds (D)

## Michigan

1 Bart Stupak (D) #
2 Peter Hoekstra (R) #
3 Paul B. Henry (R)
4 Dave Camp (R)
5 James A. Barcia (D) #
6 Fred Upton (R)
7 Nick Smith (R) #

8 Bob Carr (D)
9 Dale E. Kildee (D)
10 David E. Bonior (D)
11 Joe Knollenberg (R) #
12 Sander M. Levin (D)
13 William D. Ford (D)
14 John Conyers Jr. (D)
15 Barbara-Rose Collins (D)
16 John D. Dingell (D)

## Minnesota

1 Timothy J. Penny (D)
2 David Minge (D) #
3 Jim Ramstad (R)
4 Bruce F. Vento (D)
5 Martin Olav Sabo (D)
6 Rod Grams (R) #
7 Collin C. Peterson (D)
8 James L. Oberstar (D)

## Mississippi

1 Jamie L. Whitten (D)
2 Mike Espy (D)
3 G. V. "Sonny" Montgomery (D)
4 Mike Parker (D)
5 Gene Taylor (D)

## Missouri

1 William L. Clay (D)
2 James M. Talent (R) #
3 Richard A. Gephardt (D)
4 Ike Skelton (D)
5 Alan Wheat (D)
6 Pat Danner (D) #
7 Mel Hancock (R)
8 Bill Emerson (R)
9 Harold L. Volkmer (D)

## Montana

AL Pat Williams (D)

## Nebraska

1 Doug Bereuter (R)
2 Peter Hoagland (D)
3 Bill Barrett (R)

## Nevada

1 James Bilbray (D)
2 Barbara F. Vucanovich (R)

## New Hampshire

1 Bill Zeliff (R)
2 Dick Swett (D)

## New Jersey

1 Robert E. Andrews (D)
2 William J. Hughes (D)
3 H. James Saxton (R)
4 Christopher H. Smith (R)
5 Marge Roukema (R)
6 Frank Pallone Jr. (D)
7 Bob Franks (R) #
8 Herbert C. Klein (D) #
9 Robert G. Torricelli (D)
10 Donald M. Payne (D)
11 Dean A. Gallo (R)
12 Dick Zimmer (R)
13 Robert Menendez (D) #

## New Mexico

1 Steven H. Schiff (R)

2 Joe Skeen (R)
3 Bill Richardson (D)

## New York

1 George J. Hochbrueckner (D)
2 Rick A. Lazio (R) #
3 Peter T. King (R) #
4 David A. Levy (R) #
5 Gary L. Ackerman (D)
6 Floyd H. Flake (D)
7 Thomas J. Manton (D)
8 Jerrold Nadler (D) #
9 Charles E. Schumer (D)
10 Edolphus Towns (D)
11 Major R. Owens (D)
12 Nydia M. Velázquez (D) #
13 Susan Molinari (R)
14 Carolyn B. Maloney (D) #
15 Charles B. Rangel (D)
16 Jose E. Serrano (D)
17 Eliot L. Engel (D)
18 Nita M. Lowey (D)
19 Hamilton Fish Jr. (R)
20 Benjamin A. Gilman (R)
21 Michael R. McNulty (D)
22 Gerald B.H. Solomon (R)
23 Sherwood Boehlert (R)
24 John M. McHugh (R) #
25 James T. Walsh (R)
26 Maurice D. Hinchey (D) #
27 Bill Paxon (R)
28 Louise M. Slaughter (D)
29 John J. LaFalce (D)
30 Jack Quinn (R) #
31 Amo Houghton (R)

## North Carolina

1 Eva Clayton (D) #
2 Tim Valentine (D)
3 H. Martin Lancaster (D)
4 David Price (D)
5 Stephen L. Neal (D)
6 Howard Coble (R)
7 Charlie Rose (D)
8 W. G. "Bill" Hefner (D)
9 Alex McMillan (R)
10 Cass Ballenger (R)
11 Charles H. Taylor (R)
12 Melvin Watt (D) #

## North Dakota

AL Earl Pomeroy (D) #

## Ohio

1 David Mann (D) #
2 Bill Gradison (R)
3 Tony P. Hall (D)
4 Michael G. Oxley (R)
5 Paul E. Gillmor (R)
6 Ted Strickland (D) #
7 David L. Hobson (R)
8 John A. Boehner (R)
9 Marcy Kaptur (D)
10 Martin R. Hoke (R) #
11 Louis Stokes (D)
12 John R. Kasich (R)
13 Sherrod Brown (D) #
14 Tom Sawyer (D)
15 Deborah Pryce (R) #
16 Ralph Regula (R)
17 James A. Traficant Jr. (D)
18 Douglas Applegate (D)
19 Eric Fingerhut (D) #

## Oklahoma

1 James M. Inhofe (R)

2 Mike Synar (D)
3 Bill Brewster (D)
4 Dave McCurdy (D)
5 Ernest Jim Istook (R) #
6 Glenn English (D)

## Oregon

1 Elizabeth Furse (D) #
2 Bob Smith (R)
3 Ron Wyden (D)
4 Peter A. DeFazio (D)
5 Mike Kopetski (D)

## Pennsylvania

1 Thomas M. Foglietta (D)
2 Lucien E. Blackwell (D)
3 Robert A. Borski (D)
4 Ron Klink (D) #
5 William F. Clinger (R)
6 Tim Holden (D) #
7 Curt Weldon (R)
8 Jim Greenwood (R) #
9 Bud Shuster (R)
10 Joseph M. McDade (R)
11 Paul E. Kanjorski (D)
12 John P. Murtha (D)
13 Marjorie Margolies-Mezvinsky (D) #
14 William J. Coyne (D)
15 Paul McHale (D) #
16 Robert S. Walker (R)
17 George W. Gekas (R)
18 Rick Santorum (R)
19 Bill Goodling (R)
20 Austin J. Murphy (D)
21 Tom Ridge (R)

## Rhode Island

1 Ronald K. Machtley (R)
2 John F. Reed (D)

## South Carolina

1 Arthur Ravenel Jr. (R)
2 Floyd D. Spence (R)
3 Butler Derrick (D)
4 Bob Inglis (R) #
5 John M. Spratt Jr. (D)
6 James E. Clyburn (D) #

## South Dakota

AL Tim Johnson (D)

## Tennessee

1 James H. Quillen (R)
2 John J. "Jimmy" Duncan Jr. (R)
3 Marilyn Lloyd (D)
4 Jim Cooper (D)
5 Bob Clement (D)
6 Bart Gordon (D)
7 Don Sundquist (R)
8 John Tanner (D)
9 Harold E. Ford (D)

## Texas

1 Jim Chapman (D)
2 Charles Wilson (D)
3 Sam Johnson (R)
4 Ralph M. Hall (D)
5 John Bryant (D)
6 Joe L. Barton (R)
7 Bill Archer (R)
8 Jack Fields (R)
9 Jack Brooks (D)
10 J. J. Pickle (D)

11 Chet Edwards (D)
12 Pete Geren (D)
13 Bill Sarpalius (D)
14 Greg Laughlin (D)
15 E. "Kika" de la Garza (D)
16 Ronald D. Coleman (D)
17 Charles W. Stenholm (D)
18 Craig Washington (D)
19 Larry Combest (R)
20 Henry B. Gonzalez (D)
21 Lamar Smith (R)
22 Tom DeLay (R)
23 Henry Bonilla (R) #
24 Martin Frost (D)
25 Michael A. Andrews (D)
26 Dick Armey (R)
27 Solomon P. Ortiz (D)
28 Frank Tejeda (D) #
29 Gene Green (D) #
30 Eddie Bernice Johnson (D) #

## Utah

1 James V. Hansen (R)
2 Karen Shepherd (D) #
3 Bill Orton (D)

## Vermont

AL Bernard Sanders (I)

## Virginia

1 Herbert H. Bateman (R)
2 Owen B. Pickett (D)
3 Robert C. Scott (D) #
4 Norman Sisisky (D)
5 Lewis F. Payne Jr. (D)
6 Robert W. Goodlatte (R) #
7 Thomas J. Bliley Jr. (R)
8 James P. Moran Jr. (D)
9 Rick Boucher (D)
10 Frank R. Wolf (R)
11 Leslie L. Byrne (D) #

## Washington

1 Maria Cantwell (D) #
2 Al Swift (D)
3 Jolene Unsoeld (D)
4 Jay Inslee (D) #
5 Thomas S. Foley (D)
6 Norm Dicks (D)
7 Jim McDermott (D)
8 Jennifer Dunn (R) #
9 Mike Kreidler (D) #

## West Virginia

1 Alan B. Mollohan (D)
2 Bob Wise (D)
3 Nick J. Rahall II (D)

## Wisconsin

1 Les Aspin (D)
2 Scott L. Klug (R)
3 Steve Gunderson (R)
4 Gerald D. Kleczka (D)
5 Thomas M. Barrett (D) #
6 Tom Petri (R)
7 David R. Obey (D)
8 Toby Roth (R)
9 F. James Sensenbrenner Jr. (R)

## Wyoming

AL Craig Thomas (R)

# House Members Defeated Nov. 3

| | Terms | | Terms |
|---|---|---|---|
| Ben Erdreich, D-Ala. | 5 | Gerry Sikorski, D-Minn. | 5 |
| John J. Rhodes III, R-Ariz. | 3 | Joan Kelly Horn, D-Mo. | 1 |
| Frank Riggs, R-Calif. | 1 | Tom Coleman, R-Mo. | 8 |
| Richard Ray, D-Ga. | 5 | Ron Marlenee, R-Mont. | 8 [1] |
| John W. Cox Jr., D-Ill. | 1 | Thomas J. Downey, D-N.Y. | 9 |
| Jim Jontz, D-Ind. | 3 | Bill Green, R-N.Y. | 8 [2] |
| Dave Nagle, D-Iowa | 3 [1] | Bob McEwen, R-Ohio | 6 |
| Jerry Huckaby, D-La. | 8 [1] | Mary Rose Oakar, D-Ohio | 8 |
| Clyde C. Holloway, R-La. | 3 [1] | Peter H. Kostmayer, D-Pa. | 7 [3] |
| Tom McMillen, D-Md. | 3 [1] | Don Ritter, R-Pa. | 7 |
| Joseph D. Early, D-Mass. | 9 | Liz J. Patterson, D-S.C. | 3 |
| Nicholas Mavroules, D-Mass. | 7 | Albert J. Bustamante, D-Texas | 4 |

[1] *Denotes incumbents who were matched against incumbents.*
[2] *Elected in a special election in 1978.*
[3] *Served 1977-81; 1983-present.*

# Election-Year Turnover

In 1992, 110 members left the 435-seat House, the greatest number in any election since World War II.

| Year | Retirements [1] | Defeated in Primary | Defeated in General Election | Total Turnover [2] |
|---|---|---|---|---|
| 1946 | 32 | 18 | 52 | 107 |
| 1948 | 29 | 15 | 68 | 118 |
| 1950 | 29 | 6 | 32 | 73 |
| 1952 | 42 | 9 | 26 | 81 |
| 1954 | 24 | 6 | 22 | 56 |
| 1956 | 21 | 6 | 16 | 46 |
| 1958 | 33 | 3 | 37 | 79 |
| 1960 | 26 | 5 | 25 | 60 |
| 1962 | 34 | 12 | 22 | 68 |
| 1964 | 33 | 8 | 45 | 91 |
| 1966 | 22 | 8 | 41 | 73 |
| 1968 | 23 | 4 | 9 | 39 |
| 1970 | 29 | 10 | 12 | 56 |
| 1972 | 40 | 12 | 13 | 70 |
| 1974 | 43 | 8 | 40 | 92 |
| 1976 | 47 | 3 | 13 | 67 |
| 1978 | 49 | 5 | 19 | 77 |
| 1980 | 34 | 6 | 31 | 74 |
| 1982 | 40 | 10 | 29 | 81 |
| 1984 | 22 | 3 | 16 | 45 |
| 1986 | 38 | 2 | 6 | 50 |
| 1988 | 23 | 1 | 6 | 34 |
| 1990 | 27 | 1 | 15 | 45 |
| 1992 | 65 | 19 | 24 | 110 |

[1] *Includes retirees and those running for other offices.*
[2] *Also includes open seats due to deaths and resignations.*

SOURCE: Vital Statistics On Congress

*Continued from p. 21-A*
volatile western North Carolina 11th also remained in GOP hands, as Rep. Charles H. Taylor won by an unexpectedly comfortable 10-point margin.

Bush victories in Virginia, South Carolina and Alabama helped propel GOP House aspirants in Republican-leaning seats in those states. Virginia's 6th, which Democrat Jim Olin captured from the GOP in 1982, returned to its roots, electing conservative lawyer Bob Goodlatte to succeed the retiring Olin. In South Carolina's 4th, unheralded Republican Bob Inglis ousted Rep. Patterson. And in Alabama's 6th, redrawn to be a Republican fortress, former state GOP Chairman Spencer Bachus employed a witheringly negative campaign to dislodge Erdreich.

Republicans also made headway in Idaho and Colorado. GOP state Rep. Scott McInnis weathered not only a Clinton victory, but the Senate victory of the man replaced, 3rd District Democratic Rep. Ben Nighthorse Campbell.

In Idaho, state Sen. Michael D. Crapo won back the conservative 2nd District, where Republicans have been shut out since 1984. A job switch in Delaware sent outgoing Republican Gov. Michael N. Castle to the House to replace Democratic Rep. Thomas R. Carper, who was elected governor.

## Divided Opposition

Independent candidate Ross Perot and his criticism of the political establishment boosted some independents running for the House.

In Pennsylvania, Republican Bill Goodling — one of the top House bank overdrafters — fended off two challengers, one of them a credible independent, Thomas Humbert. Humbert managed 20 percent of the vote against Goodling, but with the Democratic nominee running poorly, Goodling held on to win with 45 percent.

In Connecticut's 3rd District, the third-party candidacy of Democratic primary loser Lynn Taborsak boosted the re-election bid of freshman Gary Franks, the House's only black Republican. Besieged by personal financial difficulties and staff turnover, Franks survived as Taborsak, running on Connecticut Gov. Lowell P. Weicker Jr.'s A Connecticut Party line, split the anti-Franks vote with Democratic nominee James Lawlor.

Like Franks, Don Young of Alaska, Barbara F. Vucanovich of Nevada and Olympia J. Snowe of Maine were held under 50 percent, but all won re-election because their Democratic challengers lost anti-incumbent votes to independent and third-party candidates.

While the much-heralded anti-incumbent sentiment failed to translate into massive losses at the polls, several congressional leaders were singed.

The Democratic House leadership was especially chastened. Fazio, Speaker Thomas S. Foley of Washington, Majority Whip Bonior and House Democratic Caucus Chairman Steny H. Hoyer of Maryland all were held to 55 percent or less. Ways and Means Committee Chairman Dan Rostenkowski, D-Ill., Minority Leader Robert H. Michel, R-Ill., and Minority Whip Gingrich won less than 60 percent. ■

# GOP's Comeback Dreams Dissolve

As they planned for the 1992 elections, Republican strategists were confident that redistricting would be a wedge helping GOP candidates cut deeply into the Democrats' enduring House majority.

But on Nov. 3, Republicans' hopes for major gains resulting from redistricting were frustrated. The party's failure to capitalize on the once-a-decade redrawing of district boundaries was a factor in the GOP's meager 10-seat House pickup.

The GOP's upbeat pre-election prognosis for profiting from redistricting was understandable. Reapportionment following the 1990 census shifted 19 House seats from slow-growth states — mainly in strong Democratic areas of the Northeast and Midwest — to fast-growth states — mainly in the conservative-leaning South and West.

But the presidential campaign proved to be a negative backdrop for many GOP House candidates, particularly in high-growth Western states. There President Bush scored poorly and Democratic challenger Bill Clinton ran well — a reverse of the top-of-the-ticket situation that has prevailed in the West for nearly a generation.

## California Dreaming

The GOP had expected California to be the jewel in the crown of House gains from redistricting. But Bush took less than one-third of the state's presidential vote, and Democrats won a solid majority of the state's 52 House seats.

The nation's largest state gained seven House seats in the 1990 reapportionment; a GOP-friendly state court approved a new map placing most of those new seats in such conservative areas as Southern California, the Central Valley and the East Bay suburbs of San Francisco. Republicans hoped to win at least five, maybe even six of those seats.

Yet Democrats countered the Republicans' seeming advantage with a crop of talented candidates, and they in turn benefited from Clinton's strong showing in the state. Some of the House races were very close: Republican Ken Calvert won by fewer than 1,000 votes in the 43rd District.

At the same time, Democrat Dan Hamburg unseated freshman Republican Rep. Frank Riggs in the 1st District. Democratic members disadvantaged by redistricting — including Vic Fazio, Richard H. Lehman and Anthony C. Beilenson — all won. Two Democratic candidates — Anna G. Eshoo in the 14th District and Bob Filner in the 50th — won in open-seat contests resulting from the retirements of Republican members. Steve Horn, winner in the 38th District, was the only Republican newcomer to fill a Democratic vacancy.

So Republicans, who talked boldly of gaining partisan parity under the new California House district map, were headed into the 103rd Congress with a 22-30 deficit in the

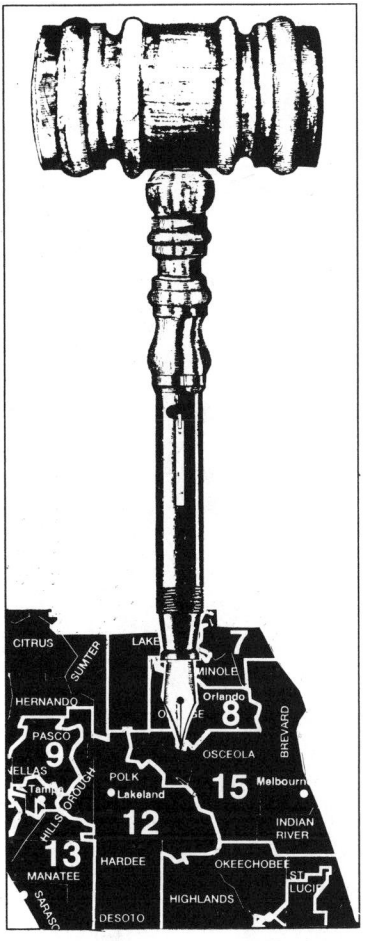

state's delegation. The old partisan breakdown was 26-19 Democratic.

## Minority Districts Prove Little Boost

In a number of states, Republicans expected to profit from legislative or judicial efforts — influenced by the Voting Rights Act — to draw House maps aimed at increasing the number of black- and Hispanic-majority districts. Typically these majority-minority districts were created by taking minority voters who had been represented by white urban Democrats; that often left those incumbents running in less-Democratic (and often more suburban) districts where they appeared more vulnerable to Republican challenge.

Thanks to mapmakers' efforts to create new districts winnable by minority candidates, 13 new blacks and six new Hispanics were elected Nov. 3 from a total of 13 states — Alabama, California, Florida, Georgia, Illinois, Louisiana, Maryland, New Jersey, New York, North Carolina, South Carolina, Texas and Virginia. (All 13 of those black House freshmen were Democrats, as were all but one of the six Hispanic freshmen.)

But the GOP fell short of its expectations for picking off white Democrats wounded in the process of drawing new minority districts.

Only three Democratic incumbents had defeats that were directly attributable to the creation of new majority-minority districts:

● In Alabama, remapping deprived Democratic Rep. Ben Erdreich of much of his heavily Democratic black constituency in Birmingham. He lost to Republican Spencer Bachus in a new 6th District that is mainly suburban and Republican-leaning.

● In Maryland's 1st District, Democratic Rep. Tom McMillen lost to GOP Rep. Wayne T. Gilchrest in a face-off forced when their districts were merged to make way for a new black-majority seat in the Washington, D.C., suburbs.

● In Louisiana, creation of the new black-majority 4th District forced Democrat Jerry Huckaby into a campaign against Republican Rep. Jim McCrery in the 5th District; Huckaby lost.

Republicans were thwarted in other states where they hoped for ripple-effect gains, however. In most of these, Democrats had controlled the redistricting process and skillfully crafted new black- and Hispanic-majority districts in ways that did not ruin the re-election prospects of white Democratic incumbents.

In North Carolina, the Democratic House delegation welcomed two new black members, Eva Clayton and Melvin Watt, who won in districts designed to their advantages. However, all six of the state's white Democratic incumbents also won re-election Nov. 3, including Tim Valentine and Stephen L. Neal. They were thought to be at

*Continued on p. 29-A*

# Congressional Districts for the 1990s

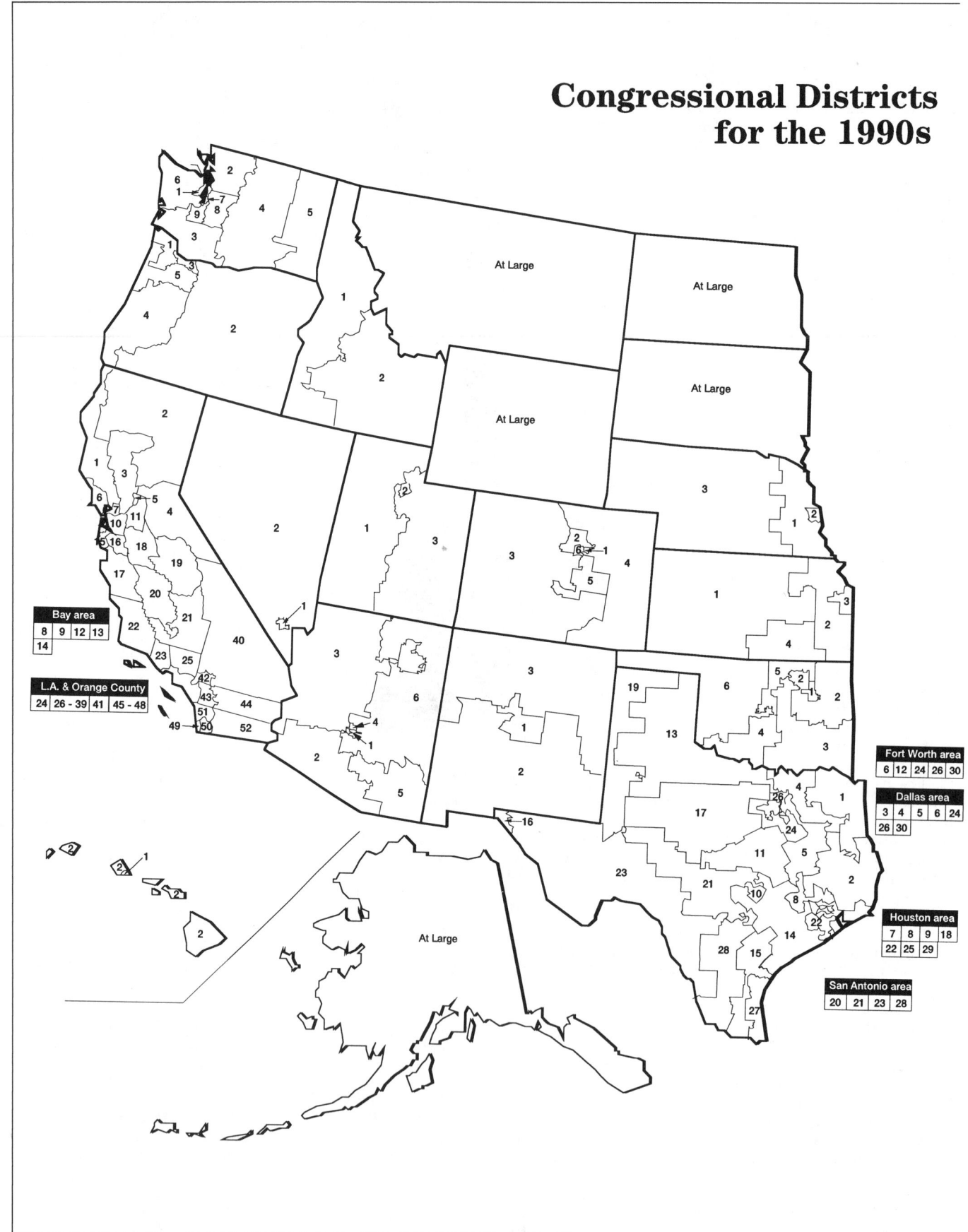

Bay area
| 8 | 9 | 12 | 13 |
| 14 |

L.A. & Orange County
| 24 | 26 - 39 | 41 | 45 - 48 |

Fort Worth area
| 6 | 12 | 24 | 26 | 30 |

Dallas area
| 3 | 4 | 5 | 6 | 24 |
| 26 | 30 |

Houston area
| 7 | 8 | 9 | 18 |
| 22 | 25 | 29 |

San Antonio area
| 20 | 21 | 23 | 28 |

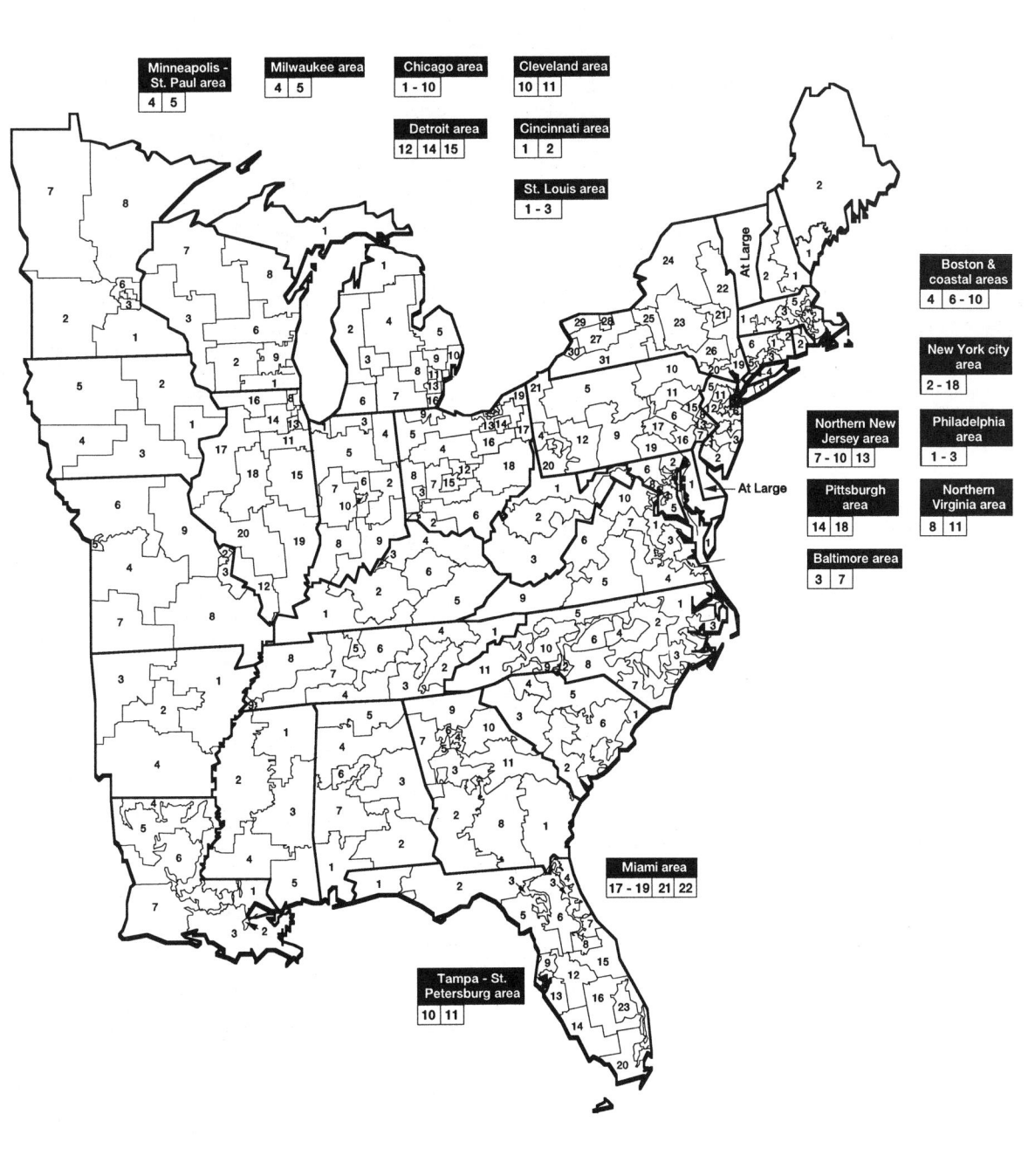

Minneapolis -
St. Paul area
4 | 5

Milwaukee area
4 | 5

Chicago area
1 - 10

Cleveland area
10 | 11

Detroit area
12 | 14 | 15

Cincinnati area
1 | 2

St. Louis area
1 - 3

Boston &
coastal areas
4 | 6 - 10

New York city
area
2 - 18

Northern New
Jersey area
7 - 10 | 13

Philadelphia
area
1 - 3

Pittsburgh
area
14 | 18

Northern
Virginia area
8 | 11

Baltimore area
3 | 7

Miami area
17 - 19 | 21 | 22

Tampa - St.
Petersburg area
10 | 11

# Redistricting in the States

Forty-three states have more than one House seat and must draw new district lines after each census and reapportionment. Below are the dates of redistricting action in these states. Following each state is its number of House seats for the 1990s; the number of seats gained or lost in 1990 reapportionment is in parentheses.

**Alabama** 7*
Map issued by federal court Jan. 27, 1992; that map became law March 27 after a map passed by the Legislature was rejected by the Justice Department.

**Arizona** 6 (+1)*
Map issued by federal court May 6, 1992.

**Arkansas** 4
Map passed Legislature March 26, 1991; governor signed April 10. Federal court upheld map Nov. 15; Supreme court upheld map June 1, 1992.

**California** 52 (+7)*
Map drawn by a special panel of retired judges approved by state Supreme Court Jan. 27, 1992; federal court Jan. 28 rejected an effort to block use of that map in 1992 pending appeal. A federal appeals court March 3 dismissed a challenge to the map.

**Colorado** 6
Map passed Legislature March 19, 1992; governor signed March 24.

**Connecticut** 6
Redistricting commission filed map with secretary of state Nov. 27, 1991; governor's signature not required.

**Florida** 23 (+4)*
Federal court approved map May 29, 1992.

**Georgia** 11 (+1)*
Map passed Legislature March 31, 1992; governor signed March 31; Justice Department approved April 2.

**Hawaii** 2
Map adopted by commission July 19, 1991; governor's signature not required.

**Idaho** 2
Map passed Legislature Jan. 21, 1992; governor signed Jan. 28.

**Illinois** 20 (-2)
Legislature failed to act by June 30, 1991 deadline. Federal court approved map Nov. 6.

**Indiana** 10
Map passed legislature June 13, 1991; governor signed June 14.

**Iowa** 5 (-1)
Map passed legislature May 11, 1991; governor signed May 30.

**Kansas** 4 (-1)
Map passed Legislature May 7, 1992; governor signed May 11. Federal court finalized that map with minor changes June 3.

**Kentucky** 6 (-1)
Map passed legislature Dec. 18, 1991; governor signed Dec. 20.

**Louisiana** 7 (-1)*
Map passed Legislature May 26, 1992; governor signed June 1. Justice Department approved July 6.

**Maine** 2
Legislature was to consider redistricting in its 1993 session; the 1992 House elections were run under the current map.

**Maryland** 8
Map passed legislature Oct. 22, 1991; governor signed Oct. 23.

**Massachusetts** 10 (-1)
Map passed legislature July 8, 1992; governor signed July 9.

**Michigan** 16 (-2)*
Federal court issued map March 23, 1992.

**Minnesota** 8
Map passed Legislature Jan. 9, 1992; vetoed by governor Jan. 10. Federal court issued map Feb. 19.

**Mississippi** 5*
Map passed Legislature Dec. 20, 1991; governor signed Dec. 20. Justice Department approved Feb. 21, 1992.

**Missouri** 9
Map passed legislature May 16, 1991; governor signed July 8.

**Nebraska** 3
Map passed Legislature June 5, 1991; governor signed June 10.

**Nevada** 2
Map passed Legislature June 11, 1991; governor signed June 20.

**New Hampshire** 2*
Map passed Legislature March 24, 1992; governor signed March 27. Justice Department approved June 12.

**New Jersey** 13 (-1)
Legislature established bipartisan commission Jan. 13, 1992; commission issued map March 20.

**New Mexico** 3
Map passed Legislature Sept. 18, 1991; governor signed Oct. 4.

**New York** 31 (-3)*
Map passed Legislature June 9, 1992; governor signed June 11. Justice Department approved July 2.

**North Carolina** 12 (+1)*
Map passed Legislature Jan. 24, 1992; Justice Deparment approved Feb. 6.

**Ohio** 19 (-2)
Map passed Legislature March 26, 1992; governor signed March 27.

**Oklahoma** 6
Map passed Legislature May 24, 1991; governor signed May 27.

**Oregon** 5
Federal court approved map Dec. 2, 1991; that map became law Dec. 16, after legislature failed to act.

**Pennsylvania** 21 (-2)
Commonwealth court judge issued map Feb. 24, 1992; state Supreme court approved it March 10.

**Rhode Island** 2
Map passed Legislature May 14, 1992; no action by governor; map became law May 22.

**South Carolina** 6*
Federal court issued map May 1, 1992.

**Tennessee** 9
Map passed Legislature May 6, 1992; governor signed May 7.

**Texas** 30 (+3)*
Map passed Legislature Aug. 25, 1991; governor signed Aug. 29. Justice Department approved Nov. 18. Federal court upheld map Dec. 24.

**Utah** 3
Map passed Legislature Oct. 31, 1991; governor signed Nov. 8.

**Virginia** 11 (+1)*
Map passed legislature Dec. 9, 1991; governor signed Dec. 11. Justice Department approved Feb. 18, 1992.

**Washington** 9 (+1)
Redistricting commission map became law Feb. 12, 1992.

**West Virginia** 3 (-1)
Map passed Legislature Oct. 11, 1991; governor signed Oct. 12. Federal court upheld map Jan. 7, 1992.

**Wisconsin** 9
Map passed Legislature April 14, 1992; governor signed April 28.

*States whose maps are reviewed by the Justice Department under Voting Rights Act provisions. Federal court-drawn maps are not subject to Justice review.*
*NOTE: The seven states with one House seat are Alaska, Delaware, Montana, North Dakota, South Dakota, Vermont and Wyoming.*

Continued from p. 25-A
risk of losing because redistricting deprived them of so many black constituents.

In Texas, the Democratic-controlled state Legislature protected the partisan interests of Democratic House incumbents while creating three new majority-minority districts (Texas gained three seats in reapportionment). Democratic Rep. Martin Frost was expected to be hurt by the drafting of a new black-majority district in Dallas and its environs, but Frost — who helped design the redistricting plan — won re-election with 60 percent of the vote. Of 19 Democratic House incumbents in Texas, the only loser was Albert G. Bustamante, who was burdened by allegations of ethical misconduct.

### A Handful Felled by New Lines

At the very least, Republicans figured that redistricting would shake up the Democratic-dominated status quo in the House. Several states drastically redrew their district lines, forcing incumbents to campaign before thousands of new voters.

Yet even as party strategists and media pundits trumpeted predictions of an anti-incumbent mood that would "clean House," the advantages of incumbency still proved strong for most members seeking re-election — even those who had to run on new playing fields because of redistricting changes.

Just a handful of unseated members could blame their defeats directly on redistricting. Georgia Democratic Rep. Richard Ray, facing thousands of new voters in a drastically revamped 3rd District, lost to Republican Mac Collins. Alabama's new map made Democrat Erdreich an instant re-election underdog; he got 45 percent of the vote.

Missouri Democratic Rep. Joan Kelly Horn, winner by a razor-thin margin in 1990, lost just a little Democratic turf in redistricting but she had none to spare; she lost by nearly 9,000 votes.

Five members were victims in incumbent-incumbent matchups: McMillen; Huckaby; Iowa Democrat Dave Nagle (who lost to GOP Rep. Jim Nussle in the 2nd District); Republican Ron Marlenee (who lost to Democrat Pat Williams in Montana's at-large district); and Republican Clyde C. Holloway (defeated by GOP colleague Richard H. Baker in Louisiana's 6th District).

All told in 1992, nine members lost in redistricting-forced incumbent-incumbent matchups. In addition to the five members defeated Nov. 3, four others lost during the primary season: Democrats Marty Russo and Terry L. Bruce in Illinois lost to William O. Lipinski and Glenn

Poshard, respectively; Democrat Harley O. Staggers Jr. lost to Alan B. Mollohan in West Virginia; and Ohio Republican Clarence E. Miller narrowly lost to Bob McEwen.

The McEwen-Miller primary in Ohio's 6th District was a bitter fight in which Miller harped on McEwen's 166 House bank overdrafts. McEwen survived but was badly weakened and lost Nov. 3 to Democrat Ted Strickland. Another incumbent brought down by a combination of unfavorable new lines and House bank overdrafts was Massachusetts Democrat Joseph D. Early, who lost to GOP state Rep. Peter I. Blute.

Incumbents undone by redistricting were outnumbered by those (mostly Democrats) who survived despite the fact that remapping had dealt them a bad hand. Democrats Lehman of California, Bob Carr of Michigan's 8th District and Gary L. Ackerman of New York's 5th District all eked out re-election victories; Iowa Republican Rep. Jim Ross Lightfoot, an underdog throughout his campaign in the drastically redrawn 3rd District, also won narrowly.

Other seemingly map-threatened members won by more comfortable margins. This group included Maryland Democratic Rep. Steny H. Hoyer, the chairman of the House Democratic Caucus. Hoyer lost most of his black constituent base to the new black-majority 4th District; much of the redrawn 5th District where he ran was new to him and more conservative than his old territory. Yet Hoyer fended off a strong challenge from Republican Lawrence J. Hogan Jr.

Another House Democratic leader put at risk by redistricting was Fazio, chairman of the Democratic Congressional Campaign Committee. He took 51 percent in California's conservative-leaning 3rd District.

### Some Bright Spots for GOP

Although nationally the GOP failed to make the redistricting-related House gains it expected, there were some bright spots for the party.

Republicans cracked the longtime Democratic hegemony in Georgia's House delegation with the unexpected help of a Democrat-drawn redistricting plan. The remap's author, state House Speaker Thomas B. Murphy, sought primarily to displace House Minority Whip Newt Gingrich. But in dismantling Gingrich's old district, the new map also disadvantaged Democratic Rep. Ray and left another suburban Atlanta district up for grabs. Ray lost; Republican John Linder narrowly won the redrawn 4th District; and Gingrich, despite tough primary and general-election competition, won again. Republicans also picked up the open 1st District, which lost black voters to the new black-majority 11th (won by Democrat Cynthia McKinney). ■

# How Other Initiatives Fared

On Nov. 3, Oregon voters rejected a controversial ballot initiative that sharply condemned homosexuality, while those in Colorado approved a measure overturning local laws designed to bar discrimination against homosexuals.

Those were among several dozen state ballot initiatives that touched on issues from increased cigarette taxes to equal rights for women. Voters sent a mixed message on homosexuality and most other questions — with the notable exception of the broad support displayed for term limits for lawmakers.

In Oregon, a proposed constitutional amendment aimed at discouraging homosexuality had attracted national attention and had drawn opposition from Democratic presidential candidate Bill Clinton. The initiative, which would have required schools to teach that homosexuality was "abnormal, wrong, unnatural and perverse," was defeated by a vote of 57 percent to 43 percent.

The less sweeping measure in Colorado, also in the form of an amendment to the state's constitution, prohibited legal claims of discrimination by homosexuals. The amendment rescinded anti-discrimination laws in three Colorado cities.

Bobbie McCallum, spokeswoman for the Equal Protection Ordinance Coalition — which lobbied against the amendment — said proponents of the initiative were successful "in selling a message that no special rights" be accorded to homosexuals. It was approved by 54 percent to 46 percent.

As in previous years, the ballot in California was loaded with initiatives. Typically, most proposals went down to defeat.

Voters rejected Proposition 167, which would have increased taxes on top wage earners to 42 percent, a 58 percent increase over existing rates. Yet voters also opposed an alternative approach to the state's fiscal crisis promoted by Republican Gov. Pete Wilson.

Wilson's initiative, which would have reduced funding for some welfare programs and allowed him more sweeping authority to cut spending, was defeated by 54 percent to 46 percent.

Californians also rejected, by 54 percent to 46 percent, an initiative that would have permitted doctor-assisted suicides under certain circumstances. And a groundbreaking measure requiring employers to provide health insurance, backed by the state's medical association, was defeated by 68 percent to 32 percent.

## Governors Rebuffed

Two other governors also took proposals directly to the people in the form of ballot initiatives. But like Wilson, they were rebuffed.

Michigan voters defeated, by 59 percent to 41 percent, a constitutional amendment backed by Republican Gov. John Engler that would have limited property tax increases.

Colorado rejected, by 56 percent to 44 percent, Democrat Roy Romer's initiative requiring a 1-cent increase in the sales tax to fund education.

Colorado approved, by 54 percent to 46 percent, an initiative promoted by a state taxpayers' group requiring voters to sign off on new tax increases. Three previous efforts by the group had failed.

By 72 percent to 28 percent, voters in Arizona approved a similar measure requiring that tax increases be backed by two-thirds of the state Legislature. In Massachusetts, an initiative to raise cigarette taxes by 25 cents a pack was approved by 54 percent to 46 percent. Revenues generated by the tax were to fund health programs.

Voters also considered the following ballot measures:

● **Abortion.** In Maryland, an initiative designed to ensure that most abortions remained legal was approved by 61 percent to 39 percent.

An Arizona initiative to restrict public funding for abortion was defeated by 69 percent to 31 percent.

● **School choice.** Voters in Colorado rejected, by 67 percent to 33 percent, a controversial initiative that would have given parents vouchers worth up to $2,400 per child for tuition at public or private schools.

The program's projected cost apparently was a factor in the outcome.

● **Death penalty.** In the District of Columbia, a tough death penalty initiative — placed on the ballot at Congress' insistence — was rejected by 67 percent to 33 percent. Voters in New Jersey approved, 73 percent to 27 percent, an initiative broadening a death penalty statute.

● **Equal rights.** In Iowa, an initiative to institute a state version of the Equal Rights Amendment was defeated by 52 percent to 48 percent.

The measure had been strongly opposed by the Christian Coalition, an organization founded by television evangelist Pat Robertson. Robertson's group also lobbied in favor of the anti-homosexual initiatives in Oregon and California. ∎

# 1992's Themes Ignored in Governors' Races

Anti-incumbency and "Year of the Woman" themes worked well in some key House and Senate races, but both messages flopped in the dozen gubernatorial contests from Vermont to Washington state Nov. 3.

All four incumbent governors succeeded in their quests to hold onto their offices in Indiana, Rhode Island, Vermont and West Virginia. Former North Carolina Democratic Gov. James B. Hunt Jr. also won back his job after an eight-year absence.

And the three women candidates vying for governorships in Montana, New Hampshire and Rhode Island lost, blunting this year's string of triumphs for female congressional candidates. Women hold the governorships of Kansas, Oregon and Texas.

The gubernatorial contests largely focused on pocketbook and ethics issues. Still, the races gained less national attention than they have in recent election years.

Larry Sabato, a professor of government at the University of Virginia, said key domestic issues that usually dominate gubernatorial feuds were front-burner issues in the 1992 presidential contest.

"The end of the Cold War finally allowed Americans to put those issues — health care, education and jobs — first at the national level," Sabato said.

Democrats and Republicans were each defending six governorships, but the Democrats had the edge going into the contests because they had the four incumbents — Evan Bayh of Indiana, Bruce Sundlun of Rhode Island, Howard Dean of Vermont and Gaston Caperton of West Virginia — seeking re-election. It was the first time this century that no GOP incumbents were on the ballot.

In the post-election alignment, Democrats picked off three gubernatorial seats held by Republicans in Delaware, Missouri and North Carolina, but lost one held by a Democrat in North Dakota, giving Democrats a net gain of two governorships.

In the end, 30 state chief executives were to be Democrats, 18 Republicans and two independents.

The Democratic gains were not enough for the party to reach the more than 2-to-1 split that Democrats enjoyed in 1986. That year, Democrats held 34 governorships to the 16 held by Republicans.

Thirty-one states went into the election with divided governments, where the same party did not control the governor's office and both legislative chambers.

The election diminished that number. At least three states with divided governments — Missouri, North Carolina and Washington — became solidly Democratic in January.

Overall, Democrats still held a sizable majority in state legislatures, despite Republican inroads Nov. 3.

Before the election, Democrats controlled 70 legislative chambers and Republicans controlled 25. Three chambers were tied; Nebraska's Legislature was unicameral and nominally nonpartisan.

But Republican gains put the GOP in control of 30 of

## Governorships

| For 1993 | | 1992 | |
|---|---|---|---|
| Democrats | 30 | Democrats | 28 |
| Republicans | 18 | Republicans | 20 |
| Independents | 2 | Independents | 2 |

| **Democrats** | |
|---|---|
| Net gain | 2 |
| Incumbents re-elected | 4 |
| Incumbents defeated | 0 |

| **Republicans** | |
|---|---|
| Net loss | 2 |
| Incumbents re-elected | 0 |
| Incumbents defeated | 0 |

the nation's 99 legislative chambers in January 1993, a net gain of five. Democrats controlled both houses in 25 states, and Republicans controlled both in eight. Sixteen states were split; three chambers were tied.

And, after brief uncertainty, the political fate of the Arkansas governorship was resolved Nov. 5. With Gov. Bill Clinton's election to the presidency, a dispute had arisen over who should succeed him because of conflicting sections in the state's 118-year-old constitution.

The constitution said a special election was necessary to fill a gubernatorial vacancy if an unexpired term had 12 months or more remaining. There were two years left in Clinton's term.

But a conflicting 1914 amendment said the lieutenant governor — in this case, Democrat Jim Guy Tucker — should fill a vacancy "for the residue of the term." Tucker wanted to succeed Clinton, but so did Democratic Arkansas Attorney General Winston Bryant, who called for a special election to fill the seat.

The Arkansas Republican Party, which has held the governorship for only six of the past 120 years, sided with Bryant in calling for an election. But Pulaski County Judge John Plegge ruled Nov. 5 that the lieutenant governor would take over. Common Cause, a nonpartisan political watchdog group, first raised the issue publicly and filed a suit seeking a clarification.

### Three Democratic Gains, One Republican

In Delaware, Rep. Thomas R. Carper became the first Democrat since 1972 to win the governorship. Carper, who had eight previous statewide election victories, easily beat Republican B. Gary Scott, a real estate executive, in a bid to fill the seat of outgoing Republican Gov. Michael N. Castle.

Carper, who had represented Delaware's at-large House seat since 1982, was heavily favored to win and swap posts with the popular Castle. Barred from seeking a third term, Castle sought and won the House seat. Scott failed to douse Carper's popularity and reputation as an able lawmaker.

In Missouri, Democratic Lt. Gov. Mel Carnahan beat Republican state Attorney General William L. Webster in the battle to succeed Republican Gov. John Ashcroft, who also could not seek another term.

Webster had won the highly publicized 1989 Supreme Court case *Webster v. Reproductive Health Services* that upheld for the first time state-imposed restrictions on abortion.

A Democrat also was elected to replace a Republican in a nasty race in North Carolina between Hunt and Republican Lt. Gov. James C. Gardner.

In North Dakota, Republicans gained their only Democratic seat in the contest to replace retiring Gov. George Sinner.

In that race, GOP businessman Edward T. Schafer beat Democratic state Attorney General Nicholas Spaeth. Schafer, the son of the former owners of the Gold Seal Co.,

# Gubernatorial Winners, Losers

Following is a summary of the results of the dozen gubernatorial races:

**DELAWARE:** Democratic Rep. Thomas R. Carper soundly beat Republican B. Gary Scott to fill the seat of outgoing Republican Gov. Michael N. Castle.

**INDIANA:** Incumbent Democratic Gov. Evan Bayh sailed to easy victory over Republican Attorney General Linley E. Pearson.

**MISSOURI:** Democratic Lt. Gov. Mel Carnahan defeated Republican Attorney General William L. Webster to succeed outgoing Republican Gov. John Ashcroft.

**MONTANA:** Republican Attorney General Marc Racicot edged out Democratic Rep. Dorothy Bradley to replace retiring Republican Gov. Stan Stephens.

**NEW HAMPSHIRE:** Republican Steve Merrill defeated Democratic state Rep. Deborah Arnie Arnesen to succeed outgoing Republican Gov. Judd Gregg.

**NORTH CAROLINA:** Former Democratic Gov. James B. Hunt Jr. regained the governor's seat after defeating Republican Lt. Gov. James C. Gardner to succeed outgoing GOP Gov. James G. Martin.

**NORTH DAKOTA:** Republican businessman Edward T. Schafer defeated Democratic Attorney General Nicholas Spaeth to succeed retiring Democratic Gov. George Sinner.

**RHODE ISLAND:** Democratic incumbent Gov. Bruce Sundlun beat back a challenge by Republican Elizabeth Ann Leonard.

**UTAH:** In a three-way race, Republican Mike Leavitt defeated Independent Merrill Cook and Democrat Stewart Hanson to fill the seat of outgoing Republican Gov. Norman H. Bangerter.

**VERMONT:** Incumbent Democratic Gov. Howard Dean easily fielded a challenge by Republican John McClaughry.

**WASHINGTON:** Former five-term Democratic congressman Mike Lowry defeated three-term Republican Attorney General Ken Eikenberry to succeed outgoing Democratic Gov. Booth Gardner.

**WEST VIRGINIA:** Democratic incumbent Gaston Caperton brushed off a challenge by Republican state Agriculture Commissioner Cleve Benedict.

---

makers of Mr. Bubble bubble bath, won by emphasizing jobs in a state that has seen its population dwindle along with jobs.

### Four Survive Anti-Incumbent Tide

Two governors dueling to keep their jobs — Bayh of Indiana and Dean of Vermont — were heavily favored because of their personal popularity and records of keeping their states' economies stable during the recession.

In Indiana, Bayh, at 36 the nation's youngest governor, reminded voters that he had maintained state services without raising taxes and helped Hoosiers gain 32,600 jobs the previous year.

His opponent, state Attorney General Linley E. Pearson, unsuccessfully attacked Bayh, son of former Sen. Birch Bayh.

Pearson warned voters of financial gloom if Bayh remained as the chief executive and accused Bayh of "cooking the books" to show the state with a budget surplus. But voters soundly rejected the claims.

In Vermont, Dean, the nation's only physician serving as governor, easily deflected a challenge by Republican state Sen. John McClaughry.

More than anything, McClaughry's chances were dashed after it was revealed that he wrote a letter to a brokerage firm urging it to take off the market a recent Vermont bond offering. In the letter, McClaughry said Dean was not committed to retiring three temporary tax increases enacted in 1991, as had been stated in the bond prospectus.

Dean took over when Republican Gov. Richard Snelling died in office, keeping Snelling's staff and adopting many of his policies. He balanced the state's budget with a combination of spending cuts and tax hikes passed under Snelling. State voters and Dean remained on a honeymoon; one Vermont bumper sticker read: "Dean: I Just Like Him."

The two other incumbents who won Nov. 3 — Caperton of West Virginia and Sundlun of Rhode Island — were seen as more vulnerable after enduring tough primary battles.

West Virginians were angered at Caperton for reneging on a 1988 no-new-taxes pledge in 1989. But in the general election, Caperton parried the tax issue by raising ethical questions about his opponent, state Agriculture Commissioner Cleve Benedict.

Caperton stressed Benedict's ties to the state's former three-term Republican Gov. Arch Moore, who is serving a prison term on charges of buying votes and taking illegal contributions. Benedict worked in the Moore administration.

In Rhode Island, Sundlun withstood an aggressive primary opponent, who said he had done little to help the state's recession-wracked economy. But in the general election, Sundlun emphasized his efforts to improve the state's economy and resolve Rhode Island's bank crisis.

### Women Candidates Failed

Sundlun's re-election bid also tested the "Year of the Woman" theme, a trend that emerged in gubernatorial contests not only in Rhode Island but also in open seats in Montana and New Hampshire.

Sundlun's challenger, Republican Elizabeth Ann Leonard, a political newcomer and car dealership owner, appeared to be a strong opponent early in the race, having handily won a tough primary. But her campaign lost momentum, saddled by difficulties raising enough money to run an effective campaign and overcome partisan barriers in the heavily Democratic state.

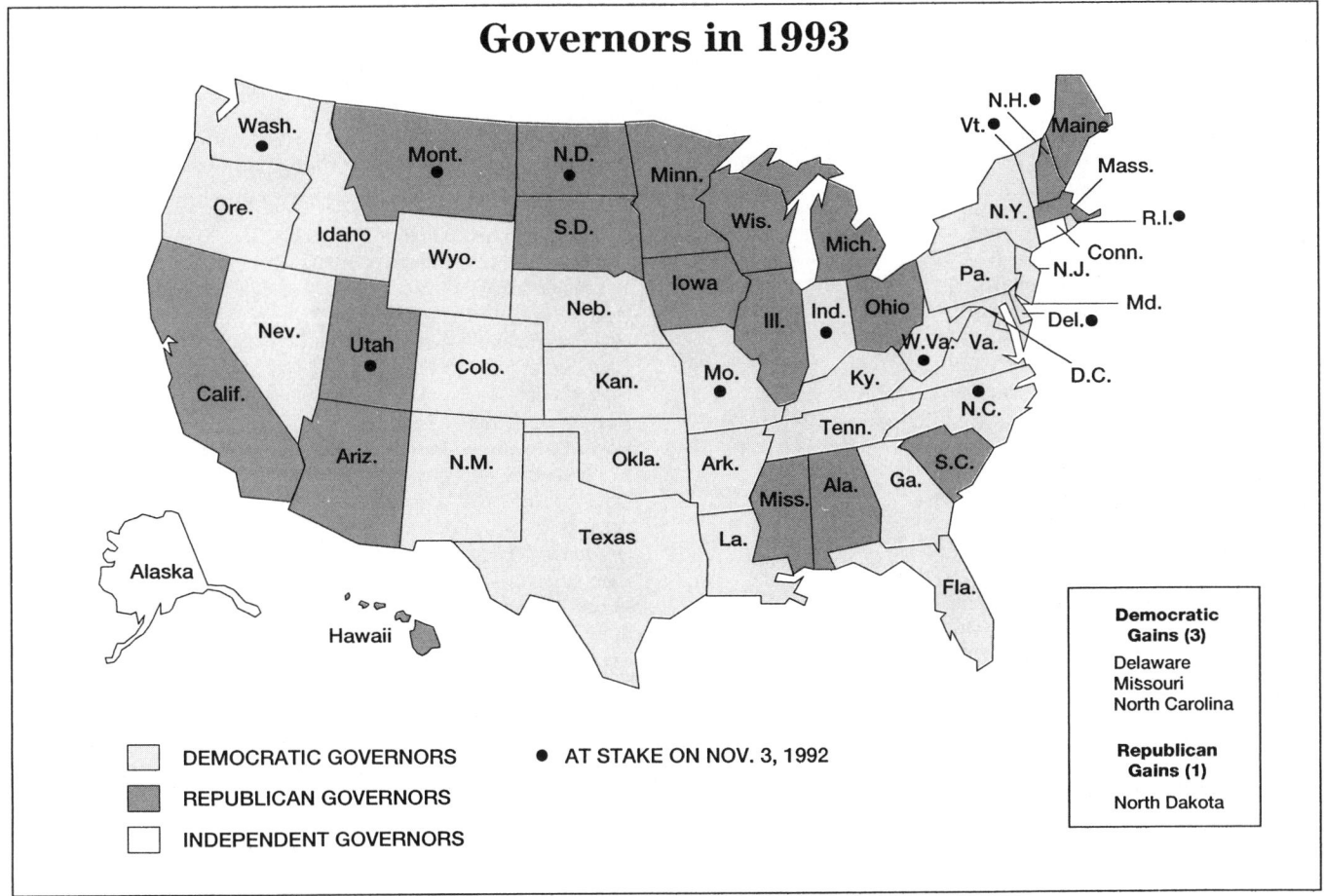

# Governors in 1993

DEMOCRATIC GOVERNORS

● AT STAKE ON NOV. 3, 1992

REPUBLICAN GOVERNORS

INDEPENDENT GOVERNORS

**Democratic Gains (3)**

Delaware
Missouri
North Carolina

**Republican Gains (1)**

North Dakota

Though female candidates in Montana (Democratic state Rep. Dorothy Bradley) and New Hampshire (Democratic state Rep. Deborah "Arnie" Arneson) launched stronger challenges, their campaigns were stanched in the end by economic issues, particularly taxes.

"The Year of the Economy overshadowed the Year of the Woman in the governors' races," said Matt Learnard, research director for the Democratic Governors' Association. "People were looking to women for change, but what it came down to was who was going to put money back in people's pockets."

## Pocketbook Issues

In Montana, the decision by Republican Gov. Stan Stephens to step down for health reasons set off a major battle between Bradley, a 16-year lawmaker who campaigned on horseback, and her Republican opponent, Attorney General Marc Racicot, over how to spend funds from a proposed 4 percent sales tax.

Both candidates wanted to use the new tax revenue to lower income and property taxes and to cover the state's budget deficit. But Bradley called for more spending on education and human services, while Racicot championed tax relief and spending cuts. The voters backed Racicot.

In New Hampshire, Arneson took the bold step of advocating the state's first-ever income tax — at 6 percent — to ease local property taxes. Though early polls suggested voters were initially receptive to her, the romance was all but dead by Election Day.

Republican Steve Merrill, a former state attorney gen-

eral and chief of staff for former Gov. John H. Sununu, rode to victory on a platform of no new taxes. Merrill succeeded Republican Judd Gregg, who sought and won the hotly contested Senate race.

Washington state was the site of another gubernatorial confrontation over taxes. But this time, former Democratic Rep. Mike Lowry beat Republican Attorney General Ken Eikenberry despite telling voters that a tax hike was possible. Lowry softened the message by offering to take a pay cut as governor.

The race between Lowry and Eikenberry presented a sharp ideological contrast. Eikenberry, a former FBI agent and attorney general for 12 years, led in early polls in which potential voters initially questioned Lowry's liberal stances. But in the end, moderate Republicans and business leaders abandoned Eikenberry as too conservative for the state.

Eikenberry's chances also were hurt when the University of Washington Board of Regents President Samuel Stroum charged Eikenberry's campaign with offering "to reappoint him" to the board "in return for a $50,000 campaign contribution."

The campaign denied the charges.

Another bitter ideological struggle was staged in Utah among a liberal Democrat, lawyer Stewart Hanson; a conservative Republican, insurance executive Mike Leavitt; and an independent, Merrill Cook.

Leavitt defeated his two opponents, but Cook took second place with 34 percent of the vote. Hanson's strong support for abortion rights and his Democratic credentials hurt him in

# 1993 Occupants of Statehouses

Listed below are the governors and the governors-elect of the 50 states and the year in which the next election for each office was to be held. The names of governors elected in November 1992 are in **boldface**.

Alabama — Guy Hunt (R) 1994
Alaska — Walter J. Hickel (I) 1994
Arizona — Fife Symington (R) 1994
Arkansas — Jim Guy Tucker (D) 1994 [1]
California — Pete Wilson (R) 1994
Colorado — Roy Romer (D) 1994
Connecticut — Lowell P. Weicker Jr. (I) 1994
**Delaware — Thomas R. Carper (D) 1996**
Florida — Lawton Chiles (D) 1994
Georgia — Zell Miller (D) 1994
Hawaii — John Waihee III (D) 1994
Idaho — Cecil D. Andrus (D) 1994
Illinois — Jim Edgar (R) 1994
**Indiana — Evan Bayh (D) 1996 [2]**
Iowa — Terry E. Branstad (R) 1994
Kansas — Joan Finney (D) 1994
Kentucky — Brereton Jones (D) 1995
Louisiana — Edwin W. Edwards (D) 1995
Maine — John R. McKernan Jr. (R) 1994
Maryland — William Donald Schaefer (D) 1994
Massachusetts — William F. Weld (R) 1994
Michigan — John Engler (R) 1994
Minnesota — Arne Carlson (R) 1994
Mississippi — Kirk Fordice (R) 1995

Missouri — **Mel Carnahan (D) 1996**
**Montana — Marc Racicot (R) 1996**
Nebraska — Ben Nelson (D) 1994
Nevada — Bob Miller (D) 1994
**New Hampshire — Steve Merrill (R) 1994**
New Jersey — James J. Florio (D) 1993
New Mexico — Bruce King (D) 1994 [2]
New York — Mario M. Cuomo (D) 1994
**North Carolina — James B. Hunt Jr. (D) 1996**
**North Dakota — Edward T. Schafer (R) 1996**
Ohio — George V. Voinovich (R) 1994
Oklahoma — David Walters (D) 1994
Oregon — Barbara Roberts (D) 1994
Pennsylvania — Robert P. Casey (D) 1994
**Rhode Island — Bruce Sundlun (D) 1994 [2]**
South Carolina — Carroll A. Campbell Jr. (R) 1994
South Dakota — George S. Mickelson (R) 1994
Tennessee — Ned McWherter (D) 1994
Texas — Ann W. Richards (D) 1994
**Utah — Mike Leavitt (R) 1996**
**Vermont — Howard Dean (D) 1994 [2]**
Virginia — L. Douglas Wilder (D) 1993
**Washington — Mike Lowry (D) 1996**
**West Virginia — Gaston Caperton (D) 1996 [2]**
Wisconsin — Tommy G. Thompson (R) 1994
Wyoming — Mike Sullivan (D) 1994

[1] *A state judge on Nov. 5 resolved competing provisions of the state constitution, ruling that Tucker would be President Clinton's successor.*
[2] *Incumbent*

this conservative and overwhelmingly Republican state.

Leavitt also was helped by outgoing Republican Gov. Norman H. Bangerter, who tapped him as his successor.

## Ethics

In Missouri, Democrat Carnahan ran ahead in pre-election polls after pounding Republican Webster for alleged ethical lapses.

Webster had entered the race as the favorite after winning the high-profile abortion restrictions case before the U.S. Supreme Court. But Webster saw his early lead slip away after Carnahan reminded voters of the attorney general's role in a troubled state workers' compensation fund.

Webster also faced criticism for taking in hundreds of thousands of dollars in campaign contributions from lawyers hired for state business.

Webster returned some of the contributions and denied wrongdoing but was never able to regain his early lead.

In North Carolina, Hunt, a Democrat and former two-term governor who had been out of office since losing a 1984 bid to unseat Sen. Jesse Helms, faced Republican Gardner in a race dominated by heated charges and countercharges of wrongdoing. The two were vying to succeed Republican Gov. James G. Martin, who was barred by law from seeking a third term.

Gardner accused Hunt of being a liar and lacking "steel in his spine." Hunt struck back, demanding that Gardner explain hundreds of thousands of dollars in unpaid business debts and back taxes.

But Hunt managed victory by largely focusing his campaign on improving the state's economy and worker retraining programs. ∎

# Election '92 Results

Following are the official 1992 vote returns for Senate, House and gubernatorial elections for all states except Minnesota. Only unofficial returns were available for Minnesota at press time. All figures were supplied by each state's election agency. The box below provides a key to party designation.

Included are write-in candidates who received at least 0.1 percent of the vote. Because of rounding and because scattered write-in votes are not listed, percentages do not always add to 100. Incumbents are marked with a bullet (●).

| | Vote Total | % |
|---|---|---|
| **ALABAMA** | | |
| **Senate** | | |
| ● Richard C. Shelby (D) | 1,022,698 | 64.8 |
| Richard Sellers (R) | 522,015 | 33.1 |
| Jerome Shockley (LIBERT) | 31,811 | 2.0 |
| Write-ins | 1,275 | .1 |
| **House** | | |
| 1 ● Sonny Callahan (R) | 128,874 | 60.2 |
| William A. Brewer (D) | 78,742 | 36.8 |
| John R. Garrett (LIBERT) | 6,548 | 3.1 |
| 2 Terry Everett (R) | 112,906 | 49.5 |
| George C. Wallace Jr. (D) | 109,335 | 47.9 |
| Glynn Reeves (LIBERT) | 3,150 | 1.4 |
| Malcolm S. Brassell (I) | 1,426 | .6 |
| Richard C. Boone (I) | 1,330 | .6 |
| 3 ● Glen Browder (D) | 119,175 | 60.3 |
| Don Sledge (R) | 73,800 | 37.4 |
| Rodric D. Templeton (LIBERT) | 4,570 | 2.3 |
| 4 ● Tom Bevill (D) | 157,907 | 68.5 |
| Martha "Mickey" Strickland (R) | 66,934 | 29.0 |
| Robert P. King (LIBERT) | 5,646 | 2.4 |
| 5 ● Robert E. "Bud" Cramer (D) | 160,060 | 65.6 |
| Terry Smith (R) | 77,951 | 31.9 |
| C. Michael Seibert (LIBERT) | 6,006 | 2.5 |
| 6 Spencer Bachus (R) | 146,599 | 52.3 |
| ● Ben Erdreich (D) | 126,062 | 45.0 |
| Carla Cloum (I) | 4,521 | 1.6 |
| Mark Bodenhausen (LIBERT) | 2,836 | 1.0 |
| 7 Earl F. Hilliard (D) | 144,320 | 69.5 |
| Kervin Jones (R) | 36,086 | 17.4 |
| James M. Lewis (I) | 12,461 | 6.0 |
| James Chambliss (I) | 11,466 | 5.5 |
| Michael Todd Mayer (LIBERT) | 2,135 | 1.0 |
| John Hawkins (SW) | 1,165 | .6 |
| Write-ins | 140 | .1 |
| **ALASKA** | | |
| **Senate** | | |
| ● Frank H. Murkowski (R) | 127,163 | 53.0 |
| Tony Smith (D) | 92,065 | 38.4 |
| Mary E. Jordan (GREEN) | 20,019 | 8.4 |
| Write-ins | 467 | .2 |

| | Vote Total | % |
|---|---|---|
| **House** | | |
| AL ● Don Young (R) | 111,849 | 46.8 |
| John S. Devens (D) | 102,378 | 42.8 |
| Michael A. States (Alaskan Independence) | 15,049 | 6.3 |
| Mike Milligan (GREEN) | 9,529 | 4.0 |
| Write-ins | 311 | .1 |
| **ARIZONA** | | |
| **Senate** | | |
| ● John McCain (R) | 771,395 | 55.8 |
| Claire Sargent (D) | 436,321 | 31.6 |
| Evan Mecham (I) | 145,361 | 10.5 |
| Kiana Delamare (LIBERT) | 22,613 | 1.6 |
| Ed Finkelstein (NA) | 6,335 | .5 |
| **House** | | |
| 1 Sam Coppersmith (D) | 130,715 | 51.3 |
| ● John J. Rhodes III (R) | 113,613 | 44.6 |
| Ted Goldstein (NL) | 10,461 | 4.1 |
| 2 ● Ed Pastor (D) | 90,693 | 66.0 |
| Don Shooter (R) | 41,257 | 30.0 |
| Dan Detaranto (LIBERT) | 5,423 | 4.0 |
| 3 ● Bob Stump (R) | 158,906 | 61.5 |
| Roger Hartstone (D) | 88,830 | 34.4 |
| Pamela Volponi (NL) | 10,767 | 4.2 |
| 4 ● Jon Kyl (R) | 156,330 | 59.2 |
| Walter R. Mybeck II (D) | 70,572 | 26.7 |
| Debbie Collings (I) | 25,553 | 9.7 |
| Tim McDermott (LIBERT) | 11,611 | 4.4 |
| 5 ● Jim Kolbe (R) | 172,867 | 66.5 |
| Jim Toevs (D) | 77,256 | 29.7 |
| Perry Willis (LIBERT) | 9,690 | 3.7 |
| 6 Karan English (D) | 124,251 | 53.0 |
| Doug Wead (R) | 97,074 | 41.4 |
| Sarah Stannard (I) | 13,047 | 5.6 |
| **ARKANSAS** | | |
| **Senate** | | |
| ● Dale Bumpers (D) | 553,635 | 60.2 |
| Mike Huckabee (R) | 366,373 | 39.8 |

| | Vote Total | % |
|---|---|---|
| **House** | | |
| 1 Blanche Lambert (D) | 149,558 | 69.8 |
| Terry Hayes (R) | 64,618 | 30.2 |
| 2 ● Ray Thornton (D) | 154,946 | 74.2 |
| Dennis Scott (R) | 53,978 | 25.8 |
| 3 Tim Hutchinson (R) | 125,295 | 50.2 |
| John VanWinkle (D) | 117,775 | 47.2 |
| Ralph P. Forbes (I) | 6,329 | 2.5 |
| 4 Jay Dickey (R) | 113,009 | 52.3 |
| W.J. "Bill" McCuen (D) | 102,918 | 47.7 |
| **CALIFORNIA** | | |
| **Senate (2-year Term)** | | |
| Dianne Feinstein (D) | 5,853,621 | 54.3 |
| ● John Seymour (R) | 4,093,488 | 38.0 |
| Gerald Horne (PFP) | 305,699 | 2.8 |
| Paul Meeuwenberg (AMI) | 281,972 | 2.6 |
| Richard B. Boddie (LIBERT) | 247,788 | 2.3 |
| **Senate (6-year Term)** | | |
| Barbara Boxer (D) | 5,173,443 | 47.9 |
| Bruce Herschensohn (R) | 4,644,139 | 43.0 |
| Genevieve Torres (PFP) | 372,816 | 3.5 |
| Jerome McCready (AMI) | 372,780 | 3.5 |
| June R. Genis (LIBERT) | 235,918 | 2.2 |
| **House** | | |
| 1 Dan Hamburg (D) | 119,676 | 47.6 |
| ● Frank Riggs (R) | 113,266 | 45.1 |
| Phil Baldwin (PFP) | 10,764 | 4.3 |
| Matthew L. Howard (LIBERT) | 7,500 | 3.0 |
| 2 ● Wally Herger (R) | 167,247 | 65.2 |
| Elliot Roy Freedman (D) | 71,780 | 28.0 |
| Harry H. Pendery (LIBERT) | 17,529 | 6.8 |
| 3 ● Vic Fazio (D) | 122,149 | 51.2 |
| H.L. "Bill" Richardson (R) | 96,092 | 40.3 |
| Ross Crain (LIBERT) | 20,444 | 8.6 |
| 4 ● John T. Doolittle (R) | 141,155 | 49.8 |
| Patricia Malberg (D) | 129,489 | 45.7 |
| Patrick Lee McHargue (LIBERT) | 12,705 | 4.5 |
| 5 ● Robert T. Matsui (D) | 158,250 | 68.6 |
| Robert S. Dinsmore (R) | 58,698 | 25.5 |
| Gordon D. Mors (AMI) | 4,745 | 2.1 |
| Chris Rufer (LIBERT) | 4,547 | 2.0 |
| Tian Harter (GREEN) | 4,316 | 1.9 |

# Abbreviations for Party Designations

| | | | | | |
|---|---|---|---|---|---|
| ACP | A Connecticut Party | GREEN | Green | NJC | New Jersey Conservative Party |
| AFP | America First Populist | I | Independent | NJI | New Jersey Independents |
| AM | American | IA | Independent American | NL | Natural Law |
| AMI | American Independent | IFC | Independents for Change | PFP | Peace and Freedom |
| C | Conservative | IP | Independent Party | POP | Populist |
| CC | Concerned Citizens | IV | Independent Voters | R | Republican |
| D | Democratic | L | Liberal | RTL | Right to Life |
| ECR | Economic Recovery | LIBERT | Libertarian | SW | Socialist Worker |
| EJ | Economic Justice | LIF | Long Island First | TCP-LI | Tax Cut Party-Long Island |
| FFL | Freedom for LaRouche | LU | Liberty Union | TIC | Tisch Independent Citizens |
| GR | Grassroots | NA | New Alliance | WL | Workers League |

| | | Vote Total | % |
|---|---|---|---|
| 6 | Lynn Woolsey (D) | 190,322 | 65.2 |
| | Bill Filante (R) | 98,171 | 33.6 |
| | Claude Heater (write-in) | 3,141 | 1.1 |
| 7 ● | George Miller (D) | 153,320 | 70.3 |
| | Dave Scholl (R) | 54,822 | 25.1 |
| | David L. Franklin (PFP) | 9,840 | 4.5 |
| 8 ● | Nancy Pelosi (D) | 191,906 | 82.5 |
| | Marc Wolin (R) | 25,693 | 11.0 |
| | Cesar G. Cadabes (PFP) | 7,572 | 3.3 |
| | James R. Elwood (LIBERT) | 7,511 | 3.2 |
| 9 ● | Ronald V. Dellums (D) | 164,265 | 71.9 |
| | G. William Hunter (R) | 53,707 | 23.5 |
| | Dave Linn (PFP) | 10,472 | 4.6 |
| 10 | Bill Baker (R) | 145,702 | 52.0 |
| | Wendell H. Williams (D) | 134,635 | 48.0 |
| 11 | Richard W. Pombo (R) | 94,453 | 47.6 |
| | Patricia Garamendi (D) | 90,539 | 45.6 |
| | Christine Roberts (LIBERT) | 13,498 | 6.8 |
| 12 ● | Tom Lantos (D) | 157,205 | 68.8 |
| | Jim Tomlin (R) | 53,278 | 23.3 |
| | Mary Weldon (PFP) | 10,142 | 4.4 |
| | George L. O'Brien (LIBERT) | 7,782 | 3.4 |
| 13 ● | Pete Stark (D) | 123,795 | 60.2 |
| | Verne Teyler (R) | 64,953 | 31.6 |
| | Roslyn A. Allen (PFP) | 16,768 | 8.2 |
| 14 | Anna G. Eshoo (D) | 146,873 | 56.7 |
| | Tom Huening (R) | 101,204 | 39.0 |
| | Chuck Olson (LIBERT) | 7,220 | 2.8 |
| | David Wald (PFP) | 3,912 | 1.5 |
| 15 ● | Norman Y. Mineta (D) | 168,617 | 63.5 |
| | Robert Wick (R) | 82,875 | 31.2 |
| | Duggan Dieterly (LIBERT) | 13,293 | 5.0 |
| | Bill Futrell (write-in) | 585 | .2 |
| 16 ● | Don Edwards (D) | 96,661 | 62.0 |
| | Ted Bundesen (R) | 49,843 | 32.0 |
| | Amani S. Kuumba (PFP) | 9,370 | 6.0 |
| 17 ● | Leon E. Panetta (D) | 151,565 | 72.0 |
| | Bill McCampbell (R) | 49,947 | 23.7 |
| | Maureen Smith (PFP) | 4,804 | 2.3 |
| | John D. Wilkes (LIBERT) | 4,051 | 1.9 |
| 18 ● | Gary Condit (D) | 139,704 | 84.7 |
| | (No Republican candidate) | | |
| | Kim R. Almstrom (LIBERT) | 25,307 | 15.3 |
| 19 ● | Richard H. Lehman (D) | 101,620 | 46.9 |
| | Tal L. Cloud (R) | 100,590 | 46.4 |
| | Dorothy L. Wells (PFP) | 13,334 | 6.2 |
| | James E. Williams Jr. (write-in) | 1,098 | .5 |
| 20 ● | Cal Dooley (D) | 72,679 | 64.9 |
| | Ed Hunt (R) | 39,388 | 35.1 |
| 21 ● | Bill Thomas (R) | 127,758 | 65.2 |
| | Deborah A. Vollmer (D) | 68,058 | 34.7 |
| | Michael David Hodges (write-in) | 149 | .1 |
| 22 | Michael Huffington (R) | 131,242 | 52.5 |
| | Gloria Ochoa (D) | 87,328 | 34.9 |
| | Mindy Lorenz (GREEN) | 23,699 | 9.5 |
| | W. Howard Dilbeck (LIBERT) | 7,553 | 3.0 |
| 23 ● | Elton Gallegly (R) | 115,504 | 54.3 |
| | Anita Perez Ferguson (D) | 88,225 | 41.4 |
| | Jay C. Wood (LIBERT) | 9,091 | 4.3 |
| 24 ● | Anthony C. Beilenson (D) | 141,742 | 55.5 |
| | Tom McClintock (R) | 99,835 | 39.1 |
| | John Paul Lindblad (PFP) | 13,690 | 5.4 |
| 25 | Howard P. ''Buck'' McKeon (R) | 113,611 | 51.9 |
| | James H. ''Gil'' Gilmartin (D) | 72,233 | 33.0 |
| | Rick Pamplin (I) | 13,930 | 6.4 |
| | Peggy Christensen (LIBERT) | 6,932 | 3.2 |
| | Charles Wilken (GREEN) | 6,919 | 3.2 |
| | Nancy Lawrence (PFP) | 5,090 | 2.3 |
| 26 ● | Howard L. Berman (D) | 73,807 | 61.0 |
| | Gary Forsch (R) | 36,453 | 30.1 |
| | Margery Hinds (PFP) | 7,180 | 5.9 |
| | Bernard Zimring (LIBERT) | 3,468 | 2.9 |
| 27 ● | Carlos J. Moorhead (R) | 105,521 | 49.7 |
| | Doug Kahn (D) | 83,805 | 39.4 |
| | Jesse A. Moorman (GREEN) | 11,003 | 5.2 |
| | Margaret L. Edwards (PFP) | 7,329 | 3.4 |
| | Dennis Decherd (LIBERT) | 4,790 | 2.3 |
| 28 ● | David Dreier (R) | 122,353 | 58.4 |
| | Al Wachtel (D) | 76,525 | 36.5 |
| | Walter Sheasby (GREEN) | 6,233 | 3.0 |
| | Thomas J. Dominy (LIBERT) | 4,271 | 2.0 |

| | | Vote Total | % |
|---|---|---|---|
| 29 ● | Henry A. Waxman (D) | 160,312 | 61.3 |
| | Mark A. Robbins (R) | 67,141 | 25.7 |
| | David Davis (I) | 15,445 | 5.9 |
| | Susan C. Davies (PFP) | 13,888 | 5.3 |
| | Felix Tsvi Rogin (LIBERT) | 4,699 | 1.8 |
| 30 | Xavier Becerra (D) | 48,800 | 58.4 |
| | Morry Waksberg (R) | 20,034 | 24.0 |
| | Blase Bonpane (GREEN) | 6,315 | 7.6 |
| | Elizabeth A. Nakano (PFP) | 6,173 | 7.4 |
| | Andrew Consalvo (LIBERT) | 2,221 | 2.7 |
| 31 ● | Matthew G. Martinez (D) | 68,324 | 62.6 |
| | Reuben D. Franco (R) | 40,873 | 37.4 |
| 32 ● | Julian C. Dixon (D) | 150,644 | 87.2 |
| | (No Republican candidate) | | |
| | Bob Weber (LIBERT) | 12,384 | 7.2 |
| | William R. Williams (PFP) | 9,782 | 5.7 |
| 33 | Lucille Roybal-Allard (D) | 32,010 | 63.0 |
| | Robert Guzman (R) | 15,428 | 30.4 |
| | Tim Delia (PFP) | 2,135 | 4.2 |
| | Dale S. Olvera (LIBERT) | 1,206 | 2.4 |
| 34 ● | Esteban E. Torres (D) | 91,738 | 61.3 |
| | J. ''Jay'' Hernandez (R) | 50,907 | 34.0 |
| | Carl M. ''Marty'' Swinney (LIBERT) | 7,072 | 4.7 |
| 35 ● | Maxine Waters (D) | 102,941 | 82.5 |
| | Nate Truman (R) | 17,417 | 14.0 |
| | Alice Mae Miles (PFP) | 2,797 | 2.2 |
| | Carin Rogers (LIBERT) | 1,618 | 1.3 |
| 36 | Jane Harman (D) | 125,751 | 48.4 |
| | Joan Milke Flores (R) | 109,684 | 42.2 |
| | Richard H. Greene (GREEN) | 13,297 | 5.1 |
| | Owen Staley (PFP) | 5,519 | 2.1 |
| | Marc F. Denny (LIBERT) | 5,504 | 2.1 |
| 37 | Walter R. Tucker (D) | 97,159 | 85.7 |
| | (No Republican candidate) | | |
| | B. Kwaku Duren (PFP) | 16,178 | 14.3 |
| 38 | Steve Horn (R) | 92,038 | 48.6 |
| | Evan Anderson Braude (D) | 82,108 | 43.4 |
| | Paul Burton (PFP) | 8,391 | 4.4 |
| | Blake Ashley (LIBERT) | 6,756 | 3.6 |
| 39 | Ed Royce (R) | 122,472 | 57.3 |
| | Molly McClanahan (D) | 81,728 | 38.2 |
| | Jack Dean (LIBERT) | 9,484 | 4.4 |
| 40 ● | Jerry Lewis (R) | 129,563 | 63.1 |
| | Donald M. Rusk (D) | 63,881 | 31.1 |
| | Margie Akin (PFP) | 11,839 | 5.8 |
| 41 | Jay C. Kim (R) | 101,753 | 59.6 |
| | Bob Baker (D) | 58,777 | 34.4 |
| | Mike Noonan (PFP) | 10,136 | 5.9 |
| 42 ● | George E. Brown Jr. (D) | 79,780 | 50.7 |
| | Dick Rutan (R) | 69,251 | 44.0 |
| | Fritz R. Ward (LIBERT) | 8,424 | 5.4 |
| 43 | Ken Calvert (R) | 88,987 | 46.7 |
| | Mark A. Takano (D) | 88,468 | 46.4 |
| | Gary R. Odom (AMI) | 6,095 | 3.2 |
| | Gene L. Berkman (LIBERT) | 4,989 | 2.6 |
| | John Schwab (write-in) | 2,100 | 1.1 |
| 44 ● | Al McCandless (R) | 110,333 | 54.2 |
| | Georgia Smith (D) | 81,693 | 40.1 |
| | Phil Turner (LIBERT) | 11,515 | 5.7 |
| 45 ● | Dana Rohrabacher (R) | 123,731 | 54.5 |
| | Patricia McCabe (D) | 88,508 | 39.0 |
| | Gary D. Copeland (LIBERT) | 14,777 | 6.5 |
| 46 ● | Robert K. Dornan (R) | 55,659 | 50.2 |
| | Robert John Banuelos (D) | 45,435 | 41.0 |
| | Richard G. Newhouse (LIBERT) | 9,712 | 8.8 |
| 47 ● | C. Christopher Cox (R) | 165,004 | 64.9 |
| | John F. Anwiler (D) | 76,924 | 30.3 |
| | Maxine B. Quirk (PFP) | 12,297 | 4.8 |
| 48 | Ron Packard (R) | 140,935 | 61.1 |
| | Michael Farber (D) | 67,415 | 29.2 |
| | Donna White (PFP) | 13,396 | 5.8 |
| | Ted Lowe (LIBERT) | 8,749 | 3.8 |
| 49 | Lynn Schenk (D) | 127,280 | 51.1 |
| | Judy Jarvis (R) | 106,170 | 42.7 |
| | John Wallner (LIBERT) | 10,706 | 4.3 |
| | Milton Zaslow (PFP) | 4,738 | 1.9 |
| 50 | Bob Filner (D) | 77,293 | 56.6 |
| | Tony Valencia (R) | 39,531 | 28.9 |
| | Barbara Hutchinson (LIBERT) | 15,489 | 11.3 |
| | Roger B. Batchelder (PFP) | 4,250 | 3.1 |

| | | Vote Total | % |
|---|---|---|---|
| 51 ● | Randy ''Duke'' Cunningham (R) | 141,890 | 56.1 |
| | Bea Herbert (D) | 85,148 | 33.7 |
| | Bill Holmes (LIBERT) | 10,309 | 4.1 |
| | Miriam E. Clark (PFP) | 10,307 | 4.1 |
| | Richard L. Roe (GREEN) | 5,328 | 2.1 |
| 52 ● | Duncan Hunter (R) | 112,995 | 52.9 |
| | Janet M. Gastil (D) | 88,076 | 41.2 |
| | Joe Shea (LIBERT) | 6,977 | 3.3 |
| | Dennis P. Gretsinger (PFP) | 5,734 | 2.7 |

## COLORADO

**Senate**

| | | Vote Total | % |
|---|---|---|---|
| | Ben Nighthorse Campbell (D) | 803,725 | 51.8 |
| | Terry Considine (R) | 662,893 | 42.7 |
| | Richard O. Grimes (Perot's Independents) | 42,455 | 2.7 |
| | Matt Noah (Christian Pro-Life) | 22,846 | 1.5 |
| | Dan Winters (I) | 20,347 | 1.3 |

**House**

| | | Vote Total | % |
|---|---|---|---|
| 1 ● | Patricia Schroeder (D) | 156,629 | 68.8 |
| | Raymond Diaz Aragon (R) | 70,902 | 31.2 |
| 2 ● | David E. Skaggs (D) | 164,790 | 60.7 |
| | Bryan Day (R) | 88,470 | 32.6 |
| | Vern Tharp (American Grassroots Alternative) | 18,101 | 6.7 |
| 3 | Scott McInnis (R) | 143,293 | 54.7 |
| | Mike Callihan (D) | 114,480 | 43.7 |
| | Ki R. Nelson (Colorado Populist) | 4,189 | 1.6 |
| 4 ● | Wayne Allard (R) | 139,884 | 57.8 |
| | Tom Redder (D) | 101,957 | 42.2 |
| 5 ● | Joel Hefley (R) | 173,096 | 71.1 |
| | Charles A. Oriez (D) | 62,550 | 25.7 |
| | Keith L. Hamburger (Colorado Libertarian) | 7,769 | 3.2 |
| 6 ● | Dan Schaefer (R) | 142,021 | 60.9 |
| | Tom Kolbe (D) | 91,073 | 39.1 |

## CONNECTICUT

**Senate**

| | | Vote Total | % |
|---|---|---|---|
| ● | Christopher J. Dodd (D, ACP) | 882,569 | 58.8 |
| | Brook Johnson (R) | 572,036 | 38.1 |
| | Richard D. Gregory (CC) | 35,315 | 2.4 |
| | Howard A. Grayson Jr. (LIBERT) | 10,741 | .7 |

**House**

| | | Vote Total | % |
|---|---|---|---|
| 1 ● | Barbara B. Kennelly (D, ACP) | 164,735 | 67.1 |
| | Philip L. Steele (R) | 75,111 | 30.6 |
| | Gary R. Garneau (CC) | 5,577 | 2.3 |
| 2 ● | Sam Gejdenson (D, ACP) | 123,291 | 50.8 |
| | Edward W. Munster (R) | 119,416 | 49.2 |
| 3 ● | Rosa DeLauro (D, ACP) | 162,568 | 65.7 |
| | Tom Scott (R) | 84,952 | 34.3 |
| 4 ● | Christopher Shays (R) | 147,816 | 67.3 |
| | Dave Schropfer (D) | 58,666 | 26.7 |
| | Al Smith (ACP) | 11,679 | 5.3 |
| | Ronald M. Fried (NL) | 1,445 | .7 |
| 5 ● | Gary Franks (R) | 104,891 | 43.7 |
| | James J. Lawlor (D) | 74,791 | 31.1 |
| | Lynn H. Taborsak (ACP) | 54,022 | 22.5 |
| | Rosita Rodriguez (CC) | 5,090 | 2.1 |
| | Bernard A. Nevas (NL) | 864 | .4 |
| | David G. LaPointe (I) | 625 | .3 |
| 6 ● | Nancy L. Johnson (R) | 166,967 | 69.7 |
| | Eugene F. Slason (D) | 60,373 | 25.2 |
| | Daniel W. Plawecki (CC) | 9,544 | 4.0 |
| | Charles Pearl (I) | 1,677 | .7 |
| | Ralph C. Economu (I) | 1,036 | .4 |

## DELAWARE

**Governor**

| | | Vote Total | % |
|---|---|---|---|
| | Thomas R. Carper (D) | 179,365 | 64.7 |
| | B. Gary Scott (R) | 90,725 | 32.8 |
| | Floyd E. McDowell Sr. (A Delaware Party) | 3,779 | 1.4 |
| | Richard A. Cohen (LIBERT) | 3,165 | 1.1 |

**House**

| | | Vote Total | % |
|---|---|---|---|
| AL | Michael N. Castle (R) | 153,037 | 55.4 |
| | S.B. Woo (D) | 117,426 | 42.5 |
| | Peggy Schmitt (LIBERT) | 5,661 | 2.1 |

## FLORIDA *

**Senate**

| | | Vote Total | % |
|---|---|---|---|
| | ● Bob Graham (D) | 3,244,299 | 65.4 |
| | Bill Grant (R) | 1,715,156 | 34.6 |

**House**

| | | Vote Total | % |
|---|---|---|---|
| 1 | ● Earl Hutto (D) | 118,753 | 52.0 |
| | Terry Ketchel (R) | 100,136 | 43.9 |
| | Barbara Ann Rodgers-Hendricks (GREEN) | 9,320 | 4.1 |
| 2 | Pete Peterson (D) | 167,151 | 73.4 |
| | Ray Wagner (R) | 60,378 | 26.5 |
| 3 | Corrine Brown (D) | 91,877 | 59.3 |
| | Don Weidner (R) | 63,070 | 40.7 |
| 4 | Tillie Fowler (R) | 135,772 | 56.7 |
| | Mattox Hair (D) | 103,484 | 43.2 |
| 5 | Karen L. Thurman (D) | 129,678 | 49.2 |
| | Tom Hogan (R) | 114,331 | 43.4 |
| | Cindy Munkittrick (I) | 19,459 | 7.4 |
| 6 | ● Cliff Stearns (R) | 144,120 | 65.4 |
| | Phil Denton (D) | 76,396 | 34.6 |
| 7 | John L. Mica (R) | 125,790 | 56.4 |
| | Dan Webster (D) | 96,926 | 43.5 |
| | Ken McCarthy (write-in) | 213 | .1 |
| 8 | ● Bill McCollum (R) | 141,925 | 68.5 |
| | Chuck Kovaleski (D) | 65,132 | 31.5 |
| 9 | ● Michael Bilirakis (R) | 157,822 | 58.9 |
| | Cheryl Davis Knapp (D) | 110,023 | 41.1 |
| 10 | ● C.W. Bill Young (R) | 149,347 | 56.6 |
| | Karen Moffitt (D) | 114,637 | 43.4 |
| 11 | ● Sam M. Gibbons (D) | 100,962 | 52.8 |
| | Mark Sharpe (R) | 77,625 | 40.6 |
| | Joe De Minico (I) | 12,729 | 6.7 |
| 12 | Charles T. Canady (R) | 100,468 | 52.1 |
| | Tom Mims (D) | 92,333 | 47.9 |
| 13 | Dan Miller (R) | 158,836 | 57.8 |
| | Rand Snell (D) | 115,741 | 42.2 |
| 14 | ● Porter J. Goss (R) | 220,324 | 82.1 |
| | (No Democratic candidate) | | |
| | James H. King (I) | 48,156 | 17.9 |
| 15 | Jim Bacchus (D) | 132,385 | 50.7 |
| | Bill Tolley (R) | 128,830 | 49.3 |
| 16 | Tom Lewis (R) | 157,253 | 60.8 |
| | John P. Comerford (D) | 101,217 | 39.2 |
| 17 | Carrie Meek (D) | 102,732 | 100.0 |
| | (No Republican candidate) | | |
| 18 | ● Ileana Ros-Lehtinen (R) | 104,715 | 66.8 |
| | Magda Montiel Davis (D) | 52,095 | 33.2 |
| 19 | ● Harry A. Johnston (D) | 177,411 | 63.1 |
| | Larry Metz (R) | 103,848 | 36.9 |
| 20 | Peter Deutsch (D) | 130,946 | 55.1 |
| | Beverly Kennedy (R) | 91,573 | 38.5 |
| | James M. Blackburn (I) | 15,340 | 6.4 |
| 21 | Lincoln Diaz-Balart (R) | Unopposed | |
| 22 | ● E. Clay Shaw Jr. (R) | 128,376 | 52.0 |
| | Gwen Margolis (D) | 91,605 | 37.1 |
| | Richard "Even" Stephens (I) | 15,467 | 6.3 |
| | Michael F. Petrie (I) | 6,311 | 2.6 |
| | Bernard Anscher (I) | 5,272 | 2.1 |
| 23 | Alcee L. Hastings (D) | 84,232 | 58.5 |
| | Ed Fielding (R) | 44,800 | 31.1 |
| | Al Woods (I) | 14,873 | 10.3 |

*Incomplete returns.*

## GEORGIA

**Senate**

| | | Vote Total | % |
|---|---|---|---|
| | ● Wyche Fowler Jr. (D) | 1,108,416 | 49.2 |
| | Paul Coverdell (R) | 1,073,282 | 47.7 |
| | Jim Hudson (LIBERT) | 69,878 | 3.1 |

**Senate (Nov. 24 runoff)**

| | | Vote Total | % |
|---|---|---|---|
| | Paul Coverdell (R) | 635,114 | 50.7 |
| | ● Wyche Fowler Jr. (D) | 618,877 | 49.4 |

**House**

| | | Vote Total | % |
|---|---|---|---|
| 1 | Jack Kingston (R) | 103,932 | 57.8 |
| | Barbara Christmas (D) | 75,808 | 42.2 |
| 2 | Sanford Bishop (D) | 95,789 | 63.7 |
| | Jim Dudley (R) | 54,593 | 36.3 |
| 3 | Mac Collins (R) | 114,107 | 54.8 |
| | ● Richard Ray (D) | 94,271 | 45.2 |
| 4 | John Linder (R) | 126,495 | 50.5 |
| | Cathey Steinberg (D) | 123,819 | 49.5 |
| 5 | ● John Lewis (D) | 147,445 | 72.1 |
| | Paul R. Stabler (R) | 56,960 | 27.9 |
| 6 | ● Newt Gingrich (R) | 158,761 | 57.7 |
| | Tony Center (D) | 116,196 | 42.3 |
| 7 | ● George "Buddy" Darden (D) | 111,374 | 57.3 |
| | Al Beverly (R) | 82,915 | 42.7 |
| 8 | ● J. Roy Rowland (D) | 108,472 | 55.7 |
| | Bob Cunningham (R) | 86,220 | 44.3 |
| 9 | Nathan Deal (D) | 113,024 | 59.2 |
| | Daniel Becker (R) | 77,919 | 40.8 |
| 10 | Don Johnson (D) | 108,426 | 53.8 |
| | Ralph Hudgens (R) | 93,059 | 46.2 |
| 11 | Cynthia McKinney (D) | 120,168 | 73.1 |
| | Woodrow Lovett (R) | 44,221 | 26.9 |

## HAWAII

**Senate**

| | | Vote Total | % |
|---|---|---|---|
| | ● Daniel K. Inouye (D) | 208,266 | 57.3 |
| | Rick Reed (R) | 97,928 | 26.9 |
| | Linda B. Martin (GREEN) | 49,921 | 13.7 |
| | Richard O. Rowland (LIBERT) | 7,547 | 2.1 |

**House**

| | | Vote Total | % |
|---|---|---|---|
| 1 | ● Neil Abercrombie (D) | 129,332 | 72.9 |
| | Warner C. Kimo Sutton (R) | 41,575 | 23.4 |
| | Rockne Hart Johnson (LIBERT) | 6,569 | 3.7 |
| 2 | ● Patsy T. Mink (D) | 131,454 | 72.6 |
| | Kamuela Price (R) | 40,070 | 22.1 |
| | Lloyd "Jeff" Mallan (LIBERT) | 9,431 | 5.2 |

## IDAHO

**Senate**

| | | Vote Total | % |
|---|---|---|---|
| | Dirk Kempthorne (R) | 270,468 | 56.5 |
| | Richard Stallings (D) | 208,036 | 43.5 |

**House**

| | | Vote Total | % |
|---|---|---|---|
| 1 | ● Larry LaRocco (D) | 140,985 | 58.1 |
| | Rachel S. Gilbert (R) | 90,983 | 37.5 |
| | John Abel (I) | 6,255 | 2.6 |
| | Henry "Sonny" Kinsey (I) | 4,567 | 1.9 |
| 2 | Michael D. Crapo (R) | 139,783 | 60.8 |
| | J.D. Williams (D) | 81,450 | 35.4 |
| | Steven L. Kauer (I) | 4,917 | 2.1 |
| | David William Mansfield (I) | 3,807 | 1.7 |

## ILLINOIS

**Senate**

| | | Vote Total | % |
|---|---|---|---|
| | Carol Moseley-Braun (D) | 2,631,229 | 53.3 |
| | Richard S. Williamson (R) | 2,126,833 | 43.1 |
| | Chad Koppie (Conservative Party of Illinois) | 100,422 | 2.0 |
| | Andrew B. Spiegel (LIBERT) | 34,527 | .7 |
| | Charles A. Winter (NL) | 15,118 | .3 |
| | Alan J. Port (NA) | 12,689 | .3 |
| | Kathleen Kaku (SW) | 10,056 | .2 |
| | John Justice (POP) | 8,656 | .2 |

**House**

| | | Vote Total | % |
|---|---|---|---|
| 1 | Bobby L. Rush (D) | 209,258 | 82.8 |
| | Jay Walker (R) | 43,453 | 17.2 |
| 2 | Mel Reynolds (D) | 182,614 | 78.1 |
| | Ron Blackstone (R) | 31,957 | 13.7 |
| | Louanner Peters (Louanner Peters Party) | 19,293 | 8.2 |
| 3 | ● William O. Lipinski (D) | 162,165 | 63.5 |
| | Harry C. Lepinske (R) | 93,128 | 36.5 |
| 4 | Luis V. Gutierrez (D) | 90,452 | 77.6 |
| | Hildegarde Rodriguez-Schieman (R) | 26,154 | 22.4 |
| 5 | ● Dan Rostenkowski (D) | 132,889 | 57.3 |
| | Elias R. "Non-Incumbent" Zenkich (R) | 90,738 | 39.1 |
| | Blaise C. Grenke (LIBERT) | 8,456 | 3.6 |
| 6 | ● Henry J. Hyde (R) | 165,009 | 65.5 |
| | Barry W. Watkins (D) | 86,891 | 34.5 |
| 7 | ● Cardiss Collins (D) | 182,811 | 81.1 |
| | Norman G. Boccio (R) | 35,346 | 15.7 |
| | Rose-Marie Love (ECR) | 4,711 | 2.1 |
| | Geri Knoll McLauchlan (NL) | 2,413 | 1.1 |
| 8 | ● Philip M. Crane (R) | 132,887 | 55.7 |
| | Sheila A. Smith (D) | 96,419 | 40.4 |
| | Joe M. Dillier (Independent Congressional) | 9,327 | 3.9 |
| 9 | ● Sidney R. Yates (D) | 162,942 | 68.0 |
| | Herb Sohn (R) | 64,760 | 27.0 |
| | Sheila A. Jones (ECR) | 12,001 | 5.0 |
| 10 | ● John Edward Porter (R) | 155,230 | 64.5 |
| | Michael J. Kennedy (D) | 85,400 | 35.5 |
| 11 | ● George E. Sangmeister (D) | 135,387 | 55.7 |
| | Robert T. Herbolsheimer (R) | 107,860 | 44.3 |
| 12 | ● Jerry F. Costello (D) | 168,762 | 71.2 |
| | Mike Starr (R) | 68,115 | 28.8 |
| 13 | ● Harris W. Fawell (R) | 179,257 | 68.4 |
| | Dennis Michael Temple (D) | 82,985 | 31.6 |
| 14 | ● Dennis Hastert (R) | 155,271 | 67.3 |
| | Jonathan Abram Reich (D) | 75,294 | 32.7 |
| 15 | ● Thomas W. Ewing (R) | 142,167 | 59.3 |
| | Charles D. Mattis (D) | 97,190 | 40.6 |
| | Gerard Archibald (write-in) | 229 | .1 |
| 16 | Donald Manzullo (R) | 142,388 | 55.6 |
| | ● John W. Cox Jr. (D) | 113,555 | 44.4 |
| 17 | Lane Evans (D) | 156,233 | 60.1 |
| | Ken Schloemer (R) | 103,719 | 39.9 |
| 18 | ● Robert H. Michel (R) | 156,533 | 57.8 |
| | Ronald C. Hawkins (R) | 114,413 | 42.2 |
| 19 | ● Glenn Poshard (D) | 187,156 | 69.1 |
| | Douglas E. Lee (R) | 83,526 | 30.9 |
| 20 | ● Richard J. Durbin (D) | 154,869 | 56.5 |
| | John M. Shimkus (R) | 119,219 | 43.5 |

## INDIANA

**Governor**

| | | Vote Total | % |
|---|---|---|---|
| | ● Evan Bayh (D) | 1,382,151 | 62.0 |
| | Linley E. Pearson (R) | 822,533 | 36.9 |
| | Mary Catherine Barton (NA) | 24,378 | 1.1 |

**Senate**

| | | Vote Total | % |
|---|---|---|---|
| | ● Daniel R. Coats (R) | 1,267,972 | 57.3 |
| | Joseph H. Hogsett (D) | 900,148 | 40.7 |
| | Steve Dillon (LIBERT) | 35,733 | 1.6 |
| | Raymond Tirado (NA) | 7,474 | .3 |

**House**

| | | Vote Total | % |
|---|---|---|---|
| 1 | ● Peter J. Visclosky (D) | 147,054 | 69.4 |
| | David J. Vucich (R) | 64,770 | 30.6 |
| 2 | ● Philip R. Sharp (D) | 130,881 | 57.1 |
| | William G. Frazier (R) | 90,593 | 39.5 |
| | Theodore Shaver (I) | 7,821 | 3.4 |
| 3 | ● Tim Roemer (D) | 121,269 | 57.4 |
| | Carl H. Baxmeyer (R) | 89,834 | 42.6 |
| 4 | ● Jill L. Long (D) | 134,907 | 62.1 |
| | Charles W. Pierson (R) | 82,468 | 37.9 |
| 5 | Steve Buyer (R) | 112,492 | 51.0 |
| | ● Jim Jontz (D) | 107,973 | 49.0 |
| 6 | ● Dan Burton (R) | 186,499 | 72.2 |
| | Natalie M. Bruner (D) | 71,952 | 27.8 |
| 7 | ● John T. Myers (R) | 129,189 | 59.5 |
| | Ellen E. Wedum (D) | 88,005 | 40.5 |
| 8 | ● Frank McCloskey (D) | 125,244 | 52.5 |
| | Richard E. Mourdock (R) | 108,054 | 45.3 |
| | John W. Taylor (I) | 3,098 | 1.3 |
| | Jimmy Gale Funkhouser Jr. (LIBERT) | 2,001 | .8 |
| 9 | ● Lee H. Hamilton (D) | 160,980 | 69.7 |
| | Michael E. Bailey (R) | 70,057 | 30.3 |
| 10 | ● Andrew Jacobs Jr. (D) | 117,604 | 64.0 |
| | Janos Horvath (R) | 64,378 | 35.0 |
| | Carolyn P. Sackett (NA) | 1,849 | 1.0 |

| | | Vote Total | % |
|---|---|---|---|

### IOWA

**Senate**

| | | Vote Total | % |
|---|---|---|---|
| ● | Charles E. Grassley (R) | 899,761 | 69.6 |
| | Jean Lloyd-Jones (D) | 351,561 | 27.2 |
| | Stuart Zimmerman (NL) | 16,403 | 1.3 |
| | Sue Atkinson (I) | 6,277 | .5 |
| | Mel Boring (I) | 5,508 | .4 |
| | Rosanne Freeburg (I) | 4,999 | .4 |
| | Carl Eric Olsen (GR) | 3,404 | .3 |
| | Richard O'Dell Hughes (I) | 2,918 | .2 |
| | Cleve Andrew Pulley (SW) | 1,370 | .1 |

**House**

| | | | Vote Total | % |
|---|---|---|---|---|
| 1 | ● | Jim Leach (R) | 178,042 | 68.1 |
| | | Jan J. Zonneveld (D) | 81,600 | 31.2 |
| | | Write-ins | 1,667 | .6 |
| 2 | ● | Jim Nussle (R) | 134,536 | 50.2 |
| | ● | Dave Nagle (D) | 131,570 | 49.1 |
| | | Albert W. Schoeman (GR) | 1,757 | .7 |
| 3 | ● | Jim Ross Lightfoot (R) | 125,931 | 48.9 |
| | | Elaine Baxter (D) | 121,063 | 47.1 |
| | | Larry Chroman (NL) | 10,181 | 4.0 |
| 4 | ● | Neal Smith (D) | 158,610 | 61.6 |
| | | Paul Lunde (R) | 94,045 | 36.5 |
| | | Jerry Yellin (NL) | 2,427 | .9 |
| | | William C. Oviatt (GR) | 2,359 | .9 |
| | | Write-ins | 152 | .1 |
| 5 | ● | Fred Grandy (R) | 196,942 | 99.3 |
| | | (No Democratic candidate) | | |
| | | Write-ins | 1,424 | .7 |

### KANSAS

**Senate**

| | | Vote Total | % |
|---|---|---|---|
| ● | Bob Dole (R) | 706,246 | 62.7 |
| | Gloria O'Dell (D) | 349,525 | 31.0 |
| | Christina Campbell-Cline (I) | 45,423 | 4.0 |
| | Mark B. Kirk (LIBERT) | 25,253 | 2.2 |

**House**

| | | | Vote Total | % |
|---|---|---|---|---|
| 1 | ● | Pat Roberts (R) | 194,912 | 68.3 |
| | | Duane West (D) | 83,620 | 29.3 |
| | | Steven A. Rosile (LIBERT) | 6,765 | 2.4 |
| 2 | ● | Jim Slattery (D) | 151,019 | 56.2 |
| | | Jim Van Slyke (R) | 109,801 | 40.8 |
| | | Arthur L. Clack (LIBERT) | 7,986 | 3.0 |
| 3 | ● | Jan Meyers (R) | 169,929 | 58.0 |
| | | Tom Love (D) | 110,071 | 37.6 |
| | | Frank Kaul (LIBERT) | 12,791 | 4.4 |
| 4 | ● | Dan Glickman (D) | 143,671 | 51.7 |
| | | Eric R. Yost (R) | 117,070 | 42.1 |
| | | Seth L. Warren (LIBERT) | 17,275 | 6.2 |

### KENTUCKY

**Senate**

| | | Vote Total | % |
|---|---|---|---|
| ● | Wendell H. Ford (D) | 836,888 | 62.9 |
| | David L. Williams (R) | 476,604 | 35.8 |
| | James A. Ridenour (LIBERT) | 17,366 | 1.3 |

**House**

| | | | Vote Total | % |
|---|---|---|---|---|
| 1 | | Tom Barlow (D) | 128,524 | 60.5 |
| | | Steve Hamrick (R) | 83,088 | 39.1 |
| | | Marvin Seat (Reform) | 962 | .5 |
| 2 | ● | William H. Natcher (D) | 126,894 | 61.4 |
| | | Bruce R. Bartley (R) | 79,684 | 38.6 |
| 3 | ● | Romano L. Mazzoli (D) | 148,066 | 52.7 |
| | | Susan B. Stokes (R) | 132,689 | 47.3 |
| 4 | ● | Jim Bunning (R) | 139,634 | 61.6 |
| | | Dr. Floyd G. Poore (D) | 86,890 | 38.4 |
| 5 | ● | Harold Rogers (R) | 115,255 | 54.6 |
| | | John Doug Hays (D) | 95,760 | 45.4 |
| 6 | | Scotty Baesler (D) | 135,613 | 60.7 |
| | | Charles W. Ellinger (R) | 87,816 | 39.3 |

### LOUISIANA [1]

**Senate**

| | | Vote Total | % |
|---|---|---|---|
| ● | John B. Breaux (D) | | Won in primary |

[1] *Louisiana primary is open to candidates of all parties. If no one gets 50 percent, the top two vote-getters meet in the general election.*


| | | Vote Total | % |
|---|---|---|---|

**House**

| | | | Vote Total | % |
|---|---|---|---|---|
| 1 | ● | Robert L. Livingston (R) | | Won in primary |
| 2 | ● | William J. Jefferson (D) | | Won in primary |
| 3 | ● | W.J. "Billy" Tauzin (D) | | Won in primary |
| 4 | | Cleo Fields (D) | 143,980 | 73.9 |
| | | Charles Jones (D) | 50,851 | 26.1 |
| 5 | ● | Jim McCrery (R) | 153,501 | 63.0 |
| | ● | Jerry Huckaby (D) | 90,079 | 37.0 |
| 6 | ● | Richard H. Baker (R) | 123,953 | 50.6 |
| | | Clyde C. Holloway (R) | 121,225 | 49.4 |
| 7 | ● | Jimmy Hayes (D) | | Won in primary |

### MAINE

**House**

| | | | Vote Total | % |
|---|---|---|---|---|
| 1 | ● | Thomas H. Andrews (D) | 232,696 | 65.0 |
| | | Linda Bean (R) | 125,236 | 35.0 |
| | | Write-ins | 216 | .1 |
| 2 | ● | Olympia J. Snowe (R) | 153,022 | 49.1 |
| | | Patrick K. McGowan (D) | 130,824 | 42.0 |
| | | Jonathan K. Carter (GREEN) | 27,526 | 8.8 |

### MARYLAND

**Senate**

| | | Vote Total | % |
|---|---|---|---|
| ● | Barbara A. Mikulski (D) | 1,307,610 | 71.0 |
| | Alan L. Keyes (R) | 533,688 | 29.0 |

**House**

| | | | Vote Total | % |
|---|---|---|---|---|
| 1 | ● | Wayne T. Gilchrest (R) | 120,084 | 51.6 |
| | ● | Tom McMillen (D) | 112,771 | 48.4 |
| 2 | ● | Helen Delich Bentley (R) | 165,443 | 65.1 |
| | | Michael C. Hickey Jr. (D) | 88,658 | 34.9 |
| 3 | ● | Benjamin L. Cardin (D) | 163,354 | 73.5 |
| | | William T.S. Bricker (R) | 58,869 | 26.5 |
| 4 | ● | Albert R. Wynn (D) | 136,902 | 75.2 |
| | | Michele Dyson (D) | 45,166 | 24.8 |
| 5 | ● | Steny H. Hoyer (D) | 118,312 | 53.0 |
| | | Lawrence J. Hogan Jr. (R) | 97,982 | 43.9 |
| | | William D. Johnston III (I) | 6,990 | 3.1 |
| 6 | ● | Roscoe G. Bartlett (R) | 125,564 | 54.2 |
| | | Thomas H. Hattery (D) | 106,224 | 45.8 |
| 7 | ● | Kweisi Mfume (D) | 152,689 | 85.3 |
| | | Kenneth Kondner (R) | 26,304 | 14.7 |
| 8 | ● | Constance A. Morella (R) | 203,377 | 72.5 |
| | | Edward J. Heffernan (D) | 77,042 | 27.5 |

### MASSACHUSETTS

**House**

| | | | Vote Total | % |
|---|---|---|---|---|
| 1 | ● | John W. Olver (D) | 135,049 | 51.5 |
| | | Patrick Larkin (R) | 113,828 | 43.4 |
| | | Louis R. Godena (Peace Jobs Justice) | 7,162 | 2.7 |
| | | Dennis M. Kelly (Pro-Democracy Reform) | 4,355 | 1.7 |
| | | Jeffrey W. Rebello (FFL) | 1,598 | .6 |
| 2 | ● | Richard E. Neal (D) | 131,215 | 53.1 |
| | | Anthony W. Ravosa Jr. (R) | 76,795 | 31.1 |
| | | Thomas R. Sheehan (For the People) | 38,963 | 15.8 |
| | | Write-ins | 190 | .1 |
| 3 | | Peter I. Blute (R) | 131,473 | 50.4 |
| | ● | Joseph D. Early (D) | 115,587 | 44.3 |
| | | Leonard J. Umina (IV) | 9,691 | 3.7 |
| | | Michael T. Moore (NL) | 4,130 | 1.6 |
| 4 | ● | Barney Frank (D) | 182,633 | 67.7 |
| | | Edward J. McCormick III (R) | 70,665 | 25.2 |
| | | Luke Lumina (IV) | 13,670 | 5.1 |
| | | Dennis J. Ingalls (FFL) | 2,797 | 1.0 |
| 5 | | Martin T. Meehan (D) | 133,844 | 52.2 |
| | | Paul W. Cronin (R) | 96,206 | 37.5 |
| | | Mary J. Farinelli (I) | 19,077 | 7.4 |
| | | David E. Coleman (I) | 7,214 | 2.8 |
| | | Write-ins | 223 | .1 |
| 6 | | Peter G. Torkildsen (R) | 159,165 | 54.8 |
| | ● | Nicholas Mavroules (D) | 130,248 | 44.9 |
| | | Write-ins | 899 | .3 |
| 7 | ● | Edward J. Markey (D) | 174,837 | 62.1 |
| | | Stephen A. Sohn (R) | 78,262 | 27.8 |
| | | Robert B. Antonelli (I) | 28,421 | 10.1 |


| | | | Vote Total | % |
|---|---|---|---|---|
| 8 | ● | Joseph P. Kennedy II (D) | 149,903 | 83.1 |
| | | (No Republican candidate) | | |
| | | Alice Harriett Nakash (I) | 30,402 | 16.8 |
| | | Write-ins | 179 | .1 |
| 9 | ● | Joe Moakley (D) | 175,550 | 69.2 |
| | | Martin D. Conboy (R) | 54,291 | 21.4 |
| | | Lawrence C. Mackin (I) | 15,637 | 6.2 |
| | | Robert W. Horan (I) | 8,084 | 3.2 |
| 10 | ● | Gerry E. Studds (D) | 189,342 | 60.8 |
| | | Daniel W. Daly (R) | 75,887 | 24.4 |
| | | Jon L. Bryan (I) | 39,265 | 12.6 |
| | | Michael P. Umina (IV) | 6,020 | 1.9 |
| | | Robert W. Knapp (FFL) | 1,106 | .4 |

### MICHIGAN

**House**

| | | | Vote Total | % |
|---|---|---|---|---|
| 1 | | Bart Stupak (D) | 144,857 | 53.9 |
| | | Philip E. Ruppe (R) | 117,056 | 43.6 |
| | | Gerald Aydlott (LIBERT) | 4,094 | 1.5 |
| | | Lyman Clark (NL) | 2,570 | 1.0 |
| 2 | ● | Peter Hoekstra (R) | 155,577 | 63.0 |
| | | John H. Miltner (D) | 86,265 | 35.0 |
| | | Dick Jacobs (LIBERT) | 4,840 | 2.0 |
| 3 | ● | Paul B. Henry (R) | 162,451 | 61.3 |
| | | Carol S. Kooistra (D) | 95,927 | 36.2 |
| | | Richard Whitelock (LIBERT) | 3,232 | 1.2 |
| | | Susan Normandin (NL) | 3,228 | 1.2 |
| 4 | ● | Dave Camp (R) | 157,337 | 62.5 |
| | | Lisa A. Donaldson (D) | 87,573 | 34.8 |
| | | Joan Dennison (TIC) | 3,344 | 1.3 |
| | | Gary R. Bradley (LIBERT) | 2,027 | .8 |
| | | Thomas E. List (NL) | 1,247 | .5 |
| 5 | | James A. Barcia (D) | 147,618 | 60.3 |
| | | Keith Muxlow (R) | 93,098 | 38.0 |
| | | Lloyd Clarke (Workers World) | 4,270 | 1.7 |
| 6 | ● | Fred Upton (R) | 144,083 | 61.8 |
| | | Andy Davis (D) | 89,020 | 38.2 |
| 7 | | Nick Smith (R) | 133,972 | 87.6 |
| | | (No Democratic candidate) | | |
| | | Kenneth L. Proctor (LIBERT) | 18,751 | 12.3 |
| | | Write-ins | 145 | .1 |
| 8 | ● | Bob Carr (D) | 135,517 | 47.6 |
| | | Dick Chrysler (R) | 131,906 | 46.3 |
| | | Frank D. McAlpine (I) | 12,155 | 4.3 |
| | | Michael E. Marotta (LIBERT) | 5,115 | 1.8 |
| 9 | ● | Dale E. Kildee (D) | 133,956 | 53.7 |
| | | Megan O'Neill (R) | 111,798 | 44.8 |
| | | Key Halverson (NL) | 1,891 | .8 |
| | | Jerome White (WL) | 1,872 | .8 |
| 10 | ● | David E. Bonior (D) | 138,193 | 53.1 |
| | | Douglas Carl (R) | 114,918 | 44.2 |
| | | David A. Weidner (LIBERT) | 7,098 | 2.7 |
| 11 | | Joe Knollenberg (R) | 168,940 | 57.6 |
| | | Walter Briggs (D) | 117,725 | 40.2 |
| | | Brian Richard Wright (LIBERT) | 4,144 | 1.4 |
| | | Henry Ogden Clark (NL) | 2,269 | .8 |
| 12 | ● | Sander M. Levin (D) | 137,514 | 52.6 |
| | | John Pappageorge (R) | 119,357 | 45.7 |
| | | Charles Hahn (LIBERT) | 2,751 | 1.1 |
| | | R.W. Montgomery (NL) | 1,724 | .7 |
| 13 | ● | William D. Ford (D) | 127,642 | 51.9 |
| | | R. Robert Geake (R) | 105,169 | 42.8 |
| | | Randall F. Roe (I) | 8,626 | 3.5 |
| | | Paul Steven Jensen (TIC) | 3,314 | 1.3 |
| | | Larry Roberts (WL) | 1,127 | .5 |
| 14 | ● | John Conyers Jr. (D) | 165,496 | 82.4 |
| | | John W. Gordon (R) | 32,036 | 15.9 |
| | | Richard R. Miller (NL) | 2,043 | 1.0 |
| | | D'Artagnan Collier (WL) | 1,296 | .6 |
| 15 | ● | Barbara-Rose Collins (D) | 148,908 | 80.5 |
| | | Charles C. Vincent (R) | 31,849 | 17.2 |
| | | James E. Harris Jr. (I) | 2,704 | 1.5 |
| | | Jane Walker Meade (NL) | 1,496 | .8 |
| 16 | ● | John D. Dingell (D) | 156,964 | 65.1 |
| | | Frank Beaumont (R) | 75,694 | 31.4 |
| | | Max J. Siegle (TIC) | 4,048 | 1.7 |
| | | Jeff Hampton (LIBERT) | 2,387 | 1.0 |
| | | Martin P. McLaughlin (WL) | 1,842 | .8 |

| | | Vote Total | % |
|---|---|---|---|

## MINNESOTA

### House

| | | Vote Total | % |
|---|---|---|---|
| 1 ● | Timothy J. Penny (D) | 206369 | 73.85 |
| | Timothy R. Droogsma (R) | 72367 | 25.9 |
| 2 | David Minge (D) | 132156 | 47.83 |
| | Cal R. Ludeman (R) | 131587 | 47.62 |
| | Stan Bentz (I) | 12146 | 4.40 |
| 3 ● | Jim Ramstad (R) | 200240 | 63.62 |
| | Paul Mandell (D) | 104606 | 33.24 |
| | Dwight Fellman (GR) | 9164 | 2.91 |
| 4 ● | Bruce F. Vento (D) | 159796 | 57.49 |
| | Ian Maitland (R) | 101744 | 36.6 |
| | James L. Willess (I) | 6732 | 2.42 |
| | Dan R. Vacek (GR) | 4418 | 1.59 |
| | Lynn Marvin Johnson (NL) | 3602 | 1.30 |
| | Jo Rothenberg (SW) | 1236 | .44 |
| 5 ● | Martin Olav Sabo (D) | 174139 | 62.84 |
| | Stephen A. Moriarty (R) | 77093 | 27.82 |
| | Russell B. Bentley (GR) | 6786 | 2.44 |
| | Sandra Coleman (NA) | 5927 | 2.14 |
| | Mary Mellen (NL) | 5499 | 1.98 |
| | Glenn Mesaros (I) | 4809 | 1.74 |
| | Christopher Nisan (SW) | 2062 | .74 |
| 6 | Rod Grams (R) | 133564 | 44.37 |
| ● | Gerry Sikorski (D) | 100016 | 33.23 |
| | Dean Barkley (I) | 48329 | 16.05 |
| | James H. Peterson (Independents for Perot) | 16411 | 5.45 |
| | Tom Firnstahl (NL) | 2400 | .80 |
| 7 ● | Collin C. Peterson (D) | 133886 | 50.42 |
| | Bernie Omann (R) | 130396 | 49.11 |
| 8 ● | James L. Oberstar (D) | 167104 | 59.04 |
| | Phil Herwig (R) | 83823 | 29.62 |
| | Harry Robb Welty (Perot Choice) | 22619 | 7.99 |
| | Floyd A. Henspeter (Term Limits Candidate) | 8602 | 3.04 |

## MISSISSIPPI

### House

| | | Vote Total | % |
|---|---|---|---|
| 1 ● | Jamie L. Whitten (D) | 121,664 | 59.5 |
| | Clyde E. Whitaker (R) | 82,952 | 40.5 |
| 2 ● | Mike Espy (D) | 133,361 | 76.4 |
| | Dorothy Benford (R) | 41,248 | 23.6 |
| 3 ● | G.V. "Sonny" Montgomery (D) | 162,864 | 81.2 |
| | Michael E. Williams (R) | 37,710 | 18.8 |
| 4 ● | Mike Parker (D) | 130,927 | 67.3 |
| | Jack L. McMillan (R) | 43,705 | 22.5 |
| | Liz Gilchrist (I) | 10,523 | 5.4 |
| | James H. Meredith (I) | 9,389 | 4.8 |
| 5 ● | Gene Taylor (D) | 120,766 | 63.2 |
| | Paul Harvey (R) | 67,619 | 35.4 |
| | Shawn O'Hara (I) | 2,673 | 1.4 |

## MISSOURI

### Governor

| | | Vote Total | % |
|---|---|---|---|
| | Mel Carnahan (D) | 1,375,425 | 58.7 |
| | William L. Webster (R) | 968,574 | 41.3 |

### Senate

| | | Vote Total | % |
|---|---|---|---|
| ● | Christopher S. Bond (R) | 1,221,901 | 51.9 |
| | Geri Rothman-Serot (D) | 1,057,967 | 44.9 |
| | Jeanne F. Bojarski (LIBERT) | 75,048 | 3.2 |

### House

| | | Vote Total | % |
|---|---|---|---|
| 1 ● | William L. Clay (D) | 158,693 | 68.1 |
| | Arthur S. Montgomery (R) | 74,482 | 31.9 |
| 2 | James M. Talent (R) | 157,594 | 50.4 |
| ● | Joan Kelly Horn (D) | 148,729 | 47.6 |
| | Jim Higgins (LIBERT) | 6,119 | 2.0 |
| 3 ● | Richard A. Gephardt (D) | 174,000 | 64.0 |
| | Mack Holekamp (R) | 90,006 | 33.1 |
| | Robert Stockhausen (LIBERT) | 7,828 | 2.9 |
| 4 ● | Ike Skelton (D) | 176,977 | 70.4 |
| | John Carley (R) | 74,475 | 29.6 |
| 5 ● | Alan Wheat (D) | 151,014 | 59.1 |
| | Edward "Gomer" Moody (R) | 93,562 | 36.6 |
| | Tom Danaher (NL) | 6,107 | 2.4 |
| | Grant Stauffer (LIBERT) | 4,629 | 1.8 |

| | | Vote Total | % |
|---|---|---|---|
| 6 | Pat Danner (D) | 148,887 | 55.4 |
| ● | Tom Coleman (R) | 119,637 | 44.6 |
| 7 ● | Mel Hancock (R) | 160,303 | 61.6 |
| | Thomas Patrick Deaton (D) | 99,762 | 38.4 |
| 8 ● | Bill Emerson (R) | 147,398 | 63.0 |
| | Thad Bullock (D) | 86,730 | 37.0 |
| 9 ● | Harold L. Volkmer (D) | 124,694 | 47.7 |
| | Rick Hardy (R) | 118,811 | 45.5 |
| | Jeff Barrow (GREEN) | 10,565 | 4.0 |
| | Duane Neil Burghard (I) | 7,265 | 2.8 |

## MONTANA

### Governor

| | | Vote Total | % |
|---|---|---|---|
| | Marc Racicot (R) | 209,401 | 51.3 |
| | Dorothy Bradley (D) | 198,421 | 48.7 |

### House

| | | Vote Total | % |
|---|---|---|---|
| AL ● | Pat Williams (D) | 203,711 | 50.5 |
| ● | Ron Marlenee (R) | 189,570 | 47.0 |
| | Jerome J. Wilverding (LIBERT) | 10,454 | 2.6 |

## NEBRASKA

### House

| | | Vote Total | % |
|---|---|---|---|
| 1 ● | Doug Bereuter (R) | 142,713 | 59.7 |
| | Gerry Finnegan (D) | 96,309 | 40.3 |
| 2 ● | Peter Hoagland (D) | 119,512 | 51.2 |
| | Ronald L. Staskiewicz (R) | 113,828 | 48.8 |
| 3 ● | Bill Barrett (R) | 170,857 | 71.7 |
| | Lowell Fisher (D) | 67,457 | 28.3 |

## NEVADA

### Senate

| | | Vote Total | % |
|---|---|---|---|
| ● | Harry Reid (D) | 253,150 | 51.0 |
| | Demar Dahl (R) | 199,413 | 40.2 |
| | "None of these candidates" | 13,154 | 2.7 |
| | Joe S. Garcia Jr. (IA) | 11,240 | 2.3 |
| | Lois Avery (NL) | 7,279 | 1.5 |
| | H. Kent Cromwell (LIBERT) | 7,222 | 1.5 |
| | Harry Tootle (POP) | 4,429 | .9 |

### House

| | | Vote Total | % |
|---|---|---|---|
| 1 ● | James Bilbray (D) | 128,278 | 57.9 |
| | J. Coy Pettyjohn (R) | 84,217 | 38.0 |
| | Scott A. Kjar (LIBERT) | 8,993 | 4.1 |
| 2 ● | Barbara F. Vucanovich (R) | 129,575 | 47.9 |
| | Pete Sferrazza (D) | 117,199 | 43.3 |
| | Daniel M. Hansen (IA) | 13,285 | 4.9 |
| | Dan Becan (LIBERT) | 7,552 | 2.8 |
| | Don Golden (POP) | 2,850 | 1.1 |

## NEW HAMPSHIRE

### Governor

| | | Vote Total | % |
|---|---|---|---|
| | Steve Merrill (R) | 289,170 | 56.0 |
| | Deborah Arnie Arnesen (D) | 206,232 | 40.0 |
| | Miriam F. Luce (LIBERT) | 20,663 | 4.0 |

### Senate

| | | Vote Total | % |
|---|---|---|---|
| | Judd Gregg (R) | 249,591 | 48.2 |
| | John Rauh (D) | 234,982 | 45.3 |
| | Katherine M. Alexander (LIBERT) | 18,214 | 3.5 |
| | Larry Brady (I) | 9,340 | 1.8 |
| | Kenneth E. Blevens Sr. (I) | 4,752 | .9 |
| | David Haight (NL) | 1,284 | .3 |

### House

| | | Vote Total | % |
|---|---|---|---|
| 1 ● | Bill Zeliff (R) | 135,936 | 53.1 |
| | Bob Preston (D) | 108,578 | 42.4 |
| | Knox Bickford (LIBERT) | 5,633 | 2.2 |
| | Richard P. Bosa (I) | 3,537 | 1.4 |
| | Linda Spitzfaden (NL) | 1,997 | .8 |
| | Write-ins | 172 | .1 |
| 2 ● | Dick Swett (D) | 157,328 | 61.7 |
| | Bill Hatch (R) | 91,126 | 35.7 |
| | John A. Lewicke (LIBERT) | 5,977 | 2.3 |
| | James J. Bingham (NL) | 657 | .3 |

## NEW JERSEY

### House

| | | Vote Total | % |
|---|---|---|---|
| 1 ● | Robert E. Andrews (D) | 153,525 | 67.3 |
| | Lee A. Solomon (R) | 65,123 | 28.6 |
| | James E. Smith (Pro-Life Pro-Family Veteran) | 3,761 | 1.7 |
| | Jerry Zeldin (LIBERT) | 2,641 | 1.2 |
| | Kenneth L. Lowndes (Pro-Life Independent Conservative) | 2,163 | 1.0 |
| | Nicholas Pastuch (AFP) | 859 | .4 |
| 2 ● | William J. Hughes (D) | 132,465 | 55.9 |
| | Frank A. LoBiondo (R) | 98,315 | 41.5 |
| | Roger W. Bacon (LIBERT) | 2,575 | 1.1 |
| | Joseph Ponczek (Anti-Tax) | 2,067 | .9 |
| | Andrea Lippi (Freedom Equality Prosperity) | 1,605 | .7 |
| 3 ● | H. James Saxton (R) | 151,368 | 59.2 |
| | Timothy E. Ryan (D) | 94,012 | 36.8 |
| | Helen L. Radder (LIBERT) | 2,711 | 1.1 |
| | Joseph A. Plonski (AFP) | 2,309 | .9 |
| | Michael S. Permuko (NJC) | 1,728 | .7 |
| | James Reilly (I) | 915 | .4 |
| | William Donald McMahon (Donald of Moorestown) | 901 | .4 |
| | Anthony J. Verderese (The Independent Party) | 749 | .3 |
| | Martin T. King (I) | 593 | .2 |
| | Frank Burke (Basic Reformed Government) | 512 | .2 |
| 4 ● | Christopher H. Smith (R) | 149,095 | 61.8 |
| | Brian M. Hughes (D) | 84,514 | 35.0 |
| | Benjamin Grindlinger (LIBERT) | 2,984 | 1.2 |
| | Patrick C. Pasculli (I) | 2,137 | .9 |
| | Agnes A. James (NJC) | 1,630 | .7 |
| | Joseph J. Notarangelo (AFP) | 865 | .4 |
| 5 ● | Marge Roukema (R) | 196,198 | 71.5 |
| | Frank R. Lucas (D) | 67,579 | 24.6 |
| | William J. Leonard (I) | 6,182 | 2.3 |
| | Michael V. Pierone (LIBERT) | 2,636 | 1.0 |
| | George Lahood (Equality Brotherhood Justice) | 994 | .4 |
| | Stuart Bacha (AFP) | 782 | .3 |
| 6 ● | Frank Pallone Jr. (D) | 118,266 | 52.3 |
| | Joseph M. Kyrillos (R) | 100,949 | 44.7 |
| | Joseph Spalletta (The People's Candidate) | 2,153 | 1.0 |
| | Bill Stewart (LIBERT) | 1,404 | .6 |
| | Peter Cerrato (Independent for Freedom) | 1,073 | .5 |
| | George P. Predham (You Gotta Believe) | 951 | .4 |
| | Simone Berg (SW) | 613 | .3 |
| | Kenneth Matto (AFP) | 411 | .2 |
| | Charles H. Dickson (Capitalist) | 273 | .1 |
| 7 | Bob Franks (R) | 132,174 | 53.3 |
| | Leonard R. Sendelsky (D) | 105,761 | 42.6 |
| | Eugene J. Gillespie Jr. (I) | 4,043 | 1.6 |
| | Bill Campbell (No Nonsense Government) | 2,612 | 1.1 |
| | Spencer Layman (LIBERT) | 1,964 | .8 |
| | John L. Kucek (AFP) | 844 | .3 |
| | Kevin Michael Criss (People's Congressional Preference) | 684 | .3 |
| 8 | Herbert C. Klein (D) | 96,742 | 47.0 |
| | Joseph L. Bubba (R) | 84,674 | 41.1 |
| | Gloria J. Kolodziej (IFC) | 16,170 | 7.9 |
| | Thomas Caslander (IFC) | 2,916 | 1.4 |
| | Carmine O. Pellosie (Independent People's Network) | 2,135 | 1.0 |
| | Louis M. Stefanelli (LIBERT) | 1,109 | .5 |
| | Rob Dominianni (Restore Public Trust) | 1,099 | .5 |
| | Jason Redrup (SW) | 392 | .2 |
| | Gregory E. Dzula (AFP) | 316 | .2 |
| | Neal A. Gorfinkle (NJI) | 275 | .1 |

| | | Vote Total | % |
|---|---|---|---|
| 9 ● | Robert G. Torricelli (D) | 139,188 | 58.3 |
| | Patrick J. Roma (R) | 88,179 | 36.9 |
| | Peter J. Russo (Clean Up Congress) | 4,491 | 1.9 |
| | Gary Novosielski (NJI) | 2,257 | 1.0 |
| | Joseph D'Alessio (AFP) | 1,606 | .7 |
| | Herbert H. Shaw (Politicians Are Crooks) | 1,369 | .6 |
| | Daniel M. Karlan (LIBERT) | 1,099 | .5 |
| | Shel Haas (An Independent Voice) | 515 | .2 |
| 10 ● | Donald M. Payne (D) | 117,287 | 78.4 |
| | Alfred D. Palermo (R) | 30,160 | 20.2 |
| | Roberto Caraballo (LIBERT) | 1,272 | .9 |
| | William T. Leonard (SW) | 913 | .6 |
| 11 ● | Dean A. Gallo (R) | 188,165 | 70.1 |
| | Ona Spiridellis (D) | 68,871 | 25.7 |
| | Richard S. Roth (LIBERT) | 3,538 | 1.3 |
| | Barry J. Fitzpatrick (Time for Change) | 3,127 | 1.2 |
| | David C. Karlen (I) | 1,882 | .7 |
| | Howard Safier (Howard Safier-Independent) | 1,711 | .6 |
| | Richard E. Hrazanek (AFP) | 1,142 | .4 |
| 12 ● | Dick Zimmer (R) | 174,216 | 63.9 |
| | Frank Abate (D) | 83,035 | 30.4 |
| | Carl J. Mayer (I) | 11,051 | 4.1 |
| | Carl Peters (LIBERT) | 1,906 | .7 |
| | Edward F. Eggert (I) | 1,804 | .7 |
| | Compton C. Pakenham (AFP) | 745 | .3 |
| 13 ● | Robert Menendez (D) | 93,670 | 64.3 |
| | Fred J. Theemling Jr. (R) | 44,529 | 30.6 |
| | Joseph D. Bonacci (Stop Tax Increases) | 2,363 | 1.6 |
| | Len Flynn (LIBERT) | 1,539 | 1.1 |
| | John E. Rummel (Communist) | 1,525 | 1.1 |
| | Jane Harris (SW) | 1,406 | 1.0 |
| | Donald K. Stoveken (AFP) | 682 | .5 |

### NEW MEXICO

**House**

| | | Vote Total | % |
|---|---|---|---|
| 1 ● | Steven H. Schiff (R) | 128,426 | 62.6 |
| | Robert J. Aragon (D) | 76,600 | 37.3 |
| | Orlin G. Cole (write-in) | 188 | .1 |
| 2 ● | Joe Skeen (R) | 94,838 | 56.4 |
| | Dan Sosa Jr. (D) | 73,157 | 43.5 |
| | David Lee Pilley (write-in) | 175 | .1 |
| 3 ● | Bill Richardson (D) | 122,850 | 67.4 |
| | F. Gregg Bemis Jr. (R) | 54,569 | 29.9 |
| | Ed Nagel (LIBERT) | 4,798 | 2.6 |

### NEW YORK

**Senate**

| | | Vote Total | % |
|---|---|---|---|
| ● | Alfonse M. D'Amato (R, C, RTL) | 3,166,994 | 49.0 |
| | Robert Abrams (D, L) | 3,086,200 | 47.8 |
| | Norma Segal (LIBERT) | 108,530 | 1.7 |
| | Mohammad Mehdi (NA) | 56,631 | .9 |
| | Stanley Nelson (NL) | 23,747 | .4 |
| | Ed Warren (SW) | 16,724 | .3 |

**House**

| | | Vote Total | % |
|---|---|---|---|
| 1 ● | George J. Hochbrueckner (D, LIF) | 117,940 | 51.7 |
| | Edward P. Romaine (R, C, RTL, TCP-LI) | 110,043 | 48.3 |
| 2 | Rick A. Lazio (R, C, TCP-LI) | 109,386 | 53.2 |
| ● | Thomas J. Downey (D, LIF) | 96,328 | 46.8 |
| 3 | Peter T. King (R, C) | 124,727 | 49.6 |
| | Steve A. Orlins (D) | 116,915 | 46.5 |
| | Louis P. Roccanova (RTL) | 6,888 | 2.7 |
| | Ben-Zion J. Heyman (L) | 3,092 | 1.2 |
| 4 | David A. Levy (R, C) | 110,710 | 50.2 |
| | Philip M. Schiliro (D, L) | 100,386 | 45.5 |
| | Vincent P. Garbitelli (RTL) | 9,548 | 4.3 |
| 5 ● | Gary L. Ackerman (D, L) | 110,476 | 52.4 |
| | Allan E. Binder (R) | 94,907 | 45.0 |
| | Andrew J. Duff (RTL) | 5,448 | 2.6 |
| 6 ● | Floyd H. Flake (D) | 96,972 | 81.0 |
| | Dianand D. Bhagwandin (R, C) | 22,687 | 19.0 |

| | | Vote Total | % |
|---|---|---|---|
| 7 ● | Thomas J. Manton (D) | 72,280 | 56.9 |
| | Dennis C. Shea (R, C) | 54,639 | 43.1 |
| 8 | Jerrold Nadler (D, L) ‡ | 138,296 | 81.2 |
| | David L. Askren (R) | 25,548 | 15.0 |
| | Margaret V. Byrnes (C) | 5,180 | 3.0 |
| | Arthur R. Block (NA) | 1,224 | .7 |
| 9 ● | Charles E. Schumer (D, L) | 116,545 | 88.6 |
| | (No Republican candidate) | | |
| | Alice E. Gaffney (C) | 14,985 | 11.4 |
| 10 ● | Edolphus Towns (D, L) | 97,509 | 95.8 |
| | (No Republican candidate) | | |
| | Owen Augustin (C) | 4,315 | 4.2 |
| 11 ● | Major R. Owens (D, L) | 80,028 | 93.6 |
| | (No Republican candidate) | | |
| | Michael Gaffney (C) | 4,287 | 5.0 |
| | Ernest N. Foster (NA) | 1,179 | 1.4 |
| 12 | Nydia Velazquez (D) | 55,926 | 76.5 |
| | Angel Diaz (R, C, RTL) | 14,976 | 20.5 |
| | Ruben Franco (L) | 1,556 | 2.1 |
| | Rafael Mendez (NA) | 609 | .8 |
| 13 ● | Susan Molinari (R, C) | 107,903 | 56.1 |
| | Sal F. Albanese (D, L) | 73,520 | 38.2 |
| | Kathleen M. Murphy (RTL) | 10,825 | 5.6 |
| 14 | Carolyn B. Maloney (D, L) | 101,652 | 50.4 |
| ● | Bill Green (R, Independent Neighbors) | 97,215 | 48.2 |
| | Abraham J. Hirschfeld (Better Eastside) | 2,970 | 1.5 |
| 15 ● | Charles B. Rangel (D) | 105,011 | 94.9 |
| | (No Republican candidate) | | |
| | Jose A. Suero (C, Independent Fusion) | 4,345 | 3.9 |
| | Jessie Fields (NA) | 1,337 | 1.2 |
| 16 ● | Jose E. Serrano (D, L) | 85,222 | 91.4 |
| | Michael Walters (R, C) | 7,975 | 8.6 |
| 17 ● | Eliot L. Engel (D, L) | 98,068 | 80.1 |
| | Martin Richman (R) | 16,511 | 13.5 |
| | Kevin Brawley (C) | 3,143 | 2.6 |
| | Martin J. O'Grady (RTL) | 3,067 | 2.5 |
| | Nana LaLuz (NL) | 1,592 | 1.3 |
| 18 ● | Nita M. Lowey (D) | 115,841 | 55.6 |
| | Joseph J. DioGuardi (R, C, RTL) | 92,687 | 44.4 |
| 19 ● | Hamilton Fish Jr. (R, C) | 139,610 | 60.1 |
| | Neil McCarthy (D) | 92,854 | 39.9 |
| 20 ● | Benjamin A. Gilman (R) | 150,301 | 66.1 |
| | Jonathan L. Levine (D) | 66,826 | 29.4 |
| | Robert F. Garrison (RTL) | 10,204 | 4.5 |
| 21 ● | Michael R. McNulty (D, C) | 166,371 | 62.7 |
| | Nancy Norman (R, L) | 91,184 | 34.4 |
| | William J. Donnelly (RTL) | 7,723 | 2.9 |
| 22 ● | Gerald B. H. Solomon (R, C, RTL) | 164,436 | 65.4 |
| | David Roberts (D) | 86,896 | 34.6 |
| 23 ● | Sherwood Boehlert (R) | 139,774 | 63.6 |
| | Paula DiPerna (D) | 61,835 | 28.2 |
| | Randall A. Terry (RTL) | 8,688 | 4.0 |
| | Geoffrey P. Grace (C) | 8,011 | 3.6 |
| | Ted F. Janowski (NL) | 1,354 | .6 |
| 24 | John M. McHugh (R, Voter Rights) | 122,257 | 60.8 |
| | Margaret M. Ravenscroft (D) | 47,675 | 23.7 |
| | Morrison J. Hosley Jr. (C, RTL) | 26,763 | 13.3 |
| | Stephen Burke (L) | 4,374 | 2.2 |
| 25 ● | James T. Walsh (R, C) | 135,076 | 55.7 |
| | Rhea Jezer (D, Common Sense) | 107,310 | 44.3 |
| 26 ● | Maurice D. Hinchey (D, L) | 119,557 | 50.4 |
| | Bob Moppert (R, C) | 110,738 | 46.7 |
| | Mary C. Dixon (RTL) | 6,821 | 2.9 |
| 27 ● | Bill Paxon (R, C, RTL) | 156,596 | 63.5 |
| | W. Douglas Call (D) | 89,906 | 36.5 |
| 28 ● | Louise M. Slaughter (D) | 140,908 | 55.2 |
| | William P. Polito (R, C) | 112,273 | 44.0 |
| | Keith R.T. Perez (EJ) | 1,897 | .7 |

| | | Vote Total | % |
|---|---|---|---|
| 29 ● | John J. LaFalce (D, L) | 128,230 | 54.5 |
| | William E. Miller Jr. (R, C) | 98,031 | 41.6 |
| | Kenneth J. Kowalski (RTL) | 7,367 | 3.1 |
| | John A. Basar Jr. (EJ) | 1,830 | .8 |
| 30 | Jack Quinn (R, Change Congress) | 125,734 | 51.7 |
| | Dennis Gorski (D, C) | 111,445 | 45.8 |
| | Mary F. Refermat (RTL) | 6,025 | 2.5 |
| 31 ● | Amo Houghton (R, C) | 150,696 | 70.6 |
| | Joseph P. Leahey (D) | 52,010 | 24.4 |
| | Gretchen S. McManus (RTL) | 10,848 | 5.1 |

### NORTH CAROLINA

**Governor**

| | | Vote Total | % |
|---|---|---|---|
| | James B. Hunt Jr. (D) | 1,368,246 | 52.7 |
| | Jim Gardner (R) | 1,121,955 | 43.2 |
| | Scott McLaughlin (LIBERT) | 104,983 | 4.1 |

**Senate**

| | | Vote Total | % |
|---|---|---|---|
| | Lauch Faircloth (R) | 1,297,892 | 50.4 |
| ● | Terry Sanford (D) | 1,194,015 | 46.3 |
| | Bobby Yates Emory (LIBERT) | 85,948 | 3.3 |

**House**

| | | Vote Total | % |
|---|---|---|---|
| 1 | Eva Clayton (D) | 116,078 | 67.0 |
| | Ted Tyler (R) | 54,457 | 31.4 |
| | C. Barry Williams (LIBERT) | 2,727 | 1.6 |
| † | Eva Clayton (D) | 118,324 | 56.7 |
| | Ted Tyler (R) | 86,273 | 41.3 |
| | C. Barry Williams (LIBERT) | 4,121 | 2.0 |
| 2 ● | Tim Valentine (D) | 113,693 | 53.7 |
| | Don Davis (R) | 93,893 | 44.4 |
| | Dennis Bryant Lubahn (LIBERT) | 3,983 | 1.9 |
| 3 ● | H. Martin Lancaster (D) | 101,739 | 54.4 |
| | Tommy Pollard (R) | 80,759 | 43.2 |
| | Mark Jackson (LIBERT) | 4,552 | 2.4 |
| 4 ● | David Price (D) | 171,299 | 64.6 |
| | LaVinia ''Vicky'' Rothrock Goudie (R) | 89,345 | 33.7 |
| | Eugene Paczelt (LIBERT) | 4,416 | 1.7 |
| 5 ● | Stephen L. Neal (D) | 117,835 | 52.7 |
| | Richard M. Burr (R) | 102,086 | 45.6 |
| | Gary Albrecht (LIBERT) | 3,758 | 1.7 |
| 6 ● | Howard Coble (R) | 162,822 | 70.8 |
| | Robin Hood (D) | 67,200 | 29.2 |
| 7 ● | Charlie Rose (D) | 92,414 | 56.7 |
| | Robert C. Anderson (R) | 66,536 | 40.8 |
| | Marc Kelley (LIBERT) | 4,151 | 2.6 |
| 8 ● | W. G. ''Bill'' Hefner (D) | 113,162 | 57.9 |
| | Coy C. Privette (R) | 71,842 | 36.8 |
| | J. Wendell Drye (LIBERT) | 10,447 | 5.4 |
| 9 ● | Alex McMillan (R) | 153,650 | 67.3 |
| | Rory Blake (D) | 74,583 | 32.7 |
| 10 ● | Cass Ballenger (R) | 149,033 | 63.4 |
| | Ben Neill (D) | 79,206 | 33.7 |
| | Jeffrey Clayton Brown (LIBERT) | 6,888 | 2.9 |
| 11 ● | Charles H. Taylor (R) | 130,158 | 54.7 |
| | John S. Stevens (D) | 108,003 | 45.4 |
| 12 | Melvin Watt (D) | 127,262 | 70.4 |
| | Barbara Gore Washington (R) | 49,402 | 27.3 |
| | Curtis Wade Krumel (LIBERT) | 4,160 | 2.3 |

### NORTH DAKOTA

**Governor**

| | | Vote Total | % |
|---|---|---|---|
| | Edward T. Schafer (R) | 176,398 | 57.9 |
| | Nicholas Spaeth (D) | 123,845 | 40.6 |
| | Harley McLain (I) | 2,614 | .9 |
| | Michael O. DuPaul (I) | 2,004 | .7 |

**Senate**

| | | Vote Total | % |
|---|---|---|---|
| ● | Kent Conrad (D) | 102,887 | 63.3 |
| | Jack Dalrymple (R) | 54,726 | 33.7 |
| | Darold Larson (I) | 4,839 | 3.0 |

‡ *Nadler was elected on the same ballot to fill the seat left vacant by the death of Ted Weiss, D.*

† *Clayton won a special election to fill the seat left vacant by the death of Walter B. Jones, D.*

| | Vote Total | % |
|---|---|---|
| **Senate** | | |
| Byron L. Dorgan (D) | 179,347 | 59.0 |
| Steve Sydness (R) | 118,162 | 38.9 |
| Tom Asbridge (I) | 6,448 | 2.1 |
| **House** | | |
| AL  Earl Pomeroy (D) | 169,273 | 56.8 |
| John T. Korsmo (R) | 117,442 | 39.4 |
| Anna Belle Bourgois (I) | 7,394 | 2.5 |
| Grady Blount (I) | 3,789 | 1.3 |

## OHIO

| | Vote Total | % |
|---|---|---|
| **Senate** | | |
| ● John Glenn (D) | 2,444,419 | 51.0 |
| Mike DeWine (R) | 2,028,300 | 42.3 |
| Martha Kathryn Grevatt (I) | 321,234 | 6.7 |
| **House** | | |
| 1  David Mann (D) | 120,190 | 51.3 |
| (No Republican candidate) | | |
| Steve Grote (I) | 101,498 | 43.3 |
| James A. Berns (I) | 12,734 | 5.4 |
| 2 ● Bill Gradison (R) | 177,720 | 70.1 |
| Thomas R. Chandler (D) | 75,924 | 29.9 |
| 3 ● Tony P. Hall (D) | 146,072 | 59.7 |
| Peter W. Davis (R) | 98,733 | 40.3 |
| 4 ● Michael G. Oxley (R) | 147,346 | 61.3 |
| Raymond M. Ball (D) | 92,608 | 38.5 |
| James R. Stahl (write-in) | 486 | .2 |
| 5 ● Paul E. Gillmor (R) | Unopposed | |
| 6 ● Ted Strickland (D) | 122,720 | 50.7 |
| ● Bob McEwen (R) | 119,252 | 49.3 |
| 7 ● David L. Hobson (R) | 164,195 | 71.3 |
| Clifford S. Heskett (D) | 66,237 | 28.7 |
| 8 ● John A. Boehner (R) | 176,362 | 74.0 |
| Fred Sennet (D) | 62,033 | 26.0 |
| 9 ● Marcy Kaptur (D) | 178,879 | 73.6 |
| Ken D. Brown (R) | 53,011 | 21.8 |
| Ed Howard (I) | 11,162 | 4.6 |
| 10  Martin R. Hoke (R) | 136,433 | 56.8 |
| ● Mary Rose Oakar (D) | 103,788 | 43.2 |
| 11 ● Louis Stokes (D) | 154,718 | 69.2 |
| Beryl E. Rothschild (R) | 43,866 | 19.6 |
| Edmund Gudenas (I) | 19,773 | 8.8 |
| Gerald C. Henley (I) | 5,267 | 2.4 |
| 12 ● John R. Kasich (R) | 170,297 | 71.2 |
| Bob Fitrakis (D) | 68,761 | 28.8 |
| 13  Sherrod Brown (D) | 134,486 | 53.3 |
| Margaret R. Mueller (R) | 88,889 | 35.2 |
| Mark Miller (I) | 20,320 | 8.1 |
| Tom Lawson (I) | 4,719 | 1.9 |
| Werner J. Lange (I) | 3,844 | 1.5 |
| 14 ● Tom Sawyer (D) | 165,335 | 67.8 |
| Robert Morgan (R) | 78,659 | 32.2 |
| 15  Deborah Pryce (R) | 110,390 | 44.1 |
| Richard Cordray (D) | 94,907 | 37.9 |
| Linda S. Reidelbach (I) | 44,906 | 17.9 |
| 16 ● Ralph Regula (R) | 158,489 | 63.7 |
| Warner D. Mendenhall (D) | 90,224 | 36.3 |
| 17 ● James A. Traficant Jr. (D) | 216,503 | 84.2 |
| Salvatore Pansino (R) | 40,743 | 15.8 |
| 18 ● Douglas Applegate (D) | 166,189 | 68.3 |
| Bill Ress (R) | 77,229 | 31.7 |
| 19  Eric D. Fingerhut (D) | 138,465 | 52.6 |
| Robert A. Gardner (R) | 124,606 | 47.4 |

## OKLAHOMA

| | Vote Total | % |
|---|---|---|
| **Senate** | | |
| ● Don Nickles (R) | 757,876 | 58.5 |
| Steve Lewis (D) | 494,350 | 38.2 |
| Roy V. Edwards (I) | 21,225 | 1.6 |
| Thomas D. Ledgerwood II (I) | 20,972 | 1.6 |
| **House** | | |
| 1 ● James M. Inhofe (R) | 119,211 | 52.8 |
| John Selph (D) | 106,619 | 47.2 |
| 2 ● Mike Synar (D) | 118,542 | 55.5 |
| Jerry Hill (R) | 87,657 | 41.1 |
| William S. Vardeman (I) | 7,314 | 3.4 |
| 3 ● Bill Brewster (D) | 155,934 | 75.1 |
| Robert W. Stokes (R) | 51,725 | 24.9 |
| 4 ● Dave McCurdy (D) | 140,841 | 70.7 |
| Howard Bell (R) | 58,235 | 29.3 |
| 5  Ernest Jim Istook (R) | 123,237 | 53.4 |
| Laurie Williams (D) | 107,579 | 46.6 |
| 6 ● Glenn English (D) | 134,734 | 67.8 |
| Bob Anthony (R) | 64,068 | 32.2 |

## OREGON

| | Vote Total | % |
|---|---|---|
| **Senate** | | |
| ● Bob Packwood (R) | 717,455 | 52.1 |
| Les AuCoin (D) | 639,851 | 46.5 |
| Write-ins | 18,727 | 1.4 |
| **House** | | |
| 1  Elizabeth Furse (D) | 152,917 | 52.0 |
| Tony Meeker (R) | 140,986 | 47.9 |
| Write-ins | 251 | .1 |
| 2 ● Bob Smith (R) | 184,163 | 67.1 |
| Denzel Ferguson (D) | 90,036 | 32.8 |
| Write-ins | 279 | .1 |
| 3 ● Ron Wyden (D) | 208,028 | 77.1 |
| Al Ritter (R) | 50,235 | 18.6 |
| Blair Bobier (LIBERT) | 11,413 | 4.2 |
| Write-ins | 203 | .1 |
| 4 ● Peter A. DeFazio (D) | 199,372 | 71.4 |
| Richard L. Schulz (R) | 79,733 | 28.5 |
| Write-ins | 194 | .1 |
| 5 ● Mike Kopetski (D) | 174,443 | 63.9 |
| Jim Seagraves (R) | 97,984 | 35.9 |
| Write-ins | 517 | .2 |

## PENNSYLVANIA

| | Vote Total | % |
|---|---|---|
| **Senate** | | |
| ● Arlen Specter (R) | 2,358,125 | 49.1 |
| Lynn Yeakel (D) | 2,224,966 | 46.3 |
| John F. Perry III (LIBERT) | 219,319 | 4.6 |
| **House** | | |
| 1 ● Thomas M. Foglietta (D) | 150,172 | 80.9 |
| Craig Snyder (R) | 35,419 | 19.1 |
| 2 ● Lucien E. Blackwell (D) | 164,355 | 76.8 |
| Larry Hollin (R) | 47,906 | 22.4 |
| Mark Wyatt (SW) | 1,666 | .8 |
| 3 ● Robert A. Borski (D) | 130,828 | 58.9 |
| Charles F. Dougherty (R) | 86,787 | 39.1 |
| John J. Hughes (I) | 4,356 | 2.0 |
| 4  Ron Klink (D) | 186,684 | 78.5 |
| Gordon R. Johnston (R) | 48,484 | 20.4 |
| Drew Ley (I) | 2,754 | 1.2 |
| 5 ● William F. Clinger (R, D) | Unopposed | |
| 6  Tim Holden (D) | 108,312 | 52.1 |
| John E. Jones (R) | 99,694 | 47.9 |
| 7 ● Curt Weldon (R) | 180,648 | 66.0 |
| Frank Daly (D) | 91,623 | 33.5 |
| William Alan Hickman (NL) | 1,627 | .6 |
| 8  Jim Greenwood (R) | 129,593 | 51.9 |
| ● Peter H. Kostmayer (D) | 114,095 | 45.7 |
| William H. Magerman (Magerman for Congress) | 5,850 | 2.3 |
| 9 ● Bud Shuster (R, D) | Unopposed | |
| 10 ● Joseph M. McDade (R, D) | 189,414 | 90.4 |
| Albert A. Smith (LIBERT) | 20,134 | 9.6 |
| 11 ● Paul E. Kanjorski (D) | 138,875 | 67.1 |
| Michael A. Fescina (R) | 68,112 | 32.9 |
| 12 ● John P. Murtha (D) | Unopposed | |
| 13  Marjorie Margolies-Mezvinsky (D) | 127,685 | 50.3 |
| Jon D. Fox (R) | 126,312 | 49.7 |
| 14 ● William J. Coyne (D) | 165,633 | 72.3 |
| Byron W. King (R) | 61,311 | 26.8 |
| Joanne S. Kuniansky (SW) | 1,300 | .6 |
| Paul Scherrer (WL) | 794 | .3 |
| 15  Paul McHale (D) | 111,419 | 52.2 |
| ● Don Ritter (R) | 99,520 | 46.7 |
| Eugene A. Nau (NL) | 2,385 | 1.1 |
| 16 ● Robert S. Walker (R) | 137,823 | 64.8 |
| Robert Peters (D) | 74,741 | 35.2 |
| 17 ● George W. Gekas (R) | 150,158 | 69.5 |
| Bill Sturges (D) | 65,881 | 30.5 |
| 18 ● Rick Santorum (R) | 154,024 | 60.6 |
| Frank A. Pecora (D) | 96,655 | 38.0 |
| Denise Winebrenner Edwards (New Independent) | 3,650 | 1.4 |
| 19 ● Bill Goodling (R) | 98,599 | 45.3 |
| Paul V. Kilker (D) | 74,798 | 34.4 |
| Thomas M. Humbert (I) | 44,190 | 20.3 |
| 20 ● Austin J. Murphy (D) | 114,898 | 50.7 |
| Bill Townsend (R) | 111,591 | 49.3 |
| 21 ● Tom Ridge (R) | 150,729 | 68.0 |
| John C. Harkins (D) | 70,802 | 32.0 |

## RHODE ISLAND

| | Vote Total | % |
|---|---|---|
| **Governor** | | |
| ● Bruce Sundlun (D) | 261,484 | 61.6 |
| Elizabeth Ann Leonard (R) | 145,590 | 34.3 |
| Joseph F. Devine (Reform '92) | 14,511 | 3.4 |
| Jack D. Potter (POP) | 1,698 | .4 |
| John J. Staradumsky (I) | 1,535 | .4 |
| **House** | | |
| 1 ● Ronald K. Machtley (R) | 135,982 | 70.1 |
| David R. Carlin Jr. (D) | 48,092 | 24.8 |
| Frederick E. Dick (Ross Perot Independent) | 6,012 | 3.1 |
| Norman J. Jacques (I) | 4,003 | 2.1 |
| 2 ● Jack Reed (D) | 144,450 | 70.7 |
| James W. Bell (R) | 49,998 | 24.5 |
| Thomas J. Ricci (I) | 6,715 | 3.3 |
| John Turnbull (Independent Thinking) | 3,250 | 1.6 |

## SOUTH CAROLINA

| | Vote Total | % |
|---|---|---|
| **Senate** | | |
| ● Ernest F. Hollings (D) | 591,030 | 50.1 |
| Thomas F. Hartnett (R) | 554,175 | 46.9 |
| Mark Johnson (LIBERT) | 22,962 | 1.9 |
| Robert Barnwell Clarkson II (AM) | 11,568 | 1.0 |
| Write-ins | 703 | .1 |
| **House** | | |
| 1 ● Arthur Ravenel Jr. (R) | 121,938 | 66.1 |
| Bill Oberst Jr. (D) | 59,908 | 32.5 |
| John R. Peeples (AM) | 2,608 | 1.4 |
| Write-ins | 95 | .1 |
| 2 ● Floyd D. Spence (R) | 148,667 | 87.6 |
| (No Democratic candidate) | | |
| Geb Sommer (LIBERT) | 20,816 | 12.3 |
| Write-ins | 187 | .1 |
| 3 ● Butler Derrick (D) | 119,119 | 61.1 |
| Jim Bland (R) | 75,660 | 38.8 |
| 4  Bob Inglis (R) | 99,879 | 50.3 |
| ● Liz J. Patterson (D) | 94,182 | 47.5 |
| Jo Jorgensen (LIBERT) | 4,286 | 2.2 |
| 5 ● John M. Spratt Jr. (D) | 112,031 | 61.2 |
| Bill Horne (R) | 70,866 | 38.7 |
| Write-ins | 189 | .1 |
| 6  James E. Clyburn (D) | 120,647 | 65.3 |
| John Chase (R) | 64,149 | 34.7 |

## SOUTH DAKOTA

| | Vote Total | % |
|---|---|---|
| **Senate** | | |
| ● Tom Daschle (D) | 217,095 | 64.9 |
| Charlene Haar (R) | 108,733 | 32.5 |
| Gus Hercules (LIBERT) | 4,353 | 1.3 |
| Kent Hyde (I) | 4,314 | 1.3 |
| **House** | | |
| AL ● Tim Johnson (D) | 230,070 | 69.1 |
| John Timmer (R) | 89,375 | 26.9 |
| Ronald Wieczorek (I) | 6,746 | 2.0 |
| Robert J. Newland (LIBERT) | 3,931 | 1.2 |
| Ann Balakier (I) | 2,780 | .8 |

| | | Vote Total | % |
|---|---|---|---|

## TENNESSEE

**House**

| 1 | ● James H. Quillen (R) | 114,797 | 67.5 |
|---|---|---|---|
| | J. Carr "Jack" Christian (D) | 47,809 | 28.1 |
| | Don Fox (I) | 4,126 | 2.4 |
| | Fred A. Hartley (I) | 3,416 | 2.0 |
| 2 | ● John J. "Jimmy" Duncan Jr. (R) | 148,377 | 72.2 |
| | Troy Goodale (D) | 52,887 | 25.7 |
| | Randon J. Krieg (I) | 4,134 | 2.0 |
| 3 | ● Marilyn Lloyd (D) | 105,693 | 48.8 |
| | Zach Wamp (R) | 102,763 | 47.5 |
| | Carol Hagan (I) | 4,433 | 2.1 |
| | Pete Melcher (I) | 2,048 | .9 |
| | Marjorie M. Martin (I) | 1,593 | .7 |
| 4 | ● Jim Cooper (D) | 98,984 | 64.1 |
| | Dale Johnson (R) | 50,340 | 32.6 |
| | Ginnia C. Fox (I) | 3,970 | 2.6 |
| | Kieven Parks (I) | 1,210 | .8 |
| 5 | ● Bob Clement (D) | 125,233 | 66.8 |
| | Tom Stone (R) | 49,417 | 26.3 |
| | Steven L. Edmondson (I) | 6,724 | 3.6 |
| | Richard H. Wyatt (I) | 3,507 | 1.9 |
| | John D. Haury (I) | 1,685 | .9 |
| | Ben Tomeo (I) | 1,002 | .5 |
| 6 | ● Bart Gordon (D) | 120,177 | 56.6 |
| | Marsha Blackburn (R) | 86,289 | 40.6 |
| | H. Scott Benson (I) | 5,952 | 2.8 |
| 7 | ● Don Sundquist (R) | 125,101 | 61.7 |
| | David R. Davis (D) | 72,062 | 35.5 |
| | Rickey Boyette (I) | 2,290 | 1.1 |
| | Jim Osburn (I) | 1,831 | .9 |
| | Francis Fredrick Tapp (I) | 1,573 | .8 |
| 8 | ● John Tanner (D) | 136,852 | 83.7 |
| | (No Republican candidate) | | |
| | Lawrence J. Barnes (I) | 9,605 | 5.9 |
| | David L. Ward (I) | 6,930 | 4.2 |
| | John E. Vinson (I) | 5,435 | 3.3 |
| | Millard J. McKissack II (I) | 4,600 | 2.8 |
| 9 | ● Harold E. Ford (D) | 123,276 | 57.9 |
| | Charles L. Black (R) | 60,606 | 28.5 |
| | Richard Liptock (I) | 14,075 | 6.6 |
| | James Vandergriff (I) | 12,265 | 5.8 |
| | William Rolen (I) | 2,517 | 1.2 |

## TEXAS

**House**

| 1 | ● Jim Chapman (D) | Unopposed | |
|---|---|---|---|
| 2 | ● Charles Wilson (D) | 118,625 | 56.1 |
| | Donna Peterson (R) | 92,176 | 43.6 |
| | Roger Northen (write-in) | 549 | .3 |
| 3 | ● Sam Johnson (R) | 201,569 | 86.1 |
| | (No Democratic candidate) | | |
| | Noel Kopala (LIBERT) | 32,570 | 13.9 |
| 4 | ● Ralph M. Hall (D) | 128,008 | 58.1 |
| | David L. Bridges (R) | 83,875 | 38.1 |
| | Steven Rothacker (LIBERT) | 8,450 | 3.8 |
| 5 | ● John Bryant (D) | 98,567 | 58.9 |
| | Richard Stokley (R) | 62,419 | 37.3 |
| | William H. Walker (LIBERT) | 6,344 | 3.8 |
| 6 | ● Joe L. Barton (R) | 189,140 | 71.9 |
| | John Dietrich (D) | 73,933 | 28.1 |
| 7 | ● Bill Archer (R) | Unopposed | |
| 8 | ● Jack Fields (R) | 179,349 | 77.0 |
| | Chas. Robinson (D) | 53,473 | 23.0 |
| 9 | ● Jack Brooks (D) | 118,690 | 53.6 |
| | Steve Stockman (R) | 96,270 | 43.5 |
| | Billy Joe Crawford (LIBERT) | 6,401 | 2.9 |
| 10 | ● J.J. Pickle (D) | 177,233 | 67.7 |
| | Herbert Spiro (R) | 68,646 | 26.2 |
| | Terry Blum (LIBERT) | 6,353 | 2.4 |
| | Jeff Davis (I) | 6,056 | 2.3 |
| | Stephen Hopkins (write-in) | 3,510 | 1.3 |
| 11 | ● Chet Edwards (D) | 119,999 | 67.4 |
| | James W. Broyles (R) | 58,033 | 32.6 |
| 12 | ● Pete Geren (D) | 125,492 | 62.8 |
| | David Hobbs (R) | 74,432 | 37.2 |

| | | Vote Total | % |
|---|---|---|---|
| 13 | ● Bill Sarpalius (D) | 117,892 | 60.3 |
| | Beau Boulter (R) | 77,514 | 39.7 |
| 14 | ● Greg Laughlin (D) | 135,930 | 68.1 |
| | Humberto J. Garza (R) | 54,412 | 27.3 |
| | Vic Vreeland (I) | 9,329 | 4.7 |
| 15 | ● E. "Kika" de la Garza (D) | 86,351 | 60.4 |
| | Tom Haughey (R) | 56,549 | 39.6 |
| 16 | ● Ronald D. Coleman (D) | 66,731 | 51.9 |
| | Chip Taberski (R) | 61,870 | 48.1 |
| 17 | ● Charles W. Stenholm (D) | 136,213 | 66.1 |
| | Jeannie Sadowski (R) | 69,958 | 33.9 |
| 18 | ● Craig Washington (D) | 111,422 | 64.7 |
| | Edward Blum (R) | 56,080 | 32.6 |
| | Gregg Lassen (LIBERT) | 4,706 | 2.7 |
| 19 | ● Larry Combest (R) | 162,057 | 77.4 |
| | Terry Lee Moser (D) | 47,325 | 22.6 |
| 20 | ● Henry B. Gonzalez (D) | Unopposed | |
| 21 | ● Lamar Smith (R) | 190,979 | 72.2 |
| | James M. Gaddy (D) | 62,827 | 23.7 |
| | William E. Grisham (LIBERT) | 10,847 | 4.1 |
| 22 | ● Tom DeLay (R) | 150,221 | 68.9 |
| | Richard Konrad (D) | 67,812 | 31.1 |
| 23 | Henry Bonilla (R) | 98,259 | 59.1 |
| | ● Albert G. Bustamante (D) | 63,797 | 38.4 |
| | David Alter (LIBERT) | 4,291 | 2.6 |
| 24 | ● Martin Frost (D) | 104,174 | 59.8 |
| | Steve Masterson (R) | 70,042 | 40.2 |
| 25 | ● Michael A. Andrews (D) | 98,975 | 56.0 |
| | Dolly Madison McKenna (R) | 73,192 | 41.4 |
| | Richard Mauk (LIBERT) | 4,710 | 2.7 |
| 26 | ● Dick Armey (R) | 150,209 | 73.1 |
| | John Wayne Caton (D) | 55,237 | 26.9 |
| 27 | ● Solomon P. Ortiz (D) | 87,022 | 55.5 |
| | Jay Kimbrough (R) | 66,853 | 42.6 |
| | Charles Henry Schoonover (LIBERT) | 2,969 | 1.9 |
| 28 | Frank Tejeda (D) | 122,457 | 87.1 |
| | (No Republican candidate) | | |
| | David C. Slatter (LIBERT) | 18,128 | 12.9 |
| 29 | ● Gene Green (D) | 64,064 | 64.9 |
| | Clark Kent Ervin (R) | 34,609 | 35.1 |
| 30 | Eddie Bernice Johnson (D) | 107,831 | 71.5 |
| | Lucy Cain (R) | 37,853 | 25.1 |
| | Ken Ashby (LIBERT) | 5,063 | 3.4 |

## UTAH

**Governor**

| | | | |
|---|---|---|---|
| Mike Leavitt (R) | | 321,713 | 42.2 |
| Merrill Cook (IP) | | 255,753 | 33.5 |
| Stewart Hanson (D) | | 177,181 | 23.2 |
| Rita Gum (POP) | | 3,593 | .5 |
| Gary R. Van Horn (AM) | | 1,492 | .2 |
| Eleanor Garcia (SW) | | 1,158 | .2 |
| Linda Metzger-Agin (I) | | 917 | .1 |
| Frank W. Richins (IA) | | 729 | .1 |

**Senate**

| | | | |
|---|---|---|---|
| Robert F. Bennett (R) | | 420,069 | 55.4 |
| Wayne Owens (D) | | 301,228 | 39.7 |
| Anita R. Morrow (POP) | | 17,549 | 2.3 |
| Maury Modine (LIBERT) | | 14,341 | 1.9 |
| Patricia Grogan (SW) | | 5,292 | .7 |

**House**

| 1 | ● James V. Hansen (R) | 160,037 | 65.3 |
|---|---|---|---|
| | Ron Holt (D) | 68,712 | 28.0 |
| | William J. "Dub" Lawrence (IP) | 16,505 | 6.7 |
| 2 | Karen Shepherd (D) | 127,738 | 50.5 |
| | Enid Greene (R) | 118,307 | 46.8 |
| | A. Peter Crane (IP) | 6,274 | 2.5 |
| | Eileen Koschak (SW) | 650 | .3 |
| 3 | ● Bill Orton (D) | 135,029 | 58.9 |
| | Richard R. Harrington (R) | 84,019 | 36.7 |
| | Wayne L. Hill (IP) | 5,764 | 2.5 |
| | Charles M. Wilson (I) | 2,068 | .9 |
| | Doug Jones (LIBERT) | 1,797 | .8 |
| | Nels J'Anthony (SW) | 384 | .2 |

| | | Vote Total | % |
|---|---|---|---|

## VERMONT

**Governor**

| | | | |
|---|---|---|---|
| ● Howard Dean (D) | | 213,523 | 74.7 |
| John McClaughry (R) | | 65,837 | 23.0 |
| Richard F. Gottlieb (LU) | | 3,120 | 1.1 |
| August "Gus" Jaccaci (NL, NA) | | 2,834 | 1.0 |
| Write-ins | | 414 | .1 |

**Senate**

| | | | |
|---|---|---|---|
| ● Patrick J. Leahy (D) | | 154,762 | 54.2 |
| James H. Douglas (R) | | 123,854 | 43.3 |
| Jerry Levy (LU) | | 5,121 | 1.8 |
| Michael B. Godeck (FFL) | | 1,780 | .6 |
| Write-ins | | 222 | .1 |

**House**

| AL | ● Bernard Sanders (I) | 162,724 | 57.8 |
|---|---|---|---|
| | Tim Philbin (R) | 86,901 | 30.9 |
| | Lewis E. Young (D) | 22,279 | 7.9 |
| | Pete Diamondstone (LU) | 3,660 | 1.3 |
| | John Dewey (NL, NA) | 3,549 | 1.3 |
| | Douglas M. Miller (FFL) | 2,049 | .7 |
| | Write-ins | 464 | .2 |

## VIRGINIA

**House**

| 1 | ● Herbert H. Bateman (R) | 133,537 | 57.5 |
|---|---|---|---|
| | Andrew H. Fox (D) | 89,814 | 38.7 |
| | Donald L. Macleay Jr. (I) | 8,677 | 3.7 |
| 2 | ● Owen B. Pickett (D) | 99,253 | 56.0 |
| | J.L. "Jim" Chapman IV (R) | 77,797 | 43.9 |
| 3 | Robert C. Scott (D) | 132,432 | 78.6 |
| | Daniel Jenkins (R) | 35,780 | 21.2 |
| | Write-ins | 261 | .2 |
| 4 | ● Norman Sisisky (D) | 147,649 | 68.4 |
| | A.J. "Tony" Zevgolis (R) | 68,286 | 31.6 |
| 5 | ● Lewis F. Payne Jr. (D) | 133,031 | 68.9 |
| | W.A. "Bill" Hurlburt (R) | 60,030 | 31.1 |
| 6 | Robert W. Goodlatte (R) | 127,309 | 60.0 |
| | Stephen Alan Musselwhite (D) | 84,618 | 39.9 |
| | Write-ins | 160 | .1 |
| 7 | ● Thomas J. Bliley Jr. (R) | 211,618 | 82.9 |
| | (No Democratic candidate) | | |
| | Gerald E. Berg (I) | 43,267 | 16.9 |
| | Write-ins | 490 | .2 |
| 8 | ● James P. Moran Jr. (D) | 138,542 | 56.1 |
| | Kyle E. McSlarrow (R) | 102,717 | 41.6 |
| | Alvin O. West (I) | 5,601 | 2.3 |
| | Write-ins | 266 | .1 |
| 9 | ● Rick Boucher (D) | 133,284 | 63.1 |
| | L. Garrett Weddle (R) | 77,985 | 36.9 |
| 10 | ● Frank R. Wolf (R) | 144,471 | 63.6 |
| | Raymond E. Vickery (D) | 75,775 | 33.4 |
| | Alan R. Ogden (I) | 6,874 | 3.0 |
| 11 | Leslie L. Byrne (D) | 114,172 | 50.0 |
| | Henry N. Butler (R) | 103,119 | 45.2 |
| | A.T. "Art" Narro (I) | 6,681 | 2.9 |
| | Perry J. Mitchell (I) | 4,155 | 1.8 |
| | Write-ins | 145 | .1 |

## WASHINGTON

**Governor**

| | | | |
|---|---|---|---|
| Mike Lowry (D) | | 1,184,315 | 52.2 |
| Ken Eikenberry (R) | | 1,086,216 | 47.8 |

**Senate**

| | | | |
|---|---|---|---|
| Patty Murray (D) | | 1,197,973 | 54.0 |
| Rod Chandler (R) | | 1,020,829 | 46.0 |

**House**

| 1 | Maria Cantwell (D) | 148,844 | 54.9 |
|---|---|---|---|
| | Gary Nelson (R) | 113,897 | 42.0 |
| | Patrick L. Ruckert (I) | 4,322 | 1.6 |
| | Anne Fleming (NL) | 4,211 | 1.6 |
| 2 | ● Al Swift (D) | 133,207 | 52.1 |
| | Jack Metcalf (R) | 107,365 | 42.0 |
| | R.M. "Robin" Dexter (I) | 8,702 | 3.4 |
| | Karen Leibrant (NL) | 6,646 | 2.6 |

|  |  | Vote Total | % |
|---|---|---|---|
| 3 • | Jolene Unsoeld (D) | 138,043 | 56.0 |
|  | Pat Fiske (R) | 108,583 | 44.0 |
| 4 | Jay Inslee (D) | 106,556 | 50.8 |
|  | Richard "Doc" Hastings (R) | 103,028 | 49.2 |
| 5 • | Thomas S. Foley (D) | 135,965 | 55.2 |
|  | John Sonneland (R) | 110,443 | 44.8 |
| 6 • | Norm Dicks (D) | 152,933 | 64.2 |
|  | Lauri J. Phillips (R) | 66,664 | 28.0 |
|  | Tom Donnelly (I) | 14,490 | 6.1 |
|  | Jim Horrigan (LIBERT) | 4,075 | 1.7 |
| 7 • | Jim McDermott (D) | 222,604 | 78.4 |
|  | Glenn C. Hampson (R) | 54,149 | 19.1 |
|  | Paul Glumaz (I) | 7,197 | 2.5 |
| 8 | Jennifer Dunn (R) | 155,874 | 60.4 |
|  | George O. Tamblyn (D) | 87,611 | 33.9 |
|  | Bob Adams (I) | 14,686 | 5.7 |
| 9 | Mike Kreidler (D) | 110,902 | 52.1 |
|  | Pete von Reichbauer (R) | 91,910 | 43.2 |
|  | Brian Wilson (I) | 6,585 | 3.1 |
|  | Timothy J. Brill (I) | 3,522 | 1.7 |

## WEST VIRGINIA

**Governor**

|  | Vote Total | % |
|---|---|---|
| • Gaston Caperton (D) | 368,302 | 56.0 |
| Cleve Benedict (R) | 240,390 | 36.6 |
| Charlotte Jean Pritt (write-in) | 48,490 | 7.4 |

**House**

|  |  | Vote Total | % |
|---|---|---|---|
| 1 • | Alan B. Mollohan (D) | Unopposed | |
| 2 • | Bob Wise (D) | 143,988 | 70.9 |
|  | Samuel A. Cravotta (R) | 59,102 | 29.1 |
| 3 • | Nick J. Rahall II (D) | 122,279 | 65.6 |
|  | Ben Waldman (R) | 64,012 | 34.4 |

## WISCONSIN

**Senate**

|  | Vote Total | % |
|---|---|---|
| Russell D. Feingold (D) | 1,290,662 | 52.6 |
| • Bob Kasten (R) | 1,129,599 | 46.0 |
| Patrick W. Johnson (I) | 16,513 | .7 |
| William Bittner (LIBERT) | 9,147 | .4 |
| Mervin A. Hanson Sr. (I) | 3,264 | .1 |
| Robert L. Kundert (I) | 2,747 | .1 |
| Joseph Selliken (I) | 2,733 | .1 |

**House**

|  |  | Vote Total | % |
|---|---|---|---|
| 1 • | Les Aspin (D) | 147,495 | 57.6 |
|  | Mark Neumann (R) | 104,352 | 40.7 |
|  | John Graf (I) | 4,391 | 1.7 |
| 2 • | Scott L. Klug (R) | 183,366 | 62.6 |
|  | Ada E. Deer (D) | 108,291 | 37.0 |
|  | Joseph E. Schumacher (I) | 1,140 | .4 |
| 3 • | Steve Gunderson (R) | 146,903 | 56.4 |
|  | Paul Sacia (D) | 108,664 | 41.7 |
|  | Jay B. Evenson (I) | 4,736 | 1.8 |

|  |  | Vote Total | % |
|---|---|---|---|
| 4 • | Gerald D. Kleczka (D) | 173,482 | 65.8 |
|  | Joseph L. Cook (R) | 84,872 | 32.2 |
|  | Daniel Slak (I) | 2,803 | 1.1 |
|  | John Washburn (LIBERT) | 2,488 | .9 |
|  | Write-ins | 158 | .1 |
| 5 | Thomas M. Barrett (D) | 162,344 | 69.3 |
|  | Donalda Ann Hammersmith (R) | 71,885 | 30.4 |
|  | Write-ins | 747 | .3 |
| 6 • | Tom Petri (R) | 143,875 | 52.9 |
|  | Peggy A. Lautenschlager (D) | 128,232 | 47.1 |
| 7 • | David R. Obey (D) | 166,200 | 64.4 |
|  | Dale R. Vannes (R) | 91,772 | 35.6 |
| 8 • | Toby Roth (R) | 191,704 | 70.1 |
|  | Catherine L. Helms (D) | 81,792 | 29.9 |
| 9 • | F. James Sensenbrenner Jr. (R) | 192,898 | 69.7 |
|  | Ingrid K. Buxton (D) | 77,362 | 28.0 |
|  | David E. Marlow (I) | 4,619 | 1.7 |
|  | Jeffrey Holt Millikin (LIBERT) | 1,881 | .7 |

## WYOMING

**House**

|  |  | Vote Total | % |
|---|---|---|---|
| AL • | Craig Thomas (R) | 113,882 | 57.8 |
|  | Jon Herschler (D) | 77,418 | 39.3 |
|  | Craig Alan McCune (LIBERT) | 5,677 | 2.9 |

# State Data on Voter and Party Registration

**ALABAMA**
(as of Aug. 1992)
No party registration
| | | |
|---|---|---|
| Total | 2,210,617 | |
| Inactive | 463,049 | |

**ALASKA**
(Oct. 1, 1992)
| | | |
|---|---|---|
| Democrats | 57,982 | 19% |
| Republicans | 66,953 | 22 |
| Other | 181,505 | 59 |
| Total | 306,440 | |

**ARIZONA**
(Aug. 1992)
| | | |
|---|---|---|
| Democrats | 762,386 | 42% |
| Republicans | 824,345 | 46 |
| Other | 207,656 | 11.5 |
| Total | 1,794,387 | |
| Inactive | 279,823 | |

**ARKANSAS**
(May 5, 1992)
No party registration
| | | |
|---|---|---|
| Total | 1,191,000 | |

**CALIFORNIA**
(Sept. 1992)
| | | |
|---|---|---|
| Democrats | 6,870,967 | 49% |
| Republicans | 5,355,305 | 38 |
| Other | 1,895,770 | 13 |
| Total | 14,122,042 | |

**COLORADO**
(Oct. 2, 1992)
| | | |
|---|---|---|
| Democrats | 652,717 | 34% |
| Republicans | 649,619 | 34 |
| Other | 602,235 | 32 |
| Total | 1,904,571 | |

**CONNECTICUT**
(Feb. 1992)
| | | |
|---|---|---|
| Democrats | 655,073 | 39% |
| Republicans | 450,578 | 27 |
| Other | 568,045 | 34 |
| Total | 1,673,696 | |

**DELAWARE**
(Oct. 19, 1992)
| | | |
|---|---|---|
| Democrats | 147,533 | 43% |
| Republicans | 125,383 | 37 |
| Other | 67,052 | 20 |
| Total | 339,968 | |

**FLORIDA**
(Aug. 3, 1992)
| | | |
|---|---|---|
| Democrats | 3,120,480 | 51% |
| Republicans | 2,488,014 | 41 |
| Other | 471,880 | 8 |
| Total | 6,080,374 | |

**GEORGIA**
(July 1992)
No party registration
| | | |
|---|---|---|
| Total | 2,871,702 | |

**HAWAII**
(Oct. 19, 1992)
No party registration
| | | |
|---|---|---|
| Total | 464,428 | |

**IDAHO**
(May 26, 1992)
No party registration
| | | |
|---|---|---|
| Total | 521,171 | |

**ILLINOIS**
(March 17, 1992)
No party registration
| | | |
|---|---|---|
| Total | 5,864,682 | |

**INDIANA**
(June 1992)
No party registration
| | | |
|---|---|---|
| Total | 2,938,366 | |

**IOWA**
(Oct. 1, 1992)
| | | |
|---|---|---|
| Democrats | 593,813 | 38% |
| Republicans | 504,349 | 32 |
| Other | 467,381 | 30 |
| Total | 1,565,543 | |

**KANSAS**
(July 1992)
| | | |
|---|---|---|
| Democrats | 370,550 | 31% |
| Republicans | 526,664 | 45 |
| Other | 284,109 | 24 |
| Total | 1,181,323 | |

**KENTUCKY**
(Oct. 13, 1992)
| | | |
|---|---|---|
| Democrats | 1,374,459 | 66% |
| Republicans | 615,732 | 30 |
| Other | 86,072 | 4 |
| Total | 2,076,263 | |

**LOUISIANA**
(Sept. 25, 1992)
| | | |
|---|---|---|
| Democrats | 1,617,129 | 72% |
| Republicans | 421,794 | 19 |
| Other | 208,373 | 9 |
| Total | 2,247,296 | |

**MAINE**
(June 1992)
| | | |
|---|---|---|
| Democrats | 289,174 | 33% |
| Republicans | 257,373 | 29 |
| Other | 329,995 | 38 |
| Total | 876,542 | |

**MARYLAND**
(Sept. 30, 1992)
| | | |
|---|---|---|
| Democrats | 1,421,399 | 61% |
| Republicans | 687,354 | 30 |
| Other | 210,236 | 9 |
| Total | 2,318,989 | |

**MASSACHUSETTS**
(Aug. 1992)
| | | |
|---|---|---|
| Democrats | 1,277,787 | 41% |
| Republicans | 426,841 | 14 |
| Other | 1,415,558 | 45 |
| Total | 3,120,186 | |

**MICHIGAN**
(Aug. 1992)
No party registration
| | | |
|---|---|---|
| Total | 5,956,403 | |

**MINNESOTA**
(Oct. 19, 1992)
No party registration
| | | |
|---|---|---|
| Total | 2,705,484 | |

**MISSISSIPPI**
(Oct. 20, 1992)
No party registration
| | | |
|---|---|---|
| Total | 1,640,150 | |

**MISSOURI**
(Aug. 4, 1992)
No party registration
| | | |
|---|---|---|
| Total | 2,769,150 | |

**MONTANA**
(June 1992)
No party registration
| | | |
|---|---|---|
| Total | 479,578 | |

**NEBRASKA**
(May 12, 1992)
| | | |
|---|---|---|
| Democrats | 371,839 | 42% |
| Republicans | 441,945 | 50 |
| Other | 71,319 | 8 |
| Total | 885,103 | |

**NEVADA**
(Aug. 1992)
| | | |
|---|---|---|
| Democrats | 261,791 | 45% |
| Republicans | 238,174 | 40 |
| Other | 86,829 | 15 |
| Total | 586,794 | |

**NEW HAMPSHIRE**
(Sept. 1992)
| | | |
|---|---|---|
| Democrats | 212,743 | 36% |
| Republicans | 248,319 | 41 |
| Other | 134,810 | 22.5 |
| Total | 595,872 | |

**NEW JERSEY**
(May 1992)
| | | |
|---|---|---|
| Democrats | 1,120,480 | 30% |
| Republicans | 765,631 | 21 |
| Other | 1,798,245 | 49 |
| Total | 3,684,356 | |

**NEW MEXICO**
(Sept. 1992)
| | | |
|---|---|---|
| Democrats | 382,078 | 59% |
| Republicans | 221,910 | 34 |
| Other | 44,874 | 7 |
| Total | 648,862 | |

**NEW YORK**
(July 1992)
| | | |
|---|---|---|
| Democrats | 3,814,070 | 47% |
| Republicans | 2,622,984 | 32 |
| Other | 1,684,358 | 21 |
| Total | 8,121,412 | |

**NORTH CAROLINA**
(Oct. 5, 1992)
| | | |
|---|---|---|
| Democrats | 2,313,520 | 61% |
| Republicans | 1,217,114 | 32 |
| Other | 286,746 | 7 |
| Total | 3,817,380 | |

**NORTH DAKOTA**
No voter registration

**OHIO**
(June 2, 1992)
No party registration
| | | |
|---|---|---|
| Democrats | 1,508,011 | 25% |
| Republicans | 1,085,756 | 18 |
| Other | 3,366,805 | 57 |
| Total | 5,960,572 | |

**OKLAHOMA**
(May 1, 1992)
| | | |
|---|---|---|
| Democrats | 1,337,196 | 64% |
| Republicans | 688,159 | 33 |
| Other | 51,759 | 3 |
| Total | 2,077,114 | |

**OREGON**
(Aug. 1992)
| | | |
|---|---|---|
| Democrats | 735,512 | 45% |
| Republicans | 604,444 | 37 |
| Other | 282,275 | 18 |
| Total | 1,622,231 | |

**PENNSYLVANIA**
(April 28, 1992)
| | | |
|---|---|---|
| Democrats | 2,710,389 | 51% |
| Republicans | 2,362,748 | 44 |
| Other | 249,919 | 5 |
| Total | 5,323,056 | |

**RHODE ISLAND**
(Sept. 15, 1992)
No party registration
| | | |
|---|---|---|
| Total | 535,012 | |

**SOUTH CAROLINA**
(Oct 17, 1992)
No party registration
| | | |
|---|---|---|
| Total | 1,535,567 | |

**SOUTH DAKOTA**
(May 18, 1992)
| | | |
|---|---|---|
| Democrats | 174,386 | 43% |
| Republicans | 200,425 | 49 |
| Other | 32,010 | 8 |
| Total | 406,821 | |

**TENNESSEE**
(June 1, 1992)
No party registration
| | | |
|---|---|---|
| Total | 2,447,529 | |

**TEXAS**
(March 1992)
No party registration
| | | |
|---|---|---|
| Total | 7,968,221 | |

**UTAH**
(Sept. 8, 1992)
No party registration
| | | |
|---|---|---|
| Total | 831,267 | |

**VERMONT**
(Sept. 8, 1992)
No party registration
| | | |
|---|---|---|
| Total | 351,839 | |

**VIRGINIA**
(Oct. 20, 1992)
No party registration
| | | |
|---|---|---|
| Total | 3,054,510 | |

**WASHINGTON**
(Sept. 25, 1992)
No party registration
| | | |
|---|---|---|
| Total | 2,583,731 | |

**WEST VIRGINIA**
(Apr. 13, 1992)
| | | |
|---|---|---|
| Democrats | 600,794 | 66% |
| Republicans | 277,798 | 31 |
| Other | 29,399 | 3 |
| Total | 907,991 | |

**WISCONSIN**
No statewide registration

**WYOMING**
(Aug. 18, 1992)
| | | |
|---|---|---|
| Democrats | 71,952 | 35% |
| Republicans | 115,598 | 55 |
| Other | 21,256 | 10 |
| Total | 208,806 | |

<u>DAY BY DAY</u>

# Clinton Maintains Control At the Democratic Convention

NEW YORK — Bill Clinton wrote the script, and the Democrats followed it.

To be sure, there were distractions, both from the audience and the actors in competing shows.

But despite former California Gov. Edmund G. "Jerry" Brown Jr.'s refusal to hop on the bandwagon or Ross Perot's stunning announcement from Dallas that he was bowing out, Clinton's reviews were good, the star was given a standing ovation, and the entire crew took the show on the road.

If Clinton couldn't control the events in Texas, he certainly called the shots inside Madison Square Garden. From start to finish, the Clinton team orchestrated a program that stressed the themes Democrats would push in the fall campaign.

There were reminders of Clinton's poor childhood, an effort to show he was in touch with the common people. There were clever and pointed attacks on President Bush and Vice President Dan Quayle.

There were consistent attempts to show that the Democratic Party had been unified and redefined in Clinton's centrist image. And there was a display of confidence, optimism and determination to end 12 years of GOP control of the White House.

Clinton arrived in New York on July 12, buoyed by a boost in the polls suggesting many Americans were pleased with the choice of Tennessee Sen. Al Gore as his running mate. Three hours after Clinton's plane touched down, there was more good news: Jesse Jackson concluded his national television show by endorsing the Arkansas governor. Jackson was less than enthusiastic, but more important was the fact that the endorsement came without Clinton having to negotiate with Jackson the way his predecessors had.

Brown remained the lone holdout, but Clinton's people never seemed overly upset by that, and it did not prevent the Democrats from presenting an image of unity and harmony. Brown's delegates, angry that he was not given a prime-time speaking slot, caused some disruptions on the convention floor, and the news-starved media gave them plenty of attention. But it did not detract from the impression that Clinton was firmly in charge.

Like the Democratic Party itself, Madison Square Garden had been redesigned for the occasion. Technicians had turned the relatively small hall into an elaborate television studio, with a huge white podium and balloons fastened to the ceiling by nets. More than half the delegates were seated not on the arena floor but in regular spectator seats on the perimeter of the arena. Lighting was used to emphasize the studio effect, brightening when applause was

R. MICHAEL JENKINS

**The candidate's speech was a crowd pleaser.**

sought and dimming to hush the crowd. Each night of the convention was planned to have at least two major events, most directly related to the central themes the Democrats wanted to project.

Monday, a large section of the program was designed to give exposure to six female Democrats who were running for Senate seats. Throughout the week women played a major role at the convention, and issues women had highlighted — abortion rights, women's health care and the Clarence Thomas-Anita F. Hill hearings — were discussed from the podium, always to loud cheers from the floor.

The Democrats chose three keynote speakers to end Monday's program. They stressed that the party had changed, they blasted the Bush administration for economic policies that they said favored the rich, and they portrayed Clinton as a candidate from modest roots who was in touch with the people.

Tuesday, the Democrats solidified their move to the center by adopting a platform devoid of many of the liberal planks and slogans that characterized previous documents.

Then Jackson took the podium. Starting slowly and deliberately, he repeated his endorsement of Clinton and then gradually increased the pitch as he berated the administration and the country for ignoring the underprivileged. By the time he finished, delegates were screaming.

Wednesday night, Brown got his turn on the podium and, as expected, he refused to endorse Clinton. Former Massachusetts Sen. Paul E. Tsongas also spoke, and while he did offer an endorsement, he warned Democrats that they would have to make hard economic choices in the days ahead.

But the real drama Wednesday came when New York Gov. Mario M. Cuomo formally nominated Clinton. Cuomo upheld his reputation for oratory, bringing the convention hall to a fever pitch with his denunciations of Bush and his salute to Clinton as the "Comeback Kid." Clinton then made a surprise appearance to thank the convention.

The stunning announcement Thursday morning that Perot would not run for president became a major topic of conversation among delegates. In their speeches Thursday night, Clinton and Gore appealed to Perot supporters to recognize that Democrats could offer the change they wanted, but otherwise stuck to the themes that had been stressed all week.

Gore took a series of swipes at Bush and Quayle. He then hushed the packed hall with an extraordinarily personal account of his son's brush with death three years earlier.

Clinton used his speech to reintroduce himself to the voters. Recounting his fatherless childhood and stressing his small-town roots, Clinton summoned Americans to a "new covenant" of shared responsibility.

What follows is a detailed diary of the Democratic National Convention. Texts of the major speeches begin on p. 54-A.

# Trying To Douse Conflicts And Focus Fire on Bush

The tone for the first half of Monday's session was set an hour before it began — and several blocks from the convention. At a caucus for his 600-plus delegates, Jerry Brown told his supporters that he wanted an open and competitive convention. He said he would not accept the Clinton camp's requirement that he endorse the nominee if he wanted a prime-time speaking slot, and he urged his troops not to give in.

Inside Madison Square Garden, the Brown delegates made their first move about 40 minutes after the convention was called to order at 5 p.m. A small group from California began waving Brown signs and shouting, "Let Jerry speak." Reporters and photographers, who until then had been busy chasing rumors and speculation (including hints that Virginia Gov. L. Douglas Wilder might join Ross Perot's presidential ticket), quickly swarmed over the Brown delegates in search of news and controversy.

The chanting spread to the Wisconsin group and to other delegations in which Brown had significant support, and it grew louder whenever Democratic Party Chairman Ronald H. Brown, who was blamed for keeping Jerry Brown off the program, stood at the podium. The sudden outbursts had the appearance of spontaneity, but most were orchestrated by Brown's lieutenants, who were linked to the delegates on the floor by message-relaying beepers.

The Clinton forces initially were caught by surprise, and it took them almost an hour to rush in reinforcements, in the form of enough Clinton signs to blanket the hall. Gradually, the Brown delegates, many hoarse from shouting, softened their protest and ended any serious attempt to disrupt the convention.

## Back to the Script

With attention back on the podium and the approach of prime-time television, convention speakers began to hit home on the themes for the night — that Bush's was a failed presidency, that Democrats offered the only real hope for change and that a united party was on the road to victory.

It fell to Oklahoma Gov. David Walters to begin warming the crowd for a night of anti-Bush rhetoric. He took the first of many pokes at Vice President Dan Quayle, who had recently instructed a student, during a school visit, to spell "potato" with an "e" on the end. Walters led the crowd in a letter-by-letter spelling of the word, urging them to "stop right there" after the second "o."

The first truly rousing welcome went to Texas Gov. Ann W. Richards, the convention chair, who introduced herself by saying, "My name is Ann Richards, and I'm pro-choice when I vote."

Richards was best known nationally for her 1988 convention keynote address, which included a pointed and personal attack on Bush. She did not mention Bush by name this time, although she referred to her earlier speech and said: "I really hate to say it. But I told you so."

She said it was natural for the delegates

R. MICHAEL JENKINS
**Bradley was a local favorite**

and other Americans to be tired of empty political promises. "We're tired of hearing about the '80s; they're over," she said. "We're tired of hearing about the Reagan era; it's over. And as far as this White House is concerned," she added, pausing briefly, "Honey, you can turn out the lights: The party's over."

## Women's Year

Handing the convention's gavel to Richards was just the prelude to what had been informally referred to as "Ladies' Night," the Democrats' attempt to showcase some of their

R. MICHAEL JENKINS
**Brown, left, and Mayor Dinkins in the New York delegation**

leading female Senate candidates. The women were introduced to the convention by Sen. Barbara A. Mikulski of Maryland, one of two women in the Senate and the only Democratic female senator.

"This is the year of the women because this is the year of change," Mikulski said. She said women have a different political perspective, rooted in a concern for families, in contrast to "12 years of Republican blue suits who are out of touch, too often out of the country and now out of ideas."

Mikulski introduced six female Senate candidates, all of whom spoke briefly from the convention floor. They were Carol Moseley Braun of Illinois, Lynn Yeakel of Pennsylvania, Rep. Barbara Boxer and Dianne Feinstein of California, Jean Lloyd-Jones of Iowa, and Gloria O'Dell of Kansas. Each had a different emphasis.

Braun, the only black woman in the group, said: "This country is challenged to recognize that in our diversity is our strength. Quality and excellence have many faces, many voices."

Boxer offered a litany of challenges facing the United States, including its relationship with other countries. "We cannot allow American jobs to be put on a fast track to Mexico, on a slow boat to China or on a jet plane to Taiwan." And, she said, "We must never allow government to get in the middle of our most private decision. I will fight for a woman's right to choose."

Yeakel was particularly critical of her Republican opponent, Arlen Specter, Anita F. Hill's chief interrogator during Clarence Thomas' confirmation hearings. She said Specter tailored his votes for re-election bids, ignored the middle class and poor, and had

"humiliated all the women of America with his shameless performance."

Feinstein, the last of the group to speak, dismissed Republicans who referred to the wave of female candidates as "just gender politics." "It's not just about gender. It's about an agenda, an agenda of change," Feinstein said.

Ron Brown's return to the podium for his speech energized Jerry Brown's delegates again. Some of them pressed toward the podium and frequently succeeded in drowning out the speaker.

But Ron Brown managed to grab the audience's attention when he talked about "a kid from Harlem" becoming party chairman and about Democratic victories in congressional and state elections since he became chairman three years ago.

Ignoring the protests, Brown said: "Never, in a generation, have we Democrats been so united," and then he mocked Bush's 1988 pledge not to raise taxes. "Read our lips: No second term," Brown said as he criticized Bush for protecting the rich, breaking promises to protect the environment and improve education, being unconcerned about domestic issues and blaming others for problems of his own making. "No second term; no second term," the delegates responded enthusiastically.

### Hitting the Key Note

Brown's speech rallied the crowd just before the keynote address or, in this case, the keynote addresses. Instead of one speaker, the Democrats opted for three.

The Garden appearance was a homecoming of sorts for Sen. Bill Bradley of New Jersey. A local favorite, Bradley had been a star forward for the New York Knicks basketball team, and a banner with his name and number hung from the rafters.

But the buildup did not necessarily suit Bradley, who delivered a serious but uninspiring speech, often having trouble overcoming the buzz of conversation in the hall. He tried, but with only limited success, to draw the crowd into a refrain of his own. Whether the subject was unemployment, the environment, post-communist Russia or race riots in Los Angeles, Bush's response was the same, Bradley said: "You waffled and wiggled and wavered."

The Bush administration has shown a propensity to inflame wounds rather than heal them, Bradley said. But Democrats are not blameless, he said, often preferring short-term fixes to long-term solutions. He urged the Democrats in New York to stand for something as they sought to regain the White House and said all Americans ought to be willing to make personal sacrifices for the greater good.

Delegates' restlessness continued as the next keynoter, Gov. Zell Miller of Georgia, began by talking about being born in the midst of the Depression in the drafty bedroom of a rented house in the Appalachian Mountains. But Miller, who had helped Clinton win overwhelming victory in Georgia's influential primary, peppered his speech with

PHOTOS BY R. MICHAEL JENKINS

**Senate candidates Jean Lloyd-Jones of Iowa, above, and Carol Moseley Braun of Illinois, right, spoke briefly. Former Rep. Barbara C. Jordan of Texas, bottom right, was the only woman among the keynote speakers.**

sure applause lines as he went after Bush and Quayle and delivered the convention's first attack on Perot.

"I know what Dan Quayle means when he says it's best for children to have two parents. You bet it is! And it would be nice for them to have trust funds, too," Miller said. "We can't all be born rich, handsome and lucky, and that's why we have the Democratic Party."

Turning to the president, Miller said whether it's high taxes, the lack of affordable health care, crime-filled streets or abandoned factories, "George Bush doesn't get it."

That's why the nation can't afford to re-elect Bush, Miller said. "If the education president gets another term, even our kids won't be able to spell potato. If the law-and-order president gets another term, the criminals will run wild because our commander in chief talks like Dirty Harry but acts like Barney Fife."

Then Miller broke what had been a Democratic reluctance to attack Perot, saying the Texas businessman who has positioned himself as a political outsider has a long history of lobbying Congress for tax breaks. "Sounds to me like instead of shaking the system up, Mr. Perot's been shaking it down. Ross says he'll clean out the barn, but he's been knee-deep in it for years." The arena roared with laughter at each line, reaching its loudest point when Miller stretched his Georgian drawl and asserted, "If Ross Perot's an outsider, folks, I'm from Brooklyn."

If Bradley largely lost the delegates and Miller enlivened them, former Rep. Barbara C. Jordan of Texas held their rapt attention.

Jordan began by noting that her previous keynote speech was delivered in the same spot in 1976, when Democrats last won the presidency. Another victory is possible this year under the rubric of change, Jordan said, but she

wondered aloud what change is in the offing.

Like Bradley, Jordan warned that Democrats have to prove themselves. "The American electorate must be persuaded to trust us, the Democrats, to govern again," she said. "Why not change from a party with a reputation of tax and spend to one with a reputation of investment and growth?" Economic growth and environmental protection can occur simultaneously, she said. It ought not be a trickle-down economy, she added, but one that permits minorities in poor neighborhoods to attain the skills they need to prosper.

Spurring economic growth and lowering the budget deficit will require everyone to make sacrifices, she said, including those on entitlements, retirees on fixed incomes, corporate executives and members of Congress.

Jordan also hailed the onset of female congressional candidates, drawing huge cheers when she quoted from French author and statesman Alexis de Tocqueville: "If I were asked to what singular substance do I mainly attribute the prosperity and growing strength of the American people, I should reply: to the superiority of their women."

★ ★ ★

# Jackson, Activists Provide Second-Night Drama

**TUESDAY**

Tuesday was platform night, at least in theory, but the debate over the party's manifesto was brief and uninspired. The real drama came later, when two activists who have the AIDS virus moved delegates to tears and when Jesse Jackson's rousing speech brought the convention to a fever pitch.

AIDS also got attention outside the hall, particularly in Times Square, where police estimated that 10,000 people attended a midday rally for AIDS sufferers.

A gathering of another sort was sponsored by the convention's women's caucus, which held a jubilant meeting to cheer Bill and Hillary Clinton. The presidential candidate was greeted at the podium by more than 50 women who are running for the House and Senate this year.

Clinton had a much less pleasant encounter with an anti-abortion activist earlier in the morning when he set out for a jog in Central Park. "What about the babies?" the activist asked, as he tried to hand Clinton a fetus in a clear plastic bag.

Democrats were keenly aware throughout the day that baseball fans across the country would skip watching the evening session in lieu of baseball's All-Star Game. Texas Railroad Commissioner Lena Guerrero began her speech by giving the score of the game in progress.

## The Platform

Clinton's overwhelming delegate strength and Democrats' frustration with three straight presidential losses helped mute any complaints over the centrist platform that clearly reflected the Clinton view of how the Democratic Party should present itself to voters.

The platform emphasized the need for economic growth, pledged to uphold law and order and to use military force overseas where necessary, called for a cutoff in welfare benefits after two years and supported the right of states to enact death penalty statutes. The platform did include more traditional Democratic viewpoints, such as protecting abortion rights, providing civil rights for homosexuals and taxing wealthy people at higher rates. *(Text of platform, p. 59-A)*

By prior agreement, delegates pledged to former Massachusetts Sen. Paul E. Tsongas were allowed to offer and debate four minority planks. But it was a debate only in the loosest sense of the word. The speeches on both sides were brief, and most speakers for Clinton's position made

R. MICHAEL JENKINS

**Jesse Jackson briefly praised Clinton, then devoted most of his Tuesday night speech to working people and the poor.**

little effort to engage in a point-by-point rebuttal.

Three of the planks ultimately were rejected by voice vote. One called for investment-related tax breaks. Another, on the deficit, called for limits on government spending, including Medicare and other politically sensitive entitlements. And a third proposed increasing the gasoline tax by 5 cents per gallon to benefit new spending on infrastructure.

The hall's electronic voting system was to decide the fate of a fourth plank, which said that a middle-class tax cut and a tax credit for families with children ought to be delayed until the deficit is under control. This had a been a key difference between Tsongas and Clinton during the campaign.

"Let us give Paul Tsongas his due," said Rep. Wayne Owens of Utah. "He has raised exponentially the intellectual and visionary level of debate in this campaign.... It is better for middle America to rebuild our economic base, to provide meaningful employment and control federal spending, than it is to give an immediate middle-class tax cut." But the plank was defeated, 963 to 2,287.

The opposition being formally dispatched, a long series of brief speeches followed, each outlining a different aspect of the platform. None of them drew much attention in the Garden, though. Brown's delegates showed their all-encompassing dissatisfaction with the platform and the convention by brandishing signs that said, "Not!" Some Clinton

delegates held aloft "pro-choice, pro-Clinton" signs.

Colorado Gov. Roy Romer, co-chairman of the platform committee, finally called for the "yeas" and "nays" on the platform, though he barely waited to hear the latter before loudly concluding, "The 1992 platform is adopted."

In an unusual maneuver, the gathering of the nation's most committed Democrats then heard from a Republican. Kathy Taylor of Hershey, Pa., said she was speaking for herself and for five other Republican women who stood with her in announcing that they would vote for Clinton "because he's pro-choice" on abortion. She denounced Bush for having struck "an unholy alliance with the most extreme anti-choice interest groups in America."

This presentation must have been particularly galling to Pennsylvania Gov. Robert P. Casey, who had unsuccessfully sought to address the convention about the abortion issue. Casey's strong anti-abortion views were at odds not only with Clinton, but with the vast majority of delegates, including many in Casey's own state who held up "Pennsylvania is pro-choice" signs during the abortion discussion.

## Bush AIDS Record Attacked

After a rousing rendition of the "Star-Spangled Banner" by Aretha Franklin, the delegates then hushed one another so they could hear from two speakers who are HIV-positive.

The first was Bob Hattoy, an environmental advocate and Clinton adviser who said he is gay. "AIDS does not discriminate. But George Bush's White House does," Hattoy said. Next was Elizabeth Glaser, who explained that she had been infected with the AIDS virus through a blood transfusion given to her while giving birth to her first child 11 years ago. She found out four years later that she had unknowingly passed on the virus to her daughter through breast milk and to her son while he was in the womb.

"Exactly four years ago, my daughter died of AIDS. She did not survive the Reagan administration," Glaser said. "I am here because my son and I may not survive four more years of leaders who say they care, but do nothing," she added, while video screens overhead showed several delegates crying as she spoke.

Former President Jimmy Carter was up next. Carter, who left the White House in 1981 with low popularity, has been enjoying a renaissance lately with his charitable works here and abroad, and was warmly received in the hall. He expressed regret that the United States was viewed by other countries as "more warlike than peace-loving," mentioning the invasions of Grenada and Panama, support for the Nicaraguan rebels and the gulf war.

Carter's most resilient trait has been his preoccupation with morality, so perhaps his most meaningful contribution to Clinton was vouching for his character. He said he had known Clinton for more than 15 years and described him as "a friend and a fine governor" who had endured "false and misleading political attacks.... He is a man of honesty and integrity."

## Jackson Raises the Roof

Jackson, as is his custom, proved to be the evening's most fiery speaker, and the Garden was packed as he spoke. Having tussled with Clinton over the direction of the party and Jackson's own role in the general election campaign, Jackson began by praising the Arkansas Democrat for having survived

MICHAEL HIRSCH

**AIDS activists, above, rallied in Times Square on July 14. Former President Jimmy Carter, right, called Clinton "a man of honesty and integrity."**

R. MICHAEL JENKINS

"a tough spring. It will make you strong for the fall.... The hopes of many depend upon your quest."

But Jackson spent most of his half-hour talking broadly about his own vision and interests. He said there is still much to be done to help working people and the poor. He said he had met youngsters in housing projects for whom "jail is a step up." Jail protects them from drive-by shootings and feeds them, and gives them access to health care and vocational training, Jackson said. "Everything they should have on the outside they only get on the inside."

Turning to immigration, Jackson said, "If we were wrong and anti-Semitic to lock the Jews out in 1939, if we were wrong to lock the Japanese-Americans up in 1942, then it's wrong to lock the Haitians out in 1992." He also spoke in biblical terms, saying Jesus was born to a homeless couple and was a child of a single mother. "But Mary had family values," Jackson said. "It was Herod, the Quayle of his day, who put no value on the family."

The Garden began to empty after Jackson's speech, and the delegates who remained seemed relatively uninterested in the talks that followed. One speaker who did manage to draw a rise from the crowd was Sen. Tom Harkin of Iowa, a former presidential candidate. "I want you to know that I may be out of the battle for myself," he said, "but I'm not out of the fight to put a Democrat in the White House in 1992." The session ended with many of the party's female congressional candidates being introduced and ushered onto the podium.

# Cuomo Delivers the Talk; Clinton Takes the Walk

**W E D N E S D A Y**

Two events dominated Wednesday night's convention session: the news that Ed Rollins, campaign manager for Ross Perot, had quit because of differences with the candidate over strategy and the prime-time nominating speech by Cuomo, the party's premier orator.

It was just an hour before the gavel fell that Rollins made his decision known, setting off lots of speculation in the news-hungry media that Perot was in a political free fall. On the floor, however, delegates seemed far more interested in the business at hand.

Democrats set to work with a tribute to the late Robert F. Kennedy and speeches by three Democratic also-rans: Sen. Bob Kerrey of Nebraska, Paul Tsongas and Jerry Brown.

The Kennedy tribute took on a somber note, reviving sad memories of both John F. and Robert F. Kennedy. Robert Kennedy's son, Rep. Joseph P. Kennedy II of Massachusetts, introduced a film about his father, and then Sen. Edward M. Kennedy, Mass., gave a rousing speech that combined tribute to his brother with a hearty endorsement of the Clinton-Gore ticket.

Kennedy told the crowd that the memory of Robert Kennedy is a "vivid fire that still lights the best and most honorable paths of public life."

"I could say many things here in support of Bill Clinton," Kennedy said. "But there is one thing that matters most. He has sought to heal, to oppose hate, to reach across the divides and make us whole again. With Bill Clinton, it is time to reject the politics of slash and burn — the evil politics that makes the face of Willie Horton more important in a national campaign than the face of a hungry child."

## The Might-Have-Beens

Like Harkin, Kerrey offered a ringing endorsement of the ticket, promising to do whatever he could to help. "I will fight as hard as I know how with every ounce of my puny body ... and every ounce of my inexhaustible will to elect Bill Clinton the next president of the United States of America."

While the barbs aimed at Quayle were the norm all week (one reporter counted six potato jokes), Kerrey offered the harshest zinger. Compared with vice presidential candidate Gore, said Kerrey, "Dan Quayle is a shiver looking for a spine to run up."

At 8 p.m. the formal presidential nominating process began, and that was when Jerry Brown, the principal Democratic holdout, got his moment on the podium — although not under the terms he had wanted. There was no prime-time, official speaking slot. Instead, he took the podium under party rules that allow anyone whose name is placed in nomination to address the delegates.

Brown had been denied a better slot

because he had refused to endorse Clinton, and he said nothing in his speech to change that. In fact, he never mentioned Clinton.

But Brown's speech followed the party's game plan, with most of it directed squarely at the Bush administration.

"Instead of government by the people, of the people and for the people, President Bush and his administration give us government of, by and for the privileged," Brown said.

Brown said he would continue his "Take Back America" coalition, though he did not specify in what form.

"We have to break the growing tie between political and economic power.... I want to fight on the side of the people who pay the bills, fight the wars and never come to our receptions," Brown said.

Tsongas, the final former presidential candidate of the night, endorsed Clinton, but he used most of his time to stress his campaign theme of fiscal conservatism and included a somber warning of disaster if his call for economic discipline is not heeded.

"You cannot redistribute wealth that you never created," he said. "You cannot be pro-jobs and anti-business at the same time.... I have said this ... but I believe it is fundamental: No goose, no golden eggs."

Tsongas got cheers for his jabs at the GOP.

"They told us it was morning in America," he said. "They told us we could have it all. They lied."

## The Roll Call Tally

But the moment most were waiting for was Cuomo's nomination of Clinton. And Cuomo did not disappoint the eager crowd of delegates.

"The ship of state is headed for the rocks," he said. "The crew knows it. The passengers know it. Only the captain of the ship — President Bush — appears not to know it. He seems to think that the ship will be saved by imperceptible undercurrents, directed by the invisible

REUTERS

**Cuomo, the party's premier orator, nominated Clinton on July 15.**

hand of some cyclical economic god."

Cuomo said prayers are always helpful, but they must be "accompanied by good works."

"We need a captain who understands that, and who will seize the wheel before it's too late," he said. "I am here tonight to offer America that new captain with a new course: Gov. Bill Clinton of Arkansas."

Cuomo recalled the victory parades after the Persian Gulf War, but said he longed for parades to celebrate accomplishments at home: "You've had your parade! It's time for change — someone smart enough to know, strong enough to do, sure enough to lead. The Comeback Kid. A new voice for America. Because I love New York, because I love America, I nominate for office of the president of the United States, the man from Hope, Ark., Gov. Bill Clinton."

The crowd went wild.

The official roll call of states followed with Alabama passing to give Arkansas the opportunity to cast the first vote. Clinton's mother, delegate Virginia Kelly, told the convention that the state cast all 48 votes for its favorite son.

The state delegations moved through the roll call with the usual descriptive expressions. Indiana's delegation introduced itself as the "the home of the next retired vice president of the United States."

The New Hampshire delegation drew

**Brown**

**Kerrey**

some cheers and laughs when its chairman told the convention the state would stick with Clinton "until the last dog dies," echoing a statement Clinton made there on the eve of the New Hampshire primary. Ohio got the honor of putting Clinton over the top.

At the end of the roll call the tally was Clinton, 3,372; Brown, 579; and Tsongas, 209. Subsequently, the nomination was approved by acclamation.

### Clinton Comes Back

The evening came to a dramatic and surprising end when the nominee answered chants of "we want Bill" by visiting the convention hall. Clinton had been watching the roll call from a party at Macy's department store two blocks away, and walked most of the way to Madison Square Garden after he saw the pandemonium that broke out when he was formally nominated. His appearance a day early was unusual, but not unprecedented, and wildly welcomed by the delegates, who cheered, chanted and stomped in appreciation while tons of confetti dropped from the ceiling.

Clinton likened his visit to the convention floor to that of John F. Kennedy in 1960 who he said "came to give a simple thank you." Clinton made a point of thanking Cuomo for his remarks, and picking up on Cuomo's phrase, promised to return Thursday to accept the nomination as "the Comeback Kid."

★ ★ ★

# Call for a New Covenant Tops Off Closing Night

**T H U R S D A Y**

On the fourth and final day of the convention — six months after the nation's first Democratic primary and more than four months before the election — Bill Clinton addressed the most pressing concern of his candidacy: How to define himself.

His introduction, by convention chairman Texas Gov. Ann W. Richards, gave a flavor to what was to follow.

"The story of Bill Clinton is truly an American story," said Richards. "Bill Clinton is not a creation of the media or this party. He is a real human being — a husband, a father, a friend."

In his 54-minute speech, some 20 minutes longer than the seemingly interminable nominating speech he gave in 1988, Clinton zeroed in on the themes the campaign reflected in the party platform. He described himself as "a product of the American middle class" who would accept the nomination "in the name of all the people who do the work, pay the taxes, raise the kids and play by the rules — the hard-working Americans who make up our forgotten middle class." He talked about his own family and an "America where 'family values' live in our actions, not just our speeches."

The speech kicked off with a salute to his campaign trail opponents, singling out each by name. The crowd re-

sponded with ovations of varying degrees, but Paul E. Tsongas received the loudest response, despite a large and unruly Jerry Brown contingent. Several voiced their displeasure with the nominee with signs such as "Something is wrong with the Clinton dream when Brownies are not included."

Before launching into the main body of the speech, Clinton stared directly into the bank of network television cameras situated in front of the main podium and told a national television audience of an estimated 22 million viewers that "unemployment only has to go up by one more person before a real recovery can begin. And Mr. President, you are that man."

For those familiar with Clinton only through the harsh glare of media coverage and monologues of late-night comedians, the Arkansas governor offered a very different image.

He spoke of growing up fatherless and of the small-town values his mother and grandparents instilled in him.

The references to his background were aimed at dispelling notions that Clinton had grown up in a privileged environment, to show he is more in touch with most Americans than Bush is, and to address questions raised about his character during the primary campaign.

### A Middle American

That point was underscored in a 14-minute biographical portrait that preceded his entrance. Produced by family friend Linda Bloodworth-Thomason, the creator of several successful television programs, the film presented an intimate look at Clinton's life, starting with black-and-white

photos of Hope, Ark., his hometown. His mother recalled that she went to the movies the night before his birth to see a film called "Tomorrow is Forever."

The crowd cheered as she told a story of how Clinton confronted his inebriated and abusive stepfather but grew hushed when Clinton described the painful ordeal of watching with his young daughter the "60 Minutes" interview about allegations that he had had affairs.

Through one-on-one interviews with his mother, half brother, Roger, and wife, Hillary, Clinton was portrayed as a devoted husband and caring father. Hillary talked of the day she met her future husband. Clinton gave his account of the day his child was born. Chelsea, an only child who was rarely seen before the convention, appeared in several home movie scenes.

With family values at a premium in current political discourse, Clinton devoted part of his remarks to countering Republicans who have attempted to seize the issue.

"Frankly, I'm fed up with politicians in Washington lecturing the rest of us about 'family values,'" he said to a boisterous ovation. "Our families have values. But our government doesn't.

"An America that includes every family. Every traditional family and every extended family. Every two-income family and every single-parent family, and every foster family."

He borrowed a theme from Jesse Jackson's 1988 convention address when he added, "I want to say something to every child in America tonight who is out there trying to grow up without a father or mother: I know how you feel. You're special, too. You matter to America."

But Clinton distanced himself from Jackson and the traditional liberal, activist government policies that many Americans associate with the party by admitting, "My fellow Democrats, it's time for us to realize that we've got some changing to do too. There is not a program in government for every problem. And if we really want government to help people, we've got to make it work again."

He termed his proposal a "New Covenant, a solemn agreement between the people and their government, based not simply on what each of us can take, but on what all of us must give to our nation."

It offers "a new choice based on old values. We offer opportunity. We demand responsibility.... The choice we offer is not conservative or liberal; in many ways it's not even Republican or Democratic. It is different. It is new.

PHOTOS BY R. MICHAEL JENKINS

**Above, the Clinton family celebrates at the end of the convention July 16, with Broadway entertainer Jennifer Holliday and South Carolina youth Reggie Jackson, who earlier in the week had sung the national anthem. Right, Al Gore gestures to the crowd after his speech accepting the vice presidential nomination.**

And it will work."

Incorporating themes developed by the Democratic Leadership Council, a centrist organization Clinton used to head, he noted that the New Covenant means "Opportunity. Responsibility. Community."

While Clinton's vision of a New Covenant may be a departure, the term is not: Massachusetts Gov. Michael S. Dukakis also referred to a covenant in his 1988 acceptance speech.

Unlike Dukakis, however, Clinton admitted that there are problems in his home state yet unsolved, saying, "No, there is no Arkansas miracle. But there are a lot of miraculous people."

Of the man who defeated Dukakis, Clinton stated, "We can do better." He added, "Mr. President, life's a lot less kind and a lot less gentle than it was before your administration took office."

Like virtually every other speaker Thursday night, Clinton could not resist the opportunity to take a poke at the vice president. Referring to Dan Quayle's recent spell-

ing gaffe, he said of his own ticket mate, "Just in case you didn't know it, that's Gore with an 'e.'"

Signs mocking Quayle were sprinkled throughout the hall. There was also an abundance of other signs with subjects including freedom for Tibet, animal rights and opposition to the use of Mylar confetti at the convention.

A handful of mischievous California Brown delegates held signs supporting Gennifer Flowers, the woman who had accused Clinton of conducting an affair with her.

Both Gore and Clinton responded to what was perhaps the convention's biggest story, the withdrawal of unannounced presidential candidate Ross Perot.

At a midday news conference in Dallas, Perot exited the presidential race after concluding "that we cannot win." He said a three-way race would be decided in the House of Representatives and that would be "disruptive to the country." Perot failed to endorse a candidate but noted that "the Democratic Party has revitalized itself."

Clinton asked Perot supporters to "join us and together we will revitalize America," in a reference to Perot's withdrawal speech.

Gore exhorted Perot backers to "stay involved. You have already changed politics for the better."

**Gore Leads Off**

The Tennessee senator's acceptance speech was less time-consuming but no less energizing than Clinton's. Taking a series of swipes at Bush and Quayle, Gore accused them of advocating tax policies that favor the rich, ignoring AIDS, embarrassing the country with weak environmental policies and allowing the nation's budget deficit to mushroom out of control. "It is time for them to go," he repeated, leading the crowd in the main refrain of his speech.

But after exciting the assembled, Gore brought some delegates to tears with the story of how his son, Albert III, nearly died after being hit by a car.

"When you've seen your 6-year-old son fighting for his life, you realize that some things matter a lot more than winning. You lose patience with the lazy assumption of so many in politics that we can always just muddle through. When you've seen your reflection in the empty stare of a boy waiting for a second breath of life, you realize that we weren't put here on earth to look out for our needs alone; we're part of something much larger than ourselves."

Using the incident as an allegory for the need to look beyond the concerns of daily life, he urged Americans "to unite our country behind a higher calling."

After ending his speech, Gore embraced his wife, Tipper, and engaged in a quick celebratory waltz to the band's rendition of Paul Simon's hit single "You Can Call Me Al." It won a raucous

R. MICHAEL JENKINS

**House Speaker Thomas S. Foley and Senate Majority Leader George J. Mitchell, at left, joined cheers for the ticket on the last night of the convention.**

reception from the crowd.

Gore's name was put in nomination by Maryland Sen. Barbara A. Mikulski, who had been on the podium Monday to introduce the Democrats' female Senate candidates.

In an apparent effort to calm any qualms among black voters toward an all-Southern white ticket, Gore's nomination was seconded by Rep. John Lewis of Georgia, a veteran of the 1960s civil rights struggles.

"Al Gore is committed to the building of an interracial democracy in America," Lewis said. "As a son of the South, he has consistently spoken out against bigotry and discrimination. . . . He can not only 'talk the talk,' but Al Gore can 'walk the walk.'"

Lewis was the only speaker of the night before the nominees to elicit a reaction from the crowd, and he whipped the delegates into a sign-waving frenzy. But the demonstration was awkwardly cut short by the unexpected and momentum-halting announcement that there would be a short recess.

Convention planners had to delay Gore's appearance because his nomination by acclamation skewed the timing of the schedule. Clinton's speech, set to directly follow Gore, was pegged for 10:15.

The disappointed delegates soon found ways to amuse themselves. The Oklahoma delegation gave its rendition of Rogers and Hammerstein's "Oklahoma" while others chanted and attempted "the wave."

When Clinton arrived, he was greeted by a sea of white pennants heralding his candidacy. For the well-choreographed finale, American flags were passed out by the hundreds. The refrain of the final song played out over the loudspeakers, "Don't Stop (Thinking About Tomorrow)" by the rock group Fleetwood Mac, seemed chosen to emphasize the generational gap between Clinton and Bush. Roger Clinton led a verse; his brother sang along without the microphone. The convention closed with Democratic dignitaries on stage, swaying and singing. ■

> **"When you've seen your 6-year-old son fighting for his life, you realize that some things matter more than winning. . . . When you've seen your reflection in the empty stare of a boy waiting for a second breath of life, you realize that we weren't put here on earth to look out for our needs alone."**
>
> **—Al Gore**

## DEMOCRATIC CONVENTION

# Nominee Clinton Describes Vision of 'New Covenant'

*On July 16, Arkansas Gov. Bill Clinton accepted the Democratic presidential nomination. Following is the Reuter text of his remarks.*

**CLINTON:** Gov. [Ann W.] Richards, Chairman [Ronald H.] Brown, Mayor [David N.] Dinkins, our great host — my fellow delegates, and my fellow Americans, I am so proud of Al Gore.

He said he came here tonight because he always wanted to do the warm-up for Elvis. Well, I ran for president this year for one reason and one reason only: I wanted to come back to this convention and finish that speech I started four years ago.

Last night [New York Gov.] Mario Cuomo taught us how a real nominating speech should be given.

He also made it clear why we have to steer our ship of state on a new course. Tonight I want to talk with you about my hope for the future, my faith in the American people and my vision of the kind of country we can build together.

I salute the good men who were my campaign — companions on the campaign trail: [Iowa Sen.] Tom Harkin. [Nebraska Sen.] Bob Kerrey [Virginia Gov.] Doug Wilder. [Former California Gov.] Jerry Brown. And [former Massachusetts Sen.] Paul Tsongas.

One sentence in the platform we built says it all: "The most important family policy, urban policy, labor policy, minority policy and foreign policy America can have is an expanding entrepreneurial economy of high-wage, high-skill jobs."

And so, in the name of all those who do the work, pay the taxes, raise the kids and play by the rules, in the name of the hardworking Americans who make up our forgotten middle class, I proudly accept your nomination for president of the United States.

I am a product of that middle class. And when I am president, you will be forgotten no more.

We meet at a special moment in history, you and I. The Cold War is over. Soviet communism has collapsed. And our values — freedom, democracy, individual rights and free enterprise — they have triumphed all around the world. And yet just as we have won the Cold War abroad, we are losing the battles for economic opportunity and social justice here at home.

Now that we have changed the world, it's time to change America.

I have news for the forces of greed and the defenders of the status quo: Your time has come and gone. It's time for a change in America.

Tonight 10 million of our fellow Americans are out of work. Tens of millions more work harder for lower pay. The incumbent president says unemployment always goes up a little before a recovery begins. But unemployment only has to go up by one more person before a real recovery can begin.

And Mr. President, you are that man.

This election is about putting power back in your hands and putting the government back on your side. It's about putting people first.

You know, I've said that all across the country. And whenever I do, someone always comes back at me, as a young man did this week at a town meeting at the Henry Street Settlement on the Lower East Side of Manhattan. He said, "That sounds good, Bill. But you're a politician. Why should I trust you?"

Tonight, as plainly as I can, I want to tell you who I am, what I believe and where I want to lead America.

I never met my father.

He was killed in a car wreck on a rainy road three months before I was born, driving from Chicago to Arkansas to see my mother.

After that, my mother had to support us. So we lived with my grandparents while she went back to Louisiana to study nursing.

I can still see her clearly tonight through the eyes of a 3-year-old: kneeling at the train station and weeping as she put me back on the train to Arkansas with my grandmother. She endured her pain because she knew her sacrifice was the only way she could support me and give me a better life.

My mother taught me. She taught me about family, and hard work, and sacrifice. She held steady through tragedy after tragedy. And she held our family, my brother and me, together through tough times. As a child, I watched her go off to work each day at a time when it wasn't always easy to be a working mother.

As an adult, I watched her fight off breast cancer. And again she has taught me a lesson in courage. And always, always she taught me to fight.

That's why I'll fight to create high-paying jobs so that parents can afford to raise their children today. That's why I'm so committed to making sure every American gets the health care that saved my mother's life.

And that women's health care gets the same attention as men's.

That's why I'll fight to make sure women in this country receive respect and dignity — whether they work in the home, out of the home or both.

You want to know where I get my fighting spirit? It all started with my mother. Thank you, mother. I love you.

When I think about opportunity for all Americans, I think about my grandfather.

He ran a country store in our little town of Hope. There were no food stamps back then, so when his customers — whether they were white or black — who worked hard and did the best they could came in with no money, well, he gave them food anyway. Just made a note of it. So did I. Before I was big enough to see over the counter, I learned from him to look up to people other folks looked down on.

My grandfather just had a high school education — a grade school education. But in that country store he taught me more about equality in the eyes of the Lord than all my professors at Georgetown; more about the intrinsic worth of every individual than all the philosophers at Oxford; more about the need for equal justice under the law than all the jurists at Yale Law School.

If you want to know where I come by the passionate commitment I have to bringing people together without regard to race, it all started with my grandfather.

I learned a lot from another person, too. A person who for more than 20 years has worked hard to help our children. Paying the price of time to make sure our schools don't fail them. Someone who traveled our state for a year, studying, learning, listening. Going to PTA meetings, school board meetings, town hall meetings. Putting together a package of school reforms recognized around the nation. Doing it all while building a distinguished legal career and being a wonderful loving mother.

That person is my wife.

Hillary taught me. She taught me that all children can learn, and that each of us has a duty to help them do it. So if you want to know why I care so much about our children and our future, it all started with Hillary. I love you.

Frankly, I'm fed up with politicians in Washington lecturing the rest of us about "family values."

Our families have values. But our government doesn't.

I want an America where "family values" live in our actions, not just in our speeches. An America that includes every family: every traditional family and every extended family, every two-parent family, every single-parent family and every foster family. Every family.

I do want to say something to the fathers in this country who have chosen to abandon their children by neglecting their child support: Take responsibility for your children, or we will force you to do so.

Because governments don't raise children; parents do. And you should.

And I want to say something to every child in America tonight who is out there trying to grow up without a father or a mother: I know how you feel. You're special, too. You matter to America. And don't you ever let anybody tell you you can't become whatever you want to be.

And if other politicians make you feel like you're not a part of their families, come on and be part of ours.

The thing that makes me angriest about what's gone wrong these last 12 years is that our government has lost touch with

our values, while politicians continue to shout about them. I'm tired of it.

I was raised to believe the American Dream was built on rewarding hard work. But we have seen the folks in Washington turn the American ethic on its head. For too long those who play by the rules and keep the faith have gotten the shaft. And those who cut corners and cut deals have been rewarded.

People are working harder than ever, spending less time with their children, working nights and weekends on the job instead of going to PTA and Little League or Scouts. And their incomes are still going down, their taxes are going up, and the costs of housing, health care and education are going through the roof. Meanwhile, more and more of our best people are falling into poverty, even though they work 40 hours a week.

Our people are pleading for change, but government is in the way. It's been hijacked by privileged, private interests. It has forgotten who really pays the bills around here. It's taking more of your money and giving you less in return.

We have got to go beyond the brain-dead politics in Washington and give our people the kind of government they deserve: a government that works for them.

The president ought to be a powerful force for progress. But right now I know how President Lincoln felt when Gen. [George B.] McClellan wouldn't attack in the Civil War. He asked him, "If you're not going to use your army, may I borrow it?" And so I say: George Bush, if you won't use your power to help America, step aside. I will.

Our country is falling behind. The president is caught in the grip of a failed economic theory. We have gone from first to 13th in the world in wages since Reagan and Bush have been in office. Four years ago, candidate Bush said America is a special place, not just "another pleasant country somewhere on the U.N. roll call, between Albania and Zimbabwe."

Now, under President Bush, America has an unpleasant economy stuck somewhere between Germany and Sri Lanka. And for most Americans, Mr. President, life's a lot less kind and a lot less gentle than it was before your administration took office.

Our country has fallen so far, so fast, that just a few months ago the Japanese prime minister actually said he felt sympathy for America. Sympathy. When I am your president, the rest of the world will not look down on us with pity but up to us with respect again.

What is George Bush doing about our economic problems?

Now four years ago he promised us 15 million new jobs by now. And he's over 14 million short. Al Gore and I can do better.

He has raised taxes on the people driving pickup trucks and lowered taxes on people riding in limousines. We can do better.

He promised to balance the budget, but he hasn't even tried. In fact, the budgets he has submitted to Congress nearly doubled the debt. Even worse, he wasted

billions and reduced our investments in education and jobs. We can do better.

So if you are sick and tired of a government that doesn't work to create jobs, if you're sick and tired of a tax system that's stacked against you, if you're sick and tired of exploding debt and reduced investments in our future, or if, like the great civil rights pioneer Fannie Lou Hamer, you're just plain old sick and tired of being sick and tired, then join with us, work with us, win with us, and we can make our country the country it was meant to be.

The choice you face is clear.

George Bush talks a good game. But he has no game plan to compete and win in the world economy. I do. He won't take on the big insurance companies to lower costs and provide health care to all Americans. I will.

He won't even implement the recommendations of his own commission on AIDS, but I will.

He won't streamline the federal government and change the way it works; cut 100,000 bureaucrats and put 100,000 new police officers on your streets of American cities, but I will.

He's never balanced a government budget, but I have. Eleven times.

He won't break the stranglehold the special interests have on our elections and lobbyists have on our government, but I will.

He won't give mothers and fathers a chance to take some time off from work when a baby's born or a parent is sick, but I will.

We're losing our farms at a rapid rate and he has no commitment to keep family farms in the family, but I do.

He's talked a lot about drugs but he hasn't helped people on the front line to wage that war on drugs and crime, but I will.

He won't take the lead in protecting the environment and creating new jobs in environmental technologies for the 21st century, but I will.

You know what else? He doesn't have Al Gore, and I do.

Just in case, just in case you didn't notice, that's Gore with an "e" on the end.

And George Bush won't guarantee a woman's right to choose. I will.

Hear me now: I am not pro-abortion. I am pro-choice, firmly. I believe this difficult and painful decision should be left to the women of America.

I hope the right to privacy can be protected and we will never again have to discuss this issue on political platforms.

But I am old enough to remember what it was like before *Roe v. Wade*, and I do not want to return to the time when we make criminals of women and their doctors.

Jobs. Education. Health care. These are not just commitments from my lips. They are the work of my life.

Our priorities are clear: We will put our people first again.

But priorities without a clear plan of action are just empty words. To turn our rhetoric into reality we've got to change the way government does business, fundamentally. Until we do, we'll continue to be

pouring billions of dollars down the drain.

The Republicans have campaigned against big government for a generation. But have you noticed? They've run big government for a generation, and they haven't changed a thing. They don't want to fix government; they still want to campaign against it. And that's all.

But, my fellow Democrats, it's time for us to realize that we've got some changing to do too. There is not a program in government for every problem. And if we really want to use government to help people, we've got to make it work again.

Because we are committed in this convention and in this platform to making these changes, we are, as Democrats, in the words that Ross Perot himself spoke today, a revitalized Democratic Party.

I am well aware that all those millions of people who rallied to Ross Perot's cause wanted to be in an army of patriots for change. Tonight I say to them: Join us and together we will revitalize America.

Now, I don't have all the answers. But I do know the old ways don't work. Trickle-down economics has sure failed. And big bureaucracies, both private and public, they fail too.

That's why we need a new approach to government. A government that offers more empowerment and less entitlement, more choices for young people in the schools they attend, in the public schools they attend. And more choices for the elderly and for people with disabilities in the long-term care they receive.

A government that is leaner, not meaner, a government that expands opportunity, not bureaucracy, a government that understands that jobs must come from growth in a vibrant and vital system of free enterprise. I call this approach a New Covenant, a solemn agreement between the people and their government, based not simply on what each of us can take, but on what all of us must give to our nation.

We offer our people a new choice based on old values. We offer opportunity. We demand responsibility. We will build an American community again. The choice we offer is not conservative or liberal; in many ways it's not even Republican or Democratic. It is different. It is new. And it will work.

It will work because it is rooted in the vision and the values of the American people. Of all the things George Bush has ever said that I disagree with, perhaps the thing that bothers me most is how he derides and degrades the American tradition of seeing and seeking a better future. He mocks it as "the vision thing."

But just remember what the Scripture says: "Where there is no vision, the people perish."

I hope — I hope nobody in this great hall tonight or in our beloved country has to go through tomorrow without a vision. I hope no one ever tries to raise a child without a vision. I hope nobody ever starts a business or plants a crop in the ground without a vision. For where there is no

vision the people perish.

One of the reasons we have so many children in so much trouble in so many places in this nation is because they have seen so little opportunity, so little responsibility, so little loving, caring community that they literally cannot imagine the life we are calling them to lead.

And so I say again, where there is no vision, America will perish.

What is the vision of our New Covenant?

An America with millions of new jobs in dozens of new industries moving confidently toward the 21st century. An America that says to entrepreneurs and business people: We will give you more incentives and more opportunity than ever before to develop the skills of your workers and create American jobs and American wealth in the new global economy.

But you must do your part; you must be responsible. American companies must act like American companies again — exporting products, not jobs.

That's what this New Covenant is all about.

An America in which the doors of college are thrown open once again to the sons and daughters of stenographers and steelworkers. We'll say: Everybody can borrow the money to go to college. But you must do your part. You must pay it back — from your paychecks, or better yet, by going back home and serving your communities.

Just think of it, think of it, millions of energetic young men and women serving their country by policing the streets or teaching the children, or caring for the sick, or working with the elderly and people with disabilities, or helping young people stay off drugs and out of gangs, giving us all a sense of new hope and limitless possibilities. That's what this New Covenant is all about.

An America in which health care is a right, not a privilege.

In which we say to all of our people: Your government has the courage — finally — to take on the health-care profiteers and make health care affordable for every family.

But you must do your part: preventive care, prenatal care, child immunization; saving lives, saving money, saving families from heartbreak. That's what the New Covenant is all about.

An America in which middle-class incomes — not middle-class taxes — are going up. An America, yes, in which the wealthiest few — those making over $200,000 a year — are asked to pay their fair share.

An America in which the rich are not soaked — but the middle class is not drowned, either.

Responsibility starts at the top; that's what the New Covenant is all about. An America where we end welfare as we know it. We will say to those on welfare, you will have and you deserve the opportunity through training and education, through child care and medical coverage, to liberate yourself.

But then, when you can, you must work, because welfare should be a second chance, not a way of life. That's what the New Covenant is all about.

An America with the world's strongest defense, ready and willing to use force, when necessary. An America at the forefront of the global effort to preserve and protect our common environment — and promoting global growth. An America that will not coddle tyrants, from Baghdad to Beijing.

An America that champions the cause of freedom and democracy, from Eastern Europe to Southern Africa, and in our own hemisphere, in Haiti and Cuba.

The end of the Cold War permits us to reduce defense spending while still maintaining the strongest defense in the world. But we must plow back every dollar of defense cuts into building American jobs right here at home.

I know well that the world needs a strong America, but we have learned that strength begins at home.

The New Covenant is about more than opportunities and responsibilities for you and your families. It's also about our common community. Tonight every one of you knows deep in your heart that we are too divided. It is time to heal America.

And so, we must say to every American: Look beyond the stereotypes that blind us. We need each other. All of us, we need each other. We don't have a person to waste. And yet, for too long politicians told the most of us that are doing all right that what's really wrong with America is the rest of us. Them. Them, the minorities. Them, the liberals. Them, the poor. Them, the homeless. Them, the people with disabilities. Them, the gays. We got to where we really "them'ed" ourselves to death. Them and them and them.

But this is America. There is no them. There is only us.

One nation, under God, indivisible, with liberty and justice for all.

That is our Pledge of Allegiance, and that's what the New Covenant is all about.

How do I know we can come together and make change happen? Because I have seen it in my own state. In Arkansas we're working together and we're making progress. No, there is no Arkansas miracle. But there are a lot of miraculous people.

And because of them, our schools are better, our wages are higher, our factories are busier, our water is cleaner, and our budget is balanced. We're moving ahead.

I wish — I wish I could say the same thing about America under the incumbent president. He took the richest country in the world and brought it down.

We took one of the poorest states in America and lifted it up.

I say all, to all those in this campaign season who would criticize Arkansas, come on down.

Especially — especially if you're from Washington — come on down. Sure, you'll see us struggling against some of the problems we haven't solved yet. But you'll also see a lot of great people doing amazing things. And you might even learn a thing or two.

In the end, my fellow Americans, this New Covenant simply asks us all to be Americans again. Old-fashioned Americans for a new time. Opportunity. Responsibility. Community. When we pull together, America will pull ahead. Throughout the whole history of this country, we have seen time and time and time again when we are united, we are unstoppable.

We can seize this moment, make it exciting and energizing and heroic to be an American again.

We can renew our faith in each other and in ourselves. We can restore our sense of unity and community. As the Scripture says, our eyes have not yet seen, nor our ears heard nor our minds imagined what we can build.

But I can't do this alone. No president can. We must do it together. It won't be easy and it won't be quick. We didn't get into this mess overnight, and we won't get out of it overnight. But we can do it with our commitment, creativity, diversity and drive.

We can do it. We can do it. We can do it.

I want every person in this hall and every person in this land to reach out and join us in a great new adventure to chart a bold new future.

As a teenager I heard John Kennedy's summons to citizenship. And then, as a student at Georgetown, I heard that call clarified by a professor named Carroll Quigley, who said to us that America was the greatest country in the history because our people have always believed in two things, that tomorrow can be better than today, and that every one of us has a personal, moral responsibility to make it so.

That kind of future entered my life the night our daughter Chelsea was born. As I stood in that delivery room, I was overcome with the thought that God had given me a blessing my own father never knew: the chance to hold my child in my arms.

Somewhere at this very moment, another child is born in America. Let it be our cause to give that child a happy home, a healthy family, a hopeful future. Let it be our cause to see that that child has the chance to live to the fullest of her God-given capacities. Let it be our cause to see that child grow up strong and secure, braced by her challenges but never struggling alone; with family and friends and a faith that in America, no one is left out; no one is left behind.

Let it be our cause that when this child is able, she gives something back to her children, her community and her country. Let it be our cause to give her a country that's coming together, not coming apart. A country of boundless hopes and endless dreams; a country that once again lifts its people and inspires the world.

Let that be our cause, our commitment and our New Covenant.

My fellow Americans, I end tonight where it all began for me: I still believe in a place called Hope. God bless you, and God bless America. ∎

# Gore on the Bush White House: 'It Is Time for Them To Go'

*On July 17, Tennessee Sen. Al Gore accepted the Democratic nomination for vice president. Following is the Reuter text of his remarks.*

**GORE:** Thank you. Thank you. Thank you very much.

I have to tell you, I've been dreaming of this moment since I was a kid growing up in Tennessee: that one day I'd have the chance to come here to Madison Square Garden and be the warm-up act for Elvis.

My friends, I thank you for your confidence expressed in the vote this evening. I pledge to pour my heart and soul into this crusade on behalf of the American people. And I accept your nomination for the vice presidency of the United States of America.

I did not seek — I did not seek this nomination nor did I expect it. But I am here to join this team because I love my country and because I believe in my heart that together, Bill Clinton and I offer the American people the best chance we have to move this nation forward in the right direction again.

I am here because the country I love has a government that is failing our people — failing the forgotten majority in your hometown and mine, those who scrimped and saved, who work hard all their lives to build a better life for their children.

I am here to renew a journey our founders began more than 200 years ago. In my lifetime, I have seen America's ideals and dreams change the world, and I believe that now is the time to bring those ideals and dreams home here to change America.

Our country is in trouble. And while George Bush and Dan Quayle have been making excuses for deadlock and delay, people in other nations inspired by the eternal promise of America have torn down the Berlin Wall, brought communism to its knees and forced a racist government in South Africa to turn away from apartheid.

Throughout the world, obstacles to liberty that many thought might stand forever turned out to simply be no match for men and women who decided in their hearts that their future could be much greater than their past would let them dream.

Their faith in the power of conscience and their confidence in the force of truth required a leap of the human spirit. Can we say truthfully that their chance for change was better than ours? And yet we face our own crisis of the spirit here and now in America. We're told we can no longer change; we've seen our better days. They even say we're history.

The cynics are having a field day be-cause across this country millions of American families have been betrayed by a government out of touch with our values and beholden to the privileged few. Millions of people — millions of people are losing faith in the very idea of democracy and are even in danger of losing heart, because they fear their lives may no longer have any deeper meaning or purpose.

But you can't kill hope that easily, not in America, not here, where a cynic is just a disappointed idealist in disguise, a dreamer yearning to dream again.

In every American, no matter how badly betrayed or poorly led, there is always hope. Even now, if you listen, you can hear the pulse of America's true spirit.

No, the American spirit isn't gone. But we vow here tonight that in November George Bush and Dan Quayle will be history.

I'm not saying they're bad people, but their approach to governing this country has badly failed. They have taxed the many to enrich the few, and it is time for them to go.

They have given us false choices, bad choices and no choice. And it is time for them to go.

They have ignored the suffering of those who are victims — of AIDS, of crime, of poverty, of ignorance, of hatred and harassment. It is time for them to go.

They have nourished and appeased tyranny, and endangered America's deepest interest while betraying our cherished ideals. It is time for them to go.

They have mortgaged our children's future to avoid the decisions they lack the courage to make. It is time for them to go.

They embarrassed our nation when the whole world was asking for American leadership in confronting the environmental crisis. It is time for them to go.

They have demeaned our democracy with the politics of distraction, denial and despair. What time is it?

**REPLY:** It is time for them to go.

**GORE:** What time is it?

**REPLY:** It is time for them to go.

**GORE:** What time is it?

**REPLY:** It is time for them to go.

The American people are disgusted with excuses and tired of blame. They know that throughout American history, each generation has passed on leadership to the next. That time has come again. The time for a new generation of leadership for the United States of America to take over from George Bush and Dan Quayle. And you know what that means for them. It is time for them to go.

Ladies and gentlemen, in 1992 our challenge is not to elect the last president of the 20th century but to elect the first president of the 21st century, President Bill Clinton.

Bill Clinton has a plan that offers real answers for the real problems of real people, a bold new economic strategy to rebuild this country and put our people back to work.

And if you want to know what Bill Clinton can do, take a look at what he has already done. For more than a decade he has been fighting against incredible odds to bring good jobs, better skills and genuine hope to one of the poorest states in our country.

A decade ago, when his state needed dramatic reform to shake up one of the poorest school systems in America, Bill Clinton took on the established interests and made Arkansas the first state to require teacher testing. He has cut classroom size, raised test scores above the national average and earned the support of both teachers and parents, who now know Bill Clinton will be the real education president for this country.

For most of the last decade, while the Republicans have been trying to use welfare to divide us, Bill Clinton has led the fight to reform the welfare system, to move people off welfare and into the work force.

And he did all this while balancing 11 budgets in a row. Let me say that again: while balancing 11 budgets in a row and giving the people of Arkansas one of the lowest tax burdens in this country. No wonder Arkansas under Bill Clinton has been creating manufacturing jobs at 10 times the national rate. And no wonder when all of the nation's governors, Republicans and Democrats alike, were asked to vote on who was the most effective governor in all the land, by an overwhelming margin they chose Bill Clinton.

What we need in America in 1992 is a president who will unleash the best in us by putting faith in the decency and good judgment of our people. A president who will challenge us to be true to our values and examine the ways in which our own attitudes are sometimes barriers to the progress we seek.

I'm convinced that America is ready to be inspired and lifted again, by leaders committed to seeking out the best in our society, developing it and strengthening it. I've spent much of my career working to protect the environment, not only because it is vital to the future of my state of Tennessee, our country and our earth but because I believe there is a fundamental link between our current relationship to the earth and the attitudes that stand in the way of human progress.

For generations we have believed that we could abuse the earth because we were somehow not really connected to it. But now we must face the truth. The task of saving the earth's environment must and will become the central organizing principle of the post-Cold War world.

And just as the false assumption that we are not connected to the earth has led to

the ecological crisis, so the equally false assumption that we are not connected to each other has led to our social crisis.

Even worse, the evil and mistaken assumption that we have no connection to those generations preceding us or those who will follow us has led to the crisis of values we face today.

Those are the connections that are missing from our politics today. Those are the bridges we must rebuild if we are to rebuild our country. And those are the values we must honor if we are to recapture that faith in the future which has always been the heart of the American Dream.

We have another challenge as well. In the wake of the Cold War, with the reemergence of ancient ethnic and racial hatreds throughout the world, the United States must once again prove that there is a better way. Just as we accepted as a people on behalf of humankind the historic mission of proving that political freedom is the best form of government and that economic freedom is the best engine of prosperity, and must now accept the obligation of proving that freedom from prejudice is the heart and soul of community, that yes, we can get along.

Yes, people of all backgrounds cannot only live together peacefully but enrich one another, celebrate diversity and come together as one. Yes, we will be one people and live the dream that will make this world free.

In the end, this election isn't about politics. It isn't even about winning, though that's what we are going to do.

This election is about the responsibilities that we owe one another, the responsibilities that we owe our children, the calling we hear to serve our country and to be part of a community larger than ourselves.

You've heard a lot in the past week about how much Bill Clinton and I have in common. Indeed, we both share the values we learned in our hometowns: individual responsibility, faith, family and the belief that hard work should be rewarded. We're both fathers with young children, children who are part of a generation whose very future is very much at stake in this election. And we're both proud of our wives, Hillary Clinton and Tipper Gore — two women who have done more for the children of this country in the last 12 years than the last two men who have sat in the Oval Office have done in their entire lifetimes.

I'm proud my father and mother could be here tonight to see me join a ticket that will make good on the best advice they ever gave me: to tell the truth and always love my country. My sister and I were born to two wonderful people who worked hard to give us a better life. 1992 is the Year of the Woman. It is also the 46th anniversary of the year my mother, born in a time when women weren't even allowed to vote, became one of the first women to graduate from Vanderbilt Law School.

My father was a teacher in a one-room school who worked his way to the United States Senate. I was 8 years old when my father's name was placed in nomination for the vice presidency before the Democratic convention in 1956. And growing up, I watched him stand courageously for civil rights and economic opportunity and a government that worked for ordinary people.

I don't know what it's like to lose a father, but I know what it's like to lose a sister and almost lose a son. I wish my late sister Nancy could be here this evening, but I am grateful beyond words for the blessings that my family has shared. Three years ago, my son Albert was struck by a car crossing the street after watching a baseball game in Baltimore. Tipper and I watched as he was thrown 30 feet in the air and scraped another 20 feet on the pavement after he hit the ground. I ran to his side and called his name, but he was limp and still, without breath or pulse. His eyes were open with the empty stare of death, and we prayed, the two of us, there in the gutter, with only my voice.

His injuries, inside and out, were massive, and for terrible days he lingered between life and death. Tipper and I spent the next 30 days and nights there at his bedside. Our family was lifted and healed, in no small measure by an incredible outpouring of love and compassion and prayers of thousands of people, most of whom we never even knew.

Albert is plenty brave and strong, and with the support of three wonderful sisters — Karenna, Kristin and Sarah — and two loving parents who helped him with his exercises every morning and prayed for him every night, he pulled through. And now, thank God, he has fully recovered, and runs and plays and torments his older sisters like any little boy.

But, ladies and gentlemen, I want to tell you this straight from my heart — that experience changed me forever. When you've seen your 6-year-old son fighting for his life, you realize that some things matter a lot more than winning. You lose patience with the lazy assumption of so many in politics that we can always just muddle through. When you've seen your reflection in the empty stare of a boy waiting for a second breath of life, you realize that we weren't put here on earth to look out for our needs alone; we are part of something much larger than ourselves. All of us are part of something much greater than we are capable of imagining.

And my friends, if you look up for a moment from the rush of your daily lives, you will hear the quiet voices of your country crying out for help. You will see your reflection in the weary eyes of those who are losing hope in America. And you will see that our democracy is lying there in the gutter, waiting for us to give it a second breath of life.

I don't care what party you're in, whether you are an independent, whether you have been tempted to give up completely on the whole political process or not, or give up on our party or not, we want you to join this common effort to unite our country behind a higher calling. If you have been supporting Ross Perot, I want to make a special plea to you this evening: Stay involved. You have already changed politics in this country for the better. Keep on fighting for change.

The time has come for all Americans to be part of the healing. In the words of the Bible, "Do not lose heart. This nation will be renewed."

In order to renew our nation, we must renew ourselves. Just as America has always transcended the hopes and dreams of every other nation on earth, so must we transcend ourselves, and in Gandhi's words, become the change we wish to see in the world.

Let those of us alive today resolve with one another that we will so conduct ourselves — in this campaign and in our lives — that 200 years from now, Americans will say of our labors that this nation and this earth were healed by people they never even knew.

I'm told that Hope, Ark., is indeed a lot like my hometown of Carthage, Tenn.: a place where people know about it when you're born and care about it when you die. That's the America Bill Clinton and I grew up in. That's the kind of nation we want our children to grow up in. Just as Hope is a community, so is America. When we bring the community of America together, we will rekindle the American spirit and renew this nation for generations to come. And the way to begin is to elect Bill Clinton president of the United States of America.

Thank you very much. ■

## THE PLATFORM

# Party Statement of Policies Mirrors Clinton's Goals

*Following is the text of the Democratic platform draft approved by the Platform Committee on June 27, 1992. It was approved without change at the convention July 14.*

Two hundred summers ago, this Democratic Party was founded by the man whose burning pen fired the spirit of the American Revolution — who once argued we should overthrow our own government every 20 years to renew our freedom and keep pace with a changing world. In 1992, the party Thomas Jefferson founded invokes his spirit of revolution anew.

Our land reverberates with a battle cry of frustration that emanates from America's very soul — from the families in our bedrock neighborhoods, from the unsung, workaday heroes of the world's greatest democracy and economy. America is on the wrong track. The American people are hurting. The American dream of expanding opportunity has faded. Middle-class families are working hard, playing by the rules, but still falling behind. Poverty has exploded. Our people are torn by divisions.

The last 12 years have been a nightmare of Republican irresponsibility and neglect. America's leadership is indifferent at home and uncertain in the world. Republican mismanagement has disarmed government as an instrument to make our economy work and support the people's most basic values, needs and hopes. The Republicans brought America a false and fragile prosperity based on borrowing, not income, and so will leave behind a mountain of public debt and a backbreaking annual burden in interest. It is wrong to borrow to spend on ourselves, leaving our children to pay our debts.

We hear the anguish and the anger of the American people. We know it is directed not just at the Republican administrations that have had power but at government itself.

Their anger is justified. We can no longer afford business as usual — neither the policies of the last 12 years of tax breaks for the rich, mismanagement, lack of leadership and cuts in services for the middle class and the poor, nor the adoption of new programs and new spending without new thinking.

It is time to listen to the grass roots of America, time to renew the spirit of citizen activism that has always been the touchstone of a free and democratic society.

Therefore we call for *a revolution in government* — to take power away from entrenched bureaucracies and narrow interests in Washington and put it back in the hands of ordinary people. We vow to make

government more decentralized, more flexible and more accountable — to reform public institutions and replace public officials who aren't leading with ones who will.

The Revolution of 1992 is about restoring America's economic greatness. We need to rebuild America by abandoning the something-for-nothing ethic of the last decade and putting people first for a change. Only a thriving economy, a strong manufacturing base and growth in creative new enterprise can generate the resources to meet the nation's pressing human and social needs. An expanding, entrepreneurial economy of high-skill, high-wage jobs is the most important family policy, urban policy, labor policy, minority policy and foreign policy America can have.

The Revolution of 1992 is about putting government back on the side of working men and women — to help those who work hard, pay their bills, play by the rules, don't lobby for tax breaks, do their best to give their kids a good education and to keep them away from drugs, who want a safe neighborhood for their families, the security of decent, productive jobs for themselves and a dignified life for their parents.

The Revolution of 1992 is about a radical change in the way government operates — not the Republican proposition that government has no role nor the old notion that there's a program for every problem, but a shift to a more efficient, flexible and results-oriented government that improves services, expands choices, and empowers citizens and communities to change our country from the bottom up. We believe in an activist government, but it must work in a different, more responsive way.

The Revolution of 1992 is about facing up to tough choices. There is no relief for America's frustration in the politics of diversion and evasion, of false choices or of no choices at all. Instead of everyone in Washington blaming one another for inaction, we will act decisively — and ask to be held accountable if we don't.

Above all the Revolution of 1992 is about restoring the basic American values that built this country and will always make it great: personal responsibility, individual liberty, tolerance, faith, family and hard work. We offer the American people not only new ideas, a new course and a new president, but a return to the enduring principles that set our nation apart: the promise of opportunity, the strength of community, the dignity of work and a decent life for senior citizens.

To make this revolution, we seek a *New Covenant* to repair the damaged bond between the American people and their govern-

ment, that will expand *opportunity*, insist upon greater individual *responsibility* in return, restore *community* and ensure *national security* in a profoundly new era.

We welcome the close scrutiny of the American people, including Americans who may have thought the Democratic Party had forgotten its way, as well as all who know us as the champion for those who have been denied a chance. With this platform we take our case for change to the American people.

### I. Opportunity

Our party's first priority is opportunity — broad-based, non-inflationary economic growth and the opportunity that flows from it. Democrats in 1992 hold nothing more important for America than an economy that offers growth and jobs for all.

President Bush, with no interest in domestic policy, has given America the slowest economic growth, the slowest income growth and the slowest jobs growth since the Great Depression. And the American people know the long Bush recession reflects not just a business cycle, but a long-term slide, so that even in a fragile recovery we're sinking. The ballooning Bush deficits hijacked capital from productive investments. Savings and loan sharks enriched themselves at their country's expense. The stock market tripled, but average incomes stalled, and poverty claimed more of our children.

We reject both the do-nothing government of the last 12 years and the big government theory that says we can hamstring business and tax and spend our way to prosperity. Instead we offer a third way. Just as we have always viewed working men and women as the bedrock of our economy, we honor business as a noble endeavor and vow to create a far better climate for firms and independent contractors of all sizes that empower their workers, revolutionize their workplaces, respect the environment, and serve their communities well.

We believe in free enterprise and the power of market forces. But economic growth will not come without a national economic strategy to invest in people. For 12 years our country has had no economic vision, leadership or strategy. It is time to put our people and our country first.

**Investing in America.** The only way to lay the foundation for renewed American prosperity is to spur both public and private investment. We must strive to close both the budget deficit and the investment gap. Our major competitors invest far more than we do in roads, bridges and the information networks and technologies of the future. We

will rebuild America by investing more in transportation, environmental technologies, defense conversion and a national information network.

To begin making our economy grow, the president and Congress should agree that savings from defense must be reinvested productively at home, including research, education and training, and other productive investments. This will sharply increase the meager 9 percent of the national budget now devoted to the future. We will create a "future budget" for investments that make us richer, to be kept separate from those parts of the budget that pay for the past and present. For the private sector, instead of a sweeping capital gains windfall to the wealthy and those who speculate, we will create an investment tax credit and a capital gains reduction for patient investors in emerging technologies and new business.

**Support for innovation.** We will take back the advantage now ceded to Japan and Germany, which invest in new technologies at higher rates than the U.S. and have the growth to show for it. We will make the R&D [research and development] tax credit permanent, double basic research in the key technologies for our future and create a civilian research agency to fast-forward their development.

**The deficit.** Addressing the deficit requires fair and shared sacrifice of all Americans for the common good. In 12 Republican years a national debt that took 200 years to accumulate has been *quadrupled*. Rising interest on that debt now swallows one tax dollar in seven. In place of the Republican supply side disaster, the Democratic investment, economic conversion and growth strategy will generate more revenues from a growing economy. We must also tackle spending by putting everything on the table; eliminate non-productive programs; achieve defense savings; reform entitlement programs to control soaring health-care costs; cut federal administrative costs by 3 percent annually for four years; limit increases in the "present budget" to the rate of growth in the average American's paycheck; apply a strict "pay as you go" rule to new non-investment spending; and make the rich pay their fair share in taxes. These choices will be made while protecting senior citizens and without further victimizing the poor. This deficit-reduction effort will encourage private savings, eliminate the budget deficit over time and permit fiscal policies that can restore America's economic health.

**Defense conversion.** Our economy needs both the people and the funds released from defense at the Cold War's end. We will help the stalwarts of that struggle — the men and women who served in our armed forces and who work in our defense industries — make the most of a new era. We will provide early notice of program changes to give communities, business and workers enough time to plan. We will honor and support our veterans. Departing military personnel, defense workers and defense support personnel will have access to job retraining, continuing education, placement and relocation assistance, early retirement benefits for military

personnel, and incentives to enter teaching, law enforcement and other vital civilian fields. Redirected national laboratories and a new civilian research agency will put defense scientists, engineers and technicians to work at critical civilian technologies. Small business defense firms will have technical assistance and transition grants and loans to help convert to civilian markets, and defense-dependent communities will have similar aid in planning and implementing conversion. We will strongly support our civilian space program, particularly environmental missions.

**The cities.** Only a robust economy will revitalize our cities. It is in all Americans' interest that the cities once again be places where hard-working families can put down roots and find good jobs, quality health care, affordable housing and decent schools. Democrats will create a new partnership to rebuild America's cities after 12 years of Republican neglect. This partnership will include consideration of the seven economic growth initiatives set forth by our nation's mayors. We will create jobs by investing significant resources to put people back to work, beginning with a summer jobs initiative and training programs for inner-city youth. We support a stronger community development program and targeted fiscal assistance to cities that need it most. A national public works investment and infrastructure program will provide jobs and strengthen our cities, suburbs, rural communities and country. We will encourage the flow of investment to inner city development and housing through targeted enterprise zones and incentives for private and public pension funds to invest in urban and rural projects. While cracking down on redlining and housing discrimination, we also support and will enforce a revitalized Community Reinvestment Act that challenges banks to lend to entrepreneurs and development projects; a national network of Community Development Banks to invest in urban and rural small businesses; and microenterprise lending for poor people seeking self-employment as an alternative to welfare.

**Agriculture and the rural community.** All Americans, producers and consumers alike, benefit when our food and fiber are produced by hundreds of thousands of family farmers receiving a fair price for their products. The abundance of our nation's food and fiber system should not be taken for granted. The revolution that lifted America to the forefront of world agriculture was achieved through a unique partnership between public and private interests. The inattention and hostility that has characterized Republican food, agriculture and rural development policies of the past 12 years has caused a crisis in rural America. The cost of Republican farm policy has been staggering, and its total failure is demonstrated by the record number of rural bankruptcies.

A sufficient and sustainable agricultural economy can be achieved through fiscally responsible programs. It is time to re-establish the private/public partnership to ensure that family farmers get a fair return for their

labor and investment, that consumers receive safe and nutritious foods, and that needed investments are made in basic research, education, rural business development, market development and infrastructure to sustain rural communities.

**Workers' rights.** Our workplaces must be revolutionized to make them more flexible and productive. We will reform the job safety laws to empower workers with greater rights and to hold employers accountable for dangers on the job. We will act against sexual harassment in the workplace. We will honor the work ethic — by expanding the earned-income tax credit so no one with children at home who works full time is still in poverty, by fighting on the side of family farmers to ensure they get a fair price for their hard work and working to sustain rural communities; by making work more valuable than welfare; and by supporting the right of workers to organize and bargain collectively without fear of intimidation or permanent replacement during labor disputes.

**Lifelong learning.** A competitive American economy requires the global market's best-educated, best-trained, most flexible work force. It's not enough to spend more on our schools; we must insist on results. We oppose the Bush administration's efforts to bankrupt the public school system — the bedrock of democracy — through private school vouchers. To help children reach school ready to learn, we will expand child health and nutrition programs and extend Head Start to all eligible children, and guarantee all children access to quality, affordable child care. We deplore the savage inequalities among public schools across the land and believe every child deserves an equal chance to a world-class education. Reallocating resources toward this goal must be a priority. We support education reforms such as site-based decision-making and public school choice, with strong protections against discrimination. We support the goal of a 90 percent graduation rate and programs to end dropouts. We will invest in educational technology and establish world-class standards in math, science and other core subjects, and support effective tests of progress to meet them. In areas where there are no registered apprenticeship programs, we will adopt a national apprenticeship-style program to ease the transition from school to work for non-college-bound students, so they can acquire skills that lead to high-wage jobs. In the new economy, opportunity will depend on lifelong learning. We will support the goal of literacy for all Americans. We will ask firms to invest in the training of all workers, not just corporate management.

**A domestic GI bill.** Over the past 12 years, skyrocketing costs and declining middle-class incomes have placed higher education out of reach for millions of Americans. It is time to revolutionize the way student loan programs are run. We will make college affordable to *all* students who are qualified to attend, *regardless of family income.* A Domestic GI Bill will enable all Americans to borrow money for college, so long as they are

willing to pay it back as a percentage of their income over time or through national service addressing unmet community needs.

**Affordable health care.** All Americans should have universal access to quality, affordable health care — not as a privilege but as a right. That requires tough controls on health costs, which are rising at two to three times the rate of inflation, terrorizing American families and businesses and depriving millions of the care they need. We will enact a uniquely American reform of the health-care system to control costs and make health care affordable; ensure quality and choice of health-care providers; cover all Americans regardless of pre-existing conditions; squeeze out waste, bureaucracy and abuse; improve primary and preventive care including child immunization and prevention of diseases like tuberculosis now becoming rampant in our cities; provide expanded education on the relationship between diet and health; expand access to mental health treatment services; provide a safety net through support of public hospitals; provide for the full range of reproductive choice — education, counseling, access to contraceptives and the right to a safe, legal abortion; expand medical research; and provide more long-term care, including home health care. We will make ending the epidemic in breast cancer a major priority, and expand reproductive health services and other special health needs of women. We must be united in declaring war on AIDS and HIV disease, implement the recommendations of the National Commission on AIDS and fully fund the Ryan White Care Act; provide targeted and honest prevention campaigns; combat HIV-related discrimination; make drug treatment available for all addicts who seek it; guarantee access to quality care; expand clinical trials for treatments and vaccines; and speed up the FDA [Food and Drug Administration] drug approval process.

**Fairness.** Growth and equity work in tandem. People should share in society's common costs according to their ability to pay. In the last decade, mounting payroll and other taxes have fallen disproportionately on the middle class. We will relieve the tax burden on middle-class Americans by forcing the rich to pay their fair share. We will provide long-overdue tax relief to families with children. To broaden opportunity, we will support fair lending practices.

**Energy efficiency and sustainable development.** We reject the Republican myth that energy efficiency and environmental protection are enemies of economic growth. We will make our economy more efficient, using less energy, reducing our dependence on foreign oil, and producing less solid and toxic waste. We will adopt a coordinated transportation policy, with a strong commitment to mass transit; encourage efficient alternative-fueled vehicles; increase our reliance on clean natural gas; promote clean coal technology; invest in R&D [research and development] on renewable energy sources; strengthen efforts to prevent air and water pollution; support incentives for domestic oil and gas operations; and push

for revenue-neutral incentives that reward conservation, prevent pollution and encourage recycling.

**Civil and equal rights.** We don't have an American to waste. Democrats will continue to lead the fight to ensure that no Americans suffer discrimination or deprivation of rights on the basis of race, gender, language, national origin, religion, age, disability, sexual orientation or other characteristics irrelevant to ability. We support ratification of the Equal Rights Amendment, affirmative action, stronger protection of voting rights for racial and ethnic minorities, including language access to voting, and continued resistance to discriminatory English-only pressure groups. We will reverse the Bush administration's assault on civil rights enforcement, and instead work to rebuild and vigorously use machinery for civil rights enforcement; support comparable remedies for women; aggressively prosecute hate crimes; strengthen legal services for the poor; deal with other nations in a way that Americans of any origin do not become scapegoats or victims of foreign policy disputes; provide civil rights protection for gay men and lesbians and an end to Defense Department discrimination; respect Native American culture and our treaty commitments; require the United States government to recognize its trustee obligations to the inhabitants of Hawaii generally and to Native Hawaiians in particular; and fully enforce the Americans with Disability Act to enable people with disabilities to achieve independence and function at their highest possible level.

**Commonwealth and territories.** We recognize the existing status of the Commonwealth of Puerto Rico and the strong economic relationship between the people of Puerto Rico and the United States. We pledge to support the right of the people of the Commonwealth of Puerto Rico to choose freely, and in concert with the U.S. Congress their relationship with the United States, either as an enhanced commonwealth, a state or an independent nation.

We pledge to the people of American Samoa, Guam, the Northern Mariana Islands and the Virgin Islands just and fair treatment under federal policies, assisting their economic and social development. We respect their right and that of the people of Palau to decide freely their future relationship with the United States and to be consulted on issues and policies that directly affect them.

## II. Responsibility

Sixty years ago, Franklin Roosevelt gave hope to a nation mired in the Great Depression. While government should promise every American the opportunity to get ahead, it was the people's responsibility, he said, to make the most of that opportunity: "Faith in America demands that we recognize the new terms of the old social contract. In the strength of great hope we must all shoulder our common load."

For 12 years, the Republicans have expected too little of our public institutions

and placed too little faith in our people. We offer a new social contract based neither on callous, do-nothing Republican neglect nor on an outdated faith in programs as the solution to every problem. We favor a third way beyond the old approaches — to put government back on the side of citizens who play by the rules. We believe that by what it says and how it conducts its business, government must once again make responsibility an instrument of national purpose. Our future as a nation depends upon the daily assumption of personal responsibility by millions of Americans from all walks of life — for the religious faith they follow, the ethics they practice, the values they instill, the pride they take in their work.

**Strengthening the family.** Governments don't raise children, people do. People who bring children into this world have a responsibility to care for them and give them values, motivation and discipline. Children should not have children. We need a national crackdown on deadbeat parents, an effective system of child-support enforcement nationwide and a systematic effort to establish paternity for every child. We must also make it easier for parents to build strong families through pay equity. Family and medical leave will ensure that workers don't have to choose between family and work. We support a family preservation program to reduce child and spousal abuse by providing preventive services and foster care to families in crisis. We favor ensuring quality and affordable child-care opportunities for working parents, and a fair and healthy start for every child, including essential prenatal and well-baby care. We support the needs of our senior citizens for productive and healthy lives, including hunger prevention, income adequacy, transportation access and abuse prevention.

**Welfare reform.** Welfare should be a second chance, not a way of life. We want to break the cycle of welfare by adhering to two simple principles: No one who is able to work can stay on welfare forever, and no one who works should live in poverty. We will continue to help those who cannot help themselves. We will offer people on welfare a new social contract. We'll invest in education and job training, and provide the child care and health care they need to go to work and achieve long-term self-sufficiency. We will give them the help they need to make the transition from welfare to work, and require people who can work to go to work within two years in available jobs either in the private sector or in community service to meet unmet needs. That will restore the covenant that welfare was meant to be: a promise of temporary help for people who have fallen on hard times.

**Choice.** Democrats stand behind the right of every woman to choose, consistent with *Roe v. Wade*, regardless of ability to pay, and support a national law to protect that right. It is a fundamental constitutional liberty that individual Americans — not government — can best take responsibility for making the most difficult and intensely personal decisions regarding reproduction. The

goal of our nation must be to make abortion less necessary, not more difficult or more dangerous. We pledge to support contraceptive research, family planning, comprehensive family life education, and policies that support healthy childbearing and enable parents to care most effectively for their children.

**Making schools work**. Education is a cooperative enterprise that can only succeed if everyone accepts and exercises personal responsibility. Students must stay in school and do their best; parents must get involved in their children's education; teachers must attain, maintain and demonstrate classroom competency; school administrators must enforce discipline and high standards of educational attainment; governments must end the inequalities that create educational ghettos among school districts and provide equal educational opportunity for all, and ensure that teachers' pay measures up to their decisive role in children's lives; and the American people should recognize education as the core of our economy, democracy and society.

**Labor-management responsibilities**. The private sector is the engine of our economy and the main source of national wealth. But it is not enough for those in the private sector just to make as much money as they can. The most irresponsible people in all of the 1980s were those at the top of the ladder, the inside traders, quick-buck artists and S&L [savings and loans] kingpins who looked out for themselves and not for the country. America's corporate leaders have a responsibility to invest in their country. CEOs [chief executive officers], who pay themselves 100 times what they pay the average worker, shouldn't get big raises unrelated to performance. If a company wants to overpay its executives and underinvest in the future or transfer jobs overseas, it shouldn't get special treatment and tax breaks from the Treasury. Managers must work with employees to make the workplace safer, more satisfying and more efficient.

Workers must also accept added responsibilities in the new economy. In return for an increased voice and a greater stake in the success of their enterprises, workers should be prepared to join in cooperative efforts to increase productivity, flexibility and quality. Government's neutrality between labor and management cannot mean neutrality about the collective bargaining process, which has been purposely crippled by Republican administrations. Our economic growth depends on processes, including collective bargaining, that permit labor and management to work together on their common interests, even as they work out their conflicts.

**Responsibility for the environment**. For ourselves and future generations, we must protect our environment. We will protect our old-growth forests, preserve critical habitats, provide a genuine "no net loss" policy on wetlands, conserve the critical resources of soil, water and air, oppose new offshore oil drilling and mineral exploration and production in our nation's many environmentally critical areas, and address ocean pollution by reducing oil and toxic waste

spills at sea. We believe America's youth can serve their country well through a civilian conservation corps. To protect the public health, we will clean up the environmental horrors at federal facilities, insist that private polluters clean up their toxic and hazardous wastes, and vigorously prosecute environmental criminals. We will oppose Republican efforts to gut the Clean Air Act in the guise of competitiveness. We will reduce the volume of solid waste and encourage the use of recycled materials while discouraging excess packaging. To avoid the mistakes of the past, we will actively support energy efficiency, recycling and pollution-prevention strategies.

**Responsible government**. Democrats in 1992 intend to lead a revolution in government, challenging it to act responsibly and be accountable, starting with the hardest and most urgent problems of the deficit and economic growth. Rather than throwing money at obsolete programs, we will eliminate unnecessary layers of management, cut administrative costs, give people more choices in the service they get and empower them to make those choices. To foster greater responsibility in government at every level, we support giving greater flexibility to our cities, counties and states in achieving federal mandates and carrying out existing programs.

**Responsible officials**. All branches of government must live by the laws the rest of us obey, determine their pay in an open manner that builds public trust and eliminate special privileges. People in public office need to be accessible to the people they represent. It's time to reform the campaign finance system, to get big money out of our politics and let the people back in. We must limit overall campaign spending and limit the disproportionate and excessive role of PACs [political action committees]. We need new voter registration laws that expand the electorate, such as universal same-day registration, along with full political rights and protections for public employees and new regulations to ensure that the airwaves truly help citizens make informed choices among candidates and policies. And we need fair political representation for all sectors of our country — including the District of Columbia, which deserves and must get statehood status.

## III. Restoring Community

The success of democracy in America depends substantially on the strength of our community institutions: families and neighborhoods, public schools, religious institutions, charitable organizations, civic groups and other voluntary associations. In these social networks, the values and character of our citizens are formed as we learn the habits and skills of self-government and acquire an understanding of our common rights and responsibilities as citizens.

Twelve years of Republican rule have undermined the spirit of mutual dependence and obligation that binds us together. Republican leaders have urged Americans to

turn inward, to pursue private interests without regard to public responsibilities. By playing racial, ethnic and gender-based politics, they have divided us against each other, created an atmosphere of blame, denial and fear, and undone the hard-fought battles for equality and fairness.

Our communities form a vital "third sector" that lies between government and the marketplace. The wisdom, energy and resources required to solve our problems are not concentrated in Washington but can be found throughout our communities, including America's nonprofit sector, which has grown rapidly over the last decade. Government's best role is to enable people and communities to solve their own problems.

America's special genius has been to forge a community of shared values from people of remarkable and diverse backgrounds. As the party of inclusion, we take special pride in our country's emergence as the world's largest and most successful multiethnic, multiracial republic. We condemn anti-Semitism, racism, homophobia, bigotry and negative stereotyping of all kinds. We must help all Americans understand the diversity of our cultural heritage. But it is also essential that we preserve and pass on to our children the common elements that hold this mosaic together as we work to make our country a land of freedom and opportunity for all.

Both Republican neglect and traditional spending programs have proven unequal to these challenges. Democrats will pursue a new course that stresses work, family and individual responsibility, and that empowers Americans to liberate themselves from poverty and dependence. We pledge to bolster the institutions of civil society and place a new emphasis on civic enterprises that seek solutions to our nation's problems. Through common, cooperative efforts we can rebuild our communities and transform our nation.

**Combating crime and drugs**. Crime is a relentless danger to our communities. Over the last decade, crime has swept through our country at an alarming rate. During the 1980s, more than 200,000 Americans were murdered, four times the number who died in Vietnam. Violent crimes rose by more than 16 percent since 1988 and nearly doubled since 1975. In our country today, a murder is committed every 25 minutes, a rape every six minutes, a burglary every 10 seconds. The pervasive fear of crime disfigures our public life and diminishes our freedom.

None suffer more than the poor: An explosive mixture of blighted prospects, drugs and exotic weaponry has turned many of our inner-city communities into combat zones. As a result, crime is not only a symptom but also a major cause of the worsening poverty and demoralization that afflicts inner city communities.

To empower America's communities, Democrats pledge to restore government as upholder of basic law and order for crime-ravaged communities. The simplest and most direct way to restore order in our cities is to put more police on the streets. America's

police are locked in an unequal struggle with crime: Since 1951 the ratio of police officers to reported crimes has reversed, from 3-to-1 to 1-to-3. We will create a Police Corps, in which participants will receive college aid in return for several years of service after graduation in a state or local police department. As we shift people and resources from defense to the civilian economy, we will create new jobs in law enforcement for those leaving the military.

We will expand drug counseling and treatment for those who need it, intensify efforts to educate our children at the earliest ages to the dangers of drug and alcohol abuse, and curb demand from the street corner to the penthouse suite, so that the United States, with 5 percent of the world's population, no longer consumes 50 percent of the world's illegal drugs.

**Community policing.** Neighborhoods and police should be partners in the war on crime. Democrats support more community policing, which uses foot patrols and storefront offices to make police officers visible fixtures in urban neighborhoods. We will combat street violence and emphasize building trust and solving the problems that breed crime.

**Firearms.** It is time to shut down the weapons bazaars in our cities. We support a reasonable waiting period to permit background checks for purchases of handguns, as well as assault weapons controls to ban the possession, sale, importation and manufacture of the most deadly assault weapons. We do not support efforts to restrict weapons used for legitimate hunting and sporting purposes. We will work for swift and certain punishment of all people who violate the country's gun laws and for stronger sentences for criminals who use guns. We will also seek to shut down the black market for guns and impose severe penalties on people who sell guns to children.

**Pursuing all crime aggressively.** In contrast to the Republican policy of leniency toward white-collar crime — which breeds cynicism in poor communities about the impartiality of our justice system — Democrats will redouble efforts to ferret out and punish those who betray the public trust, rig financial markets, misuse their depositors' money or swindle their customers.

**Further initiatives.** Democrats also favor innovative sentencing and punishment options, including community service and boot camps for first-time offenders; tougher penalties for rapists; victim-impact statements and restitution to ensure that crime victims will not be lost in the complexities of the criminal justice system; and initiatives to make our schools safe, including alternative schools for disruptive children.

**Empowering the poor and expanding the middle class.** We must further the new direction set in the Family Support Act of 1988, away from subsistence and dependence and toward work, family and personal initiative and responsibility. We advocate slower phasing out of Medicaid and other benefits to encourage work; special savings accounts to help low-income families build assets; fair lending; an indexed minimum wage; an expanded Job Corps; and an end to welfare rules that encourage family breakup and penalize individual initiative, such as the $1,000 limit on personal savings.

**Immigration.** Our nation of immigrants has been invigorated repeatedly as new people, ideas and ways of life have become part of the American tapestry. Democrats support immigration policies that promote fairness, non-discrimination and family reunification and that reflect our constitutional freedoms of speech, association and travel.

**Housing.** Safe, secure housing is essential to the institutions of community and family. We support homeownership for working families and will honor that commitment through policies to encourage affordable mortgage credit. We must also confront homelessness by renovating, preserving and expanding the stock of affordable low-income housing. We support tenant management and ownership, so public housing residents can manage their own affairs and acquire property worth protecting.

**National service.** We will create new opportunities for citizens to serve each other, their communities and their country. By mobilizing hundreds of thousands of volunteers, national service will enhance the role of ordinary citizens in solving unresolved community problems.

**The arts.** We believe in public support for the arts, including a National Endowment for the Arts that is free from political manipulation and firmly rooted in the First Amendment's freedom of expression guarantee.

## IV. Preserving Our National Security

During the past four years, we have seen the corrosive effect of foreign policies that are rooted in the past, divorced from our values, fearful of change and unable to meet its challenges. Under President Bush, crises have been managed rather than prevented; dictators like Saddam Hussein have been wooed rather than deterred; aggression by the Serbian regime against its neighbors in what was Yugoslavia has been met by American timidity rather than toughness; human rights abusers have been rewarded, not challenged; the environment has been neglected, not protected; and America's competitive edge in the global economy has been dulled, not honed. It is time for new American leadership that can meet the challenges of a changing world.

At the end of World War II, American strength had defeated tyranny and American ingenuity had overcome the Depression. Under President [Harry S] Truman, the United States led the world into a new era, redefining global security with bold approaches to tough challenges: containing communism with the NATO alliance and in Korea; building the peace through organizations such as the United Nations; and advancing global economic security through new multilateral institutions.

Nearly a half century later, we stand at another pivotal point in history. The collapse of communism does not mean the end of danger of threats to our interests. But it does pose an unprecedented opportunity to make our future more secure and prosperous. Once again, we must define a compelling vision for global leadership at the dawn of a new era.

## V. Restructuring Our Military Forces

We have not seen the end of violence, aggression and the conflicts that can threaten American interests and our hopes for a more peaceful world. What the United States needs is not the Bush administration's Cold War thinking on a smaller scale but a comprehensive restructuring of the American military enterprise to meet the threats that remain.

**Military strength.** America is the world's strongest military power, and we must remain so. A post-Cold War restructuring of American forces will produce substantial savings beyond those promised by the Bush administration, but that restructuring must be achieved without undermining our ability to meet future threats to our security. A military structure for the 1990s and beyond must be built on four pillars: *First,* a survivable nuclear force to deter any conceivable threat as we reduce our nuclear arsenals through arms control negotiations and other reciprocal action. *Second,* conventional forces shifted toward projecting power wherever our vital national interests are threatened. This means reducing the size of our forces in Europe while meeting our obligations to NATO and strengthening our rapid deployment capabilities to deal with new threats to our security posed by renegade dictators, terrorists, international drug traffickers and the local armed conflicts that can threaten the peace of entire regions. *Third,* maintenance of the two qualities that make America's military the best in the world — the superiority of our military personnel and of our technology. These qualities are vital to shortening any conflict and saving American lives. *Fourth,* intelligence capabilities redirected to develop far more sophisticated, timely and accurate analyses of the economic and political conditions that can fuel new conflicts.

**Use of force.** The United States must be prepared to use military force decisively when necessary to defend our vital interests. The burdens of collective security in a new era must be shared fairly, and we should encourage multilateral peacekeeping through the United Nations and other international efforts.

**Preventing and containing conflict.** American policy must be focused on averting military threats as well as meeting them. To halt the spread of nuclear and other weapons of mass destruction, we must lead a renewed international effort to get tough with companies that peddle nuclear and chemical warfare technologies, strengthen the International Atomic Energy Agency and enforce strong sanctions against governments that violate international restraints. A Comprehensive Test Ban would strengthen

our ability to stop the spread of nuclear weapons to other countries, which may be our greatest future security threat. We must press for strong international limits on the dangerous and wasteful flow of conventional arms to troubled regions. A U.S. troop presence should be maintained in Korea as long as North Korea presents a threat to South Korea.

## VI. Restoring America's Economic Leadership

The United States cannot be strong abroad if it is weak at home. Restoring America's global economic leadership must become a central element of our national security policies. The strength of nations, once defined in military terms, now is measured also by the skills of their workers, the imagination of their managers and the power of their technologies.

Either we develop and pursue a national plan for restoring our economy through a partnership of government, labor and business, or we slip behind the nations that are competing with us and growing. At stake are American jobs, our standard of living and the quality of life for ourselves and our children.

Economic strength — indeed our national security — is grounded on a healthy domestic economy. But we cannot be strong at home unless we are part of a vibrant and expanding global economy that recognizes human rights and seeks to improve the living standards of all the world's people. This is vital to achieving good quality, high-paying jobs for Americans.

**Trade.** Our government must work to expand trade while insisting that the conduct of world trade is fair. It must fight to uphold American interests — promoting exports, expanding trade in agricultural and other products, opening markets in major product and service sectors with our principal competitors, achieving reciprocal access. This should include renewed authority to use America's trading leverage against the most serious problems. The U.S. government also must firmly enforce U.S. laws against unfair trade.

**Trade agreements.** Multilateral trade agreements can advance our economic interests by expanding the global economy. Whether negotiating the North American Free Trade Area (NAFTA) [agreement] or completing the GATT [General Agreement on Tariffs and Trade] negotiations, our government must assure that our legitimate concerns about environmental, health and safety, and labor standards are included. Those American workers whose jobs are affected must have the benefit of effective adjustment assistance.

## VII. Promoting Democracy

Brave men and women — like the hero who stood in front of a tank in Beijing and the leader who stood on a tank in Moscow — are putting their lives on the line for democracy around the world. But as the tide of democracy rose in the former Soviet Union and in China, in the Baltics and South Africa, only reluctantly did this administration abandon the status quo and embrace the fight for freedom.

Support for democracy serves our ideals *and* our interests. A more democratic world is a world that is more peaceful and more stable. An American foreign policy of engagement for democracy must effectively address:

**Emerging democracies.** Helping to lead an international effort to assist the emerging — and still fragile — democracies in Eastern Europe and the former Soviet Union build democratic institutions in free market settings, demilitarize their societies and integrate their economies into the world trading system. Unlike the Bush administration, which waited too long to recognize the new democratic governments in the Baltic countries and the nations of the former Soviet Union, we must act decisively with our European allies to support freedom, diminish ethnic tensions, and oppose aggression in the former communist countries, such as Bosnia-Herzegovina, which are struggling to make the transition from communism to democracy. As change sweeps through the Balkans, the United States must be sensitive to the concerns of Greece regarding the use of the name Macedonia. And in the post-Cold War era, our foreign assistance programs in Africa, the Caribbean, Latin America and elsewhere should be targeted at helping democracies rather than tyrants.

**Democracy Corps.** Promoting democratic institutions by creating a Democracy Corps to send American volunteers to countries that seek legal, financial and political expertise to build democratic institutions, and support groups like the National Endowment for Democracy and Asia Foundation and others.

**China trade terms.** Conditioning of favorable trade terms for China on respect for human rights in China and Tibet, greater market access for U.S. goods, and responsible conduct on weapons proliferation.

**South Africa.** Maintenance of state and local sanctions against South Africa in support of an investment code of conduct, existing limits on deductibility of taxes paid to South Africa and diplomatic pressure until there is an irreversible, full and fair accommodation with the black majority to create a democratic government with full rights for all its citizens. We deplore the continuing violence, especially by Boipatong Township, and are concerned about the collapse of the negotiations. The U.S. government should consider reimposing federal sanctions. The Democratic Party supports the creation of a South African/American Enterprise Fund that will provide a new interim government with the use of public and private funds to help in the development of democracy in South Africa.

**Middle East peace.** Support for the peace process now under way in the Middle East, rooted in the tradition of the Camp David accords. Direct negotiations between Israel, her Arab neighbors and Palestinians, with no imposed solutions, are the only way to achieve enduring security for Israel and full peace for all parties in the region. The end of the Cold War does not alter America's deep interest in our longstanding special relationship with Israel, based on shared values, a mutual commitment to democracy and a strategic alliance that benefits both nations. The United States must act effectively as an honest broker in the peace process. It must not, as has been the case with this administration, encourage one side to believe that it will deliver unilateral concessions from the other. Jerusalem is the capital of the state of Israel and should remain an undivided city accessible to people of all faiths.

**Human rights.** Standing everywhere for the rights of individuals and respect for ethnic minorities against the repressive acts of governments — against torture, political imprisonment and all attacks on civilized standards of human freedom. This is a proud tradition of the Democratic Party, which has stood for freedom in South Africa and continues to resist oppression in Cuba. Our nation should once again promote the principle of sanctuary for politically oppressed people everywhere, be they Haitian refugees, Soviet Jews seeking U.S. help in their successful absorption into Israeli society or Vietnamese fleeing communism. Forcible return of anyone fleeing political repression is a betrayal of American values.

**Human needs.** Support for the struggle against poverty and disease in the developing world, including the heartbreaking famine in Africa. We must not replace the East-West conflict with one between North and South, a growing divide between the industrialized and developing world. Our development programs must be re-examined and restructured to assure that their benefits truly help those most in need to help themselves. At stake are the lives of millions of human beings who live in hunger, uprooted from their homes, too often without hope. The United States should work to establish a specific plan and timetable for the elimination of world hunger.

**Cyprus.** A renewed commitment to achieve a Cyprus settlement pursuant to the United Nations resolutions. This goal must now be restored to the diplomatic agenda of the United States.

**Northern Ireland.** In light of America's historic ties to the people of Great Britain and Ireland, and consistent with our country's commitment to peace, democracy and human rights around the world, a more active United States role in promoting peace and political dialogue, to bring an end to the violence and achieve a negotiated solution in Northern Ireland.

## VIII. Preserving the Global Environment

As the threat of nuclear holocaust recedes, the future of the Earth is challenged by gathering environmental crises. As governments around the world have sought the path to concerted action, the Bush administration — despite its alleged foreign policy expertise — has been more of an obstacle to progress than a leader for change, practicing

isolationism on an issue that affects us all. Democrats know we must act now to save the health of the Earth and the health of our children for generations to come.

**Addressing global warming.** The United States must become a leader, not an impediment, in the fight against global warming. We should join our European allies in agreeing to limit carbon dioxide emissions to 1990 levels by the year 2000.

**Ozone depletion.** The United States must be a world leader in finding replacements for CFCs [chlorofluorocarbons] and other ozone-depleting substances.

**Biodiversity.** We must work actively to protect the planet's biodiversity and preserve its forests. At the Rio Earth Summit, the Bush administration's failure to negotiate a biodiversity treaty it could sign was an abdication of international leadership.

**Developing nations.** We must fashion imaginative ways of engaging governments and business in the effort to encourage developing nations to preserve their environmental heritage.

**Population growth.** Explosive population growth must be controlled by working closely with other industrialized and developing nations and private organizations to fund greater family-planning efforts.

\* \* \*

As a nation and as a people, we have entered into a new era. The Republican president and his advisers are rooted in Cold War precepts and cannot think or act anew. Through almost a half century of sacrifice, constancy and strength, the American people advanced democracy's triumph in the Cold War. Only new leadership that restores our nation's greatness at home can successfully draw upon these same strengths of the American people to lead the world into a new era of peace and freedom.

In recent years we have seen brave people abroad face down tanks, defy coups and risk exodus by boat on the high seas for a chance at freedom and the kind of opportunities we call the American dream. It is time for Americans to fight against the decline of those same opportunities here at home.

Americans know that, in the end, we will all rise or fall together. To make our society one again, Democrats will restore America's founding values of family, community and common purpose.

We believe in the American people. We will challenge all Americans to give something back to their country. And they will be enriched in return, for when individuals assume responsibility, they acquire dignity. When people go to work, they rediscover a pride that was lost. When absent parents pay child support, they restore a connection they and their children need. When students work harder, they discover they can learn as well as any on Earth. When corporate managers put their workers and long-term success ahead of short-term gain, their companies do well and so do they. When the leaders we elect assume responsibility for America's problems, we will do what is right to move America forward together. ■

<u>DAY BY DAY</u>

# Time Tested Themes Mark GOP Convention

HOUSTON — The Democrats may have chosen to focus on the future and the youthful enthusiasm of their baby boomer ticket. But the Republicans who convened here did their best to persuade voters to remember the past and trust in experience.

From the rousing opening night performance of former President Ronald Reagan to the repeated calls to honor traditional family values, the Republican National Convention looked backward as much as it looked ahead.

There were frequent references to having defeated communism and having won the Persian Gulf War. Voters were asked to ignore the Democrats' attempt to remake themselves in a more moderate image and to remember instead what life was like under Jimmy Carter, the last Democratic president.

There was little moderation evident in the party platform adopted for George Bush's second term. The GOP adopted a hard-line approach opposing abortion rights and any attempt to increase taxes. On the social issues front, there were planks favoring school choice, school prayer and family values.

Bush was portrayed not so much in ideological terms but as a level-headed manager and warm family man. Reagan described him as a "steady hand on the tiller through the choppy waters of the '90s."

First Lady Barbara Bush, whose popularity dwarfed her husband's, never strayed far from his side. She boasted that the president's proudest accomplishment after a long career in public service was "that his children still come home."

There was no shortage of villains during convention week.

Bill Clinton, the Democratic presidential nominee, was described as a classic tax-and-spend liberal, a draft dodger, a neophyte on foreign affairs; in short, the "failed governor of a small state."

Congress was constantly ripped for everything from check-floating to tax-raising.

The Democratic National Convention was viewed as a sham for placing a moderate facade on a party still tied to the outmoded ideas of the 1960s and uncommitted to traditional family values. Republicans gleefully noted that Democratic congressional leaders were confined to bit parts during their own party's convention.

Finally, the delegates needed little prompting to vent their frustrations at the "liberal media" for praising Clinton, dwelling on dissension over the GOP's anti-abortion stance and overemphasizing the weak economy.

R. MICHAEL JENKINS

**Young supporters rallied behind the president and the vice president in a week meant to play up Bush's successes and redefine Quayle.**

The Republican convention's host city has been among those beset by economic woes, especially because of its ties to the depressed oil and gas industries. But after having banished the hometown Astros for nearly a month, organizers spiffed up the Astrodome in soft shades of red, white and blue. Outside the dome, 50-foot-tall banners bearing stars, stripes and the GOP's stylized elephant logo were raised.

This was a homecoming of sorts for Bush. A New Englander by birth who came to Texas to work in the oil business, he retains his residency at a Houston hotel.

Bush returned to Houston in need of a good bounce in the polls, which generally showed him trailing Clinton by close to 20 percentage points. As they had four years ago, political pundits suggested Bush had to make "the speech of his life." He needed to redefine Clinton, provide direction for his own second term and appeal to Reagan Democrats and disaffected Republicans who had flirted with supporting Texas businessman Ross Perot's independent campaign.

Party activists also sought a fresh start for Dan Quayle, widely perceived as being bumbling, gaffe-prone and ineffective. But many conservatives still viewed the vice president as a hero, and because Quayle survived attempts to dump him from the ticket during the weeks leading up to the convention, GOP strategists looked forward to remaking his image as a thoughtful, middle-class American fighting for family values.

Recognizing that a vacuum of leadership would exist after 16 years of nominating Reagan and Bush, a host of potential presidential candidates in 1996 looked forward to Houston as a place to make their mark.

By week's end, Jack F. Kemp, secretary of Housing and Urban Development, seemed to draw the widest support among the class of 1996. TV commentator and 1992 candidate Patrick J. Buchanan was the most combative and potentially divisive. And Massachusetts Gov. William F. Weld, a social and economic libertarian, became the most sought-after voice for the party's moderate wing.

Quayle seemed to solidify his standing as one of the party's most effective spokesmen on family issues, willing to poke fun at his foibles and eager to attack Democrats and the "media elite."

And Bush left Houston to reports that he had already narrowed the gap between himself and Clinton.

What follows is a detailed diary of the Republican National Convention. Texts of the major speeches begin on p. 73-A.

**MONDAY**

The first day of the convention set the tone for the week that followed: President Bush arrived in town vowing he was ready for a tough, hands-on fight with the Democrats. GOP officials blocked an abortion debate, and the conservative platform was easily approved. Patrick J. Buchanan delivered a slashing attack on Bill and Hillary Clinton. And former President Ronald Reagan gave his endorsement to Bush as the man who could carry on his legacy.

The formal opening of the convention came Monday morning, when Republican National Committee Chairman Rich Bond called the first session to order, but the real kickoff came several hours later when Bush rolled into Houston and declared that the campaign had finally begun.

In a speech delivered with gusto to a hand-picked rally, Bush told supporters to prepare "for the most stirring political comeback since Harry Truman gave 'em hell in 1948."

Bush sought to link Clinton to the Democratic Congress, which he blamed for the nation's problems — a refrain that would be played over and over throughout the week.

"They are the sultans of the status quo," Bush said of the Democratic majority in Congress. "I've held out my hand to those crazy guys only to have it bitten off. And I'm tired of it."

Lambasting Clinton as overconfident, Bush noted that Clinton had recently said he was planning his transition team. "I half expected, when I went over to the Oval Office, to find him over there measuring the drapes," Bush told the cheering, foot-stomping crowd. "I have a message for him. Put those drapes on hold; it is going to be curtain time for that ticket. And I mean it."

Vice President Quayle, in warmup remarks for the president, denounced Clinton as a "slick" politician who lacks the character to lead the nation through difficult times.

### On the Podium

The Bush-Quayle rally came between two official convention sessions — each four hours long and featuring a parade of speakers promoting Bush and denouncing Clinton.

The highlight of the morning session was a speech by Bond warning against putting the Democrats in power at both ends of Pennsylvania Avenue.

"To give the rubber-check Democrats in Congress Bill Clinton as a rubber-stamp president is a journey to disaster," he said. "We all remember

LISA QUINONES
Former President Reagan, above, gave Bush his endorsement after Buchanan, below, had whipped the crowd into a frenzy.

REUTERS

what happened last time we had a Democrat Congress and a Democrat president — double-digit everything from unemployment to inflation. This election is not a choice between left or right, but a choice between up or down."

Bond's spirited address stood out among dozens of morning speeches that dragged on and left delegates in the hall restless and inattentive.

The main order of business at the morning session was adoption of the platform, but it had already become clear that efforts to force a debate on abortion had fallen short. A majority in six delegations was required to challenge the platform's call for a constitutional ban on all abortions, but abortion rights supporters said they could muster majorities in only four delegations — Maine, Massachusetts, New Mexico and the Virgin Islands. The reason, they said, was that delegates felt it was more important to avoid embarrassing Bush than to force an open debate.

In the end the platform was approved by voice vote. There were cries of "no!" when the document was put to delegates, but no public challenge.

Between sessions, many delegates could be found in the nearby Astroarena, where patriotic exhibits adorned the walls and concessionaires sold their wares. Delegates could buy anything from Southwestern-style clothing to crystal elephants to canned armadillo meat; from buttons saying "Viva Bush" to those that said "Adulterers for Clinton."

### Reagan's Night

The convention was called back into order in the evening for a session dominated by the party's conservative wing and tributes to former President Reagan.

Buchanan began with a tribute to Reagan as the man who defeated communism and brought freedom to Eastern Europe. "Ronald Reagan made us proud to be Americans again," he said. "We never felt better about our country; and we never stood taller in the eyes of the world."

Buchanan next apppealed to his supporters to throw their support to Bush. He acknowledged the disagreements with Bush that led him to challenge the president but said the convention marked the time to unite.

"The right place for us to be now in this presidential campaign is right beside George Bush," Buchanan said.

Buchanan had whipped the crowd into a frenzy with a bitter, scathing attack on Clinton, attacking his patriotism and charging that his view of change for America would mean abortion on demand, a litmus test for the Supreme Court, homosexual rights, women in combat and discrimination against religious schools. "That's

change, all right," said Buchanan, but "it's not the kind of change we can abide in a nation that we still call God's country."

Buchanan noted that Bush had been the "youngest fighter pilot in the Pacific" during World War II and then added: "When Bill Clinton's turn came in Vietnam, he sat up in a dormitory in Oxford, England, and figured out how to dodge the draft."

Buchanan also attacked Hillary Clinton. "Hillary has compared marriage and the family as institutions to slavery and life on an Indian reservation. Well, speak for yourself, Hillary."

Buchanan's remarks were enthusiastically received in the hall, but the biggest response came for President Reagan, who described his speech as the "last chapter" in his political career. At 81, the grand patriarch of the Republican Party showed all the oratorical skills and political spirit that had made him the hero of GOP conservatives.

Reagan began with an eloquent defense of his eight-year stewardship, claiming credit for ending the Cold War and warning of dire consequences if America turned away from his legacy. He interspersed his speech with pointed jabs at the Democrats and included a strong endorsement of Bush.

"We stood tall and proclaimed that communism was destined for the ash heap of history," he said. "We never heard so much ridicule from our liberal friends. But we knew then what the liberal Democrat leaders just couldn't figure out: The sky would not fall if America restored her strength and resolve. The sky would not fall if an American president spoke the truth. The only thing that would fall was the Berlin Wall."

Reagan told the crowd that this year's campaign was extremely important and that Bush, though not a showman, was a level-headed leader who would offer a "steady hand on the tiller through the choppy waters of the '90s" and who deserved to be re-elected. He said he "warmly, genuinely, wholeheartedly" backed Bush — and Quayle.

Reagan's speech was filled with the political optimism and faith in the dream that characterized his presidency.

"The United States is unique because we are an empire of ... democracy, of free men and free markets, and of the extraordinary possibilities that lie within seemingly ordinary men and women," he said. "America's best days are yet to come."

★★★

**TUESDAY**

It was perhaps fitting that the permanent convention chairman, House Minority Leader Robert H. Michel of Illinois, played the role of master of ceremonies on Tuesday because the day was devoted to bashing the Democratic-controlled Congress, which Republicans blamed for blocked initiatives, thwarted ambition and frustration.

"We are here to tell the American people that this election is just as much about the Congress as it is about the presidency," Michel said. "The Democrats have controlled the House of Representatives now for 38 straight years, and that has to change."

He set the night's blistering tone by stating that Democrats "alone ... are responsible for the unholy mess Congress is in."

Congressional Democrats were used as a foil to highlight the president's domestic agenda and the change he has sought to implement. "The Constitution makes the president commander in chief of the Army but not commander in chief of the Congress," said keynote speaker Sen. Phil Gramm of Texas. "The Democrats who control Congress by overwhelming margins have used their majority to throttle the president's program and to strangle the nation's economy in a partisan gridlock the likes of which we have not seen before in this century."

With the big-name speakers scheduled for the evening, many delegates bypassed the morning session. Those who did attend saw many female and minority speakers.

Reps. Barbara F. Vucanovich of Nevada and Nancy L. Johnson of Connecticut joined Jose M. Casanova, chairman of the Republican National Hispanic Assembly, and Fred Brown, chairman of the National Black Republican Council. Jewish Republicans and Asian-Americans also were represented as were Republicans abroad.

But the speech that got the most attention came from a white man: California Attorney General Dan Lungren, who revived the specter of Willie Horton, the Massachusetts murderer prominently featured in Bush campaign ads used against Michael S. Dukakis in 1988.

Referring to the furlough of Horton as a symbol of Democratic leniency, Lungren called Horton "a liberal icon," whom Democrats trot out to "invite the press to worship at the altar of righteous indignation."

Saying that Democrat Bill Clinton, in his nominating speech, "didn't utter a single word about victims of crime," Lungren delivered a tough message of law and order that stressed that "Republicans refuse to confuse the victim with the victimizer."

Passions stirring outside the Astrodome countered the relative quiet of the proceedings inside. About 100 Republican teenagers besieged a Democratic news conference about 10 blocks from the hall, where party Chairman Ron Brown was showing off new Clinton campaign TV ads to reporters. Chanting "Libs go home," "We love George," and, in reference to the president's dog and Clinton's wife, "Millie not Hillie,"

Republicans blasted the Democrats' control of the House, calling them "responsible for the unholy mess."

R. MICHAEL JENKINS

the youths pounded on the walls and windows of the restaurant where the news conference took place. Republican National Committee Chairman Bond apologized the next day.

Tuesday afternoon was devoted to delegation meetings and rallies, including some that Bush and Quayle attended.

Bush also made news in an interview with the "MacNeil/Lehrer NewsHour" when he talked of shaking up his administration.

"You'll see plenty of new faces, plenty of changes in this administration," he said.

### 1992 and Beyond

The evening session again focused on change and was filled with attacks on Congress. But it was a night that spoke to 1996 as much as it did to 1992: Several Republican figures with an eye on the presidency addressed the party faithful.

Expectations were high for two presumed presidential contenders — Gramm and Housing and Urban Development Secretary Jack F. Kemp. Gramm, in particular, kept a high profile in the days preceding the convention; tickets to his "Red, White and Boots" reception Monday night were among the most coveted invitations of the week.

While awaiting Gramm and Kemp, delegates heard from three governors whose successes at home have thrust them into the national spotlight and fueled speculation about a future spot on the national ticket.

Govs. Tommy G. Thompson of Wisconsin and John Engler of Michigan delivered unemotional speeches, but Gov. William F. Weld of Massachusetts highlighted divisions between moderates and conservatives on abortion and homosexual rights when he told delegates, "I happen to think that individual freedom should extend to a woman's right to choose. I want the government out of your pocketbook and your bedroom." Crowd reaction was a mixed bag of boos and cheers.

The crowd began to warm when House Minority Whip Newt Gingrich of Georgia took up the night's refrain: "We need change in Washington. The question is which end of Pennsylvania Avenue needs to change."

For the unsure, Gingrich told them, "Give President Bush a Republican Congress to work with, and we will do more to fundamentally reform government in the first 90 days than the Democrats have done in 38 years."

### Kemp Leads the Charge

Kemp got an enthusiastic response when he credited

"The Democrats ... have used their majority to throttle the president's program."

—Sen. Phil Gramm

"It was ... our Republican presidents, Ronald Reagan and George Bush, that helped change the world."

—Jack F. Kemp, above

PHOTOS BY R. MICHAEL JENKINS

"We need change.... The question is which end of Pennsylvania Avenue needs to change."

—Rep. Newt Gingrich

Reagan and Bush for their roles in the demise of communism. "Ladies and gentleman," he told the assembled, "communism didn't fall. It was pushed. It was our ideas that did the pushing and our Republican presidents, Ronald Reagan and George Bush, that helped change the world." The most rousing ovation of the night came when Kemp added, "I loved hearing Ronald Reagan last night."

From changing the world, Kemp switched his focus to changing America. He advocated lower taxes, the creation of enterprise zones and home ownership, ideas he has long championed.

Kemp blamed the country's economic problems on Congress' refusal to enact Bush's appeals for investment tax credits, capital gains cuts, enterprise zones, a new tax credit for first-time home buyers and an increased credit for children.

Kemp concluded his speech by staring directly into the camera bank in front of the podium and exhorting the president to "give 'em hell Thursday night."

### Keynote Falls Flat

For the most part, Gramm used the keynote to bash both Congress and Clinton. Likening him to a used car salesman, Gramm said Clinton "is peddling a model from the '70s — a Carter-mobile with the axle broken and the frame bent to the left. It was a lemon for the nation in the '70s when it sent inflation through the roof and income through the floor, and it is a lemon today."

Hoping to link the Democrat to his failed predecessors on the national ticket, Gramm charged that "the Clinton plan calls for a new domestic spending spree totaling over $100 billion a year — the largest increase in American history."

He asked the crowd, "Is that the change we want?" And the answer was a resounding no, the same as it was the five other times he inquired.

Gramm also attributed change in the world order to Bush. After crediting Reagan and Bush as catalysts for change from Eastern Europe to the Middle East, the Texas senator went one step further. "It was Ronald Reagan who put the Kremlin in the cross hairs," he said, "but it was George Bush who pulled the trigger."

While Kemp received a warm reception for his efforts, Gramm's was tepid. He shared his brand of folksy humor with the crowd at the outset, when he joked about "trying to do the Lord's work in the devil's city," but he had trouble connecting with the crowd.

**W E D N E S D A Y**

Wednesday was family night at the Astrodome. The delegates heard from the candidates' wives, Barbara Bush and Marilyn Quayle, and speakers throughout the evening discussed "family values." The evening's high point came when the entire Bush clan gathered at the podium, and the president made a cameo appearance.

The Bush family's arrival was choreographed to occur in the heart of television's prime time. Later, the presidential nomination roll call seemed almost an afterthought, stretching well beyond midnight Eastern time. By then, the large network booths had emptied and were being cleaned by janitorial crews.

Outside the Astrodome, the weather, which had been remarkably comfortable as the convention began, had grown muggy. That did little to dampen the spirits at a hotel parking lot, where North Carolina and Texas partisans fought to a draw in a friendly barbecue showdown.

Throughout the day, media attention focused ever more tightly on the stakes involved in Bush's Thursday night acceptance speech and whether he had already begun planning to overhaul his Cabinet if he won. Bush, appearing at a fundraiser luncheon, predicted that the election would come down to trust. "And the American people are going to say, I trust George Bush because he's made the tough decisions and he's conducted himself with honor and decency in that office."

## Homage and Attack

Mixed among the evening's tributes to families were strong attacks on Clinton, especially for having sidestepped service in the Vietnam War and for suggesting deep defense cuts. "When you come to think of it," said television evangelist Pat Robertson, " 'Slick Willie' talks like John Wayne but acts like Gomer Pyle."

Robertson sought to portray Clinton as an enemy of the family. "When Bill Clinton talks about family values ... he is not talking about either families or values. He is talking about a radical plan to destroy the traditional family and transfer its functions to the federal government."

Many delegates were milling about during speeches by Robertson and others; they did not settle in until the address by Mary Fisher, who has tested HIV-positive. The crowd hushed as Fisher, 44, the daughter of a Detroit multimillionaire and longtime GOP fundraiser, spoke about the AIDS virus, which she had contracted from her ex-husband.

**In a day devoted to family issues, First lady Barbara Bush, right, adopted a gentle tone when talking about her husband, children and grandchildren. Earlier, delegates gave rapt attention to Mary Fisher, below, who has tested HIV-positive and spoke about the AIDS virus.**

LISA QUINONES

"I ask you ... to recognize that the AIDS virus is not a political creature," Fisher said, as she implored the delegates to show people with AIDS the same sort of compassion that she said the president and Mrs. Bush had shown toward her. "But we do the president's cause no good if we praise the American family but ignore a virus that destroys it," she said. "There is no family or community, no race or religion, no place left in America that is safe. Until we genuinely embrace this message, we are a nation at risk."

The mood turned more combative again during Marilyn Quayle's speech. She said that she and her husband, like the Democratic standard-bearers, were members of the baby boom generation, but "not everyone demonstrated, dropped out, took drugs, joined in the sexual revolution or dodged the draft."

Her speech was a call for traditional values, which she said were still compatible with women furthering their careers: "Nothing offends me more than attempts to paint Republicans as looking to turn the clock back for women. ... Political liberals hold no monopoly on respect-

REUTERS

ing women's abilities."

Barbara Bush adopted a gentler theme. She began by praising her husband as "the strongest, the most decent, the most caring, the wisest, yes, and the healthiest man I know." She described him at some length as being enraptured with his own family, saying how pleased she was that he believed his greatest accomplishment was "that his children still come home."

After 22 of the Bush's children and grandchildren were ushered onto the podium to loud applause, the president himself suddenly emerged on the stage. He was hugged by

a granddaughter and kissed by his wife as the crowd erupted with a roar and chants of "Four more years."

### Making It Official

The nominating speeches began with Labor Secretary Lynn Martin calling Democrats "whimpering naysayers" who peddle "the crass politics of fear and the false promise of change," while describing their congressmen as "aging punjabs."

She rhetorically asked a variation of the question Reagan repeated as he sought re-election in 1984: "Is America better off today than she was four years ago?"

In response, rather than dwell on the soft economy, Martin spoke of victory in the Persian Gulf War, the end of communism and Bush's commitment to make improvements on the domestic front. "Inside George Bush — inside that man is the heart of an 18-year-old fighter pilot who risked his life for this country, who did not run from responsibility then and will not now," she said. "You can't be one kind of man and another kind of president."

After a series of seconding speeches, the delegates delayed a roll call vote until Quayle's name also could be placed in nomination.

William J. Bennett, the former drug czar and one-time Education secretary, nominated the vice president. But Bennett spent considerably less time talking about Quayle than discussing his own views on how the two parties differ on family values.

LISA QUINONES

"Political liberals hold no monopoly on respecting women's abilities."

—Marilyn Quayle

He said Republicans do not believe that public schools ought to distribute condoms to students or that government should subsidize pornography and obscenity. He said fatherhood means more than getting a woman pregnant; it also entails love and sacrifice and shared responsibility.

Speaking of alternative lifestyles, Bennett said people can generally live as they wish, "and yet, we believe that some ways of living are better than others." He said the GOP was not seeking to use "traditional family values" as a wedge issue for voters, but to "honor and to affirm what is best in us." Democrats may have now made it "politically correct" to speak in favor of family values and personal morality, Bennett concluded, but "what is not so politically correct is to be precise about what you mean," as Quayle has done.

When the roll call for the presidential nomination finally began, the state presentations were, as usual, occasionally colorful and almost always long-winded — even when the state delegation's spokesman concluded by passing. The roll call was arranged so that Texas, the convention's host state and technically Bush's home, put him over the top. The final tally was 2,166 votes for Bush, 18 for Buchanan and three for others, before the nomination was approved by acclamation. New Hampshire never cast its 23 votes.

By then, the Astrodome had largely emptied. The many red, white and blue balloons that hung from the ceiling remained there, for another day.

★ ★ ★

<table>
<tr><td rowspan="8">T H U R S D A Y</td></tr>
</table>

For all the hoopla, receptions, rhetoric and spin control, the first three days of convention week were little more than prelude for the critical closing night when Bush and Quayle would make their acceptance speeches and the convention would be pronounced a success or failure.

The buildup for both addresses had been intense. Quayle's was seen as his big chance to redefine his political persona. Bush had an even greater task — to give "the speech of his life."

Neither quite lived up to the advance billing, but both delivered effective addresses that lifted the voices and spirits of the convention hall, and when both left town Friday morning, they could point to significantly better opinion polls as a sign of success.

After a stirring introduction by Senate Minority Leader Bob Dole of Kansas, Bush came out fighting against the Democratic-controlled Congress and Democratic nominee Bill Clinton.

The president offered no detailed vision for a second term but said he would propose an unspecified across-the-board tax reduction, provided Congress would also cut spending in a manner he found acceptable.

He also proposed allowing taxpayers to set aside 10 percent of their taxes to reduce the deficit, but did not specify the spending cuts he would propose to make up the revenue.

Responding to the concerns of delegates still angry over

his broken "no new taxes" pledge, Bush admitted that it had been a mistake but posed a question to the electorate. "Who do you trust in this election — the candidate who has raised taxes one time and regrets it, or the other candidate who raised taxes and fees 128 times and enjoyed it every time?"

Trust was again the issue as Bush highlighted his role

R. MICHAEL JENKINS

**Dole warmed up the crowd for the president on Aug. 20.**

as commander in chief in what is widely considered to be his strength — foreign policy. He spoke of Cold War triumph yet warned that "the Soviet bear may be gone, but there are still wolves in the woods."

These existing threats allowed Bush to tout his stewardship in the Persian Gulf War and raise questions about what his opponent would have done.

"What about the leader of the Arkansas National Guard," he mocked, "the man who hopes to be commander in chief? Well, while I bit the bullet . . . he bit his nails."

## Lawyers, Media Take Hits

Drawing on the frustration expressed by party leaders and a majority of delegates about media coverage, Bush told the audience, "You don't hear much about this good news, because the media also tends to focus only on the bad. And when the Berlin Wall fell, I half expected to see a headline: 'Wall Falls, Three Border Guards Lose Jobs.' And underneath it probably says: 'Clinton Blames Bush.' "

Bush scrutinized another institution with few defenders — the legal profession. "I am fighting to reform our legal system," he said, "to put an end to crazy lawsuits. And if that means climbing into the ring with the trial lawyers, well, let me just say, Round 1 starts tonight.

"After all — after all, my opponent's campaign is being backed by practically every trial lawyer who ever wore a tasseled loafer. He's not in the ring with them, he's in the tank."

Still, the main event was Congress- and Clinton-bashing.

In presenting his domestic agenda of open markets for American products, lower government spending, tax relief, small business opportunity, legal and health-care reform, job training, and education reform, he blamed "the gridlock Democratic Congress" for failing to enact them.

He called Congress "the master of inaction" but said "it wasn't always this way." Decrying the partisanship that has marked his relationship with the institution, he said, "I extended my hand to the congressional leaders, Democratic leaders, and they bit it."

## Defiant Quayle

In an assertive and well-received acceptance speech, Quayle defiantly answered his legion of detractors.

The vice president launched an all-out assault: "I know my critics wish I were not standing here tonight. They don't like our values. They look down on our beliefs. They're afraid of our ideas. And they know the American people stand on our side.

And that's — that's why when someone confronts them and challenges them, they will stop at nothing to destroy him, and I say to them: You have failed. I stand — I stand before you, and before the American people — unbowed, unbroken and ready to keep fighting for our beliefs."

Quayle's entrance was preceded by a short biographical video, similar to the one that introduced Clinton to the Democratic convention. The video interspersed interviews with family members, including Quayle's wife, Marilyn, and his mother.

The substance of Quayle's speech touched on the cultural themes he has employed to elevate his status and energize the party's conservative wing.

In discussing his concern for the undermining of family values, he said, "Americans try to raise their children to understand right and wrong, only to be told that every so-called 'lifestyle alternative' is morally equivalent. That is wrong."

Quayle also warned of the dangers of too many lawyers and frivolous lawsuits: "The litigation explosion has damaged our competitiveness; it has wiped out jobs; it has forced doctors to quit practicing in places where they are needed most. Every American knows this legal system is broken, and now is the time to fix it."

R. MICHAEL JENKINS

R. MICHAEL JENKINS

**As the confetti rained down, President and Mrs. Bush, above, basked in the success of the convention. Earlier, Vice President Dan Quayle, left, had shown pugnacious qualities in his acceptance speech.**

Quayle also used the occasion for some self-deprecating humor.

"For more than a month, the media have been telling us that Bill Clinton and Al Gore are 'moderates,' " he said. "If they're moderates, I'm a world champion speller."

As the evening drew to a close and Bush concluded his acceptance speech, colored confetti and red, white and blue balloons rained down on cheering delegates. Fireworks spewed from the faux sandstone pillars on the stage and huge balloons exploded over the media stand.

As Dan and Marilyn Quayle joined Bush and his wife, Barbara, on stage, a patriotic medley roused the crowd to a still-higher pitch.

It was a marked departure from the conclusion of the Democratic convention, which ended with a crowded assemblage on the podium, scored with a song by a contemporary rock group. ∎

## REPUBLICAN NATIONAL CONVENTION

# Quayle Accepts Nomination, Lauds His Running Mate

*Dan Quayle on Aug. 20 addressed the Republican National Convention to accept the nomination for vice president. Following is the Reuter transcript of his remarks.*

**QUAYLE:** Mr. Chairman, delegates to this convention and friends around America.

With gratitude and a sense of mission, once again I accept your nomination as vice president of the United States.

Tonight — tonight I am stronger, more confident and more determined than ever to re-elect our great president, George Bush.

I know my critics wish I were not standing here tonight. They don't like our values. They look down on our beliefs. They're afraid of our ideas. And they know the American people stand on our side. And that's — that's why, when someone confronts them and challenges them, they will stop at nothing to destroy him. And I say to them, I say: You have failed.

I stand — I stand before you, and before the American people — unbowed, unbroken and ready to keep fighting for our beliefs.

I come from Huntington, a small farming community in Indiana. I had an upbringing like many in my generation — a life built around family, public school, Little League, basketball and church on Sunday. My brother and I shared a room in our two-bedroom house. We walked to school together. This was life in small-town America. Our people were strong, and we believed in the traditional values of middle America.

Marilyn and I have tried to teach our children these values, like faith in God, love of family and appreciation of freedom.

We have also taught them about family issues like adoption. My parents adopted twins when I was 10 years old. We have taught our children to respect single parents and their challenges — challenges that faced my grandmother many years ago and my own sister today.

And we have taught our children about the tragedy of diseases like breast cancer, which took the life of Marilyn's mother. Marilyn and I have hosted an annual event called the Race for the Cure of Breast Cancer. Two months ago, 20,000 runners, men and women, young and old, joined in our nation's capital to race for the cure. By leading the battle against breast cancer, in memory of her mother, Marilyn has taken a family tragedy and turned it into hope for others.

Like so many Americans, for me, family comes first. When family values are undermined, our country suffers. All too often

parents struggle to instill character in their sons and daughters, only to see their values belittled and their beliefs mocked by those who look down on America. Americans try to raise their children to understand right and wrong, only to be told that every so-called "lifestyle alternative" is morally equivalent. That is wrong.

The gap — the gap between us and our opponents is a cultural divide. It is not just a difference between conservative and liberal; it is a difference between fighting for what's right and refusing to see what's wrong.

Families can also be strengthened by empowering our people — with low taxes, home ownership, parental choice in education, job training, safe streets, a clean environment and affordable health care. In all of these areas, we have a reform agenda, and it is time for Congress to get out of the way and pass the president's plan.

Speaking of reform: Our legal system — speaking of reform, our legal system is spinning out of control. The explosion of frivolous lawsuits burdens our economy and weakens our system of justice. America has 5 percent of the world's population and 70 percent of the world's lawyers.

I have nothing against lawyers — at least most of them. I'm a lawyer; I'm married to a lawyer. When we worked our way through night law school, Marilyn and I looked forward with pride to becoming part of the finest legal system in the world.

But today our country has a problem: Our legal system is costing consumers $300 billion a year. The litigation explosion has damaged our competitiveness; it has wiped out jobs; it has forced doctors to quit practicing in places where they are needed most. Every American knows this legal system is broken, and now is the time to fix it.

The President's Council on Competitiveness, which I chair, will continue to lead the charge against unnecessary federal regulation. We've worked to save jobs and to save lives. We've reformed the drug-approval process to speed up the availability of new medicines for people with life-threatening diseases like cystic fibrosis, cancer and AIDS.

And what is the response of the Democrats in Congress? They have tried to kill the Council on Competitiveness, which stands up for the American people and against the bureaucrats and the special interests. They think the Competitiveness Council should go. They don't get it. It is time for them to go.

You know, if the Democrats in Congress can't run their own restaurant, can't run their own post office and can't run their own bank, they sure can't be trusted

to run our country.

I hope everybody who watched the Democratic Convention noticed how they hid their congressional leaders. You couldn't find them anywhere. Maybe it was a slick idea to keep those Democratic congressmen and senators under wraps. But on Election Day, but on Election Day, they're going to learn a hard lesson: You can run from a TV camera; you can even run from your own delegates; but you can't hide from the voters of America.

So again — so again, there is only one thing to say about the spend-everything, block-everything, know-nothing Democratic Congress: It is time for them to go.

And it's — and it's time — and it's time to change Congress for good. Almost 16 years ago, in my first speech as a member of the House of Representatives, I proposed limiting the terms of Congress. The Democratic Congress — the Democratic Congress tells us that it is good for the country to limit Ronald Reagan and George Bush to two terms as president. I say to them, if it is good for the country to limit Ronald Reagan and George Bush to two terms, then it would be great for the country to limit the terms of senators like [Majority Leader] George [J.] Mitchell and Ted [Edward M.] Kennedy, and the rest of that liberal Democratic Congress down there in Washington.

None of the reforms — none of the reforms I've just mentioned has any support from Bill Clinton. Bill Clinton talks about change, but he can't really change America because the special interests won't let him. He can't say a word — not one single word — about legal reform because the trial lawyers won't let him. He can't support — he can't support — he can't support school choice for parents because the education lobby in Washington won't let him. He will not join the majority of Americans in supporting term limits because the Democratic Congress won't let him. And he can't fight for the traditional family because his supporters in Hollywood and the media elite won't let him.

My friends: Bill Clinton and the special interests will never run America because we won't let them.

For more — speaking of the media, for more than a month, the media have been telling us that Bill Clinton and Al Gore are "moderates."

If they're moderates, I'm a world champion speller.

We are the true voice for change, and we do not take our marching orders from the special interests. On behalf of legal reform and education reform, we've taken on the strongest forces of the status quo, and we will not back down. On behalf of deregulation and term limits, we've taken on the Democratic Congress, and we will not back down. And on behalf of family values, we've taken on Hollywood and the media elite, and we will not back down.

It's been said — it's been said, and it is true, that a leader gives his people character. And once again, America is going to

choose a leader who had judgment, experience and moral strength. Four years ago, none of us knew that the Berlin Wall would fall, the Iron Curtain would be lifted, the Baltic nations would be free, communism would be dead and buried, the Soviet Union would cease to exist and the threatening SS-18 ballistic missiles would be history. Nor did we know that we would be called upon to confront the aggression of a Middle East tyrant.

But four years ago we did know this: Whatever lay ahead, there was a clear choice to lead us. There was one man we could trust to guide our journey to a new century. And because we elected George Bush as our president, America is stronger, and the world is safer.

My friends — now, listen, listen, listen to this, listen to this, in an attempt, in an attempt to establish credibility in foreign policy, Gov. Clinton recently compared himself to former [Calif.] Gov. Ronald Reagan.

I know Ronald Reagan. Ronald Reagan is a friend of mine. And, Bill Clinton, you're no Ronald Reagan.

The Democratic — the Democratic — the Democratic nominee calls America "the mockery of the world," but he and his running mate are the only ones who believe that. To Gov. Clinton, I say this: America is the greatest nation in the world, and that's one thing you're not going to change.

These last four years, I have worked with a man who represents so much of what is good in our country, a man whose public and personal life are the embodiment of character. Every day in that Oval Office, I see the dedication of a husband, father and grandfather; the self-reliance of an entrepreneur; the courage of a Navy pilot; the dependability of a loyal friend; the compassion of a man of faith; and the wisdom of the man who married Barbara Bush.

George Bush has given us great victories abroad and performed great deeds at home. But, as Theodore Roosevelt said, the greatest victories are yet to be won, and the greatest deeds are yet to be done.

We will go on fighting for the values, the hopes and the dreams of our people. We will take this campaign to every American and to every state. We will win because of our principles; we will win because of our beliefs; and we will build an America more secure in the values of faith, family and freedom.

In these difficult times, America needs the very best: the best in character, the best in leadership and the best in judgment. And the very best is our nominee, our president, George Bush. Thank you very much. God bless you, and God bless America. ∎

## REPUBLICAN NATIONAL CONVENTION

# Bush Takes Off the Gloves, Comes Out Fighting

*On Aug. 20, President Bush accepted the Republican presidential nomination. Following is the Reuter text of his remarks.*

**BUSH:** Thank you very, very much. Thank you, so much. Thank you all very, very much. Let's go to work. Thank you. Thank you so much. Thank you all very much. Thank you. Thank you very much.

And I am proud to receive, and I am honored to accept your nomination for president of the United States.

May I thank my dear friend and our great leader [Senate Minority Leader] Bob Dole for that wonderful introduction. Let me say this: This nomination is not for me alone. It is for the ideas, principles and values that we stand for.

And my job — my job has been made easier by a leader who has taken a lot of unfair criticism, with grace and humor — Vice President Dan Quayle.

I want to talk tonight about the sharp choice that I intend to offer Americans this fall, a choice between different agendas, different directions and, yes, a choice about the character of the man you want to lead this nation.

I know that Americans have many questions — about our economy, about our country's future, even questions about me. And I'll answer them tonight.

And first, I feel great.

And I am heartened by the polls, the ones that say I look better in my jogging shorts than the governor of Arkansas.

Four years ago — four years ago, I spoke about missions — for my life and for our country. I spoke of one urgent mission — defending our security and promoting the American ideal abroad.

Just pause for a moment to reflect on what we've done.

Germany has united, and a slab of the Berlin Wall sits right outside this Astrodome.

Arabs and Israelis now sit face to face and talk peace.

And every hostage held in Lebanon is free.

The conflict — the conflict in El Salvador is over, and free elections brought democracy to Nicaragua.

Black and white South Africans cheered each other at the Olympics. The Soviet Union can only be found in history books. The captive nations of Eastern Europe and the Baltics are captive no more. And today on — today, on the rural streets of Poland, merchants sell cans of air labeled "the last breath of communism."

If I had stood before you four years ago and described this as the world we would help to build, you would have said, George Bush, you must have been smoking something, and you must have inhaled.

This convention is the first at which an American president can say: The Cold War is over, and freedom finished first.

Now, some — some — we have a lot to be proud of. A lot. Some want to rewrite history, want to skip over the struggle, claim the outcome was inevitable. And while the U.S. postwar strategy was largely bipartisan, the fact remains that the liberal, McGovern wing of the other party — including my opponent — consistently made the wrong choices.

In the '70s, they wanted a hollow Army; we wanted a strong fighting force.

In the '80s — and you remember this one — in the '80s, they wanted a nuclear freeze; we insisted on peace through strength.

And from — from Angola — from Angola to Central America, they said, let's negotiate, deliberate, procrastinate. And we said, just stand up for freedom.

And now — now the Cold War is over and they claim, hey, we were with you all the way.

No. Their — their behavior — really, their behavior reminds me of the old con man's advice to the new kid. He said, "Son, if you're being run out of town, just get out in front and make it look like a parade."

Make no mistake — make no mistake — the demise of communism wasn't a sure thing. It took the strong leadership of presidents from both parties, including Republicans like Richard [M.] Nixon, Gerald [R.] Ford and Ronald Reagan.

And — and without their vision and the support of the American people, the Soviet Union would be a strong superpower today, and we'd be facing a nuclear threat tonight.

My opponents say I spend too much time on foreign policy. As if it didn't matter that schoolchildren once hid under their desks in drills to prepare for nuclear war. I saw the chance to rid our children's dreams of the nuclear nightmare, and I did.

Over the past four years, more people have breathed the fresh air of freedom than in all of human history. I saw a chance to help, and I did. And these — these were the two defining opportunities — not of a year, not of a decade, but of an entire span of human history.

I seized those opportunities for our kids and our grandkids, and I make no apologies for that.

Now — now — now, the Soviet bear may be gone, but there are still wolves in the woods.

We saw that when [Iraqi leader]

Saddam Hussein invaded Kuwait. The Mideast might have become a nuclear powder keg — our energy supplies held hostage. So we did what was right, and what was necessary. We destroyed a threat, freed a people and locked a tyrant in the prison of his own country.

Well, well, what about the leader of the Arkansas National Guard — the man who hopes to be commander in chief? Well, while I bit the bullet, and he bit his nails, and two days — two days — two days — listen to this, now, two days after Congress voted to follow my lead, my opponent said this, and I quote directly: "I guess I would have voted with the majority if it was a close vote. But I agree with the arguments the minority made."

Now, that sounds to me like his policy can be summed up by a road sign he's probably seen on his bus tour: slippery when wet.

Look — look, this is serious business. Think about the impact of our foreign policy failures the last time the Democrats controlled both ends of Pennsylvania Avenue. Gas lines. Grain embargoes. American hostages blindfolded.

There will be more foreign policy challenges like Kuwait in the next four years. Terrorists and aggressors to stand up to; dangerous weapons to be controlled and destroyed. And freedom's fight is not finished. And I look forward to being the first president to visit a free, democratic Cuba.

Who will lead the world — who will lead the world in the face of these challenges? Not my opponent. In his acceptance speech he devoted just 65 seconds to telling us about the world.

And then he said that America was, and I quote again — I want to be fair and factual — I quote, being "ridiculed" everywhere. Well, tell that to the people around the world, for whom America is still a dream. Tell that to leaders around the world, from whom America commands respect.

Ridiculed? Ridiculed? Tell that to the men and women of Desert Storm.

Let me make — let me just make an aside comment here because of what you've been reading in the paper. This is a political year, but there's a lot of danger in the world, and you can be sure I will never let politics interfere with a foreign policy decision. Forget the election — I will do what is right for the national security of the United States of America. And that is a pledge from my heart.

Fifty years ago — 50 years ago this summer, I was 18 years of age — I see some young people in the audience tonight, and I remember how I felt in those days.

I believed deeply in this country, and we were faced with a world war. And so I made a decision to go off and fight a battle much different from political battles.

And I was scared, but I was willing. I was young, but I was ready. I had barely lived when I began to watch men die. I began to see the special place of America in the world, and I began to see, even then,

that the world would become a much smaller place, and faraway places could become more and more like America.

And 50 years later, after change of almost biblical proportions, we know that when freedom grows, America grows. And just as a strong America means a safer world, we have learned that a safer world means a stronger America.

This election is about change. But that's not unusual, because the American revolution is never-ending. Today, the pace of change is accelerating. We face new opportunities and new challenges. And the question is, who do you trust to make change work for you?

My opponent — my opponent —

My opponent says America is a nation in decline. Of our economy, he says, we are somewhere on the list beneath Germany, heading south toward Sri Lanka.

Well, don't let anyone tell you that America is second-rate, especially somebody running for president.

Maybe he hasn't heard — maybe he hasn't heard that we are still the world's largest economy. No other nation sells more outside its borders. The Germans, the British, the Japanese can't touch the productivity of you — the American worker and the American farmer.

My opponent — my opponent won't mention that. He won't remind you that interest rates are the lowest they've been in 20 years, and millions of Americans have refinanced their homes.

And you just won't hear that inflation — the thief of the middle class — has been locked in a maximum-security prison.

And you don't hear much about this good news, because the media also tends to focus only on the bad. And when the Berlin Wall fell, I half expected to see a headline: "Wall Falls, Three Border Guards Lose Jobs."

And underneath it probably says: "Clinton Blames Bush."

You don't — you don't hear a lot about progress in America. So let me tell you about some good things we've done together.

Just two weeks ago, all three nations of North America agreed to trade freely from Manitoba to Mexico. And this will bring good jobs to Main Street U.S.A.

We passed the Americans with Disabilities Act — bringing 43 million people into the economic mainstream. And I must say, it is about time. Our children will breathe easier because of our new Clean Air Act. We are rebuilding our roads, providing jobs for more than half a million Americans.

And we passed a child-care law, and we took a stand for family values by saying that when it comes to raising children, government doesn't know best, parents know best.

I have — I have fought against prejudice and anti-Semitism all my life. And I am proud that we strengthened our civil rights laws — and we did it without resorting to quotas.

And one more thing of vital importance to all. Today, cocaine use has fallen by 60 percent among young people. To the teenagers, the parents and the volunteers who are helping us battle the scourge of drugs in America, we say thank you, thank you from the bottom of our hearts.

Do I want to do more? You bet. Nothing hurts me more than to meet with soldiers home from the Persian Gulf who can't find a job. Or workers who have a job but worry that the next day will bring a pink slip. And what about parents who scrape and struggle to send their kids to college, only to find them back living at home, because they can't get work?

The world is in transition, and we are feeling that transition in our homes. The defining challenge of the '90s is to win the economic competition — to win the peace. We must be a military superpower, an economic superpower and an export superpower.

In this election — in this election, you'll hear two visions of how to do this. Theirs is to look inward, and protect what we already have. Ours is to look forward — to open new markets, prepare our people to compete, to restore our social fabric, to save and invest — so we can win.

We believe — we believe that now that the world looks more like America, it is time for America to look more like herself.

And so we offer a philosophy that puts faith in the individual, not the bureaucracy. A philosophy that empowers people to do their best so America can be at its best. In a world that is safer and freer, this is how we will build an America that is stronger, safer and more secure.

We start with a simple fact: Government is too big and spends too much.

And I've asked Congress to put a lid on mandatory spending except Social Security. And I've proposed doing away with over 200 programs and 4,000 wasteful projects and to freeze all other spending. The gridlock Democrat Congress said: "No."

So, beginning tonight, so beginning tonight, I will enforce the spending freeze on my own. And if Congress sends me a bill spending more than I asked for in my budget — I will veto it fast.

Veto it fast — faster than copies of Millie's book sold.

Congress won't cut spending but refuses to give the president the power to eliminate pork barrel projects that waste your money. Forty-three governors have that power. So I ask you, the American people: Give me a Congress that will give me the line-item veto.

Let me tell you about a recent battle I fought with Congress, in which I was aided by [House Minority Leader] Bob Michel and his troops and Bob Dole and his troops. This spring, I worked day and night to get two-thirds of its members to approve a balanced-budget amendment to the Constitution.

We almost had it, but we lost by just nine votes. Now, listen how. Just before the vote, the liberal leaders of Congress con-

vinced 12 members who cosponsored the bill to switch sides and vote no. Keep in mind, they voted against a bill they had already put their names on.

Something fishy is going on. And look at my opponent on this issue. Look at my opponent, who says he's for balanced budgets. But he came out against the amendment. He's like that on a lot of issues, first one side, then the other. He's been spotted in more places than Elvis Presley.

After all these years — after all these years, Congress has become pretty creative at finding ways to waste your money. So we need to be just as creative at finding ways to stop them. And I have a brand new idea.

Taxpayers should be given the right to check a box on their tax returns so that up to 10 percent of their payments can go for one purpose alone: to reduce the national debt.

But we also — but we also need to make sure — we need to make sure that Congress doesn't just turn around and borrow more money to spend more money. And so I will require that, for every tax dollar set aside to cut the debt, the ceilings on spending will be cut by an equal amount.

And that way — that way, we will cut both debt and spending, and take a whack out of the budget deficit.

My feelings about big government come from my experience; I spent half my adult life in the private sector. My opponent has a different experience — he's been in government nearly all his life. His passion to expand government knows no bounds.

And he's already proposed — and listen to this carefully — he has already proposed $220 billion in new spending, along with the biggest tax increase in history — $150 billion — and that's just to start.

He says he wants to tax the rich, but folks, he defines rich as anyone who has a job.

You've heard of the separation of powers. Well, my opponent practices a different theory: the power of separations. Government has the power to separate you from your wallet.

Now, let me say this. When it comes to taxes, I've learned the hard way. There's an old saying. Good judgment comes from experience, and experience comes from bad judgment. Two years ago, I made a bad call on the Democrats' tax increase. I underestimated Congress' addiction to taxes, and with my back against the wall, I agreed to a hard bargain: one tax increase one time in return for the toughest spending limits ever.

Well, it was a mistake to go along with the Democratic tax increase.

And I admit it. But here's the question for the American people. Who do you trust in this election — the candidate who has raised taxes one time and regrets it, or the other candidate, who raised taxes and fees 128 times and enjoyed it every time?

Thank you very much.

When the new — OK. When the new Congress convenes — when the new Congress convenes next January, I will propose to further reduce taxes across the board — provided we pay for these cuts with specific spending reductions that I consider appropriate, so that we do not increase the deficit.

I will also continue to fight to increase the personal exemption and to create jobs by winning a cut in capital gains taxes.

That — that will especially help small businesses. You know, they create — small businesses, they create two-thirds of the new jobs in America. But my opponent's plan for small business is clear, present and dangerous. Besides new income taxes, his plan will lead to a new payroll tax to pay for a government takeover of health care, and another new tax — and another new tax to pay for training. And that is just the beginning.

And if he gets his way, hardware stores all across America will have a new sign up: "Closed for despair." And I guess you'd say his plan really is "Elvis Economics": America will be checking into the "Heartbreak Hotel."

I believe — I believe that small business needs relief — from taxation, regulation and litigation.

And thus, I will extend for one year the freeze on paperwork and unnecessary federal regulation that I imposed last winter. There is no reason — there is no reason that federal regulations should live longer than my friend George Burns. And I — I will issue an order to get rid of any rule whose time has come — and gone.

And I see something happening in our towns and neighborhoods. Sharp lawyers are running wild. Doctors are afraid to practice medicine. And some moms and pops won't even coach Little League anymore. We must sue each other less — and care for each other more.

I am fighting to reform our legal system, to put an end to crazy lawsuits. And if that means climbing into the ring with the trial lawyers, well, let me just say, Round 1 starts tonight.

After all — after all, my opponent's campaign is being backed by practically every trial lawyer who ever wore a tasseled loafer. He's not in the ring with them, he's in the tank.

There are other things we need to do to get out economy up to speed, and prepare our kids for the next century.

We must have new incentives for research and new training for workers. Small businesses need capital and credit, and defense workers need new jobs.

And I have a plan to provide affordable health care for every American, controlling costs by cutting paperwork and lawsuits, and expanding coverage to the poorest of the poor.

We do not need my opponent's plan for a massive government takeover of health care, which would ration care and deny you the right to choose a doctor.

Who wants health care — who wants a health-care system with the efficiency of the House Post Office and the compassion of the KGB?

What about our schools? What about our schools? My opponent and I both want to change the way our kids learn. He wants to change our schools a little bit — I want to change them a lot.

Take the issue of whether parents should be able to choose the best school for their kids. My opponent says that's OK — as long as the school is run by government. And I say every parent and child should have a real choice of schools — public, private or religious.

So — so we have a clear choice to fix our problems. Do we turn to the tattered blanket of bureaucracy that other nations are tossing away? Or do we give our people the freedom and incentives to build security for themselves?

Here's what I'm fighting for:

- Open markets for American products.
- Lower government spending.
- Tax relief.
- Opportunities for small business.
- Legal and health reform.
- Job training.
- And new schools built on competition, ready for the 21st century.

Now, OK, why are these proposals not in effect today? Only one reason — the gridlock Democratic Congress.

[Reacting to chants of "clean the House"] That's a very good idea. A very good idea.

Now, I know Americans are tired of the blame game, tired of people in Washington acting like they are candidates for the next episode of "American Gladiators."

I don't like it either. Neither should you. But the truth is the truth. Our policies haven't failed; they haven't been tried.

Americans want jobs. And on Jan. 28, I put before Congress a plan to create jobs. And if it had been passed back then, 500,000 more Americans would be at work right now. But in a nation that demands action, Congress has become the master of inaction.

And it wasn't always this way. I heard President Ford tonight. I served in Congress 22 years ago. Back then, we cooperated, we didn't get personal, we put the people above everything else. Heck, we didn't even have blow-dryers in those days.

At my first inauguration, I said that people didn't send us to bicker. I extended my hand — and I think the American people know this — I extended my hand to the congressional leaders, the Democratic leaders, and they bit it.

And the House leadership — the House leadership has not changed in 38 years. It is a body caught in a hopelessly tangled web of PACs, perks, privileges, partnership and paralysis.

Every day — every day, Congress puts politics ahead of principle and above progress.

Now, let me give you just one example. Feb. 20, 1991. It was at the height of the gulf war. On that very same day, I asked American pilots to risk their lives to fly missions over Baghdad. And I also wanted

to strengthen our economic security for the future.

So that very same day, I introduced a new domestic energy strategy which would cut our dependence on foreign oil by 7 million barrels a day.

And how many days did it take to win the gulf war? Forty-three. And how many did it take Congress to pass a national energy strategy? Five hundred and thirty-two, and still counting.

I have ridden stationary bikes that can move faster than the United States House of Representatives and the United States Senate, controlled by the Democrat leadership. [Reacting to chants of "hit 'em harder"] OK. All right. You wait. I'm fixing to.

Where — where does my opponent stand with Congress?

Well, up in New York at their convention, they kept the congressional leaders away from the podium — hid them away.

They didn't want America to hear from the people who really make the decisions.

And they hid them for a very good reason — because the American people would recognize a dangerous combination: a rubber-check Congress and a rubber-stamp president.

Gov. Clinton — Gov. Clinton and Congress know that you've caught on to their lingo.

They know when they say "spending," you say, "uh-oh."

So now they have a new word, "investment." They want to invest $220 billion more of your money, but I want you to keep it.

Gov. Clinton — Gov. Clinton and Congress want to put through the largest tax increase in history, but I will not let that happen.

Gov. Clinton and Congress don't want kids to have the option of praying in school, but I do.

Clinton and Congress don't want to close legal loopholes and keep criminals behind bars, but I will.

Clinton and Congress will stack the judiciary with liberal judges who write laws they can't get approved by the voters.

Gov. Clinton — Gov. Clinton even says that [New York Gov.] Mario Cuomo belongs on the Supreme Court.

Wait a minute. Maybe not a bad idea. If you believe in judicial restraint, you probably ought to be happy.

After all, the good governor of New York can't make up his mind between chocolate and vanilla at Baskin-Robbins. We won't have another court decision for 35 years. And maybe that's all right, too.

Are my opponent and Congress really in cahoots? Look at one important question: Should we limit the terms of Congress?

Gov. Clinton says no. Congress says no. I say yes.

We tried this — look, we tried this once before, combining the Democratic governor of a small Southern state with a very liberal vice president and a Democratic Congress. America does not need Carter II.

We do not want to take America back to those days of malaise. But Americans want to know, where's proof that we will have better days in Washington?

I'll give you 150 reasons. And that's how many members of Congress are expected to leave Washington this year. Some are tainted by scandal — the voters have bounced them the way they bounced their own checks. But others are good members. Republican and Democrat. And they agree with me. The place just doesn't work anymore.

One hundred-fifty new members — from both parties — will be coming to Washington this fall.

And every one will have a fresh view of America's future.

And I pledge today to the American people, immediately after this election, I will meet with every one of these new members, before they get attacked by the PACs, overwhelmed by their staffs and cornered by some camera crew.

And I — and I will lay out my case for change. Change that matters, real change that makes a difference. Change that is right for America.

You see, there is a yearning in America, a feeling that maybe it's time to get back to our roots.

Sure, we must change, but some values are timeless.

I believe in families that stick together, fathers who stick around.

And I happen to believe very deeply in the worth of each individual human being, born or unborn.

And I believe —

And I believe — and I believe — I believe in teaching our kids the difference between what's wrong and what's right, teaching them respect for hard work and to love their neighbors.

And I believe that America will always have a special place in God's heart, as long as he has a special place in ours. And maybe —

And maybe that's why I've always believed that patriotism is not just another point of view.

There are times in every young person's life, when God introduces you to yourself. And I remember such a time.

It was back many years ago, when I stood watch at 4 a.m. up on the bridge of the USS *Finback*.

I would stand there and look out on the blackness of the sky, broken only by the sparkling stars above. And I would think about friends I lost, a country I loved and about a girl named Barbara.

And I remember those nights as clearly as any in my life.

You know, you can see things from up there that other people don't see. You can see storm clouds rise and then disappear. The first hint of the sun over the horizon, and the first outline of the shore far away.

And now, I know Americans are uneasy today, there is anxious talk around our kitchen tables. But from where I stand, I see not America's sunset, but a sunrise.

And the world changes for which we've sacrificed for a generation have finally come to pass, and with them a rare and unprecedented opportunity to pass the sweet cup of prosperity around our American table.

Are we up to it? I know we are. As I travel our land, I meet veterans who once worked the turrets of a tank and can now master the keyboards of high-tech economy.

I see teachers, blessed with the incredible American capacity for innovation, who are teaching our children a new way to learn, for a new century.

And I meet parents, some working two jobs with hectic schedules, who — who still find new ways to teach old values to steady their kids in a turbulent world.

And I take heart from what is happening in America, not from those who profess a new passion for government but from those with an old and enduring faith in the human potential.

Those who understand that the genius of America is our capacity for rebirth and renewal. America is the land where the sun is always peeking over the horizon.

And tonight I appeal to that unyielding, undying, undeniable American spirit. I ask you to consider, now that the entire world is moving our way, why would we want to go back their way?

I ask not just for your support for my agenda but for your commitment to renew and rebuild our nation — by shaking up one institution that has withstood change for over four decades.

Join me in rolling away the roadblock —

Join me in rolling away the roadblock at the other end of Pennsylvania Avenue, so that in the next four years, we will match our accomplishments outside, by building a stronger, safer, more secure America inside.

Forty-four — forty-four years ago, in another age of uncertainty, a different president embarked on a similar mission. His name was Harry S Truman.

And as he stood before his party to accept their nomination, Harry Truman knew the freedom I know this evening, the freedom to talk about what's right for America, and let the chips fall where they may.

Harry Truman said this: This is more than a political call to arms. Give me your help, not to win votes alone but to win this new crusade and keep America safe and secure for its own people.

Well, tonight I say to you, join me in our new crusade to reap the rewards of our global victory — to win the peace — so that we may make America safer and stronger for all our people.

May God bless you, and may God bless the United States of America. Thank you very much. ∎

## THE PLATFORM

# Party Stresses Family Values, Decentralized Authority

*Following is the text of the 1992 Republican Party platform.*

*It was adopted by the delegates to the national convention Aug. 17 by voice vote.*

### Preamble

Abraham Lincoln, our first Republican president, expressed the philosophy that inspires Republicans to this day: "The legitimate object of government is to do for a community of people whatever they need to have done, but cannot do at all, or cannot so well do, for themselves in their separate and individual capacities. But in all that people can individually do as well for themselves, government ought not to interfere."

We believe that most problems of human making are within the capacity of human ingenuity to solve.

For good reason, millions of new Americans have flocked to our shores: America has always been an opportunity society. Republicans have always believed that economic prosperity comes from individual enterprise, not government programs. We have defended our core principles for 138 years. But never has this country, and the world, been so receptive to our message.

The fall of the Berlin Wall symbolizes an epochal change in the way people live. More important, it liberates the way people think. We see with new clarity that centralized government bureaucracies created in this century are not the wave of the future. Never again will people trust planners and paper shufflers more than they trust themselves. We all watched as the statue of Soviet hangman Feliks Dzherzhinsky was toppled in front of Moscow's KGB headquarters by the very people his evil empire sought to enslave. Its sightless eyes symbolized the moral blindness of totalitarians around the world. They could never see the indomitable spirit of people determined to be free from government control — free to build a better future with their own heads, hands and hearts.

We Republicans saw clearly the dangers of collectivism: not only the military threat but the deeper threat to the souls of people bound in dependence. Here at home, we warned against "big government," because we knew concentrated decision-making, no matter how well-intentioned, was a danger to liberty and prosperity. Republicans stood at the rampart of freedom, defending the individual against the domineering state. While we did not always prevail, we always stood our ground, faithful to our principles and confident of history's ultimate verdict.

Our opponents declared that the dogmas of the left were the final and victorious faith. From kremlins and ivory towers, their planners proclaimed the bureaucratic millennium. But in a tragic century of illusion, Five-Year Plans and Great Leaps Forward failed to summon a Brave New World. One hundred and fifty years of slogans and manifestos came crashing down in an ironic cascade of unintended consequences. All that is left are the ruins of a failed scoundrel ideology.

As May Day lapses back into just another spring festival, the Fourth of July emerges as the common holiday of free men and women. Yet, in 1992, when the self-governing individual has overcome the paternalistic state, liberals here at home simply do not get it. Indeed, their party seeks to turn the clock back. But their ideas are old and tired. Like planets still orbiting a dying star, the believers in state power turn their faces to a distant and diminishing light.

The Democrats would revise history to rationalize a return to bigger government, higher taxes and moral relativism. The Democratic Party has forgotten its origins as a party of work, thrift and self-reliance. But they have not forgotten their art for dissembling and distortion. The Democrats are trapped in their compact with the ideology of trickle-down government, but they are clever enough to know that the voters would shun them if their true markings were revealed.

America had its rendezvous with destiny in 1980. Faced with crisis at home and abroad, Americans turned to Republican leadership in the White House. Presidents Reagan and Bush turned our nation away from the path of overtaxation, hyper-regulation and megagovernment. Instead, we moved in a new direction. We cut taxes, reduced red tape, put people above bureaucracy. And so we vanquished the idea of the almighty state as the supervisor of our daily lives. In choosing hope over fear, Americans raised a beacon, reminding the world that we are a shining city on a hill, the last best hope for man on earth.

Contrary to statist Democrat propaganda, the American people know that the 1980s were a rising tide, a magnificent decade for freedom and entrepreneurial creativity. We are confident that, knowing this, they will never consciously retreat to the bad old days of tax and spend. Our platform will clarify the choice before our fellow citizens.

We have learned that ideas do indeed have consequences. Thus, our words are important not for their prose but for what they reveal about the thinking of our president and our party.

Two years ago, President Bush described the key elements of what he called "our new paradigm," a fresh approach that aims to put new ideas to work in the service of enduring principles — principles we upheld throughout the long twilight struggle, principles George Bush has acted decisively to advance. Thus we honor the Founders and their vision.

Unlike our opponents, we are inspired by a commitment to profound change. Our mission combines timeless beliefs with a positive vision of a vigorous America: prosperous and tolerant, just and compassionate. We believe that individual freedom, hard work and personal responsibility — basic to free society — are also basic to effective government. We believe in the fundamental goodness of the American people. We believe in traditional family values and in the Judeo-Christian heritage that informs our culture. We believe in the Constitution and its guarantee of color-blind equal opportunity. We believe in free markets. We believe in constructive change, in both true conservatism and true reform. We believe government has a legitimate role to play in our national life, but government must never dominate that life.

While our goals are constant, we are willing to innovate, experiment and learn. We have learned that bigger is not better, that quantity and quality are different things, that more money does not guarantee better outcomes.

We have learned the importance of individual choice — in education, health care, child care — and that bureaucracy is the enemy of initiative and self-reliance. We believe in empowerment, including home ownership for as many as possible. We believe in decentralized authority, and a bottom-line, principled commitment to what works for people.

We believe in the American people: free men and women with faith in God, working for themselves and their families, believing in the value of every human being from the very young to the very old.

We believe the Founders intended Congress to be responsive, flexible and foresighted. After decades of Democrat misrule, the Congress is none of these things. Dominated by reactionaries, obsessed with the failed policies and structures of the past, the Democrat majority

displays a "do-nothing" doggedness: They intend to learn nothing and forget nothing. Seeking to build a better America, we seek to elect a better Congress.

Finally, we believe in a president who represents the national interest, not just the aggregation of well-connected special interests — a president who brings unity to the American purpose.

America faces many challenges. Republicans, under the strong leadership of President Bush, are responding with this bold platform of new ideas that infuses our commitment to individual freedom and market forces with an equal commitment to a decent, just way of life for every American.

With a firm faith that the American people will always choose hope over fear, we Republicans dedicate ourselves to this forward-looking agenda for America in the 1990s, transcending old, static ideas with a shared vision of hope, optimism and opportunity.

## Uniting Our Family

As the family goes, so goes the nation. Strong families and strong communities make a strong America. An old adage says, "America is great because she is good; if America ceases to be good, she will cease to be great."

Our greatness starts at home — literally. So Republicans believe government should strengthen families, not replace them. Today, more than ever, the traditional family is under assault. We believe our laws should reflect what makes our nation prosperous and wholesome: faith in God, hard work, service to others and limited government.

Parents bring reality to these principles when they pass them on to their children. As the book of Proverbs proclaims, "Train up a child in the way he should go: and when he is old, he will not depart from it."

Imagine the America we could create if all parents taught their children the importance of honesty, work, responsibility and respect for others. We would have less violence in our homes and streets; less illegal drug use; fewer teen pregnancies forcing girls and boys to be adults before they have graduated from high school. Instead, we would have an America of families, friends and communities that care about one another.

That kind of future is not a matter of chance; it is a question of personal responsibility. Barbara Bush captured the importance of that stewardship when she said, "At the end of your life you will never regret not having passed one more test, not winning one more verdict, or not closing one more deal. You will regret time not spent with a husband, a child, a friend or a parent."

The Republican Party has espoused these principles since its founding. Families built on solid, spiritual foundations are central to our party's inspiration. Families built on solid, spiritual foundations are central to our party's inspiration. At this time of great national and global transition, we renew our commitment to these fundamental principles, which will guide our family, our country, our world into the next century.

### Family: The Home of Freedom

**The rights of the family.** Our national renewal starts with the family. It is where each new generation gains its moral anchor. It is the school of citizenship, the engine of economic progress, a permanent haven when everything is changing.

Change can be good, when it liberates the energy and commitment of family members to build better futures. We welcome change that corrects the mistakes of the past, particularly those at war against the family. For more than three decades, the liberal philosophy has assaulted the family on every side.

Today, its more vocal advocates believe children should be able to sue their parents over decisions about schooling, cosmetic surgery, employment and other family matters. They deny parental authority and responsibility, fracturing the family into isolated individuals, each of them dependent upon — and helpless before — government. This is the ultimate agenda of contemporary socialism under all its masks: to liberate youth from traditional family values by replacing family functions with bureaucratic social services. That is why today's liberal Democrats are hostile toward any institution government cannot control, like private child care or religious schools.

The Republican Party responds, as it has since 1980, with an unabashed commitment to the family's economic liberty and moral rights. Republicans trust parents and believe they, not courts and lawyers, know what is best for their children. That is why we will work to ensure that the Congress and the states shall enact no law abridging the rights of the family formed by blood, marriage, adoption or legal custody — rights that are anterior and superior to those of government. Republicans oppose and resist the efforts of the Democratic Party to redefine the traditional American family.

**The right to a family.** Every child deserves a family in a home filled with love and free from abuse. Today, many children do not enjoy that right. We are determined to change that. While government cannot legislate love and compassion, we can provide the leadership to encourage the development of healthy, nurturing families. We applaud the fine example of family values and family virtue as lived by the president and the first lady.

We will promote whole, caring families by eliminating biases that have crept into our legal and tax codes. We will advance adoption through significant tax credits, insurance reforms and legal reforms. We encourage adoption for those unprepared or unwilling to bear the emotional, financial or physical demands of raising a child, and will work to revive maternity homes to ensure care for both mothers and babies.

We applaud the commitment of foster-care parents who provide family environments for foster-care children. We abhor the disgraceful bureaucratic mismanagement of foster care. Big-city mayors have spent billions on social service bureaucrats who have lost track of many children. Many have no health records, no real residence, not even the simplest personal possessions. Shuttled from house to house, they lack discipline and identity, and are ripe for lives of crime. We are determined to reform this system to help these children.

Broken homes can have a devastating emotional and economic impact upon children and are the breeding ground for gang members. We urge state legislatures to explore ways to promote marital stability. Because the intergenerational family is a vital element of social cohesion, we urge greater respect for the rights and roles of grandparents.

Republicans recognize the importance of having fathers and mothers in the home. The two-parent family still provides the best environment of stability, discipline, responsibility and character. Documentation shows that where the father has deserted his family, children are more likely to commit a crime, to drop out of school, to become violent, to become teen parents, to take illegal drugs, to become mired in poverty, or to have emotional or behavioral problems. We support the courageous efforts of single-parent families to have a stable home.

**Caring for children.** George Bush secured the American family's most important victory of the last four years: his child-care bill. He won landmark legislation — a voucher system for low-income households, allowing parents to choose what's best for their children, including care given by neighbors or churches. The Democratic Party opposed that legislation and instead sought government control of child care and fewer choices for parents.

The president also advanced equity for families that forgo a second income to care for their children at home through his Young Child Tax Credit. Congressional Democrats are already trying to repeal it.

The demands of employment and commuting often make it hard for parents to spend time with their children. Republicans advocate maximum flexibility in working and child-care arrangements so that families can make the most of their schedules. We support pro-family policies: job-sharing, telecommuting, compressed workweeks, parental leave negotiated between employer and employees, and flextime. We reject the Democrats' one-size-fits-all approach that puts mandates on employers and takes choices away from employees.

Most parents prefer in-home care of their children but often encounter government obstacles. Republicans will promote

in-home care by allowing payment annually, instead of quarterly, of income taxes by employees and withholding taxes by employers. Our proposals for tort reform, now blocked by the Democrat Congress, will prevent excessive litigation that hampers the growth of child-care opportunities. By taking care of our children, we are taking care of our future.

**Family security.** Over the last several decades, liberal Democrats have increasingly shifted economic burdens onto the American family. Indeed, the liberal Democrat tax-and-spend policies have forced millions of women into the workplace just to make ends meet. Because of their policies in Congress, fathers and mothers have a tougher time bringing home what they work so hard for.

Between 1948 and 1990, under the Democrat-controlled Congress for most of those years, federal taxes on the average family of four rose from 2 percent to 24 percent of income. When state and local levies are included, the tax burden exceeds one-third of family income. The increase in the effective federal tax rate since 1950 has now swallowed up an ever-increasing share of a family's earnings. Instead of working to improve their family's standard of living, they must work to feed government's gluttonous appetite.

This is a scandal. In the 1980s, two Republican presidents kept Democrats from making matters worse. Presidents Reagan and Bush led the way to increase the personal exemption for dependents. We pledge to go farther to restore the value, as a percentage of average household income, it had 50 years ago. The value of the dependent deduction has eroded to a fraction of its original worth to families. Republicans call for a complete restoration, in real dollars, to its original value. Rather than fatten government bureaucracies with new programs to "help" families, we want to expand the Young Child Tax Credit to $500 per child and make it available to all families with children under the age of 10.

When the Democrats establish tax policy that makes marriage more expensive than living together, they discourage traditional commitment and stable home life. We will remove the marriage penalty in the tax code, so a married couple will receive as large a standard deduction as their unmarried counterparts. Together, these changes will empower parents to care for their families in a way public services never can.

**Achieving educational excellence.** In the earliest American communities, pioneers would establish a church, then a school. Parents wanted their children to have the best possible education, to learn what they needed to know to make a better life. Virtually every newly arrived immigrant family thought of education as the American way from the back to the front of the line. Americans have come to believe that only a country that successfully educates its sons and daughters can count on a strong, competitive economy, a vibrant culture and a solid civic life.

As a result of this popular demand for education, Americans have created the most extensive and widely accessible educational system in the world. The people have insisted that primary responsibility for education properly remain with families, communities and states, although, from early times, the national government has played a role in encouraging innovation and access. In the 18th century, the Northwest Ordinance assured that school bells would ring amid frontier forests. In the 19th century, President Lincoln signed the Morrill Act establishing 50 land-grant colleges. In the 20th century, President Eisenhower signed the National Defense Education Act, providing millions with a chance at higher education; and President Nixon signed legislation that today provides federal grants and loans to half our full-time college students. In the 21st century, the promotion of educational excellence will be more crucial than ever before in our nation's history.

Recognizing what every parent knows, that our current educational system is not educating our children, President Bush is leading an educational revolution. We applaud the president's bold vision to change radically our education system. Our parents want it, our communities want it, our states want it, and our children want it — but the Democrat leadership in the House and Senate continue to thwart the will of the American people for radical change in the way we educate our children.

The Republican strategy is based on sound principle. Parents have the right to choose the best school for their children. Schools should teach right from wrong. Schools should reinforce parental authority, not replace it. We should increase flexibility from federal regulation. We should explore a new generation of break-the-mold New American Schools. Standards and assessments should be raised, not reduced to a lowest common denominator. Communities should be empowered to find what works. The pursuit of excellence in education is a fundamental goal. Good teachers should be rewarded for teaching well. Alternative certification can bring desperately needed new people into the teaching profession. America needs public, private and parochial schools.

Education is a joint responsibility of the individual, the family and the community. Parents are the first and most important teachers of their children. They should have the right not only to participate in their child's education but to choose for their children among the broadest array of educational choices, without regard to their income. We also support the right of parents to provide quality education through home-based schools.

The Bush administration has sent to Congress several legislative proposals embodying these principles. The proposals, in spite of the fact that 1,500 communities across the nation have developed local committees to support them through the America 2000 strategy, languish in the Democrat Congress. And they are opposed by special-interest unions that have a power grip on the failed policies of the past.

**Improving America by improving our schools.** For America to maintain her pre-eminence into the next century, our educational system must be revolutionized. Too many schools still teach in an outdated manner. Too many government and union rules have burdened our schools. And too much influence by lobbyists has blocked true reform. Even the most inspiring teachers are working within a system that stymies their creativity and fails to challenge their students.

**Creating the best schools in the world.** We applaud President Bush's consistent and determined leadership in setting a new direction for American education. Our overriding purpose is clear: to create the best schools in the world for our children by the turn of the century.

To do so, the president has established a bold strategy, America 2000, which challenges communities in every state to take charge to achieve our ambitious national education goals. The success of America 2000 will depend upon the local community, where implementation and ultimate responsibility rest.

We have seen real progress. Perhaps most important, though, is that President Bush has fostered a national debate on education that has challenged every American to get involved. He has called forth American traits of ingenuity and ambition to create better lives for our children. As a result, a new generation of break-the-mold new American schools is taking shape. New and tougher standards and assessments are being established for what our children should know. The number of strings attached to federal school aid is being reduced.

The president has shown unprecedented leadership for the most important education goal of all: helping middle- and low-income families enjoy the same choice of schools — public, private or religious — that families with more resources already have. The president's proposed "GI Bill for Children" will provide $1,000 scholarships to middle- and low-income families, enabling their children to attend the school of their choice. This innovative plan will not only drive schools to excel as they compete, but will also give every parent consumer power to obtain an excellent education for his or her child.

Republican leadership has nearly doubled funds for Head Start, making it possible, for the first time, for all eligible 4-year-olds to participate, should their parents choose to enroll them. The Bush administration has put a college education within reach of millions more students, young and old. The president has proposed allowing families to deduct the interest they pay on

student loans, and penalty-free withdrawal of IRA [individual retirement account] funds for educational expenses.

**Ensuring high standards in knowledge and skills.** For America to compete in a world in which 85 percent of all jobs will require high skills, we believe that students not planning to attend college need better opportunities. America's college graduates set the world pace for knowledge and skills. But we also have a strong commitment to the "forgotten half" of the students in our schools, students who will graduate from high school ill-prepared for work. We must build a well-educated, high-skills work force to ensure a new century of prosperity for America.

The president has developed a sweeping youth apprenticeship strategy to meet this goal. His plan will ensure that students meet the high standards demanded of all high school students, while training them with a skill as well. We strongly support youth apprenticeships that include a year of college, to encourage a lifetime of learning and opportunity for students.

**Our educational beliefs.** We are confident that the United States can, by the end of this decade, reach the six national education goals that President Bush and the nation's governors have established: that all children should arrive at school ready to learn; that high school graduation rates should be at least 90 percent; that all children learn challenging subject matter and become responsible citizens; that American children should be first in the world in math and science; that there must be a literate and skilled work force; and that schools must be disciplined and free of drugs and violence.

We have an uncompromising commitment to improve public education — which means assuring that our schools produce well-educated, responsible citizens — not the maintenance of a government monopoly over the means of educating. American families must be given choice in education. We value the important role played by our private, independent and parochial schools, colleges and universities. We believe that their quality is best encouraged by minimizing government regulation.

We believe distance learning is a valuable tool in the fight to bring equal educational opportunity to every student regardless of wealth or geographic location. Distance learning provides students access to the vast educational resources of our nation.

We encourage the use of modern technology to meet the goal of educational excellence. We support policies that provide access for all instructional and educational programmers to permit them to provide the greatest choice of programming and material to schools and teachers. We also support policies that will encourage the use of all advanced technologies for the delivery of educational and instructional programming in order to give schools and

teachers the greatest flexibility in providing creative and innovative instruction. We encourage local school boards to ensure review of these materials by parents and educators.

We support efforts to open the teaching profession by reforming the certification system now barring many talented men and women from the classroom.

Schools should be — as they have been traditionally — academic institutions. Families and communities err when by neglect or design they transfer to the school responsibilities that belong in the home and in the community. Schools were created to help and strengthen families, not to undermine or substitute for them.

Accordingly, we oppose programs in public schools that provide birth control or abortion services or referrals. Instead, we encourage abstinence education programs with proven track records in protecting youth from disease, pregnancy and drug use.

The critical public mission in education is to set tough, clear standards of achievement and ensure that those who educate our children are accountable for meeting them. This is not just a matter of plans or dollars. Competency testing and merit pay for teachers are essential elements of such accountability.

We are proud of our many dedicated, professional teachers and educators who have committed their lives to educating America's children. We also believe that powerful unions and liberal special interest groups should not be the driving force in educational reform.

Just as spiritual principles — our moral compass — help guide public policy, learning must have a moral basis. America must remain neutral toward particular religions, but we must not remain neutral toward religion itself or the values religion supports. Mindful of our country's Judeo-Christian heritage and rich religious pluralism, we support the right of students to engage in voluntary prayer in schools and the right of the community to do so at commencements or other occasions. We will strongly enforce the law guaranteeing equal access to school facilities. We also advocate recitation of the Pledge of Allegiance in schools as a reminder of the principles that sustain us as one nation under God.

Our ambitious vision for America works, however, only in a society of well-educated citizens. The Democratic Party, beholden to the special interests that resist change, can never accomplish the improvements in education that our schools and our children so desperately need. Indeed, they have no plan.

The Republican Party has started an education revolution. We have presented a detailed plan which is even now becoming reality. The future of our nation demands no less. The president is leading the country on an education crusade, a crusade the American people have joined.

**For healthier families: Promote**

**health, prevent disease, reform health care.** Americans receive the finest medical care in the world. We have the best health-care providers, the best hospitals and the best medical technology. People come here from Canada, from Europe, from every part of the globe, to seek procedures and treatments that are either unavailable or strictly rationed in their home countries.

But we must do better. Costs are soaring. Many Americans, responsible for children and aging parents, worry about the quality and price of care. The 1992 election presents all of us with a clear choice.

Democrats want a costly, coercive system, imported from abroad, with a budget set by Congress and policies set by bureaucrats. That is a prescription for misery. It would imperil jobs, require billions in new taxes, lower the quality of health care overall, drive health-care providers out of the profession, and result in rationing.

The congressional Democrats' health-care reform proposal would exclude themselves from coverage under their own program. They refuse to live with the scheme they are trying to force on the rest of the county.

Republicans believe government control of health care is irresponsible and ineffective. We believe health-care choices should remain in the hands of the people, not government bureaucrats. This issue truly represents a fundamental difference between the two parties.

We endorse President Bush's comprehensive health-care plan, which solves the two major problems of the current system — access and affordability — while preserving the high-quality care Americans now enjoy. The president's plan will make health care *more affordable* through tax credits and deductions that will offset insurance costs for 95 million Americans; and make health care *more accessible*, especially for small businesses, by reducing insurance costs and eliminating workers' worries of losing insurance if they change jobs. This plan will expand access to health care by:

● Creating new tax credits and deductions to help low- and middle-income Americans. These tax credits would be available in the form of vouchers for low-income people who work.

● Providing insurance security for working Americans by requiring insurers to cover pre-existing conditions.

● Making health insurance premiums fully deductible for the self-employed.

● Making it easier for small firms to purchase coverage for their employees. The proposal would allow small businesses to form health insurance purchasing pools that would make insurance more affordable. It also would guarantee the availability and renewability of insurance for small firms, set premium standards, pre-empt state mandated-benefit laws, establish minimum coverage plans, and require states to establish risk pools to spread

risks broadly across health insurers.

• Addressing the medical malpractice problem by a cap on non-economic damage recoveries in malpractice claims and an alternative dispute resolution before going to court.

In short, the president aims to make coverage available to all, guaranteed, renewable, with no preconditions. Under his plan, no one will have to go broke to get well.

The Democrats' plan stands in stark philosophical contrast. Instead of preserving individual options, it would rely on government bureaucrats. Instead of preserving quality care, it would lead to rationing and waiting lines. And instead of enhancing the health-care security of American workers, it would require a massive increase in payroll taxes that would destroy hundreds of thousands of jobs.

The Democrats' so-called play-or-pay proposal would require employers either to provide health insurance for their workers or pay a new tax that would fund in part a new government-run health program. According to a study prepared by the Urban Institute, this mandate would require new federal taxes — or new federal borrowing — of $36 billion in the first year alone. Nearly 52 million Americans who now have private health insurance would be dumped by their employers onto the government-run plan. Additional costs to employers — particularly small employers — would total an estimated $30 billion in the first year. The Republican staff of Congress' Joint Economic Committee estimates that 712,000 people would lose their jobs because of the play-or-pay mandate.

Republicans are also determined to resolve the crisis in medical liability, allowing physicians and certified midwives to deliver babies and practice in underserved areas. Meaningful medical tort reform would assure that doctors would not have to practice medicine under a cloud of potential litigation. We will reduce administrative expenses and paperwork by adopting a uniform claim and data system. We pledge our support for rehabilitation and long-term care coverage. We will curb costs through better prenatal and other preventive care. We encourage the application of the Good Samaritan law to protect health-care providers who wish to volunteer their time to provide patient care to the community. We encourage coordinated care in public programs and private insurance. We further support regulatory reforms to speed the development of new drugs and medical technology.

The health-care safety net must be secure for those who need preventive, acute and long-term care. Special consideration should be given to abolishing or reforming programs which prohibit or discourage individuals from seeking to work their way out of poverty and dependency. We will reduce paperwork burdens and redirect those resources to actual services. We will enhance access to medical care through community health centers, which provide primary care in medically underserved areas. We will modify outdated antitrust rules that prohibit hospitals from merging their resources to provide improved, cost-effective health care.

We encourage the use of telecommunications technology to link hospitals in larger communities with heath-care facilities in smaller communities. Advanced communications networks will facilitate the sharing of resources, will improve access to affordable health care through the transmission of medical imaging and diagnostics and will ensure that Americans living in rural areas have the same access to doctors and the latest medical procedures as Americans living in urban areas.

Republicans focus on health, not just health care. We want not only to treat disease and disability but to reduce and prevent them. Through funding for NIH [the National Institutes of Health], we invest in research to cure a range of diseases, from cancer to heart disease, from multiple sclerosis to lupus. We support efforts which foster early cancer detection. Even more important, we rely on individuals to lower the incidence of preventable illness and injury. A large part of our health-care costs, public and private, is caused by behavior. Good judgment can save billions of dollars — and perhaps millions of lives.

**AIDS.** The HIV/AIDS epidemic has exploded over the past decade into a crisis of tragic proportions. In our country, AIDS already has claimed more than 150,000 lives, and as many as 1 million more Americans may have been infected with the virus.

Epidemics have, throughout history, challenged governments, which have too often been powerless to combat them. Science — and human wisdom — have advanced, however, and we have met this crisis not only with a massive commitment of resources but also with a personal determination on the part of the president. That commitment and leadership will continue.

AIDS should be treated like any other communicable or sexually transmitted disease, while at the same time preserving patient confidentiality. We are committed to ensure that our nation's response to AIDS is shaped by compassion, not fear or ignorance and will oppose, as a matter of decency and honor, any discrimination against Americans who are its victims.

We encourage state legislatures to enact legislation which makes it a criminal act for anyone knowingly to transmit the AIDS virus.

We will seek to ensure that medical personnel, and the people who trust in their care, will be protected against infection.

This disease also challenges America scientifically. We must succeed in slowing the epidemic's spread. The administration has thus placed great emphasis on a variety of prevention efforts to do so. We must recognize, also, that prevention is linked ultimately to personal responsibility and moral behavior. We reject the notion that the distribution of clean needles and condoms are the solution to stopping the spread of AIDS. Education designed to curb the spread of this disease should stress marital fidelity, abstinence and a drug-free lifestyle. There must be a means for successfully treating the virus, and this has led to a threefold increase in research and steps to speed the approval process for new drugs that could make a crucial difference to those infected.

Above all, a cure must be found. We have committed enormous resources — $4.2 billion over the past four years for research alone, more than for any disease except cancer. In keeping with the American spirit, our fellow citizens with HIV/AIDS deserve our compassion and our care, and they deserve our united commitment to a cure.

**Healthy families.** Responsible families are the key to wellness. They are the best guard against infant mortality and child abuse. We support programs to help mothers and their babies get a good start in life; and we call for strong action, at all levels of government, to enforce parental responsibility with regard to alcohol, drugs and neglect.

We applaud the president's initiatives to require the involvement of more women in clinical trials and to create within NIH a center to combat breast and cervical cancer. We also call for expanded research on various diseases, common to both men and women, but whose effects on women have yet to be determined. We call for fetal protection in the workplace and in scientific research.

**The homeless.** The Bush administration has worked vigorously to address this tragedy, believing that involuntary homelessness in America is unacceptable. Accordingly, the administration has proposed $4 billion in homeless assistance, an amount cut back by the Democrat-controlled Congress. We have also implemented a Shelter Plus Care program designed to assist homeless persons who are mentally ill, chemically dependent or stricken with AIDS. Republicans remain determined to help the homeless as a matter of ethical commitment as well as sound public policy.

**Older Americans.** The interests of older Americans are addressed throughout this platform, for the elderly play an honored role in all walks of American life. From reducing inflation to fighting crime, from quality health care to a cleaner environment, the Republican agenda for all has particular relevance to those who have worked the longest and grown the wisest.

We reaffirm our commitment to a strong Social Security system. To stop penalizing grandparents and other seniors who care for children, we pledge to continue the Republican crusade to end the earnings limitation for Social Security recipients. More than ever, our nation needs

older Americans in its schools and workplaces. There should be no barriers to their full participation in our country's future. We pledge support for greater availability of long-term care and for research to combat Alzheimer's disease. Republicans also took the lead in expanding home health care in government programs, and we want to build on that accomplishment.

**Promoting cultural values.** The culture of our nation has traditionally supported those pillars on which civilized society is built: personal responsibility, morality and the family. Today, however, these pillars are under assault. Elements within the media, the entertainment industry, academia and the Democratic Party are waging a guerrilla war against American values. They deny personal responsibility, disparage traditional morality, denigrate religion and promote hostility toward the family's way of life. Children, the members of our society most vulnerable to cultural influences, are barraged with violence and promiscuity, encouraging reckless and irresponsible behavior. This undermines the authority of parents, the ones most responsible for passing on to their offspring a sense of right and wrong. The lesson our party draws is important — that all of us, individuals and corporations alike, have a responsibility to reflect the values we expect our fellow citizens to exhibit. And if children grow to adulthood reflecting not the values of their parents but the amorality with which they are bombarded, those who send such messages cannot duck culpability.

One example is the advocacy of violence against law enforcement officers, promoted by a corporation more interested in profits than the possible consequences of such a message. We believe, in the spirit of Theodore Roosevelt, that corporations — like individuals — have responsibilities to society, and that conscience alone should prevent such outrages.

We also stand united with those private organizations, such as the Boy Scouts of America, who are defending decency in fulfillment of their own moral responsibilities. We reject the irresponsible position of those corporations that have cut off contributions to such organizations because of their courageous stand for family values. Moreover, we oppose efforts by the Democratic Party to include sexual preference as a protected minority receiving preferential status under civil rights statutes at the federal, state and local level.

We oppose any legislation or law that legally recognizes same-sex marriages and allows such couples to adopt children or provide foster care.

We must recognize that the time has come for a national crusade against pornography. Some would have us believe that obscenity and pornography have no social impact. But if hard-core pornography does not cheapen the human spirit, then neither does Shakespeare elevate it. We call on federal agencies to halt the sale, under government auspices, of pornographic materials. We endorse Republican legislation, the Pornogra-

phy Victims Compensation Act, allowing victims of pornography to seek damages from those who make or sell it, especially since the Commission on Pornography, in 1986, found a direct link between pornography and violent crimes committed against women and children. We also believe that the various state legislatures should create a civil cause of action against makers and distributors of pornography when their material incites a violent crime.

Government has a responsibility, as well, to ensure that it promotes the common moral values that bind us together as a nation. We therefore condemn the use of public funds to subsidize obscenity and blasphemy masquerading as art. The fine arts, including those with public support, can certainly enrich our society. However, no artist has an inherent right to claim taxpayer support for his or her private vision of art if that vision mocks the moral and spiritual basis on which our society is founded. We believe a free market in art — with neither suppression nor favoritism by government — is the best way to foster the cultural revival our country needs.

## Individual Rights, Good Homes and Safe Streets

At a time when the rest of the world has rejected socialism, there are communities here at home where free markets have not been permitted to flourish. Decades of liberalism have left us with two economies. The pro-growth economy rewards effort, promotes thrift and supports strong families. The other economy stifles initiative and is anti-work and anti-family. In one economy, people are free to be owners and entrepreneurs. In the other economy, people are at the mercy of government. We are determined to elevate the poor into the pro-growth economy.

Republicans will lead a new national consensus around economic opportunity, greater access to property, home ownership and housing, jobs and entrepreneurship. We must bring the great promise of America to every city, every small town, and to all our people.

Our agenda for equality of opportunity runs throughout this platform and applies to all Americans. There is no such thing as segregated success. We reject the Democrats' politics of division, envy and conflict. They believe that America is split into classes and can be healed only through the redistribution of wealth. We believe in the economics of multiplication: free markets expand opportunity and wealth for all.

That is true liberation. It frees poor people not only from want but also from government control. That is why liberal Democrats have fought us every step of the way, refusing congressional action on enterprise zones until Los Angeles burned — and then mocking the expectations of the poor by gutting that critical proposal. They can kill bills, but they cannot kill hope. We are determined to pass that legislation for the sake of all who are awaiting their chance for the American Dream.

We will eliminate laws that keep Americans out of jobs, like the outdated ban on home work. The antiquated Davis-Bacon Act inflates taxpayer costs and keeps willing workers from getting jobs in federally assisted projects. It must go. Unlike the Democrats, we believe the private sector, not the federal government, should set prevailing wage rates.

As explained elsewhere in this platform, low-income families must gain control of their future through choice in their children's education.

**Rebuilding the dream.** Our party has always championed the American dream of home ownership. Abraham Lincoln wanted all families to have access to property, because it would give them a tangible stake in their family's future. As families built homes and improved the land, they built a brighter future for themselves and a legacy for their children. Lincoln's Homestead Act of 1862 did all this without enlarging government. It empowered families.

In the tradition of Lincoln, President Bush has replicated the American dream of home ownership. For first-time home buyers, he has proposed a $5,000 tax credit. For lower-income families, he has worked to restore opportunity through HOPE, his initiative to help tenants now dependent on federal aid to buy their own homes; Mortgage Revenue Bonds, to assist more than 1.9 million families to buy a first home; Low-Income Housing Tax Credits, already producing more than 420,000 decent apartments at affordable prices; and HOME, a partnership among all levels of government to help low-income families secure better housing.

For everyone, but especially for the poor, the best housing policy is non-inflationary economic growth and low interest rates, the heart of our opportunity agenda.

**Ending dependency.** Welfare is the enemy of opportunity and stable family life. Two decades ago, decisions about public assistance were taken away from states and communities and given to Washington officials. Since then, almost everything has gone wrong. Since 1965, we have spent $3.5 trillion on welfare. It brought a horrendous expansion of dependence, especially among mothers and children.

Today's welfare system is anti-work and anti-marriage. It taxes families to subsidize illegitimacy. It rewards unethical behavior and penalizes initiative. It cannot be merely tinkered with by Congress; it must be re-created by states and localities. Republican governors and legislators in several states have already launched dramatic reforms, especially with workfare and learnfare. Welfare can no longer be a check in the mail with no responsibility.

We believe fathers and mothers must be held responsible for their children. We support stronger enforcement of child support laws. We call for strong enforcement and tough penalties against welfare fraud and insist that work must be a mandatory

part of public assistance for all who are able to work. Because divorce, desertion and illegitimacy account for almost all the increase in child poverty over the last 20 years, we put the highest priority upon enforcement of family rights and responsibilities.

Among these responsibilities is the obligation to get an education — a key to avoiding dependency. Families on welfare with school-age children must be required to send them to school or provide adequate home education in keeping with various state laws in order to continue receiving public assistance. Young adult heads of welfare households should be required to complete appropriate education or training programs.

**Safe homes and streets.** One of the first duties of government is to protect the public security — to maintain law and order so that citizens are free to pursue the fruits of life and liberty. The Democrats have forsaken this solemn pledge. Instead of protecting society from hardened criminals, they blame society and refuse to hold accountable for their actions individuals who have chosen to engage in violent and criminal conduct. This has led to the state of affairs in which we find ourselves today.

Violent crime is the gravest domestic threat to our way of life. It has turned our communities into battlegrounds, playgrounds into graveyards. It threatens everyone, but especially the very young, the elderly, the weak. It destroys business and suffocates economic opportunity in struggling communities. It is a travesty that some American children have to sleep in bathtubs for protection from stray bullets. The poverty of values that justifies drive-by shootings and random violence holds us hostage and insecure, even in our own homes. We must work to develop community-help projects designed to instill a sense of responsibility and pride.

This is the legacy of a liberalism that elevates criminals' rights above victims' rights, that justifies soft-on-crime judges' approving early-release prison programs and that leaves law enforcement officers powerless to deter crime with the threat of certain punishment.

For 12 years, two Republican presidents have fought to reverse this trend, along with Republican officials in the states. They have named tough law-and-order judges, pushed for minimum mandatory sentences, expanded federal assistance to states and localities, sought to help states redress court orders on prison overcrowding, and devoted record resources that are turning the tide against drugs. They have repeatedly proposed legislation, consistently rejected by congressional Democrats, to restore the severest penalties for the most heinous crimes, to ensure swift and certain punishment, and to end the legal loopholes that let criminals go free.

Congressional Democrats reject Republican reform of the exclusionary rule that prohibits use of relevant evidence obtained in good faith and allows criminals, even murderers, to go free on a technicality. They reject our reform of habeas corpus law to prevent the appellate process from becoming a lawyers' game to thwart justice through endless appeals and procedural delays. They refuse to enact effective procedures to reinstate the death penalty for the most heinous crimes. They reject tougher, mandatory sentences for career criminals. Instead, congressional Democrats actually voted to create more loopholes for vicious thugs and fewer protections for victims of crime and have opposed mandatory restitution for victims. Their crime legislation, which we emphatically reject, cripples law enforcement by overturning over 20 United States Supreme Court cases that have helped to reduce crime and keep violent criminal offenders off the streets.

For too long our criminal justice system has carefully protected the rights of criminals and neglected the suffering of the innocent victims of crime and their families. We support the rights of crime victims to be present, heard and informed throughout the criminal justice process, and to be provided with restitution and services to aid their recovery.

We believe in giving police the resources to do their job. Law enforcement must remain primarily a state and local responsibility. With 95 percent of all violent crimes within the jurisdiction of the states, we have led efforts to increase the number of police protecting our citizens. We also support incentives to encourage personnel leaving the armed forces to continue to defend their country — against the enemy within — by entering the law enforcement profession.

Narcotics traffic drives street crime. President Bush has, for the first time, used the resources of our armed forces against the international drug trade. By our insistence, multilateral control of precursor chemicals and money laundering is now an international priority. We decry efforts by congressional Democrats to slash international anti-narcotics funding and inhibit the most vital control efforts in Peru. We support efforts to work with South and Central American leaders to eradicate crops used to produce illegal narcotics.

The Republican Party is committed to a drug-free America. During the last 12 years, we have radically reversed the Democrats' attitude of tolerance toward narcotics, vastly increased federal operations against drugs, cleaned up the military and launched mandatory testing for employees in various fields, including White House personnel. As a result, overall drug abuse is falling. We urge that states and communities emphasize anti-drug education by police officers and others in schools to educate young children to the dangers of the drug culture. Dope is no longer trendy.

We oppose legalizing or decriminalizing drugs. That is a morally abhorrent idea, the last vestige of an ill-conceived philosophy that counseled the legitimacy of permissiveness. Today, a similarly dysfunctional morality explains away drug dealing as an escape, and drive-by shootings as an act of political violence. There is no excuse for the wanton destruction of human life. We therefore support the stiffest penalties, including the death penalty, for major drug traffickers.

Drug users must face punishment, including fines and imprisonment, for contributing to the demand that makes the drug trade profitable. Among possible sanctions should be the loss of government assistance and suspension of drivers' licenses. Residents of public housing should be able to protect their families against drugs by screening out abusers and dealers. We support grass-roots action to drive dealers and crack houses out of operation.

Safe streets also mean highways that are free of drunken drivers and drivers under the influence of illegal drugs. Republicans support the toughest possible state laws to deal with drunken drivers and users of illegal drugs, who deserve no sympathy from our courts or state legislatures. We also oppose the illicit abuse of legal drugs.

White-collar crime threatens homes and families in a different way. It steals secretly, forcing up prices, rigging contracts, swindling consumers and harming the overwhelming majority of business people who play fair and obey the law. We support imprisonment for those who steal from the American people. We pledge an all-out fight against it, especially within the political machines that control many of our major cities. We will continue to bring to justice corrupt politicians and those who collude with them to plunder savings and loans.

**New members of the American family.** Our nation of immigrants continues to welcome those seeking a better life. This reflects our past, when some newcomers fled intolerance; some sought prosperity; some came as slaves. All suffered and sacrificed but hoped their children would have a better life. All searched for a shared vision — and found one in America. Today we are stronger for our diversity.

Illegal entry into the United States, on the other hand, threatens the social compact on which immigration is based. That is, the nation accepts immigrants and is enriched by their determination and values. Illegal immigration, on the other hand, undermines the integrity of border communities and already crowded urban neighborhoods. We will build on the already announced strengthening of the Border Patrol to better coordinate interdiction of illegal entrants through greater cross-border cooperation. Specifically, we will increase the size of the Border Patrol in order to meet the increasing need to stop illegal immigration and we will equip the Border Patrol with the tools, technologies and structures necessary to secure the border.

We will seek stiff penalties for those who smuggle illegal aliens into the country, and for those who produce or sell fraudulent documents. We also will reduce incentives to enter the United States by promot-

ing initiatives such as the North American Free Trade Agreement. In creating new economic opportunity in Mexico, a NAFTA removes the incentive to cross the border illegally in search of work.

**Individual rights.** The protection of individual rights is the foundation for opportunity and security.

The Republican Party is unique in this regard. Since its inception, it has respected every person, even when that proposition was not universally popular. Today, as in the day of Lincoln, we insist that no American's rights are negotiable.

That is why we declare that bigotry and prejudice have no place in American life. We denounce all who practice or promote racism, anti-Semitism or religious intolerance. We believe churches and religious schools should not be taxed; we defend the right of religious leaders to speak out on public issues; and we condemn the cowardly desecration of places of worship that has shocked our country in recent years.

Asserting equal rights for all, we support the Bush administration's vigorous enforcement of statutes to prevent illegal discrimination on account of sex, race, creed or national origin. Promoting opportunity, we reject efforts to replace equal rights with quotas or other preferential treatment. That is why President Bush fought so long against the Democrat Congress to win a civil rights bill worthy of that name.

We renew the historic Republican commitment to the rights of women, from the early days of the suffragist movement to the present. Because legal rights mean little without opportunity, we assert economic growth as the key to the continued progress of women in all fields of American life.

We believe the unborn child has a fundamental individual right to life that cannot be infringed. We therefore reaffirm our support for a human life amendment to the Constitution, and we endorse legislation to make clear that the 14th Amendment's protections apply to unborn children. We oppose using public revenues for abortion and will not fund organizations that advocate it. We commend those who provide alternatives to abortion by meeting the needs of mothers and offering adoption services. We reaffirm our support for appointment of judges who respect traditional family values and the sanctity of innocent human life.

President Bush signed into law the greatest advance ever for disabled persons: The Americans with Disabilities Act, a milestone in removing barriers to full participation in our country's life. We will fully implement it with sensitivity to the needs of small businesses, just as we have earlier legal protections for the disabled in federal programs. We oppose the non-consensual withholding of health care or treatment from any person because of handicap, age or infirmity, just as we oppose euthana-sia and assisted suicide.

We support full access to the polls, and the entire political process, by disabled voters. We will ensure that students with disabilities benefit from America 2000's new emphasis on testing for excellence and accountability for results.

Promoting the rights of the disabled requires, before all else, an expanding economy, both to advance assistive technology and to create opportunities for personal advancement. That is another reason why Republicans are committed to growth.

We reaffirm our commitment to the Fifth Amendment to the Constitution: "No person shall be . . . deprived of life, liberty, or property, without due process of law; nor shall private property be taken for public use, without just compensation." We support strong enforcement of this Takings Clause to keep citizens secure in the use and development of their property. We also seek to reduce the amount of land owned or controlled by the government, especially in the Western states. We insist upon prompt payment for private lands certified as critical for preserving essential parks and preserves.

Republicans defend the constitutional right to keep and bear arms. We call for stiff mandatory sentences for those who use firearms in a crime. We note that those who seek to disarm citizens in their homes are the same liberals who tried to disarm our nation during the Cold War and are today seeking to cut our national defense below safe levels. We applaud congressional Republicans for overturning the District of Columbia's law blaming firearm manufacturers for street crime.

We affirm the right of individuals to form, join or assist labor organizations to bargain collectively, consistent with state laws. We support the right of states to enact right-to-work laws.

A Republican Congress will amend the Hobbs Act, so that union officials will not be exempt from the law's prohibition against extortion and violence. We call for greater legal protection from violence for workers who stay on the job during strikes.

We support self-determination for Indian tribes in managing their own affairs and resources. Recognizing the government-to-government trust responsibility, we aim to end dependency fostered by federal controls. Reservations and tribal lands held in trust should be free to become enterprise zones so their people can fully share in the nation's prosperity. We will work with tribal governments to improve education, health, economic opportunity and environmental conditions. We endorse efforts to preserve the culture and languages of Native Americans and Hawaiians and to ensure their equitable participation in federal programs.

## Uniting Our Country

Over the last four years, the United States has achieved our overriding objective since the end of World War II. Com-munism and other forms of planned economies lie in the ash heap of history, defeated not only by our military strength but by the force of our ideas — democracy and free enterprise.

Now a huge international market is evolving. Combined with America's low inflation and low interest rate environment, it presents us with unprecedented economic opportunity. We commit to the proposition that the American economy will remain first in the world. This is our goal. Achieving it will ensure that our people will enjoy the jobs, benefits and economic growth to sustain the American dream for themselves and their posterity.

Republicans believe that the greatest engine for social change and economic progress is the entrepreneurial economy. We believe that America has broken down the lines of class to a greater degree than any society on earth, not because of government but because of an economic system that allows men and women to create wealth for themselves and their communities. We believe that positive change can occur and benefit all Americans if we continue to remove governmental barriers to entrepreneurship and, thus, economic growth.

Our cause embraces traditional ideals and modern realities. It both reforms and innovates. We aim to shape history through faith in one another. Because we look forward, we emphasize saving, investment and job creation. We encourage innovation and the entrepreneurial spirit that are, together, part of our national character. We both conserve and develop our natural resources. Because we have learned from the past, we are determined to change what desperately needs changing in government.

Government does not have all the answers, but we know where to find them: in the spirit of our people. We know the weapons for this battle: economic and political liberty in the pursuit of happiness. We understand that material gain improves life only if it lifts us all to pursue higher ends: self-respect, work and study, a decent life and future for our children, and a useful old age.

So we rededicate ourselves to the truths the nation keeps coming back to — the simple, spiritual truths about our family, our country, our world — for upon them we will build our more perfect union.

## Security and Opportunity in a Changing Economy

Our economy is people, not statistics. The American people, not government, rescued the United States from an economic collapse triggered by Democrats in the 1970s. Crippled by taxes, robbed by inflation, threatened by controls, stunned by interest rates, the people ended America's decline and restored hope across our country and around our world.

We launched an era of growth and prosperity such as the world had never seen: 20 million new jobs in the longest peacetime economic expansion in the his-

tory of the Republic. We curbed the size and power of the federal establishment. We lowered tax rates. We restored a sound dollar. We unleashed the might of free people to produce, compete and triumph in free markets. We gave them the tools; they completed the job.

During the 1980s and into the present decade, the U.S. economy once again became the engine of global growth. Inflation has fallen to its lowest level in 30 years. Interest rates dropped 15 percentage points. Productivity has sharply risen. Exports are booming. Despite a global downturn in late 1990, real economic growth resumed last year and has continued for five consecutive quarters. With low interest rates and low inflation, the American economy is poised for stronger growth through the rest of the 1990s. Keeping inflation and interest rates low and stable through a sound monetary policy is essential for economic growth.

These gains were made in spite of the leaders of the Democratic Party. They continue to delay and defeat the president's agenda for growth, jobs and prosperity. Spending faster than ever, they blocked Republican reforms that would have saved billions of wasted taxpayer dollars. They refused to give the president a line-item veto to curb their self-serving pork-barrel projects.

The congressional Democrat leadership killed the Taxpayer Protection Amendment for a balanced budget in the Democrat-controlled House of Representatives. It was supported by 98 percent of the Republican members; 57 percent of the Democrat members voted no. Then they rigged parliamentary procedures to forbid a vote on that amendment in the Democrat-controlled Senate. Every Republican senator voted twice to end the filibuster, while more than 70 percent of the Democrats voted twice to keep the filibuster going. Their nominee this year for the vice presidency supported the filibuster and spurned the balanced-budget amendment.

They played citizens against one another, wallowing in the politics of hate and envy to smear the wonder of social mobility. They lied about America's achievement in the 1980s, rewriting history to erase the true accomplishments of the American people.

**Keeping what you earn.** The test of economic policy is whether it promotes economic growth and expands job opportunities. Lower taxes and an expanding economy depend on long-term, consistent restraint in the growth of federal spending.

In 1990, as the deficit was threatening to balloon and further harm the economy, the president pushed for cuts in government spending overall and for caps on mandatory spending. The Democrat Congress insisted, however, on a tax hike as their price for controlling spending. In short, the Democrats held the U.S. economy — and U.S. jobs –- hostage in order to raise taxes, much as they had done to President Reagan.

Just as they did with President Reagan, the Democrat-controlled Congress promised President Bush they would abide by binding controls on federal spending; and just as with President Reagan, they broke their word. Republicans will not again agree to such a program.

This year, to create jobs and promote growth, President Bush submitted a program of tax cuts and incentives designed to get the economy moving again — a program very similar to one he had sent to Congress in early 1990.

The Democrats' response was predictable — instead of cutting taxes, they passed a $100 billion tax increase that would have smothered growth and jobs. The president, true to our Republican philosophy, vetoed this tax hike, and sustained his veto with the support of Republicans in Congress.

Now a new Democrat nominee comes forward with his plan for the economy. With a clean piece of paper, and every opportunity to end his party's romance with taxes, he has instead proposed the largest tax increase in American history. His tax increases, his proposed mandated benefits on small firms, and his further reductions in defense would cost the jobs of 2.6 million Americans. With his present spending increases, his plan would greatly increase the federal budget and the deficit.

The simple truth for the American people is this: The only safeguard between themselves and Democrat tax increases is the use of the veto by George Bush and enough Republican votes in Congress to sustain it.

The truth is that the Democrat philosophy of bigger government and rigorous redistribution of income requires them to push for ever increasing spending and ever higher taxes.

The choice is clear — between George Bush, who vetoes tax increases, and his opponent, who proposes a $150 billion tax increase.

Our Republican position is equally clear: We will oppose any attempt to increase taxes. Furthermore, Republicans believe that the taxes insisted on by the Democrats in the 1990 budget agreement were recessionary. The Democrat Congress held President Bush and indeed all Americans hostage, refusing to take even modest steps to control spending, unless taxes were increased. The American economy suffered as a result. We believe the tax increases of 1990 should ultimately be repealed.

Just as history shows that tax increases destroy jobs and economic growth, it also shows that the proper path to create jobs and growth is tax rate reduction.

We commend those congressional and senatorial candidates who pledge to oppose tax rate increases.

As the deficit comes under control, we aspire to further tax rate cuts, strengthening incentives to work, save, invest and innovate. We also support President Bush's efforts to reduce federal spending and to cap the growth of non-Social Security entitlements.

Republicans want individuals and families to control their own economic destiny. Only long-term expansion of our economy and jobs can make the American dream a reality for generations to come. That is why we demand that the Congress do what President Bush called for last January: open a new era of growth and opportunity by enacting his comprehensive plan for economic recovery, including a reduction in the capital gains tax; an investment tax allowance; a $5,000 tax credit for first-time home buyers; a needed modification of the "passive loss rule"; a $500 increase in the personal income tax exemption; making permanent the research and development tax credit; and the passage of federal enterprise zone legislation.

We support restoring the deductibility of IRAs for all Americans, including full-time homemakers, and encourage savings for education and home ownership through Family Savings Accounts. The president's Family Savings Accounts will be an impetus to the economy. Let families use their IRAs for first-time home purchases, for college education and for medical emergencies.

We will cut the capital gains tax rate to 15 percent — zero in enterprise zones — and index it so government cannot profit from inflation by taxing phantom capital gains, literally stealing from savings and pensions.

We reject the notion advanced by Democrats that this enhances the wealthy. To the contrary, it would encourage investment, create new jobs, make capital available for business expansion and contribute to economic expansion.

Reducing the tax on investment will be the biggest possible boost for the new technologies, businesses and jobs we need for the next century. If government taxes capital gains at such a high rate that there is no incentive to take risks, to build businesses, to invest, to create jobs or to better oneself, then jobs and small businesses vanish, and everyone's opportunities are diminished.

Cutting the rate, on the other hand, will help supply seed capital where it is needed most — in our poorest communities. Refusing to cut it will handcuff America in international competition and will shackle aspiring entrepreneurs in inner cities and poor rural areas. To encourage investment in new technologies, we will make permanent the research and development tax credit. For the same reason, we want to expand deductibility for investments in new plant and equipment.

**We support further tax simplification.** The tax code should create jobs for Americans, not profits for tax lawyers, lobbyists and tax shelters. Small businesses should spend more time hiring and producing, not filling out IRS forms.

**We oppose taxing religious and ethnic fraternal benefit societies** because of their vital role in fostering charity and patriotism.

**We also oppose tax withholding on savings and dividends.**

**We applaud the efforts by President Bush to help workers who change jobs by enhancing the portability of pensions.**

Leading Democrat members of Congress have called for a national sales tax, or European style value-added tax (VAT), which would take billions of dollars out of the hands of American consumers. Such a tax has been imposed on many nations in Europe and has resulted in higher prices, fewer jobs and higher levels of government spending. Republicans oppose the idea of putting a VAT on the backs of the American people.

Republicans believe in expanding the economy. Jobs and growth are our answer to the future.

**The future is the family.** The most dramatic change in the tax code in our lifetime is one that has never been explicitly enacted by Congress or reported as a specific new event. It is the gradual, year-by-year erosion of the personal exemption, until it was indexed by a Republican administration in 1986.

Republicans also led the way in the 1980s by increasing the personal exemption from $1,500 to $2,000. This platform calls for another immediate increase of $500, but in the long run we are committed to fully restoring the inflation-adjusted value of the personal exemption. This will require reductions in federal spending, which is why the best hope for tax fairness for America's families lies in a Republican Congress.

**Liberation through deregulation.** Government regulation is a hidden tax on American families, costing each household more than $5,000 every year. It stifles job creation and hobbles our national competitiveness. The "iron triangle" of special interests, federal bureaucrats and Democrat congressional staff is robbing consumers and producers alike.

We support President Bush's freeze on new regulations. We applaud his Competitiveness Council, under Vice President Quayle, for fighting the regulatory mania, saving the public $20 billion with its initial 90-day moratorium on new regulations and billions more under the current 120-day freeze. We call for a permanent moratorium until our regulatory reforms are fully in place. They include market-based regulation, cost-benefit analysis of all new rule-making, and a regulatory budget that will make Congress admit — and correct — the harm it does by legislation that destroys jobs and competitiveness.

We recognize that property rights are being endangered by government over-regulation. We reaffirm the constitutional right to private ownership of property; this right is paramount in our free society. Every rule that reduces the value of private property is what our Constitution calls a "taking." This under-the-table taxation is unfair, immoral and economically destructive. We support legislation to require full compensation of property owners who are victims of regulatory takings.

**Homeownership.** The best housing policy is a non-inflationary, growing economy that has produced low mortgage rates and has made housing more affordable.

We demand Congress enact President's Bush's housing program introduced as part of his pro-growth package in January.

Provide a $5,000 tax credit for first-time home buyers and allow them penalty-free IRA withdrawals.

Set a modified "passive loss rule" for active real estate investors.

Extend tax preferences for mortgage revenue bonds and low-income housing.

And allow deductions for losses on personal residences.

The average American's home is his or her primary asset. That asset should be completely shielded from federal taxation, allowing the homeowner to maintain it or access it as he or she sees fit. We call for the complete elimination of the capital gains tax on the sale of a principal residence.

Owning a home is not just an investment. It is a commitment to the community, a guard against crime, a statement about family life. It is a crucial component of upward mobility. To advance these goals, Republicans are determined to preserve deductibility of mortgage interest.

Bureaucratic government imposes too many regulatory barriers to affordable housing. These barriers must come down.

We applaud efforts in the states to lower property taxes, which strike hardest at the poor, the elderly, families with children and family farmers. We advocate repeal of rent-control laws, which help the affluent and hurt low-income families by causing housing shortages.

We support the FHA [Federal Housing Administration] mortgage insurance program, the Government National Mortgage Association, the VA [Department of Veterans Affairs] guarantee program and other programs that enhance housing choices for all. We urge federal departments and agencies to work with the private sector to bring foreclosed housing stock back into service as soon as possible.

We reaffirm our commitment to open housing, without quotas or controls, as part of the opportunity we seek for all.

For low-income families, the Republican Party stands for a revolution in housing by converting public housing into homes owned by low-income Americans. President Bush is eager to work closely with the states to fight and win a new conservative war on poverty. The truest measure of our success will not be how many families we add to housing assistance rolls but, rather, how many families move into the ranks of homeownership. But every part of that opportunity agenda has been thwarted by landlord Democrats in Congress. We ask the electorate: End the strangulation of divided government. Give Republicans the chance to move housing policy off the Democratic Party plantation into the mainstream of American life. Resident management and ownership of public housing reflects this American mission, not only to assure political freedom but to allow all our fellow citizens to build a better life for themselves and their children.

Congressional Democrats have consistently blocked efforts to repeal the earnings test which prevents people over age 65 from keeping their jobs and remaining productive members of the work force. The Social Security earnings test discriminates against senior citizens. These senior citizens have to pay the highest marginal tax rate of any Americans. We support repeal of the Social Security earnings test.

**Controlling government spending.** For 12 years, Republicans in the White House and Congress have battled a Democrat system corrupt and contemptuous of the American taxpayer. Our Republican presidents have vetoed one reckless bill after another. But liberal Democrats still control a rigged machine that keeps on spending the public's money.

The only solution is for the voters to end divided government so that a Republican Congress can enact the balanced-budget amendment, requiring a supermajority for any future tax increases. And since the Democrat-controlled Congress has consistently voted down a line-item veto amendment for the president to control specific wasteful pork barrel spending, a Republican Congress will adopt a line-item veto for the presidency, restore presidential power to rescind spending and to lower specific appropriations.

Deficits have grown as Democrat Congresses have converted government assistance programs into entitlements and allowed spending to become uncontrolled. A Republican Congress, working with a Republican president, will consider non-Social Security mandatory spending portions of the federal budget when looking for savings.

When legislators and bureaucrats waste tax money, they deserve to lose their jobs. When they save money, they deserve praise. When federal programs have outlived their usefulness, they deserve a decent burial. When federal judges dare to seize the power of the purse, by ordering the imposition of taxes, they should be removed from office by the procedures provided by the Constitution.

The latest Democrat scam is to raise taxes for "investment" — a code word for more government spending. A Republican Congress will foster investment where it does the most good, by individuals within the private sector.

**Job creation and small-business opportunities.** The engines of growth in a free economy are small businesses and jobs. Almost 99 percent of all businesses in America are considered small. Small business is the backbone of the American

economy. For the past 12 years it has led the way in economic growth.

Small business generates 67 percent of all new jobs. Employment in industries dominated by small business increased more than twice as fast as in industries dominated by large businesses. Small business plays a critical role in America's economic health. What happens on Main Street drives what happens on Wall Street.

To create jobs and keep small business growing, the Republican Party supports increased access to capital for business expansion, exporting, long-term investment, opportunity capital for the disadvantaged, and capital to bring new products and new technology to the market.

The Republican Party enthusiastically encourages the passage of federal enterprise zones. Enterprise zones have been effective programs for promoting growth in urban and rural America. Republicans believe that the concept of enterprise zones is based on unyielding faith in the entrepreneurial spirit of all Americans. Enterprise zones foster individual initiative and government deregulation. The states have come a long way in developing successful enterprise programs. State programs could only benefit from federal efforts. Congress should follow the lead of President Bush and HUD Secretary Jack Kemp in passing the federal enterprise zone program that will empower communities by reducing government regulation and taxation.

The implementation of enterprise zones as an incentive for job creation and business development is also essential to further job and business opportunities. These efforts are bolstered by continued support of job training and minority business development programs, which have been created and implemented by the president's administration within the last three years. This is of special import to women, who own 32 percent of the nation's businesses, most of them small ones.

Because the regulation of securities markets bars most small businesses from easy access to capital, we also support the Small Business Administration's Section 7(a) loan guarantee program and similar efforts that essentially compensate for the burdens government itself imposes upon entrepreneurs.

**Leading the information age.** The nation's telecommunications infrastructure will be essential to growth and competitiveness in the information age. The most far-reaching transformation of daily life since the harnessing of electricity will mean unprecedented opportunity for rural areas, reduced commuting, health care in the home and empowerment for the disabled.

Today, however, government policy at both the federal and state levels is standing in the way of this telecommunications progress.

Existing judicial, legislative and regulatory market allocation schemes constitute a counterproductive industrial policy by prohibiting the full participation by all providers in all segments of the telecom-

munications marketplace. We need to liberate this future-oriented technology and, in turn, empower the American people by giving consumers a truly competitive choice and lower prices.

As a result, we Republicans believe that full and open competition in the telecommunications marketplace is the most effective means for the United States to achieve our goal of having the most technologically advanced telecommunications infrastructure in the world.

**Jobs through science and technology.** We believe technology holds the key to America's future — and the future is bright. America is not in decline. America is still the land of opportunity. The new horizon is science and technology. New discoveries, new challenges and new opportunities await us. Science and technology offer us change — exciting, dramatic and positive change in the well-being of every American.

Scientific research and development in genetics, biotechnology and electronics will provide better, more affordable health care for all Americans. Distance learning, through technology, will help bring exciting, quality, affordable education to all students, even in rural areas and inner cities. Technology will help us conquer disease, protect the environment and provide a more abundant, healthier food supply. And technology will lead to better jobs and a better quality of life for all of us — and for our children and our children's children.

Scientific and technological developments in telecommunications, high-performance computers, high-speed data networks, digitization, advanced software, biotechnology, high-energy physics, advanced materials, superconductors, manufacturing processes, energy, transportation, agriculture, oceanography, atmospheric studies, geological research, space and the environment are some of the keys to increases in productivity. And increases in productivity will create economic growth and a higher standard of living for all of us. Technology is also critical to our national defense.

We believe America must make technological development one of its highest priorities. We therefore support efforts to promote science and technology — providing funding for basic research, supporting investment in emerging technologies, improving education in science and engineering, enhancing tax credits for research and development, eliminating unnecessary regulation to create competitive markets, and protecting intellectual property. We further support efforts to increase the pace of technology transfer from the government to the private sector, where the fruits of this research can be used in the free market to create new processes, products and most important, jobs.

We believe these policies will make us internationally competitive and will lead to a bright and prosperous future for our nation.

President Bush has provided leadership in this area by developing budgets allocating major new resources to scientific endeavors. The National Science Foundation, the National Institutes of Health, the National Aeronautics and Space Administration (NASA), and the research and development program in the departments of Energy and Commerce have all become budget priorities under the president's leadership. The sad fact is, however, that the Democrat Congress has cut steadily and sharply in science areas in order to expand spending on social programs. This is shortsighted; the truth is that American innovation in science and engineering will expand our economy and jobs to greater social advantage to all Americans. A Republican Congress working with President Bush would reflect our interest in advancing scientific inquiry and assuring the resulting economic benefits for all Americans.

**Space.** We are a pioneer people. Today's telecommunications revolution began with the first satellites of the Eisenhower years. So too, what we now do — or fail to do — in space will determine the future for generations to come.

That is why President Bush established the National Space Council under Vice President Quayle. Together, they rescued a floundering program, revamped NASA, opened up competition and engaged the best minds of academia and research in a twofold mission for mankind. Mission to Planet Earth will define and perhaps mitigate effects on our fragile environment. Mission from Planet Earth will open space for science and industry. Especially in this Columbian year, we hail the president's decision "to return to the moon, this time to stay, and then a journey to tomorrow, a mission to Mars."

Investments in space, though aimed at the future, pay dividends right now — in research and medicine, in international competitiveness and domestic opportunity. This must not be diverted to political pork barrels. The journey to the stars used to be a bipartisan adventure, but many Democrat officeholders have jumped ship.

Republicans, by contrast, are determined to complete space station *Freedom* within this decade. Our agenda is to lower the cost of access to space, and to broaden that access to the private sector, with a family of new launchers; to build and fly sensors for the global environment; and to advance cutting-edge capabilities like the National Aerospace Plane and single stage-to-orbit rockets, so technological breakthroughs can be quickly exploited. We will promote space-based industry and ensure that space remains a frontier for private enterprise, not a restricted preserve for government. We will continue international cooperation in space ventures and welcome Russia's cosmonauts and citizens of other nations to fly for freedom.

**Banking and job creation.** Job cre-

ation and economic growth are dependent on a healthy and competitive financial services system that can respond to the needs of the market. The Democrat Congress stalled Republican legislation to prevent the savings and loan crisis. Then, last year, the Congress refused to pass the Republican administration's comprehensive financial sector reform bill to strengthen our banking industry and let it compete, both domestically and internationally, consistent with the principles of safety and soundness.

We applaud the president's efforts to alleviate the continuing problems caused by lack of funds available to creditworthy borrowers in small businesses and the housing industry. We endorse his efforts to restrain overzealous regulators, reduce regulatory compliance costs, strengthen financial institutions through diversification and reduce unnecessary barriers to lending.

**Trade: A new world of growth.** Four years ago, the American people faced an historic decision: Compete or retreat. They chose, with President Bush, to compete in the international arena. Rather than retreat with the Democrats to the limits of yesteryear, they decided to attack the international marketplace with characteristic American vigor. Just as George Bush is a proven world leader on the military front, equally he is an economic world leader.

The results are spectacular. We have cut the trade deficit in half in just four years. The United States is again the world's top exporter. Exports drive our economy. Every $1 billion in exports creates 20,000 new jobs for Americans. Exports have created nearly 2 million new jobs at home since 1988.

We are tough free traders, battling to sweep away barriers to our exports. We are waging the Uruguay Round of the General Agreement on Tariffs and Trade (GATT) negotiations to win worldwide reductions in tariffs, elimination of subsidies and protection of American intellectual property rights. We are fighting to reduce farm subsidies in the European Community and to break up their government-industry collusion in production of civil aircraft. We firmly endorse President Bush's policy to support the Republic of China on Taiwan in international trade and her accession to GATT. Major market access gains have been made with Japan, with American manufacturing exports tripling since 1985. Throughout the world, we enforced greater compliance with U.S. trade rights. And we are making every effort to bring home a Uruguay Round agreement that is not only good for America, but great for tomorrow's entrepreneurs everywhere.

The free-trade agenda for the next four years starts with the signing of a North American Free Trade Agreement (NAFTA) with Mexico, completing the establishment of a free-trade area which already includes Canada. NAFTA will create the largest market in the world, greater than the European Community, with 360 million consumers and a total output of six trillion dollars. It means a net gain of hundreds of thousands of American jobs.

We acknowledge the possible effects on regional markets, specifically agriculture. We encourage our negotiators to be sensitive to those market concerns.

We will continue to fill the Pacific Rim with American exports, negotiating trade agreements with other Asian economies, and will complete our efforts — such as the Structural Impediments Initiative with Japan — to reduce barriers to American goods and services. And we will continue to negotiate the Enterprise for the Americas Initiative with Latin America as a first step in creating a hemispheric free-trade zone.

Congress should report to the American people the cost to workers, consumers and businesses of every Democrat trade restriction, trade tax or trade quota bill it considers. We will not tolerate their obstructing the greatest expansion of international trade in history. Republicans welcome this opportunity; for we know America's workers, thinkers and builders will make the most of it.

**International economic policy.** Twelve years ago, we unleashed a tidal wave of freedom around the world — not just political but economic liberty as well. What works in America — personal responsibility, limited government, competition — works throughout the world.

Because the world economy is interdependent, the United States has been affected by downturns elsewhere, particularly since 1990 with the crash of the Japanese stock market and Germany's economic difficulties. Now, as progress resumes, the Republican plan for global growth is vital for all nations, developed or otherwise. The continuing prosperity of our neighborhoods will depend in part upon the masterful diplomacy we have come to expect from President Bush.

Economic freedom is an essential link to our foreign policy. It means expanded trade, but it also means dynamic growth based on shared values — a coming together of nations in the commonwealth of peaceful progress. To that end, U.S. aid, whether bilateral or through international organizations, should promote market reforms, limit regulation and encourage free trade.

Chief among these market reforms should be the privatization of state-owned industries such as telecommunications, power, mining and refining. Privatization should afford American companies the opportunity to purchase some of these assets, bring competition to these countries and substantially reduce our trade deficit. The United States government should take all possible steps to assist American companies wishing to invest in privatized industries by adopting policies, rules and regulations that will equitably facilitate these ventures, especially for small businesses.

We will work with developing nations to make their economies attractive to private investment and will support innovations to guarantee repayment of their loans, including debt for equity swaps. Our experience can help them develop environmentally rational strategies for growth.

Because we uphold the family as the building block of economic progress, we protect its right in international programs and will continue to withhold funds from organizations involved in abortion.

Most important, we encourage developing nations to adopt both democracy and free markets. The two are inextricably tied and afford all people the greatest opportunities.

### Reforming Government and the Legal System

Two centuries ago, the American people created a miracle — a system of government, founded on limited authority and the rule of law, a system that made government the servant of the people. Today it is in shambles. Citizens feel overwhelmed by vast bureaucracies. Congress insulates incumbents from public judgment. Huge problems get worse while committee chairmen play partisan games. The current legal system tends to breed delay, cost, confusion and jargon — everything but justice. Many of our once-great cities are controlled by one-party machines that promote and encourage corruption and incompetence.

The Republic has not failed; the Democratic Party bosses failed the Republic.

The Republican Party, now as at its founding, challenges a debased status quo. In Congress, the states, our cities, our courtrooms, we fight for the basics of self-government.

We rely on what works, judging programs by how well they do instead of how much they spend. The Democrats believe in more government. Republicans believe in leaner, more effective government.

We decentralize authority, returning decisions to states, localities and private institutions. The Democrat bosses want to concentrate power on Capitol Hill. Republicans place it in town halls and the American home.

Republicans favor the free-enterprise system. We choose market forces — consumer rights — over red tape. The Democrats argue that government must constantly override the market. Republicans regard the worst market failure as the failure to have a market.

We replace dependency with empowerment. The Democrats see an America filled with wards of the state. Republicans see an America peopled by citizens and consumers eager for the chance to chart their own course.

We make electoral systems understandable and accountable to the voter. The Democrats fear proposals that would limit the tenure and hidden power of incumbent politicians. Republicans want the

ballot box to prevail over the cloakroom.

**Cleaning up the imperial Congress.** The Democrats have controlled the House of Representatives for 38 years — five years longer than Castro has held Cuba. They have held the Senate for 32 of those 38. Their entrenched power has produced a Congress arrogant, out of touch, hopelessly entangled in a web of PACs, perks, privileges, partisanship, paralysis and pork. No wonder they hid their congressional leaders during the Democrat convention of 1992. They didn't want Americans to remember who has been running the Congress.

The Democrats have transformed what the framers of the Constitution intended as the people's House into a pathological institution. They have grossly increased their staffing, their payrolls, their allied bureaucracies in little-known congressional agencies. Congress has ballooned to 284 congressional committees and subcommittees, almost 40,000 legislative branch employees and staff, and $2.5 billion in taxpayer financing, amounting to approximately $5 million per lawmaker per year. Incumbents have abused free mailing privileges for personal political gain. Twenty-two Democrats, with a total of 585 years in power, rule over a committee system that blocks every attempt at reform.

The Democrats have trampled the traditions of the House, rigging rules, forbidding votes on crucial amendments, denying fair apportionment of committee seats and resources. They have stacked campaign laws to benefit themselves. The Democrat leadership of the House has been tainted with scandal and has resisted efforts to investigate scandals once disclosed. Some in their leadership have resigned in well-earned disgrace.

The Democrat leadership of the Congress has turned the healthy competition of constitutional separation of powers into mean-spirited politics of innuendo and inquisition. Committee hearings are no longer for fact-finding; they are political sideshows. "Advise and consent" has been replaced by "slash and burn."

Republicans want to change all that. We reaffirm our support for a constitutional amendment to limit the number of terms House members and senators may serve. We want a citizens' Congress, free of bloated pensions and perpetual perks.

Congress must stop exempting itself from laws such as the minimum wage and the civil rights statutes, as well as laws that apply to the executive branch. The Independent Counsel Act is a case in point. It has permitted rogue prosecutors to spend tremendous amounts to hound some of the nation's finest public servants. If that act is reauthorized, it must be extended to Congress as well. Safety and health regulations, civil rights and minimum wage laws are further examples of areas where Congress has set itself apart from the people. This practice must end.

Congress must slash its own bureau-

cracy. Its employees operate in a maze of overlapping jurisdictions. A Republican Congress will cut expenses by 25 percent, reduce the number of committees and subcommittees, and assign staff in accurate proportion to party strength.

We will restore integrity to the House of Representatives, reforming its rules, allowing open debate and amendment. The committee system, both in Congress and in Democrat-controlled state legislatures, has been abused by chairpersons who have arbitrarily killed legislation that would have passed. Committees are a place for open and free discussion, not a closet for Democrats to stash Republican legislation. Democracy itself is endangered by these abuses, and Republicans condemn those practices. Both houses of Congress must guarantee protection to whistleblowers to encourage employees to report illegality, corruption, sexual harassment and discrimination.

The Democrat rulers of Congress have blocked or stalled presidential initiatives in many areas, including education, housing, crime control, economic recovery, job creation and budget reform. They care more about scoring petty partisan points for themselves and their party than about achieving real progress for the nation. To accomplish change, we need a change in Congress.

**Reforming the congressional budget process.** At the heart of the Democrats' corruption of Congress is a fraudulent budget process. They do not want the public to understand how they spend the public's money. At a time when the nation's future depends on reduction of deficits, the lords of the Capitol still play the old shell game.

Republicans vigorously support a balanced budget, a balanced-budget constitutional amendment and a line-item veto for the president.

Republicans believe this balancing of the budget should be achieved, not by increasing taxes to match spending, but by cutting spending to current levels of revenue. We prefer a balanced-budget amendment that contains a supermajority requirement to raise taxes.

We also propose procedural reforms. We support legislation that would require Congress to pass a legally binding budget before it can consider spending bills. The budget's spending ceilings shall not be exceeded without a supermajority vote of both chambers. If Congress fails to pass any appropriation bill, funding for its programs will automatically be frozen at the previous year's level. The key to prosperity for the rest of this century and for the next generation of Americans is a budget strategy that restores sanity to the budget process and checks the growth of government.

Congress should be forced to confront basic arithmetic through Truth in Counting. The Democrats measure all changes in funding against a "current services baseline," with built-in increases for inflation

and other factors. If they want a $1 million program to grow to $2 million, they then count an increase to $1.5 million as a half-million dollar cut. This is the accounting system of Wonderland, where words mean exactly what the Democrat Speaker says they mean. The double-talk must end with zero-based budgeting. We also support "sunset laws" that require government agencies to be reviewed periodically and reauthorized only if they can be rejustified.

**Cleaning up politics: The gerrymander.** After more than a half-century of distortion by power-hungry Democrats, the political system is increasingly rigged.

Throughout the 1980s, voters were cheated out of dozens of seats in the House of Representatives and in state legislatures because districts were oddly shaped to guarantee election of Democrats. It was swindle by law. We support state-level appointment of nonpartisan redistricting commissions to apply clear standards for compactness of districts, competitiveness between the parties and protection of community interests.

**Cleaning up politics: Campaign reform.** We crusade for clean elections. We support state efforts to increase voter participation but condemn Democrat attempts to perpetrate vote fraud through schemes that override the state's safeguards of orderly voter registration. And it is critical that the states retain the authority to tailor voter registration procedures to unique local circumstances.

Most of all, we condemn the Democrats' shameless plots to make taxpayers foot the bills for their campaigns. Their campaign finance bill would have given $1 billion, over six years, in subsidies to candidates. President Bush vetoed that bill. Campaign financing does need reform. It does not need a hand in the public's pocketbook.

We will require congressional candidates to raise most of their funds from individuals within their home constituencies. This will limit outside special-interest money and result in less expensive campaigns, with less padding for incumbents. To the same end, we will strengthen the role of political parties to remove pressure on candidates to spend so much time soliciting funds. We will eliminate political action committees supported by corporations, unions or trade associations, and restrict the practice of bundling.

To restore competition in elections by attacking the unfair advantages of incumbency, we will stop incumbents from warding off challengers merely by amassing huge war chests. Congressional candidates will be forbidden from carrying campaign funds from one election to the next. We will oppose arbitrary spending limits — cynical devices which hobble challengers to keep politicians in office.

We will fully implement the Supreme Court's decision in the *Beck* case, ensuring that workers have the right to stop the use

of their union dues for political or other non-collective bargaining purposes.

**Managing government in the public interest.** The focus of government must shift from quantity to quality, from spending to service. Americans should expect measurable, published standards for services provided by government at all levels. Performance standards and rules, commonplace in the private sector, must be applied to government activities as well. Because federal government employees should not be a privileged caste, we will remove the bar to garnishing their wages to ensure payment of their debts.

The Quality Revolution in American business has quietly but profoundly transformed American culture over the past decade. Millions of American workers have benefited from the more cooperative spirit the Quality Revolution has brought to tens of thousands of workplaces; and every American has benefited from the lower costs, higher quality service and greater level of competitiveness it has produced. Republicans are proud to have played a leading role in this transformation, especially through the annual Malcolm Baldrige National Quality Award, which recognizes companies that best represent the principles of quality.

The Quality Revolution in the private sector, with its concepts of continuous improvement, profound knowledge and "doing the right thing right the first time," stands in stark contrast to the outmoded practices, insensitivity and outright waste, abuse and corruption endemic in the bureaucratic welfare state. The Republican Party is firmly committed to bringing the Quality Revolution into government at every level by creating a "Quality Workers for a Quality America" coalition whose aim will be to transform the bureaucratic welfare state into a government that is customer-friendly, cost-effective and improving constantly.

Privatization is an important alternative to higher taxes and reduced services. If private enterprise can perform better and more cheaply than government, let it do so. This is especially true of properties now decaying under government control, such as public housing, where residents should have the option to manage their own projects. These citizens should have the chance to become stockholders and managers of government enterprises and to run them more efficiently as private enterprises. We applaud President Bush's initiative to allow states and localities to privatize facilities built with federal aid.

Where it advances both efficiency and safety, we will advocate privatization of airport operation and management.

We deplore the blatant political bias of the government-sponsored radio and television networks. It is especially outrageous that taxpayers are now forced to underwrite this biased broadcasting through the Corporation for Public Broadcasting (CPB). We call for sweeping reform of CPB, including greater accountability through application of the Freedom of Information Act, a one-year funding cycle and enforcement of rigorous fairness standards for all CPB-supported programming. We look forward to the day when public broadcasting is self-sufficient.

Always trusting the initiative of the American people over the ways of government, we will not initiate production of goods or delivery of services by the federal government if they can be procured from the private sector.

**We will not initiate any federal activity that can be conducted better on the state or local level.** In doing so, we reassert the crucial importance of the 10th Amendment. We oppose costly federal mandates that stifle innovation and force tax hikes upon states and localities. We require that Congress calculate the cost of mandated initiatives upon communities affected and provide adequate financial support for mandates invoked. We will continue the process of returning power to local voters by replacing federal programs with block grants.

**Reforming the legal system.** The United States, with 5 percent of the world's population, has two-thirds of the world's lawyers. Litigation has become an industry, an end in itself. The number of civil cases in federal district courts has more than tripled in the past 30 years. It now takes more than a year to resolve the average lawsuit. Delays of three to five years are commonplace.

The current legal system forces consumers to pay higher prices for everything from basic goods to medical treatment. Direct litigation and inflated insurance premiums sock American consumers for an estimated $80 billion a year. All told, our legal system costs, directly and indirectly, $300 billion a year. What it costs us in the world marketplace, by hindering our competitiveness, is beyond calculation.

We therefore endorse the president's proposals for legal reform as developed by Vice President Quayle, and we salute his principled challenge to the American Bar Association to clean up its own house. We support the Fairness Rule, to allow the winning party to a lawsuit to recover the costs of litigation from the losing party. This will discourage needless suits, freeing legal resources for people with genuine cases.

We believe complainants should have a choice of ways to settle problems through alternative dispute programs that will permit parties to pursue less costly and less complicated ways to resolve conflicts. We also call for greater use of judicial sanctions to stop frivolous lawsuits. We call for changes to the federal Racketeer Influenced and Corrupt Organizations (RICO) law to limit its use in civil litigation by requiring proof of all elements by clear and convincing proof.

We seek to restore fairness and predictability to punitive damages by placing appropriate limits on them, dividing trials into two phases to determine liability separately from damages and requiring clear proof of wrongdoing. This will go a long way to reduce insurance premiums for professional and product liability and for all malpractice, including medical, thereby lowering costs for consumers throughout the economy, while preserving the ability of injured persons to obtain damages. It will also foster the creation of new products for the American marketplace, perhaps cures for the diseases we most fear.

The Republican Party commends President Bush and Vice President Quayle for their continued leadership in helping volunteers overcome their concern that their good acts and voluntary donations of time on behalf of civic groups, community organizations and churches will result in civil liability and lawsuits. We encourage the state legislatures to pass the administration's model bill, "The Volunteerism Act."

We will throw out "junk science" by requiring courts to verify the legitimacy of persons called as expert witnesses. To restore integrity to courtroom testimony, we will ban the practice of paying fees to experts only if a successful verdict is obtained. We will maintain diversity jurisdiction for citizens of different states to ensure access to the federal courts when appropriate.

Because four-fifths of the time and cost of a lawsuit involves discovery — pretrial investigation of the facts — we will require automatic disclosure, by both sides, of basic information. We will ban abuses of the discovery process used to intimidate opponents and drive up their costs.

We will fight rising health-care costs — and equally important, help dedicated doctors to keep practicing in critical areas like obstetrics — by providing incentives for states to reform their liability laws. This will reduce the practice of "defensive medicine," requiring patients to be tested for every conceivable ailment at their own enormous expense to guard against the mere possibility of a lawsuit.

Recognizing that legal reform can solve only parts of the larger problem, we support a federal product liability law. The cost of product liability protection is a great expense to the American consumer and seriously impedes our international competitiveness. For example, a consumer pays an additional 17 percent to cover the liability insurance of an ordinary stepladder.

If 13 European nations can enact uniform product liability laws to give them a competitive edge against the United States, we can do it here, too — once we break the Democrat hold on the Congress so Republicans can put the interests of workers and consumers ahead of trial lawyers.

Some of the problems in our legal system are rooted in a declining sense of, and respect for, individual responsibility. We reaffirm that all Americans are first and finally responsible for their own behavior.

**The nation's capital.** We call for closer and responsible congressional scrutiny of the city, federal oversight of its law enforcement and courts, and tighter fiscal restraints over its expenditures. We oppose statehood as inconsistent with the original intent of the framers of the Constitution and with the need for a federal city belonging to all the people as our nation's capital.

**A new era for the territories.** We welcome greater participation in all aspects of the political process by Americans residing in Guam, the Virgin Islands, American Samoa, the Northern Marianas and Puerto Rico.

Because territorial America is far-flung and divergent, we know that any single approach to the future will not necessarily meet the needs of all. Republicans therefore emphasize respect for the wishes of those who reside in the territories regarding their relationship to the rest of the union.

We affirm the right of American citizens in the United States territories to seek the full extension of the Constitution with the accompanying rights and responsibilities, and we support all necessary legislation to permit them to do so.

The Republican Party supports the right of the United States citizens of Puerto Rico to be admitted to the union as a fully sovereign state after they freely so determine.

We recognize that the people of Guam have voted for a closer relationship with the United States of America, and we reaffirm our support of their right to mutually improve their political relationship through commonwealth.

We support American Samoa's efforts to advance toward economic self-reliance through a multi-year plan, while ensuring the protection afforded to the people of American Samoa by the original treaty of cession.

We support the full extension of rights and responsibilities under the U.S. Constitution to American citizens of the Virgin Islands.

We commend President Bush for the successful development of self-government in Micronesia and the Marshall Islands and for efforts to conclude the United Nations' last trusteeship in Palau consistent with the people's right of self-determination.

## Our Land, Food and Resources

We hold the resources of our country in stewardship. Our heritage from the past must be our legacy to generations to come. Our people have always known that, as they cherished their land and turned earth and rock into food, fiber and power. In the process, they built the world's most formidable economy, sustained by its raw materials, driven by its energy resources. They brought comfort to the home, transformed the nation and fed the world.

Agriculture and energy remain building blocks of modern life. Their vitality is crucial to the nation's growth. Indeed, to its survival. While supporting conservation, we reject the notion that there are limits to growth.

Human ingenuity is the ultimate resource, and it knows no limits. The true measure of America's economic success is not whether austerity can be shared by many, but whether prosperity can be achieved for all.

We advocate privatizing those government agencies and assets that would be more productive and better maintained in private ownership. We support efforts to decentralize government monopolies that poorly serve the public and waste taxpayers' dollars.

**Agriculture.** The Republican Party is the home of the farmer, rancher and forester. We have long championed their right to pursue growth, efficiency and competitiveness through market incentives, diversification and personal ingenuity. And for good reason. Their industry provides consumers with the highest-quality food and fiber for the smallest percentage of disposable income of any nation in the history of the world.

They have been pioneer environmentalists. They have turned over to their children and grandchildren land that has been nurtured to expand its productivity while conserving this vital resource. Even more important, they have cultivated in their homes strong family life and moral virtues.

We endorse American Samoa's time-honored land tenure system, which fosters self-reliance and strong extended family values. When we lose farmers, we lose much more than agriculture. We are committed to bringing our farm families the full benefit of a growing and diversified rural economy.

Our rural families also deserve to be brought into the mainstream of health care, with tax policies that provide all who are self-employed full deductibility of their health insurance premiums.

We stand with farmers against attempts by liberal Democrats to repeal the laws of economics by dictating price levels and restricting production. We stand with them against agriculture embargoes. We reject the notion that elected officials and bureaucrats make better farm managers than farmers themselves.

We remain strong in our support of livestock agriculture. We believe in the humane treatment of animals, but we oppose attempts by animal rights extremists to impose excessive restrictions on animal husbandry practices.

Our Omnibus Farm Bills of 1985 and 1990 gave farmers greater flexibility in decisions concerning management of their farms and marketing of their commodities. We have reduced government control and ownership of commodity inventories. Export sales and profitability have improved significantly. Agricultural debt has fallen by 30 percent. Under this president and sound Republican policies, net farm income has reached record levels.

At the same time, we cut by two-thirds the cost of government commodity programs. Only one-half of 1 percent of the federal budget is now spent on those programs. By reducing dependency on government, we have created a healthier agricultural sector. We will build upon our 1985 and 1990 legislation and repeal obsolete or unworkable statues while continuing to provide a viable base of support for U.S. farmers.

Agricultural prosperity is essential to the nation's global competitiveness. We will continue to expand the growth of American agriculture through exports, development of new products and new markets.

Commodity exports this year will hit $40 billion, a 50 percent increase over the levels of five years ago. There has never been an annual deficit in our balance of agricultural trade, and the positive balance this year will be $18 billion.

We pledge to fight unfair competition and to bring down the walls of protectionism around the world that unfairly inhibit competitiveness of U.S. farm exports. We pledge continued pressure to open world markets through the Uruguay Round, the North American Free Trade Agreement and bilateral negotiations.

We affirm that there will be no GATT agreement unless it improves opportunities for U.S. farmers to compete in world markets. We repeat our demands for cutbacks in export subsidies by the European Community and elsewhere, and we will fight the use of arbitrary health and sanitation standards to sabotage U.S. exports.

New markets for agricultural products will also be created as producers translate technological breakthroughs into new uses, such as soy oil diesel and biodegradable plastics. We support the widest possible use of ethanol in the U.S. motor fuel market, including in oxygenated fuels programs and as ethanol blends in reformulated gasolines.

In addition, the Republican Party supports increased research and development to reduce ethanol production costs and expand its use in motor fuel markets. Such use will greatly help American farmers, improve the rural economy and reduce our dependence on imported oil.

Building our farm economy requires meeting our farmers' financing needs. Critical to these needs are competitive, reasonable interests rates for U.S. producers. Under George Bush, interest rates have been dramatically reduced, thereby contributing substantially to improving the net income of American farm and ranch families. We will continue working to ensure that farmers have access to credit, with particular consideration to the needs of young and beginning farmers.

We recognize the importance of efficient, equitable transportation systems to the economic viability of agricultural exports; and we will work to achieve greater efficiencies within the U.S. maritime industry and to decrease the cost to agricul-

ture of shipping services.

We support farm conservation efforts, both those pioneered in our 1985 farm bill and entirely voluntary undertakings, which result in three times as much erosion control as those mandated by law. We support the Conservation Reserve, with more than 35 million acres now enrolled. It shows what farmers can do through incentives rather than government controls.

We value our nation's real wetlands habitat and the diversity of our native animal and plant life. We oppose, however, bureaucratic harassment of farm, ranch and timber families under statutes regarding endangered species and wetlands. When actions are required to protect an endangered species, we recognize that jobs can be lost, communities displaced and economic progress for all denied. Accordingly, prior to the implementation of a recovery plan for a species declared to be endangered, we will require the Congress to affirm the priority of the species on the endangered list and the specific measures to be taken in any recovery plan. These acts should not rest with the rubber stamp of a bureaucrat.

With regard to wetlands, following our principle that environmental protection be reasonable, land that is not truly wet would not be classified as a wetland. Protection of environmentally sensitive wetlands must not come at the price of disparaging landowners' property rights. Thus, we endorse, as President Bush has done, legislation to discourage government activities that ignore property rights. We also find intolerable the use of taxpayer funds, through the Legal Services Corporation, to attack the agricultural community.

**Power for progress.** Energy sustains life as we know it: our standard of living, the prospect for economic growth, the way our children will live in the century ahead. Republican energy policy, now as in the past, reflects the common-sense aspirations of the American people.

Our goals address our fundamental needs: an energy supply, available to all, that remains reasonably priced, secure and clean, produced by strong energy industries on which the country can rely, operating in an environmentally responsible manner and producing from domestically available energy resources to the maximum extent practicable.

Anyone older than a teenager can remember the energy upheavals of the bad old days, when political games threw the nation into a tailspin. Stranded in gasoline lines, shocked by home heating bills, shutting down factory operations, America's motorists, homeowners and workers rightly blamed official Washington for wrecking something that had always worked so efficiently that it was taken for granted.

Today, after 12 years of Republican reform, we can again have confidence in our energy policies. The average household spends 11 percent less on energy, as adjusted for inflation, than it did in 1980, because of both conservation and lower costs.

We broke the shackles of bureaucratic regulation by ending petroleum price and allocation controls, deregulating natural gas wellhead prices, and repealing restrictions on the use of clean-burning natural gas by industry and utilities. We repealed the windfall profit tax on crude oil that penalized investment in domestic oil production. We promoted free competition in an open marketplace and ended the public subsidy to the synthetic fuels program. And we broke the back of OPEC, the international energy cartel.

And, equally important, we undertook a re-evaluation of estimates of our domestic energy resource base, which the Carter administration had determined to be inadequate. The Republican administration correctly found that we can indeed continue to supply a significant amount of our domestically available energy resources, including natural gas and coal, for all energy consumption needs well into the next century.

When Iraq's dictator moved to seize the world's energy lifeline by controlling the Persian Gulf, George Bush did more than liberate Kuwait. He prevented an energy crisis and economic shutdown in America. Now his national energy strategy leads toward continued growth in the century ahead. It provides the nation with a comprehensive and balanced strategy for America's energy future. Specifically, it promotes adequate energy supplies and reduces consumer costs by relying on market forces, diversifying domestic energy sources and improving the efficiency and flexibility of energy consumption. We seek to foster greater competition and increased output, in the interest of producers and consumers alike.

The domestic oil and gas industry saves us from total dependence on unreliable foreign imports. But over the past decade, it has lost more than 300,000 jobs. Drilling rigs are still. Crippled by environmental rules and taxes, independent producers have been devastated and major companies are moving operations overseas. We will reverse that situation by allowing access, under environmental safeguards, to the coastal plain of the Arctic National Wildlife Refuge, possibly one of the largest petroleum reserves in our country, and to selected areas of the outer continental shelf (OCS). We support incentives to encourage domestic investment for onshore and OCS oil and gas exploration and development, including relief from the alternative minimum tax, credits for enhanced oil recovery and geological exploration under known geological oil fields and producing geological structures, and modified percentage depletion rules to benefit marginal production. We will ensure that royalty payments on federal lands remain consistent with changing economic conditions.

Most important, unlike Democrat no-growth fanatics, we know what is most at stake in the energy debate: the family's standard of living, including job opportunities, household income and the environment in which we live.

That is why we have been supporting complete decontrol of wellhead prices for clean natural gas, which have already declined 10 percent in the last four years while consumption increased by the same amount. We support replacing government controls with the power of the market to determine transactions between buyers and sellers of natural gas. We encourage the use of natural gas for both vehicles and electricity generation, and the expansion of research, development and demonstration for end-use natural gas technologies. We will foster more public-private partnerships to advance use of natural gas.

The Republican Party has a deep and abiding commitment to America's mining industry. We support the original intent of the Mining Law of 1872: to provide the security necessary for miners to risk capital investment on federal lands, thus preserving jobs and bolstering the domestic economy.

We support clean coal technologies to allow greater use of America's most abundant fossil fuel within standards required by the Clean Air Act. We encourage the export of U.S. coal. We support acceleration of the international transfer of coal-related technologies to boost exports for U.S. coal, in order to capitalize on America's leadership in these technologies.

We oppose any attempt to impose a carbon tax as proposed by liberal Democrats.

We endorse major national projects, like the superconducting super collider, which offer the promise of developing more efficient ways to store, transport and use energy.

We will hasten development of the next generation of nuclear power plants — one of the cleanest, safest energy sources of all. Republicans back reform of the nuclear licensing process. We will site and license a permanent waste depository and a monitored retrievable storage facility. We reject the scare tactics used against nuclear power by those who want to shut down this essential contributor to the American future.

We endorse development of renewable energy sources and research on fuel cells, conservation, hydro, solar, hydrogren and wind power as components of our overall plan for energy security and environmental quality.

**Public lands.** The millions of acres that constitute this nation's public lands must continue to provide for a number of uses. We are committed to the multiple use of our public lands. We believe that recreation, forestry, ranching, mining, oil and gas exploration, and production on our public lands can be conducted in a way compatible with their conservation. The United States has some of the richest mineral resources in the world. Our public lands should not be arbitrarily locked up and put off limits to responsible uses.

Approximately 50 percent of the lands

in the West are owned by the federal government. These lands are a deeply intermingled patchwork built of public and private ownership. In order to provide an economic base for the people of the West, a public-private cooperative partnership on these lands for multiple use in an environmentally sound manner is imperative.

**Transportation.** From its founding, the Republican Party has considered the nation's transportation system crucial to economic opportunity for all. That is why our 1860 platform endorsed the transcontinental railroad. It is why President Eisenhower signed the Interstate and Defense Highway Act, bringing America closer together and launching a lengthy economic expansion.

Today, America's transportation system is safer, more efficient, more reliable than that of any other country. It employs one of every 10 workers and accounts for $800 billion in spending. It enables us to compete in the world market and gives us more choices in our daily lives.

Under President Bush, that system has been strengthened by revolutionary legislation to pave the way into the century ahead. Providing $151 billion for highways and transit systems, it is the most extensive transportation improvement project in our nation's history — and a tremendous jobs program as well.

Highway death rates have dropped to an all-time low, largely due to better road design and stronger safety programs. This progress would be wiped out by the Democrats' draconian plan for higher Corporate Average Fuel Economy (CAFE) standards. Their national nominees want to require a 45 miles-per-gallon standard. That means unsafe vehicles, reduced consumer choice, higher car costs and a loss of 300,000 jobs in the auto industry here at home.

To reduce the congestion that still chokes urban areas, we established a National Highway System of 155,000 miles, giving states and localities greater voice in decisions about projects. It will improve connections between ports and highways, airports and railways; spur development of new airports and reduce their environmental impact; promote private investment in transportation; and foster high-tech solutions to congestion.

To keep America on the move, we assert the same principle that guides us in all other sectors of the economy: consumers benefit through competition within the private sector. That is why we will complete the job of trucking deregulation. We will also abolish the Interstate Commerce Commission, finally freeing shippers and consumers from horse-and-buggy regulation. We applaud the president's executive order that will assist communities to privatize government-controlled ventures, such as airports and toll roads.

Our tough trade campaign, along with regulatory reforms, will assure U.S. air carriers fair access to international routes and allow the U.S. merchant marine to sail over foreign protectionism. The president has proposed and will aggressively pursue a comprehensive revision of existing maritime policy.

Regulatory reform of airlines now allows more people to fly more safely, at better prices. Tough laws for drug and alcohol testing are making all modes of transportation safer than ever. Disabled persons will have greater access to the entire transportation network under the Americans with Disabilities Act.

Wherever possible, the market should allocate investment in transportation, steering the development of passenger rail, mass transit and highways to best suit consumers. States and localities should have discretion in using Highway Trust Fund revenues to construct new roads, expand existing ones or invest in mass transit facilities, as they see fit. We advocate development of high-speed rail systems, through private investment, to serve intercity travel. We also advocate development of short-haul aircraft with vertical takeoff and landing capability, to bring commerce and jobs to communities large and small.

We will continue aggressively to support development of intelligent highway systems, an efficient battery for electric cars, perfected natural gas vehicles, greater private investment in space travel and removal of regulatory impediments to intermodal transport.

Because Republicans advocate personal responsibility, we salute groups, organizations and individuals that take direct action to improve safe driving and street safety.

**Environment.** Cleaning up America is a labor of love for family, neighborhood and the nation. In the Republican tradition of conserving the past to enrich the future, we have made the United States the world's leader in environmental progress.

We spend more than any other country on environmental protection. Over the last 20 years, our country has spent $1 trillion to clean its air, water and land. We increased GNP by 70 percent while cutting lead in the air by 97 percent. Our rivers run cleaner than ever in memory. We've preserved parks, wilderness and wildlife. The price of progress is now about $115 billion a year, almost 2 percent of GNP; and that will grow to 3 percent by 2000.

Clearly we have led the world in investment in environmental protection. We have taught the world three vital lessons. First, environmental progress is integrally related to economic advancement. Second, economic growth generates the capital to pay for environmental gains. Third, private ownership and economic freedom are the best security against environmental degradation. The ghastly truth about state socialism is now exposed in what used to be the Soviet Union: dead rivers and seas, poisoned land, dying people.

Liberal Democrats think people are the problem. We know people are the solution. Respecting the people's rights and views, we applied market-based solutions to environmental problems. President Bush's landmark Clean Air Act amendments of 1990, the toughest environmental law ever enacted, uses an innovative system of emission credits to achieve its dramatic reductions. This will save $1 billion over the Democrats' command-and-control approach. Other provisions of that law will cut acid rain emissions in half, reduce toxic pollutants by 90 percent, reduce smog and speed the use of cleaner fuels.

The president's leadership has doubled spending for real wetlands and targeted 1 million acres for a wetlands reserve through his farm bill of 1990. We have collected more civil penalties from polluters in two years than in the previous 20, begun the phaseout of substances that harm the ozone layer and launched a long-term campaign to expand and improve national parks, forests and recreation areas, adding 1.5 million acres. President Bush has dramatically increased spending for cleaning up past environmental damage caused by federal facilities.

Our reforestation drive will plant 1 billion trees a year across America. Our moratorium on offshore drilling in sensitive offshore areas has bought time for technology to master environmental challenges. Our farm policies have begun a new era in sound agricultural environmentalism.

Because the environment knows no boundaries, President Bush has accelerated U.S. research on global climate change, spending $2.7 billion in the last three years and requesting $1.4 billion for 1993, more than the rest of the world put together. Under his leadership, we have assisted nations from the Third World to Eastern Europe in correcting the environmental damage inflicted by socialism. We proposed a worldwide forestry convention and gave almost half a billion dollars to forest conservation. We won debt-for-nature swaps and environmental trust funds in Latin America and the Caribbean. We secured prohibitions against unilateral export or dumping of hazardous waste. We led the international ban on trade in ivory, persuaded Japan to end drift net fishing, streamlined response to oil spills and increased environmental protection for Antarctica.

Adverse changes in climate must be the common concern of mankind. At the same time, we applaud our president for personally confronting the international bureaucrats at the Rio Conference. He refused to accept their anti-American demands for income redistribution and won instead a global climate treaty that relies on real action plans rather than arbitrary targets hostile to U.S. growth and workers.

Following his example, a Republican Senate will not ratify any treaty that moves environmental decisions beyond our democratic process or transfers beyond our shores authority over U.S. property. The Democrats' national candidates, on the other hand, insist the United States must do what our foreign competitors refuse to do: abolish 300,000 to 1,000,000 jobs to get a modest reduction in "greenhouse gases."

Environmental progress must continue in tandem with economic growth. Crippling an industry is no solution at all. Bankrupt facilities only worsen environmental situations. Unemployment is a form of pollution too, poisoning families and contaminating whole communities.

Some in our own country still refuse to face those facts. They try to hijack environmentalism, making it anti-growth and anti-jobs. Although the average family of four now pays $1,000 a year for environmental controls, liberal Democrats want to tighten the squeeze. They use junk science to foster hysteria instead of reason, demanding rigid controls, more taxes and less resource production.

However, with billions of dollars at stake in national production and jobs, not to mention our quality of life, our decisions to spend on environmental protection must not be determined by the politics of the moment. We will use scientifically respectable risk-benefit assessments to settle environmental controversies.

It is time to replace knee-jerk reactions with the kind of scientific analysis that helps businesses, individuals and communities contribute to economic and environmental progress through flexible application of laws. We must base our environmental policies on real risks to human health, determined by sound, peer-reviewed science, including procedures for what is an acceptable risk.

We will require federal agencies to promptly compensate, from their own budgets, for any taking of private property, including the denial of use.

We will legislatively overhaul the "superfund" program to speed the cleanup of hazardous waste and more efficiently use superfund dollars. We will develop greenways of parks and open space in urban areas to further improve the quality of life in our cities. We will work with U.S. industry and labor to identify promising markets abroad where America's environmental know-how can carry our success story to the rest of Planet Earth.

**Private property rights.** We reaffirm our commitment to the Fifth Amendment to the Constitution: "No person shall be . . . deprived of life, liberty, or property, without due process of law; nor shall private property be taken for public use, without just compensation." We support strong enforcement of this Takings Clause to keep citizens secure in the use and development of their property.

The right to own, use and dispose of property inheres in mankind by nature and is a fundamental political tenet of all free nations. We applaud the wisdom of the First Congress for incorporating this guarantee of individual liberty in the Bill of Rights. We remind all government officials that property rights are not granted by government; rather, government is directed by the governed to protect the rights of private property owners.

The vigilant protection of private property rights safeguards for citizens everything of value, including their right of contract to produce and sell the fruits of their labor. The historic collapse of communism and other command-and-control economies is absolute evidence of the failure of economic systems that lack a recognition of the natural rights of property owners.

We also seek to reduce the amount of land owned or controlled by the government, especially in the Western states. We insist upon prompt payment for private lands certified as critical for preserving essential parks and preserves.

## Uniting Our World

The world is now our neighborhood. Its triumphs and tragedies affect our communities, our jobs and the security of our families. That is why Republicans want America to shape the international future: because we put America first.

Not everyone does. Just 12 years ago, the forces of freedom were in tattered retreat. A failed foreign policy by a Democrat White House and Democrat-controlled Congress had left our allies uncertain, our friends betrayed, our foes emboldened. It was a frightening era, in some ways the worst of times. We all remember the flickering television images of blindfolded Americans being degraded by thugs. When voters make their choice in this year's elections, they should ask themselves: Are we safer and stronger today, in 1992, than we were in 1980, when Jimmy Carter was the Democrat president?

Republicans are proud to answer those questions. The nation's international position has not just improved since the Democrats left office. It has been transformed. Never in this century has the United States enjoyed such security from foreign enemies. With President Bush leading the free world, the Soviet empire has collapsed, as Ronald Reagan predicted, into the dustbin of history. Eastern Europe is liberated. Germany is peacefully united. The former Soviet armies are returning home. Nuclear arsenals are being cut to fractions of their former size.

A democratically elected Russian president sits in the Kremlin. Ukraine, Armenia and the Baltic States take their rightful place among the family of nations. Israel and all of its Arab neighbors talk face to face for the first time. Nicaragua and Panama celebrate democracy.

It might very well not have turned out this way. Only the naive believe that history is an inevitable tide or a series of accidents. Our crusade of a half-century, to champion freedom and civilization against the dark night of totalitarianism, is now victorious. An American president led the free world to this great triumph. George Bush was that man.

Freedom's victory begins a new chapter in the epic of America, full of both promise and peril. This different and unpredictable world demands visionary, ex-

perienced leadership, tested and strengthened, careful and cool. At stake is nothing less than our security, our prosperity and our children's future. Americans can trust President Bush with that awesome responsibility.

## The Triumph of Freedom

No other president in the long history of our country has achieved so many of the enduring objectives of American foreign policy in so short a time as has George Bush. He made it look easy, even destined. It was neither.

Building on the legacy of Ronald Reagan, George Bush saw the chance to sweep away decadent communism. He was the first Western leader to declare his determination to fashion "a Europe whole and free." He took the free world beyond containment, led the way in aiding democracy in Eastern Europe and punched holes through the rusting Iron Curtain. We all remember the joy we felt when we saw the people of Berlin dancing on top of the crumbling wall that had symbolized four decades of communist oppression.

He championed Germany's right to become again one nation and orchestrated the diplomacy to make it happen, on Western terms, in one astounding year. Foreseeing revolutionary change in the Soviet Union itself, he carefully pushed its rules to open the way to the democratic future. When crisis came, in August 1991, George Bush, in the words of Boris Yeltsin, "was the first to understand the true meaning of the victory of the Russian people" and gave his decisive backing to the cause of democracy.

The world had never before faced the disintegration of a nuclear superpower. Today, thanks in large part to President Bush's initiatives, nuclear weapons are found in only four countries of the former Soviet Union — not 14. Because of his efforts, all but Russia are giving up any claim to these weapons, and Russia has agreed to destroy the most dangerous missiles ever built. The balance of terror is fading away. The ideals of liberty, both political and economic, are the dominant moral and intellectual force around the globe.

George Bush made it happen.

Yet now that we have won the Cold War, we must also win the peace. We must not repeat the mistake of the past by throwing away victory through complacency. A new world beckons, unlike any we have ever known, filled with uncertainties. Old passions have re-emerged. New democracies struggle to decide their destiny. Nations are torn asunder. Migrants and refugees strain the social fabric of continents. Tyrants work to build nuclear, chemical and even biological weapons to threaten us and our neighbors. Drug trafficking and terrorism, often linked, menace Americans at home and abroad.

Great transitions in world affairs are rarely tidy. They challenge statesmanship,

require steadiness and wisdom. History teaches that when the United States shrinks from the world, we hasten the emergence of new dangers. Republicans remember the lesson taught by our Founders: that eternal vigilance is the price of liberty.

**Meeting the challenge.** The gulf war showed the world how much is at stake when voters choose their president. George Bush had known war firsthand. So he tried the way of peace — months of negotiations and economic sanctions — then did what a president must do. He led from powerful convictions based on American values. The United States, in a pre-eminent position of world leadership, forged a new strategy of collective engagement which invigorated the United Nations.

This was not the same United States held hostage in 1980, when the Democrats controlled both the White House and the Congress. No helpless giant here. The president charted a path that wrecked Saddam Hussein's dreams of conquest and nuclear aggression while keeping America from the quagmire of indefinite military occupation of Iraq.

President Bush, trusting the military commanders he had chosen, was commander-in-chief of one of the finest achievements in the distinguished history of our armed forces. Americans will never forget that, of the 323 congressional Democrats, only 96 voted to support Operation Desert Storm and 227 voted to oppose it. If the Democrats had prevailed, Saddam Hussein would still be in Kuwait, armed with nuclear weapons. Everyone discovered what difference a vote for president can make.

**Leadership through partnership.** A new era demands a new agenda. Our post-Cold War strategy both reflects our country's ideals and guards its interests.

Building a commonwealth of freedom differs greatly from the old concept of containment. It rests on a stable balance of power but goes beyond it to emphasize, above all, the supremacy of an idea: a common conception of how to make freedom work for all the nations moving with us into a radically changing future.

Republicans understand that objective cannot be pursued by the United States alone. We therefore have harnessed the free world's strength to American leadership. But such a strategy requires a president whose lead others will trust and follow. By forging consensus whenever possible, we multiply the impact of our nation's power and principles. But if necessary we will act alone to protect American interests. Consistent with our policy and traditions, we oppose any actions that would undermine America's sovereignty, either in political or economic terms. Leadership through partnership allows us to project American ideals and project American interests abroad, at less cost to our taxpayers.

That is how we will secure the victory

of democracy as the best guarantee of a world without war. It is how we will open the world for American business to ensure prosperity in an open international economy. And it is how we will banish the nuclear nightmare, limit the danger from weapons of mass destruction and safely manage a critical transition in our nation's defenses.

**Securing the victory of democracy.** The spread of democracy and economic liberty is the best guarantee of peace. It can mean speaking out or applying economic pressure to encourage peaceful change; aiding democratic forces; or being ready, as a last resort, to take military action where vital American interests are at stake, as when President Bush restored the rule of law to Panama. Republican presidents have used all these tools in a comprehensive, consistent campaign to promote democracy worldwide.

New tests lie ahead. On past occasions, the tide of liberty has ebbed as dictators recaptured much of what they had lost. We want freedom's wave to roll on to reach countries like China, Cuba, North Korea, Vietnam and others. We want to keep drawing attention to serious human rights violations around the world, spurring other governments to make and fulfill the promise of liberty to their people. We want to prevent any new ideology of authoritarianism from drawing any of the world's people to a grim and vengeful vision of our future.

This is the challenge we face in the next four years. It is why President Bush led the way in promoting assistance to the fledgling democracies of Eastern Europe. It is why he has persuaded Congress to invest in the democratic future of nations reborn from communism. To the peoples of those nations, and to the Russian people in particular, we declare: If you stay on the path to freedom, we stand ready to help.

We rejoice especially with the people of Latvia, Lithuania and Estonia, whose nationhood we have always upheld in law and in our hearts.

In Western Europe, we reaffirm the NATO alliance. While we reduce our troop commitments on the continent — a thousand soldiers are coming home every week — we must keep a powerful force deployed there. The United States must remain a European power in the broadest sense, able to influence the policies and events that affect the livelihood and security of future generations of Americans.

The violence in what used to be Yugoslavia is an affront to humanity. We condemn those responsible for the carnage there and call for an immediate international investigation of atrocities. We support the United Nations peacekeeping effort and urge an immediate cease-fire by all parties. The United States should continue to demand respect for international law and fundamental human rights in this agonizing conflict.

We encourage a peaceful settlement for Cyprus and respect by all parties for

the wishes of the Cypriot people.

We urge peace and justice for Northern Ireland. We welcome the newly begun process of constitutional dialogue that holds so much promise. We encourage investment and reconstruction to create opportunity for all.

In the Middle East, prospects for peace have been transformed by the determined statesmanship of George Bush. Without the leadership of President Bush, Iraq would today threaten world peace, the peace and security of the Middle East, and the very survival of Israel with a huge conventional army and nuclear weapons. Direct peace talks, on terms Israel rightly had sought for more than four decades, would not be a reality. Soviet Jewish emigration likely would have been interrupted. The rescue of Ethiopian Jewry might not have happened. And the equation of Zionism to racism still would be a grotesque stain on the United Nations.

Although much has changed for the better, the Middle East remains an area of high tensions — many unrelated to the Arab-Israeli conflict — where regional conflicts can escalate to threaten the vital interests of the United States. As Saddam Hussein's aggression against Kuwait demonstrated, heavily armed radical regimes are capable of independent aggressive action. In this environment, Israel's demonstrated strategic importance to the United States, as our most reliable and capable ally in this part of the world, is more important than ever. This strategic relationship, with its unique moral dimension, explains the understandable support Israel receives from millions of Americans who participate in our political process. The strong ties between the United States and Israel were demonstrated during the gulf war when Israel chose not to retaliate against repeated missile attacks, even though they caused severe damage and loss of life. We will continue to broaden and deepen the strategic relationship with our ally Israel — the only true democracy in the Middle East — by taking additional concrete steps to further institutionalize the partnership. This will include maintaining adequate levels of security and economic assistance; continuing our meetings on military, political and economic cooperation and coordination; pre-positioning military equipment; developing joint contingency plans; and increasing joint naval and air exercises.

Consistent with our strategic relationship, the United States should continue to provide large-scale security assistance to Israel, maintaining Israel's qualitative military advantage over any adversary or coalition of adversaries. We also will continue to negotiate with the major arms supplying nations to reach an agreement on limiting arms sales to the Middle East and preventing the proliferation of non-conventional weapons.

We applaud the president's leadership in fostering unprecedented direct talks between Israel and its Arab neighbors. The United States is prepared to use its good

offices to mediate disputes at their request. We do not believe the United States should attempt to impose a solution on the parties.

The basis for negotiations must be U.N. Security Council Resolutions 242 and 338. Peace must come from direct negotiations. It will be up to the negotiators to determine exactly what is required to satisfy these resolutions, but we firmly believe Israel has a right to exist in secure and recognized borders.

As President Bush stated in Madrid, our objective is not simply to end the state of war; rather, it is to establish real peace, one with treaties, security, diplomatic relations, trade, investment, cultural exchange, even tourism. We want the Middle East to become a place where people lead normal lives.

A meaningful peace must assure Israel's security while recognizing the legitimate rights of the Palestinian people. We oppose the creation of an independent Palestinian state. Nor will we support the creation of any political entity that would jeopardize Israel's security.

As Israelis and Palestinians negotiate interim self-government, no party will be required to commit itself to any specific final outcome of direct negotiations. Israel should not be forced to negotiate with any party. In this regard, the United States will have no dialogue with the PLO until it satisfies in full the conditions laid out by President Bush in 1990.

We believe Jerusalem should remain an undivided city, with free and unimpeded access to all holy places by people of all faiths. No genuine peace would deny Jews the right to live anywhere in the special city of Jerusalem.

Peace in the Middle East entails cooperation among all the parties in the region. To this end, we have worked to bring all of the states of the area together with Israel to hold multilateral negotiations on issues of common concern such as regional development, water, refugees, arms control and the environment. We support these forums as a means of encouraging Arab acceptance of Israel and solving common regional problems.

We continue to back legislation mandating that if the United Nations and its agencies were to deny Israel's right to participate, the United States would withhold financial support and withdraw from those bodies until their action was rectified.

Republicans believe freedom of emigration is a fundamental human right and that Jews from any nation should be free to travel to Israel. Republicans are proud that we have maintained our historic and moral commitment to the resettlement in Israel of persecuted Jews. We congratulate President Bush and Secretary [of State James A.] Baker [III] on the agreement with Israel for a generous package of loan guarantees that will provide new immigrants with needed humanitarian assistance.

We also should maintain our close ties with and generous aid for Egypt, which properly reaps the benefits of its courageous peace with Israel. We continue to support Egypt and other pro-Western states in the region against subversion and aggression and call for an end to the Arab boycott of Israel. We also support establishment of a strong central government in Lebanon, democratically elected and representative of its citizens.

We salute all the countries in the Middle East who contributed to the success of Desert Storm and share our goal of stability in the region.

With them, we hope to build upon that triumph a new future for the Middle East, founded on mutual respect and a common longing for peace. To promote this goal, we should settle for nothing less than full, unconditional, immediate and verified Iraqi compliance with all aspects of the cease-fire laid out in U.N. resolutions.

In the Western Hemisphere, as elsewhere, we must promote democratic values. We will continue to seek cooperation in the common battle against the drug lords. We will also lower barriers to trade and investment, knowing that our exports to Latin America are helping to lead our economic recovery at home.

The president's Enterprise for the Americas initiative and the North American Free Trade Agreement mean, for the United States, billions of dollars in new trade, hundreds of thousands of new jobs, and a long-term solution to the economic pressures behind illegal immigration.

We welcome positive changes, economic and political, in Mexico and salute the people of Panama on their recovery of free institutions after Operation Just Cause. We commend President Bush for the decisive military action that led to the end of the corrupt [Manuel Antonio] Noriega regime and freedom for democratically minded Panamanians.

We will uphold free and unencumbered U.S. access to the canal. We hail the patriots of El Salvador and Nicaragua, whose bravery and blood thwarted communism and Castro despite the inconstancy of congressional Democrats. Together with other members of the Organization of American States, we will work to restore democracy to Haiti.

The Monroe Doctrine remains a cardinal principle of our foreign policy, and we continue to strive toward the day when the alien ideology of communism and Fidel Castro's regime will be purged from Cuba, and Americans can welcome Cuban people back into the family of free nations. Toward that end, we support Radio and TV Martí and the spirit of Cuba Libre.

In Asia, we remain committed to the spread of political and economic liberty. We will work with Japan for common progress and maintain military presence in Japan and in Asia. We also will promote greater Japanese responsibility for self-defense and worldwide prosperity.

We reaffirm our commitment to the security of Taiwan and regard any attempt to alter its status by force as a threat to the entire region.

We adhere to the Taiwan Relations Act, the basis for continuing cooperation with those who have stood loyally with us for half a century.

Our policy toward China is based on support for democratic reform. We need to maintain the relationship with China so that we can effectively encourage such reform. We will continue to work toward the day when the Chinese people will finally complete their journey to an open society, free of the deplorable restrictions on personal liberties that still exist.

We will maintain our close relationship with the Republic of Korea, helping to deter aggression from the north. North Korea remains an outlaw state and must not be permitted to acquire nuclear weapons.

With the people of the Philippines, we will maintain our special ties of history and affection.

We support the movement in Cambodia toward peace and democracy.

We demand the fullest possible accounting for America's POWs and MIAs in Southeast Asia. The grief of their families touches all of us. We will seek complete information in all forums and from all sources. Our president has put the government of Vietnam on notice: Improved relations depends upon this goal.

In Africa, despite opposition from congressional Democrats, we armed freedom fighters and helped force the withdrawal of Cuban troops.

Now we enter the long season of building, trying to revive faith in democracy on a continent ravaged by Marxist wars, looted by local dictators and misled by socialist ideology. Political and economic liberty are the keys.

We will support responsible efforts by the international community to help end the anarchy in Somalia and to address the plight of the people of that country suffering from drought and starvation. We condemn those who are using armed force to impede food distribution.

In South Africa, the Republican policy of constructive engagement — opposing apartheid while fostering peaceful change — has been successful. That nation's prospects have been transformed for the better, though many difficulties lie ahead.

We condemn all violence against the innocent and applaud those who seek reconciliation to create a new, democratic South Africa. We encourage economic reform as crucial to both security and prosperity in the new South Africa.

We recognize that foreign aid must have a reasonable relationship to our national interests. We therefore support an ongoing review of such programs so that they can be both effectual and justified. We promote financial contribution from other democracies of the world to share the cost of the American burden for peacekeeping and foreign aid.

We support efforts by private voluntary agencies to help meet the needs of

countries newly liberated from communism and of the developing world in such areas as medical, agricultural, educational and entrepreneurial assistance.

**Opening the world to American business.** The triumph of democracy is also a victory for economic freedom. All the world over, people in search of a better life are rejecting politicians' control of their future. This will mean a broader horizon for American opportunity. The whole world has become our marketplace.

The election of 1992 will determine whether our country seizes this tremendous opportunity or retreats from it. Republicans trust individuals and families to make their own economic decisions; Democrat politicians do not. We reject their program of strangled trade, industrial policy, high taxes and regulation. We reject punitive taxes on foreign businesses in this country that only invite retaliatory taxes against U.S. businesses abroad. Trade war is the road to international depression — and for keeping American workers dependent on government handouts. We do not want to replace the arms race with a subsidies race.

Putting Americans first means keeping the national interest ahead of the special interests. It means opening the world to American goods within a system of free and expanding trade. Just as Ronald Reagan declared in Berlin, "Tear down this wall," so George Bush is dismantling the walls of protectionism in order to continue expanding our exports.

Our strong commitment to free trade also encompasses vigorous enforcement of U.S. trade laws. We expect a fair and level playing field in our trade with other nations and will work to ensure that foreign markets are just as open to our goods as U.S. markets are to theirs. In all negotiations concerning trade, we will put the interests of America first.

Throughout the world, as here at home, the Republican Party stands for growth. America's families have nothing to fear — and everything to gain — from the new era of free enterprise and prosperity that will emerge as free people compete, excel and progress.

**Banishing the nuclear nightmare.** The world has moved from the brink of disaster to the threshold of historic opportunity. For almost half a century, we lived under the shadow of nuclear destruction. Today, that specter is fading. We will not stop here. We will banish the threat of nuclear annihilation from the face of the earth — not by savaging our military, as some Democrats might insist but by building on the historic diplomatic achievements of Presidents Bush and Reagan.

This means ensuring stable command and control of the former Soviet arsenal, complete acceptance and verified implementation of all treaty obligations by the successor states to the Soviet Union, and achieving the additional 50 percent reduction in strategic forces now agreed upon.

We must assist in dismantling weapons, transforming the massive Soviet war machine into an engine of peace and civilian revival. We will cooperate with our former adversaries both to curtail proliferation and to move beyond the ABM Treaty toward effective ballistic missile defenses.

We will not permit the Soviet nuclear nightmare to be replaced by another one. Outlaw nations — North Korea, Iran, Iraq, Libya and others — lust for weapons of mass destruction. This is the nightmare of proliferation: nuclear, chemical and biological weapons that, together with ballistic missiles, can deliver death across whole continents, including our own.

We will renew and strengthen the Nuclear Nonproliferation Treaty. We will design security policies to counter proliferation dangers. We will reinforce multilateral accords like the Missile Technology Control Regime. And most important, we will develop and deploy global defenses against ballistic missiles. Despite the opposition of the Democratic Party and congressional Democrats, we will deploy an effective strategic defense system for the American people.

## America's Security

Because America won the Cold War, our homes and neighborhoods are more secure then they have been for half a century. Our children are safer. The greatest peace dividend is peace itself. For it, we thank God.

Victory was never inevitable. It was won in blood and treasure, over five decades, by the American people — from the military on the front lines to the taxpayers sustaining the forces of freedom. It was also secured, and the course of mankind profoundly changed for the better, because two successive Republican presidents, Ronald Reagan and George Bush, were dedicated to peace through strength.

"Peace through strength" was more than a slogan. It was the calculated Republican plan for, first, the survival, and then the triumph, of America. But freedom did not come cheaply, and the new world we celebrate today required great sacrifice.

In 1981 we inherited from Jimmy Carter and anti-defense Democrats a crippled military: demoralized, underfunded, ill-equipped. Republicans told the truth to the American people; they heeded our call to arms.

We restored our armed forces to their proper place in both the budget and the pride of the nation. Our men and women in uniform today are the equals of the finest soldiers, sailors and airmen who ever wore the uniform of our country.

Like earlier generations in 1918 and 1945, they won a great victory. Now, as in the aftermath of those earlier conflicts, comes the difficult task of reducing both the size and cost of defense without letting down America's guard. In the past, terrible mistakes were made, and we paid dearly for them when war came to Korea. We will not allow that to happen again.

**America challenged.** The greatest danger to America's security is here at home, among those who would leave the nation unprepared for the new realities of the post-Cold War world. The ruthless demagogues in rogue regimes are real and so are the nuclear, chemical and biological weapons they seek. The danger of nuclear proliferation is real, especially with the dispersal of nuclear know-how after the collapse of the Soviet Union. That is why the Republican Party, whose leaders, such as Dan Quayle, insisted upon fielding a new Patriot missile in the 1980s, now calls for a new generation of defense against the Scuds of tomorrow.

Rather than admit their mistakes of the past, the same liberal Democrats who sought to disarm America against the Soviet threat now compound their errors with a new campaign — half audacity, half mendacity — to leave the nation unprotected in a still dangerous world.

Republicans call for a controlled defense drawdown, not a free fall. That is why President Bush proposes to carefully reduce defense spending over the next four years by an additional $34 billion, including $18 billion in outlays, with a 25 percent reduction in personnel. He has already eliminated over 100 weapon systems. Around the world, American forces are coming home from the frontiers of the Cold War. More than 550 overseas bases are being closed or realigned. Yet U.S. forces retain the ability to meet the challenge of another Desert Storm with equal success.

U.S. defense spending already has been reduced significantly. Five years ago, it was more than a quarter of the federal budget. By 1997 it will be less than a sixth. Spending on defense and intelligence, as a proportion of gross domestic product, will be the lowest it has been since before World War II.

Yet any defense budget, however lean, is still too much for the Democrats. They want to start by cutting defense outlays over the next four years by nearly $60 billion beyond the president's cuts, throwing as many as 1 million additional Americans out of work.

And this may be just the beginning, as the Democrats use the defense budget as a bottomless piggy bank to try to beat swords into pork barrels. This is folly. It would take us back to the hollow military of the Carter era. Once American defenses are allowed to decay, they cannot be rebuilt overnight. Effective arsenals, like effective leaders, require years of patient development. And our greatest asset of all, the people on whom our security depends, deserve a constant long-term investment in their quality, morale and safety. Republicans pledge to provide it.

**America secure.** Because the United States will rely on a smaller force of offensive nuclear weapons to deter aggression in the post-Cold War era, we will maintain the triad of land, sea, and air-based strategic forces. We will continue to test the

safety, reliability and effectiveness of our nuclear weapons.

With a smaller military, modernization of conventional forces is more important than ever. Desert Storm showed the importance of "force multipliers" like smart munitions, stealth technology and night-fighting capabilities.

We will upgrade existing weapons and selectively procure those that hold the promise of dramatic forward leaps in capability. Under no circumstances will we yield our technological superiority.

We must remain ready to defend American citizens and interests wherever they may be threatened. Essential to that readiness is maintenance of a strong global navy and modernization of vital airlift and sealift capacity. We remain committed to combating terrorism in all its forms wherever it threatens U.S. citizens or interests.

Republicans will preserve the nation's access to space for defense, as well as for other purposes, and ensure that space technology does not fall into dangerous hands.

Transformed by the collapse of communism, our Strategic Defense Initiative [SDI] is now designed to provide the United States and our allies with global defenses against limited ballistic missile attacks.

SDI is the greatest investment in peace we could ever make. This system will be our shield against technoterrorism. Russia has agreed to be our partner in it, sharing early warning information and jointly moving forward to stop those who would rain death upon the innocent.

We will use missile defenses to assure threatened nations that they do not need to acquire ballistic missiles of their own. We will move beyond the ABM Treaty to deploy effective defenses with the goal of someday eliminating, not merely reducing, the threat of nuclear holocaust.

We support efforts to reduce armaments, both conventional and otherwise, but the most effective arms control of all over the long run is democracy. Free nations do not attack one another. That is why the promotion of democracy on every continent is an essential part of the Republican defense agenda.

**Managing the peace.** A new era in defense requires new approaches to management, to get more out of every dollar in a shrinking budget.

That calls for dramatically different ways of doing business. For example, President Bush's reforms in defense management and acquisition already mean massive savings — $70 billion through 1997 — without sacrificing combat capability.

Our armed forces will still depend on our superb industrial base for everything from belt buckles to submarines. We cannot lose that engineering and manufacturing capability.

This is especially true of the high technology, demonstrated in Desert Storm, that made our enemies realize they had been left behind in the race for the future.

We therefore pledge to maintain America's technological lead, preserve its defense industrial base, and maintain robust levels of investment in research and development.

We will attack the problem of waste in the military, especially at its root in the pork barrel politics of Capitol Hill. A Republican Congress will end the costly micromanagement of defense programs and reduce the number and scope of oversight committees.

We will urge the Department of Defense to encourage a broader constituency for saving and to continue genuine procurement reforms based on performance rather than unreasonable regulations imposed by the Democrat Congress. We will continue the successful effort to eliminate redundancy and streamline all facets of defense management.

We applaud the president's efforts to assist all individuals and communities adversely affected by the ongoing defense build-down, with more than 30 defense adjustment programs already in place and more than $7 billion committed to the effort in just the next two years.

**The men and women of defense.** Republicans created the all-volunteer Army, and we hail its success. We pledge to keep faith with the men and women volunteers and with their families, for they are the backbone of the nation's defense. We oppose Democrat efforts to bring back the draft, whether directly or through the subterfuge of compulsory domestic service.

The armed forces are a colorblind meritocracy, a model for the rest of our society. Its enlistees should receive preference in federal education and retraining programs. We applaud the advancement of women in the military and single out for special recognition the outstanding contribution of women in Operations Desert Shield/Desert Storm.

However, we oppose liberal Democrat attempts to place women in combat positions just to make an ideological point. Unlike the Democratic Party and its candidate, we support the continued exclusion of homosexuals from the military as a matter of good order and discipline.

The Department of Defense will not be an exception to our assertion of family values. Republicans will not tolerate sexual harassment or misconduct toward any individual in the ranks. We demand both its prevention and its punishment.

To drive home that point, we urge a halt to the sale, in military facilities, of sexually explicit materials. We call for greater consideration of the needs of families when parents are called to duty.

We must ensure that all of the various benefits, including medical, that were promised to the men and women who chose to make the military and the defense of their nation a career are fulfilled even upon retirement.

In the Republican tradition of support for America's veterans, we proposed and created a Department of Veterans Affairs

so their concerns would be represented at the Cabinet table. We affirm our support for veterans preference in federal employment and for sufficient funding to maintain the integrity of the veterans hospital and medical-care system. We strongly endorse programs to meet the needs of unemployed veterans.

**Intelligence.** Desert Storm reminded us that our intelligence community is a national asset of critical importance to our security.

Assuring the availability of timely and reliable information on regional threats and unrest, drug trafficking, terrorism, technology transfer, proliferation and a host of other issues — this is one of our highest national priorities in the post-Cold War world.

U.S. policy-makers also must have the best possible understanding of international trade, investment, industrial, financial and other developments that affect our economic security.

We must and will maintain the full range of our traditional intelligence capabilities, including covert action, to ensure our security in a dangerous and unpredictable world.

We reject the Democrat candidate's proposal to cripple U.S. intelligence and decry the deep spending cuts to the intelligence budget sponsored by Democrats in Congress.

**Proven leadership.** George Bush has been the most important architect of Western aspirations and designs for the challenging world we are now entering. His record is clear. President Bush has shown he understands how to lead in this new era, where the pre-eminent position of the United States offers new opportunities to build an international consensus on key issues. President Bush, with experienced Republican leadership, has proved he knows how to place our nation at the center of effective coalitions where our power is multiplied.

The test of international leadership is on the field, not in a playbook. The Oval Office is no place for on-the-job training — not in carrying out the presidential duty to protect and defend our nation, not in managing the arsenal of the supreme nuclear power.

There are those who talk and those who perform. George Bush has clearly performed for America, making the right calls in a series of tough decisions that helped transform the world.

Now that we have won the Cold War, we must secure the peace that follows. History has shown that the years following conflict are often critical — where the choices made can either lay the foundation for lasting peace or sow the seeds of the future war. In this period of high hopes and great challenges ahead, the nation needs the tested and experienced leadership of President Bush and the Republican Party. ∎

# Candidates Square Off in First Televised Forum

*On Oct. 11, President Bush, Arkansas Gov. Bill Clinton and independent candidate Ross Perot met at Washington University in St. Louis for the first of three televised presidential debates. Following is the Reuter transcript of that debate:*

**JIM LEHRER:** Good evening, and welcome to the first of three debates among the major candidates for president of the United States, sponsored by the Commission on Presidential Debates.

The candidates are: independent candidate Ross Perot, Governor Bill Clinton, the Democratic nominee, and President George Bush, the Republican nominee. I am Jim Lehrer of the MacNeil/Lehrer NewsHour on PBS, and I will be the moderator for this 90-minute event, which is taking place before an audience in the athletic complex on the campus of Washington University in St. Louis, Missouri.

Three journalists will be asking questions tonight. They are John Mashek of The Boston Globe, Ann Compton of ABC News and Sander Vanocur, a freelance journalist.

We will follow a format agreed to by representatives of the Clinton and Bush campaigns. That agreement contains no restrictions on the content or subject matter of the questions. Each candidate will have up to two minutes for a closing statement. The order of those, as well as the questioning, was determined by a drawing.

The first question goes to Mr. Perot. He will have two minutes to answer, to be followed by rebuttals of one minute each from Governor Clinton and then President Bush.

Gentlemen, good evening.

The first topic tonight is what separates each of you from the other. Mr. Perot, what do you believe tonight is the single most important separating issue of this campaign?

**ROSS PEROT:** I think the principal that separates me is that five and a half million people came together on their own and put me on the ballot. I was not put on the ballot by either of the two parties; I was not put on the ballot by any PAC money, by any foreign lobbyist money, by any special interest money. This is a movement that came from the people. This is the way the framers of the Constitution intended our government to be, a government that comes from the people.

Over time we have developed a government that comes at the people, that comes from the top down, where the people are more or less treated as objects to be pro-

grammed during the campaign with commercials and media events and fear messages and personal attacks and things of that nature.

The thing that separates my candidacy and makes it unique is that this came from millions of people in 50 states all over this country who wanted a candidate that worked and belonged to nobody but them. I go into this race as their servant, and I belong to them. So this comes from the people.

**LEHRER:** Governor Clinton, one minute response.

**CLINTON:** The most important distinction in this campaign is that I represent real hope for change, a departure from trickle-down economics, a departure from tax-and-spend economics to invest-and-grow. But before I can do that, I must challenge the American people to change and they must decide.

Tonight I say to the president, Mr. Bush, for 12 years you've had it your way. You've had your chance, and it didn't work. It's time to change. I want to bring that change to the American people, but we must all decide first we have the courage to change for hope and a better tomorrow.

**LEHRER:** President Bush, one minute response, sir.

**BUSH:** Well, I think one thing that distinguishes is experience. I think we've dramatically changed the world. I'll talk about that a little bit later, but the changes are mind-boggling for world peace. Kids go to bed at night without the same fear of nuclear war.

And change for change's sake isn't enough. We saw that message in the late '70s. We heard a lot about change. And what happened? The misery index went right through the roof.

But my economic program I think is the kind of change we want. And the way we're going to get it done is we're going to have a brand-new Congress. A lot of them are thrown out because of all the scandals. I'll sit down with them — Democrats and Republicans alike — and work for my agenda for American renewal, which represents real change.

But I'd say if you had to separate out, I think it's experience at this level.

**LEHRER:** Governor Clinton, how do you respond to the president — you have two minutes — on the question of experience? He says that is what distinguishes him from the other two of you.

**CLINTON:** I believe experience counts, but it's not everything. Values, judgment and the record that I have

amassed in my state also should count for something. I've worked hard to create good jobs and to educate people. My state now ranks first in the country in job growth this year, fourth in income growth, fourth in the reduction of poverty, third in overall economic performance, according to a major news magazine. That's because we believe in investing in education and in jobs.

We have to change in this country. You know, my wife, Hillary, gave me a book about a year ago in which the author defined "insanity" as just doing the same old thing over and over again and expecting a different result. We have got to have the courage to change.

Experience is important, yes. I've gotten a lot of experience in dealing with ordinary people over the last year, month. I've touched more people's lives and seen more heartbreak and hope, more pain and promise than anybody else who's run for president this year.

I think the American people deserve better than they're getting. We have gone from first to 13th in the world in wages in the last 12 years since Mr. Bush and Mr. Reagan have been in. Personal income has dropped while people have worked harder. In the last four years, there have been twice as many bankruptcies as new jobs created. We need a new approach.

The same old experience is not relevant. We're living in a new world after the Cold War, and what works in this new world is not trickle down, not government for the benefit of the privileged few, not tax and spend, but a commitment to invest in American jobs and American education, controlling American health-care costs and bringing the American people together. That is what works.

And you can have the right kind of experience and the wrong kind of experience. Mine is rooted in the real lives of real people, and it will bring real results, if we have the courage to change.

**BUSH:** I just thought of another big difference here between me — I don't believe Mr. Perot feels this way, but I know Governor Clinton did, because I want to accurately quote him. He thinks — I think he said that the country is coming apart at the seams.

Now, I know that the only way he can win is to make everybody believe the economy is worse than it is, but this country's not coming apart at the seams, for heaven's sakes. We're the United States of America. In spite of the economic problems, we're the most respected economy around the world. Many would trade for it.

We've been caught up in a global slowdown. We can do much, much better, but we ought not to try to convince the American people that America is a country that is coming apart at the seams.

I would hate to be running for president and think that the only way I could win would be to convince everybody how horrible things are. Yes, there are big problems, and yes, people are hurting, but I believe that this agenda for American renewal I have is the answer to do it. And I believe we can get it done now, whereas we didn't in the past, because you're going to have a whole brand new bunch of people in the Congress that are going to have to listen to the same American people I'm listening to.

**LEHRER:** Mr. Perot, a minute response, sir.

**PEROT:** Well, they've got a point. I don't have any experience in running up a $4 trillion debt.

I don't have any experience in gridlock government, where nobody takes responsibility for anything and everybody blames everybody else. I don't have any experience in creating the worst public school system in the industrialized world, the most violent, crime-ridden society in the industrialized world.

But I do have a lot of experience in getting things done.

So if we're at a point in history where we want to stop talking about it and do it, I've got a lot of experience in figuring out how to solve problems, making the solutions work and then moving on to the next one. I've got a lot of experience in not taking 10 years to solve a 10-minute problem.

So if it's time for action, I think I have experience that counts. If there's more time for gridlock and talk and finger-pointing, I'm the wrong man.

**LEHRER:** President Bush, the question goes to you. You have two minutes. And the question is this: Are there important issues of character separating you from these other two men?

**BUSH:** I think the American people should be the judge of that. I think character is a very important question. I said something the other day where I was accused of being like Joe McCarthy because I questioned — I put it this way: I think it's wrong to demonstrate against your own country or organize demonstrations against your own country in foreign soil. I just think it's wrong.

Maybe, they say, well, it was youthful indiscretion. I was 19 or 20 flying off an aircraft carrier, and that shaped me to be commander in chief of the armed forces. And I'm sorry, but demonstrating — it's not a question of patriotism. It's a question of character and judgment.

They get on me — Bill's gotten on me about "read my lips," and when I make a mistake, I'll admit it. But he has made — not admitted a mistake. And I just find it impossible to understand how an American can demonstrate against his own country in a foreign land, organizing demonstrations

against it, when young men are held prisoner in Hanoi or kids out of the ghetto were drafted.

Some say, well, you're old-fashioned. Maybe I am, but I just don't think that's right. Now, whether it's character or judgment, whatever it is, I have a big difference here on this issue. And so we'll just have to see how it plays out, but I — I couldn't do that, and I don't think most Americans could do that.

And they all say, well, it was a long time ago. Well, admit it then. Say, I made a terrible mistake. How could you be commander in chief of the armed forces and have some kid say, when you have to make a tough decision, as I did in Panama or in Kuwait, and then have some kid jump up and say, well, I'm not going to go; the commander in chief was organizing demonstrations halfway around the world during another era.

So there are differences. But that's about the main area where I think we have a difference. I don't know about — we'll talk about that a little with Ross here in a bit.

**LEHRER:** Mr. Perot, you have one minute.

**PEROT:** I think the American people make their own decisions on character, and, at a time when we have work to do and we need action, I think they need to clearly understand the backgrounds of each person. I think the press can play a huge role in making sure that the backgrounds are clearly presented in an objective way. Then make a decision.

Certainly, anyone in the White House should have the character to be there.

But I think it's very important to measure when and where things occurred. Did they occur when you are a young person in your formative years, or did they occur while you were a senior official in the federal government?

When you're a senior official in the federal government spending billions of dollars of taxpayers' money and you're a mature individual and you make a mistake, then that was on our ticket. If you make it as a young man, time passes.

So I would say just, you know, look at all three of us, decide who you think will do the job, pick that person in November, because, believe me, as I've said before, the party's over, and it's time for the cleanup crew. And we do have to have change, and people who never take responsibility for anything when it happens on their watch and people who are in charge —

**LEHRER:** Your time is up.

**PEROT:** — the time is up.

**LEHRER:** Time is up.

**PEROT:** More later.

**LEHRER:** Governor Clinton, you have one minute.

**CLINTON:** Ross gave a good answer, but I've got to respond directly to Mr. Bush. You have questioned my patriotism; you even brought some right-wing congressmen into the White House to plot how to attack me for going to Russia in 1969

and 1970, when over 50,000 other Americans did.

Now, I honor your service in World War II; I honor Mr. Perot's service in uniform and the service of every man and woman who ever served, including Admiral [William J.] Crowe [Jr.], who was your chairman of the Joint Chiefs and who's supporting me.

But when Joe McCarthy went around this country attacking people's patriotism, he was wrong — he was wrong. And a senator from Connecticut stood up to him named Prescott Bush.

Your father was right to stand up to Joe McCarthy; you were wrong to attack my patriotism. I was opposed to the war, but I love my country.

And we need a president who will bring this country together, not divide it. We've had enough division. I want to lead a unified country.

**ANN COMPTON:** Governor Clinton, can you lock in a level here tonight on where middle-income families can be guaranteed a tax cut or, at the very least, at what income level they can be guaranteed no tax increase?

**CLINTON:** The tax increase I have proposed triggers in at family incomes of $200,000 and above. Those are the people who in the 1980s had their incomes go up while their taxes went down.

Middle-class people, defined as people with incomes of $52,000 and down, had their incomes go down while their taxes went up in the Reagan-Bush years because of six increases in the payroll taxes. So that is where my income limit would trigger.

**COMPTON:** There will be no tax increases —

**CLINTON:** Right. My plan —

**COMPTON:** — below $200,000 —

**CLINTON:** — notwithstanding my opponent's ad, my plan triggers in at gross incomes, family incomes of $200,000 and above. Then we want to give modest middle-class tax relief to restore some fairness, especially to middle-class people with families with incomes of under $60,000.

In addition to that, the money that I raise from upper-income people and from asking foreign corporations just to pay the same income on their income earned in America that American corporations do will be used to give incentives back to upper-income people. I want to give people permanent incentives on investment tax credit, like President [John F.] Kennedy and the Congress inaugurated in the early '60s to get industry moving again: a research and development tax credit, a low-income housing tax credit, a long-term capital gains proposal for new business and business expansions.

We've got to have no more trickle down. We don't need across-the-board tax cuts for the wealthy for nothing. We need to say here's your tax incentive if you create American jobs, the old-fashioned way. I'd like to create more millionaires than were created under Mr. Bush and Mr. Reagan, but I don't want to have four years

where we have no growth in the private sector, and that's what's happened in the last four years. We're down 35,000 jobs in the private sector. We need to invest and grow, and that's what I want to do.

**LEHRER:** President Bush, one minute, sir.

**BUSH:** Well, let me — I have to correct one thing. I didn't question the man's patriotism. I questioned his judgment and his character. What he did in Moscow, that's fine. Let him explain it. He did. I accept that. What I don't accept is demonstrating and organizing demonstrations in a foreign country when your country's at war. I'm sorry. I cannot accept it.

In terms of — this one on taxes spells out the biggest difference between us. I do not believe we need to go back to the Mondale proposals or the Dukakis proposals of tax and spend. Governor Clinton says $200,000, but he also says he wants to raise $150 billion. Taxing people over $200,000 will not get you $150 billion. And then when you add in his other spending proposals, regrettably you end up socking it to the working man.

That old adage they use — we're going to soak the rich — we're going to soak the rich — it always ends up being the poor cab driver or the working man that ends up paying the bill. And so I just have a different approach. I believe the way to get the deficit down is to control the growth of mandatory spending programs, and not raise taxes on the American people. We've got a big difference there.

**LEHRER:** Mr. Perot, one minute.

**PEROT:** We've got to have a growing, expanding job base to give us a growing, expanding tax base. Right now we have a flat to deteriorating job base, and where it appears to be growing, it's minimum-wage jobs. So we've got to really rebuild our job base. That's going to take money for infrastructure and investment to do that. Our foreign competitors are doing it; we're not.

We cannot pay off the $4 trillion debt, balance the budget and have the industries of the future and the high-paying jobs in this country without having the revenue. We're going to go through a period of shared sacrifice. There's one challenge. It's got to be fair.

We've created a mess, don't have much to show for it, and we have got to fix it. And that's about all I can say in a minute.

**LEHRER:** OK. Next question goes to President Bush for a two-minute answer, and it will be asked by Sandy Vanocur.

**SANDER VANOCUR:** Mr. President, this past week your secretary of the Army, Michael Stone, said he had no plans to abide by a congressional mandate to cut U.S. forces in Europe from 150,000 to 100,000 by the end of September 1996. Now, why, almost 50 years after the end of World War II, and with the total collapse of the Soviet Union, should American taxpayers be taxed to support armies in Europe when the Europeans have plenty of money to do it for themselves?

**PRESIDENT BUSH:** Well, Sander,

that's a good question, and the answer is: For 40-some years we kept the peace. If you look at the cost of not keeping the peace in Europe, it would be exorbitant. We have reduced the number of troops that are deployed and going to be deployed. I have cut defense spending. And the reason we could do that is because of our fantastic success in winning the Cold War. We never would have got there if we had gone for the nuclear freeze crowd; we never would have got there if we had listened to those that wanted to cut defense spending.

I think it is important that the United States stay in Europe and continue to guarantee the peace. We simply cannot pull back.

Now, when anybody has a spending program they want to spend money on at home, they say, well, let's cut money out of the Defense Department. I will accept, and have accepted, the recommendations of two proven leaders, [Joint Chiefs of Staff Chairman] Gen. Colin Powell and [Defense] Secretary Dick Cheney. They feel that the levels we're operating at and the reductions that I have proposed are proper.

And so I simply do not think we should go back to the isolation days and starting blaming foreigners. We are the sole remaining superpower, and we should be that. And we have a certain disproportionate responsibility. But I would ask the American people to understand that if we make imprudent cuts, if we go too far, we risk the peace. And I don't want to do that. I've seen what it is like to see a war, to see the burdens of a war, and I don't want to see us make reckless cuts.

Because of our programs we have been able to significantly cut defense spending. But let's not cut into the muscle, and let's not cut down our insurance policy, which is participation of American forces in NATO, the greatest peacekeeping organization ever made. Today you've got problems in Europe, still bubbling along even though Europe's gone democracy's route. But we are there, and I think this insurance policy is necessary. I think it goes with world leadership, and I think the levels we've come up with are just about right.

**LEHRER:** Mr. Perot, one minute, sir.

**PEROT:** If I'm poor and you're rich, and I can get you to defend me, that's good. But when the tables get turned, I ought to do my share. Right now we spend about $300 billion a year on defense; the Japanese spend around $30 billion in Asia; the Germans spend around $30 billion in Europe. For example, Germany will spend a trillion dollars building infrastructure over the next 10 years. It's kind of easy to do if you only have to pick up a $30 billion tab to defend your country.

The European Community is in a position to pay a lot more than they have in the past. I agree with the president: When they couldn't, we should have; now that they can, they should. We sort of seem to have a desire to try to stay over there and control it. They don't want us to control it, very candidly. So it, I think, is very important for us to let them assume more and more of

the burden and for us to bring that money back here and rebuild our infrastructure, because we can only be a superpower if we are an economic superpower; and we can only be an economic superpower if we have a growing, expanding job base.

**LEHRER:** Governor Clinton, one minute, sir.

**CLINTON:** I agree with the general statement Mr. Bush made. I disagree that we need 150,000 troops to fulfill our role in Europe. We certainly must maintain an engagement there. There are certainly dangers there, there are certainly other trouble spots in the world which are closer to Europe than to the United States.

But two former defense secretaries recently issued a report saying that 100,000 or slightly fewer troops would be enough, including President [Ronald] Reagan's former defense secretary, Mr. Carlucci. Many of the military experts whom I consulted on this agreed.

We're going to have to spend more money in the future on military technology and on greater mobility, greater airlift, greater sealift, the B-22 airplane. We're going to have to do some things that are quite costly. And I simply don't believe we can afford — nor do we need — to keep 150,000 troops in Europe given how much the Red Army, now under the control of Russia, has been cut; the arms control agreement concluded between Mr. Bush and Mr. Yeltsin, something I have applauded. I don't think we need 150,000 troops.

Let me make one other point. Mr. Bush talked about taxes. He didn't tell you that he vetoed a middle-class tax cut because it would be paid for by raising taxes on the wealthy and vetoed an investment tax credit paid for by raising taxes on the wealthy.

**LEHRER:** All right. We go now to Mr. Perot for a two-minute question, and it will be asked by John Mashek.

**MASHEK:** Mr. Perot, you talked about fairness just a minute ago and sharing the pain. As part of your plan to reduce the ballooning federal deficit, you've suggested that we raise gasoline taxes 50 cents a gallon over five years. Why punish the middle-class consumer to such a degree?

**PEROT:** It's 10 cents-a-year cumulative. It finally gets to 50 cents at the end of the fifth year. I think "punish" is the wrong word. Again, see, I didn't create this problem. We're trying to solve it.

Now, if you study our international competitors, some of our international competitors collect up to $3.50 a gallon in taxes, and they use that money to build infrastructure and to create jobs. We collect 35 cents, and we don't have it to spend.

I know it's not popular, and I understand the nature of your question. But the people who will be helped the most by it are the working people who will get the jobs created because of this tax.

Why do we have to do it? Because we have so mismanaged our country over the years, and it is now time to pay the fiddler. And if we don't, we will be spending our children's money. We have spent $4 trillion

worth. An incredible number of young people are active in supporting my effort because they are deeply concerned that we have taken the American dream from them. I think it's fitting that we're on the campus of a university tonight. These young people, when they get out of this wonderful university, will have difficulty finding a job.

We've got to clean this mess up, leave this country in good shape and pass on the American dream to them. We've got to collect the taxes to do it. If there's a fairer way, I'm all ears — aah.

But — but — see, let me make it very clear. If people don't have the stomach to fix these problems, I think it's a good time to face it, November. If they do, then they will have heard the harsh reality of what we have to do. I'm not playing Lawrence Welk music tonight.

**LEHRER:** All right, Governor Clinton, you have a minute, sir.

**CLINTON:** I think Mr. Perot has confronted this deficit issue, but I think it's important to point out that we really have two deficits in America, not one. We have a budget deficit in the federal government, but we also have an investment, a jobs, an income deficit. People are working harder for less money than they were making 10 years ago, two-thirds of our people — a $1,600 drop in average income in just the last two years.

The problem I have with the Perot prescription is that almost all economists who've looked at it say that if you cut the deficit this much this quick, it will increase unemployment, it will slow down the economy. That's why I think we shouldn't do it that quickly. We have a disciplined reduction in the deficit of 50 percent over the next four years, but first get incentives to invest in this economy, put the American people back to work. We've got to invest and grow.

Nine Nobel Prize-winning economists and 500 others, including numerous Republican and Democratic business executives, have endorsed this approach because it offers the best hope to put America back to work and get our incomes rising instead of falling.

**LEHRER:** President Bush, one minute, sir.

**BUSH:** Your question was on fairness. I just disagree with Mr. Perot. I don't believe it is fair to slap a 50-cent-a-gallon tax over whatever many years on the people that have to drive for a living, people that go long distances. I don't think we need to do it.

You see, I have a fundamental difference. I agree with what he's talking about in trying to get this spending down and the discipline, although I think we ought to totally exempt Social Security. But he's talking tough medicine, and I think that's good.

I disagree with the tax-and-spend philosophy. You see, I don't think we need to tax more and spend more, and then say that's going to make the problem better. And I'm afraid that's what I think I'm hearing from Governor Clinton.

I believe what you need to do is some

of what Ross is talking about: control the growth of mandatory spending and get taxes down. He's mentioned some ways to do it — and I agree with those. I've been talking about getting a capital gains cut forever, and his friends in Congress have been telling me that's a tax break for the rich. It would stimulate investment. I'm for an investment tax allowance; I'm for a tax break for first-time homebuyers. And with this new Congress coming in, gridlock will be gone, and I'll sit down with them and say let's get this done.

But I do not want to go the tax-and-spend route.

**LEHRER:** All right, let's move on now to the subject of jobs. The first question goes to President Bush for two minutes, and John will ask that question.

**MASHEK:** Mr. President, last month you came to St. Louis to announce a very lucrative contract for McDonnell Douglas to build F-15s for Saudi Arabia. In today's Post-Dispatch, a retired saleswoman, a 75-year-old woman named Marjorie Roberts, asked if she could ask a question of the candidates. She said she wanted to register her concern about the lack of a plan to convert our defense-oriented industries into other purposes.

How would you answer her?

**BUSH:** I assume she was supportive of the decision on McDonnell Douglas; I assume she was supporting me on the decision to sell those airplanes. I think it's a good decision — took a little heat for it, but I think it was the correct decision to do. And we worked it out, and indeed we're moving forward all around the world in a much more peaceful way. So that one we came away with in creating jobs for the American people.

I would simply say to her, look, take a look at what the president has proposed on job retraining. When you cut back on defense spending, some people are going to be thrown out of work. If you throw another 50,000 kids on the street because of cutting recklessly in troop levels, you're going to put a lot more out of work. I would say to them, look at the job retraining programs that we're proposing. Therein is the best answer to her.

And another one is: Stimulate investment and savings. I mean, we've got big economic problems, but we are not coming apart at the seams; we're ready for a recovery. With interest rates down and inflation down — the cruelest tax of all, caught up in a global slowdown right now — that will change if you go with the programs I've talked about and if you help with job retraining and education.

I am a firm believer that our America 2000 education problem is the answer — a little longer run; it's going to take a while to educate. But it is a good program.

So her best help for short term is job retraining, if she was thrown out of work at a defense plant. But tell her it's not all that gloomy; we're the United States, we faced tough problems before. Look at the misery index when the Democrats had both the

White House and the Congress. It was just right through the roof.

Now, we can do better. And the way to do better is not to tax and spend but to retrain, get that control of the mandatory spending programs. I'm much more optimistic about this country than some.

**LEHRER:** Mr. Perot? Mr. Perot, you have one minute, sir.

**PEROT:** Defense industries are going to have to convert to civilian industries. Many of them are. And the sooner they start, the sooner they'll finish. And there will be a significant transition. And it's very important that we not continue to let our industrial base deteriorate.

We had someone who I'm sure regrets [having] said it, in the president's staff, said he didn't care whether we made potato chips or computer chips. Well, anybody that thinks about it cares a great deal. No. 1, you make more making computer chips than potato chips; and, No. 2, 19 out of 20 computer chips that we have in this country now come from Japan. We've given away whole industries.

So as we phase these industries over, there's a lot of intellectual talent in these industries. A lot of these people in industries can be converted to the industries of tomorrow, and that's where the high-paying jobs are. We need to have a very carefully thought-through phase-over.

Now, see, we practice 19th century capitalism. The rest of the world practices 21st century capitalism. I can't handle that in a minute, but I hope we can get back into it later. In the rest of the world, the countries and the businesses would be working together to make this transition in an intelligent way.

**LEHRER:** Governor Clinton, you have one minute, sir.

**CLINTON:** We must have a transition plan to plan to convert from a defense to a domestic economy. No other nation would have cut defense as much as we already have without that. There are 200,000 people unemployed in California alone because we have cut defense without planning to retrain them and to reinvest in the technologies of the future here at home. That is what I want to do.

This administration may say they have a plan, but the truth is they have not even released all the money, the paltry sum of money, that Congress appropriated. I want to take every dollar by which we reduce defense and reinvest it in technologies for the 21st century — in new transportation, in communication, in environmental cleanup technologies. Let's put the American people to work, and let's build the kind of high-tech, high-wage, high-growth economy that the American people deserve.

**LEHRER:** All right. The next question goes to Mr. Perot for a two-minute answer. It will be asked by Ann. Ann?

**COMPTON:** Mr. Perot, you talked a minute ago about rebuilding the job base. But is it true what Governor Clinton just said, that that means that unemployment will increase, that it will slow the economy?

And how would you specifically use the powers of the presidency to get more people back into good jobs immediately?

**PEROT:** Step one, the American people send me up there. The day after election, I'll get with congressional — we won't even wait till inauguration, and I'll ask the president to help, and I'll ask his staff to help me. And we will start putting together teams to put together — to take all the plans that exist and do something with them.

Please understand. There are great plans lying all over Washington nobody ever executes. It's like having a blueprint for a house you never built. You don't have anywhere to sleep.

Now our challenge is to take these things, do something with them. Step one, we want to put America back to work, clean up the small-business problem, have one task force at work on that. The second, you've got your big companies that are in trouble, including the defense industries — have another one on that.

Have a third task force on new industries of the future to make sure we nail those for our country and they don't wind up in Europe and Asia. Convert from 19th to 21st century capitalism.

See, we have an adversarial relationship between government and business. Our international competitors that are cleaning our plate have an intelligent relationship between government and business, and a supportive relationship.

Then have another task force on crime because, next to jobs, our people are concerned about their safety. Health care, schools — one on the debt and deficit. And finally in that 90-day period before the inauguration, put together the framework for the town hall and give the American people a Christmas present. Show them by Christmas the first cut at these plans. By the time Congress comes into session to go to work, have those plans ready to go in front of Congress. Then get off to a flying start in '93 to execute these plans.

Now, there are people in this room and people on this stage who've been in meetings when I would sit there and say, "Is this the one we're going to talk about or do something about?" Well, obviously, my orientation is let's go do it. Now, put together your plans by Christmas, be ready to go when Congress goes. Nail these things. Small business — you've got to have capital, you've got to have credit, and many of them need mentors or coaches.

And we can create more jobs there in a hurry than any other place.

**LEHRER:** Governor Clinton, one minute.

**CLINTON:** This country desperately needs a jobs program, and my first priority would be to pass a jobs program, to introduce it on the first day I was inaugurated. I would meet with the leaders of the Congress, with all the newly elected members of the Congress and as many others with whom I could meet between the time of the election and the inauguration, and we would present a jobs program.

Then we would present a plan to control health-care costs and phase in healthcare coverage for all Americans. Until we control health care costs, we're not going to control the deficit. It is the No. 1 culprit. But first we must have an aggressive jobs program.

I live in a state where manufacturing job growth has far outpaced the nation in the last few years, where we have created more private sector jobs since Mr. Bush has been president than have been created in the entire rest of the country, where Mr. Bush's labor secretary said the job growth has been enormous.

We've done it in Arkansas. Give me a chance to create these kind of jobs in America. We can do it. I know we can.

**LEHRER:** President Bush, one minute.

**BUSH:** We've got the plan announced for what we can do for small business. I've already put forward things that'll get this country working fast, some of which have been echoed here tonight — investment tax allowance, capital gains reduction, more on research and development, tax credit for first-time home buyers.

What I'm going to do is say to [White House Chief of Staff] Jim Baker when this campaign is over, all right, let's sit down now, you go in domestic affairs what you've done in foreign affairs, be kind of the economic coordinator of all the domestic side of the House, and that includes all the economic side, all the training side, and bring this program together.

We're going to have a new Congress, and we're going to say to them, you've listened to the voters the way we have. Nobody wants gridlock anymore, and so let's get the program through.

And I believe it'll work because, as Ross said, we've got the plans. The plans are all over Washington. And I've put ours together in something called the agenda for American renewal, and it makes sense, it's sensible, it creates jobs, it gets to the base of the kind of jobs we need. And so I'll just be asking for support to get that put into effect.

**LEHRER:** All right. The next question goes to Governor Clinton for two minutes. It will be asked by Sandy.

**VANOCUR:** Governor Clinton, when a president running for the first time gets into the office and wants to do something about the economy, he finds in Washington there's a person who has much more power over the economy than he does: the chairman of the Federal Reserve Board, accountable to no one.

That being the case, would you go along with proposals made by Treasury Secretary James [sic] Brady and Congressman Lee [H.] Hamilton [D-Ind.] to make the Federal Reserve Board chairman somehow more accountable to elected officials?

**CLINTON:** Well, let me say that I think that we might ought to review the terms, the way it works. But frankly, I don't think that's the problem today. We have low interest rates today. At least we

have low interest rates that the Fed can control.

Our long-term interest rates are still pretty high because of our deficit and because of our economic performance. And there was a terrible reaction internationally to Mr. Bush saying he was going to give us four more years of trickle-down economics — another across-the-board tax cut and most of it going to the wealthy, with no real guarantee of investment.

But I think the important thing — the important thing — is to use the powers the president does have on the assumption that, given the condition of this economy, we're going to keep interest rates down if we have the discipline to increase investment and reduce the debt at the same time. That is my commitment.

I think the American people are hungry for action. I think Congress is hungry for someone who will work with them instead of manipulate them, someone who will not veto a bill that has an investment tax credit, middle-class tax relief, research and development tax credits, as Mr. Bush has done. Give me a chance to do that.

I don't have to worry, I don't think, in the near term about the Federal Reserve. Their policies so far, it seems to me, are pretty sound.

**LEHRER:** President Bush, you have one minute.

**BUSH:** I don't think the Fed ought to be put under the executive branch. There is separation there; I think that's fine. [Federal Reserve Board Chairman] Alan Greenspan is respected. I've had some arguments with him about the speed at which we might have lowered rates.

But Governor Clinton, he talks about the reaction to the markets. There was a momentary fear that he might win, and the markets went phwwt, down like that.

So I don't think we can judge on — the stock market has been strong. It's been very strong since I've been president.

And they recognize we've got great difficulties. But they're also much more optimistic than the pessimists we have up here tonight.

In terms of vetoing tax bills, you're darn right. I'm going to protect the American taxpayer against the spend-and-tax Congress, and I'm going to keep on vetoing them because I don't think we are taxed too little; I think the government's spending too much. So Governor Clinton can label it "tax for the rich" or anything he wants. I'm going to protect the working man by continuing to veto and to threaten veto until we get this new Congress, and then we're going to move forward on our plan.

I've got to protect them.

**LEHRER:** Mr. Perot, one minute.

**PEROT:** Keep the Federal Reserve independent, but let's live in a world of reality. We live in a global economy, not a national economy. These interest rates we have now don't make any sense. We have a $4 trillion debt, and only in America would

you finance 70 percent of it five years or less. So 70 percent of our debt is five years or less. It's very interest-sensitive.

We have a 4 percent gap between what we pay for Treasuries and for what Germany pays for one-to-five-year treasuries. That gap is going to close because the Arabs, the Japanese and folks in this country are going to start buying German treasuries because they can get more money.

Every time our interest rates go up 1 percent, that adds $28 billion to the deficit or to the debt, whichever place you want to put it. We are sitting on a ticking bomb, folks, because we have totally mismanaged our country and we had better get it back under control. Just think in your own business if you had all of your long-term problems financed short-term. You'd go broke in a hurry.

**LEHRER:** All right. We're going to move — We're going to move to foreign affairs. The first question goes to Mr. Perot for a two-minute answer, and Sandy will ask it.

**VANOCUR:** Mr. Perot, in the post-Cold War environment, what should be the overriding U.S. national interest, and what can the United States do, and what can it afford to do to defend that national interest?

**PEROT:** Well, again, if you're not rich, you're not a superpower. So we have two that I'd put as No. 1. I have 1 and 1(a). One is we've got to have the money to be able to pay for defense.

And we've got to manufacture here. Believe it or not, folks, you can't ship it all overseas; you've got to make it here. And you can't convert from potato chips to airplanes in an emergency.

See, Willow Run could be converted from cars to airplanes in World War II because it was here. We've got to make things here. You just can't ship them overseas anymore. I hope we talk more about that.

The second thing on priorities, we've got to help Russia succeed in its revolution, and all of its republics. When we think of Russia, remember we're thinking of many countries now. We've got to help them. That's pennies on the dollar compared to renewing the Cold War.

Third, we've got all kinds of agreements on paper and some that are being executed on getting rid of nuclear warheads. Russia and its republics are out of control or, at best, in weak control right now. It's a very unstable situation. You've got every rich Middle Eastern country over there trying to buy nuclear weapons, as you well know. And that will lead to another five-star migraine headache down the road.

We really need to nail down the intercontinental ballistic missiles, the ones that can hit us from Russia. We're focused on the tactical. We've made real progress there. We've got some agreements on the nuclear. But we don't have those things put away yet. The sooner the better.

So, in terms of priorities, we've got to be financially strong. No. 2, we've got to take care of this missile situation and try to get the nuclear war behind us and give that a very high priority. And No. 3, we need to help and support Russia and the republics in every possible way to become democratic, capitalistic societies, and not just sit back and let those countries continue in turmoil because they could go back worse than things used to be — and, believe me, there are a lot of old boys in the KGB and the military that liked it better the way it used to be.

Thank you.

**LEHRER:** Governor Clinton, one minute.

**CLINTON:** In order to keep America the strongest nation in the world, we need some continuity and some change. There are three fundamental challenges. First of all, the world is still a dangerous and uncertain place. We need a new military and a new national security policy equal to the challenges of the post-Cold War era, a smaller permanent military force, but one that is more mobile, well-trained with high-technology equipment.

We need to continue the negotiations to reduce the nuclear arsenals in the Soviet Union, the former Soviet Union, and the United States. We need to stop this proliferation of weapons of mass destruction.

Second, we have to face that in this world, economic security is a whole lot of national security. Our dollar is at a low-time low against some foreign currencies; we're weak in the world. We must rebuild America's strength at home.

And, finally, we ought to be promoting the democratic impulses around the world. Democracies are our partners; they don't go to war with each other they're reliable friends in the future.

National security, economic strength, democracy.

**LEHRER:** President Bush, one minute.

**BUSH:** We still are the envy of the world in terms of our military, there's no question about that. We're the envy of the world in terms of our economy, in spite of the difficulties we're having. There's no question about that. Our exports are dramatically up.

I might say to Mr. Perot, I can understand why you might have missed it because there's so much fascination by trivia, but I worked out a deal with [Russian Republic President] Boris Yeltsin to eliminate, get rid of entirely, the most destabilizing weapons of all, the SS-18, the big intercontinental ballistic missile; I mean, that's been done. And thank God it has, because the parents of these young people around here go to bed at night without the same fear of nuclear war.

We made dramatic progress. And so we've got a good military. The question that says get a new military, get the best in the world — we got it. And they're keeping the peace, and they're respected around the world. And we are more respected, because of the way we have conducted ourselves. We didn't listen to the nuclear freeze crowd. We said peace through strength, and it worked, and the Cold War is over. And America understands that.

But we're turned so inward, we don't understand the global picture. And we are helping democracy, Ross. The Freedom Support Act is something that I got through the Congress, and it's a very good thing, because it does exactly what you say — and I think you agree with that — to help Russian democracy. And we're going to keep on doing that.

**LEHRER:** All right, next question is for Governor Clinton, and John will ask it.

**MASHEK:** Governor Clinton, you've accused the president of coddling tyrants, including those in Beijing. As president, how would you exert U.S. power to influence affairs in China?

**CLINTON:** I think our relationships with China are important, and I don't think we want to isolate China. But I think it is a mistake for us to do what this administration did when all those kids went out there carrying the Statue of Liberty in Tiananmen Square. Mr. Bush sent two people in secret to toast the Chinese leaders and basically tell them not to worry about it. They rewarded him by opening negotiations with Iran to transfer nuclear technology. That was their response to that sort of action.

Now that voices in the Congress and throughout the country have insisted that we do something about China, look what has happened. China has finally agreed to stop sending us products made with prison labor, not because we coddled them but because the administration was pushed into doing something about it. And recently the Chinese have announced that they're going to lower some barriers to our products, which they ought to do since they have a $15 billion trade surplus with the United States under Mr. Bush, the second biggest surplus of all, second to Japan.

So I would be firm. I would say if you want to continue most-favored-nation status for your government-owned industries as well as your private ones, observe human rights in the future, open your society, recognize the legitimacy of those kids that were carrying the Statute of Liberty.

If we can stand up for our economic interests, we ought to be able to pursue the democratic interests of the people in China, and over the long run they'll be more reliable partners.

**LEHRER:** President Bush, you have one minute,.

**BUSH:** Well, the administration was the first major country to stand up against the abuse in Tiananmen Square. We are the ones that worked out the prison labor deal; we are the ones that have lowered the barrier to products by [U.S. Trade Representative] Carla Hills' negotiation.

I am the one that said let's keep the MFN because you see China moving towards a free market economy. To do what the Congress and Governor Clinton is suggesting, you'd isolate and ruin Hong Kong. They are making some progress — not enough for us. We were the first ones to put

sanctions on — we still have them on on some things.

But Governor Clinton's philosophy is isolate 'em. He says don't do it, but the policies he's expounding of putting conditions on MFN and kind of humiliating them is not the way you make the kind of progress we are getting.

And I have stood up with these people, and I understand what you have to do to be strong in this situation. And it's moving — not as fast as we'd like. But you isolate China and turn them inward, and then we've made a tremendous mistake. And I'm not going to do it, and I've had to fight a lot of people that were saying human rights — and we are the ones that put the sanctions on and stood for it.

And he can insult [National Security Adviser] Gen. [Brent] Scowcroft if he wants to; he didn't go over to coddle, he went over to say you must make the very changes they're making now.

**LEHRER:** One minute, Mr. Perot.

**PEROT:** All right, so here's China, so here's your country, broken into many provinces. It has some very elderly leaders that will not be around too much longer. Capitalism is growing and thriving across big portions of China. Asia will be our largest trading partner in the future. It will be a growing and a closer relationship. We have a delicate tightwire walk that we must go through at the present time to make sure that we do not cozy up to tyrants, to make sure that they don't get the impression that they can suppress their people.

But time is our friend there, because their leaders will change in not too many years, worst case, and their country is making great progress.

One last point on the missiles. I don't want the American people to be confused. We have written agreements and we have some missiles that have been destroyed, but we have a huge number of intercontinental ballistic missiles that are still in place in Russia. The fact that you have an agreement is one thing. Till they're destroyed, some crazy person can either sell them or use them.

**LEHRER:** All right. The next question goes to President Bush for a two-minute answer, and Ann will ask it.

**COMPTON:** Mr. President, how can you watch the killing in Bosnia and the ethnic cleansing, or the starvation and anarchy in Somalia, and not want to use America's might, if not America's military, to try to end that kind of suffering?

**BUSH:** Ann, both of them are very complicated situations. And I vowed something because I learned something from Vietnam. I am not going to commit U.S. forces until I know what the mission is, till the military tells me that it can be completed, and till I know how they can come out.

We are helping. American airplanes are helping today on humanitarian relief for Sarajevo. It is America that's in the lead in helping with humanitarian relief for Somalia.

But when you go to put somebody else's son or daughter into war, I think you have got to be a little bit careful, and you have to be sure that there's a military plan that can do this. You have ancient ethnic rivalries that have cropped up as Yugoslavia's dissolved or getting dissolved, and it isn't going to be solved by sending in the 82nd Airborne, and I'm not going to do that as commander in chief.

I am going to stand by and use the moral persuasion of the United States to get satisfaction in terms of prison camps, and we're making some progress there, and in terms of getting humanitarian relief in there. And right now, as you know, the United States took the lead in a no-fly operation up there in — no-fly order up in the United Nations. We're working through the international organizations.

That's one thing I learned by forging that tremendous and greatly — highly successful coalition against [President of Iraq] Saddam Hussein, the dictator. Use — work internationally to do it.

I am very concerned about it. I am concerned about ethnic cleansing. I am concerned about a tax on Muslims, for example, over there. But I must stop short of using American force until I know how those young men and women are going to get out of there as well as get in, know what the mission is, and define it. And I think I'm on the right track.

**COMPTON:** Are you designing a mission —

**LEHRER:** Ms. — Ann, sorry, sorry. Time is up. We have to go to Mr. Perot for a one-minute response.

**PEROT:** I think if we learned anything in Vietnam, it is you first commit this nation before you commit the troops to the battlefield. We cannot send our people all over the world to solve every problem that comes up.

This is basically a problem that is a primary concern to the European Community. Certainly we care about the people, we care about the children, we care about the tragedy. But it is inappropriate for us, just because there's a problem somewhere around the world, to take the sons and daughters of working people — and make no mistake about it, our all-volunteer armed force is not made up of the sons and daughters of the beautiful people; it's the working folks who send their sons and daughters to war, with a few exceptions. It's very unlike World War II, when FDR's sons flew missions. Everybody went. It's a different world now.

It's very important that we not just, without thinking it through, just rush to every problem in the world and have our people torn to pieces.

**LEHRER:** Governor Clinton, one minute.

**CLINTON:** I agree that we cannot commit ground forces to become involved in the quagmire of Bosnia or in the tribal wars of Somalia. But I think that it's important to recognize that there are things that can be done short of that, and that we

do have interests there. There are, after all, two million refugees now because of the problems in what was Yugoslavia, the largest number since World War II, and there may be hundreds of thousands of people who will starve or freeze to death in this winter. The United States should try to work with its allies and stop it. I urged the president to support this air cover, and he did — and I applaud that. I applaud the no-fly zone, and I know that he's going back to the United Nations to try to get authority to enforce it.

I think we should stiffen the embargo on the Belgrade government, and I think we have to consider whether or not we should lift the arms embargo now on the Bosnians, since they are in no way in a fair fight with a heavily armed opponent bent on "ethnic cleansing."

We can't get involved in the quagmire, but we must do what we can.

**LEHRER:** All right, moving on now to divisions in our country, the first question goes to Governor Clinton for two minutes, and Ann will ask it.

**COMPTON:** Governor Clinton, can you tell us what your definition of the word "family" is?

**CLINTON:** A family involves at least one parent, whether natural or adoptive or foster, and children. A good family is a place where love and discipline and good values are transmuted [sic] from the elders to the children, a place where people turn for refuge, and where they know they're the most important people in the world. America has a lot of families who are in trouble today. There's been a lot of talk about family values in this campaign. I know a lot about that. I was born to a widowed mother who gave me family values, and grandparents.

I've seen the family values of my people in Arkansas. I've seen the family values of all these people in America who are out there killing themselves working harder for less in a country that's had the worst economic years in 50 years and the first decline in industrial production ever.

I think the president owes it to family values to show that he values America's families, whether they're people on welfare you're trying to move from welfare to work, the working poor whom I think deserve a tax break to lift them above poverty if they've got a child in the house and are working 40 hours a week, working families who deserve a fair tax system and the opportunity for constant retraining; they deserve a strong economy.

And I think they deserve a family and medical leave act. Seventy-two other nations have been able to do it. Mr. Bush vetoed it twice because he says we can't do something 72 other countries do, even though there was a small-business exemption.

So with all the talk about family values, I know about family values — I wouldn't be here without them. The best expression of my family values is that tonight's my 17th wedding anniversary, and I'd like to close my question by just wishing

my wife a happy anniversary, and thank you, my daughter, for being there.

**LEHRER:** President Bush, one minute.

**BUSH:** Well, I would say that one meeting that made a profound impression on me was when the mayors of the big cities, including the mayor of Los Angeles, a Democrat, came to see me, and they unanimously said the decline in urban America stems from the decline in the American family. So I do think we need to strengthen family. When Barbara holds an AIDS baby, she's showing a certain compassion for family; when she reads to children, the same thing.

I believe that discipline and respect for the law — all of these things should be taught to children, not in our schools, but families have to do that. I'm appalled at the highest — outrageous numbers of divorces. It happens in families; it's happened in ours. But it's gotten too much. And I just think that we ought to do everything we can to respect the American family. It can be a single-parent family. Those mothers need help. And one way to do it is to get these deadbeat fathers to pay their obligations to these mothers — that will help strengthen the American family.

And there's a whole bunch of other things that I can't click off in this short period of time.

**LEHRER:** All right, Mr. Perot, you have one minute.

**PEROT:** If I had to solve all the problems that face this country and I could be granted one wish as we started down the trail to rebuild the job base, the schools and so on and so forth, I would say a strong family unit in every home, where every child is loved, nurtured and encouraged. A little child before they're 18 months learns to think well of himself or herself or poorly. They develop a positive or negative self-image. At a very early age they learn how to learn. If we have children who are not surrounded with love and affection — you see, I look at my grandchildren and wonder if they'll ever learn to walk because they're always in someone's arms. And I think, my gosh, wouldn't it be wonderful if every child had that love and support. But they don't.

We will not be a great country unless we have a strong family unit in every home. And I think you can use the White House as a bully pulpit to stress the importance of these little children, particularly in their young and formative years, to mold these little precious pieces of clay so that they, too, can live rich full lives when they're grown.

**LEHRER:** New question, two-minute answer, goes to President Bush. Sandy will ask it.

**VANOCUR:** Mr. President, there's been a lot of talk about Harry Truman in this campaign, so much so that I think tomorrow I'll wake up and see him named as the next commissioner of baseball.

The thing that Mr. Truman didn't have to deal with is drugs. Americans are increasingly alarmed about drug-related crimes in cities and suburbs. And your administration

is not the first to have grappled with this.

And are you at all of a mind that maybe it ought to go to another level, if not to what's advocated by William F. Buckley, Jr. and Milton Friedman, legalization, somewhere between there and where we are now?

**BUSH:** No, I don't think that's the right answer. I don't believe legalizing narcotics is the answer. I just don't believe that's the answer. I do believe that there's some fairly good news out there. The use of cocaine, for example, by teenagers is dramatically down. But we've got to keep fighting on this war against drugs. We're doing a little better in interdiction. Many of the countries below that used to say, well, this is the United States' problem — if you'd get the demand down, then we wouldn't have the problem — are working cooperatively with the DEA [Drug Enforcement Administration] and the military. We're using the military more now in terms of interdiction. Our funding for recovery is up, recovering the addicts.

Where we're not making the progress, Sander, is in — we're making it in teenagers, and thank God, because I thought what Ross said was most appropriate about these families and these children. But where we're not making it is with the confirmed addicts. And I'll tell you one place that's working well, and that is the private sector — Jim Burke and this task force that he has, you may know about it. I'll tell the American people, but this man said I'll get you a million dollars a day in pro bono advertising, something that's very hard for the government to do. And he went out and he did it. And people are beginning to educate through this program, teaching these kids you shouldn't use drugs.

So we're still in the fight. But I must tell you, I think legalization of narcotics, or something of that nature, in the face of the medical evidence, would be totally counterproductive. And I oppose it, and I'm going to stand up and continue to oppose it.

**LEHRER:** Mr. Perot, one minute.

**PEROT:** Anytime you think you want to legalize drugs, go to a neonatal unit — if you can get in. They're between 100 percent and 200 percent capacity up and down the East Coast. And the reason is crack babies being born, babies in the hospital 42 days. Typical cost to you and me is $125,000. Again and again and again, the mother disappears in three days, and the child becomes a ward of the state because he's permanently and genetically damaged.

Just look at those little children, and if anybody can even think about legalizing drugs, they've lost me.

Now, let's look at priorities. You know, we went on the Libyan raid — do you remember that one? — because we were worried to death that [Libyan leader Muammar el-]Qaddafi might be building up chemical weapons. We've got chemical warfare being conducted against our children on the streets in this country all day every day, and we don't have the will to stamp it out.

Now, again, if I get up there, if you send me, we're going to have some blunt talks about this, and we're really going to get down

in the trenches and say, is this one you want to talk about or fix, because talk won't do it, folks. There are guys that couldn't get a job third shift in a Dairy Queen driving BMWs and Mercedes selling drugs. And these old boys are not going to quit easy.

**LEHRER:** Governor Clinton, one minute.

**CLINTON:** Like Mr. Perot, I have held crack babies in my arms. But I know more about this, I think, than anybody else up here because I have a brother who's a recovering drug addict. I'm very proud of him.

But I can tell you this. If drugs were legal, I don't think he'd be alive today. I am adamantly opposed to legalizing drugs. He is alive today because of the criminal justice system.

That's a mistake. What should we do? First, we ought to prevent more of this on the street. Thirty years ago, there were three policemen for every crime. Now there are three crimes for every policeman. We need a hundred thousand more police on the street. I have a plan for that.

Secondly, we ought to have treatment on demand.

Thirdly, we ought to have boot camps for first-time non-violent offenders so they can get discipline and treatment and education and get reconnected to the community before they're severed and sent to prison, where they can learn how to be first-class criminals.

There is a crime bill that, lamentably, was blocked from passage — once again, mostly by Republicans in the United States Senate — which would have addressed some of these problems. That crime bill is going to be one of my highest priorities next January if I become president.

**LEHRER:** Next question is to you, Mr. Perot. You have two minutes to answer it, and John will ask it.

**MASHEK:** Mr. Perot, racial division continues to tear apart our great cities, the last episode being this spring in Los Angeles.

Why is this still happening in America, and what would you do to end it?

**PEROT:** This is a relevant question here tonight. The first thing I'd do is, during political campaigns, I would urge everybody to stop trying to split this country into fragments and appeal to the differences between us and then wonder why the melting pot is all broken to pieces after November the 3rd.

We are all in this together. We ought to love one another because united teams win and divided teams lose. And if we can't love one another, we ought to get along with one another. And if you can't get there, just recognize we're all stuck with one another because nobody's going anywhere, right?

Now, that ought to get everybody back up to let's get along together and make it work. Our diversity is a strength. We've turned it into a weakness.

Now again, the White House is a bully pulpit. I think whoever is in the White House should just make it absolutely un-

conscionable and inexcusable, and if anybody's in the middle of a speech at, you know, one of these conventions, I would expect the candidate to go out and lift him off the stage if he starts preaching hate — because we don't have time for it.

See, our differences are our strengths. We have got to pull together. In athletics, we know it. See, divided teams lose; united teams win.

We have got to unite and pull together, and there's nothing we can't do. But if we sit around blowing all this energy out the window on racial strife and hatred, we are stuck with a sure loser because we have been a melting pot. We're becoming more and more of a melting pot. Let's make it a strength, not a weakness.

**LEHRER:** Governor Clinton, one minute.

**CLINTON:** I grew up in the segregated South, thankfully raised by a grandfather, with almost no formal education but with a heart of gold, who taught me early that all people were equal in the eyes of God.

I saw the winds of hatred divide people and keep the people of my state poorer than they would have been, spiritually and economically. And I've done everything I could in my public life to overcome racial divisions.

We don't have a person to waste in this country. We are being murdered economically because we have too many dropouts, we have too many low-birthweight babies, we have too many drug addicts as kids, we have too much violence, we are too divided by race, by income, by region. And I have devoted a major portion of this campaign to going across this country and looking for opportunities to go to white groups and African-American groups and Latino groups and Asian-American groups and say the same thing.

If the American people cannot be brought together, we can't turn this country around. If we can come together, nothing can stop us.

**LEHRER:** Mr. President, one minute.

**BUSH:** Well, I think Governor Clinton is committed. I do think it's fair to note — he can rebut it — but Arkansas is one of the few states that doesn't have any civil rights legislation.

I've tried to use the White House as a bully pulpit, speaking out against discrimination. We passed two very forward-looking civil rights bills. It's not going to be all done by legislation. But I do think that you need to make an appeal every time you can to eliminate racial divisions and discrimination, and I'll keep on doing that and pointing to some legislative accomplishment to back it up.

I have to take 10 seconds here at the end — the red light isn't on yet — to say to Ross Perot, please don't say to the DEA agents on the street that we don't have the will to fight drugs. Please. I have watched these people — the same for our local law enforcement people. We're backing them at every way we possibly can. But maybe you

meant that some in the country don't have the will to fight it, but those that are out there on the front line, as you know — you've been a strong backer of law enforcement — really — I just want to clear that up — have the will to fight it, and, frankly, some of them are giving their lives.

**LEHRER:** Time, Mr. President. All right. Let's go now to another subject, the subject of health. The first question for two minutes is to President Bush, and John will ask it.

**MASHEK:** Mr. President, yesterday tens of thousands of people paraded past the White House to demonstrate their concern about the disease AIDS. A celebrated member of your commission, [basketball star] Magic Johnson, quit, saying that there was too much inaction.

Where is this widespread feeling coming from that your administration is not doing enough about AIDS?

**BUSH:** Coming from the political process. We have increased funding for AIDS. We've doubled it on research and on every other aspect of it. My request for this year was $4.9 billion for AIDS — 10 times as much per AIDS victim as per cancer victim.

I think that we're showing the proper compassion and concern. So I can't tell you where it's coming from, but I am very much concerned about AIDS, and I believe that we've got the best researchers in the world out there at NIH working the problem. We're funding them — I wish there was more money — but we're funding them far more than any time in the past, and we're going to keep on doing that.

I don't know. I was a little disappointed in Magic because he came to me and I said, "Now if you see something we're not doing, get a hold of me. Call me, let me know." He went to one meeting, and then we heard that he was stepping down. So he's replaced by [GOP fundraiser] Mary Fisher who electrified the Republican convention by talking about the compassion and the concern that we feel. It was a beautiful moment, and I think she'll do a first-class job on that commission.

So I think the appeal is yes, we care. And the other thing is part of AIDS — it's one of the few diseases where behavior matters. And I once called on somebody, "Well, change your behavior. Is the behavior you're using prone to cause AIDS? Change the behavior." Next thing I know, one of these ACT-UP groups is out saying, "Bush ought to change his behavior."

You can't talk about it rationally. The extremes are hurting the AIDS cause. To go into a Catholic mass in a beautiful cathedral in New York under the cause of helping in AIDS and start throwing condoms around in the Mass, I'm sorry, I think it sets back the cause.

We cannot move to the extreme. We've got to care. We've got to continue everything we can at the federal and the local level. Barbara, I think, is doing a superb job in destroying the myth about AIDS. And all of us are in this fight together, all

of us care. Do not go to the extreme.

**LEHRER:** One minute, Mr. Perot.

**PEROT:** First, I think Mary Fisher was a great choice. We're lucky to have her heading the commission. Secondly, I think one thing that if I were sent to do the job, I would sit down with FDA [Food and Drug Administration], look at exactly where we are. Then I would really focus on let's get these things out. If you're going to die, you don't have to go through this 10-year cycle that FDA goes through on new drugs.

Believe me, people with AIDS are more than willing to take that risk. And we could be moving out to the human population a whole lot faster than we are on some of these new drugs. So I would think we can expedite the problem there.

Let me go back a minute to racial divisiveness. The all-time low in our country was the [Supreme Court] Judge [Clarence] Thomas-Anita Hill hearings, and those senators ought to be hanging their heads in shame for what they did there.

Second thing, there are not many times in your life when you get to talk to a whole country. But let me just say to all of America: If you hate people, I don't want your vote. That's how strongly I feel about it.

**LEHRER:** Governor Clinton, one minute.

**CLINTON:** Over 150,000 Americans have died of AIDS. Well over a million-and-a-quarter Americans are HIV-positive. We need to put one person in charge of the battle against AIDS to cut across all the agencies that deal with it. We need to accelerate the drug approval process. We need to fully fund the act named for that wonderful boy Ryan White to make sure we're doing everything we can on research and treatment.

And the president should lead a national effort to change behavior, to keep our children alive in the schools, responsible behavior to keep people alive. This is a matter of life and death. I have worked in my state to reduce teen pregnancy and illness among children. I know it's tough.

The reason Magic Johnson resigned from the AIDS Commission is because the statement you heard tonight from Mr. Bush is the longest and best statement he's made about it in public.

I am proud of what we did at the Democratic convention, putting two HIV-positive people on the platform, and I am proud of the leadership that I'm going to bring to this country in dealing with the AIDS crisis.

**LEHRER:** New question for Mr. Perot. You have two minutes to answer, and Ann will ask it.

**COMPTON:** Mr. Perot, even if you've got what people say are the guts to take on changes in the most popular, the most sacred of the entitlements, Medicare, people say you haven't a prayer of actually getting anything passed in Washington.

Since a president isn't a lone ranger, how in the world can you make some of those unpopular changes?

**PEROT:** Two ways. No. 1, if I get

there, it will be a very unusual and historical event — because the people, not the special interests, put me there. I will have a unique mandate. I have said again and again, and this really upsets the establishment in Washington, that we're going to inform the people in detail on the issues through an electronic town hall so that they really know what's going on.

They will want to do what's good for our country. Now, all these fellows with thousand-dollar suits and alligator shoes running up and down the halls of Congress that make policy now — the lobbyists, the PAC [political action committee] guys, the foreign lobbyists, and what-have-you — they'll be over there in the Smithsonian, you know — because we're going to get rid of them, and the Congress will be listening to the people. And the American people are willing to have fair, shared sacrifice. They're not as stupid as Washington thinks they are. The American people are bright, intelligent, caring, loving people who want a great country for their children and grandchildren. And they will make those sacrifices.

So I welcome that challenge, and just watch — because if the American people send me there, we'll get it done.

Now, everybody will faint in Washington. They've never seen anything happen in that town.

This is a town where the White House says, "Congress did it;" Congress says, "The White House did it." And I'm sitting there and saying, well, who else could be around, you know? Then when they get off by themselves, they say nobody did it.

And yet the cash register's empty, and it used to have our money, the taxpayers' money, in it, and we didn't get the results.

No, we'll get it done.

**LEHRER:** Governor, one minute.

**CLINTON:** Ross, that's a great speech, but it's not quite that simple.

I mean, look at the facts. Both parties in Washington, the president and the Congress, have cut Medicare. The average senior citizen is spending a higher percentage of income on health care today than they were in 1965, before Medicare came in.

The president's got another proposal to require them to pay $400 a year more for the next five years.

But if you don't have the guts to control costs by changing the insurance system and taking on the bureaucracies and the regulation of health care in the private and public sector, you can't fix this problem. Costs will continue to spiral.

And just remember this, folks: A lot of folks on Medicare are out there every day making the choice between food and medicine, not poor enough for Medicare-Medicaid, not wealthy enough to buy their medicine. I've met them, people like Mary Annie and Edward Davis in Nashua, N.H.. All over this country, they cannot even buy medicine.

So let's be careful. When we talk about cutting health-care costs, let's start with the insurance companies and the people

that are making a killing instead of making our people healthy.

**LEHRER:** One minute, President Bush.

**BUSH:** Well, first place, I'd like to clear up something because every four years, the Democrats go around and say, Republicans are going to cut Social Security and Medicare. They started it again.

I'm the president that stood up and said, "Don't mess with Social Security," and I'm not going to, and we haven't and we are not going to, go after the Social Security recipient.

I have one difference with Mr. Perot on that because I don't think we need to touch Social Security.

What we do need to do, though, is control the growth of these mandatory programs. And Ross properly says, OK, there's some pain in that. But Governor Clinton refuses to touch that, simply refuses. So what we've got to do is control it, let it grow for inflation, let it grow for the amount of new people added, population, and then hold the line.

And I believe that is the way you get the deficit down, not by the tax-and-spend program that we hear every four years, whether it's [Walter F.]Mondale, [Michael S.] Dukakis, whoever else it is. I just don't believe we ought to do that. So hold the line on Social Security and put a cap on the growth of the mandatory program.

**LEHRER:** New question: it is for Governor Clinton, two-minute answer. Sandy will ask it.

**VANOCUR:** Governor Clinton, Ann Compton has brought up Medicare. I remember in 1965, when [Rep.] Wilbur [D.] Mills of Arkansas, the chairman of Ways and Means, was pushing it through the Congress. The charge against it was it's socialized medicine.

**CLINTON:** Mr. Bush made that charge.

**VANOCUR:** Well, he served with him two years later, in 1967, where I first met him. The second point, though, is that it is now skyrocketing out of control. People want it. We say it's going bonkers.

Is not the Oregon plan applied to Medicaid rationing the proper way to go, even though the federal government last August ruled that it violated the Americans with Disabilities Act of 1990?

**CLINTON:** I thought the Oregon plan should at least have been allowed to be tried because at least the people in Oregon were trying to do something. Let me go back to the main point, Sandy.

Mr. Bush is trying to run against [former Democratic Presidents] Lyndon [B.] Johnson and Jimmy Carter and everybody in the world but me in this race. I have proposed a managed competition plan for health care. I will say again: You cannot control health-care costs simply by cutting Medicare.

Look what's happened. The federal government has cut Medicare and Medicaid in the last few years, states have cut Medicaid — we've done it in Arkansas un-

der budget pressures. But what happens? More and more people get on the rolls as poverty increases. If you don't control the health-care costs of the entire system, you cannot get control of it.

Look at our program. We set up a national ceiling on health-care costs tied to inflation and population growth set by health-care providers, not by the government. We provide for managed competition, not government models, in every states. And we control private and public health-care costs.

Now, just a few days ago a bipartisan commission of Republicans and Democrats — more Republicans than Democrats — said my plan will save the average family $1,200 a year more than the Bush plan will by the year 2000, $2.2 trillion in the next 12 years, $400 billion a year by the end of this decade. I've got a plan to control health-care costs. But you can't just do it by cutting Medicare; you have to take on the insurance companies, the bureaucracies. And you have to have cost controls, yes.

But keep in mind we are spending 30 percent more on health care than any country in the world, any country, and yet we have 35 million people uninsured, we have no preventing and primary care. The Oregon plan is a good start if the federal government is going to continue to abandon its responsibilities. I say if Germany can cover everybody and keep costs under inflation, if Hawaii can cover 98 percent of their people at lower health-care costs than the rest of us, if Rochester, New York, can do it with two-thirds of the cost of the rest of it, America can do it, too.

I'm tired of being told we can't. I say we can. We can do better, and we must.

**LEHRER:** President Bush, one minute.

**BUSH:** Well, I don't have time in 30 seconds, or whatever — a minute — to talk about our health-care reform plan. The Oregon plan made some good sense, but it's easy to dismiss the concerns of the disabled. As president I have to be sure that those waivers, which we're approving all over the place, are covered under the law. Maybe we can work it out. But the Americans with Disabilities Act, speaking about sound and sensible civil rights legislation, was the most foremost piece of legislation passed in modern times, and so we do have something more than a technical problem.

Governor Clinton clicked off the things — he's going to take on insurance companies and bureaucracies. He failed to take on somebody else — the malpractice suit people, those that bring these lawsuits against — these frivolous trial lawyers' lawsuits that are running the costs of medical care up $25 [billion] to $50 billion. And he refuses to put anything, controls, on these crazy lawsuits.

If you want to help somebody, don't run the costs up by making doctors have to have five or six tests, where one would do, for fear of being sued, or have somebody along the highway not stop to pick up a guy and help him because he's afraid a trial

lawyer will come along and sue him. We're suing each other too much and caring for each other too little.

**LEHRER:** Mr. Perot, one minute.

**PEROT:** We got the most expensive health-care system in the world; it ranks behind 15 other nations when we come to life expectancy, and 22 other nations when we come to infant mortality. So we don't have the best.

Pretty simple, folks — if you're paying more and you don't have the best, if all else fails, go copy the people who have the best who spend less, right?

Well, we can do better than that. Again, we've got plans lying all over the place in Washington. Nobody ever implements them.

Now I'm back to square one. If you want to stop talking about it and do it, then I'll be glad to go up there and we'll get it done.

But if you just want to keep the music going, just stay traditional this next time around, and four years from now you'll have everybody blaming everybody else for a bad health-care system.

Talk is cheap; words are plentiful; deeds are precious. Let's get on with it.

**LEHRER:** And that's exactly what we're going to do. That was, in fact, the final question and answer. We're now going to move to closing statements. Each candidate will have up to two minutes.

The order, remember, was determined by drawing, and Mr. Perot, you are first.

**PEROT:** Well, it's been a privilege to be able to talk to the American people tonight. I make no bones about it. I love this country. I love the principle it's founded on. I love the people here. I don't like to see the country's principles violated. I don't like to see the people in a deteriorating economy in a deteriorating country because our government has lost touch with the people.

The people in Washington are good people. We just have a bad system. We've got to change the system. It's time to do it because we have run up so much debt that time is no longer our friend. We've got to put our house in order.

When you go to bed tonight, look at your children. Think of their dreams. Think of your dreams as a child and ask yourself, isn't it time to stop talking about it? Isn't it time to stop creating images? Isn't it time to do it? Aren't you sick of being treated like an unprogrammed robot? Every four years, they send you all kinds of messages to tell you how to vote and then go back to business as usual.

They told you at the tax and budget summit that if you agreed to a tax increase, we could balance the budget. They didn't tell you that that same year they increased spending $1.83 for every dollar we increased taxes. That's Washington in a nutshell right there.

In the final analysis, I'm doing this for your children when you look at them tonight.

There's another group that I feel very close to, and these are the men and women who fought on the battlefield, the children — the families — of the ones who died and the people who left parts of their bodies over there. I'd never ask you to do anything for me, but I owe you this, and I'm doing it for you. And I can't tell you what it means to me at these rallies when I see you and you come up and the look in your eyes — and I know how you feel and you know how I feel. And then I think of the older people who are retired.

They grew up in the Depression. They fought and won World War II. We owe you a debt we can never repay you. And the greatest repayment I can ever give is to recreate the American dream for your children and grandchildren. I'll give you everything I have, if you want me to do it.

**LEHRER:** Governor Clinton, your closing statement.

**CLINTON:** I'd like to thank the people of St. Louis and Washington University, the Presidential Debate Commission and all those who made this night possible. And I'd like to thank those of you who are watching.

Most of all, I'd like to thank all of you who have touched me in some way over this last year, all the thousands of you whom I've seen. I'd like to thank the computer executives and the electronics executives in Silicon Valley, two-thirds of whom are Republicans who said they wanted to sign on to a change in America. I'd like to thank the hundreds of executives who came to Chicago, a third of them Republicans, who said they wanted to change. I'd like to thank the people who've started with Mr. Perot who've come on to help our campaign.

I'd like to thank all the folks around America that no one ever knows about — the woman that was holding the AIDS baby she adopted in Cedar Rapids, Iowa, who asked me to do something more for adoption; the woman who stopped along the road in Wisconsin and wept because her husband had lost his job after 27 years; all the people who are having a tough time and the people who are winning but who know how desperately we need to change.

This debate tonight has made crystal clear a challenge that is old as America — the choice between hope and fear, change or more of the same, the courage to move into a new tomorrow or to listen to the crowd who says things could be worse.

Mr. Bush has said some very compelling things tonight that don't quite square with the record. He was president for three years before he proposed a health-care plan that still hasn't been sent to Congress in total; three years before an economic plan — and he still didn't say tonight that that tax bill he vetoed raised taxes only on the rich and gave the rest of you a break — but he vetoed it anyway.

I offer a new direction. Invest in American jobs, American education, control health-care costs, bring this country together again. I want the future of this country to be as bright and brilliant as its past, and it can be if we have the courage to change.

**LEHRER:** President Bush, your closing statement.

**BUSH:** Let me tell you a little what it's like to be president. In the Oval Office, you can't predict what kind of crisis is going to come up. You have to make tough calls. You can't be on one hand this way and one hand another. You can't take different positions on these difficult issues. And then you need a philosophical — I'd call it a philosophical underpinning. Mine for foreign affairs is democracy and freedom, and look at the dramatic changes around the world. The Cold War is over. The Soviet Union is no more, and we're working with a democratic country. Poland, Hungary, Czechoslovakia, the Baltics are free.

Take a look at the Middle East. We had to stand up against a tyrant. The United States came together as we haven't in many, many years. And we kicked this man out of Kuwait. And in the process, as a result of that will and that decision and that toughness, we now have ancient enemies talking peace in the Middle East. Nobody would have dreamed it possible.

And I think the biggest dividend of making these tough calls is the fact that we are less afraid of nuclear war. Every parent out there has much less worry that their kids are going to be faced with nuclear holocaust. All this is good.

On the domestic side, what we must do is have change that empowers people — not change for the sake of change, tax and spend. We don't need to do that anymore. What we need to do is empower people. We need to invest and save. We need to do better in education. We need to do better in job retraining. We need to expand our exports, and they're going very, very well, indeed. And we need to strengthen the American family.

I hope as president that I've earned your trust. I've admitted it when I make a mistake, but then I go on and help, try to solve the problems. I hope I've earned your trust because a lot of being president is about trust and character. And I ask for your support for four more years to finish this job.

Thank you very, very much.

**LEHRER:** Don't go away yet. I just want to thank the three panelists and thank the three candidates for participating — President Bush, Governor Clinton and Mr. Perot. They will appear again together on Oct. 15 and again on Oct. 19, and next Tuesday there will be a debate among the three candidates for vice president.

And for now, from Washington University in St. Louis, Missouri, I'm Jim Lehrer. Thank you, and good night. ∎

# Voters Grill Candidates in Unprecedented Format

*On Oct. 15, President Bush, Arkansas Gov. Bill Clinton and independent candidate Ross Perot met at the University of Richmond in Richmond, Va., for the second of three televised presidential debates. ABC News correspondent Carole Simpson served as moderator. Following is the Reuter transcript of that debate:*

**SIMPSON:** Good evening and welcome to this second of three presidential debates between the major candidates for president of the United States. The candidates are the Republican nominee, President George Bush; the independent, Ross Perot; and Governor Bill Clinton, the Democratic nominee.

My name is Carole Simpson, and I will be the moderator for tonight's 90-minute debate, which is coming to you from the campus of the University of Richmond in Richmond, Va.

Now, tonight's program is unlike any other presidential debate in history. We're making history now, and it's pretty exciting. An independent polling firm has selected an audience of 209 uncommitted voters from this area. The candidates will be asked questions by these voters on a topic of their choosing — anything they want to ask about. My job as moderator is to, you know, take care of the questioning, ask questions myself if I think there needs to be continuity and balance, and sometimes I might ask the candidates to respond to what another candidate may have said.

Now, the format has been agreed to by representatives of both the Republican and Democratic campaigns, and there is no subject matter that is restricted. Anything goes. We can ask anything.

After the debate, the candidates will have an opportunity to make a closing statement.

So, President Bush, I think you said it earlier — let's get it on.

**BUSH:** Let's go.

**SIMPSON:** And I think the first question is over here.

**AUDIENCE PARTICIPANT:** Yes. I'd like to direct my question to Mr. Perot. What will you do as president to open foreign markets to fair competition from American business and to stop unfair competition here at home from foreign countries so that we can bring jobs back to the United States?

**PEROT:** That's right at the top of my agenda. We've shipped millions of jobs overseas, and we have a strange situation because we have a process in Washington

where after you've served for a while you cash in, become a foreign lobbyist, make $30,000 a month, then take a leave, work on presidential campaigns, make sure you've got good contacts and then go back out.

Now, if you just want to get down to brass tacks, first thing you ought to do is get all these folks who've got these one-way trade agreements that we've negotiated over the years and say fellas, we'll take the same deal we gave you. And they'll take gridlock right at that point because, for example, we've got international competitors who simply could not unload their cars off the ships if they had to comply — you see, if it was a two-way street, just couldn't do it. We have got to stop sending jobs overseas.

To those of you in the audience who are business people: pretty simple. If you're paying $12, $13, $14 an hour for a factory worker, and you can move your factory south of the border, pay $1 an hour for labor, hire a young — let's assume you've been in business for a long time. You've got a mature workforce. Pay $1 an hour for your labor, have no health care — that's the most expensive single element in making the car. Have no environmental controls, no pollution controls and no retirement. And you don't care about anything but making money. There will be a job-sucking sound going south.

If the people send me to Washington, the first thing I'll do is study that 2,000-page agreement and make sure it's a two-way street.

One last point here. I decided I was dumb and didn't understand it so I called a "Who's Who" of the folks that have been around it, and I said why won't everybody go south; they said it will be disruptive; I said for how long. I finally got 'em for 12 to 15 years. And I said, well, how does it stop being disruptive? And that is when their jobs come up from $1 an hour to $6 an hour, and ours go down to $6 an hour; then it's leveled again, but in the meantime you've wrecked the country with these kind of deals. We got to cut it out.

**SIMPSON:** Thank you, Mr. Perot. I see that the president has stood up, so he must have something to say about this.

**BUSH:** Carole, the thing that saved us in this global economic slowdown has been our exports, and what I'm trying to do is increase our exports. And if indeed all the jobs were going to move south because there are lower wages — there are lower wages now, and they haven't done that. And so I have just negotiated with the president of Mexico the North American Free Trade Agreement — and the prime

minister of Canada, I might add — and I want to have more of these free trade agreements, because export jobs are increasing far faster than any jobs that may have moved overseas. That's a scare tactic, because it's not that many. But any one that's here, we want to have more jobs here. And the way to do that is to increase our exports.

Some believe in protection. I don't; I believe in free and fair trade, and that's the thing that saved us. So I will keep on as president trying to get a successful conclusion to the GATT Round, the big Uruguay Round of trade, which will really open up markets for our agriculture, particularly. I want to continue to work after we get this NAFTA agreement ratified this coming year. I want to get one with Eastern Europe; I want to get one with Chile. And free and fair trade is the answer, not protection.

And, as I say, we've had tough economic times, and it's exports that have saved us, exports that have built.

**SIMPSON:** Gov. Clinton.

**CLINTON:** I'd like to answer the question, because I've actually been a governor for 12 years, so I've known a lot of people who have lost their jobs because of jobs moving overseas, and I know a lot of people whose plants have been strengthened by increasing exports.

The trick is to expand our export base and to expand trade on terms that are fair to us. It is true that our exports to Mexico, for example, have gone up and our trade deficit has gone down; it's also true that just today a record high trade deficit was announced with Japan.

So what is the answer? Let me just mention three things very quickly. No. 1, make sure that other countries are as open to our markets as our markets are to them, and, if they're not, have measures on the books that don't take forever and a day to implement.

No. 2, change the tax code. There are more deductions in the tax code for shutting plants down and moving overseas than there are for modernizing plant and equipment here. Our competitors don't do that. Emphasize and subsidize modernizing plant and equipment here, not moving plants overseas.

No. 3, stop the federal government's program that now gives low-interest loans and job training funds to companies that will actually shut down and move to other countries, but we won't do the same thing for plants that stay here.

So more trade but on fair terms — and favor investment in America.

**SIMPSON:** Thank you. I think we have a question over here.

**AUDIENCE PARTICIPANT:** This is for Gov. Clinton. In the real world, that is, outside of Washington, D.C., compensation and achievement are based on goals defined and achieved. My question is about the deficit. Would you define in specific dollar goals how much you would reduce the deficit in each of the four years of a Clinton administration and then enter into a legally binding contract with the American people, that if you did not achieve those goals that you would not seek a second term? Answer yes or no, and then comment on your answer, please.

**CLINTON:** No, and here's why. And I'll tell you exactly why. Because the deficit now has been building up for 12 years. I'll tell you exactly what I think can be done. I think we can bring it down by 50 percent in four years and grow the economy. Now, I could get rid of it in four years in theory on the books now, but to do it you'd have to raise taxes too much and cut benefits too much to people who need them, and it would even make the economy worse.

Mr. Perot will tell you, for example, that the expert he hired to analyze his plan says that it will bring the deficit down in five years but it will make unemployment bad for four more years. So my view is, sir, you have to increase investment, grow the economy and reduce the deficit by controlling health-care costs, prudent reductions in defense, cuts in domestic programs and asking the wealthiest Americans and foreign corporations to pay their fair share of taxes and investing and growing this economy.

I ask everybody to look at my economic ideas, and nine Nobel prize winners and over 500 economists and hundreds of business people, including a lot of Republicans said, this is the way you've got to go. If you don't grow the economy you can't get it done. But I can't foresee all the things that will happen, and I don't think a president should be judged solely on the deficit.

Let me also say, we're having an election today. You'll have a shot at me in four years, and you can vote me right out if you think I've done a lousy job, and I would welcome you to do that.

**SIMPSON:** Mr. President.

**BUSH:** Well, I'm a little confused here, because I don't see how you can grow the deficit down by raising people's taxes. You see, I don't think the American people are taxed too little. I think they're taxed too much. I went for one tax increase, and when I make a mistake I admit it. I said that wasn't the right thing to do.

Gov. Clinton's program wants to tax more and spend more — $150 billion in new taxes, spend another $220. I don't believe that's the way to do it.

Here's something that'll help. Give us a balanced budget amendment. He always talks about Arkansas having a balanced budget, and they do, but he has a balanced budget amendment. Have to do it. I'd like the government to have that. And I think it

would discipline not only the Congress, which needs it, but also the executive branch.

I'd like to have what 43 governors have — the line-item veto, so if the Congress can't cut, and we've got a reckless spending Congress, let the president have a shot at it by wiping out things that are pork barrel or something of that nature.

I've proposed another one. Some sophisticates think it may be a little gimmicky; I think it's good. It's a check-off. It says to you as a taxpayer — say you're going to pay a tax of 1,000 bucks or something. You can check 10 percent of that if you want to, in the one box, and that 10 percent, $100, or if you're paying $10,000, whatever it is, $1,000, check it off and make the government, make it lower the deficit by that amount.

And if the Congress won't do it, if they can't get together and negotiate how to do that, then you'd have a sequester across the board. You'd exempt Social Security — I don't want to tax or touch Social Security. I'm the president that said hey, don't mess with Social Security, and we haven't.

So I believe that we need to control the growth of mandatory spending, back to this gentleman's question. That's the main growing thing in the budget. The program that the president — two-thirds of the budget, I as president never get to look at, never get to touch. We've got to control that growth to inflation and population increase, but not raise taxes on the American people now. I just don't believe that would stimulate any kind of growth at all.

**SIMPSON:** How about you, Mr. Perot?

**PEROT:** Well, we're $4 trillion in debt. We're going into debt an additional $1 billion, little more than $1 billion every working day of the year.

Now, the thing I love about it — I'm just a businessman. I was down in Texas taking care of business, tending to my family. This situation got so bad that I decided I'd better get into it. The American people asked me to get into it. But I just find it fascinating that while we sit here tonight we will go into debt an additional $50 million in an hour and a half.

Now, it's not the Republicans' fault, of course, and it's not the Democrats' fault. And what I'm looking for is who did it? Now, they're the two folks involved, so maybe if you put them together, they did it.

Now, the facts are we have to fix it. I'm here tonight for these young people up here in the balcony from this college. When I was a young man, when I got out of the Navy I had multiple job offers. Young people with high grades can't get a job. People — the 18- to 24-year-old high school graduates 10 years ago were making more than they are now. In other words, we were down to 18 percent of them were making — 18- to 24-year-olds were making less than $12,000. Now that's up to 40 percent. And what's happened in the meantime? The dollar's gone through the floor.

Now, whose fault is that? Not the Democrats. Not the Republicans. Somewhere out there there's an extraterrestrial that's doing this to us, I guess. And everybody says they take responsibility. Somebody somewhere has to take responsibility for this.

Put it to you bluntly, American people. If you want me to be your president, we're going to face our problems. We'll deal with the problems. We'll solve our problems. We'll pay down our debt. We'll pass on the American dream to our children, and I will not leave our children a situation that they have today.

When I was a boy it took two generations to double the standard of living. Today it will take 12 generations. Our children will not see the American dream because of this debt that somebody, somewhere dropped on us.

**SIMPSON:** You're all wonderful speakers, and I know you have lots more to add, but I've talked to this audience, and they have lots of questions on other topics. Can we move to another topic, please? We have one up here, I think.

**AUDIENCE PARTICIPANT:** Yes, I'd like to address all the candidates with this question. The amount of time the candidates have spent in this campaign trashing their opponents' character and their programs is depressingly large. Why can't your discussions and proposals reflect the genuine complexity and the difficulty of the issues to try to build a consensus around the best aspects of all proposals?

**SIMPSON:** Who wants to take that one? Mr. Perot, you have an answer for everything, don't you? Go right ahead, sir.

**PEROT:** No, I don't have an answer for everything. As you all know, I've been buying 30-minute segments to talk about issues. And tomorrow night on NBC, from 10:30 to 11 Eastern, we're going to talk about how you pay the debt down, so we're going to come right down to that one. We'll be on again Saturday night, 8 to 9 o'clock on ABC. So the point is —

**BUSH:** Like [Democratic primary candidate] Jerry Brown, the 800 number.

**PEROT:** — I couldn't agree with you more, couldn't agree with you more. And I have said again and again and again, let's get off mud wrestling, let's get off personalities, and let's talk about jobs, health care, crime, the things that concern the American people. I'm spending my money — not PAC money, not foreign money, my money — to take this message to the people.

**SIMPSON:** Thank you, Mr. Perot. So that seems directed; he would say it's you gentlemen that have been doing that. Mr. Clinton, Gov. Clinton — oh, President Bush, how would you like to respond?

**BUSH:** Well, in the first place, I believe that character is a part of being president. I think you have to look at it. I think that has to be a part of a candidate for president or being president. In terms of programs, I've submitted, what, four different budgets to the United States Congress in great detail. It's so heavy they'd give you

a broken back. And everything in there says what I am for.

Now I've come out with a new agenda for America's renewal, a plan that I believe really will help stimulate the growth of this economy. My record on world affairs is pretty well known because I've been president for four years, so I feel I've been talking issues.

You know, nobody likes "who shot John," but I think the first negative campaign run in this election was by Gov. Clinton, and I'm not going to sit there and be a punching bag; I'm going to stand up and say, hey, listen, here's my side of it.

But character is an important part of the equation. The other night Gov. Clinton raised my — I don't know if you saw the debate the other night. You did — suffered through that? Well, he raised the question of my father — it was a good line, well rehearsed and well delivered. But he raised the question of my father and said, well, your father, Prescott Bush, was against McCarthy, you should be ashamed of yourself, McCarthyism. I remember something my dad told me — I was 18 years old, going to Penn Station to go on into the Navy, and he said write your mother — which I faithfully did; he said serve your country — my father was an honor, duty and country man; and he said tell the truth. And I've tried to do that in public life, all through it. That says something about character.

My argument with Gov. Clinton — you can call it mud wrestling, but I think it's fair to put in focus — is I am deeply troubled by someone who demonstrates and organizes demonstration in a foreign land when his country's at war. Probably a lot of kids here disagree with me. But that's what I feel. That's what I feel passionately about. I'm thinking of Ross Perot's running mate sitting in the jail. How would he feel about it? But maybe that's generational. I don't know.

But the big argument I have with the governor on this is this taking different positions on different issues — trying to be one thing to one person here that's opposing the NAFTA agreement and then for it — what we call waffling. And I do think that you can't turn the White House into the Waffle House. You've got to say what you're for and you've got to —

**SIMPSON:** Mr. President, I'm getting time cues and with all due respect —

**BUSH:** Excuse me. I don't want to —

**SIMPSON:** I'm sorry.

**BUSH:** I don't want to —

**SIMPSON:** Gov. Clinton.

**BUSH:** I get wound up because I feel strongly —

**SIMPSON:** Yes, you do.

**CLINTON:** Let me say first of all to you that I believe so strongly in the question you asked that I suggested this format tonight. I started doing these formats a year ago in New Hampshire, and I found that we had huge crowds because all I did was let people ask questions, and I tried to give very specific answers. I also had a program starting last year. I've been disturbed

by the tone and the tenor of this campaign. Thank goodness the networks have a fact check so I don't have to just go blue in the face anymore. Mr. Bush said once again I was going to have a $150 billion tax increase. When [Vice President Dan] Quayle said that, all the networks said, that's not true. He's got over $100 billion of tax cuts and incentives.

So I'm not going to take up your time tonight, but let me just say this. We'll have a debate in four days, and we can talk about this character thing again. But The Washington Post ran a long editorial today saying they couldn't believe Mr. Bush was making character an issue and they said he was the greatest, quote, "political chameleon" for changing his positions of all times. Now, I don't want to get into that —

**BUSH:** Please don't get into The Washington Post.

**CLINTON:** Wait a minute. Let's don't — you don't have to believe it. Here's my point. I'm not interested in his character. I want to change the character of the presidency. And I'm interested in what we can trust him to do and what you can trust me to do and what you can trust Mr. Perot to do for the next four years. So I think you're right, and I hope the rest of the night belongs to you.

**SIMPSON:** May I — I talked to this audience before you gentlemen came, and I asked them about how they felt about the tenor of the campaign. Would you like to let them know what you thought about that, when I said are you pleased with how the campaign's been going?

**AUDIENCE:** No.

**SIMPSON:** Who wants to say why you don't like the way the campaign is going? We have a gentleman back here.

**AUDIENCE PARTICIPANT:** And forgive the notes here, but I'm shy on camera.

The focus of my work as a domestic mediator is meeting the needs of the children that I work with, by way of their parents, and not the wants of their parents. And I ask the three of you, how can we, as, symbolically, the children of the future president, expect the two of you, the three of you to meet our needs, the needs in housing and in crime and you name it, as opposed to the wants of your political spin doctors and your political parties?

**SIMPSON:** So your question is?

**AUDIENCE PARTICIPANT:** Can we focus on the issues and not the personalities and the mud? I think there's a need, if we could take a poll here with the folks from Gallup perhaps, I think there's a real need here to focus at this point on the needs.

**SIMPSON:** How do you respond? How do you gentlemen respond to —

**CLINTON:** I agree with him.

**BUSH:** Let's do it.

**SIMPSON:** President Bush?

**BUSH:** Let's do it. Let's talk about programs for children.

**AUDIENCE PARTICIPANT:** Could we cross our hearts? It sounds silly here, but

could we make a commitment? You know, we're not under oath at this point, but could you make a commitment to the citizens of the United States to meet our needs, and we have many, and not yours again? I repeat that. It's a real need, I think, that we all have.

**BUSH:** I think it depends how you define it. I mean, I think in general, let's talk about these issues. Let's talk about the programs. But in the presidency, a lot goes into it. Caring goes into it. That's not particularly specific. Strength goes into it. That's not specific. Standing up against aggression. That's not specific in terms of a program. This is what a president has to do.

So in principle, though, I'll take your point and think we ought to discuss child care or whatever else it is.

**SIMPSON:** And you, too?

**CLINTON:** Ross had his hand up.

**SIMPSON:** Yes.

**PEROT:** Just no hedges, no ifs, ands and buts. I'll take the pledge because I know the American people want to talk about issues and not tabloid journalism. So I'll take the pledge and will stay on the issues.

Now, just for the record, I don't have any spin doctors. I don't have any speechwriters. Probably shows. I make those charts you see on television.

But you don't have to wonder if it's me talking. See, what you see is what you get, and if you don't like it, you got two other choices, right?

**CLINTON:** Wait a minute. I want to say just one thing now, Ross, in fairness. The ideas I express are mine. I've worked on these things for 12 years, and I'm the only person up here who hasn't been part of Washington in any way for the last 20 years. So I don't want the implication to be that somehow everything we say is just cooked up and put in our head by somebody else. I worked 12 years very hard as a governor on the real problems of real people. I'm just as sick as you are by having to wake up and figure out how to defend myself every day. I never thought I'd ever be involved in anything like this.

**PEROT:** May I finish?

**SIMPSON:** Yes, you may finish.

**PEROT:** Very briefly?

**SIMPSON:** Yes, very briefly.

**PEROT:** And I don't have any foreign money in my campaign. I don't have any foreign lobbyists on leave in my campaign. I don't have any PAC money in my campaign. I've got 5.5 million hard-working people who put me on the ballot, and I belong to them. And they're interested in what you're interested in.

I take the pledge. I've already taken the pledge on cutting the deficit in half. I never got to say that. There's a great young group, Lead or Leave, college students, young people, who don't want us to spend their money. I took the pledge we'd cut it out.

**SIMPSON:** Thank you. We have a question here.

**AUDIENCE PARTICIPANT:** Yes. I would like to get a response from all three gentlemen. And the question is, what are your plans to improve the physical infrastructure of this nation, which includes the water system, the sewer system, our transportation systems, et cetera. Thank you.

**SIMPSON:** The cities. Who's going to fix the cities and how?

**BUSH:** I'll be glad to take a shot at it.

**SIMPSON:** Please.

**BUSH:** I'm not sure that — and I can understand if you haven't seen this, because there's been a lot of hue and cry. We passed the most furthest looking transportation bill in the history of this country since Eisenhower started the interstate highways — $150 billion for improving the infrastructure. That happened when I was president. And so I'm very proud of the way that came about, and I think it's a very, very good beginning.

Like Mr. Perot, I am concerned about the deficits, and $150 billion is a lot of money, but it's awful hard to say we're going to out and spend more money when we're trying to get the deficit down. But I would cite that as a major accomplishment. We hear all the negatives. When you're president you expect this. Everybody's running against the incumbent. They can do better. Everyone knows that.

But here's something that we can take great pride in because it really does get to what you're talking about. Our home initiative — our home-ownership initiative — HOPE — that passed the Congress is a good start for having people own their own homes instead of living in these deadly tenements.

Our enterprise zones, that we hear a lot of lip service about in Congress, would bring jobs into the inner city. There's a good program. And I need the help of everybody across this country to get it passed in substantial way by the Congress.

When we went out to South Central in Los Angeles — some of you may remember the riots there. I went out there. I went to a Boy's Club. And everyone of them — the Boy's Club leaders, the ministers — all of them were saying pass enterprise zones. We go back to Washington, and very difficult to get it through the Congress. But there's going to be a new Congress. No one likes gridlock. There's going to be a new Congress because the old one — I don't want to get this man made at me — but there was a post office scandal and a bank scandal. You're going to have a lot of new members of Congress. And then you can sit down and say, help me do what we should for the cities. Help me pass these programs.

**SIMPSON:** Mr. President, aren't you threatening to veto the bill — the urban aid bill — that included enterprise zones?

**BUSH:** Sure, but the problem is, you get so many things included in a great big bill that you have to look at the overall good. That's the problem with our system. If you had a line-item veto you could knock out the pork. You could knock out the tax increases, and you could do what the peo-

ple want, and that's create enterprise zones.

**SIMPSON:** Gov. Clinton, you're chomping at the bit.

**CLINTON:** That bill pays for these urban enterprise zones by asking the wealthiest Americans to pay a little more. And that's why he wants to veto it, just like he vetoed an earlier bill this year — this is not mud slinging; this is fact slinging — a bill earlier this year — this is facts — that would have given investment tax credits and other incentives to reinvest in our cities, in our country. But it asked the wealthiest Americans to pay a little more. Mr. Perot wants to do the same thing. I agree with him. I mean, we agree with that.

But let me tell you specifically what my plan does: My plan would dedicate $20 billion a year in each of the next four years for investments in new transportation, communications, environmental clean-ups and new technologies for the 21st century. And we would target it especially in areas that have been either depressed or which have lost a lot of defense-related jobs. There are 200,000 people in California, for example, who have lost their defense-related jobs. They ought to be engaged in making high-speed rail. They ought to be engaged in breaking ground in other technologies, doing waste recycling, clean water technology and things of that kind.

We can create millions of jobs in these new technologies — more than we're going to lose in defense — if we target it. But we're investing a much smaller percentage of our income in the things you just asked about than all of our major competitors, and our wealth growth is going down as a result of it. It's making the country poorer, which is why I answered the gentleman the way I did before. We have to both bring down the deficit and get our economy going through these kinds of investments in order to get the kind of wealth and jobs and incomes we need in America.

**SIMPSON:** Mr. Perot, what about your plans for the cities? You want to tackle the economy and the deficit first.

**PEROT:** First you've got to have money to pay for these things. So you've got to create jobs. There are all kinds of ways to create jobs in the inner city. I'm not a politician, but I think I could go to Washington in a week and get everybody holding hands and get this bill signed because I talk to the Democratic leaders and they want it. I talk to the Republican leaders, and they want it. But since they're bred from childhood to fight with one another rather than get results, you know, I would be glad to drop out and spend a little time and see if we couldn't build some bridges.

Now, results is what counts. The president can't order Congress around. Congress can't order the president around. That's not bad for a guy that's never been there, right? But you have to work together.

Now, I have talked to the chairmen of the committees that want this. They're Democrats. The president wants it, but we

can't get it because we sit here in gridlock because it's a campaign year. We didn't fund a lot of other things this year, like the savings and loan mess. That's another story that we're going to pay a big price for right after the election.

The facts are, though — the facts are — the American people are hurting. These people are hurting in the inner cities. We're shipping the, quote, "low-paying jobs" overseas. What are low-paying jobs? Textiles, shoes, things like that that we say are yesterday's industries. They're tomorrow's industries in the inner cities.

Let me say in my case, if I'm out of work, I'll cut grass tomorrow to take care of my family. I'll be happy to make shoes; I'll be happy to make clothing; I'll make sausage. You just give me a job. Put those jobs in the inner cities instead of doing diplomatic deals and shipping them to China where prison labor does the work.

**SIMPSON:** Mr. Perot, everybody thought you won the first debate because you were plain-speaking and you made it sound, oh, so simple. Well, just do it. What makes you think that you're going to be able to get the Democrats and Republicans together any better than these guys?

**PEROT:** If you ask me if I could fly a fighter plane or be an astronaut, I can't. I've spent my life creating jobs. That's something I know how to do. And, very simply, in the inner city, they're starved — you see, small business is the way to jump start the inner city, not —

**SIMPSON:** Are you answering my question?

**PEROT:** You want jobs in the inner city? Do you want jobs in the inner city? Is that your question?

**SIMPSON:** No, I want you to tell me how you're going to be able to get the Republicans and Democrats in Congress to work together better than these two gentlemen.

**PEROT:** Oh, I'm sorry. Well, I've listened to both sides, and if they would talk to one another instead of throwing rocks, I think we could get a lot done. And, among other things, I would say, OK, over here in this Senate committee to the chairman who is anxious to get this bill passed, the president who is anxious, I'd say rather than just yelling at one another, why don't we find out where we're apart, try to get together, get the bill passed and give the people the benefits and not play party politics right now? And I think the press would follow that so closely that probably they would get it done.

That's the way I would do it. I doubt if they'll give me the chance, but I will drop everything and go work on it.

**SIMPSON:** OK, I have a question here.

**AUDIENCE PARTICIPANT:** My question was originally for Gov. Clinton, but I think I would welcome a response from all three candidates. As you are aware, crime is rampant in our cities. And in the Richmond area — and I'm sure it's happened elsewhere — 12-year-olds are

carrying guns to school. And I'm sure when our Founding Fathers wrote the Constitution they did not mean for the right to bear arms to apply to 12-year-olds. So I'm asking: Where do you stand on gun control, and what do you plan to do about it?

**SIMPSON:** Gov. Clinton?

**CLINTON:** I support the right to keep and bear arms. I live in a state where over half the adults have hunting or fishing licenses, or both. But I believe we have to have some way of checking handguns before they're sold, to check the criminal history, the mental health history, and the age of people who are buying them. Therefore I support the Brady bill, which would impose a national waiting period unless and until a state did what only Virginia has done now, which is to automate its records. Once you automate your records, then you don't have to have a waiting period, but at least you can check.

I also think we should have, frankly, restrictions on assault weapons whose only purpose is to kill. We need to give the police a fighting chance in our urban areas where the gangs are building up.

The third thing I would say — it doesn't bear directly on gun control, but it's very important — we need more police on the street. There is a crime bill which would put more police on the street, which was killed for this session by a filibuster in the Senate, mostly by Republican senators, and I think it's a shame it didn't pass; I think it should be made the law — but it had the Brady bill in it, the waiting period.

I also believe that we should offer college scholarships to people who will agree to work them off as police officers, and I think, as we reduce our military forces, we should let people earn military retirement by coming out and working as police officers. Thirty years ago there were three police officers on the street for every crime; today there are three crimes for every police officer.

In the communities which have had real success putting police officers near schools where kids carry weapons — to get the weapons out of the schools — are on the same blocks, you've seen crime go down. In Houston there's been a 15-percent drop in the crime rate in the last year because of the work the mayor did there in increasing the police force. So I know it can work; I've seen it happen.

**SIMPSON:** Thank you. President Bush?

**BUSH:** I think you put your finger on a major problem. I talk about strengthening the American family, and it's very hard to strengthen the family if people are scared to walk down to the corner store and, you know, send their kid down to get a loaf of bread. It's very hard.

I have been fighting for very strong anti-crime legislation — habeas corpus reform, so you don't have these endless appeals, so when somebody gets sentenced, hey, this is for real. I've been fighting for changes in the exclusionary rule so if an honest cop stops somebody and makes a

technical mistake, the criminal doesn't go away.

I'll probably get into a fight in this room with some, but I happen to think that we need stronger death penalties for those that kill police officers.

Virginia's in the lead in this, as Gov. Clinton properly said, on this identification system for firearms. I am not for national registration of firearms. Some of the states that have the toughest anti-gun laws have the highest levels of crime. I am for the right, as the governor says — I'm a sportsman, and I don't think you ought to eliminate all kinds of weapons. But I was not for the bill that he was talking about because it was not tough enough on the criminal.

I'm very pleased that the Fraternal Order of Police in Little Rock, Ark., endorsed me because I think they see I'm trying to strengthen the anti-crime legislation. We've got more money going out for local police than any previous administration.

So we've got to get it under control, and there's one last point I'd make. Drugs. We have got to win our national strategy against drugs, the fight against drugs. And we're making some progress, doing a little better on interdiction. We're not doing as well amongst the people that get to be habitual drug-users.

The good news is, and I think it's true in Richmond, teenage use is down of cocaine, substantially, 60 percent in the last couple of years. So we're making progress, but until we get that one done, we're not going to solve the neighborhood crime problem.

**SIMPSON:** Mr. Perot, there are young black males in America dying at unprecedented rates —

**PEROT:** I didn't get to make a comment on this.

**SIMPSON:** Yes, I'm getting to that.

**PEROT:** Oh, you're going to let me. Excuse me.

**SIMPSON:** The fact that homicide is the leading cause of death among young black males 15 to 24 years old. What are you going to do to get the guns off the street?

**PEROT:** On any program, and this includes crime, you'll find we have all kinds of great plans lying around that never get enacted into law and implemented. I don't care what it is — competitiveness, health care, crime, you name it. Brady Bill, I agree that it's a timid step in the right direction, but it won't fix it. So why pass a law that won't fix it?

Now, what it really boils down to is can you live — we become so preoccupied with the rights of the criminal that we've forgotten the rights of the innocent. And in our country we have evolved to a point where we've put millions of innocent people in jail, because you go to the poor neighborhoods and they've put bars on their windows and bars on their doors and put themselves in jail to protect the things that they acquired legitimately. That's where we are.

We have got to become more con-

cerned about people who play by the rules and get the balance we require. This is going to take, first, building a consensus at grassroots America. Right from the bottom up, the American people have got to say they want it. And at that point, we can pick from a variety of plans and develop new plans. And the way you get things done is bury yourselves in the room with one another, put together the best program, take it to the American people, use the electronic town hall — the kind of thing you're doing here tonight — build a consensus and then do it and then go on to the next one. But don't just sit here slow dancing for four years doing nothing.

**SIMPSON:** Thank you. Thank you, Mr. Perot.

We have a question up here.

**AUDIENCE PARTICIPANT:** Please state your position on term limits, and, if you are in favor of them, how will you get them enacted?

**BUSH:** Any order? I'll be glad to respond.

**SIMPSON:** Thank you.

**BUSH:** I strongly support term limits for members of the United States Congress. I believe it would return the government closer to the people, the way that Ross Perot is talking about. The president's terms are limited to two, a total of eight years. What's wrong with limiting the terms of members of Congress to 12? Congress has gotten kind of institutionalized. For 38 years one party has controlled the House of Representatives, and the result, a sorry little post office that can't do anything right and a bank that has more overdrafts than all the Chase Bank and Citibank put together. We've got to do something about it.

And I think you get a certain arrogance, bureaucratic arrogance, if people stay there too long. And so I favor, strongly favor, term limits.

And how to get them passed? Send us some people that will pass the idea. And I think you will. I think the American people want it now. Every place I go I talk about it, and I think they want it done. Actually, you'd have to have some amendments to the Constitution because of the way the Constitution reads.

**SIMPSON:** Thank you. Gov. Clinton.

**CLINTON:** I know they're popular, but I'm against them. I'll tell you why. I believe, No. 1, it would pose a real problem for a lot of smaller states in the Congress who have enough trouble now making sure their interests are heard. No. 2, I think it would increase the influence of unelected staff members in the Congress who have too much influence already. I want to cut the size of the congressional staffs, but I think you're going to have too much influence there with people who were never elected, who have lots of expertise.

No. 3, if the people really have a mind to change, they can. You're going to have 120 to 150 new members of Congress.

Now, let me tell you what I favor instead. I favor strict controls on how much

you can spend running for Congress, strict limits on political action committees, requirements that people running for Congress appear in open public debates like we're doing now. If you did that you could take away the incumbents' advantage because challengers like me would have a chance to run against incumbents like him for House races and Senate races, and then the voters could make up their own mind without being subject to an unfair fight.

So that's how I feel about it, and I think if we had the right kind of campaign reform, we'd get the changes you want.

**SIMPSON:** Mr. Perot, would you like to address term limitations?

**PEROT:** Yes. Let me do so first on a personal level. If the American people send me up to do this job, I intend to be there one term. I do not intend to spend one minute of one day thinking about re-election. And as a matter of principle — and my situation is unique, and I understand it — I would take absolutely no compensation; I go as their servant.

Now, I have set as strong an example as I can, then at that point when we sit down over at Capitol Hill — tomorrow night I'm going to be talking about government reform — it's a long subject, you wouldn't let me finish tonight. If you want to hear it, you get it tomorrow night — you'll hear it tomorrow night.

But we have got to reform government. If you put term limits in and don't reform government, you won't get the benefits you thought. It takes both. So we need to do the reforms and the term limits. And after we reform it, it won't be a lifetime career opportunity; good people will go serve and then go back to their homes and not become foreign lobbyists and cash in at 30,000 bucks a month and then take time off to run some president's campaign.

They're all nice people, they're just in a bad system. I don't think there are any villains, but, boy, is the system rotten.

**SIMPSON:** Thank you very much. We have a question over here.

**AUDIENCE PARTICIPANT:** I'd like to ask Gov. Clinton, do you attribute the rising costs of health care to the medical profession itself, or do you think the problem lies elsewhere? And what specific proposals do you have to tackle this problem?

**CLINTON:** I've had more people talk to me about their health-care problems, I guess, than anything else, all across America — you know, people who've lost their jobs, lost their businesses, had to give up their jobs because of sick children. So let me try to answer you in this way: Let's start with a premise. We spend 30 percent more of our income than any nation on earth on health care, and yet we insure fewer people. We have 35 million people without any insurance at all — and I see them all the time. A hundred thousand Americans a month have lost their health insurance just in the last four years.

So if you analyze where we're out of line with other countries, you come up with

the following conclusions. No. 1, we spend at least $60 billion a year on insurance, administrative cost, bureaucracy and government regulation that wouldn't be spent in any other nation. So we have to have, in my judgment, a drastic simplification of the basic health insurance policies of this country, be very comprehensive for everybody.

Employers would cover their employees, government would cover the unemployed.

No. 2, I think you have to take on specifically the insurance companies and require them to make some significant change in the way they rate people in the big community pools. I think you have to tell the pharmaceutical companies they can't keep raising drug prices at three times the rate of inflation. I think you have to take on medical fraud. I think you have to help doctors stop practicing defensive medicine. I've recommended that our doctors be given a set of national practice guidelines and that if they follow those guidelines that raises the presumption that they didn't do anything wrong.

I think you have to have a system of primary and preventive clinics in our inner cities and our rural areas so people can have access to health care.

The key is to control the cost and maintain the quality. To do that you need a system of managed competition where all of us are covered in big groups and we can choose our doctors and our hospitals, a wide range, but there is an incentive to control costs. And I think there has to be — I think Mr. Perot and I agree on this, there has to be a national commission of health care providers and health-care consumers that set ceilings to keep health costs in line with inflation, plus population growth.

Now, let me say, some people say we can't do this, but Hawaii does it. They cover 98 percent of their people and their insurance premiums are much cheaper than the rest of America, and so does Rochester, N.Y. They now have a plan to cover everybody and their premiums are two-thirds of the rest of the country.

This is very important. It's a big human problem and a devastating economic problem for America, and I'm going to send a plan to do this within the first 100 days of my presidency. It's terribly important.

**SIMPSON:** Thank you. Sorry to cut you short, but, President Bush, health-care reform.

**BUSH:** I just have to say something. I don't want to stampede. Ross was very articulate across the country. I don't want anybody to stampede to cut the president's salary off altogether. Barbara's sitting over here and I — but what I have proposed, 10 percent cut, downsize the government, and we can get that done.

She asked a question, I think, is whether the health-care profession was to blame. No. One thing to blame is these malpractice lawsuits. They're breaking the system. It costs $20 [billion] to $25 billion a

year, and I want to see those outrageous claims capped. Doctors don't dare to deliver babies sometimes because they're afraid that somebody's going to sue them. People don't dare — medical practitioners, to help somebody along the highway that are hurt because they're afraid that some lawyer's going to come along and get a big lawsuit. So you can't blame the practitioners for the health problem.

And my program is this. Keep the government as far out of it as possible, make insurance available to the poorest of the poor, through vouchers. Next, range in the income bracket through tax credits, and get on about the business of pooling insurance. A great big company can buy — Ross has got a good-sized company, been very successful. He can buy insurance cheaper than Mom and Pop's store on the corner. But if those mom-and-pop stores all get together and pool, they, too, can bring the cost of insurance down.

So I want to keep the quality of health care. That means keep government out of it. I want to do — I don't like this idea of these boards. It all sounds to me like you're going to have some government setting price. I want competition, and I want to pool the insurance and take care of it that way and have — oh, here's the other point.

I think medical care should go with the person. If you leave a business, I think your insurance should go with you to some other business. You shouldn't be worrying if you get a new job as to whether that's gonna — and part of our plan is to make it what they call portable — big word, but that means if you're working for the Jones Company and you go to the Smith Company, your insurance goes with you. I think it's a good program. I'm really excited about getting it done, too.

**SIMPSON:** Mr. Perot.

**PEROT:** We have the most expensive health-care system in the world. Twelve percent of our gross national product goes to health care. Our industrial competitors, who are beating us in competition, spend less and have better health care. Japan spends a little over 6 percent of its gross national product. Germany spends 8 percent.

It's fascinating. You've bought a front-row box seat, and you're not happy with your health care, and you're saying tonight we've got bad health care but very expensive health care. Folks, here's why: Go home and look in the mirror.

You own this country, but you have no voice in it the way it's organized now, and if you want to have a high-risk experience, comparable to bungee jumping, go into Congress sometime when they're working on this kind of legislation, when the lobbyists are running up and down the halls. Wear your safety-toe shoes when you go. And as a private citizen, believe me, you are looked on as a major nuisance.

The facts are you now have a government that comes at you. You're supposed to have a government that comes from you.

Now, there are all kinds of good ideas,

brilliant ideas, terrific ideas on health care. None of them ever get implemented because — let me give you an example. A senator runs every six years. He's got to raise 20,000 bucks a week to have enough money to run. Who's he gonna listen to — us or the folks running up and down the aisles with money, the lobbyists, the PAC money? He listens to them. Who do they represent? Health-care industry. Not us.

Now, you've got to have a government that comes from you again. You've got to reassert your ownership in this country, and you've got to completely reform our government. And at that point they'll just be like apples falling out of a tree. The programs will be good because the elected officials will be listening to — I said the other night I was all ears, and I would listen to any good idea. I think we ought to do plastic surgery on a lot of these guys so that they're all ears, too, and listen to you. Then you get what you want, and shouldn't you? You paid for it. Why shouldn't you get what you want, as opposed to what some lobbyist cuts a deal, writes a little piece in the law and he goes through. That's the way the game's played now. Till you change it, you're gonna be unhappy.

**SIMPSON:** Thank you. Gov. Clinton, you wanted one brief point in there.

**CLINTON:** One brief point. We have elections so people can make decisions about this. The point I want to make to you is, a bipartisan commission reviewed my plan and the Bush plan and there were as many Republicans as Democratic health-care experts on it. They concluded that my plan would cover everybody and his would leave 27 million behind by the year 2000, and that my plan in the next 12 years would save $2.2 trillion in public and private money to reinvest in this economy, and the average family would save $1,200 a year under the plan that I offered without any erosion in the quality of health care.

So I ask you to look at that. And you have to vote for somebody with a plan. That's what you have elections for. If people would say, well, he got elected to do this, and then the Congress says, OK, I'm going to do it. That's what the election was about.

**SIMPSON:** Brief, Gov. Clinton. Thank you. We have a question right here.

**AUDIENCE PARTICIPANT:** Yes. How has the national debt personally affected each of your lives? And if it hasn't, how can you honestly find a cure for the economic problems of the common people if you have no experience in what's ailing them?

**PEROT:** May I answer that?

**SIMPSON:** Well, Mr. Perot — yes, of course.

**PEROT:** Who do you want to start with?

**AUDIENCE PARTICIPANT:** My question is for each of you, so —

**PEROT:** It caused me to disrupt my private life and my business to get involved in this activity. That's how much I care about it. And believe me, if you knew my family and if you knew the private life I have, you would agree in a minute that that's a whole lot more fun than getting involved in politics.

But I have lived the American dream. I came from a very modest background. Nobody's been luckier than I've been, all the way across the spectrum, and the greatest riches of all are my wife and children. That's true of any family.

But I want all the children — I want these young people up here to be able to start with nothing but an idea, like I did, and build a business. But they've got to have a strong basic economy, and if you're in debt, it's like having a ball and chain around you.

I just figure, as lucky as I've been, I owe it to them, and I owe it to the future generations, and on a very personal basis, I owe it to my children and grandchildren.

**SIMPSON:** Thank you, Mr. Perot. Mr. President.

**BUSH:** Well, I think the national debt affects everybody.

**AUDIENCE PARTICIPANT:** You personally.

**BUSH:** Obviously it has a lot to do with interest rates —

**SIMPSON:** She's saying, "you personally"

**AUDIENCE PARTICIPANT:** You, on a personal basis — how has it affected you?

**SIMPSON:** Has it affected you personally?

**BUSH:** I'm sure it has. I love my grandchildren —

**AUDIENCE PARTICIPANT:** How?

**BUSH:** I want to think that they're going to be able to afford an education. I think that that's an important part of being a parent. If the question — maybe I — get it wrong. Are you suggesting that if somebody has means that the national debt doesn't affect them?

**AUDIENCE PARTICIPANT:** What I'm saying is —

**BUSH:** I'm not sure I get — help me with the question, and I'll try to answer it.

**AUDIENCE PARTICIPANT:** Well, I've had friends that have been laid off from jobs.

**BUSH:** Yeah.

**AUDIENCE PARTICIPANT:** I know people who cannot afford to pay the mortgage on their homes, their car payment. I have personal problems with the national debt. But how has it affected you, and, if you have no experience in it, how can you help us, if you don't know what we're feeling?

**SIMPSON:** I think she means more the recession — the economic problems today the country faces rather than the deficit.

**BUSH:** Well, listen, you ought to be in the White House for a day and hear what I hear and see what I see and read the mail I read and touch the people that I touch from time to time. I was in the Lomax AME Church. It's a black church just outside of Washington, D.C. And I read in the bulletin about teenage pregnancies, about the difficulties that families are having to make ends meet.

I talk to parents. I mean, you've got to care. Everybody cares if people aren't doing well.

But I don't think it's fair to say, you haven't had cancer, therefore you don't know what's it like. I don't think it's fair to say, you know, whatever it is, that if you haven't been hit by it personally. But everybody's affected by the debt; because of the tremendous interest that goes into paying on that debt everything's more expensive. Everything comes out of your pocket and my pocket. So it's that.

But I think in terms of the recession, of course you feel it when you're president of the United States. And that's why I'm trying to do something about it by stimulating the export, investing more, better education systems.

Thank you. I'm glad you clarified it.

**SIMPSON:** Gov. Clinton.

**CLINTON:** Tell me how it's affected you again.

**AUDIENCE PARTICIPANT:** Um —

**CLINTON:** You know people who've lost their jobs and lost their homes?

**AUDIENCE PARTICIPANT:** Well, yeah, uh-huh.

**CLINTON:** Well, I've been governor of a small state for 12 years. I'll tell you how it's affected me. Every year Congress and the president sign laws that make us do more things and gives us less money to do it with. I see people in my state, middle-class people — their taxes have gone up in Washington, and their services have gone down while the wealthy have gotten tax cuts.

I have seen what's happened in this last four years when — in my state, when people lose their jobs, there's a good chance I'll know them by their names. When a factory closes, I know the people who ran it. When the businesses go bankrupt, I know them.

And I've been out here for 13 months meeting in meetings just like this ever since October, with people like you all over America, people that have lost their jobs, lost their livelihood, lost their health insurance.

What I want you to understand is the national debt is not the only cause of that. It is because America has not invested in its people. It is because we have not grown. It is because we've had 12 years of trickle-down economics. We've gone from first to 12th in the world in wages. We've had four years where we've produced no private sector jobs. Most people are working harder for less money than they were making 10 years ago.

It is because we are in the grip of a failed economic theory. And this decision you're about to make better be about what kind of economic theory you want, not just people saying I'm going to go fix it, but what are we going to do?

I think what we have to do is invest in

American jobs, American education, control American health-care costs and bring the American people together again.

**AUDIENCE PARTICIPANT:** Thank you.

**SIMPSON:** Thank you, Gov. Clinton. We are a little more than halfway through this program, and I'm glad we're getting the diversity of questions that we are, and I don't want to forget these folks on the wings over here so let's go over here. Do you have a question?

**AUDIENCE PARTICIPANT:** Yes, I do. My name is Ben Smith. I work in the financial field, counseling retirees, and I'm personally concerned about three major areas.

One is, the Social Security Administration or trust fund is projected to be insolvent by the year 2036. And we funded the trust fund with IOUs in the form of Treasury bonds. The Pension Guarantee Fund, which backs up our private retirement plans for retirees, is projected to be bankrupt by the year 2026, not to mention the cutbacks by private companies. And Medicare is projected to be bankrupt maybe as soon as 1997.

And I would like from each of you a specific response as to what you intend to do for retirees relative to these issues, not generalities but specifics because I think they're very disturbing issues.

**SIMPSON:** President Bush, may we start with you?

**BUSH:** Well, the Social Security — you're an expert and I could, I'm sure, learn from you the details of the Pension Guarantee Fund and the Social Security Fund. The Social Security system was fixed [for] about five years, and I think it's projected out to be sound beyond that. So at least we have time to work with it.

But on all of these things, a sound economy is the only way to get it going. Growth in the economy is going to add to the overall prosperity and wealth. I can't give you a specific answer on Pension Guarantee Fund. All I know is that we have firm government credit to guarantee the pensions. And that is very important. But it's — the full faith and credit of the United States, in spite of our difficulties, is still pretty good. It's still the most respected credit.

So I would simply say, as these dates get close, you're going to have to reorganize and refix as we did with the Social Security Fund. And I think that's the only answer. But the more immediate answer is to do what this lady was suggesting we do, and that is to get this deficit down and get on without adding to the woes, and then restructure.

One thing I've called for that has been stymied, and I'll keep on working for it, is a whole financial reform legislation. It is absolutely essential in terms of bringing our banking system and credit system into the new age instead of having it living back in the dark ages. And it's a big fight. And I don't want to give my friend Ross another shot at me here, but I am fighting with the Congress to get this through. And you can't just go up and say I'm going to fix it. You've got some pretty strong-willed guys up there that argue with you.

But that's what the election's about. I agree with the governor. That's what the election's about. And sound fiscal policy is the best answer, I think, to all the three problems you mentioned.

**SIMPSON:** Thank you. Mr. Perot.

**PEROT:** On the broad issue here, when you're trying to solve a problem, you get the best plans. You have a raging debate about those plans. Then out of that debate, with leadership, comes consensus. Then, if the plans are huge and complex like health care, I would urge you to implement pilot programs. Like the old carpenter says, measure twice, cut once. Let's make sure this thing's as good as we all think it is at the end of the meeting.

Then finally, our government passes laws and freezes the plan in concrete. Anybody that's ever built a successful business will tell you you optimize, optimize, optimize after you've put something into effect. The reason Medicare and Medicaid are a mess is we froze them.

Everybody knows how to fix them. There are people all over the federal government, if they could just touch it with a screwdriver, could fix it.

Now, back over here. See, we've got a $4 trillion debt and only in America would you have $2.8 trillion of it, or 70 percent of it, financed five years or less. Now, that's another thing for you to think about when you go home tonight. You don't finance long-term debt with short-term money. Why did our government do it? To get the interest rates down. A 1 percent increase in interest rates in that $2.8 trillion is $28 billion a year.

Now, when you look at what Germany pays for money and what we don't pay for money, you realize there's quite a spread, right, and you realize this is a temporary thing and there's going to be another sucking sound that runs our deficit through the roof.

You know, and everybody's ducking it so I'm gonna say it, that we are not letting that surplus stay in the bank. We are not investing that surplus like a pension fund. We are spending that surplus to make the deficit look smaller to you than it really is.

Now, that — put you in jail in corporate America if you kept books that way, but in government it's just kind of the way things are. That's because it comes at you, not from you.

Now then, that money needs to be — they don't even pay interest on it. They just write a note for the interest.

**SIMPSON:** Mr. Perot, can you wrap it up?

**PEROT:** Do you want to fix the problem or sound-bite it? I understand the importance of time but see, here's how we get to this mess we're in.

**SIMPSON:** But we've got to be fair.

**PEROT:** This is just one of 1,000. Now then, to nail it, there's one way out — a growing, expanding job base. A growing, expanding job base to generate the funds and the tax revenues to pay off the mess and rebuild America. We've got to double-hit. If we're $4 trillion down, we should have everything perfect, but we don't. We've got to pay it off and build money to renew it — spend money to renew it, and that's going to take a growing, expanding job base. That is priority one in this country. Put everybody that's breathing to work. And I'd love to be out of workers and have to import them, like some of our international competitors.

**SIMPSON:** Mr. Perot, I'm sorry. I'm going to —

**PEROT:** Sorry.

**SIMPSON:** And I don't want to sound-bite you but we are trying to be fair —

**PEROT:** OK.

**SIMPSON:** — to everyone.

**PEROT:** Absolutely. I apologize.

**SIMPSON:** All right. Gov. Clinton.

**CLINTON:** I think I remember the question.

Let me say first of all, I want to answer your specific question but first of all, we all agree that there should be a growing economy. What you have to decide is who's got the best economic plan. And we all have ideas out there, and Mr. Bush has a record. So I don't want you to read my lips and I sure don't want you to read his. I do hope you will read our plans.

Now, specifically, one, on Medicare, it is not true that everyone knows how to fix it. There are different ideas — the Bush plan, the Perot plan, the Clinton — we have different ideas.

I am convinced, having studied health care for a year hard and talking to hundreds and hundreds of people all across America, that you cannot control the cost of Medicare until you control the cost of private health care and public health care, with managed competition, ceiling on cost, and radical reorganization of the insurance markets. You've got to do that; we got to get those costs down.

No. 2, with regard to Social Security, that program — a lot of you may not know this — it produces a $70 billion surplus a year. Social Security is in surplus $70 billion. Six increases in the payroll tax — that means people with incomes of $51,000 a year or less pay a disproportionally high share of the federal tax burden, which is why I want some middle-class tax relief.

What do we have to do? By the time the century turns, we have got to have our deficit under control, we have to work it of so that surplus is building up so when the baby boomers like me retire, we're OK.

No. 3, on the pension funds, I don't know as much about it, but I will say this. What I would do is to bring in the pension experts of the country, take a look at it and strengthen the pension requirements further, because it's not just enough to have the guarantee. We had a guarantee on the S&Ls, right? We had a guarantee — and what happened? You picked up a $500

billion bill because of the dumb way the federal government deregulated it.

So I think we are going to have to change and strengthen the pension requirements on private retirement plans.

**SIMPSON:** Thank you. I think we have a question here on international affairs, hopefully.

**AUDIENCE PARTICIPANT:** We've come to a position where we're in the new world order, and I'd like to know what the candidates feel our position is in this new world order, and what our responsibilities are as a superpower?

**SIMPSON:** Mr. President.

**BUSH:** Well, we have come to that position. Since I became president, 43, 44 countries have gone democratic, no longer totalitarian, no longer living under dictatorship or communist rule. This is exciting. New world order to me means freedom and democracy. I think we will have a continuing responsibility, as the only remaining superpower, to stay involved. If we pull back in some isolation and say we don't have to do our share, or more than our share, anymore, I believe you are going to just ask for conflagration that we'll get involved in in the future.

NATO, for example, has kept the peace for many, many years, and I want to see us keep fully staffed in NATO so we'll continue to guarantee the peace in Europe.

But the exciting thing is, the fear of nuclear war is down. And you hear all the bad stuff that's happened on my watch; I hope people will recognize that this is something pretty good for mankind. I hope they'll think it's good that democracy and freedom is on the move. And we're going to stay engaged, as long as I'm president, working to improve things.

You know, it's so easy now to say, hey, cut out foreign aid, we got a problem at home. I think the United States has to still have the Statue of Liberty as a symbol, caring for others. Right this very minute we're sending supplies in to help these little starving kids in Somalia. It's the United States that's taken the lead in humanitarian aid into Bosnia. We're doing this all around the world.

Yes, we've got problems at home. And I think I've got a good plan to help fix those problems at home. But because of our leadership, because we didn't listen to the freeze — the nuclear-freeze group, do you remember? freeze it, back in the late '70s — freeze, don't touch it; we're going to lock it in now or else we'll have war. President Reagan said no, peace through strength. It worked. The Soviet Union is no more, and now we're working to help them become totally democratic through the Freedom Support Act that I led on, a great Democratic ambassador, Bob Strauss, over there, Jim Baker, all of us got this thing passed — through cooperation, Ross — it worked with cooperation, and you're for that, I'm sure, helping Russia become democratic.

So the new world order to me means freedom and democracy, keep engaged, do not pull back into isolation. And we are the

United States, and we have a responsibility to lead and to guarantee the security.

If it hadn't been for us, Saddam Hussein would be sitting on top of three-fifths of the oil supply of the world and he'd have nuclear weapons. And only the United States could do this. Excuse me, Carole.

**SIMPSON:** Thank you. Mr. Perot.

**PEROT:** Well, it's cost-effective to help Russia succeed in its revolution; it's pennies on the dollar compared to going back to the Cold War. Russia is still very unstable; they could go back to square one, and worse. All the nuclear weapons are not dismantled. I am particularly concerned about the intercontinental weapons, the ones that can hit us. We've got agreements, but they are still there.

With all this instability and breaking into republics, and all the Middle Eastern countries going over there and shopping for weapons, we've got our work cut out for us. So we need to stay right on top of that and constructively help them move toward democracy and capitalism.

We have to have money to do that. We have to have our people at work. See, for 45 years we were preoccupied with the Red Army. I suggest now that our No. 1 preoccupation is red ink and our country and we've got to put our people back to work so that we can afford to do these things we want to do in Russia. We cannot be the policeman for the world any longer. We spent $300 billion a year defending the world. Germany and Japan spend around $30 billion apiece. If I can get you to defend me and I can spend all my money building industry, that's a home run for me.

Coming out of World War II it made sense. Now the other superpowers need to do their part. I'll close on this point. You can't be a superpower unless you're an economic superpower. If we're not an economic superpower, we're a used-to-be and we will no longer be a force for good throughout the world. And if nothing else gets you excited about rebuilding our industrial base, maybe that will, because job one is to put our people back to work.

**SIMPSON:** Gov. Clinton, the president mentioned Saddam Hussein. Your vice president and you have had some words about the president and Saddam Hussein. Would you care to comment?

**CLINTON:** I'd rather answer her question first, and then I'll be glad to. Because the question you ask is important. The end of the Cold War brings an incredible opportunity for change. Winds of freedom blowing around the world, Russia demilitarizing. And it also requires us to maintain some continuity — some bipartisan American commitment to certain principles. And I would just say there are three things that I would like to say. No. 1, we do have to maintain the world's strongest defense. We may differ about what the elements of that are.

I think that defense needs to be — with fewer people in permanent armed services but with greater mobility on the land, in the air and on the sea, with a real dedi-

cation to continuing development of high technology weaponry and well trained people. I think we're going to have to work to stop the proliferation of weapons of mass destruction. Got to keep going until all those nuclear weapons in Russia are gone and the other republics. No. 2, if you don't rebuild the economic strength of this country at home, we won't be a superpower. We can't have any more instances like what happened when Mr. Bush went to Japan and the Japanese prime minister said he felt sympathy for our country. We have to be the strongest economic power in the world. That's what got me into this race, so we could rebuild the American economy.

And No. 3, we need to be a force for freedom and democracy and we need to use our unique position to support freedom, whether it's in Haiti or in China or in any other place, wherever the seeds of freedom are sprouting. We can't impose it, but we need to nourish it and that's the kind of thing that I would do as president — follow those three commitments into the future.

**SIMPSON:** OK. We have a question up there.

**AUDIENCE PARTICIPANT:** Yes. We've talked a lot tonight about creating jobs. But we have an awful lot of high school graduates who don't know how to read a ruler, who cannot fill out an application for a job.

How can we create high-paying jobs with the education system we have and what would you do to change it?

**SIMPSON:** Who would like to begin — the education president?

**PEROT:** Go ahead, sir. Yeah, go ahead.

**BUSH:** I'd be delighted to, because you can't do it the old way. You can't do it with the school bureaucracy controlling everything and that's why we have a new program that I hope people have heard about. It's being worked now in 1,700 communities — bypassed Congress on this one, Ross — 1,700 communities across the country. It's called America 2000. And it literally says to the communities, re-invent the schools, not just the bricks and mortar but the curriculum and everything else. Think anew. We have a concept called the New American School Corporation where we're doing exactly that.

And so I believe that we've got to get the power in the hands of the teachers, not the teachers' union. What's happening up there?

And so our America 2000 program also says this. It says let's give parents the choice of a public, private or public school — public, private or religious school. And it works — it works in Milwaukee. Democratic woman up there — taking the lead in this. The mayor up there, on the program. And the schools that are not chosen are improved — competition does that.

So we've got to innovate through school choice. We've got to innovate through this America 2000 program. But she is absolutely right. The programs that we've been trying where you control every-

thing and mandate it from Washington don't work. The governors — and I believe Gov. Clinton was in on this — but maybe — I don't want to invoke him here. But they come to me and they say, please get the Congress to stop passing so many mandates telling us how to control things. We know better how to do it in California or Texas or wherever it is.

So this is what our program is all about. And I believe you're right on to something, that if we don't change the education we're not going to be able to compete. Federal funding for education is up substantially — Pell grants are up. But it isn't going to get the job done if we don't change K through 12.

**SIMPSON:** Gov. Clinton.

**CLINTON:** First of all, let me say that I've spent more of my time and life on this in the last 12 years than any other issue. Seventy percent of my state's money goes to the public schools, and I was really honored when Time magazine said that our schools have shown more improvement than any other state in the country except one other — they named two states showing real strides forward in the eighties. So I care a lot about this, and I've spent countless hours in schools.

But let me start with what you said. I agree with some of what Mr. Bush said, but it's nowhere near enough. We live in a world where what you earn depends on what you can learn, where the average 18-year-old will change jobs eight times in a lifetime and where none of us can promise any of you that what you now do for a living is absolutely safe from now on. Nobody running can promise that; there's too much change in the world.

So what should we do? Let me reel some things off real quick, because you said you wanted specifics. No. 1, under my program we would provide matching funds to states to teach everybody with a job to read in the next five years and give everybody with a job the chance to get a high school diploma, in big places on the job.

No. 2, we would provide two-year apprenticeship programs to high school graduates who don't go to college. And community colleges are on the job.

No. 3, we'd open the doors to college education to high school graduates without regard to income. They could borrow the money and pay it back as a percentage of their income or with a couple of years of service to our nation here at home.

No. 4, we would fully fund the Head Start program to get little kids off to a good start.

And, five, I would have an aggressive program of school reform, more choices — I favor public schools or these new charter schools — we can talk about that if you want. I don't think we should spend tax money on private schools. But I favor public school choice, and I favor radical decentralization in giving more power to better-trained principals and teachers with parent councils to control their schools.

Those things would revolutionize American education and take us to the top economically.

**SIMPSON:** Thank you.

**AUDIENCE PARTICIPANT:** What are they going to cost?

**SIMPSON:** The question is, what is it going to cost? What is it going to cost?

**CLINTON:** In six years — I budget all this in my budget, and in six years the college program would cost $8 billion over and above what — the present student loan program costs four [billion dollars]; you pay $3 billion for busted loans, because we don't have an automatic recovery system, and a billion dollars in bank fees. So the net cost would be eight billion six years from now in a trillion-plus budget — not very much.

The other stuff — all the other stuff I mentioned — costs much less than that. The Head Start program full funding would cost about five billion more. And it's all covered in my budget from — the plans that I've laid out — from raising taxes on families with incomes above $200,000 and asking foreign corporations to pay the same tax that American corporations do on the same income, from $140 billion in budget cuts, including what I think are very prudent cuts in the defense budget. It's all covered in the plan.

**SIMPSON:** Thank you. Mr. Perot, you on education, please.

**PEROT:** Yes, I've got scars to show for being around education reform. And the first word you need to say in every city and state, and just draw a line in the sand, is public schools exist for the benefit of the children. You're going to see a lot of people fall over it, because any time you're spending $199 billion dollars a year, somebody's getting it. And the children get lost in the process. So that's Step 1.

Keep in mind in 1960, when our schools were the envy of the world, we were spending $16 billion on them; now we spend more than any other nation in the world — $199 billion a year — and rank at the bottom of the industrialized world in terms of education achievement. One more time you've bought a front-row box seat and got a third-rate performance. This is a government that is not serving you.

By and large it should be local — the more local, the better. Interesting phenomenon: Small towns have good schools, big cities have terrible schools. The best people in a small town will serve on the school board; you get into big cities, it's political patronage, stepping stones — you get the job, give your relatives a janitor's job at $57,000 a year, more than the teachers make, and with luck they clean the cafeteria once a week. Now, you're paying for that. Those schools belong to you. And we put up with that.

Now, as long as we put up with that, that's what you're going to get. And these folks are just dividing up 199 billion bucks and the children get lost. If I could wish for one thing for great public schools, it would be a strong family unit in every home — nothing will ever replace that. You say, well, gee, what are you going to do about that? Well, the White House is a bully pulpit, and I think we ought to be pounding on the table every day. There's nothing — the most efficient unit of government the world will ever know is a strong loving family unit.

Next thing. You need small schools, not big schools. In a little school everybody is somebody; individualism is very important. These big factories? Everybody told me they were cost-effective. I did a study on it; they're cost-ineffective. Five thousand students — why is a high school that big? One reason. Sooner or later you get 11 more boys that can run like the devil that weigh 250 pounds and they might win district. Now, that has nothing to do with learning.

Secondly, across Texas, typically half of the school day was non-academic pursuits — in one place it was 35 percent. In Texas you could have unlimited absences to go to livestock shows. Found a boy — excuse me, but this gives the flavor — a boy in Houston kept a chicken in the bathtub in downtown Houston and missed 65 days going to livestock shows. Finally had to come back to school, the chicken lost its feathers. That's the only way we got him back.

Now, that's your tax money being wasted.

Now, neighborhood schools. It is terrible to bus tiny little children across town. And it is particularly terrible to take poor tiny little children and wait until the first grade and bus them across town to Mars, where the children know their numbers, know their letters, have had every advantage. At the end of the first day, that little child wants out.

I'll close on this. You've got to have world-class teachers, world-class books. If you ever got close to how textbooks were selected, you wouldn't want to go back the second day. I don't have time to tell you the stories.

**SIMPSON:** No, you don't.

**PEROT:** Finally, if we don't fix this, you're right. We can't have the industries of tomorrow unless we have the best educated workforce. And here you've got, for the disadvantaged children, you've got to have early childhood development. Cheapest money you'll ever spend. First contact should be with the money when she's pregnant. That little child needs to be loved and hugged and nurtured and made to feel special, like your children were. They learn to think well or poorly of themselves in the first 18 months.

**SIMPSON:** Thank you.

**AUDIENCE PARTICIPANT:** Thank you, Mr. Perot.

**PEROT:** And in the first few years they either learn how to learn or don't learn how to learn. And if they don't, they wind up in prison.

**SIMPSON:** Thank you, Mr. Perot.

**PEROT:** And it costs more to keep them in prison than it does to send them to Harvard. I rest my case.

**SIMPSON:** Thank you. President Bush, you wanted to answer.

**BUSH:** I just had a word of clarification because of something Gov. Clinton said.

My school choice program, GI Bill for Kids, does not take public money and give it to private schools. It does what the GI Bill itself did when I came out of World War II. It takes public money and gives it to families or individuals to choose the school they want. And where it's been done, those schools, like in Rochester, those schools that weren't chosen find that they then compete and do better.

So I think it's worth a shot. We've got a pilot program. It ought to be tried. School choice — public, private or religious. Not to the schools but to — you know, 46 percent of the teachers in Chicago, public school teachers, send their kids to private school.

Now, I think we ought to try to help families and see if it will do what I think — make all schools better.

**CLINTON:** I just want to mention if I could —

**SIMPSON:** Very briefly.

**CLINTON:** Very briefly. Involving the parents in the preschool education of their kids, even if they're poor and uneducated, can make a huge difference. We have a big program in my state that teaches mothers or fathers to teach their kids to get ready for school. It's the most successful thing we've ever done.

Just a fact clarification real quickly. We do not spend a higher percentage of our income on public education than every other country. There are nine countries that spend more than we do on public education. We spend more on education 'cause we spend so much more on colleges.

But if you look at public education alone and you take into account the fact that we have more racial diversity and more poverty, it makes a big difference. There are great public schools where there's public school choice, accountability and brilliant principals. I'll just mention one — the Beasley Academic Center in Chicago. I commend it to anybody. It's as good as any private school in the country.

**SIMPSON:** We have very little time left and it occurs to me that we have talked all this time and there has not been one question about some of the racial tensions and ethnic tensions in America. Is there anyone in this audience that would like to pose a question to the candidates on this?

**AUDIENCE PARTICIPANT:** What I'd like to know, and this is to any of the three of you, is aside from the recent accomplishment of your party, aside from those accomplishments in racial representation, and without citing any of your current appointments or successful elections, when do you estimate your party will both nominate and elect an Afro-American and female ticket to the presidency of the United States?

**SIMPSON:** Gov. Clinton, why don't you answer that first?

**CLINTON:** Well, I don't have any idea but I hope it will happen some time in my lifetime.

**AUDIENCE PARTICIPANT:** I do, too.

**CLINTON:** I believe that this country is electing more and more African Americans and Latinos and Asian Americans who are representing districts that are themselves not necessarily of a majority of their race. The American people are beginning to vote across racial lines, and I hope it will happen more and more.

More and more women are being elected. Look at all these women Senate candidates we have here. And you know, according to my mother and my wife and my daughter, this world would be a lot better place if women were running it most of the time.

I do think there are special experiences and judgments and backgrounds and understandings that women bring to this process, by the way. This lady said here, how have you been affected by the economy. I mean, women know what's it like to be paid an unequal amount for equal work. They know what it's like not to have flexible working hours. They know what it's like not to have family leave or child care. So I think it would be a good thing for America if it happened. And I think it will happen in my lifetime.

**SIMPSON:** OK. I'm sorry. We have just a little bit of time left. Let's try to get responses from each of them. President Bush or Mr. Perot?

**BUSH:** I think if Barbara Bush were running this year she'd be elected. But it's too late.

You don't want us to mention appointees, but when you see the quality of people in our administration, see how Colin Powell performed — I say administration, he's in the military —

**AUDIENCE PARTICIPANT:** I said when's your guess?

**BUSH:** You weren't impressed with the fact that he —

**AUDIENCE PARTICIPANT:** Excuse me. I'm extremely impressed with that.

**BUSH:** Yeah, but wouldn't that suggest to the American people, then, here's a quality person, if he decided that he could automatically get the nomination of either party?

**AUDIENCE PARTICIPANT:** Sure — I just wanted to know — yes.

**BUSH:** Huh?

**AUDIENCE PARTICIPANT:** I'm totally impressed with that. I just wanted to know is, when's your-

**BUSH:** Oh, I see.

**AUDIENCE PARTICIPANT:** When?

**BUSH:** You mean, time?

**AUDIENCE PARTICIPANT:** Yeah.

**BUSH:** I don't know — starting after four years. — No, I think you'll see —

**SIMPSON:** Mr. Perot.

**BUSH:** I think you'll see more minor-

ity candidates and women candidates coming forward.

**SIMPSON:** We have — thank you.

**BUSH:** This is supposed to be the year of the woman in the Senate. Let's see how they do. I hope a lot of them lose.

**SIMPSON:** Mr. Perot — I don't want to cut you off any more but we only have a minute left.

**PEROT:** I have a fearless forecast. A message just won't do it. Colin Powell will be on somebody's ticket four years from now — right? Right? He wanted that said — four years.

**SIMPSON:** How about a woman?

**PEROT:** Now, if won't be, Gen. Waller would be — you say, why do you keep picking military people. These are people that I just happen to know and have a high regard for. I'm sure there are hundreds of others.

**BUSH:** How about Dr. Lou Sullivan?

**PEROT:** Absolutely.

**BUSH:** Yeah, a good man.

**SIMPSON:** What about a woman?

**PEROT:** Oh, oh.

**BUSH:** My candidate's back there.

**PEROT:** OK. I can think of many.

**SIMPSON:** Many?

**PEROT:** Absolutely.

**SIMPSON:** When?

**PEROT:** All right. How about Sandra Day O'Connor as an example?

**SIMPSON:** Hm-hm.

**PEROT:** Dr. Bernadine Healy —

**SIMPSON:** Good.

**PEROT:** National Institutes of Health. I'll yield the floor.

**BUSH:** All good Republicans.

**PEROT:** Name some more.

**SIMPSON:** Thank you. I want to apologize to our audience because there were 209 people here and there were 209 questions. We only got to a fraction of them and I'm sorry to those of you that didn't get to ask your questions but we must move to the conclusion of the program.

It is time now for the two-minute closing statements, and by prior agreement President Bush will go first.

**BUSH:** May I ask for an exception because I think we owe Carole Simpson — anybody who can stand in between these three characters here and get the job done — we owe her a round of applause.

But don't take it out of my time!

**SIMPSON:** That's right.

**BUSH:** I feel strongly about it because I don't want it to come out of my time.

**SIMPSON:** Give this man more time.

**BUSH:** No, but let me just say to the American people in two and a half weeks we're going to choose who should sit in this Oval Office, who to lead the economic recovery, who to be the leader of the free world, who to get the deficit down. Three ways to do that. One is to raise taxes. One is to reduce spending — controlling that mandatory spending. Another one is to invest and save and to stimulate growth. I do not want to raise taxes. I differ with the two here on that. I'm just not going to do that.

I do believe that we need to control mandatory spending. I think we need to invest and save more. I believe that we need to educate better and retrain better. I believe that we need to export more so I'll keep working for export agreements where we can sell more abroad and I believe that we must strengthen the family. We've got to strengthen the family.

Now, let me pose this question to America. If in the next five minutes a television announcer came on and said, there is a major international crisis — there is a major threat to the world or in this country a major threat — my question is, who, if you were appointed to name one of the three of us, who would you choose? Who has the perseverance, the character, the integrity, the maturity, to get the job done?

I hope I'm that person. Thank you very, very much.

**SIMPSON:** Thank you, Mr. President. And now a closing statement from Mr. Perot.

**PEROT:** If the American people want to do it and not talk about it, then they ought to — you know, I'm one person they ought to consider. If they just want to keep slow dancing and talk about it and not do it, I'm not your name. I am results oriented. I am action oriented. I've dealt my businesses. Getting things done in three months that my competitors took 18 months to do.

Everybody says you can't do that with Congress. Sure, you can do that with Congress. Congress — they're all good people. They're all patriots but you've got to link arms and work with them. Sure, you'll have arguments. Sure, you'll have fights. We have them all day, every day. But we get the job done.

Now, I have to come back in my close to one thing because I am passionate about education. I was talking about early childhood education for disadvantaged little children. And let me tell you one specific pilot program where children who don't have a chance go to this program when they're three. Now we're going back to when the mother's pregnant and they'll start right after they're born.

Starting when they're 3 and going to this school until they're 9 and then going into the public school in the fourth grade. Ninety percent are on the honor role. Now that will change America. Those children will all go to college. They will live the American dream. And I beg the American people, any time they think about reforming education to take this piece of society that doesn't have a chance and take these little pieces of clay that can be shaped and molded and give them the same love and nurture and affection and support you give your children and teach them that they're unique and that they're precious and that there's only one person in the world like them and you will see this nation bloom. And we will have so many people who are qualified for the top job that it will be terrific.

Now, finally, if you can't pay the bills you're dead in the water. And we have got to put our nation back to work. Now, if you don't want to really do that I'm not your man. I'd go crazy sitting up there slow dancing that one. In other words, unless we're going to do it, then pick somebody who likes to talk about it.

Now, just remember when you think about me — I didn't create this mess. I've been paying taxes just like you and Lord knows, I've paid my share — over a billion in taxes. And for a guy that started out with everything he owned in the trunk of his car —

**SIMPSON:** Mr. Perot, I'm sorry —

**PEROT:** — that ain't bad.

**SIMPSON:** — once again.

**PEROT:** But it's in your hands. I wish you well. I'll see you tomorrow night —

on NBC — 10:30 to 11:00 Eastern time.

**SIMPSON:** And finally, last but not least — Gov. Clinton.

**CLINTON:** Thank you, Carole, and thank you, ladies and gentlemen.

Since I suggested this format I hope it's been good for all of you. I really tried to be faithful to your request that we answer the questions specifically and pointedly. I thought I owed that to you and I respect you for being here and for the impact you've had on making this a more positive experience.

These problems are not easy. They're not going to be solved overnight. But I want you to think about just two or three things. First of all, the people of my state have let me be their governor for 12 years because I made commitments to two things — more jobs and better schools.

Our schools are now better. Our children get off to a better start from preschool programs and smaller classes in the early grades, and we have one of the most aggressive adult education programs in the country. We talked about that. This year my state ranks first in the country in job growth, fourth in manufacturing in job growth, fourth in income growth, fourth in the decline of poverty.

I'm proud of that. It happened because I could work with people — Republicans and Democrats. That's why we've had 24 retired generals and admirals, hundreds of business people, many of them Republican, support this campaign.

You have to decide whether you want to change or not. We do not need four more years of an economic theory that doesn't work. We've had 12 years of trickle-down economics. It's time to put the American people first, to invest and grow this economy. I'm the only person here who's ever balanced a government budget and I've presented 12 of them and cut spending repeatedly. But you cannot just get there by balancing the budget. We've got to grow the economy by putting people first — real people like you.

I got into this race because I did not want my child to grow up to be part of the first generation of Americans to do worse than her parents. We're better than that. We can do better than that. I want to make America as great as it can be and I ask for your help in doing it.

Thank you very much.

**SIMPSON:** Thank you, Gov. Clinton. Ladies and gentlemen, this concludes the debate, sponsored by the Bipartisan Commission on Presidential Debates. I'd like to thank our audience of 209 uncommitted voters who may leave this evening maybe being committed, and hopefully they'll go to the polls like everyone else on November 3rd and vote.

We invite you to join us on the third and final presidential debate next Monday, October 19th, from the campus of Michigan State University in East Lansing, Michigan.

I'm Carole Simpson. Good night. ∎

# Final Debate's Dual Format Uses Moderator and Panel

*Following is the Reuter transcript of the second of three televised presidential debates. The candidates, President Bush, Arkansas Gov. Bill Clinton and Ross Perot, met Oct. 19 at Michigan State University in East Lansing, Mich.*

**JIM LEHRER:** Good evening. Welcome to this third and final debate among the three major candidates for president of the United States: Gov. Bill Clinton, the Democratic nominee; President George Bush, the Republican nominee; independent candidate Ross Perot.

I am Jim Lehrer of the "MacNeil/Lehrer NewsHour" on PBS. I will be the moderator for this debate, which is being sponsored by the Commission on Presidential Debates. It will be 90 minutes long. It is happening before an audience on the campus of Michigan State University in East Lansing.

The format was conceived by and agreed to by representatives of the Bush and Clinton campaigns, and it is somewhat different than those used in the earlier debates.

I will ask questions for the first half under rules that permit follow-ups. A panel of three other journalists will ask questions in the second half under rules that do not.

As always, each candidate will have two minutes, up to two minutes, to make a closing statement. The order of those as well as that for the formal questioning were all determined by a drawing.

Gentlemen, again welcome and again good evening.

It seems, from what some of those voters said at your Richmond debate, and from polling and other data, that each of you, fairly or not, faces serious voter concerns about the underlying credibility and believability of what each of you says you would do as president in the next four years.

Gov. Clinton, in accordance with the draw, those concerns about you are first: You are promising to create jobs, reduce the deficit, reform the health-care system, rebuild the infrastructure, guarantee college education for everyone who is qualified, among many other things, all with financial pain only for the very rich. Some people are having trouble apparently believing that is possible. Should they have that concern?

**CLINTON:** No. There are many people who believe that the only way we can get this country turned around is to tax the middle class more and punish them more, but the truth is that middle-class Americans are basically the only group of Americans who've been taxed more in the 1980s and during the last 12 years, even though their incomes have gone down. The wealthiest Americans have been taxed much less, even though their incomes have gone up.

Middle-class people will have their fair share of changing to do and many challenges to face, including the challenge of becoming constantly re-educated.

But my plan is a departure from trickle-down economics, just cutting taxes on the wealthiest Americans and getting out of the way. It's also a departure from tax-and-spend economics, because you can't tax and divide an economy that isn't growing.

I propose an American version of what works in other countries — I think we can do it better: Invest and grow.

I believe we can increase investment and reduce the deficit at the same time if we not only ask the wealthiest Americans and foreign corporations to pay their share, we also provide over $100 billion in tax relief, in terms of incentives for new plants, new small businesses, new technologies, new housing, and for middle-class families, and we have $140 billion of spending cuts. Invest and grow. Raise some more money, spend the money on tax incentives to have growth in the private sector, take the money from the defense cuts and reinvest it in new transportation and communications and environmental cleanup systems. This will work.

On this, as on so many other issues, I have a fundamental difference from the present administration. I don't believe trickle-down economics will work. Unemployment is up. Most people are working harder for less money than they were making 10 years ago. I think we can do better if we have the courage to change.

**LEHRER:** Mr. President, a response.

**BUSH:** Do I have one minute? Just the ground rules here.

**LEHRER:** Roughly one minute. We can loosen that up a little bit but go ahead.

**BUSH:** Well, he doesn't like trickle-down government but I think he's talking about the Reagan-Bush years where we created 15 million jobs. The rich are paying a bigger percent of the total tax burden. And what I don't like is trickle-down government. And therein, I think Gov. Clinton keeps talking about trickle down, trickle down, and he's still talking about spending more and taxing more.

Government — he says invest in government, grow government. Government doesn't create jobs. If they do, they're make-work jobs. It's the private sector that creates jobs. And yes, we've got too many taxes on the American people and we're spending too much.

And that's why I want to get the deficit down by controlling the growth of mandatory spending. It won't be painless. I think Mr. Perot put his finger on something there. It won't be painless but we've got to get the job done. But not by raising taxes.

Mr. and Mrs. America, when you hear him say we're going to tax only the rich, watch your wallet because his figures don't add up and he's going to sock it right to the middle-class taxpayer and lower, if he's going to pay for all the spending programs he proposes.

So we have a big difference on this trickle-down theory. I do not want any more trickle-down government. It's gotten too big. I want to do something about that.

**LEHRER:** Mr. Perot, what do you think of the governor's approach, what he just laid out?

**PEROT:** The basic problem with it, it doesn't balance the budget. If you forecast it out, we still have a significant deficit under each of their plans, as I understand them.

Our challenge is to stop the financial bleeding. If you take a patient into the hospital that's bleeding arterially, Step One is to stop the bleeding. And we are bleeding arterially.

There's only one way out of this, and that is to stop the deterioration of our job base, to have a growing, expanding job base, to give us the tax base — see, balancing the budget is not nearly as difficult as paying off the $4 trillion debt and leaving our children the American dream intact.

We have spent their money. We've got to pay it back. This is going to take fair, shared sacrifice. My plan balances the budget within six years. We didn't do it faster than that because we didn't want to disrupt the economy. We gave it off to a slow start and a fast finish to give the economy time to recover. But we faced it and we did it, and we believe it's fair, shared sacrifice.

The one thing I have done is lay it squarely on the table in front of the American people. You've had a number of occasions to see in detail what the plan is, and at least you'll understand it. I think that's fundamental in our country, that you know what you're getting into.

**LEHRER:** Governor, the word "pain" — one of the other leadership things that's put on you is that you don't speak of pain, that you speak of all things — nobody's

going to really have to suffer under your plan. You've heard what Mr. Perot has said. He's said it's got — to do the things that you want to do, you can't do it by just taking the money from the rich. That's what the president says as well.

How do you respond to that? They said the numbers don't add up.

**CLINTON:** I disagree with both of them. For one thing, let me just follow up here. I disagree with Mr. Perot that the answer is to raise — put a 50-cent gas tax on the middle class and raise more taxes on the middle class and the working poor than on the wealthy.

His own analysis says that unemployment will be slightly higher in 1995 under his plan than it is today.

And as far as what Mr. Bush says, he is the person who raised taxes on the middle class after saying he wouldn't. And just this year, Mr. Bush vetoed a tax increase on the wealthy that gave middle-class tax relief. He vetoed middle-class tax relief this year.

And furthermore, under this administration, spending has increased more than it has in the last 20 years, and he asked Congress to spend more money than it actually spent. Now, it's hard to outspend Congress but he tried to for the last three years.

So my view is the middle class is the — they've been suffering, Jim. Now, should people pay more for Medicare if they can? Yes. Should they pay more for Social Security if they get more out of it than they paid in, they're upper income people? Yes. But look what's happened to the middle class. Middle-class Americans are working harder for less money than they were making 10 years ago, and they're paying higher taxes. The tax burden on them has not gone down. It has gone up. I don't think the answer is to slow the economy down more, drive unemployment up more and undermine the health of the private sector. The answer is to invest and grow this economy. That's what works in other countries, and that's what'll work here.

**LEHRER:** As a practical matter, Mr. President, do you agree with the governor when he says that the middle class, the taxes on the middle class — do your numbers agree that the taxes on the middle class have gone up during the last —

**BUSH:** I think everybody's paying too much taxes. He refers to one tax increase. Let me remind you it was a Democratic tax increase, and I didn't want to do it, and I went along with it. And I said I make a mistake. If I make a mistake, I admit it. That's quite different than some. But I think that's the American way.

I think everyone's paying too much, but I think this idea that you can go out and — then he hits me for vetoing a tax bill. Yes, I did. And the American taxpayer ought to be glad they have a president to stand up to a spending Congress. We remember what it was like when we had a spending president and a spending Congress, and interest rates — who remembers that? They were at 21.5 percent under

Jimmy Carter, and inflation was 15. We don't want to go back to that.

And so yes, everybody's taxed too much and I want to get the taxes down, but not by signing a tax bill that's going to raise taxes on people.

**LEHRER:** Mr. President, when you said just then that you admit your mistakes and you looked at Gov. Clinton and said — what mistake is it that you want him to admit to?

**BUSH:** Well, the record in Arkansas. I mean, look at it, and that's what we're asking America to have? Now look, he says Arkansas' a poor state. They are. But in almost every category they're lagging. I'll give you an example. He talks about all the jobs he's created in one or two years. Over the last 10 years since he's been governor, they're 30 percent behind, 30 percent — they're 30 percent of the national average. On pay for teachers, on all these categories, Arkansas is right near the very bottom.

You haven't heard me mention this before, but we're getting close now, and I think it's about time I start putting things in perspective. And I'm going to do that. It's not dirty campaigning, because he's been talking about my record for a half a year here, 11 months here. So we've got to do that. I got to get it in perspective.

What's his mistake? Admit it, that Arkansas is doing very, very badly against any standard — environment, support for police officers, whatever it is.

**LEHRER:** Governor, is that true?

**CLINTON:** Mr. Bush's Bureau of Labor Statistics says that Arkansas ranks first in the country in the growth of new jobs this year, first.

**BUSH:** This year.

**CLINTON:** Fourth in manufacturing jobs, fourth in the reduction of poverty, fourth in income increase. Over the last ten years we've created manufacturing jobs much more rapidly than the national average. Over the last five years our income has grown more rapidly than the national average. We are second in tax burden, the second lowest tax burden in the country.

We have the lowest per capita state and local spending in the country. We're low spending, low tax burden. We dramatically increased investment and our jobs are growing. I wish America had that kind of record and I think most people looking at us tonight would like it if we had more jobs and a lower spending burden on the government.

**LEHRER:** Mr. Perot, if you were sitting at home now and just heard this exchange about Arkansas, who would you believe?

**PEROT:** I grew up five blocks from Arkansas. Let's put it in perspective. It's a beautiful state. It's a fairly rural state. It has a population less than Chicago or Los Angeles, about the size of Dallas and Forth Worth combined.

So I think probably we're making a mistake night after night after night to cast the nation's future on a unit that small.

**LEHRER:** Why is that a mistake?

**PEROT:** It's irrelevant.

**LEHRER:** What he did as governor of Arkansas is irrelevant?

**PEROT:** No, no, no, but I could say, you know, that I ran a small grocery store on the corner, therefore I extrapolate that into the fact that I can run Wal-Mart. That's not true.

I can't protect an Arkansas company, you notice there, Governor.

**LEHRER:** Governor?

**CLINTON:** Mr. Perot, with all respect, I think it is highly relevant, and I think that a $4 billion budget of state and federal funds is not all that small, and I think the fact that I took a state that was one of the poorest states in the country and had been for 153 years and tried my best to modernize its economy and to make the kind of changes that have generated support from people like the presidents of Apple Computer and Hewlett-Packard and some of the biggest companies in this country, 24 retired generals and admirals and hundreds of business executives, are highly relevant. And, you know, I'm frankly amazed that since you grew up five blocks from there you would think that what goes on in that state is irrelevant. I think it's been pretty impressive.

**PEROT:** It's not —

**CLINTON:** And the people who have jobs — the people who have jobs and educations and opportunities that didn't have them 10 years ago don't think it's irrelevant at all; they think it's highly relevant and they wish the rest of the country had them.

**BUSH:** I don't have a dog in this fight, but I'd like to get in on this.

**CLINTON:** Well, you think it's relevant.

**BUSH:** Gov. Clinton has to operate under a balanced budget amendment — he has to do it, that is the law. I'd like to see a balanced budget amendment for America, to protect the American taxpayers, and then that would discipline not only the executive branch but the spending Congress, the Congress that's been in control of one party, his party, for 38 years. And we almost had it done.

And that institution, the House of Representatives — everyone is yelling "Clean House!" One of the reasons is we almost had it done, and the Speaker — a very, able, decent fellow, I might add — but he twisted the arms of some of the sponsors of that legislation and had them change their vote. What's relevant here is that tool, that discipline, that he has to live by in Arkansas, and I'd like it for the American people. I want the line-item veto. I want a check-off, so if the Congress can't do it, let people check off their income tax, 10 percent of it, to compel the government to cut spending. And if they can't do it, if the Congress can't do it, let them then have to do it across the board. That's what we call a sequester. That's the discipline we need, and I'm working for that — to protect the American taxpayer against the big spenders.

**LEHRER:** Mr. President, let's move to some of the leadership concerns that have been voiced about you. And they relate to something you said in your closing statement in Richmond the other night about the president being the manager of crises. And that relates to an earlier criticism, that you began to focus on the economy, on health care, on racial divisions in this country, only after they became crises.

Is that a fair criticism?

**BUSH:** Jim, I don't think that's a fair shot. I hear it — I hear it echoed by political opponents. But I don't think it's fair. I think we've been fighting from Day One to do something about the inner cities. I'm for enterprise zones. I have had it in every single proposal I've sent to the Congress. And now we hear a lot of talk, oh, well, we all want enterprise zones, and yet the House and the Senate can't send it down without loading it up with a lot of, you know, these Christmas tree ornaments they put on the legislation.

I don't think in racial harmony that I'm a laggard on that. I've been speaking out since day one. We've gotten the Americans with Disabilities Act, which I think is one of the foremost pieces of civil rights legislation. And yes, it took me to veto two civil rights quota bills because I don't believe in quotas, and I don't think the American people believe in quotas. And I beat back the Congress on that, and then we passed a decent civil rights bill that offers guarantees against discrimination in employment.

And that is good.

I've spoken out over and over again against antisemitism and racism, and I think my record as a member of Congress speaks for itself on that.

What was the other part of it?

**LEHRER:** Well, it's just that — you've spoken to it. I mean, but the idea, not so much in specifics, but that it has to be a crisis before it gets your attention.

**BUSH:** I don't think that's true at all. I don't think that's true, but you know, let others fire away on it.

**LEHRER:** Do you think that's true, Mr. Perot?

**PEROT:** I'd like to just talk about issues, and so —

**LEHRER:** You don't think this is an issue?

**PEROT:** Well, no, but the point is that's a subjective thing. See, the subjective thing is when does President Bush react? And it would be very difficult for me to answer that in any short period of time.

**LEHRER:** Well, then, let's phrase — I'll phrase it differently, then. He said the other night in his closing words in Richmond that one of the key things that he believes the American people should decide between — among the three of you is who they want in charge if this country gets to a crisis.

Now, that's what he said, and the rap on the president is that it's only crisis time that he focuses on some of these things. So my question to you — we're going to talk

about you in a minute — my question to you —

**PEROT:** I thought you'd forgotten I was here.

**LEHRER:** No, no, no, no, no.

But my question to you is, so — if you have nothing to say about it, fine, I'll go to Gov. Clinton, but —

**PEROT:** I will let the American people decide that. I would rather not critique the two candidates.

**LEHRER:** All right. Governor, what do you think?

**CLINTON:** The only thing I would say about that is, I think that on the economy, Mr. Bush said for a long time there was no recession, and then said it would be better to do nothing than to have a compromise effort with the Congress.

He really didn't have a new economic program until over 1300 days into his presidency, and not all of his health-care initiative has been presented to the Congress even now.

I think it's important to elect a president who is committed to getting this economy going again, and who realizes we have to abandon trickle-down economics and put the American people first again, and who will send programs to the Congress in the first hundred days to deal with the critical issues that America is crying out for leadership on — jobs, incomes, the health-care crisis, the need to control the economy. Those things deserve to be dealt with from Day One. I will deal with them from Day One. They will be my first priority, not my election year concern.

**LEHRER:** Mr. President?

**BUSH:** Well, I think you're overlooking that we have had major accomplishments in the first term. But if you're talking about protecting the taxpayer against his friends in the United States Congress, go back to what it was like when you had a Democratic president and a Democratic Congress. You don't have to go back to Herbert Hoover. Go back to Jimmy Carter, and interest rates were 21 percent, inflation was 15 percent. The misery index — unemployment and inflation added together — it was invented by the Democrats — went right through the roof. We've cut it in half.

And all you hear about is how bad things are. You know, remember the question, are you better off? Well, is a home buyer better off he can refinance the home, because interest rates are down? Is the senior citizen better off because inflation is not wiping out their family's savings? I think they are. Is the guy out of work better off? Of course he's not, but he's not gonna be better off if we grow the government, if we invest, as Gov. Clinton says, invest in more government.

You've got to free up the private sector. You've got to let small businesses have more incentives. For three months — three quarters I've been fighting, three quarters been fighting to get the Congress to pass some incentives for small business. Capital gains, investment tax allowance, credit for

first-time home buyers. And it's blocked by the Congress. And then if a little of it comes my way, they load it up with Christmas trees and tax increases, and I have to stand up and favor the taxpayer.

**LEHRER:** I have to — we have to talk about Ross Perot now or he'll get me, I'm sure. Mr. Perot, on this issue that I have raised at the very beginning and we've been talking about, which is leadership, as president of the United States, it concerns — my reading of it, at least, my concerns about you, as expressed by folks in the polls and other places, it goes like this.

You had a problem with General Motors. You took your $750 million and you left. You had a problem in the spring and summer about some personal hits that you took as a potential candidate for president of the United States and you walked out.

Does that say anything relevant to how you would function as president of the United States?

**PEROT:** I think the General Motors thing is very relevant. I did everything I could to get General Motors to face its problems in the mid-'80s while it was still financially strong. They just wouldn't do it, and everybody now knows the terrible price they're paying by waiting until it's obvious to the brain-dead that they have problems.

Now, hundreds, thousands of good, decent people, whole cities up here in this state are adversely impacted because they would not move in a timely way. Our government is that point now. The thing that I am in this race for is to tap the American people on the shoulder and to say to every single one of you, fix it while we're still relatively strong. If you have a heart problem, you don't wait till a heart attack to address it.

So the General Motors experience is relevant. At the point when I could not get them to address those problems, I had created so much stress in the board, who wanted to just keep the Lawrence Welk music going, that they asked to buy my remaining shares. I sold them my remaining shares. They went their way. I went my way because it was obvious we had a complete disagreement about what should be done with the company.

But let's take my life in perspective. Again and again, on complex, difficult tasks, I have stayed the course. When I was asked by our government to do the POW project, within a year the Vietnamese had sent people into Canada to make arrangements to have me and my family killed. And I had five small children, and my family and I decided we would stay the course, and we lived with that problem for three years.

Then I got into the Texas War on Drugs program and the big-time drug dealers got all upset. Then when I had two people imprisoned in Iran, I could have left them there. I could have rationalized it. We went over, we got them out, we brought them back home. And since then, for years, I have lived with the burden of the Middle

East, where it's eye for an eye and tooth for a tooth country, in terms of their unhappiness with the fact that I was successful in that effort.

Again and again and again, in the middle of the night, at 2 or 3 o'clock in the morning, my government has called me to take extraordinary steps for Americans in distress, and again and again and again I have responded. And I didn't wilt and I didn't quit.

Now, what happened in July we've covered again and again and again. But I think in terms of the American people's concern about my commitment, I'm here tonight, folks; I never quit supporting you as you put me on the ballot in the other 26 states; and when you asked me to come back in, I came back in. And talk about not quitting, I'm spending my money on this campaign; the two parties are spending your money, taxpayer money. I put my wallet on the table for you and your children. Over $60 million at least will go into this campaign to lead the American dream to you and your children, to get this country straightened out, because if anybody owes it to you, I do. I've lived the American dream; I'd like for your children to be able to live it, too.

**LEHRER:** Governor, do you have a response to the staying-the-course question about Mr. Perot?

**CLINTON:** I don't have any criticism of Mr. Perot. I think what I'd like to talk about a minute, since you're asking the question, is the General Motors issue. I don't think there's any question that the automobile executives made some errors in the 1980s, but I also think we should look at how much productivity has increased lately, how much labor has done to increase productivity and how much management has done. And we're still losing a lot of auto jobs, in my judgment, because we don't have a national economic strategy that will build the industrial base of this country.

Just today I met with the presidents and the vice presidents of the Willow Run union here, near here. They both said they were Vietnam veterans supporting me because I had an economic program to put them back to work. We need an investment incentive to modernize plant and equipment; we've got to control the health-care costs for those people — otherwise we can't keep the manufacturing jobs here; and we need a tough trade policy that is fair, that insists on open markets and return for open markets. We ought to have a strategy that will build the economic and industrial base.

So I think Mr. Perot was right in questioning the management practices. But they didn't have much of a partner in government here as compared with the policies the Germans and the Japanese followed, and I believe we can do better. That's one of the things I want to change. I know that we can grow manufacturing jobs. We did it in my state, and we can do it nationally.

**LEHRER:** Mr. President, do you have a response?

**BUSH:** To this?

**LEHRER:** Yes.

**BUSH:** Well, I wondered, when Gov. Clinton was talking to the auto workers, whether he talked about his and Sen. Gore's favoring CAFE standards, fuel efficiency standards, of 40 miles per gallon. That would break the auto industry and throw a lot of people out of work.

As regarding Mr. Perot, I take back something I said about him. I once said, in a frivolous moment, when he got out of the race: If you can't stand the heat, buy an air-conditioning company. And I take it back, because I think — he said he made a mistake. And the thing I find is if I make a mistake, I admit it. I've never heard Gov. Clinton make a mistake.

But one mistake he's made is fuel efficiency standards at 40 to 45 miles a gallon will throw many auto workers out of work, and you can't have it both ways. There's a pattern here of appealing to the auto workers and then trying to appeal to the spotted owl crowds or the extremes in the environmental movement. You can't do it as president: you can't have a pattern of one side of the issue one day and another the next.

So my argument is not with Ross Perot; it is more with Gov. Clinton.

**LEHRER:** Governor, what about that charge? Do you want it both ways on this issue?

**CLINTON:** Let's just talk about the CAFE standards — that's the fuel efficiency standards. They are now 27.5 miles per gallon per automobile fleet. I never said — and I defy you to find where I said — I gave an extensive environmental speech in April, and I said that we ought to have a goal of raising the fuel efficiency standards to 40 miles a gallon. I think that should be a goal. I have never said we should write it into law if there is evidence that that goal cannot be achieved. The National Science Foundation did a study which said it would be difficult for us to reach fuel efficiency standards in excess of 37 miles per gallon by the year 2000.

I think we should try to raise the fuel efficiency. And let me say this. I think we ought to have incentives to do it, I think we ought to push to do it. That doesn't mean we have to write it into the law.

Look, I am a job creator, not a job destroyer. It is the Bush administration that has had no new jobs in the private sector in the last four years. In my state, we're leading the country in private sector job growth.

But it is good for America to improve fuel efficiency. We also ought to convert more vehicles to compressed natural gas. That's another way to improve the environment.

**LEHRER:** Mr. Perot, based on your experience at General Motors, where do you come down on this? This has been thrown about, back and forth, during this campaign from the very beginning about jobs and CAFE standards.

**PEROT:** Well, everybody's nibbling around the edges. Let's go to the center of the bull's-eye, the core problem. And believe me, everybody on the factory floor all over this country knows it. You implement that NAFTA, the Mexican trade agreement, where they pay people a dollar an hour, have no health care, no retirement, no pollution controls, et cetera, et cetera, et cetera, and you're going to hear a giant sucking sound of jobs being pulled out of this country right at a time when we need the tax base to pay the debt and pay down the interest on the debt and get our house back in order.

We've got to proceed very carefully on that. See, there's a lot I don't understand. I do understand business. I do understand creating jobs. I do understand how to make things work. And I got a long history of doing that.

Now, if you want to go to the core problem that faces everybody in manufacturing in this country, it's that agreement that's about to be put into practice. It's very simple. Everybody says it'll create jobs. Yes, it'll create bubble jobs.

Now, you know, watch this — listen very carefully to this. One-time surge while we build factories and ship machine tools and equipment down there. Then year after year for decades, they will have jobs. And I finally — I thought I didn't understand it — called all the experts, and they said, oh, it'll be disruptive for 12 to 15 years.

We haven't got 12 days, folks. We cannot lose those jobs. They were eventually saying, Mexican jobs will eventually come to $7.50 an hour, ours will eventually go down to $7.50 an hour. Makes you feel real good to hear that, right?

Let's think it through here. Let's be careful. I'm for free trade philosophically, but I have studied these trade agreements till the world has gone flat, and we don't have good trade agreements across the world.

I hope we'll have a chance to get into that tonight, because I can get right to the center of the bull's-eye and tell you why we're losing whole industries in this country.

**LEHRER:** Just for the record, though, Mr. Perot, I take it, then, from your answer, you do not have a position on whether or not enforcing the CAFE standards will cost jobs in the auto industry?

**PEROT:** Oh, no, it will cost jobs, but that's not — let me say this. I'd rather, if you gave me two bad choices —

**LEHRER:** Okay.

**PEROT:** I'd rather have some jobs left here than just see everything head south, see?

**LEHRER:** So that means — in other words, you agree with President Bush; is that right?

**PEROT:** No, I'm saying our principal need now is to stabilize the tax base, which is the job base, and create a growing, dynamic base. Now please, folks, if you don't hear anything else I say, remember where the — millions of people at work are our tax base.

One quick point. If you confiscate the Forbes 400 wealth, take it all, you cannot balance the budget this year. Kind of gets your head straight about where the taxes, year in and year out, have gotta come from. Millions and millions of people at work.

**LEHRER:** Yes, sir.

**BUSH:** I'm caught in the middle on NAFTA. Ross says, with great conviction, he opposes the North American Free Trade Agreement. I am for the North American Free Trade Agreement. My problem with Gov. Clinton, once again, is that one time he's gonna make up his mind, he sees some merit in it, but then he sees a lot of things wrong with it. Then the other day he says he's for it, however then we've got to pass other legislation.

When you're president of the United States, you cannot have this pattern of saying well, I'm for it but I'm on the other side of it. And it's true on this and it's true on CAFE.

Look, if Ross were right when we get a free trade agreement with Mexico, why wouldn't they have gone down there now? You have a differential in wages right now. I just have an honest philosophical difference. I think free trade is going to expand our job opportunity. I think it is exports that have saved us when we're in a global slowdown, a connected global slowdown, a recession in some countries. And it's free trade, fair trade that needs to be our hallmark, and we need more free trade agreements, not fewer.

**LEHRER:** Governor, quick answer on trade and I want to go on to something else.

**CLINTON:** I'd like to respond to that. You know, Mr. Bush was very grateful when I was among the Democrats who said he ought to have the authority to negotiate an agreement with Mexico. Neither I nor anybody else, as far a I know, agreed to give him our proxy to say that whatever he did was fine for the workers of this country and for the interests of this country.

I am the one who's in the middle on this. Mr. Perot says it's a bad deal. Mr. Bush says it's a hunky-dory deal. I say on balance it does more good than harm if, if we can get some protection for the environment so that the Mexicans have to follow their own environmental standards, their own labor law standards, and if we have a genuine commitment to reeducate and retrain the American workers who lose their jobs and reinvest in this economy.

I have a realistic approach to trade. I want more trade, and I know there are some good things in that agreement. But it can sure be made better.

Let me just point out, just today in the Los Angeles Times, Clyde Prestowitz, who was one of President Reagan's leading trade advisers and a lifelong conservative Republican, endorsed my candidacy because he knows that I'll have a free and fair trade policy, a hard-headed, realistic policy, and not get caught up in rubber-stamping everything the Bush administration did. If I wanted to do that, why would

I run for president, Jim? Anybody else can run the middle class down and run the economy in a ditch. I want to change it.

**LEHRER:** We've got about four —

**BUSH:** I think he made my case. On the one hand, it's a good deal but on the other hand I'd make it better. You can't do that as president. You can't do it on the war, where he says well, I was with the minority but I guess I would have voted with the majority.

This is my point tonight. We're talking about two weeks from now you've gotta decide who's gonna be president. And there is this pattern that has plagued in him the primaries and now about trying to have it both ways on all these issues. You can't do that. And if you make a mistake, say you made a mistake and go on about your business, trying to serve the American people.

Right now we heard it. Ross is against it. I am for it. He says on the one hand I am for it and on the other hand I may be against it.

**LEHRER:** The governor —

**CLINTON:** That's what's wrong with Mr. Bush. His whole deal is you've gotta be for it or against it, you can't make it better. I believe we can be better. I think the American people are sick and tired of either/or solutions, people being pushed in the corner, polarized to extremes.

I think they want somebody with common sense who can do what's best for the American people. And I'd be happy to discuss these other issues, but I can't believe he is accusing me of getting on both sides. He said trickle-down economics was voodoo economics; now he's its biggest practitioner.

He promised — he — you know — let me just say —

**BUSH:** But I've always said trickle-down government is bad.

**CLINTON:** I could run this string out a long time, but remember this, Jim. Those 209 Americans last Thursday night in Richmond told us they wanted us to stop talking about each other and start talking about Americans and their problems and their promise, and I think we ought to get back to that.

I'll be glad to answer any question you have, but this election ought to be about the American people.

**LEHRER:** Mr. Perot.

**PEROT:** Is there an equal time rule tonight?

**BUSH:** Yes.

**PEROT:** Or do you just keep lunging in at will? I thought we were going to have equal time, but maybe I just have to interrupt the other two. Is that the way it works?

**LEHRER:** No, it's — Mr. Perot, you're doing fine. Go ahead. Whatever you want to say, say it.

**PEROT:** Now that we've talked all around the problem about free trade, let's go again to the center of the bull's-eye.

**LEHRER:** Wait a minute. I was going to ask — I thought you wanted to respond to what we're talking about.

**PEROT:** I do, I do.

**LEHRER:** All right.

**PEROT:** I just want to make — foreign lobbyists, this whole thing. Our country has sold out to foreign lobbyists. We don't have free trade. Both parties have foreign lobbyists on leave in key roles in their campaigns. And if there's anything more unwise than that, I don't know what it is. Every debate I bring this up, and nobody ever addresses it.

I would like for them to look you in the eye and tell you why they have people representing foreign countries working on their campaigns. And you know, you've seen the list, I've seen the list, we won't go into the names, but no wonder they — if I had those people around me all day every day, telling me it was fair and free, I might believe it. But if I look at the facts as a businessman, it's so tilted, the first thing you ought to do is just say, guys, if you like these deals so well, we'll give you the deal you gave us.

Now, Japanese couldn't unload the cars in this country if they had the same restrictions we had, and on and on and on and on and on. I suggest to you that the core problem — one country spent $400 million lobbying in 1988, our country. And it goes on and on. And you look at a who's who in these campaigns around the two candidates. They're foreign lobbyists taking leave. What do you think they're going to do when the campaign's over? Go back to work at 30,000 bucks a month representing some other country. I don't believe that's in the American people's interest.

I don't have a one of them, and I haven't taken a penny of foreign money, and I never will.

**LEHRER:** Mr. President, how do you respond to that? Mr. Perot's made that charge several times. The fact that you have people working in your campaign who are paid foreign lobbyists.

**BUSH:** Most people that are lobbying are lobbying the Congress. And I don't think there's anything wrong with an honest person who happens to represent an interest of another country for making his case. That's the American way. And what you're assuming is that that makes the recipient of the lobbying corrupt or the lobbyist himself corrupt. I don't agree with that.

But if I found somebody that had a conflict of interest that would try to illegally do something as a foreign — registered lobby, the laws cover this. I don't know why — I've never understood quite why Mr. Perot was so upset about it, because one of the guys he used to have working for him, I believe, had foreign accounts. Could be wrong, but I think so.

**PEROT:** And as soon as I found it out, he went out the door.

**BUSH:** Well —

But I don't — I think you got to look at the integrity and the honor of the people that are being lobbied and those that are lobbyists. The laws protect the American taxpayer in this regard. If the laws are vio-

lated so much, but to suggest if somebody represents a foreign country on anything, that makes him corrupt or against the taxpayer, I don't agree with that.

**PEROT:** One quick relevant specific. We're getting ready to dismantle the airlines industry in our country, and none of you know it. And I doubt in all candor if the president knows it. But this deal that we're doing with BAC and USAir and KLM and Northwest, guess who's on the president's campaign big time: a guy from Northwest. This deal is terribly destructive to the U.S. airline industry. One of the largest industries in the world is the travel, tourist business. We won't be making airplanes in this country 10 years from now if we let deals like this go through.

If the president has any interest tonight, I'll detail it to you; I won't take 10 minutes tonight. All these things take a few minutes. But that's happening as we sit here today.

We hammerlock the American companies — American Airlines, Delta — the last few great we have, because we're trying to do this deal with these two European companies. And never forget, they've got Airbus over there, and it's a government-owned, privately owned, consortium across Europe. They're dying to get the commercial airline business. Japan is trying to get the commercial airline business.

I don't think there are any villains inside government on this issue, but there's sure a lot of people who don't understand business. And maybe you need somebody up there who understands when you're getting your pocket picked.

**CLINTON:** Jim.

**LEHRER:** Governor, I'm sorry, but that concludes my time with — well, you —

**CLINTON:** Why, I had a great response to that.

**LEHRER:** All right, go ahead, quick, quickly.

**CLINTON:** Just very briefly. I think Ross is right and that we do need some more restrictions on lobbyists. We ought to make them disclose the people they've given money to when they're testifying before congressional committees; we ought to close the lawyers' loopholes, they ought to have to disclose when they're really lobbying. And we ought to have to limit — we ought to have a much longer period of time, about five years, between the time when people can leave executive branch offices and then go out and start lobbying for foreign interests. I agree with that.

We've wrecked the airline industry already because of all these leveraged buyouts and all these terrible things that have happened to the airline industry. We're going to have a hard time rebuilding it.

But the real thing we got to have is a competitive economic strategy. Look what's happening to McDonnell Douglas; even Boeing is losing market share — because we let the Europeans spend $25 to $40 billion on Airbus without an appropriate competitive response.

What I want America to do is to trade more but to compete and win by investing in competitive ways. And we're in real trouble on that.

**LEHRER:** I'm going to be in real trouble if I don't bring out — it's now time —

**BUSH:** I promise it's less than 10 seconds.

**LEHRER:** Okay.

**BUSH:** I heard Gov. Clinton congratulate us on one thing — first time he said something pleasant about this administration. Productivity in this country is up, it is way up — productivity is up. And that's a good thing. There are many good ones, but I was glad he acknowledged that. Thank you.

**LEHRER:** Now we're going to move to the second half —

**PEROT:** Now give me one second —

**LEHRER:** We're going to move to the —

**PEROT:** I've volunteered. Now, look, I'm just kind of a, you know, cur dog here; I was put on the ballot by the people, not special interests. So I have to stand up for myself. Now, Jim, let me net it out. On the second debate, I offered, since both sides want the enterprise zones and we can't get together, I said I'll take a few days off and go to Washington and hold hands with you and we'll get it done; I'll take a few days off and hold hands with you and get this airlines thing straightened, because that's important to this country. That's kind of pathetic I have to do it — and nobody's called me yet to come up, I might mention.

**LEHRER:** All right, I want to bring in —

**PEROT:** But if they do — if they do, it's easy to fix. If you all want the enterprise zones, why don't we pass the dang thing and do it, right?

**LEHRER:** All right. Now we're going to bring in three other journalists to ask questions. They are Susan Rook of CNN, Gene Gibbons of Reuters and Helen Thomas of United Press International. You thought you'd never get in here, did you?

**BUSH:** Uh-uh. Uh-uh.

**LEHRER:** Okay, we're going to continue on the subject of leadership and the first question goes to Gov. Clinton for a two-minute answer. It will be asked by Helen Thomas. Helen?

**THOMAS:** Gov. Clinton, your credibility has come into question because of your different responses on the Vietnam draft. If you had it to do over again, would you put on the nation's uniform, and if elected, could you in good conscience send someone to war?

**CLINTON:** If I had it to do over again I might answer the questions a little better. You know, I'd been in public life a long time and no one had ever questioned my role and so I was asked a lot of questions about things that happened a long time ago and I don't think I answered them as well as I could have.

Going back 23 years, I don't know, Helen. I was opposed to the war. I couldn't

help that. I felt very strongly about it, and I didn't want to go at the time. It's easy to say in retrospect I would have done something differently.

President Lincoln opposed the war and there were people who said maybe he shouldn't be president, but I think he made us a pretty good president in wartime. We've had a lot of other presidents who didn't wear their country's uniform who had to order our young soldiers into battle, including President Wilson and President Roosevelt.

So the answer is I could do that. I wouldn't relish doing it but I wouldn't shrink from it. I think that the president has to be prepared to use the power of the nation when our vital interests are threatened, when our treaty commitments are at stake, when we know that something has to be done that is in the national interest, and that is a part of being president.

Could I do it? Yes, I could.

**LEHRER:** A reminder now. We're back on the St. Louis rules, which means that the governor had his answer and then each of you will have one minute to respond. Mr. President.

**BUSH:** Well, I've expressed my heartfelt difference with Gov. Clinton on organizing demonstrations while in a foreign land against your country, when young ghetto kids have been drafted and are dying.

My argument with him on — the question was about the draft — is that there's this same pattern. In New Hampshire Sen. Kerrey said you ought to level, you ought to tell the truth about it. On April 17 he said he'd bring out all the records on the draft. They have not been forthcoming. He got a deferment or he didn't. He got a notice or he didn't. And I think it's this pattern that troubles me, more than the draft. A lot of decent, honorable people felt as he did on the draft. But it's this pattern.

And again, you might be able to make amendments all the time, Governor, but you've got to, as president, you can't be on all these different sides, and you can't have this pattern of saying well, I did this or I didn't, then the facts come out and you change it.

That's my big difference with him on the draft. It wasn't failing to serve.

**LEHRER:** Your minute is up, sir.

**BUSH:** Yes, sir.

**LEHRER:** Mr. Perot, one minute.

**PEROT:** I've spent my whole adult life very close to the military. I feel very strongly about the people who go into battle for our country. I appreciate their idealism, their sacrifices. Appreciate the sacrifices their families make. That's been displayed again and again in a very tangible way.

I look on this as history. I don't look on it personally as relevant, and I consider it really a waste of time tonight, when you consider the issues that face our country right now.

**LEHRER:** All right. The next question goes to President Bush and Gene Gib-

bons will ask it. Gene.

**GIBBONS:** Mr. President, you keep saying that you made a mistake in agreeing to a tax increase to get the 1990 budget deal with Congress. But if you hadn't gotten that deal, you would have either had to get repeal of the Gramm-Rudman Deficit Control Act or cut defense spending drastically at a time when the country was building up for the gulf war, and decimate domestic discretionary spending, including such things as air traffic control.

If you had it to do all over again, sir, which of those alternatives would you choose?

**BUSH:** I wouldn't have taken any of the alternatives. I believe that — I believe I made a mistake. I did it for the very reasons you say. There was one good thing that came out of that budget agreement, and that is we put a cap on discretionary spending. One-third of the president's budget is at the president's discretion, or really the Congress, since they appropriate every time and tell a president how to spend every dime. We've put a cap on the growth of all that spending, and that's good and that's helped.

But I was wrong because I thought the tax compromise, going along with one Democratic tax increase, would help the economy. I see no evidence that it has done it.

So what would I have done? What should I have done? I should have held out for a better deal that would have protected the taxpayer and not ended up doing what we had to do, or what I thought at the time would help.

So I made a mistake, and I — you know, the difference, I think, is that I knew at the time I was going to take a lot of political flak. I knew we'd have somebody out there yelling "read my lips", and I did it because I thought it was right. And I made a mistake. That's quite different than taking a position where you know it's best for you. That wasn't best for me and I knew it in the very beginning. I thought it would be better for the country than it was. So there we are.

**LEHRER:** Mr. Perot, one minute.

**PEROT:** 101 in Leadership is be accountable for what you do. Let's go back to the tax and budget summit briefly. Nobody ever told the American people that we increased spending $1.83 for every dollar of taxes raised. That's absolutely unconscionable. Both parties carry a huge blame for that on their shoulders.

This was not a way to pay down the deficit. This was a trick on the American people. That's not leadership.

Let's go back in terms of accepting responsibility for your actions. If you create Saddam Hussein, over a ten-year period, using billions of dollars of U.S. taxpayer money, step up to the plate and say it was a mistake. If you create Noriega, using taxpayer money, step up to the plate and say it was a mistake. If you can't get your act together to pick him up one day when a Panamanian major has kidnapped

him and a Special Forces team is 400 yards away and it's a stroll across the park to get him, and if you can't get your act together, at least pick up the Panamanian major, who they then killed, step up to the plate and admit it was a mistake. That's leadership, folks.

Now, leaders will always make mistakes. We've created, and I'm not aiming at any one person here, I'm aiming at our government — nobody takes responsibility for anything. We've gotta change that.

**LEHRER:** I'm taking responsibility for saying your time's up.

**PEROT:** I'm watching the lights.

**LEHRER:** All right. Gov. Clinton, one minute, sir.

**CLINTON:** The mistake that was made was making the "read my lips" promise in the first place just to get elected, knowing what the size of the deficit was.

Knowing what the size of the deficit was, knowing there was no plan to control health-care costs and knowing that we did not have a strategy to get real economic growth back into this economy. The choices were not good then. I think at the time, the mistake that was made was signing off on the deal late on Saturday night in the middle of the night. That's just what the president did when he vetoed the Family Leave Act.

I think what he should have done is gone before the American people on the front end and said listen, I made a commitment and it was wrong. I made a mistake because I couldn't have foreseen these circumstances and this is the best deal we can work out at the time. He said it was in the public interest at the time and most everybody who was involved in it, I guess, thought it was. The real mistake was the "read my lips" promise in the first place. You just can't promise something like that just to get elected if you know there's a good chance that circumstances may overtake you.

**LEHRER:** All right, Mr. Perot, the question is for you. You have a two-minute answer, and it will be asked by Susan Rook.

**ROOK:** Mr. Perot, you've talked about going to Washington to do what the people who run this country want you to do. But it is the president's duty to lead, and often lead alone. How can you lead if you are forever seeking consensus before you act?

**PEROT:** You're talking about two different subjects. In order to lead, you first have to use the White House as a bully pulpit and lead; then you have to develop consensus or you can't get anything done, and that's where we are now. We can't get anything done.

How do you get anything done when you've got all of these political action committees, all of these thousands of registered lobbyists — 40,000 registered lobbyists, 23,000 special interest groups — and the list goes on and on and on. And the average citizen out here is just working hard every day. You've got to go to the people.

I just love the fact that everybody, par-

ticularly in the media, goes bonkers over the town hall. I guess it's because you will lose your right to tell them what to think. The point is, they'll get to decide what to think.

I love the fact that people will listen to a guy with a bad accent and a poor presentation manner talking about flip charts for 30 minutes, because they want the details. See, all the folks up there at the top said the attention span of the American people is no more than five minutes, they won't watch it. They're thirsty for it.

You want to have a new program in this country. If you get grassroots America excited about it, and if they tap Congress on the shoulder and say, "Do it, Charlie," it'll happen. And that's a whole lot different from these fellows running up and down the halls whispering in their ears now and promising campaign funds for the next election if they do it.

Now, I think that's going back to where we started. That's having a government from the people. I think that's the essence of leadership, rather than cutting deals in dark rooms in Washington.

**LEHRER:** Gov. Clinton, one minute.

**CLINTON:** Well, I believe in the town hall meetings; they started with my campaign in New Hampshire. And I think Ross Perot has done a good job in having them. And I, as you know, pushed for the debate to include the 209 American citizens who were part of it in Richmond a few days ago. I've done a lot of them, and I'll continue to do them as president.

But I'd also like to point out that I haven't been part of what we're criticizing in Washington tonight. Of the three of us, I have balanced a government budget 12 times, I have offered and passed campaign finance reform, offered, pushed for and passed in public referendum lobbyist restrictions, done the kinds of things you have to do to get legislators together not only to establish consensus but to challenge them to change.

And in 12 years as governor I guess I've taken on every interest group there was in my state at one time or another to fight for change. It can be done. That's why I tried to be so specific in this campaign to have a mandate, if elected, so that Congress will know what the American people have voted for.

**LEHRER:** President Bush, one minute.

**BUSH:** I would like the record to show the panelists that Ross Perot took the first shot at the press. My favorite bumper sticker, though, is: Annoy the Media. Re-elect President Bush. And I just had to work that in. Sorry, Helen. I'm going to pay for this later on.

Look, you have to build a consensus, but in some things — Ross mentioned Saddam Hussein. Yes, we tried, and, yes, we failed to bring him into the family of nations; he had the fourth-largest army. But then when he moved against Kuwait, I said this will not stand. And it's hard to build a consensus. We went to the U.N., we

made historic resolutions up there, the whole world was united, our Congress was dragging its feet. Gov. Clinton said, well, I might have been with the minority, let sanctions work — but I guess I would have voted with the majority.

A president can't do that. Sometimes he has to act. And in this case I'm glad we did, because if we had let sanctions work and tried to build a consensus on that, Saddam Hussein today would be in Saudi Arabia controlling the world's oil supply, and he would be there maybe with a nuclear weapon. We busted the fourth-largest army, and we did it through leadership.

**LEHRER:** All right, we're going to go on to another subject now, and the subject is priorities. The first question goes to you, President Bush, and Susan will ask it.

**ROOK:** President Bush, gentlemen, I acknowledge that all of you have women and ethnic minorities working for you and working with you. But when we look at the circle of the key people closest to you, your inner circle of advisers, we see white men only. Why? And when will that change?

**BUSH:** You don't see Margaret Tutwiler sitting in there with me today.

**ROOK:** The key people, President Bush.

**BUSH:** Huh?

**ROOK:** The key people, the people beyond the glass ceiling.

**BUSH:** I happen to think she's a key person. I think our Cabinet members are key people. I think the woman that works with me, Rose Zamaria, is about as tough as a boot out there and makes some discipline and protects the taxpayer.

Look at our Cabinet. You talk about somebody strong. Look at Carla Hills. Look at Lynn Martin, who's fighting against this glass ceiling and doing a first-class job on it. Look at our surgeon general, Dr. Novello. You can look all around and you'll see first-class, strong women.

Jim Baker's a man. Yeah, I plead guilty to that.

But look who's around with him there. I mean, this is a little defensive on your part, Susan, to be honest with you. We've got a very good record appointing women to high positions and positions of trust, and I'm not defensive at all about it. What we got to do is keep working, as the Labor Department is doing a first-class job on, to break down discrimination, to break down the glass ceiling.

And I am not apologetic at all about our record with women. We've got, I think — you know, you think about women in government, I think about women in business. Why not try to help them with my small business program to build some incentives into the system? I think we're making progress here.

You got a lot of women running for office. As I said the other night, I hope a lot of them lose because they're liberal Democrats — and we don't need more of them in the Senate or more of them in the House. But nevertheless, they're out there. And we got some very good Republican women

running. So we're making dramatic progress.

**LEHRER:** Mr. Perot, one minute.

**PEROT:** Well, I come from the computer business, and everybody knows the women are more talented than the men. So we have a long history of having a lot of talented women. One of our first officers was a woman, the chief financial officer. She was a director. And it was so far back, it was considered so odd, and even though we were a tiny, little company at the time, it made all the national magazines.

But in terms of being influenced by women and being a minority, there they are right out there, my wife and my four beautiful daughters, and I just have one son, so he and I are surrounded by women, giving — telling us what to do all the time.

And the rest of my minute, I want to make a very brief comment here in terms of Saddam Hussein. We told him that we wouldn't get involved with his border dispute, and we've never revealed those papers that were given to Ambassador Glaspie on July the 25th. I suggest, in the sense of taking responsibility for your actions, we lay those papers on the table. They're not the secrets to the nuclear bomb.

Secondly, we got upset when he took the whole thing, but to the ordinary American out there who doesn't know where the oil fields are in Kuwait, they're near the border. We told him he could take the northern part of Kuwait, and when he took the whole thing, we went nuts. And if we didn't tell him that, why won't we even let the Senate Foreign Relations Committee and the Senate Intelligence Committee see the written instructions for Ambassador Glaspie?

**BUSH:** I've got reply on that. That gets to the national honor. We did not say to Saddam Hussein, Ross, you can take the northern part of Kuwait.

**PEROT:** Well, where are the papers?

**BUSH:** That is absolutely absurd.

**PEROT:** Where are the papers?

**BUSH:** Glaspie has testified — and Glaspie's papers have been presented to the United States Senate. Please, let's be factual.

**PEROT:** If you have time, go through Nexis and Lexis, pull all the old news articles, look at what Ambassador Glaspie said all through the fall and what have you, and then look at what she and Kelly and all the others in State said at the end when they were trying to clean it up. And talk to any head of any of those key committees in the Senate. They will not let them see the written instructions given to Ambassador Glaspie. And I suggest that in a free society owned by the people, the American people ought to know what we told Ambassador Glaspie to tell Saddam Hussein, because we spent a lot of money and risked lives and lost lives in that effort, and did not accomplish most of our objectives.

We got Kuwait back to the emir but he's still not his nuclear, his chemical, his bacteriological and he's still over there,

right? I'd like to see those written instructions.

**LEHRER:** Mr. President, just to make sure that everybody knows what's going on here, when you responded directly to Mr. Perot, you violated the rule, your rules. Now —

**BUSH:** For which I apologize. When I make a mistake I say I'm sorry.

**LEHRER:** I just want to make sure everybody understands. If you all want to change the rules, we can do it.

**BUSH:** No, I don't. I apologize for it but that one got right to the national honor and I'm sorry. I just couldn't let it stand.

**LEHRER:** Gov. Clinton, you have a minute.

**CLINTON:** Susan, I don't agree that there are no women and minorities in important positions in my campaign. There are many. But I think even more relevant is my record at home. For most of my time as governor a woman was my chief of staff. An African-American was my chief cabinet officer. An African-American was my chief economic development officer.

It was interesting today. There was a story today or yesterday in The Washington Post about my economic programs and my chief budget officer and my chief economic officer were both African-Americans, even though the Post didn't mention that, which I think is a sign of progress.

The National Women's Political Caucus gave me an award, one of their Good Guy Awards, for my involvement of women in high levels of government, and I've appointed more minorities to positions of high level in government than all the governors in the history of my state combined, before me.

So that's what I'll do as president. I don't think we've got a person to waste and I think I owe the American people a White House staff, a Cabinet and appointments that look like America but that meet high standards of excellence, and that's what I'll do.

**LEHRER:** All right. Next question goes to you, Mr. Perot. It's a two-minute question and Helen will ask it. Helen?

**THOMAS:** Mr. Perot, what proof do you have that Saddam Hussein was told that he could have the — do you have any actual proof or are you asking for the papers? And also, I really came in with another question. What is this penchant you have to investigate everyone? Are those accusations correct — investigating your staff, investigating the leaders of the grassroots movement, investigating associates of your family?

**PEROT:** No. They're not correct and if you look at my life, until I got involved in this effort, I was one person. And then after the Republican dirty tricks group got through with me I'm another person, which I consider an absolutely sick operation. And all of you in the press know exactly what I'm talking about.

They investigated every single one of my children. They investigated my wife. They interviewed all of my children's

friends from childhood on. They went to extraordinary, sick lengths, and I just found it amusing that they would take two or three cases where I was involved in lawsuits and would engage an investigator — the lawyers would engage an investigator, which is common. And the only difference between me and any other businessman that has the range of businesses that I have is I haven't had that many lawsuits.

So that's just another one of those little fruit-loopy things they make up to try to, instead of facing issues, to try to redefine a person that's running against them. This goes on night and day. I will do everything I can, if I get up there, to make dirty tricks a thing of the past. One of the two groups has raised it to an art form. It's a sick art form.

Now, let's go back to Saddam Hussein. We gave Ambassador Glaspie written instructions. That's a fact. We've never let the Congress and the Foreign Relations, Senate Intelligence Committees see them. That's a fact. Ambassador Glaspie did a lot of talking right after July 25 and that's a fact and it's in all the newspapers. And you pull all of it at once and read it and I did, and it's pretty clear what she and Kelly and the other key guys around that thing thought they were doing.

Then at the end of the war, when they had to go testify about it, their stories are a total disconnect from what they said in August, September and October.

So I say this is very simple. Saddam Hussein released a tape, as you know, claiming it was a transcript of their meeting, where she said we will not become involved in your border dispute and, in effect, you can take the northern part of the country. We later said no, that's not true. I said well, this is simple. What were her written instructions? We guard those like the secrets of the atomic bomb, literally.

Now, I say whose country is this? This is ours. Who will get hurt if we lay those papers on the table? The worst thing is, again, it's a mistake. Nobody did any of this with evil intent. I just object to the fact that we cover up and hide things. Whether it's Iran-contra, Iraq-gate or you name it, it's a steady stream.

**LEHRER:** Gov. Clinton, you have one minute.

**CLINTON:** Let's take Mr. Bush for the moment at his word — he's right, we don't have any evidence at least that our government did tell Saddam Hussein he could have that part of Kuwait. And let's give him the credit he deserves for organizing Operation Desert Storm and Desert Shield. It was a remarkable event.

But let's look at where I think the real mistake was made. In 1988 when the war between Iraq and Iran ended, we knew Saddam Hussein was a tyrant; we had dealt with him because he was against Iran — the enemy of my enemy maybe is my friend.

All right, the war's over; we know he's dropping mustard gas on his own people, we know he's threatened to incinerate half of Israel. Several government departments — several — had information that he was converting our aid to military purposes and trying to develop weapons of mass destruction. But in late '89 the president signed a secret policy saying we were going to continue to try to improve relations with him, and we sent him some sort of communication on the eve of his invasion of Kuwait that we still wanted better relations.

So I think what was wrong — I give credit where credit is due — but the responsibility was in coddling Saddam Hussein when there was no reason to do it and when people at high levels in our government knew he was trying to do things that were outrageous.

**LEHRER:** Mr. President, you have a moment — a minute, I'm sorry.

**BUSH:** Well, it's awful easy when you're dealing with 90-90 hindsight. We did try to bring Saddam Hussein into the family of nations; he did have the fourth largest army. All our Arab allies out there thought we ought to do just exactly that. And when he crossed the line, I stood up and looked into the camera and I said: This aggression will not stand. And we formed a historic coalition, and we brought him down, and we destroyed the fourth-largest army. And the battlefield was searched, and there wasn't one single iota of evidence that any U.S. weapons were on that battlefield. And the nuclear capability has been searched by the United Nations, and there hasn't been one single scintilla of evidence that there's any U.S. technology involved in it.

And what you're seeing on all this Iraq-gate is a bunch of people who were wrong on the war trying to cover their necks and try to do a little revisionism. And I cannot let that stand, because it isn't true.

Yes, we had grain credits for Iraq, and there isn't any evidence that those grain credits were diverted into weaponry — none, none whatsoever.

And so I just have to say, it's fine. You can't stand there, Gov. Clinton, and say, well, I think I'd have been — I have supported the minority, let sanctions work or wish it would go away — but I would have voted with the majority. Come on, that's not leadership.

**LEHRER:** All right, the next question goes to Gov. Clinton, and Gene Gibbons will ask it. Gene?

**GIBBONS:** Governor, an important aspect of leadership is, of course, anticipating problems. During the 1988 campaign there was little or no mention of the savings and loan crisis that has cost the American people billions and billions of dollars. Now there are rumblings that a commercial bank crisis is on the horizon.

Is there such a problem, sir? If so, how bad is it and what will it cost to clean it up?

**CLINTON:** Gene, there is a problem in the sense that there are some problem banks, and on December 19th new regulations will go into effect which will in effect give the government the responsibility to close some banks that are not technically insolvent but that are plainly in trouble.

On the other hand, I don't think that we have any reason to believe that the dimensions of this crisis are anywhere near as great as the savings and loan crisis. The mistake that both parties made in Washington with the S&L business was deregulating them without proper capital requirements, proper oversight and regulation, proper training of the executives. Many people predicted what happened, and it was a disaster.

The banking system in this country is fundamentally sound with some weak banks. I think that our goal ought to be first of all not to politicize it, not to frighten people; secondly to say that we have to enforce the law in two ways.

We don't want to overreact, as the federal regulators have in my judgment, on good banks so that they've created credit crunches, that is, they have made our recession worse in the last couple of years — but we do want to act prudently with the banks that are in trouble.

We also want to say that insofar as is humanly possible the banking industry itself should pay for the cost of any bank failures; the taxpayers should not. And that will be my policy.

And I believe if we have a good, balanced approach, we can get the good banks loaning money again, end the credit crunch, have proper regulation on the ones that are in trouble, and not overreact. It is a serious problem, but I don't see it as the kind of terrible, terrible problem that the S&L problem was.

**LEHRER:** President Bush, one minute.

**BUSH:** Well, I don't believe it would be appropriate for a president to suggest that the banking system is not sound. It is sound. There are some problem banks out there. But what we need is financial reform; we need some real financial reform, banking reform, legislation. And I have proposed that. And when I am re-elected, I believe one of the first things ought to be to press a new Congress not beholden to the old ways to pass financial reform legislation that modernizes the banking system, doesn't put a lot of inhibitions on it, and protects the depositors through keeping the FDIC sound.

But I think that — I just was watching some of the proceedings of the American Bankers Association, and I think the general feeling is most of the banks are sound, certainly there's no comparison here between what happened to the S&Ls and where the banks stand right now, in my view.

**LEHRER:** Mr. Perot, one minute.

**PEROT:** Well, nobody's gotten into the real issue yet on the savings and loan again — nobody's got a business background, I guess. The whole problem came up in 1984. The president of the United States was told officially it was a $20 billion problem. These crooks — now, Willie Sut-

ton would have gone to own a savings and loan rather than rob banks, because he robbed banks because that's where the money is; owning a savings and loan is where the money was.

Now, in 1984 they were told. I believe the vice president was in charge of deregulation. Nobody touched that tar baby till the day after election in 1988 because they were flooding both parties with crooked PAC money, and it was in many cases stolen PAC money. Now, you and I never got a ride on a lot of these yachts and fancy things it bought, but you and I are paying for it. And they buried it till right after the election.

Now, if you believe The Washington Post and you believe this extensive study that's been done — and I'm reading it — right after election day this year they're going to hit us with a hundred banks, it will be a $100-billion problem. Now, if that's true, just tell me now. I'm grown up, I can deal with it, I'll pay my share. But just tell me now; don't bury until after the election twice. I say that to both political parties.

The people deserve that since we have to pick up the tab; you got the PAC money, we'll pay the tab. Just tell us.

**LEHRER:** All right, Mr. Perot, the next question — we're going into a new round here on a category just called differences, and the question goes to you, Mr. Perot, and Gene will ask it. Gene?

**GIBBONS:** Mr. Perot, aside from the deficit, what government policy or policies do you really want to do something about? What really sticks in your craw about conditions in this country — beside the deficit — that you would want to fix as president?

**PEROT:** The debt and the deficit. Well, if you watched my television show the other night, you saw it. And if you watch it Thursday, Friday, Saturday this week, you'll get more. A shameless plug there, Mr. President.

But in a nutshell we've got to reform our government or we won't get anything done. We have a government that doesn't work. All these specific examples I'm giving tonight — if you had a business like that, they'd be leading you away and boarding up the doors. We have a government that doesn't work. It's supposed to come from the people, it comes at the people. The people need to take their government back. You've got to reform Congress, they've got to be servants of the people again; you've got to reform the White House. We've got to turn this thing around. And it's a long list of specific items.

And I've covered it again and again in print and on television. But very specifically the key thing is to turn the government back to the people and take it away from the special interests and have people go to Washington to serve. Who can give themselves a 23 percent pay raise anywhere in the world except Congress? Who would have 1,200 airplanes worth $2 billion a year just to fly around in? I don't have a free, reserved parking place at National Airport, why should my servants? I don't have an

indoor gymnasium and an indoor tennis and an indoor every other thing they can think of; I don't have a place where I can go make free TV to send to my constituents to try to brainwash them to elect me the next time.

And I'm paying for all that for those guys. I'm going to be running an ad pretty soon that shows they promised us they were going to hold the line on spending at the tax and budget summit, and I'm going to show how much they've increased this little stuff they do for themselves. And it is silly putty, folks, and the American people have had enough of it.

Step One, if I get up there, we're going to clean that up. You say, how can I get Congress to do that? I'll have millions of people at my shoulder, shoulder to shoulder with me, and we will see it done work speed — because it's wrong. We've turned the country upside down.

**LEHRER:** Gov. Clinton, you have one minute. Governor?

**CLINTON:** I would just point out, on the point Mr. Perot made, I agree that we need to cut spending in Congress. I've called for a 25 percent reduction in congressional staffs and expenditures. But the White House staff increased its expenditures by considerably more than Congress has in the last four years under the Bush administration, and Congress has actually spent a billion dollars less than President Bush asked them to spend. Now, when you outspend Congress you're really swinging.

That, however, is not my only passion. The real problem in this country is that most people are working hard and falling farther behind. My passion is to pass a jobs program and get incomes up with an investment incentive program to grow jobs in the private sector, to waste less public money and invest more, to control health-care costs and provide for affordable health care for all Americans and to make sure we've got the best trained workforce in the world. That is my passion.

We've gotta get this country growing again and this economy strong again or we can't bring down the deficit. Economic growth is the key to the future of this country.

**LEHRER:** President Bush, one minute.

**BUSH:** On government reform?

**LEHRER:** Sir?

**BUSH:** Government reform?

**LEHRER:** Yes, exactly. Well, to respond to the subject that Mr. Perot mentioned.

**BUSH:** Well, how about this for a government reform policy? Reduce the White House staff by a third after or at the same time the Congress does the same thing for their staff. Term limits for members of the United States Congress. Give the government back to the people. Let's do it that way. The president has term limits. Let's limit some of these guys sitting out there tonight.

Term limits. And then how about a balanced budget amendment to the Con-

stitution? Forty-three — more than that — states have it, I believe. Let's try that. And you want to do something about all this extra spending that concerns Mr. Perot and me? Okay. How about a line-item veto? Forty-three governors have that. And give it to the president, and if the Congress isn't big enough to do it, let the president have a shot at this excess spending. A line-item veto. That means you can take a line and cut out some of the pork out of a meaningful bill.

Gov. Clinton keeps hitting me on vetoing legislation. Well, that's the only protection the taxpayer has against some of these reckless pork programs up there, and I'd rather be able to just line it right out of there and get on about passing some good stuff but leave out the garbage. Line-item veto — there's a good reform program for you.

**LEHRER:** All right.

Next question goes to Gov. Clinton. You have two minutes, Governor, and Susan will ask it.

**ROOK:** Gov. Clinton, you said that you will raise taxes on the rich, people with incomes of $200,000 a year or higher. A lot of people are saying that you will have to go lower than that, much lower. Will you make a pledge tonight below which, an income level that you will not go below? I'm looking for numbers, sir, not just a concept.

**CLINTON:** My plan — you can read my plan. My plan says that we want to raise marginal incomes on family incomes above $200,000 from 31 to 36 percent, that we want to ask foreign corporations simply to pay the same percentage of taxes on their income that American corporations play [sic] in America, that we want to use that money to provide over $100 billion in tax cuts for investment in new plant and equipment, for small business, for new technologies, and for middle class tax relief.

Now, I'll tell you this. I will not raise taxes on the middle class to pay for these programs. If the money does not come in there to pay for these programs, we will cut other government spending or we will slow down the phase-in of the programs. I am not gonna raise taxes on the middle class to pay for these programs.

Now furthermore, I am not gonna tell you "read my lips" on anything because I cannot foresee what emergencies might develop in this country. And the president said never, never, never would he raise taxes in New Jersey, and within a day Marlin Fitzwater, his spokesman, said now, that's not a promise.

So I think even he has learned that you can't say "read my lips" because you can't know what emergencies might come up. But I can tell you this. I'm not gonna raise taxes on middle class Americans to pay for the programs I've recommended. Read my plan.

And you know how you can trust me about that? Because you know, in the first debate, Mr. Bush made some news. He'd just said Jim Baker was going to be secre-

tary of State and in the first debate he said no, now he's gonna be responsible for domestic economic policy.

Well, I'll tell ya. I'll make some news in the third debate. The person responsible for domestic economic policy in my administration will be Bill Clinton. I'm gonna make those decisions, and I won't raise taxes on the middle class to pay for my programs.

**LEHRER:** President Bush, you have one minute.

**BUSH:** That's what worries me — that he's going to be responsible. He's going to do — and he would do for the United States what he's done to Arkansas. He would do for the United States what he's done to Arkansas. We do not want to be the lowest of the low. We are not a nation in decline. We are a rising nation.

Now, my problem is — I heard what he said. He said I want to take it from the rich, raise $150 billion from the rich. To get it, to get $150 billion in new taxes, you got to go down to the guy that's making $36,600. And if you want to pay for the rest of his plan, all the other spending programs, you're going to sock it to the working man.

So when you hear "tax the rich," Mr. and Mrs. America, watch your wallet. Lock your wallet because he's coming right after you just like Jimmy Carter did and just like you're going to get — you're going to end up with interest rates at 21 percent, and you're going to have inflation going through the roof.

Yes, we're having tough times, but we do not need to go back to the failed policies of the past, when you had a Democratic president and a spendthrift Democratic Congress.

**LEHRER:** Mr. Perot.

**CLINTON:** Jim, you permitted Mr. Bush to break the rules, he said, to defend the honor of the country. What about the honor of my state? We rank first in the country in job growth, we got the lowest spending, state and local, in the country, and the second lowest tax burden. And the difference between Arkansas and the United States is that we're going in the right direction and this country's going in the wrong direction. And I have to defend the honor of my state.

**LEHRER:** We've got a wash, according to my calculation. We have a wash. And we go to Mr. Perot for one minute. In other words, it's a violation of the rule, that's what I meant, Mr. Perot.

**PEROT:** So I'm the only one that's untarnished at this point?

**LEHRER:** That's right. You're clear.

**PEROT:** I'm sure I'll do it before it's over.

Key thing here, see, we all come up with images. Images don't fix anything. I think — you know, I'm starting to understand it. You stay around this long enough, you think about — if you talk about it in Washington, you think you did it. If you've been on television about it, you think you did it.

What we need is people to stop talking and start doing.

Now, our real problem here is they both have plans that will not work. The Wall Street Journal said your numbers don't add up. And you can take it out on charts, you look at all the studies the different groups have done, you go out four, five, six years, we're still drifting along with a huge deficit.

So let's come back to harsh reality, and what I — you know, everybody says, gee, Perot, you're tough. I'm saying, well, this is not as tough as World War II and it's not as tough as the revolution. And it's fair, shared sacrifice to do the right thing for our country and for our children. And it will be fun if we all work together to do it.

**LEHRER:** All right. This is the last question, and it goes to President Bush for a two-minute answer. And it will be asked by Helen.

**THOMAS:** Mr. President, why have you dropped so dramatically in the leadership polls, from the high 80s to the 40s? And you have said that you will do anything you have to do to get re-elected. What can you do in two weeks to win reelection?

**BUSH:** Well, I think the answer to why the drop, I think, has been the economy in the doldrums. Why I'll win is I think I have the best plan of the three of us up here to do something about it. Mine does not grow the government, it does not invest, have government invest.

It says we need to do better in terms of stimulating private business. We got a big philosophical difference here tonight between one who thinks the government can do all these things through tax and spend, and one who thinks it ought to go the other way.

And so I believe the answer is, I'm going to win it because I'm getting into focus my agenda for America's renewal, and also I think that Gov. Clinton's had pretty much of a free ride. On looking specifically at the Arkansas record — he keeps criticizing us, criticizing me, I'm the incumbent, fine. But he's an incumbent, and we've got to look at all the facts. They're almost at the bottom on every single category. We can't do that to the American people.

And then, Helen, I really believe where people are going to ask this question about trust, because I do think there's a pattern by Gov. Clinton of saying one thing to please one group, and then trying to please another group. And I think that pattern is a dangerous thing to suggest would work for the Oval Office. It doesn't work that way when you're president.

Truman is right. The buck stops there. And you have to make decisions even when it's against your own interest. And I've done that. It's against my political interest to say go ahead and go along with the tax increase, but I did what I thought was right at the time. So I think people are going to be looking for trust and experience.

And then, I mentioned it the other

night, I think if there's a crisis, people are going to say, well, George Bush has taken us through some tough crises, and we trust him to do that.

And so I'll make the appeal on a wide array of issues. Also I got a philosophical difference. I got to watch the clock here. I don't think we're a declining nation. The whole world has had economic problems. We're doing better than a lot of the countries in the world. And we're going to lead the way out of this economic recession across this world and economic slowdown here at home.

**LEHRER:** Mr. Perot, you have —

**BUSH:** That's why I think I'll win.

**LEHRER:** Mr. Perot — sorry, excuse me, sir. Mr. Perot, you have one minute.

**PEROT:** I'm the last one, right?

**LEHRER:** No, Gov. Clinton has a minute after you. Then we have the closing statements.

**PEROT:** One minute after you.

**LEHRER:** Right.

**PEROT:** I'm totally focused on the fact that we may have bank failures and nobody answered it. I'm totally focused on the fact that we are still evading the issue of the Glaspie papers. I'm totally focused on the fact that we still could have enterprise zones, according to both parties, but we don't. So I am still focused on gridlock, I guess.

And I am also focused on the fact that isn't it a paradox that we have the highest productivity in our workforce in the industrialized world and at the same time have the largest trade deficit, and at the same time rank behind nine other nations in what we pay our most productive people in the world, and we're losing whole industries overseas.

Now, can't somebody agree with me that the government is breaking business's legs with these trade agreements? They're breaking business's legs in a number of different ways. We have an adversarial relationship that's destroying jobs and sending them overseas while we have the finest workers in the world.

Keep in mind a factory worker has nothing to do with anything except putting it together on the factory floor. It's our obligation to make sure that we give him the finest products in the world to put together and we don't break his legs in the process.

**LEHRER:** Gov. Clinton, one minute.

**CLINTON:** I really can't believe Mr. Bush is still trying to make trust an issue after "read my lips" and 15 million new jobs and embracing what he called voodoo economics and embracing an export enhancement program for farmers he threatened to veto and going all around the country giving out money in programs that he once opposed.

But the main thing is he still didn't get it, from what he said the other night to that fine woman on our program, the 209 people in Richmond. They don't want us talking about each other. They want us to talk about the problems of this country.

I don't think he'll be re-elected because trickle-down economics is a failure and he's offering more of it, and what he's saying about my program is just not true. Look at the Republicans that have endorsed me. High-tech executives in Northern California. Look at the 24 generals and admirals, retired, that have endorsed me, including the deputy commander of Desert Storm. Look at Sarah Brady, Jim Brady's wife, President Reagan's press secretary, who endorsed me because he knuckled under to the NRA and wouldn't fight for the Brady Bill.

We've got a broad-based coalition that goes beyond party because I am going to change this country and make it better, with the help of the American people.

**LEHRER:** All right. Now, that was the final question and answer and we now go to the closing statements. Each candidate will have up to two minutes. The order was determined by a drawing. Gov. Clinton, you're first. Governor.

**CLINTON:** First, I'd like to thank the commission and my opponents for participating in these debates and making them possible. I think the real winners of the debates were the American people.

I was especially moved in Richmond a few days ago when 209 of our fellow citizens got to ask us questions. They went a long way toward reclaiming this election for the American people and taking their country back.

I want to say, since this is the last time I'll be on a platform with my opponents, that even though I disagree with Mr. Perot on how fast we can reduce the deficit and how much we can increase taxes on the middle class, I really respect what he's done in this campaign to bring the issue of deficit reduction to our attention.

I'd like to say to Mr. Bush, even though I've got profound differences with him, I do honor his service to our country. I appreciate his efforts and I wish him well. I just believe it's time to change.

I offer a new approach. It's not trickle-down economics. It's been tried for 12 years and it's failed. More people are working harder for less, 100,000 people a month losing their health insurance, unemployment going up, our economy slowing down. We can do better.

And it's not tax and spend economics. It's invest and grow, put our people first, control health care costs and provide basic health care to all Americans, have an education system second to none and revitalize the private economy.

That is my commitment to you. It is the kind of change that can open up a whole new world of opportunities to America as we enter the last decade of this century and move towards the 21st century. I want a country where people who work hard and play by the rules are rewarded, not punished. I want a country where people are coming together across the lines of race and region and income. I know we can do better.

It won't take miracles and it won't happen overnight, but we can do much, much better if we have the courage to change. Thank you very much.

**LEHRER:** President Bush, your closing statement, sir.

**BUSH:** Three weeks from now — two weeks from tomorrow, America goes to the polls and you're going to have to decide who you want to lead this country to economic recovery. On jobs — that's the No. 1 priority, and I believe my program for stimulating investment, encouraging small business, brand-new approach to education, strengthening the American family, and, yes, creating more exports is the way to go. I don't believe in trickle-down government, I don't believe in larger taxes and larger government spending.

On foreign affairs, some think it's irrelevant. I believe it's not. We're living in an interconnected world. The whole world is having economic difficulties. The U.S. is doing better than a lot. But we've got to do even better. And if a crisis comes up, I ask who has the judgment and the experience and, yes, the character to make the right decision?

And, lastly, the other night on character Gov. Clinton said it's not the character of the president but the character of the presidency. I couldn't disagree more. Horace Greeley said the only thing that endures is character. And I think it was Justice Black who talked about great nations, like great men, must keep their word.

And so the question is, who will safeguard this nation, who will safeguard our people and our children? I need your support, I ask for your support. And may God bless the United States of America.

**LEHRER:** Mr. Perot, your closing statement, sir.

**PEROT:** To the millions of fine decent people who did the unthinkable and took their country back in their own hands and put me on the ballot, let me pledge to you that tonight is just the beginning. These next two weeks we will be going full steam ahead to make sure that you get a voice and that you get your country back.

This Thursday night on ABC from 8:30 to 9, Friday night on NBC from 8 to 8:30, and Saturday night on CBS from 8 to 8:30, we'll be down in the trenches under the hood working on fixin' the old car to get it back on the road.

Now, the question is, can we win? Absolutely we can win, because it's your country. Question really is who do you want in the White House. It's that simple.

Now, you got to stop letting these people tell you who to vote for, you got to stop letting these folks in the press tell you you're throwing your vote away — you got to start using your own head.

Then the question is, can we govern? I love that one. The "we" is you and me. You bet your hat we can govern because we will be in there together and we will figure out what to do, and you won't tolerate gridlock, you won't tolerate endless meandering and wandering around, and you won't tolerate non-performance. And, believe me, anybody that knows me understands I have a very low tolerance for non-performance also. Together we can get anything done.

The president mentioned that you need the right person in a crisis. Well, folks, we got one, and that one is a financial crisis. Pretty simply, who's the best-qualified person up here on the stage to create jobs? Make your decision and vote on November the 3rd. I suggest you might consider somebody who's created jobs. Who's the best person to manage money? I suggest you pick a person who's successfully managed money. Who's the best person to get results and not talk? Look at the record and make your decision.

And, finally, who would you give your pension fund and your savings account to to manage? And, last one, who would you ask to be the trustee of your estate and take care of your children if something happened to you?

Finally, to you students up there — God bless you, I'm doing this for you: I want you to have the American dream.

To the American people, I'm doing this because I love you. That's it. Thank you very much.

**LEHRER:** All right, thank you, Mr. Perot; thank you, Mr. President; thank you, Gov. Clinton — for being with us tonight and in the previous debates. Thank you to the panel.

The only thing that is left to be said is, from Michigan State University in East Lansing, I'm Jim Lehrer, thank you and good night. ∎

# Candidates Trade Shots in Verbal 'Pingpong Game'

**HAL BRUNO:** Good evening from Atlanta and welcome to the vice presidential debate sponsored by the Nonpartisan Commission on Presidential Debates. It's being held here in the Theater for the Arts on the campus of Georgia Tech. I'm Hal Bruno from ABC News and I'm going to be moderating tonight's debate. The participants are Republican Vice President Dan Quayle, Democratic Sen. Al Gore, and retired Vice Admiral James Stockdale, who is the vice presidential nominee for independent candidate Ross Perot.

You have two minutes for an opening statement. I will then present the issues to be discussed. For each topic, the candidates will have a minute and 15 seconds to respond. Then this will be followed by a five minute discussion period in which they can ask questions of each other if they so choose.

Now, the order of response has been determined by a drawing, and we'll rotate with each topic. At the end of the debate, each candidate will have two minutes for a closing statement.

Our radio and TV audience should know that the candidates were given an equal allocation of auditorium seats for their supporters. So I'd like to ask the audience here in the theater to please refrain from applause or any partisan demonstration once the debate is under way because it takes time away from the candidates. So with that plea from your moderator let's get started.

And we'll turn first to Sen. Gore for his opening statement.

**GORE:** Good evening. It's great to be here in Atlanta for this debate where America will be showcased to the world when the 1996 Olympics are put on right here. It's appropriate because in a real sense, our discussion this evening will be about what kind of nation we want to be four years from now. It's also a pleasure to be with my two opponents this evening. Adm. Stockdale, may I say it's a special honor to share this stage with you. Those of us who served in Vietnam looked at you as a national hero even before you were awarded the congressional Medal of Honor.

And Mr. Vice President — Dan, if I may — it was 16 years ago that you and I went to the Congress on the very first day together.

I'll make you a deal this evening. If you don't try to compare [President] George Bush to Harry Truman, I won't compare you to Jack Kennedy.

Harry Truman —

**QUAYLE:** Do you remember the last time someone compared themselves to Jack Kennedy? Do you remember what they said?

**GORE:** Harry Truman, it's worth remembering, assumed the presidency when Franklin [D.] Roosevelt died here in Georgia — only one of many occasions when fate thrust a vice president into the Oval Office in a time of crisis. It's something to think about during the debate this evening. But our real discussion is going to be about change. [Arkansas Gov.] Bill Clinton and I stand for change because we don't believe our nation can stand four more years of what we've had under George Bush and Dan Quayle.

When the recession came they were like a deer caught in the headlights — paralyzed into inaction, blinded to the suffering and pain of bankruptcies and people who were unemployed. We have an environmental crisis, a health insurance crisis, substandard education. It is time for a change.

Bill Clinton and I want to get our country moving forward again, put our people back to work and create a bright future for the United States of America.

**BRUNO:** Okay, the next statement will be from Vice President Quayle.

**QUAYLE:** Well, thank you, Sen. Gore, for reminding me about my performance in the 1988 vice presidential debate. This is 1992, Bill Clinton is running against President George Bush. There are two things that I'm going to stress during this debate: One, Bill Clinton's economic plan and his agenda will make matters much, much worse — he will raise your taxes, he will increase spending, he will make government bigger, jobs will be lost; second, Bill Clinton does not have the strength nor the character to be president of the United States.

Let us look at the agendas. President Bush wants to hold the line on taxes; Bill Clinton wants to raise taxes. President Bush is for a balanced-budget amendment; Bill Clinton is opposed to it. We want to reform the legal system because it's too costly; Bill Clinton wants the status quo. We want to reform the health-care system; Bill Clinton wants to ration health care. Bill Clinton wants to empower government; we want to empower people.

In St. Louis, Mo., in June of this year, Bill Clinton said this: "America is the mockery of the world." He is wrong.

At some time during these next four years there is going to be a crisis — there will be an international crisis. I can't tell you where it's going to be; I can't even tell you the circumstances — but it will happen. We need a president who has the experience, who has been tested, who has the integrity and qualifications to handle the crisis. The president has been tested; the president has the integrity and the character. The choice is yours.

You need to have a president you can trust. Can you really trust Bill Clinton?

**BRUNO:** Adm. Stockdale, your opening statement, please, sir.

**STOCKDALE:** Who am I? Why am I here?

I'm not a politician — everybody knows that. So don't expect me to use the language of the Washington insider. Thirty-seven years in the Navy, and only one of them up there in Washington. And now I'm an academic.

The centerpiece of my life was the Vietnam War. I was there the day it started. I led the first bombing raid against North Vietnam. I was there the day it ended, and I was there for everything in between. Ten years in Vietnam, aerial combat and torture. I know things about the Vietnam War better than anybody in the world. I know some things about the Vietnam War better than anybody in the world.

And I know how governments, how American governments can be — can be courageous, and how they can be callow. And that's important. That's one thing I'm an insider on.

I was the leader of the underground of the American pilots who were shot down in prison in North Vietnam. You should know that the American character displayed in those dungeons by those fine men was a thing of beauty.

I look back on those years as the beginning of wisdom, learning everything a man can learn about the vulnerabilities and the strengths that are ours as Americans.

Why am I here tonight? I am here because I have in my brain and in my heart what it takes to lead America through tough times.

**BRUNO:** Thank you, Admiral.

I thought since you're running for vice president, that we ought to start off by talking about the vice presidency itself. The vice president presides over the Senate. He casts a deciding vote in case of a tie, but his role really depends on the assignments that are given to him by the president. However, if a president should die in office or is unable to serve for any other reason, the vice president automatically becomes president, and that has happened five times in this century.

So the proposition I put on the table

for you to discuss is this: What role would each of you like to play as vice president, what areas interest you and what are your qualifications to serve as president, if necessary?

In the case of Vice President Quayle, whom we're starting with, I suppose you'd tell us the role that you did play in the first term and which you'd like to do in a second term. Go ahead, sir.

**QUAYLE:** Well, then I won't give you that answer.

Qualifications. I've been there, Hal. I've done the job. I've been tested. I've been vice president for four years. Sen. Gore referred to us being elected to the Congress together in 1976. I've done the job. I've done many things for the president.

But even as vice president you never know exactly what your role is going to be from time to time, and let me just give you an example of where I was tested under fire and in a crisis.

President Bush was flying to Malta in 1989 to meet with [Soviet] President [Mikhail S.] Gorbachev. It was the first meeting between President Bush and President Gorbachev. They had known each other before.

A coup broke out in the Philippines. I had to go to the situation room. I had to assemble the president's advisers. I talked to [Philippine] President [Corazon C.] Aquino. I made the recommendation to the president. The president made the decision; the coup was suppressed; democracy continued in the Philippines; the situation was ended.

I've been there. And I'll tell you one other thing that qualifies you for being president — and it's this, Hal — you've got to stand up for what you believe in. And nobody has ever criticized me for not having strong beliefs.

**BRUNO:** Adm. Stockdale.

**STOCKDALE:** My association with Mr. Perot is a very personal one, and as I have stood in and finally taken his running mate position, he has granted me total autonomy. I don't take advantage of it, but I am sure that he would make me a partner in decision — in making decisions about the way to handle health care, the way to get this economy back on its feet again, in every way.

I have not had the experience of these gentlemen, but — to be any more specific — but I know I have his trust, and I intend to act in a way to keep that situation alive. Thank you.

**BRUNO:** Sen. Gore.

**GORE:** Bill Clinton understands the meaning of the words "teamwork" and "partnership." If we're successful in our efforts to gain your trust and lead this nation, we will work together to put our country back on the right track again. The experience that George Bush and Dan Quayle have been talking about includes the worst economic performance since the Great Depression. Unemployment is up; personal income is down; bankruptcies are up; housing

starts are down. How long can we continue with trickle-down economics when the record of failure is so abundantly clear?

Discussions of the vice presidency tend sometimes to focus on the crisis during which a vice president is thrust into the Oval Office, and indeed, one-third of the vice presidents who have served have been moved into the White House.

But the teamwork and partnership beforehand — and hopefully that situation never happens — how you work together is critically important. The way we work together in this campaign is one sample.

Now I'd like to say in response to Vice President Quayle — he talked about Malta and the Philippines. George Bush has concentrated on every other country in the world. When are you guys going to start worrying about our people here in the United States of America and get our country moving again?

**BRUNO:** Again, I will ask the audience: Please do not applaud, it takes time from the candidates. All right, now we have five minutes for discussion. Go ahead, Vice President Quayle.

**QUAYLE:** The answer to that is very simple: We are not going to raise taxes to create new jobs; we have a plan to create new jobs. But that wasn't the question. The question dealt with qualifications. Teamwork and partnership may be fine in the Congress, Sen. Gore — that's what Congress is all about, compromise, teamwork, working things out. But when you're president of the United States or when you're vice president and you have to fill in like I did the night of the crisis in the Philippines, you've got to make a decision; you've got to make up your mind. Bill Clinton, running for president of the United States, said this about the Persian Gulf War. He said: "Had I been in the Senate, I would have voted with the majority, if it was a close vote. But I agreed with the arguments of the minority."

You can't have it both ways; you have to make a decision. You cannot sit there in an international crisis — and sit there and say, well, on the one hand, this is okay, and, on the other hand, this is okay. You've got to make the decision. President Bush has made the decisions; he's been tested; he's got the experience; he's got the qualification; he's got the integrity to be our president for the next four years.

**BRUNO:** Thank you, Mr. Vice President. Adm. Stockdale, it's your turn to respond next, and then Sen. Gore will have his chance to respond.

**STOCKDALE:** Okay. I thought this was just an open session, this five-minute thing, and I didn't have anything to add to his. But I will —

**GORE:** Well, I'll jump in if you don't want —

**QUAYLE:** I thought anyone could jump in whenever they wanted to.

**BRUNO:** Okay, whatever pleases you gentlemen is fine with me. You're the candidates.

**QUAYLE:** But I want Adm. Stock-

dale's time.

**BRUNO:** This is not the Senate, where you can trade off time. Go ahead, Sen. Gore.

**GORE:** I'll let you all figure out the rules. I've got some points that I want to make here, and I still haven't gotten an answer to my question on when you guys are going to start worrying about this country, but I want to elaborate on it before —

**QUAYLE:** Why doesn't the Democratic Congress — why doesn't the Democratic Congress —

**BRUNO:** Mr. Vice President, let him say his thoughts, and then you can come in.

**GORE:** I was very patient in letting you get off that string of attacks. We've been listening to —

**QUAYLE:** Good points.

**GORE:** — trickle-down economics for 12 years now, and you all still support trickle-down to the very last drop. And, you know, talking about this point of concentrating on every other country in the world as opposed to the people of our country right here at home, when George Bush took former Secretary of State [James A.] Baker out of the State Department and put him in charge of the campaign and made him chief of staff in the White House, Mr. Baker, who's quite a capable man, said that for these last four years George Bush was working on the problems of the rest of the world and in the next four years he would target America.

Well, I want you to know we really appreciate that. But Bill Clinton and I will target America from day one. We won't wait four years before we concentrate on the problems in this country.

He went on to say that it's really amazing what George Bush can do when he concentrates. Well, it's time that we had a president like Bill Clinton who can concentrate and will concentrate and work on the problems of real people in this country. You know, our country is in trouble. We simply cannot continue with this philosophy of giving huge tax cuts to the very wealthy, raising taxes on middle-income families the way Bush and Quayle have done and then waiting for it to work. How much longer will it take, Dan, for trickle-down economics to work, in your theory?

**QUAYLE:** Well, we're going to have plenty of time to talk about trickle-down government, which you're for. But the question —

**GORE:** Well, I'd like to hear the answer.

**QUAYLE:** But the question is — the question is — and which you have failed to address, and that is: Why is Bill Clinton qualified to be president of the United States? You've talked about —

**GORE:** Oh, I'll be happy to answer that question —

**QUAYLE:** You've talked about Jim Baker. You've talked about trickle down-economics. You've talked about the worst economy —

**BRUNO:** Now, wait a minute. The question was about —

QUAYLE: — in 50 years.

GORE: I'll be happy to answer those. May I answer —

QUAYLE: Why is he qualified to be president of the United States?

GORE: I'll be happy to —

QUAYLE: I want to go back and make a point —

GORE: Well, you've asked me the question. If you won't answer my question, I will answer yours.

QUAYLE: I have not asked you a question. I've made a statement, that you have not told us why Bill Clinton is qualified to be president of the United States. I pointed out what he said about the Persian Gulf War. But let me repeat it for you. Here's what he said, Senator. You know full well what he said.

GORE: You want me to answer your question?

QUAYLE: I'm making a statement. Then you can answer it.

BRUNO: Can we give Adm. Stockdale a chance to come in, please —

And again, audience —

[Simultaneous conversation]

QUAYLE: [Inaudible] here's what he said. I mean, this is the Persian Gulf War — the most important event in his political lifetime and here's what Bill Clinton says. If it's a close vote, I'd vote with the majority.

BRUNO: Let's give Adm. Stockdale a chance to come in.

QUAYLE: But he was in the minority. That qualifies you for being president of the United States. I hope America is listening very closely to this debate tonight.

STOCKDALE: And I think America is seeing right now the reason this nation is in gridlock.

The trickle-downs and the tax-and-spends, or whatever you want to call them are at swords' points. We can't get this economy going. Over here we've got Dan, whose president is going to take eight years to balance the budget, and on my left, the senator, whose boss is going to get it half way balanced in four years. Ross Perot has got a plan to balance the budget five years in length from start to finish. And we're — people of the non-professional category who are just sick of this terrible thing that's happened to the country. And we've got a man who knows how to fix it, and I'm working for him.

BRUNO: I was a little bit worried that there might not be a free-flowing discussion tonight.

Let's move on to the economy. Specifically the economy was talked about at great length the other night in the presidential debate. Let's talk about a very particular aspect of the economy and that is, getting people back to work. For the average person, the great fear is losing his or her job, and many Americans have lost jobs in this recession, which also means the loss of benefits, the loss of a home, the destruction of a family's security. Specifically, how would your administration go about getting people back to work, and how

long is it going to take? And we start with Adm. Stockdale.

STOCKDALE: The lifeblood of our economy is investment. And right now when we pay $350 — we borrow $350 billion a year — it saps the money markets and the private investors are not getting their share. What we do is work on that budget by an aggressive program, not a painful program, so that we can start borrowing less money and getting more investment money on the street through entrepreneurs who can build factories, who will hire people, and maybe we'll start manufacturing goods in this country again. That's — that's my answer.

BRUNO: Okay. Sen. Gore.

GORE: Bill Clinton's top priority is putting America back to work. Bill Clinton and I will create good, high-wage jobs for our people, the same way he has done in his state. Bill Clinton has created high-wage manufacturing jobs at 10 times the national average and in fact according to the statistics coming from the Bush-Quayle Labor Department, for the last two years in a role Bill Clinton's state has been No. 1 among all 50 in the creation of jobs in the private sector.

By contrast, in the nation as a whole, during the last four years, it is the first time since the presidency of Herbert Hoover, that we have gone for a four-year period with fewer jobs at the end of that four-year period than we had at the beginning.

And look at manufacturing. We have lost 1.4 million jobs in manufacturing under George Bush and Dan Quayle. They have even — we learned two weeks ago — taken our tax dollars and subsidized the moving of U.S. factories to foreign countries.

Now don't deny it because "60 Minutes" and "Nightline" and the nation's newspapers have investigated this very carefully.

When are you going to stop using our tax dollars to shut down American factories and move 'em to foreign countries and throw Americans out of work?

BRUNO: Vice President Quayle.

QUAYLE: Senator, don't always believe what you see on television.

Let me tell you: The media have been wrong before. We have never subsidized any country — or any company to move from the United States to Latin America. You know full well the Caribbean Basin Initiative, you've supported that.

GORE: No.

QUAYLE: That is a program there —

GORE: I voted against it.

QUAYLE: You voted for it, and your record —

GORE: No.

QUAYLE: Okay. Well, we'll — we'll have a lot of interesting debate after this debate. Our people will be glad to furnish the press, if they're interested, in Sen. Gore's voting record on the Caribbean Basin Initiative. But let's talk — you know, you keep talking about trickle-down economics and all this stuff, about the worst

economy since Hoover. It is a bad economy. It's a tough economy. The question isn't — it's not who you're going to blame; what are you going to do about it? Your proposal is to raise $150 billion in taxes. To raise $220 billion in new spending.

GORE: No.

QUAYLE: How is raising taxes going to help small business? How is raising taxes going to help the farmer? How is raising taxes going to help the consumer in America? I submit to you that raising taxes will make matters much, much worse.

BRUNO: Admiral. We now throw it open for discussion. Adm. Stockdale, it's your turn to start the discussion.

STOCKDALE: Well, we've got to — we've got to clean out the barn, if I may quote my boss, and start getting this investment money on the street so we can get and encourage entrepreneurs to build factories. We — the program is out there. It's a put-together thing that requires some sacrifice, but not excessive, and we are willing to move forward in — on a five-year clip to put us back where we can start over and get — get this nation straightened out.

BRUNO: Sen. Gore, getting people back to work.

GORE: Well, the difference between the Perot-Stockdale plan and the Clinton-Gore plan is that Ross Perot's plan concentrates almost exclusively on balancing the budget and reducing the budget deficit, and the danger is that if that is the only goal it could throw our nation back into an even worse recession.

Bill Clinton and I have a detailed five-year budget plan to create good jobs, cut the budget deficit in half, and eliminate the investment deficit in order to get our economy moving forward again. We have a $20-billion infrastructure fund to create a nationwide network of high-speed rail, for example, and what are called information superhighways to open up a whole universe of knowledge for our young people and to help our universities and companies that rely on new advances in the information revolution. We also have tax incentives for investment in job-creating activities, not the kind of encouragement for short-term rip-offs like the proposal that we have had from George Bush.

But I want to return and say one more time: You have used our tax dollars to subsidize the recruitment of U.S. companies to move overseas and throw Americans out of work. In Decaturville, Tenn., not very far from my home, a factory was shut down right there when they were solicited by officials paid with U.S. taxpayers' money, and then the replacement workers in a foreign country were trained with our tax dollars and then their imports were subsidized coming back into the United States.

When are you going to stop that program?

QUAYLE: We do not have any program that encourages companies to close down here and to go and invest on foreign soil. That is absolutely outrageous. Of course American businesses do have busi-

ness abroad; we've got global competition. We want businesses to expand. Do you realize this, Senator, that [for] every job that's overseas there's three jobs back here to support that.

But never have we ever, nor would we, support the idea of someone closing down a factory here and moving overseas. That's just totally ridiculous.

**GORE:** It's going on right now; it happened in Tennessee, in Decaturville, Tenn. When George Bush went to Nashville, the employees who lost their jobs asked to meet with —

**QUAYLE:** I want to get back —

**GORE:** I talked with them. Let me tell you what they're feeling. Some of them are in their 50s and 60s. They want to know where they're going to get new jobs when their jobs have been destroyed. And there are 1.4 million manufacturing jobs that have been lost because of the policies of you and George Bush. Do you seriously believe that we ought to continue the same policies that have created the worst economy since the Great Depression?

**QUAYLE:** I hope that when you talked to those people you said: And the first thing that Bill Clinton and I are going to do is to raise $150 billion in new taxes.

**GORE:** You got that wrong, too.

**QUAYLE:** And the first — that is part of your plan.

**GORE:** No, it's not.

**QUAYLE:** — $150,000 in new taxes. Well, you're going to disavow your plan.

**GORE:** Listen, what we're proposing —

**QUAYLE:** You know what you're doing; you know what you're doing? You're pulling a Clinton.

And you know what a Clinton is? And you know what a Clinton is? A Clinton is, is what he says — he says one thing one day and another thing the next day — you try to have both sides of the issues. The fact of the matter is that you are proposing $150 billion in new taxes.

**GORE:** No.

**QUAYLE:** And I hope that you talk to the people in Tennessee —

**GORE:** No, we're not.

**QUAYLE:** — and told them that —

**GORE:** You can say it all you want, but it doesn't make it true.

**QUAYLE:** — going to have new taxes. I hope you talked to them about the fact that you were going to increase spending to $220 billion. I'm sure what you didn't talk to them about was about how we're going to reform the health-care system, like the president wants to do. He wants to go out and to reform the health-care system so that every American will have available to them affordable health insurance.

I'm sure one other thing that you didn't talk to them about, Senator, and that is legal reform, because your position on legal reform is the status quo. And yet you talk about foreign competition. Why should an American company have to spend 15 to 20 times on product liability and insurance costs compared to a com-

pany in Japan or a company in Germany or somewhere else? That's not right. We have product liability reform legislation on Capitol Hill. It will create jobs. And a Democratic Congress won't pass it.

**BRUNO:** Okay. I think it's time to move on to our next topic. All three of you gentlemen have some expertise in defense and the armed forces. Vice President Quayle and Sen. Gore both served on the Senate Armed Services Committee. Adm. Stockdale, of course, has a very distinguished military career.

With the end of the Cold War, everyone agrees that there are going to be major cuts. They've already started in the defense budget. But this country has a long history of neglecting its military needs in peacetime and then paying for it with heavy casualties when we're caught unprepared. How much of a defense cut is safe? What happens to the people who are forced to leave the military services, or if they lose their jobs because they're working in defense industries?

I think we start with Sen. Gore this time.

**GORE:** Bill Clinton and I support a strong national defense. He and I have both fought for change within the Democratic Party as well as within the country. In the aftermath of the Cold War, the definition of strong national defense has obviously changed somewhat. For example, George Bush wants to maintain at least 150,000 American soldiers in Europe, even though World War II ended 50 years ago.

Bill Clinton and I agree with so many military experts who believe that it is time for the Europeans, who are so much wealthier now and more powerful than they were at the end of World War II, to start picking up a little more of that tab themselves and not rely so exclusively on the United States taxpayers for the defense of Europe.

We believe that we can make savings in our defense budget and at the same time, improve our national security.

Now, for those who are affected by the cutbacks, whether they come from George Bush or Bill Clinton and me — the difference is, Bill Clinton and I have a defense conversion program so that those who won the Cold War will not be left out in the cold. We want to put them to work building an infrastructure and an economy here in this country for the '90s and the next century.

**BRUNO:** Vice President Quayle.

**QUAYLE:** We won the Cold War because we invested in national security. We won the Cold War because we invested in our military. We didn't win the Cold — or we won the Cold War because America had the political will and made the right decisions. Yes, we can make the cuts in defense, and we have. Bill Clinton wants to cut defense another $60 billion. I'd say to the defense workers in California and elsewhere, a $60 billion defense cut is going to cut a lot of jobs out.

Yes, we are making a conversion and

we can go to a civil space rather than having defense — or the defense industry. Well, let me say this: We would not have won the Cold War if we had listened to Sen. Gore and his crowd and had supported a nuclear freeze. If you would have supported that attitude — if you would have supported that attitude, we would not have won the Cold War. We won the Cold War because we invested and we went forward.

**BRUNO:** Mr. — Adm. Stockdale, please.

**STOCKDALE:** Yes, thanks. The numbers, in terms of the dollar cuts, as they stand on our plans now, show us almost the same as the vice president's. But we'd note that Mr. — Gov. Clinton's plan is almost twice as much a cut as either one of us. I've been through the end of World War II, and the surprise beginning of Korea, to see how we — it cost us more money because we overcut the defense budget in the first place. I don't say that —

So I think that should be eyed with great suspicion, people that are really kicking the props out from under our grand military establishment prematurely.

Now there's other differences between the Perot approach and what we see up here on either side of me, and that has to do with how we want to focus our interests, economic and military, more to the Pacific. We figure that we are generally going along with any sort of a troop removal from Europe. So that's still another face of this puzzle.

**BRUNO:** Sen. Gore, would you like to start the discussion period on this topic?

**GORE:** Yeah, I'd like to respond first to you, Adm. Stockdale. Under the details of our five-year budget plan, we do propose more in defense cuts than George Bush and Dan Quayle, but only 5 percent more. [Former Joint Chiefs Chairman] Adm. [William J.] Crowe, who I think was one of your classmates in Annapolis —

**STOCKDALE:** Oh, yes, I've known him —

**GORE:** — has endorsed —

**STOCKDALE:** — 50 years.

**GORE:** — the military portions of our plan, even though he was the chairman of the Joint Chiefs under George Bush, and John White has endorsed the economic aspects of our plan, even though I believe he was the architect of Ross Perot's economic plan.

Now when I heard George Bush say at the convention in Houston, that when he heard the phrase "we won the Cold War," it made him wonder who the "we" was. Well, I want to tell you, President Bush, the "we" is the people of the United States of America. This wasn't a partisan victory that came suddenly, a few months after you took the oath of office. This started with Harry Truman, and it was a bipartisan effort from the very beginning. George Bush taking credit for the Berlin Wall coming down is like the rooster taking credit for the sunrise.

And I want to, I want to add — I want to add one other thing, because in the de-

bate a few nights ago, I think President Bush made a very serious misstatement of fact in response to Ross Perot. It was kind of a little lecture he gave to Ross Perot when he said, "Those SS-18s are gone, Ross, that's done." He — he reached a deal with [Russian President] Boris Yeltsin to completely remove them so we can all sleep safely without any fear tonight.

But you know what? They thought they were going to get that deal, but when he took the person in charge of the negotiations out of the State Department and put him in charge of the re-election campaign, the deal unraveled, and now there is no START II deal at all. In fact there are serious problems.

Isn't it a fact, Dan, that every single one of those SS-18s is still there, in the silos, and under the START I treaty, only half of the silos are supposed to be dismantled, and there is no deal to get rid of the other half?

Didn't the president make a mistake there?

**BRUNO:** Vice President Quayle, please.

**QUAYLE:** The president does have a commitment from Boris Yeltsin to eliminate the SS-18s. That is a commitment to —

**GORE:** Is it an agreement?

**QUAYLE:** It is a commitment.

**GORE:** Oh.

**QUAYLE:** Let's talk about, let's talk about —

**GORE:** Well, he said he'd —

**BRUNO:** Let him talk, Senator.

**QUAYLE:** Lighten up here, Al.

**BRUNO:** Go ahead.

**QUAYLE:** Let's talk about getting agreements. You know, the president of the United States doesn't just negotiate with your friends in Congress; the president of the United States deals on the international scene. He's got to deal with the president of Russia; he's got to deal with the chancellor of Germany, the prime minister of Britain, the president of France, the prime minister of Japan — he's got to deal with a whole host of leaders around the world.

And the leaders sit down and they will negotiate, and they will come to agreements with people that they trust. And this is a fundamental problem with Bill Clinton, is trust and character.

It is not the issue of how he avoided military service 20-some years ago; it's the fact — it's the fact that he does not tell the truth about it. He first said he didn't get an induction notice, then we find out that he did; he said he didn't have an ROTC slot, then we find out he did; he said he didn't use Sen. [J.W.] Fulbright's office for special influence, then we find out that he did.

These are inconsistencies. Bill Clinton has trouble telling the truth. And he will have a very difficult time dealing with somebody like Yeltsin or [German] Chancellor [Helmut] Kohl or [British] Prime Minister [John] Major or [French] President [François] Mitterrand, because truth and integrity are prerequisites to being president of the United States.

**GORE:** I want to respond to that, I want to respond to that. George Bush, in case you've forgotten, Dan, said, "Read my lips — no new taxes." And you know what?

**QUAYLE:** I didn't think I was going to hear that tonight.

**GORE:** Hold on, hold on, let me finish.

**QUAYLE:** Okay.

**GORE:** He also said he wanted to be the environmental president; then he went on to say he wanted to be the education president. Then he said that he wouldn't raise taxes again — no, never, ever, ever. Then the next day his spokesman, Marlin Fitzwater, came out and said that's not a pledge. Then two weeks ago he said that after the election, if you win, then James Baker's going to go back to be secretary of State; then a week later, in the debate a few nights ago, he said, no, after the election, if we win, James Baker is going to be in charge of domestic policy.

Which is it, Dan? Is he going to — what's your role in this going to be?

**BRUNO:** Well, we'll have to move on to another topic.

**QUAYLE:** Let me —

**BRUNO:** Sorry, Mr. Vice President.

**QUAYLE:** I don't have time to respond to that?

**BRUNO:** You'll get plenty of chance to respond, so don't worry.

**QUAYLE:** Okay, you're the moderator. I was under the assumption that when the thing is like that that you get a chance to respond.

**BRUNO:** Well, we ran out of time; according to the agreement, it's time to move on. And I want to stick to the agreement.

**QUAYLE:** Okay. Well, you got the last word on that, but we'll come back to it.

**BRUNO:** But you'll have a chance — I can see what's happening here: We throw out the topic and then we drift. But that's okay, because I think it's making for a healthy exchange.

The only thing I would ask of you —

**GORE:** I'm enjoying it.

**BRUNO:** The only thing I would ask of you gentlemen is that when we get to the discussion period, whoever talks first be considerate of the others, because you have a tendency to filibuster.

**QUAYLE:** Look over there.

**BRUNO:** Okay, I'm not pointing any fingers. Let's talk about the environment — we'll get away from controversy.

Everyone wants a safe and clean environment, but there's an ongoing conflict between environmental protection and the need for economic growth and jobs. So the point I throw out on the table is, how do you resolve this conflict between protection of the environment and growth in jobs, and why has it taken so long to deal with basic problems, such as toxic waste dumps, clean air and clean water?

And, Vice President Quayle, it's your turn to start first.

**QUAYLE:** Hal, that's a false choice. You don't have to have a choice between the environment and jobs — you can have both. Look at the president's record: Clean air legislation passed the Democratic Congress because of the leadership of George Bush. It is the most comprehensive clean air act in our history. We are firmly behind preserving our environment, and we have a good record with which to stand. The question comes about: What is going to be their position when it comes to the environment? I say it's a false choice. You ought to ask somebody in Michigan, a UAW worker in Michigan, if they think increasing the CAFE standards, the fuel economy standards, to 45 miles a gallon is a good idea — 300,000 people out of work.

You ought to talk to the timber people in the Northwest, where they say that — well, we can only save the owl. Forget about jobs. You ought to talk to the coal miners. They're talking about putting a coal tax on. They're talking about a tax on utilities, a tax on gasoline and home heating oil — all sorts of taxes.

No, Hal, the choice isn't the environment and jobs. With the right policies — prudent policies — we can have both.

**BRUNO:** Adm. Stockdale.

**STOCKDALE:** I read Sen. Gore's book about the environment, and I don't see how he could possibly pay for his proposals in today's economic climate.

You know, the Marshall Plan of the environment, and so forth.

And also, I'm told by some experts that the things that he fears most might not be all that dangerous, according to some scientists. You know, you can overdo, I'm told, environmental cleaning up. If you purify the pond, the water lilies die. You know, I love this planet, and I want it to stay here, but I don't like to have it the private property of fanatics that want to overdo this thing.

**BRUNO:** Sen. Gore.

**GORE:** Bill Clinton and I believe we can create millions of new jobs by leading the environmental revolution instead of dragging our feet and bringing up the rear.

You know, Japan and Germany are both opening — proclaiming to the world now that the biggest new market in the history of world business is the market for the new products and technologies that foster economic progress without environmental destruction.

Why is the Japanese business organization — the largest one they have, the Ki Den Ren [phonetic], arguing for tougher environmental standards than those embodied in U.S. law? Why is MITI — their trade organization — calling on all Japanese corporations everywhere in the world to exceed by as much as possible the environmental standards of every country in which they're operating?

Well, maybe they're just dumb about business competition. But maybe they know something that George Bush and Dan Quayle don't know — that the future will call for greater efficiency and greater

environmental efficiency.

This is an issue that touches my basic values. I'm taught in my religious tradition that we are given dominion over the Earth, but we're required to be good stewards of the Earth, and that means to take care of it. We're not doing that now under the Bush-Quayle policies. They have gutted the Clean Air Act. They have broken his pledge to be the environmental president. Bill Clinton and I will change that.

**BRUNO:** Okay. Discussion period now. Again, leave time for each other, please. Vice President Quayle, go ahead.

**QUAYLE:** Well, I'm tempted to yield to Adm. Stockdale on this. But I — you know, the fact of the matter is is that one of the proposals that Sen. Gore has suggested is to have the taxpayers of America spend $100 billion a year on environmental projects in foreign countries —

**GORE:** That's not true —

**QUAYLE:** Foreign aid — well, Senator, it's in your book. On page 304 —

**GORE:** No, it's not.

**QUAYLE:** It is there. It is in your book. You know, Hal, I wanted to bring the Gore book tonight, because I figured he was going to pull a Bill Clinton on me, and he has. Because he's going to disavow what's in his book. It's in your book —

**GORE:** No.

**QUAYLE:** It comes out to $100 billion of foreign aid for environmental projects.

**BRUNO:** All right. Let's give him a chance to answer.

**QUAYLE:** Now, how are we going to pay for it? How are we going to pay for an extra $100 billion of the taxpayers' money for this?

**GORE:** Dan, I appreciate you reading my book very much, but you've got it wrong.

**QUAYLE:** No, I've got it right.

**GORE:** There's no such proposal.

**QUAYLE:** Okay, well, we'll find —

**BRUNO:** Let him talk, Mr. Vice President. Let the senator talk. Go ahead.

**GORE:** There is no such proposal. What I have called upon is a cooperative effort by the United States and Europe and Asia to work together in opening up new markets throughout the world for the new technologies that are necessary in order to reconcile the imperatives of economic progress with the imperatives of environmental protection. Take Mexico City, for an example. They are shutting down factories right now, not because of their economy, but because they're choking together on the air pollution. They're banning automobiles some days of the week.

Now what they want is not new laser-guided missile systems. What they want are new engines and new factories and new products that don't pollute the air and the water, but nevertheless allow them to have a decent standard of living for their people. Last year 35 percent of our exports went to developing countries, countries where the population is expanding worldwide by as much as 1 billion people every 10 years.

We cannot stick our heads in the sand and pretend that we don't face a global environmental crisis, nor should we assume that it's going to cost jobs. Quite the contrary. We are going to be able to create jobs as Japan and Germany are planning to do right now, if we have the guts to leave.

Now earlier we heard about the auto industry and the timber industry. There have been 250,000 jobs lost in the automobile industry during the Reagan-Bush-Quayle years. There have been tens of thousands of jobs lost in the timber industry. What they like to do is point the finger of blame with one hand and hand out pink slips with the other hand. They've done a poor job both with the economy and the environment.

It's time for a change.

**BRUNO:** Adm. Stockdale, you had something you wanted to say here?

**STOCKDALE:** I know that — I read where Sen. Gore's mentor had disagreed with some of the scientific data that is in his book. How do you respond to those criticisms of that sort? Do you —

**QUAYLE:** Deny it.

**GORE:** Well —

**STOCKDALE:** Do you take this into account?

**GORE:** No, I — let me respond. Thank you, Admiral, for saying that. You're talking about Roger Revelle. His family wrote a lengthy letter saying how terribly he had been misquoted and had his remarks taken completely out of context just before he died.

He believed up until the day he died — no, it's true, he died last year —

**BRUNO:** I'd ask the audience to stop, please.

**GORE:** — and just before he died, he co-authored an article which was — had statements taken completely out of context. In fact the vast majority of the world's scientists — and they have worked on this extensively — believe that we must have an effort to face up to the problems we face with the environment. And if we just stick out heads in the sand and pretend that's not real, we're not doing ourselves a favor. Even worse than that, we're telling our children and all future generations that we weren't willing to face up to this obligation.

**QUAYLE:** Hal, can I —

**GORE:** I believe that we have a mandate —

**BRUNO:** Sure. We've still got time.

**GORE:** — to try to solve this problem, particularly when we can do it while we create jobs in the process.

**BRUNO:** Go ahead, Mr. Vice President, there's still time. Not much, though.

**QUAYLE:** I know it. We've got to have a little equal time here now, Hal. In the book you also suggest taxes on, gasoline taxes on utilities, taxes on carbon, taxes on timber. There's a whole host of taxes. And I don't just — I don't believe raising taxes is the way to solve our environmental problems.

And you talk about the bad situation in the auto industry. You seem to say that the answer is: Well, I'll just make it that

much worse by increasing the CAFE standards. Yes, the auto industry is hurting, it's been hurting for a long time, and increasing the CAFE standards to 45 miles per gallon, like you and Bill Clinton are suggesting, will put, as I said, 300,000 people out of work.

**BRUNO:** Okay, let's move on now. I would like to remind the audience of one thing. Trying to stop you from applauding may be a lost cause. I didn't say anything about hissing, but I do think it is discourteous, and there's no call for that, and it reflects badly on the candidate you're supporting. So let's knock that off.

Let's go on to health care. Health-care protection has become a necessity of life in our society, yet millions of Americans are not insured and the cost of medical treatment is practically out of control.

How do you propose to control these costs, and how are you going to provide access to health care for every American?

Let's see, whose turn is it to go now?

**QUAYLE:** I think it's Adm. Stockdale's.

**BRUNO:** I think it's Adm. Stockdale's turn to go first. Go ahead, sir.

**STOCKDALE:** Well, we have excellent technical health care, but we don't administer it very well, and the escalating costs top any other budget danger in the — on the horizon, I think. And what Mr. Perot has suggested is that we try to re- — to look at the incentives; the incentives that are in our current way of doing business are what are killing us. There's — there's no incentive for a hypochondriac not to go to the — to Medicare every day. There is no incentive for a doctor to curtail the expensive tests because he's under threat of malpractice lawyers.

And so we — we just have a web of wrong-way incentives that has to be changed by some people who are in the medical profession and some other crafty people who know how to write contracts to change incentives or get — get the — the incentives situation under control.

**BRUNO:** Sen. Gore.

**GORE:** Bill Clinton and I believe that if a criminal has the right to a lawyer, every American family ought to have the right to see a doctor of their own choosing when they need to see a doctor. There are almost 40 million Americans who work full time today and yet have no health insurance whatsoever.

We are proposing to change that, not with a government-run plan, not with new taxes, but with a new approach called managed competition.

We are going to provide a standard health insurance package provided by private insurance companies and eliminate the duplication and red tape and overlap. And we're going to have cost controls to eliminate the unnecessary procedures that are costing so much money today.

There was a bipartisan commission evenly divided between Republicans and Democrats who looked at our plan and the Bush-Quayle proposal. They said ours will

save tens of billions of dollars and cover every American. The Bush proposal, by contrast, will cost us tens of billions and still leave Americans uninsured.

But what I want to know is, why has George Bush waited for three and a half years during this health insurance crisis before finally coming out with a proposal, just before the election, and he still hasn't introduced it in Congress. Why the long wait, Dan?

**BRUNO:** Mr. Vice President.

**QUAYLE:** Hal, President Bush has had his health-care reform agenda on Capitol Hill for eight months. He's had parts of it up there for years. You talk about increasing costs that the president has had on Capitol Hill — medical malpractice reform legislation — for several years. Defensive medicine and health care today cost $20.7 billion. Defense medicine defined as testing and treatment that is only necessary in case of a law suit. Wouldn't that be nice to take $20.7 billion that we're putting into our legal system and put it to preventive health care or women's health care or something else besides trial lawyers?

But no — you don't want to reform the health-care system to drive down costs through medical malpractice. What you're doing — you are talking about a government program. Your program is to ration health care. You said in your statement to see a doctor when you want to see a doctor. When you start rationing health care there's going to be a waiting line to see a doctor unless it's an emergency.

Remember when we rationed energy in this country? Waiting lines at the gasoline stations. The same thing would happen when you ration health care. The president's proposal deals with tax credits, deductions and purchasing health care in the private sector and making health care affordable and available to every single American.

**BRUNO:** Adm. Stockdale, would you like to start the discussion period?

**STOCKDALE:** Well, I'm out of ammunition on this —

**GORE:** Well, let me talk then because I've got a couple of things that I want to say.

**BRUNO:** Go ahead, Senator.

**GORE:** We still didn't get an answer to the question of why George Bush waited for three and a half years —

**QUAYLE:** He didn't wait three and a half years.

**GORE:** — during the national —

**QUAYLE:** I did answer the question.

**GORE:** — health insurance crisis before he even made a proposal. And it still hasn't been submitted to Congress in the form of legislation. I also want to respond to the question about malpractice. Do you know which state has the lowest malpractice premiums in the entire country? Bill Clinton's Arkansas does — partly because he has passed reform measures limiting the time during which malpractice suits can be filed. In fact, tort claims generally have fallen 10 percent under Bill Clinton there.

But you know, that's not the reason for this health insurance crisis. The reason is, we've had absolutely no leadership. Let me tell you about a friend of mine named Mitch Philpot from Marietta, Ga. — not far from here — who Tipper and I met with his family in Johns Hopkins Hospital. Their son, Brett, was in the bed next to our son, and they couldn't pay their medical bills. They used to live in Atlanta, but they lost their house. And while they were there, both Mitch and his wife lost their jobs because they could not get unpaid leave.

We passed legislation to give family leave under circumstances like that, exempting small business. How can you talk about family values, Dan, and twice veto the Family Medical Leave Act?

**BRUNO:** Mr. Vice President.

**QUAYLE:** Pass our Family Leave Act, because it goes to small businesses where the major problem is. Your proposal excluded small business. That's the problem.

Now, let me talk about health care and —

**GORE:** Did you require it? Did you require it?

**QUAYLE:** My turn —

**GORE:** Did you require [inaudible] — [Simultaneous conversation]

**QUAYLE:** My turn.

**GORE:** It's a free discussion.

**QUAYLE:** Take a breath, Al. Inhale.

**GORE:** It's a free discussion.

Did you require family leave in that legislation? Yes or no?

**QUAYLE:** We offered incentives to small businesses. Yes or no —

**GORE:** That's a no, isn't it?

**QUAYLE:** Was small business exempted under your proposal?

**GORE:** Yes.

**QUAYLE:** Yes. And that's where the biggest problem is —

**GORE:** Did you require it of anyone?

**QUAYLE:** I'm going to get back to the topic again —

**GORE:** Did you require it of anyone?

**QUAYLE:** — because he obviously doesn't want to talk about health insurance or health care, which you address. I was absolutely — I shouldn't say that — another Clinton. You pulled another Clinton on me because here you go again. Medical malpractice legislation has been before the Congress of the United States, and you tried to convince the American people that he is for tort reform? The biggest campaign contributors to your campaign are the trial lawyers of America.

We have a letter — and we're going to release it again to the media, if the media is interested — where the head of the trial lawyers of Arkansas said that Bill Clinton was basically in their back pocket, that Bill Clinton has always opposed tort reform of any kind. It's in the letter; we have it; we'll make it available — because Bill Clinton is not for tort reform.

I'd like to know where Bill Clinton stands on health insurance. When he was campaigning in New Hampshire, he said I

am for the pay-or-play health insurance. Pay or play, that's a 7 [percent] to 9 percent payroll tax on every worker in America that participates in this program.

**GORE:** Can I respond?

**QUAYLE:** And then, all of a sudden, this summer he says, oh, I'm not for a pay-or-play. Here we go again. Bill Clinton, one day he's for pay-or-play, the next day he's against pay or play. He does it in education. He writes Polly Williams, a Democrat state legislator in Milwaukee, Wis., saying, "I'm for choice in education;" then he goes to the NEA teachers union and says, "Sorry, I'm not for choice in education because you won't let me be for choice in education."

One time Bill Clinton says term limits — we ought to limit terms; it's ridiculous that a member of Congress can serve for 30, 40, 50 years, and you limit the terms of the president — but that's another subject.

**GORE:** We're fixing to limit one.

**QUAYLE:** It's not going to be mine; it's going to be people like you and /[Sens. Edward M.]/Kennedy and [Howard M.]Metzenbaum and George [J.] Mitchell and the rest of that Democratic Congress on Capitol Hill — that's who we're talking about.

And that's who the American people — as you well know, you've got term limits for a president; you don't have term limits for Congress, and I think it's absolutely ridiculous that we don't.

**GORE:** I want to respond to some of this.

**QUAYLE:** Here goes Bill Clinton again; he says, "Well, term limits, that's an interesting idea, I think I might be in favor of that." Then his Democratic friends in Congress say, "No, Bill, you can't be for that."

Bill Clinton has trouble telling the truth.

**GORE:** I want to respond, if I might.

**BRUNO:** Go ahead, Senator, quickly.

**GORE:** You know, in response to my question before that long laundry list, he said that they had their own family leave proposal. It was just like the proposal of your party back when Social Security was first proposed. You said: We're for it as long as it's voluntary. Same with Medicare. You said: We're for it so long as it's voluntary. Civil rights: We're for it so long as it's voluntary.

**BRUNO:** Senator, I'm going to have to ask you to wrap this one up.

**GORE:** Family leave is important enough to be required.

**BRUNO:** Okay, thanks. Coming out of health care, again trying to avoid controversy, let's talk about the abortion debate.

Abortion rights has been a bitter controversy in this country for almost 20 years. It's been heightened by the recent Supreme Court decisions. So I'll make it very simple in this question: Where do each of you stand on the issue? What actions will your president's administration take on the abortion question? Will it be a factor in the appointment of federal judges, especially to

the Supreme Court? And I believe that Sen. Gore goes first.

**GORE:** Bill Clinton and I support the right of a woman to choose.

That doesn't mean we're pro-abortion; in fact, we believe there are way too many abortions in this country. And the way to reduce them is by reducing the number of unwanted pregnancies, not vetoing family planning legislation the way George Bush has consistently done.

The reason we are pro-choice and in favor of a woman's right to privacy is because we believe that during the early stages of a pregnancy the government has no business coming in and ordering a woman to do what the government thinks is best. What Dan Quayle and George Bush and Jerry Falwell and Pat Robertson think is the right decision in a given set of circumstances is their privilege — but don't have the government order a woman to do what they think is the right thing to do.

We ought to be able to build more common ground among those who describe themselves as pro-choice and pro-life in efforts to reduce the number of unwanted pregnancies.

But, Dan, you can clear this up very simply by repeating after me: I support the right of a woman to choose. Can you say that?

**BRUNO:** Vice President Quayle, your turn.

**QUAYLE:** This issue is an issue that divides Americans deeply. I happen to be pro-life. I have been pro-life for my 16 years in public life. My objective and the president's objective is to try to reduce abortions in this country. We have 1.6 million abortions. We have more abortions in Washington, D.C., than we do live births. Why shouldn't we have more reflection upon the issue before — the decision of abortion is made. I would hope that we would agree upon that. Something like a 24-hour waiting period, parental notification.

I was in Los Angeles recently, and I talked to a woman who told me that she had an abortion when she was 17 years of age. And looking back on that, she said it was a mistake. She said — she said: I wished at that time, that I was going through this difficult time, that I had counseling to talk about the post-abortion trauma, and talk about adoption rather than abortion. Because if I had had that discussion, I would have had the child. Let's not forget that every abortion stops a beating heart. I think we have far too many abortions in this country, in this country of ours.

**BRUNO:** Adm. Stockdale.

**STOCKDALE:** I believe that a woman owns her body and what she does with it is her own business, period. Period.

**BRUNO:** That's it?

**STOCKDALE:** I don't — I, too, abhor abortions, but I don't think they should be made illegal, and I don't — and I don't

think it's a political issue. I think it's a privacy issue.

**BRUNO:** You caught me by surprise. Let's go ahead with the discussion of this issue. Sen. Gore.

**GORE:** Well, you notice in his response, that Dan did not say "I support the right of a woman to choose." That is because he and George Bush have turned over their party to Pat Buchanan and Phyllis Schlafly, who have ordered them to endorse a platform which makes all abortions illegal under any circumstances, regardless of what has led to that decision by a woman.

Even in cases of rape and incest, their platform requires that a woman be penalized, that she not be allowed to make a choice, if she believes, in consultation with her family, her doctor, and others, whoever she chooses, that she wants to have an abortion after rape or incest. They make it completely —

**QUAYLE:** Senator, do you support a 24-hour waiting period?

**GORE:** — illegal under any of those circumstances.

Now they want to waffle around —

**QUAYLE:** Do you support a 24-hour waiting period?

**GORE:** Let me finish this, briefly. Now — now you want to waffle around on it and give the impression that maybe you don't really mean what you say. But again, you can clear it up by simply repeating, "I support the right of a woman to choose." Say it.

**BRUNO:** Let him say it himself; let him say his own words. Go ahead, Mr. Vice President.

**QUAYLE:** Thank you. Talk about waffling around. This issue is a very important issue. It has been debated throughout your public life and throughout my public life, and one thing that I don't think that it is wise to do, and that is to change your position.

At one time, and most of the time in the House of Representatives, you had a pro-life position.

**GORE:** That's simply not true.

**QUAYLE:** In 1987, you wrote a letter, and we'll pass this out to the media —

**GORE:** That is simply not true.

**QUAYLE:** You wrote a letter saying that you oppose taxpayer funding of abortion. Bill Clinton has the same type of a record.

**GORE:** In some circumstances.

**QUAYLE:** You're going to qualify it now.

**GORE:** And I still do.

**QUAYLE:** And Bill Clinton, when he was governor of Arkansas, also worked with the Right-to-Life people and supported Right-to-Life positions, and now he has changed. Talk about waffling around. This is the typical type of Clinton response. Even on the issue like abortion. He's on both sides of the issue.

Take the NAFTA agreement —

**GORE:** Well, wait —

**BRUNO:** Let's stick with the ques-

tion, Mr. Vice President.

**QUAYLE:** How long did he have —

**GORE:** I know you want to change the subject, Dan, but let's stay on this one for a while.

**QUAYLE:** How long did he have to wait — or how quickly did he change his position on education? He changes his position all the time.

**GORE:** Let's stay with this issue for a while.

**QUAYLE:** Bill Clinton — Bill Clinton has trouble telling the truth. Three words he fears most in the English language —

**BRUNO:** Does anybody have any view about the appointment of judges on this?

**QUAYLE:** — Tell the truth.

**GORE:** Yeah, I want to talk about this, because the question was not about free trade or education. The question —

**QUAYLE:** Talk about waffling. You're the one who brought up the —

**GORE:** Now, I let you talk.

**QUAYLE:** — issue of waffling. He's waffled on the abortion issue.

**GORE:** I let you talk. Let me talk now. It's going to be a long evening if you're like this, now.

**QUAYLE:** Oh, no, it's not —

**GORE:** Don't change the subject —

**BRUNO:** Let's get on with it. Gentlemen, let's get on with it.

**GORE:** Don't change the subject —

**QUAYLE:** Well, answer my questions, then.

**GORE:** What you have done —

**QUAYLE:** Answer my questions. On the 24-hour waiting period — do you support that?

**GORE:** I have had the same position —

**QUAYLE:** Do you support that?

**GORE:** I have had the same position on abortion, in favor of a woman's right to choose. Do you support a woman's right to choose —

**QUAYLE:** Do you support a 24-hour waiting period to have —

**GORE:** You're still avoiding —

**QUAYLE:** How about avoiding the question?

**GORE:** — the question. Now, wait a minute. Let me tell you why this is so important. There are millions of women in this country who passionately believe in the right of a woman to privacy. And they [the Republicans] want to stack the Supreme Court with justices who will take away the right to privacy. Make no mistake about it. That is their agenda —

And if you support them, don't be surprised if that is exactly what they want to do, and that is why Dan Quayle refuses to say this evening that he supports the right of a woman to choose.

I agree with Adm. Stockdale and the vast majority of Democrats and Republicans in this country. You know, one of the reasons so many Republicans are supporting the Clinton-Gore ticket is because they've turned over the party to this right-wing extremist group which takes positions

on issues like abortion that don't even allow exceptions for rape and incest.

**BRUNO:** Senator —

**GORE:** Again, can't you just say you support the right of a woman to choose?

**BRUNO:** Could we give Adm. Stockdale a chance to jump in here if he wants to, if he dares to.

**STOCKDALE:** I would like to get in — I feel like I'm an observer at a pingpong game, where they're talking about well, you know, they're expert professional politicians that massage these intricate plots and know every nuance to 'em. And meantime, we're facing a desperate situation in our economy. I've seen the cost of living double in my lifetime. A new granddaughter was born in my family — my granddaughter — three weeks ago. And according to the statistics that we have — that is, the Perot group — the chances of her seeing a doubling of the standard of living are nil. In fact, her children will be dead before another — this standard of living is doubled. So what the heck! Let's get on with talking about something substantive.

**BRUNO:** All right. Mr. Vice President, you'll have a chance to — You'll have a chance in the closing statements.

**QUAYLE:** We need to get on —

**BRUNO:** No, let's move on to another topic.

**QUAYLE:** Just 15 seconds to respond.

**GORE:** Well, can I have 15 seconds also?

**BRUNO:** No, let's move on, gentlemen.

**QUAYLE:** I'll tell you what. If —

**BRUNO:** Let's not — we're not horse trading. We're having a debate. Let's go on. Let's talk about the cities. Because that's where a majority of Americans live, in urban areas, and they're facing a financial and social crisis. They've lost sources of tax revenue. The aid that once came from the federal and state governments has been drastically cut. There's an epidemic of drugs, crime and violence. Their streets, the schools are like war zones. It's becoming increasingly difficult to pay for public education, for transportation, for police and fire protection, the basic services that local government must provide.

Now, everybody says, talks about enterprise zones. That may be part of the solution, but what else are your administrations really going to be willing to do to help the cities?

Vice President Quayle, it's your turn to go first.

**QUAYLE:** Well, Hal, enterprise zones are important, and it's an idea that the president has been pushing, and there's been very strong reluctance on, with the Democratic Congress. We'll continue to push it.

We also want, Hal, to have home ownership. I was at a housing sub — a housing project in San Francisco several months ago and met with people that were trying to reclaim their neighborhood.

They wanted home ownership. They

didn't want handouts. And I was with the Democrat mayor of San Francisco who was there supporting our idea. But when you look at the cities and you see the problems we have with crime, drugs, lack of jobs, I also want to point out one of the fundamental problems that we have in American cities and throughout America today, and that is the breakdown of the American family.

I know some people laugh about it when I talk about the breakdown of the family, but it's true. Sixty percent of the kids that are born in our major cities today are born out of wedlock. We have too many divorces. We have too many fathers that aren't assuming their responsibility. The breakdown of the family is a contributing factor to the problems that we have in urban America.

**BRUNO:** Adm. Stockdale.

**STOCKDALE:** I think enterprise zones are good, but I think the problem is deeper than that. I think we are — you know, when I was — I ran a civilization for several years, a civilization of three to four hundred wonderful men. We had our own laws. We had our own, practically our own constitution. And I put up — I was the — I was the sovereign for a good bit of that. And I tried to analyze human predicaments in that microcosm of life in the — in the world.

And I found out that when I really got down to putting out dos and don'ts, and lots of these included; take torture for this and that, and this and that, and never take any amnesty, for reasons they all understood and went along with. But one of the — we had an acronym, BACKUS, and each one of those B-A-C-K was something for which you — you had to make them hurt you before you did it. Bowing in public, making, making — getting on the radio and so forth. But at the end it was US, BACKUS. You got the double meaning there.

But the US could be called the United States, but it was Unity Over Self, Loners Make Out. Somehow we're going to have to get some love in this country between races and between rich and poor. You have got to have leaders — and they're out there — who can do this with their bare hands, with — working with, with people on the scene.

**BRUNO:** Sen. Gore, please.

**GORE:** George Bush's urban policy has been a tale of two cities: the best of times for the very wealthy; the worst of times for everyone else. We have seen a decline in urban America under the Bush-Quayle administration. Bill Clinton and I want to change that, by creating good jobs, investing in infrastructure, new programs in job training and apprenticeship, welfare reform — to say to a mother with young children that if she gets a good job, her children are not going to lose their Medicaid benefits — incentives for investment in the inner city area, and, yes, enterprise zones. Vice President Quayle said they're important, but George Bush eliminated them from his urban plan, and then —

**QUAYLE:** Well, that's not true.

**GORE:** And then, when they were included in a plan that the Congress passed —

**QUAYLE:** We have been for enterprise zones —

**GORE:** — George Bush vetoed the enterprise zone law, the law that included them, for one reason: because that same bill raised taxes on those making more than $200,000 a year.

Let's face up to it, Dan: Your top priority really, isn't it, to make sure that the very wealthy don't have to pay any more taxes. We want to cut taxes on middle-income families and raise them on those making more than $200,000 a year.

**QUAYLE:** What plan is that?

**GORE:** And if we can take our approach, the cities will be much better off.

**BRUNO:** Let's start the discussion period right here. Go ahead.

**QUAYLE:** What plan is that that's just going to raise taxes on those making over $200,000 a year? You may call that your plan, but everyone knows that you simply can't get $150 billion in new taxes by raising the marginal tax rate to a top rate of 36 percent and only taxing those making $200,000 a year. It's absolutely ridiculous. The top 2 percent which you refer to, that gets you down to $64,000; then you have about a $40 billion shortfall — that gets you down to $36,000 a year. Everybody making more than $36,000 a year will have their taxes increased if Bill Clinton is president of the United States.

And I don't know how you're going to go to urban America and say that raising taxes is good for you. I don't know how you're going to go to urban America and say, well, the best thing that we can offer is simply to raise taxes again. This is nothing more than a tax-and-spend platform. We've seen it before. It doesn't work.

Let me tell you about a story.

**GORE:** Can I respond to some of that?

**QUAYLE:** I've got a very good example —

**GORE:** Can I respond to some of that?

**QUAYLE:** — when we talk about families here, because I was meeting with some former gang members in Phoenix and Los Angeles and Albuquerque, N.M. And when I talked to those former gang members, here's what they told [me about] why they joined the gang. They said, well, joining a gang is like joining a family. I said, joining a family? Yes, because the gang offered support, it offered leadership, it offered comfort, it was a way to get ahead.

Where have we come if joining a gang is like being a member of the family?

**BRUNO:** Sen. Gore, you wanted to respond?

**QUAYLE:** And that's why I think that families have to be strengthened, and you don't strengthen the American family by raising taxes.

**GORE:** I do want to respond to that.

**BRUNO:** Go ahead, Senator, Admiral.

**GORE:** George Bush and Dan Quayle want to protect the very wealthy. That is the group that has gotten all of the tax cuts

under the Bush-Quayle administration. Nobody here who is middle-income has gotten a tax cut because middle-income families have had tax increases under Bush and Quayle in order to finance the cuts for the very wealthy. That's what trickle-down economics is all about. And they want to continue it.

We're proposing to also require foreign corporations to pay the same taxes that American corporations do when they do business here in the United States of America. George Bush has not been willing to enforce the laws and collect those taxes. We want to close that loophole and raise more money in that way.

**BRUNO:** Senator, can we stick to the cities, sir?

**GORE:** Excuse me?

**BRUNO:** Stick to the cities.

**GORE:** All right. Well, he, he talked about ways to raise money to help the cities. What we're proposing is to invest in the infrastructure in cities and have targeted tax incentives for investment right in inner city areas. The enterprise zones represent a part of our proposal, also, and strengthening the family through welfare reform. And you know the Bush administration has cut out — has vetoed family leave, they have cut childhood immunization and college aid.

If you don't support parents and you don't support children, how — how can you say you support families?

**QUAYLE:** How about supporting parents and the right to choose where their kids go to school, Al?

Do you support that?

**GORE:** We —

**QUAYLE:** Let the parents — let the parents —

**GORE:** Do you want me to answer?

**QUAYLE:** — public or private schools?

**GORE:** Want me to answer?

**BRUNO:** Go ahead.

**GORE:** We support the public school choice, to go to any public school of your choice. What we don't support — and listen to what they're proposing — to take U.S. taxpayer dollars and subsidize private schools. Now I'm all for private schools, but to use taxpayer dollars, when the people who get these little vouchers often won't be able to afford the private school anyway, and the private school is not —

**QUAYLE:** Al, I think, I think it's important —

**GORE:** — under any obligation to admit them, that is a ripoff of the U.S. taxpayer.

**QUAYLE:** That's important. This is a very — this is a very important issue. Choice in education is a very important issue.

**BRUNO:** Let him respond.

**QUAYLE:** And he said that he was not for choosing — giving the parents the right to choose to send their children to public schools. But it's okay for the wealthy to choose to send their kids to private schools, but it's not okay for the middle class and the working poor to choose where they want to send their kids to school.

I think that it's time that all parents in America have a right to choose where they send their kids to school to get an education.

**BRUNO:** Adm. Stockdale, would you like to have the last word in this period?

**STOCKDALE:** I — I come down on the side of freedom of school choice. The — and there's a lot of misunderstandings that I've heard here tonight, that I may have the answer to. The — starting at, you know, for the last, almost a decade, we've worried about our schools officially through Washington, and the president had a meeting of all the governors, and then they tried the conventional fixes for schools — that is, to increase the certification of — requirements for the teachers, to lengthen the school day, to lengthen the school year and nothing — this is a very brief overview of the thing — but nothing happened. And it's time to change the school's structure. In schools, bureaucracy is bad and autonomy is good. The only good schools we have are those run by talented principals and devoted teachers, and they're running their own show. How many times have I thrived? You know, the best thing I had when I ran that civilization — it succeeded, and it's a landmark. The best thing I had going for me was I had no contact with Washington for all those years.

**GORE:** Could I respond?

**BRUNO:** We have to go on. What I'm about to say doesn't apply to the debate tonight; it applies to the campaign that's been going on outside this auditorium. With three weeks to go, this campaign has at times been very ugly, with the tone being set by personal negative attacks.

As candidates, how does it look from your viewpoint? And are these tactics really necessary? Adm. Stockdale — it's your turn to go first.

**STOCKDALE:** You know, I didn't have my hearing aid turned on. Tell me again.

**BRUNO:** I'm sorry, sir. I was saying that at times this campaign has been very ugly with personal negative attacks. As a candidate, how does it look from where you are, and are these tactics really necessary?

**STOCKDALE:** Nasty attacks — well, I think there is a case to be made for putting emphasis on character over these issues that we've been batting back and forth and [that] have a life of their own. Sure, you have to know where you're going with your government, but character is the big variable in the success. Character of the leaders is the big variable in the success — long-term success — of an administration.

I went to a friend of mine in New York some years ago, and he was a president of a major TV network and he said, you know, I think we have messed up this whole — this election process — it was an election year — by stressing that — putting out the dogma that issues are the thing to talk about, not character.

He said, I felt so strongly about this, I went back and read the Lincoln-Douglas debates. Read those debates. How do they come down? Douglas is all character. He knows all of the little stinky numbers these guys do. Abraham Lincoln had character. Thank God we got the right president in the Civil War.

But that is a question that is a valid one, and you know, I would like to brag about the character of my boss.

**BRUNO:** Okay, Sen. Gore.

**GORE:** This election is about the future of our country, not about personal attacks against one candidate or another. Our nation is in trouble, and it is appalling to me that with 10 million Americans out work, with the rest working harder for less money than they did four years ago, with the loss of 1.4 million manufacturing jobs in our nation, with the health-care crisis, a crisis of crime and drugs and AIDS, substandard education, that George Bush would constantly try to level personal attacks at his opponent.

Now, this, of course, just reached a new low last week when he resorted to a classic McCarthyite technique of trying to smear Bill Clinton over a trip that he took as a student along with lots of other Rhodes Scholars who were invited to go to Russia. It's a classic McCarthyite smear technique. I think the president of the United States ought to apologize. I think that he insulted the intelligence of the American people, and I'm awful proud that the American people rejected that tactic so overwhelmingly that he decided he had made a mistake. Do you think it was a mistake, too, Dan?

**BRUNO:** Okay. Vice President Quayle.

**QUAYLE:** Let me answer the question.

**BRUNO:** Go ahead.

**QUAYLE:** Hal, you said — and I wrote it down here — "personal negative attacks." Has anyone been reading my press clippings for the last four years?

But I happen to — I agree with one thing on — with Sen. Gore, and that is that we ought to look to the future, and the future is, who's going to be the next president of the United States. And is it a negative attack and a personal attack to point out that Bill Clinton has trouble telling the truth? He said that he didn't even demonstrate — he told the people in Arkansas in 1978. Then we find out he organized demonstrations. You know, I don't care whether he demonstrated or didn't demonstrate. The fact — the question is, tell the truth. Just tell us the truth.

Today, Bill Clinton — excuse me — yesterday in Philadelphia on a radio show, just yesterday on a radio show, he attacked — Admiral, he attacks Ross Perot saying the media is giving Ross Perot a free ride. The press asked him when the klieg lights are on, said what do you mean by Ross Perot getting a free ride? He says I didn't say that at all.

I mean, you can't have it both ways. No, I don't think that is a personal attack. What I find troubling with Bill Clinton is he can't tell the truth. You cannot lead this great country of ours by misleading the people.

**BRUNO:** All right, gentlemen, the control room advises me that in order to have time for your closing statements, which we certainly want, there simply is not going to be time for a discussion period on this particular topic.

So let's go to the closing statements. You have two minutes each. And we'll start with Adm. Stockdale.

**STOCKDALE:** I think the best justification for getting Ross Perot in the race again to say is that we're seeing this kind of chitchat back and forth about issues that don't concentrate on where our grandchildren — the living standards of our children and grandchildren. He is, as I have read in more than one article, a revolutionary; he's got plans out there that are going to double the speed at which this budget problem is being cared for. It was asked how, if we would squeeze down so fast that we would strangle the economy in the process. That is an art, to follow all those variables and know when to let up and to nurse this economy back together with pulls and pushes.

And there's no better man in the world to do that than that old artist, Ross Perot. And so I think that my closing statement is that I think I'm in a room with people that aren't the life of reality. The United States is in deep trouble. We've got to have somebody that can get up there and bring out the firehoses and get it stopped, and that's what we're about in the Perot campaign.

**BRUNO:** Thank you. Sen. Gore, your closing statement, sir.

**GORE:** Three weeks from today, our nation will make a fateful decision. We can continue traveling the road we have been on, which has led to higher unemployment and worse economic times, or we can reach out for change. If we choose change, it will require us to reach down inside ourselves to find the courage to take a new direction.

Sometimes it seems deceptively easy to continue with old habits even when they're no longer good for us. Trickle-down economics simply does not work. We have had an increase in all of the things that should be decreasing. Everything that should have been increasing has been going down. We have got to change direction.

Bill Clinton offers a new approach. He has been named by the other 49 governors, Republicans and Democrats alike, as the best and most effective governor in the entire United States of America.

He's moved 17,000 people off the welfare rolls and on to payrolls. He has introduced innovations in health care and education, and again, he has led the nation for the last two years in a row in the creation of jobs in the private sector.

Isn't it time for a new approach, a new generation of ideas and leadership, to put our nation's people first and to get our economy moving again?

We simply cannot stand to continue with this failed approach that is no good for us. Ultimately, it is a choice between hope and fear, a choice between the future and the past. It is time to reach out for a better nation. We are bigger than George Bush has told us we are, as a nation, and we have a much brighter future.

Give us a chance. With your help, we'll change this country, and we can't wait to get started.

**BRUNO:** Vice President Quayle.

**QUAYLE:** Thank you, Hal. I'd like to use this closing statement to talk to you about a few people that I have met in these last four years. I think of a woman in Chicago when I was talking to parents about education where she stood up and said I'm sick and tired of these schools in this city being nothing but a factory for failure. And that's why we support choice in education.

I was in Beaumont, Texas, and met with small-business people, and they wanted to reform the civil justice system because they think our legal system costs too much and there's too much of a delay in getting an answer.

I was in Middletown, Ohio, talking to a welfare woman, where she said I want to go back to work and I had a job offered to me, but I'm not going to take it because I have two children at home and the job that is offered to me doesn't have health insurance. Under President Bush's health-care reform package that woman won't have to make a choice about going back to work or health care for her children, because she'll have both.

I was in Vilnius, Lithuania, Independence Square, speaking to 10,000 people in the middle of winter. Hundreds of people came up to me and said: God bless America.

Yes, in the next four years, as I said, somewhere, some time, there's going to be a crisis, and you need to have a president that is qualified, has the experience and has been tested. Not one time during this evening, during 90 minutes, did Al Gore tell us why Bill Clinton is qualified to be president. He never answered my charges that Bill Clinton has trouble telling the truth.

The choice is yours. The American people should demand that their president tell the truth. Do you really believe — do you really believe Bill Clinton will tell the truth? And do you, do you trust Bill Clinton to be your president?

**BRUNO:** That concludes this vice presidential debate. I'd like to thank Vice President Quayle, Sen. Gore, Adm. Stockdale for being participants.

The next presidential debate is scheduled for this Thursday at 9:00 p.m. Eastern Time at the University of Richmond in Richmond, Va. To all of our viewers and listeners, thank you and good night. ■

# Clinton Hits the Ground Running

The awesome job of turning a campaign into an administration began quickly for President-elect Bill Clinton, but he approached the task with the deliberateness that marked his tenure as governor of Arkansas.

Clinton spent the first three days after the election resting and meeting with advisers before announcing that former Deputy Secretary of State Warren M. Christopher and former National Urban League President Vernon Jordan would lead his transition operation.

Christopher, who supervised the day-to-day transition operations and was eventually named secretary of State in the new administration, had won praise for his direction earlier in the year of the process that led to the selection of Sen. Al Gore, D-Tenn., as Clinton's running mate. Jordan, who was also on the vice presidential search team, was given the title of transition board chairman and assumed responsibility for the Washington side of the operation.

Christopher, talking to reporters in Arkansas on Nov. 6, said he hoped for an orderly transition process that would proceed in a "brisk but nevertheless conscientious" manner.

Clinton was under pressure to act quickly on the transition. Right after the election, clearly fatigued by his marathon campaigning, he said he found the amount of decisions to be made during the pre-inaugural period "mind-boggling."

"There's just an immense amount of work to be done, all the while trying to be faithful to our obligations to thank the people who've helped us and to maintain the kind of can-do and open and flexible culture that was so dominant in our campaign," he said Nov. 4.

Clinton said that while many decisions were still up in the air, he planned to "focus like a laser beam" on the economy.

Democrats in Congress were quick to offer a helping hand. Senate Majority Leader George J. Mitchell, D-Maine, told reporters the day after the election that he expected "a good, positive, productive working relationship" with the new administration.

"I think the one attribute that Gov. Clinton has demonstrated in his previous service as governor has been a remarkable energy and skill in dealing with the legislative branch of government in his own state," Mitchell said. "So I think there is going to be a very positive cooperative attitude and a genuine desire on the part of all concerned to move forward."

However, Republican leaders used the immediate post-election period to stake out potentially confrontational positions in anticipation of exerting some leverage on the upcoming session.

Senate Minority Leader Bob Dole, Kan., told reporters Nov. 4 that he had an election "mandate" to represent the 57 percent of voters who did not support the Clinton ticket. He warned that he would hold Clinton's feet to the fire on reducing the deficit, possibly drawing on help from independent candidate Ross Perot and his supporters.

"It's not that we're going to try to obstruct. We're not going to be stampeded either," said Dole. "It's not all going to be milk and honey for the Democrats."

Clinton soon responded by inviting Democratic leaders to Little Rock, Ark., for consultations and then visiting Washington on Nov. 18-19. He vowed to work closely with lawmakers "to close the loops on the details of our policy" so that he could unveil a consensus economic program shortly after his inauguration.

After a series of get-acquainted meetings with congressional leaders Nov. 19, during which he displayed a keen awareness of how to work the halls of Congress, Clinton said he was "very optimistic" that some agreements could be reached. He said the American people "don't expect miracles of us, but they do expect progress, and they do want us to work. They want us to work together."

Clinton continued to meet regularly with his transition team and outside advisers on a variety of issues, but November ended without him naming any members of his new administration.

The delay prompted considerable comment in the news media, with pundits questioning whether the new administration team would be in place in time to hit the ground running. Clinton shrugged off the criticism, insisting his pace was about the same as past presidents, but he promised to name his full Cabinet before Christmas.

Clinton had said all along that he would choose his economic team first, and on Dec. 10-11 he made good on his word.

For the two key appointments, he picked experienced members of Congress. Texas Sen. Lloyd Bentsen, the chairman of the Finance Committee, was named Treasury secretary, and the chairman of the House Budget Committee, Rep. Leon E. Panetta of California, was named to head the Office of Management and Budget (OMB).

In selecting Bentsen and Panetta, Clinton sent an important signal about his economic plans. The choices made it plain that he was much more concerned about the nation's long-term economic health than about the residual short-term effects of the latest recession. That represented a change, due chiefly to several key indicators that the economy was improving. It also suggested a somewhat greater emphasis on deficit reduction than Clinton seemed to embrace six months before.

By appointing individuals who, for the most part, represent mainstream thinking, Clinton reinforced his own moderate economic outlook. But he also made it clear that he planned to be his own chief economic adviser and to tap disparate points of view.

"In the end," he said Dec. 10, "I will make the ultimate decisions and be the ultimate arbiter when there has to be an arbiter."

That process was to be aided, Clinton said, by the creation of a National Economic Council — to be headed by Robert E. Rubin, co-chairman of Goldman Sachs Corp. Rubin, 54, a relative newcomer to Clinton's inner circle, played the honest broker among competing economic camps during the presidential campaign and that was to be his principal responsibility in his new job.

The first nominations also showed Clinton's primary concern to be practical politics — getting his program enacted. Bentsen and Panetta were regarded members of Congress who could be called upon to sell Clinton's ideas to their former colleagues.

In his next round of appointments, Clinton began to fulfill his pledge to select a Cabinet that represented the diversity of the country. For the 17 posts formally designated as the Cabinet, Clinton named four blacks (Com-

merce Secretary Ronald H. Brown, Energy Secretary Hazel R. O'Leary, Agriculture Secretary Mike Espy and Veterans' Affairs Secretary Jesse Brown), two Hispanics (Housing Secretary Henry G. Cisneros and Transportation Secretary Federico F. Peña) and **three** women (HHS Secretary Donna Shalala, Energy Secretary Hazel R. O'Leary, and Attorney General Janet Reno. Clinton also picked two women for jobs that he hoped to elevate to Cabinet status: Environmental Protection Agency Administrator Carol M. Browner and U.N. Representative Madeleine K. Albright.

To accommodate the new president, confirmation hearings on most of Clinton's nominees were held before the inauguration, and most were quickly confirmed in the two days after Clinton was sworn in.

The one major exception was in his selection of an attorney general. Clinton's first nomination for the post, Zoe Baird, ran into strong public opposition and withdrew because she had knowingly hired illegal immigrants as domestic help and had not paid social security taxes. Clinton's apparent second choice, Kimba Wood, also withdrew because she had hired an illegal immigrant, although she had broken no laws.

Following is a rundown of Clinton's major appointments:

## SECRETARY OF TREASURY

As Clinton's Treasury secretary, Lloyd Bentsen was expected to use his vast experience with the tax code and the federal budget to shape Clinton's economic plan and sell it to Congress and the financial markets.

By putting the chairman of the Finance Committee in his Cabinet, Clinton got one of the Senate's true titans, a conservative, business-minded Democrat who was comforting to Wall Street and adept at the ultimate insider game of tax legislating.

But in introducing the members of his economic team at a news conference on Dec. 10, Clinton seemed to take pains to deflect criticism that Bentsen, the millionaire son of a wealthy Texas landowner, understood and catered to the needs of business but not those of average taxpayers.

"I wanted someone who had the unique capacity to command the respect of Wall Street, while showing an unrelenting concern for the Americans who make their living on Main Street," Clinton said.

Bentsen's appointment capped an extraordinary rebirth for a politician who already was considered an elder statesman by the time he claimed the Finance Committee chairmanship in 1987. After waiting 16 years for power, Bentsen thrived in the job. Managing a series of major trade, budget, health and tax bills with stoic efficiency, he emerged as an effective and reliable party leader after a career largely spent promoting Texas business interests.

Bentsen surprised many observers when he surrendered his powerful position to join the Clinton administration. But it was clear that he had grown frustrated with the interminable battles between the White House and Congress during his tenure as chairman.

In 1992 alone, he saw two multibillion-dollar tax bills vetoed after months of exhaustive deal-cutting and long days of grinding floor debate. "I've heard all these stories about my being an insider," Bentsen said Dec. 10. "Let me tell you, I felt like an outsider for 12 years. And I'm tired of the gridlock."

Moving to the Treasury Department was to give Bentsen a critical role on the world financial stage at a time when major issues remained unresolved, such as the amount of assistance the United States should give Russia in its transition to a market economy. Bentsen would represent the United States at the July 1993 meeting in Tokyo of the finance ministers of industrialized nations, which was expected to focus partly on the U.S.-Japan trade and financial relationship.

Bentsen's big break came when his legislative record caught the attention of Massachusetts Gov. Michael S. Dukakis, who gave Bentsen the second spot on the Democratic ticket in 1988. Bentsen performed well throughout the campaign, using his debate with GOP vice presidential nominee Dan Quayle to deliver the most memorable line of the election — "Senator, you're no Jack Kennedy."

He toured the country talking about middle-class issues such as home ownership and the cost of a college education, and voters found his calm, confident manner appealing.

But Bentsen, a shrewd poker player, hedged his bets. Under an unusual Texas law, he was able to run simultaneously for vice president and for re-election to the Senate. After Dukakis' defeat, Bentsen returned for his fourth Senate term, with many Democrats grumbling that their ticket would have been more competitive if the No. 2 candidate had been on top.

As one of the Democrats' two chief tax-writers (the other being House Ways and Means Committee Chairman Dan Rostenkowski, D-Ill.), Bentsen proved willing to accommodate himself to prevailing political winds. A longtime proponent of a tax break on capital gains, he nonetheless was instrumental in helping the Democrats embarrass Bush on the issue in 1990, when they argued that his proposed capital gains tax cut was a giveaway to the wealthy.

When Democrats returned to the tax fairness issue in 1992, Bentsen, working with Rostenkowski and others, crafted tax legislation that contained versions of investment incentives proposed by Bush, including a modest capital gains cut. But Bentsen also insisted on a tax cut for the middle class paid for by higher rates on the wealthy that the president could not accept. Bush vetoed the bill. Clinton may have been impressed by Bentsen's handiwork, despite the veto. Wrapped into one neat package were three of the themes Clinton endorsed during his campaign — middle-class tax relief, higher taxes on upper-income earners and new tax incentives to promote business investment.

While he remained firmly committed to helping the oil and gas industry, former aides and Finance Committee observers contended that Bentsen had become more skeptical about picking winners and losers through the tax code. In addition, the deficit has made handing out expensive tax breaks for particular industries impractical.

Bentsen remained an advocate of broad-based tax incentives to stimulate business investment and personal savings. In that respect, he meshed easily with Clinton, who favored an investment tax credit that would allow businesses to write off a portion of their machinery and equipment purchases.

If Bentsen had a blind spot, it was that in his zeal to restore certain tax breaks eliminated in 1986, he was sometimes willing to accept a further increase in the deficit.

To raise the low U.S. savings rate, Bentsen crusaded to restore the tax deduction for individual retirement accounts (IRAs) to all taxpayers. Critics accused him of budget trickery when he included the expensive IRA plan in a tax bill last year. He delayed the effective date so that the revenue loss would not be felt until after five years, at

which time, said Sen. Bill Bradley, D-N.J., the deficit would "explode."

Bentsen usually stuck to the letter, if not the spirit, of the 1990 budget agreement, which required that any new tax breaks be offset over five years by other revenue-raisers.

## OMB DIRECTOR

Clinton's announcement Dec. 10 that House Budget Committee Chairman Leon E. Panetta would head the White House budget office seemed to signal a greater commitment to deficit reduction than many — including Panetta — suspected during Clinton's presidential campaign.

Panetta, one of Congress' most persistent deficit hawks, had panned the economic plan Clinton unveiled last summer, complaining that it was not a sufficiently serious attack on the deficit. Until the last stages of Clinton's selection process, even Panetta was convinced that his own honest but impolitic response had helped disqualify him from serious consideration, according to sources close to the Budget chairman.

The job of directing OMB traditionally had been one of the most important in the modern White House economic policymaking apparatus. As the source of the president's annual budgets and the only agency that collects budget data throughout the federal government, OMB came to wield tremendous influence over the broad direction of government policy.

Thanks to budget law that gave it the ultimate authority to determine when spending violates preset ceilings, OMB enabled a succession of Republican presidents to confront Democrat-dominated Congresses over fiscal policy.

Whether Panetta would continue that tradition was uncertain. Though he got high marks for knowledge, sharp elbows and doggedness in his two-term leadership of the House Budget Committee, he faced having to contend with one of the heaviest of Senate heavyweights in Treasury Secretary Bentsen.

As Panetta's deputy, Clinton named Alice M. Rivlin, a Brookings Institution scholar who was the first director of the Congressional Budget Office.

Asked about Panetta's lack of enthusiasm for Clinton's campaign stance on the deficit, Clinton told reporters that he was "going to give him a chance to teach me some math."

Clinton noted that Rivlin also had differences with him on economic matters. What he wanted, he said, were not advisers who always agreed with him, but aides "that the Congress will believe are giving them good, honest numbers and are committed to deficit reduction." He added, "You should view their selection as a decision by me that we cannot grow the economy without a very serious and credible long-term deficit-reduction program."

Panetta has been training for the OMB job almost since he came to Congress in 1977. A converted Republican who was forced to resign in 1970 as director of the Office for Civil Rights because the Nixon White House thought he was being too aggressive, Panetta was elected to Congress as a Democrat in 1976 and soon made the budget his area of expertise.

He was named to the Budget Committee in 1979 and served the maximum six years. He then tried to run for chairman, but he would have needed a rules change from the Democratic Caucus. He lost that vote in 1984.

Long before the end of the mandatory four-year waiting period before he could return to the committee, Panetta began campaigning for the chairmanship, which he took over in 1989.

Panetta immersed himself in the technical details of budgeting and became an acknowledged expert on the numbers, a skill that enabled him to play a leading role in the 1990 budget summit negotiations.

After the 1990 budget summit, Panetta earned a reputation as a dogged enforcer of the budget rules and a true believer in the critical importance of deficit reduction — often to the point of annoying his more doctrinaire Democratic colleagues. "Panetta is a Budget chairman first and a Democrat second," said one insider.

## SECRETARY OF LABOR

Labor Department watchers were hoping for a newly energized bureaucracy with a place at the Clinton economics table for Labor Secretary Robert B. Reich, whom Clinton named on Dec. 11.

Reich, 46, was a lecturer at Harvard's Kennedy School of Government, a former director of policy planning at the Federal Trade Commission under President Jimmy Carter and a close friend of Clinton's since their days as Rhodes scholars at Oxford.

During the transition period, Reich headed Clinton's economic policy planning group, though he was not an economist. During the early 1980s, Reich was one of the early advocates of providing government subsidies to build up industry. He was also a strong advocate for meshing education and job training to improve the work force. And he was more interested in raising workers' pay than corporate profits, because he believed workers strengthen the economy by spending their money.

Reich's appointment drew praise both from organized labor and from some business groups.

"It's delightful to have someone appointed who is essentially a part of the economic planning for the new president," said Robert M. McGlotten, legislative director for the AFL-CIO, which represented more than 14 million workers. McGlotten said he did not believe that the Labor secretary needed a background in labor to be effective. Clinton consulted with the AFL-CIO before making his selection public.

At the U.S. Chamber of Commerce, which represented business interests and tended to side with Presidents Bush and Ronald Reagan, Reich's nomination brought enthusiasm.

## EPA ADMINISTRATOR

For Clinton, Carol M. Browner brought crucial advantages to the EPA.

As head of Florida's Department of Environmental Regulation, she understood Clinton's concern that federal environmental rules not overburden states. As a former congressional staff member, she knew the ins and outs of Capitol Hill. And it did not hurt to have worked for Vice President-elect Gore.

"She knows, as I know, what it is like to be governed by the EPA and how awful it can be," Clinton said in announcing the appointment Dec. 11. Yet Clinton said his administration would usher in a new era of increased stature for the EPA. He said Browner would attend Cabinet meetings and that the agency will be treated "as if it were

part of the Cabinet."

"I think [the EPA] plainly should have Cabinet status," Clinton said, vowing to support legislation in Congress to elevate the agency.

Environmentalists and business groups alike applauded Browner, saying the 36-year-old was an activist with a sound sense of the politically possible.

A 1979 graduate of the University of Florida College of Law, Browner quickly rose in Washington. She worked from 1983 to 1986 at Citizen Action, a lobbying group, where she helped win passage of legislation giving citizens the "right to know" about industrial chemical releases.

The Miami native then joined the office of then-Sen. Lawton Chiles, D-Fla., as a legislative aide. There, she was involved in the complex negotiations to expand Big Cypress Natural Preserve, as well as the effort to ban offshore oil wells off the Florida Keys.

She left Chiles' office in 1986 to work as counsel for the Senate Energy and Natural Resources Committee, and later spent two years as Tennessee Sen. Al Gore's legislative director. She worked on a number of environmental issues for Gore, such as the marathon push to pass the 1990 amendments to the Clean Air Act.

As head of Florida's environmental policy, she oversaw an agency with 1,700 employees and a budget of $750 million.

## SECRETARY OF HEALTH AND HUMAN SERVICES

Clinton's choice of University of Wisconsin Chancellor Donna E. Shalala to head the vast Department of Health and Human Services came as a surprise to many.

Shalala, 51, was most often mentioned as a candidate for secretary of Education. But associates said HHS, with its vast array of public health and children's programs, was a better fit for the woman who succeeded Hillary Rodham Clinton as chairman of the board of the Children's Defense Fund, the Washington-based children's advocacy group.

Shalala was most highly regarded for her administrative skills — a necessity for running the department with the largest budget in the federal government, including Social Security, Medicare and the Public Health Service.

One of the areas in which Shalala was not an expert was health policy, one of Clinton's top priorities. But Clinton said he, not his HHS secretary, would be the key player on health reform.

As chancellor at Wisconsin, Shalala headed the nation's fourth-largest university — making her not only the first woman to head a Big Ten school, but also one of only two female heads of major research universities nationwide.

A professor of education and political science, Shalala had a background almost as diverse as the sprawling department she was been named to head.

She taught social science in Iran as a Peace Corps volunteer, served as treasurer of the firm that bailed out New York City in the mid-1970s and was an assistant secretary of the Department of Housing and Urban Development under President Jimmy Carter. As a teenager, she played baseball on a team coached by then-college student (and later New York Yankees owner) George Steinbrenner.

By all reports, Shalala is a hands-on person. One biography calls her "a workaholic who thrives on 15-hour workdays and a perfectionist who personally tested floor waxes for the new buildings at Hunter College," the New York City institution where she was president from 1980 to 1988.

At Wisconsin, she addressed the problem of undergraduates feeling neglected by personally meeting incoming freshmen at the airport, accompanying them to their dormitories, and helping them unpack. Most mornings she could be seen on campus walking her golden retriever, Bucky, while reading The New York Times and listening to a Walkman.

## WHITE HOUSE CHIEF OF STAFF

Clinton turned to his oldest friend to fill one of the most difficult and least defined administration jobs — White House chief of staff.

In naming Thomas F. McLarty III, Clinton selected a man with minimal Washington experience for what is the quintessential inside-Washington role.

Until his appointment, McLarty, who went to kindergarten with Clinton in Hope, Ark., was chairman of Arkla Inc., a natural gas company listed among the Fortune 500.

He had long been involved in Arkansas politics and had been a Clinton confidante through most of the new president's political career.

Clinton dismissed the notion that Washington credentials were crucial. He said instead that most successful White House chiefs of staff have served primarily as "honest brokers," a role he expected his childhood buddy to ably fill.

The 46-year-old corporate executive said that while he did not have Washington experience, he had learned about the nation's capital as a businessman, a former Arkansas state legislator and former chairman of the state's Democratic Party. "And I have learned something about how to make organizations work," he said.

In recent years, the chief of staff had become a power center. The job was filled with varying degrees of success, however, and was often the focus of blame for the failings of a particular administration.

John H. Sununu, Donald T. Regan, John R. Haldeman and other former chiefs of staffs came under fire for their handling of the White House staff and in some cases for inhibiting the flow of information to the president.

Hamilton Jordan, Carter's chief of staff, was widely criticized for fostering bad relations between the White House and Capitol Hill.

McLarty, however, was expected to have a style closer to that of more low-key top presidential aides, such as Howard H. Baker Jr., who served during President Ronald Reagan's second term, and Dick Cheney, who was chief of staff for President Gerald R. Ford.

"The impressive thing is that these two men know each other extremely well and have each other's confidence," said Richard Moe, a top adviser to former Vice President Walter F. Mondale. "And he has no agenda of his own, [which is] when chiefs of staff get into trouble."

McLarty had extensive involvement in Arkansas politics. At age 23, he was elected Arkansas' youngest state legislator.

He later became chairman of the Arkansas Democratic Party and had been close to a number of state politicians, including the state's two Democratic senators, David Pryor and Dale Bumpers.

McLarty took over his family's auto business after college and in 1974 was elected to Arkla's board of directors.

He went to work for the company full-time five years later and worked his way up, becoming the chairman of the board and chief executive officer in 1985.

## SECRETARY OF
## HOUSING AND URBAN DEVELOPMENT

By choosing former San Antonio Mayor Henry G. Cisneros as secretary of Housing and Urban Development (HUD), Clinton launched another politician on the comeback trail.

Cisneros drew plenty of accolades during his eight-year tenure as mayor, particularly for his attention to economic development and promotion of the city. He was touted as a rising national star, mentioned as a potential senator or governor, and seriously considered as Mondale's vice presidential running mate in 1984.

But like Clinton, Cisneros became engulfed in controversy over an extramarital affair. The affair with a campaign supporter — as well as his infant son's medical problems — contributed to Cisneros' decision not to seek re-election in 1989. It appeared that his promising political career had been cut short.

He spent the four years before Clinton's election running a financial consulting company, Cisneros Asset Management, as well as a health and benefit planning company and a communications firm.

A San Antonio native, Cisneros kept up an active schedule in civic matters, from promoting educational finance equity to increasing Hispanics' clout. He found reconciliation at home, too; his wife dropped her divorce petition in 1991 a few weeks after filing it.

While generally liberal on social issues, Cisneros as mayor put a strong emphasis on economic development. Among the public and private projects developed during his term were the Alamodome stadium, Sea World, a biotechnology park and expansion of the city's convention center.

## SECRETARY OF COMMERCE

One man most everyone expected to be part of Clinton's administration was Ronald H. Brown, the successful chairman of the Democratic National Committee (DNC) and the first black to hold the top post in either major party.

Brown's name was mentioned for several jobs, including ambassador to the United Nations, attorney general and U.S. trade representative.

Secretary of Commerce was not among these, and Clinton may have surprised many Dec. 12 by naming Brown to run the department. But the selection set up the kind of career challenge Brown had faced repeatedly.

Brown, 51, had ended the era of all-white fraternities as a student at Middlebury College in Vermont a generation earlier. He was the first African-American to serve as chief counsel on a Senate standing committee (Judiciary) and the first black partner at his Washington law firm.

Brown worked for liberals such as Massachusetts Sen. Edward M. Kennedy and civil rights leader Jesse Jackson. And he remained close to his former law school professor, New York Gov. Mario M. Cuomo.

But as DNC chairman, he was part of the effort to increase the party's mainstream appeal. And at the last two Democratic national conventions, his skills and contacts had made him a bridge between party factions.

Brown faced some criticism because of ties to certain foreign firms. As a lawyer-lobbyist with Patton, Boggs & Blow, he served a variety of corporate and foreign clients — from Japanese electronics firms to the government of Haiti under dictator Jean-Claude "Baby Doc" Duvalier.

To satisfy critics, Brown resigned from his firm and severed his ties with all former clients.

## SECRETARY OF VETERANS AFFAIRS

In naming Jesse Brown as head of the Department of Veterans Affairs (VA), Clinton chose a man who intimately knew the inner workings of the agency — both as a veteran and a lobbyist.

Brown, 48, was the executive director of Disabled American Veterans (DAV), a 1.3-million member nonprofit group of wartime disabled veterans that lobbied Congress and the executive branch on veterans issues. He occupied the top spot from 1988 to 1992, and he worked for the organization for 25 years.

Associates said Brown viewed veterans' health care as a top priority and that he also wanted veterans to receive their benefits quickly and with quality consideration of their claims. Claims backlogs made it difficult for veterans to navigate the VA system.

Brown was also interested in programs to help veterans who were homeless or dependent on drugs.

Brown served in the U.S. Marine Corps from 1963 to 1966, when he was wounded in action in Vietnam. The injury, for which he received the Purple Heart, left his right arm partially paralyzed. He began working at the DAV in 1967.

## SECRETARY OF STATE

Warren M. Christopher did not have a reputation as a deep thinker on foreign policy. But over the years he had expressed some deep-seated views on the conduct of foreign affairs that seemed likely to guide his stewardship as Bill Clinton's secretary of State.

As deputy secretary of State during the Jimmy Carter administration, Christopher asserted that international conflicts can yield to peaceful negotiations, that Congress should keep out of the day-to-day conduct of foreign policy and that the secretary of State should not have to defend his turf as the president's foreign policy spokesman.

In a 1981 speech on the "lessons of Iran," Christopher urged patience and quiet diplomacy, rather than a reliance on force, in dealing with crises.

"I believe we should grasp, as a central lesson of the crisis, the wisdom in seeking negotiated settlements to international disputes," he said.

Indeed, the shining moment in Christopher's State Department career was in 1980, when he took the lead in negotiating the release of the 52 American hostages held by Iran. But the Iranians waited until after Ronald Reagan became president on Jan. 20, 1981, before releasing the hostages.

Perhaps typically, Christopher had laboriously laid the groundwork, while others reaped the rewards. When the Senate approved a resolution praising Christopher and other State Department officials, Howell Heflin, D-Ala., called him "an unsung American hero."

After his tenure in the State Department, Christopher addressed the issue of which branch — and which department — should predominate in setting the foreign policy agenda.

In a 1982 article in Foreign Affairs magazine, he called on Congress to "recognize and accept the responsibility of the executive to conduct and manage foreign policy on a daily basis."

And Christopher said that there should be no struggle for primacy between the State Department and the National Security Council, of the sort that hamstrung most recent administrations.

"The secretary of State should be the architect of our foreign policy and sole authoritative spokesman other than the president," he wrote. "The National Security adviser should shun public attention, eschewing television appearances, press briefings and diplomatic missions abroad."

Throughout his career, Christopher was viewed as a competent, careful diplomat. He built a reputation as the quintessential trouble-shooter, taking on tasks as daunting and as varied as the negotiations over the American hostages in Iran and the investigation of the Los Angeles police force after devastating riots in spring 1992.

Yet his personal qualities — as well as his close relationship with Clinton — were at least as important in landing the nomination. Christopher impressed Clinton with his smooth management of the day-to-day operations of the Clinton transition. He also received high marks for leading the team that selected Tennessee Sen. Al Gore as Clinton's running mate.

"He's got experience, he's a superb negotiator and he's a man of good judgment," said Joseph S. Nye Jr., a former deputy under secretary of State during the Carter administration who directs the Center for International Affairs at Harvard University.

The cautious corporate attorney will need those skills as he represents the Clinton administration before a host of foreign policy troubles that have defied solution.

From Somalia to Haiti, from the instability in the former Soviet Union to the war in the former Yugoslavia, foreign crises threatened to divert the attention of the Clinton administration from its overarching objective of reviving the domestic economy.

However, Christopher was unable to shake the perception that he lacked the stature of foreign policy strategists with sterling academic credentials and the ability to formulate sweeping statements on geopolitics, such as former Secretary of State Henry Kissinger and Zbigniew Brzezinski, Carter's national security adviser.

In 1980, Christopher was a candidate to replace Cyrus R. Vance as secretary of State after Vance resigned over Carter's failed hostage rescue mission. At the time, former Rep. Benjamin S. Rosenthal, D-N.Y., called Christopher "more of a mechanic than a philosopher." He eventually was passed over for the top job; Carter selected former Sen. Edmund S. Muskie, D-Maine.

Harvard's Nye maintained that the uncertain terrain of the post-Cold War era, with its jumbled alliances and brush-fire conflicts, played to Christopher's strengths as a pragmatist. "He's not a Kissinger," Nye said. "But I'm not convinced a Kissinger would be a good thing at this time."

Hodding Carter, the State Department spokesman during the Carter administration, responded sharply to Christopher's detractors. "Excuse me, but what have the people with 'strategic vision' been writing during the past five years?" Carter asked. "It doesn't matter what the subject was — they were almost always wrong."

Christopher, known as "Chris" to his friends, also is an unprepossessing man with an almost legendary ability to keep secrets. "He would have made a great judge," said Bryce Nelson, who served as director of communications for the panel, known as the Christopher commission, that studied and then criticized the Los Angeles police.

"He's a modest public servant, the type that you rarely see at the top levels of government," Nelson said.

## DEFENSE SECRETARY

For nearly a decade, House Armed Services Chairman Les Aspin, Wis., tried to nudge the Democratic Party toward the middle of the political road on defense questions, just as Clinton did on a broader range of issues.

But aside from that general alignment of political purposes, Aspin had not been particularly close to Clinton before the Democratic National Convention in July. During the fall campaign, however, Aspin became a key adviser to Clinton on national security policy. The two men hit it off well, by several accounts, sharing a fascination with the art of forging politically viable solutions to complex policy problems.

From the time he gained the Armed Services chair in 1985, Aspin has tried unabashedly to use his position, and his mastery of the subject matter, to shape — and thus steer — policy debates in the House. His early efforts frequently were frustrated by fellow Democrats' reaction to his often-abrasive style and to his disregard for liberal orthodoxy. But beginning in late 1989, Aspin, backed by a small cadre of politically savvy aides, fostered a more congenial and productive relationship with his colleagues. In the past three years, only Senate Armed Services Committee Chairman Sam Nunn, D-Ga., has matched Aspin's ability to define the terms of public and congressional debate on military affairs.

In the past, Aspin has disclaimed interest in being secretary of Defense, saying he would be cut out of the policy game once he left that job. But this time, with a like-minded Democrat headed for the White House and the stage set for crafting a new U.S. defense stance for the post-Cold War world, he wanted the job enough to do something very uncharacteristic: He kept quiet.

In the seven weeks between Clinton's election and his announcement Dec. 22 that Aspin was his choice to head the Pentagon, two highly charged defense issues surfaced:

● A court case highlighted Clinton's campaign promise to eliminate the current policy barring homosexuals from the armed services, a pledge vigorously opposed by senior military leaders.

● Acting under U.N. auspices, President Bush ordered up to 28,000 U.S. troops to Somalia to protect humanitarian relief efforts from the prevailing anarchy. It fell to Clinton to decide how long, and in what role, U.S. forces would remain.

Both issues cast long shadows over the incoming administration, and the Somalia case touched on the questions of when U.S. military forces should be used, an issue Aspin has tried to move to the front burner. Nevertheless, presumably to avoid foreclosing Clinton's options, Aspin had maintained an unwonted silence on both matters.

But during Aspin's confirmation hearing Jan. 7, one message that came through was his belief in the use of U.S. force as an instrument of foreign policy — even for limited objectives with uncertain results.

And he remained noncommittal on Clinton's campaign promise to lift the ban on homosexuals in the military, noting that allied governments had abandoned similar bans and making no suggestion that Clinton would not keep his pledge. In the early days of Clinton's presidency, the issue of the gay ban remained in the forefront until a compromise was announced Jan. 29, which put lifting of the ban on hold until July 15.

As of early 1993, Aspin had ordered the Pentagon to draft plans for a fiscal 1994 budget that would trim at least $10.8 billion from the 1993 appropriation. And Aspin stood by his recommendation of February 1992 that U.S. forces be cut more deeply than President Bush had proposed. Compared with the plan presented by Bush's Defense secretary, Dick Cheney, Aspin had called for keeping on active duty nine Army divisions rather than 12, 10 Air Force fighter wings rather than 15, and 340 ships (including 11 aircraft carriers) rather than 450 ships (including 12 carriers).

Aspin said his proposed force would be large enough to conduct simultaneously a massive ground war in the Middle East, an aerial defense of South Korea against attack from the north, and a minor intervention on the scale of the 1989 occupation of Panama.

But Cheney, Joint Chiefs of Staff Chairman Gen. Colin L. Powell Jr. and other top brass blasted Aspin's proposed force as dangerously anemic. And they contended that his effort to calibrate the size of the force against specific potential threats ignored the uncertainties of a world no longer structured by the U.S.-Soviet standoff.

While briefing reporters Dec. 4 on the planned deployment to Somalia, Powell warned against efforts to cut the margin of U.S. strength too fine, "by those [who] want to size the force exactly plus one person against a threat they think exists now, [which] isn't the one we're going to have to deal with two days from now."

In a Sept. 21 speech, Aspin hinted strongly that he saw the current Pentagon leadership as unduly loath to use military force for limited objectives: "striking military targets or assets to influence behavior elsewhere.... [So-called smart bombs] have improved our ability to make air strikes with little if any loss of U.S. lives and with a minimum of collateral damage and loss of civilian lives on the other side," he said. "We can target communication nodes, power grids and command and control assets . . . the kinds of targets that national leadership and military commands hold dear."

Since the Vietnam War, however, U.S. military leaders have vehemently derided proposals to use force in a finely calibrated way as an instrument of diplomatic leverage.

Aspin had endorsed a plan for the anti-ballistic missile (ABM) program, known as the Strategic Defense Initiative (SDI), hammered out in 1991 by Nunn and several Republican senators, that would orient SDI toward deploying early in the next decade a limited, ground-based defense that would comply with the 1972 treaty limiting ABM systems. Aspin recommended slashing SDI by $2.5 billion, basically freezing funding at the fiscal 1993 level.

While supporting SDI research, Clinton has been ambiguous on whether he backs deployment. But in 1991, then-Sen. Al Gore vigorously opposed it. *(1991 Almanac, p. 412)*

## NATIONAL SECURITY ADVISER

In 1990, international relations scholar Anthony Lake sounded a warning to future U.S. policy-makers. "An end to the Cold War," he wrote, "does not presage an end to the rough-and-tumble of international relations as they have always been conducted."

Lake, appointed as national security adviser by Clinton, has proved more prescient than he might have imagined. He now will be facing the post-Cold War crises he forecast two years ago — including "new, war-caused famines" and dangerously increased flows of refugees — in countries such as Somalia and Bosnia-Herzegovina.

To deal with those crises, Clinton planned to rely heavily on veterans of former President Jimmy Carter's administration. During the Carter years, Lake was director of policy planning at the State Department, where his deputy was Washington attorney Samuel R. "Sandy" Berger — who will serve as Lake's top aide in the White House.

A professor of international relations at Mount Holyoke College and the author of several books on foreign affairs, Lake is expected to add intellectual firepower to Clinton's national security team.

Like Clinton, Lake carried some baggage from the Vietnam era. In 1970, he resigned his position as special assistant to National Security Adviser Henry A. Kissinger to protest the secret U.S. invasion of Cambodia.

As Clinton's foreign policy wise men during the presidential campaign, Lake and Berger made a concerted effort to heal lingering bitterness from the Democratic Party's long-running battles over foreign policy, which date back to Vietnam.

Lake had some personal fence-mending to do with the party's hawks. During the Carter administration, Lake was accused of shutting out members of the Coalition for a Democratic Majority — a conservative forerunner to the Democratic Leadership Council — from key appointments in the State Department. He has denied the accusation.

Undoubtedly, the demise of communism helped Lake and Berger bring together the party's disparate elements. Lake said, "There is a lot more common ground than there used to be in the days of the ideological wars in the party."

## SECRETARY OF TRANSPORTATION

During his eight years as mayor of Denver, Federico Peña put so much emphasis on major building projects that one critic accused him of having an "edifice complex." Peña's skill as a builder, though, is one of the main reasons that Clinton chose him to be his secretary of Transportation.

"As I said often during the campaign, we must rebuild America's infrastructure to rebuild the economy," Clinton said when he introduced Peña to the media on Christmas Eve. "Meeting these needs will be a truly monumental task, one that calls for a secretary of Transportation who knows how to build and who knows how America's cities and suburbs and rural areas work."

Fittingly, Peña's biggest edifice was in the field of transportation: a $2.7 billion airport outside Denver that is slated to open in October 1993. Working on that project gave Peña an insider's understanding of the Transportation Department, and introduced him to some of the key players in Congress on transportation issues.

Supporters such as George F. Doughty, the former aviation director in Denver, said Peña had the persistence, vision and focus needed to lift major public works projects off the blueprints and onto the ground. He also had the ability to build a consensus in support of an expensive and controversial project, said Maria Garcia Berry, an influential Denver lobbyist.

Critics of Peña's tenure as mayor, including Denver City Councilman Ted Hackworth, called him indecisive and accused him of loading his city with debt. In addition, Pierre Jimenez, the president of Hispanics of Colorado, said, "There's some suspicion on the part of community

leaders here in Denver that very few Hispanics will go to Washington" with Peña.

On the other hand, Peña was expected to be a strong advocate for minority set-asides, given his insistence on set-asides at the new Denver airport.

Peña was Clinton's second Hispanic nominee for a Cabinet post; the first was former San Antonio Mayor Henry G. Cisneros for secretary of Housing and Urban Development.

The son of a Texas cotton broker, Peña started his career in Colorado as an attorney for two Hispanic advocacy groups. He spent four years in the Colorado legislature before ousting the longtime mayor of Denver at age 36.

As mayor, Peña helped bring three major public works projects to fruition — the airport, a convention center and a baseball stadium — in addition to pushing through more than $450 million in bonds for public improvements. Floyd Ciruli, a pollster in Denver and former chairman of the Colorado Democratic Party, said Peña helped convince the public that these projects were wise investments at a time of deep regional recession. "If America's ready [to make that kind of investment], Peña's the man to do it. He will take the bit in his teeth and run hard with it," Ciruli said.

Clinton seems ready, and so do such key members of Congress as Rep. Norman Y. Mineta, D-Calif., and Sen. Max Baucus, D-Mont., the likely chairmen of the public works committees. An array of transportation and civic groups is pushing for more public works spending, too. It remained to be seen if the money could be found to finance this spending, or if Clinton and Congress were willing to push the federal government further into debt for the sake of infrastructure.

Another potential hurdle was the concern among some congressmen that a massive public-works program will fuel inflation.

James E. Landry, president of the Air Transport Association of America, said he was encouraged by Peña's wish to help the airline industry compete in the global marketplace. The industry was eager for help from the Transportation Department in opening foreign airports to American carriers, in reducing the regulatory burden and in pushing some tax relief through Congress.

The maritime industry also was clamoring for help, and Peña has expressed sympathy with that cause as well.

## U.N. REPRESENTATIVE

For Madeleine K. Albright, the third time was the charm. The Georgetown University professor spent the past three presidential campaigns serving as a top foreign policy adviser to the Democratic ticket. This time, the effort paid off.

As Bill Clinton's choice for U.N. ambassador, Albright could put to the test many of the Democratic foreign policy ideas she helped keep alive during the 1980s.

The post was especially crucial in light of the more-activist, but uncertain, role envisioned for the United Nations in the post-Cold War world. Albright, 55, said Clinton told her that "he wanted to see the United Nations not only as a peacekeeper but as a peacemaker, not only in helping to resolve disputes but also in preventing them."

Albright, who had also served for the past three years as president of the Center for National Policy, a Democratic think tank, brought to the job a long string of political and policy associations and, friends said, an ability to pull together and organize ideas.

"She has the capacity to sit through tedious meetings, to broker differences, to listen to people, to find common ground," said Robert E. Hunter, director of European Studies with the Center for Strategic and International Studies, and a longtime colleague. "In other words, when you're dealing with 160 different countries, it's the people skills that matter most, and she has them."

Sen. Richard G. Lugar of Indiana, a senior Republican on the Foreign Relations Committee, said Albright brought to the job a "very broad view on many international situations. I respect that."

But one Albright colleague, who asked not to be identified, described her as "more of a process person" and suggested that a president with weak foreign policy credentials might need a U.N. ambassador with a more clearly defined world view.

In any event, Albright, who specialized in Eastern Europe and Soviet studies, had shown an indisputable flair for exploring the world of foreign policy ideas. During the 1980s, her Georgetown home became a foreign-policy salon for Democratic experts waiting for the return of their party to the White House. She also continued to counsel congressional Democrats on foreign policy, including offering the advice that the United States should try to avert war with Iraq and rely on international sanctions.

During the 1984 campaign, Albright was foreign policy adviser to vice presidential nominee Geraldine A. Ferraro. Four years later, she was Michael S. Dukakis' chief foreign policy adviser, and she worked for Clinton, most recently as part of the national security transition team.

Born in Czechoslovakia, Albright came to the United States at age 11 when her father, Josef Korbel, a Czech diplomat, defected from the communist-controlled country while in the United States to serve on a special U.N. commission.

"You can therefore understand how proud I will be to sit at the United Nations behind the nameplate that says 'United States of America,'" she said in accepting the appointment.

## U.S. TRADE REPRESENTATIVE

Los Angeles lawyer and lobbyist Mickey Kantor needed all of his formidable negotiating skills to handle the job that good friend and Clinton handed him on Christmas Eve.

As Clinton's nominee for U.S. trade representative, Kantor, 53, took on one of the most demanding jobs in the administration with virtually nothing in his résumé to qualify him except his reported ability to bring warring sides to common ground.

Kantor's lack of international trade experience made him similar to several of his predecessors. Carla A. Hills, U.S. trade representative during the Bush administration, for example, was a Washington lawyer and a former secretary of the Department of Housing and Urban Development when Bush tapped her for the job in 1988.

Hills bequeathed enormous problems to Kantor. Top agenda items include a push to complete the long-stalled Uruguay Round of global free-trade talks and the negotiation of side agreements to the North American Free Trade Agreement with Canada and Mexico that Clinton said are needed to protect workers and the environment.

As trade representative, Kantor would have to deal with questions such as whether countries such as Japan were violating trade agreements with the United States.

Kantor served as Clinton's campaign manager, but he was shoved aside by other Clinton aides after the election in part for fear that his image as a high-powered lobbyist for some of the nation's biggest corporations would taint the transition.

His smooth orchestration of the two-day economic summit in Little Rock, Ark., on Dec. 14-15 reportedly helped heal any difficulties he might have had with Clinton.

Kantor first met Clinton in 1978, when he served with Hillary Rodham Clinton on the board of the Legal Services Corporation.

Kantor's track record in high-level Democratic politics dates to 1972, when he was staff director for the campaign of Sargent Shriver, George McGovern's running mate. Kantor later held top jobs in Alan Cranston's 1974 Senate campaign and the presidential campaigns of Edmund G. "Jerry" Brown Jr. in 1976, Jimmy Carter in 1980 and Walter Mondale in 1984. At his Los Angeles law firm, he shared the letterhead with former Democratic National Committee Chairman Charles T. Manatt.

## INTERIOR SECRETARY

The selection of former Arizona Gov. Bruce Babbitt as Interior secretary held promise of a new era of activism for a once-sleepy department, which found itself on the front lines of the battle over the management of the federal government's vast holdings of land and natural resources in the West.

Babbitt heads a sprawling department that manages more land than almost any state in the union, ranging from Alaskan wilderness to California desert, from the Grand Canyon National Park to Civil War battlefields in Virginia.

With the West becoming increasingly urbanized and its natural resources called upon to do more things for more people, Babbitt was in the center of the fierce environmental debates now raging in the West.

Babbitt was one of the foremost conservationists in the country. He cut his teeth on Western environmental issues in 1980 when, as governor of Arizona, he shepherded through the state Legislature a water-management bill that managed to placate thirsty urban areas, farm districts and mining concerns.

"The secretary of the Interior must be tough enough to stand up to powerful interests, skillful enough to integrate economic concerns and the needs for economic growth," Clinton said at the Dec. 24 news conference announcing Babbitt's nomination.

Babbitt and Clinton are of the same breed of 1980s governors who endeavored to move the Democratic Party to the center. Babbitt liked to describe himself as part of the "radical center." He and Clinton were founding members of the Democratic Leadership Council, the centrist policy group that set the tone for this year's Democratic presidential victory.

Since leaving government for private legal practice in 1987, Babbitt had immersed himself in environmental issues on national and international levels. He had been a well-regarded critic of Western water and land use policy. Babbitt was often credited with coining the term "public use" to describe how the federal lands of the West — once in the sole purvey of ranchers, miners and loggers — must accommodate environmental and recreational needs.

Babbitt said he would continue "making available the natural resources — oil and gas, timber, minerals, forage — that create good jobs and prosperous communities in the West and indeed, all over America."

In a 1991 interview with Congressional Quarterly, Babbitt said the old philosophy of multiple uses for federal land, wherein resource users are supposed to coexist with recreationalists and wildlife, "is a cop-out. The agencies say everybody can do everything everywhere, and the fact is they can't."

As expected, environmental groups were thrilled with Babbitt's selection.

"I can't think of a better choice," said George Frampton, president of the Wilderness Society. "When Bruce Babbitt moves into the secretary's office, the ghost of [Reagan Interior Secretary] James Watt will, at long last, be exorcised."

But Western private property groups were not as happy.

"I think Bruce Babbitt and Al Gore will do for us what James Watt did for the preservationists," said Charles S. Cushman, the executive director of the League of Private Property Voters, a Washington-state based group that is fighting against what it called excessive regulation of federal lands.

"We have deep concerns that Mr. Babbitt will bring in underlings from the preservation groups ... who want to eliminate resource-dependent communities of the West," Cushman said.

## CIA DIRECTOR

Attorney R. James Woolsey came to the job of central intelligence director with a résumé that marked him as one of the most prominent Democratic appointees in the GOP administrations of Ronald Reagan and President Bush. For more than a decade, he has been closely aligned with Defense Secretary Les Aspin in trying to move the Democratic Party away from its post-Vietnam aversion to military force.

A Stanford graduate, Woolsey shared with Clinton two other academic credentials: a Rhodes scholarship to Oxford and a law degree from Yale. He spent his Army service (1968-70) in the kind of Pentagon analysis job that Aspin had held shortly before him. For much of that time, he served as an adviser to the U.S. delegation to the Strategic Arms Limitation Talks (SALT).

Woolsey came into political prominence in 1983-84 as a member of the White House advisory panel chaired by Brent Scowcroft, appointed by Reagan to come up with a plan for deploying the controversial MX missile. Woolsey collaborated with Aspin, then-House member Al Gore, Tenn., and other defense-minded Democrats to shape the commission's proposal to deploy a small number of MXs while developing a small mobile missile (dubbed Midgetman).

As a gesture of Reagan's willingness to adapt U.S. arms control policy to the panel's recommendation, the president named Woolsey to the team negotiating the Strategic Arms Reduction Treaty (START) with the Soviet Union.

As Clinton's intelligence chief, the Tulsa-born Woolsey was to deal closely with two fellow Oklahomans: House Intelligence Chairman Dave McCurdy, D-Okla., and retired Adm. William J. Crowe, the former chairman of the Joint Chiefs of Staff whom Clinton named to head the President's Foreign Intelligence Advisory Board.

## SECRETARY OF ENERGY

Clinton's choice of Minnesota utilities executive Hazel R. O'Leary, 55, to be Energy secretary may have been a

surprise to the conventional wisdom, but O'Leary has what has become a familiar mix in Clinton's appointments: hands-on industry experience and a knowledge of how the federal government works.

As a black woman, O'Leary's designation also helps Clinton keep his pledge to select a Cabinet that "looks like America." Clinton recruited O'Leary — who was recommended by a friend in the energy business — amid increasing complaints from women's and minority groups about the lack of diversity in the Cabinet.

Her nomination also signaled Clinton's determination to move the nation's energy policy away from its focus on production to an emphasis on conservation as a way to lessen this country's dependence on foreign oil.

But at the same time, some industry watchers criticized the decision because O'Leary, while well-versed in energy production and conservation, lacks expertise in the area of nuclear weapons production and handling of its environmentally threatening aftermath, nuclear waste. The department is now trimming its nuclear facilities — which account for approximately two-thirds of its budget — but enormously expensive and technically challenging cleanup and disposal problems remain.

With her utility executive background, O'Leary was familiar with the problems utilities have in storing nuclear waste and supported the opening of a high-level nuclear waste dump at Yucca Mountain in Nevada — something many environmentalists and Nevadans opposed.

Clinton acknowledged the challenges facing the department but suggested Dec. 21 that he wanted the department to focus on reducing U.S. dependence on foreign oil.

O'Leary, as executive vice president of Northern States Power Co., was in effect the chief lobbyist for the utility, which serviced 1.7 million people in Wisconsin, Minnesota, Michigan and the Dakotas. She devoted much of her time to promoting innovative alternative energy sources and conservation for the utility.

"I feel that I've been training for this job for about 20 years," she said at the news conference.

She added: "I stand before you, having been 20 years in this business, to tell you we're no better off in terms of stepping back from that foreign barrel of oil than we were almost in 1974. That's unconscionable for this nation, and it's also unconscionable for those who have attempted to set the policy. It has not worked."

Before joining Northern States Power, O'Leary was vice president of O'Leary Associates, an energy consulting firm in Washington that specialized in preparing expert testimony and project financing.

But some of her most valuable experience came during the Ford and Carter administrations, where she worked in the Energy Department and its predecessor, the Federal Energy Administration. There, she was a regulator of the petroleum, natural gas and electric industries, as well as of federal energy conservation programs.

## SECRETARY OF EDUCATION

By choosing former South Carolina Gov. Richard W. Riley to head the Department of Education, Clinton has found someone similar to himself to reform the public schools.

Both Riley and Clinton were former Southern governors considered to be at the vanguard of the education reform movement.

"No issue matters more to me than education," Clinton said Dec. 21 in announcing Riley's nomination. Noting that the Department of Education does not directly teach students or pay teachers, he outlined what the department could do: "It can set benchmarks, national standards for excellence. The secretary can pull together teachers and parents, businesses and universities, to design schools . . . that meet tomorrow's needs."

Clinton praised Riley's state reform program for emphasizing preschools, better working conditions for teachers and more funding for colleges. Others agreed.

"I think it's a superb appointment of somebody who has an excellent record as an education governor," said Robert H. Atwell, president of the American Council on Education, an umbrella organization for colleges and universities. "He's a very thoughtful person and somebody who is close to Bill Clinton. What more could you ask for?"

A Democrat, Riley, 60, served as governor from 1979 to 1987. While in office, he pushed through the legislature a major school improvement bill paid for by raising the sales tax by one penny.

"It was a major achievement to get a tax increase through in South Carolina," said Neal D. Thigpen, a political scientist and commentator at Francis Marion University in Florence, S.C. Thigpen said Riley did it through personal lobbying: "He was a workhorse with the General Assembly."

The package included initiatives to boost academic standards, improve testing, upgrade teacher and principal training and provide schools with incentives to improve student performance. For example, beginning in the 1989-90 school year, the law required that all students pass an exit examination before receiving a high school diploma. And the state had begun paying for teachers and principals to take courses to improve their skills.

"The choice of Dick Riley as Education secretary signals an important and exciting change for our nation's students," said Albert Shanker, president of the American Federation of Teachers, a union representing 750,000 teachers. "As a visionary education reformer in South Carolina, Riley recognized that real changes require transforming the whole system, not just depending on a single magic bullet."

Riley said he would continue working toward the national education goals developed in 1989 by President Bush and the nation's governors. Those goals include reducing the dropout rate and making American students first-rate in math and science.

He described the Clinton education agenda as one of opportunity, "one that will give every single child a fair chance . . . one that will offer training to high school students who must compete for jobs in the future. One that will give young people a chance to serve their nation."

After Riley left office, he joined the law firm of Nelson, Mullins, Riley and Scarborough. He was a political science lecturer at Furman University, his alma mater.

Clinton had tapped Riley to work on the transition team in Washington, making recommendations for lower-level appointments.

## SECRETARY OF AGRICULTURE

In Mike Espy, Clinton found a nominee who seemed likely to please deeply divergent interests. Because Espy was the nation's first black Agriculture secretary, he was hailed as a break with tradition and in keeping with Clinton's agenda for change. But traditional, conservative

farming interests were pleased with Clinton's choice because they saw Espy as a team player with strong sympathies for the needs and interests of the agriculture community.

Espy has often been cited as a prototype of the new generation of influential black politicians. His politics were mainstream Democratic, his personal image was measured and his success was dependent on a coalition of black and white voters.

Unlike many of his older black colleagues in Congress, Espy did not begin his political career at the bully pulpit of the church or early civil rights movement. He was the well-educated product of one of the Mississippi Delta's more prominent black families. His early political experience was essentially administrative — as an assistant secretary of state in Mississippi and then as the director of the attorney general's consumer protection division.

"Our successes have come in the boardrooms and courtrooms," he said of his generation of black leaders. "My development has always been in a multiracial environment."

Espy, a former member of the House Agriculture Committee, got high marks from both Democrats and Republicans for his understanding of complex and arcane U.S. farm programs. A soft-spoken man, Espy had become adroit at getting his provisions included in farm legislation, usually through backdoor negotiations, committee sources said.

"He is not flamboyant. He's quiet; he is persistent; he is knowledgeable," said Rep. Bill Emerson, R-Mo., a panel member.

In addition to six years on the Agriculture panel, Espy had been an active member of the House Select Committee on Hunger and had chaired its domestic task force. That gave him a broad look at the nutrition programs run by the Agriculture Department, including food stamps and the National School Lunch program.

Espy's personal relationship with Clinton was also noted as crucial to Espy's ability to manage a department that was sure to see many changes. In his first term, Espy was a player in enacting legislation to create the Lower Mississippi Delta Commission, which was given two years to develop ideas to combat poverty in Mississippi and other states in the region.

Clinton chaired that commission. And Espy was one of Clinton's earliest congressional supporters in his bid for the presidency.

## ATTORNEY GENERAL

After two false starts, Clinton selected Janet Reno to head the Justice Department. Reno, 54, had been the Dade County state attorney for 15 years, managing an office of 900 workers and thousands of criminal cases. She had been elected to that post five times and had a strong reputation for integrity.

The daughter of two newspaper reporters, Reno grew up in Miami and graduated from Cornell University and Harvard Law School.

In the early 1970s, she worked briefly for the Judiciary Committee of the Florida House, then ran unsuccessfully for the Legislature in 1972.

She joined the Dade state attorney's office in 1973. She spent three years there and another two in private practice before then-Gov. Reubin Askew, D, appointed her to fill out the Dade state attorney's term in 1978. Reno's margin of victory increased steadily in each election; by the time of her fifth election she was the highest vote-getter in the county. Reno, a Democrat, held the position until joining the Cabinet.

Dade County's criminal caseload was challenging: The area, which includes Miami, was a hot spot for drug activity, violent crime and racial conflict.

Reno generally had won high marks for bringing a fair hand to her work.

Early on, many blacks criticized Reno's record on such concerns as police brutality against minorities. In 1980, her office lost a high-profile case against police officers who had fatally beaten a black man. The verdict set off race riots.

But Reno won over many of these skeptics through subsequent cases and diligent community outreach.

Reno pioneered alternative strategies to fight crime, such as a special court designed to deter young drug offenders.

She had aggressively prosecuted sexual and child abuse cases. A local rap star made the music charts with a song praising Reno's efforts to crack down on parents who did not pay child support.

However, Reno had been criticized for not being equally assertive in pursuing corrupt public officials.

Reno disputed that charge during a White House news conference Feb. 11, 1993, saying she sometimes transferred such cases to the federal system because different legal rules made it easier to obtain convictions in that arena.

Reno had not had a lot of exposure to many of the federal and constitutional legal issues she would face at the Justice Department, a factor Clinton said had initially deterred him from selecting her.

But Clinton was won over after two other choices for the job were withdrawn. Clinton's first choice for the job, corporate attorney Zoë Baird, withdrew amid public condemnation of her decision to hire two illegal aliens as domestic workers and her failure to pay required Social Security taxes. A "nanny problem" also felled Judge Kimba M. Wood, a leading contender to replace Baird. Wood also had hired an illegal alien to care for her child, but at a time when it was legal to do so.

Reno was single and had no children. "I've never hired an illegal alien. And I think I paid all my Social Security taxes," she said at the Feb. 11 news conference. ■

# VOTE STUDIES

PRESIDENTIAL SUPPORT

# Politics, Drop in Senate Support Put Bush's Ratings in Cellar

*President's 43 percent score is lowest on record;*
*even Republicans say he lacked a clear agenda*

For President Bush, 1992 was simply the worst of times. An administration that had always been dogged by meager congressional support saw its final redoubt — Senate Republicans — crack.

It was a major reason why, according to CQ's annual study of voting in Congress, Bush won a dismal 43.0 percent of the roll call votes on which he took a stand in 1992. His score — 11 percentage points below his 1991 level — was the worst performance of any president at any point in his term since CQ began keeping score 39 years ago. For every vote taken during the four years, Bush won an average of 51.8 percent — the lowest of any first-term president since CQ began tracking this variable in 1953.

Bush did even worse when measured against his own legislative priorities. None of the three major legislative requests he made in his State of the Union address — an economic stimulus package, school choice and a health-care plan — became law.

Bush's success rate in the House was only 37 percent; it was 53 percent in the Senate. Both declined from 1991.

Nicholas E. Calio, the chief White House lobbyist, said: "Obviously, first and foremost it was an election year, a highly charged partisan election year. This year was the most partisan I've ever seen."

Some political scientists agree and say Bush never had a chance, not in a campaign year.

"The basic reason for the decline is that the Democrats controlled Congress," said James Sundquist, a senior fellow at the Brookings Institution in Washington. Democrats seized control of the national agenda, with the goal of

## Guide to Vote Studies

defeating the president, he said.

In fact, some analysts and GOP lawmakers contend that many of the votes Bush lost were little more than Democratic parrying. They point to votes on lifting the "gag rule" on abortion information at federally funded health clinics and on family leave as examples of votes intended to sharpen public perceptions of the parties' differences.

But what was also striking in 1992 was the criticism Republicans leveled at Bush. This was reflected most sharply by the decline in GOP support for Bush in the Senate, from 83 percent in 1991 to 75 percent in 1992. In the House, his GOP support fell 1 point to 71 percent.

Bush's problems were most evident Oct. 8, when Senate Republicans joined Democrats to override his veto of a bill to reregulate cable TV rates — the first and only override of the administration. "That was the best evidence of his weakened position," said Sen. Mitch McConnell, R-Ky., a longtime Bush backer. "The whole year was an attempt by the majority to make [Bush] look bad."

For Rep. Tom DeLay, R-Texas, the new secretary of the House Republican Conference and an outspoken conservative, the problem was not so much a lack of support for the administration but the absence of a presidential agenda.

"In the congressional arena, many of the votes that reflected my unity with the president were often veto overrides," DeLay said. But he noted that there were few opportunities to vote for Bush initiatives. "I don't think Republicans were trying to be independent," he said. "[Yet] for two years we couldn't get the president or the

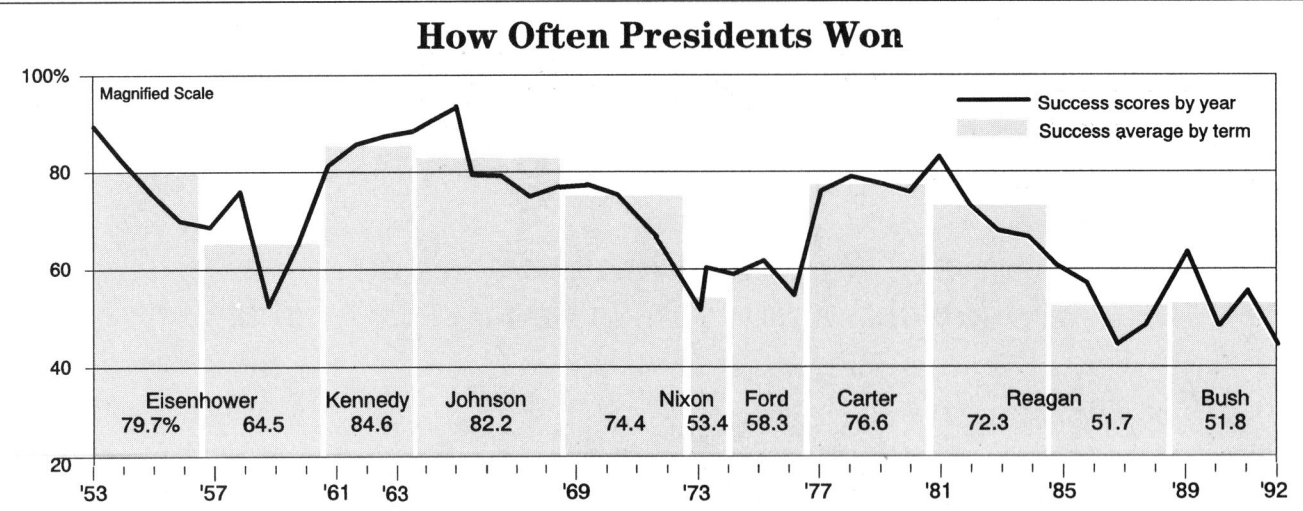

## How Often Presidents Won

**Magnified Scale**

— Success scores by year
▨ Success average by term

| Eisenhower | | Kennedy | Johnson | | Nixon | Ford | Carter | | Reagan | | Bush |
|---|---|---|---|---|---|---|---|---|---|---|---|
| 79.7% | 64.5 | 84.6 | 82.2 | 74.4 | 53.4 | 58.3 | 76.6 | | 72.3 | 51.7 | 51.8 |

'53    '57    '61  '63    '69    '73    '77    '81    '85    '89  '92

President Bush's 1992 success score of 43.0 percent is the lowest in the 41-year history of the Congressional Quarterly vote study. His four-year average is barely above the low mark set in Ronald Reagan's second term.

CQ's year-end review of the votes produced a few changes from the preliminary totals used for an Oct. 17 story.

After each session, CQ editors review all vote captions published in the magazine to see if presidential positions are correct. Some changes were made for the October story; subsequently, 10 House votes and three Senate votes were added to the study. That had the effect of lowering the average for Bush's four-year term from 51.9 percent to 51.8 percent.

A complete list of votes used in the survey is on p. 6-B. Year-by-year scores are on p. 9-B.

---

### Presidential Success

A measure of how often the president won his way on roll call votes on which he took a clear position.

### Presidential Support

A measure of how often individual members of Congress voted in accord with the president's position, regardless of whether it prevailed.

---

people around him to be dynamic on the economy or domestic policies."

History will likely bolster DeLay's observations, according to Cary R. Covington, a University of Iowa professor. Covington's studies of past presidents indicate that presidents in a minority party only win if they have a well-defined agenda that they push — something that goes beyond simply taking positions on various issues or playing defense against the opposing party's initiatives.

"I don't think Bush had a proactive agenda," Covington said. "He had a number of proposals he had put together with an eye toward the election, but it was more so that he could say he had something rather than actually having something he'd been preparing for all along. And Congress recognized that."

As the election began to look like it was Arkansas Gov. Bill Clinton's to lose, Bush's GOP support began to drift still more. Republican senatorial candidates, such as Alfonse M. D'Amato, N.Y., and Arlen Specter, Pa., campaigned on their agreement with Clinton's mantra of "change." So it was unsurprising that D'Amato's support for Bush fell 19 percentage points to 60 percent in 1992, compared with 1991; Specter's plummeted 23 percentage points to 45 percent in 1992. Other GOP senators showed similar declines.

CQ's presidential support study is based on an examination of all the roll call votes on which Bush took a clear position. This year, of the 488 recorded roll call votes in the House, CQ identified 105 on which the president took a position. Of the 270 recorded votes in the Senate, he took an unambiguous position on 60.

Those votes are the raw material for the two indicators used to measure presidential support.

● The first is presidential success. This measures how often Bush won on votes on which he took a position.

● The second measure is members' support — how often a member votes the same way as the president's position. A 100 percent score for a House member would mean that member voted to back the president's position whenever he or she voted on the 105 issues.

### A Lack of Priorities

The tone for the year was set early, in the aftermath of the State of the Union address. Bush's poll numbers were the lowest of his tenure to that point, and lawmakers looked to the speech to gauge his priorities. One widely leaked campaign memo called it the presidency's "defining event."

Using Desert Storm rhetoric, Bush presented a grab bag of requests that he said would get the economy moving.

In the main, there were three Bush themes: jump-starting the economy through tax cuts and incentives, including lowering the capital gains tax rate; a school choice proposal; and a health-care plan based on tax credits. Bush then drew a line in the sand, setting a 90-day deadline for Congress to pass his economic proposals.

Republicans immediately criticized two of the policies, the health-care and tax proposals. "We are beyond just supporting things by word of mouth," said Rep. Nancy L. Johnson, Conn., a member of the Ways and Means subcommittee on health, who complained that Republicans had not seen the proposals.

Bush was forced to hastily rewrite his 1993 budget's health plan at the request of Republicans. The plan he announced in February was vague, and he never submitted a detailed legislative package for debate in Congress.

Bush's economic plan faced similar GOP criticism. Con-

servatives such as Rep. Newt Gingrich, R-Ga., said openly that the proposal did not go far enough, and they prepared a plan featuring deeper tax cuts and slashed mandatory spending programs. They forced Bush to compromise, though the administration warned against tinkering with its plan.

House Democrats pushed for an up-or-down vote on Bush's original plan. But when the time came, it had so little support that House Republicans refused to vote for it. A compromise, backed by Gingrich and Minority Leader Robert H. Michel, R-Ill., attracted much more GOP support, but it died on a party-line vote.

In the end, Bush spent March 20, the deadline for the 90-day challenge, vetoing the Democrat-written tax bill that cleared the same day (HR 4210). The battle would be a microcosm of the year.

Bush's four-year average success rate of 51.8 percent was lower than any other president's four-year term that CQ has measured except the 51.7 percent rate President Ronald Reagan scored in his second term. But some analysts suggest that comparing Bush's term with the first term of President Richard M. Nixon is more intriguing than comparisons with Reagan.

### A Nixon-Bush Comparison

When Nixon won in 1968, he faced what was then a novelty: a Congress controlled by the opposition party. The last president in similar straits had been Zachary Taylor in 1848, although it has since happened to both Reagan and Bush.

But Nixon used a combination of hardball politics and compromise with liberal Democrats to rack up a success rate of better than 75 percent in the years before Watergate. Even in his worst year, 1973, he did not dip below 50 percent. He also judiciously wielded the veto pen, issuing 16 in 1972.

Jon R. Bond, a professor of political science at Texas A&M University, said: "Nixon was a strong conservative, no doubt about it. But in his first four years he achieved a number of victories on the floor." Nixon put his stamp on policies as liberal as wage and price controls and as conservative (at the time) as revenue sharing.

Bush, according to Bond, was unable to compromise as Nixon did, even though Bush had a reputation as a pragmatist. "Bush was never trusted by the conservatives. And he turned out to be a very conservative president" to try to retain their trust, Bond said.

Many conservative Republicans point to Bush's one major compromise — the 1990 budget agreement — as the beginning of his downfall. Stephen Moore, a congressional budget analyst at the libertarian Cato Institute in Washington, said: "The budget deal was a huge, embarrassing defeat for the president and was a defining moment for him. I believe he lost so much credibility with House and Senate Republicans that he never again had a base of trust to bring people together to win legislative battles."

That is reflected in his 1992 record on domestic issues.

R. MICHAEL JENKINS

**Bush's four-year average was 51.8 percent.**

Bush won 29 and lost 58 votes on domestic and economic issues in the House. He had a closer, but still losing, record in the Senate: 24 wins, 25 defeats.

In both chambers he had a winning record on foreign policy, a Bush strong-point.

Despite all the disagreement, Republicans still supported Bush fairly solidly. Not surprisingly, the GOP leadership most strongly backed Bush. National Republican Senatorial Committee Chairman Phil Gramm of Texas supported Bush 90 percent of the time; Minority Leader Bob Dole of Kansas was close behind at 88 percent.

The Democratic senator who backed the president most frequently was Richard C. Shelby of Alabama at 65 percent. He supported Bush more often than seven Republicans.

But there were 13 Democratic senators, including Al Gore of Tennessee, Majority Leader George J. Mitchell of Maine and Edward M. Kennedy of Massachusetts, who supported the president 25 percent of the time or less. In the House, Michel helped lead Bush supporters at 93 percent. Gingrich scored 88 percent, and new Republican Conference Chairman Dick Armey, Texas, scored 86 percent.

The House Democrat with the highest ranking was Charles W. Stenholm of Texas, who supported Bush 70 percent of the time. Five representatives — led by Craig Washington, D-Texas — voted with Bush's position less than one time in 10.

### What To Keep in Mind

CQ's presidential support analysis, taken as a whole, can aid in gauging a president's effectiveness, and it provides a useful indicator of long-term trends. But there are several caveats. The study's usefulness diminishes, for instance, as the need for detail rises. It does not measure the president's effectiveness, or members' support, except on floor votes.

Many important measures, particularly in the Senate, pass by voice vote, and thus do not count under the scoring system, which measures only roll call votes. And large differences in senators' support rankings can boil down to a handful of votes because there are so few with a clear presidential position.

The study also treats every vote the same, regardless of significance.

Said the White House's Calio: "I think in terms of [CQ's] ratings vs. our internal ratings, there is a real difference. CQ rates every vote, and there are some we don't care about. And there are some votes CQ rates as a loss, but that we considered a win because we showed veto strength. So they don't really reflect the complicated reality."

As Calio noted, the veto casts a far longer shadow than can be shown in the studies. The Democrats never brought up some bills for override votes that Bush would have won, and others were altered, or even dropped, because of a veto threat. When these things happen, although they represent a victory for Bush, they are not reflected in the president's score. ∎

> "The budget deal was a huge, embarrassing defeat for the president and was a defining moment for him."
>
> —Stephen Moore, budget analyst, the Cato Institute

# 1992 Senate Presidential Position Votes . . .

The following is a list of Senate and House votes in 1992 on which there was a clear presidential position, listed by roll call number with a brief description and categorized by topic.

| Vote # | Description |
| --- | --- |

## Domestic Policy

### 16 Victories

| | |
| --- | --- |
| 3 | Education |
| 17 | Jobless benefits |
| 28 | Energy policy |
| 30 | Higher education |
| 35 | Lumbee tribe (cloture) |
| 53 | Crime bill (cloture) |
| 88 | Campaign finance (veto) |
| 113 | Public broadcasting |
| 131 | Railroad labor |
| 145 | Jobless benefits |
| 156 | Agriculture |
| 163 | Energy policy |
| 166 | Super collider |
| 194 | Space station |
| 226 | Motor voter registration (veto) |
| 262 | Crime bill (cloture) |

### 18 Defeats

| | |
| --- | --- |
| 5 | School choice |
| 14 | Cable TV |
| 37 | Indoor radon |
| 61 | Fetal tissue/abortion |
| 66 | Fetal tissue/abortion |
| 82 | Campaign finance |
| 86 | Motor voter registration (cloture) |
| 98 | Motor voter registration |
| 101 | Highway funding |
| 112 | Public broadcasting |
| 115 | Fetal tissue/abortion |
| 151 | Interstate waste |
| 219 | Labor-HHS funding/abortion |
| 220 | Overseas military abortions |
| 225 | Cable TV |
| 232 | Family leave (veto) |
| 254 | Family planning/abortion (veto) |
| 264 | Cable TV (veto) |

## Defense and Foreign Policy

### 7 Victories

| | |
| --- | --- |
| 62 | Foreign aid |
| 139 | Russian aid |
| 148 | Russian aid |
| 214 | SDI |
| 216 | Stealth bombers |
| 252 | Foreign aid |
| 253 | START treaty |

### 4 Defeats

| | |
| --- | --- |
| 83 | Defense/*Seawolf* |
| 167 | Nuclear testing |
| 182 | SDI |
| 217 | Nuclear testing |

| Vote # | Description |
| --- | --- |

## Nominations

### 1 Victory

| | |
| --- | --- |
| 193 | Edward E. Carnes Jr. confirmation |

## Economic Affairs and Trade

### 8 Victories

| | |
| --- | --- |
| 52 | China MFN (veto) |
| 56 | Budget walls (cloture) |
| 59 | RTC funding |
| 137 | Mortgage refinancing regulation |
| 208 | Budget walls |
| 209 | Budget walls |
| 211 | Budget walls |
| 255 | China MFN (veto) |

### 6 Defeats

| | |
| --- | --- |
| 31 | China MFN |
| 51 | Taxes |
| 54 | Taxes |
| 84 | Budget rescission |
| 85 | Budget rescission |
| 240 | Taxes |

## Presidential Success, 1992

| Senate | Votes | % |
| --- | --- | --- |
| Victories | 32 | (53%) |
| Defeats | 28 | (47%) |
| **Totals:** | 60 | (100%) |
| **House** | **Votes** | **%** |
| Victories | 39 | (37%) |
| Defeats | 66 | (63%) |
| **Totals:** | 105 | (100%) |
| **1992 Congress** | **Votes** | **%** |
| Victories | 71 | (43%) |
| Defeats | 94 | (57%) |
| **Total votes:** | 165 | (100%) |

# ... And House Position Votes, by Category

| Vote # | Description |
|---|---|

| Vote # | Description |
|---|---|

## Domestic Policy

### 22 Victories

| Vote # | Description |
|---|---|
| 4 | Jobless benefits |
| 97 | Undersea research |
| 116 | Legal services/redistricting |
| 125 | Disaster relief |
| 127 | Airport funds |
| 133 | Energy policy |
| 134 | Energy policy |
| 140 | Energy policy |
| 141 | Energy policy |
| 206 | Disaster relief |
| 222 | Fetal tissue/abortion (veto) |
| 236 | Railroad labor |
| 251 | Vertical price fixing |
| 253 | Alcohol/drug abuse funds |
| 267 | Jobless benefits |
| 276 | Customs funds |
| 329 | Mining activities |
| 334 | Space station |
| 443 | Family leave (veto) |
| 447 | Indian monument |
| 452 | Family planning/abortion (veto) |
| 474 | Energy policy |

### 33 Defeats

| Vote # | Description |
|---|---|
| 19 | Fishing sanctions |
| 35 | Aviation park |
| 79 | Campaign finance |
| 95 | Family planning/abortion |
| 103 | Legal services/lobbying |
| 106 | Legal services/abortion |
| 115 | Legal services/abortion |
| 118 | Legal services/abortion |
| 121 | Shipbuilding subsidies |
| 143 | Energy policy |
| 147 | Fetal tissue/abortion |
| 163 | Overseas military abortions |
| 179 | Jobless benefits |
| 194 | Motor voter registration |
| 201 | Super collider |
| 207 | Coast Guard |
| 240 | Undersea research |
| 256 | Council on Competitiveness |
| 300 | Grazing fees |
| 313 | Cable TV |
| 325 | Davis-Bacon Act |
| 354 | Legal services/abortion |
| 366 | Housing |
| 372 | Child welfare |
| 375 | Family planning/abortion |
| 384 | School choice |
| 385 | School choice |
| 386 | Airline competition |
| 390 | Family leave |
| 398 | Cable TV |
| 455 | Montana wilderness |
| 458 | Overseas military abortions |
| 477 | Cable TV (veto) |

## Defense and Foreign Policy

### 10 Victories

| Vote # | Description |
|---|---|
| 63 | Foreign aid |
| 167 | Defense funds |
| 168 | SDI |
| 169 | SDI |
| 170 | Stealth bombers |
| 263 | SDI |
| 265 | Stealth bombers |
| 353 | TV Marti |
| 374 | Russian aid |
| 462 | Russian aid |

### 9 Defeats

| Vote # | Description |
|---|---|
| 34 | Haitian refugees |
| 155 | Defense/troops overseas |
| 156 | Defense/troops in Europe |
| 157 | Defense/troops overseas |
| 162 | Nuclear weapons |
| 164 | Nuclear testing |
| 171 | Troops overseas |
| 352 | TV Marti |
| 429 | Nuclear testing |

## Economic Affairs and Trade

### 7 Victories

| Vote # | Description |
|---|---|
| 25 | Taxes |
| 55 | Taxes (veto) |
| 66 | Budget walls |
| 174 | Budget rules |
| 281 | Budget walls |
| 283 | Budget walls |
| 395 | Securities regulation |

### 24 Defeats

| Vote # | Description |
|---|---|
| 28 | Taxes |
| 30 | Taxes |
| 31 | Taxes |
| 39 | Budget |
| 41 | Budget |
| 42 | Budget |
| 43 | China MFN (veto) |
| 54 | Taxes |
| 69 | Resolution Trust Corporation funding |
| 109 | Budget rescissions |
| 110 | Budget rescissions |
| 111 | Budget rescissions |
| 112 | Budget rescissions |
| 187 | Balanced-budget amendment |
| 242 | Social Security |
| 272 | Trade |
| 273 | Trade |
| 282 | Budget walls |
| 284 | Budget walls |
| 285 | China MFN |
| 286 | China MFN |
| 356 | Trade |
| 357 | Trade |
| 441 | China MFN (veto) |

# Leading Scorers: Bush's Support, Opposition

## Highest Scorers — Support

Those who in 1992 voted most often for President Bush's position. Scores are based on actual votes cast and ranked by percentages before rounding. Members not eligible for half the votes are not listed.

### Senate

Shelby

Gramm

| Democrats | | Republicans | |
|---|---|---|---|
| Shelby, Ala. | 65% | Gramm, Texas | 90% |
| Johnston, La. | 53 | Lugar, Ind. | 90 |
| Heflin, Ala. | 53 | Garn, Utah | 89 |
| Bentsen, Texas | 47 | Dole, Kan. | 88 |
| Bingaman, N.M. | 44 | Hatch, Utah | 88 |
| Exon, Neb. | 43 | Burns, Mont. | 85 |
| Robb, Va. | 42 | Craig, Idaho | 85 |
| Breaux, La. | 42 | Cochran, Miss. | 84 |
| Burdick, N.D. * | 41 | Mack, Fla. | 84 |
| Inouye, Hawaii | 41 | Symms, Idaho | 84 |
| Nunn, Ga. | 41 | Lott, Miss. | 83 |
| | | Simpson, Wyo. | 83 |

** Quentin N. Burdick was eligible for 40 of the 60 presidential support votes.*

### House

Stenholm

McCrery

| Democrats | | Republicans | |
|---|---|---|---|
| Stenholm, Texas | 70% | McCrery, La. | 93% |
| Barnard, Ga. | 68 | Michel, Ill. | 93 |
| Hutto, Fla. | 68 | Hansen, Utah | 92 |
| Montgomery, Miss. | 66 | Lowery, Calif. | 91 |
| Pickett, Va. | 65 | Baker, La. | 90 |
| Parker, Miss. | 63 | Ireland, Fla. | 90 |
| Hall, Texas | 63 | Kyl, Ariz. | 90 |
| Ray, Ga. | 61 | Rhodes, Ariz. | 89 |
| Skelton, Mo. | 60 | Boehner, Ohio | 88 |
| Byron, Md. | 58 | Roberts, Kan. | 88 |
| Taylor, Miss. | 58 | Oxley, Ohio | 88 |
| Geren, Texas | 58 | Gingrich, Ga. | 88 |
| | | Hopkins, Ky. | 88 |

## Highest Scorers — Opposition

Those who in 1992 voted most often against President Bush's position. Scores are based on actual votes cast and ranked by percentages before rounding. Members not eligible for half the votes are not listed.

### Senate

Lautenberg

Specter

| Democrats | | Republicans | |
|---|---|---|---|
| Lautenberg, N.J. | 78% | Specter, Pa. | 55% |
| Harkin, Iowa | 77 | Jeffords, Vt. | 53 |
| Kerry, Mass. | 77 | Hatfield, Ore. | 47 |
| Mikulski, Md. | 77 | D'Amato, N.Y. | 40 |
| Leahy, Vt. | 76 | Chafee, R.I. | 38 |
| Wellstone, Minn. | 76 | Packwood, Ore. | 38 |
| | | Cohen, Maine | 37 |
| | | Durenberger, Minn. | 34 |
| | | Kasten, Wis. | 33 |

### House

Washington

Shays

| Democrats | | Republicans | |
|---|---|---|---|
| Washington, Texas | 94% | Shays, Conn. | 60% |
| Boxer, Calif. | 92 | Snowe, Maine | 59 |
| Abercrombie, Hawaii | 91 | Morella, Md. | 59 |
| Serrano, N.Y. | 91 | Gilman, N.Y. | 59 |
| Clay, Mo. | 91 | Boehlert, N.Y. | 58 |
| AuCoin, Ore. | 89 | Green, N.Y. | 58 |
| Stokes, Ohio | 89 | Machtley, R.I. | 52 |
| Collins, Ill. | 89 | Horton, N.Y. | 48 |
| Payne, N.J. | 89 | Roukema, N.J. | 48 |
| Wolpe, Mich. | 89 | Ridge, Pa. | 48 |

## Presidential Support Definitions

Congressional Quarterly determines presidential positions on congressional votes by examining the statements made by President Bush or his authorized spokesmen. *Support* measures the percentage of the time members voted in accord with the position of the president. *Opposition* measures the percentage of the time members voted against the president's position. *Success* measures the percentage of the contested votes on which the president prevailed. Absences lowered parties' scores.

## National Security vs. Domestic Issues

The following are 1992 presidential success scores broken down into domestic and national security issues, with national security including foreign policy and defense. Scores for 1991 are in parentheses:

|  | National Security | Domestic | Average |
|---|---|---|---|
| Senate | 64% (76) | 50% (64) | 53% (69) |
| House | 43 (50) | 35 (40) | 37 (43) |
| **Average** | 51 (63) | 40 (49) | 43 (54) |

## Average Scores

Scores for 1991 are in parentheses:

| | Support | | | Opposition | |
|---|---|---|---|---|---|
| | Democrats | Republicans | | Democrats | Republicans |
| Senate | 32% (41) | 73% (83) | Senate | 65% (56) | 24% (16) |
| House | 25 (34) | 71 (72) | House | 67 (62) | 24 (25) |

## Regional Averages

Scores for 1991 are in parentheses:

| | \ Support | | | | | \ Opposition | | | |
|---|---|---|---|---|---|---|---|---|---|
| | East | West | South | Midwest | | East | West | South | Midwest |
| **Democrats** | | | | | **Democrats** | | | | |
| Senate | 27% (35) | 33% (40) | 38% (51) | 29% (35) | Senate | 72% (64) | 62% (56) | 58% (45) | 66% (61) |
| House | 20 (29) | 21 (31) | 35 (41) | 22 (31) | House | 71 (67) | 71 (63) | 57 (55) | 73 (67) |
| **Republicans** | | | | | **Republicans** | | | | |
| Senate | 71% (73) | 75% (84) | 78% (89) | 74% (84) | Senate | 36% (26) | 22% (14) | 18% (9) | 24% (14) |
| House | 62 (65) | 76 (76) | 75 (74) | 70 (74) | House | 34 (34) | 18 (22) | 20 (21) | 25 (23) |

*(CQ defines regions of the United States as follows:* **East:** *Conn., Del., Maine, Md., Mass., N.H., N.J., N.Y., Pa., R.I., Vt., W.Va.* **West:** *Alaska, Ariz., Calif., Colo., Hawaii, Idaho, Mont., Nev., N.M., Ore., Utah, Wash., Wyo.* **South:** *Ala., Ark., Fla., Ga., Ky., La., Miss., N.C., Okla., S.C., Tenn., Texas, Va.* **Midwest:** *Ill., Ind., Iowa, Kan., Mich., Minn., Mo., Neb., N.D., Ohio, S.D., Wis.)*

## Success Rate History

| Eisenhower | | Johnson | | Ford | | Reagan | |
|---|---|---|---|---|---|---|---|
| 1953 | 89.0% | 1964 | 88.0% | 1974 | 58.2% | 1981 | 82.4% |
| 1954 | 82.8 | 1965 | 93.0 | 1975 | 61.0 | 1982 | 72.4 |
| 1955 | 75.0 | 1966 | 79.0 | 1976 | 53.8 | 1983 | 67.1 |
| 1956 | 70.0 | 1967 | 79.0 | | | 1984 | 65.8 |
| 1957 | 68.0 | 1968 | 75.0 | | | 1985 | 59.9 |
| 1958 | 76.0 | | | | | 1986 | 56.1 |
| 1959 | 52.0 | **Nixon** | | **Carter** | | 1987 | 43.5 |
| 1960 | 65.0 | 1969 | 74.0% | 1977 | 75.4% | 1988 | 47.4 |
| **Kennedy** | | 1970 | 77.0 | 1978 | 78.3 | | |
| | | 1971 | 75.0 | 1979 | 76.8 | **Bush** | |
| 1961 | 81.0% | 1972 | 66.0 | 1980 | 75.1 | 1989 | 62.6% |
| 1962 | 85.4 | 1973 | 50.6 | | | 1990 | 46.8 |
| 1963 | 87.1 | 1974 | 59.6 | | | 1991 | 54.2 |
| | | | | | | 1992 | 43.0 |

# Presidential Support, Presidential Opposition: House

**1. Bush Support Score, 1992.** Percentage of 105 recorded votes in 1992 on which President Bush took a position and on which a representative voted "yea" or "nay" *in agreement* with the president's position. Failures to vote lowered both support and opposition scores.

**2. Bush Opposition Score, 1992.** Percentage of 105 recorded votes in 1992 on which President Bush took a position and on which a representative voted "yea" or "nay" *in disagreement* with the president's position. Failures to vote lowered both support and opposition scores.

**3. Bush Support Score, 1992.** Percentage of 105 recorded votes in 1992 on which President Bush took a position and on which a representative was present and voted "yea" or "nay" *in agreement* with the president's position. In this version of the study, absences were not counted; therefore, failures to vote did not lower support or opposition scores. Opposition scores, not listed here, are the inverse of the support score; i.e., the opposition score is equal to 100 percent minus the individual's support score.

[1] *Ted Weiss, D-N.Y., died Sept. 14, 1992. He was eligible for 93 presidential support votes in 1992.*

[2] *Walter B. Jones, D-N.C., died Sept. 15, 1992. He was eligible for 93 presidential support votes in 1992.*

[3] *Thomas S. Foley, D-Wash., as Speaker of the House, voted at his discretion. Foley was eligible for 10 presidential support votes in 1992.*

## KEY

† Not eligible for all presidential-support votes in 1992 or voted "present" to avoid possible conflict of interest.

Democrats    *Republicans*

*Independent*

| | 1 | 2 | 3 |
|---|---|---|---|
| **Alabama** | | | |
| 1 Callahan | 82 | 16 | 83 |
| 2 *Dickinson* | 64 | 19 | 77 |
| 3 Browder | 43 | 53 | 45 |
| 4 Bevill | 38 | 53 | 42 |
| 5 Cramer | 39 | 58 | 40 |
| 6 Erdreich | 44 | 54 | 45 |
| 7 Harris | 42 | 54 | 44 |
| **Alaska** | | | |
| AL *Young* | 75 | 22 | 77 |
| **Arizona** | | | |
| 1 *Rhodes* | 88 | 10 | 89 |
| 2 Pastor | 20 | 75 | 21 |
| 3 *Stump* | 85 | 15 | 85 |
| 4 *Kyl* | 90 | 10 | 90 |
| 5 *Kolbe* | 77 | 21 | 79 |
| **Arkansas** | | | |
| 1 Alexander | 18 | 56 | 24 |
| 2 Thornton | 34 | 62 | 36 |
| 3 *Hammerschmidt* | 80 | 15 | 84 |
| 4 Anthony | 19 | 50 | 27 |
| **California** | | | |
| 1 *Riggs* | 62 | 31 | 66 |
| 2 *Herger* | 73 | 16 | 82 |
| 3 Matsui | 26 | 71 | 26 |
| 4 Fazio | 28 | 68 | 29 |
| 5 Pelosi | 12 | 80 | 13 |
| 6 Boxer | 5 | 51 | 8 |
| 7 Miller | 14 | 77 | 16 |
| 8 Dellums | 12 | 86 | 13 |
| 9 Stark | 14 | 80 | 15 |
| 10 Edwards | 12 | 85 | 13 |
| 11 Lantos | 19 | 81 | 19 |
| 12 *Campbell* | 57 | 16 | 78 |
| 13 Mineta | 16 | 81 | 17 |
| 14 *Doolittle* | 81 | 19 | 81 |
| 15 Condit | 38 | 62 | 38 |
| 16 Panetta | 23 | 76 | 23 |
| 17 Dooley | 30 | 65 | 32 |
| 18 Lehman | 26 | 58 | 31 |
| 19 *Lagomarsino* | 81 | 12 | 87 |
| 20 *Thomas* | 66 | 17 | 79 |
| 21 *Gallegly* | 80 | 19 | 81 |
| 22 *Moorhead* | 85 | 14 | 86 |
| 23 Beilenson | 26 | 67 | 28 |
| 24 Waxman | 16 | 81 | 17 |
| 25 Roybal | 14 | 84 | 15 |
| 26 Berman | 21 | 78 | 21 |
| 27 Levine | 15 | 33 | 31 |
| 28 Dixon | 18 | 77 | 19 |
| 29 Waters | 11 | 77 | 13 |
| 30 Martinez | 16 | 79 | 17 |
| 31 Dymally | 9 | 43 | 17 |
| 32 Anderson | 34 | 61 | 36 |
| 33 *Dreier* | 84 | 13 | 86 |
| 34 Torres | 20 | 70 | 22 |
| 35 *Lewis* | 77 | 14 | 84 |
| 36 Brown | 19 | 71 | 21 |
| 37 *McCandless* | 78 | 22 | 78 |
| 38 *Dornan* | 79 | 14 | 85 |
| 39 *Dannemeyer* | 50 | 13 | 79 |
| 40 *Cox* | 78 | 15 | 84 |
| 41 *Lowery* | 75 | 8 | 91 |

| | 1 | 2 | 3 |
|---|---|---|---|
| 42 *Rohrabacher* | 74 | 26 | 74 |
| 43 *Packard* | 81 | 13 | 86 |
| 44 *Cunningham* | 82 | 13 | 86 |
| 45 *Hunter* | 80 | 19 | 81 |
| **Colorado** | | | |
| 1 Schroeder | 20 | 76 | 21 |
| 2 Skaggs | 30 | 70 | 30 |
| 3 Campbell | 27 | 45 | 37 |
| 4 *Allard* | 84 | 14 | 85 |
| 5 *Hefley* | 74 | 25 | 75 |
| 6 *Schaefer* | 82 | 17 | 83 |
| **Connecticut** | | | |
| 1 Kennelly | 22 | 77 | 22 |
| 2 Gejdenson | 16 | 84 | 16 |
| 3 DeLauro | 17 | 82 | 17 |
| 4 *Shays* | 40 | 60 | 40 |
| 5 *Franks* | 73 | 25 | 75 |
| 6 *Johnson* | 62 | 37 | 63 |
| **Delaware** | | | |
| AL Carper | 31 | 68 | 32 |
| **Florida** | | | |
| 1 Hutto | 66 | 31 | 68 |
| 2 Peterson | 27 | 69 | 28 |
| 3 Bennett | 33 | 67 | 33 |
| 4 *James* † | 75 | 25 | 75 |
| 5 *McCollum* | 73 | 22 | 77 |
| 6 *Stearns* | 79 | 19 | 81 |
| 7 Gibbons | 29 | 62 | 32 |
| 8 *Young* | 65 | 34 | 65 |
| 9 *Bilirakis* | 64 | 34 | 65 |
| 10 *Ireland* | 69 | 8 | 90 |
| 11 Bacchus | 26 | 71 | 26 |
| 12 *Lewis* | 70 | 27 | 72 |
| 13 *Goss* | 75 | 25 | 75 |
| 14 Johnston | 18 | 76 | 19 |
| 15 *Shaw* | 75 | 24 | 76 |
| 16 Smith | 16 | 72 | 18 |
| 17 Lehman | 20 | 61 | 25 |
| 18 *Ros-Lehtinen* | 61 | 36 | 63 |
| 19 Fascell | 29 | 65 | 31 |
| **Georgia** | | | |
| 1 Thomas | 42 | 45 | 48 |
| 2 Hatcher | 19 | 37 | 34 |
| 3 Ray | 50 | 32 | 61 |
| 4 Jones | 18 | 57 | 24 |
| 5 Lewis | 11 | 81 | 12 |
| 6 *Gingrich* | 76 | 10 | 88 |
| 7 Darden | 30 | 68 | 31 |
| 8 Rowland | 44 | 52 | 46 |
| 9 Jenkins | 31 | 65 | 33 |
| 10 Barnard | 44 | 21 | 68 |
| **Hawaii** | | | |
| 1 Abercrombie | 9 | 89 | 9 |
| 2 Mink | 14 | 81 | 15 |
| **Idaho** | | | |
| 1 LaRocco | 29 | 70 | 29 |
| 2 Stallings | 40 | 55 | 42 |
| **Illinois** | | | |
| 1 Hayes | 11 | 87 | 12 |
| 2 Savage | 10 | 70 | 13 |
| 3 Russo | 20 | 64 | 24 |
| 4 Sangmeister | 29 | 70 | 29 |
| 5 Lipinski | 34 | 52 | 40 |
| 6 *Hyde* | 60 | 14 | 81 |
| 7 Collins | 9 | 70 | 11 |
| 8 Rostenkowski | 18 | 71 | 20 |
| 9 Yates | 14 | 77 | 16 |
| 10 *Porter* | 62 | 33 | 65 |
| 11 Annunzio | 28 | 67 | 29 |
| 12 *Crane* | 83 | 12 | 87 |
| 13 *Fawell* | 70 | 29 | 71 |
| 14 *Hastert* | 78 | 19 | 80 |
| 15 *Ewing* | 74 | 25 | 75 |
| 16 Cox | 17 | 83 | 17 |
| 17 Evans | 11 | 88 | 12 |
| 18 *Michel* | 86 | 7 | 93 |
| 19 Bruce | 25 | 69 | 27 |
| 20 Durbin | 12 | 86 | 13 |
| 21 Costello | 32 | 65 | 33 |
| 22 Poshard | 30 | 70 | 30 |
| **Indiana** | | | |
| 1 Visclosky | 22 | 78 | 22 |
| 2 Sharp † | 20 | 77 | 21 |
| 3 Roemer | 40 | 58 | 41 |

| | 1 | 2 | 3 |
|---|---|---|---|
| 4 Long | 26 | 74 | 26 |
| 5 Jontz | 14 | 86 | 14 |
| 6 *Burton* | 75 | 23 | 77 |
| 7 *Myers* | 76 | 18 | 81 |
| 8 McCloskey | 17 | 80 | 18 |
| 9 Hamilton | 33 | 66 | 34 |
| 10 Jacobs | 21 | 77 | 21 |
| **Iowa** | | | |
| 1 *Leach* | 52 | 47 | 53 |
| 2 *Nussle* | 71 | 29 | 71 |
| 3 Nagle | 24 | 73 | 25 |
| 4 Smith | 36 | 60 | 38 |
| 5 *Lightfoot* | 78 | 15 | 84 |
| 6 *Grandy* | 78 | 19 | 80 |
| **Kansas** | | | |
| 1 *Roberts* | 87 | 11 | 88 |
| 2 Slattery | 30 | 69 | 31 |
| 3 *Meyers* | 63 | 37 | 63 |
| 4 Glickman | 27 | 71 | 27 |
| 5 *Nichols* | 73 | 17 | 81 |
| **Kentucky** | | | |
| 1 Hubbard | 33 | 50 | 40 |
| 2 Natcher | 38 | 62 | 38 |
| 3 Mazzoli | 28 | 72 | 28 |
| 4 *Bunning* | 77 | 21 | 79 |
| 5 *Rogers* | 67 | 30 | 69 |
| 6 *Hopkins* | 87 | 12 | 88 |
| 7 Perkins | 20 | 67 | 23 |
| **Louisiana** | | | |
| 1 *Livingston* | 72 | 11 | 86 |
| 2 Jefferson | 14 | 74 | 16 |
| 3 Tauzin | 55 | 42 | 57 |
| 4 *McCrery* | 77 | 6 | 93 |
| 5 Huckaby | 41 | 37 | 52 |
| 6 *Baker* | 81 | 9 | 90 |
| 7 Hayes | 43 | 40 | 52 |
| 8 *Holloway* | 70 | 21 | 77 |
| **Maine** | | | |
| 1 Andrews | 14 | 86 | 14 |
| 2 *Snowe* | 41 | 59 | 41 |
| **Maryland** | | | |
| 1 *Gilchrest* | 56 | 42 | 57 |
| 2 *Bentley* | 62 | 32 | 66 |
| 3 Cardin | 17 | 82 | 17 |
| 4 McMillen | 31 | 69 | 31 |
| 5 Hoyer | 27 | 72 | 27 |
| 6 Byron | 48 | 34 | 58 |
| 7 Mfume | 12 | 87 | 13 |
| 8 *Morella* | 39 | 56 | 41 |
| **Massachusetts** | | | |
| 1 Olver | 11 | 87 | 12 |
| 2 Neal | 14 | 85 | 14 |
| 3 Early | 17 | 75 | 19 |
| 4 Frank | 16 | 80 | 17 |
| 5 Atkins | 11 | 82 | 12 |
| 6 Mavroules | 24 | 66 | 27 |
| 7 Markey | 11 | 82 | 12 |
| 8 Kennedy | 15 | 79 | 16 |
| 9 Moakley | 15 | 71 | 18 |
| 10 Studds | 13 | 83 | 14 |
| 11 Donnelly | 19 | 68 | 22 |
| **Michigan** | | | |
| 1 Conyers | 10 | 72 | 13 |
| 2 *Pursell* | 54 | 31 | 63 |
| 3 Wolpe | 10 | 84 | 11 |
| 4 *Upton* | 57 | 43 | 57 |
| 5 *Henry* | 59 | 39 | 60 |
| 6 Carr | 30 | 67 | 31 |
| 7 Kildee | 16 | 84 | 16 |
| 8 Traxler | 10 | 40 | 19 |
| 9 *Vander Jagt* | 68 | 18 | 79 |
| 10 *Camp* | 70 | 30 | 70 |
| 11 *Davis* | 64 | 25 | 72 |
| 12 Bonior | 12 | 72 | 15 |
| 13 Collins | 12 | 79 | 14 |
| 14 Hertel | 19 | 75 | 20 |
| 15 Ford | 13 | 81 | 14 |
| 16 Dingell | 19 | 74 | 20 |
| 17 Levin | 18 | 82 | 18 |
| 18 *Broomfield* | 60 | 18 | 77 |
| **Minnesota** | | | |
| 1 Penny | 41 | 59 | 41 |
| 2 *Weber* | 62 | 13 | 82 |
| 3 *Ramstad* | 53 | 47 | 53 |
| 4 Vento | 13 | 86 | 13 |

| | 1 | 2 | 3 |
|---|---|---|---|
| 5 Sabo | 15 | 83 | 16 |
| 6 Sikorski | 13 | 84 | 14 |
| 7 Peterson | 35 | 64 | 36 |
| 8 Oberstar | 17 | 82 | 17 |
| **Mississippi** | | | |
| 1 Whitten | 27 | 36 | 42 |
| 2 Espy | 20 | 77 | 21 |
| 3 Montgomery | 66 | 34 | 66 |
| 4 Parker | 63 | 36 | 63 |
| 5 Taylor | 58 | 42 | 58 |
| **Missouri** | | | |
| 1 Clay | 9 | 86 | 9 |
| 2 Horn | 19 | 81 | 19 |
| 3 Gephardt | 16 | 76 | 18 |
| 4 Skelton | 57 | 38 | 60 |
| 5 Wheat | 12 | 88 | 12 |
| 6 *Coleman* | 63 | 37 | 63 |
| 7 *Hancock* | 81 | 19 | 81 |
| 8 *Emerson* | 76 | 24 | 76 |
| 9 Volkmer | 42 | 57 | 42 |
| **Montana** | | | |
| 1 Williams | 17 | 75 | 19 |
| 2 *Marlenee* | 68 | 22 | 76 |
| **Nebraska** | | | |
| 1 *Bereuter* | 68 | 30 | 70 |
| 2 Hoagland | 30 | 67 | 31 |
| 3 *Barrett* | 85 | 15 | 85 |
| **Nevada** | | | |
| 1 Bilbray | 31 | 68 | 32 |
| 2 *Vucanovich* | 84 | 12 | 87 |
| **New Hampshire** | | | |
| 1 *Zeliff* | 79 | 17 | 82 |
| 2 Swett | 28 | 71 | 28 |
| **New Jersey** | | | |
| 1 Andrews | 38 | 58 | 40 |
| 2 Hughes | 23 | 77 | 23 |
| 3 Pallone | 29 | 71 | 29 |
| 4 *Smith* | 61 | 38 | 62 |
| 5 Roukema | 48 | 45 | 52 |
| 6 Dwyer | 20 | 65 | 24 |
| 7 *Rinaldo* | 57 | 39 | 59 |
| 8 Roe | 30 | 61 | 33 |
| 9 Torricelli | 25 | 66 | 27 |
| 10 Payne | 10 | 85 | 11 |
| 11 *Gallo* | 71 | 26 | 74 |
| 12 *Zimmer* | 58 | 42 | 58 |
| 13 *Saxton* | 73 | 25 | 75 |
| 14 Guarini | 23 | 70 | 25 |
| **New Mexico** | | | |
| 1 *Schiff* | 67 | 31 | 68 |
| 2 *Skeen* | 76 | 24 | 76 |
| 3 Richardson | 29 | 65 | 31 |
| **New York** | | | |
| 1 Hochbrueckner | 18 | 81 | 18 |
| 2 Downey | 19 | 80 | 19 |
| 3 Mrazek | 19 | 64 | 23 |
| 4 *Lent* | 71 | 13 | 84 |
| 5 McGrath | 70 | 26 | 73 |
| 6 Flake | 10 | 76 | 12 |
| 7 Ackerman | 13 | 57 | 19 |
| 8 Scheuer | 12 | 76 | 14 |
| 9 Manton | 30 | 63 | 33 |
| 10 Schumer | 18 | 76 | 19 |
| 11 Towns | 11 | 64 | 15 |
| 12 Owens | 11 | 85 | 12 |
| 13 Solarz | 15 | 66 | 19 |
| 14 Molinari | 65 | 33 | 66 |
| 15 *Green* | 40 | 54 | 42 |
| 16 Rangel | 12 | 84 | 13 |
| 17 Weiss [1] | 14 | 76 | 15 |
| 18 Serrano | 9 | 89 | 9 |
| 19 Engel | 16 | 75 | 18 |
| 20 Lowey | 13 | 87 | 13 |
| 21 *Fish* | 54 | 43 | 56 |
| 22 *Gilman* | 41 | 58 | 41 |
| 23 McNulty | 27 | 72 | 27 |
| 24 *Solomon* | 70 | 26 | 73 |
| 25 *Boehlert* | 42 | 58 | 42 |
| 26 *Martin* | 66 | 24 | 73 |
| 27 Walsh | 64 | 35 | 64 |
| 28 McHugh | 23 | 77 | 23 |
| 29 *Horton* | 48 | 45 | 52 |
| 30 Slaughter | 16 | 84 | 16 |
| 31 *Paxon* | 80 | 20 | 80 |

| | 1 | 2 | 3 |
|---|---|---|---|
| 32 LaFalce | 27 | 70 | 27 |
| 33 Nowak | 27 | 71 | 27 |
| 34 *Houghton* | 66 | 32 | 67 |
| **North Carolina** | | | |
| 1 Jones [2] | 24 | 70 | 25 |
| 2 Valentine | 34 | 54 | 39 |
| 3 Lancaster | 46 | 52 | 47 |
| 4 Price | 25 | 74 | 25 |
| 5 Neal | 26 | 70 | 27 |
| 6 *Coble* | 75 | 25 | 75 |
| 7 Rose | 25 | 73 | 25 |
| 8 Hefner | 13 | 53 | 20 |
| 9 *McMillan* | 78 | 17 | 82 |
| 10 *Ballenger* | 69 | 27 | 72 |
| 11 *Taylor* | 76 | 19 | 80 |
| **North Dakota** | | | |
| AL Dorgan | 25 | 75 | 25 |
| **Ohio** | | | |
| 1 Luken | 35 | 57 | 38 |
| 2 *Gradison* | 76 | 24 | 76 |
| 3 Hall | 28 | 69 | 29 |
| 4 *Oxley* | 86 | 11 | 88 |
| 5 *Gillmor* | 73 | 26 | 74 |
| 6 *McEwen* | 75 | 16 | 82 |
| 7 *Hobson* | 67 | 33 | 67 |
| 8 *Boehner* | 87 | 11 | 88 |
| 9 Kaptur | 23 | 75 | 23 |
| 10 *Miller* | 87 | 13 | 87 |
| 11 Eckart | 20 | 77 | 21 |
| 12 *Kasich* | 71 | 26 | 74 |
| 13 Pease | 17 | 81 | 17 |
| 14 Sawyer | 17 | 83 | 17 |
| 15 *Wylie* | 74 | 18 | 80 |
| 16 *Regula* | 55 | 44 | 56 |
| 17 Traficant | 21 | 78 | 21 |
| 18 Applegate | 28 | 70 | 28 |
| 19 Feighan | 18 | 67 | 21 |
| 20 Oakar | 15 | 62 | 20 |
| 21 Stokes | 10 | 87 | 11 |
| **Oklahoma** | | | |
| 1 *Inhofe* | 81 | 17 | 83 |
| 2 Synar | 18 | 78 | 19 |
| 3 Brewster | 43 | 57 | 43 |
| 4 McCurdy | 42 | 51 | 45 |
| 5 *Edwards* | 67 | 15 | 81 |
| 6 English | 52 | 48 | 52 |
| **Oregon** | | | |
| 1 AuCoin | 9 | 72 | 11 |
| 2 *Smith* | 84 | 14 | 85 |
| 3 Wyden | 17 | 81 | 17 |
| 4 DeFazio | 12 | 84 | 13 |
| 5 Kopetski | 25 | 72 | 25 |
| **Pennsylvania** | | | |
| 1 Foglietta | 16 | 76 | 18 |
| 2 Blackwell | 12 | 85 | 13 |
| 3 Borski | 28 | 70 | 28 |
| 4 Kolter | 20 | 43 | 32 |
| 5 *Schulze* | 67 | 18 | 79 |
| 6 Yatron | 30 | 52 | 37 |
| 7 *Weldon* | 68 | 31 | 68 |
| 8 Kostmayer | 15 | 84 | 15 |
| 9 *Shuster* | 74 | 26 | 74 |
| 10 *McDade* | 57 | 22 | 72 |
| 11 Kanjorski | 31 | 69 | 31 |
| 12 Murtha | 39 | 54 | 42 |
| 13 *Coughlin* | 73 | 19 | 79 |
| 14 Coyne | 19 | 81 | 19 |
| 15 *Ritter* | 71 | 28 | 72 |
| 16 *Walker* | 81 | 15 | 84 |
| 17 Gekas | 74 | 20 | 79 |
| 18 *Santorum* | 70 | 28 | 72 |
| 19 *Goodling* | 72 | 28 | 72 |
| 20 Gaydos | 26 | 44 | 37 |
| 21 *Ridge* | 50 | 47 | 52 |
| 22 Murphy | 23 | 70 | 24 |
| 23 *Clinger* | 75 | 19 | 80 |
| **Rhode Island** | | | |
| 1 *Machtley* | 47 | 51 | 48 |
| 2 Reed | 14 | 86 | 14 |
| **South Carolina** | | | |
| 1 Ravenel | 58 | 40 | 59 |
| 2 *Spence* | 76 | 24 | 76 |
| 3 Derrick | 30 | 69 | 31 |
| 4 Patterson | 41 | 54 | 43 |
| 5 Spratt | 34 | 66 | 34 |
| 6 Tallon | 26 | 61 | 30 |

| | 1 | 2 | 3 |
|---|---|---|---|
| **South Dakota** | | | |
| AL Johnson | 29 | 71 | 29 |
| **Tennessee** | | | |
| 1 *Quillen* | 69 | 21 | 77 |
| 2 *Duncan* | 63 | 37 | 63 |
| 3 Lloyd | 46 | 51 | 47 |
| 4 Cooper | 42 | 56 | 43 |
| 5 Clement | 25 | 67 | 27 |
| 6 Gordon | 24 | 69 | 26 |
| 7 *Sundquist* | 77 | 20 | 79 |
| 8 Tanner | 38 | 56 | 40 |
| 9 Ford | 10 | 69 | 13 |
| **Texas** | | | |
| 1 Chapman | 31 | 64 | 33 |
| 2 Wilson | 37 | 54 | 41 |
| 3 *Johnson* | 84 | 12 | 87 |
| 4 Hall | 63 | 37 | 63 |
| 5 Bryant | 18 | 70 | 21 |
| 6 *Barton* | 77 | 13 | 85 |
| 7 *Archer* | 80 | 13 | 86 |
| 8 *Fields* | 77 | 15 | 84 |
| 9 Brooks | 30 | 62 | 33 |
| 10 Pickle | 40 | 56 | 42 |
| 11 Edwards | 43 | 56 | 43 |
| 12 Geren | 57 | 42 | 58 |
| 13 Sarpalius | 56 | 43 | 57 |
| 14 Laughlin | 41 | 48 | 46 |
| 15 de la Garza | 33 | 54 | 38 |
| 16 Coleman | 28 | 66 | 30 |
| 17 Stenholm | 68 | 29 | 70 |
| 18 Washington | 6 | 90 | 6 |
| 19 *Combest* | 79 | 21 | 79 |
| 20 Gonzalez | 23 | 77 | 23 |
| 21 *Smith* | 77 | 21 | 79 |
| 22 *DeLay* | 82 | 16 | 83 |
| 23 Bustamante | 22 | 63 | 26 |
| 24 Frost | 30 | 66 | 32 |
| 25 Andrews | 39 | 60 | 39 |
| 26 *Armey* | 85 | 13 | 86 |
| 27 Ortiz | 37 | 55 | 40 |
| **Utah** | | | |
| 1 *Hansen* | 89 | 8 | 92 |
| 2 Owens | 26 | 61 | 30 |
| 3 Orton | 55 | 42 | 57 |
| **Vermont** | | | |
| AL *Sanders* | 11 | 88 | 12 |
| **Virginia** | | | |
| 1 *Bateman* | 81 | 17 | 83 |
| 2 Pickett | 65 | 35 | 65 |
| 3 *Bliley* | 86 | 13 | 87 |
| 4 Sisisky | 49 | 50 | 50 |
| 5 Payne | 44 | 56 | 44 |
| 6 Olin | 40 | 48 | 46 |
| 7 *Allen* | 77 | 22 | 78 |
| 8 Moran | 30 | 66 | 31 |
| 9 Boucher | 21 | 78 | 21 |
| 10 *Wolf* | 78 | 22 | 78 |
| **Washington** | | | |
| 1 *Miller* | 60 | 28 | 68 |
| 2 Swift | 24 | 76 | 24 |
| 3 Unsoeld | 12 | 81 | 13 |
| 4 *Morrison* | 47 | 36 | 56 |
| 5 Foley [3] | | | |
| 6 Dicks | 36 | 61 | 37 |
| 7 McDermott | 18 | 82 | 18 |
| 8 *Chandler* | 68 | 15 | 82 |
| **West Virginia** | | | |
| 1 Mollohan | 35 | 60 | 37 |
| 2 Staggers | 16 | 65 | 20 |
| 3 Wise | 18 | 76 | 19 |
| 4 Rahall | 25 | 69 | 27 |
| **Wisconsin** | | | |
| 1 Aspin | 29 | 67 | 30 |
| 2 *Klug* | 54 | 45 | 55 |
| 3 *Gunderson* | 62 | 37 | 63 |
| 4 Kleczka | 20 | 78 | 20 |
| 5 Moody | 11 | 87 | 12 |
| 6 Petri | 67 | 33 | 67 |
| 7 Obey | 14 | 84 | 15 |
| 8 Roth | 67 | 28 | 71 |
| 9 Sensenbrenner | 69 | 30 | 70 |
| **Wyoming** | | | |
| AL *Thomas* | 77 | 22 | 78 |

| Alabama | 1 | 2 | 3 |
|---|---|---|---|
| Heflin | 53 | 47 | 53 |
| Shelby | 65 | 35 | 65 |
| **Alaska** | | | |
| *Murkowski* | 72 | 27 | 73 |
| *Stevens* | 78 | 20 | 80 |
| **Arizona** | | | |
| DeConcini | 28 | 67 | 30 |
| *McCain* | 75 | 25 | 75 |
| **Arkansas** | | | |
| Bumpers | 28 | 72 | 28 |
| Pryor | 27 | 73 | 27 |
| **California** | | | |
| Cranston | 33 | 58 | 36 |
| Seymour | 65 | 18 | 78 |
| **Colorado** | | | |
| Wirth | 33 | 52 | 39 |
| *Brown* | 75 | 25 | 75 |
| **Connecticut** | | | |
| Dodd | 32 | 68 | 32 |
| Lieberman | 37 | 63 | 37 |
| **Delaware** | | | |
| Biden | 28 | 70 | 29 |
| *Roth* | 67 | 22 | 75 |
| **Florida** | | | |
| Graham | 35 | 65 | 35 |
| *Mack* † | 83 | 16 | 84 |
| **Georgia** | | | |
| Fowler | 30 | 68 | 31 |
| Nunn | 40 | 58 | 41 |
| **Hawaii** | | | |
| Akaka | 30 | 70 | 30 |
| Inouye | 38 | 55 | 41 |
| **Idaho** | | | |
| *Craig* | 83 | 15 | 85 |
| *Symms* | 80 | 15 | 84 |
| **Illinois** | | | |
| Dixon | 32 | 50 | 39 |
| Simon | 27 | 73 | 27 |
| **Indiana** | | | |
| *Coats* | 75 | 22 | 78 |
| *Lugar* | 87 | 10 | 90 |

| Iowa | 1 | 2 | 3 |
|---|---|---|---|
| Harkin | 18 | 62 | 23 |
| *Grassley* | 70 | 30 | 70 |
| **Kansas** | | | |
| *Dole* | 88 | 12 | 88 |
| *Kassebaum* | 72 | 28 | 72 |
| **Kentucky** | | | |
| Ford | 35 | 65 | 35 |
| *McConnell* | 77 | 23 | 77 |
| **Louisiana** | | | |
| Breaux | 42 | 58 | 42 |
| Johnston | 52 | 45 | 53 |
| **Maine** | | | |
| Mitchell | 25 | 75 | 25 |
| *Cohen* | 63 | 37 | 63 |
| **Maryland** | | | |
| Mikulski | 23 | 77 | 23 |
| Sarbanes | 27 | 73 | 27 |
| **Massachusetts** | | | |
| Kennedy | 25 | 73 | 25 |
| Kerry | 23 | 77 | 23 |
| **Michigan** | | | |
| Levin | 32 | 67 | 32 |
| Riegle | 28 | 68 | 29 |
| **Minnesota** | | | |
| Wellstone | 23 | 75 | 24 |
| *Durenberger* | 63 | 33 | 66 |
| **Mississippi** | | | |
| *Cochran* | 82 | 15 | 84 |
| *Lott* | 83 | 17 | 83 |
| **Missouri** | | | |
| *Bond* | 70 | 23 | 75 |
| *Danforth* | 78 | 22 | 78 |
| **Montana** | | | |
| Baucus | 35 | 65 | 35 |
| *Burns* | 85 | 15 | 85 |
| **Nebraska** | | | |
| Exon | 43 | 57 | 43 |
| Kerrey | 25 | 58 | 30 |
| **Nevada** | | | |
| Bryan | 32 | 68 | 32 |
| Reid | 37 | 62 | 37 |

| New Hampshire | 1 | 2 | 3 |
|---|---|---|---|
| *Rudman* | 78 | 18 | 81 |
| *Smith* | 73 | 27 | 73 |
| **New Jersey** | | | |
| Bradley | 23 | 68 | 25 |
| Lautenberg | 22 | 78 | 22 |
| **New Mexico** | | | |
| Bingaman | 40 | 50 | 44 |
| *Domenici* | 82 | 18 | 82 |
| **New York** | | | |
| Moynihan | 35 | 65 | 35 |
| *D'Amato* | 58 | 38 | 60 |
| **North Carolina** | | | |
| Sanford | 22 | 67 | 25 |
| *Helms* | 62 | 15 | 80 |
| **North Dakota** | | | |
| Burdick [1] | 17 | 83 | 17 |
| Conrad | 32 | 67 | 32 |
| **Ohio** | | | |
| Glenn | 30 | 68 | 31 |
| Metzenbaum | 25 | 72 | 26 |
| **Oklahoma** | | | |
| Boren | 33 | 55 | 38 |
| *Nickles* | 77 | 20 | 79 |
| **Oregon** | | | |
| *Hatfield* | 53 | 47 | 53 |
| *Packwood* | 60 | 37 | 62 |
| **Pennsylvania** | | | |
| Wofford | 28 | 70 | 29 |
| *Specter* | 45 | 55 | 45 |
| **Rhode Island** | | | |
| Pell | 28 | 68 | 29 |
| *Chafee* | 62 | 38 | 62 |
| **South Carolina** | | | |
| Hollings | 38 | 62 | 38 |
| *Thurmond* | 78 | 22 | 78 |
| **South Dakota** | | | |
| Daschle | 25 | 75 | 25 |
| *Pressler* | 73 | 27 | 73 |
| **Tennessee** | | | |
| Gore | 22 | 47 | 32 |
| Sasser | 35 | 65 | 35 |

| Texas | 1 | 2 | 3 |
|---|---|---|---|
| Bentsen | 45 | 52 | 47 |
| *Gramm* | 90 | 10 | 90 |
| **Utah** | | | |
| *Garn* | 83 | 10 | 89 |
| *Hatch* | 82 | 12 | 88 |
| **Vermont** | | | |
| Leahy | 23 | 75 | 24 |
| *Jeffords* | 45 | 52 | 47 |
| **Virginia** | | | |
| Robb | 42 | 58 | 42 |
| *Warner* | 67 | 25 | 73 |
| **Washington** | | | |
| Adams | 25 | 75 | 25 |
| *Gorton* | 68 | 28 | 71 |
| **West Virginia** | | | |
| Byrd | 27 | 73 | 27 |
| Rockefeller | 28 | 72 | 28 |
| **Wisconsin** | | | |
| Kohl | 30 | 70 | 30 |
| *Kasten* | 63 | 32 | 67 |
| **Wyoming** | | | |
| *Simpson* | 82 | 17 | 83 |
| *Wallop* | 78 | 18 | 81 |

# Presidential Support and Opposition: Senate

**1. Bush Support Score, 1992.** Percentage of 60 recorded votes in 1992 on which President Bush took a position and on which a senator voted "yea" or "nay" *in agreement* with the president's position. Failures to vote lowered both support and opposition scores.

**2. Bush Opposition Score, 1992.** Percentage of 60 recorded votes in 1992 on which President Bush took a position and on which a senator voted "yea" or "nay" *in disagreement* with the president's position. Failures to vote lowered both support and opposition scores.

**3. Bush Support Score, 1992.** Percentage of 60 recorded votes in 1992 on which President Bush took a position and on which a senator was present and voted "yea" or "nay" *in agreement* with the president's position. In this version of the study, absences are not counted; therefore, failures to vote did not lower support or opposition scores. Opposition scores, not listed here, are the inverse of the support score; i.e., the opposition score is equal to 100 percent minus the individual's support score.

[1] *Jocelyn Birch Burdick, D-N.D., was sworn in Sept. 16, 1992, to succeed her husband, Quentin N. Burdick, D, who died Sept. 8, 1992. Quentin N. Burdick was eligible for 40 presidential support votes in 1992. His presidential support score was 35 percent; his opposition score was 50 percent; and his support score, adjusted for absences, was 41 percent in 1992. Jocelyn Birch Burdick was eligible for 18 presidential support votes in 1992.*

## CONSERVATIVE COALITION

# Southern Democrats May Score If Fading Alliance Dissolves

*Clinton may bring new power, leadership to his native region as coalition with Republicans breaks down*

The conservative coalition continued to be the congressional equivalent of an endangered species in 1992. Next year, it may become all but extinct.

For half a century, congressional action was shaped by the conservative coalition, the powerful teaming of Southern Democrats with Republicans to thwart liberal initiatives. But its influence has been fading.

Ironically, should the coalition disappear, it could well be a big victory for Southern Democrats. With Arkansas' Bill Clinton, one of their own, in the White House, they are poised to wield new power in crafting their party's agenda. If they're successful, such power will not appear as conservative coalition votes because Southerners will feel comfortable with the legislation being considered.

Southern Democrats are planning to exert their power within the Democratic Caucus, rather than by joining Republicans to block programs of the Democratic leadership.

"I see the role more as a leadership role within the Democratic Party than in a coalition with Republicans," said Chief Deputy Majority Whip Butler Derrick of South Carolina. "I think [Southern Democrats] are going to play a key role, but not in some obstructive sense. I think they will help form the consensus that will be led by the administration."

The coalition, as defined and measured by Congressional Quarterly, is a voting bloc in the House and Senate that occurs when a majority of Republicans join with a majority of Southern Democrats against a majority of Northern Democrats.

For decades, the coalition served as a check on liberal impulses in Congress. And in the early 1980s, during the first years of Ronald Reagan's presidency, the coalition was central to passing Reagan's program of federal tax cuts and steep increases in the Pentagon budget.

Since then, it has shown a steady decline, coalescing on

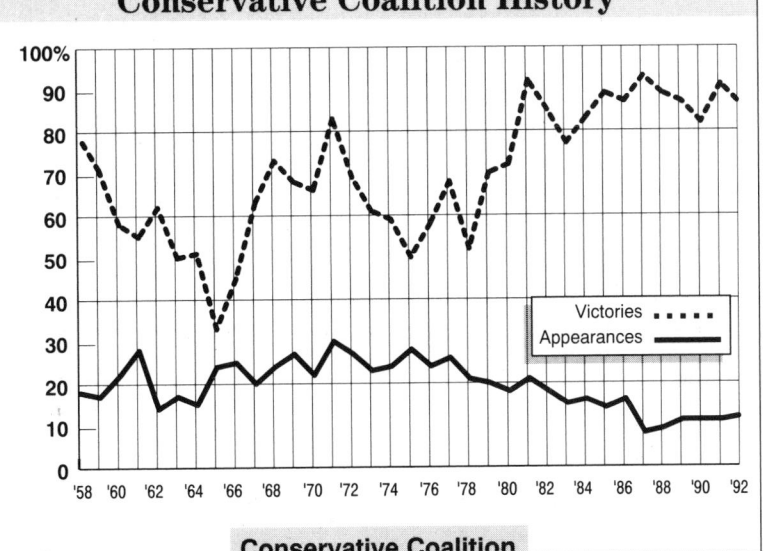

**Conservative Coalition History**

Victories ..... 
Appearances ——

**Conservative Coalition**

A voting bloc in the House and Senate consisting of a majority of Republicans and a majority of Southern Democrats, when combined against a majority of Northern Democrats.

PATT CHISHOLM

about 10 percent of floor votes in recent years. It showed a modest uptick in 1992, appearing on 12 percent of congressional floor votes, although most of the increase was due to strings of Senate votes on the energy and tax bills.

As usual, when the coalition appeared, it almost always won.

But changes in the political climate make it likely that for the next few years the coalition will become a statistical artifact.

"There is a groundswell of public opinion out there for us to move in other than in a traditionally liberal direction," said Charles W. Stenholm, D-Texas, chairman of the Conservative Democratic Forum. "Let us be a part of defining the agenda. And if we are, we will [support it]."

Even if Democrats should become dissatisfied with the direction of Clinton and Congress, the vows by Republicans to adopt a more militant and confrontational role may make it less likely for Democrats to break ranks and join the conservative coalition.

"We're going to be a very militant, forceful force," said House Minority Leader Robert H. Michel of Illinois.

### Changing Faces

Next year will be a watershed not only because of the change in the White House but also because of the changing profile of Southern Democrats in Congress. Clinton will be moving the mainstream of Democratic thought closer to the center at the same time that Southern Democrats are moving somewhat toward the left.

The November election was the first after redistricting, which added 12 House districts dominated by black voters. In each instance the results produced a black Democratic member who is expected to vote more like a Northern Democrat.

It November, there were 85 Southern Democrats elected to the House; 17 of them are black. If the newcomers follow the example o the current five black Southern

Huckaby     Erdreich     Harris

# Flight of the Boll Weevils

The mathematical imperatives of the 1992 election results will make it far more difficult for the conservative coalition to appear in the House in the 103rd Congress.

The coalition, which forms when a majority of Southern Democrats votes with a majority of Republicans against Northern Democrats, is about to lose many of its most reliable Southern members. These "Boll Weevils" have been responsible for many of the Republicans' floor victories in the past.

There will be 85 Southern Democrats in the House, the same number as this year. The composition is changing, however, with 68 whites and 17 blacks, compared with 80 whites and 5 blacks in the 102nd Congress. Most of the black members represent districts dominated by minority groups, and if historical trends hold, those members will be less likely to vote with the conservative coalition.

Assuming no absences, 43 Southern Democrats will have to cross party lines to form a conservative coalition vote. If Southern blacks vote with Northern Democrats, as has been the case in the past, 63 percent of white Southern Democrats would have to vote with the Republicans to reach the bare majority required for the conservative coalition to form. Under the same scenario for the 102nd Congress, 54 percent of such members had to join with Republicans for the coalition to appear.

The following are Southern Democrats who were strong supporters of the conservative coalition but are leaving the House:

| Member | Conservative coalition support, 1992 |
|---|---|
| Jerry Huckaby, La. | 95 percent |
| Ben Erdreich, Ala | 94 percent |
| Claude Harris, Ala. | 91 percent |
| Doug Barnard Jr., Ga. | 90 percent |
| Richard Ray, Ga. | 89 percent |
| Lindsay Thomas, Ga. | 88 percent |
| Carroll Hubbard Jr., Ky. | 87 percent |
| Charles Hatcher, Ga. | 76 percent |
| Ed Jenkins, Ga. | 76 percent |
| Liz J. Patterson, S.C. | 70 percent |
| Robin Tallon, S.C. | 70 percent |

Democrats, they will not consistently join the coalition.

When it comes to supporting the conservative coalition, each of the five current black Southern Democrats has a score ranking among the 11 lowest for all Southern Democrats. The highest support score among Southern blacks was compiled by Mike Espy of Mississippi, at 36 percent. Several of the new majority-black districts draw from rural areas, such as Espy's district, so those new members' scores may be high relative to their black Northern Democratic colleagues. But they remain unlikely to regularly join the coalition.

The drawing of minority districts in reapportionment forced several white Southern Democrats to retire or led them to defeat in November, and their new districts went Republican.

The 102nd Congress included 44 Southern Republicans; the 103rd will include 52. To a considerable extent, these Republican gains come at the expense of conservative Democrats. Replacing a conservative Democrat with a Republican may not greatly change the way a district's member votes on certain issues, but it makes it more difficult to assemble the majority of Southern Democrats required to form the conservative coalition.

The makeover of the Georgia Democratic delegation shows this phenomenon in its extreme. Seven of the eight white members of the delegation during the 102nd Congress received conservative coalition support scores greater than 75 percent. Only two of those seven remain. The new delegation will have four Republicans instead of one and seven Democrats — three blacks and four whites. And two of the four white Democrats are freshmen whose support the Democratic leadership probably can count on.

"Nathan Deal, Don Johnson are probably going to be more moderate than the people they're going to replace," said Emory University political scientist Merle Black. Deal and Johnson will replace conservatives Ed Jenkins and Doug Barnard Jr., respectively.

In Alabama, redistricting produced a newly drawn black-majority district won by black Democrat Earl F. Hilliard and a GOP-leaning 6th District won by Republican Spencer Bachus. In the process, the delegation lost two conservative Democrats — Claude Harris and Ben Erdreich — who supported the coalition more than 90 percent of the time.

Southern Democrats also face pressures toward moderation within the House. To buck the Democratic Caucus and form alliances with Republicans has its costs.

The courtly dean of the Boll Weevils, G. V. "Sonny" Montgomery, D-Miss., was almost deposed from his Veterans' Committee chairmanship earlier this month, in large part due to his conservatism and his tendency to vote with Republicans.

By the same token, cooperating with the leadership has its rewards. Of the seven newly elected Democrats named to the three choicest committees — Ways and Means, Appropriations, and Energy and Commerce — two were Southerners: Carrie Meek, Fla., who landed Appropriations, and Blanche Lambert, Ark., who won a spot on Energy and Commerce.

In giving Meek, who is black and represents a liberal constituency in the Miami area, a seat on Appropriations, the leadership-driven Steering and Policy Committee clearly saw her as a team player. Lambert, who is no Boll Weevil, won a spot on Energy and Commerce with the help of Mike Synar, D-Okla., who had the highest conservative coalition opposition score of any white Southerner.

"I have heard from the freshman class that some of the more moderate and conservative members are very upset" with their committee assignments, Stenholm said.

"There's no way you can enjoy a successful House career anymore as a conservative Southern Democrat," said Black.

Add to such changes the fact that Southern and Northern Democrats will be trying to work more closely together, and it begins to look as if the coalition, at least in the House, is on its last legs.

"The short-term impact will likely be to reduce the number of times of the conservative coalition forming," Black said. "All of these Democrats would stand to benefit enormously from a successful Democratic president."

### Senate Uncertainties

The Senate picture is less settled. Two Southern Democrats with fairly low conservative coalition support scores — Terry Sanford of North Carolina and Wyche Fowler Jr. of Georgia — lost on Nov. 3. Vice President-elect Al Gore of Tennessee tied for the lowest support score among Southern Democrats, although he missed more than half the votes. The coalition lost a generally reliable member with the departure of Lloyd Bentsen, D-Texas, to the Treasury Department.

While shifts in the roster of Southern Democrats leave the coalition in the Senate in something of a muddle, what is clear is that they are generally more moderate than their Democratic predecessors, conservative stalwarts such as John C. Stennis and James O. Eastland of Mississippi, Herman E. Talmadge of Georgia and John L. McClellan of Arkansas.

"The unreconstructed rebels have been replaced by their grandchildren, who are a lot more moderate," said University of Georgia political scientist Charles Bullock. Or, he says, they've been replaced by Republicans.

"If you're going to be elected as a Democrat, you have to be responsive to the liberal part of the electorate," Bullock said.

In 1992, the coalition appeared in 38 of 270 Senate floor votes, or 14 percent, more frequently than in the House. It prevailed on 33 of those votes for a success rate of 87 percent. But it appeared to have limited power. Of the 15 most important, or "key," votes, as determined by Congressional Quarterly, the coalition appeared twice: winning a vote to ease procedures for licensing of new nuclear power plants and losing a vote to block an amendment to the energy and water appropriations bill to impose a nuclear weapons test ban.

Perhaps the most significant appearances of the coalition occurred during consideration of appropriations bills and the budget resolution, when Southern Democrats and Republicans teamed up to block several attempts by Northern Democrats to waive budget rules and shift money from defense to domestic programs.

Many of the coalition's appearances occurred to block amendments to the national energy strategy bill (HR 776, S 2166) and the two tax bills (HR 11, HR 4210). The coalition showed up 15 times during consideration of these bills, with many of the votes reflecting regional issues.

But the frequent appearances during the energy and tax bills may also be partly attributable to the fact that the floor managers of the bills were Southern Democrats:

Finance Committee Chairman Bentsen and Energy Committee Chairman J. Bennett Johnston, D-La.

During floor votes on the energy bill — which drew criticism from environmentalists who said it was too favorable to the oil and gas and nuclear power industries — the coalition formed seven times without a defeat.

In addition to the provision on nuclear power plant licensing, the coalition preserved language to give tax breaks to the oil and gas industries, blocked environmentalists from further curbing offshore oil and gas development and stifled an attempt to mandate further use of alternative fuels.

On the tax bills, the coalition appeared eight times without a defeat. The most significant victories occurred on amendments to bar subsidiaries of U.S. companies from deducting expenses from doing business with Cuba, preserve tax breaks for oil and gas exploration and kill tax credits for employers who provide child-care facilities.

And the coalition formed, as in the past, on other legislation that dealt with social and crime issues such as gay rights, the death penalty and gun control.

> "Those very liberal members ... are going to find themselves on the outside looking in on many issues."
>
> —Rep. Butler Derrick, D-S.C.

### House Appearances

In the House, the coalition appeared on 48 votes, or 10 percent. It prevailed on 42 of those votes for victories in 88 percent of appearances. Of the 16 key votes, as determined by Congressional Quarterly, the coalition appeared on four, and it won on three of those. The only loss for the coalition on those key votes occurred on the balanced-budget amendment, which required a two-thirds margin. It failed 280-153.

But the resolve of the coalition on the budget deficit resulted in the coalition's most significant victory, which was to block attempts to tear down the so-called budget walls and shift defense spending to domestic programs.

In the two other key vote victories, the coalition saved the space station *Freedom* and repelled about $1 billion in cuts in the Strategic Defense Initiative.

Lower-profile appearances occurred on defense and foreign policy votes, the energy bill, and social and crime issues such as homosexual rights and the death penalty.

### Future Prospects

With members of Congress and academics agreeing that, at least for the immediate future, the coalition will appear less frequently, one question remains: What issues will prompt it to resurface?

Derrick expects to see it on issues such as gun control, gay rights and allowing states to enact right-to-work laws that prohibit compulsory union membership.

One early possibility could be congressional reaction to Clinton's controversial pledge to permit homosexuals in the military. The coalition could also appear if Northern Democrats decide to offer liberal amendments to bills on the floor. But if floor vehicles reflect Clinton's priorities, it is unclear whether liberals will abandon the party position.

"I think that it's going to be a year in which people are going to be working together despite some of the labels," said Rules Committee Chairman Joe Moakley, D-Mass.

Derrick predicted, "Those very liberal members . . . are going to find themselves on the outside looking in on many issues." ∎

# Leading Scorers: Conservative Coalition

High scorers in support are those who in 1992 voted most often with the conservative coalition. Opposition figures are for those who voted most often against the coalition. Scores are based on actual votes cast and ranked by percentages before rounding. Members who were not eligible for half the votes are not listed.

## Highest Scorers — Support

### Senate

**Shelby** · **Wallop** · **Conrad**

#### Southern Democrats

| | | | |
|---|---|---|---|
| Shelby, Ala. | 89% | Boren, Okla. | 77% |
| Heflin, Ala. | 89 | Bentsen, Texas | 76 |
| Ford, Ky. | 84 | Nunn, Ga. | 73 |
| Johnston, La. | 79 | Bumpers, Ark. | 71 |
| Breaux, La. | 78 | Pryor, Ark. | 66 |

#### Republicans

| | | | |
|---|---|---|---|
| Wallop, Wyo. | 100 | Helms, N.C. | 96 |
| Craig, Idaho | 97 | Burns, Mont. | 95 |
| Lott, Miss. | 97 | Hatch, Utah | 95 |
| Symms, Idaho | 97 | Thurmond, S.C. | 95 |

#### Northern Democrats

| | | | |
|---|---|---|---|
| Conrad, N.D. | 62 | Dixon, Ill. | 45 |
| Exon, Neb. | 55 | Baucus, Mont. | 45 |
| DeConcini, Ariz. | 53 | Reid, Nev. | 45 |
| Bryan, Nev. | 49 | Bingaman, N.M. | 42 |

### House

**Huckaby** · **Callahan** · **Volkmer**

#### Southern Democrats

| | | | | | | |
|---|---|---|---|---|---|---|
| Huckaby, La. | 95% | Geren, Texas | 91% | Tauzin, La. | 89% |
| Erdreich, Ala. | 94 | Harris, Ala. | 91 | Rowland, Ga. | 89 |
| Sisisky, Va. | 94 | Barnard, Ga. | 90 | Hayes, La. | 89 |
| Hall, Texas | 92 | Lloyd, Tenn. | 90 | Ray, Ga. | 89 |
| Hutto, Fla. | 91 | Stenholm, Texas | 89 | | |

#### Republicans

| | | | | | | |
|---|---|---|---|---|---|---|
| Callahan, Ala. | 100 | Spence, S.C. | 98 | Lewis, Fla. | 98 |
| Cox, Calif. | 100 | Smith, Texas | 98 | McCollum, Fla. | 98 |
| Dornan, Calif. | 100 | Schafer, Colo. | 98 | Packard, Calif. | 98 |
| Dreier, Calif. | 100 | Oxley, Ohio | 98 | Lagomarsino, | |
| Johnson, Texas | 100 | Cunningham, | | Calif. | 98 |
| Hunter, Calif. | 98 | Calif. | 98 | Gingrich, Ga. | 98 |
| Moorhead, Calif. | 98 | Baker, La. | 98 | McCrery, La. | 98 |

#### Northern Democrats

| | | | | | | |
|---|---|---|---|---|---|---|
| Volkmer, Mo. | 85 | Hamilton, Ind. | 74 | Murtha, Pa. | 71 |
| Skelton, Mo. | 85 | Campbell, Colo. | 71 | Roemer, Ind. | 71 |
| Byron, Md. | 83 | | | | |

## Highest Scorers — Opposition

**Rockefeller** · **Specter** · **Adams**

#### Southern Democrats

| | | | |
|---|---|---|---|
| Rockefeller, W.Va. | 72% | Fowler, Ga. | 43% |
| Robb, Va. | 50 | Sasser, Tenn. | 41 |
| Graham, Fla. | 47 | Byrd, W.Va. | 39 |
| Hollings, S.C. | 45 | Sanford, N.C. | 39 |

#### Republicans

| | | | |
|---|---|---|---|
| Specter, Pa. | 61 | D'Amato, N.Y. | 52 |
| Jeffords, Vt. | 60 | Packwood, Ore. | 49 |
| Cohen, Maine | 55 | Chafee, R.I. | 45 |
| Hatfield, Ore. | 53 | Durenberger, Minn. | 37 |

#### Northern Democrats

| | | | |
|---|---|---|---|
| Adams, Wash. | 95 | Kennedy, Mass. | 95 |
| Lautenberg, N.J. | 95 | Leahy, Vt. | 95 |
| Metzenbaum, Ohio | 95 | Harkin, Iowa | 93 |

**Washington** · **Green** · **Abercrombie**

#### Southern Democrats

| | | | |
|---|---|---|---|
| Washington, Texas | 93% | Jefferson, La. | 72% |
| Lewis, Ga. | 93 | Lehman, Fla. | 70 |
| Ford, Tenn. | 84 | Smith, Fla. | 68 |
| Synar, Okla. | 79 | Johnston, Fla. | 66 |
| Perkins, Ky. | 73 | Jones, Ga. | 66 |

#### Republicans

| | | | |
|---|---|---|---|
| Green, N.Y. | 64 | Ramstad, Minn. | 44 |
| Shays, Conn. | 58 | Leach, La. | 42 |
| Morella, Md. | 50 | Boehlert, N.Y. | 40 |
| Gilman, N.Y. | 44 | Roukema, N.J. | 39 |

#### Northern Democrats

| | | | |
|---|---|---|---|
| Abercrombie, Hawaii | 98 | Dellums, Calif. | 96 |
| Pelosi, Calif. | 98 | Payne, N.J. | 96 |
| Wolpe, Mich. | 98 | Serrano, N.Y. | 96 |
| Frank, Mass. | 96 | Yates, Ill. | 96 |
| Atkins, Mass. | 96 | | |

## Conservative Coalition Definitions

**Conservative coalition.** As used in this study, "conservative coalition" means a voting alliance of Republicans and Southern Democrats against the Northern Democrats in Congress. This meaning, rather than any philosophic definition of the "conservative coalition" position, provides the basis for CQ's selection of coalition votes.

**Conservative coalition support score.** Percentage of conservative coalition votes on which a member voted "yea" or "nay" *in agreement* with the position of the conservative coalition. Failures to vote, even if a member announced a stand, lower the score.

**Conservative coalition vote.** Any vote in the Senate or the House on which a majority of voting Southern Democrats and a majority of voting Republicans opposed the stand taken by a majority of voting Northern Democrats. Votes on which there was an even division within the ranks of voting Northern Democrats, Southern Democrats or Republicans are not included.

**Conservative coalition opposition score.** Percentage of conservative coalition votes on which a member voted "yea" or "nay" *in disagreement* with the position of the conservative coalition. Failures to vote, even if a member announced a stand, lower the score.

## Average Scores

Scores for 1991 are in parentheses:

| Coalition Support | Southern Democrats | | Republicans | | Northern Democrats | | Coalition Opposition | Southern Democrats | | Republicans | | Northern Democrats | |
|---|---|---|---|---|---|---|---|---|---|---|---|---|---|
| Senate | 65% | (67) | 76% | (81) | 26% | (32) | Senate | 30% | (28) | 20% | (16) | 69% | (65) |
| House | 62 | (66) | 82 | (86) | 29 | (29) | House | 30 | (30) | 13 | (10) | 64 | (67) |

## Regional Scores

Scores for 1991 are in parentheses:

### Regional Support

| | East | | West | | South | | Midwest | |
|---|---|---|---|---|---|---|---|---|
| **Democrats** | | | | | | | | |
| Senate | 21% | (24) | 32% | (41) | 65% | (67) | 28% | (35) |
| House | 25 | (27) | 28 | (26) | 62 | (66) | 32 | (34) |
| **Republicans** | | | | | | | | |
| Senate | 56% | (65) | 81% | (83) | 87% | (93) | 75% | (80) |
| House | 75 | (78) | 86 | (90) | 87 | (88) | 79 | (89) |

### Regional Opposition

| | East | | West | | South | | Midwest | |
|---|---|---|---|---|---|---|---|---|
| **Democrats** | | | | | | | | |
| Senate | 76% | (75) | 62% | (55) | 30% | (28) | 65% | (61) |
| House | 66 | (70) | 64 | (67) | 30 | (30) | 62 | (63) |
| **Republicans** | | | | | | | | |
| Senate | 40% | (33) | 14 | (13) | 8% | (5) | 23% | (18) |
| House | 20 | (20) | 8 | (7) | 8 | (5) | 17 | (10) |

*(CQ defines regions of the United States as follows:* **East:** *Conn., Del., Maine, Md., Mass., N.H., N.J., N.Y., Pa., R.I., Vt., W.Va.* **West:** *Alaska, Ariz., Calif., Colo., Hawaii, Idaho, Mont., Nev., N.M., Ore., Utah, Wash., Wyo.* **South:** *Ala., Ark., Fla., Ga., Ky., La., Miss., N.C., Okla., S.C., Tenn., Texas, Va.* **Midwest:** *Ill., Ind., Iowa, Kan., Mich., Minn., Mo., Neb., N.D., Ohio, S.D., Wis.)*

## Conservative Coalition History

Following is the percentage of the recorded votes for both chambers of Congress on which the coalition appeared and its percentage of victories:

| Year | Appearances | Victories | Year | Appearances | Victories |
|---|---|---|---|---|---|
| 1992 | 12% | 87% | 1980 | 18% | 72% |
| 1991 | 11 | 91 | 1979 | 20 | 70 |
| 1990 | 11 | 82 | 1978 | 21 | 52 |
| 1989 | 11 | 87 | 1977 | 26 | 68 |
| 1988 | 9 | 89 | 1976 | 24 | 58 |
| 1987 | 8 | 93 | 1975 | 28 | 50 |
| 1986 | 16 | 87 | 1974 | 24 | 59 |
| 1985 | 14 | 89 | 1973 | 23 | 61 |
| 1984 | 16 | 83 | 1972 | 27 | 69 |
| 1983 | 15 | 77 | 1971 | 30 | 83 |
| 1982 | 18 | 92 | 1970 | 22 | 66 |
| 1981 | 21 | 92 | 1969 | 27 | 68 |

# Conservative Coalition Vote Breakdown

Following is a list of votes, by roll call number, cast in 1992 on which a majority of Southern Democrats and a majority of Republicans voted against a majority of all other Democrats.

| House | Senate |
|---|---|

## House

### 42 Victories

| Vote # | Vote Captions |
|---|---|
| 66 | Budget walls |
| 90 | Space station funding |
| 91 | House bank scandal |
| 116 | Legal Services Corporation |
| 133 | Energy policy |
| 134 | Nuclear power |
| 140 | Strategic Petroleum Reserve |
| 141 | Nuclear waste disposal |
| 150 | Drug abuse treatment |
| 168 | SDI funding |
| 169 | SDI funding |
| 170 | B-2 bomber |
| 175 | American Folklife Center |
| 186 | Balanced-budget amendment |
| 199 | Nuclear energy research |
| 200 | Space reactor |
| 236 | Railroad labor dispute |
| 251 | Vertical price fixing |
| 259 | Funds for former presidents |
| 263 | SDI funding |
| 265 | Defense spending — B-2 bombers |
| 276 | Drug treatment funding |
| 279 | Transportation spending |
| 281 | Budget walls |
| 283 | Budget walls |
| 287 | Radioactive waste disposal |
| 296 | Interior Department overhead |
| 299 | Deer hunting |
| 302 | Timber sales |
| 304 | NEA funding |
| 327 | Tax exemptions |
| 333 | HUD overhead |
| 334 | Space station funding |
| 353 | TV Marti |
| 360 | Liquor industry taxes |
| 364 | Mortgage refinancing regulations |
| 420 | Domestic partnerships |
| 423 | Cuban trade embargo |
| 428 | Death penalty |
| 435 | Mission to Planet Earth |
| 447 | Indian monument |
| 467 | Mining royalties |

### 6 Defeats

| Vote # | Vote Captions |
|---|---|
| 142 | Hydroelectric power |
| 155 | Troops overseas |
| 171 | Troops overseas |
| 187 | Balanced-budget amendment |
| 352 | TV Marti |
| 386 | Airline competition |

## Senate

### 33 Victories

| Vote # | Vote Captions |
|---|---|
| 18 | Alternative fuels |
| 20 | Nuclear power safety |
| 22 | Refunds for natural gas consumers |
| 23 | Corporate energy consumption |
| 24 | Oil and gas exploration |
| 25 | Oil and gas exploration |
| 26 | Nuclear safety |
| 38 | Prescription drugs |
| 47 | Child care |
| 59 | Resolution Trust Corporation funding |
| 65 | Sex survey funding |
| 70 | Budget walls |
| 72 | Balanced-budget amendment |
| 74 | Legislative spending |
| 125 | Railroad labor dispute |
| 152 | Gun control |
| 153 | Commerce-Justice-State overhead |
| 155 | Rural Electrification Administration |
| 159 | Tax relief for oil and gas producers |
| 164 | Death penalty |
| 165 | Domestic partnerships |
| 192 | Edward E. Carnes Jr. confirmation |
| 193 | Edward E. Carnes Jr. confirmation |
| 208 | Budget walls |
| 209 | Budget walls |
| 211 | Budget walls |
| 216 | B-2 bombers |
| 223 | Intelligence programs funding |
| 230 | Natural gas drilling |
| 231 | Pension exemption for pilots |
| 233 | Child care |
| 235 | Tobacco advertising |
| 241 | Business in Cuba |

### 5 Defeats

| Vote # | Vote Captions |
|---|---|
| 4 | School prayer |
| 6 | Education funding |
| 217 | Nuclear testing |
| 227 | Federal charity donations |
| 252 | Foreign aid |

| | 1 | 2 | 3 |
|---|---|---|---|
| **Alabama** | | | |
| Heflin | 89 | 11 | 89 |
| Shelby | 89 | 11 | 89 |
| **Alaska** | | | |
| *Murkowski* | 82 | 13 | 86 |
| *Stevens* | 84 | 11 | 89 |
| **Arizona** | | | |
| DeConcini | 50 | 45 | 53 |
| *McCain* | 82 | 13 | 86 |
| **Arkansas** | | | |
| Bumpers | 71 | 29 | 71 |
| Pryor | 61 | 32 | 66 |
| **California** | | | |
| Cranston | 13 | 82 | 14 |
| *Seymour* | 61 | 18 | 77 |
| **Colorado** | | | |
| Wirth | 16 | 53 | 23 |
| *Brown* | 92 | 8 | 92 |
| **Connecticut** | | | |
| Dodd | 34 | 66 | 34 |
| Lieberman | 37 | 63 | 37 |
| **Delaware** | | | |
| Biden | 18 | 79 | 19 |
| *Roth* | 79 | 18 | 81 |
| **Florida** | | | |
| Graham | 53 | 47 | 53 |
| *Mack* | 82 | 13 | 86 |
| **Georgia** | | | |
| Fowler | 55 | 42 | 57 |
| Nunn | 71 | 26 | 73 |
| **Hawaii** | | | |
| Akaka | 26 | 74 | 26 |
| Inouye | 32 | 58 | 35 |
| **Idaho** | | | |
| *Craig* | 97 | 3 | 97 |
| *Symms* | 89 | 3 | 97 |
| **Illinois** | | | |
| Dixon | 39 | 47 | 45 |
| Simon | 16 | 84 | 16 |
| **Indiana** | | | |
| *Coats* | 87 | 13 | 87 |
| *Lugar* | 76 | 21 | 78 |

| | 1 | 2 | 3 |
|---|---|---|---|
| **Iowa** | | | |
| Harkin | 5 | 66 | 7 |
| *Grassley* | 68 | 32 | 68 |
| **Kansas** | | | |
| *Dole* | 92 | 8 | 92 |
| *Kassebaum* | 74 | 26 | 74 |
| **Kentucky** | | | |
| Ford | 82 | 16 | 84 |
| *McConnell* | 92 | 8 | 92 |
| **Louisiana** | | | |
| Breaux | 76 | 21 | 78 |
| Johnston | 79 | 21 | 79 |
| **Maine** | | | |
| Mitchell | 21 | 79 | 21 |
| *Cohen* | 45 | 55 | 45 |
| **Maryland** | | | |
| Mikulski | 24 | 74 | 24 |
| Sarbanes | 11 | 89 | 11 |
| **Massachusetts** | | | |
| Kennedy | 5 | 92 | 5 |
| Kerry | 8 | 89 | 8 |
| **Michigan** | | | |
| Levin | 21 | 76 | 22 |
| Riegle | 24 | 68 | 26 |
| **Minnesota** | | | |
| Wellstone | 8 | 92 | 8 |
| *Durenberger* | 63 | 37 | 63 |
| **Mississippi** | | | |
| *Cochran* | 89 | 8 | 92 |
| *Lott* | 97 | 3 | 97 |
| **Missouri** | | | |
| *Bond* | 66 | 24 | 74 |
| *Danforth* | 79 | 21 | 79 |
| **Montana** | | | |
| Baucus | 45 | 55 | 45 |
| *Burns* | 95 | 5 | 95 |
| **Nebraska** | | | |
| Exon | 55 | 45 | 55 |
| Kerrey | 18 | 58 | 24 |
| **Nevada** | | | |
| Bryan | 47 | 50 | 49 |
| Reid | 45 | 55 | 45 |

| | 1 | 2 | 3 |
|---|---|---|---|
| **New Hampshire** | | | |
| *Rudman* | 63 | 32 | 67 |
| *Smith* | 89 | 11 | 89 |
| **New Jersey** | | | |
| Bradley | 18 | 74 | 20 |
| Lautenberg | 5 | 95 | 5 |
| **New Mexico** | | | |
| Bingaman | 39 | 55 | 42 |
| *Domenici* | 89 | 11 | 89 |
| **New York** | | | |
| Moynihan | 34 | 66 | 34 |
| *D'Amato* | 42 | 45 | 48 |
| **North Carolina** | | | |
| Sanford | 53 | 34 | 61 |
| *Helms* | 71 | 3 | 96 |
| **North Dakota** | | | |
| Burdick [1] | 15 | 77 | 17 |
| Conrad | 61 | 37 | 62 |
| **Ohio** | | | |
| Glenn | 37 | 58 | 39 |
| Metzenbaum | 5 | 95 | 5 |
| **Oklahoma** | | | |
| Boren | 71 | 21 | 77 |
| *Nickles* | 87 | 11 | 89 |
| **Oregon** | | | |
| *Hatfield* | 47 | 53 | 47 |
| *Packwood* | 50 | 47 | 51 |
| **Pennsylvania** | | | |
| Wofford | 21 | 76 | 22 |
| *Specter* | 37 | 58 | 39 |
| **Rhode Island** | | | |
| Pell | 11 | 82 | 11 |
| *Chafee* | 55 | 45 | 55 |
| **South Carolina** | | | |
| Hollings | 55 | 45 | 55 |
| *Thurmond* | 95 | 5 | 95 |
| **South Dakota** | | | |
| Daschle | 37 | 63 | 37 |
| *Pressler* | 84 | 16 | 84 |
| **Tennessee** | | | |
| Gore | 13 | 34 | 28 |
| Sasser | 58 | 39 | 59 |

**Democrats**   *Republicans*

| | 1 | 2 | 3 |
|---|---|---|---|
| **Texas** | | | |
| Bentsen | 76 | 24 | 76 |
| *Gramm* | 89 | 5 | 94 |
| **Utah** | | | |
| *Garn* | 87 | 5 | 94 |
| *Hatch* | 95 | 5 | 95 |
| **Vermont** | | | |
| Leahy | 5 | 92 | 5 |
| *Jeffords* | 37 | 55 | 40 |
| **Virginia** | | | |
| Robb | 50 | 50 | 50 |
| Warner | 79 | 21 | 79 |
| **Washington** | | | |
| Adams | 5 | 95 | 5 |
| *Gorton* | 68 | 26 | 72 |
| **West Virginia** | | | |
| Byrd | 61 | 39 | 61 |
| Rockefeller | 26 | 68 | 28 |
| **Wisconsin** | | | |
| Kohl | 26 | 74 | 26 |
| *Kasten* | 61 | 32 | 66 |
| **Wyoming** | | | |
| *Simpson* | 92 | 8 | 92 |
| *Wallop* | 92 | 0 | 100 |

# Conservative Coalition
# Support and Opposition: Senate

**1. Conservative Coalition Support, 1992.** Percentage of 38 recorded votes in 1992 on which the conservative coalition appeared and on which a senator voted "yea" or "nay" *in agreement* with the position of the conservative coalition. Failures to vote lowered both support and opposition scores.

**2. Conservative Coalition Opposition, 1992.** Percentage of 38 recorded votes in 1992 on which the conservative coalition appeared and on which a senator voted "yea" or "nay" *in disagreement* with the position of the conservative coalition. Failures to vote lowered both support and opposition scores.

**3. Conservative Coalition Support, 1992.** Percentage of 38 recorded votes in 1992 on which the conservative coalition appeared and on which a senator was present and voted "yea" or "nay" *in agreement* with the position of the conservative coalition. In this version of the study, absences were not counted; therefore, failures to vote did not lower support or opposition scores. Opposition scores, not listed here, are the inverse of the support score; i.e., the opposition score is equal to 100 percent minus the individual's support score.

[1] *Jocelyn Birch Burdick, D-N.D., was sworn in Sept. 16, 1992, to succeed her husband, Quentin N. Burdick, D, who died Sept. 8, 1992. Quentin N. Burdick was eligible for 23 of 38 conservative coalition votes in 1992. His conservative coalition support score was 43 percent; his opposition score was 30 percent; and his support score, adjusted for absences, was 59 percent in 1992. Jocelyn Birch Burdick was eligible for 13 conservative coalition votes in 1992.*

# Conservative Coalition Support and Opposition: House

**1. Conservative Coalition Support, 1992.** Percentage of 48 recorded votes in 1992 on which the conservative coalition appeared and on which a representative voted "yea" or "nay" *in agreement* with the position of the conservative coalition. Failures to vote lowered both support and opposition scores.

**2. Conservative Coalition Opposition, 1992.** Percentage of 48 recorded votes in 1992 on which the conservative coalition appeared and on which a representative voted "yea" or "nay" *in disagreement* with the position of the conservative coalition. Failures to vote lowered both support and opposition scores.

**3. Conservative Coalition Support, 1992.** Percentage of 48 recorded votes in 1992 on which the conservative coalition appeared and on which a representative was present and voted "yea" or "nay" *in agreement* with the position of the conservative coalition. In this version of the study, absences were not counted; therefore, failures to vote did not lower support or opposition scores. Opposition scores, not listed here, are the inverse of the support score; i.e., the opposition score is equal to 100 percent minus the individual's support score.

[1] Ted Weiss, D-N.Y., died Sept. 14, 1992. He was eligible for 42 of 48 conservative coalition votes in 1992.

[2] Walter B. Jones, D-N.C., died Sept. 15, 1992. He was eligible for 42 of 48 conservative coalition votes in 1992.

[3] Thomas S. Foley, D-Wash., as Speaker of the House, voted at his discretion on two of 48 conservative coalition votes in 1992, for a support score of 0 percent.

| | 1 | 2 | 3 |
|---|---|---|---|
| **Alabama** | | | |
| 1 *Callahan* | 96 | 0 | 100 |
| 2 *Dickinson* | 83 | 8 | 91 |
| 3 Browder | 83 | 13 | 87 |
| 4 Bevill | 81 | 13 | 87 |
| 5 Cramer | 81 | 15 | 85 |
| 6 Erdreich | 94 | 6 | 94 |
| 7 Harris | 88 | 8 | 91 |
| **Alaska** | | | |
| AL *Young* | 85 | 10 | 89 |
| **Arizona** | | | |
| 1 *Rhodes* | 94 | 6 | 94 |
| 2 Pastor | 25 | 73 | 26 |
| 3 *Stump* | 94 | 6 | 94 |
| 4 *Kyl* | 96 | 4 | 96 |
| 5 *Kolbe* | 81 | 19 | 81 |
| **Arkansas** | | | |
| 1 Alexander | 27 | 35 | 43 |
| 2 Thornton | 67 | 23 | 74 |
| 3 *Hammerschmidt* | 92 | 4 | 96 |
| 4 Anthony | 33 | 23 | 59 |
| **California** | | | |
| 1 *Riggs* | 79 | 17 | 83 |
| 2 *Herger* | 81 | 8 | 91 |
| 3 Matsui | 29 | 67 | 30 |
| 4 Fazio | 44 | 48 | 48 |
| 5 Pelosi | 2 | 90 | 2 |
| 6 Boxer | 8 | 50 | 14 |
| 7 Miller | 13 | 77 | 14 |
| 8 Dellums | 4 | 94 | 4 |
| 9 Stark | 4 | 83 | 5 |
| 10 Edwards | 10 | 90 | 10 |
| 11 Lantos | 31 | 69 | 31 |
| 12 *Campbell* | 63 | 17 | 79 |
| 13 Mineta | 19 | 81 | 19 |
| 14 *Doolittle* | 96 | 4 | 96 |
| 15 Condit | 58 | 42 | 58 |
| 16 Panetta | 27 | 71 | 28 |
| 17 Dooley | 56 | 42 | 57 |
| 18 Lehman | 58 | 25 | 70 |
| 19 *Lagomarsino* † | 87 | 2 | 98 |
| 20 *Thomas* | 79 | 8 | 90 |
| 21 *Gallegly* | 96 | 4 | 96 |
| 22 *Moorhead* | 98 | 2 | 98 |
| 23 Beilenson | 15 | 75 | 16 |
| 24 Waxman | 13 | 85 | 13 |
| 25 Roybal | 25 | 73 | 26 |
| 26 Berman | 17 | 79 | 17 |
| 27 Levine | 13 | 48 | 21 |
| 28 Dixon | 23 | 71 | 24 |
| 29 Waters | 10 | 88 | 11 |
| 30 Martinez | 31 | 58 | 35 |
| 31 Dymally | 8 | 50 | 14 |
| 32 Anderson | 58 | 42 | 58 |
| 33 *Dreier* | 98 | 0 | 100 |
| 34 Torres | 19 | 73 | 20 |
| 35 *Lewis* | 85 | 6 | 93 |
| 36 Brown | 27 | 63 | 30 |
| 37 *McCandless* | 96 | 4 | 96 |
| 38 *Dornan* | 96 | 0 | 100 |
| 39 *Dannemeyer* | 65 | 10 | 86 |
| 40 *Cox* | 94 | 0 | 100 |
| 41 *Lowery* | 63 | 13 | 83 |

| | 1 | 2 | 3 |
|---|---|---|---|
| 42 *Rohrabacher* | 88 | 13 | 88 |
| 43 *Packard* | 90 | 2 | 98 |
| 44 *Cunningham* | 96 | 2 | 98 |
| 45 *Hunter* | 98 | 2 | 98 |
| **Colorado** | | | |
| 1 Schroeder | 29 | 69 | 30 |
| 2 Skaggs | 38 | 63 | 38 |
| 3 Campbell | 42 | 17 | 71 |
| 4 *Allard* | 83 | 17 | 83 |
| 5 *Hefley* | 90 | 8 | 91 |
| 6 *Schaefer* | 96 | 2 | 98 |
| **Connecticut** | | | |
| 1 Kennelly | 29 | 71 | 29 |
| 2 Gejdenson | 17 | 81 | 17 |
| 3 DeLauro | 25 | 73 | 26 |
| 4 *Shays* | 42 | 58 | 42 |
| 5 *Franks* | 83 | 15 | 85 |
| 6 *Johnson* | 75 | 23 | 77 |
| **Delaware** | | | |
| AL Carper | 58 | 38 | 61 |
| **Florida** | | | |
| 1 Hutto | 90 | 8 | 91 |
| 2 Peterson | 65 | 25 | 72 |
| 3 Bennett | 48 | 52 | 48 |
| 4 *James* † | 89 | 11 | 89 |
| 5 *McCollum* | 92 | 2 | 98 |
| 6 *Stearns* | 94 | 6 | 94 |
| 7 Gibbons | 58 | 35 | 62 |
| 8 *Young* | 90 | 8 | 91 |
| 9 *Bilirakis* | 85 | 15 | 85 |
| 10 *Ireland* | 63 | 2 | 97 |
| 11 Bacchus | 58 | 42 | 58 |
| 12 *Lewis* | 94 | 2 | 98 |
| 13 *Goss* | 85 | 15 | 85 |
| 14 Johnston | 33 | 65 | 34 |
| 15 *Shaw* | 92 | 6 | 94 |
| 16 Smith | 27 | 58 | 32 |
| 17 Lehman | 23 | 54 | 30 |
| 18 *Ros-Lehtinen* | 79 | 19 | 81 |
| 19 Fascell | 42 | 46 | 48 |
| **Georgia** | | | |
| 1 Thomas | 73 | 10 | 88 |
| 2 Hatcher | 40 | 13 | 76 |
| 3 Ray | 65 | 8 | 89 |
| 4 Jones | 23 | 44 | 34 |
| 5 Lewis | 6 | 83 | 7 |
| 6 *Gingrich* | 85 | 2 | 98 |
| 7 Darden | 79 | 21 | 79 |
| 8 Rowland | 85 | 10 | 89 |
| 9 Jenkins | 71 | 23 | 76 |
| 10 Barnard | 56 | 6 | 90 |
| **Hawaii** | | | |
| 1 Abercrombie | 2 | 92 | 2 |
| 2 Mink | 13 | 79 | 14 |
| **Idaho** | | | |
| 1 LaRocco | 56 | 44 | 56 |
| 2 Stallings | 65 | 29 | 69 |
| **Illinois** | | | |
| 1 Hayes | 13 | 85 | 13 |
| 2 Savage | 4 | 63 | 6 |
| 3 Russo | 23 | 63 | 27 |
| 4 Sangmeister | 48 | 52 | 48 |
| 5 Lipinski | 63 | 29 | 68 |
| 6 *Hyde* | 58 | 4 | 93 |
| 7 Collins | 13 | 65 | 16 |
| 8 Rostenkowski | 31 | 54 | 37 |
| 9 Yates | 4 | 90 | 4 |
| 10 *Porter* | 60 | 31 | 66 |
| 11 Annunzio | 40 | 52 | 43 |
| 12 *Crane* | 90 | 6 | 93 |
| 13 *Fawell* | 75 | 25 | 75 |
| 14 *Hastert* | 88 | 13 | 88 |
| 15 *Ewing* | 71 | 27 | 72 |
| 16 Cox | 29 | 71 | 29 |
| 17 Evans | 6 | 94 | 6 |
| 18 *Michel* | 88 | 4 | 95 |
| 19 Bruce | 42 | 50 | 45 |
| 20 Durbin | 21 | 77 | 21 |
| 21 Costello | 50 | 50 | 50 |
| 22 Poshard | 48 | 52 | 48 |
| **Indiana** | | | |
| 1 Visclosky | 38 | 63 | 38 |
| 2 Sharp † | 40 | 57 | 41 |
| 3 Roemer | 71 | 29 | 71 |

| | 1 | 2 | 3 |
|---|---|---|---|
| 4 Long | 44 | 56 | 44 |
| 5 Jontz | 17 | 83 | 17 |
| 6 Burton | 85 | 10 | 89 |
| 7 Myers | 90 | 10 | 90 |
| 8 McCloskey | 27 | 71 | 28 |
| 9 Hamilton | 73 | 25 | 74 |
| 10 Jacobs | 38 | 63 | 38 |

**Iowa**

| | 1 | 2 | 3 |
|---|---|---|---|
| 1 Leach | 54 | 40 | 58 |
| 2 Nussle | 65 | 35 | 65 |
| 3 Nagle | 29 | 67 | 30 |
| 4 Smith | 48 | 50 | 49 |
| 5 Lightfoot | 88 | 8 | 91 |
| 6 Grandy | 77 | 19 | 80 |

**Kansas**

| | 1 | 2 | 3 |
|---|---|---|---|
| 1 Roberts | 96 | 4 | 96 |
| 2 Slattery | 56 | 44 | 56 |
| 3 Meyers | 73 | 25 | 74 |
| 4 Glickman | 60 | 40 | 60 |
| 5 Nichols | 85 | 4 | 95 |

**Kentucky**

| | 1 | 2 | 3 |
|---|---|---|---|
| 1 Hubbard | 71 | 10 | 87 |
| 2 Natcher | 60 | 40 | 60 |
| 3 Mazzoli | 38 | 63 | 38 |
| 4 Bunning | 85 | 8 | 91 |
| 5 Rogers | 88 | 13 | 88 |
| 6 Hopkins | 92 | 4 | 96 |
| 7 Perkins | 25 | 67 | 27 |

**Louisiana**

| | 1 | 2 | 3 |
|---|---|---|---|
| 1 Livingston | 73 | 6 | 92 |
| 2 Jefferson | 25 | 65 | 28 |
| 3 Tauzin | 85 | 10 | 89 |
| 4 McCrery | 83 | 2 | 98 |
| 5 Huckaby | 73 | 4 | 95 |
| 6 Baker | 94 | 2 | 98 |
| 7 Hayes | 67 | 8 | 89 |
| 8 Holloway | 81 | 6 | 93 |

**Maine**

| | 1 | 2 | 3 |
|---|---|---|---|
| 1 Andrews | 13 | 85 | 13 |
| 2 Snowe | 69 | 31 | 69 |

**Maryland**

| | 1 | 2 | 3 |
|---|---|---|---|
| 1 Gilchrest | 71 | 27 | 72 |
| 2 Bentley | 85 | 8 | 91 |
| 3 Cardin | 27 | 71 | 28 |
| 4 McMillen | 60 | 40 | 60 |
| 5 Hoyer | 52 | 48 | 52 |
| 6 Byron | 73 | 15 | 83 |
| 7 Mfume | 13 | 88 | 13 |
| 8 Morella | 44 | 44 | 50 |

**Massachusetts**

| | 1 | 2 | 3 |
|---|---|---|---|
| 1 Olver | 10 | 90 | 10 |
| 2 Neal | 15 | 83 | 15 |
| 3 Early | 23 | 69 | 25 |
| 4 Frank | 4 | 96 | 4 |
| 5 Atkins | 4 | 94 | 4 |
| 6 Mavroules | 19 | 73 | 20 |
| 7 Markey | 8 | 88 | 9 |
| 8 Kennedy | 17 | 81 | 17 |
| 9 Moakley | 13 | 85 | 13 |
| 10 Studds | 8 | 92 | 8 |
| 11 Donnelly | 23 | 60 | 28 |

**Michigan**

| | 1 | 2 | 3 |
|---|---|---|---|
| 1 Conyers | 4 | 79 | 5 |
| 2 Pursell | 60 | 29 | 67 |
| 3 Wolpe | 2 | 88 | 2 |
| 4 Upton | 73 | 27 | 73 |
| 5 Henry | 73 | 27 | 73 |
| 6 Carr | 58 | 40 | 60 |
| 7 Kildee | 8 | 92 | 8 |
| 8 Traxler | 8 | 25 | 25 |
| 9 Vander Jagt | 77 | 8 | 90 |
| 10 Camp | 73 | 27 | 73 |
| 11 Davis | 88 | 8 | 91 |
| 12 Bonior | 10 | 71 | 13 |
| 13 Collins | 10 | 73 | 13 |
| 14 Hertel | 17 | 71 | 19 |
| 15 Ford | 17 | 69 | 20 |
| 16 Dingell | 31 | 56 | 36 |
| 17 Levin † | 30 | 70 | 30 |
| 18 Broomfield | 63 | 6 | 91 |

**Minnesota**

| | 1 | 2 | 3 |
|---|---|---|---|
| 1 Penny | 48 | 52 | 48 |
| 2 Weber | 77 | 10 | 88 |
| 3 Ramstad | 56 | 44 | 56 |
| 4 Vento | 6 | 92 | 6 |
| 5 Sabo | 8 | 92 | 8 |
| 6 Sikorski | 17 | 83 | 17 |
| 7 Peterson | 44 | 54 | 45 |
| 8 Oberstar | 15 | 85 | 15 |

**Mississippi**

| | 1 | 2 | 3 |
|---|---|---|---|
| 1 Whitten | 52 | 19 | 74 |
| 2 Espy | 35 | 63 | 36 |
| 3 Montgomery | 88 | 13 | 88 |
| 4 Parker | 88 | 13 | 88 |
| 5 Taylor | 83 | 17 | 83 |

**Missouri**

| | 1 | 2 | 3 |
|---|---|---|---|
| 1 Clay | 10 | 77 | 12 |
| 2 Horn | 35 | 65 | 35 |
| 3 Gephardt | 33 | 58 | 36 |
| 4 Skelton | 83 | 15 | 85 |
| 5 Wheat | 10 | 85 | 11 |
| 6 Coleman | 85 | 10 | 89 |
| 7 Hancock | 96 | 4 | 96 |
| 8 Emerson | 92 | 8 | 92 |
| 9 Volkmer | 81 | 15 | 85 |

**Montana**

| | 1 | 2 | 3 |
|---|---|---|---|
| 1 Williams | 33 | 56 | 37 |
| 2 Marlenee | 63 | 25 | 71 |

**Nebraska**

| | 1 | 2 | 3 |
|---|---|---|---|
| 1 Bereuter | 73 | 25 | 74 |
| 2 Hoagland | 58 | 38 | 61 |
| 3 Barrett | 85 | 13 | 87 |

**Nevada**

| | 1 | 2 | 3 |
|---|---|---|---|
| 1 Bilbray | 67 | 33 | 67 |
| 2 Vucanovich | 81 | 10 | 89 |

**New Hampshire**

| | 1 | 2 | 3 |
|---|---|---|---|
| 1 Zeliff | 92 | 8 | 92 |
| 2 Swett | 50 | 50 | 50 |

**New Jersey**

| | 1 | 2 | 3 |
|---|---|---|---|
| 1 Andrews | 50 | 48 | 51 |
| 2 Hughes | 27 | 71 | 28 |
| 3 Pallone | 33 | 67 | 33 |
| 4 Smith | 83 | 17 | 83 |
| 5 Roukema | 56 | 35 | 61 |
| 6 Dwyer | 27 | 54 | 33 |
| 7 Rinaldo | 79 | 21 | 79 |
| 8 Roe | 38 | 40 | 49 |
| 9 Torricelli | 48 | 40 | 55 |
| 10 Payne | 4 | 92 | 4 |
| 11 Gallo | 88 | 10 | 89 |
| 12 Zimmer | 67 | 33 | 67 |
| 13 Saxton | 88 | 10 | 89 |
| 14 Guarini | 38 | 52 | 42 |

**New Mexico**

| | 1 | 2 | 3 |
|---|---|---|---|
| 1 Schiff | 85 | 15 | 85 |
| 2 Skeen | 92 | 8 | 92 |
| 3 Richardson | 44 | 46 | 49 |

**New York**

| | 1 | 2 | 3 |
|---|---|---|---|
| 1 Hochbrueckner | 23 | 77 | 23 |
| 2 Downey | 21 | 73 | 22 |
| 3 Mrazek | 15 | 73 | 17 |
| 4 Lent | 75 | 4 | 95 |
| 5 McGrath | 81 | 10 | 89 |
| 6 Flake | 10 | 83 | 11 |
| 7 Ackerman | 6 | 52 | 11 |
| 8 Scheuer | 6 | 81 | 7 |
| 9 Manton | 40 | 52 | 43 |
| 10 Schumer | 13 | 81 | 13 |
| 11 Towns | 10 | 60 | 15 |
| 12 Owens | 6 | 92 | 6 |
| 13 Solarz | 10 | 71 | 13 |
| 14 Molinari | 81 | 19 | 81 |
| 15 Green | 33 | 58 | 36 |
| 16 Rangel | 15 | 81 | 15 |
| 17 Weiss [1] | 5 | 90 | 5 |
| 18 Serrano | 4 | 92 | 4 |
| 19 Engel | 25 | 73 | 26 |
| 20 Lowey | 15 | 85 | 15 |
| 21 Fish | 65 | 31 | 67 |
| 22 Gilman | 56 | 44 | 56 |
| 23 McNulty | 54 | 46 | 54 |
| 24 Solomon | 83 | 13 | 87 |
| 25 Boehlert | 58 | 40 | 60 |
| 26 Martin | 85 | 6 | 93 |
| 27 Walsh | 83 | 13 | 87 |
| 28 McHugh | 21 | 77 | 21 |
| 29 Horton | 63 | 25 | 71 |
| 30 Slaughter | 17 | 83 | 17 |
| 31 Paxon | 96 | 4 | 96 |
| 32 LaFalce | 29 | 65 | 31 |
| 33 Nowak | 29 | 69 | 30 |
| 34 Houghton | 79 | 19 | 81 |

**North Carolina**

| | 1 | 2 | 3 |
|---|---|---|---|
| 1 Jones [2] | 52 | 48 | 52 |
| 2 Valentine | 63 | 31 | 67 |
| 3 Lancaster | 75 | 25 | 75 |
| 4 Price | 52 | 48 | 52 |
| 5 Neal | 63 | 35 | 64 |
| 6 Coble | 75 | 25 | 75 |
| 7 Rose | 50 | 50 | 50 |
| 8 Hefner | 38 | 21 | 64 |
| 9 McMillan | 94 | 6 | 94 |
| 10 Ballenger | 83 | 10 | 89 |
| 11 Taylor | 88 | 10 | 89 |

**North Dakota**

| | 1 | 2 | 3 |
|---|---|---|---|
| AL Dorgan | 44 | 56 | 44 |

**Ohio**

| | 1 | 2 | 3 |
|---|---|---|---|
| 1 Luken | 46 | 44 | 51 |
| 2 Gradison | 88 | 13 | 88 |
| 3 Hall | 40 | 56 | 41 |
| 4 Oxley | 96 | 2 | 98 |
| 5 Gillmor | 90 | 6 | 93 |
| 6 McEwen | 83 | 10 | 89 |
| 7 Hobson | 88 | 13 | 88 |
| 8 Boehner | 94 | 6 | 94 |
| 9 Kaptur | 50 | 48 | 51 |
| 10 Miller | 94 | 6 | 94 |
| 11 Eckart | 38 | 63 | 38 |
| 12 Kasich | 79 | 19 | 81 |
| 13 Pease | 17 | 83 | 17 |
| 14 Sawyer | 15 | 85 | 15 |
| 15 Wylie | 79 | 15 | 84 |
| 16 Regula | 81 | 19 | 81 |
| 17 Traficant | 42 | 58 | 42 |
| 18 Applegate | 38 | 60 | 38 |
| 19 Feighan | 35 | 44 | 45 |
| 20 Oakar | 27 | 52 | 34 |
| 21 Stokes | 6 | 92 | 6 |

**Oklahoma**

| | 1 | 2 | 3 |
|---|---|---|---|
| 1 Inhofe | 92 | 4 | 96 |
| 2 Synar | 21 | 77 | 21 |
| 3 Brewster | 85 | 15 | 85 |
| 4 McCurdy | 77 | 21 | 79 |
| 5 Edwards | 79 | 4 | 95 |
| 6 English | 85 | 15 | 85 |

**Oregon**

| | 1 | 2 | 3 |
|---|---|---|---|
| 1 AuCoin | 8 | 79 | 10 |
| 2 Smith | 90 | 8 | 91 |
| 3 Wyden | 19 | 79 | 19 |
| 4 DeFazio | 21 | 75 | 22 |
| 5 Kopetski | 21 | 73 | 22 |

**Pennsylvania**

| | 1 | 2 | 3 |
|---|---|---|---|
| 1 Foglietta | 13 | 77 | 14 |
| 2 Blackwell | 6 | 94 | 6 |
| 3 Borski | 40 | 60 | 40 |
| 4 Kolter | 31 | 27 | 54 |
| 5 Schulze | 67 | 4 | 94 |
| 6 Yatron | 52 | 31 | 63 |
| 7 Weldon | 83 | 17 | 83 |
| 8 Kostmayer | 21 | 79 | 21 |
| 9 Shuster | 92 | 8 | 92 |
| 10 McDade | 65 | 13 | 84 |
| 11 Kanjorski | 46 | 54 | 46 |
| 12 Murtha | 67 | 27 | 71 |
| 13 Coughlin | 79 | 4 | 95 |
| 14 Coyne | 19 | 81 | 19 |
| 15 Ritter | 88 | 13 | 88 |
| 16 Walker | 92 | 4 | 96 |
| 17 Gekas | 83 | 13 | 87 |
| 18 Santorum | 79 | 21 | 79 |
| 19 Goodling | 81 | 19 | 81 |
| 20 Gaydos | 35 | 31 | 53 |
| 21 Ridge | 69 | 25 | 73 |
| 22 Murphy | 29 | 60 | 33 |
| 23 Clinger | 83 | 8 | 91 |

**Rhode Island**

| | 1 | 2 | 3 |
|---|---|---|---|
| 1 Machtley | 71 | 27 | 72 |
| 2 Reed | 17 | 83 | 17 |

**South Carolina**

| | 1 | 2 | 3 |
|---|---|---|---|
| 1 Ravenel | 83 | 15 | 85 |
| 2 Spence | 98 | 2 | 98 |
| 3 Derrick | 67 | 33 | 67 |
| 4 Patterson | 65 | 27 | 70 |
| 5 Spratt | 79 | 21 | 79 |
| 6 Tallon | 58 | 25 | 70 |

**South Dakota**

| | 1 | 2 | 3 |
|---|---|---|---|
| AL Johnson | 40 | 60 | 40 |

**Tennessee**

| | 1 | 2 | 3 |
|---|---|---|---|
| 1 Quillen | 77 | 15 | 84 |
| 2 Duncan | 71 | 29 | 71 |
| 3 Lloyd | 90 | 10 | 90 |
| 4 Cooper † | 74 | 23 | 76 |
| 5 Clement | 58 | 40 | 60 |
| 6 Gordon | 67 | 31 | 68 |
| 7 Sundquist | 92 | 8 | 92 |
| 8 Tanner | 77 | 21 | 79 |
| 9 Ford | 13 | 67 | 16 |

**Texas**

| | 1 | 2 | 3 |
|---|---|---|---|
| 1 Chapman | 73 | 19 | 80 |
| 2 Wilson | 77 | 19 | 80 |
| 3 Johnson | 94 | 0 | 100 |
| 4 Hall | 92 | 8 | 92 |
| 5 Bryant | 60 | 35 | 63 |
| 6 Barton | 85 | 4 | 95 |
| 7 Archer | 85 | 4 | 95 |
| 8 Fields | 88 | 4 | 95 |
| 9 Brooks | 52 | 35 | 60 |
| 10 Pickle | 73 | 27 | 73 |
| 11 Edwards | 85 | 15 | 85 |
| 12 Geren | 90 | 8 | 91 |
| 13 Sarpalius | 85 | 15 | 85 |
| 14 Laughlin | 69 | 19 | 79 |
| 15 de la Garza | 60 | 31 | 66 |
| 16 Coleman | 58 | 40 | 60 |
| 17 Stenholm | 88 | 10 | 89 |
| 18 Washington | 6 | 85 | 7 |
| 19 Combest | 94 | 6 | 94 |
| 20 Gonzalez | 38 | 63 | 38 |
| 21 Smith | 96 | 2 | 98 |
| 22 DeLay | 92 | 6 | 94 |
| 23 Bustamante | 42 | 33 | 56 |
| 24 Frost | 71 | 29 | 71 |
| 25 Andrews | 83 | 17 | 83 |
| 26 Armey | 96 | 4 | 96 |
| 27 Ortiz | 71 | 29 | 71 |

**Utah**

| | 1 | 2 | 3 |
|---|---|---|---|
| 1 Hansen | 85 | 8 | 91 |
| 2 Owens | 46 | 48 | 49 |
| 3 Orton | 67 | 31 | 68 |

**Vermont**

| | 1 | 2 | 3 |
|---|---|---|---|
| AL Sanders | 8 | 92 | 8 |

**Virginia**

| | 1 | 2 | 3 |
|---|---|---|---|
| 1 Bateman | 83 | 17 | 83 |
| 2 Pickett | 73 | 23 | 76 |
| 3 Bliley | 94 | 6 | 96 |
| 4 Sisisky | 92 | 6 | 94 |
| 5 Payne | 75 | 23 | 77 |
| 6 Olin | 46 | 31 | 59 |
| 7 Allen | 94 | 6 | 94 |
| 8 Moran | 48 | 50 | 49 |
| 9 Boucher | 44 | 56 | 44 |
| 10 Wolf | 96 | 4 | 96 |

**Washington**

| | 1 | 2 | 3 |
|---|---|---|---|
| 1 Miller | 81 | 8 | 91 |
| 2 Swift | 35 | 65 | 35 |
| 3 Unsoeld | 10 | 79 | 10 |
| 4 Morrison | 67 | 17 | 80 |
| 5 Foley [3] | | | |
| 6 Dicks | 56 | 44 | 56 |
| 7 McDermott | 13 | 88 | 13 |
| 8 Chandler | 77 | 6 | 93 |

**West Virginia**

| | 1 | 2 | 3 |
|---|---|---|---|
| 1 Mollohan | 58 | 40 | 60 |
| 2 Staggers | 33 | 54 | 38 |
| 3 Wise | 50 | 48 | 51 |
| 4 Rahall | 35 | 60 | 37 |

**Wisconsin**

| | 1 | 2 | 3 |
|---|---|---|---|
| 1 Aspin | 56 | 42 | 57 |
| 2 Klug | 67 | 33 | 67 |
| 3 Gunderson | 77 | 23 | 77 |
| 4 Kleczka | 33 | 63 | 35 |
| 5 Moody | 23 | 75 | 23 |
| 6 Petri | 73 | 25 | 74 |
| 7 Obey | 15 | 85 | 15 |
| 8 Roth | 69 | 19 | 79 |
| 9 Sensenbrenner | 65 | 35 | 65 |

**Wyoming**

| | 1 | 2 | 3 |
|---|---|---|---|
| AL Thomas | 81 | 17 | 83 |

PARTY UNITY

# Signs Point to Greater Loyalty On Both Sides of the Aisle

Partisanship was at near-record levels in Congress during this election year, particularly in the House, where almost two-thirds of the roll call votes split largely along party lines.

Party-line voting has been on the rise for several years, and there is no end in sight. As Democrats rally around their new president and Republicans fit themselves into opposition armor, partisanship could well intensify in 1993.

Election-year sniping on the House and Senate floors may account for some of the partisanship seen in the 1992 votes. But the numbers reflect a longer trend, one that predates the heated fall campaigns and appears likely to outlast them.

"The Democratic Party has gotten a lot more internally homogeneous, and Democrats and Republicans have gotten a lot more different," said David Rohde, a political science professor at Michigan State University.

The trend was most striking in the House, where 64 percent of the roll call votes split along party lines. That number is a 9-point increase from the 1991 figure of 55 percent, and matches a high recorded only once before — in 1987 — in the 38 years that Congressional Quarterly has been measuring party unity.

Fifty-three percent of Senate roll call votes fell along party lines. That is the highest percentage in three decades, save 1990, when the number was 54 percent.

Those numbers are coupled with high loyalty levels for individual members. The average Democratic lawmaker voted with the party majority 86 percent of the time, not counting absences; Republicans were only slightly behind, with an average of 83 percent. These figures are generally comparable to last year's and represent relatively high levels of loyalty historically.

The combined effect of these trends was to produce a striking number of floor victories for House Democratic leaders, who won 82 percent of the party unity votes in 1992. Senate Democrats prevailed on 57 percent of the votes that split along party lines.

Political scientists such as Barbara Sinclair of the University of California at Riverside trace the renewed force of partisan voting to the early 1980s. "We're getting the kind of party unity scores among House Democrats that we

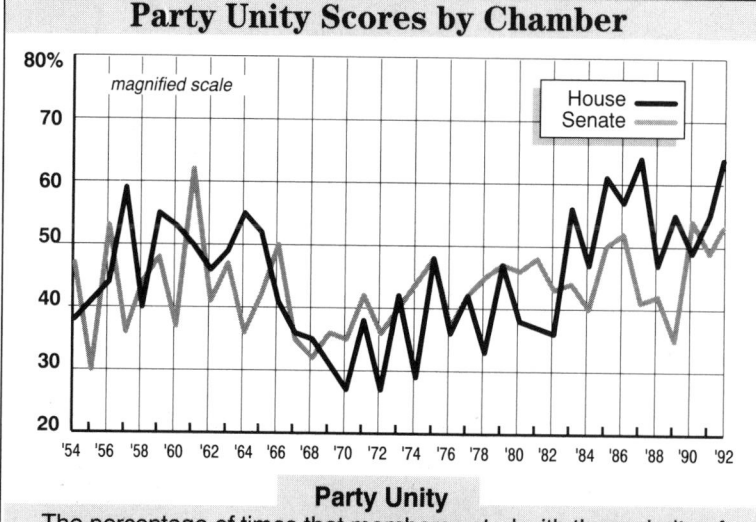

## Party Unity Scores by Chamber

magnified scale

House
Senate

'54 '56 '58 '60 '62 '64 '66 '68 '70 '72 '74 '76 '78 '80 '82 '84 '86 '88 '90 '92

### Party Unity

The percentage of times that members voted with the majority of their party, based on recorded votes on which a majority of one party voted against the majority of the other party.

PATT CHISHOLM

associate with the heights of the New Deal," Sinclair said.

Experts say it is typical for partisanship to be more evident in the House, which grants almost total procedural control to the majority party.

In the 100-member Senate, by contrast, 60 votes are needed to limit debate and force action on legislation. Since Democrats held only 57 seats in the 102nd Congress (and will have the same number in the 103rd), there are strong incentives for cooperation across party lines.

Compared with the House Speaker, the Senate majority leader also has fewer means to force discipline within party ranks.

Tom Daschle, D-S.D., who co-chairs the Democratic Policy Committee with Majority Leader George J. Mitchell, D-Maine, said a Senate leader seeking to influence individual lawmakers has "a bushel full of carrots and a few twigs."

### Presidential Politics a Factor

Particularly in the House, the percentage of partisan votes usually drops in even-numbered years, arguably because members hew closer to district desires than to party directives.

The uptick in the percentage of partisan roll calls for 1992 may reflect a combination of short- and long-term influences. In the short run, members cast votes amid unusually strong partisan acrimony over election year issues and, in the House, internal scandals involving the bank and post office. The first nine House party-unity votes of the year came on investigations into the House post office and whether the Reagan campaign in fall 1980 conspired to delay the release of American hostages being held in Iran.

Some political observers believe the high level of partisan votes reflects a deliberate strategy by Democratic leaders to frame issues along partisan lines and highlight, rather than blur, the differences between the parties.

Thomas E. Mann, director of governmental relations at the Brookings Institution, said that desire may have been more evident this year than in past election years because the Republicans appeared more vulnerable, and Clinton offered a politically acceptable alternative.

At least after their July convention, Mann said, Democratic lawmakers seemed willing to affiliate themselves with themes being articulated by their presidential nominee. "We haven't seen a Congress interested in running with the president since 1964," he said.

House Speaker Thomas S. Foley, D-Wash., suggested that President Bush's veto strategy may have helped drive up the numbers, because Republicans were less likely to support a bill destined for a veto. "The number of vetoes multiplies the number of party-line votes," he said.

### Greater Long-Term Cohesiveness

Whatever the reason for the one-year jump in partisan voting, political scientists believe the more significant factors are the long-term pressures toward greater party cohesiveness.

Democratic mavericks are found primarily among conservative-minded Southerners, who in the past often voted with Republicans. But that so-called conservative coalition continues to wane, in part because the Voting Rights Act has fundamentally altered the makeup of Southern electorates. *(Story, p. 3845)*

Additionally, the Reagan-Bush administrations pushed a strong conservative agenda that made some Southern Democrats recoil from the GOP and generally helped unite Democrats in opposition.

The party unity numbers also reflect a revival of party discipline. Sinclair said that despite early perceptions that Speaker Foley was a weak leader, he has used his clout to enforce the party will and has reaped the results in stronger party-line voting.

That policing includes conditioning choice committee assignments on voting habits, controlling floor debate through restrictive rules and using the whip structure to craft and enforce party positions on votes.

A similar insistence on party loyalty was evident in a rank-and-file challenge to Veterans' Affairs Committee Chairman G. V. "Sonny" Montgomery, D-Miss. In organizational meetings for the 103rd Congress, Montgomery came within four votes of losing his chairmanship — in large part because of his weak record on party loyalty. Montgomery opposed the majority of his party on 35 percent of the 1992 party-unity roll calls in which he voted, well above the 14 percent average.

Republican dissenters are most often members from the Northeast, which has a tradition of electing liberal Republicans to Congress. But there are fewer Republicans representing these districts, and GOP defections have declined under three consecutive Republican administrations. In 1980, for example, the average Republican party-unity score was 65 percent in the Senate, 71 percent in the House. Twelve years later, the GOP average in both chambers was 79 percent. (These scores are not adjusted for absences.)

### Looking Ahead

Success in recapturing the White House may expose some rifts among Democrats that were papered over while they battled Republican presidents. But many observers say those forces are likely to be outweighed by unifying factors.

Sinclair believes the large turnover aids party unity, because freshmen typically vote with their leadership more than the average.

All Democrats will feel some desire to support their president and prove they are up to the task of running the government. In Daschle's words: "We don't want to blow it." And for the first time in 12 years, Democratic leaders will be able to call on the president and Cabinet officers to help corral wavering members on key votes.

Mann expects to see Democratic unity scores climb higher still in 1993, perhaps to record levels, followed by some subsequent erosion.

For their part, Republicans face the challenge of presenting a coherent political alternative without being viewed as obstructionist.

In the House, early signs point to a strongly partisan tilt, at least at the top of the GOP. Texas conservative Dick Armey ousted the more moderate Jerry Lewis of California as head of the Republican Conference, and there were unsuccessful moves to replace some senior Republicans on various committees who were seen as too accommodationist.

Even if this tone holds, however, it is unclear how potent such opposition will be. Democrats have a comfortable House majority and are unlikely to need a lot of Republican votes on most issues.

GOP unity will be more critical in the Senate, where the party has 43 votes — two more than needed to block cloture.

Minority Whip Alan Simpson, R-Wyo., said that means the party can spring two members on any key cloture vote. "We're going to have a rotating release system," he said.

Being shut out of the White House tends to increase a party's cohesion. Political observers expect to see this trend in the next Senate — albeit less dramatically than in the House.

Sen. Mark O. Hatfield, R-Ore., may be a case in point. Hatfield is typically one of the more independent-minded Senate Republicans, and 1992 was no exception. He voted with the Democratic majority on more than half of the year's party unity votes.

Hatfield said those ratings reflect his long-term commitment to certain policy positions irrespective of their partisan cut. But Hatfield is concerned about the prospects of a Democratic-controlled Congress rubber-stamping dozens of proposals from Democratic-led agencies and said that scenario could lead him to vote with the Republican majority more often, provided GOP members are offering policy alternatives and not just obstruction. "It has to be a positive, constructive, loyal opposition," he said.

Lawmakers and analysts say Senate Democrats could quickly drive Republican colleagues into each other's arms if they try to speed through bills on highly partisan issues such as striker replacement, campaign finance reform or "motor voter" registration.

Simpson also predicted greater party loyalty among some senators who just survived difficult re-election battles, such as Arlen Specter of Pennsylvania, Bob Packwood of Oregon and Alfonse M. D'Amato of New York. But some of those senators are inclined to agree with Democratic positions on several issues likely to arise in the new Congress, and the GOP leadership will also have to contend with a new crop of senators approaching election battles.

"There isn't going to be a lot of percentage for the moderate Republicans to stick with their brethren unless it's on something they always believe in," said Sinclair. ■

> "We're getting the kind of party unity scores among House Democrats that we associate with the heights of the New Deal."
>
> —Barbara Sinclair, University of California at Riverside

# Leading Scorers: Party Unity

Support indicates those who in 1992 most consistently voted with their party's majority against the majority of the other party; opposition shows how often members voted against their party's majority. Scores are based on actual votes cast and ranked by percentages before rounding. Members not eligible for half the votes are not listed.

## Highest Scorers — Support

### Senate

**Kennedy**     **Craig**

| Democrats | | Republicans | |
|---|---|---|---|
| Kennedy, Mass. | 97% | Craig, Idaho | 99% |
| Sarbanes, Md. | 96 | Gramm, Texas | 98 |
| Adams, Wash. | 96 | Symms, Idaho | 97 |
| Leahy, Vt. | 96 | Lott, Miss. | 96 |
| Wellstone, Minn. | 95 | Helms, N.C. | 96 |
| Harkin, Iowa | 95 | Wallop, Wyo. | 96 |
| Metzenbaum, Ohio | 94 | Garn, Utah | 96 |
| Cranston, Calif. | 94 | Hatch, Utah | 95 |
| Gore, Tenn. | 93 | Brown, Colo. | 95 |
| Mitchell, Maine | 93 | Nickles, Okla. | 95 |

### House

**Lewis**     **Stump**

| Democrats | | Republicans | |
|---|---|---|---|
| Lewis, Ga. | 99% | Stump, Ariz. | 99% |
| Pelosi, Calif. | 99 | Armey, Texas | 99 |
| Ackerman, N.Y. | 99 | Hancock, Mo. | 98 |
| Sabo, Minn. | 98 | Moorhead, Calif. | 98 |
| Solarz, N.Y. | 98 | Crane, Ill. | 98 |
| Abercrombie, Hawaii | 98 | Schaefer, Colo. | 97 |
| Stokes, Ohio | 98 | Dannemeyer, Calif. | 97 |
| | | Doolittle, Calif. | 97 |
| | | Boehner, Ohio | 97 |

## Highest Scorers — Opposition

### Senate

**Shelby**     **Jeffords**

| Democrats | | Republicans | |
|---|---|---|---|
| Shelby, Ala. | 55% | Jeffords, Vt. | 61% |
| Heflin, Ala. | 48 | Specter, Pa. | 59 |
| Hollings, S.C. | 42 | Hatfield, Ore. | 54 |
| Boren, Okla. | 37 | Packwood, Ore. | 50 |
| Bentsen, Texas | 34 | Durenberger, Minn. | 42 |
| Johnston, La. | 33 | Chafee, R.I. | 40 |
| Nunn, Ga. | 31 | Cohen, Maine | 39 |
| Breaux, La. | 30 | D'Amato, N.Y. | 38 |
| DeConcini, Ariz. | 30 | | |
| Ford, Ky. | 30 | | |

### House

**Hutto**     **Green**

| Democrats | | Republicans | |
|---|---|---|---|
| Hutto, Fla. | 54% | Green, N.Y. | 62% |
| Hall, Texas | 51 | Gilman, N.Y. | 57 |
| Stenholm, Texas | 47 | Horton, N.Y. | 54 |
| Ray, Ga. | 46 | Morella, Md. | 51 |
| Taylor, Miss. | 42 | Boehlert, N.Y. | 49 |
| Orton, Utah | 42 | Morrison, Wash. | 44 |
| Barnard, Ga. | 41 | Snowe, Maine | 41 |
| Tauzin, La. | 40 | Fish, N.Y. | 41 |
| Jacobs, Ind. | 40 | Machtley, R.I. | 40 |

## Party-Unity Definitions

**Party-unity votes.** Recorded votes in the Senate or the House that split the parties, with a majority of voting Democrats opposing a majority of voting Republicans.

**Party-unity scores.** Percentage of party-unity votes on which a member voted "yea" or "nay" *in agreement* with a majority of his party. Failures to vote lowered scores for chambers and parties.

**Opposition-to-party scores.** Percentage of party-unity votes on which a member voted "yea" or "nay" *in disagreement* with a majority of his party. Failures to vote lowered scores for chambers and parties.

## Average Scores by Party

|  | 1992 | | 1991 | |  | 1992 | | 1991 | |
|---|---|---|---|---|---|---|---|---|---|
|  | Dem. | Rep. | Dem. | Rep. |  | Dem. | Rep. | Dem. | Rep. |
| **Party Unity** | 79% | 79% | 81% | 78% | **Opposition** | 13% | 16% | 14% | 18% |
| Senate | 77 | 79 | 80 | 81 | Senate | 18 | 17 | 17 | 17 |
| House | 79 | 79 | 81 | 77 | House | 12 | 16 | 14 | 18 |

## Sectional Support, Opposition

| SENATE | Support | Opposition | HOUSE | Support | Opposition |
|---|---|---|---|---|---|
| Northern Democrats | 82% | 13% | Northern Democrats | 82% | 9% |
| Southern Democrats | 65 | 29 | Southern Democrats | 72 | 19 |
| Northern Republicans | 77 | 20 | Northern Republicans | 77 | 18 |
| Southern Republicans | 89 | 6 | Southern Republicans | 83 | 11 |

## 1992 Victories, Defeats

|  | Senate | House | Total |
|---|---|---|---|
| Democrats won, Republicans lost | 82 | 251 | 333 |
| Republicans won, Democrats lost | 61 | 54 | 115 |

## Unanimous Voting by Parties

The number of times each party voted unanimously on 1992 party-unity votes. Scores for 1991 are in parentheses:

|  | Senate | House | Total |
|---|---|---|---|
| Democrats voted unanimously | 12 (19) | 18 (11) | 30 (30) |
| Republicans voted unanimously | 10 (15) | 47 (18) | 57 (33) |

## Party-Unity Average Scores

| Year | Democrats | Republicans | Year | Democrats | Republicans |
|---|---|---|---|---|---|
| 1992 | 79% | 79% | 1976 | 65% | 66% |
| 1991 | 81 | 78 | 1975 | 69 | 70 |
| 1990 | 81 | 74 | 1974 | 63 | 62 |
| 1989 | 81 | 73 | 1973 | 68 | 68 |
| 1988 | 79 | 73 | 1972 | 57 | 64 |
| 1987 | 81 | 74 | 1971 | 62 | 66 |
| 1986 | 78 | 71 | 1970 | 57 | 59 |
| 1985 | 79 | 75 | 1969 | 62 | 62 |
| 1984 | 74 | 72 | 1968 | 57 | 63 |
| 1983 | 76 | 74 | 1967 | 66 | 71 |
| 1982 | 72 | 71 | 1966 | 61 | 67 |
| 1981 | 69 | 76 | 1965 | 69 | 70 |
| 1980 | 68 | 70 | 1964 | 67 | 69 |
| 1979 | 69 | 72 | 1963 | 71 | 72 |
| 1978 | 64 | 67 | 1962 | 69 | 68 |
| 1977 | 67 | 70 | 1961 | 71 | 72 |

# Breakdown of Party-Unity Votes

Following are the votes, listed by roll call number, on which a majority
of Democrats voted against a majority of Republicans.

## House

### (305 of 473 votes)

| | | | | | | | | | | | | |
|---|---|---|---|---|---|---|---|---|---|---|---|---|
| 5 | 53 | 94 | 129 | 171 | 210 | 262 | 301 | 338 | 377 | 416 | 458 |
| 6 | 54 | 95 | 130 | 172 | 213 | 263 | 302 | 339 | 380 | 417 | 463 |
| 7 | 55 | 96 | 133 | 173 | 218 | 264 | 303 | 341 | 382 | 420 | 464 |
| 8 | 57 | 97 | 134 | 174 | 219 | 265 | 304 | 342 | 383 | 426 | 465 |
| 9 | 61 | 98 | 136 | 176 | 221 | 269 | 305 | 343 | 384 | 427 | 467 |
| 10 | 64 | 100 | 138 | 177 | 222 | 270 | 307 | 346 | 385 | 428 | 468 |
| 11 | 65 | 101 | 139 | 178 | 223 | 271 | 310 | 347 | 386 | 429 | 469 |
| 12 | 66 | 102 | 140 | 179 | 224 | 272 | 312 | 349 | 388 | 430 | 472 |
| 13 | 67 | 103 | 142 | 180 | 226 | 273 | 314 | 352 | 390 | 431 | 475 |
| 22 | 68 | 104 | 143 | 182 | 230 | 275 | 315 | 353 | 391 | 433 | 477 |
| 23 | 70 | 106 | 147 | 183 | 231 | 276 | 316 | 354 | 393 | 435 | 478 |
| 24 | 71 | 108 | 148 | 184 | 233 | 277 | 317 | 355 | 394 | 437 | 479 |
| 26 | 73 | 109 | 150 | 186 | 236 | 279 | 318 | 356 | 396 | 438 | 480 |
| 28 | 76 | 110 | 151 | 187 | 238 | 280 | 319 | 357 | 397 | 439 | 481 |
| 30 | 77 | 111 | 152 | 188 | 240 | 281 | 320 | 359 | 398 | 440 | 482 |
| 31 | 78 | 112 | 155 | 189 | 241 | 282 | 321 | 360 | 400 | 442 | 484 |
| 33 | 79 | 114 | 156 | 190 | 243 | 285 | 323 | 362 | 402 | 443 | 485 |
| 34 | 81 | 115 | 157 | 191 | 248 | 287 | 324 | 363 | 403 | 445 | 486 |
| 35 | 82 | 117 | 162 | 193 | 250 | 288 | 325 | 364 | 406 | 446 | 487 |
| 36 | 83 | 118 | 163 | 194 | 251 | 290 | 326 | 365 | 407 | 447 | |
| 37 | 84 | 119 | 164 | 197 | 252 | 291 | 329 | 367 | 408 | 448 | |
| 41 | 85 | 120 | 165 | 198 | 256 | 293 | 331 | 369 | 410 | 449 | |
| 42 | 88 | 123 | 166 | 200 | 257 | 294 | 332 | 370 | 411 | 452 | |
| 48 | 90 | 124 | 168 | 204 | 259 | 296 | 334 | 371 | 412 | 454 | |
| 50 | 91 | 125 | 169 | 206 | 260 | 299 | 335 | 372 | 413 | 455 | |
| 52 | 93 | 128 | 170 | 208 | 261 | 300 | 337 | 375 | 414 | 456 | |

## Senate

### (143 of 270 votes)

| | | | | | | | | | | | |
|---|---|---|---|---|---|---|---|---|---|---|---|
| 4 | 26 | 47 | 65 | 83 | 95 | 120 | 160 | 179 | 205 | 223 | 243 |
| 5 | 31 | 48 | 69 | 84 | 96 | 121 | 161 | 182 | 207 | 226 | 244 |
| 6 | 33 | 49 | 70 | 85 | 97 | 122 | 164 | 188 | 208 | 227 | 245 |
| 7 | 35 | 50 | 72 | 86 | 98 | 125 | 165 | 192 | 210 | 230 | 251 |
| 8 | 38 | 51 | 73 | 87 | 101 | 126 | 167 | 193 | 211 | 231 | 252 |
| 13 | 39 | 52 | 74 | 88 | 102 | 129 | 172 | 194 | 212 | 232 | 254 |
| 18 | 40 | 53 | 75 | 89 | 105 | 133 | 173 | 195 | 213 | 233 | 255 |
| 20 | 42 | 54 | 77 | 90 | 106 | 134 | 174 | 197 | 214 | 236 | 261 |
| 22 | 43 | 56 | 78 | 91 | 107 | 135 | 175 | 198 | 215 | 238 | 262 |
| 23 | 44 | 57 | 79 | 92 | 109 | 136 | 176 | 199 | 216 | 239 | 265 |
| 24 | 45 | 58 | 80 | 93 | 110 | 150 | 177 | 200 | 217 | 240 | 269 |
| 25 | 46 | 64 | 82 | 94 | 112 | 152 | 178 | 201 | 220 | 241 | |

## Proportion of Partisan Roll Calls

How often a majority of Democrats voted against a majority of Republicans:

| Year | House | Senate | Year | House | Senate | Year | House | Senate |
|---|---|---|---|---|---|---|---|---|
| 1954 | 38% | 47% | 1967 | 36% | 35% | 1980 | 38% | 46% |
| 1955 | 41 | 30 | 1968 | 35 | 32 | 1981 | 37 | 48 |
| 1956 | 44 | 53 | 1969 | 31 | 36 | 1982 | 36 | 43 |
| 1957 | 59 | 36 | 1970 | 27 | 35 | 1983 | 56 | 44 |
| 1958 | 40 | 44 | 1971 | 38 | 42 | 1984 | 47 | 40 |
| 1959 | 55 | 48 | 1972 | 27 | 36 | 1985 | 61 | 50 |
| 1960 | 53 | 37 | 1973 | 42 | 40 | 1986 | 57 | 52 |
| 1961 | 50 | 62 | 1974 | 29 | 44 | 1987 | 64 | 41 |
| 1962 | 46 | 41 | 1975 | 48 | 48 | 1988 | 47 | 42 |
| 1963 | 49 | 47 | 1976 | 36 | 37 | 1989 | 55 | 35 |
| 1964 | 55 | 36 | 1977 | 42 | 42 | 1990 | 49 | 54 |
| 1965 | 52 | 42 | 1978 | 33 | 45 | 1991 | 55 | 49 |
| 1966 | 41 | 50 | 1979 | 47 | 47 | 1992 | 64 | 53 |

KEY

† Not eligible for all party-unity votes in 1992 or voted "present" to avoid possible conflict of interest.

Democrats  *Republicans*

| | 1 | 2 | 3 |
|---|---|---|---|
| **Alabama** | | | |
| Heflin | 52 | 48 | 52 |
| Shelby | 45 | 55 | 45 |
| **Alaska** | | | |
| *Murkowski* | 82 | 11 | 88 |
| *Stevens* | 80 | 18 | 81 |
| **Arizona** | | | |
| DeConcini | 68 | 29 | 70 |
| *McCain* | 84 | 13 | 87 |
| **Arkansas** | | | |
| Bumpers | 69 | 29 | 71 |
| Pryor | 76 | 22 | 78 |
| **California** | | | |
| Cranston | 83 | 6 | 94 |
| Seymour | 73 | 13 | 85 |
| **Colorado** | | | |
| Wirth | 68 | 9 | 88 |
| *Brown* | 93 | 5 | 95 |
| **Connecticut** | | | |
| Dodd | 83 | 17 | 83 |
| Lieberman | 77 | 23 | 77 |
| **Delaware** | | | |
| Biden | 90 | 8 | 92 |
| *Roth* | 79 | 14 | 85 |
| **Florida** | | | |
| Graham | 73 | 27 | 73 |
| *Mack* † | 91 | 8 | 91 |
| **Georgia** | | | |
| Fowler | 73 | 20 | 79 |
| Nunn | 67 | 31 | 69 |
| **Hawaii** | | | |
| Akaka | 92 | 8 | 92 |
| Inouye | 78 | 12 | 87 |
| **Idaho** | | | |
| *Craig* | 99 | 1 | 99 |
| *Symms* | 93 | 3 | 97 |
| **Illinois** | | | |
| Dixon | 63 | 21 | 75 |
| Simon | 88 | 10 | 90 |
| **Indiana** | | | |
| *Coats* | 92 | 8 | 92 |
| *Lugar* | 86 | 12 | 88 |

| | 1 | 2 | 3 |
|---|---|---|---|
| **Iowa** | | | |
| Harkin | 66 | 3 | 95 |
| *Grassley* | 81 | 19 | 81 |
| **Kansas** | | | |
| *Dole* | 94 | 6 | 94 |
| *Kassebaum* | 76 | 22 | 77 |
| **Kentucky** | | | |
| Ford | 70 | 29 | 70 |
| *McConnell* | 91 | 8 | 92 |
| **Louisiana** | | | |
| Breaux | 68 | 29 | 70 |
| Johnston | 66 | 33 | 67 |
| **Maine** | | | |
| Mitchell | 93 | 7 | 93 |
| *Cohen* | 59 | 38 | 61 |
| **Maryland** | | | |
| Mikulski | 87 | 10 | 90 |
| Sarbanes | 96 | 4 | 96 |
| **Massachusetts** | | | |
| Kennedy | 95 | 3 | 97 |
| Kerry | 92 | 8 | 92 |
| **Michigan** | | | |
| Levin | 91 | 8 | 92 |
| Riegle | 83 | 8 | 91 |
| **Minnesota** | | | |
| Wellstone | 92 | 5 | 95 |
| *Durenberger* | 56 | 41 | 58 |
| **Mississippi** | | | |
| *Cochran* | 92 | 6 | 94 |
| *Lott* | 93 | 3 | 96 |
| **Missouri** | | | |
| *Bond* | 76 | 14 | 84 |
| *Danforth* | 77 | 20 | 79 |
| **Montana** | | | |
| Baucus | 83 | 17 | 83 |
| *Burns* | 94 | 6 | 94 |
| **Nebraska** | | | |
| Exon | 74 | 26 | 74 |
| Kerrey | 74 | 9 | 89 |
| **Nevada** | | | |
| Bryan | 78 | 22 | 78 |
| Reid | 75 | 22 | 78 |

| | 1 | 2 | 3 |
|---|---|---|---|
| **New Hampshire** | | | |
| *Rudman* | 73 | 24 | 75 |
| *Smith* | 92 | 8 | 92 |
| **New Jersey** | | | |
| Bradley | 80 | 10 | 89 |
| Lautenberg | 92 | 8 | 92 |
| **New Mexico** | | | |
| Bingaman | 70 | 23 | 75 |
| *Domenici* | 88 | 11 | 89 |
| **New York** | | | |
| Moynihan | 90 | 10 | 90 |
| *D'Amato* | 59 | 36 | 62 |
| **North Carolina** | | | |
| Sanford | 64 | 24 | 72 |
| Helms | 71 | 3 | 96 |
| **North Dakota** | | | |
| Burdick [1] | 79 | 9 | 90 |
| Conrad | 69 | 29 | 71 |
| **Ohio** | | | |
| Glenn | 83 | 17 | 83 |
| Metzenbaum | 91 | 6 | 94 |
| **Oklahoma** | | | |
| Boren | 58 | 34 | 63 |
| *Nickles* | 90 | 5 | 95 |
| **Oregon** | | | |
| *Hatfield* | 45 | 53 | 46 |
| *Packwood* | 50 | 49 | 50 |
| **Pennsylvania** | | | |
| Wofford | 90 | 8 | 92 |
| *Specter* | 41 | 57 | 41 |
| **Rhode Island** | | | |
| Pell | 83 | 9 | 90 |
| *Chafee* | 59 | 40 | 60 |
| **South Carolina** | | | |
| Hollings | 58 | 42 | 58 |
| *Thurmond* | 94 | 6 | 94 |
| **South Dakota** | | | |
| Daschle | 82 | 18 | 82 |
| *Pressler* | 91 | 9 | 91 |
| **Tennessee** | | | |
| Gore | 56 | 4 | 93 |
| Sasser | 85 | 14 | 86 |

| | 1 | 2 | 3 |
|---|---|---|---|
| **Texas** | | | |
| Bentsen | 59 | 30 | 66 |
| *Gramm* | 91 | 1 | 98 |
| **Utah** | | | |
| *Garn* | 85 | 3 | 96 |
| *Hatch* | 88 | 4 | 95 |
| **Vermont** | | | |
| Leahy | 90 | 4 | 96 |
| *Jeffords* | 36 | 58 | 39 |
| **Virginia** | | | |
| Robb | 74 | 26 | 74 |
| *Warner* | 86 | 13 | 87 |
| **Washington** | | | |
| Adams | 95 | 4 | 96 |
| *Gorton* | 80 | 18 | 81 |
| **West Virginia** | | | |
| Byrd | 74 | 25 | 75 |
| Rockefeller | 88 | 10 | 89 |
| **Wisconsin** | | | |
| Kohl | 79 | 21 | 79 |
| *Kasten* | 72 | 20 | 79 |
| **Wyoming** | | | |
| *Simpson* | 90 | 8 | 91 |
| *Wallop* | 89 | 3 | 96 |

# Party Unity
# and Party Opposition: Senate

**1. Party Unity, 1992.** Percentage of 143 party-unity recorded votes in 1992 on which a senator voted "yea" or "nay" *in agreement* with a majority of his or her party. (Party-unity roll calls are those on which a majority of voting Democrats opposed a majority of voting Republicans.) Failures to vote lowered both party-unity and party-opposition scores.

**2. Party Opposition, 1992.** Percentage of 143 party-unity recorded votes in 1992 on which a senator voted "yea" or "nay" *in disagreement* with a majority of his or her party. Failures to vote lowered both party-unity and party-opposition scores.

**3. Party Unity, 1992.** Percentage of 143 party-unity recorded votes in 1992 on which a senator was present and voted "yea" or "nay" *in agreement* with a majority of his or her party. In this version of the study, absences were not counted; therefore, failures to vote did not lower unity or opposition scores. Opposition scores, not listed here, are the inverse of the unity score; i.e., the opposition score is equal to 100 percent minus the individual's unity score.

[1] *Jocelyn Birch Burdick, D-N.D., was sworn in Sept. 16, 1992, to succeed her husband, Quentin N. Burdick, D, who died on Sept. 8, 1992. Quentin N. Burdick was eligible for 99 of 143 party-unity votes in 1992. His party-unity score was 68 percent; his opposition score was 15 percent; and his unity score, adjusted for absences, was 82 percent in 1992. Jocelyn Birch Burdick was eligible for 33 party-unity votes in 1992.*

## KEY

† Not eligible for all party-unity votes in 1992 or voted "present" to avoid possible conflict of interest.

_____

Democrats    *Republicans*

# Party Unity and Party Opposition: House

**1. Party Unity, 1992**. Percentage of 305 party-unity recorded votes in 1992 on which a representative voted "yea" or "nay" *in agreement* with a majority of his or her party. (Party-unity roll calls are those on which a majority of voting Democrats opposed a majority of voting Republicans.) Failures to vote lowered both party-unity and party-opposition scores.

**2. Party Opposition, 1992**. Percentage of 305 party-unity recorded votes in 1992 on which a representative voted "yea" or "nay" *in disagreement* with a majority of his or her party. Failures to vote lowered both party-unity and party-opposition scores.

**3. Party Unity, 1992**. Percentage of 305 party-unity recorded votes in 1992 on which a representative was present and voted "yea" or "nay" *in agreement* with a majority of his or her party. In this version of the study, absences were not counted; therefore, failures to vote did not lower unity or opposition scores. Opposition scores, not listed here, are the inverse of the unity score; i.e., the opposition score is equal to 100 percent minus the individual's unity score.

[1] *Ted Weiss, D-N.Y., died Sept. 14, 1992. He was eligible for 244 of 305 party-unity votes in 1992.*

[2] *Walter B. Jones, D-N.C., died Sept. 15, 1992. He was eligible for 244 of 305 party-unity votes in 1992.*

[3] *Bernard Sanders, I-Vt., voted as an independent. Had he voted as a Democrat, his party-unity score would have been 86 percent; his opposition score would have been 7 percent; and his unity score, adjusted for absences, would have been 92 percent.*

[4] *Thomas S. Foley, D-Wash., as Speaker of the House, voted at his discretion. He voted on 13 of the 305 party-unity votes in 1992.*

| | 1 | 2 | 3 |
|---|---|---|---|
| **Alabama** | | | |
| 1 *Callahan* | 83 | 12 | 87 |
| 2 *Dickinson* | 73 | 11 | 87 |
| 3 Browder | 75 | 23 | 77 |
| 4 Bevill | 78 | 17 | 82 |
| 5 Cramer | 75 | 23 | 76 |
| 6 Erdreich | 63 | 36 | 64 |
| 7 Harris | 71 | 27 | 72 |
| **Alaska** | | | |
| AL *Young* | 73 | 19 | 79 |
| **Arizona** | | | |
| 1 *Rhodes* | 91 | 8 | 92 |
| 2 Pastor | 89 | 9 | 91 |
| 3 *Stump* | 98 | 1 | 99 |
| 4 *Kyl* | 95 | 4 | 96 |
| 5 *Kolbe* | 84 | 13 | 87 |
| **Arkansas** | | | |
| 1 Alexander | 64 | 4 | 94 |
| 2 Thornton | 85 | 11 | 88 |
| 3 *Hammerschmidt* | 73 | 22 | 77 |
| 4 Anthony | 61 | 7 | 90 |
| **California** | | | |
| 1 *Riggs* | 71 | 17 | 81 |
| 2 *Herger* | 90 | 4 | 96 |
| 3 Matsui | 88 | 6 | 94 |
| 4 Fazio | 88 | 9 | 91 |
| 5 Pelosi | 91 | 1 | 99 |
| 6 Boxer | 50 | 4 | 92 |
| 7 Miller | 88 | 6 | 94 |
| 8 Dellums | 89 | 4 | 95 |
| 9 Stark | 81 | 6 | 93 |
| 10 Edwards | 92 | 3 | 97 |
| 11 Lantos | 90 | 6 | 94 |
| 12 *Campbell* | 70 | 13 | 84 |
| 13 Mineta | 93 | 5 | 95 |
| 14 *Doolittle* | 97 | 3 | 97 |
| 15 Condit | 61 | 36 | 63 |
| 16 Panetta | 88 | 10 | 90 |
| 17 Dooley | 77 | 18 | 81 |
| 18 Lehman | 72 | 17 | 81 |
| 19 *Lagomarsino* † | 92 | 4 | 96 |
| 20 *Thomas* | 77 | 8 | 90 |
| 21 *Gallegly* | 91 | 7 | 93 |
| 22 *Moorhead* | 97 | 2 | 98 |
| 23 Beilenson | 84 | 10 | 90 |
| 24 Waxman | 90 | 5 | 95 |
| 25 Roybal | 92 | 5 | 95 |
| 26 Berman | 89 | 5 | 94 |
| 27 Levine | 50 | 4 | 93 |
| 28 Dixon | 85 | 6 | 94 |
| 29 Waters | 82 | 4 | 96 |
| 30 Martinez | 87 | 6 | 94 |
| 31 Dymally | 51 | 2 | 97 |
| 32 Anderson | 85 | 10 | 89 |
| 33 *Dreier* | 90 | 8 | 92 |
| 34 Torres | 84 | 5 | 95 |
| 35 *Lewis* | 77 | 17 | 82 |
| 36 Brown | 88 | 5 | 95 |
| 37 *McCandless* | 90 | 9 | 91 |
| 38 *Dornan* | 88 | 4 | 95 |
| 39 *Dannemeyer* | 70 | 2 | 97 |
| 40 *Cox* | 85 | 6 | 93 |
| 41 *Lowery* | 66 | 14 | 83 |

| | 1 | 2 | 3 |
|---|---|---|---|
| 42 *Rohrabacher* | 93 | 5 | 95 |
| 43 *Packard* | 85 | 10 | 89 |
| 44 *Cunningham* | 91 | 4 | 96 |
| 45 *Hunter* | 90 | 6 | 94 |
| **Colorado** | | | |
| 1 Schroeder | 76 | 22 | 78 |
| 2 Skaggs | 88 | 10 | 89 |
| 3 Campbell | 57 | 15 | 79 |
| 4 *Allard* | 92 | 4 | 96 |
| 5 *Hefley* | 92 | 5 | 95 |
| 6 *Schaefer* | 95 | 3 | 97 |
| **Connecticut** | | | |
| 1 Kennelly | 92 | 6 | 94 |
| 2 Gejdenson | 96 | 4 | 96 |
| 3 DeLauro | 94 | 6 | 94 |
| 4 *Shays* | 62 | 38 | 62 |
| 5 *Franks* | 84 | 14 | 86 |
| 6 *Johnson* | 66 | 32 | 67 |
| **Delaware** | | | |
| AL *Carper* | 73 | 23 | 76 |
| **Florida** | | | |
| 1 Hutto | 44 | 51 | 46 |
| 2 Peterson | 76 | 15 | 84 |
| 3 Bennett | 73 | 27 | 73 |
| 4 *James* † | 93 | 7 | 93 |
| 5 *McCollum* | 89 | 8 | 92 |
| 6 *Stearns* | 92 | 4 | 96 |
| 7 Gibbons | 80 | 14 | 85 |
| 8 *Young* | 81 | 16 | 84 |
| 9 *Bilirakis* | 86 | 12 | 88 |
| 10 *Ireland* | 62 | 5 | 93 |
| 11 Bacchus | 77 | 18 | 81 |
| 12 *Lewis* | 90 | 6 | 94 |
| 13 *Goss* | 91 | 9 | 91 |
| 14 Johnston | 86 | 10 | 90 |
| 15 *Shaw* | 76 | 20 | 79 |
| 16 Smith | 86 | 5 | 95 |
| 17 Lehman | 76 | 3 | 95 |
| 18 *Ros-Lehtinen* | 73 | 24 | 75 |
| 19 Fascell | 83 | 8 | 91 |
| **Georgia** | | | |
| 1 Thomas | 60 | 19 | 76 |
| 2 Hatcher | 51 | 6 | 90 |
| 3 Ray | 42 | 36 | 54 |
| 4 Jones | 64 | 9 | 87 |
| 5 Lewis | 95 | 1 | 99 |
| 6 *Gingrich* | 82 | 5 | 94 |
| 7 Darden | 81 | 17 | 83 |
| 8 Rowland | 70 | 29 | 71 |
| 9 Jenkins | 76 | 17 | 82 |
| 10 Barnard | 32 | 23 | 59 |
| **Hawaii** | | | |
| 1 Abercrombie | 92 | 2 | 98 |
| 2 Mink | 94 | 3 | 97 |
| **Idaho** | | | |
| 1 LaRocco | 85 | 14 | 86 |
| 2 Stallings | 66 | 24 | 73 |
| **Illinois** | | | |
| 1 Hayes | 97 | 3 | 97 |
| 2 Savage | 65 | 3 | 96 |
| 3 Russo | 74 | 8 | 91 |
| 4 Sangmeister | 85 | 14 | 86 |
| 5 Lipinski | 67 | 20 | 77 |
| 6 *Hyde* | 59 | 14 | 81 |
| 7 Collins | 85 | 2 | 97 |
| 8 Rostenkowski | 90 | 6 | 94 |
| 9 Yates | 88 | 2 | 97 |
| 10 *Porter* | 73 | 23 | 76 |
| 11 Annunzio | 83 | 8 | 92 |
| 12 *Crane* | 94 | 2 | 98 |
| 13 *Fawell* | 86 | 13 | 87 |
| 14 *Hastert* | 89 | 10 | 90 |
| 15 *Ewing* | 80 | 17 | 82 |
| 16 Cox | 91 | 9 | 91 |
| 17 Evans | 95 | 5 | 95 |
| 18 *Michel* | 82 | 13 | 87 |
| 19 Bruce | 81 | 14 | 85 |
| 20 Durbin | 93 | 5 | 95 |
| 21 Costello | 78 | 18 | 81 |
| 22 Poshard | 79 | 20 | 80 |
| **Indiana** | | | |
| 1 Visclosky | 91 | 9 | 91 |
| 2 Sharp | 78 | 15 | 84 |
| 3 Roemer | 70 | 29 | 71 |

| | 1 | 2 | 3 |
|---|---|---|---|
| 4 Long | 89 | 11 | 89 |
| 5 Jontz | 89 | 11 | 89 |
| 6 Burton | 94 | 4 | 96 |
| 7 Myers | 70 | 27 | 72 |
| 8 McCloskey | 93 | 5 | 95 |
| 9 Hamilton | 79 | 20 | 80 |
| 10 Jacobs | 59 | 39 | 60 |

**Iowa**

| | 1 | 2 | 3 |
|---|---|---|---|
| 1 Leach | 65 | 33 | 66 |
| 2 Nussle | 89 | 10 | 90 |
| 3 Nagle | 85 | 8 | 91 |
| 4 Smith | 83 | 11 | 89 |
| 5 Lightfoot | 81 | 13 | 86 |
| 6 Grandy | 81 | 16 | 84 |

**Kansas**

| | 1 | 2 | 3 |
|---|---|---|---|
| 1 Roberts | 93 | 4 | 96 |
| 2 Slattery | 73 | 23 | 76 |
| 3 Meyers | 76 | 20 | 79 |
| 4 Glickman | 78 | 21 | 79 |
| 5 Nichols | 81 | 11 | 88 |

**Kentucky**

| | 1 | 2 | 3 |
|---|---|---|---|
| 1 Hubbard | 56 | 34 | 62 |
| 2 Natcher | 89 | 11 | 89 |
| 3 Mazzoli | 90 | 10 | 90 |
| 4 Bunning | 89 | 6 | 94 |
| 5 Rogers | 80 | 19 | 81 |
| 6 Hopkins | 93 | 4 | 96 |
| 7 Perkins | 70 | 9 | 89 |

**Louisiana**

| | 1 | 2 | 3 |
|---|---|---|---|
| 1 Livingston | 66 | 17 | 79 |
| 2 Jefferson | 81 | 5 | 95 |
| 3 Tauzin | 55 | 37 | 60 |
| 4 McCrery | 74 | 6 | 93 |
| 5 Huckaby | 50 | 28 | 64 |
| 6 Baker | 88 | 5 | 95 |
| 7 Hayes | 49 | 28 | 64 |
| 8 Holloway | 82 | 6 | 94 |

**Maine**

| | 1 | 2 | 3 |
|---|---|---|---|
| 1 Andrews | 90 | 8 | 92 |
| 2 Snowe | 58 | 41 | 59 |

**Maryland**

| | 1 | 2 | 3 |
|---|---|---|---|
| 1 Gilchrest | 68 | 29 | 71 |
| 2 Bentley | 77 | 19 | 80 |
| 3 Cardin | 93 | 5 | 95 |
| 4 McMillen | 82 | 17 | 82 |
| 5 Hoyer | 89 | 8 | 92 |
| 6 Byron | 56 | 31 | 64 |
| 7 Mfume | 90 | 6 | 94 |
| 8 Morella | 46 | 48 | 49 |

**Massachusetts**

| | 1 | 2 | 3 |
|---|---|---|---|
| 1 Olver | 93 | 5 | 95 |
| 2 Neal | 90 | 5 | 95 |
| 3 Early | 82 | 11 | 88 |
| 4 Frank | 93 | 5 | 95 |
| 5 Atkins | 82 | 7 | 93 |
| 6 Mavroules | 85 | 5 | 95 |
| 7 Markey | 91 | 3 | 97 |
| 8 Kennedy | 85 | 7 | 93 |
| 9 Moakley | 89 | 2 | 97 |
| 10 Studds | 93 | 4 | 96 |
| 11 Donnelly | 78 | 8 | 91 |

**Michigan**

| | 1 | 2 | 3 |
|---|---|---|---|
| 1 Conyers | 69 | 4 | 94 |
| 2 Pursell | 65 | 24 | 73 |
| 3 Wolpe | 90 | 3 | 97 |
| 4 Upton | 78 | 22 | 78 |
| 5 Henry | 78 | 19 | 80 |
| 6 Carr | 78 | 18 | 81 |
| 7 Kildee | 96 | 4 | 96 |
| 8 Traxler | 48 | 1 | 97 |
| 9 Vander Jagt | 70 | 18 | 80 |
| 10 Camp | 85 | 14 | 86 |
| 11 Davis | 55 | 30 | 65 |
| 12 Bonior | 79 | 3 | 97 |
| 13 Collins | 84 | 3 | 97 |
| 14 Hertel | 83 | 4 | 95 |
| 15 Ford | 88 | 2 | 97 |
| 16 Dingell | 87 | 6 | 94 |
| 17 Levin † | 96 | 4 | 96 |
| 18 Broomfield | 62 | 18 | 78 |

**Minnesota**

| | 1 | 2 | 3 |
|---|---|---|---|
| 1 Penny | 60 | 37 | 62 |
| 2 Weber | 71 | 9 | 89 |
| 3 Ramstad | 78 | 22 | 78 |
| 4 Vento | 95 | 4 | 96 |

| | 1 | 2 | 3 |
|---|---|---|---|
| 5 Sabo | 96 | 2 | 98 |
| 6 Sikorski | 82 | 15 | 84 |
| 7 Peterson | 82 | 17 | 83 |
| 8 Oberstar | 94 | 5 | 95 |

**Mississippi**

| | 1 | 2 | 3 |
|---|---|---|---|
| 1 Whitten | 60 | 10 | 85 |
| 2 Espy | 88 | 9 | 91 |
| 3 Montgomery | 65 | 35 | 65 |
| 4 Parker | 62 | 37 | 63 |
| 5 Taylor | 57 | 42 | 58 |

**Missouri**

| | 1 | 2 | 3 |
|---|---|---|---|
| 1 Clay | 80 | 9 | 90 |
| 2 Horn | 91 | 9 | 91 |
| 3 Gephardt | 88 | 4 | 96 |
| 4 Skelton | 66 | 31 | 68 |
| 5 Wheat | 93 | 3 | 97 |
| 6 Coleman | 76 | 19 | 80 |
| 7 Hancock | 98 | 2 | 98 |
| 8 Emerson | 84 | 15 | 85 |
| 9 Volkmer | 70 | 26 | 73 |

**Montana**

| | 1 | 2 | 3 |
|---|---|---|---|
| 1 Williams | 77 | 14 | 85 |
| 2 Marlenee | 79 | 10 | 89 |

**Nebraska**

| | 1 | 2 | 3 |
|---|---|---|---|
| 1 Bereuter | 77 | 21 | 79 |
| 2 Hoagland | 88 | 10 | 89 |
| 3 Barrett | 91 | 8 | 92 |

**Nevada**

| | 1 | 2 | 3 |
|---|---|---|---|
| 1 Bilbray | 81 | 19 | 81 |
| 2 Vucanovich | 84 | 13 | 86 |

**New Hampshire**

| | 1 | 2 | 3 |
|---|---|---|---|
| 1 Zeliff | 88 | 6 | 93 |
| 2 Swett | 75 | 24 | 76 |

**New Jersey**

| | 1 | 2 | 3 |
|---|---|---|---|
| 1 Andrews | 78 | 18 | 81 |
| 2 Hughes | 83 | 17 | 83 |
| 3 Pallone | 82 | 18 | 82 |
| 4 Smith | 61 | 37 | 62 |
| 5 Roukema | 66 | 30 | 69 |
| 6 Dwyer | 76 | 6 | 93 |
| 7 Rinaldo | 60 | 38 | 62 |
| 8 Roe | 77 | 9 | 89 |
| 9 Torricelli | 82 | 10 | 89 |
| 10 Payne | 92 | 3 | 97 |
| 11 Gallo | 73 | 24 | 75 |
| 12 Zimmer | 83 | 17 | 83 |
| 13 Saxton | 79 | 18 | 82 |
| 14 Guarini | 83 | 10 | 89 |

**New Mexico**

| | 1 | 2 | 3 |
|---|---|---|---|
| 1 Schiff | 72 | 26 | 74 |
| 2 Skeen | 67 | 32 | 68 |
| 3 Richardson | 83 | 10 | 90 |

**New York**

| | 1 | 2 | 3 |
|---|---|---|---|
| 1 Hochbrueckner | 94 | 5 | 95 |
| 2 Downey | 91 | 5 | 95 |
| 3 Mrazek | 73 | 5 | 94 |
| 4 Lent | 69 | 19 | 79 |
| 5 McGrath | 60 | 33 | 65 |
| 6 Flake | 87 | 3 | 97 |
| 7 Ackerman | 76 | 1 | 99 |
| 8 Scheuer | 86 | 4 | 96 |
| 9 Manton | 84 | 9 | 91 |
| 10 Schumer | 90 | 5 | 96 |
| 11 Towns | 70 | 4 | 95 |
| 12 Owens | 89 | 4 | 96 |
| 13 Solarz | 74 | 2 | 98 |
| 14 Molinari | 77 | 21 | 78 |
| 15 Green | 36 | 59 | 38 |
| 16 Rangel | 90 | 4 | 96 |
| 17 Weiss [1] | 88 | 2 | 97 |
| 18 Serrano | 90 | 3 | 97 |
| 19 Engel | 85 | 5 | 95 |
| 20 Lowey | 96 | 3 | 97 |
| 21 Fish | 56 | 40 | 59 |
| 22 Gilman | 42 | 57 | 43 |
| 23 McNulty | 87 | 10 | 90 |
| 24 Solomon | 88 | 9 | 91 |
| 25 Boehlert | 50 | 49 | 51 |
| 26 Martin | 69 | 16 | 81 |
| 27 Walsh | 65 | 33 | 66 |
| 28 McHugh | 90 | 7 | 93 |
| 29 Horton | 42 | 50 | 46 |
| 30 Slaughter | 96 | 3 | 97 |
| 31 Paxon | 94 | 5 | 95 |

| | 1 | 2 | 3 |
|---|---|---|---|
| 32 LaFalce | 86 | 9 | 91 |
| 33 Nowak | 86 | 8 | 92 |
| 34 Houghton | 64 | 33 | 66 |

**North Carolina**

| | 1 | 2 | 3 |
|---|---|---|---|
| 1 Jones [2] | 81 | 9 | 90 |
| 2 Valentine | 60 | 29 | 68 |
| 3 Lancaster | 73 | 24 | 75 |
| 4 Price | 91 | 8 | 92 |
| 5 Neal | 75 | 18 | 80 |
| 6 Coble | 92 | 8 | 92 |
| 7 Rose | 88 | 9 | 91 |
| 8 Hefner | 61 | 8 | 89 |
| 9 McMillan | 83 | 14 | 86 |
| 10 Ballenger | 90 | 6 | 94 |
| 11 Taylor | 89 | 8 | 92 |

**North Dakota**

| | 1 | 2 | 3 |
|---|---|---|---|
| AL Dorgan | 78 | 20 | 79 |

**Ohio**

| | 1 | 2 | 3 |
|---|---|---|---|
| 1 Luken † | 72 | 21 | 78 |
| 2 Gradison | 79 | 20 | 79 |
| 3 Hall | 80 | 11 | 88 |
| 4 Oxley | 86 | 10 | 90 |
| 5 Gillmor | 75 | 21 | 78 |
| 6 McEwen | 85 | 7 | 92 |
| 7 Hobson | 85 | 15 | 85 |
| 8 Boehner | 94 | 3 | 97 |
| 9 Kaptur | 86 | 10 | 89 |
| 10 Miller | 91 | 8 | 92 |
| 11 Eckart | 85 | 9 | 91 |
| 12 Kasich | 71 | 25 | 74 |
| 13 Pease | 89 | 9 | 91 |
| 14 Sawyer | 95 | 3 | 97 |
| 15 Wylie | 74 | 20 | 78 |
| 16 Regula | 73 | 27 | 73 |
| 17 Traficant | 89 | 9 | 91 |
| 18 Applegate | 79 | 20 | 80 |
| 19 Feighan | 73 | 6 | 92 |
| 20 Oakar | 79 | 5 | 94 |
| 21 Stokes | 92 | 2 | 98 |

**Oklahoma**

| | 1 | 2 | 3 |
|---|---|---|---|
| 1 Inhofe | 92 | 4 | 96 |
| 2 Synar | 91 | 7 | 93 |
| 3 Brewster | 75 | 22 | 77 |
| 4 McCurdy | 67 | 24 | 74 |
| 5 Edwards | 68 | 6 | 92 |
| 6 English | 64 | 35 | 65 |

**Oregon**

| | 1 | 2 | 3 |
|---|---|---|---|
| 1 AuCoin | 73 | 5 | 94 |
| 2 Smith | 93 | 5 | 95 |
| 3 Wyden | 90 | 8 | 92 |
| 4 DeFazio | 85 | 7 | 93 |
| 5 Kopetski | 90 | 7 | 93 |

**Pennsylvania**

| | 1 | 2 | 3 |
|---|---|---|---|
| 1 Foglietta | 83 | 3 | 97 |
| 2 Blackwell | 90 | 4 | 96 |
| 3 Borski | 91 | 8 | 92 |
| 4 Kolter | 56 | 7 | 89 |
| 5 Schulze | 66 | 16 | 80 |
| 6 Yatron | 72 | 11 | 87 |
| 7 Weldon | 82 | 16 | 84 |
| 8 Kostmayer | 90 | 9 | 91 |
| 9 Shuster | 86 | 10 | 89 |
| 10 McDade | 51 | 27 | 66 |
| 11 Kanjorski | 85 | 15 | 85 |
| 12 Murtha | 81 | 13 | 86 |
| 13 Coughlin | 62 | 17 | 79 |
| 14 Coyne | 96 | 3 | 97 |
| 15 Ritter | 76 | 22 | 78 |
| 16 Walker | 93 | 4 | 96 |
| 17 Gekas | 90 | 6 | 93 |
| 18 Santorum | 80 | 16 | 83 |
| 19 Goodling | 83 | 14 | 86 |
| 20 Gaydos | 61 | 10 | 85 |
| 21 Ridge | 72 | 21 | 77 |
| 22 Murphy | 64 | 32 | 67 |
| 23 Clinger | 71 | 24 | 75 |

**Rhode Island**

| | 1 | 2 | 3 |
|---|---|---|---|
| 1 Machtley | 58 | 38 | 60 |
| 2 Reed | 94 | 5 | 95 |

**South Carolina**

| | 1 | 2 | 3 |
|---|---|---|---|
| 1 Ravenel | 63 | 35 | 64 |
| 2 Spence | 82 | 17 | 83 |
| 3 Derrick | 87 | 12 | 88 |
| 4 Patterson | 65 | 33 | 66 |
| 5 Spratt | 83 | 15 | 85 |
| 6 Tallon | 67 | 15 | 82 |

**South Dakota**

| | 1 | 2 | 3 |
|---|---|---|---|
| AL Johnson | 81 | 17 | 83 |

**Tennessee**

| | 1 | 2 | 3 |
|---|---|---|---|
| 1 Quillen | 69 | 23 | 75 |
| 2 Duncan | 87 | 12 | 88 |
| 3 Lloyd | 65 | 29 | 70 |
| 4 Cooper † | 75 | 22 | 77 |
| 5 Clement | 75 | 15 | 83 |
| 6 Gordon | 86 | 10 | 89 |
| 7 Sundquist | 83 | 11 | 89 |
| 8 Tanner | 71 | 26 | 73 |
| 9 Ford | 69 | 7 | 91 |

**Texas**

| | 1 | 2 | 3 |
|---|---|---|---|
| 1 Chapman | 74 | 17 | 82 |
| 2 Wilson | 66 | 19 | 77 |
| 3 Johnson | 85 | 9 | 91 |
| 4 Hall | 49 | 50 | 49 |
| 5 Bryant | 82 | 10 | 89 |
| 6 Barton | 84 | 5 | 94 |
| 7 Archer | 85 | 10 | 89 |
| 8 Fields | 89 | 4 | 95 |
| 9 Brooks | 85 | 10 | 89 |
| 10 Pickle | 75 | 20 | 79 |
| 11 Edwards | 75 | 23 | 77 |
| 12 Geren | 59 | 38 | 61 |
| 13 Sarpalius | 66 | 34 | 66 |
| 14 Laughlin | 65 | 23 | 74 |
| 15 de la Garza | 80 | 13 | 86 |
| 16 Coleman | 82 | 10 | 89 |
| 17 Stenholm | 52 | 47 | 53 |
| 18 Washington | 80 | 4 | 95 |
| 19 Combest | 82 | 17 | 83 |
| 20 Gonzalez | 94 | 6 | 94 |
| 21 Smith | 85 | 9 | 91 |
| 22 DeLay | 90 | 7 | 93 |
| 23 Bustamante | 82 | 7 | 93 |
| 24 Frost | 82 | 11 | 88 |
| 25 Andrews | 73 | 24 | 75 |
| 26 Armey | 95 | 1 | 99 |
| 27 Ortiz | 81 | 16 | 84 |

**Utah**

| | 1 | 2 | 3 |
|---|---|---|---|
| 1 Hansen | 81 | 9 | 90 |
| 2 Owens | 75 | 17 | 81 |
| 3 Orton | 56 | 41 | 58 |

**Vermont**

| | 1 | 2 | 3 |
|---|---|---|---|
| AL Sanders [3] | -- | -- | -- |

**Virginia**

| | 1 | 2 | 3 |
|---|---|---|---|
| 1 Bateman | 70 | 28 | 72 |
| 2 Pickett | 68 | 30 | 70 |
| 3 Bliley | 89 | 8 | 92 |
| 4 Sisisky | 71 | 28 | 72 |
| 5 Payne | 76 | 23 | 77 |
| 6 Olin | 71 | 17 | 81 |
| 7 Allen | 94 | 4 | 95 |
| 8 Moran | 83 | 10 | 89 |
| 9 Boucher | 86 | 9 | 90 |
| 10 Wolf | 86 | 13 | 86 |

**Washington**

| | 1 | 2 | 3 |
|---|---|---|---|
| 1 Miller | 71 | 16 | 81 |
| 2 Swift | 91 | 7 | 93 |
| 3 Unsoeld | 93 | 4 | 96 |
| 4 Morrison | 46 | 36 | 56 |
| 5 Foley [4] | | | |
| 6 Dicks | 85 | 11 | 89 |
| 7 McDermott | 94 | 4 | 96 |
| 8 Chandler | 66 | 9 | 89 |

**West Virginia**

| | 1 | 2 | 3 |
|---|---|---|---|
| 1 Mollohan | 81 | 14 | 85 |
| 2 Staggers | 70 | 14 | 83 |
| 3 Wise | 84 | 8 | 91 |
| 4 Rahall | 79 | 17 | 82 |

**Wisconsin**

| | 1 | 2 | 3 |
|---|---|---|---|
| 1 Aspin | 84 | 11 | 88 |
| 2 Klug | 73 | 24 | 75 |
| 3 Gunderson | 67 | 32 | 68 |
| 4 Kleczka | 93 | 4 | 96 |
| 5 Moody | 86 | 11 | 89 |
| 6 Petri | 73 | 27 | 73 |
| 7 Obey | 93 | 5 | 95 |
| 8 Roth | 83 | 15 | 85 |
| 9 Sensenbrenner | 90 | 9 | 91 |

**Wyoming**

| | 1 | 2 | 3 |
|---|---|---|---|
| AL Thomas | 83 | 12 | 87 |

## VOTING PARTICIPATION

# Despite Election-Year Demands, Absence Rate Stayed Low

Facing an election year that would force record numbers out of office, few members dared to skip roll calls to campaign back home.

Most of the time, they didn't need to; the votes were scheduled to accommodate them.

Members made it to more than 93 percent of the roll calls this year. The high averages for an election year — 95 percent for the Senate and 93 percent for the House — illustrate that floor votes rank high on congressional priority lists, even in campaign season.

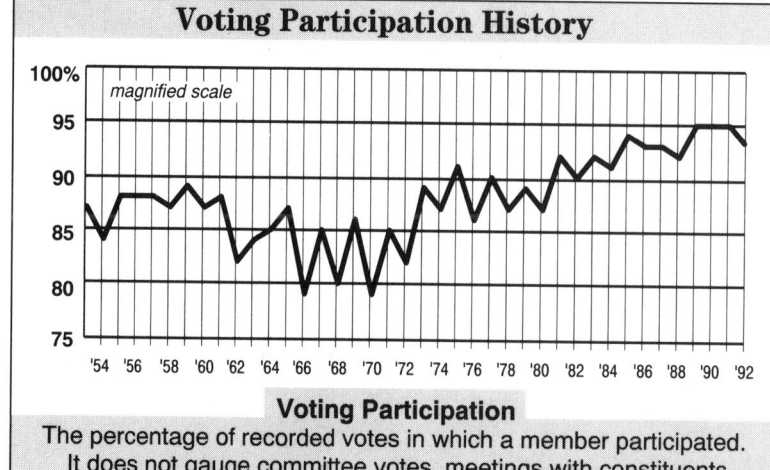

**Voting Participation History**

100%
95
90
85
80
75

*magnified scale*

'54 '56 '58 '60 '62 '64 '66 '68 '70 '72 '74 '76 '78 '80 '82 '84 '86 '88 '90 '92

**Voting Participation**
The percentage of recorded votes in which a member participated. It does not gauge committee votes, meetings with constituents or other member activities.

PATT CHISHOLM

"If you're an incumbent who can't manage to reacquaint yourself with your district [on non-voting days], then you have a problem," says Michael J. Malbin, director of the State University of New York's Center for Legislative Studies.

**Evaluating Scores**

Traditionally, voting participation scores have been used to indicate how diligently members attend to legislative duties. But political scientists say the quantitative measurement cannot show whether a member is an activist, shepherding bills from introduction to passage, or a significant force in committee.

In this year of the woman, of the career politician upset, of House reapportionment and of check-overdraft embarrassments for more than 250 members, the 102nd Congress' voting participation rate fell only 2 points, from 95.4 percent to 93.4 percent, in its second and final session.

In previous decades, voting records typically declined in even-numbered years, sometimes by as much as 8 points. But in the past two elections, members seem to have figured out ways to keep a high profile at home while being present on the floor, and scores have remained relatively constant.

A few campaigns suffered when members failed to avoid multiple absences. Democratic Sen.-elect Ben Nighthorse Campbell of Colorado lost a significant chunk of his lead over businessman and former state Sen. Terry Considine just before the election when Considine focused on Campbell's absences from Congress. Dick Wadhams, who ran the Republican's campaign, says voting participation was "one of the most lethal issues." Considine's ads called Campbell a "phantom congressman" because he voted by proxy in committee and often missed floor votes. (Campbell wound up missing 28 percent of floor votes.) At one point in October, Considine pulled even with Campbell in pre-election polls.

"Ben was caught between a rock and a hard place," according to press secretary Carol Knight, but he chose to make no formal response and wound up with 55 percent of the vote.

Part of the reason for the high voting rates is that in recent years the congressional leadership has made it easier to be present for votes. It schedules few votes on Mondays and Fridays, "stacks" votes back-to-back on Tuesday, Wednesday and Thursday, and promises no votes on several evenings each week.

In addition to using the CQ score (which excludes quorum calls), scholars suggest looking at what members do in committee, how they garner support for their initiatives and how effectively they work with other members. However, they warn that the scheduling of most floor votes Tuesday through Thursday sometimes interferes with the natural pace of legislating.

James A. Thurber, director of the Center for Congressional and Presidential Studies at American University, believes the "almost random" House schedule — ranging from Monday sessions of less than three hours to nine-hour-long Wednesday and Thursday sessions — conflicts with committee work. University of Kansas political science Professor Burdett Loomis agrees: "Sometimes things are ripe for a vote and the [committee] process gets interrupted . . . in a sense it's kind of like holding back the tide."

Some scholars find fault with the scores' sole focus on floor votes rather than committee votes because the bulk of research and negotiations occurs in committees. "You can find hundreds of committee votes that are more important than a floor vote," says Loomis, because opportunities to make major changes in legislative language are relatively rare on the floor.

Floor votes are important in forcing all members to take a position on an issue, Loomis says, but "some votes are simply there as political traps. The minority would like to push the majority to vote on difficult issues." But, he adds, "if a member misses a vote that's important to the district or on an important issue . . . that's a responsible thing to bring up in a campaign."

Despite their caveats, political scientists are well aware that a low score plastered across a constituent's TV screen can be politically potent. "It's hard to understand why

members otherwise show up for [House] Journal votes," says Malbin.

Nearly three dozen members kept any such ads at bay by missing no votes and scoring 100 percent. Among them, Rep. William H. Natcher, D-Ky., continued his tradition: He has attended every vote since he took office in 1953.

This year a few perfect scorers used the ratings to show they were hard-working incumbents. Other high scorers had backup ammunition when they launched into negative campaigns.

Victorious 99 percent scorers Sen. Daniel R. Coats, R-Ind., and Rep. Bill Sarpalius, D-Texas, used their opponents' absences to their own advantage.

Coats damaged Indiana Secretary of State Joe L. Hogsett's campaign just weeks before the election with a controversial staged segment called, "Where's Joe?" The commercial insinuated that the Democratic officeholder skipped work for nearly a week while campaigning for Congress.

In his race for Texas' 13th District, Sarpalius pulled a four-year-old skeleton from former Rep. Beau Boulter's closet. Sarpalius publicized that his Republican opponent missed 85 percent of House votes while he ran against Sen. Lloyd Bentsen in 1988.

### Eyes on a Different Prize

"Looking at the voting participation rate doesn't answer any questions," Malbin says. "It gives you a reason to look further."

Reviewing the year's political news may help to explain why many members failed to vote. Fifty-six percent scorer Tennessee Sen. Al Gore, D, campaigned for the Clinton-Gore presidential ticket. Sens. Tom Harkin, D-Iowa, and Bob Kerrey, D-Neb., sought the presidential nomination, and had 74 percent and 84 percent participation ratings, although their attendance significantly improved after they ended their candidacies last March.

With two Senate seats on the ballot, California lost some representation. Rep. Barbara Boxer claimed a Democratic Senate seat but had to miss a lot of votes in the process, ending up with a 55 percent participation rate. Incumbent Republican John Seymour (84 percent) failed in his bid for a Senate seat; so did Democratic Rep. Mel Levine (54 percent), who was beaten by Boxer in the primary.

Ten of the 13 House members who sought another office this year ranked below average in voting participation. But some managed to keep their scores high: Byron L. Dorgan, D-N.D., scored 98 percent, and Thomas R. Carper, D-Del., scored 97 percent; both won resoundingly. Wisconsin Rep. Jim Moody, who lost to Russell Feingold in a Democratic primary, scored 97 percent.

Serious health problems kept some members away from their chambers. Rep. Bob Traxler, D-Mich., suffered severe injuries in a Capitol Hill mugging. Sen. Jesse Helms, R-N.C., Rep. Doug Barnard, D-Ga., and Rep. W. G. "Bill" Hefner, D-N.C., underwent bypass surgery.

### Retirements Lower the Average

Departing members accounted for a significant portion of the bottom ranks. Members who retired — a postwar record number — voted on average almost 8.5 percent fewer times than those who will return in 1993. Re-elected House members ranked 95.3 percent, but retiring representatives scored 86.5 percent, lower than any average congressional voting record in the past decade. Returning sen-

## Scores for Retiring Members

### Senate

| Member | Score | Member | Score |
|---|---|---|---|
| Brock Adams, D-Wash. | 99% | Alan Cranston, D-Calif. | 90 |
| Warren Rudman, R-N.H. | 95 | Tim Wirth, D-Colo. | 79 |
| Steve Symms, R-Idaho | 94 | | |
| Jake Garn, R-Utah | 92 | | |
| Jocelyn Birch Burdick, D-N.D. | 90 | Avg.: retirees | 91.3 |
| | | Avg.: returning senators | 96.5 |

### House

| Member | Score | Member | Score |
|---|---|---|---|
| Charles E. Bennett, D-Fla. | 100 | Norman F. Lent, R-N.Y. | 88 |
| Craig T. James, R-Fla. | 100 | Jim Olin, D-Va. | 88 |
| Claude Harris, D-Ala. | 99 | John Miller, R-Wash. | 87 |
| George F. Allen, R-Va. | 99 | David O'B. Martin, R-N.Y. | 87 |
| Matthew J. Rinaldo, R-N.J. | 98 | Brian Donnelly, D-Mass. | 86 |
| Edward R. Roybal, D-Calif. | 97 | Robert A. Roe, D-N.J. | 86 |
| Matthew F. McHugh, D-N.Y. | 97 | Gus Yatron, D-Pa. | 85 |
| Don J. Pease, D-Ohio | 97 | Robert W. Davis, R-Mich. | 84 |
| Larry J. Hopkins, R-Ky. | 97 | Dick Schulze, R-Pa. | 84 |
| John Paul Hammerschmidt, R-Ark. | 96 | Bill Dickinson, R-Ala. | 84 |
| Glenn M. Anderson, D-Calif. | 95 | Bernard J. Dwyer, D-N.J. | 83 |
| Chalmers P. Wylie, R-Ohio | 95 | William S. Broomfield, R-Mich. | 82 |
| Dennis E. Eckart, D-Ohio | 95 | Vin Weber, R-Minn. | 81 |
| Raymond J. McGrath, R-N.Y. | 94 | Edward F. Feighan, D-Ohio | 81 |
| Henry J. Nowak, D-N.Y. | 94 | Robin Tallon, D-S.C. | 81 |
| Ed Jenkins, D-Ga. | 93 | Lindsay Thomas, D-Ga. | 80 |
| Howard Wolpe, D-Mich. | 93 | Carl C. Perkins, D-Ky. | 80 |
| Frank J. Guarini, D-N.J. | 93 | Bill Lowery, R-Calif. | 79 |
| Charles Luken, D-Ohio | 93 | Lawrence Coughlin, R-Pa. | 79 |
| Dante B. Fascell, D-Fla. | 92 | William Lehman, D-Fla. | 78 |
| Frank Horton, R-N.Y. | 92 | Robert J. Mrazek, D-N.Y. | 76 |
| James H. Scheuer, D-N.Y. | 91 | Joseph M. Gaydos, D-Pa. | 75 |
| Lawrence J. Smith, D-Fla. | 90 | Andy Ireland, R-Fla. | 69 |
| Frank Annunzio, D-Ill. | 90 | Doug Barnard Jr., D-Ga. | 57 |
| Carl D. Pursell, R-Mich. | 89 | Mervyn M. Dymally, D-Calif. | 52 |
| Dennis M. Hertel, D-Mich. | 89 | Bob Traxler, D-Mich. | 50 |
| | | Avg.: House retirees | 86.5 |
| | | Avg.: Returning members | 95.3 |

ators earned 96.5 percent and retiring ones ranked 91.3 percent.

Some declared retirees this year ranked floor votes lower than their other congressional interests. While they engaged in their last hurrah, half the House's outgoing crew scored below 90 percent this year.

Fifty-two percent scorer Rep. Mervyn M. Dymally, D-Calif., missed votes while traveling to Somalia and other African nations, conducting Congress' first hearing on the crisis, and fighting a serious illness, according to office spokesman Marwan Burgan. Dymally gave up his seat to work for his daughter Lynn's candidacy in California's 37th District.

Rep. Andy Ireland, R-Fla., with a 69 percent participation rate, decided to work in his district. Ireland says he missed procedural and partisan votes so that he could do constituent service. "I thought that since I was going out I could better use my time," he says. ■

# Voting Participation: House

**1. Voting Participation, 1992.** Percentage of 473 recorded votes in 1992 on which a representative voted "yea" or "nay."

**2. Voting Participation, 1992.** Percentage of 449 recorded votes in 1992 on which a representative voted "yea" or "nay." In this version of the study, votes of approval of the House Journal were not included.

[1] Ted Weiss, D-N.Y., died Sept. 14, 1992. He was eligible for 379 votes in 1992, 356 not including votes to approve the Journal.

[2] Walter B. Jones, D-N.C., died Sept. 15, 1992. He was eligible for 379 votes in 1992, 356 not including votes to approve the Journal.

[3] Thomas S. Foley, D-Wash., as Speaker of the House, voted at his discretion.

## KEY

† Not eligible for all recorded votes in 1992 or voted "present" to avoid a possible conflict of interest.

\# Members absent a day or more in 1992 due to illness or illness or death in family.

Democrats  *Republicans*
*Independent*

| | 1 | 2 |
|---|---|---|
| **Alabama** | | |
| 1 *Callahan* | 96 | 97 |
| 2 *Dickinson* | 84 | 85 |
| 3 Browder | 98 | 98 |
| 4 Bevill | 94 | 94 |
| 5 Cramer | 99 | 99 |
| 6 Erdreich | 99 | 99 |
| 7 Harris | 99 | 99 |
| **Alaska** | | |
| AL *Young* | 92 | 93 |
| **Arizona** | | |
| 1 *Rhodes* | 99 | 99 |
| 2 Pastor | 98 | 98 |
| 3 *Stump* | 99 | 99 |
| 4 *Kyl* | 99 | 99 |
| 5 *Kolbe* | 97 | 97 |
| **Arkansas** | | |
| 1 Alexander | 70 | 72 |
| 2 Thornton | 96 | 97 |
| 3 *Hammerschmidt* | 96 | 96 |
| 4 Anthony | 68 | 68 |
| **California** | | |
| 1 *Riggs* | 89 | 91 |
| 2 *Herger* | 94 | 94 |
| 3 Matsui # | 94 | 94 |
| 4 Fazio | 97 | 97 |
| 5 Pelosi | 93 | 94 |
| 6 Boxer | 55 | 55 |
| 7 Miller | 93 | 93 |
| 8 Dellums | 93 | 95 |
| 9 Stark | 88 | 88 |
| 10 Edwards | 96 | 96 |
| 11 Lantos | 95 | 95 |
| 12 *Campbell* | 85 | 85 |
| 13 Mineta | 98 | 98 |
| 14 *Doolittle* | 99 | 99 |
| 15 Condit | 97 | 98 |
| 16 Panetta | 98 | 98 |
| 17 Dooley | 95 | 95 |
| 18 Lehman | 90 | 91 |
| 19 *Lagomarsino* † | 96 | 96 |
| 20 *Thomas* | 88 | 88 |
| 21 *Gallegly* | 97 | 97 |
| 22 *Moorhead* | 99 | 99 |
| 23 Beilenson | 94 | 94 |
| 24 Waxman | 95 | 95 |
| 25 Roybal | 97 | 98 |
| 26 Berman | 93 | 94 |
| 27 Levine | 54 | 55 |
| 28 Dixon | 92 | 94 |
| 29 Waters | 87 | 88 |
| 30 Martinez | 92 | 92 |
| 31 Dymally | 52 | 52 |
| 32 Anderson | 95 | 95 |
| 33 *Dreier* | 98 | 98 |
| 34 Torres | 89 | 90 |
| 35 *Lewis* | 95 | 95 |
| 36 Brown | 93 | 93 |
| 37 *McCandless* | 99 | 99 |
| 38 *Dornan* | 92 | 94 |
| 39 *Dannemeyer* | 72 | 73 |
| 40 *Cox* | 92 | 93 |
| 41 *Lowery* | 79 | 81 |

| | 1 | 2 |
|---|---|---|
| 42 *Rohrabacher* | 98 | 98 |
| 43 *Packard* | 96 | 95 |
| 44 *Cunningham* | 94 | 94 |
| 45 *Hunter* | 94 | 96 |
| **Colorado** | | |
| 1 Schroeder | 97 | 98 |
| 2 Skaggs | 99 | 99 |
| 3 Campbell | 72 | 73 |
| 4 *Allard* | 97 | 98 |
| 5 *Hefley* | 97 | 97 |
| 6 *Schaefer* | 99 | 99 |
| **Connecticut** | | |
| 1 Kennelly | 98 | 98 |
| 2 Gejdenson | 99 | 99 |
| 3 DeLauro | 99 | 99 |
| 4 *Shays* | 100 | 100 |
| 5 *Franks* | 98 | 98 |
| 6 *Johnson* | 97 | 97 |
| **Delaware** | | |
| AL Carper | 97 | 98 |
| **Florida** | | |
| 1 Hutto | 95 | 96 |
| 2 Peterson # | 91 | 90 |
| 3 Bennett | 100 | 100 |
| 4 *James* † | 100 | 100 |
| 5 *McCollum* | 96 | 97 |
| 6 *Stearns* # | 96 | 96 |
| 7 Gibbons | 95 | 95 |
| 8 *Young* # | 97 | 98 |
| 9 *Bilirakis* # | 97 | 98 |
| 10 *Ireland* | 69 | 69 |
| 11 Bacchus | 96 | 96 |
| 12 *Lewis* | 96 | 96 |
| 13 *Goss* | 100 | 100 |
| 14 Johnston | 96 | 96 |
| 15 *Shaw* | 96 | 96 |
| 16 Smith | 90 | 90 |
| 17 Lehman | 78 | 78 |
| 18 *Ros-Lehtinen* | 97 | 97 |
| 19 Fascell | 92 | 92 |
| **Georgia** | | |
| 1 Thomas | 80 | 80 |
| 2 Hatcher | 60 | 59 |
| 3 Ray | 80 | 81 |
| 4 Jones | 71 | 71 |
| 5 Lewis | 97 | 96 |
| 6 *Gingrich* # | 87 | 87 |
| 7 Darden | 97 | 98 |
| 8 Rowland | 98 | 98 |
| 9 Jenkins | 93 | 93 |
| 10 Barnard # | 57 | 57 |
| **Hawaii** | | |
| 1 Abercrombie | 96 | 98 |
| 2 Mink | 98 | 98 |
| **Idaho** | | |
| 1 LaRocco | 99 | 99 |
| 2 Stallings | 90 | 90 |
| **Illinois** | | |
| 1 Hayes | 99 | 99 |
| 2 Savage | 69 | 71 |
| 3 Russo | 82 | 83 |
| 4 Sangmeister # | 98 | 98 |
| 5 Lipinski # | 86 | 86 |
| 6 *Hyde* # | 74 | 73 |
| 7 Collins | 86 | 86 |
| 8 Rostenkowski | 96 | 96 |
| 9 Yates # | 90 | 90 |
| 10 *Porter* | 95 | 96 |
| 11 Annunzio | 90 | 90 |
| 12 *Crane* | 95 | 95 |
| 13 *Fawell* | 99 | 99 |
| 14 *Hastert* | 98 | 98 |
| 15 *Ewing* | 96 | 96 |
| 16 Cox | 99 | 100 |
| 17 Evans | 99 | 99 |
| 18 *Michel* | 95 | 95 |
| 19 Bruce # | 95 | 95 |
| 20 Durbin | 99 | 99 |
| 21 Costello # | 96 | 96 |
| 22 Poshard | 99 | 99 |
| **Indiana** | | |
| 1 Visclosky | 99 | 99 |
| 2 Sharp † | 95 | 95 |
| 3 Roemer | 99 | 99 |

| District | Name | 1 | 2 |
| --- | --- | --- | --- |
| 4 | Long | 100 | 100 |
| 5 | Jontz | 100 | 100 |
| 6 | Burton | 98 | 98 |
| 7 | Myers | 97 | 97 |
| 8 | McCloskey | 97 | 97 |
| 9 | Hamilton | 99 | 99 |
| 10 | Jacobs | 98 | 99 |

**Iowa**

| District | Name | 1 | 2 |
| --- | --- | --- | --- |
| 1 | Leach † | 98 | 99 |
| 2 | Nussle | 99 | 99 |
| 3 | Nagle | 94 | 95 |
| 4 | Smith | 95 | 95 |
| 5 | Lightfoot # | 95 | 95 |
| 6 | Grandy | 96 | 96 |

**Kansas**

| District | Name | 1 | 2 |
| --- | --- | --- | --- |
| 1 | Roberts | 97 | 97 |
| 2 | Slattery | 97 | 97 |
| 3 | Meyers | 97 | 98 |
| 4 | Glickman | 99 | 99 |
| 5 | Nichols | 94 | 94 |

**Kentucky**

| District | Name | 1 | 2 |
| --- | --- | --- | --- |
| 1 | Hubbard | 91 | 91 |
| 2 | Natcher | 100 | 100 |
| 3 | Mazzoli | 100 | 100 |
| 4 | Bunning | 95 | 95 |
| 5 | Rogers | 98 | 98 |
| 6 | Hopkins | 97 | 97 |
| 7 | Perkins | 80 | 81 |

**Louisiana**

| District | Name | 1 | 2 |
| --- | --- | --- | --- |
| 1 | Livingston | 84 | 85 |
| 2 | Jefferson | 85 | 86 |
| 3 | Tauzin # | 92 | 92 |
| 4 | McCrery | 80 | 79 |
| 5 | Huckaby | 79 | 78 |
| 6 | Baker | 93 | 94 |
| 7 | Hayes | 77 | 77 |
| 8 | Holloway | 89 | 90 |

**Maine**

| District | Name | 1 | 2 |
| --- | --- | --- | --- |
| 1 | Andrews | 99 | 99 |
| 2 | Snowe | 99 | 99 |

**Maryland**

| District | Name | 1 | 2 |
| --- | --- | --- | --- |
| 1 | Gilchrest | 97 | 98 |
| 2 | Bentley | 96 | 96 |
| 3 | Cardin | 98 | 98 |
| 4 | McMillen | 99 | 99 |
| 5 | Hoyer # | 97 | 98 |
| 6 | Byron | 90 | 90 |
| 7 | Mfume | 97 | 98 |
| 8 | Morella | 95 | 96 |

**Massachusetts**

| District | Name | 1 | 2 |
| --- | --- | --- | --- |
| 1 | Olver | 98 | 98 |
| 2 | Neal | 95 | 96 |
| 3 | Early | 92 | 92 |
| 4 | Frank | 96 | 96 |
| 5 | Atkins | 89 | 89 |
| 6 | Mavroules | 89 | 90 |
| 7 | Markey # | 95 | 95 |
| 8 | Kennedy | 92 | 93 |
| 9 | Moakley | 91 | 92 |
| 10 | Studds | 97 | 97 |
| 11 | Donnelly | 86 | 87 |

**Michigan**

| District | Name | 1 | 2 |
| --- | --- | --- | --- |
| 1 | Conyers | 75 | 75 |
| 2 | Pursell | 89 | 90 |
| 3 | Wolpe | 93 | 93 |
| 4 | Upton | 99 | 99 |
| 5 | Henry | 98 | 98 |
| 6 | Carr | 96 | 97 |
| 7 | Kildee | 100 | 100 |
| 8 | Traxler | 50 | 51 |
| 9 | Vander Jagt | 88 | 88 |
| 10 | Camp | 99 | 99 |
| 11 | Davis | 84 | 85 |
| 12 | Bonior | 80 | 81 |
| 13 | Collins | 86 | 86 |
| 14 | Hertel | 89 | 90 |
| 15 | Ford | 92 | 93 |
| 16 | Dingell | 94 | 95 |
| 17 | Levin † | 100 | 100 |
| 18 | Broomfield | 82 | 82 |

**Minnesota**

| District | Name | 1 | 2 |
| --- | --- | --- | --- |
| 1 | Penny # | 97 | 97 |
| 2 | Weber | 81 | 82 |
| 3 | Ramstad | 100 | 100 |
| 4 | Vento | 99 | 99 |
| 5 | Sabo | 97 | 97 |
| 6 | Sikorski | 97 | 97 |
| 7 | Peterson | 99 | 99 |
| 8 | Oberstar | 99 | 99 |

**Mississippi**

| District | Name | 1 | 2 |
| --- | --- | --- | --- |
| 1 | Whitten | 70 | 71 |
| 2 | Espy | 96 | 97 |
| 3 | Montgomery | 99 | 99 |
| 4 | Parker | 99 | 99 |
| 5 | Taylor | 99 | 99 |

**Missouri**

| District | Name | 1 | 2 |
| --- | --- | --- | --- |
| 1 | Clay | 90 | 90 |
| 2 | Horn | 100 | 100 |
| 3 | Gephardt | 91 | 92 |
| 4 | Skelton | 97 | 98 |
| 5 | Wheat | 96 | 97 |
| 6 | Coleman | 95 | 95 |
| 7 | Hancock | 99 | 99 |
| 8 | Emerson | 99 | 99 |
| 9 | Volkmer | 96 | 96 |

**Montana**

| District | Name | 1 | 2 |
| --- | --- | --- | --- |
| 1 | Williams | 92 | 92 |
| 2 | Marlenee | 89 | 90 |

**Nebraska**

| District | Name | 1 | 2 |
| --- | --- | --- | --- |
| 1 | Bereuter | 98 | 98 |
| 2 | Hoagland | 99 | 99 |
| 3 | Barrett | 99 | 99 |

**Nevada**

| District | Name | 1 | 2 |
| --- | --- | --- | --- |
| 1 | Bilbray | 99 | 99 |
| 2 | Vucanovich | 97 | 97 |

**New Hampshire**

| District | Name | 1 | 2 |
| --- | --- | --- | --- |
| 1 | Zeliff | 94 | 95 |
| 2 | Swett | 98 | 98 |

**New Jersey**

| District | Name | 1 | 2 |
| --- | --- | --- | --- |
| 1 | Andrews | 97 | 97 |
| 2 | Hughes | 99 | 99 |
| 3 | Pallone | 99 | 99 |
| 4 | Smith | 97 | 98 |
| 5 | Roukema | 95 | 95 |
| 6 | Dwyer | 83 | 82 |
| 7 | Rinaldo | 98 | 98 |
| 8 | Roe | 86 | 87 |
| 9 | Torricelli | 91 | 91 |
| 10 | Payne | 95 | 96 |
| 11 | Gallo | 98 | 98 |
| 12 | Zimmer | 99 | 100 |
| 13 | Saxton | 97 | 98 |
| 14 | Guarini | 93 | 93 |

**New Mexico**

| District | Name | 1 | 2 |
| --- | --- | --- | --- |
| 1 | Schiff | 97 | 97 |
| 2 | Skeen | 99 | 99 |
| 3 | Richardson | 92 | 92 |

**New York**

| District | Name | 1 | 2 |
| --- | --- | --- | --- |
| 1 | Hochbrueckner | 99 | 99 |
| 2 | Downey | 96 | 96 |
| 3 | Mrazek | 76 | 78 |
| 4 | Lent | 88 | 88 |
| 5 | McGrath | 94 | 94 |
| 6 | Flake | 89 | 90 |
| 7 | Ackerman | 76 | 76 |
| 8 | Scheuer | 91 | 91 |
| 9 | Manton | 92 | 93 |
| 10 | Schumer | 94 | 95 |
| 11 | Towns | 77 | 77 |
| 12 | Owens | 93 | 94 |
| 13 | Solarz | 76 | 76 |
| 14 | Molinari | 98 | 98 |
| 15 | Green | 96 | 96 |
| 16 | Rangel | 93 | 95 |
| 17 | Weiss [1] | 91 | 92 |
| 18 | Serrano | 92 | 93 |
| 19 | Engel # | 90 | 91 |
| 20 | Lowey | 99 | 99 |
| 21 | Fish | 96 | 96 |
| 22 | Gilman | 99 | 99 |
| 23 | McNulty | 95 | 96 |
| 24 | Solomon | 97 | 97 |
| 25 | Boehlert | 99 | 99 |
| 26 | Martin | 87 | 88 |
| 27 | Walsh | 98 | 98 |
| 28 | McHugh | 97 | 98 |
| 29 | Horton | 92 | 92 |
| 30 | Slaughter | 99 | 99 |
| 31 | Paxon | 99 | 99 |
| 32 | LaFalce | 94 | 96 |
| 33 | Nowak | 94 | 95 |
| 34 | Houghton | 97 | 97 |

**North Carolina**

| District | Name | 1 | 2 |
| --- | --- | --- | --- |
| 1 | Jones [2] | 89 | 90 |
| 2 | Valentine | 91 | 92 |
| 3 | Lancaster | 97 | 98 |
| 4 | Price | 99 | 99 |
| 5 | Neal | 95 | 96 |
| 6 | Coble | 99 | 99 |
| 7 | Rose | 98 | 98 |
| 8 | Hefner # | 69 | 70 |
| 9 | McMillan | 97 | 97 |
| 10 | Ballenger | 96 | 96 |
| 11 | Taylor | 96 | 96 |

**North Dakota**

| District | Name | 1 | 2 |
| --- | --- | --- | --- |
| AL | Dorgan | 98 | 98 |

**Ohio**

| District | Name | 1 | 2 |
| --- | --- | --- | --- |
| 1 | Luken † | 93 | 93 |
| 2 | Gradison | 98 | 98 |
| 3 | Hall | 93 | 94 |
| 4 | Oxley | 97 | 97 |
| 5 | Gillmor | 97 | 97 |
| 6 | McEwen | 92 | 92 |
| 7 | Hobson | 99 | 99 |
| 8 | Boehner | 97 | 97 |
| 9 | Kaptur | 96 | 95 |
| 10 | Miller | 99 | 99 |
| 11 | Eckart | 95 | 95 |
| 12 | Kasich | 97 | 97 |
| 13 | Pease | 97 | 98 |
| 14 | Sawyer | 99 | 99 |
| 15 | Wylie | 95 | 95 |
| 16 | Regula | 99 | 99 |
| 17 | Traficant | 98 | 98 |
| 18 | Applegate | 98 | 98 |
| 19 | Feighan | 81 | 82 |
| 20 | Oakar | 83 | 83 |
| 21 | Stokes | 96 | 96 |

**Oklahoma**

| District | Name | 1 | 2 |
| --- | --- | --- | --- |
| 1 | Inhofe | 97 | 97 |
| 2 | Synar | 97 | 97 |
| 3 | Brewster | 98 | 99 |
| 4 | McCurdy | 92 | 92 |
| 5 | Edwards | 73 | 75 |
| 6 | English | 99 | 98 |

**Oregon**

| District | Name | 1 | 2 |
| --- | --- | --- | --- |
| 1 | AuCoin | 78 | 80 |
| 2 | Smith | 98 | 98 |
| 3 | Wyden | 97 | 98 |
| 4 | DeFazio | 93 | 93 |
| 5 | Kopetski | 97 | 98 |

**Pennsylvania**

| District | Name | 1 | 2 |
| --- | --- | --- | --- |
| 1 | Foglietta | 85 | 85 |
| 2 | Blackwell | 93 | 94 |
| 3 | Borski | 99 | 99 |
| 4 | Kolter | 64 | 64 |
| 5 | Schulze | 84 | 84 |
| 6 | Yatron | 85 | 85 |
| 7 | Weldon | 97 | 98 |
| 8 | Kostmayer | 99 | 99 |
| 9 | Shuster | 96 | 96 |
| 10 | McDade # | 78 | 78 |
| 11 | Kanjorski | 100 | 100 |
| 12 | Murtha | 92 | 92 |
| 13 | Coughlin | 79 | 80 |
| 14 | Coyne | 99 | 99 |
| 15 | Ritter | 98 | 98 |
| 16 | Walker | 97 | 97 |
| 17 | Gekas | 95 | 95 |
| 18 | Santorum # | 96 | 96 |
| 19 | Goodling | 98 | 98 |
| 20 | Gaydos | 75 | 76 |
| 21 | Ridge | 91 | 92 |
| 22 | Murphy | 93 | 93 |
| 23 | Clinger | 96 | 96 |

**Rhode Island**

| District | Name | 1 | 2 |
| --- | --- | --- | --- |
| 1 | Machtley | 97 | 98 |
| 2 | Reed | 99 | 99 |

**South Carolina**

| District | Name | 1 | 2 |
| --- | --- | --- | --- |
| 1 | Ravenel | 98 | 98 |
| 2 | Spence | 99 | 99 |
| 3 | Derrick | 99 | 99 |
| 4 | Patterson | 98 | 98 |
| 5 | Spratt | 99 | 99 |
| 6 | Tallon | 81 | 81 |

**South Dakota**

| District | Name | 1 | 2 |
| --- | --- | --- | --- |
| AL | Johnson | 99 | 99 |

**Tennessee**

| District | Name | 1 | 2 |
| --- | --- | --- | --- |
| 1 | Quillen | 91 | 91 |
| 2 | Duncan | 99 | 99 |
| 3 | Lloyd | 95 | 95 |
| 4 | Cooper † | 98 | 98 |
| 5 | Clement # | 91 | 91 |
| 6 | Gordon # | 96 | 96 |
| 7 | Sundquist | 95 | 95 |
| 8 | Tanner | 98 | 98 |
| 9 | Ford | 76 | 76 |

**Texas**

| District | Name | 1 | 2 |
| --- | --- | --- | --- |
| 1 | Chapman | 92 | 94 |
| 2 | Wilson | 85 | 86 |
| 3 | Johnson # | 95 | 96 |
| 4 | Hall | 99 | 99 |
| 5 | Bryant | 92 | 92 |
| 6 | Barton | 91 | 92 |
| 7 | Archer | 96 | 96 |
| 8 | Fields | 95 | 95 |
| 9 | Brooks | 96 | 96 |
| 10 | Pickle | 96 | 96 |
| 11 | Edwards | 99 | 99 |
| 12 | Geren | 98 | 98 |
| 13 | Sarpalius | 99 | 99 |
| 14 | Laughlin | 89 | 89 |
| 15 | de la Garza | 93 | 93 |
| 16 | Coleman | 91 | 92 |
| 17 | Stenholm | 97 | 97 |
| 18 | Washington | 82 | 85 |
| 19 | Combest | 99 | 98 |
| 20 | Gonzalez | 100 | 100 |
| 21 | Smith | 94 | 95 |
| 22 | DeLay | 97 | 98 |
| 23 | Bustamante | 87 | 86 |
| 24 | Frost | 93 | 94 |
| 25 | Andrews | 98 | 98 |
| 26 | Armey | 97 | 97 |
| 27 | Ortiz | 96 | 96 |

**Utah**

| District | Name | 1 | 2 |
| --- | --- | --- | --- |
| 1 | Hansen | 90 | 91 |
| 2 | Owens | 90 | 90 |
| 3 | Orton | 97 | 97 |

**Vermont**

| District | Name | 1 | 2 |
| --- | --- | --- | --- |
| AL | Sanders | 94 | 96 |

**Virginia**

| District | Name | 1 | 2 |
| --- | --- | --- | --- |
| 1 | Bateman | 97 | 98 |
| 2 | Pickett | 98 | 98 |
| 3 | Bliley | 98 | 98 |
| 4 | Sisisky | 98 | 98 |
| 5 | Payne | 99 | 99 |
| 6 | Olin | 88 | 87 |
| 7 | Allen | 99 | 99 |
| 8 | Moran # | 93 | 94 |
| 9 | Boucher | 96 | 96 |
| 10 | Wolf | 99 | 99 |

**Washington**

| District | Name | 1 | 2 |
| --- | --- | --- | --- |
| 1 | Miller | 87 | 88 |
| 2 | Swift | 98 | 98 |
| 3 | Unsoeld | 97 | 98 |
| 4 | Morrison | 83 | 83 |
| 5 | Foley [3] | | |
| 6 | Dicks | 96 | 96 |
| 7 | McDermott | 98 | 98 |
| 8 | Chandler | 75 | 75 |

**West Virginia**

| District | Name | 1 | 2 |
| --- | --- | --- | --- |
| 1 | Mollohan | 96 | 97 |
| 2 | Staggers | 85 | 85 |
| 3 | Wise | 93 | 94 |
| 4 | Rahall | 96 | 97 |

**Wisconsin**

| District | Name | 1 | 2 |
| --- | --- | --- | --- |
| 1 | Aspin | 95 | 95 |
| 2 | Klug | 97 | 98 |
| 3 | Gunderson | 99 | 99 |
| 4 | Kleczka | 96 | 96 |
| 5 | Moody | 97 | 98 |
| 6 | Petri | 99 | 99 |
| 7 | Obey | 98 | 98 |
| 8 | Roth | 96 | 96 |
| 9 | Sensenbrenner # | 99 | 99 |

**Wyoming**

| District | Name | 1 | 2 |
| --- | --- | --- | --- |
| AL | Thomas | 96 | 96 |

| State / Senator | 1 | 2 |
|---|---|---|
| **Alabama** | | |
| Heflin | 100 | 100 |
| Shelby | 100 | 100 |
| **Alaska** | | |
| *Murkowski* | 93 | 93 |
| *Stevens* # | 98 | 98 |
| **Arizona** | | |
| DeConcini † | 97 | 97 |
| *McCain* | 98 | 98 |
| **Arkansas** | | |
| Bumpers | 97 | 98 |
| Pryor | 94 | 94 |
| **California** | | |
| Cranston | 90 | 90 |
| Seymour | 84 | 85 |
| **Colorado** | | |
| Wirth | 79 | 79 |
| *Brown* | 99 | 99 |
| **Connecticut** | | |
| Dodd | 99 | 99 |
| Lieberman | 100 | 100 |
| **Delaware** | | |
| Biden | 97 | 97 |
| *Roth* # | 89 | 89 |
| **Florida** | | |
| Graham | 100 | 100 |
| *Mack* † | 98 | 98 |
| **Georgia** | | |
| Fowler | 96 | 95 |
| Nunn | 98 | 98 |
| **Hawaii** | | |
| Akaka | 100 | 100 |
| Inouye # | 91 | 91 |
| **Idaho** | | |
| *Craig* | 99 | 98 |
| *Symms* | 94 | 94 |
| **Illinois** | | |
| Dixon | 86 | 85 |
| Simon | 99 | 99 |
| **Indiana** | | |
| *Coats* | 99 | 99 |
| *Lugar* | 97 | 97 |
| **Iowa** | | |
| Harkin | 74 | 74 |
| *Grassley* | 100 | 100 |
| **Kansas** | | |
| *Dole* | 99 | 100 |
| *Kassebaum* | 98 | 98 |
| **Kentucky** | | |
| Ford | 99 | 99 |
| *McConnell* | 99 | 99 |
| **Louisiana** | | |
| Breaux | 97 | 97 |
| Johnston | 98 | 98 |
| **Maine** | | |
| Mitchell | 100 | 100 |
| *Cohen* | 99 | 98 |
| **Maryland** | | |
| Mikulski | 97 | 98 |
| Sarbanes | 100 | 100 |
| **Massachusetts** | | |
| Kennedy | 99 | 98 |
| Kerry | 99 | 99 |
| **Michigan** | | |
| Levin | 99 | 98 |
| Riegle # | 94 | 94 |
| **Minnesota** | | |
| Wellstone | 96 | 96 |
| *Durenberger* | 96 | 96 |
| **Mississippi** | | |
| *Cochran* | 98 | 98 |
| *Lott* | 98 | 98 |
| **Missouri** | | |
| *Bond* | 90 | 89 |
| *Danforth* | 97 | 97 |
| **Montana** | | |
| Baucus | 99 | 99 |
| *Burns* | 100 | 100 |
| **Nebraska** | | |
| Exon | 99 | 99 |
| Kerrey | 84 | 83 |
| **Nevada** | | |
| Bryan | 99 | 99 |
| Reid | 97 | 97 |
| **New Hampshire** | | |
| *Rudman* | 95 | 95 |
| *Smith* | 100 | 100 |
| **New Jersey** | | |
| Bradley | 91 | 91 |
| Lautenberg | 100 | 100 |
| **New Mexico** | | |
| Bingaman | 94 | 94 |
| *Domenici* | 99 | 99 |
| **New York** | | |
| Moynihan | 100 | 100 |
| *D'Amato* | 96 | 96 |
| **North Carolina** | | |
| Sanford | 84 | 84 |
| *Helms* # | 63 | 63 |
| **North Dakota** | | |
| Burdick [1] | 90 | 90 |
| Conrad # | 99 | 98 |
| **Ohio** | | |
| Glenn | 99 | 99 |
| Metzenbaum # | 97 | 97 |
| **Oklahoma** | | |
| Boren | 90 | 90 |
| *Nickles* | 97 | 97 |
| **Oregon** | | |
| *Hatfield* # | 98 | 98 |
| *Packwood* | 98 | 98 |
| **Pennsylvania** | | |
| Wofford | 97 | 97 |
| *Specter* | 96 | 96 |
| **Rhode Island** | | |
| Pell | 93 | 94 |
| *Chafee* | 98 | 98 |
| **South Carolina** | | |
| Hollings | 100 | 100 |
| *Thurmond* | 100 | 100 |
| **South Dakota** | | |
| Daschle | 100 | 100 |
| *Pressler* | 100 | 100 |
| **Tennessee** | | |
| Gore | 56 | 57 |
| Sasser | 99 | 99 |
| **Texas** | | |
| Bentsen | 92 | 92 |
| *Gramm* | 94 | 94 |
| **Utah** | | |
| *Garn* | 92 | 92 |
| *Hatch* # | 93 | 92 |
| **Vermont** | | |
| Leahy | 94 | 94 |
| *Jeffords* | 93 | 93 |
| **Virginia** | | |
| Robb | 100 | 100 |
| *Warner* | 96 | 95 |
| **Washington** | | |
| Adams | 99 | 98 |
| *Gorton* | 98 | 98 |
| **West Virginia** | | |
| Byrd | 99 | 99 |
| Rockefeller | 98 | 98 |
| **Wisconsin** | | |
| Kohl † | 100 | 100 |
| *Kasten* | 91 | 91 |
| **Wyoming** | | |
| *Simpson* | 98 | 98 |
| *Wallop* | 94 | 94 |

# Voting Participation: Senate

**1. Voting Participation, 1992.** Percentage of 270 recorded votes in 1992 on which a senator voted "yea" or "nay."

**2. Voting Participation, 1992.** Percentage of 265 recorded votes in 1992 on which a senator voted "yea" or "nay." In this version of the study, votes to instruct the sergeant at arms to request the attendance of absent senators are not included.

*NOTE: Scores are rounded to nearest percentage, except that no scores are rounded up to 100 percent. Members with a 100 percent score participated in all recorded votes for which they were eligible.*

[1] *Jocelyn Birch Burdick, D-N.D., was sworn in Sept. 16, 1992, to succeed her husband, Quentin N. Burdick, D, who died Sept. 8, 1992. Quentin N. Burdick was eligible for 189 votes in 1992, 186 not including sergeant at arms votes. His participation score on both measures was 78 percent. Jocelyn Birch Burdick was eligible for 63 votes in 1992, 62 not including sergeant at arms votes.*

# Veto Cloud Loomed Large Over 1992 Floor Fights

*Bush's support bloc held together through most confrontations, but suffered defeats on cable TV, budget amendment*

Vote-counters in the House and Senate spend most of their time looking for the 50 percent-plus-one it takes to prevail on a floor amendment or on passage of a bill.

But as the Democrats who controlled both chambers set their sights on winning the White House in 1992, many of the key floor confrontations involved efforts to win a two-thirds majority to override a veto by President Bush, or the supermajority of 60 needed in the Senate to shut off a Republican-led filibuster.

Until the very end of the year, Bush and his allies among the minority GOP found a way to prevail on most of those confrontations. On such touchstone issues as abortion, family leave and campaign finance, Democratic sponsors occasionally mustered two-thirds support in one chamber only to fall short in the other. The president was able to keep a string of 35 successful vetoes alive until the last week of the 102nd Congress.

Then came the cable TV reregulation bill (S 12), which had bipartisan support despite Bush's opposition. He vetoed the bill, as promised, but on Oct. 3 the Senate voted 74-25 and the House voted 303-114 — the first time since Bush became president that Congress enacted a bill into law over his objections.

On one earlier occasion, Bush was poised to rally a supermajority to his side but was rebuffed by the Democratic leadership. The vote occurred on a proposed constitutional amendment to require a balanced federal budget, which requires a three-fifths majority in each chamber to be sent to the states for ratification. Although it appeared to have bipartisan support, 150 House Democrats ultimately stayed with their leaders. The 280-153 vote for the measure was nine short of the number required for adoption.

Following is a rundown of the key votes of 1992.

## KEY SENATE VOTES

### 1. School Choice

Despite talk of improving public schools with national goals, standards and testing, along with new "break the

---

## How CQ Picks Votes

Since 1945, Congressional Quarterly has selected a series of key votes on major issues of the year.

An issue is judged by the extent that it represents:
- A matter of major controversy.
- A matter of presidential or political power.
- A matter of potentially great impact on the nation and lives of Americans.

For each group of related votes on an issue, one key vote usually is chosen — one that, in the opinion of CQ editors, was most important in determining the outcome.

Charts showing how each member of Congress voted on these issues can be found as follows:

---

mold" schools, the 1992 debate over elementary and secondary education hinged on one inflammatory issue: school choice. It would have sent public funds to some private schools.

Although Congress traditionally has worked on a bipartisan basis to pass education legislation, the Democratic school improvement bill (S 2) became a political battleground this election year, with President Bush trying to assert his "education president" label and Democrats striving to prove otherwise. The school choice issue was the main point of friction.

Bush and Education Secretary Lamar Alexander argued for a year that all children should be able to vote with their feet, leaving bad schools for better schools, which would in turn spur schools to improve through the competition for students. But opponents said that using federal funds for private schools would undermine public schools and the students left in them.

Choice opponents won a decisive victory Jan. 23 when the Senate declined to support even the smallest demonstration program of private school choice.

After a generally partisan debate over the basic philosophy of public education, the Senate rejected a sharply scaled-back amendment to set up six demonstration projects in which federal school aid could be used to allow low-income students to attend the schools of their parents' choice. Despite the administration's backing, the amendment failed, 36-57 (R 33-6; D 3-51; ND 2-35; SD 1-16).

Offered by Sen. Orrin G. Hatch, R-Utah, the amendment proposed spending $30 million on the program, far less than the nationwide choice plan outlined in Bush's America 2000 program for elementary and secondary education. Hatch and other choice proponents had hoped that by limiting the amendment to a small demonstration program, Democratic senators might be willing to try it.

But Senate Democrats said from the outset that they would not allow the administration to get a foot in the "choice" door. Only three Democrats voted for Hatch's amendment: Bill Bradley, N.J., John B. Breaux, La., and Joseph I. Lieberman, Conn. Six of the Senate's 43 Republicans voted against it.

The Senate vote had larger consequences for school choice advocates. The lack of support for even the scaled-back Hatch proposal prompted House Education and Labor Chairman William D. Ford, D-Mich., to dump unilaterally a compromise school choice provision that he had previously agreed to in committee. Ford said that if the Senate bill did not have public money for private school choice, then the House would not either.

A House-Senate conference report on S 2 — minus any school choice language — eventually died in the Senate in the face of a Republican filibuster threat.

## 2. Nuclear Energy

Congress administered a political booster shot to the beleaguered nuclear power industry in 1992 by approving a streamlined federal licensing process that could make it easier to build new nuclear power plants.

The Senate was the first chamber to approve the new licensing rules, adopting them by voice vote after rejecting an alternative by Sen. Bob Graham, D-Fla., that was opposed by the industry.

The once-thriving U.S. nuclear industry has seen its fortunes wane in recent years. Highly publicized accidents at Three Mile Island, near Harrisburg, Pa., and at the former Soviet Union's Chernobyl nuclear plant have shaken public confidence in the safety of nuclear power. Nuclear power has sometimes proved costlier than anticipated, and experts are struggling to determine the best way to dispose of radioactive nuclear waste.

But there is still substantial congressional support for nuclear power, especially in light of the 1990 amendments to the Clean Air Act, which set new limits on air pollution from other power sources such as coal-fired plants.

Nuclear power advocates are seeking regulatory changes they say will advance the industry. Among them was licensing reform.

In the past, the Nuclear Regulatory Commission (NRC) used a two-step process that required applicants first to win a construction license, then an operation license.

But industry officials complained this system has been abused by nuclear critics to delay plant operations and drive up costs. Industry officials have sought a combined construction and operation license that would force regulators to rule on controversial issues up front — and presumably protect investment in a plant from eleventh-hour opposition.

The NRC in 1989 issued a rule to create such a combined license, but it has been challenged in court. While that case advanced, the administration and congressional supporters sought legislation to authorize the new one-step licensing process.

Senate Energy Committee Chairman J. Bennett Johnston, D-La., included the proposal in his committee's omnibus energy bill (S 2166), over the strong opposition of environmental groups. The new process generally would cut out a second full public hearing that was required before a plant was allowed to operate. Environmentalists and other critics argued that the change could increase the possibility of approving unsafe nuclear plants and undermine public confidence in the licensing system.

During floor debate on the energy bill in February, Graham challenged the licensing proposal and offered an alternative. His proposal also would have created a one-step licensing process, but with greater guarantees for a second public hearing if critics raised valid safety concerns or new information.

But Johnston undercut support for Graham's proposal by slightly modifying his original bill to include some additional guarantees of public participation. In the key vote, Johnston moved to table (and thus kill) Graham's proposal. He prevailed 52-43: R 31-11; D 21-32 (ND 9-27, SD 12-5).

Senators then adopted the revised Johnston language by voice vote.

The Senate vote paved the way for similar action in the House, where the nuclear industry traditionally has enjoyed solid support. The House passed identical licensing language, virtually ensuring victory for the proposal if the energy bill passed. The energy bill, with the new one-step licensing provisions, cleared Congress and was signed into law in October.

The licensing change has little practical effect for now, as no new plants are on order. But the change stands to increase investor confidence in nuclear plants and provides an important symbolic win for industry.

## 3. Budget Walls

Senate Democratic leaders were confident early in the year that they would mount an effective election-year challenge to President Bush by passing economic measures with a Democratic stamp and forcing Bush to veto them.

ROBERT T SAVIDGE

A key to that strategy was a bill to knock down the budget "walls" between defense and domestic appropriations, allowing a shift of defense savings into cash-short domestic programs. They calculated that while a Bush veto of such a bill was virtually certain, it would sharpen the differences between what they saw as their invest-in-America policy and Bush's outmoded Cold War priorities.

But like their House counterparts, Senate leaders failed to reckon on trouble in their ranks. Before they could confront Bush, they had to unite Senate Democrats to overcome strong GOP opposition, and in the end they could not do it.

When Senate leaders tried to stop a filibuster against the measure March 26, they were defeated by virtually unanimous Republican opposition combined with the same Democratic coalition that would undo House Democratic leaders' plans to pass a walls bill five days later — conservative defense and deficit hawks joined with moderate and liberal Democrats worried about losing hometown defense jobs.

The bill (S 2399), drawn up by Budget Committee Chairman Jim Sasser, D-Tenn., would have changed the terms of the 1990 budget agreement to allow defense savings to be used for purposes other than deficit reduction. Senate appropriators, limited by increasingly tight spending caps, wanted the extra money to help keep domestic programs even with inflation or give them a boost.

Proponents argued that the Soviet threat that had justified the level of defense spending agreed to in the 1990 budget deal no longer existed. The money, they said, should go to other needs. "Are we going to move decisively to invest a portion of our peace dividend?" asked Sasser.

"Or are we going to maintain Cold War policy and Cold War sacrifices after the Cold War is over?"

"What peace dividend?" retorted John C. Danforth, R-Mo., who noted that the current-year deficit was estimated to be as high as $400 billion or more. "How can we talk about an election-year gift to the American people when we're broke?"

Sasser argued that the bill would simply authorize a shift of money that could have been spent anyway from one spending category to another, with no net impact on the deficit.

But even fellow Democrats disputed him. "There's only one guaranteed result to a change in the budget deal, and that's to increase the deficit," said Senate Armed Services Committee Chairman Sam Nunn, D-Ga. "If we pass this amendment . . . the defense budget will become the equivalent of the House bank."

In the end, Senate Majority Leader George J. Mitchell, D-Maine, was unable to shut down a filibuster against the measure. Mitchell and Sasser came up 10 votes short of the 60 they needed to move the bill forward. The motion to invoke cloture (and thereby end the filibuster) was rejected, 50-48: R 3-40; D 47-8 (ND 35-3, SD 12-5).

## 4. Fetal Tissue Research

Of all the abortion-related issues the 102nd Congress grappled with, none hit as close to home as whether to lift the Bush administration's ban on research using tissue from aborted fetuses.

Abortion opponents, including Bush, supported the ban because they feared the research, if successful, could encourage women to have abortions. But that was by no means a universal view among those who opposed abortion. Even some of the Congress's strongest abortion foes — such as Sens. Strom Thurmond, R-S.C., and Mark O. Hatfield, R-Ore. — opposed the ban. They argued that it was wrong to refuse to fund research that scientists said had the potential to provide treatments or even cures for such ailments as diabetes, Parkinson's disease and Alzheimer's disease. And they hammered their message home by citing the plights of friends and relatives who were waiting for a miracle; people such as Thurmond's daughter, Julie, who has diabetes, and former Rep. Morris K. Udall, D-Ariz., whose Parkinson's disease forced his retirement.

By early 1992, it became clear to abortion foes who supported the ban that they needed to provide an alternative if they were to avert legislative defeat. That alternative, provided during Senate floor consideration in late March of legislation to reauthorize the National Institutes of Health (which contained language to overturn the ban), came in the form of an amendment offered by Rep. Orrin G. Hatch, R-Utah. Hatch's amendment would have allowed the research to go forward, but instead of using remains from elective abortions, it would have created a series of "banks" to collect tissue from miscarriages and tubal pregnancies. Hatch was backed by experts who said such remains could provide enough tissue to allow the research effort to proceed.

Advocates of unfettered fetal tissue research produced experts of their own who said that tissue from miscarriages and tubal pregnancies is often diseased and unusable for research, and that it was not possible to harvest tissue fast enough from such unplanned events as miscarriages. Their argument prevailed overwhelmingly in the Senate, which rejected Hatch's amendment March 31 on a vote of 23-77: R 20-23; D 3-54 (ND 1-39, SD 2-15).

But while opponents of the ban won the battle, the staunch abortion foes won the war. Bush created the tissue banks by executive order in May and vetoed the NIH bill (HR 2507) in June, and the House failed to override. The Senate in October tried to take up yet another NIH bill that would have required researchers first to seek samples from the tissue banks but, if tissue was not readily available, would then allow them to use samples from abortions. That bill died in an end-of-session filibuster.

## 5. Campaign Finance

Passing a campaign finance bill was nothing new for the Senate; it had done so in each of the previous two Congresses. But sending a bill to the White House, as the Senate did April 30, was a new experience for many. Only 10 of the senators who voted for the bill (S 3) had been in the chamber in 1974, when the last campaign finance overhaul was enacted.

The 1992 experience, however, was academic. A veto had been guaranteed since Day One.

The Senate had passed S 3 in May 1991. The only question in 1992 was whether House and Senate conferees would try to somehow bridge the chasms that separated the chambers' bills and the gulf separating the parties to produce a bill that the president might sign. In the end, they did not. Instead, Democrats in both chambers found common ground by letting each chamber write its own rules. But that plan left out Republican views, and President Bush vetoed the bill May 9.

The Democrats believe the way to reform the congressional system is to limit campaign spending. To accomplish this within the framework of the 1976 Supreme Court decision in *Buckley v. Valeo*, the bill would have provided federal funds to candidates who agreed to comply with the spending limits and other restrictions.

The bill would have established a complex formula for determining spending ceilings depending on state population. The highest would have been $8.9 million for a candidate from a large state with a contested primary and general election; the low, $636,500, for a candidate from a small state with a primary but no general election opponent.

Candidates who agreed to obey the limit would get benefits, including cut-rate postage and up to 20 percent of the spending cap in broadcast vouchers.

Most Republicans opposed the tenets of the bill. They believe spending limits would put challengers at a disadvantage, and they strongly objected to public funding.

One key Senate provision that changed significantly between 1991 and 1992 concerned contributions from political action committees (PACs).

The 1991 version of S 3 contained a prohibition on PAC participation in Senate campaigns. It was one provision that appealed to Republicans, who had grown tired of watching PAC contributions flow to the party that controlled Congress. Democrats went along with the proposal;

it was accepted without a vote or even much debate.

But in 1992, when it was evident that the bill would clear Congress, Senate Democrats looked to their conferees to quietly dilute the ban. While not as dependent on PAC money as their House counterparts, Democratic senators who felt they could do without the politically risky "special interest" money had already kicked the habit. The others apparently felt they could not do without it.

So, without fuss, the conference changed the Senate provision to allow some contributions, limiting them to $2,500 per PAC per election (half the current cap). PAC contributions could not total more than 20 percent of the limit for a particular state.

The Senate approved the conference report April 30 on a 58-42 vote, with two Republicans switching their votes from the previous year to oppose the bill because of the PAC provision. Three Democrats changed their positions to support the measure.

When the bill came back with a veto message, only one senator switched his vote: John McCain, R-Ariz., had voted for the conference report but supported the veto. The override on May 13 was 57-42: R 3-40; D 54-2 (ND 39-0; SD 15-2).

That was nine votes short of overriding the veto. "We'll be back again and again until we get it passed into law," vowed David L. Boren, D-Okla., chief Senate sponsor of the measure.

## 6. Ex-Soviet Aid

While support for U.S. aid to the former Soviet republics was stronger in the Senate than in the House, there was still a great deal of reluctance among Senators to help the former superpower. A number of senators felt strongly that the United States should use the opportunity to impose stringent conditions on any such assistance. They argued that U.S. tax-payers should not have been asked to send their money to nations that still posed a military threat or  acted in other ways contrary to U.S. interests.

But the administration and other proponents of the legislation countered that any conditions would slow the distribution of the urgently needed assistance and possibly undermine the reform governments that it was intended to help. These fledgling regimes, while not perfect, were described as far friendlier to the United States than any replacement regime would be if they failed.

Perhaps the biggest obstacle to Senate approval of aid was the continued presence of about 100,000 former Soviet troops in the Baltic states of Lithuania, Latvia and Estonia. While Russian President Boris N. Yeltsin said it was the intention of the Commonwealth of Independent States to remove the troops eventually, the gradual withdrawal was not fast enough for Baltic supporters in Congress. They argued that these countries had never been part of the Soviet Union and that the troops represented an occupation force. The Russians countered that they could not withdraw the troops more quickly because they lacked housing and jobs for the soldiers and because the country needed first to get its economy in order.

When the ex-Soviet aid package came to the Senate floor July 1, Dennis DeConcini, D-Ariz., and Larry Pressler, R-S.D., offered an amendment to prohibit the United States from giving economic aid to Russia until the president certified that Moscow was making "significant progress" in withdrawing forces from the Baltics.

Backers of the bill said the amendment, if approved, would nullify the commitment of aid to Russia because the president would not be able to make such a certification. Foreign Relations Committee Chairman Claiborne Pell, D-R.I., tried to modify the amendment by proposing a one-year delay in the certification requirement.

Pressler then made a motion to table (or kill) Pell's amendment for a grace period on the aid restriction. On this key vote, the motion was rejected 35-60: R 11-30; D 24-30 (ND 14-24, SD 10-6). Pell's amendment was then adopted by voice vote.

It was a turning point toward passage of aid with few strings attached. Most subsequent attempts to place conditions on the aid were blocked and the bill (S 2532) was subsequently passed by a vote of 76-20.

## 7. Unemployment Compensation

For months, the House and the Senate had tried to persuade President Bush to extend emergency unemployment benefits for the long-term jobless. Existing authorization of extended benefits was due to expire July 4, 1992, and people exhausting state benefits after that date would not be eligible for federal benefits.

**Bentsen**

President Bush repeatedly complained about the price of continuing the emergency program, which had cost $2.7 billion. But when the national unemployment rate leaped three-tenths of a percent in June — to 7.8 percent, the highest rate in eight years — Bush softened his opposition considerably. Congress promptly moved on a $5.5 billion bill (HR 5260 — PL 102-318) extending benefits for the long-term jobless.

It may have been the final unemployment bill Congress would have to consider: Besides the emergency benefits, HR 5260 included a permanent change in the compensation system that was expected to make further extension bills unnecessary.

Because the usual mechanism releasing extended unemployment compensation was relatively restrictive, Congress had stepped in twice during the past year to override the regular extension system with emergency benefits. Under the regular system, jobless workers became eligible for state-federal extended benefits after they used up 26 weeks of state benefits, but only when statewide unemployment rates reached a certain trigger level. The bill changed the state-federal trigger, allowing the extended benefits to flow more quickly without intervention by Congress.

When the June unemployment rate was announced July 2, Bush's first reaction was that it was "not good news" but that he might still veto an unemployment bill if it cost too much. By the end of the day, however, Bush referred to HR 5260 as "an important safeguard for workers who still can't find jobs as the economy continues to grow."

The House-Senate conference report to HR 5260 had been written largely by Senate Finance Chairman Lloyd Bentsen, D-Texas, and represented a compromise between

Bush and the original, $5.8 billion House version.

Bentsen's bill also contained fewer permanent changes to the unemployment system. Bentsen's version provided unemployed workers in 15 states with 26 extra weeks of benefits and workers in all other states and the District of Columbia with 20 extra weeks until March 6, 1993. Those benefits went into effect when workers exhausted their state compensation without finding a job.

The change in the trigger for non-emergency extended benefits also went into effect: It would kick in March 7, 1993, the day after the emergency program expired.

The permanent change in the unemployment system was something Bush had vowed that he would not accept, but the higher unemployment numbers forced him to cave. The Senate on July 2 promptly cleared the conference report, 93-3 (R 37-3; D 56-0; ND 40-0; SD 16-0). Bush signed the bill the next day.

## 8. Strategic Defense Initiative

The Senate ratified the basic stand it had taken in 1991, funding a version of the Strategic Defense Initiative (SDI) that was aimed at deploying a ground-based, anti-missile defense system. However, with the budget tight and the Soviet threat defunct, a majority of senators voted to rein in SDI spending.

On Aug. 7, the Senate in effect supported an amendment that would have sliced $1 billion in SDI funding from the defense authorization bill (S 3114). The key vote was on a motion to table (and thus kill) the amendment. The motion failed 43-49: R 34-5; D 9-44 (ND 4-33, SD 5-11).

The strong show of sentiment to reduce SDI funding even below the $4.3 billion proposed by the Armed Services Committee blocked action on the overall defense bill for more than a month. SDI opponents refused to back down; SDI supporters, backed by a veto threat from President Bush, refused to permit the Senate to proceed to the next procedural step — a vote on the amendment to cut the funding.

Senate leaders warned that the stalemate could kill the entire defense measure, leaving the Pentagon to rely on a stopgap appropriations bill. On Sept. 17, the Senate backed away from the SDI confrontation, settling on a $3.8 billion SDI research compromise engineered by Armed Services Committee Chairman Sam Nunn, D-Ga. The final version of the bill (HR 5006 — PL 102-484), as crafted by a House-Senate conference committee, included $4.05 billion for SDI. The compromise defense appropriations bill (HR 5504) incorporated the $3.8 billion compromise on SDI funding.

The Aug. 7 vote to slash SDI may have marked the start of a third phase in SDI's contentious political history in the Senate.

President Ronald Reagan launched the program in 1983, offering it as a revolutionary program to liberate the nation from the Soviet nuclear missile threat. In the first phase of the SDI debate, through 1986, Congress routinely reduced the SDI budget from Reagan's request but rejected proposals for deeper cuts that would have restricted the program to laboratory research.

In the second phase, between 1987 and 1992, the SDI debate turned on the role of space-based weapons. Republican conservatives, led by Sen. Malcolm Wallop, R-Wyo., sought an extensive system of space-based interceptors that could destroy Soviet missiles in the first few minutes of flight, before they could swamp the defense with multiple warheads and swarms of decoys. But that goal was challenged as provocative and technically questionable by centrist Democrats, including Nunn and House Armed Services Committee Chairman Les Aspin, Wis.

Nunn and Aspin instead promoted a more modest anti-missile defense intended to protect U.S. territory, overseas forces and allies against "limited" attacks by a Third World country or by a renegade military unit.

In a series of votes between 1987 and 1991, Congress essentially endorsed the Nunn-Aspin approach: It repeatedly forced unwilling Republican administrations to respect the prohibition on space-based weapons tests included in the 1972 U.S.-Soviet treaty limiting anti-ballistic missile defenses. And in 1991, the Senate recast Bush's SDI program to focus on near-term, ground-based defenses and to defer the space-based weapons.

In 1992, liberal Democrats still opposed to such a limited defense conceded that they had lost that fight. So when the Senate took up the Armed Services Committee's $4.3 billion recommendation for SDI — compared with the the $5.4 billion requested by Bush — Jim Sasser, D-Tenn., and Dale Bumpers, D-Ark., proposed the $1 billion cut to $3.3 billion.

## 9. Nuclear Test Ban

Symbolically closing the books on the Cold War, the Senate voted to end nuclear weapons testing. The more significant of two votes on the subject came Sept. 18, when the Senate approved, 55-40, an amendment to the fiscal 1993 defense authorization bill (HR 5006) that would have imposed a nine-month halt to nuclear testing, to be followed by a permanent test ban after the end of fiscal 1996.

For four decades, a test ban was largely a distant dream of liberal activists. Every president from Dwight D. Eisenhower to Ronald Reagan proclaimed an eventual end to testing as a national goal, but only Jimmy Carter accorded the goal more than lip service.

In fiscal 1986 through 1988, the House annually had approved an amendment to the defense authorization bill that would have barred tests of nuclear weapons with an explosive punch greater than 1,000 tons of TNT. But those votes were largely symbolic, taken on the assumption the Senate would reject any significant nuclear test limitations.

And, indeed, so long as the Soviet nuclear threat was intact, a majority of senators seemed to accept the contention of Pentagon and Energy Department nuclear weapons specialists: that continuous testing was required to check on the safety and reliability of weapons already in the U.S. stockpile.

But with the disintegration of the Soviet Union — and with Russian President Boris N. Yeltsin observing a self-imposed nuclear test moratorium — test ban proponents this year stepped up their efforts to terminate the U.S. testing program.

For the first time, they were supported by Senate Armed Services Committee Chairman Sam Nunn, D-Ga., who echoed what had long been one of the liberals' arguments: That a halt to testing might give Washington more

diplomatic leverage to dissuade other countries from trying to develop nuclear weapons.

On Aug. 3, the Senate approved 68-26 an amendment by Mark O. Hatfield, R-Ore., to the fiscal 1993 energy and water appropriations bill (HR 5373) to impose a nine-month testing halt followed in 1996 by a permanent ban. But that vote overstated Senate support for the proposal because several opponents voted for the amendment for tactical reasons.

On Sept. 18, Hatfield offered a similar amendment to the defense authorization bill. It was approved 55-40: R 13-29; D 42-11 (ND 35-3; SD 7-8).

In the end, a halt to nuclear testing was enacted as part of the energy and water spending bill, and the sensitive provision then was dropped from the defense bill.

**Hatfield**

Despite the administration's vocal opposition to the test ban, President Bush signed the energy and water measure (PL 102-377), which also included funds for the politically appealing superconducting super collider, an atom smasher being built in Texas that was eagerly sought by the administration.

## 10. Family and Medical Leave

After 32 vetoes by President Bush, the Senate finally had the votes needed to override his objections. With two votes more than necessary, the Senate on Sept. 24 overrode the president's veto of the Family and Medical Leave Act (S 5), a bill to require large companies to grant unpaid leave to employees for family and medical emergencies. It was the first time in four years the Senate had mustered a two-thirds override majority.

Although the House later sustained the family leave veto, the Senate vote presaged the decline of Bush's power in Congress. And it showed the bipartisan political appeal of an issue that directly targeted middle-age, middle-class families. The measure would have granted unpaid leave of up to 12 weeks to workers for the birth or adoption of a child or the illness of a close family member. Democrats and a number of Republicans generally supported it because of this "pro-family" bent.

And while most Republicans opposed the bill because of its mandates on business, the override vote demonstrated the frustration of many within GOP ranks over Bush's refusal to negotiate a compromise with Democrats.

Just one year earlier, the Senate had approved with 65 votes — two short of what it took to override a veto — a compromise bill worked out by Democrat Christopher J. Dodd of Connecticut and Republican Christopher S. Bond of Missouri. At that time, two Democratic senators were off campaigning for president, and one was out sick. They all said they supported the bill, however, so it appeared that they would prevail if the president maintained his veto stance.

For the next year, Dodd and Bond tried to pull the administration on board. Seeking to take business interests into account, they agreed to exempt the highest-paid 10 percent of an employer's work force and to restrict eligibility for leave to employees who had worked at least 25 hours a week for the previous 12 months.

As it was, the bill would apply only to those businesses with more than 50 workers, exempting more than 95 percent of all employers (the largest 5 percent of businesses employ 60 percent of all workers).

But White House officials refused to budge. "They were not willing to deal," Bond complained. As the election neared, and as Democratic nominee Bill Clinton stepped up his campaign references to the family leave bill, Senate Democrats decided to make their push on the eve of the Republican convention in August. But GOP leaders threatened to block Dodd's effort to force a roll call vote. Instead, senators adopted the House-Senate conference report by voice vote, delaying the showdown until after the promised veto.

And as promised, Bush vetoed the bill Sept. 22, sending it back to Capitol Hill. Although Dodd and Bond appeared to have the votes, they worried about Bush peeling away important conservatives, such as Daniel R. Coats, R-Ind., who had come on board in support of a "family values" bill.

But unlike nine previous Senate override votes, Bush could not sway the one or two votes he needed. With 99 senators voting on Sept. 24, the family leave sponsors prevailed, 68-31: R 14-28; D 54-3 (ND 40-0, SD 14-3).

As expected, three senators who were absent for the 1991 vote voted to override: Tom Harkin, D-Iowa, Bob Kerrey, D-Neb., and David Pryor, D-Ark. The lone Republican to switch over to the president's side — Ted Stevens of Alaska — was offset by a Democratic switch, David L. Boren of Oklahoma.

The House on Sept. 30 voted to sustain the veto, 258-169, killing the bill for the year. In that chamber, Republican opponents were able to convince conservative Democrats that the measure would burden businesses with unnecessary mandates.

In 1993, however, the bill is likely to become law. President-elect Bill Clinton has promised to sign a family leave bill during his first 100 days in office. Still to be determined is whether Congress will send him the same bill sent to Bush, or whether emboldened Democrats will try to expand the bill's reach.

## 11. Taxes/Urban Aid

It was the second tax bill of the year — and the second one that appeared predestined for a veto. In came Senate Majority Leader Bob Dole, R-Kan., late on Sept. 25 with an amendment to shed several tax increases in the $32 billion bill (HR 11) in hopes of pleasing President Bush and maybe saving the measure.

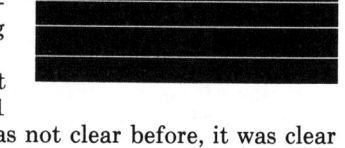

But Dole's amendment failed 34-59: R 31-8; D 3-51 (ND 1-38, SD 2-13). If it was not clear before, it was clear then that the bill was doomed.

The demise of the Dole amendment offers a microcosmic glimpse into why Congress and Bush — despite mutual agreement about the need to stimulate the economy and to give tax incentives to blighted inner cities — could not overcome deep divisions that killed this bill and stunted tax policy-making throughout much of the last four years.

Dole's amendment would have eliminated two tax raising provisions — a limit on itemized deductions and a phaseout of the personal exemption for upper-income taxpayers — that the White House had said it opposed.

To offset the $7.7 billion revenue loss caused by removing the provisions, the amendment also would have scaled

back assistance for inner cities, removed a tax break for contributions to individual retirement accounts (IRAs) and shortened to 12 months from 15 months the extension provided for a dozen expiring tax provisions.

The basic problem that Dole was trying to address was one that lay below the surface as the bill progressed through Congress throughout the late summer and early fall.

After trying to tag Bill Clinton as a tax-and-spender because of his support for a slew of mostly minor revenue provisions during his tenure as Arkansas governor, Bush was refusing to open himself to the same charge by supporting anything resembling a tax increase. So Dole was trying to get the two most obvious tax increases out of the bill. "The president of the United States is not going to sign a tax increase 30 days before the election," he told the Senate.

But in cutting the tax increases, Dole also had to cut back on the tax breaks in the bill. And Senate Finance Committee Chairman Lloyd Bentsen, D-Texas, the architect of the IRA provisions, did not appreciate that — Bentsen's opinion carried a lot of weight among fellow Democrats. The vote against Dole's amendment went largely along party lines.

Dole's amendment had an additional problem. It would have lowered from 125 to 30 the number of enterprise zones created by the bill, severely cutting back on the tax assistance for inner cities that had been the original justification for doing the bill.

In short, the Senate discovered that it was impossible to do all it wanted in the bill without tax increases. But it also proved impossible to win Bush's support for a bill with new taxes, regardless of what else it contained. With the failure of the Dole amendment, it became clear there was no overcoming that basic impediment.

## 12. Abortion Counseling

By the time the Senate finally took its first roll call vote on a bill to overturn the "gag rule" prohibiting abortion counseling in federally funded family-planning clinics, the ultimate fate of the bill was no longer in doubt. Repeated votes in the House had made clear that, while a majority of members opposed the counseling ban, a two-thirds supermajority was not attainable to override a certain Bush veto.

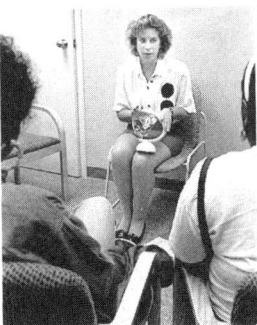
R. MICHAEL JENKINS

Still, there was more than the usual amount of interest when the Senate on Oct. 1 cast its override vote on a bill (S 323) to overturn the ban and reauthorize the federal family-planning program. It was the first time the Senate had taken a roll call vote on the measure. Both the original bill, approved in July 1991, and the conference report on the measure, approved Sept. 14, had passed on voice votes. Congress watchers also were interested in whether the Senate would, for only the second time in the Bush presidency, muster the two-thirds override margin. (The first time came only a week earlier, when the chamber voted to override Bush's veto of a bill to require employers to provide unpaid family and medical leave.)

It appeared that the Senate would have little difficulty attaining the two-thirds majority to override. Ever since abortion became a major congressional issue in the 1970s, the Senate had traditionally been more sympathetic to abortion rights forces, while the House had generally leaned towards abortion foes. But the Supreme Court's 1989 decision in *Webster v. Reproductive Health Services*, which gave states some leeway in restricting abortions, rejuvenated abortion rights forces in both chambers. As a result, the House shifted to a more abortion rights stance and the Senate moved even further into that camp.

But supporters of the bill to overturn the gag rule remained worried. Bush aides had been amazingly successful over the previous four years in getting Senate Republicans to stand by the president even when they did not agree with his veto. And it was not entirely clear how many Democrats with mixed abortion voting records would go for the override.

But the Senate vote on Oct. 1 left few doubts about where senators stood. The vote was 73-26: R 20-23; D 53-3 (ND 40-0, SD 13-3) — seven more than needed to override. A day later, however, the House surprised no one when members voted to sustain Bush's veto.

## 13. Foreign Aid

After President Bush and Israeli Prime Minister Yitzhak Rabin agreed in August on a package of loan guarantees for Jerusalem, Senate approval of the fiscal 1993 foreign aid appropriations bill (HR 5368 — PL 102-391 — H Rept 102-585) was virtually assured.

The Senate has long been a wellspring of support for Israel, and the authorization of the five-year program of loan guarantees — on top of the $3 billion usually provided Israel in the foreign aid bill — made the measure palatable for senators even during an election year focused on domestic concerns.

In the key vote Oct. 1, the Senate passed the $26.5 billion foreign aid appropriations bill, 87-12: R 35-8; D 52-4 (ND 39-1, SD 13-3).

It marked the first time in two years that the Senate had approved an aid bill. The fiscal 1992 measure became embroiled in a bitter battle between the Bush administration and Israeli government over loan guarantees.

Despite the chronic unpopularity of foreign aid, there were only a few attempts to cut the funding. Sen. Jesse Helms, R-N.C., failed in a bid to cut funding by 10 percent.

Nor was there opposition to the loan guarantees or to the bill's other major initiative, $12.3 billion in new financing for the International Monetary Fund.

But the measure addressed a host of issues arising from the breakup of the former Soviet Union and the bitter ethnic conflicts exploding in many parts of the world.

The legislation put the Senate squarely on the side of Bosnia-Herzegovina in the Yugoslav civil war by authorizing the president to provide up to $50 million in U.S. defense equipment for the country. Sen. Joseph R. Biden Jr., D-Del., who sponsored the amendment, said that 100,000 Bosnians might be "frozen while under Serbian seige" during the coming winter if Western nations ignored their plight. "Are we truly to adjourn, having done nothing?" he asked his colleagues.

The measure did not require the president to take action, and the United Nations would have to lift its arms embargo on former Yugoslavia for any arms to be provided.

Still, Bush administration officials expressed concern that the introduction of more weapons into the region would only fuel the Yugoslav conflict, although they did not actively oppose Biden's amendment.

The legislation also earmarked $55 million in refugee aid and other assistance for victims of the fighting in former Yugoslavia.

Although the Senate fully funded the Bush administration request for $417 million in aid for the former Soviet Union, it imposed restrictions on the assistance program. The measure stipulated that no U.S. aid could be provided to Russia — except for humanitarian assistance — unless Moscow either removed its troops from the three Baltic States or negotiated an agreement for withrawing its forces.

The bill also barred most assistance to Russia unless the president certified that Moscow had ceased military exports to Iran. The amendment, offered by Helms, came in response to reports that Russia had sold Iran submarines over the objections of the United States. The restrictions were relaxed significantly by House-Senate conferees in the final version of the bill.

## 14. Cable Reregulation

Never had the Bush administration worked so hard to whip up support to sustain a veto — only to get whipped so badly.

When the Senate on Oct. 5 voted to override President Bush's veto of a bill to reregulate the cable television industry, followed by similar House action hours later, the president lost his first veto confrontation with Congress after 35 successes. The Senate vote was 74-25, more than the two-thirds majority needed to override the veto; R 24-18; D 50-7 (ND 36-4, SD 14-3).

By casting the showdown as a critical test of presidential loyalty, White House advisers misjudged more than Bush's slumping popularity. They also misread members' awareness of the American public's desire for inexpensive television viewing.

Bush viewed the legislation as an unfair encroachment on the business prerogatives of a successful private industry. He also agreed with cable industry arguments that the bill had become laden with special-interest provisions to help broadcasters and the home satellite-dish industry, and that those provisions would make cable rates rise, not fall.

But lawmakers from both parties saw cable television as an unregulated monopoly, and their votes responded to heavy lobbying by broadcasters and consumer groups who complained of a 61 percent average increase in cable rates since the industry was deregulated in 1987.

The legislation (S 12 — PL 102-385) required the Federal Communications Commission to regulate rates for the lowest-priced package of programming subscribed to by the nation's 56 million cable viewers. It also took steps to help competitors such as home satellite-dish programmers compete with the $20 billion cable industry.

Bush, his Chief of Staff James A. Baker III and Senate Republican leader Bob Dole of Kansas worked hard to persuade enough senators to abandon their support for the legislation. The Senate had adopted the conference report Sept. 22 on a 74-25 vote.

In fact, the administration came close to winning the 34 senators needed to sustain the veto, falling just one or two votes short at one point. When it became apparent that the votes could not be mustered, senators who agreed to switch were released from their commitments. As a result,

the override vote was unchanged from the Sept. 22 vote on the conference report.

That the Democratic-controlled Congress denied Bush a perfect veto record — a rarity in modern times — took on heightened importance at a time when the president was struggling to gain ground against Democratic presidential challenger Bill Clinton.

"On this particular bill, [Bush] had very little to trade with, other than loyalty to the party and loyalty to him. And he didn't get it," said James A. Thurber, director of the Center for Congressional and Presidential Studies at American University.

## 15. Western Water Bill

The usually solid wall of unanimity among Western senators cracked a bit in the 102nd Congress under the powerful force of water.

In the waning days of the session, Congress approved, and President Bush signed, a huge omnibus water bill (HR 429 — PL 102-575) that had provisions affecting every Western state. The 40-title bill garnered interest from every Western quarter but, in the end, the battle came down to one title.

Title 34, long pushed by Sen. Bill Bradley, D-N.J., sought to revamp the operations of the Central Valley Project (CVP) in California, the federal government's largest irrigation and power project. Environmentalists and urban interests maintained that some way had to be found to reallocate the CVP's water, 85 percent of which was being sold at heavily discounted rates to 23,000 farming operations.

The CVP had always been blamed for environmental problems: changed stream flows, declining salmon populations and diminishing wildfowl habitat. Then a six-year drought in California started to pinch urban families and businesses who complained of being subject to rationing and high rates while nearby farmers got water for much less.

Along with George Miller, D-Calif., chairman of the House Interior and Insular Affairs Committee, and J. Bennett Johnston, D-La., chairman of the Senate Energy and Natural Resources Committee, Bradley fashioned a CVP title that would transfer more water to fish and wildlife purposes; allow urban users to buy project water from willing sellers; and shorten long-term water contracts to enhance flexibility in water distribution.

But Bradley had an implacable opponent on the measure: California Republican John Seymour, who argued that Bradley's proposal would hurt his supporters among the state's powerful farming interests.

In most situations, Seymour could have counted on aid from his fellow Western conservatives, but this time he received scant help. For example, Jake Garn, the retiring Republican from Utah, was consumed with getting the long-sought authorization to complete the massive Central Utah Irrigation Project, a measure also in the bill. Garn

was not about to let a lone senator kill off the entire bill, and he said so on a number of occasions.

Seymour's main ally was Republican Gov. Pete Wilson, who once held Seymour's seat and who as governor had appointed Seymour as his replacement in the Senate.

When the conference report came to the Senate floor Oct. 8, Seymour fought with all the dilatory weapons afforded him by the Senate.

He helped Alfonse M. D'Amato, R-N.Y., who mounted an all-night filibuster on another, unrelated bill. And he insisted that the clerk read the entire 396-page bill, a procedure that took hours of precious Senate time in the closing days of the session.

But again Seymour got little support from his Western brethren. Even as the bill was making its way to the floor, word got out that Garn and other senators had met with White House Chief of Staff James A. Baker III to lobby against a veto.

**D'Amato**

When it became clear that he did not have the votes to prevent Senate leaders from invoking cloture, Seymour caved. He agreed to a deal in which the Senate would approve a symbolic bill that incorporated the California farm community's wish list. But because that bill moved on the next-to-last day of the session, it died when the House failed to act.

The Senate, meanwhile, finally adopted the conference report on HR 429 on Oct. 8. The vote was 83-8: R 30-8; D 53-0 (ND 38-0, SD 15-0). Only two other Westerners joined Seymour in opposing the bill: Republicans Hank Brown of Colorado and Larry E. Craig of Idaho.

President Bush signed the measure Oct. 30 in the midst of his unsuccessful campaign for re-election. The move was widely seen as an attempt to win favor in Utah and other Western states, even at the sacrifice of California.

## KEY HOUSE VOTES

### 1. Taxes

When the House passed the first tax bill of the year (HR 4210) on Feb. 27, it was more of an election-year manifesto for the Democratic Party than serious legislation. Even so, party leaders clearly underestimated the difficulty they would have persuading their own rank and file to go along with a measure that promised higher taxes on the rich to finance a tax cut for the middle class.

Finding themselves short of a majority hours before the scheduled vote, House Democratic leaders resorted to a hard-nosed appeal, arguing that their party had made tax cuts for the middle class its rallying cry and could not turn back.

It worked — but just barely. A Democratic substitute amendment by Ways and Means Chairman Dan Rostenkowski, Ill., carried 221-210: R 1-164; D 219-46 (ND 156-27, SD 63-19); I 1-0. The bill (HR 4210) subsequently passed 221-209.

Many members said the bill was inadequate, either because the tax cut was too meager, or because it was the wrong policy in an era of massive deficits. Another contingent of Democrats feared voting for the higher taxes on upper-income earners that their leaders contended would bring greater fairness to the tax code, but which would

have kicked in for individuals with taxable incomes as low as $85,000.

Democrats were divided from the start about whether the central feature of their bill should have been middle-class tax relief or help for the economy. Trying to accomplish both, Rostenkowski included provisions to help the real estate industry and other sectors of the economy.

But Democratic leaders, in particular Majority Leader Richard A. Gephardt, Mo., saw the vote and the bill as an opportunity to put President Bush in a political bind: They hoped he would have to choose between opposing the middle-class tax cut or raising taxes — something he vowed never to repeat after signing a tax increase in 1990.

In a heated speech during floor debate on the bill, Gephardt said, "The question in this bill is: Where does the money go? Who do you stand for? Who do you fight for?"

Before the vote, the White House and House Republicans did their best to parry any political advantage for the Democrats, arguing that the bill was a straightforward tax increase that would do little to help the economy and would probably even hurt it. In solidarity with Bush, every House Republican but one voted against the Democratic package.

The Democrat's slim victory underscored the feeling that the bill was doomed to result in an election-year standoff with Bush, who was promising to veto any bill raising taxes. A month later, presented with the final version of the tax bill, Bush did just as he promised. And the Democrats' manifesto, endorsing higher taxes on the rich to pay for lower taxes on the middle class, was done for the year.

### 2. House Bank Overdrafts

On the surface, the House was in unanimous agreement: It voted 426-0 in the early morning hours of March 13 to reveal the names of all who overdrew their House bank accounts.

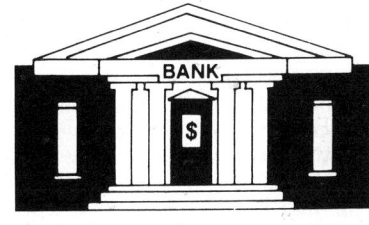

In fact, members could not have been more divided over an issue that paralyzed the House for weeks, embarrassed hundreds of members and several Cabinet members, increased public disdain for Congress, gave the executive branch unprecedented access to intimate details of members' personal finances, prompted the House to reform its internal operations and eventually helped end the careers of many members from both parties.

The issue was divisive from its inception on Sept. 18, 1991, when the General Accounting Office revealed that despite past reform attempts, the members-only House bank allowed members to routinely overdraw their checking accounts.

Activist Republicans, especially a group of freshmen known as the Gang of Seven, drove the process from the beginning. Both parties' leaders tried to end the matter by scolding members for continuing to overdraw their accounts. But the activists said that was not enough, and in October successfully pushed for the bank to be closed and for the Committee on Standards of Official Conduct to open an ethics inquiry.

After a five-month investigation, the ethics committee on March 5 proposed revealing the names of only the 24

worst offenders — those the panel decided had "abused their banking privileges" by routinely overdrawing their accounts by significant amounts during 3¼ years studied by the panel.

Again the Republicans, who with fewer members in office had less to lose, balked. Under the committee's proposal, more than 300 members who overdrew their accounts, including some with hundreds of overdrafts, could have remained anonymous. Although a bipartisan subcommittee of the ethics panel had approved the proposal unanimously, four GOP members of the full committee dissented, calling the proposal a whitewash.

Democratic leaders tried to rally their members behind the committee's proposal as the week of March 9 opened. They received no help from Republican Leader Robert H. Michel, Ill., who after a GOP leadership meeting March 10 broke his silence to endorse "full disclosure" — publicizing the names and overdraft totals of each current and former member who overdrew. President Bush backed full disclosure March 11.

Rank and file Democrats quickly began distancing themselves from the ethics committee's proposal. At a whip organization meeting March 12, Speaker Thomas S. Foley, D-Wash., was pummeled by members who either favored full disclosure or saw the fight as a sure loser. The leadership relented.

Closed-door meetings to work out the details and explain the ramifications of full disclosure to members went into the evening. The final debate did not begin until 8:25 p.m., when Sergeant at Arms Jack Russ, who ran the House bank and cashed some of his own bad checks there, resigned.

There was no longer any question what would happen, although members made speeches into the night about what they were doing. The ethics committee proposal to name the abusers (H Res 393) was taken up first, and it was approved 391-36 at 11 p.m., assuring those with fewer overdrafts that the most serious cases would be spotlighted. The full disclosure resolution (H Res 396) was not approved until 1:15 a.m. the next day.

Throughout the night, the mood was somber. "As of today," ethics member Fred Grandy, R-Iowa, told his colleagues, "your talk show hosts have a topic; as of today, your opponent has an issue and your constituents have a reason to support term limitations." Members opposed to full disclosure voiced doubts, but voted yes anyway. "I hope it will be clear to the country that we are not hiding any information, embarrassing as it may be, misleading as it may be, in many cases unjust to members as it may be; we are going to release it," Foley said.

**Grandy**

After an arduous appeals process, the committee on April 1 cited 17 current and five former members for abusing their banking privileges, and on April 16 revealed the names of 252 current members and 51 former members who overdrew their accounts. A week after all the names came out, the Justice Department's special counsel investigating the scandal for criminal wrongdoing, Malcolm R. Wilkey, subpoenaed the bank's records, prompting another weeklong fight over how much to disclose. Again, the Republicans won under the aegis of full disclosure, 347-64, on April 29.

In September, Wilkey resuscitated the issue for fall campaigns when he began sending members letters telling them

their records were no longer under scrutiny. Controversy over checks helped account for perhaps a third of the 96 members who retired or were denied re-election this year.

On. Dec. 16, Wilkey issued a report calling for a criminal investigation of a few unspecified members and former members, and the Justice Department announced that it had opened such an inquiry.

## 3. Budget Walls

After President Bush challenged Congress to pass his economic agenda in a combative State of the Union address Jan. 28, House Democratic leaders decided to try to retake the political momentum by confronting him over a series of economic issues. In addition to a tax bill and a budget resolution that would spell out their — not his — priorities, leaders planned to move quickly to knock down the budget "walls" that prohibited shifting defense money to domestic spending programs.

The 1990 budget summit agreement walled off defense, domestic and international appropriations into separate, inviolable categories. While nothing barred Congress from further reducing defense, the savings could only be used for deficit reduction, a psychological barrier that White House negotiators hoped would safeguard defense funds from a Congress that might want to raid defense for domestic projects.

But the disintegration of the Soviet Union and the collapse of the once-potent Soviet military strengthened a conviction among Democratic leaders that the priorities set by the 1990 summit were obsolete. Democratic strategists believed that shifting defense funds to cash-short domestic programs would draw a clear distinction between Democrats and Republicans during the presidential election year — demonstrating that Democrats were committed to investing in critical home-front programs, while the Bush White House and congressional Republicans were still locked in outmoded Cold War thinking. Bush had threatened to veto any bill to knock down the walls, but Democratic leaders figured a veto would draw the political distinctions that much more sharply.

But the leadership failed to reckon on dissension in the ranks. Trouble surfaced early when conservative Democrats on the House Budget Committee forced the panel to produce two budgets: a walls-down, leadership budget that devoted most defense savings to domestic programs; and a walls-up, conservative budget that would use any defense cuts for deficit reduction. The leadership budget would prevail only if the House passed a separate bill to knock down the walls.

Worried about support among their rank and file, Democratic leaders repeatedly postponed a scheduled vote on a bill (HR 3732), drawn up by Government Operations Committee Chairman John Conyers Jr., D-Mich., to eliminate the budget walls. When they finally brought the bill to a vote, members rejected Conyers overwhelmingly, 187-238: R 0-162; D 186-76 (ND 151-28, SD 35-48); I 1-0.

**Conyers**

The anatomy of the Democratic coalition against the walls bill was a study in strange bedfellows. On one side were mostly conservative deficit hawks worried about budget discipline and defense hawks concerned about opening the floodgates between defense and

domestic spending categories. On the other were members, including moderates and liberals, who worried that a cut in defense funds would mean a loss of hometown defense jobs.

The vote was one of several occasions during the year when House Democratic leaders miscalculated the strength of conservative "boll weevil" Democrats, led by Charles W. Stenholm of Texas. On this and other key issues, conservative Democrats were able to briefly form a working majority with unified House Republicans to push the House in a more fiscally conservative direction than Democratic leaders wanted it to go.

## 4. RTC Financing

Three years into the government's cleanup of hundreds of failed savings and loan institutions, Congress allowed the salvage operation to grind to a halt in April 1992.

Leary of angry voters and worried about the ever-rising cost, the House overwhelmingly refused to pump any more taxpayer money into the effort — though it was obvious to all that the refusal was nothing more than a costly postponement.

Multiple factors contributed to the House decision — including partisanship, gamesmanship and outright fear. From the beginnings of the thrift bailout in 1989 through the fall of 1991, Congress had pumped $80 billion into the Resolution Trust Corporation (RTC). More than half of that sum had come from taxpayers; a bit over $30 billion was ponied up by the thrift industry itself.

In November 1991, the first $80 billion was gone and hundreds of dead and dying thrifts remained to be shut down. So Congress reluctantly voted to give the RTC an additional $25 billion, with the stipulation that any amount that remained unspent on April 1, 1992, would revert to the Treasury. When April came, about $18 billion was returned, and the RTC's ability to close institutions and pay off depositors (or pay other banks or thrifts to take over failed thrifts) effectively came to an end.

Many members had hoped that agreement could be reached on a package of management and policy reforms for the RTC — a huge agency that created controversy with nearly every decision it made. Some critics thought it moved too slowly to reduce its huge inventory of loans and securities taken from failed thrifts; others accused it of dumping real estate on an already weakened market, or of cutting special deals with a privileged few investors.

Still others complained that other government policies — not decisions by the RTC — were causing some weak thrifts to be needlessly closed. House Republicans, led by Bill McCollum of Florida, rallied to that cause, refusing to support additional money for the RTC unless banking laws were changed to allow some weakened thrifts to be kept open.

Most Democrats saw the GOP plan as yet another instance of forbearance — the sort of policy that contributed to the crisis in the first place — and refused. (House Republican Whip Newt Gingrich of Georgia had his own gambit: He wanted to use the RTC bill to force a vote on a GOP economic stimulus package.) The result was a stalemate in the House.

On March 26, the Senate voted 52-42 in favor of a bill (S 2482) that incorporated a Bush administration request for $25 billion more for the RTC, plus restoration of the unused appropriation from the previous November. That amount would be enough, administration officials assured Congress, to conclude the cleanup. Two weeks earlier, the House Banking Committee approved a similar measure (HR 4241), but it proved impossible to line up enough votes for it to pass on the floor.

House leaders then decided to bring up a very narrow bill (HR 4704) that merely would have restored the unused $18 billion. McCollum was not allowed to offer an amendment, and Republicans decided to abandon the bill — despite administration pleas for support. With little GOP backing for spending taxpayer money on such an unpopular cause, Democrats also voted "no." The bill went down overwhelmingly on April 1, 125-298: R 45-117; D 80-180 (ND 47-130, SD 33-50); I 0-1.

The stalemate continued for the balance of the year. The House did not try to bring the bill up again, and the administration did not press the matter with any noticeable vigor.

## 5. Campaign Finance

Context was everything for the 1992 campaign finance bill. For House Democrats, under siege all spring for a series of scandals, the bill became a centerpiece of their efforts to claim the mantle of reform. On April 9, the chamber resuscitated a bill to overhaul campaign law for the first time in 18 years. Just hours later, the House voted to turn the chamber's internal operations over to a professional administrator and voted three times on resolutions to keep the heat on an internal investigation of problems at the House Post Office.

The broader context, however, was decades of wrangling between Democrats and Republicans over which party would be advantaged by a new system. Here Republicans had the last say, because President Bush made good on his oft-repeated veto threats in May, and the bill died.

At the beginning of the year, it was not clear that there would be any campaign finance bill for the House to vote on. In the first session, both chambers had passed legislation to change the financing practices for congressional campaigns. But the Senate and House bills were incompatible — the Senate provided publicly funded broadcast vouchers to candidates, while the House proposed matching funds for its candidates — and Democrats in the two chambers had wide differences in sensitive areas such as political action committee (PAC) contributions. Both bills were veto bait for Bush.

In that environment, there was little incentive to make the tough choices required to reach a conference accord and send it to the House floor. But with the House bank scandal generating headlines and public esteem for the House falling precipitously, the climate changed and Democrats rushed to the conference table.

House negotiators gave up any hope that the House and Senate would agree on one public funding formula, which made drafting a conference report a simple task of essentially stapling the two bills together.

The final bill would have set a $600,000 optional spending limit for House races in primary and general elections. Candidates who agreed to obey the limit would get benefits, including cut-rate postage and up to $200,000 in public

funds doled out to match the first $200 of each individual contribution.

Republicans dubbed the measure another congressional perk. They said a spending limit would benefit incumbents, most of whom are Democrats, at the expense of challengers who have to compete against the taxpayer-financed communications network that House members enjoy. Republicans also objected to the public funding, which Minority Whip Newt Gingrich, R-Ga., called "a new House bank with a new line of credit."

Republicans and outside reform advocates found common ground on the PAC issue. For different reasons, both would have preferred that PACs, which traditionally favor incumbents, be locked out of participation in congressional campaigns. Democrats wanted no part of that. For House campaigns, the bill left intact the current $5,000-per-PAC limit on campaign donations, although it would have placed a $200,000 aggregate cap on how much a candidate could accept from PACs.

When the conference report made it to the House floor on April 9, party positions were already staked out. The bill's promise that public financing provisions would have to be worked out later gave Southern Democrats the cover they needed, and few members crossed party lines. The House adopted the conference report 259-165: R 19-145; D 239-20 (ND 171-6, SD 68-14); I 1-0.

Subsequent action was equally predictable: the Senate passed the bill April 30 and the president vetoed the bill May 9. The Senate override attempt failed.

# 6. Abortion Counseling

Though ultimately unsuccessful, congressional efforts in 1992 to overturn the "gag rule" prohibiting abortion counseling in federally funded family-planning clinics aptly illustrated both how far abortion rights supporters had come and how far they still had to go.

For more than a decade, the House was a stronghold for abortion opponents. In the late 1970s and early 1980s, House members took the lead in imposing a series of restrictions on the procedure, mostly on funding matters.

But the Supreme Court's 1989 decision in *Webster v. Reproductive Health Services* changed all that. Just as 1973's *Roe v. Wade*, which created a nationwide right to abortion, galvanized forces opposed to the procedure, so *Webster*, which gave states more latitude to restrict abortion access, helped rejuvenate abortion rights activists. Since the decision, however, House abortion rights forces could manage to muster only a majority to overturn a variety of abortion-related restrictions, never the two-thirds needed to override repeated vetoes by anti-abortion stalwart President Bush.

The key abortion counseling vote of the year came April 30 on final passage of legislation to reauthorize the federal family planning program, Title X of the Public Health Service Act. It showed how far abortion rights backers had come. Approval of the measure (HR 3090) marked the first time since 1984 that the chamber had voted to reauthorize the program. The last time sponsors tried to do so, in 1985, the bill received only 214 votes, less than a majority and far less than the two-thirds needed for passage under the fast-track procedure sponsors used at the time. This time the vote for passage was a strong 268-150: R 55-105; D 212-45 (ND 146-28, SD 66-17); I 1-0.

But the vote also signaled that, while abortion rights

forces might have turned things around in the House, even on their strongest issues they remained unable to overturn any of the federal government's existing anti-abortion policies — as long as Bush stood by his veto promise. Many abortion foes in both parties opposed the abortion counseling rules, upheld by the Supreme Court in 1991, on the grounds that they violated free speech guarantees and medical ethics. But even with those added votes, the total was 11 short of the number needed to override Bush's promised veto.

And, in fact, the House on Oct. 2 subsequently sustained Bush's veto on a 266-148 vote.

# 7. National Energy Strategy

There was little drama about the outcome of the May 27 House vote on a massive energy bill even before members passed the legislation 381-37: R 135-23; D 245-14 (ND 173-2, SD 72-12); I 1-0.

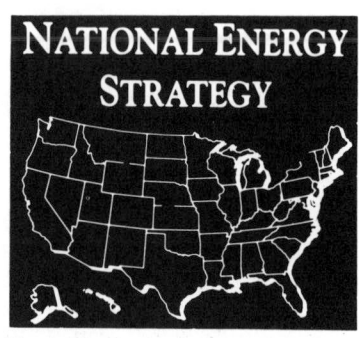

But the vote on the House bill (HR 776) was among the most important of 1992, virtually ensuring that Congress would make its first major attempt in more than a decade to curb U.S. dependence on foreign oil.

The 102nd Congress convened in the midst of the Persian Gulf crisis, which highlighted the economic and human cost of the nation's enormous thirst for oil. Not surprisingly, energy policy quickly shot to the top of the political agenda with scores of politicians clamoring for new measures to reduce oil imports.

The Bush administration outlined its policy prescriptions in a massive "National Energy Strategy" almost two years in the making. Many lawmakers peddled their own proposals, attacking the Bush plan as overly generous to oil and gas producers and the nuclear industry while slighting conservation and renewable energy.

Sen. J. Bennett Johnston, D-La., who chairs the Senate Energy Committee, quickly moved a sweeping energy bill through his committee. Environmentalists and other critics blocked it from coming to the floor late in 1991, but Johnston returned early in 1992 with a revised version. That bill, which did not include controversial proposals to allow drilling in Alaska's Arctic National Wildlife Refuge or mandate greater automobile fuel economy, easily passed the Senate in February. The legislation included measures to promote conservation and renewable energy, spur competition in the electricity industry, make it easier to build natural gas pipelines and nuclear power plants, and promote cars that run on non-gasoline fuels.

House leaders then stepped up efforts to deliver a parallel energy bill. Although Rep. Philip R. Sharp, D-Ind., already had steered such a bill through the Energy and Commerce subcommittee he chairs, it was no simple matter to get the bill to the floor.

After the full Energy and Commerce Committee approved the legislation, it was referred to eight additional House panels. Critics complained that delays would kill the bill or that the result would be an incoherent or politically

doomed patchwork, particularly as committees such as Interior and Merchant Marine and Fisheries added large and controversial restrictions on production sought by environmentalists. The Ways and Means Committee added a package of energy-related tax measures that included tax breaks for independent oil and gas drillers as well as renewable energy and some non-gasoline fuels.

But House Speaker Thomas S. Foley, D-Wash., set a deadline for the panels, and the Rules Committee subsequently trimmed some of the controversial additions. Other conflicts were resolved after key floor votes, and the finished product, while more pleasing to environmentalists, was very similar to the Senate bill.

Once the House acted, the political pressure for the Democratic-led Congress to send a finished product to the White House helped propel the massive bills through a difficult conference committee.

Lopsided votes in both chambers for energy legislation reflect policy weaknesses as well as strengths: the final version is expected to cap rather than decrease the country's growing oil imports, and many lawmakers say it does not go far enough either in aiding domestic production or, alternately, in curbing consumption. However the legislation was considered a balanced effort bound to reverse the laissez faire attitude on energy policy that dominated the 1980s and set the groundwork for additional efforts to cut oil imports.

## 8. Strategic Defense Initiative

In its first clear test of sentiment on the issue, the House on June 5 in effect backed deployment of a ground-based anti-missile defense.

The key vote came when the House rejected an amendment to the fiscal 1993 defense authorization bill (HR 5006 — PL 102-484) that would have reduced funding for the Strategic Defense Initiative (SDI) by almost $1 billion, to $3.3 billion. The vote was 161-211: R 11-134; D 149-77 (ND 125-31, SD 24-46); I 1-0.

Through 1991, the annual House action on SDI basically consisted of members staking out the lowest possible funding figure, anticipating that the Senate would approve a larger budget for the program and that a compromise sum would be hammered out in conference.

Liberal arms control activists, led by California Democrats Ronald V. Dellums and Barbara Boxer, repeatedly had proposed substantial cuts in SDI spending that were designed to limit the program to laboratory research. But the House routinely had rejected their initiatives by substantial margins. Instead, the House annually approved more modest reductions in SDI spending that would not have fundamentally reshaped the program.

In 1991, the Senate recast SDI to focus on the relatively early deployment of a ground-based anti-missile defense, consistent with the 1972 U.S.-Soviet treaty limiting anti-ballistic missile systems. The Senate action was essentially incorporated into the conference report on the fiscal 1992 defense authorization bill. SDI critics objected that the procedure had deprived House members of any opportunity to debate the revamped SDI mission.

**Durbin**

In 1992, the House Armed Services Committee brought to the House floor a fiscal 1993 authorization bill that backed $4.3 billion for the revised version of SDI, compared with the $5.4 billion requested. Illinois Democrat Richard J. Durbin offered the amendment to trim $938 million from the committee's recommendation. But members rejected this first opportunity to dissent from the SDI compromise favored by Armed Services Chairman Les Aspin, D-Wis.

During House debate July 2 on the companion defense appropriations bill (HR 5504), a Durbin amendment that would have cut $700 million from SDI was rejected by a much closer vote of 201-217. In the interval between the two votes, the House had narrowly voted to reject a constitutional amendment to require a balanced federal budget. That contentious debate had boosted the pressure on members to demonstrate their willingness to cut spending, a factor that may have motivated some of the 26 members who voted against Durbin's SDI amendment on June 5 but then supported him on July 2.

## 9. Balanced-Budget Amendment

For a decade, advocates of a constitutional amendment requiring a balanced budget had failed to convince their colleagues that such a move was just the sort of strong medicine Congress and the White House needed to bring the federal deficit under control. The high-water mark for advocates had come in 1982, when the Senate passed an amendment by  slightly more than the two-thirds majority needed for passage. The House tried in 1982 and again in 1986, but defeated the measure both times.

In May 1992, however, amendment supporters seemed to be gaining converts. Despite the budget agreement hammered out in 1990, deficits had continued to grow; the White House budget office was estimating a fiscal 1992 deficit of roughly $400 billion. Meanwhile, public regard for Congress and its ability to handle the nation's finances was sinking during a critical election year. Democrats who had long opposed the idea were changing their minds out of sheer desperation, and longtime deficit hawk Charles W. Stenholm, D-Texas, had no trouble collecting the 218 signatures he needed on a petititon that allowed the amendment (HJ Res 290) to bypass the committee bottleneck that had often stopped it from coming to the House floor.

But just when it looked like backers were sure to rally the support they needed in the House and the Senate, opponents began to fight back.

A psychological turning point came when Senate Appropriations Chairman Robert C. Byrd, D-W.Va., announced his adamant opposition and his intent to filibuster the measure in the Senate. Byrd argued that the amendment would shift fiscal power from Congress to the White House and to the federal courts, which could wind up ordering Congress to make specific spending cuts or tax increases. Byrd's stature and success record in the Senate were such that his announcement alone seemed to turn the tide. Opponents in the House then set about to sow doubt and fear among backers who might not have thought

through all the implications of the amendment.

House Budget Chairman Leon E. Panetta, D-Calif., unveiled detailed spending-cut and tax-increase scenarios designed to show just how painful it would be to implement a balanced-budget amendment by 1997, when most thought an amendment would take effect. House Democratic leaders took a different tack, offering a substitute amendment that would require a balanced budget but exempt Social Security. Organized labor launched a nationwide campaign, warning that the "balanced-budget hoax would hurt all of us" by raising taxes and cutting government benefits.

**Panetta**

Still, passage seemed likely barely a week before the June 11 House vote. In the end, though, the lobbying by Democratic leaders and outside interest groups, plus a creeping uneasiness about tinkering with the Constitution, gave opponents a nine-vote victory margin. The amendment was rejected, 280-153: R 164-2; D 116-150 (ND 52-130, SD 64-20); I 0-1.

## 10. Superconducting Super Collider

Growing opposition to the costly superconducting super collider reached a critical mass in June, when the House voted to kill the massive science project that is expected to cost at least $8.3 billion. The vote was 232-181: R 79-79; D 152-102 (ND 126-49, SD 26-53); I 1-0.

Although the House eventually reversed the decision and agreed to continue funding the project in fiscal 1993, the vote was a shocking blow to project supporters and left the endeavor on precarious political ground.

The super collider is a giant atom smasher being built underground in Waxahachie, Texas, by the Energy Department. It is designed to produce high-speed particle collisions that scientists say could unlock the fundamental secrets of matter, as well as provide valuable technological spinoffs.

But some critics are skeptical of these claims, while others say the project is simply too expensive at a time when lawmakers are struggling to find money to pay for human services and other pressing needs, including smaller science projects.

Before the June vote, Congress had already appropriated roughly $1 billion for the project.

Opponents had been gaining ground in the House and had predicted a particularly close vote on the project in 1992, when House appropriators earmarked $484 million to keep building the collider. But even sponsors of the amendment to kill the project did not expect their June 17 victory.

Timing played an important role. It was the first key spending vote after the House narrowly defeated a proposed constitutional amendment to require a balanced budget, and many lawmakers found it hard to justify approving hundreds of millions for the super collider so soon after speechifying against the deficit. The project also drew the ire of urban liberals, who had lost an earlier fight to transfer defense dollars to domestic needs and urban aid.

The atom smasher became a particularly tempting target because some of the Texas lawmakers arguing for the costly project had also been prominent advocates of balanced-budget proposals, and the delegation had mostly opposed increased spending for urban aid.

That mood faded, accounting for part of the reason the House later reversed itself, agreeing to provide an additional $517 million for the collider, after the Senate restored funding in its version of the energy and water spending bill. That was less than the $650 million President Bush had requested for fiscal 1993, but more than the $484 million initially approved by House appropriators.

While Texas receives the most direct benefits from the super collider, managers have broadened support for the project by spreading research and procurement contracts across a wide array of states. Moreover, President-elect Bill Clinton has said he supports the project.

Nevertheless, the House vote continues to cast a shadow on the super collider's prospects. The flip-flop hurts the Energy Department's chances of attracting Japanese or other foreign support for the project, which in turn could erode congressional support. And even some supporters have warned that they may not be able to continue backing the project in light of budget constraints.

## 11. Urban Aid

Congress' first concrete response to the devastating April riots in Los Angeles came when the House passed a $494.7 million supplemental appropriations bill May 14. The measure was designed to direct small-business loans and emergency grants to L.A. and to Chicago, where the recent collapse of a tunnel beneath the Chicago

River had flooded the city's downtown.

The House bill turned out to be just the opening bid, however. One week later, the Senate quadrupled the size of the measure to nearly $2 billion by adding money for a nationwide program of urban aid. The extra money was to go for summer youth jobs, a Head Start summer program for preschool children, a summer-school program for disadvantaged neighborhoods and the administration-backed "Weed and Seed" program, which aimed to "weed" drug dealers and and other criminals out of inner-city neighborhoods and "seed" the areas with social programs.

Senate backers, including some Republicans, fought off attempts to strip out the nearly $1.5 billion they added to the House bill and defeated a move to force Congress to cut other spending to pay for the programs. Virtually all of the money was to be provided on an "emergency" basis, exempt from spending caps set in the 1990 budget agreement.

Despite a White House veto threat over the size of the bill, House-Senate conferees June 5 decided to keep all the Senate add-ons and leave the bill's price tag at $2 billion. Participants in negotiations between the White House and key members of Congress said last-minute insistence on the full amount by Senate Majority Leader George J. Mitchell, D-Maine, blocked a compromise on a smaller amount, but Mitchell flatly denied the account.

In the end, it wasn't the veto threat from President Bush that forced the bill to slim down, it was strong GOP

opposition and intransigence among rank-and-file Democrats in the House. Some Democratic leaders wanted to send Bush the $2 billion conference report and force him to issue what they assumed would be a politically embarrassing veto. But when House vote-counters ran a whip check, they found that many members objected to the size of the bill, either because it would have added $2 billion to the deficit or because rural and suburban members thought it sent too much to the inner cities.

Bowing to reality, leaders accepted a White House compromise that cut the bill to $1.1 billion. The conference report was adopted by the House on June 18, seven weeks after the riots, by a vote of 249-168: R 43-117; D 205-51 (ND 158-17, SD 47-34); I 1-0. The Senate cleared the measure by voice vote later the same day.

While the supplemental was intended as part of a broader urban aid initiative, in the end it contained the only money that Congress would provide to inner cities in 1992 as a response to the L.A. riots. The other big urban aid proposal that grew out of the riots — a plan to set up dozens of "enterprise zones" where investors and businesses would get special tax breaks and other federal assistance — was finally incorporated in the tax bill (HR 11) Congress cleared just before adjournment. Bush vetoed that bill on Nov. 4.

## 12. Cable Reregulation

The House and Senate votes to override a bill (S 12) to reregulate cable television prices and services represented a stunning defeat for the cable industry and the Bush administration. But the first confirmation that Bush was on the losing side of the issue — and headed toward his first override — came July 23 on a crucial amendment by Rep. W. J. "Billy" Tauzin, D-La.

To Tauzin, along with cable bill sponsor Edward J. Markey, D-Mass., the amendment was the difference between making a serious attempt to improve cable industry competition or passing a halfhearted rate regulation bill.

Would-be competitors to the $20 billion cable industry, such as the home satellite and "wireless" cable systems, had long complained of being effectively locked out of access to cable programs through high prices and exclusive deals. Tauzin's amendment to the House bill (HR 4850) sought to ban cable programmers from discriminating against cable competitors in the price, terms and conditions of sales of their product. It also barred most exclusive contracts between cable operators and vendors.

The House approved the Tauzin amendment, 338-68: R 116-45; D 221-23 (ND 152-18, SD 69-5); I 1-0. The bill as amended by Tauzin subsequently passed the House, 340-73.

Most remarkable about the overwhelming House approval for the amendment was the political clout of the opposition. Urging defeat of the amendment was the Bush administration, the cable lobby, Energy and Commerce Chairman John D. Dingell, D-Mich., and various members of the House leadership.

Dingell supported the cable industry position that Tauzin would unfairly encroach on private business decisions, and during full committee markup of the bill he had the wording struck from the version approved by Markey's subcommittee. Dingell also argued that the provision would cause the bill to be referred to the Judiciary Committee, thus slowing down and possibly killing the entire measure.

The floor vote to replace the Tauzin language took place in the early evening hours of July 23. With little else to do but hear the discussion on the two amendments, members packed the House chamber for the debate between Tauzin and his opponent, Thomas J. Manton, D-N.Y.

Manton had offered a weaker substitute to the Tauzin amendment that was favored by the cable industry. He called Tauzin's amendment "far-reaching and radical" because it would set a government-mandated price for programming and cause program creators to lose control over their product.

Apart from the formidable opposition from Manton, Dingell and House leaders, Tauzin was saddled with the task of selling distinctions between his and Manton's amendments that were complex and difficult to discern.

Tauzin instead launched into an impassioned speech about the future of television, arguing that competition to cable would never arrive unless some controls were put on cable's program pricing policies and increasing market power.

Just as the cable television industry relied on free network broadcasts when it was in its infancy, Tauzin said, cable's competitors now need government help to purchase cable programs at fairer prices.

The House rejected Manton's substitute, 162-247, and subsequently voted to adopt the Tauzin amendment. The surprisingly large margin for Tauzin's amendment made it clear that the cable industry was heading for a big defeat — and that Bush's perfect veto record was in peril.

## 13. Space Station *Freedom*

In what may have been its last major vote on whether to keep the NASA space station *Freedom*, the House on July 29 turned back an attempt by a key Appropriations subcommittee chairman to abandon the manned-exploration venture.

The House had voted three times in 13 months to preserve the controversial space station, expected to cost from $30 billion to $40 billion by the year 2000. The latest vote came July 29 on the fiscal 1993 appropriations bill (HR 5679) for the departments of Veterans Affairs and Housing and Urban Development and independent agencies (VA-HUD). The $86.8 billion bill, as reported out of the Appropriations Committee, provided $1.73 billion for the space station, $305 million less than its fiscal 1992 appropriation. President Bush, a strong and vocal supporter of the project, had sought $2.25 billion for fiscal 1993.

But Congress had been struggling in the past two years to control high-cost science projects, pare the federal budget deficit and keep its spending bills within limits set by the 1990 budget agreement with the White House. Those budget problems only heightened lawmakers' awareness of big-ticket science projects — the space station and the superconducting super collider being the biggest — whose missions and eventual paybacks were not easy to justify.

Cost concerns forced NASA to scale back the space station two years ago, and it has come under fire from many scientists who feel it is poorly designed and incapable of serious scientific research.

According to NASA officials, the *Freedom* project would allow scientists to study how humans react to long periods in the weightless environment of outer space, thus providing the United States with a steppingstone for planetary exploration.

But members of Congress supported the project largely because of the jobs it generates across the country and in their districts. Before the House vote, NASA officials played that angle hard, passing out maps of the country that showed exactly where the space station contract money and jobs would go.

Bob Traxler, D-Mich., chairman of the VA-HUD Appropriations Subcommittee that oversees NASA funding, tried to kill the space station in 1991 by leaving it out of the committee recommendation. But at the urging of Bush, NASA officials and space industry lobbyists, the full House subsequently voted 240-173 to restore the money.

**Traxler**

This year, Traxler waited until the bill went to the floor to make his move to cut *Freedom*'s congressional lifeline. He fared no better. Again, under intense lobbying from the White House, industry officials and NASA Director Daniel Goldin, the House rejected Traxler's motion to strike, 181-237: R 38-127; D 142-110 (ND 115-59, SD 27-51); I 1-0.

Space station advocates now say they doubt that the project will be subjected in the future to such a thorough going over.

If the budget "walls" separating domestic and defense spending come down next year, as scheduled, there could be less of a pinch on space and science funding from other domestic programs. And the two leading House critics of space station funding, Traxler and New York's Bill Green, the ranking Republican on the VA-HUD panel, are not returning to Congress.

Traxler's successor as VA-HUD chairman is Louis Stokes, D-Ohio, whose state benefited greatly from the space station, receiving $101 million in contracts and 253 jobs. Although Stokes supported Traxler's amendment to kill *Freedom*, his opposition appears to be far less entrenched.

## 14. Ex-Soviet Aid

In an election year when foreign policy was shunned by both parties, one piece of international legislation stood out. After months of wrangling, Congress approved a massive package authorizing technical, financial and other assistance to the former republics of the Soviet Union.

What made the measure remarkable was that passage came against the backdrop of an extremely partisan session in which the recession-plagued U.S. economy was the main focus. Both Democrats and Republicans were reluctant to devote too much attention to foreign issues when constituents were hurting back home. This was especially true in the House, where most of the 435 members were running for re-election.

In addition, Democrats were eager to blame Republican economic policies of the previous 12 years for many of the

nation's domestic troubles. They argued that President Bush's proclivity toward foreign affairs was further evidence of his detachment from the problems of average Americans.

Given these conditions, it was no surprise that Bush's plan to join several other western industrial nations to aid the former republics, in the wake of the Soviet Union's collapse, was not warmly embraced even though some congressional leaders had previously urged him to take such action.

House Democrats, led by Majority Whip David E. Bonior, D-Mich., insisted that agreement be reached on a number of domestic fronts — including extension of jobless benefits, increased urban aid and job-creation legislation — before they would vote on the ex-Soviet aid package. That package, which Bush called his No. 1 foreign policy initiative, called for a $12.3 billion increase in the U.S. commitment to the International Monetary

**Bonior**

Fund, $410 million in bilateral humanitarian, economic and other assistance, and about $800 million to help dismantle the former Soviet nuclear arsenal.

Squabbling over domestic issues delayed House consideration of the aid bill long past the mid-June deadline for passage that Bush had requested. The president had hoped to get the aid in place before a visit by Russian President Boris N. Yeltsin to Washington on June 16-17.

It was not until early August that House leaders finally agreed to bring to the floor the legislation (HR 4547) that had been marked up by the Foreign Affairs Committee two months earlier. Paving the way for consideration was an extension of jobless benefits, as well as a tentative administration agreement with Bonior to speed up public works spending and to support loan guarantees for urban areas.

While these assurances were enough to win leadership backing, there was still great reluctance among rank-and-file members to vote for such a large foreign aid package before the election. In an unusually united effort, Democratic and Republican House leaders took to the floor to persuade members that the United States would be the long-term beneficiary of secure successor states to the former Soviet Union. They argued that a collapse of reform efforts in the republics could mean a return to totalitarianism and perhaps greater threats to U.S. security and a greater need for more defense spending. Conversely, sponsors argued, successful new free-market economies would mean more business opportunities for U.S. companies.

Leaders drew on a formidable group of aid proponents — including former presidents Ronald Reagan, Jimmy Carter, Gerald R. Ford and Richard M. Nixon, as well as a coalition of business, farm and disarmament groups — to help win passage of the bill. The legislation passed Aug. 6 by a vote of 255-164: R 94-68; D 161-95 (ND 115-63, SD 46-32); I 0-1.

## 15. Foreign Aid

A year after the House appeared to sour on foreign assistance, it voted to send President Bush a $26.3 billion foreign aid appropriations bill for fiscal 1993. In addition to continuing funding for foreign aid programs, the measure included $12.3 billion in new financing for the Interna-

tional Monetary Fund and guarantees for $10 billion in commercial loans for Israel (HR 5368, PL 102-391 — H Rept 102-585).

In the key vote Oct. 5, the House voted overwhelmingly to adopt the conference report for the $26.3 billion spending bill, 312-105: R 104-58; D 208-46 (ND 152-20, SD 56-26); I 0-1.

In October 1991, with lawmakers caught up in an "America first" mood, the House had overwhelmingly rejected a two-year foreign aid authorization bill. With the domestic economy slumping and congressional elections on the horizon, the Bush administration feared that foreign aid would become an even harder sell in 1992.

Congress also failed to complete action on a companion foreign aid appropriations measure in 1991, forcing lawmakers to approve continuing resolutions to fund the program. The fiscal 1992 bill had become tangled in a dispute between the White House and the government of Israel over Jerusalem's request for loan guarantees.

The turnabout came in part because the fiscal 1993 bill slashed actual foreign aid spending, even though it included new programs for Israel and the IMF. The bill cut $1.1 billion from the administration request, largely by eliminating military assistance grants for Turkey, Greece and Portugal and replacing them with low-interest loans.

The conference report also afforded House members their first opportunity to vote for loan guarantees for Israel, a popular program with members of both parties.

The five-year program for Israel provided U.S. guarantees — not loans or direct aid — intended to help Jerusalem secure favorable rates on commercial loans. U.S. taxpayers will not be asked to provide any funding for the program unless Israel defaults on the loans. Similarly, the $12.3 billion in new financing for the IMF entails no budgetary outlays.

Rep. David R. Obey, D-Wis., chairman of the House Appropriations Subcommittee on Foreign Operations, said that any aid bill not viewed as fiscally prudent would have drawn intense opposition from anxious lawmakers.

"It's a very tight bill and we gave people some arguments to take home and defend," Obey said after the House vote. In June, the House had voted 297-124 for the underlying appropriations bill. That measure, which did not include the loan guarantees, had reduced the administration request by $1.3 billion.

The legislation continued a long-term downward spiral in foreign aid funding. Excluding the one-time appropriation for the International Monetary Fund, the final version provided $1.4 billion less than the fiscal 1991 bill — the last one to clear Congress.

---

## 16. Western Water Bill

Nowhere were the conflicts in the way the West uses its water more starkly illustrated than in the House's battle over a single key provision of the 1992 omnibus Western water projects bill (HR 429 — PL 102-575). As crafted by Interior Committee Chairman George Miller, D-Calif., the proposal was an attempt to redirect the purpose of the Central Valley Project (CVP) in California to reflect urban and environmental values.

**Miller**

The CVP is the largest irrigation project run by the Interior Department's Bureau of Reclamation. It controls one-fifth of the state's usable water supply.

Criticism of the half-century-old project had been building for years and was exacerbated by the ongoing California drought. The CVP historically supplied its water mainly to some 23,000 Central Valley farming operations, which used the water to grow much of California's fabled produce in otherwise arid land. Farmers got the water at rates far below those paid by the other 85 percent of the state's economy — due to subsidies from federal taxpayers.

The result, environmentalists charged, was wasteful farming practices that led to polluted runoff and water diverted from other valuable uses, such as the state's now-decimated salmon fishery.

Miller, from urbanized Contra Costa County just north of the valley, used the omnibus Western water bill to transform the Central Valley Project. His proposal sought to make the CVP protect fish and wildlife and make more water available to outside users. Contracts to farmers would remain short-term until the ecological health of the region improved.

The valley's farmers cried foul. They said disrupting their decades-old system of cheap water would cost jobs, make their farms more risky investments and hurt consumers with higher food prices.

They were supported by Republican California Gov. Pete Wilson and by rural lawmakers such as Republican Bill Thomas, who represented the southern tip of the valley, and Democrat Calvin Dooley, whose family has been farming in the valley for four generations.

But a phalanx of other state interests lined up behind Miller: most of the state's urban county governments, the big metropolitan water district of Los Angeles, corporate business groups and environmentalists.

**Wilson**

Thomas, Dooley and others complained that the Miller provisions would have had no chance of approval if they were not tied to the 40-title omnibus measure, a must-pass bill for other Western states. But Miller said that was the point: The huge package had widespread support, containing as it did grandiose water projects such as the Central Utah Project and smaller but locally popular provisions dishing out largess to every Western state. Few wanted to see the whole thing sink on the opposition of a handful of California Farm Belt lawmakers.

The showdown came in the early morning hours of Oct. 6, when the House-Senate conference report came before the House. Thomas offered a motion to kick the bill back to committee and strip out all the Central Valley provisions. "If you vote yes . . . the hostages will be set free," Thomas said, referring to the other titles of the bill.

But the House was unmoved, rejecting Thomas' motion to recommit the bill to committee, 159-244: R 117-41; 42-202 (ND 15-152, SD 27-50); I 0-1. Members then adopted the conference report by voice vote.

# HOUSE VOTES 1, 2, 3, 4, 5, 6, 7, 8

*Following are 1992 votes selected by Congressional Quarterly as key votes (explanations of key votes, p. 35-B). Original vote number is provided in parentheses.*

**1. HR 4210. 1992 Tax Bill/Democratic Substitute.** Rosten-kowski, D-Ill., substitute to give workers a temporary tax credit worth up to $400 for couples and $200 for individuals a year to be paid for with a 10 percent surtax on millionaires and a new top income tax rate of 35 percent for individuals with taxable income higher than $85,000 and couples with more than $145,000. The package includes indexing of capital gains and other provisions designed to spur economic growth. Adopted 221-210: R 1-164; D 219-46 (ND 156-27, SD 63-19); I 1-0, Feb. 27, 1992. (House vote 30). A "nay" was a vote in support of the president's position.

**2. H Res 396. Further Disclosure of House Bank Abuses/ Adoption.** Adoption of the resolution to disclose the name of any member or former member who wrote a check that exceeded his balance at the House bank and the number of insufficient funds checks written by each from July 1, 1988, to Oct. 3, 1991. Adopted 426-0: R 165-0; D 260-0 (ND 178-0, SD 82-0); I 1-0, March 13, 1992 (House vote 45) (in the session that began, and the Congressional Record dated, March 12, 1992).

**3. HR 3732. Eliminate Budget Walls/Passage.** Passage of the bill to modify the 1990 Budget Enforcement Act to knock down the walls that prohibit shifting funds between defense, international and domestic appropriations. Rejected 187-238: R 0-162; D 186-76 (ND 151-28, SD 35-48); I 1-0, March 31, 1992 (House vote 66) A "nay" was a vote in support of the president's position.

**4. HR 4704. RTC Financing/Passage.** Passage of the bill to provide the Resolution Trust Corporation with about $17 billion to resolve failed savings and loan institutions by eliminating the April 1, 1992, expiration date on $25 billion provided in November 1991. Rejected 125-298: R 45-117; D 80-180 (ND 47-130, SD 33-50); I 0-1, April 1, 1992 (House vote 69). A "yea" was a vote in support of the president's position.

**5. S 3. Campaign Finance Reform/Conference Report.** Adoption of the conference report to limit spending in congressional campaigns by providing incentives to candidates to agree to voluntary spending limits, restricting contributions from political action committees (PACs) and restricting "soft money" raised and spent by state parties in federal elections. The bill would create a separate system for House and Senate campaigns. Adopted 259-165: R 19-145; D 239-20 (ND 171-6, SD 68-14); I 1-0, April 9, 1992 (House vote 79). A "nay" was a vote in support of the president's position.

**6. HR 3090. Family Planning Reauthorization/Passage.** Passage of the bill to reauthorize Title X of the Public Health Service Act for five years through fiscal 1997. The bill would overturn the administration's ban on abortion counseling at federally funded family planning clinics. Passed 268-150: R 55-105; D 212-45 (ND 146-28, SD 66-17); I 1-0, April 30, 1992 (House vote 95). A "nay" was a vote in support of the president's position. (The text of HR 3090 was subsequently inserted into a Senate bill, S 323.)

**7. HR 776. National Energy Policy/Passage.** Passage of the bill to promote increased domestic energy production and conservation; promote the wider use of alternative motor fuels; streamline the nuclear plant licensing process; restrict state powers to regulate gas production; ban certain new offshore oil and gas drilling; overhaul federal laws governing electric utilities; and provide tax incentives for renewable energy. Passed 381-37: R 135-23; D 245-14 (ND 173-2, SD 72-12); I 1-0, May 27, 1992 (House vote 144).

**8. HR 5006. Fiscal 1993 Defense Authorization/Strategic Defense Initiative.** Durbin, D-Ill., amendment to reduce funding for the Strategic Defense Initiative by $937.5 million — from the $4.3 billion in the bill to $3.3 billion. Rejected 161-211: R 11-134; D 149-77 (ND 125-31, SD 24-46); I 1-0, June 5, 1992 (House vote 169). A "nay" was a vote in support of the president's position.

## KEY

Y Voted for (yea).
# Paired for.
+ Announced for.
N Voted against (nay).
X Paired against.
— Announced against.
P Voted "present."
C Voted "present" to avoid possible conflict of interest.
? Did not vote or otherwise make a position known.

*Democrats* **Republicans**
*Independent*

| | 1 | 2 | 3 | 4 | 5 | 6 | 7 | 8 |
|---|---|---|---|---|---|---|---|---|
| **ALABAMA** | | | | | | | | |
| 1 *Callahan* | N | Y | N | N | N | N | Y | N |
| 2 *Dickinson* | X | Y | N | N | N | Y | Y | N |
| 3 Browder | Y | Y | N | N | Y | Y | Y | N |
| 4 Bevill | Y | Y | Y | N | Y | Y | Y | Y |
| 5 Cramer | Y | Y | Y | Y | Y | Y | Y | N |
| 6 Erdreich | Y | Y | N | Y | Y | Y | Y | N |
| 7 Harris | Y | Y | N | N | Y | Y | Y | N |
| **ALASKA** | | | | | | | | |
| AL *Young* | N | Y | N | N | N | N | Y | N |
| **ARIZONA** | | | | | | | | |
| 1 *Rhodes* | N | Y | N | Y | N | N | Y | N |
| 2 Pastor | Y | Y | Y | N | Y | Y | Y | Y |
| 3 *Stump* | N | N | N | N | N | N | N | N |
| 4 *Kyl* | N | Y | N | N | N | N | Y | N |
| 5 *Kolbe* | N | Y | N | N | N | N | Y | N |
| **ARKANSAS** | | | | | | | | |
| 1 Alexander | Y | Y | Y | Y | Y | Y | Y | N |
| 2 Thornton | Y | Y | Y | N | Y | Y | Y | N |
| 3 *Hammerschmidt* | N | N | N | N | N | N | N | N |
| 4 Anthony | Y | Y | N | Y | Y | Y | ? | ? |
| **CALIFORNIA** | | | | | | | | |
| 1 *Riggs* | N | Y | N | N | N | Y | Y | N |
| 2 *Herger* | N | Y | N | N | N | N | N | X |
| 3 Matsui | Y | Y | Y | Y | Y | Y | Y | Y |
| 4 Fazio | Y | Y | Y | Y | Y | Y | Y | Y |
| 5 Pelosi | Y | Y | Y | N | Y | Y | Y | ? |
| 6 Boxer | Y | Y | # | N | Y | Y | Y | ? |
| 7 Miller | Y | ? | Y | N | Y | Y | Y | Y |
| 8 Dellums | N | Y | Y | N | Y | Y | Y | Y |
| 9 Stark | Y | Y | Y | N | Y | Y | Y | Y |
| 10 Edwards | Y | Y | Y | Y | Y | Y | Y | Y |
| 11 Lantos | Y | Y | Y | Y | Y | Y | Y | N |
| 12 *Campbell* | N | Y | N | N | Y | ? | ? | ? |
| 13 Mineta | Y | Y | Y | N | Y | Y | Y | Y |
| 14 *Doolittle* | N | Y | N | N | N | N | N | N |
| 15 Condit | N | Y | N | N | Y | Y | Y | N |
| 16 Panetta | Y | Y | Y | N | Y | Y | Y | Y |
| 17 Dooley | Y | Y | N | N | Y | ? | Y | Y |
| 18 Lehman | N | Y | Y | N | Y | Y | Y | ? |
| 19 *Lagomarsino* | N | Y | N | N | N | N | # | N |
| 20 *Thomas* | N | Y | N | Y | N | Y | Y | ? |
| 21 *Gallegly* | N | Y | N | N | N | N | Y | N |
| 22 *Moorhead* | N | Y | N | N | N | N | Y | N |
| 23 Beilenson | N | Y | Y | Y | Y | Y | Y | # |
| 24 Waxman | Y | Y | Y | Y | Y | Y | Y | Y |
| 25 Roybal | Y | Y | Y | Y | Y | Y | Y | Y |
| 26 Berman | Y | Y | Y | Y | Y | Y | Y | Y |
| 27 Levine | Y | Y | # | ? | ? | Y | ? | ? |
| 28 Dixon | Y | Y | Y | ? | Y | Y | Y | Y |
| 29 Waters | Y | Y | Y | N | Y | + | Y | Y |
| 30 Martinez | Y | Y | Y | N | Y | ? | ? | Y |
| 31 Dymally | Y | Y | ? | ? | Y | Y | Y | ? |
| 32 Anderson | Y | Y | Y | Y | Y | Y | Y | N |
| 33 *Dreier* | N | Y | N | N | N | N | Y | N |
| 34 Torres | Y | Y | Y | Y | Y | Y | Y. | |
| 35 *Lewis* | N | Y | ? | Y | N | Y | Y | N |
| 36 Brown | Y | Y | Y | Y | Y | Y | Y | Y |
| 37 *McCandless* | N | Y | N | N | N | N | Y | N |
| 38 *Dornan* | N | Y | X | N | N | N | Y | N |
| 39 *Dannemeyer* | N | + | N | — | ? | ? | ? | ? |
| 40 *Cox* | N | Y | N | N | N | N | Y | N |
| 41 *Lowery* | N | Y | N | N | N | N | Y | N |

ND Northern Democrats   SD Southern Democrats

| | 1 | 2 | 3 | 4 | 5 | 6 | 7 | 8 |
|---|---|---|---|---|---|---|---|---|
| 42 *Rohrabacher* | N | Y | N | N | N | N | Y | N |
| 43 *Packard* | N | Y | N | N | N | N | X | N |
| 44 *Cunningham* | N | Y | N | N | N | N | Y | N |
| 45 *Hunter* | N | Y | N | N | N | N | N | N |
| **COLORADO** | | | | | | | | |
| 1 Schroeder | N | Y | Y | N | Y | Y | Y | Y |
| 2 Skaggs | Y | Y | Y | Y | Y | Y | Y | Y |
| 3 *Campbell* | Y | Y | N | N | Y | ? | Y | N |
| 4 *Allard* | N | Y | N | N | N | N | Y | N |
| 5 *Hefley* | N | Y | N | N | N | N | Y | N |
| 6 *Schaefer* | N | Y | N | N | N | Y | Y | N |
| **CONNECTICUT** | | | | | | | | |
| 1 Kennelly | Y | Y | Y | N | Y | Y | Y | Y |
| 2 Gejdenson | Y | Y | N | N | Y | Y | Y | Y |
| 3 DeLauro | Y | Y | Y | N | Y | # | Y | Y |
| 4 *Shays* | N | Y | Y | Y | Y | Y | Y | Y |
| 5 *Franks* | N | Y | N | Y | Y | Y | Y | Y |
| 6 *Johnson* | N | Y | N | Y | N | Y | Y | N |
| **DELAWARE** | | | | | | | | |
| AL Carper | N | Y | N | Y | Y | Y | Y | Y |
| **FLORIDA** | | | | | | | | |
| 1 *Hutto* | N | Y | N | N | N | N | Y | N |
| 2 Peterson | Y | Y | N | Y | Y | Y | Y | Y |
| 3 Bennett | Y | Y | Y | N | Y | Y | Y | Y |
| 4 *James* | N | N | N | N | N | N | Y | N |
| 5 *McCollum* | N | Y | N | N | N | N | Y | N |
| 6 *Stearns* | N | Y | N | N | N | N | N | N |
| 7 Gibbons | Y | Y | Y | N | Y | Y | Y | Y |
| 8 *Young* | N | Y | N | N | N | Y | Y | N |
| 9 *Bilirakis* | N | Y | N | N | N | N | Y | N |
| 10 *Ireland* | N | Y | N | Y | N | N | Y | ? |
| 11 Bacchus | Y | Y | N | Y | Y | Y | Y | Y |
| 12 *Lewis* | N | Y | N | N | N | N | Y | N |
| 13 *Goss* | N | Y | N | N | N | N | Y | N |
| 14 Johnston | Y | Y | Y | Y | Y | Y | Y | Y |
| 15 *Shaw* | N | Y | N | N | N | N | Y | N |
| 16 Smith | Y | Y | Y | N | Y | # | Y | Y |
| 17 Lehman | Y | ? | Y | Y | Y | Y | Y | Y |
| 18 *Ros—Lehtinen* | N | Y | N | N | N | N | Y | ? |
| 19 Fascell | Y | Y | Y | Y | Y | Y | Y | N |
| **GEORGIA** | | | | | | | | |
| 1 *Thomas* | N | N | N | N | N | Y | Y | N |
| 2 Hatcher | Y | Y | Y | N | Y | Y | Y | ? |
| 3 Ray | ? | Y | N | N | Y | N | Y | X |
| 4 Jones | Y | Y | Y | Y | Y | Y | Y | Y |
| 5 Lewis | Y | Y | Y | Y | Y | Y | Y | ? |
| 6 *Gingrich* | N | Y | N | N | N | N | Y | N |
| 7 *Darden* | Y | Y | N | Y | Y | N | Y | N |
| 8 Rowland | N | Y | N | Y | Y | N | Y | N |
| 9 Jenkins | Y | Y | N | N | Y | Y | Y | N |
| 10 Barnard | N | Y | N | ? | ? | N | Y | N |
| **HAWAII** | | | | | | | | |
| 1 Abercrombie | Y | Y | Y | N | Y | Y | Y | Y |
| 2 Mink | Y | Y | Y | N | Y | Y | Y | ? |
| **IDAHO** | | | | | | | | |
| 1 LaRocco | Y | Y | N | N | Y | Y | Y | Y |
| 2 Stallings | N | Y | N | N | Y | Y | Y | Y |
| **ILLINOIS** | | | | | | | | |
| 1 Hayes | Y | Y | Y | Y | Y | Y | Y | Y |
| 2 Savage | Y | ? | Y | N | Y | Y | Y | Y |
| 3 Russo | N | Y | Y | N | ? | Y | Y | Y |
| 4 Sangmeister | Y | Y | Y | Y | Y | Y | Y | Y |
| 5 Lipinski | Y | Y | Y | N | Y | N | Y | N |
| 6 *Hyde* | N | Y | N | N | N | N | Y | N |
| 7 Collins | Y | ? | Y | N | Y | Y | # | # |
| 8 Rostenkowski | Y | Y | Y | N | Y | Y | Y | Y |
| 9 Yates | Y | Y | Y | ? | Y | Y | Y | Y |
| 10 *Porter* | N | Y | N | Y | N | Y | Y | # |
| 11 Annunzio | Y | Y | Y | N | Y | N | Y | N |
| 12 *Crane* | N | N | N | N | N | N | N | N |
| 13 *Fawell* | N | Y | N | Y | N | Y | Y | N |
| 14 *Hastert* | N | Y | N | N | N | N | Y | N |
| 15 *Ewing* | N | Y | N | N | N | N | Y | N |
| 16 *Cox* | N | Y | Y | N | Y | Y | Y | Y |
| 17 Evans | Y | Y | Y | Y | Y | Y | Y | Y |
| 18 *Michel* | N | Y | N | N | N | ? | N | N |
| 19 Bruce | Y | Y | Y | N | Y | Y | Y | + |
| 20 Durbin | Y | Y | Y | Y | Y | Y | Y | Y |
| 21 Costello | Y | Y | Y | N | ? | N | Y | N |
| 22 Poshard | Y | Y | Y | N | Y | N | Y | Y |
| **INDIANA** | | | | | | | | |
| 1 Visclosky | Y | Y | N | N | Y | Y | Y | Y |
| 2 Sharp | Y | Y | N | N | Y | Y | Y | Y |
| 3 Roemer | N | Y | N | N | Y | Y | Y | N |

52-B — 1992 CQ ALMANAC

| | 1 | 2 | 3 | 4 | 5 | 6 | 7 | 8 |
|---|---|---|---|---|---|---|---|---|
| 4 Long | N | Y | N | N | Y | Y | N | Y |
| 5 Jontz | Y | Y | Y | N | Y | Y | Y | Y |
| 6 ***Burton*** | N | Y | N | N | N | N | Y | N |
| 7 ***Myers*** | N | Y | N | N | N | N | Y | N |
| 8 McCloskey | Y | Y | Y | N | Y | Y | Y | N |
| 9 Hamilton | N | Y | N | N | Y | Y | Y | N |
| 10 Jacobs | Y | Y | N | N | Y | Y | Y | Y |
| **IOWA** | | | | | | | | |
| 1 ***Leach*** | N | Y | N | Y | Y | Y | Y | Y |
| 2 ***Nussle*** | N | Y | N | N | N | N | Y | Y |
| 3 Nagle | Y | Y | Y | N | N | Y | Y | Y |
| 4 Smith | Y | Y | Y | N | ? | Y | Y | N |
| 5 ***Lightfoot*** | N | Y | N | N | N | N | Y | N |
| 6 ***Grandy*** | N | Y | N | Y | N | N | Y | N |
| **KANSAS** | | | | | | | | |
| 1 ***Roberts*** | N | Y | N | N | N | N | Y | N |
| 2 Slattery | Y | Y | N | N | Y | Y | Y | Y |
| 3 ***Meyers*** | N | Y | N | Y | N | Y | Y | N |
| 4 Glickman | Y | Y | N | N | Y | Y | Y | Y |
| 5 ***Nichols*** | N | Y | N | N | N | Y | Y | ? |
| **KENTUCKY** | | | | | | | | |
| 1 Hubbard | Y | Y | N | N | Y | Y | Y | ? |
| 2 Natcher | Y | Y | Y | N | Y | Y | Y | N |
| 3 Mazzoli | Y | Y | N | N | Y | N | Y | Y |
| 4 ***Bunning*** | N | Y | ? | N | N | N | Y | N |
| 5 ***Rogers*** | N | Y | N | N | N | N | Y | N |
| 6 ***Hopkins*** | N | Y | N | N | N | N | Y | N |
| 7 Perkins | Y | Y | Y | ? | N | N | Y | Y |
| **LOUISIANA** | | | | | | | | |
| 1 ***Livingston*** | N | Y | N | N | N | N | N | ? |
| 2 Jefferson | Y | Y | Y | N | Y | Y | Y | Y |
| 3 Tauzin | N | Y | N | N | N | N | Y | N |
| 4 ***McCrery*** | N | Y | N | Y | N | N | Y | N |
| 5 Huckaby | Y | Y | N | N | N | Y | Y | N |
| 6 ***Baker*** | N | Y | N | Y | N | N | N | N |
| 7 Hayes | N | Y | N | N | N | N | Y | N |
| 8 ***Holloway*** | N | Y | N | N | N | N | Y | N |
| **MAINE** | | | | | | | | |
| 1 Andrews | Y | Y | Y | N | Y | Y | Y | Y |
| 2 ***Snowe*** | Y | Y | N | N | Y | Y | Y | N |
| **MARYLAND** | | | | | | | | |
| 1 ***Gilchrest*** | N | Y | N | Y | N | Y | Y | N |
| 2 ***Bentley*** | ? | Y | N | N | N | ? | ? | N |
| 3 Cardin | Y | Y | Y | Y | Y | Y | Y | Y |
| 4 McMillen | N | Y | N | Y | Y | Y | Y | N |
| 5 Hoyer | Y | Y | Y | Y | Y | Y | Y | N |
| 6 Byron | Y | Y | N | N | Y | Y | Y | ? |
| 7 Mfume | Y | Y | Y | N | Y | Y | Y | Y |
| 8 ***Morella*** | N | Y | N | Y | Y | Y | Y | # |
| **MASSACHUSETTS** | | | | | | | | |
| 1 Olver | Y | Y | Y | N | Y | Y | Y | Y |
| 2 Neal | Y | Y | Y | N | Y | Y | Y | Y |
| 3 Early | N | Y | Y | N | Y | Y | Y | Y |
| 4 Frank | Y | Y | Y | N | Y | Y | Y | Y |
| 5 Atkins | Y | Y | Y | N | Y | Y | Y | Y |
| 6 Mavroules | Y | Y | Y | Y | Y | N | Y | Y |
| 7 Markey | Y | Y | Y | Y | Y | Y | Y | Y |
| 8 Kennedy | Y | Y | Y | Y | Y | Y | Y | Y |
| 9 Moakley | Y | Y | Y | Y | Y | Y | Y | Y |
| 10 Studds | Y | Y | Y | N | Y | Y | Y | Y |
| 11 Donnelly | Y | Y | Y | N | Y | N | ? | Y |
| **MICHIGAN** | | | | | | | | |
| 1 Conyers | Y | + | Y | N | Y | Y | Y | Y |
| 2 ***Pursell*** | N | Y | N | ? | N | Y | Y | ? |
| 3 Wolpe | Y | Y | Y | N | Y | Y | Y | ? |
| 4 ***Upton*** | N | Y | N | N | N | Y | Y | N |
| 5 ***Henry*** | N | Y | N | N | N | N | Y | N |
| 6 Carr | N | Y | Y | N | N | Y | Y | Y |
| 7 Kildee | Y | Y | Y | N | Y | N | Y | Y |
| 8 Traxler | Y | Y | Y | Y | Y | ? | Y | ? |
| 9 ***Vander Jagt*** | N | Y | N | N | N | N | Y | ? |
| 10 ***Camp*** | N | Y | N | N | N | N | Y | N |
| 11 ***Davis*** | N | Y | N | N | N | N | Y | N |
| 12 Bonior | Y | Y | Y | Y | Y | Y | Y | Y |
| 13 Collins | Y | ? | Y | N | Y | + | Y | Y |
| 14 Hertel | Y | Y | Y | N | Y | Y | Y | ? |
| 15 Ford | Y | Y | Y | Y | Y | Y | Y | Y |
| 16 Dingell | Y | Y | Y | ? | Y | Y | Y | ? |
| 17 Levin | Y | Y | Y | Y | Y | Y | Y | Y |
| 18 ***Broomfield*** | N | Y | N | N | N | N | Y | ? |
| **MINNESOTA** | | | | | | | | |
| 1 Penny | Y | Y | N | N | Y | Y | N | Y |
| 2 ***Weber*** | N | Y | N | N | N | N | Y | N |
| 3 ***Ramstad*** | N | Y | N | N | N | Y | Y | N |
| 4 Vento | Y | Y | Y | Y | Y | Y | Y | Y |

| | 1 | 2 | 3 | 4 | 5 | 6 | 7 | 8 |
|---|---|---|---|---|---|---|---|---|
| 5 Sabo | N | Y | Y | Y | Y | Y | Y | Y |
| 6 Sikorski | Y | Y | Y | N | Y | Y | Y | Y |
| 7 Peterson | N | Y | Y | N | Y | N | Y | Y |
| 8 Oberstar | Y | Y | Y | Y | Y | N | Y | Y |
| **MISSISSIPPI** | | | | | | | | |
| 1 Whitten | ? | ? | Y | Y | ? | N | Y | ? |
| 2 Espy | Y | Y | N | N | Y | Y | Y | Y |
| 3 Montgomery | N | Y | N | Y | Y | N | N | N |
| 4 Parker | N | Y | N | Y | Y | N | Y | N |
| 5 Taylor | N | Y | N | N | N | N | Y | N |
| **MISSOURI** | | | | | | | | |
| 1 Clay | Y | Y | Y | N | Y | Y | Y | Y |
| 2 Horn | Y | Y | Y | N | Y | Y | Y | Y |
| 3 Gephardt | Y | Y | Y | Y | Y | Y | Y | Y |
| 4 Skelton | N | Y | X | N | Y | N | Y | N |
| 5 Wheat | Y | Y | Y | N | Y | Y | Y | Y |
| 6 ***Coleman*** | N | Y | N | N | N | Y | Y | N |
| 7 ***Hancock*** | N | Y | N | N | N | N | N | N |
| 8 ***Emerson*** | N | Y | N | N | N | N | Y | N |
| 9 Volkmer | Y | Y | N | N | Y | N | Y | Y |
| **MONTANA** | | | | | | | | |
| 1 Williams | Y | Y | Y | N | Y | Y | Y | ? |
| 2 ***Marlenee*** | N | Y | N | N | Y | X | N | Y |
| **NEBRASKA** | | | | | | | | |
| 1 ***Bereuter*** | N | Y | N | Y | N | Y | Y | N |
| 2 Hoagland | Y | Y | N | Y | Y | Y | Y | N |
| 3 ***Barrett*** | N | Y | N | Y | N | N | Y | N |
| **NEVADA** | | | | | | | | |
| 1 Bilbray | Y | Y | N | N | Y | Y | Y | N |
| 2 ***Vucanovich*** | N | Y | N | N | N | N | N | ? |
| **NEW HAMPSHIRE** | | | | | | | | |
| 1 ***Zeliff*** | N | Y | N | N | N | Y | Y | N |
| 2 Swett | N | Y | Y | N | Y | Y | Y | N |
| **NEW JERSEY** | | | | | | | | |
| 1 Andrews | N | Y | Y | N | Y | Y | Y | N |
| 2 Hughes | N | Y | Y | N | Y | Y | Y | Y |
| 3 Pallone | N | Y | Y | N | Y | Y | Y | Y |
| 4 ***Smith*** | N | Y | N | ? | Y | N | Y | N |
| 5 ***Roukema*** | N | Y | N | Y | N | Y | Y | Y |
| 6 Dwyer | N | Y | Y | N | Y | Y | Y | Y |
| 7 ***Rinaldo*** | N | Y | N | N | Y | N | Y | N |
| 8 Roe | N | Y | Y | N | Y | N | Y | N |
| 9 Torricelli | N | Y | Y | N | Y | Y | Y | N |
| 10 Payne | Y | Y | Y | N | Y | Y | Y | Y |
| 11 ***Gallo*** | N | Y | N | Y | N | Y | Y | N |
| 12 ***Zimmer*** | N | Y | N | N | Y | Y | Y | N |
| 13 ***Saxton*** | N | Y | N | ? | N | N | Y | N |
| 14 Guarini | Y | Y | Y | N | Y | Y | Y | N |
| **NEW MEXICO** | | | | | | | | |
| 1 ***Schiff*** | N | Y | N | N | N | Y | Y | N |
| 2 ***Skeen*** | N | Y | N | Y | N | Y | Y | N |
| 3 Richardson | Y | Y | N | N | Y | Y | Y | N |
| **NEW YORK** | | | | | | | | |
| 1 Hochbrueckner | Y | Y | Y | N | Y | Y | Y | Y |
| 2 Downey | Y | Y | Y | N | Y | Y | Y | Y |
| 3 Mrazek | N | Y | Y | ? | Y | Y | Y | Y |
| 4 ***Lent*** | N | Y | N | N | N | N | Y | ? |
| 5 ***McGrath*** | N | Y | N | N | N | N | Y | N |
| 6 Flake | Y | Y | Y | N | Y | Y | Y | ? |
| 7 Ackerman | Y | Y | Y | Y | Y | Y | Y | ? |
| 8 Scheuer | Y | Y | Y | N | Y | Y | Y | ? |
| 9 Manton | Y | Y | Y | Y | Y | N | Y | Y |
| 10 Schumer | Y | Y | Y | Y | Y | Y | Y | Y |
| 11 Towns | Y | Y | Y | N | Y | Y | Y | Y |
| 12 Owens | Y | Y | Y | N | Y | Y | Y | Y |
| 13 Solarz | Y | Y | Y | Y | Y | Y | Y | Y |
| 14 ***Molinari*** | N | Y | N | N | N | Y | Y | N |
| 15 ***Green*** | N | Y | N | Y | Y | Y | Y | ? |
| 16 Rangel | Y | Y | Y | N | Y | Y | Y | Y |
| 17 Vacancy | | | | | | | | |
| 18 Serrano | Y | Y | Y | N | Y | Y | Y | Y |
| 19 Engel | Y | Y | Y | N | Y | Y | Y | Y |
| 20 Lowey | Y | Y | Y | N | Y | Y | Y | Y |
| 21 ***Fish*** | N | Y | N | N | Y | Y | Y | N |
| 22 ***Gilman*** | N | Y | N | N | Y | Y | Y | N |
| 23 McNulty | Y | Y | Y | N | Y | Y | Y | N |
| 24 ***Solomon*** | N | Y | N | N | N | N | Y | N |
| 25 ***Boehlert*** | N | Y | N | Y | Y | Y | Y | N |
| 26 ***Martin*** | N | Y | N | N | ? | Y | Y | N |
| 27 ***Walsh*** | N | Y | N | Y | N | N | Y | N |
| 28 McHugh | Y | Y | Y | Y | Y | Y | Y | Y |
| 29 ***Horton*** | N | Y | N | N | N | Y | Y | N |
| 30 Slaughter | Y | Y | Y | N | Y | Y | Y | Y |
| 31 ***Paxon*** | N | Y | N | N | N | N | Y | N |

| | 1 | 2 | 3 | 4 | 5 | 6 | 7 | 8 |
|---|---|---|---|---|---|---|---|---|
| 32 LaFalce | Y | Y | Y | N | Y | N | Y | Y |
| 33 Nowak | Y | Y | Y | N | Y | N | Y | Y |
| 34 ***Houghton*** | N | Y | N | Y | N | Y | Y | N |
| **NORTH CAROLINA** | | | | | | | | |
| 1 Vacancy | | | | | | | | |
| 2 Valentine | Y | Y | N | ? | Y | Y | Y | Y |
| 3 Lancaster | N | Y | N | N | Y | Y | Y | N |
| 4 Price | Y | Y | Y | Y | Y | Y | Y | Y |
| 5 Neal | Y | Y | ? | Y | Y | Y | Y | Y |
| 6 ***Coble*** | N | Y | N | N | N | N | Y | N |
| 7 Rose | Y | Y | Y | Y | Y | Y | Y | Y |
| 8 Hefner | Y | Y | Y | N | Y | Y | Y | ? |
| 9 ***McMillan*** | N | Y | N | Y | N | Y | Y | N |
| 10 ***Ballenger*** | N | Y | N | N | N | Y | X | N |
| 11 ***Taylor*** | N | Y | — | N | N | N | Y | N |
| **NORTH DAKOTA** | | | | | | | | |
| AL Dorgan | Y | Y | N | N | Y | Y | Y | Y |
| **OHIO** | | | | | | | | |
| 1 Luken | Y | Y | N | N | Y | N | Y | ? |
| 2 ***Gradison*** | N | Y | N | Y | N | Y | Y | N |
| 3 Hall | Y | Y | Y | N | Y | N | Y | Y |
| 4 ***Oxley*** | N | Y | N | N | N | N | Y | N |
| 5 ***Gillmor*** | N | Y | N | Y | N | N | Y | N |
| 6 ***McEwen*** | N | Y | N | N | N | X | Y | N |
| 7 ***Hobson*** | N | Y | N | N | N | Y | Y | N |
| 8 ***Boehner*** | N | Y | N | N | N | N | Y | N |
| 9 Kaptur | Y | Y | Y | N | Y | Y | Y | Y |
| 10 ***Miller*** | N | Y | N | N | N | N | Y | N |
| 11 Eckart | Y | Y | Y | N | Y | Y | Y | Y |
| 12 ***Kasich*** | N | Y | N | N | N | N | Y | N |
| 13 Pease | Y | Y | Y | Y | Y | Y | Y | Y |
| 14 Sawyer | Y | Y | Y | N | Y | Y | Y | Y |
| 15 ***Wylie*** | N | Y | N | Y | N | N | Y | N |
| 16 ***Regula*** | N | Y | N | N | N | Y | Y | N |
| 17 Traficant | N | Y | Y | N | N | Y | Y | Y |
| 18 Applegate | Y | Y | Y | N | N | N | Y | Y |
| 19 Feighan | Y | Y | Y | Y | Y | Y | Y | ? |
| 20 Oakar | Y | Y | Y | N | Y | N | ? | Y |
| 21 Stokes | Y | Y | Y | N | Y | Y | Y | Y |
| **OKLAHOMA** | | | | | | | | |
| 1 ***Inhofe*** | N | Y | N | N | N | N | N | N |
| 2 Synar | Y | Y | Y | Y | Y | Y | N | Y |
| 3 Brewster | Y | Y | N | N | Y | Y | Y | N |
| 4 McCurdy | N | Y | N | Y | Y | Y | Y | N |
| 5 ***Edwards*** | N | Y | N | N | N | N | N | N |
| 6 English | N | Y | N | N | Y | Y | N | N |
| **OREGON** | | | | | | | | |
| 1 AuCoin | Y | Y | Y | N | Y | Y | Y | Y |
| 2 ***Smith*** | N | Y | N | N | N | N | N | N |
| 3 Wyden | Y | Y | Y | N | Y | Y | Y | Y |
| 4 DeFazio | Y | Y | Y | N | Y | Y | Y | Y |
| 5 Kopetski | Y | Y | Y | N | Y | Y | Y | + |
| **PENNSYLVANIA** | | | | | | | | |
| 1 Foglietta | Y | Y | Y | N | Y | Y | Y | Y |
| 2 Blackwell | Y | Y | Y | N | Y | Y | Y | Y |
| 3 Borski | Y | Y | Y | N | Y | N | Y | N |
| 4 Kolter | Y | Y | Y | N | Y | ? | Y | ? |
| 5 ***Schulze*** | N | Y | N | N | N | N | Y | N |
| 6 Yatron | Y | Y | N | N | Y | N | Y | N |
| 7 ***Weldon*** | N | Y | N | N | N | N | Y | N |
| 8 Kostmayer | Y | Y | Y | N | Y | Y | Y | Y |
| 9 ***Shuster*** | N | Y | N | N | N | N | Y | N |
| 10 ***McDade*** | N | Y | N | Y | N | ? | ? | ? |
| 11 Kanjorski | Y | Y | Y | N | Y | N | Y | Y |
| 12 Murtha | Y | Y | N | Y | Y | N | Y | N |
| 13 ***Coughlin*** | N | Y | N | Y | N | Y | Y | N |
| 14 Coyne | Y | Y | Y | Y | Y | Y | Y | Y |
| 15 ***Ritter*** | N | Y | N | N | N | N | Y | N |
| 16 ***Walker*** | N | Y | N | N | N | N | Y | N |
| 17 ***Gekas*** | N | Y | N | N | N | Y | Y | N |
| 18 ***Santorum*** | N | Y | N | N | N | N | Y | N |
| 19 ***Goodling*** | N | Y | N | N | N | N | Y | Y |
| 20 Gaydos | Y | Y | Y | N | N | ? | Y | ? |
| 21 ***Ridge*** | N | Y | N | N | Y | Y | Y | Y |
| 22 Murphy | Y | Y | Y | N | N | N | Y | Y |
| 23 ***Clinger*** | N | Y | N | Y | N | Y | N | — |
| **RHODE ISLAND** | | | | | | | | |
| 1 ***Machtley*** | N | Y | N | N | Y | Y | Y | N |
| 2 Reed | Y | Y | Y | N | Y | Y | Y | Y |
| **SOUTH CAROLINA** | | | | | | | | |
| 1 ***Ravenel*** | N | Y | N | N | N | Y | Y | N |
| 2 ***Spence*** | N | Y | N | N | N | N | Y | N |
| 3 Derrick | Y | Y | N | Y | Y | Y | Y | Y |
| 4 Patterson | N | Y | N | N | Y | Y | Y | — |
| 5 Spratt | Y | Y | N | Y | Y | Y | Y | N |
| 6 Tallon | Y | Y | Y | N | Y | N | Y | Y |

| | 1 | 2 | 3 | 4 | 5 | 6 | 7 | 8 |
|---|---|---|---|---|---|---|---|---|
| **SOUTH DAKOTA** | | | | | | | | |
| AL Johnson | Y | Y | Y | Y | Y | Y | Y | N |
| **TENNESSEE** | | | | | | | | |
| 1 ***Quillen*** | N | Y | N | N | N | N | Y | N |
| 2 ***Duncan*** | N | Y | N | N | Y | N | N | Y |
| 3 Lloyd | N | Y | N | N | Y | Y | Y | N |
| 4 Cooper | N | Y | N | N | Y | Y | Y | N |
| 5 Clement | Y | Y | N | N | Y | Y | Y | N |
| 6 Gordon | Y | Y | N | N | Y | Y | Y | Y |
| 7 ***Sundquist*** | N | Y | N | N | N | N | Y | N |
| 8 Tanner | Y | Y | N | N | Y | Y | Y | N |
| 9 Ford | Y | Y | Y | N | Y | Y | Y | Y |
| **TEXAS** | | | | | | | | |
| 1 Chapman | Y | Y | Y | N | Y | Y | N | N |
| 2 Wilson | Y | Y | N | N | ? | Y | Y | N |
| 3 ***Johnson*** | N | Y | N | N | N | N | N | N |
| 4 Hall | N | Y | N | N | N | N | N | N |
| 5 Bryant | Y | Y | Y | N | Y | Y | Y | Y |
| 6 ***Barton*** | N | Y | N | N | N | N | Y | N |
| 7 ***Archer*** | N | Y | N | N | N | N | N | N |
| 8 ***Fields*** | N | Y | N | N | N | ? | N | — |
| 9 Brooks | Y | Y | ? | Y | Y | Y | Y | ? |
| 10 Pickle | Y | Y | N | Y | Y | Y | Y | N |
| 11 Edwards | Y | Y | N | N | Y | Y | Y | N |
| 12 Geren | N | Y | N | Y | N | Y | Y | N |
| 13 Sarpalius | N | Y | N | Y | N | N | N | N |
| 14 Laughlin | Y | Y | N | Y | Y | Y | Y | ? |
| 15 de la Garza | # | Y | Y | N | Y | N | N | ? |
| 16 Coleman | Y | Y | Y | Y | Y | Y | Y | N |
| 17 Stenholm | Y | Y | N | Y | Y | N | N | N |
| 18 Washington | Y | Y | Y | N | Y | Y | Y | Y |
| 19 ***Combest*** | N | Y | N | N | N | N | N | N |
| 20 Gonzalez | Y | Y | Y | Y | Y | Y | N | Y |
| 21 ***Smith*** | N | Y | N | N | N | Y | N | N |
| 22 ***DeLay*** | N | Y | N | N | N | N | N | N |
| 23 Bustamante | Y | Y | Y | N | Y | Y | N | X |
| 24 Frost | Y | Y | Y | N | N | Y | Y | N |
| 25 Andrews | Y | Y | N | N | Y | Y | N | N |
| 26 ***Armey*** | N | Y | N | N | N | N | N | N |
| 27 Ortiz | Y | Y | N | N | Y | N | N | N |
| **UTAH** | | | | | | | | |
| 1 ***Hansen*** | N | Y | N | Y | N | N | Y | N |
| 2 Owens | Y | Y | N | N | Y | Y | Y | Y |
| 3 Orton | Y | Y | N | N | Y | N | Y | Y |
| **VERMONT** | | | | | | | | |
| AL *Sanders* | Y | Y | Y | N | Y | Y | Y | Y |
| **VIRGINIA** | | | | | | | | |
| 1 ***Bateman*** | N | Y | N | Y | N | N | Y | N |
| 2 Pickett | N | Y | N | Y | N | Y | Y | N |
| 3 ***Bliley*** | N | Y | N | Y | N | N | Y | N |
| 4 Sisisky | Y | Y | N | Y | N | Y | Y | N |
| 5 Payne | Y | Y | N | Y | Y | Y | Y | N |
| 6 Olin | Y | Y | N | Y | N | Y | Y | ? |
| 7 ***Allen*** | N | Y | N | N | N | Y | Y | N |
| 8 Moran | Y | ? | Y | Y | Y | Y | Y | Y |
| 9 Boucher | Y | Y | Y | N | Y | Y | Y | Y |
| 10 ***Wolf*** | N | Y | N | Y | N | N | Y | N |
| **WASHINGTON** | | | | | | | | |
| 1 ***Miller*** | N | Y | N | Y | Y | Y | Y | ? |
| 2 Swift | Y | Y | Y | Y | Y | Y | Y | Y |
| 3 Unsoeld | Y | Y | Y | N | Y | Y | Y | ? |
| 4 ***Morrison*** | N | Y | N | Y | Y | Y | Y | ? |
| 5 Foley | Y | Y | | | | | | |
| 6 Dicks | Y | Y | Y | Y | Y | Y | Y | N |
| 7 McDermott | Y | Y | Y | N | Y | Y | Y | Y |
| 8 ***Chandler*** | N | Y | N | Y | N | Y | Y | N |
| **WEST VIRGINIA** | | | | | | | | |
| 1 Mollohan | Y | Y | Y | N | Y | N | Y | N |
| 2 Staggers | Y | Y | Y | N | Y | N | Y | Y |
| 3 Wise | Y | Y | Y | N | Y | Y | Y | Y |
| 4 Rahall | Y | Y | Y | N | Y | N | Y | Y |
| **WISCONSIN** | | | | | | | | |
| 1 Aspin | Y | Y | Y | Y | Y | Y | Y | N |
| 2 ***Klug*** | N | Y | N | N | Y | Y | Y | Y |
| 3 ***Gunderson*** | N | Y | N | N | N | N | Y | N |
| 4 Kleczka | Y | Y | Y | Y | Y | Y | Y | Y |
| 5 Moody | Y | Y | Y | N | Y | Y | Y | Y |
| 6 ***Petri*** | N | Y | N | N | Y | N | Y | N |
| 7 Obey | N | Y | Y | Y | Y | Y | Y | Y |
| 8 ***Roth*** | N | Y | N | N | N | N | Y | X |
| 9 ***Sensenbrenner*** | N | Y | N | N | N | N | Y | Y |
| **WYOMING** | | | | | | | | |
| AL ***Thomas*** | N | Y | N | Y | N | Y | Y | Y |

Southern states - Ala., Ark., Fla., Ga., Ky., La., Miss., N.C., Okla., S.C., Tenn., Texas, Va.
Omitted votes are quorum calls, which CQ does not include in its vote charts.

**9. HJ Res 290. Balanced-Budget Constitutional Amendment/Passage.** Passage of the joint resolution to propose a constitutional amendment that would prohibit deficit spending unless a three-fifths majority of both chambers of Congress approved a specific deficit amount or there was a declaration of war (or national military emergency) enacted into law; require the president to submit a balanced budget each fiscal year; and require a three-fifths majority of both chambers of Congress to increase the public debt. The amendment would take effect in fiscal 1998 or the second year after ratification, whichever is later. Rejected 280-153: R 164-2; D 116-150 (ND 52-130, SD 64-20); I 0-1, June 11, 1992 (House vote 187). A two-thirds majority of those present and voting of both chambers (289 in this case) is required to propose an amendment to the Constitution. A "yea" was a vote in support of the president's position.

**10. HR 5373. Fiscal 1993 Energy and Water Appropriations/Superconducting Super Collider.** Eckart, D-Ohio, amendment to cut $450 million of the $483.7 million provided for the superconducting super collider, leaving approximately $34 million to shut down the project. Adopted 232-181: R 79-79; D 152-102 (ND 126-49, SD 26-53); I 1-0, June 17, 1992 (House vote 201). A "nay" was a vote in support of the president's position.

**11. HR 5132. Fiscal 1992 Disaster Relief Supplemental Appropriations/Conference Report.** Adoption of the conference report to provide $1,075,510,000 in new budget authority in fiscal 1992 for disaster assistance and loans to respond to the Los Angeles riots and Chicago flooding. The $1.1 billion also includes $500 million for Summer Youth Employment. The funds are designated as emergency spending, thus exempt from the spending caps of the 1990 Budget Enforcement Act. Adopted 249-168: R 43-117; D 205-51 (ND 158-17, SD 47-34); I 1-0, June 18, 1992 (House vote 206). A "yea" was a vote in support of the president's position.

**12. HR 4850. Cable Television Reregulation/Program Access.** Tauzin, D-La., amendment to give satellite distributors and other potential cable competitors lower-priced access to cable programming. Adopted 338-68: R 116-45; D 221-23 (ND 152-18, SD 69-5); I 1-0, July 23, 1992 (House vote 311).

**13. HR 5679. Fiscal 1993 VA, Housing and Urban Development, Independent Agencies Appropriations/Space Station Cuts.** Traxler, D-Mich., amendment to cut $1.2 billion of the $1.73 billion in the bill for NASA's space station *Freedom*, leaving $525 million to close down the program. Rejected 181-237: R 38-127; D 142-110 (ND 115-59, SD 27-51); I 1-0, July 29, 1992 (House vote 334). A "nay" was a vote in support of the president's position.

**14. HR 4547. Russian Aid/Passage.** Passage of the bill to provide aid to the former republics of the Soviet Union. The bill also increases the U.S. contribution to the International Monetary Fund by $12.3 billion and includes numerous other measures to boost aid to the former republics. Passed 255-164: R 94-68; D 161-95 (ND 115-63, SD 46-32); I 0-1, Aug. 6, 1992 (House vote 374). A "yea" was a vote in support of the president's position.

**15. HR 5368. Fiscal 1993 Foreign Operations Appropriations/Conference Report.** Adoption of the conference report to provide $26.26 billion for foreign aid in fiscal 1993. The administration requested $27.43 billion. The bill would provide $10 billion in loan guarantees for Israel and increase the U.S. contribution to International Monetary Fund by $12.3 billion. Adopted 312-105: R 104-58; D 208-46 (ND 152-20, SD 56-26); I 0-1, Oct. 5, 1992 (House vote 470).

**16. HR 429. Western Water Bill/Central Valley Project.** Thomas, R-Calif., motion to recommit to conference the conference report with instructions to report it back after deleting the reform of the Central Valley Project in California. Motion rejected 159-244: R 117-41; D 42-202 (ND 15-152, SD 27-50); I 0-1, Oct. 6, 1992 (House vote 480; in the session that began and the Congressional Record dated Oct. 5). (The conference report subsequently was adopted by voice vote.)

## KEY

| | |
|---|---|
| Y | Voted for (yea). |
| # | Paired for. |
| + | Announced for. |
| N | Voted against (nay). |
| X | Paired against. |
| — | Announced against. |
| P | Voted "present." |
| C | Voted "present" to avoid possible conflict of interest. |
| ? | Did not vote or otherwise make a position known. |

Democrats **Republicans**
*Independent*

| | 9 | 10 | 11 | 12 | 13 | 14 | 15 | 16 |
|---|---|---|---|---|---|---|---|---|
| **ALABAMA** | | | | | | | | |
| 1 *Callahan* | Y | N | N | Y | N | N | N | Y |
| 2 *Dickinson* | Y | N | N | Y | N | ? | N | ? |
| 3 Browder | Y | N | N | Y | N | N | N | Y |
| 4 Bevill | Y | N | Y | Y | N | ? | N | Y |
| 5 Cramer | Y | N | N | Y | N | Y | N | Y |
| 6 Erdreich | Y | N | N | Y | N | N | N | N |
| 7 Harris | Y | N | N | Y | N | N | Y | Y |
| **ALASKA** | | | | | | | | |
| AL *Young* | Y | N | ? | Y | N | Y | Y | Y |
| **ARIZONA** | | | | | | | | |
| 1 *Rhodes* | Y | N | N | N | N | Y | N | N |
| 2 Pastor | N | Y | Y | N | Y | N | Y | N |
| 3 *Stump* | Y | N | N | N | N | N | N | Y |
| 4 *Kyl* | Y | N | N | N | N | N | N | Y |
| 5 *Kolbe* | Y | N | N | Y | Y | Y | Y | N |
| **ARKANSAS** | | | | | | | | |
| 1 Alexander | N | N | Y | Y | ? | Y | Y | ? |
| 2 Thornton | N | N | Y | Y | N | Y | Y | N |
| 3 *Hammerschmidt* | Y | N | N | Y | N | Y | N | Y |
| 4 Anthony | Y | N | Y | ? | Y | Y | Y | N |
| **CALIFORNIA** | | | | | | | | |
| 1 *Riggs* | Y | N | N | Y | N | N | Y | N |
| 2 *Herger* | Y | Y | N | N | N | N | N | Y |
| 3 Matsui | N | N | Y | Y | N | Y | Y | N |
| 4 Fazio | N | N | Y | N | Y | N | Y | Y |
| 5 Pelosi | N | Y | Y | Y | Y | Y | Y | N |
| 6 Boxer | N | Y | Y | Y | ? | N | # | ? |
| 7 Miller | N | Y | Y | Y | Y | Y | Y | N |
| 8 Dellums | N | Y | Y | Y | Y | Y | Y | N |
| 9 Stark | N | Y | Y | Y | Y | Y | N | N |
| 10 Edwards | N | Y | Y | Y | N | Y | N | N |
| 11 Lantos | N | Y | Y | Y | Y | Y | Y | Y |
| 12 *Campbell* | Y | Y | Y | N | Y | N | Y | Y |
| 13 Mineta | N | N | Y | Y | N | Y | Y | N |
| 14 *Doolittle* | Y | Y | N | N | N | N | N | Y |
| 15 Condit | Y | Y | Y | Y | Y | N | N | Y |
| 16 Panetta | N | Y | Y | Y | Y | N | Y | Y |
| 17 Dooley | Y | Y | Y | Y | Y | N | N | Y |
| 18 Lehman | N | Y | Y | Y | N | Y | Y | Y |
| 19 *Lagomarsino* | Y | N | N | N | N | Y | Y | Y |
| 20 *Thomas* | Y | Y | N | Y | N | Y | Y | Y |
| 21 *Gallegly* | Y | Y | N | N | N | N | N | Y |
| 22 *Moorhead* | Y | N | N | Y | N | N | N | Y |
| 23 Beilenson | N | Y | Y | Y | Y | Y | Y | N |
| 24 Waxman | N | Y | Y | Y | N | Y | Y | N |
| 25 Roybal | N | Y | Y | Y | Y | N | ? | N |
| 26 Berman | N | Y | Y | N | Y | N | Y | N |
| 27 Levine | N | N | Y | ? | N | Y | Y | Y |
| 28 Dixon | N | Y | Y | Y | N | Y | Y | Y |
| 29 Waters | N | Y | Y | Y | N | Y | Y | Y |
| 30 Martinez | N | Y | Y | Y | Y | N | Y | N |
| 31 Dymally | N | ? | Y | ? | N | N | Y | N |
| 32 Anderson | N | Y | Y | Y | Y | Y | Y | N |
| 33 *Dreier* | Y | N | N | Y | N | N | N | Y |
| 34 Torres | N | Y | Y | Y | N | Y | Y | N |
| 35 *Lewis* | Y | Y | Y | Y | Y | Y | Y | N |
| 36 Brown | N | Y | Y | Y | Y | N | Y | N |
| 37 *McCandless* | Y | Y | N | Y | N | N | N | Y |
| 38 *Dornan* | Y | N | N | N | N | N | N | Y |
| 39 *Dannemeyer* | Y | N | N | N | N | N | N | Y |
| 40 *Cox* | Y | N | N | N | N | N | N | Y |
| 41 Lowery | Y | Y | Y | Y | N | Y | Y | Y |

| | 9 | 10 | 11 | 12 | 13 | 14 | 15 | 16 |
|---|---|---|---|---|---|---|---|---|
| 42 *Rohrabacher* | Y | Y | N | N | N | N | N | Y |
| 43 *Packard* | Y | N | N | N | N | N | N | Y |
| 44 *Cunningham* | Y | N | N | Y | N | N | Y | Y |
| 45 *Hunter* | Y | N | N | Y | N | Y | Y | Y |
| **COLORADO** | | | | | | | | |
| 1 Schroeder | N | Y | Y | N | Y | Y | Y | N |
| 2 Skaggs | N | N | Y | N | Y | Y | Y | N |
| 3 Campbell | Y | Y | Y | N | ? | N | Y | Y |
| 4 *Allard* | Y | N | N | N | N | Y | Y | Y |
| 5 *Hefley* | Y | N | N | N | N | Y | Y | Y |
| 6 *Schaefer* | Y | N | N | N | N | N | N | Y |
| **CONNECTICUT** | | | | | | | | |
| 1 Kennelly | N | Y | Y | N | Y | Y | Y | N |
| 2 Gejdenson | N | Y | Y | N | Y | N | Y | N |
| 3 DeLauro | N | Y | Y | Y | N | N | Y | N |
| 4 *Shays* | Y | N | Y | N | Y | Y | Y | N |
| 5 *Franks* | Y | N | Y | N | N | N | Y | Y |
| 6 *Johnson* | Y | Y | Y | Y | N | Y | Y | Y |
| **DELAWARE** | | | | | | | | |
| AL Carper | Y | Y | N | N | N | Y | Y | N |
| **FLORIDA** | | | | | | | | |
| 1 Hutto | Y | Y | N | Y | N | N | N | Y |
| 2 Peterson | Y | Y | N | + | N | Y | N | |
| 3 Bennett | Y | Y | Y | Y | Y | N | N | |
| 4 *James* | Y | N | Y | N | N | N | Y | N |
| 5 *McCollum* | Y | Y | N | Y | N | N | Y | Y |
| 6 *Stearns* | Y | N | Y | N | N | ? | N | Y |
| 7 Gibbons | N | Y | Y | Y | N | Y | Y | N |
| 8 *Young* | Y | N | N | N | Y | N | Y | N |
| 9 *Bilirakis* | Y | N | N | Y | N | N | N | Y |
| 10 *Ireland* | Y | N | Y | N | Y | ? | Y | |
| 11 Bacchus | Y | N | Y | Y | Y | N | Y | N |
| 12 *Lewis* | Y | N | N | Y | N | N | N | Y |
| 13 *Goss* | Y | N | N | N | N | N | N | Y |
| 14 Johnston | Y | Y | Y | Y | Y | Y | Y | N |
| 15 *Shaw* | Y | N | Y | N | N | Y | Y | Y |
| 16 Smith | N | Y | Y | N | Y | N | Y | Y |
| 17 Lehman | N | N | Y | ? | Y | Y | Y | ? |
| 18 *Ros—Lehtinen* | Y | Y | Y | N | N | N | Y | Y |
| 19 Fascell | N | N | Y | Y | N | Y | Y | N |
| **GEORGIA** | | | | | | | | |
| 1 Thomas | Y | N | Y | ? | ? | Y | Y | Y |
| 2 Hatcher | Y | ? | Y | ? | ? | ? | Y | ? |
| 3 Ray | Y | N | N | ? | Y | N | N | Y |
| 4 Jones | Y | # | ? | ? | Y | Y | Y | ? |
| 5 Lewis | N | Y | Y | N | Y | Y | Y | N |
| 6 *Gingrich* | Y | N | Y | N | N | N | N | Y |
| 7 Darden | Y | N | N | N | N | N | N | N |
| 8 Rowland | Y | N | Y | N | N | Y | N | Y |
| 9 Jenkins | Y | N | ? | ? | Y | N | Y | N |
| 10 Barnard | Y | N | Y | N | N | ? | ? | ? |
| **HAWAII** | | | | | | | | |
| 1 Abercrombie | N | Y | Y | Y | N | Y | Y | N |
| 2 Mink | N | Y | Y | N | Y | Y | Y | N |
| **IDAHO** | | | | | | | | |
| 1 LaRocco | Y | N | Y | Y | Y | Y | Y | N |
| 2 Stallings | Y | N | Y | Y | ? | Y | Y | Y |
| **ILLINOIS** | | | | | | | | |
| 1 Hayes | N | Y | Y | Y | N | Y | N | Y |
| 2 Savage | N | Y | Y | Y | ? | N | N | N |
| 3 Russo | N | Y | Y | Y | N | Y | Y | N |
| 4 Sangmeister | Y | Y | Y | Y | N | N | N | N |
| 5 Lipinski | Y | Y | Y | Y | N | N | ? | N |
| 6 *Hyde* | Y | N | ? | ? | ? | Y | Y | Y |
| 7 Collins | N | Y | Y | N | Y | N | N | N |
| 8 Rostenkowski | N | Y | Y | Y | Y | Y | ? | N |
| 9 Yates | N | Y | Y | ? | Y | Y | Y | ? |
| 10 *Porter* | Y | Y | Y | Y | Y | Y | Y | N |
| 11 Annunzio | N | Y | Y | Y | N | Y | Y | ? |
| 12 *Crane* | Y | ? | ? | N | N | N | N | Y |
| 13 *Fawell* | Y | N | N | N | Y | Y | Y | N |
| 14 *Hastert* | Y | Y | Y | Y | Y | Y | Y | N |
| 15 *Ewing* | Y | N | Y | Y | Y | Y | Y | N |
| 16 *Cox* | Y | Y | Y | Y | Y | Y | Y | N |
| 17 Evans | N | Y | Y | Y | Y | Y | Y | N |
| 18 *Michel* | Y | ? | Y | Y | Y | Y | Y | N |
| 19 Bruce | Y | Y | Y | Y | Y | Y | Y | N |
| 20 Durbin | N | Y | Y | Y | N | Y | Y | N |
| 21 Costello | Y | Y | Y | Y | N | N | N | N |
| 22 Poshard | Y | Y | Y | Y | Y | N | Y | N |
| **INDIANA** | | | | | | | | |
| 1 Visclosky | N | Y | N | Y | N | Y | Y | N |
| 2 Sharp | Y | Y | Y | Y | Y | Y | Y | ? |
| 3 Roemer | Y | N | Y | N | N | N | N | N |

ND  Northern Democrats  SD  Southern Democrats

| | 9 | 10 | 11 | 12 | 13 | 14 | 15 | 16 |
|---|---|---|---|---|---|---|---|---|
| 4 Long | Y | Y | Y | Y | Y | Y | Y | N |
| 5 Jontz | Y | Y | Y | Y | Y | N | N | N |
| 6 ***Burton*** | Y | Y | N | N | Y | N | Y | Y |
| 7 ***Myers*** | Y | N | N | N | N | N | N | Y |
| 8 McCloskey | Y | N | Y | Y | Y | Y | Y | N |
| 9 Hamilton | N | Y | Y | Y | Y | Y | Y | N |
| 10 Jacobs | Y | Y | Y | Y | Y | N | N | N |
| **IOWA** | | | | | | | | |
| 1 ***Leach*** | Y | Y | Y | Y | Y | Y | Y | N |
| 2 ***Nussle*** | Y | Y | N | Y | Y | Y | N | Y |
| 3 Nagle | N | N | Y | Y | N | Y | Y | N |
| 4 Smith | N | N | Y | Y | Y | Y | Y | N |
| 5 ***Lightfoot*** | Y | N | N | Y | N | Y | Y | Y |
| 6 ***Grandy*** | Y | Y | N | Y | Y | Y | Y | Y |
| **KANSAS** | | | | | | | | |
| 1 ***Roberts*** | Y | Y | N | Y | N | Y | N | Y |
| 2 Slattery | N | Y | ? | Y | N | Y | Y | N |
| 3 ***Meyers*** | Y | Y | N | Y | N | Y | Y | N |
| 4 Glickman | Y | Y | ? | Y | N | Y | Y | N |
| 5 ***Nichols*** | Y | Y | ? | Y | N | Y | N | Y |
| **KENTUCKY** | | | | | | | | |
| 1 Hubbard | Y | ? | ? | Y | N | N | N | Y |
| 2 Natcher | Y | N | Y | Y | N | Y | Y | N |
| 3 Mazzoli | Y | N | Y | Y | Y | N | Y | N |
| 4 ***Bunning*** | Y | Y | N | Y | N | N | N | Y |
| 5 ***Rogers*** | Y | N | N | Y | Y | N | N | Y |
| 6 ***Hopkins*** | Y | N | N | N | N | Y | N | N |
| 7 Perkins | N | N | Y | Y | N | N | N | Y |
| **LOUISIANA** | | | | | | | | |
| 1 ***Livingston*** | Y | N | N | Y | N | Y | Y | Y |
| 2 Jefferson | N | Y | Y | Y | ? | N | Y | N |
| 3 Tauzin | Y | N | N | Y | ? | N | N | Y |
| 4 ***McCrery*** | Y | N | N | Y | N | Y | Y | Y |
| 5 Huckaby | Y | N | N | Y | N | N | N | Y |
| 6 ***Baker*** | Y | N | N | Y | N | N | N | Y |
| 7 Hayes | Y | N | N | Y | ? | N | N | N |
| 8 ***Holloway*** | Y | N | N | Y | N | N | N | Y |
| **MAINE** | | | | | | | | |
| 1 Andrews | N | Y | Y | Y | Y | Y | Y | N |
| 2 ***Snowe*** | Y | Y | N | Y | Y | N | Y | N |
| **MARYLAND** | | | | | | | | |
| 1 ***Gilchrest*** | Y | N | Y | Y | N | N | Y | N |
| 2 ***Bentley*** | Y | N | N | Y | N | Y | Y | Y |
| 3 Cardin | N | ? | Y | Y | N | Y | Y | N |
| 4 McMillen | Y | N | Y | Y | N | Y | Y | N |
| 5 Hoyer | Y | N | Y | Y | N | Y | Y | N |
| 6 Byron | Y | N | Y | Y | N | Y | Y | Y |
| 7 Mfume | N | Y | Y | Y | Y | N | Y | N |
| 8 ***Morella*** | Y | Y | Y | Y | N | Y | Y | N |
| **MASSACHUSETTS** | | | | | | | | |
| 1 Olver | N | Y | Y | Y | Y | Y | Y | N |
| 2 Neal | N | Y | Y | Y | Y | N | Y | N |
| 3 Early | Y | Y | Y | ? | Y | N | Y | N |
| 4 Frank | N | Y | Y | Y | Y | Y | Y | N |
| 5 Atkins | N | Y | Y | Y | Y | N | ? | N |
| 6 Mavroules | N | N | Y | Y | N | Y | Y | N |
| 7 Markey | N | Y | Y | Y | Y | Y | Y | N |
| 8 Kennedy | Y | Y | Y | Y | Y | Y | Y | N |
| 9 Moakley | N | Y | Y | Y | Y | Y | Y | N |
| 10 Studds | N | Y | Y | Y | Y | Y | Y | N |
| 11 Donnelly | Y | Y | Y | Y | Y | N | N | N |
| **MICHIGAN** | | | | | | | | |
| 1 Conyers | N | Y | Y | ? | ? | N | Y | N |
| 2 ***Pursell*** | Y | N | N | Y | Y | N | Y | Y |
| 3 Wolpe | N | Y | Y | Y | Y | Y | Y | N |
| 4 ***Upton*** | Y | Y | Y | Y | Y | Y | Y | N |
| 5 ***Henry*** | Y | Y | N | Y | Y | Y | N | Y |
| 6 Carr | Y | Y | N | Y | N | N | Y | N |
| 7 Kildee | N | Y | Y | Y | Y | Y | Y | N |
| 8 Traxler | ? | ? | ? | ? | Y | ? | Y | ? |
| 9 ***Vander Jagt*** | Y | N | N | Y | N | Y | Y | Y |
| 10 ***Camp*** | Y | Y | N | Y | N | Y | Y | Y |
| 11 ***Davis*** | Y | N | Y | Y | N | Y | ? | ? |
| 12 Bonior | N | ? | ? | N | N | Y | Y | N |
| 13 Collins | N | Y | Y | Y | ? | N | Y | N |
| 14 Hertel | N | N | Y | Y | Y | Y | Y | N |
| 15 Ford | N | Y | Y | ? | Y | Y | Y | N |
| 16 Dingell | N | Y | Y | Y | Y | Y | Y | N |
| 17 Levin | N | Y | Y | Y | Y | Y | Y | N |
| 18 ***Broomfield*** | Y | ? | N | Y | N | Y | Y | Y |
| **MINNESOTA** | | | | | | | | |
| 1 Penny | Y | Y | N | Y | Y | Y | Y | N |
| 2 ***Weber*** | Y | ? | Y | Y | N | Y | Y | Y |
| 3 ***Ramstad*** | Y | Y | N | Y | Y | N | Y | N |
| 4 Vento | N | Y | Y | Y | Y | Y | Y | N |

| | 9 | 10 | 11 | 12 | 13 | 14 | 15 | 16 |
|---|---|---|---|---|---|---|---|---|
| 5 Sabo | N | Y | Y | Y | Y | Y | Y | N |
| 6 Sikorski | Y | Y | Y | Y | Y | Y | ? | N |
| 7 Peterson | Y | Y | N | Y | Y | Y | Y | N |
| 8 Oberstar | N | Y | Y | Y | Y | Y | Y | N |
| **MISSISSIPPI** | | | | | | | | |
| 1 Whitten | Y | N | Y | Y | N | Y | Y | N |
| 2 Espy | Y | ? | Y | Y | Y | N | Y | Y |
| 3 Montgomery | Y | N | N | Y | Y | Y | N | N |
| 4 Parker | Y | Y | N | N | Y | Y | Y | Y |
| 5 Taylor | Y | Y | N | Y | N | N | N | Y |
| **MISSOURI** | | | | | | | | |
| 1 Clay | N | Y | Y | Y | Y | N | Y | N |
| 2 Horn | N | Y | Y | Y | Y | Y | Y | N |
| 3 Gephardt | N | N | Y | Y | N | Y | Y | N |
| 4 Skelton | Y | N | N | Y | Y | Y | Y | Y |
| 5 Wheat | N | Y | Y | Y | Y | N | Y | N |
| 6 ***Coleman*** | Y | Y | N | Y | N | Y | N | Y |
| 7 ***Hancock*** | Y | Y | N | N | N | N | N | Y |
| 8 ***Emerson*** | Y | N | N | Y | N | Y | Y | Y |
| 9 Volkmer | Y | N | N | Y | N | N | N | Y |
| **MONTANA** | | | | | | | | |
| 1 Williams | N | Y | Y | Y | Y | N | N | N |
| 2 ***Marlenee*** | Y | Y | N | Y | Y | N | N | Y |
| **NEBRASKA** | | | | | | | | |
| 1 ***Bereuter*** | Y | Y | N | Y | Y | Y | Y | Y |
| 2 Hoagland | Y | Y | Y | Y | Y | Y | Y | N |
| 3 ***Barrett*** | Y | Y | N | Y | N | Y | N | Y |
| **NEVADA** | | | | | | | | |
| 1 Bilbray | Y | Y | Y | Y | Y | Y | Y | N |
| 2 ***Vucanovich*** | Y | N | Y | Y | N | Y | Y | N |
| **NEW HAMPSHIRE** | | | | | | | | |
| 1 ***Zeliff*** | Y | Y | Y | N | N | Y | Y | Y |
| 2 Swett | Y | Y | N | Y | Y | Y | Y | N |
| **NEW JERSEY** | | | | | | | | |
| 1 Andrews | Y | N | Y | N | N | N | Y | N |
| 2 Hughes | N | Y | N | Y | Y | N | Y | N |
| 3 Pallone | Y | Y | Y | Y | Y | Y | Y | N |
| 4 ***Smith*** | Y | N | Y | Y | N | Y | Y | N |
| 5 ***Roukema*** | Y | Y | N | N | Y | Y | Y | N |
| 6 Dwyer | N | N | Y | Y | Y | # | Y | ? |
| 7 ***Rinaldo*** | Y | Y | Y | N | Y | Y | Y | N |
| 8 Roe | N | N | Y | Y | N | Y | Y | N |
| 9 Torricelli | Y | N | Y | Y | N | Y | Y | N |
| 10 Payne | N | Y | Y | Y | Y | N | Y | N |
| 11 ***Gallo*** | Y | N | Y | Y | N | Y | Y | Y |
| 12 ***Zimmer*** | Y | Y | N | Y | Y | N | Y | N |
| 13 ***Saxton*** | Y | Y | N | Y | N | Y | Y | Y |
| 14 Guarini | N | Y | Y | Y | N | Y | X | N |
| **NEW MEXICO** | | | | | | | | |
| 1 ***Schiff*** | Y | N | Y | Y | N | Y | Y | Y |
| 2 ***Skeen*** | Y | N | Y | Y | N | Y | Y | Y |
| 3 Richardson | Y | N | Y | Y | N | Y | Y | N |
| **NEW YORK** | | | | | | | | |
| 1 Hochbrueckner | N | N | Y | Y | N | Y | Y | Y |
| 2 Downey | N | Y | Y | Y | N | Y | Y | N |
| 3 Mrazek | N | Y | Y | Y | N | Y | ? | N |
| 4 ***Lent*** | Y | Y | Y | N | N | Y | Y | Y |
| 5 ***McGrath*** | Y | Y | Y | N | N | Y | Y | N |
| 6 Flake | N | Y | Y | Y | Y | N | Y | N |
| 7 Ackerman | N | Y | Y | Y | Y | Y | Y | N |
| 8 Scheuer | N | Y | Y | Y | Y | Y | Y | N |
| 9 Manton | N | N | Y | Y | N | Y | Y | N |
| 10 Schumer | N | ? | # | Y | Y | Y | Y | N |
| 11 Towns | N | Y | Y | Y | ? | N | Y | N |
| 12 Owens | N | Y | Y | Y | Y | N | Y | N |
| 13 Solarz | N | Y | Y | ? | ? | Y | Y | ? |
| 14 ***Molinari*** | Y | Y | N | N | Y | Y | Y | Y |
| 15 ***Green*** | N | N | Y | Y | Y | Y | Y | N |
| 16 Rangel | N | N | Y | Y | Y | N | Y | N |
| 17 Vacancy | | | | | | | | |
| 18 Serrano | N | Y | Y | Y | Y | N | Y | N |
| 19 Engel | N | N | Y | Y | N | Y | Y | N |
| 20 Lowey | N | N | Y | Y | Y | Y | Y | N |
| 21 ***Fish*** | Y | Y | Y | N | Y | Y | Y | Y |
| 22 ***Gilman*** | N | Y | Y | Y | N | Y | Y | N |
| 23 McNulty | N | N | Y | Y | N | Y | Y | N |
| 24 ***Solomon*** | Y | Y | N | Y | Y | N | N | N |
| 25 ***Boehlert*** | Y | Y | Y | Y | N | Y | Y | N |
| 26 ***Martin*** | Y | Y | Y | Y | N | Y | Y | Y |
| 27 ***Walsh*** | Y | N | Y | Y | N | N | Y | Y |
| 28 McHugh | N | N | Y | Y | Y | Y | Y | N |
| 29 ***Horton*** | Y | Y | Y | N | N | Y | Y | N |
| 30 Slaughter | N | Y | Y | Y | Y | Y | Y | N |
| 31 ***Paxon*** | Y | Y | N | Y | N | N | Y | Y |

| | 9 | 10 | 11 | 12 | 13 | 14 | 15 | 16 |
|---|---|---|---|---|---|---|---|---|
| 32 LaFalce | N | Y | Y | Y | Y | Y | Y | N |
| 33 Nowak | N | Y | Y | Y | Y | Y | Y | N |
| 34 ***Houghton*** | Y | N | Y | Y | N | Y | Y | N |
| **NORTH CAROLINA** | | | | | | | | |
| 1 Vacancy | | | | | | | | |
| 2 Valentine | Y | Y | N | Y | — | N | N | Y |
| 3 Lancaster | Y | Y | N | Y | Y | Y | Y | N |
| 4 Price | Y | Y | Y | Y | Y | Y | Y | N |
| 5 Neal | Y | Y | Y | Y | Y | N | N | N |
| 6 ***Coble*** | Y | Y | N | Y | Y | N | Y | Y |
| 7 Rose | N | Y | Y | Y | N | Y | Y | ? |
| 8 Hefner | ? | ? | ? | Y | Y | N | N | N |
| 9 ***McMillan*** | Y | Y | N | Y | N | ? | Y | Y |
| 10 ***Ballenger*** | Y | Y | N | Y | Y | N | N | Y |
| 11 ***Taylor*** | Y | N | N | Y | N | Y | Y | Y |
| **NORTH DAKOTA** | | | | | | | | |
| AL Dorgan | Y | Y | N | Y | Y | N | Y | N |
| **OHIO** | | | | | | | | |
| 1 Luken | Y | Y | Y | N | Y | ? | Y | Y |
| 2 ***Gradison*** | Y | Y | N | N | N | Y | Y | Y |
| 3 Hall | Y | Y | Y | N | N | Y | Y | ? |
| 4 ***Oxley*** | Y | N | N | N | N | Y | N | Y |
| 5 ***Gillmor*** | Y | Y | N | Y | N | Y | Y | Y |
| 6 ***McEwen*** | Y | N | N | Y | N | ? | N | Y |
| 7 ***Hobson*** | Y | N | N | N | N | Y | Y | Y |
| 8 ***Boehner*** | Y | N | N | N | N | Y | Y | Y |
| 9 Kaptur | N | N | Y | Y | Y | N | Y | N |
| 10 ***Miller*** | Y | N | N | N | N | Y | N | Y |
| 11 Eckart | Y | Y | Y | Y | Y | Y | Y | ? |
| 12 ***Kasich*** | Y | N | Y | Y | Y | N | Y | N |
| 13 Pease | N | Y | N | Y | Y | Y | Y | N |
| 14 Sawyer | N | Y | Y | Y | Y | Y | Y | N |
| 15 ***Wylie*** | Y | Y | N | Y | N | Y | Y | Y |
| 16 ***Regula*** | Y | Y | N | Y | N | Y | Y | Y |
| 17 Traficant | N | N | Y | Y | N | N | N | N |
| 18 Applegate | N | Y | N | Y | N | N | N | N |
| 19 Feighan | Y | Y | ? | ? | N | Y | Y | N |
| 20 Oakar | N | N | Y | Y | N | N | Y | N |
| 21 Stokes | N | N | Y | Y | Y | N | Y | N |
| **OKLAHOMA** | | | | | | | | |
| 1 ***Inhofe*** | Y | Y | N | Y | N | N | Y | Y |
| 2 Synar | N | Y | Y | Y | Y | Y | Y | N |
| 3 Brewster | Y | N | N | Y | N | Y | Y | N |
| 4 McCurdy | Y | Y | Y | Y | N | Y | Y | Y |
| 5 ***Edwards*** | Y | Y | N | Y | N | N | Y | ? |
| 6 English | Y | Y | Y | Y | N | N | N | Y |
| **OREGON** | | | | | | | | |
| 1 AuCoin | N | Y | Y | Y | Y | N | Y | N |
| 2 ***Smith*** | Y | N | N | Y | N | N | N | Y |
| 3 Wyden | N | Y | Y | Y | Y | Y | Y | N |
| 4 DeFazio | Y | N | Y | Y | Y | N | N | N |
| 5 Kopetski | N | N | Y | N | N | N | Y | N |
| **PENNSYLVANIA** | | | | | | | | |
| 1 Foglietta | N | Y | Y | Y | Y | N | Y | ? |
| 2 Blackwell | N | Y | Y | ? | Y | N | Y | N |
| 3 Borski | N | N | Y | Y | Y | N | Y | N |
| 4 Kolter | Y | ? | ? | ? | N | Y | Y | ? |
| 5 ***Schulze*** | Y | ? | Y | Y | N | ? | N | ? |
| 6 Yatron | Y | N | Y | Y | N | Y | Y | ? |
| 7 ***Weldon*** | Y | Y | N | Y | N | Y | N | N |
| 8 Kostmayer | N | Y | N | Y | Y | Y | Y | N |
| 9 ***Shuster*** | Y | Y | N | Y | Y | N | N | Y |
| 10 ***McDade*** | Y | X | Y | Y | N | Y | Y | ? |
| 11 Kanjorski | N | Y | Y | Y | Y | N | N | N |
| 12 Murtha | N | N | Y | Y | Y | Y | Y | N |
| 13 ***Coughlin*** | Y | Y | Y | ? | N | Y | Y | Y |
| 14 Coyne | N | N | Y | Y | Y | Y | Y | N |
| 15 ***Ritter*** | Y | Y | N | Y | N | Y | Y | Y |
| 16 ***Walker*** | Y | N | N | Y | N | Y | N | Y |
| 17 ***Gekas*** | Y | N | N | Y | N | Y | Y | Y |
| 18 ***Santorum*** | Y | N | N | Y | N | N | N | N |
| 19 ***Goodling*** | Y | Y | N | N | Y | N | N | ? |
| 20 Gaydos | N | Y | Y | Y | N | ? | N | ? |
| 21 ***Ridge*** | Y | ? | N | Y | N | N | Y | Y |
| 22 Murphy | N | # | N | Y | Y | X | N | N |
| 23 ***Clinger*** | Y | N | Y | Y | N | Y | Y | Y |
| **RHODE ISLAND** | | | | | | | | |
| 1 ***Machtley*** | Y | Y | Y | Y | Y | N | Y | N |
| 2 Reed | N | Y | Y | Y | Y | N | Y | N |
| **SOUTH CAROLINA** | | | | | | | | |
| 1 ***Ravenel*** | Y | Y | N | Y | Y | Y | Y | N |
| 2 ***Spence*** | Y | N | N | Y | N | N | N | Y |
| 3 Derrick | Y | N | Y | Y | Y | Y | Y | N |
| 4 Patterson | Y | Y | N | Y | Y | N | N | N |
| 5 Spratt | Y | Y | Y | Y | Y | Y | Y | N |
| 6 Tallon | N | Y | Y | ? | N | Y | Y | Y |

| | 9 | 10 | 11 | 12 | 13 | 14 | 15 | 16 |
|---|---|---|---|---|---|---|---|---|
| **SOUTH DAKOTA** | | | | | | | | |
| AL Johnson | Y | N | N | Y | Y | Y | Y | N |
| **TENNESSEE** | | | | | | | | |
| 1 ***Quillen*** | Y | X | X | Y | N | N | Y | N |
| 2 ***Duncan*** | Y | Y | N | Y | Y | N | N | Y |
| 3 Lloyd | Y | N | Y | Y | N | N | N | N |
| 4 Cooper | Y | N | Y | Y | N | Y | Y | N |
| 5 Clement | Y | Y | Y | Y | Y | ? | ? | ? |
| 6 Gordon | Y | Y | Y | Y | Y | ? | Y | N |
| 7 ***Sundquist*** | Y | Y | N | Y | N | N | Y | Y |
| 8 Tanner | Y | Y | Y | Y | N | N | N | Y |
| 9 Ford | N | Y | Y | Y | Y | ? | Y | N |
| **TEXAS** | | | | | | | | |
| 1 Chapman | Y | N | N | Y | N | N | N | N |
| 2 Wilson | Y | N | Y | ? | N | ? | Y | N |
| 3 ***Johnson*** | Y | N | N | N | N | Y | Y | Y |
| 4 Hall | Y | N | N | Y | N | N | N | Y |
| 5 Bryant | Y | N | Y | Y | N | N | Y | N |
| 6 ***Barton*** | Y | N | N | N | N | N | N | Y |
| 7 ***Archer*** | Y | N | N | N | N | N | N | Y |
| 8 ***Fields*** | Y | N | N | N | N | N | N | Y |
| 9 Brooks | N | N | Y | Y | N | Y | N | N |
| 10 Pickle | Y | N | Y | Y | N | Y | Y | N |
| 11 Edwards | Y | N | N | Y | N | Y | Y | Y |
| 12 Geren | Y | N | N | Y | N | N | Y | Y |
| 13 Sarpalius | Y | N | N | Y | N | N | N | N |
| 14 Laughlin | Y | N | N | ? | N | Y | Y | N |
| 15 de la Garza | Y | N | Y | Y | N | Y | Y | N |
| 16 Coleman | N | N | Y | N | N | Y | Y | Y |
| 17 Stenholm | Y | N | N | Y | N | Y | Y | Y |
| 18 Washington | N | Y | N | Y | Y | N | Y | N |
| 19 ***Combest*** | Y | N | N | Y | N | N | N | N |
| 20 Gonzalez | N | N | Y | Y | Y | N | N | N |
| 21 ***Smith*** | Y | N | Y | Y | N | Y | Y | Y |
| 22 ***DeLay*** | Y | N | N | ? | N | N | N | Y |
| 23 Bustamante | N | N | Y | Y | N | Y | Y | N |
| 24 Frost | Y | N | Y | ? | N | Y | Y | N |
| 25 Andrews | Y | N | N | Y | N | Y | Y | N |
| 26 ***Armey*** | Y | N | N | N | N | N | N | Y |
| 27 Ortiz | Y | N | Y | Y | N | N | Y | N |
| **UTAH** | | | | | | | | |
| 1 ***Hansen*** | Y | N | N | ? | N | Y | N | N |
| 2 Owens | Y | Y | Y | Y | Y | Y | Y | N |
| 3 Orton | Y | Y | N | N | Y | Y | Y | N |
| **VERMONT** | | | | | | | | |
| AL *Sanders* | N | Y | Y | Y | Y | N | N | N |
| **VIRGINIA** | | | | | | | | |
| 1 ***Bateman*** | Y | N | Y | Y | N | Y | Y | Y |
| 2 Pickett | N | N | N | N | N | Y | Y | Y |
| 3 ***Bliley*** | Y | N | N | N | N | Y | Y | Y |
| 4 Sisisky | Y | Y | N | Y | N | Y | Y | Y |
| 5 Payne | Y | N | N | Y | Y | Y | Y | Y |
| 6 Olin | N | N | N | N | Y | Y | Y | Y |
| 7 ***Allen*** | Y | N | N | Y | N | N | N | Y |
| 8 Moran | Y | N | Y | Y | N | Y | Y | N |
| 9 Boucher | N | N | N | Y | N | Y | N | N |
| 10 ***Wolf*** | Y | Y | N | Y | N | Y | Y | Y |
| **WASHINGTON** | | | | | | | | |
| 1 ***Miller*** | Y | N | N | N | N | Y | Y | N |
| 2 Swift | N | Y | Y | Y | N | Y | Y | N |
| 3 Unsoeld | N | Y | Y | Y | Y | Y | Y | N |
| 4 ***Morrison*** | Y | N | Y | Y | N | Y | Y | Y |
| 5 Foley | N | | | | | Y | | |
| 6 Dicks | N | N | Y | Y | N | Y | Y | N |
| 7 McDermott | N | Y | Y | Y | Y | Y | Y | N |
| 8 ***Chandler*** | Y | N | ? | Y | N | Y | ? | ? |
| **WEST VIRGINIA** | | | | | | | | |
| 1 Mollohan | N | N | Y | Y | N | Y | Y | N |
| 2 Staggers | N | Y | Y | Y | Y | N | ? | Y |
| 3 Wise | Y | Y | Y | Y | N | Y | Y | N |
| 4 Rahall | N | Y | Y | Y | N | N | N | N |
| **WISCONSIN** | | | | | | | | |
| 1 Aspin | N | N | Y | N | N | Y | Y | N |
| 2 ***Klug*** | Y | Y | Y | N | N | N | Y | N |
| 3 ***Gunderson*** | Y | Y | N | Y | N | Y | Y | N |
| 4 Kleczka | N | Y | Y | Y | Y | N | N | N |
| 5 Moody | Y | Y | N | Y | Y | N | Y | N |
| 6 ***Petri*** | Y | Y | N | Y | N | N | N | N |
| 7 Obey | N | Y | Y | Y | Y | Y | Y | N |
| 8 ***Roth*** | Y | Y | N | Y | N | N | N | Y |
| 9 ***Sensenbrenner*** | Y | Y | N | Y | N | N | N | Y |
| **WYOMING** | | | | | | | | |
| AL ***Thomas*** | Y | N | N | ? | N | Y | N | Y |

Southern states - Ala., Ark., Fla., Ga., Ky., La., Miss., N.C., Okla., S.C., Tenn., Texas, Va.
Omitted votes are quorum calls, which CQ does not include in its vote charts.

| | 1 | 2 | 3 | 4 | 5 | 6 | 7 | 8 |
|---|---|---|---|---|---|---|---|---|
| **ALABAMA** | | | | | | | | |
| Heflin | N | Y | N | N | Y | Y | Y | Y |
| *Shelby* | N | Y | N | N | N | Y | Y | Y |
| **ALASKA** | | | | | | | | |
| *Murkowski* | Y | Y | N | N | N | N | Y | Y |
| *Stevens* | Y | ? | N | N | N | N | Y | Y |
| **ARIZONA** | | | | | | | | |
| DeConcini | ? | Y | Y | N | Y | Y | Y | N |
| *McCain* | Y | Y | N | Y | Y | N | Y | Y |
| **ARKANSAS** | | | | | | | | |
| Bumpers | N | Y | Y | N | Y | Y | Y | N |
| Pryor | N | Y | Y | N | Y | Y | Y | N |
| **CALIFORNIA** | | | | | | | | |
| Cranston | N | N | Y | N | Y | N | Y | N |
| *Seymour* | Y | N | N | N | N | Y | Y | Y |
| **COLORADO** | | | | | | | | |
| Wirth | N | Y | Y | N | Y | N | Y | ? |
| *Brown* | Y | Y | N | N | N | N | N | Y |
| **CONNECTICUT** | | | | | | | | |
| Dodd | N | Y | N | N | Y | Y | Y | N |
| Lieberman | Y | Y | N | N | N | Y | Y | N |
| **DELAWARE** | | | | | | | | |
| Biden | N | N | Y | N | Y | N | Y | N |
| *Roth* | Y | Y | N | N | N | ? | ? | Y |
| **FLORIDA** | | | | | | | | |
| Graham | N | N | Y | N | Y | Y | Y | N |
| *Mack* | Y | Y | N | N | N | N | Y | Y |
| **GEORGIA** | | | | | | | | |
| Fowler | N | N | Y | N | Y | Y | Y | N |
| Nunn | N | Y | N | N | Y | N | Y | Y |
| **HAWAII** | | | | | | | | |
| Akaka | N | N | Y | N | Y | N | Y | N |
| Inouye | N | \# | Y | N | Y | N | Y | N |
| **IDAHO** | | | | | | | | |
| *Craig* | Y | Y | N | Y | N | Y | N | Y |
| *Symms* | Y | Y | N | Y | N | Y | N | Y |
| **ILLINOIS** | | | | | | | | |
| Dixon | N | N | ? | N | Y | Y | Y | Y |
| Simon | N | N | Y | N | Y | N | Y | Y |
| **INDIANA** | | | | | | | | |
| *Coats* | Y | Y | N | Y | N | N | Y | Y |
| *Lugar* | Y | N | N | Y | N | N | Y | Y |

| | 1 | 2 | 3 | 4 | 5 | 6 | 7 | 8 |
|---|---|---|---|---|---|---|---|---|
| **IOWA** | | | | | | | | |
| Harkin | ? | \*X | + | N | Y | N | Y | N |
| *Grassley* | Y | N | N | Y | N | N | Y | N |
| **KANSAS** | | | | | | | | |
| *Dole* | Y | Y | N | N | N | N | Y | Y |
| *Kassebaum* | Y | Y | N | N | N | N | Y | N |
| **KENTUCKY** | | | | | | | | |
| Ford | N | Y | Y | Y | Y | Y | Y | N |
| *McConnell* | Y | Y | N | N | N | N | Y | N |
| **LOUISIANA** | | | | | | | | |
| Breaux | Y | Y | Y | N | Y | Y | Y | N |
| Johnston | N | Y | Y | Y | Y | N | Y | N |
| **MAINE** | | | | | | | | |
| Mitchell | N | N | Y | N | Y | N | Y | N |
| *Cohen* | N | N | N | N | N | N | Y | Y |
| **MARYLAND** | | | | | | | | |
| Mikulski | N | N | Y | N | Y | N | Y | N |
| Sarbanes | N | N | Y | N | Y | Y | Y | N |
| **MASSACHUSETTS** | | | | | | | | |
| Kennedy | N | N | Y | N | Y | N | Y | N |
| Kerry | N | N | Y | N | Y | N | Y | N |
| **MICHIGAN** | | | | | | | | |
| Levin | N | N | Y | N | Y | N | Y | N |
| Riegle | N | ? | Y | N | Y | Y | Y | N |
| **MINNESOTA** | | | | | | | | |
| Wellstone | N | N | Y | N | Y | N | Y | − |
| *Durenberger* | Y | N | N | Y | Y | N | Y | Y |
| **MISSISSIPPI** | | | | | | | | |
| *Cochran* | Y | Y | N | N | Y | N | Y | Y |
| *Lott* | Y | Y | N | N | N | N | Y | Y |
| **MISSOURI** | | | | | | | | |
| *Bond* | ? | Y | N | N | N | N | Y | Y |
| Danforth | Y | Y | N | N | N | N | Y | Y |
| **MONTANA** | | | | | | | | |
| Baucus | N | N | Y | N | Y | N | Y | N |
| Burns | N | Y | N | Y | N | Y | N | Y |
| **NEBRASKA** | | | | | | | | |
| Exon | N | Y | N | Y | N | Y | N | Y |
| Kerrey | ? | ? | Y | N | Y | N | Y | N |
| **NEVADA** | | | | | | | | |
| Bryan | N | N | Y | N | Y | N | Y | N |
| Reid | N | N | Y | N | Y | Y | Y | N |

| | 1 | 2 | 3 | 4 | 5 | 6 | 7 | 8 |
|---|---|---|---|---|---|---|---|---|
| **NEW HAMPSHIRE** | | | | | | | | |
| *Rudman* | Y | Y | N | N | N | N | Y | Y |
| *Smith* | Y | Y | N | Y | N | Y | Y | Y |
| **NEW JERSEY** | | | | | | | | |
| Bradley | Y | Y | Y | N | Y | ? | Y | N |
| Lautenberg | N | N | Y | N | Y | Y | Y | N |
| **NEW MEXICO** | | | | | | | | |
| Bingaman | N | Y | Y | N | Y | N | Y | N |
| *Domenici* | Y | Y | N | N | N | N | Y | Y |
| **NEW YORK** | | | | | | | | |
| Moynihan | N | N | Y | N | Y | N | Y | N |
| *D'Amato* | + | N | N | Y | N | Y | Y | Y |
| **NORTH CAROLINA** | | | | | | | | |
| Sanford | N | Y | Y | N | Y | ? | ? | N |
| *Helms* | Y | Y | N | Y | N | + | ? | + |
| **NORTH DAKOTA** | | | | | | | | |
| Burdick | N | Y | Y | N | Y | N | Y | ? |
| Conrad | N | Y | Y | N | Y | N | Y | N |
| **OHIO** | | | | | | | | |
| Glenn | N | N | Y | N | Y | N | Y | N |
| Metzenbaum | N | N | Y | N | ? | ? | Y | N |
| **OKLAHOMA** | | | | | | | | |
| Boren | N | N | Y | N | Y | N | Y | N |
| *Nickles* | Y | Y | N | Y | N | Y | Y | Y |
| **OREGON** | | | | | | | | |
| *Hatfield* | N | N | N | N | N | N | Y | N |
| *Packwood* | Y | N | Y | N | N | Y | Y | Y |
| **PENNSYLVANIA** | | | | | | | | |
| Wofford | N | Y | Y | N | Y | N | Y | N |
| *Specter* | N | Y | Y | N | N | Y | Y | Y |
| **RHODE ISLAND** | | | | | | | | |
| Pell | N | N | Y | N | Y | N | Y | N |
| *Chafee* | N | N | N | N | N | N | Y | N |
| **SOUTH CAROLINA** | | | | | | | | |
| Hollings | N | Y | Y | N | N | Y | Y | Y |
| *Thurmond* | Y | Y | N | N | N | N | Y | Y |
| **SOUTH DAKOTA** | | | | | | | | |
| Daschle | N | N | Y | N | Y | N | Y | N |
| *Pressler* | Y | Y | N | Y | N | Y | Y | Y |
| **TENNESSEE** | | | | | | | | |
| Gore | N | N | Y | N | Y | Y | Y | ? |
| Sasser | N | Y | Y | N | Y | N | Y | N |

| | 1 | 2 | 3 | 4 | 5 | 6 | 7 | 8 |
|---|---|---|---|---|---|---|---|---|
| **TEXAS** | | | | | | | | |
| Bentsen | N | Y | Y | N | Y | N | Y | Y |
| *Gramm* | Y | Y | N | Y | N | Y | Y | Y |
| **UTAH** | | | | | | | | |
| *Garn* | + | Y | N | N | N | N | Y | ? |
| *Hatch* | Y | Y | N | Y | N | N | Y | + |
| **VERMONT** | | | | | | | | |
| Leahy | N | N | Y | N | Y | N | Y | N |
| *Jeffords* | N | N | N | N | Y | N | Y | N |
| **VIRGINIA** | | | | | | | | |
| Robb | N | N | N | N | Y | N | Y | N |
| *Warner* | Y | Y | N | N | N | N | ? | Y |
| **WASHINGTON** | | | | | | | | |
| Adams | N | N | Y | N | Y | N | Y | N |
| *Gorton* | + | Y | N | N | N | N | Y | Y |
| **WEST VIRGINIA** | | | | | | | | |
| Byrd | N | N | Y | N | Y | N | Y | N |
| Rockefeller | N | N | Y | N | Y | N | Y | N |
| **WISCONSIN** | | | | | | | | |
| Kohl | N | N | Y | N | Y | N | Y | N |
| *Kasten* | Y | N | N | Y | N | Y | Y | + |
| **WYOMING** | | | | | | | | |
| *Simpson* | Y | Y | N | N | N | N | Y | Y |
| *Wallop* | Y | Y | N | Y | N | Y | Y | Y |

ND  Northern Democrats    SD  Southern Democrats     Southern states - Ala., Ark., Fla., Ga., Ky., La., Miss., N.C., Okla., S.C., Tenn., Texas, Va.

**1. S 2. Elementary and Secondary Education/School Choice.** Hatch, R-Utah, amendment to authorize $30 million for six demonstration projects to give low-income parents money to pay for enrolling a child at the public or private school of their choice, including religiously affiliated schools. Rejected 36-57: R 33-6; D 3-51 (ND 2-35, SD 1-16), Jan. 23, 1992 (Senate vote 5). A "yea" was a vote in support of the president's position.

**2. S 2166. National Energy Policy/NRC Hearings.** Johnston, D-La., motion to table (kill) the Graham, D-Fla., amendment to the Johnston amendment, to require the Nuclear Regulatory Commission (NRC) to conduct full adjudicatory hearings on serious new safety issues or major construction deficiencies before operation of new power reactors. Motion agreed to 52-43: R 31-11; D 21-32 (ND 9-27, SD 12-5), Feb. 6, 1992 (Senate vote 20).

**3. S 2399. Eliminate Budget Fire Walls/Cloture.** Mitchell, D-Maine, motion to invoke cloture (thus limiting debate) on the motion to proceed to the bill to modify the 1990 Budget Enforcement Act to knock down the walls that prohibit shifting funds between defense and domestic appropriations. Motion rejected 50-48: R 3-40; D 47-8 (ND 35-3, SD 12-5), March 26, 1992 (Senate vote 56). A three-fifths majority vote (60) of the total Senate is required to invoke cloture. A "nay" was a vote in support of the president's position.

**4. HR 2507. National Institutes of Health Reauthorization/Fetal Tissue Research.** Hatch, R-Utah, amendment to replace provisions that lift the ban on fetal tissue transplant research, including tissue from induced abortions, with provisions to establish a registry for a nonprofit bank of tissue from spontaneous abortions and ectopic pregnancies. Rejected 23-77: R 20-23; D 3-54 (ND 1-39, SD 2-15), March 31, 1992 (Senate vote 61). A "yea" was a vote in support of the president's position.

**5. S 3. Campaign Finance/Veto Override.** Passage, over President Bush's May 9 veto, of the bill to limit spending in congressional campaigns by providing incentives to candidates to agree to voluntary spending limits, restricting money from political action committees (PACs) and restricting "soft money" raised by state parties in federal elections. Rejected 57-42: R 3-40; D 54-2 (ND 39-0, SD 15-2), May 13, 1992 (Senate vote 88). A two-thirds majority of those present and voting (66 in this case) is required to override a veto. A "nay" was a vote in support of the president's position.

**6. S 2532. Aid for Former Soviet Republics/Russian Troops in Baltic States.** Pressler, R-S.D., motion to table (kill) the Pell, D-R.I., amendment to the DeConcini, D-Ariz., amendment to give a one-year grace period before imposing DeConcini provisions to suspend aid until the president certifies that Russia has significantly withdrawn armed forces from the Baltic States. Motion rejected 35-60: R 11-30; D 24-30 (ND 14-24, SD 10-6), July 1, 1992 (Senate vote 139). A "nay" was a vote in support of the president's position. (The Pell amendment subsequently was adopted by voice vote.)

**7. HR 5260. Extended Unemployment Benefits/Conference Report.** Adoption of the conference report to provide 20 or 26 weeks of extended unemployment benefits between July 4, 1992, and March 6, 1993, if the national unemployment rate stays above 7 percent. After March 6, 1993, states could use a new 6.5 percent unemployment rate to trigger 13 weeks of extended benefits. Passed 93-3: R 37-3; D 56-0 (ND 40-0, SD 16-0), July 2, 1992 (Senate vote 145). A "yea" was a vote in support of the president's position.

**8. S 3114. Fiscal 1993 Defense Authorization/Strategic Defense Initiative.** Warner, R-Va., motion to table (kill) the Sasser, D-Tenn., amendment to cut the Strategic Defense Initiative by $1 billion from the committee level of $4.3 billion. Motion rejected 43-49: R 34-5; D 9-44 (ND 4-33, SD 5-11), Aug. 7, 1992 (Senate vote 182). A "yea" was a vote in support of the president's position.

### KEY

Y  Voted for (yea).
\#  Paired for.
+  Announced for.
N  Voted against (nay).
X  Paired against.
−  Announced against.
P  Voted ''present.''
C  Voted ''present'' to avoid possible conflict of interest.
?  Did not vote or otherwise make a position known.

Democrats   *Republicans*

| | 9 | 10 | 11 | 12 | 13 | 14 | 15 |
|---|---|---|---|---|---|---|---|
| **ALABAMA** | | | | | | | |
| Heflin | N | N | N | Y | Y | Y | Y |
| Shelby | N | N | Y | Y | Y | N | Y |
| **ALASKA** | | | | | | | |
| *Murkowski* | Y | Y | ? | Y | Y | Y | ? |
| *Stevens* | N | N | Y | Y | Y | N | Y |
| **ARIZONA** | | | | | | | |
| DeConcini | Y | Y | N | Y | Y | N | Y |
| *McCain* | N | Y | Y | N | Y | Y | Y |
| **ARKANSAS** | | | | | | | |
| Bumpers | Y | Y | N | Y | N | Y | Y |
| Pryor | Y | Y | N | Y | N | Y | Y |
| **CALIFORNIA** | | | | | | | |
| Cranston | Y | Y | ? | Y | Y | N | Y |
| *Seymour* | ? | ? | ? | Y | Y | N | N |
| **COLORADO** | | | | | | | |
| Wirth | ? | Y | N | Y | Y | N | Y |
| *Brown* | N | N | Y | Y | Y | N | N |
| **CONNECTICUT** | | | | | | | |
| Dodd | Y | Y | N | Y | Y | Y | Y |
| Lieberman | Y | Y | N | Y | Y | Y | Y |
| **DELAWARE** | | | | | | | |
| Biden | Y | Y | N | Y | Y | Y | Y |
| *Roth* | N | Y | N | Y | N | Y | Y |
| **FLORIDA** | | | | | | | |
| Graham | Y | Y | N | Y | Y | Y | Y |
| *Mack* | N | N | Y | N | Y | P | Y |
| **GEORGIA** | | | | | | | |
| Fowler | Y | Y | N | Y | Y | Y | Y |
| Nunn | N | Y | N | Y | Y | Y | Y |
| **HAWAII** | | | | | | | |
| Akaka | Y | Y | N | Y | Y | Y | Y |
| Inouye | Y | Y | N | Y | Y | Y | Y |
| **IDAHO** | | | | | | | |
| *Craig* | N | N | Y | N | N | N | N |
| *Symms* | N | N | Y | N | N | N | Y |
| **ILLINOIS** | | | | | | | |
| Dixon | N | Y | N | Y | Y | Y | Y |
| Simon | Y | Y | N | Y | Y | Y | Y |
| **INDIANA** | | | | | | | |
| *Coats* | N | Y | Y | N | Y | Y | Y |
| *Lugar* | N | N | Y | Y | Y | N | Y |
| **IOWA** | | | | | | | |
| Harkin | Y | Y | N | Y | Y | Y | Y |
| *Grassley* | Y | N | N | N | Y | Y | Y |
| **KANSAS** | | | | | | | |
| *Dole* | N | N | Y | N | Y | N | Y |
| *Kassebaum* | Y | N | Y | Y | Y | Y | N |
| **KENTUCKY** | | | | | | | |
| Ford | Y | Y | N | N | Y | Y | Y |
| *McConnell* | N | N | N | Y | Y | Y | Y |
| **LOUISIANA** | | | | | | | |
| Breaux | N | Y | N | N | Y | Y | Y |
| Johnston | N | Y | N | N | Y | Y | Y |
| **MAINE** | | | | | | | |
| Mitchell | Y | Y | N | Y | Y | Y | Y |
| *Cohen* | N | Y | N | Y | Y | Y | N |
| **MARYLAND** | | | | | | | |
| Mikulski | Y | Y | N | Y | Y | Y | Y |
| Sarbanes | Y | Y | N | Y | Y | Y | Y |
| **MASSACHUSETTS** | | | | | | | |
| Kennedy | Y | Y | N | Y | Y | Y | Y |
| Kerry | Y | Y | N | Y | Y | Y | Y |
| **MICHIGAN** | | | | | | | |
| Levin | Y | Y | N | Y | Y | Y | Y |
| Riegle | Y | Y | N | Y | Y | Y | Y |
| **MINNESOTA** | | | | | | | |
| Wellstone | Y | Y | N | Y | Y | Y | Y |
| *Durenberger* | N | Y | Y | N | Y | Y | Y |
| **MISSISSIPPI** | | | | | | | |
| *Cochran* | N | N | Y | N | Y | Y | Y |
| *Lott* | N | N | Y | N | Y | N | Y |
| **MISSOURI** | | | | | | | |
| *Bond* | Y | Y | ? | Y | Y | Y | ? |
| *Danforth* | Y | Y | N | N | Y | Y | Y |
| **MONTANA** | | | | | | | |
| Baucus | Y | Y | N | Y | Y | Y | Y |
| *Burns* | N | N | Y | N | N | N | Y |
| **NEBRASKA** | | | | | | | |
| Exon | Y | Y | N | Y | Y | Y | C |
| Kerrey | Y | Y | N | Y | Y | Y | Y |
| **NEVADA** | | | | | | | |
| Bryan | N | N | Y | N | Y | Y | Y |
| Reid | N | Y | N | Y | Y | N | Y |
| **NEW HAMPSHIRE** | | | | | | | |
| *Rudman* | N | N | Y | Y | Y | N | N |
| *Smith* | N | N | Y | N | N | N | N |
| **NEW JERSEY** | | | | | | | |
| Bradley | Y | Y | N | Y | Y | Y | Y |
| Lautenberg | Y | Y | N | Y | Y | Y | Y |
| **NEW MEXICO** | | | | | | | |
| Bingaman | ? | Y | N | Y | Y | Y | Y |
| *Domenici* | N | N | Y | N | Y | Y | Y |
| **NEW YORK** | | | | | | | |
| Moynihan | Y | Y | N | Y | Y | Y | Y |
| *D'Amato* | Y | Y | Y | Y | Y | Y | Y |
| **NORTH CAROLINA** | | | | | | | |
| Sanford | Y | Y | N | Y | Y | Y | ? |
| *Helms* | N | N | Y | N | N | N | N |
| **NORTH DAKOTA** | | | | | | | |
| Burdick | Y | Y | N | Y | Y | Y | Y |
| Conrad | Y | Y | N | Y | Y | Y | Y |
| **OHIO** | | | | | | | |
| Glenn | Y | Y | N | Y | Y | Y | Y |
| Metzenbaum | Y | Y | N | Y | Y | Y | Y |
| **OKLAHOMA** | | | | | | | |
| Boren | ? | Y | ? | Y | Y | N | Y |
| *Nickles* | N | N | N | Y | N | Y | N |
| **OREGON** | | | | | | | |
| *Hatfield* | Y | Y | Y | Y | Y | Y | Y |
| *Packwood* | Y | Y | N | Y | Y | N | Y |
| **PENNSYLVANIA** | | | | | | | |
| Wofford | Y | Y | N | Y | Y | Y | Y |
| *Specter* | Y | Y | N | Y | Y | Y | Y |
| **RHODE ISLAND** | | | | | | | |
| Pell | Y | Y | N | Y | Y | Y | Y |
| *Chafee* | Y | Y | Y | Y | Y | N | Y |
| **SOUTH CAROLINA** | | | | | | | |
| Hollings | N | N | Y | N | Y | N | Y |
| *Thurmond* | N | N | Y | N | Y | N | N |
| **SOUTH DAKOTA** | | | | | | | |
| Daschle | Y | Y | N | Y | Y | Y | Y |
| *Pressler* | Y | N | Y | N | Y | Y | Y |
| **TENNESSEE** | | | | | | | |
| Gore | ? | Y | ? | ? | ? | Y | ? |
| Sasser | Y | Y | N | Y | Y | Y | Y |
| **TEXAS** | | | | | | | |
| Bentsen | N | Y | N | Y | Y | Y | Y |
| *Gramm* | N | N | Y | N | Y | N | Y |
| **UTAH** | | | | | | | |
| *Garn* | N | N | Y | N | N | N | Y |
| *Hatch* | N | N | Y | N | Y | Y | Y |
| **VERMONT** | | | | | | | |
| Leahy | Y | Y | N | Y | Y | Y | ? |
| *Jeffords* | Y | Y | Y | Y | Y | Y | ? |
| **VIRGINIA** | | | | | | | |
| Robb | N | Y | N | Y | Y | Y | Y |
| *Warner* | N | N | Y | Y | Y | Y | Y |
| **WASHINGTON** | | | | | | | |
| Adams | Y | Y | N | Y | Y | Y | Y |
| *Gorton* | N | N | Y | Y | Y | Y | Y |
| **WEST VIRGINIA** | | | | | | | |
| Byrd | Y | Y | N | Y | N | Y | Y |
| Rockefeller | Y | Y | N | Y | Y | Y | Y |
| **WISCONSIN** | | | | | | | |
| Kohl | Y | Y | N | Y | Y | Y | Y |
| *Kasten* | Y | N | ? | N | Y | Y | ? |
| **WYOMING** | | | | | | | |
| *Simpson* | N | N | Y | Y | Y | Y | Y |
| *Wallop* | N | N | Y | N | N | N | Y |

ND  Northern Democrats    SD  Southern Democrats    Southern states - Ala., Ark., Fla., Ga., Ky., La., Miss., N.C., Okla., S.C., Tenn., Texas, Va.

**9. S 3114. Fiscal 1993 Defense Authorization/Nuclear Testing Moratorium.** Hatfield, R-Ore., amendment to the Cohen, R-Maine, amendment. The Hatfield amendment would impose a nine-month moratorium on nuclear testing until July 1, 1993; allow limited testing between July 1, 1993, and Jan. 1, 1997; require reports to Congress on the remaining weapons in the U.S. stockpile, proposed safety improvements and tests, and plans for a comprehensive test ban by Sept. 30, 1996; and, contingent on certain factors, prohibit nuclear tests after Sept. 30, 1996, unless a foreign state conducts a test. The Cohen amendment would impose a three-month testing moratorium, allow limited testing until 1998, and impose a test ban in 1998; the president could waive that ban for one year to negotiate a comprehensive test ban. Adopted 55-40: R 13-29; D 42-11 (ND 35-3, SD 7-8), Sept. 18, 1992 (Senate vote 217). The Cohen amendment, as amended by the Hatfield amendment, subsequently was adopted by voice vote. A "nay" was a vote in support of the president's position.

**10. S 5. Family and Medical Leave/Veto Override.** Passage, over President Bush's Sept. 22 veto, of the bill to require companies with more than 50 employees to provide workers with up to 12 weeks of unpaid leave for family emergencies. Passed (thus cleared for House action) 68-31: R 14-28; D 54-3 (ND 40-0, SD 14-3), Sept. 24, 1992 (Senate vote 232). A two-thirds majority of those present and voting (66 in this case) is required to override a veto. A "nay" was a vote in support of the president's position.

**11. HR 11. Tax Bill/Enterprise Zones.** Dole, R-Kan., amendment to eliminate provisions making permanent the existing cap on itemized deductions and the phaseout of the personal exemption for upper-income taxpayers; to cut the number of tax enterprise zones from 125 to 30; and to limit the Individual Retirement Account deduction. Rejected 34-59: R 31-8; D 3-51 (ND 1-38, SD 2-13), Sept. 25, 1992 (Senate vote 240). A "yea" was a vote in support of the president's position.

**12. S 323. Family Planning Amendments/Veto Override.** Passage, over President Bush's Sept. 25 veto, of the bill to reauthorize Title X of the Public Health Service Act for five years through fiscal 1997. The bill would overturn the administration's ban on abortion counseling at federally funded family planning clinics. Passed (thus cleared for House action) 73-26: R 20-23; D 53-3 (ND 40-0, SD 13-3), Oct. 1, 1992 (Senate vote 254). A two-thirds majority of those present and voting (66 in this case) is required to override a veto. A "nay" was a vote in support of the president's position.

**13. HR 5368. Fiscal 1993 Foreign Operations Appropriations/Passage.** Passage of the bill to provide $26.5 billion in new budget authority for foreign assistance and related programs in fiscal 1993. The administration requested $27.3 billion. Passed 87-12: R 35-8; D 52-4 (ND 39-1, SD 13-3), Oct. 1, 1992 (Senate vote 256).

**14. S 12. Cable Television Reregulation/Veto Override.** Passage, over President Bush's Oct. 3 veto, of the bill to improve competition in the cable industry by giving the Federal Communications Commission authority over basic rates and giving broadcasters the right to charge cable operators for the use of over-the-air signals. Passed (thus cleared for House action) 74-25: R 24-18; D 50-7 (ND 36-4, SD 14-3), Oct. 5, 1992 (Senate vote 264). A two-thirds majority of those present and voting (67 in this case) is required to override a veto. A "nay" was a vote in support of the president's position.

**15. HR 429. Western Water Bill/Conference Report.** Adoption of the conference report to reauthorize Bureau of Reclamation construction programs, including authorization for completing the Central Utah Project and reforms for the Central Valley Project in California. Adopted (thus clearing the bill for the president) 83-8: R 30-8; D 53-0 (ND 38-0, SD 15-0), Oct. 8, 1992 (Senate vote 267).

# PUBLIC LAWS

# Public Laws, 102nd Congress, 2nd Session

**PL 102-244 (HR 4095)** Increase the number of weeks for which benefits are payable under the Emergency Unemployment Compensation Act of 1991. Introduced by ROSTENKOWSKI, D-Ill., Jan. 22, 1992. House Ways and Means reported, amended, Jan. 29 (H Rept 102-427). House passed, amended, under suspension of the rules, Feb. 4. Senate passed Feb. 4. President signed Feb. 7, 1992.

**PL 102-245 (HR 1989)** Authorize appropriations for the National Institute of Standards and Technology and the Technology Administration of the Department of Commerce. Introduced by VALENTINE, D-N.C., April 23, 1991. House Science, Space and Technology reported, amended, June 26 (H Rept 102-134). House passed, amended, July 16. Senate Commerce, Science and Transportation discharged. Senate passed, amended, Nov. 27. House agreed to Senate amendment, under suspension of the rules, Jan. 28. President signed Feb. 14, 1992.

**PL 102-246 (S 1415)** Provide for additional membership on the Library of Congress Trust Fund Board. Introduced by PELL, D-R.I., June 27, 1991. Senate Rules and Administration reported Oct. 3. Senate passed Oct. 4. House passed, under suspension of the rules, Feb. 4. President signed Feb. 18, 1992.

**PL 102-247 (HR 2927)** Provide for the establishment of the St. Croix, Virgin Islands, Historical Park and Ecological Preserve. Introduced by De LUGO, D-Virgin Islands, July 17, 1991. House Interior and Insular Affairs reported, amended, Nov. 5 (H Rept 102-285). House passed, amended, under suspension of the rules, Nov. 5. Senate Energy and Natural Resources reported, amended, Nov. 25 (S Rept 102-243). Senate passed, amended, Jan. 31. House agreed to Senate amendment, under suspension of the rules, Feb. 4. President signed Feb. 24, 1992.

**PL 102-248 (HR 543)** Establish the Manzanar National Historic Site in California. Introduced by LEVINE, D-Calif., Jan. 16, 1991. House Interior and Insular Affairs reported, amended, June 24 (H Rept 102-125). House passed, amended, under suspension of the rules, June 24. Senate Energy and Natural Resources, reported, amended, Nov. 23 (S Rept 102-236). Senate passed, amended, Nov. 26. House considered Senate amendments, under suspension of the rules, Feb. 18. House agreed to Senate amendments, under suspension of the rules, Feb. 19. President signed March 3, 1992.

**PL 102-249 (HR 476)** Designate certain rivers in Michigan as components of the National Wild and Scenic Rivers System. Introduced by KILDEE, D-Mich., Jan. 10, 1991. House Interior and Insular Affairs reported, amended, June 3 (H Rept 102-84). House passed, amended, under suspension of the rules, June 3. Senate Energy and Natural Resources reported, amended, Nov. 23 (S Rept 102-240). Senate passed, amended, Feb. 7. House agreed to Senate amendments, under suspension of the rules, Feb. 18. President signed March 3, 1992.

**PL 102-250 (HR 355)** Amend the Reclamation States Drought Assistance Act of 1988 to extend the period of time during which drought assistance may be provided by the secretary of the Interior. Introduced by LEHMAN, D-Calif., Jan. 3, 1991. House Interior and Insular Affairs reported, amended, March 15 (H Rept 102-21, Part I). House Merchant Marine and Fisheries discharged. House passed, amended, March 21. Senate Energy and Natural Resources, reported, amended, Oct. 8 (S Rept 102-185). Senate passed, amended, Oct. 31. House disagreed to Senate amendment and asked for a conference Nov. 20. Senate receded from its amendment Nov. 27. Senate passed, amended, Nov. 27. House agreed to Senate amendment Feb. 19. President signed March 5, 1992.

**PL 102-251 (HR 3866)** Provide for the designation of the Flower Garden Banks National Marine Sanctuary. Introduced by ORTIZ, D-Texas, Nov. 22, 1991. House passed, under suspension of the rules, Nov. 23. Senate passed, amended, Nov. 27. House agreed to Senate amendment, under suspension of the rules, Jan. 28. President signed March 9, 1992.

**PL 102-252 (H J Res 395)** Designate Feb. 6, 1992, as National Women and Girls in Sports Day. Introduced by SNOWE, R-Maine, Jan. 30, 1992. House Post Office and Civil Service discharged. House passed Feb. 5. Senate Judiciary reported Feb. 27. Senate passed Feb. 27. President signed March 10, 1992.

**PL 102-253 (H J Res 350)** Designate March 1992 as Irish-American Heritage Month. Introduced by MANTON, D-N.Y., Oct. 16, 1991. House Post Office and Civil Service discharged. House passed Feb. 5. Senate Judiciary reported Feb. 27. Senate passed Feb. 27. President signed March 10, 1992.

**PL 102-254 (H J Res 343)** Designate March 12, 1992, as Girl Scouts of the United States of America 80th Anniversary Day. Introduced by SLAUGHTER, D-N.Y., Oct. 3, 1991. House Post Office and Civil Service discharged. House passed Feb. 5. Senate Judiciary reported Feb. 27. Senate passed Feb. 27. President signed March 11, 1992.

**PL 102-255 (HR 4113)** Permit the transfer before the expiration of the otherwise applicable 60-day congressional review period of the obsolete training aircraft carrier USS *Lexington* to the city of Corpus Christi, Texas, for use as a naval museum and memorial. Introduced by ORTIZ, D-Texas, Jan. 24, 1992. House Armed Services, reported, amended, Feb. 20. House passed, amended, under suspension of the rules, Feb. 25. Senate passed Feb. 26. President signed March 12, 1992.

**PL 102-256 (HR 2092)** Carry out obligations of the United States under the United Nations Charter and other international agreements pertaining to the protection of human rights by establishing a civil action for recovery of damages from an individual who engages in torture or extrajudicial killing. Introduced by YATRON, D-Pa., April 24, 1991. House Judiciary reported, amended, Nov. 25 (H Rept 102-367, Part I). House passed, amended, under suspension of the rules, Nov. 25. Senate passed March 3. President signed March 12, 1992.

**PL 102-257 (S J Res 176)** Designate March 19, 1992, as National Women in Agriculture Day. Introduced by DIXON, D-Ill., July 10, 1991. Senate Judiciary reported Oct. 31. Senate passed Nov. 1. House Post Office and Civil Service discharged. House passed March 11. President signed March 17, 1992.

**PL 102-258 (S 996)** Authorize and direct the secretary of the Interior to terminate a reservation of use and occupancy at the Buffalo National River. Introduced by BUMPERS, D-Ark., May 7, 1991. Senate Energy and Natural Resources reported July 25 (S Rept 102-120). Senate passed July 31. House Interior and Insular Affairs reported March 2 (H Rept 102-448). House passed, under suspension of the rules, March 3. President signed March 19, 1992.

**PL 102-259 (S 2184)** Establish the Morris K. Udall Scholarship and Excellence in National Environmental Policy Foundation. Introduced by DeCONCINI, D-Ariz., Feb. 4, 1992. Senate passed Feb. 4. House passed, under suspension of the rules, March 3. President signed March 19, 1992.

**PL 102-260 (H J Res 446)** Waive certain enrollment requirements with respect to HR 4210 of the 102nd Congress. Introduced by GEPHARDT, D-Mo., March 19, 1992. House passed March 19. Senate passed March 19. President signed March 20, 1992.

**PL 102-261 (S 1467)** Designate the Federal Building and U.S. Courthouse at 15 Lee St. in Montgomery, Ala., as the Frank M. Johnson Jr. Federal Building and U.S. Courthouse. Introduced by HEFLIN, D-Ala., July 11, 1991. Senate Environment and Public Works discharged. Senate passed Oct. 30. House Public Works and Transportation reported, amended, Feb. 26 (H Rept 102-445). House passed, amended, under suspension of the rules, March 3. Senate agreed to House amendments March 5. President signed March 20, 1992.

**PL 102-262 (S 1889)** Designate the Federal Building and U.S. Courthouse located at 111 S. Wolcott in Casper, Wyo., as the Ewing T. Kerr Federal Building and U.S. Courthouse. Introduced by SIMPSON, R-Wyo., Oct. 29, 1991. Senate Environment and Public Works discharged. Senate passed Oct. 30. House Public Works and Transportation reported, amended, Feb. 26 (H Rept

102-444). House passed, amended, under suspension of the rules, March 3. Senate agreed to House amendments March 5. President signed March 20, 1992.

**PL 102-263 (S J Res 240)** Designate March 25, 1992, as Greek Independence Day: A National Day of Celebration of Greek and American Democracy. Introduced by SPECTER, R-Pa., Jan. 23, 1992. Senate Judiciary reported Feb 27. Senate passed Feb. 27. House Post Office and Civil Service discharged. House passed March 11. President signed March 20, 1992.

**PL 102-264 (H J Res 284)** Designate the second week in April as National Public Safety Telecommunications Week. Introduced by MARKEY, D-Mass., June 25, 1991. House Post Office and Civil Service discharged. House passed, amended, Oct. 9. Senate Judiciary discharged. Senate passed March 17. President signed March 26, 1992.

**PL 102-265 (S 2324)** Amend the Food Stamp Act of 1977 to make a technical correction relating to exclusions from income under the food stamp program. Introduced by LEAHY, D-Vt., March 5, 1992. Senate passed March 5. House Passed March 11. President signed March 26, 1992.

**PL 102-266 (H J Res 456)** Make further continuing appropriations for fiscal 1992. Introduced by WHITTEN, D-Miss., March 30, 1992. House Appropriations discharged. House passed, amended, March 31. Senate passed, amended, April 1. House agreed to Senate amendments April 1. President signed April 1, 1992.

**PL 102-267 (H J Res 272)** Proclaim March 20, 1992, as National Agriculture Day. Introduced by de la GARZA, D-Texas, June 18, 1991. House Post Office and Civil Service discharged. House passed March 11. Senate Judiciary discharged. Senate passed March 20. President signed April 2, 1992.

**PL 102-268 (H J Res 410)** Designate April 14, 1992, as Education and Sharing Day, USA. Introduced by GEPHARDT, D-Mo., Feb. 11, 1992. House Post Office and Civil Service discharged. House passed March 11. Senate Judiciary discharged. Senate passed April 1. President signed April 13, 1992.

**PL 102-269 (S J Res 246)** Designate April 15, 1992, as National Recycling Day. Introduced by LIEBERMAN, D-Conn., Jan. 31, 1992. Senate Judiciary reported Feb. 27. Senate passed Feb. 27. House Post Office and Civil Service discharged. House passed April 8. President signed April 15, 1992.

**PL 102-270 (S J Res 271)** Express the sense of the Congress regarding the peace process in Liberia and authorizing reprogramming of existing foreign aid appropriations for limited assistance to support this process. Introduced by SIMPSON, R-Wyo., March 13, 1992. Senate passed March 13. House passed, under suspension of the rules, April 7. President signed April 16, 1992.

**PL 102-271 (S 606)** Amend the Wild and Scenic Rivers Act by designating certain segments of the Allegheny River in the state of Pennsylvania as a component of the National Wild and Scenic Rivers System. Introduced by HEINZ, R-Pa., March 7, 1991. Senate Energy and Natural Resources reported, amended, Nov. 23 (S Rept 102-232). Senate passed, amended, Nov. 26. House considered, under suspension of the rules, Feb. 18. House passed, amended, under suspension of the rules, Feb. 19. Senate agreed to House amendment April 8. President signed April 20, 1992.

**PL 102-272 (HR 3686)** Amend Title 28, U.S. Code, to make changes in the places of holding court in the Eastern District of North Carolina. Introduced by COBLE, R-N.C., Oct. 31, 1991. House Judiciary reported Nov. 25 (H Rept 102-369). House passed, under suspension of the rules, Nov. 25. Senate Judiciary reported April 8. Senate passed April 8. President signed April 21, 1992.

**PL 102-273 (HR 4449)** Authorize jurisdictions receiving funds for fiscal 1992 under the HOME Investment Partnership Act that are allocated for new construction to use the funds, at the discretion of the jurisdiction, for other eligible activities under the act and to amend the Stewart B. McKinney Homeless Assistance Amendments Act of 1988 to authorize local governments that have financed housing projects that have been provided a Section 8 financial adjustment factor to use recaptured amounts available from refinancing of the projects for housing activities. Introduced by FRANK, D-Mass., March 12, 1992. House passed, under sus-

pension of the rules, March 17. Senate passed April 8. President signed April 21, 1992.

**PL 102-274 (S 985)** Assure the people of the Horn of Africa the right to food and the other basic necessities of life and to promote peace and development in the region. Introduced by SIMON, D-Ill., April 25, 1991. Senate Foreign Relations reported, amended, June 27. Senate passed, amended, July 16. House passed, amended, under suspension of the rules, April 7. Senate agreed to House amendment April 8. President signed April 21, 1992.

**PL 102-275 (S 1743)** Amend the Wild and Scenic Rivers Act by designating certain rivers in the state of Arkansas as components of the National Wild and Scenic Rivers System. Introduced by BUMPERS, D-Ark., Sept. 24, 1991. Senate Energy and Natural Resources reported, amended, Nov. 12 (S Rept 102-210). Senate passed, amended, Nov. 26. House Interior and Insular Affairs reported, amended, March 30 (H Rept 102-473). House passed, amended, under suspension of the rules, March 30. Senate agreed to House amendments April 8. President signed April 22, 1992.

**PL 102-276 (HR 4572)** Direct the secretary of Health and Human Services to waive certain requirements under the Medicaid program during 1992 and 1993 for health maintenance organizations operated by the Dayton Area Health Plan in Dayton, Ohio. Introduced by HALL, D-Ohio, March 25, 1992. House Energy and Commerce reported, amended, April 9 (H Rept 102-494). House passed, amended, April 10. Senate passed April 10. President signed April 28, 1992.

**PL 102-277 (H J Res 402)** Approve the location of a memorial to George Mason. Introduced by MORAN, D-Va., Feb. 4, 1992. House Interior and Insular Affairs reported March 30 (H Rept 102-472). House passed, under suspension of the rules, March 30. Senate Rules and Administration discharged. Senate passed April 10. President signed April 28, 1992.

**PL 102-278 (S J Res 174)** Designate the month of May 1992 as National Amyotrophic Lateral Sclerosis Awareness Month. Introduced by GRAHAM, D-Fla., July 8, 1991. Senate Judiciary reported Oct. 31. Senate passed Nov. 1. House Post Office and Civil Service discharged. House passed April 30. President signed May 9, 1992.

**PL 102-279 (S J Res 222)** Designate 1992 as the Year of Reconciliation between American Indians and non-Indians. Introduced by DASCHLE, D-S.D., Oct. 30, 1991. Senate Judiciary discharged. Senate passed March 17. House Post Office and Civil Service discharged. House passed April 30. President signed May 9, 1992.

**PL 102-280 (H J Res 430)** Designate May 4, 1992, through May 10, 1992, as Public Service Recognition Week. Introduced by MORAN, D-Va., Feb. 27, 1992. House Post Office and Civil Service discharged. House passed April 30. Senate passed May 5. President signed May 11, 1992.

**PL 102-281 (HR 3337)** Require the secretary of the Treasury to mint a coin in commemoration of the 200th anniversary of the White House. Introduced by BAKER, R-La., Sept. 16, 1991. House passed, amended, under suspension of the rules, Nov. 26. Senate passed, amended, Nov. 27. House considered, under suspension of the rules, Feb. 18. House failed to agree to Senate amendments, under suspension of the rules, Feb. 19. House recommitted conference report April 1 (H Rept 102-454). House agreed to conference report April 8 (H Rept 102-485). Senate agreed to conference report April 28. President signed May 13, 1992.

**PL 102-282 (HR 2454)** Authorize the secretary of Health and Human Services to impose debarments and other penalties for illegal activities involving the approval of abbreviated drug applications under the Federal Food, Drug and Cosmetic Act. Introduced by DINGELL, D-Mich., May 23, 1991. House Energy and Commerce reported, amended, Oct. 24 (H Rept 102-272). House considered, under suspension of rules, Oct. 28. House passed, amended, under suspension of the rules, Oct. 31. Senate Labor and Human Resources discharged. Senate passed, amended, April 10. House agreed to Senate amendments, under suspension of the rules, April 28. President signed May 13, 1992.

**PL 102-283 (H J Res 425)** Designate May 10, 1992, as Infant Mortality Awareness Day. Introduced by HARRIS, D-Ala.,

Feb. 26, 1992. House Post Office and Civil Service discharged. House passed April 30. Senate passed May 7. President signed May 14, 1992.

**PL 102-284 (S J Res 251)** Designate the month of May 1992 as National Huntington's Disease Awareness Month. Introduced by KASSEBAUM, R-Kan., Feb. 6, 1992. Senate Judiciary discharged. Senate passed May 5. House Post Office and Civil Service discharged. House passed May 7. President signed May 14, 1992.

**PL 102-285 (HR 2763)** Enhance geologic mapping of the United States. Introduced by RAHALL, D-W.Va., June 25, 1991. House Interior and Insular Affairs reported, amended, Nov. 19 (H Rept 102-333). House passed, amended, under suspension of the rules, Nov. 19. Senate Energy and Natural Resources discharged. Senate passed, amended, March 31. House agreed to Senate amendments April 30. President signed May 18, 1992.

**PL 102-286 (HR 4184)** Designate the Department of Veterans Affairs Medical Center located in Northampton, Mass., as the Edward P. Boland Department of Veterans Affairs Medical Center. Introduced by NEAL, D-Mass., Feb. 5, 1992. House Veterans' Affairs reported March 19 (H Rept 102-458). House passed, under suspension of the rules, April 7. Senate Veterans' Affairs discharged. Senate passed April 30. President signed May 18, 1992.

**PL 102-287 (H J Res 466)** Designate April 26, 1992, through May 2, 1992, as National Crime Victims' Rights Week. Introduced by GEKAS, R-Pa., April 8, 1992. House Post Office and Civil Service discharged. House passed April 30. Senate passed May 5. President signed May 18, 1992.

**PL 102-288 (H J Res 388)** Designate the month of May 1992 as National Foster Care Month. Introduced by MATSUI, D-Calif., Jan. 3, 1992. House Post Office and Civil Service discharged. House passed April 30. Senate Judiciary discharged. Senate passed May 13. President signed May 19, 1992.

**PL 102-289 (HR 4774)** Provide flexibility to the secretary of Agriculture to carry out food assistance programs in certain countries. Introduced by ROSE, D-N.C., April 7, 1992. House Agriculture reported April 9 (H Rept 102-496). House passed, under suspension of the rules, May 5. Senate passed May 7. President signed May 20, 1992.

**PL 102-290 (H J Res 371)** Designate May 31 through June 6, 1992, as a Week for the National Observance of the 50th Anniversary of World War II. Introduced by MYERS, R-Ind., Nov. 7, 1991. House Post Office and Civil Service discharged. House passed April 30. Senate passed May 7. President signed May 20, 1992.

**PL 102-291 (S 2378)** Amend Title 38, U.S. Code, to extend certain authorities relating to the administration of veterans laws. Introduced by CRANSTON, D-Calif., March 20, 1992. Senate Veterans' Affairs discharged. Senate passed, amended, April 30. House passed May 7. President signed May 20, 1992.

**PL 102-292 (S 1182)** Transfer jurisdiction of certain public lands in the state of Utah to the Forest Service. Introduced by GARN, R-Utah, May 24, 1991. Senate Energy and Natural Resources reported, amended, Nov. 12 (S Rept 102-206). Senate passed, amended, Nov. 23. House Interior and Insular Affairs reported May 11 (H Rept 102-517). House passed, under suspension of the rules, May 12. President signed May 26, 1992.

**PL 102-293 (S 452)** Authorize a transfer of administrative jurisdiction over certain land to the secretary of the Interior. Introduced by DASCHLE, D-S.D., Feb. 20, 1991. Senate Energy and Natural Resources reported, amended, Nov. 19 (S Rept 102-220). Senate passed, amended, Nov. 26. House Interior and Insular Affairs reported May 11 (H Rept 102-516). House passed, under suspension of the rules, May 12. President signed May 27, 1992.

**PL 102-294 (S 749)** Rename and expand the boundaries of the Mound City Group National Monument in Ohio. Introduced by METZENBAUM, D-Ohio, March 21, 1991. Senate Energy and Natural Resources reported, amended, July 15 (S Rept 102-108). Senate passed, amended, Sept. 23. House Interior and Insular Affairs reported April 7 (H Rept 102-483). House passed, under suspension of the rules, May 12. President signed May 27, 1992.

**PL 102-295 (S 838)** Amend the Child Abuse Prevention and Treatment Act to revise and extend programs under such act.

Introduced by DODD, D-Conn., April 17, 1991. Senate Labor and Human Resources reported, amended, Sept. 27 (S Rept 102-164). Senate passed, amended, Nov. 7. House Education and Labor discharged. House passed, amended, April 7. Senate agreed to House amendment April 9. President signed May 28, 1992.

**PL 102-296 (S J Res 254)** Commending the New York Stock Exchange on the occasion of its bicentennial. Introduced by MOYNIHAN, D-N.Y., Feb. 7, 1992. Senate Judiciary reported Feb. 27. Senate passed Feb. 27. House Post Office and Civil Service discharged. House passed May 14. President signed May 28, 1992.

**PL 102-297 (S 2569)** Amend Title 10, U.S. Code, to make the vice chairman of the Joint Chiefs of Staff a member of the Joint Chiefs of Staff, to provide joint duty credit for certain service and to provide for the temporary continuation of the current deputy national security adviser in a flag officer grade in the Navy. Introduced by NUNN, D-Ga., April 9, 1992. Senate Armed Services reported April 9 (S Rept 102-270). Senate passed April 28. House Armed Services discharged. House passed, amended, May 20. Senate agreed to House amendments May 21. President signed June 2, 1992.

**PL 102-298 (HR 4990)** Rescind certain budget authority proposed to be rescinded in special messages transmitted to the Congress by the president in accordance with Title X of the Congressional Budget and Impoundment Control Act of 1974, as amended. Introduced by WHITTEN, D-Miss., April 28, 1992. House Appropriations reported, amended, April 29 (H Rept 102-505). House passed, amended, May 7. Senate passed, amended, May 12. Conference report filed in the House on May 20 (H Rept 102-530). House agreed to conference report May 21. Senate agreed to conference report May 21. President signed June 4, 1992.

**PL 102-299 (S 870)** Authorize inclusion of a tract of land in the Golden Gate National Recreation Area, California. Introduced by CRANSTON, D-Calif., April 18, 1991. Senate Energy and Natural Resources reported, amended, Oct. 8 (S Rept 102-182). Senate passed, amended, Oct. 16. House Interior and Insular Affairs reported, amended, March 24 (H Rept 102-467). House passed, amended, under suspension of the rules, March 24. Senate agreed to House amendment May 21. President signed June 9, 1992.

**PL 102-300 (S 2783)** Amend the Federal Food, Drug, and Cosmetic Act with respect to medical devices. Introduced by KENNEDY, D-Mass., May 21, 1992. Senate passed May 21. House passed May 28. President signed June 16, 1992.

**PL 102-301 (HR 2556)** Entitled the Los Padres Condor Range and River Protection Act. Introduced by LAGOMARSINO, R-Calif., June 5, 1991. House Interior and Insular Affairs reported, amended, Nov. 6 (H Rept 102-290, Part I). House passed, amended, under suspension of the rules, Nov. 12, 1991. Senate Energy and Natural Resources reported June 2 (S Rept 102-291). Senate passed June 4. President signed June 19, 1992.

**PL 102-302 (HR 5132)** Make dire emergency supplemental appropriations for disaster assistance to meet urgent needs because of calamities such as those which occurred in Los Angeles and Chicago, for the fiscal year ending Sept. 30, 1992. Introduced by WHITTEN, D-Miss., May 12, 1992. House Appropriations reported May 12 (H Rept 102-518). House passed May 14. Senate Appropriations reported, amended, May 19. Senate considered May 20. Senate passed, amended, May 21. Conference report filed in the House on June 17 (H Rept 102-577). House agreed to conference report June 18. House receded and concurred in Senate amendment June 18. House receded and concurred with amendments in Senate amendments June 18. Senate agreed to conference report June 18. Senate agreed to House amendments to Senate amendments June 18. President signed June 22, 1992.

**PL 102-303 (H J Res 445)** Designate June 1992 as National Scleroderma Awareness Month. Introduced by DWYER, D-N.J., March 18, 1992. House Post Office and Civil Service discharged. House passed June 5. Senate passed June 9. President signed June 23, 1992.

**PL 102-304 (HR 1642)** Establish in the state of Texas the Palo Alto Battlefield National Historic Site. Introduced by ORTIZ, D-Texas, March 22, 1991. House Interior and Insular Affairs reported, amended, June 3 (H Rept 102-86). House passed,

amended, under suspension of the rules, June 3. Senate Energy and Natural Resources reported May 21 (H Rept 102-285). Senate passed June 4. President signed June 23, 1992.

**PL 102-305 (H J Res 442)** Designate May 16, 1992, through May 22, 1992, as National Awareness Week for Lifesaving Techniques. Introduced by YOUNG, R-Fla., March 17, 1992. House Post Office and Civil Service discharged. House passed, amended, June 5. Senate passed June 9. President signed June 23, 1992.

**PL 102-306 (H J Res 517)** Provide for a settlement of the railroad labor-management disputes between certain railroads and certain of their employees. Introduced by ECKART, D-Ohio, June 25, 1992. House passed June 25. Senate passed June 25. President signed June 26, 1992.

**PL 102-307 (S 756)** Amend Title 17, U.S. Code, the copyright renewal provisions. Introduced by by DeCONCINI, D-Ariz., March 21, 1991. Senate Judiciary reported, amended, Oct. 22 (S Rept 102-194). Senate passed, amended, Nov. 25. House passed, amended, June 4. Senate agreed to House amendment June 4. President signed June 26, 1992.

**PL 102-308 (S 2703)** Authorize the president to appoint Gen. Thomas C. Richards to the Office of Administrator of the Federal Aviation Administration. Introduced by FORD, D-Ky., May 13, 1992. Senate Commerce, Science and Transportation discharged. Senate passed June 9. House passed, under suspension of the rules, June 22. President signed June 26, 1992.

**PL 102-309 (H J Res 470)** Designate the month of September 1992 as National Spina Bifida Awareness Month. Introduced by BROOMFIELD, R-Mich., April 9, 1992. House Post Office and Civil Service discharged. House passed June 5. Senate passed June 11. President signed June 30, 1992.

**PL 102-310 (S 2905)** Provide a four-month extension of the transition rule for separate capitalization of savings associations' subsidiaries. Introduced by RIEGLE, D-Mich., June 29, 1992. Senate passed June 29. House passed June 30. President signed July 1, 1992.

**PL 102-311 (HR 4548)** Authorize contributions to United Nations peacekeeping activities. Introduced by FASCELL, D-Fla., March 24, 1992. House passed, amended, under suspension of the rules, June 15. Senate passed June 23. President signed July 2, 1992.

**PL 102-312 (HR 3041)** Designate the federal building located at 1520 Market Street, St. Louis, Mo., as the L. Douglas Abram Federal Building. Introduced by CLAY, D-Mo., July 25, 1991. House Public Works and Transportation reported Feb. 26 (H Rept 102-441). House passed, under suspension of the rules, March 3. Senate Environment and Public Works discharged. Senate passed June 23. President signed July 2, 1992.

**PL 102-313 (HR 2818)** Designate the Federal building located at 78 Center Street in Pittsfield, Mass., as the Silvio O. Conte Federal Building. Introduced by OLVER, D-Mass., June 27, 1991. House Public Works and Transportation reported Feb. 26 (H Rept 102-440). House passed, under suspension of the rules, March 3. Senate Environment and Public Works discharged. Senate passed June 23. President signed July 2, 1992.

**PL 102-314 (HR 3711)** Authorize grants to be made to state programs designed to provide resources to persons who are nutritionally at risk in the form of fresh, nutritious unprepared foods. Introduced by KILDEE, D-Mich., Nov. 5, 1991. House Education and Labor reported, amended, May 28 (H Rept 102-540, Part I). House Agriculture reported, amended, June 4 (H Rept 102-540, Part II). House passed, amended, under suspension of the rules, June 22. Senate passed June 23. President signed July 2, 1992.

**PL 102-315 (H J Res 499)** Designate July 2, 1992, as National Literacy Day. Introduced by PAYNE, D-N.J., May 28, 1992. House Post Office and Civil Service discharged. House passed June 25. Senate passed June 30. President signed July 2, 1992.

**PL 102-316 (H J Res 509)** Extend through Sept. 30, 1992, the period in which there remains available for obligation certain amounts appropriated for the Bureau of Indian Affairs for the school operations costs of bureau-funded schools. YATES, D-Ill., June 18, 1992. House Appropriations discharged. House passed June 18. Senate passed June 23. President signed July 2, 1992.

**PL 102-317 (S 2901)** Direct the secretary of Health and

Human Services to extend the waiver granted to the Tennessee Primary Care Network of the enrollment mix requirement under the Medicaid program. Introduced by SASSER, D-Tenn., June 26, 1992. Senate passed June 26. House passed June 30. President signed July 2, 1992.

**PL 102-318 (HR 5260)** Extend the Emergency Unemployment Compensation Program, to revise the trigger provisions contained in the extended unemployment compensation program. Introduced by ROSTENKOWSKI, D-Ill., May 26, 1992. House Ways and Means reported June 2 (H Rept 102-543, Part I). House Government Operations reported June 9 (H Rept 102-543, Part II). House passed, amended, June 9. Senate Finance reported, amended, June 15. Senate considered June 18. Senate passed, amended, June 19. House agreed to conference reported July 2 (H Rept 102-650). Senate agreed to conference report July 2. President signed July 3, 1992.

**PL 102-319 (H J Res 459)** Designate the week beginning July 26, 1992, as Lyme Disease Awareness Week. HOCHBRUECKNER, D-N.Y., April 1, 1992. House Post Office and Civil Service discharged. House passed June 25. Senate passed June 26. President signed July 8, 1992.

**PL 102-320 (S 1254)** Increase the authorized acreage limit for the Assateague Island National Seashore on the Maryland mainland. Introduced by SARBANES, D-Md., June 11, 1991. Senate Energy and Natural Resources reported, amended, Oct. 8 (S Rept 102-184). Senate passed, amended, Oct. 16. House Interior and Insular Affairs reported, amended, March 24 (H Rept 102-468). House passed, amended, under suspension of the rules, March 24, 1992. Senate agreed to House amendment with amendment April 9. House agreed to Senate amendment to the House amendment, under suspension of the rules, June 29. President signed July 10, 1992.

**PL 102-321 (S 1306)** Amend Title V of the Public Health Service Act to revise and extend certain programs, and to restructure the Alcohol, Drug Abuse and Mental Health Administration. Introduced by KENNEDY, D-Mass., June 17, 1991. Senate Labor and Human Resources reported, amended, July 30 (S Rept 102-131). Senate passed, amended, Aug. 2, 1991. House passed, amended, March 24. Conference report filed in the House May 14 (H Rept 102-522). House failed to agree to conference report, under suspension of the rules, May 19. House recommitted conference report May 28. Conference report filed in the House June 3 (H Rept 102-546). Senate considered conference report June 4. Senate agreed to conference report June 9. House agreed to conference report July 1. President signed July 10, 1992.

**PL 102-322 (HR 5412)** Authorize the transfer of certain naval vessels to Greece and Taiwan. Introduced by FASCELL, D-Fla., June 17, 1992. House passed, amended, under suspension of the rules, June 22. Senate Armed Services reported July 1. Senate passed July 2. President signed July 19, 1992.

**PL 102-323 (S J Res 324)** Commend the NASA Langley Research Center on the celebration of its 75th anniversary on July 17, 1992. Introduced by SIMPSON, R-Wyo., June 26, 1992. Senate passed June 26. House Science, Space and Technology discharged. House passed July 2. President signed July 20, 1992.

**PL 102-324 (S 2780)** Amend the Food Security Act of 1985 to remove certain easement requirements under the conservation reserve program. Introduced by LEAHY, D-Vt., May 21, 1992. Senate passed May 21. House Agriculture reported June 30 (H Rept 102-636). House passed July 1. President signed July 22, 1992.

**PL 102-325 (S 1150)** Reauthorize the Higher Education Act of 1965. Introduced by PELL, D-R.I., May 23, 1991. Senate Labor and Human Resources reported, amended, Nov. 12 (S Rept 102-204). Senate considered Feb. 20. Senate passed, amended, Feb. 21. House passed, amended, March 26. Conference report filed in the House June 29 (H Rept 102-630). Senate agreed to conference report June 30. House agreed to conference report July 8. President signed July 23, 1992.

**PL 102-326 (HR 158)** Designate the facility on Highway 64 East in Hiddenite, N.C., as the Zora Leah S. Thomas Post Office. Introduced by NEAL, D-N.C., Jan. 3, 1991. House passed, amended, under suspension of the rules, July 15. Senate Govern-

mental Affairs discharged. Senate passed July 2, 1992. President signed July 23, 1992.

**PL 102-327 (HR 4505)** Designate the facility of the U.S. Postal Service at 20 S. Montgomery St. in Trenton, N.J., as the Arthur J. Holland United States Post Office Building. Introduced by SMITH, R-N.J., March 18, 1992. House passed, under suspension of the rules, June 22. Senate Governmental Affairs discharged. Senate passed July 2. President signed July 23, 1992.

**PL 102-328 (HR 479)** Amend the National Trails System Act to designate the California National Historic Trail and the Pony Express National Historic Trail as components of the National Trails System. Introduced by BEREUTER, R-Neb., Jan. 11, 1991. House Interior and Insular Affairs reported, amended, May 6 (H Rept 102-48). House considered, under suspension of the rules, May 7. House passed, amended, under suspension of the rules, May 8. Senate Energy and Natural Resources reported July 15 (S Rept 102-319). Senate passed July 21. President signed Aug. 3, 1992.

**PL 102-329 (HR 5343)** Make technical amendments to the American Technology Pre-eminence Act of 1991 and the Fair Packaging and Labeling Act with respect to their treatment of the SI metric system. Introduced by BROWN, D-Calif., June 9, 1992. House Science, Space and Technology reported, amended, June 18 (H Rept 102-581, Part I). House passed, amended, under suspension of the rules, June 29. Senate Commerce, Science, and Transportation discharged. Senate passed July 21. President signed Aug. 3, 1992.

**PL 102-330 (S 2938)** Authorize the Architect of the Capitol to acquire certain property. Introduced by MITCHELL, D-Maine, July 1, 1992. Senate passed July 1. House passed, amended, July 2. Senate agreed to House amendment July 21. President signed Aug. 3, 1992.

**PL 102-331 (S J Res 92)** Designate July 28, 1992, as Buffalo Soldiers Day. Introduced by KASSEBAUM, R-Kan., March 12, 1991. Senate Judiciary discharged. Senate passed June 26, 1991. House Post Office and Civil Service discharged. House passed July 24, 1992. President signed Aug. 3, 1992.

**PL 102-332 (S J Res 295)** Designate Sept. 10, 1992, as National D.A.R.E. Day. Introduced by DeCONCINI, D-Ariz., April 30, 1992. Senate Judiciary reported June 25. Senate passed June 26. House Post Office and Civil Service discharged. House passed July 21. President signed Aug. 3, 1992.

**PL 102-333 (S J Res 310)** Designate Aug. 1, 1992, as Helsinki Human Rights Day. Introduced by DeCONCINI, D-Ariz., May 21, 1992. Senate Judiciary discharged. Senate passed June 16. House passed, under suspension of the rules, July 27. President signed Aug. 4, 1992.

**PL 102-334 (S 2641)** Partially restore obligation authority authorized in the Intermodal Surface Transportation Efficiency Act of 1992. Introduced by MOYNIHAN, D-N.Y., April 30, 1992. Senate passed April 30. House passed, under suspension of the rules, July 28. President signed Aug. 6, 1992.

**PL 102-335 (HR 3836)** Provide for the management of federal lands containing the Pacific yew to ensure a sufficient supply of taxol, a cancer-treating drug made from the Pacific yew. Introduced by STUDDS, D-Mass., Nov. 20, 1991. House Merchant Marine and Fisheries Committee reported, amended, June 9, 1992 (H Rept 102-552, Part I). House Interior and Insular Affairs Committee reported, amended, July 7 (H Rept 102-552, Part II). House Agriculture Committee reported, amended, July 7 (H Rept 102-552, Part III). House passed, under suspension of the rules, as amended, July 7. Senate passed July 23. President signed Aug. 7, 1992.

**PL 102-336 (HR 5059)** Extend the boundaries of the grounds of the National Gallery of Art to include the National Sculpture Garden. Introduced by CLAY, D-Mo., May 5, 1992. House passed, under suspension of the rules, July 21. Senate passed July 27. President signed Aug. 7, 1992.

**PL 102-337 (S 2917)** Amend the National School Lunch Act to authorize the secretary of Agriculture to provide financial and other assistance to the University of Mississippi, in cooperation with the University of Southern Mississippi, to establish and maintain a food service management institute. Introduced by

COCHRAN, R-Miss., June 30. Senate Agriculture, Nutrition and Forestry Committee discharged June 30. Senate passed July 2. House passed, under suspension of the rules, July 28. President signed Aug. 7, 1992.

**PL 102-338 (HR 4026)** Formulate a plan for the management of natural and cultural resources on the Zuni Indian Reservation, on the lands of the Ramah Band of the Navajo Tribe of Indians, and the Navajo Nation, and in other areas within the Zuni River watershed and upstream from the Zuni Indian Reservation. Introduced by RICHARDSON, D-N.M., Nov. 26, 1991. House Interior and Insular Affairs Committee passed July 27, 1992 (H Rept 102-726). Passed House, amended, under suspension of the rules, July 27. Passed Senate July 29. President signed Aug. 11, 1992.

**PL 102-339 (HR 5566)** Provide additional time to negotiate settlement of a land dispute in South Carolina. Introduced by SPRATT, D-S.C., July 7, 1992. Passed House, under suspension of the rules, July 27. Passed Senate July 30. President signed Aug. 11, 1992.

**PL 102-340 (S J Res 270)** Designate Aug. 15, 1992, as 82nd Airborne Division 50th Anniversary Recognition Day. Introduced by THURMOND, R-S.C., March 13, 1992. Senate Judiciary discharged July 2. Senate passed July 2. House Post Office and Civil Service discharged Aug. 6. House passed Aug. 6. President signed Aug. 12, 1992.

**PL 102-341 (HR 5487)** Provide for appropriations for Agriculture, Rural Development, Food and Drug Administration, and related agencies' programs for the fiscal year ending Sept. 30, 1993. Introduced by WHITTEN, D-Miss., June 25, 1992. House Appropriations reported June 25 (H Rept 102-617). House passed, amended, June 30. Senate Appropriations passed, amended, July 23 (S Rept 102-334). Senate passed, amended, July 28. House and Senate conferees agreed on the conference report Aug. 6. Conference report filed in the House on Aug. 7 (H Rept 102-815). House agreed to conference report Aug. 11. House receded and concurred in Senate amendments Aug. 11. House receded and concurred with amendments in Senate amendments Aug. 11. Senate agreed to conference report Aug. 11. President signed Aug. 14, 1992.

**PL 102-342 (S 2759)** Amend the National School Lunch Act to improve the nutritional well-being of children under age 6 living in homeless shelters. Introduced by LEAHY, D-Vt., May 20, 1992. Senate passed May 20. House Education and Labor reported, amended, July 1 (H Rept 102-645). House passed, amended, under suspension of the rules, July 28. Senate agreed to House amendments July 30. President signed Aug. 14, 1992.

**PL 102-343 (S 959)** Establish a commission to commemorate the 250th anniversary of the birth of Thomas Jefferson. Introduced by WARNER, R-Va., April 25, 1991. Senate Judiciary reported, amended, Nov. 6 (no written report). Senate passed, amended, Nov. 15. House Post Office and Civil Service discharged Nov. 18. House passed, amended, July 28, 1992. Senate agreed to the House amendment July 30, 1992. President signed Aug. 17, 1992.

**PL 102-344 (HR 4312)** Amend the Voting Rights Act of 1965 with respect to bilingual election requirements. Introduced by SERRANO, D-N.Y., Feb. 25, 1992. House Judiciary reported, amended, July 8 (H Rept 102-655). House passed, amended, July 24. Senate passed Aug. 7. President signed Aug. 26, 1992.

**PL 102-345 (HR 5481)** Amend the Federal Aviation Act of 1958 relating to administrative assessment of civil penalties. Introduced by OBERSTAR, D-Minn., June 24, 1992. House Public Works and Transportation reported, amended, July 21 (H Rept 102-671). House passed, amended, Aug. 3. Senate passed Aug. 12. President signed Aug. 26, 1992.

**PL 102-346 (S 544)** Amend the Food, Agriculture, Conservation and Trade Act of 1990 to provide protection to animal research facilities from illegal acts. Introduced by HEFLIN, D-Ala., March 5, 1991. Senate Agriculture, Nutrition and Forestry discharged. Senate passed, amended, Oct. 16. House Agriculture discharged. House passed, amended, Aug. 4, 1992. Senate agreed to House amendments Aug. 7. President signed Aug. 26, 1992.

**PL 102-347 (S 807)** Permit Mount Olivet Cemetery Association of Salt Lake City, Utah, to lease a certain tract of land for a

period of not more than 70 years. Introduced by HATCH, R-Utah, April 11, 1991. Reported by Senate Energy and Natural Resources Nov. 12 (S Rept 102-205). Senate passed Nov. 23. House Interior and Insular Affairs reported Aug. 10, 1992 (H Rept 102-821). House passed, under suspension of the rules, Aug. 10. President signed Aug. 26, 1992.

**PL 102-348 (S 1770)** Convey certain surplus real property located in the Black Hills National Forest to the Black Hills Workshop and Training Center. Introduced by DASCHLE, D-S.D., Sept. 27, 1991. Senate Energy and Natural Resources reported, amended, Nov. 23 (H Rept 102-234). Senate passed, amended, Nov. 26. House Government Operations discharged. House passed, amended, Aug. 4, 1992. Senate agreed to House amendment Aug. 6. President signed Aug. 26, 1992.

**PL 102-349 (S 1963)** Amend Section 992 of Title 28, U.S. Code, to provide that a member of the U.S. Sentencing Commission whose term has expired may continue to serve until a successor is appointed or until the expiration of the next session of Congress. Introduced by BIDEN, D-Del., Nov. 13, 1991. Senate Judiciary discharged. Senate passed, amended, Jan. 31, 1992. House Judiciary reported Aug. 10 (H Rept 102-827). House passed, under suspension of the rules, Aug. 11. President signed Aug. 26, 1992.

**PL 102-350 (S 2079)** Establish the Marsh-Billings National Historical Park in the state of Vermont. Introduced by JEFFORDS, R-Vt., Nov. 26, 1991. Senate Energy and Natural Resources reported, amended, June 2, 1992 (S Rept 102-290). Senate passed, amended, June 4. House Interior and Insular Affairs reported, amended, June 9 (H Rept 102- 678). House passed, amended, under suspension of the rules, July 27. Senate agreed to House amendment Aug. 6. President signed Aug. 26, 1992.

**PL 102-351 (S 3001)** Amend the Food Stamp Act of 1977 to prevent a reduction in the adjusted cost of the thrifty food plan during fiscal 1993. Introduced by DOMENICI, R-N.M., July 22, 1992. Senate Agriculture, Nutrition and Forestry discharged. Senate passed July 28. House Agriculture discharged. House passed Aug. 12. President signed Aug. 26, 1992.

**PL 102-352 (S 3112)** Amend the Public Health Service Act to make certain technical corrections. Introduced by KENNEDY, D-Mass., July 30, 1992. Senate passed July 30. House passed Aug. 10. President signed Aug. 26, 1992.

**PL 102-353 (S 3163)** Amend the federal Food, Drug and Cosmetic Act to coordinate federal and state regulation of wholesale drug distribution. Introduced by KENNEDY, D-Mass., Aug. 10, 1992. Senate passed Aug. 11. House passed Aug. 12. President signed Aug. 26, 1992.

**PL 102-354 (HR 2549)** Make technical corrections to Chapter 5 of Title 5, U.S. Code. Introduced by FRANK, D-Mass., June 5, 1991. House Judiciary reported, amended, Nov. 25 (H Rept 102-372). House passed, amended, under suspension of the rules, Nov. 25. Senate Judiciary reported July 31, 1992 (no written report). Senate passed Aug. 6. President signed Aug. 26, 1992.

**PL 102-355 (HR 2926)** Amend the act of May 17, 1954, relating to the Jefferson National Expansion Memorial to authorize increased funding for the East St. Louis portion of the memorial. Introduced by COSTELLO, D-Ill., July 17, 1991. House Administration discharged. House Interior and Insular Affairs reported, amended, March 24, 1992 (H Rept 102-465). House passed, under suspension of the rules, March 24. Senate Energy and Natural Resources reported, amended, March 26 (S Rept 102-288). Senate passed, amended, July 20. House agreed to Senate amendment Aug. 6. President signed Aug. 26, 1992.

**PL 102-356 (HR 2977)** Authorize appropriations for public broadcasting. Introduced by MARKEY, D-Mass., July 23, 1991. House Energy and Commerce reported, amended, Nov. 23 (H Rept 102-363). House passed, amended, under suspension of the rules, Nov. 25. Senate Commerce, Science and Transportation discharged. Senate passed, amended, June 3, 1992. House agreed to Senate amendment Aug. 4. President signed Aug. 26, 1992.

**PL 102-357 (HR 3795)** Amend Title 28, U.S. Code, to establish three divisions in the Central Judicial District of California. Introduced by BROWN, D-Calif., Nov. 18, 1991. House Judiciary reported Aug. 3, 1992 (H Rept 102-772). House passed, under

suspension of the rules, Aug. 3. Senate passed, Aug. 6. President signed Aug. 26, 1992.

**PL 102-358 (HR 4437)** Authorize funds for the implementation of the settlement agreement reached between the Pueblo de Cochiti and the U.S. Army Corps of Engineers under the authority of PL 100-202. Introduced by RICHARDSON, D-N.M., March 11, 1992. House Interior and Insular Affairs reported July 21 (H Rept 102-681, Part I). House passed July 27. Senate passed July 31. President signed Aug. 26, 1992.

**PL 102-359 (HR 5560)** Extend for one year the National Commission on Time and Learning. Introduced by KILDEE, D-Mich., July 7, 1992. House Education and Labor discharged. House passed July 8. Senate Labor and Human Resources discharged. Senate passed Aug. 7. President signed Aug. 26, 1992.

**PL 102-360 (HR 5623)** Waive the period of congressional review for certain District of Columbia acts. Introduced by DELLUMS, D-Calif., July 21, 1992. House District of Columbia reported July 23 (H Rept 192-706). House passed July 29. Senate Governmental Affairs discharged. Senate passed Aug. 12. President signed Aug. 26, 1992.

**PL 102-361 (HR 5688)** Amend Title 28, U.S. Code, to authorize the appointment of additional bankruptcy judges. Introduced by BROOKS, D-Texas, July 23, 1992. House Judiciary reported, amended, July 23 (H Rept 102-825). House passed, amended, under suspension of the rules, Aug. 10. Senate passed Aug. 12. President signed Aug. 26, 1992.

**PL 102-362 (H J Res 411)**, Designate the week of Sept. 13, 1992, through Sept. 19, 1992, as National Rehabilitation Week. Introduced by McDADE, R-Pa., Feb. 18, 1992. House Post Office and Civil Service discharged. House passed July 21. Senate Judiciary discharged. Senate passed Aug. 11. President signed Aug. 26, 1992.

**PL 102-363 (H J Res 507)** Approve the extension of nondiscriminatory treatment with respect to the products of the Republic of Albania. Introduced by GEPHARDT, D-Mo., June 16, 1992. House Ways and Means reported June 16. House passed, under suspension of the rules, Aug. 3. Senate passed Aug. 11. President signed Aug. 26, 1992.

**PL 102-364 (H J Res 492)** Designate September 1992 as Childhood Cancer Month. Introduced by ROE, D-N.J., May 21, 1992. House Post Office and Civil Service discharged. House passed Aug. 6. Senate Judiciary discharged. Senate passed Aug. 12. President signed Sept. 2, 1992.

**PL 102-365 (HR 2607)** Authorize activities under the Federal Railroad Safety Act of 1970 for fiscal 1992 through 1994. Introduced by SWIFT, D-Wash., June 11, 1991. House Energy and Commerce reported, amended, Sept. 16 (H Rept 102-205). House passed, amended, under suspension of the rules, Sept. 23. Senate Commerce, Science and Transportation discharged. Senate passed, amended, March 18, 1992. House agreed to Senate amendment with amendments pursuant to H J Res 516 July 21, 1992. Senate agreed to House amendments to Senate amendment with amendment Aug. 12. President signed Sept. 3, 1992.

**PL 102-366 (HR 4111)** Amend the Small Business Act to provide additional loan assistance to small businesses. Introduced by LaFALCE, D-N.Y., Jan. 24, 1992. House Small Business Committee reported, amended, April 9 (H Rept 102-492). House passed, amended, May 14. Senate Small Business discharged. Senate passed, amended, Aug. 11. House agreed to Senate amendments with amendment Aug. 11. Senate agreed to House amendment to Senate amendment Aug. 12. President signed Sept. 4, 1992.

**PL 102-367 (HR 3033)** Amend the Job Training Partnership Act to strengthen the program of employment and training assistance under the act. Introduced by PERKINS, D-Ky., July 25, 1991. House Education and Labor reported, amended, Oct. 7 (H Rept 102-240). House passed, amended, under suspension of the rules, Oct. 9. Senate passed, amended, April 30, 1992. Conference report filed in the House Aug. 6 (H Rept 102-811). Senate agreed to conference report Aug. 7. House agreed to conference report, under suspension of the rules, Aug. 11. President signed Sept. 7, 1992.

**PL 102-368 (HR 5620)** Provide for supplemental appropriations, transfers and rescissions for the fiscal year ending Sept. 30, 1992. Introduced by WHITTEN, D-Miss., July 21, 1992. House Appropriations reported July 21 (H Rept 102-672). House passed, amended, July 28. Senate Appropriations Committee reported, amended, Sept. 10 (S Rept 102-395). Senate passed, amended, Sept. 15. Senate insisted on its amendments and asked for a conference. House disagreed to Senate amendments Nos. 1-68 and agreed to Senate amendment No. 69 with an amendment Sept. 18. Senate receded from its amendments Nos. 1-68 and agreed to House amendment to Senate amendment No. 69 Sept. 18. President signed Sept. 23, 1992.

**PL 102-369 (H J Res 413)** Designate Sept. 13, 1992, as Commodore John Barry Day. Introduced by GILMAN, R-N.Y., Feb. 19, 1992. House Post Office and Civil Service discharged. House passed Sept. 10. Senate passed Sept. 10. President signed Sept. 24, 1992.

**PL 102-370 (S J Res 303)** Designate October 1992 as National Breast Cancer Awareness Month. Introduced by PELL, D-R.I., May 13, 1992. Senate Judiciary reported June 25 (no written report). Senate passed June 26. House Post Office and Civil Service discharged. House passed Sept. 10. President signed Sept. 24, 1992.

**PL 102-371 (HR 4551)** Amend the Civil Liberties Act of 1988 to increase the authorization for the trust fund under that act. Introduced by GEPHARDT, D-Mo., March 24, 1992. House Judiciary reported, amended, Sept. 14 (H Rept 102-863). House passed, amended, under suspension of the rules, Sept. 14. Senate passed Sept. 16. President signed Sept. 27, 1992.

**PL 102-372 (S 680)** Amend the International Travel Act of 1961 to assist in the growth of international travel and tourism into the United States. Introduced by ROCKEFELLER, D-W.Va., March 14, 1991. Senate Commerce, Science and Transportation reported, amended, Sept. 13 (S Rept 102-150). Senate passed, amended, Oct. 24. House Energy and Commerce discharged. House passed, amended, Nov. 23. Senate agreed to House amendments with amendment Aug. 12, 1992. House agreed to Senate amendment to House amendments, under suspension of the rules, Sept. 15. President signed Sept. 30, 1992.

**PL 102-373 (S J Res 337)** Designate Sept. 18, 1992, as National POW/MIA Recognition Day, and authorize display of the National League of Families POW/MIA flag. Introduced by KERRY, D-Mass., Sept. 15, 1992. Senate Judiciary discharged Sept. 15. Senate passed Sept. 15. House passed Sept. 16. President signed Sept. 30, 1992.

**PL 102-374 (S 1607)** Provide for the settlement of water rights claims of the Northern Cheyenne Tribe. Introduced by BURNS, R-Mont., July 31, 1991. Senate Indian Affairs reported, amended, July 29, 1992 (S Rept 102-347). Senate passed, amended, Aug. 7. House Interior and Insular Affairs reported Sept. 22 (H Rept 102-894). House passed, under suspension of the rules, Sept. 22. President signed Sept. 30, 1992.

**PL 102-375 (HR 2967)** Amend the Older Americans Act of 1965 to authorize appropriations for fiscal 1992 through 1995; authorize a 1993 National Conference on Aging; and amend the Native Americans Programs Act of 1974 to authorize appropriations for fiscal 1992 through 1995. Introduced by MARTINEZ, D-Calif., July 23, 1991. House Education and Labor reported, amended, Sept. 11 (H Rept 102-199). House passed, amended, Sept. 12. Senate Labor and Human Resources discharged. Senate passed, amended, Nov. 12. House agreed to Senate amendment with an amendment, pursuant to H Res 433, April 9, 1992. Senate concurred with amendment to the House amendment to the Senate amendment Sept. 15. House agreed to Senate amendment to House amendment to Senate amendment, under suspension of the rules, Sept. 22. President signed Sept. 30, 1992.

**PL 102-376 (H J Res 553)** Provide for continuing appropriations for fiscal 1993. Introduced by WHITTEN, D-Miss., Sept. 24, 1992. House passed Sept. 30. Senate passed Sept. 30. President signed Oct. 1, 1992.

**PL 102-377 (HR 5373)** Provide for appropriations for energy and water development for the fiscal year ending Sept. 30, 1993. Introduced by BEVILL, D-Ala., June 11, 1992. House

Appropriations reported June 11 (H Rept 102-555). House passed, amended, June 17. Senate Appropriations reported, amended, July 27 (S Rept 102-344). Senate passed, amended, Aug. 3. House disagreed to Senate amendments and agreed to a conference Sept. 9. Conference report filed in the House Sept. 15 (H Rept 102-866). House agreed to conference report Sept. 17. House receded and concurred in Senate amendments. House receded and concurred with amendments in Senate amendments. House receded and concurred with an amendment in Senate amendment. Senate agreed to conference report Sept. 24. Senate agreed to House amendments to Senate amendments Sept. 24. President signed Oct. 2, 1992.

**PL 102-378 (HR 2850)** Make technical and conforming changes in Title 5, U.S. Code, and the Federal Employees Pay Comparability Act of 1990. Introduced by CLAY, D-Mo., July 10, 1991. House passed, under suspension of the rules, March 17, 1992. Senate Governmental Affairs reported, amended, June 30 (no written report). Senate passed, amended, Aug. 6. House agreed to Senate amendment Sept. 2. President signed Oct. 2, 1992.

**PL 102-379 (HR 5126)** Direct the secretary of the Treasury to mint coins in commemoration of the 100th anniversary of the beginning of the protection of Civil War battlefields. Introduced by VENTO, D-Minn., May 7, 1992. House passed, under suspension of the rules, July 1. Senate Banking, Housing and Urban Affairs discharged. Senate passed Sept. 19. President signed Oct. 5, 1992.

**PL 102-380 (HR 5428)** Provide for appropriations for military construction for the Defense Department for the fiscal year ending Sept. 30, 1993. Introduced by HEFNER, D-N.C., June 18, 1992. House Appropriations reported June 18 (H Rept 102-580). House passed, amended, June 23. Senate Appropriations reported, amended, July 31 (S Rept 102-355). Senate passed, amended, Aug. 5. House disagreed to Senate amendments and agreed to a conference Sept. 9. Conference report filed in House on Sept. 22 (H Rept 102-888). House agreed to conference report Sept. 24. House receded and concurred in Senate amendment. House receded and concurred with amendments in Senate amendments. Senate agreed to conference report Sept. 25. Senate agreed to House amendments to Senate amendments Sept. 25. President signed Oct. 5, 1992.

**PL 102-381 (HR 5503)** Provide for appropriations for the Department of the Interior and related agencies for the fiscal year ending Sept. 30, 1993. Introduced by YATES, D-Ill., June 29, 1992. House Appropriations reported June 29 (H Rept 102-626). House passsed, amended, July 23. Senate Appropriations reported, amended, July 29 (S Rept 102-345). Senate passed, amended, Aug. 6. House disagreed to Senate amendments and agreed to a conference Sept. 10. Conference report filed in the House on Sept. 24 (H Rept 102-901). House agreed to conference report Sept. 30. Senate agreed to conference report Sept. 30. President signed Oct. 5, 1992.

**PL 102-382 (HR 6056)** Provide for appropriations for the government of the District of Columbia and other activities chargeable in whole or in part against the revenues of said District for the fiscal year ending Sept. 30, 1993. Introduced by DIXON, D-Calif., Sept. 30, 1992. House Appropriations discharged. House passed Sept. 30. Senate passed Sept. 30. President signed Oct. 5, 1992.

**PL 102-383 (S 1731)** Establish the policy of the United States with respect to Hong Kong. Introduced by McCONNELL, R-Ky., Sept. 20, 1991. Senate Foreign Relations reported, amended, May 7, 1992 (no written report). Senate passed, amended, May 21. House passed, amended, under suspension of the rules, Aug. 11. Senate agreed to House amendments Sept. 17. President signed Oct. 5, 1992.

**PL 102-384 (S 3175)** Improve the administrative provisions and make technical corrections in the National Community and Service Act of 1990. Introduced by KENNEDY, D-Mass., Aug. 11, 1992. Senate passed Aug. 12. House passed, under suspension of the rules, Sept. 16. President signed Oct. 5, 1992.

**PL 102-385 (S 12)** Amend Title VI of the Communications Act of 1934 to ensure carriage on cable television of local news and other programming and to restore the right of local regulatory authorities to regulate cable television rates. Introduced by DAN-

FORTH, R-Mo., Jan. 14, 1991. Senate Commerce, Science and Transportation reported, amended, June 28 (S Rept 102-92). Senate passed, amended, Jan. 31, 1992. House passed, amended, July 23. Senate disagreed to House amendments and agreed to a conference Aug. 12. Conference report filed in the House on Sept. 14 (H Rept 102-862). House agreed to conference report Sept. 17. Senate agreed to conference report Sept. 22. President vetoed Oct. 3. Senate passed over veto Oct. 5. House passed over veto Oct. 5. Became public law without presidential approval Oct. 5, 1992.

**PL 102-386 (HR 2194)** Amend the Solid Waste Disposal Act to clarify provisions concerning the application of certain requirements and sanctions to federal facilities. Introduced by ECKART, D-Ohio, May 2, 1991. House passed, amended, under suspension of the rules, June 24. Senate passed, amended, Oct. 24. House disagreed to the Senate amendment and agreed to a conference Feb. 4, 1992. Conference report filed in the House on Sept. 22 (H Rept 102-886). House agreed to conference report Sept. 23. Senate agreed to conference report Sept. 23. President signed Oct. 6, 1992.

**PL 102-387 (H J Res 560)** Waive certain enrollment requirements with respect to any appropriations bill for the remainder of the 102nd Congress. Introduced by GEPHARDT, D-Mo., Oct. 4, 1992. House passed Oct. 4. Senate passed Oct. 5. President signed Oct. 6, 1992.

**PL 102-388 (HR 5518)** Provide for appropriations for the Department of Transportation and related agencies for the fiscal year ending Sept. 30, 1993. Introduced by LEHMAN, D-Fla., July 1, 1992. House Appropriations reported July 1 (H Rept 102-639). House passed, amended, July 9. Senate Appropriations passed, amended, July 30 (S Rept 102-351). Senate passed Aug. 5. House disagreed to Senate amendments and agreed to a conference Sept. 9. Conference report filed in the House on Sept. 28 (H Rept 102-924). House agreed to conference report Oct. 1. House receded and concurred in Senate amendments Oct. 1. House receded and concurred with amendments in Senate amendments Oct. 1. Senate agreed to conference report Oct. 1. Senate agreed to House amendments to Senate amendments Oct. 1. President signed Oct. 6, 1992.

**PL 102-389 (HR 5679)** Provide for appropriations for the departments of Veterans Affairs and Housing and Urban Development, and for sundry independent agencies, boards, commissions, corporations, and offices for the fiscal year ending Sept. 30, 1993. Introduced by TRAXLER, D-Mich., July 23, 1992. House Appropriations reported July 23 (H Rept 102-710). House passed, amended, July 29. Senate Appropriations reported, amended, Aug. 3 (S Rept 102-356). Senate passed, amended, Sept. 9. House disagreed to Senate amendments and agreed to a conference Sept. 15. Conference report filed in the House on Sept. 24 (H Rept 102-902). House agreed to conference report Sept. 25. House receded and concurred in Senate amendments Sept. 25. House receded and concurred with amendments in Senate amendments Sept. 25. House insisted on its disagreement to Senate amendments Sept. 25. Senate agreed to conference report Sept. 25. Senate agreed to House amendments to Senate amendments Sept. 25. Senate receded from its amendment Sept. 25. President signed Oct. 6, 1992.

**PL 102-390 (HR 3654)** Provide for the minting of commemorative coins to support the 1996 Atlanta Centennial Olympic Games and the programs of the U.S. Olympic Committee. Introduced by BARNARD, D-Ga., Oct. 29, 1991. House passed, amended, under suspension of the rules, July 1, 1992. Senate Banking, Housing and Urban Affairs discharged. Senate passed Sept. 19. President signed Oct. 6, 1992.

**PL 102-391 (HR 5368)** Provide for appropriations for foreign operations, export financing, and related programs for the fiscal year ending Sept. 30, 1993. Introduced by OBEY, D-Wis., June 10, 1992. House Appropriations reported, amended, June 18 (H Rept 102-585). House passed, amended, June 25. Senate Appropriations reported, amended, Sept. 23 (S Rept 102-419). Senate passed, amended, Oct. 1. House disagreed to Senate amendments and agreed to a conference Oct. 1. Conference report filed in the House (H Rept 102-1011). House agreed to conference report Oct. 5. Senate agreed to conference report Oct. 5. President signed Oct. 6, 1992.

**PL 102-392 (HR 5427)** Provide for appropriations for the legislative branch for the fiscal year ending Sept. 30, 1993. Introduced by FAZIO, D-Calif., June 18, 1992. House Appropriations reported June 18 (H Rept 102-579). House passed, amended, June 24. Senate Appropriations reported, amended, Sept. 23 (S Rept 102-418). Senate passed, amended, Oct. 1. House disagreed to the Senate amendments and agreed to a conference Oct. 2. Conference report filed in the House on Oct. 3 (H Rept 102-1007). House agreed to the conference report Oct. 4. Senate agreed to the conference report Oct. 5. President signed Oct. 6, 1992.

**PL 102-393 (HR 5488)** Provide for appropriations for the Treasury Department, the U.S. Postal Service, the Executive Office of the President, and certain independent agencies, for the fiscal year ending Sept. 30, 1993. Introduced by ROYBAL, D-Calif., June 25, 1992. House Appropriations reported June 25 (H Rept 102-618). House passed, amended, July 1. Senate Appropriations reported, amended, July 31 (S Rept 102-353). Senate passed, amended, Sept. 10. House disagreed to the Senate amendments and agreed to a conference Sept. 15. Conference report filed in the House on Sept. 28 (H Rept 102-919). House agreed to the conference report Oct. 1. President signed Oct. 6, 1992.

**PL 102-394 (HR 5677)** Provide for appropriations for the departments of Health and Human Services, Labor, and Education, and related agencies, for the fiscal year ending Sept. 30, 1993. Introduced by NATCHER, D-Ky., July 23, 1992. House Appropriations reported July 23 (H Rept 102-708). House passed, amended, July 28. Senate Appropriations reported, amended, Sept. 10 (S Rept 102-397). Senate passed, amended, Sept. 18. House disagreed to the Senate amendments and agreed to a conference Sept. 22. Conference report filed in the House Oct. 1 (H Rept 102-974). House agreed to conference report Oct. 3. House receded and concurred in Senate amendments Oct. 3. House receded and concurred with amendments in Senate amendments Oct. 3. Senate agreed to the conference report Oct. 3. Senate agreed to House amendments to Senate amendments Oct. 3. President signed Oct. 6, 1992.

**PL 102-395 (HR 5678)** Provide for appropriations for the departments of Commerce, Justice and State, the judiciary, and related agencies for the fiscal year ending Sept. 30, 1993. Introduced by SMITH, D-Iowa, July 23, 1992. House Appropriations reported July 23 (H Rept 102-710). House passed, amended, July 29. Senate Appropriations reported, amended, Aug. 3 (S Rept 102-356). Senate passed, amended, Sept. 9. House disagreed to Senate amendments and agreed to a conference Sept. 15. Conference report filed in the House on Sept. 24 (H Rept 102-902). House agreed to the conference report Sept. 25. House receded and concurred in Senate amendments Sept. 25. House receded and concurred with amendments in Senate amendments Sept. 25. House insisted on its disagreement to Senate amendment Sept. 25. Senate agreed to conference report Sept. 25. Senate agreed to House amendments to Senate amendments Sept. 25. Senate receded from its amendment Sept. 25. President signed Oct. 6, 1992.

**PL 102-396 (HR 5504)** Provide for appropriations for the Department of Defense for the fiscal year ending Sept. 30, 1993. Introduced by MURTHA, D-Pa., June 29, 1992. House Appropriations reported June 29 (H Rept 102-627). House passed, amended, July 2. Senate Appropriations reported, amended, Sept. 17 (S Rept 102-408). Senate passed, amended, Sept. 23. House disagreed to Senate amendments and agreed to a conference Sept. 24. Conference report filed in the House on Oct. 5 (H Rept 102-1015). House agreed to the conference report Oct. 5. Senate agreed to the conference report Oct. 5. President signed Oct. 6, 1992.

**PL 102-397 (S 1766)** Relating to the jurisdiction of the U.S. Capitol Police. Introduced by FORD, D-Ky., Sept. 26, 1991. Senate passed Sept. 26. House Administration discharged. House passed, amended, July 7, 1992. House insisted on its amendments and asked for a conference July 7. Senate agreed to House amendments with amendment July 21. House disagreed to Senate amendment to House amendments and asked for a further conference Aug. 12. Senate receded from its amendment to the House amendments Sept. 17. Senate agreed to House amendments with further amendments Sept. 17. House agreed to Senate amendments to House amendments Sept. 22. President signed Oct. 6, 1992.

**PL 102-398 (S J Res 23)** To consent to certain amendments enacted by the Legislature of the state of Hawaii to the Hawaiian Homes Commission Act of 1920. Introduced by INOUYE, D-Hawaii, Jan. 14, 1991. Senate Energy and Natural Resources reported, amended, Nov. 23 (S Rept 102-235). Senate passed, amended, Nov. 26. House passed, under suspension of the rules, Sept. 22, 1992. President signed Oct. 6, 1992.

**PL 102-399 (HR 5058)** Authorize appropriations for the American Folklife Center for fiscal 1993-97. Introduced by CLAY, D-Mo., May 5, 1992. House failed to suspend the rules and pass HR 5058 on June 9. House Administration discharged. House passed, amended, Sept. 24. Senate passed Sept. 29. President signed Oct. 7, 1992.

**PL 102-400 (HR 5399)** Amend the U.S. Commission on Civil Rights Act of 1983 to provide an authorization of appropriations. Introduced by EDWARDS, D-Calif., June 16, 1992. House Judiciary reported Aug. 3 (H Rept 102-770). House passed, under suspension of the rules, Aug. 3. Senate Judiciary reported Sept. 17 (no written report). Senate passed Sept. 29. President signed Oct. 7, 1992.

**PL 102-401 (HR 5630)** Amend the Head Start Act to expand services provided by Head Start programs, to expand the authority of the secretary of Health and Human Services to reduce the amount of matching funds required to be provided by particular Head Start agencies and to authorize the purchase of Head Start facilities. Introduced by MARTINEZ, D-Calif., July 21, 1992. House Education and Labor reported, amended, July 31 (H Rept 102-763). House passed, amended, under suspension of the rules, Aug. 3. Senate Labor and Human Resources discharged. Senate passed Sept. 24. President signed Oct. 7, 1992.

**PL 102-402 (HR 1435)** Direct the secretary of the Army to transfer jurisdiction over the Rocky Mountain Arsenal, Colo., to the secretary of the Interior. Introduced by SCHROEDER, D-Colo., March 13, 1991. House Armed Services reported, amended, March 20, 1992 (H Rept 102-463, Part I). House considered, under suspension of the rules, July 7. House Merchant Marine and Fisheries reported, amended, July 7 (H Rept 102-463, Part II). House passed, amended, under suspension of the rules, July 7. Senate passed, amended, Sept. 18. House agreed to Senate amendments Sept. 25. President signed Oct. 9, 1992.

**PL 102-403 (HR 3379)** Amend Section 574 of Title 5, U.S. Code, relating to the authorities of the Administrative Conference. Introduced by FRANK, D-Mass., Sept. 24, 1991. House Judiciary reported Nov. 25 (H Rept 102-371). House passed, under suspension of the rules, Nov. 25. Senate Judiciary reported June 25, 1992. Senate passed Sept. 17. Enrolled bill returned to the House, pursuant to H Con Res 366 Oct. 2. Presented to the president Oct. 5. President signed Oct. 9, 1992.

**PL 102-404 (S 1216)** Provide for the deferral of enforced departure and the granting of lawful temporary residence status in the United States to certain classes of non-immigrant aliens of the People's Republic of China. Introduced by GORTON, R-Wash., June 4, 1991. Senate Judiciary reported, amended, May 7, 1992. Senate passed, amended, May 21. House Judiciary reported, amended, Aug. 10 (H Rept 102-826). House passed, amended, under suspension of the rules, Aug. 10. Senate agreed to House amendments Sept. 23. President signed Oct. 9, 1992.

**PL 102-405 (S 2344)** Improve the provision of health-care and other services to veterans by the Department of Veterans Affairs. Introduced by CRANSTON, D-Calif., March 11, 1992. Senate passed March 11. House passed, amended, under suspension of the rules, May 12. Conference report filed in the House on Sept. 17 (H Rept 102-871). House agreed to conference report Sept. 24. Senate agreed to conference report Sept. 25. President signed Oct. 9, 1992.

**PL 102-406 (HR 2448)** Provide for the minting of coins in commemoration of Benjamin Franklin and to enact a fire service bill of rights. Introduced by WELDON, R-Pa., May 23, 1991. House passed, amended, under suspension of the rules, Oct. 3, 1992. Senate passed Oct. 7. President signed Oct. 12, 1992.

**PL 102-407 (HR 1628)** Authorize the construction of a monument in the District of Columbia or its environs to honor Thomas Paine and for other purposes. Introduced by LOWEY, D-N.Y., March 21, 1991. House passed, under suspension of the rules, July 21, 1992. Senate passed Oct. 1. President signed Oct. 13, 1992.

**PL 102-408 (HR 3508)** Amend the Public Health Service Act to revise and extend certain programs relating to the education of individuals as health professionals. Introduced by WAXMAN, D-Calif., Oct. 3, 1991. House Energy and Commerce reported, amended, Oct. 25 (H Rept 102-275). House passed, amended, under suspension of the rules, Nov. 12. Senate passed, amended, Nov. 26. Senate agreed to conference report Sept. 25, 1992. Conference report filed in the House on Sept. 29 (H Rept 102-925). House agreed to conference report, under suspension of the rules, Sept. 29. President signed Oct. 13, 1992.

**PL 102-409 (HR 4178)** Amend the Public Health Service Act to provide for a program to carry out research on the drug known as diethylstilbestrol, to educate health professionals and the public on the drug and to provide for certain longitudinal studies regarding individuals who have been exposed to the drug. Introduced by SLAUGHTER, D-N.Y., Feb. 5, 1992. House Energy and Commerce reported, amended, Aug. 10 (H Rept 102-817). House passed, amended, under suspension of the rules, Aug. 10. Senate passed Sept. 30. President signed Oct. 13, 1992.

**PL 102-410 (HR 5673)** Amend the Public Health Service Act to revise and extend the programs of the Agency for Health Care Policy and Research. Introduced by WAXMAN, D-Calif., July 22, 1992. House Energy and Commerce reported, amended, Sept. 22 (H Rept 102-892). House considered, under suspension of the rules, Sept. 22. House passed, amended, under suspension of the rules, Sept. 24. Senate passed Sept. 30. President signed Oct. 13, 1992.

**PL 102-411 (HR 5925)** Amend Title VII of the Civil Rights Act of 1964 to establish a revolving fund for use by the Equal Employment Opportunity Commission to provide education, technical assistance and training relating to the laws administered by the commission. Introduced by FORD, D-Mich., Sept. 10, 1992. House passed, under suspension of the rules, Sept. 16. Senate passed Oct. 2. President signed Oct. 14, 1992.

**PL 102-412 (H J Res 320)** Authorize the government of the District of Columbia to establish, in the District of Columbia or its environs, a memorial to African-Americans who served with Union forces during the Civil War. Introduced by NORTON, D-D.C., Aug. 2, 1991. House passed, amended, under suspension of the rules, June 9, 1992. Senate passed Oct. 1. President signed Oct. 14, 1992.

**PL 102-413 (H J Res 542)** Designate the week beginning Nov. 9, 1992, as Hire a Veteran Week. Introduced by BROWN, D-Calif., Aug. 12, 1992. House passed Sept. 30. Senate passed Oct. 3. President signed Oct. 14, 1992.

**PL 102-414 (S 3195)** Require the secretary of the Treasury to mint coins in commemoration of the 50th anniversary of the United States' involvement in World War II. Introduced by GLENN, D-Ohio, Aug. 12, 1992. Senate passed Sept. 19. House passed, under suspension of the rules, Sept. 29. President signed Oct. 14, 1992.

**PL 102-415 (HR 3157)** Provide for the settlement of certain claims under the Alaska Native Claims Settlement Act. Introduced by YOUNG, R-Alaska, July 31, 1991. House Interior and Insular Affairs reported, amended, July 21, 1992 (H Rept 102-673). House passed, amended, under suspension of the rules, July 27. Senate passed Sept. 9. Senate proceedings vacated Sept. 10. Senate passed Oct. 1. President signed Oct. 14, 1992.

**PL 102-416 (HR 2144)** Provide for the restoration of the federal trust relationship with and assistance to the terminated tribes of California Indians and the individual members thereof; to extend federal recognition to certain Indian tribes in California; to establish administrative procedures and guidelines to clarify the status of certain Indian tribes in California; and to establish a federal commission on policies and programs affecting California Indians. Introduced by MILLER, D-Calif., April 30, 1991. House considered, under suspension of the rules, Aug. 11, 1992. House passed, amended, under suspension of the rules, Aug. 12. Senate Indian Affairs reported, amended, Sept. 29 (S Rept 102-441). Senate passed, amended, Oct. 2. House agreed to Senate amend-

ments, under suspension of the rules, Oct. 3. President signed Oct. 14, 1992.

**PL 102-417 (HR 2324)** Amend Title 28, U.S. Code, with respect to witness fees. Introduced by HUGHES, D-N.J., May 14, 1991. House Judiciary reported Aug. 2 (H Rept 102-194). House passed, under suspension of the rules, Nov. 18. Senate Judiciary reported, amended, June 25, 1992. Senate passed, amended, Aug. 6. House agreed to Senate amendments Oct. 3. President signed Oct. 14, 1992.

**PL 102-418 (S J Res 287)** Designate the week of Oct. 4, 1992, through Oct. 10, 1992, as Mental Illness Awareness Week. Introduced by SIMON, D-Ill., April 1, 1992. Senate Judiciary reported June 25. Senate passed June 26. House passed Sept. 30. President signed Oct. 14, 1992.

**PL 102-419 (HR 2321)** Establish the Dayton Aviation Heritage National Historical Park in the state of Ohio. Introduced by HALL, D-Ohio, May 14, 1991. House Interior and Insular Affairs reported, amended, March 2, 1992 (H Rept 102-449). House considered, under suspension of the rules, March 3. House passed, amended, under suspension of the rules, March 4. Senate passed, amended, Sept. 9. Senate proceedings vacated Sept. 10. Senate Energy and Natural Resources reported, amended, Sept. 24 (S Rept 102-462). Senate passed, amended, Oct. 1. House agreed to Senate amendments pursuant to H Res 596 on Oct. 4. President signed Oct. 16, 1992.

**PL 102-420 (HR 5258)** Provide for the withdrawal of most-favored-nation status from the Federal Republic of Yugoslavia and to provide for the restoration of such status if certain conditions are fulfilled. Introduced by WOLF, R-Va., May 21, 1992. House Ways and Means reported Sept. 18 (H Rept 102-880). House passed, under suspension of the rules, Sept. 22. Senate passed, amended, Sept. 30. House agreed to Senate amendments, under suspension of the rules, Oct. 6. President signed Oct. 16, 1992.

**PL 102-421 (HR 5483)** Modify the provisions of the Education of the Deaf Act Amendments of 1988. Introduced by OWENS, D-N.Y., June 24, 1992. House Education and Labor reported, amended, Aug. 10 (H Rept 102-818). House passed, amended, under suspension of the rules, Aug. 10. Senate passed, amended, Oct. 5. House agreed to Senate amendments, under suspension of the rules, Oct. 6. President signed Oct. 16, 1992.

**PL 102-422 (S 1880)** Amend the District of Columbia Spouse Equity Act of 1988. Introduced by LEVIN, D-Mich., Oct. 25, 1991. Senate Governmental Affairs reported Aug. 10, 1992 (S Rept 102-366). Senate passed Sept. 25. House passed, under suspension of the rules, Sept. 29. President signed Oct. 16, 1992.

**PL 102-423 (S 3007)** Authorize financial assistance for the construction and maintenance of the Mary McLeod Bethune Memorial Fine Arts Center. Introduced by GRAHAM, D-Fla., July 22, 1992. Senate passed July 22. House passed, under suspension of the rules, Sept. 29. President signed Oct. 16, 1992.

**PL 102-424 (S J Res 305)** Designate October 1992 as Polish-American Heritage Month. Introduced by SIMON, D-Ill., May 14, 1992. Senate Judiciary reported June 25. Senate passed June 26. House passed Sept. 30. President signed Oct. 16, 1992.

**PL 102-425 (S J Res 319)** Designate the second Sunday in October of 1992 as National Children's Day. Introduced by KASSEBAUM, R-Kan., June 18, 1992. Senate Judiciary reported June 25. Senate passed June 26. House passed Sept. 30. President signed Oct. 16, 1992.

**PL 102-426 (HR 4016)** Amend the Comprehensive Environmental Response, Compensation and Liability Act of 1980 to require the federal government, before termination of federal activities on any real property owned by the government, to identify real property where no hazardous substance was stored, released or disposed of. Introduced by PANETTA, D-Calif., on Nov. 26, 1991. House Energy and Commerce reported, amended, Aug. 6, 1992 (H Rept 102-814). House passed, amended, under suspension of the rules, Aug. 10. Senate passed, amended, Sept. 18. Conference report filed in the House on Oct. 3 (H Rept 102-986). Senate agreed to conference report Oct. 5. House agreed to conference report, under suspension of the rules, Oct. 6. President signed Oct. 19, 1992.

**PL 102-427 (HR 3665)** Establish the Little River Canyon

National Preserve in Alabama. Introduced by BEVILL, D-Ala., on Oct. 29, 1991. House Interior and Insular Affairs reported, amended, April 7, 1992 (H Rept 102-482). House passed, amended, under suspension of the rules, April 7. Senate Energy and Natural Resources reported, amended, Sept. 24 (S Rept 102-472). Senate passed, amended, Oct. 1. House agreed to Senate amendment Oct. 3. President signed Oct. 21, 1992.

**PL 102-428 (HR 5237)** Amend the Rural Electrification Act of 1936 to improve the provision of electric and telephone service in rural areas. Introduced by ENGLISH, D-Okla., on May 21, 1992. House Agriculture reported, amended, Aug. 4 (H Rept 102-782, Part I). House considered, under suspension of the rules, Aug. 4. House passed, amended, under suspension of the rules, Aug. 5. Senate passed, amended, Oct. 5. House agreed to Senate amendment, under suspension of the rules, Oct. 6. President signed Oct. 21, 1992.

**PL 102-429 (HR 5739)** Reauthorize the Export-Import Bank of the United States. Introduced by OAKAR, D-Ohio, on July 31, 1992. House passed, under suspension of the rules, Aug. 4. Senate passed, amended, Aug. 12. Conference report filed in the House on Oct. 4 (H Rept 102-1010). House agreed to conference report Oct. 6. Senate agreed to conference report Oct. 8. President signed Oct. 21, 1992.

**PL 102-430 (HR 1216)** Modify the boundaries of the Indiana Dunes National Lakeshore. Introduced by VISCLOSKY, D-Ind., on Feb. 28, 1991. House Interior and Insular Affairs reported, amended, July 15 (H Rept 102-151). House passed, amended, under suspension of the rules, July 15. Senate Energy and Natural Resources reported, amended, July 23, 1992 (S Rept 102-340). Senate passed, amended, July 29. House agreed to Senate amendment with amendments pursuant to H Res 605 on Oct. 6. Senate agreed to House amendments to Senate amendments Oct. 8. President signed Oct. 23, 1992.

**PL 102-431 (HR 2181)** Permit the secretary of the Interior to acquire by exchange lands in the Cuyahoga National Recreation Area that are owned by the state of Ohio. Introduced by SAWYER, D-Ohio, May 1, 1991. House Interior and Insular Affairs reported, amended, Sept. 23 (H Rept 102-211). House passed, amended, under suspension of the rules, Sept. 24. Senate Energy and Natural Resources reported Sept. 24, 1992. Senate passed Oct. 7, 1992. President signed Oct. 23, 1992.

**PL 102-432 (HR 2431)** Amend the Wild and Scenic Rivers Act by designating a segment of the Lower Merced River in California as a component of the National Wild and Scenic Rivers System. Introduced by CONDIT, D-Calif., May 22, 1991. House Interior and Insular Affairs reported, amended, Nov. 22 (H Rept 102-349). House passed, amended, under suspension of the rules, Nov. 23. Senate passed, amended, April 9, 1992. House agreed to Senate amendment with amendment Sept. 29. Senate agreed to House amendment to Senate amendment Oct. 7. President signed Oct. 23, 1992.

**PL 102-433 (HR 3118)** Designate Federal Office Building No. 9 at 1900 E St. N.W., Washington, D.C., as the Theodore Roosevelt Federal Building. Introduced by GILMAN, R-N.Y., on July 31, 1991. House Public Works and Transportation reported Feb. 26, 1992 (H Rept 102-438). House passed, under suspension of the rules, March 3. Senate passed Oct. 7. President signed Oct. 23, 1992.

**PL 102-434 (HR 3818)** Designate the building at 80 N. Hughey Ave. in Orlando, Fla., as the George C. Young U.S. Courthouse and Federal Building. Introduced by McCOLLUM, R-Fla., on Nov. 19, 1991. House Public Works and Transportation reported Feb. 26, 1992 (H Rept 102-443). House passed, under suspension of the rules, March 3. Senate passed Oct. 7. President signed Oct. 23, 1992.

**PL 102-435 (HR 4281)** Designate the federal building and courthouse to be constructed at 5th and Ross streets in Santa Ana, Calif., as the Ronald Reagan Federal Building and Courthouse. Introduced by COX, R-Calif., on Feb. 20, 1992. House Public Works and Transportation reported, amended, Sept. 25 (H Rept 102-917). House passed, amended, under suspension of the rules, Sept. 29. Senate passed Oct. 7. President signed Oct. 23, 1992.

**PL 102-436 (HR 4489)** Provide for a land exchange with

Tacoma, Wash. Introduced by DICKS, D-Wash., March 18, 1992. House Interior and Insular Affairs reported, amended, Sept. 29 (H Rept 102-946). House passed, amended, under suspension of the rules, Sept. 29. Senate passed Oct. 7. President signed Oct. 23, 1992.

**PL 102-437 (HR 4539)** Designate the general mail facility of the U.S. Postal Service in Gulfport, Miss., as the Larkin I. Smith General Mail Facility and the building of the U.S. Postal Service in Poplarville, Miss., as the Larkin I. Smith Post Office Building. Introduced by TAYLOR, D-Miss., March 20, 1992. House passed, amended, under suspension of the rules, Aug. 4. Senate Governmental Affairs reported Sept. 18. Senate passed Oct. 5. President signed Oct. 23, 1992.

**PL 102-438 (HR 4771)** Designate the facility under construction for use by the U.S. Postal Service at FM 1098 Loop in Prairie View, Texas, as the Esel D. Bell Post Office Building. Introduced by LAUGHLIN, D-Texas, April 3, 1992. House passed, amended, under suspension of the rules, June 22. Senate passed Oct. 8. President signed Oct. 23, 1992.

**PL 102-439 (HR 4999)** Authorize additional appropriations for implementation of the development plan for Pennsylvania Avenue between the Capitol and the White House. Introduced by KOSTMAYER, D-Pa., April 28, 1992. House Interior and Insular Affairs reported June 15 (H Rept 102-562). House passed, amended, under suspension of the rules, June 15. Senate Energy and Natural Resources reported Sept. 24. Senate passed Oct. 7. President signed Oct. 23, 1992.

**PL 102-440 (HR 5013)** Promote the conservation of wild exotic birds, to provide for the Great Lakes Fish and Wildlife Tissue Bank, to reauthorize the Fish and Wildlife Conservation Act of 1980, to reauthorize the African Elephant Conservation Act and for other purposes. Introduced by STUDDS, D-Mass., April 29, 1992. House Merchant Marine and Fisheries reported, amended, July 29 (H Rept 102-749, Part I). House Ways and Means reported July 31 (H Rept 102-749, Part II). House passed, amended, under suspension of the rules, Aug. 11. Senate passed, amended, Sept. 30. House agreed to Senate amendments Oct. 5. President signed Oct. 23, 1992.

**PL 102-441 (HR 5122)** Relating to the settlement of the water rights claims of the Jicarilla Apache Tribe. Introduced by RICHARDSON, D-N.M., May 7, 1992. House Interior and Insular Affairs reported, amended, Sept. 29 (H Rept 102-955). House passed, amended, under suspension of the rules, Sept. 29. Senate passed Oct. 7. President signed Oct. 23, 1992.

**PL 102-442 (HR 5222)** Designate the federal building and U.S. courthouse at 204 S. Main St. in South Bend, Ind., as the Robert A. Grant Federal Building and U.S. Courthouse. Introduced by ROEMER, D-Ind., May 20, 1992. House Public Works and Transportation reported June 24 (H Rept 102-612). House passed, under suspension of the rules, July 28. Senate passed Oct. 7. President signed Oct. 23, 1992.

**PL 102-443 (HR 5291)** Provide for the temporary use of certain lands in South Gate, Calif., for elementary school purposes. Introduced by MARTINEZ, D-Calif., May 28, 1992. House Interior and Insular Affairs reported, amended, July 23 (H Rept 102-689). House passed, amended, under suspension of the rules, July 27. Senate passed Oct. 8. President signed Oct. 23, 1992.

**PL 102-444 (HR 5328)** Amend Title 35, U.S. Code, with respect to the late payment of maintenance fees. Introduced by McCOLLUM, R-Fla., June 4, 1992. House Judiciary reported, amended, Oct. 3 (H Rept 102-993). House passed, amended, under suspension of the rules, Oct. 3. Senate passed Oct. 7. President signed Oct. 23, 1992.

**PL 102-445 (HR 5431)** Designate the federal building at 200 Federal Plaza in Paterson, N.J., as the Robert A. Roe Federal Building. Introduced by MINETA, D-Calif., June 18, 1992. House Public Works and Transportation reported July 9 (H Rept 102-660). House passed, under suspension of the rules, July 28. Senate passed Oct. 7. President signed Oct. 23, 1992.

**PL 102-446 (HR 5432)** Designate the federal building and U.S. courthouse at the corner of College Avenue and Mountain Street in Fayetteville, Ark., as the John Paul Hammerschmidt Federal Building and U.S. Courthouse. Introduced by SHUSTER,

R-Pa., June 18, 1992. House Public Works and Transportation reported July 9 (H Rept 102-661). House passed, under suspension of the rules, July 28. Senate passed Oct. 7. President signed Oct. 23, 1992.

**PL 102-447 (HR 5453)** Designate the Central Square facility of the U.S. Postal Service in Cambridge, Mass., as the Clifton Merriman Post Office Building. Introduced by KENNEDY, D-Mass., June 22, 1992. House passed, under suspension of the rules, Aug. 4. Senate Governmental Affairs reported Sept. 18. Senate passed Oct. 5. President signed Oct. 23, 1992.

**PL 102-448 (HR 5479)** Designate the facility of the U.S. Postal Service at 1100 Wythe St. in Alexandria, Va., as the Helen Day United States Post Office Building. Introduced by MORAN, D-Va., June 24, 1992. House passed, under suspension of the rules, Aug. 4. Senate passed Oct. 8. President signed Oct. 23, 1992.

**PL 102-449 (HR 5491)** Designate the Department of Veterans Affairs medical center in Marlin, Texas, as the Thomas T. Connally Department of Veterans Affairs Medical Center. Introduced by EDWARDS, D-Texas, June 25, 1992. House Veterans' Affairs reported July 24 (H Rept 102-715). House passed, under suspension of the rules, Aug. 4. Senate passed Oct. 8. President signed Oct. 23, 1992.

**PL 102-450 (HR 5572)** Designate May of each year as Asian/Pacific American Heritage Month. Introduced by HORTON, R-N.Y., July 8, 1992. House Post Office and Civil Service reported Sept. 30 (H Rept 102-957). House passed, under suspension of the rules, Oct. 4. Senate passed Oct. 7. President signed Oct. 23, 1992.

**PL 102-451 (HR 5575)** Authorize certain uses of real property acquired by the Architect of the Capitol for use by the Librarian of Congress. Introduced by ROSE, D-N.C., July 8, 1992. House Administration reported, amended, Oct. 2 (H Rept 102-979). House passed, amended, under suspension of the rules, Oct. 2. Senate passed Oct. 7. President signed Oct. 23, 1992.

**PL 102-452 (HR 5602)** Grant the consent of the Congress to the Interstate Rail Passenger Network Compact. Introduced by McCLOSKEY, D-Ind., July 9, 1992. House Judiciary reported Oct. 2 (H Rept 102-983). House passed, under suspension of the rules, Oct. 3. Senate passed Oct. 7. President signed Oct. 23, 1992.

**PL 102-453 (HR 5605)** Authorize and direct land ownership consolidation in the Cedar Rapids Watershed, Mount Daker-Snoqualmie National Forest, Wash. Introduced by McDERMOTT, D-Wash., July 9, 1992. House Agriculture reported, amended, Sept. 29 (H Rept 102-937, Part I). House passed, amended, under suspension of the rules, Sept. 29. Senate passed Oct. 8. President signed Oct. 23, 1992.

**PL 102-454 (HR 5751)** Provide for the distribution within the United States of certain materials prepared by the United States Information Agency. Introduced by FASCELL, D-Fla., Aug. 3, 1992. House passed, under suspension of the rules, Aug. 10. Senate passed Oct. 5. President signed Oct. 23, 1992.

**PL 102-455 (HR 5831)** Designate the federal building at Main and Church streets in Victoria, Texas, as the Martin Luther King Jr. Federal Building. Introduced by LAUGHLIN, D-Texas, on Aug. 12, 1992. House Public Works and Transportation reported, amended, Sept. 25 (H Rept 102-914). House passed, amended, under suspension of the rules, Sept. 29. Senate passed Oct. 7. President signed Oct. 23, 1992.

**PL 102-456 (HR 6000)** Redesignate Springer Mountain National Recreation Area as Ed Jenkins National Recreation Area. Introduced by BARNARD, D-Ga., Sept. 23, 1992. House Agriculture reported Sept. 29 (H Rept 102-935). House passed, under suspension of the rules, Sept. 29. Senate passed Oct. 8. President signed Oct. 23, 1992.

**PL 102-457 (HR 6049)** Amend the Congressional Award Act to revise and extend authorities for the Congressional Award Board. Introduced by OWENS, D-N.Y., Sept. 28, 1992. House passed, under suspension of the rules, Oct. 2. Senate passed Oct. 7. President signed Oct. 23, 1992.

**PL 102-458 (HR 6072)** Direct expedited negotiated settlement of the land rights of the Kenai Natives Association Inc., under Section 14(h)(3) of the Alaska Native Claims Settlement Act, by directing land acquisition and exchange negotiations by

the secretary of the Interior and certain Alaska Native corporations involving lands and interests in lands held by the United States and such corporations. Introduced by YOUNG, R-Alaska, Sept. 30, 1992. House passed, under suspension of the rules, Oct. 3. Senate passed Oct. 8. President signed Oct. 23, 1992.

**PL 102-459 (HR 6165)** Amend certain provisions of law relating to establishment, in the District of Columbia or its environs, of a memorial to honor Thomas Paine. Introduced by LOWEY, D-N.Y., Oct. 5, 1992. House passed Oct. 6. Senate passed Oct. 8. President signed Oct. 23, 1992.

**PL 102-460 (HR 6179)** Amend the Wild and Scenic Rivers Act. Introduced by KOSTMAYER, D-Pa., Oct. 5, 1992. House passed, under suspension of the rules, Oct. 6. Senate passed Oct. 8. President signed Oct. 23, 1992.

**PL 102-461 (HR 6184)** Amend the National Trails System Act to designate the American Discovery Trail for study to determine the feasibility and desirability of its designation as a national trail. Introduced by BYRON, D-Md., Oct. 5, 1992. House passed Oct. 6. Senate passed Oct. 8. President signed Oct. 23, 1992.

**PL 102-462 (H J Res 353)** Designate the week beginning Jan. 3, 1993, as Braille Literacy Week. Introduced by BALLENGER, R-N.C., Oct. 17, 1991. House passed, amended, Sept. 16, 1992. Senate Judiciary reported Oct. 5. Senate passed Oct. 8. President signed Oct. 23, 1992.

**PL 102-463 (H J Res 399)** Designate the week beginning Nov. 1, 1992, as National Medical Staff Services Awareness Week. Introduced by DUNCAN, R-Tenn., Feb. 4, 1992. House passed Oct. 6. Senate passed Oct. 8. President signed Oct. 23, 1992.

**PL 102-464 (H J Res 457)** Designate Jan. 16, 1993, as Religious Freedom Day. Introduced by BLILEY, R-Va., March 31, 1992. House passed June 25. Senate Judiciary reported Oct. 5. Senate passed Oct. 8. President signed Oct. 23, 1992.

**PL 102-465 (H J Res 467)** Designate Oct. 24, 1992, through Nov. 1, 1992, as National Red Ribbon Week for a Drug-Free America. Introduced by HORN, D-Mo., April 8, 1992. House passed Sept. 16. Senate passed Oct. 8. President signed Oct. 23, 1992.

**PL 102-466 (H J Res 471)** Designate Sept. 16, 1992, as National Occupational Therapy Day. Introduced by SOLARZ, D-N.Y., April 9, 1992. House passed Oct. 6. Senate passed Oct. 8. President signed Oct. 23, 1992.

**PL 102-467 (H J Res 484)** Designate the week beginning Feb. 14, 1993, as National Visiting Nurse Associations Week. Introduced by OAKAR, D-Ohio, May 14, 1992. House passed Sept. 30. Senate passed Oct. 8. President signed Oct. 23, 1992.

**PL 102-468 (H J Res 489)** Designate Feb. 21, 1993, through Feb. 27, 1993, as American Wine Appreciation Week. Introduced by FAZIO, D-Calif., May 21, 1992. House passed Oct. 6. Senate passed Oct. 8. President signed Oct. 23, 1992.

**PL 102-469 (H J Res 500)** Designate March 1993 as Irish-American Heritage Month. Introduced by MANTON, D-N.Y., June 1, 1992. House passed Sept 30. Senate Judiciary reported Oct. 5. Senate passed Oct. 8. President signed Oct. 23, 1992.

**PL 102-470 (H J Res 520)** Designate the month of October 1992 as Country Music Month. Introduced by CLEMENT, D-Tenn., June 30, 1992. House passed Sept 16. Senate Judiciary reported Oct. 5. Senate passed Oct. 8. President signed Oct. 23, 1992.

**PL 102-471 (H J Res 523)** Designate Oct. 8, 1992, as National Firefighters Day. Introduced by WELDON, R-Pa., July 2, 1992. House passed Sept 30. Senate Judiciary reported Oct. 5. Senate passed Oct. 8. President signed Oct. 23, 1992.

**PL 102-472 (H J Res 529)** Support the planting of 500 redwood trees from California in Spain in commemoration of the quincentenary of the voyage of Christopher Columbus and designate the trees as a gift to the people of Spain. Introduced by PASTOR, D-Ariz., July 9, 1992. House passed Oct. 4. Senate passed Oct. 7. President signed Oct. 23, 1992.

**PL 102-473 (H J Res 543)** Designate Nov. 30, 1992, through Dec. 6, 1992, as National Education First Week. Introduced by FAZIO, D-Calif., Aug. 12, 1992. House passed Oct. 6. Senate passed Oct. 8. President signed Oct. 23, 1992.

**PL 102-474 (H J Res 547)** Designate May 2, 1993, through May 8, 1993, as National Walking Week. Introduced by RITTER, R-Pa., Aug. 12, 1992. House passed Oct. 6. Senate passed Oct. 8. President signed Oct. 23, 1992.

**PL 102-475 (H J Res 563)** Provide for the convening of the first session of the 103rd Congress. Introduced by GEPHARDT, D-Mo., Oct. 5, 1992. House passed Oct. 6. Senate passed Oct. 7. President signed Oct. 23, 1992.

**PL 102-476 (S 1146)** Establish a national advanced technician training program, utilizing the resources of the nation's two-year associate-degree granting colleges to expand the pool of skilled technicians in strategic advanced-technology fields, to increase the productivity of the nation's industries and to improve the competitiveness of the United States in international trade. Introduced by MIKULSKI, D-Md., May 23, 1991. Senate passed, amended, Oct. 2, 1992. House passed Oct. 3. President signed Oct. 23, 1992.

**PL 102-477 (S 1530)** Authorize the integration of employment, training and related services provided by Indian tribes. Introduced by SIMON, D-Ill., July 23, 1991. Senate Indian Affairs reported, amended, Oct. 15 (S Rept 102-188). Senate passed, amended, Oct. 30. House Interior and Insular Affairs reported, amended, Sept. 24, 1992 (H Rept 102-905). House passed, amended, under suspension of the rules, Sept. 29. Senate agreed to House amendment Oct. 7. President signed Oct. 23, 1992.

**PL 102-478 (S 2625)** Designate the U.S. courthouse being constructed at 400 Cooper St. in Camden, N.J., as the Mitchell H. Cohen United States Courthouse. Introduced by LAUTENBERG, D-N.J., April 28, 1992. Senate passed July 21. House passed Oct. 6. President signed Oct. 23, 1992.

**PL 102-479 (S 2661)** Authorize the striking of a medal commemorating the 250th anniversary of the founding of the American Philosophical Society and the birth of Thomas Jefferson. Introduced by MOYNIHAN, D-N.Y., May 6, 1992. Senate passed Sept. 23. House passed, under suspension of the rules, Oct. 3. President signed Oct. 23, 1992.

**PL 102-480 (S 2834)** Designate the U.S. Post Office Building at 100 Main St., Millsboro, Del., as the John J. Williams Post Office Building. Introduced by ROTH, R-Del., June 11, 1992. Senate Governmental Affairs reported June 30. Senate passed July 2. House passed, under suspension of the rules, Oct. 4. President signed Oct. 23, 1992.

**PL 102-481 (S J Res 166)** Designate the week of Oct. 4. 1992, through Oct. 10, 1992, as National Customer Service Week. Introduced by DOLE, R-Kan., June 20, 1991. Senate passed April 29, 1992. House passed Oct. 6. President signed Oct. 23, 1992.

**PL 102-482 (S J Res 218)** Designate the year 1993 as the Year of American Craft: A Celebration of the Creative Work of the Hand. Introduced by MITCHELL, D-Maine, Oct. 24, 1991. Senate Judiciary reported Feb. 27, 1992. Senate passed Feb. 27. House passed Sept. 30. President signed Oct. 23, 1992.

**PL 102-483 (S J Res 252 )** Designate the week of April 18, 1993, through April 24, 1993, as National Credit Education Week. Introduced by DIXON, D-Ill., Feb. 6, 1992. Senate Judiciary reported June 25. Senate passed June 26. House passed Sept. 30. President signed Oct. 23, 1992.

**PL 102-484 (HR 5006)** Authorize appropriations for fiscal 1992 for military functions of the Department of Defense and prescribe military personnel levels for fiscal 1993. Introduced by ASPIN, D-Wis., April 29, 1992. House Armed Services reported, amended, May 19 (H Rept 102-527). House considered June 3 and 4. House passed, amended, June 5. Senate passed, amended, Sept. 19. Conference report filed in the House Oct. 1 (H Rept 102-966). House agreed to conference report Oct. 3. Senate agreed to conference report Oct. 5. President signed Oct. 23, 1992.

**PL 102-485 (HR 6050)** Facilitate recovery from recent disasters by providing greater flexibility for depository institutions and their regulators and for other purposes. House passed, under suspension of the rules, Oct. 3. Senate passed Oct. 8. Introduced by GONZALEZ, D-Texas, Sept. 29, 1992. President signed Oct. 23, 1992.

**PL 102-486 (HR 776)** Provide for improved energy efficiency. Introduced by SHARP, D-Ind., Feb. 4, 1991. House Energy and Commerce reported, amended, March 30, 1992 (H Rept 102-

474, Part I). House Science, Space and Technology reported, amended, May 1 (H Rept 102-474, Part II). House Public Works and Transportation reported, amended, May 1 (H Rept 102-474, Part III). House Foreign Affairs reported, amended, May 4 (H Rept 102-474, Part IV). House Government Operations reported, amended, May 5 (H Rept 102-474, Part V). House Ways and Means reported, amended, May 5 (H Rept 102-474, Part VI). House Judiciary reported, amended, May 5 (H Rept 102-474, Part VII). House Interior and Insular Affairs reported, amended, May 5 (H Rept 102-474, Part VIII). House Merchant Marine and Fisheries reported, amended, May 5 (H Rept 102-474, Part IX). House considered May 20 and 21. House passed, amended, May 27. Senate Finance reported, amended, June 18. Senate considered July 29. Senate passed, amended, July 30. Conference report filed in the House on Oct. 5 (H Rept 102-1018). House agreed to conference report Oct. 5. Senate agreed to conference report Oct. 8. President signed Oct. 24, 1992.

**PL 102-487 (HR 2263)** Amend Chapter 45 of Title 5, U.S. Code, to authorize awards for cost savings disclosures. Introduced by KASICH, R-Ohio, May 8, 1991. House Post Office and Civil Service reported, amended, Nov. 22 (H Rept 102-356). House passed, amended, under suspension of the rules, Nov. 25. Senate Governmental Affairs reported, amended, Aug. 10, 1992. Senate passed, amended, Sept. 24. House agreed to Senate amendments Oct. 4. President signed Oct. 24, 1992.

**PL 102-488 (HR 2896)** Authorize the secretary of the Interior to revise the boundaries of the Minuteman National Historical Park in Massachusetts. Introduced by ATKINS, D-Mass., July 16, 1991. House Interior and Insular Affairs reported Oct. 28 (H Rept 102-276). House passed, amended, under suspension of the rules, Oct. 28. Senate Energy and Natural Resources reported July 23, 1992 (H Rept 102-330). Senate passed Oct. 7. President signed Oct. 24, 1992.

**PL 102-489 (HR 3638)** Make technical amendments to the law that authorizes the modification of the boundaries of the Alaska Maritime National Wildlife Refuge. Introduced by YOUNG, R-Alaska, Oct. 24, 1991. House Merchant Marine and Fisheries reported Nov. 22 (H Rept 102-350). House considered, under suspension of the rules, Nov. 23. House passed, under suspension of the rules, Nov. 27. Senate Energy and Natural Resources reported Sept. 24, 1992 (S Rept 102-467). Senate passed Oct. 7. President signed Oct. 24, 1992.

**PL 102-490 (HR 3673)** Authorize a research program through the National Science Foundation on the treatment of contaminated water through membrane processes. Introduced by PACKARD, R-Calif., Oct. 30, 1991. House Science, Space and Technology reported, amended, June 16, 1992 (H Rept 102-566). House passed, amended, under suspension of the rules, June 29. Senate passed Oct. 7. President signed Oct. 24, 1992.

**PL 102-491 (HR 4398)** Remove outdated limitations on the acquisition or construction of branch buildings by Federal Reserve banks that are necessary for bank branch expansion if the acquisition or construction is approved by the Board of Governors of the Federal Reserve System. Introduced by ERDREICH, D-Ala., March 5, 1992. House passed, under suspension of the rules, June 30. Senate passed Oct. 8. President signed Oct. 24, 1992.

**PL 102-492 (HR 4412)** Amend Title 17, U.S. Code, relating to fair use of copyrighted works. Introduced by HUGHES, D-N.J., March 5, 1992. House Judiciary reported, amended, Aug. 11 (H Rept 102-836). House passed, amended, under suspension of the rules, Aug. 11. Senate passed Oct. 7. President signed Oct. 24, 1992.

**PL 102-493 (HR 4773)** Provide for reporting of pregnancy success rates of assisted reproductive technology programs and for the certification of embryo laboratories. Introduced by WYDEN, D-Ore., April 3, 1992. House Energy and Commerce reported, amended, June 29 (H Rept 102-624). House passed, amended, under suspension of the rules, June 29. Senate Labor and Human Resources reported Oct. 1 (S Rept 102-452). Senate passed Oct. 8. President signed Oct. 24, 1992.

**PL 102-494 (HR 4841)** Grant the consent of the Congress to the New Hampshire-Maine Interstate School Compact. Introduced by SWETT, D-N.H., April 9, 1992. House Judiciary re-

ported Sept. 17 (H Rept 102-874). House passed, under suspension of the rules, Sept. 22. Senate passed Oct. 2. President signed Oct. 24, 1992.

**PL 102-495 (HR 4844)** Restore Olympic National Park and the Elwha River ecosystem and fisheries in Washington. Introduced by SWIFT, D-Wash., April 9, 1992. House passed, amended, under suspension of the rules, Oct. 6. Senate passed Oct. 7. President signed Oct. 24, 1992.

**PL 102-496 (HR 5095)** Authorize appropriations for fiscal 1993 for intelligence and intelligence-related activities of the U.S. government and the Central Intelligence Agency Retirement and Disability System. Introduced by McCURDY, D-Okla., May 7, 1992. House Intelligence reported, amended, June 2 (H Rept 102-544, Part I). House Armed Services reported June 17 (H Rept 102-544, Part II). House passed, amended, June 25. Senate passed, amended, Sept. 23. Conference report filed in the House on Oct. 1 (H Rept 102-963). House agreed to the conference report Oct. 2. Senate agreed to the conference report Oct. 2. President signed Oct. 24, 1992.

**PL 102-497 (HR 5686)** Make technical amendments to certain federal Indian statutes. Introduced by RHODES, R-Ariz., July 23, 1992. House Interior and Insular Affairs reported Aug. 3 (H Rept 102-774). House passed, amended, under suspension of the rules, Aug. 3. Senate Indian Affairs reported, amended, Sept. 28 (S Rept 102-428). Senate passed, amended, Oct. 1. House agreed to Senate amendments, under suspension of the rules, Oct. 3. President signed Oct. 24, 1992.

**PL 102-498 (HR 6014)** Designate certain land in the state of Missouri owned by the United States and administered by the secretary of Agriculture as part of the Mark Twain National Forest. Introduced by VOLKMER, D-Mo., Sept. 24, 1992. House Agriculture reported Sept. 29 (H Rept 102-936). House passed, under suspension of the rules, Sept. 29. Senate passed Oct. 7. President signed Oct. 24, 1992.

**PL 102-499 (HR 6047)** Amend the U.S. Information and Educational Exchange Act of 1948, the Foreign Service Act of 1980 and other provisions of law to make certain changes in administrative authorities. Introduced by BERMAN, D-Calif., Sept. 28, 1992. House passed, amended, under suspension of the rules, Oct. 2. Senate passed Oct. 7. President signed Oct. 24, 1992.

**PL 102-500 (HR 6164)** Amend the John F. Kennedy Center Act to authorize appropriations for maintenance, repair, alteration and other services necessary for the John F. Kennedy Center for the Performing Arts. Introduced by ROE, D-N.J., Oct. 5, 1992. House passed Oct. 6. Senate passed Oct. 7. President signed Oct. 24, 1992.

**PL 102-501 (HR 6183)** Amend the Public Health Service Act to provide protection from legal liability for certain health-care professionals providing services pursuant to such act. Introduced by WYDEN, D-Ore., Oct. 5, 1992. House passed Oct. 6. Senate passed Oct. 8. President signed Oct. 24, 1992.

**PL 102-502 (H J Res 271)** Authorize the Go For Broke National Veterans Association Foundation to establish a memorial to Japanese-American Veterans in the District of Columbia or its environs. Introduced by MINETA, D-Calif., June 12, 1991. House Administration reported, amended, July 27, 1992 (H Rept 102-727). House passed, amended, under suspension of the rules, July 28. Senate Energy and Natural Resources reported Sept. 24. Senate passed Oct. 7. President signed Oct. 24, 1992.

**PL 102-503 (H J Res 409)** Designate Jan. 16, 1993, as National Good Teen Day. Introduced by TRAFICANT, D-Ohio, Feb. 5, 1992. House passed Sept. 10. Senate passed Oct. 8. President signed Oct. 24, 1992.

**PL 102-504 (H J Res 429)** Designate May 2, 1993, through May 9, 1993, as Be Kind to Animals and National Pet Week. Introduced by GUARINI, D-N.J., Feb. 27, 1992. House passed, amended, June 5. Senate passed Oct. 8. President signed Oct. 24, 1992.

**PL 102-505 (H J Res 458)** Designate the week beginning Oct. 25, 1992, as World Population Awareness Week. Introduced by MOODY, D-Wis., March 31, 1992. House passed Oct. 6. Senate passed Oct. 8. President signed Oct. 24, 1992.

**PL 102-506 (S 1145)** Amend the Ethics in Government Act

of 1978 to remove the limitation on the authorization of appropriations for the Office of Government Ethics. Introduced by LEVIN, D-Mich., May 23, 1991. Senate Governmental Affairs reported July 30 (S Rept 102-132). Senate passed Aug. 2. House passed, amended, Aug. 4, 1992. Senate agreed to House amendment Oct. 7. President signed Oct. 24, 1992.

**PL 102-507 (S 1577)** Amend the Alzheimer's Disease and Related Dementias Service Research Act of 1986 to reauthorize the act. Introduced by METZENBAUM, D-Ohio, July 29, 1991. Senate Labor and Human Resources reported, amended, Nov. 25 (S Rept 102-242). Senate passed, amended, Nov. 26. House passed, amended, Oct. 6, 1992. Senate agreed to House amendment Oct. 7. President signed Oct. 24, 1992.

**PL 102-508 (S 1583)** Amend the Natural Gas Pipeline Safety Act of 1968 and the Hazardous Liquid Pipeline Safety Act of 1979 to authorize appropriations and to improve pipeline safety. Introduced by EXON, D-Neb., July 29, 1991. Senate Commerce, Science and Transportation reported, amended, Sept. 16 (S Rept 102-152). Senate passed, amended, Oct. 7. House passed, amended, Sept. 15, 1992. Senate agreed to House amendments with amendment Oct. 5. House agreed to Senate amendment to House amendments, under suspension of the rules, Oct. 6. President signed Oct. 24, 1992.

**PL 102-509 (S 2201)** Authorize the admission to the United States of certain scientists of the Commonwealth of Independent States as employment-based immigrants under the Immigration and Nationality Act. Introduced by BROWN, D-Colo., Feb. 6, 1992. Senate Judiciary reported, amended, April 8. Senate passed, amended, May 20. House Judiciary reported Sept. 21 (H Rept 102-881, Part I). House, passed, amended, under suspension of the rules, Sept. 21. Senate agreed to House amendments Oct. 2. President signed Oct. 24, 1992.

**PL 102-510 (S 2322)** Increase the rates of compensation for veterans with service-connected disabilities and the rates of dependency and indemnity compensation for the survivors of certain disabled veterans. Introduced by CRANSTON, D-Calif., March 5, 1992. Senate Veterans' Affairs reported, amended, July 20 (S Rept 102-322). Senate passed, amended, July 28. House passed, amended, Aug. 4. Senate agreed to House amendments with amendment Sept. 22. House agreed to Senate amendment to House amendments Sept. 30. President signed Oct. 24, 1992.

**PL 102-511 (S 2532)** Enact the Freedom for Russia and Emerging Eurasian Democracies and Open Markets Support Act. Introduced by PELL, D-R.I., April 7, 1992. Senate Foreign Relations reported, amended, June 2 (H Rept 102-292). Senate considered June 29, July 1. Senate passed, amended, July 2. House passed, amended, Aug. 6. Conference report filed in the House on Oct. 1 (H Rept 102-964). House agreed to conference report Oct. 3. President signed Oct. 24, 1992.

**PL 102-512 (S 2875)** Amend the Child Nutrition Act of 1966 to enhance competition among infant-formula manufacturers and to reduce the per-unit costs of infant formula for the special supplemental food program for women, infants and children (WIC). Introduced by LEAHY, D-Vt., June 18, 1992. Senate passed, amended, Oct. 5. House passed Oct. 6. President signed Oct. 24, 1992.

**PL 102-513 (S 3224)** Designate the U.S. courthouse to be constructed in Fargo, N.D., as the Quentin N. Burdick U.S. Courthouse. Introduced by MOYNIHAN, D-N.Y., Sept. 10, 1992. Senate passed Sept. 10. House passed Oct. 6. President signed Oct. 24, 1992.

**PL 102-514 (S 3279)** Extend the authorization for use of official mail in the location and recovery of missing children. Introduced by METZENBAUM, D-Ohio, Sept. 26, 1992. Senate passed Sept. 26. House passed Sept. 30. President signed Oct. 24, 1992.

**PL 102-515 (S 3312)** Enact the Cancer Registries Amendment Act. Introduced by LEAHY, D-Vt., Oct. 2, 1992. Senate passed Oct. 2. House passed, amended, Oct. 6. Senate agreed to House amendments Oct. 7. President signed Oct. 24, 1992.

**PL 102-516 (S J Res 304)** Designate the week of Jan. 3, 1993, as National Law Enforcement Training Week. Introduced by ROTH, R-Del., May 14, 1992. Senate Judiciary reported June 25.

Senate passed June 26. House passed Oct. 6. President signed Oct. 24, 1992.

**PL 102-517 (S J Res 309)** Designate the week beginning Nov. 8, 1992, as National Women Veterans Recognition Week. Introduced by CRANSTON, D-Calif., May 21, 1992. Senate Judiciary reported June 25. Senate passed June 26. House passed Oct. 6. President signed Oct. 24, 1992.

**PL 102-518 (S J Res 318)** Designate Nov. 13, 1992, as Vietnam Veterans Memorial 10th Anniversary Day. Introduced by KERRY, D-Mass., June 18, 1992. Senate Judiciary reported June 25. Senate passed June 26. House passed Oct. 6. President signed Oct. 24, 1992.

**PL 102-519 (HR 4542)** Prevent and deter auto theft. Introduced by SCHUMER, D-N.Y., March 24, 1992. House Judiciary reported, amended, Aug. 12 (H Rept 102-851, Part I). House Energy and Commerce reported, amended, Sept. 22 (H Rept 102-851, Part II). House Ways and Means reported, amended, Sept. 23 (H Rept 102-851, Part III). House passed, amended, under suspension of the rules, Oct. 6. Senate passed Oct. 8. President signed Oct. 25, 1992.

**PL 102-520 (HR 5862)** Amend Title I of the Omnibus Crime Control and Safe Streets Act of 1968 to ensure an equitable and timely distribution of benefits to public safety officers. Introduced by MANTON, D-N.Y., Aug. 12, 1992. House Judiciary reported Oct. 3 (H Rept 102-994). House passed, amended, under suspension of the rules, Oct. 3. Senate passed Oct. 7. President signed Oct. 25, 1992.

**PL 102-521 (S 1002)** Impose a criminal penalty for flight to avoid payment of arrearages in child support. Introduced by SHELBY, D-Ala., May 8, 1991. Senate Judiciary reported, amended, Sept. 17, 1992. Senate passed, amended, Sept. 18. House passed, amended, Oct. 3. Senate agreed to House amendment Oct. 7. President signed Oct. 25, 1992.

**PL 102-522 (HR 2042)** Authorize appropriations for activities under the Federal Fire Prevention and Control Act of 1974. Introduced by BOUCHER, D-Va., April 24, 1991. House Science, Space, and Technology reported May 15 (H Rept 102-62). House passed, under suspension of the rules, June 3. Senate passed, amended, Sept. 29, 1992. House agreed to Senate amendments Oct. 2. President signed Oct. 26, 1992.

**PL 102-523 (HR 5419)** Amend the Marine Mammal Protection Act of 1972 to authorize the secretary of State to enter into international agreements to establish a global moratorium to prohibit harvesting tuna with purse seine nets or to encircle dolphins or other marine mammals. Introduced by STUDDS, D-Mass., June 17, 1992. House Merchant Marine and Fisheries reported, amended, July 28 (H Rept 102-746, Part I). House Ways and Means reported, amended, July 31 (H Rept 102-746, Part II). House considered, under suspension of the rules, Sept. 22. House passed, amended, under suspension of the rules, Sept. 24. Senate passed Oct. 8. President signed Oct. 26, 1992.

**PL 102-524 (S 2044)** Assist Native Americans in ensuring the survival and continuing vitality of their languages. Introduced by INOUYE, D-Hawaii, Nov. 25, 1991. Senate Indian Affairs reported, amended, July 27, 1992 (S Rept 102-343). Senate passed, amended, Aug. 5. House passed, amended, under suspension of the rules, Oct. 2. Senate agreed to House amendment Oct. 5. President signed Oct. 26, 1992.

**PL 102-525 (S 2890)** Provide for the establishment of the Civil Rights in Education: the Brown v. Board of Education National Historic Site in Kansas. Introduced by DOLE, R-Kan., June 24, 1992. Senate Energy and Natural Resources reported, amended, Sept. 24 (S Rept 102-468). Senate passed, amended, Oct. 1. House considered, under suspension of the rules, Oct. 4. House passed, amended, under suspension of the rules, Oct. 6. Senate agreed to House amendment Oct. 8. President signed Oct. 26, 1992.

**PL 102-526 (S 3006)** Provide for the expeditious disclosure of records relevant to the assassination of President John F. Kennedy. Introduced by GLENN, D-Ohio, July 22, 1992. Senate Governmental Affairs reported July 22 (S Rept 102-328). Senate passed, amended, July 27. House passed Sept. 30. President signed Oct. 26, 1992.

**PL 102-527 (HR 1252)** Authorize the State Justice Institute

to analyze and disseminate information regarding the admissibility and quality of testimony of witnesses with expertise relating to battered women, and to develop and disseminate training materials to increase the use of such experts to provide testimony in criminal trials of battered women, particularly in cases involving indigent women. Introduced by MORELLA, R-Md., March 5, 1991. House Judiciary reported, amended, Oct. 3, 1992 (H Rept 102-991). House passed, amended, under suspension of the rules, Oct. 3. Senate passed Oct. 7. President signed Oct. 27, 1992.

**PL 102-528 (HR 1253)** Amend the State Justice Institute Act of 1984 to carry out research and develop judicial training curricula relating to child custody litigation. Introduced by MORELLA, R-Md., March 5, 1991. House Judiciary reported, Oct. 3, 1992 (H Rept 102-992). House passed, under suspension of the rules, Oct. 3. Senate passed Oct. 7. President signed Oct. 27, 1992.

**PL 102-529 (HR 2660)** Authorize appropriations for the United States Holocaust Memorial Council and for other purposes. Introduced by YATES, D-Ill., June 17, 1991. House Interior and Insular Affairs reported, amended, June 15, 1992 (H Rept 102-563, Part I). House passed, amended, under suspension of the rules, June 16. Senate passed Oct. 7. President signed Oct. 27, 1992.

**PL 102-530 (HR 3475)** Assist businesses in providing women with opportunities in apprenticeship and non-traditional occupations. Introduced by MORELLA, R-Md., Oct. 2, 1991. House passed, under suspension of the rules, Sept. 29, 1992. Senate passed Oct. 7. President signed Oct. 27, 1992.

**PL 102-531 (HR 3635)** Amend the Public Health Service Act to revise and extend the program of block grants for preventive health and health services. Introduced by WAXMAN, D-Calif., Oct. 24, 1991. House Energy and Commerce reported, amended, Nov. 15 (H Rept 102-318). House passed, amended, under suspension of the rules, Nov. 19. Senate passed, amended, Nov. 27. Conference report filed in the House Oct. 5, 1992 (H Rept 102-1019). House agreed to conference report, under suspension of the rules, Oct. 6. Senate agreed to conference report Oct. 7. President signed Oct. 27, 1992.

**PL 102-532 (HR 4059)** Amend the Agricultural Trade Development and Assistance Act of 1954 to authorize additional functions within the Enterprise for the Americas Initiative. Introduced by de la GARZA, D-Texas, Nov. 26, 1991. House Agriculture reported, amended, July 16, 1992 (H Rept 102-667, Part I). House passed, amended, under suspension of the rules, Oct. 2. Senate passed Oct. 7. President signed Oct. 27, 1992.

**PL 102-533 (HR 4250)** Authorize appropriations for the National Railroad Passenger Corporation. Introduced by SWIFT, D-Wash., Feb. 19, 1992. House Energy and Commerce reported, amended, May 6 (H Rept 102-513). House passed, amended, under suspension of the rules, Aug. 11. Senate passed, amended, Aug. 12. Conference report filed in the House Oct. 3 (H Rept 102-990). House agreed to the conference report, under suspension of the rules, Oct. 4. Senate agreed to the conference report Oct. 7. President signed Oct. 27, 1992.

**PL 102-534 (HR 5716)** Extend for two years the authorizations of appropriations for certain programs under Title I of the Omnibus Crime Control and Safe Streets Act of 1968. Introduced by SCHUMER, D-N.Y., July 29, 1992. House Judiciary reported Sept. 22 (H Rept 102-884). House considered, under suspension of the rules, Sept. 22. House passed, amended, under suspension of the rules, Sept. 24. Senate passed Oct. 7. President signed Oct. 27, 1992.

**PL 102-535 (HR 5763)** Provide equitable treatment to producers of sugar cane subject to proportionate shares. Introduced by HUCKABY, D-La., Aug. 4, 1992. House Agriculture reported, amended, Aug. 10 (H Rept 102-831). House passed, amended, under suspension of the rules, Aug. 10. Senate passed Oct. 5. President signed Oct. 27, 1992.

**PL 102-536 (HR 5853)** Designate segments of the Great Egg Harbor River and its tributaries in New Jersey as components of the National Wild and Scenic Rivers System. Introduced by HUGHES, D-N.J., Aug. 12, 1992. House Interior and Insular Affairs reported, amended, Sept. 29 (H Rept 102-952). House passed, amended, under suspension of the rules, Sept. 29. Senate passed Oct. 7. President signed Oct. 27, 1992.

**PL 102-537 (HR 6022)** Amend the Fair Credit Reporting Act to require the inclusion in consumer reports of information provided to consumer reporting agencies regarding the failure of a consumer to pay overdue child support. Introduced by LaROCCO, D-Idaho, Sept. 24, 1992. House passed, amended, under suspension of the rules, Sept. 29. Senate passed Oct. 5. President signed Oct. 27, 1992.

**PL 102-538 (HR 6180)** Authorize appropriations for the National Telecommunications and Information Administration. Introduced by MARKEY, D-Mass., Oct. 5, 1992. House passed Oct. 6. Senate passed Oct. 8. President signed Oct. 27, 1992.

**PL 102-539 (HR 6182)** Amend the Public Health Service Act to establish the authority for the regulation of mammograpy services and radiological equipment. Introduced by DINGELL, D-Mich., Oct. 5, 1992. House passed, under suspension of the rules, Oct. 6. Senate passed Oct. 7. President signed Oct. 27, 1992.

**PL 102-540 (H J Res 503)** Acknowledge the sacrifices that military families have made in behalf of the nation and designate Nov. 23, 1992, as National Military Families Recognition Day. Introduced by ESPY, D-Miss., June 9, 1992. House passed Sept. 30. Senate Judiciary reported Oct. 5. Senate passed Oct. 8. President signed Oct. 27, 1992.

**PL 102-541 (S 225)** Expand the boundaries of the Fredericksburg and Spotsylvania County Battlefields Memorial National Military Park, Virginia. Introduced by WARNER, R-Va., Jan. 16, 1991. Senate Energy and Natural Resources reported, amended, July 23 (S Rept 102-335). Senate passed, amended, July 29. House passed Oct. 3. President signed Oct. 27, 1992.

**PL 102-542 (S 759)** Amend certain trademark laws to clarify that states, instrumentalities of states, and officers and employees of states acting in their official capacity are subject to suit in federal court by any person for infringement of trademarks and that all the remedies can be obtained in such suit that can be obtained in a suit against a private entity. Introduced by DeCONCINI, D-Ariz., March 21, 1991. Senate Judiciary reported May 12, 1992 (S Rept 102-280). Senate passed, amended, June 12. House passed Oct. 3. President signed Oct. 27, 1992.

**PL 102-543 (S 1664)** Establish the Keweenaw National Historic Park. Introduced by LEVIN, D-Mich., Aug. 2, 1991. Senate Energy and Natural Resources reported, amended, Sept. 24, 1992 (S Rept 102-480). Senate passed, amended, Oct. 1. House passed, under suspension of the rules, Oct. 6. President signed Oct. 27, 1992.

**PL 102-544 (S 2964)** Grant the consent of the Congress to a supplemental compact or agreement between Pennsylvania and New Jersey concerning the Delaware River Port Authority. Introduced by SPECTER, R-Pa., July 2, 1992. Senate Judiciary reported Aug. 12. Senate passed Aug. 12. House passed Oct. 6. President signed Oct. 27, 1992.

**PL 102-545 (S 3134)** Expand the production and distribution of educational and instructional video programming and supporting educational materials for preschool and elementary school children as a tool to improve school readiness, to develop and distribute educational and instructional video programming and support materials for parents, child-care providers, and educators of young children, and to expand services provided by Head Start programs. Introduced by KENNEDY, D-Mass., Aug. 5, 1992. Senate Labor and Human Resources reported, amended, Sept. 24. Senate passed, amended, Oct. 1. House passed, amended, under suspension of the rules, Oct. 6. Senate agreed to House amendment Oct. 7. President signed Oct. 27, 1992.

**PL 102-546 (HR 707)** Improve the regulation of futures trading and authorize appropriations for the Commodity Futures Trading Commission. Introduced by ENGLISH, D-Okla., Jan. 29, 1991. House Agriculture reported, amended, March 1 (H Rept 102-6). House passed, amended, under suspension of the rules, March 5. Senate passed, amended, April 18. Conference report filed in the House Oct. 2, 1992 (H Rept 102-978). House agreed to conference report Oct. 2. Senate agreed to conference report Oct. 8. President signed Oct. 28, 1992.

**PL 102-547 (HR 939)** Provide eligibility to members of the selected reserve for the Veterans Home Loan Program. Introduced by STAGGERS, D-W.Va., Feb. 6, 1991. House Veterans' Affairs

reported, amended, Nov. 6 (H Rept 102-292, Part I). House Ways and Means reported, amended, Feb. 14, 1992 (H Rept 102-292, Part II). House passed, amended, under suspension of the rules, March 3. Senate passed, amended, Oct. 1. House agreed to Senate amendments with amendment Oct. 6. Senate agreed to House amendment to Senate amendments Oct. 7. President signed Oct. 28, 1992.

**PL 102-548 (HR 3598)** Amend Title 49, U.S. Code, to provide for verification of weights. Introduced by BENTLEY, R-Md., Oct. 22, 1991. House passed, amended, under suspension of the rules, Oct. 4, 1992. Senate passed Oct. 7. President signed Oct. 28, 1992.

**PL 102-549 (HR 4996)** Extend the authorities of the Overseas Private Investment Corporation. Introduced by GEJDENSON, D-Conn., April 28, 1992. House Foreign Affairs reported, amended, June 5 (H Rept 102-551). House considered June 17. House passed, amended, Aug. 5. Senate passed, amended, Oct. 1. Conference report filed in the House Oct. 5 (H Rept 102-1026). House agreed to conference report Oct. 6. Senate agreed to conference report Oct. 8. President signed Oct. 28, 1992.

**PL 102-550 (HR 5334)** Amend and extend certain laws relating to housing and community development. Introduced by GONZALEZ, D-Texas, June 5, 1992. House Banking, Finance and Urban Affairs reported, amended, July 30 (H Rept 102-760). House passed, amended, Aug. 5. Senate passed, amended, Sept. 10. Conference report filed in the House Oct. 5 (H Rept 102-1017). House agreed to conference report Oct. 5. Senate agreed to conference report Oct. 8. President signed Oct. 28, 1992.

**PL 102-551 (HR 5954)** Amend the Rural Electrification Act of 1936 to clarify the status of the Rural Telephone Bank and its accounting policies. Introduced by ENGLISH, D-Okla., Sept. 16, 1992. House Agriculture reported, amended, Sept. 29 (H Rept 102-943). House passed, amended, under suspension of the rules, Sept. 29. Senate passed, amended, Oct. 5. House agreed to Senate amendments Oct. 6. President signed Oct. 28, 1992.

**PL 102-552 (HR 6125)** Enhance the financial safety and soundness of the banks and associations of the Farm Credit System. Introduced by de la GARZA, D-Texas, Oct. 3, 1992. House passed Oct. 4. Senate passed Oct. 7. President signed Oct. 28, 1992.

**PL 102-553 (HR 6128)** Amend the United States Warehouse Act to provide for the use of electronic cotton warehouse receipts and for other purposes. Introduced by de la GARZA, D-Texas, Oct. 3, 1992. House passed Oct. 4. Senate passed Oct. 7. President signed Oct. 28, 1992.

**PL 102-554 (HR 6129)** Amend the Consolidated Farm and Rural Development Act to establish a program to aid beginning farmers and ranchers and to improve the operation of the Farmers Home Administration and to amend the Farm Credit Act. Introduced by de la GARZA, D-Texas, Oct. 3, 1992. House passed Oct. 4. Senate passed Oct. 8. President signed Oct. 28, 1992.

**PL 102-555 (HR 6133)** Enable the United States to maintain its leadership in land remote sensing by providing data continuity for the Landsat program, and establish a new national land remote sensing policy. Introduced by BROWN, D-Calif., Oct. 5, 1992. House passed Oct. 6. Senate passed Oct. 7. President signed Oct. 28, 1992.

**PL 102-556 (HR 6191)** Protect the public interest and the future development of pay-per-call technology by providing for the regulation and oversight of the applications and growth of the pay-per-call industry. Introduced by SWIFT, D-Wash., Oct. 5, 1992. House passed Oct. 6. Senate passed Oct. 7. President signed Oct. 28, 1992.

**PL 102-557 (H J Res 546)** Designate Feb. 4, 1993, and Feb. 3, 1994, as National Women and Girls in Sports Day. Introduced by MOLINARI, R-N.Y., Aug. 12, 1992. House passed Sept 30. Senate Judiciary reported Oct. 5. Senate passed Oct. 8. President signed Oct. 28, 1992.

**PL 102-558 (S 347)** Amend the Defense Production Act of 1950 to revitalize the defense industrial base of the United States. Introduced by RIEGLE, D-Mich., Feb. 5, 1991. Senate passed, amended, Feb. 21. House passed, amended, Oct. 10. Conference report filed in the House Oct. 5 (H Rept 102-1028). House agreed to conference report Oct. 6, 1992. Senate agreed to conference

report Oct. 8. President signed Oct. 28, 1992.

**PL 102-559 (S 474)** Prohibit sports gambling under state law. Introduced by DeCONCINI, D-Ariz., Feb. 22, 1991. Senate Judiciary reported, amended, Nov. 26 (S Rept 102-248). Senate passed, amended, June 2, 1992. House passed, amended, under suspension of the rules, Oct. 6. Senate agreed to House amendments Oct. 7. President signed Oct. 28, 1992.

**PL 102-560 (S 758)** Clarify that states, instrumentalities of states, and officers and employees of states acting in their official capacity are subject to suit in federal court by any person for infringement of patents and plant variety protections, and that all the remedies can be obtained in such suit that can be obtained in a suit against a private entity. Introduced by DeCONCINI, D-Ariz., March 21, 1991. Senate Judiciary reported May 12, 1992 (S Rept 102-280). Senate passed June 12. House passed Oct. 3. President signed Oct. 28, 1992.

**PL 102-561 (S 893)** Amend Title 18, U.S. Code, to impose criminal sanctions for violation of software copyright. Introduced by HATCH, R-Utah, April 23, 1991. Senate Judiciary reported April 7, 1992 (S Rept 102-268). Senate passed, amended, June 4. House Judiciary reported, amended, Oct. 3 (H Rept 102-997). House passed, amended, under suspension of the rules, Oct. 3. Senate agreed to House amendments Oct. 8. President signed Oct. 28, 1992.

**PL 102-562 (S 1439)** Authorize and direct the secretary of the Interior to convey certain lands in Livingston Parish, La. Introduced by JOHNSTON, D-La., July 9, 1991. Senate Energy and Natural Resources reported, amended, May 21, 1992 (S Rept 102-284). Senate passed, amended, June 12. House Interior and Insular Affairs reported, amended, Sept. 29 (H Rept 102-948). House passed, amended, under suspension of the rules, Sept. 29. Senate agreed to House amendments Oct. 8. President signed Oct. 28, 1992.

**PL 102-563 (S 1623)** Amend Title 17, U.S. Code, to implement a royalty payment system and serial copy management system for digital audio recording and prohibit certain copyright infringement actions. Introduced by DeCONCINI, D-Ariz., Aug. 1, 1991. Senate Judiciary reported, amended, Nov. 27 (S Rept 102-294). Senate passed, amended, June 17, 1992. House passed, amended, Sept. 22. Senate agreed to House amendment Oct. 7. President signed Oct. 28, 1992.

**PL 102-564 (S 2941)** Provide the administrator of the Small Business Administration continued authority to administer the small business innovation research program. Introduced by RUDMAN, R-N.H., July 2, 1992. Senate passed, amended, Oct. 3. House passed, under suspension of the rules, Oct. 6. President signed Oct. 28, 1992.

**PL 102-565 (S 3309)** Amend the Peace Corps Act to authorize appropriations for the Peace Corps for fiscal 1993 and to establish a Peace Corps foreign exchange fluctuations account. Introduced by CRANSTON, D-Calif., Oct. 2, 1992. Senate passed Oct. 2. House passed Oct. 6. President signed Oct. 28, 1992.

**PL 102-566 (S 3327)** Amend the Agricultural Adjustment Act of 1938 to permit the acre-for-acre transfer of an acreage allotment or quota for certain commodities. Introduced by FORD, D-Ky., Oct. 5, 1992. Senate passed Oct. 5. House passed Oct. 6. President signed Oct. 28, 1992.

**PL 102-567 (HR 2130)** Authorize appropriations for the National Oceanic and Atmospheric Administration for fiscal 1992. Introduced by HERTEL, D-Mich., April 30, 1991. House Merchant Marine and Fisheries reported, amended, June 26 (H Rept 102-133, Part I). House Ways and Means reported, amended, July 11 (H Rept 102-133, Part II). House passed, amended, Nov. 20. Senate passed, amended, Aug. 12, 1992. House agreed to Senate amendments with an amendment pursuant to H Res 610 on Oct. 6. Senate agreed to House amendment to Senate amendments Oct. 7. President signed Oct. 29, 1992.

**PL 102-568 (HR 5008)** Amend Title 38, U.S. Code, to reform the formula for payment of dependency and indemnity compensation to survivors of veterans who died from service-connected causes. Introduced by APPLEGATE, D-Ohio, April 29, 1992. House Veterans' Affairs reported, amended, July 29 (H Rept 102-753, Part I). House Ways and Means reported Aug. 6 (H Rept

102-753, Part II). House passed, amended, under suspension of the rules, Aug. 10. Senate passed, amended, Sept. 22. House agreed to Senate amendments with amendments Oct. 3. Senate agreed to House amendments to Senate amendments Oct. 7. President signed Oct. 29, 1992.

**PL 102-569 (HR 5482)** Revise and extend the programs of the Rehabilitation Act of 1973. Introduced by OWENS, D-N.Y., June 24, 1992. House Education and Labor reported, amended, Aug. 10 (H Rept 102-822). House passed, amended, under suspension of the rules, Aug. 10. Senate passed, amended, Aug. 12. Conference report filed in the House Oct. 1 (H Rept 102-973). House agreed to conference report, under suspension of the rules, Oct. 2. Senate agreed to conference report Oct. 5. President signed Oct. 29, 1992.

**PL 102-570 (HR 5809)** Authorize the secretary of the Interior to construct and operate an interpretive center for the Ridgefield National Wildlife Refuge in Clark County, Wash. Introduced by UNSOELD, D-Wash., April 10, 1992. House Merchant Marine and Fisheries reported, amended, Sept. 29 (H Rept 102-928). House passed, amended, under suspension of the rules, Sept. 29. Senate passed Oct. 7. President signed Oct. 29, 1992.

**PL 102-571 (HR 6181)** Amend the Federal Food, Drug and Cosmetic Act to authorize human drug application, prescription drug establishment and prescription drug product fees. Introduced by DINGELL, D-Mich., Oct. 5, 1992. House passed Oct. 6. Senate passed Oct. 7. President signed Oct. 29, 1992.

**PL 102-572 (S 1569)** Implement the recommendations of the Federal Courts Study Committee. Introduced by HEFLIN, D-Ala., July 26, 1991. Senate Judiciary reported, amended, July 27, 1992 (S Rept 102-342). Senate passed, amended, Aug. 3. House passed, amended, Oct. 3. Senate agreed to House amendments Oct. 7. President signed Oct. 29, 1992.

**PL 102-573 (S 2481)** Amend the Indian Health Care Improvement Act to authorize appropriations for Indian health programs. Introduced by INOUYE, D-Hawaii, March 25, 1992. Senate Indian Affairs reported, amended, Aug. 27 (S Rept 102-392). Senate passed, amended, Sept. 18. House considered, under suspension of the rules Oct. 2. House passed, amended, under suspension of the rules, Oct. 3. Senate agreed to House amendments Oct. 7. President signed Oct. 29, 1992.

**PL 102-574 (S 2679)** Promote the recovery of Hawaii tropical forests. Introduced by AKAKA, D-Hawaii, May 7, 1992. Senate passed, amended, Sept. 30. House passed Oct. 2. President signed Oct. 29, 1992.

**PL 102-575 (HR 429)** Authorize additional appropriations for the construction of the Buffalo Bill Dam and Reservoir, Shoshone Project, Pick-Sloan Missouri Basin program, Wyoming, and for other purposes. Introduced by THOMAS, R-Wyo., Jan. 3, 1991. House Interior and Insular Affairs reported, amended, June 18 (H Rept 102-114, Part I). House passed, amended, June 20. Senate Energy and Natural Resources reported, amended, March 31, 1992 (S Rept 102-267). Senate passed, amended, April 10. House agreed to Senate amendment with amendment June 18. Senate agreed to House amendment to Senate amendment with amendment July 31. Conference report filed in the House Oct. 5 (H Rept 102-1016). House agreed to conference report Oct. 6. Senate agreed to conference report Oct. 8. President signed Oct. 30, 1992.

**PL 102-576 (HR 2032)** Amend the act of May 15, 1965, authorizing the secretary of the Interior to designate the Nez Perce National Historical Park in Idaho. Introduced by WILLIAMS, D-Mont., April 23, 1991. House Interior and Insular Affairs reported, amended, Oct. 21 (H Rept 102-258). House considered, under suspension of the rules, Oct. 21. House passed, amended, under suspension of the rules, Oct. 22. Senate passed, amended, Nov. 27. House agreed to Senate amendments with amendment pursuant to H Res 504 on June 29, 1992. Senate agreed to House amendment to Senate amendment Oct. 8. President signed Oct. 30, 1992.

**PL 102-577 (H J Res 422)** Designate November 1992 as Neurofibromatosis Awareness Month. Introduced by SCHEUER, D-N.Y., Feb. 25, 1992. House passed, amended, Sept. 10. Senate passed Oct. 8. President signed Oct. 30, 1992.

**PL 102-578 (S 775)** Increase the rates of compensation for

veterans with service-connected disabilities and the rates of dependency and indemnity compensation for the survivors of certain disabled veterans. Introduced by CRANSTON, D-Calif., March 22, 1991. Senate Veterans' Affairs reported, amended, Aug. 2 (S Rept 102-139). Senate passed, amended, Nov. 20. House passed, amended, Sept. 30, 1992. Senate agreed to House amendments Oct. 7. President signed Oct. 30, 1992.

**PL 102-579 (S 1671)** Withdraw certain public lands and otherwise provide for the operation of the Waste Isolation Pilot Plant in Eddy County, N.M. Introduced by DOMENICI, R-N.M., Aug. 2, 1991. Senate Energy and Natural Resources reported, amended, Oct. 28 (S Rept 102-196). Senate passed, amended, Nov. 5. House passed, amended, July 21, 1992. Conference report filed in the House Oct. 6 (H Rept 102-1037). House agreed to conference report, under suspension of the rules, Oct. 6. Senate agreed to conference report Oct. 8. President signed Oct. 30, 1992.

**PL 102-580 (HR 6167)** Provide for the conservation and development of water and related resources and authorize the U.S. Army Corps of Engineers civil works program to construct various projects for improvements to the nation's infrastructure. Introduced by ROE, D-N.J., Oct. 5, 1992. House passed, under suspension of the rules, Oct. 6. Senate passed Oct. 8. President signed Oct. 31, 1992.

**PL 102-581 (HR 6168)** Amend the Airport and Airway Improvement Act of 1982 to authorize appropriations for the portion of fiscal 1993 ending before May 1, 1993, and amend Title XIII of the Federal Aviation Act of 1958 relating to aviation insurance. Introduced by OBERSTAR, D-Minn., Oct. 5, 1992. House passed Oct. 6. Senate passed Oct. 8. President signed Oct. 31, 1992.

**PL 102-582 (HR 2152)** Enhance the effectiveness of the United Nations international drift net fishery conservation program. Introduced by STUDDS, D-Mass., April 30, 1991. House Merchant Marine and Fisheries reported, amended, Oct. 22 (H Rept 102-262, Part I). House Ways and Means reported, amended, Feb. 19, 1992 (H Rept 102-262, Part II). House passed, amended, under suspension of the rules, Feb. 25. Senate passed, amended, July 31. House agreed to Senate amendment with amendments pursuant to H Res 548 on Aug. 10. Senate agreed to House amendments to Senate amendment with amendment Aug. 12. House agreed to Senate amendment to House amendments to Senate amendment, under suspension of the rules, Oct. 4. President signed Nov. 2, 1992.

**PL 102-583 (HR 6187)** Amend the Foreign Assistance Act of 1961 with respect to international narcotic control programs and activities. Introduced by FASCELL, D-Fla., Oct. 5, 1992. House passed Oct. 6. Senate passed Oct. 7. President signed Nov. 2, 1992.

**PL 102-584 (S 2572)** Authorize an exchange of lands in Arkansas and Idaho. Introduced by BUMPERS, D-Ark., April 9, 1992. Senate Energy and Natural Resources reported, amended, Aug. 12 (S Rept 102-371). Senate passed, amended, Sept. 10. House Merchant Marine and Fisheries reported, amended, Sept. 29 (H Rept 102-931, Part I). House Agriculture reported Sept. 29 (H Rept 102-931, Part II). House Interior and Insular Affairs reported, amended, Sept. 29 (H Rept 102-931, Part III). House passed, amended, under suspension of the rules, Sept. 29. Senate agreed to House amendment Oct. 7. President signed Nov. 2, 1992.

**PL 102-585 (HR 5193)** Improve the delivery of health-care services to eligible veterans and clarify the authority of the secretary of Veterans Affairs. Introduced by MONTGOMERY, D-Miss., May 18, 1992. House Veterans' Affairs reported July 24 (H Rept 102-714, Part I). House passed, under suspension of the rules, Aug. 4. Senate passed, amended, Oct. 1. House agreed to Senate amendments with amendment Oct. 6. Senate agreed to House amendment to Senate amendments Oct. 8. President signed Nov. 4, 1992.

**PL 102-586 (HR 5194)** Amend the Juvenile Justice and Delinquency Prevention Act of 1974 to authorize appropriations for fiscal 1993-96. Introduced by MARTINEZ, D-Calif., May 18, 1992. House Education and Labor reported, amended, July 29 (H Rept 102-756). House passed, amended, under suspension of the rules, Aug. 3. Senate passed, amended, Sept. 25. House agreed to Senate amendment with amendment pursuant to H Res 594 Oct.

2. Senate agreed to House amendment to Senate amendment Oct. 7. President signed Nov. 4, 1992.

**PL 102-587 (HR 5617)** Provide congressional approval of a governing international fishery agreement. Introduced by STUDDS, D-Mass., July 9, 1992. House Merchant Marine and Fisheries reported Sept. 29 (H Rept 102-927). House passed, amended, under suspension of the rules, Oct. 6. Senate passed Oct. 7. President signed Nov. 4, 1992.

**PL 102-588 (HR 6135)** Authorize appropriations to the National Aeronautics and Space Administration for research and development, space flight, control and data communications, construction of facilities, research and program management, and inspector general. Introduced by BROWN, D-Calif., Oct. 5, 1992. House passed Oct. 6. Senate passed Oct. 7. President signed Nov. 4, 1992.

**PL 102-589 (HR 5377)** Amend the Cash Management Improvement Act of 1990 to provide adequate time for implementation of that act. Introduced by CONYERS, D-Mich., June 11, 1992. House passed, under suspension of the rules, July 21. Senate passed, amended, Oct. 2. House agreed to Senate amendment Oct. 3. President signed Nov. 10, 1992.

**PL 102-590 (HR 5400)** Establish in the Department of Veterans Affairs a program of comprehensive services for homeless veterans. Introduced by STAGGERS, D-W.Va., June 16, 1992. House Veterans' Affairs reported, amended, July 24 (H Rept 102-721). House passed, amended, under suspension of the rules, July 27. Senate passed, amended, Sept. 8. House agreed to Senate amendments with amendment Oct. 3. Senate agreed to House amendment to Senate amendment to Senate amendments Oct. 7. President signed Nov. 10, 1992. ■

# CONGRESS
# AND
# ITS MEMBERS

# The Legislative Process in Brief

*(Parliamentary terms used below are defined in the glossary, p. 6-D)*

## Introduction of Bills

A House member (including the resident commissioner of Puerto Rico and non-voting delegates of the District of Columbia, Guam, the Virgin Islands and American Samoa) may introduce any one of several types of bills and resolutions by handing it to the clerk of the House or placing it in a box called the hopper.

A senator first gains recognition of the presiding officer to announce the introduction of a bill. If objection is offered by any senator, the introduction of the bill is postponed until the following day.

As the next step in either the House or Senate, the bill is numbered, referred to committee, labeled with the sponsor's name and sent to the Government Printing Office so that copies can be made for subsequent study and action. Senate bills may be jointly sponsored and carry several senators' names.

Until 1978, the House limited the number of members who could cosponsor any one bill; the ceiling was eliminated at the beginning of the 96th Congress.

A bill written in the executive branch and proposed as an administration measure usually is introduced by the chairman of the congressional committee that has jurisdiction over the subject.

**Bills**—Prefixed with HR in the House, S in the Senate, followed by a number. Used as the form for most legislation, whether general or special, public or private.

**Joint Resolutions**—Designated H J Res or S J Res. Subject to the same procedure as bills, with the exception of a joint resolution proposing an amendment to the Constitution. The latter must be approved by two-thirds of both houses and is thereupon sent directly to the administrator of general services for submission to the states for ratification instead of being presented to the president for his approval.

**Concurrent Resolutions**—Designated H Con Res or S Con Res. Used for matters affecting the operations of both houses. These resolutions do not become law.

**Resolutions**—Designated H Res or S Res. Used for a matter concerning the operation of either house alone and adopted only by the chamber in which it originates.

## Committee Action

With few exceptions, bills are referred to the appropriate standing committees. The job of referral formally is the responsibility of the Speaker of the House and the presiding officer of the Senate, but this task usually is carried out on their behalf by the parliamentarians of the House and Senate.

Precedent, statute and the jurisdictional mandates of the committees as set forth in the rules of the House and Senate determine which committees receive what kinds of bills. An exception is the referral of private bills, which are sent to whatever committee is designated by their sponsors.

Bills are technically considered "read for the first time" when referred to House committees.

When a bill reaches a committee, it is placed on the committee's calendar. At that time the bill comes under the sharpest congressional focus. Its chances for passage are quickly determined; the great majority of bills falls by the legislative roadside.

Failure of a committee to act on a bill is equivalent to killing it; the measure can be withdrawn from the committee's purview only by a discharge petition signed by a majority of the House membership on House bills or by adoption of a special resolution in the Senate. Discharge attempts rarely succeed.

The first committee action taken on a bill usually is a request for comment on it by interested government agencies. The committee chairman may assign the bill to a subcommittee for study and hearings, or it may be considered by the full committee. Hearings may be public, closed (executive session) or both. After considering a bill, a subcommittee reports to the full committee its recommendations for action and any proposed amendments.

The full committee then votes on its recommendation to the House or Senate. This procedure is called "ordering a bill reported."

Occasionally a committee may order a bill reported unfavorably; most of the time a report, submitted by the committee chairman to the House or Senate, calls for favorable action on the measure since the committee can effectively "kill" a bill by simply not taking any action.

After the bill is reported, the committee chairman instructs the staff to prepare a written report. The report describes the bill's purposes and scope, explains the committee revisions, notes proposed changes in existing law and, usually, includes the views of the executive branch agencies consulted. Often committee members opposing a bill include dissenting views in the report.

Usually, the committee "marks up" or proposes amendments to the bill. If they are substantial and the measure is complicated, the committee may order a "clean bill" introduced, which will embody the proposed amendments. The original bill then is put aside and the clean bill, with a new number, is reported to the floor.

The chamber must approve, alter or reject the committee amendments before the bill itself can be put to a vote.

## Floor Action

After a bill is reported back to the house where it originated, it is placed on the calendar.

There are five legislative calendars in the House, issued in one cumulative calendar titled *Calendars of the United States House of Representatives and History of Legislation*. The House calendars are:

*The Union Calendar* to which are referred bills raising revenues, general appropriations bills and any measures directly or indirectly appropriating money or property. It is the Calendar of the Committee of the Whole House on the State of the Union.

*The House Calendar* to which are referred bills of pub-

lic character not raising revenue or appropriating money or property.

*The Consent Calendar* to which are referred bills of a non-controversial nature that are passed without debate when the Consent Calendar is called on the first and third Mondays of each month.

*The Private Calendar* to which are referred bills for relief in the nature of claims against the United States or private immigration bills that are passed without debate when the Private Calendar is called the first and third Tuesdays of each month.

*The Discharge Calendar* to which are referred motions to discharge committees when the necessary signatures are signed to a discharge petition.

There is only one legislative calendar in the Senate and one "executive calendar" for treaties and nominations submitted to the Senate. When the Senate Calendar is called, each senator is limited to five minutes' debate on each bill.

**Debate.** A bill is brought to debate by varying procedures. If it is a routine measure, it may await the call of the calendar. If it is urgent or important, it can be taken up in the Senate either by unanimous consent or by a majority vote. The majority leader, in consultation with the minority leader and others, schedules the bills that will be taken up for debate.

In the House, precedence is granted if a special rule is obtained from the Rules Committee. A request for a special rule usually is made by the chairman of the committee that favorably reported the bill, supported by the bill's sponsor and other committee members. The request, considered by the Rules Committee in the same way that other committees consider legislative measures, is in the form of a resolution providing for immediate consideration of the bill.

The Rules Committee reports the resolution to the House, where it is debated and voted upon in the same fashion as regular bills. If the Rules Committee should fail to report a rule requested by a committee, there are several ways to bring the bill to the House floor — under suspension of the rules, on Calendar Wednesday or by a discharge motion.

The resolutions providing special rules are important because they specify how long the bill may be debated and whether it may be amended from the floor. If floor amendments are banned, the bill is considered under a "closed rule," which permits only members of the committee that first reported the measure to the House to alter its language, subject to chamber acceptance.

When a bill is debated under an "open rule," amendments may be offered from the floor. Committee amendments always are taken up first but may be changed, like all amendments up to the second degree; that is, an amendment to an amendment to an amendment is not in order.

Duration of debate in the House depends on whether the bill is under discussion by the House proper or before the House when it is sitting as the Committee of the Whole House on the State of the Union.

In the House, the amount of time for debate either is determined by special rule or is allocated with an hour for each member if the measure is under consideration without a rule.

In the Committee of the Whole, the amount of time agreed on for general debate is equally divided between proponents and opponents. At the end of general discussion, the bill is read section by section for amendment. Debate on an amendment is limited to five minutes for each side; this is called the "five-minute rule." In practice,

amendments regularly are debated more than 10 minutes, with members gaining the floor by offering pro forma amendments or obtaining unanimous consent to speak longer than five minutes.

Senate debate usually is unlimited. It can be halted only by unanimous consent or by "cloture," which requires a three-fifths majority of the entire Senate or, in the case of a proposed change in the Senate rules, a two-thirds vote.

The House considers almost all important bills within a parliamentary framework known as the Committee of the Whole. It is not a committee as the word usually is understood; it is the full House meeting under another name for the purpose of speeding action on legislation.

Technically, the House sits as the Committee of the Whole when it considers any tax measure or bill dealing with public appropriations. It also can resolve itself into the Committee of the Whole if a member moves to do so and the motion is carried. The Speaker appoints a member to serve as the chairman.

The rules of the House permit the Committee of the Whole to meet when a quorum of 100 members is present on the floor and to amend and act on bills, within certain time limitations. When the Committee of the Whole has acted, it "rises," the Speaker returns as the presiding officer of the House and the member appointed chairman of the Committee of the Whole reports the action of the committee and its recommendations.

The Committee of the Whole cannot pass a bill; it reports the measure to the full House with whatever changes it has approved. The full House then may pass or reject the bill — or, on occasion, recommit the bill to committee. Amendments adopted in the Committee of the Whole may be put to a second vote in the full House.

**Votes.** Voting on bills may occur repeatedly before they are finally approved or rejected. The House votes on the rule for the bill and on various amendments to the bill. Voting on amendments often is a more illuminating test of a bill's support than is the final tally. Sometimes members approve final passage of bills after vigorously supporting amendments that, if adopted, would scuttle the legislation.

The Senate has three different methods of voting: an untabulated voice vote, a standing vote (called a division) and a recorded roll call to which members answer "yea" or "nay" when their names are called.

The House also employs voice and standing votes, but since January 1973 yeas and nays have been recorded by an electronic voting device, eliminating the need for time-consuming roll calls.

Another method of voting, used in the House only, is the teller vote. Traditionally, members filed up the center aisle past counters; only vote totals were announced. Since 1971, one-fifth of a quorum can demand that the votes of individual members be recorded, thereby forcing them to take a public position on amendments to key bills.

After amendments to a bill have been voted upon, a vote may be taken on a motion to recommit the bill to committee. If carried, this vote removes the bill from the chamber's calendar and is usually a death blow to the bill. If the motion is unsuccessful, the bill then is "read for the third time." An actual reading usually is dispensed with. Until 1965, an opponent of a bill could delay this move by objecting and asking for a full reading of an engrossed (certified in final form) copy of the bill. After the "third reading," the vote on final passage is taken.

The final vote may be followed by a motion to reconsider, and this motion may be followed by a move to lay the

motion on the table. Usually, those voting for the bill's passage vote for the tabling motion, thus safeguarding the final passage action. With that, the bill has been formally passed by the chamber. While a motion to reconsider a Senate vote is pending on a bill, the measure cannot be sent to the House.

# Action in Second House

After a bill is passed, it is sent to the other chamber. This body may then take one of several steps. It may pass the bill as is — accepting the other chamber's language. It may send the bill to committee for scrutiny or alteration, or reject the entire bill, advising the other house of its actions. Or it simply may ignore the bill submitted while it continues work on its own version of the proposed legislation. Frequently, one chamber may approve a version of a bill that is greatly at variance with the version passed by the other house, and then substitute its contents for the language of the other, retaining only the latter's bill number.

A provision of the Legislative Reorganization Act of 1970 permits a separate House vote on any non-germane amendment added by the Senate to a House-passed bill and requires a majority vote to retain the amendment. Previously, the House was forced to act on the bill as a whole; the only way to defeat the non-germane amendment was to reject the entire bill.

Often, the second chamber makes only minor changes. If these are readily agreed to by the other house, the bill then is sent to the president.

If the opposite chamber significantly alters the bill submitted to it, however, the measure usually is "sent to conference." The chamber that has possession of the "papers" (engrossed bill, engrossed amendments, messages of transmittal) requests a conference and the other chamber must agree to it. If the second house does not agree, the bill dies.

# Conference, Final Action

**Conference.** A conference reconciles the differences between House and Senate versions of a legislative bill. The conferees usually are senior members appointed by the presiding officers of the two houses, from the committees that managed the bills. Under this arrangement the conferees of one house have the duty of trying to maintain their chamber's position in the face of amending actions by the conferees (also referred to as "managers") of the other house.

The number of conferees from each chamber varies, depending upon the length or complexity of the bill involved. A majority vote controls the action of each group; a large representation does not give one chamber a voting advantage over the other.

Theoretically, conferees are not allowed to write new legislation in reconciling the two versions before them, but this curb sometimes is bypassed. Many bills have been put into acceptable compromise form only after new language was provided by the conferees.

The 1970 Reorganization Act attempted to tighten restrictions on conferees by forbidding them to introduce any language on a topic that neither chamber sent to conference or to modify any topic beyond the scope of the differing versions of the bill.

Frequently, the ironing out of difficulties takes days or even weeks. As a conference proceeds, conferees reconcile differences between the versions. Generally, they grant concessions only insofar as they are sure that the chamber they represent will accept the compromises.

Occasionally, uncertainty over how either house will react, or the refusal of a chamber to back down on a disputed amendment, results in an impasse, and the bills die in conference even though each was approved by its sponsoring chamber.

Conferees may go back to their respective chambers for further instructions, when they report certain portions in disagreement. Then the chamber concerned can either "recede and concur" in the amendment of the other house or "insist on its amendment."

When the conferees have reached agreement, they prepare a conference report embodying their recommendations. The report, in document form, must be submitted to each house.

The conference report must be adopted by each house; adoption of the report is approval of the compromise bill. The chamber which asked for a conference yields to the other chamber the opportunity to vote first.

**Final Steps.** After a bill has been passed by both the House and Senate in identical form, all of the original papers are sent to the enrolling clerk of the chamber in which the bill originated. He then prepares an enrolled bill, which is printed on parchment paper.

When this bill has been certified as correct by the secretary of the Senate or the clerk of the House, depending on which chamber originated the bill, it is signed first (no matter whether it originated in the Senate or House) by the Speaker of the House and then by the president of the Senate. It is next sent to the White House to await action.

If the president approves the bill, he signs it, dates it and usually writes the word "approved" on the document. If he does not sign it within 10 days (Sundays excepted) and Congress is in session, the bill becomes law without his signature. Should Congress adjourn before the 10 days expire, and the president fails to sign the measure, it does not become law. This procedure is called the pocket veto.

A president vetoes a bill by refusing to sign it and, before the 10-day period expires, returning it to Congress with a message stating his reasons. The message is sent to the chamber that originated the bill. If no action is taken on the message, the bill dies.

Congress, however, can attempt to override the veto and enact the bill, "the objections of the president to the contrary notwithstanding." Overriding a veto requires a two-thirds vote of those present, who must number a quorum and vote by roll call.

Debate can precede this vote, with motions permitted to lay the message on the table, postpone action on it or refer it to committee. If the president's veto is overridden in both houses, the bill becomes law. Otherwise, it is dead.

When bills are passed finally and signed, or passed over a veto, they are given law numbers in numerical order as they become law. There are two series of numbers, one for public and one for private laws, starting at the number "1" for each two-year term of Congress. They are then identified by law number and by Congress — for esample, Private Law 21, 97th Congress; Public Law 250, 97th Congress (or PL 97-250). ∎

# Glossary of Congressional Terms

**Act**—The term for legislation once it has passed both houses of Congress and has been signed by the president or passed over his veto, thus becoming law. *(See also Veto, Pocket Veto.)*

Also used in parliamentary terminology for a bill that has been passed by one house and engrossed. *(See Engrossed Bill.)*

**Adjournment Sine Die**—Adjournment without definitely fixing a day for reconvening; literally, "adjournment without a day." Usually used to connote the final adjournment of a session of Congress. A session can continue until noon, Jan. 3, of the following year, when, under the 20th Amendment to the Constitution, it automatically terminates. Both houses must agree to a concurrent resolution for either house to adjourn for more than three days.

**Adjournment to a Day Certain**—Adjournment under a motion or resolution that fixes the next time of meeting. Under the Constitution, neither house can adjourn for more than three days without the concurrence of the other. A session of Congress is not ended by adjournment to a day certain.

**Amendment**—A proposal of a member of Congress to alter the language, provisions or stipulations in a bill or in another amendment. An amendment usually is printed, debated and voted upon in the same manner as a bill.

**Amendment in the Nature of a Substitute**—Usually an amendment that seeks to replace the entire text of a bill. Passage of this type of amendment strikes out everything after the enacting clause and inserts a new version of the bill. An amendment in the nature of a substitute also can refer to an amendment that replaces a large portion of the text of a bill.

**Appeal**—A member's challenge of a ruling or decision made by the presiding officer of the chamber. In the Senate, the senator appeals to members of the chamber to override the decision. If carried by a majority vote, the appeal nullifies the chair's ruling. In the House, the decision of the Speaker traditionally has been final; seldom are there appeals to the members to reverse the Speaker's stand. To appeal a ruling is considered an attack on the Speaker.

**Appropriations Bill**—A bill that gives legal authority to spend or obligate money from the Treasury. The Constitution disallows money to be drawn from the Treasury "but in Consequence of Appropriations made by Law."

By congressional custom, an appropriations bill originates in the House, and it is not supposed to be considered by the full House or Senate until a related measure authorizing the funding is enacted. An appropriations bill grants the actual money approved by authorization bills, but not necessarily the full amount permissible under the authorization. The 1985 Gramm-Rudman anti-deficit law stipulated that the House is to pass by June 30 the last regular appropriations bill for the fiscal year starting the following Oct. 1. (There is no such deadline for the Senate.) However, for decades appropriations often have not been final until well after the fiscal year begins, requiring a succession of stopgap bills to continue the government's functions. In addition, much federal spending — about half of all budget authority, notably that for Social Security and interest on the federal debt — does not require annual appropriations; those programs exist under permanent appropriations. *(See also Authorization, Budget Process, Backdoor Spending Authority, Entitlement Program.)*

In addition to general appropriations bills, there are two specialized types. *(See Continuing Resolution, Supplemental Appropriations Bill.)*

**Authorization**—Basic, substantive legislation that establishes or continues the legal operation of a federal program or agency, either indefinitely or for a specific period of time, or which sanctions a particular type of obligation or expenditure. An authorization normally is a prerequisite for an appropriation or other kind of budget authority. Under the rules of both chambers, the appropriation for a program or agency may not be considered until its authorization has been considered (although this requirement is often waived). An authorization sets the maximum amount of funds that can be given to a program or agency, but sometimes it merely authorizes "such sums as may be necessary." *(See also Backdoor Spending Authority.)*

**Backdoor Spending Authority**—Budget authority provided in legislation outside the normal appropriations process. The most common forms of backdoor spending are borrowing authority, contract authority, entitlements and loan guarantees that commit the government to payments of principal and interest on loans — such as Guaranteed Student Loans — made by banks or other private lenders. Loan guarantees result in actual outlays only when there is a default by the borrower.

In some cases, such as interest on the public debt, a permanent appropriation is provided that becomes available without further action by Congress.

**Bills**—Most legislative proposals before Congress are in the form of bills and are designated by HR in the House of Representatives or S in the Senate, according to the house in which they originate, and by a number assigned in the order in which they are introduced during the two-year period of a congressional term. "Public bills" deal with general questions and become public laws if approved by Congress and signed by the president. "Private bills" deal with individual matters such as claims against the government, immigration and naturalization cases or land titles, and become private laws if approved and signed. *(See also Concurrent Resolution, Joint Resolution, Resolution.)*

**Bills Introduced**—In both the House and Senate, any number of members may join in introducing a single bill or resolution. The first member listed is the sponsor of the bill, and all subsequent members listed are the bill's cosponsors.

Many bills are committee bills and are introduced under the name of the chairman of the committee or subcommittee. All appropriations bills fall into this category. A committee frequently holds hearings on a number of related bills and may agree to one of them or to an entirely new bill. *(See also Report, Clean Bill, By Request.)*

**Bills Referred**—When introduced, a bill is referred to the committee or committees that have jurisdiction over the subject with which the bill is concerned. Under the standing rules of the House and Senate, bills are referred by the Speaker in the House and by the presiding officer in the Senate. In practice, the House and Senate parliamentarians act for these officials and refer the vast majority of bills.

**Borrowing Authority**—Statutory authority that permits a federal agency to incur obligations and make payments for specified purposes with borrowed money.

**Budget**—The document sent to Congress by the president early each year estimating government revenue and expenditures for the ensuing fiscal year.

**Budget Act**—The common name for the Congressional Budget and Impoundment Control Act of 1974, which established the current budget process and created the Congressional Budget Office. The act also put limits on presidential authority to spend appropriated money. *(See Impoundments, Budget Process.)*

**Budget Authority**—Authority to enter into obligations that will result in immediate or future outlays involving federal funds. The basic forms of budget authority are appropriations, contract authority and borrowing authority. Budget authority may be classified by (1) the period of availability (one-year, multiple-year or without a time limitation), (2) the timing of congressional action (current or permanent) or (3) the manner of determining the amount available (definite or indefinite).

**Budget process** — Congress in 1990 overhauled its budget procedures for the third time since it created the congressional

budget process in 1974. The 1990 Budget Enforcement Act departed from its predecessor budget laws by holding Congress harmless until fiscal 1994 for budget-deficit increases that it did not explicitly cause.

If the deficit increased because of recession, war or specifically exempted programs, that would no longer trigger the automatic spending cuts ("sequester") threatened by the Gramm-Rudman antideficit law, enacted in 1985 and amended in 1987.

The new budget rules did require, however, that spending programs be hit with a sequester if Congress exceeded pre-agreed caps on discretionary spending (appropriations bills) or violated new "pay-as-you-go" rules for mandatory spending (entitlement programs such as Medicare or food stamps) or tax cuts. *(See also Sequester Order.)*

Discretionary spending was divided into three categories — domestic, defense and international — for fiscal years 1991-93. Each category had a spending cap, and money could not be taken from one category to increase another. For fiscal years 1994-95, the three categories were to be collapsed into a single pot of money with a single cap.

For taxes and entitlements, the pay-as-you-go plan required that new entitlement spending or tax cuts be deficit-neutral. If Congress cut taxes, created a new entitlement program or expanded eligibility or benefits for an existing program, it had to offset the cost or subject entitlement spending programs to a sequester.

The 1990 law made minor changes in the timetable for presidential submission of budgets and for congressional approval of budget resolutions and reconciliation bills, two mechanisms created by the Congressional Budget and Impoundment Control Act of 1974. The president was given until the first Monday in February to submit his proposed budget. Congressional budget resolutions, due by April 15 annually, set guidelines for congressional action on spending and tax measures; they were to be adopted by the House and Senate but not signed by the president and did not have the force of law. Reconciliation bills, due by June 15, made the actual changes in existing law to meet budget resolution goals.

**Budget Resolution**—A concurrent resolution passed by both houses of Congress, but not requiring the president's signature, setting forth or revising the congressional budget for each of three fiscal years. The budget resolution sets forth various budget totals and functional allocations and may include reconciliation instructions. *(See Functions, Reconciliation.)*

**By Request**—A phrase used when a senator or representative introduces a bill at the request of an executive agency or private organization but does not necessarily endorse the legislation.

**Calendar**—An agenda or list of business awaiting possible action by each chamber. The House uses five legislative calendars. *(See Consent, Discharge, House, Private and Union Calendar.)*

In the Senate, all legislative matters reported from committee go on one calendar. They are listed there in the order in which committees report them or the Senate places them on the calendar, but they may be called up out of order by the majority leader, either by obtaining unanimous consent of the Senate or by a motion to call up a bill. The Senate also uses one non-legislative calendar; this is used for treaties and nominations. *(See Executive Calendar.)*

**Calendar Wednesday**—A procedure in the House, now rarely used, whereby committees, on Wednesdays, may be called in the order in which they appear in Rule X of the House, for the purpose of bringing up any of their bills from either the House or the Union Calendar, except bills that are privileged. General debate is limited to two hours. Bills called up from the Union Calendar are considered in Committee of the Whole. Calendar Wednesday is not observed during the last two weeks of a session and may be dispensed with at other times by a two-thirds vote. This procedure is now routinely is dispensed with by unanimous consent.

**Call of the Calendar**—Senate bills that are not brought up for debate by a motion, unanimous consent or a unanimous consent agreement are brought before the Senate for action when the calendar listing them is "called." Bills must be called in the order listed. Measures considered by this method usually are non-controversial, and debate on the bill and any proposed amendments is limited to a total of five minutes for each senator.

**Chamber**—The meeting place for the membership of either the House or the Senate; also the membership of the House or Senate meeting as such.

**Clean Bill**—Frequently after a committee has finished a major revision of a bill, one of the committee members, usually the chairman, will assemble the changes and what is left of the original bill into a new measure and introduce it as a "clean bill." The revised measure, which is given a new number, then is referred back to the committee, which reports it to the floor for consideration. This often is a timesaver, as committee-recommended changes in a clean bill do not have to be considered and voted on by the chamber. Reporting a clean bill also protects committee amendments that could be subject to points of order concerning germaneness.

**Clerk of the House**—Chief administrative officer of the House of Representatives, with duties corresponding to those of the secretary of the Senate. *(See also Secretary of the Senate.)*

**Cloture**—The process by which a filibuster can be ended in the Senate other than by unanimous consent. A motion for cloture can apply to any measure before the Senate, including a proposal to change the chamber's rules. A cloture motion requires the signatures of 16 senators to be introduced. To end a filibuster, the cloture motion must obtain the votes of three-fifths of the entire Senate membership (60 if there are no vacancies), except when the filibuster is against a proposal to amend the standing rules of the Senate and a two-thirds vote of senators present and voting is required. The cloture request is put to a roll call vote one hour after the Senate meets on the second day following introduction of the motion. If approved, cloture limits each senator to one hour of debate. The bill or amendment in question comes to a final vote after 30 hours of consideration (including debate time and the time it takes to conduct roll calls, quorum calls and other procedural motions). *(See Filibuster.)*

**Committee**—A division of the House or Senate that prepares legislation for action by the parent chamber or makes investigations as directed by the parent chamber.

There are several types of committees. *(See Standing and Select or Special Committees.)* Most standing committees are divided into subcommittees, which study legislation, hold hearings and report bills, with or without amendments, to the full committee. Only the full committee can report legislation for action by the House or Senate.

**Committee of the Whole**—The working title of what is formally "The Committee of the Whole House [of Representatives] on the State of the Union." The membership is composed of all House members sitting as a committee. Any 100 members who are present on the floor of the chamber to consider legislation comprise a quorum of the committee. Any legislation, however, must first have passed through the regular legislative or Appropriations committee and have been placed on the calendar.

Technically, the Committee of the Whole considers only bills directly or indirectly appropriating money, authorizing appropriations or involving taxes or charges on the public. Because the Committee of the Whole need number only 100 representatives, a quorum is more readily attained, and legislative business is expedited. Before 1971, members' positions were not individually recorded on votes taken in the Committee of the Whole. *(See Teller Vote.)*

When the full House resolves itself into the Committee of the Whole, it replaces the Speaker with a "chairman." A measure is debated and amendments may be proposed, with votes on amendments as needed. *(See Five-Minute Rule.)*

When the committee completes its work on the measure, it dissolves itself by "rising." The Speaker returns, and the chairman of the Committee of the Whole reports to the House that the committee's work has been completed. At this time members may demand a roll call vote on any amendment adopted in the Committee of the Whole. The final vote is on passage of the legislation.

**Committee Veto**—A requirement added to a few statutes directing that certain policy directives by an executive department or agency be reviewed by certain congressional committees before they are implemented. Under common practice, the government department or agency and the committees involved are expected to reach a consensus before the directives are carried out. *(See also Legislative Veto.)*

**Concurrent Resolution**—A concurrent resolution, designated H Con Res or S Con Res, must be adopted by both houses, but it is not sent to the president for approval and therefore does not have the force of law. A concurrent resolution, for example, is used to fix the time for adjournment of a Congress. It also is used as the vehicle for expressing the sense of Congress on a foreign policy or domestic issue, and it serves as the vehicle for coordinated decisions on the federal budget under the 1974 Congressional Budget and Impoundment Control Act. *(See also Bills, Joint Resolution, Resolution.)*

**Conference**—A meeting between the representatives of the House and the Senate to reconcile differences between the two houses on provisions of a bill passed by both chambers. Members of the conference committee are appointed by the Speaker and the presiding officer of the Senate and are called "managers" for their respective chambers. A majority of the managers for each house must reach agreement on the provisions of the bill (often a compromise between the versions of the two chambers) before it can be considered by either chamber in the form of a "conference report." When the conference report goes to the floor, it cannot be amended, and, if it is not approved by both chambers, the bill may go back to conference under certain situations, or a new conference must be convened. Many rules and informal practices govern the conduct of conference committees.

Bills that are passed by both houses with only minor differences need not be sent to conference. Either chamber may "concur" in the other's amendments, completing action on the legislation. Sometimes leaders of the committees of jurisdiction work out an informal compromise instead of having a formal conference. *(See Custody of the Papers.)*

**Confirmations**—*(See Nominations.)*

**Congressional Record**—The daily, printed account of proceedings in both the House and Senate chambers, showing substantially verbatim debate, statements and a record of floor action. Highlights of legislative and committee action are embodied in a Daily Digest section of the Record, and members are entitled to have their extraneous remarks printed in an appendix known as "Extension of Remarks." Members may edit and revise remarks made on the floor during debate, and quotations from debate reported by the press are not always found in the Record.

The Congressional Record provides a way to distinguish remarks spoken on the floor of the House and Senate from undelivered speeches. In the Senate, all speeches, articles and other matter that members insert in the Record without actually reading them on the floor are set off by large black dots, or bullets. However, a loophole allows a member to avoid the bulleting if he delivers any portion of the speech in person. In the House, undelivered speeches and other material are printed in a distinctive typeface. *(See also Journal)*

**Congressional Terms of Office**—Normally begin on Jan. 3 of the year following a general election and are two years for representatives and six years for senators. Representatives elected in special elections are sworn in for the remainder of a term. A person may be appointed to fill a Senate vacancy and serves until a successor is elected; the successor serves until the end of the term applying to the vacant seat.

**Consent Calendar**—Members of the House may place on this calendar most bills on the Union or House Calendar that are considered to be non-controversial. Bills on the Consent Calendar normally are called on the first and third Mondays of each month. On the first occasion that a bill is called in this manner, consideration may be blocked by the objection of any member. The second time, if there are three objections, the bill is stricken from the Consent Calendar. If fewer than three members object, the bill is given immediate consideration.

A bill on the Consent Calendar may be postponed in another way. A member may ask that the measure be passed over "without prejudice." In that case, no objection is recorded against the bill, and its status on the Consent Calendar remains unchanged. A bill stricken from the Consent Calendar remains on the Union or House Calendar.

**Continuing Resolution**—A joint resolution, cleared by Congress and signed by the president (when the new fiscal year is about to begin or has begun), to provide new budget authority for federal agencies and programs to continue in operation until the regular appropriations acts are enacted. The continuing resolution usually specifies a maximum rate at which an agency may incur obligations, based on the rate of the prior year, the president's budget request or an appropriations bill passed by either or both houses of Congress but not yet enacted. Continuing resolutions also are called "CRs" or continuing appropriations.

**Contract Authority**—Budget authority contained in an authorization bill that permits the federal government to enter into contracts or other obligations for future payments from funds not yet appropriated by Congress. The assumption is that funds will be available for payment in a subsequent appropriation act.

**Controllable Budget Items**—In federal budgeting, this term refers to programs for which the budget authority or outlays during a fiscal year can be controlled without changing existing, substantive law. The concept "relatively uncontrollable under current law" includes outlays for open-ended programs and fixed costs such as interest on the public debt, Social Security benefits, veterans' benefits and outlays to liquidate prior-year obligations. More and more spending for federal programs has become uncontrollable or relatively uncontrollable.

**Correcting Recorded Votes**—Rules prohibit members from changing their votes after the result has been announced. But, occasionally, hours, days or months after a vote has been taken, a member may announce he was "incorrectly recorded." In the Senate, a request to change one's vote almost always receives unanimous consent. In the House, members are prohibited from changing their votes if tallied by the electronic voting system. If the vote was taken by roll call, a change is permissible if consent is granted.

**Cosponsor**—*(See Bills Introduced.)*

**Current Services Estimates**—Estimated budget authority and outlays for federal programs and operations for the forthcoming fiscal year based on continuation of existing levels of service without policy changes. These estimates of budget authority and outlays, accompanied by the underlying economic and policy assumptions upon which they are based, are transmitted by the president to Congress when the budget is submitted.

**Custody of the Papers**—To reconcile differences between the House and Senate versions of a bill, a conference may be arranged. The chamber with "custody of the papers" — the engrossed bill, engrossed amendments, messages of transmittal — is the only body empowered to request the conference. By custom, the chamber that asks for a conference is the last to act on the conference report once agreement has been reached on the bill by the conferees.

Custody of the papers sometimes is manipulated to ensure that a particular chamber acts either first or last on the conference report.

**Deferral**—Executive branch action to defer, or delay, the spending of appropriated money. The 1974 Congressional Budget and Impoundment Control Act requires a special message from the president to Congress reporting a proposed deferral of spending. Deferrals may not extend beyond the end of the fiscal year in which the message is transmitted. A federal district court in 1986 struck down the president's authority to defer spending for policy reasons; the ruling was upheld by a federal appeals court in 1987. Congress can prohibit proposed deferrals by enacting a law doing so; most often, cancellations of proposed deferrals are included in appropriations bills. *(See also Rescission.)*

**Dilatory Motion**—A motion made for the purpose of killing

time and preventing action on a bill or amendment. House rules outlaw dilatory motions, but enforcement is largely within the discretion of the Speaker or chairman of the Committee of the Whole. The Senate does not have a rule banning dilatory motions, except under cloture.

**Discharge a Committee**—Occasionally, attempts are made to relieve a committee from jurisdiction over a measure before it. This is attempted more often in the House than in the Senate, and the procedure rarely is successful.

In the House, if a committee does not report a bill within 30 days after the measure is referred to it, any member may file a discharge motion. Once offered, the motion is treated as a petition needing the signatures of a majority of members (218 if there are no vacancies). After the required signatures have been obtained, there is a delay of seven days. Thereafter, on the second and fourth Mondays of each month, except during the last six days of a session, any member who has signed the petition must be recognized, if he so desires, to move that the committee be discharged. Debate on the motion to discharge is limited to 20 minutes, and, if the motion is carried, consideration of the bill becomes a matter of high privilege.

If a resolution to consider a bill is held up in the Rules Committee for more than seven legislative days, any member may enter a motion to discharge the committee. The motion is handled like any other discharge petition in the House. Occasionally, to expedite non-controversial legislative business, a committee is discharged by unanimous consent of the House, and a petition is not required. (*Senate procedure, see Discharge Resolution.*)

**Discharge Calendar**—The House calendar to which motions to discharge committees are referred when they have the required number of signatures (218) and are awaiting floor action.

**Discharge Petition**—(*See Discharge a Committee.*)

**Discharge Resolution**—In the Senate, a special motion that any senator may introduce to relieve a committee from consideration of a bill before it. The resolution can be called up for Senate approval or disapproval in the same manner as any other Senate business. (*House procedure, see Discharge a Committee.*)

**Division of a Question for Voting**—A practice that is more common in the Senate but also used in the House whereby a member may demand a division of an amendment or a motion for purposes of voting. Where an amendment or motion can be divided, the individual parts are voted on separately when a member demands a division. This procedure occurs most often during the consideration of conference reports.

**Division Vote**—(*See Standing Vote.*)

**Enacting Clause**—Key phrase in bills beginning, "Be it enacted by the Senate and House of Representatives . . ." A successful motion to strike it from legislation kills the measure.

**Engrossed Bill**—The final copy of a bill as passed by one chamber, with the text as amended by floor action and certified by the clerk of the House or the secretary of the Senate.

**Enrolled Bill**—The final copy of a bill that has been passed in identical form by both chambers. It is certified by an officer of the house of origin (clerk of the House or secretary of the Senate) and then sent on for the signatures of the House Speaker, the Senate president pro tempore and the president of the United States. An enrolled bill is printed on parchment.

**Entitlement Program**—A federal program that guarantees a certain level of benefits to persons or other entities who meet requirements set by law, such as Social Security, farm price supports or unemployment benefits. It thus leaves no discretion with Congress on how much money to appropriate, and some entitlements carry permanent appropriations.

**Executive Calendar**—This is a non-legislative calendar in the Senate on which presidential documents such as treaties and nominations are listed.

**Executive Document**—A document, usually a treaty, sent to the Senate by the president for consideration or approval. Executive documents are identified for each session of Congress according to the following pattern: Executive A, 97th Congress, 1st Session; Executive B, and so on. They are referred to committee in the same manner as other measures. Unlike legislative documents, however, treaties do not die at the end of a Congress but remain "live" proposals until acted on by the Senate or withdrawn by the president.

**Executive Session**—A meeting of a Senate or House committee (or occasionally of either chamber) that only its members may attend. Witnesses regularly appear at committee meetings in executive session — for example, Defense Department officials during presentations of classified defense information. Other members of Congress may be invited, but the public and press are not allowed to attend.

**Expenditures**—The actual spending of money as distinguished from the appropriation of funds. Expenditures are made by the disbursing officers of the administration; appropriations are made only by Congress. The two are rarely identical in any fiscal year. In addition to some current budget authority, expenditures may represent budget authority made available one, two or more years earlier.

**Filibuster**—A time-delaying tactic associated with the Senate and used by a minority in an effort to prevent a vote on a bill or amendment that probably would pass if voted upon directly. The most common method is to take advantage of the Senate's rules permitting unlimited debate, but other forms of parliamentary maneuvering may be used. The stricter rules of the House make filibusters more difficult, but delaying tactics are employed occasionally through various procedural devices allowed by House rules. (*Senate filibusters, see Cloture.*)

**Fiscal Year**—Financial operations of the government are carried out in a 12-month fiscal year, beginning on Oct. 1 and ending on Sept. 30. The fiscal year carries the date of the calendar year in which it ends. (From fiscal year 1844 to fiscal year 1976, the fiscal year began July 1 and ended the following June 30.)

**Five-Minute Rule**—A debate-limiting rule of the House that is invoked when the House sits as the Committee of the Whole. Under the rule, a member offering an amendment is allowed to speak five minutes in its favor, and an opponent of the amendment is allowed to speak five minutes in opposition. Debate is then closed. In practice, amendments regularly are debated more than 10 minutes, with members gaining the floor by offering pro forma amendments or obtaining unanimous consent to speak longer than five minutes. (*See Strike Out the Last Word.*)

**Floor Manager**—A member who has the task of steering legislation through floor debate and the amendment process to a final vote in the House or the Senate. Floor managers usually are chairmen or ranking members of the committee that reported the bill. Managers are responsible for apportioning the debate time granted supporters of the bill. The ranking minority member of the committee normally apportions time for the minority party's participation in the debate.

**Frank**—A member's facsimile signature, which is used on envelopes in lieu of stamps, for the member's official outgoing mail. The "franking privilege" is the right to send mail postage-free.

**Germane**—Pertaining to the subject matter of the measure at hand. All House amendments must be germane to the bill being considered. The Senate requires that amendments be germane when they are proposed to general appropriations bills or to bills being considered once cloture has been adopted or, frequently, when the Senate is proceeding under a unanimous consent agreement placing a time limit on consideration of a bill. The 1974 budget act also requires that amendments to concurrent budget resolutions be germane. In the House, floor debate must be germane, and the first three hours of debate each day in the Senate must be germane to the pending business.

**Gramm-Rudman-Hollings Deficit Reduction Act**—(See Budget Process, Sequestration.)

**Grandfather Clause**—A provision that exempts persons or other entities already engaged in an activity from rules or legislation affecting that activity. Grandfather clauses sometimes are added to legislation in order to avoid antagonizing groups with established interests in the activities affected.

**Hearings**—Committee sessions for taking testimony from witnesses. At hearings on legislation, witnesses usually include specialists, government officials and spokespersons for individuals or entities affected by the bill or bills under study. Hearings related to special investigations bring forth a variety of witnesses. Committees sometimes use their subpoena power to summon reluctant witnesses. The public and press may attend open hearings but are barred from closed, or "executive," hearings. The vast majority of hearings are open to the public. (See Executive Session.)

**Hold-Harmless Clause**—A provision added to legislation to ensure that recipients of federal funds do not receive less in a future year than they did in the current year if a new formula for allocating funds authorized in the legislation would result in a reduction to the recipients. This clause has been used most often to soften the impact of sudden reductions in federal grants.

**Hopper**—Box on House clerk's desk where members deposit bills and resolutions to introduce them. (See also Bills Introduced.)

**Hour Rule**—A provision in the rules of the House that permits one hour of debate time for each member on amendments debated in the House of Representatives sitting as the House. Therefore, the House normally amends bills while sitting as the Committee of the Whole, where the five-minute rule on amendments operates. (See Committee of the Whole, Five-Minute Rule.)

**House**—The House of Representatives, as distinct from the Senate, although each body is a "house" of Congress.

**House as in Committee of the Whole**—A procedure that can be used to expedite consideration of certain measures such as continuing resolutions and, when there is debate, private bills. The procedure only can be invoked with the unanimous consent of the House or a rule from the Rules Committee and has procedural elements of both the House sitting as the House of Representatives, such as the Speaker presiding and the previous question motion being in order, and the House sitting as the Committee of the Whole, such as the five-minute rule pertaining.

**House Calendar**—A listing for action by the House of public bills that do not directly or indirectly appropriate money or raise revenue.

**Immunity**—The constitutional privilege of members of Congress to make verbal statements on the floor and in committee for which they cannot be sued or arrested for slander or libel. Also, freedom from arrest while traveling to or from sessions of Congress or on official business. Members in this status may be arrested only for treason, felonies or a breach of the peace, as defined by congressional manuals.

**Joint Committee**—A committee composed of a specified number of members of both the House and Senate. A joint committee may be investigative or research-oriented, an example of the latter being the Joint Economic Committee. Others have housekeeping duties such as the joint committees on Printing and on the Library of Congress.

**Joint Resolution**—A joint resolution, designated H J Res or S J Res, requires the approval of both houses and the signature of the president, just as a bill does, and has the force of law if approved. There is no practical difference between a bill and a joint resolution. A joint resolution generally is used to deal with a limited matter such as a single appropriation.

Joint resolutions also are used to propose amendments to the Constitution. They do not require a presidential signature but become a part of the Constitution when three-fourths of the states have ratified them.

**Journal**—The official record of the proceedings of the House and Senate. The Journal records the actions taken in each chamber, but, unlike the Congressional Record, it does not include the substantially verbatim report of speeches, debates, statements and the like.

**Law**—An act of Congress that has been signed by the president or passed over his veto by Congress. Public bills, when signed, become public laws, and are cited by the letters PL and a hyphenated number. The number before the hyphen corresponds to the Congress, and the one or more digits after the hyphen refer to the numerical sequence in which the president signed the bills during that Congress. Private bills, when signed, become private laws. (See also Pocket Veto, Slip Laws, Statutes at Large, U.S. Code.)

**Legislative Day**—The "day" extending from the time either house meets after an adjournment until the time it next adjourns. Because the House normally adjourns from day to day, legislative days and calendar days usually coincide. But in the Senate, a legislative day may, and frequently does, extend over several calendar days. (See Recess.)

**Legislative Veto**—A procedure, held unconstitutional by the Supreme Court, permitting either the House or Senate, or both chambers, to review proposed executive branch regulations or actions and to block or modify those with which they disagreed.

The specifics of the procedure varied, but Congress generally provided for a legislative veto by including in a bill a provision that administrative rules or action taken to implement the law were to go into effect at the end of a designated period of time unless blocked by either or both houses of Congress. Another version of the veto provided for congressional reconsideration and rejection of regulations already in effect.

The Supreme Court in 1983 struck down the legislative veto as an unconstitutional violation of the lawmaking procedure provided in the Constitution.

**Loan Guarantees**—Loans to third parties for which the federal government in the event of default guarantees, in whole or in part, the repayment of principal or interest to a lender or holder of a security.

**Lobby**—A group seeking to influence the passage or defeat of legislation. Originally the term referred to persons frequenting the lobbies or corridors of legislative chambers to speak to lawmakers.

The definition of a lobby and the activity of lobbying is a matter of differing interpretation. By some definitions, lobbying is limited to direct attempts to influence lawmakers through personal interviews and persuasion. Under other definitions, lobbying includes attempts at indirect, or "grass-roots," influence, such as persuading members of a group to write or visit their district's representative and state's senators or attempting to create a climate of opinion favorable to a desired legislative goal.

The right to attempt to influence legislation is based on the First Amendment to the Constitution, which says Congress shall make no law abridging the right of the people "to petition the government for a redress of grievances."

**Majority Leader**—Floor leader for the majority party in each chamber. In the Senate, in consultation with the minority leader and his colleagues, the majority leader directs the legislative schedule for the chamber. He also is his party's spokesperson and chief strategist. In the House, the majority leader is second to the Speaker in the majority party's leadership and serves as his party's legislative strategist.

**Majority Whip**—In effect, the assistant majority leader, in either the House or Senate. His job is to help marshal majority forces in support of party strategy and legislation.

**Manual**—The official handbook in each house prescribing in detail its organization, procedures and operations.

**Marking Up a Bill**—Going through the contents of a piece of

legislation in committee or subcommittee to, for example, consider its provisions in large and small portions, act on amendments to provisions and proposed revisions to the language, and insert new sections and phraseology. If the bill is extensively amended, the committee's version may be introduced as a separate bill, with a new number, before being considered by the full House or Senate. *(See Clean Bill.)*

**Minority Leader**—Floor leader for the minority party in each chamber. *(See also Majority Leader.)*

**Minority Whip**—Performs duties of whip for the minority party. *(See also Majority Whip.)*

**Morning Hour**—The time set aside at the beginning of each legislative day for the consideration of regular, routine business. The "hour" is of indefinite duration in the House, where it is rarely used.

In the Senate, it is the first two hours of a session following an adjournment, as distinguished from a recess. The morning hour can be terminated earlier if the morning business has been completed. Business includes such matters as messages from the president, communications from the heads of departments, messages from the House, the presentation of petitions, reports of standing and select committees and the introduction of bills and resolutions. During the first hour of the morning hour in the Senate, no motion to proceed to the consideration of any bill on the calendar is in order except by unanimous consent. During the second hour, motions can be made but must be decided without debate. Senate committees may meet while the Senate conducts morning hour.

**Motion**—In the House or Senate chamber, a request by a member to institute any one of a wide array of parliamentary actions. He "moves" for a certain procedure, such as the consideration of a measure. The precedence of motions, and whether they are debatable, is set forth in the House and Senate manuals.

**Nominations**—Presidential appointments to office subject to Senate confirmation. Although most nominations win quick Senate approval, some are controversial and become the topic of hearings and debate. Sometimes senators object to appointees for patronage reasons — for example, when a nomination to a local federal job is made without consulting the senators of the state concerned. In some situations a senator may object that the nominee is "personally obnoxious" to him. Usually other senators join in blocking such appointments out of courtesy to their colleagues. *(See Senatorial Courtesy.)*

**One-Minute Speeches**—Addresses by House members at the beginning of a legislative day. The speeches may cover any subject but are limited to one minute's duration.

**Outlays**—Payments made (generally through the issuance of checks or disbursement of cash) to liquidate obligations. Outlays during a fiscal year may be for the payment of obligations incurred in prior years or in the same year.

**Override a Veto**—If the president disapproves a bill and sends it back to Congress with his objections, Congress may try to override his veto and enact the bill into law. Neither house is required to attempt to override a veto. The override of a veto requires a recorded vote with a two-thirds majority of those present and voting in each chamber. The question put to each house is: "Shall the bill pass, the objections of the president to the contrary notwithstanding?" *(See also Pocket Veto, Veto.)*

**Oversight Committee**—A congressional committee, or designated subcommittee of a committee, that is charged with general oversight of one or more federal agencies' programs and activities. Usually, the oversight panel for a particular agency also is the authorizing committee for that agency's programs and operations.

**Pair**—A voluntary, informal arrangement that two lawmakers, usually on opposite sides of an issue, make on recorded votes. In many cases the result is to subtract a vote from each side, with no effect on the outcome. Pairs are not authorized in the rules of either house, are not counted in tabulating the final result and

have no official standing. However, members pairing are identified in the Congressional Record, along with their positions on such votes, if known. A member who expects to be absent for a vote can pair with a member who plans to vote, with the latter agreeing to withhold his vote.

There are three types of pairs: 1) A live pair involves a member who is present for a vote and another who is absent. The member in attendance votes and then withdraws the vote, announcing that he has a live pair with colleague "X" and stating how the two members would have voted, one in favor, the other opposed. A live pair may affect the outcome of a closely contested vote, since it subtracts one "yea" or one "nay" from the final tally. A live pair may cover one or several specific issues. 2) A general pair, widely used in the House, does not entail any arrangement between two members and does not affect the vote. Members who expect to be absent notify the clerk that they wish to make a general pair. Each member then is paired with another desiring a pair, and their names are listed in the Congressional Record. The member may or may not be paired with another taking the opposite position, and no indication of how the members would have voted is given. 3) A specific pair is similar to a general pair, except that the opposing stands of the two members are identified and printed in the Record.

**Petition**—A request or plea sent to one or both chambers from an organization or private citizens' group asking support of particular legislation or favorable consideration of a matter not yet receiving congressional attention. Petitions are referred to appropriate committees.

**Pocket Veto**—The act of the president in withholding his approval of a bill after Congress has adjourned. When Congress is in session, a bill becomes law without the president's signature if he does not act upon it within 10 days, excluding Sundays, from the time he gets it. But if Congress adjourns sine die within that 10-day period, the bill will die even if the president does not formally veto it.

The Supreme Court in 1986 agreed to decide whether the president can pocket veto a bill during recesses and between sessions of the same Congress or only between Congresses. The justices in 1987 declared the case moot, however, because the bill in question was invalid once the case reached the court. *(See also Veto.)*

**Point of Order**—An objection raised by a member that the chamber is departing from rules governing its conduct of business. The objector cites the rule violated, the chair sustaining his objection if correctly made. Order is restored by the chair's suspending proceedings of the chamber until it conforms to the prescribed "order of business."

**President of the Senate**—Under the Constitution, the vice president of the United States presides over the Senate. In his absence, the president pro tempore, or a senator designated by the president pro tempore, presides over the chamber.

**President Pro Tempore**—The chief officer of the Senate in the absence of the vice president; literally, but loosely, the president for a time. The president pro tempore is elected by his fellow senators, and the recent practice has been to elect the senator of the majority party with the longest period of continuous service.

**Previous Question**—A motion for the previous question, when carried, has the effect of cutting off all debate, preventing the offering of further amendments and forcing a vote on the pending matter. In the House, the previous question is not permitted in the Committee of the Whole. The motion for the previous question is a debate-limiting device and is not in order in the Senate.

**Printed Amendment**—A House rule guarantees five minutes of floor debate in support and five minutes in opposition, and no other debate time, on amendments printed in the Congressional Record at least one day prior to the amendment's consideration in the Committee of the Whole. In the Senate, while amendments may be submitted for printing, they have no parliamentary standing or status. An amendment submitted for printing in the Senate,

however, may be called up by any senator.

**Private Calendar**—In the House, private bills dealing with individual matters such as claims against the government, immigration or land titles are put on this calendar. The private calendar must be called on the first Tuesday of each month, and the Speaker may call it on the third Tuesday of each month as well.

When a private bill is before the chamber, two members may block its consideration, which recommits the bill to committee. Backers of a recommitted private bill have recourse. The measure can be put into an "omnibus claims bill" — several private bills rolled into one. As with any bill, no part of an omnibus claims bill may be deleted without a vote. When the private bill goes back to the House floor in this form, it can be deleted from the omnibus bill only by majority vote.

**Privileged Questions**—The order in which bills, motions and other legislative measures are considered on the floor of the Senate and House is governed by strict priorities. A motion to table, for instance, is more privileged than a motion to recommit. Thus, if a member moves to recommit a bill to committee for further consideration, another member could supersede the first action by moving to table it, and a vote would occur first on the motion to table (or kill) the motion to recommit. A motion to adjourn is considered "of the highest privilege" and would have to be considered before virtually any other motion. *(See also Questions of Privilege.)*

**Pro Forma Amendment**—*(See Strike Out the Last Word.)*

**Public Laws**—*(See Law.)*

**Questions of Privilege**—These are matters affecting members of Congress individually or collectively. Matters affecting the rights, safety, dignity and integrity of proceedings of the House or Senate as a whole are questions of privilege in both chambers.

Questions involving individual members are called questions of "personal privilege." A member rising to ask a question of personal privilege is given precedence over almost all other proceedings. For instance, if a member feels that he has been improperly impugned in comments by another member, he can immediately demand to be heard on the floor on a question of personal privilege. An annotation in the House rules points out that the privilege rests primarily on the Constitution, which gives him a conditional immunity from arrest and an unconditional freedom to speak in the House. *(See also Privileged Questions.)*

**Quorum**—The number of members whose presence is necessary for the transaction of business. In the Senate and House, it is a majority of the membership. A quorum is 100 in the Committee of the Whole House. If a point of order is made that a quorum is not present, the only business that is in order is either a motion to adjourn or a motion to direct the sergeant-at-arms to request the attendance of absentees.

**Readings of Bills**—Traditional parliamentary procedure required bills to be read three times before they were passed. This custom is of little modern significance. Normally a bill is considered to have its first reading when it is introduced and printed, by title, in the Congressional Record. In the House, its second reading comes when floor consideration begins. (This is the most likely point at which there is an actual reading of the bill, if there is any.) The second reading in the Senate is supposed to occur on the legislative day after the measure is introduced, but before it is referred to committee. The third reading (again, usually by title) takes place when floor action has been completed on amendments.

**Recess**—Distinguished from adjournment in that a recess does not end a legislative day and therefore does not interrupt unfinished business. The rules in each house set forth certain matters to be taken up and disposed of at the beginning of each legislative day. The House usually adjourns from day to day. The Senate often recesses, thus meeting on the same legislative day for several calendar days or even weeks at a time.

**Recognition**—The power of recognition of a member is lodged in the Speaker of the House and the presiding officer of the Senate. The presiding officer names the member to speak first when two or more members simultaneously request recognition.

**Recommit to Committee**—A motion, made on the floor after a bill has been debated, to return it to the committee that reported it. If approved, recommittal usually is considered a death blow to the bill. In the House, a motion to recommit can be made only by a member opposed to the bill, and, in recognizing a member to make the motion, the Speaker gives preference to members of the minority party over majority-party members.

A motion to recommit may include instructions to the committee to report the bill again with specific amendments or by a certain date. Or the instructions may direct that a particular study be made, with no definite deadline for further action. If the recommittal motion includes instructions to "report the bill back forthwith" and the motion is adopted, floor action on the bill continues; the committee does not actually reconsider the legislation.

**Reconciliation**—The 1974 budget act provides for a "reconciliation" procedure for bringing existing tax and spending laws into conformity with ceilings enacted in the congressional budget resolution. Under the procedure, Congress instructs designated legislative committees to approve measures adjusting revenues and expenditures by a certain amount. The committees have a deadline by which they must report the legislation, but they have the discretion of deciding what changes are to be made. The recommendations of the various committees are consolidated without change by the Budget committees into an omnibus reconciliation bill, which then must be considered and approved by both houses of Congress. The orders to congressional committees to report recommendations for reconciliation bills are called reconciliation instructions, and they are contained in the budget resolution. Reconciliation instructions are not binding, but Congress must meet annual Gramm-Rudman deficit targets to avoid the automatic spending cuts of sequestration, which means it must also meet the goal of reconciliation. *(See also Budget Resolution, Sequestration.)*

**Reconsider a Vote**—A motion to reconsider the vote by which an action was taken has, until it is disposed of, the effect of putting the action in abeyance. In the Senate, the motion can be made only by a member who voted on the prevailing side of the original question or by a member who did not vote at all. In the House, it can be made only by a member on the prevailing side.

A common practice in the Senate after close votes on an issue is a motion to reconsider, followed by a motion to table the motion to reconsider. On this motion to table, senators vote as they voted on the original question, which allows the motion to table to prevail, assuming there are no switches. The matter then is finally closed and further motions to reconsider are not entertained. In the House, as a routine precaution, a motion to reconsider usually is made every time a measure is passed. Such a motion almost always is tabled immediately, thus shutting off the possibility of future reconsideration, except by unanimous consent.

Motions to reconsider must be entered in the Senate within the next two days of actual session after the original vote has been taken. In the House, they must be entered either on the same day or on the next succeeding day the House is in session.

**Recorded Vote**—A vote upon which each member's stand is individually made known. In the Senate, this is accomplished through a roll call of the entire membership, to which each senator on the floor must answer "yea," "nay" or "present." Since January 1973, the House has used an electronic voting system for recorded votes, including yea-and-nay votes formerly taken by roll calls.

When not required by the Constitution, a recorded vote can be obtained on questions in the House on the demand of one-fifth (44 members) of a quorum or one-fourth (25) of a quorum in the Committee of the Whole. *(See Yeas and Nays.)*

**Report**—Both a verb and a noun as a congressional term. A committee that has been examining a bill referred to it by the parent chamber "reports" its findings and recommendations to the chamber when it completes consideration and returns the measure. The process is called "reporting" a bill.

A "report" is the document setting forth the committee's explanation of its action. Senate and House reports are numbered separately and are designated S Rept or H Rept. When a commit-

tee report is not unanimous, the dissenting committee members may file a statement of their views, called minority or dissenting views and referred to as a minority report. Members in disagreement with some provisions of a bill may file additional or supplementary views. Sometimes a bill is reported without a committee recommendation.

Adverse reports occasionally are submitted by legislative committees. However, when a committee is opposed to a bill, it usually fails to report the bill at all. Some laws require that committee reports — favorable or adverse — be made.

**Rescission**—An item in an appropriations bill rescinding or canceling budget authority previously appropriated but not spent. Also, the repeal of a previous appropriation by Congress at the request of the president to cut spending or because the budget authority no longer is needed. Under the 1974 budget act, however, unless Congress approves a rescission within 45 days of continuous session after receipt of the proposal, the funds must be made available for obligation. *(See also Deferral.)*

**Resolution**—A "simple" resolution, designated H Res or S Res, deals with matters entirely within the prerogatives of one house or the other. It requires neither passage by the other chamber nor approval by the president, and it does not have the force of law. Most resolutions deal with the rules or procedures of one house. They also are used to express the sentiments of a single house such as condolences to the family of a deceased member or to comment on foreign policy or executive business. A simple resolution is the vehicle for a "rule" from the House Rules Committee. *(See also Concurrent and Joint Resolutions, Rules.)*

**Rider**—An amendment, usually not germane, that its sponsor hopes to get through more easily by including it in other legislation. Riders become law if the bills embodying them are enacted. Amendments providing legislative directives in appropriations bills are outstanding examples of riders, though technically legislation is banned from appropriations bills.

The House, unlike the Senate, has a strict germaneness rule; thus, riders usually are Senate devices to get legislation enacted quickly or to bypass lengthy House consideration and, possibly, opposition.

**Rules**—A rule is a standing order governing the conduct of House or Senate business and listed among the permanent rules of either chamber. The rules deal with issues such as duties of officers, the order of business, admission to the floor, parliamentary procedures on handling amendments and voting and jurisdictions of committees.

In the House, a rule also may be a resolution reported by its Rules Committee to govern the handling of a particular bill on the floor. The committee may report a "rule," also called a "special order," in the form of a simple resolution. If the resolution is adopted by the House, the temporary rule becomes as valid as any standing rule and lapses only after action has been completed on the measure to which it pertains. A rule sets the time limit on general debate. It also may waive points of order against provisions of the bill in question such as non-germane language or against certain amendments intended to be proposed to the bill from the floor. It may even forbid all amendments or all amendments except those proposed by the legislative committee that handled the bill. In this instance, it is known as a "closed" rule as opposed to an "open" rule, which puts no limitation on floor amendments, thus leaving the bill completely open to alteration by the adoption of germane amendments.

**Secretary of the Senate**—Chief administrative officer of the Senate, responsible for overseeing the duties of Senate employees, educating Senate pages, administering oaths, overseeing the registration of lobbyists and handling other tasks necessary for the continuing operation of the Senate. *(See also Clerk of the House.)*

**Select or Special Committee**—A committee set up for a special purpose and, usually, for a limited time by resolution of either the House or Senate. Most special committees are investigative and lack legislative authority: legislation is not referred to them, and they cannot report bills to their parent chamber. *(See also Standing Committees.)*

**Senatorial Courtesy**—Sometimes referred to as "the courtesy of the Senate," it is a general practice — with no written rule — applied to consideration of executive nominations. Generally, it means that nominations from a state are not to be confirmed unless they have been approved by the senators of the president's party of that state, with other senators following their colleagues' lead in the attitude they take toward consideration of such nominations. *(See Nominations.)*

**Sequester order** — Under procedures put in place by the 1985 Gramm-Rudman antideficit law, Congress was threatened with year-end, across-the-board spending cuts known as a sequester if the deficit exceeded a pre-set maximum. The Budget Enforcement Act of 1990 effectively did away with that form of sequester for fiscal years 1991-93, replacing it with a series of targeted "mini-sequesters." *(See also Budget Process.)*

For fiscal 1991-93, discretionary spending in any of the 13 regular appropriations bills that exceeded the cap for its particular category (domestic, defense or international) would trigger a sequester in that category only. For fiscal 1994-95, however, the three categories were collapsed into a single pot of money, which meant that a sequester would affect all discretionary spending. The sequester would take place 15 days after adjournment.

New "pay-as-you-go" rules required that mandatory spending (entitlement programs such as Medicare and food stamps) and tax cuts be deficit-neutral. If Congress cut taxes, expanded existing entitlement programs or created new entitlements, the cost had to be offset. If there was no offset, a sequester of all non-exempt entitlement programs would take place 15 days after Congress adjourns.

Two other types of sequesters affected supplemental appropriations bills. A supplemental that exceeded discretionary spending limits and was enacted before July 1 would trigger a "within-session" sequester within 15 days of enactment. That sequester would require a cutback in spending for the offending category during the current fiscal year.

A supplemental that exceeded the caps and was enacted after June 30 would trigger a "look-back" sequester, which would reduce the cap for the offending category for the next fiscal year by the amount of the excess spending.

**Sine Die**—*(See Adjournment Sine Die.)*

**Slip Laws**—The first official publication of a bill that has been enacted and signed into law. Each is published separately in unbound single-sheet or pamphlet form. *(See also Law, Statutes at Large, U.S. Code.)*

**Speaker**—The presiding officer of the House of Representatives, selected by the caucus of the party to which he belongs and formally elected by the whole House.

**Special Session**—A session of Congress after it has adjourned sine die, completing its regular session. Special sessions are convened by the president.

**Spending Authority**—The 1974 budget act defines spending authority as borrowing authority, contract authority and entitlement authority for which budget authority is not provided in advance by appropriation acts.

**Sponsor**—*(See Bills Introduced.)*

**Standing Committees**—Committees that are permanently established by House and Senate rules. The standing committees of the House were last reorganized by the committee reorganization of 1974. The last major realignment of Senate committees was in the committee system reorganization of 1977. The standing committees are legislative committees — legislation may be referred to them and they may report bills and resolutions to their parent chambers. *(See also Select or Special Committees.)*

**Standing Vote**—A non-recorded vote used in both the House and Senate. (A standing vote also is called a division vote.) Members in favor of a proposal stand and are counted by the presiding officer. Then members opposed stand and are counted. There is no record of how individual members voted.

**Statutes at Large**—A chronological arrangement of the laws enacted in each session of Congress. Though indexed, the laws are not arranged by subject matter, and there is not an indication of how they changed previously enacted laws. *(See also Law, Slip Laws, U.S. Code.)*

**Strike From the Record**—Remarks made on the House floor may offend some member, who moves that the offending words be "taken down" for the Speaker's cognizance, and then expunged from the debate as published in the Congressional Record.

**Strike Out the Last Word**—A motion whereby a House member is entitled to speak for five minutes on an amendment then being debated by the chamber. A member gains recognition from the chair by moving to "strike out the last word" of the amendment or section of the bill under consideration. The motion is pro forma, requires no vote and does not change the amendment being debated.

**Substitute**—A motion, amendment or entire bill introduced in place of the pending legislative business. Passage of a substitute measure kills the original measure by supplanting it. The substitute also may be amended. *(See also Amendment in the Nature of a Substitute.)*

**Supplemental Appropriations Bill**—Legislation appropriating funds after the regular annual appropriations bill for a federal department or agency has been enacted. A supplemental appropriation provides additional budget authority beyond original estimates for programs or activities, including new programs authorized after the enactment of the regular appropriation act, for which the need for funds is too urgent to be postponed until enactment of the next year's regular appropriation bill.

**Suspend the Rules**—Often a time-saving procedure for passing bills in the House. The wording of the motion, which may be made by any member recognized by the Speaker, is: "I move to suspend the rules and pass the bill . . ." A favorable vote by two-thirds of those present is required for passage. Debate is limited to 40 minutes and no amendments from the floor are permitted. If a two-thirds favorable vote is not attained, the bill may be considered later under regular procedures. The suspension procedure is in order every Monday and Tuesday and is intended to be reserved for non-controversial bills.

**Table a Bill**—Motions to table, or to "lay on the table," are used to block or kill amendments or other parliamentary questions. When approved, a tabling motion is considered the final disposition of that issue. One of the most widely used parliamentary procedures, the motion to table is not debatable, and adoption requires a simple majority vote.

In the Senate, however, different language sometimes is used. The motion may be worded to let a bill "lie on the table," perhaps for subsequent "picking up." This motion is more flexible, keeping the bill pending for later action, if desired. Tabling motions on amendments are effective debate-ending devices in the Senate.

**Teller Vote**—This is a largely moribund House procedure in the Committee of the Whole. Members file past tellers and are counted as for or against a measure, but they are not recorded individually. In the House, tellers are ordered upon demand of one-fifth of a quorum. This is 44 in the House, 20 in the Committee of the Whole.

The House also has a recorded teller vote, now largely supplanted by the electronic voting procedure, under which the votes of each member are made public just as they would be on a recorded vote.

**Treaties**—Executive proposals — in the form of resolutions of ratification — which must be submitted to the Senate for approval by two-thirds of the senators present. Treaties are normally sent to the Foreign Relations Committee for scrutiny before the Senate takes action. Foreign Relations has jurisdiction over all treaties, regardless of the subject matter. Treaties are read three times and debated on the floor in much the same manner as legislative proposals. After approval by the Senate, treaties are formally ratified by the president.

**Trust Funds**—Funds collected and used by the federal government for carrying out specific purposes and programs according to terms of a trust agreement or statute such as the Social Security and unemployment compensation trust funds. Such funds are administered by the government in a fiduciary capacity and are not available for the general purposes of the government.

**Unanimous Consent**—Proceedings of the House or Senate and action on legislation often take place upon the unanimous consent of the chamber, whether or not a rule of the chamber is being violated. Unanimous consent is used to expedite floor action and frequently is used in a routine fashion such as by a senator requesting the unanimous consent of the Senate to have specified members of his staff present on the floor during debate on a specific amendment.

**Unanimous Consent Agreement**—A device used in the Senate to expedite legislation. Much of the Senate's legislative business, dealing with both minor and controversial issues, is conducted through unanimous consent or unanimous consent agreements. On major legislation, such agreements usually are printed and transmitted to all senators in advance of floor debate. Once agreed to, they are binding on all members unless the Senate, by unanimous consent, agrees to modify them. An agreement may list the order in which various bills are to be considered, specify the length of time bills and contested amendments are to be debated and when they are to be voted upon and, frequently, require that all amendments introduced be germane to the bill under consideration.

In this regard, unanimous consent agreements are similar to the "rules" issued by the House Rules Committee for bills pending in the House.

**Union Calendar**—Bills that directly or indirectly appropriate money or raise revenue are placed on this House calendar according to the date they are reported from committee.

**U.S. Code**—A consolidation and codification of the general and permanent laws of the United States arranged by subject under 50 titles, the first six dealing with general or political subjects, and the other 44 alphabetically arranged from agriculture to war. The U.S. Code is updated annually, and a new set of bound volumes is published every six years. *(See also Law, Slip Laws, Statutes at Large.)*

**Veto**—Disapproval by the president of a bill or joint resolution (other than one proposing an amendment to the Constitution). When Congress is in session, the president must veto a bill within 10 days, excluding Sundays, after he has received it; otherwise, it becomes law without his signature. When the president vetoes a bill, he returns it to the house of origin along with a message stating his objections. *(See also Pocket Veto, Override a Veto.)*

**Voice Vote**—In either the House or Senate, members answer "aye" or "no" in chorus, and the presiding officer decides the result. The term also is used loosely to indicate action by unanimous consent or without objection.

**Whip**—*(See Majority and Minority Whip.)*

**Without Objection**—Used in lieu of a vote on non-controversial motions, amendments or bills that may be passed in either the House or Senate if no member voices an objection.

**Yeas and Nays**—The Constitution requires that yea-and-nay votes be taken and recorded when requested by one-fifth of the members present. In the House, the Speaker determines whether one-fifth of the members present requested a vote. In the Senate, practice requires only 11 members. The Constitution requires the yeas and nays on a veto override attempt. *(See Recorded Vote.)*

**Yielding**—When a member has been recognized to speak, no other member may speak unless he obtains permisssion from the member recognized. This permission is called yielding and usually is requested in the form, "Will the gentleman (or gentlelady) yield to me?" While this activity occasionally is seen in the Senate, the Senate has no rule or practice to parcel out time. ■

# TEXT

# Bush Assures Australia of U.S. Commitment to Pacific Rim

*President Bush on Jan. 2 addressed a special session of the Australian Parliament in Canberra. Following is the Reuter transcript of his remarks:*

Thank you, Mr. Speaker, Mr. President, Mr. Prime Minister, and the leader of the Opposition, Mr. Leader, members and senators. It is a deep and wonderful honor for me to be here, and I am very, very grateful for the honor of appearing before this house of the Australian Parliament.

I know that the members have gone to extraordinary lengths to arrange this special session, and I think the people in our country will appreciate this very, very much.

I want to offer special greetings and thanks to the members of the Australian/ U.S.A. Parliamentary Group, who have done so much to deepen the friendship between our countries.

Let me just make an initial observation, if I might. You have a wonderfully vigorous political climate. That has got to be the classic understatement of the year.

And I see this rough and tumble that goes forth like this, and I thank God for the presidential system at home, but nevertheless —

Let me make this observation, though. I feel very fortunate to have known several of your members from both sides of the aisle over the years. And amidst all the intensity and emotion brought forth in these chambers, I've always been impressed by the united message that your leaders have sent to my country. Even when out of office or in the opposition, they've always placed Australia's interest ahead of personal interest. And that says something very positive, very important, about your great country.

That's certainly one reason that any visitor from the United States cannot but help feel a warm kinship with Australia. Both of our young nations were seen by explorers and pioneers and immigrants as destinations of freedom and opportunity. Our cultures reflect an extraordinary diversity, from British and Irish to Italian and Polish, to Vietnamese and Cambodian. And this Parliament building displays an original copy of the Magna Carta, I'm told, one of only four such manuscripts to have survived to this day. The U.S. National Archives is home to another of those original manuscripts.

And I can think of no more powerful symbol of our shared commitments to the rights of the individual, to the rule of law and to the government of consent, by consent of the people.

With our common ancestries and shared ideals, Americans and Australians also find other similarities. Each of our countries spans a continent rich in agriculture and minerals resources; spectacular natural beauty abounds in fantastic variety in both our nations as well. And, to be frank, our people think big. And their biggest ideas are the ones we share — the belief in the indivisibility of human freedom and the willingness to struggle and sacrifice for the peace and security of other nations.

This year marks the 50th anniversary of the fateful battle of the Coral Sea. And we remember the courage and the fighting skill of the Australian and American naval forces. Their valor spared Australia from invasion and stemmed the tide of totalitarianism.

In Korea and Vietnam, Australians and Americans again joined forces. Their sacrifices were not in vain. [South] Korea is a democracy, setting a standard for free market development worldwide. Long-suffering Cambodia now has the hope of a durable peace and free elections. Even Vietnam is opening to the world, seeking reintegration with the dynamic market economies of the region.

In the Persian Gulf we stood together against Saddam Hussein's aggression. Indeed, the first two coalition partners in a joint boarding exercise to enforce the United Nations' resolutions were Australians from the HMAS *Darwin* and Americans from the USS *Brewerton*.

During the war the joint defense facilities here in Australia played an invaluable role in detecting launches of Iraqi Scud missiles. And today two of the three navies represented in operations enforcing the embargo against Iraq are those of Australia and the United States of America.

But even as we recall our struggles and successes, we must now look forward to the opportunity to shape our shared destiny.

First, we face together the challenge of economic opportunity and growth, creating jobs for our people and for their families.

And, second, we face new but no less exacting challenges to our security — the threats of regional conflicts and proliferation of the weapons of mass destruction.

And, third, we face the exciting task of fostering the remarkable momentum for democracy and freedom that swept the world these past few years.

A strong America has been central to the triumph of free markets and free people, and I am confident that the United States will continue to have the conviction and the capacity to be a force for good and that a new era of economic opportunity will unfold with enhanced opportunities for peace.

The coming era promises unparalleled potential for economic growth in the nations of the Pacific.

In 1990 the Asia-Pacific region accounted for a total of $300 billion in two-way commerce with the United States, a total nearly one-third larger than America's volume of trade across the Atlantic. This region is the fastest-growing market in the world, and still there are voices on both sides of the Pacific calling for economic isolationism.

And while for some nations, including Australia and the United States, these are tough, hard economic times, we both know protectionism is a fundamentally bankrupt notion. Make no mistake, America will continue to stand for open trade and open markets. And trade means jobs, means good jobs — at home and abroad, and I'm sure it comes as no surprise that my highest priority as president of the United States is to promote economic growth and jobs for our people.

And that goal is fully consistent with economic growth and jobs for Australians. And you and I know that open markets generate growth, that international trade is not simply a zero-sum game.

And you also know that the nations who share the rewards of a vibrant and growing international trading system must also share the responsibilities.

Australia has stood as a true leader in efforts to achieve success in the Uruguay Round of the [General Agreement on Tariffs and Trade] GATT negotiations, and you brought great skill and energy in seeking deep cuts in trade-distorting agricultural subsidies.

Progress on agriculture is the key to the success of the GATT talks. And your farmers are not alone in feeling the pain caused by the heavy subsidies of the European Community [EC]. Our wheat production dropped by almost 30 percent last year.

But I am also aware of the concern such United States' trade programs as this Export Enhancement Program [EEP] can cause Australian farmers. Our EEP program has one and only one objective, and that is to force the EC to stop its avalanche of subsidized exports.

And the fact is that the EC subsidizes over 10 times the amount of farm exports that we do. And, moreover, our program seeks to minimize the effects on Australia and other non-subsidizing nations.

While I don't like having to use these remedies, I will safeguard the interests of American farmers. And without EEP the European Community would absorb additional markets, forcing out those who can compete fairly, farmers in countries like

Australia and the United States.

We both know, all of us know, that the real answer is what our two governments are doing — working hard for a historic new GATT arrangement that cuts back subsidies, especially for exports. And that's why the U.S. is committed to working with GATT Director [Arthur] Dunkel's new text.

We believe his draft moves us closer to finally concluding an agreement. While not perfect, it makes an important contribution. And the international trading system is too important to pass up this opportunity.

I trust and hope that Australia and other Pacific nations will join us to instill additional momentum in the Uruguay Round negotiations when they resume later this month.

This is the best comprehensive approach that we can offer to our hard-working farmers and ranchers.

We also see the potential for using regional organizations to expand and indeed liberalize trade around the globe. We are especially encouraged by Australia's leadership in the APEC, in the Asia-Pacific Economic Cooperation process.

The success of the November APEC ministerial in Seoul [South Korea] was proof that APEC is emerging as the economic forum in the Pacific, and is increasingly fostering a sense of community around the Pacific Rim.

North America — Mexico, the United States and Canada — is part of this community.

And so let me just assure you, every one of you, both sides of this aisle, that the North America Free Trade Agreement will not become an exclusive trading bloc. It will lower internal barriers without raising external barriers. And our growth will help stimulate yours just as growth in Asia will spur our exports.

We also can do more bilaterally to expand trade, and that's why I'm proposing a United States-Australia trade and investment framework agreement, one way to enhance our already strong economic engagement. And that's our agenda, to expand exports and growth through reducing trade barriers, whether globally, regionally or bilaterally.

Clearly with the dramatic changes in the world, we must adapt to new security realities as well, but let me simply pledge to you, our friends, no matter what changes may come about in the defense expenditures in the United States or in the nature of the threats to international peace, the U.S.-Australian alliance is fundamental to the stability of the Asia-Pacific region.

I understand that there is some concern in Asia about America's commitment, given our imminent departure from Subic Bay [Naval Station] in the Philippines. Let me put it plainly. I have served in Asia personally in time of war and in time of peace, and with changing times, our posture is going to change to suit different needs. But our role and our purpose as a Pacific power will remain constant. It is

important that the people of Australia understand this. We intend to remain engaged no matter whatever the changing security arrangements of our time.

And yes, we've talked about it here today with the prime minister [Paul Keating], with the leader of the opposition [Dr. John Hewson], with others. The Cold War is over, but the threat of communism, which for so many decades occupied our energies, is now replaced by the instabilities of ethnic rivalries and regional conflicts.

And yes, the Soviet Union as we've known it is history. It's a new era, but like Australia, the United States has fought three wars in Asia over the past 50 years, and we know that our security is inextricably linked to stability across the Pacific, and we will not put that security and stability at risk.

I can assure you that the United States intends to retain the appropriate military presence to protect its allies and to counter threats to peace. Just recently in the Persian Gulf, we witnessed that the dangerous combination of volatile regional conflicts and weapons of mass destruction requires our constant attention.

And so, I salute Australia's leadership in stemming the threat of chemical, biological and nuclear weapons. It's your children and the children of the entire world who will grow up in a safer world, thanks to such efforts.

Australia and the United States are also working to end another longstanding and tragic regional conflict. Our combined initiatives in the United Nations have been major factors in the progress toward peace and free elections in Cambodia. Both of us have now re-established official representation in Phnom Penh in order to move the peace process forward.

Australia is making an additional contribution by sending a senior military officer to head the U.N. peacekeeping force in Cambodia. And I am proud of our collective efforts to end the nightmare in Cambodia and usher in a new era of hope and rebuilding.

And finally, American and Australian aspirations for the future are evident in our increasing cooperation on such matters as environmental protection, educational and social issues. We can take pride in our governments' joint actions toward conservation of the tropical forests, protecting endangered species and promoting technologies for clean-burning coal. Australia also plays a leading role in the international fight against illicit drugs. And I know I speak for millions of American parents in expressing thanks for your efforts to fight drug abuse, to fight drug trafficking.

I believe the next generations of Australians and Americans will grow even closer. I see no threat to that at all. And I foresee a steady expansion of travel and cultural exchanges in years to come. Australia's natural beauty, of which I've seen regrettably little this trip, is really sensational, a powerful magnet for American tourists.

But more than this, it is the spirit of

your country that earns Australia so much admiration in our country, in America, and indeed around the world. Your artists' contributions to film and dance and music have whetted our appetites for more and more things Australian. U.S. television carries Australian-rules football, and many Americans enjoy the rough and tumble of hardhitting with reckless abandon.

We have something similar — we call it politics in the United States.

But I credit the clear air of Australia for its effect on one of the freshest minds now working in Washington, and I'm speaking about our secretary of Education, Lamar Alexander. In 1987, after completing eight years as governor of Tennessee, Lamar took his wife and children to spend a half a year in this beautiful country. And now that he's joined my Cabinet as secretary of Education, Lamar Alexander is working for revolutionary changes to improve our schools. And this, too, is part of our program to make America competitive and strong and help it grow.

Secretary Alexander is promoting innovative ideas that he saw in practice right here in Australia — for instance, the large measure of freedom that Australians have in choosing among private and religious or state-operated schools. And when we succeed with some of these reforms, we'll thank pathfinders such as Australians for their example.

Of course, we've always shared fraternal ties and the spirit of freedom ever since an American vessel named *Philadelphia* became the first trading ship to call at Sydney's Port Jackson in 1792. Almost a century later, Mark Twain visited Australia and spoke for all Americans when he said, "You have a spirit of independence here which cannot be overpraised."

And 50 years ago, in the Coral Sea, Australians and Americans paid a high price for freedom, but they proved to the world that the future belongs to the brave and the bold. For the half century since, we have deepened our friendship, our economic interdependence and our collaboration on mutual defense. And now more clearly than ever, we can see a hopeful future for the far-flung kinsmen of Australia and America and for all who share those fundamental ideals that we hold dear.

We're prepared to work as partners in the next century, to break new ground for freedom, cooperation and economic progress.

For me this has been a great honor. For Barbara and me, it has been a sheer pleasure to be with you all here for these short 2½ days. But this hospitality of the Australian people is indescribable. I couldn't possibly tell you how emotional I feel about it.

So let me simply say thank you again for the extraordinary honor of allowing me to address this distinguished Parliament. May your debates be lively and full of friendship and affection, as they once in a while are. And may God bless you all. And may the Lord smile on the kinship and friendship of Australia and the United States of America. Thank you very, very much. ∎

## TRADE TALKS

# Outline of Mutual Agreement To End U.S. - Japan Discord

*At the conclusion of President Bush's talks in Tokyo, Japan and the United States jointly issued an "action plan" to help erase friction caused by the huge trade imbalance between the countries. Following is a summary of the main points. References to the fiscal year refer to the Japanese fiscal year, which runs from April 1 to March 31:*

**Auto parts:** Japanese automobile manufacturers set goals to procure $19 billion in auto parts from the United States by fiscal year 1994, up from $10 billion in 1990.

Car factories of Japanese affiliates in the United States set a goal of $15 billion in purchases, up from about $7 billion. Japanese imports of parts from the United States would double to $4 billion.

Japanese automakers operating in the United States are expected to increase their local procurement of parts from 50 percent to about 70 percent by 1994, with a corresponding decrease in imports from Japan from 50 percent to about 30 percent.

**Research and development:** Japanese automakers expect to expand research and development centers in the United States from 1,400 employees to 2,200 employees in "the near future." Japanese automakers also pledged to assist U.S. parts suppliers to develop long-term business relationships with Japan.

**Auto sales:** The Japanese agreed to sell U.S.-made cars in their dealerships, setting a target of about 20,000 more a year — beyond the roughly 35,000 a year now sold — and made it clear that their dealers can sell autos made by more than one manufacturer.

Japanese automakers pledged an increased willingness to handle and help expand sale of U.S. cars and announced cooperative measures, including providing space to display U.S. automobiles at seven showrooms in the metropolitan Tokyo area. The Japanese government said it would increase budgetary allocations for such events as foreign automobile shows in Japan.

**Electronics imports:** A group of 23 Japanese auto, electronics and machine industries also agreed to import $10 billion more from other countries in fiscal year 1993 than they did in fiscal 1990.

**Incentives for trade:** The Japanese government announced tax and financial incentives to promote imports to, and investments in, Japan, such as low-interest loans.

In addition, 88 companies and 22 industrial associations, which account for approximately 50 percent of Japanese trade, expressed support, and most made voluntary plans, to promote imports and local procurement when operating outside Japan.

**Competitiveness study:** Japan's Fair Trade Commission will study the competitiveness of the automobile parts, glass and paper products industries.

**Uruguay trade talks:** The Japanese government stated its determination to successfully conclude the Uruguay Round of multilateral trade talks and to negotiate improved market access for goods and services. But the Japanese government did not explicitly say it will ease its ban on rice imports.

**Computers:** The Japanese government will initiate a plan to expand public sector purchases of foreign computer products and services in fair and open competition, but no specific measures were announced.

The government reaffirmed its commitment to make "further efforts" for increased market access in semiconductors and long-term cooperative relationships between Japanese and U.S. companies.

**Paper and glass:** The United States and Japanese governments said they would agree by the end of March on measures to "substantially increase" market access for foreign firms exporting paper products to Japan.

The government also will work to "substantially increase" market access for competitive imports of flat glass, including encouraging Japanese companies to increase imports and facilitating the efforts of foreign firms to increase imports of flat glass.

**Certification problems:** In addition to the automotive standards issues, Japan's Office of the Trade and Investment Ombudsman has resolved or will resolve 49 non-auto complaints about standards, certification, testing and important procedures issues raised by American companies. The steps are to improve market access by U.S. exporters in areas such as industrial machinery, chemicals, transportation equipment, processed food, cosmetics and pharmaceuticals. ■

## JAPANESE TRADE TALKS

# Automakers Praise 'First Step' But Lament Lack of Progress

*At the conclusion of the Japanese-American talks, several American auto executives met with reporters to discuss results. They included Ford Chairman Harold "Red" Poling, General Motors Chairman Robert Stempel and Jack Reilly, chairman of the Parts Manufacturers Association and of Tenneco. Following are excerpts from the Reuter transcript:*

**Q:** Can you tell us, gentlemen, each of you — do you feel that you're going home essentially empty-handed?

**STEMPEL:** . . . I think what we did today was start a process. We spent a lot of time in meetings. As you know, the automotive side was very active. I think the president was very clear on that when he indicated that the first steps were in place. We've had lengthy discussions, hard discussions. We did not have an automotive agreement. And the Japanese were very clear on that. . . . We had the beginning of a process.

And the process from their side was a first step. Red [Poling] put forth, on behalf of all of us, a very strong proposal, very clearly supporting the president when he said that we really have to work on this chronic trade imbalance. And our proposal was somewhat different, and we feel that it is a first step and a very important step. Red and I will be taking some actions here to again have a follow-up meeting on this. . . .

**POLING:** I would characterize it as good news and bad news. The good news is I think that this is one of the first times that we've had business and government in the United States coordinating their efforts on a serious national problem. I think that's very positive.

Second, I would say that I believe the message was conveyed to the Japanese of the seriousness of the problem in the strongest language possible. I think the president indicated that it was a serious problem, that progress had to be made, and that all resources would be used to assure that progress was made.

[Commerce Secretary Robert A.] Mosbacher reinforced that in every meeting that we participated in, and in the detail, the discussions with the government officials, [Commerce Under Secretary for International Trade J.] Michael Farren was equally firm. So I think that's the good news.

The bad news is, I think, the proposals that are on the table, as far as the auto industry is concerned, are inadequate, and as Bob indicated the agreement is that a process is in place and additional work has to be done.

**REILLY:** . . . My comment would be that I think on the parts issue there was some progress, but it was definitely insufficient. . . .

**Q:** Mr. Poling, I believe we heard you say when you were leaving that, you were quoted as saying, "I am not smiling."

**POLING:** That's right.

**Q:** You obviously are not very happy with what you heard here, and I was told that you were probably the strongest of all in your wording to the Japanese. Why are you not happy?

**POLING:** I would have been pleased if I had seen an indication of a commitment on the part of the Japanese to a specific objective in terms of a reduction in the imbalance of trade with our country. The fact that we did not have that leaves me unsmiling.

\* \* \*

**Q:** Can you tell us exactly — when you say there was no agreement — what were the issues, what did you put on the table, and what were the issues they did not agree upon, and was this proposal in the name of the administration, the White House?

**STEMPEL:** You heard the president today. You heard him very strongly say that the chronic trade imbalance between the United States and Japan has to be corrected. He made that very clear. . . . And certainly the industry made that very clear. We were not satisfied that that issue of the trade imbalance was fully addressed. What has happened is clearly a recognition on both sides that the trade imbalance is something that cannot be dismissed. We've agreed that we have to go after that aggressively. . . .

**Q:** Can you just tell us specifically — specifically what proposals were you putting on the table they rejected?

**POLING:** They did not reject it. . . . We have suggested that it would be appropriate for Japan to initiate actions to get the balance of trade reasonably in balance over a period of five years, starting with the 20 percent reduction in 1992. That was the specific proposal. They did not reject it. They did not respond.

**Q:** What is your level of dissatisfaction? Are you dissatisfied enough that you will urge [Sen. Donald W.] Riegle [Jr., D-Mich.] and [House Majority Leader Richard A.] Gephardt [D-Mo.] to [push forward with] their bill? [The bill would require Japan to reduce its trade deficit with the United State by 20 percent per year in each of the next five years and would set a limit on sales of Japanese autos in the United States.]

**POLING:** I would like to see a little more about the process and what is accomplished as a result of the process. I think that the alternative of legislative action is always there. I would like to think that we can accomplish it without it.

**STEMPEL:** I think that's our clear view. We definitely want to accomplish this. Both Red and I feel if we can do it on a country-to-

country basis, industry-to-industry basis, we are far better off than fences and regulation. So clearly, we're going to work to that end.

**Q:** . . . Are [Gephardt and Riegle] going to go ahead with this?

**POLING:** My guess is they'll go ahead.

\* \* \*

**Q:** I just wondered if you all felt it was worthwhile having made this trip?

**POLING:** From my standpoint, and I'll let Bob and Jack speak for themselves, I think it was positive. I have felt for some time that we have not had the relationship between business and government in the United States in the interests of our country's goals, and I think it's time we get it. I think we have begun. And from that standpoint, I think it was very positive.

**STEMPEL:** I would agree with that. I think this was an important first step. We generally see the Japanese government and industry together in our country when they come in to do business with the U.S. For Red and myself, this was the first time we had the full support of the U.S. Department of Commerce and the president, and so it's very positive in the sense that we acted as one and really came with some strength. . . .

**REILLY:** My comment would be not only is it positive, I think it was absolutely critical, and a step in the right direction. . . .

**Q:** Would you say that the figures in the proposal of the Japanese side were a surprise to you? [Japanese automakers will seek to buy $19 billion annually in U.S. auto parts by 1994 and boost imports of U.S. autos by 20,000 a year.] Would you describe them as almost embarrassingly low?

**POLING:** You're pretty close.

\* \* \*

**Q:** Mr. Reilly or Mr. Poling, do you believe as a result of what the president has styled a successful trade mission, and your own statement that it's an important beginning, that it would render what Congressman Gephardt says he might introduce, the Gephardt plan on [trade] deficit reduction, do you think that would be counterproductive?

**POLING:** No, I don't think it would render it counterproductive. I think that unless action is taken by Japan to address the serious problem of the bilateral deficit, that risk is always there. And the longer it takes for a specific action to be proposed, the greater the risk.

**STEMPEL:** The issue of the Congress acting, I think, is a natural reaction to the fact that they are seeing their constituents out of work, out of jobs, seeing manufacturing decay, and obviously want to do something. . . .

So we are concerned about that. I think it's very natural for them to take a protectionist stance.

I think history has shown us that protective trade barriers are not the best thing for a free global trade system. Certainly the president today was very eloquent on that point, pointing out that it was much better to have free and fair trade, unencumbered by rules and restrictions. So we very clearly are in favor of that. ∎

## THE STATE OF THE UNION

# Bush Reviews Planned Cuts, Offers Economic Spurs

*Sounding patriotic note, president calls on Congress to pass his pending proposals in key areas*

*Following is the text of President Bush's State of the Union address, delivered to a joint session of Congress on Jan. 28.*

Mr. Speaker, Mr. President, distinguished members of Congress, honored guests and fellow citizens: Thank you very much for that warm reception.

You know, the big buildup this address has had, I wanted to make sure it would be a big hit, but I couldn't convince Barbara to deliver it for me.

I see the Speaker and the vice president are laughing. They saw what I did in Japan, and they're just happy they're sitting behind me.

I mean to speak tonight of big things, of big changes and the promises they hold, and of some big problems and how together we can solve them and move our country forward as the undisputed leader of the age.

We gather tonight at a dramatic and deeply promising time in our history and in the history of man on Earth.

For in the past 12 months, the world has known changes of almost biblical proportions. And even now, months after the failed coup that doomed a failed system, I am not sure we have absorbed the full impact, the full import of what happened. But communism died this year.

Even as president, with the most fascinating possible vantage point, there were times when I was so busy helping to manage progress and helping to lead change, that I didn't always show the joy that was in my heart.

But the biggest thing that has happened in the world in my life — in our lives — is this: By the grace of God, America won the Cold War.

I mean to speak this evening of the changes that can take place in our country now that we can stop making the sacrifices we had to make when we had an avowed enemy that was a superpower. Now we can look homeward even more and move to set right what needs to be set right.

And I will speak of those things.

But let me tell you something I've been thinking these past few months. It's a kind of roll call of honor. For the Cold War didn't "end" — it was won.

And I think of those who won it, in places like Korea and Vietnam. And some of

them didn't come back. And back then, they were heroes; but this year they were victors.

The long roll call — all the G.I. Joes and Janes, all the ones who fought faithfully for freedom, who hit the ground and sucked the dust and knew their share of horror.

This may seem frivolous — I don't mean it so — but it's moving to me how the world saw them.

The world saw not only their special valor but their special style — their rambunctious, optimistic bravery, their do-or-die unity unhampered by class or race or region. What a group we've put forth, for generations now — from the ones who wrote "Kilroy was here" on the walls of German stalags to those who left signs in the Iraq desert that said "I saw Elvis." What a group of kids we've sent out into the world.

And there's another to be singled out — though it may seem inelegant. I mean a mass of people called "the American taxpayer." No one ever thinks to thank the American people who pay a country's bills or an alliance's bills. But for half a century now the American people have shouldered the burden and paid taxes that were higher than they would have been to support a defense that was bigger than it would have been if imperial communism had never existed.

But it did. Doesn't anymore.

And here is a fact that I wouldn't mind the world acknowledging: The American taxpayer bore the brunt of the burden and deserves a hunk of the glory.

And so now, for the first time in 35 years, our strategic bombers stand down. No longer are they on round-the-clock alert. Tomorrow our children will go to school and study history and how plants grow. And they won't have, as my children did, air raid drills in which they crawl under their desks and cover their heads in case of nuclear war. My grandchildren don't have to do that and won't have the bad dreams children had once in decades past. There are still threats. But the long, drawn-out dread is over.

A year ago tonight I spoke to you at a moment of high peril. American forces had just unleashed Operation Desert Storm. And after 40 days in the desert skies and four days on the ground, the men and women of America's armed forces and our allies accomplished the goals that I declared and you endorsed:

We liberated Kuwait.

Soon after, the Arab world and Israel sat down to talk seriously and comprehensively about peace — an historic first. And soon after that, at Christmas, the last American hostages came home. Our policies were vindicated.

Much good can come from the prudent use of power. And much good can come of this: A world once divided into two armed camps now recognizes one sole and pre-eminent power — the United States of America.

And they regard this with no dread. For the world trusts us with power — and the world is right. They trust us to be fair and restrained; they trust us to be on the side of decency. And they trust us to do what's right.

I use those words advisedly. A few days after the war began, I received a telegram from Joanne Speicher, the wife of the first pilot killed in the gulf, Lt. Cmdr. Scott Speicher. Even in her grief, she wanted me to know that some day when her children were old enough, she would tell them "that their father went away to war because it was the right thing to do."

And she said it all: It was the right thing to do.

And we did it together. There were honest differences here in this chamber. But when the war began, you put partisanship aside and we supported our troops.

This is still a time for pride — but this is no time to boast. For problems face us, and we must stand together once again and solve them — and not let our country down.

Two years ago, I began planning cuts in military spending that reflected the changes of the new era. But now, this year, with imperial communism gone, that process can be accelerated.

Tonight I can tell you of dramatic changes in our strategic nuclear force. These are actions we are taking on our own — because they are the right thing to do.

After completing 20 planes for which we have begun procurement, we will shut down further production of the B-2 bomber.

We will cancel the small ICBM [intercontinental ballistic missile] program. We will cease production of new warheads for our sea-based ballistic missiles. We will stop all new production of the Peacekeeper missile. And we will not purchase any more

advanced cruise missiles.

This weekend I will meet at Camp David with Boris Yeltsin of the Russian Federation. I have informed President Yeltsin that if the Commonwealth — the former Soviet Union — will eliminate all land-based multiple warhead ballistic missiles, I will do the following:

We will eliminate all Peacekeeper missiles. We will reduce the number of warheads on Minuteman missiles to one and reduce the number of warheads on our sea-based missiles by about one-third. And we will convert a substantial portion of our strategic bombers to primarily conventional use.

President Yeltsin's early response has been very positive, and I expect our talk at Camp David to be fruitful.

I want you to know that for half a century, American presidents have longed to make such decisions and say such words. But even in the midst of celebration we must keep caution as a friend.

For the world is still a dangerous place. Only the dead have seen the end of conflict. And though yesterday's challenges are behind us, tomorrow's are being born.

The secretary of Defense recommended these cuts after consultation with the Joint Chiefs of Staff. And I make them with confidence. But do not misunderstand me.

The reductions I have approved will save us an additional $50 billion over the next five years. By 1997 we will have cut defense by 30 percent since I took office. These cuts are deep and you must know my resolve: this deep and no deeper.

To do less would be insensible to progress — but to do more would be ignorant of history.

We must not go back to the days of "the hollow army." We cannot repeat the mistakes made twice in this century, when armistice was followed by recklessness and defense was purged as if the world were permanently safe.

I remind you this evening that I have asked for your support in funding a program to protect our country from limited nuclear missile attack. We must have this protection because too many people in too many countries have access to nuclear arms.

And I urge you again to pass the Strategic Defense Initiative — SDI.

There are those who say that now we can turn away from the world, that we have no special role, no special place.

But we are the United States of America, the leader of the West that has become the leader of the world.

As long as I am president, I will continue to lead in support of freedom everywhere — not out of arrogance, not out of altruism, but for the safety and security of our children.

This is a fact: Strength in the pursuit of peace is no vice; isolationism in the pursuit of security is no virtue.

Now to our troubles at home. They are not all economic, but the primary problem is our economy. And there are some good signs: Inflation, that thief, is down; and interest rates are down. But unemployment is too high, some industries are in trouble, and growth is not what it should be.

Let me tell you right from the start and right from the heart: I know we're in hard times, but I know something else — this will not stand.

My friends in this chamber, we can bring the same courage and sense of common purpose to the economy that we brought to Desert Storm. And we can defeat hard times together.

I believe you will help. One reason is that you're patriots, and you want the best for your country. And I believe that in your hearts you want to put partisanship aside and get the job done — because it's the right thing to do.

The power of America rests in a stirring but simple idea — that people will do great things if only you set them free.

Well, we're going to set the economy free, for if this age of miracles and wonders has taught us anything, it's that if we can change the world, we can change America.

We must encourage investment. We must make it easier for people to invest money and create new products, new industries and new jobs. We must clear away the obstacles to growth — high taxes, high regulation, red tape and, yes, wasteful government spending.

None of this will happen with a snap of the fingers — but it will happen. And the test of a plan isn't whether it's called new or dazzling. The American people aren't impressed by gimmicks; they're smarter on this score than all of us in this room. The only test of a plan is, is it sound and will it work.

We must have a short-term plan to address our immediate needs and heat up the economy. And we need a longer-term plan to keep the combustion going and to guarantee our place in the world economy.

There are certain things that a president can do without Congress — and I am going to do them.

I have this evening asked major Cabinet departments and federal agencies to institute a 90-day moratorium on any new federal regulations that could hinder growth.

In those 90 days, major departments and agencies will carry out a top-to-bottom review of all regulations, old and new, to stop the ones that will hurt growth and speed up those that will help growth.

Further, for the untold number of hard-working, responsible American workers and businessmen and women who've been forced to go without needed bank loans — the banking credit crunch must end.

I won't neglect my responsibility for sound regulations that serve the public good, but regulatory overkill must be stopped.

And I have instructed our government regulators to stop it.

I have directed Cabinet departments and federal agencies to speed up pro-growth expenditures as quickly as possible. This should put an extra $10 billion into the economy in the next six months. And our new transportation bill provides more than $150 billion for construction and maintenance projects that are vital to our growth and well-being. That means jobs building roads, jobs building bridges and jobs building railways.

And I have this evening directed the secretary of the Treasury to change the federal tax withholding tables. With this change, millions of Americans from whom the government withholds more than necessary can now choose to have the government withhold less from their paychecks. Something tells me a number of taxpayers may take us up on this one. This initiative could return about $25 billion back into our economy over the next 12 months — money people can use to help pay for clothing, college or to get a new car.

And, finally, working with the Federal Reserve, we will continue to support monetary policy that keeps both interest rates and inflation down.

These are the things that I can do.

And now, members of Congress, let me tell you what you can do for your country.

You must pass the other elements of my plan to meet our economic needs. Everyone knows that investment spurs recovery. And I am proposing this evening a change in the alternative minimum tax and the creation of a new 15 percent investment tax allowance.

This will encourage businesses to accelerate investment and bring people back to work.

Real estate has led our economy out of almost all the tough times we've ever had. Once building starts, carpenters and plumbers work, people buy homes and take out mortgages.

My plan would modify the passive-loss rule for active real estate developers.

And it would make it easier for pension plans to purchase real estate.

For those Americans who dream of buying a first home and who can't quite afford it, my plan would allow first-time buyers to withdraw savings from IRA without penalty — and provide a $5,000 tax credit for the first purchase of that home.

And, finally, my immediate plan calls on Congress to give crucial help to people who own a home, to everyone who has a business, or a farm, or a single investment.

This time, at this hour, I cannot take no for an answer. You must cut the capital gains tax on the people of our country.

Never has an issue been more demagogued by its opponents.

But the demagogues are wrong — and they know it. Sixty percent of the people who benefit from lower capital gains have incomes under $50,000. A cut in the capital gains tax increases jobs and helps just about everyone in our country.

And so I'm asking you to cut the capital gains tax to a maximum of 15.4 percent.

And I'll tell you, those of you who say,

oh, no, someone who's comfortable may benefit from this. You kind of remind me of the old definition of the Puritan, who wouldn't sleep at night worrying that somehow someone somewhere was out having a good time.

The opponents of this measure — and those who've authored various so-called soak-the-rich bills that are floating around this chamber — should be reminded of something: When they aim at the big guy they usually hit the little guy. And maybe it's time that stopped.

This then is my short-term plan. Your part, members of Congress, requires enactment of these common-sense proposals that will have a strong effect on the economy without breaking the budget agreement and without raising tax rates.

While my plan is being passed and kicking in, we've got to care for those in trouble today. I have provided up to $4.4 billion in my budget to extend federal unemployment benefits. I ask for congressional action right away. And I thank the committee —

Well, at last.

And let's be frank — let me level with you. I know, and you know, that my plan is unveiled in a political season. And I know, and you know, that everything I propose will be viewed by some in merely partisan terms. But I ask you to know what is in my heart: And my aim is to increase our nation's good. And I am doing what I think is right; I am proposing what I know will help.

I pride myself that I am a prudent man, and I believe that patience is a virtue. But I understand that politics is for some a game — and that sometimes the game is to stop all progress and then decry the lack of improvement.

But let me tell you: Far more important than my political future — and far more important than yours — is the well-being of our country.

And members of this chamber are practical people, and I know you won't resent some practical advice: When people put their party's fortunes, whatever the party, whatever side of this aisle, before the public good, they court defeat not only for their country, but for themselves. And they will certainly deserve it.

And I submit my plan tomorrow. And I am asking you to pass it by March 20. And I ask the American people to let you know they want this action by March 20.

From the day after that, if it must be: The battle is joined.

And you know when principle is at stake, I relish a good fair fight.

I said my plan has two parts, and it does. And it is the second part that is the heart of the matter. For it's not enough to get an immediate burst. We need long-term improvement in our economic position.

We all know that the key to our economic future is to ensure that America continues as the economic leader of the world. We have that in our power.

Here, then, is my long-term plan to guarantee our future.

First, trade: We will work to break down the walls that stop world trade. We will work to open markets everywhere. And in our major trade negotiations, I will continue pushing to eliminate tariffs and subsidies that damage America's farmers and workers.

And we'll get more good American jobs within our own hemisphere through the North American Free Trade Agreement and through the Enterprise for the Americas Initiative.

But changes are here, and more are coming. The workplace of the future will demand more highly skilled workers than ever — more people who are computer literate, highly educated.

And we must be the world's leader in education. And we must revolutionize America's schools.

My America 2000 education strategy will help us reach that goal. My plan will give parents more choice, give teachers more flexibility and help communities create New American schools.

Thirty states across the nation have established America 2000 programs. Hundreds of cities and towns have joined in.

And now Congress must join this great movement: Pass my proposals for New American schools.

That was my second long-term proposal.

And here's my third: We must make common-sense investments that will help us compete long term in the marketplace. We must encourage research and development. And my plan is to make the R&D [research and development] tax credit permanent and to provide record levels of support — over $76 billion this year alone — for people who will explore the promise of emerging technologies.

Fourth, we must do something about crime and drugs.

And it is time for a major renewed investment in fighting violent street crime. It saps our strength and hurts our faith in our society and in our future together.

Surely a tired woman on her way to work at 6 in the morning on a subway deserves the right to get there safely.

And surely it's true that everyone who changes his or her life because of crime — from those afraid to go out at night to those afraid to walk in the parks they pay for — surely these people have been denied a basic civil right.

It is time to restore it.

Congress, pass my comprehensive crime bill.

It is tough on criminals and supportive of police — and it has been languishing in these hallowed halls for years now. Pass it. Help your country.

And, fifth, I ask you tonight to fund our HOPE housing proposal and to pass my enterprise zone legislation, which will get businesses into the inner city. We must empower the poor with the pride that comes from owning a home, getting a job, becoming a part of things.

My plan would encourage real estate construction by extending tax incentives for mortgage revenue bonds and low-income housing.

And I ask tonight for record expenditures for the program that helps children born into want move into excellence: Head Start.

Step six: We must reform our health-care system.

For this, too, bears on whether or not we can compete in the world. American health costs have been exploding. This year America will spend over $800 billion on health. And that's expected to grow to 1.6 trillion by the end of the decade. We simply cannot afford this.

The cost of health care shows up not only in your family budget but in the price of everything we buy and everything we sell. When health coverage for a fellow on an assembly line costs thousands of dollars, the cost goes into the products he makes — and you pay the bill.

We must make a choice.

Now, some pretend we can have it both ways. They call it "play or pay." But that expensive approach is unstable. It will mean higher taxes, fewer jobs and eventually a system under complete government control.

Really, there are only two options: We can move toward a nationalized system — which will restrict patient choice — a system which will restrict patient choice in picking a doctor and force the government to ration services arbitrarily — and what we'll get is patients in long lines, indifferent service and a huge new tax burden; or we can reform our own private health-care system, which still gives us, for all its flaws, the best-quality health care in the world.

Well, let's build on our strengths.

My plan provides insurance security for all Americans — while preserving and increasing the idea of choice. We make basic health insurance affordable for all low-income people not now covered. And we do it by providing a health insurance tax credit of up to $3,750 for each low-income family.

And the middle class gets new help too. And, by reforming the health insurance market, my plan assures that Americans will have access to basic health insurance even if they change jobs or develop serious health problems.

We must bring costs under control, preserve quality, preserve choice and reduce the people's nagging daily worry about health insurance. My plan, the details of which I will announce very shortly, does just that.

And, seventh, we must get the federal deficit under control.

We now have in law enforceable spending caps and a requirement that we pay for the programs we create.

There are those in Congress who would ease that discipline now. But I cannot let them do it — and I won't.

My plan would freeze all domestic discretionary budget authority — which means "no more next year than this year."

I will not tamper with Social Security.

But I would put real caps on the growth of uncontrolled spending. And I would also freeze federal domestic government employment.

And with the help of Congress, my plan will get rid of 246 programs that don't deserve federal funding.

Some of them have noble titles, but none of them is indispensable. We can get rid of each and every one of them.

You know, it's time we rediscovered a "home truth" the American people have never forgotten: This government is too big and spends too much.

I call upon Congress to adopt a measure that will help put an end to the annual ritual of filling the budget with pork-barrel appropriations. Every year the press has a field day making fun of outrageous examples — Lawrence Welk museum, research grant for Belgian endive.

We all know how these things get into the budget. And maybe you need someone to help you say no. I know how to say it. And I know what I need to make it stick. Give me the same thing 43 governors have — the line item veto and let me help you control spending.

We must put an end to unfinanced federal government mandates. These are the requirements Congress puts on our cities, counties and states — without supplying the money.

And if Congress passes a mandate, it should be forced to pay for it and balance the cost with savings elsewhere. After all, a mandate just increases someone else's burden — and that means higher taxes at the state and local level.

Step eight: Congress should enact the bold reform proposals that are still awaiting congressional action — bank reform, civil justice reform, tort reform and my national energy strategy.

Finally, we must strengthen the family — because it is the family that has the greatest bearing on our future.

When Barbara holds an AIDS baby in her arms and reads to children, she's saying to every person in this country: Family matters.

And I am announcing tonight a new Commission on America's Urban Families. I've asked Missouri's governor, John Ashcroft, to be chairman, former Dallas Mayor Annette Strauss to be co-chair. You know, I had mayors from the League of Cities in the other day at the White House, and they told me something striking. They said that every one of them, Republicans and Democrats, agreed on one thing: that the major cause of the problems of the cities is the dissolution of the family.

And they asked for this commission, and they were right to ask, because it's time to determine what we can do to keep families together, strong and sound.

There's one thing we can do right away: Ease the burden of rearing a child. I ask you tonight to raise the personal exemption by $500 per child for every family. For a family with four kids, that's an increase of $2,000. And this is a good start in the right direction, and it's what we can afford.

It's time to allow families to deduct the interest they pay on student loans.

I am asking you to do just that. And I'm asking you to allow people to use money from their IRAs to pay medical and education expenses — all without penalties.

And I'm asking for more. Ask American parents what they dislike about how things are in our country and chances are good that pretty soon they'll get to welfare. Americans are the most generous people on earth. But we have to go back to the insight of [President] Franklin Roosevelt who, when he spoke of what became the welfare program, warned that it must not become "a narcotic" and a "subtle destroyer" of the spirit.

Welfare was never meant to be a lifestyle; it was never meant to be a habit; it was never supposed to be passed from generation to generation like a legacy.

It's time to replace the assumptions of the welfare state and help reform the welfare system.

States throughout the country are beginning to operate with new assumptions: that when able-bodied people receive government assistance, they have responsibilities to the taxpayer, a responsibility to seek work, education or job training; a responsibility to get their lives in order; a responsibility to hold their families together and refrain from having children out of wedlock — and a responsibility to obey the law.

We are going to help this movement. Often, state reform requires waiving certain federal regulations. I will act to make that process easier and quicker for every state that asks our help.

And I want to add, as we make these changes, we work together to improve this system, that our intention isn't scapegoating or fingerpointing. If you can read the papers or watch TV, you know there's been a rise these days in a certain kind of bitterness, racist comments, anti-Semitism, an increased sense of division.

Really, this is not us — this is not who we are. And this is not acceptable.

And so you have my plan for America. And I am asking for big things — but I believe in my heart you will do what's right.

And, you know, it's kind of an American tradition to show a certain skepticism toward our democratic institutions. I myself have sometimes thought the aging process could be delayed if it had to make its way through Congress.

You will deliberate, and you will discuss, and that is fine. But, my friends, the people cannot wait. They need help now.

And there is a mood among us. People are worried, there has been talk of decline. Someone even said our workers are lazy and uninspired.

And I thought, really, you go tell Neil Armstrong standing on the moon, tell the men and women who put him there, tell the American farmer who feeds his country and the world. Tell the men and women of Desert Storm.

Moods come and go, but greatness endures. Ours does. And maybe for a moment it's good to remember what, in the dailiness of our lives, we forget:

We are still and ever the freest nation on earth — the kindest nation on earth — the strongest nation on earth — and we have always risen to the occasion.

And we are going to lift this nation out of hard times inch by inch and day by day, and those who would stop us had better step aside — because I look at hard times and I make this vow: This will not stand.

And so we move on together, a rising nation, the once and future miracle that is still, this night, the hope of the world.

Thank you. God bless you. And God bless our beloved country. Thank you very, very much. ∎

---

## DEMOCRATIC RESPONSE

# Foley Counters Bush's Speech

*Following President Bush's State of the Union address, House Speaker Thomas S. Foley of Washington delivered the Democratic response.*

My fellow Americans, tonight I speak for the Democratic Party. But I also speak for working families and the middle class; for those who worked hard to move ahead but now find themselves falling behind; for so many of strength and spirit and skill who watch with increasing uncertainty as so many of their hopes have been threatened.

This should be America's high noon.

But instead, after winning both a war in the Persian Gulf a year ago and the historic struggle of the last half century against communism, we face an ominous, persistent recession, which reminds us anew of President Kennedy's warning that "This nation cannot be strong abroad if it is weak at home."

At home in America today, thousands wait on a frozen morning outside a hotel in Chicago for just a chance to apply for a job, no matter what the work or wages.

At home in America today, the largest automaker in the world, which once seemed to be the most secure of all corporations, announces that it will have to lay off 75,000 people in order to survive.

At home in America today, the average earnings increase of our workers has declined from first in the world to 10th. This year, millions more of our workers find themselves unemployed and their family's health uninsured. Many state governments are slashing education and other services and raising taxes. The nations whose freedom we protected in the past continue to

surpass us in high-paying jobs and the industries of the future.

The standard of living of the American people is a first and fundamental measure of the state of the American union.

So the urgent, overriding task of 1992 is to restore growth and jobs. And the great challenge of the 1990s is to reclaim our industrial edge, revive our economic leadership and make America once more the most prosperous and powerful economy on Earth.

For too long, we were told to wait — that things would get better on their own. There was even an effort to talk us out of the recession — or to tell us that it wasn't really happening at all.

But the truth finally became all too painful — and all too clear. The supply-side, trickle-down decade of the 1980s finally led to an economy in decline and left us month after month with a national administration adrift in domestic policy, seemingly without ideas and without apparent commitment or energy to move America ahead.

In the midst of this recession, the administration even resisted extending unemployment benefits; Congress had to pass it three times last year before the president would sign it.

Today, before the president had sent his message, Congress took action to renew that extension, and we now welcome the president's support.

For many months, Democrats have set forth an agenda for change. We have proposed a tax cut for the middle class to help lift the consumer demand that fuels our economy. We have demanded policies to bring down the trade barriers that lock American products out of markets from Europe to Asia. We have called for national health insurance to make health care a fundamental right of all Americans.

Here, too, we will seek common ground with the president and the Republicans. To achieve all this and more, we will work with him and with them to do what is best for the country.

But we will also stand our ground when basic principles are at stake. We will not agree to do the wrong thing simply for the sake of doing something. In short, we seek a fundamental change from the unsuccessful economic polices of the past 12 years.

When we say a middle-class tax cut, we mean exactly that — not more of the tax cuts of the 1980s, which gave most of the benefits to the very few and left most of our people actually paying more in taxes.

We will insist that this time the benefits must go to working families, not to the privileged.

We will insist that a middle-class tax cut be paid for not by taking money that should go to schools and health care but by calling on the richest of our citizens at long last to pay their fair share.

We will oppose any effort to misuse the present crisis as an excuse to repeat the worst errors of the last decade. Then we

sowed the seeds of the recession we are now in; we must not go down that path again.

During the past two administrations, there have been consistent efforts to undo government protection of public health and safety. Today the hurt of the unemployed is no excuse to undermine regulatory rules that protect their families and all of us from pollution, deceptive advertising, unsafe food and medicine, workplace injury and death. This is not the way to create jobs or make American business prosperous.

Nor will we accept the kind of capital gains tax cut that will lead largely to accelerated profit-taking, not accelerated investment. One can play a lot of games with statistics, but the bottom line is that two-thirds of all the money from the administration's capital gains tax cut would go to the richest 1 percent of taxpayers. Instead, we need targeted incentives to reward companies that build and buy now — that hire instead of laying off.

The president said tonight that when you aim at the well-off, you usually hit the little guy. The truth is: For 12 years they have been promising to help the little guy — and then giving all the breaks to the well-off. And it is time that that stopped.

As Democrats, our purpose is not just to end this recession but to begin a new time of economic growth and progress.

So we will propose a new commitment to civilian technology and research. For half a century, American weapons were the best in the world. As we enter the new century, America must build the best consumer and industrial products.

We will pursue a trade policy that opens markets on equal terms so that when we buy from Europe and Asia, they will be buying from us as well. We will demand far-reaching changes in education and training so that our students will be first, not last, among the industrial nations in science and math — and so our workers will have the skills and the change to compete successfully with anyone, anywhere.

We will also fight for fundamental change in the area of health care.

Today, millions of Americans have no health insurance at all. And even those who do have no assurance that they are safe. People worry that if they get sick, their coverage will be canceled. Premiums and out-of-pocket costs continue to multiply. Workers who lose their jobs suddenly find their children without health insurance.

This issue will be a test of our national character.

Few Americans realize that the United States and South Africa are the only economically advanced nations that do not guarantee the health care of their people.

We will fight to change that in this Congress — and in the next one, as long as it takes — because lives and health are at stake, and so is the financial health of America's families.

It is not enough to make minor changes — to tinker at the edges while tolerating basic flaws. We want to replace the status quo, not protect it. We want to

help the middle-class family — not tax its health-care benefits.

It is time for national health insurance. It is time to cover every American. It is time to control costs.

Because otherwise we will continue to pay more and more for less and less.

And soon, the burden will break the budgets of middle-class families, of business and of government at every level.

Health care is one of the great unfinished tasks of our society. Almost 60 years ago, America decided that people should age with dignity — and we passed Social Security. Now we must decide that families will live with dignity — and pass national health insurance.

Finally, there are other, urgent issues of basic justice that also go to our character as a nation. So we will oppose any effort from any quarter to widen and exploit racial division — or lessen our commitment to break down the barriers and at long last fulfill the pledge that millions of us make every day, from the schoolhouses of America to the floor of the House of Representatives: that we shall be "one nation, under God, indivisible, with liberty and justice for all." Appeals to race should have no place in our politics or our national life.

We will stand for another civil right of every American — the civil right to be protected from violence and crime.

Election after election, we hear tough talk; this year, we will pass tougher laws if the president will ask the Republicans in the Senate to stop filibustering the crime bill that has already been passed by the House of Representatives.

We will stand — and we will fight — for a woman's right to choose. If the Supreme Court removes the guarantees of choice from the Constitution of the United States, this Congress will write it into the laws of the United States.

We will stand for day care and family leave so that workers who take time off to help a sick parent or child will no longer risk their jobs.

In closing, let me reaffirm our essential resolve, which is to make America work again. For when the economy is wrong, nothing else is right.

We cannot undo all the mistakes of the past 12 years in a single year or in a single Congress.

The administration has waited a long time to act. Over and over, we have said we can fight this recession, and we will. We can change this nation fundamentally — and we have to.

It is true — the Cold War is over, the Old World past; the old ways of thinking and leading will not do.

It is time now to turn our attention to our own land and to our own people — to rebuild its economic strength and standard of life, to master the very different challenges of this new era.

Only a few times have Americans stood at so decisive a turning point. Now, with all of us working together, let's get this nation moving again. ∎

# Bush Outlines Health Plan, Attacks Other Approaches

### But Democrats, quick to respond, say Bush plan does not go far enough to control patient costs

*President Bush outlined his health-care proposals in a speech in Cleveland on Feb. 6. Congressional Democrats quickly criticized the plan as deficient, saying it would help doctors and insurance companies but would do little to ease health costs for patients. They said Bush's proposals did not deal with basic problems such as affordability of health insurance, the ability to retain insurance when workers change jobs and the soaring costs of health care. Following are excerpts from the Reuter transcript of the president's remarks.*

... People who know northern Ohio know that this region's on the move [in health care]. In addition to the world-renowned Cleveland Clinic, now the city's No. 1 employer, northern Ohio is also home to some of the most innovative approaches to health care.... Communities across the country can follow your lead to create workable solutions to health-care challenges.

And I had a briefing in Washington from the leaders of these organizations. And that really is why I've chosen to come to Cleveland this morning to address the health-care crisis in our country and lay out my four-point program for comprehensive health-care reform.

Reform is urgent, for more reasons than one. Right now far too many Americans are uninsured, and those who are insured pay too much for health care, and we are going to do, do something about that.

The one thing this crisis isn't about — and I was reminded of this in my visit to the hospital just now — the one thing it is not about is the quality of care. American health care is first-rate, it is the best in the entire world, and right now the vast majority of Americans have access to that health-care system. But the cost has skyrocketed, from $74 billion in 1970 to $800 billion today, and if we keep going at the same rate, that $800 billion will double to $1.6 trillion by the year 2000.

These numbers alone would make the case for reform. They tell us there's a connection we simply can't ignore between what we pay for health care and the long-term health of our economy.

But cold statistics don't show us the worry that people feel. The all too familiar fear about what happens to their health care if they change jobs, or worse still, if they lose their jobs. And in these hard times, we simply cannot accept the fact that one in every seven Americans is uninsured.

There's a better way, and my plan puts the emphasis on expanding access while preserving choice people now have over the type of health-care coverage and health care they receive.

My plan will give Americans a greater sense of security, help ease the fears that so many Americans have that changing jobs will cost them their health coverage.

And the key here is portability — changing the system to ensure people that they'll always have access to health insurance, no matter where they work. And finally, my plan will help cut costs. It helps us make health insurance more affordable, and more affordable means more accessible.

And my plan will preserve what works and reform what doesn't, and, above all, it will ensure every American universal access to affordable health insurance.

We stand at a crossroads. We can move forward dramatically, reform our market-based system, or we can force ourselves to swallow a cure worse than the disease.

Some people have scribbled out a prescription for disaster. They want to nationalize our health system, put the government in control of the system. You let government control the prices, let government ration the kind of health care people get, let government tell people looking for care how much they'll get, what kind and when.

Nationalized systems cover everyone, but keep in mind the drawbacks that come with a nationalized system. Long waiting lists for surgery. Shortages of high-tech equipment responsible for so many of the miracles of modern medicine. Let me cite just one example for you.

The Cleveland Clinic performs 10 coronary bypass surgeries a day, I'm told; high-tech, high-quality surgery, without any wait.

But if you live in British Columbia [Canada], the wait for coronary bypass surgery is six months. It is no wonder so many people from abroad come to American hospitals for surgery.

And when you nationalize health care you push costs higher, far higher. Some studies estimate that nationalized health care would cost the average American fam-ily a huge new tax burden. For the nation, a staggering $250 [billion] to $500 billion a year in new taxes.

Such a massive tax increase is simply unacceptable, and the American people should not be asked to accept it. And for that price you get the worst of both worlds. No one has an incentive to control costs, and everyone pays.

But there are other proposals out there that sound simple but are every bit as harmful. One's called play or pay. Each employer must play, meaning provide insurance for employees, or pay a payroll tax to finance government health coverage.

Businessmen and women tell me horror stories about health-care costs spiraling out of control.

Well, play or pay will leave a lot of small businesses, businesses struggling on the edge of survival right now, with a tough choice. They can cut workers' wages to pay for mandated health care, they can fire some workers to cover the workers they keep, or they can raise prices and pass along the cost to the consumer.

Some studies put the cost in jobs lost under play or pay as high as a half a million or more. Lower wages, lost jobs, higher costs, anyway you look at it that's the wrong choice for America.

Now strip away the rhetoric, strip it out of there, and play or pay just creates a backdoor route to nationalized health care, and it encourages employers to stop offering benefits, throw the problem in the government's lap and dump millions of fully insured workers into a public plan like Medicaid.

And because new employer taxes in play or pay don't pay for the program, the American taxpayer will obviously foot the bill, and I am not about to let that happen. You won't hear this from the people pushing play or pay. Ask them about the side effects of their proposal and they'll say take two aspirin and call me after the election.

I don't believe people want to be shoveled into some new health-care bureaucracy. They want good health. A large part of the answer is prevention, and every one of us can make changes in our behavior to reduce the risk of disease and illness, and pardon me for being just a little bit old-fashioned, but what we're talking about is behavior, drugs, alcohol abuse, risky sexual behavior. You know what I'm talking about. And there's nothing

wrong with discussing that, trying to do better in this field.

Tomorrow in San Diego I'll focus in more detail on the ways prevention can help people live healthier lives and help keep our economy healthy, too. But today I want to focus on the health-care system, on this comprehensive market-based reform plan I have.

The fact is, we do not have to create a new government bureaucracy to give Americans access to affordable quality health care. We need a system that delivers, a system that works for America, a system that puts quality care within reach of every American family.

Our system should be built on choice, not central control. It should keep costs down and open up access. But above all, it should allow all Americans to rest secure when it comes to health care, to ease their worry, that if they change jobs, if they or their kids develop serious health problems, they'll still be able to count on the coverage they need.

Now, my comprehensive four-point plan meets every one of these common-sense tests, and here's how it works.

Point one. We will make health care more accessible by making health insurance more affordable.

For low-income individuals and families, I propose a health insurance credit up to $3,750 a year to guarantee people, even people too poor to file taxes, the ability to purchase private health insurance. That will give these families a certificate or voucher to be used strictly for health care, worth more than $300 a month. And they can use it to buy into the plan their employers offer but they could never afford, or they can shop for whatever private plan suits them best. That's the American commitment to choice at its best.

For middle-income individuals and families, I purpose a health insurance tax deduction of $3,750.

American families with incomes under $80,000 will receive new help from either the credit or the tax deduction. And let me tell you what that means: new help to purchase health insurance for 95 million Americans.

And once again, this insurance will be portable. People who change jobs would have insurance regardless of their health — and this is important — or regardless of their family's health.

But best of all, my plan will bring health-care coverage to almost 30 million uninsured Americans — security to people who far too long have had to do without. And that's the first point in this four-point plan. Access.

Point two. We will cut the runaway costs of health care by making the system more efficient. Today I'm asking you to learn a new acronym — HIN, health insurance networks. Insurance costs obey the law of large numbers. The larger the group being insured, the lower the cost per individual. Pooling. Pooling lowers insurance costs, and significantly cuts administrative costs.

HINs will provide incentives for small companies to do what Cleveland's Cozy Group has done when it brought 10,000 small businesses together to make a joint

"The fact is, we do not have to create a new government bureaucracy to give Americans access to affordable quality health care. We need a system ... that puts quality care within reach of every American family."

—President Bush

purchase of health care. The nation should listen and follow.

Another way to drive costs down — make everyone a better health-care consumer. Right now most people pay more attention to the price of toothpaste than the comparative costs of health care. People don't waste much time thinking about the costs of their care, but in the end, we all pay the price.

We need to follow the lead of initiatives like Cleveland Health Quality Choice, programs that give people shopping for health care a kind of bluebook for medical costs. Innovations like these will help all of us keep the costs of quality health care as low as possible.

Point three. We will wring out waste and excess in the present system.

We've targeted medical malpractice for reform. It is time to put an end to these astronomical, sky's-the-limit lawsuits. You shouldn't have to pay a lawyer when you go to the doctor.... Our doctors, the most able and dedicated in the entire world, shouldn't be living in fear of these outrageous lawsuits. And high malpractice premiums mean higher doctors' bills, higher hospital costs, costs passed along not only to the patient but to every single American taxpayer.

Now, I have challenged the health insurance industry to cut red tape, to share common forms, to simplify and speed up claims processing. And here's a challenge for the next four years. There is no reason almost all health insurance claims can't be processed electronically. That single step would eliminate a mountain of health-care paperwork and pare back costs.

We've got to attack the excesses of mandated benefits. When states now order health insurers to cover 1,000 different types of treatment, something's gone wrong. Next thing they'll be covering manicures for Millie. It's gone too far, and I think everybody knows it, and we should challenge the states to do something about the excessive mandates that shoot these costs right up through the roof.

Fourth and finally, we will get the growth in government health programs under control.

Right now, government health-care programs can claim a dubious distinction. They are the fastest-growing parts in the federal budget.

For those of you interested in history, go back and listen to what was said about these programs at their inception. Go back and hear the rhetoric on the floor of the United States Congress. And now compare that to what actually has happened in these costs.

This year alone, Medicaid — this year alone, let me repeat that, Medicaid costs will increase by 38 percent. We will not, repeat, not cut benefits. We can make real savings simply by reducing this huge rate of increase. We must bring runaway costs under control. Smart, sensible efficiencies will help our reform plan pay for itself.

The federal government should also give states flexibility to design these new universal-access programs for the poor, programs that will provide quality services to all their citizens.

I've just met with Gov. [George V.] Voinovich [R-Ohio] and the rest of the governors. Regardless of party, Democrat, Republican, it doesn't matter, they want flexibility, and we must give it to them. Right here in Ohio, your governor has proposed health-care reforms that will do for this state what we want to do on the federal level.

States should be able to use new federal resources to design programs that work, not some one-size-fits-all solution imposed by Washington, D.C.

Providing affordable care, efficient care, wringing out excess and waste, and controlling federal growth. These four points will create the kind of market-based reform plan that will give Americans the kind of health care they want and deserve and put an end to the worry that keeps them awake at night.

Remember what people want. People want quality care, care they can afford, and care they can count on, care they can rely on.

I keep coming back to what works for this country. Think about the challenges that we face as a nation. Anyone who is concerned about competitiveness has to see controlling health-care costs as key to a healthy economy.

We've got to make certain our reform corrects our weaknesses without destroying our strengths. And when we talk about health care, we're talking about matters of the most personal nature, in some cases literally life and death, and decisions that go with them.

We don't need to put government between patients and their doctors. We don't need to create another wasteful federal bureaucracy.

As president I simply will not let that happen. We need common sense, comprehensive health-care reform, and we need it now.

And my plan I really believe is the right plan, a plan that meets our obligation to all Americans by putting hope and health within their reach....  ■

# Bush Asks Nation's Support For Aid To Former Soviets

*President Bush presented his assistance package for the nations of the former Soviet Union to the congressional leadership on April 1. Following is a Reuter transcript of the statement Bush made at the White House after presenting the package.*

I have a statement that is a little longer than the normal, but let me just say that I have just met with the congressional leadership to request their bipartisan backing for a new, comprehensive and integrated program to support the struggle of freedom under way in Russia, Ukraine and the other new states that have replaced the Soviet Union.

The revolution in these states is a defining moment in history, with profound consequences for America's own national interest. The stakes are as high for us now as any that we have faced in this century, and our adversary for 45 years, the one nation that posed a worldwide threat to freedom and peace, is now seeking to join the community of democratic nations. A victory for democracy and freedom in the former U.S.S.R. creates the possibility of a new world of peace for our children and grandchildren.

But if this democratic revolution is defeated, it could plunge us into a world more dangerous in some respects than the dark years of the Cold War.

America must meet this challenge, joining with those who stood beside us in the battle against imperial communism: Germany, the United Kingdom, Japan, France, Canada, Italy and other allies. Together, we won the Cold War, and today we must win the peace.

This effort will require new resources from the industrial democracies, but nothing like the price we would pay if democracy and reform failed in Russia and Ukraine and Belarus and Armenia and the states of central Asia.

It will require the commitment of a united America strengthened by a consensus that transcends even the heated partisanship of a presidential election campaign.

And today I call upon Congress, Republicans and Democrats alike, and the American people, to stand behind this united effort. Our national effort must be part of a global effort. I've been in contact with [German] Chancellor [Helmut] Kohl, [British] Prime Minister [John] Major, [French] President [François] Mitterrand, other key allies, to discuss our plans and to assure them of the high priority I place on the success of this endeavor.

To this end, I would like to announce today a plan to support democracy in the states of the former Soviet Union. This is a complex set of issues which took months to sort out, working within the administration, working with our major allies and with the leaders of the new independent states of the former Soviet Union. A number of things had to come together to make sure we got it right. Let me give you a little bit of the history.

I asked Secretary [of State James A.] Baker [III] to outline our fundamental approach in his Dec. 12 speech at Princeton. I spoke again on the need to embrace Russia and the other new states of the former Soviet Union in my Jan. 22 speech at the Washington conference to coordinate the humanitarian assistance. On Feb. 1, [Russian President] Boris [N.] Yeltsin and I discussed these issues at Camp David, and that same day [Treasury] Secretary [Nicholas F.] Brady met with Boris Yeltsin's key economic adviser, Yegor Gaidar, to discuss how we could support Russian reforms.

A week later Jim Baker followed up during his meeting with Kozyrev, [Russian] Foreign Minister [Andrei V.] Kozyrev and Boris Yeltsin in Moscow. And just yesterday the IMF [International Monetary Fund] reached tentative agreement with Russia on its market reform program.

After weeks of intensive consultations in the G-7 [group of seven leading industrial nations], Chancellor Kohl currently serving as chairman of the G-7, has announced today G-7 support for an IMF program for Russia. The program that I'm announcing today builds on this progress and includes three major components.

First, the United States has been working with its Western allies and the international financial institutions on an unprecedented multilateral program to support reform in the newly independent states. The success of this program will depend upon their commitment to reform and their willingness to work with the international community.

Russia is exhibiting that commitment, and I'm announcing today that the U.S. is prepared to join in a substantial multilateral financial assistance package in support of Russia's reforms. We're working to develop, with our allies and the IMF, a $6 billion currency stabilization fund, to help maintain confidence in the Russian ruble.

The U.S. will also join in a multilateral effort to marshal roughly $18 billion in financial support in 1992 to assist Russian efforts to stabilize and restructure their economy. We've been working with the Russian government for three months to help it develop an economic reform plan to permit the major industrialized countries to provide support.

We will work to complete action on this approximately $24 billion package by the end of April, and I pledge the full cooperation of the United States in this effort.

Second, the United States will also act to broaden its own capacity to extend assistance to the new states. I am transmitting to Congress a comprehensive bill — the Freedom Support Act — to mobilize the executive branch, the Congress, and indeed, our private sector, around a comprehensive and integrated package of support for the new states.

Now, this package will authorize a U.S. quota increase of $12 billion for the IMF, which is critical to supporting Russia and the other new states. The IMF and World Bank will be the primary sources of funding for the major financial assistance needs of the new governments.

The U.S. quota increase for the IMF was specifically assumed in the budget agreement and does not require a budget outlay.

Support my existing authority to work with the G-7 and the IMF to put together this stabilization program for Russia, and support possible subsequent programs for other states of the former Soviet Union, as they embark on landmark reforms, including up to $3 billion for stabilization funds.

It would also repeal restrictive Cold War legislation so that American business can compete on an even footing in these new markets. And I'm determined that American business be given the chance to invest in trade with the new states, and to that end, I've also directed that the United States negotiate trade and bilateral investment in tax treaties with these countries just as soon as possible.

Significant new trade relationships can create jobs right here in this country.

The package will broaden the use of $500 million appropriated by Congress last year to encompass not only the safe dismantling and destruction of nuclear weapons but also the broader goals of nuclear plant safety, demilitarization and defense conversion.

It will also establish a major people-to-people program between the United States and the states of the former Soviet Union to create the type of lasting personal bonds among our peoples and Russian understanding of democratic institutions so critical to long-term peace.

This effort will complement our existing programs to bring hundreds of busi-

nessmen to the United States from the Commonwealth [of Independent States] and then send hundreds of Peace Corps volunteers to the new states.

In sending this authorization legislation to Congress, I call upon the Congress to act concurrently to provide the appropriations necessary to make these authorizations a reality.

Third, in the addition to the $3.75 billion already extended by the [United States] since January 1991, I am announcing today $1.1 billion in new Commodity Credit Corporation credit guarantees for the purchase of American agricultural products; $600 million of that will go for U.S. sales to Russia and an additional $500 million for U.S. sales to Ukraine and other states.

Now, let me close on a personal note. I think every day about the challenge of securing a peaceful future for the American future. And I believe very strongly that President Yeltsin's reform program holds the greatest hope for the future of the Russian people, and for the security of the American people, as we define a new relationship with that great country.

President Yeltsin has taken some very courageous steps for democracy and free markets. And I am convinced that it is in our own national interest to support him strongly.

For more than 45 years, the highest responsibility of nine American presidents, Democrats and Republicans, was to wage and win the Cold War. It was my privilege to work with [former President] Ronald Reagan on these broad programs, and now, to lead the American people in winning the peace by embracing the people so recently freed from tyranny, to welcome them into the community of democratic nations.

I know there are those who say we should pull back, concentrate our energies, our interest and our resources on our pressing domestic problems, and they are, they are very important.

But I ask them to think of the consequences here at home of peace in the world. We've got to act now.

And if we turn away, if we do not do what we can to help democracy succeed in the lands of the old Soviet Union, our failure to act will carry a far higher price, and if we face up to the challenge, matching the courage of President Yeltsin, of Ukrainian President [Leonid M.] Kravchuk, of Armenian President [Levon A.] Ter-Petrosyan.

And many other future generations of Americans will thank us for having had the foresight and the conviction to stand up for democracy and work for peace in this decade and into the next century.

That is the end of this statement. I'll be glad to take just a handful of questions, and then Jim Baker and Secretary Brady will — I think Secretary Brady will go into more detail on the legislation, and Secretary Brady and others will be available. I think [Agriculture Secretary Edward R.] Madigan will talk to you about the agricultural sector of it. ∎

# Text of McHugh's Statement On Releasing 22 Names

*On April 1, Rep. Matthew F. McHugh, D-N.Y., released the names of the 22 biggest abusers of the House bank. He was acting chairman of the Committee on Standards of Official Conduct for this investigation. Following is the text of his statement.*

Mr. Speaker, pursuant to HR 236 and HR 393, I am today disclosing the names and pertinent account information on those current and former members of the House of Representatives who, between July 1, 1988, and Oct. 3, 1991, were found to have abused their banking privileges at the so-called House bank.

HR 236 directed the Committee on Standards of Official Conduct to investigate the use and operations of the House bank and to determine, among other things, whether any members or former members abused their banking privileges. As defined by that resolution, individuals abused banking privileges by "routinely and repeatedly writing checks for which their accounts did not have, by a significant amount, sufficient funds on deposit to cover."

On March 10, 1992, the committee reported to the House its findings and recommendations (H Rept. 102-452). Among them was a preliminary finding that 24 accounts had been involved in abuse of banking privileges. The committee report described the criteria the committee had used to identify those accounts. In substance, the committee determined that a member routinely and repeatedly overdrafted an account by a significant amount if he or she overdrew the account by more than the member's next month's net salary deposit at least once per month in 20 percent of the months the member had an account at the House bank.

In its report the committee recommended that, after each of the 24 account-holders had been given an opportunity to be heard in executive session, the names and pertinent account information should be publicly disclosed for those who were finally determined by the committee to have met the criteria established by HR 236. On March 12, 1992, the House adopted HR 393, which ordered such disclosure not less than 10 days after its adoption.

A subcommittee designated by the full committee then afforded those among the 24 who requested a hearing the opportunity to be heard. The subcommittee concluded that two account-holders should not be included on the final list of those to be disclosed. The reasons for excluding them included the following:

(1) One member was excluded from the list because a number of wire transfers he had initiated to move funds into his House account were, upon further investigation by the General Accounting Office, determined to be timely received and recorded by the House bank's agent. The subcommittee concluded that since the member had arranged for funds to be transferred by wire in time to avoid certain overdrafts, a number of months previously attributed to him should be excluded. This removed him from the list.

(2) One member documented, and the General Accounting Office substantiated, a House bank error which treated certain checks as overdrafts. The correction of the error reduced the number of months in which the negative balance exceeded the next net salary deposit to below 20 percent of the months at issue.

The subcommittee believes that although the following individuals abused their banking privileges, as abuse is defined in HR 236, their intent to abuse such privileges is by no means clear. The subcommittee reached its conclusions based on the resolution's definition of abuse, the practices of the House bank and the records available to it. It did not consider the intent of members. However, given the informal nature of the House bank's operations, including its longtime practice of honoring overdrafts and its lack of written rules and regulations, the subcommittee cannot say the people on this list intended to abuse banking privileges.

It should be noted, for example, that some members have cited a statute stating that members are entitled to be paid on the last day of each month. The subcommittee believes that the actual practice of the House bank in crediting member accounts on the first business day of each month is controlling on this point. The committee notes in this connection that members were advised by the *Congressional Handbook* distributed by the Committee on House Administration that they would be paid on the first business day of the month, and members' monthly bank statements reflect that practice. However, some members may have relied on the statute in writing checks.

The subcommittee also notes that some members arranged with the House bank to have voluntary transfers made from their gross pay and this arrangement had the effect of reducing their net salary deposit each month, the threshold established by the subcommittee for determining significant overdrafts. Voluntary transfers, which were deducted by the House bank from gross salary before the net salary was credited to a member's account, had the effect of putting a member at some disadvantage for purposes of this inquiry. ∎

# Leaders, Special Counsel Exchange Letters

A subpoena for records of the defunct House bank, issued April 21 by a grand jury at the request of Malcolm R. Wilkey, special counsel to the attorney general, raised concerns among House members about the constitutional separation of powers, rights of privacy and potential leaks of information. The House voted April 29 to comply with the subpoena, but only after days of internal debate and an exchange of letters among leaders seeking to clarify the situation. Following is the text of the letters.

## Special Counsel Wilkey Seeks Ethics Committee Records

March 31, 1992

The Honorable Matthew F. McHugh
Chairman, Subcommittee Conducting
the House Bank Inquiry
Committee on Standards of Official
Conduct

Dear Mr. Chairman:

As you may know, I have been appointed Special Counsel to the Attorney General to conduct a preliminary inquiry concerning the operation of the Office of the Sergeant-at-Arms of the House of Representatives, in particular, the facility known as the House bank, to determine whether there have been violations of criminal law. In connection with this inquiry, I request that you provide me copies of all documents specifically referenced in the House Report of the Committee on Standards of Official Conduct, No. 102-452, 102d Cong., 2nd Sess. (dated March 10, 1992).

Also, I ask you to provide copies of all interim and any other reports regarding the House bank by the Committee on Standards of Official Conduct, subcommittee conducting the House bank inquiry and their members or staff, as well as, by the General Accounting Office, and any other congressional committees investigating the House bank, together with the supporting working papers. This would include, but not be limited to, statistical analyses, correspondence, the 1990 and 1991 reports by the National Bank of Washington and Riggs National Bank to the Speaker regarding the House bank, proposed regulations relating to the House bank, and transcripts of testimony by witnesses before the subcommittee, together with task force reports to the House Administration Committee.

Finally, I ask that you [sic] to provide

access to all other documents not specifically described above but relied upon by the subcommittee or the committee in its inquiry into the operation of the bank of the Sergeant-at-Arms of the House of Representatives.

Your earliest cooperation would be appreciated.

Sincerely,

Malcolm Wilkey

## Speaker Foley Declines To Provide Records

April 20, 1992

Dear Judge Wilkey:

I write to follow up on our meeting last week with the Attorney General in which I indicated my desire to consult further with the House parliamentarian and talk with Mr. Michel before providing a further response to your proposal for access to records of the former House bank.

The parliamentarian continues to advise that it would be inconsistent with the House rules for me to provide the copies of records you seek without a vote of the House. Also, as I indicated at that meeting, the sweeping scope of your documentary request is such that I could not in conscience comply without consulting the House, whatever the rules might dictate.

Accordingly, I believe that your documentary request must be considered by the Hosue, which reconvenes next week. Mr. Michel agrees with this course of action.

In the meantime, I am informed that you have taken up the offer Messrs. Gephardt, Brooks, McHugh and I made in the meeting to begin interviewing the staff of the former bank concerning the general nature of its operations. It is our hope that these interviews will allow you to narrow the focus of your preliminary inquiry.

With high regard, I am

Sincerely yours,

Thomas S. Foley
The Speaker

## Wilkey Outlines Records He Seeks

April 21, 1992

Dear Mr. Speaker:

I thank you for your letter of 20 April,

setting forth your proposed course of action in regard to the House banking facility records. I also thank you for facilitating our interviews with the recent staff of the former bank.

Since there has been an exchange of several letters beginning the 1st of April and the conference on the 13th, let me state clearly what we need immediately, and why we need it.

First, why we need it:

1. I am charged with inquiring into possible criminal law violations. The House committee specifically did not do this, nor were they asked to do it. My inquiry therefore has a purpose and reference points completely different from those of the House.

2. It is impossible to obtain an accurate picture of the bank's overall operations without full access to its records. For example, there may have been differential handling of the accounts.

3. Countless members of the House itself have claimed that there were gross irregularities in the way the bank was managed. Customarily when a bank is closed because of such allegations investigators have access to the complete records. When reviewing the operations of a bank which is conceded to have been abused, no request or subpoena for such basic records as checks and bank statements can be dismissed as over-broad.

4. We have received demands from members of the House and from the public by letters and through the media that there be an investigation of the former bank with reference to the criminal laws. Nothing less than a complete look at the records — with reference to the criminal law — will satisfy the American people. The honor of the House and the interest of citizens demand no less.

Second, what we now need:

1. The rolls of the microfilm or microfiche, reputedly 41 in number, which presumably contain all the checks handled by the bank during the 39-month period in question. There is no other source which contains nearly as complete a picture of the bank's operations, which is first priority and fundamental to our inquiry.

2. In order to restate my position at our meeting of the 13th, and to avoid any confusion in the House as to what we need to begin work at this time, we have determined that the clearest and most unequivocal way to proceed is by a simple subpoena for the microfilm alone. I am not asking for any of the deliberative records of the committee. I do not intend this to be

seen as an abandonment of my request for all documents relevant to this matter. I think that by having all of those documents, my work can proceed more quickly. I would welcome a decision by you or the House to provide us with all of those documents.

Perhaps a third point — how we intend to handle these records — would be helpful to you and the House.

As I stated in our conference on the 13th, since reviewing the overall operation of the bank can be done with complete information on only the accounts originally listed by the committee as having some irregularity, therefore, the data on the approximately 170 accounts not listed can be returned as soon as these can be segregated, without prejudice to asking for these again if this becomes necessary. As the inquiry proceeds, I intend to return data concerning any accounts where we have determined that information on any particular accounts is no longer relevant to our inquiry.

This letter is being delivered with a grand jury subpoena because the record of our letter exchanges and conference should be capsuled into one clear statement in order to focus the attention of the House on exactly what we need for our inquiry and why we need it. If one thing emerged from the phone call of your House counsel this morning, it was that this matter, under discussion since 1 April, will be more easily decided with the clarification this subpoena provides. And further, with a subpoena the secrecy of grand jury proceedings and the provisions of the Right to Financial Privacy Act will apply to the banking records.

In our conference I expressed the view that the flood of allegations regarding the banking operation required a preliminary inquiry to resolve any question of criminal conduct. I also expressed my belief that the vast majority of House members, if not all, will be found to have committed no crime, but I can only make such determination by reviewing the bank's records. Surely the great majority of the House desires to furnish the essential information to do this.

With continued high regard,

Sincerely,

Malcolm R. Wilkey

## Foley Describes Concerns To Members

April 24, 1992

Dear Colleague:

I write to bring you up to date concerning the activities of the Special Counsel to the Attorney General, Judge Malcolm R. Wilkey, who is conducting a preliminary inquiry into the operations of the former House bank. I will focus particularly on the steps Judge Wilkey has taken to obtain access to all bank documents and the bipartisan leadership's response.

Judge Wilkey sought on an informal basis access to virtually all bank records in the possession of the Committee on Standards of Official Conduct. On April 21, despite the assurances of the bipartisan House leadership that the House would take up this matter promptly upon its return next week, Judge Wilkey sought the same records by subpoenas. The records include all banking transactions over a 39-month period — every single check (whether it caused an overdraft or not) deposit slips and monthly statements — of each member or former member of the House, whether he or she had overdrafts or not. The subpoenas also seek every check of every person who used the former bank during that period: employees, members of the press, members' spouses, and even some members of the public.

It is important to understand the events that led up to the present situation and what will follow. The bipartisan leadership sought a meeting with Attorney General Barr and Judge Wilkey, which occurred on April 13. At that time, I advised the Attorney General and Judge Wilkey that the House leadership would support cooperation with the preliminary inquiry directed by Judge Wilkey, but with a clear understanding that the procedures of the House and the rights of individual members would have to be fully respected.

This position required, in my view, the following:

— that the nature of the preliminary inquiry be properly defined so that the House and its individual members could be satisfied that it fell within the appropriate jurisdiction of the Department of Justice. This meant, specifically, that the investigation could not proceed on the terms Judge Wilkey had proposed to us, an in public statements, i.e. as an open-ended and undefined inquiry into the general financial activities of all members of the House of Representatives. I therefore asked him to narrow his request accordingly;

— that, even if properly defined, this inquiry would respect the most basic principles governing the relationship between two co-equal branches of government — particularly where each branch is controlled by a different political party and the inquiry will be conducted during a presidential election year. This, in turn, underscores the importance of full security during the department's preliminary review to avoid "leaks" or any other manipulation of confidential data that might inspire the suspicion of partisan motivation; and

— that it is our expectation that the inquiry would be conducted expeditiously and in accordance with appropriate legal process.

Following that meeting, on April 20, I forwarded to Judge Wilkey, on behalf of myself and the Republican leader, a letter informing him of advice I had received from the parliamentarian that House rules would prohibit turning over the records of the former bank in response to his request. I added that, whatever the rules might dictate, I could not in conscience comply with the sweeping and unprecedented scope of his documentary request.

On April 21, Judge Wilkey responded with the issuance of subpoenas for microfilm copies of all bank records during the 39-month period involved in the earlier review of the Committee on Standards of Official Conduct. Although Judge Wilkey now states that he would eliminate from the scope of his preliminary review records relating to the 170 members who had no overdrafts, the plain language of the subpoenas requests all bank records contained on the microfilm rolls.

It was apparently Judge Wilkey's belief that the issuance of subpoenas at this time would contribute to an expedited inquiry with full application of the secrecy afforded by law to grand jury proceedings and the Right to Financial Privacy Act. Be that as it may, it was, in my view, unhelpful to the resolution of this matter and inconsistent with the principles I have expressed directly to the Attorney General, for Judge Wilkey to have acted so precipitously at a time when the House was not in session and communication with members is all the more difficult.

Upon the House's return, I will promptly convene the bipartisan leadership to expeditiously consider recommendations for appropriate action that accommodates the legitimate interests of the Department of Justice, the House, its members and the public. Any such action must reflect the principles set out above, which are crucial to the constitutional structure of government, individual rights assured to all citizens, and the expectation of the public that the legal process will be impartial and fair.

Sincerely,

Thomas S. Foley
The Speaker

## GOP Leader Michel Describes Situation to Republicans

April 24, 1992

Dear Republican Colleague:

The Speaker, by his "Dear Colleague" of today, informed you that Special Counsel to the Attorney General, Judge Malcolm Wilkey, has by subpoena sought records of the House bank.

Let me say at the outset that my position has been to provide Judge Wilkey with access to the documents in the possession of the Committee on Standards of Official Conduct which are relevant to the investi-

gation. Judge Wilkey has instead sought to subpoena copies of all checks and deposits of the House bank, which are contained on microfilm and microfiche.

One issue is how you segregate overdraft records of all those who used the House bank (members, former members, press, staff) from those with no overdrafts. Checks on the microfilm and microfiche appear in a random manner, not by account.

The extent of the subpoena request must be discussed with the bipartisan leadership group as well as all members before we act in the House. While I want to reserve final judgment, and subject to meeting with our leadership, members of the Committee on Standards of Official Conduct and our conference, I believe we can provide Judge Wilkey with copies of all checks which resulted in an overdraft without prejudice to how the House may decide to respond at a later date. At the same time, each member or former member would receive copies of their account records which are turned over to Judge Wilkey while we immediatley begin a process to segregate all accounts. Finally, the Committee on Standards of Official Conduct should reach a determination immediately on whether an overdraft of $10,000 results in an obligation that must be reported on a financial disclosure form.

I realize this is a difficult and complex issue, but members should be advised that we are now proceeding with a criminal investigation, not just an internal House review. We must proceed prudently and expeditiously with all the facts and options before us.

Sincerely,

Bob Michel
Republican Leader

---

### Wilkey Writes to Members

April 27, 1992

To the Honorable Members of the House of Representatives:

This letter is addressed to all of you to correct some misapprehensions about the purpose and scope of the Department of Justice preliminary inquiry which I am conducting. I hope each of you has read my letter of 21 April to Speaker Foley with copy to Mr. Michel. There I set forth as precisely as is possible at this stage what we need, why we need it, and how we propose to handle the microfilm/microfiche.

What we need and why we need it is really no different from any inquiry into any troubled financial institution after it is closed. This banking facility may have had a unique clientele, but its records vital to any inquiry — deposits, checks, statements, daily tally sheets — are no different from any other bank. It is impossible to

make any meaningful examination without these. We believe they are on the microfilm.

This is what the subpoena asks for — and nothing else. Contrary to the assertion that our original request has been greatly broadened, the opposite is true. My original request letter listed in detail all those records to which the House committee had enjoyed access. We believe we should have equal access to do our job. In order to expedite matters, at the 13 April conference we *narrowed* our request to the 41 rolls of microfilm only. The subpoena asks just for this.

The subpoena was sent, with an accompanying letter, not only to narrow our immediate request, but also to focus attention of the House on exactly what was covered. Speaker Foley had stated that under Rule L he felt obliged to lay our request, like a subpoena, before the House. After an exchange of several letters and a conference at which only a few members were present, we wanted to make clear exactly what was before the House — a subpoena for 41 rolls of microfilm, none other.

It is true that these 41 rolls contain most of the records of the bank's operations, including checks and perhaps statements of all its depositors and those who used its facilities. That would be so of any bank. The depositors (members) in this bank are in no different position from that in which they would be if they had used a failed S&L or a fraudulently operated BCCI. All customers' records are necessarily commingled on the microfilm. It is necessary to have this to make any examination of the bank's overall operation, which is our first priority.

It took months for ten GAO accountants to give the House committee even a partial view for limited purposes of the bank's operations. The House cannot give us on a timely basis the accounts of only those members with overdrawn checks. With FBI techniques we expect to do the necessary reproduction and segregation in a very few weeks. At the conference on 13 April I offered to have a House custodian accompany the microfilm records, observe the process of duplication, and take back the microfilm when it was done. I also offered to return the records, when duplicated and segregated, of those members who are not listed as having overdrafts. This last procedure we can still follow under the rules governing a grand jury subpoena.

It is claimed that no U.S. government money has been involved. Who *knows* this? The Sergeant-At-Arms had at least two Treasury accounts on which he could draw. He drew on both by a Treasury check, as an authorized U.S. Government disbursing officer. Treasury checks are customarily used to draw on U.S. government funds. The only case in point in the D.C. Circuit holds that these funds continue to be the property of the government until actually disbursed by the Surgeant-At-Arms. *Romney v. U.S.*, 167 F.2d 521 (D.C. Cir. 1948).

It has been claimed that there have been no violations of law in the operation of the House banking facility. How can anyone possible make such a claim? There has been no investigation focused on possible criminal law violations. The House committee was not charged with this responsibility, was not legally competent to do so, and specifically shielded itself from knowledge of certain facts which might be relevant in a criminal inquiry. As a matter of fact, our preliminary inquiry has already unearthed evidence that a classic check kiting scheme may have occurred.

It is claimed that not a penny was "lost" due to the thousands of overdraft checks. What is meant by "lost"? This term does not necessarily include misapplication or conversion. Further, there are a number of criminal law violations in which "loss" is not a necessary element at all.

One claim that has *not* been asserted is that these banking facility records are in any way, shape, form or fashion connected with the deliberative or legislative functions of the House, and thus involve the Speech or Debate clause, nor could there be such a claim. All legitimate functions of this banking facility probably could have been performed by an automatic teller machine. And let it be noted that we are not asking for any deliberative records of the House committee.

There have been suggestions that we could be furnished with all documents really relevant to our investigation, sometimes accompanied by the definition of "relevant" as being only the overdraft checks. This would be totally inadequate for any inquiry into the overall operations of the bank by its employees. It would be inadequate even for any inquiry into the account of a member with 700 overdrafts, for we would need all other checks, deposits, statements to gain an accurate picture of what the overdrafts meant, or that they really existed.

More fundamentally, "relevance" for the purpose of inquiry into possible criminal law violations is always determined initially by those responsible for conducting the investigation, not the objects of the inquiry. A moment's thought should convince anyone that the opposite system simply would not work.

It has been claimed that the Grand Jury subpoena sweeps too broadly, and does so without publicly detailing the specific criminal charges which form the basis of the inquiry. This claim is totally contrary to the time-honored function of the grand jury:

> ... the grand jury "can investigate merely on suspicion that the law is being violated, or even just because it wants assurance that it is not." *United States v. Morton Salt Co.*, 338 U.S. 632, 642-643 (1950). The function of the grand jury is to inquire into all information that might possibly bear on its investigation until it has identified an offense or has satisfied itself that none has occurred. As a necessary consequence of its investigatory func-

tion, the grand jury paints a broad brush. "A grand jury investigation 'is not fully carried out until every available clue has been run down and all witnesses examined in every proper way to find if a crime has been committed.'" *Branzburg v. Hayes,* 408 U.S. 665, 701 (1972), quoting *United States v. Stone,* 429 F. 2d 183, 140 (CA2 1970).

A grand jury subpoena is thus much different from a subpoena issued in the context of a prospective criminal trial, where a specific offense has been identified and a particular defendant charged. "[T]he identity of the offender, and the precise nature of the offense, if there be one, normally are developed at the conclusion of the grand jury's labors, not at the beginning." *Blair v. United States,* 250 U.S. 273, 282 (1919). In short, the Government cannot be required to justify the issuance of a grand jury subpoena by presenting evidence sufficient to establish probable cause because the very purpose of requesting the information is to ascertain whether probable cause exists. See *Hale v. Henkel,* 201 U.S. 43, 65 (1906).

*United States v. R. Enterprises, Inc. et al.,* 498 U.S. ___, 112 L. Ed. 2d 795, 805, 111 S. Ct. 722, 726 (1991).

I go back to where I started. We are conducting an inquiry into the operation of a troubled bank which has closed. We need the usual records. The clientele may be different, but that does not alter the nature of our inquiry, nor the records needed. In our America the criminal law knows no specially privileged groups.

I reiterate my sincere belief that there will be few, if any, criminal law violations found. But no one will know until a full impartial inquiry is made.

Respectfully,

Malcolm R. Wilkey

## Michel Tells Foley Republicans Support Compliance

April 28, 1992

Dear Mr. Speaker:

After consulting with my leadership it is my belief that the House of Representatives should provide Judge Wilkey with the documents as requested in the subpoena of April 21, 1992.

It is also my belief that in the House resolution to consider this action further steps be taken. The resolution should direct that every effort be made to provide members with copies of all records on their accounts which are turned over to Judge Wilkey. As you know, many members have been unable to reconstruct their own accounts based on their own records. It is important that members have access to the same information that is being provided to Judge Wilkey.

Furthermore, the resolution should direct the Committee on Standards and Official Conduct to determine whether an overdraft of $10,000 results in an obligation that must be reported on financial disclosure forms. The committee should be instructed to make this determination before the May 15 filing deadline for disclosure forms.

These are my thoughts for a determination of the matter. Please let me know how I can assist in bringing this matter to a close by Thursday.

Sincerely,

Bob Michel

## Michel Seeks Clarification From Wilkey

April 29, 1992

Dear Judge Wilkey:

I would like a clarification of your intent in regards to the records of the approximately 170 accounts which had no overdrafts. I understood previously to your letter of April 21, 1992, that you were in no way interested in these accounts. In the letter of the 21st, however, you indicate that the records of the non-overdrafted accounts would be returned to the House "without prejudice to asking for these again if this becomes necessary." I believe there needs to be some clarification here.

As you are aware, I think it important that persons representing the House be present as the records of the House are copied. Furthermore, duplicates of account-holder records turned over to you should also be furnished to the account holder. Please advise me if these requests can be accommodated.

A paramount concern, of course, is the integrity and confidentiality of these records which will be in your possession. I seek your personal assurance that all necessary steps will be taken to ensure their safekeeping, free from improper disclosure.

I thank you for your attention to these matters.

Sincerely,

Robert H. Michel

## Wilkey Offers Assurances to Michel

April 29, 1992

Dear Mr. Michel:

Re: The 170 Non-Involved Accounts

It is evident that there is confusion both among members and the public over our having access to the accounts of members not involved with overdrafts. As you are aware, all of the records are commingled and thus it is necessary to have all the microfilm to review the overall operation of the bank and even to evaluate completely one account.

We have no interest in or need for the data on the 170 accounts on the facts we now know. If this changes, we would expect to make a specific showing of need at that time after a thorough review of data previously furnished.

We have technological facilities which will enable us to separate the 170 as a group from the other accounts as a group quickly. We will return these to the House unorganized, uncollated, and unreviewed by us. The House may have its representatives present while this is being done. All of the above procedures I offered to carry out at the conference on 13 April.

We will duplicate the checks, deposit slips, and account statements (if such appear) of the members' overdraft accounts, and return same to the House for distribution to the individual members.

We will meticulously guard the confidentiality and integrity of all these records, being aware that they are not only covered by grand jury secrecy but are the personal records of members of a coordinate branch of government.

Cordially,

Malcolm R. Wilkey                    ■

# Leaks in Hill and Keating Cases A Mystery to Senate Counsel

*Despite a four-month investigation, a Senate special counsel has failed to identify the sources of leaked confidential information regarding Anita F. Hill's sexual harassment charges against Supreme Court nominee Clarence Thomas.*

*In a report to the Senate, the special counsel, New York lawyer Peter J. Fleming Jr., also reported that he could not identify the source of numerous leaks involving the Senate Ethics Committee inquiry into five senators' relationships with Charles S. Keating, president of the failed Lincoln Savings and Loan Association.*

*Following are excerpts from the report, including a detailed chronology of events leading to the Anita Hill leak and the concluding section devoted to a discussion of the general issue of leaked documents.*

## A. Senate Documents

The results of the investigation established:

1. On September 23, 1991, Anita F. Hill telefaxed a statement of her allegations of sexual harassment to the Judiciary Committee. The document was signed and dated September 23, 1991. It did not appear to be notarized.

2. On September 25, 1991, Anita F. Hill telefaxed an identical statement to the Judiciary Committee with typographical errors corrected. It was signed and dated September 25, 1991. It did not appear to be notarized.

3. On September 25, 1991, James Brudney, a staff person for Senator [Howard M.] Metzenbaum [D-Ohio], asked Anita F. Hill to send him either a copy of her statement or a written description of her allegations. Anita F. Hill telefaxed an exact copy of her September 25, 1991, statement to the Judiciary Committee to Brudney on that day. It was not signed or dated or notarized.

4. Anita F. Hill did not supply a copy of her statement to any other person or organization until after the October 6 publication of her allegations in Newsday and on National Public Radio.

5. An FBI report, containing Form 302 interviews of Anita F. Hill, Clarence Thomas, and others, was received by the Judiciary Committee on September 25, 1991.

6. Hard copy of the FBI report on Anita F. Hill's allegations was not disseminated outside the Senate in whole or in part.

7. The contents of the FBI report were not disseminated outside the Senate in whole or in part, contrary to the impression created by published and broadcast reports of Anita F. Hill's allegations.

8. An unauthorized disclosure of hard copy of Anita F. Hill's written allegations to the Judiciary Committee played a significant role in the publication of Anita F. Hill's allegations on National Public Radio.

9. Contrary to some public speculation, Judge Susan Hoerchner [workers compensation judge of Norwalk, Calif.] was not responsible for the . . . October 6 publication of Anita F. Hill's allegations.

10. The inquiry of the Select Committee on Ethics was permeated by disclosures of committee-sensitive information. The disclosures were both partisan and strategic in nature.

11. We are unable to identify any source of these disclosures. The evidence indicates there were multiple sources.

## B. Phelps

1. Timothy M. Phelps is a reporter for Newsday who covered the nomination proceedings of Judge Clarence Thomas to the Supreme Court.

2. Prior to September 27, 1991, Phelps heard rumors of sexual harassment allegations associated with Clarence Thomas.

3. Prior to September 27, 1991, Phelps spoke to Anita F. Hill about Thomas' nomination but did not associate Hill with the sexual harassment rumors.

4. On September 27, 1991, Phelps learned from "sources" that the Federal Bureau of Investigation had "reopened its background investigation of Thomas to check opponents' allegations of personal misconduct." We have not identified Phelps' "sources."

5. On or about October 2, 1991, Phelps determined Anita F. Hill was a likely complainant making allegations of sexual harassment against Thomas.

6. On October 5, 1991, Phelps spoke with Senator [Paul] Simon, [D-Ill.] about Hill's allegations. The senator did not make unauthorized disclosures to Phelps.

7. On the evening of October 5, 1991, Newsday published a story by Phelps quoting a "source who has seen [Hill's] statement to the FBI."

8. Phelps did not have hard copy of the FBI report or Hill's statement.

9. The information provided by Phelps' "source" derived from Hill's statement, and not from the FBI report.

10. We have not been able to identify Phelps' "source."

## C. Totenberg

1. Nina Totenberg is the legal affairs correspondent for National Public Radio.

2. Prior to September 27, 1991, Totenberg heard rumors of sexual harassment associated with Thomas but did not speak to Anita F. Hill.

3. On or before Wednesday, October 2, 1991, Totenberg obtained hard copy of a document which contained the contents of Hill's statement to the Judiciary Committee. The document originated from the Senate.

4. Totenberg spoke to Hill on October 3, 4, and 5, 1991.

5. Hill did not solicit publication of her allegations by Totenberg.

6. Prior to the afternoon of October 5, 1991, Hill refused to discuss the details of her allegations on tape unless Totenberg demonstrated possession of Hill's statement.

7. On Saturday afternoon, October 5, 1991, Totenberg read the first page of her document to Hill. Hill recognized it as her statement and said so; she then agreed to be interviewed on tape.

8. Totenberg delayed reading the document until Saturday afternoon because she was not sure it was genuine. Totenberg was not sure her document was genuine either because it was signed and dated but not notarized, or because it was not signed or dated or notarized.

9. On October 6, 1991, Totenberg broadcast a report on Hill's allegations and the Judiciary Committee's handling of those allegations.

10. Although she quoted sources purporting to describe the FBI report, Totenberg did not have access to the FBI report.

11. We do not know if the document was signed or dated or whether it was an unsigned and undated document because Totenberg destroyed it and would not answer questions.

12. We are unable to identify the Senate source of the document delivered to Totenberg.

## D. Keating

1. On July 12, 1990, The Washington Times reported Special Counsel Robert Bennett's likely recommendation to the Ethics Committee regarding the five senators under investigation by the Committee.

2. Prior to the disclosure leading to the July 12, 1990, article, Bennett's preliminary views were known only to the members of the Ethics Committee, staff assisting the Ethics Committee, and Bennett and his staff.

3. The committee-sensitive information contained in the July 12, 1990, article

was not provided to The Washington Times by counsel for the five senators.

4. On September 29, 1990, The New York Times published an article disclosing Bennett's preliminary recommendations transmitted in a September 10, 1990, written report to the Ethics Committee. The report was a committee-sensitive document.

5. Prior to the September 29, 1990, article, all counsel for the five senators were generally aware of Bennett's recommendation as to their own clients.

6. The New York Times article, on its face, excludes the possibility that counsel for the five senators were the sources of the information contained in that article. The article states that it is based on "several congressional officials," none of whom can be identified.

7. Documents produced to Special Counsel during the ethics investigation were disclosed to the press in October 1990. These documents were committee-sensitive documents and were distributed in an attempt to influence the proceedings.

8. The source or sources of these documents cannot be determined.

9. Committee deliberations were reported in the press throughout the proceedings. These reports disclosed confidential committee-sensitive information and varied as to their accuracy. We have been unable to identify the source of these articles.

10. On July 15, 1990, Senator [Jesse] Helms [R-N.C.] advised the committee that he was prepared to issue as his own report a report prepared by Bennett and transmitted to the committee.

11. The Bennett report was transmitted to the committee as a confidential document for use by the committee as a working draft for its own final report.

12. On August 5, 1990, Senator Helms issued his own report on the Cranston matter.

13. Senator Helms stated publicly that his own report was based on what he considered to be the "generally excellent" draft of Bennett.

* * *

## IX. General Issues

S Res 202, by its very nature, implicates issues of importance which may well transcend the specific question of who, if anyone, was responsible for the unauthorized disclosure of information from Senate documents in connection with the Ethics Committee's investigation or the nomination of Judge Thomas.

1. Does the Senate, historically an institution of open debate, have any need or right to confidentiality?

2. If so, should the Senate condone breaches of confidentiality?

3. Does the media's claim of its own right of confidentiality take primacy over the Senate's right to police itself?

### A. Confidentiality

Its history shows the fundamental policy of the Senate to be one of open debate and public access to information. With rare exceptions, the Senate has conducted all of its legislative proceedings since 1795 in open session. Since 1929, the Senate has provided for open sessions on the floor for the consideration of nominations and treaties, both of which previously had been treated in confidence. In accord with this fundamental policy, the Senate has acted to make its proceedings fully accessible. Under the Constitution, the Senate "keeps a Journal of its Proceedings, and from time to time publishes the same, excepting such parts as may in their judgment require Secrecy." Since 1802, the Senate has provided the press with special access to the chamber. In 1848, the Senate began directly arranging for publication of Senate floor debate, culminating in the initiation of the Congressional Record beginning in 1873. Since 1986, the Senate's floor proceedings have been broadcast over radio and television.

The Senate also opens the majority of its committee proceedings to the public. By Senate rule, all meetings, including meetings to conduct hearings, of Senate committees "shall be open to the public," unless a committee votes to close a particular meeting or limited series of them for one of several prescribed reasons. Senate rules likewise create a presumption for the broadcast of committee hearings by radio and television.

All of this, however, cannot mean that confidentiality is never required and, when imposed, is not to be respected. As expressed by one member, there is the hope that by "ridding the government of unnecessary secrecy, there will be greater respect for the times when confidentiality is essential." In particular situations, and for valid reasons, identifiable and significant interests warrant an institutional judgment that confidentiality is essential to the appropriate discharge of institutional responsibility. Certain of these interests are particularly relevant to the matters which are the subject of the investigation mandated by S Res 202.

### 1. Citizen Interests

Private citizens have both an interest and a right to communicate with elected representatives with the assurance of confidentiality. The First Amendment guarantees the right of the public to "petition the Government for a redress of grievances." As the Supreme Court has stated, "this right is implicit in 'the very idea of government, republican in form'" *McDonald v. Smith,* (quoting *United States v. Cruikshank,* and this right to petition the government "requires stringent protection" and "substantial 'breathing space.'" *(New York Times Co. v. Sullivan).*

James Madison's remarks when the First Amendment was proposed manifest the intent that the Petition Clause guarantee the right of the people to "communicate their will," not only by "publicly address[ing] their representatives," but also by "privately advise[ing] them." Public values are served by promising confidentiality in order to encourage a citizen's free exchange of ideas with elected representatives. The Senate has an obligation to take all steps necessary to maintain the confidentiality of communications from those private citizens who request it. Indeed, Senate access to relevant but sensitive personal information often will depend upon assurances of confidentiality. It seems certain that breaches of confidentiality by the Senate will diminish the willingness of individuals to come forward.

Nor can the Senate ignore the substantial personal cost imposed on private citizens whose confidentiality is breached. Members and staff persons, because of the positions they occupy and the role they play in the formulation of policy, have no more right to breach a promise of confidentiality than does any other individual or entity in our society. Simple fairness requires that the Senate keep its promises, and that obligation runs to all who work within the institution regardless of rank or status.

A duty of fairness runs also to those who may be the subject of untested allegations delivered to the Senate in confidence. We cannot distinguish the principles which should govern the investigation of a nominee for the United States Supreme Court from the principles which govern any governmental investigation, including grand jury proceedings, where confidentiality is required in order to assure "that persons who are accused but exonerated . . . will not be held up to public ridicule." *(Douglas Oil Co. of California v. Petrol Stops Northwest).*

### 2. Institutional Interest

The Senate itself requires "breathing space" in order to encourage candid internal consideration of sensitive matters and alternative policies. As with any organization, plain speaking and individual candor within the Senate depend upon institutional acceptance of the importance of confidentiality in given circumstances. The Supreme Court has observed that "human experience teaches that those who expect public dissemination of their remarks may well temper candor with a concern for appearances and for their own interests to the detriment of the decision-making process," and has found the importance of protecting from public disclosure "communications from high Government officials to those who advise and assist them in the performance of their manifold duties . . . too plain to require further discussion." *(United States v. Nixon).*

An appropriate degree of confidentiality therefore is essential if the historic value of public access is to be maintained and if plain speaking and candid internal debate is to be encouraged. Beyond even those considerations, some degree of confidentiality must be respected if there is to be cooperation between the executive and legislative branches. Information of vital importance to the Senate often is within

the possession of the executive branch, and much of that information may be subject to concerns of confidentiality. The risk of unauthorized disclosure of confidential information has become a substantial impediment to open cooperation between the two branches, which are, after all, charged by the American public with the obligation to govern effectively. Officials in both the executive and the legislative branches have focused on the risk or actual instance of unauthorized disclosure by Congress as a reason which justifies unilateral decision by the executive branch to willfully withhold information from the Congress.

Finally, there is the question of public confidence. Violation of what the public perceives as accepted norms of conduct, including breaches of confidentiality, breeds a loss of faith and respect for the Senate. Any disagreement on this point evidences a serious misunderstanding of our people's sense of fairness and what is right. There must be concern for the argument, frequently heard, that the Senate cannot be trusted to legislate rules of public conduct when the Senate itself is unable or unwilling to act with appropriate care. The Senate is more than an institution. The Senate is a public example of proper conduct. A failure of the Senate to act in accord with its own rules, and within ordinary norms of decency, will surely produce an erosion in public confidence which is essential to effective representative government.

## B. Leaking

The practice of leaking destroys these interests in confidentiality. If it is correct, as The New York Times opined — "the Senate runs on leaks" — then its members must ask if this should continue. Institutional behavior begins with the members. It is they who are responsible for the sense of ethics and the environment within which staff persons work. How the Senate runs is up to its members.

There exists in any institution, whether written or not, a contract between employer and employee that information confidential to the institution shall not become public property. In the Senate, it is a contract which serves the public interest because it provides an environment within which open discourse can lead to the consensual resolution of issues. Leaking breaks that contract.

It is difficult to find a policy consideration which would justify institutional acceptance of leaking. The members of this institution should not be deceived. Leaking is viewed publicly as partisan and political. It is not viewed as honorable or productive or in the public interest. We agree with the words of Senator [George J.] Mitchell [D-Maine] when, on October 24, 1991, he stated:

> Every leak is to be condemned. Every leak is to be deplored. The end does not justify the means. And a leak which harms the opponent is

just as wrong as a leak which harms a friend. A leak which injures a cause I oppose is just as wrong as a leak which injures a cause I favor.

Those who leak violate more than institutional trust. He or she violates the confidence and friendship of those with whom they work. By demanding confidentiality as the price of disclosure, the anonymous source of a leak casts an unfair shadow of suspicion over all who have or are suspected to have had access to the same information. Throughout the course of this investigation, we have met and questioned tens of unusual men and women, many on the threshold of their careers, each possessed with intelligence, a high quotient of decency, and a true dedication to the commonweal. While their views undoubtedly differ on matters of public consequence, we have no doubt their views are well-informed and heartfelt. We speak of Senate staff persons and of those private persons who, far more than most Americans, give of their time and minds to issues, the resolution of which shall affect all of our futures. We speak also of the members of the Senate to whom too little public credit is given for carrying out the responsibilities of governance, the burden of which few of us are willing to assume. By condemning the anonymous source, the Senate will protect those who keep their trust. Each deserves this much.

A Senate in which leaking is tolerated, and even approved, will inevitably become a Senate within which free speech truly is inhibited. The expression of ideas in the course of reasonable debate will be stifled for fear that one's ideas — perhaps unpopular or contrarian — will become the fodder of public dialogue and criticism through anonymous disclosures. If the Senate implicitly condones the practice, it shall impair the freedom of open and honest debate and, over time, shall diminish and even lose its ability to decide the great issues that face us. It is this which provides the real threat to that freedom of speech for which the First Amendment stands.

It is precisely to this issue that Circuit Judge [James L.] Buckley recently spoke in *Lamprecht v. FCC*. In *Lamprecht*, preliminary drafts of the majority and dissenting opinions in a sensitive case were leaked in connection with the Thomas nomination. The final opinion of the court was issued on February 19, 1992. In words endorsed specifically by six of the other 11 circuit court judges, Judge Buckley wrote:

> The seriousness of this violation cannot be overstated. Each member of this panel has been aggrieved by it, as have the parties who brought this case to us for adjudication. Moreover, because one or more of their number has been guilty of a willful breach of trust, this incident must cast a shadow over the dozen or more able young law clerks who had become privy to the preliminary drafts.

The hemorrhaging of confidential information has become endemic in the legislative and executive branches of our government, with untold costs to their ability to function. It is essential that we prevent this disease from invading the judiciary, as this would inevitably undermine the public confidence that is one of the major strengths of our legal system.

S Res 202 squarely confronted the practice of leaking. It is for the Senate to determine whether the intent of S Res 202 is to become the rule of this institution.

The argument is made that leaks serve the public interest as a means of monitoring the conduct of public officials. It is a view based upon a presumption that respect for any idea of confidentiality will result in abuse of the public trust. We question this view, which, we believe, increasingly has shackled and therefore diminished the ability of government to reach reasoned decisions. We believe history shows that, as a nation, we fared better when a presumption of trust was the rule.

## C. The Media

The media view leaking from a different perspective. It may fairly be said the American media are addicted to leaks. They argue that leaks are essential to fulfilling their obligation as public watchdog. The passage of S Res 202 placed the Senate's interest in confidentiality on a collision course with this point of view.

### 1. The Journalists

Early in this investigation, we requested interviews of Phelps and Totenberg, the journalists who authored and broadcast the October 6 disclosures. Our requests were rejected publicly in print and on the air. Accordingly, subpoenas were issued to these and other journalists for testimony and documents. The media's response was swift, universal, exaggerated, inaccurate, and unfair to the Senate.

### 2. Decision To Subpoena Journalists

The decision to subpoena journalists was made independently by Special Counsel and his staff. No member was consulted. No member approved the decision. Under the rules enacted to govern this investigation, the president pro tempore was required to authorize the subpoenas because they clearly sought relevant evidence. Nor could the Rules Committee block the subpoenas. Its power was limited to ruling on objections to questions already asked. Ultimately, it exercised that power against Special Counsel.

### 3. Reasons

The journalists possessed the evidence which was most relevant to fulfilling the mandate of S Res 202. The law affords no testimonial privilege. The Supreme Court

has never recognized the privilege which the journalists claimed. Lower federal courts have never recognized the privilege where the evidence sought was relevant and a reasonable effort had been made to obtain that evidence from other sources. Further, a cloud of suspicion hung over the members of this institution and their staff persons. We believed — and continue to believe — that the interests of this institution and the public interest required that all lawful means be employed to lift that cloud and determine the truth.

The First Amendment does not elevate journalists to a position above all other citizens. Called upon to give relevant testimony in a proper forum, the law requires that journalists do so. Our position on this issue is fully set forth in papers submitted to the Rules Committee, copies of which are incorporated by reference as a part of this report. We there cited the words of then Circuit Judge Potter Stewart, in *Garland v. Torre*.

But freedom of the press, precious and vital though it is to a free society, is not an absolute.

Freedom of the press, hard-won over the centuries by men of courage, is basic to a free society. But basic too are courts of justice, armed with the power to discover the truth. The concept that it is the duty of a witness to testify in a court of law has roots fully as deep in our history as does the guarantee of a free press.

Without question, the exaction of this duty impinges, if not always, upon the First Amendment freedoms of the witness. Material sacrifice and the invasion of personal privacy are implicit in its performance. The freedom to choose whether to speak or to be silent disappears. But the personal sacrifice involved is a part of the necessary contribution of the individual to the welfare of the public.

If an additional First Amendment liberty — the freedom of the press — is here involved, we do not hesitate to conclude that it too must give place under the Constitution to a paramount public interest in the fair administration of justice.

The Supreme Court has spoken most recently on this issue in *Branzburg v. Hayes*, where Mr. Justice [Byron R.] White wrote:

We are admonished that refusal to provide a First Amendment reporter's privilege will undermine the freedom of the press to collect and disseminate news. But this is not the lesson history teaches us. As noted previously, the common law recognized no such privilege, and the constitutional argument was not even asserted until 1958. From the beginning of our country the press has

operated without constitutional protection for press informants, and the press has flourished. The existing constitutional rules have not been a serious obstacle to either the development or retention of confidential news sources by the press.

There has since evolved in the lower federal courts a standard which requires the balancing of two considerations. The first consideration is whether identification of the confidential source is central to the determination of the issue at hand. The second consideration is whether the party requesting disclosure has made reasonable efforts to obtain the same information from alternative sources.

Both considerations were satisfied in this investigation. There is no doubt that identification of confidential sources is relevant and goes to the very heart of the mandate of S Res 202. Nor can there be any claim of a failure to exhaust alternative sources of information. In excess of 200 witnesses were questioned in both matters, all under the penal sanction of 18 U.S.C. 1001. These included senators and staff persons with access or reasonably possible access to the information in question in both matters, private counsel in the Keating investigation, private sector individuals, Anita Hill herself, and each member of the executive branch, including the White House, the Department of Justice, and the FBI, who had access or reasonably possible access to the information in question in the Thomas matter.

Just as there exists a conflict between the Senate's right of confidentiality and the media's pursuit of the news, there exists a tension between a journalist's choice of silence and the rule of law which governs all citizens. This tension cannot and should not be eased or resolved by accommodation. History teaches that enforcement of the law has provided the appropriate and lasting means for either the validation or change of existing law. The appropriate process has been judicial. If journalists are to receive a testimonial protection not accorded other citizens, then this protection must spring either from informed judicial decision or legislative enactment of appropriate shield laws.

A free and democratic society does not rest on the notion that all information shall be made available for public debate. It is worthwhile to remember that the framers themselves insisted on privacy for the deliberations from which our Constitution itself emerged. For reasons already stated, confidential deliberation is a necessary component of conscientious governance. A balance must be maintained between a multitude of competing interests. It is this truth which the media ignore in their claim of primacy.

Senate acceptance of the media's insistence that their interests are foremost, and acquiescence in the media's claim of a superior right, will sanction the continued ability and perhaps even the right of sena-

tors and staff persons to disclose confidential information with a certainty that their anonymity will be secure. This is a thoughtless proposition, which the passage of S Res 202 seemed clearly to reject.

Further, when we consider the needs of this institution, it is difficult to find a policy consideration which can justify anonymity as a legitimate demand by those who seek to disclose confidential Senate information. If the decision to breach confidence is based upon a genuine perception of the public interest, then no person should wish to be anonymous. The decision to speak with attribution lends both weight and honor to the claim that it is the public interest which is at heart. From Boston Harbor to the streets of Selma, open protest has been our people's way of effecting change.

DATED: May 4, 1992
Respectfully submitted,
PETER FLEMING JR.
Temporary Special Independent Counsel

Mark O'Donoghue
Samuel Rosenthal
Michelle Rice

Associate Counsel

# Bush, Democratic Leaders Agree to Work Together

*In response to the riots in Los Angeles, President Bush and congressional leaders agreed May 12 to try to fashion compromise legislation to address the social and economic problems of American cities.*

*The day before their meeting, Democratic leaders sent Bush a letter outlining their approach to the problem. Following is the text of the May 11 letter, which was signed by Senate Majority Leader George J. Mitchell, D-Maine, House Speaker Thomas S. Foley, D-Wash., and House Majority Leader Dick Gephardt, D-Mo.*

Dear Mr. President,

We commend you for visiting Los Angeles last week. The presence and concern of the President are important to Americans in a time of crisis.

The events in Los Angeles have focused national attention on the serious economic and social problems in urban areas.

The conditions present in Los Angeles exist in most of our nations's urban areas. They present a challenge to our society. That requires an immediate response to the situation in Los Angeles and a longer term strategy that addresses the fundamental problems in many of our cities.

The creation of jobs, and the opportunity and hope that come with a job, are vital to the recovery of Los Angeles and the renewal of our urban areas. The personal safety of residents of urban areas is crucial to the rejuvenation and vibrancy of neighborhoods.

We know that we and you disagree on some aspects of this matter.

Americans undoubtedly also have different perspectives on the best approaches to these problems. But on one thing we can all agree: No one benefits if differences of opinion paralyze our society's response.

We therefore propose the following actions and invite you to join with us in gaining their enactment.

— People need jobs. The surface Transportation Act of 1991 provided the largest public works authorization in our history. Nearly all of the required money is in a Trust Fund. States have indicated that they could use another $1 billion on approved projects this year. States will be able to spend the full $25.7 billion authorized for the next fiscal year. We urge you to revise your FY 1993 budget request to provide for the full authorization. This would increase available funds by $3.6 billion.

— In addition, the Housing Reauthorization bill now pending in Congress, including the Community Development Block Grant, and the Head Start summer program, will create jobs and empower urban residents by providing increased affordable housing and expanding local community development activities.

We can begin to improve this beginning, first, with consultation, among Members of the Congressional Black Caucus, community leaders in Los Angeles and other affected urban areas; and, second, by recognizing that other long-term measures, now stalled because of politics or paralysis, must be broken free and moved to the front of the nation's agenda. Specifically, we refer to the need for cooperation between the Executive Branch and Congress on behalf of broad-based economic growth that will provide jobs, opportunity and justice for all Americans. It has often been said, and we would do well to remember today, that a good job is the best social program for everyone in our society.

These measures, by themselves, will not solve all the problems. Much more will be needed. But we believe they represent an important start.

Without order, there cannot be the stable communities that nurture stable families. The foundation for personal responsibility is formed only within a stable family structure. There is a broad core of agreement between us on which we can build, and we write you in the same spirit you expressed in a news conference before leaving to visit Los Angeles.

You told Americans then that the challenge is not one of assigning blame, but whether we, as a country, have not done enough for those left behind. You said you were not satisfied that we had. We share those sentiments.

Americans need to know that their President and Congress, whatever their differences, can work together to meet urgent national needs. We want to do so. We believe we can. We believe incentives for economic growth and restoration; the urgent need to combat crime and random violence; and a deeper commitment by government, business, and individuals to constructive, supportive family policy; all these constitute a common ground.

We invite you to join us in moving expeditiously in a bipartisan fashion on these important initiatives.

## Bush Statement

*The following day, May 12, President Bush outlined his urban agenda in a written statement. Following is the text:*

Today I am discussing with Congress a strategy to bring hope and opportunity to distressed communities. Our action is based on bedrock American values — personal responsibility, work and family. We must end the cycle of dependency and give all Americans a place at the table of economic opportunity.

Clearly, the time has come to set aside old ideas and try something new. We in government have a responsibility to act now to guarantee a hopeful future for the children of this nation — a future where people are safe, neighborhoods can flourish, children can learn and jobs can be created.

All Americans share the common goals of equal opportunity, advancement, and upward mobility. But the American Dream is hindered by too many obstacles: unsafe cities, slow economic growth, an out-of-date education system and dependency-creating government programs.

We must start with policies that refocus programs to serve those who are most needy, and increase the effectiveness of government services through innovation, competition and choice. Our approach is a radical break with the policies of the past. But as Abraham Lincoln once said, "It is time to think and act anew."

My action plan consists of six core components:

(1) "Weed and Seed": Our families cannot thrive and jobs cannot flourish in a climate of lawlessness and fear. Our "Weed and Seed" initiative to combat crime wins back our inner cities by "weeding out" gang leaders, drug dealers and career criminals and "seeding" communities with expanded employment, educational and social services.

(2) HOPE: When people lack jobs, opportunity or ownership of property, they have little or no stake in their communities. Our HOPE (Homeownership and Opportunity for People Everywhere) initiative fosters a sense of community pride by offering inner-city residents a chance for homeownership and management of public housing.

(3) Enterprise Zones: We must spark an economic revival in urban America to create jobs and opportunity. Our enterprise zones initiative encourages businesses to re-enter our inner cities by creating tax credits, expanding capital investment and bringing regulatory relief to some of the nation's most economically depressed areas.

(4) Education Reform: It is time to reform and improve American education. Our education reform strategy — America 2000 — envisions an America in which all parents have the choice of the best schools available — public, private or parochial.

(5) Welfare Reform: While no one disputes that government has an obligation to provide a safety net to those in need, there is too much emphasis on programs that penalize ambition, promote alienation and destroy individual dignity. We must encourage family formation and allow individuals to fulfill their potential for a productive, meaningful life.

(6) Youth Jobs: Youth apprenticeships and Job Training 2000 — The health of our cities and our economy depend on a skilled work force and facilitating the transportation of students from school to work. Prompt enactment of our proposals can help provide job opportunities and training this summer. ∎

## ADDRESS TO CONGRESS

# 'There Will Be No More Lies,' Yeltsin Vows to the Nation

### Russian pledges action on POWs, asks American support, saying 'there is no alternative to reform'

*On June 17, Russian President Boris N. Yeltsin addressed a joint meeting of the House and Senate. Following is the Reuter transcript of his remarks, delivered through an interpreter:*

Mr. Speaker, Mr. President, members of Congress, ladies and gentlemen:

It is indeed a great honor for me to address the Congress of the great land of freedom as the first-ever, over 1,000 years of history of Russia, popularly elected president, as a citizen of the great country which has made its choice in favor of liberty and democracy.

For many years, our two nations were the two poles, the two opposites. They wanted to make us implacable enemies. That affected the destinies of the world in a most tragic way.

The world was shaken by the storms of confrontation. It was close to exploding; close to perishing beyond salvation.

That evil scenario is becoming a thing of the past. Reason begins to triumph over madness. We have left behind the period when America and Russia looked at each other through gun sights, ready to pull the trigger at any time.

Despite what we saw in the well-known American film, "The Day After," it can be said today, tomorrow will be a day of peace, less of fear and more of hope for the happiness of our children.

The world can sigh in relief. The idol of communism, which spread everywhere social strife, animosity and unparalleled brutality, which instilled fear in humanity, has collapsed.

It has collapsed never to rise again. I am here to assure you, we will not let it rise again in our land.

I am glad that the people of Russia have found strength to shake off the crushing burden of the totalitarian system. I am proud that I am addressing you on behalf of the great people whose dignity is restored.

I admire ordinary Russian men and women who, in spite of severe trials, have preserved their intellectual integrity and are enduring tremendous hardships for the

R. MICHAEL JENKINS

**Addressing Congress June 17, Yeltsin vowed to account for any American POWs in the former Soviet Union.**

sake of the revival of their country.

Russia has made its final choice in favor of a civilized way of life, common sense and universal human heritage. I am convinced that our people will reach that goal. There is no people on this earth who could be harmed by the air of freedom. There are no exceptions to that rule.

Liberty sets the mind free, fosters independence and unorthodox thinking and ideas. But it does not offer instant prosperity or happiness and wealth to everyone. This is something that politicians in particular must keep in mind. Even the most benevolent intentions will inevitably be abandoned and committed to oblivion if they are not translated into everyday efforts.

Our experience of the recent years has conclusively pointed that out. Liberty will not be fooled. There can be no coexistence between democracy and a totalitarian state system. There can be no coexistence between market economy and powers who control everything and everyone.

There can be no coexistence between a

civic society, which is pluralist by definition, and communist intolerance to dissent. The experience of the past decade has taught us: Communism has no human face. Freedom and communism are incompatible.

You will recall August 1991, when for three days Russia was under the dark cloud of dictatorship.

I addressed the Muscovites who were defending the White House of Russia. I addressed all the people of Russia. I addressed them standing on top of the tank whose crew had disobeyed criminal orders.

I will be candid with you: At that moment, I feared. But I had no fear for myself. I feared for the future of democracy in Russia and throughout the world. Because I was aware what could happen if we failed to win.

Citizens of Russia upheld their freedom and did not allow the continuation of the 75 years of nightmare. From this high rostrum I want to express our sincere thanks and gratitude to President Bush and to the American people for their invaluable moral support for the just cause of the people of Russia.

Last year citizens of Russia passed another difficult test of maturity. We chose to forgo vengeance and the intoxicating craving for summary justice over the fallen collossus known under the name of the CPSU [Communist Party of the Soviet Union].

There was no replay of history. The Communist Party citadel, next to the Kremlin, the Communist Bastille, was not destroyed. There was not a hint of violence against Communists in Russia. People simply brushed off the venomous dust of the past and went about their business.

There were no lynch law trials in Russia. The doings of the Communist Party over many years have been referred to the constitutional court of the Russian Federation. I am confident that its verdict will be fair.

Russia has seen for itself that any delay in strengthening the foundations of freedom and democracy can throw the society far back. For us the ominous lesson of the past is relevant today as never before. It was precisely in a devastated country, with an economy in near paralysis, that

Bolshevism succeeded in building a totalitarian regime, creating a gigantic war machine and an insatiable military-industrial complex.

## Economic and Political Reforms

This must not be allowed to happen again. That is why economic and political reforms are the primary tasks for Russia today. We are facing the challenges that no one has ever faced before at any one time.

We must carry through unprecedented reforms in the economy, which over the seven decades has been stripped of all market infrastructure; lay the foundations for democracy; and restore the rule of law in the country that for scores of years was poisoned with political strife and political oppression.

We have no right to fail in this most difficult endeavor, for there will be no second try, as in sports. Our predecessors have used them all up. The reforms must succeed.

I am given strength by the support of the majority of the citizens of Russia. The people of Russia are aware that there is no alternative to reform, and that this is very important.

My job, as everybody else's in Russia, is not an easy one. But in everything I do, I have the reliable and invaluable support of my wife, and of my entire large family.

Today I am telling you what I tell my fellow countrymen: I will not go back on the reforms. And it is practically impossible to topple Yeltsin in Russia. I am in good health, and I will not say "uncle" before I make the reforms irreversible.

We realize our great responsibility for the success of our changes, not only toward the people of Russia but also toward the citizens of America and of the entire world.

Today the freedom of America is being upheld in Russia. Should the reforms fail, it will cost hundreds of billions to upset that failure.

## New Arms Treaty

Yesterday we concluded an unprecedented agreement on cutting down strategic offensive arsenals. They will be reduced radically in two phases, not by 30 or 40 percent, as negotiated previously over 15 years. They will be slashed to less than one-third of today's strength — from 21,000 nuclear warheads on both sides down to 6,000 to 7,000 by the year 2000. And it has taken us only five months to negotiate. And I fervently hope that George Bush and myself will be there in the year 2000 to preside over that.

We have simply no right to miss this unique opportunity, the more so that arms and the future of Russian reforms designed to make impossible any restoration of the totalitarian dictatorship in Russia are so dramatically interrelated.

I am here to say that we have the firm determination and the political will to move forward. We have proved that by what we have done.

It is Russia that has put an end to the imperial policies and was the first to recog-

nize the independence of the Baltic republics.

Russia is a founding member of the Commonwealth of Independent States, which has averted uncontrolled disintegration of the former empire and the threat of a general interethnic blood bath.

Russia has granted tangible powers to its autonomous republics. The treaty of federation has been signed, and our nation has escaped the fate of the Soviet Union.

Russia has preserved its unity. It was Russia that substantially slowed down the flywheel of militarization and is doing all it can to stop it altogether.

I am formally announcing that, without waiting for the treaty to be signed, we have begun taking off alert the heavy SS-18 missiles targeted on the United States of America.

And the defense minister of Russia is here in this room to confirm that.

Russia has brought its policies toward a number of countries in line with its solemn declarations of the recent years. We have stopped arms deliveries to Afghanistan, where the senseless military adventure has taken thousands of Russian and hundreds of thousands of Afghan lives.

With external props removed, the puppet regime collapsed.

We have corrected the well-known imbalances in relations with Cuba. At present that country is one of our Latin American partners. Our commerce with Cuba is based on universally accepted principles and world prices.

## An End to Double Standards

It is Russia that once and for all has done away with double standards in foreign policy. We are firmly resolved not to lie any more, either to our negotiating partners, or to the Russian or American or any other people.

There will be no more lies — ever.

The same applies to biological weapons experiments and the facts that have been revealed about American prisoners of war, the KAL 007 flight and many other things. That list could be continued.

The archives of the KGB and the Communist Party Central Committee are being opened.

Moreover, we are inviting the cooperation of the United States and other nations to investigate these dark pages.

I promise you that each and every document in each and every archive will be examined in order to investigate the fate of every American unaccounted for. As president of Russia, I assure you that even if one American has been detained in my country, and can still be found, I will find him; I will get him back to his family.

*(sustained applause)*

I thank you for the applause. I could see everybody rise.

Some of you who have just risen here to applaud me have also written in the press that until Yeltsin gets things done and gets all the jobs done, there should be no Freedom Support Act passing through the Congress.

Well, I don't really quite understand you, ladies and gentlemen. This matter has been investigated, and is being investigated. Yeltsin has already opened the archives, and is inviting you to join us in investigating the fate of each and every unaccounted American.

So now you are telling me, first, do the job, and then we shall support you in passing that act? I don't quite understand you.

We have made tangible moves to make contact between Russia and foreign business communities much easier. Under the recent legislation, foreign nationals who privatize a facility or a building in Russia are given property rights to the plot of land on which they are located.

Legislation on bankruptcy has been recently enacted.

Mandatory sale of foreign currency to the state, at an artificially low rate of exchange, has been ended.

We are ready to bring our legal practice, as much as possible, in line with world standards, of course on the basis of symmetry with each country.

We are inviting the private sector of the United States to invest in the unique and untapped Russian market. And I am saying: Do not be late.

## U.S. Policy

Now that the period of global confrontation is behind us, I call upon you to take a fresh look at the current policy of the United States toward Russia, and also to take a fresh look at the longer-term prospects of our relations.

Russia is a different country today. Sometimes the obsolete standards brought into being by a different era are artificially imposed on new realities.

True, that equally applies to us. Let us together, therefore, master the art of reconciling differences on the basis of partnership, which is the most efficient and democratic way.

This would come naturally both for the Russians and the Americans. If this is done, many of the problems which are now impeding mutual advantageous cooperation between Russia and the United States will become irrelevant, and I mean legislative frameworks too.

It will not be a wasteful endeavor. On the contrary, it will promote a more efficient solution of your problems, as well as of ours. And of course it will create new jobs, in Russia as well as in the United States.

History is giving us a chance to fulfill President [Woodrow] Wilson's dream, namely, to make the world safe for democracy.

More than 30 years ago, President [John F.] Kennedy addressed these words to humanity: "My fellow citizens of the world, ask not what America can do for you, but what together we can do for the freedom of man."

I believe that his inspired call for working together toward a democratic world is addressed above all to our two peoples, to the people of America and to

the people of Russia.

Partnership and friendship of our two largest democracies, in strengthening democracy, is indeed a great goal.

Joining the world community, we wish to preserve our identity, our own image and history, promote culture, strengthen moral standards of our people.

We find relevant the warning of the great Russian philosopher, Berdyaev, who said to negate Russia in the name of humankind is to rob humankind.

At the same time, Russia does not aspire to change the world in its own image. It is the fundamental principle of the new Russia to be generous and to share experience, moral values and emotional warmth, rather than to impose and curse.

It is the tradition of the Russian people to repay kindness with kindness. This is the bedrock of the Russian lifestyle, the underlying truth revealed by the great Russian culture.

Free and democratic Russia will remain committed to this tenet. Today, free and democratic Russia is extending its hand of friendship to the people of America. Acting on the will of the people of Russia, I am inviting you, and through you, the people of the United States, to join us in partnership in the quest for freedom and justice in the 21st century.

The Russo-American dialogue has gone through many a dramatic moment. But the peoples of Russia and America have never gone to war against each other. Even in the darkest periods, our affinity prevailed over our hatred.

In this context, I would like to recall something that took place 50 years ago. The unprecedented war, world war, was waging. Russia, which was bleeding white, and all our people were looking forward to the opening of the second front. And it was opened, first and foremost, thanks to the active stance taken by President [Franklin D.] Roosevelt and by the entire American people.

Sometimes I think that if today, like during that war, a second but peaceful front could be opened to promote democratic market reforms, their success would be guaranteed early.

The passing by Congress of the Freedom Support Act could become the first step in that direction.

Today legislation promoting reforms is much more important than appropriation of funds.

May I express the hope that the United States Congress, as the staunch advocate of freedom, will remain faithful to its strategic course on this occasion as well.

Members of Congress, every man is a man of his own time. No exception is ever made for anyone, whether an ordinary citizen or the president. Much experience has been gained; many things have been reassessed.

I would like now to conclude my statement with the words from a song by Irving Berlin, an American of Russian descent: God bless America, to which I add, and Russia. ∎

## JOINT NEWS CONFERENCE

# Bush, Yeltsin Announce Accord On Speeding Arms Reductions

*Following is the Reuter transcript of the joint announcement June 16 by President Bush and Russian President Boris N. Yeltsin on the new strategic arms agreement and on the POW/MIA question. Yeltsin spoke through an interpreter.*

**PRESIDENT BUSH:** . . . Let me just say that I'm pleased to announce that President Yeltsin and I have just reached an extraordinary agreement on two areas of vital importance to our countries and to the world. First, we have agreed on far-reaching new strategic arms reductions, building on the agreement reached with Russia, Ukraine, Kazakhstan and Belarus. Our two countries are now agreeing to even further dramatic strategic arms reductions substantially below the levels determined by START [Strategic Arms Reduction Treaty].

We have agreed to eliminate the world's most dangerous weapons, heavy

---

**"With this agreement, the nuclear nightmare recedes more and more for ourselves, for our children and for our grandchildren."**

**—President Bush**

---

ICBMs [intercontinental ballistic missiles], and all other multiple-warhead ICBMs, and dramatically reduce our total strategic nuclear weapons.

Those dramatic reductions will take place in two phases. They will be completed no later than the year 2003 and may be completed as early as the year 2000 if the United States can assist Russia in the required destruction of ballistic missile systems.

With this agreement, the nuclear nightmare recedes more and more for ourselves, for our children and for our grandchildren.

Just a few years ago, the United States was planning a strategic nuclear stockpile of about 13,000 warheads. Now President Yeltsin and I have agreed that both sides will go down to 3,000 to 3,500 warheads, with each nation determining its own force structure within that range.

And I'd like to point out that this fundamental agreement, which in earlier years could not have been completed even in a decade, has been completed in only five

months.

Our ability to reach this agreement so quickly is a tribute to the new relationship between the United States and Russia and to the personal leadership of our guest, Boris Yeltsin.

In the near future, the United States and Russia will record our agreement in a brief treaty document that President Yeltsin and I will sign and submit for ratification in our countries.

President Yeltsin and I have also agreed to work together, along with the allies and other interested states, to develop a concept for a global protection system against limited ballistic missile attack.

And we will explore a senior group — or we will establish a senior group — to explore practical steps toward that end, including the sharing of early warning and cooperation in developing ballistic missile defense capabilities and technologies.

This group will also explore the development of a legal basis for cooperation, including new treaties and agreements, and possible changes to existing treaties and agreements necessary to implement the global protection system.

That group is headed by [State Department Policy Planning Director] Dennis Ross for the United States [and] will first meet in Moscow within the next 30 days.

In conclusion, these are remarkable steps for our two countries, a departure from the tensions and the suspicions of the past, and a tangible, important expression of our new relationship. They also hold major promise for a future world protected against the danger of limited ballistic missile attack.

### Yeltsin Responds

**PRESIDENT YELTSIN:** Mr. President, ladies and gentlemen, I'd like to add a few words to what President Bush has just announced here.

What we have achieved is an unparalleled and probably an unexpected thing for you and for the whole world. You are the first to hear about this historic decision, which has been reached today after just five months of negotiations. We are in fact meeting a sharp, dramatic reduction in the total number for the two sides of the number of nuclear warheads, from 21,000 to 6,000 or 7,000 for the United States of America and Russia.

Indeed, we have been able to cut over those five months of negotiations the total number of nuclear warheads to one-third, while it took 15 years under the START treaty to make some reductions.

This is an expression of the funda-

mental change in the political and economic relations between the United States of America and Russia.

It is also an expression and a proof of the personal trust and confidence that has been established between the presidents of these countries, President Bush of the United States of America and [the] president of Russia, and these things have been achieved without deception, without anybody wishing to gain unilateral advantages.

This is a result of the trust entertained by the president of democratic Russia toward America and by the president of the United States toward the new Russia.

This is the result of a carefully measured balance of security. We were not going in for numbers, for just 1,000, 2,000 or 3,000 pieces. Rather we have established a record for each country to elect the number, the figure that it will consider appropriate for its own defense and security.

As I have told you, the total number will go down from 21,000 to 6,000 for the two sides. Under the first phase, the reductions for the two sides will be down to the 3,800-to-4,250 bracket: including ICBMs, 1,250; and heavy missiles, 650; SLBMs, 2,250. Under the second phase we shall go down to, respectively, 3,000 and 3,500, including total reduction and destruction of heavy missiles.

Land-based MIRVs [multiple warhead missiles] will be reduced as well. SLBMs [submarine-launched ballistic missiles] will go down to 1,750.

Each country will elect the figure that it will consider appropriate to ensure its defense and security.

Thus we are departing from the ominous parity where each country was exerting every effort to stay in line, which has led Russia, for instance, to have half of its population living below the poverty line. We cannot afford it, and therefore we must have a minimum-security level to deal with any possible eventuality which might arise anywhere in the world and threaten our security.

But we know one thing: We shall not fight against each other. This is a solemn undertaking that we are taking today, and it will be reflected as a matter of partnership and friendship in the charter that we are going to sign.

Our proposal is to cut the process of destruction from the proposed 13 years down to nine years. So the things that I have been mentioning before will materialize by the year 2000.

I am happy to be involved here in this historic occasion, and I will also hope that I will be as happy when this thing materializes and President Bush and I will be celebrating together the implementation of that agreement in the year 2000.

I thank you.

I want to add that these figures have been agreed with and ratified by the secretary for Defense, Mr. [Dick] Cheney, and the defense minister, Pavel Grachev, of the Russian Federation.

I thank you.

**P:** And I would only add to that my gratitude to the secretary of State, to Mr. [Andrei V.] Kozyrev, his counterpart, and also to Gen. [Brent] Scowcroft and others that have worked on this and accomplished all this in record time. . . .

**Q:** Would you explain for people who might not understand why friends who trust each other and who do not plan to attack would still need 7,000 nuclear warheads —

**P:** What I'm saying is, we've moved dramatically down from 13,000. It's going to be a — this will be seen as an enormous move forward toward the relaxation of tension and toward the friendship that we feel for each other.

The elimination of these — the most destabilizing of weapons — is extraordinarily positive. And the fact that each country at this juncture in history retains some nuclear weapons speaks for itself.

Who knows what lies out there ahead? But certainly I agree with what President Yeltsin said, that there is no animosity. The Cold War days are over, and he came here in a spirit of forward movement on these arms control agreements, and that speaks for itself.

**YELTSIN:** I would like to amplify on that.

I would say that in response to your question that the technical and financial resources that are required in order to destroy, dismantle and reduce the total number of warheads and missiles from 21,000 to 6,000 or 7,000 is enormous, and this is the only thing that conditions this figure.

## American POWs

**Q:** [Question on the status of possible American POWs in Russia].

**P:** . . . . President Yeltsin and I discussed this morning the issue that is of the highest priority for our administration and, I know, for every American — the fate of American POWs and MIAs from World War II, Korea, the Cold War period and Vietnam.

President Yeltsin informed me for the first time that Russia may have information about the fate of some of our servicemen from Vietnam. And he said the Russian government is pursuing this information vigorously, just as we speak.

And with us today are President Yeltsin's adviser, Dmitri Volkogonov over here, and our able former ambassador to the U.S.S.R., Ambassador Malcolm Toon. Now they are the co-chairs of the Joint U.S.-Russian Commission on POW-MIAs, and they've met during the last few months along with the members of the United States Congress who are also part of this bipartisan U.S. delegation to unearth information on American POWs and MIAs from 1945 on, and Russian POWs and MIAs from the Afghan war.

President Yeltsin and I have instructed both of these gentlemen to begin immediately a joint U.S.-Russian pursuit of the latest information — it was given to me today.

I have asked Ambassador Toon to return immediately to Moscow to work on this issue, and I want to assure all Americans, and particularly those families of the American POWs and MIAs, that we will spare no effort in working with our Russian colleagues to investigate all information in the Russian archives concerning our servicemen.

And while we do not have any specific information to make public today, I pledge to keep the American people informed of developments on this issue as we find out more about these latest leads.

And let me just point out that the forthcoming comments by President Yeltsin are just one more sign of this improved new relationship between Russia and the United States of America. For him to go back and dig into these records, without fear of embarrassment, is of enormous consequence to the people of the United States of America.

And I salute him for this. He has told me he will go the last mile to find whatever . . . [information exists about] American POWs and MIAs, and to clear this record once and for all, and in so many other fields this demonstrates his leadership and the period of change that we are saluting and I saluted here today on the South Lawn of the White House. So we're very grateful to you, Mr. President.

**YELTSIN:** I will only add a couple of points, Mr. President.

Our commission, headed and chaired by Dmitri Volkogonov, has been meeting for several months now, and it has already met with some success, and I can promise that the joint commission which will be established following this press conference will be working hard and will report to the American public all the information that will be found in the archives that we are going to open for it, in . . . [opening] the archives in the KGB, in the Central Committee of the Communist Party, regarding the fate of American POWs and MIAs.

**Q:** Do you agree it's possible some of those Americans may still be alive?

**P:** I would simply say that this — I have no evidence of that, but the cooperation that is, has been extended, and again is being extended by the president of Russia will guarantee to the American people that if anyone's alive, that person, those people would be found. And equally as important to the loved ones is the accounting for any possible MIA.

And so we have no evidence of anyone being alive, but I would simply say again that this, this is the best way to get to the bottom of it, and this new approach by the president of Russia to go into these archives and to try to find missing records will be the best assurance that I can give the American people that the truth will, will be revealed, finally.

**Q:** Is there a danger of raising false hopes?

**P:** You got to be careful of that, yeah. ∎

## PRESIDENTIAL ADDRESS

# Bush: U.S. 'Second to None' In Environmental Effort

*Following is the text of President Bush's formal remarks at the Earth Summit in Rio de Janeiro, Brazil, on June 12:*

**PRESIDENT BUSH:** .... This is truly an historic gathering.

And the Chinese have a proverb, if a man cheats the Earth, the Earth will cheat man. And the idea of sustaining the planet so that it may sustain us is as old as life itself. We must leave this Earth in better condition than we found it.

And today this old truth must be applied to new threats facing the resources which sustain us all — the atmosphere and the ocean, the stratosphere and the biosphere. Our village is truly global. Some find the challenges ahead overwhelming. I believe that their pessimism is unfounded.

Twenty years ago, at the Stockholm Conference, the chief concern of our predecessors was the horrible threat of nuclear war, the ultimate pollutant. No more. Upon my return from Rio, I will meet with Russian President [Boris N.] Yeltsin in Washington, and the subject we will discuss is cooperation, not confrontation.

Twenty years ago, some spoke of the limits to growth, and today we realize that growth is the engine of change, and the friend of the environment. Today an unprecedented era of peace, freedom and stability makes concerted action on the environment possible as never before.

This summit is but one key step in the process of international cooperation on environment and development. The United States will work to carry forward the promise of Rio. And because as important as the road to Rio has been, what matters more is the road from Rio.

There are those who say that cooperation between developed and developing countries is impossible. Well, let them come to Latin America, where debt-for-nature swaps are protecting forests in Costa Rica and funding pollution control in Chile. There are those who say that it takes state control to protect the environment. Well, let them go to Eastern Europe, where the poisoned bodies of children now pay for the sins of fallen dictators, and only the new breeze of freedom is allowing for cleanup.

There are those who say that change can never come because the interests of the status quo are too powerful. Well, let them come right here to Brazil, where President [Fernando] Collor [de Mello] is forging a new approach that recognizes the economic value of sustaining the rain forest.

There are those who say that economic growth and environmental protection cannot be compatible. Well, let them come to the United States, where in the 20 years since Stockholm, our economy has grown by 57 percent and yet we've cut the lead going into the air by 97 percent, the carbon monoxide by 41 percent, the particulates by 59 percent. We've cleaned up our water and preserved our parks, wilderness and wildlife.

There are those who say that the leaders of the world do not care about the Earth and the environment. Well, let them all come here to Rio.

Mr. President, we have come to Rio. We've not only seen the concern; we share it. We not only care; we're taking action.

We come to Rio with an action plan on climate change. It stresses energy efficiency, cleaner air, reforestation, new technology. And I'm happy to report that I've just signed that framework convention on climate change.

And today I invite my colleagues from the industrialized world to join in a prompt start on the convention's implementation. I propose that our countries meet by Jan. 1 to lay out our national plans for meeting the specific commitments in the framework convention. Let us join in translating the words spoken here into concrete action to protect the planet.

We come to Rio with a proposal to double global forest assistance, and we stand ready to work together, respecting national sovereignty, on new strategies for forests for the future.

As a down payment, we will double U.S. forest bilateral assistance next year and we will reform at home, phasing out clear-cutting as a standard practice on U.S. national forests and working to plant 1 billion trees a year.

We come to Rio with an extensive program of technology cooperation. We stand ready, government and private sector, to help spread green technology and launch a new generation of clean growth. We come to Rio recognizing that the developing countries must play a role in protecting the global environment but will need assistance in pursuing this cleaner growth.

So we stand ready to increase U.S. international environmental aid by 66 percent above the 1990 levels, on top of the more than $2.5 billion that we provide through the world's development banks for Agenda 21 projects.

We come to Rio with more scientific knowledge about the environment than ever before and with the wisdom that there is much, much we [can] do that's not yet known. And we stand ready to share our science and to lead the world in a program of continued research.

We come to Rio prepared to continue America's unparalleled efforts to preserve species and habitat. And let me be clear: Our efforts to protect biodiversity itself will exceed, will exceed the requirements of the treaty. But that proposed agreement threatens to retard biotechnology and undermine the protection of ideas, and unlike the climate agreement, its financing scheme will not work. And it is never easy, it is never easy to stand alone on principle, but sometimes leadership requires that you do. And now is such a time.

Let's face it, there has been some criticism of the United States, but I must tell you, we come to Rio proud of what we have accomplished, and committed to extending the record on American leadership on the environment. In the United States we have the world's tightest air quality standards on cars and factories, the most advanced laws for protecting lands and waters, and the most open processes for public participation.

And now for a simple truth. America's record on environmental protection is second to none, so I did not come here to apologize. We come to press on with deliberate purpose and forceful action, and such action will demonstrate our continuing commitment to leadership and to international cooperation on the environment.

We believe that the road to Rio must point toward both environmental protection and economic growth, environment and development, and by now it's clear [that] to sustain development we must protect the environment and to protect the environment we must sustain development.

It's been said that we don't inherit the Earth from our ancestors, we borrow it from our children, and when our children look back on this time and this place they will be grateful that we met at Rio and they will certainly be pleased with the intentions stated and the commitments made. But they will judge us by the actions we take from this day forward. Let us not disappoint them.

Mr. President, once again my congratulations to you, sir; Mr. [U.N.] Secretary General [Boutros Boutros-Ghali], our sincere thanks, and thank you all very, very much. ∎

## ABORTION

# Supreme Court's Decision On Pennsylvania Case

*Following are excerpts from the U.S. Supreme Court's June 29 opinions in the cases of* Planned Parenthood v. Casey *and* Casey v. Planned Parenthood. *The main opinion was written by Justice Sandra Day O'Connor on behalf of herself and Justices Anthony M. Kennedy and David H. Souter. Separate opinions concurring in part and dissenting in part were filed by Justices Harry A. Blackmun and John Paul Stevens. Chief Justice William H. Rehnquist wrote an opinion, joined by Justices Byron R. White, Antonin Scalia and Clarence Thomas, dissenting from the majority's upholding of the 1973 case* Roe v. Wade, *which set out the right of a woman to obtain an abortion.*

### O'Connor's Majority Opinion

Liberty finds no refuge in a jurisprudence of doubt. Yet 19 years after our holding that the Constitution protects a woman's right to terminate her pregnancy in its early stages, *Roe v. Wade*, 410 U.S. 113 (1973), that definition of liberty is still questioned. Joining the respondents as amicus curiae, the United States, as it has done in five other cases in the last decade, again asks us to overrule *Roe....*

The Court of Appeals found it necessary to follow an elaborate course of reasoning ... to determine whether the statute enacted by Pennsylvania meets constitutional standards. And at oral arguments in this Court, the attorney for the parties challenging the statute took the position that none of the enactments can be upheld without overruling *Roe v. Wade.* We disagree with that analysis; but we acknowledge that our decisions after *Roe* cast doubt upon the meaning and reach of its holding. Further, the Chief Justice admits that he would overrule the central holding of *Roe* and adopt the rational relationship test as the sole criterion of constitutionality. State and federal courts as well as legislatures throughout the Union must have guidance as they seek to address this subject in conformance with the Constitution. Given these premises, we find it imperative to review once more the principles that define the rights of the woman and the legitimate authority of the State respecting termination of pregnancies by abortion procedures.

After considering the fundamental constitutional questions resolved by *Roe*, principles of institutional integrity, and the rule of stare decisis, we are led to conclude this: The essential holding of *Roe v. Wade* should be retained and once again reaffirmed.

It must be stated at the outset and with clarity that *Roe*'s essential holding, the holding we reaffirm, has three parts. First is a recognition of the right of the woman to choose to have an abortion before viability and to obtain it without undue interference from the State. Before viability, the State's interests are not strong enough to support a prohibition of abortion or the imposition of a substantial obstacle to the woman's effective right to elect the procedure. Second is a confirmation of the State's power to restrict abortions after fetal viability, if the law contains exceptions for pregnancies which endanger a woman's life or health. And third is the principle that the State has legitimate interests from the outset of the pregnancy in protecting the health of the woman and the life of the fetus that may become a child. These principles do not contradict one another, and we adhere to each....

Constitutional protection of the woman's decision to terminate her pregnancy derives from the Due Process Clause of the Fourteenth Amendment. It declares that no State shall "deprive any person of life, liberty, or property, without due process of law." The controlling word in the case before us is "liberty.". . .

Neither the Bill of Rights nor the specific practices of States at the time of the adoption of the Fourteenth Amendment marks the outer limits of the substantive sphere of liberty which the Fourteenth Amendment protects.... As the second Justice Harlan recognized:

"The full scope of the liberty guaranteed by the Due Process Clause cannot be found in or limited by the precise terms of the specific guarantees elsewhere provided in the Constitution. This liberty ... is a rational continuum which, broadly speaking, includes a freedom from all substantial arbitrary impositions and purposeless restraints ... and which also recognizes, what a reasonable and sensitive judgment must, that certain interests require particularly careful scrutiny of the state needs asserted to justify their abridgment. . . ."

The inescapable fact is that adjudication of substantive due process claims may call upon the Court in interpreting the Constitution to exercise that same capacity which, by tradition, courts always have exercised: reasoned judgment. Its boundaries are not susceptible of expression as a simple rule. That does not mean we are free to invalidate state policy choices with which we disagree; yet neither does it permit us to shrink from the duties of our office. As Justice Harlan observed:

"Due process has not been reduced to any formula; its content cannot be determined by reference to any code. The best that can be said is that through the course of this Court's decisions it has represented the balance which our Nation, built upon postulates of respect for the liberty of the individual, has struck between that liberty and the demands of organized society ... The balance of which I speak is the balance struck by this country, having regard to what history teaches are the traditions from which it developed and as well as the traditions from which it broke. That tradition is a living thing. A decision of the Court which radically departs from it could not long survive, while a decision which builds on what has survived is likely to be sound. No formula could serve as a substitute, in this area, for judgment and restraint."

\* \* \*

... Men and women of good conscience can disagree, and we suppose some always shall disagree, about the profound moral and spiritual implications of terminating a pregnancy, even in its earliest stage. Some of us as individuals find abortion offensive to our most basic principles of morality, but that cannot control our decision. Our obligation is to define the liberty of all, not to mandate our own moral code. The underlying constitutional issue is whether the State can resolve these philosophic questions in such a definitive way that a woman lacks all choice in the matter, except perhaps in those rare circumstances in which the pregnancy is itself a danger to her own life or health, or is the result of rape or incest....

Our law affords constitutional protection to personal decisions relating to marriage, procreation, contraception, family relationships, child rearing and education ... These matters, involving the most intimate and personal choices a person may make in a lifetime, choices central to personal dignity and autonomy, are central to the liberty protected by the Fourteenth Amendment. At the heart of liberty is the right to define one's own concept of existence, of meaning, of the universe, and of the mystery of human life. Beliefs about these matters could not define the attributes of personhood were they formed under compulsion of the State.

These considerations begin our analysis of the woman's interest in terminating

her pregnancy but cannot end it, for this reason: Though the abortion decision may originate within the zone of conscience and belief, it is more than a philosophic exercise. Abortion is a unique act. It is an act fraught with consequences for others: for the woman who must live with the implications of her decision; for the persons who perform and assist in the procedure; for the spouse, family and society which must confront the knowledge that these procedures exist ... and, depending on one's beliefs, for the life or potential life that is aborted.

That is because the liberty of the woman is at stake in a sense unique to the human condition and so unique to the law. The mother who carries a child to full term is subject to anxieties, to physical constraints, to pain that only she must bear. That these sacrifices have from the beginning of the human race been endured by women with a pride that ennobles her in the eyes of others, and gives to the infant a bond of love, cannot alone be grounds for the State to insist she make the sacrifice. Her suffering is too intimate and personal for the State to insist, without more, upon its own vision of the woman's role, however dominant that vision has been in the course of our history and our culture. The destiny of the woman must be shaped to a large extent on her own conception of her spiritual imperatives and her place in society. . . .

In some critical respects the abortion decision is of the same character as the decision to use contraception, to which [Court decisions] afford constitutional protection. . . . They support the reasoning in *Roe* relating to the woman's liberty because they involve personal decisions concerning not only the meaning of procreation but also human responsibility and respect for it. As with abortion, reasonable people will have differences of opinion about these matters. One view is based on such reverence for the wonder of creation that any pregnancy ought to be welcomed and carried to full term no matter how difficult it will be to provide for the child and ensure its well-being. Another is that the inability to provide for the nurture and care of the infant is a cruelty to the child and an anguish to the parent. . . . The same concerns are present when the woman confronts the reality that, perhaps despite her attempts to avoid it, she has become pregnant.

It was this dimension of personal liberty that *Roe* sought to protect ... arguments which in their ultimate formulation conclude that *Roe* should be overruled ... are outweighed by the explication of individual liberty we have given combined with the force of stare decisis. . . .

So in this case we may inquire whether *Roe*'s central rule has been found unworkable; whether the rule's limitation on state power could be removed without serious inequity to those who have relied upon it or significant damage to the stability of the society governed by the rule in question; whether the law's growth in the intervening years has left *Roe*'s central rule a doctrinal

anachronism discounted by society; and whether *Roe*'s premises of fact have so far changed in the ensuing two decades as to render its central holding somehow irrelevant or unjustifiable in dealing with the issue it addressed.

Although *Roe* has engendered opposition, it has in no sense proved "unworkable" ... representing as it does a simple limitation beyond which a state law is unenforceable. . . .

To eliminate the issue of reliance ... would be simply to refuse to face the fact that for two decades of economic and social developments, people have organized intimate relationships and made choices that define their views of themselves and their places in society, in reliance on the availability of abortion in the event that contraception should fail. . . . The Constitution serves human values, and while the effect of reliance on *Roe* cannot be exactly measured, neither can the certain cost of overruling *Roe* for people who have ordered their thinking and living around that case be dismissed. . . .

No evolution of legal principle has left *Roe*'s doctrinal footings weaker than they were in 1973. No development of constitutional law since the case was decided has implicitly or explicitly left *Roe* behind as a mere survivor of obsolete constitutional thinking ... one could classify *Roe* as sui generis ... then there clearly has been no erosion of its central determination. . . .

We have seen how time has overtaken some of *Roe*'s factual assumptions ... but these facts ... have no bearing on the validity of *Roe*'s central holding, that viability marks the earliest point at which the State's interest in fetal life is constitutionally adequate to justify a legislative ban on non-therapeutic abortions. The soundness or unsoundness of that constitutional judgment in no sense turns on whether viability occurs at approximately 28 weeks, as was usual at the time of *Roe*, at 23 to 24 weeks, as it sometimes does today, or at some moment even slightly earlier in pregnancy, as it may if fetal respiratory capacity can somehow be enhanced in the future. Whenever it may occur, the attainment of viability may continue to serve as the critical fact ... which is to say no change in *Roe*'s factual underpinning has left its central holding obsolete, and none supports an argument for overruling it. . . .

The sum of the precedential inquiry to this point shows *Roe*'s underpinnings unweakened in any way affecting its central holding. While it has engendered disapproval, it has not been unworkable. An entire generation has come of age free to assume *Roe*'s concept of liberty in defining the capacity of women to act in society, and to make reproductive decisions; no erosion of principle going to liberty or personal autonomy has left *Roe*'s central holding a doctrinal remnant; *Roe* portends no developments at odds with other precedent for the analysis of personal liberty; and no changes of fact have rendered viability more or less appropriate as the point at

which the balance of interests tips. Within the balance of normal stare decisis analysis, then, and subject to the considerations on which it customarily turns, the stronger argument is for affirming *Roe*'s central holding, with whatever degree of personal reluctance any of us may have, not for overruling it. . . .

The Court's duty in the present case is clear. In 1973 it confronted the already-divisive issue of governmental power to limit personal choice to undergo abortion, for which it provided a new resolution based on the due process guaranteed by the Fourteenth Amendment. Whether or not a new social consensus is developing on that issue, its divisiveness is no less today than in 1973, and pressure to overrule the decision, like pressure to retain it, has grown only more intense. A decision to overrule *Roe*'s essential holding under the existing circumstances would address error, if error there was, at the cost of both profound and unnecessary damage to the Court's legitimacy, and to the Nation's commitment to the rule of law. It is therefore imperative to adhere to the essence of *Roe*'s original decision, and we do so today. . . .

From what we have said so far it follows that it is a constitutional liberty of the woman to have some freedom to terminate her pregnancy. . . . The woman's liberty is not so unlimited, however, that from the outset the State cannot show its concern for the life of the unborn, and at a later point in fetal development the State's interest in life has sufficient force so that the right of the woman to terminate the pregnancy can be restricted.

That brings us, of course, to the point where much criticism has been directed at *Roe,* a criticism that always inheres when the Court draws a specific rule from what in the Constitution is but a general standard. We conclude, however, that the urgent claims of the woman to retain the ultimate control over her destiny and her body, claims implicit in the meaning of liberty, require us to perform that function. Liberty must not be extinguished for the want of a line that is clear. . . .

We conclude the line should be drawn at viability, so that before that time the woman has a right to choose to terminate her pregnancy. . . .

On the other side of the equation is the interest of the State in the protection of potential life. . . . It must be remembered that *Roe v. Wade* speaks with clarity in establishing not only the woman's liberty but also the State's "important and legitimate interest in potential life."

\* \* \*

*Roe* established a trimester framework to govern abortion regulations. Under this elaborate but rigid construct, almost no regulation at all is permitted during the first trimester of pregnancy; regulations designed to protect the woman's health, but not to further the State's interest in potential life, are permitted during the second trimester; and during the third trimes-

ter, when the fetus is viable, prohibitions are permitted provided the life or health of the mother is not at stake.

The trimester framework no doubt was erected to ensure that the woman's right to choose not become so subordinate to the State's interest in promoting fetal life that her choice exists in theory but not in fact. We do not agree, however, that the trimester approach is necessary to accomplish this objective. A framework of this rigidity was unnecessary and in its later interpretation sometimes contradicted the State's permissible exercise of powers.

Though the woman has the right to choose to terminate or continue her pregnancy before viability, it does not at all follow that the State is prohibited from taking steps to ensure that this choice is thoughtful and informed....

We reject the trimester framework, which we do not consider to be a part of the essential holding of *Roe*.... The trimester framework suffers from these basic flaws: In its formulation it misconceives the nature of the pregnant woman's interest; and in practice it undervalues the State's interest in potential life, as recognized in *Roe*....

The very notion that the State has substantial interest in potential life leads to the conclusion that not all regulations must be deemed unwarranted. Not all burdens on the right to decide whether to terminate a pregnancy will be undue. In our view, the undue-burden standard is the appropriate means of reconciling the State's interest with the woman's constitutionally protected liberty....

A finding of undue burden is a shorthand for the conclusion that a state regulation has the purpose or effect of placing a substantial obstacle in the path of a woman seeking an abortion of a non-viable fetus....

We give this summary:

(a) To protect the central right recognized by *Roe v. Wade* while at the same time accommodating the State's profound interest in potential life, we will employ the undue burden analysis....

(b) We reject the rigid trimester framework of *Roe v. Wade* ... throughout pregnancy, the State may take measures to ensure that the woman's choice is informed, and measures designed to advance this interest will not be invalidated as long as their purpose is to persuade the woman to choose childbirth over abortion....

(c) As with any medical procedure, the State may enact regulations to further health or safety of a woman seeking an abortion....

(d) Our adoption of undue burden ... does not disturb the central holding of *Roe v. Wade,* and we reaffirm that holding.

(e) We also affirm *Roe*'s holding that "subsequent to viability, the State in promoting its interest in the potentiality of human life may, if it chooses, regulate, and even proscribe, abortion except where it is necessary, in appropriate medical judgment, for the preservation of the life or

health of the mother...."

The Court of Appeals applied what it believed to be the undue-burden standard and upheld each of the provisions except for the notification requirement. We agree generally with this conclusion....

We ... conclude that, as construed by the Court of Appeals, the medical emergency definition imposes no undue burden on a woman's abortion right....

We are left with the argument that the various aspects of the informed consent requirement are unconstitutional because they place barriers in the way of abortion on demand. Even the broadest reading of *Roe,* however, has not suggested that there is a constitutional right to abortion on demand. Rather, the right protected by *Roe* is a right to decide to terminate a pregnancy free of undue interference by the State. Because the informed consent requirement facilitates the wise exercise of that right it cannot be classified as an interference with the right *Roe* protects....

In well-functioning marriages, spouses discuss important intimate decisions such as whether to bear a child. But there are millions of women in this country who are victims of regular physical and psychological abuse at the hands of their husbands.... Many may fear that notifying their husbands [of a pregnancy] will provoke further instances of ... abuse. And many women who are pregnant as a result of sexual assaults by their husbands will be unable to avail themselves of the exception for spousal sexual assault....

The spousal notification requirement is thus likely to prevent a significant number of women from obtaining abortion.... We must not blind ourselves to the fact that the significant number of women who fear for their safety and the safety of their children are likely to be deterred from procuring an abortion as surely as if the Commonwealth had outlawed abortion in all cases....

The husband's interest in the life of the child his wife is carrying does not permit the State to empower him with this troubling degree of authority over his wife.... A State may not give to a man the kind of dominion over his wife that parents exercise over their children....

Section 3209 embodies a view of marriage consonant with the common-law status of married women but repugnant to our present understanding of marriage and the nature of the rights secured by the Constitutions. Women do not lose their constitutionally protected liberty when they marry. The Constitution protects all individuals, male or female, married or unmarried, from the abuse of governmental power, even where that power is employed for the supposed benefit of a member of the individual's family. These considerations confirm our conclusion that section 3209 is invalid....

Except in a medical emergency, an unemancipated young woman under 18 may not obtain an abortion unless she and one of her parents (or guardian) provides in-

formed consent.... If neither a parent nor guardian provides consent, a court may authorize the performance of an abortion upon a determination that the young woman is mature and capable of giving informed consent ... or that an abortion would be in her best interests....

Our Constitution is a covenant running from the first generation of Americans to us and then to future generations. It is a coherent succession. Each generation must learn anew that the Constitution's written terms embody ideas and aspirations that must survive more ages than one. We accept our responsibility not to retreat from interpreting the full meaning of the covenant in light of all of our precedents. We invoke it once again to define the freedom guaranteed by the Constitution's own promise, the promise of liberty.

## Stevens' Opinion

... The societal costs of overturning *Roe* at this date would be enormous. *Roe* is an integral part of a correct understanding of both the concept of liberty and the basic equality of men and women....

[The following of precedents) also provides a sufficient basis for my agreement with the joint opinion's reaffirmation of *Roe*'s post-viability analysis.

Specifically, I accept the proposition that if the state is interested in protecting fetal life after viability, it may go so far as to proscribe abortion during that period, except when it is necessary to preserve the life or health of the mother.

I also accept what is implicit in the court's analysis, namely, a reaffirmation of *Roe*'s explanation of why the state's obligation to protect the life or health of the mother must take precedence over any duty to the unborn. The court in *Roe* carefully considered, and rejected, the state's argument "that the fetus is a 'person'" within the language and meaning of the Fourteenth Amendment....

Thus, as a matter of federal constitutional law, a developing organism that is not yet a "person" does not have what is sometimes described as a "right to life." This has been and, by the court's holding today, remains a fundamental premise of our constitutional law governing reproductive autonomy....

## Blackmun's Opinion

Three years ago, in *Webster v. Reproductive Health Services,* four members of this court appeared poised to "cast into darkness the hopes and visions of every woman in this country" who has come to believe that the Constitution guaranteed her the right to reproductive choice.

All that remained between the promise of *Roe* and the darkness of the plurality was a single, flickering flame. Decisions since *Webster* gave little reason to hope that this flame would cast much light. But now, just when so many expected the darkness to fall, the flame has grown bright.

I do not underestimate the significance of today's joint opinion. Yet I remain

steadfast in my belief that the right to reproductive choice is entitled to the full protection afforded by this court before *Webster.* And I fear for the darkness as four justices anxiously await the single vote necessary to extinguish the light.

Make no mistake, the joint opinion of Justices O'Connor, Kennedy and Souter is an act of personal courage and constitutional principle. In contrast to previous decisions in which Justices O'Connor and Kennedy postponed reconsideration of *Roe v. Wade,* the authors of the joint opinion today join Justice Stevens and me in concluding that "the essential holding of *Roe* should be retained and once again reaffirmed."

In brief, five members of this court today recognize that the Constitution protects a woman's right to terminate her pregnancy in its early stages. A fervent view of individual liberty and the force of [court precedents] have led the court to this conclusion.

Today a majority reaffirms that the Due Process Clause of the Fourth Amendment establishes "a realm of personal liberty which the government may not enter...."

## Blackmun on Rehnquist

At long last, the chief justice admits it. Gone are the contentions that the issue need not be (or has not been) considered. There, on the first page, for all to see, is that which was expected: "We believe that Roe was wrongly decided, and that it can and should be overruled consistently with our traditional approach to (precedent) in constitutional cases."

If there is much reason to applaud the advances made by the joint opinion today, there is far more to fear from the chief justice's opinion. The chief justice's criticism of *Roe* follows from his stunted conception of individual liberty.... This constricted view is reinforced by the chief justice's exclusive reliance on tradition as a source of fundamental rights....

In the chief justice's world, a woman considering whether to terminate a pregnancy is entitled to no more protection than adulterers, murderers and so-called sexual deviates. Given the chief justice's exclusive reliance on tradition, people using contraceptives seem the next likely candidate for his list of outcasts.

Even more shocking than the chief justice's cramped notion of individual liberty is his complete omission of any discussion of the effects that compelled childbirth and motherhood have on women's lives....

In one sense, the court's approach is worlds apart from that of the chief justice and Justice (Antonin) Scalia. And yet, in another sense, the distance between the two approaches is short — the distance is but a single vote.

I am 83 years old. I cannot remain on this court forever, and when I do step down, the confirmation process for my successor well may focus on the issue before us today. That, I regret, may be exactly where the choice between the two worlds will be made.

## Rehnquist's Dissent

The joint opinion, following its newly-minted variation on stare decisis, retains the outer shell of *Roe v. Wade,* 410 U.S. 113 (1973), but beats a wholesale retreat from the substance of that case. We believe that Roe was wrongly decided, and that it can and should be overruled consistently with our traditional approach to stare decisis in constitutional cases....

But, as the Court of Appeals found, the state of our post-*Roe* decisional law dealing with the regulation of abortion is confusing and uncertain, indicating that a reexamination of that line of cases is in order.... Unfortunately for those who must apply this Court's decisions, the reexamination undertaken today leaves the Court no less divided than beforehand.

In *Roe v. Wade,* the Court recognized a "guarantee of personal privacy" which "is broad enough to encompass a woman's decision whether or not to terminate her pregnancy." (410 U.S., at 152-153.) We are now of the view that, in terming this right fundamental, the Court in *Roe* read the earlier opinions upon which it based its decision much too broadly. Unlike marriage, procreation and contraception, abortion "involves the purposeful termination of potential life." *Harris v. McRae,* 448 U.S. 297, 325 (1980). The abortion decision must therefore "be recognized as sui generis, different in kind from the others that the Court has protected under the rubric of personal or family privacy and autonomy." *Thornburgh v. American College of Obstetricians and Gynecologists,* supra, at 792 (White, J., dissenting). One cannot ignore the fact that a woman is not isolated in her pregnancy, and that the decision to abort necessarily involves the destruction of a fetus. See *Michael H. v. Gerald D.,* supra, at 124, n. 4 (To look "at the act which is assertedly the subject of a liberty interest in isolation from its effect upon other people [is] like inquiring whether there is a liberty interest in firing a gun where the case at hand happens to involve its discharge into another person's body")....

We think, therefore, both in view of this history and of our decided cases dealing with substantive liberty under the Due Process Clause, that the Court was mistaken in *Roe* when it classified a woman's decision to terminate her pregnancy as a "fundamental right" that could be abridged only in a manner which withstood "strict scrutiny...."

We believe that the sort of constitutionally imposed abortion code of the type illustrated by our decisions following *Roe* is inconsistent "with the notion of a Constitution cast in general terms, as ours is, and usually speaking in general principles, as ours does." The court in *Roe* reached too far when it analogized the right to abort a fetus to the rights involved in *Pierce, Meyer, Loving,* and *Griswold,* and thereby deemed the right to abortion fundamental....

Whatever the "central holding" of *Roe* that is left after the joint opinion finishes dissecting it is surely not the result of that

principle. While purporting to adhere to precedent, the joint opinion instead revises it. *Roe* continues to exist, but only in the way a storefront on a western movie set exists: a mere facade to give the illusion of reality....

In our view, authentic principles of stare decisis do not require that any portion of the reasoning in *Roe* be kept intact....

Our constitutional watch does not cease merely because we have spoken before on an issue; when it becomes clear that a prior constitutional interpretation is unsound we are obliged to reexamine the question.

The joint opinion discusses several stare decisis factors which, it asserts, point toward retaining a portion of *Roe.* Two of these factors are that the main "factual underpinning" of *Roe* has remained the same, and that its doctrinal foundation is no weaker now than it was in 1973. Of course, what might be called the basic facts which gave rise to Roe have remained the same — women become pregnant, there is a point somewhere, depending on medical technology, where a fetus becomes viable, and women give birth to children. But this is only to say that the same facts which gave rise to Roe will continue to give rise to similar cases. It is not a reason, in and of itself, why those cases must be decided in the same incorrect manner as was the first case to deal with the question. And surely there is no requirement, in considering whether to depart from stare decisis in a constitutional case, that a decision be more wrong now than it was at the time it was rendered. If that were true, the most outlandish constitutional decision could survive forever, based simply on the fact that it was no more outlandish later than it was when originally rendered.

The joint opinion thus turns to what can only be described as an unconventional — and unconvincing — notion of reliance, a view based on the surmise that the availability of abortion since *Roe* has led to "two decades of economic and social developments" that would be undercut if the error of *Roe* were recognized. The joint opinion's assertions of this fact is undeveloped and totally conclusory. In fact, one cannot be sure to what economic and social developments the opinion is referring. Surely it is dubious to suggest that women have reached their "places in society" in reliance upon *Roe,* rather than as a result of their determination to obtain higher education and compete with men in the job market, and of society's increasing recognition of their ability to fill positions that were previously thought to be reserved only for men.

In the end, having failed to put forth any evidence to prove any true reliance, the joint opinion's argument is based solely on generalized assertions about the national psyche, on a belief that the people of this country have grown accustomed to the *Roe* decision over the last 19 years and have "ordered their thinking and living around"

it. As an initial matter, one might inquire how the joint opinion can view the "central holding" of *Roe* as so deeply rooted in our constitutional culture, when it so casually uproots and disposes of that same decision's trimester framework. Furthermore, at various points in the past, the same could have been said about this Court's erroneous decisions that the Constitution allowed "separate but equal" treatment of minorities, see *Plessy v. Ferguson*, 163 U.S. 537 (1896), or that "liberty" under the Due Process Clause protected "freedom of contract." . . . The "separate but equal" doctrine lasted 58 years after *Plessy*, and *Lochner*'s protection of contractual freedom lasted 32 years. However, the simple fact that a generation or more had grown used to these major decisions did not prevent the Court from correcting its errors in those cases, nor should it prevent us from correctly interpreting the Constitution here. . . .

Apparently realizing that conventional stare decisis principles do not support its position, the joint opinion advances a belief that retaining a portion of *Roe* is necessary to protect the "legitimacy of this court." Because the Court must take care to render decisions "grounded truly in principle," and not simply as political and social compromises . . . the joint opinion properly declares it to be this Court's duty to ignore the public criticism and protest that may arise as a result of a decision. Few would quarrel with this statement although it may be doubted that Members of this Court, holding their tenure as they do during constitutional "good behavior," are at all likely to be intimidated by such public protests. . . .

But just as the Court should not respond to that sort of protest by retreating from the decision simply to allay the concerns of the protesters, it should likewise not respond by determining to adhere to the decision at all costs lest it seem to be retreating under fire. Public protests should not alter the normal application of stare decisis, lest perfectly lawful protest activity be penalized by the Court itself.

Taking the joint opinion on its own terms, we doubt that its distinction between *Roe*, on the one hand, and *Plessy* and *Lochner*, on the other, withstands analysis. . . .

There are other reasons why the joint opinion's discussion of legitimacy is unconvincing as well. In assuming that the Court is perceived as "surrendering to political pressure" when it overrules a controversial decision, ante, at 25, the joint opinion forgets that there are two sides to any controversy. The joint opinion asserts that, in order to protect its legitimacy, the Court must refrain from overruling a controversial decision lest it be viewed as favoring those who oppose the decision. But a decision to adhere to prior precedent is subject to the same criticism, for in such a case one can easily argue that the Court is responding to those who have demonstrated in favor of the original decision. . . .

The sum of the joint opinion's labors in the name of stare decisis and "legitimacy" is this: *Roe v. Wade* stands as a sort of judicial Potemkin Village, which may be pointed out to passers-by as a monument to the importance of adhering to precedent. But behind the facade, an entirely new method of analysis, without any roots in constitutional law, is imported to decide the constitutionality of state laws regulating abortion. Neither stare decisis nor "legitimacy" are truly served by such an effort. . . .

A woman's interest in having an abortion is a form of liberty protected by the Due Process Clause, but States may regulate abortion procedures in ways rationally related to a legitimate state interest.

The question before us is therefore whether the spousal notification requirement rationally furthers any legitimate state interests. We conclude that it does. First, a husband's interests in procreation within marriage and in the potential life of his unborn child are certainly substantial ones. . . . The State itself has legitimate interests both in protecting these interests of the father and in protecting the potential life of the fetus, and the spousal notification requirement is reasonably related to advancing those state interests. By providing that a husband will usually know of his spouse's intent to have an abortion, the provision makes it more likely that the husband will participate in deciding the fate of his unborn child, a possibility that might otherwise have been denied him. This participation might in some cases result in a decision to proceed with the pregnancy. . . .

In our view, the spousal notice requirement is a rational attempt by the State to improve truthful communication between spouses and encourage collaborative decisionmaking, and thereby fosters marital integrity. . . .

For the reasons stated, we therefore would hold that each of the challenged provisions of the Pennsylvania statute is consistent with the Constitution. It bears emphasis that our conclusion in this regard does not carry with it any necessary approval of these regulations. Our task is, as always, to decide only whether the challenged provisions of a law comport with the United States Constitution. If, as we believe, these do, their wisdom as a matter of public policy is for the people of Pennsylvania to decide.

## Scalia's Opinion

The States may, if they wish, permit abortion on demand, but the Constitution does not require them to do so. The permissibility of abortion, and the limitations upon it, are to be resolved like the most important questions in our democracy: by citizens trying to persuade one another and then voting. As the Court acknowledges, "where reasonable people disagree the government can adopt one position or the other." *Ante*, at 8. The Court is correct in adding the qualification that this "assumes a state of affairs in which the choice does not intrude upon a protected liberty," *ante*, at 9 — but the crucial part of that qualification is the penultimate word. A State's choice between two positions on which reasonable people can disagree is constitutional even when (as is often the case) it intrudes upon a "liberty" in the absolute sense. Laws against bigamy, for example — which entire societies of reasonable people disagree with — intrude upon men and women's liberty to marry and live with one another. But bigamy happens not to be a liberty specially "protected" by the Constitution.

That is, quite simply, the issue in this case: not whether the power of a woman to abort her unborn child is a "liberty" in the absolute sense; or even whether it is a liberty of great importance to many women. Of course it is both. The issue is whether it is a liberty protected by the Constitution of the United States. I am sure it is not. I reach that conclusion not because of anything so exalted as my views concerning the "concept of existence, of meaning, of the universe, and of the mystery of human life." *Ibid.* Rather, I reach it for same reason I reach the conclusion that bigamy is not constitutionally protected — because of two simple facts: 1) the Constitution says absolutely nothing about it, and 2) the longstanding traditions of American society having permitted it to be legally proscribed. . . .

There is a poignant aspect to today's opinion. Its length, and what might be called its epic tone, suggest that its authors believe they are bringing to an end a troublesome era in the history of our Nation and of our Court. . . .

Quite to the contrary, by foreclosing all democratic outlet for the deep passions this issue arouses, by banishing the issue from the political forum that gives all participants, even the losers, the satisfaction of a fair hearing and an honest fight, by continuing the imposition of a rigid national rule instead of allowing for regional differences, the Court merely prolongs and intensifies the anguish.

We should get out of this area, where we have no right to be, and where we do neither ourselves nor the country any good by remaining. ■

ETHICS

# GOP, Democratic Reports On House Post Office

*A task force of the House Administration Committee was unable to agree on a unified report of its investigation into the House Post Office, so each party's contingent issued its own report. The House voted July 22 to send both reports to the ethics committee and to make its files available to the Justice Department.*

*The task force was evenly divided between the parties. Pat Roberts of Kansas led the Republicans, who included Bill Thomas of California and Bill Barrett of Nebraska. Democrats were led by Charlie Rose of North Carolina; other members were Al Swift of Washington and Gerald D. Kleczka of Wisconsin.*

*Following are overview sections from each report.*

---

### Republican Task Force Report — Overview

---

#### Management and Operation

The investigation found a Post Office in disarray. The Post Office followed few of the standard procedures of the USPS [United States Postal Service]. Management in the House Post Office was incapable of carrying out the responsibilities and tasks assigned.

The Acting Postmaster, Michael Shinay, stated he found conditions chaotic, the offices cluttered and in disorder, a "bunker mentality" among otherwise hard-working employees, as well as a lack of management control and no written procedures to guide day-to-day activities. Mr. Shinay found there was little sense of responsibility with respect to daily work time and attendance and that many office positions allotted had insufficient duties to justify a full-time assignment. Other positions were found to be assigned to activities only indirectly related to normal Post Office responsibilities, such as the telex and Visa services.

In 1972, the annual payroll cost of the House Post Office was approximately $911,000. By 1991, the cost had risen to $3,920,655, a 400 [330] percent increase. These staff expansions were attributed to increased incoming mail that increased the workload. However, there are major discrepancies between the House Post Office estimates of mail volume and USPS mail counts.

*Based upon Postmaster [Robert V.] Rota's records, the incoming mail volume skyrocketed from 52 million pieces in 1977 to 225 million in 1985. However, mail volume records from the USPS show Mr. Rota's overcount was 160 million in 1985. His overcount of the incoming mail to the House from 1985 through 1991 was in most cases in excess of 100 million pieces of mail per year.*

*In just one year, the Postmaster's count was 350 percent of the actual USPS mail count.*

These huge discrepancies underscore the fact that mail volume reports were used in part to justify an increasing patronage employment system. It also underscores the Postmaster's dilemma. The House Post Office was in such bad shape in terms of productivity, absenteeism, incompetence, employee morale, and politicization that Mr. Rota had to more than double the mail count in order to justify enough extra and temporary employees to keep up with the actual mail flow.

In 1990, a plan to reorganize the House Post Office was submitted to the House Administration Subcommittee on Personnel and Police. The original proposal would have cost $1,246,102 and would have created 55 additional positions in the Post Office. The plan was considered in two stages and the subcommittee cut the proposal by 57 [56.2] percent to $546,096 and reduced the number of new positions from 55 to nine.

No one exercised institutional oversight over the Post Office. In regard to policy, operations and favors for Members, it appears that Postmaster Rota did exactly what certain Members asked him to do and clearly believed he was doing what was expected of him.

Numerous interviewees, including Postmaster Rota, testified to major difficulties with the way employees were hired, disciplined, suspended or terminated. For example, a House Post Office employee on several occasions exhibited bizarre behavior that included disrobing. Yet, it was his supervisor who was reprimanded because she took action to stop the disruption.

Postmaster Rota and his staff had virtually no authority to hire or fire patronage employees. Instead, he was directed by the Democratic Patronage Committee in job assignments, promotions and disciplinary actions.

Of the 160 full-time House Post Office employees, two have been identified as Republican appointments. As positions became open in the House Post Office or positions were mandated, the Postmaster would await word from the Democratic Personnel Committee on the individual to be appointed. Individuals were assigned these positions, not based upon their experience or qualifications, but on the Member's request. Some employees appointed were illiterate and incapable of carrying out assigned tasks, leaving work to be done by other employees, thereby adding to the need for more employees.

Simply stated, the more powerful the patron or sponsor of the individual, the less control Postmaster Rota or others would have over the employee. This inability to appoint qualified and competent individuals led to a lack of professionalism, inefficiency,

incompetency, abuse and absenteeism.

Substantial payments of overtime for time not worked were made, with individuals able to certify overtime (including their own) without supervision. A few employees were consistently absent from the House Post Office during working hours and two were consistently identified as being "no show" or "ghost" employees.

Employees felt strongly that there were major racial tensions in the House Post Office, with black employees stating they were overlooked for promotion or advancement. Other witnesses testified to unsafe working conditions including harassment, threats, verbal abuse and fighting.

#### Alleged Improper Activities.

● **Drugs.** Alleged illegal drug activity is under investigation by the DOJ [Department of Justice] and the Capitol Police. As of the date of this report, two former Post Office employees have been indicted for drug-related offenses and each has entered into a plea agreement with the U.S. Attorney.

However, the Task Force determined there was little, if any, implementation of current Capitol Hill drug policy or any program of education and rehabilitation. Witnesses complained about lack of response to reported drug use and drug paraphernalia. Complaints by two female employees, who received direct threats of physical harm to them and their families as a result of reporting alleged drug use and sales, were ignored. This matter was not resolved until the complaints were brought to the attention of the Task Force.

● **Embezzlement.** The theft of government property and embezzlement of funds is under investigation by the U.S. Attorney. Four Post Office employees have been indicted and have entered into plea agreements relating to the theft of nearly $34,000. The lack of management controls, including the retention of excess cash and an ineffective audit policy, led to these crimes.

● **Misuse of the Postmaster's Frank.** Many allegations have been made regarding the alleged use of the Postmaster's frank for non-official mailings. The Acting Postmaster's record of use of the Postmaster's frank reveals a dramatic difference in comparison with Mr. Rota's. Acting Postmaster Shinay's franking use has averaged approximately $500 per month for State Department telexes. Mr. Rota's franking costs averaged close to $4,000 a month.

Both Joanna O'Rourke, Chief of Staff, and Nancy Collins, Deputy Postmaster, stated in their first interview with House Administration Committee Democratic staff that they knew some Members' mail went out under the Postmaster's frank. Corroborating records were not available and the Task Force did not have access to Ms. O'Rourke or Mr. Rota under oath.

Copies of the internal correspondence of the Hill, including Republican legislative "Dear Colleague" letters, were sent to Democratic leadership and a select group of lobbyists throughout the city. Congressional Records, Federal Registers, congressional

calendars, newspapers, magazines and other highly in-demand publications were mailed to this group under the frank, as well as being distributed to House offices, at no cost to the senders or the recipients.

● **The Postmaster's Express Mail Account.** An Express Mail Federal agency account was established for Congress in 1978. Identified as P-300 for the House, the account was closely controlled by Postmaster Rota with approved mailings restricted to relatively few Members and House Officers.

Testimony indicated that the P-300 account was used for personal matters. A review of Express Mail forms between 1989 and 1990 shows that a number of Members and House Officers made use of the P-300 account. In addition to Express Mail originating in Washington, USPS records indicate widespread use at the congressional district level.

The USPS reported that for the third fiscal quarter of 1990, approximately $2,000 was spent from the P-300 account. The USPS reported that for the fourth fiscal quarter, the quarter just prior to the 1990 election, approximately $37,000 was spent.

● **Check Cashing and Stamps for Cash.** The failure of the Postmaster to remit all Postal funds on a daily basis and the improper requisition of stamps permitted the accumulation of excess cash available for check cashing at the House Post Office.

The total accountability on July 9, 1991, was $442,812.92, and of that amount, $47,299.56 was in cash, despite USPS regulations forbidding cash retention of more than $100. Approximately $29,000 in cash was in the office of James Smith, the Assistant Postmaster for Accountable Papers. This contrasts with a USPS recommended total House Post Office accountability of $195,000.

Witnesses described Mr. Smith's office as littered with stamps and money. Stamps and cash were kept in desk drawers, on the desk and even on the floor as well as in the safe.

An internal audit found a shortage of between $1,000 and $5,000, but there is no record of this shortage having been reported to the Postmaster or outside postal authorities.

Due to the lack of a standard or understood policy, check acceptance and cashing practices varied among counter clerks. Personal checks, campaign committee checks, cash and vouchers were accepted as payment for Postal charges and services as long as the individual had a House identification card. The Task Force also received testimony that personal checks and payroll checks were being cashed. Numerous House Post Office employees stated they had received cash for personal or payroll checks from the counter clerks.

There would appear to be no practical way to determine from existing records which checks were used to purchase stamps as opposed to being negotiated for cash.

Witnesses stated some Members of Congress, certain former Members, lobbyists, and personal friends of Postmaster Rota used the House Post Office as a "personal bank." All of these alleged transactions were approved by Mr. Rota, Ms. O'Rourke or Mr. Smith behind closed doors. Since the Task Force did not have access to any of the above named individuals under oath, the allegations could not be verified.

There have been various reports of stamps being exchanged for cash to Members and others by Post Office personnel. This matter is the subject of a continuing Grand Jury investigation.

● **Misuse of House Employees for Campaign Purposes.** The House Post Office set up and serviced Post Office boxes for the campaign committees of certain Members of Congress at the Brentwood U.S. Post Office facility. The Postmaster would assist the Members in setting up the boxes, and the passport couriers would regularly pick up the mail and bring it back to the House, bypassing security scanners. The mail was then delivered to the Members' offices.

The boxes are a concern when House employees are utilized to service campaign collection and distribution.

The Task Force was unable to determine the total number of boxes serviced by the House Post Office. Mr. Rota estimated as many as 25 boxes could have existed. The couriers had direct knowledge of boxes maintained for: Rep. Nicholas Mavroules [D-Mass.], Rep. Dennis [M.] Hertel [D-Mich.], Rep. Jim Moody [D-Wis.], Rep. Mary Rose Oakar [D-Ohio], and Rep. Edward [F.] Feighan [D-Ohio].

In addition to the above, records and correspondence from the House Post Office show courier service for: Rep. Jan Meyers [R-Kan.] and former Members Fernand [J.] St Germain [D-R.I.], Samuel [S.] Stratton [D-N.Y.], and Mario Biaggi [D-N.Y.]; the American Leaders Fund (a leadership PAC [political action committee] controlled by Rep. Dan Rostenkowski [D-Ill.]); and two individuals, Ralph Welch and Bob Hamilton.

● **Personal and Member Abuse of Post Office Resources.** Witnesses stated that Post Office vehicles were used for non-official business. The vehicles were reported to have been used to drive Members, former Members and lobbyists to the airport. Couriers stated they were often asked to drop off packages at various destinations in the city. While a log of miles, departures, destinations and arrivals was allegedly kept, the only log book obtained by the Task Force contained a record of mileage only from Nov. 25, 1991, to May 23, 1992, and did not record destinations.

Several employees stated that the Director of Transportation, Jerry Carter, also acted as Mr. Rota's personal driver and that other drivers drove special errands at Mr. Rota's request.

House Post Office personnel were sometimes directed by supervisors to perform "favors" for various Member offices. The Task Force received reports that employees were asked to answer telephones during staff parties and fund-raising receptions. In certain instances, calendars were reportedly sent to the Post Office to be stamped with the Member's signature by House Post Office employees. These calendars allegedly were sent to the Member's congressional district under the Postmaster's frank.

Witnesses testified that certain lobbyists had access to parking spaces in underground garage space allotted to Members and staff. Mr. Rota had 10 spaces allotted, of which seven were listed as "vacant." Employees stated lobbyists and former Members were helped in regard to personal transportation and obtaining tickets for air and train travel.

House Post Office Chief of Staff, Joanna O'Rourke, maintained a "flower fund" containing profits from a Post Office vending machine. The vending machine or "flower fund" was used to send flowers when an employee had a death in the family.

According to early interviews conducted by House Administration Democratic Staff, O'Rourke kept the cash from the fund in her desk. Later an account was opened at the Congressional Credit Union in her name.

● **Capitol Police Criminal Investigation.** There are conflicting statements and allegations regarding the specific roles played by the Capitol Police, House Post Office staff, the Counsel to the Clerk, Capitol Police Attorney, Sergeant at Arms and House Democratic leadership from June 6, 1991, to July 10, 1991, when the Capitol Police are [sic] informed they would no longer lead the investigation.

Captain [Max] Kennedy and former Chief [Frank A.] Kerrigan stated their belief that the investigation by the Capitol Police was being conducted in a professional manner until it was slowed and eventually suspended at the initiation of Clerk's Counsel Steven Ross. The Police noted the six-week delay in time from the original audit by the Capitol Police on May 29, to the second audit of July 9, 1991. In addition, serious drug-use allegations made at the time of the audits went uninvestigated for many months.

The last witness to appear before the Task Force, former Chief Kerrigan, has alleged Mr. Ross threatened the Capitol Police with the withdrawal of support for pending pay raises and retirement reform unless the Capitol Police withdrew to a supporting role.

Mr. Ross stated that he in no way attempted to impede the investigation, but was concerned about the rights of House Post Office employees, the need for a professional audit by U.S. Postal Inspectors and the question of relationship between the Capitol Police and the Department of Justice.

---

## Democratic Task Force Report — Summary of Findings

### Personnel

● **Ghost Employees.** The Task Force is aware of allegations raised in the media concerning so-called "ghost employees." After extensive investigation, the Task Force has found no conclusive evidence that any employee of the House Post Office was a ghost employee. Despite these charges, which the Task Force considers attributable to either political motives or employee jealousy, the Task Force is recommending that the circumstances of

one present employee's work habits be reviewed by the Committee on Standards [of Official Conduct — the ethics committee].

● **Overtime.** The Task Force determined that the Post Office lacked a consistent policy for the awarding of overtime, resulting in several inappropriate or abusive practices. Managers were allowed to approve their own overtime, one employee was able to approve overtime for her two daughters, and there were several instances where overtime was continually awarded for hours not actually worked. The Committee strongly notes the need for a consistent, written overtime policy for the House Post Office and is recommending that the supervisors who apparently awarded overtime in inappropriate circumstances be reviewed by the Committee on Standards.

● **Employment Policy/Patronage.** The Task Force heard consistent and abundant testimony that the patronage system caused a substantial portion of the dysfunction which the Task Force found in the House Post Office. The patronage system resulted in an attitude of indifference toward assigned functions, low workplace morale, and low productivity among many of the Post Office employees. The Committee believes that the elimination of the patronage system will allow employee concerns to be more adequately addressed.

● **Employee Leave.** The Task Force found that those with authority to grant leave in the House Post Office failed to faithfully and consistently administer the leave policy mandated by the Committee on House Administration. Post Office employees were granted excessive amounts of leave, both paid and unpaid.

● **Worker's Compensation.** The Task Force was not presented with any evidence of excessive use, or fraudulent filing of workman's compensation claims. However, the Task Force did not find any evidence of efforts by House Post Office management to reduce the risks of injury inherent in that workplace, and thereby reduce the number and size of the legitimate worker's compensation claims.

## Operations

● **Check Cashing.** The Task Force heard allegations that stamp counter clerks cashed checks for individuals, and that Members were allowed to cash campaign checks. Task Force attempts to investigate these allegations were hampered by Department of Justice hindering as well as poor recordkeeping in the Post Office. It appears that the Deputy Postmaster and Chief of Staff permitted an arbitrary check cashing policy. The Task Force found no evidence to prove the allegations concerning the practice of redeeming campaign checks or official vouchers for cash. The Assistant Postmaster for Accountable Papers, in response to questioning, offered no indication that this occurred.

● **Post Office Boxes.** The Task Force determined that many Members kept post office boxes in local post offices to receive campaign mail, a practice entirely consistent with federal law and House rules. The Task Force focused on the pickup and delivery of mail from the boxes by House Post Office employees. The Committee does not believe the conduct of any Members contravened any federal statute or House Rule. While the Committee believes that Members may continue to hold these boxes, the Committee also believes that, as a matter of policy, Post Office employees should no longer be used to pick up the mail received into the boxes.

● **State Department Services.** The House Post Office, in cooperation with the Department of State, provides coordinated services to House Members, such as facilitating passport and visa applications. The Task Force found that these activities provide a legitimate service to the House of Representatives and are a legitimate use of House Post Office employees.

● **Loaned Employees.** The Task Force heard testimony that House Post Office employees were asked by supervisors to perform activities for Members outside of the Post Office. These activities are not a recommended use of Post Office employees, and the Committee believes this practice will disappear with the demise of the patronage system.

● **Postmaster's Mailing List.** Former Postmaster Rota maintained a list of individuals to whom he regularly provided information intended for Members. Insofar as the letters went to non-Members, the Committee considers this to be clearly inappropriate, but the practice ended with Mr. Rota's resignation.

● **Postmaster's Frank.** The Postmaster has been accorded the privilege to frank mail, and the Task Force found that Postmaster Rota would allow Members to send mail under his frank, a violation of House regulations adopted in 1991. Because no records are kept as to destination of mail, it has been impossible to determine the full extent of his misuse, or which Members benefited.

● **Orange Bags/D-DOP Bags.** The Task Force has found that both the Orange Bag Service and the Direct District Office Pouch (D-DOP) to be an effective way to transport communications between a Member's Washington office and that Member's district office.

● **Flower Fund.** The "Flower Fund" represented the proceeds from a soft drink vending machine located in the House Post Office, and was intended to be used to purchase flowers for employees who were sick or who had a death in the family. Instead, the fund was used as a personal petty cash account, maintained in a haphazard manner by Ms. Joanna O'Rourke, Chief of Staff of the House Post Office. Since May 11, 1992, the House Restaurant System has been operating all vending machines in the House Complex, and the Flower Fund has been eliminated.

● **P-300 Account.** The Postmaster maintained a "P-300" account that was apparently used as an express mail account, although no witnesses were able to properly define its use or purpose. In a situation similar to that involving use of the Postmaster's frank by Members, it seems as though the Postmaster did not properly control the use of the account. However, since this account has been closed, no further action is warranted.

● **Stamp Exchange Practices.** The Task Force investigated allegations made in the press that individuals exchanged stamps for cash at the House Post Office. The Task Force found instances where individuals exchanged old stamps for new stamps, either because the old stamps were damaged, or because the individual wanted special commemorative stamps. The Task Force found no evidence that any exchange of stamps for cash ever took place at the House Post Office, and considers those allegations to be unfounded.

● **Personal Loans.** The Task Force found that it was common for the Assistant to the Postmaster for Accountable Papers, Mr. James Smith, to make loans of from $10 to $200 to various employees. Mr. Smith claims to have always used his personal funds as the source of these loans, but given the constant state of chaos of Mr. Smith's office, it is impossible to determine if that is indeed the case.

● **Non-Official Transportation.** The Task Force found that Post Office employees and vehicles were used to run errands unrelated to any official business of the Post Office. Such errands included making pickups and deliveries of items, as well as transporting Members, former Members, the Postmaster, and others. New policies should be implemented prohibiting this practice.

● **Security.** During the course of the review of the Office of the Postmaster's operations, several security and safety weaknesses were noted. The Task Force findings, along with recommendations for improvements, were forwarded to the Acting Postmaster on June 17, 1992.

## Suspected Improper Activities

● **Drugs.** The Task Force heard rumors of drug use and sales at the House Post Office. The possession and/or sale of drugs is criminal in nature, and the Task Force was not constituted to conduct a criminal investigation. Thus, the Task Force did not investigate the details of these rumors, apart from the effect these activities might have upon the management and operation of the post office. Witnesses before the Task Force were neither able to confirm nor deny these rumors.

● **Embezzlement.** The initial investigation into the House Post Office began with the admitted embezzlement by a stamp counter clerk, and since then, three additional stamp counter clerks have pled guilty to embezzlement, and one supervisor has pled guilty to covering up the embezzlement. The Task Force found that controls placed upon stamp counter clerks were nearly non-existent. The clerks had too much autonomy and responsibility, there was no accounting or auditing process in place, and the clerks were neither screened nor trained properly. Changes should be made to correct these problems. ∎

# Bush Outlines New Plan For Economic Renewal

*Following is the Reuter transcript of President Bush's speech Sept. 10 before the Detroit Economic Club.*

**PRESIDENT BUSH:** .... This morning I'm here for a very serious speech, serious business. And I'm releasing today an agenda for the American renewal. And I've come here today to introduce it to you and to the nation. And my agenda diagnoses the economic problems that our nation faces, lays out the principles that should guide us in the years ahead and explains the integrated approach that I'm pursuing to meet the challenge.

Over the past weeks I've been discussing certain elements of my economic agenda and in the weeks ahead I will be expanding on those and other ideas.

The document that I'm releasing today shows how the pieces all fit together, but let's begin today by stepping back, taking stock of where we are as a great nation in the broader sweep of history.

The American people have just completed the greatest mission in the lifetime of our country, the triumph of Democratic capitalism over imperial communism. And today this year, for the first time since December of 1941, the United States is not engaged in a war, hot or cold. And throughout history, at the close of prolonged and costly wars, victors have confronted the problem of securing a new basis for peace and prosperity.

The American people recognize that we stand at such a watershed and we sense the epic changes at work in the world and in the economy, the uneasiness that stirs the democracies who served as our partners in the long struggle. And we feel the uneasiness in our own homes, our own communities, and we see the difficulties of our neighbors and friends who have felt change most directly. And we know that while we face an era of great opportunity, we face great risks as well if we fail to make the right choices, if we fail to engage this new world wisely.

But America has always possessed unique powers. And foremost among them is the power of regeneration — to transform uncertainty into opportunity. Only in America do we have the people, the talents, the principles and ideals to fully embrace the world that opens before us. For America to be safe and strong, we must meet the defining challenge of the 1990s — to win the economic competition, to win the peace, and we must be a military superpower, an economic superpower, an export superpower.

My agenda for renewal asks that we look forward, to open new markets, prepare our people to work, strengthen our families, save and invest, so that we can win. Our renewal depends on economic growth, but growth not for the few at the expense of the many, not for the present at the expense of the future....

We know that the clumsy hand of government is no match for the uplifting hand of the marketplace. My international economic and trade strategy will guarantee our position as an export superpower, extending our global economic reach in tandem with our security presence to stretch beyond our borders so that we can create more jobs within our borders. At the same time we need to foster at home the capabilities that will keep us in the lead.

Radical changes in our education system to prepare our children for a constantly changing workplace, incentives for the entrepreneurs and new technologies to sharpen our competitive edge — job training, health care reform — to promote the economic security of our working men and women, and new approaches for reaching out to those who have been left behind, since in the century ahead we will need the talent and the energy of every single American.

And finally, because our greatest strengths flow not from government but from the personal initiative of free men and women, my agenda aims to check the growth of government and, in some important ways, to reverse it. Together, the components of this new agenda should renew America according to her most cherished principles. And this renewed America will be empowered towards a grand goal — nearly double the size of our economy to $10 trillion by the early years of the next century. To place this agenda in a larger context, let me turn briefly to five profound changes now at work in our economy.

## Five Major Changes

When Americans gather around the kitchen table at night and talk about how they'll meet a mortgage or pay the doctor's bill, they're feeling these changes in their daily lives. And before the changes have run their course, they will have forever altered the way Americans buy and sell, work and create.

The first great change in our economy is ironically caused by our very success in ending the Cold War. In the short run, deductions in defense spending have meant painful layoffs in many industries, and we are taking steps to ease this transition. But in the medium and long run, deductions in defense will free up priceless skills and technologies for peacetime growth.

Second, most of our industries are transforming themselves from old-style hierarchies into flatter organizations with fewer layers between customer and executive. The new organizations emphasize a skill-based work force, lean production, shorter production cycles, from castings to computers. This is a revolution as dramatic as the one made earlier this century when Henry Ford led the country from craft-based production to mass manufacturing.

While these changes are essential to maintaining our competitive edge, they've come with a cost. Everyone in this room knows that. Layoffs, cutbacks among both white- and blue-collar workers. These hard-working people need reassurance not only about their economic security but about preserving the sense of self-worth that only work can provide.

The third change. While the 1980s brought us the greatest peacetime expansion in our history, the boom also led too many of us to take on too much debt. And we've been paying that down, that debt, and lower interest rates have helped us do that. And the process is largely over, but consumers and companies remain cautious.

The fourth change involves our financial system. We entered the '80s with a 50-year-old banking system designed for the days when tellers wore green eyeshades, not for an era when billions, billions of investment dollars crossed borders at the speed of light. In the late '70s record interest rates and inflation rates rocked this anachronistic system. The less efficient institutions could not survive, obligating the federal government to protect the savings of millions of Americans.

Now, this process of paying debt down is nearing its end. Our financial system will become more flexible and efficient, but for now lenders are cautious, and despite low interest rates, small business can still find it hard to get the credit.

But the most far-reaching of these five changes is the emergence of a global economy. No nation is an island today. One out of every six manufacturing jobs is directly tied to exports. The crops sown from one out of every three acres of farmland are sold abroad.

Consider some implications of this global economy. When growth slows abroad, as it has recently, our own growth slows as well. And America will only grow in the next century if we can compete globally in every part of the world....

## Strengths and Weaknesses

Now, in drafting an agenda for America's future, we had to assess our strengths as well as our weaknesses. Conveniently, the other side has discovered many weaknesses and very few strengths. And of course they might find temporary political gain in portraying America as past her prime, over the hill. But they have no more right to argue for partisan purposes that our economy is weaker than it is. And I have to understand our problems.

Our strengths are real. Now here are some facts.

The misery index, the sum of inflation and unemployment, is 10.8 percent, down from 19.6 percent in 1980. Inflation stands at about 3 percent. Interest rates are at a 20-year low. The purchasing power of Americans gives us the highest standard of

living in the world. And we enjoy the highest home ownership rate of all major industrialized countries.

And we send 68 percent of our children on to higher education, more than any other country, and well above Germany's 32 percent and Japan's 30 percent. And with 5 percent of the world's population, we produce 25 percent of the world's total output, and 37 percent of its high-tech products.

I don't mean to suggest that all is well, that we don't need to lead and manage the changes that are transforming our economy. But you can't chart the stars if you think the sky is falling down.

Over the past 12 years we have almost doubled the size of our economy. It's as if we created two extra economies the size of Germany's from scratch.

And how will we meet our goals? Before you hear the specifics of this agenda, let me tell you a little bit about what I believe, because change, if it is to be a force for good, must be guided by principles. And the principles [that] must guide change are the principles that never change.

I believe we are a nation of special individuals, not special interests. Individuals draw their enduring strength from their families, from their neighbors and communities, not from the government. And so I believe we must never ask government to do what families and neighbors and individuals can better do for themselves and for one another.

I believe, because I've seen it. Economic growth comes from the small-business woman who takes a risk on a new product, from the computer hacker working in a garage in a cluttered way, from the Merit Scholar in south L.A. — south central — with a future as big as his dreams. And I believe government owes it to them and to you to keep tax rates low and make them even lower, to keep money sound, to limit government spending and regulations and to open the way for greater competition and freer trade.

But I do not believe, as some might, that government's obligation ends there. As a conservative, I believe that government can help people, offer them hope and opportunity by giving them the means and the confidence to make the decisions that matter in life. . . .

## Agenda for the Future

From now on, if America is to lead the world, we need a leader who knows the territory. And my agenda for America renewal calls for action on six interconnected fronts. There's no single cause of our present situation. There can be no single cure. The whole of our agenda will be, must be, greater than the sum of its parts.

First, challenging the world. During the Cold War, we built a global security structure with military alliances across the Atlantic and the Pacific and in the same way, the post-Cold War era requires a strategic economic and trade policy, global in scope, and built on our foundation as an economic and export superpower. We are uniquely positioned to achieve this goal. As the largest fully integrated market in the world, we wield leverage with other countries that want access to our market. And as both a Pacific and European power, we are tied to the largest and most rapidly growing economies across both oceans.

And as the strongest nation in our hemisphere, we are looked to for leadership by free economies emerging from Chile, all the way up to Mexico.

The same holds true for the newly born economies of Eastern Europe and the former Soviet Union, where our values, our products, even our language carry a unique appeal. In Moscow today, the lines at McDonald's are longer than the lines at Lenin's tomb. And the key to America's growth, expansion and innovation has always been our openness to trade, investment, ideas and people. And as this openness is at last being reciprocated around the world, we find ourselves again at a special advantage.

The next steps in my strategic trade policy are to secure congressional approval of the North American Free Trade Agreement and to complete the global trade negotiations, the GATT Round, creating high-wage American jobs and expanding the pool of customers hungry for the fruits of American labor.

Let me emphasize, these agreements are steps, not ends in themselves. And so I want to announce today that it is my goal to develop a strategic network of free trade agreements with Latin America, with Poland, Hungary and Czechoslovakia, and with countries across the Pacific. And then as these external barriers fall, I believe we can help reduce internal barriers to competition as well. In North America, Western Europe, Japan and elsewhere, greater competition will encourage entrepreneurial capitalism at the expense of government power and entrenched interests, spurring unprecedented economic growth.

Traveling around the country, I've seen it happen already, particularly in some small businesses, as they strengthen themselves for international competition. . . .

But a business is only as efficient, as resilient, as innovative as the people who keep its books and build its products and devise its strategy. Materials, machines, methods, they'll come and go. But the American worker will remain the key to our economic security.

## Education and Training

And that brings me then to the second part of our agenda: preparing our children.

The workplace of the 21st century will be constantly changing. I've heard that from many business people sitting right here at the tables in this hall.

We must prepare the American people for a lifetime of learning to keep a step ahead of that process of change. Developed nations need developing minds. The burden will fall on our educational system. As in the past, education should be the ladder that children can climb to better themselves.

Our current school system is not up to the task. Designed for the 19th century, it will collapse under the weight of the 21st. And our educational establishment is caught in the same time warp, where standing still means falling behind.

Money alone is not the answer. The United States already spends more per pupil than any other country but Switzerland. The answer is a radical overhaul of the system itself. And if we want to change our country, we simply have got to change our schools.

The catalyst for change, the one reform that drives all others, is school choice, giving children scholarship so that all parents have the freedom to choose which schools will best serve their children. Competition is the principle that must underlie education reform, to break the establishment's monopoly on the system. And competition will not work unless parents are allowed to choose their children's schools, whether it's the public school across town or the parochial school across the street.

Consider just one statistic. In Chicago, 46 percent of public school teachers send their children to private schools. Clearly they know something about monopoly education that my opponent doesn't. And our different approaches to education reform reveal the grand canyon that divides me and my opponent.

You see the same contrast in child care or health care and a host of other issues. My opponent prefers uniformity to variety and choice, relying on these government bureaucracies to offer one-size-fits-all service. And I don't want to pull everyone down to make everyone equal. I want to give everyone the tools to climb as high as they can dream.

And even as we fix our schools, the question remains: Will there be good jobs for the kids? And that's the third part of this agenda — sharpening business's competitive edge. I learned my economics the way most of you did — a lot of late-night sweating over a balance sheet or P&L statement, trying to meet a payroll. And I saw that if people are allowed to keep more of what they produce, they will produce more. It's common sense. And when capital is taxed lightly, there's more of it. And when it's taxed heavily, it becomes scarce, available only to those who are already wealthy, who need it least of all.

That's not the kind of economy that I want. And if capital were more abundant, labor would be more in demand, wages would rise, unemployment lines would shrink, and that is the kind of economy that I want.

And that's why I want enterprise zones in our inner cities and in our rural areas, and that's why I want to make this research and development, this R&D tax credit permanent, and that's why I want to cut the capital gains tax and index it for inflation.

Those are the fundamentals. I also see three other ways to sharpen the competitive edge in American business. First, strengthening small business by cutting taxes, making sure that credit is available, and by lifting the dead weight of govern-

ment regulation.

Second, supporting civilian R&D by bringing the development, production and marketing of technology closer to the consumer.

And third, reforming our legal system. Every year American business and consumers spend up to $200 billion just in direct costs to lawyers, far more than our competitors in Japan and Europe, and my product liability reform and Access To Justice Act will restore rationality to the system and stop undermining the American worker.

This is a fact. We will never lead the world in the 21st century until we learn to sue each other less and care for each other more.

And the fourth part of my agenda [is] promoting economic security for working men and women. Again common sense shows the way. True security will come only by developing individual capability, not dependency, and that independence in turn comes through the private sector, not the government. Government's role will be to ease the individual's adjustment to a fast-changing marketplace.

The average worker today will change jobs, it's estimated, 10 times over the course of his or her working life. And so we need a wider and more flexible range of job training and placement services for both the young and old, the blue- and white-collar worker. And now especially for our workers from the defense industries.

## Health Care

Pensions must be portable. Health care must be affordable. Our health-care system today, I think everyone here would agree, provides the best care, but at an unacceptable price.

More than 30 million Americans have no health insurance. Health-care costs are the fastest-rising part of our budget for government, businesses and yes, families. And my reforms get to the base of these problems while preserving and building on our system's strengths: Our state-of-the-art care, openness to innovation and consumer choice. And taken together, my reforms cut health-care costs by $394 billion over five years.

And my opponent's plan could eventually place a full 13 percent of our economy under the control of the federal government, meaning more bureaucracy, rationed care, inefficient service, and in the end higher costs.

We must enhance competition and market forces, not restrict them. We must preserve individual choice, not hand decision-making over to the centralized bureaucracies. We must reduce the burden on employers and employees, not bury them in a tide of new taxes and government regulations.

The programs I've outlined and that are detailed in this agenda are based on the principles that will empower all Americans to make their own choices and better their lives.

But I believe we need to do more for some of our citizens who've been left behind. And that is the fifth component of this agenda, leaving no one behind.

The American dream is nothing more

than the belief that all Americans can make a better life for their children. The dream has made us the most dynamic society in the world. It's yet another strength we can draw upon for the challenge ahead.

And so we must give every American a shot at making good on the dream. And I reject the shopworn logic that sees poverty as a simple lack of income, a kind of economic shortfall that can be replaced with a government check.

A conservative philosophy of empowerment must have at its foundation the creation of character, through the ownership of property, through the dignity of work, and that means sweeping away a nightmare of crime from our cities, building a core of property owners, creating business incentives and making individual discipline and self-reliance the goal of all of our programs.

## Role of Government

I call the final component of my agenda "right-sizing government." You'll recognize it. I take the term from the business world, which has a lot to teach those of us in government. At a time when companies across the country have been restructuring, increasing efficiency, all to prepare for the economic competition of tomorrow, the federal government faces an obligation to do the same.

Today the federal government spends nearly 24 cents of every dollar . . . of the nation's income. And that's the fact. Government is too big and spends too much. And the size and structure of government are relics of a different age — artifacts more suited to the dilemmas of 50 years ago than the problems of today. Every institution in our society has learned that by pushing power down through organizations, by using technology to speed the flow of information, you don't just save money, you improve productivity. And it's time for the government to do the same. And I will streamline the government, consolidating agencies, tightening budgets and cutting the salaries of highly paid federal employees. And I'll start by cutting the White House budget 33 percent if the Congress cuts its own budget by the same amount.

You might say, why the linkage? Well, with fewer congressional staff badgering us for endless reports and endless visits to Capitol Hill, I know we can cut costs by that amount.

And I'll cut the salaries of all federal employees earning more than $75,000 by 5 percent. Taxpayers have tightened their belts. The better-paid federal workers should do the same. The agenda I published today contains specific proposals to cut the fat, got a cap on the growth of mandatory spending, without touching Social Security, a freeze on domestic spending, a balanced-budget amendment, a line-item veto.

And a new mechanism, disciplinary mechanism, a checkoff box on tax returns to give the taxpayer the power to cut the deficit. I will fight to reduce spending and spur growth so we can get this budget in balance. And unlike my opponent, I do not believe the American people are under-

taxed. Quite the opposite. I am committed to cutting taxes across the board.

My cap on the growth of mandatory spending allows for population growth and inflation. It specifically exempts Social Security. But that cap alone, with those caveats will save about $300 billion over five years. And if we use just $130 billion in specific spending cuts that I have already proposed . . . we could cut income tax rates by 1 percentage point across the board, reduce the small-business tax rate from 15 percent to 10 percent and reduce the tax on capital gains. That's the direction I want to go. Tax less, spend less, cut the deficit and redirect our current spending to serve the interests of all Americans.

I honestly believe that this is the way, the only way, to control the size of the federal government. And the facts are painful, but plain. For congressmen, spending is power. And they will exercise that power until they have spent every last dime they can squeeze from the working men and women of America. And it's as simple as this: Raising taxes won't cut the deficit. . . .

In the agenda published today, you'll find 13 proposals that I intend to achieve in the first year of my second term. I present them as a single program, a unified strategy to make change work for America. And over the last three years I've shown how Americans can change the world. And we've made a respectable start managing the change at home.

Our primary task now is to target America. And I intend to fight for this agenda, to fight as hard as I can. And with a new Congress that can have as many as 150 new members, I am optimistic. If Congress balks, we'll move forward anyway, just as I've done with education, regulatory and welfare reform. I'll work with our great governors, with the state and local governments, with the private sector, with anyone who shares the urge to renew our country.

The American people know that the events of recent years have shaken the world. At the close of the Cold War, we can achieve peace, prosperity and promise at home. And the American people want that. The American people deserve that. And I want America to seize this moment. I want to stimulate entrepreneurial capitalism, not punish it. I want to empower people to make their own choices, not yoke them to new bureaucracies. I want a government that spends less, regulates less and taxes less, and I will fight without hesitation for a free flow of trade and capital and ideas around the world because Americans never retreat; we always compete. . . .

I know that times have been very, very difficult for many Americans. The world that we knew as children, no matter what your age, will never be the same. America will change. That's our destiny. How it will change will soon be decided, and I ask, as you consider the choice that you face, to consider carefully whose agenda for change best fits America's principles, our national experience and our hopes for lasting peace and prosperity. ∎

# President-Elect Clinton Reassures Allies

*On Nov. 4, President-elect Bill Clinton addressed the media assembled in Little Rock, Ark. Following is the text of his remarks:*

Today I want to reaffirm the essential continuity of American foreign policy and my desire to seek bipartisan support for our role in the world.

During the transition that is now beginning, I urge America's friends and foes alike to recognize, as I do, that America has only one president at a time, that America's foreign policy remains solely in his hands, that even as America's administrations change, America's fundamental interests do not, that the greatest gesture of good will any nation can make toward me is to continue their full cooperation during this period with our one president, George Bush, and that the greatest mistake any adversary could make would be to doubt America's resolve during this period of transition.

I look forward to working closely with President Bush to ensure continuity in global affairs of interest to all Americans, from continued progress in the Mideast peace talks to completing negotiations on the details of the START [Strategic Arms Reduction Treaty] II arms control agreement, to making progress toward a good agreement on our world trade talks, to bolstering Russia's fledgling democracy, to working toward peaceful resolution of the conflict in the republics of the former Yugoslavia, to assisting the victims of famine in Somalia.

I also look forward to getting to work on the hard and vital task of restoring our nation's economic strength. Today I say to our financial and business leaders that although change is on the horizon, we understand the need to pursue stability even as we pursue new growth.

The changes I seek will strengthen America's market systems, not weaken them.

And to the people of our great nation, for whom we pledge to get up every morning and work hard to bring the economic opportunity that was at the core of the Clinton-Gore campaign, I say that the task has already begun. It will not be easy, but we will spare no effort to restore growth, jobs and incomes to the American people.

Let me also stress the stakes and the opportunities in the months and years that lie ahead. The Cold War is won. Now we have a chance to build a new peace. We have entered a global economy. Now we have the opportunity to master its competitive challenges rather than let these changes undermine our strength. We have become a diverse people of many colors and languages and beliefs. Now we have the obligation to ensure that our diversity is a source of strength and pride to all of us here at home and around the world.

We've become a nation of 250 million Americans. Now we have the opportunity, the duty, and the imperative to see that we do not leave even one of those 250 million behind as we move toward the next century.

We have entered a period of great challenge and extraordinary opportunity for our nation. I am confident we can make it a proud time in our history, proud for the families who are raising this nation's next generation, proud for the workers and businesses who are America's life blood, proud for the men and women who wear America's uniforms, and proud for the peoples of other nations living today in freedom, or in fear, who draw strength from American ideals, and share our vision of a peaceful and more prosperous world.

America has called upon me to be our next president. But our forebears call on all of us at this moment to honor their efforts, their sacrifices, their ideals and their lives, by working hard and working together to improve this good and great nation as much for our children, and our children's children, as those who preceded us did for us. They call on us to take our dreams and our hopes, and make them real.

Thank you, and God bless America. ∎

# 'America Will Answer the Call' On Somalia, Bush Says

## President announces Marines have been dispatched to Mogadishu 'For one reason only: to enable the starving to be fed'

*Following is the Reuter transcript of President Bush's Dec. 4 address to the nation on the situation in Somalia.*

**PRESIDENT BUSH:** I want to talk to you today about the tragedy in Somalia, and about a mission that can ease suffering and save lives. Every American has seen the shocking images from Somalia; the scope of suffering there is hard to imagine. Already, over a quarter-million people, as many people as live in Buffalo, New York, have died in the Somali famine. In the months ahead, five times that number — 1.5 million people — could starve to death.

For many months now, the United States has been actively engaged in the massive international relief effort to ease Somalia's suffering. All told, America has sent Somalia 200,000 tons of food, more than half the world total. This summer, the distribution system broke down. Truck convoys from Somalia's ports were blocked. Sufficient food failed to reach the starving in the interior of Somalia.

And so in August we took additional action in concert with the United Nations. We sent in the U.S. Air Force to help fly food to the towns. To date, American pilots have flown over 1,400 flights, delivering over 17,000 tons of food aid. And when the U.N. authorized 3,500 U.N. guards to protect the relief operation, we flew in the first of them, 500 soldiers from Pakistan.

But in the months since then, the security situation has grown worse. The U.N. has been prevented from deploying its initial commitment of troops. In many cases, food from relief flights is being looted upon landing. Food convoys have been hijacked, aid workers assaulted, ships with food have been subject to artillery attacks that prevented them from docking.

There is no government in Somalia. Law and order have broken down. Anarchy prevails. One image tells the story: Imagine 7,000 tons of food aid literally bursting out of a warehouse on a dock in Mogadishu while Somalis starve less than a kilometer away because relief workers cannot run the gantlet of armed gangs roving the city.

Confronted with these conditions, relief groups called for outside troops to provide security so they could feed people. It's now clear that military support is necessary to ensure the safe delivery of the food Somalis need to survive.

It was this situation which led us to tell the United Nations that the United States would be willing to provide more help to enable relief to be delivered. Last night the United Nations Security Council, by unanimous vote and after the tireless efforts of Secretary-General [Boutros] Boutros-Ghali, welcomed the United States' offer to lead a coalition to get the food through.

After consulting with my advisers, with world leaders and the congressional leadership, I have today told Secretary-General Boutros-Ghali that America will answer the call. I have given the order to [Defense] Secretary [Dick] Cheney to move a substantial American force into Somalia. As I speak, a Marine amphibious ready group, which we maintain at sea, is offshore Mogadishu. These troops will be joined by elements of the First Marine Expeditionary Force based out of Camp Pendleton, California, and by the Army's 10th Mountain Division out of Fort Drum, New York.

These and other American forces will assist in Operation Restore Hope. They are America's finest. They will perform this mission with courage and compassion and they will succeed.

The people of Somalia, especially the children of Somalia, need our help. We're able to ease their suffering. We must help them live. We must give them hope. America must act.

In taking this action I want to emphasize that I understand the United States alone cannot right the world's wrongs, but we also know that some crises in the world cannot be resolved without American involvement. That American action is often necessary as a catalyst for broader involvement in the community of nations. Only the United States has the global reach to place a large security force on the ground in such a distant place, quickly and efficiently, and thus save thousands of innocents from death. We will not, however, be acting alone.

I expect forces from about a dozen countries to join us in this mission. When we see Somalia's children starving, all of America hurts. We've tried to help in many ways, and make no mistake about it — now we and our allies will ensure that aid gets through. And here is what we and our coalition partners will do.

First, we will create a secure environment in the hardest-hit parts of Somalia, so that food can move from ships overland to the people in the countryside now devastated by starvation. And second, once we have created that secure environment, we will withdraw our troops, handing the security mission back to a regular U.N. peacekeeping force.

Our mission has a limited objective — to open the supply routes, to get the food moving and to prepare the way for a U.N. peacekeeping force to keep it moving.

This operation is not open-ended. We will not stay one day longer than is absolutely necessary. And let me be very clear. Our mission is humanitarian, but we will not tolerate armed gangs ripping off their own people, condemning them to death by starvation. General [Joseph P.] Hoar and his troops have the authority to take whatever military action is necessary to safeguard the lives of our troops and the lives of Somalia's people.

The outlaw elements in Somalia must understand this is serious business. We will accomplish our mission. We have no intent to remain in Somalia with fighting forces, but we are determined to do it right, to secure an environment that will allow food to get to the starving people of Somalia. To the people of Somalia I promise this: We do not plan to dictate political outcomes. We respect your sovereignty and independence.

Based on my conversations with other coalition leaders, I can state with confidence we come to your country for one reason only: to enable the starving to be fed.

And let me say to the men and women of our armed forces, we're asking you to do a difficult and dangerous job. As commander in chief, I assure you you will have our full support to get the job done. And we will bring you home as soon as possible.

And finally, let me close with a message to the families of the men and women who take part in this mission.

I understand it is difficult to see your loved ones go, to send them off knowing they will not be home for the holidays. But the humanitarian mission they undertake is in the finest traditions of service.

And so to every sailor, soldier, airman and Marine who is involved in this mission, let me say, you're doing God's work. We will not fail.

Thank you and may God bless the United States of America. ∎

## UNITED NATIONS

# U.N. Council Resolves To Ensure 'Secure Environment' in Somalia

*Following is the text of the U. N. Security Council Resolution 794, adopted Dec. 3, on the use of troops in Somalia:*

THE SECURITY COUNCIL,

REAFFIRMING its Resolutions 733 (1992) of 23 January 1992, 746 (1992) of 17 March 1992, 751 (1992) of 24 April 1992, 767 (1992) of 27 July 1992, and 775 (1992) of 28 August 1992,

RECOGNIZING the unique character of the present situation in Somalia and mindful of its deteriorating, complex and extraordinary nature, requiring an immediate and exceptional response,

DETERMINING that the magnitude of the human tragedy caused by the conflict in Somalia, further exacerbated by the obstacles being created to the distribution of humanitarian assistance, constitutes a threat to international peace and security,

GRAVELY ALARMED by the deterioration of the humanitarian situation in Somalia and UNDERLINING the urgent need for the quick delivery of humanitarian assistance in the whole country,

NOTING the efforts of the League of Arab States, the Organization of African Unity, and in particular the proposal made by its chairman at the 47th regular session of the General Assembly for the organization of an international conference, and the Organization of the Islamic Conference and other regional agencies and arrangements to promote reconciliation and political settlement in Somalia and to address the humanitarian needs of the people of that country,

COMMENDING the ongoing efforts of the United Nations, its specialized agencies and humanitarian organizations and of non-governmental organizations and of states to ensure delivery of humanitarian assistance in Somalia,

RESPONDING to the urgent calls from Somalia for the international community to take measures to ensure the delivery of humanitarian assistance in Somalia,

EXPRESSING GRAVE ALARM at continuing reports of widespread violations of international humanitarian law occurring in Somalia, including reports of violence and threats of violence against personnel participating lawfully in impartial humanitarian relief activities; deliberate attacks on non-combatants, relief consignments and vehicles, and medical relief facilities; and impeding the delivery of food and medical supplies essential for the survival of the civilian population,

DISMAYED by the continuation of conditions that impede the delivery of humanitarian supplies to destinations within Somalia, and in particular reports of looting of relief supplies destined for starving people, attacks on aircraft and ships bringing in humanitarian relief supplies, and attacks on the Pakistani UNOSOM [United Nations Operation in Somalia] contingent in Mogadishu,

TAKING NOTE with appreciation of the letters of the Secretary-General of 24 November 1992 (S/24859) and of 29 November (S/24868),

SHARING the Secretary-General's assessment that the situation in Somalia is intolerable and that it has become necessary to review the basic premises and principles of the U.N. effort in Somalia, and that UNOSOM's existing course would not in present circumstances be an adequate response to the tragedy in Somalia,

DETERMINED to establish as soon as possible the necessary conditions for the delivery of humanitarian assistance wherever needed in Somalia, in conformity with resolutions 751 (1992) and 767 (1992),

NOTING the offer by member States aimed at establishing a secure environment for humanitarian relief operations in Somalia as soon as possible,

DETERMINED FURTHER to restore peace, stability, and law and order with a view to facilitating the process of a political settlement under the auspices of the United Nations, aimed at national reconciliation in Somalia, and encouraging the Secretary-General and his Special Representative to undertake at all stages work at the national and regional levels to promote these objectives;

RECOGNIZING that the people of Somalia bear ultimate responsibility for the reconstruction of their own country,

1. REAFFIRMS its demand that all parties, movements and factions in Somalia immediately cease hostilities, maintain a cease-fire throughout the country, and cooperate with the Special Representative of the Secretary-General as well as with the military forces to be established pursuant to the authorization given in paragraph 10 below in order to promote the process of relief distribution, reconciliation and political settlement in Somalia;

2. DEMANDS that all parties, movements and factions in Somalia take all measures necessary to facilitate the efforts of the United Nations, its specialized agencies and humanitarian organizations to provide urgent humanitarian assistance to the affected population in Somalia;

3. ALSO DEMANDS that all parties, movements and factions in Somalia take all measures necessary to ensure the safety of United Nations and all other personnel engaged in the delivery of humanitarian asssitance, including the military forces to be established pursuant to the authorization given in paragraph 10 below.

4. FURTHER DEMANDS that all parties, movements and factions in Somalia immediately cease and desist from all breaches of international humanitarian law, including from actions such as those described above;

5. STRONGLY CONDEMNS all violations of international humanitarian law occurring in Somalia, including in particular the deliberate impeding of the delivery of food and medical supplies essential for the survival of the civilian population, and AFFIRMS that those who commit or order the commission of such acts will be held individually responsible of such acts;

6. DECIDES that the operations and the further deployment of the 3,500 personnel of the United Nations Operation in Somalia ... authorized by paragraph 3 of Resolution 775 (1992) should proceed at the discretion of the Secretary-General in the light of his assessment of conditions on the ground; and requests him to keep the [Security] Council informed and to make such recommendations as may be appropriate for the fulfillment of its mandate where conditions permit;

7. ENDORSES the recommendations by the Secretary-General in his letter (S/24868) that action under Chapter VII of the Charter of the United Nations should be taken in order to establish a secure environment for humanitarian relief operations in Somalia as soon as possible;

8. WELCOMES the offer by member States described in the Secretary-General's letter to the Council of 29 November 1992 concerning the establishment of an operation to create such a secure environment;

9. WELCOMES also offers by other member States to participate in that operation;

10. Acting under Chapter VII of the Charter of the United Nations, AUTHORIZES the Secretary-General and member States cooperating to implement the offer referred to in paragraph 8 above to use all necessary means to establish as soon as possible a secure environment for humanitarian relief operations in Somalia;

11. CALLS upon all member States which are in a position to do so to provide military forces and to make additional contributions, in cash or in kind, in accordance with paragraph 10 above, and REQUESTS the Secretary-General to establish a fund through which the contributions, where appropriate, could be channeled to the States or operations concerned;

12. AUTHORIZES the Secretary-General and the member States concerned to make the necessary arrangements for the unified command and control of the forces involved, which will reflect the offer referred to in paragraph 8 above;

13. REQUESTS the Secretary-General and the member States acting under paragraph 10 above to establish appropriate mechanisms for coordination between the United Nations and their military forces;

14. DECIDES to appoint an ad hoc

commission composed of members of the Security Council to report to the Council on the implementation of this resolution;

15. INVITES the Secretary-General to attach a small UNOSOM liaison staff to the Field Headquarters of the unified command;

16. Acting under Chapters VII and VIII of the Charter, CALLS upon States, nationally or through regional agencies or arrangements, to use such measures as may be necessary to ensure strict implementation of paragraph 5 of resolution 733 (1992);

17. REQUESTS all States, in particular those in the region, to provide appropriate support for the actions undertaken by States, nationally or through regional agencies or arrangements, pursuant to this and other relevant resolutions;

18. REQUESTS the Secretary-General and, as appropriate, the States concerned, to report to the Council on a regular basis, the first such report to be made no later than 15 days after the adoption of this resolution, on the implementation of this resolution and the attainment of the objective of establishing a secure environment so as to enable the Council to make the necessary decision for a prompt transition to continued peacekeeping operations;

19. REQUESTS the Secretary-General to submit a plan to the Council initially within 15 days after the adoption of this resolution, to ensure that UNOSOM will be able to fulfill its mandate upon the withdrawal of the unified command;

20. INVITES the Secretary-General and his Special Representative to continue their efforts to achieve a political settlement in Somalia;

21. DECIDES to remain actively seized of the matter.

## Clinton's Comments

*Following is the text of a statement issued Dec. 3 by President-elect Bill Clinton:*

U.N. Security Council Resolution 794 is a historic and welcome step to assist the people of Somalia. By voting to authorize all necessary means to establish a secure environment for humanitarian relief operations in Somalia, the United Nations has provided new hope for the millions of Somalis at risk of starvation.

I commend President Bush for taking the lead in this important humanitarian effort. I appreciate his keeping me informed of developments as he makes decisions regarding possible courses of action for the United States under this new Security Council resolution. ∎

## HOUSE BANK

# Wilkey Issues His Final Report On Members' Bank Scandal

*Justice Department's special counsel finds evidence of criminal conduct, recommends full investigation*

*On Dec. 16, Special Counsel Malcom R. Wilkey issued his final report on a preliminary inquiry into the House bank scandal. Following are excerpts from the report.*

### I. Introduction

The United States House of Representatives has maintained a banking facility (sometimes referred to as the "House Bank") since approximately 1830 to facilitate paying salaries to the Members. Its lengthy, and periodically troubled, existence had been largely unknown to the citizenry until recently, when the problems with extensive overdrafting became visible. The public outcry engendered by these disclosures resulted in the closing of the banking facility at the end of 1991. However, there still remained many unanswered questions about whether any Members had committed crimes in the course of their use of the bank, whether any of the bank's employees had committed any crimes in their running of the bank, and whether any money of the United States had been misappropriated through the operation of the bank.

While it appeared at the outset of my preliminary inquiry that some criminal activity had occurred at the House Bank, it was also clear that many of the accusations of criminal conduct on the part of individual Members were unjustified. In the atmosphere of the time, neither the press nor the public was inclined to make the distinction between conduct based on a misunderstanding of the rules, conduct which was obviously unethical, and conduct which might violate the criminal laws. Since it appeared that the vast majority of the Members of the House would fall into the categories of either innocent of any intentional wrongdoing or responsible for only ethical violations, and since most of the 435 Members were immediately faced with primary elections and the general election in November, it seemed only the fair and

decent thing to establish as our first priority the identification of those Members whose bank records and other evidence did not indicate a violation of federal criminal laws. I recognize full well that the normal course of an inquiry or investigation, looking ultimately toward criminal indictments of the wrongdoers, usually focuses on the worst offenders first, and lets the others, innocent as they may be, drop unnoticed by the wayside. I believe that the unique clientele of this bank — the only depositors being Members of the House — called for a reversal of the usual priorities.

So we began the process of thoroughly reviewing each and every account in which there were one or more overdrafts [1] identified by the House Ethics Committee, some 329 accounts in all. By 1 September 1992, when I made my interim report to you, we had just reached the point at which we could safely say that slightly more than half the accounts we were examining gave no evidence of any prosecutable criminal violation. On most of the remaining accounts it appeared that we would be able to reach the same conclusion over the next few weeks.

Therefore, since the equities in notifying over half the Members involved seemed to outweigh the temporary uncertainty of the public about the status of those Members not first notified, I sent out a large number of letters in early September notifying Members that their accounts showed no evidence of any prosecutable criminal violation. I stressed in the letter and in the press release of the Department that our review of these accounts was a continuing process, that most of the other Members would rather quickly receive a similar letter, and that the time element involved really now depended on the complexity of the accounts and our ability to secure information from the Members themselves, and from other banks and financial institutional besides the House Bank.

While this method of proceeding doubtless caused temporary anxiety among those Members up for re-election who had not yet received a letter, still it appeared that this anxiety was dissipated rather quickly as the Members and the public began to realize that we were engaged in a continuing process. By the date of the November election I had sent clearance letters to all but nine of the Members seeking re-election. If I had not adopted the priority of first clearing the innocent and then proceeding to more intensive examination of other cases, by usual prosecutorial methods we might well have secured one or more indictments by the middle of September, but we would have been in no position to assure the other Members and the public as to who was clearly innocent. Then the question in September and October to these Members would have been, not: Have you received a letter yet? but: Have you been indicted yet? This would have been grossly unfair to the vast majority of the Members of the House, particularly those seeking re-election, who would ultimately be informed that there was no evidence of any criminal violation on the records we had examined. According to the records actual criminal conduct by some Members appears to have taken place, but it is quite limited. This corresponds to the opinion I formed at the outset, and conveyed to you and to the House leadership.

\* \* \*

### VIII. Misconceptions

A. *No public funds were ever used or lost.*

The Sergeant at Arms was a U.S. Treasury Disbursing Officer, the position which gave him access to, and control of, and accountability for the money involved here. As discussed above in Section IV, the funds in the House Bank remained funds of the United States until actually paid to the Member or for his account.

The only way the Sergeant at Arms could obtain money for use in the House check-cashing facility was to write a green Treasury check, which was cashed at a commercial bank, just as an individual Government employee would do with his salary check. When an individual Government employee cashes his salary check, he draws upon Government funds, not his own. This is what the Sergeant at

Arms did, i.e., he wrote a green Treasury check and presented it for cash at NBW/Riggs several days each week, thus drawing upon Treasury funds. Or he wrote a similar check to the Federal Reserve to pay for the Members' House Bank checks presented.

The Sergeant at Arms did not maintain an "account" at Riggs or NBW. Rather, he used those institutions only as a check-cashing facility like that of the House Bank itself, not as we are accustomed to dealing with our personal accounts in an ordinary bank. If there had been an "ordinary account" at the Riggs, the Sergeant at Arms would have written a check on the Riggs Bank on that account. He did not. He wrote a Treasury check on a Treasury account. For convenience, arrangements were worked out with first NBW, then Riggs, but the Sergeant at Arms' check could have been cashed any morning at any bank.

The "Account" which each individual Member had with the Sergeant at Arms was simply a bookkeeping entry showing that the Member had a right to ask the Sergeant at Arms to obtain for him an amount of money up to a certain figure, i.e., usually the remainder of the salary which was owed him for that month. The Sergeant at Arms satisfied this request by payment out of the cash that he kept on hand, or, in the case of "House Bank checks" coming to the Sergeant at Arms through the Federal Reserve System, by drawing a Treasury check in payment to the Federal Reserve for the total of House Bank checks presented each day. Under applicable case law, this money belonged to the United States until the Sergeant at Arms actually disbursed it.

B. *It was a Members' cooperative, underwritten by Members' own deposits.*

The House check cashing facility in the office of the Sergeant at Arms was not a "cooperative" in any sense of the word. The individual Members simply agreed individually with the Sergeant at Arms by signing a prescribed form to leave their salary funds, otherwise due and payable to them by a Treasury check, in the Treasury, until the individual Member requested the Sergeant at Arms by a "check" drawn on the "House Bank" to furnish the Member either cash or satisfy a "check" drawn to a third party. The obligations ran between the individual Member and the U.S. Government via the facility provided by the Sergeant at Arms.

Certainly the Members did not provide the $721,000 plus annual overhead to operate this facility. This money came out of taxpayer dollars.

C. *No checks were ever really "bounced."*

There certainly were. The abuse of the facility by some Members grew so bad that they were advised that their checks would not be honored unless their remaining balance with the Sergeant at Arms was sufficient to cover that specific check. There is no evidence that a House Bank teller ever embarrassed a Member by refusing to cash his check at the teller's cage, but in some instances Members were invited by the teller to see the Sergeant at Arms or the Bank Director before the check was honored (if it ever was). When the abuse became too aggravated, checks written on the banking facility to third parties were sometimes returned through the Federal Reserve System marked "Refer to Maker."

In addition, commercial bank checks which had been cashed or deposited at the House Bank were regularly returned through Riggs and earlier through NBW when there were insufficient funds in the commercial bank accounts.

D. *No Member was notified of his overdrafts and therefore was innocent of any intentional abuse.*

It is true that some Members were never notified that their checks on the Sergeant at Arms facility had overdrawn their accounts. These were the instances near the end of the month in which the overdraft was of small consequence and would clearly be covered by the next salary check of the Member due the first of the coming month.

The habitual overdrafters were habitually notified. One clerk customarily devoted most of her time to making phone calls to the Members' offices, notifying them of overdrafts and inviting them to come in and settle up.

E. *There was no kiting of checks.*

Check kiting is commonly defined as the writing of one check knowing there are insufficient funds in the account drawn upon, and the attempted replenishment by a second check drawn on another account with insufficient funds. The key to a check kite is the advantage of the "float," the time necessary to clear a check from one bank to another.

This did occur in a number of Members' accounts. Whether it occurred with the intent necessary to

constitute a provable criminal offense can only be determined by a close examination of the individual Member's account. Some Members did write checks on the House Bank with insufficient funds remaining in their accounts to cover the checks, and then attempted to make up the insufficiency by a check drawn on a commercial bank, which likewise did not have sufficient funds to cover it.

If a Member had the intent to run a check-kiting scheme, the method of operation of the House check cashing facility offered a golden opportunity. The practice was not to reject the checks drawn by Members when they had insufficient funds, but to put them in a drawer and term them "throwouts." The Member would then be called and asked to make up his deficiency. It might be several days or weeks before he did that, and when he did, in some instances he presented a check on an outside commercial bank which was likewise insufficient.

Thus the House banking facility offered two great advantages: first, an additional period of delay before he had to make good the original bad check, and secondly, and perhaps most importantly, the comforting knowledge that his original bad check would never be sent back through channels without him knowing about it and having a chance to cover it. Regular commercial bank check-kiting schemers never have these protections.

F. *There has been no violation of law because not a penny was "lost."*

There are a number of crimes, including misapplication and conversion of funds, in which the element of loss is not necessary at all to prove the crime. For example, simply because embezzled money has been replaced does not mean that an embezzlement has not taken place at a given point in time.

In the last analysis, money is like other forms of property. To have legal title to it is one aspect; to enjoy the use of it is another. The use of money, the use of a limousine, the use of a house, has an easily determined value. To acquire the use of money without paying for it would constitute a profit to the user, and a loss to whoever was deprived of the use during that period of time.

G. *The review by the House Ethics Committee found no criminal violations.*

The House Ethics Committee was not charged with the responsibility of

inquiring into possible criminal law violations, was not legally competent to do so, and specifically shielded itself from knowledge of certain facts which might be relevant in a criminal inquiry. Criminal inquiries are the responsibility of the Executive Branch. Given the attitude of a few Members of the House manifested by their systematic abuse of the check-cashing facility, can anyone imagine the attitude and practices which might have been displayed by a growing number of Members in future years, if this inquiry looking toward specific criminal violations had not been undertaken? If the Executive Branch had shirked its duty, the Legislative Branch, with some reason, might have come to consider itself a specially privileged group under the criminal law.

H. *All overdrafting is a crime and should be prosecuted.*

To date, no action or practice relating to the House Bank has aroused more intense public outcry, or more critical commentary by the media, than Members' overdrafting practices at the House Bank. The general perception that Members were able to engage, for extended periods, in a practice forbidden to the general public has prompted some members of the public to conclude that Members who engaged in overdrafting must have committed criminal violations.

To the contrary, in the circumstances of a particular case, an overdraft may be either a legitimate method of borrowing money, or an illegitimate and criminal method of obtaining it through the connivance of the person from whom it is obtained or even through the sole conduct of the overdrafter. To determine which of these conclusions would be correct, one must examine a host of factors, such as the financial institution's policies and practices concerning overdrafting, the manner in which the individual conducted the overdrafting, and the extent of knowledge by the overdrafter and the financial institution's personnel concerning the true state of the overdrafter's finances.

Both law and commercial practice recognize that overdrafting can create a legitimate lending relationship between the customer and the financial institution on which the overdrafted check has been drawn. An overdraft is in effect a loan. That loan can be the result of an express policy, such as the overdraft protection many commercial banks offer. A loan can also be implied from the practice of a particular financial institution in honoring checks for which the bank is aware there are insufficient funds.

The House Bank routinely honored most checks written by Members whether or not there were sufficient funds to cover them. This practice effectively limited the Members' potential criminal liability. When an overdraft is honored by a financial institution rather than being returned without being paid ("bounced"), there is ordinarily no violation of the [Washington] D.C. bad check law.

The D.C. law requires proof that, at the time the check was written or presented, the person knew he did not have either sufficient funds on deposit or credit at the bank to cover the check. If the bank honors the check, the overdrafter can argue that obviously he had sufficient "credit" at the bank to cover the check, or it would not have been honored. By honoring literally thousands of checks that most commercial banks would have returned for insufficient funds, the House Bank permitted Members to engage in conduct that would have been impossible (and, in some circumstances, even criminal) for the general public.

In addition, the D.C. statute requires proof not only that a person wrote or delivered a check for which there were insufficient funds or credit at the institution on which the check is drawn, but also that the person knew, at the time he wrote or delivered the check, that he had insufficient funds or credit. Under this statute, many Members could legitimately claim that they did not know, at the time they wrote checks on their House Bank accounts, that they had insufficient funds or credit there. Since the monthly account statement issued by the House Bank did not list negative balances — a practice that commercial banks and bank examiners would have considered intolerable — it would be difficult in most instances to prove that a Member actually knew that there were insufficient funds in the account when the check was written or presented.

For these reasons, we decided, in the vast majority of cases, that the evidence relating to overdrafts written by the Member was insufficient to warrant further investigation for Federal criminal violations. In appropriate circumstances, however, certain conduct by a Member that relates to overdrafting at the House Bank may warrant such further investigation.

## IX. Results of the Preliminary Inquiry

Three hundred and twenty-nine accounts at the House banking facility were identified by the Ethics Committee as having one or more overdrafts and were subject to our review. Commencing 9 September 1992 I wrote to certain account holders advising them that "based on the evidence we have reviewed there is no basis for pursuing a further inquiry regarding possible criminal violations concerning your account." The "clearance letter" is limited to activities associated with the use of the House banking facility. It also contains a proviso allowing for further investigation if other evidence comes to light. Moreover, the clearance letter does not address the moral or ethical propriety of the Members' use of their accounts by only whether criminal conduct was apparent. In some instances the inquiry uncovered evidence that civil, rather than criminal, violations may have occurred. In those instances I have referred the matter to the appropriate agency. As of the date of this Report, the vast majority of account holders have received a letter from me advising each of my conclusion that no further criminal inquiry is warranted.

Of course, to date not all account holders have received a clearance letter. In some cases further investigation may clear up quickly any outstanding questions about the accounts. One of the unforeseen reasons for delay in clearing a number of accounts has been the delay of certain Members themselves in furnishing specific information requested.

As to others, including some former House employees, I am recommending that a full investigation be conducted. In those instances where my preliminary inquiry has uncovered evidence of possible criminal conduct, only a full investigation can determine whether indictment and prosecution is appropriate.

Part II of this Final Report, based in part on Grand Jury information, discusses in detail the legal authorities on which we have proceeded, and refers to full scale investigations. It cannot be publicly disclosed and is therefore bound separately for your consideration. ∎

[1] As used in this Report, "overdraft" refers to a check drawn on a bank in which there were not sufficient funds to cover it, but [which] the bank paid anyway; "bounced" refers to a check drawn on a bank where there were not sufficient funds to cover it, and the bank returned the check unpaid.

## IRAN-CONTRA

# Bush Cites 'Policy Differences' In Granting Six Pardons

*Following is the text of President Bush's Dec. 24, 1992, proclamation granting a pardon to six people indicted in the Iran-contra affair.*

Today I am exercising my power under the Constitution to pardon former Secretary of Defense Caspar Weinberger and others for their conduct related to the Iran-Contra affair.

For more than 6 years now, the American people have invested enormous resources into what has become the most thoroughly investigated matter of its kind in our history. During that time, the last American hostage has come home to freedom, worldwide terrorism has declined, the people of Nicaragua have elected a democratic government, and the Cold War has ended in victory for the American people and the cause of freedom we championed.

In the mid 1980's, however, the outcome of these struggles was far from clear. Some of the best and most dedicated of our countrymen were called upon to step forward. Secretary Weinberger was among the foremost.

Caspar Weinberger is a true American patriot. He has rendered long and extraordinary service to our country. He served for 4 years in the Army during World War II where his bravery earned him a Bronze Star. He gave up a lucrative career in private life to accept a series of public positions in the late 1960's and 1970's, including Chairman of the Federal Trade Commission, Director of the Office of Management and Budget, and Secretary of Health, Education and Welfare. Caspar Weinberger was one of the principal architects of the downfall of the Berlin Wall and the Soviet Union. He directed the military renaissance in this country that led to the breakup of the communist bloc and a new birth of freedom and democracy. Upon his resignation in 1987, Caspar Weinberger was awarded the highest civilian medal our Nation can bestow on one of its citizens, the Presidential Medal of Freedom.

Secretary Weinberger's legacy will endure beyond the ending of the Cold War. The military readiness of this Nation that he in large measure created could not have been better displayed than it was 2 years ago in the Persian Gulf and today in Somalia.

As Secretary Weinberger's pardon request noted, it is a bitter irony that on the day the first charges against Secretary Weinberger were filed, Russian President Boris Yeltsin arrived in the United States to celebrate the end of the Cold War. I am pardoning him not just out of compassion or to spare a 75-year-old patriot the torment of lengthy and costly legal proceedings, but to make it possible for him to receive the honor he deserves for his extraordinary service to our country.

Moreover, on a somewhat more personal note, I cannot ignore the debilitating illnesses faced by Caspar Weinberger and his wife. When he resigned as Secretary of Defense, it was because of his wife's cancer. In the years since he left public service, her condition has not improved. In addition, since that time, he also has become ill. Nevertheless, Caspar Weinberger has been a pillar of strength for his wife; this pardon will enable him to be by her side undistracted by the ordeal of a costly and arduous trial.

I have also decided to pardon five other individuals for their conduct related to the Iran-Contra affair: [former Assistant Secretary of State] Elliott Abrams, [former CIA official] Duane Clarridge, [former CIA official] Alan Fiers, [former CIA official] Clair George, and [former National Security Adviser] Robert McFarlane. First, the common denominator of their motivation--whether their actions were right or wrong--was patriotism. Second, they did not profit or seek to profit from their conduct. Third, each has a record of long and distinguished service to this country. And finally, all five have already paid a price--in depleted savings, lost careers, anguished families--grossly disproportionate to any misdeeds or errors of judgment they may have committed.

The prosecutions of the individuals I am pardoning represent what I believe is a profoundly troubling development in the political and legal climate of our country: the criminalization of policy differences. These differences should be addressed in the political arena, without the Damocles sword of criminality hanging over the heads of some of the combatants. The proper target is the President, not his subordinates; the proper forum is the voting booth, not the courtroom.

In recent years, the use of criminal processes in policy disputes has become all too common. It is my hope that the action I am taking today will begin to restore these disputes to the battleground where they properly belong.

In addition, the actions of the men I am pardoning took place within the larger Cold War struggle. At home, we had a long, sometimes heated debate about how that struggle should be waged. Now the Cold War is over. When earlier wars have ended, Presidents have historically used their power to pardon to put bitterness behind us and look to the future. This healing tradition reaches at least from James Madison's pardon of Lafitte's pirates after the War of 1812, to Andrew Johnson's pardon of soldiers who had fought for the Confederacy, to Harry Truman's and Jimmy Carter's pardons of those who violated the selective service laws in World War II and Vietnam.

In many cases, the offenses pardoned by these Presidents were at least as serious as those I am pardoning today. The actions of those pardoned and the decisions to pardon them raised important issues of conscience, the rule of law, and the relationship under our Constitution between the government and the governed. Notwithstanding the seriousness of these issues and the passions they aroused, my predecessors acted because it was time for the country to move on. Today I do the same.

Some may argue that this decision will prevent full disclosure of some new key fact to the American people. That is not true. This matter has been investigated exhaustively. The Tower Board, the Joint Congressional Committee charged with investigating the Iran-Contra affair, and the Independent Counsel have looked into every aspect of this matter. The Tower Board interviewed more than 80 people and reviewed thousands of documents. The Joint Congressional Committee interviewed more than 500 people and reviewed more than 300,000 pages of material. Lengthy committee hearings were held and broadcast on national television to millions of Americans. And as I have noted, the Independent Counsel investigation has gone on for more than 6 years, and it has cost more than $31 million.

Moreover, the Independent Counsel stated last September that he had completed the active phase of his investigation. He will have the opportunity to place his full assessment of the facts in the public record when he submits his final report. While no impartial person has seriously suggested that my own role in this matter is legally questionable, I have further requested that the Independent Counsel provide me with a copy of my sworn testimony to his office, which I am prepared to release immediately. And I understand Secretary Weinberger has requested the release of all of his notes pertaining to the Iran-Contra matter.

For more than 30 years in public service, I have tried to follow three precepts: honor, decency, and fairness. I know, from all those years of service, that the American people believe in fairness and fair play. In granting these pardons today, I am doing what I believe honor, decency, and fairness require.

NOW, THEREFORE, I, George Bush, President of the United States of America, pursuant to my power under Article II, Section 2, of the Constitution, do hereby grant a full, complete, and unconditional pardon to Elliott Abrams, Duane R. Clarridge, Alan Fiers, Clair George, Robert C. McFarlane, and Caspar Weinberger for all offenses charged or prosecuted by Independent Counsel Lawrence E. Walsh or other members of his office, or committed by these individuals and within the jurisdiction of that office.

IN WITNESS WHEREOF, I have hereunto set my hand this twenty-fourth day of December, in the year of our Lord nineteen hundred and ninety-two, and of the Independence of the United States of America the two hundred and seventeenth. ■

# INTEREST GROUP RATINGS

# Voters Respond to '91 Group Ratings

Amid voter discontent and a growing wave of anti-incumbent sentiment, the 1991 interest group ratings proved more important to voters than in most years.

For nearly half a century, voters' coalitions had used the annual ratings — compiled by interest groups on the basis of how members voted on issues important to them — as a quick reference for judging familiar members. But for 1992, as voters sorted through charges of wrongdoing and wrestled with the attractiveness of "outsider" candidates, interest groups believed voters would look increasingly to the ratings to clarify the picture. *(Votes, p. 10-F; scores, this page.)*

"There's such an anti-incumbency sentiment out there that I am sure that the ratings will be key," said Christine Russell, House liaison for the U.S. Chamber of Commerce.

According to AFL-CIO officials, the number of requests by union locals for copies of ratings had increased since the last congressional election cycle in 1990. After distributing 40,000 copies of the ratings, the AFL-CIO was forced to print more of its score cards.

Interest group members typically used the ratings when choosing which incumbents to endorse. Endorsements could be very valuable to campaigns because they came with access to sometimes hundreds of thousands of voters. Groups provided phone banks, mailings and other services to the candidates they endorsed.

All members whose cumulative average was 70 percent or higher received an endorsement from the Chamber in an election year, Russell said.

Campaign contributions were also affected by interest group ratings. "I'd be surprised if there's any affiliate that doesn't look at the ratings before writing a check," said Jo Ellen Deutsch, government affairs manager at the Association of Flight Attendants.

Congressional Quarterly annually publishes the interest group ratings provided by Americans for Democratic Action (ADA), the American Conservative Union (ACU), the AFL-CIO and the Chamber.

Though often flawed and limited in how they can be used, the ratings can be good indicators of certain trends. "A rating can give us decent information about relative preferences within a given Congress," Keith Krehbiel, a Stanford University political scientist, said. "They are reasonable reflections of general policy predispositions."

## Established Trends

Despite the signs of increased importance, the 1991 ratings followed the pattern of past years.

As was almost always the case, the AFL-CIO, which selected 12 key votes, and the Chamber of Commerce, which chose 10 in each chamber, took opposing views on economic issues. They opposed each other on the extension of unemploy-

### Party Scores

*Average scores for members of each party in each chamber, as computed by CQ research staff.*

| | House | Senate |
|---|---|---|
| **Americans for Democratic Action** | | |
| Democrats | 67% | 75% |
| Republicans | 14 | 18 |
| **American Conservative Union** | | |
| Democrats | 18 | 22 |
| Republicans | 82 | 76 |
| **AFL-CIO** | | |
| Democrats | 83 | 78 |
| Republicans | 24 | 29 |
| **Chamber of Commerce** | | |
| Democrats | 32 | 20 |
| Republicans | 83 | 73 |

ment benefits, family and medical leave, fast-track consideration for the president's trade agreements, conditional most-favored-nation status for China and revisions of the Davis-Bacon Act, which set wage standards for federal contracts.

In a rare convergence of views, business and labor both let senators know that they opposed campaign finance reform legislation, although for very different reasons. The Chamber opposed public financing of campaigns, and the AFL-CIO opposed bans on political action committee contributions.

The ADA and the ACU used 20 and 19 votes, respectively, to evaluate members. The votes presented age-old confrontations over civil rights, the death penalty, defense spending and abortion, as well as over such more current issues as the authorization of the use of force in the Persian Gulf and the nomination of Clarence Thomas to the Supreme Court.

In 1991 Congress increasingly supported labor over business. The Chamber's 1-9 Senate record was the worst score in either chamber, and the AFL-CIO's 10-2 success rate in the House stood out as the most successful record among the groups. The ratings indicated that labor had gained support since 1990, when its House record was 7-5, and that business had lost friends from the previous year; in 1990 the Chamber record in the Senate was a somewhat higher 4-8.

The 10 labor victories included extending unemployment benefits, revising wage standard laws, easing rules governing employment discrimination suits and passing a landmark highway bill with the potential to create at least 2 million jobs.

But the good House voting record was not enough to influence enactment on some issues. Three AFL-CIO wins came on bills threatened with vetoes: the Family Medical Leave Act (HR 2), the striker replacement bill (HR 5) and the Flight Attendant Duty Time Act (HR 14), which limits the hours in a flight attendant's workday.

ACU's lack of success (four of 19 in the House, eight of 19 in the Senate) surprised few. Illustrating the dwindling power of conservatives in Congress, the ACU continued to have a relatively poor success rate in both chambers.

In addition to indicating trends, ratings highlighted members who diverged from party or regional patterns. For example, the score cards in 1991 showed that three Southern Democratic senators — North Carolinian Terry Sanford and Tennesseans Jim Sasser and Al Gore — often took more liberal positions than their regional colleagues.

John Lewis, D-Ga., was the only House member with a zero rating from the Chamber of Commerce.

In some cases, ratings could be used as election-time ammunition against members. The scores could become fodder for opponents anxious to show that incumbents were out of touch with their constituents. ∎

# How Four Interest Groups Rated Members in 1991

Following are the positions advocated by four major interest groups on congressional votes they used to rate members in 1991.

A "Y" or "N" indicates whether the group favored a yea or nay vote; "won" or "lost" indicates whether the group's position prevailed.

The term "Southern Democrats" applies to members from Ala., Ark., Fla., Ga., Ky., La., Miss., N.C., Okla., S.C., Tenn., Texas and Va.

## Americans for Democratic Action

*Since 1947, ADA ratings served as a standard, if sometimes disputed, measure of liberalism. The ADA based its ratings on 20 Senate votes and 20 House votes.*

### Senate Votes

**The ADA supported:**

Continuing international sanctions rather than authorizing the use of force to pressure Iraq to withdraw from Kuwait *(Vote 1)*. Y-lost

Disapproving the president's request to extend for two years fast-track procedures that required legislation implementing trade agreements to be considered within 60 days without amendment *(Vote 86)*. Y-lost

Allowing racial minorities to challenge death penalty sentences by using statistics that showed a disproportionate number of their race were condemned to die *(Vote 102)*. N Motion to strike provisions-lost

Rejecting the death penalty as a maximum sentence in favor of mandatory life imprisonment without the possibility of release *(Vote 107)*. Y-lost

Requiring waiting period of five business days before handgun purchases and mandatory background check of prospective handgun buyers *(Vote 115)*. Y-won

Invoking cloture (thus limiting debate) on a proposal to allow eligible citizens to register to vote when they applied for or renewed driver's licenses *(Vote 140)*. Y-lost

Passage of the bill prohibiting the president from renewing most-favored-nation (MFN) trade status for China unless he certified that China had improved its record on human rights and weapons proliferation *(Vote 142)*. Y-won

Prohibiting multiple missile interceptor sites and deployment of space-based missile sensors banned by the 1972 anti-ballistic missile treaty; keeping the Strategic De-

fense Initiative (SDI) in the research and development stage *(Vote 168)*. Y-lost

Invoking cloture (thus limiting debate) on a proposal allowing military personnel and their dependents to obtain privately paid abortions in overseas military facilities *(Vote 177)*. Y-lost

Waiving the Budget Act to transfer $3.15 billion in budget authority from the Defense Department to education and other assistance programs, including Head Start and a low-income fuel fund *(Vote 182)*. Y-lost

Prohibiting employers from granting preferential treatment in hiring, pay or other job conditions based on race, color, religion, sex or national origin *(Vote 187)*. N to designate germane-won

Cutting $3.2 billion from the Air Force's procurement account, halting production of the B-2 bomber at 15 planes *(Vote 206)*. N Motion to table-lost

Passage, over President Bush's veto, the bill designating an estimated $6.3 billion in emergency spending to extend unemployment benefits for up to 20 additional weeks through July 4, 1992 *(Vote 221)*. Y-lost

**The ADA opposed:**

Eliminating taxpayer funding of presidential campaigns and mail subsidies for political parties *(Vote 73)*. Y Motion to table-won

Limiting the ability of death row prisoners to file federal habeas corpus petitions by restricting the time they had to file petitions and the grounds for challenges to their sentences, and allowing the courts to dismiss petitions if the court decided the prisoner had a "full and fair" hearing on his claim at the state level. *(Vote 108)*. N-lost

Prohibiting federally funded facilities that assisted pregnant women from advising them, on request, of all legal and medical options, including abortion *(Vote 128)*. N-won

Allowing health-care professionals to test patients for the human immunodeficiency virus (HIV), the AIDS virus, before invasive medical procedures *(Vote 162)*. Y Motion to table-lost

Confirming President Bush's nomination of Clarence Thomas to be an associate justice of the U.S. Supreme Court *(Vote 220)*. N-lost

Invoking cloture (thus limiting debate) on the national energy policy bill that allowed drilling in the Arctic National Wildlife Refuge, mandated that federal and private vehicle fleets use alternative fuels, directed the secretary of Transportation to adopt new corporate average fuel economy standards, restructured electric utility regulations, streamlined the licensing process for nuclear power plants and enacted other programs related to energy production and consumption. *(Vote 242)*. N-won

Prohibiting the National Endowment for the Arts from using funds to promote, disseminate or produce materials that depicted or described, in a patently offensive way,

sexual or excretory activities or organs *(Vote 241).* Y Motion to table-won

## House Votes

### The ADA supported:

Continuing international sanctions rather than authorizing the use of force to pressure Iraq to withdraw from Kuwait *(Vote 8).* Y-lost

Passage of the bill to require a seven-day waiting period for handgun purchases, allowing local law enforcement authorities to check the background of prospective buyers to see if they had a criminal record or mental illness *(Vote 83).* Y-won

Terminating the Strategic Defense Initiative (SDI) organization and permitting only basic research on it in fiscal 1992, with funding at $1.1 billion *(Vote 97).* Y-lost

Reducing by $8 billion the amount that could be spent in fiscal 1992 to deploy U.S. forces in Europe, Japan or South Korea *(Vote 101).* Y-lost

Allowing privately paid-for abortions to be performed in overseas military hospitals *(Vote 109).* Y-won

Disapproving the president's request for a two-year renewal of fast-track procedures that required legislation implementing trade agreements to be considered within 60 days without amendment *(Vote 115).* Y-lost

Providing for unlimited punitive damages for discrimination based on sex, religion or disability; banning sex discrimination in private contracts; defining "business necessity" as a practice that bears a substantial and demonstrable relationship to job performance *(Vote 127).* Y-lost

Passage of the bill reversing or modifying six Supreme Court decisions that narrowed the reach and remedies of job discrimination laws *(Vote 131).* Y-won

Cutting $260 million from the budget to complete development of an MX intercontinental ballistic missile that could be launched from a rail car *(Vote 144).* Y-lost

Passage of the bill prohibiting the president from renewing most-favored-nation (MFN) trade status for China unless he certified that China had improved its record on human rights and weapons proliferation *(Vote 205).* Y-won

Passage of the bill prohibiting employers from hiring permanent replacements for union-represented workers striking over economic issues *(Vote 213).* Y-won

Passage of the bill to permanently extend unemployment benefits for up to 20 additional weeks and to designate as emergency spending an estimated $6.3 billion through fiscal 1996. *(Vote 267).* Y-won

Rejecting the death penalty as a maximum sentence in favor of mandatory life imprisonment without the possibility of parole *(Vote 311).* Y-lost

Banning the ownership, shipping or sale of 13 types of semiautomatic assault weapons and automatic loading devices *(Vote 318).* N Motion to strike provisions-lost

Allowing death row prisoners to raise certain race-bias claims in habeas corpus appeals *(Vote 324).* N Motion to strike provisions-lost

Providing $1.39 billion in supplemental spending for the Head Start preschool programs; the Woman, Infants and

Children nutrition program; and the childhood immunization program *(Vote 347).* Y-won

### The ADA opposed:

Restoring space station funding and offsetting the cost by freezing every other space program and cutting public housing subsidies *(Vote 141).* N-lost

Eliminating the law that prohibited U.S. aid to Pakistan if it attempted to increase its nuclear arsenal *(Vote 151).* N-won

Prohibiting the National Endowment for the Arts from funding projects that depicted or described, in a patently offensive way, sexual or excretory activities or organs *(Vote 308).* Y to table-lost

Substituting a ban on consideration of race in sentencing for a provision allowing racial minorities to challenge death penalty sentences by using statistics that showed a disproportionate number of their race were condemned to die *(Vote 322).* N-lost

## ADA Scores

A complete list of individual scores begins on page 10-F.

### Senate Highs and Lows

**High scorers.** Four Northern Democrats scored 100 percent: Harkin, Iowa; Metzenbaum, Ohio; Sarbanes, Md.; Simon, Ill. Seven Northern Democrats scored 95 percent.

Highest among Southern Democrats were Sanford, N.C., and Sasser, Tenn., with 90 percent. Gore, Tenn., and Bumpers, Ark., followed with 75 and 70 percent, respectively.

The highest-scoring Republicans were Cohen, Maine, and Jeffords, Vt., with 65 percent.

**Low scorers.** Three Republicans — Gramm, Texas; McConnell, Ky.; and Nickles, Okla. — scored 0 percent. Twelve scored 5 percent.

Among Southern Democrats, Pryor, Ark., and Breaux, La., scored lowest with 30 percent. Alabamans Shelby and Heflin each scored 35 percent.

Northern Democrats Exon, Neb., and DeConcini, Ariz., scored lowest of that group with 50 percent.

### House Highs and Lows

**High scorers.** Twenty-one Northern Democrats scored 100 percent. Twenty-two Northern Democrats; the lone independent, Sanders, Vermont; and one Southern Democrat, Washington, Texas, scored 95 percent.

Other Southern Democrat high scorers were Smith, Fla., with 90 percent; and Jefferson, La., and Lewis, Ga., who tied with 85 percent.

Green, N.Y., scored highest among Republicans with 75 percent. Morella, Md., received 65 percent. Shays, Conn.; Gilman, N.Y.; and Leach, Iowa, followed with 60 percent.

**Low scorers.** Thirty-five Republicans scored 0 percent. Thirty-three scored 5 percent.

Louisianans Huckaby and Tauzin and Texan Laughlin scored lowest among Southern Democrats with 10 percent.

Lowest scoring among Northern Democrats were Byron, Md., and Orton, Utah, with 25 percent; Skelton, Mo., followed with 30 percent.

## American Conservative Union

*The ACU sought "to mobilize resources of responsible conservative thought across the country and further the general cause of conservatism." It based its ratings on 19 Senate and 19 House votes.*

### Senate Votes

**The ACU supported:**

Authorizing the use of military force if Iraq did not withdraw from Kuwait and comply with U.N. Security Council resolutions by Jan. 15 *(Vote 2).* Y-won

Freezing budget authority and outlays for all fiscal 1992 discretionary spending at fiscal 1991 levels in order to reduce the deficit *(Vote 47).* N Motion to table-lost

Requiring U.S. economic assistance to Latin America to be used to promote free-market policies *(Vote 60).* Y-lost

Permitting federal prosecutors to seek the death penalty for anyone who used a firearm in the commission of a murder if the weapon had moved in interstate or foreign commerce *(Vote 109).* Y-won

Replacing Brady bill provisions requiring a seven-day waiting period for handgun purchases with provisions requiring within two years an instant background checking system *(Vote 113).* Y-lost

Prohibiting federally funded clinics from performing an abortion for a minor unless a parent or guardian had been given 48 hours' notice *(Vote 131).* Y-won

Allowing health-care professionals to test patients for the human immunodeficiency virus (HIV), the AIDS virus, before invasive medical procedures *(Vote 162).* N Motion to table-won

Cutting the Legal Services Corporation by $48.41 million and transfering the fund to the FBI *(Vote 163).* N Motion to table-lost

Confirming President Bush's nomination of Clarence Thomas to be an associate justice of the U.S. Supreme Court *(Vote 220).* Y-won

Prohibiting the National Endowment for the Arts from using funds to promote, disseminate or produce materials that depicted or described, in a patently offensive way, sexual or excretory activities or organs *(Vote 241).* N Motion to table-lost

Invoking cloture (thus limiting debate) on the National Energy Policy bill that allowed drilling in the Arctic National Wildlife Refuge, mandated that federal and private vehicle fleets use alternative fuels, directed the secretary of Transportation to adopt new corporate average fuel economy standards, restructured electric utility regulations, streamlined the licensing process for nuclear power plants and enacted other programs related to energy production and consumption *(Vote 242).* Y-lost

**The ACU opposed:**

Passage of the bill that set voluntary campaign spending limits tied to incentives including vouchers for broadcast time, mail subsidies and public funding *(Vote 85).* N-lost

Allowing racial minorities to challenge death penalty sentences by using statistics that showed a disproportionate number of their race were condemned to die *(Vote 102).* Y Motion to strike-won

Raising senators' pay from $101,900 to $125,100, banning senators' honoraria and limiting outside earned income to 15 percent of a senator's base pay *(Vote 133).* N-lost

Prohibiting multiple missile interceptor sites and deployment of space-based missile sensors banned by the 1972 anti-ballistic missile treaty; keeping the Strategic Defense Initiative (SDI) in the research and development stage *(Vote 168).* N-won

Reducing the authorization for the Strategic Defense Initiative (SDI) by $1.4 billion to $3.2 billion *(Vote 171).* Y Motion to table-won

Providing an estimated $6.3 billion for up to 20 additional weeks of unemployment benefits based on a state's average total unemployment rate *(Vote 213).* N-lost

Authorizing $25 billion in fiscal 1992-93 for foreign economic and military assistance including funds for the United Nations Population Fund; overturning the administration's Mexico City policy that prohibited funding for international organizations that performed or promoted abortions for family planning *(Vote 219).* N-lost

Reversing or modifying six Supreme Court decisions that narrowed the reach and remedies of job discrimination laws *(Vote 238).* N-lost

### House Votes

**The ACU supported:**

Authorizing the use of military force if Iraq did not withdraw from Kuwait and comply with U.N. Security Council resolutions by Jan. 15 *(Vote 9).* Y-won

Negotiating an agreement with the Soviet Union that allowed the research, development, testing and deployment of defenses against ballistic missiles of all ranges *(Vote 47).* Y-lost

Cutting domestic discretionary spending for 1992 to levels below Democrats' and the president's budget proposals *(Vote 68).* Y-lost

Requiring the secretary of State to seek reimbursement for the costs necessary to tear down and rebuild the bug-riddled U.S. Embassy in Moscow *(Vote 91).* Y-lost

Requiring random drug testing for all State Department employees *(Vote 93).* Y-lost

Authorizing the administration's defense request, which increased Strategic Defense Initiative (SDI) funding and provided $3.2 billion for the procurement of four new B-2 bombers *(Vote 99).* Y-lost

Reducing fiscal 1992 funding for the House official mail costs to the fiscal 1991 level of $59 million *(Vote 133).* Y-lost

Prohibiting aid to the South African Communist Party and other communist groups in South Africa *(Vote 183).* Y-won

Eliminating all of the fiscal 1992 funding for the National Endowment for the Arts *(Vote 192).* Y-lost

Lowering the threshold of eligibility for capital punishment from "intent to kill" to showing "a reckless disregard for life" *(Vote 313).* Y-won

Limiting the ability of death row prisoners to file federal habeas corpus petitions by restricting the time they had to file petitions and the grounds for challenges to their sentences, and allowing the courts to dismiss petitions if the court decided the prisoner had a "full and fair" hearing at the state level *(Vote 316).* Y-lost

Substituting a ban on consideration of race in sentencing for a provision allowing racial minorities to challenge death penalty sentences by using statistics that showed a disproportionate number of their race were condemned to die *(Vote 322).* Y-won

### The ACU opposed:

Passage of the bill requiring a waiting period of seven days before handgun purchases for a background check of prospective handgun buyers *(Vote 83).* N-lost

Approving the $1.59 trillion (in budget authority) budget blueprint that conformed to the discretionary spending caps and the pay-as-you-go requirements set by the 1990 budget agreement *(Vote 112).* N-lost

Passage of the bill reversing or modifying six Supreme Court decisions that narrowed the reach and remedies of job discrimination laws *(Vote 131).* N-lost

Preserving the $20 million in funding for the United Nations Population Fund, which supported family planning programs in many countries *(Vote 148).* N-lost

Passage of the bill prohibiting employers from hiring permanent replacements for union-represented workers striking over economic issues *(Vote 213).* N-lost

Passing the bill designating an estimated $6.3 billion in emergency spending to extend unemployment benefits to long-term unemployed workers for up to 20 additional weeks through fiscal 1996 *(Vote 267).* N-lost

Passage of the bill requiring employers to give unpaid leave to workers caring for a newborn or adopted child or sick relative *(Vote 393).* N-lost

## ACU Scores

A complete list of individual scores begins on page 10-F.

### Senate Highs and Lows

**High scorers.** Two Republicans received perfect 100 percent scores: Coats, Ind., and Helms, N.C. Gramm, Texas; Nickles, Okla.; and Wallop, Wyo., each scored 95 percent.

Shelby, Ala., led Democrats with 76 percent. The next-highest Southern Democrat was Hollings, S.C., with 62 percent; Heflin, Ala., and Breaux, La., followed with 57 percent.

The highest-scoring Northern Democratic was Dixon, Ill., who had 52 percent.

**Low scorers.** Eight Northern Democrats shared the lowest rung with 0 percent. Ten Northern Democrats scored 5 percent.

Also with 5 percent was the lowest-scoring Southern Democrat: Sasser, Tenn. Next lowest were Sanford, N.C.; Pryor, Ark.; and Gore, Tenn., who scored 10, 11 and 14 percent, respectively.

Among Republicans, Jeffords, Vt., scored lowest with 10 percent. Chafee, R.I., and Hatfield, Ore., had 24 percent.

### House Highs and Lows

**High scorers.** Thirty-four Republicans received perfect scores of 100 percent. Eighteen Republicans scored 95 percent.

Hall, Texas, led Southern Democrats with 90 percent. Taylor, Miss., received the next-highest score among Southern Democrats with 84 percent. Hutto, Fla., and Hayes, La., followed with 80 percent.

Among Northern Democrats, Orton, Utah, scored highest with 63 percent, followed by Condit, Calif., with 58 percent.

**Low scorers.** Seventy-seven Northern Democrats and nine Southern Democrats scored 0 percent. Twenty Northern Democrats and one Southern Democrat scored 5 percent.

Morella, Md., was the lowest-scoring Republican with 15 percent. Green, N.Y., scored next-lowest among Republicans, with 25 percent.

## AFL-CIO

*The umbrella group for organized labor, which had rated members of Congress since 1955, said its ratings represented "votes for or against the interest of workers." The AFL-CIO based its ratings on 12 Senate votes and 12 House votes.*

### Senate Votes

### The AFL-CIO supported:

Prohibiting the increased use of helpers (semiskilled workers who were paid less than the prevailing wage rate for skilled work) in federally funded construction projects *(Vote 35).* N Motion to strike-won

Reducing the Social Security payroll tax and financing the program on a pay-as-you-go basis *(Vote 46).* N Motion to table-lost

Disapproving the president's request to extend for two years fast-track procedures that required legislation implementing trade agreements to be considered within 60 days without amendment *(Vote 86).* Y-lost

Invoking cloture (thus limiting debate) on a proposal to allow eligible citizens to register to vote when they applied for or renewed driver's licenses *(Vote 140).* Y-lost

Passage of the bill prohibiting the president from renewing most-favored-nation trade status for China unless he certified that China had improved its record on human rights, weapons proliferation and fair trade *(Vote 142).* Y-won

Requiring employers to give unpaid leave to workers caring for a newborn or adopted child or sick relative but raising the number of hours an employee must work in order

to be eligible *(Vote 215)*. Y-won

Passing, over President Bush's veto, the bill designating an estimated $6.3 billion in emergency spending to extend unemployment benefits for up to 20 additional weeks through July 4, 1992 *(Vote 221)*. Y-lost

Passage of the bill reversing or modifying six Supreme Court decisions that narrowed the reach and remedies of job discrimination laws *(Vote 238)*. Y-won

### The AFL-CIO opposed:

Passage of the bill that set voluntary campaign spending limits tied to incentives including vouchers for broadcast time, mail subsidies and public funding *(Vote 85)*. N-lost

Eliminating cargo-preference and cash purchase requirements in the fiscal 1992-93 foreign aid authorization bill *(Vote 146)*. Y to table-won

Confirming President Bush's nomination of Clarence Thomas to be an associate justice of the U.S. Supreme Court *(Vote 220)*. N-lost

Eliminating the "pension losers" provision that provided limited payments to individuals whose plans were terminated prior to the enactment of the Employee Retirement Security Act *(Vote 248)*. Y to table-lost

### House Votes

### The AFL-CIO supported:

Prohibiting the increased use of helpers (semiskilled workers who were paid less than the prevailing wage rate for skilled work) in federally funded construction projects *(Vote 34)*. N Motion to strike-won

Disapproving the president's request for a two-year renewal of fast-track procedures that required legislation implementing trade agreements to be considered within 60 days without amendment *(Vote 115)*. Y-lost

Passage of the bill reversing or modifying six Supreme Court decisions that narrowed the reach and remedies of job discrimination laws *(Vote 131)*. Y-won

Requiring countries that received U.S. cash assistance to spend an equivalent amount to buy U.S. goods and services; requiring half of the cargo shipped by sea to go on U.S.-flag vessels *(Vote 150)*. N Motion to strike-won

Disapproving President Bush's waiver of the legislation barring most-favored-nation (MFN) trade status to China *(Vote 203)*. Y-won

Passage of the bill prohibiting employers from hiring permanent replacements for union-represented workers striking over economic issues *(Vote 213)*. Y-won

Passage of the bill requiring the Department of Transportation to issue regulations limiting the amount of time airline attendants could be required to work *(Vote 250)*. Y-won

Passage of the bill designating an estimated $6.3 billion in emergency spending to extend unemployment benefits for up to 20 additional weeks through fiscal 1996 *(Vote 267)*. Y-won

Passage of the bill to authorize $151 billion for highway and mass transit programs in fiscal 1992-97 and extend the gas tax set to expire in fiscal 1995 through fiscal 1999 *(Vote 338)*. Y-won

Passage of the bill requiring employers to give unpaid leave to workers caring for a newborn or adopted child or sick relative *(Vote 393)*. Y-won

Passage, over President Bush's veto, of the bill to provide $205 billion in new budget authority for the Departments of Labor, Health and Human Services, and Education and related agencies; and blocking enforcement of the administration rule barring abortion counseling in federally funded family planning clinics *(Vote 403)*. Y-lost

### The AFL-CIO opposed:

Requiring candidates to raise at least half of all their campaign money from people living in their districts; cutting the amount political action committees could give candidates from $5,000 to $1,000 *(Vote 425)*. N-won

## AFL-CIO Scores

A complete list of individual scores begins on page 10-F.

### Senate Highs and Lows

**High scorers.** Eight Northern Democrats and one Southern Democrat scored 92 percent. Tennesseans Gore and Sasser followed Sanford, N.C., the Southern Democrats' highest scorer, with 83 percent. Packwood, Ore., and D'Amato, N.Y., were the highest-scoring Republicans, with 67 percent.

**Low scorers.** Pressler, R-S.D., scored lowest with 8 percent. Fifteen Republicans followed with 17 percent. Among the Democrats, Boren, Okla., scored lowest with 42 percent; Nunn, Ga., and Kohl, Wis., followed with 58 percent.

### House Highs and Lows

**High scorers.** Seventy Democrats, seven Southern Democrats and 63 Northern Democrats and independent Sanders, Vt., received perfect scores of 100 percent. Gilman, N.Y., led Republicans with 92 percent. Horton, N.Y., followed with 83 percent.

**Low scorers.** Fourteen Republicans received 0 percent. Thirty-six scored 8 percent.

Hall, Texas; Huckaby, La.; Montgomery, Miss.; and Stenholm, Texas, scored lowest among Democrats with 17 percent. Four other Southern Democrats ranked next lowest with 33 percent.

Orton, Utah, also with 33 percent, received the lowest score among the Northern Democrats. Penny, Minn., followed with 42 percent.

## U.S. Chamber of Commerce

*The Chamber selected votes it said provided "a fair representation of floor votes on issues important to*

*business — including large and small firms." Ten Senate and 10 House votes were chosen for the study.*

## Senate Votes

### The Chamber supported:

Reducing the Social Security payroll tax and financing the program on a pay-as-you-go basis *(Vote 46)*. N Motion to table-lost

Indexing capital gains and cutting the capital gains tax rate from 28 percent to 19.6 percent for assets held more than three years in order to reduce the cost of capital, stimulate economic growth, and create new jobs *(Vote 202)*. Y to table point of order against-lost

Allowing Senate employees the same rights as private-sector workers to remedy infringements on civil rights with jury trials and punitive damages *(Vote 237)*. N Motion to table-lost

Invoking cloture (thus limiting debate) on the National Energy Policy bill to allow drilling in the Arctic National Wildlife Refuge, mandate that federal and private vehicle fleets use alternative fuels, direct the secretary of Transportation to adopt new corporate average fuel economy standards, restructure electric utility regulations, streamline the licensing process for nuclear power plants, and enact other programs related to energy production and consumption *(Vote 242)*. Y-lost

### The Chamber opposed:

Prohibiting the increased use of helpers (semiskilled workers who are paid less than the prevailing wage rate for skilled work) in federally funded construction projects *(Vote 35)*. Y to strike-lost

Invoking cloture (thus limiting debate) on a proposal to tighten the ban on vertical price fixing, which occurred when a manufacturer conspired with a retailer to force a competing merchant to charge at least a certain price for goods or face a cutoff of supplies *(Vote 53)*. N-lost

Passage of the bill that set voluntary campaign spending limits tied to incentives including vouchers for broadcast time, mail subsidies and public funding *(Vote 85)*. N-lost

Disapproving the president's request for a two-year renewal of fast-track procedures directing congressional consideration of trade agreements *(Vote 86)*. N-won

Passage of the bill prohibiting the president from renewing most-favored-nation trade status for China unless he certified that China had improved its record on human rights, weapons proliferation and fair trade *(Vote 142)*. N-lost

Requiring employers to give unpaid leave to workers caring for a newborn or adopted child or sick relative but raising the number of hours an employee must work in order to be eligible *(Vote 215)*. N-lost

## House Votes

### The Chamber supported:

Keeping domestic discretionary spending about $7.5 billion lower than the budget agreement caps and cutting entitlement programs including Medicare over five years *(Vote 69)*. Y-won

Exempting small manufacturers who lacked market power from vertical price fixing bans *(Vote 304)*. Y-won

Approving the extension of non-discriminatory treatment, most-favored-nation (MFN) trade status, for the republics of the former Soviet Union *(Vote 410)*. Y-won

### The Chamber opposed:

Revisions of the Davis-Bacon Act prohibiting the increased use of helpers (semiskilled workers paid less than the prevailing wage rate for skilled work) in federally funded construction projects *(Vote 34)*. Y Motion to strike-lost

Disapproving the president's request to extend for two years fast-track procedures that required legislation implementing trade agreements to be considered within 60 days without amendment *(Vote 115)*. N-won

Passage of the bill reversing or modifying six Supreme Court decisions that narrowed the reach and remedies of job discrimination laws *(Vote 131)*. N-lost

Passage of the bill prohibiting employers from hiring permanent replacements for union-represented workers striking over economic issues *(Vote 213)*. N-lost

Replacing provisions designating unemployment benefits as emergency spending with provisions that increased the federal unemployment tax on employers to pay for extended benefits *(Vote 264)*. N-won

Providing $500,000 in emergency supplemental appropriations for a National Academy of Sciences wetlands delineation study *(Vote 348)*. N-won

Passage of the bill requiring employers to give unpaid leave to workers caring for a newborn or adopted child or sick relative *(Vote 393)*. N-lost

## Chamber Scores

A complete list of individual scores begins on page 10-F.

### Senate Highs and Lows

**High scorers.** Five Republicans scored 100 percent; six followed with 90 percent. Boren, Okla., scored highest among Southern Democrats with 56 percent. Pryor, Ark., followed with 50 percent. Lieberman, Conn., was the highest scorer among Northern Democrats with 30 percent.

**Low scorers.** Three Northern Democrats — Glenn, Ohio; Levin, Mich.; and Wofford, Pa. — and one Southern Democrat — Sasser, Tenn. — scored lowest with 0 percent. Twelve Northern Democrats and three Southern Democrats received scores of 10 percent.

Jeffords, Vt., scored lowest among Republicans with 22 percent.

### House Highs and Lows

**High scorers.** Forty-four Republicans scored 100 percent. Forty-two had 90 percent. Stenholm, Texas, and Hutto, Fla., led Southern Democrats with 90 percent each. LaRocco, Idaho, led Northern Democrats with 60 percent.

**Low scorers.** Lewis, Ga., with a 0 score, was the chamber's only absolute opponent. Next to Lewis, the lowest-scoring Southern Democrats were Erdreich, Ala., and Gonzalez, Texas, each scoring 10 percent.

Twenty Northern Democrats also scored 10 percent.

The lowest Republican was Gilman, N.Y., with 20 percent. ■

# Interest Group Ratings: House

**ADA (Americans for Democratic Action)** — The percentage of time each representative voted in accordance with the ADA position on 20 selected votes in 1991. The percentages were compiled by the ADA. Failure to vote lowered scores.

**AFL-CIO (American Federation of Labor-Congress of Industrial Organizations)** — The percentage of time each representative voted in favor of the AFL-CIO position on 12 selected votes in 1991. The percentages were compiled by the AFL-CIO. Failure to vote did not lower scores.

**CCUS (Chamber of Commerce of the United States)** — The percentage of time each representative voted with the Chamber's position on 10 selected votes in 1991. The percentages were compiled by the Chamber. Failure to vote did not lower scores.

**ACU (American Conservative Union)** — The percentage of time each representative voted with the ACU position on 19 selected votes in 1991. The percentages were compiled by the ACU. Failure to vote did not lower scores.

[1] *Ed Pastor, D-Ariz, was sworn in Oct. 3, 1991, to succeed Morris K. Udall, D, who resigned May 4, 1991. Pastor was rated on six votes by the ADA, four votes by the AFL-CIO, four votes by the CCUS and four votes by the ACU. Udall was not rated by any of the groups.*

[2] *Thomas W. Ewing, R-Ill., was sworn in July 10, 1991, to succeed Edward Madigan, R, who resigned March 8, 1991, after being confirmed as secretary of Agriculture. Ewing was rated on nine votes by the ADA, four votes by the AFL-CIO, six votes by the CCUS and six votes by the ACU. Madigan received a perfect score from the ACU for his gulf war vote. He was not rated by the other groups.*

[3] *John W. Olver, D-Mass., was sworn in June 18, 1991, to succeed Silvio O. Conte, R, who died Feb. 8, 1991. Olver was rated on nine votes by the ADA, eight by the AFL-CIO, six by the CCUS and eight by the ACU. Conte received a 0 percent score from the ACU for his gulf war vote. He was not rated by other groups.*

[4] *Lucien E. Blackwell, D-Pa., was sworn in Nov. 13, 1991, to succeed William H. Gray III, D, who resigned Sept. 11, 1991. Blackwell was rated on three votes by the AFL-CIO and on one vote by the ACU. Gray was rated on 11 votes by the ADA (85). He was not rated by the other groups.*

[5] *Sam Johnson, R-Texas, was sworn in May 22, 1991, to succeed Steve Bartlett, R, who resigned March 11, 1991. Johnson was rated on 16 votes by the ADA, 11 votes by the AFL-CIO, eight by the CCUS and 12 by the ACU. Bartlett was not rated by any of the groups.*

[6] *George F. Allen, R-Va., was sworn in Nov. 12, 1991, to succeed D. French Slaughter Jr., R, who resigned Nov. 5, 1991. Allen was rated on three votes by the AFL-CIO and on one by the ACU. Slaughter was rated on 13 votes by the ADA (5). He was not rated by any other group.*

[7] *Thomas S. Foley, D-Wash., as Speaker of the House, voted at his discretion. Foley was rated on three votes by the AFL-CIO (100) and on three by the ACU.*

## KEY

ADA — Americans for Democratic Action

AFL-CIO — American Federation of Labor-Congress of Industrial Organizations

CCUS — Chamber of Commerce of the United States

ACU — American Conservative Union

Democrats **Republicans**
*Independent*

| | ADA | AFL-CIO | CCUS | ACU |
|---|---|---|---|---|
| **Alabama** | | | | |
| 1 *Callahan* | 0 | 17 | 90 | 100 |
| 2 *Dickinson* | 5 | 9 | 90 | 85 |
| 3 Browder | 30 | 82 | 56 | 50 |
| 4 Bevill | 35 | 92 | 30 | 42 |
| 5 Cramer | 40 | 83 | 40 | 40 |
| 6 Erdreich | 40 | 92 | 10 | 45 |
| 7 Harris | 35 | 83 | 40 | 55 |
| **Alaska** | | | | |
| AL *Young* | 10 | 55 | 67 | 67 |
| **Arizona** | | | | |
| 1 *Rhodes* | 0 | 0 | 90 | 100 |
| 2 Pastor [1] | 83 | 100 | 25 | 0 |
| 3 *Stump* | 0 | 0 | 90 | 100 |
| 4 *Kyl* | 5 | 8 | 90 | 100 |
| 5 *Kolbe* | 10 | 17 | 100 | 80 |
| **Arkansas** | | | | |
| 1 Alexander | 55 | 82 | 33 | 19 |
| 2 Thornton | 40 | 92 | 50 | 15 |
| 3 *Hammerschmidt* | 0 | 17 | 100 | 89 |
| 4 Anthony | 65 | 58 | 70 | 16 |
| **California** | | | | |
| 1 *Riggs* | 30 | 25 | 90 | 65 |
| 2 *Herger* | 5 | 18 | 89 | 100 |
| 3 Matsui | 70 | 80 | 25 | 0 |
| 4 Fazio | 75 | 83 | 30 | 0 |
| 5 Pelosi | 90 | 92 | 20 | 0 |
| 6 Boxer | 80 | 100 | 25 | 0 |
| 7 Miller | 95 | 100 | 20 | 0 |
| 8 Dellums | 90 | 100 | 20 | 0 |
| 9 Stark | 100 | 100 | 20 | 0 |
| 10 Edwards | 95 | 100 | 20 | 0 |
| 11 Lantos | 75 | 100 | 11 | 11 |
| 12 *Campbell* | 25 | 25 | 70 | 70 |
| 13 Mineta | 90 | 100 | 20 | 0 |
| 14 *Doolittle* | 5 | 9 | 78 | 100 |
| 15 Condit | 60 | 92 | 40 | 58 |
| 16 Panetta | 80 | 83 | 30 | 5 |
| 17 Dooley | 60 | 75 | 50 | 10 |
| 18 Lehman | 60 | 100 | 30 | 25 |
| 19 *Lagomarsino* | 10 | 8 | 90 | 85 |
| 20 *Thomas* | 10 | 18 | 100 | 79 |
| 21 *Gallegly* | 10 | 8 | 90 | 85 |
| 22 *Moorhead* | 5 | 8 | 90 | 100 |
| 23 Beilenson | 80 | 67 | 30 | 0 |
| 24 Waxman | 90 | 83 | 10 | 0 |
| 25 Roybal | 80 | 91 | 22 | 0 |
| 26 Berman | 85 | 82 | 22 | 11 |
| 27 Levine | 65 | 100 | 20 | 15 |
| 28 Dixon | 85 | 100 | 20 | 0 |
| 29 Waters | 90 | 100 | 11 | 0 |
| 30 Martinez | 65 | 100 | 20 | 11 |
| 31 Dymally | 75 | 91 | 13 | 0 |
| 32 Anderson | 70 | 83 | 30 | 20 |
| 33 *Dreier* | 0 | 0 | 90 | 100 |
| 34 Torres | 80 | 92 | 20 | 5 |
| 35 *Lewis* | 0 | 18 | 100 | 83 |
| 36 Brown | 70 | 92 | 20 | 15 |
| 37 *McCandless* | 5 | 8 | 90 | 90 |
| 38 *Dornan* | 10 | 18 | 88 | 95 |
| 39 *Dannemeyer* | 10 | 8 | 90 | 100 |
| 40 *Cox* | 10 | 8 | 80 | 100 |
| 41 *Lowery* | 5 | 17 | 100 | 90 |

| | ADA | AFL-CIO | CCUS | ACU |
|---|---|---|---|---|
| 42 *Rohrabacher* | 15 | 17 | 90 | 100 |
| 43 *Packard* | 5 | 8 | 90 | 95 |
| 44 *Cunningham* | 5 | 17 | 90 | 95 |
| 45 *Hunter* | 5 | 27 | 78 | 100 |
| **Colorado** | | | | |
| 1 Schroeder | 90 | 83 | 30 | 0 |
| 2 Skaggs | 85 | 75 | 40 | 0 |
| 3 Campbell | 55 | 92 | 40 | 45 |
| 4 *Allard* | 0 | 0 | 100 | 95 |
| 5 *Hefley* | 10 | 25 | 90 | 100 |
| 6 *Schaefer* | 5 | 17 | 90 | 95 |
| **Connecticut** | | | | |
| 1 Kennelly | 80 | 83 | 20 | 0 |
| 2 Gejdenson | 95 | 100 | 20 | 0 |
| 3 DeLauro | 95 | 92 | 20 | 0 |
| 4 *Shays* | 60 | 42 | 70 | 50 |
| 5 *Franks* | 15 | 25 | 100 | 85 |
| 6 *Johnson* | 35 | 42 | 70 | 55 |
| **Delaware** | | | | |
| AL *Carper* | 55 | 92 | 40 | 20 |
| **Florida** | | | | |
| 1 Hutto | 15 | 33 | 90 | 80 |
| 2 Peterson | 55 | 75 | 40 | 15 |
| 3 Bennett | 60 | 83 | 20 | 35 |
| 4 *James* | 25 | 25 | 80 | 85 |
| 5 *McCollum* | 10 | 18 | 89 | 90 |
| 6 *Stearns* | 25 | 33 | 70 | 90 |
| 7 Gibbons | 60 | 58 | 30 | 16 |
| 8 *Young* | 30 | 8 | 80 | 85 |
| 9 *Bilirakis* | 15 | 8 | 80 | 89 |
| 10 *Ireland* | 0 | 0 | 100 | 95 |
| 11 Bacchus | 50 | 83 | 33 | 20 |
| 12 *Lewis* | 10 | 17 | 90 | 90 |
| 13 *Goss* | 5 | 8 | 80 | 90 |
| 14 Johnston | 80 | 91 | 22 | 11 |
| 15 *Shaw* | 0 | 17 | 100 | 90 |
| 16 Smith | 90 | 100 | 22 | 0 |
| 17 Lehman | 55 | 80 | 14 | 0 |
| 18 *Ros-Lehtinen* | 40 | 42 | 50 | 70 |
| 19 Fascell | 65 | 83 | 30 | 10 |
| **Georgia** | | | | |
| 1 Thomas | 35 | 58 | 70 | 47 |
| 2 Hatcher | 45 | 60 | 50 | 35 |
| 3 Ray | 25 | 36 | 70 | 60 |
| 4 Jones | 65 | 83 | 33 | 25 |
| 5 Lewis | 85 | 92 | 0 | 0 |
| 6 *Gingrich* | 5 | 17 | 100 | 100 |
| 7 Darden | 40 | 58 | 60 | 35 |
| 8 Rowland | 35 | 45 | 67 | 42 |
| 9 Jenkins | 25 | 67 | 67 | 25 |
| 10 Barnard | 15 | 33 | 78 | 55 |
| **Hawaii** | | | | |
| 1 Abercrombie | 100 | 100 | 10 | 0 |
| 2 Mink | 100 | 100 | 20 | 0 |
| **Idaho** | | | | |
| 1 LaRocco | 45 | 64 | 60 | 16 |
| 2 Stallings | 45 | 67 | 40 | 25 |
| **Illinois** | | | | |
| 1 Hayes | 100 | 100 | 20 | 0 |
| 2 Savage | 90 | 92 | 22 | 0 |
| 3 Russo | 70 | 92 | 20 | 20 |
| 4 Sangmeister | 60 | 82 | 22 | 15 |
| 5 Lipinski | 45 | 75 | 20 | 30 |
| 6 *Hyde* | 10 | 17 | 70 | 80 |
| 7 Collins | 90 | 100 | 20 | 0 |
| 8 Rostenkowski | 45 | 73 | 30 | 16 |
| 9 Yates | 95 | 100 | 22 | 6 |
| 10 *Porter* | 30 | 17 | 80 | 80 |
| 11 Annunzio | 55 | 75 | 40 | 16 |
| 12 *Crane* | 0 | 0 | 89 | 100 |
| 13 *Fawell* | 15 | 8 | 100 | 84 |
| 14 *Hastert* | 0 | 8 | 100 | 95 |
| 15 *Ewing* [2] | 0 | 13 | 100 | 100 |
| 16 Cox | 90 | 75 | 30 | 0 |
| 17 Evans | 100 | 100 | 20 | 5 |
| 18 *Michel* | 0 | 10 | 100 | 89 |
| 19 Bruce | 70 | 100 | 30 | 20 |
| 20 Durbin | 95 | 92 | 30 | 5 |
| 21 Costello | 55 | 83 | 30 | 15 |
| 22 Poshard | 65 | 75 | 30 | 25 |
| **Indiana** | | | | |
| 1 Visclosky | 80 | 92 | 30 | 10 |
| 2 Sharp | 75 | 75 | 40 | 5 |
| 3 Roemer | 50 | 67 | 40 | 30 |

| | ADA | AFL-CIO | CCUS | ACU |
|---|---|---|---|---|
| 4 Long | 70 | 75 | 40 | 10 |
| 5 Jontz | 90 | 83 | 10 | 10 |
| 6 ***Burton*** | 5 | 17 | 80 | 100 |
| 7 ***Myers*** | 0 | 17 | 90 | 70 |
| 8 McCloskey | 90 | 83 | 20 | 0 |
| 9 Hamilton | 65 | 58 | 50 | 15 |
| 10 Jacobs | 80 | 91 | 20 | 20 |
| **Iowa** | | | | |
| 1 ***Leach*** | 60 | 42 | 70 | 35 |
| 2 ***Nussle*** | 20 | 8 | 90 | 85 |
| 3 Nagle | 85 | 92 | 20 | 10 |
| 4 Smith | 55 | 82 | 40 | 11 |
| 5 ***Lightfoot*** | 0 | 8 | 100 | 100 |
| 6 ***Grandy*** | 25 | 17 | 100 | 85 |
| **Kansas** | | | | |
| 1 ***Roberts*** | 5 | 0 | 90 | 83 |
| 2 Slattery | 40 | 67 | 50 | 40 |
| 3 ***Meyers*** | 25 | 33 | 70 | 75 |
| 4 Glickman | 50 | 67 | 33 | 32 |
| 5 ***Nichols*** | 5 | 8 | 100 | 95 |
| **Kentucky** | | | | |
| 1 Hubbard | 40 | 92 | 40 | 50 |
| 2 Natcher | 50 | 100 | 30 | 20 |
| 3 Mazzoli | 65 | 67 | 20 | 10 |
| 4 ***Bunning*** | 10 | 8 | 90 | 100 |
| 5 ***Rogers*** | 10 | 25 | 90 | 79 |
| 6 ***Hopkins*** | 0 | 0 | 67 | 90 |
| 7 Perkins | 75 | 100 | 30 | 15 |
| **Louisiana** | | | | |
| 1 ***Livingston*** | 0 | 8 | 100 | 90 |
| 2 Jefferson | 85 | 92 | 20 | 0 |
| 3 Tauzin | 10 | 50 | 80 | 70 |
| 4 ***McCrery*** | 0 | 8 | 90 | 85 |
| 5 Huckaby | 10 | 17 | 89 | 67 |
| 6 ***Baker*** | 0 | 8 | 100 | 95 |
| 7 Hayes | 20 | 50 | 67 | 80 |
| 8 ***Holloway*** | 5 | 20 | 75 | 100 |
| **Maine** | | | | |
| 1 Andrews | 100 | 92 | 20 | 0 |
| 2 ***Snowe*** | 35 | 67 | 40 | 55 |
| **Maryland** | | | | |
| 1 ***Gilchrest*** | 20 | 17 | 90 | 70 |
| 2 ***Bentley*** | 25 | 50 | 40 | 60 |
| 3 Cardin | 75 | 92 | 30 | 0 |
| 4 McMillen | 50 | 75 | 40 | 15 |
| 5 Hoyer | 80 | 92 | 30 | 0 |
| 6 Byron | 25 | 58 | 60 | 45 |
| 7 Mfume | 100 | 100 | 20 | 5 |
| 8 ***Morella*** | 65 | 67 | 60 | 15 |
| **Massachusetts** | | | | |
| 1 Olver [3] | 100 | 100 | 33 | 0 |
| 2 Neal | 90 | 100 | 20 | 5 |
| 3 Early | 85 | 92 | 10 | 30 |
| 4 Frank | 100 | 83 | 20 | 5 |
| 5 Atkins | 90 | 83 | 30 | 0 |
| 6 Mavroules | 85 | 92 | 20 | 10 |
| 7 Markey | 100 | 100 | 20 | 0 |
| 8 Kennedy | 95 | 100 | 20 | 0 |
| 9 Moakley | 90 | 100 | 20 | 5 |
| 10 Studds | 90 | 100 | 20 | 0 |
| 11 Donnelly | 75 | 82 | 33 | 15 |
| **Michigan** | | | | |
| 1 Conyers | 95 | 100 | 20 | 0 |
| 2 ***Pursell*** | 25 | 25 | 100 | 79 |
| 3 Wolpe | 100 | 100 | 20 | 0 |
| 4 ***Upton*** | 25 | 25 | 100 | 80 |
| 5 ***Henry*** | 30 | 25 | 80 | 65 |
| 6 Carr | 75 | 58 | 40 | 21 |
| 7 Kildee | 95 | 92 | 10 | 5 |
| 8 Traxler | 80 | 92 | 10 | 16 |
| 9 ***Vander Jagt*** | 0 | 17 | 100 | 90 |
| 10 ***Camp*** | 15 | 8 | 100 | 80 |
| 11 ***Davis*** | 20 | 64 | 40 | 53 |
| 12 Bonior | 95 | 100 | 20 | 0 |
| 13 Collins | 100 | 100 | 20 | 0 |
| 14 Hertel | 95 | 92 | 20 | 0 |
| 15 Ford | 95 | 100 | 13 | 0 |
| 16 Dingell | 65 | 92 | 22 | 22 |
| 17 Levin | 100 | 100 | 30 | 0 |
| 18 ***Broomfield*** | 15 | 8 | 100 | 84 |
| **Minnesota** | | | | |
| 1 Penny | 50 | 42 | 60 | 30 |
| 2 ***Weber*** | 5 | 8 | 90 | 85 |
| 3 ***Ramstad*** | 25 | 33 | 80 | 85 |
| 4 Vento | 90 | 92 | 10 | 0 |

| | ADA | AFL-CIO | CCUS | ACU |
|---|---|---|---|---|
| 5 Sabo | 90 | 92 | 10 | 0 |
| 6 Sikorski | 95 | 92 | 20 | 0 |
| 7 Peterson | 65 | 67 | 40 | 15 |
| 8 Oberstar | 85 | 83 | 20 | 11 |
| **Mississippi** | | | | |
| 1 Whitten | 25 | 75 | 60 | 33 |
| 2 Espy | 65 | 75 | 50 | 16 |
| 3 Montgomery | 5 | 17 | 90 | 70 |
| 4 Parker | 20 | 33 | 80 | 75 |
| 5 Taylor | 15 | 33 | 80 | 84 |
| **Missouri** | | | | |
| 1 Clay | 90 | 100 | 20 | 0 |
| 2 Horn | 85 | 100 | 30 | 10 |
| 3 Gephardt | 75 | 92 | 30 | 0 |
| 4 Skelton | 30 | 67 | 60 | 47 |
| 5 Wheat | 100 | 100 | 10 | 0 |
| 6 ***Coleman*** | 5 | 25 | 90 | 75 |
| 7 ***Hancock*** | 5 | 8 | 90 | 100 |
| 8 ***Emerson*** | 15 | 25 | 90 | 85 |
| 9 Volkmer | 35 | 75 | 40 | 42 |
| **Montana** | | | | |
| 1 Williams | 65 | 73 | 44 | 20 |
| 2 ***Marlenee*** | 10 | 18 | 88 | 94 |
| **Nebraska** | | | | |
| 1 ***Bereuter*** | 10 | 17 | 100 | 85 |
| 2 Hoagland | 50 | 83 | 10 | 15 |
| 3 ***Barrett*** | 0 | 8 | 90 | 89 |
| **Nevada** | | | | |
| 1 Bilbray | 35 | 100 | 20 | 40 |
| 2 ***Vucanovich*** | 0 | 9 | 78 | 100 |
| **New Hampshire** | | | | |
| 1 ***Zeliff*** | 10 | 8 | 100 | 80 |
| 2 Swett | 45 | 92 | 30 | 40 |
| **New Jersey** | | | | |
| 1 Andrews | 70 | 92 | 10 | 15 |
| 2 Hughes | 70 | 92 | 33 | 26 |
| 3 Pallone | 60 | 92 | 10 | 30 |
| 4 ***Smith*** | 45 | 75 | 40 | 60 |
| 5 ***Roukema*** | 35 | 55 | 67 | 50 |
| 6 Dwyer | 80 | 100 | 20 | 5 |
| 7 ***Rinaldo*** | 35 | 67 | 30 | 55 |
| 8 Roe | 70 | 83 | 20 | 10 |
| 9 Torricelli | 60 | 92 | 30 | 20 |
| 10 Payne | 95 | 100 | 20 | 0 |
| 11 ***Gallo*** | 20 | 42 | 90 | 60 |
| 12 ***Zimmer*** | 20 | 42 | 70 | 70 |
| 13 ***Saxton*** | 10 | 27 | 67 | 74 |
| 14 Guarini | 55 | 82 | 20 | 15 |
| **New Mexico** | | | | |
| 1 ***Schiff*** | 20 | 33 | 80 | 65 |
| 2 ***Skeen*** | 0 | 17 | 90 | 85 |
| 3 Richardson | 50 | 92 | 30 | 20 |
| **New York** | | | | |
| 1 Hochbrueckner | 75 | 100 | 20 | 0 |
| 2 Downey | 85 | 92 | 20 | 0 |
| 3 Mrazek | 70 | 90 | 17 | 0 |
| 4 ***Lent*** | 10 | 25 | 90 | 74 |
| 5 ***McGrath*** | 35 | 67 | 40 | 55 |
| 6 Flake | 100 | 100 | 20 | 0 |
| 7 Ackerman | 85 | 100 | 20 | 10 |
| 8 Scheuer | 100 | 100 | 10 | 0 |
| 9 Manton | 80 | 92 | 20 | 10 |
| 10 Schumer | 85 | 92 | 20 | 0 |
| 11 Towns | 90 | 100 | 13 | 0 |
| 12 Owens | 100 | 100 | 11 | 0 |
| 13 Solarz | 75 | 83 | 20 | 10 |
| 14 ***Molinari*** | 30 | 58 | 70 | 70 |
| 15 ***Green*** | 75 | 67 | 30 | 25 |
| 16 Rangel | 95 | 100 | 20 | 0 |
| 17 Weiss | 90 | 100 | 11 | 0 |
| 18 Serrano | 100 | 100 | 10 | 0 |
| 19 Engel | 90 | 100 | 30 | 15 |
| 20 Lowey | 100 | 100 | 20 | 0 |
| 21 ***Fish*** | 45 | 75 | 40 | 35 |
| 22 ***Gilman*** | 60 | 92 | 20 | 30 |
| 23 McNulty | 80 | 100 | 10 | 10 |
| 24 ***Solomon*** | 15 | 45 | 56 | 90 |
| 25 ***Boehlert*** | 45 | 75 | 40 | 40 |
| 26 ***Martin*** | 5 | 27 | 90 | 76 |
| 27 ***Walsh*** | 25 | 50 | 70 | 63 |
| 28 McHugh | 85 | 83 | 20 | 5 |
| 29 ***Horton*** | 50 | 83 | 50 | 30 |
| 30 Slaughter | 95 | 100 | 20 | 5 |
| 31 ***Paxon*** | 10 | 17 | 80 | 85 |

| | ADA | AFL-CIO | CCUS | ACU |
|---|---|---|---|---|
| 32 LaFalce | 90 | 83 | 30 | 10 |
| 33 Nowak | 85 | 92 | 20 | 10 |
| 34 ***Houghton*** | 20 | 50 | 70 | 70 |
| **North Carolina** | | | | |
| 1 Jones | 40 | 90 | 33 | 28 |
| 2 Valentine | 25 | 58 | 70 | 55 |
| 3 Lancaster | 40 | 58 | 60 | 40 |
| 4 Price | 60 | 83 | 50 | 10 |
| 5 Neal | 55 | 64 | 50 | 30 |
| 6 ***Coble*** | 15 | 25 | 80 | 90 |
| 7 Rose | 70 | 92 | 40 | 0 |
| 8 Hefner | 55 | 91 | 40 | 10 |
| 9 ***McMillan*** | 15 | 25 | 100 | 85 |
| 10 ***Ballenger*** | 10 | 17 | 90 | 95 |
| 11 ***Taylor*** | 10 | 17 | 90 | 90 |
| **North Dakota** | | | | |
| AL Dorgan | 75 | 75 | 40 | 25 |
| **Ohio** | | | | |
| 1 Luken | 35 | 50 | 60 | 50 |
| 2 ***Gradison*** | 10 | 8 | 90 | 84 |
| 3 Hall | 75 | 75 | 30 | 10 |
| 4 ***Oxley*** | 5 | 8 | 100 | 80 |
| 5 ***Gillmor*** | 10 | 25 | 70 | 65 |
| 6 ***McEwen*** | 5 | 17 | 90 | 100 |
| 7 ***Hobson*** | 10 | 25 | 80 | 80 |
| 8 ***Boehner*** | 0 | 0 | 100 | 95 |
| 9 Kaptur | 85 | 82 | 30 | 5 |
| 10 ***Miller*** | 10 | 18 | 78 | 100 |
| 11 Eckart | 85 | 92 | 20 | 0 |
| 12 ***Kasich*** | 15 | 8 | 100 | 85 |
| 13 Pease | 75 | 83 | 20 | 0 |
| 14 Sawyer | 90 | 92 | 30 | 0 |
| 15 ***Wylie*** | 10 | 17 | 100 | 84 |
| 16 ***Regula*** | 20 | 58 | 60 | 55 |
| 17 Traficant | 85 | 100 | 20 | 15 |
| 18 Applegate | 45 | 92 | 20 | 45 |
| 19 Feighan | 95 | 92 | 20 | 0 |
| 20 Oakar | 85 | 92 | 20 | 0 |
| 21 Stokes | 100 | 100 | 22 | 0 |
| **Oklahoma** | | | | |
| 1 ***Inhofe*** | 5 | 9 | 90 | 100 |
| 2 Synar | 90 | 75 | 30 | 0 |
| 3 Brewster | 20 | 67 | 60 | 45 |
| 4 McCurdy | 30 | 64 | 60 | 26 |
| 5 ***Edwards*** | 10 | 18 | 90 | 95 |
| 6 English | 35 | 67 | 40 | 50 |
| **Oregon** | | | | |
| 1 AuCoin | 95 | 92 | 20 | 5 |
| 2 ***Smith*** | 5 | 17 | 90 | 85 |
| 3 Wyden | 85 | 83 | 30 | 5 |
| 4 DeFazio | 80 | 100 | 20 | 11 |
| 5 Kopetski | 75 | 83 | 20 | 5 |
| **Pennsylvania** | | | | |
| 1 Foglietta | 95 | 100 | 11 | 0 |
| 2 Blackwell [4] | | 100 | | 0 |
| 3 Borski | 60 | 91 | 10 | 30 |
| 4 Kolter | 50 | 92 | 30 | 28 |
| 5 ***Schulze*** | 10 | 36 | 89 | 89 |
| 6 Yatron | 40 | 89 | 13 | 33 |
| 7 ***Weldon*** | 30 | 55 | 60 | 65 |
| 8 Kostmayer | 85 | 92 | 22 | 0 |
| 9 ***Shuster*** | 15 | 42 | 90 | 95 |
| 10 ***McDade*** | 30 | 56 | 44 | 65 |
| 11 Kanjorski | 50 | 92 | 10 | 25 |
| 12 Murtha | 40 | 92 | 30 | 26 |
| 13 ***Coughlin*** | 30 | 50 | 60 | 65 |
| 14 Coyne | 80 | 83 | 20 | 0 |
| 15 ***Ritter*** | 10 | 33 | 100 | 90 |
| 16 ***Walker*** | 5 | 8 | 90 | 100 |
| 17 ***Gekas*** | 5 | 25 | 100 | 90 |
| 18 ***Santorum*** | 15 | 42 | 80 | 80 |
| 19 ***Goodling*** | 20 | 25 | 70 | 73 |
| 20 Gaydos | 60 | 100 | 30 | 25 |
| 21 ***Ridge*** | 15 | 58 | 90 | 70 |
| 22 Murphy | 50 | 82 | 33 | 39 |
| 23 ***Clinger*** | 15 | 42 | 90 | 70 |
| **Rhode Island** | | | | |
| 1 ***Machtley*** | 45 | 58 | 50 | 47 |
| 2 Reed | 95 | 92 | 20 | 0 |
| **South Carolina** | | | | |
| 1 ***Ravenel*** | 25 | 58 | 70 | 75 |
| 2 ***Spence*** | 10 | 25 | 80 | 95 |
| 3 Derrick | 70 | 75 | 70 | 37 |
| 4 Patterson | 45 | 67 | 60 | 45 |
| 5 Spratt | 50 | 83 | 30 | 21 |
| 6 Tallon | 35 | 75 | 40 | 55 |

| | ADA | AFL-CIO | CCUS | ACU |
|---|---|---|---|---|
| **South Dakota** | | | | |
| AL Johnson | 65 | 83 | 40 | 20 |
| **Tennessee** | | | | |
| 1 ***Quillen*** | 5 | 33 | 80 | 90 |
| 2 ***Duncan*** | 20 | 33 | 80 | 100 |
| 3 Lloyd | 30 | 82 | 33 | 50 |
| 4 Cooper | 35 | 42 | 70 | 40 |
| 5 Clement | 50 | 75 | 40 | 20 |
| 6 Gordon | 60 | 92 | 40 | 15 |
| 7 ***Sundquist*** | 0 | 17 | 100 | 90 |
| 8 Tanner | 30 | 42 | 67 | 50 |
| 9 Ford | 80 | 100 | 14 | 0 |
| **Texas** | | | | |
| 1 Chapman | 30 | 67 | 44 | 26 |
| 2 Wilson | 25 | 82 | 50 | 30 |
| 3 ***Johnson*** [5] | 0 | 0 | 100 | 100 |
| 4 Hall | 5 | 17 | 80 | 90 |
| 5 Bryant | 80 | 92 | 33 | 11 |
| 6 ***Barton*** | 10 | 8 | 90 | 90 |
| 7 ***Archer*** | 0 | 0 | 100 | 95 |
| 8 ***Fields*** | 0 | 8 | 100 | 100 |
| 9 Brooks | 55 | 92 | 30 | 17 |
| 10 Pickle | 45 | 55 | 56 | 16 |
| 11 Edwards | 40 | 75 | 50 | 35 |
| 12 Geren | 15 | 50 | 70 | 60 |
| 13 Sarpalius | 25 | 42 | 60 | 70 |
| 14 Laughlin | 10 | 67 | 60 | 55 |
| 15 de la Garza | 45 | 58 | 40 | 32 |
| 16 Coleman | 60 | 92 | 40 | 10 |
| 17 Stenholm | 5 | 17 | 90 | 70 |
| 18 Washington | 95 | 100 | 11 | 0 |
| 19 ***Combest*** | 0 | 8 | 90 | 95 |
| 20 Gonzalez | 75 | 100 | 10 | 0 |
| 21 ***Smith*** | 5 | 25 | 70 | 84 |
| 22 ***DeLay*** | 5 | 9 | 90 | 100 |
| 23 Bustamante | 60 | 91 | 40 | 5 |
| 24 Frost | 65 | 100 | 20 | 20 |
| 25 Andrews | 30 | 58 | 50 | 35 |
| 26 ***Armey*** | 0 | 0 | 100 | 100 |
| 27 Ortiz | 30 | 64 | 56 | 26 |
| **Utah** | | | | |
| 1 ***Hansen*** | 0 | 0 | 100 | 100 |
| 2 Owens | 70 | 75 | 40 | 11 |
| 3 Orton | 25 | 33 | 60 | 63 |
| **Vermont** | | | | |
| AL Sanders | 95 | 100 | 10 | 15 |
| **Virginia** | | | | |
| 1 ***Bateman*** | 10 | 17 | 100 | 80 |
| 2 Pickett | 25 | 58 | 60 | 35 |
| 3 ***Bliley*** | 0 | 17 | 100 | 95 |
| 4 Sisisky | 30 | 73 | 67 | 39 |
| 5 Payne | 35 | 58 | 70 | 50 |
| 6 Olin | 45 | 58 | 50 | 30 |
| 7 ***Allen*** [6] | | 33 | | 100 |
| 8 Moran | 70 | 83 | 40 | 10 |
| 9 Boucher | 65 | 75 | 40 | 10 |
| 10 ***Wolf*** | 15 | 17 | 80 | 80 |
| **Washington** | | | | |
| 1 ***Miller*** | 25 | 42 | 80 | 70 |
| 2 Swift | 90 | 83 | 30 | 0 |
| 3 Unsoeld | 90 | 100 | 10 | 5 |
| 4 ***Morrison*** | 25 | 33 | 70 | 65 |
| 5 Foley [7] | | 100 | | 0 |
| 6 Dicks | 70 | 82 | 38 | 5 |
| 7 McDermott | 95 | 83 | 20 | 0 |
| 8 ***Chandler*** | 10 | 17 | 90 | 79 |
| **West Virginia** | | | | |
| 1 Mollohan | 50 | 92 | 20 | 30 |
| 2 Staggers | 80 | 92 | 20 | 10 |
| 3 Wise | 70 | 100 | 30 | 5 |
| 4 Rahall | 65 | 100 | 11 | 21 |
| **Wisconsin** | | | | |
| 1 Aspin | 60 | 75 | 33 | 32 |
| 2 ***Klug*** | 35 | 33 | 80 | 55 |
| 3 ***Gunderson*** | 20 | 33 | 100 | 80 |
| 4 Kleczka | 85 | 91 | 11 | 0 |
| 5 Moody | 95 | 82 | 30 | 6 |
| 6 ***Petri*** | 10 | 8 | 90 | 85 |
| 7 Obey | 85 | 92 | 20 | 15 |
| 8 ***Roth*** | 20 | 8 | 80 | 100 |
| 9 ***Sensenbrenner*** | 20 | 17 | 100 | 90 |
| **Wyoming** | | | | |
| AL ***Thomas*** | 0 | 0 | 100 | 95 |

| Alabama | ADA | AFL-CIO | CCUS | ACU |
|---|---|---|---|---|
| Heflin | 35 | 67 | 40 | 57 |
| Shelby | 35 | 67 | 40 | 76 |
| **Alaska** | | | | |
| *Murkowski* | 5 | 42 | 60 | 86 |
| *Stevens* | 10 | 42 | 60 | 76 |
| **Arizona** | | | | |
| DeConcini | 50 | 67 | 20 | 45 |
| *McCain* | 5 | 17 | 70 | 86 |
| **Arkansas** | | | | |
| Bumpers | 70 | 67 | 20 | 24 |
| Pryor | 30 | 80 | 50 | 11 |
| **California** | | | | |
| Cranston | 85 | 90 | 13 | 0 |
| *Seymour* | 15 | 33 | 100 | 86 |
| **Colorado** | | | | |
| Wirth | 85 | 83 | 30 | 14 |
| *Brown* | 10 | 17 | 80 | 90 |
| **Connecticut** | | | | |
| Dodd | 75 | 92 | 20 | 24 |
| Lieberman | 65 | 83 | 30 | 25 |
| **Delaware** | | | | |
| Biden | 90 | 83 | 20 | 5 |
| Roth | 20 | 25 | 60 | 81 |
| **Florida** | | | | |
| Graham | 65 | 75 | 20 | 38 |
| *Mack* | 15 | 50 | 70 | 90 |
| **Georgia** | | | | |
| Fowler | 65 | 64 | 22 | 33 |
| Nunn | 50 | 58 | 40 | 48 |
| **Hawaii** | | | | |
| Akaka | 90 | 92 | 20 | 5 |
| Inouye | 80 | 92 | 20 | 14 |
| **Idaho** | | | | |
| *Craig* | 5 | 25 | 100 | 86 |
| *Symms* | 5 | 17 | 100 | 90 |
| **Illinois** | | | | |
| Dixon | 55 | 67 | 10 | 52 |
| Simon | 100 | 75 | 10 | 0 |
| **Indiana** | | | | |
| *Coats* | 5 | 25 | 80 | 100 |
| *Lugar* | 10 | 17 | 90 | 76 |

| Iowa | ADA | AFL-CIO | CCUS | ACU |
|---|---|---|---|---|
| Harkin | 100 | 90 | 14 | 0 |
| *Grassley* | 15 | 17 | 60 | 81 |
| **Kansas** | | | | |
| *Dole* | 5 | 17 | 80 | 86 |
| *Kassebaum* | 35 | 17 | 80 | 62 |
| **Kentucky** | | | | |
| Ford | 50 | 75 | 10 | 47 |
| *McConnell* | 0 | 17 | 90 | 90 |
| **Louisiana** | | | | |
| Breaux | 30 | 67 | 40 | 57 |
| Johnston | 40 | 75 | 40 | 52 |
| **Maine** | | | | |
| Mitchell | 90 | 83 | 30 | 5 |
| *Cohen* | 65 | 42 | 40 | 43 |
| **Maryland** | | | | |
| Mikulski | 90 | 83 | 20 | 10 |
| Sarbanes | 100 | 92 | 10 | 0 |
| **Massachusetts** | | | | |
| Kennedy | 95 | 83 | 20 | 0 |
| Kerry | 95 | 83 | 20 | 5 |
| **Michigan** | | | | |
| Levin | 90 | 75 | 0 | 5 |
| Riegle | 90 | 83 | 10 | 14 |
| **Minnesota** | | | | |
| Wellstone | 95 | 83 | 20 | 5 |
| *Durenberger* | 35 | 33 | 50 | 48 |
| **Mississippi** | | | | |
| *Cochran* | 5 | 25 | 80 | 76 |
| *Lott* | 5 | 27 | 78 | 86 |
| **Missouri** | | | | |
| *Bond* | 20 | 27 | 70 | 81 |
| *Danforth* | 20 | 25 | 70 | 60 |
| **Montana** | | | | |
| Baucus | 70 | 58 | 20 | 24 |
| *Burns* | 5 | 17 | 90 | 86 |
| **Nebraska** | | | | |
| Exon | 50 | 67 | 20 | 38 |
| Kerrey | 75 | 78 | 29 | 5 |
| **Nevada** | | | | |
| Bryan | 70 | 83 | 20 | 38 |
| Reid | 65 | 92 | 10 | 33 |

| New Hampshire | ADA | AFL-CIO | CCUS | ACU |
|---|---|---|---|---|
| *Rudman* | 15 | 17 | 60 | 71 |
| *Smith* | 10 | 17 | 70 | 90 |
| **New Jersey** | | | | |
| Bradley | 90 | 75 | 10 | 10 |
| Lautenberg | 95 | 67 | 10 | 5 |
| **New Mexico** | | | | |
| Bingaman | 65 | 67 | 20 | 19 |
| *Domenici* | 10 | 17 | 90 | 76 |
| **New York** | | | | |
| Moynihan | 95 | 92 | 10 | 0 |
| *D'Amato* | 15 | 67 | 50 | 86 |
| **North Carolina** | | | | |
| Sanford | 90 | 92 | 10 | 10 |
| *Helms* | 5 | 20 | 88 | 100 |
| **North Dakota** | | | | |
| Burdick | 90 | 83 | 20 | 14 |
| Conrad | 75 | 75 | 20 | 43 |
| **Ohio** | | | | |
| Glenn | 90 | 75 | 0 | 10 |
| Metzenbaum | 100 | 83 | 10 | 0 |
| **Oklahoma** | | | | |
| Boren | 45 | 42 | 56 | 45 |
| *Nickles* | 0 | 25 | 100 | 95 |
| **Oregon** | | | | |
| *Hatfield* | 60 | 58 | 50 | 24 |
| *Packwood* | 50 | 67 | 60 | 43 |
| **Pennsylvania** | | | | |
| Wofford [1] | 79 | 89 | 0 | 22 |
| *Specter* | 40 | 58 | 50 | 71 |
| **Rhode Island** | | | | |
| Pell | 90 | 83 | 22 | 0 |
| *Chafee* | 60 | 45 | 40 | 24 |
| **South Carolina** | | | | |
| Hollings | 55 | 75 | 40 | 62 |
| *Thurmond* | 10 | 25 | 70 | 90 |
| **South Dakota** | | | | |
| Daschle | 85 | 83 | 10 | 24 |
| *Pressler* | 5 | 8 | 80 | 86 |
| **Tennessee** | | | | |
| Gore | 75 | 83 | 20 | 14 |
| Sasser | 90 | 83 | 0 | 5 |

| Texas | ADA | AFL-CIO | CCUS | ACU |
|---|---|---|---|---|
| Bentsen | 50 | 67 | 20 | 30 |
| *Gramm* | 0 | 17 | 89 | 95 |
| **Utah** | | | | |
| *Garn* | 10 | 25 | 70 | 84 |
| *Hatch* | 10 | 25 | 90 | 86 |
| **Vermont** | | | | |
| Leahy | 95 | 92 | 20 | 5 |
| *Jeffords* | 65 | 50 | 22 | 10 |
| **Virginia** | | | | |
| Robb | 60 | 67 | 10 | 43 |
| *Warner* | 20 | 25 | 80 | 76 |
| **Washington** | | | | |
| Adams | 95 | 92 | 20 | 10 |
| Gorton | 30 | 17 | 80 | 67 |
| **West Virginia** | | | | |
| Byrd | 65 | 83 | 10 | 33 |
| Rockefeller | 90 | 75 | 10 | 5 |
| **Wisconsin** | | | | |
| Kohl | 90 | 58 | 20 | 24 |
| *Kasten* | 15 | 42 | 100 | 86 |
| **Wyoming** | | | | |
| *Simpson* | 10 | 17 | 80 | 80 |
| *Wallop* | 5 | 25 | 90 | 95 |

ND  Northern Democrats     SD  Southern Democrats

Southern states - Ala., Ark., Fla., Ga., Ky., La., Miss., N.C., Okla., S.C., Tenn., Texas, Va.

# Interest Group Ratings: Senate

**ADA (Americans for Democratic Action)** — The percentage of time each senator voted in accordance with the ADA position on 20 selected votes in 1991. The percentages were compiled by the ADA. Failure to vote lowered scores.

**AFL-CIO (American Federation of Labor-Congress of Industrial Organizations)** — The percentage of time each senator voted in favor of the AFL-CIO position on 12 selected votes in 1991. The percentages were compiled by the AFL-CIO. Failure to vote did not lower scores.

**CCUS (Chamber of Commerce of the United States)** — The percentage of time each senator voted with the Chamber's position on 10 selected votes in 1991. The percentages were compiled by the Chamber. Failure to vote did not lower scores.

**ACU (American Conservative Union)** — The percentage of time each senator voted with the ACU position on 19 selected votes in 1991. The percentages were compiled by the ACU. Failure to vote did not lower scores.

[1] *Harris Wofford, D-Pa., was sworn in May 9, 1991, to succeed John Heinz, R, who died in a plane crash April 4, 1991. Wofford was rated on 17 votes by the ADA, nine votes by the AFL-CIO, five votes by the CCUS and on 14 votes by the ACU. Heinz received a perfect score from the ACU for his gulf war vote. Heinz was not rated by the other groups.*

# HOUSE ROLL CALL VOTES

**2. HR 3866. Maritime Boundary Agreement With Russia.** Jones, D-N.C., motion to suspend the rules and adopt the concurrent resolution (H Con Res 268) to make technical corrections to the bill and change all references in the agreement to reflect the dissolution of the Soviet Union so that the 1990 agreement would apply to the United States and Russia. Motion agreed to 390-0: R 154-0; D 235-0 (ND 159-0, SD 76-0); I 1-0, Jan. 28, 1992. A two-thirds majority of those present and voting (260 in this case) was required for passage under suspension of the rules.

**3. HR 1989. American Technology Pre-eminence.** Valentine, D-N.C., motion to suspend the rules and agree to the Senate amendment to the bill to authorize funds for federal programs intended to help U.S. high-technology companies compete in world markets. Motion agreed to (thus clearing the bill for the president) 392-1: R 155-0; D 236-1 (ND 161-1, SD 75-0); I 1-0, Jan. 28, 1992. A two-thirds majority of those present and voting (262 in this case) was required for passage under suspension of the rules.

**4. HR 4095. Unemployment Benefits Extension/Passage.** Rostenkowski, D-Ill., motion to suspend the rules and pass the bill to provide $2.7 billion to extend unemployment benefits an additional 13 weeks for a total of 33 weeks in high-unemployment states and 26 weeks in all other states and change the expiration date of the emergency benefits from June 13 to July 4, 1992. Motion agreed to 404-8: R 151-8; D 252-0 (ND 175-0, SD 77-0); I 1-0, Feb. 4, 1992. A "yea" was a vote in support of the president's position.

**5. H Res 340. Investigation of the House Post Office/Previous Question.** Gephardt, D-Mo., motion to order the previous question (thus limiting debate and the possibility of amendment) on the adoption of the resolution to direct the House Administration Committee to conduct an investigation into drug dealing and financial embezzlement at the House Post Office. Motion agreed to 253-162: R 0-161; D 252-1 (ND 171-1, SD 81-0); I 1-0, Feb. 5, 1992.

**6. H Res 340. Investigation of the House Post Office.** Adoption of the resolution to direct the House Administration Committee to conduct an investigation into drug dealing and financial embezzlement at the House Post Office. Adopted 254-160: R 1-160; D 252-0 (ND 172-0, SD 80-0); I 1-0, Feb. 5, 1992.

**7. H Res 341. Investigation of the House Post Office/Select Committee.** Gephardt, D-Mo., motion to table (kill) the Lewis, R-Calif., resolution to create a bipartisan select committee to investigate allegations of drug dealing and financial embezzlement at the House Post Office. Motion agreed to 250-161: R 0-160; D 249-1 (ND 169-0, SD 80-1); I 1-0, Feb. 5, 1992.

**8. H Res 342. "October Surprise" Investigation/Sentencing Investigation.** Gephardt, D-Mo., motion to table (kill) the resolution to establish a Bipartisan Legal Advisory Group to investigate whether the chief counsel to the House Committee on Foreign Affairs acted with proper authorization concerning the reduced sentencing of Dirk Stoffberg, a convicted arms dealer, by a U.S. District Court. Stoffberg provided information to the Foreign Affairs Committee concerning whether the 1980 Reagan campaign conspired to delay the release of 52 American hostages in Iran to forestall an "October Surprise" by the Carter administration that could have affected the 1980 election. Motion agreed to 249-160: R 0-160; D 248-0 (ND 169-0, SD 79-0); I 1-0, Feb. 5, 1992.

**9. H Res 258. "October Surprise" Investigation/Previous Question.** Derrick, D-S.C., motion to order the previous question (thus limiting debate and the possibility of amendment) on the rule (H Res 303) to provide for House floor consideration of the resolution to authorize the Speaker to appoint 13 House members to a task force to investigate allegations that the 1980 Reagan campaign conspired to delay the release of 52 American hostages in Iran until after the 1980 election. Motion agreed to 251-161: R 0-160; D 250-1 (ND 170-1, SD 80-0); I 1-0, Feb. 5, 1992.

## KEY

| | |
|---|---|
| Y | Voted for (yea). |
| # | Paired for. |
| + | Announced for. |
| N | Voted against (nay). |
| X | Paired against. |
| − | Announced against. |
| P | Voted "present." |
| C | Voted "present" to avoid possible conflict of interest. |
| ? | Did not vote or otherwise make a position known. |

Democrats   **Republicans**
*Independent*

| | 2 | 3 | 4 | 5 | 6 | 7 | 8 | 9 |
|---|---|---|---|---|---|---|---|---|
| **ALABAMA** | | | | | | | | |
| 1 *Callahan* | Y | Y | Y | N | N | N | N | N |
| 2 *Dickinson* | Y | Y | Y | N | N | N | N | N |
| 3 Browder | Y | Y | Y | Y | Y | Y | Y | Y |
| 4 Bevill | Y | Y | Y | Y | Y | Y | Y | Y |
| 5 Cramer | Y | Y | Y | Y | Y | Y | Y | Y |
| 6 Erdreich | Y | Y | Y | Y | Y | Y | Y | Y |
| 7 Harris | Y | Y | Y | Y | Y | Y | Y | Y |
| **ALASKA** | | | | | | | | |
| AL *Young* | ? | ? | Y | N | N | N | N | N |
| **ARIZONA** | | | | | | | | |
| 1 *Rhodes* | Y | Y | Y | N | N | N | N | N |
| 2 Pastor | Y | Y | Y | Y | Y | Y | Y | Y |
| 3 *Stump* | Y | Y | N | N | N | N | N | N |
| 4 *Kyl* | Y | Y | Y | N | N | N | N | N |
| 5 *Kolbe* | Y | Y | Y | N | N | N | N | N |
| **ARKANSAS** | | | | | | | | |
| 1 Alexander | Y | Y | Y | Y | Y | Y | Y | Y |
| 2 Thornton | Y | Y | Y | Y | Y | Y | Y | Y |
| 3 *Hammerschmidt* | Y | Y | Y | N | N | N | N | N |
| 4 Anthony | Y | Y | Y | Y | Y | Y | Y | Y |
| **CALIFORNIA** | | | | | | | | |
| 1 *Riggs* | Y | Y | Y | N | N | N | N | N |
| 2 *Herger* | Y | Y | Y | N | N | N | N | N |
| 3 Matsui | Y | Y | Y | Y | Y | Y | Y | Y |
| 4 Fazio | Y | Y | Y | Y | Y | Y | Y | Y |
| 5 Pelosi | Y | Y | Y | Y | Y | Y | Y | Y |
| 6 Boxer | Y | Y | Y | Y | Y | Y | Y | Y |
| 7 Miller | Y | Y | Y | Y | Y | Y | Y | Y |
| 8 Dellums | ? | ? | Y | Y | Y | Y | Y | Y |
| 9 Stark | Y | Y | Y | Y | Y | Y | ? | ? |
| 10 Edwards | Y | Y | ? | ? | ? | ? | ? | ? |
| 11 Lantos | ? | ? | Y | ? | ? | ? | ? | ? |
| 12 *Campbell* | Y | Y | Y | N | N | N | N | N |
| 13 Mineta | Y | Y | Y | Y | Y | ? | Y | Y |
| 14 *Doolittle* | Y | Y | N | N | N | N | N | N |
| 15 Condit | Y | Y | Y | Y | Y | Y | Y | Y |
| 16 Panetta | Y | Y | Y | Y | Y | Y | Y | Y |
| 17 Dooley | ? | ? | Y | Y | Y | Y | Y | Y |
| 18 Lehman | Y | Y | Y | Y | Y | Y | Y | Y |
| 19 *Lagomarsino* | Y | Y | N | N | N | N | N | N |
| 20 *Thomas* | Y | Y | ? | X | X | X | X | X |
| 21 *Gallegly* | Y | Y | N | N | N | N | N | N |
| 22 *Moorhead* | Y | Y | Y | N | N | N | N | N |
| 23 Beilenson | Y | Y | Y | Y | Y | Y | Y | Y |
| 24 Waxman | Y | Y | Y | Y | Y | Y | Y | Y |
| 25 Roybal | Y | Y | Y | Y | Y | Y | Y | Y |
| 26 Berman | Y | Y | Y | Y | Y | Y | Y | Y |
| 27 Levine | ? | ? | Y | ? | ? | ? | ? | ? |
| 28 Dixon | Y | Y | Y | Y | Y | Y | Y | Y |
| 29 Waters | Y | Y | Y | ? | ? | Y | Y | Y |
| 30 Martinez | Y | Y | + | Y | Y | Y | Y | Y |
| 31 Dymally | ? | ? | + | # | # | # | ? | # |
| 32 Anderson | Y | Y | Y | Y | Y | Y | Y | Y |
| 33 *Dreier* | Y | Y | Y | N | N | N | N | N |
| 34 Torres | Y | Y | Y | Y | Y | Y | Y | Y |
| 35 *Lewis* | Y | Y | Y | N | N | N | N | N |
| 36 Brown | Y | Y | Y | Y | Y | Y | Y | Y |
| 37 *McCandless* | Y | Y | Y | N | N | N | N | N |
| 38 *Dornan* | Y | Y | N | N | N | N | N | N |
| 39 *Dannemeyer* | ? | ? | − | − | − | − | − | − |
| 40 *Cox* | Y | Y | Y | N | N | N | N | N |
| 41 *Lowery* | Y | Y | Y | N | N | N | N | N |

| | 2 | 3 | 4 | 5 | 6 | 7 | 8 | 9 |
|---|---|---|---|---|---|---|---|---|
| 42 *Rohrabacher* | Y | Y | Y | N | N | N | N | N |
| 43 *Packard* | Y | Y | Y | N | N | N | N | N |
| 44 *Cunningham* | ? | ? | Y | N | N | N | N | N |
| 45 *Hunter* | Y | Y | Y | N | N | N | N | N |
| **COLORADO** | | | | | | | | |
| 1 Schroeder | Y | Y | Y | Y | Y | Y | Y | Y |
| 2 Skaggs | Y | Y | Y | Y | Y | Y | Y | Y |
| 3 Campbell | ? | ? | Y | Y | Y | Y | Y | Y |
| 4 *Allard* | Y | Y | N | N | N | N | N | N |
| 5 *Hefley* | Y | Y | Y | N | N | N | N | N |
| 6 *Schaefer* | Y | Y | Y | N | N | N | N | N |
| **CONNECTICUT** | | | | | | | | |
| 1 Kennelly | Y | Y | Y | Y | Y | Y | Y | Y |
| 2 Gejdenson | Y | Y | Y | Y | Y | Y | Y | Y |
| 3 DeLauro | Y | Y | Y | Y | Y | Y | Y | Y |
| 4 *Shays* | Y | Y | N | N | N | N | N | N |
| 5 *Franks* | Y | Y | Y | N | N | N | N | N |
| 6 *Johnson* | Y | Y | N | N | N | N | N | N |
| **DELAWARE** | | | | | | | | |
| AL Carper | Y | Y | Y | Y | Y | Y | Y | Y |
| **FLORIDA** | | | | | | | | |
| 1 *Hutto* | Y | Y | ? | ? | ? | ? | ? | ? |
| 2 Peterson | Y | Y | Y | Y | Y | Y | Y | Y |
| 3 Bennett | Y | Y | Y | Y | N | Y | Y | Y |
| 4 *James* | Y | Y | Y | N | N | N | N | N |
| 5 *McCollum* | Y | Y | Y | N | N | N | N | N |
| 6 *Stearns* | Y | Y | N | N | N | N | N | N |
| 7 Gibbons | Y | Y | ? | Y | Y | Y | Y | Y |
| 8 *Young* | Y | Y | Y | N | N | N | N | N |
| 9 *Bilirakis* | Y | Y | ? | N | N | N | N | N |
| 10 *Ireland* | Y | Y | N | N | N | N | N | ? |
| 11 Bacchus | Y | Y | Y | Y | Y | Y | Y | Y |
| 12 *Lewis* | Y | Y | Y | N | N | N | N | N |
| 13 *Goss* | Y | Y | N | N | N | N | N | N |
| 14 Johnston | Y | Y | Y | Y | Y | Y | Y | Y |
| 15 *Shaw* | Y | Y | Y | Y | Y | Y | Y | Y |
| 16 Smith | Y | Y | Y | Y | Y | Y | Y | Y |
| 17 Lehman | Y | Y | Y | Y | Y | Y | Y | Y |
| 18 *Ros-Lehtinen* | Y | Y | N | N | N | N | N | N |
| 19 Fascell | Y | Y | Y | Y | Y | Y | Y | Y |
| **GEORGIA** | | | | | | | | |
| 1 Thomas | Y | Y | Y | ? | ? | ? | ? | ? |
| 2 Hatcher | Y | Y | Y | Y | Y | Y | Y | Y |
| 3 Ray | Y | Y | Y | Y | Y | Y | Y | Y |
| 4 Jones | Y | Y | Y | Y | Y | Y | Y | Y |
| 5 Lewis | Y | Y | Y | Y | Y | Y | Y | Y |
| 6 *Gingrich* | Y | Y | Y | N | N | N | N | N |
| 7 Darden | Y | Y | Y | Y | Y | Y | Y | Y |
| 8 Rowland | Y | Y | Y | Y | Y | Y | Y | Y |
| 9 Jenkins | Y | Y | Y | Y | Y | Y | Y | Y |
| 10 Barnard | Y | Y | Y | Y | Y | Y | Y | Y |
| **HAWAII** | | | | | | | | |
| 1 Abercrombie | Y | Y | Y | Y | Y | Y | Y | Y |
| 2 Mink | Y | Y | Y | Y | Y | Y | Y | Y |
| **IDAHO** | | | | | | | | |
| 1 LaRocco | Y | Y | Y | Y | Y | Y | Y | Y |
| 2 Stallings | Y | Y | Y | Y | Y | Y | Y | Y |
| **ILLINOIS** | | | | | | | | |
| 1 Hayes | Y | Y | Y | Y | Y | Y | Y | Y |
| 2 Savage | Y | Y | Y | Y | Y | Y | Y | Y |
| 3 Russo | Y | Y | Y | Y | Y | Y | Y | Y |
| 4 Sangmeister | Y | Y | Y | Y | Y | Y | Y | Y |
| 5 Lipinski | Y | Y | Y | Y | Y | Y | Y | Y |
| 6 *Hyde* | Y | Y | Y | N | N | N | N | N |
| 7 Collins | Y | Y | Y | Y | Y | Y | Y | Y |
| 8 Rostenkowski | Y | Y | Y | Y | Y | Y | Y | Y |
| 9 Yates | Y | Y | Y | Y | Y | Y | Y | Y |
| 10 *Porter* | + | + | Y | N | N | N | N | N |
| 11 Annunzio | Y | Y | Y | Y | Y | Y | Y | Y |
| 12 *Crane* | Y | Y | N | N | N | N | N | N |
| 13 *Fawell* | Y | Y | Y | N | N | N | N | N |
| 14 *Hastert* | ? | ? | Y | N | N | N | N | N |
| 15 *Ewing* | Y | Y | Y | N | N | N | N | N |
| 16 *Cox* | Y | Y | Y | Y | Y | Y | Y | Y |
| 17 Evans | Y | Y | Y | Y | Y | Y | Y | Y |
| 18 *Michel* | Y | Y | Y | N | N | N | N | N |
| 19 Bruce | Y | Y | Y | Y | Y | Y | Y | Y |
| 20 Durbin | Y | Y | Y | Y | Y | Y | Y | Y |
| 21 Costello | Y | Y | Y | Y | Y | Y | Y | Y |
| 22 Poshard | Y | Y | Y | Y | Y | Y | Y | Y |
| **INDIANA** | | | | | | | | |
| 1 Visclosky | Y | Y | Y | Y | Y | Y | Y | Y |
| 2 Sharp | Y | Y | Y | Y | Y | Y | Y | Y |
| 3 Roemer | Y | Y | Y | Y | Y | Y | Y | Y |

ND   Northern Democrats       SD   Southern Democrats

| | 2 | 3 | 4 | 5 | 6 | 7 | 8 | 9 |
|---|---|---|---|---|---|---|---|---|
| 4 Long | Y | Y | Y | Y | Y | Y | Y | Y |
| 5 Jontz | Y | Y | Y | Y | Y | Y | Y | Y |
| 6 ***Burton*** | Y | Y | N | N | N | N | N | N |
| 7 ***Myers*** | Y | Y | N | N | N | N | N | N |
| 8 McCloskey | Y | Y | Y | Y | Y | Y | Y | Y |
| 9 Hamilton | Y | Y | Y | Y | Y | Y | Y | Y |
| 10 Jacobs | Y | Y | Y | N | Y | Y | Y | N |
| **IOWA** | | | | | | | | |
| 1 ***Leach*** | Y | Y | Y | N | N | N | N | N |
| 2 ***Nussle*** | Y | Y | Y | N | N | N | N | N |
| 3 Nagle | ? | Y | Y | Y | Y | Y | Y | Y |
| 4 Smith | Y | Y | Y | Y | Y | Y | Y | Y |
| 5 ***Lightfoot*** | Y | Y | Y | N | N | ? | ? | ? |
| 6 ***Grandy*** | Y | Y | Y | N | N | N | N | N |
| **KANSAS** | | | | | | | | |
| 1 ***Roberts*** | Y | Y | Y | N | N | N | N | N |
| 2 Slattery | Y | Y | Y | Y | Y | Y | Y | Y |
| 3 ***Meyers*** | Y | Y | Y | N | N | N | N | N |
| 4 Glickman | Y | Y | Y | Y | Y | Y | Y | Y |
| 5 ***Nichols*** | Y | Y | Y | N | N | N | N | N |
| **KENTUCKY** | | | | | | | | |
| 1 Hubbard | Y | Y | Y | Y | Y | Y | Y | Y |
| 2 Natcher | Y | Y | Y | Y | Y | Y | Y | Y |
| 3 Mazzoli | Y | Y | Y | Y | Y | Y | Y | Y |
| 4 ***Bunning*** | Y | Y | Y | N | N | N | N | N |
| 5 ***Rogers*** | Y | Y | Y | N | N | N | N | N |
| 6 ***Hopkins*** | Y | Y | Y | N | N | N | N | N |
| 7 Perkins | Y | Y | Y | Y | Y | Y | Y | Y |
| **LOUISIANA** | | | | | | | | |
| 1 ***Livingston*** | Y | Y | Y | N | N | N | N | N |
| 2 Jefferson | ? | ? | ? | Y | Y | Y | Y | Y |
| 3 Tauzin | ? | ? | Y | Y | Y | Y | Y | Y |
| 4 ***McCrery*** | Y | Y | Y | N | N | N | N | N |
| 5 Huckaby | Y | Y | Y | Y | Y | Y | Y | Y |
| 6 ***Baker*** | Y | Y | Y | N | N | N | N | N |
| 7 Hayes | Y | Y | Y | Y | Y | Y | ? | Y |
| 8 ***Holloway*** | Y | Y | Y | N | N | N | N | N |
| **MAINE** | | | | | | | | |
| 1 Andrews | Y | Y | Y | Y | Y | Y | Y | Y |
| 2 ***Snowe*** | Y | Y | Y | N | N | N | N | N |
| **MARYLAND** | | | | | | | | |
| 1 ***Gilchrest*** | Y | Y | Y | N | N | N | N | N |
| 2 ***Bentley*** | Y | Y | Y | N | N | N | ? | N |
| 3 Cardin | Y | Y | Y | Y | Y | Y | Y | Y |
| 4 McMillen | Y | Y | Y | Y | Y | Y | Y | Y |
| 5 Hoyer | Y | Y | Y | Y | Y | Y | Y | Y |
| 6 Byron | Y | Y | Y | Y | Y | Y | Y | Y |
| 7 Mfume | Y | Y | Y | Y | Y | Y | Y | Y |
| 8 ***Morella*** | Y | Y | Y | N | N | N | N | N |
| **MASSACHUSETTS** | | | | | | | | |
| 1 Olver | Y | Y | Y | Y | Y | Y | Y | Y |
| 2 Neal | Y | Y | Y | Y | Y | Y | Y | Y |
| 3 Early | Y | Y | Y | Y | Y | Y | Y | Y |
| 4 Frank | ? | ? | Y | Y | Y | Y | Y | Y |
| 5 Atkins | Y | Y | Y | Y | Y | Y | Y | Y |
| 6 Mavroules | Y | Y | Y | Y | Y | Y | Y | Y |
| 7 Markey | Y | Y | ? | ? | ? | ? | ? | Y |
| 8 Kennedy | Y | Y | Y | Y | Y | Y | Y | Y |
| 9 Moakley | Y | Y | Y | Y | Y | Y | Y | Y |
| 10 Studds | Y | Y | Y | Y | Y | Y | Y | Y |
| 11 Donnelly | ? | ? | Y | Y | Y | Y | Y | Y |
| **MICHIGAN** | | | | | | | | |
| 1 Conyers | Y | Y | Y | Y | Y | Y | Y | Y |
| 2 ***Pursell*** | Y | Y | Y | N | N | ? | N | N |
| 3 Wolpe | + | Y | Y | Y | Y | Y | Y | Y |
| 4 ***Upton*** | Y | Y | Y | N | N | N | N | N |
| 5 ***Henry*** | Y | Y | Y | N | N | N | N | N |
| 6 Carr | ? | Y | Y | Y | Y | ? | Y | Y |
| 7 Kildee | Y | Y | Y | Y | Y | Y | Y | Y |
| 8 Traxler | Y | Y | Y | Y | Y | Y | Y | Y |
| 9 ***Vander Jagt*** | Y | Y | Y | N | N | N | N | N |
| 10 ***Camp*** | Y | Y | Y | N | N | N | N | N |
| 11 ***Davis*** | Y | Y | Y | N | N | N | N | N |
| 12 Bonior | Y | Y | Y | Y | Y | Y | Y | Y |
| 13 Collins | Y | Y | Y | Y | Y | Y | Y | Y |
| 14 Hertel | Y | Y | Y | Y | Y | Y | Y | Y |
| 15 Ford | Y | Y | Y | Y | Y | ? | Y | Y |
| 16 Dingell | Y | Y | Y | Y | Y | Y | Y | Y |
| 17 Levin | Y | Y | Y | Y | Y | Y | Y | Y |
| 18 ***Broomfield*** | Y | Y | Y | N | N | N | N | N |
| **MINNESOTA** | | | | | | | | |
| 1 Penny | Y | N | Y | Y | Y | Y | Y | Y |
| 2 ***Weber*** | Y | Y | Y | N | N | N | N | N |
| 3 ***Ramstad*** | Y | Y | Y | N | N | N | N | N |
| 4 Vento | Y | Y | Y | Y | Y | Y | Y | Y |
| 5 Sabo | ? | ? | Y | Y | Y | Y | Y | Y |
| 6 Sikorski | Y | Y | Y | Y | Y | Y | Y | Y |
| 7 Peterson | Y | Y | Y | Y | Y | Y | Y | Y |
| 8 Oberstar | Y | Y | Y | Y | Y | Y | Y | Y |
| **MISSISSIPPI** | | | | | | | | |
| 1 Whitten | Y | Y | ? | ? | ? | ? | ? | ? |
| 2 Espy | Y | Y | Y | Y | Y | Y | Y | Y |
| 3 Montgomery | Y | Y | Y | Y | Y | Y | Y | Y |
| 4 Parker | Y | Y | Y | Y | Y | Y | Y | Y |
| 5 Taylor | Y | Y | Y | Y | Y | Y | Y | Y |
| **MISSOURI** | | | | | | | | |
| 1 Clay | Y | Y | Y | ? | ? | ? | ? | ? |
| 2 Horn | Y | Y | Y | Y | Y | Y | Y | Y |
| 3 Gephardt | Y | Y | Y | Y | Y | Y | Y | Y |
| 4 Skelton | Y | Y | Y | Y | Y | Y | Y | Y |
| 5 Wheat | Y | Y | Y | Y | Y | Y | Y | Y |
| 6 ***Coleman*** | Y | Y | Y | N | N | N | N | N |
| 7 ***Hancock*** | Y | Y | Y | N | N | N | N | N |
| 8 ***Emerson*** | Y | Y | Y | N | N | N | N | N |
| 9 Volkmer | Y | Y | Y | Y | Y | Y | Y | Y |
| **MONTANA** | | | | | | | | |
| 1 Williams | Y | Y | Y | Y | Y | Y | Y | Y |
| 2 ***Marlenee*** | Y | Y | Y | N | N | N | N | N |
| **NEBRASKA** | | | | | | | | |
| 1 ***Bereuter*** | Y | Y | Y | N | N | N | N | N |
| 2 Hoagland | Y | Y | Y | Y | Y | Y | Y | Y |
| 3 ***Barrett*** | Y | Y | Y | N | ? | N | N | N |
| **NEVADA** | | | | | | | | |
| 1 Bilbray | Y | Y | Y | Y | Y | Y | Y | Y |
| 2 ***Vucanovich*** | Y | Y | Y | N | N | N | N | N |
| **NEW HAMPSHIRE** | | | | | | | | |
| 1 ***Zeliff*** | Y | Y | Y | N | N | N | N | N |
| 2 Swett | ? | ? | Y | Y | Y | Y | Y | Y |
| **NEW JERSEY** | | | | | | | | |
| 1 Andrews | Y | Y | Y | Y | Y | Y | ? | Y |
| 2 Hughes | Y | Y | Y | Y | Y | Y | Y | Y |
| 3 Pallone | Y | Y | Y | Y | Y | Y | Y | Y |
| 4 ***Smith*** | Y | Y | Y | N | N | N | N | N |
| 5 ***Roukema*** | Y | Y | Y | N | N | N | N | N |
| 6 Dwyer | Y | Y | Y | Y | Y | Y | Y | Y |
| 7 ***Rinaldo*** | Y | Y | Y | N | N | N | N | N |
| 8 Roe | Y | Y | Y | Y | Y | Y | Y | Y |
| 9 Torricelli | ? | ? | Y | Y | Y | Y | Y | Y |
| 10 Payne | Y | Y | Y | Y | Y | Y | Y | Y |
| 11 ***Gallo*** | Y | Y | Y | N | N | N | N | N |
| 12 ***Zimmer*** | Y | Y | Y | N | N | N | N | N |
| 13 ***Saxton*** | Y | Y | Y | N | N | N | N | N |
| 14 Guarini | Y | Y | Y | Y | Y | Y | Y | Y |
| **NEW MEXICO** | | | | | | | | |
| 1 ***Schiff*** | ? | ? | Y | N | N | N | N | N |
| 2 ***Skeen*** | Y | Y | Y | N | N | N | N | N |
| 3 Richardson | Y | Y | Y | Y | Y | Y | Y | Y |
| **NEW YORK** | | | | | | | | |
| 1 Hochbrueckner | ? | ? | Y | Y | Y | Y | Y | Y |
| 2 Downey | Y | Y | Y | Y | Y | Y | Y | Y |
| 3 Mrazek | ? | ? | ? | ? | ? | ? | ? | ? |
| 4 ***Lent*** | ? | ? | Y | N | N | N | N | N |
| 5 ***McGrath*** | Y | Y | Y | N | N | N | N | N |
| 6 Flake | Y | Y | Y | Y | Y | Y | Y | Y |
| 7 Ackerman | Y | Y | Y | Y | Y | Y | Y | Y |
| 8 Scheuer | ? | ? | Y | Y | Y | Y | Y | Y |
| 9 Manton | Y | Y | Y | Y | Y | Y | Y | Y |
| 10 Schumer | Y | Y | Y | Y | Y | Y | Y | Y |
| 11 Towns | Y | Y | Y | Y | Y | Y | Y | Y |
| 12 Owens | Y | Y | Y | Y | Y | Y | Y | Y |
| 13 Solarz | Y | Y | Y | Y | Y | Y | Y | Y |
| 14 ***Molinari*** | Y | Y | Y | N | N | N | N | N |
| 15 ***Green*** | Y | Y | Y | N | N | N | N | N |
| 16 Rangel | Y | Y | Y | Y | Y | Y | Y | Y |
| 17 Weiss | Y | Y | Y | Y | Y | Y | Y | Y |
| 18 Serrano | Y | Y | Y | Y | Y | Y | Y | Y |
| 19 Engel | Y | Y | Y | Y | Y | Y | Y | Y |
| 20 Lowey | Y | Y | Y | Y | Y | Y | Y | Y |
| 21 ***Fish*** | Y | Y | Y | N | N | N | N | N |
| 22 ***Gilman*** | Y | Y | Y | N | N | N | N | N |
| 23 McNulty | Y | Y | Y | Y | Y | Y | Y | Y |
| 24 ***Solomon*** | Y | Y | Y | N | N | N | N | N |
| 25 ***Boehlert*** | Y | Y | Y | N | N | N | N | N |
| 26 ***Martin*** | Y | Y | Y | N | N | N | N | N |
| 27 ***Walsh*** | Y | Y | Y | N | N | N | N | N |
| 28 McHugh | Y | Y | Y | Y | Y | Y | Y | Y |
| 29 ***Horton*** | Y | Y | Y | N | N | N | N | N |
| 30 Slaughter | Y | Y | Y | Y | Y | Y | Y | Y |
| 31 ***Paxon*** | Y | Y | Y | N | N | N | N | N |
| 32 LaFalce | Y | Y | Y | Y | Y | Y | Y | Y |
| 33 Nowak | Y | Y | Y | Y | Y | Y | Y | Y |
| 34 ***Houghton*** | Y | Y | Y | N | N | N | N | N |
| **NORTH CAROLINA** | | | | | | | | |
| 1 Jones | Y | Y | Y | Y | Y | Y | Y | Y |
| 2 Valentine | Y | Y | Y | Y | Y | Y | Y | Y |
| 3 Lancaster | Y | ? | Y | Y | Y | Y | Y | Y |
| 4 Price | Y | Y | Y | Y | Y | Y | Y | Y |
| 5 Neal | Y | Y | Y | Y | Y | Y | Y | Y |
| 6 ***Coble*** | Y | Y | Y | N | N | N | N | N |
| 7 Rose | Y | Y | Y | Y | Y | Y | Y | Y |
| 8 Hefner | Y | Y | Y | Y | Y | Y | Y | Y |
| 9 ***McMillan*** | Y | Y | Y | N | N | N | N | N |
| 10 ***Ballenger*** | Y | Y | Y | N | N | N | N | N |
| 11 ***Taylor*** | Y | Y | Y | N | N | N | N | N |
| **NORTH DAKOTA** | | | | | | | | |
| AL Dorgan | Y | Y | Y | Y | Y | Y | Y | Y |
| **OHIO** | | | | | | | | |
| 1 Luken | Y | Y | Y | Y | Y | Y | Y | Y |
| 2 ***Gradison*** | Y | Y | Y | N | N | N | N | N |
| 3 Hall | Y | Y | Y | Y | Y | Y | Y | Y |
| 4 ***Oxley*** | Y | Y | Y | N | N | N | N | N |
| 5 ***Gillmor*** | Y | Y | Y | N | N | N | N | N |
| 6 ***McEwen*** | Y | Y | Y | N | N | N | N | N |
| 7 ***Hobson*** | Y | Y | Y | N | N | N | N | N |
| 8 ***Boehner*** | Y | Y | Y | N | N | N | N | N |
| 9 Kaptur | Y | Y | Y | Y | Y | Y | Y | Y |
| 10 ***Miller*** | Y | Y | Y | N | N | N | N | N |
| 11 Eckart | Y | Y | Y | Y | Y | Y | # | # |
| 12 ***Kasich*** | Y | Y | Y | N | N | N | N | N |
| 13 Pease | Y | Y | Y | Y | Y | Y | Y | Y |
| 14 Sawyer | Y | Y | Y | Y | Y | Y | Y | Y |
| 15 ***Wylie*** | Y | Y | Y | N | N | N | N | N |
| 16 ***Regula*** | Y | Y | Y | N | N | N | N | N |
| 17 Traficant | Y | Y | Y | Y | Y | Y | Y | Y |
| 18 Applegate | Y | Y | Y | Y | Y | Y | Y | Y |
| 19 Feighan | ? | ? | Y | Y | Y | Y | Y | Y |
| 20 Oakar | ? | ? | Y | Y | Y | Y | Y | Y |
| 21 Stokes | Y | Y | Y | Y | Y | Y | Y | Y |
| **OKLAHOMA** | | | | | | | | |
| 1 ***Inhofe*** | Y | Y | Y | N | N | N | N | N |
| 2 Synar | Y | Y | Y | Y | Y | Y | Y | Y |
| 3 Brewster | Y | Y | Y | Y | Y | Y | Y | Y |
| 4 McCurdy | ? | ? | Y | Y | Y | Y | ? | Y |
| 5 ***Edwards*** | ? | ? | Y | N | N | N | N | N |
| 6 English | ? | ? | Y | Y | Y | Y | Y | Y |
| **OREGON** | | | | | | | | |
| 1 AuCoin | ? | ? | Y | Y | Y | Y | Y | Y |
| 2 ***Smith*** | Y | Y | Y | N | N | N | N | N |
| 3 Wyden | Y | Y | Y | Y | Y | Y | Y | Y |
| 4 DeFazio | Y | Y | Y | Y | Y | Y | # | ? |
| 5 Kopetski | Y | Y | Y | Y | Y | Y | Y | Y |
| **PENNSYLVANIA** | | | | | | | | |
| 1 Foglietta | Y | Y | Y | Y | Y | Y | Y | Y |
| 2 Blackwell | Y | Y | Y | Y | Y | Y | Y | Y |
| 3 Borski | Y | Y | Y | Y | Y | Y | Y | Y |
| 4 Kolter | Y | Y | ? | ? | ? | ? | ? | ? |
| 5 ***Schulze*** | Y | Y | Y | N | N | N | N | N |
| 6 Yatron | Y | Y | Y | Y | Y | Y | Y | Y |
| 7 ***Weldon*** | Y | Y | Y | N | N | N | N | N |
| 8 Kostmayer | Y | Y | Y | Y | Y | Y | Y | Y |
| 9 ***Shuster*** | Y | Y | Y | N | N | N | N | N |
| 10 ***McDade*** | ? | ? | ? | N | N | N | N | N |
| 11 Kanjorski | Y | Y | Y | Y | Y | Y | Y | Y |
| 12 Murtha | Y | Y | Y | Y | Y | Y | Y | Y |
| 13 ***Coughlin*** | Y | Y | Y | N | N | N | N | N |
| 14 Coyne | Y | Y | Y | Y | Y | Y | Y | Y |
| 15 ***Ritter*** | Y | Y | Y | N | N | N | N | N |
| 16 ***Walker*** | Y | Y | Y | N | N | N | N | N |
| 17 ***Gekas*** | Y | Y | Y | N | N | N | N | N |
| 18 ***Santorum*** | Y | Y | Y | N | N | N | N | N |
| 19 ***Goodling*** | Y | Y | Y | N | N | N | N | N |
| 20 Gaydos | Y | Y | Y | ? | ? | ? | ? | ? |
| 21 ***Ridge*** | ? | Y | Y | N | N | N | N | N |
| 22 Murphy | Y | Y | Y | Y | Y | Y | Y | Y |
| 23 ***Clinger*** | Y | Y | Y | N | N | N | N | N |
| **RHODE ISLAND** | | | | | | | | |
| 1 ***Machtley*** | Y | Y | Y | N | N | N | N | N |
| 2 Reed | Y | Y | Y | Y | Y | Y | Y | Y |
| **SOUTH CAROLINA** | | | | | | | | |
| 1 ***Ravenel*** | Y | Y | Y | N | N | N | N | N |
| 2 ***Spence*** | Y | Y | Y | N | N | N | N | N |
| 3 Derrick | Y | Y | Y | Y | Y | Y | Y | Y |
| 4 Patterson | Y | Y | Y | Y | Y | Y | Y | Y |
| 5 Spratt | Y | Y | Y | Y | Y | Y | Y | Y |
| 6 Tallon | Y | Y | Y | Y | Y | Y | Y | Y |
| **SOUTH DAKOTA** | | | | | | | | |
| AL Johnson | Y | Y | Y | Y | Y | Y | Y | Y |
| **TENNESSEE** | | | | | | | | |
| 1 ***Quillen*** | Y | Y | Y | N | N | N | N | N |
| 2 ***Duncan*** | Y | Y | Y | N | N | N | N | N |
| 3 Lloyd | + | Y | Y | Y | Y | Y | Y | Y |
| 4 Cooper | Y | Y | Y | Y | Y | Y | Y | Y |
| 5 Clement | Y | Y | + | Y | Y | Y | Y | Y |
| 6 Gordon | Y | Y | ? | Y | Y | Y | Y | Y |
| 7 ***Sundquist*** | Y | Y | Y | N | N | N | N | N |
| 8 Tanner | Y | Y | ? | Y | Y | Y | Y | Y |
| 9 Ford | Y | Y | ? | Y | Y | Y | Y | Y |
| **TEXAS** | | | | | | | | |
| 1 Chapman | Y | Y | Y | Y | Y | Y | Y | Y |
| 2 Wilson | Y | Y | Y | Y | Y | Y | Y | Y |
| 3 ***Johnson*** | Y | Y | N | ? | ? | ? | X | X |
| 4 Hall | Y | Y | Y | Y | Y | Y | Y | Y |
| 5 Bryant | Y | Y | Y | Y | Y | Y | Y | Y |
| 6 ***Barton*** | Y | Y | ? | N | N | N | N | N |
| 7 ***Archer*** | Y | Y | N | N | N | N | N | N |
| 8 ***Fields*** | Y | Y | Y | N | N | N | N | N |
| 9 Brooks | Y | Y | Y | Y | Y | Y | Y | Y |
| 10 Pickle | Y | Y | Y | Y | Y | Y | Y | Y |
| 11 Edwards | Y | Y | Y | Y | Y | Y | Y | Y |
| 12 Geren | Y | Y | Y | Y | Y | Y | Y | Y |
| 13 Sarpalius | Y | Y | Y | Y | Y | Y | Y | Y |
| 14 Laughlin | Y | Y | Y | Y | Y | Y | Y | Y |
| 15 de la Garza | ? | ? | Y | Y | Y | Y | Y | ? |
| 16 Coleman | ? | ? | Y | ? | ? | ? | ? | ? |
| 17 Stenholm | Y | Y | Y | Y | Y | Y | Y | Y |
| 18 Washington | Y | Y | Y | Y | Y | Y | Y | Y |
| 19 ***Combest*** | Y | Y | N | N | N | N | N | N |
| 20 Gonzalez | Y | Y | Y | Y | Y | Y | Y | Y |
| 21 ***Smith*** | Y | Y | Y | N | N | N | N | N |
| 22 ***DeLay*** | Y | Y | N | N | N | N | N | N |
| 23 Bustamante | ? | ? | Y | Y | Y | Y | Y | Y |
| 24 Frost | Y | Y | Y | Y | ? | Y | Y | Y |
| 25 Andrews | Y | Y | Y | Y | Y | Y | Y | Y |
| 26 ***Armey*** | Y | Y | N | N | N | N | N | N |
| 27 Ortiz | Y | ? | Y | Y | Y | Y | Y | Y |
| **UTAH** | | | | | | | | |
| 1 ***Hansen*** | Y | Y | Y | N | N | N | N | N |
| 2 Owens | ? | ? | Y | Y | Y | Y | Y | Y |
| 3 Orton | Y | Y | Y | Y | Y | Y | Y | Y |
| **VERMONT** | | | | | | | | |
| AL *Sanders* | Y | Y | Y | Y | Y | Y | Y | Y |
| **VIRGINIA** | | | | | | | | |
| 1 ***Bateman*** | Y | Y | Y | N | N | N | N | N |
| 2 Pickett | Y | Y | Y | Y | Y | Y | Y | Y |
| 3 ***Bliley*** | Y | Y | Y | N | N | N | N | N |
| 4 Sisisky | Y | Y | Y | Y | Y | Y | Y | Y |
| 5 Payne | Y | Y | Y | Y | Y | Y | Y | Y |
| 6 Olin | ? | ? | Y | Y | Y | Y | Y | Y |
| 7 ***Allen*** | Y | Y | Y | N | N | N | N | N |
| 8 Moran | Y | Y | Y | Y | Y | Y | Y | Y |
| 9 Boucher | Y | Y | Y | Y | Y | Y | Y | Y |
| 10 ***Wolf*** | Y | ? | Y | N | N | N | N | N |
| **WASHINGTON** | | | | | | | | |
| 1 ***Miller*** | ? | ? | ? | ? | N | N | N | N |
| 2 Swift | Y | Y | Y | Y | Y | Y | Y | Y |
| 3 Unsoeld | Y | Y | Y | Y | Y | Y | Y | Y |
| 4 ***Morrison*** | ? | Y | ? | ? | ? | ? | ? | ? |
| 5 Foley | | | | | | | | |
| 6 Dicks | Y | Y | Y | Y | Y | Y | Y | Y |
| 7 McDermott | Y | Y | Y | Y | Y | Y | Y | Y |
| 8 ***Chandler*** | Y | Y | Y | N | N | N | N | N |
| **WEST VIRGINIA** | | | | | | | | |
| 1 Mollohan | Y | Y | Y | Y | Y | Y | Y | Y |
| 2 Staggers | Y | Y | Y | Y | Y | Y | Y | Y |
| 3 Wise | ? | ? | Y | Y | Y | Y | Y | Y |
| 4 Rahall | Y | Y | ? | Y | Y | Y | Y | Y |
| **WISCONSIN** | | | | | | | | |
| 1 Aspin | ? | ? | Y | Y | Y | Y | Y | Y |
| 2 ***Klug*** | Y | Y | Y | N | N | N | N | N |
| 3 ***Gunderson*** | Y | Y | Y | N | N | N | N | N |
| 4 Kleczka | ? | Y | Y | Y | Y | Y | Y | Y |
| 5 Moody | Y | Y | Y | Y | Y | Y | Y | Y |
| 6 ***Petri*** | Y | Y | Y | N | N | N | N | N |
| 7 Obey | Y | Y | Y | Y | Y | Y | Y | Y |
| 8 ***Roth*** | Y | Y | Y | N | N | N | N | N |
| 9 ***Sensenbrenner*** | Y | Y | Y | N | N | N | N | N |
| **WYOMING** | | | | | | | | |
| AL ***Thomas*** | Y | Y | Y | N | N | N | N | N |

Southern states - Ala., Ark., Fla., Ga., Ky., La., Miss., N.C., Okla., S.C., Tenn., Texas, Va.
Omitted votes are quorum calls, which CQ does not include in its vote charts.

**10. H Res 258. "October Surprise" Investigation/Rule.** Adoption of the resolution (H Res 303) to provide for House floor consideration of the resolution to authorize the Speaker to appoint 13 House members to a task force to investigate allegations that the 1980 Reagan campaign conspired to delay the release of 52 American hostages in Iran until after the 1980 election. Adopted 247-158: R 0-158; D 246-0 (ND 169-0, SD 77-0); I 1-0, Feb. 5, 1992.

**11. H Res 258. "October Surprise" Investigation/Appeal Chair's Ruling.** Derrick, D-S.C., motion to table (kill) the Walker, R-Pa., appeal of the chair's ruling that the McEwen, R-Ohio, point of order that the resolution to establish a task force to investigate allegations concerning the release of the American hostages in Iran in 1981 was not properly funded, was out of order. Motion agreed to 227-150: R 0-150; D 226-0 (ND 151-0, SD 75-0); I 1-0, Feb. 5, 1992.

**12. H Res 258. "October Surprise" Investigation.** Michel, R-Ill., substitute amendment to create a task force to investigate alleged attempts by either the 1980 Reagan campaign or the Carter administration to affect the timing of the release of 52 American hostages in Iran during the 1980 election. Rejected 158-249: R 158-0; D 0-248 (ND 0-168, SD 0-80); I 0-1, Feb. 5, 1992.

**13. H Res 258. "October Surprise" Investigation.** Adoption of the resolution to authorize the Speaker to appoint 13 House members to a task force to investigate allegations that the 1980 Reagan campaign conspired to delay the release of 52 American hostages in Iran until after the 1980 election. Adopted 217-192: R 0-158; D 216-34 (ND 156-13, SD 60-21); I 1-0, Feb. 5, 1992.

**14. S 606. Allegheny Wild and Scenic River Systems.** Vento, D-Minn., motion to suspend the rules and pass the bill to designate segments of the Allegheny River in Pennsylvania as components of the National Wild and Scenic Rivers System. Motion agreed to 409-3: R 156-3; D 252-0 (ND 171-0, SD 81-0); I 1-0, Feb. 19, 1992. A two-thirds majority of those present and voting (275 in this case) was required for passage under suspension of the rules.

**15. HR 543. Manzanar National Historic Site.** Vento, D-Minn., motion to suspend the rules and concur in the Senate amendments to the bill to designate as a National Historic Site the Manzanar War Relocation Center in California, which held 10,000 Japanese-Americans during World War II. Motion agreed to (thus clearing the bill for the president) 400-13: R 147-13; D 252-0 (ND 171-0, SD 81-0); I 1-0, Feb. 19, 1992. A two-thirds majority of those present and voting (276 in this case) was required for passage under suspension of the rules.

**16. HR 3337. Omnibus Coin Act.** Torres, D-Calif., motion to suspend the rules and concur in the Senate amendments to the bill to mint coins in commemoration of various events, including the 200th anniversary of the White House, the 1994 USA World Cup and the Christopher Columbus Quincentenary. The bill would also require the redesign of the reverse of all U.S. coins. Motion rejected 172-241: R 45-114; D 126-127 (ND 84-87, SD 42-40); I 1-0, Feb. 19, 1992. A two-thirds majority of those present and voting (276 in this case) was required for passage under suspension of the rules.

**17. HR 3490. Pay-Per-Call Telephone Regulation/Passage.** Swift, D-Wash., motion to suspend the rules and pass the bill to direct the Federal Communications Commission to regulate the 900 pay-per-call telephone industry to protect consumers from fraud. Motion agreed to 381-31: R 127-30; D 253-1 (ND 172-1, SD 81-0); I 1-0; Feb. 25, 1992. A two-thirds majority of those present and voting (275 in this case) was required for passage under suspension of the rules.

## KEY

| | |
|---|---|
| Y | Voted for (yea). |
| # | Paired for. |
| + | Announced for. |
| N | Voted against (nay). |
| X | Paired against. |
| − | Announced against. |
| P | Voted "present." |
| C | Voted "present" to avoid possible conflict of interest. |
| ? | Did not vote or otherwise make a position known. |

Democrats  **Republicans**
*Independent*

| | 10 | 11 | 12 | 13 | 14 | 15 | 16 | 17 |
|---|---|---|---|---|---|---|---|---|
| **ALABAMA** | | | | | | | | |
| 1 *Callahan* | N | N | Y | N | Y | Y | Y | Y |
| 2 *Dickinson* | N | N | Y | N | Y | Y | Y | ? |
| 3 Browder | Y | Y | N | Y | Y | Y | N | Y |
| 4 Bevill | Y | Y | N | Y | Y | Y | N | Y |
| 5 Cramer | Y | Y | ? | N | Y | Y | N | Y |
| 6 Erdreich | Y | Y | N | Y | Y | Y | N | Y |
| 7 Harris | Y | Y | N | N | Y | Y | Y | Y |
| **ALASKA** | | | | | | | | |
| AL *Young* | N | N | Y | N | Y | Y | N | Y |
| **ARIZONA** | | | | | | | | |
| 1 *Rhodes* | N | N | Y | N | Y | Y | N | Y |
| 2 Pastor | Y | Y | N | Y | Y | Y | Y | Y |
| 3 *Stump* | N | N | Y | N | N | N | N | N |
| 4 *Kyl* | N | N | Y | N | Y | Y | N | Y |
| 5 *Kolbe* | N | N | Y | N | Y | Y | Y | N |
| **ARKANSAS** | | | | | | | | |
| 1 Alexander | Y | Y | N | Y | Y | Y | Y | Y |
| 2 Thornton | Y | Y | N | Y | Y | Y | Y | Y |
| 3 *Hammerschmidt* | N | N | Y | N | Y | Y | N | Y |
| 4 Anthony | Y | Y | N | N | Y | Y | Y | + |
| **CALIFORNIA** | | | | | | | | |
| 1 *Riggs* | N | N | Y | N | Y | Y | N | N |
| 2 *Herger* | N | N | Y | N | Y | Y | N | Y |
| 3 Matsui | Y | Y | N | Y | Y | Y | Y | Y |
| 4 Fazio | Y | Y | N | Y | Y | Y | Y | Y |
| 5 Pelosi | Y | Y | N | Y | Y | Y | Y | Y |
| 6 Boxer | Y | Y | N | Y | ? | ? | ? | Y |
| 7 Miller | Y | ? | N | Y | Y | Y | Y | Y |
| 8 Dellums | Y | Y | N | Y | Y | Y | Y | Y |
| 9 Stark | ? | ? | ? | ? | Y | Y | N | Y |
| 10 Edwards | ? | ? | ? | ? | Y | Y | N | Y |
| 11 Lantos | ? | ? | ? | ? | ? | ? | ? | Y |
| 12 *Campbell* | N | N | Y | N | Y | Y | Y | Y |
| 13 Mineta | Y | Y | N | Y | Y | Y | Y | Y |
| 14 *Doolittle* | N | N | Y | N | Y | Y | N | Y |
| 15 Condit | Y | Y | N | N | Y | Y | N | Y |
| 16 Panetta | Y | Y | N | Y | Y | Y | N | Y |
| 17 Dooley | Y | Y | N | Y | Y | Y | Y | Y |
| 18 Lehman | Y | Y | N | Y | Y | Y | Y | Y |
| 19 *Lagomarsino* | N | N | Y | N | Y | Y | N | Y |
| 20 *Thomas* | X | ? | # | X | Y | Y | N | Y |
| 21 *Gallegly* | N | N | Y | N | + | + | − | Y |
| 22 *Moorhead* | N | N | Y | N | Y | Y | N | Y |
| 23 Beilenson | Y | Y | N | Y | Y | Y | N | Y |
| 24 Waxman | Y | Y | N | Y | Y | Y | Y | Y |
| 25 Roybal | Y | Y | N | Y | Y | Y | Y | Y |
| 26 Berman | Y | Y | N | Y | Y | Y | Y | Y |
| 27 Levine | ? | ? | ? | ? | ? | ? | ? | ? |
| 28 Dixon | Y | Y | N | Y | Y | Y | Y | Y |
| 29 Waters | Y | Y | N | Y | Y | Y | N | Y |
| 30 Martinez | Y | Y | N | Y | Y | Y | Y | Y |
| 31 Dymally | ? | ? | ? | + | ? | ? | ? | Y |
| 32 Anderson | Y | Y | N | Y | Y | Y | N | Y |
| 33 *Dreier* | N | N | Y | N | ? | ? | ? | N |
| 34 Torres | Y | ? | N | Y | Y | Y | Y | Y |
| 35 *Lewis* | N | N | Y | N | Y | Y | N | Y |
| 36 Brown | Y | Y | N | Y | Y | Y | Y | Y |
| 37 *McCandless* | N | N | Y | N | Y | Y | N | Y |
| 38 *Dornan* | N | N | Y | N | Y | Y | N | N |
| 39 *Dannemeyer* | − | − | + | − | − | − | − | + |
| 40 *Cox* | N | N | Y | N | Y | Y | N | Y |
| 41 Lowery | N | N | Y | N | Y | Y | N | ? |

| | 10 | 11 | 12 | 13 | 14 | 15 | 16 | 17 |
|---|---|---|---|---|---|---|---|---|
| 42 *Rohrabacher* | N | N | Y | N | Y | Y | N | Y |
| 43 *Packard* | N | N | Y | N | Y | Y | N | ? |
| 44 *Cunningham* | N | N | Y | N | Y | Y | N | ? |
| 45 *Hunter* | N | N | Y | N | Y | N | N | Y |
| **COLORADO** | | | | | | | | |
| 1 Schroeder | Y | Y | N | Y | Y | Y | Y | Y |
| 2 Skaggs | Y | Y | N | Y | Y | Y | Y | Y |
| 3 Campbell | Y | Y | N | N | Y | Y | Y | Y |
| 4 *Allard* | N | N | Y | N | Y | Y | N | Y |
| 5 *Hefley* | N | N | Y | N | Y | Y | N | Y |
| 6 *Schaefer* | N | N | Y | N | Y | Y | N | Y |
| **CONNECTICUT** | | | | | | | | |
| 1 Kennelly | Y | Y | N | Y | Y | Y | N | Y |
| 2 Gejdenson | Y | Y | N | Y | Y | Y | Y | Y |
| 3 DeLauro | Y | Y | N | Y | Y | Y | Y | Y |
| 4 *Shays* | N | N | Y | N | Y | Y | Y | Y |
| 5 *Franks* | N | N | Y | N | Y | Y | N | Y |
| 6 *Johnson* | N | N | Y | N | Y | Y | Y | Y |
| **DELAWARE** | | | | | | | | |
| AL Carper | Y | Y | N | N | Y | Y | Y | Y |
| **FLORIDA** | | | | | | | | |
| 1 Hutto | ? | ? | ? | ? | Y | Y | N | Y |
| 2 Peterson | Y | Y | N | Y | Y | Y | N | Y |
| 3 Bennett | Y | Y | N | Y | Y | Y | N | Y |
| 4 *James* | N | N | Y | N | Y | Y | N | Y |
| 5 *McCollum* | N | N | Y | N | Y | Y | N | Y |
| 6 *Stearns* | N | N | Y | N | N | N | N | Y |
| 7 Gibbons | Y | Y | N | Y | Y | Y | N | Y |
| 8 *Young* | N | N | Y | N | Y | Y | N | Y |
| 9 *Bilirakis* | N | N | Y | N | Y | Y | N | Y |
| 10 *Ireland* | ? | ? | ? | ? | Y | Y | Y | N |
| 11 Bacchus | Y | Y | N | Y | Y | Y | Y | Y |
| 12 *Lewis* | N | N | Y | N | Y | Y | N | Y |
| 13 *Goss* | N | N | Y | N | Y | Y | N | N |
| 14 Johnston | Y | Y | N | Y | Y | Y | Y | Y |
| 15 *Shaw* | N | ? | Y | N | Y | Y | N | Y |
| 16 Smith | Y | Y | N | Y | Y | Y | Y | Y |
| 17 Lehman | Y | Y | N | Y | Y | Y | Y | Y |
| 18 *Ros−Lehtinen* | N | N | Y | N | Y | Y | N | Y |
| 19 Fascell | Y | Y | N | Y | Y | Y | Y | Y |
| **GEORGIA** | | | | | | | | |
| 1 Thomas | ? | ? | ? | ? | Y | Y | Y | Y |
| 2 Hatcher | Y | Y | N | Y | Y | Y | Y | Y |
| 3 Ray | Y | Y | N | N | ? | ? | ? | Y |
| 4 Jones | Y | ? | N | Y | N | Y | N | Y |
| 5 Lewis | Y | Y | N | Y | Y | Y | Y | Y |
| 6 *Gingrich* | N | N | Y | N | Y | Y | N | Y |
| 7 Darden | Y | Y | N | Y | Y | Y | Y | Y |
| 8 Rowland | Y | Y | N | Y | Y | Y | Y | Y |
| 9 Jenkins | Y | ? | N | Y | Y | Y | Y | Y |
| 10 Barnard | Y | Y | N | Y | Y | Y | Y | Y |
| **HAWAII** | | | | | | | | |
| 1 Abercrombie | Y | Y | N | Y | Y | Y | N | Y |
| 2 Mink | Y | Y | N | Y | Y | Y | N | Y |
| **IDAHO** | | | | | | | | |
| 1 LaRocco | Y | Y | N | Y | Y | Y | N | Y |
| 2 Stallings | Y | Y | N | Y | Y | Y | Y | Y |
| **ILLINOIS** | | | | | | | | |
| 1 Hayes | Y | Y | N | Y | Y | Y | N | Y |
| 2 Savage | Y | Y | N | Y | ? | ? | ? | Y |
| 3 Russo | Y | ? | N | Y | Y | Y | N | Y |
| 4 Sangmeister | Y | Y | N | N | Y | Y | Y | Y |
| 5 Lipinski | Y | Y | N | N | ? | ? | ? | Y |
| 6 *Hyde* | N | N | Y | N | Y | Y | N | N |
| 7 Collins | Y | Y | N | Y | ? | ? | ? | Y |
| 8 Rostenkowski | Y | Y | N | Y | Y | Y | N | Y |
| 9 Yates | Y | Y | N | Y | Y | Y | N | Y |
| 10 *Porter* | N | N | Y | N | Y | Y | N | N |
| 11 Annunzio | Y | Y | N | Y | Y | Y | Y | Y |
| 12 *Crane* | N | N | Y | N | N | N | N | ? |
| 13 *Fawell* | N | N | Y | N | Y | Y | N | Y |
| 14 *Hastert* | N | N | Y | N | Y | Y | N | Y |
| 15 *Ewing* | N | N | Y | N | N | N | N | N |
| 16 Cox | Y | Y | N | Y | Y | Y | Y | Y |
| 17 Evans | Y | Y | N | Y | Y | Y | Y | Y |
| 18 *Michel* | N | N | Y | N | Y | Y | N | Y |
| 19 Bruce | Y | Y | N | Y | Y | Y | Y | Y |
| 20 Durbin | Y | Y | N | Y | Y | Y | N | Y |
| 21 Costello | Y | Y | N | Y | Y | Y | N | Y |
| 22 Poshard | Y | Y | N | Y | Y | Y | N | Y |
| **INDIANA** | | | | | | | | |
| 1 Visclosky | Y | Y | N | Y | Y | Y | N | Y |
| 2 Sharp | Y | ? | N | Y | Y | Y | N | Y |
| 3 Roemer | Y | Y | N | Y | Y | Y | N | Y |

ND Northern Democrats    SD Southern Democrats

| | 10 | 11 | 12 | 13 | 14 | 15 | 16 | 17 |
|---|---|---|---|---|---|---|---|---|
| 4 Long | Y | Y | N | Y | Y | Y | N | Y |
| 5 Jontz | Y | Y | N | Y | Y | Y | N | Y |
| 6 ***Burton*** | N | N | Y | N | Y | Y | N | N |
| 7 ***Myers*** | N | N | Y | N | Y | Y | N | Y |
| 8 McCloskey | Y | ? | N | Y | Y | Y | N | Y |
| 9 Hamilton | Y | Y | N | Y | Y | Y | N | Y |
| 10 Jacobs | Y | ? | N | Y | Y | Y | N | Y |
| **IOWA** | | | | | | | | |
| 1 ***Leach*** | N | N | Y | N | Y | Y | N | Y |
| 2 ***Nussle*** | N | N | Y | N | Y | Y | N | N |
| 3 Nagle | Y | Y | N | Y | Y | Y | N | Y |
| 4 Smith | Y | ? | N | Y | Y | Y | Y | Y |
| 5 ***Lightfoot*** | ? | ? | ? | ? | Y | Y | N | Y |
| 6 ***Grandy*** | N | N | Y | N | Y | Y | N | N |
| **KANSAS** | | | | | | | | |
| 1 ***Roberts*** | N | N | Y | N | Y | Y | N | Y |
| 2 Slattery | Y | Y | N | Y | Y | Y | Y | Y |
| 3 ***Meyers*** | N | N | Y | N | Y | Y | Y | Y |
| 4 Glickman | Y | Y | N | Y | Y | Y | N | Y |
| 5 ***Nichols*** | N | N | Y | N | Y | N | N | N |
| **KENTUCKY** | | | | | | | | |
| 1 Hubbard | Y | Y | N | Y | Y | Y | Y | Y |
| 2 Natcher | Y | Y | N | Y | Y | Y | N | Y |
| 3 Mazzoli | Y | Y | N | Y | Y | Y | N | Y |
| 4 ***Bunning*** | N | ? | Y | N | Y | Y | Y | Y |
| 5 ***Rogers*** | N | ? | Y | N | Y | Y | N | Y |
| 6 ***Hopkins*** | N | N | Y | N | Y | Y | N | Y |
| 7 Perkins | Y | Y | N | N | Y | Y | N | Y |
| **LOUISIANA** | | | | | | | | |
| 1 ***Livingston*** | N | N | Y | N | Y | Y | N | Y |
| 2 Jefferson | Y | Y | N | Y | Y | Y | N | Y |
| 3 Tauzin | Y | Y | N | N | Y | Y | Y | Y |
| 4 ***McCrery*** | N | N | Y | N | Y | Y | Y | Y |
| 5 Huckaby | Y | Y | N | N | Y | Y | Y | Y |
| 6 ***Baker*** | N | N | Y | N | Y | Y | Y | Y |
| 7 Hayes | Y | Y | N | N | Y | Y | Y | Y |
| 8 ***Holloway*** | N | N | Y | N | Y | N | N | Y |
| **MAINE** | | | | | | | | |
| 1 Andrews | Y | Y | N | Y | Y | Y | N | Y |
| 2 ***Snowe*** | N | N | Y | N | Y | Y | N | Y |
| **MARYLAND** | | | | | | | | |
| 1 ***Gilchrest*** | N | N | Y | N | Y | Y | Y | Y |
| 2 ***Bentley*** | N | N | Y | N | Y | Y | N | ? |
| 3 Cardin | Y | Y | N | Y | Y | Y | Y | Y |
| 4 McMillen | Y | ? | N | Y | Y | Y | Y | Y |
| 5 Hoyer | Y | Y | N | Y | Y | Y | Y | Y |
| 6 Byron | Y | Y | N | N | Y | Y | N | Y |
| 7 Mfume | Y | Y | N | Y | Y | Y | N | Y |
| 8 ***Morella*** | N | N | Y | N | Y | Y | Y | Y |
| **MASSACHUSETTS** | | | | | | | | |
| 1 Olver | Y | Y | N | Y | Y | Y | N | Y |
| 2 Neal | Y | Y | N | Y | Y | Y | N | Y |
| 3 Early | Y | Y | N | Y | Y | Y | Y | Y |
| 4 Frank | Y | Y | N | Y | Y | Y | Y | Y |
| 5 Atkins | Y | Y | N | Y | Y | Y | Y | Y |
| 6 Mavroules | Y | Y | N | Y | Y | Y | Y | ? |
| 7 Markey | Y | Y | N | Y | Y | Y | Y | Y |
| 8 Kennedy | Y | Y | N | Y | Y | Y | N | Y |
| 9 Moakley | Y | Y | N | Y | ? | ? | ? | Y |
| 10 Studds | Y | Y | N | Y | Y | Y | Y | Y |
| 11 Donnelly | Y | Y | N | Y | Y | Y | N | Y |
| **MICHIGAN** | | | | | | | | |
| 1 Conyers | Y | ? | N | Y | Y | Y | Y | Y |
| 2 ***Pursell*** | N | ? | Y | N | Y | Y | N | Y |
| 3 Wolpe | Y | Y | N | Y | Y | Y | N | Y |
| 4 ***Upton*** | N | N | Y | N | Y | Y | N | Y |
| 5 ***Henry*** | N | N | Y | N | Y | Y | N | Y |
| 6 Carr | Y | Y | N | Y | Y | Y | N | Y |
| 7 Kildee | Y | Y | N | Y | Y | Y | Y | Y |
| 8 Traxler | Y | Y | N | Y | Y | Y | Y | Y |
| 9 ***Vander Jagt*** | N | N | Y | N | Y | Y | Y | ? |
| 10 ***Camp*** | N | N | Y | N | Y | Y | N | Y |
| 11 ***Davis*** | N | ? | Y | N | Y | Y | N | Y |
| 12 Bonior | Y | Y | N | Y | Y | Y | Y | Y |
| 13 Collins | Y | Y | N | Y | Y | Y | Y | Y |
| 14 Hertel | Y | ? | N | Y | Y | Y | N | Y |
| 15 Ford | Y | Y | ? | Y | Y | Y | Y | Y |
| 16 Dingell | Y | ? | N | Y | Y | Y | Y | Y |
| 17 Levin | Y | Y | N | Y | Y | Y | N | Y |
| 18 ***Broomfield*** | N | N | Y | N | Y | Y | N | Y |
| **MINNESOTA** | | | | | | | | |
| 1 Penny | Y | Y | N | N | Y | Y | N | N |
| 2 ***Weber*** | N | N | Y | N | Y | Y | N | Y |
| 3 ***Ramstad*** | N | N | Y | N | Y | Y | N | Y |
| 4 Vento | Y | Y | N | Y | Y | Y | N | Y |

| | 10 | 11 | 12 | 13 | 14 | 15 | 16 | 17 |
|---|---|---|---|---|---|---|---|---|
| 5 Sabo | Y | ? | N | Y | Y | Y | N | Y |
| 6 Sikorski | Y | Y | N | Y | Y | Y | N | Y |
| 7 Peterson | Y | Y | N | Y | Y | Y | Y | Y |
| 8 Oberstar | Y | ? | N | Y | Y | Y | N | Y |
| **MISSISSIPPI** | | | | | | | | |
| 1 Whitten | ? | ? | ? | ? | ? | ? | ? | ? |
| 2 Espy | Y | Y | N | Y | Y | Y | Y | Y |
| 3 Montgomery | Y | Y | N | N | Y | Y | N | Y |
| 4 Parker | Y | Y | N | N | Y | Y | N | Y |
| 5 Taylor | Y | Y | N | N | Y | Y | N | Y |
| **MISSOURI** | | | | | | | | |
| 1 Clay | ? | ? | ? | ? | Y | Y | Y | Y |
| 2 Horn | Y | Y | N | Y | Y | Y | N | Y |
| 3 Gephardt | Y | Y | N | Y | Y | Y | Y | Y |
| 4 Skelton | Y | Y | N | N | Y | Y | N | Y |
| 5 Wheat | Y | Y | N | Y | Y | Y | N | Y |
| 6 ***Coleman*** | N | ? | Y | N | Y | Y | Y | Y |
| 7 ***Hancock*** | N | N | Y | N | Y | N | N | N |
| 8 ***Emerson*** | N | N | Y | N | Y | Y | N | Y |
| 9 Volkmer | Y | Y | N | N | Y | Y | N | Y |
| **MONTANA** | | | | | | | | |
| 1 Williams | Y | Y | N | Y | Y | Y | Y | Y |
| 2 ***Marlenee*** | N | N | Y | N | Y | Y | Y | Y |
| **NEBRASKA** | | | | | | | | |
| 1 ***Bereuter*** | N | N | Y | N | Y | Y | N | Y |
| 2 Hoagland | Y | Y | N | Y | Y | Y | N | Y |
| 3 ***Barrett*** | N | N | Y | N | Y | Y | N | N |
| **NEVADA** | | | | | | | | |
| 1 Bilbray | Y | Y | N | Y | Y | Y | N | Y |
| 2 ***Vucanovich*** | N | N | Y | N | Y | Y | Y | N |
| **NEW HAMPSHIRE** | | | | | | | | |
| 1 ***Zeliff*** | N | N | Y | N | Y | N | N | N |
| 2 Swett | Y | ? | N | Y | Y | Y | N | Y |
| **NEW JERSEY** | | | | | | | | |
| 1 Andrews | Y | Y | N | Y | Y | Y | Y | Y |
| 2 Hughes | Y | Y | N | Y | Y | Y | N | Y |
| 3 Pallone | Y | Y | N | Y | Y | Y | Y | Y |
| 4 ***Smith*** | N | N | Y | N | Y | Y | N | Y |
| 5 ***Roukema*** | N | N | Y | N | Y | Y | N | Y |
| 6 Dwyer | Y | Y | N | Y | Y | Y | N | Y |
| 7 ***Rinaldo*** | N | N | Y | N | Y | Y | Y | Y |
| 8 Roe | Y | Y | N | Y | Y | Y | Y | Y |
| 9 Torricelli | Y | Y | N | Y | Y | Y | Y | Y |
| 10 Payne | Y | Y | N | Y | Y | Y | Y | Y |
| 11 ***Gallo*** | N | N | Y | N | Y | Y | Y | Y |
| 12 ***Zimmer*** | N | N | Y | N | Y | Y | N | Y |
| 13 ***Saxton*** | N | N | Y | N | Y | Y | N | Y |
| 14 Guarini | Y | Y | N | Y | Y | Y | Y | Y |
| **NEW MEXICO** | | | | | | | | |
| 1 ***Schiff*** | N | N | Y | N | ? | ? | ? | Y |
| 2 ***Skeen*** | N | N | Y | N | Y | Y | Y | Y |
| 3 Richardson | Y | Y | N | Y | Y | Y | Y | Y |
| **NEW YORK** | | | | | | | | |
| 1 Hochbrueckner | Y | Y | N | Y | Y | Y | Y | Y |
| 2 Downey | Y | ? | N | Y | Y | Y | N | Y |
| 3 Mrazek | ? | ? | ? | ? | ? | ? | ? | ? |
| 4 ***Lent*** | N | ? | Y | N | Y | Y | Y | Y |
| 5 ***McGrath*** | N | N | Y | N | Y | Y | N | Y |
| 6 Flake | Y | Y | ? | ? | Y | Y | Y | Y |
| 7 Ackerman | Y | Y | N | Y | ? | ? | ? | Y |
| 8 Scheuer | Y | Y | N | Y | Y | Y | N | Y |
| 9 Manton | Y | Y | N | Y | Y | Y | Y | Y |
| 10 Schumer | Y | Y | N | Y | Y | Y | Y | Y |
| 11 Towns | Y | ? | N | Y | Y | Y | Y | Y |
| 12 Owens | Y | Y | N | Y | Y | Y | Y | Y |
| 13 Solarz | Y | Y | N | Y | Y | Y | Y | Y |
| 14 ***Molinari*** | N | N | Y | N | Y | Y | N | Y |
| 15 ***Green*** | N | N | Y | N | Y | Y | Y | Y |
| 16 Rangel | Y | Y | N | Y | Y | Y | Y | Y |
| 17 Weiss | Y | Y | N | Y | Y | Y | Y | Y |
| 18 Serrano | Y | Y | N | Y | Y | Y | Y | ? |
| 19 Engel | Y | Y | N | Y | Y | Y | N | ? |
| 20 Lowey | Y | Y | N | Y | Y | Y | Y | Y |
| 21 ***Fish*** | N | N | Y | N | Y | Y | Y | Y |
| 22 ***Gilman*** | N | N | Y | N | Y | Y | Y | Y |
| 23 McNulty | Y | Y | N | N | Y | Y | Y | Y |
| 24 ***Solomon*** | N | N | Y | N | Y | Y | N | Y |
| 25 ***Boehlert*** | N | N | Y | N | Y | Y | Y | Y |
| 26 ***Martin*** | N | N | Y | N | Y | Y | N | Y |
| 27 ***Walsh*** | N | N | Y | N | Y | Y | N | Y |
| 28 McHugh | Y | Y | N | Y | Y | Y | N | Y |
| 29 ***Horton*** | N | N | Y | N | Y | Y | Y | Y |
| 30 Slaughter | Y | Y | N | Y | Y | Y | N | Y |
| 31 ***Paxon*** | N | N | Y | N | Y | Y | N | Y |

| | 10 | 11 | 12 | 13 | 14 | 15 | 16 | 17 |
|---|---|---|---|---|---|---|---|---|
| 32 LaFalce | Y | Y | N | Y | Y | Y | N | Y |
| 33 Nowak | Y | Y | N | Y | Y | Y | Y | Y |
| 34 ***Houghton*** | N | N | Y | N | Y | Y | N | N |
| **NORTH CAROLINA** | | | | | | | | |
| 1 Jones | Y | Y | N | Y | Y | Y | Y | Y |
| 2 Valentine | Y | ? | N | N | Y | Y | Y | Y |
| 3 Lancaster | Y | ? | N | Y | Y | Y | Y | Y |
| 4 Price | Y | Y | N | Y | Y | Y | N | Y |
| 5 Neal | Y | Y | N | Y | Y | Y | N | Y |
| 6 ***Coble*** | N | N | Y | N | Y | N | N | N |
| 7 Rose | Y | Y | N | Y | Y | Y | Y | Y |
| 8 Hefner | Y | Y | N | Y | Y | Y | Y | Y |
| 9 ***McMillan*** | N | N | Y | N | Y | Y | N | Y |
| 10 ***Ballenger*** | N | N | Y | N | Y | Y | N | N |
| 11 ***Taylor*** | N | N | Y | N | Y | Y | N | N |
| **NORTH DAKOTA** | | | | | | | | |
| AL Dorgan | Y | Y | N | Y | Y | Y | N | Y |
| **OHIO** | | | | | | | | |
| 1 Luken | + | Y | ? | ? | Y | Y | N | Y |
| 2 ***Gradison*** | N | N | Y | N | Y | Y | N | N |
| 3 Hall | Y | Y | N | Y | Y | Y | Y | Y |
| 4 ***Oxley*** | N | ? | Y | N | Y | Y | Y | Y |
| 5 ***Gillmor*** | N | N | Y | N | ? | Y | Y | Y |
| 6 ***McEwen*** | N | N | Y | N | Y | Y | N | Y |
| 7 ***Hobson*** | N | N | Y | N | Y | Y | Y | Y |
| 8 ***Boehner*** | N | N | Y | N | Y | Y | N | N |
| 9 Kaptur | Y | Y | N | Y | Y | Y | Y | Y |
| 10 ***Miller*** | N | N | Y | N | Y | Y | N | Y |
| 11 Eckart | # | ? | X | # | Y | Y | N | Y |
| 12 ***Kasich*** | N | N | Y | N | Y | Y | N | Y |
| 13 Pease | Y | Y | N | Y | Y | Y | N | Y |
| 14 Sawyer | Y | Y | N | Y | Y | Y | Y | Y |
| 15 ***Wylie*** | N | N | Y | N | Y | Y | Y | Y |
| 16 ***Regula*** | N | N | Y | N | Y | Y | N | Y |
| 17 Traficant | Y | Y | N | Y | Y | Y | N | Y |
| 18 Applegate | Y | Y | N | Y | Y | Y | N | Y |
| 19 Feighan | Y | Y | N | Y | Y | Y | N | Y |
| 20 Oakar | Y | Y | N | Y | Y | Y | N | Y |
| 21 Stokes | Y | Y | N | Y | Y | Y | Y | Y |
| **OKLAHOMA** | | | | | | | | |
| 1 ***Inhofe*** | N | N | Y | N | Y | Y | N | Y |
| 2 Synar | Y | ? | N | Y | Y | Y | Y | Y |
| 3 Brewster | Y | Y | N | Y | Y | Y | N | Y |
| 4 McCurdy | Y | Y | N | Y | Y | Y | N | Y |
| 5 ***Edwards*** | N | N | Y | N | Y | Y | N | Y |
| 6 English | Y | Y | N | N | Y | Y | N | Y |
| **OREGON** | | | | | | | | |
| 1 AuCoin | Y | Y | N | Y | Y | Y | Y | Y |
| 2 ***Smith*** | N | N | Y | N | Y | Y | N | Y |
| 3 Wyden | Y | Y | N | Y | Y | Y | Y | + |
| 4 DeFazio | # | ? | X | # | Y | Y | Y | Y |
| 5 Kopetski | Y | Y | N | Y | Y | Y | Y | Y |
| **PENNSYLVANIA** | | | | | | | | |
| 1 Foglietta | Y | ? | N | Y | Y | Y | Y | Y |
| 2 Blackwell | ? | Y | N | Y | ? | ? | ? | Y |
| 3 Borski | Y | Y | N | Y | Y | Y | Y | Y |
| 4 Kolter | ? | ? | ? | ? | Y | Y | Y | ? |
| 5 ***Schulze*** | N | ? | Y | N | Y | Y | N | Y |
| 6 Yatron | Y | Y | N | Y | Y | Y | N | Y |
| 7 ***Weldon*** | N | N | Y | N | Y | Y | Y | Y |
| 8 Kostmayer | Y | Y | N | Y | Y | Y | N | Y |
| 9 ***Shuster*** | N | N | Y | N | Y | Y | N | Y |
| 10 ***McDade*** | N | N | ? | ? | Y | Y | Y | Y |
| 11 Kanjorski | Y | Y | N | Y | Y | Y | N | Y |
| 12 Murtha | Y | Y | N | Y | Y | Y | N | ? |
| 13 ***Coughlin*** | N | N | Y | N | Y | Y | N | Y |
| 14 Coyne | Y | Y | N | Y | Y | Y | N | Y |
| 15 ***Ritter*** | N | ? | Y | N | Y | Y | N | Y |
| 16 ***Walker*** | N | N | Y | N | Y | Y | N | N |
| 17 ***Gekas*** | N | N | Y | N | Y | Y | Y | Y |
| 18 ***Santorum*** | N | N | ? | ? | Y | Y | N | Y |
| 19 ***Goodling*** | N | N | Y | N | Y | Y | N | Y |
| 20 Gaydos | ? | ? | ? | ? | Y | Y | N | Y |
| 21 ***Ridge*** | N | N | Y | N | Y | Y | Y | Y |
| 22 Murphy | Y | Y | N | Y | Y | Y | N | Y |
| 23 ***Clinger*** | N | N | Y | N | Y | Y | N | Y |
| **RHODE ISLAND** | | | | | | | | |
| 1 ***Machtley*** | N | N | Y | N | Y | Y | Y | Y |
| 2 Reed | Y | Y | N | Y | Y | Y | Y | Y |
| **SOUTH CAROLINA** | | | | | | | | |
| 1 ***Ravenel*** | N | N | Y | N | Y | Y | N | Y |
| 2 ***Spence*** | N | N | Y | N | Y | Y | N | Y |
| 3 Derrick | Y | Y | N | Y | Y | Y | N | Y |
| 4 Patterson | Y | Y | N | N | Y | Y | N | Y |
| 5 Spratt | Y | Y | N | Y | Y | Y | N | Y |
| 6 Tallon | Y | Y | N | Y | Y | Y | N | Y |

| | 10 | 11 | 12 | 13 | 14 | 15 | 16 | 17 |
|---|---|---|---|---|---|---|---|---|
| **SOUTH DAKOTA** | | | | | | | | |
| AL Johnson | Y | ? | N | Y | Y | Y | Y | Y |
| **TENNESSEE** | | | | | | | | |
| 1 ***Quillen*** | N | N | Y | N | Y | Y | N | Y |
| 2 ***Duncan*** | N | N | Y | N | Y | N | N | Y |
| 3 Lloyd | Y | Y | N | N | Y | Y | N | Y |
| 4 Cooper | Y | Y | N | Y | Y | Y | N | Y |
| 5 Clement | Y | Y | N | Y | Y | Y | Y | Y |
| 6 Gordon | Y | Y | N | Y | Y | Y | N | Y |
| 7 ***Sundquist*** | N | N | Y | N | Y | Y | Y | Y |
| 8 Tanner | Y | Y | N | Y | Y | Y | N | Y |
| 9 Ford | Y | Y | N | Y | Y | Y | Y | Y |
| **TEXAS** | | | | | | | | |
| 1 Chapman | Y | ? | N | Y | ? | Y | N | Y |
| 2 Wilson | Y | Y | N | N | Y | Y | Y | Y |
| 3 ***Johnson*** | X | ? | # | X | Y | Y | N | Y |
| 4 Hall | ? | Y | N | N | Y | Y | N | Y |
| 5 Bryant | Y | Y | N | Y | Y | Y | N | Y |
| 6 ***Barton*** | N | N | Y | N | Y | Y | N | Y |
| 7 ***Archer*** | N | N | Y | N | Y | Y | N | N |
| 8 ***Fields*** | N | N | Y | N | Y | Y | N | Y |
| 9 Brooks | Y | Y | N | N | Y | Y | Y | Y |
| 10 Pickle | ? | Y | N | Y | Y | Y | N | Y |
| 11 Edwards | Y | Y | N | Y | Y | Y | N | Y |
| 12 Geren | Y | Y | N | N | Y | Y | Y | Y |
| 13 Sarpalius | Y | Y | N | Y | Y | Y | Y | Y |
| 14 Laughlin | Y | Y | N | Y | Y | Y | N | Y |
| 15 de la Garza | ? | Y | N | Y | ? | ? | ? | Y |
| 16 Coleman | ? | ? | ? | ? | Y | Y | Y | ? |
| 17 Stenholm | Y | Y | N | N | Y | Y | N | Y |
| 18 Washington | Y | Y | N | Y | Y | ? | Y | ? |
| 19 ***Combest*** | N | N | Y | N | Y | Y | Y | Y |
| 20 Gonzalez | Y | Y | N | Y | Y | Y | Y | Y |
| 21 ***Smith*** | N | N | Y | N | Y | Y | Y | Y |
| 22 ***DeLay*** | ? | N | Y | N | Y | Y | N | N |
| 23 Bustamante | Y | Y | N | Y | Y | Y | Y | Y |
| 24 Frost | ? | Y | N | Y | Y | Y | Y | Y |
| 25 Andrews | Y | Y | N | Y | Y | Y | N | Y |
| 26 ***Armey*** | ? | N | Y | N | Y | Y | N | Y |
| 27 Ortiz | Y | Y | N | Y | Y | Y | Y | Y |
| **UTAH** | | | | | | | | |
| 1 ***Hansen*** | N | N | Y | N | ? | ? | ? | Y |
| 2 Owens | Y | ? | N | Y | Y | Y | Y | Y |
| 3 Orton | Y | Y | N | Y | Y | Y | N | Y |
| **VERMONT** | | | | | | | | |
| AL *Sanders* | Y | Y | N | Y | Y | Y | Y | Y |
| **VIRGINIA** | | | | | | | | |
| 1 ***Bateman*** | N | N | Y | N | Y | Y | N | Y |
| 2 Pickett | Y | Y | N | Y | Y | Y | Y | Y |
| 3 ***Bliley*** | N | N | Y | N | Y | Y | N | Y |
| 4 Sisisky | Y | Y | N | Y | Y | Y | Y | Y |
| 5 Payne | Y | Y | N | Y | Y | Y | Y | Y |
| 6 Olin | Y | Y | N | Y | Y | Y | N | Y |
| 7 ***Allen*** | N | N | Y | N | Y | N | N | Y |
| 8 Moran | Y | Y | N | Y | Y | Y | N | Y |
| 9 Boucher | Y | Y | N | Y | Y | Y | Y | Y |
| 10 ***Wolf*** | N | N | Y | N | Y | Y | N | Y |
| **WASHINGTON** | | | | | | | | |
| 1 ***Miller*** | N | N | Y | N | Y | Y | ? | ? |
| 2 Swift | Y | Y | N | Y | Y | Y | Y | Y |
| 3 Unsoeld | Y | Y | N | Y | Y | Y | N | Y |
| 4 ***Morrison*** | ? | ? | + | – | Y | Y | N | Y |
| 5 Foley | | | | | | | | |
| 6 Dicks | Y | Y | N | Y | Y | Y | N | Y |
| 7 McDermott | Y | Y | N | Y | Y | Y | N | Y |
| 8 ***Chandler*** | N | N | Y | N | ? | ? | ? | Y |
| **WEST VIRGINIA** | | | | | | | | |
| 1 Mollohan | Y | Y | N | Y | Y | Y | N | Y |
| 2 Staggers | Y | ? | N | Y | Y | Y | Y | Y |
| 3 Wise | Y | Y | N | Y | Y | Y | N | Y |
| 4 Rahall | Y | Y | N | N | Y | Y | N | Y |
| **WISCONSIN** | | | | | | | | |
| 1 Aspin | Y | Y | N | Y | Y | Y | Y | Y |
| 2 ***Klug*** | N | N | Y | N | Y | Y | N | Y |
| 3 ***Gunderson*** | N | N | Y | N | Y | Y | Y | Y |
| 4 Kleczka | Y | Y | N | Y | Y | Y | N | Y |
| 5 Moody | Y | Y | N | Y | Y | Y | N | Y |
| 6 ***Petri*** | N | N | Y | N | Y | Y | Y | Y |
| 7 Obey | Y | Y | N | Y | Y | Y | N | Y |
| 8 ***Roth*** | N | N | Y | N | Y | Y | N | + |
| 9 ***Sensenbrenner*** | N | N | Y | N | Y | Y | N | N |
| **WYOMING** | | | | | | | | |
| AL ***Thomas*** | N | N | Y | N | Y | Y | Y | Y |

Southern states - Ala., Ark., Fla., Ga., Ky., La., Miss., N.C., Okla., S.C., Tenn., Texas, Va.
Omitted votes are quorum calls, which CQ does not include in its vote charts.

**18. HR 4113. Expedited Transfer of the USS *Lexington*/ Passage.** Bennett, D-Fla., motion to suspend the rules and pass the bill to waive the 60-day congressional review period and allow the Navy to transfer the aircraft carrier USS *Lexington* to the city of Corpus Christi, Texas, to be used as a naval memorial. Motion agreed to 414-0: R 157-0; D 256-0 (ND 175-0, SD 81-0); I 1-0; Feb. 25, 1992. A two-thirds majority of those present and voting (276 in this case) was required for passage under suspension of the rules.

**19. HR 2152. Drift Net Fishing Sanctions/Passage.** Studds, D-Mass., motion to suspend the rules and pass the bill to impose sanctions on nations that use drift net fishing after Dec. 31, 1992. Motion agreed to 412-0: R 157-0; D 254-0 (ND 173-0, SD 81-0); I 1-0; Feb. 25, 1992. A two-thirds majority of those present and voting (276 in this case) was required for passage under suspension of the rules. A "nay" was a vote in support of the president's position.

**20. H Con Res 239. Commend the People of Lithuania/ Passage.** Hamilton, D-Ind., motion to suspend the rules and pass the concurrent resolution commending the people of Lithuania for their peaceful transition to democracy and a free-market economy. Motion agreed to 411-0: R 157-0; D 253-0 (ND 172-0, SD 81-0); I 1-0; Feb. 25, 1992. A two-thirds majority of those present and voting (274 in this case) was required for passage under suspension of the rules.

**21. H J Res 414. Honor Drug War Casualties/Passage.** Feighan, D-Ohio, motion to suspend the rules and pass the joint resolution to honor those who have lost their lives in the war against drugs. Motion agreed to 410-0: R 155-0; D 254-0 (ND 173-0, SD 81-0); I 1-0; Feb. 25, 1992. A two-thirds majority of those present and voting (274 in this case) was required for passage under suspension of the rules.

**22. Procedural Motion.** Approval of the House Journal of Tuesday, Feb. 25. Motion agreed to 282-115: R 44-108; D 238-7 (ND 160-7, SD 78-0); I 0-0; Feb. 26, 1992.

**23. HR 4210. 1992 Tax Bill/Appeal Chair's Ruling.** Derrick, D-S.C., motion to table (kill) the Solomon, R-N.Y., appeal of the chair's ruling, rejecting the Solomon point of order against the rule (H Res 374) providing for House floor consideration of the tax bill for not including a motion to recommit with instructions. Motion agreed to 256-157: R 0-157; D 255-0 (ND 175-0, SD 80-0); I 1-0; Feb. 26, 1992.

**24. HR 4210. 1992 Tax Bill/Rule.** Adoption of the rule (H Res 374) to provide for House floor consideration of the bill to provide tax changes and economic incentives designed to stimulate the economy. Adopted 244-178: R 0-161; D 244-16 (ND 164-14, SD 80-2); I 0-1; Feb. 26, 1992.

**25. HR 4210. 1992 Tax Bill/Substitute.** Gephardt, D-Mo., substitute amendment incorporating the tax and economic growth proposals contained in President Bush's State of the Union address and fiscal 1993 budget, including an increase in the personal exemption by $500 for taxpayers with children, a reduction in the capital gains rate to 15.4 percent and a two-year $5,000 tax credit for first-time home buyers. Rejected 1-427: R 0-163; D 1-263 (ND 1-181, SD 0-82); I 0-1, Feb. 26, 1992. A "nay" was a vote in support of the president's position.

## KEY

| | |
|---|---|
| Y | Voted for (yea). |
| # | Paired for. |
| + | Announced for. |
| N | Voted against (nay). |
| X | Paired against. |
| − | Announced against. |
| P | Voted "present." |
| C | Voted "present" to avoid possible conflict of interest. |
| ? | Did not vote or otherwise make a position known. |

Democrats **Republicans**
*Independent*

| | 18 | 19 | 20 | 21 | 22 | 23 | 24 | 25 |
|---|---|---|---|---|---|---|---|---|
| **ALABAMA** | | | | | | | | |
| 1 *Callahan* | Y | Y | Y | Y | N | N | N | N |
| 2 *Dickinson* | ? | ? | ? | ? | ? | ? | X | ? |
| 3 Browder | Y | Y | Y | Y | Y | Y | Y | N |
| 4 Bevill | Y | Y | Y | Y | Y | Y | Y | N |
| 5 Cramer | Y | Y | Y | Y | Y | Y | Y | N |
| 6 Erdreich | Y | Y | Y | Y | Y | N | N | N |
| 7 Harris | Y | Y | Y | Y | Y | Y | Y | N |
| **ALASKA** | | | | | | | | |
| AL *Young* | Y | Y | Y | Y | N | N | N | N |
| **ARIZONA** | | | | | | | | |
| 1 *Rhodes* | Y | Y | Y | N | N | N | N | N |
| 2 Pastor | Y | Y | Y | Y | Y | Y | Y | N |
| 3 *Stump* | Y | Y | Y | N | N | N | N | N |
| 4 *Kyl* | Y | Y | Y | Y | N | N | N | N |
| 5 *Kolbe* | Y | Y | Y | N | N | N | N | N |
| **ARKANSAS** | | | | | | | | |
| 1 Alexander | Y | Y | Y | Y | Y | Y | Y | N |
| 2 Thornton | Y | Y | Y | Y | Y | Y | Y | N |
| 3 *Hammerschmidt* | Y | Y | Y | Y | N | N | N | N |
| 4 Anthony | + | + | + | + | Y | Y | Y | N |
| **CALIFORNIA** | | | | | | | | |
| 1 *Riggs* | Y | Y | Y | N | N | N | N | N |
| 2 *Herger* | Y | Y | Y | N | N | N | N | N |
| 3 Matsui | Y | Y | Y | Y | Y | Y | Y | N |
| 4 Fazio | Y | Y | Y | Y | Y | Y | Y | N |
| 5 Pelosi | Y | Y | Y | Y | Y | Y | Y | N |
| 6 Boxer | Y | Y | Y | Y | ? | Y | Y | N |
| 7 Miller | Y | Y | Y | Y | Y | Y | Y | N |
| 8 Dellums | Y | Y | Y | Y | Y | Y | Y | N |
| 9 Stark | Y | Y | Y | Y | Y | Y | Y | N |
| 10 Edwards | Y | Y | Y | Y | Y | Y | Y | N |
| 11 Lantos | Y | Y | Y | Y | Y | Y | Y | N |
| 12 *Campbell* | Y | Y | Y | N | N | N | N | N |
| 13 Mineta | Y | Y | Y | Y | Y | Y | Y | N |
| 14 *Doolittle* | Y | Y | Y | N | N | N | N | N |
| 15 Condit | Y | Y | Y | Y | Y | Y | Y | N |
| 16 Panetta | Y | Y | Y | Y | Y | Y | Y | N |
| 17 Dooley | Y | Y | Y | ? | Y | Y | Y | N |
| 18 Lehman | Y | Y | Y | Y | Y | Y | Y | N |
| 19 *Lagomarsino* | Y | Y | Y | N | N | N | N | N |
| 20 *Thomas* | Y | Y | Y | N | N | N | N | N |
| 21 *Gallegly* | Y | Y | Y | N | N | N | N | N |
| 22 *Moorhead* | Y | Y | Y | N | N | N | N | N |
| 23 Beilenson | Y | Y | Y | Y | Y | Y | Y | N |
| 24 Waxman | Y | Y | Y | Y | Y | Y | Y | N |
| 25 Roybal | Y | Y | Y | Y | Y | Y | Y | N |
| 26 Berman | Y | Y | Y | Y | Y | Y | Y | N |
| 27 Levine | ? | ? | ? | ? | Y | Y | Y | N |
| 28 Dixon | Y | Y | Y | Y | Y | Y | Y | N |
| 29 Waters | Y | Y | Y | ? | Y | Y | Y | N |
| 30 Martinez | Y | Y | Y | Y | Y | Y | Y | N |
| 31 Dymally | Y | Y | Y | Y | Y | Y | # | N |
| 32 Anderson | Y | Y | Y | ? | Y | Y | Y | N |
| 33 *Dreier* | Y | Y | Y | N | N | N | N | N |
| 34 Torres | Y | Y | Y | Y | Y | Y | Y | N |
| 35 *Lewis* | Y | Y | Y | N | N | N | N | N |
| 36 Brown | Y | Y | Y | Y | Y | Y | Y | N |
| 37 *McCandless* | Y | Y | Y | N | N | N | N | N |
| 38 *Dornan* | Y | Y | Y | Y | N | N | N | N |
| 39 *Dannemeyer* | + | + | + | + | − | − | − | − |
| 40 *Cox* | Y | Y | Y | Y | N | N | N | N |
| 41 *Lowery* | ? | ? | ? | ? | ? | N | N | N |

| | 18 | 19 | 20 | 21 | 22 | 23 | 24 | 25 |
|---|---|---|---|---|---|---|---|---|
| 42 *Rohrbacher* | Y | Y | Y | N | N | N | N | N |
| 43 *Packard* | Y | Y | Y | Y | N | N | N | N |
| 44 *Cunningham* | ? | ? | ? | ? | N | N | N | N |
| 45 *Hunter* | Y | Y | Y | N | N | N | N | N |
| **COLORADO** | | | | | | | | |
| 1 Schroeder | Y | Y | Y | Y | N | Y | Y | N |
| 2 Skaggs | Y | Y | Y | Y | Y | Y | Y | N |
| 3 Campbell | Y | Y | Y | Y | Y | N | N | N |
| 4 *Allard* | Y | Y | Y | N | N | N | N | N |
| 5 *Hefley* | Y | Y | Y | N | N | N | N | N |
| 6 *Schaefer* | Y | Y | Y | N | ? | N | N | N |
| **CONNECTICUT** | | | | | | | | |
| 1 Kennelly | Y | Y | Y | Y | Y | Y | Y | N |
| 2 Gejdenson | Y | Y | Y | Y | Y | Y | Y | N |
| 3 DeLauro | Y | Y | Y | Y | Y | Y | Y | N |
| 4 *Shays* | Y | Y | Y | N | N | N | N | N |
| 5 *Franks* | Y | Y | Y | N | N | N | N | N |
| 6 *Johnson* | Y | Y | Y | N | Y | N | N | N |
| **DELAWARE** | | | | | | | | |
| AL Carper | Y | Y | Y | Y | Y | Y | Y | N |
| **FLORIDA** | | | | | | | | |
| 1 Hutto | Y | Y | Y | Y | Y | Y | Y | N |
| 2 Peterson | Y | Y | Y | Y | Y | Y | Y | N |
| 3 Bennett | Y | Y | Y | Y | Y | Y | Y | N |
| 4 *James* | Y | Y | Y | N | N | N | N | N |
| 5 *McCollum* | Y | Y | Y | N | N | N | N | N |
| 6 *Stearns* | Y | Y | Y | N | N | N | N | N |
| 7 Gibbons | Y | Y | Y | ? | Y | Y | Y | N |
| 8 *Young* | Y | Y | Y | N | N | N | N | N |
| 9 *Bilirakis* | Y | Y | Y | N | N | N | N | N |
| 10 *Ireland* | Y | Y | Y | ? | N | N | N | N |
| 11 Bacchus | Y | Y | Y | Y | Y | Y | Y | N |
| 12 *Lewis* | Y | Y | Y | Y | N | N | N | N |
| 13 *Goss* | Y | Y | Y | N | N | N | N | N |
| 14 Johnston | Y | Y | Y | Y | Y | Y | Y | N |
| 15 *Shaw* | Y | Y | Y | Y | N | N | N | N |
| 16 Smith | Y | Y | Y | Y | Y | Y | Y | N |
| 17 Lehman | Y | Y | Y | Y | Y | Y | Y | N |
| 18 *Ros−Lehtinen* | Y | Y | Y | N | N | N | N | N |
| 19 Fascell | Y | Y | Y | ? | Y | Y | Y | N |
| **GEORGIA** | | | | | | | | |
| 1 Thomas | Y | Y | Y | Y | Y | Y | Y | N |
| 2 Hatcher | Y | Y | Y | Y | Y | Y | Y | N |
| 3 Ray | Y | Y | Y | Y | ? | N | N | N |
| 4 Jones | Y | Y | Y | Y | ? | Y | Y | N |
| 5 Lewis | Y | Y | Y | Y | Y | Y | Y | N |
| 6 *Gingrich* | Y | Y | Y | N | ? | N | N | N |
| 7 Darden | Y | Y | Y | Y | Y | Y | Y | N |
| 8 Rowland | Y | Y | Y | Y | Y | Y | Y | N |
| 9 Jenkins | Y | Y | Y | Y | Y | Y | Y | N |
| 10 Barnard | Y | Y | Y | Y | Y | Y | Y | N |
| **HAWAII** | | | | | | | | |
| 1 Abercrombie | Y | Y | Y | Y | Y | Y | Y | N |
| 2 Mink | Y | Y | Y | Y | Y | Y | Y | N |
| **IDAHO** | | | | | | | | |
| 1 LaRocco | Y | Y | Y | Y | Y | Y | Y | N |
| 2 Stallings | Y | Y | Y | Y | Y | Y | Y | N |
| **ILLINOIS** | | | | | | | | |
| 1 Hayes | Y | Y | Y | Y | Y | Y | Y | N |
| 2 Savage | Y | Y | Y | Y | ? | ? | ? | N |
| 3 Russo | Y | Y | Y | Y | ? | Y | Y | N |
| 4 Sangmeister | Y | Y | Y | Y | Y | Y | Y | N |
| 5 Lipinski | Y | Y | Y | Y | Y | Y | Y | N |
| 6 *Hyde* | Y | Y | Y | Y | N | ? | N | N |
| 7 Collins | ? | ? | ? | ? | Y | Y | Y | N |
| 8 Rostenkowski | Y | Y | Y | Y | Y | Y | Y | N |
| 9 Yates | Y | Y | Y | Y | Y | N | N | N |
| 10 *Porter* | Y | Y | Y | Y | N | N | N | N |
| 11 Annunzio | Y | Y | Y | Y | Y | Y | Y | N |
| 12 *Crane* | ? | ? | ? | ? | N | N | N | N |
| 13 *Fawell* | Y | Y | Y | N | N | N | N | N |
| 14 *Hastert* | Y | Y | Y | N | N | N | N | N |
| 15 *Ewing* | Y | Y | Y | N | N | N | N | N |
| 16 Cox | Y | Y | Y | Y | Y | Y | Y | N |
| 17 Evans | Y | Y | Y | Y | Y | Y | Y | N |
| 18 *Michel* | Y | Y | Y | N | N | N | N | N |
| 19 Bruce | Y | Y | Y | Y | Y | Y | Y | N |
| 20 Durbin | Y | Y | Y | Y | Y | Y | Y | N |
| 21 Costello | Y | Y | Y | Y | Y | Y | Y | N |
| 22 Poshard | Y | Y | Y | Y | Y | Y | Y | N |
| **INDIANA** | | | | | | | | |
| 1 Visclosky | Y | Y | Y | Y | Y | Y | Y | N |
| 2 Sharp | Y | Y | Y | Y | ? | ? | ? | N |
| 3 Roemer | Y | Y | Y | Y | Y | N | N | N |

ND  Northern Democrats    SD  Southern Democrats

| | 18 | 19 | 20 | 21 | 22 | 23 | 24 | 25 |
|---|---|---|---|---|---|---|---|---|
| 4 Long | Y | Y | Y | Y | Y | Y | Y | N |
| 5 Jontz | Y | Y | Y | Y | Y | Y | Y | N |
| 6 ***Burton*** | Y | Y | Y | Y | N | N | N | N |
| 7 ***Myers*** | Y | Y | Y | Y | Y | N | N | N |
| 8 McCloskey | Y | Y | Y | Y | Y | Y | Y | N |
| 9 Hamilton | Y | Y | Y | Y | Y | Y | N | N |
| 10 Jacobs | Y | Y | Y | Y | N | Y | Y | N |
| **IOWA** | | | | | | | | |
| 1 ***Leach*** | Y | Y | Y | Y | N | N | N | N |
| 2 ***Nussle*** | Y | Y | Y | Y | N | N | N | N |
| 3 Nagle | Y | Y | Y | Y | Y | Y | Y | N |
| 4 Smith | Y | Y | Y | Y | Y | Y | Y | N |
| 5 ***Lightfoot*** | Y | Y | Y | Y | N | N | N | N |
| 6 ***Grandy*** | Y | Y | Y | Y | N | N | N | N |
| **KANSAS** | | | | | | | | |
| 1 ***Roberts*** | Y | Y | Y | Y | N | N | N | N |
| 2 Slattery | Y | Y | Y | Y | Y | Y | Y | N |
| 3 ***Meyers*** | Y | Y | Y | Y | N | N | N | N |
| 4 Glickman | Y | Y | Y | Y | Y | Y | Y | N |
| 5 ***Nichols*** | Y | Y | Y | Y | Y | N | N | N |
| **KENTUCKY** | | | | | | | | |
| 1 Hubbard | Y | Y | Y | Y | Y | Y | Y | N |
| 2 Natcher | Y | Y | Y | Y | Y | Y | Y | N |
| 3 Mazzoli | Y | Y | Y | Y | Y | Y | Y | N |
| 4 ***Bunning*** | Y | Y | Y | Y | N | N | N | N |
| 5 ***Rogers*** | Y | Y | Y | Y | N | N | N | N |
| 6 ***Hopkins*** | Y | Y | Y | Y | N | N | N | N |
| 7 Perkins | Y | Y | Y | Y | Y | Y | Y | N |
| **LOUISIANA** | | | | | | | | |
| 1 ***Livingston*** | Y | Y | Y | Y | Y | N | N | N |
| 2 Jefferson | Y | Y | Y | Y | Y | Y | Y | N |
| 3 Tauzin | Y | Y | Y | Y | Y | ? | Y | N |
| 4 ***McCrery*** | Y | Y | Y | Y | N | N | N | N |
| 5 Huckaby | Y | Y | Y | Y | Y | Y | Y | N |
| 6 ***Baker*** | Y | Y | Y | Y | N | N | N | N |
| 7 Hayes | Y | Y | Y | Y | ? | Y | Y | N |
| 8 ***Holloway*** | Y | Y | Y | Y | N | N | N | N |
| **MAINE** | | | | | | | | |
| 1 Andrews | Y | Y | Y | Y | Y | Y | Y | N |
| 2 ***Snowe*** | Y | Y | Y | Y | Y | N | N | N |
| **MARYLAND** | | | | | | | | |
| 1 ***Gilchrest*** | Y | Y | Y | Y | N | N | N | N |
| 2 ***Bentley*** | ? | ? | ? | ? | N | N | N | N |
| 3 Cardin | Y | Y | Y | Y | Y | Y | Y | N |
| 4 McMillen | Y | Y | Y | Y | Y | Y | Y | N |
| 5 Hoyer | Y | Y | Y | Y | ? | ? | ? | N |
| 6 Byron | Y | Y | Y | Y | Y | Y | Y | N |
| 7 Mfume | Y | Y | Y | Y | Y | Y | Y | N |
| 8 ***Morella*** | Y | Y | Y | Y | N | ? | N | N |
| **MASSACHUSETTS** | | | | | | | | |
| 1 Olver | Y | Y | Y | Y | ? | Y | Y | N |
| 2 Neal | Y | Y | Y | Y | Y | Y | Y | N |
| 3 Early | Y | Y | Y | Y | Y | Y | N | N |
| 4 Frank | Y | ? | Y | Y | Y | Y | Y | N |
| 5 Atkins | Y | Y | Y | Y | Y | Y | Y | N |
| 6 Mavroules | ? | ? | Y | Y | Y | Y | Y | N |
| 7 Markey | Y | Y | Y | Y | Y | Y | Y | N |
| 8 Kennedy | Y | Y | Y | Y | Y | Y | N | N |
| 9 Moakley | Y | Y | Y | Y | Y | Y | Y | N |
| 10 Studds | Y | Y | Y | Y | Y | Y | Y | N |
| 11 Donnelly | Y | Y | Y | Y | Y | Y | Y | N |
| **MICHIGAN** | | | | | | | | |
| 1 Conyers | Y | Y | Y | Y | Y | Y | Y | N |
| 2 ***Pursell*** | Y | Y | Y | Y | N | N | N | N |
| 3 Wolpe | Y | Y | ? | Y | Y | Y | Y | N |
| 4 ***Upton*** | Y | Y | Y | Y | N | N | N | N |
| 5 ***Henry*** | Y | Y | Y | Y | N | N | N | N |
| 6 Carr | Y | Y | Y | Y | Y | Y | N | N |
| 7 Kildee | Y | Y | Y | Y | Y | Y | Y | N |
| 8 Traxler | Y | Y | Y | Y | Y | Y | Y | N |
| 9 ***Vander Jagt*** | ? | ? | ? | ? | ? | ? | ? | N |
| 10 ***Camp*** | Y | Y | Y | Y | N | N | N | N |
| 11 ***Davis*** | Y | Y | Y | Y | Y | N | N | N |
| 12 Bonior | Y | Y | Y | Y | Y | Y | Y | N |
| 13 Collins | Y | Y | Y | Y | Y | Y | Y | N |
| 14 Hertel | Y | Y | Y | Y | Y | Y | Y | N |
| 15 Ford | Y | Y | Y | Y | Y | Y | Y | N |
| 16 Dingell | Y | Y | Y | Y | Y | Y | Y | N |
| 17 Levin | Y | Y | Y | Y | Y | Y | Y | N |
| 18 ***Broomfield*** | Y | Y | Y | Y | Y | N | N | N |
| **MINNESOTA** | | | | | | | | |
| 1 Penny | Y | Y | Y | Y | N | Y | Y | N |
| 2 ***Weber*** | Y | Y | Y | Y | N | N | N | N |
| 3 ***Ramstad*** | Y | Y | Y | Y | N | N | N | N |
| 4 Vento | Y | Y | Y | Y | Y | Y | Y | N |

| | 18 | 19 | 20 | 21 | 22 | 23 | 24 | 25 |
|---|---|---|---|---|---|---|---|---|
| 5 Sabo | Y | Y | Y | Y | Y | Y | Y | N |
| 6 Sikorski | Y | Y | Y | Y | N | Y | Y | N |
| 7 Peterson | Y | Y | Y | Y | Y | Y | Y | N |
| 8 Oberstar | Y | Y | Y | Y | Y | Y | Y | N |
| **MISSISSIPPI** | | | | | | | | |
| 1 Whitten | ? | ? | ? | ? | ? | ? | ? | ? |
| 2 Espy | Y | Y | Y | Y | Y | Y | Y | N |
| 3 Montgomery | Y | Y | Y | Y | Y | Y | Y | N |
| 4 Parker | Y | Y | Y | Y | Y | Y | Y | N |
| 5 Taylor | Y | Y | Y | Y | Y | Y | N | N |
| **MISSOURI** | | | | | | | | |
| 1 Clay | Y | Y | Y | Y | N | Y | Y | N |
| 2 Horn | Y | Y | Y | Y | Y | Y | Y | N |
| 3 Gephardt | Y | Y | Y | Y | Y | Y | Y | N |
| 4 Skelton | Y | Y | Y | Y | Y | Y | Y | N |
| 5 Wheat | Y | Y | ? | Y | Y | Y | Y | N |
| 6 ***Coleman*** | Y | Y | Y | Y | N | N | N | N |
| 7 ***Hancock*** | Y | Y | Y | Y | N | N | N | N |
| 8 ***Emerson*** | Y | Y | Y | Y | Y | N | N | N |
| 9 Volkmer | Y | Y | Y | Y | Y | Y | Y | N |
| **MONTANA** | | | | | | | | |
| 1 Williams | Y | Y | Y | Y | Y | Y | N | N |
| 2 ***Marlenee*** | Y | Y | Y | Y | N | N | N | N |
| **NEBRASKA** | | | | | | | | |
| 1 ***Bereuter*** | Y | Y | Y | Y | N | N | N | N |
| 2 Hoagland | Y | Y | Y | Y | Y | Y | Y | N |
| 3 ***Barrett*** | Y | Y | Y | Y | N | N | N | N |
| **NEVADA** | | | | | | | | |
| 1 Bilbray | Y | Y | Y | Y | Y | Y | Y | N |
| 2 ***Vucanovich*** | Y | Y | Y | Y | N | N | N | N |
| **NEW HAMPSHIRE** | | | | | | | | |
| 1 ***Zeliff*** | Y | Y | Y | Y | N | N | N | N |
| 2 Swett | Y | Y | Y | Y | Y | Y | Y | N |
| **NEW JERSEY** | | | | | | | | |
| 1 Andrews | Y | Y | Y | Y | Y | Y | Y | N |
| 2 Hughes | Y | Y | Y | Y | Y | Y | N | N |
| 3 Pallone | Y | Y | Y | Y | Y | Y | Y | N |
| 4 ***Smith*** | Y | Y | Y | Y | ? | N | N | N |
| 5 ***Roukema*** | Y | Y | Y | Y | N | N | N | N |
| 6 Dwyer | Y | Y | Y | Y | Y | Y | Y | N |
| 7 ***Rinaldo*** | Y | Y | Y | Y | Y | N | N | N |
| 8 Roe | Y | Y | Y | Y | Y | Y | Y | N |
| 9 Torricelli | Y | Y | Y | Y | Y | Y | Y | N |
| 10 Payne | Y | Y | Y | Y | Y | Y | Y | N |
| 11 ***Gallo*** | Y | Y | Y | Y | N | N | N | N |
| 12 ***Zimmer*** | Y | Y | Y | Y | N | N | N | N |
| 13 ***Saxton*** | Y | Y | Y | Y | N | N | N | N |
| 14 Guarini | Y | Y | Y | Y | Y | Y | Y | N |
| **NEW MEXICO** | | | | | | | | |
| 1 ***Schiff*** | Y | Y | Y | Y | N | N | N | N |
| 2 ***Skeen*** | Y | Y | Y | Y | N | N | N | N |
| 3 Richardson | Y | Y | Y | Y | Y | Y | Y | N |
| **NEW YORK** | | | | | | | | |
| 1 Hochbrueckner | Y | Y | Y | Y | Y | Y | Y | N |
| 2 Downey | Y | Y | Y | Y | Y | Y | Y | N |
| 3 Mrazek | Y | Y | ? | ? | ? | Y | Y | N |
| 4 ***Lent*** | Y | Y | Y | ? | N | N | N | N |
| 5 ***McGrath*** | Y | Y | Y | Y | Y | N | N | N |
| 6 Flake | Y | Y | Y | Y | Y | Y | Y | N |
| 7 Ackerman | Y | Y | Y | Y | Y | Y | Y | N |
| 8 Scheuer | Y | Y | Y | Y | Y | Y | Y | N |
| 9 Manton | Y | Y | Y | Y | Y | Y | Y | N |
| 10 Schumer | Y | Y | Y | Y | Y | Y | Y | N |
| 11 Towns | Y | Y | Y | Y | Y | Y | Y | N |
| 12 Owens | Y | Y | Y | Y | Y | Y | Y | N |
| 13 Solarz | Y | Y | Y | Y | Y | Y | Y | N |
| 14 ***Molinari*** | Y | Y | Y | Y | N | N | N | N |
| 15 ***Green*** | Y | Y | Y | Y | Y | N | N | N |
| 16 Rangel | Y | Y | ? | Y | Y | Y | Y | N |
| 17 Weiss | Y | Y | Y | Y | Y | Y | Y | N |
| 18 Serrano | Y | Y | Y | Y | Y | Y | Y | N |
| 19 Engel | ? | ? | ? | ? | ? | Y | Y | N |
| 20 Lowey | Y | Y | Y | Y | Y | Y | Y | N |
| 21 ***Fish*** | Y | Y | Y | Y | Y | N | N | N |
| 22 ***Gilman*** | Y | Y | Y | Y | Y | N | N | N |
| 23 McNulty | Y | Y | Y | Y | Y | Y | Y | N |
| 24 ***Solomon*** | Y | Y | Y | Y | N | N | N | N |
| 25 ***Boehlert*** | Y | Y | Y | Y | N | N | N | N |
| 26 ***Martin*** | Y | Y | Y | Y | N | N | N | N |
| 27 ***Walsh*** | Y | Y | Y | Y | Y | N | N | N |
| 28 McHugh | Y | Y | Y | Y | Y | Y | Y | N |
| 29 ***Horton*** | Y | Y | Y | Y | Y | N | N | N |
| 30 Slaughter | Y | Y | Y | Y | Y | Y | Y | N |
| 31 ***Paxon*** | Y | Y | Y | Y | N | N | N | N |

| | 18 | 19 | 20 | 21 | 22 | 23 | 24 | 25 |
|---|---|---|---|---|---|---|---|---|
| 32 LaFalce | Y | Y | Y | Y | Y | Y | Y | N |
| 33 Nowak | Y | Y | Y | Y | Y | ? | Y | N |
| 34 ***Houghton*** | Y | Y | Y | Y | ? | N | N | N |
| **NORTH CAROLINA** | | | | | | | | |
| 1 Jones | Y | Y | Y | Y | Y | Y | Y | N |
| 2 Valentine | Y | Y | Y | Y | Y | Y | ? | ? |
| 3 Lancaster | Y | Y | Y | Y | Y | Y | Y | N |
| 4 Price | Y | Y | Y | Y | Y | Y | Y | N |
| 5 Neal | Y | Y | Y | Y | Y | Y | Y | N |
| 6 ***Coble*** | Y | Y | Y | Y | N | N | N | N |
| 7 Rose | Y | Y | Y | Y | Y | Y | Y | N |
| 8 Hefner | Y | Y | Y | Y | Y | Y | Y | N |
| 9 ***McMillan*** | Y | Y | Y | Y | N | N | N | N |
| 10 ***Ballenger*** | Y | Y | Y | Y | N | N | N | N |
| 11 ***Taylor*** | Y | Y | Y | + | N | N | N | N |
| **NORTH DAKOTA** | | | | | | | | |
| AL Dorgan | Y | Y | Y | Y | Y | Y | N | N |
| **OHIO** | | | | | | | | |
| 1 Luken | Y | Y | Y | Y | Y | Y | Y | N |
| 2 ***Gradison*** | Y | Y | Y | Y | Y | N | N | N |
| 3 Hall | Y | Y | Y | Y | Y | Y | Y | N |
| 4 ***Oxley*** | Y | Y | Y | Y | Y | ? | N | N |
| 5 ***Gillmor*** | Y | Y | Y | Y | Y | N | N | N |
| 6 ***McEwen*** | Y | Y | Y | Y | N | N | N | N |
| 7 ***Hobson*** | Y | Y | Y | Y | ? | N | N | N |
| 8 ***Boehner*** | Y | Y | Y | Y | N | N | N | N |
| 9 Kaptur | Y | Y | Y | Y | Y | Y | Y | N |
| 10 ***Miller*** | Y | Y | Y | Y | N | N | N | N |
| 11 Eckart | Y | Y | Y | Y | Y | ? | Y | N |
| 12 ***Kasich*** | Y | Y | Y | Y | ? | N | N | N |
| 13 Pease | Y | Y | Y | Y | ? | Y | Y | N |
| 14 Sawyer | Y | Y | Y | Y | Y | Y | Y | N |
| 15 ***Wylie*** | Y | Y | Y | Y | Y | N | N | N |
| 16 ***Regula*** | Y | Y | Y | Y | N | N | N | N |
| 17 Traficant | Y | Y | Y | Y | Y | Y | Y | N |
| 18 Applegate | Y | Y | Y | Y | Y | Y | Y | N |
| 19 Feighan | Y | Y | Y | Y | Y | Y | Y | N |
| 20 Oakar | Y | Y | Y | Y | Y | Y | Y | N |
| 21 Stokes | Y | Y | Y | Y | Y | Y | Y | N |
| **OKLAHOMA** | | | | | | | | |
| 1 ***Inhofe*** | Y | Y | Y | Y | N | N | N | N |
| 2 Synar | Y | Y | Y | Y | Y | Y | Y | N |
| 3 Brewster | Y | Y | Y | Y | ? | Y | Y | N |
| 4 McCurdy | Y | Y | Y | Y | Y | Y | Y | N |
| 5 ***Edwards*** | Y | Y | Y | Y | Y | N | N | N |
| 6 English | Y | Y | Y | Y | Y | Y | Y | N |
| **OREGON** | | | | | | | | |
| 1 AuCoin | Y | Y | Y | Y | Y | Y | N | N |
| 2 ***Smith*** | Y | Y | Y | Y | N | N | N | N |
| 3 Wyden | ? | + | ? | ? | Y | Y | N | N |
| 4 DeFazio | Y | Y | Y | Y | Y | Y | Y | N |
| 5 Kopetski | Y | Y | Y | Y | Y | Y | Y | N |
| **PENNSYLVANIA** | | | | | | | | |
| 1 Foglietta | Y | Y | Y | Y | Y | Y | Y | N |
| 2 Blackwell | Y | Y | Y | Y | Y | Y | Y | N |
| 3 Borski | Y | Y | Y | Y | Y | Y | Y | N |
| 4 Kolter | ? | ? | ? | ? | Y | Y | Y | N |
| 5 ***Schulze*** | Y | Y | Y | Y | Y | N | N | N |
| 6 Yatron | Y | Y | Y | Y | Y | Y | Y | N |
| 7 ***Weldon*** | Y | Y | Y | Y | N | N | N | N |
| 8 Kostmayer | Y | Y | Y | Y | Y | Y | Y | N |
| 9 ***Shuster*** | Y | Y | Y | Y | Y | N | N | N |
| 10 ***McDade*** | Y | Y | Y | Y | N | N | N | N |
| 11 Kanjorski | Y | Y | Y | Y | Y | Y | Y | N |
| 12 Murtha | ? | ? | ? | ? | Y | Y | Y | N |
| 13 ***Coughlin*** | Y | Y | Y | Y | ? | N | N | N |
| 14 Coyne | Y | Y | Y | Y | Y | Y | Y | N |
| 15 ***Ritter*** | Y | Y | Y | Y | Y | N | N | N |
| 16 ***Walker*** | Y | Y | Y | Y | N | N | N | N |
| 17 ***Gekas*** | Y | Y | Y | Y | N | N | N | N |
| 18 ***Santorum*** | Y | Y | Y | Y | N | N | N | N |
| 19 ***Goodling*** | Y | Y | Y | Y | N | N | N | N |
| 20 Gaydos | Y | Y | Y | Y | Y | ? | Y | N |
| 21 ***Ridge*** | Y | Y | Y | Y | N | N | N | N |
| 22 Murphy | Y | Y | Y | Y | N | Y | Y | N |
| 23 ***Clinger*** | Y | Y | Y | Y | Y | N | N | N |
| **RHODE ISLAND** | | | | | | | | |
| 1 ***Machtley*** | Y | Y | Y | Y | N | N | N | N |
| 2 Reed | Y | Y | Y | Y | Y | Y | Y | N |
| **SOUTH CAROLINA** | | | | | | | | |
| 1 ***Ravenel*** | Y | Y | Y | Y | Y | N | N | N |
| 2 ***Spence*** | Y | Y | Y | Y | Y | N | N | N |
| 3 Derrick | Y | Y | Y | Y | Y | Y | Y | N |
| 4 Patterson | Y | Y | Y | Y | Y | Y | Y | N |
| 5 Spratt | Y | Y | Y | Y | Y | Y | Y | N |
| 6 Tallon | Y | Y | Y | Y | Y | Y | Y | N |

| | 18 | 19 | 20 | 21 | 22 | 23 | 24 | 25 |
|---|---|---|---|---|---|---|---|---|
| **SOUTH DAKOTA** | | | | | | | | |
| AL Johnson | Y | Y | Y | Y | Y | Y | Y | N |
| **TENNESSEE** | | | | | | | | |
| 1 ***Quillen*** | Y | Y | Y | Y | Y | N | N | N |
| 2 ***Duncan*** | Y | Y | Y | Y | N | N | N | N |
| 3 Lloyd | Y | Y | Y | Y | Y | Y | Y | N |
| 4 Cooper | Y | Y | Y | Y | Y | Y | Y | N |
| 5 Clement | Y | Y | Y | Y | Y | Y | Y | N |
| 6 Gordon | Y | Y | Y | Y | Y | Y | Y | N |
| 7 ***Sundquist*** | Y | Y | Y | Y | N | N | N | N |
| 8 Tanner | Y | Y | Y | Y | Y | Y | Y | N |
| 9 Ford | Y | Y | Y | Y | Y | Y | Y | N |
| **TEXAS** | | | | | | | | |
| 1 Chapman | Y | Y | Y | Y | Y | Y | Y | N |
| 2 Wilson | Y | Y | Y | Y | Y | Y | Y | N |
| 3 ***Johnson*** | Y | Y | Y | Y | Y | N | N | N |
| 4 Hall | Y | Y | Y | Y | Y | Y | Y | N |
| 5 Bryant | Y | Y | Y | Y | Y | Y | Y | N |
| 6 ***Barton*** | Y | Y | Y | Y | N | N | N | N |
| 7 ***Archer*** | Y | Y | Y | Y | Y | ? | N | N |
| 8 ***Fields*** | Y | Y | Y | Y | ? | N | N | N |
| 9 Brooks | Y | Y | Y | Y | Y | Y | Y | N |
| 10 Pickle | Y | Y | Y | Y | Y | Y | Y | N |
| 11 Edwards | Y | Y | Y | Y | Y | Y | Y | N |
| 12 Geren | Y | Y | Y | Y | Y | Y | Y | N |
| 13 Sarpalius | Y | Y | Y | Y | Y | Y | Y | N |
| 14 Laughlin | Y | Y | Y | Y | Y | Y | Y | N |
| 15 de la Garza | Y | Y | Y | Y | Y | Y | Y | N |
| 16 Coleman | ? | ? | ? | ? | ? | ? | ? | ? |
| 17 Stenholm | Y | Y | Y | Y | Y | Y | Y | N |
| 18 Washington | ? | ? | ? | ? | ? | Y | Y | N |
| 19 ***Combest*** | Y | Y | Y | Y | Y | N | N | N |
| 20 Gonzalez | Y | Y | Y | Y | Y | Y | Y | N |
| 21 ***Smith*** | Y | Y | Y | Y | ? | ? | ? | ? |
| 22 ***DeLay*** | Y | Y | Y | Y | N | N | N | N |
| 23 Bustamante | Y | Y | Y | Y | Y | Y | Y | N |
| 24 Frost | Y | Y | Y | Y | Y | Y | Y | N |
| 25 Andrews | Y | Y | Y | Y | Y | Y | Y | N |
| 26 ***Armey*** | Y | Y | Y | Y | N | N | N | N |
| 27 Ortiz | Y | Y | Y | Y | Y | Y | Y | N |
| **UTAH** | | | | | | | | |
| 1 ***Hansen*** | Y | Y | Y | Y | ? | N | N | N |
| 2 Owens | Y | Y | Y | Y | Y | Y | Y | N |
| 3 Orton | Y | Y | Y | Y | Y | Y | Y | Y |
| **VERMONT** | | | | | | | | |
| AL *Sanders* | Y | Y | Y | Y | ? | Y | N | N |
| **VIRGINIA** | | | | | | | | |
| 1 ***Bateman*** | Y | Y | Y | Y | Y | N | N | N |
| 2 Pickett | Y | Y | Y | Y | Y | Y | Y | N |
| 3 ***Bliley*** | Y | Y | Y | Y | N | N | N | N |
| 4 Sisisky | Y | Y | Y | Y | Y | Y | Y | N |
| 5 Payne | Y | Y | Y | Y | Y | Y | Y | N |
| 6 Olin | Y | Y | Y | Y | Y | Y | Y | N |
| 7 ***Allen*** | Y | Y | Y | Y | N | N | N | N |
| 8 Moran | Y | Y | Y | Y | Y | Y | Y | N |
| 9 Boucher | Y | Y | Y | Y | Y | Y | Y | N |
| 10 ***Wolf*** | Y | Y | Y | Y | N | N | N | N |
| **WASHINGTON** | | | | | | | | |
| 1 ***Miller*** | ? | ? | ? | ? | N | N | N | N |
| 2 Swift | Y | Y | Y | Y | Y | ? | Y | N |
| 3 Unsoeld | Y | Y | Y | Y | Y | Y | Y | N |
| 4 ***Morrison*** | Y | Y | Y | Y | Y | N | N | N |
| 5 Foley | | | | | | | | |
| 6 Dicks | Y | Y | Y | Y | Y | Y | Y | N |
| 7 McDermott | Y | Y | Y | Y | ? | Y | Y | N |
| 8 ***Chandler*** | Y | Y | Y | Y | P | N | N | N |
| **WEST VIRGINIA** | | | | | | | | |
| 1 Mollohan | Y | Y | Y | Y | ? | Y | Y | N |
| 2 Staggers | Y | Y | Y | Y | Y | Y | Y | N |
| 3 Wise | Y | Y | Y | Y | Y | Y | Y | N |
| 4 Rahall | Y | Y | Y | Y | ? | Y | Y | N |
| **WISCONSIN** | | | | | | | | |
| 1 Aspin | Y | Y | Y | Y | Y | Y | Y | N |
| 2 ***Klug*** | Y | Y | Y | Y | N | N | N | N |
| 3 ***Gunderson*** | Y | Y | Y | Y | Y | N | N | N |
| 4 Kleczka | Y | Y | Y | Y | Y | Y | Y | N |
| 5 Moody | Y | Y | Y | Y | ? | Y | Y | N |
| 6 ***Petri*** | Y | Y | Y | Y | Y | N | N | N |
| 7 Obey | Y | P | Y | Y | Y | Y | N | N |
| 8 ***Roth*** | + | + | + | + | N | N | N | N |
| 9 ***Sensenbrenner*** | Y | Y | Y | Y | N | N | N | N |
| **WYOMING** | | | | | | | | |
| AL ***Thomas*** | Y | Y | Y | Y | N | N | N | N |

Southern states - Ala., Ark., Fla., Ga., Ky., La., Miss., N.C., Okla., S.C., Tenn., Texas, Va.
Omitted votes are quorum calls, which CQ does not include in its vote charts.

**26. Procedural Motion.** Approval of the House Journal of Wednesday, Feb. 26. Motion agreed to 285-115: R 45-110; D 240-5 (ND 161-5, SD 79-0); I 0-0, Feb. 27, 1992.

**28. HR 4210. 1992 Tax Bill/Republican Substitute.** Archer, R-Texas, substitute amendment to implement a seven-point plan that included a cut in the capital gains tax rate, a $5,000 two-year tax credit and penalty-free withdrawals from Individual Retirement Accounts for first-time home buyers, passive loss deductions for real estate developers, an increase in the rate of depreciation for business equipment and new rules encouraging real estate investment by pension funds. Rejected 166-264: R 152-13; D 14-250 (ND 5-177, SD 9-73); I 0-1, Feb. 27, 1992. A "yea" was a vote in support of the president's position.

**30. HR 4210. 1992 Tax Bill/Democratic Substitute.** Rostenkowski, D-Ill., substitute amendment to give workers a temporary tax credit worth up to $400 for couples and $200 for individuals a year to be paid for with a 10 percent surtax on millionaires and a new top income tax rate of 35 percent on individuals with taxable income higher than $85,000 and couples above $145,000. The package also included indexing of capital gains, passive loss deductions for real estate developers, permanent extension of certain tax breaks, penalty-free withdrawals from Individual Retirement Accounts for first homes and medical and educational expenses, and other provisions designed to provide economic growth. Adopted 221-210: R 1-164; D 219-46 (ND 156-27, SD 63-19); I 1-0, Feb. 27, 1992. A "nay" was a vote in support of the president's position.

**31. HR 4210. 1992 Tax Bill/Passage.** Passage of the bill to give workers a temporary tax credit worth up to $400 for couples and $200 for individuals a year to be paid for with a 10 percent surtax on millionaires and a new top income tax rate of 35 percent on individuals with taxable income higher than $85,000 and couples above $145,000. The package included indexing of capital gains, passive loss deductions for real estate developers, permanent extension of certain tax breaks, penalty-free withdrawals from Individual Retirement Accounts for first homes and medical and educational expenses, and other provisions designed to spur economic growth. Passed 221-209: R 1-163; D 219-46 (ND 156-27, SD 63-19); I 1-0, Feb. 27, 1992. A "nay" was a vote in support of the president's position.

**32. HR 3844. Haitian Refugee Protection/Extended Protections.** Conyers, D-Mich., amendment to grant temporary protected status for Haitians in the custody of the United States until democracy returned to Haiti, even if they arrived after Feb. 5. Rejected 96-304: R 1-154; D 94-150 (ND 82-88, SD 12-62); I 1-0, Feb. 27, 1992.

**33. HR 3844. Haitian Refugee Protection/Reimbursement.** Shaw, R-Fla., amendment to authorize reimbursement by the federal government to state and local governments for the incremental costs associated with Haitians permitted to enter the United States under the bill. Adopted 241-144: R 138-11; D 103-132 (ND 76-89, SD 27-43; I 0-1), Feb. 27, 1992.

**34. HR 3844. Haitian Refugee Protection/Passage.** Passage of the bill to suspend for six months the repatriation of Haitians who were in the custody of the United States before Feb. 5, 1992; require the administration to report on the fate of repatriated Haitians; provide 2,000 refugee admission slots to Haitians; and prohibit the admission to the United States of any person involved in the September 1991 coup in Haiti. Passed 217-165: R 18-131; D 198-34 (ND 150-12, SD 48-22); I 1-0, Feb. 27, 1992. A "nay" was a vote in support of the president's position.

**35. HR 2321. Dayton Aviation Heritage Park.** Vento, D-Minn., motion to suspend the rules and pass the bill to establish the Dayton (Ohio) Aviation Heritage National Historical Park to preserve sites and structures associated with the Wright Brothers and aviation development. Motion agreed to 278-133: R 63-93; D 214-40 (ND 157-18, SD 57-22); I 1-0, March 4, 1992. A two-thirds majority of those present and voting (274 in this case) was required for passage under suspension of the rules. A "nay" was a vote in support of the president's position.

## KEY

| | |
|---|---|
| Y | Voted for (yea). |
| # | Paired for. |
| + | Announced for. |
| N | Voted against (nay). |
| X | Paired against. |
| − | Announced against. |
| P | Voted "present." |
| C | Voted "present" to avoid possible conflict of interest. |
| ? | Did not vote or otherwise make a position known. |

Democrats   ***Republicans***
*Independent*

| | 26 | 28 | 30 | 31 | 32 | 33 | 34 | 35 |
|---|---|---|---|---|---|---|---|---|
| **ALABAMA** | | | | | | | | |
| 1 *Callahan* | N | Y | N | N | N | Y | N | N |
| 2 *Dickinson* | ? | # | ? | X | ? | ? | ? | Y |
| 3 Browder | Y | Y | N | Y | N | N | N | Y |
| 4 Bevill | Y | N | Y | N | N | N | N | Y |
| 5 Cramer | Y | Y | Y | N | N | N | N | Y |
| 6 Erdreich | Y | N | Y | N | N | N | N | Y |
| 7 Harris | Y | N | Y | Y | N | N | N | Y |
| **ALASKA** | | | | | | | | |
| AL *Young* | N | Y | N | N | N | Y | N | Y |
| **ARIZONA** | | | | | | | | |
| 1 *Rhodes* | N | Y | N | N | N | ? | ? | Y |
| 2 Pastor | Y | Y | Y | Y | Y | Y | Y | Y |
| 3 *Stump* | N | Y | N | N | N | Y | N | N |
| 4 *Kyl* | ? | Y | N | N | N | Y | N | N |
| 5 *Kolbe* | N | Y | N | N | N | Y | N | Y |
| **ARKANSAS** | | | | | | | | |
| 1 Alexander | ? | N | Y | Y | ? | ? | ? | Y |
| 2 Thornton | Y | N | Y | Y | ? | ? | Y | ? |
| 3 *Hammerschmidt* | Y | Y | N | N | N | Y | N | Y |
| 4 Anthony | Y | N | Y | Y | N | X | Y | Y |
| **CALIFORNIA** | | | | | | | | |
| 1 *Riggs* | ? | Y | N | N | Y | Y | Y | Y |
| 2 *Herger* | N | Y | N | N | ? | ? | ? | N |
| 3 Matsui | Y | N | Y | Y | Y | Y | Y | Y |
| 4 Fazio | Y | N | Y | Y | Y | Y | Y | Y |
| 5 Pelosi | Y | N | Y | Y | Y | Y | Y | Y |
| 6 Boxer | Y | N | Y | Y | Y | Y | Y | ? |
| 7 Miller | Y | N | Y | Y | N | N | Y | Y |
| 8 Dellums | Y | N | N | N | Y | Y | Y | Y |
| 9 Stark | Y | N | Y | Y | Y | ? | Y | Y |
| 10 Edwards | Y | N | Y | Y | Y | N | Y | Y |
| 11 Lantos | Y | N | Y | Y | Y | Y | Y | Y |
| 12 *Campbell* | N | Y | N | N | N | Y | N | N |
| 13 Mineta | Y | N | Y | Y | Y | N | Y | Y |
| 14 *Doolittle* | N | Y | N | N | N | N | N | Y |
| 15 Condit | Y | N | N | N | Y | Y | N | N |
| 16 Panetta | Y | N | Y | Y | Y | Y | Y | Y |
| 17 Dooley | Y | N | Y | Y | Y | Y | Y | Y |
| 18 Lehman | Y | N | N | N | Y | Y | Y | Y |
| 19 *Lagomarsino* | N | Y | N | N | N | Y | N | N |
| 20 *Thomas* | N | Y | N | N | ? | # | X | Y |
| 21 *Gallegly* | N | Y | N | N | N | Y | N | N |
| 22 *Moorhead* | N | Y | N | N | N | Y | N | N |
| 23 Beilenson | Y | N | N | N | N | N | Y | Y |
| 24 Waxman | Y | N | Y | Y | N | N | Y | Y |
| 25 Roybal | Y | N | Y | Y | N | Y | N | Y |
| 26 Berman | ? | N | Y | Y | Y | Y | Y | Y |
| 27 Levine | Y | N | Y | Y | ? | ? | ? | ? |
| 28 Dixon | ? | N | Y | Y | Y | Y | Y | Y |
| 29 Waters | ? | N | Y | Y | Y | Y | Y | Y |
| 30 Martinez | Y | N | Y | Y | N | Y | N | Y |
| 31 Dymally | Y | N | Y | Y | ? | ? | ? | Y |
| 32 Anderson | Y | N | Y | Y | N | Y | N | Y |
| 33 *Dreier* | N | Y | N | N | N | Y | N | N |
| 34 Torres | ? | N | Y | Y | ? | ? | ? | Y |
| 35 *Lewis* | N | Y | N | N | N | Y | N | Y |
| 36 Brown | Y | N | Y | N | Y | N | Y | Y |
| 37 *McCandless* | N | Y | N | N | N | Y | N | N |
| 38 *Dornan* | ? | Y | N | N | N | Y | N | Y |
| 39 *Dannemeyer* | N | Y | N | N | ? | ? | ? | ? |
| 40 *Cox* | N | Y | N | N | N | Y | N | N |
| 41 *Lowery* | N | Y | N | N | N | Y | N | N |

| | 26 | 28 | 30 | 31 | 32 | 33 | 34 | 35 |
|---|---|---|---|---|---|---|---|---|
| 42 *Rohrabacher* | N | Y | N | N | N | Y | N | N |
| 43 *Packard* | Y | Y | N | N | N | Y | N | Y |
| 44 *Cunningham* | N | Y | N | N | N | N | N | N |
| 45 *Hunter* | N | Y | N | N | N | Y | N | N |
| **COLORADO** | | | | | | | | |
| 1 Schroeder | N | N | N | N | Y | N | Y | N |
| 2 Skaggs | Y | N | Y | N | Y | N | Y | N |
| 3 Campbell | Y | N | Y | Y | N | Y | N | Y |
| 4 *Allard* | N | Y | N | N | N | N | N | N |
| 5 *Hefley* | N | Y | N | N | N | N | N | N |
| 6 *Schaefer* | N | Y | N | N | N | Y | N | N |
| **CONNECTICUT** | | | | | | | | |
| 1 Kennelly | Y | N | Y | Y | Y | N | Y | Y |
| 2 Gejdenson | Y | N | Y | Y | Y | Y | Y | Y |
| 3 DeLauro | Y | N | Y | Y | Y | N | Y | Y |
| 4 *Shays* | N | Y | N | N | N | N | N | N |
| 5 *Franks* | N | Y | N | N | N | N | N | N |
| 6 *Johnson* | Y | Y | N | N | N | Y | Y | Y |
| **DELAWARE** | | | | | | | | |
| AL *Carper* | Y | N | N | N | N | N | N | Y |
| **FLORIDA** | | | | | | | | |
| 1 *Hutto* | Y | Y | N | N | N | Y | N | N |
| 2 Peterson | Y | N | Y | N | Y | Y | Y | Y |
| 3 Bennett | Y | Y | Y | Y | Y | Y | Y | Y |
| 4 *James* | N | Y | N | N | N | N | N | N |
| 5 *McCollum* | N | Y | N | N | N | Y | N | N |
| 6 *Stearns* | N | Y | N | N | N | N | N | N |
| 7 Gibbons | Y | N | Y | Y | Y | Y | Y | ? |
| 8 *Young* | N | N | N | N | N | Y | N | N |
| 9 *Bilirakis* | N | Y | N | N | N | Y | N | ? |
| 10 *Ireland* | N | Y | N | N | N | Y | N | Y |
| 11 Bacchus | Y | N | Y | Y | N | Y | N | Y |
| 12 *Lewis* | N | N | N | N | N | Y | N | N |
| 13 *Goss* | N | Y | N | N | N | Y | N | N |
| 14 Johnston | Y | N | Y | Y | N | Y | ? | Y |
| 15 *Shaw* | N | Y | N | N | N | Y | N | Y |
| 16 Smith | Y | N | Y | Y | Y | N | Y | Y |
| 17 Lehman | Y | N | Y | Y | Y | Y | Y | Y |
| 18 *Ros−Lehtinen* | N | Y | N | N | N | Y | Y | ? |
| 19 Fascell | Y | N | Y | Y | N | Y | Y | ? |
| **GEORGIA** | | | | | | | | |
| 1 Thomas | ? | N | N | N | N | N | N | Y |
| 2 Hatcher | Y | N | Y | Y | ? | ? | ? | Y |
| 3 Ray | ? | X | X | ? | ? | ? | ? | N |
| 4 Jones | Y | N | Y | Y | Y | Y | Y | Y |
| 5 Lewis | Y | N | Y | Y | N | Y | N | Y |
| 6 *Gingrich* | N | Y | N | N | N | ? | ? | Y |
| 7 Darden | Y | N | Y | N | Y | N | Y | Y |
| 8 Rowland | Y | N | N | N | N | N | N | X |
| 9 Jenkins | Y | N | Y | Y | N | N | Y | Y |
| 10 Barnard | Y | N | N | N | ? | ? | ? | Y |
| **HAWAII** | | | | | | | | |
| 1 Abercrombie | Y | N | Y | Y | Y | Y | Y | Y |
| 2 Mink | Y | N | Y | Y | Y | Y | Y | Y |
| **IDAHO** | | | | | | | | |
| 1 LaRocco | Y | N | Y | Y | N | N | Y | Y |
| 2 Stallings | Y | N | N | N | ? | ? | ? | Y |
| **ILLINOIS** | | | | | | | | |
| 1 Hayes | Y | N | Y | Y | N | N | Y | Y |
| 2 Savage | ? | N | Y | Y | Y | N | Y | ? |
| 3 Russo | Y | N | N | N | ? | ? | ? | Y |
| 4 Sangmeister | Y | Y | Y | Y | N | Y | N | Y |
| 5 Lipinski | Y | N | Y | N | Y | N | Y | N |
| 6 *Hyde* | Y | N | N | N | N | Y | ? | Y |
| 7 Collins | Y | N | Y | Y | N | Y | N | Y |
| 8 Rostenkowski | Y | N | Y | ? | ? | ? | ? | Y |
| 9 Yates | Y | N | Y | Y | N | Y | ? | Y |
| 10 *Porter* | Y | N | N | N | N | Y | N | N |
| 11 Annunzio | Y | N | Y | N | Y | N | Y | Y |
| 12 *Crane* | ? | Y | N | N | N | Y | N | N |
| 13 *Fawell* | N | Y | N | N | N | N | N | N |
| 14 *Hastert* | N | Y | N | N | N | N | N | N |
| 15 *Ewing* | Y | N | N | N | N | N | N | N |
| 16 Cox | N | Y | Y | Y | N | Y | Y | Y |
| 17 Evans | Y | N | Y | Y | Y | N | Y | Y |
| 18 *Michel* | N | Y | N | N | N | Y | N | Y |
| 19 Bruce | Y | N | Y | N | Y | N | Y | Y |
| 20 Durbin | Y | N | Y | Y | Y | N | Y | Y |
| 21 Costello | Y | N | Y | N | Y | N | Y | N |
| 22 Poshard | Y | N | Y | N | Y | N | Y | N |
| **INDIANA** | | | | | | | | |
| 1 Visclosky | Y | N | Y | N | N | N | Y | Y |
| 2 Sharp | Y | N | Y | Y | N | N | Y | Y |
| 3 Roemer | Y | N | N | N | N | N | Y | N |

ND  Northern Democrats    SD  Southern Democrats

| | 26 | 28 | 30 | 31 | 32 | 33 | 34 | 35 |
|---|---|---|---|---|---|---|---|---|
| 4 Long | Y | N | N | N | N | Y | Y | Y |
| 5 Jontz | Y | N | Y | Y | Y | Y | Y | Y |
| 6 ***Burton*** | N | Y | N | N | N | ? | ? | N |
| 7 ***Myers*** | Y | Y | N | N | N | Y | N | Y |
| 8 McCloskey | Y | N | Y | Y | N | N | Y | Y |
| 9 Hamilton | Y | N | N | N | N | N | Y | Y |
| 10 Jacobs | N | N | Y | Y | Y | N | Y | N |
| **IOWA** | | | | | | | | |
| 1 ***Leach*** | N | Y | N | N | N | Y | N | Y |
| 2 ***Nussle*** | N | N | N | N | N | Y | N | N |
| 3 Nagle | Y | N | Y | Y | Y | Y | Y | Y |
| 4 Smith | Y | N | Y | Y | Y | N | Y | Y |
| 5 ***Lightfoot*** | N | N | N | N | N | Y | N | Y |
| 6 ***Grandy*** | N | Y | N | N | N | Y | N | N |
| **KANSAS** | | | | | | | | |
| 1 ***Roberts*** | N | Y | N | N | N | N | N | N |
| 2 Slattery | Y | N | Y | Y | N | N | Y | N |
| 3 ***Meyers*** | ? | Y | N | N | N | N | N | N |
| 4 Glickman | Y | N | Y | Y | N | N | Y | Y |
| 5 ***Nichols*** | Y | Y | N | N | N | N | N | N |
| **KENTUCKY** | | | | | | | | |
| 1 Hubbard | Y | N | Y | Y | N | N | Y | N |
| 2 Natcher | Y | N | Y | Y | N | N | Y | N |
| 3 Mazzoli | Y | N | Y | Y | N | N | Y | Y |
| 4 ***Bunning*** | N | Y | N | N | N | Y | N | N |
| 5 ***Rogers*** | N | N | N | N | N | N | Y | Y |
| 6 ***Hopkins*** | N | Y | N | N | N | Y | N | N |
| 7 Perkins | Y | N | Y | Y | N | N | Y | Y |
| **LOUISIANA** | | | | | | | | |
| 1 ***Livingston*** | Y | Y | N | N | N | Y | N | ? |
| 2 Jefferson | Y | N | Y | Y | Y | Y | Y | Y |
| 3 Tauzin | Y | N | N | N | N | N | N | Y |
| 4 ***McCrery*** | N | Y | N | N | N | Y | N | N |
| 5 Huckaby | Y | N | Y | Y | N | N | Y | Y |
| 6 ***Baker*** | N | Y | N | N | N | Y | N | N |
| 7 Hayes | Y | N | N | N | N | N | Y | Y |
| 8 ***Holloway*** | ? | Y | N | N | N | Y | N | N |
| **MAINE** | | | | | | | | |
| 1 Andrews | Y | N | Y | Y | Y | Y | Y | N |
| 2 ***Snowe*** | N | N | Y | Y | N | Y | N | N |
| **MARYLAND** | | | | | | | | |
| 1 ***Gilchrest*** | N | Y | N | N | N | Y | N | Y |
| 2 ***Bentley*** | N | Y | N | ? | N | Y | N | N |
| 3 Cardin | Y | N | Y | Y | N | Y | Y | Y |
| 4 McMillen | Y | N | N | N | N | Y | Y | Y |
| 5 Hoyer | Y | N | Y | Y | N | ? | # | Y |
| 6 Byron | Y | N | Y | Y | N | N | N | N |
| 7 Mfume | ? | N | Y | Y | Y | Y | Y | Y |
| 8 ***Morella*** | N | Y | N | N | N | N | Y | Y |
| **MASSACHUSETTS** | | | | | | | | |
| 1 Olver | Y | N | Y | Y | Y | Y | Y | Y |
| 2 Neal | Y | N | Y | Y | Y | Y | Y | Y |
| 3 Early | Y | N | N | N | Y | N | Y | Y |
| 4 Frank | Y | N | Y | Y | Y | N | Y | Y |
| 5 Atkins | Y | N | Y | Y | Y | Y | Y | Y |
| 6 Mavroules | Y | N | Y | Y | N | Y | Y | Y |
| 7 Markey | Y | N | Y | Y | Y | N | Y | Y |
| 8 Kennedy | Y | N | Y | Y | Y | Y | Y | Y |
| 9 Moakley | ? | N | Y | Y | Y | Y | ? | Y |
| 10 Studds | Y | N | Y | Y | Y | Y | Y | Y |
| 11 Donnelly | Y | N | Y | Y | N | Y | Y | Y |
| **MICHIGAN** | | | | | | | | |
| 1 Conyers | Y | N | Y | Y | Y | N | Y | Y |
| 2 ***Pursell*** | N | N | N | N | N | N | N | Y |
| 3 Wolpe | Y | N | Y | Y | Y | Y | Y | Y |
| 4 ***Upton*** | N | Y | N | N | N | N | Y | Y |
| 5 ***Henry*** | N | Y | N | N | N | Y | N | N |
| 6 Carr | ? | N | N | N | N | N | N | Y |
| 7 Kildee | Y | N | Y | Y | Y | N | Y | Y |
| 8 Traxler | Y | N | Y | Y | Y | Y | Y | Y |
| 9 ***Vander Jagt*** | Y | Y | N | N | N | Y | N | Y |
| 10 ***Camp*** | N | Y | N | N | N | Y | N | N |
| 11 ***Davis*** | Y | Y | N | N | N | ? | ? | Y |
| 12 Bonior | Y | N | Y | Y | Y | N | Y | Y |
| 13 Collins | ? | N | Y | Y | Y | N | Y | Y |
| 14 Hertel | Y | N | Y | Y | N | N | Y | ? |
| 15 Ford | Y | N | Y | Y | # | X | # | Y |
| 16 Dingell | ? | N | Y | Y | N | N | Y | Y |
| 17 Levin | Y | N | Y | Y | Y | N | Y | Y |
| 18 ***Broomfield*** | P | Y | N | N | N | Y | N | Y |
| **MINNESOTA** | | | | | | | | |
| 1 Penny | Y | N | Y | Y | Y | Y | Y | N |
| 2 ***Weber*** | N | Y | N | N | N | Y | Y | ? |
| 3 ***Ramstad*** | N | Y | N | N | N | Y | N | N |
| 4 Vento | Y | N | Y | Y | Y | Y | Y | Y |

| | 26 | 28 | 30 | 31 | 32 | 33 | 34 | 35 |
|---|---|---|---|---|---|---|---|---|
| 5 Sabo | Y | N | N | N | Y | N | Y | Y |
| 6 Sikorski | N | N | Y | Y | Y | Y | Y | Y |
| 7 Peterson | Y | N | N | N | Y | Y | ? | Y |
| 8 Oberstar | Y | N | Y | Y | Y | Y | Y | ? |
| **MISSISSIPPI** | | | | | | | | |
| 1 Whitten | ? | ? | ? | ? | ? | ? | ? | ? |
| 2 Espy | Y | N | Y | Y | Y | N | Y | Y |
| 3 Montgomery | Y | N | N | N | N | Y | N | Y |
| 4 Parker | Y | N | N | N | N | Y | N | Y |
| 5 Taylor | Y | N | N | N | N | N | N | N |
| **MISSOURI** | | | | | | | | |
| 1 Clay | N | N | Y | Y | Y | N | Y | Y |
| 2 Horn | Y | N | Y | Y | N | N | Y | N |
| 3 Gephardt | Y | N | Y | Y | N | N | Y | Y |
| 4 Skelton | Y | N | N | N | N | N | N | Y |
| 5 Wheat | Y | N | Y | Y | Y | N | Y | Y |
| 6 ***Coleman*** | N | Y | N | N | N | Y | N | N |
| 7 ***Hancock*** | N | Y | N | N | N | Y | N | N |
| 8 ***Emerson*** | N | Y | N | N | N | Y | N | Y |
| 9 Volkmer | Y | N | Y | Y | N | Y | N | Y |
| **MONTANA** | | | | | | | | |
| 1 Williams | Y | N | Y | Y | N | # | # | Y |
| 2 ***Marlenee*** | N | Y | N | N | ? | ? | X | Y |
| **NEBRASKA** | | | | | | | | |
| 1 ***Bereuter*** | N | Y | N | N | N | N | N | Y |
| 2 Hoagland | Y | N | Y | Y | N | N | Y | Y |
| 3 ***Barrett*** | N | Y | N | N | N | Y | N | N |
| **NEVADA** | | | | | | | | |
| 1 Bilbray | Y | N | Y | Y | N | N | Y | Y |
| 2 ***Vucanovich*** | N | Y | N | N | N | Y | N | N |
| **NEW HAMPSHIRE** | | | | | | | | |
| 1 ***Zeliff*** | N | Y | N | N | N | Y | N | ? |
| 2 Swett | Y | N | N | N | N | Y | Y | N |
| **NEW JERSEY** | | | | | | | | |
| 1 Andrews | Y | N | N | N | N | Y | Y | Y |
| 2 Hughes | Y | N | N | N | N | N | Y | N |
| 3 Pallone | Y | Y | N | N | Y | Y | Y | N |
| 4 ***Smith*** | Y | Y | N | N | N | Y | Y | Y |
| 5 ***Roukema*** | N | Y | N | N | N | Y | N | N |
| 6 Dwyer | Y | N | N | N | N | Y | Y | Y |
| 7 ***Rinaldo*** | Y | Y | N | N | N | Y | Y | N |
| 8 Roe | Y | N | N | N | Y | Y | Y | Y |
| 9 Torricelli | Y | N | N | N | N | Y | Y | Y |
| 10 Payne | Y | N | Y | Y | Y | N | Y | Y |
| 11 ***Gallo*** | N | Y | N | N | ? | ? | X | N |
| 12 ***Zimmer*** | N | Y | N | N | N | Y | N | N |
| 13 ***Saxton*** | N | N | N | N | N | Y | N | N |
| 14 Guarini | Y | N | Y | Y | N | Y | Y | Y |
| **NEW MEXICO** | | | | | | | | |
| 1 ***Schiff*** | Y | Y | N | N | N | Y | N | ? |
| 2 ***Skeen*** | Y | Y | N | N | N | Y | N | Y |
| 3 Richardson | Y | N | Y | Y | ? | ? | ? | Y |
| **NEW YORK** | | | | | | | | |
| 1 Hochbrueckner | Y | N | Y | Y | N | Y | Y | Y |
| 2 Downey | Y | N | Y | Y | Y | Y | Y | Y |
| 3 Mrazek | Y | N | N | N | N | Y | Y | Y |
| 4 ***Lent*** | Y | Y | N | N | N | Y | N | Y |
| 5 ***McGrath*** | Y | Y | N | N | N | Y | N | Y |
| 6 Flake | Y | N | Y | Y | Y | N | Y | Y |
| 7 Ackerman | Y | N | Y | Y | Y | Y | N | Y |
| 8 Scheuer | ? | N | Y | Y | Y | Y | Y | Y |
| 9 Manton | Y | N | Y | Y | N | N | Y | Y |
| 10 Schumer | Y | N | Y | Y | N | N | Y | Y |
| 11 Towns | ? | N | Y | Y | Y | Y | N | Y |
| 12 Owens | Y | N | Y | Y | Y | N | Y | Y |
| 13 Solarz | Y | N | Y | Y | Y | N | Y | Y |
| 14 ***Molinari*** | N | Y | N | N | N | Y | N | Y |
| 15 ***Green*** | Y | N | N | N | N | Y | Y | Y |
| 16 Rangel | ? | N | Y | Y | Y | N | Y | Y |
| 17 Weiss | Y | N | Y | Y | Y | N | Y | ? |
| 18 Serrano | Y | N | Y | Y | Y | N | Y | Y |
| 19 Engel | Y | N | Y | Y | Y | N | Y | Y |
| 20 Lowey | Y | N | Y | Y | Y | Y | Y | Y |
| 21 ***Fish*** | Y | Y | N | N | N | Y | Y | Y |
| 22 ***Gilman*** | Y | Y | N | N | Y | Y | Y | Y |
| 23 McNulty | Y | N | Y | Y | Y | N | Y | Y |
| 24 ***Solomon*** | N | Y | N | N | N | Y | N | N |
| 25 ***Boehlert*** | N | Y | N | N | N | Y | N | Y |
| 26 ***Martin*** | Y | Y | N | N | N | Y | N | Y |
| 27 ***Walsh*** | Y | Y | N | N | N | Y | N | Y |
| 28 McHugh | Y | N | Y | Y | N | Y | Y | Y |
| 29 ***Horton*** | Y | Y | N | N | N | Y | N | Y |
| 30 Slaughter | Y | N | Y | Y | N | N | Y | Y |
| 31 ***Paxon*** | N | Y | N | N | N | Y | N | N |

| | 26 | 28 | 30 | 31 | 32 | 33 | 34 | 35 |
|---|---|---|---|---|---|---|---|---|
| 32 LaFalce | Y | N | Y | Y | N | Y | Y | Y |
| 33 Nowak | Y | N | Y | Y | N | Y | Y | Y |
| 34 ***Houghton*** | Y | Y | N | N | N | Y | N | N |
| **NORTH CAROLINA** | | | | | | | | |
| 1 Jones | Y | N | Y | Y | Y | Y | Y | Y |
| 2 Valentine | Y | N | Y | Y | N | N | N | N |
| 3 Lancaster | Y | N | N | N | N | Y | Y | Y |
| 4 Price | Y | N | Y | Y | N | N | Y | Y |
| 5 Neal | Y | N | Y | Y | N | ? | Y | ? |
| 6 ***Coble*** | N | Y | N | N | N | Y | N | N |
| 7 Rose | Y | N | Y | Y | N | Y | Y | Y |
| 8 Hefner | Y | N | Y | Y | N | N | Y | Y |
| 9 ***McMillan*** | N | Y | N | N | N | Y | N | N |
| 10 ***Ballenger*** | N | Y | N | N | — | + | — | Y |
| 11 ***Taylor*** | N | Y | N | N | ? | ? | X | Y |
| **NORTH DAKOTA** | | | | | | | | |
| AL Dorgan | Y | N | Y | Y | N | N | Y | N |
| **OHIO** | | | | | | | | |
| 1 Luken | Y | N | Y | Y | N | N | Y | Y |
| 2 ***Gradison*** | Y | Y | N | N | N | Y | N | Y |
| 3 Hall | Y | N | Y | Y | N | N | Y | Y |
| 4 ***Oxley*** | Y | Y | N | N | N | Y | N | Y |
| 5 ***Gillmor*** | Y | Y | N | N | N | Y | N | Y |
| 6 ***McEwen*** | N | Y | N | N | N | Y | N | Y |
| 7 ***Hobson*** | N | Y | N | N | N | Y | N | Y |
| 8 ***Boehner*** | N | Y | N | N | ? | ? | X | Y |
| 9 Kaptur | Y | N | Y | Y | N | Y | Y | Y |
| 10 ***Miller*** | N | Y | N | N | N | Y | N | Y |
| 11 Eckart | Y | N | Y | Y | N | N | Y | Y |
| 12 ***Kasich*** | Y | Y | N | N | N | Y | N | Y |
| 13 Pease | Y | N | Y | Y | N | N | Y | Y |
| 14 Sawyer | Y | N | Y | Y | N | Y | Y | Y |
| 15 ***Wylie*** | Y | Y | N | N | N | Y | N | Y |
| 16 ***Regula*** | N | N | N | N | N | Y | N | Y |
| 17 Traficant | Y | N | N | N | N | N | Y | Y |
| 18 Applegate | Y | N | Y | Y | N | N | Y | Y |
| 19 Feighan | Y | N | Y | Y | N | N | Y | Y |
| 20 Oakar | Y | N | Y | Y | Y | N | Y | Y |
| 21 Stokes | Y | N | Y | Y | Y | N | Y | Y |
| **OKLAHOMA** | | | | | | | | |
| 1 ***Inhofe*** | N | Y | N | N | N | Y | N | N |
| 2 Synar | Y | N | Y | Y | N | N | Y | Y |
| 3 Brewster | Y | Y | Y | Y | N | N | N | N |
| 4 McCurdy | Y | N | N | N | N | N | Y | N |
| 5 ***Edwards*** | ? | Y | N | N | N | Y | N | N |
| 6 English | Y | Y | N | N | N | Y | N | N |
| **OREGON** | | | | | | | | |
| 1 AuCoin | Y | N | Y | Y | X | # | # | Y |
| 2 ***Smith*** | N | Y | N | N | N | ? | ? | N |
| 3 Wyden | Y | N | Y | Y | N | Y | Y | Y |
| 4 DeFazio | Y | N | Y | Y | N | N | Y | Y |
| 5 Kopetski | Y | N | Y | Y | Y | N | Y | Y |
| **PENNSYLVANIA** | | | | | | | | |
| 1 Foglietta | Y | N | Y | Y | Y | N | ? | Y |
| 2 Blackwell | Y | N | Y | Y | Y | N | Y | Y |
| 3 Borski | Y | N | Y | Y | N | N | Y | Y |
| 4 Kolter | ? | N | Y | Y | ? | ? | ? | Y |
| 5 ***Schulze*** | Y | Y | N | N | N | Y | N | Y |
| 6 Yatron | Y | N | Y | Y | Y | Y | Y | Y |
| 7 ***Weldon*** | N | Y | N | N | N | Y | N | N |
| 8 Kostmayer | Y | N | Y | Y | N | N | Y | Y |
| 9 ***Shuster*** | Y | Y | N | N | N | N | N | N |
| 10 ***McDade*** | N | Y | N | N | N | ? | ? | ? |
| 11 Kanjorski | Y | N | Y | Y | N | Y | N | Y |
| 12 Murtha | ? | N | Y | Y | N | Y | Y | Y |
| 13 ***Coughlin*** | N | Y | N | N | N | N | N | Y |
| 14 Coyne | Y | N | Y | Y | Y | Y | Y | Y |
| 15 ***Ritter*** | Y | Y | N | N | N | Y | N | N |
| 16 ***Walker*** | N | Y | N | N | N | Y | N | N |
| 17 ***Gekas*** | N | Y | N | N | N | Y | N | N |
| 18 ***Santorum*** | N | Y | N | N | N | Y | N | N |
| 19 ***Goodling*** | N | N | N | N | N | Y | N | N |
| 20 Gaydos | ? | N | Y | Y | N | N | N | Y |
| 21 ***Ridge*** | N | N | N | N | N | Y | N | N |
| 22 Murphy | N | N | Y | Y | N | N | ? | Y |
| 23 ***Clinger*** | Y | Y | N | N | N | Y | N | Y |
| **RHODE ISLAND** | | | | | | | | |
| 1 ***Machtley*** | N | N | N | N | N | Y | Y | N |
| 2 Reed | Y | N | Y | Y | N | N | Y | Y |
| **SOUTH CAROLINA** | | | | | | | | |
| 1 ***Ravenel*** | Y | Y | N | N | N | Y | N | N |
| 2 ***Spence*** | Y | Y | N | N | N | Y | N | N |
| 3 Derrick | Y | N | Y | Y | N | N | Y | Y |
| 4 Patterson | Y | N | N | N | N | N | N | N |
| 5 Spratt | Y | N | Y | Y | N | N | Y | Y |
| 6 Tallon | Y | N | Y | Y | ? | ? | ? | Y |

| | 26 | 28 | 30 | 31 | 32 | 33 | 34 | 35 |
|---|---|---|---|---|---|---|---|---|
| **SOUTH DAKOTA** | | | | | | | | |
| AL Johnson | Y | N | Y | Y | N | Y | Y | N |
| **TENNESSEE** | | | | | | | | |
| 1 ***Quillen*** | Y | Y | N | N | ? | X | X | Y |
| 2 ***Duncan*** | N | Y | N | N | N | Y | N | N |
| 3 Lloyd | Y | N | N | N | N | ? | ? | N |
| 4 Cooper | Y | N | N | N | N | N | Y | Y |
| 5 Clement | Y | Y | Y | Y | Y | N | Y | N |
| 6 Gordon | Y | N | Y | Y | N | N | Y | Y |
| 7 ***Sundquist*** | ? | Y | N | N | N | Y | N | N |
| 8 Tanner | Y | Y | Y | Y | N | Y | N | N |
| 9 Ford | Y | N | Y | Y | Y | Y | Y | Y |
| **TEXAS** | | | | | | | | |
| 1 Chapman | ? | N | Y | Y | N | N | N | N |
| 2 Wilson | Y | N | Y | Y | N | N | Y | Y |
| 3 ***Johnson*** | Y | Y | N | N | N | Y | N | N |
| 4 Hall | Y | N | N | N | N | Y | N | N |
| 5 Bryant | Y | N | Y | Y | N | N | Y | Y |
| 6 ***Barton*** | N | Y | N | N | N | Y | N | N |
| 7 ***Archer*** | Y | Y | N | N | N | Y | N | N |
| 8 ***Fields*** | N | Y | N | N | N | Y | N | N |
| 9 Brooks | Y | N | Y | Y | N | N | Y | Y |
| 10 Pickle | Y | N | Y | Y | N | N | Y | Y |
| 11 Edwards | Y | N | Y | Y | N | N | Y | Y |
| 12 Geren | Y | N | N | N | ? | ? | ? | N |
| 13 Sarpalius | Y | N | N | N | N | N | ? | N |
| 14 Laughlin | Y | N | Y | Y | N | ? | ? | N |
| 15 de la Garza | ? | ? | # | # | ? | ? | ? | Y |
| 16 Coleman | Y | N | Y | Y | ? | ? | ? | Y |
| 17 Stenholm | Y | N | Y | Y | N | Y | N | N |
| 18 Washington | Y | N | Y | Y | Y | N | Y | Y |
| 19 ***Combest*** | Y | Y | N | N | N | Y | N | N |
| 20 Gonzalez | Y | N | Y | Y | Y | N | Y | Y |
| 21 ***Smith*** | N | Y | N | N | N | Y | N | N |
| 22 ***DeLay*** | N | Y | N | N | N | Y | N | Y |
| 23 Bustamante | Y | N | Y | Y | Y | N | Y | Y |
| 24 Frost | Y | N | Y | Y | N | N | Y | ? |
| 25 Andrews | Y | N | Y | Y | N | N | Y | Y |
| 26 ***Armey*** | N | Y | N | N | N | Y | N | N |
| 27 Ortiz | Y | N | Y | Y | ? | ? | # | Y |
| **UTAH** | | | | | | | | |
| 1 ***Hansen*** | N | Y | N | N | N | Y | N | N |
| 2 Owens | Y | Y | Y | Y | Y | N | Y | Y |
| 3 Orton | Y | Y | Y | Y | ? | ? | # | N |
| **VERMONT** | | | | | | | | |
| AL *Sanders* | ? | N | Y | Y | Y | N | Y | Y |
| **VIRGINIA** | | | | | | | | |
| 1 ***Bateman*** | Y | Y | N | N | N | Y | N | Y |
| 2 Pickett | Y | N | N | N | N | N | N | Y |
| 3 ***Bliley*** | N | Y | N | N | N | Y | N | N |
| 4 Sisisky | Y | N | Y | Y | N | Y | Y | Y |
| 5 Payne | Y | N | Y | Y | N | Y | Y | N |
| 6 Olin | Y | N | Y | Y | N | Y | Y | Y |
| 7 ***Allen*** | N | Y | N | N | N | Y | N | N |
| 8 Moran | Y | Y | Y | Y | Y | Y | Y | Y |
| 9 Boucher | Y | N | Y | Y | N | Y | N | Y |
| 10 ***Wolf*** | N | Y | N | N | N | Y | N | Y |
| **WASHINGTON** | | | | | | | | |
| 1 ***Miller*** | N | Y | N | N | N | Y | Y | N |
| 2 Swift | Y | N | Y | Y | N | Y | Y | Y |
| 3 Unsoeld | Y | N | Y | Y | N | Y | Y | Y |
| 4 ***Morrison*** | Y | Y | N | N | N | Y | Y | N |
| 5 Foley | | | Y | Y | | | | |
| 6 Dicks | Y | N | Y | Y | ? | ? | ? | Y |
| 7 McDermott | Y | N | Y | Y | Y | Y | Y | Y |
| 8 ***Chandler*** | N | Y | N | N | ? | ? | ? | N |
| **WEST VIRGINIA** | | | | | | | | |
| 1 Mollohan | Y | N | Y | Y | N | Y | Y | Y |
| 2 Staggers | Y | N | Y | Y | N | N | Y | Y |
| 3 Wise | Y | N | Y | Y | N | Y | Y | Y |
| 4 Rahall | Y | N | Y | Y | N | Y | Y | Y |
| **WISCONSIN** | | | | | | | | |
| 1 Aspin | Y | N | Y | Y | N | ? | ? | Y |
| 2 ***Klug*** | Y | Y | N | N | N | Y | N | N |
| 3 ***Gunderson*** | Y | Y | N | N | N | Y | N | Y |
| 4 Kleczka | Y | N | Y | Y | N | ? | # | Y |
| 5 Moody | Y | N | Y | Y | Y | Y | Y | Y |
| 6 ***Petri*** | ? | N | N | N | N | N | N | N |
| 7 Obey | Y | N | N | N | N | N | Y | Y |
| 8 ***Roth*** | N | Y | N | N | N | N | N | N |
| 9 ***Sensenbrenner*** | N | Y | N | N | N | N | N | N |
| **WYOMING** | | | | | | | | |
| AL ***Thomas*** | Y | Y | N | N | N | Y | N | N |

Southern states - Ala., Ark., Fla., Ga., Ky., La., Miss., N.C., Okla., S.C., Tenn., Texas, Va.
Omitted votes are quorum calls, which CQ does not include in its vote charts.

**36. H Con Res 287. Fiscal 1993 Budget Resolution/ Previous Question.** Derrick, D-S.C., motion to order the previous question (thus limiting debate and possibility of amendment) on adoption of the rule (H Res 386) to provide for House floor consideration of the resolution to set budget levels for fiscal 1993. Motion agreed to 248-172: R 0-161; D 247-11 (ND 171-5, SD 76-6); I 1-0, March 4, 1992.

**37. H Con Res 287. Fiscal 1993 Budget Resolution/Rule.** Adoption of the rule (H Res 386) to provide for House floor consideration of the budget resolution to set budget levels for fiscal 1993. Adopted 239-182: R 0-161; D 238-21 (ND 169-8, SD 69-13); I 1-0, March 4, 1992.

**38. H Con Res 287. Fiscal 1993 Budget Resolution/ Spending Freeze.** Dannemeyer, R-Calif., substitute amendment to hold domestic discretionary spending for fiscal 1993 at fiscal 1992 levels; cut Medicare and Medicaid entitlement programs by $138.4 billion over five years; cut international affairs programs by 25 percent; and reduce the interest cost on the national debt by issuing low-interest securities. Rejected 60-344: R 57-99; D 3-244 (ND 2-164, SD 1-80); I 0-1, March 4, 1992.

**39. H Con Res 287. Fiscal 1993 Budget Resolution/President's Budget.** Gradison, R-Ohio, substitute amendment incorporating the president's fiscal 1993 budget, including the president's short-term economic stimulus package, a defense cut of $7.9 billion in fiscal 1993, a $32.2 billion cut in entitlement spending over five years and a $3.6 billion reduction in revenues in fiscal 1993. Rejected 42-370: R 42-119; D 0-250 (ND 0-169, SD 0-81); I 0-1, March 4, 1992. A "yea" was a vote in support of the president's position.

**40. H Con Res 287. Fiscal 1993 Budget Resolution/Black Caucus Budget.** Towns, D-N.Y., substitute amendment to halve annual military spending within four years, shifting the savings to domestic programs. The substitute also provided a tax cut for middle-income taxpayers by increasing taxes on the wealthy and corporations. Rejected 77-342: R 0-160; D 76-182 (ND 66-109, SD 10-73); I 1-0, March 5, 1992.

**41. H Con Res 287. Fiscal 1993 Budget Resolution/"Plan A."** Adoption of sections one, two and four of the budget resolution (Plan "A") to set fiscal 1993 budget levels. Plan A allowed for the possibility that a separate bill (HR 3732) be enacted to modify the 1990 Budget Enforcement Act to remove the prohibition on shifting money from defense to domestic programs. Plan A doubled the president's defense cuts, splitting proceeds between deficit reduction and domestic spending in a ratio of 25 to 75, and set: budget authority, $1.525 trillion; outlays, $1.505 trillion; revenues, $1.173 trillion; deficit, $331 billion. Adopted 215-201: R 0-157; D 214-44 (ND 155-20, SD 59-24); I 1-0, March 5, 1992. A "nay" was a vote in support of the president's position.

**42. H Con Res 287. Fiscal 1993 Budget Resolution/"Plan B."** Adoption of section three of the budget resolution (Plan "B") to set budget levels for fiscal 1993. Plan B provided for the possibility that a separate bill (HR 3732) not be enacted to remove the prohibition in budget law on shifting money from defense to domestic programs. Plan B doubled the president's defense cuts with the savings going to deficit reduction and set: budget authority, $1.513 trillion; outlays, $1.498 trillion; revenues, $1.173 trillion; deficit, $325 billion. Adopted 224-191: R 5-151; D 219-39 (ND 153-23, SD 66-16); I 0-1, March 5, 1992. A "nay" was a vote in support of the president's position.

**43. HR 2212. Conditional MFN for China in 1992/Veto override.** Passage, over President Bush's March 2 veto, of the bill to prohibit the president from granting most-favored-nation (MFN) status to China for the 12-month period beginning July 3, 1992, unless he reported that China had accounted for and released prisoners detained because of the 1989 pro-democracy protest and that China had made significant progress in preventing human rights abuses, remedying unfair trade practices and limiting weapons proliferation. Passed (thus sending the bill to the Senate) 357-61: R 110-51; D 246-10 (ND 167-8, SD 79-2); I 1-0, March 11, 1992. A "nay" was a vote supporting the president's position.

## KEY

| | |
|---|---|
| Y | Voted for (yea). |
| # | Paired for. |
| + | Announced for. |
| N | Voted against (nay). |
| X | Paired against. |
| − | Announced against. |
| P | Voted "present." |
| C | Voted "present" to avoid possible conflict of interest. |
| ? | Did not vote or otherwise make a position known. |

Democrats  *Republicans*
*Independent*

| | 36 | 37 | 38 | 39 | 40 | 41 | 42 | 43 |
|---|---|---|---|---|---|---|---|---|
| **ALABAMA** | | | | | | | | |
| 1 Callahan | N | N | Y | Y | N | N | N | N |
| 2 Dickinson | N | N | Y | Y | N | N | N | N |
| 3 Browder | Y | Y | N | N | N | Y | Y | Y |
| 4 Bevill | Y | Y | N | N | N | Y | Y | Y |
| 5 Cramer | Y | Y | N | N | N | Y | Y | Y |
| 6 Erdreich | Y | Y | N | N | N | Y | Y | Y |
| 7 Harris | Y | Y | N | N | N | Y | Y | Y |
| **ALASKA** | | | | | | | | |
| AL Young | N | N | N | N | N | N | N | N |
| **ARIZONA** | | | | | | | | |
| 1 Rhodes | N | N | Y | N | N | N | N | Y |
| 2 Pastor | Y | Y | N | N | Y | Y | Y | Y |
| 3 Stump | N | N | Y | N | N | N | N | Y |
| 4 Kyl | N | N | Y | N | N | N | N | Y |
| 5 Kolbe | N | N | N | N | N | N | N | N |
| **ARKANSAS** | | | | | | | | |
| 1 Alexander | Y | Y | N | N | Y | Y | Y | N |
| 2 Thornton | Y | Y | N | N | Y | Y | Y | Y |
| 3 Hammerschmidt | N | N | Y | N | N | N | N | ? |
| 4 Anthony | Y | Y | N | N | N | Y | Y | Y |
| **CALIFORNIA** | | | | | | | | |
| 1 Riggs | N | N | N | N | N | N | N | Y |
| 2 Herger | N | N | N | N | N | N | N | Y |
| 3 Matsui | Y | Y | N | N | Y | Y | Y | N |
| 4 Fazio | Y | Y | N | N | Y | Y | Y | Y |
| 5 Pelosi | Y | Y | N | N | Y | Y | Y | Y |
| 6 Boxer | Y | Y | N | N | Y | Y | Y | Y |
| 7 Miller | Y | Y | N | Y | Y | Y | Y | # |
| 8 Dellums | Y | Y | N | N | Y | Y | Y | Y |
| 9 Stark | Y | Y | N | N | Y | Y | Y | Y |
| 10 Edwards | Y | Y | N | Y | Y | Y | Y | Y |
| 11 Lantos | Y | Y | N | N | Y | Y | Y | Y |
| 12 Campbell | N | N | N | N | N | N | N | N |
| 13 Mineta | Y | Y | N | N | Y | Y | Y | Y |
| 14 Doolittle | N | N | Y | N | N | N | N | Y |
| 15 Condit | Y | Y | N | N | N | N | N | Y |
| 16 Panetta | Y | Y | N | N | Y | N | Y | Y |
| 17 Dooley | Y | Y | N | N | ? | + | # | Y |
| 18 Lehman | Y | Y | ? | N | Y | Y | Y | Y |
| 19 Lagomarsino | N | N | N | N | N | N | N | Y |
| 20 Thomas | N | N | Y | N | N | N | N | N |
| 21 Gallegly | N | N | Y | N | N | N | N | Y |
| 22 Moorhead | N | N | Y | N | N | N | N | Y |
| 23 Beilenson | Y | Y | N | N | Y | Y | Y | Y |
| 24 Waxman | Y | Y | N | N | Y | Y | Y | Y |
| 25 Roybal | Y | Y | N | N | Y | Y | Y | Y |
| 26 Berman | Y | Y | N | N | Y | Y | Y | Y |
| 27 Levine | ? | ? | ? | ? | N | Y | Y | ? |
| 28 Dixon | Y | Y | N | N | Y | Y | Y | Y |
| 29 Waters | Y | Y | N | N | Y | Y | Y | Y |
| 30 Martinez | Y | Y | N | Y | Y | Y | Y | Y |
| 31 Dymally | Y | Y | ? | ? | # | ? | ? | Y |
| 32 Anderson | Y | Y | N | N | Y | Y | Y | Y |
| 33 Dreier | N | N | Y | N | N | N | N | N |
| 34 Torres | Y | Y | ? | ? | Y | Y | Y | Y |
| 35 Lewis | N | N | Y | N | N | N | N | N |
| 36 Brown | Y | Y | ? | N | Y | Y | Y | N |
| 37 McCandless | N | N | N | N | N | N | N | N |
| 38 Dornan | N | N | Y | N | N | N | N | N |
| 39 Dannemeyer | N | N | Y | N | ? | ? | ? | + |
| 40 Cox | N | N | Y | N | N | N | N | Y |
| 41 Lowery | N | N | N | N | N | N | N | N |

| | 36 | 37 | 38 | 39 | 40 | 41 | 42 | 43 |
|---|---|---|---|---|---|---|---|---|
| 42 Rohrabacher | N | N | Y | N | N | N | N | Y |
| 43 Packard | N | N | Y | N | N | N | ? | Y |
| 44 Cunningham | N | N | N | N | N | N | ? | Y |
| 45 Hunter | N | N | Y | N | N | N | N | Y |
| **COLORADO** | | | | | | | | |
| 1 Schroeder | Y | Y | N | N | Y | Y | Y | Y |
| 2 Skaggs | Y | Y | N | N | Y | Y | Y | Y |
| 3 Campbell | N | N | N | N | N | N | N | Y |
| 4 Allard | N | N | N | N | N | N | N | N |
| 5 Hefley | N | N | N | N | N | N | N | Y |
| 6 Schaefer | N | N | N | N | N | N | N | Y |
| **CONNECTICUT** | | | | | | | | |
| 1 Kennelly | Y | Y | N | N | N | N | N | Y |
| 2 Gejdenson | Y | Y | N | N | N | N | N | Y |
| 3 DeLauro | Y | Y | N | N | N | N | N | Y |
| 4 Shays | N | N | Y | N | N | N | Y | N |
| 5 Franks | N | N | N | N | N | N | N | N |
| 6 Johnson | N | N | Y | N | N | N | N | N |
| **DELAWARE** | | | | | | | | |
| AL Carper | Y | Y | N | N | N | Y | Y | Y |
| **FLORIDA** | | | | | | | | |
| 1 Hutto | N | N | N | N | N | N | N | Y |
| 2 Peterson | Y | Y | N | N | N | Y | Y | Y |
| 3 Bennett | N | N | N | N | N | N | N | Y |
| 4 James | N | N | N | N | N | N | N | Y |
| 5 McCollum | N | N | Y | N | N | N | N | Y |
| 6 Stearns | N | N | Y | N | N | N | N | Y |
| 7 Gibbons | Y | Y | N | N | Y | Y | Y | Y |
| 8 Young | N | N | Y | N | N | N | N | Y |
| 9 Bilirakis | ? | N | N | N | N | N | N | Y |
| 10 Ireland | N | N | ? | ? | ? | ? | ? | N |
| 11 Bacchus | Y | Y | N | N | N | Y | Y | Y |
| 12 Lewis | N | N | Y | N | N | N | N | Y |
| 13 Goss | N | N | N | N | N | N | N | Y |
| 14 Johnston | Y | Y | N | N | N | Y | Y | Y |
| 15 Shaw | N | N | N | N | N | N | N | N |
| 16 Smith | Y | Y | ? | N | Y | Y | Y | Y |
| 17 Lehman | Y | Y | N | N | Y | Y | Y | Y |
| 18 Ros—Lehtinen | ? | ? | ? | ? | ? | N | N | Y |
| 19 Fascell | Y | Y | N | N | Y | Y | Y | Y |
| **GEORGIA** | | | | | | | | |
| 1 Thomas | Y | Y | N | N | N | ? | ? | Y |
| 2 Hatcher | Y | Y | N | N | N | Y | Y | Y |
| 3 Ray | Y | Y | N | N | N | Y | Y | Y |
| 4 Jones | Y | Y | N | N | N | Y | Y | Y |
| 5 Lewis | Y | Y | N | N | Y | Y | Y | Y |
| 6 Gingrich | N | N | Y | N | N | N | N | Y |
| 7 Darden | Y | Y | N | N | N | Y | Y | Y |
| 8 Rowland | Y | Y | N | N | N | Y | Y | Y |
| 9 Jenkins | Y | Y | N | N | N | Y | Y | Y |
| 10 Barnard | N | N | N | N | N | N | N | Y |
| **HAWAII** | | | | | | | | |
| 1 Abercrombie | Y | Y | N | N | Y | Y | Y | Y |
| 2 Mink | Y | Y | N | N | Y | Y | Y | Y |
| **IDAHO** | | | | | | | | |
| 1 LaRocco | Y | Y | N | N | N | Y | Y | Y |
| 2 Stallings | Y | Y | N | N | N | Y | Y | Y |
| **ILLINOIS** | | | | | | | | |
| 1 Hayes | Y | Y | N | N | Y | Y | Y | Y |
| 2 Savage | ? | ? | ? | ? | ? | Y | Y | ? |
| 3 Russo | Y | Y | ? | N | ? | ? | ? | ? |
| 4 Sangmeister | Y | Y | N | N | N | Y | Y | Y |
| 5 Lipinski | Y | Y | N | N | ? | ? | ? | Y |
| 6 Hyde | ? | ? | ? | ? | N | N | N | Y |
| 7 Collins | Y | Y | N | N | Y | ? | # | # |
| 8 Rostenkowski | Y | Y | ? | N | Y | Y | Y | Y |
| 9 Yates | ? | ? | ? | ? | # | ? | ? | Y |
| 10 Porter | N | N | Y | N | N | N | N | N |
| 11 Annunzio | Y | Y | N | N | X | Y | Y | Y |
| 12 Crane | N | N | N | N | N | N | N | N |
| 13 Fawell | N | N | N | N | N | N | N | N |
| 14 Hastert | N | N | N | N | N | N | N | N |
| 15 Ewing | N | N | N | N | N | N | N | N |
| 16 Cox | Y | Y | N | N | N | N | N | Y |
| 17 Evans | Y | Y | N | N | Y | Y | Y | Y |
| 18 Michel | N | N | N | N | N | N | N | N |
| 19 Bruce | Y | Y | N | N | N | Y | Y | Y |
| 20 Durbin | Y | Y | N | N | Y | Y | Y | Y |
| 21 Costello | Y | Y | N | N | N | Y | Y | Y |
| 22 Poshard | Y | Y | N | N | N | Y | Y | Y |
| **INDIANA** | | | | | | | | |
| 1 Visclosky | Y | Y | N | N | N | N | N | Y |
| 2 Sharp | ? | ? | N | N | N | Y | Y | Y |
| 3 Roemer | Y | Y | N | N | N | N | N | N |

ND  Northern Democrats     SD  Southern Democrats

| | 36 | 37 | 38 | 39 | 40 | 41 | 42 | 43 |
|---|---|---|---|---|---|---|---|---|
| 4 Long | Y | Y | N | N | N | Y | Y | Y |
| 5 Jontz | Y | Y | N | N | N | N | N | Y |
| 6 ***Burton*** | N | N | Y | N | N | N | N | Y |
| 7 ***Myers*** | N | N | N | N | N | N | N | N |
| 8 McCloskey | Y | Y | N | ? | N | Y | Y | Y |
| 9 Hamilton | Y | Y | N | N | N | Y | Y | Y |
| 10 Jacobs | N | N | N | N | Y | — | N | Y |
| **IOWA** | | | | | | | | |
| 1 ***Leach*** | N | N | N | N | N | N | N | N |
| 2 ***Nussle*** | N | N | N | N | N | N | N | N |
| 3 Nagle | Y | Y | N | N | Y | Y | Y | Y |
| 4 Smith | Y | Y | N | N | N | Y | N | N |
| 5 ***Lightfoot*** | N | N | N | N | N | N | N | N |
| 6 ***Grandy*** | N | N | Y | N | N | N | Y | N |
| **KANSAS** | | | | | | | | |
| 1 ***Roberts*** | N | N | N | N | N | N | N | N |
| 2 Slattery | Y | Y | N | N | N | Y | Y | Y |
| 3 ***Meyers*** | N | N | N | N | N | N | N | Y |
| 4 Glickman | Y | Y | N | N | N | Y | Y | Y |
| 5 ***Nichols*** | N | N | N | N | N | N | N | N |
| **KENTUCKY** | | | | | | | | |
| 1 Hubbard | Y | N | N | N | N | Y | Y | Y |
| 2 Natcher | Y | Y | N | N | N | Y | Y | Y |
| 3 Mazzoli | Y | Y | N | N | N | Y | Y | Y |
| 4 ***Bunning*** | N | N | N | N | N | N | N | Y |
| 5 ***Rogers*** | N | N | N | N | N | N | N | Y |
| 6 ***Hopkins*** | N | N | ? | Y | N | N | N | Y |
| 7 Perkins | Y | Y | N | N | Y | Y | Y | Y |
| **LOUISIANA** | | | | | | | | |
| 1 ***Livingston*** | N | N | Y | N | ? | ? | ? | N |
| 2 Jefferson | Y | Y | N | N | Y | Y | Y | Y |
| 3 Tauzin | Y | Y | N | N | N | N | Y | Y |
| 4 ***McCrery*** | N | N | N | Y | N | N | N | N |
| 5 Huckaby | Y | Y | N | N | N | N | Y | Y |
| 6 ***Baker*** | N | N | Y | Y | N | ? | ? | N |
| 7 Hayes | Y | Y | N | N | N | N | N | Y |
| 8 ***Holloway*** | N | N | Y | N | N | N | N | Y |
| **MAINE** | | | | | | | | |
| 1 Andrews | Y | Y | N | N | N | Y | Y | Y |
| 2 ***Snowe*** | N | N | N | N | N | N | N | Y |
| **MARYLAND** | | | | | | | | |
| 1 ***Gilchrest*** | N | N | N | Y | N | N | N | Y |
| 2 ***Bentley*** | N | N | N | N | N | N | N | Y |
| 3 Cardin | Y | Y | N | N | N | Y | Y | Y |
| 4 McMillen | Y | Y | N | N | N | Y | Y | Y |
| 5 Hoyer | Y | Y | N | N | N | Y | Y | Y |
| 6 Byron | N | N | N | N | N | N | N | Y |
| 7 Mfume | Y | Y | N | N | Y | Y | Y | Y |
| 8 ***Morella*** | N | N | N | N | N | N | Y | Y |
| **MASSACHUSETTS** | | | | | | | | |
| 1 Olver | Y | Y | N | N | Y | Y | Y | Y |
| 2 Neal | Y | N | N | N | Y | Y | Y | Y |
| 3 Early | Y | N | N | N | Y | Y | Y | Y |
| 4 Frank | Y | Y | N | N | Y | Y | Y | Y |
| 5 Atkins | Y | Y | N | N | Y | Y | Y | Y |
| 6 Mavroules | Y | Y | N | N | N | Y | Y | Y |
| 7 Markey | Y | Y | N | N | Y | Y | Y | Y |
| 8 Kennedy | Y | Y | N | N | Y | Y | Y | Y |
| 9 Moakley | Y | Y | N | N | Y | Y | Y | Y |
| 10 Studds | Y | Y | N | N | Y | Y | Y | Y |
| 11 Donnelly | Y | Y | N | N | N | Y | Y | Y |
| **MICHIGAN** | | | | | | | | |
| 1 Conyers | Y | Y | N | N | Y | Y | Y | Y |
| 2 ***Pursell*** | N | N | Y | N | N | N | N | Y |
| 3 Wolpe | Y | Y | N | N | N | Y | Y | Y |
| 4 ***Upton*** | N | N | N | N | N | N | N | Y |
| 5 ***Henry*** | N | N | Y | N | N | N | N | Y |
| 6 Carr | Y | Y | ? | N | N | N | N | Y |
| 7 Kildee | Y | Y | N | N | Y | Y | Y | Y |
| 8 Traxler | Y | Y | N | N | Y | Y | Y | Y |
| 9 ***Vander Jagt*** | N | N | N | N | N | N | N | N |
| 10 ***Camp*** | N | N | N | N | N | N | N | Y |
| 11 ***Davis*** | N | N | ? | N | N | ? | ? | N |
| 12 Bonior | Y | Y | N | N | Y | Y | Y | Y |
| 13 Collins | Y | Y | N | N | Y | Y | Y | Y |
| 14 Hertel | ? | Y | N | N | N | Y | N | Y |
| 15 Ford | Y | Y | N | N | Y | Y | Y | Y |
| 16 Dingell | Y | Y | N | N | N | Y | Y | Y |
| 17 Levin | Y | Y | N | N | N | Y | Y | Y |
| 18 ***Broomfield*** | N | N | N | N | N | N | N | Y |
| **MINNESOTA** | | | | | | | | |
| 1 Penny | Y | Y | Y | N | N | Y | Y | Y |
| 2 ***Weber*** | ? | ? | ? | ? | N | N | N | Y |
| 3 ***Ramstad*** | N | N | N | N | N | N | N | Y |
| 4 Vento | Y | Y | N | N | Y | Y | Y | Y |

| | 36 | 37 | 38 | 39 | 40 | 41 | 42 | 43 |
|---|---|---|---|---|---|---|---|---|
| 5 Sabo | Y | Y | N | N | Y | Y | Y | Y |
| 6 Sikorski | Y | Y | N | N | N | Y | Y | Y |
| 7 Peterson | Y | Y | N | N | Y | Y | Y | Y |
| 8 Oberstar | Y | Y | N | N | Y | Y | Y | Y |
| **MISSISSIPPI** | | | | | | | | |
| 1 Whitten | ? | ? | ? | ? | ? | ? | ? | ? |
| 2 Espy | Y | Y | N | N | Y | Y | Y | Y |
| 3 Montgomery | N | N | N | N | N | N | N | Y |
| 4 Parker | Y | Y | N | N | N | N | Y | Y |
| 5 Taylor | N | N | N | N | N | N | N | Y |
| **MISSOURI** | | | | | | | | |
| 1 Clay | Y | Y | N | N | Y | Y | Y | Y |
| 2 Horn | Y | Y | N | N | N | Y | Y | Y |
| 3 Gephardt | Y | Y | ? | N | N | Y | Y | Y |
| 4 Skelton | N | N | N | N | N | N | N | Y |
| 5 Wheat | Y | Y | N | N | Y | Y | Y | Y |
| 6 ***Coleman*** | N | N | N | N | N | N | N | Y |
| 7 ***Hancock*** | N | N | Y | N | N | N | N | Y |
| 8 ***Emerson*** | N | N | Y | N | N | N | N | Y |
| 9 Volkmer | Y | Y | N | N | N | Y | Y | Y |
| **MONTANA** | | | | | | | | |
| 1 Williams | Y | Y | N | N | N | Y | N | N |
| 2 ***Marlenee*** | N | N | ? | N | N | N | N | N |
| **NEBRASKA** | | | | | | | | |
| 1 ***Bereuter*** | N | N | N | N | N | N | N | Y |
| 2 Hoagland | Y | Y | N | N | N | Y | Y | Y |
| 3 ***Barrett*** | N | N | N | N | N | N | N | N |
| **NEVADA** | | | | | | | | |
| 1 Bilbray | Y | Y | N | N | N | Y | Y | Y |
| 2 ***Vucanovich*** | N | N | Y | Y | N | N | N | N |
| **NEW HAMPSHIRE** | | | | | | | | |
| 1 ***Zeliff*** | N | N | Y | N | N | N | N | Y |
| 2 Swett | Y | Y | N | N | N | Y | Y | Y |
| **NEW JERSEY** | | | | | | | | |
| 1 Andrews | Y | Y | N | N | N | N | N | Y |
| 2 Hughes | Y | Y | N | N | N | N | N | Y |
| 3 Pallone | Y | Y | N | N | N | N | N | Y |
| 4 ***Smith*** | N | N | N | N | N | N | N | Y |
| 5 ***Roukema*** | N | N | N | N | N | N | N | Y |
| 6 Dwyer | Y | Y | N | N | N | Y | Y | Y |
| 7 ***Rinaldo*** | N | N | N | N | N | N | N | Y |
| 8 Roe | Y | Y | N | N | N | Y | Y | Y |
| 9 Torricelli | Y | Y | N | N | N | Y | Y | Y |
| 10 Payne | Y | Y | N | N | Y | Y | Y | Y |
| 11 ***Gallo*** | N | N | N | N | N | N | N | Y |
| 12 ***Zimmer*** | N | N | Y | N | N | N | N | Y |
| 13 ***Saxton*** | N | N | N | N | N | N | N | Y |
| 14 Guarini | Y | Y | N | N | N | Y | Y | Y |
| **NEW MEXICO** | | | | | | | | |
| 1 ***Schiff*** | N | N | N | N | N | N | N | Y |
| 2 ***Skeen*** | N | N | N | N | N | N | N | Y |
| 3 Richardson | Y | Y | N | N | N | Y | Y | Y |
| **NEW YORK** | | | | | | | | |
| 1 Hochbrueckner | Y | Y | N | N | N | Y | Y | Y |
| 2 Downey | Y | Y | N | N | N | Y | Y | Y |
| 3 Mrazek | Y | Y | ? | ? | N | Y | Y | Y |
| 4 ***Lent*** | N | N | N | N | N | N | N | N |
| 5 ***McGrath*** | N | N | N | N | N | N | N | Y |
| 6 Flake | Y | Y | ? | ? | Y | Y | Y | ? |
| 7 Ackerman | Y | Y | N | N | N | Y | Y | Y |
| 8 Scheuer | Y | Y | N | N | Y | Y | Y | Y |
| 9 Manton | Y | Y | N | N | N | Y | Y | Y |
| 10 Schumer | Y | Y | N | N | N | Y | Y | Y |
| 11 Towns | Y | Y | N | N | Y | Y | Y | Y |
| 12 Owens | Y | Y | N | N | Y | Y | Y | Y |
| 13 Solarz | Y | Y | N | N | N | Y | Y | Y |
| 14 ***Molinari*** | N | N | N | N | N | N | N | Y |
| 15 ***Green*** | N | N | N | N | N | N | N | Y |
| 16 Rangel | Y | Y | N | N | Y | Y | Y | Y |
| 17 Weiss | Y | Y | N | N | Y | Y | Y | Y |
| 18 Serrano | Y | Y | N | N | Y | Y | Y | Y |
| 19 Engel | Y | Y | N | N | N | Y | Y | Y |
| 20 Lowey | Y | Y | N | N | N | Y | Y | Y |
| 21 ***Fish*** | N | N | N | N | N | N | N | Y |
| 22 ***Gilman*** | N | N | N | N | N | N | N | Y |
| 23 McNulty | Y | Y | N | N | N | Y | Y | Y |
| 24 ***Solomon*** | N | N | Y | Y | N | N | N | N |
| 25 ***Boehlert*** | N | N | N | N | N | N | N | Y |
| 26 ***Martin*** | N | N | N | N | N | N | N | Y |
| 27 ***Walsh*** | N | N | N | N | N | N | N | Y |
| 28 McHugh | Y | Y | N | N | N | Y | Y | Y |
| 29 ***Horton*** | N | N | N | N | N | N | N | Y |
| 30 Slaughter | Y | Y | N | N | N | Y | Y | Y |
| 31 ***Paxon*** | N | N | N | N | N | N | N | Y |

| | 36 | 37 | 38 | 39 | 40 | 41 | 42 | 43 |
|---|---|---|---|---|---|---|---|---|
| 32 LaFalce | Y | Y | N | N | N | Y | Y | Y |
| 33 Nowak | + | + | — | — | N | Y | Y | Y |
| 34 ***Houghton*** | N | N | N | Y | N | N | N | Y |
| **NORTH CAROLINA** | | | | | | | | |
| 1 Jones | ? | Y | N | N | N | Y | Y | Y |
| 2 Valentine | Y | N | N | N | N | N | Y | ? |
| 3 Lancaster | Y | N | N | N | N | N | N | Y |
| 4 Price | Y | Y | N | N | N | Y | Y | Y |
| 5 Neal | ? | ? | ? | ? | N | Y | Y | Y |
| 6 ***Coble*** | N | N | N | Y | N | N | N | Y |
| 7 Rose | Y | Y | N | N | N | N | Y | Y |
| 8 Hefner | Y | Y | N | N | N | Y | Y | Y |
| 9 ***McMillan*** | N | N | N | Y | N | N | N | Y |
| 10 ***Ballenger*** | N | N | Y | Y | N | N | N | Y |
| 11 ***Taylor*** | N | N | N | N | N | N | N | Y |
| **NORTH DAKOTA** | | | | | | | | |
| AL Dorgan | Y | Y | N | N | N | N | N | Y |
| **OHIO** | | | | | | | | |
| 1 Luken | Y | Y | N | N | N | N | Y | Y |
| 2 ***Gradison*** | N | N | N | Y | N | N | N | N |
| 3 Hall | Y | Y | N | N | N | Y | Y | Y |
| 4 ***Oxley*** | N | N | N | Y | N | N | N | N |
| 5 ***Gillmor*** | N | N | N | N | N | N | N | N |
| 6 ***McEwen*** | N | N | Y | Y | N | N | N | Y |
| 7 ***Hobson*** | N | N | N | N | N | N | N | Y |
| 8 ***Boehner*** | N | N | N | N | N | ? | N | Y |
| 9 Kaptur | Y | Y | N | N | N | Y | Y | Y |
| 10 ***Miller*** | N | N | Y | Y | N | N | N | Y |
| 11 Eckart | Y | Y | N | N | N | Y | Y | Y |
| 12 ***Kasich*** | N | N | N | Y | N | N | N | ? |
| 13 Pease | Y | Y | N | N | N | Y | Y | Y |
| 14 Sawyer | Y | Y | N | N | N | Y | Y | Y |
| 15 ***Wylie*** | N | N | N | Y | N | N | N | X |
| 16 ***Regula*** | N | N | N | N | N | N | ? | Y |
| 17 Traficant | Y | Y | N | N | Y | Y | Y | Y |
| 18 Applegate | Y | Y | N | N | N | N | N | Y |
| 19 Feighan | Y | Y | N | N | N | Y | Y | Y |
| 20 Oakar | Y | Y | N | — | Y | Y | Y | Y |
| 21 Stokes | Y | Y | N | N | Y | Y | Y | Y |
| **OKLAHOMA** | | | | | | | | |
| 1 ***Inhofe*** | N | N | Y | Y | N | N | N | Y |
| 2 Synar | Y | Y | N | N | N | Y | Y | Y |
| 3 Brewster | Y | Y | N | N | N | Y | Y | Y |
| 4 McCurdy | Y | Y | N | N | N | Y | Y | Y |
| 5 ***Edwards*** | N | N | Y | N | N | N | N | Y |
| 6 English | Y | N | N | N | N | N | N | Y |
| **OREGON** | | | | | | | | |
| 1 AuCoin | Y | Y | N | N | Y | Y | Y | Y |
| 2 ***Smith*** | N | N | N | N | N | N | N | Y |
| 3 Wyden | Y | Y | N | N | Y | Y | Y | N |
| 4 DeFazio | Y | Y | N | N | Y | Y | Y | Y |
| 5 Kopetski | Y | Y | N | N | Y | Y | Y | N |
| **PENNSYLVANIA** | | | | | | | | |
| 1 Foglietta | Y | Y | N | N | Y | Y | Y | Y |
| 2 Blackwell | Y | Y | N | N | Y | Y | Y | Y |
| 3 Borski | Y | Y | N | N | N | Y | Y | Y |
| 4 Kolter | Y | Y | N | N | N | Y | Y | Y |
| 5 ***Schulze*** | N | N | Y | Y | N | N | N | Y |
| 6 Yatron | Y | Y | N | N | N | Y | Y | Y |
| 7 ***Weldon*** | N | N | N | N | N | N | N | Y |
| 8 Kostmayer | Y | Y | N | N | N | Y | Y | Y |
| 9 ***Shuster*** | N | N | Y | N | N | N | N | N |
| 10 ***McDade*** | ? | ? | ? | ? | N | N | N | N |
| 11 Kanjorski | Y | Y | N | N | N | Y | Y | Y |
| 12 Murtha | Y | Y | N | N | N | Y | Y | Y |
| 13 ***Coughlin*** | N | N | ? | Y | N | N | N | N |
| 14 Coyne | Y | Y | N | N | Y | Y | Y | Y |
| 15 ***Ritter*** | N | N | N | N | N | N | N | Y |
| 16 ***Walker*** | N | N | Y | N | N | N | N | Y |
| 17 ***Gekas*** | N | N | N | N | N | N | N | N |
| 18 ***Santorum*** | N | N | N | Y | N | N | Y | Y |
| 19 ***Goodling*** | N | N | N | Y | N | N | N | Y |
| 20 Gaydos | Y | Y | ? | ? | N | Y | Y | Y |
| 21 ***Ridge*** | N | N | N | N | N | N | N | Y |
| 22 Murphy | Y | Y | N | N | N | Y | Y | Y |
| 23 ***Clinger*** | N | N | ? | Y | N | N | N | Y |
| **RHODE ISLAND** | | | | | | | | |
| 1 ***Machtley*** | N | N | N | N | N | N | N | Y |
| 2 Reed | Y | Y | N | N | N | N | N | Y |
| **SOUTH CAROLINA** | | | | | | | | |
| 1 ***Ravenel*** | N | N | Y | N | N | N | N | Y |
| 2 ***Spence*** | N | N | Y | N | N | N | N | Y |
| 3 Derrick | Y | Y | N | N | N | Y | Y | Y |
| 4 Patterson | Y | Y | N | N | N | N | Y | Y |
| 5 Spratt | Y | Y | N | N | N | Y | Y | Y |
| 6 Tallon | Y | Y | N | N | N | Y | Y | Y |

| | 36 | 37 | 38 | 39 | 40 | 41 | 42 | 43 |
|---|---|---|---|---|---|---|---|---|
| **SOUTH DAKOTA** | | | | | | | | |
| AL Johnson | Y | Y | N | N | N | Y | Y | Y |
| **TENNESSEE** | | | | | | | | |
| 1 ***Quillen*** | N | N | Y | Y | ? | ? | X | N |
| 2 ***Duncan*** | N | N | N | N | N | N | N | Y |
| 3 Lloyd | Y | N | N | N | N | N | Y | Y |
| 4 Cooper | Y | Y | N | N | N | Y | Y | Y |
| 5 Clement | Y | Y | N | N | N | Y | Y | Y |
| 6 Gordon | Y | Y | ? | ? | N | Y | Y | Y |
| 7 ***Sundquist*** | N | N | Y | Y | ? | ? | ? | N |
| 8 Tanner | Y | Y | N | N | N | Y | Y | Y |
| 9 Ford | Y | Y | N | N | Y | Y | Y | Y |
| **TEXAS** | | | | | | | | |
| 1 Chapman | Y | Y | N | N | N | N | N | Y |
| 2 Wilson | Y | Y | N | ? | N | Y | Y | Y |
| 3 ***Johnson*** | N | N | Y | N | N | N | N | Y |
| 4 Hall | Y | N | N | N | N | N | N | Y |
| 5 Bryant | Y | Y | N | N | N | Y | Y | Y |
| 6 ***Barton*** | N | N | Y | Y | N | N | N | Y |
| 7 ***Archer*** | N | N | Y | N | N | N | N | N |
| 8 ***Fields*** | N | N | Y | N | N | N | N | N |
| 9 Brooks | Y | Y | N | N | N | Y | Y | Y |
| 10 Pickle | Y | Y | N | N | N | Y | Y | Y |
| 11 Edwards | Y | ? | N | N | N | N | N | Y |
| 12 Geren | Y | Y | N | N | N | N | N | Y |
| 13 Sarpalius | Y | Y | N | N | N | N | Y | Y |
| 14 Laughlin | Y | Y | N | N | N | N | N | Y |
| 15 de la Garza | Y | Y | N | N | N | Y | Y | Y |
| 16 Coleman | Y | Y | N | N | N | N | N | ? |
| 17 Stenholm | Y | Y | N | N | N | Y | Y | Y |
| 18 Washington | Y | Y | N | N | Y | Y | Y | Y |
| 19 ***Combest*** | N | N | Y | N | N | N | N | Y |
| 20 Gonzalez | Y | Y | N | N | N | Y | Y | Y |
| 21 ***Smith*** | N | N | Y | Y | N | N | N | Y |
| 22 ***DeLay*** | N | N | Y | N | N | N | N | N |
| 23 Bustamante | Y | Y | N | N | N | Y | Y | Y |
| 24 Frost | Y | Y | N | N | N | Y | Y | Y |
| 25 Andrews | Y | Y | N | N | N | Y | Y | Y |
| 26 ***Armey*** | N | ? | Y | N | N | N | N | N |
| 27 Ortiz | Y | Y | N | N | X | ? | ? | ? |
| **UTAH** | | | | | | | | |
| 1 ***Hansen*** | N | N | Y | Y | N | N | N | N |
| 2 Owens | Y | Y | ? | ? | ? | ? | ? | Y |
| 3 Orton | Y | N | N | N | N | N | N | Y |
| **VERMONT** | | | | | | | | |
| AL *Sanders* | Y | Y | N | N | Y | Y | N | Y |
| **VIRGINIA** | | | | | | | | |
| 1 ***Bateman*** | N | N | N | N | N | N | N | N |
| 2 Pickett | Y | N | N | N | N | N | N | N |
| 3 ***Bliley*** | N | N | Y | N | N | N | N | Y |
| 4 Sisisky | N | N | N | N | N | N | N | Y |
| 5 Payne | Y | Y | N | N | N | Y | Y | Y |
| 6 Olin | Y | Y | N | N | N | Y | Y | Y |
| 7 ***Allen*** | N | N | N | N | N | N | N | Y |
| 8 Moran | Y | Y | N | N | N | Y | Y | Y |
| 9 Boucher | Y | Y | N | N | N | Y | Y | Y |
| 10 ***Wolf*** | N | N | N | N | N | N | N | Y |
| **WASHINGTON** | | | | | | | | |
| 1 ***Miller*** | N | N | N | Y | N | N | N | Y |
| 2 Swift | Y | Y | N | N | Y | Y | Y | Y |
| 3 Unsoeld | Y | Y | N | N | Y | Y | Y | Y |
| 4 ***Morrison*** | N | N | N | N | N | N | Y | Y |
| 5 Foley | | | | | | Y | Y | |
| 6 Dicks | N | N | N | N | N | Y | Y | Y |
| 7 McDermott | Y | Y | N | N | Y | Y | Y | Y |
| 8 ***Chandler*** | N | N | N | Y | ? | ? | X | Y |
| **WEST VIRGINIA** | | | | | | | | |
| 1 Mollohan | Y | Y | N | N | N | Y | Y | Y |
| 2 Staggers | Y | Y | N | N | N | N | N | Y |
| 3 Wise | Y | Y | N | N | N | Y | Y | Y |
| 4 Rahall | Y | Y | N | N | Y | Y | Y | Y |
| **WISCONSIN** | | | | | | | | |
| 1 Aspin | Y | Y | N | N | N | Y | Y | Y |
| 2 ***Klug*** | N | N | N | N | N | N | N | Y |
| 3 ***Gunderson*** | N | N | N | N | N | N | N | Y |
| 4 Kleczka | Y | Y | N | N | N | Y | Y | Y |
| 5 Moody | Y | Y | N | N | N | Y | Y | Y |
| 6 ***Petri*** | N | N | N | N | N | N | N | Y |
| 7 Obey | Y | Y | N | N | N | Y | Y | Y |
| 8 ***Roth*** | N | N | N | N | N | N | N | Y |
| 9 ***Sensenbrenner*** | N | N | Y | N | N | N | N | Y |
| **WYOMING** | | | | | | | | |
| AL ***Thomas*** | N | N | Y | N | N | N | N | Y |

Southern states - Ala., Ark., Fla., Ga., Ky., La., Miss., N.C., Okla., S.C., Tenn., Texas, Va.
Omitted votes are quorum calls, which CQ does not include in its vote charts.

**44. H Res 393. Limited Disclosure of Bank Abuses/Adoption.** Adoption of the resolution to disclose the names of the 24 people — 19 current House members and five former members — who routinely and repeatedly wrote checks that exceeded their balances at the House Bank by significant amounts from July 1, 1988, to Oct. 3, 1991, and details of their check-floating history. Adopted 391-36: R 135-30; D 255-6 (ND 177-2, SD 78-4); I 1-0, March 12, 1992.

**45. H Res 396. Further Disclosure of House Bank Abuses/Adoption.** Adoption of the resolution to disclose the name of all members or former members who wrote checks that exceeded their balance at the House Bank and the number of insufficient fund checks written by each from July 1, 1988, to Oct. 3, 1991. Adopted 426-0: R 165-0; D 260-0 (ND 178-0, SD 82-0); I 1-0, March 13, 1992 (in the session that began, and the Congressional Record dated, March 12, 1992).

**46. H Res 397. Reconstruction of House Bank Accounts/Committee Referral.** Gephardt, D-Mo., motion to refer to the Committee on Standards of Official Conduct the Edwards, R-Okla., resolution to instruct the Speaker, within 20 days, to have the account histories of every current and former member at the House Bank for the period from July 1, 1988, to Oct. 3, 1991, fully reconstructed and the names and details released. Motion rejected 150-275: R 43-122; D 107-152 (ND 75-102, SD 32-50); I 0-1, March 13, 1992 (in the session that began, and the Congressional Record dated, March 12, 1992).

**47. H Res 397. Reconstruction of House Bank Accounts/Account History.** Gephardt, D-Mo., motion to commit to the Committee on Standards of Official Conduct the Edwards, R-Okla., resolution to instruct the Speaker, within 20 days, to have the account histories of every current and former member at the House Bank for the period from July 1, 1988, to Oct. 3, 1991, fully reconstructed and the names and details released. Motion agreed to 244-133: R 83-58; D 160-75 (ND 111-51, SD 49-24); I 1-0, March 13, 1992 (in the session that began, and the Congressional Record dated, March 12, 1992).

**48. Procedural Motion.** Approval of the House Journal of Tuesday, March 17. Motion agreed to 289-106: R 48-100; D 240-6 (ND 160-6, SD 80-0); I 1-0, March 18, 1992.

**49. HR 4210. 1992 Tax Bill/Motion to Instruct Conferees.** Walker, R-Pa., motion to table (kill) the Archer, R-Texas, motion to instruct the House conferees on the 1992 tax bill to insist that the House provisions to create a new top income tax rate of 35 percent and the Senate provisions to create a new top income rate of 36 percent be dropped from the bill. Motion rejected 0-409: R 0-154; D 0-254 (ND 0-171, SD 0-83); I 0-1, March 18, 1992.

**50. HR 4210. 1992 Tax Bill/Motion to Instruct Conferees.** Rostenkowski, D-Ill., substitute amendment to the Archer, R-Texas, motion to instruct the House conferees on the 1992 tax bill. The substitute changed the instructions to ones that instructed the House conferees to insist on provisions that provided significant middle-class tax relief, rather than instructions to not agree to the House provisions to create a new top income tax rate of 35 percent and the Senate provisions to create a new top income rate of 36 percent. Adopted 206-200: R 1-154; D 204-46 (ND 143-24, SD 61-22); I 1-0, March 18, 1992. (Subsequently, the Archer motion as modified by the Rostenkowski amendment was adopted by voice vote.)

**51. HR 3209. Federal Employee Reservist Benefit Extension.** Ackerman, D-N.Y., motion to suspend the rules and pass the bill to ensure that the level of compensation for federal employees ordered to military duty during the Persian Gulf War is not less than their pay as federal employees and for other purposes. Motion agreed to 354-57: R 104-52; D 249-5 (ND 167-4, SD 82-1); I 1-0, March 18, 1992. A two-thirds majority of those present and voting (274 in this case) was required for passage under suspension of the rules.

## KEY

Y Voted for (yea).
\# Paired for.
+ Announced for.
N Voted against (nay).
X Paired against.
- Announced against.
P Voted "present."
C Voted "present" to avoid possible conflict of interest.
? Did not vote or otherwise make a position known.

Democrats  *Republicans*
*Independent*

| | 44 | 45 | 46 | 47 | 48 | 49 | 50 | 51 |
|---|---|---|---|---|---|---|---|---|
| **ALABAMA** | | | | | | | | |
| 1 *Callahan* | Y | Y | N | N | N | N | N | N |
| 2 *Dickinson* | Y | Y | N | ? | N | Y | N | N |
| 3 Browder | Y | Y | N | Y | N | Y | N | Y |
| 4 Bevill | Y | Y | N | Y | Y | N | N | Y |
| 5 Cramer | Y | Y | N | Y | Y | N | N | Y |
| 6 Erdreich | Y | Y | N | N | Y | N | Y | Y |
| 7 Harris | Y | Y | N | N | Y | N | Y | Y |
| **ALASKA** | | | | | | | | |
| AL *Young* | Y | Y | Y | ? | N | N | N | Y |
| **ARIZONA** | | | | | | | | |
| 1 *Rhodes* | Y | Y | Y | N | N | N | N | N |
| 2 Pastor | Y | Y | Y | Y | Y | N | Y | Y |
| 3 *Stump* | Y | Y | N | N | N | N | N | N |
| 4 *Kyl* | N | Y | Y | N | N | N | N | N |
| 5 *Kolbe* | Y | Y | Y | N | N | N | N | N |
| **ARKANSAS** | | | | | | | | |
| 1 Alexander | Y | Y | Y | Y | Y | N | Y | Y |
| 2 Thornton | Y | Y | Y | Y | Y | N | Y | Y |
| 3 *Hammerschmidt* | Y | Y | N | Y | Y | ? | N | Y |
| 4 Anthony | Y | Y | Y | Y | Y | ? | Y | Y |
| **CALIFORNIA** | | | | | | | | |
| 1 *Riggs* | N | Y | Y | Y | ? | N | N | N |
| 2 *Herger* | Y | Y | N | N | N | N | N | N |
| 3 Matsui | Y | Y | Y | Y | Y | N | Y | Y |
| 4 Fazio | Y | Y | Y | Y | Y | N | Y | Y |
| 5 Pelosi | Y | Y | Y | Y | Y | N | Y | Y |
| 6 Boxer | Y | Y | Y | Y | Y | N | Y | Y |
| 7 Miller | ? | ? | ? | ? | ? | ? | ? | ? |
| 8 Dellums | Y | Y | Y | Y | ? | # | Y | |
| 9 Stark | Y | Y | ? | ? | N | Y | Y | Y |
| 10 Edwards | Y | Y | Y | ? | Y | N | Y | Y |
| 11 Lantos | Y | Y | Y | Y | Y | N | Y | Y |
| 12 *Campbell* | Y | Y | N | N | N | N | N | N |
| 13 Mineta | Y | Y | N | Y | N | Y | N | Y |
| 14 *Doolittle* | N | Y | N | Y | N | N | N | N |
| 15 Condit | Y | Y | N | Y | Y | N | Y | Y |
| 16 Panetta | Y | Y | N | Y | N | Y | N | Y |
| 17 Dooley | Y | Y | ? | ? | Y | N | Y | Y |
| 18 Lehman | Y | Y | N | Y | Y | N | Y | Y |
| 19 *Lagomarsino* | Y | Y | N | N | N | N | N | N |
| 20 *Thomas* | Y | Y | N | N | N | N | N | N |
| 21 *Gallegly* | Y | Y | N | N | N | N | N | N |
| 22 *Moorhead* | Y | Y | N | N | N | N | N | N |
| 23 Beilenson | Y | Y | N | Y | N | Y | N | Y |
| 24 Waxman | Y | Y | N | Y | N | Y | N | Y |
| 25 Roybal | Y | Y | Y | Y | Y | N | Y | Y |
| 26 Berman | Y | Y | Y | Y | Y | N | Y | Y |
| 27 Levine | Y | Y | N | N | Y | ? | ? | ? |
| 28 Dixon | Y | Y | Y | Y | Y | N | Y | Y |
| 29 Waters | Y | Y | Y | Y | Y | N | Y | Y |
| 30 Martinez | Y | Y | Y | Y | Y | N | Y | Y |
| 31 Dymally | Y | Y | N | ? | N | Y | N | Y |
| 32 Anderson | Y | Y | Y | Y | Y | N | Y | Y |
| 33 *Dreier* | Y | Y | N | N | N | N | N | N |
| 34 Torres | Y | Y | Y | Y | Y | N | Y | Y |
| 35 *Lewis* | Y | Y | N | N | N | N | N | N |
| 36 Brown | Y | Y | Y | ? | Y | N | Y | Y |
| 37 *McCandless* | Y | Y | N | ? | N | N | N | Y |
| 38 *Dornan* | N | Y | Y | N | N | N | N | N |
| 39 *Dannemeyer* | + | + | - | + | - | - | - | + |
| 40 *Cox* | Y | Y | N | N | N | N | N | Y |
| 41 *Lowery* | Y | Y | N | N | ? | ? | ? | ? |

| | 44 | 45 | 46 | 47 | 48 | 49 | 50 | 51 |
|---|---|---|---|---|---|---|---|---|
| 42 *Rohrabacher* | N | Y | N | Y | ? | ? | ? | ? |
| 43 *Packard* | N | Y | N | N | Y | N | N | N |
| 44 *Cunningham* | Y | N | N | N | N | N | N | Y |
| 45 *Hunter* | Y | Y | N | ? | ? | ? | ? | ? |
| **COLORADO** | | | | | | | | |
| 1 Schroeder | Y | Y | Y | N | N | N | N | Y |
| 2 Skaggs | Y | Y | Y | Y | N | Y | N | Y |
| 3 Campbell | Y | Y | N | ? | Y | N | Y | Y |
| 4 *Allard* | N | Y | N | N | N | N | N | N |
| 5 *Hefley* | Y | Y | Y | N | N | N | N | Y |
| 6 *Schaefer* | Y | Y | N | Y | N | N | N | Y |
| **CONNECTICUT** | | | | | | | | |
| 1 Kennelly | Y | Y | Y | Y | Y | N | Y | Y |
| 2 Gejdenson | Y | Y | Y | Y | Y | N | Y | Y |
| 3 DeLauro | Y | Y | N | Y | Y | N | Y | Y |
| 4 *Shays* | Y | Y | Y | Y | N | N | N | Y |
| 5 *Franks* | Y | Y | N | Y | N | N | N | Y |
| 6 *Johnson* | Y | Y | Y | Y | N | N | N | Y |
| **DELAWARE** | | | | | | | | |
| AL Carper | Y | Y | N | Y | ? | N | N | Y |
| **FLORIDA** | | | | | | | | |
| 1 Hutto | Y | Y | N | N | N | N | N | Y |
| 2 Peterson | Y | Y | N | Y | N | Y | N | Y |
| 3 Bennett | Y | Y | N | Y | N | Y | N | Y |
| 4 *James* | N | Y | N | N | N | N | N | N |
| 5 *McCollum* | Y | Y | N | N | N | N | N | Y |
| 6 *Stearns* | Y | Y | N | N | N | N | N | N |
| 7 Gibbons | Y | Y | Y | Y | Y | N | Y | Y |
| 8 *Young* | Y | Y | N | N | N | N | N | N |
| 9 *Bilirakis* | Y | Y | N | N | N | N | N | N |
| 10 *Ireland* | Y | Y | N | Y | ? | ? | ? | ? |
| 11 Bacchus | N | Y | N | Y | N | Y | N | Y |
| 12 *Lewis* | Y | Y | N | N | N | N | N | N |
| 13 *Goss* | Y | Y | Y | N | N | N | N | N |
| 14 Johnston | Y | Y | Y | Y | N | Y | N | Y |
| 15 *Shaw* | Y | Y | N | N | N | N | N | Y |
| 16 Smith | Y | Y | Y | Y | N | Y | N | Y |
| 17 Lehman | Y | ? | ? | ? | Y | N | Y | Y |
| 18 *Ros—Lehtinen* | Y | Y | N | Y | N | N | N | Y |
| 19 Fascell | Y | Y | Y | Y | Y | N | Y | Y |
| **GEORGIA** | | | | | | | | |
| 1 Thomas | Y | Y | N | N | Y | N | N | Y |
| 2 Hatcher | Y | Y | N | Y | Y | N | Y | Y |
| 3 Ray | Y | Y | N | N | Y | N | N | Y |
| 4 Jones | N | Y | N | Y | Y | N | Y | Y |
| 5 Lewis | Y | Y | Y | Y | Y | N | Y | Y |
| 6 *Gingrich* | Y | Y | N | Y | N | N | N | N |
| 7 Darden | Y | Y | Y | Y | Y | N | Y | Y |
| 8 Rowland | Y | Y | N | Y | Y | N | Y | Y |
| 9 Jenkins | Y | Y | N | N | Y | N | N | Y |
| 10 Barnard | Y | Y | N | N | N | N | N | Y |
| **HAWAII** | | | | | | | | |
| 1 Abercrombie | Y | Y | Y | Y | Y | N | Y | Y |
| 2 Mink | Y | Y | N | N | Y | N | Y | Y |
| **IDAHO** | | | | | | | | |
| 1 LaRocco | Y | Y | N | Y | Y | N | Y | Y |
| 2 Stallings | Y | Y | N | Y | N | N | Y | Y |
| **ILLINOIS** | | | | | | | | |
| 1 Hayes | Y | Y | Y | Y | N | Y | Y | Y |
| 2 Savage | ? | ? | ? | ? | ? | ? | ? | ? |
| 3 Russo | Y | Y | N | N | ? | ? | ? | ? |
| 4 Sangmeister | Y | Y | Y | Y | N | Y | N | Y |
| 5 Lipinski | Y | Y | N | N | ? | ? | ? | ? |
| 6 *Hyde* | Y | Y | N | Y | N | Y | N | Y |
| 7 Collins | ? | ? | ? | ? | ? | ? | ? | ? |
| 8 Rostenkowski | Y | Y | N | N | N | N | N | Y |
| 9 Yates | Y | Y | ? | ? | ? | ? | ? | ? |
| 10 *Porter* | Y | Y | N | N | + | - | - | - |
| 11 Annunzio | Y | Y | Y | ? | Y | N | Y | Y |
| 12 *Crane* | Y | Y | N | N | ? | N | N | N |
| 13 *Fawell* | Y | Y | Y | N | N | N | N | Y |
| 14 *Hastert* | Y | Y | Y | Y | N | N | N | Y |
| 15 *Ewing* | Y | Y | N | Y | ? | ? | N | N |
| 16 Cox | Y | Y | N | N | N | N | N | Y |
| 17 Evans | Y | Y | N | Y | N | Y | N | Y |
| 18 *Michel* | Y | Y | Y | N | N | N | N | Y |
| 19 Bruce | Y | Y | N | N | + | - | + | + |
| 20 Durbin | Y | Y | N | Y | N | Y | N | Y |
| 21 Costello | Y | Y | N | Y | N | Y | N | Y |
| 22 Poshard | Y | Y | N | N | Y | N | N | Y |
| **INDIANA** | | | | | | | | |
| 1 Visclosky | Y | Y | Y | Y | Y | N | Y | N |
| 2 Sharp | Y | Y | N | Y | N | Y | N | Y |
| 3 Roemer | N | Y | N | N | Y | N | N | Y |

ND Northern Democrats  SD Southern Democrats

| | 44 | 45 | 46 | 47 | 48 | 49 | 50 | 51 |
|---|---|---|---|---|---|---|---|---|
| 4 Long | Y | Y | N | N | Y | N | N | Y |
| 5 Jontz | Y | Y | N | N | Y | N | Y | Y |
| 6 ***Burton*** | N | Y | N | Y | N | N | N | Y |
| 7 ***Myers*** | Y | Y | N | N | Y | N | N | Y |
| 8 McCloskey | Y | Y | N | Y | Y | N | Y | Y |
| 9 Hamilton | Y | Y | N | N | Y | N | N | Y |
| 10 Jacobs | Y | Y | N | ? | N | N | Y | Y |
| **IOWA** | | | | | | | | |
| 1 ***Leach*** | Y | Y | N | ? | N | N | N | Y |
| 2 ***Nussle*** | Y | Y | N | Y | N | N | N | N |
| 3 Nagle | Y | Y | N | N | Y | N | Y | Y |
| 4 Smith | Y | Y | Y | Y | Y | N | Y | Y |
| 5 ***Lightfoot*** | N | Y | N | Y | N | N | N | N |
| 6 ***Grandy*** | Y | Y | Y | Y | N | N | N | N |
| **KANSAS** | | | | | | | | |
| 1 ***Roberts*** | N | Y | N | N | N | N | ? | N |
| 2 Slattery | Y | Y | N | Y | Y | N | N | Y |
| 3 ***Meyers*** | N | Y | Y | Y | Y | N | N | Y |
| 4 Glickman | Y | Y | N | Y | Y | N | Y | Y |
| 5 ***Nichols*** | N | Y | N | N | Y | N | N | N |
| **KENTUCKY** | | | | | | | | |
| 1 Hubbard | Y | Y | N | N | Y | N | N | Y |
| 2 Natcher | Y | Y | Y | Y | Y | N | Y | Y |
| 3 Mazzoli | Y | Y | Y | Y | Y | N | Y | Y |
| 4 ***Bunning*** | N | Y | N | Y | N | N | N | Y |
| 5 ***Rogers*** | Y | Y | N | Y | N | N | N | N |
| 6 ***Hopkins*** | Y | Y | N | N | N | N | N | N |
| 7 Perkins | Y | Y | N | N | Y | N | Y | Y |
| **LOUISIANA** | | | | | | | | |
| 1 ***Livingston*** | Y | Y | N | N | Y | N | N | N |
| 2 Jefferson | Y | Y | Y | Y | Y | N | Y | Y |
| 3 Tauzin | Y | Y | N | Y | Y | N | N | Y |
| 4 ***McCrery*** | Y | Y | Y | ? | N | N | N | Y |
| 5 Huckaby | Y | Y | N | Y | Y | N | Y | Y |
| 6 ***Baker*** | Y | Y | Y | Y | N | N | N | N |
| 7 Hayes | Y | Y | N | Y | Y | N | N | Y |
| 8 ***Holloway*** | Y | Y | Y | Y | ? | N | N | Y |
| **MAINE** | | | | | | | | |
| 1 Andrews | Y | Y | N | Y | Y | N | Y | Y |
| 2 ***Snowe*** | Y | Y | N | Y | Y | N | Y | Y |
| **MARYLAND** | | | | | | | | |
| 1 ***Gilchrest*** | Y | Y | N | Y | N | N | N | Y |
| 2 ***Bentley*** | Y | Y | N | Y | N | N | N | Y |
| 3 Cardin | Y | Y | Y | Y | Y | N | Y | Y |
| 4 McMillen | Y | Y | N | Y | Y | N | N | Y |
| 5 Hoyer | Y | Y | N | Y | ? | N | Y | Y |
| 6 Byron | Y | Y | N | Y | Y | N | N | N |
| 7 Mfume | Y | Y | N | Y | ? | N | Y | Y |
| 8 ***Morella*** | Y | Y | N | Y | N | N | N | Y |
| **MASSACHUSETTS** | | | | | | | | |
| 1 Olver | Y | Y | N | N | Y | N | Y | Y |
| 2 Neal | Y | Y | N | N | Y | N | Y | Y |
| 3 Early | Y | Y | N | N | Y | N | Y | Y |
| 4 Frank | Y | Y | Y | Y | Y | N | Y | Y |
| 5 Atkins | Y | Y | N | N | Y | N | Y | Y |
| 6 Mavroules | Y | Y | Y | ? | Y | N | Y | Y |
| 7 Markey | Y | Y | N | Y | Y | N | Y | Y |
| 8 Kennedy | Y | Y | N | N | Y | N | Y | Y |
| 9 Moakley | Y | Y | N | Y | Y | N | Y | Y |
| 10 Studds | Y | Y | N | N | Y | N | Y | Y |
| 11 Donnelly | Y | Y | Y | Y | Y | N | ? | Y |
| **MICHIGAN** | | | | | | | | |
| 1 Conyers | Y | + | Y | Y | Y | N | Y | Y |
| 2 ***Pursell*** | Y | Y | Y | ? | Y | N | N | Y |
| 3 Wolpe | Y | Y | Y | Y | Y | N | Y | Y |
| 4 ***Upton*** | Y | Y | N | Y | N | N | N | Y |
| 5 ***Henry*** | Y | Y | N | Y | N | N | N | Y |
| 6 Carr | Y | Y | N | N | Y | N | N | Y |
| 7 Kildee | Y | Y | N | Y | Y | N | Y | Y |
| 8 Traxler | Y | Y | Y | ? | Y | N | Y | Y |
| 9 ***Vander Jagt*** | Y | Y | N | N | N | N | N | Y |
| 10 ***Camp*** | N | Y | N | Y | N | N | N | Y |
| 11 ***Davis*** | Y | Y | N | N | ? | ? | ? | ? |
| 12 Bonior | Y | Y | Y | Y | Y | N | Y | Y |
| 13 Collins | ? | ? | ? | ? | Y | N | Y | Y |
| 14 Hertel | Y | Y | Y | Y | ? | N | Y | Y |
| 15 Ford | Y | Y | Y | Y | Y | N | Y | Y |
| 16 Dingell | Y | Y | Y | Y | Y | N | Y | Y |
| 17 Levin | Y | Y | Y | Y | Y | N | Y | Y |
| 18 ***Broomfield*** | Y | Y | N | Y | Y | N | N | Y |
| **MINNESOTA** | | | | | | | | |
| 1 Penny | Y | Y | N | Y | Y | N | N | N |
| 2 ***Weber*** | Y | Y | N | ? | Y | N | N | Y |
| 3 ***Ramstad*** | Y | Y | N | N | N | N | N | Y |
| 4 Vento | Y | Y | Y | Y | Y | N | Y | Y |

| | 44 | 45 | 46 | 47 | 48 | 49 | 50 | 51 |
|---|---|---|---|---|---|---|---|---|
| 5 Sabo | Y | Y | Y | Y | Y | N | Y | Y |
| 6 Sikorski | Y | Y | N | Y | N | N | Y | Y |
| 7 Peterson | Y | Y | N | Y | Y | N | N | Y |
| 8 Oberstar | Y | Y | Y | Y | Y | N | Y | Y |
| **MISSISSIPPI** | | | | | | | | |
| 1 Whitten | ? | ? | ? | ? | ? | ? | ? | ? |
| 2 Espy | Y | Y | N | N | Y | N | Y | Y |
| 3 Montgomery | Y | Y | N | Y | Y | N | N | Y |
| 4 Parker | Y | Y | N | Y | Y | N | N | Y |
| 5 Taylor | Y | Y | N | N | Y | N | N | Y |
| **MISSOURI** | | | | | | | | |
| 1 Clay | Y | Y | Y | Y | N | N | Y | Y |
| 2 Horn | Y | Y | N | Y | Y | N | Y | Y |
| 3 Gephardt | Y | Y | Y | Y | Y | N | Y | Y |
| 4 Skelton | Y | Y | N | N | Y | N | N | Y |
| 5 Wheat | Y | Y | N | N | Y | N | Y | Y |
| 6 ***Coleman*** | Y | Y | Y | ? | N | N | N | Y |
| 7 ***Hancock*** | Y | Y | N | N | N | N | N | N |
| 8 ***Emerson*** | Y | Y | N | N | N | N | N | Y |
| 9 Volkmer | Y | Y | N | N | Y | N | Y | Y |
| **MONTANA** | | | | | | | | |
| 1 Williams | Y | Y | N | Y | Y | N | Y | Y |
| 2 ***Marlenee*** | Y | Y | N | Y | N | N | N | N |
| **NEBRASKA** | | | | | | | | |
| 1 ***Bereuter*** | Y | Y | N | N | N | N | N | Y |
| 2 Hoagland | Y | Y | N | Y | Y | N | Y | Y |
| 3 ***Barrett*** | Y | Y | N | N | N | N | N | N |
| **NEVADA** | | | | | | | | |
| 1 Bilbray | Y | Y | N | Y | Y | N | Y | Y |
| 2 ***Vucanovich*** | Y | Y | Y | ? | N | N | N | N |
| **NEW HAMPSHIRE** | | | | | | | | |
| 1 ***Zeliff*** | Y | Y | Y | Y | N | N | N | N |
| 2 Swett | Y | Y | Y | Y | Y | N | N | Y |
| **NEW JERSEY** | | | | | | | | |
| 1 Andrews | Y | Y | N | N | Y | N | N | Y |
| 2 Hughes | Y | Y | N | Y | Y | N | N | Y |
| 3 Pallone | Y | Y | N | N | Y | N | N | Y |
| 4 ***Smith*** | N | Y | N | Y | ? | N | N | Y |
| 5 ***Roukema*** | Y | Y | Y | Y | N | N | N | Y |
| 6 Dwyer | Y | Y | Y | Y | Y | N | Y | Y |
| 7 ***Rinaldo*** | Y | Y | N | Y | Y | N | N | Y |
| 8 Roe | Y | Y | Y | Y | Y | N | Y | Y |
| 9 Torricelli | Y | Y | Y | ? | Y | N | Y | Y |
| 10 Payne | Y | Y | Y | Y | Y | N | Y | Y |
| 11 ***Gallo*** | Y | Y | Y | Y | N | N | N | Y |
| 12 ***Zimmer*** | N | Y | N | Y | N | N | N | Y |
| 13 ***Saxton*** | Y | Y | Y | Y | N | N | N | Y |
| 14 Guarini | Y | Y | N | N | Y | N | Y | Y |
| **NEW MEXICO** | | | | | | | | |
| 1 ***Schiff*** | Y | Y | N | N | Y | N | N | Y |
| 2 ***Skeen*** | Y | Y | N | N | Y | N | N | Y |
| 3 Richardson | Y | Y | N | Y | Y | N | Y | Y |
| **NEW YORK** | | | | | | | | |
| 1 Hochbrueckner | Y | Y | N | N | Y | N | Y | Y |
| 2 Downey | Y | Y | N | N | Y | N | Y | Y |
| 3 Mrazek | Y | Y | N | N | Y | N | N | Y |
| 4 ***Lent*** | Y | Y | N | ? | Y | N | N | Y |
| 5 ***McGrath*** | Y | Y | N | N | N | N | N | Y |
| 6 Flake | Y | Y | Y | Y | Y | N | Y | Y |
| 7 Ackerman | Y | Y | Y | Y | Y | N | Y | Y |
| 8 Scheuer | Y | Y | Y | Y | ? | N | Y | Y |
| 9 Manton | Y | Y | Y | Y | Y | N | Y | Y |
| 10 Schumer | Y | Y | N | N | Y | N | Y | Y |
| 11 Towns | Y | Y | Y | Y | Y | N | Y | Y |
| 12 Owens | Y | Y | Y | ? | ? | N | Y | Y |
| 13 Solarz | Y | Y | N | N | Y | N | Y | Y |
| 14 ***Molinari*** | Y | Y | N | Y | N | N | N | Y |
| 15 ***Green*** | Y | Y | N | Y | Y | N | N | N |
| 16 Rangel | Y | Y | Y | Y | Y | N | Y | Y |
| 17 Weiss | Y | Y | Y | Y | Y | N | Y | Y |
| 18 Serrano | Y | Y | Y | Y | Y | N | Y | Y |
| 19 Engel | Y | Y | N | Y | Y | N | Y | Y |
| 20 Lowey | Y | Y | N | Y | Y | N | Y | Y |
| 21 ***Fish*** | Y | Y | N | Y | Y | N | N | Y |
| 22 ***Gilman*** | N | Y | N | N | Y | N | N | Y |
| 23 McNulty | Y | Y | N | Y | Y | N | Y | Y |
| 24 ***Solomon*** | Y | Y | N | N | N | N | N | Y |
| 25 ***Boehlert*** | Y | Y | N | Y | N | N | N | Y |
| 26 ***Martin*** | Y | Y | N | Y | N | N | N | Y |
| 27 ***Walsh*** | Y | Y | N | Y | N | N | N | Y |
| 28 McHugh | Y | Y | Y | Y | Y | N | Y | Y |
| 29 ***Horton*** | Y | Y | N | Y | Y | N | N | Y |
| 30 Slaughter | Y | Y | N | Y | Y | N | Y | Y |
| 31 ***Paxon*** | Y | Y | Y | Y | N | N | N | Y |

| | 44 | 45 | 46 | 47 | 48 | 49 | 50 | 51 |
|---|---|---|---|---|---|---|---|---|
| 32 LaFalce | Y | Y | N | Y | Y | N | Y | Y |
| 33 Nowak | Y | Y | N | Y | Y | N | Y | Y |
| 34 ***Houghton*** | Y | Y | N | Y | Y | N | N | Y |
| **NORTH CAROLINA** | | | | | | | | |
| 1 Jones | Y | Y | Y | ? | Y | N | Y | Y |
| 2 Valentine | Y | Y | N | N | Y | N | N | N |
| 3 Lancaster | Y | Y | N | N | Y | N | Y | Y |
| 4 Price | Y | Y | Y | ? | Y | N | Y | Y |
| 5 Neal | Y | Y | N | Y | Y | N | Y | Y |
| 6 ***Coble*** | Y | Y | Y | ? | N | N | N | N |
| 7 Rose | Y | Y | Y | Y | Y | N | Y | Y |
| 8 Hefner | Y | Y | Y | ? | Y | N | Y | Y |
| 9 ***McMillan*** | Y | Y | Y | Y | N | N | N | N |
| 10 ***Ballenger*** | Y | Y | Y | Y | N | N | N | N |
| 11 ***Taylor*** | Y | Y | N | Y | N | N | N | Y |
| **NORTH DAKOTA** | | | | | | | | |
| AL Dorgan | Y | Y | N | N | N | N | Y | Y |
| **OHIO** | | | | | | | | |
| 1 Luken | Y | Y | N | Y | Y | N | Y | Y |
| 2 ***Gradison*** | Y | Y | N | ? | Y | N | N | Y |
| 3 Hall | Y | Y | N | N | Y | N | Y | Y |
| 4 ***Oxley*** | Y | Y | Y | Y | Y | N | N | Y |
| 5 ***Gillmor*** | Y | Y | N | ? | Y | N | N | Y |
| 6 ***McEwen*** | Y | Y | N | N | N | N | N | Y |
| 7 ***Hobson*** | Y | Y | Y | Y | N | N | N | N |
| 8 ***Boehner*** | N | Y | Y | Y | N | N | N | N |
| 9 Kaptur | Y | Y | N | Y | Y | N | Y | Y |
| 10 ***Miller*** | Y | Y | Y | N | N | N | N | Y |
| 11 Eckart | Y | Y | N | N | Y | N | Y | Y |
| 12 ***Kasich*** | Y | Y | N | Y | Y | N | N | Y |
| 13 Pease | Y | Y | N | Y | Y | N | ? | Y |
| 14 Sawyer | Y | Y | N | Y | Y | N | Y | Y |
| 15 ***Wylie*** | Y | Y | N | Y | Y | N | N | Y |
| 16 ***Regula*** | Y | Y | N | N | N | N | N | Y |
| 17 Traficant | Y | Y | N | Y | Y | N | N | Y |
| 18 Applegate | N | Y | N | Y | Y | N | Y | Y |
| 19 Feighan | Y | Y | Y | Y | Y | ? | ? | Y |
| 20 Oakar | Y | Y | N | Y | Y | N | Y | Y |
| 21 Stokes | Y | Y | Y | Y | Y | N | Y | Y |
| **OKLAHOMA** | | | | | | | | |
| 1 ***Inhofe*** | N | Y | N | Y | N | N | N | Y |
| 2 Synar | Y | Y | N | Y | Y | N | Y | Y |
| 3 Brewster | Y | Y | N | Y | Y | N | Y | Y |
| 4 McCurdy | Y | Y | Y | Y | Y | N | Y | Y |
| 5 ***Edwards*** | Y | Y | N | N | ? | ? | X | ? |
| 6 English | Y | Y | N | Y | Y | N | Y | Y |
| **OREGON** | | | | | | | | |
| 1 AuCoin | Y | Y | N | N | ? | ? | ? | ? |
| 2 ***Smith*** | N | Y | N | Y | N | N | N | N |
| 3 Wyden | Y | Y | N | N | Y | N | Y | Y |
| 4 DeFazio | Y | Y | N | N | Y | N | Y | Y |
| 5 Kopetski | Y | Y | Y | Y | Y | N | Y | Y |
| **PENNSYLVANIA** | | | | | | | | |
| 1 Foglietta | Y | Y | Y | ? | Y | N | Y | Y |
| 2 Blackwell | Y | Y | Y | ? | Y | N | Y | Y |
| 3 Borski | Y | Y | Y | Y | Y | N | Y | Y |
| 4 Kolter | Y | Y | N | Y | Y | N | Y | Y |
| 5 ***Schulze*** | Y | Y | N | ? | Y | N | N | N |
| 6 Yatron | Y | Y | N | Y | Y | N | Y | Y |
| 7 ***Weldon*** | Y | Y | N | N | N | N | N | Y |
| 8 Kostmayer | Y | Y | N | N | Y | N | Y | Y |
| 9 ***Shuster*** | Y | Y | Y | ? | Y | N | N | Y |
| 10 ***McDade*** | Y | Y | Y | ? | Y | N | N | Y |
| 11 Kanjorski | Y | Y | N | N | Y | N | Y | Y |
| 12 Murtha | Y | Y | Y | Y | Y | N | Y | Y |
| 13 ***Coughlin*** | Y | Y | N | Y | N | N | N | Y |
| 14 Coyne | Y | Y | Y | Y | Y | N | Y | Y |
| 15 ***Ritter*** | Y | Y | N | Y | Y | N | N | Y |
| 16 ***Walker*** | N | Y | Y | Y | N | N | N | N |
| 17 ***Gekas*** | N | Y | N | N | N | N | N | Y |
| 18 ***Santorum*** | N | Y | N | Y | N | N | N | Y |
| 19 ***Goodling*** | Y | Y | N | Y | N | N | N | Y |
| 20 Gaydos | Y | Y | Y | Y | Y | N | Y | Y |
| 21 ***Ridge*** | Y | Y | Y | Y | N | N | N | Y |
| 22 Murphy | Y | Y | N | Y | N | N | Y | Y |
| 23 ***Clinger*** | Y | Y | N | ? | Y | N | N | N |
| **RHODE ISLAND** | | | | | | | | |
| 1 ***Machtley*** | Y | Y | N | N | ? | N | N | Y |
| 2 Reed | Y | Y | N | N | Y | N | Y | Y |
| **SOUTH CAROLINA** | | | | | | | | |
| 1 ***Ravenel*** | Y | Y | N | N | Y | N | N | Y |
| 2 ***Spence*** | Y | Y | N | N | Y | N | N | Y |
| 3 Derrick | Y | Y | N | Y | Y | N | Y | Y |
| 4 Patterson | Y | Y | N | Y | Y | N | N | Y |
| 5 Spratt | Y | Y | N | Y | Y | N | Y | Y |
| 6 Tallon | Y | Y | N | N | ? | N | Y | Y |

| | 44 | 45 | 46 | 47 | 48 | 49 | 50 | 51 |
|---|---|---|---|---|---|---|---|---|
| **SOUTH DAKOTA** | | | | | | | | |
| AL Johnson | Y | Y | N | N | Y | N | Y | Y |
| **TENNESSEE** | | | | | | | | |
| 1 ***Quillen*** | N | Y | N | ? | Y | N | N | Y |
| 2 ***Duncan*** | N | Y | N | N | N | N | N | N |
| 3 Lloyd | Y | Y | N | Y | Y | N | N | Y |
| 4 Cooper | Y | Y | N | Y | Y | N | N | Y |
| 5 Clement | Y | Y | Y | N | Y | N | Y | Y |
| 6 Gordon | Y | Y | N | Y | Y | N | Y | Y |
| 7 ***Sundquist*** | N | Y | N | N | N | N | N | Y |
| 8 Tanner | Y | Y | N | N | Y | N | Y | Y |
| 9 Ford | Y | Y | Y | ? | ? | ? | ? | ? |
| **TEXAS** | | | | | | | | |
| 1 Chapman | Y | Y | N | N | Y | N | Y | Y |
| 2 Wilson | Y | Y | N | Y | Y | N | Y | Y |
| 3 ***Johnson*** | Y | Y | N | Y | Y | N | N | N |
| 4 Hall | Y | Y | N | N | Y | N | N | Y |
| 5 Bryant | Y | Y | Y | Y | Y | N | Y | Y |
| 6 ***Barton*** | Y | Y | N | N | ? | ? | ? | ? |
| 7 ***Archer*** | Y | Y | N | Y | Y | N | N | N |
| 8 ***Fields*** | Y | Y | N | N | N | N | N | N |
| 9 Brooks | Y | Y | Y | Y | Y | N | Y | Y |
| 10 Pickle | Y | Y | Y | Y | Y | N | Y | Y |
| 11 Edwards | Y | Y | N | N | Y | N | Y | Y |
| 12 Geren | Y | Y | N | N | Y | N | N | Y |
| 13 Sarpalius | Y | Y | N | N | Y | N | N | Y |
| 14 Laughlin | Y | Y | Y | ? | Y | N | Y | Y |
| 15 de la Garza | Y | Y | Y | ? | Y | N | Y | Y |
| 16 Coleman | ? | Y | Y | Y | ? | N | Y | Y |
| 17 Stenholm | Y | Y | N | N | Y | N | Y | Y |
| 18 Washington | N | Y | Y | ? | ? | N | Y | Y |
| 19 ***Combest*** | Y | Y | N | ? | Y | N | N | Y |
| 20 Gonzalez | N | Y | N | Y | Y | N | Y | Y |
| 21 ***Smith*** | Y | Y | N | N | ? | N | N | N |
| 22 ***DeLay*** | N | Y | N | N | N | N | N | N |
| 23 Bustamante | Y | Y | Y | ? | Y | N | Y | Y |
| 24 Frost | Y | Y | N | Y | Y | N | Y | Y |
| 25 Andrews | Y | Y | Y | Y | Y | N | Y | Y |
| 26 ***Armey*** | N | Y | N | N | N | N | N | N |
| 27 Ortiz | Y | Y | N | Y | Y | N | Y | Y |
| **UTAH** | | | | | | | | |
| 1 ***Hansen*** | Y | Y | Y | ? | Y | N | N | Y |
| 2 Owens | Y | Y | N | N | Y | N | N | ? |
| 3 Orton | Y | Y | N | Y | Y | N | N | Y |
| **VERMONT** | | | | | | | | |
| AL *Sanders* | Y | Y | N | Y | Y | N | Y | Y |
| **VIRGINIA** | | | | | | | | |
| 1 ***Bateman*** | Y | Y | N | Y | Y | N | N | Y |
| 2 Pickett | Y | Y | N | N | Y | N | N | Y |
| 3 ***Bliley*** | Y | Y | Y | Y | N | N | N | Y |
| 4 Sisisky | Y | Y | N | N | Y | N | Y | Y |
| 5 Payne | Y | Y | Y | Y | Y | N | N | Y |
| 6 Olin | Y | Y | N | ? | Y | N | N | Y |
| 7 ***Allen*** | N | Y | Y | Y | ? | N | N | Y |
| 8 Moran | ? | ? | ? | ? | Y | N | N | Y |
| 9 Boucher | Y | Y | N | Y | Y | N | Y | Y |
| 10 ***Wolf*** | Y | Y | N | N | N | N | N | Y |
| **WASHINGTON** | | | | | | | | |
| 1 ***Miller*** | Y | Y | N | Y | ? | ? | ? | ? |
| 2 Swift | Y | Y | Y | Y | Y | N | Y | Y |
| 3 Unsoeld | Y | Y | Y | Y | Y | N | Y | Y |
| 4 ***Morrison*** | Y | Y | N | Y | Y | N | N | Y |
| 5 Foley | Y | Y | Y | Y | | | | |
| 6 Dicks | Y | Y | Y | Y | Y | N | Y | Y |
| 7 McDermott | Y | Y | Y | Y | Y | N | Y | Y |
| 8 ***Chandler*** | Y | Y | N | Y | N | N | N | Y |
| **WEST VIRGINIA** | | | | | | | | |
| 1 Mollohan | Y | Y | Y | Y | Y | N | Y | Y |
| 2 Staggers | Y | Y | N | N | Y | N | Y | Y |
| 3 Wise | Y | Y | N | Y | Y | N | Y | Y |
| 4 Rahall | Y | Y | N | Y | Y | N | Y | Y |
| **WISCONSIN** | | | | | | | | |
| 1 Aspin | Y | Y | Y | ? | Y | N | Y | Y |
| 2 ***Klug*** | Y | Y | N | N | Y | N | N | Y |
| 3 ***Gunderson*** | Y | Y | Y | ? | Y | N | N | Y |
| 4 Kleczka | Y | Y | Y | ? | Y | N | Y | Y |
| 5 Moody | Y | Y | N | N | Y | N | Y | Y |
| 6 ***Petri*** | Y | Y | N | N | Y | N | N | N |
| 7 Obey | Y | Y | Y | Y | Y | N | Y | Y |
| 8 ***Roth*** | Y | Y | Y | Y | N | N | N | N |
| 9 ***Sensenbrenner*** | Y | Y | N | Y | N | N | N | N |
| **WYOMING** | | | | | | | | |
| AL ***Thomas*** | Y | Y | N | ? | Y | N | N | Y |

Southern states - Ala., Ark., Fla., Ga., Ky., La., Miss., N.C., Okla., S.C., Tenn., Texas, Va.
Omitted votes are quorum calls, which CQ does not include in its vote charts.

**52. Procedural Motion.** Approval of the House Journal of Thursday, March 19. Approved 263-110: R 40-104; D 223-6 (ND 149-5, SD 74-1); I 0-0, March 20, 1992.

**53. HR 4210. 1992 Tax Bill/Rule.** Adoption of the rule (H Res 402) to waive all points of order and provide for House floor consideration of the conference report to create a 20 percent tax credit against Social Security taxes paid by middle-income families, to be replaced in 1994 by a permanent $300-a-child tax credit. The credits would be paid for by adding a new top tax rate of 36 percent and a 10 percent surtax on millionaires. The conference report also provided for a graduated capital gains tax cut. Taxpayers could deduct up to $2,000 per year contributed to individual retirement accounts; qualified taxpayers could make penalty-free withdrawals for first-time home purchases or for medical or educational expenses. Adopted 244-151: R 0-150; D 243-1 (ND 166-1, SD 77-0); I 1-0, March 20, 1992.

**54. HR 4210. 1992 Tax Bill/Conference Report.** Adoption of the conference report to create a 20 percent tax credit against Social Security taxes paid by middle-income families, to be replaced in 1994 by a permanent $300-a-child tax credit. The credits would be paid for by adding a new top tax rate of 36 percent and a 10 percent surtax on millionaires. The conference report also provided for a graduated capital gains tax cut. Taxpayers could deduct up to $2,000 per year contributed to individual retirement accounts; qualified taxpayers could make penalty-free withdrawals for first-time home purchases or for medical or educational expenses. Adopted 211-189: R 1-149; D 209-40 (ND 149-23, SD 60-17); I 1-0, March 20, 1992. A "nay" was a vote in support of the president's position.

**55. HR 4210. 1992 Tax Bill/Veto Override.** Passage, over President Bush's March 20 veto, of the $77.5 billion tax bill to create a 20 percent tax credit against Social Security taxes paid by middle-income families, to be replaced in 1994 by a permanent $300-a-child tax credit. The credits would be paid for by adding a new top income tax rate of 36 percent and a 10 percent surtax on millionaires. The conference report also provided for a graduated capital gains tax cut. Taxpayers could deduct up to $2,000 per year contributed to individual retirement accounts; qualified taxpayers could make penalty-free withdrawals for first-time home purchases or for medical or educational expenses. Rejected 211-215: R 1-163; D 209-52 (ND 150-29, SD 59-23); I 1-0, March 25, 1992. A "nay" was a vote in support of the president's position.

**56. HR 3553. Higher Education Act Reauthorization/Recipient Requirements.** Henry, R-Mich., amendment to require that federal financial student aid recipients be high school graduates or have a general equivalency diploma. Rejected 28-385: R 28-133; D 0-251 (ND 0-171, SD 0-80); I 0-1, March 26, 1992.

**57. HR 3553. Higher Education Act Reauthorization/Sallie Mae.** Gradison, R-Ohio, amendment to establish the Treasury Department as the financial safety and soundness regulator for the Student Loan Marketing Association (Sallie Mae). Rejected 181-232: R 102-56; D 79-175 (ND 40-133, SD 39-42); I 0-1, March 26, 1992.

**58. HR 3553. Higher Education Act Reauthorization/Allow Pell Grants to Prisoners.** Towns, D-N.Y., substitute amendment to the Coleman, R-Mo., amendment to allow state and federal prisoners to receive Pell grants but place restrictions on which prisoners could receive grants and under what conditions the grants could be used. Towns would prohibit prisoners on death row, prisoners with life sentences without parole and habitual criminals from receiving Pell grants. The Coleman amendment prohibited Pell grants from going to state and federal prisoners. Rejected 85-314: R 12-139; D 72-175 (ND 59-109, SD 13-66); I 1-0, March 26, 1992.

**59. HR 3553. Higher Education Act Reauthorization/Prohibit Pell Grants to Prisoners.** Coleman, R-Mo., amendment to prohibit Pell grants from going to state and federal prisoners. Adopted 351-39: R 142-6; D 209-32 (ND 138-26, SD 71-6); I 0-1, March 26, 1992.

## KEY

Y  Voted for (yea).
#  Paired for.
+  Announced for.
N  Voted against (nay).
X  Paired against.
−  Announced against.
P  Voted "present."
C  Voted "present" to avoid possible conflict of interest.
?  Did not vote or otherwise make a position known.

Democrats **Republicans** *Independent*

| | 52 | 53 | 54 | 55 | 56 | 57 | 58 | 59 |
|---|---|---|---|---|---|---|---|---|
| **ALABAMA** | | | | | | | | |
| 1 *Callahan* | N | N | ? | N | N | Y | N | N |
| 2 *Dickinson* | ? | ? | ? | N | N | Y | N | Y |
| 3 Browder | Y | Y | Y | Y | ? | Y | N | Y |
| 4 Bevill | Y | Y | Y | Y | N | Y | N | ? |
| 5 Cramer | Y | Y | Y | Y | N | Y | N | Y |
| 6 Erdreich | Y | Y | Y | Y | N | Y | N | Y |
| 7 Harris | Y | Y | Y | Y | N | Y | N | Y |
| **ALASKA** | | | | | | | | |
| AL *Young* | N | N | N | N | N | N | N | Y |
| **ARIZONA** | | | | | | | | |
| 1 *Rhodes* | N | N | N | N | Y | N | Y | Y |
| 2 Pastor | Y | Y | Y | Y | N | N | N | Y |
| 3 *Stump* | N | N | N | N | Y | N | N | Y |
| 4 *Kyl* | N | N | N | N | Y | N | Y | Y |
| 5 *Kolbe* | N | N | N | N | Y | N | Y | Y |
| **ARKANSAS** | | | | | | | | |
| 1 Alexander | Y | Y | Y | Y | N | N | N | Y |
| 2 Thornton | Y | Y | Y | Y | N | N | N | Y |
| 3 *Hammerschmidt* | Y | N | N | N | N | N | N | Y |
| 4 Anthony | Y | Y | Y | Y | N | N | N | Y |
| **CALIFORNIA** | | | | | | | | |
| 1 *Riggs* | N | N | N | N | N | N | N | Y |
| 2 *Herger* | N | N | N | N | N | Y | N | Y |
| 3 Matsui | Y | Y | Y | Y | N | N | N | Y |
| 4 Fazio | Y | Y | Y | Y | N | N | N | Y |
| 5 Pelosi | ? | Y | Y | Y | N | N | N | Y |
| 6 Boxer | ? | Y | Y | Y | N | ? | ? | ? |
| 7 Miller | ? | # | # | Y | N | N | Y | N |
| 8 Dellums | ? | Y | Y | Y | N | N | Y | N |
| 9 Stark | Y | Y | N | N | ? | ? | ? | ? |
| 10 Edwards | Y | Y | Y | Y | N | N | Y | N |
| 11 Lantos | Y | Y | Y | Y | N | N | Y | N |
| 12 *Campbell* | ? | ? | X | N | Y | N | Y | N |
| 13 Mineta | Y | Y | Y | Y | N | N | N | Y |
| 14 *Doolittle* | N | N | N | N | Y | N | Y | Y |
| 15 Condit | Y | Y | N | N | Y | N | N | Y |
| 16 Panetta | Y | Y | Y | Y | N | N | N | Y |
| 17 Dooley | Y | Y | Y | Y | N | N | N | Y |
| 18 Lehman | Y | Y | N | N | N | N | N | Y |
| 19 *Lagomarsino* | N | N | N | N | N | Y | N | Y |
| 20 *Thomas* | ? | X | ? | N | N | Y | N | Y |
| 21 *Gallegly* | N | N | N | N | Y | Y | N | Y |
| 22 *Moorhead* | N | N | N | N | N | Y | N | Y |
| 23 Beilenson | Y | Y | N | N | N | Y | Y | Y |
| 24 Waxman | Y | Y | Y | Y | N | N | Y | Y |
| 25 Roybal | ? | Y | Y | Y | N | N | Y | N |
| 26 Berman | Y | Y | Y | Y | N | N | Y | Y |
| 27 Levine | ? | ? | ? | ? | ? | ? | ? | ? |
| 28 Dixon | Y | Y | Y | Y | N | N | N | Y |
| 29 Waters | Y | ? | Y | Y | N | N | Y | N |
| 30 Martinez | Y | Y | Y | Y | ? | ? | ? | ? |
| 31 Dymally | ? | # | ? | Y | N | N | Y | ? |
| 32 Anderson | Y | Y | Y | Y | N | N | N | Y |
| 33 *Dreier* | Y | N | N | N | Y | N | Y | Y |
| 34 Torres | Y | Y | Y | Y | N | N | Y | N |
| 35 *Lewis* | N | N | N | N | N | Y | N | Y |
| 36 Brown | Y | Y | Y | Y | N | N | N | Y |
| 37 *McCandless* | N | N | N | N | N | N | N | N |
| 38 *Dornan* | ? | N | N | N | Y | N | Y | N |
| 39 *Dannemeyer* | − | − | − | − | + | + | + | − |
| 40 *Cox* | N | N | N | N | N | Y | N | Y |
| 41 *Lowery* | ? | N | N | N | N | N | N | Y |

| | 52 | 53 | 54 | 55 | 56 | 57 | 58 | 59 |
|---|---|---|---|---|---|---|---|---|
| 42 *Rohrabacher* | N | N | N | N | Y | N | Y | N |
| 43 *Packard* | Y | N | N | N | N | Y | N | Y |
| 44 *Cunningham* | N | N | N | N | N | Y | N | Y |
| 45 *Hunter* | ? | N | N | N | N | N | N | Y |
| **COLORADO** | | | | | | | | |
| 1 Schroeder | N | Y | Y | Y | N | Y | N | Y |
| 2 Skaggs | Y | ? | # | Y | N | Y | N | Y |
| 3 Campbell | Y | Y | Y | Y | N | N | N | Y |
| 4 *Allard* | N | N | N | N | Y | Y | N | Y |
| 5 *Hefley* | N | N | N | N | Y | N | Y | Y |
| 6 *Schaefer* | N | N | N | N | N | Y | N | Y |
| **CONNECTICUT** | | | | | | | | |
| 1 Kennelly | Y | Y | Y | Y | N | Y | − | + |
| 2 Gejdenson | Y | Y | Y | Y | N | N | N | Y |
| 3 DeLauro | Y | Y | Y | Y | N | N | N | Y |
| 4 *Shays* | N | N | N | N | N | Y | N | Y |
| 5 *Franks* | N | N | N | N | Y | N | Y | Y |
| 6 *Johnson* | Y | N | N | N | N | ? | ? | ? |
| **DELAWARE** | | | | | | | | |
| AL Carper | Y | Y | N | N | N | Y | Y | Y |
| **FLORIDA** | | | | | | | | |
| 1 Hutto | Y | Y | N | N | N | N | N | Y |
| 2 Peterson | Y | Y | Y | # | ? | X | ? | ? |
| 3 Bennett | Y | Y | Y | Y | N | Y | N | Y |
| 4 *James* | N | N | N | N | N | Y | N | Y |
| 5 *McCollum* | N | N | N | N | N | Y | N | Y |
| 6 *Stearns* | N | N | N | N | Y | N | Y | Y |
| 7 Gibbons | Y | Y | Y | Y | N | N | N | Y |
| 8 *Young* | N | N | N | N | N | ? | ? | ? |
| 9 *Bilirakis* | N | N | N | N | N | Y | N | Y |
| 10 *Ireland* | N | N | N | N | N | Y | N | Y |
| 11 Bacchus | Y | Y | Y | Y | N | Y | N | Y |
| 12 *Lewis* | N | N | N | N | N | Y | N | Y |
| 13 *Goss* | N | N | N | N | N | Y | N | Y |
| 14 Johnston | Y | Y | Y | Y | N | Y | N | Y |
| 15 *Shaw* | Y | N | N | N | N | Y | N | Y |
| 16 Smith | Y | Y | Y | Y | N | N | N | Y |
| 17 Lehman | ? | ? | ? | Y | N | N | N | ? |
| 18 *Ros-Lehtinen* | N | N | N | N | N | N | N | Y |
| 19 Fascell | Y | Y | Y | Y | N | N | N | Y |
| **GEORGIA** | | | | | | | | |
| 1 Thomas | ? | ? | ? | N | ? | N | N | Y |
| 2 Hatcher | ? | ? | # | Y | N | N | N | Y |
| 3 Ray | Y | Y | N | N | N | Y | N | Y |
| 4 Jones | Y | Y | N | N | N | Y | N | Y |
| 5 Lewis | Y | Y | Y | Y | N | N | Y | N |
| 6 *Gingrich* | N | N | X | N | Y | N | N | Y |
| 7 Darden | Y | Y | Y | Y | N | N | N | Y |
| 8 Rowland | Y | Y | Y | Y | N | Y | N | Y |
| 9 Jenkins | Y | Y | Y | Y | ? | ? | ? | ? |
| 10 Barnard | ? | ? | X | N | N | Y | N | Y |
| **HAWAII** | | | | | | | | |
| 1 Abercrombie | ? | Y | Y | Y | N | N | Y | N |
| 2 Mink | Y | Y | Y | Y | N | Y | Y | Y |
| **IDAHO** | | | | | | | | |
| 1 LaRocco | Y | Y | Y | Y | N | N | N | Y |
| 2 Stallings | Y | N | N | N | N | Y | N | Y |
| **ILLINOIS** | | | | | | | | |
| 1 Hayes | Y | Y | Y | Y | N | N | Y | N |
| 2 Savage | ? | Y | Y | Y | N | N | N | Y |
| 3 Russo | ? | ? | ? | N | ? | ? | ? | ? |
| 4 Sangmeister | Y | Y | Y | Y | N | N | N | Y |
| 5 Lipinski | ? | ? | ? | Y | N | N | N | Y |
| 6 *Hyde* | ? | N | N | N | N | Y | N | Y |
| 7 Collins | ? | # | # | Y | N | N | Y | N |
| 8 Rostenkowski | Y | Y | Y | Y | N | N | N | Y |
| 9 Yates | Y | Y | Y | Y | N | N | Y | N |
| 10 *Porter* | N | N | N | N | N | Y | N | Y |
| 11 Annunzio | Y | Y | Y | Y | N | N | N | Y |
| 12 *Crane* | N | N | N | N | N | Y | N | Y |
| 13 *Fawell* | N | N | N | N | N | Y | N | Y |
| 14 *Hastert* | N | − | N | N | N | Y | N | Y |
| 15 *Ewing* | Y | N | N | N | ? | Y | N | ? |
| 16 Cox | Y | Y | Y | Y | N | N | N | Y |
| 17 Evans | Y | Y | Y | Y | N | N | Y | N |
| 18 *Michel* | N | N | N | N | N | Y | N | Y |
| 19 Bruce | + | + | + | Y | N | N | N | Y |
| 20 Durbin | Y | Y | Y | Y | N | N | N | Y |
| 21 Costello | Y | Y | Y | + | N | N | ? | Y |
| 22 Poshard | Y | Y | Y | Y | N | N | N | Y |
| **INDIANA** | | | | | | | | |
| 1 Visclosky | Y | Y | Y | Y | ? | Y | N | Y |
| 2 Sharp | Y | Y | Y | Y | N | N | N | Y |
| 3 Roemer | Y | Y | N | N | N | N | N | Y |

ND Northern Democrats  SD Southern Democrats

| | 52 | 53 | 54 | 55 | 56 | 57 | 58 | 59 |
|---|---|---|---|---|---|---|---|---|
| 4 Long | Y | Y | N | N | N | N | N | Y |
| 5 Jontz | Y | Y | Y | Y | N | Y | Y | N |
| 6 ***Burton*** | N | N | N | N | N | N | N | Y |
| 7 ***Myers*** | Y | N | N | N | N | N | N | Y |
| 8 McCloskey | Y | Y | Y | Y | ? | N | N | Y |
| 9 Hamilton | Y | Y | N | N | N | Y | N | Y |
| 10 Jacobs | N | Y | Y | Y | N | Y | Y | N |
| **IOWA** | | | | | | | | |
| 1 ***Leach*** | N | N | N | N | N | Y | N | Y |
| 2 ***Nussle*** | N | N | N | N | N | Y | N | Y |
| 3 Nagle | Y | ? | Y | Y | N | N | N | Y |
| 4 Smith | Y | Y | Y | Y | N | N | N | Y |
| 5 ***Lightfoot*** | N | N | N | N | N | Y | N | Y |
| 6 ***Grandy*** | N | N | N | N | N | + | N | Y |
| **KANSAS** | | | | | | | | |
| 1 ***Roberts*** | N | N | N | N | N | N | ? | ? |
| 2 Slattery | Y | Y | N | N | N | Y | N | Y |
| 3 ***Meyers*** | N | N | N | N | N | Y | N | Y |
| 4 Glickman | Y | Y | Y | Y | N | Y | N | Y |
| 5 ***Nichols*** | Y | N | N | N | N | N | N | Y |
| **KENTUCKY** | | | | | | | | |
| 1 Hubbard | Y | Y | Y | Y | N | N | N | Y |
| 2 Natcher | Y | Y | Y | Y | N | N | N | Y |
| 3 Mazzoli | Y | Y | Y | Y | N | N | N | Y |
| 4 ***Bunning*** | N | N | N | N | N | N | ? | ? |
| 5 ***Rogers*** | N | N | N | N | N | Y | N | Y |
| 6 ***Hopkins*** | N | N | N | N | Y | N | N | Y |
| 7 Perkins | ? | Y | Y | Y | N | N | N | Y |
| **LOUISIANA** | | | | | | | | |
| 1 ***Livingston*** | ? | ? | ? | N | N | Y | N | Y |
| 2 Jefferson | Y | Y | Y | Y | N | N | Y | N |
| 3 Tauzin | Y | Y | N | N | N | N | N | Y |
| 4 ***McCrery*** | N | N | N | N | Y | Y | N | Y |
| 5 Huckaby | ? | ? | ? | Y | N | Y | N | Y |
| 6 ***Baker*** | ? | X | ? | N | N | Y | N | Y |
| 7 Hayes | ? | ? | ? | N | N | Y | N | Y |
| 8 ***Holloway*** | ? | ? | ? | N | N | Y | N | Y |
| **MAINE** | | | | | | | | |
| 1 Andrews | Y | Y | Y | Y | N | N | N | Y |
| 2 ***Snowe*** | Y | N | Y | Y | N | N | N | Y |
| **MARYLAND** | | | | | | | | |
| 1 ***Gilchrest*** | N | N | N | N | N | N | N | Y |
| 2 ***Bentley*** | N | N | N | N | N | N | Y | Y |
| 3 Cardin | Y | Y | Y | Y | N | Y | N | Y |
| 4 McMillen | Y | Y | N | N | N | N | N | Y |
| 5 Hoyer | Y | Y | Y | Y | N | N | N | Y |
| 6 Byron | Y | Y | Y | N | N | Y | N | Y |
| 7 Mfume | Y | Y | Y | Y | N | N | Y | N |
| 8 ***Morella*** | N | N | N | N | N | N | N | Y |
| **MASSACHUSETTS** | | | | | | | | |
| 1 Olver | Y | Y | Y | Y | N | N | N | Y |
| 2 Neal | Y | Y | Y | Y | N | N | N | Y |
| 3 Early | Y | Y | N | N | N | N | N | Y |
| 4 Frank | Y | Y | Y | Y | N | N | ? | ? |
| 5 Atkins | Y | Y | Y | Y | N | Y | N | ? |
| 6 Mavroules | Y | Y | Y | Y | N | N | N | Y |
| 7 Markey | Y | Y | Y | Y | N | N | Y | Y |
| 8 Kennedy | Y | Y | Y | Y | N | N | Y | N |
| 9 Moakley | Y | Y | Y | Y | N | N | N | Y |
| 10 Studds | Y | Y | Y | Y | N | N | N | Y |
| 11 Donnelly | Y | Y | Y | Y | ? | N | ? | ? |
| **MICHIGAN** | | | | | | | | |
| 1 Conyers | ? | Y | Y | Y | N | N | Y | ? |
| 2 ***Pursell*** | ? | ? | ? | N | N | Y | N | Y |
| 3 Wolpe | Y | Y | Y | Y | N | N | Y | Y |
| 4 ***Upton*** | N | N | N | N | Y | Y | N | Y |
| 5 ***Henry*** | N | N | N | N | Y | Y | N | Y |
| 6 Carr | Y | Y | N | N | N | N | N | Y |
| 7 Kildee | Y | Y | Y | Y | N | N | Y | Y |
| 8 Traxler | Y | Y | Y | Y | N | N | N | Y |
| 9 ***Vander Jagt*** | N | N | N | N | N | N | ? | ? |
| 10 ***Camp*** | N | N | N | N | N | N | N | Y |
| 11 ***Davis*** | Y | N | N | N | N | N | N | Y |
| 12 Bonior | Y | Y | Y | Y | N | N | Y | Y |
| 13 Collins | Y | Y | Y | Y | N | N | Y | N |
| 14 Hertel | ? | Y | Y | Y | N | N | N | Y |
| 15 Ford | ? | ? | Y | Y | N | N | Y | Y |
| 16 Dingell | Y | Y | Y | Y | N | N | N | Y |
| 17 Levin | Y | Y | Y | Y | N | N | N | Y |
| 18 ***Broomfield*** | Y | N | N | N | Y | N | N | Y |
| **MINNESOTA** | | | | | | | | |
| 1 Penny | Y | Y | Y | N | N | Y | N | Y |
| 2 ***Weber*** | ? | N | N | N | N | N | N | Y |
| 3 ***Ramstad*** | N | N | N | N | N | N | N | Y |
| 4 Vento | Y | Y | Y | Y | N | N | Y | Y |

| | 52 | 53 | 54 | 55 | 56 | 57 | 58 | 59 |
|---|---|---|---|---|---|---|---|---|
| 5 Sabo | Y | Y | Y | Y | N | N | Y | Y |
| 6 Sikorski | N | Y | Y | Y | N | N | N | Y |
| 7 Peterson | Y | Y | N | N | N | Y | Y | Y |
| 8 Oberstar | Y | Y | Y | Y | N | N | Y | Y |
| **MISSISSIPPI** | | | | | | | | |
| 1 Whitten | ? | ? | ? | ? | ? | ? | ? | ? |
| 2 Espy | Y | Y | Y | Y | N | N | N | Y |
| 3 Montgomery | Y | Y | N | N | N | Y | N | Y |
| 4 Parker | Y | Y | N | N | N | Y | N | Y |
| 5 Taylor | Y | Y | N | N | N | Y | N | Y |
| **MISSOURI** | | | | | | | | |
| 1 Clay | N | Y | Y | Y | ? | N | Y | Y |
| 2 Horn | Y | Y | Y | Y | N | N | N | Y |
| 3 Gephardt | Y | Y | Y | Y | N | N | N | Y |
| 4 Skelton | Y | Y | N | N | N | N | N | Y |
| 5 Wheat | Y | Y | Y | Y | N | N | N | Y |
| 6 ***Coleman*** | N | N | N | N | N | N | N | Y |
| 7 ***Hancock*** | N | N | N | N | N | Y | N | Y |
| 8 ***Emerson*** | N | N | N | N | N | N | N | Y |
| 9 Volkmer | Y | Y | Y | Y | N | Y | N | Y |
| **MONTANA** | | | | | | | | |
| 1 Williams | Y | Y | Y | Y | N | N | Y | Y |
| 2 ***Marlenee*** | ? | ? | X | N | N | N | N | Y |
| **NEBRASKA** | | | | | | | | |
| 1 ***Bereuter*** | N | N | N | N | N | Y | N | Y |
| 2 Hoagland | Y | Y | Y | Y | N | Y | N | Y |
| 3 ***Barrett*** | N | N | N | N | N | N | N | Y |
| **NEVADA** | | | | | | | | |
| 1 Bilbray | Y | Y | Y | Y | N | Y | N | Y |
| 2 ***Vucanovich*** | N | N | N | N | N | N | N | Y |
| **NEW HAMPSHIRE** | | | | | | | | |
| 1 ***Zeliff*** | N | N | N | N | Y | Y | N | Y |
| 2 Swett | Y | Y | N | N | N | N | N | Y |
| **NEW JERSEY** | | | | | | | | |
| 1 Andrews | Y | Y | N | N | N | N | N | Y |
| 2 Hughes | Y | N | N | N | N | N | N | Y |
| 3 Pallone | Y | Y | N | N | N | N | N | Y |
| 4 ***Smith*** | Y | N | N | N | N | Y | ? | ? |
| 5 ***Roukema*** | N | N | N | N | Y | Y | N | Y |
| 6 Dwyer | Y | Y | N | N | N | Y | N | Y |
| 7 ***Rinaldo*** | Y | N | N | N | N | Y | N | Y |
| 8 Roe | ? | ? | N | N | N | N | N | Y |
| 9 Torricelli | Y | Y | Y | Y | ? | Y | N | Y |
| 10 Payne | Y | Y | Y | Y | N | N | Y | N |
| 11 ***Gallo*** | ? | N | N | N | N | Y | N | Y |
| 12 ***Zimmer*** | N | N | N | N | Y | Y | N | Y |
| 13 ***Saxton*** | ? | N | N | N | N | Y | N | Y |
| 14 Guarini | Y | Y | Y | Y | N | Y | N | Y |
| **NEW MEXICO** | | | | | | | | |
| 1 ***Schiff*** | Y | N | N | N | N | Y | N | Y |
| 2 ***Skeen*** | Y | N | N | N | N | Y | N | Y |
| 3 Richardson | Y | Y | Y | Y | N | Y | N | Y |
| **NEW YORK** | | | | | | | | |
| 1 Hochbrueckner | Y | Y | Y | Y | N | Y | N | Y |
| 2 Downey | Y | Y | Y | Y | N | N | N | Y |
| 3 Mrazek | ? | ? | ? | N | ? | ? | ? | ? |
| 4 ***Lent*** | Y | N | N | N | N | Y | N | Y |
| 5 ***McGrath*** | N | N | N | N | N | Y | N | Y |
| 6 Flake | Y | Y | Y | Y | N | N | Y | N |
| 7 Ackerman | Y | Y | Y | Y | N | N | N | Y |
| 8 Scheuer | Y | Y | Y | Y | N | N | Y | N |
| 9 Manton | ? | ? | # | Y | N | N | N | Y |
| 10 Schumer | Y | Y | Y | Y | N | Y | Y | Y |
| 11 Towns | Y | Y | Y | Y | N | N | Y | N |
| 12 Owens | Y | Y | Y | Y | N | N | Y | N |
| 13 Solarz | Y | Y | Y | Y | N | N | Y | Y |
| 14 ***Molinari*** | N | N | N | N | N | N | N | Y |
| 15 ***Green*** | Y | N | N | N | N | Y | Y | Y |
| 16 Rangel | Y | Y | Y | Y | N | N | Y | N |
| 17 Weiss | ? | Y | Y | # | N | N | Y | N |
| 18 Serrano | Y | Y | Y | Y | N | N | Y | N |
| 19 Engel | Y | Y | Y | Y | N | N | N | Y |
| 20 Lowey | Y | Y | Y | Y | N | N | Y | Y |
| 21 ***Fish*** | Y | N | N | N | N | Y | N | Y |
| 22 ***Gilman*** | Y | N | N | N | N | N | N | Y |
| 23 McNulty | Y | Y | Y | Y | N | N | N | Y |
| 24 ***Solomon*** | N | N | N | N | N | N | N | Y |
| 25 ***Boehlert*** | N | N | N | N | N | N | N | Y |
| 26 ***Martin*** | N | N | N | N | N | N | N | Y |
| 27 ***Walsh*** | N | N | N | N | N | Y | N | Y |
| 28 McHugh | Y | Y | Y | Y | N | N | N | Y |
| 29 ***Horton*** | Y | N | N | N | N | N | Y | Y |
| 30 Slaughter | Y | Y | Y | Y | N | N | N | Y |
| 31 ***Paxon*** | N | N | N | N | N | Y | N | Y |

| | 52 | 53 | 54 | 55 | 56 | 57 | 58 | 59 |
|---|---|---|---|---|---|---|---|---|
| 32 LaFalce | ? | Y | Y | Y | N | N | N | Y |
| 33 Nowak | Y | Y | Y | Y | N | N | Y | Y |
| 34 ***Houghton*** | Y | N | N | N | N | Y | N | Y |
| **NORTH CAROLINA** | | | | | | | | |
| 1 Jones | Y | Y | Y | Y | N | N | N | Y |
| 2 Valentine | Y | Y | Y | Y | N | Y | N | Y |
| 3 Lancaster | Y | Y | Y | N | N | Y | Y | Y |
| 4 Price | Y | Y | Y | Y | N | N | Y | Y |
| 5 Neal | Y | Y | Y | Y | N | Y | N | Y |
| 6 ***Coble*** | N | N | N | N | N | Y | N | Y |
| 7 Rose | Y | Y | Y | Y | N | N | N | Y |
| 8 Hefner | Y | Y | Y | Y | N | Y | N | Y |
| 9 ***McMillan*** | N | N | N | N | Y | Y | N | Y |
| 10 ***Ballenger*** | N | N | N | N | Y | Y | N | Y |
| 11 ***Taylor*** | N | N | N | N | Y | N | N | Y |
| **NORTH DAKOTA** | | | | | | | | |
| AL Dorgan | Y | Y | Y | Y | N | Y | N | Y |
| **OHIO** | | | | | | | | |
| 1 Luken | Y | Y | Y | N | N | N | N | Y |
| 2 ***Gradison*** | Y | N | N | N | Y | Y | ? | ? |
| 3 Hall | Y | Y | Y | Y | N | N | N | Y |
| 4 ***Oxley*** | Y | N | N | N | N | Y | N | Y |
| 5 ***Gillmor*** | Y | N | N | N | N | Y | N | Y |
| 6 ***McEwen*** | N | N | N | N | N | N | Y | N |
| 7 ***Hobson*** | N | N | N | N | N | Y | Y | N |
| 8 ***Boehner*** | N | N | N | N | N | N | ? | ? |
| 9 Kaptur | Y | Y | Y | Y | N | Y | N | Y |
| 10 ***Miller*** | N | N | N | N | N | N | N | Y |
| 11 Eckart | Y | Y | Y | Y | N | Y | N | Y |
| 12 ***Kasich*** | Y | N | N | N | N | Y | N | Y |
| 13 Pease | Y | Y | Y | Y | N | Y | Y | N |
| 14 Sawyer | Y | Y | Y | Y | N | N | N | Y |
| 15 ***Wylie*** | ? | ? | ? | N | N | Y | N | Y |
| 16 ***Regula*** | N | N | N | N | N | Y | Y | Y |
| 17 Traficant | Y | Y | N | N | N | N | N | Y |
| 18 Applegate | Y | Y | Y | Y | N | N | N | Y |
| 19 Feighan | Y | Y | Y | Y | N | N | N | Y |
| 20 Oakar | Y | Y | Y | Y | N | N | N | Y |
| 21 Stokes | Y | Y | Y | Y | N | N | Y | N |
| **OKLAHOMA** | | | | | | | | |
| 1 ***Inhofe*** | N | N | N | N | N | Y | N | Y |
| 2 Synar | Y | Y | Y | Y | N | N | N | Y |
| 3 Brewster | ? | Y | Y | Y | N | N | N | Y |
| 4 McCurdy | Y | Y | N | N | N | Y | N | Y |
| 5 ***Edwards*** | ? | ? | ? | N | N | N | N | Y |
| 6 English | Y | Y | N | N | N | Y | N | Y |
| **OREGON** | | | | | | | | |
| 1 AuCoin | ? | Y | Y | ? | ? | ? | ? | ? |
| 2 ***Smith*** | N | N | N | N | N | N | N | Y |
| 3 Wyden | Y | Y | Y | Y | N | Y | N | Y |
| 4 DeFazio | Y | Y | Y | Y | N | N | Y | Y |
| 5 Kopetski | Y | Y | Y | Y | N | Y | Y | N |
| **PENNSYLVANIA** | | | | | | | | |
| 1 Foglietta | Y | Y | Y | Y | N | N | Y | N |
| 2 Blackwell | ? | Y | Y | Y | N | N | Y | N |
| 3 Borski | Y | Y | Y | Y | N | N | N | Y |
| 4 Kolter | Y | Y | Y | Y | N | ? | ? | ? |
| 5 ***Schulze*** | Y | N | N | N | N | N | N | Y |
| 6 Yatron | Y | Y | Y | Y | N | N | ? | ? |
| 7 ***Weldon*** | N | N | N | N | N | N | N | Y |
| 8 Kostmayer | Y | Y | Y | Y | N | N | Y | Y |
| 9 ***Shuster*** | N | N | N | N | N | Y | N | Y |
| 10 ***McDade*** | N | N | N | N | N | N | N | Y |
| 11 Kanjorski | Y | Y | Y | Y | N | N | N | Y |
| 12 Murtha | Y | Y | Y | Y | N | N | N | Y |
| 13 ***Coughlin*** | N | N | N | N | Y | Y | ? | ? |
| 14 Coyne | Y | Y | Y | Y | N | N | Y | Y |
| 15 ***Ritter*** | Y | N | N | N | N | Y | N | Y |
| 16 ***Walker*** | N | N | N | N | Y | N | Y | Y |
| 17 ***Gekas*** | N | N | N | N | Y | Y | N | Y |
| 18 ***Santorum*** | ? | N | N | N | N | ? | ? | X |
| 19 ***Goodling*** | N | N | N | N | N | N | N | Y |
| 20 Gaydos | ? | Y | Y | Y | N | ? | N | ? |
| 21 ***Ridge*** | N | N | N | N | N | N | N | ? |
| 22 Murphy | N | Y | Y | Y | N | N | N | Y |
| 23 ***Clinger*** | Y | N | N | N | N | Y | N | Y |
| **RHODE ISLAND** | | | | | | | | |
| 1 ***Machtley*** | N | N | N | N | N | N | N | Y |
| 2 Reed | ? | Y | Y | Y | N | N | N | Y |
| **SOUTH CAROLINA** | | | | | | | | |
| 1 ***Ravenel*** | Y | N | N | N | N | N | N | Y |
| 2 ***Spence*** | N | N | N | N | N | Y | N | Y |
| 3 Derrick | Y | Y | Y | Y | N | N | N | Y |
| 4 Patterson | Y | Y | N | N | N | N | N | Y |
| 5 Spratt | Y | Y | Y | Y | N | Y | N | Y |
| 6 Tallon | Y | Y | Y | Y | N | N | N | Y |

| | 52 | 53 | 54 | 55 | 56 | 57 | 58 | 59 |
|---|---|---|---|---|---|---|---|---|
| **SOUTH DAKOTA** | | | | | | | | |
| AL Johnson | Y | Y | Y | Y | N | Y | Y | Y |
| **TENNESSEE** | | | | | | | | |
| 1 ***Quillen*** | N | N | N | N | N | N | Y | N |
| 2 ***Duncan*** | Y | N | N | N | N | Y | N | Y |
| 3 Lloyd | N | Y | N | N | N | Y | N | Y |
| 4 Cooper | Y | Y | N | N | N | Y | Y | Y |
| 5 Clement | Y | Y | Y | Y | N | N | Y | Y |
| 6 Gordon | Y | Y | Y | Y | N | N | N | Y |
| 7 ***Sundquist*** | N | N | N | N | N | N | Y | ? |
| 8 Tanner | Y | Y | Y | Y | N | Y | Y | Y |
| 9 Ford | Y | Y | Y | ? | N | N | Y | Y |
| **TEXAS** | | | | | | | | |
| 1 Chapman | Y | Y | Y | Y | N | Y | N | Y |
| 2 Wilson | Y | Y | Y | Y | N | N | ? | ? |
| 3 ***Johnson*** | Y | N | N | N | Y | N | N | Y |
| 4 Hall | Y | Y | N | N | N | Y | N | Y |
| 5 Bryant | Y | Y | Y | Y | N | N | N | Y |
| 6 ***Barton*** | N | N | N | N | Y | Y | N | Y |
| 7 ***Archer*** | Y | N | N | N | N | Y | N | Y |
| 8 ***Fields*** | N | N | N | N | N | Y | N | Y |
| 9 Brooks | Y | Y | Y | Y | N | N | N | Y |
| 10 Pickle | Y | Y | Y | Y | N | Y | N | Y |
| 11 Edwards | Y | Y | Y | Y | N | Y | N | Y |
| 12 Geren | Y | Y | N | N | N | Y | N | Y |
| 13 Sarpalius | Y | Y | N | N | N | Y | N | Y |
| 14 Laughlin | ? | ? | ? | Y | N | ? | ? | ? |
| 15 de la Garza | Y | Y | Y | Y | N | N | N | Y |
| 16 Coleman | Y | Y | Y | Y | N | N | N | Y |
| 17 Stenholm | Y | Y | Y | N | N | Y | N | ? |
| 18 Washington | Y | Y | Y | Y | N | N | Y | N |
| 19 ***Combest*** | Y | N | N | N | N | Y | N | Y |
| 20 Gonzalez | Y | Y | Y | Y | N | N | N | N |
| 21 ***Smith*** | ? | ? | ? | N | N | Y | ? | ? |
| 22 ***DeLay*** | N | N | N | N | Y | N | N | Y |
| 23 Bustamante | Y | Y | Y | Y | N | N | N | Y |
| 24 Frost | Y | Y | Y | Y | N | N | N | Y |
| 25 Andrews | Y | Y | Y | Y | N | Y | N | Y |
| 26 ***Armey*** | N | N | N | N | ? | # | ? | ? |
| 27 Ortiz | Y | Y | Y | Y | N | N | N | Y |
| **UTAH** | | | | | | | | |
| 1 ***Hansen*** | Y | N | N | N | N | Y | N | Y |
| 2 Owens | Y | Y | N | N | N | N | N | Y |
| 3 Orton | ? | ? | X | N | N | Y | N | Y |
| **VERMONT** | | | | | | | | |
| AL *Sanders* | ? | Y | Y | Y | N | N | Y | N |
| **VIRGINIA** | | | | | | | | |
| 1 ***Bateman*** | Y | N | N | N | N | Y | N | Y |
| 2 Pickett | Y | Y | N | N | N | N | N | Y |
| 3 ***Bliley*** | N | N | N | N | N | Y | N | Y |
| 4 Sisisky | Y | Y | N | N | N | N | N | Y |
| 5 Payne | Y | Y | Y | Y | N | Y | N | Y |
| 6 Olin | Y | Y | Y | Y | N | N | Y | N |
| 7 ***Allen*** | N | N | N | N | N | Y | N | Y |
| 8 Moran | Y | Y | Y | Y | N | N | Y | Y |
| 9 Boucher | Y | Y | Y | Y | N | Y | N | Y |
| 10 ***Wolf*** | N | N | N | N | N | Y | N | Y |
| **WASHINGTON** | | | | | | | | |
| 1 ***Miller*** | N | ? | N | X | − | + | − | + |
| 2 Swift | Y | Y | Y | Y | N | N | N | Y |
| 3 Unsoeld | Y | Y | Y | Y | N | N | Y | Y |
| 4 ***Morrison*** | ? | ? | ? | N | − | + | − | + |
| 5 Foley | | | Y | Y | | | | |
| 6 Dicks | Y | Y | Y | Y | N | N | N | Y |
| 7 McDermott | Y | Y | Y | Y | N | Y | Y | Y |
| 8 ***Chandler*** | ? | X | ? | N | N | Y | N | Y |
| **WEST VIRGINIA** | | | | | | | | |
| 1 Mollohan | ? | Y | Y | Y | N | N | N | Y |
| 2 Staggers | Y | Y | Y | Y | N | N | N | Y |
| 3 Wise | Y | Y | Y | Y | N | N | N | Y |
| 4 Rahall | Y | Y | Y | Y | N | N | N | N |
| **WISCONSIN** | | | | | | | | |
| 1 Aspin | Y | Y | Y | Y | N | N | N | Y |
| 2 ***Klug*** | Y | N | N | N | N | Y | N | Y |
| 3 ***Gunderson*** | Y | N | N | N | N | N | N | Y |
| 4 Kleczka | Y | Y | Y | Y | N | N | ? | # |
| 5 Moody | Y | Y | Y | Y | N | N | Y | ? |
| 6 ***Petri*** | Y | N | N | N | Y | Y | N | Y |
| 7 Obey | Y | Y | Y | Y | N | N | N | Y |
| 8 ***Roth*** | N | N | N | N | N | Y | N | Y |
| 9 ***Sensenbrenner*** | N | N | N | N | Y | Y | N | Y |
| **WYOMING** | | | | | | | | |
| AL ***Thomas*** | Y | N | N | N | N | N | N | Y |

Southern states - Ala., Ark., Fla., Ga., Ky., La., Miss., N.C., Okla., S.C., Tenn., Texas, Va.
Omitted votes are quorum calls, which CQ does not include in its vote charts.

**61. HR 3553. Higher Education Act Reauthorization/ Race Discrimination.** Rohrabacher, R-Calif., amendment to express the sense of Congress that institutions of higher learning should not discriminate based on race in admissions, particularly with regard to Asian-Americans. Rejected 94-276: R 88-47; D 6-228 (ND 4-158, SD 2-70); I 0-1, March 26, 1992.

**62. HR 3553. Higher Education Act Reauthorization/ Passage.** Passage of the bill to reauthorize through fiscal 1997 the Higher Education Act of 1965 that governed federal financial aid to post-secondary students. Passed 365-3: R 129-3; D 235-0 (ND 162-0, SD 73-0); I 1-0, March 26, 1992.

**63. H J Res 456. Fiscal 1992 Foreign Aid Continuing Appropriations/Passage.** Passage of the joint resolution to fund foreign aid for the remainder of the fiscal year through Sept. 30, 1992. Most programs would be funded at either the fiscal 1991 level or the level in the House-passed bill for fiscal 1992, whichever was lower. The bill did not include the loan guarantees for Israel but provided an increase in $270 million for U.N. peacekeeping activities and gave the administration greater flexibility to direct aid to the former republics of the Soviet Union. Passed 275-131: R 87-70; D 188-60 (ND 137-30, SD 51-30); I 0-1, March 31, 1992. A "yea" was a vote in support of the president's position.

**64. HR 3732. Eliminate Budget Walls/Rule.** Derrick, D-S.C., motion to order the previous question (thus ending debate and the possibility of amendment) on adoption of the rule (H Res 410) to provide for House floor consideration of the bill to modify the 1990 Budget Enforcement Act (PL 101-508). Motion agreed to 242-177: R 0-161; D 241-16 (ND 167-8, SD 74-8); I 1-0, March 31, 1992.

**65. HR 3732. Eliminate Budget Walls/Motion To Recommit.** Solomon, R-N.Y., motion to recommit to a bipartisan select committee the bill to modify the 1990 Budget Enforcement Act (PL 101-508), with instructions to report it back to the House with provisions that reform the budget process by reducing government spending and the deficit. Motion rejected 162-262: R 162-0; D 0-261 (ND 0-178, SD 0-83); I 0-1, March 31, 1992.

**66. HR 3732. Eliminate Budget Walls/Passage.** Passage of the bill to modify the 1990 Budget Enforcement Act (PL 101-508) to knock down the walls that prohibit the shifting of funds between defense, international and domestic appropriations. Rejected 187-238: R 0-162; D 186-76 (ND 151-28, SD 35-48); I 1-0, March 31, 1992. A "nay" was a vote in support of the president's position.

**67. HR 4704. RTC Financing/Rule.** Adoption of the rule (H Res 412) to provide for House floor consideration of the bill to provide the Resolution Trust Corporation with about $17 billion to resolve failed savings and loan institutions by eliminating the April 1, 1992, expiration date on $25 billion provided in November 1991 of which $8 billion has been spent. Adopted 228-193: R 29-135; D 199-57 (ND 133-42, SD 66-15); I 0-1, April 1, 1992.

**68. HR 4704. RTC Financing/Motion To Recommit.** Johnson, R-Texas, motion to recommit to the House Banking Committee (thus killing) the bill to provide the Resolution Trust Corporation with about $17 billion to resolve failed savings and loan institutions by eliminating the April 1, 1992, expiration date on the $25 billion, provided in November 1991, of which $8 billion has been spent. Motion rejected 173-247: R 128-33; D 45-213 (ND 32-144, SD 13-69); I 0-1, April 1, 1992.

## KEY

| | |
|---|---|
| Y | Voted for (yea). |
| # | Paired for. |
| + | Announced for. |
| N | Voted against (nay). |
| X | Paired against. |
| − | Announced against. |
| P | Voted "present." |
| C | Voted "present" to avoid possible conflict of interest. |
| ? | Did not vote or otherwise make a position known. |

Democrats  **Republicans**
*Independent*

| | 61 | 62 | 63 | 64 | 65 | 66 | 67 | 68 |
|---|---|---|---|---|---|---|---|---|
| **ALABAMA** | | | | | | | | |
| 1 Callahan | N | Y | Y | N | Y | N | N | Y |
| 2 Dickinson | N | Y | Y | N | N | N | N | Y |
| 3 Browder | N | Y | Y | Y | N | N | Y | N |
| 4 Bevill | ? | ? | Y | Y | N | Y | Y | N |
| 5 Cramer | N | Y | Y | Y | N | Y | N | N |
| 6 Erdreich | N | Y | Y | Y | N | Y | N | N |
| 7 Harris | N | Y | Y | N | N | N | N | N |
| **ALASKA** | | | | | | | | |
| AL *Young* | Y | Y | Y | N | Y | N | N | N |
| **ARIZONA** | | | | | | | | |
| 1 *Rhodes* | Y | Y | Y | N | Y | N | N | N |
| 2 Pastor | − | Y | Y | Y | N | Y | Y | N |
| 3 *Stump* | Y | N | N | N | Y | N | N | Y |
| 4 *Kyl* | Y | Y | Y | N | Y | N | N | N |
| 5 *Kolbe* | Y | Y | Y | N | Y | N | N | N |
| **ARKANSAS** | | | | | | | | |
| 1 Alexander | N | Y | N | Y | N | Y | Y | N |
| 2 Thornton | N | Y | N | ? | N | Y | Y | N |
| 3 *Hammerschmidt* | Y | Y | N | N | Y | N | N | Y |
| 4 Anthony | N | Y | N | Y | N | Y | Y | N |
| **CALIFORNIA** | | | | | | | | |
| 1 *Riggs* | Y | ? | Y | N | Y | N | N | Y |
| 2 *Herger* | ? | ? | N | N | Y | N | N | Y |
| 3 Matsui | N | Y | Y | Y | N | Y | Y | N |
| 4 Fazio | N | Y | Y | Y | N | Y | Y | N |
| 5 Pelosi | N | Y | Y | Y | N | Y | Y | N |
| 6 Boxer | ? | ? | ? | ? | ? | # | N | N |
| 7 Miller | N | Y | Y | Y | N | Y | Y | N |
| 8 Dellums | N | Y | Y | Y | N | Y | Y | N |
| 9 Stark | ? | ? | Y | Y | N | Y | Y | N |
| 10 Edwards | N | Y | Y | Y | N | Y | Y | N |
| 11 Lantos | N | Y | Y | Y | N | Y | Y | N |
| 12 *Campbell* | Y | Y | Y | N | Y | N | N | Y |
| 13 Mineta | N | Y | Y | Y | N | Y | Y | N |
| 14 *Doolittle* | Y | N | N | N | Y | N | N | Y |
| 15 Condit | N | Y | N | N | N | N | Y | N |
| 16 Panetta | N | Y | Y | Y | N | Y | Y | N |
| 17 Dooley | N | Y | Y | Y | N | Y | Y | N |
| 18 Lehman | N | Y | Y | Y | N | Y | Y | N |
| 19 *Lagomarsino* | Y | Y | N | N | Y | N | N | N |
| 20 *Thomas* | ? | ? | N | N | Y | N | N | N |
| 21 *Gallegly* | Y | Y | N | N | Y | N | N | Y |
| 22 *Moorhead* | Y | Y | N | N | Y | N | N | Y |
| 23 Beilenson | N | Y | Y | Y | N | Y | Y | N |
| 24 Waxman | ? | ? | Y | Y | N | Y | Y | N |
| 25 Roybal | N | Y | Y | Y | N | Y | Y | N |
| 26 Berman | ? | ? | Y | Y | N | Y | Y | N |
| 27 Levine | ? | ? | ? | ? | ? | # | ? | ? |
| 28 Dixon | N | Y | Y | ? | N | Y | ? | ? |
| 29 Waters | N | Y | Y | Y | N | Y | ? | N |
| 30 Martinez | ? | ? | Y | Y | N | Y | Y | N |
| 31 Dymally | N | Y | Y | Y | N | Y | Y | ? |
| 32 Anderson | N | Y | Y | Y | N | Y | Y | N |
| 33 *Dreier* | Y | Y | N | N | Y | N | N | Y |
| 34 Torres | N | Y | Y | Y | N | Y | Y | N |
| 35 *Lewis* | Y | Y | ? | ? | ? | ? | N | Y |
| 36 Brown | N | Y | Y | Y | N | Y | Y | N |
| 37 *McCandless* | ? | ? | N | N | Y | N | N | Y |
| 38 *Dornan* | ? | Y | ? | ? | ? | X | N | Y |
| 39 *Dannemeyer* | + | − | N | N | Y | N | − | + |
| 40 *Cox* | Y | Y | N | N | Y | N | N | Y |
| 41 *Lowery* | Y | Y | ? | N | Y | N | N | Y |

| | 61 | 62 | 63 | 64 | 65 | 66 | 67 | 68 |
|---|---|---|---|---|---|---|---|---|
| 42 *Rohrabacher* | Y | Y | N | N | Y | N | N | Y |
| 43 *Packard* | Y | Y | N | N | Y | N | N | Y |
| 44 *Cunningham* | Y | Y | N | N | Y | N | N | Y |
| 45 *Hunter* | Y | Y | N | N | Y | N | N | Y |
| **COLORADO** | | | | | | | | |
| 1 Schroeder | N | Y | N | Y | N | Y | N | N |
| 2 Skaggs | N | Y | Y | Y | N | Y | Y | N |
| 3 Campbell | N | Y | Y | Y | N | N | Y | N |
| 4 *Allard* | N | N | N | N | Y | N | N | Y |
| 5 *Hefley* | Y | Y | N | N | Y | N | N | Y |
| 6 *Schaefer* | N | Y | N | N | Y | N | N | Y |
| **CONNECTICUT** | | | | | | | | |
| 1 Kennelly | − | + | Y | Y | N | Y | Y | ? |
| 2 Gejdenson | N | Y | Y | Y | N | Y | Y | N |
| 3 DeLauro | N | Y | Y | Y | N | Y | Y | N |
| 4 *Shays* | N | Y | Y | N | N | N | Y | N |
| 5 *Franks* | N | Y | Y | N | Y | N | N | N |
| 6 *Johnson* | ? | ? | Y | N | Y | N | Y | N |
| **DELAWARE** | | | | | | | | |
| AL Carper | N | Y | Y | N | N | N | Y | N |
| **FLORIDA** | | | | | | | | |
| 1 Hutto | N | Y | N | N | N | N | N | Y |
| 2 Peterson | ? | ? | Y | Y | N | Y | N | Y |
| 3 Bennett | N | Y | Y | Y | N | Y | Y | N |
| 4 *James* | N | Y | N | N | Y | N | N | N |
| 5 *McCollum* | Y | Y | N | N | Y | N | N | N |
| 6 *Stearns* | Y | Y | N | N | Y | N | N | Y |
| 7 Gibbons | N | Y | Y | Y | N | Y | Y | N |
| 8 *Young* | ? | ? | N | N | Y | N | N | N |
| 9 *Bilirakis* | Y | Y | N | N | Y | N | N | N |
| 10 *Ireland* | Y | Y | Y | N | Y | N | N | ? |
| 11 Bacchus | N | Y | Y | Y | N | Y | Y | N |
| 12 *Lewis* | N | Y | N | N | Y | N | N | Y |
| 13 *Goss* | Y | Y | N | N | Y | N | N | N |
| 14 Johnston | N | Y | Y | Y | N | Y | Y | N |
| 15 *Shaw* | N | Y | N | N | Y | N | N | Y |
| 16 Smith | N | Y | Y | Y | N | Y | Y | N |
| 17 Lehman | ? | ? | Y | Y | N | Y | Y | N |
| 18 Ros−Lehtinen | Y | Y | Y | N | Y | N | N | N |
| 19 Fascell | N | Y | Y | Y | N | Y | Y | N |
| **GEORGIA** | | | | | | | | |
| 1 Thomas | ? | ? | Y | Y | N | Y | Y | N |
| 2 Hatcher | N | Y | Y | Y | N | Y | Y | N |
| 3 Ray | N | Y | N | Y | N | N | N | N |
| 4 Jones | N | Y | Y | Y | N | Y | Y | N |
| 5 Lewis | N | Y | Y | Y | N | Y | Y | N |
| 6 *Gingrich* | Y | Y | Y | N | Y | N | N | Y |
| 7 Darden | N | Y | N | Y | N | Y | N | N |
| 8 Rowland | N | Y | N | Y | N | N | N | N |
| 9 Jenkins | ? | ? | Y | Y | N | Y | N | N |
| 10 Barnard | N | Y | N | Y | N | N | N | N |
| **HAWAII** | | | | | | | | |
| 1 Abercrombie | N | Y | Y | Y | N | Y | Y | N |
| 2 Mink | N | Y | Y | Y | N | Y | Y | Y |
| **IDAHO** | | | | | | | | |
| 1 LaRocco | N | Y | Y | Y | N | N | N | N |
| 2 Stallings | N | Y | Y | Y | N | N | Y | N |
| **ILLINOIS** | | | | | | | | |
| 1 Hayes | N | Y | Y | Y | N | Y | Y | N |
| 2 Savage | N | Y | N | Y | N | Y | ? | N |
| 3 Russo | ? | ? | N | Y | N | Y | Y | N |
| 4 Sangmeister | N | Y | Y | Y | N | Y | Y | N |
| 5 Lipinski | Y | Y | Y | Y | N | Y | Y | N |
| 6 *Hyde* | Y | Y | ? | N | Y | N | N | N |
| 7 Collins | N | Y | P | Y | N | Y | N | N |
| 8 Rostenkowski | N | Y | Y | Y | N | Y | Y | N |
| 9 Yates | N | Y | Y | Y | N | Y | Y | N |
| 10 *Porter* | N | Y | Y | N | Y | N | N | N |
| 11 Annunzio | N | Y | Y | Y | N | Y | N | N |
| 12 *Crane* | Y | N | N | N | Y | N | N | N |
| 13 *Fawell* | N | Y | Y | N | Y | N | N | N |
| 14 *Hastert* | Y | Y | N | N | Y | N | N | N |
| 15 *Ewing* | ? | ? | Y | N | Y | N | N | N |
| 16 *Cox* | Y | Y | N | N | Y | N | N | N |
| 17 Evans | N | Y | Y | Y | N | Y | Y | N |
| 18 *Michel* | Y | Y | Y | N | Y | N | N | N |
| 19 Bruce | N | Y | Y | N | N | Y | Y | N |
| 20 Durbin | N | Y | Y | Y | N | Y | Y | N |
| 21 Costello | N | Y | Y | Y | N | Y | Y | N |
| 22 Poshard | N | Y | N | Y | N | Y | Y | Y |
| **INDIANA** | | | | | | | | |
| 1 Visclosky | N | Y | Y | Y | N | N | Y | N |
| 2 Sharp | N | Y | Y | N | N | N | Y | N |
| 3 Roemer | N | Y | N | Y | N | N | Y | Y |

| | 61 | 62 | 63 | 64 | 65 | 66 | 67 | 68 |
|---|---|---|---|---|---|---|---|---|
| 4 Long | N | Y | Y | Y | N | N | Y | N |
| 5 Jontz | N | Y | N | Y | N | Y | N | Y |
| 6 ***Burton*** | ? | ? | Y | N | Y | N | N | Y |
| 7 ***Myers*** | Y | Y | N | N | Y | N | Y | N |
| 8 McCloskey | N | Y | Y | Y | N | Y | Y | N |
| 9 Hamilton | N | Y | Y | Y | N | N | Y | N |
| 10 Jacobs | N | Y | N | N | N | N | N | Y |
| **IOWA** | | | | | | | | |
| 1 ***Leach*** | N | Y | Y | N | Y | N | Y | N |
| 2 ***Nussle*** | N | Y | N | N | Y | N | N | Y |
| 3 Nagle | N | Y | + | Y | N | Y | Y | N |
| 4 Smith | N | Y | Y | Y | N | Y | Y | N |
| 5 ***Lightfoot*** | Y | Y | Y | N | Y | N | N | Y |
| 6 ***Grandy*** | Y | Y | N | N | Y | N | N | N |
| **KANSAS** | | | | | | | | |
| 1 ***Roberts*** | ? | ? | N | N | Y | N | N | Y |
| 2 Slattery | N | Y | N | Y | N | N | N | Y |
| 3 ***Meyers*** | Y | Y | Y | N | Y | N | Y | N |
| 4 Glickman | N | Y | + | Y | N | N | N | Y |
| 5 ***Nichols*** | Y | Y | N | N | Y | N | N | Y |
| **KENTUCKY** | | | | | | | | |
| 1 Hubbard | N | Y | N | Y | N | N | Y | N |
| 2 Natcher | N | Y | Y | Y | N | Y | Y | N |
| 3 Mazzoli | N | Y | N | Y | N | N | Y | N |
| 4 ***Bunning*** | ? | ? | ? | ? | ? | ? | N | Y |
| 5 ***Rogers*** | Y | Y | N | N | Y | N | N | Y |
| 6 ***Hopkins*** | Y | Y | N | N | Y | N | N | Y |
| 7 Perkins | N | Y | N | Y | N | Y | ? | ? |
| **LOUISIANA** | | | | | | | | |
| 1 ***Livingston*** | Y | Y | Y | N | Y | N | Y | Y |
| 2 Jefferson | N | Y | Y | Y | N | Y | Y | N |
| 3 Tauzin | N | Y | Y | N | N | N | N | Y |
| 4 ***McCrery*** | ? | ? | Y | N | Y | N | N | Y |
| 5 Huckaby | N | Y | Y | Y | N | N | Y | N |
| 6 ***Baker*** | ? | ? | Y | N | Y | N | N | Y |
| 7 Hayes | N | Y | N | N | N | N | Y | N |
| 8 ***Holloway*** | Y | Y | N | N | Y | N | N | Y |
| **MAINE** | | | | | | | | |
| 1 Andrews | N | Y | Y | Y | N | Y | N | Y |
| 2 ***Snowe*** | N | Y | N | N | Y | N | N | Y |
| **MARYLAND** | | | | | | | | |
| 1 ***Gilchrest*** | N | Y | Y | N | Y | N | N | N |
| 2 ***Bentley*** | Y | Y | Y | N | Y | N | N | Y |
| 3 Cardin | N | Y | Y | N | N | Y | Y | N |
| 4 McMillen | N | Y | Y | Y | N | N | Y | N |
| 5 Hoyer | N | Y | Y | Y | N | Y | Y | N |
| 6 Byron | N | Y | N | Y | N | N | Y | N |
| 7 Mfume | N | Y | Y | Y | N | Y | N | Y |
| 8 ***Morella*** | N | Y | Y | N | Y | N | Y | N |
| **MASSACHUSETTS** | | | | | | | | |
| 1 Olver | N | Y | Y | Y | N | Y | Y | Y |
| 2 Neal | N | Y | Y | Y | N | Y | Y | N |
| 3 Early | N | Y | N | Y | N | Y | Y | N |
| 4 Frank | N | Y | Y | Y | N | Y | Y | Y |
| 5 Atkins | N | Y | Y | Y | N | Y | N | Y |
| 6 Mavroules | N | Y | Y | Y | N | Y | Y | N |
| 7 Markey | N | ? | Y | Y | N | Y | Y | N |
| 8 Kennedy | N | Y | Y | Y | N | Y | N | N |
| 9 Moakley | N | Y | Y | Y | N | Y | Y | N |
| 10 Studds | N | Y | Y | Y | N | Y | Y | N |
| 11 Donnelly | ? | ? | Y | Y | N | Y | Y | N |
| **MICHIGAN** | | | | | | | | |
| 1 Conyers | N | Y | Y | Y | N | Y | N | N |
| 2 ***Pursell*** | ? | ? | Y | N | Y | N | Y | Y |
| 3 Wolpe | ? | ? | Y | Y | N | Y | Y | N |
| 4 ***Upton*** | Y | Y | Y | N | Y | N | N | Y |
| 5 ***Henry*** | Y | Y | N | N | Y | N | N | Y |
| 6 Carr | N | Y | Y | Y | N | Y | Y | N |
| 7 Kildee | N | Y | Y | Y | N | Y | Y | Y |
| 8 Traxler | ? | ? | Y | Y | N | Y | Y | N |
| 9 ***Vander Jagt*** | Y | Y | ? | N | Y | N | N | Y |
| 10 ***Camp*** | Y | Y | Y | N | Y | N | N | Y |
| 11 ***Davis*** | ? | ? | Y | N | Y | N | N | Y |
| 12 Bonior | N | Y | Y | Y | N | Y | Y | N |
| 13 Collins | N | Y | Y | Y | N | Y | N | Y |
| 14 Hertel | N | Y | Y | Y | N | Y | Y | N |
| 15 Ford | N | Y | Y | Y | N | Y | Y | Y |
| 16 Dingell | N | Y | Y | Y | N | Y | Y | ? |
| 17 Levin | N | Y | Y | Y | N | Y | Y | N |
| 18 ***Broomfield*** | Y | Y | Y | N | Y | N | N | Y |
| **MINNESOTA** | | | | | | | | |
| 1 Penny | Y | Y | Y | Y | N | N | N | Y |
| 2 ***Weber*** | Y | Y | ? | N | Y | N | N | Y |
| 3 ***Ramstad*** | Y | Y | Y | N | Y | N | N | Y |
| 4 Vento | N | Y | Y | Y | N | Y | Y | N |

| | 61 | 62 | 63 | 64 | 65 | 66 | 67 | 68 |
|---|---|---|---|---|---|---|---|---|
| 5 Sabo | N | Y | Y | Y | N | Y | Y | N |
| 6 Sikorski | N | Y | Y | Y | N | Y | N | N |
| 7 Peterson | N | Y | Y | Y | N | Y | Y | N |
| 8 Oberstar | N | Y | Y | Y | N | Y | Y | N |
| **MISSISSIPPI** | | | | | | | | |
| 1 Whitten | ? | ? | ? | Y | N | Y | Y | N |
| 2 Espy | N | Y | Y | Y | N | N | Y | ? |
| 3 Montgomery | N | Y | N | Y | N | N | Y | N |
| 4 Parker | N | Y | Y | N | N | N | Y | N |
| 5 Taylor | N | Y | N | N | N | N | N | Y |
| **MISSOURI** | | | | | | | | |
| 1 Clay | N | Y | ? | Y | N | Y | Y | N |
| 2 Horn | N | Y | Y | Y | N | Y | Y | N |
| 3 Gephardt | N | Y | Y | Y | N | Y | Y | N |
| 4 Skelton | N | Y | ? | ? | ? | X | Y | N |
| 5 Wheat | N | Y | Y | Y | N | Y | Y | N |
| 6 ***Coleman*** | Y | Y | N | N | Y | N | N | Y |
| 7 ***Hancock*** | Y | Y | N | N | Y | N | N | Y |
| 8 ***Emerson*** | Y | Y | N | N | Y | N | N | Y |
| 9 Volkmer | N | Y | N | Y | N | N | Y | N |
| **MONTANA** | | | | | | | | |
| 1 Williams | N | Y | N | Y | N | Y | Y | Y |
| 2 ***Marlenee*** | Y | Y | N | N | Y | N | N | Y |
| **NEBRASKA** | | | | | | | | |
| 1 ***Bereuter*** | Y | Y | Y | N | Y | N | Y | N |
| 2 Hoagland | N | Y | Y | Y | N | N | Y | N |
| 3 ***Barrett*** | ? | ? | N | N | Y | N | N | N |
| **NEVADA** | | | | | | | | |
| 1 Bilbray | N | Y | Y | Y | N | N | N | N |
| 2 ***Vucanovich*** | Y | Y | Y | N | Y | N | N | Y |
| **NEW HAMPSHIRE** | | | | | | | | |
| 1 ***Zeliff*** | Y | Y | N | N | Y | N | N | Y |
| 2 Swett | N | Y | Y | N | N | Y | N | Y |
| **NEW JERSEY** | | | | | | | | |
| 1 Andrews | N | Y | Y | Y | N | Y | Y | N |
| 2 Hughes | N | Y | N | Y | N | Y | N | Y |
| 3 Pallone | N | Y | Y | Y | N | Y | Y | N |
| 4 ***Smith*** | ? | ? | Y | N | Y | N | ? | ? |
| 5 ***Roukema*** | N | Y | N | N | Y | N | Y | N |
| 6 Dwyer | ? | ? | Y | Y | N | Y | Y | N |
| 7 ***Rinaldo*** | N | Y | Y | N | Y | N | Y | Y |
| 8 Roe | N | Y | ? | Y | N | Y | Y | N |
| 9 Torricelli | ? | ? | Y | Y | N | Y | Y | N |
| 10 Payne | N | Y | Y | Y | N | Y | N | N |
| 11 ***Gallo*** | N | Y | Y | N | Y | N | N | N |
| 12 ***Zimmer*** | Y | Y | Y | N | Y | N | N | Y |
| 13 ***Saxton*** | N | Y | Y | N | Y | N | N | ? |
| 14 Guarini | N | Y | N | Y | N | Y | Y | N |
| **NEW MEXICO** | | | | | | | | |
| 1 ***Schiff*** | Y | Y | Y | N | Y | N | Y | Y |
| 2 ***Skeen*** | N | Y | Y | N | Y | N | Y | Y |
| 3 Richardson | N | Y | Y | Y | N | N | Y | N |
| **NEW YORK** | | | | | | | | |
| 1 Hochbrueckner | N | Y | Y | Y | N | Y | Y | N |
| 2 Downey | N | Y | Y | Y | N | Y | Y | N |
| 3 Mrazek | ? | ? | Y | Y | N | Y | ? | ? |
| 4 ***Lent*** | N | Y | Y | N | Y | N | N | Y |
| 5 ***McGrath*** | Y | Y | Y | N | Y | N | N | Y |
| 6 Flake | N | Y | Y | Y | N | Y | N | Y |
| 7 Ackerman | N | Y | Y | Y | N | Y | Y | N |
| 8 Scheuer | N | Y | Y | Y | N | Y | Y | N |
| 9 Manton | N | Y | Y | Y | N | Y | Y | N |
| 10 Schumer | N | Y | Y | Y | N | Y | Y | N |
| 11 Towns | N | Y | ? | Y | N | Y | Y | N |
| 12 Owens | N | Y | Y | Y | N | Y | N | N |
| 13 Solarz | N | Y | Y | Y | N | Y | Y | N |
| 14 ***Molinari*** | Y | Y | Y | N | Y | N | Y | Y |
| 15 ***Green*** | Y | Y | Y | N | Y | N | Y | N |
| 16 Rangel | N | Y | Y | Y | N | Y | Y | N |
| 17 Weiss | N | Y | Y | Y | N | Y | Y | N |
| 18 Serrano | N | Y | ? | ? | N | Y | N | N |
| 19 Engel | N | Y | Y | Y | N | Y | N | N |
| 20 Lowey | N | Y | Y | Y | N | Y | Y | N |
| 21 ***Fish*** | N | Y | Y | N | Y | N | N | Y |
| 22 ***Gilman*** | N | Y | Y | N | Y | N | N | Y |
| 23 McNulty | N | Y | Y | Y | N | Y | Y | N |
| 24 ***Solomon*** | Y | ? | N | N | Y | N | Y | Y |
| 25 ***Boehlert*** | N | Y | Y | N | Y | N | Y | N |
| 26 ***Martin*** | N | Y | Y | N | Y | N | N | Y |
| 27 ***Walsh*** | N | Y | Y | N | Y | N | N | N |
| 28 McHugh | N | Y | Y | Y | N | Y | Y | N |
| 29 ***Horton*** | N | Y | Y | N | Y | N | Y | N |
| 30 Slaughter | ? | Y | Y | Y | − | Y | Y | N |
| 31 ***Paxon*** | Y | ? | Y | N | Y | N | N | Y |

| | 61 | 62 | 63 | 64 | 65 | 66 | 67 | 68 |
|---|---|---|---|---|---|---|---|---|
| 32 LaFalce | N | + | Y | Y | N | Y | Y | N |
| 33 Nowak | N | Y | Y | Y | N | Y | ? | N |
| 34 ***Houghton*** | N | Y | Y | N | Y | N | N | N |
| **NORTH CAROLINA** | | | | | | | | |
| 1 Jones | N | Y | Y | Y | N | Y | Y | N |
| 2 Valentine | N | Y | N | Y | N | N | ? | ? |
| 3 Lancaster | N | Y | Y | Y | N | N | N | N |
| 4 Price | N | Y | Y | Y | N | Y | Y | N |
| 5 Neal | Y | Y | N | ? | ? | ? | Y | N |
| 6 ***Coble*** | Y | Y | Y | N | Y | N | N | Y |
| 7 Rose | N | Y | Y | Y | N | Y | Y | N |
| 8 Hefner | N | Y | N | Y | N | Y | Y | N |
| 9 ***McMillan*** | Y | Y | Y | N | Y | N | Y | N |
| 10 ***Ballenger*** | + | + | N | N | Y | N | Y | Y |
| 11 ***Taylor*** | Y | Y | − | − | + | − | N | Y |
| **NORTH DAKOTA** | | | | | | | | |
| AL Dorgan | N | Y | N | N | N | N | N | N |
| **OHIO** | | | | | | | | |
| 1 Luken | N | Y | Y | Y | N | N | Y | N |
| 2 ***Gradison*** | ? | ? | Y | N | Y | N | Y | N |
| 3 Hall | N | Y | Y | Y | N | Y | Y | N |
| 4 ***Oxley*** | Y | Y | N | N | Y | N | Y | Y |
| 5 ***Gillmor*** | Y | Y | Y | N | Y | N | N | N |
| 6 ***McEwen*** | ? | ? | N | N | Y | N | N | Y |
| 7 ***Hobson*** | Y | Y | Y | N | Y | N | N | Y |
| 8 ***Boehner*** | ? | ? | Y | N | Y | N | N | Y |
| 9 Kaptur | N | Y | Y | Y | N | Y | N | N |
| 10 ***Miller*** | N | Y | N | N | Y | N | N | Y |
| 11 Eckart | N | Y | Y | Y | N | Y | N | N |
| 12 ***Kasich*** | N | Y | Y | N | Y | N | N | Y |
| 13 Pease | N | Y | N | Y | N | Y | Y | N |
| 14 Sawyer | N | Y | Y | Y | N | Y | Y | N |
| 15 ***Wylie*** | N | ? | Y | N | Y | N | Y | N |
| 16 ***Regula*** | N | Y | N | N | Y | N | Y | Y |
| 17 Traficant | N | Y | N | Y | N | Y | Y | N |
| 18 Applegate | N | Y | N | Y | N | Y | N | Y |
| 19 Feighan | ? | ? | ? | ? | N | Y | ? | N |
| 20 Oakar | N | Y | ? | Y | N | Y | Y | N |
| 21 Stokes | N | Y | Y | Y | N | Y | Y | N |
| **OKLAHOMA** | | | | | | | | |
| 1 ***Inhofe*** | Y | Y | Y | N | Y | N | N | Y |
| 2 Synar | − | + | Y | Y | N | Y | Y | N |
| 3 Brewster | N | Y | Y | Y | N | N | Y | N |
| 4 McCurdy | N | Y | Y | Y | N | N | ? | N |
| 5 ***Edwards*** | N | Y | N | N | Y | N | N | Y |
| 6 English | N | Y | N | Y | N | N | N | Y |
| **OREGON** | | | | | | | | |
| 1 AuCoin | X | ? | Y | Y | N | Y | N | N |
| 2 ***Smith*** | N | Y | N | N | Y | N | N | Y |
| 3 Wyden | N | Y | Y | Y | N | Y | N | Y |
| 4 DeFazio | N | Y | N | Y | N | Y | N | Y |
| 5 Kopetski | N | Y | Y | Y | N | Y | Y | N |
| **PENNSYLVANIA** | | | | | | | | |
| 1 Foglietta | N | Y | Y | Y | N | Y | Y | N |
| 2 Blackwell | N | Y | Y | Y | N | Y | N | N |
| 3 Borski | N | Y | Y | Y | N | Y | Y | N |
| 4 Kolter | ? | ? | Y | Y | N | Y | Y | N |
| 5 ***Schulze*** | Y | Y | N | N | Y | N | N | Y |
| 6 Yatron | ? | ? | Y | Y | N | N | Y | N |
| 7 ***Weldon*** | Y | Y | N | N | Y | N | N | Y |
| 8 Kostmayer | N | Y | Y | Y | N | Y | Y | Y |
| 9 ***Shuster*** | N | Y | N | N | Y | N | N | Y |
| 10 ***McDade*** | N | Y | Y | N | Y | N | N | N |
| 11 Kanjorski | N | Y | N | Y | N | Y | N | N |
| 12 Murtha | N | Y | Y | Y | N | N | Y | N |
| 13 ***Coughlin*** | ? | ? | Y | N | Y | N | Y | N |
| 14 Coyne | N | Y | Y | Y | N | Y | Y | N |
| 15 ***Ritter*** | Y | Y | Y | N | Y | N | N | Y |
| 16 ***Walker*** | Y | Y | N | N | Y | N | N | Y |
| 17 ***Gekas*** | N | Y | N | N | Y | N | N | Y |
| 18 ***Santorum*** | ? | ? | Y | N | Y | N | N | Y |
| 19 ***Goodling*** | N | Y | N | N | Y | N | N | Y |
| 20 Gaydos | N | Y | ? | ? | N | Y | Y | N |
| 21 ***Ridge*** | ? | ? | Y | N | Y | N | N | Y |
| 22 Murphy | N | Y | ? | Y | N | Y | N | Y |
| 23 ***Clinger*** | N | Y | Y | N | Y | N | Y | Y |
| **RHODE ISLAND** | | | | | | | | |
| 1 ***Machtley*** | N | Y | Y | N | Y | N | N | ? |
| 2 Reed | N | Y | Y | Y | N | Y | Y | N |
| **SOUTH CAROLINA** | | | | | | | | |
| 1 ***Ravenel*** | Y | Y | Y | N | Y | N | Y | Y |
| 2 ***Spence*** | N | Y | N | N | Y | N | N | Y |
| 3 Derrick | N | Y | Y | Y | N | N | Y | N |
| 4 Patterson | N | Y | N | Y | N | Y | Y | N |
| 5 Spratt | N | Y | Y | Y | N | N | Y | N |
| 6 Tallon | N | Y | Y | Y | N | Y | Y | N |

| | 61 | 62 | 63 | 64 | 65 | 66 | 67 | 68 |
|---|---|---|---|---|---|---|---|---|
| **SOUTH DAKOTA** | | | | | | | | |
| AL Johnson | Y | Y | Y | Y | N | Y | Y | N |
| **TENNESSEE** | | | | | | | | |
| 1 ***Quillen*** | Y | Y | N | N | Y | N | N | Y |
| 2 ***Duncan*** | Y | Y | N | N | Y | N | N | Y |
| 3 Lloyd | N | Y | N | Y | N | N | Y | Y |
| 4 Cooper | N | Y | Y | N | N | N | Y | N |
| 5 Clement | N | Y | Y | Y | N | N | Y | N |
| 6 Gordon | N | Y | Y | Y | N | N | Y | N |
| 7 ***Sundquist*** | Y | Y | Y | N | Y | N | N | Y |
| 8 Tanner | N | Y | N | Y | N | N | Y | Y |
| 9 Ford | N | Y | Y | Y | N | Y | Y | Y |
| **TEXAS** | | | | | | | | |
| 1 Chapman | N | Y | N | Y | N | Y | Y | N |
| 2 Wilson | ? | ? | Y | Y | N | N | Y | N |
| 3 ***Johnson*** | N | Y | Y | N | Y | N | N | Y |
| 4 Hall | N | Y | N | N | N | N | N | Y |
| 5 Bryant | N | Y | N | Y | N | Y | Y | N |
| 6 ***Barton*** | # | ? | N | N | Y | N | N | Y |
| 7 ***Archer*** | ? | ? | N | N | Y | N | N | Y |
| 8 ***Fields*** | Y | Y | ? | ? | Y | N | N | Y |
| 9 Brooks | N | Y | ? | ? | ? | ? | Y | N |
| 10 Pickle | N | Y | Y | Y | N | N | Y | N |
| 11 Edwards | N | Y | Y | Y | N | N | Y | N |
| 12 Geren | N | Y | N | Y | N | N | Y | N |
| 13 Sarpalius | N | Y | N | Y | N | N | Y | N |
| 14 Laughlin | ? | ? | Y | Y | N | N | Y | N |
| 15 de la Garza | N | Y | Y | Y | N | Y | Y | N |
| 16 Coleman | N | Y | Y | Y | N | Y | Y | N |
| 17 Stenholm | ? | ? | Y | Y | N | N | Y | N |
| 18 Washington | N | Y | P | Y | N | Y | ? | N |
| 19 ***Combest*** | Y | Y | N | N | Y | N | N | Y |
| 20 Gonzalez | N | Y | N | Y | N | Y | Y | N |
| 21 ***Smith*** | ? | ? | Y | N | Y | N | N | Y |
| 22 ***DeLay*** | Y | Y | N | N | Y | N | N | Y |
| 23 Bustamante | N | Y | Y | Y | N | Y | Y | N |
| 24 Frost | N | Y | Y | Y | N | Y | Y | N |
| 25 Andrews | N | Y | Y | Y | N | N | Y | N |
| 26 ***Armey*** | ? | ? | N | N | Y | N | N | Y |
| 27 Ortiz | N | Y | ? | Y | N | N | Y | N |
| **UTAH** | | | | | | | | |
| 1 ***Hansen*** | N | Y | N | N | Y | N | N | Y |
| 2 Owens | N | Y | Y | N | N | N | Y | N |
| 3 Orton | N | Y | Y | Y | N | N | N | N |
| **VERMONT** | | | | | | | | |
| AL *Sanders* | N | Y | N | Y | N | Y | N | N |
| **VIRGINIA** | | | | | | | | |
| 1 ***Bateman*** | Y | Y | Y | N | Y | N | Y | Y |
| 2 Pickett | N | Y | N | Y | N | N | Y | N |
| 3 ***Bliley*** | ? | ? | Y | N | Y | N | Y | Y |
| 4 Sisisky | ? | ? | Y | Y | N | N | Y | N |
| 5 Payne | N | Y | Y | Y | N | N | Y | N |
| 6 Olin | ? | ? | Y | Y | N | N | Y | N |
| 7 ***Allen*** | Y | Y | N | N | Y | N | N | Y |
| 8 Moran | Y | Y | Y | Y | N | Y | N | Y |
| 9 Boucher | ? | Y | N | Y | N | Y | Y | N |
| 10 ***Wolf*** | Y | Y | Y | N | Y | N | N | Y |
| **WASHINGTON** | | | | | | | | |
| 1 ***Miller*** | + | + | Y | N | Y | N | N | Y |
| 2 Swift | N | Y | Y | Y | N | Y | Y | N |
| 3 Unsoeld | N | Y | Y | Y | N | Y | Y | N |
| 4 ***Morrison*** | − | + | Y | N | Y | N | N | Y |
| 5 Foley | | | | | | | | |
| 6 Dicks | N | Y | Y | Y | N | Y | Y | N |
| 7 McDermott | N | Y | Y | Y | N | Y | Y | N |
| 8 ***Chandler*** | N | Y | Y | N | Y | N | N | Y |
| **WEST VIRGINIA** | | | | | | | | |
| 1 Mollohan | N | Y | ? | Y | N | Y | Y | N |
| 2 Staggers | N | Y | N | Y | N | Y | N | N |
| 3 Wise | N | Y | N | Y | N | Y | Y | N |
| 4 Rahall | N | Y | N | Y | N | Y | N | Y |
| **WISCONSIN** | | | | | | | | |
| 1 Aspin | N | Y | Y | Y | N | Y | Y | N |
| 2 ***Klug*** | N | Y | Y | N | Y | N | N | Y |
| 3 ***Gunderson*** | N | Y | N | N | Y | N | N | Y |
| 4 Kleczka | N | Y | Y | Y | N | Y | Y | N |
| 5 Moody | Y | Y | Y | Y | N | Y | Y | Y |
| 6 ***Petri*** | Y | Y | N | N | Y | N | N | N |
| 7 Obey | N | Y | Y | Y | N | Y | Y | N |
| 8 ***Roth*** | Y | Y | N | N | Y | N | N | Y |
| 9 ***Sensenbrenner*** | Y | Y | N | N | Y | N | N | Y |
| **WYOMING** | | | | | | | | |
| AL ***Thomas*** | Y | Y | N | N | Y | N | N | Y |

Southern states - Ala., Ark., Fla., Ga., Ky., La., Miss., N.C., Okla., S.C., Tenn., Texas, Va.
Omitted votes are quorum calls, which CQ does not include in its vote charts.

## KEY

Y   Voted for (yea).
#   Paired for.
+   Announced for.
N   Voted against (nay).
X   Paired against.
−   Announced against.
P   Voted "present."
C   Voted "present" to avoid possible conflict of interest.
?   Did not vote or otherwise make a position known.

**Democrats**  ***Republicans***
*Independent*

**69. HR 4704. RTC Financing/Passage.** Passage of the bill to provide the Resolution Trust Corporation with about $17 billion to resolve failed savings and loan institutions by eliminating the April 1, 1992, expiration date on the $25 billion, provided November 1991, of which $8 billion had been spent. The $17 billion was expected to provide the RTC with funding through September 1992, but more money would be needed after that. Rejected 125-298: R 45-117; D 80-180 (ND 47-130, SD 33-50); I 0-1, April 1, 1992. A "yea" was a vote in support of the president's position.

**70. HR 3337. Omnibus Commemorative Coin Bill/Recommit Conference Report.** McCandless, R-Calif., motion to recommit to the joint House-Senate conference committee the conference report on the bill to mint coins in commemoration of various events, with instructions to House conferees to disagree to the Senate amendment requiring redesigns of the reverse sides of the half dollar and the quarter. Motion agreed to 206-199: R 137-19; D 69-179 (ND 39-130, SD 30-49); I 0-1, April 1, 1992.

**71. HR 2039. Legal Services Corporation Reauthorization/Rule.** Adoption of the rule (H Res 413) to provide for House floor consideration of the bill to reauthorize through fiscal 1996 such sums as necessary for the Legal Services Corporation to help give legal assistance to the poor in civil cases. Adopted 263-146: R 14-146; D 248-0 (ND 168-0, SD 80-0); I 1-0, April 2, 1992.

**72. HR 4276. Historic Sites Selection Procedures.** Vento, D-Minn., motion to suspend the rules and pass the bill to prohibit the Interior Department from using National Park Service funds earmarked in appropriations bills for any project to preserve historic American sites unless the project was specifically authorized by a law enacted after this bill. Motion agreed to 381-0: R 145-0; D 235-0 (ND 158-0, SD 77-0); I 1-0, April 7, 1992. A two-thirds majority of those present and voting (254 in this case) was required for passage under suspension of the rules.

**73. Procedural Motion.** Approval of the House Journal of Tuesday, April 7. Approved 282-120: R 45-115; D 236-5 (ND 160-4, SD 76-1); I 1-0, April 8, 1992.

**74. HR 3337. Commemorative Coins/Conference Report.** Adoption of the conference report to mint coins in commemoration of the 200th anniversary of the White House, the 500th anniversary of Christopher Columbus' voyage, the 1994 World Cup Soccer Games, James Madison and the Bill of Rights, and to mint a silver medal for Persian Gulf War veterans. The bill did not include provisions to redesign the reverse sides of the half dollar and the quarter. Adopted 414-0: R 159-0; D 254-0 (ND 174-0, SD 80-0); I 1-0, April 8, 1992.

**75. S 3. Campaign Finance Reform/Motion To Recommit.** Thomas, R-Calif., motion to recommit to the House-Senate conference committee the conference report to give House and Senate candidates incentives to agree to campaign spending limits, with instructions to report it back with provisions to prohibit House members from using the frank or their official House allowance for mass mailings outside their current congressional districts. Motion agreed to 408-8: R 161-0; D 246-8 (ND 171-2, SD 75-6); I 1-0, April 8, 1992.

**76. Procedural Motion.** Approval of the House Journal of Wednesday, April 8. Approved 283-121: R 46-115; D 236-6 (ND 156-6, SD 80-0); I 1-0, April 9, 1992.

| | 69 | 70 | 71 | 72 | 73 | 74 | 75 | 76 |
|---|---|---|---|---|---|---|---|---|
| **ALABAMA** | | | | | | | | |
| 1 *Callahan* | N | Y | N | Y | N | Y | Y | N |
| 2 *Dickinson* | N | Y | N | Y | ? | Y | Y | N |
| 3 Browder | N | N | Y | Y | Y | Y | Y | Y |
| 4 Bevill | N | ? | Y | Y | Y | Y | Y | Y |
| 5 Cramer | N | Y | Y | Y | Y | Y | Y | Y |
| 6 Erdreich | N | N | Y | Y | Y | Y | Y | Y |
| 7 Harris | N | Y | Y | Y | Y | Y | Y | Y |
| **ALASKA** | | | | | | | | |
| AL *Young* | N | Y | N | Y | N | Y | Y | N |
| **ARIZONA** | | | | | | | | |
| 1 *Rhodes* | Y | Y | N | Y | N | Y | Y | N |
| 2 Pastor | N | N | Y | Y | Y | Y | Y | Y |
| 3 *Stump* | N | N | N | ? | N | Y | Y | N |
| 4 *Kyl* | Y | Y | N | Y | ? | Y | Y | N |
| 5 *Kolbe* | N | N | N | Y | N | Y | Y | N |
| **ARKANSAS** | | | | | | | | |
| 1 Alexander | Y | Y | Y | ? | ? | Y | N | Y |
| 2 Thornton | N | N | ? | Y | ? | ? | ? | Y |
| 3 *Hammerschmidt* | Y | N | N | ? | Y | Y | Y | Y |
| 4 Anthony | Y | Y | Y | Y | ? | Y | Y | Y |
| **CALIFORNIA** | | | | | | | | |
| 1 *Riggs* | N | Y | N | Y | ? | ? | Y | N |
| 2 *Herger* | N | Y | N | ? | N | Y | Y | N |
| 3 Matsui | Y | N | Y | Y | Y | Y | Y | Y |
| 4 Fazio | Y | N | Y | Y | Y | Y | Y | Y |
| 5 Pelosi | N | N | ? | Y | Y | Y | Y | Y |
| 6 Boxer | N | Y | ? | Y | ? | Y | Y | Y |
| 7 Miller | N | N | Y | Y | Y | Y | Y | Y |
| 8 Dellums | N | N | ? | Y | Y | Y | Y | Y |
| 9 Stark | N | Y | Y | Y | Y | Y | Y | Y |
| 10 Edwards | Y | N | Y | Y | Y | Y | Y | Y |
| 11 Lantos | N | N | Y | ? | Y | Y | Y | Y |
| 12 *Campbell* | N | Y | N | Y | N | Y | Y | N |
| 13 Mineta | Y | N | Y | Y | Y | Y | Y | Y |
| 14 *Doolittle* | N | Y | N | Y | N | Y | Y | N |
| 15 Condit | N | N | ? | Y | Y | Y | Y | Y |
| 16 Panetta | Y | Y | Y | Y | Y | Y | Y | Y |
| 17 Dooley | N | N | Y | Y | Y | Y | Y | Y |
| 18 Lehman | N | N | Y | Y | Y | Y | ? | Y |
| 19 *Lagomarsino* | N | Y | N | Y | N | Y | Y | N |
| 20 *Thomas* | Y | Y | N | Y | N | Y | Y | N |
| 21 *Gallegly* | N | Y | N | Y | N | Y | Y | N |
| 22 *Moorhead* | N | Y | N | Y | N | Y | ? | N |
| 23 Beilenson | Y | N | Y | Y | Y | Y | Y | Y |
| 24 Waxman | N | N | Y | Y | Y | Y | Y | Y |
| 25 Roybal | Y | N | Y | Y | Y | Y | Y | Y |
| 26 Berman | Y | N | Y | ? | Y | ? | Y | Y |
| 27 Levine | ? | ? | ? | Y | ? | ? | Y | Y |
| 28 Dixon | ? | ? | ? | Y | ? | ? | ? | Y |
| 29 Waters | N | N | ? | ? | Y | Y | Y | ? |
| 30 Martinez | N | Y | Y | Y | Y | Y | Y | Y |
| 31 Dymally | ? | ? | ? | ? | Y | Y | Y | Y |
| 32 Anderson | Y | N | Y | Y | Y | Y | Y | Y |
| 33 *Dreier* | N | Y | N | Y | N | Y | Y | N |
| 34 Torres | Y | N | Y | ? | Y | ? | Y | Y |
| 35 *Lewis* | Y | ? | N | Y | N | Y | Y | N |
| 36 Brown | Y | N | Y | Y | Y | Y | Y | Y |
| 37 *McCandless* | N | Y | N | Y | N | Y | Y | N |
| 38 *Dornan* | N | Y | N | ? | ? | Y | Y | N |
| 39 *Dannemeyer* | − | + | ? | Y | N | Y | ? | N |
| 40 *Cox* | N | Y | N | Y | N | Y | Y | N |
| 41 *Lowery* | N | Y | N | ? | N | Y | Y | N |

| | 69 | 70 | 71 | 72 | 73 | 74 | 75 | 76 |
|---|---|---|---|---|---|---|---|---|
| 42 *Rohrabacher* | N | Y | N | Y | N | Y | Y | N |
| 43 *Packard* | N | Y | N | Y | N | Y | Y | N |
| 44 *Cunningham* | N | Y | N | Y | N | Y | Y | N |
| 45 *Hunter* | N | Y | N | ? | N | Y | Y | N |
| **COLORADO** | | | | | | | | |
| 1 Schroeder | N | N | Y | Y | Y | Y | Y | Y |
| 2 Skaggs | Y | N | Y | Y | Y | Y | Y | Y |
| 3 Campbell | N | ? | Y | Y | Y | Y | Y | Y |
| 4 *Allard* | N | N | N | N | N | Y | Y | N |
| 5 *Hefley* | N | Y | N | Y | N | Y | Y | N |
| 6 *Schaefer* | N | Y | N | Y | N | Y | Y | N |
| **CONNECTICUT** | | | | | | | | |
| 1 Kennelly | N | N | Y | Y | Y | Y | Y | Y |
| 2 Gejdenson | N | N | Y | Y | Y | Y | Y | Y |
| 3 DeLauro | N | N | Y | Y | Y | Y | Y | Y |
| 4 *Shays* | Y | Y | N | Y | Y | Y | Y | N |
| 5 *Franks* | Y | Y | N | ? | N | Y | Y | N |
| 6 *Johnson* | Y | Y | Y | Y | Y | Y | Y | Y |
| **DELAWARE** | | | | | | | | |
| AL Carper | Y | Y | Y | Y | Y | Y | Y | Y |
| **FLORIDA** | | | | | | | | |
| 1 Hutto | N | Y | Y | Y | Y | Y | Y | Y |
| 2 Peterson | N | Y | Y | ? | Y | Y | Y | Y |
| 3 Bennett | N | N | Y | Y | Y | Y | Y | Y |
| 4 *James* | N | Y | C | N | Y | Y | Y | N |
| 5 *McCollum* | N | Y | Y | Y | N | Y | Y | Y |
| 6 *Stearns* | N | Y | N | ? | N | Y | Y | N |
| 7 Gibbons | N | N | Y | Y | Y | Y | Y | Y |
| 8 *Young* | N | N | N | Y | N | Y | Y | N |
| 9 *Bilirakis* | N | Y | N | ? | ? | ? | ? | N |
| 10 *Ireland* | Y | ? | N | ? | ? | Y | Y | N |
| 11 Bacchus | N | N | Y | Y | Y | Y | Y | Y |
| 12 *Lewis* | N | Y | N | Y | N | Y | Y | N |
| 13 *Goss* | N | Y | N | Y | N | Y | Y | N |
| 14 Johnston | Y | N | Y | Y | Y | Y | Y | Y |
| 15 *Shaw* | Y | Y | N | ? | N | Y | Y | N |
| 16 Smith | Y | Y | Y | Y | Y | Y | Y | Y |
| 17 Lehman | Y | ? | Y | Y | Y | Y | Y | Y |
| 18 *Ros—Lehtinen* | N | Y | N | Y | N | Y | Y | N |
| 19 Fascell | Y | N | Y | Y | Y | Y | Y | Y |
| **GEORGIA** | | | | | | | | |
| 1 Thomas | N | N | Y | Y | Y | Y | Y | Y |
| 2 Hatcher | N | N | Y | Y | Y | Y | Y | Y |
| 3 Ray | N | Y | Y | Y | N | Y | Y | Y |
| 4 Jones | N | N | Y | N | Y | Y | Y | Y |
| 5 Lewis | Y | N | Y | Y | Y | Y | Y | Y |
| 6 *Gingrich* | Y | Y | N | Y | N | Y | Y | N |
| 7 Darden | N | N | Y | Y | ? | Y | Y | Y |
| 8 Rowland | N | Y | Y | Y | Y | Y | Y | Y |
| 9 Jenkins | Y | N | Y | Y | Y | Y | Y | Y |
| 10 Barnard | Y | N | ? | Y | Y | Y | Y | Y |
| **HAWAII** | | | | | | | | |
| 1 Abercrombie | N | N | Y | Y | Y | Y | Y | Y |
| 2 Mink | N | N | Y | Y | Y | Y | Y | Y |
| **IDAHO** | | | | | | | | |
| 1 LaRocco | N | N | Y | Y | Y | Y | Y | Y |
| 2 Stallings | N | N | Y | Y | Y | Y | Y | Y |
| **ILLINOIS** | | | | | | | | |
| 1 Hayes | N | N | Y | ? | Y | Y | Y | Y |
| 2 Savage | N | N | Y | Y | Y | Y | Y | Y |
| 3 Russo | N | Y | ? | Y | Y | Y | Y | ? |
| 4 Sangmeister | N | Y | Y | Y | Y | Y | Y | Y |
| 5 Lipinski | N | N | Y | Y | Y | Y | Y | Y |
| 6 *Hyde* | N | Y | N | Y | N | Y | Y | N |
| 7 Collins | N | N | Y | Y | Y | Y | Y | Y |
| 8 Rostenkowski | N | Y | Y | Y | Y | Y | Y | Y |
| 9 Yates | Y | ? | Y | Y | Y | Y | Y | ? |
| 10 *Porter* | Y | Y | N | Y | N | Y | Y | N |
| 11 Annunzio | N | Y | Y | Y | Y | Y | Y | Y |
| 12 *Crane* | N | Y | N | Y | N | Y | Y | N |
| 13 *Fawell* | Y | Y | N | Y | N | Y | Y | N |
| 14 *Hastert* | N | Y | N | Y | N | Y | Y | N |
| 15 *Ewing* | N | Y | N | Y | N | Y | Y | N |
| 16 Cox | N | N | Y | Y | Y | Y | Y | Y |
| 17 Evans | N | N | Y | Y | Y | Y | Y | Y |
| 18 *Michel* | Y | ? | N | Y | N | Y | Y | N |
| 19 Bruce | N | Y | Y | Y | Y | Y | Y | Y |
| 20 Durbin | N | N | Y | Y | Y | Y | Y | Y |
| 21 Costello | N | N | Y | ? | ? | ? | ? | ? |
| 22 Poshard | N | Y | Y | Y | Y | Y | N | Y |
| **INDIANA** | | | | | | | | |
| 1 Visclosky | N | N | Y | Y | Y | Y | Y | Y |
| 2 Sharp | N | Y | Y | Y | Y | Y | Y | Y |
| 3 Roemer | N | Y | Y | Y | Y | Y | Y | Y |

ND   Northern Democrats      SD   Southern Democrats

| | 69 | 70 | 71 | 72 | 73 | 74 | 75 | 76 |
|---|---|---|---|---|---|---|---|---|
| 4 Long | N | N | Y | Y | Y | Y | Y | Y |
| 5 Jontz | N | N | Y | Y | Y | Y | Y | Y |
| 6 ***Burton*** | N | Y | N | Y | N | Y | Y | N |
| 7 ***Myers*** | N | Y | N | ? | Y | Y | Y | Y |
| 8 McCloskey | N | N | Y | Y | Y | Y | Y | Y |
| 9 Hamilton | N | Y | Y | Y | Y | Y | Y | Y |
| 10 Jacobs | N | Y | Y | Y | N | Y | N | N |
| **IOWA** | | | | | | | | |
| 1 ***Leach*** | Y | Y | N | Y | N | Y | Y | N |
| 2 ***Nussle*** | N | Y | N | Y | N | Y | Y | N |
| 3 Nagle | N | N | Y | Y | Y | Y | Y | Y |
| 4 Smith | N | Y | Y | Y | Y | Y | Y | ? |
| 5 ***Lightfoot*** | N | Y | N | Y | N | Y | Y | N |
| 6 ***Grandy*** | Y | Y | Y | Y | N | Y | Y | N |
| **KANSAS** | | | | | | | | |
| 1 ***Roberts*** | N | Y | N | Y | N | Y | Y | N |
| 2 Slattery | N | Y | Y | Y | Y | Y | Y | Y |
| 3 ***Meyers*** | Y | N | N | Y | N | Y | Y | N |
| 4 Glickman | N | Y | Y | Y | Y | Y | Y | Y |
| 5 ***Nichols*** | N | Y | N | Y | Y | Y | Y | Y |
| **KENTUCKY** | | | | | | | | |
| 1 Hubbard | N | N | Y | Y | Y | Y | Y | Y |
| 2 Natcher | N | N | Y | Y | Y | Y | Y | Y |
| 3 Mazzoli | N | Y | Y | Y | Y | Y | Y | Y |
| 4 ***Bunning*** | N | Y | N | Y | N | Y | Y | N |
| 5 ***Rogers*** | N | Y | N | Y | N | Y | Y | N |
| 6 ***Hopkins*** | N | N | N | ? | N | Y | Y | N |
| 7 Perkins | ? | ? | Y | Y | Y | Y | Y | Y |
| **LOUISIANA** | | | | | | | | |
| 1 ***Livingston*** | N | N | Y | Y | Y | Y | Y | Y |
| 2 Jefferson | N | N | Y | ? | ? | ? | ? | Y |
| 3 Tauzin | N | N | Y | Y | Y | Y | Y | Y |
| 4 ***McCrery*** | Y | Y | N | Y | Y | Y | Y | Y |
| 5 Huckaby | N | Y | ? | Y | Y | Y | Y | Y |
| 6 ***Baker*** | Y | Y | N | Y | N | Y | Y | N |
| 7 Hayes | N | Y | Y | ? | Y | Y | ? | Y |
| 8 ***Holloway*** | N | Y | N | Y | N | Y | Y | N |
| **MAINE** | | | | | | | | |
| 1 Andrews | N | N | Y | Y | Y | Y | Y | Y |
| 2 ***Snowe*** | N | Y | N | Y | Y | Y | Y | Y |
| **MARYLAND** | | | | | | | | |
| 1 ***Gilchrest*** | Y | Y | N | Y | Y | Y | Y | N |
| 2 ***Bentley*** | N | Y | N | Y | N | Y | Y | N |
| 3 Cardin | Y | N | Y | Y | Y | Y | Y | Y |
| 4 McMillen | Y | N | Y | Y | Y | Y | Y | Y |
| 5 Hoyer | Y | N | Y | Y | Y | Y | Y | Y |
| 6 Byron | N | Y | Y | Y | Y | Y | Y | Y |
| 7 Mfume | N | N | Y | ? | ? | ? | Y | Y |
| 8 ***Morella*** | Y | N | N | Y | Y | Y | Y | N |
| **MASSACHUSETTS** | | | | | | | | |
| 1 Olver | N | N | Y | Y | Y | Y | Y | Y |
| 2 Neal | N | N | Y | Y | ? | Y | Y | Y |
| 3 Early | N | N | Y | Y | Y | Y | Y | Y |
| 4 Frank | N | N | Y | Y | Y | Y | Y | Y |
| 5 Atkins | N | N | Y | Y | Y | Y | Y | Y |
| 6 Mavroules | Y | N | ? | Y | Y | Y | Y | Y |
| 7 Markey | Y | N | Y | Y | Y | Y | Y | Y |
| 8 Kennedy | Y | N | Y | Y | Y | Y | Y | ? |
| 9 Moakley | Y | N | Y | Y | Y | Y | Y | Y |
| 10 Studds | N | N | ? | Y | Y | Y | Y | Y |
| 11 Donnelly | N | N | Y | Y | Y | Y | Y | Y |
| **MICHIGAN** | | | | | | | | |
| 1 Conyers | N | N | Y | Y | Y | Y | Y | ? |
| 2 ***Pursell*** | ? | ? | Y | Y | Y | Y | Y | Y |
| 3 Wolpe | N | N | Y | Y | Y | Y | Y | Y |
| 4 ***Upton*** | N | N | N | Y | N | Y | Y | N |
| 5 ***Henry*** | N | Y | N | Y | N | Y | Y | N |
| 6 Carr | N | N | Y | Y | Y | Y | Y | Y |
| 7 Kildee | N | N | Y | Y | Y | Y | Y | Y |
| 8 Traxler | Y | N | Y | Y | Y | Y | Y | Y |
| 9 ***Vander Jagt*** | N | Y | N | ? | N | Y | Y | Y |
| 10 ***Camp*** | N | Y | N | Y | N | Y | Y | N |
| 11 ***Davis*** | N | ? | N | Y | N | Y | Y | Y |
| 12 Bonior | Y | N | Y | Y | Y | Y | Y | Y |
| 13 Collins | N | N | Y | Y | Y | Y | Y | Y |
| 14 Hertel | N | ? | ? | Y | Y | Y | Y | Y |
| 15 Ford | Y | N | Y | Y | ? | Y | Y | Y |
| 16 Dingell | ? | Y | Y | Y | Y | Y | Y | Y |
| 17 Levin | Y | Y | Y | Y | Y | Y | Y | Y |
| 18 ***Broomfield*** | N | Y | N | Y | Y | Y | Y | Y |
| **MINNESOTA** | | | | | | | | |
| 1 Penny | N | Y | Y | Y | Y | Y | Y | Y |
| 2 ***Weber*** | N | Y | N | Y | N | ? | Y | N |
| 3 ***Ramstad*** | N | Y | Y | Y | N | Y | Y | N |
| 4 Vento | Y | N | Y | Y | Y | Y | Y | Y |
| 5 Sabo | Y | N | Y | Y | Y | Y | ? | Y |
| 6 Sikorski | N | N | Y | Y | N | Y | Y | N |
| 7 Peterson | N | N | Y | Y | Y | Y | Y | Y |
| 8 Oberstar | Y | N | Y | Y | Y | Y | Y | Y |
| **MISSISSIPPI** | | | | | | | | |
| 1 Whitten | Y | ? | Y | ? | ? | ? | ? | ? |
| 2 Espy | N | N | Y | Y | Y | Y | Y | Y |
| 3 Montgomery | Y | N | Y | Y | Y | Y | Y | Y |
| 4 Parker | Y | N | Y | Y | Y | ? | Y | Y |
| 5 Taylor | N | Y | Y | Y | Y | Y | Y | Y |
| **MISSOURI** | | | | | | | | |
| 1 Clay | N | N | Y | Y | N | Y | Y | N |
| 2 Horn | N | N | Y | Y | Y | Y | Y | Y |
| 3 Gephardt | Y | N | Y | Y | Y | Y | Y | ? |
| 4 Skelton | N | Y | Y | Y | Y | Y | Y | Y |
| 5 Wheat | N | N | Y | Y | Y | Y | Y | Y |
| 6 ***Coleman*** | N | Y | N | Y | N | Y | Y | N |
| 7 ***Hancock*** | N | Y | N | Y | N | Y | Y | N |
| 8 ***Emerson*** | N | Y | N | Y | N | Y | Y | N |
| 9 Volkmer | N | Y | Y | Y | Y | Y | Y | Y |
| **MONTANA** | | | | | | | | |
| 1 Williams | N | N | Y | Y | Y | Y | Y | Y |
| 2 ***Marlenee*** | N | Y | N | ? | N | Y | Y | N |
| **NEBRASKA** | | | | | | | | |
| 1 ***Bereuter*** | Y | Y | N | Y | N | Y | Y | N |
| 2 Hoagland | Y | N | Y | Y | Y | Y | Y | ? |
| 3 ***Barrett*** | Y | Y | N | Y | N | Y | Y | N |
| **NEVADA** | | | | | | | | |
| 1 Bilbray | N | N | Y | Y | Y | Y | Y | Y |
| 2 ***Vucanovich*** | N | Y | N | Y | N | Y | Y | ? |
| **NEW HAMPSHIRE** | | | | | | | | |
| 1 ***Zeliff*** | N | Y | N | Y | N | Y | Y | N |
| 2 Swett | N | N | Y | Y | Y | Y | Y | Y |
| **NEW JERSEY** | | | | | | | | |
| 1 Andrews | N | N | Y | Y | Y | Y | Y | Y |
| 2 Hughes | N | Y | Y | Y | Y | Y | Y | Y |
| 3 Pallone | N | N | Y | Y | Y | Y | Y | Y |
| 4 ***Smith*** | ? | ? | N | Y | Y | Y | Y | Y |
| 5 ***Roukema*** | Y | Y | N | Y | N | Y | Y | N |
| 6 Dwyer | N | Y | ? | Y | Y | Y | Y | Y |
| 7 ***Rinaldo*** | N | Y | Y | Y | Y | Y | Y | Y |
| 8 Roe | N | ? | Y | Y | Y | Y | ? | Y |
| 9 Torricelli | N | N | Y | Y | Y | Y | Y | Y |
| 10 Payne | N | ? | Y | ? | Y | Y | Y | Y |
| 11 ***Gallo*** | Y | Y | N | Y | N | Y | Y | N |
| 12 ***Zimmer*** | N | Y | N | Y | N | Y | Y | N |
| 13 ***Saxton*** | ? | ? | N | Y | N | Y | Y | N |
| 14 Guarini | N | N | Y | Y | Y | Y | Y | ? |
| **NEW MEXICO** | | | | | | | | |
| 1 ***Schiff*** | N | Y | N | Y | Y | Y | Y | Y |
| 2 ***Skeen*** | Y | Y | N | Y | Y | Y | Y | Y |
| 3 Richardson | N | N | Y | Y | Y | Y | Y | Y |
| **NEW YORK** | | | | | | | | |
| 1 Hochbrueckner | N | Y | Y | Y | Y | Y | Y | Y |
| 2 Downey | N | Y | Y | Y | Y | Y | Y | Y |
| 3 Mrazek | ? | ? | ? | ? | ? | ? | ? | ? |
| 4 ***Lent*** | N | ? | N | Y | Y | Y | Y | Y |
| 5 ***McGrath*** | N | Y | N | Y | Y | Y | Y | Y |
| 6 Flake | N | N | Y | ? | Y | Y | Y | ? |
| 7 Ackerman | Y | N | ? | ? | Y | Y | Y | Y |
| 8 Scheuer | N | N | Y | Y | Y | Y | Y | Y |
| 9 Manton | Y | N | Y | ? | Y | Y | Y | Y |
| 10 Schumer | Y | N | Y | Y | Y | Y | Y | Y |
| 11 Towns | N | N | Y | ? | Y | Y | Y | Y |
| 12 Owens | N | N | Y | Y | Y | Y | Y | Y |
| 13 Solarz | Y | N | Y | ? | ? | Y | Y | Y |
| 14 ***Molinari*** | N | Y | N | ? | N | Y | Y | N |
| 15 ***Green*** | Y | Y | N | Y | Y | Y | Y | Y |
| 16 Rangel | N | N | Y | ? | ? | ? | ? | Y |
| 17 Weiss | Y | N | Y | Y | Y | Y | Y | ? |
| 18 Serrano | N | N | Y | ? | ? | ? | ? | Y |
| 19 Engel | N | N | Y | Y | Y | Y | Y | Y |
| 20 Lowey | N | N | Y | ? | ? | Y | Y | ? |
| 21 ***Fish*** | N | N | Y | Y | Y | Y | Y | Y |
| 22 ***Gilman*** | N | N | Y | Y | Y | Y | Y | Y |
| 23 McNulty | N | N | Y | Y | Y | Y | Y | Y |
| 24 ***Solomon*** | N | Y | N | Y | N | Y | Y | ? |
| 25 ***Boehlert*** | Y | N | Y | Y | N | Y | Y | N |
| 26 ***Martin*** | N | Y | N | Y | N | Y | Y | ? |
| 27 ***Walsh*** | Y | Y | N | Y | N | Y | Y | N |
| 28 McHugh | Y | N | Y | Y | Y | Y | Y | Y |
| 29 ***Horton*** | N | ? | Y | Y | Y | Y | Y | Y |
| 30 Slaughter | N | Y | Y | ? | Y | Y | Y | Y |
| 31 ***Paxon*** | N | Y | N | Y | N | Y | Y | N |
| 32 LaFalce | N | N | Y | Y | Y | Y | Y | Y |
| 33 Nowak | N | N | ? | Y | Y | Y | Y | Y |
| 34 ***Houghton*** | Y | Y | N | Y | Y | Y | Y | Y |
| **NORTH CAROLINA** | | | | | | | | |
| 1 Jones | Y | N | Y | Y | Y | Y | Y | Y |
| 2 Valentine | ? | ? | ? | Y | Y | Y | Y | Y |
| 3 Lancaster | N | N | Y | Y | Y | Y | Y | Y |
| 4 Price | Y | N | Y | Y | Y | Y | Y | Y |
| 5 Neal | Y | N | Y | Y | Y | Y | Y | ? |
| 6 ***Coble*** | N | Y | N | Y | N | Y | Y | N |
| 7 Rose | Y | Y | Y | Y | Y | Y | Y | Y |
| 8 Hefner | N | Y | Y | Y | Y | Y | Y | Y |
| 9 ***McMillan*** | Y | N | N | Y | N | Y | Y | N |
| 10 ***Ballenger*** | N | Y | N | Y | N | Y | Y | N |
| 11 ***Taylor*** | N | Y | N | Y | N | Y | Y | N |
| **NORTH DAKOTA** | | | | | | | | |
| AL Dorgan | N | Y | Y | Y | Y | Y | Y | N |
| **OHIO** | | | | | | | | |
| 1 Luken | N | N | Y | Y | Y | Y | Y | Y |
| 2 ***Gradison*** | Y | Y | N | Y | Y | Y | Y | N |
| 3 Hall | N | N | Y | Y | Y | Y | Y | Y |
| 4 ***Oxley*** | N | Y | N | Y | Y | Y | Y | N |
| 5 ***Gillmor*** | Y | Y | N | Y | Y | ? | ? | Y |
| 6 ***McEwen*** | N | Y | ? | ? | N | Y | Y | N |
| 7 ***Hobson*** | N | Y | N | Y | N | Y | Y | N |
| 8 ***Boehner*** | N | Y | ? | Y | N | ? | Y | N |
| 9 Kaptur | N | N | Y | Y | Y | Y | Y | Y |
| 10 ***Miller*** | N | Y | N | Y | N | Y | Y | N |
| 11 Eckart | N | N | Y | Y | Y | Y | Y | Y |
| 12 ***Kasich*** | N | Y | N | Y | Y | Y | Y | Y |
| 13 Pease | Y | N | Y | Y | Y | Y | Y | Y |
| 14 Sawyer | N | ? | Y | Y | Y | Y | Y | Y |
| 15 ***Wylie*** | Y | Y | N | Y | Y | Y | Y | Y |
| 16 ***Regula*** | N | Y | N | Y | N | Y | Y | N |
| 17 Traficant | N | N | Y | Y | Y | Y | Y | Y |
| 18 Applegate | N | ? | Y | Y | Y | Y | Y | Y |
| 19 Feighan | Y | N | Y | ? | ? | Y | Y | ? |
| 20 Oakar | N | ? | Y | ? | Y | Y | Y | Y |
| 21 Stokes | N | N | Y | Y | Y | Y | Y | Y |
| **OKLAHOMA** | | | | | | | | |
| 1 ***Inhofe*** | N | Y | N | Y | N | Y | Y | N |
| 2 Synar | Y | N | Y | Y | Y | Y | Y | Y |
| 3 Brewster | N | N | Y | Y | Y | Y | Y | Y |
| 4 McCurdy | Y | Y | Y | Y | Y | Y | Y | Y |
| 5 ***Edwards*** | N | Y | N | ? | N | Y | Y | N |
| 6 English | N | Y | Y | Y | Y | Y | Y | Y |
| **OREGON** | | | | | | | | |
| 1 AuCoin | N | N | Y | Y | Y | Y | Y | Y |
| 2 ***Smith*** | N | Y | N | Y | N | Y | Y | N |
| 3 Wyden | N | N | Y | Y | Y | Y | Y | Y |
| 4 DeFazio | N | N | Y | Y | Y | Y | Y | Y |
| 5 Kopetski | N | N | Y | Y | Y | Y | Y | Y |
| **PENNSYLVANIA** | | | | | | | | |
| 1 Foglietta | N | N | ? | ? | Y | Y | Y | Y |
| 2 Blackwell | N | N | Y | Y | ? | Y | Y | Y |
| 3 Borski | N | N | Y | Y | Y | Y | Y | Y |
| 4 Kolter | N | Y | Y | Y | Y | Y | Y | Y |
| 5 ***Schulze*** | N | Y | ? | ? | Y | Y | Y | Y |
| 6 Yatron | N | Y | Y | Y | Y | Y | Y | Y |
| 7 ***Weldon*** | N | N | N | Y | N | Y | Y | N |
| 8 Kostmayer | N | Y | Y | Y | Y | Y | Y | ? |
| 9 ***Shuster*** | N | Y | N | Y | N | Y | Y | N |
| 10 ***McDade*** | Y | Y | N | ? | N | Y | Y | N |
| 11 Kanjorski | N | Y | Y | Y | Y | Y | Y | Y |
| 12 Murtha | Y | N | Y | Y | Y | Y | Y | Y |
| 13 ***Coughlin*** | Y | Y | N | Y | N | Y | Y | N |
| 14 Coyne | Y | N | Y | Y | Y | Y | Y | Y |
| 15 ***Ritter*** | N | Y | N | Y | Y | Y | Y | Y |
| 16 ***Walker*** | N | Y | N | Y | N | Y | Y | N |
| 17 ***Gekas*** | N | Y | N | Y | N | Y | Y | N |
| 18 ***Santorum*** | N | Y | N | Y | Y | Y | Y | Y |
| 19 ***Goodling*** | N | Y | N | Y | N | Y | Y | N |
| 20 Gaydos | N | Y | Y | Y | Y | Y | Y | Y |
| 21 ***Ridge*** | N | Y | N | Y | N | Y | Y | ? |
| 22 Murphy | N | N | Y | ? | N | Y | Y | N |
| 23 ***Clinger*** | Y | Y | N | Y | Y | Y | Y | N |
| **RHODE ISLAND** | | | | | | | | |
| 1 ***Machtley*** | N | N | Y | Y | N | Y | Y | N |
| 2 Reed | N | N | Y | Y | Y | Y | Y | Y |
| **SOUTH CAROLINA** | | | | | | | | |
| 1 ***Ravenel*** | N | Y | N | Y | Y | Y | Y | Y |
| 2 ***Spence*** | N | Y | Y | Y | N | Y | Y | Y |
| 3 Derrick | Y | N | Y | Y | Y | Y | Y | Y |
| 4 Patterson | N | Y | Y | ? | Y | Y | Y | Y |
| 5 Spratt | Y | N | Y | Y | Y | Y | Y | Y |
| 6 Tallon | N | N | Y | Y | Y | Y | Y | Y |
| **SOUTH DAKOTA** | | | | | | | | |
| AL Johnson | Y | N | Y | Y | Y | Y | Y | Y |
| **TENNESSEE** | | | | | | | | |
| 1 ***Quillen*** | N | N | N | Y | Y | Y | Y | Y |
| 2 ***Duncan*** | N | Y | N | Y | N | ? | Y | N |
| 3 Lloyd | N | Y | Y | Y | Y | Y | Y | Y |
| 4 Cooper | N | Y | Y | Y | Y | Y | Y | Y |
| 5 Clement | N | N | Y | Y | Y | Y | Y | Y |
| 6 Gordon | N | N | Y | Y | Y | Y | Y | Y |
| 7 ***Sundquist*** | N | N | N | ? | N | Y | Y | N |
| 8 Tanner | N | Y | Y | Y | Y | Y | Y | Y |
| 9 Ford | N | Y | Y | Y | Y | Y | Y | ? |
| **TEXAS** | | | | | | | | |
| 1 Chapman | N | N | Y | Y | Y | Y | N | ? |
| 2 Wilson | N | N | Y | Y | ? | Y | Y | Y |
| 3 ***Johnson*** | N | Y | N | Y | Y | Y | Y | Y |
| 4 Hall | N | ? | Y | Y | Y | Y | Y | Y |
| 5 Bryant | N | N | Y | Y | Y | Y | Y | Y |
| 6 ***Barton*** | N | Y | N | Y | N | Y | Y | N |
| 7 ***Archer*** | N | Y | N | Y | Y | Y | Y | Y |
| 8 ***Fields*** | N | Y | N | Y | N | Y | Y | N |
| 9 Brooks | Y | N | Y | Y | Y | Y | N | Y |
| 10 Pickle | Y | N | Y | Y | P | Y | Y | Y |
| 11 Edwards | N | N | Y | Y | Y | Y | Y | Y |
| 12 Geren | Y | Y | Y | Y | Y | Y | Y | Y |
| 13 Sarpalius | Y | N | Y | Y | Y | Y | N | Y |
| 14 Laughlin | Y | Y | Y | Y | Y | Y | Y | Y |
| 15 de la Garza | N | Y | Y | Y | Y | Y | Y | Y |
| 16 Coleman | Y | N | Y | Y | Y | Y | Y | Y |
| 17 Stenholm | Y | N | Y | Y | Y | Y | Y | Y |
| 18 Washington | N | N | ? | ? | Y | Y | N | Y |
| 19 ***Combest*** | N | Y | N | Y | Y | Y | Y | Y |
| 20 Gonzalez | Y | N | Y | Y | Y | Y | Y | Y |
| 21 ***Smith*** | N | Y | N | Y | N | Y | Y | N |
| 22 ***DeLay*** | N | Y | N | Y | N | Y | Y | N |
| 23 Bustamante | N | N | Y | Y | Y | Y | Y | Y |
| 24 Frost | N | Y | Y | Y | Y | Y | N | Y |
| 25 Andrews | N | Y | Y | Y | Y | Y | Y | Y |
| 26 ***Armey*** | N | Y | N | Y | N | Y | Y | N |
| 27 Ortiz | N | N | Y | Y | Y | Y | Y | Y |
| **UTAH** | | | | | | | | |
| 1 ***Hansen*** | Y | Y | N | Y | N | Y | Y | N |
| 2 Owens | N | N | Y | Y | Y | Y | Y | Y |
| 3 Orton | N | Y | Y | Y | Y | Y | Y | Y |
| **VERMONT** | | | | | | | | |
| AL *Sanders* | N | N | Y | Y | Y | Y | Y | Y |
| **VIRGINIA** | | | | | | | | |
| 1 ***Bateman*** | Y | Y | ? | Y | Y | Y | Y | Y |
| 2 Pickett | Y | N | Y | Y | ? | Y | Y | Y |
| 3 ***Bliley*** | Y | Y | N | Y | N | Y | Y | N |
| 4 Sisisky | Y | N | Y | Y | Y | Y | Y | Y |
| 5 Payne | Y | Y | Y | Y | Y | Y | Y | Y |
| 6 Olin | Y | Y | Y | Y | Y | Y | Y | Y |
| 7 ***Allen*** | N | Y | N | Y | N | Y | Y | N |
| 8 Moran | Y | N | ? | Y | Y | Y | Y | Y |
| 9 Boucher | N | Y | Y | Y | Y | Y | Y | Y |
| 10 ***Wolf*** | Y | Y | N | Y | N | Y | Y | N |
| **WASHINGTON** | | | | | | | | |
| 1 ***Miller*** | Y | Y | N | Y | N | Y | ? | N |
| 2 Swift | Y | N | Y | Y | Y | Y | Y | Y |
| 3 Unsoeld | N | N | Y | Y | Y | Y | Y | Y |
| 4 ***Morrison*** | Y | N | N | Y | Y | + | + | Y |
| 5 Foley | | | | | | | | |
| 6 Dicks | Y | N | Y | Y | Y | Y | Y | Y |
| 7 McDermott | N | N | Y | Y | Y | Y | Y | Y |
| 8 ***Chandler*** | Y | Y | N | Y | N | Y | Y | N |
| **WEST VIRGINIA** | | | | | | | | |
| 1 Mollohan | N | N | Y | Y | Y | Y | Y | Y |
| 2 Staggers | N | Y | Y | Y | Y | Y | Y | Y |
| 3 Wise | N | Y | Y | Y | Y | Y | Y | Y |
| 4 Rahall | N | N | Y | Y | Y | Y | Y | Y |
| **WISCONSIN** | | | | | | | | |
| 1 Aspin | Y | Y | Y | Y | Y | Y | Y | Y |
| 2 ***Klug*** | N | Y | N | Y | Y | Y | Y | Y |
| 3 ***Gunderson*** | N | Y | N | Y | Y | Y | Y | Y |
| 4 Kleczka | Y | N | Y | Y | Y | Y | Y | ? |
| 5 Moody | N | N | Y | Y | Y | Y | Y | Y |
| 6 ***Petri*** | N | N | N | Y | Y | Y | Y | Y |
| 7 Obey | Y | ? | Y | Y | Y | Y | Y | Y |
| 8 ***Roth*** | N | Y | N | Y | N | Y | Y | N |
| 9 ***Sensenbrenner*** | N | Y | N | Y | N | Y | Y | N |
| **WYOMING** | | | | | | | | |
| AL ***Thomas*** | Y | Y | N | Y | Y | Y | Y | Y |

Southern states - Ala., Ark., Fla., Ga., Ky., La., Miss., N.C., Okla., S.C., Tenn., Texas, Va.
Omitted votes are quorum calls, which CQ does not include in its vote charts.

**77. S 3. Campaign Finance Reform/Previous Question.** Gejdenson, D-Conn., motion to order the previous question (thus limiting debate and the possibility of amendment) on the adoption of the conference report to limit spending in congressional campaigns by providing incentives to candidates to agree to voluntary spending limits, restricting money that candidates can accept from political action committees (PACs), and restricting "soft money" raised and spent by state parties in federal elections. Motion agreed to 260-161: R 6-158; D 253-3 (ND 170-3, SD 83-0); I 1-0, April 9, 1992.

**78. S 3. Campaign Finance Reform/Motion to Recommit.** Walsh, R-N.Y., motion to recommit to the Conference Committee the conference report to limit spending in congressional campaigns by providing incentives to candidates to agree to voluntary spending limits, with instructions to report it back to the House after stripping all sections from the bill that allow for public financing of subsidies to congressional campaigns. Motion rejected 179-243: R 154-10; D 25-232 (ND 12-163, SD 13-69); I 0-1, April 9, 1992.

**79. S 3. Campaign Finance Reform/Conference Report.** Adoption of the conference report to limit spending in congressional campaigns by providing incentives to candidates to agree to voluntary spending limits, restricting money that candidates can accept from political action committees (PACs) and restricting "soft money" raised and spent by state parties in federal elections. The bill created a separate system for House and Senate campaigns, and none of the provisions of the bill became effective until the cost of public financing was offset by subsequent legislation. Adopted 259-165: R 19-145; D 239-20 (ND 171-6, SD 68-14); I 1-0, April 9, 1992. A "nay" was a vote supporting the president's position.

**80. H Res 430. House Post Office Investigation.** Adoption of the resolution to condemn any attempt to interfere with the ad hoc investigation into the allegations of drug dealing and financial embezzlement at the House Post Office. Adopted 417-1: R 160-0; D 256-1 (ND 176-0, SD 80-1); I 1-0, April 9, 1992.

**81. H Res 431. Investigation of Reported Illegal Hiring Practices.** Gephardt, D-Mo., motion to table (kill) the Riggs, R-Calif., resolution to require an investigation by a bipartisan ad hoc Standards of Official Conduct Committee into the published reports of illegal hiring practices and ghost employees in the House of Representatives. Motion agreed to 231-181: R 1-158; D 229-23 (ND 159-14, SD 70-9); I 1-0, April 9, 1992.

**82. H Res 423. Administrative Operation of the House/ Rule.** Adoption of the rule (H Res 427) to provide for House floor consideration of the resolution to transfer administrative and financial functions from the clerk, sergeant at arms and doorkeeper to a newly created director of non-legislative and financial services to be appointed jointly by the Speaker and majority and minority leaders. Adopted 257-159: R 0-159; D 256-0 (ND 176-0, SD 80-0); I 1-0, April 9, 1992.

**83. H Res 423. Administrative Operations of the House/Substitute.** Michel, R-Ill., substitute amendment to make changes to both legislative and administrative procedures, including the creation of a chief financial officer and an inspector general; the elimination of the office of the doorkeeper and the postmaster; require that party ratio on committees reflect the ratio in the whole House; eliminate proxy voting in committees; to cut committee staff size by 50 percent; and to increase the president's ability to rescind previous appropriations. Rejected 159-254: R 159-0; D 0-253 (ND 0-171, SD 0-82); I 0-1, April 9, 1992.

**84. H Res 423. Administrative Operation of the House/Adoption.** Adoption of the resolution to transfer administrative and financial functions from the sergeant at arms, doorkeeper and clerk to a newly created director of non-legislative and financial services; to create an inspector general to conduct periodic audits of the House; to eliminate designated perquisites in the House; and abolish the House postmaster. Adopted 269-81: R 16-78; D 252-3 (ND 171-2, SD 81-1); I 1-0, April 9, 1992.

## KEY

| | |
|---|---|
| Y | Voted for (yea). |
| # | Paired for. |
| + | Announced for. |
| N | Voted against (nay). |
| X | Paired against. |
| − | Announced against. |
| P | Voted "present." |
| C | Voted "present" to avoid possible conflict of interest. |
| ? | Did not vote or otherwise make a position known. |

Democrats   *Republicans*
*Independent*

| | 77 | 78 | 79 | 80 | 81 | 82 | 83 | 84 |
|---|---|---|---|---|---|---|---|---|
| **ALABAMA** | | | | | | | | |
| 1 *Callahan* | N | Y | N | Y | N | N | Y | N |
| 2 *Dickinson* | N | Y | N | Y | N | N | Y | N |
| 3 Browder | Y | N | Y | Y | Y | Y | N | Y |
| 4 Bevill | Y | N | Y | Y | Y | Y | N | Y |
| 5 Cramer | Y | N | Y | Y | Y | Y | N | Y |
| 6 Erdreich | Y | N | Y | Y | N | Y | N | Y |
| 7 Harris | Y | N | Y | Y | Y | Y | N | Y |
| **ALASKA** | | | | | | | | |
| AL *Young* | N | Y | N | ? | ? | ? | # | ? |
| **ARIZONA** | | | | | | | | |
| 1 *Rhodes* | N | Y | N | Y | N | N | Y | N |
| 2 Pastor | Y | N | Y | Y | Y | Y | N | Y |
| 3 *Stump* | N | Y | N | N | N | N | Y | N |
| 4 *Kyl* | N | Y | N | Y | N | N | Y | P |
| 5 *Kolbe* | N | Y | N | Y | N | N | Y | P |
| **ARKANSAS** | | | | | | | | |
| 1 Alexander | Y | N | Y | Y | Y | Y | N | Y |
| 2 Thornton | Y | N | Y | Y | Y | Y | N | Y |
| 3 *Hammerschmidt* | N | Y | N | Y | N | N | Y | N |
| 4 Anthony | Y | N | Y | ? | Y | Y | N | Y |
| **CALIFORNIA** | | | | | | | | |
| 1 *Riggs* | N | Y | N | Y | N | N | Y | P |
| 2 *Herger* | N | Y | N | Y | N | N | Y | N |
| 3 Matsui | Y | N | Y | Y | Y | Y | N | Y |
| 4 Fazio | Y | N | Y | Y | Y | Y | N | Y |
| 5 Pelosi | Y | N | Y | Y | Y | Y | N | Y |
| 6 Boxer | Y | N | Y | Y | Y | Y | N | Y |
| 7 Miller | Y | N | Y | Y | Y | Y | N | Y |
| 8 Dellums | Y | N | Y | Y | Y | Y | N | Y |
| 9 Stark | Y | N | Y | Y | Y | Y | N | Y |
| 10 Edwards | Y | N | Y | Y | Y | Y | N | Y |
| 11 Lantos | Y | N | Y | Y | Y | Y | N | Y |
| 12 *Campbell* | N | Y | N | Y | N | N | Y | P |
| 13 Mineta | Y | N | Y | Y | Y | Y | N | Y |
| 14 *Doolittle* | N | Y | N | Y | N | N | Y | P |
| 15 Condit | Y | Y | Y | Y | Y | Y | N | Y |
| 16 Panetta | Y | N | Y | Y | Y | Y | N | Y |
| 17 Dooley | Y | N | Y | Y | Y | Y | N | Y |
| 18 Lehman | Y | N | Y | Y | Y | Y | N | Y |
| 19 *Lagomarsino* | N | Y | N | Y | N | N | Y | N |
| 20 *Thomas* | N | Y | N | N | N | N | Y | P |
| 21 *Gallegly* | N | Y | N | Y | N | N | Y | N |
| 22 *Moorhead* | N | Y | N | Y | N | N | Y | N |
| 23 Beilenson | Y | N | Y | Y | Y | Y | N | Y |
| 24 Waxman | Y | N | Y | Y | Y | Y | N | Y |
| 25 Roybal | Y | N | Y | Y | Y | Y | N | Y |
| 26 Berman | Y | N | Y | Y | Y | Y | N | Y |
| 27 Levine | ? | ? | ? | ? | ? | ? | ? | ? |
| 28 Dixon | Y | N | Y | Y | Y | Y | N | Y |
| 29 Waters | Y | N | Y | Y | Y | Y | N | Y |
| 30 Martinez | Y | N | Y | Y | Y | Y | N | Y |
| 31 Dymally | ? | N | Y | Y | ? | Y | X | # |
| 32 Anderson | Y | N | Y | Y | Y | Y | N | Y |
| 33 *Dreier* | N | Y | N | Y | N | N | Y | N |
| 34 Torres | Y | N | Y | Y | Y | Y | N | Y |
| 35 *Lewis* | N | Y | N | Y | N | N | Y | P |
| 36 Brown | Y | N | Y | Y | Y | Y | N | Y |
| 37 *McCandless* | N | Y | N | Y | N | N | Y | N |
| 38 *Dornan* | N | Y | N | Y | N | X | # | X |
| 39 *Dannemeyer* | ? | ? | ? | ? | ? | ? | ? | ? |
| 40 *Cox* | N | Y | N | Y | N | N | Y | P |
| 41 *Lowery* | N | Y | N | Y | N | N | Y | P |

| | 77 | 78 | 79 | 80 | 81 | 82 | 83 | 84 |
|---|---|---|---|---|---|---|---|---|
| 42 *Rohrabacher* | N | Y | N | Y | N | N | Y | P |
| 43 *Packard* | N | Y | N | Y | N | N | Y | N |
| 44 *Cunningham* | N | Y | N | Y | N | N | Y | N |
| 45 *Hunter* | N | Y | N | Y | N | N | Y | P |
| **COLORADO** | | | | | | | | |
| 1 Schroeder | Y | N | Y | Y | Y | Y | N | Y |
| 2 Skaggs | Y | N | Y | Y | Y | Y | N | Y |
| 3 Campbell | Y | N | Y | Y | Y | Y | N | Y |
| 4 *Allard* | N | Y | N | Y | N | N | Y | N |
| 5 *Hefley* | N | Y | N | Y | N | N | Y | N |
| 6 *Schaefer* | N | Y | N | Y | N | N | Y | N |
| **CONNECTICUT** | | | | | | | | |
| 1 Kennelly | Y | N | Y | Y | Y | Y | N | Y |
| 2 Gejdenson | Y | N | Y | Y | Y | Y | N | Y |
| 3 DeLauro | Y | N | Y | Y | Y | Y | N | Y |
| 4 *Shays* | N | N | Y | Y | N | N | Y | Y |
| 5 *Franks* | N | Y | N | Y | N | N | Y | N |
| 6 *Johnson* | N | Y | N | Y | N | N | Y | P |
| **DELAWARE** | | | | | | | | |
| AL Carper | Y | N | Y | Y | Y | Y | N | Y |
| **FLORIDA** | | | | | | | | |
| 1 Hutto | Y | Y | N | Y | N | N | Y | N |
| 2 Peterson | Y | N | Y | Y | Y | Y | N | Y |
| 3 Bennett | Y | N | Y | Y | N | Y | N | Y |
| 4 *James* | N | Y | N | Y | N | N | Y | N |
| 5 *McCollum* | N | Y | N | Y | N | N | Y | P |
| 6 *Stearns* | N | Y | N | N | N | N | Y | N |
| 7 Gibbons | Y | N | Y | Y | Y | Y | N | Y |
| 8 *Young* | N | Y | N | Y | N | N | Y | N |
| 9 *Bilirakis* | N | Y | N | N | N | N | Y | N |
| 10 *Ireland* | N | Y | N | Y | N | N | Y | N |
| 11 Bacchus | Y | N | Y | Y | Y | Y | N | Y |
| 12 *Lewis* | N | Y | N | Y | N | N | Y | P |
| 13 *Goss* | N | Y | N | Y | N | N | Y | N |
| 14 Johnston | Y | N | Y | Y | Y | Y | N | Y |
| 15 *Shaw* | N | Y | N | Y | N | N | Y | P |
| 16 Smith | Y | N | Y | Y | Y | Y | N | Y |
| 17 Lehman | Y | N | Y | Y | Y | Y | N | Y |
| 18 *Ros—Lehtinen* | N | Y | N | Y | N | N | Y | P |
| 19 Fascell | Y | N | Y | Y | Y | Y | N | Y |
| **GEORGIA** | | | | | | | | |
| 1 Thomas | Y | N | Y | Y | Y | Y | N | Y |
| 2 Hatcher | Y | N | Y | Y | Y | Y | N | Y |
| 3 Ray | Y | N | Y | Y | Y | Y | N | Y |
| 4 Jones | Y | N | Y | Y | Y | Y | N | Y |
| 5 Lewis | Y | ? | Y | Y | Y | Y | N | Y |
| 6 *Gingrich* | N | Y | N | Y | N | ? | Y | P |
| 7 Darden | Y | N | Y | Y | Y | Y | N | Y |
| 8 Rowland | Y | N | Y | Y | Y | Y | N | Y |
| 9 Jenkins | Y | N | Y | Y | Y | Y | N | Y |
| 10 Barnard | ? | ? | ? | ? | ? | ? | X | # |
| **HAWAII** | | | | | | | | |
| 1 Abercrombie | Y | N | Y | Y | Y | Y | N | Y |
| 2 Mink | Y | N | Y | Y | Y | Y | N | Y |
| **IDAHO** | | | | | | | | |
| 1 LaRocco | Y | N | Y | Y | Y | Y | N | Y |
| 2 Stallings | Y | N | Y | Y | Y | Y | N | Y |
| **ILLINOIS** | | | | | | | | |
| 1 Hayes | Y | N | Y | Y | Y | Y | N | Y |
| 2 Savage | Y | N | Y | Y | Y | Y | N | Y |
| 3 Russo | ? | ? | ? | ? | ? | ? | ? | ? |
| 4 Sangmeister | Y | N | Y | Y | Y | Y | N | Y |
| 5 Lipinski | Y | N | Y | Y | Y | Y | N | Y |
| 6 *Hyde* | N | Y | N | Y | N | N | Y | N |
| 7 Collins | Y | N | Y | Y | Y | Y | N | Y |
| 8 Rostenkowski | Y | N | Y | Y | Y | Y | ? | Y |
| 9 Yates | ? | ? | ? | ? | ? | # | X | ? |
| 10 *Porter* | N | Y | N | Y | N | N | Y | N |
| 11 Annunzio | Y | N | Y | Y | Y | Y | N | Y |
| 12 *Crane* | N | Y | N | Y | N | N | Y | N |
| 13 *Fawell* | N | Y | N | Y | N | N | Y | P |
| 14 *Hastert* | N | Y | N | Y | N | N | Y | P |
| 15 *Ewing* | N | Y | N | Y | N | N | Y | N |
| 16 Cox | Y | N | Y | Y | Y | Y | N | Y |
| 17 Evans | Y | N | Y | Y | Y | Y | N | Y |
| 18 *Michel* | N | Y | N | Y | N | N | Y | ? |
| 19 Bruce | Y | N | Y | Y | Y | Y | N | Y |
| 20 Durbin | Y | N | Y | Y | Y | Y | N | Y |
| 21 Costello | ? | ? | ? | ? | ? | ? | ? | ? |
| 22 Poshard | Y | N | Y | Y | Y | Y | N | Y |
| **INDIANA** | | | | | | | | |
| 1 Visclosky | Y | N | Y | Y | Y | Y | N | Y |
| 2 Sharp | Y | N | Y | Y | Y | Y | N | Y |
| 3 Roemer | Y | N | Y | Y | Y | Y | N | Y |

ND Northern Democrats   SD Southern Democrats

| | 77 | 78 | 79 | 80 | 81 | 82 | 83 | 84 |
|---|---|---|---|---|---|---|---|---|
| 4 Long | Y | N | Y | Y | Y | Y | N | Y |
| 5 Jontz | Y | N | Y | Y | Y | Y | N | Y |
| 6 ***Burton*** | N | Y | N | ? | N | N | Y | P |
| 7 ***Myers*** | N | Y | N | Y | N | N | Y | N |
| 8 McCloskey | Y | N | Y | Y | Y | Y | N | Y |
| 9 Hamilton | Y | N | Y | Y | N | Y | N | Y |
| 10 Jacobs | N | N | Y | Y | N | Y | N | Y |
| **IOWA** | | | | | | | | |
| 1 ***Leach*** | Y | N | Y | Y | N | N | Y | P |
| 2 ***Nussle*** | N | Y | N | Y | N | N | Y | P |
| 3 Nagle | Y | Y | N | Y | Y | Y | N | Y |
| 4 Smith | ? | ? | ? | ? | ? | ? | ? | ? |
| 5 ***Lightfoot*** | N | Y | N | Y | N | N | Y | P |
| 6 ***Grandy*** | N | Y | N | Y | N | N | Y | N |
| **KANSAS** | | | | | | | | |
| 1 ***Roberts*** | N | Y | N | Y | N | N | Y | N |
| 2 Slattery | Y | N | Y | Y | N | Y | N | Y |
| 3 ***Meyers*** | N | Y | N | Y | N | N | Y | N |
| 4 Glickman | Y | N | Y | Y | N | Y | N | Y |
| 5 ***Nichols*** | N | Y | N | Y | N | N | Y | N |
| **KENTUCKY** | | | | | | | | |
| 1 Hubbard | Y | N | Y | Y | Y | Y | N | Y |
| 2 Natcher | Y | N | Y | Y | Y | Y | N | Y |
| 3 Mazzoli | Y | N | Y | Y | Y | Y | N | Y |
| 4 ***Bunning*** | N | Y | N | Y | N | N | Y | N |
| 5 ***Rogers*** | N | Y | N | Y | N | N | Y | Y |
| 6 ***Hopkins*** | N | Y | N | Y | N | N | Y | N |
| 7 Perkins | Y | N | N | Y | Y | Y | N | N |
| **LOUISIANA** | | | | | | | | |
| 1 ***Livingston*** | N | Y | N | Y | N | N | Y | P |
| 2 Jefferson | Y | N | Y | Y | Y | Y | N | Y |
| 3 Tauzin | Y | Y | N | Y | N | Y | N | Y |
| 4 ***McCrery*** | N | Y | N | Y | N | N | Y | P |
| 5 Huckaby | Y | Y | N | Y | N | ? | N | Y |
| 6 ***Baker*** | N | Y | N | Y | N | N | Y | N |
| 7 Hayes | Y | Y | N | Y | N | Y | N | Y |
| 8 ***Holloway*** | N | Y | N | Y | N | N | Y | P |
| **MAINE** | | | | | | | | |
| 1 Andrews | Y | N | Y | Y | Y | Y | N | Y |
| 2 ***Snowe*** | Y | Y | Y | Y | N | N | Y | N |
| **MARYLAND** | | | | | | | | |
| 1 ***Gilchrest*** | N | Y | N | Y | N | N | Y | N |
| 2 ***Bentley*** | N | Y | N | Y | N | N | Y | N |
| 3 Cardin | Y | N | Y | Y | Y | Y | N | Y |
| 4 McMillen | Y | N | Y | Y | Y | Y | N | Y |
| 5 Hoyer | Y | N | Y | Y | Y | Y | N | Y |
| 6 Byron | Y | Y | Y | Y | Y | Y | N | Y |
| 7 Mfume | Y | N | Y | Y | Y | Y | N | Y |
| 8 ***Morella*** | N | N | Y | Y | N | N | Y | Y |
| **MASSACHUSETTS** | | | | | | | | |
| 1 Olver | Y | N | Y | Y | Y | Y | N | Y |
| 2 Neal | Y | N | Y | Y | Y | Y | N | Y |
| 3 Early | Y | Y | Y | Y | Y | Y | N | Y |
| 4 Frank | Y | N | Y | Y | Y | Y | N | Y |
| 5 Atkins | Y | N | Y | Y | Y | Y | N | Y |
| 6 Mavroules | Y | N | Y | Y | Y | Y | N | Y |
| 7 Markey | Y | N | Y | Y | Y | Y | N | Y |
| 8 Kennedy | Y | ? | Y | Y | Y | Y | N | Y |
| 9 Moakley | Y | N | Y | Y | Y | Y | N | Y |
| 10 Studds | Y | N | Y | Y | Y | Y | N | Y |
| 11 Donnelly | Y | N | Y | Y | Y | Y | N | Y |
| **MICHIGAN** | | | | | | | | |
| 1 Conyers | Y | N | Y | Y | Y | Y | N | Y |
| 2 ***Pursell*** | N | Y | N | Y | N | N | Y | P |
| 3 Wolpe | Y | N | Y | Y | Y | Y | N | Y |
| 4 ***Upton*** | N | Y | N | Y | N | N | Y | P |
| 5 ***Henry*** | N | Y | N | Y | N | N | Y | P |
| 6 Carr | Y | Y | N | Y | Y | Y | N | Y |
| 7 Kildee | Y | N | Y | Y | Y | Y | N | Y |
| 8 Traxler | Y | N | Y | Y | Y | Y | N | Y |
| 9 ***Vander Jagt*** | N | Y | N | Y | ? | N | Y | P |
| 10 ***Camp*** | N | Y | N | Y | N | N | Y | N |
| 11 ***Davis*** | N | Y | N | Y | N | N | Y | N |
| 12 Bonior | Y | N | Y | Y | Y | Y | N | Y |
| 13 Collins | Y | N | Y | Y | Y | Y | N | Y |
| 14 Hertel | ? | N | Y | Y | Y | Y | N | ? |
| 15 Ford | Y | N | Y | Y | Y | Y | N | Y |
| 16 Dingell | ? | ? | Y | Y | ? | ? | ? | ? |
| 17 Levin | Y | N | Y | Y | Y | Y | N | Y |
| 18 ***Broomfield*** | N | Y | N | Y | N | N | Y | P |
| **MINNESOTA** | | | | | | | | |
| 1 Penny | Y | N | Y | Y | N | Y | N | Y |
| 2 ***Weber*** | N | Y | N | ? | ? | ? | ? | ? |
| 3 ***Ramstad*** | N | Y | N | Y | N | N | Y | Y |
| 4 Vento | Y | N | Y | Y | Y | Y | N | Y |

| | 77 | 78 | 79 | 80 | 81 | 82 | 83 | 84 |
|---|---|---|---|---|---|---|---|---|
| 5 Sabo | Y | N | Y | Y | Y | Y | N | Y |
| 6 Sikorski | Y | N | Y | Y | Y | Y | N | Y |
| 7 Peterson | Y | N | Y | Y | Y | Y | N | Y |
| 8 Oberstar | Y | N | Y | Y | Y | Y | N | Y |
| **MISSISSIPPI** | | | | | | | | |
| 1 Whitten | ? | ? | ? | ? | ? | ? | ? | ? |
| 2 Espy | Y | N | Y | Y | Y | Y | N | Y |
| 3 Montgomery | Y | Y | Y | Y | Y | Y | N | Y |
| 4 Parker | Y | Y | Y | Y | Y | Y | N | Y |
| 5 Taylor | Y | Y | N | Y | N | Y | N | Y |
| **MISSOURI** | | | | | | | | |
| 1 Clay | Y | N | Y | Y | Y | Y | N | Y |
| 2 Horn | Y | N | Y | Y | Y | Y | N | Y |
| 3 Gephardt | Y | N | Y | Y | Y | Y | N | Y |
| 4 Skelton | Y | N | Y | Y | Y | Y | N | Y |
| 5 Wheat | ? | N | Y | Y | Y | Y | N | Y |
| 6 ***Coleman*** | N | Y | N | Y | N | N | Y | N |
| 7 ***Hancock*** | N | Y | N | Y | N | N | Y | N |
| 8 ***Emerson*** | N | Y | N | Y | N | N | Y | Y |
| 9 Volkmer | Y | Y | Y | Y | Y | Y | N | Y |
| **MONTANA** | | | | | | | | |
| 1 Williams | Y | N | Y | Y | N | Y | N | Y |
| 2 ***Marlenee*** | Y | Y | Y | Y | N | N | Y | P |
| **NEBRASKA** | | | | | | | | |
| 1 ***Bereuter*** | N | Y | N | Y | N | N | Y | P |
| 2 Hoagland | Y | N | Y | Y | Y | Y | N | Y |
| 3 ***Barrett*** | N | Y | N | Y | N | N | Y | P |
| **NEVADA** | | | | | | | | |
| 1 Bilbray | Y | N | Y | Y | Y | Y | N | Y |
| 2 ***Vucanovich*** | N | Y | N | Y | N | N | Y | N |
| **NEW HAMPSHIRE** | | | | | | | | |
| 1 ***Zeliff*** | N | Y | N | ? | ? | ? | # | X |
| 2 Swett | Y | N | Y | Y | Y | Y | N | Y |
| **NEW JERSEY** | | | | | | | | |
| 1 Andrews | Y | N | Y | Y | N | Y | N | Y |
| 2 Hughes | Y | N | Y | Y | Y | Y | N | ? |
| 3 Pallone | Y | N | Y | Y | N | Y | N | Y |
| 4 ***Smith*** | N | Y | Y | Y | N | N | Y | N |
| 5 ***Roukema*** | N | Y | N | Y | N | N | Y | N |
| 6 Dwyer | Y | N | Y | Y | Y | Y | ? | ? |
| 7 ***Rinaldo*** | N | Y | Y | Y | N | N | Y | Y |
| 8 Roe | Y | N | Y | Y | Y | Y | N | Y |
| 9 Torricelli | Y | N | Y | Y | Y | Y | N | Y |
| 10 Payne | Y | N | Y | Y | Y | Y | N | Y |
| 11 ***Gallo*** | N | Y | N | Y | N | N | Y | N |
| 12 ***Zimmer*** | N | N | Y | Y | N | N | Y | N |
| 13 ***Saxton*** | N | Y | N | Y | N | N | Y | N |
| 14 Guarini | Y | N | Y | Y | Y | Y | N | Y |
| **NEW MEXICO** | | | | | | | | |
| 1 ***Schiff*** | N | Y | N | Y | N | N | Y | N |
| 2 ***Skeen*** | N | Y | N | Y | N | N | Y | N |
| 3 Richardson | Y | N | Y | Y | Y | Y | N | Y |
| **NEW YORK** | | | | | | | | |
| 1 Hochbrueckner | Y | N | Y | Y | Y | Y | N | Y |
| 2 Downey | Y | N | Y | Y | Y | Y | N | Y |
| 3 Mrazek | Y | N | Y | Y | Y | Y | N | Y |
| 4 ***Lent*** | N | Y | N | Y | N | N | Y | N |
| 5 ***McGrath*** | N | Y | N | Y | Y | N | Y | Y |
| 6 Flake | Y | N | Y | Y | Y | Y | N | Y |
| 7 Ackerman | Y | N | Y | Y | Y | Y | N | Y |
| 8 Scheuer | Y | N | Y | Y | Y | Y | N | Y |
| 9 Manton | Y | N | Y | Y | Y | Y | N | Y |
| 10 Schumer | Y | N | Y | Y | Y | Y | N | Y |
| 11 Towns | Y | N | Y | Y | Y | Y | N | Y |
| 12 Owens | Y | N | Y | Y | Y | Y | N | Y |
| 13 Solarz | Y | N | Y | Y | Y | Y | N | Y |
| 14 ***Molinari*** | N | Y | N | Y | N | N | Y | N |
| 15 ***Green*** | Y | N | Y | Y | N | N | Y | P |
| 16 Rangel | Y | N | Y | Y | Y | Y | N | Y |
| 17 Weiss | Y | N | Y | Y | Y | Y | N | Y |
| 18 Serrano | Y | N | Y | Y | Y | Y | N | Y |
| 19 Engel | Y | N | Y | Y | Y | Y | N | Y |
| 20 Lowey | Y | N | Y | Y | Y | Y | N | Y |
| 21 ***Fish*** | Y | Y | Y | Y | N | N | Y | P |
| 22 ***Gilman*** | N | N | Y | Y | N | N | Y | Y |
| 23 McNulty | Y | N | Y | Y | Y | Y | N | Y |
| 24 ***Solomon*** | N | Y | N | Y | N | N | Y | P |
| 25 ***Boehlert*** | N | N | Y | Y | N | N | Y | N |
| 26 ***Martin*** | ? | ? | ? | ? | ? | ? | ? | ? |
| 27 ***Walsh*** | N | Y | N | Y | N | N | Y | N |
| 28 McHugh | Y | N | Y | Y | ? | Y | N | Y |
| 29 ***Horton*** | N | Y | N | Y | N | N | Y | N |
| 30 Slaughter | Y | N | Y | Y | Y | Y | N | Y |
| 31 ***Paxon*** | N | Y | N | Y | N | N | Y | N |

| | 77 | 78 | 79 | 80 | 81 | 82 | 83 | 84 |
|---|---|---|---|---|---|---|---|---|
| 32 LaFalce | Y | N | Y | Y | Y | Y | N | Y |
| 33 Nowak | Y | N | Y | Y | Y | Y | N | Y |
| 34 ***Houghton*** | N | Y | N | Y | N | N | Y | N |
| **NORTH CAROLINA** | | | | | | | | |
| 1 Jones | Y | N | Y | Y | Y | Y | N | Y |
| 2 Valentine | Y | N | Y | Y | Y | Y | N | Y |
| 3 Lancaster | Y | N | Y | Y | Y | Y | N | Y |
| 4 Price | Y | N | Y | Y | Y | Y | N | Y |
| 5 Neal | Y | N | Y | Y | Y | Y | N | Y |
| 6 ***Coble*** | N | Y | N | Y | N | N | Y | P |
| 7 Rose | Y | N | Y | Y | Y | Y | N | Y |
| 8 Hefner | Y | N | Y | Y | Y | Y | N | Y |
| 9 ***McMillan*** | N | Y | N | Y | N | N | Y | P |
| 10 ***Ballenger*** | N | Y | N | Y | N | N | Y | P |
| 11 ***Taylor*** | N | Y | N | Y | N | N | Y | P |
| **NORTH DAKOTA** | | | | | | | | |
| AL Dorgan | Y | N | Y | Y | Y | Y | N | Y |
| **OHIO** | | | | | | | | |
| 1 Luken | Y | N | Y | Y | Y | Y | N | Y |
| 2 ***Gradison*** | N | Y | N | Y | N | N | Y | N |
| 3 Hall | Y | N | Y | Y | ? | Y | N | Y |
| 4 ***Oxley*** | N | Y | N | Y | N | N | Y | N |
| 5 ***Gillmor*** | N | Y | N | Y | N | N | Y | P |
| 6 ***McEwen*** | N | Y | N | Y | N | N | Y | N |
| 7 ***Hobson*** | N | Y | N | Y | N | N | Y | N |
| 8 ***Boehner*** | N | Y | N | Y | N | N | Y | P |
| 9 Kaptur | Y | N | Y | Y | Y | Y | N | Y |
| 10 ***Miller*** | N | Y | N | Y | N | N | Y | N |
| 11 Eckart | Y | N | Y | Y | Y | Y | N | Y |
| 12 ***Kasich*** | N | Y | N | Y | N | N | Y | N |
| 13 Pease | Y | N | Y | Y | Y | Y | N | Y |
| 14 Sawyer | Y | Y | Y | Y | Y | Y | N | Y |
| 15 ***Wylie*** | N | Y | N | Y | N | N | Y | P |
| 16 ***Regula*** | N | Y | N | Y | N | N | Y | Y |
| 17 Traficant | Y | Y | N | Y | Y | Y | N | Y |
| 18 Applegate | N | Y | N | Y | Y | Y | N | N |
| 19 Feighan | Y | N | Y | Y | Y | Y | N | Y |
| 20 Oakar | Y | N | Y | Y | Y | Y | ? | Y |
| 21 Stokes | Y | N | Y | Y | Y | Y | N | Y |
| **OKLAHOMA** | | | | | | | | |
| 1 ***Inhofe*** | N | Y | N | Y | N | N | Y | N |
| 2 Synar | Y | N | Y | Y | Y | Y | N | Y |
| 3 Brewster | Y | N | Y | Y | Y | Y | N | Y |
| 4 McCurdy | Y | N | Y | Y | Y | Y | N | Y |
| 5 ***Edwards*** | N | Y | N | Y | N | N | Y | N |
| 6 English | Y | N | Y | Y | Y | Y | N | Y |
| **OREGON** | | | | | | | | |
| 1 AuCoin | Y | N | Y | ? | Y | Y | N | Y |
| 2 ***Smith*** | N | Y | N | Y | N | N | Y | N |
| 3 Wyden | Y | N | Y | Y | Y | Y | N | Y |
| 4 DeFazio | Y | N | Y | Y | Y | Y | N | Y |
| 5 Kopetski | Y | N | Y | Y | Y | Y | N | Y |
| **PENNSYLVANIA** | | | | | | | | |
| 1 Foglietta | Y | N | Y | Y | Y | Y | N | Y |
| 2 Blackwell | Y | N | Y | Y | Y | Y | N | Y |
| 3 Borski | Y | N | Y | Y | Y | Y | N | Y |
| 4 Kolter | Y | N | Y | Y | N | Y | N | Y |
| 5 ***Schulze*** | N | Y | N | Y | N | N | Y | P |
| 6 Yatron | Y | Y | Y | Y | N | Y | N | Y |
| 7 ***Weldon*** | N | Y | N | Y | N | N | Y | N |
| 8 Kostmayer | Y | N | Y | Y | Y | Y | N | Y |
| 9 ***Shuster*** | N | Y | N | Y | N | N | Y | N |
| 10 ***McDade*** | N | Y | N | Y | N | N | Y | P |
| 11 Kanjorski | Y | N | Y | Y | Y | Y | N | Y |
| 12 Murtha | Y | N | Y | Y | Y | Y | N | Y |
| 13 ***Coughlin*** | N | Y | N | Y | N | N | Y | P |
| 14 Coyne | Y | N | Y | Y | Y | Y | N | Y |
| 15 ***Ritter*** | N | Y | N | Y | N | N | Y | Y |
| 16 ***Walker*** | N | Y | N | Y | N | N | Y | P |
| 17 ***Gekas*** | N | Y | N | Y | N | N | Y | N |
| 18 ***Santorum*** | N | Y | N | Y | N | N | Y | P |
| 19 ***Goodling*** | N | Y | N | Y | N | N | Y | P |
| 20 Gaydos | Y | N | N | Y | Y | Y | N | Y |
| 21 ***Ridge*** | N | Y | Y | Y | N | N | Y | N |
| 22 Murphy | N | Y | N | Y | N | Y | N | Y |
| 23 ***Clinger*** | N | Y | N | Y | N | N | Y | N |
| **RHODE ISLAND** | | | | | | | | |
| 1 ***Machtley*** | N | Y | Y | Y | N | N | Y | Y |
| 2 Reed | Y | N | Y | Y | Y | Y | N | Y |
| **SOUTH CAROLINA** | | | | | | | | |
| 1 ***Ravenel*** | N | Y | N | Y | ? | N | Y | N |
| 2 ***Spence*** | N | Y | N | Y | N | N | Y | P |
| 3 Derrick | Y | N | Y | Y | Y | Y | N | Y |
| 4 Patterson | Y | Y | Y | Y | Y | Y | N | Y |
| 5 Spratt | Y | N | Y | Y | Y | Y | N | Y |
| 6 Tallon | Y | N | Y | Y | Y | Y | N | Y |

| | 77 | 78 | 79 | 80 | 81 | 82 | 83 | 84 |
|---|---|---|---|---|---|---|---|---|
| **SOUTH DAKOTA** | | | | | | | | |
| AL Johnson | Y | N | Y | Y | Y | Y | N | Y |
| **TENNESSEE** | | | | | | | | |
| 1 ***Quillen*** | N | Y | N | Y | N | N | Y | Y |
| 2 ***Duncan*** | N | Y | Y | Y | N | N | Y | Y |
| 3 Lloyd | Y | N | Y | Y | N | Y | N | Y |
| 4 Cooper | Y | N | Y | Y | Y | Y | N | Y |
| 5 Clement | Y | N | Y | Y | Y | Y | N | Y |
| 6 Gordon | Y | N | Y | Y | Y | Y | N | Y |
| 7 ***Sundquist*** | N | Y | N | Y | N | N | Y | Y |
| 8 Tanner | Y | N | Y | Y | Y | Y | N | Y |
| 9 Ford | Y | N | Y | Y | Y | Y | N | Y |
| **TEXAS** | | | | | | | | |
| 1 Chapman | Y | N | Y | Y | Y | Y | N | Y |
| 2 Wilson | Y | N | ? | Y | ? | Y | N | Y |
| 3 ***Johnson*** | N | Y | N | Y | N | N | Y | P |
| 4 Hall | Y | Y | N | Y | N | Y | N | Y |
| 5 Bryant | Y | N | Y | Y | ? | ? | N | Y |
| 6 ***Barton*** | N | Y | N | Y | N | N | Y | P |
| 7 ***Archer*** | N | Y | N | Y | N | N | Y | N |
| 8 ***Fields*** | N | Y | N | Y | N | N | Y | P |
| 9 Brooks | Y | N | Y | Y | Y | Y | N | Y |
| 10 Pickle | Y | Y | Y | Y | Y | Y | N | Y |
| 11 Edwards | Y | N | Y | Y | Y | Y | N | Y |
| 12 Geren | Y | Y | N | Y | N | Y | N | Y |
| 13 Sarpalius | Y | Y | N | Y | Y | Y | N | Y |
| 14 Laughlin | Y | N | Y | ? | ? | ? | ? | ? |
| 15 de la Garza | Y | N | Y | Y | Y | Y | N | Y |
| 16 Coleman | Y | N | Y | Y | Y | Y | N | Y |
| 17 Stenholm | Y | N | Y | Y | Y | Y | N | Y |
| 18 Washington | Y | N | Y | N | Y | Y | N | Y |
| 19 ***Combest*** | N | Y | N | Y | N | N | Y | N |
| 20 Gonzalez | Y | N | Y | Y | Y | Y | N | Y |
| 21 ***Smith*** | N | Y | N | Y | N | N | Y | P |
| 22 ***DeLay*** | N | Y | N | Y | N | N | Y | P |
| 23 Bustamante | Y | N | Y | Y | Y | Y | N | Y |
| 24 Frost | Y | N | N | Y | Y | Y | N | Y |
| 25 Andrews | Y | N | Y | Y | Y | Y | N | Y |
| 26 ***Armey*** | N | Y | N | Y | N | N | Y | N |
| 27 Ortiz | Y | N | Y | Y | Y | Y | N | Y |
| **UTAH** | | | | | | | | |
| 1 ***Hansen*** | N | Y | N | Y | N | N | Y | P |
| 2 Owens | Y | N | Y | Y | Y | Y | N | Y |
| 3 Orton | Y | Y | Y | Y | Y | Y | N | Y |
| **VERMONT** | | | | | | | | |
| AL *Sanders* | Y | N | Y | Y | Y | Y | N | Y |
| **VIRGINIA** | | | | | | | | |
| 1 ***Bateman*** | N | Y | N | Y | N | N | Y | P |
| 2 Pickett | Y | N | N | Y | ? | Y | N | Y |
| 3 ***Bliley*** | N | Y | N | Y | N | N | Y | P |
| 4 Sisisky | Y | N | N | Y | Y | Y | N | Y |
| 5 Payne | Y | N | Y | Y | Y | Y | N | Y |
| 6 Olin | Y | N | N | Y | Y | Y | N | Y |
| 7 ***Allen*** | N | Y | N | Y | N | N | Y | P |
| 8 Moran | Y | N | Y | Y | Y | Y | N | Y |
| 9 Boucher | Y | N | Y | Y | Y | Y | N | Y |
| 10 ***Wolf*** | N | Y | N | Y | N | N | Y | P |
| **WASHINGTON** | | | | | | | | |
| 1 ***Miller*** | N | N | Y | Y | N | N | Y | Y |
| 2 Swift | Y | N | Y | Y | Y | Y | N | Y |
| 3 Unsoeld | Y | N | Y | Y | Y | Y | N | Y |
| 4 ***Morrison*** | N | Y | Y | Y | N | N | ? | ? |
| 5 Foley | | | | | | | | Y |
| 6 Dicks | Y | N | Y | Y | Y | Y | N | Y |
| 7 McDermott | Y | N | Y | Y | Y | Y | N | Y |
| 8 ***Chandler*** | N | Y | N | Y | N | N | Y | P |
| **WEST VIRGINIA** | | | | | | | | |
| 1 Mollohan | Y | N | Y | Y | Y | Y | ? | Y |
| 2 Staggers | Y | N | Y | Y | Y | Y | N | Y |
| 3 Wise | Y | N | Y | Y | Y | Y | N | Y |
| 4 Rahall | Y | N | Y | Y | Y | Y | N | Y |
| **WISCONSIN** | | | | | | | | |
| 1 Aspin | Y | N | Y | Y | Y | Y | N | Y |
| 2 ***Klug*** | Y | N | Y | Y | N | N | Y | P |
| 3 ***Gunderson*** | N | Y | N | Y | N | N | Y | P |
| 4 Kleczka | Y | N | Y | Y | Y | Y | N | Y |
| 5 Moody | Y | N | Y | Y | N | Y | N | Y |
| 6 ***Petri*** | N | N | Y | Y | N | N | Y | Y |
| 7 Obey | Y | N | Y | Y | Y | Y | N | Y |
| 8 ***Roth*** | N | Y | N | Y | N | N | Y | N |
| 9 ***Sensenbrenner*** | N | Y | N | Y | N | N | Y | N |
| **WYOMING** | | | | | | | | |
| AL ***Thomas*** | N | Y | N | Y | N | N | Y | N |

Southern states - Ala., Ark., Fla., Ga., Ky., La., Miss., N.C., Okla., S.C., Tenn., Texas, Va.
Omitted votes are quorum calls, which CQ does not include in its vote charts.

**85. H Res 434. Recuse House Counsel in House Post Office Investigation.** Gephardt, D-Mo., motion to table (kill) the Walker, R-Pa., resolution to direct the clerk of the House to recuse his counsel from legal requests made by the Justice Department concerning its investigation of alleged drug dealing and financial embezzlement at the House Post Office. Motion agreed to 239-170: R 0-159; D 238-11 (ND 166-2, SD 72-9); I 1-0, April 9, 1992.

**86. HR 2967. Older Americans Act Reauthorization/Floor Procedures.** Adoption of the resolution (H Res 425) to permit consideration under suspension of the rules of a resolution to agree to a House amendment to the Senate amendments to the bill to reauthorize the Older Americans Act through fiscal 1995. Adopted 269-139: R 105-52; D 164-86 (ND 114-55, SD 50-31); I 0-1, April 9, 1992.

**87. HR 2967. Older Americans Act Reauthorization/Adoption.** Ford, D-Mich., motion to suspend the rules and adopt the resolution (H Res 434) to agree to a House amendment to the Senate amendments to the bill to reauthorize the Older Americans Act through fiscal 1995. The bill waived the 1990 Budget Agreement pay-as-you-go requirements for the provisions in the bill that revised the Social Security Earnings Test at an estimated cost of $7.3 billion over five years to double the amount a person between the age of 65 through 69 could earn without having their Social Security retirement benefits reduced. Motion agreed to 340-68: R 127-30; D 212-38 (ND 144-26, SD 68-12); I 1-0, April 9, 1992.

**88. Procedural Motion.** Approval of the House Journal of Tuesday, April 28. Approved 291-113: R 46-110; D 244-3 (ND 163-3, SD 81-0); I 1-0, April 29, 1992.

**89. HR 4364. Fiscal 1993-95 NASA Reauthorization/Rule.** Adoption of the rule (H Res 432) to provide for House floor consideration of the bill to authorize $15.3 billion in fiscal 1993 and $47.3 billion for fiscal 1993-95 for the National Aeronautics and Space Administration (NASA). The bill provided $2.3 billion for the space station *Freedom* and mandated that "core" programs be funded before discretionary programs. Adopted 419-0: R 159-0; D 259-0 (ND 177-0, SD 82-0); I 1-0, April 29, 1992.

**90. HR 4364. Fiscal 1993-95 NASA Reauthorization/Space Station *Freedom*** Roemer, D-Ind., amendment to cut $2.3 billion to terminate space station *Freedom*, transferring $1.1 billion of the funds to other NASA programs and using the rest to reduce the deficit. Rejected 159-254: R 30-128; D 128-126 (ND 106-69, SD 22-57); I 1-0, April 29, 1992.

**91. H Res 440. Refer House Bank Records Subpoena to Court.** Adoption of the Gephardt, D-Mo., resolution to ask the U.S. District Court to decide which records of the now-closed House bank should be provided in response to subpoenas issued at the behest of the Justice Department's special counsel, Malcolm R. Wilkey, in connection with the investigation of possible criminal violations at the bank. Rejected 131-284: R 0-160; D 131-123 (ND 98-77, SD 33-46); I 0-1, April 29, 1992.

**92. H Res 441. Provide House Bank Records to Special Counsel.** Adoption of the Michel, R-Ill., resolution to provide the special counsel investigating possible criminal violations at the recently closed House bank with microfilm records showing virtually all transactions at the bank for a recent 39-month period, including all checks, deposits, balance statements and daily settlement sheets (where bank officials listed member overdrafts). The 39-month period was the subject of the House ethics committee's inquiry into the overdraft scandal. The microfilm in question was the subject of two subpoenas issued at the behest of the Justice Department's special counsel, Malcolm R. Wilkey, though the resolution refers only to Wilkey's requests for the evidence and does not mention the subpoenas. Adopted 347-64: R 160-0; D 186-64 (ND 123-49, SD 63-15); I 1-0, April 29, 1992.

## KEY

| | |
|---|---|
| Y | Voted for (yea). |
| # | Paired for. |
| + | Announced for. |
| N | Voted against (nay). |
| X | Paired against. |
| − | Announced against. |
| P | Voted "present." |
| C | Voted "present" to avoid possible conflict of interest. |
| ? | Did not vote or otherwise make a position known. |

Democrats **Republicans**
*Independent*

| | 85 | 86 | 87 | 88 | 89 | 90 | 91 | 92 |
|---|---|---|---|---|---|---|---|---|
| **ALABAMA** | | | | | | | | |
| 1 *Callahan* | N | Y | Y | ? | ? | ? | ? | ? |
| 2 *Dickinson* | N | N | Y | N | Y | N | N | Y |
| 3 Browder | Y | N | Y | Y | Y | N | N | Y |
| 4 Bevill | Y | Y | Y | Y | Y | N | Y | Y |
| 5 Cramer | Y | N | Y | Y | Y | N | N | Y |
| 6 Erdreich | N | Y | Y | Y | Y | N | Y | Y |
| 7 Harris | Y | N | Y | Y | Y | N | N | Y |
| **ALASKA** | | | | | | | | |
| AL *Young* | ? | ? | ? | N | Y | N | N | Y |
| **ARIZONA** | | | | | | | | |
| 1 *Rhodes* | N | N | Y | N | Y | N | N | Y |
| 2 Pastor | Y | Y | Y | Y | Y | N | Y | Y |
| 3 *Stump* | N | N | Y | N | Y | N | N | Y |
| 4 *Kyl* | N | N | Y | N | Y | N | N | Y |
| 5 *Kolbe* | N | N | N | N | Y | N | N | Y |
| **ARKANSAS** | | | | | | | | |
| 1 Alexander | Y | Y | Y | ? | ? | ? | ? | ? |
| 2 Thornton | Y | Y | Y | Y | Y | N | Y | Y |
| 3 *Hammerschmidt* | N | N | Y | Y | Y | N | N | Y |
| 4 Anthony | Y | Y | Y | Y | Y | Y | Y | Y |
| **CALIFORNIA** | | | | | | | | |
| 1 *Riggs* | N | Y | Y | N | Y | N | N | Y |
| 2 *Herger* | N | Y | Y | N | Y | N | N | Y |
| 3 Matsui | Y | N | N | Y | Y | N | N | Y |
| 4 Fazio | Y | N | Y | Y | N | N | Y | Y |
| 5 Pelosi | Y | N | Y | Y | Y | Y | Y | N |
| 6 Boxer | Y | Y | Y | Y | Y | N | Y | N |
| 7 Miller | Y | N | Y | Y | Y | Y | Y | N |
| 8 Dellums | Y | Y | Y | Y | Y | Y | Y | N |
| 9 Stark | Y | Y | Y | ? | Y | Y | Y | N |
| 10 Edwards | Y | N | Y | Y | Y | N | Y | N |
| 11 Lantos | Y | Y | Y | Y | Y | N | Y | Y |
| 12 *Campbell* | N | Y | Y | N | Y | N | N | Y |
| 13 Mineta | Y | Y | Y | Y | Y | N | Y | Y |
| 14 *Doolittle* | N | Y | N | N | Y | N | N | Y |
| 15 Condit | N | N | N | Y | Y | Y | Y | Y |
| 16 Panetta | Y | N | Y | Y | Y | Y | Y | Y |
| 17 Dooley | Y | N | Y | Y | Y | Y | Y | Y |
| 18 Lehman | Y | Y | Y | ? | Y | Y | Y | Y |
| 19 *Lagomarsino* | N | Y | Y | N | Y | N | N | Y |
| 20 *Thomas* | N | N | N | N | Y | N | N | Y |
| 21 *Gallegly* | N | Y | Y | N | Y | N | N | Y |
| 22 *Moorhead* | N | Y | Y | N | Y | N | N | Y |
| 23 Beilenson | Y | N | N | Y | Y | Y | Y | N |
| 24 Waxman | ? | Y | Y | Y | Y | N | Y | N |
| 25 Roybal | Y | Y | Y | Y | Y | N | Y | Y |
| 26 Berman | Y | Y | Y | Y | Y | N | Y | Y |
| 27 Levine | ? | ? | ? | ? | ? | ? | ? | ? |
| 28 Dixon | Y | Y | Y | Y | Y | N | Y | Y |
| 29 Waters | Y | Y | Y | ? | Y | Y | Y | ? |
| 30 Martinez | Y | Y | Y | Y | Y | N | Y | Y |
| 31 Dymally | ? | ? | ? | ? | Y | N | ? | N |
| 32 Anderson | Y | Y | Y | Y | Y | N | N | Y |
| 33 *Dreier* | N | N | N | N | Y | N | N | Y |
| 34 Torres | Y | Y | Y | Y | Y | N | Y | N |
| 35 *Lewis* | N | Y | N | N | Y | N | N | Y |
| 36 Brown | Y | N | Y | Y | Y | Y | Y | N |
| 37 *McCandless* | N | Y | Y | N | Y | N | N | Y |
| 38 *Dornan* | ? | ? | ? | Y | Y | N | N | Y |
| 39 *Dannemeyer* | ? | ? | ? | ? | ? | ? | ? | ? |
| 40 *Cox* | N | Y | Y | N | Y | N | N | Y |
| 41 *Lowery* | N | Y | Y | ? | Y | N | N | Y |

| | 85 | 86 | 87 | 88 | 89 | 90 | 91 | 92 |
|---|---|---|---|---|---|---|---|---|
| 42 *Rohrabacher* | N | N | N | Y | N | N | N | Y |
| 43 *Packard* | N | Y | Y | Y | Y | N | N | Y |
| 44 *Cunningham* | N | N | N | N | Y | N | N | Y |
| 45 *Hunter* | N | Y | N | N | Y | N | N | Y |
| **COLORADO** | | | | | | | | |
| 1 Schroeder | Y | N | N | Y | Y | Y | N | Y |
| 2 Skaggs | Y | N | N | Y | Y | Y | Y | N |
| 3 *Campbell* | Y | N | Y | ? | Y | Y | Y | Y |
| 4 *Allard* | N | Y | N | N | Y | N | N | Y |
| 5 *Hefley* | N | Y | Y | N | Y | N | N | Y |
| 6 *Schaefer* | N | Y | N | N | Y | N | N | Y |
| **CONNECTICUT** | | | | | | | | |
| 1 Kennelly | Y | Y | Y | Y | Y | N | Y | Y |
| 2 Gejdenson | Y | Y | Y | Y | Y | N | Y | Y |
| 3 DeLauro | Y | Y | Y | Y | Y | N | Y | Y |
| 4 *Shays* | N | Y | Y | N | Y | N | Y | Y |
| 5 *Franks* | N | N | Y | N | Y | N | Y | Y |
| 6 *Johnson* | N | N | N | Y | Y | N | N | Y |
| **DELAWARE** | | | | | | | | |
| AL Carper | Y | N | Y | Y | Y | N | N | Y |
| **FLORIDA** | | | | | | | | |
| 1 Hutto | Y | N | Y | Y | Y | N | N | Y |
| 2 Peterson | Y | N | Y | Y | Y | N | N | Y |
| 3 Bennett | N | N | N | Y | Y | Y | N | Y |
| 4 *James* | N | Y | N | N | Y | N | N | Y |
| 5 *McCollum* | N | N | N | N | Y | N | N | Y |
| 6 *Stearns* | N | N | Y | N | Y | N | N | Y |
| 7 Gibbons | Y | Y | Y | Y | Y | N | N | Y |
| 8 *Young* | N | Y | Y | N | Y | N | N | Y |
| 9 *Bilirakis* | N | Y | N | N | Y | N | N | Y |
| 10 *Ireland* | N | N | N | ? | ? | ? | ? | ? |
| 11 Bacchus | Y | N | Y | Y | Y | N | N | Y |
| 12 *Lewis* | N | N | N | N | Y | N | N | Y |
| 13 *Goss* | N | Y | Y | N | Y | N | N | Y |
| 14 Johnston | Y | N | Y | Y | Y | Y | Y | N |
| 15 *Shaw* | N | N | Y | N | Y | N | N | Y |
| 16 Smith | Y | Y | Y | ? | Y | Y | ? | ? |
| 17 Lehman | ? | ? | ? | Y | Y | Y | Y | Y |
| 18 *Ros—Lehtinen* | N | Y | Y | N | Y | N | N | ? |
| 19 Fascell | Y | Y | Y | Y | Y | ? | Y | Y |
| **GEORGIA** | | | | | | | | |
| 1 Thomas | Y | Y | Y | Y | Y | N | N | Y |
| 2 Hatcher | Y | Y | Y | Y | Y | Y | N | Y |
| 3 Ray | Y | N | Y | Y | Y | N | N | Y |
| 4 Jones | Y | Y | Y | Y | Y | Y | N | Y |
| 5 Lewis | Y | Y | Y | Y | Y | N | Y | N |
| 6 *Gingrich* | N | Y | N | N | Y | N | N | Y |
| 7 Darden | Y | Y | Y | Y | Y | N | N | Y |
| 8 Rowland | Y | Y | Y | Y | Y | N | N | Y |
| 9 Jenkins | Y | Y | Y | Y | Y | N | Y | N |
| 10 Barnard | ? | ? | ? | ? | ? | ? | ? | ? |
| **HAWAII** | | | | | | | | |
| 1 Abercrombie | Y | N | Y | Y | Y | Y | Y | N |
| 2 Mink | Y | Y | Y | Y | Y | Y | Y | N |
| **IDAHO** | | | | | | | | |
| 1 LaRocco | Y | N | Y | Y | Y | Y | Y | Y |
| 2 Stallings | Y | Y | Y | Y | Y | N | N | Y |
| **ILLINOIS** | | | | | | | | |
| 1 Hayes | Y | N | Y | Y | Y | Y | Y | N |
| 2 Savage | Y | Y | Y | ? | ? | ? | ? | ? |
| 3 Russo | ? | ? | ? | Y | Y | Y | # | N |
| 4 Sangmeister | Y | Y | Y | Y | Y | N | N | Y |
| 5 Lipinski | Y | Y | Y | Y | Y | N | N | Y |
| 6 *Hyde* | N | N | Y | N | Y | N | N | Y |
| 7 Collins | Y | N | Y | ? | Y | Y | Y | N |
| 8 Rostenkowski | Y | Y | Y | Y | Y | ? | Y | N |
| 9 Yates | ? | ? | ? | Y | Y | Y | Y | N |
| 10 *Porter* | N | N | N | N | Y | Y | N | Y |
| 11 Annunzio | ? | ? | ? | Y | Y | X | Y | N |
| 12 *Crane* | N | N | N | N | Y | N | N | Y |
| 13 *Fawell* | N | N | Y | N | Y | N | N | Y |
| 14 *Hastert* | N | Y | N | Y | Y | N | N | Y |
| 15 *Ewing* | N | N | N | ? | Y | N | N | Y |
| 16 Cox | Y | N | N | Y | Y | Y | Y | Y |
| 17 Evans | Y | Y | Y | Y | Y | Y | Y | Y |
| 18 *Michel* | N | Y | N | N | Y | N | N | Y |
| 19 Bruce | Y | Y | Y | Y | Y | N | N | Y |
| 20 Durbin | Y | N | Y | Y | Y | N | Y | N |
| 21 Costello | ? | ? | ? | Y | Y | Y | Y | N |
| 22 Poshard | Y | Y | Y | Y | Y | N | Y | Y |
| **INDIANA** | | | | | | | | |
| 1 Visclosky | Y | N | N | Y | Y | Y | Y | N |
| 2 Sharp | Y | N | Y | Y | Y | Y | N | ? |
| 3 Roemer | Y | Y | Y | Y | Y | Y | N | Y |

ND Northern Democrats   SD Southern Democrats

| | 85 | 86 | 87 | 88 | 89 | 90 | 91 | 92 |
|---|---|---|---|---|---|---|---|---|
| 4 Long | Y | N | Y | Y | Y | Y | Y | Y |
| 5 Jontz | Y | Y | Y | Y | Y | Y | N | Y |
| 6 ***Burton*** | N | N | N | N | Y | N | N | Y |
| 7 ***Myers*** | N | N | Y | Y | Y | N | N | Y |
| 8 McCloskey | Y | Y | Y | Y | Y | Y | Y | N |
| 9 Hamilton | Y | N | N | Y | Y | Y | N | Y |
| 10 Jacobs | N | N | N | N | Y | Y | N | Y |
| **IOWA** | | | | | | | | |
| 1 ***Leach*** | N | Y | Y | N | Y | Y | N | Y |
| 2 ***Nussle*** | N | N | Y | N | Y | N | N | Y |
| 3 Nagle | Y | Y | Y | Y | Y | N | Y | N |
| 4 Smith | ? | ? | ? | Y | Y | Y | Y | N |
| 5 ***Lightfoot*** | N | Y | Y | N | Y | N | N | Y |
| 6 ***Grandy*** | N | N | Y | N | Y | Y | N | Y |
| **KANSAS** | | | | | | | | |
| 1 ***Roberts*** | N | N | Y | N | Y | N | N | Y |
| 2 Slattery | Y | N | N | Y | Y | N | N | Y |
| 3 ***Meyers*** | N | Y | Y | N | Y | N | N | Y |
| 4 Glickman | Y | N | N | Y | Y | Y | N | Y |
| 5 ***Nichols*** | N | N | N | Y | Y | N | N | Y |
| **KENTUCKY** | | | | | | | | |
| 1 Hubbard | N | Y | Y | Y | Y | N | N | Y |
| 2 Natcher | Y | Y | Y | Y | Y | Y | Y | N |
| 3 Mazzoli | Y | N | N | Y | Y | Y | N | Y |
| 4 ***Bunning*** | N | Y | Y | N | Y | N | N | Y |
| 5 ***Rogers*** | N | Y | Y | N | Y | N | N | Y |
| 6 ***Hopkins*** | N | N | N | N | Y | N | N | Y |
| 7 Perkins | Y | Y | Y | Y | Y | N | Y | N |
| **LOUISIANA** | | | | | | | | |
| 1 ***Livingston*** | N | N | Y | Y | Y | N | N | Y |
| 2 Jefferson | Y | Y | Y | Y | Y | N | Y | Y |
| 3 Tauzin | N | Y | Y | Y | Y | N | N | Y |
| 4 ***McCrery*** | N | Y | Y | Y | Y | N | N | Y |
| 5 Huckaby | N | Y | Y | Y | Y | N | N | Y |
| 6 ***Baker*** | N | Y | Y | N | Y | N | N | Y |
| 7 Hayes | N | Y | Y | Y | Y | N | Y | Y |
| 8 ***Holloway*** | N | Y | Y | N | Y | N | N | Y |
| **MAINE** | | | | | | | | |
| 1 Andrews | Y | N | Y | Y | Y | Y | N | Y |
| 2 ***Snowe*** | N | Y | Y | Y | Y | N | N | Y |
| **MARYLAND** | | | | | | | | |
| 1 ***Gilchrest*** | N | Y | Y | N | Y | N | N | Y |
| 2 ***Bentley*** | N | Y | Y | N | Y | N | N | Y |
| 3 Cardin | Y | Y | Y | Y | Y | N | Y | Y |
| 4 McMillen | Y | N | Y | Y | Y | N | N | Y |
| 5 Hoyer | Y | N | Y | Y | Y | N | Y | Y |
| 6 Byron | Y | N | Y | Y | Y | N | N | Y |
| 7 Mfume | Y | Y | Y | Y | Y | Y | Y | Y |
| 8 ***Morella*** | N | Y | Y | N | Y | N | N | Y |
| **MASSACHUSETTS** | | | | | | | | |
| 1 Olver | Y | Y | Y | Y | Y | Y | Y | Y |
| 2 Neal | Y | Y | Y | Y | Y | N | N | Y |
| 3 Early | ? | ? | ? | Y | Y | Y | N | Y |
| 4 Frank | Y | Y | Y | Y | Y | Y | Y | P |
| 5 Atkins | Y | Y | N | Y | Y | Y | Y | Y |
| 6 Mavroules | Y | Y | Y | Y | Y | Y | N | Y |
| 7 Markey | Y | Y | Y | Y | Y | Y | Y | Y |
| 8 Kennedy | Y | N | N | Y | Y | N | N | Y |
| 9 Moakley | Y | Y | Y | Y | Y | Y | Y | Y |
| 10 Studds | Y | Y | Y | Y | Y | Y | N | Y |
| 11 Donnelly | Y | N | Y | Y | Y | Y | N | Y |
| **MICHIGAN** | | | | | | | | |
| 1 Conyers | Y | N | Y | ? | Y | Y | Y | N |
| 2 ***Pursell*** | N | N | N | Y | Y | Y | N | Y |
| 3 Wolpe | Y | N | Y | Y | Y | Y | Y | N |
| 4 ***Upton*** | N | Y | Y | N | Y | Y | N | Y |
| 5 ***Henry*** | N | Y | Y | N | Y | Y | N | Y |
| 6 Carr | Y | Y | Y | Y | Y | N | N | Y |
| 7 Kildee | Y | Y | Y | Y | Y | Y | N | Y |
| 8 Traxler | Y | Y | Y | Y | Y | N | ? | Y |
| 9 ***Vander Jagt*** | N | Y | Y | N | Y | N | N | Y |
| 10 ***Camp*** | N | Y | Y | N | Y | Y | N | Y |
| 11 ***Davis*** | N | Y | Y | N | Y | N | N | Y |
| 12 Bonior | Y | Y | Y | Y | Y | Y | Y | N |
| 13 Collins | Y | Y | Y | Y | Y | Y | Y | N |
| 14 Hertel | Y | Y | Y | Y | Y | Y | Y | N |
| 15 Ford | Y | Y | Y | Y | Y | Y | Y | N |
| 16 Dingell | ? | ? | ? | Y | Y | N | Y | Y |
| 17 Levin | Y | Y | Y | Y | Y | Y | N | Y |
| 18 ***Broomfield*** | N | Y | Y | Y | Y | N | N | Y |
| **MINNESOTA** | | | | | | | | |
| 1 Penny | Y | N | N | Y | Y | Y | N | Y |
| 2 ***Weber*** | ? | ? | ? | N | Y | N | N | Y |
| 3 ***Ramstad*** | N | Y | Y | N | Y | Y | N | Y |
| 4 Vento | Y | N | N | Y | Y | Y | Y | N |

| | 85 | 86 | 87 | 88 | 89 | 90 | 91 | 92 |
|---|---|---|---|---|---|---|---|---|
| 5 Sabo | Y | N | N | Y | Y | Y | Y | N |
| 6 Sikorski | Y | Y | Y | N | Y | Y | N | Y |
| 7 Peterson | Y | Y | Y | Y | Y | Y | N | Y |
| 8 Oberstar | Y | N | N | Y | Y | Y | Y | N |
| **MISSISSIPPI** | | | | | | | | |
| 1 Whitten | ? | ? | ? | Y | Y | N | ? | ? |
| 2 Espy | Y | Y | Y | Y | Y | Y | N | Y |
| 3 Montgomery | Y | N | Y | Y | Y | N | N | Y |
| 4 Parker | Y | N | N | Y | Y | N | N | Y |
| 5 Taylor | N | Y | Y | Y | Y | N | N | Y |
| **MISSOURI** | | | | | | | | |
| 1 Clay | Y | N | Y | ? | Y | N | Y | N |
| 2 Horn | Y | N | Y | Y | Y | N | N | Y |
| 3 Gephardt | Y | Y | N | Y | Y | N | Y | Y |
| 4 Skelton | Y | Y | Y | Y | Y | Y | N | Y |
| 5 Wheat | Y | Y | Y | Y | Y | N | Y | P |
| 6 ***Coleman*** | N | Y | Y | ? | Y | ? | N | Y |
| 7 ***Hancock*** | N | N | N | N | Y | N | N | Y |
| 8 ***Emerson*** | N | Y | Y | N | Y | N | N | Y |
| 9 Volkmer | Y | Y | Y | Y | Y | N | N | Y |
| **MONTANA** | | | | | | | | |
| 1 Williams | Y | Y | Y | Y | Y | Y | N | Y |
| 2 ***Marlenee*** | N | Y | Y | ? | ? | ? | ? | ? |
| **NEBRASKA** | | | | | | | | |
| 1 ***Bereuter*** | N | N | N | N | Y | Y | N | Y |
| 2 Hoagland | Y | N | N | Y | Y | Y | N | Y |
| 3 ***Barrett*** | N | N | N | N | Y | N | N | Y |
| **NEVADA** | | | | | | | | |
| 1 Bilbray | Y | Y | Y | Y | Y | N | N | Y |
| 2 ***Vucanovich*** | N | Y | Y | N | Y | N | N | Y |
| **NEW HAMPSHIRE** | | | | | | | | |
| 1 ***Zeliff*** | ? | ? | ? | N | Y | N | N | Y |
| 2 Swett | Y | N | Y | Y | Y | Y | N | Y |
| **NEW JERSEY** | | | | | | | | |
| 1 Andrews | Y | Y | Y | Y | Y | N | N | Y |
| 2 Hughes | Y | N | N | Y | Y | Y | Y | Y |
| 3 Pallone | Y | Y | Y | Y | Y | Y | N | Y |
| 4 ***Smith*** | N | Y | Y | Y | Y | N | N | Y |
| 5 ***Roukema*** | N | Y | Y | N | Y | Y | N | Y |
| 6 Dwyer | ? | ? | ? | Y | Y | Y | N | Y |
| 7 ***Rinaldo*** | N | Y | Y | Y | Y | N | N | Y |
| 8 Roe | Y | ? | Y | Y | Y | N | Y | ? |
| 9 Torricelli | Y | Y | Y | Y | Y | N | Y | Y |
| 10 Payne | Y | Y | Y | Y | Y | Y | Y | N |
| 11 ***Gallo*** | N | Y | Y | N | Y | N | N | Y |
| 12 ***Zimmer*** | N | Y | Y | N | Y | Y | N | Y |
| 13 ***Saxton*** | N | Y | Y | N | Y | N | N | Y |
| 14 Guarini | Y | Y | N | Y | Y | Y | Y | N |
| **NEW MEXICO** | | | | | | | | |
| 1 ***Schiff*** | N | Y | Y | Y | Y | N | N | Y |
| 2 ***Skeen*** | N | Y | Y | Y | Y | N | N | Y |
| 3 Richardson | Y | Y | Y | Y | Y | N | Y | Y |
| **NEW YORK** | | | | | | | | |
| 1 Hochbrueckner | Y | Y | Y | Y | Y | N | N | Y |
| 2 Downey | Y | Y | Y | Y | Y | N | N | Y |
| 3 Mrazek | Y | Y | Y | ? | ? | N | N | Y |
| 4 ***Lent*** | N | ? | Y | ? | Y | N | N | Y |
| 5 ***McGrath*** | N | Y | Y | Y | Y | N | N | Y |
| 6 Flake | Y | Y | Y | Y | Y | Y | Y | N |
| 7 Ackerman | Y | Y | Y | Y | Y | Y | Y | Y |
| 8 Scheuer | Y | Y | Y | Y | Y | N | Y | Y |
| 9 Manton | ? | ? | ? | Y | Y | N | Y | Y |
| 10 Schumer | Y | Y | Y | Y | Y | Y | N | Y |
| 11 Towns | Y | Y | Y | Y | Y | N | Y | N |
| 12 Owens | Y | Y | Y | Y | Y | Y | Y | N |
| 13 Solarz | Y | Y | Y | Y | Y | Y | N | Y |
| 14 ***Molinari*** | N | Y | Y | N | Y | Y | N | Y |
| 15 ***Green*** | N | N | N | Y | Y | Y | N | Y |
| 16 Rangel | Y | Y | Y | Y | Y | N | Y | N |
| 17 Weiss | Y | Y | Y | Y | Y | Y | Y | N |
| 18 Serrano | Y | Y | Y | Y | Y | Y | Y | N |
| 19 Engel | Y | Y | Y | Y | Y | N | N | Y |
| 20 Lowey | Y | Y | Y | Y | Y | Y | N | Y |
| 21 ***Fish*** | N | Y | Y | Y | Y | N | N | Y |
| 22 ***Gilman*** | N | Y | Y | Y | Y | N | N | Y |
| 23 McNulty | Y | Y | Y | Y | Y | Y | N | Y |
| 24 ***Solomon*** | N | Y | Y | N | Y | Y | N | Y |
| 25 ***Boehlert*** | N | Y | Y | N | Y | N | N | Y |
| 26 ***Martin*** | ? | ? | ? | N | Y | N | N | Y |
| 27 ***Walsh*** | N | Y | Y | N | Y | N | N | Y |
| 28 McHugh | Y | N | Y | Y | Y | N | Y | Y |
| 29 ***Horton*** | N | Y | Y | Y | Y | N | N | Y |
| 30 Slaughter | Y | Y | Y | Y | Y | Y | Y | Y |
| 31 ***Paxon*** | N | Y | Y | N | Y | N | N | Y |

| | 85 | 86 | 87 | 88 | 89 | 90 | 91 | 92 |
|---|---|---|---|---|---|---|---|---|
| 32 LaFalce | Y | Y | Y | Y | Y | Y | N | Y |
| 33 Nowak | Y | Y | Y | Y | Y | N | N | Y |
| 34 ***Houghton*** | N | Y | Y | Y | Y | Y | N | Y |
| **NORTH CAROLINA** | | | | | | | | |
| 1 Jones | Y | N | ? | Y | Y | N | Y | N |
| 2 Valentine | Y | N | N | Y | Y | N | N | Y |
| 3 Lancaster | Y | Y | Y | Y | Y | Y | N | Y |
| 4 Price | Y | N | Y | Y | Y | Y | Y | Y |
| 5 Neal | Y | Y | Y | Y | Y | Y | Y | Y |
| 6 ***Coble*** | N | Y | Y | N | Y | Y | N | Y |
| 7 Rose | Y | Y | Y | Y | Y | Y | Y | N |
| 8 Hefner | Y | Y | Y | Y | Y | Y | N | Y |
| 9 ***McMillan*** | N | N | N | N | Y | N | N | Y |
| 10 ***Ballenger*** | N | Y | Y | N | Y | N | N | Y |
| 11 ***Taylor*** | N | Y | Y | N | Y | N | N | Y |
| **NORTH DAKOTA** | | | | | | | | |
| AL Dorgan | Y | Y | Y | Y | Y | Y | N | Y |
| **OHIO** | | | | | | | | |
| 1 Luken | Y | N | N | Y | Y | Y | N | Y |
| 2 ***Gradison*** | N | ? | ? | Y | Y | N | N | Y |
| 3 Hall | Y | Y | Y | Y | Y | N | N | Y |
| 4 ***Oxley*** | N | N | Y | N | Y | N | N | Y |
| 5 ***Gillmor*** | N | Y | Y | Y | Y | ? | N | Y |
| 6 ***McEwen*** | N | N | Y | N | Y | Y | N | Y |
| 7 ***Hobson*** | N | Y | Y | N | Y | N | N | Y |
| 8 ***Boehner*** | N | Y | Y | N | Y | N | N | Y |
| 9 Kaptur | Y | Y | Y | Y | Y | N | N | Y |
| 10 ***Miller*** | N | Y | Y | N | Y | Y | N | Y |
| 11 Eckart | Y | Y | Y | Y | Y | Y | Y | Y |
| 12 ***Kasich*** | N | N | Y | Y | Y | Y | N | Y |
| 13 Pease | Y | N | N | Y | Y | Y | Y | Y |
| 14 Sawyer | Y | Y | Y | Y | Y | Y | Y | Y |
| 15 ***Wylie*** | N | Y | Y | Y | Y | Y | N | Y |
| 16 ***Regula*** | N | Y | Y | N | Y | N | N | Y |
| 17 Traficant | Y | Y | Y | Y | Y | N | Y | N |
| 18 Applegate | Y | Y | Y | Y | Y | N | Y | Y |
| 19 Feighan | Y | Y | Y | Y | Y | N | N | Y |
| 20 Oakar | Y | Y | Y | Y | Y | N | Y | Y |
| 21 Stokes | Y | Y | Y | Y | Y | N | Y | N |
| **OKLAHOMA** | | | | | | | | |
| 1 ***Inhofe*** | N | Y | Y | N | Y | N | N | Y |
| 2 Synar | Y | N | Y | Y | Y | Y | Y | N |
| 3 Brewster | Y | N | Y | Y | Y | N | Y | Y |
| 4 McCurdy | Y | N | N | Y | Y | N | Y | Y |
| 5 ***Edwards*** | N | Y | Y | N | Y | N | Y | Y |
| 6 English | Y | Y | Y | Y | Y | N | N | Y |
| **OREGON** | | | | | | | | |
| 1 AuCoin | Y | Y | Y | ? | ? | # | X | ? |
| 2 ***Smith*** | N | Y | Y | N | Y | N | N | Y |
| 3 Wyden | Y | Y | Y | Y | Y | Y | N | Y |
| 4 DeFazio | Y | Y | Y | Y | Y | N | Y | Y |
| 5 Kopetski | Y | Y | Y | Y | Y | N | Y | N |
| **PENNSYLVANIA** | | | | | | | | |
| 1 Foglietta | ? | ? | ? | Y | Y | Y | Y | N |
| 2 Blackwell | Y | Y | Y | Y | Y | Y | Y | N |
| 3 Borski | Y | Y | Y | Y | Y | Y | Y | Y |
| 4 Kolter | Y | Y | Y | ? | Y | ? | ? | ? |
| 5 ***Schulze*** | N | N | N | Y | Y | ? | ? | ? |
| 6 Yatron | Y | Y | Y | Y | Y | Y | Y | Y |
| 7 ***Weldon*** | N | Y | Y | N | ? | N | N | Y |
| 8 Kostmayer | Y | N | Y | Y | Y | Y | N | Y |
| 9 ***Shuster*** | N | Y | ? | N | Y | N | N | Y |
| 10 ***McDade*** | N | Y | Y | ? | ? | ? | ? | ? |
| 11 Kanjorski | Y | Y | Y | Y | Y | Y | Y | Y |
| 12 Murtha | Y | Y | Y | Y | Y | N | Y | N |
| 13 ***Coughlin*** | N | Y | Y | N | Y | N | N | Y |
| 14 Coyne | Y | Y | Y | Y | Y | Y | Y | Y |
| 15 ***Ritter*** | N | Y | Y | Y | Y | N | N | Y |
| 16 ***Walker*** | N | N | N | N | Y | N | N | Y |
| 17 ***Gekas*** | N | Y | Y | N | Y | N | N | Y |
| 18 ***Santorum*** | N | Y | Y | Y | Y | N | N | Y |
| 19 ***Goodling*** | N | Y | Y | N | Y | N | N | Y |
| 20 Gaydos | Y | Y | Y | ? | Y | N | Y | Y |
| 21 ***Ridge*** | N | Y | Y | N | Y | N | N | Y |
| 22 Murphy | Y | Y | Y | ? | ? | ? | ? | ? |
| 23 ***Clinger*** | N | N | N | Y | Y | N | N | Y |
| **RHODE ISLAND** | | | | | | | | |
| 1 ***Machtley*** | N | Y | Y | N | Y | N | N | Y |
| 2 Reed | Y | Y | Y | Y | Y | Y | N | Y |
| **SOUTH CAROLINA** | | | | | | | | |
| 1 ***Ravenel*** | N | Y | Y | Y | Y | N | N | Y |
| 2 ***Spence*** | N | Y | Y | Y | Y | N | N | Y |
| 3 Derrick | Y | Y | Y | Y | Y | Y | N | Y |
| 4 Patterson | Y | N | Y | Y | Y | Y | N | Y |
| 5 Spratt | Y | Y | Y | Y | Y | Y | N | Y |
| 6 Tallon | Y | Y | Y | Y | Y | N | N | Y |

| | 85 | 86 | 87 | 88 | 89 | 90 | 91 | 92 |
|---|---|---|---|---|---|---|---|---|
| **SOUTH DAKOTA** | | | | | | | | |
| AL Johnson | Y | N | Y | Y | Y | Y | N | Y |
| **TENNESSEE** | | | | | | | | |
| 1 ***Quillen*** | N | Y | Y | N | Y | N | N | Y |
| 2 ***Duncan*** | N | N | N | Y | Y | Y | N | Y |
| 3 Lloyd | Y | Y | Y | Y | Y | N | N | Y |
| 4 Cooper | Y | N | N | Y | Y | N | N | Y |
| 5 Clement | Y | Y | Y | Y | Y | N | Y | Y |
| 6 Gordon | Y | Y | Y | Y | Y | Y | N | Y |
| 7 ***Sundquist*** | N | Y | Y | ? | ? | N | N | Y |
| 8 Tanner | Y | Y | Y | Y | Y | N | Y | Y |
| 9 Ford | Y | Y | Y | Y | Y | N | Y | N |
| **TEXAS** | | | | | | | | |
| 1 Chapman | Y | Y | Y | Y | Y | N | N | Y |
| 2 Wilson | Y | Y | Y | Y | Y | N | N | Y |
| 3 ***Johnson*** | N | N | N | Y | Y | N | N | Y |
| 4 Hall | N | Y | Y | Y | Y | N | N | Y |
| 5 Bryant | Y | N | Y | Y | Y | N | N | Y |
| 6 ***Barton*** | N | N | N | N | Y | N | N | Y |
| 7 ***Archer*** | N | N | N | Y | Y | N | N | Y |
| 8 ***Fields*** | N | N | Y | N | Y | N | N | Y |
| 9 Brooks | Y | Y | Y | Y | Y | N | Y | N |
| 10 Pickle | Y | Y | Y | Y | Y | N | Y | Y |
| 11 Edwards | Y | N | N | Y | Y | N | Y | N |
| 12 Geren | N | N | N | Y | Y | N | N | Y |
| 13 Sarpalius | Y | N | Y | Y | Y | N | N | Y |
| 14 Laughlin | ? | ? | ? | Y | Y | N | Y | N |
| 15 de la Garza | Y | Y | Y | Y | Y | N | N | Y |
| 16 Coleman | Y | Y | Y | Y | Y | N | N | Y |
| 17 Stenholm | Y | N | N | Y | Y | N | N | Y |
| 18 Washington | Y | Y | Y | ? | Y | N | Y | N |
| 19 ***Combest*** | N | Y | Y | Y | Y | N | N | Y |
| 20 Gonzalez | Y | Y | Y | Y | Y | N | Y | N |
| 21 ***Smith*** | N | N | Y | N | Y | N | N | Y |
| 22 ***DeLay*** | N | N | N | N | Y | N | N | Y |
| 23 Bustamante | Y | N | Y | Y | Y | N | N | Y |
| 24 Frost | Y | N | Y | Y | Y | N | Y | Y |
| 25 Andrews | Y | N | Y | Y | Y | N | N | Y |
| 26 ***Armey*** | N | N | N | N | Y | N | N | Y |
| 27 Ortiz | Y | Y | Y | Y | Y | N | N | Y |
| **UTAH** | | | | | | | | |
| 1 ***Hansen*** | N | Y | Y | Y | Y | N | N | Y |
| 2 Owens | Y | Y | Y | Y | Y | Y | N | Y |
| 3 Orton | Y | N | N | Y | Y | Y | Y | Y |
| **VERMONT** | | | | | | | | |
| AL *Sanders* | Y | N | Y | Y | Y | Y | N | Y |
| **VIRGINIA** | | | | | | | | |
| 1 ***Bateman*** | N | N | N | Y | Y | N | N | Y |
| 2 Pickett | Y | N | N | Y | Y | — | — | + |
| 3 ***Bliley*** | N | N | N | Y | Y | N | N | Y |
| 4 Sisisky | Y | Y | Y | Y | Y | N | N | Y |
| 5 Payne | Y | N | N | Y | Y | Y | Y | Y |
| 6 Olin | Y | N | N | Y | Y | ? | ? | ? |
| 7 ***Allen*** | N | N | Y | N | Y | N | N | Y |
| 8 Moran | Y | Y | Y | Y | Y | N | Y | Y |
| 9 Boucher | Y | Y | Y | Y | Y | N | N | Y |
| 10 ***Wolf*** | N | N | N | N | Y | N | N | Y |
| **WASHINGTON** | | | | | | | | |
| 1 ***Miller*** | N | Y | Y | N | Y | N | N | Y |
| 2 Swift | ? | N | N | Y | Y | N | Y | N |
| 3 Unsoeld | Y | N | Y | Y | Y | Y | Y | N |
| 4 ***Morrison*** | ? | ? | ? | Y | Y | N | N | Y |
| 5 Foley | | | | | | | Y | |
| 6 Dicks | Y | Y | Y | Y | Y | N | Y | Y |
| 7 McDermott | Y | N | Y | Y | Y | N | Y | N |
| 8 ***Chandler*** | N | N | N | N | Y | N | N | Y |
| **WEST VIRGINIA** | | | | | | | | |
| 1 Mollohan | Y | Y | Y | Y | Y | N | N | Y |
| 2 Staggers | Y | Y | Y | ? | Y | Y | N | Y |
| 3 Wise | Y | Y | Y | Y | Y | N | N | Y |
| 4 Rahall | Y | Y | Y | Y | Y | N | N | Y |
| **WISCONSIN** | | | | | | | | |
| 1 Aspin | Y | N | Y | Y | Y | Y | N | Y |
| 2 ***Klug*** | N | Y | Y | Y | Y | N | N | Y |
| 3 ***Gunderson*** | N | Y | Y | Y | Y | N | N | Y |
| 4 Kleczka | Y | Y | Y | Y | Y | Y | Y | Y |
| 5 Moody | Y | N | Y | Y | Y | N | N | Y |
| 6 ***Petri*** | N | Y | Y | Y | Y | N | N | Y |
| 7 Obey | Y | Y | Y | Y | Y | Y | Y | Y |
| 8 ***Roth*** | N | Y | Y | Y | Y | N | N | Y |
| 9 ***Sensenbrenner*** | N | Y | Y | N | Y | N | N | Y |
| **WYOMING** | | | | | | | | |
| AL ***Thomas*** | N | Y | Y | N | Y | N | N | Y |

Southern states - Ala., Ark., Fla., Ga., Ky., La., Miss., N.C., Okla., S.C., Tenn., Texas, Va.
Omitted votes are quorum calls, which CQ does not include in its vote charts.

**93. H Res 429. Temporary Committee Funding.** Adoption of the resolution to continue funding for the committees of the House through May 31, 1992. Funding would have expired at midnight on April 30 without the resolution. Adopted 312-86: R 71-80; D 240-6 (ND 162-5, SD 78-1); I 1-0, April 30, 1992.

**94. HR 3090. Family Planning Reauthorization/Rule.** Adoption of the rule (H Res 442) to provide for House floor consideration of the bill to reauthorize Title X of the Public Health Service Act for five years through fiscal 1997. The bill overturned the administration's "gag rule" and thus allowed abortion counseling at federally funded family planning clinics at the patient's request and in a non-directive manner. Adopted 273-146: R 28-128; D 244-18 (ND 168-11, SD 76-7); I 1-0, April 30, 1992.

**95. HR 3090. Family Planning Reauthorization.** Passage of the bill to reauthorize Title X of the Public Health Service Act for five years through fiscal 1997. The bill overturned the administration's "gag rule" and thus allowed abortion counseling at federally funded family planning clinics, but only at the patient's request and in a non-directive manner. Passed 268-150: R 55-105; D 212-45 (ND 146-28, SD 66-17); I 1-0, April 30, 1992. A "nay" was a vote supporting the president's position. (After passage the House called up and passed S 323 after striking all but the enacting clause and inserting the text of HR 3090 as passed by the House.)

**96. Procedural Motion.** Approval of the House Journal of Tuesday, May 5. Approved 259-106: R 44-102; D 215-4 (ND 139-4, SD 76-0); I 0-0, May 6, 1992.

**97. HR 3247. National Undersea Research Program.** Hughes, D-N.J., motion to suspend the rules and pass the bill to establish an Office of Undersea Research within the National Oceanic and Atmospheric Administration to award research proposals to study ocean and large lake ecosystems. The bill authorized $172 million for fiscal 1992-96. Motion rejected 255-133: R 43-108; D 212-25 (ND 146-13, SD 66-12); I 0-0, May 6, 1992. A two-thirds majority of those present and voting (259 in this case) was required for passage under suspension of the rules. A "nay" was a vote in support of the president's position.

**98. HR 2039. Legal Services Corporation (LSC) Reauthorization/Rule.** Adoption of the rule (H Res 444) to provide for House floor consideration of the bill to reauthorize through fiscal 1996 such sums as necessary for the Legal Services Corporation to help give legal assistance to the poor in civil cases. Adopted 238-167: R 0-161; D 238-6 (ND 161-4, SD 77-2); I 0-0, May 6, 1992. (The House on April 2 approved a rule (H Res 413) to provide for general debate on the bill. This rule governed debate of amendments to the bill.)

**99. HR 2039. Legal Services Corporation (LSC) Reauthorization.** Brooks, D-Texas, en bloc amendment to incorporate several amendments, including those to waive the 60 percent attorney requirement for governing bodies that receive LSC funds, provide fired or suspended LSC employees the right to an independent due process hearing, clarify that the LSC may provide grants for less than 12 months for programs starting after a new year, require non-LSC funds be accounted separately from federal funds, and for other purposes. Adopted 410-3: R 158-3; D 252-0 (ND 171-0, SD 81-0); I 0-0, May 6, 1992.

**100. HR 2039. Legal Services Corporation (LSC) Reauthorization/Outreach Activities.** Brooks, D-Texas, amendment as modified to allow Legal Services Corporation outreach activities to be sponsored by church groups. Adopted 263-150: R 33-127; D 230-23 (ND 169-4, SD 61-19); I 0-0, May 6, 1992.

## KEY

Y Voted for (yea).
\# Paired for.
+ Announced for.
N Voted against (nay).
X Paired against.
— Announced against.
P Voted "present."
C Voted "present" to avoid possible conflict of interest.
? Did not vote or otherwise make a position known.

*Democrats*  **Republicans**
*Independent*

| | 93 | 94 | 95 | 96 | 97 | 98 | 99 | 100 |
|---|---|---|---|---|---|---|---|---|
| **ALABAMA** | | | | | | | | |
| 1 *Callahan* | ? | N | N | ? | ? | N | Y | N |
| 2 *Dickinson* | ? | Y | Y | N | N | N | Y | N |
| 3 Browder | Y | Y | Y | Y | Y | Y | Y | Y |
| 4 Bevill | Y | Y | Y | Y | Y | Y | Y | Y |
| 5 Cramer | Y | Y | Y | Y | Y | Y | Y | Y |
| 6 Erdreich | N | Y | Y | Y | Y | Y | Y | Y |
| 7 Harris | Y | Y | Y | Y | Y | Y | Y | Y |
| **ALASKA** | | | | | | | | |
| AL *Young* | Y | Y | N | N | N | Y | N | N |
| **ARIZONA** | | | | | | | | |
| 1 *Rhodes* | N | N | N | N | N | N | Y | N |
| 2 Pastor | Y | Y | Y | Y | Y | Y | Y | Y |
| 3 *Stump* | N | N | N | N | N | N | Y | N |
| 4 *Kyl* | N | N | N | N | N | N | Y | N |
| 5 *Kolbe* | N | Y | Y | N | N | N | Y | N |
| **ARKANSAS** | | | | | | | | |
| 1 Alexander | Y | Y | Y | ? | Y | Y | Y | Y |
| 2 Thornton | Y | Y | Y | Y | Y | Y | Y | Y |
| 3 *Hammerschmidt* | Y | N | N | Y | N | N | Y | N |
| 4 Anthony | Y | Y | Y | Y | Y | Y | Y | Y |
| **CALIFORNIA** | | | | | | | | |
| 1 *Riggs* | + | + | Y | ? | ? | N | Y | N |
| 2 *Herger* | N | N | N | N | N | N | Y | N |
| 3 Matsui | Y | Y | Y | Y | Y | Y | Y | Y |
| 4 Fazio | Y | Y | Y | Y | Y | Y | Y | Y |
| 5 Pelosi | Y | Y | Y | Y | Y | Y | Y | Y |
| 6 Boxer | Y | Y | Y | ? | ? | Y | ? | ? |
| 7 Miller | ? | Y | Y | Y | Y | Y | Y | Y |
| 8 Dellums | ? | Y | Y | ? | Y | Y | Y | Y |
| 9 Stark | Y | Y | Y | Y | Y | Y | Y | Y |
| 10 Edwards | Y | Y | Y | Y | Y | Y | Y | Y |
| 11 Lantos | Y | Y | Y | Y | Y | Y | Y | Y |
| 12 *Campbell* | N | Y | Y | ? | ? | ? | ? | ? |
| 13 Mineta | Y | Y | Y | Y | Y | Y | Y | Y |
| 14 *Doolittle* | N | N | N | N | N | N | Y | N |
| 15 Condit | Y | Y | Y | N | N | Y | Y | Y |
| 16 Panetta | Y | Y | Y | Y | Y | Y | Y | Y |
| 17 Dooley | Y | Y | ? | ? | Y | Y | Y | Y |
| 18 Lehman | Y | Y | Y | Y | Y | Y | Y | Y |
| 19 *Lagomarsino* | N | N | N | N | N | N | Y | N |
| 20 *Thomas* | ? | N | Y | N | Y | N | Y | N |
| 21 *Gallegly* | N | N | N | N | N | N | Y | N |
| 22 *Moorhead* | N | N | N | N | N | N | Y | N |
| 23 Beilenson | Y | Y | Y | Y | Y | Y | Y | Y |
| 24 Waxman | Y | Y | Y | Y | Y | Y | Y | Y |
| 25 Roybal | Y | Y | Y | Y | Y | Y | Y | Y |
| 26 Berman | Y | Y | Y | Y | Y | Y | Y | Y |
| 27 Levine | Y | Y | Y | Y | Y | Y | Y | Y |
| 28 Dixon | ? | Y | Y | ? | ? | Y | Y | Y |
| 29 Waters | Y | Y | + | + | + | + | + | + |
| 30 Martinez | Y | Y | Y | Y | Y | Y | Y | Y |
| 31 Dymally | ? | Y | Y | ? | ? | ? | ? | Y |
| 32 Anderson | Y | Y | Y | Y | Y | Y | Y | Y |
| 33 *Dreier* | N | N | N | N | N | N | Y | N |
| 34 Torres | Y | Y | Y | + | + | + | Y | + |
| 35 *Lewis* | Y | N | Y | N | N | N | Y | N |
| 36 Brown | Y | Y | Y | Y | Y | Y | Y | Y |
| 37 *McCandless* | Y | N | Y | N | N | N | Y | N |
| 38 *Dornan* | N | N | N | N | N | N | Y | N |
| 39 *Dannemeyer* | ? | ? | N | Y | N | N | Y | N |
| 40 *Cox* | N | N | ? | N | ? | N | N | N |
| 41 *Lowery* | Y | ? | N | ? | N | N | Y | N |

| | 93 | 94 | 95 | 96 | 97 | 98 | 99 | 100 |
|---|---|---|---|---|---|---|---|---|
| 42 *Rohrabacher* | N | N | N | Y | N | N | Y | N |
| 43 *Packard* | N | N | N | Y | N | N | Y | N |
| 44 *Cunningham* | N | N | N | N | N | N | Y | N |
| 45 *Hunter* | N | N | N | N | N | N | Y | Y |
| **COLORADO** | | | | | | | | |
| 1 Schroeder | Y | Y | Y | N | N | Y | Y | Y |
| 2 Skaggs | Y | Y | Y | Y | Y | Y | Y | Y |
| 3 *Campbell* | ? | ? | ? | Y | Y | Y | Y | Y |
| 4 *Allard* | N | N | N | ? | ? | N | Y | N |
| 5 *Hefley* | N | N | N | N | N | N | Y | N |
| 6 *Schaefer* | N | N | N | ? | ? | N | Y | N |
| **CONNECTICUT** | | | | | | | | |
| 1 Kennelly | Y | Y | Y | Y | Y | Y | Y | Y |
| 2 Gejdenson | Y | Y | Y | Y | Y | Y | Y | Y |
| 3 DeLauro | Y | Y | \# | Y | Y | Y | Y | Y |
| 4 *Shays* | N | Y | N | N | N | Y | Y | Y |
| 5 *Franks* | N | N | Y | N | N | N | Y | N |
| 6 *Johnson* | ? | Y | Y | Y | Y | N | Y | Y |
| **DELAWARE** | | | | | | | | |
| AL Carper | Y | Y | Y | Y | Y | Y | Y | Y |
| **FLORIDA** | | | | | | | | |
| 1 Hutto | ? | N | N | N | N | Y | N | N |
| 2 Peterson | Y | Y | Y | Y | Y | Y | Y | Y |
| 3 Bennett | Y | N | N | Y | N | N | Y | N |
| 4 *James* | N | N | N | N | N | C | C | C |
| 5 *McCollum* | N | N | N | Y | N | N | Y | N |
| 6 *Stearns* | N | N | N | Y | N | N | Y | N |
| 7 Gibbons | Y | Y | Y | Y | Y | Y | Y | Y |
| 8 *Young* | N | N | N | N | N | N | Y | N |
| 9 *Bilirakis* | N | N | N | N | N | N | Y | N |
| 10 *Ireland* | ? | ? | N | N | N | N | ? | N |
| 11 Bacchus | Y | Y | Y | Y | Y | Y | Y | Y |
| 12 *Lewis* | Y | N | N | N | N | N | Y | N |
| 13 *Goss* | N | N | N | N | N | N | Y | N |
| 14 Johnston | Y | Y | Y | Y | Y | Y | Y | Y |
| 15 *Shaw* | N | N | N | N | N | N | Y | N |
| 16 Smith | ? | ? | \# | Y | Y | Y | Y | Y |
| 17 Lehman | ? | Y | Y | Y | Y | Y | Y | Y |
| 18 *Ros—Lehtinen* | N | N | N | N | N | Y | N | N |
| 19 Fascell | Y | Y | Y | Y | Y | ? | Y | Y |
| **GEORGIA** | | | | | | | | |
| 1 Thomas | Y | Y | Y | Y | Y | Y | Y | Y |
| 2 Hatcher | Y | Y | Y | Y | Y | Y | Y | Y |
| 3 Ray | Y | Y | N | Y | Y | Y | Y | N |
| 4 Jones | Y | Y | Y | Y | Y | ? | Y | Y |
| 5 Lewis | Y | Y | Y | Y | Y | Y | Y | Y |
| 6 *Gingrich* | Y | N | N | N | N | N | Y | N |
| 7 Darden | Y | Y | Y | Y | Y | Y | Y | Y |
| 8 Rowland | Y | Y | Y | Y | Y | Y | Y | Y |
| 9 Jenkins | Y | Y | Y | N | Y | Y | Y | Y |
| 10 Barnard | ? | ? | ? | Y | Y | N | ? | ? |
| **HAWAII** | | | | | | | | |
| 1 Abercrombie | Y | Y | Y | + | + | Y | Y | Y |
| 2 Mink | Y | Y | Y | Y | Y | Y | Y | Y |
| **IDAHO** | | | | | | | | |
| 1 LaRocco | Y | Y | Y | Y | Y | Y | Y | Y |
| 2 Stallings | Y | Y | Y | Y | Y | Y | Y | Y |
| **ILLINOIS** | | | | | | | | |
| 1 Hayes | Y | Y | Y | Y | Y | Y | Y | Y |
| 2 Savage | ? | Y | Y | ? | ? | Y | Y | Y |
| 3 Russo | Y | Y | Y | Y | Y | Y | Y | Y |
| 4 Sangmeister | Y | Y | Y | Y | Y | Y | Y | Y |
| 5 Lipinski | Y | Y | N | ? | Y | Y | Y | Y |
| 6 *Hyde* | ? | N | N | N | N | N | Y | Y |
| 7 Collins | Y | Y | Y | Y | Y | Y | Y | Y |
| 8 Rostenkowski | Y | Y | Y | Y | Y | Y | Y | Y |
| 9 Yates | ? | Y | Y | Y | Y | Y | Y | Y |
| 10 *Porter* | N | N | Y | N | N | N | Y | Y |
| 11 Annunzio | Y | Y | Y | Y | Y | Y | Y | Y |
| 12 *Crane* | N | N | N | N | N | N | N | N |
| 13 *Fawell* | N | N | Y | N | N | N | Y | N |
| 14 *Hastert* | Y | N | N | ? | N | Y | N | N |
| 15 *Ewing* | N | N | N | ? | ? | N | Y | ? |
| 16 *Cox* | Y | Y | Y | Y | Y | Y | Y | Y |
| 17 Evans | Y | Y | Y | Y | Y | Y | Y | Y |
| 18 *Michel* | Y | ? | N | N | N | N | Y | N |
| 19 Bruce | Y | Y | Y | Y | Y | Y | Y | Y |
| 20 Durbin | Y | Y | Y | Y | Y | Y | Y | Y |
| 21 Costello | Y | N | N | Y | N | Y | Y | Y |
| 22 Poshard | Y | N | N | Y | N | Y | Y | Y |
| **INDIANA** | | | | | | | | |
| 1 Visclosky | N | Y | Y | ? | Y | Y | Y | Y |
| 2 Sharp | Y | Y | Y | Y | ? | Y | Y | Y |
| 3 Roemer | Y | Y | Y | + | + | + | Y | Y |

ND  Northern Democrats    SD  Southern Democrats

| | 93 | 94 | 95 | 96 | 97 | 98 | 99 | 100 |
|---|---|---|---|---|---|---|---|---|
| 4 Long | Y | Y | Y | Y | Y | Y | Y | Y |
| 5 Jontz | Y | Y | Y | Y | Y | Y | Y | Y |
| 6 ***Burton*** | N | N | N | N | N | N | Y | N |
| 7 ***Myers*** | Y | N | N | Y | N | N | Y | N |
| 8 McCloskey | Y | Y | Y | Y | Y | Y | Y | Y |
| 9 Hamilton | Y | Y | Y | Y | Y | Y | Y | Y |
| 10 Jacobs | N | N | Y | N | Y | N | Y | Y |
| **IOWA** | | | | | | | | |
| 1 ***Leach*** | N | N | Y | N | N | N | Y | Y |
| 2 ***Nussle*** | N | N | N | N | N | N | Y | N |
| 3 Nagle | Y | Y | Y | Y | Y | Y | Y | Y |
| 4 Smith | Y | Y | Y | Y | Y | Y | Y | Y |
| 5 ***Lightfoot*** | N | N | N | N | N | N | Y | N |
| 6 ***Grandy*** | Y | N | N | N | N | N | Y | N |
| **KANSAS** | | | | | | | | |
| 1 ***Roberts*** | N | N | N | ? | ? | N | Y | N |
| 2 Slattery | Y | Y | Y | Y | Y | Y | Y | Y |
| 3 ***Meyers*** | Y | Y | Y | ? | N | N | Y | N |
| 4 Glickman | Y | Y | Y | Y | N | Y | Y | Y |
| 5 ***Nichols*** | N | N | Y | Y | N | N | Y | N |
| **KENTUCKY** | | | | | | | | |
| 1 Hubbard | Y | Y | Y | Y | N | Y | Y | Y |
| 2 Natcher | Y | Y | Y | Y | Y | Y | Y | Y |
| 3 Mazzoli | Y | Y | N | Y | Y | Y | Y | Y |
| 4 ***Bunning*** | N | N | N | N | N | N | Y | N |
| 5 ***Rogers*** | Y | N | N | N | N | N | Y | N |
| 6 ***Hopkins*** | N | N | N | N | N | N | Y | N |
| 7 Perkins | Y | Y | N | Y | Y | Y | Y | Y |
| **LOUISIANA** | | | | | | | | |
| 1 ***Livingston*** | Y | N | N | Y | N | N | Y | N |
| 2 Jefferson | Y | Y | Y | ? | ? | ? | Y | Y |
| 3 Tauzin | Y | N | N | Y | Y | Y | Y | N |
| 4 ***McCrery*** | N | N | N | N | N | N | Y | N |
| 5 Huckaby | Y | Y | Y | Y | Y | Y | Y | N |
| 6 ***Baker*** | N | N | N | ? | ? | ? | Y | N |
| 7 Hayes | Y | Y | N | Y | Y | Y | Y | N |
| 8 ***Holloway*** | N | N | N | N | N | N | Y | N |
| **MAINE** | | | | | | | | |
| 1 Andrews | Y | Y | Y | Y | Y | Y | Y | Y |
| 2 ***Snowe*** | Y | Y | Y | Y | Y | N | Y | Y |
| **MARYLAND** | | | | | | | | |
| 1 ***Gilchrest*** | Y | ? | Y | N | Y | N | Y | Y |
| 2 ***Bentley*** | Y | N | ? | N | Y | N | Y | N |
| 3 Cardin | Y | Y | Y | Y | Y | Y | Y | Y |
| 4 McMillen | Y | Y | Y | Y | Y | Y | Y | Y |
| 5 Hoyer | Y | Y | Y | Y | Y | Y | Y | Y |
| 6 Byron | Y | Y | Y | ? | ? | ? | ? | ? |
| 7 Mfume | Y | Y | Y | ? | ? | Y | Y | Y |
| 8 ***Morella*** | Y | Y | Y | Y | Y | N | Y | Y |
| **MASSACHUSETTS** | | | | | | | | |
| 1 Olver | Y | Y | Y | Y | Y | Y | Y | Y |
| 2 Neal | Y | Y | Y | ? | ? | ? | Y | Y |
| 3 Early | Y | Y | Y | Y | Y | Y | Y | Y |
| 4 Frank | Y | Y | Y | Y | Y | Y | Y | Y |
| 5 Atkins | N | Y | Y | Y | Y | Y | Y | Y |
| 6 Mavroules | Y | N | N | ? | Y | Y | Y | Y |
| 7 Markey | Y | Y | Y | Y | Y | Y | Y | Y |
| 8 Kennedy | Y | Y | Y | Y | Y | Y | Y | Y |
| 9 Moakley | Y | Y | Y | ? | ? | ? | ? | ? |
| 10 Studds | Y | Y | Y | Y | Y | Y | Y | Y |
| 11 Donnelly | Y | Y | N | ? | ? | ? | Y | Y |
| **MICHIGAN** | | | | | | | | |
| 1 Conyers | Y | Y | Y | Y | Y | ? | Y | Y |
| 2 ***Pursell*** | Y | Y | Y | Y | Y | N | Y | N |
| 3 Wolpe | ? | Y | Y | Y | Y | Y | Y | Y |
| 4 ***Upton*** | N | N | Y | N | Y | N | Y | N |
| 5 ***Henry*** | N | N | N | N | Y | N | Y | N |
| 6 Carr | Y | Y | Y | ? | Y | Y | Y | Y |
| 7 Kildee | Y | Y | N | Y | Y | Y | Y | Y |
| 8 Traxler | Y | Y | ? | Y | Y | Y | Y | Y |
| 9 ***Vander Jagt*** | Y | N | N | ? | ? | ? | Y | N |
| 10 ***Camp*** | N | N | N | N | Y | N | Y | N |
| 11 ***Davis*** | Y | N | N | Y | Y | N | ? | Y |
| 12 Bonior | Y | Y | Y | Y | Y | Y | Y | Y |
| 13 Collins | ? | Y | + | Y | Y | Y | Y | Y |
| 14 Hertel | Y | ? | Y | Y | Y | Y | ? | Y |
| 15 Ford | Y | Y | Y | ? | Y | Y | Y | Y |
| 16 Dingell | Y | Y | Y | ? | Y | Y | Y | Y |
| 17 Levin | Y | Y | Y | Y | Y | Y | Y | Y |
| 18 ***Broomfield*** | Y | N | N | Y | Y | N | Y | N |
| **MINNESOTA** | | | | | | | | |
| 1 Penny | Y | Y | Y | Y | Y | Y | Y | Y |
| 2 ***Weber*** | N | N | N | ? | ? | N | Y | N |
| 3 ***Ramstad*** | N | Y | Y | N | N | N | Y | Y |
| 4 Vento | Y | Y | Y | Y | Y | Y | Y | Y |
| 5 Sabo | Y | Y | Y | Y | Y | Y | Y | Y |
| 6 Sikorski | Y | Y | Y | ? | Y | Y | Y | Y |
| 7 Peterson | Y | N | N | Y | Y | Y | Y | Y |
| 8 Oberstar | Y | N | N | Y | Y | Y | Y | Y |
| **MISSISSIPPI** | | | | | | | | |
| 1 Whitten | Y | Y | N | ? | ? | Y | Y | Y |
| 2 Espy | Y | Y | Y | Y | N | Y | Y | Y |
| 3 Montgomery | Y | Y | N | Y | N | Y | Y | N |
| 4 Parker | Y | Y | N | Y | N | Y | Y | N |
| 5 Taylor | Y | N | N | Y | N | Y | Y | N |
| **MISSOURI** | | | | | | | | |
| 1 Clay | Y | Y | Y | N | Y | Y | Y | Y |
| 2 Horn | N | Y | Y | Y | Y | Y | Y | Y |
| 3 Gephardt | Y | Y | Y | Y | Y | Y | Y | Y |
| 4 Skelton | Y | Y | N | Y | N | Y | Y | N |
| 5 Wheat | ? | Y | Y | Y | Y | Y | ? | Y |
| 6 ***Coleman*** | Y | N | Y | N | N | N | Y | N |
| 7 ***Hancock*** | N | N | N | N | N | N | Y | ? |
| 8 ***Emerson*** | Y | N | N | N | N | N | Y | N |
| 9 Volkmer | Y | N | N | Y | Y | Y | Y | Y |
| **MONTANA** | | | | | | | | |
| 1 Williams | Y | Y | Y | Y | Y | Y | Y | Y |
| 2 ***Marlenee*** | ? | ? | X | N | N | N | Y | N |
| **NEBRASKA** | | | | | | | | |
| 1 ***Bereuter*** | Y | N | Y | N | N | N | Y | Y |
| 2 Hoagland | Y | Y | Y | Y | Y | Y | Y | Y |
| 3 ***Barrett*** | Y | N | N | N | N | N | Y | N |
| **NEVADA** | | | | | | | | |
| 1 Bilbray | Y | Y | Y | Y | Y | Y | Y | Y |
| 2 ***Vucanovich*** | Y | N | N | N | N | N | Y | N |
| **NEW HAMPSHIRE** | | | | | | | | |
| 1 ***Zeliff*** | Y | N | Y | N | N | N | Y | N |
| 2 Swett | Y | Y | Y | Y | N | Y | Y | Y |
| **NEW JERSEY** | | | | | | | | |
| 1 Andrews | Y | Y | Y | Y | Y | Y | Y | Y |
| 2 Hughes | Y | Y | Y | Y | Y | Y | Y | Y |
| 3 Pallone | Y | Y | Y | Y | Y | Y | Y | Y |
| 4 ***Smith*** | Y | N | N | Y | Y | N | Y | Y |
| 5 ***Roukema*** | Y | Y | Y | N | N | N | Y | N |
| 6 Dwyer | Y | Y | Y | Y | Y | Y | Y | Y |
| 7 ***Rinaldo*** | Y | N | N | Y | Y | N | Y | Y |
| 8 Roe | Y | Y | N | ? | Y | Y | Y | Y |
| 9 Torricelli | Y | Y | Y | Y | Y | Y | Y | Y |
| 10 Payne | Y | Y | Y | ? | Y | Y | Y | Y |
| 11 ***Gallo*** | Y | Y | Y | N | Y | N | Y | N |
| 12 ***Zimmer*** | N | N | Y | N | N | N | Y | N |
| 13 ***Saxton*** | Y | N | N | N | Y | N | Y | N |
| 14 Guarini | Y | Y | Y | Y | Y | Y | Y | Y |
| **NEW MEXICO** | | | | | | | | |
| 1 ***Schiff*** | Y | N | Y | N | N | N | Y | N |
| 2 ***Skeen*** | Y | N | Y | Y | N | N | Y | Y |
| 3 Richardson | Y | Y | Y | Y | Y | Y | Y | Y |
| **NEW YORK** | | | | | | | | |
| 1 Hochbrueckner | Y | Y | Y | Y | Y | Y | Y | Y |
| 2 Downey | Y | Y | Y | Y | Y | Y | Y | Y |
| 3 Mrazek | Y | Y | Y | ? | ? | Y | Y | Y |
| 4 ***Lent*** | Y | N | N | Y | Y | N | Y | N |
| 5 ***McGrath*** | Y | N | N | Y | Y | N | Y | N |
| 6 Flake | Y | Y | Y | Y | Y | Y | Y | Y |
| 7 Ackerman | Y | Y | Y | Y | Y | Y | Y | Y |
| 8 Scheuer | Y | Y | Y | Y | Y | Y | Y | Y |
| 9 Manton | Y | Y | N | Y | Y | Y | Y | Y |
| 10 Schumer | Y | Y | Y | Y | Y | Y | Y | Y |
| 11 Towns | ? | Y | Y | ? | Y | Y | Y | Y |
| 12 Owens | Y | Y | Y | Y | Y | Y | Y | Y |
| 13 Solarz | Y | Y | Y | Y | Y | Y | Y | Y |
| 14 ***Molinari*** | N | N | Y | N | N | N | Y | Y |
| 15 ***Green*** | Y | Y | Y | Y | Y | N | Y | Y |
| 16 Rangel | Y | Y | Y | ? | Y | Y | Y | Y |
| 17 Weiss | Y | Y | Y | Y | Y | Y | Y | Y |
| 18 Serrano | Y | Y | Y | Y | Y | Y | Y | Y |
| 19 Engel | Y | Y | Y | ? | Y | Y | Y | Y |
| 20 Lowey | Y | Y | Y | ? | Y | Y | Y | Y |
| 21 ***Fish*** | Y | Y | Y | Y | Y | N | Y | Y |
| 22 ***Gilman*** | Y | Y | Y | Y | Y | N | Y | Y |
| 23 McNulty | Y | Y | Y | Y | Y | Y | Y | Y |
| 24 ***Solomon*** | N | N | N | N | N | N | Y | N |
| 25 ***Boehlert*** | Y | Y | Y | N | Y | N | Y | Y |
| 26 ***Martin*** | Y | N | Y | N | Y | N | Y | N |
| 27 ***Walsh*** | Y | N | N | Y | N | N | Y | Y |
| 28 McHugh | Y | Y | Y | Y | Y | Y | Y | Y |
| 29 ***Horton*** | Y | Y | Y | Y | Y | N | Y | Y |
| 30 Slaughter | Y | Y | Y | Y | Y | Y | Y | Y |
| 31 ***Paxon*** | N | N | N | N | Y | N | Y | N |
| 32 LaFalce | Y | Y | N | Y | Y | Y | Y | Y |
| 33 Nowak | Y | Y | N | ? | ? | ? | Y | Y |
| 34 ***Houghton*** | Y | Y | Y | Y | Y | N | Y | Y |
| **NORTH CAROLINA** | | | | | | | | |
| 1 Jones | Y | Y | Y | ? | ? | ? | Y | Y |
| 2 Valentine | Y | Y | Y | ? | ? | ? | ? | ? |
| 3 Lancaster | Y | Y | Y | Y | Y | Y | Y | Y |
| 4 Price | Y | Y | Y | Y | Y | Y | Y | Y |
| 5 Neal | Y | Y | Y | Y | Y | Y | Y | Y |
| 6 ***Coble*** | N | N | N | N | N | N | Y | N |
| 7 Rose | Y | Y | Y | Y | Y | Y | Y | Y |
| 8 Hefner | Y | Y | Y | Y | Y | Y | Y | Y |
| 9 ***McMillan*** | Y | Y | Y | N | N | N | Y | Y |
| 10 ***Ballenger*** | ? | N | Y | N | N | N | Y | N |
| 11 ***Taylor*** | N | N | N | N | N | N | Y | N |
| **NORTH DAKOTA** | | | | | | | | |
| AL Dorgan | Y | Y | Y | Y | N | Y | Y | Y |
| **OHIO** | | | | | | | | |
| 1 Luken | Y | Y | N | Y | Y | Y | Y | Y |
| 2 ***Gradison*** | N | ? | Y | Y | N | N | Y | Y |
| 3 Hall | Y | Y | N | ? | Y | Y | Y | N |
| 4 ***Oxley*** | Y | N | N | Y | N | N | Y | N |
| 5 ***Gillmor*** | Y | N | N | Y | N | N | Y | N |
| 6 ***McEwen*** | N | N | X | N | N | N | Y | N |
| 7 ***Hobson*** | N | N | Y | N | N | N | Y | N |
| 8 ***Boehner*** | N | N | N | N | N | N | Y | N |
| 9 Kaptur | Y | Y | Y | Y | Y | Y | Y | Y |
| 10 ***Miller*** | Y | N | N | N | N | N | Y | N |
| 11 Eckart | Y | Y | Y | ? | ? | ? | ? | Y |
| 12 ***Kasich*** | N | N | N | Y | N | N | Y | N |
| 13 Pease | Y | Y | Y | Y | Y | Y | Y | Y |
| 14 Sawyer | Y | Y | Y | Y | Y | Y | Y | Y |
| 15 ***Wylie*** | ? | N | N | Y | N | N | Y | Y |
| 16 ***Regula*** | Y | Y | Y | N | N | N | Y | N |
| 17 Traficant | Y | Y | Y | Y | Y | Y | Y | Y |
| 18 Applegate | Y | N | N | Y | Y | Y | Y | Y |
| 19 Feighan | ? | Y | Y | ? | ? | ? | Y | Y |
| 20 Oakar | Y | Y | N | Y | Y | Y | Y | Y |
| 21 Stokes | Y | Y | Y | Y | Y | Y | Y | Y |
| **OKLAHOMA** | | | | | | | | |
| 1 ***Inhofe*** | N | N | N | N | N | N | Y | N |
| 2 Synar | Y | Y | Y | Y | Y | Y | Y | Y |
| 3 Brewster | Y | Y | Y | ? | Y | Y | Y | Y |
| 4 McCurdy | ? | Y | Y | Y | Y | Y | Y | Y |
| 5 ***Edwards*** | ? | N | N | N | N | N | Y | N |
| 6 English | Y | Y | Y | Y | Y | Y | Y | N |
| **OREGON** | | | | | | | | |
| 1 AuCoin | Y | Y | Y | ? | ? | ? | ? | ? |
| 2 ***Smith*** | N | N | N | N | N | N | Y | N |
| 3 Wyden | Y | Y | Y | Y | Y | Y | Y | Y |
| 4 DeFazio | Y | Y | Y | Y | Y | Y | Y | Y |
| 5 Kopetski | Y | Y | Y | Y | Y | Y | Y | ? |
| **PENNSYLVANIA** | | | | | | | | |
| 1 Foglietta | Y | Y | Y | ? | ? | Y | Y | Y |
| 2 Blackwell | ? | Y | Y | Y | Y | Y | Y | Y |
| 3 Borski | Y | Y | N | Y | Y | Y | Y | Y |
| 4 Kolter | ? | ? | ? | ? | Y | ? | Y | ? |
| 5 ***Schulze*** | Y | N | N | Y | N | N | Y | N |
| 6 Yatron | Y | Y | N | ? | ? | ? | ? | ? |
| 7 ***Weldon*** | N | N | N | N | N | N | Y | N |
| 8 Kostmayer | Y | Y | Y | Y | Y | Y | Y | Y |
| 9 ***Shuster*** | Y | N | N | N | N | N | Y | N |
| 10 ***McDade*** | ? | ? | ? | ? | ? | ? | ? | ? |
| 11 Kanjorski | Y | N | N | Y | Y | Y | Y | Y |
| 12 Murtha | Y | Y | N | Y | Y | Y | Y | Y |
| 13 ***Coughlin*** | Y | Y | Y | ? | N | N | Y | Y |
| 14 Coyne | Y | Y | Y | Y | Y | Y | Y | Y |
| 15 ***Ritter*** | N | N | N | Y | N | N | Y | N |
| 16 ***Walker*** | N | N | N | N | N | N | Y | N |
| 17 ***Gekas*** | ? | N | Y | N | N | N | Y | N |
| 18 ***Santorum*** | Y | N | N | Y | N | N | Y | N |
| 19 ***Goodling*** | N | N | N | N | N | N | Y | — |
| 20 Gaydos | Y | Y | ? | Y | N | Y | Y | Y |
| 21 ***Ridge*** | N | N | Y | N | Y | N | Y | Y |
| 22 Murphy | N | N | N | N | Y | Y | Y | N |
| 23 ***Clinger*** | Y | N | Y | Y | Y | N | Y | Y |
| **RHODE ISLAND** | | | | | | | | |
| 1 ***Machtley*** | N | Y | Y | N | Y | N | Y | Y |
| 2 Reed | Y | Y | Y | Y | Y | Y | Y | Y |
| **SOUTH CAROLINA** | | | | | | | | |
| 1 ***Ravenel*** | Y | Y | Y | Y | Y | N | Y | Y |
| 2 ***Spence*** | Y | N | N | Y | Y | N | Y | Y |
| 3 Derrick | Y | Y | Y | Y | Y | Y | Y | Y |
| 4 Patterson | Y | Y | Y | Y | N | Y | Y | Y |
| 5 Spratt | Y | Y | Y | Y | Y | Y | Y | ? |
| 6 Tallon | Y | N | N | Y | Y | Y | Y | Y |
| **SOUTH DAKOTA** | | | | | | | | |
| AL Johnson | Y | Y | Y | Y | Y | Y | Y | Y |
| **TENNESSEE** | | | | | | | | |
| 1 ***Quillen*** | Y | N | N | N | N | N | Y | N |
| 2 ***Duncan*** | N | N | N | N | N | N | Y | N |
| 3 Lloyd | ? | Y | Y | Y | N | Y | Y | Y |
| 4 Cooper | Y | Y | Y | Y | Y | Y | Y | Y |
| 5 Clement | Y | Y | Y | Y | Y | Y | Y | Y |
| 6 Gordon | Y | Y | Y | Y | Y | Y | Y | Y |
| 7 ***Sundquist*** | N | N | N | ? | ? | N | Y | N |
| 8 Tanner | Y | Y | Y | Y | Y | Y | Y | N |
| 9 Ford | Y | Y | Y | ? | ? | ? | ? | ? |
| **TEXAS** | | | | | | | | |
| 1 Chapman | Y | Y | Y | ? | ? | Y | Y | Y |
| 2 Wilson | Y | Y | Y | ? | ? | ? | Y | N |
| 3 ***Johnson*** | Y | N | N | Y | N | N | Y | N |
| 4 Hall | Y | N | N | Y | N | Y | Y | N |
| 5 Bryant | Y | Y | Y | Y | Y | Y | Y | Y |
| 6 ***Barton*** | Y | N | N | ? | N | N | Y | N |
| 7 ***Archer*** | Y | N | N | ? | N | N | Y | N |
| 8 ***Fields*** | ? | ? | ? | N | N | N | Y | N |
| 9 Brooks | Y | Y | Y | Y | Y | Y | Y | Y |
| 10 Pickle | Y | Y | Y | Y | Y | Y | Y | Y |
| 11 Edwards | Y | Y | Y | Y | Y | Y | Y | N |
| 12 Geren | Y | Y | Y | Y | Y | Y | Y | Y |
| 13 Sarpalius | Y | Y | N | Y | N | Y | Y | N |
| 14 Laughlin | Y | Y | Y | Y | Y | Y | Y | N |
| 15 de la Garza | Y | Y | N | Y | Y | Y | Y | Y |
| 16 Coleman | Y | Y | Y | Y | Y | Y | Y | Y |
| 17 Stenholm | Y | N | N | Y | N | Y | Y | N |
| 18 Washington | Y | Y | Y | Y | Y | Y | Y | Y |
| 19 ***Combest*** | Y | N | N | Y | N | N | Y | N |
| 20 Gonzalez | Y | Y | Y | Y | Y | Y | Y | Y |
| 21 ***Smith*** | Y | N | Y | N | N | N | Y | N |
| 22 ***DeLay*** | N | N | N | ? | N | N | Y | N |
| 23 Bustamante | Y | Y | Y | Y | Y | Y | Y | Y |
| 24 Frost | Y | Y | Y | Y | Y | Y | Y | Y |
| 25 Andrews | Y | Y | Y | Y | Y | Y | Y | N |
| 26 ***Armey*** | N | N | N | N | N | N | N | N |
| 27 Ortiz | Y | Y | N | Y | Y | Y | Y | Y |
| **UTAH** | | | | | | | | |
| 1 ***Hansen*** | Y | N | N | Y | N | N | Y | N |
| 2 Owens | Y | Y | Y | Y | Y | Y | Y | Y |
| 3 Orton | Y | Y | N | Y | N | Y | Y | N |
| **VERMONT** | | | | | | | | |
| AL *Sanders* | Y | Y | Y | + | + | + | + | + |
| **VIRGINIA** | | | | | | | | |
| 1 ***Bateman*** | Y | N | N | Y | Y | N | Y | N |
| 2 Pickett | Y | Y | Y | Y | Y | Y | Y | Y |
| 3 ***Bliley*** | Y | N | N | N | N | N | Y | N |
| 4 Sisisky | Y | Y | Y | Y | Y | Y | Y | Y |
| 5 Payne | Y | Y | Y | Y | Y | Y | Y | Y |
| 6 Olin | Y | Y | Y | Y | Y | Y | Y | Y |
| 7 ***Allen*** | N | N | Y | N | N | N | Y | N |
| 8 Moran | Y | Y | Y | Y | Y | Y | Y | + |
| 9 Boucher | Y | Y | Y | Y | Y | Y | Y | Y |
| 10 ***Wolf*** | N | N | N | N | N | N | Y | N |
| **WASHINGTON** | | | | | | | | |
| 1 ***Miller*** | Y | Y | Y | N | Y | N | Y | N |
| 2 Swift | Y | Y | Y | Y | Y | Y | Y | Y |
| 3 Unsoeld | Y | Y | Y | Y | Y | Y | Y | Y |
| 4 ***Morrison*** | Y | Y | Y | Y | Y | N | Y | N |
| 5 Foley | | | | | | | | |
| 6 Dicks | Y | Y | Y | Y | Y | Y | Y | Y |
| 7 McDermott | ? | Y | Y | Y | Y | Y | Y | Y |
| 8 ***Chandler*** | N | Y | Y | N | N | N | Y | N |
| **WEST VIRGINIA** | | | | | | | | |
| 1 Mollohan | Y | N | N | ? | ? | N | Y | Y |
| 2 Staggers | Y | Y | N | Y | Y | Y | Y | Y |
| 3 Wise | Y | Y | Y | Y | Y | Y | ? | Y |
| 4 Rahall | Y | Y | N | Y | N | Y | Y | Y |
| **WISCONSIN** | | | | | | | | |
| 1 Aspin | Y | Y | Y | Y | Y | Y | Y | Y |
| 2 ***Klug*** | N | Y | Y | Y | Y | N | Y | Y |
| 3 ***Gunderson*** | Y | N | N | Y | Y | N | Y | N |
| 4 Kleczka | Y | Y | Y | Y | Y | Y | Y | Y |
| 5 Moody | Y | Y | Y | Y | Y | Y | Y | Y |
| 6 ***Petri*** | N | N | N | Y | N | N | Y | N |
| 7 Obey | Y | Y | Y | Y | Y | Y | Y | Y |
| 8 ***Roth*** | Y | N | N | N | N | N | Y | N |
| 9 ***Sensenbrenner*** | N | N | N | N | N | N | Y | N |
| **WYOMING** | | | | | | | | |
| AL ***Thomas*** | N | N | Y | Y | N | N | Y | N |

Southern states - Ala., Ark., Fla., Ga., Ky., La., Miss., N.C., Okla., S.C., Tenn., Texas, Va.
Omitted votes are quorum calls, which CQ does not include in its vote charts.

**101. HR 2039. Legal Services Corporation (LSC) Reauthorization/Competitive Bidding.** McCollum, R-Fla., amendment to change the bill's study of a competitive bidding system for distributing LSC funds to a requirement that 10 percent of the funds in fiscal 1993-94 be provided to test a competitive bidding system. Rejected 170-251: R 149-14; D 21-236 (ND 6-168, SD 15-68); I 0-1, May 6, 1992.

**102. HR 2039. Legal Services Corporation (LSC) Reauthorization/Attorney's Fees.** Stenholm, D-Texas, amendment to prohibit the recovery of attorney's fees from non-governmental defendants. Rejected 178-240: R 142-21; D 36-218 (ND 14-158, SD 22-60); I 0-1, May 6, 1992.

**103. HR 2039. Legal Services Corporation (LSC) Reauthorization/Lobbying.** Frank, D-Mass., substitute amendment to the Gekas, R-Pa., amendment to ban only non-corporation public funds for grass-roots lobbying. The Gekas amendment expanded the bill's ban on lobbying and applied the lobbying restrictions to all corporation, private or public funds. Adopted 222-196: R 12-149; D 209-47 (ND 160-14, SD 49-33); I 1-0, May 6, 1992. A "nay" was a vote in support of the president's position.

**104. HR 2039. Legal Services Corporation (LSC) Reauthorization/Lobbying Restrictions.** Gekas, R-Pa., amendment as amended by the Frank, D-Mass., amendment to ban the use of non-corporation public funds for grass-roots lobbying. The original Gekas amendment expanded the bill's ban on lobbying and applied the lobbying restrictions to all corporation, private or public funds. Adopted 221-196: R 25-136; D 196-59 (ND 124-49, SD 72-10); I 0-1, May 6, 1992.

**105. HR 2039. Legal Services Corporation (LSC) Reauthorization/LSC Procedures.** Fish, R-N.Y., amendment to ensure that the corporation had sufficient time to investigate and evaluate allegations made against recipient agencies, clarify that the corporation must consider personal privacy rights of clients during an investigation and require corporation recipients to keep separate accounts for federal and non-federal funds. Adopted 410-2: R 160-0; D 249-2 (ND 167-1, SD 82-1); I 1-0, May 6, 1992.

**106. HR 2039. Legal Services Corporation (LSC) Reauthorization/Restrict Litigation.** McCollum, R-Fla., amendment to extend prohibitions on the use of LSC funds for certain kinds of cases, such as abortion-related litigation or redistricting, to cover all public and private funds. The amendment also changed the definition of "alternative corporation" to make it more difficult to use mirror corporations to avoid restrictions in the bill. Rejected 156-257: R 133-28; D 23-228 (ND 6-164, SD 17-64); I 0-1, May 6, 1992. A "yea" was a vote in support of the president's position.

**107. H Con Res 287. Fiscal 1993 Budget Resolution/Balanced Budget Constitutional Amendment.** Gradison, R-Ohio, motion to instruct the House conferees to include Senate provisions relating to the adoption of a joint resolution proposing an amendment to the Constitution for a federal balanced budget. Motion agreed to 322-66: R 150-1; D 172-64 (ND 106-56, SD 66-8); I 0-1, May 6, 1992.

**108. Procedural Motion.** Approval of the House Journal of Wednesday, May 6. Approved 262-122: R 34-116; D 228-6 (ND 153-6, SD 75-0); I 0-0, May 7, 1992.

## KEY

Y Voted for (yea).
\# Paired for.
+ Announced for.
N Voted against (nay).
X Paired against.
− Announced against.
P Voted "present."
C Voted "present" to avoid possible conflict of interest.
? Did not vote or otherwise make a position known.

———

**Democrats** ***Republicans***
*Independent*

| | 101 | 102 | 103 | 104 | 105 | 106 | 107 | 108 |
|---|---|---|---|---|---|---|---|---|
| **ALABAMA** | | | | | | | | |
| 1 *Callahan* | Y | Y | N | N | Y | Y | Y | N |
| 2 *Dickinson* | Y | Y | N | N | Y | Y | N | N |
| 3 Browder | N | ? | N | Y | Y | N | Y | Y |
| 4 Bevill | N | N | N | Y | Y | N | ? | Y |
| 5 Cramer | N | N | N | Y | Y | N | Y | Y |
| 6 Erdreich | N | N | N | Y | Y | N | Y | Y |
| 7 Harris | N | N | N | Y | N | N | Y | Y |
| **ALASKA** | | | | | | | | |
| AL *Young* | Y | N | ? | N | Y | Y | Y | ? |
| **ARIZONA** | | | | | | | | |
| 1 *Rhodes* | Y | Y | N | N | Y | Y | Y | N |
| 2 Pastor | N | N | Y | N | Y | N | Y | + |
| 3 *Stump* | Y | Y | N | N | Y | Y | Y | N |
| 4 *Kyl* | Y | Y | N | N | Y | Y | Y | N |
| 5 *Kolbe* | Y | Y | N | N | Y | Y | Y | N |
| **ARKANSAS** | | | | | | | | |
| 1 Alexander | N | N | Y | Y | Y | N | N | Y |
| 2 Thornton | N | N | Y | Y | Y | N | Y | Y |
| 3 *Hammerschmidt* | Y | Y | N | N | Y | Y | Y | Y |
| 4 Anthony | N | N | Y | Y | Y | N | Y | Y |
| **CALIFORNIA** | | | | | | | | |
| 1 *Riggs* | Y | N | N | N | Y | N | Y | N |
| 2 *Herger* | Y | Y | N | N | Y | Y | Y | N |
| 3 Matsui | N | N | Y | Y | Y | N | N | Y |
| 4 Fazio | N | N | Y | Y | Y | N | Y | Y |
| 5 Pelosi | N | N | Y | Y | Y | N | N | Y |
| 6 Boxer | ? | ? | ? | ? | ? | ? | ? | ? |
| 7 Miller | N | N | Y | Y | Y | N | N | Y |
| 8 Dellums | N | N | Y | N | Y | N | N | ? |
| 9 Stark | N | N | Y | Y | Y | N | N | Y |
| 10 Edwards | N | N | Y | Y | Y | N | N | Y |
| 11 Lantos | N | N | Y | Y | Y | N | Y | Y |
| 12 *Campbell* | ? | ? | ? | ? | ? | ? | ? | ? |
| 13 Mineta | N | N | Y | Y | Y | ? | N | Y |
| 14 *Doolittle* | Y | Y | N | N | Y | Y | Y | N |
| 15 Condit | N | N | Y | Y | Y | N | Y | Y |
| 16 Panetta | N | N | Y | Y | Y | N | Y | Y |
| 17 Dooley | N | N | Y | Y | Y | N | Y | Y |
| 18 Lehman | Y | Y | N | Y | Y | N | N | Y |
| 19 *Lagomarsino* | Y | Y | N | N | Y | Y | Y | N |
| 20 *Thomas* | Y | Y | N | N | Y | Y | Y | N |
| 21 *Gallegly* | Y | Y | N | N | Y | Y | Y | N |
| 22 *Moorhead* | Y | Y | N | N | Y | Y | Y | N |
| 23 Beilenson | N | N | Y | N | Y | ? | ? | Y |
| 24 Waxman | N | N | Y | N | Y | N | N | Y |
| 25 Roybal | N | N | Y | N | Y | N | N | Y |
| 26 Berman | N | N | Y | N | Y | N | N | Y |
| 27 Levine | N | N | ? | ? | ? | ? | ? | ? |
| 28 Dixon | N | N | Y | Y | Y | N | N | Y |
| 29 Waters | − | − | + | − | + | − | − | + |
| 30 Martinez | N | N | Y | N | Y | N | N | Y |
| 31 Dymally | N | N | Y | N | Y | N | ? | Y |
| 32 Anderson | N | N | Y | Y | Y | N | Y | Y |
| 33 *Dreier* | Y | Y | N | N | Y | Y | Y | N |
| 34 Torres | − | − | Y | N | Y | N | Y | + |
| 35 *Lewis* | Y | Y | N | N | Y | Y | Y | N |
| 36 Brown | N | N | Y | ? | N | ? | N | Y |
| 37 *McCandless* | Y | Y | N | N | Y | Y | Y | N |
| 38 *Dornan* | Y | Y | N | N | Y | Y | Y | N |
| 39 *Dannemeyer* | Y | Y | N | N | Y | Y | Y | N |
| 40 *Cox* | Y | N | N | Y | Y | N | Y | N |
| 41 *Lowery* | Y | Y | N | N | Y | Y | Y | N |

| | 101 | 102 | 103 | 104 | 105 | 106 | 107 | 108 |
|---|---|---|---|---|---|---|---|---|
| 42 *Rohrabacher* | Y | Y | N | N | Y | Y | Y | N |
| 43 *Packard* | Y | Y | N | N | Y | Y | Y | N |
| 44 *Cunningham* | Y | Y | N | N | Y | Y | Y | N |
| 45 *Hunter* | Y | Y | N | ? | Y | Y | Y | N |
| **COLORADO** | | | | | | | | |
| 1 Schroeder | N | N | Y | Y | Y | N | Y | N |
| 2 Skaggs | N | N | Y | Y | Y | N | Y | Y |
| 3 Campbell | N | N | Y | Y | Y | N | Y | Y |
| 4 *Allard* | Y | Y | N | N | Y | Y | Y | N |
| 5 *Hefley* | Y | Y | N | N | Y | Y | Y | N |
| 6 *Schaefer* | Y | Y | N | N | Y | Y | Y | N |
| **CONNECTICUT** | | | | | | | | |
| 1 Kennelly | N | N | Y | Y | Y | N | Y | Y |
| 2 Gejdenson | N | N | Y | Y | Y | N | Y | Y |
| 3 DeLauro | N | N | Y | Y | Y | N | Y | Y |
| 4 *Shays* | N | N | Y | Y | Y | N | Y | Y |
| 5 *Franks* | Y | Y | N | N | Y | Y | Y | Y |
| 6 *Johnson* | Y | N | Y | Y | Y | Y | Y | Y |
| **DELAWARE** | | | | | | | | |
| AL Carper | N | N | Y | Y | Y | N | Y | ? |
| **FLORIDA** | | | | | | | | |
| 1 Hutto | Y | Y | N | Y | Y | Y | Y | N |
| 2 Peterson | N | N | Y | Y | Y | N | Y | Y |
| 3 Bennett | N | N | N | Y | N | Y | N | Y |
| 4 *James* | C | C | C | C | C | C | Y | N |
| 5 *McCollum* | Y | Y | N | N | Y | Y | Y | N |
| 6 *Stearns* | Y | Y | N | N | Y | Y | Y | N |
| 7 Gibbons | N | N | Y | Y | N | Y | N | Y |
| 8 *Young* | Y | Y | N | N | Y | Y | ? | N |
| 9 *Bilirakis* | Y | Y | N | Y | Y | Y | ? | N |
| 10 *Ireland* | Y | Y | N | N | Y | Y | Y | ? |
| 11 Bacchus | N | N | Y | Y | N | Y | N | Y |
| 12 *Lewis* | Y | Y | N | N | Y | Y | ? | N |
| 13 *Goss* | N | N | Y | Y | Y | Y | Y | N |
| 14 Johnston | N | N | Y | Y | Y | N | N | Y |
| 15 *Shaw* | Y | Y | N | N | Y | Y | Y | Y |
| 16 Smith | N | N | Y | N | N | N | N | Y |
| 17 Lehman | N | N | Y | Y | Y | N | N | ? |
| 18 *Ros—Lehtinen* | Y | Y | N | N | Y | N | Y | N |
| 19 Fascell | N | N | Y | Y | Y | N | N | Y |
| **GEORGIA** | | | | | | | | |
| 1 Thomas | N | N | Y | Y | Y | N | Y | Y |
| 2 Hatcher | N | N | Y | Y | Y | N | Y | Y |
| 3 Ray | Y | Y | Y | Y | Y | Y | Y | Y |
| 4 Jones | N | N | Y | Y | Y | N | Y | Y |
| 5 Lewis | N | N | Y | Y | Y | N | N | Y |
| 6 *Gingrich* | Y | Y | N | N | Y | Y | Y | N |
| 7 Darden | N | N | Y | Y | Y | N | ? | Y |
| 8 Rowland | Y | Y | N | Y | Y | Y | ? | ? |
| 9 Jenkins | Y | Y | N | N | Y | N | ? | ? |
| 10 Barnard | Y | Y | N | Y | Y | Y | Y | Y |
| **HAWAII** | | | | | | | | |
| 1 Abercrombie | N | N | Y | N | Y | N | N | Y |
| 2 Mink | N | N | Y | N | Y | N | N | Y |
| **IDAHO** | | | | | | | | |
| 1 LaRocco | N | N | Y | Y | Y | N | Y | Y |
| 2 Stallings | N | Y | Y | Y | Y | N | Y | Y |
| **ILLINOIS** | | | | | | | | |
| 1 Hayes | N | N | Y | N | Y | N | N | Y |
| 2 Savage | N | N | Y | N | N | N | N | ? |
| 3 Russo | N | N | Y | N | Y | N | N | Y |
| 4 Sangmeister | N | N | Y | Y | Y | N | Y | Y |
| 5 Lipinski | N | N | N | N | Y | N | Y | Y |
| 6 *Hyde* | Y | Y | N | Y | Y | Y | Y | N |
| 7 Collins | N | N | Y | N | N | N | N | + |
| 8 Rostenkowski | N | N | Y | Y | Y | N | Y | Y |
| 9 Yates | N | N | Y | Y | Y | N | ? | Y |
| 10 *Porter* | Y | Y | N | Y | Y | Y | Y | Y |
| 11 Annunzio | N | N | Y | Y | Y | N | ? | Y |
| 12 *Crane* | Y | Y | N | N | Y | Y | Y | N |
| 13 *Fawell* | Y | Y | N | Y | Y | Y | Y | Y |
| 14 *Hastert* | Y | Y | N | N | Y | Y | Y | N |
| 15 *Ewing* | Y | Y | N | N | Y | Y | Y | Y |
| 16 Cox | N | N | Y | Y | Y | N | N | ? |
| 17 Evans | N | N | Y | Y | Y | N | N | Y |
| 18 *Michel* | Y | Y | N | N | Y | Y | ? | N |
| 19 Bruce | N | N | Y | Y | Y | N | Y | + |
| 20 Durbin | N | N | Y | Y | Y | N | Y | Y |
| 21 Costello | N | N | Y | Y | Y | N | Y | Y |
| 22 Poshard | N | N | Y | Y | Y | N | Y | Y |
| **INDIANA** | | | | | | | | |
| 1 Visclosky | N | N | Y | Y | Y | N | N | Y |
| 2 Sharp | N | N | Y | Y | Y | N | Y | Y |
| 3 Roemer | N | N | Y | Y | Y | N | Y | Y |

ND  Northern Democrats     SD  Southern Democrats

| | 101 | 102 | 103 | 104 | 105 | 106 | 107 | 108 |
|---|---|---|---|---|---|---|---|---|
| 4 Long | N | N | Y | Y | Y | N | Y | Y |
| 5 Jontz | N | N | Y | N | Y | N | Y | Y |
| 6 ***Burton*** | Y | Y | N | N | Y | Y | Y | N |
| 7 ***Myers*** | Y | Y | N | N | Y | Y | Y | Y |
| 8 McCloskey | N | N | Y | Y | Y | N | Y | Y |
| 9 Hamilton | N | N | Y | Y | Y | N | Y | Y |
| 10 Jacobs | N | N | Y | Y | Y | N | Y | N |
| **IOWA** | | | | | | | | |
| 1 ***Leach*** | N | N | Y | Y | Y | N | Y | ? |
| 2 ***Nussle*** | Y | Y | N | N | Y | Y | Y | N |
| 3 Nagle | N | N | Y | Y | Y | N | N | Y |
| 4 Smith | N | N | Y | Y | Y | N | N | Y |
| 5 ***Lightfoot*** | Y | Y | N | N | Y | Y | Y | N |
| 6 ***Grandy*** | Y | Y | N | N | Y | Y | Y | N |
| **KANSAS** | | | | | | | | |
| 1 ***Roberts*** | Y | Y | N | N | Y | Y | Y | N |
| 2 Slattery | N | N | Y | Y | Y | N | Y | Y |
| 3 ***Meyers*** | Y | Y | Y | Y | Y | N | Y | N |
| 4 Glickman | N | N | Y | Y | Y | N | Y | Y |
| 5 ***Nichols*** | Y | Y | N | N | Y | Y | Y | Y |
| **KENTUCKY** | | | | | | | | |
| 1 Hubbard | N | Y | N | Y | Y | N | Y | Y |
| 2 Natcher | N | N | Y | Y | Y | N | Y | Y |
| 3 Mazzoli | N | N | Y | Y | Y | Y | Y | Y |
| 4 ***Bunning*** | Y | Y | N | N | Y | Y | Y | N |
| 5 ***Rogers*** | Y | Y | N | N | Y | Y | Y | N |
| 6 ***Hopkins*** | Y | Y | N | N | Y | Y | Y | N |
| 7 Perkins | N | N | Y | N | Y | N | N | Y |
| **LOUISIANA** | | | | | | | | |
| 1 ***Livingston*** | Y | Y | N | N | Y | Y | Y | N |
| 2 Jefferson | N | N | Y | N | Y | N | N | Y |
| 3 Tauzin | Y | Y | N | Y | Y | Y | Y | Y |
| 4 ***McCrery*** | Y | Y | N | N | Y | Y | Y | N |
| 5 Huckaby | N | Y | N | Y | Y | Y | Y | Y |
| 6 ***Baker*** | Y | Y | N | N | Y | Y | Y | N |
| 7 Hayes | N | N | N | Y | Y | Y | ? | Y |
| 8 ***Holloway*** | Y | Y | N | N | Y | Y | Y | N |
| **MAINE** | | | | | | | | |
| 1 Andrews | N | N | Y | N | Y | N | N | Y |
| 2 ***Snowe*** | Y | N | N | N | Y | N | Y | N |
| **MARYLAND** | | | | | | | | |
| 1 ***Gilchrest*** | Y | Y | N | Y | Y | Y | Y | ? |
| 2 ***Bentley*** | Y | Y | N | N | Y | Y | Y | N |
| 3 Cardin | N | N | Y | N | N | N | P | Y |
| 4 McMillen | N | N | Y | Y | Y | N | Y | Y |
| 5 Hoyer | N | N | Y | Y | Y | N | Y | Y |
| 6 Byron | # | # | X | ? | ? | # | ? | ? |
| 7 Mfume | N | N | Y | N | Y | N | Y | Y |
| 8 ***Morella*** | N | N | Y | Y | Y | N | Y | ? |
| **MASSACHUSETTS** | | | | | | | | |
| 1 Olver | N | N | Y | Y | Y | N | Y | Y |
| 2 Neal | N | N | Y | Y | Y | N | Y | Y |
| 3 Early | N | N | Y | Y | Y | N | Y | Y |
| 4 Frank | N | N | Y | Y | Y | N | N | Y |
| 5 Atkins | N | N | Y | Y | Y | N | Y | Y |
| 6 Mavroules | N | N | Y | Y | Y | N | + | Y |
| 7 Markey | N | N | Y | Y | Y | N | Y | Y |
| 8 Kennedy | N | N | Y | Y | Y | ? | ? | Y |
| 9 Moakley | ? | ? | ? | ? | ? | ? | ? | ? |
| 10 Studds | N | N | Y | Y | Y | N | Y | Y |
| 11 Donnelly | Y | N | Y | Y | Y | N | Y | Y |
| **MICHIGAN** | | | | | | | | |
| 1 Conyers | N | N | Y | N | ? | N | N | Y |
| 2 ***Pursell*** | Y | Y | N | N | Y | Y | Y | Y |
| 3 Wolpe | N | N | Y | Y | Y | N | N | Y |
| 4 ***Upton*** | Y | Y | N | Y | Y | N | Y | N |
| 5 ***Henry*** | Y | Y | N | Y | Y | N | Y | N |
| 6 Carr | N | N | Y | Y | Y | N | Y | Y |
| 7 Kildee | N | N | Y | Y | Y | N | Y | Y |
| 8 Traxler | N | N | Y | Y | Y | N | Y | Y |
| 9 ***Vander Jagt*** | Y | Y | N | N | Y | N | Y | Y |
| 10 ***Camp*** | Y | Y | N | N | Y | Y | Y | N |
| 11 ***Davis*** | Y | N | N | N | Y | Y | ? | N |
| 12 Bonior | N | N | Y | Y | Y | N | N | Y |
| 13 Collins | N | N | Y | Y | Y | N | N | Y |
| 14 Hertel | N | N | Y | Y | Y | N | N | Y |
| 15 Ford | N | N | Y | Y | Y | N | N | Y |
| 16 Dingell | N | N | Y | Y | Y | N | N | Y |
| 17 Levin | N | N | Y | Y | Y | N | Y | Y |
| 18 ***Broomfield*** | Y | Y | N | N | ? | ? | ? | P |
| **MINNESOTA** | | | | | | | | |
| 1 Penny | N | N | N | Y | Y | N | Y | Y |
| 2 ***Weber*** | Y | Y | ? | ? | ? | ? | ? | ? |
| 3 ***Ramstad*** | N | N | Y | Y | Y | Y | N | N |
| 4 Vento | N | N | Y | Y | Y | N | N | Y |

| | 101 | 102 | 103 | 104 | 105 | 106 | 107 | 108 |
|---|---|---|---|---|---|---|---|---|
| 5 Sabo | N | N | Y | Y | Y | N | N | Y |
| 6 Sikorski | N | N | Y | Y | Y | N | Y | N |
| 7 Peterson | N | N | Y | Y | Y | N | Y | Y |
| 8 Oberstar | N | N | Y | Y | Y | N | N | Y |
| **MISSISSIPPI** | | | | | | | | |
| 1 Whitten | N | N | ? | ? | ? | ? | ? | Y |
| 2 Espy | N | N | Y | Y | Y | N | Y | Y |
| 3 Montgomery | Y | Y | N | Y | Y | Y | Y | Y |
| 4 Parker | Y | Y | N | Y | Y | Y | Y | Y |
| 5 Taylor | Y | Y | N | Y | Y | Y | Y | Y |
| **MISSOURI** | | | | | | | | |
| 1 Clay | N | N | Y | N | Y | N | N | N |
| 2 Horn | N | N | Y | Y | Y | N | Y | Y |
| 3 Gephardt | N | N | Y | Y | Y | N | Y | Y |
| 4 Skelton | Y | Y | N | N | Y | Y | Y | Y |
| 5 Wheat | N | N | Y | N | Y | N | N | Y |
| 6 ***Coleman*** | Y | Y | N | N | Y | Y | Y | N |
| 7 ***Hancock*** | Y | Y | N | N | Y | Y | Y | N |
| 8 ***Emerson*** | Y | Y | N | N | Y | Y | Y | N |
| 9 Volkmer | N | Y | N | Y | Y | Y | Y | Y |
| **MONTANA** | | | | | | | | |
| 1 Williams | N | N | Y | Y | Y | N | Y | ? |
| 2 ***Marlenee*** | Y | Y | N | N | Y | Y | Y | N |
| **NEBRASKA** | | | | | | | | |
| 1 ***Bereuter*** | Y | Y | N | N | Y | Y | Y | N |
| 2 Hoagland | N | N | Y | N | Y | N | Y | Y |
| 3 ***Barrett*** | Y | Y | N | N | Y | Y | Y | N |
| **NEVADA** | | | | | | | | |
| 1 Bilbray | N | N | N | Y | Y | N | Y | Y |
| 2 ***Vucanovich*** | Y | Y | N | N | ? | Y | Y | N |
| **NEW HAMPSHIRE** | | | | | | | | |
| 1 ***Zeliff*** | Y | Y | N | N | Y | Y | Y | N |
| 2 Swett | N | N | Y | Y | Y | N | Y | Y |
| **NEW JERSEY** | | | | | | | | |
| 1 Andrews | N | N | Y | Y | Y | N | Y | Y |
| 2 Hughes | N | N | Y | Y | Y | N | N | Y |
| 3 Pallone | N | N | Y | Y | Y | N | Y | Y |
| 4 ***Smith*** | Y | Y | N | N | Y | Y | Y | Y |
| 5 ***Roukema*** | Y | Y | N | N | Y | N | Y | N |
| 6 Dwyer | N | N | Y | Y | Y | N | Y | Y |
| 7 ***Rinaldo*** | Y | N | N | N | Y | Y | Y | Y |
| 8 Roe | N | N | Y | Y | Y | N | ? | ? |
| 9 Torricelli | N | N | Y | Y | Y | N | Y | Y |
| 10 Payne | N | N | Y | N | Y | N | N | Y |
| 11 ***Gallo*** | Y | Y | N | N | Y | N | Y | ? |
| 12 ***Zimmer*** | Y | N | N | N | Y | N | Y | N |
| 13 ***Saxton*** | Y | Y | N | N | Y | Y | Y | N |
| 14 Guarini | Y | N | N | Y | Y | N | Y | ? |
| **NEW MEXICO** | | | | | | | | |
| 1 ***Schiff*** | N | Y | N | N | Y | N | Y | N |
| 2 ***Skeen*** | Y | Y | N | N | Y | Y | Y | N |
| 3 Richardson | N | N | Y | Y | Y | N | Y | Y |
| **NEW YORK** | | | | | | | | |
| 1 Hochbrueckner | N | N | Y | Y | Y | N | Y | Y |
| 2 Downey | N | N | Y | Y | Y | N | N | Y |
| 3 Mrazek | N | N | Y | Y | ? | N | N | Y |
| 4 ***Lent*** | Y | Y | N | N | Y | Y | ? | Y |
| 5 ***McGrath*** | N | Y | N | N | Y | Y | Y | Y |
| 6 Flake | N | N | Y | Y | Y | N | ? | ? |
| 7 Ackerman | N | N | Y | Y | Y | N | ? | Y |
| 8 Scheuer | N | N | Y | Y | Y | N | N | Y |
| 9 Manton | N | ? | Y | Y | Y | N | Y | Y |
| 10 Schumer | N | N | Y | Y | Y | N | N | Y |
| 11 Towns | N | N | Y | N | Y | N | N | Y |
| 12 Owens | N | N | Y | N | Y | N | N | Y |
| 13 Solarz | N | N | Y | Y | Y | N | N | Y |
| 14 ***Molinari*** | Y | Y | N | N | Y | N | Y | N |
| 15 ***Green*** | N | N | Y | Y | Y | N | N | Y |
| 16 Rangel | N | N | Y | Y | ? | N | N | ? |
| 17 Weiss | N | N | Y | N | Y | N | N | Y |
| 18 Serrano | N | N | Y | N | Y | N | N | Y |
| 19 Engel | N | N | Y | Y | Y | N | Y | Y |
| 20 Lowey | N | N | Y | Y | Y | N | Y | Y |
| 21 ***Fish*** | Y | Y | N | N | Y | N | ? | Y |
| 22 ***Gilman*** | N | N | Y | Y | Y | N | Y | Y |
| 23 McNulty | N | N | Y | Y | Y | N | Y | Y |
| 24 ***Solomon*** | Y | Y | N | N | Y | Y | Y | N |
| 25 ***Boehlert*** | N | N | Y | Y | Y | N | Y | N |
| 26 ***Martin*** | Y | Y | N | N | Y | Y | Y | N |
| 27 ***Walsh*** | N | N | N | N | Y | Y | Y | N |
| 28 McHugh | N | Y | Y | Y | ? | N | N | Y |
| 29 ***Horton*** | Y | N | Y | Y | Y | N | ? | Y |
| 30 Slaughter | N | N | Y | Y | Y | N | Y | Y |
| 31 ***Paxon*** | Y | Y | N | N | Y | Y | Y | N |

| | 101 | 102 | 103 | 104 | 105 | 106 | 107 | 108 |
|---|---|---|---|---|---|---|---|---|
| 32 LaFalce | N | Y | Y | Y | Y | Y | Y | Y |
| 33 Nowak | N | N | Y | ? | Y | N | Y | Y |
| 34 ***Houghton*** | N | Y | N | N | Y | N | Y | Y |
| **NORTH CAROLINA** | | | | | | | | |
| 1 Jones | N | N | Y | Y | Y | N | Y | Y |
| 2 Valentine | ? | ? | ? | ? | ? | ? | ? | ? |
| 3 Lancaster | N | N | Y | Y | Y | N | Y | Y |
| 4 Price | N | N | Y | Y | Y | N | Y | Y |
| 5 Neal | N | N | Y | Y | Y | N | Y | Y |
| 6 ***Coble*** | Y | Y | N | N | Y | Y | Y | N |
| 7 Rose | N | Y | Y | Y | Y | N | Y | Y |
| 8 Hefner | N | N | N | Y | Y | N | Y | Y |
| 9 ***McMillan*** | Y | Y | N | N | Y | Y | Y | ? |
| 10 ***Ballenger*** | Y | Y | N | N | Y | Y | Y | N |
| 11 ***Taylor*** | Y | Y | N | N | Y | Y | Y | N |
| **NORTH DAKOTA** | | | | | | | | |
| AL Dorgan | N | N | N | N | Y | N | Y | Y |
| **OHIO** | | | | | | | | |
| 1 Luken | N | N | Y | Y | Y | N | Y | Y |
| 2 ***Gradison*** | Y | Y | N | Y | Y | N | Y | Y |
| 3 Hall | N | Y | Y | Y | Y | N | Y | Y |
| 4 ***Oxley*** | Y | Y | N | N | Y | Y | Y | N |
| 5 ***Gillmor*** | Y | Y | N | N | Y | Y | Y | Y |
| 6 ***McEwen*** | Y | Y | N | N | Y | Y | Y | N |
| 7 ***Hobson*** | Y | Y | N | N | Y | Y | Y | N |
| 8 ***Boehner*** | Y | Y | N | N | Y | Y | Y | N |
| 9 Kaptur | N | N | Y | Y | Y | N | Y | Y |
| 10 ***Miller*** | Y | Y | N | N | Y | Y | Y | ? |
| 11 Eckart | N | N | Y | N | Y | N | Y | Y |
| 12 ***Kasich*** | Y | Y | N | N | Y | Y | Y | Y |
| 13 Pease | N | N | Y | N | Y | N | N | Y |
| 14 Sawyer | N | N | Y | Y | Y | N | Y | Y |
| 15 ***Wylie*** | Y | Y | N | N | Y | N | Y | Y |
| 16 ***Regula*** | Y | Y | N | N | Y | Y | Y | N |
| 17 Traficant | N | N | Y | Y | Y | N | Y | Y |
| 18 Applegate | N | Y | Y | Y | N | Y | Y | Y |
| 19 Feighan | N | N | Y | N | Y | N | Y | ? |
| 20 Oakar | N | N | Y | Y | Y | N | Y | Y |
| 21 Stokes | N | N | Y | N | Y | N | N | Y |
| **OKLAHOMA** | | | | | | | | |
| 1 ***Inhofe*** | Y | Y | N | N | Y | Y | Y | N |
| 2 Synar | N | N | Y | N | Y | N | Y | Y |
| 3 Brewster | N | N | Y | Y | Y | N | Y | Y |
| 4 McCurdy | N | N | Y | Y | Y | ? | ? | ? |
| 5 ***Edwards*** | Y | Y | N | N | Y | Y | Y | ? |
| 6 English | N | Y | N | Y | Y | Y | Y | Y |
| **OREGON** | | | | | | | | |
| 1 AuCoin | X | X | # | ? | ? | X | ? | ? |
| 2 ***Smith*** | Y | Y | N | Y | Y | Y | Y | N |
| 3 Wyden | N | N | Y | N | Y | N | Y | Y |
| 4 DeFazio | N | N | Y | N | Y | N | Y | Y |
| 5 Kopetski | N | N | Y | N | Y | N | Y | Y |
| **PENNSYLVANIA** | | | | | | | | |
| 1 Foglietta | N | N | Y | N | Y | N | N | Y |
| 2 Blackwell | N | N | Y | N | Y | N | N | Y |
| 3 Borski | N | N | Y | Y | Y | N | Y | Y |
| 4 Kolter | ? | ? | ? | ? | ? | ? | ? | ? |
| 5 ***Schulze*** | Y | Y | N | N | Y | Y | Y | Y |
| 6 Yatron | ? | ? | ? | ? | ? | ? | ? | ? |
| 7 ***Weldon*** | Y | Y | N | N | Y | Y | ? | N |
| 8 Kostmayer | N | N | Y | Y | Y | N | Y | Y |
| 9 ***Shuster*** | Y | Y | N | N | Y | Y | Y | N |
| 10 ***McDade*** | ? | ? | ? | ? | ? | ? | ? | N |
| 11 Kanjorski | N | Y | Y | Y | Y | Y | N | Y |
| 12 Murtha | N | N | Y | Y | ? | ? | ? | Y |
| 13 ***Coughlin*** | Y | Y | N | N | Y | Y | ? | N |
| 14 Coyne | N | N | Y | Y | Y | N | N | Y |
| 15 ***Ritter*** | Y | Y | N | N | Y | Y | Y | Y |
| 16 ***Walker*** | Y | Y | N | N | Y | Y | Y | N |
| 17 ***Gekas*** | N | Y | N | N | Y | Y | ? | N |
| 18 ***Santorum*** | Y | Y | N | N | Y | Y | Y | Y |
| 19 ***Goodling*** | Y | Y | N | N | Y | Y | Y | N |
| 20 Gaydos | N | Y | Y | Y | Y | N | Y | ? |
| 21 ***Ridge*** | Y | N | N | N | Y | N | Y | N |
| 22 Murphy | Y | Y | Y | Y | Y | N | Y | N |
| 23 ***Clinger*** | Y | Y | N | Y | Y | Y | Y | N |
| **RHODE ISLAND** | | | | | | | | |
| 1 ***Machtley*** | N | N | Y | Y | Y | N | Y | N |
| 2 Reed | N | N | Y | Y | Y | N | Y | Y |
| **SOUTH CAROLINA** | | | | | | | | |
| 1 ***Ravenel*** | Y | Y | N | N | Y | N | Y | Y |
| 2 ***Spence*** | Y | Y | N | N | Y | Y | Y | Y |
| 3 Derrick | N | N | Y | Y | Y | N | Y | Y |
| 4 Patterson | N | N | N | Y | Y | N | Y | Y |
| 5 Spratt | N | N | Y | Y | Y | N | Y | ? |
| 6 Tallon | N | N | Y | Y | Y | N | ? | Y |

| | 101 | 102 | 103 | 104 | 105 | 106 | 107 | 108 |
|---|---|---|---|---|---|---|---|---|
| **SOUTH DAKOTA** | | | | | | | | |
| AL Johnson | N | N | N | N | Y | Y | Y | Y |
| **TENNESSEE** | | | | | | | | |
| 1 ***Quillen*** | Y | Y | N | N | Y | Y | Y | N |
| 2 ***Duncan*** | Y | Y | N | N | Y | Y | Y | N |
| 3 Lloyd | N | N | N | N | Y | N | Y | Y |
| 4 Cooper | N | N | Y | Y | Y | N | Y | Y |
| 5 Clement | N | N | Y | Y | Y | N | Y | Y |
| 6 Gordon | N | N | Y | Y | Y | N | Y | Y |
| 7 ***Sundquist*** | Y | Y | N | N | Y | Y | Y | N |
| 8 Tanner | N | Y | N | N | Y | N | Y | Y |
| 9 Ford | ? | ? | ? | ? | Y | N | Y | Y |
| **TEXAS** | | | | | | | | |
| 1 Chapman | N | N | Y | Y | Y | N | Y | ? |
| 2 Wilson | Y | Y | N | Y | Y | N | Y | ? |
| 3 ***Johnson*** | Y | Y | N | N | Y | Y | Y | ? |
| 4 Hall | Y | Y | N | Y | Y | Y | Y | Y |
| 5 Bryant | N | N | Y | Y | Y | N | Y | Y |
| 6 ***Barton*** | Y | Y | N | N | Y | Y | Y | N |
| 7 ***Archer*** | Y | Y | N | N | Y | Y | Y | Y |
| 8 ***Fields*** | Y | Y | N | N | Y | Y | Y | N |
| 9 Brooks | N | N | Y | Y | Y | N | N | Y |
| 10 Pickle | Y | N | N | N | Y | N | Y | Y |
| 11 Edwards | Y | Y | N | Y | Y | Y | Y | Y |
| 12 Geren | N | Y | N | Y | Y | Y | Y | Y |
| 13 Sarpalius | Y | Y | N | Y | Y | Y | Y | Y |
| 14 Laughlin | N | Y | N | Y | Y | N | Y | Y |
| 15 de la Garza | N | Y | Y | Y | Y | N | Y | ? |
| 16 Coleman | N | N | Y | Y | Y | N | Y | Y |
| 17 Stenholm | Y | Y | N | Y | Y | Y | Y | Y |
| 18 Washington | N | N | Y | N | N | N | N | ? |
| 19 ***Combest*** | Y | Y | N | N | Y | Y | Y | Y |
| 20 Gonzalez | N | N | Y | Y | Y | N | N | Y |
| 21 ***Smith*** | Y | Y | N | N | Y | Y | Y | N |
| 22 ***DeLay*** | Y | Y | N | N | Y | Y | Y | N |
| 23 Bustamante | N | N | Y | Y | Y | N | Y | Y |
| 24 Frost | N | N | Y | Y | Y | N | Y | Y |
| 25 Andrews | N | N | Y | Y | Y | N | Y | Y |
| 26 ***Armey*** | Y | Y | N | N | Y | Y | Y | N |
| 27 Ortiz | N | N | Y | Y | Y | ? | Y | Y |
| **UTAH** | | | | | | | | |
| 1 ***Hansen*** | Y | Y | N | N | Y | Y | Y | Y |
| 2 Owens | N | N | Y | N | Y | N | Y | Y |
| 3 Orton | Y | Y | N | N | Y | Y | Y | Y |
| **VERMONT** | | | | | | | | |
| AL *Sanders* | N | N | Y | N | Y | N | N | ? |
| **VIRGINIA** | | | | | | | | |
| 1 ***Bateman*** | Y | Y | N | Y | Y | Y | ? | Y |
| 2 Pickett | N | N | Y | Y | Y | N | Y | Y |
| 3 ***Bliley*** | Y | Y | N | N | Y | Y | Y | N |
| 4 Sisisky | N | N | Y | Y | Y | N | Y | Y |
| 5 Payne | N | N | N | Y | Y | N | Y | ? |
| 6 Olin | N | N | Y | Y | Y | N | ? | Y |
| 7 ***Allen*** | Y | Y | N | N | Y | Y | Y | N |
| 8 Moran | N | N | Y | Y | Y | N | ? | Y |
| 9 Boucher | N | N | Y | Y | Y | N | Y | Y |
| 10 ***Wolf*** | Y | Y | N | N | Y | Y | Y | N |
| **WASHINGTON** | | | | | | | | |
| 1 ***Miller*** | Y | Y | N | N | Y | Y | Y | ? |
| 2 Swift | N | N | Y | Y | Y | N | Y | Y |
| 3 Unsoeld | N | N | Y | N | Y | N | N | Y |
| 4 ***Morrison*** | Y | Y | N | N | Y | Y | Y | Y |
| 5 Foley | | | | | | | | |
| 6 Dicks | N | N | Y | Y | Y | N | Y | Y |
| 7 McDermott | N | N | Y | Y | Y | N | Y | Y |
| 8 ***Chandler*** | Y | Y | N | N | Y | Y | Y | N |
| **WEST VIRGINIA** | | | | | | | | |
| 1 Mollohan | N | N | Y | Y | Y | N | Y | Y |
| 2 Staggers | N | Y | N | Y | Y | N | Y | Y |
| 3 Wise | N | N | Y | Y | Y | N | Y | Y |
| 4 Rahall | N | N | Y | Y | Y | N | N | Y |
| **WISCONSIN** | | | | | | | | |
| 1 Aspin | N | N | Y | Y | Y | N | Y | Y |
| 2 ***Klug*** | Y | Y | N | N | Y | N | Y | ? |
| 3 ***Gunderson*** | Y | Y | N | Y | Y | Y | Y | Y |
| 4 Kleczka | N | ? | Y | Y | Y | N | Y | Y |
| 5 Moody | N | N | Y | N | Y | N | Y | N |
| 6 ***Petri*** | Y | N | N | N | Y | Y | Y | Y |
| 7 Obey | N | N | Y | Y | Y | N | Y | Y |
| 8 ***Roth*** | Y | Y | N | N | Y | Y | Y | N |
| 9 ***Sensenbrenner*** | Y | Y | N | N | Y | Y | Y | N |
| **WYOMING** | | | | | | | | |
| AL ***Thomas*** | Y | Y | N | Y | Y | Y | Y | N |

Southern states - Ala., Ark., Fla., Ga., Ky., La., Miss., N.C., Okla., S.C., Tenn., Texas, Va.
Omitted votes are quorum calls, which CQ does not include in its vote charts.

**109. HR 4990. Fiscal 1992 Rescissions/Appeal Ruling of Chair.** Derrick, D-S.C., motion to table (kill) the Solomon, R-N.Y., appeal of the ruling of the chair that rejected the Solomon point of order against the rule (H Res 447) to provide for House floor consideration of the bill to rescind previously approved budget authority for fiscal 1992 for prohibiting a motion to recommit with instructions. Motion agreed to 253-161: R 0-161; D 252-0 (ND 169-0, SD 83-0); I 1-0, May 7, 1992. A "nay" was a vote in support of the president's position.

**110. HR 4990. Fiscal 1992 Rescissions/Order Previous Question.** Derrick, D-S.C., motion to order the previous question (thus limiting debate and the possibility of amendment) on the rule (H Res 447) to provide for House floor consideration of the bill to rescind previously approved budget authority for fiscal 1992. Motion agreed to 257-160: R 4-159; D 252-1 (ND 170-1, SD 82-0); I 1-0, May 7, 1992. A "nay" was a vote in support of the president's position.

**111. HR 4990. Fiscal 1992 Rescissions/Rule.** Adoption of the rule (H Res 447) for House floor consideration of the bill to rescind previously approved budget authority for fiscal 1992. Adopted 240-178: R 8-154; D 231-24 (ND 164-8, SD 67-16); I 1-0, May 7, 1992. A "nay" was a vote in support of the president's position.

**112. HR 4990. Fiscal 1992 Rescissions/President's Proposals.** Fawell, R-Ill., amendment to substitute $5.66 billion of the president's rescissions for the rescissions recommended by the House Appropriations Committee. The president's proposal rescinded funding for both a second and third *Seawolf* nuclear submarine, a total of nearly $3 billion. The committee's bill rescinded funding only for a third submarine, a total of $1.9 billion. Rejected 150-266: R 133-29; D 17-236 (ND 10-161, SD 7-75); I 0-1, May 7, 1992. A "yea" was a vote in support of the president's position.

**113. HR 4990. Fiscal 1992 Rescissions/Passage.** Passage of the bill to rescind $5,804,621,975 in previously approved budget authority for fiscal 1992, including $4.9 billion in defense, $733.9 million in domestic programs and $123.8 million in foreign aid. The bill rejected the president's rescission of the second and third *Seawolf* nuclear submarines and canceled funding only for the second submarine. In accordance with the Congressional Budget Act of 1974, the administration requested rescissions totaling $5,662,972,690. The bill did not address the president's fourth rescission package of $2.2 billion. Passed 412-2: R 159-1; D 252-1 (ND 170-1, SD 82-0); I 1-0, May 7, 1992.

**114. Procedural Motion.** Approval of the House Journal of Monday, May 11. Approved 252-116: R 42-113; D 210-3 (ND 142-3, SD 68-0); I 0-0, May 12, 1992.

**115. HR 2039. Legal Services Corporation (LSC) Reauthorization/Abortion Cases.** Gekas, R-Pa., amendment to prohibit agencies that receive funds from the LSC from engaging in litigation or lobbying regarding abortion. Rejected 188-216: R 124-35; D 64-180 (ND 39-128, SD 25-52); I 0-1, May 12, 1992. A "yea" was a vote in support of the president's position.

**116. HR 2039. Legal Services Corporation (LSC) Reauthorization/Redistricting Cases.** Stenholm, D-Texas, amendment to prohibit agencies that receive LSC funds from engaging in any redistricting activities, including local and judicial redistricting. The original bill allowed LSC-funded agencies to participate in local and judicial activities but not federal or state. Adopted 286-123: R 154-5; D 132-117 (ND 68-101, SD 64-16); I 0-1, May 12, 1992. A "yea" was a vote in support of the president's position.

## KEY

| | |
|---|---|
| Y | Voted for (yea). |
| # | Paired for. |
| + | Announced for. |
| N | Voted against (nay). |
| X | Paired against. |
| − | Announced against. |
| P | Voted "present." |
| C | Voted "present" to avoid possible conflict of interest. |
| ? | Did not vote or otherwise make a position known. |

Democrats  **Republicans**  *Independent*

| | 109 | 110 | 111 | 112 | 113 | 114 | 115 | 116 |
|---|---|---|---|---|---|---|---|---|
| **ALABAMA** | | | | | | | | |
| 1 *Callahan* | N | N | N | Y | Y | N | Y | Y |
| 2 *Dickinson* | N | N | N | Y | Y | N | Y | ? |
| 3 Browder | Y | Y | Y | N | Y | Y | N | Y |
| 4 Bevill | Y | Y | Y | N | Y | Y | N | Y |
| 5 Cramer | Y | Y | Y | N | Y | Y | N | Y |
| 6 Erdreich | Y | Y | Y | N | Y | Y | N | Y |
| 7 Harris | Y | Y | Y | N | Y | Y | N | Y |
| **ALASKA** | | | | | | | | |
| AL *Young* | N | N | N | Y | Y | N | Y | Y |
| **ARIZONA** | | | | | | | | |
| 1 *Rhodes* | N | N | N | Y | Y | N | Y | Y |
| 2 Pastor | # | + | + | − | + | Y | N | N |
| 3 *Stump* | N | N | N | Y | Y | N | Y | Y |
| 4 *Kyl* | N | N | N | Y | Y | N | Y | Y |
| 5 *Kolbe* | N | N | N | Y | Y | N | Y | Y |
| **ARKANSAS** | | | | | | | | |
| 1 Alexander | Y | Y | Y | N | Y | ? | ? | ? |
| 2 Thornton | Y | Y | Y | N | Y | Y | Y | Y |
| 3 *Hammerschmidt* | N | N | N | Y | Y | Y | Y | Y |
| 4 Anthony | Y | Y | Y | N | Y | Y | N | Y |
| **CALIFORNIA** | | | | | | | | |
| 1 *Riggs* | N | N | N | Y | Y | N | Y | Y |
| 2 *Herger* | N | N | N | Y | Y | N | Y | Y |
| 3 Matsui | Y | Y | Y | N | Y | Y | N | N |
| 4 Fazio | Y | Y | Y | N | Y | Y | N | N |
| 5 Pelosi | Y | Y | Y | N | Y | Y | N | N |
| 6 Boxer | ? | ? | ? | ? | ? | ? | N | N |
| 7 Miller | Y | Y | Y | N | Y | Y | N | N |
| 8 Dellums | Y | Y | Y | N | Y | Y | N | N |
| 9 Stark | Y | Y | Y | N | Y | Y | N | N |
| 10 Edwards | Y | Y | Y | N | Y | Y | N | N |
| 11 Lantos | Y | Y | Y | N | Y | Y | N | N |
| 12 *Campbell* | ? | ? | ? | ? | ? | N | N | Y |
| 13 Mineta | Y | Y | Y | N | Y | Y | N | N |
| 14 *Doolittle* | N | N | N | Y | Y | N | Y | Y |
| 15 Condit | Y | Y | N | Y | Y | Y | N | Y |
| 16 Panetta | Y | Y | Y | N | Y | Y | N | N |
| 17 Dooley | Y | Y | Y | N | Y | Y | N | N |
| 18 Lehman | Y | Y | Y | N | Y | ? | N | N |
| 19 *Lagomarsino* | N | N | N | Y | Y | N | Y | Y |
| 20 *Thomas* | N | N | N | Y | Y | N | Y | Y |
| 21 *Gallegly* | N | N | N | Y | Y | N | Y | Y |
| 22 *Moorhead* | N | N | N | Y | Y | N | Y | Y |
| 23 Beilenson | Y | Y | Y | N | Y | Y | N | N |
| 24 Waxman | Y | Y | Y | N | Y | ? | N | N |
| 25 Roybal | Y | Y | Y | N | Y | ? | N | N |
| 26 Berman | Y | Y | Y | N | Y | Y | N | N |
| 27 Levine | ? | ? | ? | ? | ? | ? | ? | ? |
| 28 Dixon | Y | Y | Y | N | Y | ? | N | N |
| 29 Waters | + | + | + | − | + | Y | ? | N |
| 30 Martinez | Y | Y | Y | N | Y | Y | N | N |
| 31 Dymally | Y | Y | Y | N | Y | ? | ? | ? |
| 32 Anderson | Y | Y | Y | N | Y | Y | N | N |
| 33 *Dreier* | N | N | N | Y | Y | N | Y | Y |
| 34 Torres | Y | Y | Y | N | Y | ? | N | N |
| 35 *Lewis* | N | N | N | N | Y | N | Y | Y |
| 36 Brown | Y | Y | Y | N | Y | Y | N | N |
| 37 *McCandless* | N | N | N | Y | Y | N | Y | Y |
| 38 *Dornan* | N | N | N | Y | Y | N | Y | Y |
| 39 *Dannemeyer* | − | − | − | + | + | ? | ? | ? |
| 40 *Cox* | N | N | N | Y | Y | N | Y | Y |
| 41 Lowery | N | N | N | Y | Y | N | Y | Y |

| | 109 | 110 | 111 | 112 | 113 | 114 | 115 | 116 |
|---|---|---|---|---|---|---|---|---|
| 42 *Rohrabacher* | N | N | N | Y | Y | N | Y | Y |
| 43 *Packard* | N | N | N | Y | Y | Y | Y | Y |
| 44 *Cunningham* | N | N | N | Y | Y | N | Y | Y |
| 45 *Hunter* | N | N | N | Y | Y | N | Y | Y |
| **COLORADO** | | | | | | | | |
| 1 Schroeder | Y | Y | Y | N | Y | ? | N | N |
| 2 Skaggs | Y | Y | Y | N | Y | Y | N | N |
| 3 Campbell | Y | Y | Y | ? | ? | Y | N | Y |
| 4 *Allard* | N | N | N | Y | Y | N | Y | Y |
| 5 *Hefley* | N | N | N | Y | Y | N | Y | Y |
| 6 *Schaefer* | N | N | N | Y | Y | N | Y | Y |
| **CONNECTICUT** | | | | | | | | |
| 1 Kennelly | Y | Y | Y | N | Y | Y | N | N |
| 2 Gejdenson | Y | Y | Y | N | Y | Y | N | N |
| 3 DeLauro | Y | Y | Y | N | Y | Y | N | N |
| 4 *Shays* | N | N | N | N | Y | N | Y | N |
| 5 *Franks* | N | Y | Y | N | Y | N | N | Y |
| 6 *Johnson* | N | Y | Y | N | Y | N | N | Y |
| **DELAWARE** | | | | | | | | |
| AL Carper | Y | Y | N | N | Y | Y | N | Y |
| **FLORIDA** | | | | | | | | |
| 1 Hutto | Y | Y | N | Y | Y | Y | Y | Y |
| 2 Peterson | Y | Y | Y | N | Y | Y | N | Y |
| 3 Bennett | Y | Y | Y | N | Y | Y | Y | Y |
| 4 *James* | N | N | N | Y | Y | N | C | C |
| 5 *McCollum* | N | N | N | Y | Y | N | Y | Y |
| 6 *Stearns* | N | N | N | Y | Y | N | Y | Y |
| 7 Gibbons | Y | Y | Y | Y | Y | Y | N | N |
| 8 *Young* | N | N | N | Y | Y | N | Y | Y |
| 9 *Bilirakis* | N | N | N | Y | Y | N | Y | Y |
| 10 *Ireland* | N | N | N | Y | Y | N | Y | Y |
| 11 Bacchus | Y | Y | Y | N | Y | Y | N | N |
| 12 *Lewis* | N | N | N | Y | Y | N | Y | Y |
| 13 *Goss* | N | N | N | Y | Y | N | Y | Y |
| 14 Johnston | Y | Y | Y | N | Y | Y | N | N |
| 15 *Shaw* | N | N | N | Y | Y | N | Y | Y |
| 16 Smith | Y | Y | Y | N | Y | Y | N | N |
| 17 Lehman | ? | ? | ? | ? | ? | ? | Y | N |
| 18 *Ros−Lehtinen* | N | N | N | Y | Y | N | Y | Y |
| 19 Fascell | Y | Y | Y | N | Y | ? | Y | N |
| **GEORGIA** | | | | | | | | |
| 1 Thomas | Y | Y | Y | N | Y | Y | N | Y |
| 2 Hatcher | Y | Y | Y | N | Y | Y | N | Y |
| 3 Ray | Y | Y | Y | Y | Y | Y | Y | Y |
| 4 Jones | Y | Y | Y | N | Y | Y | N | Y |
| 5 Lewis | Y | Y | Y | N | Y | Y | N | N |
| 6 *Gingrich* | N | N | N | Y | Y | N | Y | Y |
| 7 Darden | Y | Y | Y | N | Y | Y | N | Y |
| 8 Rowland | Y | Y | Y | N | Y | Y | N | Y |
| 9 Jenkins | Y | Y | Y | N | Y | ? | ? | Y |
| 10 Barnard | Y | Y | N | ? | ? | ? | ? | Y |
| **HAWAII** | | | | | | | | |
| 1 Abercrombie | Y | Y | Y | N | Y | Y | N | N |
| 2 Mink | Y | Y | Y | N | Y | Y | N | Y |
| **IDAHO** | | | | | | | | |
| 1 LaRocco | Y | Y | Y | N | Y | Y | N | Y |
| 2 Stallings | Y | Y | Y | N | Y | Y | N | Y |
| **ILLINOIS** | | | | | | | | |
| 1 Hayes | Y | Y | Y | N | Y | Y | N | N |
| 2 Savage | Y | Y | Y | N | Y | ? | N | N |
| 3 Russo | ? | Y | Y | Y | Y | Y | Y | N |
| 4 Sangmeister | Y | Y | Y | N | Y | Y | N | N |
| 5 Lipinski | Y | Y | Y | N | Y | Y | Y | N |
| 6 *Hyde* | N | N | N | Y | Y | N | Y | ? |
| 7 Collins | # | Y | Y | N | Y | Y | ? | X |
| 8 Rostenkowski | Y | Y | Y | N | Y | Y | N | N |
| 9 Yates | Y | Y | Y | N | Y | Y | N | N |
| 10 *Porter* | N | N | N | Y | Y | N | Y | Y |
| 11 Annunzio | Y | Y | Y | N | Y | Y | N | N |
| 12 *Crane* | N | N | N | Y | Y | N | Y | Y |
| 13 *Fawell* | N | N | N | Y | Y | N | Y | Y |
| 14 *Hastert* | N | N | N | Y | Y | N | Y | Y |
| 15 *Ewing* | N | N | N | Y | Y | N | Y | Y |
| 16 Cox | Y | Y | Y | N | Y | Y | N | N |
| 17 Evans | Y | Y | Y | N | Y | Y | N | N |
| 18 *Michel* | N | N | N | Y | Y | N | Y | Y |
| 19 Bruce | Y | Y | Y | N | Y | Y | N | N |
| 20 Durbin | Y | Y | Y | N | Y | Y | N | N |
| 21 Costello | Y | Y | Y | N | Y | Y | N | N |
| 22 Poshard | Y | Y | Y | N | Y | Y | Y | Y |
| **INDIANA** | | | | | | | | |
| 1 Visclosky | Y | Y | Y | N | Y | Y | N | Y |
| 2 Sharp | Y | Y | Y | N | Y | Y | N | N |
| 3 Roemer | Y | Y | Y | N | Y | Y | Y | Y |

ND  Northern Democrats   SD  Southern Democrats

| | 109 | 110 | 111 | 112 | 113 | 114 | 115 | 116 |
|---|---|---|---|---|---|---|---|---|
| 4 Long | Y | Y | Y | N | Y | Y | N | Y |
| 5 Jontz | Y | Y | N | Y | Y | Y | N | N |
| 6 ***Burton*** | N | N | N | Y | Y | N | Y | Y |
| 7 ***Myers*** | N | N | N | N | Y | Y | Y | Y |
| 8 McCloskey | Y | Y | Y | N | Y | Y | N | N |
| 9 Hamilton | Y | Y | Y | N | Y | Y | N | Y |
| 10 Jacobs | Y | N | N | N | Y | ? | N | Y |
| **IOWA** | | | | | | | | |
| 1 ***Leach*** | N | N | N | Y | Y | N | N | N |
| 2 ***Nussle*** | N | N | N | Y | Y | N | Y | Y |
| 3 Nagle | Y | Y | Y | N | Y | Y | N | Y |
| 4 Smith | Y | Y | Y | N | Y | Y | N | Y |
| 5 ***Lightfoot*** | N | N | N | N | Y | N | # | # |
| 6 ***Grandy*** | N | N | N | Y | Y | N | Y | Y |
| **KANSAS** | | | | | | | | |
| 1 ***Roberts*** | N | N | N | Y | Y | N | Y | Y |
| 2 Slattery | Y | Y | Y | N | Y | Y | Y | N |
| 3 ***Meyers*** | N | N | N | Y | Y | N | N | Y |
| 4 Glickman | Y | Y | Y | Y | Y | Y | N | Y |
| 5 ***Nichols*** | N | N | N | Y | Y | Y | N | Y |
| **KENTUCKY** | | | | | | | | |
| 1 Hubbard | Y | Y | N | Y | Y | Y | N | Y |
| 2 Natcher | Y | Y | Y | N | Y | Y | Y | Y |
| 3 Mazzoli | Y | Y | Y | N | Y | Y | Y | N |
| 4 ***Bunning*** | N | N | N | Y | Y | N | Y | Y |
| 5 ***Rogers*** | N | N | N | Y | Y | N | Y | Y |
| 6 ***Hopkins*** | N | N | N | Y | Y | N | Y | Y |
| 7 Perkins | Y | Y | Y | N | Y | Y | Y | N |
| **LOUISIANA** | | | | | | | | |
| 1 ***Livingston*** | N | N | N | N | + | Y | Y | Y |
| 2 Jefferson | Y | Y | Y | N | Y | ? | ? | ? |
| 3 Tauzin | Y | Y | N | N | Y | Y | Y | Y |
| 4 ***McCrery*** | N | N | N | Y | Y | Y | Y | Y |
| 5 Huckaby | Y | Y | N | N | Y | Y | Y | Y |
| 6 ***Baker*** | N | N | N | Y | Y | N | Y | Y |
| 7 Hayes | Y | Y | Y | N | Y | ? | ? | Y |
| 8 ***Holloway*** | X | N | N | Y | Y | N | Y | Y |
| **MAINE** | | | | | | | | |
| 1 Andrews | Y | Y | Y | N | Y | Y | N | N |
| 2 ***Snowe*** | N | N | N | Y | Y | Y | N | Y |
| **MARYLAND** | | | | | | | | |
| 1 ***Gilchrest*** | N | N | N | Y | Y | N | N | Y |
| 2 ***Bentley*** | N | N | N | Y | Y | N | Y | Y |
| 3 Cardin | Y | Y | Y | N | Y | Y | N | N |
| 4 McMillen | Y | Y | Y | N | Y | Y | N | Y |
| 5 Hoyer | Y | Y | Y | N | Y | Y | N | N |
| 6 Byron | ? | ? | ? | ? | ? | ? | ? | # |
| 7 Mfume | Y | Y | Y | N | Y | ? | N | N |
| 8 ***Morella*** | N | N | N | Y | Y | ? | N | Y |
| **MASSACHUSETTS** | | | | | | | | |
| 1 Olver | Y | Y | Y | N | Y | Y | N | N |
| 2 Neal | Y | Y | Y | N | Y | ? | Y | Y |
| 3 Early | Y | Y | Y | N | Y | Y | Y | Y |
| 4 Frank | Y | Y | Y | N | Y | Y | N | N |
| 5 Atkins | Y | Y | N | Y | Y | Y | N | N |
| 6 Mavroules | Y | Y | Y | N | Y | Y | Y | Y |
| 7 Markey | Y | Y | Y | N | Y | Y | N | N |
| 8 Kennedy | Y | Y | Y | Y | N | Y | N | N |
| 9 Moakley | ? | ? | ? | ? | ? | ? | ? | ? |
| 10 Studds | Y | Y | Y | N | Y | Y | N | N |
| 11 Donnelly | Y | Y | Y | N | Y | ? | Y | Y |
| **MICHIGAN** | | | | | | | | |
| 1 Conyers | Y | Y | Y | N | Y | Y | N | N |
| 2 ***Pursell*** | N | N | N | Y | Y | Y | N | Y |
| 3 Wolpe | Y | Y | Y | N | Y | Y | N | N |
| 4 ***Upton*** | N | N | N | Y | Y | N | Y | Y |
| 5 ***Henry*** | N | N | N | Y | Y | N | Y | Y |
| 6 Carr | Y | Y | Y | N | Y | Y | Y | Y |
| 7 Kildee | Y | Y | Y | N | Y | Y | Y | N |
| 8 Traxler | Y | Y | Y | N | Y | Y | N | N |
| 9 ***Vander Jagt*** | N | N | N | Y | Y | Y | Y | Y |
| 10 ***Camp*** | N | N | N | Y | Y | N | Y | Y |
| 11 ***Davis*** | N | N | N | Y | N | N | Y | Y |
| 12 Bonior | Y | Y | Y | N | Y | Y | N | N |
| 13 Collins | Y | Y | Y | N | Y | Y | N | N |
| 14 Hertel | Y | Y | Y | N | Y | Y | N | N |
| 15 Ford | Y | Y | Y | N | Y | ? | N | N |
| 16 Dingell | Y | Y | Y | N | Y | Y | N | Y |
| 17 Levin | Y | Y | Y | N | Y | Y | N | N |
| 18 ***Broomfield*** | N | N | N | Y | ? | Y | Y | Y |
| **MINNESOTA** | | | | | | | | |
| 1 Penny | Y | Y | Y | Y | Y | Y | Y | Y |
| 2 ***Weber*** | ? | ? | ? | ? | ? | N | ? | Y |
| 3 ***Ramstad*** | N | N | N | Y | Y | Y | N | Y |
| 4 Vento | Y | Y | Y | N | Y | Y | N | N |

| | 109 | 110 | 111 | 112 | 113 | 114 | 115 | 116 |
|---|---|---|---|---|---|---|---|---|
| 5 Sabo | Y | Y | Y | N | Y | Y | N | N |
| 6 Sikorski | Y | Y | Y | N | Y | N | N | N |
| 7 Peterson | Y | Y | Y | N | Y | Y | Y | Y |
| 8 Oberstar | Y | Y | Y | N | Y | Y | N | N |
| **MISSISSIPPI** | | | | | | | | |
| 1 Whitten | Y | Y | Y | N | Y | ? | ? | ? |
| 2 Espy | Y | Y | Y | N | Y | ? | N | N |
| 3 Montgomery | Y | Y | Y | N | Y | Y | Y | Y |
| 4 Parker | Y | Y | Y | N | Y | Y | Y | Y |
| 5 Taylor | Y | Y | Y | N | Y | Y | Y | Y |
| **MISSOURI** | | | | | | | | |
| 1 Clay | Y | Y | Y | N | Y | N | N | N |
| 2 Horn | Y | Y | Y | N | Y | Y | N | Y |
| 3 Gephardt | Y | Y | Y | N | Y | Y | N | N |
| 4 Skelton | Y | Y | Y | N | Y | Y | Y | Y |
| 5 Wheat | Y | Y | Y | N | Y | Y | N | N |
| 6 ***Coleman*** | N | N | N | Y | Y | N | Y | Y |
| 7 ***Hancock*** | N | N | N | Y | Y | N | Y | Y |
| 8 ***Emerson*** | N | N | N | Y | Y | N | Y | Y |
| 9 Volkmer | Y | Y | Y | N | Y | ? | Y | Y |
| **MONTANA** | | | | | | | | |
| 1 Williams | Y | Y | Y | N | Y | Y | N | N |
| 2 ***Marlenee*** | N | N | N | Y | Y | ? | Y | Y |
| **NEBRASKA** | | | | | | | | |
| 1 ***Bereuter*** | N | N | N | Y | Y | ? | ? | ? |
| 2 Hoagland | Y | Y | Y | N | Y | Y | N | N |
| 3 ***Barrett*** | N | N | N | N | Y | N | N | Y |
| **NEVADA** | | | | | | | | |
| 1 Bilbray | Y | Y | Y | N | Y | Y | Y | Y |
| 2 ***Vucanovich*** | N | N | N | Y | Y | N | Y | Y |
| **NEW HAMPSHIRE** | | | | | | | | |
| 1 ***Zeliff*** | N | N | N | Y | Y | N | Y | Y |
| 2 Swett | Y | Y | N | Y | Y | Y | N | N |
| **NEW JERSEY** | | | | | | | | |
| 1 Andrews | Y | Y | Y | N | Y | Y | N | Y |
| 2 Hughes | Y | Y | Y | N | Y | Y | N | Y |
| 3 Pallone | Y | Y | Y | N | Y | Y | N | N |
| 4 ***Smith*** | N | N | N | N | Y | Y | Y | Y |
| 5 ***Roukema*** | N | N | N | Y | Y | N | N | Y |
| 6 Dwyer | Y | Y | Y | N | Y | Y | N | N |
| 7 ***Rinaldo*** | N | N | N | N | Y | Y | Y | Y |
| 8 Roe | Y | Y | Y | N | Y | ? | Y | N |
| 9 Torricelli | Y | Y | Y | N | Y | Y | ? | N |
| 10 Payne | Y | Y | Y | N | Y | Y | N | N |
| 11 ***Gallo*** | N | N | N | Y | Y | N | N | Y |
| 12 ***Zimmer*** | N | N | N | Y | Y | N | N | Y |
| 13 ***Saxton*** | N | N | N | Y | Y | N | Y | Y |
| 14 Guarini | Y | Y | Y | N | Y | Y | Y | Y |
| **NEW MEXICO** | | | | | | | | |
| 1 ***Schiff*** | N | N | N | Y | Y | ? | Y | Y |
| 2 ***Skeen*** | N | N | Y | N | Y | Y | Y | Y |
| 3 Richardson | Y | Y | Y | N | Y | Y | N | Y |
| **NEW YORK** | | | | | | | | |
| 1 Hochbrueckner | Y | Y | Y | N | Y | Y | N | N |
| 2 Downey | Y | Y | Y | N | Y | Y | N | N |
| 3 Mrazek | Y | Y | Y | N | Y | ? | ? | ? |
| 4 ***Lent*** | N | N | Y | Y | Y | Y | Y | Y |
| 5 ***McGrath*** | N | N | N | Y | Y | Y | Y | Y |
| 6 Flake | ? | ? | ? | N | Y | Y | N | N |
| 7 Ackerman | Y | Y | Y | N | Y | Y | ? | ? |
| 8 Scheuer | Y | Y | Y | N | Y | ? | N | N |
| 9 Manton | Y | Y | Y | N | Y | Y | Y | Y |
| 10 Schumer | Y | Y | Y | N | Y | Y | N | N |
| 11 Towns | Y | Y | Y | N | Y | Y | N | N |
| 12 Owens | Y | Y | Y | N | Y | Y | N | N |
| 13 Solarz | Y | Y | Y | N | Y | Y | N | N |
| 14 ***Molinari*** | N | N | N | Y | Y | N | N | N |
| 15 ***Green*** | N | N | N | Y | Y | Y | N | N |
| 16 Rangel | Y | Y | Y | N | Y | Y | N | N |
| 17 Weiss | Y | Y | Y | N | Y | ? | N | N |
| 18 Serrano | Y | Y | Y | N | Y | Y | N | N |
| 19 Engel | Y | Y | Y | N | Y | ? | X | X |
| 20 Lowey | Y | Y | Y | N | Y | ? | N | N |
| 21 ***Fish*** | N | N | N | Y | Y | Y | Y | Y |
| 22 ***Gilman*** | N | N | N | N | Y | Y | N | Y |
| 23 McNulty | Y | Y | Y | N | Y | Y | Y | Y |
| 24 ***Solomon*** | N | N | N | Y | Y | N | Y | Y |
| 25 ***Boehlert*** | N | N | N | Y | Y | N | N | N |
| 26 ***Martin*** | N | N | N | Y | Y | N | Y | Y |
| 27 ***Walsh*** | N | Y | Y | N | Y | N | Y | Y |
| 28 McHugh | Y | Y | Y | N | Y | Y | N | Y |
| 29 ***Horton*** | N | N | N | Y | Y | Y | N | N |
| 30 Slaughter | Y | Y | Y | N | Y | Y | N | N |
| 31 ***Paxon*** | N | N | N | Y | Y | N | Y | Y |

| | 109 | 110 | 111 | 112 | 113 | 114 | 115 | 116 |
|---|---|---|---|---|---|---|---|---|
| 32 LaFalce | Y | Y | Y | N | Y | ? | Y | Y |
| 33 Nowak | Y | Y | Y | N | Y | ? | Y | Y |
| 34 ***Houghton*** | N | N | N | Y | Y | Y | N | Y |
| **NORTH CAROLINA** | | | | | | | | |
| 1 Jones | Y | Y | Y | N | Y | Y | N | Y |
| 2 Valentine | ? | ? | ? | ? | ? | ? | Y | Y |
| 3 Lancaster | Y | Y | Y | N | Y | Y | N | Y |
| 4 Price | Y | Y | Y | N | Y | Y | N | Y |
| 5 Neal | Y | Y | Y | N | Y | Y | N | Y |
| 6 ***Coble*** | N | N | N | Y | Y | N | Y | Y |
| 7 Rose | Y | Y | Y | N | Y | Y | N | Y |
| 8 Hefner | Y | Y | Y | N | Y | Y | N | Y |
| 9 ***McMillan*** | N | N | N | Y | Y | N | Y | Y |
| 10 ***Ballenger*** | N | N | N | ? | ? | N | Y | Y |
| 11 ***Taylor*** | N | N | N | Y | Y | N | Y | Y |
| **NORTH DAKOTA** | | | | | | | | |
| AL Dorgan | Y | Y | Y | N | Y | Y | N | Y |
| **OHIO** | | | | | | | | |
| 1 Luken | Y | Y | Y | N | Y | Y | Y | Y |
| 2 ***Gradison*** | N | N | N | N | Y | N | N | Y |
| 3 Hall | Y | Y | Y | N | Y | Y | Y | N |
| 4 ***Oxley*** | N | N | N | N | Y | N | Y | Y |
| 5 ***Gillmor*** | N | N | N | N | Y | Y | Y | Y |
| 6 ***McEwen*** | N | N | N | Y | Y | ? | ? | ? |
| 7 ***Hobson*** | N | N | N | Y | Y | N | Y | Y |
| 8 ***Boehner*** | N | N | N | Y | Y | N | Y | Y |
| 9 Kaptur | Y | Y | Y | N | Y | Y | Y | N |
| 10 ***Miller*** | N | N | N | N | Y | N | Y | Y |
| 11 Eckart | Y | Y | Y | N | Y | Y | N | Y |
| 12 ***Kasich*** | N | N | N | Y | Y | Y | Y | Y |
| 13 Pease | Y | Y | Y | N | Y | Y | N | N |
| 14 Sawyer | Y | Y | Y | N | Y | Y | N | N |
| 15 ***Wylie*** | N | N | N | Y | Y | Y | Y | Y |
| 16 ***Regula*** | N | N | N | N | Y | N | Y | Y |
| 17 Traficant | Y | Y | Y | N | Y | Y | N | Y |
| 18 Applegate | Y | Y | Y | N | Y | Y | Y | Y |
| 19 Feighan | ? | Y | Y | N | Y | ? | N | N |
| 20 Oakar | Y | Y | Y | ? | ? | ? | ? | ? |
| 21 Stokes | Y | Y | Y | N | Y | ? | N | N |
| **OKLAHOMA** | | | | | | | | |
| 1 ***Inhofe*** | N | N | N | Y | Y | N | Y | Y |
| 2 Synar | Y | Y | Y | N | Y | Y | N | N |
| 3 Brewster | Y | Y | Y | N | Y | Y | N | Y |
| 4 McCurdy | Y | Y | Y | N | Y | Y | N | Y |
| 5 ***Edwards*** | N | N | N | Y | Y | N | Y | Y |
| 6 English | Y | Y | Y | N | Y | Y | Y | Y |
| **OREGON** | | | | | | | | |
| 1 AuCoin | ? | ? | ? | ? | ? | ? | X | ? |
| 2 ***Smith*** | N | N | N | Y | Y | N | Y | Y |
| 3 Wyden | Y | Y | Y | N | Y | Y | N | N |
| 4 DeFazio | Y | Y | Y | N | Y | Y | N | N |
| 5 Kopetski | Y | Y | Y | N | Y | Y | N | N |
| **PENNSYLVANIA** | | | | | | | | |
| 1 Foglietta | Y | Y | Y | N | Y | ? | N | N |
| 2 Blackwell | Y | Y | Y | N | Y | Y | N | N |
| 3 Borski | Y | Y | Y | N | Y | Y | Y | Y |
| 4 Kolter | ? | ? | ? | ? | ? | ? | ? | ? |
| 5 ***Schulze*** | N | N | N | Y | Y | ? | Y | Y |
| 6 Yatron | ? | ? | ? | ? | ? | Y | Y | Y |
| 7 ***Weldon*** | N | N | N | Y | Y | N | Y | Y |
| 8 Kostmayer | Y | Y | Y | N | Y | Y | N | N |
| 9 ***Shuster*** | N | N | N | Y | Y | N | Y | Y |
| 10 ***McDade*** | N | N | N | N | Y | ? | Y | Y |
| 11 Kanjorski | Y | Y | Y | N | Y | Y | Y | Y |
| 12 Murtha | Y | Y | Y | N | Y | Y | Y | Y |
| 13 ***Coughlin*** | N | N | N | Y | Y | N | N | Y |
| 14 Coyne | Y | Y | Y | N | Y | Y | N | N |
| 15 ***Ritter*** | N | N | N | Y | Y | Y | Y | Y |
| 16 ***Walker*** | N | N | N | Y | Y | N | Y | Y |
| 17 ***Gekas*** | N | N | N | Y | Y | N | Y | Y |
| 18 ***Santorum*** | N | N | N | Y | Y | Y | Y | Y |
| 19 ***Goodling*** | N | N | N | Y | Y | ? | Y | Y |
| 20 Gaydos | Y | Y | Y | N | Y | ? | Y | Y |
| 21 ***Ridge*** | N | N | N | Y | Y | N | N | Y |
| 22 Murphy | Y | Y | Y | N | Y | Y | N | Y |
| 23 ***Clinger*** | N | N | N | Y | Y | Y | Y | Y |
| **RHODE ISLAND** | | | | | | | | |
| 1 ***Machtley*** | N | Y | Y | N | Y | N | N | Y |
| 2 Reed | Y | Y | Y | N | Y | Y | N | N |
| **SOUTH CAROLINA** | | | | | | | | |
| 1 ***Ravenel*** | N | N | N | N | Y | Y | N | Y |
| 2 ***Spence*** | N | N | N | Y | Y | Y | Y | Y |
| 3 Derrick | Y | Y | Y | N | Y | Y | N | Y |
| 4 Patterson | Y | Y | N | Y | Y | Y | N | Y |
| 5 Spratt | Y | Y | Y | N | Y | Y | N | Y |
| 6 Tallon | Y | Y | Y | N | Y | ? | ? | ? |

| | 109 | 110 | 111 | 112 | 113 | 114 | 115 | 116 |
|---|---|---|---|---|---|---|---|---|
| **SOUTH DAKOTA** | | | | | | | | |
| AL Johnson | Y | Y | Y | N | Y | Y | Y | Y |
| **TENNESSEE** | | | | | | | | |
| 1 ***Quillen*** | N | N | N | N | Y | N | Y | Y |
| 2 ***Duncan*** | N | N | N | Y | Y | Y | Y | Y |
| 3 Lloyd | Y | Y | Y | N | Y | Y | N | Y |
| 4 Cooper | Y | Y | Y | Y | Y | Y | Y | Y |
| 5 Clement | Y | Y | Y | N | Y | ? | Y | Y |
| 6 Gordon | Y | Y | Y | N | Y | Y | N | Y |
| 7 ***Sundquist*** | N | N | N | Y | Y | N | Y | Y |
| 8 Tanner | Y | Y | N | N | Y | Y | N | Y |
| 9 Ford | Y | Y | Y | N | Y | Y | N | N |
| **TEXAS** | | | | | | | | |
| 1 Chapman | Y | Y | Y | N | Y | ? | N | Y |
| 2 Wilson | Y | Y | Y | N | Y | Y | N | Y |
| 3 ***Johnson*** | N | N | N | Y | Y | Y | Y | Y |
| 4 Hall | Y | Y | N | N | Y | Y | Y | Y |
| 5 Bryant | Y | Y | Y | N | Y | ? | ? | ? |
| 6 ***Barton*** | N | N | N | Y | Y | N | Y | N |
| 7 ***Archer*** | N | N | ? | Y | Y | Y | Y | Y |
| 8 ***Fields*** | N | N | N | Y | Y | N | Y | Y |
| 9 Brooks | Y | ? | Y | N | Y | Y | N | Y |
| 10 Pickle | Y | Y | Y | N | Y | Y | N | Y |
| 11 Edwards | Y | Y | Y | N | Y | Y | Y | Y |
| 12 Geren | Y | Y | Y | N | Y | ? | Y | Y |
| 13 Sarpalius | Y | Y | Y | N | Y | ? | Y | Y |
| 14 Laughlin | Y | Y | Y | N | Y | Y | Y | Y |
| 15 de la Garza | Y | Y | Y | N | Y | Y | Y | N |
| 16 Coleman | Y | Y | Y | N | Y | Y | N | N |
| 17 Stenholm | Y | Y | N | Y | Y | Y | Y | Y |
| 18 Washington | Y | Y | Y | N | Y | ? | N | N |
| 19 ***Combest*** | N | N | N | Y | Y | Y | Y | Y |
| 20 Gonzalez | Y | Y | Y | N | Y | Y | N | N |
| 21 ***Smith*** | N | N | N | Y | Y | N | Y | Y |
| 22 ***DeLay*** | N | N | N | Y | Y | ? | Y | Y |
| 23 Bustamante | Y | Y | Y | N | Y | Y | N | N |
| 24 Frost | Y | Y | Y | N | Y | ? | N | N |
| 25 Andrews | Y | Y | Y | N | Y | Y | N | Y |
| 26 ***Armey*** | N | N | N | Y | Y | ? | # | Y |
| 27 Ortiz | Y | Y | Y | N | Y | Y | Y | N |
| **UTAH** | | | | | | | | |
| 1 ***Hansen*** | N | N | N | Y | Y | Y | Y | Y |
| 2 Owens | Y | Y | Y | N | Y | Y | N | N |
| 3 Orton | Y | Y | N | Y | Y | Y | Y | Y |
| **VERMONT** | | | | | | | | |
| AL *Sanders* | Y | Y | Y | N | Y | ? | N | N |
| **VIRGINIA** | | | | | | | | |
| 1 ***Bateman*** | N | N | N | Y | Y | Y | Y | Y |
| 2 Pickett | Y | Y | N | Y | Y | Y | N | Y |
| 3 ***Bliley*** | N | N | N | Y | Y | N | Y | Y |
| 4 Sisisky | Y | Y | N | N | Y | Y | N | Y |
| 5 Payne | Y | Y | N | N | Y | Y | N | Y |
| 6 Olin | Y | Y | N | N | Y | Y | N | Y |
| 7 ***Allen*** | N | N | N | Y | Y | N | Y | Y |
| 8 Moran | Y | Y | Y | N | Y | Y | N | Y |
| 9 Boucher | Y | Y | Y | N | Y | Y | N | Y |
| 10 ***Wolf*** | N | N | N | Y | Y | N | Y | Y |
| **WASHINGTON** | | | | | | | | |
| 1 ***Miller*** | X | N | N | Y | Y | N | N | Y |
| 2 Swift | Y | Y | Y | N | Y | Y | N | Y |
| 3 Unsoeld | Y | Y | Y | N | Y | Y | N | N |
| 4 ***Morrison*** | N | N | N | Y | Y | Y | N | Y |
| 5 Foley | | | | | | | | |
| 6 Dicks | Y | Y | Y | N | Y | Y | N | Y |
| 7 McDermott | Y | Y | Y | N | Y | Y | N | N |
| 8 ***Chandler*** | N | N | N | Y | Y | N | N | Y |
| **WEST VIRGINIA** | | | | | | | | |
| 1 Mollohan | Y | Y | Y | N | Y | ? | Y | Y |
| 2 Staggers | Y | ? | Y | N | Y | ? | ? | ? |
| 3 Wise | Y | Y | Y | N | Y | ? | — | — |
| 4 Rahall | Y | Y | Y | N | Y | ? | Y | Y |
| **WISCONSIN** | | | | | | | | |
| 1 Aspin | Y | Y | Y | N | Y | Y | N | Y |
| 2 ***Klug*** | N | N | N | Y | Y | Y | N | Y |
| 3 ***Gunderson*** | N | N | N | Y | Y | Y | N | Y |
| 4 Kleczka | Y | Y | Y | N | Y | Y | N | Y |
| 5 Moody | Y | Y | Y | N | Y | Y | N | N |
| 6 ***Petri*** | N | N | N | Y | Y | Y | Y | Y |
| 7 Obey | Y | Y | Y | N | Y | Y | N | Y |
| 8 ***Roth*** | N | N | N | Y | Y | Y | Y | Y |
| 9 ***Sensenbrenner*** | N | N | N | Y | Y | N | Y | Y |
| **WYOMING** | | | | | | | | |
| AL ***Thomas*** | N | N | N | Y | Y | N | Y | Y |

Southern states - Ala., Ark., Fla., Ga., Ky., La., Miss., N.C., Okla., S.C., Tenn., Texas, Va.
Omitted votes are quorum calls, which CQ does not include in its vote charts.

**117. HR 2039. Legal Services Corporation (LSC) Reauthorization/Recommit With Instructions.** McCollum, R-Fla., motion to recommit to House Judiciary Committee the bill to reauthorize the LSC, with instructions to report it back with a substitute amendment to require a competitive bidding test for distributing LSC funds; prohibit agencies that receive LSC funds from engaging in all redistricting and abortion-related activities; expand the bill's ban on lobbying; prohibit recovery of attorneys' fees from non-governmental defendants; and for other purposes. Rejected 173-236: R 137-22; D 36-213 (ND 15-154, SD 21-59); I 0-1, May 12, 1992.

**118. HR 2039. Legal Services Corporation (LSC) Reauthorization/Passage.** Passage of the bill to reauthorize through fiscal 1996 such sums as necessary for the LSC to help give legal assistance to the poor in civil cases. Passed 253-154: R 27-130; D 225-24 (ND 161-9, SD 64-15); I 1-0, May 12, 1992. A "nay" was a vote in support of the president's position.

**119. HR 2056. Penalties for Foreign Shipbuilding Subsidies/Rule.** Adoption of rule (H Res 443) to provide for House floor consideration of bill to require ships entering U.S. ports to certify that their construction or repair was not subsidized by a foreign government or face countervailing anti-dumping duties. The bill repealed the Coast Guard user fees on recreational boats established in the 1990 Budget Enforcement Act (PL 101-508). Adopted 290-125: R 39-122; D 250-3 (ND 170-2, SD 80-1); I 1-0, May 13, 1992.

**120. HR 2056. Penalties for Foreign Shipbuilding Subsidies/Motion to Recommit.** Archer, R-Texas, motion to recommit the bill to deter foreign governments from subsidizing construction of commercial ships and repeal Coast Guard user fees on recreational boats to the House Ways and Means Committee, with instructions to report it back to the House after stripping provisions to impose countervailing anti-dumping duties on ships constructed or repaired with subsidies from a foreign government, leaving only the fees repeal in the bill. Motion rejected 179-237: R 118-42; D 61-194 (ND 28-145, SD 33-49); I 0-1, May 13, 1992.

**121. HR 2056. Penalties for Foreign Shipbuilding Subsidies/Passage.** Passage of bill to require ships entering U.S. ports to certify that their construction or repair had not been subsidized by a foreign government or face countervailing anti-dumping duties. The bill repealed the Coast Guard user fees on recreational boats established in the 1990 Budget Enforcement Act (PL 101-508). Passed 339-78: R 103-57; D 235-21 (ND 163-11, SD 72-10); I 1-0, May 13, 1992. A "nay" was a vote in support of the president's position.

**122. HR 4111. Small Business Loan Guarantees/Passage.** Passage of bill to authorize federal guarantees for up to $5 billion in loans for fiscal 1992 for the Small Business Administration's 7(a) Loan Program. The authorization increased to $6 billion in fiscal 1993 and $7 billion fiscal 1994. The bill permitted up to 10 percent of the authorization to be used for special pilot programs and allowed an increase of $200 million a year for existing authorization for development company loan and debenture guarantees. Passed 399-2: R 153-2; D 245-0 (ND 165-0, SD 80-0); I 1-0, May 14, 1992.

**123. HR 5132. Fiscal 1992 Disaster Relief Supplemental Appropriations/Order Previous Question.** Beilenson, D-Calif., motion to order the previous question (thus ending debate and the possibility of amendment) on the rule (H Res 454) to provide for floor consideration of the bill to provide $494,650,000 in new budget authority in fiscal 1992 for disaster assistance and loans to respond to the Los Angeles riots and the Chicago tunnel collapse and subsequent flooding. Motion agreed to 262-139: R 20-136; D 241-3 (ND 166-2, SD 75-1); I 1-0, May 14, 1992.

**124. HR 5132. Fiscal 1992 Disaster Relief Supplemental Appropriations/Rule.** Adoption of the rule (H Res 454) to provide for floor consideration of the bill to provide $494,650,000 in new budget authority in fiscal 1992 for disaster assistance and loans to respond to the Los Angeles riots and the Chicago tunnel collapse and subsequent flooding. Adopted 298-106: R 71-85; D 226-21 (ND 157-12, SD 69-9); I 1-0, May 14, 1992.

## KEY

Y Voted for (yea).
\# Paired for.
\+ Announced for.
N Voted against (nay).
X Paired against.
— Announced against.
P Voted "present."
C Voted "present" to avoid possible conflict of interest.
? Did not vote or otherwise make a position known.

Democrats **Republicans** *Independent*

| | 117 | 118 | 119 | 120 | 121 | 122 | 123 | 124 |
|---|---|---|---|---|---|---|---|---|
| **ALABAMA** | | | | | | | | |
| 1 *Callahan* | Y | N | Y | N | Y | N | N | N |
| 2 *Dickinson* | Y | N | N | N | Y | N | N | N |
| 3 Browder | N | Y | Y | N | Y | Y | Y | Y |
| 4 Bevill | N | Y | Y | N | Y | Y | Y | Y |
| 5 Cramer | N | Y | Y | N | Y | Y | Y | Y |
| 6 Erdreich | N | Y | Y | N | Y | Y | Y | Y |
| 7 Harris | N | Y | Y | N | Y | Y | Y | Y |
| **ALASKA** | | | | | | | | |
| AL *Young* | Y | N | Y | Y | Y | Y | N | Y |
| **ARIZONA** | | | | | | | | |
| 1 *Rhodes* | Y | N | N | Y | N | Y | N | Y |
| 2 Pastor | N | Y | Y | N | Y | Y | Y | Y |
| 3 *Stump* | Y | N | N | Y | Y | Y | N | N |
| 4 *Kyl* | Y | N | N | Y | N | Y | N | Y |
| 5 *Kolbe* | Y | N | N | Y | N | ? | N | N |
| **ARKANSAS** | | | | | | | | |
| 1 Alexander | ? | ? | Y | N | Y | Y | Y | Y |
| 2 Thornton | N | Y | Y | N | Y | Y | Y | Y |
| 3 *Hammerschmidt* | Y | N | Y | N | Y | Y | N | Y |
| 4 Anthony | N | Y | Y | Y | Y | ? | ? | ? |
| **CALIFORNIA** | | | | | | | | |
| 1 *Riggs* | N | Y | N | N | N | Y | N | Y |
| 2 *Herger* | Y | N | N | Y | N | Y | N | Y |
| 3 Matsui | N | Y | Y | N | Y | Y | Y | Y |
| 4 Fazio | N | Y | Y | N | Y | Y | Y | Y |
| 5 Pelosi | N | Y | Y | N | Y | Y | Y | Y |
| 6 Boxer | N | Y | Y | N | Y | Y | Y | Y |
| 7 Miller | N | Y | Y | ? | Y | Y | Y | Y |
| 8 Dellums | N | Y | Y | N | Y | Y | Y | Y |
| 9 Stark | N | Y | Y | N | Y | Y | Y | Y |
| 10 Edwards | N | Y | ? | N | Y | Y | Y | Y |
| 11 Lantos | N | Y | Y | N | Y | Y | Y | Y |
| 12 *Campbell* | N | N | N | Y | N | N | Y | Y |
| 13 Mineta | N | Y | Y | N | Y | Y | Y | Y |
| 14 *Doolittle* | Y | N | N | Y | N | Y | N | N |
| 15 Condit | N | Y | Y | N | Y | Y | Y | Y |
| 16 Panetta | N | Y | Y | N | Y | Y | Y | Y |
| 17 Dooley | N | Y | Y | N | Y | Y | Y | Y |
| 18 Lehman | N | N | Y | N | Y | Y | Y | Y |
| 19 *Lagomarsino* | Y | N | N | Y | Y | Y | N | Y |
| 20 *Thomas* | Y | N | Y | Y | Y | Y | N | Y |
| 21 *Gallegly* | Y | N | N | Y | Y | Y | N | Y |
| 22 *Moorhead* | Y | N | N | Y | N | Y | N | Y |
| 23 Beilenson | N | Y | Y | N | Y | Y | Y | Y |
| 24 Waxman | N | Y | Y | N | Y | Y | Y | Y |
| 25 Roybal | N | Y | Y | N | Y | Y | Y | ? |
| 26 Berman | N | Y | Y | Y | Y | Y | Y | Y |
| 27 Levine | ? | ? | ? | ? | ? | ? | ? | ? |
| 28 Dixon | N | Y | Y | N | Y | Y | Y | Y |
| 29 Waters | N | Y | Y | N | Y | Y | Y | Y |
| 30 Martinez | N | Y | Y | N | Y | Y | Y | Y |
| 31 Dymally | ? | ? | # | ? | ? | ? | ? | ? |
| 32 Anderson | N | Y | Y | N | Y | Y | Y | ? |
| 33 *Dreier* | Y | N | N | Y | N | Y | N | Y |
| 34 Torres | N | Y | Y | N | Y | Y | Y | Y |
| 35 *Lewis* | Y | N | N | N | Y | Y | N | Y |
| 36 Brown | N | Y | Y | N | Y | Y | Y | Y |
| 37 *McCandless* | Y | N | N | Y | N | Y | N | Y |
| 38 *Dornan* | Y | N | N | N | N | Y | N | N |
| 39 *Dannemeyer* | ? | ? | ? | ? | ? | ? | ? | ? |
| 40 *Cox* | Y | N | N | Y | N | Y | N | Y |
| 41 *Lowery* | Y | ? | Y | N | Y | Y | Y | Y |
| **ALABAMA (cont.)** | | | | | | | | |
| 42 *Rohrabacher* | Y | N | N | Y | Y | Y | N | N |
| 43 *Packard* | Y | N | Y | N | Y | Y | X | X |
| 44 *Cunningham* | ? | N | Y | N | Y | Y | N | N |
| 45 *Hunter* | Y | N | Y | N | Y | N | N | N |
| **COLORADO** | | | | | | | | |
| 1 Schroeder | N | Y | Y | N | Y | Y | Y | Y |
| 2 Skaggs | N | Y | Y | N | Y | Y | Y | Y |
| 3 .Campbell | N | Y | Y | N | Y | Y | Y | Y |
| 4 *Allard* | Y | N | N | Y | N | N | N | N |
| 5 *Hefley* | Y | N | N | Y | N | N | N | N |
| 6 *Schaefer* | Y | N | Y | Y | Y | Y | N | N |
| **CONNECTICUT** | | | | | | | | |
| 1 Kennelly | N | Y | Y | N | Y | Y | Y | Y |
| 2 Gejdenson | N | Y | Y | N | Y | Y | Y | Y |
| 3 DeLauro | N | Y | Y | N | Y | Y | Y | Y |
| 4 *Shays* | N | N | N | Y | N | Y | Y | N |
| 5 *Franks* | Y | N | N | Y | N | Y | Y | Y |
| 6 *Johnson* | N | Y | N | N | Y | ? | N | Y |
| **DELAWARE** | | | | | | | | |
| AL Carper | N | Y | Y | N | Y | Y | Y | N |
| **FLORIDA** | | | | | | | | |
| 1 Hutto | Y | N | Y | Y | Y | Y | Y | Y |
| 2 Peterson | N | Y | Y | Y | Y | Y | Y | Y |
| 3 Bennett | N | Y | Y | Y | Y | Y | Y | Y |
| 4 *James* | C | C | N | Y | Y | N | N | N |
| 5 *McCollum* | Y | N | N | Y | Y | N | N | N |
| 6 *Stearns* | Y | N | N | Y | Y | N | N | N |
| 7 Gibbons | N | Y | Y | N | Y | Y | ? | Y |
| 8 *Young* | Y | N | Y | N | Y | Y | N | Y |
| 9 *Bilirakis* | Y | N | N | N | Y | N | N | Y |
| 10 *Ireland* | Y | N | N | ? | ? | N | N | N |
| 11 Bacchus | N | Y | Y | N | Y | Y | Y | Y |
| 12 *Lewis* | Y | N | N | Y | N | Y | N | N |
| 13 *Goss* | Y | N | N | Y | N | N | N | N |
| 14 Johnston | N | Y | Y | N | Y | Y | Y | Y |
| 15 *Shaw* | Y | N | Y | Y | Y | Y | N | Y |
| 16 Smith | N | Y | Y | N | Y | N | Y | Y |
| 17 Lehman | N | Y | Y | N | Y | Y | Y | Y |
| 18 *Ros-Lehtinen* | Y | N | Y | N | Y | N | N | Y |
| 19 Fascell | N | Y | N | N | Y | Y | Y | Y |
| **GEORGIA** | | | | | | | | |
| 1 Thomas | Y | Y | Y | Y | Y | Y | ? | Y |
| 2 Hatcher | N | Y | ? | ? | ? | ? | ? | ? |
| 3 Ray | Y | Y | Y | N | Y | Y | Y | N |
| 4 Jones | N | Y | Y | N | Y | Y | Y | Y |
| 5 Lewis | N | Y | Y | N | Y | Y | Y | Y |
| 6 *Gingrich* | Y | N | N | Y | N | Y | N | Y |
| 7 Darden | N | N | Y | N | Y | Y | Y | Y |
| 8 Rowland | N | Y | Y | N | Y | Y | Y | Y |
| 9 Jenkins | N | Y | Y | N | Y | Y | Y | Y |
| 10 Barnard | Y | N | Y | Y | Y | Y | Y | Y |
| **HAWAII** | | | | | | | | |
| 1 Abercrombie | N | Y | Y | N | Y | Y | Y | Y |
| 2 Mink | N | Y | Y | Y | Y | Y | Y | Y |
| **IDAHO** | | | | | | | | |
| 1 LaRocco | N | Y | Y | N | Y | Y | Y | Y |
| 2 Stallings | N | Y | Y | N | Y | Y | Y | Y |
| **ILLINOIS** | | | | | | | | |
| 1 Hayes | N | Y | Y | N | Y | Y | Y | Y |
| 2 Savage | N | Y | Y | N | Y | Y | Y | Y |
| 3 Russo | N | Y | Y | N | Y | Y | Y | Y |
| 4 Sangmeister | N | Y | ? | ? | ? | ? | ? | ? |
| 5 Lipinski | N | Y | Y | N | Y | Y | Y | Y |
| 6 *Hyde* | ? | ? | N | Y | N | Y | N | Y |
| 7 Collins | X | # | Y | N | Y | Y | ? | ? |
| 8 Rostenkowski | N | Y | Y | N | Y | Y | Y | Y |
| 9 Yates | N | Y | Y | N | Y | Y | Y | Y |
| 10 *Porter* | N | Y | N | N | Y | Y | Y | Y |
| 11 Annunzio | N | Y | Y | N | Y | Y | Y | Y |
| 12 *Crane* | Y | N | N | N | N | N | N | N |
| 13 *Fawell* | Y | N | Y | N | Y | Y | N | Y |
| 14 *Hastert* | Y | N | N | Y | N | Y | N | Y |
| 15 *Ewing* | Y | N | N | Y | N | Y | N | Y |
| 16 Cox | N | Y | Y | N | Y | Y | Y | Y |
| 17 Evans | N | Y | Y | N | Y | Y | Y | Y |
| 18 *Michel* | Y | N | N | Y | N | Y | N | Y |
| 19 Bruce | N | Y | Y | N | Y | Y | Y | Y |
| 20 Durbin | N | Y | Y | N | Y | Y | Y | Y |
| 21 Costello | Y | Y | Y | N | Y | Y | Y | Y |
| 22 Poshard | Y | Y | Y | N | Y | Y | Y | Y |
| **INDIANA** | | | | | | | | |
| 1 Visclosky | N | Y | Y | N | Y | Y | Y | Y |
| 2 Sharp | N | Y | Y | N | Y | Y | Y | Y |
| 3 Roemer | Y | Y | Y | N | Y | Y | Y | Y |

ND Northern Democrats    SD Southern Democrats

| | 117 | 118 | 119 | 120 | 121 | 122 | 123 | 124 |
|---|---|---|---|---|---|---|---|---|
| 4 Long | N | Y | Y | Y | Y | Y | Y | Y |
| 5 Jontz | N | Y | Y | N | Y | Y | Y | Y |
| 6 ***Burton*** | Y | N | N | Y | Y | Y | N | N |
| 7 ***Myers*** | Y | N | N | Y | N | Y | N | Y |
| 8 McCloskey | N | Y | Y | N | Y | Y | Y | Y |
| 9 Hamilton | N | Y | Y | Y | Y | Y | N | N |
| 10 Jacobs | N | Y | N | N | Y | Y | N | N |
| **IOWA** | | | | | | | | |
| 1 ***Leach*** | N | Y | N | Y | Y | Y | Y | Y |
| 2 ***Nussle*** | Y | N | N | Y | N | Y | N | Y |
| 3 Nagle | N | Y | Y | Y | N | Y | Y | Y |
| 4 Smith | N | Y | Y | N | Y | Y | ? | Y |
| 5 ***Lightfoot*** | # | X | ? | ? | ? | ? | ? | ? |
| 6 ***Grandy*** | Y | N | N | Y | N | Y | N | N |
| **KANSAS** | | | | | | | | |
| 1 ***Roberts*** | Y | N | N | Y | N | Y | N | N |
| 2 Slattery | N | Y | Y | Y | N | Y | Y | Y |
| 3 ***Meyers*** | Y | Y | N | Y | Y | Y | N | Y |
| 4 Glickman | N | Y | Y | Y | Y | Y | Y | Y |
| 5 ***Nichols*** | Y | N | N | Y | N | Y | N | N |
| **KENTUCKY** | | | | | | | | |
| 1 Hubbard | N | Y | Y | Y | N | Y | Y | N |
| 2 Natcher | N | Y | Y | N | Y | Y | Y | Y |
| 3 Mazzoli | N | N | Y | N | Y | Y | Y | Y |
| 4 ***Bunning*** | Y | N | N | Y | N | Y | N | N |
| 5 ***Rogers*** | Y | N | N | Y | N | Y | N | N |
| 6 ***Hopkins*** | Y | N | N | Y | N | Y | N | Y |
| 7 Perkins | N | Y | Y | N | Y | Y | Y | Y |
| **LOUISIANA** | | | | | | | | |
| 1 ***Livingston*** | Y | N | Y | N | Y | Y | N | Y |
| 2 Jefferson | ? | ? | Y | N | Y | Y | Y | Y |
| 3 Tauzin | Y | N | Y | N | Y | Y | ? | ? |
| 4 ***McCrery*** | Y | N | ? | ? | ? | ? | ? | ? |
| 5 Huckaby | Y | N | Y | Y | Y | Y | Y | Y |
| 6 ***Baker*** | Y | N | N | N | Y | Y | N | N |
| 7 Hayes | N | Y | Y | Y | Y | Y | Y | Y |
| 8 ***Holloway*** | Y | N | N | N | Y | Y | N | N |
| **MAINE** | | | | | | | | |
| 1 Andrews | N | Y | Y | N | Y | Y | Y | Y |
| 2 ***Snowe*** | Y | Y | Y | N | Y | Y | N | Y |
| **MARYLAND** | | | | | | | | |
| 1 ***Gilchrest*** | N | Y | N | N | Y | Y | N | Y |
| 2 ***Bentley*** | Y | N | Y | N | Y | Y | N | N |
| 3 Cardin | N | Y | Y | N | Y | Y | Y | Y |
| 4 McMillen | N | Y | Y | N | Y | Y | Y | Y |
| 5 Hoyer | N | Y | Y | N | Y | Y | ? | Y |
| 6 Byron | Y | N | Y | N | Y | ? | Y | Y |
| 7 Mfume | N | Y | Y | N | Y | Y | Y | Y |
| 8 ***Morella*** | N | Y | N | N | Y | Y | N | Y |
| **MASSACHUSETTS** | | | | | | | | |
| 1 Olver | N | Y | Y | N | Y | Y | Y | Y |
| 2 Neal | N | Y | Y | N | Y | Y | Y | Y |
| 3 Early | N | Y | Y | N | Y | Y | Y | Y |
| 4 Frank | N | Y | Y | Y | Y | Y | Y | Y |
| 5 Atkins | N | Y | Y | N | Y | Y | Y | Y |
| 6 Mavroules | N | Y | Y | N | Y | Y | Y | Y |
| 7 Markey | N | Y | Y | N | Y | Y | Y | Y |
| 8 Kennedy | N | Y | Y | N | Y | Y | Y | Y |
| 9 Moakley | ? | ? | ? | ? | ? | ? | ? | ? |
| 10 Studds | N | Y | Y | N | Y | Y | Y | Y |
| 11 Donnelly | N | Y | Y | N | Y | Y | Y | Y |
| **MICHIGAN** | | | | | | | | |
| 1 Conyers | N | Y | Y | N | Y | Y | ? | N |
| 2 ***Pursell*** | Y | N | N | Y | Y | Y | ? | ? |
| 3 Wolpe | N | Y | Y | N | Y | Y | Y | Y |
| 4 ***Upton*** | Y | N | N | Y | Y | Y | N | N |
| 5 ***Henry*** | Y | N | N | Y | Y | ? | ? | ? |
| 6 Carr | N | Y | Y | N | Y | Y | Y | Y |
| 7 Kildee | N | Y | Y | N | Y | Y | Y | Y |
| 8 Traxler | N | Y | Y | N | Y | Y | Y | Y |
| 9 ***Vander Jagt*** | Y | N | Y | Y | Y | ? | ? | ? |
| 10 ***Camp*** | Y | N | Y | Y | Y | Y | N | N |
| 11 ***Davis*** | Y | N | Y | N | Y | ? | N | Y |
| 12 Bonior | N | Y | Y | N | Y | Y | Y | Y |
| 13 Collins | N | Y | Y | N | Y | + | Y | Y |
| 14 Hertel | N | Y | Y | N | Y | Y | Y | Y |
| 15 Ford | N | Y | Y | N | Y | ? | Y | Y |
| 16 Dingell | N | Y | Y | N | Y | Y | Y | Y |
| 17 Levin | N | Y | Y | N | Y | Y | Y | Y |
| 18 ***Broomfield*** | Y | N | N | Y | Y | Y | Y | ? |
| **MINNESOTA** | | | | | | | | |
| 1 Penny | N | Y | Y | Y | Y | Y | Y | N |
| 2 ***Weber*** | Y | N | N | Y | N | Y | N | N |
| 3 ***Ramstad*** | N | Y | N | Y | Y | Y | N | N |
| 4 Vento | N | Y | Y | N | Y | Y | Y | Y |

| | 117 | 118 | 119 | 120 | 121 | 122 | 123 | 124 |
|---|---|---|---|---|---|---|---|---|
| 5 Sabo | N | Y | Y | N | Y | Y | Y | Y |
| 6 Sikorski | N | Y | Y | N | Y | Y | Y | Y |
| 7 Peterson | N | Y | Y | Y | Y | Y | Y | Y |
| 8 Oberstar | N | Y | Y | N | Y | Y | Y | Y |
| **MISSISSIPPI** | | | | | | | | |
| 1 Whitten | ? | ? | Y | N | Y | Y | Y | Y |
| 2 Espy | N | Y | Y | N | Y | Y | ? | Y |
| 3 Montgomery | Y | N | Y | N | Y | Y | Y | Y |
| 4 Parker | Y | N | ? | ? | ? | Y | Y | Y |
| 5 Taylor | Y | N | Y | N | Y | Y | Y | Y |
| **MISSOURI** | | | | | | | | |
| 1 Clay | N | Y | Y | N | Y | Y | Y | Y |
| 2 Horn | N | Y | Y | N | Y | Y | Y | Y |
| 3 Gephardt | N | Y | Y | N | Y | Y | Y | Y |
| 4 Skelton | Y | N | Y | N | Y | Y | Y | Y |
| 5 Wheat | N | Y | Y | N | Y | Y | Y | Y |
| 6 ***Coleman*** | Y | N | N | Y | Y | Y | N | N |
| 7 ***Hancock*** | Y | N | N | Y | Y | Y | N | N |
| 8 ***Emerson*** | Y | N | Y | N | Y | Y | N | N |
| 9 Volkmer | N | N | Y | N | Y | Y | Y | Y |
| **MONTANA** | | | | | | | | |
| 1 Williams | N | Y | Y | Y | N | Y | Y | Y |
| 2 ***Marlenee*** | Y | N | N | Y | Y | Y | N | N |
| **NEBRASKA** | | | | | | | | |
| 1 ***Bereuter*** | ? | ? | N | Y | N | Y | N | N |
| 2 Hoagland | N | Y | Y | N | Y | Y | Y | Y |
| 3 ***Barrett*** | Y | N | N | Y | N | Y | N | N |
| **NEVADA** | | | | | | | | |
| 1 Bilbray | N | Y | Y | N | Y | Y | Y | Y |
| 2 ***Vucanovich*** | Y | N | N | Y | Y | Y | N | N |
| **NEW HAMPSHIRE** | | | | | | | | |
| 1 ***Zeliff*** | Y | N | N | Y | Y | Y | N | Y |
| 2 Swett | N | Y | Y | N | Y | Y | Y | Y |
| **NEW JERSEY** | | | | | | | | |
| 1 Andrews | N | Y | Y | N | Y | Y | Y | Y |
| 2 Hughes | N | Y | Y | N | Y | Y | Y | N |
| 3 Pallone | N | Y | Y | N | Y | Y | Y | Y |
| 4 ***Smith*** | Y | N | Y | Y | Y | Y | N | Y |
| 5 ***Roukema*** | Y | N | X | # | ? | Y | N | N |
| 6 Dwyer | N | Y | Y | N | Y | Y | Y | Y |
| 7 ***Rinaldo*** | Y | N | N | N | Y | Y | N | Y |
| 8 Roe | N | Y | Y | N | Y | Y | Y | Y |
| 9 Torricelli | N | Y | Y | N | Y | Y | Y | Y |
| 10 Payne | N | Y | Y | N | Y | Y | Y | N |
| 11 ***Gallo*** | N | N | N | Y | N | Y | N | N |
| 12 ***Zimmer*** | N | Y | N | Y | N | Y | N | N |
| 13 ***Saxton*** | Y | N | Y | N | Y | Y | N | N |
| 14 Guarini | N | Y | Y | N | Y | Y | Y | Y |
| **NEW MEXICO** | | | | | | | | |
| 1 ***Schiff*** | N | Y | N | Y | N | Y | N | N |
| 2 ***Skeen*** | Y | N | Y | N | Y | Y | Y | Y |
| 3 Richardson | N | Y | Y | N | Y | Y | Y | Y |
| **NEW YORK** | | | | | | | | |
| 1 Hochbrueckner | N | Y | Y | N | Y | Y | Y | Y |
| 2 Downey | N | Y | Y | N | Y | Y | Y | Y |
| 3 Mrazek | ? | ? | ? | ? | ? | Y | Y | Y |
| 4 ***Lent*** | Y | N | Y | N | Y | Y | N | Y |
| 5 ***McGrath*** | Y | N | Y | N | Y | Y | Y | Y |
| 6 Flake | N | Y | Y | N | Y | Y | Y | Y |
| 7 Ackerman | ? | ? | Y | N | Y | Y | Y | Y |
| 8 Scheuer | ? | Y | Y | N | Y | Y | Y | Y |
| 9 Manton | N | Y | Y | N | N | Y | Y | Y |
| 10 Schumer | N | Y | Y | N | ? | Y | Y | Y |
| 11 Towns | N | Y | Y | N | Y | Y | Y | Y |
| 12 Owens | N | Y | Y | N | Y | Y | Y | Y |
| 13 Solarz | N | Y | Y | N | Y | Y | Y | Y |
| 14 ***Molinari*** | N | N | N | Y | Y | Y | N | Y |
| 15 ***Green*** | N | Y | N | Y | N | Y | Y | Y |
| 16 Rangel | N | Y | Y | N | Y | Y | Y | # |
| 17 Weiss | N | Y | Y | N | N | Y | Y | Y |
| 18 Serrano | N | Y | Y | N | Y | Y | Y | Y |
| 19 Engel | ? | ? | ? | N | Y | Y | Y | Y |
| 20 Lowey | N | Y | Y | N | Y | Y | Y | Y |
| 21 ***Fish*** | N | Y | Y | Y | Y | Y | Y | Y |
| 22 ***Gilman*** | N | + | Y | N | Y | Y | Y | Y |
| 23 McNulty | N | Y | Y | N | Y | Y | Y | Y |
| 24 ***Solomon*** | Y | N | N | Y | Y | Y | N | Y |
| 25 ***Boehlert*** | N | Y | Y | N | Y | Y | ? | Y |
| 26 ***Martin*** | Y | N | N | Y | Y | Y | N | Y |
| 27 ***Walsh*** | Y | Y | N | Y | Y | Y | N | Y |
| 28 McHugh | N | Y | Y | N | Y | Y | Y | Y |
| 29 ***Horton*** | N | Y | Y | N | Y | Y | Y | Y |
| 30 Slaughter | N | Y | Y | N | Y | Y | Y | Y |
| 31 ***Paxon*** | Y | N | N | Y | Y | Y | N | N |

| | 117 | 118 | 119 | 120 | 121 | 122 | 123 | 124 |
|---|---|---|---|---|---|---|---|---|
| 32 LaFalce | Y | Y | Y | Y | Y | Y | Y | Y |
| 33 Nowak | N | Y | Y | N | Y | Y | Y | Y |
| 34 ***Houghton*** | N | Y | N | Y | Y | Y | Y | Y |
| **NORTH CAROLINA** | | | | | | | | |
| 1 Jones | N | Y | Y | N | Y | Y | ? | ? |
| 2 Valentine | Y | N | Y | Y | Y | Y | Y | N |
| 3 Lancaster | N | Y | Y | N | Y | Y | Y | Y |
| 4 Price | N | Y | Y | Y | Y | Y | Y | Y |
| 5 Neal | N | Y | Y | N | Y | Y | Y | Y |
| 6 ***Coble*** | Y | N | N | Y | Y | Y | N | N |
| 7 Rose | N | Y | Y | Y | Y | Y | Y | Y |
| 8 Hefner | N | Y | Y | N | Y | Y | Y | Y |
| 9 ***McMillan*** | Y | N | N | Y | Y | Y | N | Y |
| 10 ***Ballenger*** | Y | N | N | Y | Y | Y | N | N |
| 11 ***Taylor*** | Y | N | Y | N | Y | Y | N | Y |
| **NORTH DAKOTA** | | | | | | | | |
| AL Dorgan | N | Y | Y | Y | Y | Y | Y | Y |
| **OHIO** | | | | | | | | |
| 1 Luken | N | Y | Y | N | Y | ? | ? | ? |
| 2 ***Gradison*** | N | Y | Y | Y | N | Y | N | Y |
| 3 Hall | N | Y | Y | N | Y | Y | Y | Y |
| 4 ***Oxley*** | Y | N | N | Y | N | Y | N | N |
| 5 ***Gillmor*** | Y | N | N | Y | Y | Y | N | N |
| 6 ***McEwen*** | ? | ? | N | Y | N | Y | N | N |
| 7 ***Hobson*** | Y | N | N | Y | Y | Y | N | N |
| 8 ***Boehner*** | Y | N | Y | N | Y | Y | N | Y |
| 9 Kaptur | N | Y | Y | N | Y | Y | Y | Y |
| 10 ***Miller*** | Y | N | N | Y | N | Y | N | N |
| 11 Eckart | N | Y | N | Y | Y | Y | Y | Y |
| 12 ***Kasich*** | Y | ? | N | Y | Y | Y | N | Y |
| 13 Pease | N | Y | Y | N | Y | Y | Y | Y |
| 14 Sawyer | N | Y | Y | N | Y | Y | Y | Y |
| 15 ***Wylie*** | Y | Y | N | Y | N | Y | N | Y |
| 16 ***Regula*** | Y | Y | N | N | Y | Y | N | Y |
| 17 Traficant | N | Y | Y | N | Y | Y | Y | Y |
| 18 Applegate | Y | N | Y | N | Y | Y | ? | N |
| 19 Feighan | N | Y | Y | N | Y | ? | Y | Y |
| 20 Oakar | ? | ? | Y | N | Y | ? | ? | ? |
| 21 Stokes | N | Y | Y | N | Y | Y | Y | Y |
| **OKLAHOMA** | | | | | | | | |
| 1 ***Inhofe*** | Y | N | N | Y | N | Y | N | N |
| 2 Synar | N | Y | Y | Y | Y | Y | Y | Y |
| 3 Brewster | N | Y | Y | Y | Y | Y | Y | Y |
| 4 McCurdy | N | Y | Y | Y | Y | Y | Y | Y |
| 5 ***Edwards*** | Y | N | N | Y | N | Y | N | N |
| 6 English | Y | Y | Y | Y | N | Y | Y | Y |
| **OREGON** | | | | | | | | |
| 1 AuCoin | ? | ? | ? | X | ? | ? | # | ? |
| 2 ***Smith*** | Y | N | N | Y | N | Y | N | Y |
| 3 Wyden | N | Y | Y | N | Y | Y | Y | Y |
| 4 DeFazio | N | Y | Y | N | Y | Y | Y | Y |
| 5 Kopetski | N | Y | Y | N | Y | Y | Y | Y |
| **PENNSYLVANIA** | | | | | | | | |
| 1 Foglietta | N | Y | Y | N | Y | Y | Y | Y |
| 2 Blackwell | N | Y | Y | N | Y | Y | Y | Y |
| 3 Borski | N | Y | Y | N | Y | ? | Y | Y |
| 4 Kolter | ? | ? | ? | ? | ? | ? | ? | ? |
| 5 ***Schulze*** | Y | N | Y | N | Y | Y | N | Y |
| 6 Yatron | Y | Y | Y | N | Y | Y | Y | Y |
| 7 ***Weldon*** | Y | N | Y | N | Y | Y | N | Y |
| 8 Kostmayer | N | Y | Y | Y | Y | Y | Y | Y |
| 9 ***Shuster*** | Y | N | N | Y | Y | Y | N | N |
| 10 ***McDade*** | Y | N | Y | Y | Y | Y | Y | Y |
| 11 Kanjorski | Y | Y | Y | N | Y | Y | Y | Y |
| 12 Murtha | Y | Y | Y | N | Y | Y | Y | Y |
| 13 ***Coughlin*** | Y | N | N | N | N | Y | N | Y |
| 14 Coyne | N | Y | Y | N | Y | Y | Y | Y |
| 15 ***Ritter*** | Y | N | Y | N | Y | Y | N | N |
| 16 ***Walker*** | Y | N | N | Y | Y | Y | N | N |
| 17 ***Gekas*** | Y | N | N | N | Y | Y | N | N |
| 18 ***Santorum*** | Y | N | ? | ? | ? | ? | ? | ? |
| 19 ***Goodling*** | Y | N | N | N | Y | Y | N | N |
| 20 Gaydos | N | Y | Y | N | Y | Y | Y | Y |
| 21 ***Ridge*** | N | Y | Y | N | Y | Y | N | N |
| 22 Murphy | Y | N | Y | N | Y | ? | ? | Y |
| 23 ***Clinger*** | Y | N | N | Y | Y | Y | N | Y |
| **RHODE ISLAND** | | | | | | | | |
| 1 ***Machtley*** | N | Y | Y | Y | Y | Y | N | N |
| 2 Reed | N | Y | Y | N | Y | Y | Y | Y |
| **SOUTH CAROLINA** | | | | | | | | |
| 1 ***Ravenel*** | Y | Y | Y | Y | Y | Y | Y | Y |
| 2 ***Spence*** | Y | N | Y | Y | Y | Y | N | Y |
| 3 Derrick | N | Y | Y | N | Y | Y | Y | Y |
| 4 Patterson | N | Y | Y | N | Y | Y | Y | N |
| 5 Spratt | N | Y | Y | N | Y | Y | Y | Y |
| 6 Tallon | ? | ? | Y | Y | Y | Y | Y | N |

| | 117 | 118 | 119 | 120 | 121 | 122 | 123 | 124 |
|---|---|---|---|---|---|---|---|---|
| **SOUTH DAKOTA** | | | | | | | | |
| AL Johnson | Y | Y | Y | N | Y | Y | Y | Y |
| **TENNESSEE** | | | | | | | | |
| 1 ***Quillen*** | Y | N | Y | N | Y | Y | N | Y |
| 2 ***Duncan*** | Y | N | N | N | Y | Y | N | N |
| 3 Lloyd | N | Y | Y | N | Y | Y | ? | ? |
| 4 Cooper | N | Y | Y | N | Y | Y | Y | Y |
| 5 Clement | Y | Y | ? | N | Y | Y | Y | Y |
| 6 Gordon | N | ? | Y | N | Y | Y | Y | Y |
| 7 ***Sundquist*** | Y | N | N | Y | Y | ? | N | N |
| 8 Tanner | Y | Y | Y | N | Y | Y | Y | Y |
| 9 Ford | N | Y | Y | N | Y | Y | Y | Y |
| **TEXAS** | | | | | | | | |
| 1 Chapman | N | Y | Y | Y | Y | ? | Y | Y |
| 2 Wilson | Y | N | Y | Y | N | ? | Y | ? |
| 3 ***Johnson*** | Y | N | N | Y | N | Y | N | N |
| 4 Hall | Y | N | Y | Y | Y | Y | Y | N |
| 5 Bryant | ? | ? | ? | ? | ? | Y | Y | Y |
| 6 ***Barton*** | Y | N | N | Y | N | Y | Y | N |
| 7 ***Archer*** | Y | N | N | Y | N | Y | N | N |
| 8 ***Fields*** | Y | N | N | Y | N | Y | N | N |
| 9 Brooks | N | Y | Y | N | Y | Y | Y | Y |
| 10 Pickle | N | Y | Y | N | Y | Y | Y | Y |
| 11 Edwards | Y | Y | Y | Y | Y | Y | Y | Y |
| 12 Geren | Y | Y | Y | Y | Y | Y | Y | Y |
| 13 Sarpalius | Y | N | Y | Y | Y | Y | Y | Y |
| 14 Laughlin | Y | Y | Y | Y | Y | Y | Y | ? |
| 15 de la Garza | N | Y | Y | Y | Y | Y | Y | Y |
| 16 Coleman | N | Y | Y | N | Y | Y | Y | Y |
| 17 Stenholm | Y | N | Y | Y | N | Y | Y | N |
| 18 Washington | N | Y | Y | N | Y | Y | N | N |
| 19 ***Combest*** | Y | N | N | Y | N | Y | N | N |
| 20 Gonzalez | N | Y | Y | N | Y | Y | Y | Y |
| 21 ***Smith*** | Y | N | N | Y | Y | Y | N | N |
| 22 ***DeLay*** | Y | N | N | Y | N | Y | N | N |
| 23 Bustamante | N | Y | Y | Y | Y | Y | Y | Y |
| 24 Frost | N | Y | Y | N | Y | Y | Y | Y |
| 25 Andrews | N | Y | Y | Y | N | Y | Y | N |
| 26 ***Armey*** | Y | N | N | Y | N | N | N | N |
| 27 Ortiz | N | Y | Y | Y | Y | Y | Y | Y |
| **UTAH** | | | | | | | | |
| 1 ***Hansen*** | Y | N | N | Y | N | Y | N | N |
| 2 Owens | N | Y | Y | N | Y | Y | Y | Y |
| 3 Orton | Y | N | Y | N | Y | Y | Y | N |
| **VERMONT** | | | | | | | | |
| AL *Sanders* | N | Y | Y | N | Y | Y | Y | Y |
| **VIRGINIA** | | | | | | | | |
| 1 ***Bateman*** | Y | N | Y | N | Y | Y | N | Y |
| 2 Pickett | N | Y | Y | N | Y | Y | Y | Y |
| 3 ***Bliley*** | Y | N | N | Y | Y | Y | N | N |
| 4 Sisisky | N | Y | Y | N | Y | Y | Y | Y |
| 5 Payne | N | Y | Y | N | Y | Y | Y | Y |
| 6 Olin | N | Y | Y | N | Y | Y | Y | Y |
| 7 ***Allen*** | Y | N | N | N | Y | Y | N | N |
| 8 Moran | N | Y | Y | N | Y | ? | Y | Y |
| 9 Boucher | N | Y | Y | Y | N | Y | Y | Y |
| 10 ***Wolf*** | Y | N | N | Y | Y | Y | N | N |
| **WASHINGTON** | | | | | | | | |
| 1 ***Miller*** | Y | Y | N | Y | N | ? | ? | ? |
| 2 Swift | N | Y | Y | Y | Y | Y | Y | Y |
| 3 Unsoeld | N | Y | Y | N | Y | Y | Y | Y |
| 4 ***Morrison*** | Y | N | N | Y | Y | Y | N | Y |
| 5 Foley | | | | | | | | |
| 6 Dicks | N | Y | Y | Y | Y | Y | Y | Y |
| 7 McDermott | N | Y | Y | N | Y | Y | Y | Y |
| 8 ***Chandler*** | Y | N | N | Y | N | Y | N | Y |
| **WEST VIRGINIA** | | | | | | | | |
| 1 Mollohan | Y | N | Y | N | Y | Y | Y | Y |
| 2 Staggers | ? | ? | ? | ? | ? | ? | ? | ? |
| 3 Wise | — | + | Y | N | Y | Y | Y | Y |
| 4 Rahall | Y | N | Y | Y | N | Y | Y | Y |
| **WISCONSIN** | | | | | | | | |
| 1 Aspin | N | Y | Y | Y | N | Y | Y | N |
| 2 ***Klug*** | Y | Y | N | Y | Y | Y | N | Y |
| 3 ***Gunderson*** | Y | Y | Y | Y | Y | Y | N | N |
| 4 Kleczka | N | Y | Y | N | Y | Y | Y | Y |
| 5 Moody | N | Y | Y | N | Y | Y | Y | N |
| 6 ***Petri*** | Y | N | Y | Y | Y | Y | N | N |
| 7 Obey | N | Y | Y | Y | Y | Y | Y | Y |
| 8 ***Roth*** | Y | N | N | N | Y | Y | N | N |
| 9 ***Sensenbrenner*** | Y | N | N | Y | N | Y | N | N |
| **WYOMING** | | | | | | | | |
| AL ***Thomas*** | Y | N | N | Y | Y | Y | N | N |

Southern states - Ala., Ark., Fla., Ga., Ky., La., Miss., N.C., Okla., S.C., Tenn., Texas, Va.
Omitted votes are quorum calls, which CQ does not include in its vote charts.

**125. HR 5132. Fiscal 1992 Disaster Relief Supplemental Appropriations/Passage.** Passage of the bill to provide $494,650,000 in new budget authority in fiscal 1992 for disaster assistance and loans to respond to the Los Angeles riots and the Chicago tunnel collapse and subsequent flooding to be administered by the Small Business Administration and the Federal Emergency Management Agency. The funds were designated as emergency spending, thus exempt from the spending caps of the 1990 Budget Enforcement Act. Passed 244-162: R 44-110; D 199-52 (ND 155-17, SD 44-35); I 1-0, May 14, 1992. A "yea" was a vote in support of the president's position.

**126. H Res 456. House Post Office Subpoenas.** Adoption of the Walker, R-Pa., resolution to direct the Speaker to produce the five subpoenas issued on May 6 by the Department of Justice to three House members and two House employees concerning the criminal investigation of the House Post Office and to explain what delayed the timely consideration of the subpoenas. Adopted 324-3: R 125-0; D 198-3 (ND 133-1, SD 65-2); I 1-0, May 14, 1992.

**127. HR 4691. Airport and Airway Improvement/ Passage.** Passage of the bill to authorize $19.3 billion for fiscal 1993-94 for the construction and improvement of airports, modernization of the nation's air traffic control system, and Federal Aviation Administration operations. Passed 410-2: R 156-1; D 253-1 (ND 172-1, SD 81-0); I 1-0, May 19, 1992. A "yea" was a vote in support of the president's position.

**128. S 1306. Alcohol, Drug Abuse and Mental Health Administration Reorganization/Passage.** Waxman, D-Calif., motion to suspend the rules and pass the bill to reauthorize the federal substance abuse and mental health programs for fiscal 1993-94. The bill would split the block grant for mental health and substance abuse services into two separate grants, transfer the research arm of the Alcohol, Drug Abuse and Mental Health Administration to the National Institutes of Health, and provide more money to rural areas under state funding formulas. Motion rejected 264-148: R 50-110; D 213-38 (ND 163-7, SD 50-31); I 1-0, May 19, 1992. A two-thirds majority of those present and voting (276 in this case) was required for passage under suspension of the rules.

**129. Procedural Motion.** Approval of the House Journal of Tuesday, May 19. Approved 287-115: R 42-110; D 244-5 (ND 164-5, SD 80-0); I 1-0, May 20, 1992.

**130. H Res 460. Financial Management of the House/Ruling of the Chair.** Gephardt, D-Mo., motion to table (kill) the Santorum, R-Pa., appeal of the chair's ruling that the Santorum privileged resolution to direct the Speaker to have a third party perform financial and performance audits of the Capitol Preservation Commission account and the House Contingent account, was not a privileged resolution addressing the rights and integrity of the House and thus out of order. Motion agreed to 262-149: R 10-149; D 251-0 (ND 171-0, SD 80-0); I 1-0, May 20, 1992. (The chair's ruling was subsequently upheld, and the Santorum privileged resolution was ruled out of order.)

**131. H Con Res 320. Congressional Recognition of the 27th Constitutional Amendment/Adoption.** Brooks, D-Texas, motion to suspend the rules and adopt the concurrent resolution to provide formal congressional recognition of the ratification of the 27th amendment to the Constitution, which provides that a congressional pay raise shall not take effect until an intervening election has occurred. Motion agreed to 414-3: R 161-0; D 252-3 (ND 173-1, SD 79-2); I 1-0, May 20, 1992. A two-thirds majority of those present and voting (278 in this case) was required for passage under suspension of the rules.

**132. HR 776. National Energy Policy/Performance Standards.** Atkins, D-Mass., amendment to require manufacturers to meet national performance standards for faucets, water closets, urinals and showerheads to conserve energy and water. The bill sets standards only for showerheads. Adopted 328-79: R 89-71; D 238-8 (ND 164-4, SD 74-4); I 1-0, May 20, 1992.

## KEY

| | |
|---|---|
| Y | Voted for (yea). |
| # | Paired for. |
| + | Announced for. |
| N | Voted against (nay). |
| X | Paired against. |
| − | Announced against. |
| P | Voted "present." |
| C | Voted "present" to avoid possible conflict of interest. |
| ? | Did not vote or otherwise make a position known. |

*Democrats*   **Republicans**
*Independent*

| | 125 | 126 | 127 | 128 | 129 | 130 | 131 | 132 |
|---|---|---|---|---|---|---|---|---|
| **ALABAMA** | | | | | | | | |
| 1 *Callahan* | N | Y | Y | Y | Y | N | Y | N |
| 2 *Dickinson* | ? | ? | Y | Y | N | Y | N | ? |
| 3 Browder | N | Y | Y | Y | Y | Y | Y | Y |
| 4 Bevill | Y | ? | Y | Y | Y | Y | Y | Y |
| 5 Cramer | N | Y | Y | Y | Y | Y | Y | Y |
| 6 Erdreich | N | Y | Y | Y | Y | Y | Y | Y |
| 7 Harris | N | Y | Y | Y | Y | Y | Y | Y |
| **ALASKA** | | | | | | | | |
| AL *Young* | N | Y | Y | Y | N | Y | Y | N |
| **ARIZONA** | | | | | | | | |
| 1 *Rhodes* | N | Y | Y | N | Y | N | Y | N |
| 2 Pastor | Y | Y | Y | Y | Y | Y | Y | Y |
| 3 *Stump* | N | Y | Y | N | N | N | Y | N |
| 4 *Kyl* | N | Y | Y | N | N | N | Y | N |
| 5 *Kolbe* | N | Y | Y | N | Y | N | Y | N |
| **ARKANSAS** | | | | | | | | |
| 1 Alexander | Y | ? | Y | Y | Y | Y | Y | Y |
| 2 Thornton | Y | Y | Y | Y | Y | Y | Y | Y |
| 3 *Hammerschmidt* | N | Y | Y | Y | Y | Y | Y | N |
| 4 Anthony | # | ? | ? | # | ? | # | ? | ? |
| **CALIFORNIA** | | | | | | | | |
| 1 *Riggs* | N | Y | Y | N | N | N | Y | N |
| 2 *Herger* | N | Y | Y | N | N | N | Y | ? |
| 3 Matsui | Y | Y | Y | Y | Y | Y | Y | Y |
| 4 Fazio | Y | Y | Y | Y | Y | Y | Y | Y |
| 5 Pelosi | Y | ? | Y | Y | Y | Y | Y | Y |
| 6 Boxer | Y | ? | ? | ? | ? | ? | ? | ? |
| 7 Miller | Y | ? | Y | Y | ? | Y | Y | Y |
| 8 Dellums | Y | Y | Y | Y | Y | Y | Y | Y |
| 9 Stark | Y | Y | Y | Y | Y | Y | Y | Y |
| 10 Edwards | Y | Y | Y | Y | P | Y | Y | Y |
| 11 Lantos | Y | Y | Y | Y | Y | Y | Y | Y |
| 12 *Campbell* | Y | Y | ? | ? | N | N | Y | Y |
| 13 Mineta | Y | ? | Y | Y | Y | Y | Y | Y |
| 14 *Doolittle* | N | Y | Y | N | N | N | N | N |
| 15 Condit | Y | Y | Y | Y | Y | Y | Y | Y |
| 16 Panetta | Y | Y | Y | Y | Y | Y | Y | Y |
| 17 Dooley | Y | Y | Y | Y | Y | Y | Y | Y |
| 18 Lehman | Y | ? | Y | Y | Y | Y | Y | Y |
| 19 *Lagomarsino* | N | Y | Y | N | N | N | Y | N |
| 20 *Thomas* | N | ? | Y | N | ? | N | Y | N |
| 21 *Gallegly* | N | ? | Y | N | Y | N | Y | N |
| 22 *Moorhead* | N | Y | Y | N | N | N | Y | N |
| 23 Beilenson | Y | ? | Y | Y | Y | Y | Y | Y |
| 24 Waxman | Y | Y | Y | Y | Y | Y | Y | Y |
| 25 Roybal | Y | ? | Y | Y | Y | Y | Y | Y |
| 26 Berman | Y | ? | Y | Y | Y | Y | Y | Y |
| 27 Levine | ? | ? | ? | ? | ? | ? | ? | ? |
| 28 Dixon | Y | Y | Y | Y | Y | Y | Y | Y |
| 29 Waters | Y | Y | Y | Y | Y | Y | ? | Y |
| 30 Martinez | Y | Y | Y | Y | Y | Y | Y | Y |
| 31 Dymally | ? | ? | Y | Y | Y | Y | Y | Y |
| 32 Anderson | Y | Y | ? | ? | Y | Y | Y | Y |
| 33 *Dreier* | N | Y | Y | N | Y | N | Y | N |
| 34 Torres | Y | Y | Y | Y | Y | Y | Y | Y |
| 35 *Lewis* | N | Y | Y | N | Y | N | Y | N |
| 36 Brown | Y | ? | Y | Y | Y | Y | Y | Y |
| 37 *McCandless* | N | Y | Y | N | N | N | Y | N |
| 38 *Dornan* | N | Y | Y | N | Y | N | Y | N |
| 39 *Dannemeyer* | ? | ? | ? | ? | N | N | Y | N |
| 40 *Cox* | N | Y | Y | N | N | N | Y | N |
| 41 *Lowery* | Y | Y | Y | Y | N | N | Y | N |

| | 125 | 126 | 127 | 128 | 129 | 130 | 131 | 132 |
|---|---|---|---|---|---|---|---|---|
| 42 *Rohrabacher* | N | Y | Y | N | N | N | Y | N |
| 43 *Packard* | X | ? | Y | N | Y | N | Y | N |
| 44 *Cunningham* | N | ? | Y | N | N | N | Y | N |
| 45 *Hunter* | N | Y | Y | N | N | N | Y | N |
| **COLORADO** | | | | | | | | |
| 1 Schroeder | Y | Y | Y | N | N | Y | Y | Y |
| 2 Skaggs | Y | Y | Y | N | Y | Y | Y | Y |
| 3 *Campbell* | Y | ? | Y | Y | Y | Y | Y | Y |
| 4 *Allard* | N | Y | Y | N | N | N | Y | N |
| 5 *Hefley* | N | ? | Y | N | N | N | Y | N |
| 6 *Schaefer* | N | ? | Y | N | N | N | Y | N |
| **CONNECTICUT** | | | | | | | | |
| 1 Kennelly | Y | Y | Y | Y | Y | Y | Y | Y |
| 2 Gejdenson | Y | ? | Y | Y | Y | Y | Y | Y |
| 3 DeLauro | Y | Y | Y | Y | Y | Y | Y | Y |
| 4 *Shays* | N | Y | Y | N | N | Y | Y | Y |
| 5 *Franks* | Y | Y | Y | N | N | Y | Y | Y |
| 6 *Johnson* | N | Y | Y | Y | N | N | Y | Y |
| **DELAWARE** | | | | | | | | |
| AL Carper | N | Y | Y | Y | Y | Y | Y | Y |
| **FLORIDA** | | | | | | | | |
| 1 Hutto | N | Y | Y | N | Y | Y | Y | Y |
| 2 Peterson | N | Y | Y | N | Y | Y | Y | Y |
| 3 Bennett | Y | Y | Y | N | Y | Y | Y | Y |
| 4 *James* | N | Y | Y | N | N | N | Y | Y |
| 5 *McCollum* | N | Y | Y | N | N | N | Y | Y |
| 6 *Stearns* | N | Y | Y | N | N | N | Y | Y |
| 7 Gibbons | Y | ? | Y | N | Y | Y | Y | Y |
| 8 *Young* | N | Y | Y | N | N | N | Y | Y |
| 9 *Bilirakis* | N | Y | Y | N | N | N | Y | Y |
| 10 *Ireland* | Y | ? | Y | N | N | N | Y | N |
| 11 Bacchus | Y | Y | Y | Y | Y | Y | Y | Y |
| 12 *Lewis* | N | Y | Y | N | N | N | Y | Y |
| 13 *Goss* | Y | Y | Y | N | N | N | Y | Y |
| 14 Johnston | Y | Y | Y | Y | Y | Y | Y | Y |
| 15 *Shaw* | N | Y | Y | N | N | N | Y | Y |
| 16 Smith | Y | Y | Y | Y | Y | Y | Y | Y |
| 17 Lehman | Y | ? | Y | Y | Y | Y | Y | Y |
| 18 *Ros—Lehtinen* | Y | Y | Y | N | N | N | Y | Y |
| 19 Fascell | Y | Y | Y | N | Y | Y | Y | Y |
| **GEORGIA** | | | | | | | | |
| 1 Thomas | ? | ? | Y | Y | Y | Y | Y | Y |
| 2 Hatcher | ? | ? | ? | ? | Y | Y | Y | Y |
| 3 Ray | N | ? | Y | Y | Y | Y | Y | Y |
| 4 Jones | Y | ? | ? | ? | ? | ? | ? | ? |
| 5 Lewis | Y | Y | Y | Y | Y | Y | Y | Y |
| 6 *Gingrich* | N | Y | Y | N | N | N | Y | Y |
| 7 Darden | N | Y | Y | Y | Y | Y | Y | Y |
| 8 Rowland | N | Y | Y | Y | Y | Y | Y | Y |
| 9 Jenkins | N | Y | Y | Y | ? | Y | Y | Y |
| 10 Barnard | Y | ? | Y | Y | Y | Y | Y | Y |
| **HAWAII** | | | | | | | | |
| 1 Abercrombie | Y | N | Y | Y | ? | Y | Y | Y |
| 2 Mink | Y | Y | Y | Y | Y | Y | Y | Y |
| **IDAHO** | | | | | | | | |
| 1 LaRocco | Y | Y | Y | N | Y | Y | Y | Y |
| 2 Stallings | Y | Y | Y | N | Y | Y | Y | Y |
| **ILLINOIS** | | | | | | | | |
| 1 Hayes | Y | Y | Y | Y | Y | Y | Y | Y |
| 2 Savage | Y | Y | Y | Y | Y | Y | Y | Y |
| 3 Russo | Y | Y | Y | Y | Y | Y | Y | Y |
| 4 Sangmeister | # | ? | Y | Y | Y | Y | Y | Y |
| 5 Lipinski | Y | Y | Y | Y | Y | Y | Y | Y |
| 6 *Hyde* | Y | ? | Y | N | N | N | Y | Y |
| 7 Collins | ? | ? | Y | Y | Y | Y | Y | Y |
| 8 Rostenkowski | Y | ? | Y | Y | Y | Y | Y | Y |
| 9 Yates | Y | ? | Y | Y | Y | Y | Y | Y |
| 10 *Porter* | Y | Y | Y | N | Y | ? | Y | Y |
| 11 Annunzio | Y | Y | Y | Y | Y | Y | Y | Y |
| 12 *Crane* | N | ? | N | N | N | N | Y | N |
| 13 *Fawell* | Y | Y | Y | N | N | N | Y | Y |
| 14 *Hastert* | Y | Y | Y | N | N | N | Y | Y |
| 15 *Ewing* | N | Y | Y | N | Y | N | Y | N |
| 16 Cox | Y | Y | Y | Y | Y | Y | Y | Y |
| 17 Evans | Y | Y | Y | Y | Y | Y | Y | Y |
| 18 *Michel* | Y | Y | Y | N | N | Y | Y | Y |
| 19 Bruce | Y | Y | Y | Y | Y | Y | Y | Y |
| 20 Durbin | Y | Y | Y | Y | Y | Y | Y | Y |
| 21 Costello | Y | Y | Y | Y | Y | Y | Y | Y |
| 22 Poshard | Y | Y | Y | Y | N | N | Y | Y |
| **INDIANA** | | | | | | | | |
| 1 Visclosky | N | Y | Y | Y | Y | Y | Y | Y |
| 2 Sharp | Y | Y | Y | Y | Y | Y | Y | Y |
| 3 Roemer | N | Y | Y | Y | Y | Y | Y | Y |

ND Northern Democrats   SD Southern Democrats

| | 125 | 126 | 127 | 128 | 129 | 130 | 131 | 132 |
|---|---|---|---|---|---|---|---|---|
| 4 Long | Y | Y | Y | Y | Y | Y | Y | Y |
| 5 Jontz | Y | Y | Y | Y | Y | Y | Y | Y |
| 6 ***Burton*** | N | Y | Y | N | N | N | Y | N |
| 7 ***Myers*** | N | Y | Y | N | Y | N | Y | N |
| 8 McCloskey | Y | Y | Y | Y | Y | Y | Y | Y |
| 9 Hamilton | Y | Y | Y | Y | Y | Y | Y | Y |
| 10 Jacobs | Y | Y | Y | Y | N | Y | Y | Y |
| **IOWA** | | | | | | | | |
| 1 ***Leach*** | Y | Y | Y | Y | N | N | Y | C |
| 2 ***Nussle*** | N | Y | Y | Y | N | N | Y | N |
| 3 Nagle | Y | Y | Y | Y | Y | ? | Y | Y |
| 4 Smith | Y | Y | Y | Y | Y | Y | N | Y |
| 5 ***Lightfoot*** | ? | ? | Y | N | N | N | Y | N |
| 6 ***Grandy*** | N | ? | ? | ? | ? | X | ? | ? |
| **KANSAS** | | | | | | | | |
| 1 ***Roberts*** | N | ? | Y | N | N | N | Y | N |
| 2 Slattery | N | Y | Y | Y | Y | Y | Y | Y |
| 3 ***Meyers*** | N | Y | Y | N | N | N | Y | Y |
| 4 Glickman | N | Y | Y | Y | Y | Y | Y | N |
| 5 ***Nichols*** | N | Y | Y | N | Y | N | Y | N |
| **KENTUCKY** | | | | | | | | |
| 1 Hubbard | N | Y | Y | Y | Y | Y | Y | N |
| 2 Natcher | Y | Y | Y | Y | Y | Y | Y | Y |
| 3 Mazzoli | Y | Y | Y | N | Y | Y | Y | Y |
| 4 ***Bunning*** | N | ? | Y | N | N | N | Y | N |
| 5 ***Rogers*** | N | Y | Y | N | N | N | Y | N |
| 6 ***Hopkins*** | Y | ? | Y | N | N | N | Y | N |
| 7 Perkins | Y | N | Y | Y | ? | Y | N | Y |
| **LOUISIANA** | | | | | | | | |
| 1 ***Livingston*** | N | Y | Y | N | ? | ? | Y | N |
| 2 Jefferson | Y | Y | Y | Y | Y | Y | Y | Y |
| 3 Tauzin | N | Y | Y | N | Y | Y | Y | Y |
| 4 ***McCrery*** | ? | ? | Y | N | N | N | Y | Y |
| 5 Huckaby | N | Y | Y | N | Y | Y | Y | Y |
| 6 ***Baker*** | N | Y | Y | N | N | N | Y | N |
| 7 Hayes | N | ? | Y | N | Y | Y | Y | Y |
| 8 ***Holloway*** | N | Y | Y | N | N | N | Y | N |
| **MAINE** | | | | | | | | |
| 1 Andrews | Y | Y | Y | Y | Y | Y | Y | Y |
| 2 ***Snowe*** | N | Y | Y | N | Y | N | Y | Y |
| **MARYLAND** | | | | | | | | |
| 1 ***Gilchrest*** | Y | Y | Y | Y | ? | N | Y | Y |
| 2 ***Bentley*** | N | Y | Y | Y | ? | N | Y | Y |
| 3 Cardin | Y | Y | Y | Y | Y | Y | Y | Y |
| 4 McMillen | Y | Y | Y | Y | Y | Y | Y | Y |
| 5 Hoyer | Y | Y | Y | Y | Y | + | Y | Y |
| 6 Byron | Y | Y | Y | Y | Y | Y | Y | Y |
| 7 Mfume | Y | Y | Y | Y | Y | Y | Y | Y |
| 8 ***Morella*** | Y | Y | Y | Y | ? | ? | Y | Y |
| **MASSACHUSETTS** | | | | | | | | |
| 1 Olver | Y | Y | Y | Y | Y | Y | Y | Y |
| 2 Neal | Y | ? | Y | Y | Y | Y | Y | ? |
| 3 Early | Y | ? | Y | N | Y | Y | Y | Y |
| 4 Frank | Y | Y | Y | Y | Y | Y | Y | Y |
| 5 Atkins | Y | ? | N | Y | Y | Y | Y | Y |
| 6 Mavroules | Y | Y | Y | Y | Y | Y | Y | Y |
| 7 Markey | Y | Y | ? | ? | Y | Y | Y | Y |
| 8 Kennedy | Y | Y | Y | Y | Y | Y | Y | Y |
| 9 Moakley | ? | ? | Y | Y | Y | Y | Y | Y |
| 10 Studds | Y | Y | Y | Y | Y | Y | Y | Y |
| 11 Donnelly | Y | Y | ? | ? | ? | Y | Y | Y |
| **MICHIGAN** | | | | | | | | |
| 1 Conyers | Y | Y | Y | Y | Y | Y | Y | ? |
| 2 ***Pursell*** | X | ? | ? | ? | ? | N | Y | Y |
| 3 Wolpe | Y | Y | Y | Y | Y | Y | Y | ? |
| 4 ***Upton*** | Y | Y | Y | Y | N | N | Y | Y |
| 5 ***Henry*** | ? | ? | Y | N | N | N | Y | Y |
| 6 Carr | N | Y | Y | Y | Y | Y | Y | Y |
| 7 Kildee | Y | Y | Y | Y | Y | Y | Y | Y |
| 8 Traxler | Y | ? | Y | Y | Y | Y | Y | Y |
| 9 ***Vander Jagt*** | ? | ? | Y | N | Y | N | Y | N |
| 10 ***Camp*** | N | Y | Y | N | N | N | Y | Y |
| 11 ***Davis*** | Y | Y | Y | N | N | Y | Y | Y |
| 12 Bonior | Y | Y | Y | Y | Y | Y | Y | Y |
| 13 Collins | Y | Y | Y | Y | Y | Y | Y | Y |
| 14 Hertel | Y | Y | Y | Y | Y | Y | Y | ? |
| 15 Ford | Y | Y | Y | Y | Y | Y | Y | Y |
| 16 Dingell | Y | Y | Y | Y | Y | Y | Y | Y |
| 17 Levin | Y | Y | Y | C | Y | Y | Y | Y |
| 18 ***Broomfield*** | N | Y | ? | X | Y | N | Y | N |
| **MINNESOTA** | | | | | | | | |
| 1 Penny | N | Y | Y | Y | Y | Y | Y | N |
| 2 ***Weber*** | N | Y | ? | N | N | N | Y | Y |
| 3 ***Ramstad*** | N | Y | Y | N | N | N | Y | Y |
| 4 Vento | Y | Y | Y | Y | Y | Y | Y | Y |

| | 125 | 126 | 127 | 128 | 129 | 130 | 131 | 132 |
|---|---|---|---|---|---|---|---|---|
| 5 Sabo | Y | Y | Y | Y | Y | Y | Y | Y |
| 6 Sikorski | Y | Y | Y | Y | N | Y | Y | Y |
| 7 Peterson | N | Y | Y | Y | Y | Y | Y | Y |
| 8 Oberstar | Y | Y | Y | Y | Y | Y | Y | Y |
| **MISSISSIPPI** | | | | | | | | |
| 1 Whitten | Y | Y | Y | Y | Y | Y | ? | ? |
| 2 Espy | Y | Y | Y | Y | Y | Y | Y | Y |
| 3 Montgomery | Y | ? | Y | Y | Y | Y | Y | Y |
| 4 Parker | N | Y | Y | Y | Y | Y | Y | Y |
| 5 Taylor | N | Y | Y | Y | Y | Y | Y | Y |
| **MISSOURI** | | | | | | | | |
| 1 Clay | Y | ? | Y | N | N | Y | Y | ? |
| 2 Horn | Y | Y | Y | Y | Y | Y | Y | Y |
| 3 Gephardt | Y | Y | ? | ? | Y | Y | Y | Y |
| 4 Skelton | N | Y | Y | Y | Y | Y | Y | Y |
| 5 Wheat | Y | Y | Y | Y | Y | Y | Y | Y |
| 6 ***Coleman*** | N | ? | Y | N | N | N | + | Y |
| 7 ***Hancock*** | N | Y | Y | N | N | N | Y | N |
| 8 ***Emerson*** | N | Y | Y | N | N | N | Y | Y |
| 9 Volkmer | N | Y | Y | Y | Y | Y | Y | Y |
| **MONTANA** | | | | | | | | |
| 1 Williams | N | Y | Y | Y | Y | Y | Y | N |
| 2 ***Marlenee*** | N | ? | ? | Y | ? | N | Y | N |
| **NEBRASKA** | | | | | | | | |
| 1 ***Bereuter*** | N | ? | Y | N | N | N | Y | N |
| 2 Hoagland | Y | Y | Y | Y | Y | Y | Y | Y |
| 3 ***Barrett*** | N | Y | Y | N | N | N | Y | N |
| **NEVADA** | | | | | | | | |
| 1 Bilbray | Y | Y | Y | Y | Y | Y | Y | Y |
| 2 ***Vucanovich*** | N | ? | Y | N | N | N | Y | N |
| **NEW HAMPSHIRE** | | | | | | | | |
| 1 ***Zeliff*** | ? | ? | Y | N | N | N | Y | N |
| 2 Swett | Y | Y | Y | Y | Y | Y | Y | Y |
| **NEW JERSEY** | | | | | | | | |
| 1 Andrews | Y | Y | Y | Y | Y | Y | Y | Y |
| 2 Hughes | Y | Y | Y | Y | Y | Y | Y | Y |
| 3 Pallone | Y | Y | Y | Y | Y | Y | Y | Y |
| 4 ***Smith*** | Y | Y | Y | Y | Y | N | Y | Y |
| 5 ***Roukema*** | N | Y | Y | N | N | N | Y | Y |
| 6 Dwyer | Y | ? | Y | Y | Y | Y | Y | Y |
| 7 ***Rinaldo*** | Y | Y | Y | Y | Y | N | Y | Y |
| 8 Roe | Y | ? | Y | ? | ? | ? | Y | Y |
| 9 Torricelli | Y | ? | Y | Y | Y | ? | Y | Y |
| 10 Payne | Y | Y | Y | Y | ? | Y | Y | ? |
| 11 ***Gallo*** | Y | Y | Y | Y | N | N | Y | Y |
| 12 ***Zimmer*** | N | Y | Y | N | N | N | Y | Y |
| 13 ***Saxton*** | Y | Y | Y | Y | N | Y | Y | Y |
| 14 Guarini | Y | Y | Y | Y | Y | Y | Y | Y |
| **NEW MEXICO** | | | | | | | | |
| 1 ***Schiff*** | Y | Y | Y | N | Y | N | Y | N |
| 2 ***Skeen*** | Y | Y | Y | N | Y | N | Y | N |
| 3 Richardson | Y | Y | Y | Y | Y | Y | Y | Y |
| **NEW YORK** | | | | | | | | |
| 1 Hochbrueckner | Y | Y | Y | Y | Y | Y | Y | Y |
| 2 Downey | Y | ? | Y | Y | Y | Y | Y | Y |
| 3 Mrazek | Y | Y | Y | Y | Y | Y | Y | Y |
| 4 ***Lent*** | Y | Y | Y | Y | N | N | Y | Y |
| 5 ***McGrath*** | Y | Y | Y | Y | Y | Y | Y | Y |
| 6 Flake | Y | Y | Y | Y | Y | Y | Y | Y |
| 7 Ackerman | Y | ? | Y | Y | Y | Y | Y | Y |
| 8 Scheuer | Y | ? | Y | Y | Y | Y | Y | Y |
| 9 Manton | Y | Y | Y | Y | ? | Y | Y | Y |
| 10 Schumer | Y | Y | Y | Y | Y | Y | Y | Y |
| 11 Towns | Y | Y | Y | Y | Y | Y | Y | Y |
| 12 Owens | Y | Y | Y | Y | Y | Y | Y | Y |
| 13 Solarz | Y | Y | Y | Y | Y | Y | Y | Y |
| 14 ***Molinari*** | N | Y | Y | Y | N | N | Y | Y |
| 15 ***Green*** | Y | Y | Y | Y | Y | N | Y | Y |
| 16 Rangel | Y | ? | Y | N | ? | Y | Y | Y |
| 17 Weiss | Y | ? | Y | Y | Y | Y | Y | Y |
| 18 Serrano | Y | ? | Y | Y | Y | Y | Y | Y |
| 19 Engel | Y | Y | Y | Y | ? | ? | ? | Y |
| 20 Lowey | Y | Y | Y | Y | Y | Y | Y | Y |
| 21 ***Fish*** | Y | Y | Y | N | Y | N | Y | Y |
| 22 ***Gilman*** | Y | Y | Y | Y | Y | N | Y | Y |
| 23 McNulty | Y | Y | Y | Y | Y | Y | Y | Y |
| 24 ***Solomon*** | N | Y | Y | N | N | N | Y | Y |
| 25 ***Boehlert*** | Y | Y | Y | Y | N | N | Y | Y |
| 26 ***Martin*** | N | Y | Y | N | N | N | Y | Y |
| 27 ***Walsh*** | ? | ? | Y | Y | N | N | Y | Y |
| 28 McHugh | Y | ? | Y | Y | Y | Y | Y | Y |
| 29 ***Horton*** | Y | Y | Y | Y | Y | N | Y | Y |
| 30 Slaughter | Y | Y | Y | Y | Y | Y | Y | Y |
| 31 ***Paxon*** | N | Y | Y | N | N | N | Y | Y |

| | 125 | 126 | 127 | 128 | 129 | 130 | 131 | 132 |
|---|---|---|---|---|---|---|---|---|
| 32 LaFalce | Y | Y | Y | Y | Y | Y | Y | Y |
| 33 Nowak | Y | Y | Y | Y | Y | Y | Y | Y |
| 34 ***Houghton*** | Y | ? | Y | Y | ? | ? | Y | Y |
| **NORTH CAROLINA** | | | | | | | | |
| 1 Jones | ? | ? | Y | Y | Y | Y | Y | Y |
| 2 Valentine | N | Y | Y | Y | Y | Y | Y | Y |
| 3 Lancaster | Y | Y | Y | Y | Y | Y | Y | Y |
| 4 Price | Y | Y | Y | Y | Y | Y | Y | Y |
| 5 Neal | Y | Y | Y | Y | Y | Y | Y | Y |
| 6 ***Coble*** | N | Y | Y | N | N | N | Y | N |
| 7 Rose | N | Y | Y | Y | Y | Y | Y | Y |
| 8 Hefner | N | Y | Y | Y | Y | Y | Y | Y |
| 9 ***McMillan*** | N | Y | Y | Y | N | N | Y | Y |
| 10 ***Ballenger*** | N | + | Y | N | N | N | Y | Y |
| 11 ***Taylor*** | N | Y | Y | N | N | N | Y | N |
| **NORTH DAKOTA** | | | | | | | | |
| AL Dorgan | Y | ? | Y | Y | Y | Y | Y | Y |
| **OHIO** | | | | | | | | |
| 1 Luken | ? | ? | Y | Y | Y | Y | Y | Y |
| 2 ***Gradison*** | N | ? | Y | N | ? | N | Y | Y |
| 3 Hall | Y | Y | Y | Y | Y | Y | Y | Y |
| 4 ***Oxley*** | N | Y | Y | Y | Y | N | Y | N |
| 5 ***Gillmor*** | N | Y | Y | N | Y | N | Y | Y |
| 6 ***McEwen*** | N | Y | Y | N | N | N | Y | N |
| 7 ***Hobson*** | N | Y | Y | Y | N | N | Y | Y |
| 8 ***Boehner*** | N | Y | Y | N | N | N | Y | N |
| 9 Kaptur | Y | Y | Y | Y | Y | Y | Y | Y |
| 10 ***Miller*** | N | Y | Y | Y | N | N | Y | N |
| 11 Eckart | Y | Y | Y | Y | Y | Y | Y | Y |
| 12 ***Kasich*** | Y | Y | Y | Y | Y | N | Y | Y |
| 13 Pease | Y | Y | Y | Y | Y | Y | Y | Y |
| 14 Sawyer | Y | Y | Y | Y | Y | Y | Y | Y |
| 15 ***Wylie*** | Y | Y | Y | N | Y | N | ? | ? |
| 16 ***Regula*** | N | Y | Y | N | N | N | Y | Y |
| 17 Traficant | Y | ? | Y | Y | Y | Y | Y | Y |
| 18 Applegate | N | Y | Y | Y | Y | Y | Y | Y |
| 19 Feighan | Y | Y | ? | ? | Y | Y | Y | Y |
| 20 Oakar | ? | ? | Y | ? | ? | ? | ? | ? |
| 21 Stokes | Y | Y | Y | Y | Y | Y | + | Y |
| **OKLAHOMA** | | | | | | | | |
| 1 ***Inhofe*** | N | Y | Y | N | N | N | Y | N |
| 2 Synar | Y | Y | Y | Y | Y | Y | Y | Y |
| 3 Brewster | N | Y | Y | Y | Y | Y | Y | Y |
| 4 McCurdy | Y | Y | ? | ? | Y | Y | Y | Y |
| 5 ***Edwards*** | N | Y | ? | ? | ? | ? | ? | ? |
| 6 English | Y | Y | Y | N | Y | Y | Y | Y |
| **OREGON** | | | | | | | | |
| 1 AuCoin | ? | ? | ? | # | ? | ? | ? | ? |
| 2 ***Smith*** | N | Y | Y | N | N | N | Y | N |
| 3 Wyden | Y | Y | Y | Y | Y | Y | Y | Y |
| 4 DeFazio | Y | Y | Y | Y | Y | Y | Y | Y |
| 5 Kopetski | Y | Y | ? | ? | Y | Y | Y | Y |
| **PENNSYLVANIA** | | | | | | | | |
| 1 Foglietta | Y | Y | Y | Y | Y | Y | Y | Y |
| 2 Blackwell | Y | Y | Y | Y | ? | ? | Y | Y |
| 3 Borski | Y | Y | Y | Y | Y | Y | Y | Y |
| 4 Kolter | ? | ? | Y | Y | Y | Y | ? | ? |
| 5 ***Schulze*** | Y | Y | Y | N | Y | N | Y | Y |
| 6 Yatron | Y | ? | Y | Y | Y | Y | Y | Y |
| 7 ***Weldon*** | N | Y | Y | N | N | N | Y | Y |
| 8 Kostmayer | Y | Y | Y | Y | Y | Y | Y | Y |
| 9 ***Shuster*** | N | ? | Y | N | N | N | Y | N |
| 10 ***McDade*** | Y | ? | Y | Y | N | N | Y | Y |
| 11 Kanjorski | Y | Y | Y | Y | Y | Y | Y | Y |
| 12 Murtha | Y | Y | Y | Y | Y | Y | Y | Y |
| 13 ***Coughlin*** | Y | Y | Y | Y | ? | N | Y | N |
| 14 Coyne | Y | Y | Y | Y | Y | Y | Y | Y |
| 15 ***Ritter*** | N | Y | Y | N | Y | N | Y | Y |
| 16 ***Walker*** | N | Y | Y | N | N | N | Y | N |
| 17 ***Gekas*** | Y | Y | Y | N | N | N | Y | Y |
| 18 ***Santorum*** | ? | ? | Y | N | Y | N | Y | Y |
| 19 ***Goodling*** | N | ? | Y | N | N | N | Y | Y |
| 20 Gaydos | N | ? | Y | Y | Y | Y | Y | Y |
| 21 ***Ridge*** | N | Y | Y | N | N | N | Y | Y |
| 22 Murphy | N | ? | Y | Y | N | Y | Y | ? |
| 23 ***Clinger*** | N | Y | Y | Y | Y | N | Y | Y |
| **RHODE ISLAND** | | | | | | | | |
| 1 ***Machtley*** | N | ? | Y | Y | N | N | Y | Y |
| 2 Reed | Y | ? | Y | Y | Y | Y | Y | Y |
| **SOUTH CAROLINA** | | | | | | | | |
| 1 ***Ravenel*** | Y | Y | Y | N | Y | N | Y | Y |
| 2 ***Spence*** | N | Y | Y | Y | Y | N | Y | Y |
| 3 Derrick | Y | Y | Y | Y | Y | Y | Y | Y |
| 4 Patterson | N | + | Y | Y | Y | Y | Y | Y |
| 5 Spratt | Y | Y | Y | Y | Y | Y | Y | Y |
| 6 Tallon | N | Y | Y | Y | Y | Y | Y | Y |

| | 125 | 126 | 127 | 128 | 129 | 130 | 131 | 132 |
|---|---|---|---|---|---|---|---|---|
| **SOUTH DAKOTA** | | | | | | | | |
| AL Johnson | N | Y | Y | Y | Y | Y | Y | Y |
| **TENNESSEE** | | | | | | | | |
| 1 ***Quillen*** | N | ? | Y | Y | N | N | ? | ? |
| 2 ***Duncan*** | N | + | Y | N | N | N | Y | N |
| 3 Lloyd | ? | ? | Y | Y | Y | Y | Y | Y |
| 4 Cooper | Y | Y | Y | Y | Y | ? | Y | Y |
| 5 Clement | Y | Y | Y | Y | Y | Y | Y | Y |
| 6 Gordon | Y | Y | Y | Y | Y | Y | Y | Y |
| 7 ***Sundquist*** | N | Y | Y | Y | N | N | Y | Y |
| 8 Tanner | N | Y | Y | Y | Y | Y | Y | Y |
| 9 Ford | Y | Y | Y | Y | Y | Y | Y | Y |
| **TEXAS** | | | | | | | | |
| 1 Chapman | N | Y | Y | N | Y | Y | Y | ? |
| 2 Wilson | N | Y | Y | N | Y | Y | ? | ? |
| 3 ***Johnson*** | N | Y | Y | N | Y | N | Y | N |
| 4 Hall | N | Y | Y | N | Y | Y | Y | N |
| 5 Bryant | N | Y | Y | N | Y | Y | Y | Y |
| 6 ***Barton*** | N | Y | Y | N | N | N | Y | N |
| 7 ***Archer*** | N | Y | Y | N | Y | N | Y | N |
| 8 ***Fields*** | N | Y | Y | N | ? | N | Y | N |
| 9 Brooks | Y | Y | Y | N | Y | Y | Y | Y |
| 10 Pickle | Y | Y | Y | N | Y | Y | Y | Y |
| 11 Edwards | N | Y | Y | N | Y | Y | Y | Y |
| 12 Geren | N | Y | Y | N | Y | Y | Y | N |
| 13 Sarpalius | N | Y | Y | N | Y | Y | Y | Y |
| 14 Laughlin | ? | ? | Y | N | Y | Y | Y | Y |
| 15 de la Garza | Y | Y | Y | N | Y | Y | Y | Y |
| 16 Coleman | Y | Y | Y | N | Y | Y | Y | Y |
| 17 Stenholm | N | ? | Y | N | Y | Y | Y | N |
| 18 Washington | N | ? | Y | N | Y | ? | N | Y |
| 19 ***Combest*** | N | Y | Y | N | Y | Y | Y | N |
| 20 Gonzalez | Y | N | Y | Y | Y | Y | Y | Y |
| 21 ***Smith*** | Y | Y | Y | N | N | N | Y | Y |
| 22 ***DeLay*** | N | Y | Y | N | N | ? | Y | N |
| 23 Bustamante | Y | Y | Y | Y | Y | Y | Y | ? |
| 24 Frost | Y | Y | Y | N | Y | Y | Y | Y |
| 25 Andrews | Y | Y | Y | N | Y | Y | Y | Y |
| 26 ***Armey*** | N | Y | Y | N | N | N | Y | N |
| 27 Ortiz | Y | Y | Y | N | Y | Y | Y | Y |
| **UTAH** | | | | | | | | |
| 1 ***Hansen*** | N | Y | Y | N | Y | N | Y | Y |
| 2 Owens | Y | Y | Y | Y | Y | Y | Y | Y |
| 3 Orton | N | ? | Y | Y | Y | Y | Y | N |
| **VERMONT** | | | | | | | | |
| AL *Sanders* | Y | Y | Y | Y | Y | Y | Y | Y |
| **VIRGINIA** | | | | | | | | |
| 1 ***Bateman*** | N | Y | Y | Y | Y | N | Y | Y |
| 2 Pickett | N | Y | Y | Y | Y | Y | Y | Y |
| 3 ***Bliley*** | N | Y | Y | Y | N | N | Y | N |
| 4 Sisisky | N | Y | Y | Y | Y | Y | Y | Y |
| 5 Payne | N | Y | Y | Y | Y | Y | Y | Y |
| 6 Olin | Y | Y | Y | Y | ? | Y | Y | Y |
| 7 ***Allen*** | N | Y | ? | N | N | N | Y | N |
| 8 Moran | Y | Y | Y | Y | Y | Y | Y | Y |
| 9 Boucher | Y | Y | Y | Y | Y | ? | Y | Y |
| 10 ***Wolf*** | N | Y | Y | N | N | N | Y | Y |
| **WASHINGTON** | | | | | | | | |
| 1 ***Miller*** | ? | ? | Y | Y | N | Y | Y | Y |
| 2 Swift | Y | Y | Y | Y | Y | Y | Y | Y |
| 3 Unsoeld | Y | Y | Y | Y | Y | Y | Y | Y |
| 4 ***Morrison*** | Y | ? | Y | Y | Y | N | Y | Y |
| 5 Foley | | | | | | | | |
| 6 Dicks | Y | ? | Y | Y | Y | Y | Y | Y |
| 7 McDermott | Y | ? | Y | Y | Y | Y | Y | Y |
| 8 ***Chandler*** | Y | ? | Y | Y | N | N | Y | Y |
| **WEST VIRGINIA** | | | | | | | | |
| 1 Mollohan | Y | Y | Y | Y | Y | Y | Y | Y |
| 2 Staggers | ? | ? | Y | Y | Y | Y | Y | Y |
| 3 Wise | Y | Y | Y | Y | Y | Y | Y | Y |
| 4 Rahall | Y | Y | Y | Y | Y | Y | Y | Y |
| **WISCONSIN** | | | | | | | | |
| 1 Aspin | Y | Y | Y | Y | Y | Y | Y | Y |
| 2 ***Klug*** | Y | Y | Y | N | Y | N | Y | Y |
| 3 ***Gunderson*** | N | Y | Y | N | Y | N | Y | Y |
| 4 Kleczka | Y | ? | Y | Y | Y | Y | Y | ? |
| 5 Moody | N | Y | Y | Y | Y | Y | Y | Y |
| 6 ***Petri*** | N | Y | Y | N | Y | N | Y | Y |
| 7 Obey | Y | Y | Y | Y | Y | Y | Y | Y |
| 8 ***Roth*** | N | ? | Y | N | Y | N | Y | N |
| 9 ***Sensenbrenner*** | N | Y | Y | N | N | N | Y | N |
| **WYOMING** | | | | | | | | |
| AL ***Thomas*** | N | Y | Y | Y | N | N | Y | N |

Southern states - Ala., Ark., Fla., Ga., Ky., La., Miss., N.C., Okla., S.C., Tenn., Texas, Va.
Omitted votes are quorum calls, which CQ does not include in its vote charts.

**133. HR 776. National Energy Policy/Octane Replacement.** Jontz, D-Ind., amendment to require the secretary of Energy to establish an octane replacement program to increase the use of domestically produced, renewable, non-petroleum octane enhancers such as ethanol. The amendment would also create a system for the use of marketable octane credits for gasoline sold in the United States. Rejected 198-211: R 46-112; D 151-99 (ND 115-56, SD 36-43); I 1-0, May 20, 1992. A 'nay' was a vote in support of the president's position.

**134. HR 776. National Energy Policy/Nuclear Plants.** Clement, D-Tenn., amendment on nuclear power plant licensing to make it significantly more difficult to force a second public hearing before a new plant would be allowed to operate. Adopted 254-160: R 144-18; D 110-141 (ND 47-124, SD 63-17); I 0-1, May 20, 1992. A 'yea' was a vote in support of the president's position.

**135. HR 776. National Energy Policy/Natural Gas.** Markey, D-Mass., amendment to prohibit state pro-rationing of natural gas for the purpose of raising prices. Adopted 238-169: R 94-63; D 143-106 (ND 124-45, SD 19-61); I 1-0, May 20, 1992.

**136. HR 4990. Fiscal 1992 Rescissions/Rule.** Adoption of the rule (H Res 462) to waive all points of order against and provide for House floor consideration of the conference report to rescind $8,158,305,054 in previously approved budget authority for fiscal 1992. Adopted 267-142: R 18-137; D 248-5 (ND 169-5, SD 79-0); I 1-0, May 21, 1992.

**137. HR 4990. Fiscal 1992 Rescissions/Conference Report.** Adoption of the conference report to rescind $8,158,305,054 in previously approved budget authority for fiscal 1992, including $7.2 billion in defense, $761 million in domestic programs and $164 million in foreign aid. The bill would rescind $500 million for the B-2 bomber, $200 million for the Strategic Defense Initiative, and terminate the third but not the second *Seawolf* nuclear submarine. The administration had requested rescissions totaling $7,862,772,690. Adopted 404-11: R 157-1; D 246-10 (ND 166-9, SD 80-1); I 1-0, May 21, 1992.

**138. H Con Res 287. Fiscal 1993 Budget Resolution/Rule.** Adoption of the rule (H Res 463) to waive all points of order against and provide for House floor consideration of the conference report to set budget levels for the fiscal year ending Sept. 30, 1993: budget authority, $1.516 trillion; outlays, $1.500 trillion; revenues, $1.173 trillion; deficit, $327 billion. Adopted 253-160: R 0-159; D 252-1 (ND 172-0, SD 80-1); I 1-0, May 21, 1992.

**139. H Con Res 287. Fiscal 1993 Budget Resolution/Conference Report.** Adoption of the conference report to set budget levels for the fiscal year ending Sept. 30, 1993: budget authority, $1.516 trillion; outlays, $1.500 trillion; revenues, $1.173 trillion; deficit, $327 billion. Adopted 209-207: R 0-159; D 209-47 (ND 143-34, SD 66-13); I 0-1, May 21, 1992.

**140. HR 776. National Energy Policy/Strategic Petroleum Reserve.** Rostenkowski, D-Ill., amendment to strike the provisions of the bill to require oil importers and refiners to set aside 1 percent of their crude oil for the Strategic Petroleum Reserve (SPR) or make cash payments to fill the SPR, if enough oil is not acquired to fill the reserve through other means at a rate of 150,000 barrels per day. Adopted 263-135: R 141-9; D 122-125 (ND 60-106, SD 62-19); I 0-1, May 27, 1992. A "yea" was a vote in support of the president's position.

## KEY

Y   Voted for (yea).
#   Paired for.
+   Announced for.
N   Voted against (nay).
X   Paired against.
−   Announced against.
P   Voted "present."
C   Voted "present" to avoid possible conflict of interest.
?   Did not vote or otherwise make a position known.

Democrats   **Republicans**
*Independent*

| | 133 | 134 | 135 | 136 | 137 | 138 | 139 | 140 |
|---|---|---|---|---|---|---|---|---|
| **ALABAMA** | | | | | | | | |
| 1 *Callahan* | N | Y | N | N | Y | N | N | Y |
| 2 *Dickinson* | Y | Y | ? | N | N | N | N | Y |
| 3 Browder | N | Y | N | Y | Y | Y | Y | N |
| 4 Bevill | N | Y | N | Y | Y | Y | Y | Y |
| 5 Cramer | N | Y | N | Y | Y | Y | N | Y |
| 6 Erdreich | N | Y | N | Y | Y | Y | Y | Y |
| 7 Harris | N | Y | N | Y | Y | Y | Y | N |
| **ALASKA** | | | | | | | | |
| AL *Young* | N | Y | N | N | Y | N | N | Y |
| **ARIZONA** | | | | | | | | |
| 1 *Rhodes* | N | Y | N | N | Y | N | N | Y |
| 2 Pastor | + | Y | N | Y | Y | Y | Y | N |
| 3 *Stump* | N | Y | N | N | Y | N | N | Y |
| 4 *Kyl* | N | Y | N | N | Y | N | N | Y |
| 5 *Kolbe* | N | Y | Y | N | Y | N | N | Y |
| **ARKANSAS** | | | | | | | | |
| 1 Alexander | Y | Y | N | Y | Y | Y | Y | ? |
| 2 Thornton | Y | Y | N | Y | Y | Y | Y | Y |
| 3 *Hammerschmidt* | Y | Y | N | Y | Y | Y | Y | Y |
| 4 Anthony | ? | # | X | ? | ? | ? | # | # |
| **CALIFORNIA** | | | | | | | | |
| 1 *Riggs* | N | N | Y | N | Y | N | N | Y |
| 2 *Herger* | ? | Y | Y | N | Y | N | N | Y |
| 3 Matsui | N | N | N | Y | Y | Y | Y | ? |
| 4 Fazio | N | N | N | Y | Y | Y | Y | Y |
| 5 Pelosi | Y | N | Y | Y | Y | Y | Y | Y |
| 6 Boxer | ? | X | # | ? | ? | ? | ? | X |
| 7 Miller | N | N | Y | N | Y | N | N | Y |
| 8 Dellums | Y | N | Y | N | Y | N | N | N |
| 9 Stark | N | N | Y | N | Y | N | N | Y |
| 10 Edwards | N | N | Y | Y | Y | Y | Y | N |
| 11 Lantos | Y | N | Y | Y | Y | Y | Y | N |
| 12 *Campbell* | N | N | N | ? | ? | ? | ? | ? |
| 13 Mineta | N | N | N | Y | Y | Y | Y | N |
| 14 *Doolittle* | N | Y | Y | N | Y | N | N | Y |
| 15 Condit | Y | N | Y | Y | Y | Y | Y | Y |
| 16 Panetta | Y | N | N | Y | Y | Y | Y | Y |
| 17 Dooley | Y | Y | Y | Y | Y | Y | Y | Y |
| 18 Lehman | N | Y | N | Y | Y | Y | Y | Y |
| 19 *Lagomarsino* | N | Y | Y | N | Y | N | N | # |
| 20 *Thomas* | N | N | N | N | Y | N | N | Y |
| 21 *Gallegly* | N | Y | Y | N | Y | N | N | Y |
| 22 *Moorhead* | N | Y | Y | N | Y | N | N | Y |
| 23 Beilenson | N | N | Y | Y | Y | Y | Y | N |
| 24 Waxman | N | Y | Y | Y | Y | Y | Y | N |
| 25 Roybal | N | N | Y | Y | Y | Y | Y | N |
| 26 Berman | Y | N | Y | Y | Y | Y | Y | Y |
| 27 Levine | ? | X | ? | ? | ? | ? | ? | X |
| 28 Dixon | N | N | Y | Y | Y | Y | Y | N |
| 29 Waters | Y | N | Y | Y | Y | Y | ? | N |
| 30 Martinez | Y | N | Y | Y | Y | Y | Y | N |
| 31 Dymally | Y | N | ? | ? | ? | # | Y | N |
| 32 Anderson | N | Y | N | Y | Y | Y | Y | Y |
| 33 *Dreier* | N | N | Y | N | Y | N | N | Y |
| 34 Torres | + | N | Y | Y | Y | Y | Y | N |
| 35 *Lewis* | N | Y | N | N | Y | N | N | Y |
| 36 Brown | N | N | Y | Y | Y | Y | Y | N |
| 37 *McCandless* | N | Y | Y | N | Y | N | N | Y |
| 38 *Dornan* | N | Y | Y | N | Y | N | N | Y |
| 39 *Dannemeyer* | N | Y | N | Y | N | Y | ? | ? |
| 40 *Cox* | N | Y | N | Y | Y | N | N | Y |
| 41 *Lowery* | ? | Y | Y | N | Y | N | N | Y |

| | 133 | 134 | 135 | 136 | 137 | 138 | 139 | 140 |
|---|---|---|---|---|---|---|---|---|
| 42 *Rohrabacher* | N | Y | Y | N | Y | N | N | Y |
| 43 *Packard* | N | Y | Y | N | ? | ? | X | ? |
| 44 *Cunningham* | N | Y | N | Y | N | N | N | Y |
| 45 *Hunter* | N | Y | Y | N | Y | N | N | Y |
| **COLORADO** | | | | | | | | |
| 1 Schroeder | Y | N | N | Y | Y | Y | N | Y |
| 2 Skaggs | N | N | N | Y | Y | Y | Y | Y |
| 3 Campbell | N | N | N | Y | Y | Y | Y | Y |
| 4 *Allard* | N | Y | N | N | Y | N | N | Y |
| 5 *Hefley* | Y | Y | N | N | Y | N | N | Y |
| 6 *Schaefer* | N | Y | N | N | Y | N | N | Y |
| **CONNECTICUT** | | | | | | | | |
| 1 Kennelly | N | N | Y | Y | Y | Y | Y | N |
| 2 Gejdenson | Y | N | Y | Y | Y | Y | Y | N |
| 3 DeLauro | N | N | Y | Y | Y | Y | Y | N |
| 4 *Shays* | N | N | Y | Y | Y | N | N | Y |
| 5 *Franks* | N | Y | Y | Y | Y | N | N | Y |
| 6 *Johnson* | N | Y | Y | N | Y | N | N | Y |
| **DELAWARE** | | | | | | | | |
| AL Carper | Y | Y | Y | Y | Y | Y | Y | N |
| **FLORIDA** | | | | | | | | |
| 1 Hutto | N | Y | N | Y | Y | Y | Y | Y |
| 2 Peterson | N | Y | N | Y | Y | Y | Y | Y |
| 3 Bennett | N | N | Y | Y | Y | Y | Y | N |
| 4 *James* | N | Y | Y | N | Y | N | N | Y |
| 5 *McCollum* | N | Y | Y | N | Y | N | N | ? |
| 6 *Stearns* | N | Y | Y | N | Y | N | N | Y |
| 7 Gibbons | ? | ? | Y | Y | Y | Y | Y | Y |
| 8 *Young* | N | Y | Y | N | Y | N | N | N |
| 9 *Bilirakis* | N | Y | N | N | Y | N | N | Y |
| 10 *Ireland* | N | Y | N | ? | Y | N | N | Y |
| 11 Bacchus | N | N | Y | Y | Y | Y | Y | Y |
| 12 *Lewis* | N | Y | Y | N | N | N | N | + |
| 13 *Goss* | N | Y | Y | N | Y | N | N | Y |
| 14 Johnston | Y | N | Y | Y | Y | Y | Y | Y |
| 15 *Shaw* | N | Y | Y | N | Y | N | N | Y |
| 16 Smith | Y | N | Y | Y | Y | Y | Y | N |
| 17 Lehman | ? | N | Y | Y | Y | Y | Y | N |
| 18 *Ros−Lehtinen* | N | N | Y | N | Y | N | N | Y |
| 19 Fascell | Y | Y | N | Y | Y | Y | Y | ? |
| **GEORGIA** | | | | | | | | |
| 1 Thomas | Y | Y | N | Y | Y | Y | Y | Y |
| 2 Hatcher | Y | Y | N | Y | Y | ? | ? | Y |
| 3 Ray | N | Y | N | Y | ? | Y | # | Y |
| 4 Jones | ? | ? | ? | ? | ? | ? | ? | N |
| 5 Lewis | Y | N | Y | Y | Y | Y | Y | N |
| 6 *Gingrich* | N | Y | N | Y | N | N | N | Y |
| 7 Darden | Y | Y | N | Y | Y | Y | Y | Y |
| 8 Rowland | N | Y | N | Y | Y | Y | Y | Y |
| 9 Jenkins | Y | Y | N | Y | Y | Y | ? | Y |
| 10 Barnard | Y | Y | N | Y | Y | N | Y | N |
| **HAWAII** | | | | | | | | |
| 1 Abercrombie | Y | N | Y | Y | Y | Y | Y | N |
| 2 Mink | N | N | Y | Y | Y | Y | Y | N |
| **IDAHO** | | | | | | | | |
| 1 LaRocco | Y | N | N | Y | Y | Y | Y | Y |
| 2 Stallings | Y | Y | N | Y | Y | Y | Y | Y |
| **ILLINOIS** | | | | | | | | |
| 1 Hayes | Y | N | Y | Y | Y | Y | N | Y |
| 2 Savage | Y | N | Y | Y | Y | Y | N | N |
| 3 Russo | Y | Y | Y | N | Y | Y | N | ? |
| 4 Sangmeister | Y | Y | Y | Y | Y | Y | Y | Y |
| 5 Lipinski | Y | Y | Y | Y | Y | Y | Y | Y |
| 6 *Hyde* | Y | Y | Y | ? | ? | ? | N | Y |
| 7 Collins | N | Y | Y | ? | ? | ? | ? | X |
| 8 Rostenkowski | Y | Y | Y | Y | Y | Y | Y | Y |
| 9 Yates | Y | Y | Y | Y | Y | Y | Y | N |
| 10 *Porter* | Y | Y | N | Y | N | N | N | Y |
| 11 Annunzio | Y | N | Y | Y | Y | Y | Y | Y |
| 12 *Crane* | N | Y | N | N | Y | N | N | + |
| 13 *Fawell* | N | Y | Y | N | N | N | N | Y |
| 14 *Hastert* | N | Y | N | N | Y | N | N | Y |
| 15 *Ewing* | N | Y | N | N | Y | N | N | Y |
| 16 *Cox* | Y | N | Y | Y | Y | Y | N | Y |
| 17 Evans | Y | N | Y | Y | Y | Y | N | Y |
| 18 *Michel* | N | Y | Y | N | Y | N | N | Y |
| 19 Bruce | Y | N | Y | Y | Y | Y | Y | + |
| 20 Durbin | Y | N | Y | Y | Y | Y | Y | Y |
| 21 Costello | Y | N | Y | Y | Y | Y | Y | N |
| 22 Poshard | Y | N | N | Y | Y | Y | Y | Y |
| **INDIANA** | | | | | | | | |
| 1 Visclosky | N | N | Y | Y | Y | Y | N | Y |
| 2 Sharp | Y | N | Y | Y | Y | Y | N | Y |
| 3 Roemer | Y | Y | Y | Y | Y | Y | N | Y |

ND  Northern Democrats     SD  Southern Democrats

| | 133 | 134 | 135 | 136 | 137 | 138 | 139 | 140 |
|---|---|---|---|---|---|---|---|---|
| 4 Long | Y | N | Y | Y | Y | Y | Y | Y |
| 5 Jontz | Y | N | Y | Y | Y | Y | Y | N |
| 6 ***Burton*** | Y | Y | N | N | Y | N | N | ? |
| 7 ***Myers*** | Y | Y | N | Y | Y | N | N | Y |
| 8 McCloskey | Y | N | Y | Y | ? | Y | Y | N |
| 9 Hamilton | ? | Y | N | Y | Y | Y | Y | N |
| 10 Jacobs | N | N | Y | Y | Y | Y | N | N |
| **IOWA** | | | | | | | | |
| 1 ***Leach*** | ? | Y | Y | N | Y | N | N | Y |
| 2 ***Nussle*** | Y | Y | N | N | Y | N | N | Y |
| 3 Nagle | Y | Y | Y | Y | Y | Y | N | Y |
| 4 Smith | Y | Y | N | Y | Y | Y | N | Y |
| 5 ***Lightfoot*** | Y | Y | Y | Y | Y | N | N | Y |
| 6 ***Grandy*** | ? | ? | ? | ? | Y | N | N | Y |
| **KANSAS** | | | | | | | | |
| 1 ***Roberts*** | N | Y | N | N | Y | N | N | Y |
| 2 Slattery | Y | N | N | Y | Y | Y | Y | N |
| 3 ***Meyers*** | Y | Y | N | N | Y | N | N | Y |
| 4 Glickman | Y | N | N | Y | Y | Y | Y | Y |
| 5 ***Nichols*** | N | Y | N | N | Y | N | N | Y |
| **KENTUCKY** | | | | | | | | |
| 1 Hubbard | Y | Y | N | Y | Y | N | N | Y |
| 2 Natcher | N | Y | N | Y | Y | Y | Y | Y |
| 3 Mazzoli | Y | N | Y | Y | Y | Y | Y | N |
| 4 ***Bunning*** | N | Y | N | N | Y | N | N | Y |
| 5 ***Rogers*** | N | N | N | N | Y | N | N | Y |
| 6 ***Hopkins*** | N | Y | N | N | Y | N | N | Y |
| 7 Perkins | Y | N | Y | Y | Y | Y | Y | Y |
| **LOUISIANA** | | | | | | | | |
| 1 ***Livingston*** | N | Y | N | Y | Y | N | N | Y |
| 2 Jefferson | N | Y | N | Y | Y | Y | Y | Y |
| 3 Tauzin | N | Y | N | Y | Y | Y | N | Y |
| 4 ***McCrery*** | N | Y | N | ? | ? | ? | ? | Y |
| 5 Huckaby | N | Y | N | Y | Y | Y | Y | Y |
| 6 ***Baker*** | N | Y | N | N | Y | N | N | Y |
| 7 Hayes | N | Y | N | Y | Y | Y | N | Y |
| 8 ***Holloway*** | Y | Y | N | N | Y | N | N | # |
| **MAINE** | | | | | | | | |
| 1 Andrews | N | N | Y | Y | Y | Y | Y | N |
| 2 ***Snowe*** | N | N | Y | Y | Y | N | N | Y |
| **MARYLAND** | | | | | | | | |
| 1 ***Gilchrest*** | Y | N | Y | N | Y | N | N | Y |
| 2 ***Bentley*** | Y | Y | Y | N | Y | N | N | ? |
| 3 Cardin | Y | N | Y | Y | Y | Y | Y | Y |
| 4 McMillen | Y | Y | Y | Y | Y | Y | Y | N |
| 5 Hoyer | Y | Y | Y | Y | Y | Y | Y | Y |
| 6 Byron | N | Y | Y | Y | Y | Y | N | Y |
| 7 Mfume | Y | Y | Y | Y | Y | Y | Y | N |
| 8 ***Morella*** | N | Y | Y | N | Y | N | N | N |
| **MASSACHUSETTS** | | | | | | | | |
| 1 Olver | Y | N | Y | Y | Y | Y | Y | N |
| 2 Neal | Y | N | Y | Y | Y | Y | Y | N |
| 3 Early | N | N | Y | N | Y | Y | Y | N |
| 4 Frank | N | N | Y | N | Y | Y | Y | N |
| 5 Atkins | Y | N | Y | Y | Y | Y | Y | N |
| 6 Mavroules | Y | N | Y | Y | Y | Y | Y | N |
| 7 Markey | N | N | Y | Y | Y | Y | Y | N |
| 8 Kennedy | Y | N | Y | N | N | Y | Y | N |
| 9 Moakley | Y | N | Y | Y | Y | Y | Y | N |
| 10 Studds | N | N | Y | Y | Y | Y | Y | N |
| 11 Donnelly | N | Y | Y | Y | Y | Y | Y | ? |
| **MICHIGAN** | | | | | | | | |
| 1 Conyers | Y | N | Y | Y | Y | ? | N | N |
| 2 ***Pursell*** | N | Y | ? | N | Y | N | N | Y |
| 3 Wolpe | Y | N | Y | ? | Y | ? | Y | N |
| 4 ***Upton*** | N | Y | Y | N | Y | N | N | Y |
| 5 ***Henry*** | N | Y | Y | N | Y | N | N | Y |
| 6 Carr | N | Y | Y | Y | Y | Y | N | ? |
| 7 Kildee | Y | N | Y | Y | Y | Y | Y | N |
| 8 Traxler | ? | ? | ? | Y | Y | Y | Y | N |
| 9 ***Vander Jagt*** | N | Y | N | N | Y | N | N | Y |
| 10 ***Camp*** | N | Y | Y | N | Y | N | N | Y |
| 11 ***Davis*** | ? | Y | N | N | ? | N | N | Y |
| 12 Bonior | N | N | N | Y | Y | Y | Y | N |
| 13 Collins | N | Y | N | Y | Y | Y | Y | N |
| 14 Hertel | N | N | Y | Y | Y | Y | Y | N |
| 15 Ford | Y | ? | ? | Y | Y | Y | Y | N |
| 16 Dingell | N | Y | N | Y | Y | Y | Y | N |
| 17 Levin | Y | N | Y | Y | Y | Y | Y | N |
| 18 ***Broomfield*** | N | Y | Y | ? | ? | ? | ? | Y |
| **MINNESOTA** | | | | | | | | |
| 1 Penny | Y | N | Y | N | Y | Y | Y | N |
| 2 ***Weber*** | Y | Y | ? | ? | Y | N | N | Y |
| 3 ***Ramstad*** | Y | N | Y | N | Y | N | N | Y |
| 4 Vento | Y | N | N | Y | Y | Y | Y | N |

| | 133 | 134 | 135 | 136 | 137 | 138 | 139 | 140 |
|---|---|---|---|---|---|---|---|---|
| 5 Sabo | Y | N | Y | Y | Y | Y | Y | N |
| 6 Sikorski | Y | N | Y | Y | N | Y | Y | N |
| 7 Peterson | Y | N | Y | Y | Y | Y | N | Y |
| 8 Oberstar | Y | N | Y | Y | Y | Y | Y | N |
| **MISSISSIPPI** | | | | | | | | |
| 1 Whitten | ? | ? | ? | Y | Y | Y | Y | ? |
| 2 Espy | Y | Y | N | Y | Y | Y | Y | Y |
| 3 Montgomery | N | Y | N | Y | Y | Y | Y | Y |
| 4 Parker | N | Y | N | Y | Y | Y | Y | Y |
| 5 Taylor | Y | N | N | Y | Y | Y | Y | N |
| **MISSOURI** | | | | | | | | |
| 1 Clay | Y | N | N | Y | Y | Y | Y | N |
| 2 Horn | Y | N | Y | Y | Y | Y | Y | N |
| 3 Gephardt | Y | N | N | Y | Y | Y | Y | N |
| 4 Skelton | Y | Y | N | Y | Y | Y | Y | Y |
| 5 Wheat | Y | N | Y | Y | Y | Y | Y | N |
| 6 ***Coleman*** | Y | Y | Y | N | Y | N | N | N |
| 7 ***Hancock*** | N | Y | N | N | Y | N | N | Y |
| 8 ***Emerson*** | Y | Y | N | N | Y | N | N | Y |
| 9 Volkmer | Y | Y | Y | Y | Y | Y | N | Y |
| **MONTANA** | | | | | | | | |
| 1 Williams | Y | N | ? | Y | Y | Y | Y | Y |
| 2 ***Marlenee*** | Y | Y | N | N | Y | N | N | Y |
| **NEBRASKA** | | | | | | | | |
| 1 ***Bereuter*** | Y | Y | Y | N | Y | N | N | Y |
| 2 Hoagland | Y | N | N | Y | Y | Y | Y | Y |
| 3 ***Barrett*** | Y | Y | N | N | Y | N | N | Y |
| **NEVADA** | | | | | | | | |
| 1 Bilbray | Y | N | N | Y | Y | Y | Y | Y |
| 2 ***Vucanovich*** | N | N | N | N | Y | N | N | Y |
| **NEW HAMPSHIRE** | | | | | | | | |
| 1 ***Zeliff*** | N | Y | Y | N | Y | N | N | Y |
| 2 Swett | Y | N | Y | Y | Y | Y | N | N |
| **NEW JERSEY** | | | | | | | | |
| 1 Andrews | Y | Y | Y | Y | Y | Y | N | Y |
| 2 Hughes | Y | Y | Y | Y | Y | Y | Y | N |
| 3 Pallone | Y | N | Y | Y | Y | Y | Y | N |
| 4 ***Smith*** | Y | Y | Y | Y | Y | N | N | Y |
| 5 ***Roukema*** | N | Y | Y | N | Y | N | N | N |
| 6 Dwyer | Y | Y | Y | Y | Y | ? | ? | N |
| 7 ***Rinaldo*** | N | Y | Y | Y | Y | N | N | Y |
| 8 Roe | Y | ? | ? | Y | Y | Y | N | N |
| 9 Torricelli | Y | Y | Y | Y | Y | Y | Y | ? |
| 10 Payne | ? | ? | ? | Y | Y | Y | Y | N |
| 11 ***Gallo*** | Y | Y | Y | Y | Y | N | N | Y |
| 12 ***Zimmer*** | Y | Y | Y | N | Y | N | N | Y |
| 13 ***Saxton*** | Y | Y | Y | N | Y | N | N | Y |
| 14 Guarini | N | Y | Y | Y | Y | Y | Y | ? |
| **NEW MEXICO** | | | | | | | | |
| 1 ***Schiff*** | N | Y | N | Y | Y | N | N | Y |
| 2 ***Skeen*** | Y | Y | N | Y | Y | N | N | Y |
| 3 Richardson | Y | N | N | Y | Y | Y | Y | Y |
| **NEW YORK** | | | | | | | | |
| 1 Hochbrueckner | Y | N | Y | Y | Y | Y | Y | N |
| 2 Downey | N | N | Y | Y | Y | Y | Y | N |
| 3 Mrazek | N | N | Y | Y | Y | Y | Y | N |
| 4 ***Lent*** | N | Y | Y | N | Y | N | N | Y |
| 5 ***McGrath*** | N | Y | Y | N | Y | N | N | ? |
| 6 Flake | Y | N | Y | Y | Y | Y | Y | N |
| 7 Ackerman | N | N | Y | Y | Y | Y | Y | N |
| 8 Scheuer | Y | N | Y | Y | Y | Y | Y | — |
| 9 Manton | N | Y | Y | Y | Y | Y | Y | ? |
| 10 Schumer | Y | N | Y | Y | Y | Y | Y | N |
| 11 Towns | N | Y | Y | Y | Y | Y | Y | ? |
| 12 Owens | Y | N | Y | Y | Y | Y | Y | N |
| 13 Solarz | N | N | Y | Y | Y | Y | Y | N |
| 14 ***Molinari*** | N | Y | Y | N | Y | N | N | Y |
| 15 ***Green*** | N | N | Y | Y | Y | N | N | N |
| 16 Rangel | Y | ? | Y | Y | Y | Y | Y | Y |
| 17 Weiss | N | N | Y | Y | Y | Y | Y | N |
| 18 Serrano | Y | N | Y | Y | Y | Y | Y | N |
| 19 Engel | Y | N | Y | Y | Y | Y | Y | N |
| 20 Lowey | N | N | Y | Y | Y | Y | Y | N |
| 21 ***Fish*** | N | N | Y | N | Y | N | N | N |
| 22 ***Gilman*** | N | N | Y | N | Y | N | N | N |
| 23 McNulty | N | Y | Y | Y | Y | Y | Y | Y |
| 24 ***Solomon*** | N | Y | Y | N | Y | N | N | Y |
| 25 ***Boehlert*** | N | N | Y | N | Y | N | N | N |
| 26 ***Martin*** | Y | Y | Y | N | Y | N | N | ? |
| 27 ***Walsh*** | Y | Y | Y | Y | Y | N | N | Y |
| 28 McHugh | Y | N | Y | Y | Y | Y | Y | N |
| 29 ***Horton*** | Y | Y | Y | ? | Y | N | N | Y |
| 30 Slaughter | Y | N | Y | Y | Y | Y | Y | N |
| 31 ***Paxon*** | N | Y | Y | N | Y | N | N | Y |

| | 133 | 134 | 135 | 136 | 137 | 138 | 139 | 140 |
|---|---|---|---|---|---|---|---|---|
| 32 LaFalce | N | N | Y | Y | Y | Y | Y | N |
| 33 Nowak | N | N | Y | Y | Y | Y | Y | N |
| 34 ***Houghton*** | N | N | ? | Y | Y | N | N | Y |
| **NORTH CAROLINA** | | | | | | | | |
| 1 Jones | Y | Y | N | Y | Y | Y | Y | Y |
| 2 Valentine | Y | Y | N | Y | Y | Y | N | Y |
| 3 Lancaster | Y | Y | N | Y | Y | Y | Y | Y |
| 4 Price | Y | Y | Y | Y | Y | Y | Y | N |
| 5 Neal | Y | N | Y | ? | Y | Y | N | Y |
| 6 ***Coble*** | N | Y | Y | N | Y | N | N | Y |
| 7 Rose | Y | Y | Y | ? | Y | Y | Y | N |
| 8 Hefner | Y | Y | Y | Y | Y | Y | Y | Y |
| 9 ***McMillan*** | N | Y | N | N | Y | N | N | Y |
| 10 ***Ballenger*** | N | Y | Y | N | Y | N | N | Y |
| 11 ***Taylor*** | N | Y | N | N | Y | N | N | Y |
| **NORTH DAKOTA** | | | | | | | | |
| AL Dorgan | Y | N | N | Y | Y | Y | N | Y |
| **OHIO** | | | | | | | | |
| 1 Luken | Y | N | Y | Y | Y | Y | Y | Y |
| 2 ***Gradison*** | N | Y | N | N | Y | N | N | Y |
| 3 Hall | Y | Y | Y | Y | Y | Y | Y | N |
| 4 ***Oxley*** | N | Y | Y | N | Y | N | N | + |
| 5 ***Gillmor*** | Y | Y | Y | N | Y | N | N | Y |
| 6 ***McEwen*** | Y | Y | Y | N | Y | N | N | Y |
| 7 ***Hobson*** | N | Y | Y | N | Y | N | N | Y |
| 8 ***Boehner*** | Y | Y | N | N | Y | N | N | Y |
| 9 Kaptur | N | N | Y | Y | Y | Y | Y | ? |
| 10 ***Miller*** | Y | Y | N | N | Y | N | N | Y |
| 11 Eckart | N | N | Y | Y | Y | Y | Y | N |
| 12 ***Kasich*** | Y | N | Y | N | Y | N | N | Y |
| 13 Pease | Y | N | N | Y | Y | Y | Y | Y |
| 14 Sawyer | Y | N | Y | ? | Y | Y | Y | Y |
| 15 ***Wylie*** | ? | ? | ? | N | Y | N | N | Y |
| 16 ***Regula*** | N | Y | Y | Y | Y | N | N | Y |
| 17 Traficant | Y | N | Y | Y | Y | Y | N | Y |
| 18 Applegate | Y | N | Y | Y | Y | Y | N | Y |
| 19 Feighan | Y | N | Y | Y | Y | Y | Y | Y |
| 20 Oakar | ? | ? | ? | ? | ? | ? | ? | ? |
| 21 Stokes | Y | N | Y | Y | Y | Y | N | N |
| **OKLAHOMA** | | | | | | | | |
| 1 ***Inhofe*** | N | Y | N | N | Y | N | N | Y |
| 2 Synar | N | N | N | Y | Y | Y | Y | N |
| 3 Brewster | N | Y | N | Y | Y | Y | Y | Y |
| 4 McCurdy | N | Y | N | Y | Y | Y | Y | Y |
| 5 ***Edwards*** | ? | ? | ? | N | Y | N | N | Y |
| 6 English | N | Y | N | Y | Y | Y | N | Y |
| **OREGON** | | | | | | | | |
| 1 AuCoin | ? | ? | ? | # | ? | ? | ? | N |
| 2 ***Smith*** | N | Y | N | N | Y | N | N | Y |
| 3 Wyden | N | N | Y | Y | Y | Y | Y | N |
| 4 DeFazio | Y | N | Y | Y | N | Y | Y | Y |
| 5 Kopetski | Y | N | N | Y | Y | Y | Y | Y |
| **PENNSYLVANIA** | | | | | | | | |
| 1 Foglietta | N | Y | Y | Y | Y | Y | Y | Y |
| 2 Blackwell | Y | Y | Y | Y | Y | Y | Y | Y |
| 3 Borski | Y | Y | Y | Y | Y | Y | Y | Y |
| 4 Kolter | ? | ? | ? | Y | Y | Y | N | Y |
| 5 ***Schulze*** | N | Y | Y | N | Y | N | N | ? |
| 6 Yatron | Y | Y | N | Y | Y | Y | Y | N |
| 7 ***Weldon*** | N | Y | Y | N | Y | N | N | Y |
| 8 Kostmayer | Y | N | Y | Y | Y | Y | Y | Y |
| 9 ***Shuster*** | N | Y | Y | N | Y | N | N | Y |
| 10 ***McDade*** | N | Y | ? | Y | Y | N | N | ? |
| 11 Kanjorski | Y | Y | Y | Y | Y | Y | Y | N |
| 12 Murtha | Y | Y | N | Y | Y | Y | Y | Y |
| 13 ***Coughlin*** | N | Y | Y | N | Y | N | N | Y |
| 14 Coyne | N | N | Y | Y | Y | Y | Y | Y |
| 15 ***Ritter*** | N | Y | Y | Y | Y | N | N | Y |
| 16 ***Walker*** | N | Y | Y | N | Y | N | N | Y |
| 17 ***Gekas*** | Y | N | Y | N | Y | N | N | Y |
| 18 ***Santorum*** | N | Y | Y | N | Y | N | N | Y |
| 19 ***Goodling*** | Y | N | Y | Y | Y | N | N | Y |
| 20 Gaydos | ? | ? | ? | Y | Y | Y | Y | Y |
| 21 ***Ridge*** | Y | Y | Y | N | Y | N | N | Y |
| 22 Murphy | Y | Y | ? | Y | Y | Y | Y | N |
| 23 ***Clinger*** | N | Y | N | N | Y | N | N | Y |
| **RHODE ISLAND** | | | | | | | | |
| 1 ***Machtley*** | N | N | Y | Y | Y | N | N | Y |
| 2 Reed | N | N | Y | Y | Y | Y | Y | N |
| **SOUTH CAROLINA** | | | | | | | | |
| 1 ***Ravenel*** | Y | Y | N | N | Y | N | N | Y |
| 2 ***Spence*** | N | Y | N | N | Y | N | N | Y |
| 3 Derrick | Y | Y | N | Y | Y | Y | Y | Y |
| 4 Patterson | N | Y | N | Y | Y | Y | Y | Y |
| 5 Spratt | Y | Y | Y | Y | Y | Y | Y | Y |
| 6 Tallon | N | Y | Y | Y | Y | Y | Y | Y |

| | 133 | 134 | 135 | 136 | 137 | 138 | 139 | 140 |
|---|---|---|---|---|---|---|---|---|
| **SOUTH DAKOTA** | | | | | | | | |
| AL Johnson | Y | N | Y | Y | Y | Y | Y | N |
| **TENNESSEE** | | | | | | | | |
| 1 ***Quillen*** | ? | # | ? | X | ? | X | X | Y |
| 2 ***Duncan*** | N | Y | N | N | Y | N | N | Y |
| 3 Lloyd | Y | Y | N | Y | Y | Y | Y | Y |
| 4 Cooper | N | Y | Y | Y | Y | Y | Y | N |
| 5 Clement | Y | Y | N | Y | Y | Y | Y | Y |
| 6 Gordon | Y | Y | Y | Y | + | Y | Y | N |
| 7 ***Sundquist*** | N | Y | N | N | Y | N | N | Y |
| 8 Tanner | Y | Y | N | Y | Y | Y | Y | Y |
| 9 Ford | Y | N | Y | ? | Y | Y | Y | Y |
| **TEXAS** | | | | | | | | |
| 1 Chapman | N | Y | N | ? | Y | Y | N | Y |
| 2 Wilson | Y | Y | N | Y | Y | Y | Y | Y |
| 3 ***Johnson*** | N | Y | N | N | Y | N | N | Y |
| 4 Hall | N | Y | N | Y | Y | Y | N | Y |
| 5 Bryant | Y | N | N | Y | Y | Y | Y | Y |
| 6 ***Barton*** | N | Y | N | N | Y | N | N | Y |
| 7 ***Archer*** | N | Y | N | N | Y | N | N | Y |
| 8 ***Fields*** | N | Y | N | N | Y | N | N | Y |
| 9 Brooks | N | Y | N | Y | Y | Y | Y | Y |
| 10 Pickle | N | N | N | Y | Y | Y | Y | Y |
| 11 Edwards | Y | Y | N | Y | Y | Y | Y | Y |
| 12 Geren | N | Y | N | Y | Y | ? | N | Y |
| 13 Sarpalius | Y | Y | N | Y | Y | Y | Y | Y |
| 14 Laughlin | ? | Y | N | Y | Y | Y | Y | Y |
| 15 de la Garza | Y | Y | N | Y | Y | Y | Y | Y |
| 16 Coleman | N | Y | N | Y | Y | Y | Y | Y |
| 17 Stenholm | N | Y | N | Y | Y | Y | Y | Y |
| 18 Washington | Y | N | N | Y | N | Y | Y | N |
| 19 ***Combest*** | N | Y | N | N | Y | N | N | Y |
| 20 Gonzalez | N | N | N | Y | Y | Y | Y | Y |
| 21 ***Smith*** | N | Y | N | N | Y | N | N | Y |
| 22 ***DeLay*** | N | Y | N | N | Y | N | N | ? |
| 23 Bustamante | N | Y | N | Y | Y | Y | Y | Y |
| 24 Frost | N | Y | N | Y | Y | Y | Y | Y |
| 25 Andrews | N | Y | N | Y | Y | Y | Y | Y |
| 26 ***Armey*** | N | Y | N | N | Y | N | N | Y |
| 27 Ortiz | N | Y | N | Y | Y | Y | Y | Y |
| **UTAH** | | | | | | | | |
| 1 ***Hansen*** | Y | Y | N | N | Y | N | N | Y |
| 2 Owens | Y | N | N | Y | Y | Y | N | N |
| 3 Orton | N | Y | N | Y | Y | Y | N | Y |
| **VERMONT** | | | | | | | | |
| AL *Sanders* | Y | N | Y | Y | Y | Y | N | N |
| **VIRGINIA** | | | | | | | | |
| 1 ***Bateman*** | N | Y | N | N | Y | N | N | Y |
| 2 Pickett | N | Y | N | Y | Y | Y | N | Y |
| 3 ***Bliley*** | N | Y | N | N | Y | N | N | Y |
| 4 Sisisky | N | Y | N | Y | Y | Y | Y | Y |
| 5 Payne | N | Y | N | Y | Y | Y | N | Y |
| 6 Olin | N | Y | ? | Y | Y | Y | Y | N |
| 7 ***Allen*** | N | Y | Y | N | Y | N | N | Y |
| 8 Moran | N | ? | ? | Y | Y | Y | + | Y |
| 9 Boucher | N | N | Y | Y | Y | Y | Y | N |
| 10 ***Wolf*** | N | Y | Y | N | Y | N | N | Y |
| **WASHINGTON** | | | | | | | | |
| 1 ***Miller*** | N | Y | Y | N | Y | N | N | Y |
| 2 Swift | N | Y | Y | Y | Y | Y | Y | N |
| 3 Unsoeld | Y | N | Y | Y | Y | Y | Y | N |
| 4 ***Morrison*** | Y | Y | N | ? | ? | ? | ? | Y |
| 5 Foley | | | | | | | Y | |
| 6 Dicks | Y | Y | N | Y | Y | Y | Y | Y |
| 7 McDermott | Y | N | Y | Y | N | Y | Y | Y |
| 8 ***Chandler*** | N | Y | Y | N | Y | N | N | Y |
| **WEST VIRGINIA** | | | | | | | | |
| 1 Mollohan | N | N | N | Y | Y | Y | Y | ? |
| 2 Staggers | Y | N | N | N | N | Y | N | Y |
| 3 Wise | N | N | N | Y | Y | Y | Y | Y |
| 4 Rahall | Y | N | N | Y | Y | Y | N | Y |
| **WISCONSIN** | | | | | | | | |
| 1 Aspin | Y | N | Y | Y | Y | Y | Y | N |
| 2 ***Klug*** | Y | Y | Y | N | Y | N | N | Y |
| 3 ***Gunderson*** | Y | Y | Y | N | Y | N | N | Y |
| 4 Kleczka | Y | N | Y | Y | Y | Y | Y | Y |
| 5 Moody | Y | N | Y | Y | Y | Y | Y | N |
| 6 ***Petri*** | Y | Y | Y | N | Y | N | N | Y |
| 7 Obey | Y | N | Y | Y | Y | Y | Y | N |
| 8 ***Roth*** | Y | Y | Y | N | Y | N | N | Y |
| 9 ***Sensenbrenner*** | Y | Y | Y | N | Y | N | N | Y |
| **WYOMING** | | | | | | | | |
| AL ***Thomas*** | N | Y | N | N | Y | N | N | Y |

Southern states - Ala., Ark., Fla., Ga., Ky., La., Miss., N.C., Okla., S.C., Tenn., Texas, Va.
Omitted votes are quorum calls, which CQ does not include in its vote charts.

**141. HR 776. National Energy Policy/Low-Level Nuclear Waste.** Gejdenson, D-Conn., amendment to establish tougher requirements for the disposal of low-level radioactive waste, including reclassifying some of this waste as high-level waste and requiring that low-level waste dumps be located in low-density population areas. Rejected 117-293: R 16-142; D 100-151 (ND 87-81, SD 13-70); I 1-0, May 27, 1992. A "nay" was a vote in support of the president's position.

**142. HR 776. National Energy Policy/Hydroelectric Projects.** Dingell, D-Mich., substitute amendment to the Miller, D-Calif., amendment to give states and other federal agencies more control in protecting rivers against the Federal Energy Regulatory Commission in the licensing of hydroelectric projects but not as much control as originally proposed by the Miller amendment. Rejected 195-221: R 118-40; D 77-180 (ND 35-139, SD 42-41); I 0-1, May 27, 1992.

**143. HR 776. National Energy Policy/Hydroelectric Projects.** Miller, D-Calif., amendment to give states a veto power over Federal Energy Regulatory Commission licensing of hydroelectric projects by prohibiting the federal licensing of projects prohibited by state law; and for other purposes. Adopted 318-98: R 78-80; D 239-18 (ND 163-11, SD 76-7); I 1-0, May 27, 1992. A "nay" was a vote in support of the president's position.

**144. HR 776. National Energy Policy/Passage.** Passage of the bill to promote increased domestic energy production and conservation; promote the wider use of alternative motor fuels; streamline the nuclear plant licensing process; restrict state powers to regulate gas production; ban certain new offshore oil and gas drilling; overhaul federal laws governing electric utilities; provide tax incentives for renewable energy; and for other purposes. Passed 381-37: R 135-23; D 245-14 (ND 173-2, SD 72-12); I 1-0, May 27, 1992.

**145. H Res 471. Disclosing House Bank Records.** Adoption of the Gephardt, D-Mo., resolution to provide Malcolm R. Wilkey, the Justice Department's special counsel investigating possible criminal violations at the House bank, with additional bank records he had requested and to authorize a leadership group to respond to further requests. Adopted 396-5: R 153-0; D 242-5 (ND 166-3, SD 76-2); I 1-0, May 28, 1992.

**146. HR 2507. National Institutes of Health Reauthorization/Rule.** Adoption of the rule (H Res 466) to waive all points of order against and provide for House floor consideration of the conference report to reauthorize and amend the programs of NIH through fiscal 1996. The conference report lifted the ban on fetal tissue transplant research using fetal tissue obtained from induced abortions. Adopted 308-100: R 88-70; D 219-30 (ND 149-19, SD 70-11); I 1-0, May 28, 1992.

**147. HR 2507. National Institutes of Health Reauthorization/Conference Report.** Adoption of the conference report to reauthorize and amend the programs of NIH through fiscal 1996, including fiscal 1993 funding of $2.2 billion for the National Cancer Institute and $1.4 billion for the Heart, Lung and Blood Institute. The conference report lifted the ban on fetal tissue transplant research using fetal tissue obtained from induced abortions. Adopted 260-148: R 43-116; D 216-32 (ND 148-19, SD 68-13); I 1-0, May 28, 1992. A "nay" was a vote supporting the president's position.

**148. H Res 379. Committee Funding for 1992.** Gaydos, D-Pa., motion to order the previous question (thus limiting debate and the possibility of amendment) on the Gaydos substitute amendment to freeze funding for the operations of all standing and select committees of the House at the 1991 level of $55 million for the second session of the 102nd Congress. The resolution provided for a 4.9 percent increase to $57.8 million. Nussle, R-Iowa, attempted to defeat the previous question in order to offer an amendment that would have provided for a 5 percent cut. Motion agreed to 254-146: R 7-145; D 246-1 (ND 166-1, SD 80-0); I 1-0, May 28, 1992. (The Gaydos amendment was subsequently adopted by voice vote.)

## KEY

| | |
|---|---|
| Y | Voted for (yea). |
| # | Paired for. |
| + | Announced for. |
| N | Voted against (nay). |
| X | Paired against. |
| − | Announced against. |
| P | Voted "present." |
| C | Voted "present" to avoid possible conflict of interest. |
| ? | Did not vote or otherwise make a position known. |

Democrats **Republicans** *Independent*

| | 141 | 142 | 143 | 144 | 145 | 146 | 147 | 148 |
|---|---|---|---|---|---|---|---|---|
| **ALABAMA** | | | | | | | | |
| 1 *Callahan* | N | Y | Y | Y | Y | N | N | Y |
| 2 *Dickinson* | N | Y | Y | Y | Y | N | N | N |
| 3 Browder | N | N | Y | Y | Y | Y | Y | Y |
| 4 Bevill | N | Y | Y | Y | Y | Y | Y | Y |
| 5 Cramer | N | N | Y | Y | Y | Y | Y | Y |
| 6 Erdreich | N | N | Y | Y | Y | Y | Y | Y |
| 7 Harris | N | Y | Y | Y | Y | Y | Y | Y |
| **ALASKA** | | | | | | | | |
| AL *Young* | N | Y | N | Y | Y | N | N | ? |
| **ARIZONA** | | | | | | | | |
| 1 *Rhodes* | N | Y | N | Y | Y | N | N | N |
| 2 Pastor | N | N | Y | Y | Y | Y | Y | Y |
| 3 *Stump* | N | Y | N | N | Y | N | N | N |
| 4 *Kyl* | N | Y | N | Y | Y | N | N | N |
| 5 *Kolbe* | N | Y | N | Y | Y | Y | Y | N |
| **ARKANSAS** | | | | | | | | |
| 1 Alexander | ? | ? | ? | Y | Y | ? | ? | ? |
| 2 Thornton | N | Y | Y | Y | Y | N | N | Y |
| 3 *Hammerschmidt* | N | Y | Y | N | Y | N | N | Y |
| 4 Anthony | X | # | ? | ? | ? | ? | ? | ? |
| **CALIFORNIA** | | | | | | | | |
| 1 *Riggs* | N | N | Y | Y | ? | Y | Y | N |
| 2 *Herger* | N | Y | N | N | Y | N | N | N |
| 3 Matsui | ? | N | Y | Y | Y | Y | Y | Y |
| 4 Fazio | N | N | Y | Y | Y | Y | + | Y |
| 5 Pelosi | Y | N | Y | Y | Y | Y | + | Y |
| 6 Boxer | # | ? | ? | ? | ? | ? | # | ? |
| 7 Miller | Y | N | Y | Y | Y | Y | Y | Y |
| 8 Dellums | Y | N | Y | Y | Y | Y | Y | Y |
| 9 Stark | Y | N | Y | Y | Y | Y | Y | ? |
| 10 Edwards | Y | N | Y | Y | Y | Y | Y | Y |
| 11 Lantos | N | N | Y | Y | Y | Y | Y | Y |
| 12 *Campbell* | ? | ? | ? | ? | ? | ? | ? | ? |
| 13 Mineta | Y | N | Y | Y | Y | Y | Y | Y |
| 14 *Doolittle* | N | Y | N | N | Y | N | N | N |
| 15 Condit | N | N | Y | Y | Y | Y | Y | Y |
| 16 Panetta | N | N | Y | Y | Y | Y | Y | Y |
| 17 Dooley | N | N | Y | Y | Y | Y | Y | Y |
| 18 Lehman | N | N | Y | Y | Y | Y | Y | Y |
| 19 *Lagomarsino* | ? | ? | ? | # | ? | ? | X | ? |
| 20 *Thomas* | N | Y | N | Y | Y | Y | Y | N |
| 21 *Gallegly* | N | Y | Y | Y | Y | Y | N | N |
| 22 *Moorhead* | N | Y | N | Y | Y | N | N | N |
| 23 Beilenson | Y | N | Y | Y | Y | Y | Y | Y |
| 24 Waxman | Y | N | Y | Y | Y | Y | Y | Y |
| 25 Roybal | Y | N | Y | Y | Y | Y | Y | Y |
| 26 Berman | Y | N | Y | Y | Y | Y | Y | Y |
| 27 Levine | # | ? | ? | ? | ? | ? | # | ? |
| 28 Dixon | Y | N | Y | Y | ? | ? | ? | ? |
| 29 Waters | Y | N | Y | Y | Y | Y | Y | Y |
| 30 Martinez | X | ? | ? | ? | Y | Y | Y | Y |
| 31 Dymally | ? | N | Y | Y | N | ? | ? | ? |
| 32 Anderson | N | Y | N | Y | Y | Y | Y | Y |
| 33 *Dreier* | N | Y | Y | Y | Y | Y | N | N |
| 34 Torres | Y | N | Y | Y | + | Y | Y | Y |
| 35 *Lewis* | N | Y | N | Y | Y | Y | Y | N |
| 36 Brown | N | Y | ? | Y | Y | Y | Y | Y |
| 37 *McCandless* | N | Y | N | Y | Y | N | N | N |
| 38 *Dornan* | N | Y | N | Y | Y | N | N | N |
| 39 *Dannemeyer* | ? | ? | ? | ? | ? | ? | ? | ? |
| 40 *Cox* | N | Y | N | Y | Y | N | N | N |
| 41 *Lowery* | N | Y | N | Y | Y | N | N | N |
| **42 *Rohrabacher*** | N | Y | N | Y | Y | N | N | N |
| 43 *Packard* | X | ? | ? | X | ? | ? | X | ? |
| 44 *Cunningham* | N | Y | N | Y | Y | N | N | N |
| 45 *Hunter* | N | Y | N | N | Y | N | N | ? |
| **COLORADO** | | | | | | | | |
| 1 Schroeder | Y | N | Y | Y | Y | Y | + | Y |
| 2 Skaggs | N | N | Y | Y | Y | Y | Y | Y |
| 3 Campbell | N | Y | Y | Y | ? | ? | ? | ? |
| 4 *Allard* | N | Y | N | Y | Y | N | N | N |
| 5 *Hefley* | N | Y | N | Y | Y | N | N | N |
| 6 *Schaefer* | N | Y | N | Y | Y | N | N | N |
| **CONNECTICUT** | | | | | | | | |
| 1 Kennelly | Y | N | Y | Y | Y | Y | Y | Y |
| 2 Gejdenson | Y | N | Y | Y | Y | Y | Y | Y |
| 3 DeLauro | Y | N | Y | Y | Y | Y | Y | Y |
| 4 *Shays* | Y | N | Y | Y | Y | Y | Y | Y |
| 5 *Franks* | Y | N | Y | Y | Y | N | Y | N |
| 6 *Johnson* | Y | N | Y | Y | Y | Y | Y | N |
| **DELAWARE** | | | | | | | | |
| AL Carper | N | N | Y | Y | Y | Y | Y | Y |
| **FLORIDA** | | | | | | | | |
| 1 Hutto | N | Y | Y | Y | Y | N | N | Y |
| 2 Peterson | N | N | Y | Y | Y | Y | Y | Y |
| 3 Bennett | N | N | Y | Y | Y | Y | Y | Y |
| 4 *James* | N | Y | Y | Y | Y | N | N | N |
| 5 *McCollum* | N | Y | Y | Y | Y | N | N | N |
| 6 *Stearns* | N | Y | N | Y | Y | N | N | N |
| 7 Gibbons | N | Y | Y | Y | Y | Y | Y | Y |
| 8 *Young* | N | Y | Y | Y | Y | N | N | N |
| 9 *Bilirakis* | N | Y | Y | Y | Y | N | N | N |
| 10 *Ireland* | ? | Y | N | Y | Y | N | N | N |
| 11 Bacchus | N | N | Y | Y | Y | Y | Y | Y |
| 12 *Lewis* | N | Y | Y | Y | Y | Y | Y | Y |
| 13 *Goss* | N | Y | N | Y | Y | N | N | N |
| 14 Johnston | N | N | Y | Y | Y | Y | Y | Y |
| 15 *Shaw* | N | Y | Y | Y | Y | N | N | N |
| 16 Smith | N | N | Y | Y | Y | Y | Y | Y |
| 17 Lehman | N | N | Y | Y | Y | Y | Y | Y |
| 18 *Ros−Lehtinen* | N | Y | Y | Y | Y | N | N | N |
| 19 Fascell | N | N | Y | Y | Y | Y | Y | Y |
| **GEORGIA** | | | | | | | | |
| 1 Thomas | N | Y | Y | Y | Y | Y | Y | Y |
| 2 Hatcher | N | Y | Y | Y | ? | ? | ? | ? |
| 3 Ray | N | Y | Y | Y | Y | Y | N | ? |
| 4 Jones | N | Y | Y | Y | Y | Y | Y | Y |
| 5 Lewis | Y | N | Y | Y | Y | Y | Y | Y |
| 6 *Gingrich* | N | Y | Y | Y | Y | N | N | N |
| 7 Darden | N | Y | Y | Y | Y | Y | Y | Y |
| 8 Rowland | N | Y | Y | Y | Y | Y | Y | Y |
| 9 Jenkins | N | N | Y | Y | Y | Y | Y | Y |
| 10 Barnard | N | Y | Y | Y | Y | ? | ? | ? |
| **HAWAII** | | | | | | | | |
| 1 Abercrombie | Y | N | Y | Y | Y | Y | Y | Y |
| 2 Mink | N | N | Y | Y | Y | Y | + | Y |
| **IDAHO** | | | | | | | | |
| 1 LaRocco | N | N | Y | Y | Y | Y | Y | Y |
| 2 Stallings | N | N | Y | Y | N | N | N | Y |
| **ILLINOIS** | | | | | | | | |
| 1 Hayes | N | N | Y | Y | Y | Y | Y | Y |
| 2 Savage | N | N | Y | Y | Y | Y | Y | Y |
| 3 Russo | N | N | Y | Y | Y | Y | Y | Y |
| 4 Sangmeister | N | N | Y | Y | Y | ? | Y | Y |
| 5 Lipinski | N | Y | Y | Y | Y | Y | Y | Y |
| 6 *Hyde* | N | Y | N | Y | N | N | N | N |
| 7 Collins | # | ? | ? | # | ? | ? | Y | Y |
| 8 Rostenkowski | N | Y | Y | Y | Y | Y | Y | Y |
| 9 Yates | Y | N | Y | N | Y | Y | Y | Y |
| 10 *Porter* | N | N | Y | Y | Y | Y | Y | Y |
| 11 Annunzio | N | N | Y | Y | N | Y | Y | Y |
| 12 *Crane* | N | Y | N | Y | N | N | N | N |
| 13 *Fawell* | N | Y | Y | Y | Y | Y | Y | N |
| 14 *Hastert* | N | Y | N | Y | Y | N | N | N |
| 15 *Ewing* | N | Y | Y | Y | Y | N | N | N |
| 16 Cox | Y | N | Y | Y | Y | Y | Y | Y |
| 17 Evans | N | N | Y | Y | Y | Y | Y | Y |
| 18 *Michel* | ? | ? | ? | ? | ? | ? | ? | ? |
| 19 Bruce | + | + | + | + | + | + | + | + |
| 20 Durbin | Y | N | Y | Y | Y | Y | Y | Y |
| 21 Costello | N | N | Y | Y | Y | Y | Y | Y |
| 22 Poshard | N | N | Y | Y | N | N | N | Y |
| **INDIANA** | | | | | | | | |
| 1 Visclosky | N | Y | Y | Y | Y | Y | Y | Y |
| 2 Sharp | C | Y | Y | Y | Y | Y | Y | Y |
| 3 Roemer | N | N | Y | Y | N | N | N | Y |

ND   Northern Democrats   SD   Southern Democrats

| | 141 | 142 | 143 | 144 | 145 | 146 | 147 | 148 |
|---|---|---|---|---|---|---|---|---|
| 4 Long | N | N | Y | N | Y | Y | Y | Y |
| 5 Jontz | Y | N | Y | Y | Y | Y | Y | Y |
| 6 ***Burton*** | N | Y | N | Y | Y | N | N | N |
| 7 ***Myers*** | N | Y | N | Y | Y | Y | N | N |
| 8 McCloskey | Y | Y | Y | Y | N | Y | Y | Y |
| 9 Hamilton | N | Y | Y | Y | Y | Y | Y | Y |
| 10 Jacobs | Y | Y | Y | Y | Y | Y | Y | N |
| **IOWA** | | | | | | | | |
| 1 ***Leach*** | N | N | Y | Y | Y | N | Y | N |
| 2 ***Nussle*** | N | Y | N | Y | Y | N | N | N |
| 3 Nagle | N | N | Y | Y | Y | Y | Y | Y |
| 4 Smith | N | Y | Y | Y | Y | Y | Y | Y |
| 5 ***Lightfoot*** | N | Y | N | Y | Y | N | N | N |
| 6 ***Grandy*** | N | Y | N | Y | Y | Y | N | N |
| **KANSAS** | | | | | | | | |
| 1 ***Roberts*** | N | Y | N | Y | Y | N | N | N |
| 2 Slattery | N | N | Y | Y | Y | Y | Y | Y |
| 3 ***Meyers*** | N | N | Y | Y | Y | Y | Y | N |
| 4 Glickman | N | N | Y | Y | Y | Y | Y | Y |
| 5 ***Nichols*** | N | Y | N | Y | Y | Y | N | N |
| **KENTUCKY** | | | | | | | | |
| 1 Hubbard | N | Y | Y | Y | Y | Y | Y | Y |
| 2 Natcher | Y | N | Y | Y | Y | Y | Y | Y |
| 3 Mazzoli | Y | N | Y | Y | Y | Y | N | Y |
| 4 ***Bunning*** | N | Y | N | Y | Y | N | N | ? |
| 5 ***Rogers*** | N | Y | N | Y | Y | N | N | N |
| 6 ***Hopkins*** | N | Y | N | Y | ? | Y | N | N |
| 7 Perkins | N | N | Y | Y | ? | Y | Y | Y |
| **LOUISIANA** | | | | | | | | |
| 1 ***Livingston*** | N | Y | N | N | ? | ? | X | ? |
| 2 Jefferson | Y | N | Y | Y | Y | Y | Y | Y |
| 3 Tauzin | N | Y | N | Y | Y | N | N | Y |
| 4 ***McCrery*** | N | Y | N | Y | ? | Y | N | N |
| 5 Huckaby | N | Y | Y | Y | Y | Y | Y | Y |
| 6 ***Baker*** | N | Y | N | N | Y | Y | N | N |
| 7 Hayes | N | Y | N | Y | Y | Y | Y | Y |
| 8 ***Holloway*** | N | Y | N | Y | Y | N | N | N |
| **MAINE** | | | | | | | | |
| 1 Andrews | Y | N | Y | Y | Y | Y | Y | Y |
| 2 ***Snowe*** | Y | N | Y | Y | Y | Y | Y | N |
| **MARYLAND** | | | | | | | | |
| 1 ***Gilchrest*** | N | N | Y | Y | Y | Y | Y | Y |
| 2 ***Bentley*** | ? | ? | ? | ? | Y | Y | Y | N |
| 3 Cardin | Y | N | Y | Y | Y | Y | Y | Y |
| 4 McMillen | N | Y | Y | Y | Y | Y | Y | Y |
| 5 Hoyer | N | N | Y | Y | Y | Y | Y | Y |
| 6 Byron | N | N | Y | Y | Y | Y | Y | Y |
| 7 Mfume | Y | N | Y | Y | Y | Y | Y | Y |
| 8 ***Morella*** | N | N | Y | Y | Y | Y | Y | Y |
| **MASSACHUSETTS** | | | | | | | | |
| 1 Olver | Y | N | Y | Y | Y | Y | Y | ? |
| 2 Neal | Y | N | Y | Y | Y | Y | Y | Y |
| 3 Early | Y | N | Y | Y | Y | Y | Y | Y |
| 4 Frank | Y | N | Y | Y | Y | Y | Y | Y |
| 5 Atkins | Y | N | Y | Y | Y | Y | Y | Y |
| 6 Mavroules | ? | N | Y | Y | Y | Y | Y | Y |
| 7 Markey | Y | Y | Y | Y | Y | Y | Y | Y |
| 8 Kennedy | Y | N | Y | Y | Y | Y | Y | Y |
| 9 Moakley | Y | N | Y | Y | Y | Y | Y | Y |
| 10 Studds | Y | N | Y | Y | Y | Y | Y | Y |
| 11 Donnelly | ? | ? | ? | ? | ? | ? | ? | ? |
| **MICHIGAN** | | | | | | | | |
| 1 Conyers | N | Y | N | Y | Y | Y | Y | Y |
| 2 ***Pursell*** | Y | Y | Y | Y | Y | Y | Y | N |
| 3 Wolpe | Y | N | Y | Y | Y | Y | Y | Y |
| 4 ***Upton*** | Y | Y | Y | Y | Y | Y | Y | N |
| 5 ***Henry*** | N | N | Y | Y | Y | Y | Y | N |
| 6 Carr | N | Y | N | Y | Y | Y | Y | Y |
| 7 Kildee | Y | N | Y | Y | Y | Y | Y | Y |
| 8 Traxler | N | N | Y | Y | ? | ? | ? | ? |
| 9 ***Vander Jagt*** | N | Y | Y | Y | Y | Y | N | N |
| 10 ***Camp*** | Y | Y | N | Y | Y | Y | N | N |
| 11 ***Davis*** | N | Y | N | Y | ? | N | N | N |
| 12 Bonior | Y | Y | Y | Y | Y | Y | Y | Y |
| 13 Collins | N | Y | N | Y | Y | + | # | + |
| 14 Hertel | Y | N | Y | Y | Y | Y | Y | Y |
| 15 Ford | N | Y | N | Y | Y | Y | Y | Y |
| 16 Dingell | N | Y | N | Y | Y | Y | Y | Y |
| 17 Levin | N | N | Y | Y | Y | Y | Y | Y |
| 18 ***Broomfield*** | N | Y | Y | Y | Y | Y | N | N |
| **MINNESOTA** | | | | | | | | |
| 1 Penny | N | N | Y | N | Y | N | N | Y |
| 2 ***Weber*** | Y | Y | Y | Y | Y | N | N | N |
| 3 ***Ramstad*** | N | N | Y | Y | Y | N | N | N |
| 4 Vento | N | N | Y | Y | Y | Y | Y | Y |

| | 141 | 142 | 143 | 144 | 145 | 146 | 147 | 148 |
|---|---|---|---|---|---|---|---|---|
| 5 Sabo | N | N | Y | Y | Y | Y | Y | Y |
| 6 Sikorski | Y | N | Y | Y | Y | Y | Y | Y |
| 7 Peterson | N | N | Y | Y | Y | N | Y | Y |
| 8 Oberstar | N | N | Y | Y | Y | Y | Y | Y |
| **MISSISSIPPI** | | | | | | | | |
| 1 Whitten | N | Y | Y | Y | ? | Y | Y | Y |
| 2 Espy | N | Y | Y | Y | Y | Y | Y | Y |
| 3 Montgomery | N | Y | Y | N | Y | Y | Y | Y |
| 4 Parker | N | Y | Y | Y | Y | N | N | Y |
| 5 Taylor | N | Y | Y | Y | Y | N | N | Y |
| **MISSOURI** | | | | | | | | |
| 1 Clay | Y | N | Y | Y | Y | Y | Y | Y |
| 2 Horn | N | N | Y | Y | Y | Y | Y | Y |
| 3 Gephardt | N | N | Y | Y | Y | Y | Y | Y |
| 4 Skelton | N | Y | Y | Y | Y | Y | N | Y |
| 5 Wheat | Y | N | Y | Y | Y | Y | Y | Y |
| 6 ***Coleman*** | N | Y | Y | Y | Y | Y | Y | N |
| 7 ***Hancock*** | N | Y | N | N | Y | N | N | N |
| 8 ***Emerson*** | N | Y | N | Y | Y | N | N | N |
| 9 Volkmer | N | Y | Y | Y | Y | N | N | Y |
| **MONTANA** | | | | | | | | |
| 1 Williams | N | N | Y | Y | Y | Y | Y | Y |
| 2 ***Marlenee*** | N | Y | N | N | Y | Y | N | N |
| **NEBRASKA** | | | | | | | | |
| 1 ***Bereuter*** | N | N | Y | Y | Y | Y | N | N |
| 2 Hoagland | N | N | Y | Y | Y | Y | Y | Y |
| 3 ***Barrett*** | N | Y | N | Y | Y | Y | N | N |
| **NEVADA** | | | | | | | | |
| 1 Bilbray | N | N | Y | Y | Y | Y | Y | Y |
| 2 ***Vucanovich*** | N | N | N | N | Y | N | N | N |
| **NEW HAMPSHIRE** | | | | | | | | |
| 1 ***Zeliff*** | N | Y | N | Y | Y | N | N | N |
| 2 Swett | N | Y | Y | Y | Y | Y | Y | Y |
| **NEW JERSEY** | | | | | | | | |
| 1 Andrews | Y | N | Y | Y | Y | Y | Y | Y |
| 2 Hughes | Y | N | Y | Y | Y | Y | Y | Y |
| 3 Pallone | Y | N | Y | Y | Y | Y | Y | Y |
| 4 ***Smith*** | N | N | Y | Y | Y | Y | N | N |
| 5 ***Roukema*** | N | Y | Y | Y | Y | Y | Y | N |
| 6 Dwyer | N | N | Y | Y | Y | Y | Y | Y |
| 7 ***Rinaldo*** | N | N | Y | Y | Y | N | N | N |
| 8 Roe | N | Y | Y | Y | ? | Y | N | Y |
| 9 Torricelli | ? | N | Y | Y | Y | Y | Y | Y |
| 10 Payne | Y | N | Y | Y | Y | Y | Y | Y |
| 11 ***Gallo*** | N | Y | Y | Y | Y | Y | Y | N |
| 12 ***Zimmer*** | N | N | Y | Y | Y | N | Y | N |
| 13 ***Saxton*** | N | N | Y | Y | Y | N | N | N |
| 14 Guarini | ? | X | Y | Y | Y | Y | Y | Y |
| **NEW MEXICO** | | | | | | | | |
| 1 ***Schiff*** | N | N | Y | Y | Y | N | N | N |
| 2 ***Skeen*** | N | N | N | Y | Y | Y | Y | N |
| 3 Richardson | Y | N | Y | Y | Y | Y | Y | Y |
| **NEW YORK** | | | | | | | | |
| 1 Hochbrueckner | Y | N | Y | Y | Y | Y | Y | Y |
| 2 Downey | Y | N | Y | Y | Y | Y | Y | Y |
| 3 Mrazek | Y | N | Y | Y | Y | Y | Y | Y |
| 4 ***Lent*** | N | Y | N | Y | ? | ? | ? | ? |
| 5 ***McGrath*** | N | Y | N | Y | Y | Y | N | Y |
| 6 Flake | Y | N | Y | Y | P | Y | Y | Y |
| 7 Ackerman | Y | N | Y | Y | Y | Y | Y | Y |
| 8 Scheuer | N | N | Y | Y | Y | Y | Y | Y |
| 9 Manton | N | Y | N | Y | ? | ? | ? | ? |
| 10 Schumer | Y | N | Y | Y | Y | Y | Y | Y |
| 11 Towns | ? | Y | N | Y | Y | Y | Y | Y |
| 12 Owens | Y | N | Y | Y | Y | Y | Y | Y |
| 13 Solarz | Y | N | Y | Y | Y | Y | Y | Y |
| 14 ***Molinari*** | Y | Y | N | Y | Y | Y | Y | N |
| 15 ***Green*** | N | N | Y | Y | Y | Y | Y | N |
| 16 Rangel | Y | N | Y | Y | Y | Y | Y | Y |
| 17 Weiss | Y | N | Y | Y | Y | Y | Y | Y |
| 18 Serrano | Y | N | Y | Y | Y | Y | Y | Y |
| 19 Engel | Y | N | Y | Y | Y | Y | Y | Y |
| 20 Lowey | Y | N | Y | Y | Y | Y | Y | Y |
| 21 ***Fish*** | Y | N | Y | Y | Y | Y | N | N |
| 22 ***Gilman*** | Y | N | Y | Y | Y | Y | Y | N |
| 23 McNulty | Y | Y | Y | Y | Y | Y | Y | Y |
| 24 ***Solomon*** | N | N | Y | Y | Y | Y | N | N |
| 25 ***Boehlert*** | Y | N | Y | Y | Y | Y | Y | Y |
| 26 ***Martin*** | N | Y | Y | Y | Y | Y | N | N |
| 27 ***Walsh*** | Y | N | Y | Y | Y | Y | N | ? |
| 28 McHugh | Y | N | Y | Y | Y | Y | Y | Y |
| 29 ***Horton*** | N | N | Y | Y | Y | Y | Y | Y |
| 30 Slaughter | Y | N | Y | Y | Y | Y | Y | Y |
| 31 ***Paxon*** | N | Y | N | Y | Y | N | N | N |

| | 141 | 142 | 143 | 144 | 145 | 146 | 147 | 148 |
|---|---|---|---|---|---|---|---|---|
| 32 LaFalce | N | N | Y | Y | Y | Y | N | Y |
| 33 Nowak | Y | N | Y | Y | Y | N | Y | Y |
| 34 ***Houghton*** | Y | Y | N | Y | Y | Y | Y | N |
| **NORTH CAROLINA** | | | | | | | | |
| 1 Jones | N | Y | Y | Y | Y | Y | Y | Y |
| 2 Valentine | N | Y | Y | Y | Y | Y | Y | Y |
| 3 Lancaster | N | Y | Y | Y | Y | Y | Y | Y |
| 4 Price | N | Y | Y | Y | Y | Y | Y | Y |
| 5 Neal | Y | N | Y | Y | Y | Y | Y | Y |
| 6 ***Coble*** | N | Y | N | Y | Y | N | N | N |
| 7 Rose | Y | N | Y | Y | Y | Y | Y | Y |
| 8 Hefner | N | Y | Y | Y | ? | Y | Y | Y |
| 9 ***McMillan*** | N | Y | N | Y | Y | Y | N | N |
| 10 ***Ballenger*** | N | Y | ? | X | Y | N | N | N |
| 11 ***Taylor*** | N | Y | N | Y | Y | N | N | N |
| **NORTH DAKOTA** | | | | | | | | |
| AL Dorgan | Y | N | Y | Y | Y | Y | Y | Y |
| **OHIO** | | | | | | | | |
| 1 Luken | Y | N | Y | Y | Y | N | N | Y |
| 2 ***Gradison*** | N | Y | Y | Y | Y | Y | Y | N |
| 3 Hall | Y | N | Y | Y | Y | Y | N | Y |
| 4 ***Oxley*** | N | Y | N | Y | Y | Y | N | N |
| 5 ***Gillmor*** | N | Y | Y | Y | Y | Y | Y | N |
| 6 ***McEwen*** | N | Y | N | Y | Y | Y | N | ? |
| 7 ***Hobson*** | N | Y | Y | Y | Y | Y | Y | N |
| 8 ***Boehner*** | N | Y | N | Y | Y | Y | N | N |
| 9 Kaptur | Y | N | Y | Y | Y | Y | Y | Y |
| 10 ***Miller*** | N | Y | N | Y | Y | N | N | N |
| 11 Eckart | N | Y | Y | Y | Y | Y | Y | Y |
| 12 ***Kasich*** | N | Y | N | Y | Y | N | N | N |
| 13 Pease | N | N | Y | Y | Y | Y | Y | Y |
| 14 Sawyer | N | N | Y | Y | Y | Y | Y | Y |
| 15 ***Wylie*** | N | Y | Y | Y | Y | N | N | N |
| 16 ***Regula*** | N | Y | Y | Y | Y | N | N | N |
| 17 Traficant | N | Y | Y | Y | Y | Y | Y | Y |
| 18 Applegate | Y | N | Y | Y | Y | Y | Y | Y |
| 19 Feighan | Y | N | Y | Y | Y | Y | Y | Y |
| 20 Oakar | ? | ? | ? | ? | ? | ? | ? | ? |
| 21 Stokes | Y | N | Y | Y | Y | Y | Y | Y |
| **OKLAHOMA** | | | | | | | | |
| 1 ***Inhofe*** | N | Y | N | N | Y | Y | N | ? |
| 2 Synar | N | N | Y | N | Y | Y | Y | Y |
| 3 Brewster | N | Y | Y | Y | Y | Y | Y | Y |
| 4 McCurdy | Y | N | Y | Y | Y | Y | Y | Y |
| 5 ***Edwards*** | N | Y | N | N | Y | N | N | ? |
| 6 English | N | Y | Y | N | Y | Y | Y | Y |
| **OREGON** | | | | | | | | |
| 1 AuCoin | Y | N | Y | Y | Y | Y | Y | Y |
| 2 ***Smith*** | N | ? | N | N | Y | N | N | N |
| 3 Wyden | Y | N | Y | Y | Y | Y | Y | Y |
| 4 DeFazio | N | N | Y | Y | Y | Y | Y | Y |
| 5 Kopetski | N | Y | N | Y | Y | Y | Y | Y |
| **PENNSYLVANIA** | | | | | | | | |
| 1 Foglietta | Y | N | Y | Y | Y | Y | Y | Y |
| 2 Blackwell | Y | N | Y | Y | Y | Y | Y | Y |
| 3 Borski | Y | N | Y | Y | Y | N | Y | Y |
| 4 Kolter | N | N | Y | Y | Y | N | N | ? |
| 5 ***Schulze*** | N | Y | N | Y | Y | N | N | N |
| 6 Yatron | N | N | Y | Y | Y | N | N | Y |
| 7 ***Weldon*** | N | N | Y | Y | Y | Y | N | N |
| 8 Kostmayer | Y | N | Y | Y | Y | Y | Y | Y |
| 9 ***Shuster*** | N | Y | N | Y | Y | Y | Y | N |
| 10 ***McDade*** | ? | ? | ? | ? | ? | N | N | N |
| 11 Kanjorski | N | N | Y | Y | Y | N | N | Y |
| 12 Murtha | N | Y | Y | Y | Y | N | Y | Y |
| 13 ***Coughlin*** | N | Y | Y | Y | Y | Y | N | N |
| 14 Coyne | N | N | Y | Y | Y | Y | Y | Y |
| 15 ***Ritter*** | N | Y | N | Y | Y | Y | Y | N |
| 16 ***Walker*** | N | Y | N | Y | Y | Y | N | N |
| 17 ***Gekas*** | Y | Y | N | Y | Y | Y | N | N |
| 18 ***Santorum*** | N | Y | Y | Y | Y | Y | N | N |
| 19 ***Goodling*** | N | Y | Y | Y | Y | N | N | N |
| 20 Gaydos | N | N | Y | Y | Y | N | N | Y |
| 21 ***Ridge*** | N | N | Y | Y | Y | Y | Y | N |
| 22 Murphy | N | N | Y | Y | Y | Y | N | Y |
| 23 ***Clinger*** | N | Y | N | N | Y | N | N | N |
| **RHODE ISLAND** | | | | | | | | |
| 1 ***Machtley*** | N | N | Y | Y | Y | Y | Y | N |
| 2 Reed | Y | N | Y | Y | Y | Y | Y | Y |
| **SOUTH CAROLINA** | | | | | | | | |
| 1 ***Ravenel*** | N | N | Y | Y | Y | Y | Y | N |
| 2 ***Spence*** | N | Y | N | Y | Y | Y | N | N |
| 3 Derrick | N | Y | Y | Y | Y | Y | Y | Y |
| 4 Patterson | N | Y | Y | Y | Y | Y | Y | Y |
| 5 Spratt | N | N | Y | Y | Y | Y | Y | Y |
| 6 Tallon | N | N | Y | Y | Y | N | Y | Y |

| | 141 | 142 | 143 | 144 | 145 | 146 | 147 | 148 |
|---|---|---|---|---|---|---|---|---|
| **SOUTH DAKOTA** | | | | | | | | |
| AL Johnson | Y | N | Y | Y | Y | Y | Y | Y |
| **TENNESSEE** | | | | | | | | |
| 1 ***Quillen*** | N | N | Y | Y | Y | N | N | N |
| 2 ***Duncan*** | N | Y | Y | N | Y | N | N | N |
| 3 Lloyd | N | Y | Y | Y | Y | Y | Y | Y |
| 4 Cooper | N | Y | Y | Y | Y | Y | Y | Y |
| 5 Clement | N | Y | Y | Y | Y | Y | Y | Y |
| 6 Gordon | N | N | Y | Y | Y | Y | Y | Y |
| 7 ***Sundquist*** | N | Y | Y | Y | Y | N | N | N |
| 8 Tanner | N | N | Y | Y | Y | Y | Y | Y |
| 9 Ford | Y | Y | Y | Y | Y | Y | Y | Y |
| **TEXAS** | | | | | | | | |
| 1 Chapman | N | Y | Y | N | ? | Y | Y | Y |
| 2 Wilson | N | N | Y | Y | Y | Y | Y | Y |
| 3 ***Johnson*** | N | Y | N | N | Y | N | N | Y |
| 4 Hall | N | Y | N | N | Y | N | Y | Y |
| 5 Bryant | Y | N | Y | Y | Y | Y | Y | Y |
| 6 ***Barton*** | N | Y | N | Y | Y | N | N | N |
| 7 ***Archer*** | N | Y | N | N | ? | N | N | N |
| 8 ***Fields*** | N | Y | N | N | Y | N | N | N |
| 9 Brooks | N | N | Y | Y | Y | Y | Y | Y |
| 10 Pickle | N | N | Y | Y | Y | Y | Y | Y |
| 11 Edwards | N | Y | N | Y | Y | Y | Y | Y |
| 12 Geren | N | Y | Y | Y | Y | Y | Y | Y |
| 13 Sarpalius | N | Y | N | N | Y | N | N | Y |
| 14 Laughlin | N | Y | Y | Y | Y | Y | Y | Y |
| 15 de la Garza | Y | N | Y | N | Y | N | N | Y |
| 16 Coleman | Y | N | Y | Y | Y | Y | Y | Y |
| 17 Stenholm | N | Y | N | N | Y | N | N | Y |
| 18 Washington | Y | N | Y | Y | N | ? | Y | Y |
| 19 ***Combest*** | N | Y | N | N | Y | Y | N | N |
| 20 Gonzalez | N | N | Y | N | N | Y | Y | Y |
| 21 ***Smith*** | N | Y | Y | Y | Y | Y | Y | N |
| 22 ***DeLay*** | N | Y | N | N | Y | N | N | N |
| 23 Bustamante | N | N | Y | N | Y | Y | Y | Y |
| 24 Frost | N | N | Y | Y | Y | Y | Y | Y |
| 25 Andrews | N | N | Y | N | Y | Y | Y | Y |
| 26 ***Armey*** | N | Y | N | N | Y | N | N | N |
| 27 Ortiz | Y | Y | Y | N | Y | Y | N | Y |
| **UTAH** | | | | | | | | |
| 1 ***Hansen*** | N | Y | N | Y | Y | ? | N | N |
| 2 Owens | N | N | Y | Y | Y | Y | Y | Y |
| 3 Orton | N | Y | N | Y | Y | N | N | Y |
| **VERMONT** | | | | | | | | |
| AL *Sanders* | Y | N | Y | Y | Y | Y | Y | Y |
| **VIRGINIA** | | | | | | | | |
| 1 ***Bateman*** | N | Y | N | Y | Y | Y | N | N |
| 2 Pickett | N | N | N | Y | Y | Y | Y | Y |
| 3 ***Bliley*** | N | Y | N | Y | Y | Y | N | N |
| 4 Sisisky | N | N | Y | Y | Y | Y | Y | Y |
| 5 Payne | N | Y | Y | Y | Y | Y | Y | Y |
| 6 Olin | N | N | Y | Y | Y | Y | Y | Y |
| 7 ***Allen*** | N | N | Y | Y | Y | N | N | N |
| 8 Moran | N | N | Y | Y | Y | Y | Y | Y |
| 9 Boucher | N | Y | Y | Y | Y | Y | Y | Y |
| 10 ***Wolf*** | N | Y | Y | Y | Y | N | N | N |
| **WASHINGTON** | | | | | | | | |
| 1 ***Miller*** | N | N | Y | Y | Y | Y | Y | N |
| 2 Swift | N | Y | N | Y | Y | Y | Y | Y |
| 3 Unsoeld | Y | N | Y | Y | Y | Y | Y | Y |
| 4 ***Morrison*** | N | N | Y | Y | Y | Y | Y | N |
| 5 Foley | | | | | | | | |
| 6 Dicks | N | Y | Y | Y | Y | Y | Y | ? |
| 7 McDermott | Y | N | Y | Y | Y | Y | Y | Y |
| 8 ***Chandler*** | N | N | N | Y | Y | Y | Y | N |
| **WEST VIRGINIA** | | | | | | | | |
| 1 Mollohan | N | Y | Y | Y | Y | N | N | Y |
| 2 Staggers | N | N | Y | Y | Y | Y | Y | Y |
| 3 Wise | N | Y | Y | Y | Y | Y | Y | Y |
| 4 Rahall | Y | N | Y | Y | Y | N | N | Y |
| **WISCONSIN** | | | | | | | | |
| 1 Aspin | Y | N | Y | Y | Y | Y | Y | Y |
| 2 ***Klug*** | N | N | Y | Y | Y | Y | Y | N |
| 3 ***Gunderson*** | N | Y | Y | Y | Y | N | N | N |
| 4 Kleczka | N | N | Y | Y | Y | Y | Y | Y |
| 5 Moody | N | N | Y | Y | Y | Y | Y | Y |
| 6 ***Petri*** | N | N | Y | Y | Y | Y | N | N |
| 7 Obey | N | N | Y | Y | Y | Y | Y | Y |
| 8 ***Roth*** | N | Y | Y | Y | Y | N | N | N |
| 9 ***Sensenbrenner*** | N | N | Y | Y | Y | N | N | N |
| **WYOMING** | | | | | | | | |
| AL ***Thomas*** | N | Y | Y | Y | Y | Y | N | N |

Southern states - Ala., Ark., Fla., Ga., Ky., La., Miss., N.C., Okla., S.C., Tenn., Texas, Va.
Omitted votes are quorum calls, which CQ does not include in its vote charts.

## KEY

Y  Voted for (yea).
#  Paired for.
+  Announced for.
N  Voted against (nay).
X  Paired against.
−  Announced against.
P  Voted ''present.''
C  Voted ''present'' to avoid possible conflict of interest.
?  Did not vote or otherwise make a position known.

Democrats    **Republicans**
*Independent*

---

**149. H Res 379. Committee Funding for 1992/Funding Freeze.** Adoption of the resolution to freeze funding for the operations of all standing and select committees of the House at the 1991 level of $55 million for the second session of the 102nd Congress. The committees of the House had requested an increase to $61.5 million. Adopted 323-76: R 78-74; D 244-2 (ND 165-2, SD 79-0); I 1-0, May 28, 1992.

**150. S 1306. Alcohol, Drug Abuse and Mental Health Administration Reorganization.** Gingrich, R-Ga., motion to recommit to the conference committee the conference report, with instructions to report it back to the House with a prohibition on the use of federal funds to buy clean needles or syringes for distribution to drug addicts to use illegal drugs. Motion agreed to 214-157: R 135-6; D 79-150 (ND 36-117, SD 43-33); I 0-1, May 28, 1992. (Hence, the conference report was sent back to conference for further consideration.)

**151. Procedural Motion.** Approval of the House Journal of Tuesday, June 2. Approved 248-97: R 40-93; D 207-4 (ND 136-4, SD 71-0); I 1-0, June 3, 1992.

**152. HR 5006. Fiscal 1993 Defense Authorization/Rule.** Adoption of the rule (H Res 474) to provide for House floor consideration of the bill to authorize $274 billion for defense programs in fiscal 1993. Adopted 257-136: R 26-125; D 230-11 (ND 154-10, SD 76-1); I 1-0, June 3, 1992.

**153. HR 5132. Fiscal 1992 Disaster Relief Supplemental Appropriations/Instruct Conferees.** McDade, R-Pa., motion to instruct the House conferees on the fiscal 1992 disaster relief supplemental to accept the Senate amendment expressing the sense of the Senate in favor of urban enterprise zones. Motion agreed to 372-21: R 149-1; D 223-19 (ND 150-17, SD 73-2); I 0-1, June 3, 1992.

**154. HR 5006. Fiscal 1993 Defense Authorization/Burden Sharing.** Kasich, R-Ohio, amendment to direct the president to achieve agreements by the end of fiscal 1994 with NATO nations and South Korea to assume a greater share of the costs of U.S. military installations, reallocating the savings to activities at military installations in the United States. The amendment reduced by 5 percent in fiscal 1993 and 10 percent in fiscal 1994 the amount available for the operation and maintenance for overseas basing activities. Adopted 396-9: R 150-7; D 245-2 (ND 166-2, SD 79-0); I 1-0, June 3, 1992.

**155. HR 5006. Fiscal 1993 Defense Authorization/Troops Overseas.** Frank, D-Mass., amendment to reduce the authorization level in the bill by $3.5 billion by accelerated withdrawal of U.S. forces or equipment in Europe, Japan and South Korea or an increased level of host-nation support. Adopted 220-185: R 39-117; D 180-68 (ND 146-24, SD 34-44); I 1-0, June 3, 1992. A "nay" was a vote in support of the president's position.

**156. HR 5006. Fiscal 1993 Defense Authorization/Troops in Europe.** Schroeder, D-Colo., amendment to reduce the maximum number of military personnel in Europe to 100,000 by the end of fiscal 1995. The current authorization level of 235,700 would remain in fiscal 1992-95. Adopted 241-162: R 34-120; D 206-42 (ND 162-9, SD 44-33); I 1-0, June 3, 1992. A 'nay' was a vote in support of the president's position.

| | 149 | 150 | 151 | 152 | 153 | 154 | 155 | 156 |
|---|---|---|---|---|---|---|---|---|
| **ALABAMA** | | | | | | | | |
| 1 *Callahan* | N | Y | Y | Y | Y | Y | N | N |
| 2 *Dickinson* | Y | N | N | Y | Y | N | N | N |
| 3 Browder | Y | Y | Y | Y | Y | Y | N | N |
| 4 Bevill | Y | Y | Y | Y | Y | Y | N | N |
| 5 Cramer | Y | N | Y | Y | Y | Y | N | N |
| 6 Erdreich | Y | Y | Y | Y | Y | Y | N | N |
| 7 Harris | Y | Y | Y | Y | Y | Y | N | N |
| **ALASKA** | | | | | | | | |
| AL *Young* | ? | ? | N | Y | Y | Y | N | N |
| **ARIZONA** | | | | | | | | |
| 1 *Rhodes* | Y | N | N | N | Y | Y | N | N |
| 2 Pastor | Y | N | Y | Y | Y | Y | Y | Y |
| 3 *Stump* | Y | N | N | N | Y | Y | N | N |
| 4 *Kyl* | Y | N | N | N | Y | Y | N | N |
| 5 *Kolbe* | Y | N | N | N | Y | Y | N | N |
| **ARKANSAS** | | | | | | | | |
| 1 Alexander | ? | ? | Y | Y | Y | Y | N | N |
| 2 Thornton | Y | N | Y | Y | Y | Y | N | Y |
| 3 *Hammerschmidt* | Y | Y | Y | Y | Y | Y | N | N |
| 4 Anthony | # | ? | ? | ? | ? | ? | ? | ? |
| **CALIFORNIA** | | | | | | | | |
| 1 *Riggs* | N | Y | ? | ? | ? | ? | ? | ? |
| 2 *Herger* | N | Y | N | N | Y | Y | N | N |
| 3 Matsui | Y | N | Y | Y | Y | Y | Y | Y |
| 4 Fazio | Y | N | Y | Y | Y | Y | N | Y |
| 5 Pelosi | Y | N | Y | Y | Y | Y | Y | Y |
| 6 Boxer | ? | ? | ? | ? | ? | ? | # | ? |
| 7 Miller | Y | N | Y | N | Y | Y | Y | Y |
| 8 Dellums | Y | N | ? | ? | Y | Y | Y | Y |
| 9 Stark | ? | ? | Y | Y | Y | Y | Y | Y |
| 10 Edwards | Y | N | Y | Y | Y | Y | Y | Y |
| 11 Lantos | Y | N | Y | Y | Y | Y | N | Y |
| 12 *Campbell* | ? | ? | ? | ? | ? | ? | ? | ? |
| 13 Mineta | Y | N | ? | Y | Y | Y | Y | Y |
| 14 *Doolittle* | N | Y | N | N | Y | Y | N | N |
| 15 Condit | Y | Y | Y | Y | Y | Y | Y | Y |
| 16 Panetta | Y | N | Y | Y | Y | Y | Y | Y |
| 17 Dooley | Y | N | Y | Y | Y | Y | Y | Y |
| 18 Lehman | Y | ? | ? | ? | ? | ? | ? | ? |
| 19 *Lagomarsino* | ? | ? | ? | ? | ? | ? | ? | ? |
| 20 *Thomas* | Y | Y | X | ? | X | ? | X | ? |
| 21 *Gallegly* | Y | Y | ? | ? | Y | Y | N | N |
| 22 *Moorhead* | N | Y | N | N | Y | N | N | N |
| 23 Beilenson | Y | ? | Y | Y | Y | Y | Y | Y |
| 24 Waxman | Y | N | ? | ? | ? | Y | # | Y |
| 25 Roybal | Y | N | ? | ? | ? | ? | Y | Y |
| 26 Berman | Y | N | ? | ? | ? | Y | Y | Y |
| 27 Levine | ? | ? | ? | ? | ? | ? | ? | ? |
| 28 Dixon | ? | ? | Y | Y | Y | Y | Y | N |
| 29 Waters | Y | N | ? | ? | ? | ? | Y | Y |
| 30 Martinez | Y | N | ? | ? | ? | ? | Y | Y |
| 31 Dymally | # | X | ? | ? | ? | ? | ? | ? |
| 32 Anderson | Y | N | Y | Y | Y | Y | Y | Y |
| 33 *Dreier* | N | Y | ? | ? | ? | ? | ? | ? |
| 34 Torres | Y | N | + | + | + | + | Y | Y |
| 35 *Lewis* | Y | ? | ? | ? | ? | ? | ? | ? |
| 36 Brown | ? | ? | Y | Y | Y | Y | Y | Y |
| 37 *McCandless* | Y | Y | N | Y | Y | N | N | N |
| 38 *Dornan* | ? | Y | ? | X | ? | ? | X | ? |
| 39 *Dannemeyer* | ? | ? | ? | ? | ? | ? | ? | ? |
| 40 *Cox* | N | Y | ? | ? | ? | Y | N | ? |
| 41 *Lowery* | Y | Y | N | N | Y | N | N | N |

| | 149 | 150 | 151 | 152 | 153 | 154 | 155 | 156 |
|---|---|---|---|---|---|---|---|---|
| 42 *Rohrabacher* | N | Y | ? | ? | ? | Y | Y | Y |
| 43 *Packard* | X | ? | Y | N | Y | Y | N | N |
| 44 *Cunningham* | Y | Y | ? | ? | ? | Y | N | N |
| 45 *Hunter* | N | Y | N | N | N | N | N | N |
| **COLORADO** | | | | | | | | |
| 1 Schroeder | Y | Y | N | Y | Y | Y | Y | Y |
| 2 Skaggs | Y | N | Y | Y | Y | Y | N | Y |
| 3 *Campbell* | ? | ? | Y | Y | Y | Y | Y | Y |
| 4 *Allard* | N | Y | ? | N | Y | Y | Y | N |
| 5 *Hefley* | N | ? | N | N | Y | N | Y | N |
| 6 *Schaefer* | Y | ? | N | N | Y | N | N | N |
| **CONNECTICUT** | | | | | | | | |
| 1 Kennelly | Y | N | ? | Y | Y | Y | Y | Y |
| 2 Gejdenson | Y | N | Y | Y | Y | Y | Y | Y |
| 3 DeLauro | Y | X | Y | Y | Y | Y | Y | Y |
| 4 *Shays* | N | Y | N | Y | Y | Y | N | N |
| 5 *Franks* | N | Y | N | N | Y | N | N | N |
| 6 *Johnson* | Y | Y | ? | Y | Y | Y | N | N |
| **DELAWARE** | | | | | | | | |
| AL Carper | Y | Y | Y | Y | Y | Y | Y | Y |
| **FLORIDA** | | | | | | | | |
| 1 Hutto | Y | Y | Y | Y | Y | Y | N | N |
| 2 Peterson | Y | Y | Y | Y | Y | Y | N | Y |
| 3 Bennett | Y | Y | Y | Y | Y | Y | Y | Y |
| 4 *James* | N | Y | N | N | Y | Y | N | N |
| 5 *McCollum* | N | Y | N | N | Y | N | N | N |
| 6 *Stearns* | N | Y | N | N | Y | N | N | N |
| 7 Gibbons | Y | Y | ? | Y | Y | Y | Y | N |
| 8 *Young* | N | Y | N | N | Y | N | N | N |
| 9 *Bilirakis* | Y | Y | N | Y | Y | Y | N | N |
| 10 *Ireland* | N | Y | ? | N | ? | Y | ? | ? |
| 11 Bacchus | Y | Y | Y | Y | Y | Y | N | N |
| 12 *Lewis* | N | Y | N | N | Y | Y | N | N |
| 13 *Goss* | N | Y | N | Y | Y | Y | N | N |
| 14 Johnston | Y | Y | Y | Y | ? | Y | Y | Y |
| 15 *Shaw* | N | Y | Y | N | Y | Y | N | N |
| 16 Smith | Y | Y | ? | Y | Y | Y | Y | Y |
| 17 Lehman | Y | N | Y | Y | Y | Y | Y | Y |
| 18 *Ros—Lehtinen* | N | Y | N | N | Y | Y | N | N |
| 19 Fascell | Y | Y | Y | Y | ? | Y | N | N |
| **GEORGIA** | | | | | | | | |
| 1 Thomas | Y | N | ? | Y | Y | Y | N | N |
| 2 Hatcher | ? | ? | Y | Y | Y | Y | N | N |
| 3 Ray | ? | ? | Y | Y | Y | Y | N | N |
| 4 Jones | Y | N | Y | Y | Y | Y | ? | ? |
| 5 Lewis | Y | N | Y | Y | Y | Y | Y | Y |
| 6 *Gingrich* | N | Y | N | N | Y | N | N | N |
| 7 Darden | Y | N | Y | Y | Y | Y | N | Y |
| 8 Rowland | Y | N | Y | Y | Y | Y | N | N |
| 9 Jenkins | Y | N | Y | Y | Y | Y | N | Y |
| 10 Barnard | ? | ? | Y | Y | Y | Y | N | N |
| **HAWAII** | | | | | | | | |
| 1 Abercrombie | N | N | Y | Y | Y | Y | Y | Y |
| 2 Mink | Y | N | Y | Y | Y | Y | Y | Y |
| **IDAHO** | | | | | | | | |
| 1 LaRocco | Y | Y | Y | Y | Y | Y | Y | Y |
| 2 Stallings | Y | Y | Y | Y | Y | Y | Y | Y |
| **ILLINOIS** | | | | | | | | |
| 1 Hayes | Y | N | Y | N | Y | Y | Y | Y |
| 2 Savage | Y | N | ? | N | Y | Y | Y | Y |
| 3 Russo | Y | N | ? | ? | ? | ? | ? | ? |
| 4 Sangmeister | Y | Y | Y | Y | Y | Y | Y | Y |
| 5 Lipinski | Y | Y | Y | Y | Y | Y | Y | Y |
| 6 *Hyde* | Y | Y | N | Y | Y | N | N | N |
| 7 Collins | Y | ? | Y | Y | Y | Y | Y | Y |
| 8 Rostenkowski | Y | N | Y | Y | Y | Y | Y | Y |
| 9 Yates | Y | N | Y | N | Y | Y | Y | Y |
| 10 *Porter* | Y | Y | N | N | Y | Y | N | N |
| 11 Annunzio | Y | N | Y | Y | Y | Y | Y | Y |
| 12 *Crane* | N | Y | N | N | Y | N | N | N |
| 13 *Fawell* | N | Y | N | N | Y | Y | N | N |
| 14 *Hastert* | Y | N | N | N | Y | Y | N | N |
| 15 *Ewing* | N | Y | N | N | Y | Y | N | N |
| 16 Cox | Y | N | Y | N | Y | Y | N | N |
| 17 Evans | Y | N | Y | N | Y | Y | Y | Y |
| 18 *Michel* | ? | ? | N | N | Y | N | N | N |
| 19 Bruce | + | + | Y | Y | Y | Y | Y | Y |
| 20 Durbin | Y | N | Y | Y | Y | Y | Y | Y |
| 21 Costello | Y | N | Y | Y | Y | Y | N | Y |
| 22 Poshard | Y | Y | Y | Y | Y | Y | N | N |
| **INDIANA** | | | | | | | | |
| 1 Visclosky | Y | Y | Y | Y | Y | Y | Y | Y |
| 2 Sharp | Y | N | Y | Y | Y | ? | Y | Y |
| 3 Roemer | Y | Y | Y | Y | N | Y | N | N |

ND  Northern Democrats    SD  Southern Democrats

| | 149 | 150 | 151 | 152 | 153 | 154 | 155 | 156 |
|---|---|---|---|---|---|---|---|---|
| 4 Long | Y | N | Y | Y | Y | Y | N | Y |
| 5 Jontz | Y | N | Y | Y | Y | Y | Y | Y |
| 6 ***Burton*** | N | Y | N | N | Y | Y | N | N |
| 7 ***Myers*** | N | Y | Y | N | N | Y | Y | N |
| 8 McCloskey | Y | N | Y | Y | Y | Y | Y | Y |
| 9 Hamilton | Y | Y | Y | Y | Y | Y | N | Y |
| 10 Jacobs | N | N | N | Y | Y | Y | Y | Y |
| **IOWA** | | | | | | | | |
| 1 ***Leach*** | N | ? | ? | N | Y | Y | Y | Y |
| 2 ***Nussle*** | N | Y | ? | N | Y | Y | Y | Y |
| 3 Nagle | Y | N | ? | Y | Y | Y | ? | Y |
| 4 Smith | Y | N | ? | Y | Y | Y | N | Y |
| 5 ***Lightfoot*** | Y | Y | ? | N | Y | Y | N | Y |
| 6 ***Grandy*** | N | N | N | N | Y | Y | Y | Y |
| **KANSAS** | | | | | | | | |
| 1 ***Roberts*** | Y | Y | N | N | Y | Y | N | N |
| 2 Slattery | Y | Y | Y | Y | Y | Y | N | Y |
| 3 ***Meyers*** | N | Y | Y | N | Y | Y | N | N |
| 4 Glickman | Y | Y | Y | Y | Y | Y | Y | Y |
| 5 ***Nichols*** | Y | Y | Y | N | Y | Y | N | N |
| **KENTUCKY** | | | | | | | | |
| 1 Hubbard | Y | Y | ? | ? | ? | ? | ? | ? |
| 2 Natcher | Y | N | Y | Y | Y | Y | N | Y |
| 3 Mazzoli | Y | Y | Y | Y | Y | Y | N | Y |
| 4 ***Bunning*** | ? | ? | N | N | Y | Y | N | N |
| 5 ***Rogers*** | Y | Y | N | N | Y | Y | N | Y |
| 6 ***Hopkins*** | Y | Y | N | N | Y | Y | N | N |
| 7 Perkins | Y | N | ? | ? | ? | ? | ? | ? |
| **LOUISIANA** | | | | | | | | |
| 1 ***Livingston*** | ? | ? | N | ? | Y | Y | N | N |
| 2 Jefferson | Y | N | ? | Y | Y | Y | Y | Y |
| 3 Tauzin | Y | Y | ? | Y | Y | Y | Y | Y |
| 4 ***McCrery*** | Y | Y | N | N | Y | Y | N | N |
| 5 Huckaby | Y | Y | Y | Y | Y | Y | N | N |
| 6 ***Baker*** | N | Y | N | N | Y | Y | N | N |
| 7 Hayes | Y | Y | Y | ? | ? | ? | ? | ? |
| 8 ***Holloway*** | N | Y | N | N | Y | Y | N | Y |
| **MAINE** | | | | | | | | |
| 1 Andrews | Y | N | Y | Y | N | Y | Y | Y |
| 2 ***Snowe*** | N | Y | Y | N | Y | Y | Y | Y |
| **MARYLAND** | | | | | | | | |
| 1 ***Gilchrest*** | Y | Y | N | N | Y | Y | Y | N |
| 2 ***Bentley*** | Y | Y | N | N | Y | Y | N | N |
| 3 Cardin | Y | N | Y | Y | Y | Y | Y | Y |
| 4 McMillen | Y | Y | ? | Y | Y | Y | Y | Y |
| 5 Hoyer | Y | N | Y | Y | Y | Y | N | Y |
| 6 Byron | Y | N | Y | Y | Y | N | N | N |
| 7 Mfume | Y | N | ? | Y | Y | Y | Y | Y |
| 8 ***Morella*** | Y | N | N | Y | Y | Y | Y | Y |
| **MASSACHUSETTS** | | | | | | | | |
| 1 Olver | Y | N | Y | N | Y | Y | Y | Y |
| 2 Neal | Y | N | ? | N | Y | Y | Y | Y |
| 3 Early | Y | ? | ? | N | Y | Y | Y | Y |
| 4 Frank | Y | N | Y | Y | Y | Y | Y | Y |
| 5 Atkins | Y | N | Y | N | Y | Y | Y | Y |
| 6 Mavroules | Y | N | ? | Y | Y | Y | Y | Y |
| 7 Markey | Y | N | Y | Y | Y | Y | Y | Y |
| 8 Kennedy | Y | N | Y | Y | Y | Y | Y | Y |
| 9 Moakley | Y | N | Y | Y | Y | Y | Y | Y |
| 10 Studds | Y | N | Y | Y | Y | Y | Y | Y |
| 11 Donnelly | ? | ? | Y | Y | Y | Y | Y | Y |
| **MICHIGAN** | | | | | | | | |
| 1 Conyers | Y | N | Y | Y | N | Y | Y | Y |
| 2 ***Pursell*** | N | Y | Y | N | Y | Y | Y | N |
| 3 Wolpe | Y | N | Y | Y | Y | Y | Y | Y |
| 4 ***Upton*** | N | Y | N | N | Y | Y | Y | Y |
| 5 ***Henry*** | N | Y | N | N | Y | Y | Y | Y |
| 6 Carr | Y | Y | Y | Y | Y | Y | Y | Y |
| 7 Kildee | Y | N | Y | Y | Y | Y | Y | Y |
| 8 Traxler | ? | ? | ? | ? | ? | ? | ? | ? |
| 9 ***Vander Jagt*** | Y | ? | Y | Y | Y | Y | Y | N |
| 10 ***Camp*** | N | Y | N | N | Y | Y | Y | N |
| 11 ***Davis*** | Y | Y | N | Y | Y | Y | N | N |
| 12 Bonior | Y | N | Y | Y | Y | Y | Y | Y |
| 13 Collins | + | — | Y | Y | Y | Y | Y | Y |
| 14 Hertel | Y | N | Y | Y | Y | Y | Y | Y |
| 15 Ford | Y | N | Y | Y | N | Y | Y | Y |
| 16 Dingell | Y | ? | ? | Y | N | Y | Y | Y |
| 17 Levin | Y | C | Y | Y | Y | Y | Y | Y |
| 18 ***Broomfield*** | Y | ? | Y | N | Y | Y | N | N |
| **MINNESOTA** | | | | | | | | |
| 1 Penny | Y | Y | Y | Y | Y | Y | Y | Y |
| 2 ***Weber*** | N | Y | ? | N | Y | Y | N | N |
| 3 ***Ramstad*** | Y | Y | N | N | Y | Y | Y | N |
| 4 Vento | Y | N | Y | Y | Y | Y | Y | Y |
| 5 Sabo | Y | N | Y | Y | Y | Y | Y | Y |
| 6 Sikorski | Y | N | N | Y | Y | Y | Y | Y |
| 7 Peterson | Y | N | Y | Y | Y | Y | Y | Y |
| 8 Oberstar | Y | N | Y | Y | Y | Y | Y | Y |
| **MISSISSIPPI** | | | | | | | | |
| 1 Whitten | Y | N | Y | Y | Y | Y | ? | ? |
| 2 Espy | Y | N | Y | Y | Y | Y | Y | Y |
| 3 Montgomery | Y | N | Y | Y | Y | Y | N | N |
| 4 Parker | Y | N | Y | Y | Y | Y | N | N |
| 5 Taylor | Y | N | Y | Y | Y | Y | N | N |
| **MISSOURI** | | | | | | | | |
| 1 Clay | Y | ? | Y | Y | N | Y | Y | Y |
| 2 Horn | Y | N | Y | Y | Y | Y | Y | Y |
| 3 Gephardt | Y | N | Y | Y | Y | Y | Y | Y |
| 4 Skelton | Y | Y | Y | Y | Y | N | N | N |
| 5 Wheat | Y | N | Y | Y | Y | Y | Y | Y |
| 6 ***Coleman*** | Y | Y | N | N | Y | Y | N | N |
| 7 ***Hancock*** | N | Y | N | N | Y | Y | N | N |
| 8 ***Emerson*** | Y | Y | N | N | Y | Y | N | N |
| 9 Volkmer | Y | Y | ? | Y | Y | Y | N | Y |
| **MONTANA** | | | | | | | | |
| 1 Williams | Y | N | Y | Y | Y | Y | Y | Y |
| 2 ***Marlenee*** | N | ? | N | N | Y | Y | N | N |
| **NEBRASKA** | | | | | | | | |
| 1 ***Bereuter*** | N | Y | N | N | Y | Y | N | N |
| 2 Hoagland | Y | N | Y | Y | Y | Y | N | Y |
| 3 ***Barrett*** | Y | Y | N | N | Y | Y | N | N |
| **NEVADA** | | | | | | | | |
| 1 Bilbray | Y | Y | Y | N | Y | Y | N | Y |
| 2 ***Vucanovich*** | N | Y | N | N | Y | Y | N | N |
| **NEW HAMPSHIRE** | | | | | | | | |
| 1 ***Zeliff*** | N | Y | N | N | Y | Y | Y | N |
| 2 Swett | Y | Y | Y | Y | Y | Y | Y | Y |
| **NEW JERSEY** | | | | | | | | |
| 1 Andrews | Y | N | ? | N | Y | ? | ? | ? |
| 2 Hughes | Y | N | Y | N | Y | Y | Y | Y |
| 3 Pallone | Y | N | Y | Y | Y | Y | Y | Y |
| 4 ***Smith*** | Y | Y | Y | N | Y | Y | N | N |
| 5 ***Roukema*** | Y | ? | ? | N | Y | Y | Y | Y |
| 6 Dwyer | Y | ? | Y | Y | Y | Y | Y | Y |
| 7 ***Rinaldo*** | Y | Y | Y | N | Y | Y | N | N |
| 8 Roe | Y | ? | Y | Y | Y | Y | Y | Y |
| 9 Torricelli | Y | ? | Y | Y | Y | Y | Y | N |
| 10 Payne | Y | N | Y | Y | Y | Y | Y | Y |
| 11 ***Gallo*** | Y | Y | N | N | Y | Y | N | N |
| 12 ***Zimmer*** | N | Y | N | N | Y | Y | Y | Y |
| 13 ***Saxton*** | N | Y | N | N | Y | Y | N | N |
| 14 Guarini | Y | N | Y | Y | Y | Y | Y | Y |
| **NEW MEXICO** | | | | | | | | |
| 1 ***Schiff*** | Y | Y | ? | Y | Y | Y | Y | N |
| 2 ***Skeen*** | Y | Y | Y | Y | Y | Y | N | N |
| 3 Richardson | Y | N | Y | Y | Y | Y | N | Y |
| **NEW YORK** | | | | | | | | |
| 1 Hochbrueckner | Y | Y | Y | Y | Y | Y | Y | Y |
| 2 Downey | Y | N | Y | Y | N | Y | Y | Y |
| 3 Mrazek | Y | N | Y | Y | Y | Y | Y | Y |
| 4 ***Lent*** | ? | ? | ? | N | Y | Y | N | N |
| 5 ***McGrath*** | Y | Y | Y | Y | Y | Y | N | N |
| 6 Flake | Y | N | Y | Y | Y | Y | Y | Y |
| 7 Ackerman | Y | N | ? | # | Y | Y | Y | Y |
| 8 Scheuer | Y | N | ? | Y | Y | Y | Y | Y |
| 9 Manton | ? | ? | Y | Y | Y | Y | Y | Y |
| 10 Schumer | Y | N | ? | Y | Y | Y | Y | Y |
| 11 Towns | Y | N | ? | Y | Y | ? | ? | ? |
| 12 Owens | Y | N | ? | Y | N | Y | Y | Y |
| 13 Solarz | Y | N | Y | Y | Y | Y | Y | Y |
| 14 ***Molinari*** | Y | Y | N | N | Y | Y | N | N |
| 15 ***Green*** | Y | N | Y | Y | Y | Y | Y | Y |
| 16 Rangel | Y | Y | ? | Y | Y | Y | Y | Y |
| 17 Weiss | Y | N | Y | Y | N | Y | Y | Y |
| 18 Serrano | Y | Y | Y | Y | Y | Y | Y | Y |
| 19 Engel | Y | N | Y | Y | Y | Y | Y | Y |
| 20 Lowey | Y | Y | Y | Y | Y | Y | Y | Y |
| 21 ***Fish*** | Y | Y | Y | N | Y | Y | N | N |
| 22 ***Gilman*** | Y | Y | Y | N | Y | Y | N | N |
| 23 McNulty | Y | Y | Y | Y | Y | Y | Y | Y |
| 24 ***Solomon*** | Y | Y | N | N | Y | Y | N | N |
| 25 ***Boehlert*** | Y | Y | N | Y | Y | Y | N | Y |
| 26 ***Martin*** | Y | Y | N | N | Y | N | N | N |
| 27 ***Walsh*** | ? | ? | Y | N | Y | Y | N | N |
| 28 McHugh | Y | N | Y | Y | Y | Y | N | Y |
| 29 ***Horton*** | Y | Y | Y | Y | Y | Y | N | N |
| 30 Slaughter | Y | N | Y | Y | Y | Y | Y | Y |
| 31 ***Paxon*** | N | Y | N | N | Y | Y | N | N |
| 32 LaFalce | Y | N | Y | Y | Y | Y | Y | Y |
| 33 Nowak | Y | N | ? | Y | Y | Y | Y | Y |
| 34 ***Houghton*** | Y | Y | Y | N | Y | Y | N | N |
| **NORTH CAROLINA** | | | | | | | | |
| 1 Jones | Y | Y | ? | ? | Y | Y | N | Y |
| 2 Valentine | Y | N | Y | Y | Y | Y | Y | Y |
| 3 Lancaster | Y | N | Y | Y | Y | Y | N | N |
| 4 Price | Y | N | Y | Y | Y | Y | Y | Y |
| 5 Neal | Y | N | Y | Y | Y | Y | Y | Y |
| 6 ***Coble*** | N | Y | N | N | Y | Y | Y | N |
| 7 Rose | Y | N | Y | Y | Y | Y | Y | Y |
| 8 Hefner | Y | N | ? | ? | ? | ? | ? | ? |
| 9 ***McMillan*** | N | Y | N | N | Y | Y | N | N |
| 10 ***Ballenger*** | N | Y | N | N | Y | Y | Y | N |
| 11 ***Taylor*** | N | Y | N | N | Y | Y | N | N |
| **NORTH DAKOTA** | | | | | | | | |
| AL Dorgan | Y | N | Y | Y | Y | Y | Y | Y |
| **OHIO** | | | | | | | | |
| 1 Luken | Y | Y | Y | Y | Y | Y | Y | Y |
| 2 ***Gradison*** | N | Y | Y | N | Y | Y | N | N |
| 3 Hall | Y | N | ? | Y | Y | Y | Y | Y |
| 4 ***Oxley*** | Y | Y | N | N | Y | Y | N | ? |
| 5 ***Gillmor*** | Y | Y | Y | N | Y | Y | N | Y |
| 6 ***McEwen*** | X | ? | ? | ? | ? | Y | N | Y |
| 7 ***Hobson*** | Y | Y | N | N | Y | Y | Y | N |
| 8 ***Boehner*** | N | Y | N | N | Y | Y | N | N |
| 9 Kaptur | Y | N | Y | Y | Y | Y | Y | Y |
| 10 ***Miller*** | N | Y | ? | N | Y | Y | N | N |
| 11 Eckart | Y | N | ? | Y | Y | Y | Y | Y |
| 12 ***Kasich*** | Y | Y | Y | N | Y | Y | N | Y |
| 13 Pease | Y | N | Y | Y | N | Y | N | Y |
| 14 Sawyer | Y | N | Y | Y | Y | Y | Y | Y |
| 15 ***Wylie*** | Y | Y | Y | N | Y | Y | Y | N |
| 16 ***Regula*** | N | Y | N | N | Y | Y | Y | N |
| 17 Traficant | Y | Y | Y | Y | Y | Y | Y | Y |
| 18 Applegate | Y | Y | Y | Y | Y | Y | Y | Y |
| 19 Feighan | Y | N | ? | ? | ? | Y | Y | Y |
| 20 Oakar | ? | ? | ? | ? | ? | ? | ? | ? |
| 21 Stokes | Y | N | ? | Y | Y | Y | Y | Y |
| **OKLAHOMA** | | | | | | | | |
| 1 ***Inhofe*** | ? | ? | ? | N | Y | Y | N | N |
| 2 Synar | Y | N | Y | Y | N | Y | Y | Y |
| 3 Brewster | Y | N | Y | Y | Y | Y | Y | Y |
| 4 McCurdy | Y | N | Y | Y | Y | Y | Y | Y |
| 5 ***Edwards*** | ? | ? | ? | N | Y | Y | N | N |
| 6 English | Y | Y | Y | Y | ? | Y | N | Y |
| **OREGON** | | | | | | | | |
| 1 AuCoin | Y | N | Y | N | Y | Y | Y | Y |
| 2 ***Smith*** | N | Y | N | N | Y | Y | N | N |
| 3 Wyden | Y | N | Y | N | Y | Y | Y | Y |
| 4 DeFazio | Y | N | Y | ? | Y | Y | Y | Y |
| 5 Kopetski | Y | N | Y | Y | Y | Y | Y | Y |
| **PENNSYLVANIA** | | | | | | | | |
| 1 Foglietta | Y | N | Y | Y | Y | Y | N | Y |
| 2 Blackwell | Y | N | Y | Y | Y | Y | Y | Y |
| 3 Borski | Y | N | Y | Y | Y | Y | Y | Y |
| 4 Kolter | ? | ? | Y | Y | Y | ? | ? | ? |
| 5 ***Schulze*** | N | ? | Y | N | Y | Y | N | N |
| 6 Yatron | Y | ? | Y | Y | Y | Y | Y | Y |
| 7 ***Weldon*** | N | Y | N | N | Y | Y | N | N |
| 8 Kostmayer | Y | N | Y | Y | Y | Y | Y | Y |
| 9 ***Shuster*** | Y | Y | N | N | Y | Y | N | N |
| 10 ***McDade*** | Y | Y | N | Y | Y | Y | ? | ? |
| 11 Kanjorski | Y | N | Y | Y | Y | Y | Y | Y |
| 12 Murtha | ? | ? | Y | Y | Y | Y | N | N |
| 13 ***Coughlin*** | Y | Y | ? | N | Y | Y | N | N |
| 14 Coyne | Y | N | Y | Y | Y | Y | Y | Y |
| 15 ***Ritter*** | N | Y | Y | N | Y | Y | Y | Y |
| 16 ***Walker*** | N | Y | N | N | Y | Y | Y | N |
| 17 ***Gekas*** | N | Y | N | N | Y | Y | N | N |
| 18 ***Santorum*** | Y | Y | Y | N | Y | Y | N | Y |
| 19 ***Goodling*** | Y | Y | N | N | Y | Y | N | N |
| 20 Gaydos | Y | ? | ? | Y | Y | Y | Y | Y |
| 21 ***Ridge*** | N | Y | ? | ? | ? | Y | Y | N |
| 22 Murphy | Y | ? | N | N | Y | Y | Y | Y |
| 23 ***Clinger*** | Y | Y | Y | N | ? | Y | N | N |
| **RHODE ISLAND** | | | | | | | | |
| 1 ***Machtley*** | Y | Y | N | N | Y | Y | N | N |
| 2 Reed | Y | N | Y | Y | Y | Y | Y | Y |
| **SOUTH CAROLINA** | | | | | | | | |
| 1 ***Ravenel*** | Y | Y | Y | Y | Y | Y | N | Y |
| 2 ***Spence*** | Y | Y | N | N | Y | N | N | N |
| 3 Derrick | Y | N | Y | # | Y | Y | Y | Y |
| 4 Patterson | Y | Y | Y | Y | Y | Y | Y | N |
| 5 Spratt | Y | Y | ? | Y | Y | Y | N | Y |
| 6 Tallon | Y | N | Y | Y | Y | Y | Y | Y |
| **SOUTH DAKOTA** | | | | | | | | |
| AL Johnson | Y | Y | Y | Y | Y | Y | Y | Y |
| **TENNESSEE** | | | | | | | | |
| 1 ***Quillen*** | N | Y | ? | Y | Y | Y | N | N |
| 2 ***Duncan*** | N | Y | N | N | Y | Y | Y | N |
| 3 Lloyd | Y | Y | Y | Y | Y | Y | N | N |
| 4 Cooper | Y | N | Y | Y | Y | Y | Y | N |
| 5 Clement | Y | Y | Y | Y | Y | Y | Y | Y |
| 6 Gordon | Y | Y | ? | Y | ? | Y | Y | Y |
| 7 ***Sundquist*** | Y | Y | ? | N | Y | Y | N | N |
| 8 Tanner | Y | N | Y | Y | Y | Y | N | Y |
| 9 Ford | Y | N | Y | Y | Y | Y | Y | Y |
| **TEXAS** | | | | | | | | |
| 1 Chapman | Y | ? | Y | Y | Y | Y | Y | Y |
| 2 Wilson | Y | ? | Y | Y | Y | Y | Y | Y |
| 3 ***Johnson*** | Y | Y | ? | N | Y | Y | N | N |
| 4 Hall | Y | Y | Y | N | Y | Y | N | Y |
| 5 Bryant | Y | Y | Y | Y | Y | Y | Y | Y |
| 6 ***Barton*** | Y | ? | ? | N | Y | Y | N | N |
| 7 ***Archer*** | Y | Y | Y | N | Y | Y | N | N |
| 8 ***Fields*** | N | Y | N | N | Y | Y | N | N |
| 9 Brooks | Y | # | Y | Y | Y | Y | Y | N |
| 10 Pickle | Y | Y | Y | Y | Y | Y | N | N |
| 11 Edwards | Y | Y | Y | Y | Y | Y | N | N |
| 12 Geren | Y | Y | Y | Y | Y | Y | N | N |
| 13 Sarpalius | Y | Y | Y | Y | Y | Y | N | Y |
| 14 Laughlin | Y | Y | Y | Y | Y | Y | N | N |
| 15 de la Garza | Y | Y | Y | Y | Y | Y | N | Y |
| 16 Coleman | Y | Y | Y | Y | Y | Y | N | Y |
| 17 Stenholm | Y | Y | Y | Y | Y | Y | Y | Y |
| 18 Washington | Y | N | ? | ? | N | Y | Y | Y |
| 19 ***Combest*** | Y | Y | Y | N | Y | Y | N | N |
| 20 Gonzalez | Y | Y | Y | Y | Y | Y | N | N |
| 21 ***Smith*** | Y | Y | N | N | Y | Y | N | N |
| 22 ***DeLay*** | Y | Y | N | N | Y | Y | N | Y |
| 23 Bustamante | Y | Y | Y | Y | Y | Y | N | Y |
| 24 Frost | Y | Y | Y | Y | Y | Y | Y | Y |
| 25 Andrews | Y | Y | Y | Y | Y | Y | N | Y |
| 26 ***Armey*** | N | Y | N | N | Y | Y | N | N |
| 27 Ortiz | ? | Y | Y | Y | Y | Y | N | Y |
| **UTAH** | | | | | | | | |
| 1 ***Hansen*** | N | Y | Y | N | Y | N | N | N |
| 2 Owens | Y | N | Y | Y | Y | Y | Y | Y |
| 3 Orton | Y | Y | Y | Y | Y | Y | Y | Y |
| **VERMONT** | | | | | | | | |
| AL *Sanders* | Y | N | Y | Y | N | Y | Y | Y |
| **VIRGINIA** | | | | | | | | |
| 1 ***Bateman*** | Y | Y | Y | Y | Y | N | N | N |
| 2 Pickett | Y | Y | Y | Y | ? | Y | N | N |
| 3 ***Bliley*** | Y | Y | N | Y | Y | Y | N | N |
| 4 Sisisky | Y | Y | Y | Y | Y | Y | N | Y |
| 5 Payne | Y | # | Y | Y | Y | Y | N | N |
| 6 Olin | Y | Y | Y | Y | Y | Y | N | N |
| 7 ***Allen*** | N | Y | N | Y | Y | Y | N | N |
| 8 Moran | Y | N | Y | Y | Y | Y | Y | ? |
| 9 Boucher | Y | Y | Y | Y | Y | Y | Y | Y |
| 10 ***Wolf*** | Y | Y | N | Y | Y | Y | N | Y |
| **WASHINGTON** | | | | | | | | |
| 1 ***Miller*** | N | Y | ? | N | Y | Y | N | Y |
| 2 Swift | Y | N | Y | Y | Y | Y | Y | Y |
| 3 Unsoeld | Y | N | Y | Y | Y | Y | Y | Y |
| 4 ***Morrison*** | Y | ? | Y | Y | Y | ? | N | Y |
| 5 Foley | | | | | | | | |
| 6 Dicks | Y | N | Y | Y | Y | Y | N | N |
| 7 McDermott | Y | N | Y | Y | Y | Y | Y | Y |
| 8 ***Chandler*** | N | ? | N | N | Y | Y | N | N |
| **WEST VIRGINIA** | | | | | | | | |
| 1 Mollohan | Y | Y | Y | Y | Y | Y | N | N |
| 2 Staggers | Y | Y | ? | Y | Y | Y | Y | Y |
| 3 Wise | Y | Y | Y | Y | Y | Y | Y | Y |
| 4 Rahall | Y | Y | Y | Y | Y | Y | N | N |
| **WISCONSIN** | | | | | | | | |
| 1 Aspin | Y | N | Y | Y | Y | Y | N | Y |
| 2 ***Klug*** | Y | Y | Y | N | Y | Y | Y | N |
| 3 ***Gunderson*** | Y | Y | Y | N | Y | Y | Y | Y |
| 4 Kleczka | Y | Y | Y | Y | Y | Y | N | ? |
| 5 Moody | Y | N | Y | Y | Y | Y | Y | Y |
| 6 ***Petri*** | N | Y | Y | N | Y | Y | N | Y |
| 7 Obey | Y | N | Y | Y | N | Y | Y | Y |
| 8 ***Roth*** | N | Y | N | N | Y | Y | Y | Y |
| 9 ***Sensenbrenner*** | N | Y | N | N | Y | Y | Y | Y |
| **WYOMING** | | | | | | | | |
| AL ***Thomas*** | Y | Y | N | N | Y | Y | N | N |

Southern states - Ala., Ark., Fla., Ga., Ky., La., Miss., N.C., Okla., S.C., Tenn., Texas, Va.
Omitted votes are quorum calls, which CQ does not include in its vote charts.

**157. HR 5006. Fiscal 1993 Defense Authorization/ Troops Overseas.** Gephardt, D-Mo., amendment to reduce by 40 percent below the fiscal 1992 level the number of U.S. military personnel stationed outside the United States by the end of fiscal 1995. The amendment provided for a waiver in the event of war or a presidential declaration of an emergency. Adopted 225-177: R 20-136; D 204-41 (ND 161-8, SD 43-33); I 1-0, June 3, 1992. A 'nay' was a vote in support of the president's position.

**158. HR 5006. Fiscal 1993 Defense Authorization/ Nuclear Stockpile.** Evans, D-Ill., amendment to require the president to submit an unclassified annual report on the U.S. nuclear weapons stockpile and inventory of tritium and fissile material. The amendment allowed the president to waive this requirement with a certification that the member states of the Commonwealth of Independent States had not negotiated in good faith on a reciprocal release. Rejected 83-318: R 0-155; D 82-163 (ND 74-93, SD 8-70); I 1-0, June 3, 1992.

**160. HR 5006. Fiscal 1993 Defense Authorization/ Nuclear Weapons.** Aspin, D-Wis., amendment to increase the authorization level for programs to reduce the nuclear weapons of the former Soviet Union from $400 million to $650 million; authorize the transfer of $60 million from the procurement accounts of Defense agencies to a nuclear non-proliferation technology initiative through the Defense Advanced Research Projects Agency and the Department of Energy; authorize the transfer of $40 million from the working capital accounts of the Department of Defense for international non-proliferation activities; and require a report by the secretary of Defense on nuclear non-proliferation activities. Adopted 356-54: R 125-36; D 230-18 (ND 160-13, SD 70-5); I 1-0, June 4, 1992.

**162. HR 5006. Fiscal 1993 Defense Authorization/ Nuclear Weapons.** Mavroules, D-Mass., amendment to call for further nuclear weapons reductions in the United States and other nuclear states including the former Soviet republics, France, the United Kingdom and China; call for accelerated nuclear reductions under the Strategic Arms Reduction Treaty(START); and call for an end to the production of plutonium and highly enriched uranium by 1995. Adopted 278-135: R 45-115; D 232-20 (ND 172-4, SD 60-16); I 1-0, June 4, 1992. A "nay" was a vote in support of the president's position.

**163. HR 5006. Fiscal 1993 Defense Authorization/ Abortions in Military Hospitals.** AuCoin, D-Ore., amendment to allow military personnel stationed outside the United States to obtain abortions in military hospitals, provided they pay the full cost. Adopted 216-193: R 34-125; D 181-68 (ND 130-44, SD 51-24); I 1-0, June 4, 1992. A "nay" was a vote in support of the president's position.

**164. HR 5006. Fiscal 1993 Defense Authorization/ Nuclear Weapons Testing.** Kopetski, D-Ore., amendment to provide a one-year moratorium on nuclear weapons testing unless the president certified that any of the former republics of the Soviet Union had conducted a nuclear weapons test during the period. Adopted 237-167: R 24-134; D 212-33 (ND 165-7, SD 47-26); I 1-0, June 4, 1992. A "nay" was a vote in support of the president's position.

**165. HR 5006. Fiscal 1993 Defense Authorization/ Defense Industry Conversion.** Hopkins, R-Ky., amendment to the Frost, D-Texas, amendment to give the secretary of Defense discretion in implementing the provisions of the Frost amendment that require defense contractors to give hiring preferences and provide early retirement protection to defense workers as a condition for future contracts. The amendment also made job training programs contingent on a joint Defense and Labor department study on the re-employment potential of defense workers. Rejected 147-235: R 145-5; D 2-229 (ND 1-156, SD 1-73); I 0-1, June 4, 1992.

**166. HR 5006. Fiscal 1993 Defense Authorization/ Defense Industry Conversion.** Frost, D-Texas, amendment to provide $1 billion for defense reinvestment and economic conversion activities. Adopted 275-105: R 43-104; D 231-1 (ND 156-1, SD 75-0); I 1-0, June 4, 1992.

## KEY

| | |
|---|---|
| Y | Voted for (yea). |
| # | Paired for. |
| + | Announced for. |
| N | Voted against (nay). |
| X | Paired against. |
| − | Announced against. |
| P | Voted "present." |
| C | Voted "present" to avoid possible conflict of interest. |
| ? | Did not vote or otherwise make a position known. |

**Democrats** *Republicans*
*Independent*

| | 157 | 158 | 160 | 162 | 163 | 164 | 165 | 166 |
|---|---|---|---|---|---|---|---|---|
| **ALABAMA** | | | | | | | | |
| 1 *Callahan* | N | N | Y | N | N | N | Y | N |
| 2 *Dickinson* | N | N | Y | N | Y | N | Y | N |
| 3 Browder | N | N | Y | Y | N | Y | N | Y |
| 4 Bevill | N | N | Y | N | N | N | N | Y |
| 5 Cramer | N | N | Y | Y | N | N | N | Y |
| 6 Erdreich | N | N | Y | Y | Y | N | N | Y |
| 7 Harris | N | N | Y | N | N | N | N | Y |
| **ALASKA** | | | | | | | | |
| AL *Young* | N | N | N | N | N | N | Y | Y |
| **ARIZONA** | | | | | | | | |
| 1 *Rhodes* | N | N | Y | N | N | N | Y | N |
| 2 Pastor | Y | N | Y | Y | Y | Y | N | Y |
| 3 *Stump* | N | N | N | N | N | N | Y | N |
| 4 *Kyl* | N | N | Y | N | N | N | Y | N |
| 5 *Kolbe* | N | N | Y | N | Y | N | Y | N |
| **ARKANSAS** | | | | | | | | |
| 1 Alexander | Y | N | Y | Y | Y | Y | N | Y |
| 2 Thornton | Y | N | Y | Y | N | Y | N | Y |
| 3 *Hammerschmidt* | N | N | N | N | N | N | Y | N |
| 4 Anthony | ? | ? | ? | ? | ? | # | ? | ? |
| **CALIFORNIA** | | | | | | | | |
| 1 *Riggs* | ? | ? | Y | Y | Y | N | Y | ? |
| 2 *Herger* | N | N | N | N | X | ? | ? | |
| 3 Matsui | Y | N | Y | Y | Y | Y | N | Y |
| 4 Fazio | Y | N | Y | Y | Y | Y | N | Y |
| 5 Pelosi | Y | Y | Y | Y | Y | Y | ? | Y |
| 6 Boxer | # | ? | Y | Y | Y | Y | N | Y |
| 7 Miller | Y | Y | Y | Y | Y | Y | ? | Y |
| 8 Dellums | Y | Y | Y | Y | Y | Y | N | Y |
| 9 Stark | Y | Y | Y | Y | Y | Y | N | Y |
| 10 Edwards | Y | Y | Y | Y | Y | Y | N | Y |
| 11 Lantos | Y | Y | Y | Y | Y | Y | N | Y |
| 12 *Campbell* | ? | ? | ? | ? | ? | ? | ? | ? |
| 13 Mineta | Y | Y | Y | Y | Y | Y | N | Y |
| 14 *Doolittle* | N | N | N | N | N | N | Y | N |
| 15 Condit | N | N | Y | Y | Y | Y | N | Y |
| 16 Panetta | Y | N | Y | Y | Y | Y | N | Y |
| 17 Dooley | Y | N | Y | Y | Y | Y | N | Y |
| 18 Lehman | ? | ? | ? | ? | ? | ? | ? | ? |
| 19 *Lagomarsino* | ? | ? | Y | N | N | N | Y | N |
| 20 *Thomas* | X | ? | ? | X | # | X | ? | X |
| 21 *Gallegly* | N | N | Y | N | N | N | Y | N |
| 22 *Moorhead* | N | N | N | N | N | N | Y | N |
| 23 Beilenson | Y | Y | Y | Y | Y | Y | ? | # |
| 24 Waxman | Y | Y | Y | Y | Y | Y | N | Y |
| 25 Roybal | Y | Y | Y | Y | Y | Y | N | Y |
| 26 Berman | Y | Y | Y | Y | Y | Y | N | Y |
| 27 Levine | ? | ? | ? | ? | ? | ? | ? | ? |
| 28 Dixon | Y | Y | Y | Y | Y | Y | N | Y |
| 29 Waters | Y | Y | Y | Y | Y | Y | N | Y |
| 30 Martinez | Y | Y | Y | Y | Y | Y | N | Y |
| 31 Dymally | ? | ? | Y | Y | Y | ? | ? | ? |
| 32 Anderson | Y | N | Y | Y | Y | Y | N | Y |
| 33 *Dreier* | ? | ? | Y | N | N | N | Y | N |
| 34 Torres | + | Y | Y | Y | Y | Y | N | Y |
| 35 *Lewis* | ? | ? | Y | N | N | N | Y | N |
| 36 Brown | Y | N | Y | Y | Y | Y | N | Y |
| 37 *McCandless* | N | N | Y | N | N | Y | N | Y |
| 38 *Dornan* | X | ? | N | N | N | N | Y | N |
| 39 *Dannemeyer* | ? | ? | ? | ? | ? | ? | ? | ? |
| 40 *Cox* | N | N | N | N | N | N | Y | N |
| 41 *Lowery* | N | N | N | N | N | N | Y | N |

| | 157 | 158 | 160 | 162 | 163 | 164 | 165 | 166 |
|---|---|---|---|---|---|---|---|---|
| 42 *Rohrabacher* | Y | N | Y | N | Y | N | Y | N |
| 43 *Packard* | N | N | Y | N | N | N | Y | Y |
| 44 *Cunningham* | N | N | Y | N | N | N | Y | Y |
| 45 *Hunter* | N | N | Y | N | N | N | Y | N |
| **COLORADO** | | | | | | | | |
| 1 Schroeder | Y | Y | Y | Y | Y | Y | N | Y |
| 2 Skaggs | Y | N | Y | Y | Y | Y | N | Y |
| 3 Campbell | N | N | Y | Y | Y | Y | N | Y |
| 4 *Allard* | N | N | N | N | N | N | Y | N |
| 5 *Hefley* | Y | ? | Y | N | N | N | Y | N |
| 6 *Schaefer* | N | N | N | N | N | N | Y | N |
| **CONNECTICUT** | | | | | | | | |
| 1 Kennelly | Y | N | Y | Y | Y | Y | N | Y |
| 2 Gejdenson | Y | N | Y | Y | Y | Y | N | Y |
| 3 DeLauro | Y | N | Y | Y | Y | Y | N | Y |
| 4 *Shays* | Y | Y | Y | Y | Y | Y | Y | Y |
| 5 *Franks* | N | N | N | Y | N | Y | Y | Y |
| 6 *Johnson* | N | N | Y | N | Y | N | Y | Y |
| **DELAWARE** | | | | | | | | |
| AL Carper | Y | N | Y | Y | Y | Y | N | Y |
| **FLORIDA** | | | | | | | | |
| 1 Hutto | N | N | Y | N | N | N | N | Y |
| 2 Peterson | N | N | Y | Y | Y | Y | N | Y |
| 3 Bennett | Y | N | Y | Y | Y | Y | N | Y |
| 4 *James* | N | N | Y | N | N | N | Y | N |
| 5 *McCollum* | N | N | Y | N | N | N | Y | N |
| 6 *Stearns* | N | N | N | N | N | N | Y | N |
| 7 Gibbons | N | N | ? | ? | ? | ? | ? | ? |
| 8 *Young* | N | N | Y | N | N | N | Y | N |
| 9 *Bilirakis* | N | N | N | Y | N | Y | Y | Y |
| 10 *Ireland* | N | N | Y | N | N | N | Y | ? |
| 11 Bacchus | N | N | Y | Y | Y | Y | N | Y |
| 12 *Lewis* | N | N | Y | N | N | N | Y | N |
| 13 *Goss* | N | N | N | N | N | N | Y | N |
| 14 Johnston | Y | N | Y | Y | Y | Y | N | Y |
| 15 *Shaw* | N | N | N | N | N | N | Y | N |
| 16 Smith | Y | Y | Y | Y | Y | Y | N | Y |
| 17 Lehman | Y | Y | Y | Y | Y | Y | N | Y |
| 18 *Ros−Lehtinen* | N | N | Y | Y | N | Y | Y | Y |
| 19 Fascell | N | N | Y | Y | Y | Y | N | Y |
| **GEORGIA** | | | | | | | | |
| 1 Thomas | N | N | Y | N | Y | Y | N | Y |
| 2 Hatcher | ? | N | Y | ? | ? | ? | ? | ? |
| 3 Ray | N | N | N | N | N | Y | N | Y |
| 4 Jones | ? | ? | ? | ? | ? | ? | ? | ? |
| 5 Lewis | Y | Y | Y | Y | Y | Y | N | Y |
| 6 *Gingrich* | N | N | N | N | N | N | Y | N |
| 7 Darden | Y | N | Y | Y | Y | Y | N | Y |
| 8 Rowland | N | N | Y | Y | Y | Y | N | Y |
| 9 Jenkins | Y | N | Y | Y | Y | Y | N | Y |
| 10 Barnard | N | N | Y | N | N | N | Y | Y |
| **HAWAII** | | | | | | | | |
| 1 Abercrombie | Y | Y | Y | Y | Y | Y | N | Y |
| 2 Mink | Y | N | Y | Y | Y | Y | N | Y |
| **IDAHO** | | | | | | | | |
| 1 LaRocco | Y | N | Y | Y | Y | Y | N | Y |
| 2 Stallings | Y | N | Y | N | Y | N | Y | N |
| **ILLINOIS** | | | | | | | | |
| 1 Hayes | Y | Y | Y | Y | Y | Y | N | Y |
| 2 Savage | Y | Y | Y | Y | Y | Y | N | Y |
| 3 Russo | ? | ? | Y | Y | N | Y | N | Y |
| 4 Sangmeister | Y | Y | Y | Y | N | Y | N | Y |
| 5 Lipinski | Y | Y | Y | N | N | N | N | Y |
| 6 *Hyde* | N | N | Y | N | N | N | Y | N |
| 7 Collins | Y | Y | Y | Y | Y | Y | ? | ? |
| 8 Rostenkowski | Y | Y | Y | Y | Y | Y | N | Y |
| 9 Yates | Y | Y | Y | Y | Y | Y | N | Y |
| 10 *Porter* | N | N | Y | N | Y | Y | + | − |
| 11 Annunzio | Y | N | Y | N | Y | N | N | Y |
| 12 *Crane* | N | N | N | N | N | N | Y | N |
| 13 *Fawell* | Y | N | Y | Y | Y | Y | N | Y |
| 14 *Hastert* | N | N | N | N | N | N | Y | N |
| 15 *Ewing* | Y | N | N | N | N | N | N | Y |
| 16 Cox | Y | Y | Y | Y | Y | Y | N | Y |
| 17 Evans | Y | Y | Y | Y | Y | Y | N | Y |
| 18 *Michel* | N | N | N | N | N | N | Y | N |
| 19 Bruce | Y | Y | + | Y | N | Y | N | Y |
| 20 Durbin | Y | Y | Y | Y | Y | Y | N | Y |
| 21 Costello | Y | N | Y | N | Y | N | N | Y |
| 22 Poshard | Y | N | N | N | Y | N | N | Y |
| **INDIANA** | | | | | | | | |
| 1 Visclosky | Y | N | Y | Y | Y | Y | N | Y |
| 2 Sharp | Y | N | Y | ? | Y | ? | N | Y |
| 3 Roemer | Y | N | N | Y | N | Y | N | Y |

ND Northern Democrats          SD Southern Democrats

| | 157 | 158 | 160 | 162 | 163 | 164 | 165 | 166 |
|---|---|---|---|---|---|---|---|---|
| 4 Long | Y | N | Y | Y | Y | Y | N | Y |
| 5 Jontz | Y | Y | N | Y | Y | Y | N | Y |
| 6 ***Burton*** | N | N | N | N | N | N | ? | ? |
| 7 ***Myers*** | N | N | Y | N | N | N | Y | N |
| 8 McCloskey | Y | N | Y | Y | Y | Y | N | Y |
| 9 Hamilton | Y | N | Y | Y | Y | Y | N | Y |
| 10 Jacobs | Y | Y | Y | Y | Y | Y | N | Y |
| **IOWA** | | | | | | | | |
| 1 ***Leach*** | Y | N | Y | Y | Y | Y | Y | Y |
| 2 ***Nussle*** | Y | N | Y | Y | N | N | Y | N |
| 3 Nagle | Y | N | Y | Y | Y | Y | N | Y |
| 4 Smith | Y | N | Y | Y | Y | N | N | Y |
| 5 ***Lightfoot*** | N | N | Y | N | N | N | Y | N |
| 6 ***Grandy*** | N | N | Y | Y | N | N | Y | N |
| **KANSAS** | | | | | | | | |
| 1 ***Roberts*** | N | N | Y | N | N | N | Y | N |
| 2 Slattery | Y | N | Y | Y | Y | Y | ? | ? |
| 3 ***Meyers*** | N | N | Y | Y | Y | Y | Y | Y |
| 4 Glickman | Y | N | Y | Y | Y | Y | N | Y |
| 5 ***Nichols*** | N | N | Y | N | ? | ? | ? | ? |
| **KENTUCKY** | | | | | | | | |
| 1 Hubbard | ? | ? | ? | ? | ? | ? | ? | ? |
| 2 Natcher | Y | N | Y | Y | N | Y | N | Y |
| 3 Mazzoli | Y | N | Y | Y | N | Y | N | Y |
| 4 ***Bunning*** | N | N | Y | N | N | N | Y | N |
| 5 ***Rogers*** | N | N | N | N | N | N | Y | N |
| 6 ***Hopkins*** | N | N | N | N | N | N | Y | N |
| 7 Perkins | ? | ? | N | Y | N | Y | N | Y |
| **LOUISIANA** | | | | | | | | |
| 1 ***Livingston*** | N | N | Y | N | N | N | Y | N |
| 2 Jefferson | Y | Y | Y | Y | Y | Y | N | Y |
| 3 Tauzin | ? | N | Y | N | N | N | N | Y |
| 4 ***McCrery*** | N | N | Y | N | N | N | Y | N |
| 5 Huckaby | N | N | Y | Y | N | N | N | Y |
| 6 ***Baker*** | N | N | Y | N | N | N | Y | N |
| 7 Hayes | ? | ? | Y | Y | N | N | N | Y |
| 8 ***Holloway*** | N | N | N | N | N | N | Y | N |
| **MAINE** | | | | | | | | |
| 1 Andrews | Y | Y | Y | Y | Y | Y | N | Y |
| 2 ***Snowe*** | N | N | Y | Y | Y | N | N | Y |
| **MARYLAND** | | | | | | | | |
| 1 ***Gilchrest*** | N | N | Y | Y | Y | Y | Y | Y |
| 2 ***Bentley*** | N | N | Y | N | N | N | Y | Y |
| 3 Cardin | Y | N | Y | Y | Y | Y | N | Y |
| 4 McMillen | Y | N | Y | Y | Y | Y | N | Y |
| 5 Hoyer | Y | N | Y | Y | Y | Y | N | Y |
| 6 Byron | N | N | Y | N | N | ? | ? | ? |
| 7 Mfume | Y | N | Y | Y | Y | Y | N | Y |
| 8 ***Morella*** | Y | N | Y | Y | Y | Y | + | + |
| **MASSACHUSETTS** | | | | | | | | |
| 1 Olver | Y | Y | Y | Y | Y | Y | N | Y |
| 2 Neal | Y | Y | Y | Y | N | Y | N | Y |
| 3 Early | Y | N | Y | Y | N | Y | N | Y |
| 4 Frank | Y | Y | Y | Y | Y | Y | N | Y |
| 5 Atkins | Y | Y | Y | Y | Y | Y | N | Y |
| 6 Mavroules | Y | N | Y | Y | N | Y | N | Y |
| 7 Markey | Y | Y | Y | Y | Y | Y | N | Y |
| 8 Kennedy | Y | Y | Y | Y | Y | Y | N | Y |
| 9 Moakley | # | ? | Y | Y | N | Y | N | Y |
| 10 Studds | Y | Y | Y | Y | Y | Y | N | Y |
| 11 Donnelly | Y | Y | Y | Y | N | Y | N | Y |
| **MICHIGAN** | | | | | | | | |
| 1 Conyers | Y | Y | Y | Y | Y | Y | N | ? |
| 2 ***Pursell*** | N | N | Y | N | N | Y | ? | ? |
| 3 Wolpe | Y | Y | Y | Y | Y | Y | ? | ? |
| 4 ***Upton*** | N | N | Y | Y | N | Y | Y | N |
| 5 ***Henry*** | N | N | Y | Y | N | Y | Y | N |
| 6 Carr | Y | N | Y | Y | Y | Y | Y | N |
| 7 Kildee | Y | N | Y | Y | N | Y | N | Y |
| 8 Traxler | ? | ? | ? | ? | ? | ? | ? | ? |
| 9 ***Vander Jagt*** | N | N | Y | ? | ? | ? | ? | ? |
| 10 ***Camp*** | N | N | Y | Y | N | N | Y | N |
| 11 ***Davis*** | N | N | Y | N | N | N | Y | N |
| 12 Bonior | Y | Y | Y | Y | N | Y | N | Y |
| 13 Collins | Y | Y | N | Y | Y | Y | N | Y |
| 14 Hertel | Y | N | Y | Y | N | Y | ? | ? |
| 15 Ford | Y | Y | Y | Y | Y | Y | N | Y |
| 16 Dingell | Y | N | Y | N | Y | ? | ? | ? |
| 17 Levin | Y | N | Y | Y | Y | Y | N | Y |
| 18 ***Broomfield*** | N | N | Y | Y | N | N | Y | N |
| **MINNESOTA** | | | | | | | | |
| 1 Penny | Y | N | Y | Y | N | Y | N | Y |
| 2 ***Weber*** | N | N | Y | N | N | N | Y | N |
| 3 ***Ramstad*** | N | N | Y | Y | Y | N | Y | N |
| 4 Vento | Y | N | Y | Y | Y | Y | N | Y |

| | 157 | 158 | 160 | 162 | 163 | 164 | 165 | 166 |
|---|---|---|---|---|---|---|---|---|
| 5 Sabo | Y | N | Y | Y | Y | Y | N | Y |
| 6 Sikorski | Y | Y | Y | Y | Y | Y | N | Y |
| 7 Peterson | Y | N | Y | Y | N | Y | ? | Y |
| 8 Oberstar | Y | Y | Y | Y | N | Y | N | Y |
| **MISSISSIPPI** | | | | | | | | |
| 1 Whitten | ? | ? | Y | Y | ? | ? | ? | ? |
| 2 Espy | Y | N | Y | Y | Y | Y | N | Y |
| 3 Montgomery | N | N | Y | Y | N | N | N | Y |
| 4 Parker | N | N | Y | Y | N | N | N | Y |
| 5 Taylor | N | N | Y | Y | N | N | N | Y |
| **MISSOURI** | | | | | | | | |
| 1 Clay | Y | Y | Y | Y | Y | Y | N | Y |
| 2 Horn | Y | N | Y | Y | Y | Y | N | Y |
| 3 Gephardt | Y | N | Y | Y | Y | Y | N | Y |
| 4 Skelton | N | N | Y | Y | N | N | N | Y |
| 5 Wheat | Y | Y | Y | Y | Y | Y | N | Y |
| 6 ***Coleman*** | N | N | Y | N | N | N | Y | Y |
| 7 ***Hancock*** | N | N | N | N | N | N | Y | N |
| 8 ***Emerson*** | N | N | Y | N | N | N | Y | ? |
| 9 Volkmer | Y | N | N | Y | N | Y | N | Y |
| **MONTANA** | | | | | | | | |
| 1 Williams | Y | N | Y | Y | Y | Y | N | Y |
| 2 ***Marlenee*** | N | N | Y | N | N | N | Y | N |
| **NEBRASKA** | | | | | | | | |
| 1 ***Bereuter*** | N | N | Y | N | N | N | Y | N |
| 2 Hoagland | Y | N | Y | Y | Y | Y | N | Y |
| 3 ***Barrett*** | N | N | Y | N | N | N | Y | N |
| **NEVADA** | | | | | | | | |
| 1 Bilbray | Y | N | Y | Y | N | N | ? | ? |
| 2 ***Vucanovich*** | N | N | Y | N | N | N | Y | N |
| **NEW HAMPSHIRE** | | | | | | | | |
| 1 ***Zeliff*** | N | N | N | N | Y | N | Y | N |
| 2 Swett | Y | Y | Y | Y | Y | Y | N | Y |
| **NEW JERSEY** | | | | | | | | |
| 1 Andrews | ? | ? | N | N | Y | N | N | Y |
| 2 Hughes | Y | N | Y | Y | Y | Y | N | Y |
| 3 Pallone | Y | N | Y | Y | Y | Y | N | Y |
| 4 ***Smith*** | Y | N | Y | Y | N | Y | Y | Y |
| 5 ***Roukema*** | N | N | Y | Y | Y | Y | N | Y |
| 6 Dwyer | Y | N | Y | Y | Y | Y | ? | Y |
| 7 ***Rinaldo*** | N | N | ? | ? | X | N | Y | Y |
| 8 Roe | ? | ? | Y | Y | N | Y | N | Y |
| 9 Torricelli | Y | N | Y | Y | Y | Y | N | Y |
| 10 Payne | Y | Y | Y | Y | Y | Y | N | Y |
| 11 ***Gallo*** | N | N | Y | N | Y | N | Y | N |
| 12 ***Zimmer*** | Y | N | Y | N | Y | N | Y | N |
| 13 ***Saxton*** | N | N | Y | N | N | N | Y | N |
| 14 Guarini | Y | N | Y | Y | Y | Y | N | Y |
| **NEW MEXICO** | | | | | | | | |
| 1 ***Schiff*** | N | N | Y | N | Y | N | Y | Y |
| 2 ***Skeen*** | N | N | Y | N | N | N | Y | N |
| 3 Richardson | Y | N | Y | Y | Y | N | N | Y |
| **NEW YORK** | | | | | | | | |
| 1 Hochbrueckner | Y | Y | Y | Y | Y | Y | N | Y |
| 2 Downey | Y | Y | Y | Y | Y | Y | N | Y |
| 3 Mrazek | Y | Y | Y | Y | Y | Y | N | Y |
| 4 ***Lent*** | N | N | Y | N | N | N | Y | Y |
| 5 ***McGrath*** | N | N | Y | N | N | N | Y | Y |
| 6 Flake | Y | N | Y | Y | Y | Y | N | Y |
| 7 Ackerman | Y | N | ? | ? | ? | ? | ? | ? |
| 8 Scheuer | Y | Y | Y | Y | Y | Y | ? | ? |
| 9 Manton | Y | N | Y | Y | N | Y | N | Y |
| 10 Schumer | Y | N | Y | Y | Y | Y | N | Y |
| 11 Towns | ? | ? | Y | Y | Y | Y | N | Y |
| 12 Owens | Y | Y | ? | Y | Y | Y | ? | ? |
| 13 Solarz | Y | N | Y | Y | Y | Y | N | Y |
| 14 ***Molinari*** | N | N | Y | N | Y | N | Y | N |
| 15 ***Green*** | Y | N | Y | Y | Y | Y | ? | ? |
| 16 Rangel | Y | ? | Y | Y | Y | Y | N | Y |
| 17 Weiss | Y | Y | Y | Y | Y | Y | N | Y |
| 18 Serrano | Y | Y | Y | Y | Y | Y | N | Y |
| 19 Engel | Y | N | ? | Y | Y | Y | N | Y |
| 20 Lowey | Y | N | Y | Y | Y | Y | N | Y |
| 21 ***Fish*** | N | N | Y | Y | N | Y | Y | Y |
| 22 ***Gilman*** | N | N | Y | Y | Y | Y | N | Y |
| 23 McNulty | Y | N | Y | Y | N | Y | N | Y |
| 24 ***Solomon*** | N | N | N | N | N | N | Y | N |
| 25 ***Boehlert*** | N | N | Y | Y | Y | Y | N | Y |
| 26 ***Martin*** | N | N | Y | N | N | N | Y | N |
| 27 ***Walsh*** | N | N | N | Y | N | Y | Y | N |
| 28 McHugh | Y | N | Y | Y | Y | Y | N | Y |
| 29 ***Horton*** | ? | ? | Y | Y | Y | N | Y | Y |
| 30 Slaughter | Y | Y | Y | Y | Y | Y | N | Y |
| 31 ***Paxon*** | N | N | Y | N | N | N | Y | Y |

| | 157 | 158 | 160 | 162 | 163 | 164 | 165 | 166 |
|---|---|---|---|---|---|---|---|---|
| 32 LaFalce | Y | N | Y | Y | N | Y | N | Y |
| 33 Nowak | Y | N | ? | Y | N | Y | N | Y |
| 34 ***Houghton*** | N | N | Y | N | Y | N | Y | N |
| **NORTH CAROLINA** | | | | | | | | |
| 1 Jones | Y | N | Y | Y | Y | Y | N | Y |
| 2 Valentine | N | N | N | Y | Y | Y | N | Y |
| 3 Lancaster | N | N | Y | Y | Y | N | ? | Y |
| 4 Price | Y | N | Y | Y | Y | Y | N | Y |
| 5 Neal | Y | N | Y | Y | Y | Y | N | Y |
| 6 ***Coble*** | N | N | N | N | N | N | Y | N |
| 7 Rose | Y | N | Y | Y | ? | ? | N | Y |
| 8 Hefner | ? | ? | ? | ? | ? | ? | ? | ? |
| 9 ***McMillan*** | N | N | Y | N | N | N | Y | N |
| 10 ***Ballenger*** | N | N | Y | N | N | N | Y | N |
| 11 ***Taylor*** | N | N | N | Y | N | Y | Y | N |
| **NORTH DAKOTA** | | | | | | | | |
| AL Dorgan | Y | — | Y | Y | Y | Y | N | Y |
| **OHIO** | | | | | | | | |
| 1 Luken | Y | N | Y | Y | N | Y | N | Y |
| 2 ***Gradison*** | N | N | Y | N | N | N | Y | N |
| 3 Hall | Y | N | Y | Y | N | Y | N | Y |
| 4 ***Oxley*** | N | N | Y | N | N | N | Y | N |
| 5 ***Gillmor*** | Y | N | Y | N | N | N | Y | Y |
| 6 ***McEwen*** | N | N | Y | N | N | N | Y | N |
| 7 ***Hobson*** | N | N | Y | Y | N | N | Y | Y |
| 8 ***Boehner*** | N | N | Y | N | N | N | Y | N |
| 9 Kaptur | Y | N | Y | Y | N | Y | N | Y |
| 10 ***Miller*** | N | N | Y | Y | N | N | Y | N |
| 11 Eckart | Y | Y | Y | Y | Y | Y | N | Y |
| 12 ***Kasich*** | N | N | Y | Y | N | N | Y | Y |
| 13 Pease | Y | N | Y | Y | Y | Y | N | Y |
| 14 Sawyer | Y | N | Y | Y | Y | Y | N | Y |
| 15 ***Wylie*** | N | N | ? | ? | ? | ? | ? | ? |
| 16 ***Regula*** | Y | N | Y | Y | N | Y | Y | Y |
| 17 Traficant | Y | Y | N | Y | Y | Y | N | Y |
| 18 Applegate | Y | N | Y | Y | Y | Y | N | Y |
| 19 Feighan | Y | N | ? | Y | ? | Y | ? | ? |
| 20 Oakar | ? | ? | Y | Y | ? | ? | ? | ? |
| 21 Stokes | Y | Y | Y | Y | Y | Y | N | Y |
| **OKLAHOMA** | | | | | | | | |
| 1 ***Inhofe*** | N | N | N | N | N | N | Y | N |
| 2 Synar | Y | Y | Y | Y | Y | Y | N | Y |
| 3 Brewster | Y | N | N | Y | Y | Y | N | Y |
| 4 McCurdy | Y | N | Y | Y | Y | Y | N | Y |
| 5 ***Edwards*** | Y | N | Y | N | N | N | ? | ? |
| 6 English | Y | N | Y | Y | N | Y | N | Y |
| **OREGON** | | | | | | | | |
| 1 AuCoin | Y | N | Y | Y | Y | Y | N | Y |
| 2 ***Smith*** | N | N | N | N | N | N | Y | N |
| 3 Wyden | Y | Y | Y | Y | Y | Y | N | Y |
| 4 DeFazio | Y | Y | Y | Y | Y | Y | N | Y |
| 5 Kopetski | Y | Y | Y | Y | Y | Y | N | Y |
| **PENNSYLVANIA** | | | | | | | | |
| 1 Foglietta | Y | Y | Y | Y | Y | Y | N | Y |
| 2 Blackwell | Y | Y | Y | Y | Y | Y | N | Y |
| 3 Borski | Y | N | Y | Y | Y | Y | N | Y |
| 4 Kolter | ? | ? | N | Y | N | Y | ? | ? |
| 5 ***Schulze*** | N | N | Y | N | N | N | Y | N |
| 6 Yatron | Y | N | Y | Y | N | Y | N | Y |
| 7 ***Weldon*** | N | N | Y | Y | N | N | Y | Y |
| 8 Kostmayer | Y | Y | Y | Y | Y | Y | N | Y |
| 9 ***Shuster*** | N | N | Y | N | N | N | Y | N |
| 10 ***McDade*** | ? | ? | Y | Y | N | N | Y | Y |
| 11 Kanjorski | Y | Y | Y | Y | Y | Y | N | Y |
| 12 Murtha | N | N | Y | Y | N | N | ? | ? |
| 13 ***Coughlin*** | N | N | Y | N | Y | N | Y | Y |
| 14 Coyne | Y | Y | Y | Y | Y | Y | N | Y |
| 15 ***Ritter*** | N | N | Y | Y | N | N | Y | Y |
| 16 ***Walker*** | N | N | N | N | N | N | Y | N |
| 17 ***Gekas*** | N | N | N | N | N | N | Y | N |
| 18 ***Santorum*** | N | N | Y | Y | N | N | Y | Y |
| 19 ***Goodling*** | N | N | Y | Y | N | N | Y | Y |
| 20 Gaydos | Y | ? | N | ? | ? | ? | ? | ? |
| 21 ***Ridge*** | N | N | Y | Y | N | N | Y | Y |
| 22 Murphy | Y | N | N | Y | N | Y | N | Y |
| 23 ***Clinger*** | N | N | Y | N | N | — | + | — |
| **RHODE ISLAND** | | | | | | | | |
| 1 ***Machtley*** | N | N | Y | Y | Y | N | Y | Y |
| 2 Reed | Y | N | Y | Y | Y | Y | N | Y |
| **SOUTH CAROLINA** | | | | | | | | |
| 1 ***Ravenel*** | N | N | Y | Y | N | N | Y | Y |
| 2 ***Spence*** | N | N | Y | N | N | N | Y | Y |
| 3 Derrick | Y | N | Y | N | Y | Y | N | Y |
| 4 Patterson | N | N | Y | Y | Y | N | N | Y |
| 5 Spratt | N | N | Y | Y | Y | Y | N | Y |
| 6 Tallon | Y | N | ? | ? | Y | Y | N | Y |

| | 157 | 158 | 160 | 162 | 163 | 164 | 165 | 166 |
|---|---|---|---|---|---|---|---|---|
| **SOUTH DAKOTA** | | | | | | | | |
| AL Johnson | Y | N | Y | Y | Y | Y | N | Y |
| **TENNESSEE** | | | | | | | | |
| 1 ***Quillen*** | N | N | N | N | N | N | Y | N |
| 2 ***Duncan*** | Y | N | N | N | N | N | Y | N |
| 3 Lloyd | N | N | Y | N | Y | N | N | Y |
| 4 Cooper | N | N | Y | N | Y | Y | N | Y |
| 5 Clement | Y | N | Y | Y | Y | Y | N | Y |
| 6 Gordon | Y | N | Y | Y | Y | Y | N | Y |
| 7 ***Sundquist*** | N | N | Y | N | N | N | Y | N |
| 8 Tanner | N | N | Y | Y | Y | N | N | Y |
| 9 Ford | Y | N | Y | Y | Y | Y | N | Y |
| **TEXAS** | | | | | | | | |
| 1 Chapman | Y | N | Y | N | Y | N | N | Y |
| 2 Wilson | Y | N | Y | N | Y | N | N | Y |
| 3 ***Johnson*** | N | N | N | N | N | N | Y | N |
| 4 Hall | Y | N | N | N | N | N | N | Y |
| 5 Bryant | Y | N | Y | Y | Y | ? | N | Y |
| 6 ***Barton*** | N | N | Y | N | N | N | Y | N |
| 7 ***Archer*** | N | N | Y | N | N | N | Y | N |
| 8 ***Fields*** | N | N | Y | N | N | N | Y | N |
| 9 Brooks | Y | N | Y | Y | Y | N | N | Y |
| 10 Pickle | Y | N | Y | Y | Y | Y | N | Y |
| 11 Edwards | N | N | ? | Y | Y | Y | N | Y |
| 12 Geren | Y | N | Y | N | Y | N | N | Y |
| 13 Sarpalius | Y | N | Y | Y | N | N | N | Y |
| 14 Laughlin | N | N | Y | N | N | N | N | Y |
| 15 de la Garza | Y | N | Y | Y | N | ? | ? | ? |
| 16 Coleman | Y | N | Y | Y | Y | Y | N | Y |
| 17 Stenholm | N | N | Y | Y | N | N | N | Y |
| 18 Washington | Y | Y | Y | Y | Y | Y | N | Y |
| 19 ***Combest*** | N | N | N | N | N | N | Y | N |
| 20 Gonzalez | N | Y | Y | Y | Y | Y | N | Y |
| 21 ***Smith*** | N | N | Y | N | N | N | Y | N |
| 22 ***DeLay*** | N | N | N | N | N | N | Y | N |
| 23 Bustamante | Y | N | ? | # | ? | # | ? | ? |
| 24 Frost | Y | N | Y | Y | Y | Y | N | Y |
| 25 Andrews | Y | N | Y | N | Y | N | N | Y |
| 26 ***Armey*** | N | N | N | N | N | N | Y | N |
| 27 Ortiz | Y | N | Y | Y | N | N | N | Y |
| **UTAH** | | | | | | | | |
| 1 ***Hansen*** | N | N | Y | N | N | N | Y | N |
| 2 Owens | Y | Y | Y | Y | Y | Y | N | Y |
| 3 Orton | Y | N | Y | Y | N | Y | N | Y |
| **VERMONT** | | | | | | | | |
| AL *Sanders* | Y | Y | Y | Y | Y | Y | N | Y |
| **VIRGINIA** | | | | | | | | |
| 1 ***Bateman*** | N | N | Y | N | N | N | Y | N |
| 2 Pickett | N | N | ? | Y | Y | N | N | Y |
| 3 ***Bliley*** | N | N | N | N | N | N | Y | N |
| 4 Sisisky | N | N | Y | N | Y | N | N | Y |
| 5 Payne | N | N | Y | N | Y | Y | N | Y |
| 6 Olin | N | N | ? | ? | ? | ? | ? | ? |
| 7 ***Allen*** | N | N | N | N | N | N | Y | N |
| 8 Moran | Y | Y | Y | Y | Y | Y | N | Y |
| 9 Boucher | Y | N | Y | Y | Y | Y | N | Y |
| 10 ***Wolf*** | N | N | Y | N | N | N | Y | N |
| **WASHINGTON** | | | | | | | | |
| 1 ***Miller*** | N | N | Y | N | Y | N | ? | ? |
| 2 Swift | Y | N | Y | Y | Y | Y | N | ? |
| 3 Unsoeld | Y | Y | Y | Y | Y | Y | ? | ? |
| 4 ***Morrison*** | Y | N | Y | Y | Y | Y | ? | ? |
| 5 Foley | | | | | | | | |
| 6 Dicks | N | N | Y | Y | Y | Y | N | Y |
| 7 McDermott | Y | Y | Y | Y | Y | Y | N | Y |
| 8 ***Chandler*** | N | N | Y | N | Y | N | Y | Y |
| **WEST VIRGINIA** | | | | | | | | |
| 1 Mollohan | N | N | Y | Y | N | Y | N | Y |
| 2 Staggers | Y | Y | Y | Y | N | Y | N | Y |
| 3 Wise | Y | N | Y | Y | Y | Y | N | Y |
| 4 Rahall | N | N | N | Y | N | Y | N | Y |
| **WISCONSIN** | | | | | | | | |
| 1 Aspin | Y | N | Y | Y | Y | Y | N | Y |
| 2 ***Klug*** | N | N | Y | Y | Y | Y | Y | N |
| 3 ***Gunderson*** | Y | N | Y | Y | Y | Y | Y | N |
| 4 Kleczka | Y | N | Y | Y | N | Y | N | Y |
| 5 Moody | Y | Y | Y | Y | Y | Y | N | Y |
| 6 ***Petri*** | Y | N | N | Y | N | Y | Y | Y |
| 7 Obey | Y | Y | Y | Y | Y | Y | N | Y |
| 8 ***Roth*** | Y | N | N | N | N | Y | Y | N |
| 9 ***Sensenbrenner*** | Y | N | N | N | N | N | Y | N |
| **WYOMING** | | | | | | | | |
| AL ***Thomas*** | N | N | Y | N | N | N | Y | N |

Southern states - Ala., Ark., Fla., Ga., Ky., La., Miss., N.C., Okla., S.C., Tenn., Texas, Va.
Omitted votes are quorum calls, which CQ does not include in its vote charts.

## KEY

Y   Voted for (yea).
#   Paired for.
+   Announced for.
N   Voted against (nay).
X   Paired against.
−   Announced against.
P   Voted "present."
C   Voted "present" to avoid possible conflict of interest.
?   Did not vote or otherwise make a position known.

Democrats   **Republicans**
*Independent*

---

**167. HR 5006. Fiscal 1993 Defense Authorization/Funding Levels.** Dellums, D-Calif., amendment to reduce the total authorization in the bill by 10 percent. Rejected 90-283: R 4-142; D 85-141 (ND 76-79, SD 9-62); I 1-0, June 4, 1992. A "nay" was a vote in support of the president's position.

**168. HR 5006. Fiscal 1993 Defense Authorization/Strategic Defense Initiative.** Dellums, D-Calif., amendment to limit funding for ballistic missile defense, principally the Strategic Defense Initiative (SDI), to a level of $2.3 billion, compared with $4.3 billion in the bill; repeal the Missile Defense Act of 1991; and terminate the Strategic Defense Initiative Organization. Rejected 117-248: R 2-142; D 114-106 (ND 104-48, SD 10-58); I 1-0, June 5, 1992. A "nay" was a vote in support of the president's position.

**169. HR 5006. Fiscal 1993 Defense Authorization/Strategic Defense Initiative.** Durbin, D-Ill., amendment to reduce funding for the Strategic Defense Initiative (SDI) by $937.5 million from the $4.3 billion in the bill to $3.3 billion. Rejected 161-211: R 11-134; D 149-77 (ND 125-31, SD 24-46); I 1-0, June 5, 1992. A "nay" was a vote in support of the president's position.

**170. HR 5006. Fiscal 1993 Defense Authorization/B-2 Aircraft.** Andrews, D-Maine, amendment to prohibit the production of any new B-2 aircraft by cutting $2.7 billion, allowing only for B-2 expenditures associated with research, development and the deployment of the 15 B-2s funded before fiscal 1992. Rejected 162-212: R 22-123; D 139-89 (ND 120-38, SD 19-51); I 1-0, June 5, 1992. A "nay" was a vote in support of the president's position.

**171. HR 5006. Fiscal 1993 Defense Authorization/Troops Overseas.** Separate vote in the full House at the request of Solomon, R-N.Y., on the Frank, D-Mass., amendment to reduce the authorization level in the bill by $3.5 billion by the accelerated withdrawal of U.S. forces or equipment from Europe, Japan and South Korea or by an increased level of host-nation support. Adopted 202-164: R 32-110; D 169-54 (ND 137-18, SD 32-36); I 1-0, June 5, 1992. A "nay" was a vote in support of the president's position.

**172. HR 5006. Fiscal 1993 Defense Authorization/Passage.** Passage of the bill to authorize $270 billion for defense programs in fiscal 1993, including $4.3 billion for the Strategic Defense Initiative (SDI) and $4 billion for the B-2 bomber. The bill provides an authorization level $11 billion less than the administration's proposal, $20.4 billion less than appropriated in fiscal 1992, $18.4 billion less than the level set in the 1990 Budget Enforcement Act and $7 billion less than the level set in the 1993 budget resolution. Passed 198-168: R 30-112; D 167-56 (ND 104-51, SD 63-5); I 1-0, June 5, 1992.

**173. Procedural Motion.** Approval of the House Journal of Friday, June 5. Approved 231-116: R 32-112; D 199-4 (ND 137-4, SD 62-0); I 0-0, June 9, 1992.

**174. HR 5333. Balanced Budget.** Conyers, D-Mich., motion to suspend the rules and pass the bill to require the president to submit and the House and Senate Budget committees to report a fiscal 1994 budget that would provide for a balanced budget by fiscal 1998. Motion rejected 199-220: R 10-151; D 189-68 (ND 144-31, SD 45-37); I 0-1, June 9, 1992. A two-thirds majority of those present and voting (280 in this case) was required for passage under suspension of the rules. A "nay" was a vote in support of the president's position.

| | 167 | 168 | 169 | 170 | 171 | 172 | 173 | 174 |
|---|---|---|---|---|---|---|---|---|
| **ALABAMA** | | | | | | | | |
| 1 *Callahan* | N | N | N | N | Y | N | ? | N |
| 2 *Dickinson* | N | N | N | N | Y | N | N | N |
| 3 Browder | N | N | N | N | Y | N | Y | N |
| 4 Bevill | N | N | N | N | Y | N | Y | Y |
| 5 Cramer | N | N | N | N | Y | N | Y | N |
| 6 Erdreich | N | N | N | N | Y | N | Y | N |
| 7 Harris | N | N | N | N | Y | N | Y | N |
| **ALASKA** | | | | | | | | |
| AL *Young* | N | ? | N | N | N | N | N | N |
| **ARIZONA** | | | | | | | | |
| 1 *Rhodes* | N | N | N | N | N | N | N | N |
| 2 Pastor | N | Y | Y | Y | Y | Y | Y | Y |
| 3 *Stump* | N | N | N | N | N | N | N | N |
| 4 *Kyl* | N | N | N | N | N | N | N | N |
| 5 *Kolbe* | N | N | N | N | Y | Y | N | N |
| **ARKANSAS** | | | | | | | | |
| 1 Alexander | N | ? | N | ? | ? | ? | ? | Y |
| 2 Thornton | N | N | N | N | Y | ? | Y | Y |
| 3 *Hammerschmidt* | N | N | N | ? | ? | ? | Y | N |
| 4 Anthony | X | ? | ? | ? | ? | ? | ? | ? |
| **CALIFORNIA** | | | | | | | | |
| 1 *Riggs* | N | N | N | Y | N | Y | ? | N |
| 2 *Herger* | ? | X | X | X | ? | X | ? | N |
| 3 Matsui | N | Y | Y | N | Y | Y | Y | Y |
| 4 Fazio | N | N | Y | N | N | Y | Y | Y |
| 5 Pelosi | ? | # | ? | ? | ? | X | ? | Y |
| 6 Boxer | Y | Y | Y | Y | Y | N | Y | Y |
| 7 Miller | ? | ? | ? | ? | ? | ? | Y | Y |
| 8 Dellums | Y | Y | Y | Y | Y | N | N | Y |
| 9 Stark | Y | Y | Y | Y | Y | N | Y | Y |
| 10 Edwards | Y | Y | Y | Y | Y | N | Y | Y |
| 11 Lantos | N | N | Y | Y | Y | Y | Y | Y |
| 12 *Campbell* | ? | ? | ? | ? | ? | ? | N | N |
| 13 Mineta | Y | Y | Y | Y | Y | N | Y | Y |
| 14 *Doolittle* | N | N | N | N | N | N | N | N |
| 15 Condit | N | Y | Y | Y | Y | Y | Y | N |
| 16 Panetta | N | Y | Y | Y | Y | Y | Y | Y |
| 17 Dooley | N | Y | Y | N | Y | Y | Y | Y |
| 18 Lehman | ? | ? | ? | ? | ? | ? | ? | Y |
| 19 *Lagomarsino* | N | N | N | N | N | N | N | N |
| 20 *Thomas* | ? | X | ? | ? | ? | X | N | N |
| 21 *Gallegly* | N | N | N | N | N | N | N | N |
| 22 *Moorhead* | N | N | N | N | N | N | N | N |
| 23 Beilenson | ? | # | # | ? | ? | ? | Y | Y |
| 24 Waxman | Y | Y | Y | Y | Y | N | Y | Y |
| 25 Roybal | Y | Y | Y | N | Y | N | Y | Y |
| 26 Berman | N | N | Y | Y | Y | Y | Y | Y |
| 27 Levine | ? | ? | ? | ? | ? | ? | ? | ? |
| 28 Dixon | Y | ? | ? | N | Y | Y | Y | Y |
| 29 Waters | Y | Y | Y | Y | Y | N | N | Y |
| 30 Martinez | N | Y | Y | N | Y | Y | Y | Y |
| 31 Dymally | # | ? | ? | ? | ? | ? | ? | Y |
| 32 Anderson | Y | N | N | N | Y | N | Y | N |
| 33 *Dreier* | N | N | N | N | N | N | Y | Y |
| 34 Torres | N | ? | Y | N | Y | Y | Y | Y |
| 35 *Lewis* | N | N | N | N | N | N | N | N |
| 36 Brown | N | ? | ? | ? | ? | Y | Y | Y |
| 37 *McCandless* | N | N | N | N | N | N | N | N |
| 38 *Dornan* | N | N | N | N | N | N | N | N |
| 39 *Dannemeyer* | ? | ? | ? | ? | ? | ? | N | N |
| 40 *Cox* | N | N | N | N | N | N | N | Y |
| 41 *Lowery* | N | N | N | N | N | ? | N | N |

| | 167 | 168 | 169 | 170 | 171 | 172 | 173 | 174 |
|---|---|---|---|---|---|---|---|---|
| 42 *Rohrabacher* | N | N | N | Y | N | N | N | N |
| 43 *Packard* | N | N | N | N | N | N | N | N |
| 44 *Cunningham* | N | N | N | N | N | N | N | N |
| 45 *Hunter* | N | N | N | N | N | N | N | N |
| **COLORADO** | | | | | | | | |
| 1 Schroeder | Y | Y | Y | Y | Y | Y | ? | Y |
| 2 Skaggs | Y | Y | Y | N | Y | Y | Y | Y |
| 3 *Campbell* | N | ? | N | Y | ? | ? | ? | Y |
| 4 *Allard* | N | N | N | N | N | N | N | N |
| 5 *Hefley* | N | N | N | N | N | N | N | N |
| 6 *Schaefer* | N | N | N | N | N | N | N | N |
| **CONNECTICUT** | | | | | | | | |
| 1 Kennelly | Y | N | Y | Y | Y | Y | Y | Y |
| 2 Gejdenson | N | Y | Y | Y | Y | Y | Y | Y |
| 3 DeLauro | N | N | Y | Y | Y | Y | Y | Y |
| 4 *Shays* | Y | Y | Y | Y | Y | N | Y | Y |
| 5 *Franks* | N | N | N | N | N | N | N | N |
| 6 *Johnson* | N | N | N | N | Y | N | Y | N |
| **DELAWARE** | | | | | | | | |
| AL Carper | N | Y | Y | N | Y | Y | Y | Y |
| **FLORIDA** | | | | | | | | |
| 1 *Hutto* | N | N | N | N | Y | ? | ? | |
| 2 Peterson | N | N | Y | N | Y | Y | Y | Y |
| 3 Bennett | N | N | Y | Y | Y | Y | Y | N |
| 4 *James* | N | N | N | Y | Y | N | N | N |
| 5 *McCollum* | N | N | N | N | N | N | N | N |
| 6 *Stearns* | N | N | N | N | N | N | N | N |
| 7 Gibbons | ? | ? | Y | Y | N | Y | Y | Y |
| 8 *Young* | N | N | N | N | N | N | N | N |
| 9 *Bilirakis* | N | N | N | N | N | Y | N | N |
| 10 *Ireland* | ? | ? | ? | ? | ? | ? | N | Y |
| 11 Bacchus | N | N | Y | Y | Y | Y | Y | Y |
| 12 *Lewis* | N | N | N | N | N | N | N | N |
| 13 *Goss* | N | N | N | N | N | N | N | N |
| 14 Johnston | N | Y | Y | Y | Y | # | Y | Y |
| 15 *Shaw* | Y | Y | Y | Y | Y | N | Y | Y |
| 16 Smith | Y | Y | Y | Y | Y | Y | Y | Y |
| 17 Lehman | ? | ? | ? | ? | ? | ? | Y | Y |
| 18 *Ros−Lehtinen* | N | N | N | N | N | N | N | N |
| 19 Fascell | N | N | N | N | Y | Y | Y | Y |
| **GEORGIA** | | | | | | | | |
| 1 Thomas | N | N | N | N | Y | N | Y | N |
| 2 Hatcher | ? | ? | ? | ? | ? | ? | ? | Y |
| 3 Ray | N | X | X | N | Y | ? | Y | Y |
| 4 Jones | ? | ? | ? | ? | ? | ? | ? | N |
| 5 Lewis | Y | ? | ? | ? | ? | ? | Y | Y |
| 6 *Gingrich* | N | N | N | N | N | N | N | N |
| 7 Darden | N | N | N | N | N | N | Y | Y |
| 8 Rowland | N | N | N | N | N | N | Y | Y |
| 9 Jenkins | N | N | N | N | Y | Y | Y | Y |
| 10 Barnard | N | N | N | N | N | N | Y | N |
| **HAWAII** | | | | | | | | |
| 1 Abercrombie | Y | ? | Y | Y | Y | Y | ? | Y |
| 2 Mink | Y | ? | ? | ? | ? | ? | ? | Y |
| **IDAHO** | | | | | | | | |
| 1 LaRocco | N | N | Y | Y | Y | Y | Y | Y |
| 2 *Stallings* | N | N | Y | Y | Y | ? | ? | ? |
| **ILLINOIS** | | | | | | | | |
| 1 Hayes | Y | Y | Y | Y | Y | N | Y | Y |
| 2 Savage | Y | Y | Y | Y | Y | N | ? | Y |
| 3 Russo | Y | Y | Y | Y | ? | ? | Y | Y |
| 4 Sangmeister | N | N | Y | Y | Y | Y | Y | Y |
| 5 Lipinski | N | N | N | Y | Y | Y | Y | Y |
| 6 *Hyde* | N | N | N | N | N | N | N | N |
| 7 Collins | # | # | # | ? | ? | X | Y | Y |
| 8 Rostenkowski | Y | ? | ? | ? | ? | ? | Y | Y |
| 9 Yates | Y | Y | Y | Y | Y | N | Y | Y |
| 10 *Porter* | − | X | # | + | + | # | − | N |
| 11 Annunzio | X | N | N | N | Y | N | Y | Y |
| 12 *Crane* | N | N | N | N | N | N | N | N |
| 13 *Fawell* | N | N | N | Y | N | N | N | N |
| 14 *Hastert* | N | N | N | N | N | N | N | N |
| 15 *Ewing* | N | N | N | N | N | N | N | N |
| 16 Cox | Y | Y | Y | Y | Y | Y | Y | Y |
| 17 Evans | Y | Y | Y | Y | Y | Y | Y | Y |
| 18 *Michel* | ? | N | N | N | N | N | N | N |
| 19 Bruce | Y | Y | Y | Y | Y | N | Y | Y |
| 20 Durbin | Y | Y | Y | N | Y | N | Y | Y |
| 21 Costello | N | N | N | Y | Y | Y | Y | Y |
| 22 Poshard | N | Y | Y | Y | Y | Y | Y | Y |
| **INDIANA** | | | | | | | | |
| 1 Visclosky | N | N | Y | Y | Y | Y | Y | N |
| 2 Sharp | N | N | N | Y | Y | Y | Y | Y |
| 3 Roemer | N | N | Y | Y | Y | Y | Y | Y |

ND   Northern Democrats       SD   Southern Democrats

| | 167 | 168 | 169 | 170 | 171 | 172 | 173 | 174 |
|---|---|---|---|---|---|---|---|---|
| 4 Long | N | Y | Y | Y | N | Y | Y | Y |
| 5 Jontz | Y | Y | Y | Y | Y | Y | Y | Y |
| 6 ***Burton*** | N | N | N | N | N | N | N | N |
| 7 ***Myers*** | N | N | N | N | Y | N | Y | N |
| 8 McCloskey | Y | N | N | Y | Y | Y | Y | Y |
| 9 Hamilton | N | N | N | N | N | Y | Y | Y |
| 10 Jacobs | Y | Y | Y | Y | Y | Y | ? | Y |
| **IOWA** | | | | | | | | |
| 1 ***Leach*** | Y | Y | Y | Y | Y | N | N | N |
| 2 ***Nussle*** | Y | N | Y | Y | Y | N | N | N |
| 3 Nagle | N | Y | Y | Y | Y | N | ? | Y |
| 4 Smith | N | N | N | N | N | Y | Y | Y |
| 5 ***Lightfoot*** | N | N | N | N | N | N | N | N |
| 6 ***Grandy*** | N | N | N | N | Y | Y | N | N |
| **KANSAS** | | | | | | | | |
| 1 ***Roberts*** | N | N | N | N | N | N | N | N |
| 2 Slattery | N | N | Y | N | Y | Y | Y | Y |
| 3 ***Meyers*** | N | N | N | Y | N | N | N | N |
| 4 Glickman | N | Y | Y | N | Y | Y | Y | Y |
| 5 ***Nichols*** | ? | ? | ? | ? | ? | ? | ? | N |
| **KENTUCKY** | | | | | | | | |
| 1 Hubbard | ? | ? | ? | ? | ? | ? | ? | N |
| 2 Natcher | N | N | N | N | Y | Y | Y | N |
| 3 Mazzoli | Y | Y | Y | Y | Y | Y | Y | Y |
| 4 ***Bunning*** | N | N | N | N | N | N | N | N |
| 5 ***Rogers*** | N | N | N | N | N | N | N | N |
| 6 ***Hopkins*** | N | N | N | N | N | N | N | N |
| 7 Perkins | Y | Y | Y | Y | Y | Y | ? | N |
| **LOUISIANA** | | | | | | | | |
| 1 ***Livingston*** | N | ? | ? | ? | ? | ? | N | N |
| 2 Jefferson | Y | N | Y | Y | Y | Y | Y | Y |
| 3 Tauzin | N | N | N | N | Y | N | ? | N |
| 4 ***McCrery*** | N | N | N | N | N | N | N | N |
| 5 Huckaby | N | N | N | N | N | Y | Y | Y |
| 6 ***Baker*** | N | N | N | N | N | N | N | N |
| 7 Hayes | N | N | N | N | ? | ? | ? | N |
| 8 ***Holloway*** | N | N | N | Y | X | # | N | N |
| **MAINE** | | | | | | | | |
| 1 Andrews | Y | Y | Y | Y | Y | Y | Y | N |
| 2 ***Snowe*** | N | N | N | Y | Y | Y | N | N |
| **MARYLAND** | | | | | | | | |
| 1 ***Gilchrest*** | N | N | N | N | Y | Y | ? | ? |
| 2 ***Bentley*** | N | N | N | N | N | N | N | N |
| 3 Cardin | N | N | Y | Y | Y | Y | Y | N |
| 4 McMillen | N | N | N | N | Y | Y | Y | Y |
| 5 Hoyer | N | N | N | N | N | Y | Y | Y |
| 6 Byron | ? | ? | ? | ? | ? | ? | ? | ? |
| 7 Mfume | Y | Y | Y | Y | Y | N | Y | Y |
| 8 ***Morella*** | + | X | # | # | + | − | N | N |
| **MASSACHUSETTS** | | | | | | | | |
| 1 Olver | Y | Y | Y | Y | Y | N | Y | Y |
| 2 Neal | Y | Y | Y | Y | Y | N | ? | Y |
| 3 Early | Y | Y | Y | Y | Y | N | Y | Y |
| 4 Frank | Y | Y | Y | Y | Y | Y | Y | N |
| 5 Atkins | Y | Y | Y | Y | Y | N | Y | Y |
| 6 Mavroules | N | Y | Y | Y | Y | Y | ? | Y |
| 7 Markey | Y | Y | Y | Y | Y | Y | Y | Y |
| 8 Kennedy | Y | Y | Y | Y | Y | Y | ? | Y |
| 9 Moakley | N | Y | Y | Y | Y | Y | Y | Y |
| 10 Studds | Y | Y | Y | Y | Y | N | Y | Y |
| 11 Donnelly | N | Y | Y | Y | Y | Y | Y | Y |
| **MICHIGAN** | | | | | | | | |
| 1 Conyers | Y | Y | Y | Y | Y | N | Y | Y |
| 2 ***Pursell*** | ? | ? | ? | ? | ? | ? | ? | N |
| 3 Wolpe | # | # | ? | ? | ? | ? | Y | Y |
| 4 ***Upton*** | N | N | N | N | Y | N | N | N |
| 5 ***Henry*** | Y | N | N | Y | Y | N | N | N |
| 6 Carr | ? | N | Y | N | Y | Y | Y | Y |
| 7 Kildee | Y | Y | Y | Y | Y | Y | Y | Y |
| 8 Traxler | ? | ? | ? | Y | ? | ? | ? | ? |
| 9 ***Vander Jagt*** | ? | ? | ? | ? | ? | ? | Y | N |
| 10 ***Camp*** | N | N | N | N | Y | N | N | N |
| 11 ***Davis*** | ? | N | N | N | N | Y | ? | N |
| 12 Bonior | Y | Y | Y | Y | Y | Y | ? | ? |
| 13 Collins | Y | Y | Y | Y | Y | Y | Y | Y |
| 14 Hertel | ? | ? | ? | ? | ? | ? | ? | N |
| 15 Ford | Y | ? | Y | # | Y | Y | Y | Y |
| 16 Dingell | ? | ? | ? | ? | ? | # | Y | Y |
| 17 Levin | N | Y | Y | Y | Y | Y | Y | Y |
| 18 ***Broomfield*** | ? | ? | ? | ? | ? | ? | N | N |
| **MINNESOTA** | | | | | | | | |
| 1 Penny | N | Y | Y | Y | Y | Y | Y | Y |
| 2 ***Weber*** | N | N | N | N | N | N | ? | ? |
| 3 ***Ramstad*** | N | N | N | Y | Y | N | N | Y |
| 4 Vento | Y | Y | Y | Y | Y | N | Y | Y |
| 5 Sabo | Y | Y | Y | Y | Y | Y | Y | N |
| 6 Sikorski | Y | Y | Y | Y | Y | N | N | Y |
| 7 Peterson | N | Y | Y | Y | Y | Y | Y | N |
| 8 Oberstar | Y | Y | Y | Y | Y | N | ? | Y |
| **MISSISSIPPI** | | | | | | | | |
| 1 Whitten | ? | ? | ? | ? | N | Y | Y | N |
| 2 Espy | N | Y | Y | Y | Y | Y | Y | N |
| 3 Montgomery | N | N | N | N | N | Y | Y | N |
| 4 Parker | N | N | N | N | N | Y | Y | N |
| 5 Taylor | N | N | N | N | N | Y | ? | N |
| **MISSOURI** | | | | | | | | |
| 1 Clay | Y | Y | Y | Y | Y | N | N | Y |
| 2 Horn | N | Y | Y | Y | Y | Y | Y | Y |
| 3 Gephardt | ? | Y | Y | N | Y | Y | Y | Y |
| 4 Skelton | N | N | N | N | N | Y | ? | N |
| 5 Wheat | Y | Y | Y | Y | Y | N | Y | Y |
| 6 ***Coleman*** | N | N | N | N | N | Y | N | Y |
| 7 ***Hancock*** | N | N | N | N | N | N | N | N |
| 8 ***Emerson*** | N | N | N | N | N | N | N | N |
| 9 Volkmer | N | N | Y | N | N | N | Y | Y |
| **MONTANA** | | | | | | | | |
| 1 Williams | Y | ? | ? | ? | ? | ? | Y | Y |
| 2 ***Marlenee*** | N | N | Y | N | N | N | N | Y |
| **NEBRASKA** | | | | | | | | |
| 1 ***Bereuter*** | N | N | N | Y | N | N | N | N |
| 2 Hoagland | N | N | N | N | N | Y | Y | Y |
| 3 ***Barrett*** | N | N | N | N | N | N | N | N |
| **NEVADA** | | | | | | | | |
| 1 Bilbray | X | N | N | N | N | N | Y | Y |
| 2 ***Vucanovich*** | N | ? | ? | ? | ? | ? | N | N |
| **NEW HAMPSHIRE** | | | | | | | | |
| 1 ***Zeliff*** | N | N | N | N | N | N | N | N |
| 2 Swett | N | N | N | Y | Y | Y | ? | Y |
| **NEW JERSEY** | | | | | | | | |
| 1 Andrews | N | N | N | N | N | Y | Y | Y |
| 2 Hughes | N | N | Y | Y | Y | N | Y | Y |
| 3 Pallone | N | N | Y | N | Y | Y | Y | Y |
| 4 ***Smith*** | N | N | N | N | N | N | ? | N |
| 5 ***Roukema*** | N | N | Y | Y | Y | N | N | N |
| 6 Dwyer | ? | Y | Y | N | ? | ? | Y | N |
| 7 ***Rinaldo*** | N | N | N | N | N | N | Y | N |
| 8 Roe | ? | N | N | ? | ? | ? | Y | Y |
| 9 Torricelli | N | N | N | N | Y | Y | Y | Y |
| 10 Payne | Y | Y | Y | Y | Y | N | Y | Y |
| 11 ***Gallo*** | N | N | N | N | N | N | N | N |
| 12 ***Zimmer*** | N | N | N | Y | Y | N | N | Y |
| 13 ***Saxton*** | N | N | N | N | N | N | N | N |
| 14 Guarini | N | N | N | Y | Y | Y | Y | Y |
| **NEW MEXICO** | | | | | | | | |
| 1 ***Schiff*** | N | N | N | Y | Y | Y | Y | N |
| 2 ***Skeen*** | N | N | N | N | N | N | Y | N |
| 3 Richardson | N | N | N | Y | Y | Y | ? | Y |
| **NEW YORK** | | | | | | | | |
| 1 Hochbrueckner | N | Y | Y | N | Y | Y | Y | Y |
| 2 Downey | N | Y | Y | N | Y | Y | Y | N |
| 3 Mrazek | N | Y | Y | Y | Y | Y | Y | N |
| 4 ***Lent*** | N | ? | ? | ? | ? | ? | Y | N |
| 5 ***McGrath*** | N | N | N | N | N | N | Y | N |
| 6 Flake | Y | ? | ? | Y | Y | Y | ? | Y |
| 7 Ackerman | ? | # | ? | ? | ? | # | Y | Y |
| 8 Scheuer | ? | # | ? | ? | # | ? | Y | Y |
| 9 Manton | N | N | Y | Y | Y | Y | Y | Y |
| 10 Schumer | Y | Y | Y | Y | Y | Y | Y | N |
| 11 Towns | Y | Y | Y | Y | Y | N | ? | Y |
| 12 Owens | # | Y | Y | Y | Y | N | Y | Y |
| 13 Solarz | Y | Y | Y | Y | Y | Y | Y | Y |
| 14 ***Molinari*** | N | N | N | N | N | Y | N | N |
| 15 ***Green*** | ? | ? | ? | ? | ? | X | ? | N |
| 16 Rangel | Y | Y | Y | Y | Y | N | ? | N |
| 17 Weiss | Y | Y | Y | Y | Y | N | Y | N |
| 18 Serrano | Y | Y | Y | Y | Y | N | Y | N |
| 19 Engel | N | Y | Y | Y | Y | Y | ? | Y |
| 20 Lowey | Y | Y | Y | Y | Y | Y | Y | Y |
| 21 ***Fish*** | N | N | N | Y | N | Y | Y | N |
| 22 ***Gilman*** | N | N | N | N | N | N | Y | N |
| 23 McNulty | N | N | N | Y | Y | Y | Y | Y |
| 24 ***Solomon*** | N | N | N | N | N | N | N | N |
| 25 ***Boehlert*** | N | N | N | N | N | N | N | N |
| 26 ***Martin*** | N | N | N | N | N | N | ? | N |
| 27 ***Walsh*** | N | N | N | N | N | N | Y | N |
| 28 McHugh | N | Y | Y | Y | N | Y | ? | N |
| 29 ***Horton*** | ? | N | N | N | ? | ? | Y | N |
| 30 Slaughter | N | Y | Y | Y | Y | Y | Y | Y |
| 31 ***Paxon*** | N | N | N | N | N | N | N | N |
| 32 LaFalce | N | Y | Y | Y | Y | N | ? | Y |
| 33 Nowak | N | Y | Y | Y | Y | Y | ? | Y |
| 34 ***Houghton*** | N | N | N | N | N | Y | Y | N |
| **NORTH CAROLINA** | | | | | | | | |
| 1 Jones | N | N | Y | N | N | Y | Y | Y |
| 2 Valentine | N | N | Y | N | N | Y | ? | N |
| 3 Lancaster | N | N | N | N | N | Y | Y | Y |
| 4 Price | N | N | Y | Y | Y | Y | ? | Y |
| 5 Neal | N | N | Y | N | Y | Y | ? | Y |
| 6 ***Coble*** | N | N | N | Y | Y | Y | N | N |
| 7 Rose | N | Y | Y | N | Y | Y | Y | N |
| 8 Hefner | ? | ? | ? | ? | ? | ? | ? | ? |
| 9 ***McMillan*** | N | N | N | N | N | Y | N | N |
| 10 ***Ballenger*** | N | N | N | N | Y | Y | N | N |
| 11 ***Taylor*** | N | N | N | N | N | Y | N | N |
| **NORTH DAKOTA** | | | | | | | | |
| AL Dorgan | N | Y | Y | Y | Y | Y | Y | Y |
| **OHIO** | | | | | | | | |
| 1 Luken | N | ? | ? | ? | ? | ? | Y | N |
| 2 ***Gradison*** | N | N | N | N | N | N | N | N |
| 3 Hall | N | Y | Y | Y | Y | Y | Y | Y |
| 4 ***Oxley*** | N | N | N | N | N | Y | N | N |
| 5 ***Gillmor*** | N | N | N | N | N | N | Y | N |
| 6 ***McEwen*** | N | N | N | N | N | N | Y | N |
| 7 ***Hobson*** | N | N | N | N | Y | N | N | N |
| 8 ***Boehner*** | N | N | N | N | N | N | N | N |
| 9 Kaptur | N | N | Y | N | Y | Y | Y | Y |
| 10 ***Miller*** | N | N | N | N | N | N | N | N |
| 11 Eckart | Y | Y | Y | N | Y | Y | ? | Y |
| 12 ***Kasich*** | N | N | N | N | N | Y | ? | Y |
| 13 Pease | Y | Y | Y | Y | N | N | Y | Y |
| 14 Sawyer | N | Y | Y | Y | Y | Y | ? | Y |
| 15 ***Wylie*** | N | N | N | N | Y | N | Y | N |
| 16 ***Regula*** | N | N | N | N | Y | N | N | N |
| 17 Traficant | Y | Y | Y | Y | Y | Y | Y | Y |
| 18 Applegate | Y | Y | Y | Y | Y | N | Y | N |
| 19 Feighan | ? | ? | ? | ? | ? | ? | Y | Y |
| 20 Oakar | ? | ? | Y | Y | Y | Y | Y | Y |
| 21 Stokes | Y | Y | Y | Y | Y | N | N | Y |
| **OKLAHOMA** | | | | | | | | |
| 1 ***Inhofe*** | N | N | N | N | N | N | ? | ? |
| 2 Synar | Y | Y | Y | Y | Y | Y | Y | Y |
| 3 Brewster | N | N | N | N | Y | Y | ? | N |
| 4 McCurdy | N | N | N | N | Y | Y | ? | N |
| 5 ***Edwards*** | ? | N | N | N | N | N | N | N |
| 6 English | N | N | N | N | Y | N | Y | N |
| **OREGON** | | | | | | | | |
| 1 AuCoin | Y | Y | Y | Y | Y | N | ? | Y |
| 2 ***Smith*** | N | N | N | N | N | N | N | N |
| 3 Wyden | Y | Y | Y | Y | Y | N | P | Y |
| 4 DeFazio | Y | Y | Y | Y | Y | N | Y | Y |
| 5 Kopetski | Y | Y | + | Y | Y | Y | Y | Y |
| **PENNSYLVANIA** | | | | | | | | |
| 1 Foglietta | Y | Y | Y | Y | Y | Y | ? | N |
| 2 Blackwell | Y | Y | Y | Y | Y | N | ? | Y |
| 3 Borski | N | N | N | N | Y | Y | Y | Y |
| 4 Kolter | ? | ? | ? | ? | ? | ? | Y | Y |
| 5 ***Schulze*** | N | N | N | Y | N | N | Y | N |
| 6 Yatron | N | N | N | N | Y | Y | Y | Y |
| 7 ***Weldon*** | N | N | N | N | N | Y | ? | N |
| 8 Kostmayer | Y | Y | Y | Y | Y | N | Y | Y |
| 9 ***Shuster*** | N | N | N | N | N | N | N | N |
| 10 ***McDade*** | N | ? | ? | N | N | N | N | ? |
| 11 Kanjorski | N | Y | Y | N | Y | Y | Y | Y |
| 12 Murtha | N | N | N | N | N | Y | Y | Y |
| 13 ***Coughlin*** | N | N | N | N | N | N | ? | N |
| 14 Coyne | Y | Y | Y | Y | Y | Y | Y | Y |
| 15 ***Ritter*** | N | N | N | N | Y | Y | Y | N |
| 16 ***Walker*** | N | N | N | N | Y | N | N | N |
| 17 ***Gekas*** | N | N | N | N | N | N | N | N |
| 18 ***Santorum*** | N | N | N | Y | N | N | N | N |
| 19 ***Goodling*** | N | N | Y | N | N | Y | ? | N |
| 20 Gaydos | ? | ? | ? | ? | ? | ? | ? | Y |
| 21 ***Ridge*** | N | N | Y | Y | Y | N | ? | N |
| 22 Murphy | ? | Y | Y | Y | Y | N | N | Y |
| 23 ***Clinger*** | − | − | − | − | − | − | ? | N |
| **RHODE ISLAND** | | | | | | | | |
| 1 ***Machtley*** | N | N | N | N | N | Y | N | N |
| 2 Reed | N | Y | Y | Y | Y | Y | Y | Y |
| **SOUTH CAROLINA** | | | | | | | | |
| 1 ***Ravenel*** | N | N | N | N | N | Y | Y | N |
| 2 ***Spence*** | N | N | N | N | N | N | ? | N |
| 3 Derrick | N | N | Y | Y | Y | Y | Y | N |
| 4 Patterson | − | − | − | + | + | + | Y | Y |
| 5 Spratt | N | N | N | N | N | Y | Y | Y |
| 6 Tallon | N | N | Y | Y | Y | Y | Y | Y |
| **SOUTH DAKOTA** | | | | | | | | |
| AL Johnson | N | N | N | Y | Y | Y | Y | Y |
| **TENNESSEE** | | | | | | | | |
| 1 ***Quillen*** | N | N | N | N | N | Y | N | N |
| 2 ***Duncan*** | N | N | Y | Y | Y | N | N | N |
| 3 Lloyd | N | N | N | N | N | Y | ? | Y |
| 4 Cooper | N | N | N | N | ? | ? | Y | Y |
| 5 Clement | N | N | N | Y | Y | Y | ? | Y |
| 6 Gordon | N | N | Y | Y | Y | Y | Y | Y |
| 7 ***Sundquist*** | N | N | N | N | N | N | N | N |
| 8 Tanner | N | N | N | N | Y | Y | Y | N |
| 9 Ford | Y | Y | Y | Y | Y | N | ? | N |
| **TEXAS** | | | | | | | | |
| 1 Chapman | N | N | N | N | Y | Y | Y | Y |
| 2 Wilson | N | N | N | N | N | Y | Y | N |
| 3 ***Johnson*** | N | N | N | N | N | N | N | N |
| 4 Hall | N | N | N | N | N | Y | Y | N |
| 5 Bryant | Y | Y | Y | N | Y | Y | Y | Y |
| 6 ***Barton*** | N | N | N | N | N | N | Y | N |
| 7 ***Archer*** | N | N | N | N | N | N | Y | N |
| 8 ***Fields*** | − | − | − | − | − | − | N | N |
| 9 Brooks | N | ? | ? | ? | ? | ? | Y | Y |
| 10 Pickle | N | N | N | N | N | Y | P | Y |
| 11 Edwards | N | N | N | N | N | Y | ? | N |
| 12 Geren | N | N | N | N | N | Y | Y | N |
| 13 Sarpalius | N | N | N | N | N | Y | Y | N |
| 14 Laughlin | ? | ? | ? | ? | ? | ? | Y | Y |
| 15 de la Garza | ? | ? | ? | ? | ? | ? | Y | Y |
| 16 Coleman | N | N | N | N | N | Y | Y | Y |
| 17 Stenholm | N | N | N | N | Y | Y | Y | N |
| 18 Washington | Y | Y | Y | Y | Y | N | ? | Y |
| 19 ***Combest*** | N | N | N | N | N | Y | Y | N |
| 20 Gonzalez | N | Y | Y | N | Y | Y | Y | Y |
| 21 ***Smith*** | N | N | N | N | N | N | N | N |
| 22 ***DeLay*** | N | N | N | N | N | N | N | N |
| 23 Bustamante | X | ? | X | X | ? | # | Y | Y |
| 24 Frost | N | N | N | N | Y | Y | Y | Y |
| 25 Andrews | N | N | N | N | N | Y | Y | N |
| 26 ***Armey*** | N | N | N | N | N | N | N | N |
| 27 Ortiz | N | N | N | N | N | Y | Y | Y |
| **UTAH** | | | | | | | | |
| 1 ***Hansen*** | N | N | N | N | N | N | N | N |
| 2 Owens | N | N | Y | Y | Y | N | Y | ? |
| 3 Orton | N | N | Y | Y | Y | N | Y | Y |
| **VERMONT** | | | | | | | | |
| AL *Sanders* | Y | Y | Y | Y | Y | Y | ? | N |
| **VIRGINIA** | | | | | | | | |
| 1 ***Bateman*** | N | N | N | N | N | Y | Y | N |
| 2 Pickett | N | N | N | N | N | Y | Y | Y |
| 3 ***Bliley*** | N | N | N | N | N | N | N | N |
| 4 Sisisky | N | N | N | N | N | Y | Y | Y |
| 5 Payne | N | N | N | Y | N | Y | Y | N |
| 6 Olin | ? | ? | ? | ? | ? | ? | Y | N |
| 7 ***Allen*** | N | N | N | N | N | N | N | N |
| 8 Moran | ? | N | Y | N | N | Y | Y | Y |
| 9 Boucher | N | N | Y | Y | Y | Y | Y | Y |
| 10 ***Wolf*** | N | N | N | N | N | N | N | N |
| **WASHINGTON** | | | | | | | | |
| 1 ***Miller*** | ? | ? | ? | ? | ? | ? | ? | ? |
| 2 Swift | N | Y | Y | Y | Y | Y | Y | Y |
| 3 Unsoeld | ? | ? | ? | ? | ? | X | Y | Y |
| 4 ***Morrison*** | ? | ? | ? | ? | ? | ? | Y | N |
| 5 Foley | | | | | | | | |
| 6 Dicks | N | N | N | N | N | Y | Y | Y |
| 7 McDermott | Y | Y | Y | Y | Y | N | Y | Y |
| 8 ***Chandler*** | N | N | N | N | ? | ? | N | N |
| **WEST VIRGINIA** | | | | | | | | |
| 1 Mollohan | N | N | N | N | Y | N | Y | N |
| 2 Staggers | Y | Y | Y | Y | Y | Y | Y | Y |
| 3 Wise | N | N | Y | Y | Y | Y | ? | Y |
| 4 Rahall | Y | Y | Y | Y | Y | N | Y | Y |
| **WISCONSIN** | | | | | | | | |
| 1 Aspin | N | N | N | N | N | Y | Y | Y |
| 2 ***Klug*** | N | N | Y | Y | Y | N | N | Y |
| 3 ***Gunderson*** | N | N | N | N | Y | Y | Y | N |
| 4 Kleczka | N | Y | Y | Y | N | Y | Y | Y |
| 5 Moody | Y | Y | Y | Y | Y | N | Y | Y |
| 6 ***Petri*** | N | N | N | Y | N | N | Y | N |
| 7 Obey | Y | Y | Y | Y | Y | Y | Y | Y |
| 8 ***Roth*** | N | X | X | ? | ? | ? | Y | N |
| 9 ***Sensenbrenner*** | N | N | Y | Y | Y | N | N | N |
| **WYOMING** | | | | | | | | |
| AL ***Thomas*** | N | N | Y | N | N | N | N | N |

Southern states - Ala., Ark., Fla., Ga., Ky., La., Miss., N.C., Okla., S.C., Tenn., Texas, Va.
Omitted votes are quorum calls, which CQ does not include in its vote charts.

**175. HR 5058. American Folklife Center Authorization.** Clay, D-Mo., motion to suspend the rules and pass the bill to authorize $8 million over the next five years for an American Folklife Center. Motion rejected 137-280: R 10-151; D 126-129 (ND 99-75, SD 27-54); I 1-0, June 9, 1992. A two-thirds majority of those present and voting (278 in this case) was required for passage under suspension of the rules.

**176. HR 5260. Unemployment Benefits Extension/ Previous Question.** Derrick, D-S.C., motion to order the previous question (thus limiting debate and the possibility of amendment) on adoption of the rule (H Res 475) to provide for House floor consideration of the bill to further extend the temporary extension of unemployment benefits for workers who exhausted their regular benefits. The bill extended the right to 20 or 26 weeks of added benefits for laid-off workers from the expiration deadline of July 4 to Jan. 1, 1993, or the month after the month in which the three-month average unemployment rate fell below 6.5 percent. Motion agreed to 232-182: R 0-157; D 231-25 (ND 165-9, SD 66-16); I 1-0, June 9, 1992.

**177. HR 5260. Unemployment Benefits Extension/Rule.** Adoption of the rule (H Res 475) to provide for House floor consideration of the bill to further extend the temporary extension of unemployment benefits for workers who exhausted their regular benefits. The bill extended the right to 20 or 26 weeks of added benefits for laid-off workers from the expiration deadline of July 4 to to Jan. 1, 1993, or the month after the month in which the three-month average unemployment rate fell below 6.5 percent. Adopted 225-182: R 0-158; D 224-24 (ND 159-11, SD 65-13); I 1-0, June 9, 1992.

**178. HR 5260. Unemployment Benefits Extension/Recommital Motion.** Archer, R-Texas, motion to recommit the bill to extend unemployment benefits to the Ways and Means Committee, with instructions to report it back with an amendment that changes the provisions of the bill to be consistent with the 1990 Budget Agreement. Motion rejected 191-219: R 157-0; D 34-218 (ND 8-167, SD 26-51); I 0-1, June 9, 1992.

**179. HR 5260. Unemployment Benefits Extension/ Passage.** Passage of the bill to provide $5.8 billion to extend the temporary extension of unemployment benefits of 20 or 26 weeks of additional benefits for workers who exhausted their regular benefits set to expire on July 4 until Jan. 1, 1993, or the month after the month in which the three-month average unemployment rate fells below 6.5 percent. The bill also made permanent changes so that extended benefits automatically kicked in during periods of high unemployment. The costs of the bill were offset by a change in estimated tax payments; eliminating business tax deductions for corporate executive compensation over $1 million; and a phaseout of certain personal exemptions. The bill required a waiver of the 1990 Budget Agreement because the revenues would not come in during the same year as outlays. Passed 261-150: R 25-131; D 235-19 (ND 170-5, SD 65-14); I 1-0, June 9, 1992. A "nay" was a vote in support of the president's position.

**180. Procedural Motion.** Approval of the House Journal of Tuesday, June 9. Approved. 277-122: R 38-117; D 239-5 (ND 160-5, SD 79-0); I 0-0, June 10, 1992.

**181. H J Res 290. Balanced Budget Constitutional Amendment/Rule.** Adoption of the rule (H Res 450) to provide for House floor consideration of the joint resolution to propose a constitutional amendment to mandate a balanced federal budget. Adopted 326-91: R 157-2; D 169-88 (ND 98-77, SD 71-11); I 0-1, June 10, 1992.

**182. Procedural Motion.** Approval of the House Journal of Wednesday, June 10. Approved 284-112: R 48-107; D 236-5 (ND 164-5, SD 72-0); I 0-0, June 11, 1992.

## KEY

| | |
|---|---|
| Y | Voted for (yea). |
| # | Paired for. |
| + | Announced for. |
| N | Voted against (nay). |
| X | Paired against. |
| − | Announced against. |
| P | Voted "present." |
| C | Voted "present" to avoid possible conflict of interest. |
| ? | Did not vote or otherwise make a position known. |

Democrats **Republicans**
*Independent*

| | 175 | 176 | 177 | 178 | 179 | 180 | 181 | 182 |
|---|---|---|---|---|---|---|---|---|
| **ALABAMA** | | | | | | | | |
| 1 *Callahan* | N | N | N | Y | N | Y | Y | Y |
| 2 *Dickinson* | N | N | ? | ? | ? | N | Y | N |
| 3 Browder | N | Y | Y | N | Y | Y | Y | Y |
| 4 Bevill | N | Y | Y | N | Y | Y | Y | Y |
| 5 Cramer | N | N | N | Y | Y | Y | Y | Y |
| 6 Erdreich | N | N | Y | Y | Y | Y | Y | Y |
| 7 Harris | N | N | N | Y | Y | Y | Y | Y |
| **ALASKA** | | | | | | | | |
| AL *Young* | N | N | N | Y | N | Y | N | Y |
| **ARIZONA** | | | | | | | | |
| 1 *Rhodes* | N | N | N | Y | N | N | Y | Y |
| 2 Pastor | N | Y | Y | N | Y | Y | Y | Y |
| 3 *Stump* | N | N | N | Y | N | N | Y | N |
| 4 *Kyl* | N | N | N | Y | N | N | Y | N |
| 5 *Kolbe* | N | N | N | Y | N | N | Y | N |
| **ARKANSAS** | | | | | | | | |
| 1 Alexander | Y | Y | Y | N | Y | Y | Y | ? |
| 2 Thornton | N | Y | Y | N | Y | Y | Y | Y |
| 3 *Hammerschmidt* | N | N | N | Y | N | Y | Y | Y |
| 4 Anthony | ? | ? | ? | ? | ? | ? | ? | ? |
| **CALIFORNIA** | | | | | | | | |
| 1 *Riggs* | N | N | N | Y | N | ? | Y | N |
| 2 *Herger* | N | N | N | Y | N | N | Y | N |
| 3 Matsui | Y | Y | Y | N | Y | Y | Y | Y |
| 4 Fazio | Y | Y | Y | N | Y | Y | Y | Y |
| 5 Pelosi | Y | Y | Y | N | Y | Y | Y | Y |
| 6 Boxer | N | Y | Y | N | Y | Y | N | Y |
| 7 Miller | Y | Y | Y | N | Y | Y | Y | Y |
| 8 Dellums | Y | Y | Y | N | Y | Y | Y | Y |
| 9 Stark | Y | Y | Y | N | Y | Y | N | Y |
| 10 Edwards | Y | Y | Y | N | Y | Y | N | Y |
| 11 Lantos | Y | Y | Y | N | Y | Y | N | Y |
| 12 *Campbell* | N | N | N | Y | N | N | Y | N |
| 13 Mineta | Y | Y | Y | N | Y | Y | N | Y |
| 14 *Doolittle* | N | N | N | Y | N | N | Y | N |
| 15 Condit | N | N | N | Y | N | Y | Y | Y |
| 16 Panetta | N | Y | Y | N | Y | Y | Y | Y |
| 17 Dooley | N | Y | Y | N | Y | Y | Y | Y |
| 18 Lehman | N | Y | Y | N | Y | Y | Y | Y |
| 19 *Lagomarsino* | N | N | N | Y | N | N | Y | N |
| 20 *Thomas* | Y | N | N | Y | N | Y | Y | N |
| 21 *Gallegly* | N | N | N | Y | N | N | Y | N |
| 22 *Moorhead* | N | N | N | Y | N | N | Y | N |
| 23 Beilenson | Y | Y | Y | N | Y | ? | N | Y |
| 24 Waxman | Y | Y | Y | N | Y | Y | N | Y |
| 25 Roybal | Y | Y | Y | N | Y | Y | Y | Y |
| 26 Berman | Y | Y | Y | N | Y | Y | N | Y |
| 27 Levine | ? | ? | ? | ? | ? | ? | ? | Y |
| 28 Dixon | Y | Y | Y | N | Y | Y | Y | Y |
| 29 Waters | Y | Y | Y | N | Y | Y | Y | ? |
| 30 Martinez | Y | Y | Y | N | Y | Y | Y | Y |
| 31 Dymally | ? | ? | ? | X | # | ? | ? | Y |
| 32 Anderson | N | Y | Y | N | Y | Y | Y | Y |
| 33 *Dreier* | N | N | N | Y | N | N | Y | N |
| 34 Torres | Y | Y | Y | N | Y | ? | N | Y |
| 35 *Lewis* | N | N | N | Y | N | N | Y | N |
| 36 Brown | Y | Y | Y | N | Y | Y | Y | Y |
| 37 *McCandless* | N | N | N | Y | N | N | Y | N |
| 38 *Dornan* | N | N | N | Y | N | N | Y | ? |
| 39 *Dannemeyer* | N | N | N | Y | N | ? | N | N |
| 40 *Cox* | N | N | N | Y | N | Y | Y | N |
| 41 *Lowery* | Y | ? | ? | # | X | ? | Y | N |

| | 175 | 176 | 177 | 178 | 179 | 180 | 181 | 182 |
|---|---|---|---|---|---|---|---|---|
| 42 *Rohrabacher* | N | N | N | Y | N | Y | Y | Y |
| 43 *Packard* | N | N | N | Y | N | N | Y | Y |
| 44 *Cunningham* | N | N | N | Y | N | N | Y | Y |
| 45 *Hunter* | N | N | N | Y | N | N | Y | ? |
| **COLORADO** | | | | | | | | |
| 1 Schroeder | N | Y | Y | N | Y | N | N | N |
| 2 Skaggs | N | Y | Y | N | Y | Y | Y | Y |
| 3 Campbell | ? | ? | ? | ? | ? | ? | ? | ? |
| 4 *Allard* | N | N | N | Y | N | N | Y | N |
| 5 *Hefley* | N | N | N | Y | ? | N | Y | N |
| 6 *Schaefer* | N | N | N | Y | N | N | Y | N |
| **CONNECTICUT** | | | | | | | | |
| 1 Kennelly | Y | Y | Y | N | Y | Y | N | Y |
| 2 Gejdenson | N | Y | Y | N | Y | Y | Y | Y |
| 3 DeLauro | N | Y | Y | N | Y | Y | Y | Y |
| 4 *Shays* | N | N | N | Y | N | N | Y | N |
| 5 *Franks* | N | N | N | Y | N | Y | Y | N |
| 6 *Johnson* | N | N | N | Y | N | N | Y | N |
| **DELAWARE** | | | | | | | | |
| AL Carper | N | Y | N | N | Y | Y | Y | Y |
| **FLORIDA** | | | | | | | | |
| 1 Hutto | ? | ? | ? | ? | ? | ? | ? | Y |
| 2 Peterson | N | Y | Y | N | Y | Y | Y | Y |
| 3 Bennett | N | N | Y | N | Y | Y | Y | N |
| 4 *James* | N | N | N | Y | N | Y | Y | N |
| 5 *McCollum* | N | N | N | Y | N | Y | Y | N |
| 6 *Stearns* | N | N | N | Y | N | N | Y | N |
| 7 Gibbons | N | Y | N | Y | Y | Y | Y | Y |
| 8 *Young* | N | N | N | Y | N | ? | N | Y |
| 9 *Bilirakis* | N | N | N | Y | N | Y | Y | N |
| 10 *Ireland* | N | N | N | Y | N | ? | ? | ? |
| 11 Bacchus | N | Y | Y | N | Y | Y | Y | Y |
| 12 *Lewis* | N | N | N | Y | N | N | Y | N |
| 13 *Goss* | N | N | N | Y | N | N | Y | N |
| 14 Johnston | Y | Y | Y | N | Y | Y | Y | Y |
| 15 *Shaw* | N | N | N | Y | N | Y | Y | N |
| 16 Smith | N | Y | Y | N | Y | Y | Y | Y |
| 17 Lehman | Y | Y | ? | ? | ? | ? | N | Y |
| 18 *Ros−Lehtinen* | N | N | N | Y | N | N | Y | N |
| 19 Fascell | Y | Y | Y | N | Y | Y | N | Y |
| **GEORGIA** | | | | | | | | |
| 1 Thomas | N | Y | Y | Y | N | Y | Y | Y |
| 2 Hatcher | Y | Y | Y | N | Y | Y | Y | Y |
| 3 Ray | N | N | Y | Y | Y | Y | Y | Y |
| 4 Jones | Y | Y | Y | Y | Y | Y | Y | Y |
| 5 Lewis | Y | Y | Y | N | Y | Y | Y | Y |
| 6 *Gingrich* | N | N | N | Y | N | N | Y | N |
| 7 Darden | N | Y | Y | Y | Y | Y | Y | Y |
| 8 Rowland | N | Y | Y | Y | Y | Y | Y | Y |
| 9 Jenkins | N | Y | Y | Y | Y | Y | Y | Y |
| 10 Barnard | N | Y | N | Y | N | Y | Y | Y |
| **HAWAII** | | | | | | | | |
| 1 Abercrombie | Y | Y | Y | N | Y | ? | N | Y |
| 2 Mink | Y | Y | Y | N | Y | Y | N | Y |
| **IDAHO** | | | | | | | | |
| 1 LaRocco | N | Y | Y | N | Y | Y | Y | Y |
| 2 Stallings | ? | ? | ? | ? | ? | ? | Y | Y |
| **ILLINOIS** | | | | | | | | |
| 1 Hayes | Y | Y | Y | N | Y | Y | N | Y |
| 2 Savage | Y | Y | ? | N | Y | ? | N | ? |
| 3 Russo | Y | Y | Y | N | Y | Y | Y | Y |
| 4 Sangmeister | N | Y | Y | N | Y | Y | Y | Y |
| 5 Lipinski | Y | Y | Y | N | Y | Y | Y | Y |
| 6 *Hyde* | N | N | N | Y | N | Y | Y | N |
| 7 Collins | Y | Y | Y | N | Y | Y | Y | Y |
| 8 Rostenkowski | Y | Y | Y | N | Y | Y | Y | Y |
| 9 Yates | Y | Y | Y | N | Y | Y | N | Y |
| 10 *Porter* | N | N | N | Y | N | N | Y | N |
| 11 Annunzio | Y | Y | Y | N | Y | Y | Y | Y |
| 12 *Crane* | N | N | N | Y | N | N | Y | N |
| 13 *Fawell* | N | N | N | Y | N | N | Y | N |
| 14 *Hastert* | N | N | N | Y | N | N | Y | N |
| 15 *Ewing* | N | N | N | Y | N | N | Y | N |
| 16 Cox | N | Y | Y | N | Y | N | Y | N |
| 17 Evans | Y | Y | Y | N | Y | Y | N | Y |
| 18 *Michel* | N | N | N | Y | N | N | Y | N |
| 19 Bruce | N | Y | Y | N | Y | Y | Y | Y |
| 20 Durbin | N | Y | Y | N | Y | Y | Y | Y |
| 21 Costello | N | Y | Y | N | Y | Y | Y | Y |
| 22 Poshard | N | Y | Y | N | Y | Y | Y | Y |
| **INDIANA** | | | | | | | | |
| 1 Visclosky | N | Y | Y | N | Y | Y | Y | Y |
| 2 Sharp | Y | Y | ? | N | Y | Y | Y | Y |
| 3 Roemer | N | Y | Y | N | Y | Y | Y | Y |

ND  Northern Democrats    SD  Southern Democrats

| | 175 | 176 | 177 | 178 | 179 | 180 | 181 | 182 |
|---|---|---|---|---|---|---|---|---|
| 4 Long | N | Y | Y | N | N | Y | Y | Y |
| 5 Jontz | Y | Y | Y | N | Y | Y | Y | Y |
| 6 ***Burton*** | N | N | N | Y | N | N | Y | N |
| 7 ***Myers*** | N | N | N | Y | N | Y | Y | Y |
| 8 McCloskey | Y | Y | Y | N | Y | Y | Y | Y |
| 9 Hamilton | N | N | Y | N | Y | Y | Y | Y |
| 10 Jacobs | N | N | Y | N | Y | N | Y | N |
| **IOWA** | | | | | | | | |
| 1 ***Leach*** | N | N | N | Y | N | N | Y | N |
| 2 ***Nussle*** | N | N | N | Y | N | N | Y | N |
| 3 Nagle | Y | Y | Y | N | Y | ? | N | Y |
| 4 Smith | Y | Y | Y | N | Y | Y | N | Y |
| 5 ***Lightfoot*** | N | N | N | Y | N | N | Y | N |
| 6 ***Grandy*** | N | N | N | Y | N | N | Y | N |
| **KANSAS** | | | | | | | | |
| 1 ***Roberts*** | N | N | N | Y | N | N | Y | N |
| 2 Slattery | N | Y | Y | N | Y | Y | Y | Y |
| 3 ***Meyers*** | N | N | N | Y | N | ? | Y | N |
| 4 Glickman | N | Y | Y | N | Y | Y | Y | Y |
| 5 ***Nichols*** | N | ? | ? | ? | ? | ? | ? | ? |
| **KENTUCKY** | | | | | | | | |
| 1 Hubbard | N | Y | Y | N | Y | Y | Y | Y |
| 2 Natcher | N | Y | Y | N | Y | Y | Y | Y |
| 3 Mazzoli | Y | Y | Y | N | Y | Y | Y | Y |
| 4 ***Bunning*** | N | N | N | Y | N | N | Y | N |
| 5 ***Rogers*** | N | N | N | Y | Y | N | Y | N |
| 6 ***Hopkins*** | N | N | N | Y | N | N | Y | N |
| 7 Perkins | Y | Y | Y | N | Y | Y | N | ? |
| **LOUISIANA** | | | | | | | | |
| 1 ***Livingston*** | N | N | N | Y | N | N | ? | ? |
| 2 Jefferson | ? | Y | Y | N | Y | Y | Y | Y |
| 3 Tauzin | N | N | Y | Y | Y | Y | Y | Y |
| 4 ***McCrery*** | N | N | N | Y | N | N | Y | N |
| 5 Huckaby | N | N | Y | N | Y | Y | Y | Y |
| 6 ***Baker*** | N | N | N | Y | N | N | Y | N |
| 7 Hayes | N | N | Y | Y | Y | Y | Y | Y |
| 8 ***Holloway*** | N | N | N | Y | N | N | Y | N |
| **MAINE** | | | | | | | | |
| 1 Andrews | N | Y | Y | N | Y | Y | N | Y |
| 2 ***Snowe*** | N | N | N | Y | Y | Y | Y | Y |
| **MARYLAND** | | | | | | | | |
| 1 ***Gilchrest*** | ? | ? | ? | ? | ? | N | Y | N |
| 2 ***Bentley*** | N | N | N | Y | N | N | Y | N |
| 3 Cardin | N | Y | Y | N | Y | Y | N | Y |
| 4 McMillen | Y | N | N | N | Y | Y | Y | Y |
| 5 Hoyer | Y | Y | Y | N | Y | Y | Y | Y |
| 6 Byron | ? | ? | ? | ? | ? | ? | ? | Y |
| 7 Mfume | N | Y | Y | N | Y | Y | N | Y |
| 8 ***Morella*** | Y | N | N | Y | N | Y | N | Y |
| **MASSACHUSETTS** | | | | | | | | |
| 1 Olver | Y | Y | Y | N | Y | Y | Y | Y |
| 2 Neal | N | Y | Y | N | Y | Y | N | Y |
| 3 Early | N | Y | Y | N | Y | Y | Y | Y |
| 4 Frank | Y | Y | Y | N | Y | Y | N | Y |
| 5 Atkins | Y | Y | Y | N | Y | Y | Y | Y |
| 6 Mavroules | Y | Y | Y | N | Y | Y | Y | Y |
| 7 Markey | Y | Y | Y | N | Y | Y | Y | Y |
| 8 Kennedy | Y | Y | ? | N | Y | Y | Y | Y |
| 9 Moakley | Y | Y | Y | N | Y | Y | N | Y |
| 10 Studds | Y | Y | Y | N | Y | Y | N | Y |
| 11 Donnelly | Y | Y | Y | N | Y | Y | Y | Y |
| **MICHIGAN** | | | | | | | | |
| 1 Conyers | Y | Y | Y | N | Y | Y | N | Y |
| 2 ***Pursell*** | N | N | N | Y | N | N | Y | Y |
| 3 Wolpe | Y | Y | Y | N | Y | Y | Y | Y |
| 4 ***Upton*** | N | N | N | Y | Y | N | Y | N |
| 5 ***Henry*** | N | N | N | Y | Y | N | Y | N |
| 6 Carr | N | ? | ? | Y | Y | Y | Y | ? |
| 7 Kildee | Y | Y | Y | N | Y | Y | N | Y |
| 8 Traxler | ? | ? | ? | ? | ? | ? | N | ? |
| 9 ***Vander Jagt*** | N | ? | N | Y | N | Y | Y | Y |
| 10 ***Camp*** | N | N | N | Y | N | N | Y | N |
| 11 ***Davis*** | N | N | N | Y | Y | ? | ? | ? |
| 12 Bonior | ? | Y | Y | N | Y | ? | ? | ? |
| 13 Collins | Y | Y | Y | N | Y | Y | N | Y |
| 14 Hertel | Y | Y | Y | N | Y | Y | N | Y |
| 15 Ford | Y | Y | Y | N | Y | Y | Y | Y |
| 16 Dingell | Y | Y | Y | N | Y | Y | N | Y |
| 17 Levin | N | Y | Y | N | Y | Y | Y | Y |
| 18 ***Broomfield*** | N | N | N | Y | N | Y | Y | Y |
| **MINNESOTA** | | | | | | | | |
| 1 Penny | N | Y | N | Y | N | Y | Y | Y |
| 2 ***Weber*** | ? | ? | ? | ? | ? | ? | N | ? |
| 3 ***Ramstad*** | N | N | N | Y | N | N | Y | N |
| 4 Vento | Y | Y | Y | N | Y | Y | N | Y |

| | 175 | 176 | 177 | 178 | 179 | 180 | 181 | 182 |
|---|---|---|---|---|---|---|---|---|
| 5 Sabo | Y | Y | Y | N | Y | Y | N | Y |
| 6 Sikorski | Y | Y | Y | N | Y | N | Y | N |
| 7 Peterson | N | Y | Y | N | Y | Y | Y | Y |
| 8 Oberstar | Y | Y | Y | N | Y | Y | Y | Y |
| **MISSISSIPPI** | | | | | | | | |
| 1 Whitten | Y | Y | Y | N | Y | Y | Y | Y |
| 2 Espy | Y | Y | Y | N | Y | Y | Y | Y |
| 3 Montgomery | N | Y | Y | Y | N | Y | Y | Y |
| 4 Parker | N | Y | N | Y | N | Y | Y | Y |
| 5 Taylor | N | Y | N | Y | N | Y | Y | Y |
| **MISSOURI** | | | | | | | | |
| 1 Clay | Y | Y | ? | N | Y | N | N | N |
| 2 Horn | N | Y | Y | N | Y | Y | Y | Y |
| 3 Gephardt | Y | Y | Y | N | Y | Y | Y | Y |
| 4 Skelton | N | Y | Y | N | Y | Y | Y | Y |
| 5 Wheat | Y | Y | Y | N | Y | ? | ? | Y |
| 6 ***Coleman*** | N | N | N | Y | Y | N | Y | Y |
| 7 ***Hancock*** | N | N | N | Y | N | N | Y | N |
| 8 ***Emerson*** | Y | N | N | Y | N | N | Y | Y |
| 9 Volkmer | N | Y | Y | N | Y | Y | Y | Y |
| **MONTANA** | | | | | | | | |
| 1 Williams | Y | Y | Y | N | Y | Y | Y | ? |
| 2 ***Marlenee*** | N | N | N | Y | N | N | N | N |
| **NEBRASKA** | | | | | | | | |
| 1 ***Bereuter*** | Y | N | N | Y | N | N | Y | N |
| 2 Hoagland | Y | Y | Y | N | Y | Y | ? | Y |
| 3 ***Barrett*** | Y | N | N | Y | N | N | Y | N |
| **NEVADA** | | | | | | | | |
| 1 Bilbray | N | N | N | N | Y | Y | Y | Y |
| 2 ***Vucanovich*** | N | N | N | Y | N | N | Y | N |
| **NEW HAMPSHIRE** | | | | | | | | |
| 1 ***Zeliff*** | N | N | N | Y | N | N | Y | N |
| 2 Swett | N | Y | Y | N | Y | Y | N | Y |
| **NEW JERSEY** | | | | | | | | |
| 1 Andrews | N | N | N | N | Y | Y | Y | Y |
| 2 Hughes | N | Y | N | Y | Y | Y | N | Y |
| 3 Pallone | N | N | N | N | Y | Y | Y | Y |
| 4 ***Smith*** | N | N | N | Y | Y | Y | Y | Y |
| 5 ***Roukema*** | N | N | N | Y | Y | N | Y | N |
| 6 Dwyer | N | Y | Y | N | Y | Y | N | Y |
| 7 ***Rinaldo*** | N | N | N | Y | Y | Y | Y | Y |
| 8 Roe | N | Y | Y | N | Y | Y | Y | Y |
| 9 Torricelli | N | Y | Y | N | Y | Y | Y | Y |
| 10 Payne | Y | Y | Y | N | Y | Y | N | Y |
| 11 ***Gallo*** | N | N | N | Y | N | N | Y | N |
| 12 ***Zimmer*** | N | N | N | Y | N | N | Y | N |
| 13 ***Saxton*** | N | N | N | Y | N | N | Y | N |
| 14 Guarini | N | Y | Y | N | Y | Y | Y | Y |
| **NEW MEXICO** | | | | | | | | |
| 1 ***Schiff*** | N | N | N | Y | N | Y | Y | Y |
| 2 ***Skeen*** | N | N | N | Y | N | Y | Y | Y |
| 3 Richardson | N | Y | Y | N | Y | Y | N | Y |
| **NEW YORK** | | | | | | | | |
| 1 Hochbrueckner | Y | Y | Y | N | Y | Y | Y | Y |
| 2 Downey | Y | Y | Y | N | Y | Y | N | Y |
| 3 Mrazek | Y | Y | Y | N | Y | Y | Y | Y |
| 4 ***Lent*** | N | N | N | Y | N | Y | Y | Y |
| 5 ***McGrath*** | N | N | N | Y | N | Y | Y | Y |
| 6 Flake | Y | Y | Y | N | Y | Y | Y | Y |
| 7 Ackerman | N | Y | Y | N | Y | Y | N | Y |
| 8 Scheuer | Y | Y | Y | N | Y | Y | N | Y |
| 9 Manton | Y | Y | Y | N | Y | Y | Y | Y |
| 10 Schumer | N | Y | Y | N | Y | Y | N | Y |
| 11 Towns | Y | Y | Y | N | Y | Y | N | Y |
| 12 Owens | Y | Y | Y | N | Y | Y | N | Y |
| 13 Solarz | Y | Y | Y | N | Y | Y | Y | Y |
| 14 ***Molinari*** | N | N | N | Y | N | N | Y | N |
| 15 ***Green*** | Y | N | N | Y | Y | Y | Y | Y |
| 16 Rangel | N | Y | Y | N | Y | Y | N | ? |
| 17 Weiss | Y | Y | Y | N | Y | Y | N | Y |
| 18 Serrano | N | Y | Y | N | Y | Y | N | Y |
| 19 Engel | N | Y | Y | N | Y | Y | N | Y |
| 20 Lowey | N | Y | Y | N | Y | Y | N | Y |
| 21 ***Fish*** | N | N | N | Y | N | Y | Y | Y |
| 22 ***Gilman*** | N | N | N | Y | Y | Y | Y | Y |
| 23 McNulty | N | Y | Y | Y | Y | Y | Y | Y |
| 24 ***Solomon*** | N | N | N | Y | N | Y | N | N |
| 25 ***Boehlert*** | Y | N | N | Y | Y | N | Y | N |
| 26 ***Martin*** | N | N | N | ? | ? | N | Y | N |
| 27 ***Walsh*** | N | N | N | Y | N | Y | Y | Y |
| 28 McHugh | Y | Y | Y | N | Y | Y | Y | Y |
| 29 ***Horton*** | Y | N | N | Y | N | Y | Y | Y |
| 30 Slaughter | N | Y | Y | N | Y | ? | N | Y |
| 31 ***Paxon*** | N | N | N | Y | Y | N | Y | N |

| | 175 | 176 | 177 | 178 | 179 | 180 | 181 | 182 |
|---|---|---|---|---|---|---|---|---|
| 32 LaFalce | Y | Y | Y | N | Y | Y | Y | Y |
| 33 Nowak | Y | Y | Y | N | Y | Y | Y | Y |
| 34 ***Houghton*** | N | N | N | Y | N | Y | Y | Y |
| **NORTH CAROLINA** | | | | | | | | |
| 1 Jones | Y | Y | Y | ? | ? | Y | Y | Y |
| 2 Valentine | N | Y | N | Y | N | Y | Y | Y |
| 3 Lancaster | Y | Y | Y | Y | Y | Y | Y | Y |
| 4 Price | Y | Y | Y | N | Y | Y | Y | ? |
| 5 Neal | N | Y | N | Y | Y | Y | Y | ? |
| 6 ***Coble*** | N | N | N | Y | N | N | Y | N |
| 7 Rose | Y | Y | Y | N | Y | Y | Y | Y |
| 8 Hefner | ? | ? | ? | ? | ? | ? | ? | ? |
| 9 ***McMillan*** | N | N | N | Y | N | N | Y | N |
| 10 ***Ballenger*** | N | N | N | Y | N | N | Y | N |
| 11 ***Taylor*** | N | N | N | Y | N | N | Y | N |
| **NORTH DAKOTA** | | | | | | | | |
| AL Dorgan | N | Y | Y | N | Y | Y | Y | Y |
| **OHIO** | | | | | | | | |
| 1 Luken | N | N | N | N | Y | Y | Y | Y |
| 2 ***Gradison*** | N | N | N | Y | N | N | Y | Y |
| 3 Hall | N | Y | Y | N | Y | Y | Y | ? |
| 4 ***Oxley*** | N | N | N | Y | N | N | Y | Y |
| 5 ***Gillmor*** | N | N | N | Y | N | N | Y | Y |
| 6 ***McEwen*** | N | N | N | Y | N | Y | Y | Y |
| 7 ***Hobson*** | N | N | N | Y | N | N | Y | N |
| 8 ***Boehner*** | N | N | N | Y | N | N | Y | N |
| 9 Kaptur | N | Y | Y | N | Y | Y | Y | Y |
| 10 ***Miller*** | N | N | N | Y | N | N | Y | N |
| 11 Eckart | N | Y | Y | N | Y | Y | Y | Y |
| 12 ***Kasich*** | N | N | N | Y | N | Y | Y | Y |
| 13 Pease | Y | Y | Y | N | Y | Y | Y | Y |
| 14 Sawyer | Y | Y | Y | N | Y | Y | Y | Y |
| 15 ***Wylie*** | N | N | N | Y | N | Y | Y | Y |
| 16 ***Regula*** | N | N | N | Y | Y | N | Y | N |
| 17 Traficant | N | Y | Y | N | Y | Y | N | Y |
| 18 Applegate | N | Y | Y | N | Y | Y | Y | ? |
| 19 Feighan | N | Y | Y | N | Y | ? | Y | Y |
| 20 Oakar | Y | Y | Y | N | Y | Y | Y | Y |
| 21 Stokes | Y | Y | Y | N | Y | Y | N | Y |
| **OKLAHOMA** | | | | | | | | |
| 1 ***Inhofe*** | ? | ? | ? | # | X | ? | ? | N |
| 2 Synar | N | Y | Y | N | Y | Y | N | Y |
| 3 Brewster | N | Y | ? | N | N | Y | Y | Y |
| 4 McCurdy | N | Y | Y | N | Y | Y | Y | Y |
| 5 ***Edwards*** | N | N | N | Y | N | N | Y | ? |
| 6 English | N | Y | Y | Y | N | Y | Y | Y |
| **OREGON** | | | | | | | | |
| 1 AuCoin | Y | N | N | Y | Y | ? | N | Y |
| 2 ***Smith*** | N | N | N | Y | Y | N | Y | N |
| 3 Wyden | N | Y | Y | N | Y | Y | Y | Y |
| 4 DeFazio | N | Y | N | Y | Y | Y | Y | ? |
| 5 Kopetski | Y | Y | Y | N | Y | Y | N | Y |
| **PENNSYLVANIA** | | | | | | | | |
| 1 Foglietta | Y | Y | Y | N | Y | Y | N | Y |
| 2 Blackwell | Y | Y | Y | N | Y | Y | N | Y |
| 3 Borski | N | Y | Y | N | Y | Y | N | Y |
| 4 Kolter | Y | Y | Y | N | Y | Y | Y | Y |
| 5 ***Schulze*** | N | N | N | Y | N | Y | Y | Y |
| 6 Yatron | N | Y | Y | N | Y | Y | Y | Y |
| 7 ***Weldon*** | N | N | N | Y | Y | N | Y | N |
| 8 Kostmayer | Y | Y | Y | N | Y | Y | N | Y |
| 9 ***Shuster*** | N | N | N | Y | N | N | Y | N |
| 10 ***McDade*** | ? | ? | ? | ? | ? | ? | ? | N |
| 11 Kanjorski | N | Y | Y | N | Y | Y | N | Y |
| 12 Murtha | Y | Y | Y | N | Y | Y | Y | Y |
| 13 ***Coughlin*** | N | N | N | Y | N | N | Y | ? |
| 14 Coyne | Y | Y | Y | N | Y | Y | N | Y |
| 15 ***Ritter*** | N | N | N | Y | N | Y | Y | Y |
| 16 ***Walker*** | N | N | N | Y | N | N | Y | N |
| 17 ***Gekas*** | N | N | N | Y | Y | N | Y | N |
| 18 ***Santorum*** | N | N | N | Y | N | N | Y | Y |
| 19 ***Goodling*** | N | N | N | Y | N | N | Y | N |
| 20 Gaydos | Y | Y | Y | N | Y | Y | Y | ? |
| 21 ***Ridge*** | N | N | N | Y | Y | N | Y | N |
| 22 Murphy | Y | Y | Y | N | Y | N | Y | Y |
| 23 ***Clinger*** | Y | N | N | Y | N | Y | Y | N |
| **RHODE ISLAND** | | | | | | | | |
| 1 ***Machtley*** | N | N | N | Y | Y | N | Y | N |
| 2 Reed | N | Y | Y | N | Y | Y | Y | Y |
| **SOUTH CAROLINA** | | | | | | | | |
| 1 ***Ravenel*** | N | N | N | Y | N | Y | Y | Y |
| 2 ***Spence*** | N | N | N | Y | N | N | Y | Y |
| 3 Derrick | N | Y | Y | N | Y | ? | Y | Y |
| 4 Patterson | N | Y | Y | Y | Y | Y | Y | Y |
| 5 Spratt | N | Y | Y | N | Y | Y | Y | Y |
| 6 Tallon | N | Y | Y | N | Y | Y | Y | ? |

| | 175 | 176 | 177 | 178 | 179 | 180 | 181 | 182 |
|---|---|---|---|---|---|---|---|---|
| **SOUTH DAKOTA** | | | | | | | | |
| AL Johnson | Y | Y | Y | N | Y | ? | Y | Y |
| **TENNESSEE** | | | | | | | | |
| 1 ***Quillen*** | N | N | N | Y | N | N | Y | N |
| 2 ***Duncan*** | N | N | N | Y | N | Y | Y | Y |
| 3 Lloyd | N | N | N | Y | Y | Y | Y | Y |
| 4 Cooper | N | Y | Y | N | Y | Y | Y | Y |
| 5 Clement | N | Y | Y | Y | Y | Y | Y | Y |
| 6 Gordon | N | Y | Y | N | Y | Y | Y | Y |
| 7 ***Sundquist*** | N | ? | N | Y | N | N | Y | N |
| 8 Tanner | N | Y | Y | N | Y | Y | Y | Y |
| 9 Ford | Y | Y | Y | ? | Y | Y | Y | Y |
| **TEXAS** | | | | | | | | |
| 1 Chapman | N | Y | Y | N | Y | Y | Y | ? |
| 2 Wilson | N | Y | ? | N | Y | Y | Y | ? |
| 3 ***Johnson*** | N | N | N | Y | N | N | Y | Y |
| 4 Hall | N | N | N | Y | N | Y | Y | Y |
| 5 Bryant | N | Y | Y | N | Y | Y | Y | Y |
| 6 ***Barton*** | N | N | N | Y | N | N | Y | N |
| 7 ***Archer*** | N | N | N | Y | N | Y | Y | Y |
| 8 ***Fields*** | N | N | N | Y | N | N | Y | N |
| 9 Brooks | Y | Y | Y | N | Y | Y | N | Y |
| 10 Pickle | Y | Y | Y | N | Y | Y | Y | Y |
| 11 Edwards | N | N | ? | N | Y | Y | Y | Y |
| 12 Geren | N | N | N | Y | N | Y | Y | Y |
| 13 Sarpalius | N | Y | Y | Y | N | Y | Y | Y |
| 14 Laughlin | N | Y | N | Y | N | Y | Y | ? |
| 15 de la Garza | Y | Y | Y | N | Y | Y | Y | ? |
| 16 Coleman | Y | Y | Y | N | Y | Y | Y | Y |
| 17 Stenholm | N | Y | N | Y | N | Y | Y | Y |
| 18 Washington | Y | Y | Y | N | Y | ? | N | ? |
| 19 ***Combest*** | N | N | N | Y | N | Y | Y | Y |
| 20 Gonzalez | Y | Y | Y | N | Y | Y | N | Y |
| 21 ***Smith*** | N | N | N | Y | N | N | Y | N |
| 22 ***DeLay*** | N | N | N | Y | N | N | Y | N |
| 23 Bustamante | Y | N | Y | N | Y | Y | Y | Y |
| 24 Frost | Y | Y | Y | N | Y | Y | Y | Y |
| 25 Andrews | N | Y | Y | N | Y | Y | Y | Y |
| 26 ***Armey*** | N | N | N | Y | N | N | Y | N |
| 27 Ortiz | Y | N | Y | N | Y | Y | Y | Y |
| **UTAH** | | | | | | | | |
| 1 ***Hansen*** | N | N | N | Y | N | N | Y | N |
| 2 Owens | ? | ? | ? | ? | ? | ? | Y | Y |
| 3 Orton | N | Y | Y | N | N | Y | N | Y |
| **VERMONT** | | | | | | | | |
| AL *Sanders* | Y | Y | Y | N | Y | ? | N | ? |
| **VIRGINIA** | | | | | | | | |
| 1 ***Bateman*** | N | N | N | Y | N | Y | Y | Y |
| 2 Pickett | N | Y | Y | N | N | Y | N | Y |
| 3 ***Bliley*** | N | N | N | Y | N | N | Y | N |
| 4 Sisisky | N | Y | Y | X | # | Y | Y | Y |
| 5 Payne | N | Y | Y | N | Y | Y | Y | Y |
| 6 Olin | N | Y | Y | N | Y | Y | N | Y |
| 7 ***Allen*** | N | N | N | Y | N | N | ? | N |
| 8 Moran | Y | N | ? | ? | Y | Y | Y | Y |
| 9 Boucher | Y | Y | Y | N | Y | Y | Y | Y |
| 10 ***Wolf*** | N | N | N | Y | N | N | Y | N |
| **WASHINGTON** | | | | | | | | |
| 1 ***Miller*** | ? | ? | ? | ? | ? | N | Y | N |
| 2 Swift | Y | Y | Y | N | Y | Y | N | Y |
| 3 Unsoeld | Y | Y | Y | N | Y | Y | N | Y |
| 4 ***Morrison*** | N | N | N | Y | Y | Y | Y | ? |
| 5 Foley | | | | | | | | |
| 6 Dicks | Y | Y | Y | N | Y | Y | N | Y |
| 7 McDermott | Y | Y | Y | N | Y | Y | Y | Y |
| 8 ***Chandler*** | N | N | N | Y | N | N | Y | N |
| **WEST VIRGINIA** | | | | | | | | |
| 1 Mollohan | N | Y | Y | N | Y | Y | Y | Y |
| 2 Staggers | N | Y | Y | N | Y | Y | Y | Y |
| 3 Wise | N | Y | Y | N | Y | Y | Y | Y |
| 4 Rahall | Y | Y | Y | N | Y | Y | Y | Y |
| **WISCONSIN** | | | | | | | | |
| 1 Aspin | Y | Y | Y | N | Y | Y | Y | Y |
| 2 ***Klug*** | N | N | N | Y | N | N | Y | N |
| 3 ***Gunderson*** | N | N | N | Y | N | Y | Y | Y |
| 4 Kleczka | Y | Y | Y | N | Y | Y | Y | Y |
| 5 Moody | N | Y | Y | N | Y | Y | Y | Y |
| 6 ***Petri*** | N | N | N | Y | N | Y | Y | Y |
| 7 Obey | Y | Y | Y | N | Y | Y | N | Y |
| 8 ***Roth*** | N | N | N | Y | N | N | Y | N |
| 9 ***Sensenbrenner*** | N | N | N | Y | N | N | Y | N |
| **WYOMING** | | | | | | | | |
| AL ***Thomas*** | N | N | N | Y | N | Y | Y | Y |

Southern states - Ala., Ark., Fla., Ga., Ky., La., Miss., N.C., Okla., S.C., Tenn., Texas, Va.
Omitted votes are quorum calls, which CQ does not include in its vote charts.

**183. H J Res 290. Balanced-Budget Constitutional Amendment/Spending Limit and Line-Item Veto.** Kyl, R-Ariz., substitute to propose a constitutional amendment that prohibited total outlays from exceeding total revenues for each fiscal year and prohibit total outlays from exceeding 19 percent of the gross national product for each fiscal year, unless a three-fifths majority in each chamber voted to permit a deficit. It granted the president line-item veto authority for all spending measures. Rejected 170-258: R 152-13; D 18-244 (ND 6-173, SD 12-71); I 0-1, June 11, 1992.

**184. H J Res 290. Balanced-Budget Constitutional Amendment/Tax Increase Limit.** Barton, R-Texas, substitute to propose a constitutional amendment that required the president to submit and Congress to approve a budget in which outlays did not exceed revenues unless a three-fifths majority in each chamber approved a specified deficit. Rejected 200-227: R 155-9; D 45-217 (ND 8-172, SD 37-45); I 0-1, June 11, 1992.

**185. H J Res 290. Balanced-Budget Constitutional Amendment/Majority Vote and Social Security Exemption.** Gephardt, D-Mo., amendment in the nature of a substitute to propose a constitutional amendment that required the president to submit and Congress to adopt a balanced budget in the first year after ratification unless there is a declaration of a national urgency by the president that was approved by a majority vote of both chambers of Congress; prohibit Congress from approving higher expenditures than recommended by the president in a fiscal year; and exempt Social Security from deficit calculations. Rejected 103-327: R 2-164; D 101-162 (ND 72-109, SD 29-53); I 0-1, June 11, 1992.

**186. H J Res 290. Balanced-Budget Constitutional Amendment/Substitute.** Stenholm, D-Texas, amendment in the nature of a substitute to propose a constitutional amendment that prohibited deficit spending unless a three-fifths majority of both chambers of Congress approved a specific deficit amount or there was a declaration of war or a declaration of national military emergency enacted into law. Adopted 279-153: R 164-2; D 115-150 (ND 52-129, SD 63-21); I 0-1, June 11, 1992.

**187. H J Res 290. Balanced-Budget Constitutional Amendment/Passage.** Passage of the joint resolution to propose a constitutional amendment prohibiting deficit spending unless a three-fifths majority of both chambers of Congress approved a specific deficit amount or there was a declaration of war or a declaration of national military emergency enacted into law; required the president to submit a balanced budget each fiscal year; and required a three-fifths majority of both chambers of Congress to increase the public debt. Rejected 280-153: R 164-2; D 116-150 (ND 52-130, SD 64-20); I 0-1, June 11, 1992. A two-thirds majority of those present and voting of both chambers (289 in this case) was required to propose an amendment to the Constitution. A "yea" was a vote in support of the president's position.

**188. Procedural Motion.** Approval of the House Journal of Monday, June 15. Approved 276-113: R 46-108; D 229-5 (ND 157-5, SD 72-0); I 1-0, June 16, 1992.

**189. S 250. National "Motor Voter" Registration/Appeal Chair's Ruling.** Wheat, D-Mo., motion to table (kill) the Solomon, R-N.Y., appeal of the ruling of the chair rejecting the Solomon point of order against the rule (H Res 480) for prohibiting a motion to recommit with instructions. Motion agreed to 250-158: R 0-158; D 249-0 (ND 172-0, SD 77-0); I 1-0, June 16, 1992.

**190. S 250. National "Motor Voter" Registration/Order Previous Question.** Wheat, D-Mo., motion to order the previous question (thus limiting debate and the possibility of amendment) on adoption of the rule (H Res 480) to provide for floor consideration of the bill to require states to permit voter registration simultaneously with application for public documents such as a driver's license, marriage license or hunting permit. Motion agreed to 256-163: R 1-162; D 254-1 (ND 173-1, SD 81-0); I 1-0, June 16, 1992.

## KEY

| | |
|---|---|
| Y | Voted for (yea). |
| # | Paired for. |
| + | Announced for. |
| N | Voted against (nay). |
| X | Paired against. |
| − | Announced against. |
| P | Voted "present." |
| C | Voted "present" to avoid possible conflict of interest. |
| ? | Did not vote or otherwise make a position known. |

**Democrats**  ***Republicans***
*Independent*

| | 183 | 184 | 185 | 186 | 187 | 188 | 189 | 190 |
|---|---|---|---|---|---|---|---|---|
| **ALABAMA** | | | | | | | | |
| 1 *Callahan* | Y | Y | N | Y | Y | Y | N | N |
| 2 *Dickinson* | Y | Y | N | Y | Y | ? | ? | N |
| 3 Browder | N | Y | Y | Y | Y | Y | Y | Y |
| 4 Bevill | N | Y | Y | Y | Y | Y | Y | Y |
| 5 Cramer | N | Y | Y | Y | Y | Y | Y | Y |
| 6 Erdreich | Y | Y | N | Y | Y | Y | Y | Y |
| 7 Harris | N | Y | N | Y | Y | Y | Y | Y |
| **ALASKA** | | | | | | | | |
| AL *Young* | Y | Y | N | Y | Y | N | N | N |
| **ARIZONA** | | | | | | | | |
| 1 *Rhodes* | Y | Y | N | Y | Y | N | N | N |
| 2 Pastor | N | N | N | N | N | Y | Y | Y |
| 3 *Stump* | Y | Y | N | Y | N | N | Y | Y |
| 4 *Kyl* | Y | Y | N | Y | Y | N | N | N |
| 5 *Kolbe* | Y | Y | N | Y | Y | N | N | N |
| **ARKANSAS** | | | | | | | | |
| 1 Alexander | N | N | N | N | N | ? | Y | Y |
| 2 Thornton | N | N | Y | N | N | ? | Y | Y |
| 3 *Hammerschmidt* | Y | Y | N | Y | Y | Y | N | N |
| 4 Anthony | ? | ? | ? | Y | Y | ? | Y | Y |
| **CALIFORNIA** | | | | | | | | |
| 1 *Riggs* | Y | Y | N | Y | Y | N | N | N |
| 2 *Herger* | Y | Y | N | Y | N | N | N | N |
| 3 Matsui | N | N | N | N | N | Y | Y | Y |
| 4 Fazio | N | N | N | N | N | Y | Y | Y |
| 5 Pelosi | N | N | N | N | N | Y | Y | Y |
| 6 Boxer | N | N | Y | N | N | ? | Y | Y |
| 7 Miller | N | N | N | N | N | Y | Y | Y |
| 8 Dellums | N | N | N | N | N | Y | Y | Y |
| 9 Stark | N | N | N | N | N | Y | Y | Y |
| 10 Edwards | N | N | N | N | N | Y | Y | Y |
| 11 Lantos | N | N | Y | N | N | Y | Y | Y |
| 12 *Campbell* | Y | Y | N | Y | Y | N | N | N |
| 13 Mineta | N | N | N | N | N | Y | Y | Y |
| 14 *Doolittle* | Y | Y | N | Y | Y | N | N | N |
| 15 Condit | Y | Y | Y | Y | Y | Y | Y | Y |
| 16 Panetta | N | N | N | N | N | Y | Y | Y |
| 17 Dooley | N | N | N | N | Y | Y | Y | Y |
| 18 Lehman | N | N | N | N | Y | Y | Y | Y |
| 19 *Lagomarsino* | Y | Y | N | Y | Y | N | N | N |
| 20 *Thomas* | Y | Y | N | Y | Y | N | ? | N |
| 21 *Gallegly* | Y | Y | N | Y | N | N | N | N |
| 22 *Moorhead* | Y | Y | N | Y | Y | N | N | N |
| 23 Beilenson | N | N | N | N | N | Y | Y | Y |
| 24 Waxman | N | N | N | N | N | Y | Y | Y |
| 25 Roybal | N | N | N | N | N | Y | Y | Y |
| 26 Berman | N | N | N | N | N | Y | Y | Y |
| 27 Levine | N | N | N | N | N | ? | ? | ? |
| 28 Dixon | N | N | N | N | N | Y | Y | Y |
| 29 Waters | N | N | N | N | N | Y | Y | Y |
| 30 Martinez | N | N | N | N | N | Y | Y | Y |
| 31 Dymally | N | N | N | N | N | Y | Y | Y |
| 32 Anderson | N | N | Y | Y | Y | Y | Y | Y |
| 33 *Dreier* | Y | Y | N | Y | Y | N | Y | N |
| 34 Torres | N | N | N | Y | N | Y | Y | Y |
| 35 *Lewis* | Y | Y | N | Y | Y | N | N | N |
| 36 Brown | N | N | Y | N | N | Y | Y | Y |
| 37 *McCandless* | Y | Y | N | Y | Y | N | N | N |
| 38 *Dornan* | Y | Y | N | Y | Y | N | N | N |
| 39 *Dannemeyer* | Y | Y | N | Y | N | N | N | N |
| 40 *Cox* | Y | Y | N | Y | Y | N | N | N |
| 41 *Lowery* | Y | Y | N | Y | Y | ? | ? | ? |

| | 183 | 184 | 185 | 186 | 187 | 188 | 189 | 190 |
|---|---|---|---|---|---|---|---|---|
| 42 *Rohrabacher* | Y | Y | N | Y | Y | N | N | N |
| 43 *Packard* | Y | Y | N | Y | Y | N | N | N |
| 44 *Cunningham* | Y | Y | N | Y | Y | N | N | N |
| 45 *Hunter* | Y | Y | N | Y | Y | N | N | N |
| **COLORADO** | | | | | | | | |
| 1 Schroeder | N | N | Y | N | N | N | Y | Y |
| 2 Skaggs | N | N | Y | N | N | Y | Y | Y |
| 3 Campbell | ? | N | Y | Y | Y | ? | Y | Y |
| 4 *Allard* | Y | Y | N | Y | N | N | N | N |
| 5 *Hefley* | Y | Y | N | Y | N | N | N | N |
| 6 *Schaefer* | Y | Y | N | Y | Y | ? | N | N |
| **CONNECTICUT** | | | | | | | | |
| 1 Kennelly | N | N | N | N | N | Y | Y | Y |
| 2 Gejdenson | N | N | N | N | N | Y | Y | Y |
| 3 DeLauro | N | N | Y | N | N | Y | Y | Y |
| 4 *Shays* | Y | Y | N | Y | Y | N | N | N |
| 5 *Franks* | Y | Y | N | Y | Y | N | N | N |
| 6 *Johnson* | Y | Y | N | Y | Y | N | N | N |
| **DELAWARE** | | | | | | | | |
| AL Carper | N | Y | N | Y | Y | Y | Y | Y |
| **FLORIDA** | | | | | | | | |
| 1 Hutto | Y | Y | N | Y | Y | Y | Y | Y |
| 2 Peterson | N | Y | Y | Y | Y | Y | Y | Y |
| 3 Bennett | Y | N | N | Y | Y | Y | Y | Y |
| 4 *James* | Y | Y | N | Y | N | N | N | N |
| 5 *McCollum* | Y | Y | N | Y | Y | N | N | N |
| 6 *Stearns* | Y | Y | N | Y | Y | N | N | N |
| 7 Gibbons | N | N | Y | Y | Y | Y | Y | Y |
| 8 *Young* | Y | Y | N | Y | Y | ? | N | N |
| 9 *Bilirakis* | Y | Y | Y | Y | Y | N | N | N |
| 10 *Ireland* | Y | ? | N | Y | N | N | N | N |
| 11 Bacchus | Y | Y | Y | Y | Y | Y | Y | Y |
| 12 *Lewis* | Y | Y | Y | Y | Y | N | N | N |
| 13 *Goss* | Y | Y | N | Y | N | N | N | N |
| 14 Johnston | N | N | N | Y | Y | Y | Y | Y |
| 15 *Shaw* | Y | Y | N | Y | Y | N | N | N |
| 16 Smith | N | N | N | N | N | Y | Y | Y |
| 17 Lehman | N | N | N | N | N | Y | Y | Y |
| 18 *Ros—Lehtinen* | Y | Y | N | Y | Y | N | N | N |
| 19 Fascell | N | N | N | N | N | Y | Y | Y |
| **GEORGIA** | | | | | | | | |
| 1 Thomas | N | Y | N | Y | Y | Y | Y | Y |
| 2 Hatcher | N | Y | N | Y | Y | Y | Y | Y |
| 3 Ray | N | Y | N | Y | Y | ? | ? | ? |
| 4 Jones | N | N | N | Y | Y | Y | ? | ? |
| 5 Lewis | N | N | N | N | N | Y | Y | Y |
| 6 *Gingrich* | Y | Y | N | Y | Y | N | N | N |
| 7 Darden | N | Y | N | Y | Y | Y | Y | Y |
| 8 Rowland | N | Y | N | Y | Y | Y | Y | Y |
| 9 Jenkins | N | Y | N | Y | Y | Y | Y | Y |
| 10 Barnard | N | Y | N | Y | Y | Y | Y | Y |
| **HAWAII** | | | | | | | | |
| 1 Abercrombie | N | N | N | N | N | Y | Y | Y |
| 2 Mink | N | N | N | N | N | Y | Y | Y |
| **IDAHO** | | | | | | | | |
| 1 LaRocco | N | N | Y | Y | Y | Y | Y | Y |
| 2 Stallings | N | N | Y | Y | Y | Y | Y | Y |
| **ILLINOIS** | | | | | | | | |
| 1 Hayes | N | N | N | N | N | Y | Y | Y |
| 2 Savage | N | N | N | N | N | ? | ? | ? |
| 3 Russo | N | N | N | N | N | Y | Y | Y |
| 4 Sangmeister | N | Y | Y | Y | Y | Y | Y | Y |
| 5 Lipinski | N | N | N | N | N | Y | Y | Y |
| 6 *Hyde* | Y | Y | N | Y | Y | N | N | N |
| 7 Collins | N | N | N | N | N | Y | Y | Y |
| 8 Rostenkowski | N | N | N | N | N | Y | Y | Y |
| 9 Yates | N | N | N | N | N | Y | Y | Y |
| 10 *Porter* | Y | Y | N | Y | N | N | N | N |
| 11 Annunzio | N | N | N | N | N | Y | Y | Y |
| 12 *Crane* | Y | Y | N | Y | N | N | ? | N |
| 13 *Fawell* | Y | Y | N | Y | Y | N | N | N |
| 14 *Hastert* | Y | Y | N | Y | Y | N | N | N |
| 15 *Ewing* | Y | Y | N | Y | Y | N | N | N |
| 16 Cox | N | Y | Y | Y | Y | Y | Y | Y |
| 17 Evans | N | N | N | N | N | Y | Y | Y |
| 18 *Michel* | Y | Y | N | Y | Y | ? | N | N |
| 19 Bruce | N | N | N | Y | Y | Y | Y | Y |
| 20 Durbin | N | N | Y | Y | Y | Y | Y | Y |
| 21 Costello | N | N | N | N | N | Y | Y | Y |
| 22 Poshard | Y | N | Y | Y | Y | Y | Y | Y |
| **INDIANA** | | | | | | | | |
| 1 Visclosky | N | N | N | N | N | Y | Y | Y |
| 2 Sharp | N | N | N | Y | Y | Y | ? | ? |
| 3 Roemer | N | N | Y | Y | Y | Y | Y | Y |

ND  Northern Democrats      SD  Southern Democrats

| | 183 | 184 | 185 | 186 | 187 | 188 | 189 | 190 |
|---|---|---|---|---|---|---|---|---|
| 4 Long | N | N | Y | Y | Y | Y | Y | Y |
| 5 Jontz | N | N | Y | Y | Y | Y | Y | Y |
| 6 ***Burton*** | Y | Y | N | Y | Y | N | N | N |
| 7 ***Myers*** | N | Y | N | Y | Y | Y | N | N |
| 8 McCloskey | N | N | N | Y | Y | Y | Y | Y |
| 9 Hamilton | N | N | Y | N | N | Y | Y | Y |
| 10 Jacobs | N | N | N | Y | Y | N | Y | N |
| **IOWA** | | | | | | | | |
| 1 ***Leach*** | Y | Y | N | Y | Y | N | N | N |
| 2 ***Nussle*** | Y | Y | N | Y | Y | N | N | N |
| 3 Nagle | N | N | N | N | N | Y | Y | Y |
| 4 Smith | N | N | N | N | N | Y | Y | Y |
| 5 ***Lightfoot*** | Y | Y | N | Y | Y | N | N | N |
| 6 ***Grandy*** | Y | N | N | Y | Y | N | N | N |
| **KANSAS** | | | | | | | | |
| 1 ***Roberts*** | Y | Y | N | Y | Y | N | N | N |
| 2 Slattery | N | Y | N | N | N | Y | Y | Y |
| 3 ***Meyers*** | Y | Y | N | Y | Y | N | N | N |
| 4 Glickman | N | N | N | Y | Y | Y | Y | Y |
| 5 ***Nichols*** | Y | Y | N | Y | Y | Y | N | N |
| **KENTUCKY** | | | | | | | | |
| 1 Hubbard | Y | Y | N | Y | Y | ? | ? | ? |
| 2 Natcher | N | N | Y | Y | Y | Y | Y | Y |
| 3 Mazzoli | N | N | Y | Y | Y | Y | Y | Y |
| 4 ***Bunning*** | Y | Y | N | Y | Y | N | N | N |
| 5 ***Rogers*** | Y | Y | N | Y | Y | N | N | N |
| 6 ***Hopkins*** | Y | Y | N | Y | Y | N | N | N |
| 7 Perkins | N | N | N | N | N | ? | ? | Y |
| **LOUISIANA** | | | | | | | | |
| 1 ***Livingston*** | Y | Y | N | Y | Y | Y | N | N |
| 2 Jefferson | N | N | Y | N | N | ? | Y | Y |
| 3 Tauzin | Y | Y | N | Y | Y | Y | Y | Y |
| 4 ***McCrery*** | Y | Y | N | Y | Y | N | N | N |
| 5 Huckaby | N | N | N | Y | Y | Y | Y | Y |
| 6 ***Baker*** | Y | Y | N | Y | Y | N | N | N |
| 7 Hayes | Y | Y | Y | Y | Y | Y | Y | Y |
| 8 ***Holloway*** | Y | Y | N | Y | Y | N | N | N |
| **MAINE** | | | | | | | | |
| 1 Andrews | N | N | N | N | N | Y | Y | Y |
| 2 ***Snowe*** | Y | Y | N | Y | Y | Y | N | N |
| **MARYLAND** | | | | | | | | |
| 1 ***Gilchrest*** | Y | Y | N | Y | Y | N | N | N |
| 2 ***Bentley*** | Y | Y | N | Y | Y | N | N | N |
| 3 Cardin | N | N | N | N | N | Y | Y | Y |
| 4 McMillen | N | Y | Y | Y | Y | Y | Y | Y |
| 5 Hoyer | N | N | Y | Y | Y | Y | Y | Y |
| 6 Byron | N | N | N | Y | Y | Y | Y | Y |
| 7 Mfume | N | N | N | N | N | Y | Y | Y |
| 8 ***Morella*** | N | N | N | Y | Y | N | N | N |
| **MASSACHUSETTS** | | | | | | | | |
| 1 Olver | N | N | Y | N | N | Y | Y | Y |
| 2 Neal | N | N | Y | N | N | Y | Y | Y |
| 3 Early | N | N | Y | Y | Y | Y | Y | Y |
| 4 Frank | N | N | N | N | N | Y | Y | Y |
| 5 Atkins | N | N | N | N | N | Y | Y | Y |
| 6 Mavroules | N | N | N | N | N | Y | Y | Y |
| 7 Markey | N | N | Y | N | N | Y | Y | Y |
| 8 Kennedy | N | N | Y | Y | Y | Y | Y | Y |
| 9 Moakley | N | N | N | N | N | Y | Y | Y |
| 10 Studds | N | N | N | N | N | Y | Y | Y |
| 11 Donnelly | N | N | N | Y | Y | ? | Y | Y |
| **MICHIGAN** | | | | | | | | |
| 1 Conyers | N | N | N | N | N | ? | ? | Y |
| 2 ***Pursell*** | N | Y | N | Y | Y | Y | N | N |
| 3 Wolpe | N | N | N | N | N | ? | ? | ? |
| 4 ***Upton*** | Y | Y | N | Y | Y | N | N | N |
| 5 ***Henry*** | N | N | N | Y | Y | N | N | N |
| 6 Carr | N | N | Y | Y | Y | Y | Y | Y |
| 7 Kildee | N | N | N | N | N | Y | Y | Y |
| 8 Traxler | ? | ? | ? | ? | ? | ? | ? | ? |
| 9 ***Vander Jagt*** | Y | Y | N | Y | Y | N | N | N |
| 10 ***Camp*** | Y | Y | N | Y | Y | N | N | N |
| 11 ***Davis*** | ? | Y | N | Y | Y | N | N | N |
| 12 Bonior | ? | ? | Y | N | N | ? | # | # |
| 13 Collins | N | N | N | N | N | Y | Y | Y |
| 14 Hertel | N | N | Y | N | N | Y | Y | Y |
| 15 Ford | N | N | N | N | N | Y | Y | Y |
| 16 Dingell | N | N | Y | N | N | Y | Y | Y |
| 17 Levin | N | N | N | N | N | Y | Y | Y |
| 18 ***Broomfield*** | Y | Y | N | Y | Y | Y | N | N |
| **MINNESOTA** | | | | | | | | |
| 1 Penny | N | N | N | Y | Y | Y | Y | Y |
| 2 ***Weber*** | Y | Y | N | Y | Y | Y | N | N |
| 3 ***Ramstad*** | Y | Y | N | Y | Y | N | N | N |
| 4 Vento | N | N | N | N | N | Y | Y | Y |

| | 183 | 184 | 185 | 186 | 187 | 188 | 189 | 190 |
|---|---|---|---|---|---|---|---|---|
| 5 Sabo | N | N | N | N | N | Y | Y | Y |
| 6 Sikorski | N | N | N | Y | Y | N | Y | Y |
| 7 Peterson | N | N | N | Y | Y | Y | Y | Y |
| 8 Oberstar | N | N | N | N | N | Y | Y | Y |
| **MISSISSIPPI** | | | | | | | | |
| 1 Whitten | N | ? | ? | Y | Y | ? | Y | Y |
| 2 Espy | N | N | N | Y | Y | Y | Y | Y |
| 3 Montgomery | N | Y | N | Y | Y | Y | Y | Y |
| 4 Parker | Y | Y | N | Y | Y | Y | Y | Y |
| 5 Taylor | Y | Y | Y | Y | Y | Y | Y | Y |
| **MISSOURI** | | | | | | | | |
| 1 Clay | N | N | N | N | N | N | Y | Y |
| 2 Horn | N | N | Y | N | N | Y | Y | Y |
| 3 Gephardt | N | N | Y | N | N | Y | Y | Y |
| 4 Skelton | N | N | N | Y | Y | Y | Y | Y |
| 5 Wheat | N | N | N | N | N | Y | Y | Y |
| 6 ***Coleman*** | Y | Y | N | Y | Y | N | N | N |
| 7 ***Hancock*** | Y | Y | N | Y | Y | N | N | N |
| 8 ***Emerson*** | Y | Y | N | Y | Y | N | N | N |
| 9 Volkmer | N | N | Y | Y | Y | Y | Y | Y |
| **MONTANA** | | | | | | | | |
| 1 Williams | N | N | N | N | N | Y | Y | ? |
| 2 ***Marlenee*** | Y | Y | N | Y | Y | ? | ? | ? |
| **NEBRASKA** | | | | | | | | |
| 1 ***Bereuter*** | Y | Y | N | Y | Y | N | N | N |
| 2 Hoagland | N | N | Y | Y | Y | Y | Y | Y |
| 3 ***Barrett*** | Y | Y | N | Y | Y | N | N | N |
| **NEVADA** | | | | | | | | |
| 1 Bilbray | Y | N | Y | Y | Y | Y | Y | Y |
| 2 ***Vucanovich*** | Y | Y | Y | Y | Y | N | N | N |
| **NEW HAMPSHIRE** | | | | | | | | |
| 1 ***Zeliff*** | Y | Y | N | Y | Y | N | N | N |
| 2 Swett | Y | Y | Y | Y | Y | Y | Y | Y |
| **NEW JERSEY** | | | | | | | | |
| 1 Andrews | Y | Y | Y | Y | Y | Y | Y | Y |
| 2 Hughes | N | N | N | N | N | Y | Y | Y |
| 3 Pallone | Y | Y | Y | Y | Y | Y | Y | Y |
| 4 ***Smith*** | Y | Y | N | Y | Y | Y | N | N |
| 5 ***Roukema*** | N | N | N | Y | Y | N | N | N |
| 6 Dwyer | N | N | N | N | N | Y | Y | Y |
| 7 ***Rinaldo*** | Y | Y | N | Y | Y | Y | N | N |
| 8 Roe | N | N | Y | N | N | Y | Y | Y |
| 9 Torricelli | N | N | Y | Y | Y | ? | ? | Y |
| 10 Payne | N | N | N | N | N | Y | Y | Y |
| 11 ***Gallo*** | Y | Y | N | Y | Y | N | N | N |
| 12 ***Zimmer*** | Y | Y | N | Y | Y | N | N | N |
| 13 ***Saxton*** | Y | Y | N | Y | Y | N | N | N |
| 14 Guarini | N | N | N | N | N | Y | Y | Y |
| **NEW MEXICO** | | | | | | | | |
| 1 ***Schiff*** | Y | Y | N | Y | Y | Y | N | N |
| 2 ***Skeen*** | Y | Y | N | Y | Y | Y | N | N |
| 3 Richardson | N | N | Y | Y | Y | Y | Y | Y |
| **NEW YORK** | | | | | | | | |
| 1 Hochbrueckner | N | N | Y | N | N | Y | Y | Y |
| 2 Downey | N | N | N | N | N | Y | Y | Y |
| 3 Mrazek | N | N | N | N | N | Y | Y | Y |
| 4 ***Lent*** | Y | Y | N | Y | Y | Y | N | N |
| 5 ***McGrath*** | Y | Y | N | Y | Y | Y | ? | N |
| 6 Flake | N | N | N | N | N | Y | Y | Y |
| 7 Ackerman | N | N | Y | N | N | Y | Y | Y |
| 8 Scheuer | N | N | N | N | N | Y | Y | Y |
| 9 Manton | N | N | Y | N | N | Y | Y | Y |
| 10 Schumer | N | N | N | N | N | ? | Y | Y |
| 11 Towns | N | N | N | N | N | ? | ? | Y |
| 12 Owens | N | N | N | N | N | Y | Y | Y |
| 13 Solarz | N | N | N | N | N | ? | Y | Y |
| 14 ***Molinari*** | Y | Y | N | Y | Y | N | N | N |
| 15 ***Green*** | N | N | N | N | N | Y | N | N |
| 16 Rangel | N | N | N | N | N | ? | Y | Y |
| 17 Weiss | N | N | N | N | N | Y | Y | Y |
| 18 Serrano | N | N | N | N | N | Y | Y | Y |
| 19 Engel | N | N | Y | N | N | Y | Y | Y |
| 20 Lowey | N | N | N | N | N | Y | Y | Y |
| 21 ***Fish*** | Y | Y | N | Y | Y | Y | N | N |
| 22 ***Gilman*** | N | N | N | N | N | Y | N | N |
| 23 McNulty | N | N | Y | N | N | Y | Y | Y |
| 24 ***Solomon*** | Y | Y | N | Y | Y | N | N | N |
| 25 ***Boehlert*** | N | N | N | Y | Y | N | N | N |
| 26 ***Martin*** | Y | Y | N | Y | Y | Y | N | N |
| 27 ***Walsh*** | N | Y | N | Y | Y | Y | N | N |
| 28 McHugh | N | N | N | N | N | Y | Y | Y |
| 29 ***Horton*** | N | N | N | Y | Y | Y | N | N |
| 30 Slaughter | N | N | N | N | N | Y | Y | Y |
| 31 ***Paxon*** | Y | Y | N | Y | Y | N | N | N |

| | 183 | 184 | 185 | 186 | 187 | 188 | 189 | 190 |
|---|---|---|---|---|---|---|---|---|
| 32 LaFalce | N | N | N | N | N | ? | Y | Y |
| 33 Nowak | N | N | N | N | N | Y | Y | Y |
| 34 ***Houghton*** | Y | Y | N | Y | Y | Y | N | N |
| **NORTH CAROLINA** | | | | | | | | |
| 1 Jones | N | N | Y | N | Y | Y | Y | Y |
| 2 Valentine | N | Y | N | Y | Y | Y | Y | Y |
| 3 Lancaster | N | N | Y | Y | Y | Y | Y | Y |
| 4 Price | N | N | Y | Y | Y | Y | Y | Y |
| 5 Neal | N | N | N | Y | Y | Y | Y | Y |
| 6 ***Coble*** | Y | Y | N | Y | Y | N | N | N |
| 7 Rose | N | N | Y | N | N | Y | Y | Y |
| 8 Hefner | ? | ? | ? | ? | ? | ? | ? | ? |
| 9 ***McMillan*** | Y | Y | N | Y | Y | N | N | N |
| 10 ***Ballenger*** | Y | Y | N | Y | Y | N | N | N |
| 11 ***Taylor*** | Y | Y | N | Y | Y | N | N | N |
| **NORTH DAKOTA** | | | | | | | | |
| AL Dorgan | N | N | N | Y | Y | Y | Y | Y |
| **OHIO** | | | | | | | | |
| 1 Luken | N | Y | N | Y | Y | Y | Y | Y |
| 2 ***Gradison*** | Y | Y | N | Y | Y | Y | N | N |
| 3 Hall | N | N | N | Y | Y | Y | Y | Y |
| 4 ***Oxley*** | Y | Y | N | Y | Y | N | N | N |
| 5 ***Gillmor*** | Y | Y | N | Y | Y | Y | N | N |
| 6 ***McEwen*** | Y | Y | N | Y | Y | N | N | N |
| 7 ***Hobson*** | Y | Y | N | Y | Y | N | N | N |
| 8 ***Boehner*** | Y | Y | N | Y | Y | N | N | N |
| 9 Kaptur | N | N | Y | N | N | Y | Y | Y |
| 10 ***Miller*** | Y | Y | N | Y | Y | N | N | N |
| 11 Eckart | N | N | Y | Y | Y | Y | Y | Y |
| 12 ***Kasich*** | Y | Y | N | Y | Y | Y | N | N |
| 13 Pease | N | N | N | N | N | Y | Y | Y |
| 14 Sawyer | N | N | N | N | N | Y | Y | Y |
| 15 ***Wylie*** | Y | Y | N | Y | Y | Y | N | N |
| 16 ***Regula*** | Y | Y | N | Y | Y | N | N | N |
| 17 Traficant | N | N | N | N | N | Y | Y | Y |
| 18 Applegate | N | N | Y | N | N | Y | Y | Y |
| 19 Feighan | N | N | Y | Y | Y | Y | Y | Y |
| 20 Oakar | N | N | Y | N | N | Y | Y | Y |
| 21 Stokes | N | N | N | N | N | Y | Y | Y |
| **OKLAHOMA** | | | | | | | | |
| 1 ***Inhofe*** | Y | Y | N | Y | Y | N | N | N |
| 2 Synar | N | N | N | N | N | ? | Y | Y |
| 3 Brewster | N | N | N | Y | Y | Y | Y | Y |
| 4 McCurdy | N | N | N | Y | Y | Y | Y | Y |
| 5 ***Edwards*** | Y | Y | N | Y | Y | N | N | N |
| 6 English | N | Y | Y | Y | Y | Y | Y | Y |
| **OREGON** | | | | | | | | |
| 1 AuCoin | N | N | N | N | N | Y | Y | Y |
| 2 ***Smith*** | Y | Y | N | Y | Y | N | N | N |
| 3 Wyden | N | N | N | N | N | Y | Y | Y |
| 4 DeFazio | N | N | Y | Y | Y | Y | Y | Y |
| 5 Kopetski | N | N | Y | N | N | Y | Y | Y |
| **PENNSYLVANIA** | | | | | | | | |
| 1 Foglietta | N | N | N | N | N | Y | Y | Y |
| 2 Blackwell | N | N | N | N | N | Y | Y | Y |
| 3 Borski | N | N | N | N | N | Y | Y | Y |
| 4 Kolter | N | N | Y | Y | Y | Y | Y | Y |
| 5 ***Schulze*** | Y | Y | N | Y | Y | Y | N | N |
| 6 Yatron | N | N | Y | Y | Y | Y | Y | Y |
| 7 ***Weldon*** | Y | Y | N | Y | Y | ? | N | N |
| 8 Kostmayer | N | N | Y | N | N | Y | Y | Y |
| 9 ***Shuster*** | Y | ? | N | Y | Y | N | N | N |
| 10 ***McDade*** | N | Y | N | Y | Y | N | N | N |
| 11 Kanjorski | N | N | N | N | N | Y | Y | Y |
| 12 Murtha | N | N | Y | N | N | ? | Y | Y |
| 13 ***Coughlin*** | Y | Y | N | Y | Y | N | N | N |
| 14 Coyne | N | N | N | N | N | Y | Y | Y |
| 15 ***Ritter*** | Y | Y | N | Y | Y | Y | N | N |
| 16 ***Walker*** | Y | Y | N | Y | Y | N | N | N |
| 17 ***Gekas*** | Y | Y | N | Y | Y | ? | N | N |
| 18 ***Santorum*** | Y | Y | N | Y | Y | ? | N | N |
| 19 ***Goodling*** | Y | Y | N | Y | Y | N | N | N |
| 20 Gaydos | N | N | Y | N | N | Y | Y | Y |
| 21 ***Ridge*** | Y | Y | N | Y | Y | N | N | N |
| 22 Murphy | N | N | Y | N | N | N | Y | Y |
| 23 ***Clinger*** | Y | Y | N | Y | Y | Y | N | N |
| **RHODE ISLAND** | | | | | | | | |
| 1 ***Machtley*** | Y | Y | N | Y | Y | N | N | N |
| 2 Reed | N | N | Y | N | N | Y | Y | Y |
| **SOUTH CAROLINA** | | | | | | | | |
| 1 ***Ravenel*** | Y | Y | N | Y | Y | Y | N | N |
| 2 ***Spence*** | Y | Y | N | Y | Y | Y | N | N |
| 3 Derrick | N | N | N | Y | Y | Y | Y | Y |
| 4 Patterson | N | Y | N | Y | Y | Y | Y | Y |
| 5 Spratt | N | N | N | Y | Y | ? | ? | Y |
| 6 Tallon | N | N | N | N | N | Y | Y | Y |

| | 183 | 184 | 185 | 186 | 187 | 188 | 189 | 190 |
|---|---|---|---|---|---|---|---|---|
| **SOUTH DAKOTA** | | | | | | | | |
| AL Johnson | N | N | Y | Y | Y | Y | Y | Y |
| **TENNESSEE** | | | | | | | | |
| 1 ***Quillen*** | Y | Y | N | Y | Y | ? | X | X |
| 2 ***Duncan*** | Y | Y | N | Y | Y | ? | N | N |
| 3 Lloyd | N | Y | N | Y | Y | ? | ? | Y |
| 4 Cooper | Y | Y | Y | Y | Y | Y | Y | Y |
| 5 Clement | N | Y | N | Y | Y | Y | Y | Y |
| 6 Gordon | N | N | Y | Y | Y | Y | Y | Y |
| 7 ***Sundquist*** | Y | Y | N | Y | Y | N | N | N |
| 8 Tanner | N | Y | N | Y | Y | Y | Y | Y |
| 9 Ford | N | N | N | N | N | Y | Y | Y |
| **TEXAS** | | | | | | | | |
| 1 Chapman | N | N | Y | Y | Y | Y | Y | Y |
| 2 Wilson | N | Y | Y | Y | Y | Y | Y | ? |
| 3 ***Johnson*** | Y | Y | N | Y | Y | Y | N | N |
| 4 Hall | Y | Y | Y | Y | Y | Y | Y | Y |
| 5 Bryant | N | N | N | Y | Y | Y | Y | Y |
| 6 ***Barton*** | Y | Y | N | Y | Y | N | N | N |
| 7 ***Archer*** | Y | Y | N | Y | Y | N | N | N |
| 8 ***Fields*** | Y | Y | N | Y | Y | N | N | N |
| 9 Brooks | N | N | N | N | N | Y | Y | Y |
| 10 Pickle | N | N | N | Y | Y | Y | Y | Y |
| 11 Edwards | N | Y | N | Y | Y | Y | Y | Y |
| 12 Geren | Y | Y | N | Y | Y | Y | Y | Y |
| 13 Sarpalius | N | Y | Y | Y | Y | Y | Y | Y |
| 14 Laughlin | N | Y | N | Y | Y | Y | Y | Y |
| 15 de la Garza | N | N | Y | Y | Y | Y | Y | Y |
| 16 Coleman | N | N | Y | N | N | Y | Y | Y |
| 17 Stenholm | N | Y | N | Y | Y | Y | Y | Y |
| 18 Washington | N | N | N | N | N | Y | Y | Y |
| 19 ***Combest*** | Y | Y | N | Y | Y | Y | N | N |
| 20 Gonzalez | N | N | Y | N | N | Y | Y | Y |
| 21 ***Smith*** | Y | Y | N | Y | Y | ? | ? | N |
| 22 ***DeLay*** | Y | Y | N | Y | Y | N | N | N |
| 23 Bustamante | N | N | Y | N | N | Y | Y | Y |
| 24 Frost | N | N | Y | Y | Y | Y | Y | Y |
| 25 Andrews | N | N | N | Y | Y | Y | Y | Y |
| 26 ***Armey*** | Y | Y | N | Y | Y | N | N | N |
| 27 Ortiz | N | N | N | Y | Y | Y | ? | Y |
| **UTAH** | | | | | | | | |
| 1 ***Hansen*** | Y | Y | N | Y | Y | N | N | N |
| 2 Owens | N | N | N | Y | Y | Y | Y | Y |
| 3 Orton | N | N | N | Y | Y | Y | Y | Y |
| **VERMONT** | | | | | | | | |
| AL *Sanders* | N | N | N | N | N | Y | Y | Y |
| **VIRGINIA** | | | | | | | | |
| 1 ***Bateman*** | Y | Y | N | Y | Y | Y | N | N |
| 2 Pickett | N | N | N | N | N | Y | Y | Y |
| 3 ***Bliley*** | Y | Y | N | Y | Y | N | N | N |
| 4 Sisisky | N | Y | N | Y | Y | Y | Y | Y |
| 5 Payne | N | Y | N | Y | Y | Y | Y | Y |
| 6 Olin | N | N | N | N | N | Y | Y | Y |
| 7 ***Allen*** | Y | Y | N | Y | Y | N | N | N |
| 8 Moran | N | N | Y | Y | Y | ? | Y | Y |
| 9 Boucher | N | N | Y | N | N | Y | Y | Y |
| 10 ***Wolf*** | Y | Y | N | Y | Y | N | N | N |
| **WASHINGTON** | | | | | | | | |
| 1 ***Miller*** | Y | Y | N | Y | Y | N | N | N |
| 2 Swift | N | N | N | N | N | Y | Y | Y |
| 3 Unsoeld | N | N | N | N | N | ? | Y | Y |
| 4 ***Morrison*** | N | N | N | Y | Y | Y | N | Y |
| 5 Foley | | | | | N | | | |
| 6 Dicks | N | N | N | N | N | Y | Y | Y |
| 7 McDermott | N | N | N | N | N | Y | Y | Y |
| 8 ***Chandler*** | Y | Y | N | Y | Y | N | N | N |
| **WEST VIRGINIA** | | | | | | | | |
| 1 Mollohan | N | N | N | N | N | ? | ? | Y |
| 2 Staggers | N | N | N | N | N | Y | Y | Y |
| 3 Wise | N | N | Y | Y | Y | ? | Y | ? |
| 4 Rahall | N | N | Y | N | N | ? | Y | Y |
| **WISCONSIN** | | | | | | | | |
| 1 Aspin | N | N | Y | N | N | Y | Y | Y |
| 2 ***Klug*** | Y | Y | N | Y | Y | N | N | N |
| 3 ***Gunderson*** | N | Y | N | Y | Y | Y | N | N |
| 4 Kleczka | N | N | Y | N | N | Y | Y | Y |
| 5 Moody | N | N | N | Y | Y | Y | Y | Y |
| 6 ***Petri*** | Y | Y | N | Y | Y | Y | N | N |
| 7 Obey | N | N | Y | N | N | Y | Y | Y |
| 8 ***Roth*** | Y | Y | N | Y | Y | Y | N | N |
| 9 ***Sensenbrenner*** | Y | Y | N | Y | Y | N | N | N |
| **WYOMING** | | | | | | | | |
| AL ***Thomas*** | Y | Y | N | Y | Y | Y | N | N |

Southern states - Ala., Ark., Fla., Ga., Ky., La., Miss., N.C., Okla., S.C., Tenn., Texas, Va.
Omitted votes are quorum calls, which CQ does not include in its vote charts.

**191. S 250. National "Motor Voter" Registration/Rule.** Adoption of the rule (H Res 480) to provide for House floor consideration of the bill to require states to permit voter registration simultaneously with application for public documents such as a driver's license, marriage license or hunting permit. Adopted 264-157: R 6-157; D 257-0 (ND 175-0, SD 82-0); I 1-0, June 16, 1992.

**193. S 250. National "Motor Voter" Registration/Discretionary Program.** Thomas, R-Calif., substitute amendment to eliminate the requirements in the bill and provide $25 million in fiscal 1992-94 for block grants to states to enhance voter registration. Rejected 133-290: R 131-33; D 2-256 (ND 1-176, SD 1-80); I 0-1, June 16, 1992.

**194. S 250. National "Motor Voter" Registration/Passage.** Passage of the bill to require states to permit voter registration simultaneously with applying for public certificates such as a driver's license, marriage license or hunting permit. Passed (thus clearing for the president) 268-153: R 28-135; D 239-18 (ND 171-6, SD 68-12); I 1-0, June 16, 1992. A "nay" was a vote in support of the president's position.

**195. HR 5373. Fiscal 1993 Energy and Water Appropriations/Rule.** Adoption of the rule (H Res 485) to waive certain points of order against and provide for floor consideration of the bill to provide $21,795,636,000 for energy and water development in fiscal 1993. Adopted 377-44: R 118-41; D 258-3 (ND 176-3, SD 82-0); I 1-0, June 17, 1992.

**197. HR 5373. Fiscal 1993 Energy and Water Appropriations/Casino Beach Project.** Burton, R-Ind., amendment to eliminate the $110,000 provided to continue preconstruction engineering and design of the Casino Beach project in Chicago by the Army Corps of Engineers. The project involved the construction of a jetty to help combat erosion along Lake Shore Drive. Rejected 104-323: R 87-77; D 17-245 (ND 8-171, SD 9-74); I 0-1, June 17, 1992.

**198. HR 5373. Fiscal 1993 Energy and Water Appropriations/Red River Waterway.** Burton, R-Ind., amendment to eliminate the $2.8 million provided to complete a feasibility study for the Red River Waterway from Shreveport, La., to Daingerfield, Texas. Rejected 105-319: R 90-72; D 15-246 (ND 11-169, SD 4-77); I 0-1, June 17, 1992.

**199. HR 5373. Fiscal 1993 Energy and Water Appropriations/Advanced Liquid Metal Reactor.** Wolpe, D-Mich., amendment to reduce the nuclear energy research and development program by $34 million, thereby eliminating funding for the advanced liquid metal reactor, which was exploring conversion of nuclear waste to energy. Rejected 141-282: R 26-136; D 114-146 (ND 102-77, SD 12-69); I 1-0, June 17, 1992.

**200. HR 5373. Fiscal 1993 Energy and Water Appropriations/Space Reactor.** Wolpe, D-Mich., amendment to eliminate the $26 million in funding for the SP-100 space reactor program. Rejected 189-233: R 37-125; D 151-108 (ND 128-50, SD 23-58); I 1-0, June 17, 1992.

## KEY

Y  Voted for (yea).
#  Paired for.
+  Announced for.
N  Voted against (nay).
X  Paired against.
—  Announced against.
P  Voted "present."
C  Voted "present" to avoid possible conflict of interest.
?  Did not vote or otherwise make a position known.

Democrats  **Republicans**  *Independent*

| | 191 | 193 | 194 | 195 | 197 | 198 | 199 | 200 |
|---|---|---|---|---|---|---|---|---|
| **ALABAMA** | | | | | | | | |
| 1 *Callahan* | N | Y | N | Y | N | N | N | N |
| 2 *Dickinson* | N | Y | N | Y | N | N | N | N |
| 3 Browder | Y | N | Y | N | N | N | N | N |
| 4 Bevill | Y | N | Y | N | N | N | N | N |
| 5 Cramer | Y | N | Y | N | N | N | N | N |
| 6 Erdreich | Y | N | Y | N | N | N | N | N |
| 7 Harris | Y | N | Y | N | N | N | N | N |
| **ALASKA** | | | | | | | | |
| AL *Young* | N | Y | N | Y | N | N | N | N |
| **ARIZONA** | | | | | | | | |
| 1 *Rhodes* | N | Y | N | Y | N | Y | N | N |
| 2 Pastor | Y | N | Y | N | Y | N | Y | Y |
| 3 *Stump* | N | Y | N | N | Y | N | N | N |
| 4 *Kyl* | N | Y | N | N | Y | Y | N | N |
| 5 *Kolbe* | N | Y | N | Y | N | N | N | N |
| **ARKANSAS** | | | | | | | | |
| 1 Alexander | Y | N | Y | Y | N | N | N | N |
| 2 Thornton | Y | N | Y | Y | N | N | N | N |
| 3 *Hammerschmidt* | N | Y | N | Y | N | N | N | N |
| 4 Anthony | Y | N | Y | Y | N | N | N | N |
| **CALIFORNIA** | | | | | | | | |
| 1 *Riggs* | N | Y | Y | N | N | N | N | N |
| 2 *Herger* | N | Y | N | ? | N | N | Y | Y |
| 3 Matsui | Y | N | Y | Y | N | N | N | N |
| 4 Fazio | Y | N | Y | Y | N | N | N | N |
| 5 Pelosi | Y | N | Y | Y | N | N | Y | Y |
| 6 Boxer | Y | N | Y | Y | N | N | Y | Y |
| 7 Miller | Y | N | Y | Y | N | N | Y | Y |
| 8 Dellums | Y | N | Y | Y | N | N | Y | Y |
| 9 Stark | Y | N | Y | Y | N | N | Y | Y |
| 10 Edwards | Y | N | Y | Y | N | N | Y | Y |
| 11 Lantos | Y | N | Y | Y | N | N | Y | Y |
| 12 *Campbell* | N | Y | N | Y | Y | Y | N | N |
| 13 Mineta | Y | N | Y | Y | N | N | N | N |
| 14 *Doolittle* | N | Y | N | Y | N | N | N | N |
| 15 Condit | Y | N | Y | Y | Y | Y | Y | Y |
| 16 Panetta | Y | N | Y | Y | N | N | Y | Y |
| 17 Dooley | Y | N | Y | Y | N | N | Y | Y |
| 18 Lehman | Y | N | Y | Y | N | N | Y | Y |
| 19 *Lagomarsino* | N | Y | N | Y | N | N | N | N |
| 20 *Thomas* | N | Y | N | N | N | N | N | N |
| 21 *Gallegly* | N | Y | N | Y | Y | Y | N | N |
| 22 *Moorhead* | N | Y | N | Y | Y | N | N | N |
| 23 Beilenson | Y | N | Y | Y | N | N | Y | Y |
| 24 Waxman | Y | N | Y | Y | N | N | Y | Y |
| 25 Roybal | Y | N | Y | Y | N | N | N | N |
| 26 Berman | Y | N | Y | Y | N | N | Y | Y |
| 27 Levine | ? | N | Y | Y | N | N | N | N |
| 28 Dixon | Y | N | Y | Y | N | N | N | N |
| 29 Waters | Y | N | Y | Y | N | N | Y | Y |
| 30 Martinez | Y | N | Y | Y | N | N | N | N |
| 31 Dymally | Y | N | Y | Y | N | N | N | N |
| 32 Anderson | Y | N | Y | Y | N | N | N | N |
| 33 *Dreier* | N | Y | N | N | Y | Y | N | N |
| 34 Torres | Y | N | Y | Y | N | N | N | N |
| 35 *Lewis* | N | Y | N | N | N | N | N | N |
| 36 Brown | Y | N | Y | Y | N | N | N | N |
| 37 *McCandless* | N | Y | N | N | N | N | N | N |
| 38 *Dornan* | N | Y | N | N | Y | Y | N | N |
| 39 *Dannemeyer* | N | Y | N | N | Y | Y | N | N |
| 40 *Cox* | N | Y | N | N | Y | N | N | N |
| 41 *Lowery* | N | Y | N | Y | N | ? | ? | ? |
| 42 *Rohrabacher* | N | Y | N | Y | N | N | N | N |
| 43 *Packard* | N | Y | N | Y | N | N | N | N |
| 44 *Cunningham* | N | Y | N | Y | N | N | N | N |
| 45 *Hunter* | N | Y | N | N | N | Y | N | N |
| **COLORADO** | | | | | | | | |
| 1 Schroeder | Y | N | Y | Y | N | N | Y | Y |
| 2 Skaggs | Y | N | Y | Y | N | N | N | Y |
| 3 Campbell | Y | N | Y | Y | N | Y | N | N |
| 4 *Allard* | N | Y | N | Y | Y | Y | N | N |
| 5 *Hefley* | N | Y | N | N | Y | Y | N | N |
| 6 *Schaefer* | N | Y | N | N | Y | Y | N | N |
| **CONNECTICUT** | | | | | | | | |
| 1 Kennelly | Y | N | Y | Y | N | N | Y | Y |
| 2 Gejdenson | Y | N | Y | Y | N | N | Y | Y |
| 3 DeLauro | Y | N | Y | Y | N | N | Y | Y |
| 4 *Shays* | N | N | Y | Y | Y | Y | Y | Y |
| 5 *Franks* | N | Y | N | N | N | Y | N | N |
| 6 Johnson | N | Y | Y | Y | N | Y | N | Y |
| **DELAWARE** | | | | | | | | |
| AL Carper | Y | N | Y | Y | N | N | N | Y |
| **FLORIDA** | | | | | | | | |
| 1 Hutto | Y | N | Y | N | N | N | N | N |
| 2 Peterson | Y | N | Y | Y | N | N | N | N |
| 3 Bennett | Y | N | Y | N | N | N | Y | N |
| 4 *James* | N | N | N | Y | Y | N | N | N |
| 5 *McCollum* | N | Y | N | Y | Y | N | N | N |
| 6 *Stearns* | N | Y | N | Y | Y | Y | Y | N |
| 7 Gibbons | Y | N | Y | N | N | N | N | N |
| 8 *Young* | N | Y | N | Y | N | N | N | ? |
| 9 *Bilirakis* | N | Y | Y | Y | N | N | N | N |
| 10 *Ireland* | N | N | N | ? | N | Y | N | N |
| 11 Bacchus | Y | N | Y | N | N | N | N | N |
| 12 *Lewis* | N | N | N | N | Y | N | N | N |
| 13 *Goss* | N | Y | N | Y | Y | Y | Y | Y |
| 14 Johnston | Y | N | Y | Y | Y | N | Y | Y |
| 15 *Shaw* | N | Y | Y | N | N | N | N | N |
| 16 Smith | Y | N | Y | N | N | N | N | ? |
| 17 Lehman | Y | N | Y | N | N | N | N | N |
| 18 *Ros—Lehtinen* | N | Y | Y | N | N | N | Y | Y |
| 19 Fascell | Y | N | Y | Y | N | ? | ? | N |
| **GEORGIA** | | | | | | | | |
| 1 Thomas | Y | N | Y | N | N | N | N | N |
| 2 Hatcher | Y | N | Y | N | N | N | N | N |
| 3 Ray | ? | ? | ? | Y | Y | Y | Y | Y |
| 4 Jones | Y | N | Y | N | Y | N | ? | ? |
| 5 Lewis | Y | N | Y | Y | N | N | Y | Y |
| 6 *Gingrich* | N | Y | N | ? | Y | Y | N | N |
| 7 Darden | Y | N | Y | N | N | N | N | N |
| 8 Rowland | Y | N | Y | N | N | N | N | N |
| 9 Jenkins | Y | N | Y | N | N | N | N | N |
| 10 Barnard | Y | N | Y | N | N | N | N | N |
| **HAWAII** | | | | | | | | |
| 1 Abercrombie | Y | N | Y | N | N | N | Y | Y |
| 2 Mink | Y | N | Y | Y | N | N | Y | Y |
| **IDAHO** | | | | | | | | |
| 1 LaRocco | Y | N | Y | N | N | N | N | N |
| 2 Stallings | Y | N | Y | N | N | N | N | N |
| **ILLINOIS** | | | | | | | | |
| 1 Hayes | Y | N | Y | N | N | N | N | N |
| 2 Savage | ? | N | Y | ? | N | N | Y | Y |
| 3 Russo | Y | N | Y | Y | N | N | N | Y |
| 4 Sangmeister | Y | N | Y | Y | N | N | N | Y |
| 5 Lipinski | Y | N | N | N | N | N | N | N |
| 6 *Hyde* | N | Y | N | Y | N | N | N | N |
| 7 Collins | Y | N | Y | N | N | N | N | N |
| 8 Rostenkowski | Y | N | Y | N | N | N | N | N |
| 9 Yates | Y | N | Y | Y | N | N | N | N |
| 10 *Porter* | N | Y | N | X | N | N | N | Y |
| 11 Annunzio | Y | N | Y | Y | N | N | N | N |
| 12 *Crane* | N | Y | N | N | N | N | N | N |
| 13 *Fawell* | N | Y | N | N | N | Y | N | N |
| 14 *Hastert* | N | Y | N | Y | N | N | N | N |
| 15 *Ewing* | N | Y | N | Y | N | N | N | Y |
| 16 Cox | Y | N | Y | Y | N | N | N | N |
| 17 Evans | Y | N | Y | N | N | N | N | N |
| 18 *Michel* | N | Y | N | N | N | N | N | N |
| 19 Bruce | Y | N | Y | N | N | N | N | N |
| 20 Durbin | Y | N | Y | Y | N | N | N | N |
| 21 Costello | Y | N | Y | Y | N | N | Y | Y |
| 22 Poshard | Y | N | Y | N | N | N | N | N |
| **INDIANA** | | | | | | | | |
| 1 Visclosky | Y | N | N | Y | N | N | N | N |
| 2 Sharp | Y | N | Y | Y | Y | Y | N | Y |
| 3 Roemer | Y | N | Y | N | Y | N | Y | N |

ND  Northern Democrats    SD  Southern Democrats

| | 191 | 193 | 194 | 195 | 197 | 198 | 199 | 200 |
|---|---|---|---|---|---|---|---|---|
| 4 Long | Y | N | Y | Y | N | N | N | Y |
| 5 Jontz | Y | N | Y | Y | N | Y | Y | Y |
| 6 ***Burton*** | N | Y | N | N | Y | Y | Y | Y |
| 7 ***Myers*** | N | Y | N | Y | N | N | N | N |
| 8 McCloskey | Y | N | Y | Y | N | N | Y | Y |
| 9 Hamilton | Y | N | Y | Y | Y | Y | N | N |
| 10 Jacobs | Y | N | Y | Y | Y | Y | Y | Y |
| **IOWA** | | | | | | | | |
| 1 ***Leach*** | N | N | Y | Y | Y | Y | N | ? |
| 2 ***Nussle*** | N | Y | N | Y | Y | Y | Y | Y |
| 3 Nagle | Y | N | Y | Y | N | N | N | N |
| 4 Smith | Y | N | Y | Y | N | N | N | N |
| 5 ***Lightfoot*** | N | Y | N | Y | N | N | N | N |
| 6 ***Grandy*** | N | Y | N | N | Y | N | N | Y |
| **KANSAS** | | | | | | | | |
| 1 ***Roberts*** | N | Y | N | N | Y | Y | N | N |
| 2 Slattery | Y | N | Y | Y | Y | N | Y | Y |
| 3 ***Meyers*** | N | Y | Y | N | Y | Y | N | Y |
| 4 Glickman | Y | N | Y | Y | Y | N | N | Y |
| 5 ***Nichols*** | N | Y | N | Y | Y | Y | N | N |
| **KENTUCKY** | | | | | | | | |
| 1 Hubbard | ? | ? | ? | ? | ? | ? | ? | ? |
| 2 Natcher | Y | N | Y | Y | N | N | N | N |
| 3 Mazzoli | Y | N | Y | Y | N | N | N | N |
| 4 ***Bunning*** | N | Y | N | N | Y | Y | N | N |
| 5 ***Rogers*** | N | Y | N | Y | N | N | N | N |
| 6 ***Hopkins*** | N | Y | Y | N | Y | Y | N | N |
| 7 Perkins | Y | N | Y | Y | N | N | N | N |
| **LOUISIANA** | | | | | | | | |
| 1 ***Livingston*** | N | Y | N | Y | N | N | N | N |
| 2 Jefferson | Y | N | Y | Y | N | N | N | Y |
| 3 Tauzin | Y | N | Y | Y | N | N | N | Y |
| 4 ***McCrery*** | N | Y | N | Y | N | N | N | N |
| 5 Huckaby | Y | N | Y | Y | N | N | N | N |
| 6 ***Baker*** | N | Y | N | Y | Y | N | N | N |
| 7 Hayes | Y | N | Y | Y | N | N | N | N |
| 8 ***Holloway*** | N | Y | N | Y | Y | N | N | N |
| **MAINE** | | | | | | | | |
| 1 Andrews | Y | N | Y | Y | N | N | Y | Y |
| 2 ***Snowe*** | N | Y | N | N | Y | Y | Y | Y |
| **MARYLAND** | | | | | | | | |
| 1 ***Gilchrest*** | N | Y | Y | ? | Y | Y | Y | Y |
| 2 ***Bentley*** | N | Y | N | Y | Y | Y | N | N |
| 3 Cardin | Y | N | Y | Y | N | N | N | N |
| 4 McMillen | Y | N | Y | Y | N | N | N | N |
| 5 Hoyer | Y | N | Y | Y | N | N | N | N |
| 6 Byron | Y | N | N | Y | N | N | N | N |
| 7 Mfume | Y | N | Y | N | N | Y | N | Y |
| 8 ***Morella*** | Y | N | Y | N | N | N | N | N |
| **MASSACHUSETTS** | | | | | | | | |
| 1 Olver | Y | N | Y | Y | N | N | Y | Y |
| 2 Neal | Y | N | Y | Y | N | N | Y | Y |
| 3 Early | Y | N | Y | Y | N | N | Y | Y |
| 4 Frank | Y | N | Y | Y | N | N | Y | Y |
| 5 Atkins | Y | N | Y | Y | N | N | N | Y |
| 6 Mavroules | Y | N | Y | Y | N | N | N | Y |
| 7 Markey | Y | N | Y | Y | N | N | Y | Y |
| 8 Kennedy | Y | N | Y | Y | N | N | Y | Y |
| 9 Moakley | Y | N | Y | Y | N | N | N | Y |
| 10 Studds | Y | N | Y | Y | N | N | Y | Y |
| 11 Donnelly | Y | N | N | Y | N | N | Y | Y |
| **MICHIGAN** | | | | | | | | |
| 1 Conyers | Y | N | Y | Y | N | N | Y | Y |
| 2 ***Pursell*** | N | N | N | Y | N | N | N | N |
| 3 Wolpe | ? | ? | ? | N | N | N | Y | Y |
| 4 ***Upton*** | N | N | N | Y | Y | Y | N | Y |
| 5 ***Henry*** | N | N | N | Y | Y | Y | N | Y |
| 6 Carr | Y | N | Y | Y | N | N | N | N |
| 7 Kildee | Y | N | Y | Y | N | N | Y | Y |
| 8 Traxler | ? | ? | ? | ? | ? | ? | ? | ? |
| 9 ***Vander Jagt*** | N | Y | N | Y | N | Y | N | Y |
| 10 ***Camp*** | N | Y | N | Y | Y | Y | Y | Y |
| 11 ***Davis*** | N | Y | N | Y | N | N | N | N |
| 12 Bonior | # | X | # | ? | ? | ? | ? | ? |
| 13 Collins | Y | N | Y | Y | N | N | Y | Y |
| 14 Hertel | Y | N | Y | Y | N | N | Y | Y |
| 15 Ford | Y | N | Y | Y | N | N | N | Y |
| 16 Dingell | Y | N | Y | Y | N | N | N | Y |
| 17 Levin | Y | N | Y | Y | N | N | Y | Y |
| 18 ***Broomfield*** | N | ? | ? | Y | Y | ? | ? | N |
| **MINNESOTA** | | | | | | | | |
| 1 Penny | Y | N | Y | Y | Y | Y | Y | Y |
| 2 ***Weber*** | N | Y | N | Y | N | Y | Y | N |
| 3 ***Ramstad*** | N | N | Y | N | Y | Y | Y | Y |
| 4 Vento | Y | N | Y | Y | N | N | Y | Y |
| 5 Sabo | Y | N | Y | Y | N | N | Y | N |
| 6 Sikorski | Y | N | Y | Y | N | N | Y | Y |
| 7 Peterson | Y | N | Y | Y | N | N | N | Y |
| 8 Oberstar | Y | N | Y | Y | N | N | Y | Y |
| **MISSISSIPPI** | | | | | | | | |
| 1 Whitten | Y | N | Y | Y | N | N | N | N |
| 2 Espy | Y | N | Y | ? | N | N | Y | Y |
| 3 Montgomery | Y | N | Y | Y | N | N | N | N |
| 4 Parker | Y | N | Y | Y | N | N | N | Y |
| 5 Taylor | Y | N | Y | Y | N | N | N | N |
| **MISSOURI** | | | | | | | | |
| 1 Clay | Y | N | Y | Y | N | N | Y | Y |
| 2 Horn | Y | N | Y | Y | N | N | Y | Y |
| 3 Gephardt | Y | N | Y | Y | N | N | N | N |
| 4 Skelton | Y | N | Y | Y | N | N | N | Y |
| 5 Wheat | Y | N | Y | Y | N | N | Y | Y |
| 6 ***Coleman*** | N | Y | N | Y | N | N | N | N |
| 7 ***Hancock*** | N | Y | N | N | Y | Y | N | N |
| 8 ***Emerson*** | N | Y | N | Y | N | N | N | N |
| 9 Volkmer | ? | N | N | Y | N | N | N | N |
| **MONTANA** | | | | | | | | |
| 1 Williams | Y | N | Y | Y | N | N | N | Y |
| 2 ***Marlenee*** | ? | N | N | Y | Y | Y | Y | Y |
| **NEBRASKA** | | | | | | | | |
| 1 ***Bereuter*** | N | Y | N | N | N | N | N | N |
| 2 Hoagland | Y | N | Y | Y | N | N | N | # |
| 3 ***Barrett*** | N | Y | N | Y | Y | Y | N | N |
| **NEVADA** | | | | | | | | |
| 1 Bilbray | Y | N | Y | N | N | N | N | N |
| 2 ***Vucanovich*** | N | Y | N | N | N | N | N | N |
| **NEW HAMPSHIRE** | | | | | | | | |
| 1 ***Zeliff*** | N | N | N | N | Y | Y | N | N |
| 2 Swett | Y | N | Y | Y | N | N | Y | Y |
| **NEW JERSEY** | | | | | | | | |
| 1 Andrews | Y | N | Y | Y | N | N | Y | Y |
| 2 Hughes | Y | N | Y | Y | N | N | Y | Y |
| 3 Pallone | Y | N | Y | Y | N | N | Y | Y |
| 4 ***Smith*** | N | Y | Y | Y | N | N | N | N |
| 5 ***Roukema*** | N | N | N | Y | N | N | Y | Y |
| 6 Dwyer | Y | N | Y | Y | N | N | N | N |
| 7 ***Rinaldo*** | N | N | Y | Y | N | N | N | N |
| 8 Roe | Y | N | Y | Y | N | N | N | N |
| 9 Torricelli | Y | N | Y | Y | N | N | N | N |
| 10 Payne | Y | N | Y | Y | N | N | Y | Y |
| 11 ***Gallo*** | N | Y | N | Y | N | N | N | N |
| 12 ***Zimmer*** | N | N | Y | N | Y | Y | N | N |
| 13 ***Saxton*** | N | Y | N | Y | N | N | N | N |
| 14 Guarini | Y | N | Y | Y | N | Y | Y | Y |
| **NEW MEXICO** | | | | | | | | |
| 1 ***Schiff*** | N | Y | N | Y | N | Y | N | N |
| 2 ***Skeen*** | N | Y | N | N | N | N | N | N |
| 3 Richardson | Y | N | Y | Y | N | N | Y | Y |
| **NEW YORK** | | | | | | | | |
| 1 Hochbrueckner | Y | N | Y | Y | N | N | N | Y |
| 2 Downey | Y | N | Y | Y | N | N | Y | Y |
| 3 Mrazek | Y | N | Y | Y | N | N | Y | Y |
| 4 ***Lent*** | N | Y | N | Y | N | N | N | N |
| 5 ***McGrath*** | N | Y | Y | Y | N | N | N | N |
| 6 Flake | Y | N | Y | Y | N | N | Y | N |
| 7 Ackerman | Y | ? | ? | Y | N | N | Y | Y |
| 8 Scheuer | Y | N | Y | Y | N | N | Y | Y |
| 9 Manton | Y | N | Y | Y | N | N | N | Y |
| 10 Schumer | Y | N | Y | Y | N | N | N | ? |
| 11 Towns | Y | N | Y | Y | N | N | Y | Y |
| 12 Owens | Y | N | Y | Y | N | N | Y | Y |
| 13 Solarz | Y | N | Y | Y | N | N | Y | Y |
| 14 ***Molinari*** | N | Y | Y | Y | N | Y | N | Y |
| 15 ***Green*** | N | N | Y | Y | N | N | N | N |
| 16 Rangel | Y | N | Y | Y | N | N | Y | N |
| 17 Weiss | Y | N | Y | Y | N | N | Y | Y |
| 18 Serrano | Y | N | Y | Y | N | N | Y | Y |
| 19 Engel | Y | N | Y | Y | N | N | Y | Y |
| 20 Lowey | Y | N | Y | Y | N | N | Y | Y |
| 21 ***Fish*** | N | N | Y | Y | N | N | Y | N |
| 22 ***Gilman*** | Y | N | Y | Y | N | N | Y | N |
| 23 McNulty | Y | N | Y | Y | N | N | N | N |
| 24 ***Solomon*** | N | Y | N | Y | Y | Y | N | Y |
| 25 ***Boehlert*** | Y | N | Y | N | N | N | Y | Y |
| 26 ***Martin*** | N | Y | X | Y | ? | N | N | N |
| 27 ***Walsh*** | Y | N | Y | Y | N | N | N | N |
| 28 McHugh | Y | N | Y | Y | N | N | N | N |
| 29 ***Horton*** | Y | N | Y | Y | N | N | N | N |
| 30 Slaughter | Y | N | Y | Y | N | N | Y | Y |
| 31 ***Paxon*** | N | Y | N | Y | Y | Y | N | N |
| 32 LaFalce | Y | N | Y | Y | N | N | N | Y |
| 33 Nowak | Y | N | Y | Y | N | N | N | Y |
| 34 ***Houghton*** | ? | Y | N | Y | N | N | N | N |
| **NORTH CAROLINA** | | | | | | | | |
| 1 Jones | Y | N | Y | Y | N | N | N | N |
| 2 Valentine | Y | N | N | Y | N | N | N | N |
| 3 Lancaster | Y | Y | # | Y | N | N | Y | Y |
| 4 Price | Y | N | Y | Y | N | N | N | N |
| 5 Neal | Y | N | Y | Y | N | N | N | N |
| 6 ***Coble*** | N | N | N | Y | Y | Y | Y | Y |
| 7 Rose | Y | N | Y | Y | N | N | N | N |
| 8 Hefner | ? | ? | ? | ? | ? | ? | ? | ? |
| 9 ***McMillan*** | N | Y | N | Y | Y | Y | N | Y |
| 10 ***Ballenger*** | N | Y | N | Y | Y | Y | N | N |
| 11 ***Taylor*** | N | N | N | Y | Y | Y | N | N |
| **NORTH DAKOTA** | | | | | | | | |
| AL Dorgan | Y | N | Y | Y | N | N | N | Y |
| **OHIO** | | | | | | | | |
| 1 Luken | Y | N | Y | Y | N | Y | Y | Y |
| 2 ***Gradison*** | N | Y | N | Y | Y | Y | N | N |
| 3 Hall | Y | N | Y | Y | N | N | Y | Y |
| 4 ***Oxley*** | N | N | N | Y | Y | Y | N | N |
| 5 ***Gillmor*** | N | Y | N | Y | Y | N | N | N |
| 6 ***McEwen*** | N | Y | N | Y | N | Y | N | N |
| 7 ***Hobson*** | N | Y | N | Y | Y | Y | N | N |
| 8 ***Boehner*** | N | Y | N | Y | N | Y | N | N |
| 9 Kaptur | ? | N | Y | Y | N | N | N | N |
| 10 ***Miller*** | N | Y | N | Y | Y | Y | N | N |
| 11 Eckart | Y | N | Y | Y | N | N | N | Y |
| 12 ***Kasich*** | N | Y | N | Y | N | Y | N | N |
| 13 Pease | Y | N | Y | Y | N | N | Y | Y |
| 14 Sawyer | Y | N | Y | Y | N | N | Y | Y |
| 15 ***Wylie*** | N | Y | N | Y | Y | Y | N | N |
| 16 ***Regula*** | N | Y | N | Y | N | N | Y | N |
| 17 Traficant | Y | N | Y | Y | N | N | N | N |
| 18 Applegate | Y | Y | Y | Y | N | N | N | N |
| 19 Feighan | Y | N | Y | Y | N | N | Y | N |
| 20 Oakar | Y | N | Y | Y | N | N | N | N |
| 21 Stokes | Y | N | Y | Y | N | N | Y | Y |
| **OKLAHOMA** | | | | | | | | |
| 1 ***Inhofe*** | N | Y | N | Y | Y | N | N | N |
| 2 Synar | Y | N | Y | Y | N | N | Y | Y |
| 3 Brewster | Y | N | N | Y | N | N | Y | Y |
| 4 McCurdy | Y | N | Y | Y | Y | N | Y | N |
| 5 ***Edwards*** | N | Y | N | Y | N | ? | N | N |
| 6 English | Y | N | Y | Y | N | N | Y | Y |
| **OREGON** | | | | | | | | |
| 1 AuCoin | Y | N | Y | Y | N | N | Y | Y |
| 2 ***Smith*** | N | Y | N | Y | N | Y | N | N |
| 3 Wyden | Y | N | Y | Y | N | N | Y | Y |
| 4 DeFazio | Y | N | Y | Y | N | N | Y | Y |
| 5 Kopetski | Y | N | Y | Y | N | N | Y | Y |
| **PENNSYLVANIA** | | | | | | | | |
| 1 Foglietta | Y | N | Y | Y | N | N | Y | Y |
| 2 Blackwell | Y | N | Y | Y | N | N | Y | Y |
| 3 Borski | Y | N | Y | Y | N | N | Y | Y |
| 4 Kolter | Y | N | Y | Y | N | N | N | N |
| 5 ***Schulze*** | N | Y | N | Y | Y | Y | N | N |
| 6 Yatron | Y | N | Y | Y | N | N | N | N |
| 7 ***Weldon*** | N | Y | N | Y | Y | Y | N | N |
| 8 Kostmayer | Y | N | Y | Y | N | N | Y | Y |
| 9 ***Shuster*** | N | Y | N | Y | N | N | N | N |
| 10 ***McDade*** | N | Y | N | Y | N | N | N | N |
| 11 Kanjorski | Y | N | Y | Y | N | N | N | Y |
| 12 Murtha | Y | N | Y | Y | N | N | N | N |
| 13 ***Coughlin*** | N | Y | N | Y | N | N | N | N |
| 14 Coyne | Y | N | Y | Y | N | N | N | Y |
| 15 ***Ritter*** | N | Y | N | N | Y | Y | N | N |
| 16 ***Walker*** | N | Y | N | Y | Y | Y | N | N |
| 17 ***Gekas*** | N | Y | N | N | Y | Y | N | N |
| 18 ***Santorum*** | N | Y | Y | Y | Y | Y | Y | Y |
| 19 ***Goodling*** | N | Y | N | Y | Y | N | N | N |
| 20 Gaydos | Y | N | Y | Y | N | N | ? | Y |
| 21 ***Ridge*** | N | N | N | N | N | Y | ? | N |
| 22 Murphy | Y | N | Y | Y | N | N | Y | N |
| 23 ***Clinger*** | N | Y | N | Y | N | N | N | N |
| **RHODE ISLAND** | | | | | | | | |
| 1 ***Machtley*** | N | N | Y | Y | N | N | Y | Y |
| 2 Reed | Y | N | Y | Y | N | N | Y | Y |
| **SOUTH CAROLINA** | | | | | | | | |
| 1 ***Ravenel*** | N | Y | N | Y | Y | N | N | N |
| 2 ***Spence*** | N | Y | N | Y | Y | Y | N | N |
| 3 Derrick | Y | N | Y | Y | N | N | N | N |
| 4 Patterson | Y | N | Y | Y | Y | N | N | Y |
| 5 Spratt | Y | N | Y | Y | N | N | N | Y |
| 6 Tallon | Y | N | Y | Y | N | N | N | N |
| **SOUTH DAKOTA** | | | | | | | | |
| AL Johnson | Y | N | Y | Y | N | N | N | N |
| **TENNESSEE** | | | | | | | | |
| 1 ***Quillen*** | X | # | X | # | ? | ? | ? | X |
| 2 ***Duncan*** | N | Y | N | N | Y | Y | N | Y |
| 3 Lloyd | Y | N | Y | Y | N | N | N | N |
| 4 Cooper | Y | N | Y | Y | Y | N | N | N |
| 5 Clement | Y | N | Y | Y | Y | N | Y | Y |
| 6 Gordon | Y | N | Y | Y | N | N | N | N |
| 7 ***Sundquist*** | N | Y | N | Y | Y | Y | N | N |
| 8 Tanner | Y | N | Y | Y | Y | Y | N | Y |
| 9 Ford | Y | N | Y | Y | N | ? | N | Y |
| **TEXAS** | | | | | | | | |
| 1 Chapman | Y | N | Y | Y | N | N | N | N |
| 2 Wilson | Y | N | Y | Y | N | N | N | N |
| 3 ***Johnson*** | N | Y | N | Y | N | N | N | N |
| 4 Hall | Y | N | Y | Y | N | N | N | N |
| 5 Bryant | Y | ? | ? | Y | N | N | N | N |
| 6 ***Barton*** | N | Y | N | Y | N | N | N | N |
| 7 ***Archer*** | N | Y | N | Y | Y | Y | N | N |
| 8 ***Fields*** | N | Y | N | Y | Y | N | N | N |
| 9 Brooks | Y | N | Y | Y | N | N | N | N |
| 10 Pickle | Y | N | Y | Y | N | N | N | N |
| 11 Edwards | Y | N | Y | Y | N | N | Y | Y |
| 12 Geren | Y | N | Y | Y | N | N | N | N |
| 13 Sarpalius | Y | N | Y | Y | N | N | N | N |
| 14 Laughlin | Y | N | Y | Y | N | N | N | N |
| 15 de la Garza | Y | N | Y | Y | N | N | N | Y |
| 16 Coleman | Y | N | Y | Y | N | N | N | N |
| 17 Stenholm | Y | N | N | Y | N | N | N | Y |
| 18 Washington | Y | N | Y | Y | N | N | Y | Y |
| 19 ***Combest*** | N | Y | N | Y | Y | N | N | N |
| 20 Gonzalez | Y | N | Y | Y | N | N | N | N |
| 21 ***Smith*** | N | Y | N | Y | Y | Y | N | N |
| 22 ***DeLay*** | N | Y | N | N | Y | N | N | N |
| 23 Bustamante | Y | N | Y | Y | N | N | N | N |
| 24 Frost | Y | N | Y | Y | N | N | N | N |
| 25 Andrews | Y | N | Y | Y | Y | N | N | N |
| 26 ***Armey*** | N | Y | N | Y | Y | Y | N | N |
| 27 Ortiz | Y | N | Y | Y | N | N | N | N |
| **UTAH** | | | | | | | | |
| 1 ***Hansen*** | N | Y | N | Y | Y | N | N | N |
| 2 Owens | Y | ? | ? | Y | N | N | Y | Y |
| 3 Orton | Y | N | Y | Y | N | N | Y | Y |
| **VERMONT** | | | | | | | | |
| AL *Sanders* | Y | N | Y | Y | N | N | Y | Y |
| **VIRGINIA** | | | | | | | | |
| 1 ***Bateman*** | N | N | N | Y | N | N | N | N |
| 2 Pickett | Y | N | N | Y | N | N | N | N |
| 3 ***Bliley*** | N | Y | N | Y | N | N | N | N |
| 4 Sisisky | Y | N | Y | Y | N | N | N | N |
| 5 Payne | Y | N | Y | Y | N | N | N | Y |
| 6 Olin | Y | N | N | Y | Y | N | N | N |
| 7 ***Allen*** | N | N | N | Y | Y | Y | N | Y |
| 8 Moran | Y | N | Y | Y | N | N | N | N |
| 9 Boucher | Y | N | Y | Y | N | N | N | N |
| 10 ***Wolf*** | N | Y | N | Y | N | N | N | N |
| **WASHINGTON** | | | | | | | | |
| 1 ***Miller*** | N | N | Y | ? | Y | Y | N | N |
| 2 Swift | Y | N | Y | Y | N | N | N | Y |
| 3 Unsoeld | Y | N | Y | Y | N | N | Y | Y |
| 4 ***Morrison*** | Y | N | Y | Y | N | N | N | N |
| 5 Foley | | | | | | | | |
| 6 Dicks | Y | N | Y | Y | N | N | Y | N |
| 7 McDermott | Y | N | Y | Y | N | N | Y | Y |
| 8 ***Chandler*** | N | N | Y | Y | Y | Y | N | N |
| **WEST VIRGINIA** | | | | | | | | |
| 1 Mollohan | Y | N | Y | Y | N | N | N | N |
| 2 Staggers | Y | N | Y | Y | Y | N | Y | Y |
| 3 Wise | Y | N | Y | Y | N | N | Y | N |
| 4 Rahall | Y | N | Y | Y | N | N | Y | N |
| **WISCONSIN** | | | | | | | | |
| 1 Aspin | Y | N | Y | Y | N | N | N | Y |
| 2 ***Klug*** | N | N | Y | Y | Y | Y | Y | Y |
| 3 ***Gunderson*** | N | Y | N | Y | N | N | N | Y |
| 4 Kleczka | Y | N | Y | Y | N | N | N | Y |
| 5 Moody | Y | N | Y | Y | N | Y | Y | Y |
| 6 ***Petri*** | N | Y | N | Y | N | Y | Y | Y |
| 7 Obey | Y | N | Y | Y | ? | N | Y | Y |
| 8 ***Roth*** | N | Y | N | Y | Y | Y | Y | Y |
| 9 ***Sensenbrenner*** | N | Y | N | N | Y | Y | Y | Y |
| **WYOMING** | | | | | | | | |
| AL ***Thomas*** | N | Y | N | Y | Y | N | N | Y |

Southern states - Ala., Ark., Fla., Ga., Ky., La., Miss., N.C., Okla., S.C., Tenn., Texas, Va.
Omitted votes are quorum calls, which CQ does not include in its vote charts.

## KEY

- Y  Voted for (yea).
- #  Paired for.
- +  Announced for.
- N  Voted against (nay).
- X  Paired against.
- −  Announced against.
- P  Voted "present."
- C  Voted "present" to avoid possible conflict of interest.
- ?  Did not vote or otherwise make a position known.

Democrats  **Republicans**
*Independent*

**201. HR 5373. Fiscal 1993 Energy and Water Appropriations/Superconducting Super Collider.** Eckart, D-Ohio, amendment to cut $450 million of the $483.7 million provided for the superconducting super collider, leaving approximately $34 million to shut down the project. Adopted 232-181: R 79-79; D 152-102 (ND 126-49, SD 26-53); I 1-0, June 17, 1992. A "nay" was a vote in support of the president's position.

**202. HR 5373. Fiscal 1993 Energy and Water Appropriations/Departmental Administration.** Penny, D-Minn., amendment to cut funding for the administrative account of the Department of Energy by 5 percent, or about $21 million. Adopted 404-12: R 151-9; D 252-3 (ND 173-1, SD 79-2); I 1-0, June 17, 1992.

**203. HR 5373. Fiscal 1993 Energy and Water Appropriations/Passage.** Passage of the bill to provide $21.3 billion in new budget authority for energy and water development for fiscal 1993. The administration requested $22,419,288,000. Passed 365-51: R 125-36; D 240-14 (ND 166-8, SD 74-6); I 0-1, June 17, 1992.

**204. Procedural Motion.** Approval of the House Journal of Wednesday, June 17. Approved 284-107: R 52-102; D 231-5 (ND 158-5, SD 73-0); I 1-0, June 18, 1992.

**205. H Con Res 192. Joint Committee on the Organization of Congress.** Adoption of the concurrent resolution to create a temporary House-Senate committee to study and recommend reforms in the operations of Congress by Dec. 31, 1993. The resolution also authorized an interim report to the House no later than Nov. 6, 1992. Adopted 412-4: R 161-0; D 250-4 (ND 174-2, SD 76-2); I 1-0, June 18, 1992.

**206. HR 5132. Fiscal 1992 Disaster Relief Supplemental Appropriations/Conference Report.** Adoption of the conference report to provide $1,075,510,000 in new budget authority in fiscal 1992 for disaster assistance and loans to respond to the Los Angeles riots and Chicago flooding. The $1.1 billion also included $500 million for the nationwide Summer Youth Employment program. The funds were designated as emergency spending, thus exempt from the spending caps of the 1990 Budget Enforcement Act, but none of the money could be spent unless the president concurred in the emergency designation. Adopted 249-168: R 43-117; D 205-51 (ND 158-17, SD 47-34); I 1-0, June 18, 1992. A "yea" was a vote in support of the president's position.

**207. HR 5055. Coast Guard Authorization.** Passage of the bill to authorize $3.6 billion for the Coast Guard in fiscal 1993 for operation and maintenance, acquisition, construction and improvements, research and development, and other purposes. Passed 304-22: R 104-21; D 199-1 (ND 140-1, SD 59-0); I 1-0, June 22, 1992. A 'nay' was a vote in support of the president's position.

**208. Procedural Motion.** Approval of the House Journal of Thursday, June 18. Approved 229-100: R 34-96; D 194-4 (ND 136-3, SD 58-1); I 1-0, June 22, 1992.

| | 201 | 202 | 203 | 204 | 205 | 206 | 207 | 208 |
|---|---|---|---|---|---|---|---|---|
| **ALABAMA** | | | | | | | | |
| 1 *Callahan* | N | Y | Y | Y | Y | N | Y | Y |
| 2 *Dickinson* | N | Y | Y | ? | Y | N | Y | N |
| 3 Browder | N | Y | Y | Y | Y | N | Y | Y |
| 4 Bevill | N | Y | Y | Y | Y | Y | Y | Y |
| 5 Cramer | N | Y | Y | Y | Y | N | Y | Y |
| 6 Erdreich | N | Y | Y | Y | Y | N | ? | ? |
| 7 Harris | N | Y | Y | Y | Y | N | ? | ? |
| **ALASKA** | | | | | | | | |
| AL *Young* | N | Y | Y | ? | ? | ? | Y | N |
| **ARIZONA** | | | | | | | | |
| 1 *Rhodes* | N | Y | Y | N | Y | N | ? | ? |
| 2 Pastor | Y | Y | Y | Y | Y | Y | Y | Y |
| 3 *Stump* | N | Y | N | N | Y | N | N | N |
| 4 *Kyl* | N | Y | Y | N | Y | N | Y | N |
| 5 *Kolbe* | N | Y | Y | N | Y | N | Y | N |
| **ARKANSAS** | | | | | | | | |
| 1 Alexander | N | Y | Y | ? | ? | Y | ? | ? |
| 2 Thornton | N | Y | Y | Y | Y | Y | Y | Y |
| 3 *Hammerschmidt* | N | Y | Y | Y | Y | N | Y | Y |
| 4 Anthony | N | Y | Y | ? | Y | Y | ? | ? |
| **CALIFORNIA** | | | | | | | | |
| 1 *Riggs* | N | Y | Y | N | Y | N | ? | ? |
| 2 *Herger* | Y | Y | Y | N | Y | N | ? | ? |
| 3 Matsui | N | Y | Y | Y | Y | Y | Y | Y |
| 4 Fazio | N | Y | Y | Y | Y | Y | Y | Y |
| 5 Pelosi | Y | Y | Y | Y | Y | Y | Y | Y |
| 6 Boxer | Y | Y | Y | Y | Y | Y | ? | ? |
| 7 Miller | Y | Y | Y | Y | Y | Y | Y | Y |
| 8 Dellums | Y | Y | Y | Y | Y | Y | Y | Y |
| 9 Stark | Y | Y | N | Y | Y | Y | ? | ? |
| 10 Edwards | Y | Y | Y | Y | Y | Y | Y | Y |
| 11 Lantos | Y | Y | Y | Y | Y | Y | Y | Y |
| 12 *Campbell* | Y | Y | N | N | Y | N | Y | N |
| 13 Mineta | N | Y | Y | Y | Y | Y | Y | Y |
| 14 *Doolittle* | Y | Y | Y | N | Y | N | N | N |
| 15 Condit | Y | Y | Y | Y | Y | Y | Y | Y |
| 16 Panetta | Y | Y | Y | Y | Y | Y | Y | Y |
| 17 Dooley | Y | Y | Y | Y | Y | Y | Y | Y |
| 18 Lehman | Y | Y | Y | Y | Y | Y | ? | ? |
| 19 *Lagomarsino* | N | Y | N | Y | N | N | Y | N |
| 20 *Thomas* | Y | Y | N | N | N | N | Y | N |
| 21 *Gallegly* | N | Y | N | Y | N | N | ? | ? |
| 22 *Moorhead* | N | Y | N | N | Y | N | Y | N |
| 23 Beilenson | Y | Y | Y | ? | Y | Y | Y | Y |
| 24 Waxman | Y | Y | Y | Y | Y | Y | Y | Y |
| 25 Roybal | Y | Y | Y | Y | Y | Y | Y | Y |
| 26 Berman | Y | Y | Y | Y | Y | Y | Y | Y |
| 27 Levine | N | Y | Y | Y | Y | Y | ? | ? |
| 28 Dixon | N | Y | Y | Y | Y | Y | Y | Y |
| 29 Waters | Y | Y | Y | Y | Y | Y | Y | Y |
| 30 Martinez | Y | Y | Y | Y | Y | Y | Y | Y |
| 31 Dymally | ? | ? | ? | Y | Y | Y | ? | ? |
| 32 Anderson | N | Y | Y | Y | Y | Y | ? | ? |
| 33 *Dreier* | N | Y | N | Y | N | N | Y | N |
| 34 Torres | N | Y | Y | Y | Y | Y | ? | ? |
| 35 *Lewis* | Y | N | Y | N | Y | N | Y | Y |
| 36 Brown | N | Y | Y | Y | Y | Y | ? | ? |
| 37 *McCandless* | Y | Y | Y | N | Y | N | Y | N |
| 38 *Dornan* | N | Y | Y | ? | Y | N | Y | N |
| 39 *Dannemeyer* | N | Y | N | N | Y | N | N | N |
| 40 *Cox* | N | Y | N | Y | N | N | Y | N |
| 41 *Lowery* | Y | N | Y | N | Y | Y | ? | ? |
| 42 *Rohrabacher* | Y | Y | Y | N | Y | N | Y | N |
| 43 *Packard* | N | Y | Y | Y | Y | N | Y | Y |
| 44 *Cunningham* | N | Y | Y | N | Y | N | Y | Y |
| 45 *Hunter* | N | Y | Y | ? | Y | N | Y | N |
| **COLORADO** | | | | | | | | |
| 1 Schroeder | Y | Y | Y | N | Y | Y | Y | Y |
| 2 Skaggs | N | Y | Y | Y | Y | Y | Y | Y |
| 3 Campbell | Y | Y | Y | Y | Y | Y | ? | ? |
| 4 *Allard* | N | Y | N | N | Y | N | N | N |
| 5 *Hefley* | Y | Y | N | Y | N | N | Y | N |
| 6 *Schaefer* | N | Y | N | Y | N | N | Y | N |
| **CONNECTICUT** | | | | | | | | |
| 1 Kennelly | Y | Y | Y | Y | Y | Y | ? | ? |
| 2 Gejdenson | Y | Y | Y | Y | Y | Y | Y | Y |
| 3 DeLauro | Y | Y | Y | Y | Y | Y | Y | Y |
| 4 *Shays* | Y | Y | Y | N | Y | N | Y | N |
| 5 *Franks* | N | Y | N | Y | N | N | Y | N |
| 6 *Johnson* | Y | Y | Y | N | Y | Y | ? | ? |
| **DELAWARE** | | | | | | | | |
| AL Carper | Y | Y | Y | Y | Y | N | ? | ? |
| **FLORIDA** | | | | | | | | |
| 1 Hutto | Y | Y | Y | Y | Y | Y | Y | Y |
| 2 Peterson | Y | Y | Y | Y | Y | N | Y | Y |
| 3 Bennett | Y | Y | Y | Y | Y | Y | Y | Y |
| 4 *James* | Y | Y | Y | N | Y | N | N | N |
| 5 *McCollum* | Y | Y | N | Y | N | N | ? | ? |
| 6 *Stearns* | Y | Y | N | N | Y | N | Y | N |
| 7 Gibbons | N | Y | Y | Y | Y | Y | ? | ? |
| 8 *Young* | N | Y | Y | Y | Y | N | Y | Y |
| 9 *Bilirakis* | N | Y | N | Y | N | N | N | N |
| 10 *Ireland* | N | Y | N | Y | Y | N | N | N |
| 11 Bacchus | N | Y | Y | Y | Y | N | ? | ? |
| 12 *Lewis* | Y | N | N | Y | N | N | N | N |
| 13 *Goss* | Y | N | N | Y | N | N | N | N |
| 14 Johnston | Y | Y | Y | Y | Y | Y | ? | ? |
| 15 *Shaw* | Y | Y | Y | Y | Y | N | Y | Y |
| 16 Smith | Y | Y | Y | Y | Y | Y | ? | ? |
| 17 Lehman | N | Y | Y | Y | Y | Y | Y | Y |
| 18 *Ros−Lehtinen* | Y | Y | Y | Y | Y | Y | Y | N |
| 19 Fascell | N | Y | Y | Y | Y | Y | Y | Y |
| **GEORGIA** | | | | | | | | |
| 1 Thomas | N | Y | Y | Y | Y | Y | Y | Y |
| 2 Hatcher | ? | Y | Y | Y | Y | Y | ? | ? |
| 3 Ray | N | Y | Y | ? | N | Y | ? | ? |
| 4 Jones | # | ? | ? | ? | ? | ? | ? | ? |
| 5 Lewis | Y | Y | Y | Y | Y | Y | Y | Y |
| 6 *Gingrich* | N | Y | Y | N | Y | Y | ? | ? |
| 7 *Darden* | N | Y | Y | N | Y | Y | Y | Y |
| 8 Rowland | N | Y | Y | Y | N | Y | ? | ? |
| 9 Jenkins | N | Y | Y | Y | ? | Y | Y | Y |
| 10 Barnard | N | Y | Y | Y | Y | Y | Y | Y |
| **HAWAII** | | | | | | | | |
| 1 Abercrombie | Y | Y | Y | Y | N | Y | Y | Y |
| 2 Mink | Y | Y | Y | Y | Y | Y | Y | Y |
| **IDAHO** | | | | | | | | |
| 1 LaRocco | N | Y | Y | Y | Y | Y | Y | Y |
| 2 Stallings | N | Y | Y | Y | Y | Y | ? | ? |
| **ILLINOIS** | | | | | | | | |
| 1 Hayes | Y | Y | Y | Y | Y | Y | Y | Y |
| 2 Savage | Y | Y | N | ? | Y | Y | ? | ? |
| 3 Russo | Y | Y | Y | Y | Y | Y | Y | Y |
| 4 Sangmeister | Y | Y | Y | Y | Y | Y | Y | Y |
| 5 Lipinski | Y | Y | Y | Y | Y | Y | Y | Y |
| 6 *Hyde* | N | Y | Y | Y | ? | Y | Y | Y |
| 7 Collins | Y | Y | Y | Y | Y | Y | Y | Y |
| 8 Rostenkowski | Y | Y | Y | Y | Y | Y | ? | ? |
| 9 Yates | Y | Y | Y | Y | Y | Y | Y | Y |
| 10 *Porter* | Y | Y | Y | N | Y | N | Y | Y |
| 11 Annunzio | Y | Y | Y | Y | Y | Y | Y | Y |
| 12 *Crane* | ? | ? | X | ? | ? | ? | N | N |
| 13 *Fawell* | N | Y | N | N | Y | N | N | N |
| 14 *Hastert* | Y | Y | Y | N | Y | N | ? | ? |
| 15 *Ewing* | Y | N | Y | N | Y | N | N | N |
| 16 Cox | Y | Y | Y | Y | Y | Y | Y | Y |
| 17 Evans | Y | Y | Y | Y | Y | Y | Y | Y |
| 18 *Michel* | ? | Y | Y | N | Y | Y | ? | N |
| 19 Bruce | Y | Y | Y | Y | Y | Y | Y | Y |
| 20 Durbin | Y | Y | Y | Y | Y | Y | Y | Y |
| 21 Costello | Y | Y | Y | Y | Y | Y | Y | Y |
| 22 Poshard | Y | Y | Y | Y | Y | Y | Y | Y |
| **INDIANA** | | | | | | | | |
| 1 Visclosky | Y | Y | Y | Y | Y | N | Y | Y |
| 2 Sharp | Y | Y | Y | Y | Y | Y | Y | Y |
| 3 Roemer | N | Y | Y | Y | Y | N | Y | Y |

ND Northern Democrats   SD Southern Democrats

| | 201 | 202 | 203 | 204 | 205 | 206 | 207 | 208 |
|---|---|---|---|---|---|---|---|---|
| 4 Long | Y | Y | Y | Y | Y | Y | Y | Y |
| 5 Jontz | Y | Y | N | Y | Y | Y | Y | Y |
| 6 ***Burton*** | Y | Y | N | N | Y | N | N | N |
| 7 ***Myers*** | N | N | Y | Y | Y | N | Y | Y |
| 8 McCloskey | N | Y | Y | Y | Y | Y | Y | Y |
| 9 Hamilton | Y | Y | Y | Y | Y | Y | Y | Y |
| 10 Jacobs | Y | Y | N | N | Y | Y | Y | N |
| **IOWA** | | | | | | | | |
| 1 ***Leach*** | Y | Y | Y | N | Y | Y | Y | N |
| 2 ***Nussle*** | Y | Y | Y | N | Y | N | N | N |
| 3 Nagle | N | Y | Y | Y | Y | Y | Y | Y |
| 4 Smith | N | Y | Y | Y | Y | Y | Y | Y |
| 5 ***Lightfoot*** | N | Y | Y | N | Y | N | Y | N |
| 6 ***Grandy*** | Y | Y | Y | N | Y | N | N | N |
| **KANSAS** | | | | | | | | |
| 1 ***Roberts*** | Y | Y | N | N | Y | N | ? | ? |
| 2 Slattery | Y | Y | Y | ? | ? | ? | Y | Y |
| 3 ***Meyers*** | Y | Y | Y | N | Y | N | N | N |
| 4 Glickman | Y | Y | Y | ? | ? | ? | Y | Y |
| 5 ***Nichols*** | Y | Y | Y | ? | ? | ? | ? | ? |
| **KENTUCKY** | | | | | | | | |
| 1 Hubbard | ? | ? | ? | ? | ? | ? | Y | Y |
| 2 Natcher | N | Y | Y | Y | Y | Y | Y | Y |
| 3 Mazzoli | N | Y | Y | Y | Y | Y | Y | Y |
| 4 ***Bunning*** | Y | Y | Y | N | Y | N | Y | N |
| 5 ***Rogers*** | N | Y | Y | N | Y | N | ? | ? |
| 6 ***Hopkins*** | N | Y | Y | N | Y | N | Y | N |
| 7 Perkins | N | Y | Y | ? | Y | Y | ? | ? |
| **LOUISIANA** | | | | | | | | |
| 1 ***Livingston*** | N | N | N | N | Y | N | ? | ? |
| 2 Jefferson | Y | Y | Y | Y | Y | Y | Y | Y |
| 3 Tauzin | N | Y | Y | Y | Y | N | Y | Y |
| 4 ***McCrery*** | N | Y | Y | Y | Y | N | Y | N |
| 5 Huckaby | N | Y | Y | Y | Y | N | Y | N |
| 6 ***Baker*** | N | N | N | N | Y | N | Y | N |
| 7 Hayes | N | Y | Y | Y | Y | N | Y | Y |
| 8 ***Holloway*** | N | Y | Y | N | Y | N | Y | N |
| **MAINE** | | | | | | | | |
| 1 Andrews | Y | Y | Y | Y | Y | Y | Y | Y |
| 2 ***Snowe*** | Y | Y | Y | Y | Y | N | Y | Y |
| **MARYLAND** | | | | | | | | |
| 1 ***Gilchrest*** | N | Y | Y | N | Y | Y | Y | N |
| 2 ***Bentley*** | N | Y | Y | N | Y | N | Y | N |
| 3 Cardin | ? | ? | ? | Y | Y | Y | Y | Y |
| 4 McMillen | N | Y | Y | Y | Y | Y | Y | Y |
| 5 Hoyer | N | Y | Y | Y | Y | Y | Y | Y |
| 6 Byron | N | Y | Y | Y | Y | Y | Y | Y |
| 7 Mfume | Y | Y | Y | Y | Y | Y | Y | Y |
| 8 ***Morella*** | Y | Y | Y | Y | Y | Y | Y | N |
| **MASSACHUSETTS** | | | | | | | | |
| 1 Olver | Y | Y | Y | Y | Y | Y | Y | Y |
| 2 Neal | Y | Y | Y | Y | Y | Y | Y | Y |
| 3 Early | Y | Y | Y | Y | Y | Y | Y | Y |
| 4 Frank | Y | Y | Y | Y | Y | Y | Y | Y |
| 5 Atkins | Y | Y | Y | Y | Y | Y | Y | Y |
| 6 Mavroules | N | Y | Y | Y | Y | Y | ? | ? |
| 7 Markey | Y | Y | Y | Y | Y | Y | Y | Y |
| 8 Kennedy | Y | Y | Y | Y | Y | Y | ? | ? |
| 9 Moakley | Y | Y | Y | Y | Y | Y | Y | Y |
| 10 Studds | Y | Y | Y | Y | Y | Y | Y | Y |
| 11 Donnelly | Y | Y | Y | Y | Y | Y | ? | ? |
| **MICHIGAN** | | | | | | | | |
| 1 Conyers | Y | Y | Y | Y | Y | Y | Y | Y |
| 2 ***Pursell*** | N | Y | Y | Y | Y | N | Y | Y |
| 3 Wolpe | Y | Y | Y | Y | Y | Y | Y | Y |
| 4 ***Upton*** | Y | Y | Y | N | Y | Y | Y | N |
| 5 ***Henry*** | Y | Y | Y | N | Y | N | N | N |
| 6 Carr | Y | Y | Y | Y | Y | N | Y | Y |
| 7 Kildee | Y | Y | Y | Y | Y | Y | Y | Y |
| 8 Traxler | ? | ? | ? | ? | ? | ? | ? | ? |
| 9 ***Vander Jagt*** | N | Y | Y | Y | Y | N | Y | Y |
| 10 ***Camp*** | Y | Y | Y | N | Y | N | Y | N |
| 11 ***Davis*** | N | Y | Y | Y | Y | Y | ? | ? |
| 12 Bonior | ? | ? | ? | ? | ? | ? | ? | ? |
| 13 Collins | Y | Y | Y | Y | Y | Y | Y | Y |
| 14 Hertel | N | Y | Y | ? | Y | Y | Y | Y |
| 15 Ford | Y | Y | Y | ? | Y | Y | Y | Y |
| 16 Dingell | Y | Y | Y | Y | Y | Y | Y | Y |
| 17 Levin | Y | Y | Y | Y | Y | Y | Y | Y |
| 18 ***Broomfield*** | ? | ? | ? | Y | Y | N | Y | ? |
| **MINNESOTA** | | | | | | | | |
| 1 Penny | Y | Y | Y | Y | Y | N | Y | Y |
| 2 ***Weber*** | ? | ? | ? | ? | ? | Y | Y | N |
| 3 ***Ramstad*** | Y | Y | N | N | Y | N | N | N |
| 4 Vento | Y | Y | Y | Y | Y | Y | Y | Y |

| | 201 | 202 | 203 | 204 | 205 | 206 | 207 | 208 |
|---|---|---|---|---|---|---|---|---|
| 5 Sabo | Y | Y | Y | Y | Y | Y | Y | Y |
| 6 Sikorski | Y | Y | N | N | Y | Y | Y | N |
| 7 Peterson | Y | Y | Y | Y | Y | N | Y | Y |
| 8 Oberstar | Y | Y | Y | Y | Y | Y | Y | Y |
| **MISSISSIPPI** | | | | | | | | |
| 1 Whitten | N | Y | Y | ? | ? | Y | Y | ? |
| 2 Espy | ? | Y | Y | Y | Y | Y | ? | ? |
| 3 Montgomery | N | Y | Y | Y | Y | N | Y | Y |
| 4 Parker | Y | Y | Y | Y | Y | N | Y | Y |
| 5 Taylor | Y | Y | Y | Y | Y | N | Y | Y |
| **MISSOURI** | | | | | | | | |
| 1 Clay | Y | Y | Y | N | Y | Y | Y | Y |
| 2 Horn | Y | Y | Y | Y | Y | Y | Y | Y |
| 3 Gephardt | N | Y | Y | Y | Y | Y | Y | ? |
| 4 Skelton | N | Y | Y | ? | Y | N | ? | ? |
| 5 Wheat | Y | Y | Y | Y | Y | Y | Y | Y |
| 6 ***Coleman*** | Y | Y | Y | Y | Y | N | Y | Y |
| 7 ***Hancock*** | Y | Y | N | N | Y | N | N | N |
| 8 ***Emerson*** | N | Y | Y | N | Y | N | Y | N |
| 9 Volkmer | N | Y | Y | Y | Y | N | Y | Y |
| **MONTANA** | | | | | | | | |
| 1 Williams | Y | Y | Y | ? | Y | Y | Y | Y |
| 2 ***Marlenee*** | Y | Y | N | N | Y | N | ? | ? |
| **NEBRASKA** | | | | | | | | |
| 1 ***Bereuter*** | Y | Y | Y | N | Y | N | Y | N |
| 2 Hoagland | Y | Y | Y | Y | Y | Y | Y | Y |
| 3 ***Barrett*** | Y | Y | Y | N | Y | N | Y | N |
| **NEVADA** | | | | | | | | |
| 1 Bilbray | Y | Y | N | Y | Y | Y | Y | Y |
| 2 ***Vucanovich*** | N | Y | N | N | Y | Y | Y | N |
| **NEW HAMPSHIRE** | | | | | | | | |
| 1 ***Zeliff*** | Y | Y | N | ? | Y | Y | Y | N |
| 2 Swett | Y | Y | Y | Y | Y | N | Y | Y |
| **NEW JERSEY** | | | | | | | | |
| 1 Andrews | N | Y | Y | Y | Y | Y | Y | Y |
| 2 Hughes | Y | Y | Y | Y | Y | N | Y | Y |
| 3 Pallone | Y | Y | Y | Y | Y | Y | Y | Y |
| 4 ***Smith*** | N | Y | Y | Y | Y | Y | Y | Y |
| 5 ***Roukema*** | Y | Y | Y | N | Y | N | ? | ? |
| 6 Dwyer | N | Y | Y | Y | Y | Y | Y | Y |
| 7 ***Rinaldo*** | Y | Y | Y | Y | Y | Y | Y | Y |
| 8 Roe | N | Y | Y | Y | Y | Y | Y | Y |
| 9 Torricelli | N | Y | Y | Y | Y | Y | Y | Y |
| 10 Payne | Y | Y | Y | Y | Y | Y | ? | ? |
| 11 ***Gallo*** | N | Y | Y | N | Y | Y | ? | ? |
| 12 ***Zimmer*** | Y | Y | Y | ? | Y | N | Y | N |
| 13 ***Saxton*** | Y | Y | Y | N | Y | N | Y | N |
| 14 Guarini | Y | Y | Y | Y | ? | Y | Y | Y |
| **NEW MEXICO** | | | | | | | | |
| 1 ***Schiff*** | N | Y | Y | N | Y | Y | Y | Y |
| 2 ***Skeen*** | N | N | N | Y | Y | Y | Y | Y |
| 3 Richardson | N | Y | Y | Y | Y | Y | Y | Y |
| **NEW YORK** | | | | | | | | |
| 1 Hochbrueckner | N | Y | Y | Y | Y | Y | ? | ? |
| 2 Downey | Y | Y | Y | Y | Y | Y | Y | Y |
| 3 Mrazek | Y | Y | Y | Y | Y | Y | Y | Y |
| 4 ***Lent*** | Y | Y | Y | Y | Y | Y | ? | ? |
| 5 ***McGrath*** | Y | Y | Y | Y | Y | Y | ? | ? |
| 6 Flake | Y | Y | Y | Y | Y | Y | Y | Y |
| 7 Ackerman | Y | Y | Y | Y | Y | Y | ? | ? |
| 8 Scheuer | Y | Y | Y | Y | Y | Y | Y | Y |
| 9 Manton | N | Y | Y | Y | Y | Y | ? | ? |
| 10 Schumer | ? | ? | ? | ? | ? | # | ? | ? |
| 11 Towns | Y | Y | Y | Y | Y | Y | Y | Y |
| 12 Owens | Y | Y | Y | Y | Y | Y | ? | ? |
| 13 Solarz | Y | Y | Y | Y | Y | Y | Y | Y |
| 14 ***Molinari*** | Y | Y | Y | N | Y | N | Y | Y |
| 15 ***Green*** | N | Y | Y | Y | Y | Y | Y | Y |
| 16 Rangel | N | Y | Y | Y | N | Y | Y | Y |
| 17 Weiss | Y | Y | Y | Y | Y | Y | ? | ? |
| 18 Serrano | Y | Y | Y | Y | Y | Y | Y | Y |
| 19 Engel | N | Y | Y | ? | Y | Y | Y | Y |
| 20 Lowey | N | Y | Y | ? | Y | Y | Y | Y |
| 21 ***Fish*** | Y | N | Y | Y | Y | Y | Y | Y |
| 22 ***Gilman*** | Y | Y | Y | Y | Y | Y | Y | Y |
| 23 McNulty | N | Y | Y | Y | Y | Y | Y | Y |
| 24 ***Solomon*** | Y | Y | N | N | Y | N | N | N |
| 25 ***Boehlert*** | Y | Y | Y | N | Y | Y | Y | N |
| 26 ***Martin*** | Y | Y | Y | N | Y | Y | ? | ? |
| 27 ***Walsh*** | N | Y | Y | Y | Y | Y | Y | N |
| 28 McHugh | N | Y | Y | Y | Y | Y | Y | Y |
| 29 ***Horton*** | Y | Y | Y | Y | Y | Y | Y | Y |
| 30 Slaughter | Y | Y | Y | Y | Y | Y | Y | Y |
| 31 ***Paxon*** | Y | Y | Y | N | Y | N | Y | N |

| | 201 | 202 | 203 | 204 | 205 | 206 | 207 | 208 |
|---|---|---|---|---|---|---|---|---|
| 32 LaFalce | Y | Y | Y | Y | Y | Y | Y | Y |
| 33 Nowak | Y | Y | Y | ? | Y | Y | Y | Y |
| 34 ***Houghton*** | N | Y | Y | Y | Y | Y | ? | ? |
| **NORTH CAROLINA** | | | | | | | | |
| 1 Jones | ? | ? | ? | Y | Y | Y | Y | Y |
| 2 Valentine | Y | Y | Y | Y | Y | N | Y | Y |
| 3 Lancaster | Y | Y | Y | Y | Y | N | Y | Y |
| 4 Price | Y | Y | Y | Y | Y | Y | ? | ? |
| 5 Neal | Y | Y | Y | Y | Y | Y | ? | ? |
| 6 ***Coble*** | Y | Y | N | N | Y | N | Y | N |
| 7 Rose | Y | Y | Y | Y | Y | Y | Y | Y |
| 8 Hefner | ? | ? | ? | ? | ? | ? | ? | ? |
| 9 ***McMillan*** | Y | Y | Y | Y | Y | N | ? | N |
| 10 ***Ballenger*** | Y | Y | Y | N | Y | N | Y | N |
| 11 ***Taylor*** | N | Y | Y | N | Y | N | Y | N |
| **NORTH DAKOTA** | | | | | | | | |
| AL Dorgan | Y | Y | Y | Y | Y | N | N | Y |
| **OHIO** | | | | | | | | |
| 1 Luken | Y | Y | Y | Y | Y | Y | Y | Y |
| 2 ***Gradison*** | Y | Y | Y | Y | Y | N | Y | Y |
| 3 Hall | Y | Y | Y | Y | Y | Y | Y | Y |
| 4 ***Oxley*** | N | Y | N | Y | Y | N | Y | N |
| 5 ***Gillmor*** | Y | Y | Y | Y | Y | N | ? | ? |
| 6 ***McEwen*** | N | Y | Y | N | Y | N | Y | N |
| 7 ***Hobson*** | N | Y | Y | N | Y | N | Y | N |
| 8 ***Boehner*** | N | Y | Y | N | Y | N | Y | N |
| 9 Kaptur | N | Y | Y | Y | Y | Y | Y | Y |
| 10 ***Miller*** | N | Y | Y | N | Y | N | Y | N |
| 11 Eckart | Y | Y | Y | Y | Y | Y | Y | Y |
| 12 ***Kasich*** | N | Y | Y | Y | Y | Y | Y | Y |
| 13 Pease | Y | Y | Y | Y | Y | N | ? | ? |
| 14 Sawyer | Y | Y | Y | Y | Y | Y | Y | Y |
| 15 ***Wylie*** | Y | Y | Y | Y | Y | N | Y | Y |
| 16 ***Regula*** | Y | Y | Y | N | Y | N | Y | N |
| 17 Traficant | N | Y | Y | Y | Y | Y | Y | Y |
| 18 Applegate | Y | Y | Y | Y | Y | N | Y | Y |
| 19 Feighan | Y | Y | Y | ? | Y | ? | ? | ? |
| 20 Oakar | N | Y | Y | Y | Y | Y | Y | Y |
| 21 Stokes | N | Y | Y | Y | Y | Y | Y | Y |
| **OKLAHOMA** | | | | | | | | |
| 1 ***Inhofe*** | Y | Y | Y | N | Y | N | Y | N |
| 2 Synar | Y | Y | Y | Y | Y | Y | ? | ? |
| 3 Brewster | N | Y | N | Y | Y | N | Y | Y |
| 4 McCurdy | Y | Y | Y | Y | Y | N | Y | Y |
| 5 ***Edwards*** | Y | Y | Y | N | Y | N | ? | ? |
| 6 English | Y | Y | Y | Y | Y | Y | Y | Y |
| **OREGON** | | | | | | | | |
| 1 AuCoin | Y | Y | Y | Y | Y | Y | Y | Y |
| 2 ***Smith*** | N | Y | Y | N | Y | N | Y | N |
| 3 Wyden | Y | Y | Y | Y | Y | Y | ? | ? |
| 4 DeFazio | N | Y | Y | Y | Y | Y | ? | ? |
| 5 Kopetski | N | Y | Y | Y | Y | Y | + | + |
| **PENNSYLVANIA** | | | | | | | | |
| 1 Foglietta | Y | Y | Y | Y | Y | Y | ? | ? |
| 2 Blackwell | Y | Y | Y | Y | Y | Y | Y | Y |
| 3 Borski | N | Y | Y | Y | Y | Y | ? | ? |
| 4 Kolter | ? | ? | ? | ? | Y | ? | Y | Y |
| 5 ***Schulze*** | ? | Y | Y | Y | Y | Y | Y | Y |
| 6 Yatron | N | Y | Y | Y | Y | Y | Y | Y |
| 7 ***Weldon*** | Y | Y | Y | N | Y | N | ? | ? |
| 8 Kostmayer | Y | Y | Y | Y | Y | Y | ? | ? |
| 9 ***Shuster*** | Y | Y | Y | N | Y | N | Y | N |
| 10 ***McDade*** | X | ? | # | Y | Y | Y | ? | ? |
| 11 Kanjorski | Y | Y | Y | Y | Y | Y | Y | Y |
| 12 Murtha | N | Y | Y | Y | Y | Y | Y | Y |
| 13 ***Coughlin*** | Y | Y | Y | N | Y | Y | Y | N |
| 14 Coyne | N | Y | Y | ? | Y | Y | Y | Y |
| 15 ***Ritter*** | Y | + | Y | Y | Y | N | ? | Y |
| 16 ***Walker*** | N | Y | Y | N | Y | N | ? | N |
| 17 ***Gekas*** | N | Y | Y | N | Y | N | ? | ? |
| 18 ***Santorum*** | N | Y | Y | Y | Y | N | Y | N |
| 19 ***Goodling*** | Y | Y | Y | N | Y | N | Y | N |
| 20 Gaydos | Y | Y | Y | ? | Y | Y | ? | ? |
| 21 ***Ridge*** | ? | Y | Y | N | Y | N | Y | Y |
| 22 Murphy | # | ? | ? | N | Y | N | Y | N |
| 23 ***Clinger*** | N | Y | Y | Y | Y | Y | Y | Y |
| **RHODE ISLAND** | | | | | | | | |
| 1 ***Machtley*** | Y | Y | Y | N | Y | Y | Y | Y |
| 2 Reed | Y | Y | N | ? | Y | Y | Y | Y |
| **SOUTH CAROLINA** | | | | | | | | |
| 1 ***Ravenel*** | Y | Y | Y | Y | Y | N | Y | Y |
| 2 ***Spence*** | N | Y | Y | Y | Y | N | Y | N |
| 3 Derrick | N | Y | Y | Y | Y | Y | ? | ? |
| 4 Patterson | Y | Y | Y | Y | Y | N | Y | Y |
| 5 Spratt | Y | Y | Y | Y | Y | Y | Y | Y |
| 6 Tallon | Y | Y | Y | Y | Y | Y | ? | ? |

| | 201 | 202 | 203 | 204 | 205 | 206 | 207 | 208 |
|---|---|---|---|---|---|---|---|---|
| **SOUTH DAKOTA** | | | | | | | | |
| AL Johnson | N | Y | Y | Y | Y | N | Y | Y |
| **TENNESSEE** | | | | | | | | |
| 1 ***Quillen*** | X | ? | ? | ? | ? | X | Y | N |
| 2 ***Duncan*** | Y | Y | Y | N | Y | N | N | Y |
| 3 Lloyd | N | Y | Y | Y | Y | Y | ? | ? |
| 4 Cooper | N | Y | Y | Y | Y | Y | Y | Y |
| 5 Clement | Y | Y | Y | Y | Y | Y | Y | Y |
| 6 Gordon | Y | Y | Y | Y | Y | Y | Y | Y |
| 7 ***Sundquist*** | Y | Y | Y | N | Y | N | Y | N |
| 8 Tanner | Y | Y | Y | Y | Y | Y | ? | ? |
| 9 Ford | Y | Y | ? | Y | Y | Y | Y | Y |
| **TEXAS** | | | | | | | | |
| 1 Chapman | N | Y | Y | Y | Y | N | Y | Y |
| 2 Wilson | N | Y | Y | ? | Y | Y | Y | Y |
| 3 ***Johnson*** | N | N | N | Y | Y | N | N | N |
| 4 Hall | N | Y | N | Y | Y | N | Y | Y |
| 5 Bryant | N | Y | Y | Y | Y | Y | ? | ? |
| 6 ***Barton*** | N | N | N | ? | Y | N | ? | ? |
| 7 ***Archer*** | N | Y | Y | N | Y | N | ? | Y |
| 8 ***Fields*** | N | Y | N | N | Y | N | Y | N |
| 9 Brooks | N | Y | Y | Y | Y | Y | Y | Y |
| 10 Pickle | N | Y | Y | Y | Y | Y | Y | Y |
| 11 Edwards | N | Y | N | ? | Y | N | Y | Y |
| 12 Geren | N | Y | N | Y | Y | N | Y | Y |
| 13 Sarpalius | N | Y | Y | Y | Y | N | Y | Y |
| 14 Laughlin | N | Y | Y | Y | Y | N | Y | Y |
| 15 de la Garza | N | Y | Y | Y | Y | Y | Y | Y |
| 16 Coleman | N | Y | Y | Y | Y | Y | ? | ? |
| 17 Stenholm | N | Y | N | Y | Y | N | Y | Y |
| 18 Washington | Y | Y | Y | ? | N | N | ? | ? |
| 19 ***Combest*** | N | Y | N | Y | Y | N | N | Y |
| 20 Gonzalez | N | N | Y | Y | N | Y | Y | Y |
| 21 ***Smith*** | N | Y | N | N | Y | Y | Y | N |
| 22 ***DeLay*** | N | Y | N | N | Y | N | ? | ? |
| 23 Bustamante | N | Y | Y | Y | Y | Y | Y | Y |
| 24 Frost | N | Y | N | Y | Y | Y | Y | Y |
| 25 Andrews | N | Y | Y | Y | Y | N | Y | Y |
| 26 ***Armey*** | N | Y | N | N | Y | N | ? | ? |
| 27 Ortiz | N | Y | Y | Y | Y | Y | Y | Y |
| **UTAH** | | | | | | | | |
| 1 ***Hansen*** | N | Y | Y | Y | Y | N | ? | ? |
| 2 Owens | Y | Y | Y | Y | Y | Y | Y | Y |
| 3 Orton | Y | Y | Y | Y | Y | N | Y | Y |
| **VERMONT** | | | | | | | | |
| AL *Sanders* | Y | Y | N | Y | Y | Y | Y | Y |
| **VIRGINIA** | | | | | | | | |
| 1 ***Bateman*** | N | Y | Y | Y | Y | Y | ? | ? |
| 2 Pickett | N | Y | Y | ? | Y | N | Y | Y |
| 3 ***Bliley*** | N | Y | Y | N | Y | N | Y | N |
| 4 Sisisky | Y | Y | Y | Y | Y | N | Y | Y |
| 5 Payne | N | Y | Y | Y | Y | N | Y | Y |
| 6 Olin | N | Y | Y | Y | Y | N | Y | Y |
| 7 ***Allen*** | N | Y | N | N | Y | N | N | N |
| 8 Moran | N | N | Y | Y | + | Y | Y | Y |
| 9 Boucher | N | Y | Y | Y | Y | N | ? | Y |
| 10 ***Wolf*** | Y | Y | Y | N | Y | N | Y | N |
| **WASHINGTON** | | | | | | | | |
| 1 ***Miller*** | N | Y | Y | N | Y | N | Y | N |
| 2 Swift | Y | ? | ? | Y | Y | Y | Y | Y |
| 3 Unsoeld | Y | Y | Y | Y | Y | Y | Y | Y |
| 4 ***Morrison*** | N | Y | Y | Y | Y | Y | ? | ? |
| 5 Foley | | | | | | | | |
| 6 Dicks | N | Y | Y | Y | Y | Y | Y | Y |
| 7 McDermott | Y | Y | Y | Y | Y | Y | Y | Y |
| 8 ***Chandler*** | N | Y | Y | ? | ? | ? | Y | N |
| **WEST VIRGINIA** | | | | | | | | |
| 1 Mollohan | N | Y | Y | Y | Y | Y | ? | ? |
| 2 Staggers | Y | Y | Y | Y | Y | Y | Y | Y |
| 3 Wise | Y | Y | Y | Y | Y | Y | ? | ? |
| 4 Rahall | Y | N | Y | Y | Y | Y | ? | ? |
| **WISCONSIN** | | | | | | | | |
| 1 Aspin | N | Y | Y | Y | Y | Y | ? | ? |
| 2 ***Klug*** | Y | Y | Y | N | Y | Y | ? | ? |
| 3 ***Gunderson*** | Y | Y | Y | Y | Y | N | ? | Y |
| 4 Kleczka | Y | Y | Y | Y | Y | Y | Y | Y |
| 5 Moody | Y | Y | N | Y | Y | N | Y | ? |
| 6 ***Petri*** | Y | Y | N | Y | Y | N | N | Y |
| 7 Obey | Y | Y | Y | Y | Y | Y | Y | Y |
| 8 ***Roth*** | Y | Y | N | Y | Y | N | ? | ? |
| 9 ***Sensenbrenner*** | Y | Y | N | N | Y | N | N | N |
| **WYOMING** | | | | | | | | |
| AL ***Thomas*** | N | Y | Y | N | Y | N | N | N |

Southern states - Ala., Ark., Fla., Ga., Ky., La., Miss., N.C., Okla., S.C., Tenn., Texas, Va.
Omitted votes are quorum calls, which CQ does not include in its vote charts.

## KEY

Y   Voted for (yea).
\#   Paired for.
\+   Announced for.
N   Voted against (nay).
X   Paired against.
—   Announced against.
P   Voted "present."
C   Voted "present" to avoid possible conflict of interest.
?   Did not vote or otherwise make a position known.

Democrats   **Republicans**
*Independent*

**209. Procedural Motion.** Walker, R-Pa., motion to adjourn. Motion rejected 17-379: R 16-142; D 1-236 (ND 1-160, SD 0-76); I 0-1, June 23, 1992.

**210. HR 5428. Fiscal 1993 Military Construction Appropriations/Order Previous Question.** Hall, D-Ohio, motion to order the previous question (thus limiting debate and the possibility of amendment) on adoption of the rule (H Res 498) to waive certain points of order against and provide for House floor consideration of the bill to provide $8.56 billion in new budget authority for military construction and family housing for the Department of Defense in fiscal 1993. Motion agreed to 269-143: R 17-142; D 251-1 (ND 171-1, SD 80-0); I 1-0, June 23, 1992.

**211. HR 5428. Fiscal 1993 Military Construction Appropriations/Rule.** Adoption of the rule (H Res 498) to waive certain points of order against and provide for House floor consideration of the bill to provide $8.56 billion in new budget authority for military construction and family housing for the Department of Defense in fiscal 1993. Adopted 381-34: R 128-33; D 252-1 (ND 172-1, SD 80-0); I 1-0, June 23, 1992.

**213. HR 5428. Fiscal 1993 Military Construction Appropriations/Camp McCain Roads.** Burton, R-Ind., amendment to cut the $19 million provided for defense access roads to Camp McCain in Mississippi. Rejected 143-276: R 109-53; D 34-222 (ND 32-143, SD 2-79); I 0-1, June 23, 1992.

**214. HR 5428. Fiscal 1993 Military Construction Appropriations/Reduce Funding.** Dorgan, D-N.D., amendment to cut the new budget authority provided in the bill by 1 percent, or about $85 million. Adopted 266-156: R 102-62; D 163-94 (ND 129-46, SD 34-48); I 1-0, June 23, 1992.

**215. HR 5428. Fiscal 1993 Military Construction Appropriations/Report to House.** Thomas, D-Ga., motion to rise from the Committee of the Whole and report the bill back to the House. Motion agreed to 417-0: R 161-0; D 255-0 (ND 173-0, SD 82-0); I 1-0, June 23, 1992.

**216. HR 5428. Fiscal 1993 Military Construction Appropriations/Third Reading.** Thomas, D-Ga., motion on engrossment and third reading of the bill to provide $8.47 billion in new budget authority for military construction and family housing for the Department of Defense in fiscal 1993. Motion agreed to 412-8: R 154-8; D 257-0 (ND 175-0, SD 82-0); I 1-0, June 23, 1992.

**217. HR 5428. Fiscal 1993 Military Construction Appropriations/Passage.** Passage of the bill to provide $8.47 billion in new budget authority for military construction, family housing and base closure for the Department of Defense in fiscal 1993. The administration requested $8,273,003,000. Passed 390-33: R 136-27; D 253-6 (ND 170-6, SD 83-0); I 1-0, June 23, 1992.

| | 209 | 210 | 211 | 213 | 214 | 215 | 216 | 217 |
|---|---|---|---|---|---|---|---|---|
| **ALABAMA** | | | | | | | | |
| 1 *Callahan* | N | Y | Y | N | N | ? | Y | Y |
| 2 *Dickinson* | N | N | Y | N | N | Y | Y | Y |
| 3 Browder | N | Y | Y | N | N | Y | Y | Y |
| 4 Bevill | N | Y | Y | N | N | Y | Y | Y |
| 5 Cramer | N | Y | Y | N | N | Y | Y | Y |
| 6 Erdreich | N | Y | Y | N | Y | Y | Y | Y |
| 7 Harris | N | Y | Y | N | N | Y | Y | Y |
| **ALASKA** | | | | | | | | |
| AL *Young* | N | Y | Y | N | N | Y | Y | Y |
| **ARIZONA** | | | | | | | | |
| 1 *Rhodes* | N | N | Y | Y | Y | Y | Y | Y |
| 2 Pastor | N | Y | Y | N | N | Y | Y | Y |
| 3 *Stump* | N | N | N | Y | Y | Y | Y | Y |
| 4 *Kyl* | N | N | Y | Y | Y | Y | Y | Y |
| 5 *Kolbe* | N | N | Y | N | N | Y | Y | Y |
| **ARKANSAS** | | | | | | | | |
| 1 Alexander | N | ? | ? | N | N | Y | Y | Y |
| 2 Thornton | N | Y | Y | N | N | Y | Y | Y |
| 3 *Hammerschmidt* | N | N | N | N | N | Y | Y | Y |
| 4 Anthony | N | Y | Y | N | N | Y | Y | Y |
| **CALIFORNIA** | | | | | | | | |
| 1 *Riggs* | N | N | Y | N | N | Y | Y | Y |
| 2 *Herger* | N | N | Y | Y | Y | Y | Y | Y |
| 3 Matsui | Y | Y | Y | N | Y | Y | Y | ? |
| 4 Fazio | N | Y | Y | N | N | Y | Y | Y |
| 5 Pelosi | N | Y | Y | N | Y | Y | Y | Y |
| 6 Boxer | N | Y | Y | N | Y | Y | Y | Y |
| 7 Miller | N | Y | Y | N | Y | Y | Y | Y |
| 8 Dellums | ? | Y | Y | N | Y | Y | Y | Y |
| 9 Stark | N | Y | Y | N | Y | Y | Y | N |
| 10 Edwards | N | Y | Y | N | Y | Y | ? | Y |
| 11 Lantos | N | Y | Y | N | Y | Y | Y | Y |
| 12 *Campbell* | N | N | Y | Y | Y | Y | Y | Y |
| 13 Mineta | N | Y | Y | N | N | Y | Y | Y |
| 14 *Doolittle* | Y | N | Y | Y | Y | Y | Y | N |
| 15 Condit | N | Y | Y | N | Y | Y | Y | Y |
| 16 Panetta | N | Y | Y | N | Y | Y | Y | Y |
| 17 Dooley | N | Y | Y | N | N | Y | Y | Y |
| 18 Lehman | N | Y | Y | N | N | Y | Y | Y |
| 19 *Lagomarsino* | N | N | Y | N | Y | N | Y | Y |
| 20 *Thomas* | N | N | Y | Y | Y | Y | Y | Y |
| 21 *Gallegly* | N | N | Y | N | Y | N | Y | Y |
| 22 *Moorhead* | N | N | Y | N | Y | N | Y | Y |
| 23 Beilenson | N | Y | Y | N | Y | Y | Y | N |
| 24 Waxman | N | Y | Y | N | Y | Y | Y | Y |
| 25 Roybal | N | Y | Y | N | N | Y | Y | Y |
| 26 Berman | N | Y | Y | N | Y | ? | Y | Y |
| 27 Levine | ? | ? | ? | ? | Y | Y | Y | Y |
| 28 Dixon | ? | Y | Y | N | Y | Y | Y | Y |
| 29 Waters | ? | ? | ? | N | Y | ? | Y | Y |
| 30 Martinez | ? | Y | Y | N | Y | Y | Y | Y |
| 31 Dymally | N | ? | Y | N | Y | Y | Y | Y |
| 32 Anderson | N | Y | Y | N | N | Y | Y | Y |
| 33 *Dreier* | N | N | Y | Y | Y | Y | Y | N |
| 34 Torres | N | Y | Y | N | Y | Y | Y | Y |
| 35 *Lewis* | N | N | Y | N | N | Y | Y | Y |
| 36 Brown | N | Y | Y | N | Y | Y | Y | Y |
| 37 *McCandless* | N | N | Y | N | N | Y | Y | Y |
| 38 *Dornan* | N | N | ? | Y | N | Y | Y | Y |
| 39 *Dannemeyer* | Y | N | N | Y | Y | Y | N | Y |
| 40 *Cox* | Y | N | Y | Y | Y | Y | Y | Y |
| 41 *Lowery* | N | Y | Y | N | N | Y | Y | Y |

| | 209 | 210 | 211 | 213 | 214 | 215 | 216 | 217 |
|---|---|---|---|---|---|---|---|---|
| 42 *Rohrabacher* | N | N | Y | Y | Y | Y | N | Y |
| 43 *Packard* | N | N | Y | Y | N | Y | Y | Y |
| 44 *Cunningham* | N | N | Y | Y | N | Y | Y | Y |
| 45 *Hunter* | N | N | Y | N | Y | Y | ? | Y |
| **COLORADO** | | | | | | | | |
| 1 Schroeder | N | Y | Y | N | N | Y | Y | Y |
| 2 Skaggs | N | Y | Y | N | N | Y | Y | Y |
| 3 Campbell | ? | Y | Y | N | Y | Y | Y | Y |
| 4 *Allard* | Y | N | N | Y | Y | Y | Y | N |
| 5 *Hefley* | Y | N | N | Y | N | Y | Y | Y |
| 6 *Schaefer* | N | N | N | Y | N | Y | Y | Y |
| **CONNECTICUT** | | | | | | | | |
| 1 Kennelly | N | Y | Y | N | Y | Y | Y | Y |
| 2 Gejdenson | N | Y | Y | N | N | Y | Y | Y |
| 3 DeLauro | N | Y | Y | N | Y | Y | Y | Y |
| 4 *Shays* | N | N | Y | Y | Y | Y | Y | Y |
| 5 *Franks* | N | N | Y | Y | Y | Y | Y | Y |
| 6 *Johnson* | N | N | Y | Y | Y | Y | Y | Y |
| **DELAWARE** | | | | | | | | |
| AL Carper | N | Y | Y | Y | Y | Y | Y | Y |
| **FLORIDA** | | | | | | | | |
| 1 Hutto | N | Y | Y | N | N | Y | Y | Y |
| 2 Peterson | N | Y | Y | N | N | Y | Y | Y |
| 3 Bennett | N | Y | Y | N | N | Y | Y | Y |
| 4 *James* | N | N | N | Y | N | Y | Y | Y |
| 5 *McCollum* | ? | N | Y | N | N | Y | Y | Y |
| 6 *Stearns* | N | N | Y | Y | N | Y | Y | Y |
| 7 Gibbons | N | Y | Y | N | N | Y | Y | Y |
| 8 *Young* | N | N | N | N | N | Y | Y | Y |
| 9 *Bilirakis* | N | N | Y | Y | Y | Y | Y | Y |
| 10 *Ireland* | N | N | N | Y | N | Y | Y | Y |
| 11 Bacchus | ? | Y | Y | N | Y | Y | Y | Y |
| 12 *Lewis* | N | N | Y | Y | Y | Y | Y | Y |
| 13 *Goss* | N | N | N | Y | Y | Y | Y | N |
| 14 Johnston | N | Y | Y | N | Y | Y | Y | Y |
| 15 *Shaw* | N | N | Y | Y | Y | Y | Y | Y |
| 16 Smith | N | Y | Y | N | Y | Y | Y | Y |
| 17 Lehman | ? | Y | Y | N | N | Y | Y | Y |
| 18 *Ros—Lehtinen* | N | N | Y | Y | N | Y | Y | Y |
| 19 Fascell | N | Y | Y | N | N | Y | Y | Y |
| **GEORGIA** | | | | | | | | |
| 1 Thomas | N | Y | Y | N | N | Y | Y | Y |
| 2 Hatcher | N | Y | Y | N | N | Y | Y | Y |
| 3 Ray | N | Y | Y | N | N | Y | Y | Y |
| 4 Jones | ? | ? | ? | ? | ? | ? | ? | ? |
| 5 Lewis | N | Y | Y | N | Y | Y | Y | Y |
| 6 *Gingrich* | N | N | Y | Y | Y | Y | Y | ? |
| 7 Darden | N | Y | Y | N | N | Y | Y | Y |
| 8 Rowland | N | Y | Y | N | N | Y | Y | Y |
| 9 Jenkins | N | Y | Y | N | N | Y | Y | Y |
| 10 Barnard | N | Y | Y | N | N | Y | Y | Y |
| **HAWAII** | | | | | | | | |
| 1 Abercrombie | N | Y | Y | N | Y | Y | Y | Y |
| 2 Mink | N | Y | Y | N | N | Y | Y | Y |
| **IDAHO** | | | | | | | | |
| 1 LaRocco | N | Y | Y | Y | Y | Y | Y | Y |
| 2 Stallings | ? | ? | ? | ? | ? | ? | ? | ? |
| **ILLINOIS** | | | | | | | | |
| 1 Hayes | N | Y | Y | N | Y | Y | Y | Y |
| 2 Savage | ? | Y | Y | N | Y | Y | Y | Y |
| 3 Russo | N | Y | Y | N | Y | Y | Y | N |
| 4 Sangmeister | N | Y | Y | N | Y | Y | Y | Y |
| 5 Lipinski | N | Y | Y | N | Y | Y | Y | Y |
| 6 *Hyde* | N | N | Y | N | Y | Y | Y | Y |
| 7 Collins | N | Y | Y | N | Y | Y | Y | Y |
| 8 Rostenkowski | N | Y | Y | N | Y | Y | Y | Y |
| 9 Yates | N | Y | Y | N | N | Y | Y | Y |
| 10 *Porter* | N | N | Y | Y | Y | Y | Y | Y |
| 11 Annunzio | N | Y | Y | N | Y | Y | Y | Y |
| 12 *Crane* | Y | N | N | Y | Y | Y | Y | N |
| 13 *Fawell* | N | N | Y | Y | Y | Y | Y | N |
| 14 *Hastert* | N | N | Y | Y | Y | Y | Y | Y |
| 15 *Ewing* | N | N | Y | N | Y | Y | Y | Y |
| 16 Cox | N | Y | Y | N | Y | Y | Y | Y |
| 17 Evans | N | Y | Y | N | N | Y | Y | Y |
| 18 *Michel* | N | N | N | N | N | Y | Y | Y |
| 19 Bruce | N | Y | Y | N | N | Y | Y | Y |
| 20 Durbin | N | Y | Y | N | N | Y | Y | Y |
| 21 Costello | N | Y | Y | N | Y | Y | Y | Y |
| 22 Poshard | N | Y | Y | Y | Y | Y | Y | Y |
| **INDIANA** | | | | | | | | |
| 1 Visclosky | N | Y | Y | N | N | Y | Y | Y |
| 2 Sharp | N | Y | Y | Y | Y | Y | Y | Y |
| 3 Roemer | N | Y | Y | Y | Y | Y | Y | Y |

ND Northern Democrats   SD Southern Democrats

| | 209 | 210 | 211 | 213 | 214 | 215 | 216 | 217 |
|---|---|---|---|---|---|---|---|---|
| 4 Long | N | Y | Y | N | N | Y | Y | Y |
| 5 Jontz | N | Y | Y | Y | Y | Y | Y | Y |
| 6 ***Burton*** | N | N | N | Y | Y | Y | Y | Y |
| 7 ***Myers*** | N | N | Y | N | Y | Y | Y | N |
| 8 McCloskey | N | Y | Y | N | Y | Y | Y | Y |
| 9 Hamilton | N | Y | Y | Y | Y | Y | Y | Y |
| 10 Jacobs | N | N | Y | Y | Y | Y | Y | N |
| **IOWA** | | | | | | | | |
| 1 ***Leach*** | N | N | Y | Y | Y | Y | Y | Y |
| 2 ***Nussle*** | N | N | Y | Y | Y | Y | Y | N |
| 3 Nagle | N | Y | Y | N | N | Y | Y | Y |
| 4 Smith | N | Y | Y | N | N | Y | Y | Y |
| 5 ***Lightfoot*** | N | Y | Y | N | N | Y | Y | Y |
| 6 ***Grandy*** | N | N | Y | Y | Y | Y | Y | Y |
| **KANSAS** | | | | | | | | |
| 1 ***Roberts*** | N | N | N | Y | Y | Y | Y | N |
| 2 Slattery | N | Y | Y | Y | Y | Y | Y | Y |
| 3 ***Meyers*** | N | N | Y | Y | Y | Y | N | N |
| 4 Glickman | N | Y | Y | Y | Y | Y | Y | Y |
| 5 ***Nichols*** | N | N | Y | Y | Y | Y | Y | Y |
| **KENTUCKY** | | | | | | | | |
| 1 Hubbard | N | Y | Y | N | Y | Y | Y | Y |
| 2 Natcher | N | Y | Y | N | N | Y | Y | Y |
| 3 Mazzoli | N | Y | Y | N | N | Y | Y | Y |
| 4 ***Bunning*** | N | N | Y | Y | Y | Y | Y | Y |
| 5 ***Rogers*** | N | N | Y | Y | Y | Y | Y | Y |
| 6 ***Hopkins*** | N | N | Y | Y | Y | Y | Y | Y |
| 7 Perkins | ? | ? | ? | N | N | Y | Y | Y |
| **LOUISIANA** | | | | | | | | |
| 1 ***Livingston*** | Y | N | Y | N | N | N | Y | Y |
| 2 Jefferson | N | Y | Y | N | Y | Y | Y | Y |
| 3 Tauzin | N | Y | Y | N | Y | Y | Y | Y |
| 4 ***McCrery*** | N | N | Y | N | Y | Y | Y | Y |
| 5 Huckaby | N | Y | Y | N | Y | Y | Y | Y |
| 6 ***Baker*** | N | N | N | N | N | Y | Y | Y |
| 7 Hayes | N | Y | Y | N | Y | Y | Y | Y |
| 8 ***Holloway*** | N | N | N | N | N | Y | Y | Y |
| **MAINE** | | | | | | | | |
| 1 Andrews | N | Y | Y | Y | Y | Y | Y | Y |
| 2 ***Snowe*** | N | N | Y | Y | Y | Y | Y | Y |
| **MARYLAND** | | | | | | | | |
| 1 ***Gilchrest*** | ? | N | Y | Y | Y | Y | Y | Y |
| 2 ***Bentley*** | N | N | Y | N | N | Y | Y | Y |
| 3 Cardin | N | Y | Y | N | N | Y | Y | Y |
| 4 McMillen | N | Y | Y | N | Y | Y | Y | Y |
| 5 Hoyer | N | Y | Y | N | N | Y | Y | Y |
| 6 Byron | N | Y | Y | N | Y | Y | Y | Y |
| 7 Mfume | N | Y | Y | Y | Y | Y | Y | Y |
| 8 ***Morella*** | N | N | Y | Y | Y | Y | Y | Y |
| **MASSACHUSETTS** | | | | | | | | |
| 1 Olver | N | Y | Y | N | Y | Y | Y | Y |
| 2 Neal | N | Y | Y | N | Y | Y | Y | Y |
| 3 Early | N | Y | Y | N | N | Y | Y | Y |
| 4 Frank | N | Y | Y | N | Y | Y | Y | Y |
| 5 Atkins | N | Y | Y | N | Y | Y | Y | Y |
| 6 Mavroules | N | Y | Y | N | N | Y | Y | Y |
| 7 Markey | N | Y | Y | N | Y | Y | Y | Y |
| 8 Kennedy | N | Y | Y | N | Y | Y | Y | Y |
| 9 Moakley | N | Y | Y | N | Y | Y | Y | Y |
| 10 Studds | N | Y | Y | N | Y | Y | Y | Y |
| 11 Donnelly | N | Y | Y | N | Y | Y | Y | Y |
| **MICHIGAN** | | | | | | | | |
| 1 Conyers | N | Y | Y | N | ? | ? | Y | Y |
| 2 ***Pursell*** | N | N | Y | Y | Y | Y | N | N |
| 3 Wolpe | N | Y | Y | Y | Y | Y | Y | Y |
| 4 ***Upton*** | N | N | Y | Y | Y | Y | Y | N |
| 5 ***Henry*** | N | N | Y | Y | Y | Y | Y | N |
| 6 Carr | N | Y | Y | N | N | Y | Y | Y |
| 7 Kildee | N | Y | Y | N | Y | Y | Y | Y |
| 8 Traxler | ? | ? | ? | ? | ? | ? | ? | ? |
| 9 ***Vander Jagt*** | N | ? | Y | N | Y | Y | Y | Y |
| 10 ***Camp*** | N | N | Y | Y | Y | Y | Y | N |
| 11 ***Davis*** | ? | N | Y | N | N | Y | Y | Y |
| 12 Bonior | ? | ? | ? | ? | ? | ? | ? | ? |
| 13 Collins | ? | Y | Y | N | Y | Y | Y | Y |
| 14 Hertel | N | Y | Y | N | N | Y | Y | Y |
| 15 Ford | N | Y | Y | N | N | Y | Y | Y |
| 16 Dingell | N | Y | Y | N | Y | Y | Y | Y |
| 17 Levin | N | Y | Y | N | Y | Y | Y | Y |
| 18 ***Broomfield*** | N | N | Y | Y | Y | Y | Y | Y |
| **MINNESOTA** | | | | | | | | |
| 1 Penny | N | Y | Y | Y | Y | Y | Y | Y |
| 2 ***Weber*** | Y | N | Y | N | Y | Y | Y | Y |
| 3 ***Ramstad*** | N | N | Y | Y | Y | Y | Y | N |
| 4 Vento | N | Y | Y | Y | Y | Y | Y | Y |
| 5 Sabo | N | Y | Y | N | N | Y | Y | Y |
| 6 Sikorski | N | Y | Y | Y | Y | Y | Y | Y |
| 7 Peterson | N | Y | Y | N | Y | Y | Y | Y |
| 8 Oberstar | N | Y | Y | N | Y | Y | Y | Y |
| **MISSISSIPPI** | | | | | | | | |
| 1 Whitten | N | Y | Y | N | N | Y | Y | Y |
| 2 Espy | N | Y | Y | N | Y | Y | Y | Y |
| 3 Montgomery | N | Y | Y | N | N | Y | Y | Y |
| 4 Parker | N | Y | Y | N | Y | Y | Y | Y |
| 5 Taylor | N | Y | Y | N | N | Y | Y | Y |
| **MISSOURI** | | | | | | | | |
| 1 Clay | N | Y | Y | N | Y | Y | Y | Y |
| 2 Horn | N | Y | Y | N | Y | Y | Y | Y |
| 3 Gephardt | N | Y | Y | N | N | Y | Y | Y |
| 4 Skelton | ? | Y | Y | N | N | Y | Y | Y |
| 5 Wheat | N | Y | Y | N | Y | Y | Y | Y |
| 6 ***Coleman*** | N | N | N | Y | Y | Y | Y | Y |
| 7 ***Hancock*** | Y | N | N | Y | Y | Y | Y | N |
| 8 ***Emerson*** | N | N | Y | Y | Y | Y | Y | Y |
| 9 Volkmer | N | Y | Y | N | Y | Y | Y | Y |
| **MONTANA** | | | | | | | | |
| 1 Williams | N | ? | Y | N | N | Y | Y | Y |
| 2 ***Marlenee*** | ? | ? | ? | ? | Y | Y | Y | ? |
| **NEBRASKA** | | | | | | | | |
| 1 ***Bereuter*** | N | Y | Y | N | Y | Y | Y | Y |
| 2 Hoagland | N | Y | Y | N | Y | Y | Y | Y |
| 3 ***Barrett*** | N | N | Y | Y | Y | Y | Y | Y |
| **NEVADA** | | | | | | | | |
| 1 Bilbray | N | Y | Y | N | Y | Y | Y | Y |
| 2 ***Vucanovich*** | N | N | Y | Y | N | Y | Y | Y |
| **NEW HAMPSHIRE** | | | | | | | | |
| 1 ***Zeliff*** | N | N | Y | Y | Y | Y | Y | N |
| 2 Swett | N | Y | Y | N | Y | Y | Y | Y |
| **NEW JERSEY** | | | | | | | | |
| 1 Andrews | N | Y | Y | N | N | Y | Y | Y |
| 2 Hughes | N | Y | Y | N | Y | Y | Y | Y |
| 3 Pallone | N | Y | Y | N | N | Y | Y | Y |
| 4 ***Smith*** | N | N | Y | N | N | Y | Y | Y |
| 5 ***Roukema*** | N | Y | Y | N | Y | Y | Y | Y |
| 6 Dwyer | N | Y | ? | N | N | Y | Y | Y |
| 7 ***Rinaldo*** | N | N | Y | Y | Y | Y | Y | Y |
| 8 Roe | N | Y | Y | N | N | Y | Y | Y |
| 9 Torricelli | N | Y | Y | N | Y | Y | Y | Y |
| 10 Payne | ? | ? | ? | ? | ? | Y | Y | Y |
| 11 ***Gallo*** | N | N | Y | N | N | Y | Y | Y |
| 12 ***Zimmer*** | N | N | Y | Y | Y | Y | Y | Y |
| 13 ***Saxton*** | N | N | Y | N | N | Y | Y | Y |
| 14 Guarini | N | Y | Y | N | Y | Y | Y | Y |
| **NEW MEXICO** | | | | | | | | |
| 1 ***Schiff*** | N | N | Y | N | N | Y | Y | Y |
| 2 ***Skeen*** | N | Y | Y | N | N | Y | Y | Y |
| 3 Richardson | N | Y | Y | N | N | ? | Y | Y |
| **NEW YORK** | | | | | | | | |
| 1 Hochbrueckner | N | Y | Y | N | Y | Y | Y | Y |
| 2 Downey | N | Y | Y | N | Y | Y | Y | Y |
| 3 Mrazek | N | Y | Y | N | Y | Y | Y | Y |
| 4 ***Lent*** | ? | N | Y | ? | N | Y | Y | Y |
| 5 ***McGrath*** | N | N | Y | N | N | Y | Y | Y |
| 6 Flake | N | Y | ? | N | Y | Y | Y | Y |
| 7 Ackerman | N | Y | Y | N | Y | Y | Y | Y |
| 8 Scheuer | N | ? | Y | Y | Y | Y | Y | N |
| 9 Manton | N | Y | Y | N | Y | Y | Y | Y |
| 10 Schumer | N | Y | Y | N | Y | Y | Y | Y |
| 11 Towns | ? | Y | Y | N | Y | Y | Y | Y |
| 12 Owens | N | Y | Y | N | Y | Y | Y | Y |
| 13 Solarz | N | Y | Y | N | Y | Y | Y | Y |
| 14 ***Molinari*** | N | N | Y | N | Y | Y | Y | Y |
| 15 ***Green*** | N | N | Y | N | N | Y | Y | Y |
| 16 Rangel | N | Y | Y | N | Y | Y | Y | Y |
| 17 Weiss | N | Y | Y | N | Y | Y | Y | Y |
| 18 Serrano | N | Y | Y | N | Y | Y | Y | Y |
| 19 Engel | N | Y | Y | N | Y | Y | Y | Y |
| 20 Lowey | N | Y | Y | N | Y | Y | Y | Y |
| 21 ***Fish*** | N | Y | Y | Y | N | Y | Y | Y |
| 22 ***Gilman*** | N | N | Y | Y | Y | Y | Y | Y |
| 23 McNulty | ? | ? | ? | ? | ? | ? | ? | ? |
| 24 ***Solomon*** | N | N | Y | Y | Y | Y | Y | Y |
| 25 ***Boehlert*** | N | N | Y | Y | Y | Y | Y | Y |
| 26 ***Martin*** | N | N | Y | N | N | Y | Y | Y |
| 27 ***Walsh*** | N | N | Y | N | N | Y | Y | Y |
| 28 McHugh | N | Y | Y | N | N | Y | Y | Y |
| 29 ***Horton*** | N | Y | Y | N | Y | Y | Y | Y |
| 30 Slaughter | N | Y | Y | Y | Y | Y | Y | Y |
| 31 ***Paxon*** | N | N | Y | Y | Y | Y | Y | Y |
| 32 LaFalce | N | Y | Y | ? | ? | ? | ? | ? |
| 33 Nowak | N | Y | Y | N | Y | Y | Y | Y |
| 34 ***Houghton*** | N | N | Y | N | Y | Y | Y | Y |
| **NORTH CAROLINA** | | | | | | | | |
| 1 Jones | N | Y | Y | N | Y | Y | Y | Y |
| 2 Valentine | ? | Y | Y | N | Y | Y | Y | Y |
| 3 Lancaster | N | Y | Y | N | N | Y | Y | Y |
| 4 Price | N | Y | Y | N | Y | Y | Y | Y |
| 5 Neal | N | Y | Y | N | Y | Y | Y | Y |
| 6 ***Coble*** | N | N | N | N | Y | Y | Y | Y |
| 7 Rose | N | Y | Y | N | N | Y | Y | Y |
| 8 Hefner | ? | ? | ? | ? | ? | ? | ? | ? |
| 9 ***McMillan*** | N | N | Y | N | N | Y | Y | Y |
| 10 ***Ballenger*** | N | N | Y | Y | Y | Y | Y | Y |
| 11 ***Taylor*** | N | N | N | Y | Y | Y | Y | Y |
| **NORTH DAKOTA** | | | | | | | | |
| AL Dorgan | N | Y | Y | Y | Y | Y | Y | Y |
| **OHIO** | | | | | | | | |
| 1 Luken | N | Y | Y | Y | Y | Y | Y | Y |
| 2 ***Gradison*** | N | N | Y | Y | Y | Y | Y | Y |
| 3 Hall | N | Y | Y | N | N | Y | Y | Y |
| 4 ***Oxley*** | N | N | Y | N | N | Y | Y | N |
| 5 ***Gillmor*** | N | N | Y | N | N | Y | Y | Y |
| 6 ***McEwen*** | N | N | Y | Y | Y | Y | Y | Y |
| 7 ***Hobson*** | N | N | Y | Y | Y | Y | Y | Y |
| 8 ***Boehner*** | N | N | N | Y | Y | Y | Y | Y |
| 9 Kaptur | ? | Y | Y | N | N | Y | Y | Y |
| 10 ***Miller*** | N | N | Y | Y | Y | Y | Y | Y |
| 11 Eckart | N | Y | Y | N | Y | Y | Y | Y |
| 12 ***Kasich*** | N | N | Y | Y | Y | Y | Y | Y |
| 13 Pease | ? | Y | Y | Y | Y | Y | Y | Y |
| 14 Sawyer | N | Y | Y | N | Y | Y | Y | Y |
| 15 ***Wylie*** | N | N | N | Y | Y | Y | Y | N |
| 16 ***Regula*** | N | Y | Y | Y | Y | Y | Y | Y |
| 17 Traficant | N | Y | Y | N | Y | Y | Y | Y |
| 18 Applegate | N | Y | N | Y | Y | Y | Y | Y |
| 19 Feighan | ? | Y | Y | N | Y | Y | Y | Y |
| 20 Oakar | N | Y | Y | N | Y | Y | Y | Y |
| 21 Stokes | N | Y | Y | N | Y | Y | Y | Y |
| **OKLAHOMA** | | | | | | | | |
| 1 ***Inhofe*** | N | N | N | Y | N | Y | Y | Y |
| 2 Synar | N | Y | Y | N | Y | Y | Y | Y |
| 3 Brewster | N | Y | Y | Y | Y | Y | Y | Y |
| 4 McCurdy | N | Y | Y | ? | N | Y | Y | Y |
| 5 ***Edwards*** | ? | ? | ? | ? | ? | ? | ? | ? |
| 6 English | N | Y | Y | Y | N | Y | Y | Y |
| **OREGON** | | | | | | | | |
| 1 AuCoin | N | Y | Y | N | Y | Y | Y | Y |
| 2 ***Smith*** | N | N | N | Y | Y | Y | Y | Y |
| 3 Wyden | N | Y | Y | N | Y | Y | Y | Y |
| 4 DeFazio | N | Y | Y | N | Y | Y | Y | Y |
| 5 Kopetski | N | Y | Y | N | Y | Y | Y | Y |
| **PENNSYLVANIA** | | | | | | | | |
| 1 Foglietta | ? | Y | Y | N | N | Y | Y | Y |
| 2 Blackwell | N | Y | Y | N | Y | Y | Y | Y |
| 3 Borski | N | Y | Y | N | N | Y | Y | Y |
| 4 Kolter | N | Y | Y | N | N | Y | Y | Y |
| 5 ***Schulze*** | Y | ? | Y | Y | Y | Y | Y | Y |
| 6 Yatron | N | Y | Y | N | Y | Y | Y | Y |
| 7 ***Weldon*** | N | N | Y | Y | Y | Y | Y | Y |
| 8 Kostmayer | N | Y | Y | N | Y | Y | Y | Y |
| 9 ***Shuster*** | N | N | Y | N | N | Y | Y | Y |
| 10 ***McDade*** | N | N | Y | N | N | Y | Y | Y |
| 11 Kanjorski | N | Y | Y | N | N | Y | Y | Y |
| 12 Murtha | N | Y | Y | N | N | Y | Y | Y |
| 13 ***Coughlin*** | N | ? | Y | N | N | ? | Y | Y |
| 14 Coyne | N | Y | Y | N | Y | Y | Y | Y |
| 15 ***Ritter*** | N | N | Y | Y | Y | Y | Y | Y |
| 16 ***Walker*** | N | N | Y | Y | Y | Y | N | N |
| 17 ***Gekas*** | N | N | N | Y | Y | Y | Y | Y |
| 18 ***Santorum*** | N | N | Y | Y | Y | Y | Y | N |
| 19 ***Goodling*** | N | Y | Y | N | N | Y | Y | Y |
| 20 Gaydos | N | Y | Y | N | N | Y | Y | Y |
| 21 ***Ridge*** | ? | ? | ? | ? | ? | ? | ? | ? |
| 22 Murphy | N | Y | Y | N | Y | Y | Y | N |
| 23 ***Clinger*** | Y | Y | Y | N | N | Y | Y | Y |
| **RHODE ISLAND** | | | | | | | | |
| 1 ***Machtley*** | N | N | Y | N | N | Y | Y | Y |
| 2 Reed | N | Y | Y | N | Y | Y | Y | Y |
| **SOUTH CAROLINA** | | | | | | | | |
| 1 ***Ravenel*** | N | Y | ? | N | Y | Y | Y | Y |
| 2 ***Spence*** | N | N | Y | N | N | Y | Y | Y |
| 3 Derrick | N | Y | Y | N | Y | Y | Y | Y |
| 4 Patterson | N | Y | Y | N | Y | Y | Y | Y |
| 5 Spratt | N | Y | Y | N | Y | Y | Y | Y |
| 6 Tallon | N | Y | Y | N | Y | Y | Y | Y |
| **SOUTH DAKOTA** | | | | | | | | |
| AL Johnson | N | Y | Y | N | Y | Y | Y | Y |
| **TENNESSEE** | | | | | | | | |
| 1 ***Quillen*** | N | N | Y | Y | Y | Y | Y | Y |
| 2 ***Duncan*** | N | N | N | Y | Y | Y | Y | N |
| 3 Lloyd | N | Y | Y | N | N | Y | Y | Y |
| 4 Cooper | N | Y | Y | N | Y | Y | Y | Y |
| 5 Clement | N | Y | Y | N | Y | Y | Y | Y |
| 6 Gordon | N | Y | Y | N | Y | Y | Y | Y |
| 7 ***Sundquist*** | N | N | Y | Y | N | Y | Y | Y |
| 8 Tanner | N | Y | Y | N | N | Y | Y | Y |
| 9 Ford | ? | ? | ? | ? | ? | ? | Y | Y |
| **TEXAS** | | | | | | | | |
| 1 Chapman | ? | Y | Y | N | N | Y | Y | Y |
| 2 Wilson | N | Y | Y | N | N | Y | Y | Y |
| 3 ***Johnson*** | Y | N | Y | Y | Y | Y | Y | Y |
| 4 Hall | N | Y | Y | N | Y | Y | Y | Y |
| 5 Bryant | N | Y | Y | N | Y | Y | Y | Y |
| 6 ***Barton*** | N | N | Y | Y | N | Y | N | Y |
| 7 ***Archer*** | N | N | Y | Y | Y | Y | N | N |
| 8 ***Fields*** | Y | N | N | Y | Y | Y | Y | N |
| 9 Brooks | N | Y | Y | N | N | Y | ? | Y |
| 10 Pickle | N | Y | Y | N | Y | Y | Y | Y |
| 11 Edwards | N | Y | Y | N | N | Y | Y | Y |
| 12 Geren | N | Y | Y | N | N | Y | Y | Y |
| 13 Sarpalius | N | Y | Y | N | N | Y | Y | Y |
| 14 Laughlin | N | Y | Y | N | N | Y | Y | Y |
| 15 de la Garza | N | Y | Y | N | N | Y | Y | Y |
| 16 Coleman | N | Y | Y | N | N | Y | Y | Y |
| 17 Stenholm | N | Y | Y | N | Y | Y | Y | Y |
| 18 Washington | ? | Y | Y | N | N | Y | Y | Y |
| 19 ***Combest*** | N | Y | Y | N | N | Y | Y | Y |
| 20 Gonzalez | N | Y | Y | N | N | Y | Y | Y |
| 21 ***Smith*** | N | N | Y | Y | Y | Y | Y | Y |
| 22 ***DeLay*** | Y | Y | Y | N | N | Y | Y | Y |
| 23 Bustamante | N | Y | Y | N | N | Y | Y | Y |
| 24 Frost | N | Y | Y | N | Y | Y | Y | Y |
| 25 Andrews | N | Y | Y | N | Y | Y | Y | Y |
| 26 ***Armey*** | Y | N | N | Y | Y | Y | Y | N |
| 27 Ortiz | N | Y | Y | N | N | Y | Y | Y |
| **UTAH** | | | | | | | | |
| 1 ***Hansen*** | N | N | Y | Y | N | Y | Y | Y |
| 2 Owens | N | Y | Y | Y | Y | Y | Y | Y |
| 3 Orton | N | Y | Y | Y | Y | Y | Y | Y |
| **VERMONT** | | | | | | | | |
| AL *Sanders* | N | Y | Y | N | Y | Y | Y | Y |
| **VIRGINIA** | | | | | | | | |
| 1 ***Bateman*** | N | Y | Y | N | N | Y | Y | Y |
| 2 Pickett | N | Y | Y | N | N | Y | Y | Y |
| 3 ***Bliley*** | N | N | Y | Y | Y | Y | Y | Y |
| 4 Sisisky | N | Y | Y | N | N | Y | Y | Y |
| 5 Payne | N | Y | Y | N | N | Y | Y | Y |
| 6 Olin | N | Y | Y | N | Y | Y | Y | Y |
| 7 ***Allen*** | ? | N | N | Y | Y | Y | Y | Y |
| 8 Moran | N | Y | Y | N | N | Y | Y | Y |
| 9 Boucher | N | Y | Y | N | N | Y | Y | Y |
| 10 ***Wolf*** | N | N | Y | N | N | Y | Y | Y |
| **WASHINGTON** | | | | | | | | |
| 1 ***Miller*** | N | ? | Y | Y | Y | Y | Y | Y |
| 2 Swift | N | Y | Y | N | N | Y | Y | Y |
| 3 Unsoeld | N | Y | Y | N | Y | Y | Y | Y |
| 4 ***Morrison*** | N | Y | Y | N | N | Y | Y | Y |
| 5 Foley | | | | | | | | |
| 6 Dicks | N | Y | Y | N | N | Y | Y | Y |
| 7 McDermott | ? | Y | Y | N | Y | Y | ? | Y |
| 8 ***Chandler*** | N | N | Y | Y | Y | Y | Y | Y |
| **WEST VIRGINIA** | | | | | | | | |
| 1 Mollohan | N | Y | Y | N | N | Y | Y | Y |
| 2 Staggers | N | Y | Y | N | Y | Y | Y | Y |
| 3 Wise | ? | Y | Y | N | Y | Y | Y | Y |
| 4 Rahall | N | Y | Y | N | Y | Y | Y | Y |
| **WISCONSIN** | | | | | | | | |
| 1 Aspin | N | Y | Y | N | N | Y | Y | Y |
| 2 ***Klug*** | N | N | Y | Y | Y | Y | Y | Y |
| 3 ***Gunderson*** | Y | N | Y | N | Y | Y | Y | Y |
| 4 Kleczka | N | Y | Y | N | Y | Y | Y | Y |
| 5 Moody | N | Y | Y | Y | Y | Y | Y | Y |
| 6 ***Petri*** | N | N | N | Y | Y | Y | Y | Y |
| 7 Obey | N | Y | Y | N | N | Y | Y | Y |
| 8 ***Roth*** | N | N | N | Y | Y | Y | Y | N |
| 9 ***Sensenbrenner*** | N | N | N | Y | Y | Y | N | N |
| **WYOMING** | | | | | | | | |
| AL ***Thomas*** | N | N | Y | Y | Y | Y | Y | Y |

Southern states - Ala., Ark., Fla., Ga., Ky., La., Miss., N.C., Okla., S.C., Tenn., Texas, Va.
Omitted votes are quorum calls, which CQ does not include in its vote charts.

**218. Procedural Motion.** Approval of the House Journal of Monday, June 22. Approved 271-123: R 35-119; D 235-4 (ND 158-4, SD 77-0); I 1-0, June 23, 1992.

**219. Procedural Motion.** Walker, R-Pa., motion to adjourn. Motion rejected 131-264: R 125-33; D 6-230 (ND 5-156, SD 1-74); I 0-1, June 23, 1992.

**220. Procedural Motion.** Hoyer, D-Md., motion to adjourn. Motion agreed to 336-49: R 99-46; D 236-3 (ND 164-1, SD 72-2); I 1-0, June 23, 1992.

**221. Procedural Motion.** Approval of the House Journal of Tuesday, June 23. Approved 266-130: R 33-124; D 233-6 (ND 156-6, SD 77-0); I 0-0, June 24, 1992.

**222. HR 2507. National Institutes of Health (NIH) Reauthorization/Veto Override.** Passage, over President Bush's June 23 veto, of the bill to reauthorize and amend the programs of NIH through fiscal 1996, including fiscal 1993 funding of $2.2 billion for the National Cancer Institute and $1.4 billion for the Heart, Lung and Blood Institute. The bill lifted the ban on fetal tissue transplant research using fetal tissue obtained from induced abortions. Rejected 271-156: R 44-121; D 226-35 (ND 156-22, SD 70-13); I 1-0, June 24, 1992. A two-thirds majority of those present and voting (285 in this case) of both chambers was required to override a veto. A "nay" was a vote supporting the president's position.

**223. HR 5427. Fiscal 1993 Legislative Branch Appropriations/Order Previous Question.** Derrick, D-S.C., motion to order the previous question (thus limiting debate and the possibility of amendment) on adoption of the rule (H Res 499) to provide for House floor consideration of the bill to provide $1.8 billion in new budget authority for the operations of Congress and legislative branch agencies in fiscal 1993. The Senate was to add funding for its operations. Motion agreed to 254-171: R 0-165; D 253-6 (ND 173-4, SD 80-2); I 1-0, June 24, 1992.

**224. HR 5427. Fiscal 1993 Legislative Branch Appropriations/Rule.** Adoption of the rule (H Res 499) to provide for House floor consideration of the bill to provide $1.8 billion in new budget authority for the operations of the House and legislative branch agencies in fiscal 1993. The Senate wwas to add funding for its operations. Adopted 244-179: R 0-163; D 243-16 (ND 164-12, SD 79-4); I 1-0, June 24, 1992.

**225. HR 5427. Fiscal 1993 Legislative Branch Appropriations/Rescind Unspent Funds.** Swett, D-N.H, amendment to rescind $6.8 million in unspent funds appropriated in fiscal 1991 for the House. Adopted 426-0: R 166-0; D 259-0 (ND 177-0, SD 82-0); I 1-0, June 24, 1992.

## KEY

Y Voted for (yea).
\# Paired for.
+ Announced for.
N Voted against (nay).
X Paired against.
— Announced against.
P Voted "present."
C Voted "present" to avoid possible conflict of interest.
? Did not vote or otherwise make a position known.

*Democrats* **Republicans** *Independent*

| | 218 | 219 | 220 | 221 | 222 | 223 | 224 | 225 |
|---|---|---|---|---|---|---|---|---|
| **ALABAMA** | | | | | | | | |
| 1 *Callahan* | Y | Y | N | N | N | N | N | Y |
| 2 *Dickinson* | N | Y | Y | N | Y | N | N | Y |
| 3 Browder | Y | N | Y | Y | Y | Y | Y | Y |
| 4 Bevill | Y | N | Y | Y | Y | Y | Y | Y |
| 5 Cramer | Y | N | Y | Y | Y | Y | Y | Y |
| 6 Erdreich | Y | N | Y | Y | Y | N | Y | Y |
| 7 Harris | Y | N | Y | Y | Y | Y | Y | Y |
| **ALASKA** | | | | | | | | |
| AL *Young* | N | Y | N | N | N | N | N | Y |
| **ARIZONA** | | | | | | | | |
| 1 *Rhodes* | N | Y | ? | N | N | N | N | Y |
| 2 Pastor | Y | N | Y | ? | Y | Y | Y | Y |
| 3 *Stump* | N | Y | N | N | N | N | N | Y |
| 4 *Kyl* | N | Y | N | N | N | N | N | Y |
| 5 *Kolbe* | N | Y | N | N | Y | N | N | Y |
| **ARKANSAS** | | | | | | | | |
| 1 Alexander | ? | ? | ? | ? | Y | Y | Y | Y |
| 2 Thornton | Y | N | Y | Y | Y | Y | Y | Y |
| 3 *Hammerschmidt* | Y | N | N | N | N | N | N | Y |
| 4 Anthony | Y | N | Y | Y | Y | Y | Y | Y |
| **CALIFORNIA** | | | | | | | | |
| 1 *Riggs* | N | Y | N | N | Y | N | N | Y |
| 2 *Herger* | N | Y | N | N | N | N | N | Y |
| 3 Matsui | Y | N | Y | Y | Y | Y | Y | Y |
| 4 Fazio | Y | N | Y | Y | Y | Y | Y | Y |
| 5 Pelosi | Y | N | Y | Y | Y | Y | Y | Y |
| 6 Boxer | Y | N | Y | Y | Y | Y | Y | Y |
| 7 Miller | Y | N | Y | Y | Y | Y | Y | Y |
| 8 Dellums | Y | N | Y | Y | Y | Y | Y | Y |
| 9 Stark | Y | N | Y | Y | Y | Y | ? | Y |
| 10 Edwards | Y | N | Y | Y | Y | Y | Y | Y |
| 11 Lantos | Y | N | Y | Y | Y | Y | Y | Y |
| 12 *Campbell* | N | N | N | N | N | N | N | Y |
| 13 Mineta | Y | N | Y | Y | Y | Y | Y | Y |
| 14 *Doolittle* | N | Y | N | N | N | N | N | Y |
| 15 Condit | Y | N | Y | Y | Y | N | N | Y |
| 16 Panetta | N | Y | Y | Y | Y | N | N | Y |
| 17 Dooley | Y | N | Y | Y | Y | Y | Y | Y |
| 18 Lehman | Y | N | Y | Y | Y | Y | Y | Y |
| 19 *Lagomarsino* | N | Y | N | N | N | N | N | Y |
| 20 *Thomas* | N | Y | N | N | N | N | N | Y |
| 21 *Gallegly* | N | Y | Y | N | N | N | N | Y |
| 22 *Moorhead* | N | Y | Y | N | N | N | N | Y |
| 23 Beilenson | Y | N | Y | Y | Y | Y | Y | Y |
| 24 Waxman | Y | N | Y | Y | Y | Y | Y | Y |
| 25 Roybal | Y | N | Y | Y | Y | Y | Y | Y |
| 26 Berman | ? | N | Y | Y | Y | Y | Y | Y |
| 27 Levine | Y | N | Y | Y | Y | Y | Y | Y |
| 28 Dixon | Y | N | Y | Y | Y | Y | Y | Y |
| 29 Waters | Y | N | Y | Y | Y | Y | Y | Y |
| 30 Martinez | Y | ? | Y | Y | Y | Y | Y | Y |
| 31 Dymally | Y | ? | ? | ? | ? | Y | Y | Y |
| 32 Anderson | Y | N | Y | Y | Y | Y | Y | Y |
| 33 *Dreier* | N | Y | N | Y | Y | N | N | Y |
| 34 Torres | Y | N | Y | Y | Y | Y | Y | Y |
| 35 *Lewis* | N | Y | Y | N | N | N | N | Y |
| 36 Brown | Y | N | Y | Y | Y | Y | Y | Y |
| 37 *McCandless* | N | Y | Y | N | N | N | N | Y |
| 38 *Dornan* | N | Y | N | N | N | N | N | Y |
| 39 *Dannemeyer* | N | Y | Y | N | N | N | N | Y |
| 40 *Cox* | N | Y | ? | N | N | N | N | Y |
| 41 *Lowery* | N | Y | ? | N | N | N | N | Y |

| | 218 | 219 | 220 | 221 | 222 | 223 | 224 | 225 |
|---|---|---|---|---|---|---|---|---|
| 42 *Rohrabacher* | N | Y | Y | N | N | N | N | Y |
| 43 *Packard* | Y | Y | Y | Y | N | N | N | Y |
| 44 *Cunningham* | N | Y | Y | N | N | N | N | Y |
| 45 *Hunter* | ? | Y | ? | ? | N | N | N | Y |
| **COLORADO** | | | | | | | | |
| 1 Schroeder | N | N | Y | N | Y | Y | Y | Y |
| 2 Skaggs | Y | N | Y | Y | Y | Y | Y | Y |
| 3 Campbell | ? | N | Y | Y | Y | Y | Y | N |
| 4 *Allard* | N | Y | N | N | N | N | N | Y |
| 5 *Hefley* | N | Y | N | N | N | N | N | Y |
| 6 *Schaefer* | N | Y | N | N | N | N | N | Y |
| **CONNECTICUT** | | | | | | | | |
| 1 Kennelly | Y | N | Y | Y | Y | Y | Y | Y |
| 2 Gejdenson | Y | N | Y | Y | Y | Y | Y | Y |
| 3 DeLauro | Y | N | Y | Y | Y | Y | Y | Y |
| 4 *Shays* | N | N | Y | Y | Y | N | N | Y |
| 5 *Franks* | N | Y | N | N | N | N | N | Y |
| 6 *Johnson* | N | Y | Y | N | Y | N | N | Y |
| **DELAWARE** | | | | | | | | |
| AL Carper | Y | N | Y | Y | Y | Y | N | Y |
| **FLORIDA** | | | | | | | | |
| 1 Hutto | Y | N | Y | Y | N | Y | Y | Y |
| 2 Peterson | Y | N | Y | Y | Y | Y | Y | Y |
| 3 Bennett | Y | N | Y | N | Y | N | N | Y |
| 4 *James* | N | N | N | N | N | N | N | Y |
| 5 *McCollum* | N | Y | Y | N | N | N | N | Y |
| 6 *Stearns* | N | Y | Y | N | N | N | N | Y |
| 7 Gibbons | Y | N | Y | Y | Y | Y | Y | Y |
| 8 *Young* | N | Y | Y | N | N | N | N | Y |
| 9 *Bilirakis* | N | Y | Y | N | N | N | N | Y |
| 10 *Ireland* | N | Y | ? | N | N | N | N | Y |
| 11 Bacchus | Y | N | Y | Y | Y | Y | Y | Y |
| 12 *Lewis* | N | Y | Y | N | N | N | N | Y |
| 13 *Goss* | N | N | N | N | N | N | N | Y |
| 14 Johnston | Y | N | ? | Y | Y | Y | Y | Y |
| 15 *Shaw* | N | Y | Y | N | N | N | N | Y |
| 16 Smith | Y | N | Y | Y | Y | Y | Y | Y |
| 17 Lehman | ? | ? | ? | Y | Y | Y | Y | Y |
| 18 *Ros—Lehtinen* | N | N | N | N | N | N | N | Y |
| 19 Fascell | Y | N | Y | Y | Y | Y | Y | Y |
| **GEORGIA** | | | | | | | | |
| 1 Thomas | Y | N | Y | ? | Y | Y | Y | Y |
| 2 Hatcher | Y | N | Y | Y | Y | Y | Y | Y |
| 3 Ray | Y | N | Y | ? | N | Y | Y | Y |
| 4 Jones | ? | ? | ? | ? | \# | ? | ? | ? |
| 5 Lewis | Y | N | Y | Y | Y | Y | Y | Y |
| 6 *Gingrich* | N | Y | N | N | N | N | N | Y |
| 7 Darden | Y | N | Y | Y | Y | Y | Y | Y |
| 8 Rowland | Y | N | Y | Y | Y | Y | Y | Y |
| 9 Jenkins | Y | N | ? | Y | Y | Y | N | Y |
| 10 Barnard | ? | ? | ? | Y | Y | Y | Y | Y |
| **HAWAII** | | | | | | | | |
| 1 Abercrombie | Y | N | Y | Y | Y | Y | Y | Y |
| 2 Mink | Y | N | Y | Y | Y | Y | Y | Y |
| **IDAHO** | | | | | | | | |
| 1 LaRocco | Y | N | Y | Y | Y | Y | Y | Y |
| 2 Stallings | ? | ? | ? | Y | N | Y | Y | Y |
| **ILLINOIS** | | | | | | | | |
| 1 Hayes | Y | N | Y | Y | Y | Y | Y | Y |
| 2 Savage | Y | N | Y | ? | Y | ? | ? | Y |
| 3 Russo | Y | N | Y | Y | Y | Y | Y | Y |
| 4 Sangmeister | Y | N | Y | Y | Y | Y | Y | Y |
| 5 Lipinski | Y | N | Y | Y | Y | Y | Y | Y |
| 6 *Hyde* | Y | ? | ? | Y | N | N | N | Y |
| 7 Collins | Y | N | Y | Y | Y | Y | Y | Y |
| 8 Rostenkowski | Y | N | Y | Y | Y | Y | Y | Y |
| 9 Yates | ? | ? | ? | Y | Y | Y | Y | Y |
| 10 *Porter* | Y | Y | N | N | Y | N | N | Y |
| 11 Annunzio | Y | N | Y | Y | Y | Y | Y | Y |
| 12 *Crane* | N | Y | N | N | N | N | N | Y |
| 13 *Fawell* | N | N | N | Y | N | N | N | Y |
| 14 *Hastert* | N | Y | Y | N | N | N | N | Y |
| 15 *Ewing* | N | Y | N | Y | N | N | N | Y |
| 16 Cox | Y | N | Y | Y | Y | Y | Y | Y |
| 17 Evans | Y | N | Y | Y | Y | Y | Y | Y |
| 18 *Michel* | N | Y | Y | N | N | N | N | Y |
| 19 Bruce | Y | N | Y | Y | Y | Y | Y | Y |
| 20 Durbin | Y | N | Y | Y | Y | Y | Y | Y |
| 21 Costello | Y | N | Y | Y | Y | Y | Y | Y |
| 22 Poshard | Y | N | Y | Y | N | Y | N | Y |
| **INDIANA** | | | | | | | | |
| 1 Visclosky | Y | N | Y | Y | Y | Y | Y | Y |
| 2 Sharp | Y | N | ? | Y | Y | Y | Y | Y |
| 3 Roemer | Y | N | Y | Y | Y | Y | Y | Y |

ND   Northern Democrats   SD   Southern Democrats

| | 218 | 219 | 220 | 221 | 222 | 223 | 224 | 225 |
|---|---|---|---|---|---|---|---|---|
| 4 Long | Y | N | Y | Y | Y | Y | Y | Y |
| 5 Jontz | Y | N | Y | Y | Y | Y | Y | Y |
| 6 ***Burton*** | N | Y | N | N | N | N | N | Y |
| 7 ***Myers*** | Y | Y | Y | Y | N | N | N | Y |
| 8 McCloskey | Y | N | Y | ? | Y | Y | Y | Y |
| 9 Hamilton | Y | N | Y | Y | Y | Y | Y | Y |
| 10 Jacobs | N | N | Y | N | Y | N | N | Y |
| **IOWA** | | | | | | | | |
| 1 ***Leach*** | N | N | N | N | Y | N | N | Y |
| 2 ***Nussle*** | N | Y | ? | N | N | N | N | Y |
| 3 Nagle | ? | N | Y | ? | Y | Y | Y | Y |
| 4 Smith | Y | ? | Y | Y | Y | Y | Y | Y |
| 5 ***Lightfoot*** | N | Y | N | N | N | N | N | Y |
| 6 ***Grandy*** | N | Y | Y | N | N | N | N | Y |
| **KANSAS** | | | | | | | | |
| 1 ***Roberts*** | N | Y | Y | N | N | N | N | Y |
| 2 Slattery | Y | N | Y | Y | Y | Y | Y | Y |
| 3 ***Meyers*** | N | Y | Y | N | Y | N | N | Y |
| 4 Glickman | Y | N | Y | Y | Y | Y | Y | Y |
| 5 ***Nichols*** | Y | Y | Y | Y | N | N | N | Y |
| **KENTUCKY** | | | | | | | | |
| 1 Hubbard | Y | N | Y | Y | Y | Y | Y | Y |
| 2 Natcher | Y | N | Y | Y | Y | Y | Y | Y |
| 3 Mazzoli | Y | N | Y | Y | N | Y | Y | Y |
| 4 ***Bunning*** | N | Y | Y | N | N | N | N | Y |
| 5 ***Rogers*** | N | Y | Y | N | N | N | N | Y |
| 6 ***Hopkins*** | N | Y | Y | N | N | N | N | Y |
| 7 Perkins | Y | N | Y | Y | Y | Y | Y | Y |
| **LOUISIANA** | | | | | | | | |
| 1 ***Livingston*** | N | Y | Y | Y | N | N | N | Y |
| 2 Jefferson | ? | ? | Y | Y | Y | Y | Y | Y |
| 3 Tauzin | Y | N | Y | Y | N | Y | Y | Y |
| 4 ***McCrery*** | N | Y | Y | ? | N | N | N | Y |
| 5 Huckaby | Y | N | Y | Y | Y | Y | Y | Y |
| 6 ***Baker*** | N | Y | N | N | N | N | N | Y |
| 7 Hayes | Y | N | Y | Y | N | Y | Y | Y |
| 8 ***Holloway*** | N | Y | N | N | N | ? | N | Y |
| **MAINE** | | | | | | | | |
| 1 Andrews | Y | N | Y | Y | Y | Y | Y | Y |
| 2 ***Snowe*** | Y | Y | Y | Y | Y | N | N | Y |
| **MARYLAND** | | | | | | | | |
| 1 ***Gilchrest*** | N | Y | N | N | Y | N | ? | Y |
| 2 ***Bentley*** | N | Y | Y | N | Y | N | N | Y |
| 3 Cardin | Y | N | Y | Y | Y | Y | Y | Y |
| 4 McMillen | Y | N | Y | Y | Y | Y | Y | Y |
| 5 Hoyer | Y | N | Y | Y | Y | Y | Y | Y |
| 6 Byron | Y | N | Y | Y | Y | Y | Y | Y |
| 7 Mfume | Y | N | Y | ? | Y | Y | Y | Y |
| 8 ***Morella*** | N | N | Y | ? | Y | N | N | Y |
| **MASSACHUSETTS** | | | | | | | | |
| 1 Olver | Y | N | Y | Y | Y | Y | Y | Y |
| 2 Neal | Y | N | Y | Y | Y | Y | Y | Y |
| 3 Early | Y | N | Y | Y | Y | N | N | Y |
| 4 Frank | Y | N | Y | Y | Y | Y | Y | Y |
| 5 Atkins | Y | N | Y | Y | Y | N | N | Y |
| 6 Mavroules | ? | N | Y | Y | Y | Y | Y | Y |
| 7 Markey | ? | ? | Y | Y | Y | Y | Y | Y |
| 8 Kennedy | Y | N | Y | Y | Y | Y | Y | Y |
| 9 Moakley | Y | N | Y | Y | Y | Y | Y | Y |
| 10 Studds | Y | N | Y | Y | Y | Y | Y | Y |
| 11 Donnelly | Y | N | Y | Y | Y | Y | Y | Y |
| **MICHIGAN** | | | | | | | | |
| 1 Conyers | Y | ? | Y | Y | Y | Y | Y | Y |
| 2 ***Pursell*** | N | Y | ? | N | Y | N | N | Y |
| 3 Wolpe | Y | N | Y | Y | Y | Y | Y | Y |
| 4 ***Upton*** | N | Y | Y | N | Y | N | N | Y |
| 5 ***Henry*** | N | Y | Y | N | Y | N | N | Y |
| 6 Carr | Y | N | Y | Y | Y | Y | Y | Y |
| 7 Kildee | Y | N | Y | Y | Y | Y | Y | Y |
| 8 Traxler | ? | ? | ? | ? | Y | Y | ? | ? |
| 9 ***Vander Jagt*** | Y | Y | ? | Y | N | N | N | Y |
| 10 ***Camp*** | N | Y | Y | N | N | N | N | Y |
| 11 ***Davis*** | ? | Y | ? | ? | N | N | N | Y |
| 12 Bonior | ? | ? | ? | ? | ? | ? | ? | ? |
| 13 Collins | Y | N | Y | ? | Y | Y | Y | Y |
| 14 Hertel | Y | ? | ? | ? | Y | Y | Y | Y |
| 15 Ford | Y | N | Y | ? | Y | Y | Y | Y |
| 16 Dingell | Y | N | Y | Y | Y | Y | Y | Y |
| 17 Levin | Y | N | Y | Y | Y | Y | Y | Y |
| 18 ***Broomfield*** | N | Y | ? | Y | N | N | N | Y |
| **MINNESOTA** | | | | | | | | |
| 1 Penny | Y | Y | Y | N | N | Y | Y | Y |
| 2 ***Weber*** | N | Y | Y | N | N | N | N | Y |
| 3 ***Ramstad*** | N | N | N | N | N | N | N | Y |
| 4 Vento | Y | N | ? | Y | Y | Y | Y | Y |

| | 218 | 219 | 220 | 221 | 222 | 223 | 224 | 225 |
|---|---|---|---|---|---|---|---|---|
| 5 Sabo | Y | N | Y | Y | Y | Y | Y | Y |
| 6 Sikorski | N | N | Y | N | Y | Y | Y | Y |
| 7 Peterson | Y | N | Y | Y | N | Y | N | Y |
| 8 Oberstar | Y | ? | Y | Y | N | Y | Y | Y |
| **MISSISSIPPI** | | | | | | | | |
| 1 Whitten | Y | N | N | ? | Y | Y | Y | Y |
| 2 Espy | Y | N | Y | Y | Y | Y | Y | Y |
| 3 Montgomery | Y | N | Y | Y | Y | Y | Y | Y |
| 4 Parker | Y | N | Y | Y | N | Y | Y | Y |
| 5 Taylor | Y | N | N | Y | N | Y | Y | Y |
| **MISSOURI** | | | | | | | | |
| 1 Clay | Y | N | ? | N | Y | Y | Y | Y |
| 2 Horn | Y | N | Y | Y | Y | Y | Y | Y |
| 3 Gephardt | Y | N | Y | Y | Y | Y | Y | Y |
| 4 Skelton | Y | N | Y | Y | N | Y | Y | Y |
| 5 Wheat | Y | N | Y | ? | Y | Y | Y | Y |
| 6 ***Coleman*** | N | Y | Y | N | Y | N | N | Y |
| 7 ***Hancock*** | N | Y | N | N | N | N | N | Y |
| 8 ***Emerson*** | N | N | N | N | N | N | N | Y |
| 9 Volkmer | Y | N | Y | Y | N | Y | Y | Y |
| **MONTANA** | | | | | | | | |
| 1 Williams | Y | ? | ? | Y | Y | Y | N | Y |
| 2 ***Marlenee*** | N | Y | Y | N | N | N | N | Y |
| **NEBRASKA** | | | | | | | | |
| 1 ***Bereuter*** | N | N | N | N | N | N | N | Y |
| 2 Hoagland | Y | N | Y | Y | Y | Y | Y | Y |
| 3 ***Barrett*** | N | Y | Y | N | N | N | N | Y |
| **NEVADA** | | | | | | | | |
| 1 Bilbray | Y | N | Y | Y | Y | Y | Y | Y |
| 2 ***Vucanovich*** | N | Y | N | N | N | N | N | Y |
| **NEW HAMPSHIRE** | | | | | | | | |
| 1 ***Zeliff*** | N | N | Y | N | N | N | N | Y |
| 2 Swett | Y | N | Y | Y | Y | Y | Y | Y |
| **NEW JERSEY** | | | | | | | | |
| 1 Andrews | Y | N | Y | Y | Y | Y | Y | Y |
| 2 Hughes | Y | N | Y | Y | Y | Y | Y | Y |
| 3 Pallone | Y | N | Y | Y | Y | Y | Y | Y |
| 4 ***Smith*** | Y | N | Y | Y | N | N | N | Y |
| 5 ***Roukema*** | N | N | Y | N | Y | N | N | Y |
| 6 Dwyer | ? | N | Y | Y | Y | Y | Y | Y |
| 7 ***Rinaldo*** | Y | Y | Y | Y | N | N | N | Y |
| 8 Roe | Y | Y | ? | Y | N | Y | Y | Y |
| 9 Torricelli | Y | N | Y | Y | Y | Y | Y | Y |
| 10 Payne | Y | N | Y | Y | Y | Y | Y | Y |
| 11 ***Gallo*** | N | Y | Y | N | Y | N | N | Y |
| 12 ***Zimmer*** | N | Y | Y | N | Y | N | N | Y |
| 13 ***Saxton*** | N | Y | Y | N | N | N | N | Y |
| 14 Guarini | Y | N | Y | Y | Y | Y | Y | Y |
| **NEW MEXICO** | | | | | | | | |
| 1 ***Schiff*** | ? | Y | Y | N | N | N | N | Y |
| 2 ***Skeen*** | Y | Y | Y | Y | Y | N | N | Y |
| 3 Richardson | Y | ? | Y | Y | Y | Y | Y | Y |
| **NEW YORK** | | | | | | | | |
| 1 Hochbrueckner | Y | N | Y | Y | Y | Y | Y | Y |
| 2 Downey | ? | ? | Y | Y | Y | Y | Y | Y |
| 3 Mrazek | ? | N | Y | Y | Y | Y | Y | ? |
| 4 ***Lent*** | N | N | Y | N | N | N | N | Y |
| 5 ***McGrath*** | Y | Y | Y | ? | N | N | N | Y |
| 6 Flake | Y | N | Y | ? | # | Y | Y | Y |
| 7 Ackerman | Y | N | Y | Y | Y | Y | Y | Y |
| 8 Scheuer | Y | N | Y | Y | Y | Y | Y | Y |
| 9 Manton | ? | ? | Y | Y | N | Y | Y | Y |
| 10 Schumer | Y | N | Y | ? | ? | ? | ? | ? |
| 11 Towns | Y | N | Y | Y | Y | Y | Y | Y |
| 12 Owens | Y | N | Y | Y | Y | Y | Y | Y |
| 13 Solarz | Y | N | Y | Y | Y | ? | ? | Y |
| 14 ***Molinari*** | N | Y | Y | N | Y | N | N | Y |
| 15 ***Green*** | Y | N | Y | Y | Y | N | N | Y |
| 16 Rangel | Y | ? | ? | Y | Y | Y | Y | Y |
| 17 Weiss | Y | N | Y | ? | Y | Y | Y | Y |
| 18 Serrano | ? | ? | Y | ? | Y | Y | Y | Y |
| 19 Engel | Y | N | Y | ? | + | Y | Y | Y |
| 20 Lowey | Y | N | Y | Y | Y | Y | Y | Y |
| 21 ***Fish*** | Y | Y | ? | Y | N | N | N | Y |
| 22 ***Gilman*** | Y | N | N | Y | Y | N | N | Y |
| 23 McNulty | ? | ? | ? | ? | ? | ? | ? | ? |
| 24 ***Solomon*** | N | Y | N | N | N | N | N | Y |
| 25 ***Boehlert*** | N | N | Y | N | Y | N | N | Y |
| 26 ***Martin*** | P | Y | Y | N | N | N | N | Y |
| 27 ***Walsh*** | ? | Y | Y | N | N | N | N | Y |
| 28 McHugh | ? | ? | ? | Y | Y | Y | Y | Y |
| 29 ***Horton*** | Y | Y | ? | Y | Y | N | N | Y |
| 30 Slaughter | Y | N | Y | Y | Y | Y | Y | Y |
| 31 ***Paxon*** | N | Y | Y | N | N | N | N | Y |

| | 218 | 219 | 220 | 221 | 222 | 223 | 224 | 225 |
|---|---|---|---|---|---|---|---|---|
| 32 LaFalce | ? | ? | ? | Y | N | Y | Y | Y |
| 33 Nowak | Y | N | Y | Y | N | Y | Y | Y |
| 34 ***Houghton*** | Y | Y | Y | Y | Y | N | N | Y |
| **NORTH CAROLINA** | | | | | | | | |
| 1 Jones | Y | N | Y | Y | Y | Y | Y | Y |
| 2 Valentine | ? | N | Y | Y | Y | Y | Y | Y |
| 3 Lancaster | Y | N | Y | Y | Y | Y | Y | Y |
| 4 Price | Y | N | Y | Y | Y | Y | Y | Y |
| 5 Neal | Y | N | Y | ? | Y | Y | Y | Y |
| 6 ***Coble*** | N | N | N | N | N | N | N | Y |
| 7 Rose | Y | N | Y | Y | Y | Y | Y | Y |
| 8 Hefner | ? | ? | ? | ? | ? | ? | ? | ? |
| 9 ***McMillan*** | N | Y | Y | N | N | N | N | Y |
| 10 ***Ballenger*** | N | Y | N | N | N | N | N | Y |
| 11 ***Taylor*** | N | Y | N | N | N | N | N | Y |
| **NORTH DAKOTA** | | | | | | | | |
| AL Dorgan | Y | N | ? | Y | Y | Y | Y | Y |
| **OHIO** | | | | | | | | |
| 1 Luken | Y | N | Y | Y | N | Y | Y | Y |
| 2 ***Gradison*** | Y | Y | Y | N | Y | N | N | Y |
| 3 Hall | ? | N | Y | Y | N | Y | Y | Y |
| 4 ***Oxley*** | ? | ? | Y | N | N | N | N | Y |
| 5 ***Gillmor*** | Y | Y | Y | ? | Y | N | N | Y |
| 6 ***McEwen*** | N | Y | N | N | N | N | ? | Y |
| 7 ***Hobson*** | N | Y | N | N | Y | N | N | Y |
| 8 ***Boehner*** | N | Y | Y | N | N | N | N | Y |
| 9 Kaptur | Y | N | Y | Y | Y | Y | Y | Y |
| 10 ***Miller*** | N | N | Y | N | N | N | N | Y |
| 11 Eckart | ? | Y | Y | Y | Y | Y | Y | Y |
| 12 ***Kasich*** | Y | Y | ? | Y | N | N | N | Y |
| 13 Pease | Y | N | Y | Y | Y | Y | Y | Y |
| 14 Sawyer | Y | N | Y | Y | Y | Y | Y | Y |
| 15 ***Wylie*** | Y | Y | Y | Y | N | N | N | Y |
| 16 ***Regula*** | N | Y | Y | N | Y | N | N | Y |
| 17 Traficant | Y | N | Y | Y | Y | Y | Y | Y |
| 18 Applegate | Y | N | Y | Y | Y | Y | Y | Y |
| 19 Feighan | Y | N | Y | Y | Y | Y | Y | Y |
| 20 Oakar | Y | N | Y | Y | Y | Y | Y | Y |
| 21 Stokes | Y | N | Y | Y | Y | Y | Y | Y |
| **OKLAHOMA** | | | | | | | | |
| 1 ***Inhofe*** | ? | Y | N | N | N | N | N | Y |
| 2 Synar | Y | N | Y | Y | Y | Y | Y | Y |
| 3 Brewster | Y | N | Y | Y | Y | Y | Y | Y |
| 4 McCurdy | Y | N | Y | Y | Y | Y | Y | Y |
| 5 ***Edwards*** | ? | ? | ? | ? | X | N | N | Y |
| 6 English | Y | ? | Y | Y | Y | Y | Y | Y |
| **OREGON** | | | | | | | | |
| 1 AuCoin | Y | N | ? | Y | Y | Y | Y | Y |
| 2 ***Smith*** | N | Y | Y | N | N | N | N | Y |
| 3 Wyden | Y | N | Y | Y | Y | Y | Y | Y |
| 4 DeFazio | Y | N | Y | Y | Y | Y | Y | Y |
| 5 Kopetski | Y | N | Y | Y | Y | Y | Y | Y |
| **PENNSYLVANIA** | | | | | | | | |
| 1 Foglietta | Y | N | Y | Y | Y | Y | Y | Y |
| 2 Blackwell | Y | N | Y | Y | Y | Y | Y | Y |
| 3 Borski | Y | N | Y | Y | Y | Y | Y | Y |
| 4 Kolter | Y | N | Y | ? | N | Y | Y | Y |
| 5 ***Schulze*** | Y | ? | Y | Y | N | N | N | Y |
| 6 Yatron | Y | N | Y | Y | Y | Y | Y | Y |
| 7 ***Weldon*** | N | N | N | N | N | N | N | Y |
| 8 Kostmayer | Y | N | Y | Y | Y | Y | Y | Y |
| 9 ***Shuster*** | N | Y | Y | N | Y | N | N | Y |
| 10 ***McDade*** | N | N | ? | N | N | N | N | Y |
| 11 Kanjorski | Y | N | Y | Y | N | Y | Y | Y |
| 12 Murtha | Y | N | Y | Y | Y | Y | Y | Y |
| 13 ***Coughlin*** | N | Y | Y | ? | N | N | N | Y |
| 14 Coyne | Y | N | Y | Y | Y | Y | Y | Y |
| 15 ***Ritter*** | Y | ? | ? | Y | N | N | N | Y |
| 16 ***Walker*** | N | Y | N | N | N | N | ? | Y |
| 17 ***Gekas*** | N | Y | N | N | N | N | N | Y |
| 18 ***Santorum*** | N | Y | N | N | N | N | N | Y |
| 19 ***Goodling*** | N | N | Y | N | N | N | N | Y |
| 20 Gaydos | Y | N | Y | ? | N | Y | Y | Y |
| 21 ***Ridge*** | ? | ? | ? | N | Y | N | N | Y |
| 22 Murphy | N | Y | Y | N | N | Y | Y | Y |
| 23 ***Clinger*** | Y | Y | Y | Y | N | N | N | Y |
| **RHODE ISLAND** | | | | | | | | |
| 1 ***Machtley*** | ? | ? | Y | N | Y | N | N | Y |
| 2 Reed | Y | N | Y | Y | Y | Y | Y | Y |
| **SOUTH CAROLINA** | | | | | | | | |
| 1 ***Ravenel*** | Y | Y | Y | Y | Y | N | N | Y |
| 2 ***Spence*** | ? | Y | Y | N | N | N | N | Y |
| 3 Derrick | Y | N | Y | Y | Y | Y | Y | Y |
| 4 Patterson | Y | N | Y | Y | Y | Y | N | Y |
| 5 Spratt | Y | Y | Y | Y | Y | Y | Y | Y |
| 6 Tallon | Y | ? | Y | Y | Y | Y | Y | Y |

| | 218 | 219 | 220 | 221 | 222 | 223 | 224 | 225 |
|---|---|---|---|---|---|---|---|---|
| **SOUTH DAKOTA** | | | | | | | | |
| AL Johnson | Y | N | Y | Y | Y | Y | Y | Y |
| **TENNESSEE** | | | | | | | | |
| 1 ***Quillen*** | N | Y | Y | N | N | N | N | Y |
| 2 ***Duncan*** | N | Y | Y | N | N | N | N | Y |
| 3 Lloyd | Y | N | Y | Y | Y | Y | N | Y |
| 4 Cooper | Y | N | Y | Y | Y | Y | Y | Y |
| 5 Clement | Y | N | Y | Y | Y | Y | Y | Y |
| 6 Gordon | Y | N | Y | Y | Y | Y | Y | Y |
| 7 ***Sundquist*** | N | Y | Y | N | N | N | N | Y |
| 8 Tanner | Y | N | Y | Y | Y | Y | Y | Y |
| 9 Ford | Y | N | Y | Y | Y | Y | Y | Y |
| **TEXAS** | | | | | | | | |
| 1 Chapman | Y | ? | ? | Y | Y | Y | Y | Y |
| 2 Wilson | Y | N | Y | Y | Y | Y | Y | Y |
| 3 ***Johnson*** | Y | Y | Y | Y | N | N | N | Y |
| 4 Hall | Y | N | Y | Y | Y | Y | Y | Y |
| 5 Bryant | Y | N | Y | Y | Y | Y | Y | Y |
| 6 ***Barton*** | N | N | N | N | N | N | N | Y |
| 7 ***Archer*** | Y | N | N | Y | N | N | N | Y |
| 8 ***Fields*** | ? | ? | N | N | N | N | N | Y |
| 9 Brooks | Y | N | Y | Y | Y | Y | Y | Y |
| 10 Pickle | Y | N | Y | Y | Y | Y | Y | Y |
| 11 Edwards | Y | N | Y | Y | Y | Y | Y | Y |
| 12 Geren | Y | N | Y | Y | Y | Y | Y | Y |
| 13 Sarpalius | Y | N | Y | Y | N | Y | Y | Y |
| 14 Laughlin | Y | N | Y | Y | Y | Y | Y | Y |
| 15 de la Garza | Y | N | Y | Y | N | Y | Y | Y |
| 16 Coleman | Y | N | Y | Y | Y | Y | Y | Y |
| 17 Stenholm | Y | N | Y | Y | N | Y | Y | Y |
| 18 Washington | ? | ? | ? | ? | Y | ? | Y | ? |
| 19 ***Combest*** | Y | N | ? | Y | N | N | N | Y |
| 20 Gonzalez | Y | N | Y | Y | Y | Y | Y | Y |
| 21 ***Smith*** | N | N | Y | N | Y | N | N | Y |
| 22 ***DeLay*** | N | Y | N | N | N | N | N | Y |
| 23 Bustamante | Y | N | Y | Y | Y | Y | Y | Y |
| 24 Frost | Y | N | ? | Y | Y | Y | Y | Y |
| 25 Andrews | Y | N | Y | Y | Y | Y | Y | Y |
| 26 ***Armey*** | N | Y | N | N | N | N | N | Y |
| 27 Ortiz | Y | N | Y | Y | N | Y | Y | Y |
| **UTAH** | | | | | | | | |
| 1 ***Hansen*** | N | N | Y | ? | N | N | N | Y |
| 2 Owens | Y | N | Y | Y | Y | Y | Y | Y |
| 3 Orton | Y | N | Y | Y | N | Y | Y | Y |
| **VERMONT** | | | | | | | | |
| AL *Sanders* | Y | N | Y | ? | Y | Y | Y | Y |
| **VIRGINIA** | | | | | | | | |
| 1 ***Bateman*** | Y | Y | Y | Y | N | N | N | Y |
| 2 Pickett | Y | N | Y | Y | Y | Y | Y | Y |
| 3 ***Bliley*** | N | Y | Y | N | N | N | N | Y |
| 4 Sisisky | Y | N | Y | Y | Y | Y | Y | Y |
| 5 Payne | Y | N | Y | Y | Y | Y | Y | Y |
| 6 Olin | Y | N | ? | Y | Y | Y | Y | Y |
| 7 ***Allen*** | N | Y | Y | N | N | N | N | Y |
| 8 Moran | Y | N | Y | Y | Y | Y | Y | Y |
| 9 Boucher | Y | N | Y | Y | Y | Y | Y | Y |
| 10 ***Wolf*** | N | Y | Y | N | N | N | N | Y |
| **WASHINGTON** | | | | | | | | |
| 1 ***Miller*** | N | Y | Y | N | Y | N | N | Y |
| 2 Swift | Y | N | Y | Y | Y | Y | Y | Y |
| 3 Unsoeld | Y | N | Y | Y | Y | Y | Y | Y |
| 4 ***Morrison*** | Y | N | N | Y | Y | N | N | Y |
| 5 Foley | | | | | Y | | | |
| 6 Dicks | Y | N | Y | Y | Y | Y | Y | Y |
| 7 McDermott | Y | N | Y | Y | Y | Y | Y | Y |
| 8 ***Chandler*** | N | N | Y | N | Y | N | N | Y |
| **WEST VIRGINIA** | | | | | | | | |
| 1 Mollohan | Y | N | Y | Y | N | Y | Y | Y |
| 2 Staggers | ? | ? | Y | Y | Y | Y | Y | Y |
| 3 Wise | Y | N | Y | Y | Y | Y | Y | Y |
| 4 Rahall | Y | Y | N | Y | N | Y | Y | Y |
| **WISCONSIN** | | | | | | | | |
| 1 Aspin | Y | N | Y | Y | Y | Y | Y | Y |
| 2 ***Klug*** | N | Y | ? | N | Y | N | N | Y |
| 3 ***Gunderson*** | Y | Y | Y | Y | N | N | N | Y |
| 4 Kleczka | Y | N | Y | Y | Y | Y | Y | Y |
| 5 Moody | Y | N | Y | Y | Y | Y | Y | Y |
| 6 ***Petri*** | Y | N | ? | Y | N | N | N | Y |
| 7 Obey | Y | N | Y | Y | Y | Y | Y | Y |
| 8 ***Roth*** | Y | Y | N | N | N | N | N | Y |
| 9 ***Sensenbrenner*** | N | Y | Y | N | N | N | N | Y |
| **WYOMING** | | | | | | | | |
| AL ***Thomas*** | N | Y | Y | N | N | N | N | Y |

Southern states - Ala., Ark., Fla., Ga., Ky., La., Miss., N.C., Okla., S.C., Tenn., Texas, Va.
Omitted votes are quorum calls, which CQ does not include in its vote charts.

**226. HR 5427. Fiscal 1993 Legislative Branch Appropriations/General Accounting Office.** Cox, R-Calif., amendment to cut the appropriations for the GAO from $442 million to $333 million. Rejected 134-292: R 128-37; D 6-254 (ND 3-174, SD 3-80); I 0-1, June 24, 1992.

**227. HR 5427. Fiscal 1993 Legislative Branch Appropriations/Franked Mass Mailings.** Thomas, R-Calif., amendment to change the effective date rescinding authority for members to frank mass mailings outside their districts from Oct. 1, 1992, to the date of the enactment of the bill. Adopted 417-2: R 165-0; D 251-2 (ND 173-1, SD 78-1); I 1-0, June 24, 1992.

**229. HR 5427. Fiscal 1993 Legislative Branch Appropriations/Mail Costs.** Lightfoot, R-Iowa, motion to recommit the bill to the House Appropriations Committee, with instructions to report it back to the House after cutting $5.3 million from the account for the official mail costs of the House, reducing it from $53 million to $47.7 million. Motion agreed to 376-45: R 163-0; D 212-45 (ND 145-32, SD 67-13); I 1-0, June 24, 1992.

**230. HR 5427. Fiscal 1993 Legislative Branch Appropriations/Passage.** Passage of the bill to provide $1.8 billion in new budget authority for the operations of the House and legislative branch agencies in fiscal 1993. The amounts did not include the activities of the Senate that were to be inserted later when the bill was considered by that chamber. The budget request was for $2,104,436,000. Passed 279-143: R 32-132; D 246-11 (ND 169-8, SD 77-3); I 1-0, June 24, 1992.

**231. HR 5368. Fiscal 1993 Foreign Operations Appropriations/Rule.** Adoption of the rule (H Res 501) to provide for House floor consideration of the bill to provide $13.8 billion in new budget authority for foreign military and economic assistance and export financing in fiscal 1993. Adopted 246-177: R 0-163; D 245-14 (ND 168-10, SD 77-4); I 1-0, June 25, 1992.

**232. HR 5368. Fiscal 1993 Foreign Operations Appropriations/Reduce Funding.** Appropriations Committee substitute amendment to reduce the president's $15.1 billion request by $1.3 billion to a level of $13.8 billion. Adopted 418-2: R 161-1; D 256-1 (ND 175-1, SD 81-0); I 1-0, June 25, 1992.

**233. HR 5368. Fiscal 1993 Foreign Operations Appropriations/Development Assistance.** Burton, R-Ind., amendment to cut the development assistance account by $24 million. The administration requested $24 million for development assistance to India, but the bill does not have an earmark. Adopted 219-200: R 127-35; D 92-164 (ND 55-123, SD 37-41); I 0-1, June 25, 1992.

**234. HR 5368. Fiscal 1993 Foreign Operations Appropriations/Recommit With Instructions.** Myers, R-Ind., motion to recommit to the House Appropriations Committee the bill, with instructions to report it back to the House after cutting $35,882,400 in multilateral and bilateral economic assistance and eliminating $223,390,300 in callable loans to the International Bank for Reconstruction and Development. Motion agreed to 392-28: R 161-3; D 230-25 (ND 155-22, SD 75-3); I 1-0, June 25, 1992.

## KEY

Y   Voted for (yea).
\#   Paired for.
+   Announced for.
N   Voted against (nay).
X   Paired against.
—   Announced against.
P   Voted "present."
C   Voted "present" to avoid possible conflict of interest.
?   Did not vote or otherwise make a position known.

Democrats   **Republicans**
*Independent*

| | 226 | 227 | 229 | 230 | 231 | 232 | 233 | 234 |
|---|---|---|---|---|---|---|---|---|
| **ALABAMA** | | | | | | | | |
| 1 *Callahan* | Y | Y | Y | N | N | Y | Y | Y |
| 2 *Dickinson* | Y | Y | ? | N | N | ? | Y | Y |
| 3 Browder | N | Y | Y | Y | Y | Y | Y | Y |
| 4 Bevill | N | Y | Y | Y | Y | Y | Y | Y |
| 5 Cramer | N | Y | Y | Y | Y | Y | Y | Y |
| 6 Erdreich | Y | Y | Y | N | Y | Y | Y | Y |
| 7 Harris | N | Y | Y | Y | Y | Y | Y | Y |
| **ALASKA** | | | | | | | | |
| AL *Young* | N | Y | Y | Y | N | Y | Y | Y |
| **ARIZONA** | | | | | | | | |
| 1 *Rhodes* | Y | Y | Y | N | N | Y | Y | Y |
| 2 Pastor | N | Y | Y | Y | Y | Y | N | Y |
| 3 *Stump* | Y | Y | N | N | N | Y | Y | Y |
| 4 *Kyl* | Y | Y | Y | N | N | Y | Y | Y |
| 5 *Kolbe* | Y | Y | Y | N | N | Y | Y | Y |
| **ARKANSAS** | | | | | | | | |
| 1 Alexander | N | ? | ? | ? | Y | Y | N | Y |
| 2 Thornton | N | Y | Y | Y | Y | Y | N | Y |
| 3 *Hammerschmidt* | N | Y | N | N | N | Y | N | Y |
| 4 Anthony | N | Y | Y | Y | Y | Y | N | ? |
| **CALIFORNIA** | | | | | | | | |
| 1 *Riggs* | Y | Y | Y | N | N | N | Y | N |
| 2 *Herger* | Y | Y | Y | N | N | Y | Y | Y |
| 3 Matsui | N | Y | Y | Y | Y | Y | N | Y |
| 4 Fazio | N | Y | N | Y | Y | Y | Y | Y |
| 5 Pelosi | N | Y | Y | Y | Y | Y | N | N |
| 6 Boxer | N | Y | N | Y | Y | N | N | Y |
| 7 Miller | N | Y | Y | Y | Y | Y | Y | Y |
| 8 Dellums | N | Y | N | Y | Y | N | N | N |
| 9 Stark | N | Y | Y | Y | Y | Y | N | N |
| 10 Edwards | N | Y | Y | Y | Y | Y | N | Y |
| 11 Lantos | N | Y | Y | Y | Y | Y | N | Y |
| 12 *Campbell* | Y | Y | Y | N | N | Y | N | Y |
| 13 Mineta | N | Y | Y | Y | Y | N | N | Y |
| 14 *Doolittle* | Y | Y | Y | N | N | Y | Y | Y |
| 15 Condit | N | Y | Y | Y | Y | Y | N | Y |
| 16 Panetta | N | Y | Y | Y | Y | Y | N | Y |
| 17 Dooley | N | Y | Y | Y | Y | Y | N | Y |
| 18 Lehman | N | Y | Y | Y | Y | Y | N | Y |
| 19 *Lagomarsino* | Y | Y | Y | N | N | Y | Y | Y |
| 20 *Thomas* | Y | Y | Y | N | Y | Y | Y | Y |
| 21 *Gallegly* | Y | Y | Y | N | N | Y | Y | Y |
| 22 *Moorhead* | Y | Y | Y | N | N | Y | Y | Y |
| 23 Beilenson | N | Y | Y | Y | Y | N | N | N |
| 24 Waxman | N | ? | Y | Y | Y | Y | N | N |
| 25 Roybal | N | Y | N | Y | Y | Y | N | Y |
| 26 Berman | N | Y | Y | Y | Y | N | N | N |
| 27 Levine | N | Y | N | Y | Y | Y | N | N |
| 28 Dixon | N | Y | Y | Y | Y | Y | N | Y |
| 29 Waters | N | Y | N | Y | Y | N | N | Y |
| 30 Martinez | N | Y | Y | Y | Y | N | N | Y |
| 31 Dymally | ? | ? | N | Y | Y | Y | N | N |
| 32 Anderson | N | Y | Y | Y | Y | Y | N | Y |
| 33 *Dreier* | Y | Y | Y | N | N | Y | Y | Y |
| 34 Torres | N | Y | Y | Y | Y | Y | N | Y |
| 35 *Lewis* | Y | Y | Y | N | Y | Y | Y | Y |
| 36 Brown | N | Y | Y | Y | Y | N | N | Y |
| 37 *McCandless* | Y | Y | Y | N | N | Y | Y | Y |
| 38 *Dornan* | Y | Y | Y | N | N | Y | Y | Y |
| 39 *Dannemeyer* | Y | Y | Y | N | N | Y | Y | Y |
| 40 *Cox* | Y | Y | Y | N | N | Y | Y | Y |
| 41 *Lowery* | ? | Y | Y | Y | ? | ? | Y | Y |

| | 226 | 227 | 229 | 230 | 231 | 232 | 233 | 234 |
|---|---|---|---|---|---|---|---|---|
| 42 *Rohrabacher* | Y | Y | Y | N | N | Y | Y | Y |
| 43 *Packard* | Y | Y | Y | N | N | Y | Y | Y |
| 44 *Cunningham* | Y | Y | Y | N | N | Y | Y | Y |
| 45 *Hunter* | Y | Y | Y | N | N | Y | Y | Y |
| **COLORADO** | | | | | | | | |
| 1 Schroeder | N | Y | Y | Y | Y | Y | N | Y |
| 2 Skaggs | N | Y | Y | Y | Y | Y | N | Y |
| 3 Campbell | N | Y | Y | Y | Y | Y | N | ? |
| 4 *Allard* | Y | Y | Y | N | N | Y | Y | Y |
| 5 *Hefley* | Y | Y | Y | N | N | Y | Y | Y |
| 6 *Schaefer* | Y | Y | Y | N | N | Y | Y | Y |
| **CONNECTICUT** | | | | | | | | |
| 1 Kennelly | N | Y | Y | Y | Y | Y | N | Y |
| 2 Gejdenson | N | Y | Y | Y | Y | Y | N | Y |
| 3 DeLauro | N | Y | Y | Y | Y | Y | Y | Y |
| 4 *Shays* | N | Y | Y | N | N | Y | Y | Y |
| 5 *Franks* | Y | Y | Y | N | N | Y | Y | Y |
| 6 *Johnson* | Y | Y | N | N | N | Y | Y | Y |
| **DELAWARE** | | | | | | | | |
| AL Carper | N | Y | Y | Y | N | Y | N | Y |
| **FLORIDA** | | | | | | | | |
| 1 Hutto | N | Y | Y | Y | N | Y | Y | Y |
| 2 Peterson | N | Y | Y | Y | Y | Y | N | Y |
| 3 Bennett | N | Y | Y | Y | Y | Y | Y | Y |
| 4 *James* | Y | Y | Y | N | N | Y | Y | Y |
| 5 *McCollum* | Y | Y | Y | N | N | Y | Y | Y |
| 6 *Stearns* | Y | Y | Y | N | N | Y | Y | Y |
| 7 Gibbons | N | Y | Y | Y | Y | Y | N | Y |
| 8 *Young* | N | Y | Y | N | N | Y | Y | Y |
| 9 *Bilirakis* | Y | Y | Y | N | N | Y | Y | Y |
| 10 *Ireland* | N | Y | Y | N | N | Y | Y | Y |
| 11 Bacchus | N | Y | Y | Y | Y | Y | N | Y |
| 12 *Lewis* | Y | Y | Y | N | N | Y | Y | Y |
| 13 *Goss* | Y | Y | Y | N | N | Y | Y | Y |
| 14 Johnston | N | Y | Y | Y | Y | Y | N | Y |
| 15 *Shaw* | Y | Y | Y | N | N | Y | Y | Y |
| 16 Smith | N | Y | Y | Y | Y | Y | N | Y |
| 17 Lehman | N | Y | N | Y | Y | Y | N | N |
| 18 *Ros—Lehtinen* | Y | Y | Y | N | N | Y | Y | Y |
| 19 Fascell | N | Y | N | Y | Y | Y | N | N |
| **GEORGIA** | | | | | | | | |
| 1 Thomas | N | Y | Y | Y | Y | Y | N | Y |
| 2 Hatcher | N | Y | Y | ? | Y | N | ? | Y |
| 3 Ray | N | Y | Y | Y | Y | Y | Y | Y |
| 4 Jones | ? | ? | ? | ? | ? | ? | ? | ? |
| 5 Lewis | N | Y | N | Y | Y | Y | N | Y |
| 6 *Gingrich* | Y | Y | Y | N | N | Y | Y | Y |
| 7 Darden | N | Y | Y | Y | Y | Y | N | Y |
| 8 Rowland | N | Y | Y | Y | Y | Y | N | Y |
| 9 Jenkins | N | Y | Y | Y | Y | Y | N | Y |
| 10 Barnard | N | Y | Y | Y | ? | ? | ? | ? |
| **HAWAII** | | | | | | | | |
| 1 Abercrombie | N | Y | N | Y | Y | Y | Y | Y |
| 2 Mink | N | Y | Y | Y | Y | Y | N | Y |
| **IDAHO** | | | | | | | | |
| 1 LaRocco | N | Y | Y | Y | Y | Y | N | Y |
| 2 Stallings | N | Y | Y | Y | Y | N | Y | Y |
| **ILLINOIS** | | | | | | | | |
| 1 Hayes | N | N | N | Y | Y | Y | N | N |
| 2 Savage | N | N | N | N | N | N | N | N |
| 3 Russo | N | Y | Y | Y | Y | Y | Y | Y |
| 4 Sangmeister | N | Y | Y | Y | Y | Y | N | Y |
| 5 Lipinski | N | Y | Y | Y | Y | Y | Y | Y |
| 6 *Hyde* | Y | ? | ? | ? | N | Y | Y | Y |
| 7 Collins | N | Y | N | Y | Y | N | N | N |
| 8 Rostenkowski | N | Y | Y | Y | Y | Y | N | N |
| 9 Yates | N | Y | Y | Y | Y | Y | N | N |
| 10 *Porter* | Y | Y | Y | N | N | Y | Y | Y |
| 11 Annunzio | N | Y | Y | Y | Y | Y | Y | Y |
| 12 *Crane* | Y | Y | N | N | N | Y | Y | Y |
| 13 *Fawell* | Y | Y | Y | N | N | Y | Y | Y |
| 14 *Hastert* | Y | Y | Y | N | N | Y | Y | Y |
| 15 *Ewing* | Y | Y | Y | N | Y | Y | Y | Y |
| 16 Cox | N | Y | Y | Y | Y | Y | N | Y |
| 17 Evans | N | Y | Y | Y | Y | Y | N | Y |
| 18 *Michel* | Y | Y | Y | N | N | Y | Y | Y |
| 19 Bruce | N | Y | Y | Y | Y | Y | N | Y |
| 20 Durbin | N | Y | Y | Y | Y | Y | N | Y |
| 21 Costello | N | Y | Y | Y | Y | Y | Y | Y |
| 22 Poshard | N | Y | Y | Y | Y | Y | N | Y |
| **INDIANA** | | | | | | | | |
| 1 Visclosky | N | Y | N | Y | Y | Y | N | Y |
| 2 Sharp | N | Y | Y | N | Y | Y | N | Y |
| 3 Roemer | N | Y | Y | Y | Y | Y | N | Y |

ND Northern Democrats   SD Southern Democrats

| | 226 | 227 | 229 | 230 | 231 | 232 | 233 | 234 |
|---|---|---|---|---|---|---|---|---|
| 4 Long | N | Y | Y | Y | Y | Y | N | Y |
| 5 Jontz | N | Y | Y | Y | Y | Y | N | Y |
| 6 ***Burton*** | Y | Y | Y | N | N | Y | Y | Y |
| 7 ***Myers*** | Y | Y | Y | N | N | Y | N | Y |
| 8 McCloskey | N | Y | Y | Y | Y | Y | N | Y |
| 9 Hamilton | N | Y | Y | Y | Y | Y | N | Y |
| 10 Jacobs | N | Y | Y | N | N | Y | Y | Y |
| **IOWA** | | | | | | | | |
| 1 ***Leach*** | N | Y | Y | N | N | Y | N | N |
| 2 ***Nussle*** | Y | Y | Y | N | N | Y | Y | Y |
| 3 Nagle | N | Y | N | N | Y | Y | N | Y |
| 4 Smith | N | Y | Y | Y | Y | Y | N | Y |
| 5 ***Lightfoot*** | Y | Y | Y | N | N | Y | Y | Y |
| 6 ***Grandy*** | Y | Y | Y | N | N | Y | Y | Y |
| **KANSAS** | | | | | | | | |
| 1 ***Roberts*** | Y | Y | Y | N | N | Y | Y | Y |
| 2 Slattery | N | Y | Y | N | Y | Y | Y | Y |
| 3 ***Meyers*** | Y | Y | Y | N | N | Y | Y | Y |
| 4 Glickman | N | Y | Y | N | Y | Y | N | Y |
| 5 ***Nichols*** | Y | Y | Y | N | N | Y | Y | Y |
| **KENTUCKY** | | | | | | | | |
| 1 Hubbard | N | Y | Y | Y | N | Y | Y | Y |
| 2 Natcher | N | Y | Y | Y | Y | Y | N | Y |
| 3 Mazzoli | N | Y | Y | Y | Y | Y | N | Y |
| 4 ***Bunning*** | Y | Y | Y | N | N | Y | Y | Y |
| 5 ***Rogers*** | Y | Y | Y | N | N | Y | Y | Y |
| 6 ***Hopkins*** | Y | Y | Y | N | N | Y | Y | Y |
| 7 Perkins | N | Y | N | Y | Y | Y | N | Y |
| **LOUISIANA** | | | | | | | | |
| 1 ***Livingston*** | Y | Y | Y | Y | N | Y | N | Y |
| 2 Jefferson | N | Y | Y | Y | Y | Y | N | Y |
| 3 Tauzin | N | Y | Y | Y | Y | Y | Y | Y |
| 4 ***McCrery*** | Y | Y | Y | N | N | Y | Y | Y |
| 5 Huckaby | N | Y | Y | Y | Y | Y | ? | Y |
| 6 ***Baker*** | Y | Y | Y | N | N | Y | Y | Y |
| 7 Hayes | N | Y | Y | Y | Y | Y | Y | Y |
| 8 ***Holloway*** | Y | Y | Y | N | N | Y | Y | Y |
| **MAINE** | | | | | | | | |
| 1 Andrews | N | Y | Y | Y | Y | Y | N | Y |
| 2 ***Snowe*** | N | Y | Y | N | N | Y | Y | Y |
| **MARYLAND** | | | | | | | | |
| 1 ***Gilchrest*** | N | Y | Y | N | N | Y | N | Y |
| 2 ***Bentley*** | N | Y | Y | Y | N | Y | N | Y |
| 3 Cardin | N | Y | Y | Y | Y | Y | N | Y |
| 4 McMillen | N | Y | Y | Y | Y | Y | N | Y |
| 5 Hoyer | N | Y | Y | Y | Y | Y | Y | Y |
| 6 Byron | N | Y | Y | Y | Y | Y | Y | Y |
| 7 Mfume | N | Y | Y | Y | Y | Y | N | Y |
| 8 ***Morella*** | N | Y | Y | Y | N | Y | N | Y |
| **MASSACHUSETTS** | | | | | | | | |
| 1 Olver | N | Y | Y | Y | Y | Y | N | Y |
| 2 Neal | N | Y | Y | Y | Y | Y | N | Y |
| 3 Early | Y | Y | Y | Y | N | Y | Y | Y |
| 4 Frank | N | Y | Y | Y | Y | Y | N | Y |
| 5 Atkins | N | Y | Y | Y | Y | Y | N | Y |
| 6 Mavroules | N | Y | Y | Y | Y | Y | N | Y |
| 7 Markey | N | Y | Y | Y | Y | ? | N | Y |
| 8 Kennedy | N | Y | Y | Y | Y | Y | N | N |
| 9 Moakley | N | Y | Y | Y | Y | Y | N | Y |
| 10 Studds | N | Y | Y | Y | Y | Y | N | Y |
| 11 Donnelly | N | Y | Y | Y | Y | Y | N | Y |
| **MICHIGAN** | | | | | | | | |
| 1 Conyers | N | Y | N | Y | Y | Y | Y | N |
| 2 ***Pursell*** | Y | Y | Y | N | N | Y | N | Y |
| 3 Wolpe | N | Y | Y | Y | Y | Y | N | Y |
| 4 ***Upton*** | Y | Y | Y | N | N | Y | Y | Y |
| 5 ***Henry*** | Y | Y | Y | N | N | Y | Y | Y |
| 6 Carr | N | Y | Y | Y | Y | Y | N | Y |
| 7 Kildee | N | Y | Y | Y | Y | Y | N | Y |
| 8 Traxler | ? | ? | ? | ? | ? | ? | ? | Y |
| 9 ***Vander Jagt*** | Y | Y | Y | N | N | Y | Y | Y |
| 10 ***Camp*** | Y | Y | Y | N | N | Y | Y | Y |
| 11 ***Davis*** | N | Y | Y | Y | N | Y | N | Y |
| 12 Bonior | ? | ? | ? | ? | ? | ? | ? | ? |
| 13 Collins | N | Y | N | Y | Y | Y | N | Y |
| 14 Hertel | N | Y | Y | Y | Y | Y | N | Y |
| 15 Ford | N | Y | Y | Y | Y | Y | N | Y |
| 16 Dingell | N | Y | N | Y | Y | Y | N | Y |
| 17 Levin | N | Y | Y | Y | Y | Y | N | Y |
| 18 ***Broomfield*** | N | Y | Y | Y | N | Y | N | Y |
| **MINNESOTA** | | | | | | | | |
| 1 Penny | N | Y | Y | Y | Y | Y | Y | Y |
| 2 ***Weber*** | Y | Y | Y | N | N | Y | Y | Y |
| 3 ***Ramstad*** | Y | Y | Y | N | N | Y | Y | Y |
| 4 Vento | N | Y | Y | Y | Y | Y | N | Y |
| 5 Sabo | N | Y | Y | Y | Y | Y | N | Y |
| 6 Sikorski | N | Y | Y | Y | Y | Y | N | Y |
| 7 Peterson | N | Y | Y | Y | Y | Y | Y | Y |
| 8 Oberstar | N | Y | Y | Y | Y | Y | N | Y |
| **MISSISSIPPI** | | | | | | | | |
| 1 Whitten | Y | Y | Y | Y | Y | Y | ? | Y |
| 2 Espy | N | Y | Y | Y | Y | Y | Y | Y |
| 3 Montgomery | N | Y | Y | Y | Y | Y | Y | Y |
| 4 Parker | N | Y | Y | Y | Y | Y | Y | Y |
| 5 Taylor | N | Y | Y | Y | Y | Y | Y | Y |
| **MISSOURI** | | | | | | | | |
| 1 Clay | N | Y | N | Y | Y | Y | N | Y |
| 2 Horn | N | Y | Y | Y | Y | Y | Y | Y |
| 3 Gephardt | N | Y | Y | Y | Y | Y | N | Y |
| 4 Skelton | N | Y | Y | Y | Y | Y | Y | Y |
| 5 Wheat | N | Y | N | Y | Y | Y | N | N |
| 6 ***Coleman*** | Y | Y | Y | N | N | ? | Y | Y |
| 7 ***Hancock*** | Y | Y | Y | N | N | Y | Y | Y |
| 8 ***Emerson*** | Y | Y | Y | N | N | Y | Y | Y |
| 9 Volkmer | N | Y | Y | Y | Y | Y | Y | Y |
| **MONTANA** | | | | | | | | |
| 1 Williams | N | Y | Y | Y | N | Y | Y | Y |
| 2 ***Marlenee*** | Y | Y | Y | N | N | Y | Y | Y |
| **NEBRASKA** | | | | | | | | |
| 1 ***Bereuter*** | Y | Y | Y | N | N | Y | N | Y |
| 2 Hoagland | N | Y | Y | Y | Y | Y | N | Y |
| 3 ***Barrett*** | Y | Y | Y | N | N | Y | Y | Y |
| **NEVADA** | | | | | | | | |
| 1 Bilbray | N | Y | Y | Y | Y | Y | Y | Y |
| 2 ***Vucanovich*** | Y | Y | Y | Y | N | Y | Y | Y |
| **NEW HAMPSHIRE** | | | | | | | | |
| 1 ***Zeliff*** | Y | Y | Y | N | N | Y | Y | Y |
| 2 Swett | N | Y | Y | Y | Y | Y | Y | Y |
| **NEW JERSEY** | | | | | | | | |
| 1 Andrews | N | Y | Y | Y | Y | Y | Y | Y |
| 2 Hughes | N | Y | Y | Y | Y | Y | Y | Y |
| 3 Pallone | N | Y | Y | N | Y | Y | N | Y |
| 4 ***Smith*** | Y | Y | Y | Y | N | Y | Y | Y |
| 5 ***Roukema*** | N | Y | Y | N | N | Y | Y | Y |
| 6 Dwyer | N | Y | Y | Y | # | ? | ? | ? |
| 7 ***Rinaldo*** | Y | Y | Y | Y | N | Y | N | Y |
| 8 Roe | N | Y | N | Y | Y | Y | N | ? |
| 9 Torricelli | Y | Y | Y | Y | Y | Y | Y | Y |
| 10 Payne | N | Y | N | Y | Y | Y | Y | N |
| 11 ***Gallo*** | N | Y | Y | Y | N | Y | Y | Y |
| 12 ***Zimmer*** | Y | Y | Y | N | N | Y | Y | Y |
| 13 ***Saxton*** | Y | Y | Y | N | N | Y | Y | Y |
| 14 Guarini | N | Y | N | Y | Y | Y | Y | Y |
| **NEW MEXICO** | | | | | | | | |
| 1 ***Schiff*** | N | Y | Y | Y | N | Y | Y | Y |
| 2 ***Skeen*** | Y | Y | Y | Y | N | Y | Y | Y |
| 3 Richardson | N | Y | Y | Y | Y | Y | ? | ? |
| **NEW YORK** | | | | | | | | |
| 1 Hochbrueckner | N | Y | Y | Y | Y | Y | N | Y |
| 2 Downey | N | Y | Y | Y | Y | Y | N | Y |
| 3 Mrazek | N | Y | Y | Y | Y | Y | N | Y |
| 4 ***Lent*** | N | Y | Y | Y | N | Y | N | Y |
| 5 ***McGrath*** | N | Y | Y | Y | N | Y | N | Y |
| 6 Flake | N | Y | N | Y | Y | Y | Y | Y |
| 7 Ackerman | N | ? | ? | ? | Y | Y | N | Y |
| 8 Scheuer | N | Y | Y | Y | Y | Y | N | Y |
| 9 Manton | N | Y | Y | Y | Y | Y | N | Y |
| 10 Schumer | ? | ? | ? | ? | ? | Y | Y | Y |
| 11 Towns | N | Y | N | Y | Y | Y | N | N |
| 12 Owens | N | Y | N | Y | Y | Y | N | N |
| 13 Solarz | N | Y | Y | Y | Y | Y | N | N |
| 14 ***Molinari*** | Y | Y | Y | Y | N | Y | N | Y |
| 15 ***Green*** | N | Y | Y | Y | N | Y | N | N |
| 16 Rangel | N | Y | N | Y | Y | Y | N | Y |
| 17 Weiss | N | Y | N | Y | Y | Y | N | N |
| 18 Serrano | N | Y | N | Y | Y | Y | N | Y |
| 19 Engel | N | Y | Y | Y | Y | Y | N | Y |
| 20 Lowey | N | Y | Y | Y | Y | Y | N | Y |
| 21 ***Fish*** | Y | Y | Y | Y | N | Y | N | Y |
| 22 ***Gilman*** | N | Y | Y | Y | N | Y | N | Y |
| 23 McNulty | ? | ? | ? | ? | Y | Y | N | Y |
| 24 ***Solomon*** | Y | Y | Y | N | N | Y | Y | Y |
| 25 ***Boehlert*** | N | Y | Y | Y | N | Y | N | Y |
| 26 ***Martin*** | Y | Y | Y | N | N | Y | ? | Y |
| 27 ***Walsh*** | Y | Y | Y | N | N | Y | N | Y |
| 28 McHugh | N | Y | Y | Y | Y | Y | N | N |
| 29 ***Horton*** | N | Y | Y | Y | N | Y | N | Y |
| 30 Slaughter | N | Y | Y | Y | Y | Y | N | Y |
| 31 ***Paxon*** | Y | Y | Y | N | N | Y | Y | Y |
| 32 LaFalce | N | Y | Y | Y | Y | Y | N | Y |
| 33 Nowak | N | Y | Y | Y | Y | Y | N | Y |
| 34 ***Houghton*** | N | Y | Y | Y | N | Y | N | Y |
| **NORTH CAROLINA** | | | | | | | | |
| 1 Jones | N | Y | N | Y | Y | Y | N | Y |
| 2 Valentine | N | Y | Y | Y | Y | Y | Y | Y |
| 3 Lancaster | N | Y | Y | Y | Y | Y | N | Y |
| 4 Price | N | Y | Y | Y | Y | Y | N | Y |
| 5 Neal | N | Y | Y | Y | Y | Y | Y | Y |
| 6 ***Coble*** | Y | Y | Y | N | N | Y | Y | Y |
| 7 Rose | N | Y | N | Y | Y | Y | N | Y |
| 8 Hefner | ? | ? | ? | ? | ? | ? | ? | ? |
| 9 ***McMillan*** | Y | Y | Y | N | N | Y | N | Y |
| 10 ***Ballenger*** | Y | Y | Y | N | N | Y | Y | Y |
| 11 ***Taylor*** | Y | Y | Y | N | N | Y | Y | Y |
| **NORTH DAKOTA** | | | | | | | | |
| AL Dorgan | N | Y | Y | Y | Y | Y | Y | Y |
| **OHIO** | | | | | | | | |
| 1 Luken | N | Y | Y | Y | Y | Y | Y | Y |
| 2 ***Gradison*** | N | Y | Y | N | N | Y | Y | Y |
| 3 Hall | N | Y | Y | Y | Y | Y | N | Y |
| 4 ***Oxley*** | Y | Y | Y | N | N | Y | N | Y |
| 5 ***Gillmor*** | Y | Y | Y | N | N | Y | Y | Y |
| 6 ***McEwen*** | Y | Y | Y | N | N | Y | Y | Y |
| 7 ***Hobson*** | Y | Y | Y | N | N | Y | Y | Y |
| 8 ***Boehner*** | Y | Y | Y | N | N | Y | Y | Y |
| 9 Kaptur | N | Y | Y | Y | Y | Y | N | Y |
| 10 ***Miller*** | Y | Y | Y | N | N | Y | Y | Y |
| 11 Eckart | N | Y | Y | Y | Y | ? | Y | Y |
| 12 ***Kasich*** | N | Y | Y | N | N | Y | Y | Y |
| 13 Pease | N | Y | Y | Y | Y | Y | N | N |
| 14 Sawyer | N | Y | Y | Y | Y | Y | N | Y |
| 15 ***Wylie*** | Y | Y | Y | N | N | Y | Y | Y |
| 16 ***Regula*** | N | Y | Y | N | N | Y | Y | Y |
| 17 Traficant | N | Y | Y | Y | N | P | Y | Y |
| 18 Applegate | N | Y | Y | Y | N | Y | Y | Y |
| 19 Feighan | N | Y | Y | Y | Y | Y | N | Y |
| 20 Oakar | N | Y | Y | Y | Y | Y | N | Y |
| 21 Stokes | N | Y | N | Y | Y | Y | N | Y |
| **OKLAHOMA** | | | | | | | | |
| 1 ***Inhofe*** | Y | Y | Y | N | N | Y | Y | Y |
| 2 Synar | N | Y | N | Y | Y | Y | N | Y |
| 3 Brewster | N | Y | Y | Y | Y | Y | N | Y |
| 4 McCurdy | N | Y | Y | Y | Y | Y | Y | Y |
| 5 ***Edwards*** | Y | Y | Y | N | N | Y | Y | Y |
| 6 English | N | ? | Y | Y | Y | Y | Y | Y |
| **OREGON** | | | | | | | | |
| 1 AuCoin | N | Y | Y | Y | Y | Y | N | Y |
| 2 ***Smith*** | Y | Y | Y | N | N | Y | Y | Y |
| 3 Wyden | N | Y | Y | Y | Y | Y | Y | Y |
| 4 DeFazio | N | Y | N | Y | Y | Y | N | Y |
| 5 Kopetski | N | Y | Y | Y | Y | Y | N | Y |
| **PENNSYLVANIA** | | | | | | | | |
| 1 Foglietta | N | Y | N | Y | Y | Y | N | Y |
| 2 Blackwell | N | Y | N | Y | Y | Y | Y | Y |
| 3 Borski | N | Y | Y | Y | Y | Y | N | Y |
| 4 Kolter | N | Y | Y | Y | Y | Y | Y | Y |
| 5 ***Schulze*** | Y | Y | Y | Y | N | Y | ? | ? |
| 6 Yatron | N | Y | Y | Y | Y | Y | Y | Y |
| 7 ***Weldon*** | Y | Y | Y | N | N | Y | Y | Y |
| 8 Kostmayer | N | Y | Y | Y | Y | Y | N | Y |
| 9 ***Shuster*** | Y | Y | Y | Y | N | Y | Y | Y |
| 10 ***McDade*** | N | Y | Y | ? | ? | ? | ? | ? |
| 11 Kanjorski | N | Y | Y | Y | Y | Y | N | Y |
| 12 Murtha | N | Y | Y | Y | Y | Y | N | Y |
| 13 ***Coughlin*** | N | Y | Y | Y | N | Y | N | Y |
| 14 Coyne | N | Y | Y | Y | Y | Y | N | Y |
| 15 ***Ritter*** | N | Y | Y | N | N | Y | Y | Y |
| 16 ***Walker*** | Y | Y | Y | N | N | Y | Y | Y |
| 17 ***Gekas*** | Y | Y | Y | N | X | Y | Y | Y |
| 18 ***Santorum*** | Y | Y | Y | N | N | Y | Y | Y |
| 19 ***Goodling*** | Y | Y | Y | N | N | Y | Y | Y |
| 20 Gaydos | N | ? | Y | Y | N | Y | Y | Y |
| 21 ***Ridge*** | Y | Y | Y | N | N | Y | Y | Y |
| 22 Murphy | Y | Y | Y | N | Y | Y | Y | Y |
| 23 ***Clinger*** | N | Y | Y | N | N | Y | N | Y |
| **RHODE ISLAND** | | | | | | | | |
| 1 ***Machtley*** | N | Y | Y | N | N | Y | Y | Y |
| 2 Reed | N | Y | Y | Y | Y | Y | Y | Y |
| **SOUTH CAROLINA** | | | | | | | | |
| 1 ***Ravenel*** | N | Y | Y | N | N | Y | Y | Y |
| 2 ***Spence*** | N | Y | Y | N | N | Y | N | Y |
| 3 Derrick | N | Y | Y | Y | Y | Y | N | Y |
| 4 Patterson | N | Y | Y | Y | Y | Y | Y | Y |
| 5 Spratt | N | Y | Y | Y | Y | Y | N | Y |
| 6 Tallon | N | Y | ? | ? | ? | ? | ? | ? |
| **SOUTH DAKOTA** | | | | | | | | |
| AL Johnson | N | Y | Y | Y | Y | Y | Y | Y |
| **TENNESSEE** | | | | | | | | |
| 1 ***Quillen*** | Y | Y | Y | N | N | Y | Y | Y |
| 2 ***Duncan*** | Y | Y | Y | N | N | Y | Y | Y |
| 3 Lloyd | N | Y | Y | Y | Y | Y | Y | Y |
| 4 Cooper | N | Y | Y | Y | Y | Y | Y | Y |
| 5 Clement | N | Y | Y | Y | Y | Y | N | Y |
| 6 Gordon | N | Y | Y | Y | Y | Y | Y | Y |
| 7 ***Sundquist*** | Y | Y | Y | N | N | Y | Y | Y |
| 8 Tanner | N | Y | Y | Y | Y | Y | Y | Y |
| 9 Ford | Y | Y | Y | Y | Y | Y | N | Y |
| **TEXAS** | | | | | | | | |
| 1 Chapman | N | Y | Y | Y | Y | Y | Y | Y |
| 2 Wilson | N | Y | ? | ? | N | Y | Y | Y |
| 3 ***Johnson*** | Y | Y | Y | N | N | Y | Y | Y |
| 4 Hall | N | Y | Y | Y | Y | Y | Y | Y |
| 5 Bryant | N | Y | Y | Y | Y | Y | N | Y |
| 6 ***Barton*** | Y | Y | Y | N | N | Y | Y | Y |
| 7 ***Archer*** | Y | Y | Y | N | N | Y | Y | Y |
| 8 ***Fields*** | Y | Y | Y | N | N | Y | Y | Y |
| 9 Brooks | N | ? | Y | Y | Y | Y | Y | Y |
| 10 Pickle | N | Y | Y | Y | Y | Y | Y | Y |
| 11 Edwards | N | Y | Y | Y | Y | Y | N | Y |
| 12 Geren | N | Y | Y | Y | Y | Y | Y | Y |
| 13 Sarpalius | N | Y | Y | N | Y | Y | N | Y |
| 14 Laughlin | N | Y | Y | Y | Y | Y | ? | ? |
| 15 de la Garza | N | Y | Y | Y | Y | Y | N | Y |
| 16 Coleman | N | Y | Y | Y | Y | Y | N | Y |
| 17 Stenholm | N | Y | Y | Y | Y | Y | Y | Y |
| 18 Washington | N | N | N | Y | Y | Y | N | N |
| 19 ***Combest*** | Y | Y | Y | N | N | Y | Y | Y |
| 20 Gonzalez | N | Y | N | Y | Y | Y | N | Y |
| 21 ***Smith*** | Y | Y | Y | N | N | Y | Y | Y |
| 22 ***DeLay*** | Y | Y | Y | N | N | Y | Y | Y |
| 23 Bustamante | N | Y | N | Y | Y | Y | N | Y |
| 24 Frost | N | Y | Y | Y | Y | Y | N | Y |
| 25 Andrews | N | Y | Y | Y | Y | Y | Y | Y |
| 26 ***Armey*** | Y | Y | Y | N | N | Y | Y | Y |
| 27 Ortiz | N | Y | Y | Y | Y | Y | Y | Y |
| **UTAH** | | | | | | | | |
| 1 ***Hansen*** | Y | Y | Y | N | N | Y | Y | Y |
| 2 Owens | N | Y | Y | Y | N | Y | Y | Y |
| 3 Orton | N | Y | Y | Y | Y | Y | Y | Y |
| **VERMONT** | | | | | | | | |
| AL *Sanders* | N | Y | Y | Y | Y | Y | N | Y |
| **VIRGINIA** | | | | | | | | |
| 1 ***Bateman*** | N | Y | Y | Y | N | Y | P | Y |
| 2 Pickett | N | Y | N | N | Y | Y | N | Y |
| 3 ***Bliley*** | Y | Y | Y | N | N | Y | N | Y |
| 4 Sisisky | N | Y | Y | Y | Y | Y | Y | Y |
| 5 Payne | N | Y | Y | Y | Y | Y | N | Y |
| 6 Olin | N | ? | N | Y | Y | Y | N | Y |
| 7 ***Allen*** | Y | Y | Y | N | N | Y | Y | Y |
| 8 Moran | N | Y | Y | Y | Y | Y | Y | Y |
| 9 Boucher | N | Y | Y | Y | Y | Y | N | Y |
| 10 ***Wolf*** | N | Y | ? | N | N | Y | Y | Y |
| **WASHINGTON** | | | | | | | | |
| 1 ***Miller*** | Y | Y | Y | N | N | Y | Y | Y |
| 2 Swift | N | Y | Y | Y | Y | Y | N | Y |
| 3 Unsoeld | N | Y | N | Y | Y | Y | N | N |
| 4 ***Morrison*** | N | Y | Y | Y | N | Y | Y | Y |
| 5 Foley | | | | | | | | |
| 6 Dicks | N | Y | Y | Y | Y | Y | N | Y |
| 7 McDermott | N | Y | N | Y | Y | Y | N | Y |
| 8 ***Chandler*** | Y | Y | Y | N | N | Y | Y | Y |
| **WEST VIRGINIA** | | | | | | | | |
| 1 Mollohan | N | Y | Y | Y | Y | Y | N | Y |
| 2 Staggers | N | Y | Y | Y | Y | Y | N | Y |
| 3 Wise | N | Y | Y | Y | Y | Y | N | Y |
| 4 Rahall | N | N | Y | Y | N | Y | N | Y |
| **WISCONSIN** | | | | | | | | |
| 1 Aspin | N | Y | Y | Y | Y | Y | N | Y |
| 2 ***Klug*** | Y | Y | Y | N | N | Y | Y | Y |
| 3 ***Gunderson*** | Y | Y | Y | N | N | Y | Y | Y |
| 4 Kleczka | N | Y | Y | Y | Y | Y | N | Y |
| 5 Moody | N | Y | Y | Y | Y | Y | Y | Y |
| 6 ***Petri*** | Y | Y | Y | N | N | Y | Y | Y |
| 7 Obey | N | Y | Y | Y | Y | Y | N | Y |
| 8 ***Roth*** | N | Y | Y | N | N | Y | Y | Y |
| 9 ***Sensenbrenner*** | Y | Y | Y | N | N | Y | Y | Y |
| **WYOMING** | | | | | | | | |
| AL ***Thomas*** | Y | Y | Y | N | N | Y | Y | Y |

Southern states - Ala., Ark., Fla., Ga., Ky., La., Miss., N.C., Okla., S.C., Tenn., Texas, Va.
Omitted votes are quorum calls, which CQ does not include in its vote charts.

**235. HR 5368. Fiscal 1993 Foreign Operations Appropriations/Passage.** Passage of the bill to provide $13.76 billion in new budget authority for foreign military and economic assistance and export financing in fiscal 1993. The administration requested $15,112,798,602. Passed 297-124: R 92-72; D 205-51 (ND 153-25, SD 52-26); I 0-1, June 25, 1992.

**236. H J Res 517. Railroad Labor Dispute/Passage.** Passage of the joint resolution to provide for a 38-day cooling-off and negotiating period for unresolved labor disputes between certain railroads and certain railroad employees on strike. If there was no initial agreement, the parties submitted to an arbitrator their last best offers for rates of pay, rules and working conditions in the form of a contract. If agreement was not reached, the arbitrator selected one offer that was binding on the parties. The president could reject the arbitrator's decision. Passed 248-140: R 136-15; D 112-124 (ND 52-111, SD 60-13); I 0-1, June 25, 1992. A "yea" was a vote in support of the president's position.

**238. HR 3247. National Undersea Research Program/Funding Levels.** Hughes, D-N.J., amendment to the Walker, R-Pa., amendment to authorize $23 million in fiscal 1993 and allow for an increase of $2.1 million for each of the subsequent fiscal years. The Walker amendment froze the authorization at $17.2 million for the next five fiscal years. The bill authorized $172 million for fiscal 1992-96. Adopted 245-86: R 50-78; D 194-8 (ND 136-4, SD 58-4); I 1-0, June 29, 1992.

**239. HR 3247. National Undersea Research Program/Funding Levels.** Walker, R-Pa., amendment as amended by the Hughes, D-N.J., amendment, to authorize $23 million in fiscal 1993 and allow for an increase of $2.1 million for each of the subsequent fiscal years. Adopted 350-0: R 139-0; D 210-0 (ND 149-0, SD 61-0); I 1-0, June 29, 1992.

**240. HR 3247. National Undersea Research Program/Passage.** Passage of the bill to authorize funds to establish an Office of Undersea Research within the National Oceanic and Atmospheric Administration to award research proposals to study ocean and large lake ecosystems. Passed 265-86: R 59-80; D 205-6 (ND 145-2, SD 60-4); I 1-0, June 29, 1992. A 'nay' was a vote in support of the president's position.

**241. HR 5260. Unemployment Benefits Extension/Motion to Instruct.** Archer, R-Texas, motion to instruct the House conferees to make the bill comply with the pay-as-you-go rules of the Budget Enforcement Act of 1990. Motion agreed to 180-170: R 140-0; D 40-169 (ND 13-131, SD 27-38); I 0-1, June 29, 1992.

**242. HR 5429. Independent Social Security Administration.** Rostenkowski, D-Ill., motion to suspend the rules and pass the bill to establish the Social Security Administration as an independent agency. Motion agreed to 350-8: R 134-8; D 215-0 (ND 148-0, SD 67-0); I 1-0, June 29, 1992. A two-thirds majority of those present and voting (239 in this case) was required for passage under suspension of the rules. A "nay" was a vote supporting the president's position.

**243. HR 5487. Fiscal 1993 Agriculture Appropriations/Cooperative State Research Grants.** Fawell, R-Ill., amendment to cut the $57,688,000 for special research grants by the Cooperative State Research Service which administers funds to state agricultural experiment stations to conduct agricultural research. Rejected 126-295: R 96-68; D 30-226 (ND 18-159, SD 12-67); I 0-1, June 30, 1992.

## KEY

| | |
|---|---|
| Y | Voted for (yea). |
| # | Paired for. |
| + | Announced for. |
| N | Voted against (nay). |
| X | Paired against. |
| − | Announced against. |
| P | Voted "present." |
| C | Voted "present" to avoid possible conflict of interest. |
| ? | Did not vote or otherwise make a position known. |

Democrats   *Republicans*   *Independent*

| | 235 | 236 | 238 | 239 | 240 | 241 | 242 | 243 |
|---|---|---|---|---|---|---|---|---|
| **ALABAMA** | | | | | | | | |
| 1 *Callahan* | Y | Y | Y | Y | Y | Y | Y | Y |
| 2 *Dickinson* | N | Y | ? | ? | ? | ? | ? | Y |
| 3 Browder | Y | Y | Y | Y | Y | Y | Y | N |
| 4 Bevill | N | Y | ? | ? | ? | ? | ? | ? |
| 5 Cramer | Y | Y | Y | Y | Y | Y | Y | Y |
| 6 Erdreich | Y | Y | Y | Y | Y | Y | Y | N |
| 7 Harris | Y | Y | Y | Y | Y | Y | Y | N |
| **ALASKA** | | | | | | | | |
| AL *Young* | Y | N | Y | Y | Y | Y | Y | N |
| **ARIZONA** | | | | | | | | |
| 1 *Rhodes* | Y | Y | Y | Y | N | Y | Y | Y |
| 2 Pastor | Y | N | Y | Y | Y | Y | Y | N |
| 3 *Stump* | N | Y | ? | Y | N | Y | Y | Y |
| 4 *Kyl* | Y | Y | N | Y | N | Y | Y | Y |
| 5 *Kolbe* | Y | Y | ? | ? | ? | ? | ? | Y |
| **ARKANSAS** | | | | | | | | |
| 1 Alexander | Y | ? | ? | ? | ? | ? | ? | N |
| 2 Thornton | Y | ? | Y | Y | Y | N | Y | N |
| 3 *Hammerschmidt* | N | Y | − | + | − | + | N | N |
| 4 Anthony | ? | ? | Y | Y | Y | N | Y | N |
| **CALIFORNIA** | | | | | | | | |
| 1 *Riggs* | Y | Y | ? | Y | Y | Y | Y | Y |
| 2 *Herger* | N | Y | ? | ? | ? | Y | ? | Y |
| 3 Matsui | Y | Y | Y | Y | Y | N | Y | N |
| 4 Fazio | Y | Y | Y | Y | Y | N | Y | N |
| 5 Pelosi | Y | N | Y | Y | Y | N | Y | N |
| 6 Boxer | Y | N | Y | Y | Y | N | Y | N |
| 7 Miller | Y | N | Y | Y | Y | N | Y | N |
| 8 Dellums | Y | N | Y | Y | Y | N | Y | N |
| 9 Stark | N | N | Y | Y | Y | N | Y | N |
| 10 Edwards | Y | N | Y | Y | Y | N | ? | N |
| 11 Lantos | Y | N | Y | Y | Y | N | Y | N |
| 12 *Campbell* | Y | ? | ? | ? | ? | ? | ? | Y |
| 13 Mineta | Y | N | ? | ? | # | ? | ? | N |
| 14 *Doolittle* | N | N | Y | N | Y | Y | Y | Y |
| 15 Condit | N | N | N | Y | N | Y | Y | N |
| 16 Panetta | Y | Y | ? | Y | Y | N | Y | N |
| 17 Dooley | N | Y | ? | Y | Y | N | Y | N |
| 18 Lehman | N | Y | ? | ? | ? | ? | N | N |
| 19 *Lagomarsino* | N | Y | N | Y | N | Y | Y | Y |
| 20 *Thomas* | N | ? | ? | X | ? | ? | Y |  |
| 21 *Gallegly* | N | Y | N | Y | N | Y | Y | Y |
| 22 *Moorhead* | N | Y | N | Y | N | Y | Y | Y |
| 23 Beilenson | Y | Y | ? | ? | ? | ? | ? | N |
| 24 Waxman | Y | N | Y | Y | Y | ? | Y | N |
| 25 Roybal | Y | N | Y | Y | N | Y | N | N |
| 26 Berman | Y | ? | ? | Y | Y | N | Y | N |
| 27 Levine | Y | ? | ? | ? | ? | ? | N | N |
| 28 Dixon | Y | N | Y | Y | Y | N | Y | N |
| 29 Waters | Y | N | Y | Y | Y | N | Y | N |
| 30 Martinez | Y | N | Y | Y | Y | N | Y | N |
| 31 Dymally | Y | N | ? | ? | ? | ? | ? | ? |
| 32 Anderson | Y | Y | ? | ? | ? | ? | ? | N |
| 33 *Dreier* | N | Y | N | Y | N | Y | Y | Y |
| 34 Torres | Y | N | + | + | + | − | + | N |
| 35 *Lewis* | Y | Y | ? | Y | Y | Y | Y | N |
| 36 Brown | Y | N | Y | Y | Y | N | Y | N |
| 37 *McCandless* | N | Y | N | Y | N | Y | Y | Y |
| 38 *Dornan* | Y | N | Y | N | Y | N | Y | Y |
| 39 *Dannemeyer* | N | Y | N | Y | N | Y | Y | Y |
| 40 *Cox* | Y | Y | ? | ? | ? | ? | ? | Y |
| 41 *Lowery* | Y | Y | N | Y | ? | Y | Y | ? |

| | 235 | 236 | 238 | 239 | 240 | 241 | 242 | 243 |
|---|---|---|---|---|---|---|---|---|
| 42 *Rohrabacher* | N | N | Y | Y | Y | N | Y | Y |
| 43 *Packard* | N | Y | N | Y | N | Y | Y | Y |
| 44 *Cunningham* | Y | Y | N | Y | N | Y | Y | Y |
| 45 *Hunter* | Y | Y | N | Y | N | Y | Y | Y |
| **COLORADO** | | | | | | | | |
| 1 Schroeder | Y | + | Y | Y | Y | N | Y | N |
| 2 Skaggs | Y | Y | Y | Y | Y | N | Y | N |
| 3 Campbell | Y | ? | ? | ? | ? | ? | ? | N |
| 4 *Allard* | Y | Y | N | Y | N | Y | Y | Y |
| 5 *Hefley* | N | Y | Y | Y | N | Y | Y | Y |
| 6 *Schaefer* | N | Y | Y | Y | N | Y | Y | Y |
| **CONNECTICUT** | | | | | | | | |
| 1 Kennelly | Y | N | Y | Y | Y | N | Y | N |
| 2 Gejdenson | Y | N | Y | Y | Y | N | Y | N |
| 3 DeLauro | Y | N | Y | Y | Y | N | Y | N |
| 4 *Shays* | Y | N | Y | Y | Y | Y | Y | N |
| 5 *Franks* | Y | Y | ? | ? | ? | ? | ? | Y |
| 6 *Johnson* | Y | N | Y | Y | Y | Y | Y | Y |
| **DELAWARE** | | | | | | | | |
| AL Carper | Y | Y | Y | Y | Y | Y | Y | Y |
| **FLORIDA** | | | | | | | | |
| 1 Hutto | N | Y | Y | Y | Y | Y | Y | Y |
| 2 Peterson | Y | Y | Y | Y | Y | N | Y | N |
| 3 Bennett | N | Y | Y | Y | N | Y | Y | Y |
| 4 *James* | N | Y | N | Y | N | Y | Y | Y |
| 5 McCollum | Y | Y | Y | Y | Y | Y | Y | Y |
| 6 *Stearns* | N | Y | Y | Y | N | Y | Y | N |
| 7 Gibbons | N | Y | Y | Y | Y | N | Y | N |
| 8 *Young* | N | Y | Y | Y | N | Y | Y | N |
| 9 *Bilirakis* | Y | N | Y | Y | Y | N | Y | N |
| 10 *Ireland* | N | Y | ? | ? | ? | ? | ? | Y |
| 11 Bacchus | Y | Y | ? | ? | ? | N | Y | N |
| 12 *Lewis* | N | Y | Y | Y | N | Y | Y | Y |
| 13 *Goss* | N | Y | Y | Y | Y | N | Y | Y |
| 14 Johnston | Y | Y | ? | ? | ? | ? | ? | Y |
| 15 *Shaw* | Y | Y | Y | Y | Y | N | Y | Y |
| 16 Smith | Y | N | ? | ? | ? | ? | N | Y |
| 17 Lehman | Y | Y | Y | Y | Y | N | Y | N |
| 18 *Ros-Lehtinen* | Y | Y | Y | Y | Y | N | Y | N |
| 19 Fascell | Y | Y | Y | Y | Y | N | Y | N |
| **GEORGIA** | | | | | | | | |
| 1 Thomas | Y | ? | Y | Y | Y | N | Y | N |
| 2 Hatcher | ? | ? | Y | Y | Y | N | Y | N |
| 3 Ray | N | Y | ? | ? | ? | ? | ? | Y |
| 4 Jones | ? | ? | ? | ? | ? | ? | ? | Y |
| 5 Lewis | Y | N | ? | ? | ? | ? | ? | Y |
| 6 *Gingrich* | Y | Y | ? | ? | ? | ? | ? | Y |
| 7 Darden | Y | Y | ? | ? | ? | ? | ? | Y |
| 8 Rowland | N | Y | Y | Y | Y | N | Y | N |
| 9 Jenkins | Y | Y | Y | Y | Y | N | Y | N |
| 10 Barnard | ? | ? | Y | Y | Y | Y | Y | N |
| **HAWAII** | | | | | | | | |
| 1 Abercrombie | Y | X | ? | Y | Y | N | Y | N |
| 2 Mink | Y | N | Y | Y | Y | N | Y | N |
| **IDAHO** | | | | | | | | |
| 1 LaRocco | Y | N | ? | ? | ? | ? | N | N |
| 2 Stallings | Y | N | Y | Y | Y | N | Y | N |
| **ILLINOIS** | | | | | | | | |
| 1 Hayes | Y | N | Y | Y | Y | N | Y | N |
| 2 Savage | N | ? | ? | ? | ? | ? | N | N |
| 3 Russo | N | N | Y | Y | Y | N | Y | N |
| 4 Sangmeister | N | Y | Y | Y | Y | N | Y | N |
| 5 Lipinski | Y | Y | Y | Y | Y | N | Y | N |
| 6 *Hyde* | N | ? | N | Y | Y | Y | Y | N |
| 7 Collins | Y | N | Y | Y | Y | N | Y | N |
| 8 Rostenkowski | Y | ? | ? | Y | Y | N | Y | N |
| 9 Yates | Y | N | Y | Y | Y | N | Y | N |
| 10 *Porter* | Y | Y | N | Y | Y | Y | Y | Y |
| 11 Annunzio | Y | N | Y | Y | Y | N | Y | N |
| 12 *Crane* | N | Y | N | Y | N | Y | Y | Y |
| 13 *Fawell* | N | Y | N | Y | N | Y | Y | Y |
| 14 *Hastert* | N | Y | N | Y | N | Y | Y | Y |
| 15 *Ewing* | Y | N | Y | Y | N | Y | N | N |
| 16 *Cox* | Y | N | Y | Y | Y | N | Y | N |
| 17 Evans | Y | N | Y | ? | N | Y | N | N |
| 18 *Michel* | N | Y | N | Y | Y | Y | N | N |
| 19 Bruce | Y | Y | Y | Y | Y | N | Y | N |
| 20 Durbin | Y | Y | Y | Y | Y | N | Y | N |
| 21 Costello | N | Y | Y | Y | ? | N | Y | N |
| 22 Poshard | N | Y | Y | Y | Y | N | Y | N |
| **INDIANA** | | | | | | | | |
| 1 Visclosky | Y | N | Y | Y | Y | N | Y | N |
| 2 Sharp | Y | Y | Y | Y | Y | N | Y | N |
| 3 Roemer | N | Y | Y | Y | Y | Y | Y | N |

ND Northern Democrats   SD Southern Democrats

| | 235 | 236 | 238 | 239 | 240 | 241 | 242 | 243 |
|---|---|---|---|---|---|---|---|---|
| 4 Long | Y | N | Y | Y | Y | N | Y | N |
| 5 Jontz | N | N | Y | Y | Y | N | Y | N |
| 6 *Burton* | Y | Y | N | Y | N | Y | Y | Y |
| 7 *Myers* | N | Y | N | Y | N | Y | Y | N |
| 8 McCloskey | Y | N | Y | Y | Y | N | Y | N |
| 9 Hamilton | Y | Y | Y | Y | Y | N | Y | N |
| 10 Jacobs | N | N | Y | Y | Y | N | Y | N |
| **IOWA** | | | | | | | | |
| 1 *Leach* | Y | Y | N | Y | N | Y | Y | N |
| 2 *Nussle* | N | Y | N | Y | N | Y | Y | Y |
| 3 Nagle | Y | N | Y | Y | Y | N | Y | N |
| 4 Smith | Y | N | Y | Y | Y | N | Y | N |
| 5 *Lightfoot* | Y | Y | N | Y | N | Y | Y | N |
| 6 *Grandy* | Y | Y | N | Y | N | Y | Y | N |
| **KANSAS** | | | | | | | | |
| 1 *Roberts* | N | Y | N | Y | N | Y | Y | N |
| 2 Slattery | Y | Y | Y | Y | Y | N | Y | N |
| 3 *Meyers* | Y | Y | N | Y | N | Y | Y | Y |
| 4 Glickman | Y | Y | Y | Y | Y | N | Y | Y |
| 5 *Nichols* | N | Y | N | Y | N | Y | Y | Y |
| **KENTUCKY** | | | | | | | | |
| 1 Hubbard | N | Y | Y | Y | Y | N | Y | N |
| 2 Natcher | Y | Y | Y | Y | Y | N | Y | N |
| 3 Mazzoli | N | Y | Y | Y | Y | N | Y | N |
| 4 *Bunning* | N | Y | N | Y | N | Y | Y | Y |
| 5 *Rogers* | N | Y | ? | ? | ? | ? | ? | N |
| 6 *Hopkins* | N | Y | ? | ? | ? | Y | Y | Y |
| 7 Perkins | N | N | ? | ? | ? | ? | ? | ? |
| **LOUISIANA** | | | | | | | | |
| 1 *Livingston* | Y | ? | ? | ? | ? | ? | ? | N |
| 2 Jefferson | Y | N | Y | Y | Y | N | Y | N |
| 3 Tauzin | N | Y | Y | Y | Y | Y | Y | N |
| 4 *McCrery* | Y | Y | N | Y | N | Y | Y | N |
| 5 Huckaby | N | Y | ? | ? | ? | ? | ? | ? |
| 6 *Baker* | N | ? | N | Y | N | Y | Y | N |
| 7 Hayes | N | Y | Y | Y | Y | Y | Y | N |
| 8 *Holloway* | N | ? | N | Y | N | Y | Y | N |
| **MAINE** | | | | | | | | |
| 1 Andrews | Y | N | Y | Y | Y | N | Y | N |
| 2 *Snowe* | Y | Y | Y | Y | Y | Y | Y | N |
| **MARYLAND** | | | | | | | | |
| 1 *Gilchrest* | Y | Y | Y | Y | Y | Y | Y | N |
| 2 *Bentley* | N | Y | Y | Y | Y | Y | Y | Y |
| 3 Cardin | Y | Y | Y | Y | Y | N | Y | Y |
| 4 McMillen | Y | Y | Y | Y | Y | Y | Y | N |
| 5 Hoyer | Y | Y | Y | Y | Y | N | Y | N |
| 6 Byron | Y | Y | Y | Y | Y | Y | Y | N |
| 7 Mfume | Y | N | Y | Y | Y | N | Y | N |
| 8 *Morella* | Y | Y | ? | Y | Y | Y | Y | N |
| **MASSACHUSETTS** | | | | | | | | |
| 1 Olver | Y | N | ? | ? | ? | ? | ? | N |
| 2 Neal | Y | N | Y | Y | Y | N | Y | N |
| 3 Early | N | N | Y | Y | Y | N | Y | N |
| 4 Frank | Y | Y | ? | ? | ? | ? | ? | N |
| 5 Atkins | Y | N | Y | Y | Y | N | Y | Y |
| 6 Mavroules | Y | N | Y | Y | Y | N | Y | N |
| 7 Markey | Y | Y | Y | Y | Y | N | Y | N |
| 8 Kennedy | Y | N | ? | ? | ? | ? | ? | N |
| 9 Moakley | Y | N | Y | Y | Y | N | Y | N |
| 10 Studds | Y | Y | ? | ? | ? | ? | ? | N |
| 11 Donnelly | Y | ? | Y | Y | Y | N | Y | N |
| **MICHIGAN** | | | | | | | | |
| 1 Conyers | Y | N | ? | ? | ? | ? | ? | N |
| 2 *Pursell* | Y | Y | Y | Y | Y | Y | Y | N |
| 3 Wolpe | Y | N | Y | Y | Y | N | Y | N |
| 4 *Upton* | Y | Y | Y | Y | Y | Y | Y | N |
| 5 *Henry* | Y | Y | Y | Y | Y | Y | Y | N |
| 6 Carr | Y | Y | Y | Y | Y | Y | Y | N |
| 7 Kildee | Y | N | Y | Y | Y | N | Y | N |
| 8 Traxler | Y | ? | ? | ? | ? | ? | ? | ? |
| 9 *Vander Jagt* | Y | ? | Y | Y | Y | Y | Y | N |
| 10 *Camp* | Y | Y | Y | Y | Y | Y | Y | N |
| 11 *Davis* | Y | Y | Y | Y | Y | Y | Y | N |
| 12 Bonior | ? | ? | ? | ? | ? | ? | ? | ? |
| 13 Collins | Y | N | Y | Y | Y | N | Y | N |
| 14 Hertel | Y | N | Y | Y | Y | N | Y | N |
| 15 Ford | Y | N | ? | Y | Y | ? | Y | N |
| 16 Dingell | Y | Y | Y | Y | Y | N | Y | N |
| 17 Levin | Y | Y | Y | Y | Y | N | Y | N |
| 18 *Broomfield* | Y | ? | Y | Y | Y | ? | ? | Y |
| **MINNESOTA** | | | | | | | | |
| 1 Penny | Y | N | Y | Y | Y | Y | Y | Y |
| 2 *Weber* | Y | ? | N | Y | N | Y | Y | N |
| 3 *Ramstad* | N | Y | N | Y | N | Y | Y | Y |
| 4 Vento | Y | N | Y | Y | Y | N | Y | N |

| | 235 | 236 | 238 | 239 | 240 | 241 | 242 | 243 |
|---|---|---|---|---|---|---|---|---|
| 5 Sabo | Y | N | ? | ? | ? | ? | ? | N |
| 6 Sikorski | Y | N | ? | ? | ? | ? | ? | N |
| 7 Peterson | Y | N | Y | Y | Y | N | Y | N |
| 8 Oberstar | Y | N | Y | Y | Y | N | Y | N |
| **MISSISSIPPI** | | | | | | | | |
| 1 Whitten | Y | ? | Y | Y | Y | N | Y | N |
| 2 Espy | Y | N | Y | Y | Y | N | Y | N |
| 3 Montgomery | N | Y | N | Y | Y | Y | Y | N |
| 4 Parker | Y | Y | N | Y | N | Y | Y | N |
| 5 Taylor | N | Y | Y | Y | Y | Y | Y | N |
| **MISSOURI** | | | | | | | | |
| 1 Clay | Y | N | Y | Y | Y | N | Y | N |
| 2 Horn | Y | Y | Y | Y | Y | N | Y | Y |
| 3 Gephardt | Y | Y | Y | Y | Y | N | Y | N |
| 4 Skelton | Y | Y | Y | Y | Y | N | Y | N |
| 5 Wheat | Y | N | Y | Y | Y | N | Y | N |
| 6 *Coleman* | N | Y | Y | Y | Y | Y | Y | N |
| 7 *Hancock* | N | Y | N | Y | N | Y | Y | Y |
| 8 *Emerson* | N | Y | Y | Y | N | Y | Y | N |
| 9 Volkmer | N | N | Y | Y | Y | N | Y | N |
| **MONTANA** | | | | | | | | |
| 1 Williams | Y | N | ? | ? | ? | ? | ? | ? |
| 2 *Marlenee* | N | N | ? | ? | ? | ? | ? | N |
| **NEBRASKA** | | | | | | | | |
| 1 *Bereuter* | Y | Y | N | Y | N | Y | Y | N |
| 2 Hoagland | Y | Y | Y | Y | Y | N | Y | N |
| 3 *Barrett* | N | Y | N | Y | N | Y | Y | N |
| **NEVADA** | | | | | | | | |
| 1 Bilbray | Y | Y | Y | Y | Y | N | Y | N |
| 2 *Vucanovich* | N | Y | Y | Y | N | Y | Y | N |
| **NEW HAMPSHIRE** | | | | | | | | |
| 1 *Zeliff* | Y | Y | — | + | — | + | + | Y |
| 2 Swett | Y | Y | N | Y | Y | Y | Y | Y |
| **NEW JERSEY** | | | | | | | | |
| 1 Andrews | Y | N | Y | Y | Y | ? | ? | Y |
| 2 Hughes | N | Y | Y | Y | Y | N | Y | N |
| 3 Pallone | Y | N | Y | Y | Y | N | Y | Y |
| 4 *Smith* | N | Y | Y | Y | Y | Y | Y | N |
| 5 *Roukema* | Y | Y | Y | Y | Y | Y | Y | N |
| 6 Dwyer | ? | ? | ? | ? | ? | ? | ? | N |
| 7 *Rinaldo* | Y | Y | Y | Y | Y | Y | Y | Y |
| 8 Roe | ? | ? | Y | Y | Y | N | Y | N |
| 9 Torricelli | Y | N | ? | ? | ? | ? | Y | N |
| 10 Payne | Y | N | Y | Y | Y | N | Y | N |
| 11 *Gallo* | Y | Y | Y | Y | Y | Y | Y | N |
| 12 *Zimmer* | Y | Y | N | Y | N | Y | Y | Y |
| 13 *Saxton* | Y | Y | Y | Y | Y | Y | Y | N |
| 14 Guarini | N | # | Y | Y | Y | ? | Y | N |
| **NEW MEXICO** | | | | | | | | |
| 1 *Schiff* | Y | N | N | Y | Y | Y | Y | N |
| 2 *Skeen* | Y | Y | Y | Y | Y | Y | Y | N |
| 3 Richardson | ? | ? | Y | Y | Y | N | Y | N |
| **NEW YORK** | | | | | | | | |
| 1 Hochbrueckner | Y | N | Y | Y | Y | N | Y | N |
| 2 Downey | Y | Y | ? | Y | Y | N | Y | N |
| 3 Mrazek | Y | N | Y | Y | Y | N | Y | N |
| 4 *Lent* | Y | Y | ? | ? | ? | Y | Y | Y |
| 5 *McGrath* | Y | ? | ? | ? | ? | ? | ? | Y |
| 6 Flake | Y | N | ? | ? | ? | ? | ? | N |
| 7 Ackerman | Y | N | ? | ? | ? | ? | ? | N |
| 8 Scheuer | Y | N | Y | Y | Y | N | Y | N |
| 9 Manton | Y | Y | Y | Y | Y | N | Y | N |
| 10 Schumer | Y | ? | Y | Y | Y | N | Y | Y |
| 11 Towns | Y | Y | Y | Y | Y | N | Y | N |
| 12 Owens | Y | N | ? | ? | ? | ? | ? | ? |
| 13 Solarz | Y | Y | ? | ? | ? | ? | ? | N |
| 14 *Molinari* | Y | Y | ? | ? | ? | ? | ? | Y |
| 15 *Green* | Y | Y | Y | Y | Y | ? | ? | N |
| 16 Rangel | Y | N | Y | Y | Y | N | Y | N |
| 17 Weiss | Y | N | + | + | + | — | + | N |
| 18 Serrano | Y | N | Y | Y | Y | N | Y | N |
| 19 Engel | Y | N | ? | ? | ? | ? | ? | N |
| 20 Lowey | Y | N | Y | Y | Y | N | Y | N |
| 21 *Fish* | Y | Y | N | Y | Y | Y | Y | Y |
| 22 *Gilman* | Y | N | Y | Y | Y | Y | Y | N |
| 23 McNulty | Y | N | Y | Y | Y | N | Y | N |
| 24 *Solomon* | N | N | N | Y | N | Y | Y | Y |
| 25 *Boehlert* | Y | Y | Y | Y | Y | Y | Y | N |
| 26 *Martin* | Y | ? | Y | Y | Y | Y | Y | N |
| 27 *Walsh* | Y | N | Y | Y | N | Y | Y | Y |
| 28 McHugh | Y | Y | Y | Y | Y | N | Y | N |
| 29 *Horton* | Y | N | Y | Y | Y | Y | Y | N |
| 30 Slaughter | Y | N | Y | Y | Y | N | Y | N |
| 31 *Paxon* | Y | Y | Y | Y | Y | Y | Y | N |

| | 235 | 236 | 238 | 239 | 240 | 241 | 242 | 243 |
|---|---|---|---|---|---|---|---|---|
| 32 LaFalce | Y | N | Y | Y | Y | N | Y | N |
| 33 Nowak | Y | Y | Y | Y | Y | N | Y | N |
| 34 *Houghton* | Y | Y | N | Y | Y | Y | Y | N |
| **NORTH CAROLINA** | | | | | | | | |
| 1 Jones | N | Y | Y | Y | Y | N | Y | N |
| 2 Valentine | N | Y | Y | Y | Y | Y | Y | N |
| 3 Lancaster | Y | Y | Y | Y | Y | Y | Y | N |
| 4 Price | Y | Y | Y | Y | Y | N | Y | N |
| 5 Neal | N | Y | Y | Y | Y | Y | Y | N |
| 6 *Coble* | Y | Y | N | Y | N | Y | Y | Y |
| 7 Rose | Y | Y | Y | Y | Y | N | Y | N |
| 8 Hefner | ? | ? | ? | ? | ? | ? | ? | ? |
| 9 *McMillan* | Y | Y | ? | ? | ? | ? | ? | Y |
| 10 *Ballenger* | Y | + | N | Y | N | Y | Y | Y |
| 11 *Taylor* | Y | Y | — | + | — | + | + | Y |
| **NORTH DAKOTA** | | | | | | | | |
| AL Dorgan | Y | N | N | Y | Y | N | Y | N |
| **OHIO** | | | | | | | | |
| 1 Luken | Y | N | ? | Y | Y | N | Y | Y |
| 2 *Gradison* | N | Y | N | Y | Y | Y | N | Y |
| 3 Hall | Y | Y | Y | Y | Y | N | Y | N |
| 4 *Oxley* | N | Y | — | + | — | + | Y | Y |
| 5 *Gillmor* | N | Y | ? | ? | Y | Y | Y | Y |
| 6 *McEwen* | Y | Y | N | Y | N | Y | Y | N |
| 7 *Hobson* | Y | Y | N | Y | Y | Y | Y | Y |
| 8 *Boehner* | Y | Y | ? | Y | N | Y | Y | N |
| 9 Kaptur | Y | N | Y | Y | Y | N | Y | N |
| 10 *Miller* | N | Y | N | Y | N | Y | N | Y |
| 11 Eckart | Y | Y | N | Y | Y | N | Y | N |
| 12 *Kasich* | Y | Y | ? | Y | N | Y | Y | Y |
| 13 Pease | N | Y | Y | Y | Y | N | Y | N |
| 14 Sawyer | Y | Y | Y | Y | Y | N | Y | N |
| 15 *Wylie* | N | Y | N | Y | N | Y | N | Y |
| 16 *Regula* | N | Y | N | Y | Y | Y | Y | N |
| 17 Traficant | N | N | Y | Y | Y | N | Y | N |
| 18 Applegate | N | N | Y | Y | Y | N | Y | N |
| 19 Feighan | Y | N | ? | Y | Y | N | Y | N |
| 20 Oakar | Y | N | ? | Y | Y | N | Y | N |
| 21 Stokes | Y | N | Y | Y | Y | N | Y | N |
| **OKLAHOMA** | | | | | | | | |
| 1 *Inhofe* | Y | Y | N | Y | N | Y | Y | Y |
| 2 Synar | Y | Y | Y | Y | Y | N | Y | N |
| 3 Brewster | Y | Y | Y | Y | Y | Y | Y | N |
| 4 McCurdy | Y | Y | ? | ? | ? | ? | ? | N |
| 5 *Edwards* | Y | Y | N | Y | N | Y | Y | N |
| 6 English | N | Y | Y | Y | Y | Y | Y | N |
| **OREGON** | | | | | | | | |
| 1 AuCoin | Y | N | Y | Y | Y | N | Y | N |
| 2 *Smith* | N | Y | N | Y | N | Y | Y | N |
| 3 Wyden | Y | Y | Y | Y | Y | N | Y | N |
| 4 DeFazio | N | N | Y | Y | Y | N | Y | N |
| 5 Kopetski | Y | N | Y | Y | Y | N | Y | N |
| **PENNSYLVANIA** | | | | | | | | |
| 1 Foglietta | Y | — | Y | Y | Y | N | Y | N |
| 2 Blackwell | Y | N | Y | Y | Y | N | Y | N |
| 3 Borski | Y | N | Y | Y | Y | N | Y | N |
| 4 Kolter | N | N | Y | Y | Y | ? | ? | N |
| 5 *Schulze* | ? | ? | ? | Y | Y | Y | Y | Y |
| 6 Yatron | Y | N | Y | Y | Y | N | Y | N |
| 7 *Weldon* | N | N | Y | Y | Y | Y | Y | Y |
| 8 Kostmayer | Y | N | Y | Y | Y | N | Y | N |
| 9 *Shuster* | N | Y | N | Y | N | Y | Y | Y |
| 10 *McDade* | ? | ? | Y | Y | Y | Y | Y | N |
| 11 Kanjorski | Y | N | Y | Y | Y | N | Y | N |
| 12 Murtha | Y | N | Y | Y | Y | N | Y | N |
| 13 *Coughlin* | Y | Y | ? | Y | N | Y | Y | N |
| 14 Coyne | Y | N | Y | Y | Y | N | Y | N |
| 15 *Ritter* | Y | Y | N | Y | N | Y | Y | Y |
| 16 *Walker* | N | Y | N | Y | N | Y | N | Y |
| 17 *Gekas* | Y | ? | ? | ? | ? | ? | ? | ? |
| 18 *Santorum* | Y | N | N | Y | N | Y | Y | Y |
| 19 *Goodling* | N | Y | N | Y | N | Y | Y | N |
| 20 Gaydos | N | N | ? | ? | ? | ? | ? | Y |
| 21 *Ridge* | Y | Y | Y | Y | Y | Y | Y | N |
| 22 Murphy | N | N | ? | ? | ? | N | Y | Y |
| 23 *Clinger* | Y | Y | Y | Y | Y | Y | Y | N |
| **RHODE ISLAND** | | | | | | | | |
| 1 *Machtley* | Y | Y | Y | Y | Y | Y | Y | N |
| 2 Reed | Y | N | Y | Y | Y | N | Y | N |
| **SOUTH CAROLINA** | | | | | | | | |
| 1 *Ravenel* | Y | Y | Y | Y | Y | Y | Y | Y |
| 2 *Spence* | N | Y | Y | Y | Y | Y | Y | N |
| 3 Derrick | Y | Y | Y | Y | Y | N | Y | N |
| 4 Patterson | N | Y | N | Y | N | N | Y | Y |
| 5 Spratt | Y | Y | Y | Y | Y | N | Y | N |
| 6 Tallon | ? | ? | Y | Y | Y | N | Y | N |

| | 235 | 236 | 238 | 239 | 240 | 241 | 242 | 243 |
|---|---|---|---|---|---|---|---|---|
| **SOUTH DAKOTA** | | | | | | | | |
| AL Johnson | Y | N | Y | Y | Y | Y | Y | Y |
| **TENNESSEE** | | | | | | | | |
| 1 *Quillen* | N | Y | N | Y | N | Y | Y | N |
| 2 *Duncan* | N | Y | ? | Y | N | Y | Y | Y |
| 3 Lloyd | N | Y | ? | ? | Y | Y | Y | Y |
| 4 Cooper | Y | Y | Y | Y | Y | N | Y | Y |
| 5 Clement | Y | Y | ? | ? | ? | N | Y | Y |
| 6 Gordon | Y | Y | Y | Y | Y | N | Y | N |
| 7 *Sundquist* | Y | Y | ? | Y | N | Y | Y | N |
| 8 Tanner | N | Y | + | + | + | N | Y | N |
| 9 Ford | Y | ? | ? | ? | ? | ? | ? | N |
| **TEXAS** | | | | | | | | |
| 1 Chapman | N | Y | Y | Y | Y | N | Y | N |
| 2 Wilson | Y | N | ? | ? | ? | ? | ? | ? |
| 3 *Johnson* | Y | Y | N | Y | N | Y | Y | Y |
| 4 Hall | N | Y | N | Y | N | Y | Y | N |
| 5 Bryant | Y | N | ? | ? | ? | ? | ? | N |
| 6 *Barton* | N | Y | ? | ? | ? | ? | ? | Y |
| 7 *Archer* | N | Y | N | Y | N | Y | Y | Y |
| 8 *Fields* | N | Y | Y | Y | Y | Y | Y | N |
| 9 Brooks | N | Y | Y | Y | Y | N | Y | N |
| 10 Pickle | Y | N | ? | ? | ? | ? | ? | N |
| 11 Edwards | Y | Y | Y | Y | Y | N | Y | N |
| 12 Geren | N | Y | Y | Y | Y | Y | Y | N |
| 13 Sarpalius | N | Y | Y | Y | N | Y | Y | N |
| 14 Laughlin | ? | ? | ? | ? | ? | ? | Y | N |
| 15 de la Garza | Y | Y | ? | ? | ? | ? | ? | N |
| 16 Coleman | Y | N | Y | Y | Y | N | Y | N |
| 17 Stenholm | Y | Y | ? | ? | ? | ? | ? | Y |
| 18 Washington | Y | N | Y | ? | Y | N | Y | N |
| 19 *Combest* | N | Y | N | Y | N | Y | Y | N |
| 20 Gonzalez | Y | N | Y | Y | Y | N | Y | N |
| 21 *Smith* | Y | Y | N | Y | N | Y | Y | N |
| 22 *DeLay* | N | Y | N | Y | N | Y | Y | Y |
| 23 Bustamante | Y | N | Y | Y | Y | N | Y | N |
| 24 Frost | Y | Y | Y | Y | Y | N | Y | N |
| 25 Andrews | Y | Y | Y | Y | Y | N | Y | Y |
| 26 *Armey* | N | Y | N | Y | N | Y | Y | Y |
| 27 Ortiz | Y | Y | Y | Y | Y | N | Y | N |
| **UTAH** | | | | | | | | |
| 1 *Hansen* | N | Y | ? | ? | ? | ? | ? | Y |
| 2 Owens | Y | ? | Y | Y | Y | Y | Y | Y |
| 3 Orton | Y | Y | Y | Y | N | Y | Y | Y |
| **VERMONT** | | | | | | | | |
| AL *Sanders* | N | N | Y | Y | Y | N | Y | N |
| **VIRGINIA** | | | | | | | | |
| 1 *Bateman* | Y | Y | Y | Y | Y | Y | Y | N |
| 2 Pickett | Y | Y | Y | Y | Y | Y | Y | N |
| 3 *Bliley* | Y | Y | N | Y | N | Y | Y | N |
| 4 Sisisky | Y | Y | Y | Y | Y | Y | Y | N |
| 5 Payne | Y | Y | Y | Y | Y | Y | Y | Y |
| 6 Olin | Y | N | Y | Y | Y | Y | Y | N |
| 7 *Allen* | N | Y | N | Y | N | Y | Y | Y |
| 8 Moran | Y | Y | Y | Y | Y | N | Y | N |
| 9 Boucher | Y | Y | Y | Y | Y | N | Y | N |
| 10 *Wolf* | Y | Y | N | Y | N | Y | Y | N |
| **WASHINGTON** | | | | | | | | |
| 1 *Miller* | Y | Y | ? | Y | Y | Y | Y | Y |
| 2 Swift | Y | Y | Y | Y | Y | N | Y | N |
| 3 Unsoeld | Y | N | Y | Y | Y | ? | Y | N |
| 4 *Morrison* | Y | ? | ? | ? | ? | ? | ? | N |
| 5 Foley | | | | | | | | |
| 6 Dicks | Y | Y | Y | Y | Y | N | Y | N |
| 7 McDermott | Y | N | Y | Y | Y | N | Y | N |
| 8 *Chandler* | Y | Y | ? | ? | ? | ? | ? | N |
| **WEST VIRGINIA** | | | | | | | | |
| 1 Mollohan | N | N | Y | Y | Y | N | Y | N |
| 2 Staggers | Y | ? | ? | ? | ? | ? | ? | Y |
| 3 Wise | Y | N | ? | Y | Y | N | Y | N |
| 4 Rahall | N | N | ? | ? | ? | ? | ? | N |
| **WISCONSIN** | | | | | | | | |
| 1 Aspin | Y | ? | Y | Y | Y | Y | Y | N |
| 2 *Klug* | Y | Y | N | Y | Y | Y | Y | Y |
| 3 *Gunderson* | N | N | N | Y | Y | Y | Y | N |
| 4 Kleczka | Y | Y | Y | Y | Y | N | Y | N |
| 5 Moody | Y | N | Y | Y | Y | N | Y | N |
| 6 *Petri* | N | Y | N | Y | N | Y | Y | Y |
| 7 Obey | Y | N | Y | Y | Y | N | Y | N |
| 8 *Roth* | N | Y | N | Y | N | Y | Y | Y |
| 9 *Sensenbrenner* | N | Y | N | Y | N | Y | Y | Y |
| **WYOMING** | | | | | | | | |
| AL *Thomas* | N | N | N | Y | N | Y | Y | Y |

Southern states - Ala., Ark., Fla., Ga., Ky., La., Miss., N.C., Okla., S.C., Tenn., Texas, Va.
Omitted votes are quorum calls, which CQ does not include in its vote charts.

**244. HR 5487. Fiscal 1993 Agriculture Appropriations/ Watershed and Flood Prevention, Wetlands.** Jontz, D-Ind., amendment to cut $46,357,000 from watershed and flood prevention operations and provide funding for the Wetlands Reserve Program. Rejected 109-308: R 45-119; D 63-189 (ND 55-121, SD 8-68); I 1-0, June 30, 1992.

**245. HR 5487. Fiscal 1993 Agriculture Appropriations/ Water Quality Incentives.** Jontz, D-Ind., amendment to add $23.25 million for the Water Quality Incentive Program. Rejected 18-396: R 4-158; D 14-237 (ND 13-163, SD 1-74); I 0-1, June 30, 1992.

**246. HR 5487. Fiscal 1993 Agriculture Appropriations/ Food for Peace.** Miller, R-Wash., amendment to reduce the $343.1 million in funding for Title I of PL 480, the Food for Peace program, by $25 million. Adopted 410-4: R 162-1; D 247-3 (ND 173-2, SD 74-1); I 1-0, June 30, 1992. (Before adoption the Miller amendment was amended by a Kasich, R-Ohio, amendment. Miller would have originally cut $242.4 million.)

**247. HR 5487. Fiscal 1993 Agriculture Appropriations/ Debt Restructuring.** Glickman, D-Kan., amendment to reduce the amount the president can forgive for debt restructuring under the Enterprise for the Americas initiative from $69.5 million to $34.5 million. Rejected 78-333: R 23-141; D 54-192 (ND 40-131, SD 14-61); I 1-0, June 30, 1992.

**248. HR 5487. Fiscal 1993 Agriculture Appropriations/ Overhead Spending.** Smith, R-Texas, amendment to cut overhead spending for all agencies in the bill except the Food and Drug Administration by 10 percent. Adopted 214-191: R 125-39; D 88-152 (ND 64-104, SD 24-48); I 1-0, June 30, 1992.

**249. HR 5487. Fiscal 1993 Agriculture Appropriations/ Tobacco Promotion Abroad.** Separate vote at the request of Owens, D-Utah, on the Owens amendment to prohibit funds for the Market Promotion Program from going to promote tobacco sales abroad. In fiscal 1992, $3.5 million of the program's funds went to a group called the Tobacco Associates, which promoted the sale of U.S. tobacco products abroad. Adopted 331-82: R 123-41; D 207-41 (ND 163-9, SD 44-32); I 1-0, June 30, 1992.

**250. HR 5487. Fiscal 1993 Agriculture Appropriations/ Passage.** Passage of the bill to provide $59 billion in new budget authority for Agriculture, rural development and related agencies for fiscal year 1993. The administration requested $60.4 million. Passed 312-99: R 79-85; D 232-14 (ND 159-12, SD 73-2); I 1-0, June 30, 1992.

**251. S 429. Vertical Price Fixing/Conference Report.** Adoption of the conference report to amend the Sherman Antitrust Act of 1890 to tighten the ban on vertical price fixing, which occurred when a manufacturer conspires with a retailer to force a competing merchant to charge at least a certain price for goods or face a cutoff of supplies. The bill lowered the standard of evidence needed to get a resale price maintenance case to a jury trial. Rejected 175-225: R 9-152; D 165-73 (ND 137-27, SD 28-46); I 1-0, July 1, 1992. A "nay" was a vote in support of the president's position.

### KEY

| | |
|---|---|
| Y | Voted for (yea). |
| # | Paired for. |
| + | Announced for. |
| N | Voted against (nay). |
| X | Paired against. |
| — | Announced against. |
| P | Voted "present." |
| C | Voted "present" to avoid possible conflict of interest. |
| ? | Did not vote or otherwise make a position known. |

Democrats **Republicans** *Independent*

| | 244 | 245 | 246 | 247 | 248 | 249 | 250 | 251 |
|---|---|---|---|---|---|---|---|---|
| **ALABAMA** | | | | | | | | |
| 1 *Callahan* | N | N | Y | N | Y | Y | N | N |
| 2 *Dickinson* | N | N | Y | N | Y | Y | N | N |
| 3 Browder | N | N | Y | N | N | Y | Y | N |
| 4 Bevill | ? | ? | ? | ? | ? | ? | ? | ? |
| 5 Cramer | N | N | Y | N | N | Y | Y | N |
| 6 Erdreich | N | N | Y | ? | Y | Y | Y | N |
| 7 Harris | N | N | Y | N | N | Y | Y | N |
| **ALASKA** | | | | | | | | |
| AL *Young* | N | N | Y | N | N | N | N | N |
| **ARIZONA** | | | | | | | | |
| 1 *Rhodes* | N | N | Y | N | N | Y | N | N |
| 2 Pastor | N | N | Y | N | N | N | Y | N |
| 3 *Stump* | N | N | Y | N | N | N | N | N |
| 4 *Kyl* | N | N | Y | N | Y | N | N | N |
| 5 *Kolbe* | N | N | Y | N | Y | Y | N | N |
| **ARKANSAS** | | | | | | | | |
| 1 Alexander | N | N | N | N | N | N | Y | Y |
| 2 Thornton | N | N | Y | N | N | N | Y | N |
| 3 *Hammerschmidt* | N | N | Y | N | N | N | Y | N |
| 4 Anthony | N | N | ? | ? | ? | N | Y | ? |
| **CALIFORNIA** | | | | | | | | |
| 1 *Riggs* | N | N | Y | N | N | Y | Y | N |
| 2 *Herger* | N | N | Y | N | N | N | Y | N |
| 3 Matsui | N | N | Y | ? | ? | ? | ? | Y |
| 4 Fazio | N | N | Y | N | Y | Y | Y | Y |
| 5 Pelosi | Y | N | N | N | Y | Y | Y | Y |
| 6 Boxer | Y | N | ? | ? | ? | Y | Y | Y |
| 7 Miller | Y | N | Y | N | Y | Y | Y | Y |
| 8 Dellums | Y | N | N | N | Y | Y | Y | Y |
| 9 Stark | Y | N | Y | N | ? | Y | N | Y |
| 10 Edwards | N | N | Y | N | N | Y | Y | Y |
| 11 Lantos | N | N | Y | N | Y | Y | Y | Y |
| 12 *Campbell* | Y | N | Y | N | Y | Y | N | N |
| 13 Mineta | N | N | Y | N | Y | Y | Y | Y |
| 14 *Doolittle* | N | N | Y | N | Y | N | N | N |
| 15 Condit | N | N | Y | Y | Y | Y | Y | N |
| 16 Panetta | N | N | Y | N | Y | Y | Y | Y |
| 17 Dooley | N | N | Y | N | N | Y | Y | Y |
| 18 Lehman | N | N | Y | N | N | Y | Y | Y |
| 19 *Lagomarsino* | N | N | Y | N | Y | N | N | N |
| 20 *Thomas* | N | N | Y | N | N | N | N | N |
| 21 *Gallegly* | N | N | Y | N | Y | N | N | N |
| 22 *Moorhead* | N | N | Y | N | Y | N | N | N |
| 23 Beilenson | Y | Y | Y | N | Y | Y | N | Y |
| 24 Waxman | Y | Y | Y | N | Y | Y | Y | Y |
| 25 Roybal | N | N | Y | N | Y | Y | Y | Y |
| 26 Berman | Y | N | Y | N | Y | Y | Y | Y |
| 27 Levine | Y | N | Y | N | Y | Y | Y | Y |
| 28 Dixon | N | N | Y | N | N | Y | Y | Y |
| 29 Waters | Y | N | Y | N | N | Y | Y | Y |
| 30 Martinez | N | N | Y | N | Y | N | Y | ? |
| 31 Dymally | ? | ? | ? | ? | ? | ? | ? | ? |
| 32 Anderson | N | N | Y | N | Y | Y | Y | Y |
| 33 *Dreier* | Y | N | Y | Y | Y | N | N | N |
| 34 Torres | N | N | Y | N | Y | Y | Y | Y |
| 35 *Lewis* | N | N | Y | N | Y | Y | N | N |
| 36 Brown | Y | Y | Y | N | N | Y | N | Y |
| 37 *McCandless* | N | N | Y | Y | Y | Y | N | N |
| 38 *Dornan* | N | N | Y | N | Y | N | N | N |
| 39 *Dannemeyer* | Y | N | Y | Y | Y | N | N | N |
| 40 *Cox* | N | N | Y | N | Y | Y | N | N |
| 41 *Lowery* | ? | N | Y | N | N | Y | Y | ? |

| | 244 | 245 | 246 | 247 | 248 | 249 | 250 | 251 |
|---|---|---|---|---|---|---|---|---|
| 42 *Rohrabacher* | N | N | Y | N | Y | Y | N | N |
| 43 *Packard* | N | N | Y | N | Y | Y | N | N |
| 44 *Cunningham* | N | N | Y | N | Y | Y | N | N |
| 45 *Hunter* | N | N | Y | N | Y | N | N | N |
| **COLORADO** | | | | | | | | |
| 1 Schroeder | N | N | Y | ? | Y | Y | N | Y |
| 2 Skaggs | N | N | Y | N | N | Y | Y | Y |
| 3 Campbell | N | N | Y | N | Y | Y | Y | Y |
| 4 *Allard* | N | N | ? | N | Y | N | N | N |
| 5 *Hefley* | Y | N | N | Y | Y | N | N | N |
| 6 *Schaefer* | N | N | Y | N | N | N | N | N |
| **CONNECTICUT** | | | | | | | | |
| 1 Kennelly | N | N | Y | N | N | Y | Y | Y |
| 2 Gejdenson | N | N | Y | N | Y | Y | Y | Y |
| 3 DeLauro | N | N | Y | N | Y | Y | Y | Y |
| 4 *Shays* | Y | N | Y | Y | Y | Y | N | Y |
| 5 *Franks* | Y | N | Y | Y | Y | Y | Y | N |
| 6 *Johnson* | N | N | Y | N | Y | Y | Y | N |
| **DELAWARE** | | | | | | | | |
| AL Carper | Y | N | Y | N | Y | Y | Y | Y |
| **FLORIDA** | | | | | | | | |
| 1 Hutto | N | N | Y | N | Y | Y | Y | N |
| 2 Peterson | N | N | Y | N | N | N | Y | N |
| 3 Bennett | Y | N | Y | Y | Y | Y | Y | N |
| 4 *James* | N | N | Y | Y | Y | Y | N | N |
| 5 *McCollum* | N | N | Y | N | Y | N | N | N |
| 6 *Stearns* | Y | N | Y | Y | Y | N | N | N |
| 7 Gibbons | N | N | Y | N | N | N | Y | N |
| 8 *Young* | N | N | Y | N | Y | Y | Y | N |
| 9 *Bilirakis* | N | N | Y | Y | Y | Y | Y | N |
| 10 *Ireland* | N | N | ? | N | Y | Y | N | N |
| 11 Bacchus | N | N | Y | N | Y | Y | Y | Y |
| 12 *Lewis* | N | N | Y | N | Y | N | N | N |
| 13 *Goss* | N | N | Y | N | Y | Y | N | N |
| 14 Johnston | Y | N | N | N | Y | Y | Y | N |
| 15 *Shaw* | N | N | Y | Y | Y | Y | N | N |
| 16 Smith | N | N | Y | N | Y | Y | Y | Y |
| 17 Lehman | ? | N | Y | N | ? | Y | Y | ? |
| 18 *Ros—Lehtinen* | N | N | Y | N | Y | Y | N | N |
| 19 Fascell | N | N | Y | N | ? | ? | ? | ? |
| **GEORGIA** | | | | | | | | |
| 1 Thomas | N | N | ? | N | ? | N | Y | N |
| 2 Hatcher | N | ? | Y | N | N | Y | Y | N |
| 3 Ray | N | N | Y | Y | Y | Y | N | N |
| 4 Jones | ? | ? | ? | ? | ? | ? | ? | ? |
| 5 Lewis | N | N | Y | N | Y | Y | Y | Y |
| 6 *Gingrich* | N | N | Y | N | Y | Y | N | N |
| 7 Darden | N | N | Y | N | Y | Y | Y | N |
| 8 Rowland | N | N | N | N | N | Y | Y | N |
| 9 Jenkins | N | N | Y | N | N | N | Y | N |
| 10 Barnard | N | N | N | N | N | Y | Y | N |
| **HAWAII** | | | | | | | | |
| 1 Abercrombie | N | N | Y | N | N | N | Y | Y |
| 2 Mink | N | N | Y | N | N | Y | Y | Y |
| **IDAHO** | | | | | | | | |
| 1 LaRocco | N | N | Y | N | Y | Y | Y | N |
| 2 Stallings | N | N | Y | N | Y | Y | Y | N |
| **ILLINOIS** | | | | | | | | |
| 1 Hayes | Y | N | Y | N | N | Y | Y | Y |
| 2 Savage | N | N | Y | N | N | Y | Y | ? |
| 3 Russo | N | N | Y | N | Y | Y | Y | Y |
| 4 Sangmeister | N | N | Y | N | N | Y | Y | Y |
| 5 Lipinski | Y | N | Y | N | Y | Y | Y | Y |
| 6 *Hyde* | N | N | Y | N | N | Y | N | Y |
| 7 Collins | N | N | Y | N | N | Y | Y | Y |
| 8 Rostenkowski | N | N | Y | N | N | Y | Y | ? |
| 9 Yates | N | N | Y | N | Y | Y | Y | Y |
| 10 *Porter* | Y | Y | Y | N | Y | N | N | Y |
| 11 Annunzio | N | N | Y | N | N | Y | Y | Y |
| 12 *Crane* | Y | N | Y | Y | Y | Y | N | N |
| 13 *Fawell* | Y | N | Y | N | Y | Y | N | N |
| 14 *Hastert* | N | N | Y | N | N | N | N | N |
| 15 *Ewing* | Y | N | Y | N | Y | Y | N | N |
| 16 Cox | N | N | Y | N | Y | Y | N | N |
| 17 Evans | N | N | Y | N | Y | Y | Y | Y |
| 18 *Michel* | N | N | Y | N | N | Y | N | N |
| 19 Bruce | N | N | Y | N | Y | Y | Y | Y |
| 20 Durbin | N | N | Y | N | Y | Y | Y | Y |
| 21 Costello | N | N | Y | N | Y | Y | Y | Y |
| 22 Poshard | N | N | Y | N | Y | Y | Y | Y |
| **INDIANA** | | | | | | | | |
| 1 Visclosky | N | N | Y | N | N | Y | Y | Y |
| 2 Sharp | N | Y | Y | N | Y | Y | Y | Y |
| 3 Roemer | N | N | Y | Y | Y | Y | Y | N |

ND Northern Democrats    SD Southern Democrats

| | 244 | 245 | 246 | 247 | 248 | 249 | 250 | 251 |
|---|---|---|---|---|---|---|---|---|
| 4 Long | Y | Y | Y | Y | Y | Y | Y | N |
| 5 Jontz | Y | Y | Y | Y | Y | Y | N | Y |
| 6 **Burton** | Y | N | Y | N | Y | Y | N | N |
| 7 **Myers** | N | N | Y | N | N | Y | Y | N |
| 8 McCloskey | N | N | Y | N | N | Y | Y | N |
| 9 Hamilton | N | N | Y | N | N | N | Y | N |
| 10 Jacobs | Y | N | Y | Y | Y | Y | N | Y |
| **IOWA** | | | | | | | | |
| 1 **Leach** | Y | N | Y | N | Y | Y | Y | N |
| 2 **Nussle** | Y | N | Y | N | Y | Y | N | N |
| 3 Nagle | Y | N | Y | N | N | N | Y | Y |
| 4 Smith | N | N | N | N | N | Y | Y | Y |
| 5 **Lightfoot** | N | N | Y | N | Y | Y | Y | N |
| 6 **Grandy** | Y | Y | Y | N | Y | Y | N | N |
| **KANSAS** | | | | | | | | |
| 1 **Roberts** | N | N | Y | N | Y | Y | N | N |
| 2 Slattery | N | N | Y | Y | Y | Y | N | N |
| 3 **Meyers** | Y | N | Y | N | Y | Y | N | N |
| 4 Glickman | N | N | Y | Y | Y | Y | Y | Y |
| 5 **Nichols** | N | N | Y | N | Y | Y | N | N |
| **KENTUCKY** | | | | | | | | |
| 1 Hubbard | N | N | Y | Y | N | N | N | N |
| 2 Natcher | N | N | Y | N | N | N | Y | Y |
| 3 Mazzoli | Y | N | Y | Y | Y | Y | Y | Y |
| 4 **Bunning** | N | N | Y | N | Y | N | Y | N |
| 5 **Rogers** | N | N | Y | Y | N | N | Y | N |
| 6 **Hopkins** | N | N | Y | N | Y | N | N | N |
| 7 Perkins | ? | ? | ? | ? | ? | ? | ? | ? |
| **LOUISIANA** | | | | | | | | |
| 1 **Livingston** | N | N | Y | N | ? | ? | ? | N |
| 2 Jefferson | N | N | Y | N | N | Y | Y | N |
| 3 Tauzin | N | N | Y | N | N | Y | Y | N |
| 4 **McCrery** | Y | N | Y | N | Y | Y | Y | N |
| 5 Huckaby | ? | ? | ? | ? | ? | ? | ? | ? |
| 6 **Baker** | Y | N | Y | ? | Y | Y | Y | N |
| 7 Hayes | Y | N | Y | N | N | Y | Y | N |
| 8 **Holloway** | N | N | Y | N | Y | N | Y | N |
| **MAINE** | | | | | | | | |
| 1 Andrews | Y | N | Y | Y | N | Y | Y | Y |
| 2 **Snowe** | Y | N | Y | N | Y | Y | N | N |
| **MARYLAND** | | | | | | | | |
| 1 **Gilchrest** | Y | N | Y | N | N | Y | Y | N |
| 2 **Bentley** | N | N | Y | N | N | N | Y | Y |
| 3 Cardin | Y | N | Y | N | N | Y | Y | Y |
| 4 McMillen | Y | N | Y | N | Y | Y | Y | Y |
| 5 Hoyer | N | N | Y | N | N | N | Y | Y |
| 6 Byron | N | N | Y | N | Y | Y | Y | N |
| 7 Mfume | Y | N | Y | N | Y | Y | Y | Y |
| 8 **Morella** | Y | N | Y | N | N | Y | Y | N |
| **MASSACHUSETTS** | | | | | | | | |
| 1 Olver | Y | N | Y | N | Y | Y | Y | Y |
| 2 Neal | N | N | Y | N | Y | Y | Y | Y |
| 3 Early | N | N | Y | Y | N | Y | Y | Y |
| 4 Frank | N | N | Y | N | Y | Y | Y | Y |
| 5 Atkins | Y | N | Y | N | Y | Y | Y | Y |
| 6 Mavroules | N | N | Y | N | N | Y | Y | ? |
| 7 Markey | N | N | Y | N | Y | Y | Y | Y |
| 8 Kennedy | Y | N | Y | N | Y | Y | ? | Y |
| 9 Moakley | N | N | Y | N | N | Y | Y | Y |
| 10 Studds | N | N | Y | N | Y | Y | Y | Y |
| 11 Donnelly | N | N | Y | Y | Y | Y | N | Y |
| **MICHIGAN** | | | | | | | | |
| 1 Conyers | Y | N | Y | N | N | Y | Y | ? |
| 2 **Pursell** | N | N | Y | N | Y | Y | N | N |
| 3 Wolpe | Y | N | Y | N | N | Y | Y | Y |
| 4 **Upton** | Y | N | Y | N | Y | Y | Y | N |
| 5 **Henry** | Y | N | Y | N | Y | Y | N | N |
| 6 Carr | N | N | Y | N | N | Y | Y | N |
| 7 Kildee | N | N | Y | N | N | Y | Y | Y |
| 8 Traxler | ? | ? | ? | ? | ? | ? | ? | ? |
| 9 **Vander Jagt** | N | N | Y | N | Y | N | Y | N |
| 10 **Camp** | N | N | Y | N | Y | N | Y | N |
| 11 **Davis** | N | N | Y | N | Y | Y | Y | ? |
| 12 Bonior | ? | ? | ? | ? | ? | ? | ? | ? |
| 13 Collins | N | N | Y | N | N | Y | Y | Y |
| 14 Hertel | N | N | Y | N | N | Y | Y | Y |
| 15 Ford | N | N | Y | N | ? | Y | Y | Y |
| 16 Dingell | N | N | Y | N | N | Y | Y | Y |
| 17 Levin | N | N | Y | N | N | Y | Y | Y |
| 18 **Broomfield** | N | N | Y | N | Y | Y | N | ? |
| **MINNESOTA** | | | | | | | | |
| 1 Penny | N | N | Y | Y | Y | Y | N | N |
| 2 **Weber** | N | N | Y | N | N | N | Y | N |
| 3 **Ramstad** | Y | Y | Y | Y | Y | Y | N | N |
| 4 Vento | Y | Y | Y | N | Y | Y | Y | Y |

| | 244 | 245 | 246 | 247 | 248 | 249 | 250 | 251 |
|---|---|---|---|---|---|---|---|---|
| 5 Sabo | N | N | Y | N | N | Y | Y | Y |
| 6 Sikorski | Y | Y | Y | N | Y | Y | N | Y |
| 7 Peterson | Y | N | Y | N | N | Y | Y | N |
| 8 Oberstar | N | N | Y | N | N | Y | Y | Y |
| **MISSISSIPPI** | | | | | | | | |
| 1 Whitten | N | N | Y | N | N | N | Y | ? |
| 2 Espy | N | N | Y | N | N | N | Y | N |
| 3 Montgomery | N | N | Y | N | N | Y | Y | N |
| 4 Parker | N | N | Y | N | N | N | Y | N |
| 5 Taylor | N | N | Y | ? | N | Y | Y | N |
| **MISSOURI** | | | | | | | | |
| 1 Clay | N | N | Y | N | N | Y | Y | Y |
| 2 Horn | N | N | Y | Y | Y | Y | Y | N |
| 3 Gephardt | N | N | Y | N | N | ? | Y | Y |
| 4 Skelton | N | N | ? | ? | N | Y | Y | N |
| 5 Wheat | N | N | Y | Y | ? | Y | Y | Y |
| 6 **Coleman** | N | N | Y | N | N | N | Y | N |
| 7 **Hancock** | Y | N | Y | Y | Y | Y | N | N |
| 8 **Emerson** | N | N | Y | N | N | N | Y | N |
| 9 Volkmer | N | N | Y | Y | Y | Y | Y | Y |
| **MONTANA** | | | | | | | | |
| 1 Williams | ? | ? | ? | ? | ? | ? | ? | ? |
| 2 **Marlenee** | N | N | Y | N | N | Y | Y | N |
| **NEBRASKA** | | | | | | | | |
| 1 **Bereuter** | N | N | N | N | N | Y | Y | N |
| 2 Hoagland | Y | N | N | Y | N | Y | Y | Y |
| 3 **Barrett** | N | N | Y | N | N | Y | Y | N |
| **NEVADA** | | | | | | | | |
| 1 Bilbray | N | N | Y | N | Y | Y | Y | Y |
| 2 **Vucanovich** | N | N | Y | N | Y | Y | Y | N |
| **NEW HAMPSHIRE** | | | | | | | | |
| 1 **Zeliff** | N | N | Y | Y | Y | Y | N | N |
| 2 Swett | N | N | Y | N | Y | Y | Y | Y |
| **NEW JERSEY** | | | | | | | | |
| 1 Andrews | Y | N | Y | Y | Y | Y | Y | Y |
| 2 Hughes | Y | N | Y | Y | Y | Y | N | Y |
| 3 Pallone | Y | N | Y | N | Y | Y | N | Y |
| 4 **Smith** | Y | N | Y | N | Y | Y | Y | Y |
| 5 **Roukema** | Y | N | Y | N | Y | Y | N | N |
| 6 Dwyer | Y | N | Y | N | N | Y | Y | ? |
| 7 **Rinaldo** | Y | N | Y | N | Y | Y | Y | Y |
| 8 Roe | N | N | Y | N | ? | ? | Y | ? |
| 9 Torricelli | Y | N | Y | N | N | Y | Y | Y |
| 10 Payne | Y | N | Y | N | N | Y | Y | Y |
| 11 **Gallo** | N | N | Y | N | N | N | Y | N |
| 12 **Zimmer** | Y | N | Y | N | Y | Y | N | N |
| 13 **Saxton** | Y | N | Y | N | Y | N | N | N |
| 14 Guarini | N | N | Y | N | Y | Y | Y | Y |
| **NEW MEXICO** | | | | | | | | |
| 1 **Schiff** | N | N | Y | N | Y | Y | Y | N |
| 2 **Skeen** | N | N | Y | N | N | Y | Y | N |
| 3 Richardson | Y | N | Y | N | Y | Y | Y | Y |
| **NEW YORK** | | | | | | | | |
| 1 Hochbrueckner | N | N | Y | N | N | Y | Y | Y |
| 2 Downey | N | N | Y | N | N | Y | Y | Y |
| 3 Mrazek | Y | N | Y | N | N | Y | Y | N |
| 4 **Lent** | N | N | Y | N | Y | Y | N | N |
| 5 **McGrath** | N | N | Y | N | Y | N | N | Y |
| 6 Flake | N | N | Y | N | N | Y | Y | Y |
| 7 Ackerman | N | N | ? | ? | ? | ? | ? | ? |
| 8 Scheuer | N | N | Y | ? | ? | ? | ? | ? |
| 9 Manton | N | N | Y | N | Y | Y | Y | Y |
| 10 Schumer | Y | N | Y | N | N | Y | Y | Y |
| 11 Towns | N | N | Y | N | N | Y | Y | Y |
| 12 Owens | ? | ? | Y | N | N | Y | Y | Y |
| 13 Solarz | Y | Y | Y | N | N | Y | Y | Y |
| 14 **Molinari** | Y | N | Y | N | Y | Y | N | N |
| 15 **Green** | N | N | Y | N | N | N | Y | N |
| 16 Rangel | N | N | Y | N | N | Y | Y | Y |
| 17 Weiss | Y | N | Y | N | N | Y | Y | Y |
| 18 Serrano | N | N | Y | N | N | Y | Y | Y |
| 19 Engel | N | N | Y | N | Y | Y | Y | Y |
| 20 Lowey | N | N | Y | N | Y | Y | Y | Y |
| 21 **Fish** | N | N | Y | N | Y | Y | Y | N |
| 22 **Gilman** | Y | N | Y | N | N | Y | Y | Y |
| 23 McNulty | N | N | Y | N | N | Y | Y | Y |
| 24 **Solomon** | N | N | Y | N | Y | Y | N | N |
| 25 **Boehlert** | Y | N | Y | N | Y | Y | Y | N |
| 26 **Martin** | N | ? | Y | N | Y | Y | Y | N |
| 27 **Walsh** | Y | N | Y | Y | Y | Y | N | N |
| 28 McHugh | N | N | Y | Y | N | Y | Y | Y |
| 29 **Horton** | N | N | Y | N | N | N | Y | ? |
| 30 Slaughter | N | N | Y | N | Y | Y | Y | Y |
| 31 **Paxon** | N | N | Y | N | Y | Y | Y | N |

| | 244 | 245 | 246 | 247 | 248 | 249 | 250 | 251 |
|---|---|---|---|---|---|---|---|---|
| 32 LaFalce | N | N | Y | N | N | Y | Y | Y |
| 33 Nowak | N | N | Y | N | N | Y | Y | Y |
| 34 **Houghton** | N | N | Y | N | N | N | Y | N |
| **NORTH CAROLINA** | | | | | | | | |
| 1 Jones | N | N | Y | Y | Y | N | Y | Y |
| 2 Valentine | N | N | Y | Y | Y | N | Y | N |
| 3 Lancaster | Y | N | Y | N | Y | N | Y | N |
| 4 Price | N | N | Y | N | N | N | Y | Y |
| 5 Neal | N | N | Y | Y | Y | N | Y | N |
| 6 **Coble** | N | N | Y | Y | Y | N | Y | N |
| 7 Rose | N | N | Y | N | N | N | Y | Y |
| 8 Hefner | ? | ? | ? | ? | ? | ? | ? | ? |
| 9 **McMillan** | N | N | Y | N | Y | N | Y | N |
| 10 **Ballenger** | N | N | Y | N | Y | N | N | N |
| 11 **Taylor** | N | N | Y | N | Y | N | Y | N |
| **NORTH DAKOTA** | | | | | | | | |
| AL Dorgan | ? | N | Y | Y | Y | Y | Y | Y |
| **OHIO** | | | | | | | | |
| 1 Luken | N | N | Y | N | Y | Y | Y | Y |
| 2 **Gradison** | N | N | Y | N | Y | Y | N | N |
| 3 Hall | N | N | Y | N | N | Y | Y | ? |
| 4 **Oxley** | N | N | Y | N | Y | Y | N | N |
| 5 **Gillmor** | N | N | Y | N | Y | N | Y | N |
| 6 **McEwen** | N | N | Y | N | Y | N | N | N |
| 7 **Hobson** | N | N | Y | N | Y | Y | Y | N |
| 8 **Boehner** | N | N | Y | N | Y | N | Y | N |
| 9 Kaptur | N | N | Y | Y | N | Y | Y | Y |
| 10 **Miller** | N | ? | Y | N | Y | Y | Y | N |
| 11 Eckart | N | N | Y | Y | N | Y | Y | Y |
| 12 **Kasich** | N | N | Y | N | Y | Y | Y | N |
| 13 Pease | N | N | Y | N | N | Y | Y | Y |
| 14 Sawyer | N | N | Y | N | N | Y | Y | Y |
| 15 **Wylie** | N | N | Y | N | Y | Y | N | N |
| 16 **Regula** | N | N | Y | N | Y | Y | Y | N |
| 17 Traficant | N | N | Y | Y | Y | Y | Y | Y |
| 18 Applegate | N | N | Y | Y | Y | Y | Y | Y |
| 19 Feighan | N | N | Y | N | ? | Y | Y | Y |
| 20 Oakar | N | N | Y | N | N | Y | Y | Y |
| 21 Stokes | N | N | Y | N | N | Y | Y | Y |
| **OKLAHOMA** | | | | | | | | |
| 1 **Inhofe** | N | N | Y | N | Y | Y | N | N |
| 2 Synar | N | N | Y | N | N | Y | Y | Y |
| 3 Brewster | N | N | Y | Y | N | N | Y | N |
| 4 McCurdy | Y | N | Y | N | Y | Y | Y | N |
| 5 **Edwards** | N | N | Y | N | Y | Y | N | N |
| 6 English | Y | Y | Y | Y | N | Y | Y | N |
| **OREGON** | | | | | | | | |
| 1 AuCoin | Y | N | Y | N | N | Y | Y | Y |
| 2 **Smith** | N | N | Y | N | N | N | Y | N |
| 3 Wyden | Y | N | Y | N | N | Y | Y | Y |
| 4 DeFazio | N | N | Y | N | N | Y | Y | Y |
| 5 Kopetski | N | N | Y | N | N | Y | Y | Y |
| **PENNSYLVANIA** | | | | | | | | |
| 1 Foglietta | Y | N | Y | N | N | Y | Y | Y |
| 2 Blackwell | N | N | Y | N | N | Y | Y | Y |
| 3 Borski | Y | Y | Y | N | Y | Y | Y | Y |
| 4 Kolter | N | ? | Y | Y | ? | ? | ? | ? |
| 5 **Schulze** | Y | N | Y | N | Y | Y | N | N |
| 6 Yatron | N | N | Y | N | N | Y | Y | Y |
| 7 **Weldon** | Y | N | Y | N | Y | Y | N | N |
| 8 Kostmayer | Y | Y | Y | N | Y | Y | Y | Y |
| 9 **Shuster** | N | N | Y | N | Y | Y | N | N |
| 10 **McDade** | N | N | Y | N | N | Y | Y | Y |
| 11 Kanjorski | N | N | Y | Y | Y | Y | Y | N |
| 12 Murtha | N | N | Y | N | N | Y | Y | Y |
| 13 **Coughlin** | N | N | Y | N | N | Y | Y | N |
| 14 Coyne | N | N | Y | N | N | Y | Y | Y |
| 15 **Ritter** | Y | N | Y | N | Y | Y | N | N |
| 16 **Walker** | Y | N | Y | N | Y | N | N | N |
| 17 **Gekas** | ? | ? | ? | ? | ? | ? | ? | ? |
| 18 **Santorum** | N | N | Y | N | Y | Y | N | N |
| 19 **Goodling** | N | N | Y | N | N | Y | Y | N |
| 20 Gaydos | N | N | Y | Y | Y | Y | Y | ? |
| 21 **Ridge** | Y | ? | Y | N | Y | Y | Y | N |
| 22 Murphy | N | Y | Y | N | Y | Y | Y | Y |
| 23 **Clinger** | N | N | Y | N | N | Y | Y | N |
| **RHODE ISLAND** | | | | | | | | |
| 1 **Machtley** | N | N | Y | N | Y | Y | Y | N |
| 2 Reed | Y | N | Y | Y | Y | Y | Y | Y |
| **SOUTH CAROLINA** | | | | | | | | |
| 1 **Ravenel** | Y | N | Y | N | Y | N | Y | N |
| 2 **Spence** | N | N | Y | Y | Y | N | Y | N |
| 3 Derrick | N | N | Y | Y | N | Y | Y | N |
| 4 Patterson | N | N | Y | Y | Y | Y | Y | N |
| 5 Spratt | N | N | Y | N | Y | N | Y | Y |
| 6 Tallon | ? | ? | ? | ? | ? | ? | ? | ? |

| | 244 | 245 | 246 | 247 | 248 | 249 | 250 | 251 |
|---|---|---|---|---|---|---|---|---|
| **SOUTH DAKOTA** | | | | | | | | |
| AL Johnson | Y | N | Y | Y | N | Y | Y | N |
| **TENNESSEE** | | | | | | | | |
| 1 **Quillen** | N | N | Y | N | Y | N | Y | N |
| 2 **Duncan** | N | N | Y | Y | Y | Y | N | N |
| 3 Lloyd | N | N | Y | N | N | Y | Y | N |
| 4 Cooper | N | N | Y | N | Y | Y | Y | Y |
| 5 Clement | N | N | Y | Y | Y | N | Y | Y |
| 6 Gordon | N | N | Y | N | N | Y | Y | N |
| 7 **Sundquist** | N | N | Y | N | Y | N | Y | N |
| 8 Tanner | N | N | Y | Y | Y | N | Y | N |
| 9 Ford | N | N | Y | N | Y | Y | ? | Y |
| **TEXAS** | | | | | | | | |
| 1 Chapman | N | N | Y | N | N | Y | Y | Y |
| 2 Wilson | ? | ? | ? | N | N | Y | Y | Y |
| 3 **Johnson** | N | N | Y | N | Y | Y | Y | N |
| 4 Hall | N | N | Y | N | Y | N | Y | N |
| 5 Bryant | Y | N | Y | N | N | Y | Y | N |
| 6 **Barton** | N | N | Y | N | Y | Y | Y | N |
| 7 **Archer** | N | N | Y | N | Y | Y | N | N |
| 8 **Fields** | N | N | Y | N | Y | Y | Y | N |
| 9 Brooks | N | ? | Y | N | N | Y | Y | Y |
| 10 Pickle | N | N | Y | N | Y | Y | Y | Y |
| 11 Edwards | N | N | Y | N | N | Y | Y | Y |
| 12 Geren | N | N | Y | N | Y | N | Y | N |
| 13 Sarpalius | N | N | Y | N | N | N | Y | N |
| 14 Laughlin | N | N | Y | N | N | N | Y | Y |
| 15 de la Garza | N | N | Y | N | N | Y | Y | N |
| 16 Coleman | N | N | Y | N | N | Y | Y | N |
| 17 Stenholm | N | N | Y | N | Y | Y | Y | N |
| 18 Washington | ? | ? | Y | N | N | Y | Y | Y |
| 19 **Combest** | N | N | Y | N | N | N | Y | N |
| 20 Gonzalez | N | N | Y | N | N | Y | Y | Y |
| 21 **Smith** | N | N | Y | N | Y | Y | Y | N |
| 22 **DeLay** | N | N | Y | N | Y | N | N | N |
| 23 Bustamante | N | N | Y | ? | ? | ? | ? | ? |
| 24 Frost | N | N | Y | N | N | Y | Y | Y |
| 25 Andrews | N | N | Y | N | Y | Y | Y | Y |
| 26 **Armey** | Y | N | Y | N | Y | Y | N | N |
| 27 Ortiz | N | N | Y | N | N | Y | Y | Y |
| **UTAH** | | | | | | | | |
| 1 **Hansen** | N | N | Y | N | Y | Y | N | N |
| 2 Owens | Y | Y | Y | N | Y | Y | Y | N |
| 3 Orton | N | N | Y | Y | Y | Y | N | N |
| **VERMONT** | | | | | | | | |
| AL *Sanders* | Y | N | Y | Y | Y | Y | Y | Y |
| **VIRGINIA** | | | | | | | | |
| 1 **Bateman** | N | N | Y | N | N | N | Y | N |
| 2 Pickett | N | N | Y | N | Y | Y | Y | N |
| 3 **Bliley** | N | N | Y | N | Y | N | Y | N |
| 4 Sisisky | N | N | Y | Y | Y | N | Y | N |
| 5 Payne | N | N | Y | N | Y | N | Y | N |
| 6 Olin | N | N | Y | N | ? | Y | Y | N |
| 7 **Allen** | N | N | Y | Y | Y | N | N | N |
| 8 Moran | N | N | Y | N | ? | ? | ? | N |
| 9 Boucher | N | N | ? | N | N | N | Y | Y |
| 10 **Wolf** | N | N | Y | N | N | Y | N | N |
| **WASHINGTON** | | | | | | | | |
| 1 **Miller** | Y | N | Y | N | Y | Y | N | N |
| 2 Swift | N | N | Y | N | N | N | Y | Y |
| 3 Unsoeld | N | N | Y | N | N | Y | Y | Y |
| 4 **Morrison** | N | N | Y | N | N | Y | Y | N |
| 5 Foley | | | | | | | | |
| 6 Dicks | N | N | Y | N | N | Y | Y | Y |
| 7 McDermott | Y | N | Y | N | N | Y | Y | Y |
| 8 **Chandler** | N | N | Y | N | Y | Y | Y | N |
| **WEST VIRGINIA** | | | | | | | | |
| 1 Mollohan | N | N | Y | ? | N | N | Y | N |
| 2 Staggers | Y | N | Y | N | N | Y | ? | ? |
| 3 Wise | N | N | Y | N | N | N | ? | Y |
| 4 Rahall | N | N | Y | Y | N | Y | Y | N |
| **WISCONSIN** | | | | | | | | |
| 1 Aspin | Y | N | Y | N | Y | Y | Y | Y |
| 2 **Klug** | Y | N | Y | N | Y | Y | Y | N |
| 3 **Gunderson** | N | N | Y | N | N | Y | Y | N |
| 4 Kleczka | Y | N | Y | N | Y | Y | Y | Y |
| 5 Moody | Y | N | Y | Y | Y | Y | Y | N |
| 6 **Petri** | Y | N | Y | Y | Y | Y | N | N |
| 7 Obey | N | N | Y | Y | N | Y | Y | Y |
| 8 **Roth** | N | N | Y | Y | Y | Y | N | N |
| 9 **Sensenbrenner** | Y | N | Y | Y | Y | Y | N | N |
| **WYOMING** | | | | | | | | |
| AL **Thomas** | N | N | Y | N | N | Y | N | N |

Southern states - Ala., Ark., Fla., Ga., Ky., La., Miss., N.C., Okla., S.C., Tenn., Texas, Va.
Omitted votes are quorum calls, which CQ does not include in its vote charts.

**252. S 1306. Alcohol, Drug Abuse and Mental Health Administration Reorganization/Rule.** Adoption of the rule (H Res 479) to waive all points of order against and provide for House floor consideration of the conference report to reauthorize the federal substance abuse and mental health programs for fiscal 1993-94. Adopted 266-138: R 36-122; D 229-16 (ND 168-7, SD 61-9); I 1-0, July 1, 1992.

**253. S 1306. Alcohol, Drug Abuse and Mental Health Administration Reorganization/Conference Report.** Adoption of the conference report to reauthorize the federal substance abuse and mental health programs for fiscal 1993-94. The bill split the block grant for mental health and substance abuse services into two separate grants, transferred the research arm of the Alcohol, Drug Abuse and Mental Health Administration to the National Institutes of Health, and provided more money to rural areas under state funding formulas. The revised conference report included a prohibition on the use of federal funds to buy clean needles or syringes for distribution to drug addicts to use illegal drugs. Adopted 358-60: R 124-38; D 233-22 (ND 172-4, SD 61-18); I 1-0, July 1, 1992. A "yea" was a vote in support of the president's position.

**254. HR 5488. Fiscal 1993 Treasury, Postal Service Appropriations/Rule.** Adoption of the rule (H Res 505) to waive certain points of order against and provide for House floor consideration of the bill to provide $22.8 billion in new budget authority for the Treasury Department, the U.S. Postal Service, the Executive Office of the President and certain independent agencies in fiscal 1993. Adopted 397-11: R 148-10; D 248-1 (ND 170-1, SD 78-0); I 1-0, July 1, 1992.

**255. HR 5488. Fiscal 1993 Treasury, Postal Service Appropriations/Administrative Account Cuts.** Penny, D-Minn., amendment to cut $26 million from several administrative accounts in the bill. Adopted 388-27: R 153-10; D 234-17 (ND 162-10, SD 72-7); I 1-0, July 1, 1992.

**256. HR 5488. Fiscal 1993 Treasury, Postal Service Appropriations/Restore Council on Competitiveness.** Mc-Dade, R-Pa., amendment to eliminate the prohibition in the bill and allow the use of funds for the White House Council on Competitiveness, chaired by Vice President Dan Quayle. Rejected 183-236: R 154-10; D 29-225 (ND 7-166, SD 22-59); I 0-1, July 1, 1992. A "yea" was a vote in support of the president's position.

**257. HR 5488. Fiscal 1993 Treasury, Postal Service Appropriations/Executive Office Cuts.** Wolf, R-Va., amendment to the Wise, D-W.Va., amendment to provide a 1 percent cut for the Executive Office of the President, rather than the 5.7 percent cut provided in the Wise amendment. Rejected 160-256: R 139-23; D 21-232 (ND 8-165, SD 13-67); I 0-1, July 1, 1992.

**258. HR 5488. Fiscal 1993 Treasury, Postal Service Appropriations/Executive Office Cuts.** Wise, D-W.Va., amendment to provide a 5.7 percent cut for the Executive Office of the President. Adopted 330-87: R 87-75; D 242-12 (ND 169-5, SD 73-7); I 1-0, July 1, 1992.

**259. HR 5488. Fiscal 1993 Treasury, Postal Service Appropriations/Former Presidents.** Jacobs, D-Ind., amendment to cut $1.6 million from the account providing funds to former presidents. Rejected 202-205: R 76-83; D 125-122 (ND 90-80, SD 35-42); I 1-0, July 1, 1992.

## KEY

| | |
|---|---|
| Y | Voted for (yea). |
| # | Paired for. |
| + | Announced for. |
| N | Voted against (nay). |
| X | Paired against. |
| − | Announced against. |
| P | Voted "present." |
| C | Voted "present" to avoid possible conflict of interest. |
| ? | Did not vote or otherwise make a position known. |

Democrats **Republicans** *Independent*

| | 252 | 253 | 254 | 255 | 256 | 257 | 258 | 259 |
|---|---|---|---|---|---|---|---|---|
| **ALABAMA** | | | | | | | | |
| 1 *Callahan* | N | Y | Y | Y | Y | Y | N | N |
| 2 *Dickinson* | N | N | Y | Y | Y | Y | N | N |
| 3 Browder | Y | Y | Y | Y | N | N | Y | Y |
| 4 Bevill | ? | Y | Y | Y | N | N | Y | Y |
| 5 Cramer | Y | Y | Y | Y | N | N | Y | Y |
| 6 Erdreich | Y | Y | Y | Y | N | Y | N | Y |
| 7 Harris | Y | Y | Y | Y | N | N | Y | Y |
| **ALASKA** | | | | | | | | |
| AL *Young* | Y | N | Y | Y | Y | Y | N | N |
| **ARIZONA** | | | | | | | | |
| 1 *Rhodes* | N | Y | Y | Y | Y | Y | N | N |
| 2 Pastor | Y | Y | Y | Y | N | N | Y | Y |
| 3 *Stump* | N | N | N | Y | Y | Y | N | Y |
| 4 *Kyl* | N | Y | Y | Y | Y | Y | N | Y |
| 5 *Kolbe* | N | Y | Y | Y | Y | Y | Y | Y |
| **ARKANSAS** | | | | | | | | |
| 1 Alexander | ? | Y | Y | N | N | N | Y | N |
| 2 Thornton | Y | Y | Y | Y | N | N | Y | Y |
| 3 *Hammerschmidt* | N | Y | Y | N | Y | N | Y | N |
| 4 Anthony | ? | ? | ? | Y | N | N | Y | Y |
| **CALIFORNIA** | | | | | | | | |
| 1 *Riggs* | ? | Y | ? | Y | Y | Y | Y | Y |
| 2 *Herger* | N | N | Y | Y | Y | Y | Y | Y |
| 3 Matsui | Y | Y | Y | Y | N | N | Y | N |
| 4 Fazio | Y | Y | Y | Y | N | N | Y | Y |
| 5 Pelosi | Y | Y | Y | N | N | N | Y | Y |
| 6 Boxer | ? | ? | ? | ? | ? | ? | ? | ? |
| 7 Miller | Y | Y | Y | Y | N | N | Y | Y |
| 8 Dellums | Y | Y | Y | Y | N | N | Y | Y |
| 9 Stark | Y | Y | Y | Y | N | N | Y | Y |
| 10 Edwards | Y | Y | Y | Y | N | N | Y | Y |
| 11 Lantos | Y | Y | Y | Y | N | N | Y | Y |
| 12 *Campbell* | N | Y | Y | Y | N | N | Y | N |
| 13 Mineta | Y | Y | Y | Y | N | N | Y | N |
| 14 *Doolittle* | N | N | N | Y | Y | Y | Y | Y |
| 15 Condit | Y | Y | Y | Y | N | Y | N | Y |
| 16 Panetta | Y | Y | Y | Y | N | N | Y | N |
| 17 Dooley | Y | Y | Y | Y | N | N | Y | Y |
| 18 Lehman | Y | Y | Y | Y | N | N | Y | Y |
| 19 *Lagomarsino* | Y | Y | Y | Y | Y | Y | Y | N |
| 20 *Thomas* | N | Y | Y | Y | N | Y | Y | N |
| 21 *Gallegly* | Y | Y | Y | Y | Y | Y | Y | Y |
| 22 *Moorhead* | N | Y | Y | Y | Y | Y | Y | Y |
| 23 Beilenson | Y | Y | Y | Y | N | N | Y | N |
| 24 Waxman | Y | Y | ? | Y | N | N | Y | Y |
| 25 Roybal | Y | Y | Y | N | N | Y | N | N |
| 26 Berman | Y | Y | Y | Y | N | N | Y | N |
| 27 Levine | Y | Y | Y | ? | ? | ? | Y | N |
| 28 Dixon | Y | Y | Y | N | N | Y | N | Y |
| 29 Waters | Y | Y | Y | Y | N | N | Y | Y |
| 30 Martinez | Y | Y | Y | Y | N | N | Y | Y |
| 31 Dymally | ? | ? | ? | ? | ? | ? | ? | ? |
| 32 Anderson | Y | Y | ? | Y | N | Y | N | N |
| 33 *Dreier* | N | Y | N | Y | N | Y | N | N |
| 34 Torres | + | + | + | + | − | − | + | − |
| 35 *Lewis* | N | Y | Y | Y | N | Y | N | N |
| 36 Brown | Y | Y | Y | Y | N | N | N | N |
| 37 *McCandless* | N | Y | Y | Y | Y | Y | Y | N |
| 38 *Dornan* | N | N | N | Y | Y | N | N | N |
| 39 *Dannemeyer* | N | N | N | Y | Y | Y | Y | Y |
| 40 *Cox* | N | ? | N | Y | Y | N | Y | N |
| 41 *Lowery* | N | Y | Y | Y | N | Y | N | N |

| | 252 | 253 | 254 | 255 | 256 | 257 | 258 | 259 |
|---|---|---|---|---|---|---|---|---|
| 42 *Rohrabacher* | N | Y | Y | Y | Y | Y | Y | Y |
| 43 *Packard* | N | Y | Y | Y | Y | Y | Y | N |
| 44 *Cunningham* | N | Y | Y | Y | Y | Y | Y | N |
| 45 *Hunter* | N | N | ? | Y | Y | Y | Y | Y |
| **COLORADO** | | | | | | | | |
| 1 Schroeder | Y | N | Y | ? | N | N | Y | Y |
| 2 Skaggs | Y | Y | Y | Y | N | N | Y | N |
| 3 Campbell | Y | Y | Y | Y | N | N | Y | N |
| 4 *Allard* | N | N | N | Y | Y | Y | Y | Y |
| 5 *Hefley* | N | N | N | Y | Y | Y | Y | Y |
| 6 *Schaefer* | N | N | Y | Y | Y | Y | Y | N |
| **CONNECTICUT** | | | | | | | | |
| 1 Kennelly | Y | Y | Y | Y | N | N | Y | N |
| 2 Gejdenson | Y | Y | Y | Y | N | N | Y | N |
| 3 DeLauro | Y | Y | Y | Y | N | N | Y | N |
| 4 *Shays* | N | Y | N | Y | N | N | Y | N |
| 5 *Franks* | N | Y | Y | Y | Y | Y | N | N |
| 6 *Johnson* | ? | Y | Y | Y | Y | Y | Y | N |
| **DELAWARE** | | | | | | | | |
| AL Carper | N | N | Y | Y | N | N | Y | Y |
| **FLORIDA** | | | | | | | | |
| 1 Hutto | Y | N | Y | Y | Y | Y | Y | Y |
| 2 Peterson | N | N | Y | Y | N | Y | Y | Y |
| 3 Bennett | N | N | Y | Y | N | N | Y | Y |
| 4 *James* | N | N | Y | Y | Y | N | Y | N |
| 5 *McCollum* | N | Y | Y | Y | Y | Y | N | N |
| 6 *Stearns* | N | N | Y | Y | Y | Y | Y | N |
| 7 Gibbons | N | N | Y | Y | N | N | Y | Y |
| 8 *Young* | N | N | Y | N | Y | N | Y | N |
| 9 *Bilirakis* | N | N | Y | Y | Y | Y | Y | N |
| 10 *Ireland* | ? | N | Y | Y | N | N | Y | N |
| 11 Bacchus | N | N | Y | N | N | N | Y | Y |
| 12 *Lewis* | N | N | Y | Y | Y | Y | N | N |
| 13 *Goss* | N | N | Y | Y | Y | Y | Y | N |
| 14 Johnston | Y | N | Y | N | N | N | Y | N |
| 15 *Shaw* | ? | ? | Y | Y | Y | Y | N | N |
| 16 Smith | N | N | Y | Y | Y | N | Y | N |
| 17 Lehman | Y | N | Y | N | N | Y | N | ? |
| 18 *Ros-Lehtinen* | N | N | ? | # | ? | ? | ? | ? |
| 19 Fascell | N | N | Y | N | Y | N | Y | Y |
| **GEORGIA** | | | | | | | | |
| 1 Thomas | N | Y | Y | Y | Y | N | Y | N |
| 2 Hatcher | ? | Y | Y | N | N | Y | N | N |
| 3 Ray | Y | Y | Y | Y | Y | N | Y | N |
| 4 Jones | ? | Y | Y | Y | N | N | Y | N |
| 5 Lewis | Y | Y | Y | Y | N | N | Y | Y |
| 6 *Gingrich* | ? | Y | ? | Y | Y | Y | Y | Y |
| 7 Darden | Y | Y | Y | Y | N | N | N | Y |
| 8 Rowland | Y | Y | Y | Y | N | N | Y | N |
| 9 Jenkins | Y | Y | Y | Y | N | N | Y | N |
| 10 Barnard | ? | ? | ? | ? | ? | ? | ? | ? |
| **HAWAII** | | | | | | | | |
| 1 Abercrombie | Y | Y | Y | Y | N | N | Y | N |
| 2 Mink | Y | Y | Y | N | N | N | Y | N |
| **IDAHO** | | | | | | | | |
| 1 LaRocco | Y | Y | Y | Y | N | N | Y | Y |
| 2 Stallings | Y | Y | Y | Y | N | N | Y | Y |
| **ILLINOIS** | | | | | | | | |
| 1 Hayes | Y | Y | Y | Y | N | N | Y | N |
| 2 Savage | Y | Y | N | Y | N | N | Y | N |
| 3 Russo | Y | Y | ? | Y | N | N | Y | N |
| 4 Sangmeister | Y | Y | Y | Y | N | N | Y | N |
| 5 Lipinski | Y | Y | Y | Y | N | N | Y | N |
| 6 *Hyde* | N | Y | Y | Y | Y | ? | ? | ? |
| 7 Collins | Y | Y | Y | Y | N | N | Y | N |
| 8 Rostenkowski | Y | Y | Y | Y | N | N | Y | N |
| 9 Yates | Y | Y | Y | Y | N | N | Y | N |
| 10 *Porter* | N | Y | Y | Y | N | Y | N | N |
| 11 Annunzio | Y | Y | Y | Y | N | N | Y | N |
| 12 *Crane* | N | N | N | Y | Y | Y | N | N |
| 13 *Fawell* | N | Y | Y | Y | N | Y | N | N |
| 14 *Hastert* | N | Y | Y | Y | Y | Y | N | N |
| 15 *Ewing* | N | Y | Y | Y | Y | Y | N | N |
| 16 Cox | Y | Y | Y | Y | N | N | Y | N |
| 17 Evans | Y | Y | Y | Y | N | N | Y | N |
| 18 *Michel* | Y | Y | Y | N | Y | N | N | N |
| 19 Bruce | Y | Y | Y | Y | N | N | Y | Y |
| 20 Durbin | Y | Y | Y | Y | N | N | Y | N |
| 21 Costello | Y | Y | Y | Y | N | N | Y | N |
| 22 Poshard | Y | Y | Y | Y | N | N | Y | Y |
| **INDIANA** | | | | | | | | |
| 1 Visclosky | Y | Y | Y | Y | N | N | Y | Y |
| 2 Sharp | Y | Y | Y | Y | N | N | Y | Y |
| 3 Roemer | Y | Y | Y | Y | N | N | Y | Y |

ND Northern Democrats    SD Southern Democrats

| | 252 | 253 | 254 | 255 | 256 | 257 | 258 | 259 |
|---|---|---|---|---|---|---|---|---|
| 4 Long | Y | Y | Y | Y | N | N | Y | Y |
| 5 Jontz | Y | Y | Y | Y | N | N | Y | Y |
| 6 ***Burton*** | N | N | Y | Y | Y | Y | N | Y |
| 7 ***Myers*** | Y | Y | Y | Y | Y | Y | N | N |
| 8 McCloskey | Y | Y | Y | Y | N | N | Y | Y |
| 9 Hamilton | Y | Y | Y | Y | N | N | Y | Y |
| 10 Jacobs | Y | Y | Y | Y | N | N | Y | Y |
| **IOWA** | | | | | | | | |
| 1 ***Leach*** | N | Y | Y | Y | N | N | Y | Y |
| 2 ***Nussle*** | Y | Y | Y | Y | Y | N | Y | Y |
| 3 Nagle | Y | Y | Y | Y | ? | N | Y | N |
| 4 Smith | Y | Y | Y | Y | N | Y | N | N |
| 5 ***Lightfoot*** | N | Y | Y | Y | Y | Y | N | N |
| 6 ***Grandy*** | N | Y | Y | Y | Y | Y | Y | Y |
| **KANSAS** | | | | | | | | |
| 1 ***Roberts*** | N | Y | Y | Y | Y | Y | Y | N |
| 2 Slattery | Y | Y | Y | Y | N | N | Y | Y |
| 3 ***Meyers*** | N | Y | Y | Y | Y | Y | Y | Y |
| 4 Glickman | Y | Y | Y | Y | N | N | Y | Y |
| 5 ***Nichols*** | N | Y | Y | Y | Y | Y | Y | Y |
| **KENTUCKY** | | | | | | | | |
| 1 Hubbard | N | Y | Y | Y | N | Y | N | Y |
| 2 Natcher | Y | Y | Y | N | N | Y | N | N |
| 3 Mazzoli | Y | Y | Y | Y | N | N | Y | Y |
| 4 ***Bunning*** | N | Y | Y | Y | Y | Y | N | Y |
| 5 ***Rogers*** | N | Y | Y | Y | Y | Y | N | Y |
| 6 ***Hopkins*** | N | Y | Y | Y | Y | Y | N | ? |
| 7 Perkins | ? | ? | ? | N | N | N | Y | N |
| **LOUISIANA** | | | | | | | | |
| 1 ***Livingston*** | N | Y | Y | Y | Y | N | N | N |
| 2 Jefferson | Y | Y | Y | Y | N | N | Y | Y |
| 3 Tauzin | Y | Y | Y | Y | Y | N | Y | Y |
| 4 ***McCrery*** | N | Y | Y | Y | Y | Y | Y | Y |
| 5 Huckaby | Y | Y | Y | Y | Y | N | Y | Y |
| 6 ***Baker*** | N | ? | N | Y | Y | Y | Y | Y |
| 7 Hayes | ? | Y | Y | Y | Y | N | Y | N |
| 8 ***Holloway*** | N | Y | Y | Y | Y | Y | Y | Y |
| **MAINE** | | | | | | | | |
| 1 Andrews | Y | Y | Y | Y | N | N | Y | Y |
| 2 ***Snowe*** | ? | Y | Y | Y | Y | N | Y | Y |
| **MARYLAND** | | | | | | | | |
| 1 ***Gilchrest*** | N | Y | Y | Y | N | Y | Y | Y |
| 2 ***Bentley*** | N | Y | Y | Y | Y | Y | N | N |
| 3 Cardin | Y | Y | Y | Y | N | N | Y | N |
| 4 McMillen | Y | Y | Y | Y | N | N | Y | Y |
| 5 Hoyer | Y | Y | Y | N | N | N | Y | N |
| 6 Byron | Y | Y | Y | Y | Y | N | Y | N |
| 7 Mfume | Y | Y | Y | Y | N | N | Y | Y |
| 8 ***Morella*** | Y | Y | Y | Y | N | Y | N | N |
| **MASSACHUSETTS** | | | | | | | | |
| 1 Olver | Y | Y | Y | Y | N | N | Y | Y |
| 2 Neal | Y | Y | Y | Y | N | N | Y | Y |
| 3 Early | Y | Y | Y | N | N | Y | Y | N |
| 4 Frank | Y | Y | Y | Y | N | N | Y | Y |
| 5 Atkins | Y | Y | Y | Y | N | N | Y | Y |
| 6 Mavroules | Y | Y | Y | Y | N | N | Y | Y |
| 7 Markey | Y | Y | Y | Y | N | N | Y | Y |
| 8 Kennedy | Y | Y | Y | Y | N | N | Y | N |
| 9 Moakley | Y | Y | Y | Y | N | N | N | Y |
| 10 Studds | Y | Y | Y | Y | N | N | Y | Y |
| 11 Donnelly | Y | Y | Y | Y | N | N | Y | Y |
| **MICHIGAN** | | | | | | | | |
| 1 Conyers | Y | Y | Y | Y | N | N | Y | Y |
| 2 ***Pursell*** | N | Y | Y | Y | Y | Y | Y | Y |
| 3 Wolpe | Y | Y | Y | Y | N | N | Y | N |
| 4 ***Upton*** | N | Y | Y | Y | Y | N | Y | Y |
| 5 ***Henry*** | N | Y | Y | Y | Y | N | Y | Y |
| 6 Carr | N | Y | Y | N | N | Y | Y | Y |
| 7 Kildee | Y | Y | Y | Y | N | N | Y | Y |
| 8 Traxler | ? | ? | ? | ? | ? | ? | ? | ? |
| 9 ***Vander Jagt*** | Y | Y | Y | Y | Y | N | Y | N |
| 10 ***Camp*** | Y | Y | Y | Y | Y | N | Y | Y |
| 11 ***Davis*** | Y | Y | Y | Y | Y | Y | N | N |
| 12 Bonior | ? | ? | ? | ? | ? | ? | ? | ? |
| 13 Collins | Y | Y | Y | Y | N | N | Y | N |
| 14 Hertel | Y | Y | Y | N | N | N | N | N |
| 15 Ford | Y | Y | Y | N | N | N | Y | N |
| 16 Dingell | Y | Y | Y | Y | N | N | Y | ? |
| 17 Levin | Y | Y | Y | Y | N | N | Y | Y |
| 18 ***Broomfield*** | Y | Y | Y | N | Y | N | N | ? |
| **MINNESOTA** | | | | | | | | |
| 1 Penny | Y | Y | Y | Y | N | N | Y | Y |
| 2 ***Weber*** | N | Y | Y | Y | Y | Y | N | N |
| 3 ***Ramstad*** | N | Y | Y | Y | Y | N | Y | Y |
| 4 Vento | Y | Y | Y | Y | N | N | Y | Y |

| | 252 | 253 | 254 | 255 | 256 | 257 | 258 | 259 |
|---|---|---|---|---|---|---|---|---|
| 5 Sabo | Y | Y | Y | Y | N | N | Y | N |
| 6 Sikorski | Y | Y | Y | Y | N | N | Y | Y |
| 7 Peterson | Y | Y | Y | Y | N | N | Y | Y |
| 8 Oberstar | Y | Y | Y | Y | N | N | Y | N |
| **MISSISSIPPI** | | | | | | | | |
| 1 Whitten | Y | Y | Y | ? | N | Y | N | N |
| 2 Espy | Y | Y | Y | Y | N | N | Y | N |
| 3 Montgomery | Y | Y | Y | Y | Y | Y | N | N |
| 4 Parker | Y | Y | Y | Y | Y | Y | Y | N |
| 5 Taylor | Y | Y | Y | Y | N | N | Y | Y |
| **MISSOURI** | | | | | | | | |
| 1 Clay | Y | Y | Y | Y | N | N | Y | N |
| 2 Horn | Y | Y | Y | Y | N | N | Y | Y |
| 3 Gephardt | Y | Y | Y | Y | N | N | Y | N |
| 4 Skelton | Y | Y | Y | Y | Y | N | Y | N |
| 5 Wheat | Y | Y | Y | Y | N | N | Y | N |
| 6 ***Coleman*** | N | Y | Y | Y | Y | Y | Y | Y |
| 7 ***Hancock*** | N | N | Y | Y | Y | Y | Y | Y |
| 8 ***Emerson*** | N | Y | Y | Y | Y | Y | Y | Y |
| 9 Volkmer | Y | Y | Y | Y | N | Y | Y | Y |
| **MONTANA** | | | | | | | | |
| 1 Williams | Y | Y | Y | Y | Y | N | Y | N |
| 2 ***Marlenee*** | N | Y | ? | Y | Y | N | N | N |
| **NEBRASKA** | | | | | | | | |
| 1 ***Bereuter*** | Y | Y | Y | Y | Y | Y | Y | Y |
| 2 Hoagland | Y | Y | Y | Y | N | N | Y | N |
| 3 ***Barrett*** | Y | Y | Y | Y | Y | Y | Y | Y |
| **NEVADA** | | | | | | | | |
| 1 Bilbray | N | N | Y | Y | N | N | Y | Y |
| 2 ***Vucanovich*** | N | N | N | Y | Y | Y | N | N |
| **NEW HAMPSHIRE** | | | | | | | | |
| 1 ***Zeliff*** | N | Y | Y | Y | Y | N | Y | N |
| 2 Swett | Y | Y | Y | Y | N | N | Y | Y |
| **NEW JERSEY** | | | | | | | | |
| 1 Andrews | Y | Y | Y | Y | N | N | Y | Y |
| 2 Hughes | N | Y | Y | Y | N | N | Y | Y |
| 3 Pallone | Y | Y | Y | Y | N | N | Y | Y |
| 4 ***Smith*** | Y | Y | Y | Y | Y | Y | ? | N |
| 5 ***Roukema*** | N | Y | Y | Y | N | N | Y | N |
| 6 Dwyer | Y | Y | Y | N | N | N | Y | N |
| 7 ***Rinaldo*** | N | Y | Y | Y | N | Y | Y | Y |
| 8 Roe | Y | Y | Y | Y | N | N | Y | N |
| 9 Torricelli | Y | Y | Y | Y | N | N | Y | Y |
| 10 Payne | Y | Y | Y | Y | N | N | Y | N |
| 11 ***Gallo*** | N | Y | Y | Y | Y | Y | N | N |
| 12 ***Zimmer*** | N | Y | Y | Y | Y | N | Y | Y |
| 13 ***Saxton*** | N | Y | Y | Y | Y | Y | N | N |
| 14 Guarini | Y | Y | Y | Y | N | N | Y | Y |
| **NEW MEXICO** | | | | | | | | |
| 1 ***Schiff*** | N | Y | Y | Y | Y | Y | N | N |
| 2 ***Skeen*** | Y | Y | Y | Y | Y | Y | N | N |
| 3 Richardson | ? | ? | ? | ? | ? | ? | ? | ? |
| **NEW YORK** | | | | | | | | |
| 1 Hochbrueckner | Y | Y | Y | Y | N | N | Y | N |
| 2 Downey | Y | Y | Y | Y | N | N | Y | N |
| 3 Mrazek | Y | Y | Y | Y | N | Y | Y | N |
| 4 ***Lent*** | Y | Y | Y | Y | Y | Y | N | N |
| 5 ***McGrath*** | Y | Y | Y | Y | Y | Y | N | ? |
| 6 Flake | Y | Y | Y | Y | N | N | Y | N |
| 7 Ackerman | ? | Y | Y | ? | ? | ? | ? | ? |
| 8 Scheuer | Y | Y | Y | Y | N | N | Y | Y |
| 9 Manton | Y | Y | Y | Y | N | N | Y | N |
| 10 Schumer | Y | Y | Y | Y | N | N | Y | Y |
| 11 Towns | Y | Y | Y | Y | N | N | Y | Y |
| 12 Owens | Y | Y | Y | Y | N | N | Y | Y |
| 13 Solarz | Y | Y | Y | Y | N | ? | ? | ? |
| 14 ***Molinari*** | N | Y | Y | Y | Y | Y | N | Y |
| 15 ***Green*** | Y | Y | Y | N | Y | Y | N | N |
| 16 Rangel | N | Y | Y | N | N | N | Y | Y |
| 17 Weiss | Y | Y | Y | Y | N | N | Y | N |
| 18 Serrano | Y | Y | Y | Y | N | N | Y | ? |
| 19 Engel | Y | Y | Y | Y | N | N | Y | N |
| 20 Lowey | Y | Y | Y | Y | N | N | Y | Y |
| 21 ***Fish*** | N | Y | Y | ? | ? | ? | ? | ? |
| 22 ***Gilman*** | Y | Y | Y | N | N | Y | N | N |
| 23 McNulty | N | Y | Y | Y | N | N | Y | N |
| 24 ***Solomon*** | N | N | Y | Y | Y | Y | N | N |
| 25 ***Boehlert*** | Y | Y | Y | Y | N | Y | Y | N |
| 26 ***Martin*** | Y | Y | Y | Y | Y | Y | N | N |
| 27 ***Walsh*** | N | Y | Y | Y | Y | Y | Y | N |
| 28 McHugh | Y | Y | Y | Y | N | N | Y | N |
| 29 ***Horton*** | Y | Y | Y | Y | Y | Y | N | N |
| 30 Slaughter | Y | Y | Y | Y | N | N | Y | Y |
| 31 ***Paxon*** | N | Y | Y | Y | Y | Y | N | N |

| | 252 | 253 | 254 | 255 | 256 | 257 | 258 | 259 |
|---|---|---|---|---|---|---|---|---|
| 32 LaFalce | Y | Y | Y | Y | N | N | Y | N |
| 33 Nowak | Y | Y | Y | Y | N | N | Y | Y |
| 34 ***Houghton*** | N | Y | ? | Y | Y | Y | N | N |
| **NORTH CAROLINA** | | | | | | | | |
| 1 Jones | Y | Y | Y | Y | N | N | Y | N |
| 2 Valentine | Y | Y | Y | Y | N | N | Y | Y |
| 3 Lancaster | Y | Y | Y | Y | Y | N | Y | Y |
| 4 Price | Y | Y | Y | Y | N | N | Y | N |
| 5 Neal | Y | Y | Y | Y | N | N | Y | N |
| 6 ***Coble*** | N | Y | Y | Y | Y | Y | Y | Y |
| 7 Rose | Y | Y | Y | Y | N | N | Y | N |
| 8 Hefner | ? | ? | ? | ? | ? | ? | ? | ? |
| 9 ***McMillan*** | Y | Y | Y | Y | Y | Y | Y | N |
| 10 ***Ballenger*** | N | Y | Y | Y | Y | Y | N | N |
| 11 ***Taylor*** | N | Y | Y | Y | Y | Y | N | N |
| **NORTH DAKOTA** | | | | | | | | |
| AL Dorgan | Y | Y | Y | Y | N | N | Y | Y |
| **OHIO** | | | | | | | | |
| 1 Luken | Y | Y | Y | Y | N | N | Y | N |
| 2 ***Gradison*** | Y | Y | Y | Y | Y | Y | N | N |
| 3 Hall | Y | Y | Y | Y | N | N | Y | Y |
| 4 ***Oxley*** | Y | Y | Y | Y | Y | Y | N | N |
| 5 ***Gillmor*** | N | Y | Y | Y | Y | Y | N | ? |
| 6 ***McEwen*** | N | Y | Y | Y | Y | Y | Y | Y |
| 7 ***Hobson*** | N | Y | Y | Y | Y | Y | Y | N |
| 8 ***Boehner*** | N | Y | Y | Y | Y | Y | N | N |
| 9 Kaptur | Y | Y | Y | Y | N | N | Y | Y |
| 10 ***Miller*** | Y | Y | Y | N | Y | Y | N | N |
| 11 Eckart | Y | Y | Y | Y | N | N | Y | Y |
| 12 ***Kasich*** | Y | Y | Y | Y | Y | Y | Y | Y |
| 13 Pease | Y | Y | Y | Y | N | N | Y | Y |
| 14 Sawyer | Y | Y | Y | Y | N | N | Y | N |
| 15 ***Wylie*** | ? | Y | Y | Y | Y | Y | Y | N |
| 16 ***Regula*** | N | Y | Y | Y | Y | Y | N | N |
| 17 Traficant | Y | Y | Y | Y | N | N | Y | N |
| 18 Applegate | N | Y | Y | Y | N | N | Y | Y |
| 19 Feighan | Y | Y | Y | Y | N | N | Y | Y |
| 20 Oakar | Y | Y | ? | Y | N | N | Y | N |
| 21 Stokes | Y | Y | Y | Y | N | N | Y | N |
| **OKLAHOMA** | | | | | | | | |
| 1 ***Inhofe*** | N | Y | Y | Y | Y | Y | N | Y |
| 2 Synar | Y | Y | Y | Y | N | N | Y | N |
| 3 Brewster | Y | Y | ? | Y | Y | N | Y | N |
| 4 McCurdy | Y | Y | Y | Y | N | N | Y | N |
| 5 ***Edwards*** | N | Y | Y | Y | Y | Y | N | Y |
| 6 English | Y | Y | Y | Y | Y | N | Y | Y |
| **OREGON** | | | | | | | | |
| 1 AuCoin | Y | Y | ? | Y | N | N | Y | Y |
| 2 ***Smith*** | N | Y | Y | Y | Y | Y | N | Y |
| 3 Wyden | Y | Y | Y | Y | N | N | Y | Y |
| 4 DeFazio | Y | Y | Y | Y | N | N | Y | Y |
| 5 Kopetski | Y | Y | Y | Y | N | N | Y | Y |
| **PENNSYLVANIA** | | | | | | | | |
| 1 Foglietta | Y | Y | Y | Y | N | N | Y | Y |
| 2 Blackwell | Y | Y | Y | Y | N | N | Y | Y |
| 3 Borski | Y | Y | Y | Y | N | N | Y | N |
| 4 Kolter | Y | Y | Y | Y | N | N | Y | ? |
| 5 ***Schulze*** | N | Y | Y | Y | Y | Y | N | N |
| 6 Yatron | Y | Y | Y | Y | N | N | Y | Y |
| 7 ***Weldon*** | N | Y | Y | Y | Y | Y | Y | Y |
| 8 Kostmayer | Y | Y | Y | Y | N | Y | Y | N |
| 9 ***Shuster*** | N | N | Y | Y | Y | Y | Y | N |
| 10 ***McDade*** | Y | Y | Y | N | Y | Y | N | N |
| 11 Kanjorski | Y | Y | Y | Y | N | N | Y | N |
| 12 Murtha | Y | Y | Y | Y | N | N | Y | N |
| 13 ***Coughlin*** | Y | Y | Y | Y | Y | Y | N | N |
| 14 Coyne | Y | Y | Y | Y | Y | N | Y | N |
| 15 ***Ritter*** | N | Y | Y | Y | Y | Y | Y | Y |
| 16 ***Walker*** | Y | Y | Y | Y | Y | Y | Y | N |
| 17 ***Gekas*** | ? | ? | ? | ? | Y | Y | Y | Y |
| 18 ***Santorum*** | N | Y | Y | Y | Y | Y | Y | Y |
| 19 ***Goodling*** | Y | Y | Y | Y | Y | Y | Y | Y |
| 20 Gaydos | Y | Y | ? | Y | N | N | Y | Y |
| 21 ***Ridge*** | N | Y | ? | Y | Y | Y | Y | N |
| 22 Murphy | Y | N | Y | Y | N | N | Y | ? |
| 23 ***Clinger*** | N | Y | Y | Y | Y | Y | N | N |
| **RHODE ISLAND** | | | | | | | | |
| 1 ***Machtley*** | N | Y | Y | Y | N | N | Y | N |
| 2 Reed | Y | Y | Y | Y | N | N | Y | Y |
| **SOUTH CAROLINA** | | | | | | | | |
| 1 ***Ravenel*** | Y | Y | Y | Y | N | Y | Y | N |
| 2 ***Spence*** | N | Y | Y | Y | Y | Y | N | N |
| 3 Derrick | Y | Y | Y | Y | N | N | Y | N |
| 4 Patterson | Y | Y | Y | Y | N | N | Y | Y |
| 5 Spratt | Y | Y | Y | Y | N | N | Y | N |
| 6 Tallon | ? | ? | ? | ? | ? | ? | ? | ? |

| | 252 | 253 | 254 | 255 | 256 | 257 | 258 | 259 |
|---|---|---|---|---|---|---|---|---|
| **SOUTH DAKOTA** | | | | | | | | |
| AL Johnson | Y | Y | Y | Y | Y | N | Y | Y |
| **TENNESSEE** | | | | | | | | |
| 1 ***Quillen*** | N | Y | Y | N | Y | Y | N | N |
| 2 ***Duncan*** | ? | N | Y | Y | Y | Y | Y | Y |
| 3 Lloyd | Y | Y | Y | Y | N | N | Y | N |
| 4 Cooper | Y | Y | Y | Y | N | Y | Y | Y |
| 5 Clement | Y | Y | Y | Y | N | N | Y | Y |
| 6 Gordon | Y | Y | Y | Y | N | N | Y | N |
| 7 ***Sundquist*** | N | Y | Y | Y | Y | Y | N | Y |
| 8 Tanner | Y | Y | Y | Y | N | N | Y | Y |
| 9 Ford | Y | Y | Y | Y | N | N | Y | Y |
| **TEXAS** | | | | | | | | |
| 1 Chapman | ? | N | Y | Y | N | N | Y | ? |
| 2 Wilson | ? | Y | Y | ? | N | N | Y | N |
| 3 ***Johnson*** | N | N | Y | Y | Y | Y | N | N |
| 4 Hall | Y | N | Y | Y | Y | N | Y | Y |
| 5 Bryant | Y | N | Y | Y | N | N | Y | N |
| 6 ***Barton*** | N | N | Y | Y | Y | Y | N | N |
| 7 ***Archer*** | N | N | Y | Y | Y | Y | N | N |
| 8 ***Fields*** | N | N | Y | Y | Y | Y | N | Y |
| 9 Brooks | Y | Y | Y | Y | N | N | Y | N |
| 10 Pickle | Y | Y | Y | N | Y | Y | N | N |
| 11 Edwards | Y | N | Y | Y | Y | N | Y | N |
| 12 Geren | Y | Y | Y | Y | Y | N | Y | Y |
| 13 Sarpalius | Y | N | Y | Y | Y | N | Y | Y |
| 14 Laughlin | Y | N | Y | Y | N | N | Y | N |
| 15 de la Garza | Y | Y | Y | Y | N | Y | Y | N |
| 16 Coleman | Y | N | Y | N | N | N | Y | N |
| 17 Stenholm | Y | Y | Y | Y | Y | Y | Y | Y |
| 18 Washington | Y | N | Y | Y | N | N | Y | ? |
| 19 ***Combest*** | N | N | Y | Y | Y | Y | N | Y |
| 20 Gonzalez | N | Y | Y | N | N | N | Y | N |
| 21 ***Smith*** | N | N | Y | Y | Y | Y | N | N |
| 22 ***DeLay*** | N | N | Y | Y | Y | Y | N | Y |
| 23 Bustamante | ? | ? | ? | ? | X | ? | ? | ? |
| 24 Frost | ? | Y | Y | Y | N | N | Y | N |
| 25 Andrews | Y | N | Y | Y | N | N | Y | Y |
| 26 ***Armey*** | N | N | Y | Y | Y | Y | N | Y |
| 27 Ortiz | ? | Y | Y | Y | N | N | Y | Y |
| **UTAH** | | | | | | | | |
| 1 ***Hansen*** | N | Y | Y | Y | Y | Y | Y | Y |
| 2 Owens | Y | Y | Y | Y | N | N | Y | N |
| 3 Orton | Y | Y | Y | Y | N | N | Y | Y |
| **VERMONT** | | | | | | | | |
| AL *Sanders* | Y | Y | Y | Y | N | N | Y | Y |
| **VIRGINIA** | | | | | | | | |
| 1 ***Bateman*** | N | N | Y | Y | Y | Y | N | N |
| 2 Pickett | Y | Y | Y | Y | Y | N | Y | N |
| 3 ***Bliley*** | Y | Y | Y | Y | Y | Y | N | N |
| 4 Sisisky | Y | Y | Y | Y | Y | N | Y | N |
| 5 Payne | Y | Y | Y | Y | N | N | Y | N |
| 6 Olin | Y | Y | Y | Y | N | ? | ? | ? |
| 7 ***Allen*** | N | Y | Y | Y | Y | Y | Y | N |
| 8 Moran | Y | Y | Y | N | N | N | Y | Y |
| 9 Boucher | Y | Y | Y | Y | N | N | Y | N |
| 10 ***Wolf*** | N | Y | Y | N | Y | Y | N | N |
| **WASHINGTON** | | | | | | | | |
| 1 ***Miller*** | N | Y | Y | Y | Y | ? | Y | Y |
| 2 Swift | Y | Y | Y | Y | N | N | Y | N |
| 3 Unsoeld | Y | Y | Y | Y | N | N | Y | N |
| 4 ***Morrison*** | N | Y | Y | Y | Y | Y | Y | Y |
| 5 Foley | | | | | | | | |
| 6 Dicks | Y | Y | Y | Y | N | N | Y | N |
| 7 McDermott | Y | Y | Y | Y | N | N | Y | Y |
| 8 ***Chandler*** | N | Y | Y | Y | Y | Y | Y | Y |
| **WEST VIRGINIA** | | | | | | | | |
| 1 Mollohan | Y | Y | Y | Y | N | N | Y | N |
| 2 Staggers | Y | Y | Y | Y | N | N | Y | Y |
| 3 Wise | Y | Y | Y | Y | N | N | Y | Y |
| 4 Rahall | Y | Y | Y | Y | N | N | Y | Y |
| **WISCONSIN** | | | | | | | | |
| 1 Aspin | Y | Y | Y | Y | N | N | Y | N |
| 2 ***Klug*** | N | Y | Y | Y | Y | Y | Y | Y |
| 3 ***Gunderson*** | Y | Y | Y | Y | Y | Y | Y | Y |
| 4 Kleczka | Y | Y | Y | Y | N | N | Y | N |
| 5 Moody | Y | Y | Y | Y | N | N | Y | Y |
| 6 ***Petri*** | N | Y | Y | Y | Y | N | Y | Y |
| 7 Obey | Y | Y | Y | Y | N | N | Y | N |
| 8 ***Roth*** | N | N | Y | Y | Y | N | N | Y |
| 9 ***Sensenbrenner*** | N | N | N | Y | Y | N | Y | Y |
| **WYOMING** | | | | | | | | |
| AL ***Thomas*** | Y | Y | Y | Y | Y | Y | Y | Y |

Southern states - Ala., Ark., Fla., Ga., Ky., La., Miss., N.C., Okla., S.C., Tenn., Texas, Va.
Omitted votes are quorum calls, which CQ does not include in its vote charts.

**260. HR 5488. Fiscal 1993 Treasury, Postal Service Appropriations/New Jersey Project.** Burton, R-Ind., amendment to cut $15 million for a parking garage in Newark, N.J. Rejected 89-313: R 88-67; D 1-246 (ND 1-169, SD 0-77); I 0-0, July 1, 1992.

**261. HR 5488. Fiscal 1993 Treasury Appropriations/Report to the House.** Roybal, D-Calif., motion to rise from the Committee of the Whole and report the bill back to the House. Motion agreed to 222-180: R 8-149; D 213-31 (ND 156-11, SD 57-20); I 1-0, July 1, 1992.

**262. HR 5488. Fiscal 1993 Treasury Appropriations/Passage.** Passage of the bill to provide $22.7 billion in new budget authority for the Treasury Department, U.S. Postal Service and related agencies in fiscal 1993. The administration requested $23,043,981,000. Passed 237-166: R 11-146; D 226-20 (ND 157-11, SD 69-9); I 0-0, July 1, 1992.

**263. HR 5504. Fiscal 1993 Defense Appropriations/Strategic Defense Initiative.** Durbin, D-Ill., amendment to cut $700 million from the Strategic Defense Initiative (SDI) without affecting funding for theater missile defenses. Rejected 201-217: R 26-135; D 174-82 (ND 143-33, SD 31-49); I 1-0, July 2, 1992. A "nay" was a vote in support of the president's position.

**264. HR 5504. Fiscal 1993 Defense Appropriations/Roybal Foundation.** Burton, R-Ind., amendment to cut the $10 million in funding for the Edward R. Roybal Foundation. Adopted 218-200: R 137-28; D 81-171 (ND 47-126, SD 34-45); I 0-1, July 2, 1992.

**265. HR 5504. Fiscal 1993 Defense Appropriations/B-2 Procurement.** Penny, D-Minn., amendment to reduce the Air Force procurement account by $2.7 billion, the amount earmarked to purchase four more B-2 bombers. Rejected 173-248: R 27-138; D 145-110 (ND 123-52, SD 22-58); I 1-0, July 2, 1992. A "nay" was a vote in support of the president's position.

**266. HR 5504. Fiscal 1993 Defense Appropriations/Passage.** Passage of the bill to provide $251.9 billion in new budget authority for the Department of Defense for military personnel, operation and maintenance, procurement, and research and development in fiscal 1993. Passed 328-94: R 124-41; D 204-52 (ND 129-47, SD 75-5); I 0-1, July 2, 1992.

**267. HR 5260. Extended Unemployment Benefits/Conference Report.** Adoption of the conference report to provide 20 weeks or 26 weeks of extended unemployment benefits between July 4, 1992, and March 6, 1993, as long as the national unemployment rate stayed above 7 percent. After March 6, 1993, states had the option of using a new 6.5 percent unemployment rate to trigger 13 weeks of extended benefits. Adopted 396-23: R 142-21; D 253-2 (ND 175-1, SD 78-1); I 1-0, July 2, 1992. A "yea" was a vote in support of the president's position.

## KEY

| | |
|---|---|
| Y | Voted for (yea). |
| # | Paired for. |
| + | Announced for. |
| N | Voted against (nay). |
| X | Paired against. |
| − | Announced against. |
| P | Voted "present." |
| C | Voted "present" to avoid possible conflict of interest. |
| ? | Did not vote or otherwise make a position known. |

**Democrats** *Republicans*
*Independent*

| | 260 | 261 | 262 | 263 | 264 | 265 | 266 | 267 |
|---|---|---|---|---|---|---|---|---|
| **ALABAMA** | | | | | | | | |
| 1 *Callahan* | N | N | N | N | Y | N | Y | Y |
| 2 *Dickinson* | Y | N | N | N | Y | N | Y | Y |
| 3 Browder | N | Y | Y | N | Y | N | Y | Y |
| 4 Bevill | N | Y | Y | N | Y | N | Y | Y |
| 5 Cramer | N | Y | Y | N | Y | N | Y | Y |
| 6 Erdreich | N | N | N | N | Y | N | Y | Y |
| 7 Harris | N | N | Y | N | Y | N | Y | Y |
| **ALASKA** | | | | | | | | |
| AL *Young* | N | N | N | N | N | N | N | Y |
| **ARIZONA** | | | | | | | | |
| 1 *Rhodes* | N | N | N | N | Y | N | Y | Y |
| 2 Pastor | N | Y | Y | Y | ? | Y | Y | Y |
| 3 *Stump* | Y | N | N | N | Y | N | N | N |
| 4 *Kyl* | Y | N | N | N | Y | N | N | Y |
| 5 *Kolbe* | N | N | N | N | Y | N | Y | Y |
| **ARKANSAS** | | | | | | | | |
| 1 Alexander | N | N | Y | N | ? | ? | Y | Y |
| 2 Thornton | N | Y | Y | N | N | Y | Y | Y |
| 3 *Hammerschmidt* | N | N | N | N | N | N | Y | N |
| 4 Anthony | N | ? | ? | Y | N | Y | Y | Y |
| **CALIFORNIA** | | | | | | | | |
| 1 *Riggs* | ? | N | N | N | Y | Y | Y | Y |
| 2 *Herger* | Y | N | N | N | N | N | N | Y |
| 3 Matsui | N | Y | Y | N | N | Y | Y | Y |
| 4 Fazio | N | Y | Y | N | N | Y | Y | Y |
| 5 Pelosi | N | Y | Y | Y | N | Y | Y | Y |
| 6 Boxer | ? | ? | ? | Y | Y | N | Y | Y |
| 7 Miller | N | Y | Y | Y | N | Y | Y | Y |
| 8 Dellums | N | Y | Y | Y | N | Y | Y | Y |
| 9 Stark | N | Y | Y | ? | N | Y | N | Y |
| 10 Edwards | N | Y | Y | N | Y | N | ? | ? |
| 11 Lantos | N | Y | Y | N | Y | N | Y | Y |
| 12 *Campbell* | Y | Y | N | N | N | N | Y | Y |
| 13 Mineta | N | Y | Y | N | Y | N | Y | N |
| 14 *Doolittle* | Y | N | N | N | Y | N | N | N |
| 15 Condit | N | Y | Y | N | Y | N | Y | Y |
| 16 Panetta | N | Y | Y | N | N | Y | Y | Y |
| 17 Dooley | N | Y | Y | N | Y | N | Y | Y |
| 18 Lehman | N | Y | Y | Y | Y | Y | Y | Y |
| 19 *Lagomarsino* | Y | N | N | N | Y | N | N | Y |
| 20 *Thomas* | N | N | N | Y | N | N | Y | Y |
| 21 *Gallegly* | Y | N | N | N | N | N | Y | Y |
| 22 *Moorhead* | Y | N | N | N | N | N | N | Y |
| 23 Beilenson | N | Y | Y | N | N | Y | Y | Y |
| 24 Waxman | N | ? | Y | Y | N | Y | N | Y |
| 25 Roybal | N | Y | Y | N | N | N | Y | Y |
| 26 Berman | N | Y | Y | Y | Y | Y | Y | Y |
| 27 Levine | N | Y | Y | N | N | Y | Y | Y |
| 28 Dixon | N | Y | Y | N | N | Y | Y | Y |
| 29 Waters | N | Y | Y | N | N | Y | N | Y |
| 30 Martinez | N | Y | Y | N | ? | N | Y | Y |
| 31 Dymally | ? | ? | ? | ? | ? | ? | ? | ? |
| 32 Anderson | N | Y | Y | N | N | N | Y | Y |
| 33 *Dreier* | Y | N | N | N | Y | N | N | N |
| 34 Torres | − | + | + | Y | N | Y | N | Y |
| 35 *Lewis* | N | N | N | N | N | N | Y | Y |
| 36 Brown | N | Y | Y | N | N | N | Y | Y |
| 37 *McCandless* | N | N | N | N | Y | N | N | Y |
| 38 *Dornan* | Y | N | N | N | N | N | N | Y |
| 39 *Dannemeyer* | Y | N | N | N | N | N | N | N |
| 40 *Cox* | N | N | N | ? | Y | N | N | Y |
| 41 *Lowery* | ? | ? | ? | ? | N | N | Y | Y |

ND Northern Democrats    SD Southern Democrats

| | 260 | 261 | 262 | 263 | 264 | 265 | 266 | 267 |
|---|---|---|---|---|---|---|---|---|
| 42 *Rohrabacher* | Y | N | N | N | Y | N | Y | Y |
| 43 *Packard* | N | N | N | Y | N | N | N | N |
| 44 *Cunningham* | Y | N | N | N | Y | N | Y | Y |
| 45 *Hunter* | Y | N | N | N | Y | N | Y | Y |
| **COLORADO** | | | | | | | | |
| 1 Schroeder | N | Y | Y | Y | N | Y | N | Y |
| 2 Skaggs | N | Y | Y | N | Y | Y | Y | Y |
| 3 Campbell | N | Y | Y | N | ? | ? | ? | ? |
| 4 *Allard* | Y | N | N | N | Y | N | N | N |
| 5 *Hefley* | Y | N | N | N | Y | N | Y | Y |
| 6 *Schaefer* | N | N | N | N | Y | N | Y | Y |
| **CONNECTICUT** | | | | | | | | |
| 1 Kennelly | N | Y | Y | N | Y | N | Y | Y |
| 2 Gejdenson | N | Y | Y | Y | N | Y | Y | Y |
| 3 DeLauro | N | Y | Y | N | Y | Y | Y | Y |
| 4 *Shays* | N | Y | Y | Y | Y | Y | N | Y |
| 5 *Franks* | Y | N | N | N | Y | N | Y | Y |
| 6 *Johnson* | Y | N | N | N | Y | N | Y | Y |
| **DELAWARE** | | | | | | | | |
| AL Carper | N | Y | Y | Y | Y | N | Y | Y |
| **FLORIDA** | | | | | | | | |
| 1 Hutto | N | N | N | N | Y | N | Y | Y |
| 2 Peterson | N | Y | Y | N | N | N | Y | Y |
| 3 Bennett | N | N | Y | Y | N | Y | Y | Y |
| 4 *James* | Y | N | N | Y | N | Y | N | Y |
| 5 *McCollum* | Y | N | N | N | Y | N | N | Y |
| 6 *Stearns* | Y | N | N | N | N | N | N | Y |
| 7 Gibbons | N | Y. | Y | Y | N | Y | Y | Y |
| 8 *Young* | Y | N | N | N | Y | N | Y | Y |
| 9 *Bilirakis* | Y | N | N | N | N | N | Y | Y |
| 10 *Ireland* | Y | N | N | N | Y | N | Y | Y |
| 11 Bacchus | N | Y | Y | N | Y | Y | Y | Y |
| 12 *Lewis* | Y | N | N | N | Y | N | Y | Y |
| 13 *Goss* | Y | N | N | N | N | N | Y | Y |
| 14 Johnston | N | ? | Y | Y | N | Y | N | Y |
| 15 *Shaw* | N | N | N | N | Y | N | Y | Y |
| 16 Smith | ? | ? | ? | # | ? | ? | ? | ? |
| 17 Lehman | ? | Y | Y | Y | N | Y | Y | Y |
| 18 *Ros-Lehtinen* | ? | ? | X | N | N | N | N | Y |
| 19 Fascell | N | Y | Y | N | N | N | Y | Y |
| **GEORGIA** | | | | | | | | |
| 1 *Thomas* | ? | ? | ? | N | N | N | Y | ? |
| 2 Hatcher | N | Y | Y | N | N | N | Y | Y |
| 3 Ray | N | N | N | N | N | Y | Y | Y |
| 4 Jones | Y | Y | Y | Y | Y | Y | Y | Y |
| 5 Lewis | N | Y | Y | Y | N | Y | Y | Y |
| 6 *Gingrich* | N | N | N | N | N | Y | Y | Y |
| 7 *Darden* | N | Y | Y | N | N | Y | Y | Y |
| 8 Rowland | N | N | N | N | Y | N | Y | Y |
| 9 Jenkins | N | Y | Y | N | Y | N | Y | Y |
| 10 Barnard | ? | ? | ? | ? | ? | ? | ? | ? |
| **HAWAII** | | | | | | | | |
| 1 Abercrombie | ? | ? | ? | Y | N | Y | Y | Y |
| 2 Mink | N | Y | Y | Y | N | Y | Y | Y |
| **IDAHO** | | | | | | | | |
| 1 LaRocco | N | Y | Y | N | Y | N | Y | Y |
| 2 Stallings | N | N | Y | Y | Y | N | Y | Y |
| **ILLINOIS** | | | | | | | | |
| 1 Hayes | N | Y | Y | Y | N | Y | Y | Y |
| 2 Savage | N | ? | ? | ? | ? | ? | N | Y |
| 3 Russo | N | Y | Y | Y | N | Y | Y | Y |
| 4 Sangmeister | N | N | Y | N | Y | N | Y | Y |
| 5 Lipinski | N | Y | Y | N | N | N | Y | Y |
| 6 *Hyde* | ? | ? | ? | N | N | N | N | Y |
| 7 Collins | N | Y | Y | # | ? | ? | ? | ? |
| 8 Rostenkowski | N | Y | Y | N | N | N | Y | Y |
| 9 Yates | N | Y | Y | Y | N | Y | Y | Y |
| 10 *Porter* | Y | N | N | N | Y | N | Y | Y |
| 11 Annunzio | N | N | Y | N | N | N | Y | Y |
| 12 *Crane* | Y | N | N | N | Y | N | N | N |
| 13 *Fawell* | Y | N | N | N | Y | Y | N | Y |
| 14 *Hastert* | N | N | N | N | Y | N | N | Y |
| 15 *Ewing* | Y | N | N | Y | Y | N | Y | Y |
| 16 Cox | N | Y | Y | Y | Y | N | Y | Y |
| 17 Evans | N | Y | Y | Y | N | Y | Y | Y |
| 18 *Michel* | N | N | N | N | Y | N | Y | Y |
| 19 Bruce | N | Y | Y | Y | Y | Y | Y | Y |
| 20 Durbin | N | Y | Y | Y | Y | Y | Y | Y |
| 21 Costello | N | Y | Y | Y | Y | Y | Y | Y |
| 22 Poshard | N | Y | Y | Y | Y | Y | Y | Y |
| **INDIANA** | | | | | | | | |
| 1 Visclosky | N | Y | Y | N | Y | Y | Y | Y |
| 2 Sharp | ? | ? | ? | Y | Y | Y | Y | Y |
| 3 Roemer | N | Y | N | N | Y | Y | Y | Y |

**268. HR 11. Urban Aid and Tax Bill.** Rostenkowski, D-Ill., motion to suspend the rules and pass the bill to provide tax incentives for the establishment of 50 enterprise zones in distressed urban and rural areas and; extend certain expiring tax provisions; and enact provisions to raise revenue to offset the costs of the bill. Motion agreed to 356-55: R 158-6; D 198-48 (ND 129-39, SD 69-9); I 0-1, July 2, 1992. A two-thirds majority of those present and voting (274 in this case) was required for passage under suspension of the rules.

**269. Procedural Motion.** Approval of the House Journal of Tuesday, July 7. Approved 242-115: R 38-109; D 204-6 (ND 142-5, SD 62-1); I 0-0, July 8, 1992.

**270. HR 5100. Trade Bill/Order Previous Question.** Derrick, D-S.C., motion to order the previous question (thus ending debate and the possibility of amendment) on the rule (H Res 510) to provide for House floor consideration of the bill to reauthorize for five years the Super 301 authority under the Trade Act of 1974. Motion agreed to 247-167: R 0-163; D 246-4 (ND 168-2, SD 78-2); I 1-0, July 8, 1992.

**271. HR 5100. Trade Bill/Rule.** Adoption of the rule (H Res 510) to provide for House floor consideration of the bill to reauthorize for five years the Super 301 authority under the Trade Act of 1974. Adopted 252-163: R 2-162; D 249-1 (ND 171-0, SD 78-1); I 1-0, July 8, 1992.

**272. HR 5100. Trade Bill/Auto Trade With Japan.** Gephardt, D-Mo., en bloc amendments to direct the U.S. trade representative to negotiate an agreement with Japan to enforce a limit on imports of Japanese automobiles into the United States, and to monitor and enforce a Japanese commitment to increase use of U.S.-made parts in autos produced in the United States by Japanese-owned companies. Adopted 260-166: R 36-128; D 223-38 (ND 161-20, SD 62-18); I 1-0, July 8, 1992. A "nay" was a vote in support of the president's position.

**273. HR 5100. Trade Bill/Passage.** Passage of the bill to reauthorize for five years the Super 301 authority under the Trade Act of 1974, which required the U.S. trade representative (USTR) to annually identify countries with trade barriers to U.S. goods and target them for negotiations and possible retaliation; require the USTR to negotiate with Japan a voluntary annual limit on imports of Japanese cars into the United States; and require the USTR to initiate Super 301 investigations of Japan. Passed 280-145: R 34-130; D 245-15 (ND 176-5, SD 69-10); I 1-0, July 8, 1992. A "nay" was a vote in support of the president's position.

**274. S 1150. Higher Education Act Reauthorization/ Conference Report.** Adoption of the conference report to reauthorize through fiscal 1997 the Higher Education Act of 1965. The bill provided for a demonstration program to make direct federal loans to students; allowed all students to borrow up to the maximum amount allowed under the Guaranteed Student Loan program; allowed all parents to borrow up to the total college cost minus other financial aid through the Parent Loans to Undergraduate Students (PLUS) program; and increased the maximum Pell grant award from $2,400 to $3,700 for the 1993-94 school year. Adopted 419-7: R 156-7; D 262-0 (ND 180-0, SD 82-0); I 1-0, July 8, 1992.

**275. HR 5517. Fiscal 1993 District of Columbia Appropriations/Report to the House.** Dixon, D-Calif., motion to rise from the Committee of the Whole and report back to the House the bill to provide $714 million in federal funds for the District of Columbia and approve the spending of $3,954,141,000 in funds raised from local taxes for the District of Columbia in fiscal 1993. The administration requested $713,237,000 in federal funds and approval for spending of $3,953,658,000 in funds raised from local taxes. The bill prohibited the use of federal funds for abortions except to save the life of the woman, but would place no prohibitions on the use of locally raised funds. Motion agreed to 231-181: R 14-142; D 216-39 (ND 166-11, SD 50-28); I 1-0, July 8, 1992. (The bill was subsequently passed by voice vote.)

## KEY

| Y | Voted for (yea). |
|---|---|
| # | Paired for. |
| + | Announced for. |
| N | Voted against (nay). |
| X | Paired against. |
| − | Announced against. |
| P | Voted "present." |
| C | Voted "present" to avoid possible conflict of interest. |
| ? | Did not vote or otherwise make a position known. |

**Democrats**   ***Republicans***
*Independent*

| | 268 | 269 | 270 | 271 | 272 | 273 | 274 | 275 |
|---|---|---|---|---|---|---|---|---|
| **ALABAMA** | | | | | | | | |
| 1 *Callahan* | Y | Y | N | N | N | N | Y | N |
| 2 *Dickinson* | Y | ? | N | N | N | N | Y | N |
| 3 Browder | Y | Y | Y | Y | Y | Y | Y | N |
| 4 Bevill | Y | Y | Y | Y | Y | Y | Y | Y |
| 5 Cramer | Y | Y | Y | Y | Y | Y | Y | N |
| 6 Erdreich | Y | Y | Y | Y | Y | Y | Y | N |
| 7 Harris | Y | ? | Y | Y | Y | Y | Y | N |
| **ALASKA** | | | | | | | | |
| AL *Young* | Y | N | N | N | Y | N | Y | N |
| **ARIZONA** | | | | | | | | |
| 1 *Rhodes* | Y | N | N | N | N | N | Y | N |
| 2 Pastor | Y | Y | Y | Y | Y | Y | Y | Y |
| 3 *Stump* | Y | N | N | N | N | N | N | N |
| 4 *Kyl* | Y | N | N | N | N | N | Y | N |
| 5 *Kolbe* | Y | N | N | N | N | N | Y | Y |
| **ARKANSAS** | | | | | | | | |
| 1 Alexander | Y | ? | ? | ? | ? | ? | ? | ? |
| 2 Thornton | Y | Y | Y | Y | Y | Y | Y | Y |
| 3 *Hammerschmidt* | Y | Y | N | N | N | N | Y | N |
| 4 Anthony | Y | Y | Y | Y | N | Y | Y | ? |
| **CALIFORNIA** | | | | | | | | |
| 1 *Riggs* | Y | N | N | N | N | N | Y | N |
| 2 *Herger* | Y | N | N | N | N | N | Y | N |
| 3 Matsui | Y | Y | Y | Y | N | Y | Y | Y |
| 4 Fazio | Y | Y | Y | Y | Y | Y | Y | Y |
| 5 Pelosi | Y | Y | Y | Y | Y | Y | Y | Y |
| 6 Boxer | Y | Y | Y | Y | Y | Y | Y | Y |
| 7 Miller | Y | Y | Y | Y | Y | Y | Y | Y |
| 8 Dellums | Y | ? | Y | Y | Y | Y | Y | Y |
| 9 Stark | Y | ? | Y | Y | Y | Y | Y | Y |
| 10 Edwards | ? | Y | Y | Y | Y | Y | Y | Y |
| 11 Lantos | Y | Y | Y | Y | Y | Y | Y | Y |
| 12 *Campbell* | N | N | N | N | N | Y | Y | Y |
| 13 Mineta | N | Y | Y | Y | Y | Y | Y | Y |
| 14 *Doolittle* | Y | N | N | N | N | N | N | N |
| 15 Condit | Y | ? | Y | Y | Y | Y | Y | Y |
| 16 Panetta | N | Y | Y | Y | N | Y | Y | Y |
| 17 Dooley | Y | Y | Y | Y | N | Y | Y | Y |
| 18 Lehman | Y | Y | Y | Y | Y | Y | Y | Y |
| 19 *Lagomarsino* | Y | N | N | N | N | N | Y | N |
| 20 *Thomas* | Y | N | N | N | N | N | Y | N |
| 21 *Gallegly* | Y | N | N | N | Y | N | Y | N |
| 22 *Moorhead* | Y | ? | N | N | N | N | Y | N |
| 23 Beilenson | N | Y | Y | Y | N | Y | Y | Y |
| 24 Waxman | Y | Y | Y | Y | N | Y | Y | Y |
| 25 Roybal | Y | Y | Y | Y | Y | Y | Y | Y |
| 26 Berman | Y | Y | Y | Y | N | Y | Y | Y |
| 27 Levine | Y | Y | Y | Y | N | Y | Y | Y |
| 28 Dixon | Y | ? | Y | N | Y | Y | Y | Y |
| 29 Waters | Y | ? | ? | ? | Y | Y | Y | Y |
| 30 Martinez | P | Y | Y | Y | Y | Y | Y | Y |
| 31 Dymally | ? | ? | Y | Y | Y | Y | Y | Y |
| 32 Anderson | Y | Y | Y | Y | Y | Y | Y | Y |
| 33 *Dreier* | Y | N | N | N | N | N | Y | N |
| 34 Torres | Y | ? | Y | Y | Y | Y | Y | Y |
| 35 *Lewis* | Y | N | N | N | N | N | Y | N |
| 36 Brown | Y | Y | Y | Y | Y | Y | Y | Y |
| 37 *McCandless* | Y | N | N | N | N | N | Y | N |
| 38 *Dornan* | Y | Y | N | N | N | N | Y | N |
| 39 *Dannemeyer* | Y | N | N | N | N | N | N | N |
| 40 *Cox* | Y | Y | N | N | N | N | Y | ? |
| 41 *Lowery* | Y | ? | N | N | N | N | Y | N |

| | 268 | 269 | 270 | 271 | 272 | 273 | 274 | 275 |
|---|---|---|---|---|---|---|---|---|
| 42 *Rohrabacher* | Y | N | N | N | N | N | Y | N |
| 43 *Packard* | Y | N | N | N | N | N | Y | N |
| 44 *Cunningham* | Y | N | N | N | N | N | Y | N |
| 45 *Hunter* | Y | N | N | N | Y | N | Y | N |
| **COLORADO** | | | | | | | | |
| 1 Schroeder | N | N | Y | Y | Y | Y | Y | Y |
| 2 Skaggs | N | ? | Y | Y | Y | Y | Y | Y |
| 3 Campbell | ? | Y | Y | Y | Y | Y | Y | Y |
| 4 *Allard* | Y | N | N | N | N | N | N | N |
| 5 *Hefley* | Y | N | N | N | N | N | N | N |
| 6 *Schaefer* | Y | N | N | N | N | N | N | N |
| **CONNECTICUT** | | | | | | | | |
| 1 Kennelly | Y | Y | Y | Y | Y | Y | Y | Y |
| 2 Gejdenson | Y | Y | Y | Y | Y | Y | Y | Y |
| 3 DeLauro | Y | Y | Y | Y | Y | Y | Y | Y |
| 4 *Shays* | Y | N | N | N | N | N | Y | Y |
| 5 *Franks* | Y | N | N | N | N | N | Y | Y |
| 6 *Johnson* | Y | N | N | N | N | N | Y | Y |
| **DELAWARE** | | | | | | | | |
| AL Carper | Y | Y | Y | ? | Y | Y | Y | N |
| **FLORIDA** | | | | | | | | |
| 1 Hutto | Y | Y | Y | Y | N | Y | Y | N |
| 2 Peterson | Y | Y | Y | Y | Y | Y | Y | Y |
| 3 Bennett | Y | Y | N | Y | Y | Y | Y | Y |
| 4 *James* | Y | N | N | N | N | N | N | N |
| 5 *McCollum* | Y | N | N | N | N | N | Y | N |
| 6 *Stearns* | Y | N | N | N | N | N | N | N |
| 7 Gibbons | Y | ? | Y | N | N | Y | Y | Y |
| 8 *Young* | Y | N | N | N | N | N | Y | N |
| 9 *Bilirakis* | Y | N | N | N | N | N | Y | N |
| 10 *Ireland* | Y | N | N | N | N | N | Y | N |
| 11 Bacchus | Y | Y | Y | N | N | Y | Y | N |
| 12 *Lewis* | N | ? | X | X | X | X | ? | N |
| 13 *Goss* | Y | N | N | N | N | N | N | N |
| 14 Johnston | Y | Y | Y | Y | Y | Y | Y | Y |
| 15 *Shaw* | Y | N | N | N | N | N | Y | N |
| 16 Smith | ? | Y | Y | Y | ? | ? | Y | Y |
| 17 Lehman | ? | Y | Y | Y | Y | Y | Y | Y |
| 18 *Ros–Lehtinen* | Y | N | N | N | N | N | Y | N |
| 19 Fascell | Y | Y | Y | Y | Y | Y | Y | Y |
| **GEORGIA** | | | | | | | | |
| 1 Thomas | ? | Y | Y | Y | Y | Y | Y | N |
| 2 Hatcher | Y | ? | ? | ? | ? | ? | ? | ? |
| 3 Ray | Y | Y | Y | Y | Y | Y | Y | N |
| 4 Jones | Y | Y | Y | Y | Y | Y | Y | ? |
| 5 Lewis | Y | Y | Y | Y | Y | Y | Y | Y |
| 6 *Gingrich* | Y | N | N | N | N | N | Y | N |
| 7 *Darden* | Y | ? | Y | Y | Y | Y | Y | Y |
| 8 Rowland | Y | Y | Y | Y | Y | Y | Y | N |
| 9 Jenkins | Y | Y | Y | Y | Y | Y | Y | Y |
| 10 Barnard | ? | ? | Y | N | N | N | Y | N |
| **HAWAII** | | | | | | | | |
| 1 Abercrombie | Y | Y | Y | Y | Y | Y | Y | Y |
| 2 Mink | Y | Y | Y | Y | Y | Y | Y | Y |
| **IDAHO** | | | | | | | | |
| 1 LaRocco | Y | Y | Y | Y | Y | Y | Y | Y |
| 2 Stallings | Y | Y | Y | Y | Y | Y | Y | N |
| **ILLINOIS** | | | | | | | | |
| 1 Hayes | N | Y | Y | Y | Y | Y | Y | Y |
| 2 Savage | N | ? | ? | ? | Y | Y | Y | Y |
| 3 Russo | Y | Y | Y | Y | Y | Y | Y | Y |
| 4 Sangmeister | Y | Y | Y | Y | Y | Y | Y | Y |
| 5 Lipinski | Y | ? | Y | Y | Y | Y | Y | Y |
| 6 *Hyde* | Y | N | N | N | N | ? | ? | ? |
| 7 Collins | ? | Y | Y | Y | Y | Y | Y | Y |
| 8 Rostenkowski | Y | Y | Y | Y | N | Y | Y | N |
| 9 Yates | N | Y | Y | Y | Y | Y | Y | Y |
| 10 *Porter* | Y | N | N | N | N | N | Y | N |
| 11 Annunzio | N | Y | Y | Y | Y | Y | Y | Y |
| 12 *Crane* | Y | N | N | N | N | N | N | N |
| 13 *Fawell* | Y | N | N | N | N | N | Y | N |
| 14 *Hastert* | Y | ? | N | N | Y | N | Y | N |
| 15 *Ewing* | Y | N | N | N | N | N | Y | N |
| 16 *Cox* | Y | Y | Y | Y | Y | Y | Y | Y |
| 17 Evans | N | Y | Y | Y | Y | Y | Y | Y |
| 18 *Michel* | Y | N | N | N | N | N | Y | N |
| 19 Bruce | Y | Y | Y | Y | Y | Y | Y | Y |
| 20 Durbin | Y | Y | Y | Y | Y | Y | Y | Y |
| 21 Costello | Y | Y | Y | Y | Y | Y | Y | Y |
| 22 Poshard | Y | Y | Y | Y | Y | Y | Y | N |
| **INDIANA** | | | | | | | | |
| 1 Visclosky | Y | Y | Y | Y | Y | Y | Y | Y |
| 2 Sharp | Y | Y | Y | Y | Y | Y | Y | Y |
| 3 Roemer | Y | Y | Y | Y | Y | Y | Y | Y |

ND  Northern Democrats     SD  Southern Democrats

| | 268 | 269 | 270 | 271 | 272 | 273 | 274 | 275 |
|---|---|---|---|---|---|---|---|---|
| 4 Long | N | Y | Y | Y | Y | Y | Y | Y |
| 5 Jontz | N | Y | Y | Y | Y | Y | Y | Y |
| 6 ***Burton*** | N | N | N | N | Y | Y | N | N |
| 7 ***Myers*** | N | Y | N | N | N | N | Y | N |
| 8 McCloskey | Y | Y | Y | Y | Y | Y | Y | Y |
| 9 Hamilton | Y | Y | Y | Y | Y | Y | Y | Y |
| 10 Jacobs | Y | N | N | Y | Y | Y | Y | Y |
| **IOWA** | | | | | | | | |
| 1 ***Leach*** | Y | N | N | N | N | N | Y | N |
| 2 ***Nussle*** | Y | N | N | N | N | N | Y | N |
| 3 Nagle | Y | ? | Y | Y | Y | Y | Y | Y |
| 4 Smith | Y | Y | Y | Y | N | Y | Y | Y |
| 5 ***Lightfoot*** | Y | N | N | N | N | N | Y | N |
| 6 ***Grandy*** | Y | N | N | N | N | N | Y | N |
| **KANSAS** | | | | | | | | |
| 1 ***Roberts*** | Y | N | N | N | N | N | Y | N |
| 2 Slattery | Y | ? | ? | ? | Y | Y | Y | Y |
| 3 ***Meyers*** | Y | N | N | N | N | N | Y | N |
| 4 Glickman | Y | Y | Y | Y | Y | Y | Y | Y |
| 5 ***Nichols*** | Y | Y | N | N | N | N | Y | N |
| **KENTUCKY** | | | | | | | | |
| 1 Hubbard | Y | Y | Y | Y | Y | Y | Y | N |
| 2 Natcher | Y | Y | Y | Y | Y | Y | Y | Y |
| 3 Mazzoli | Y | Y | Y | Y | Y | Y | Y | Y |
| 4 ***Bunning*** | Y | N | N | N | N | N | Y | N |
| 5 ***Rogers*** | Y | N | N | N | Y | Y | Y | N |
| 6 ***Hopkins*** | Y | N | N | N | N | N | Y | N |
| 7 Perkins | Y | ? | Y | Y | Y | Y | Y | Y |
| **LOUISIANA** | | | | | | | | |
| 1 ***Livingston*** | Y | N | N | N | N | N | Y | N |
| 2 Jefferson | Y | ? | ? | ? | Y | Y | Y | Y |
| 3 Tauzin | Y | Y | Y | Y | Y | Y | Y | Y |
| 4 ***McCrery*** | Y | N | N | N | N | N | Y | N |
| 5 Huckaby | Y | Y | Y | Y | Y | Y | Y | N |
| 6 ***Baker*** | Y | ? | N | N | N | N | Y | N |
| 7 Hayes | Y | Y | Y | Y | Y | Y | Y | N |
| 8 ***Holloway*** | Y | N | N | N | Y | Y | Y | N |
| **MAINE** | | | | | | | | |
| 1 Andrews | Y | Y | Y | Y | Y | Y | Y | Y |
| 2 ***Snowe*** | Y | Y | N | N | Y | Y | Y | N |
| **MARYLAND** | | | | | | | | |
| 1 ***Gilchrest*** | Y | N | N | N | N | N | Y | N |
| 2 ***Bentley*** | Y | N | N | N | Y | Y | Y | N |
| 3 Cardin | Y | Y | Y | Y | Y | Y | Y | Y |
| 4 McMillen | Y | Y | Y | Y | Y | Y | Y | Y |
| 5 Hoyer | Y | Y | Y | Y | Y | Y | Y | Y |
| 6 Byron | Y | Y | Y | ? | Y | Y | Y | N |
| 7 Mfume | Y | Y | Y | Y | Y | Y | Y | Y |
| 8 ***Morella*** | Y | N | N | N | N | N | Y | Y |
| **MASSACHUSETTS** | | | | | | | | |
| 1 Olver | Y | Y | Y | Y | Y | Y | Y | Y |
| 2 Neal | Y | Y | Y | Y | Y | Y | Y | Y |
| 3 Early | N | Y | Y | Y | Y | Y | Y | Y |
| 4 Frank | N | Y | ? | ? | Y | Y | Y | Y |
| 5 Atkins | N | Y | Y | Y | Y | Y | Y | Y |
| 6 Mavroules | Y | Y | Y | Y | Y | Y | Y | Y |
| 7 Markey | ? | Y | Y | Y | Y | Y | Y | Y |
| 8 Kennedy | Y | Y | Y | Y | Y | Y | Y | Y |
| 9 Moakley | Y | Y | Y | Y | Y | Y | Y | Y |
| 10 Studds | Y | Y | Y | Y | Y | Y | Y | Y |
| 11 Donnelly | Y | ? | Y | Y | Y | Y | Y | Y |
| **MICHIGAN** | | | | | | | | |
| 1 Conyers | Y | Y | Y | Y | Y | Y | Y | Y |
| 2 ***Pursell*** | Y | ? | N | N | N | N | Y | N |
| 3 Wolpe | Y | Y | Y | Y | Y | Y | Y | Y |
| 4 ***Upton*** | Y | N | N | N | N | Y | Y | N |
| 5 ***Henry*** | Y | N | N | N | Y | Y | Y | N |
| 6 Carr | N | Y | Y | Y | Y | Y | Y | Y |
| 7 Kildee | Y | Y | Y | Y | Y | Y | Y | Y |
| 8 Traxler | ? | ? | ? | ? | # | # | ? | ? |
| 9 ***Vander Jagt*** | Y | Y | N | N | N | N | Y | N |
| 10 ***Camp*** | Y | N | N | N | N | N | Y | N |
| 11 ***Davis*** | Y | Y | N | N | Y | Y | Y | N |
| 12 Bonior | ? | ? | ? | ? | Y | Y | Y | ? |
| 13 Collins | ? | Y | Y | Y | Y | Y | Y | Y |
| 14 Hertel | N | Y | Y | Y | Y | Y | Y | Y |
| 15 Ford | N | Y | Y | Y | Y | Y | Y | ? |
| 16 Dingell | N | ? | Y | Y | Y | Y | Y | Y |
| 17 Levin | Y | Y | Y | Y | Y | Y | Y | Y |
| 18 ***Broomfield*** | ? | Y | N | N | N | N | Y | ? |
| **MINNESOTA** | | | | | | | | |
| 1 Penny | N | Y | Y | Y | N | Y | Y | N |
| 2 ***Weber*** | Y | ? | N | N | N | N | Y | N |
| 3 ***Ramstad*** | Y | N | N | N | N | N | Y | N |
| 4 Vento | Y | Y | Y | Y | Y | Y | Y | Y |

| | 268 | 269 | 270 | 271 | 272 | 273 | 274 | 275 |
|---|---|---|---|---|---|---|---|---|
| 5 Sabo | Y | Y | Y | Y | Y | Y | Y | Y |
| 6 Sikorski | Y | N | Y | Y | Y | Y | Y | Y |
| 7 Peterson | Y | Y | Y | Y | Y | Y | Y | Y |
| 8 Oberstar | N | Y | Y | Y | Y | Y | Y | Y |
| **MISSISSIPPI** | | | | | | | | |
| 1 Whitten | Y | ? | ? | Y | Y | ? | Y | ? |
| 2 Espy | Y | ? | ? | Y | Y | Y | Y | Y |
| 3 Montgomery | Y | Y | Y | Y | Y | Y | Y | N |
| 4 Parker | Y | Y | Y | Y | Y | Y | Y | N |
| 5 Taylor | N | N | Y | N | Y | Y | Y | N |
| **MISSOURI** | | | | | | | | |
| 1 Clay | N | N | Y | Y | Y | Y | Y | Y |
| 2 Horn | Y | Y | Y | Y | Y | Y | Y | Y |
| 3 Gephardt | Y | Y | Y | Y | Y | Y | Y | Y |
| 4 Skelton | Y | Y | Y | Y | Y | Y | Y | N |
| 5 Wheat | Y | ? | Y | Y | Y | Y | Y | Y |
| 6 ***Coleman*** | Y | N | N | N | Y | Y | Y | N |
| 7 ***Hancock*** | Y | N | N | N | N | N | Y | N |
| 8 ***Emerson*** | Y | N | N | N | Y | N | Y | N |
| 9 Volkmer | Y | Y | Y | Y | Y | Y | Y | N |
| **MONTANA** | | | | | | | | |
| 1 Williams | ? | ? | Y | Y | Y | Y | Y | Y |
| 2 ***Marlenee*** | Y | N | N | N | N | N | Y | N |
| **NEBRASKA** | | | | | | | | |
| 1 ***Bereuter*** | Y | N | N | N | N | N | Y | N |
| 2 Hoagland | Y | Y | Y | Y | Y | Y | Y | Y |
| 3 ***Barrett*** | Y | N | N | N | N | N | Y | N |
| **NEVADA** | | | | | | | | |
| 1 Bilbray | Y | Y | Y | Y | Y | Y | Y | Y |
| 2 ***Vucanovich*** | Y | N | N | N | N | N | Y | N |
| **NEW HAMPSHIRE** | | | | | | | | |
| 1 ***Zeliff*** | Y | N | N | N | N | N | Y | N |
| 2 Swett | N | Y | Y | Y | Y | Y | Y | Y |
| **NEW JERSEY** | | | | | | | | |
| 1 Andrews | Y | Y | Y | Y | Y | Y | Y | Y |
| 2 Hughes | Y | Y | Y | Y | Y | Y | Y | Y |
| 3 Pallone | Y | Y | Y | Y | Y | Y | Y | Y |
| 4 ***Smith*** | Y | Y | N | N | Y | Y | Y | N |
| 5 ***Roukema*** | Y | N | N | N | Y | Y | Y | N |
| 6 Dwyer | ? | Y | Y | Y | Y | Y | Y | Y |
| 7 ***Rinaldo*** | Y | ? | N | N | Y | Y | Y | N |
| 8 Roe | ? | ? | Y | Y | Y | Y | Y | ? |
| 9 Torricelli | Y | Y | Y | Y | Y | Y | Y | Y |
| 10 Payne | Y | ? | Y | Y | Y | Y | Y | Y |
| 11 ***Gallo*** | Y | N | N | N | N | N | Y | Y |
| 12 ***Zimmer*** | Y | N | N | N | N | N | Y | N |
| 13 ***Saxton*** | Y | N | N | N | N | N | Y | N |
| 14 Guarini | Y | Y | Y | Y | Y | Y | Y | Y |
| **NEW MEXICO** | | | | | | | | |
| 1 ***Schiff*** | Y | Y | N | N | N | N | Y | N |
| 2 ***Skeen*** | Y | Y | N | N | N | N | Y | N |
| 3 Richardson | Y | Y | Y | Y | Y | Y | Y | Y |
| **NEW YORK** | | | | | | | | |
| 1 Hochbrueckner | Y | Y | Y | Y | Y | Y | Y | Y |
| 2 Downey | Y | Y | Y | Y | N | Y | Y | Y |
| 3 Mrazek | ? | ? | Y | Y | N | Y | Y | Y |
| 4 ***Lent*** | Y | ? | ? | ? | ? | ? | ? | ? |
| 5 ***McGrath*** | Y | Y | N | Y | N | Y | Y | ? |
| 6 Flake | Y | Y | Y | Y | Y | Y | Y | Y |
| 7 Ackerman | N | Y | Y | Y | Y | Y | ? | ? |
| 8 Scheuer | N | Y | Y | Y | Y | Y | Y | Y |
| 9 Manton | Y | Y | Y | Y | Y | Y | Y | Y |
| 10 Schumer | Y | Y | Y | Y | N | Y | Y | Y |
| 11 Towns | Y | Y | Y | Y | Y | Y | Y | Y |
| 12 Owens | N | Y | Y | Y | Y | Y | Y | Y |
| 13 Solarz | Y | ? | Y | Y | Y | Y | Y | Y |
| 14 ***Molinari*** | Y | N | N | N | N | N | Y | N |
| 15 ***Green*** | Y | Y | N | N | N | N | Y | Y |
| 16 Rangel | Y | ? | Y | Y | Y | Y | Y | Y |
| 17 Weiss | N | ? | # | # | Y | Y | Y | Y |
| 18 Serrano | Y | Y | Y | Y | Y | Y | Y | Y |
| 19 Engel | Y | ? | ? | ? | Y | Y | Y | Y |
| 20 Lowey | Y | ? | Y | Y | Y | Y | Y | Y |
| 21 ***Fish*** | Y | Y | N | N | N | N | Y | ? |
| 22 ***Gilman*** | Y | Y | N | N | Y | Y | Y | Y |
| 23 McNulty | Y | Y | Y | Y | Y | Y | Y | Y |
| 24 ***Solomon*** | N | N | N | N | N | N | Y | N |
| 25 ***Boehlert*** | Y | N | N | N | Y | Y | Y | Y |
| 26 ***Martin*** | Y | ? | N | N | N | N | Y | N |
| 27 ***Walsh*** | Y | Y | N | N | Y | Y | Y | N |
| 28 McHugh | N | ? | Y | Y | N | N | Y | Y |
| 29 ***Horton*** | Y | Y | N | N | Y | Y | Y | ? |
| 30 Slaughter | Y | Y | Y | Y | Y | Y | Y | Y |
| 31 ***Paxon*** | Y | N | N | N | N | N | Y | N |

| | 268 | 269 | 270 | 271 | 272 | 273 | 274 | 275 |
|---|---|---|---|---|---|---|---|---|
| 32 LaFalce | N | ? | ? | Y | Y | Y | Y | Y |
| 33 Nowak | Y | ? | ? | Y | Y | Y | Y | Y |
| 34 ***Houghton*** | Y | Y | N | N | N | N | Y | N |
| **NORTH CAROLINA** | | | | | | | | |
| 1 Jones | Y | Y | Y | Y | Y | Y | Y | Y |
| 2 Valentine | Y | Y | Y | Y | N | N | Y | N |
| 3 Lancaster | Y | ? | Y | Y | Y | Y | Y | N |
| 4 Price | Y | Y | Y | Y | Y | Y | Y | ? |
| 5 Neal | Y | Y | Y | Y | N | Y | Y | Y |
| 6 ***Coble*** | Y | N | N | N | N | N | Y | N |
| 7 Rose | Y | Y | Y | Y | Y | Y | Y | Y |
| 8 Hefner | ? | ? | ? | ? | ? | ? | ? | ? |
| 9 ***McMillan*** | Y | N | N | N | N | N | Y | N |
| 10 ***Ballenger*** | Y | N | N | N | N | N | Y | N |
| 11 ***Taylor*** | Y | N | N | N | N | N | Y | N |
| **NORTH DAKOTA** | | | | | | | | |
| AL Dorgan | Y | Y | Y | Y | Y | Y | Y | Y |
| **OHIO** | | | | | | | | |
| 1 Luken | Y | ? | Y | Y | Y | Y | Y | Y |
| 2 ***Gradison*** | Y | Y | N | N | N | N | Y | N |
| 3 Hall | Y | ? | Y | Y | Y | Y | Y | N |
| 4 ***Oxley*** | Y | N | N | N | N | N | Y | N |
| 5 ***Gillmor*** | Y | Y | N | N | N | N | Y | N |
| 6 ***McEwen*** | ? | N | N | N | N | N | Y | N |
| 7 ***Hobson*** | Y | N | N | N | N | N | Y | N |
| 8 ***Boehner*** | Y | N | N | N | N | N | Y | N |
| 9 Kaptur | Y | Y | Y | Y | Y | Y | Y | Y |
| 10 ***Miller*** | Y | N | N | N | N | N | Y | N |
| 11 Eckart | Y | Y | Y | Y | Y | Y | Y | Y |
| 12 ***Kasich*** | Y | ? | N | N | N | Y | Y | N |
| 13 Pease | Y | Y | Y | Y | Y | Y | Y | Y |
| 14 Sawyer | Y | Y | Y | Y | Y | Y | Y | Y |
| 15 ***Wylie*** | Y | Y | N | N | N | N | Y | N |
| 16 ***Regula*** | Y | N | N | N | Y | Y | Y | N |
| 17 Traficant | N | Y | Y | Y | Y | Y | Y | Y |
| 18 Applegate | Y | Y | N | Y | Y | Y | Y | Y |
| 19 Feighan | Y | Y | Y | Y | Y | Y | Y | Y |
| 20 Oakar | Y | Y | Y | Y | Y | Y | Y | Y |
| 21 Stokes | Y | Y | Y | Y | Y | Y | Y | Y |
| **OKLAHOMA** | | | | | | | | |
| 1 ***Inhofe*** | Y | N | N | N | N | N | Y | N |
| 2 Synar | Y | Y | Y | Y | N | Y | Y | Y |
| 3 Brewster | Y | Y | Y | Y | Y | Y | Y | Y |
| 4 McCurdy | N | Y | N | Y | N | Y | Y | Y |
| 5 ***Edwards*** | Y | N | N | N | Y | N | Y | N |
| 6 English | Y | Y | Y | Y | Y | Y | Y | N |
| **OREGON** | | | | | | | | |
| 1 AuCoin | Y | Y | Y | Y | Y | Y | Y | Y |
| 2 ***Smith*** | Y | N | N | N | N | N | Y | N |
| 3 Wyden | Y | Y | Y | Y | N | Y | Y | Y |
| 4 DeFazio | N | Y | Y | Y | Y | Y | Y | Y |
| 5 Kopetski | Y | Y | Y | Y | N | N | Y | Y |
| **PENNSYLVANIA** | | | | | | | | |
| 1 Foglietta | Y | ? | Y | Y | Y | Y | Y | Y |
| 2 Blackwell | Y | Y | Y | Y | Y | Y | Y | Y |
| 3 Borski | Y | Y | Y | Y | Y | Y | Y | Y |
| 4 Kolter | ? | Y | Y | Y | Y | Y | Y | Y |
| 5 ***Schulze*** | Y | Y | N | Y | N | Y | Y | ? |
| 6 Yatron | Y | Y | Y | Y | Y | Y | Y | Y |
| 7 ***Weldon*** | Y | N | N | N | Y | Y | Y | N |
| 8 Kostmayer | N | Y | Y | Y | Y | Y | Y | Y |
| 9 ***Shuster*** | Y | N | N | N | Y | Y | Y | N |
| 10 ***McDade*** | Y | N | N | N | Y | Y | Y | N |
| 11 Kanjorski | N | Y | Y | Y | Y | Y | Y | Y |
| 12 Murtha | Y | Y | Y | Y | Y | Y | Y | Y |
| 13 ***Coughlin*** | Y | N | N | N | N | N | Y | Y |
| 14 Coyne | Y | Y | Y | Y | Y | Y | Y | Y |
| 15 ***Ritter*** | Y | Y | N | N | Y | Y | Y | N |
| 16 ***Walker*** | Y | N | N | N | N | N | Y | N |
| 17 ***Gekas*** | Y | N | N | N | N | N | Y | N |
| 18 ***Santorum*** | Y | N | N | N | Y | Y | Y | N |
| 19 ***Goodling*** | Y | N | N | N | Y | N | Y | N |
| 20 Gaydos | Y | Y | Y | Y | Y | Y | Y | Y |
| 21 ***Ridge*** | Y | ? | ? | N | Y | Y | Y | N |
| 22 Murphy | N | N | Y | Y | Y | Y | Y | Y |
| 23 ***Clinger*** | Y | Y | N | N | N | N | Y | N |
| **RHODE ISLAND** | | | | | | | | |
| 1 ***Machtley*** | Y | N | N | N | N | N | Y | Y |
| 2 Reed | Y | Y | Y | Y | Y | Y | Y | Y |
| **SOUTH CAROLINA** | | | | | | | | |
| 1 ***Ravenel*** | Y | Y | N | N | Y | Y | Y | N |
| 2 ***Spence*** | Y | N | N | N | Y | N | Y | N |
| 3 Derrick | Y | Y | Y | Y | Y | Y | Y | Y |
| 4 Patterson | Y | ? | Y | Y | Y | Y | Y | N |
| 5 Spratt | Y | Y | Y | Y | Y | Y | Y | N |
| 6 Tallon | Y | Y | Y | Y | Y | Y | Y | N |

| | 268 | 269 | 270 | 271 | 272 | 273 | 274 | 275 |
|---|---|---|---|---|---|---|---|---|
| **SOUTH DAKOTA** | | | | | | | | |
| AL Johnson | Y | Y | Y | Y | Y | Y | Y | Y |
| **TENNESSEE** | | | | | | | | |
| 1 ***Quillen*** | Y | N | N | N | N | N | Y | N |
| 2 ***Duncan*** | Y | N | N | N | Y | Y | Y | N |
| 3 Lloyd | Y | ? | Y | Y | N | Y | Y | N |
| 4 Cooper | Y | Y | Y | Y | N | Y | Y | Y |
| 5 Clement | Y | Y | Y | Y | Y | Y | Y | Y |
| 6 Gordon | Y | Y | Y | Y | N | Y | Y | Y |
| 7 ***Sundquist*** | Y | N | N | N | N | N | Y | N |
| 8 Tanner | Y | Y | Y | Y | Y | N | Y | Y |
| 9 Ford | Y | ? | Y | Y | Y | Y | Y | Y |
| **TEXAS** | | | | | | | | |
| 1 Chapman | Y | ? | Y | Y | Y | Y | Y | Y |
| 2 Wilson | N | ? | Y | Y | Y | Y | Y | Y |
| 3 ***Johnson*** | Y | Y | N | N | N | N | Y | ? |
| 4 Hall | N | ? | Y | Y | Y | N | Y | N |
| 5 Bryant | Y | Y | Y | Y | Y | Y | Y | Y |
| 6 ***Barton*** | Y | N | N | N | N | N | Y | N |
| 7 ***Archer*** | Y | Y | N | N | N | N | Y | ? |
| 8 ***Fields*** | Y | ? | N | N | N | N | Y | N |
| 9 Brooks | N | Y | Y | Y | Y | ? | Y | Y |
| 10 Pickle | Y | Y | Y | Y | N | Y | Y | Y |
| 11 Edwards | Y | Y | Y | Y | Y | Y | Y | Y |
| 12 Geren | Y | ? | Y | Y | Y | Y | Y | Y |
| 13 Sarpalius | Y | Y | Y | Y | Y | Y | Y | N |
| 14 Laughlin | Y | ? | Y | Y | Y | Y | Y | N |
| 15 de la Garza | Y | Y | Y | Y | Y | Y | Y | Y |
| 16 Coleman | ? | Y | Y | Y | N | Y | Y | Y |
| 17 Stenholm | N | Y | Y | Y | N | N | Y | N |
| 18 Washington | N | ? | ? | ? | Y | Y | Y | Y |
| 19 ***Combest*** | Y | Y | N | N | Y | Y | Y | N |
| 20 Gonzalez | N | Y | Y | Y | Y | Y | Y | Y |
| 21 ***Smith*** | Y | N | N | N | N | N | Y | N |
| 22 ***DeLay*** | Y | ? | N | N | N | N | N | N |
| 23 Bustamante | ? | Y | Y | Y | Y | Y | Y | Y |
| 24 Frost | Y | ? | Y | Y | Y | Y | Y | Y |
| 25 Andrews | Y | Y | Y | Y | N | Y | Y | N |
| 26 ***Armey*** | Y | N | N | N | N | N | N | N |
| 27 Ortiz | Y | Y | Y | ? | Y | Y | Y | N |
| **UTAH** | | | | | | | | |
| 1 ***Hansen*** | Y | N | N | N | N | N | Y | N |
| 2 Owens | Y | Y | Y | Y | Y | Y | Y | Y |
| 3 Orton | Y | Y | Y | Y | Y | Y | Y | Y |
| **VERMONT** | | | | | | | | |
| AL *Sanders* | N | ? | Y | Y | Y | Y | Y | Y |
| **VIRGINIA** | | | | | | | | |
| 1 ***Bateman*** | Y | Y | N | N | N | N | Y | N |
| 2 Pickett | Y | Y | Y | Y | N | N | Y | Y |
| 3 ***Bliley*** | Y | N | N | N | N | N | Y | Y |
| 4 Sisisky | Y | Y | Y | Y | Y | Y | Y | Y |
| 5 Payne | Y | Y | Y | Y | Y | Y | Y | Y |
| 6 Olin | N | Y | Y | Y | N | N | Y | Y |
| 7 ***Allen*** | Y | N | N | N | N | N | Y | N |
| 8 Moran | Y | Y | Y | Y | ? | Y | Y | Y |
| 9 Boucher | Y | Y | Y | Y | Y | Y | Y | Y |
| 10 ***Wolf*** | Y | N | N | N | N | N | Y | N |
| **WASHINGTON** | | | | | | | | |
| 1 ***Miller*** | Y | ? | N | N | N | N | Y | N |
| 2 Swift | Y | Y | Y | Y | N | N | Y | Y |
| 3 Unsoeld | N | Y | Y | Y | Y | Y | Y | Y |
| 4 ***Morrison*** | Y | Y | N | N | N | N | Y | N |
| 5 Foley | | | | | | | | |
| 6 Dicks | Y | Y | Y | Y | N | N | Y | Y |
| 7 McDermott | Y | Y | Y | Y | N | N | Y | Y |
| 8 ***Chandler*** | Y | ? | N | N | N | N | Y | N |
| **WEST VIRGINIA** | | | | | | | | |
| 1 Mollohan | N | ? | ? | Y | Y | Y | Y | Y |
| 2 Staggers | Y | Y | Y | Y | Y | Y | Y | N |
| 3 Wise | N | ? | ? | ? | Y | Y | Y | Y |
| 4 Rahall | N | Y | Y | Y | Y | Y | Y | Y |
| **WISCONSIN** | | | | | | | | |
| 1 Aspin | Y | ? | ? | Y | Y | Y | Y | Y |
| 2 ***Klug*** | Y | ? | N | N | N | N | Y | Y |
| 3 ***Gunderson*** | Y | Y | N | N | N | N | Y | Y |
| 4 Kleczka | Y | Y | Y | Y | Y | Y | Y | Y |
| 5 Moody | Y | ? | Y | Y | Y | Y | Y | Y |
| 6 ***Petri*** | N | Y | N | N | N | Y | Y | N |
| 7 Obey | N | Y | Y | Y | Y | Y | Y | Y |
| 8 ***Roth*** | Y | Y | N | N | N | N | Y | N |
| 9 ***Sensenbrenner*** | Y | N | N | N | N | Y | Y | N |
| **WYOMING** | | | | | | | | |
| AL ***Thomas*** | Y | N | N | N | N | N | Y | N |

Southern states - Ala., Ark., Fla., Ga., Ky., La., Miss., N.C., Okla., S.C., Tenn., Texas, Va.
Omitted votes are quorum calls, which CQ does not include in its vote charts.

**276. HR 3562. Transfers of Customs Forfeiture Funds/Passage.** Guarini, D-N.J., motion to suspend the rules and pass the bill to require that unobligated funds in excess of $15 million remaining in the Customs Forfeiture Fund at the end of each fiscal year be transferred to the Department of Health and Human Services for prison drug treatment programs and for assistance to hospital trauma centers. Motion rejected 173-243: R 6-153; D 166-90 (ND 132-45, SD 34-45); I 1-0, July 8, 1992. A two-thirds majority of those present and voting (277 in this case) was required for passage under suspension of the rules. A "nay" was a vote in support of the president's position.

**277. HR 5518. Fiscal 1993 Transportation Appropriations/Rule.** Adoption of the rule (H Res 513) to provide for House floor consideration of the bill to provide $13 billion in new budget authority for the Department of Transportation and related agencies. Adopted 269-149: R 20-141; D 248-8 (ND 171-4, SD 77-4); I 1-0, July 9, 1992.

**278. HR 5518. Fiscal 1993 Transportation Appropriations/Passenger Facility Charges.** Oberstar, D-Minn., en bloc amendment to strike provisions in the bill that prohibited airports from imposing passenger facility charges on "frequent flier" awards or other airline bonus program certificates; that prohibited the Federal Aviation Administration from planning and executing a passenger manifest program that applied only to U.S. airlines; and that prohibited the FAA from issuing regulations mandating a criminal background records check program for airline or airport employees. Rejected 68-348: R 34-125; D 34-222 (ND 24-152, SD 10-70); I 0-1, July 9, 1992.

**279. HR 5518. Fiscal 1993 Transportation Appropriations/Temporary Matching Requirements Waiver.** Mineta, D-Calif., amendment to permit the Federal Transit Administration to waive state and local matching requirements for certain mass transit programs in fiscal 1993, provided the state or locality paid the matching amount later. Rejected 184-229: R 4-157; D 179-72 (ND 145-28, SD 34-44); I 1-0, July 9, 1992.

**280. HR 5518. Fiscal 1993 Transportation Appropriations/Administrative Costs Spending Cuts.** Smith, R-Texas, amendment to cut the non-personnel administrative costs of each agency in the bill by approximately 10 percent, for a total of $59 million. Rejected 175-236: R 114-48; D 60-188 (ND 36-135, SD 24-53); I 1-0, July 9, 1992.

**281. HR 5518. Fiscal 1993 Transportation Appropriations/Deficit Reduction.** Michel, R-Ill., amendment to require that any savings achieved in any discretionary spending program as a result of this bill or any other appropriations bill were to be used to reduce the federal deficit. Adopted 268-143: R 160-0; D 108-142 (ND 54-119, SD 54-23); I 0-1, July 9, 1992. A "yea" was a vote in support of the president's position.

**282. HR 5518. Fiscal 1993 Transportation Appropriations/Budget Fire Walls.** Obey, D-Wis., amendment to transfer $400 million from the international discretionary spending budget to several domestic transportation programs; and to increase by $2.6 billion the amount of fiscal 1993 funding that could be obligated from the Highway Trust Fund and the Airport and Airway Trust Fund. Adopted 213-190: R 16-139; D 196-51 (ND 143-28, SD 53-23); I 1-0, July 9, 1992. A "nay" was a vote in support of the president's position.

**283. HR 5518. Fiscal 1993 Transportation Appropriations/Recommit With Instructions.** Michel, R-Ill., motion to recommit to the House Appropriations Committee the bill, with instructions to report it back to the House with an amendment to require that any savings achieved in any discretionary spending program as a result of this bill or any other appropriations bill were to be used to reduce the federal deficit. Motion agreed to 268-115: R 149-0; D 119-114 (ND 67-93, SD 52-21); I 0-1, July 9, 1992. A "yea" was a vote in support of the president's position.

## KEY

| | 276 | 277 | 278 | 279 | 280 | 281 | 282 | 283 |
|---|---|---|---|---|---|---|---|---|
| **ALABAMA** | | | | | | | | |
| 1 *Callahan* | N | N | N | N | N | Y | N | Y |
| 2 *Dickinson* | N | Y | N | N | Y | Y | Y | Y |
| 3 Browder | N | Y | N | Y | N | Y | Y | Y |
| 4 Bevill | N | Y | N | Y | N | Y | Y | Y |
| 5 Cramer | N | Y | N | Y | N | Y | Y | Y |
| 6 Erdreich | N | Y | Y | Y | Y | Y | Y | Y |
| 7 Harris | N | Y | N | Y | N | Y | N | Y |
| **ALASKA** | | | | | | | | |
| AL *Young* | N | N | Y | N | N | Y | N | Y |
| **ARIZONA** | | | | | | | | |
| 1 *Rhodes* | N | N | N | N | Y | Y | N | Y |
| 2 Pastor | N | Y | N | Y | N | Y | N | Y |
| 3 *Stump* | N | N | N | Y | N | Y | N | Y |
| 4 *Kyl* | N | N | Y | N | Y | Y | N | Y |
| 5 *Kolbe* | N | N | N | N | Y | Y | N | Y |
| **ARKANSAS** | | | | | | | | |
| 1 Alexander | ? | Y | N | ? | ? | Y | Y | Y |
| 2 Thornton | N | Y | N | ? | N | Y | Y | Y |
| 3 *Hammerschmidt* | N | Y | Y | N | N | Y | Y | Y |
| 4 Anthony | ? | Y | N | N | N | Y | N | Y |
| **CALIFORNIA** | | | | | | | | |
| 1 *Riggs* | N | ? | N | N | N | Y | N | Y |
| 2 *Herger* | N | N | N | N | Y | Y | N | Y |
| 3 Matsui | Y | Y | N | Y | N | N | Y | N |
| 4 Fazio | Y | Y | N | Y | N | N | Y | Y |
| 5 Pelosi | Y | Y | N | Y | N | N | Y | Y |
| 6 Boxer | Y | Y | N | Y | ? | ? | ? | ? |
| 7 Miller | N | Y | N | Y | N | N | Y | N |
| 8 Dellums | Y | Y | N | Y | N | N | Y | N |
| 9 Stark | Y | Y | N | ? | ? | ? | ? | ? |
| 10 Edwards | Y | Y | N | Y | N | N | Y | N |
| 11 Lantos | Y | Y | N | Y | N | N | Y | N |
| 12 *Campbell* | N | N | N | N | Y | Y | N | Y |
| 13 Mineta | Y | Y | Y | Y | N | N | Y | N |
| 14 *Doolittle* | N | N | Y | N | N | Y | N | Y |
| 15 Condit | N | Y | N | Y | N | Y | Y | Y |
| 16 Panetta | N | Y | N | Y | N | Y | Y | Y |
| 17 Dooley | N | Y | N | Y | N | Y | Y | Y |
| 18 Lehman | N | Y | N | Y | N | Y | Y | Y |
| 19 *Lagomarsino* | N | N | N | N | N | Y | N | Y |
| 20 *Thomas* | N | N | N | N | N | Y | N | Y |
| 21 *Gallegly* | N | N | N | N | Y | Y | N | Y |
| 22 *Moorhead* | N | N | N | N | Y | Y | N | Y |
| 23 Beilenson | N | N | Y | Y | Y | Y | N | Y |
| 24 Waxman | Y | Y | Y | N | N | N | N | N |
| 25 Roybal | Y | Y | N | Y | N | N | Y | N |
| 26 Berman | Y | Y | N | N | N | N | N | N |
| 27 Levine | Y | Y | N | N | N | N | N | N |
| 28 Dixon | Y | Y | N | Y | N | N | Y | N |
| 29 Waters | Y | Y | N | Y | N | N | Y | N |
| 30 Martinez | Y | Y | N | Y | N | N | Y | N |
| 31 Dymally | Y | Y | N | Y | N | N | Y | N |
| 32 Anderson | N | Y | Y | Y | N | N | Y | N |
| 33 *Dreier* | N | N | N | N | Y | Y | N | Y |
| 34 Torres | Y | Y | N | Y | N | N | Y | N |
| 35 *Lewis* | N | N | N | N | N | N | X | ? |
| 36 Brown | Y | Y | N | Y | N | N | Y | N |
| 37 *McCandless* | N | N | N | N | N | Y | N | Y |
| 38 *Dornan* | N | N | N | N | N | Y | N | Y |
| 39 *Dannemeyer* | N | N | N | Y | N | Y | N | Y |
| 40 *Cox* | N | N | N | N | N | Y | N | Y |
| 41 *Lowery* | N | ? | ? | ? | N | Y | ? | ? |

| | 276 | 277 | 278 | 279 | 280 | 281 | 282 | 283 |
|---|---|---|---|---|---|---|---|---|
| 42 *Rohrabacher* | N | N | N | N | N | Y | N | Y |
| 43 *Packard* | N | N | N | N | Y | Y | N | Y |
| 44 *Cunningham* | N | N | N | N | Y | Y | N | Y |
| 45 *Hunter* | N | N | N | Y | N | Y | N | Y |
| **COLORADO** | | | | | | | | |
| 1 Schroeder | Y | Y | N | N | N | Y | Y | Y |
| 2 Skaggs | Y | Y | N | N | N | Y | Y | Y |
| 3 Campbell | Y | Y | ? | ? | ? | ? | ? | ? |
| 4 *Allard* | N | N | Y | N | Y | Y | N | Y |
| 5 *Hefley* | N | N | N | N | Y | Y | N | Y |
| 6 *Schaefer* | N | N | N | N | Y | Y | N | Y |
| **CONNECTICUT** | | | | | | | | |
| 1 Kennelly | Y | Y | N | Y | N | Y | Y | Y |
| 2 Gejdenson | Y | Y | N | N | N | Y | Y | Y |
| 3 DeLauro | Y | Y | N | Y | N | Y | Y | Y |
| 4 *Shays* | N | Y | N | Y | N | Y | N | Y |
| 5 *Franks* | N | N | N | Y | N | Y | N | Y |
| 6 *Johnson* | N | N | N | N | Y | Y | N | Y |
| **DELAWARE** | | | | | | | | |
| AL Carper | N | Y | N | N | Y | Y | N | Y |
| **FLORIDA** | | | | | | | | |
| 1 Hutto | N | N | N | Y | N | Y | N | Y |
| 2 Peterson | Y | Y | N | Y | N | Y | Y | Y |
| 3 Bennett | N | Y | N | Y | N | Y | N | Y |
| 4 *James* | N | N | N | N | N | Y | N | Y |
| 5 *McCollum* | N | N | Y | N | Y | Y | N | Y |
| 6 *Stearns* | N | N | N | N | N | Y | N | Y |
| 7 Gibbons | Y | Y | N | ? | ? | Y | Y | Y |
| 8 *Young* | N | Y | N | N | N | Y | N | Y |
| 9 *Bilirakis* | N | N | N | N | Y | Y | N | Y |
| 10 *Ireland* | N | N | N | N | Y | Y | N | Y |
| 11 Bacchus | Y | Y | Y | Y | Y | Y | N | Y |
| 12 *Lewis* | N | N | N | N | N | Y | N | Y |
| 13 *Goss* | N | N | Y | N | Y | Y | N | Y |
| 14 Johnston | Y | Y | N | N | N | Y | N | Y |
| 15 *Shaw* | N | N | N | N | N | Y | N | Y |
| 16 Smith | Y | Y | N | N | N | Y | N | ? |
| 17 Lehman | Y | Y | Y | Y | N | N | Y | N |
| 18 *Ros—Lehtinen* | N | N | N | N | Y | Y | N | Y |
| 19 Fascell | Y | Y | Y | Y | N | N | Y | N |
| **GEORGIA** | | | | | | | | |
| 1 Thomas | N | Y | N | N | N | Y | N | Y |
| 2 Hatcher | ? | ? | ? | ? | ? | ? | ? | ? |
| 3 Ray | N | N | ? | ? | ? | # | X | ? |
| 4 Jones | Y | Y | N | N | N | N | Y | N |
| 5 Lewis | Y | Y | N | Y | N | N | Y | N |
| 6 *Gingrich* | N | N | N | N | Y | Y | N | Y |
| 7 Darden | Y | Y | N | N | N | Y | N | Y |
| 8 Rowland | N | N | N | N | N | Y | N | ? |
| 9 Jenkins | Y | Y | N | N | N | Y | N | Y |
| 10 Barnard | N | ? | ? | ? | ? | ? | ? | ? |
| **HAWAII** | | | | | | | | |
| 1 Abercrombie | Y | Y | Y | Y | N | N | Y | N |
| 2 Mink | Y | Y | N | Y | N | N | Y | N |
| **IDAHO** | | | | | | | | |
| 1 LaRocco | N | Y | N | N | N | Y | Y | Y |
| 2 Stallings | N | Y | N | Y | Y | Y | N | Y |
| **ILLINOIS** | | | | | | | | |
| 1 Hayes | Y | Y | N | N | N | Y | N | ? |
| 2 Savage | Y | ? | Y | ? | N | N | Y | ? |
| 3 Russo | Y | Y | N | Y | N | N | Y | Y |
| 4 Sangmeister | N | Y | Y | Y | N | Y | Y | Y |
| 5 Lipinski | N | Y | Y | N | N | Y | Y | Y |
| 6 *Hyde* | ? | N | N | N | N | ? | ? | ? |
| 7 Collins | Y | Y | N | N | N | N | Y | N |
| 8 Rostenkowski | Y | Y | Y | Y | N | Y | Y | ? |
| 9 Yates | Y | Y | N | Y | N | N | Y | N |
| 10 *Porter* | N | N | N | N | Y | Y | N | Y |
| 11 Annunzio | Y | Y | N | N | N | Y | N | N |
| 12 *Crane* | N | N | N | N | N | Y | N | Y |
| 13 *Fawell* | N | N | N | N | Y | Y | N | Y |
| 14 *Hastert* | N | N | N | N | Y | Y | N | Y |
| 15 *Ewing* | N | N | N | N | Y | Y | N | Y |
| 16 Cox | Y | Y | N | N | Y | Y | Y | Y |
| 17 Evans | Y | Y | Y | N | N | Y | N | Y |
| 18 *Michel* | N | Y | N | N | N | Y | N | Y |
| 19 Bruce | N | Y | N | Y | N | Y | Y | Y |
| 20 Durbin | Y | Y | N | Y | N | Y | Y | Y |
| 21 Costello | N | Y | N | Y | N | Y | Y | Y |
| 22 Poshard | N | Y | N | Y | N | Y | Y | Y |
| **INDIANA** | | | | | | | | |
| 1 Visclosky | N | Y | N | N | N | Y | N | Y |
| 2 Sharp | N | Y | N | N | N | Y | N | Y |
| 3 Roemer | N | Y | N | Y | N | Y | N | Y |

| | 276 | 277 | 278 | 279 | 280 | 281 | 282 | 283 |
|---|---|---|---|---|---|---|---|---|
| 4 Long | Y | Y | N | Y | N | Y | Y | Y |
| 5 Jontz | Y | Y | N | Y | Y | N | Y | Y |
| 6 ***Burton*** | N | N | N | N | Y | Y | N | Y |
| 7 ***Myers*** | N | N | N | N | N | Y | N | Y |
| 8 McCloskey | N | ? | N | Y | Y | N | Y | N |
| 9 Hamilton | N | Y | N | Y | N | N | Y | N |
| 10 Jacobs | Y | Y | N | Y | Y | Y | N | Y |
| **IOWA** | | | | | | | | |
| 1 ***Leach*** | N | N | N | N | Y | Y | N | Y |
| 2 ***Nussle*** | N | N | N | N | Y | Y | N | Y |
| 3 Nagle | Y | Y | N | Y | N | N | Y | Y |
| 4 Smith | Y | Y | N | Y | N | N | Y | N |
| 5 ***Lightfoot*** | N | N | N | N | N | Y | N | ? |
| 6 ***Grandy*** | N | N | N | N | Y | Y | N | Y |
| **KANSAS** | | | | | | | | |
| 1 ***Roberts*** | N | N | N | N | Y | Y | N | Y |
| 2 Slattery | Y | Y | N | N | Y | Y | N | Y |
| 3 ***Meyers*** | N | N | Y | N | Y | Y | N | Y |
| 4 Glickman | N | Y | N | N | N | Y | Y | Y |
| 5 ***Nichols*** | N | N | N | N | Y | Y | N | Y |
| **KENTUCKY** | | | | | | | | |
| 1 Hubbard | N | Y | N | Y | ? | ? | ? | ? |
| 2 Natcher | N | Y | N | N | N | Y | Y | Y |
| 3 Mazzoli | N | Y | N | Y | N | N | Y | Y |
| 4 ***Bunning*** | N | N | N | N | Y | Y | N | Y |
| 5 ***Rogers*** | N | N | N | N | N | Y | N | Y |
| 6 ***Hopkins*** | N | N | N | N | Y | Y | N | Y |
| 7 Perkins | Y | Y | N | Y | N | N | Y | N |
| **LOUISIANA** | | | | | | | | |
| 1 ***Livingston*** | N | N | ? | N | N | Y | N | Y |
| 2 Jefferson | Y | Y | N | Y | Y | N | Y | ? |
| 3 Tauzin | Y | Y | N | N | N | Y | N | Y |
| 4 ***McCrery*** | N | N | N | N | Y | Y | N | Y |
| 5 Huckaby | N | Y | N | N | Y | ? | ? | ? |
| 6 ***Baker*** | N | N | N | N | Y | Y | ? | ? |
| 7 Hayes | Y | Y | ? | ? | ? | ? | ? | ? |
| 8 ***Holloway*** | N | N | N | N | Y | Y | N | Y |
| **MAINE** | | | | | | | | |
| 1 Andrews | Y | Y | N | Y | N | N | Y | N |
| 2 ***Snowe*** | N | N | N | N | Y | Y | N | Y |
| **MARYLAND** | | | | | | | | |
| 1 ***Gilchrest*** | N | N | N | N | Y | Y | N | Y |
| 2 ***Bentley*** | N | N | Y | Y | N | Y | Y | Y |
| 3 Cardin | Y | Y | N | Y | N | N | Y | N |
| 4 McMillen | Y | Y | N | Y | Y | Y | N | Y |
| 5 Hoyer | Y | Y | N | Y | N | N | Y | N |
| 6 Byron | N | Y | N | N | Y | Y | N | Y |
| 7 Mfume | Y | Y | N | Y | Y | Y | Y | N |
| 8 ***Morella*** | N | N | N | N | N | Y | N | Y |
| **MASSACHUSETTS** | | | | | | | | |
| 1 Olver | Y | Y | N | Y | Y | N | Y | N |
| 2 Neal | Y | Y | N | Y | N | N | Y | N |
| 3 Early | Y | Y | Y | N | N | N | ? | ? |
| 4 Frank | Y | Y | N | Y | N | N | N | N |
| 5 Atkins | Y | Y | N | Y | Y | N | Y | N |
| 6 Mavroules | Y | Y | N | Y | N | Y | Y | Y |
| 7 Markey | Y | Y | N | Y | N | N | Y | N |
| 8 Kennedy | Y | Y | N | Y | Y | N | Y | N |
| 9 Moakley | Y | Y | N | Y | N | N | Y | N |
| 10 Studds | Y | Y | N | Y | N | N | Y | N |
| 11 Donnelly | Y | Y | N | Y | N | N | Y | N |
| **MICHIGAN** | | | | | | | | |
| 1 Conyers | Y | N | N | Y | N | N | Y | N |
| 2 ***Pursell*** | N | N | N | N | Y | Y | ? | ? |
| 3 Wolpe | Y | Y | N | Y | N | N | Y | N |
| 4 ***Upton*** | N | N | Y | N | Y | Y | N | Y |
| 5 ***Henry*** | N | N | N | N | Y | Y | N | Y |
| 6 Carr | N | Y | N | N | N | N | Y | N |
| 7 Kildee | Y | Y | N | Y | N | N | Y | N |
| 8 Traxler | ? | ? | ? | ? | ? | ? | ? | ? |
| 9 ***Vander Jagt*** | Y | N | N | N | Y | Y | N | Y |
| 10 ***Camp*** | N | N | N | N | Y | Y | N | Y |
| 11 ***Davis*** | N | Y | N | N | N | Y | N | Y |
| 12 Bonior | ? | ? | ? | Y | ? | N | Y | N |
| 13 Collins | Y | Y | N | Y | N | N | Y | N |
| 14 Hertel | Y | Y | N | N | N | N | Y | N |
| 15 Ford | ? | Y | N | Y | N | N | Y | N |
| 16 Dingell | Y | Y | N | Y | N | N | Y | N |
| 17 Levin | N | Y | N | Y | N | N | Y | N |
| 18 ***Broomfield*** | ? | N | N | N | N | Y | N | Y |
| **MINNESOTA** | | | | | | | | |
| 1 Penny | N | Y | N | N | Y | Y | N | Y |
| 2 ***Weber*** | N | N | N | N | Y | Y | N | ? |
| 3 ***Ramstad*** | N | N | N | N | Y | Y | N | Y |
| 4 Vento | Y | Y | Y | Y | N | N | Y | N |

| | 276 | 277 | 278 | 279 | 280 | 281 | 282 | 283 |
|---|---|---|---|---|---|---|---|---|
| 5 Sabo | Y | Y | N | Y | N | N | Y | N |
| 6 Sikorski | Y | Y | N | Y | N | Y | Y | Y |
| 7 Peterson | Y | Y | N | Y | N | N | Y | Y |
| 8 Oberstar | Y | Y | Y | Y | N | N | Y | N |
| **MISSISSIPPI** | | | | | | | | |
| 1 Whitten | ? | Y | N | N | N | Y | Y | Y |
| 2 Espy | Y | Y | N | Y | N | N | Y | N |
| 3 Montgomery | N | Y | N | N | N | Y | N | Y |
| 4 Parker | N | Y | N | N | N | Y | Y | Y |
| 5 Taylor | N | N | N | N | N | Y | N | Y |
| **MISSOURI** | | | | | | | | |
| 1 Clay | Y | Y | N | Y | N | N | Y | N |
| 2 Horn | Y | Y | N | Y | Y | Y | Y | Y |
| 3 Gephardt | Y | Y | Y | Y | N | N | Y | N |
| 4 Skelton | N | Y | N | Y | N | Y | Y | Y |
| 5 Wheat | Y | Y | N | Y | N | N | Y | N |
| 6 ***Coleman*** | N | N | N | N | Y | Y | Y | Y |
| 7 ***Hancock*** | N | N | Y | N | Y | Y | N | Y |
| 8 ***Emerson*** | N | Y | Y | N | N | Y | Y | Y |
| 9 Volkmer | N | Y | N | N | N | Y | Y | Y |
| **MONTANA** | | | | | | | | |
| 1 Williams | Y | Y | Y | Y | N | N | Y | N |
| 2 ***Marlenee*** | N | N | Y | Y | Y | ? | X | ? |
| **NEBRASKA** | | | | | | | | |
| 1 ***Bereuter*** | N | N | N | N | N | Y | N | Y |
| 2 Hoagland | N | Y | N | N | Y | Y | Y | Y |
| 3 ***Barrett*** | N | N | N | N | Y | Y | N | Y |
| **NEVADA** | | | | | | | | |
| 1 Bilbray | Y | Y | N | Y | N | Y | Y | Y |
| 2 ***Vucanovich*** | N | N | Y | N | Y | Y | N | Y |
| **NEW HAMPSHIRE** | | | | | | | | |
| 1 ***Zeliff*** | N | N | N | N | Y | Y | N | Y |
| 2 Swett | N | Y | N | Y | N | N | Y | N |
| **NEW JERSEY** | | | | | | | | |
| 1 Andrews | N | Y | Y | Y | N | N | Y | N |
| 2 Hughes | Y | Y | N | N | N | N | Y | Y |
| 3 Pallone | N | Y | N | Y | Y | Y | Y | Y |
| 4 ***Smith*** | N | N | N | N | N | Y | Y | Y |
| 5 ***Roukema*** | N | N | Y | N | Y | Y | # | ? |
| 6 Dwyer | Y | Y | N | Y | N | N | Y | N |
| 7 ***Rinaldo*** | N | N | N | N | N | Y | Y | Y |
| 8 Roe | ? | Y | Y | Y | N | N | Y | N |
| 9 Torricelli | Y | Y | N | Y | N | Y | Y | Y |
| 10 Payne | Y | Y | N | Y | N | N | Y | N |
| 11 ***Gallo*** | N | N | N | N | N | Y | N | Y |
| 12 ***Zimmer*** | N | N | N | N | Y | Y | N | Y |
| 13 ***Saxton*** | N | N | N | N | Y | Y | N | Y |
| 14 Guarini | Y | Y | N | Y | Y | Y | Y | N |
| **NEW MEXICO** | | | | | | | | |
| 1 ***Schiff*** | N | Y | N | N | Y | Y | N | Y |
| 2 ***Skeen*** | N | Y | N | N | N | Y | N | Y |
| 3 Richardson | Y | Y | N | N | N | N | Y | Y |
| **NEW YORK** | | | | | | | | |
| 1 Hochbrueckner | Y | Y | N | Y | N | Y | Y | Y |
| 2 Downey | Y | Y | N | N | N | N | Y | Y |
| 3 Mrazek | Y | Y | N | Y | N | N | Y | N |
| 4 ***Lent*** | ? | ? | ? | ? | ? | ? | ? | ? |
| 5 ***McGrath*** | Y | Y | N | N | N | Y | N | Y |
| 6 Flake | Y | Y | N | Y | N | N | Y | N |
| 7 Ackerman | ? | ? | ? | ? | ? | ? | ? | ? |
| 8 Scheuer | Y | N | N | Y | Y | N | N | N |
| 9 Manton | Y | Y | N | N | N | Y | Y | ? |
| 10 Schumer | Y | Y | N | Y | N | N | N | Y |
| 11 Towns | Y | Y | N | # | ? | X | # | ? |
| 12 Owens | Y | Y | N | Y | N | N | N | N |
| 13 Solarz | Y | ? | ? | ? | ? | ? | ? | ? |
| 14 ***Molinari*** | N | Y | Y | N | Y | Y | Y | Y |
| 15 ***Green*** | N | N | N | N | N | Y | N | Y |
| 16 Rangel | Y | Y | N | Y | N | N | Y | N |
| 17 Weiss | Y | Y | N | Y | N | N | # | ? |
| 18 Serrano | Y | Y | N | Y | N | N | Y | N |
| 19 Engel | Y | N | N | Y | N | N | Y | Y |
| 20 Lowey | Y | Y | N | Y | N | N | Y | Y |
| 21 ***Fish*** | ? | Y | N | N | Y | Y | N | Y |
| 22 ***Gilman*** | Y | N | Y | N | Y | Y | N | Y |
| 23 McNulty | Y | Y | N | N | N | N | Y | N |
| 24 ***Solomon*** | N | N | N | N | Y | Y | N | Y |
| 25 ***Boehlert*** | Y | Y | N | N | Y | Y | Y | Y |
| 26 ***Martin*** | N | N | N | N | N | Y | N | Y |
| 27 ***Walsh*** | N | N | N | N | Y | Y | N | Y |
| 28 McHugh | Y | Y | N | N | N | N | N | N |
| 29 ***Horton*** | ? | Y | N | N | N | Y | N | Y |
| 30 Slaughter | Y | Y | N | Y | N | N | Y | Y |
| 31 ***Paxon*** | N | N | N | N | Y | Y | N | Y |

| | 276 | 277 | 278 | 279 | 280 | 281 | 282 | 283 |
|---|---|---|---|---|---|---|---|---|
| 32 LaFalce | Y | Y | N | Y | N | N | Y | ? |
| 33 Nowak | Y | Y | Y | Y | N | N | Y | Y |
| 34 ***Houghton*** | Y | N | N | N | Y | Y | N | Y |
| **NORTH CAROLINA** | | | | | | | | |
| 1 Jones | Y | Y | Y | Y | N | Y | Y | N |
| 2 Valentine | N | Y | N | N | N | N | Y | N |
| 3 Lancaster | Y | Y | N | N | Y | Y | N | Y |
| 4 Price | Y | Y | N | N | N | Y | Y | Y |
| 5 Neal | Y | Y | N | N | Y | Y | Y | Y |
| 6 ***Coble*** | N | N | N | N | N | Y | N | Y |
| 7 Rose | N | Y | N | N | N | N | Y | Y |
| 8 Hefner | ? | ? | ? | ? | ? | ? | ? | ? |
| 9 ***McMillan*** | N | N | N | N | N | Y | N | Y |
| 10 ***Ballenger*** | N | N | Y | N | Y | Y | N | Y |
| 11 ***Taylor*** | N | N | Y | N | N | Y | N | Y |
| **NORTH DAKOTA** | | | | | | | | |
| AL Dorgan | Y | Y | N | N | Y | Y | N | Y |
| **OHIO** | | | | | | | | |
| 1 Luken | Y | Y | N | N | Y | Y | N | Y |
| 2 ***Gradison*** | N | N | Y | N | Y | Y | N | Y |
| 3 Hall | N | Y | N | Y | N | Y | Y | Y |
| 4 ***Oxley*** | N | — | — | N | N | Y | N | Y |
| 5 ***Gillmor*** | N | N | Y | N | Y | Y | N | Y |
| 6 ***McEwen*** | N | N | N | N | Y | Y | N | Y |
| 7 ***Hobson*** | N | N | Y | N | N | Y | N | Y |
| 8 ***Boehner*** | N | N | N | N | Y | Y | N | Y |
| 9 Kaptur | Y | Y | N | Y | Y | Y | Y | Y |
| 10 ***Miller*** | N | N | N | N | Y | Y | N | Y |
| 11 Eckart | Y | Y | N | Y | Y | Y | Y | Y |
| 12 ***Kasich*** | N | N | N | N | Y | Y | N | Y |
| 13 Pease | Y | Y | N | N | N | N | Y | N |
| 14 Sawyer | Y | Y | N | Y | N | Y | Y | Y |
| 15 ***Wylie*** | N | N | N | N | Y | Y | N | Y |
| 16 ***Regula*** | N | N | N | N | N | Y | N | Y |
| 17 Traficant | Y | Y | Y | Y | N | N | Y | N |
| 18 Applegate | N | Y | Y | Y | N | Y | Y | ? |
| 19 Feighan | Y | Y | N | Y | N | Y | Y | Y |
| 20 Oakar | Y | Y | N | Y | N | N | Y | N |
| 21 Stokes | Y | Y | N | Y | N | N | Y | N |
| **OKLAHOMA** | | | | | | | | |
| 1 ***Inhofe*** | N | N | Y | N | Y | Y | N | Y |
| 2 Synar | Y | Y | N | Y | N | N | Y | — |
| 3 Brewster | N | Y | N | N | Y | Y | Y | Y |
| 4 McCurdy | Y | Y | N | N | Y | Y | N | Y |
| 5 ***Edwards*** | N | N | N | N | Y | Y | N | ? |
| 6 English | Y | Y | Y | N | N | Y | Y | Y |
| **OREGON** | | | | | | | | |
| 1 AuCoin | Y | Y | N | Y | N | N | Y | N |
| 2 ***Smith*** | N | N | N | N | Y | Y | N | Y |
| 3 Wyden | Y | Y | N | Y | N | N | Y | N |
| 4 DeFazio | Y | Y | Y | Y | N | N | Y | N |
| 5 Kopetski | Y | Y | N | Y | N | N | Y | N |
| **PENNSYLVANIA** | | | | | | | | |
| 1 Foglietta | Y | Y | N | Y | N | N | Y | N |
| 2 Blackwell | Y | Y | N | Y | N | N | Y | N |
| 3 Borski | Y | Y | Y | Y | N | N | Y | N |
| 4 Kolter | N | Y | N | Y | ? | N | Y | N |
| 5 ***Schulze*** | ? | N | ? | ? | ? | ? | ? | ? |
| 6 Yatron | N | Y | N | ? | ? | ? | ? | ? |
| 7 ***Weldon*** | N | N | N | N | Y | Y | N | Y |
| 8 Kostmayer | Y | Y | N | Y | N | N | Y | N |
| 9 ***Shuster*** | N | Y | Y | N | N | Y | Y | Y |
| 10 ***McDade*** | Y | N | N | N | N | Y | N | Y |
| 11 Kanjorski | N | Y | Y | Y | N | Y | Y | Y |
| 12 Murtha | N | Y | N | N | N | Y | Y | Y |
| 13 ***Coughlin*** | N | N | N | N | N | Y | N | Y |
| 14 Coyne | Y | Y | N | Y | N | N | Y | N |
| 15 ***Ritter*** | N | N | N | N | Y | Y | N | Y |
| 16 ***Walker*** | N | N | N | N | Y | Y | N | Y |
| 17 ***Gekas*** | N | N | Y | N | Y | Y | N | Y |
| 18 ***Santorum*** | N | N | N | N | Y | Y | N | Y |
| 19 ***Goodling*** | N | N | Y | N | Y | Y | N | Y |
| 20 Gaydos | N | Y | ? | ? | ? | ? | ? | ? |
| 21 ***Ridge*** | N | N | N | N | Y | Y | N | ? |
| 22 Murphy | Y | Y | N | Y | Y | Y | Y | N |
| 23 ***Clinger*** | N | Y | Y | N | Y | Y | Y | Y |
| **RHODE ISLAND** | | | | | | | | |
| 1 ***Machtley*** | N | N | N | N | N | Y | N | Y |
| 2 Reed | Y | Y | N | Y | Y | N | Y | N |
| **SOUTH CAROLINA** | | | | | | | | |
| 1 ***Ravenel*** | N | N | N | Y | N | Y | N | ? |
| 2 ***Spence*** | N | N | N | N | N | Y | N | Y |
| 3 Derrick | N | Y | N | Y | N | Y | Y | Y |
| 4 Patterson | N | Y | N | N | Y | Y | N | Y |
| 5 Spratt | N | Y | N | N | Y | Y | N | Y |
| 6 Tallon | N | Y | N | N | N | Y | Y | Y |

| | 276 | 277 | 278 | 279 | 280 | 281 | 282 | 283 |
|---|---|---|---|---|---|---|---|---|
| **SOUTH DAKOTA** | | | | | | | | |
| AL Johnson | N | Y | N | Y | N | Y | Y | Y |
| **TENNESSEE** | | | | | | | | |
| 1 ***Quillen*** | N | Y | N | Y | N | Y | Y | Y |
| 2 ***Duncan*** | N | N | Y | N | Y | Y | N | Y |
| 3 Lloyd | N | Y | N | N | Y | N | Y | Y |
| 4 Cooper | Y | Y | Y | Y | Y | Y | N | Y |
| 5 Clement | N | Y | Y | Y | Y | Y | Y | Y |
| 6 Gordon | N | Y | N | N | Y | ? | Y | Y |
| 7 ***Sundquist*** | N | N | Y | N | N | Y | N | Y |
| 8 Tanner | N | Y | N | Y | Y | Y | N | Y |
| 9 Ford | Y | Y | N | Y | N | N | Y | N |
| **TEXAS** | | | | | | | | |
| 1 Chapman | N | Y | N | N | N | N | Y | Y |
| 2 Wilson | N | Y | N | N | ? | Y | Y | Y |
| 3 ***Johnson*** | N | N | ? | X | ? | ? | ? | ? |
| 4 Hall | N | Y | N | N | Y | Y | Y | N |
| 5 Bryant | Y | Y | N | N | N | Y | ? | ? |
| 6 ***Barton*** | N | N | N | N | Y | Y | N | Y |
| 7 ***Archer*** | ? | ? | ? | ? | ? | ? | ? | ? |
| 8 ***Fields*** | N | N | N | N | N | Y | N | Y |
| 9 Brooks | N | Y | N | N | N | Y | Y | N |
| 10 Pickle | N | Y | N | N | N | Y | N | Y |
| 11 Edwards | N | Y | N | Y | Y | Y | ? | Y |
| 12 Geren | N | Y | N | N | N | Y | N | Y |
| 13 Sarpalius | Y | Y | N | N | Y | Y | Y | N |
| 14 Laughlin | Y | Y | N | N | N | Y | Y | Y |
| 15 de la Garza | Y | Y | Y | Y | N | Y | Y | Y |
| 16 Coleman | N | Y | N | N | N | N | Y | N |
| 17 Stenholm | N | Y | N | N | Y | Y | N | Y |
| 18 Washington | Y | ? | N | Y | N | N | Y | N |
| 19 ***Combest*** | N | Y | N | N | Y | Y | N | Y |
| 20 Gonzalez | Y | Y | Y | N | N | Y | Y | N |
| 21 ***Smith*** | N | N | N | N | Y | Y | N | Y |
| 22 ***DeLay*** | N | N | N | N | N | Y | N | Y |
| 23 Bustamante | N | Y | N | Y | N | Y | Y | Y |
| 24 Frost | N | Y | N | N | N | N | Y | N |
| 25 Andrews | N | Y | N | N | Y | Y | N | Y |
| 26 ***Armey*** | N | N | N | N | Y | Y | N | Y |
| 27 Ortiz | Y | Y | N | Y | N | Y | Y | Y |
| **UTAH** | | | | | | | | |
| 1 ***Hansen*** | N | N | N | N | Y | Y | N | Y |
| 2 Owens | N | ? | N | Y | N | Y | N | ? |
| 3 Orton | N | Y | N | N | Y | Y | N | Y |
| **VERMONT** | | | | | | | | |
| AL *Sanders* | Y | Y | N | Y | Y | N | Y | N |
| **VIRGINIA** | | | | | | | | |
| 1 ***Bateman*** | N | Y | N | N | N | Y | N | Y |
| 2 Pickett | N | Y | Y | N | N | Y | N | Y |
| 3 ***Bliley*** | N | N | N | N | Y | Y | N | Y |
| 4 Sisisky | ? | N | N | N | Y | Y | N | Y |
| 5 Payne | N | Y | Y | N | N | Y | Y | Y |
| 6 Olin | N | Y | N | Y | N | Y | N | Y |
| 7 ***Allen*** | N | N | N | N | Y | Y | N | Y |
| 8 Moran | Y | Y | N | Y | N | Y | Y | Y |
| 9 Boucher | Y | Y | N | Y | N | Y | Y | Y |
| 10 ***Wolf*** | N | N | N | N | N | Y | N | Y |
| **WASHINGTON** | | | | | | | | |
| 1 ***Miller*** | N | N | N | N | N | Y | N | Y |
| 2 Swift | Y | Y | Y | Y | N | N | Y | N |
| 3 Unsoeld | Y | Y | N | Y | N | N | Y | ? |
| 4 ***Morrison*** | N | N | N | N | N | Y | Y | ? |
| 5 Foley | | | | | | | | |
| 6 Dicks | N | Y | N | Y | N | Y | N | Y |
| 7 McDermott | Y | Y | N | Y | N | N | Y | Y |
| 8 ***Chandler*** | N | Y | N | N | Y | Y | N | Y |
| **WEST VIRGINIA** | | | | | | | | |
| 1 Mollohan | Y | Y | N | N | N | N | Y | Y |
| 2 Staggers | Y | Y | N | Y | N | N | Y | N |
| 3 Wise | Y | Y | N | Y | N | N | Y | N |
| 4 Rahall | N | Y | N | Y | N | N | Y | N |
| **WISCONSIN** | | | | | | | | |
| 1 Aspin | N | Y | N | Y | Y | Y | Y | Y |
| 2 ***Klug*** | N | N | N | N | Y | Y | N | Y |
| 3 ***Gunderson*** | N | N | N | N | Y | Y | Y | Y |
| 4 Kleczka | Y | Y | N | Y | N | N | Y | Y |
| 5 Moody | Y | Y | N | Y | Y | N | Y | ? |
| 6 ***Petri*** | N | Y | Y | N | Y | Y | Y | Y |
| 7 Obey | Y | Y | N | N | N | N | Y | N |
| 8 ***Roth*** | N | N | N | N | Y | Y | Y | Y |
| 9 ***Sensenbrenner*** | N | N | Y | N | Y | Y | N | Y |
| **WYOMING** | | | | | | | | |
| AL ***Thomas*** | N | N | N | N | N | Y | N | Y |

Southern states - Ala., Ark., Fla., Ga., Ky., La., Miss., N.C., Okla., S.C., Tenn., Texas, Va.
Omitted votes are quorum calls, which CQ does not include in its vote charts.

## KEY

| | |
|---|---|
| Y | Voted for (yea). |
| # | Paired for. |
| + | Announced for. |
| N | Voted against (nay). |
| X | Paired against. |
| − | Announced against. |
| P | Voted "present." |
| C | Voted "present" to avoid possible conflict of interest. |
| ? | Did not vote or otherwise make a position known. |

**Democrats**  ***Republicans***
*Independent*

**284. HR 5518. Fiscal 1993 Transportation Appropriations/Passage.** Passage of the bill to provide $13 billion in new budget authority for the Department of Transportation and related agencies in fiscal 1993. Passed 306-74: R 83-66; D 222-8 (ND 152-6, SD 70-2); I 1-0, July 9, 1992. A "nay" was a vote in support of the president's position.

**285. H J Res 502. Disapproval of MFN for China in 1992.** Passage of the joint resolution to disapprove President Bush's waiver of the Jackson-Vanik amendment to the 1974 trade act with respect to China in 1992. Passed 258-135: R 76-79; D 181-56 (ND 121-41, SD 60-15); I 1-0, July 21, 1992. A "nay" was a vote in support of the president's position.

**286. HR 5318. Conditional MFN for China in 1993.** Passage of the bill to prohibit the president from waiving the Jackson-Vanik amendment to the 1974 trade act for Chinese state-owned enterprises in 1993 unless he certified that China had released and accounted for all prisoners from the Tiananmen Square demonstrations in 1989 and had made significant progress in resolving concerns over human rights violations, trade violations and weapons non-proliferation. Passed 339-62: R 112-47; D 226-15 (ND 157-7, SD 69-8); I 1-0, July 21, 1992. A "nay" was a vote in support of the president's position.

**287. HR 2637. Waste Isolation Pilot Plant Land Withdrawal/Transuranic Radioactive Waste Disposal.** Richardson, D-N.M., amendment to prohibit testing the disposal of transuranic radioactive waste at the Waste Isolation Pilot Plant in southeastern New Mexico until the Environmental Protection Agency certified that the plant was in compliance with regulations regarding the handling and disposal of radioactive wastes. Rejected 148-253: R 26-132; D 121-121 (ND 96-69, SD 25-52); I 1-0, July 21, 1992.

**288. HR 2637. Waste Isolation Pilot Plant Land Withdrawal/Line-Item Veto.** Walker, R-Pa., amendment to give the president the line-item veto for appropriations concerning the Waste Isolation Pilot Plant program. Rejected 144-248: R 135-20; D 9-227 (ND 2-162, SD 7-65); I 0-1, July 21, 1992.

**289. HR 2637. Waste Isolation Pilot Plant Land Withdrawal/Passage.** Passage of the bill to authorize the transfer from public use of federal land managed by the Bureau of Land Management in southeastern New Mexico to the Department of Energy for the Waste Isolation Pilot Plant for the disposal of transuranic radioactive waste. Passed 382-10: R 151-6; D 230-4 (ND 158-4, SD 72-0); I 1-0, July 21, 1992.

**290. HR 5503. Fiscal 1993 Interior Appropriations/Order Previous Question.** Gordon, D-Tenn., motion to order the previous question (thus limiting debate and the possibility of amendment) on adoption of the rule (H Res 517) to govern floor consideration of the bill to provide $12.7 billion in new budget authority for the Department of the Interior and related agencies in fiscal 1993. Motion agreed to 236-171: R 0-159; D 235-12 (ND 165-6, SD 70-6); I 1-0, July 22, 1992.

**291. HR 5503. Fiscal 1993 Interior Appropriations/Rule.** Adoption of the rule (H Res 517) to govern floor consideration of the bill to provide $12.7 billion in new budget authority for the Department of the Interior and related agencies in fiscal 1993. Adopted 255-154: R 8-152; D 246-2 (ND 170-2, SD 76-0); I 1-0, July 22, 1992.

| | 284 | 285 | 286 | 287 | 288 | 289 | 290 | 291 |
|---|---|---|---|---|---|---|---|---|
| **ALABAMA** | | | | | | | | |
| 1 *Callahan* | Y | N | N | N | Y | Y | N | N |
| 2 *Dickinson* | Y | N | Y | N | ? | Y | N | N |
| 3 Browder | Y | Y | Y | N | N | Y | Y | Y |
| 4 Bevill | Y | Y | Y | N | N | Y | Y | Y |
| 5 Cramer | Y | Y | Y | N | N | Y | Y | Y |
| 6 Erdreich | Y | Y | Y | N | N | Y | Y | Y |
| 7 Harris | Y | Y | Y | N | N | Y | Y | Y |
| **ALASKA** | | | | | | | | |
| AL *Young* | Y | Y | N | N | N | Y | N | N |
| **ARIZONA** | | | | | | | | |
| 1 *Rhodes* | Y | Y | Y | N | Y | Y | N | N |
| 2 Pastor | Y | Y | Y | N | Y | Y | Y | Y |
| 3 *Stump* | N | N | N | N | Y | N | N | N |
| 4 *Kyl* | N | Y | Y | N | Y | N | N | N |
| 5 *Kolbe* | Y | N | N | N | Y | Y | N | N |
| **ARKANSAS** | | | | | | | | |
| 1 Alexander | Y | Y | Y | N | Y | N | ? | Y |
| 2 Thornton | Y | Y | Y | N | N | Y | Y | Y |
| 3 *Hammerschmidt* | N | N | N | N | Y | Y | N | N |
| 4 Anthony | Y | Y | Y | N | N | Y | Y | Y |
| **CALIFORNIA** | | | | | | | | |
| 1 *Riggs* | Y | Y | Y | N | Y | Y | N | N |
| 2 *Herger* | Y | Y | Y | N | Y | N | Y | Y |
| 3 Matsui | Y | N | N | N | N | Y | Y | Y |
| 4 Fazio | Y | N | Y | N | N | Y | Y | Y |
| 5 Pelosi | Y | Y | Y | N | Y | N | Y | Y |
| 6 Boxer | ? | ? | ? | Y | N | Y | Y | Y |
| 7 Miller | Y | ? | N | N | N | Y | Y | ? |
| 8 Dellums | Y | Y | Y | ? | N | Y | Y | Y |
| 9 Stark | ? | Y | Y | Y | N | Y | Y | Y |
| 10 Edwards | Y | Y | Y | N | N | Y | Y | Y |
| 11 Lantos | Y | Y | Y | N | Y | N | Y | Y |
| 12 *Campbell* | N | N | N | N | Y | Y | N | N |
| 13 Mineta | Y | Y | N | N | N | Y | Y | Y |
| 14 *Doolittle* | N | Y | N | N | N | Y | N | N |
| 15 Condit | N | Y | N | N | N | Y | N | Y |
| 16 Panetta | ? | Y | Y | N | Y | Y | Y | Y |
| 17 Dooley | Y | Y | Y | N | N | Y | Y | Y |
| 18 Lehman | Y | ? | Y | N | N | Y | Y | Y |
| 19 *Lagomarsino* | N | N | Y | N | Y | Y | N | N |
| 20 *Thomas* | N | N | N | N | Y | Y | N | N |
| 21 *Gallegly* | N | Y | N | Y | N | Y | N | N |
| 22 *Moorhead* | N | N | Y | N | Y | N | N | N |
| 23 Beilenson | Y | Y | Y | N | Y | N | Y | Y |
| 24 Waxman | Y | Y | Y | N | Y | N | Y | Y |
| 25 Roybal | Y | Y | Y | N | N | Y | Y | Y |
| 26 Berman | Y | Y | Y | N | ? | Y | Y | Y |
| 27 Levine | Y | Y | Y | N | Y | Y | Y | Y |
| 28 Dixon | Y | Y | Y | N | N | Y | Y | Y |
| 29 Waters | Y | Y | Y | N | N | Y | Y | Y |
| 30 Martinez | Y | Y | Y | N | N | Y | Y | Y |
| 31 Dymally | Y | N | Y | N | N | Y | Y | Y |
| 32 Anderson | Y | N | Y | N | N | Y | Y | Y |
| 33 *Dreier* | N | N | N | N | Y | Y | N | N |
| 34 Torres | Y | Y | Y | N | Y | N | Y | Y |
| 35 Lewis | X | N | Y | N | Y | Y | N | N |
| 36 Brown | Y | ? | Y | N | N | Y | Y | Y |
| 37 *McCandless* | Y | Y | N | N | Y | Y | N | N |
| 38 *Dornan* | N | ? | Y | N | Y | N | N | N |
| 39 *Dannemeyer* | N | ? | Y | N | Y | N | N | N |
| 40 *Cox* | N | Y | N | Y | Y | Y | ? | ? |
| 41 *Lowery* | X | N | Y | N | Y | Y | ? | ? |

| | 284 | 285 | 286 | 287 | 288 | 289 | 290 | 291 |
|---|---|---|---|---|---|---|---|---|
| 42 *Rohrabacher* | N | Y | N | Y | N | Y | N | N |
| 43 *Packard* | N | N | N | Y | Y | Y | ? | N |
| 44 *Cunningham* | N | Y | N | Y | Y | Y | N | N |
| 45 *Hunter* | N | Y | Y | N | Y | N | N | N |
| **COLORADO** | | | | | | | | |
| 1 Schroeder | Y | Y | Y | Y | N | Y | Y | Y |
| 2 Skaggs | Y | N | Y | N | N | Y | Y | Y |
| 3 Campbell | ? | ? | ? | N | N | Y | Y | Y |
| 4 *Allard* | N | N | N | N | Y | N | N | N |
| 5 *Hefley* | N | Y | N | N | Y | N | N | N |
| 6 *Schaefer* | Y | Y | N | N | Y | Y | N | N |
| **CONNECTICUT** | | | | | | | | |
| 1 Kennelly | Y | N | Y | N | Y | Y | Y | Y |
| 2 Gejdenson | Y | Y | Y | N | N | Y | Y | Y |
| 3 DeLauro | Y | Y | Y | N | Y | Y | Y | Y |
| 4 *Shays* | N | N | Y | N | Y | N | Y | Y |
| 5 *Franks* | N | Y | Y | ? | ? | ? | N | N |
| 6 *Johnson* | Y | N | N | N | N | Y | N | N |
| **DELAWARE** | | | | | | | | |
| AL Carper | Y | Y | Y | N | N | Y | Y | Y |
| **FLORIDA** | | | | | | | | |
| 1 Hutto | Y | Y | Y | N | N | Y | Y | Y |
| 2 Peterson | + | + | + | − | + | + | + | + |
| 3 Bennett | Y | Y | Y | N | Y | Y | Y | Y |
| 4 *James* | N | Y | Y | N | Y | N | N | N |
| 5 *McCollum* | Y | Y | Y | N | Y | N | N | N |
| 6 *Stearns* | N | Y | Y | N | Y | Y | N | N |
| 7 Gibbons | Y | N | Y | Y | N | Y | Y | Y |
| 8 *Young* | Y | Y | Y | N | N | Y | N | N |
| 9 *Bilirakis* | Y | N | Y | N | N | Y | N | N |
| 10 *Ireland* | N | X | N | ? | ? | ? | N | N |
| 11 Bacchus | Y | Y | Y | N | N | Y | Y | Y |
| 12 *Lewis* | N | Y | Y | N | Y | Y | N | N |
| 13 *Goss* | N | N | N | N | Y | N | N | N |
| 14 Johnston | Y | ? | ? | N | N | Y | Y | Y |
| 15 *Shaw* | Y | N | N | N | Y | Y | N | N |
| 16 Smith | ? | Y | Y | N | N | Y | Y | Y |
| 17 Lehman | Y | Y | Y | ? | ? | Y | Y | Y |
| 18 *Ros−Lehtinen* | Y | Y | Y | N | Y | Y | N | N |
| 19 Fascell | Y | Y | Y | N | Y | Y | Y | Y |
| **GEORGIA** | | | | | | | | |
| 1 Thomas | Y | Y | Y | N | N | Y | Y | Y |
| 2 Hatcher | ? | ? | ? | ? | ? | ? | ? | ? |
| 3 Ray | ? | ? | ? | ? | ? | ? | ? | ? |
| 4 Jones | ? | ? | ? | ? | ? | ? | ? | ? |
| 5 Lewis | Y | ? | ? | ? | ? | ? | ? | ? |
| 6 *Gingrich* | Y | ? | ? | ? | ? | ? | ? | ? |
| 7 Darden | Y | Y | Y | N | N | Y | Y | Y |
| 8 Rowland | ? | Y | Y | N | N | Y | Y | Y |
| 9 Jenkins | Y | Y | N | N | Y | Y | Y | Y |
| 10 Barnard | # | Y | Y | N | N | Y | Y | Y |
| **HAWAII** | | | | | | | | |
| 1 Abercrombie | Y | Y | Y | N | N | Y | Y | N |
| 2 Mink | Y | Y | Y | N | Y | N | Y | Y |
| **IDAHO** | | | | | | | | |
| 1 LaRocco | Y | N | Y | N | N | Y | Y | Y |
| 2 Stallings | Y | N | Y | N | N | Y | Y | Y |
| **ILLINOIS** | | | | | | | | |
| 1 Hayes | ? | Y | Y | Y | N | Y | Y | Y |
| 2 Savage | ? | ? | ? | Y | N | Y | Y | Y |
| 3 Russo | ? | Y | Y | N | Y | ? | ? | ? |
| 4 Sangmeister | Y | Y | Y | N | N | Y | Y | Y |
| 5 Lipinski | ? | ? | ? | ? | ? | ? | ? | Y |
| 6 *Hyde* | ? | ? | ? | ? | ? | ? | ? | ? |
| 7 Collins | Y | Y | Y | N | Y | Y | Y | Y |
| 8 Rostenkowski | ? | N | Y | N | N | Y | Y | Y |
| 9 Yates | Y | Y | Y | N | Y | N | Y | Y |
| 10 *Porter* | N | Y | Y | Y | Y | Y | N | N |
| 11 Annunzio | Y | Y | Y | N | N | Y | Y | Y |
| 12 *Crane* | N | N | N | N | Y | N | N | N |
| 13 *Fawell* | N | N | N | Y | Y | N | N | N |
| 14 *Hastert* | N | N | N | N | Y | N | N | N |
| 15 *Ewing* | N | N | N | N | Y | Y | N | N |
| 16 Cox | Y | Y | N | N | Y | Y | Y | Y |
| 17 Evans | Y | Y | Y | Y | N | Y | Y | Y |
| 18 *Michel* | Y | N | N | N | N | Y | N | N |
| 19 Bruce | Y | Y | Y | N | N | Y | Y | Y |
| 20 Durbin | Y | ? | ? | ? | ? | ? | Y | ? |
| 21 Costello | Y | Y | Y | N | Y | N | Y | Y |
| 22 Poshard | Y | Y | Y | N | Y | N | Y | Y |
| **INDIANA** | | | | | | | | |
| 1 Visclosky | Y | Y | Y | N | Y | Y | Y | Y |
| 2 Sharp | Y | N | Y | N | N | Y | Y | Y |
| 3 Roemer | Y | N | N | N | N | Y | Y | Y |

ND Northern Democrats    SD Southern Democrats

| | 284 | 285 | 286 | 287 | 288 | 289 | 290 | 291 |
|---|---|---|---|---|---|---|---|---|
| 4 Long | Y | Y | Y | Y | N | Y | Y | Y |
| 5 Jontz | Y | Y | Y | Y | N | N | Y | Y |
| 6 ***Burton*** | N | Y | Y | N | Y | Y | N | N |
| 7 ***Myers*** | Y | Y | N | N | N | Y | N | N |
| 8 McCloskey | Y | ? | ? | ? | ? | ? | Y | Y |
| 9 Hamilton | Y | N | Y | N | N | Y | Y | Y |
| 10 Jacobs | Y | N | Y | N | N | Y | N | N |
| **IOWA** | | | | | | | | |
| 1 ***Leach*** | Y | N | N | Y | Y | Y | N | N |
| 2 ***Nussle*** | N | N | N | N | Y | Y | N | N |
| 3 Nagle | Y | N | Y | Y | N | Y | Y | Y |
| 4 Smith | Y | N | N | N | N | Y | Y | Y |
| 5 ***Lightfoot*** | ? | N | N | N | Y | Y | N | N |
| 6 ***Grandy*** | N | N | N | N | N | Y | N | N |
| **KANSAS** | | | | | | | | |
| 1 ***Roberts*** | N | N | N | N | Y | Y | N | N |
| 2 Slattery | N | N | Y | N | N | Y | Y | ? |
| 3 ***Meyers*** | Y | N | Y | Y | Y | Y | N | N |
| 4 Glickman | Y | N | Y | Y | N | Y | Y | Y |
| 5 ***Nichols*** | N | N | N | N | Y | Y | N | N |
| **KENTUCKY** | | | | | | | | |
| 1 Hubbard | ? | Y | Y | N | Y | Y | Y | Y |
| 2 Natcher | Y | N | Y | N | N | Y | Y | Y |
| 3 Mazzoli | Y | Y | Y | Y | N | Y | Y | Y |
| 4 ***Bunning*** | Y | Y | Y | N | Y | Y | N | N |
| 5 ***Rogers*** | Y | Y | Y | N | N | Y | N | N |
| 6 ***Hopkins*** | N | Y | Y | N | Y | Y | N | N |
| 7 Perkins | Y | ? | ? | ? | ? | ? | ? | ? |
| **LOUISIANA** | | | | | | | | |
| 1 ***Livingston*** | N | N | N | N | Y | Y | N | N |
| 2 Jefferson | ? | Y | Y | Y | N | Y | Y | Y |
| 3 Tauzin | Y | Y | Y | N | Y | Y | N | Y |
| 4 ***McCrery*** | ? | N | N | N | Y | Y | N | N |
| 5 Huckaby | ? | N | Y | N | N | Y | Y | Y |
| 6 ***Baker*** | ? | N | N | N | Y | Y | N | N |
| 7 Hayes | ? | Y | Y | N | N | Y | Y | Y |
| 8 ***Holloway*** | N | Y | Y | N | Y | Y | N | N |
| **MAINE** | | | | | | | | |
| 1 Andrews | Y | Y | Y | Y | N | Y | Y | Y |
| 2 ***Snowe*** | Y | Y | Y | Y | Y | Y | N | N |
| **MARYLAND** | | | | | | | | |
| 1 ***Gilchrest*** | Y | Y | Y | N | Y | Y | N | N |
| 2 ***Bentley*** | Y | Y | Y | N | N | Y | N | N |
| 3 Cardin | Y | Y | Y | N | N | Y | Y | Y |
| 4 McMillen | Y | Y | Y | Y | N | Y | Y | Y |
| 5 Hoyer | Y | Y | Y | N | N | Y | Y | Y |
| 6 Byron | Y | Y | Y | N | N | Y | ? | ? |
| 7 Mfume | Y | Y | Y | Y | N | Y | Y | Y |
| 8 ***Morella*** | Y | Y | Y | Y | N | Y | N | N |
| **MASSACHUSETTS** | | | | | | | | |
| 1 Olver | Y | Y | Y | Y | N | Y | Y | Y |
| 2 Neal | Y | Y | Y | Y | N | Y | Y | Y |
| 3 Early | ? | Y | Y | N | N | Y | Y | Y |
| 4 Frank | Y | Y | Y | Y | N | Y | Y | Y |
| 5 Atkins | Y | ? | ? | ? | ? | ? | Y | Y |
| 6 Mavroules | Y | Y | Y | N | N | Y | Y | Y |
| 7 Markey | Y | Y | Y | Y | N | Y | Y | Y |
| 8 Kennedy | Y | Y | Y | Y | N | Y | Y | Y |
| 9 Moakley | Y | Y | Y | N | N | Y | Y | Y |
| 10 Studds | Y | ? | Y | Y | N | Y | Y | Y |
| 11 Donnelly | Y | Y | Y | N | N | Y | Y | Y |
| **MICHIGAN** | | | | | | | | |
| 1 Conyers | Y | ? | ? | ? | ? | ? | Y | Y |
| 2 ***Pursell*** | X | Y | Y | N | Y | Y | N | N |
| 3 Wolpe | Y | Y | Y | Y | N | N | Y | Y |
| 4 ***Upton*** | Y | Y | Y | N | Y | Y | N | N |
| 5 ***Henry*** | Y | Y | Y | N | N | Y | N | N |
| 6 Carr | Y | ? | Y | N | N | Y | Y | Y |
| 7 Kildee | Y | Y | Y | Y | N | Y | Y | Y |
| 8 Traxler | ? | Y | Y | ? | ? | ? | ? | ? |
| 9 ***Vander Jagt*** | Y | N | Y | N | Y | Y | N | N |
| 10 ***Camp*** | Y | N | Y | N | Y | Y | N | N |
| 11 ***Davis*** | Y | Y | ? | N | Y | Y | N | N |
| 12 Bonior | Y | Y | Y | Y | N | Y | Y | Y |
| 13 Collins | Y | Y | Y | Y | N | Y | Y | Y |
| 14 Hertel | Y | Y | Y | Y | N | Y | Y | Y |
| 15 Ford | Y | Y | Y | N | N | Y | Y | Y |
| 16 Dingell | Y | N | Y | N | N | Y | Y | Y |
| 17 Levin | Y | Y | Y | Y | N | Y | Y | Y |
| 18 ***Broomfield*** | Y | N | Y | N | Y | Y | N | N |
| **MINNESOTA** | | | | | | | | |
| 1 Penny | N | N | Y | N | N | Y | Y | Y |
| 2 ***Weber*** | N | N | Y | N | Y | Y | N | N |
| 3 ***Ramstad*** | N | Y | Y | Y | Y | Y | N | N |
| 4 Vento | Y | Y | Y | Y | ? | ? | Y | Y |

| | 284 | 285 | 286 | 287 | 288 | 289 | 290 | 291 |
|---|---|---|---|---|---|---|---|---|
| 5 Sabo | Y | Y | Y | Y | N | Y | Y | Y |
| 6 Sikorski | Y | Y | Y | Y | N | Y | Y | Y |
| 7 Peterson | Y | N | N | N | N | Y | Y | Y |
| 8 Oberstar | Y | Y | Y | Y | N | Y | Y | Y |
| **MISSISSIPPI** | | | | | | | | |
| 1 Whitten | Y | ? | Y | N | N | Y | Y | Y |
| 2 Espy | Y | Y | Y | N | N | Y | Y | Y |
| 3 Montgomery | Y | N | N | N | N | Y | Y | Y |
| 4 Parker | Y | Y | Y | N | N | Y | N | Y |
| 5 Taylor | Y | Y | N | N | N | Y | Y | ? |
| **MISSOURI** | | | | | | | | |
| 1 Clay | Y | Y | Y | N | N | Y | Y | Y |
| 2 Horn | Y | Y | Y | N | N | Y | Y | Y |
| 3 Gephardt | Y | Y | Y | N | N | Y | ? | ? |
| 4 Skelton | ? | Y | Y | N | N | Y | Y | Y |
| 5 Wheat | Y | Y | Y | Y | N | Y | Y | Y |
| 6 ***Coleman*** | Y | Y | Y | N | Y | Y | N | N |
| 7 ***Hancock*** | N | N | N | N | Y | Y | N | N |
| 8 ***Emerson*** | Y | N | Y | N | Y | Y | X | X |
| 9 Volkmer | Y | N | Y | N | N | Y | Y | Y |
| **MONTANA** | | | | | | | | |
| 1 Williams | Y | N | Y | N | N | Y | ? | Y |
| 2 ***Marlenee*** | ? | N | N | N | Y | Y | N | N |
| **NEBRASKA** | | | | | | | | |
| 1 ***Bereuter*** | Y | N | Y | N | Y | Y | N | N |
| 2 Hoagland | Y | N | Y | N | N | Y | Y | Y |
| 3 ***Barrett*** | Y | N | N | N | Y | Y | N | N |
| **NEVADA** | | | | | | | | |
| 1 Bilbray | Y | Y | Y | Y | N | N | Y | Y |
| 2 ***Vucanovich*** | N | N | N | Y | Y | N | N | N |
| **NEW HAMPSHIRE** | | | | | | | | |
| 1 ***Zeliff*** | N | Y | Y | N | Y | Y | N | N |
| 2 Swett | Y | Y | Y | Y | N | Y | Y | Y |
| **NEW JERSEY** | | | | | | | | |
| 1 Andrews | Y | Y | Y | Y | N | Y | Y | Y |
| 2 Hughes | Y | N | Y | Y | N | Y | Y | Y |
| 3 Pallone | N | Y | Y | Y | N | Y | Y | Y |
| 4 ***Smith*** | Y | Y | Y | Y | Y | Y | N | N |
| 5 ***Roukema*** | # | # | ? | N | N | Y | N | N |
| 6 Dwyer | Y | Y | Y | N | N | Y | Y | Y |
| 7 ***Rinaldo*** | Y | N | Y | Y | Y | Y | N | N |
| 8 Roe | Y | N | ? | ? | ? | ? | Y | Y |
| 9 Torricelli | Y | ? | ? | ? | ? | ? | Y | Y |
| 10 Payne | Y | Y | Y | Y | N | Y | Y | Y |
| 11 ***Gallo*** | N | N | Y | N | Y | Y | N | N |
| 12 ***Zimmer*** | N | Y | Y | Y | Y | Y | N | N |
| 13 ***Saxton*** | N | N | Y | N | Y | Y | N | N |
| 14 Guarini | Y | N | Y | Y | N | Y | Y | Y |
| **NEW MEXICO** | | | | | | | | |
| 1 ***Schiff*** | Y | Y | Y | N | N | Y | N | N |
| 2 ***Skeen*** | Y | Y | Y | N | N | Y | N | N |
| 3 Richardson | Y | Y | Y | Y | N | N | Y | Y |
| **NEW YORK** | | | | | | | | |
| 1 Hochbrueckner | Y | Y | Y | Y | N | Y | Y | Y |
| 2 Downey | Y | Y | Y | Y | N | Y | Y | Y |
| 3 Mrazek | Y | ? | ? | ? | N | Y | Y | Y |
| 4 ***Lent*** | ? | N | Y | N | ? | ? | N | N |
| 5 ***McGrath*** | Y | N | Y | N | Y | Y | N | N |
| 6 Flake | Y | Y | Y | Y | N | Y | Y | Y |
| 7 Ackerman | # | Y | Y | ? | ? | ? | Y | Y |
| 8 Scheuer | Y | N | Y | Y | N | Y | Y | Y |
| 9 Manton | ? | Y | Y | N | N | Y | Y | Y |
| 10 Schumer | Y | Y | Y | Y | N | Y | Y | Y |
| 11 Towns | ? | ? | ? | ? | ? | ? | # | # |
| 12 Owens | Y | Y | Y | Y | N | Y | Y | Y |
| 13 Solarz | # | N | Y | Y | ? | ? | Y | Y |
| 14 ***Molinari*** | Y | Y | Y | N | Y | Y | N | N |
| 15 ***Green*** | Y | N | Y | Y | N | Y | N | Y |
| 16 Rangel | Y | Y | Y | Y | N | Y | Y | Y |
| 17 Weiss | ? | Y | Y | — | N | Y | Y | Y |
| 18 Serrano | Y | Y | Y | Y | N | Y | Y | Y |
| 19 Engel | Y | Y | Y | Y | N | Y | Y | Y |
| 20 Lowey | Y | Y | Y | Y | N | Y | Y | Y |
| 21 ***Fish*** | Y | Y | Y | Y | Y | Y | N | Y |
| 22 ***Gilman*** | Y | Y | Y | Y | N | N | N | Y |
| 23 McNulty | Y | Y | Y | N | N | Y | Y | Y |
| 24 ***Solomon*** | N | Y | N | Y | Y | Y | N | N |
| 25 ***Boehlert*** | Y | Y | Y | Y | N | Y | N | Y |
| 26 ***Martin*** | Y | N | Y | N | N | Y | N | N |
| 27 ***Walsh*** | Y | Y | Y | Y | N | Y | N | N |
| 28 McHugh | Y | Y | Y | Y | N | Y | Y | Y |
| 29 ***Horton*** | Y | Y | Y | ? | ? | ? | N | N |
| 30 Slaughter | Y | Y | Y | Y | N | Y | Y | Y |
| 31 ***Paxon*** | Y | Y | Y | N | Y | Y | N | N |

| | 284 | 285 | 286 | 287 | 288 | 289 | 290 | 291 |
|---|---|---|---|---|---|---|---|---|
| 32 LaFalce | ? | Y | + | + | — | + | Y | Y |
| 33 Nowak | Y | N | Y | Y | N | Y | Y | Y |
| 34 ***Houghton*** | Y | N | Y | N | Y | Y | N | N |
| **NORTH CAROLINA** | | | | | | | | |
| 1 Jones | Y | Y | Y | Y | N | Y | Y | Y |
| 2 Valentine | Y | Y | Y | Y | N | Y | Y | Y |
| 3 Lancaster | Y | ? | Y | N | N | Y | Y | Y |
| 4 Price | Y | Y | Y | N | N | Y | Y | Y |
| 5 Neal | Y | Y | Y | N | N | Y | Y | Y |
| 6 ***Coble*** | N | Y | Y | N | Y | Y | N | N |
| 7 Rose | Y | Y | Y | Y | N | Y | Y | Y |
| 8 Hefner | ? | Y | Y | N | N | Y | Y | Y |
| 9 ***McMillan*** | N | Y | Y | N | Y | Y | N | N |
| 10 ***Ballenger*** | N | Y | Y | N | Y | Y | N | N |
| 11 ***Taylor*** | Y | Y | Y | N | Y | Y | N | N |
| **NORTH DAKOTA** | | | | | | | | |
| AL Dorgan | N | N | Y | Y | Y | Y | N | Y |
| **OHIO** | | | | | | | | |
| 1 Luken | N | N | Y | N | N | Y | Y | Y |
| 2 ***Gradison*** | N | N | N | N | Y | Y | N | N |
| 3 Hall | Y | Y | Y | ? | ? | ? | ? | Y |
| 4 ***Oxley*** | N | N | N | N | Y | Y | N | N |
| 5 ***Gillmor*** | Y | N | Y | Y | Y | Y | N | N |
| 6 ***McEwen*** | N | ? | ? | N | Y | Y | N | N |
| 7 ***Hobson*** | Y | N | Y | N | Y | Y | N | N |
| 8 ***Boehner*** | N | N | N | N | Y | Y | N | N |
| 9 Kaptur | Y | Y | Y | N | N | Y | Y | Y |
| 10 ***Miller*** | N | N | Y | N | Y | Y | N | N |
| 11 Eckart | Y | Y | Y | N | ? | ? | Y | Y |
| 12 ***Kasich*** | N | Y | Y | N | ? | Y | N | N |
| 13 Pease | Y | N | Y | N | N | Y | Y | Y |
| 14 Sawyer | Y | Y | Y | N | N | Y | Y | Y |
| 15 ***Wylie*** | N | N | N | N | Y | Y | N | N |
| 16 ***Regula*** | Y | N | Y | N | Y | Y | N | Y |
| 17 Traficant | Y | Y | Y | N | N | Y | Y | Y |
| 18 Applegate | ? | Y | Y | Y | N | Y | Y | Y |
| 19 Feighan | Y | ? | ? | ? | ? | ? | ? | ? |
| 20 Oakar | Y | Y | Y | Y | N | Y | Y | Y |
| 21 Stokes | Y | Y | Y | N | N | Y | Y | Y |
| **OKLAHOMA** | | | | | | | | |
| 1 ***Inhofe*** | N | N | Y | N | Y | Y | N | N |
| 2 Synar | # | Y | Y | N | N | Y | Y | Y |
| 3 Brewster | Y | N | Y | N | N | Y | Y | ? |
| 4 McCurdy | Y | Y | Y | N | N | Y | Y | Y |
| 5 ***Edwards*** | ? | Y | Y | N | Y | Y | N | N |
| 6 English | Y | N | Y | Y | N | Y | Y | Y |
| **OREGON** | | | | | | | | |
| 1 AuCoin | Y | N | Y | Y | N | Y | ? | Y |
| 2 ***Smith*** | N | N | N | N | Y | Y | N | N |
| 3 Wyden | Y | N | Y | Y | N | Y | Y | Y |
| 4 DeFazio | Y | Y | Y | Y | N | Y | ? | Y |
| 5 Kopetski | Y | N | N | Y | N | Y | Y | Y |
| **PENNSYLVANIA** | | | | | | | | |
| 1 Foglietta | Y | Y | Y | Y | N | Y | Y | Y |
| 2 Blackwell | Y | Y | Y | Y | N | Y | Y | Y |
| 3 Borski | Y | Y | Y | N | N | Y | Y | Y |
| 4 Kolter | Y | ? | ? | ? | ? | ? | ? | Y |
| 5 ***Schulze*** | X | Y | Y | N | Y | Y | N | N |
| 6 Yatron | ? | Y | Y | N | N | Y | Y | Y |
| 7 ***Weldon*** | Y | Y | Y | Y | Y | Y | N | N |
| 8 Kostmayer | Y | Y | Y | N | N | Y | Y | Y |
| 9 ***Shuster*** | Y | N | N | N | Y | Y | N | N |
| 10 ***McDade*** | Y | N | Y | N | N | Y | N | Y |
| 11 Kanjorski | Y | Y | Y | N | N | Y | Y | Y |
| 12 Murtha | Y | Y | Y | N | N | ? | Y | Y |
| 13 ***Coughlin*** | Y | ? | ? | ? | ? | ? | ? | ? |
| 14 Coyne | Y | Y | Y | Y | N | Y | Y | Y |
| 15 ***Ritter*** | Y | Y | Y | N | Y | Y | N | N |
| 16 ***Walker*** | N | Y | Y | N | Y | Y | N | N |
| 17 ***Gekas*** | Y | Y | Y | N | Y | Y | N | N |
| 18 ***Santorum*** | Y | N | Y | N | Y | Y | N | N |
| 19 ***Goodling*** | Y | N | Y | Y | Y | Y | N | N |
| 20 Gaydos | ? | Y | Y | N | N | Y | N | ? |
| 21 ***Ridge*** | X | Y | Y | ? | ? | ? | N | N |
| 22 Murphy | Y | N | Y | Y | Y | Y | Y | Y |
| 23 ***Clinger*** | Y | N | N | N | Y | Y | N | N |
| **RHODE ISLAND** | | | | | | | | |
| 1 ***Machtley*** | Y | ? | Y | Y | Y | Y | N | Y |
| 2 Reed | Y | N | Y | Y | N | Y | Y | Y |
| **SOUTH CAROLINA** | | | | | | | | |
| 1 ***Ravenel*** | ? | Y | Y | N | Y | Y | N | N |
| 2 ***Spence*** | Y | Y | Y | N | Y | Y | N | N |
| 3 Derrick | Y | Y | Y | N | N | Y | Y | Y |
| 4 Patterson | Y | Y | Y | N | N | Y | Y | Y |
| 5 Spratt | Y | Y | Y | N | N | Y | Y | Y |
| 6 Tallon | Y | Y | Y | N | ? | ? | ? | ? |

| | 284 | 285 | 286 | 287 | 288 | 289 | 290 | 291 |
|---|---|---|---|---|---|---|---|---|
| **SOUTH DAKOTA** | | | | | | | | |
| AL Johnson | Y | N | N | Y | N | Y | Y | Y |
| **TENNESSEE** | | | | | | | | |
| 1 ***Quillen*** | Y | Y | Y | N | Y | Y | N | Y |
| 2 ***Duncan*** | Y | Y | Y | N | Y | Y | N | N |
| 3 Lloyd | Y | Y | Y | N | N | Y | Y | Y |
| 4 Cooper | Y | Y | Y | N | N | Y | Y | Y |
| 5 Clement | Y | Y | Y | N | N | Y | Y | Y |
| 6 Gordon | Y | Y | Y | N | N | Y | Y | Y |
| 7 ***Sundquist*** | Y | N | Y | N | Y | Y | N | N |
| 8 Tanner | Y | Y | Y | N | N | Y | Y | Y |
| 9 Ford | Y | ? | ? | ? | ? | ? | ? | Y |
| **TEXAS** | | | | | | | | |
| 1 Chapman | Y | Y | Y | Y | N | Y | ? | Y |
| 2 Wilson | Y | Y | Y | Y | ? | ? | N | Y |
| 3 ***Johnson*** | X | N | N | Y | Y | Y | N | N |
| 4 Hall | Y | N | N | N | Y | Y | N | Y |
| 5 Bryant | ? | Y | Y | Y | N | Y | Y | Y |
| 6 ***Barton*** | N | Y | Y | N | Y | Y | N | N |
| 7 ***Archer*** | ? | N | N | N | Y | Y | N | N |
| 8 ***Fields*** | N | ? | Y | N | Y | Y | N | N |
| 9 Brooks | Y | N | N | Y | N | Y | Y | ? |
| 10 Pickle | Y | N | Y | N | N | Y | Y | Y |
| 11 Edwards | Y | Y | Y | Y | N | Y | Y | Y |
| 12 Geren | Y | N | Y | Y | N | Y | Y | Y |
| 13 Sarpalius | Y | N | N | N | N | Y | Y | Y |
| 14 Laughlin | Y | Y | N | Y | N | Y | Y | Y |
| 15 de la Garza | Y | Y | Y | Y | N | Y | Y | Y |
| 16 Coleman | Y | Y | Y | Y | N | Y | Y | Y |
| 17 Stenholm | N | N | N | N | N | Y | Y | Y |
| 18 Washington | Y | Y | Y | Y | ? | ? | Y | Y |
| 19 ***Combest*** | N | Y | Y | N | Y | Y | N | N |
| 20 Gonzalez | Y | Y | Y | Y | N | Y | Y | Y |
| 21 ***Smith*** | N | Y | Y | N | Y | Y | N | N |
| 22 ***DeLay*** | Y | N | N | N | Y | Y | N | N |
| 23 Bustamante | Y | Y | Y | Y | N | Y | Y | Y |
| 24 Frost | Y | Y | Y | Y | N | Y | Y | Y |
| 25 Andrews | Y | N | Y | N | N | Y | Y | Y |
| 26 ***Armey*** | N | N | N | N | Y | Y | N | N |
| 27 Ortiz | Y | Y | Y | Y | N | Y | Y | Y |
| **UTAH** | | | | | | | | |
| 1 ***Hansen*** | Y | N | N | N | N | Y | N | N |
| 2 Owens | ? | Y | ? | Y | N | Y | Y | Y |
| 3 Orton | Y | N | Y | N | N | Y | Y | Y |
| **VERMONT** | | | | | | | | |
| AL *Sanders* | Y | Y | Y | Y | N | Y | Y | Y |
| **VIRGINIA** | | | | | | | | |
| 1 ***Bateman*** | Y | N | N | N | Y | Y | N | N |
| 2 Pickett | N | N | N | N | N | Y | Y | Y |
| 3 ***Bliley*** | Y | Y | Y | N | Y | Y | N | N |
| 4 Sisisky | Y | Y | Y | N | ? | ? | Y | Y |
| 5 Payne | Y | N | Y | N | N | Y | Y | Y |
| 6 Olin | Y | Y | Y | N | N | Y | Y | Y |
| 7 ***Allen*** | Y | Y | Y | N | Y | Y | N | N |
| 8 Moran | Y | Y | Y | N | N | Y | Y | Y |
| 9 Boucher | Y | Y | Y | N | ? | ? | Y | Y |
| 10 ***Wolf*** | Y | Y | Y | N | Y | Y | N | N |
| **WASHINGTON** | | | | | | | | |
| 1 ***Miller*** | Y | N | Y | N | Y | Y | N | N |
| 2 Swift | Y | N | Y | N | N | Y | Y | Y |
| 3 Unsoeld | # | Y | Y | Y | N | Y | Y | Y |
| 4 ***Morrison*** | ? | ? | ? | ? | ? | ? | N | N |
| 5 Foley | | | | | | | | |
| 6 Dicks | ? | N | Y | N | N | Y | Y | Y |
| 7 McDermott | Y | N | N | Y | N | Y | Y | Y |
| 8 ***Chandler*** | Y | N | Y | N | Y | Y | N | N |
| **WEST VIRGINIA** | | | | | | | | |
| 1 Mollohan | Y | ? | Y | N | N | Y | Y | Y |
| 2 Staggers | Y | Y | Y | N | N | Y | Y | Y |
| 3 Wise | Y | ? | Y | N | N | Y | Y | Y |
| 4 Rahall | Y | Y | Y | Y | N | Y | Y | Y |
| **WISCONSIN** | | | | | | | | |
| 1 Aspin | Y | Y | Y | N | ? | ? | Y | Y |
| 2 ***Klug*** | Y | N | Y | Y | Y | Y | N | N |
| 3 ***Gunderson*** | N | Y | Y | Y | N | Y | N | N |
| 4 Kleczka | Y | Y | Y | N | N | Y | Y | Y |
| 5 Moody | Y | Y | Y | Y | N | Y | Y | Y |
| 6 ***Petri*** | N | N | Y | Y | Y | Y | N | N |
| 7 Obey | Y | Y | Y | Y | N | Y | Y | Y |
| 8 ***Roth*** | Y | Y | Y | N | Y | Y | N | N |
| 9 ***Sensenbrenner*** | N | Y | Y | Y | Y | N | N | N |
| **WYOMING** | | | | | | | | |
| AL ***Thomas*** | Y | N | Y | N | Y | Y | N | N |

Southern states - Ala., Ark., Fla., Ga., Ky., La., Miss., N.C., Okla., S.C., Tenn., Texas, Va.
Omitted votes are quorum calls, which CQ does not include in its vote charts.

## KEY

Y Voted for (yea).
\# Paired for.
+ Announced for.
N Voted against (nay).
X Paired against.
− Announced against.
P Voted "present."
C Voted "present" to avoid possible conflict of interest.
? Did not vote or otherwise make a position known.

*Democrats* **Republicans**
*Independent*

**292. H Res 518. House Post Office Investigation Report.** Adoption of the resolution to direct the House Administration Committee to transmit to the Committee on Standards of Official Conduct and the Justice Department the committee report and all records of the task force conducting an investigation of the House Post Office. Adopted 414-0: R 159-0; D 254-0 (ND 176-0, SD 78-0); I 1-0, July 22, 1992.

**293. H Res 519. Violations of Confidentiality in the House Post Office Investigation.** Rose, D-N.C., motion to table (kill) the Thomas, R-Calif., privileged resolution to direct the ethics committee to conduct an investigation into confidentiality violations during the House Administration Task Force's investigation. Motion agreed to 233-176: R 0-158; D 232-18 (ND 158-15, SD 74-3); I 1-0, July 22, 1992.

**294. H Res 520. Public Release of All Records on the House Post Office Investigation.** Rose, D-N.C., motion to table (kill) the Walker, R-Pa., amendment to direct the House Administration Committee to make public all the records of the task force that investigated the House Post Office. Motion agreed to 207-200: R 0-158; D 206-42 (ND 147-25, SD 59-17); I 1-0, July 22, 1992.

**295. HR 5503. Fiscal 1993 Interior Appropriations/Timucuan Park and Preserve.** Bennett, D-Fla., amendment to transfer $2 million from the National Park Service construction account to the National Park Service land acquisition account with the intention that the funds be used for the Timucuan National Historical Park and Ecological Preserve in Florida. Rejected 74-344: R 20-142; D 54-201 (ND 33-144, SD 21-57); I 0-1, July 22, 1992.

**296. HR 5503. Fiscal 1993 Interior Appropriations/Administrative Overhead.** Dorgan, D-N.D., amendment to cut $48 million from the administrative overhead cost for selected agencies covered by the bill. Adopted 257-162: R 137-23; D 119-139 (ND 75-103, SD 44-36); I 1-0, July 22, 1992.

**298. HR 5503. Fiscal 1993 Interior Appropriations/National Endowment for the Arts.** Crane, R-Ill., amendment to cut the $179 million in the bill for the National Endowment for the Arts. Rejected 85-329: R 72-88; D 13-240 (ND 3-171, SD 10-69); I 0-1, July 22, 1992.

**299. HR 5503. Fiscal 1993 Interior Appropriations/Hunting at Mason Neck National Wildlife Refuge.** Brewster, D-Okla., amendment to allow the use of funds by the Fish and Wildlife Service to supervise deer hunting at the Mason Neck National Wildlife Refuge in southern Fairfax County, Va. Adopted 255-160: R 140-20; D 115-139 (ND 60-114, SD 55-25); I 0-1, July 22, 1992.

**300. HR 5503. Fiscal 1993 Interior Appropriations/Grazing Fees.** Stenholm, D-Texas, amendment to strike the provisions that would raise livestock grazing fees for ranchers using Bureau of Land Management and Forest Service lands. Rejected 164-245: R 95-67; D 69-177 (ND 37-131, SD 32-46); I 0-1, July 22, 1992. A 'yea' was a vote in support of the president's position.

| | 292 | 293 | 294 | 295 | 296 | 298 | 299 | 300 |
|---|---|---|---|---|---|---|---|---|
| **ALABAMA** | | | | | | | | |
| 1 *Callahan* | Y | N | N | N | Y | Y | Y | Y |
| 2 *Dickinson* | Y | N | N | N | Y | Y | Y | Y |
| 3 Browder | Y | Y | Y | N | N | N | Y | N |
| 4 Bevill | Y | Y | Y | N | N | N | Y | ? |
| 5 Cramer | Y | Y | Y | N | Y | N | Y | N |
| 6 Erdreich | Y | N | N | N | Y | N | Y | N |
| 7 Harris | Y | Y | Y | N | N | N | Y | N |
| **ALASKA** | | | | | | | | |
| AL *Young* | Y | N | N | Y | N | Y | Y | Y |
| **ARIZONA** | | | | | | | | |
| 1 *Rhodes* | Y | N | N | N | Y | N | Y | Y |
| 2 Pastor | Y | Y | Y | N | N | N | Y | Y |
| 3 *Stump* | Y | N | N | Y | Y | Y | Y | Y |
| 4 *Kyl* | Y | N | N | Y | Y | Y | Y | Y |
| 5 *Kolbe* | Y | N | N | N | Y | N | Y | Y |
| **ARKANSAS** | | | | | | | | |
| 1 Alexander | Y | Y | ? | ? | N | N | Y | N |
| 2 Thornton | Y | Y | Y | N | N | N | Y | Y |
| 3 *Hammerschmidt* | Y | N | N | N | N | Y | Y | Y |
| 4 Anthony | Y | Y | ? | N | N | N | N | N |
| **CALIFORNIA** | | | | | | | | |
| 1 *Riggs* | Y | N | N | N | Y | Y | ? | Y |
| 2 *Herger* | Y | N | N | N | Y | Y | Y | Y |
| 3 Matsui | Y | Y | Y | N | Y | N | N | N |
| 4 Fazio | Y | Y | Y | N | N | N | N | N |
| 5 Pelosi | Y | Y | Y | N | N | N | N | N |
| 6 Boxer | Y | N | Y | N | N | N | N | N |
| 7 Miller | Y | Y | Y | N | Y | N | N | N |
| 8 Dellums | Y | Y | Y | N | N | N | N | N |
| 9 Stark | Y | Y | Y | Y | N | N | N | N |
| 10 Edwards | Y | Y | Y | N | N | N | N | N |
| 11 Lantos | Y | Y | Y | N | Y | N | N | N |
| 12 *Campbell* | Y | N | N | N | Y | N | Y | N |
| 13 Mineta | Y | Y | Y | N | N | N | N | N |
| 14 *Doolittle* | Y | N | N | N | Y | Y | Y | Y |
| 15 Condit | Y | Y | Y | N | Y | N | Y | Y |
| 16 Panetta | Y | Y | Y | N | N | N | N | N |
| 17 Dooley | Y | Y | Y | N | Y | N | N | N |
| 18 Lehman | Y | Y | Y | N | Y | N | Y | Y |
| 19 *Lagomarsino* | Y | N | N | N | Y | Y | Y | Y |
| 20 *Thomas* | Y | N | N | N | Y | Y | Y | Y |
| 21 *Gallegly* | Y | N | N | N | Y | Y | Y | Y |
| 22 *Moorhead* | Y | N | N | N | Y | Y | Y | Y |
| 23 Beilenson | Y | Y | Y | N | N | N | N | N |
| 24 Waxman | Y | Y | Y | N | N | N | N | N |
| 25 Roybal | Y | Y | Y | N | N | N | N | N |
| 26 Berman | Y | Y | Y | N | N | N | N | N |
| 27 Levine | Y | Y | Y | N | N | N | N | Y |
| 28 Dixon | Y | Y | Y | N | N | N | N | N |
| 29 Waters | Y | Y | Y | N | N | N | N | N |
| 30 Martinez | ? | Y | Y | N | N | N | N | N |
| 31 Dymally | Y | Y | Y | Y | N | ? | ? | ? |
| 32 Anderson | Y | Y | Y | N | N | N | N | N |
| 33 *Dreier* | Y | N | N | N | Y | Y | Y | Y |
| 34 Torres | Y | Y | Y | N | N | N | N | N |
| 35 *Lewis* | Y | N | N | N | N | N | Y | Y |
| 36 Brown | Y | Y | Y | N | N | N | N | N |
| 37 *McCandless* | Y | N | N | N | Y | Y | Y | Y |
| 38 *Dornan* | Y | N | N | N | Y | Y | Y | Y |
| 39 *Dannemeyer* | Y | N | N | N | Y | Y | Y | Y |
| 40 *Cox* | ? | ? | ? | ? | ? | ? | ? | ? |
| 41 *Lowery* | ? | N | N | N | N | N | Y | N |

| | 292 | 293 | 294 | 295 | 296 | 298 | 299 | 300 |
|---|---|---|---|---|---|---|---|---|
| 42 *Rohrabacher* | Y | N | N | N | Y | Y | Y | Y |
| 43 *Packard* | Y | N | N | N | Y | Y | Y | Y |
| 44 *Cunningham* | Y | N | N | N | Y | Y | Y | Y |
| 45 *Hunter* | Y | N | N | Y | Y | Y | Y | Y |
| **COLORADO** | | | | | | | | |
| 1 Schroeder | Y | Y | Y | N | Y | N | N | N |
| 2 Skaggs | Y | Y | Y | N | N | N | N | Y |
| 3 Campbell | Y | Y | Y | N | Y | N | Y | Y |
| 4 *Allard* | Y | N | N | N | Y | N | Y | Y |
| 5 *Hefley* | Y | N | N | N | N | Y | Y | Y |
| 6 *Schaefer* | Y | N | N | N | Y | N | Y | Y |
| **CONNECTICUT** | | | | | | | | |
| 1 Kennelly | Y | Y | Y | N | N | N | N | N |
| 2 Gejdenson | Y | Y | Y | Y | N | N | N | N |
| 3 DeLauro | Y | Y | Y | N | N | N | N | N |
| 4 *Shays* | Y | N | N | N | N | N | N | N |
| 5 *Franks* | Y | N | N | N | Y | N | Y | N |
| 6 *Johnson* | Y | N | N | N | Y | ? | Y | N |
| **DELAWARE** | | | | | | | | |
| AL Carper | Y | Y | N | Y | Y | N | N | N |
| **FLORIDA** | | | | | | | | |
| 1 Hutto | Y | Y | N | Y | Y | Y | Y | Y |
| 2 Peterson | + | + | + | + | + | − | − | + |
| 3 Bennett | Y | Y | Y | Y | N | Y | N | N |
| 4 *James* | Y | N | N | Y | Y | Y | Y | Y |
| 5 *McCollum* | Y | N | N | Y | Y | Y | Y | Y |
| 6 *Stearns* | Y | N | N | N | Y | Y | Y | Y |
| 7 Gibbons | Y | Y | Y | Y | Y | N | N | N |
| 8 *Young* | Y | N | N | Y | N | Y | N | N |
| 9 *Bilirakis* | Y | N | N | N | Y | N | Y | Y |
| 10 *Ireland* | Y | ? | ? | Y | Y | N | Y | N |
| 11 Bacchus | Y | N | N | Y | Y | N | N | N |
| 12 *Lewis* | Y | N | N | Y | Y | Y | Y | Y |
| 13 *Goss* | Y | N | N | N | Y | N | Y | Y |
| 14 Johnston | Y | Y | Y | N | Y | N | N | N |
| 15 *Shaw* | Y | N | N | Y | Y | N | Y | Y |
| 16 Smith | Y | Y | Y | N | N | N | N | N |
| 17 Lehman | Y | Y | ? | N | ? | N | N | N |
| 18 *Ros—Lehtinen* | Y | N | N | N | N | N | N | N |
| 19 Fascell | Y | Y | Y | N | N | N | N | N |
| **GEORGIA** | | | | | | | | |
| 1 Thomas | ? | ? | ? | ? | ? | ? | ? | ? |
| 2 Hatcher | ? | ? | ? | ? | ? | ? | ? | ? |
| 3 Ray | ? | ? | ? | ? | ? | ? | ? | ? |
| 4 Jones | Y | Y | Y | N | N | N | N | N |
| 5 Lewis | Y | Y | Y | N | N | N | N | N |
| 6 *Gingrich* | ? | ? | ? | ? | ? | ? | ? | ? |
| 7 Darden | Y | N | N | N | N | N | N | N |
| 8 Rowland | Y | Y | Y | N | N | N | Y | N |
| 9 Jenkins | Y | Y | Y | N | N | N | Y | N |
| 10 Barnard | Y | ? | N | N | Y | N | N | N |
| **HAWAII** | | | | | | | | |
| 1 Abercrombie | Y | Y | Y | N | N | N | N | N |
| 2 Mink | Y | Y | Y | N | N | N | N | N |
| **IDAHO** | | | | | | | | |
| 1 LaRocco | Y | Y | Y | N | Y | N | Y | Y |
| 2 Stallings | Y | N | Y | N | Y | N | Y | Y |
| **ILLINOIS** | | | | | | | | |
| 1 Hayes | Y | Y | Y | Y | N | N | N | N |
| 2 Savage | Y | Y | Y | N | N | N | ? | N |
| 3 Russo | Y | Y | N | Y | N | N | N | ? |
| 4 Sangmeister | Y | N | Y | N | Y | N | N | N |
| 5 Lipinski | Y | N | Y | N | Y | N | Y | N |
| 6 *Hyde* | ? | ? | ? | ? | ? | ? | ? | ? |
| 7 Collins | Y | Y | Y | N | N | N | N | N |
| 8 Rostenkowski | Y | Y | Y | N | N | N | N | ? |
| 9 Yates | Y | Y | Y | N | N | N | N | N |
| 10 *Porter* | Y | Y | Y | N | Y | N | N | N |
| 11 Annunzio | Y | Y | Y | Y | N | N | N | ? |
| 12 *Crane* | Y | N | N | N | Y | Y | Y | Y |
| 13 *Fawell* | Y | N | N | N | Y | N | N | N |
| 14 *Hastert* | Y | N | N | N | Y | Y | Y | N |
| 15 *Ewing* | Y | N | N | N | Y | Y | Y | Y |
| 16 *Cox* | Y | N | N | N | Y | N | Y | N |
| 17 Evans | Y | Y | Y | N | N | N | N | Y |
| 18 *Michel* | Y | N | N | N | Y | N | Y | Y |
| 19 Bruce | Y | N | N | N | N | N | N | N |
| 20 Durbin | Y | Y | Y | N | Y | N | N | Y |
| 21 Costello | Y | N | N | N | N | N | N | N |
| 22 Poshard | Y | N | N | N | N | N | Y | N |
| **INDIANA** | | | | | | | | |
| 1 Visclosky | Y | Y | Y | N | Y | N | N | N |
| 2 Sharp | Y | N | N | N | Y | N | Y | N |
| 3 Roemer | Y | N | N | N | Y | N | Y | N |

ND Northern Democrats    SD Southern Democrats

| | 292 | 293 | 294 | 295 | 296 | 298 | 299 | 300 |
|---|---|---|---|---|---|---|---|---|
| 4 Long | Y | Y | Y | N | Y | N | N | Y |
| 5 Jontz | Y | Y | Y | N | N | N | Y | N |
| 6 ***Burton*** | Y | N | N | N | Y | Y | Y | N |
| 7 ***Myers*** | Y | N | N | N | N | N | Y | N |
| 8 McCloskey | Y | Y | Y | Y | N | N | N | N |
| 9 Hamilton | Y | N | N | Y | Y | N | Y | N |
| 10 Jacobs | Y | N | N | Y | Y | N | N | N |
| **IOWA** | | | | | | | | |
| 1 ***Leach*** | Y | N | N | N | Y | N | Y | N |
| 2 ***Nussle*** | Y | N | N | N | Y | N | Y | Y |
| 3 Nagle | Y | Y | Y | N | N | N | N | Y |
| 4 Smith | Y | Y | Y | N | N | N | N | N |
| 5 ***Lightfoot*** | Y | N | N | N | Y | Y | Y | Y |
| 6 ***Grandy*** | Y | N | N | N | Y | N | Y | Y |
| **KANSAS** | | | | | | | | |
| 1 ***Roberts*** | Y | N | N | N | Y | Y | Y | Y |
| 2 Slattery | Y | Y | Y | N | Y | N | Y | N |
| 3 ***Meyers*** | Y | N | N | N | Y | N | N | N |
| 4 Glickman | Y | Y | N | N | Y | N | Y | N |
| 5 ***Nichols*** | Y | N | N | N | Y | Y | Y | Y |
| **KENTUCKY** | | | | | | | | |
| 1 Hubbard | Y | Y | N | Y | Y | N | Y | Y |
| 2 Natcher | Y | Y | Y | N | N | N | N | N |
| 3 Mazzoli | Y | N | N | N | Y | N | N | N |
| 4 ***Bunning*** | Y | N | N | N | Y | Y | Y | Y |
| 5 ***Rogers*** | Y | N | N | N | Y | N | Y | Y |
| 6 ***Hopkins*** | Y | N | N | N | Y | N | Y | Y |
| 7 Perkins | ? | ? | ? | Y | N | N | Y | Y |
| **LOUISIANA** | | | | | | | | |
| 1 ***Livingston*** | Y | N | N | Y | N | Y | Y | Y |
| 2 Jefferson | Y | Y | Y | N | N | N | N | N |
| 3 Tauzin | Y | Y | ? | N | Y | Y | Y | N |
| 4 ***McCrery*** | Y | N | N | N | Y | N | Y | N |
| 5 Huckaby | Y | Y | N | N | Y | N | Y | N |
| 6 ***Baker*** | Y | N | N | N | Y | Y | Y | Y |
| 7 Hayes | Y | Y | N | N | Y | N | Y | Y |
| 8 ***Holloway*** | Y | N | N | N | Y | Y | Y | Y |
| **MAINE** | | | | | | | | |
| 1 Andrews | Y | N | N | N | Y | N | N | N |
| 2 ***Snowe*** | Y | N | N | N | Y | N | Y | N |
| **MARYLAND** | | | | | | | | |
| 1 ***Gilchrest*** | Y | N | N | Y | Y | N | N | N |
| 2 ***Bentley*** | Y | N | N | N | Y | N | Y | Y |
| 3 Cardin | Y | Y | Y | N | N | N | N | N |
| 4 McMillen | Y | Y | N | N | Y | N | Y | N |
| 5 Hoyer | Y | Y | Y | N | N | ? | N | N |
| 6 Byron | Y | Y | N | N | N | N | Y | Y |
| 7 Mfume | Y | Y | Y | N | Y | N | N | N |
| 8 ***Morella*** | Y | N | N | Y | N | N | N | N |
| **MASSACHUSETTS** | | | | | | | | |
| 1 Olver | Y | Y | Y | N | Y | N | Y | N |
| 2 Neal | Y | Y | Y | N | N | N | N | N |
| 3 Early | Y | Y | Y | N | N | N | N | N |
| 4 Frank | Y | Y | Y | N | N | N | N | N |
| 5 Atkins | Y | Y | Y | N | N | N | N | N |
| 6 Mavroules | Y | Y | N | N | N | N | N | N |
| 7 Markey | Y | Y | Y | N | N | N | N | N |
| 8 Kennedy | Y | Y | Y | N | Y | N | N | N |
| 9 Moakley | Y | Y | Y | N | N | N | N | N |
| 10 Studds | Y | Y | Y | N | N | N | N | N |
| 11 Donnelly | Y | Y | Y | N | N | N | Y | N |
| **MICHIGAN** | | | | | | | | |
| 1 Conyers | Y | ? | Y | N | N | N | N | N |
| 2 ***Pursell*** | Y | N | N | N | Y | N | Y | Y |
| 3 Wolpe | Y | Y | Y | N | N | N | N | N |
| 4 ***Upton*** | Y | N | N | N | Y | N | Y | N |
| 5 ***Henry*** | Y | N | N | N | Y | N | Y | N |
| 6 Carr | Y | Y | Y | N | N | N | Y | Y |
| 7 Kildee | Y | Y | Y | N | N | N | Y | N |
| 8 Traxler | Y | Y | Y | N | N | ? | ? | ? |
| 9 ***Vander Jagt*** | Y | N | N | N | Y | N | Y | Y |
| 10 ***Camp*** | Y | N | N | N | Y | N | Y | Y |
| 11 ***Davis*** | ? | ? | ? | N | Y | N | Y | Y |
| 12 Bonior | Y | Y | Y | N | Y | N | N | N |
| 13 Collins | Y | ? | ? | ? | ? | ? | ? | ? |
| 14 Hertel | Y | Y | Y | N | N | N | N | N |
| 15 Ford | Y | Y | ? | Y | N | N | ? | N |
| 16 Dingell | Y | Y | Y | Y | N | N | Y | N |
| 17 Levin | Y | Y | Y | N | Y | N | N | N |
| 18 ***Broomfield*** | Y | N | N | N | Y | N | N | N |
| **MINNESOTA** | | | | | | | | |
| 1 Penny | Y | Y | N | N | Y | N | Y | N |
| 2 ***Weber*** | ? | ? | ? | N | ? | N | Y | Y |
| 3 ***Ramstad*** | Y | N | N | N | Y | N | Y | N |
| 4 Vento | Y | Y | Y | Y | N | N | N | N |

| | 292 | 293 | 294 | 295 | 296 | 298 | 299 | 300 |
|---|---|---|---|---|---|---|---|---|
| 5 Sabo | Y | Y | Y | N | N | N | N | N |
| 6 Sikorski | Y | Y | Y | Y | Y | N | N | N |
| 7 Peterson | Y | Y | Y | N | Y | N | Y | Y |
| 8 Oberstar | Y | Y | Y | Y | N | N | Y | N |
| **MISSISSIPPI** | | | | | | | | |
| 1 Whitten | Y | Y | Y | N | N | N | Y | Y |
| 2 Espy | Y | Y | Y | N | N | N | Y | Y |
| 3 Montgomery | Y | Y | Y | Y | Y | N | Y | Y |
| 4 Parker | Y | Y | Y | Y | Y | N | Y | Y |
| 5 Taylor | Y | Y | N | Y | Y | Y | Y | Y |
| **MISSOURI** | | | | | | | | |
| 1 Clay | Y | Y | Y | N | N | N | N | N |
| 2 Horn | Y | Y | Y | N | Y | N | N | N |
| 3 Gephardt | ? | ? | ? | ? | ? | ? | ? | ? |
| 4 Skelton | Y | Y | Y | Y | Y | Y | Y | Y |
| 5 Wheat | Y | Y | ? | N | N | N | N | N |
| 6 ***Coleman*** | Y | N | N | N | Y | N | N | Y |
| 7 ***Hancock*** | Y | N | N | N | Y | Y | Y | Y |
| 8 ***Emerson*** | Y | N | N | Y | Y | Y | Y | Y |
| 9 Volkmer | Y | Y | Y | Y | Y | N | Y | Y |
| **MONTANA** | | | | | | | | |
| 1 Williams | Y | Y | N | N | Y | N | Y | Y |
| 2 ***Marlenee*** | Y | N | N | N | N | Y | Y | Y |
| **NEBRASKA** | | | | | | | | |
| 1 ***Bereuter*** | Y | N | N | N | Y | N | Y | N |
| 2 Hoagland | Y | Y | Y | N | N | N | N | N |
| 3 ***Barrett*** | Y | N | N | N | Y | N | Y | Y |
| **NEVADA** | | | | | | | | |
| 1 Bilbray | Y | Y | Y | N | Y | N | N | Y |
| 2 ***Vucanovich*** | Y | N | N | N | Y | Y | Y | Y |
| **NEW HAMPSHIRE** | | | | | | | | |
| 1 ***Zeliff*** | Y | N | N | N | Y | N | Y | N |
| 2 Swett | Y | Y | N | N | Y | N | Y | N |
| **NEW JERSEY** | | | | | | | | |
| 1 Andrews | Y | Y | N | N | Y | N | N | Y |
| 2 Hughes | Y | Y | N | Y | Y | N | Y | N |
| 3 Pallone | Y | Y | N | N | Y | N | Y | N |
| 4 ***Smith*** | Y | N | N | N | Y | N | Y | N |
| 5 ***Roukema*** | Y | N | N | N | Y | N | N | N |
| 6 Dwyer | ? | ? | ? | N | N | N | N | Y |
| 7 ***Rinaldo*** | Y | N | N | N | Y | N | N | N |
| 8 Roe | Y | Y | ? | N | N | N | N | N |
| 9 Torricelli | Y | Y | Y | Y | N | N | N | ? |
| 10 Payne | Y | Y | Y | N | N | N | N | N |
| 11 ***Gallo*** | Y | N | N | N | Y | N | Y | N |
| 12 ***Zimmer*** | Y | N | N | N | Y | N | Y | N |
| 13 ***Saxton*** | Y | N | N | N | Y | N | Y | N |
| 14 Guarini | Y | Y | Y | N | Y | N | Y | N |
| **NEW MEXICO** | | | | | | | | |
| 1 ***Schiff*** | Y | N | N | N | N | N | Y | Y |
| 2 ***Skeen*** | Y | N | N | N | N | N | Y | Y |
| 3 Richardson | Y | Y | Y | N | N | N | N | Y |
| **NEW YORK** | | | | | | | | |
| 1 Hochbrueckner | Y | Y | Y | N | N | N | N | N |
| 2 Downey | Y | Y | Y | N | N | N | N | N |
| 3 Mrazek | Y | Y | Y | Y | N | N | N | N |
| 4 ***Lent*** | Y | N | N | N | Y | Y | Y | Y |
| 5 ***McGrath*** | Y | N | N | N | Y | Y | Y | Y |
| 6 Flake | Y | Y | Y | N | Y | N | N | N |
| 7 Ackerman | Y | Y | Y | N | N | N | N | N |
| 8 Scheuer | Y | ? | Y | N | N | N | N | N |
| 9 Manton | Y | Y | Y | N | N | N | N | N |
| 10 Schumer | Y | Y | Y | N | Y | N | N | N |
| 11 Towns | Y | Y | Y | N | N | N | N | N |
| 12 Owens | Y | Y | Y | Y | N | N | N | N |
| 13 Solarz | Y | Y | Y | N | N | N | N | ? |
| 14 ***Molinari*** | Y | N | N | N | Y | N | Y | N |
| 15 ***Green*** | Y | N | N | N | N | N | N | N |
| 16 Rangel | Y | Y | Y | Y | Y | N | N | ? |
| 17 Weiss | Y | Y | Y | N | N | N | N | N |
| 18 Serrano | Y | Y | Y | N | N | N | N | N |
| 19 Engel | Y | Y | Y | N | Y | N | N | N |
| 20 Lowey | Y | Y | Y | N | Y | N | N | N |
| 21 ***Fish*** | Y | N | N | N | Y | N | Y | N |
| 22 ***Gilman*** | Y | N | N | N | Y | N | Y | N |
| 23 McNulty | Y | Y | Y | N | N | N | Y | N |
| 24 ***Solomon*** | Y | N | N | N | Y | Y | Y | N |
| 25 ***Boehlert*** | Y | N | N | N | N | N | Y | N |
| 26 ***Martin*** | Y | N | N | N | Y | N | Y | Y |
| 27 ***Walsh*** | Y | N | N | N | Y | N | Y | Y |
| 28 McHugh | Y | Y | Y | N | N | N | N | N |
| 29 ***Horton*** | Y | N | N | N | N | N | Y | N |
| 30 Slaughter | Y | Y | Y | N | Y | N | N | N |
| 31 ***Paxon*** | Y | N | N | N | Y | N | Y | Y |

| | 292 | 293 | 294 | 295 | 296 | 298 | 299 | 300 |
|---|---|---|---|---|---|---|---|---|
| 32 LaFalce | Y | Y | Y | N | Y | N | N | N |
| 33 Nowak | Y | Y | Y | N | Y | N | N | N |
| 34 ***Houghton*** | Y | N | N | N | N | N | Y | Y |
| **NORTH CAROLINA** | | | | | | | | |
| 1 Jones | Y | Y | Y | N | Y | N | Y | N |
| 2 Valentine | Y | Y | N | N | Y | N | Y | Y |
| 3 Lancaster | Y | Y | Y | N | Y | N | Y | Y |
| 4 Price | Y | Y | Y | N | Y | N | N | N |
| 5 Neal | Y | Y | Y | N | Y | N | Y | N |
| 6 ***Coble*** | Y | N | N | N | Y | Y | Y | Y |
| 7 Rose | Y | Y | Y | Y | N | N | Y | N |
| 8 Hefner | Y | Y | Y | N | N | N | Y | N |
| 9 ***McMillan*** | Y | N | N | N | Y | N | Y | N |
| 10 ***Ballenger*** | Y | N | N | N | Y | N | Y | Y |
| 11 ***Taylor*** | Y | N | N | N | Y | Y | Y | Y |
| **NORTH DAKOTA** | | | | | | | | |
| AL Dorgan | Y | Y | N | N | Y | N | Y | Y |
| **OHIO** | | | | | | | | |
| 1 Luken | Y | Y | Y | N | Y | N | N | N |
| 2 ***Gradison*** | Y | N | N | N | Y | N | Y | N |
| 3 Hall | Y | Y | Y | N | N | N | Y | Y |
| 4 ***Oxley*** | Y | N | N | N | Y | Y | Y | Y |
| 5 ***Gillmor*** | Y | N | N | N | Y | N | Y | Y |
| 6 ***McEwen*** | Y | N | N | N | Y | ? | Y | Y |
| 7 ***Hobson*** | Y | N | N | N | Y | N | Y | N |
| 8 ***Boehner*** | Y | N | N | N | Y | Y | Y | Y |
| 9 Kaptur | Y | Y | Y | N | Y | N | Y | N |
| 10 ***Miller*** | Y | N | N | Y | Y | Y | Y | Y |
| 11 Eckart | Y | Y | Y | N | N | N | Y | N |
| 12 ***Kasich*** | Y | N | N | N | Y | N | N | N |
| 13 Pease | Y | Y | Y | N | N | N | N | N |
| 14 Sawyer | Y | Y | Y | N | N | N | N | N |
| 15 ***Wylie*** | Y | N | N | N | Y | N | N | N |
| 16 ***Regula*** | Y | N | N | N | N | N | N | N |
| 17 Traficant | Y | Y | Y | Y | N | N | N | N |
| 18 Applegate | Y | Y | Y | N | N | N | Y | N |
| 19 Feighan | ? | ? | ? | ? | ? | ? | ? | ? |
| 20 Oakar | Y | Y | Y | N | N | N | N | ? |
| 21 Stokes | Y | Y | Y | N | N | N | N | N |
| **OKLAHOMA** | | | | | | | | |
| 1 ***Inhofe*** | Y | N | N | N | Y | Y | Y | Y |
| 2 Synar | Y | Y | Y | N | N | N | N | N |
| 3 Brewster | Y | Y | Y | N | Y | N | Y | Y |
| 4 McCurdy | Y | Y | Y | N | Y | N | Y | Y |
| 5 ***Edwards*** | Y | N | N | N | Y | Y | Y | Y |
| 6 English | Y | Y | N | Y | Y | N | Y | Y |
| **OREGON** | | | | | | | | |
| 1 AuCoin | Y | Y | Y | N | N | N | N | Y |
| 2 ***Smith*** | Y | N | N | N | Y | Y | Y | Y |
| 3 Wyden | Y | Y | Y | N | Y | N | Y | N |
| 4 DeFazio | Y | Y | Y | N | Y | N | Y | Y |
| 5 Kopetski | Y | Y | Y | Y | N | N | Y | Y |
| **PENNSYLVANIA** | | | | | | | | |
| 1 Foglietta | Y | Y | Y | N | N | N | N | N |
| 2 Blackwell | Y | Y | Y | N | N | N | N | N |
| 3 Borski | Y | Y | Y | N | Y | N | N | N |
| 4 Kolter | ? | ? | ? | ? | ? | ? | ? | ? |
| 5 ***Schulze*** | Y | N | N | N | Y | Y | Y | Y |
| 6 Yatron | Y | ? | Y | N | Y | N | Y | N |
| 7 ***Weldon*** | Y | N | N | N | Y | N | Y | N |
| 8 Kostmayer | Y | Y | Y | N | N | N | Y | N |
| 9 ***Shuster*** | Y | N | N | N | Y | Y | Y | Y |
| 10 ***McDade*** | Y | N | N | N | N | N | Y | N |
| 11 Kanjorski | Y | Y | Y | N | Y | N | Y | N |
| 12 Murtha | ? | ? | ? | N | N | N | Y | N |
| 13 ***Coughlin*** | ? | ? | ? | ? | ? | ? | ? | ? |
| 14 Coyne | Y | Y | Y | N | N | N | N | N |
| 15 ***Ritter*** | Y | N | N | N | Y | N | Y | N |
| 16 ***Walker*** | Y | N | N | N | Y | Y | ? | N |
| 17 ***Gekas*** | Y | N | N | N | Y | Y | Y | N |
| 18 ***Santorum*** | Y | N | N | N | Y | N | Y | N |
| 19 ***Goodling*** | Y | N | N | N | Y | Y | Y | Y |
| 20 Gaydos | Y | Y | Y | ? | N | N | Y | ? |
| 21 ***Ridge*** | Y | N | N | Y | Y | N | Y | N |
| 22 Murphy | Y | Y | ? | N | N | N | Y | N |
| 23 ***Clinger*** | Y | N | N | N | Y | N | Y | N |
| **RHODE ISLAND** | | | | | | | | |
| 1 ***Machtley*** | Y | N | N | N | Y | N | N | N |
| 2 Reed | Y | Y | N | N | N | N | N | N |
| **SOUTH CAROLINA** | | | | | | | | |
| 1 ***Ravenel*** | Y | N | N | N | Y | N | Y | N |
| 2 ***Spence*** | Y | N | N | Y | Y | N | Y | Y |
| 3 Derrick | Y | Y | Y | N | Y | N | N | N |
| 4 Patterson | Y | Y | N | N | Y | N | N | N |
| 5 Spratt | Y | ? | Y | N | Y | N | Y | N |
| 6 Tallon | ? | ? | ? | ? | ? | ? | ? | ? |

| | 292 | 293 | 294 | 295 | 296 | 298 | 299 | 300 |
|---|---|---|---|---|---|---|---|---|
| **SOUTH DAKOTA** | | | | | | | | |
| AL Johnson | Y | Y | Y | N | N | N | N | Y |
| **TENNESSEE** | | | | | | | | |
| 1 ***Quillen*** | Y | N | N | N | N | Y | Y | Y |
| 2 ***Duncan*** | Y | N | N | N | Y | Y | N | N |
| 3 Lloyd | Y | Y | Y | N | Y | N | Y | N |
| 4 Cooper | ? | Y | N | N | Y | N | N | N |
| 5 Clement | Y | Y | Y | N | Y | N | Y | N |
| 6 Gordon | Y | Y | Y | N | N | N | Y | N |
| 7 ***Sundquist*** | Y | N | N | N | Y | Y | Y | Y |
| 8 Tanner | Y | Y | Y | N | Y | Y | Y | N |
| 9 Ford | Y | Y | Y | N | N | N | N | N |
| **TEXAS** | | | | | | | | |
| 1 Chapman | Y | Y | Y | N | Y | N | Y | Y |
| 2 Wilson | Y | Y | N | N | N | N | Y | N |
| 3 ***Johnson*** | Y | N | N | N | Y | Y | Y | Y |
| 4 Hall | Y | Y | N | N | N | Y | Y | Y |
| 5 Bryant | Y | Y | Y | Y | Y | N | Y | N |
| 6 ***Barton*** | Y | N | N | N | Y | Y | Y | Y |
| 7 ***Archer*** | Y | N | N | N | Y | Y | Y | N |
| 8 ***Fields*** | Y | N | N | N | Y | Y | Y | Y |
| 9 Brooks | Y | Y | Y | Y | N | N | Y | N |
| 10 Pickle | Y | Y | Y | Y | N | N | Y | Y |
| 11 Edwards | Y | Y | Y | N | Y | N | Y | Y |
| 12 Geren | Y | Y | Y | N | Y | N | Y | Y |
| 13 Sarpalius | Y | Y | Y | N | Y | Y | Y | Y |
| 14 Laughlin | Y | Y | Y | N | Y | Y | Y | Y |
| 15 de la Garza | Y | Y | Y | Y | Y | N | Y | Y |
| 16 Coleman | Y | Y | Y | N | N | N | Y | N |
| 17 Stenholm | Y | Y | N | N | Y | Y | Y | Y |
| 18 Washington | Y | Y | Y | N | N | N | N | N |
| 19 ***Combest*** | Y | N | N | N | Y | Y | Y | Y |
| 20 Gonzalez | Y | Y | Y | N | N | N | N | N |
| 21 ***Smith*** | Y | N | N | N | Y | Y | Y | N |
| 22 ***DeLay*** | Y | N | N | N | Y | Y | Y | Y |
| 23 Bustamante | Y | Y | Y | N | N | N | Y | Y |
| 24 Frost | Y | Y | Y | N | Y | N | Y | Y |
| 25 Andrews | Y | Y | Y | N | Y | N | Y | N |
| 26 ***Armey*** | Y | N | N | N | Y | Y | Y | Y |
| 27 Ortiz | Y | Y | Y | Y | N | N | Y | Y |
| **UTAH** | | | | | | | | |
| 1 ***Hansen*** | Y | N | N | N | N | Y | Y | Y |
| 2 Owens | Y | Y | Y | N | Y | N | Y | Y |
| 3 Orton | Y | Y | Y | N | Y | Y | Y | Y |
| **VERMONT** | | | | | | | | |
| AL *Sanders* | Y | Y | Y | N | Y | N | N | N |
| **VIRGINIA** | | | | | | | | |
| 1 ***Bateman*** | Y | N | N | N | N | N | N | Y |
| 2 Pickett | Y | Y | Y | Y | N | N | Y | Y |
| 3 ***Bliley*** | Y | N | N | N | Y | Y | N | Y |
| 4 Sisisky | Y | Y | Y | Y | N | N | Y | Y |
| 5 Payne | Y | Y | Y | N | N | N | N | N |
| 6 Olin | Y | Y | Y | N | Y | N | N | Y |
| 7 ***Allen*** | Y | N | N | N | Y | Y | Y | Y |
| 8 Moran | Y | Y | Y | N | N | N | N | ? |
| 9 Boucher | Y | Y | Y | N | N | N | Y | N |
| 10 ***Wolf*** | Y | ? | ? | Y | N | N | Y | Y |
| **WASHINGTON** | | | | | | | | |
| 1 ***Miller*** | Y | N | N | Y | Y | N | N | N |
| 2 Swift | Y | Y | Y | N | N | N | Y | Y |
| 3 Unsoeld | Y | Y | Y | N | N | N | Y | N |
| 4 ***Morrison*** | Y | N | N | N | N | N | Y | Y |
| 5 Foley | | | | | | | | |
| 6 Dicks | Y | Y | Y | N | N | N | Y | N |
| 7 McDermott | Y | Y | Y | Y | N | N | N | N |
| 8 ***Chandler*** | Y | N | N | N | Y | N | Y | Y |
| **WEST VIRGINIA** | | | | | | | | |
| 1 Mollohan | Y | Y | Y | N | N | ? | Y | N |
| 2 Staggers | Y | N | N | N | Y | N | Y | Y |
| 3 Wise | Y | N | Y | N | Y | N | Y | N |
| 4 Rahall | Y | N | N | N | N | N | Y | N |
| **WISCONSIN** | | | | | | | | |
| 1 Aspin | Y | Y | Y | N | Y | N | N | N |
| 2 ***Klug*** | Y | N | N | N | Y | N | Y | N |
| 3 ***Gunderson*** | Y | N | N | N | N | N | Y | Y |
| 4 Kleczka | Y | Y | Y | N | Y | N | N | N |
| 5 Moody | Y | Y | N | N | Y | N | N | N |
| 6 ***Petri*** | Y | N | N | N | Y | Y | Y | N |
| 7 Obey | Y | Y | Y | N | N | N | N | N |
| 8 ***Roth*** | Y | N | N | N | Y | Y | Y | Y |
| 9 ***Sensenbrenner*** | Y | N | N | N | Y | Y | Y | N |
| **WYOMING** | | | | | | | | |
| AL ***Thomas*** | Y | N | N | N | N | N | Y | Y |

Southern states - Ala., Ark., Fla., Ga., Ky., La., Miss., N.C., Okla., S.C., Tenn., Texas, Va.
Omitted votes are quorum calls, which CQ does not include in its vote charts.

**74-H** — 1992 CQ ALMANAC

## KEY

Y Voted for (yea).
\# Paired for.
\+ Announced for.
N Voted against (nay).
X Paired against.
\- Announced against.
P Voted "present."
C Voted "present" to avoid possible conflict of interest.
? Did not vote or otherwise make a position known.

Democrats   *Republicans*
*Independent*

**301. HR 5503. Fiscal 1993 Interior Appropriations/Bureau of Indian Affairs.** Duncan, R-Tenn., amendment to cut funding for the Bureau of Indian Affairs by $79.8 million to the 1992 level of about $1.5 billion. Rejected 135-266: R 104-49; D 31-216 (ND 12-157, SD 19-59); I 0-1, July 23, 1992.

**302. HR 5503. Fiscal 1993 Interior Appropriations/Timber Sales.** Dicks, D-Wash., substitute amendment to the Jontz, D-Ind., amendment to reduce by $8 million rather than the $16.8 million in the Jontz amendment the appropriation for the National Forest System accounts related to timber sales. The Dicks amendment cut the timber harvest administration account rather than directly reducing the timber sales, as Jontz's amendment proposed. Adopted 212-206: R 110-51; D 102-154 (ND 50-125, SD 52-29); I 0-1, July 23, 1992. (The Jontz amendment as amended was subsequently adopted by voice vote.)

**303. HR 5503. Fiscal 1993 Interior Appropriations/Fossil Energy Research and Development.** Walker, R-Pa., amendment to cut by $25.7 million funding for the Energy Department's fossil energy research and development program to the levels authorized in the House-passed energy bill, HR 776, for coal liquefaction and fuel cells. Rejected 158-262: R 107-55; D 51-206 (ND 41-137, SD 10-69); I 0-1, July 23, 1992.

**304. HR 5503. Fiscal 1993 Interior Appropriations/National Endowment for the Arts.** Stearns, R-Fla., amendment to cut the $179 million for the National Endowment for the Arts by $3 million to the 1992 level. Adopted 251-171: R 154-9; D 97-161 (ND 44-134, SD 53-27); I 0-1, July 23, 1992.

**305. HR 5503. Fiscal 1993 Interior Appropriations/Funding Levels.** Burton, R-Ind., amendment to reduce the overall funding level in the bill by 1 percent to the 1992 level. Rejected 197-218: R 143-18; D 54-199 (ND 24-151, SD 30-48); I 0-1, July 23, 1992.

**306. HR 5503. Fiscal 1993 Interior Appropriations/Passage.** Passage of the bill to provide $12.7 billion in new budget authority for the Department of the Interior and related agencies in fiscal 1993, including the Forest Service, the Department of Energy, the Indian Health Service, the Smithsonian Institution, and the National Foundation on the Arts and the Humanities. The administration requested $12,224,546,000. Passed 329-94: R 82-81; D 246-13 (ND 173-5, SD 73-8); I 1-0, July 23, 1992.

**307. H Res 526. Public Release of Records on the House Post Office Investigation.** Kleczka, D-Wis., motion to table (kill) the Walker, R-Pa., privileged resolution to direct the House Administration Committee to make public all the records of the task force investigating the House Post Office. Motion agreed to 223-196: R 0-162; D 222-34 (ND 155-22, SD 67-12); I 1-0, July 23, 1992.

**308. HR 4850. Cable Television Regulation/State Powers.** Oxley, R-Ohio, amendment to authorize only state regulatory commissions to regulate cable rates when there is a lack of effective competition, rather than the Federal Communications Commission (FCC). Under the bill the FCC would establish rate regulations, and state commissions could administer them. Rejected 83-327: R 77-82; D 6-244 (ND 3-172, SD 3-72); I 0-1, July 23, 1992.

| | 301 | 302 | 303 | 304 | 305 | 306 | 307 | 308 |
|---|---|---|---|---|---|---|---|---|
| **ALABAMA** | | | | | | | | |
| 1 *Callahan* | Y | Y | N | Y | Y | Y | N | Y |
| 2 *Dickinson* | Y | Y | N | Y | Y | Y | N | Y |
| 3 Browder | N | Y | N | Y | N | Y | Y | N |
| 4 Bevill | N | Y | N | Y | N | Y | Y | N |
| 5 Cramer | N | N | N | Y | N | Y | Y | N |
| 6 Erdreich | N | Y | N | Y | N | Y | Y | N |
| 7 Harris | N | Y | N | Y | N | Y | Y | N |
| **ALASKA** | | | | | | | | |
| AL *Young* | ? | Y | N | Y | Y | N | N | N |
| **ARIZONA** | | | | | | | | |
| 1 *Rhodes* | N | Y | Y | Y | Y | Y | N | Y |
| 2 Pastor | N | Y | N | N | N | Y | Y | N |
| 3 *Stump* | Y | Y | Y | Y | Y | N | N | N |
| 4 *Kyl* | N | Y | Y | Y | Y | N | N | N |
| 5 *Kolbe* | N | Y | Y | Y | Y | Y | N | Y |
| **ARKANSAS** | | | | | | | | |
| 1 Alexander | ? | Y | N | N | N | Y | Y | N |
| 2 Thornton | N | Y | N | Y | N | Y | Y | Y |
| 3 *Hammerschmidt* | Y | Y | Y | Y | Y | Y | N | Y |
| 4 Anthony | N | Y | N | N | ? | Y | Y | N |
| **CALIFORNIA** | | | | | | | | |
| 1 *Riggs* | N | Y | Y | Y | Y | Y | N | Y |
| 2 *Herger* | Y | Y | Y | Y | Y | N | N | Y |
| 3 Matsui | N | N | Y | N | N | Y | Y | N |
| 4 Fazio | N | Y | N | N | N | Y | Y | N |
| 5 Pelosi | N | N | N | N | N | Y | Y | N |
| 6 Boxer | N | N | N | N | N | Y | Y | N |
| 7 Miller | N | N | Y | N | N | Y | Y | N |
| 8 Dellums | N | N | Y | N | N | Y | Y | N |
| 9 Stark | ? | N | N | N | N | Y | Y | N |
| 10 Edwards | N | N | N | N | N | Y | Y | N |
| 11 Lantos | N | N | N | N | N | Y | Y | N |
| 12 *Campbell* | Y | Y | N | Y | Y | N | N | Y |
| 13 Mineta | N | Y | N | N | N | Y | Y | N |
| 14 *Doolittle* | Y | Y | Y | Y | Y | N | N | Y |
| 15 Condit | Y | Y | Y | Y | Y | Y | N | Y |
| 16 Panetta | N | N | Y | N | N | Y | Y | N |
| 17 Dooley | N | Y | Y | Y | Y | Y | Y | N |
| 18 Lehman | N | Y | N | Y | N | Y | Y | N |
| 19 *Lagomarsino* | Y | Y | N | Y | Y | Y | N | Y |
| 20 *Thomas* | Y | Y | Y | Y | Y | N | N | Y |
| 21 *Gallegly* | Y | Y | N | Y | Y | N | N | Y |
| 22 *Moorhead* | Y | Y | Y | Y | Y | N | N | Y |
| 23 Beilenson | N | N | N | N | N | Y | Y | N |
| 24 Waxman | N | N | Y | N | N | Y | Y | N |
| 25 Roybal | N | Y | N | Y | N | Y | Y | N |
| 26 Berman | N | N | Y | N | N | Y | Y | N |
| 27 Levine | N | N | N | N | N | Y | Y | ? |
| 28 Dixon | ? | Y | N | N | N | Y | Y | N |
| 29 Waters | N | N | Y | N | N | Y | Y | N |
| 30 Martinez | N | N | N | Y | N | ? | Y | N |
| 31 Dymally | N | N | ? | N | N | Y | ? | ? |
| 32 Anderson | N | N | N | N | N | Y | Y | N |
| 33 *Dreier* | Y | Y | Y | Y | Y | N | N | Y |
| 34 Torres | N | N | N | N | N | Y | Y | N |
| 35 *Lewis* | Y | Y | N | Y | N | Y | N | Y |
| 36 Brown | N | N | N | N | N | Y | Y | N |
| 37 *McCandless* | ? | Y | Y | Y | Y | Y | N | Y |
| 38 *Dornan* | Y | Y | Y | Y | Y | N | N | Y |
| 39 *Dannemeyer* | Y | Y | Y | Y | Y | N | N | Y |
| 40 *Cox* | ? | Y | Y | Y | Y | N | N | Y |
| 41 *Lowery* | Y | Y | N | N | ? | Y | N | Y |

| | 301 | 302 | 303 | 304 | 305 | 306 | 307 | 308 |
|---|---|---|---|---|---|---|---|---|
| 42 *Rohrabacher* | Y | N | Y | Y | Y | N | N | Y |
| 43 *Packard* | Y | Y | Y | Y | Y | N | N | N |
| 44 *Cunningham* | ? | Y | Y | Y | Y | N | N | N |
| 45 *Hunter* | Y | Y | Y | Y | Y | N | N | Y |
| **COLORADO** | | | | | | | | |
| 1 Schroeder | N | N | N | N | Y | Y | Y | N |
| 2 Skaggs | N | N | N | N | N | Y | Y | N |
| 3 Campbell | N | N | N | N | N | Y | Y | N |
| 4 *Allard* | Y | Y | Y | Y | Y | N | N | N |
| 5 *Hefley* | Y | Y | Y | Y | Y | N | N | N |
| 6 *Schaefer* | Y | Y | Y | Y | Y | N | N | N |
| **CONNECTICUT** | | | | | | | | |
| 1 Kennelly | N | N | N | N | N | Y | Y | N |
| 2 Gejdenson | N | N | N | N | N | Y | Y | N |
| 3 DeLauro | N | N | N | N | N | Y | Y | N |
| 4 *Shays* | Y | N | Y | Y | N | Y | N | N |
| 5 *Franks* | Y | N | Y | N | Y | Y | N | Y |
| 6 *Johnson* | Y | Y | N | Y | N | Y | N | Y |
| **DELAWARE** | | | | | | | | |
| AL Carper | ? | ? | Y | Y | Y | Y | N | N |
| **FLORIDA** | | | | | | | | |
| 1 Hutto | N | N | Y | Y | Y | N | Y | N |
| 2 Peterson | + | − | + | + | + | + | + | − |
| 3 Bennett | N | N | Y | Y | Y | Y | Y | N |
| 4 *James* | Y | N | Y | Y | N | Y | N | N |
| 5 *McCollum* | Y | N | N | Y | Y | N | N | N |
| 6 *Stearns* | Y | Y | Y | Y | Y | N | N | N |
| 7 Gibbons | Y | N | N | Y | N | Y | Y | N |
| 8 *Young* | Y | N | Y | Y | Y | Y | N | N |
| 9 *Bilirakis* | Y | N | Y | Y | Y | N | N | N |
| 10 *Ireland* | Y | Y | Y | Y | ? | N | N | Y |
| 11 Bacchus | Y | N | N | Y | Y | N | N | N |
| 12 *Lewis* | Y | N | Y | Y | Y | N | N | N |
| 13 *Goss* | Y | N | Y | Y | Y | N | N | N |
| 14 Johnston | N | N | N | Y | N | Y | Y | N |
| 15 *Shaw* | N | N | Y | Y | Y | N | N | N |
| 16 Smith | N | N | N | N | N | Y | Y | N |
| 17 Lehman | N | N | N | N | N | Y | Y | ? |
| 18 *Ros—Lehtinen* | N | N | Y | Y | Y | N | N | N |
| 19 Fascell | N | N | N | N | N | Y | Y | N |
| **GEORGIA** | | | | | | | | |
| 1 Thomas | ? | ? | ? | ? | ? | ? | ? | ? |
| 2 Hatcher | N | Y | ? | ? | ? | Y | ? | ? |
| 3 Ray | ? | ? | ? | ? | ? | ? | ? | ? |
| 4 Jones | N | N | N | N | N | Y | Y | N |
| 5 Lewis | N | N | N | N | N | Y | Y | N |
| 6 *Gingrich* | Y | Y | Y | Y | Y | N | N | N |
| 7 Darden | N | Y | N | Y | N | Y | Y | N |
| 8 Rowland | Y | N | N | Y | N | Y | Y | N |
| 9 Jenkins | N | Y | N | Y | Y | Y | Y | N |
| 10 Barnard | Y | Y | N | Y | Y | Y | Y | Y |
| **HAWAII** | | | | | | | | |
| 1 Abercrombie | N | N | N | N | Y | Y | Y | N |
| 2 Mink | N | N | Y | N | N | Y | Y | N |
| **IDAHO** | | | | | | | | |
| 1 LaRocco | N | Y | N | Y | N | Y | Y | N |
| 2 Stallings | N | Y | N | Y | N | Y | Y | N |
| **ILLINOIS** | | | | | | | | |
| 1 Hayes | N | N | N | N | N | Y | Y | N |
| 2 Savage | N | Y | N | N | ? | Y | Y | N |
| 3 Russo | N | N | N | N | Y | Y | Y | N |
| 4 Sangmeister | N | N | N | N | N | Y | Y | N |
| 5 Lipinski | N | N | N | Y | N | Y | Y | N |
| 6 *Hyde* | ? | ? | ? | ? | ? | ? | ? | ? |
| 7 Collins | N | N | N | N | N | Y | Y | N |
| 8 Rostenkowski | N | N | N | N | N | Y | Y | N |
| 9 Yates | N | N | N | N | N | Y | Y | ? |
| 10 *Porter* | N | N | Y | Y | N | Y | N | N |
| 11 Annunzio | N | N | N | ? | N | Y | Y | N |
| 12 *Crane* | Y | Y | Y | Y | Y | N | N | N |
| 13 *Fawell* | Y | N | Y | Y | N | Y | N | Y |
| 14 *Hastert* | Y | N | Y | Y | Y | N | N | N |
| 15 *Ewing* | Y | N | Y | Y | Y | N | N | N |
| 16 Cox | N | N | N | N | N | Y | Y | N |
| 17 Evans | N | N | N | N | N | Y | Y | N |
| 18 *Michel* | ? | Y | N | Y | Y | Y | N | N |
| 19 Bruce | N | N | N | Y | N | Y | Y | N |
| 20 Durbin | N | N | N | N | N | Y | Y | N |
| 21 Costello | N | N | N | Y | N | Y | Y | N |
| 22 Poshard | N | N | N | Y | N | Y | Y | N |
| **INDIANA** | | | | | | | | |
| 1 Visclosky | N | Y | N | N | N | Y | Y | N |
| 2 Sharp | N | N | N | Y | N | Y | Y | N |
| 3 Roemer | Y | Y | Y | Y | Y | Y | N | N |

ND Northern Democrats   SD Southern Democrats

| | 301 | 302 | 303 | 304 | 305 | 306 | 307 | 308 |
|---|---|---|---|---|---|---|---|---|
| 4 Long | N | Y | N | Y | Y | Y | Y | N |
| 5 Jontz | N | N | N | N | Y | Y | Y | N |
| 6 ***Burton*** | Y | Y | Y | Y | Y | N | N | Y |
| 7 ***Myers*** | N | Y | N | Y | Y | N | N | N |
| 8 McCloskey | N | N | N | Y | N | Y | Y | N |
| 9 Hamilton | N | N | N | Y | Y | Y | N | N |
| 10 Jacobs | N | N | Y | Y | Y | N | N | N |
| **IOWA** | | | | | | | | |
| 1 ***Leach*** | Y | N | Y | N | Y | N | N | N |
| 2 ***Nussle*** | Y | N | Y | Y | Y | N | N | N |
| 3 Nagle | ? | ? | N | N | N | Y | Y | N |
| 4 Smith | N | Y | N | N | N | Y | Y | N |
| 5 ***Lightfoot*** | Y | Y | N | Y | Y | Y | N | N |
| 6 ***Grandy*** | Y | Y | Y | Y | Y | N | N | N |
| **KANSAS** | | | | | | | | |
| 1 ***Roberts*** | Y | Y | Y | Y | Y | N | N | Y |
| 2 Slattery | N | N | N | Y | N | Y | N | N |
| 3 ***Meyers*** | N | N | Y | Y | N | Y | N | N |
| 4 Glickman | N | N | Y | Y | N | Y | N | N |
| 5 ***Nichols*** | Y | Y | Y | Y | Y | N | N | Y |
| **KENTUCKY** | | | | | | | | |
| 1 Hubbard | N | Y | N | Y | Y | N | N | N |
| 2 Natcher | N | Y | N | N | N | Y | Y | N |
| 3 Mazzoli | N | N | N | N | N | Y | N | N |
| 4 ***Bunning*** | Y | Y | N | Y | Y | N | N | N |
| 5 ***Rogers*** | Y | Y | N | Y | N | Y | N | N |
| 6 ***Hopkins*** | Y | Y | N | Y | Y | Y | N | N |
| 7 Perkins | N | Y | N | N | N | Y | Y | N |
| **LOUISIANA** | | | | | | | | |
| 1 ***Livingston*** | N | Y | N | Y | N | Y | N | N |
| 2 Jefferson | N | Y | Y | N | N | Y | Y | N |
| 3 Tauzin | N | Y | N | Y | Y | N | Y | N |
| 4 ***McCrery*** | Y | Y | Y | Y | Y | Y | N | Y |
| 5 Huckaby | N | Y | N | Y | Y | Y | N | N |
| 6 ***Baker*** | Y | Y | Y | Y | Y | N | N | Y |
| 7 Hayes | N | Y | N | Y | N | Y | Y | N |
| 8 ***Holloway*** | Y | Y | Y | Y | Y | N | N | N |
| **MAINE** | | | | | | | | |
| 1 Andrews | N | N | N | N | ? | Y | N | N |
| 2 ***Snowe*** | N | Y | Y | Y | Y | Y | N | N |
| **MARYLAND** | | | | | | | | |
| 1 ***Gilchrest*** | N | N | Y | Y | Y | Y | N | N |
| 2 ***Bentley*** | Y | Y | N | Y | Y | Y | N | Y |
| 3 Cardin | N | N | N | N | N | Y | Y | N |
| 4 McMillen | Y | N | N | Y | N | Y | N | N |
| 5 Hoyer | N | Y | N | N | N | Y | Y | N |
| 6 Byron | Y | Y | N | Y | N | Y | Y | N |
| 7 Mfume | ? | N | N | N | N | Y | Y | N |
| 8 ***Morella*** | X | — | Y | N | N | Y | N | N |
| **MASSACHUSETTS** | | | | | | | | |
| 1 Olver | N | N | N | N | N | Y | Y | N |
| 2 Neal | N | N | N | N | N | Y | Y | N |
| 3 Early | N | N | N | N | N | Y | Y | N |
| 4 Frank | N | N | Y | N | N | Y | Y | N |
| 5 Atkins | N | N | N | N | N | Y | Y | N |
| 6 Mavroules | N | N | N | N | N | Y | Y | N |
| 7 Markey | N | N | Y | N | N | Y | Y | N |
| 8 Kennedy | N | N | N | N | N | Y | Y | N |
| 9 Moakley | N | N | N | N | N | Y | Y | N |
| 10 Studds | N | N | Y | N | N | Y | Y | N |
| 11 Donnelly | N | N | N | N | N | Y | Y | N |
| **MICHIGAN** | | | | | | | | |
| 1 Conyers | ? | N | Y | N | N | Y | Y | ? |
| 2 ***Pursell*** | Y | N | N | Y | Y | N | N | N |
| 3 Wolpe | N | N | Y | N | N | Y | Y | N |
| 4 ***Upton*** | Y | N | Y | Y | Y | N | N | N |
| 5 ***Henry*** | Y | N | Y | Y | Y | N | N | N |
| 6 Carr | N | N | N | N | N | Y | Y | N |
| 7 Kildee | N | Y | N | N | N | Y | Y | N |
| 8 Traxler | ? | ? | ? | ? | ? | ? | ? | N |
| 9 ***Vander Jagt*** | Y | Y | Y | Y | Y | Y | N | N |
| 10 ***Camp*** | N | Y | Y | Y | Y | N | N | N |
| 11 ***Davis*** | N | Y | N | Y | N | Y | N | N |
| 12 Bonior | N | Y | N | N | N | Y | Y | N |
| 13 Collins | N | N | N | N | N | Y | Y | N |
| 14 Hertel | N | N | N | N | N | Y | Y | N |
| 15 Ford | ? | ? | N | N | N | Y | Y | N |
| 16 Dingell | N | N | N | N | N | Y | Y | N |
| 17 Levin | N | N | N | N | N | Y | Y | N |
| 18 ***Broomfield*** | N | N | Y | N | Y | N | N | Y |
| **MINNESOTA** | | | | | | | | |
| 1 Penny | Y | N | Y | Y | Y | Y | N | N |
| 2 ***Weber*** | N | Y | N | Y | Y | Y | N | ? |
| 3 ***Ramstad*** | Y | N | Y | Y | Y | N | N | N |
| 4 Vento | N | N | Y | N | N | Y | Y | N |

| | 301 | 302 | 303 | 304 | 305 | 306 | 307 | 308 |
|---|---|---|---|---|---|---|---|---|
| 5 Sabo | N | Y | N | N | N | Y | Y | N |
| 6 Sikorski | N | N | Y | N | Y | Y | Y | N |
| 7 Peterson | N | Y | N | N | N | Y | Y | N |
| 8 Oberstar | N | Y | N | N | N | Y | Y | N |
| **MISSISSIPPI** | | | | | | | | |
| 1 Whitten | N | Y | N | Y | N | Y | Y | N |
| 2 Espy | N | Y | N | N | N | Y | Y | N |
| 3 Montgomery | N | Y | N | Y | Y | Y | Y | N |
| 4 Parker | Y | Y | Y | Y | N | Y | Y | N |
| 5 Taylor | Y | Y | N | Y | Y | N | N | N |
| **MISSOURI** | | | | | | | | |
| 1 Clay | N | Y | N | N | N | Y | Y | N |
| 2 Horn | N | N | N | Y | N | Y | Y | N |
| 3 Gephardt | N | Y | N | N | N | Y | Y | N |
| 4 Skelton | N | Y | N | Y | Y | N | Y | N |
| 5 Wheat | N | N | N | N | N | Y | Y | N |
| 6 ***Coleman*** | Y | Y | N | Y | Y | Y | N | N |
| 7 ***Hancock*** | Y | Y | Y | Y | Y | N | N | N |
| 8 ***Emerson*** | Y | Y | N | Y | Y | Y | N | Y |
| 9 Volkmer | N | Y | N | Y | Y | Y | Y | N |
| **MONTANA** | | | | | | | | |
| 1 Williams | N | Y | N | N | N | Y | N | N |
| 2 ***Marlenee*** | ? | Y | N | Y | Y | N | N | N |
| **NEBRASKA** | | | | | | | | |
| 1 ***Bereuter*** | N | Y | Y | Y | Y | Y | N | N |
| 2 Hoagland | N | N | Y | N | N | Y | Y | N |
| 3 ***Barrett*** | N | Y | Y | Y | Y | N | N | Y |
| **NEVADA** | | | | | | | | |
| 1 Bilbray | N | N | N | Y | N | Y | Y | N |
| 2 ***Vucanovich*** | N | Y | N | Y | Y | N | N | N |
| **NEW HAMPSHIRE** | | | | | | | | |
| 1 ***Zeliff*** | Y | N | Y | Y | Y | N | N | Y |
| 2 Swett | Y | N | Y | Y | Y | Y | N | N |
| **NEW JERSEY** | | | | | | | | |
| 1 Andrews | N | Y | N | N | N | Y | Y | N |
| 2 Hughes | N | N | N | Y | Y | Y | N | N |
| 3 Pallone | N | N | Y | N | N | Y | N | N |
| 4 ***Smith*** | Y | N | Y | Y | Y | Y | N | N |
| 5 ***Roukema*** | Y | N | N | Y | Y | Y | N | N |
| 6 Dwyer | N | N | N | N | N | Y | Y | N |
| 7 ***Rinaldo*** | Y | N | N | Y | Y | Y | N | Y |
| 8 Roe | N | Y | N | N | N | Y | Y | Y |
| 9 Torricelli | Y | N | N | Y | Y | Y | Y | N |
| 10 Payne | N | N | Y | N | N | Y | Y | N |
| 11 ***Gallo*** | N | Y | N | Y | N | Y | N | Y |
| 12 ***Zimmer*** | Y | N | Y | Y | Y | N | N | Y |
| 13 ***Saxton*** | Y | N | Y | Y | Y | N | N | Y |
| 14 Guarini | Y | N | N | N | N | Y | Y | N |
| **NEW MEXICO** | | | | | | | | |
| 1 ***Schiff*** | N | Y | Y | Y | Y | Y | N | N |
| 2 ***Skeen*** | N | Y | N | Y | N | Y | N | N |
| 3 Richardson | N | N | Y | N | N | Y | Y | N |
| **NEW YORK** | | | | | | | | |
| 1 Hochbrueckner | N | N | N | N | N | Y | Y | N |
| 2 Downey | N | N | N | N | N | Y | Y | N |
| 3 Mrazek | N | N | N | N | N | Y | Y | N |
| 4 ***Lent*** | Y | Y | N | Y | Y | Y | N | Y |
| 5 ***McGrath*** | N | Y | N | Y | Y | Y | N | N |
| 6 Flake | N | N | N | N | N | Y | Y | N |
| 7 Ackerman | N | N | N | N | N | Y | Y | N |
| 8 Scheuer | N | N | Y | N | N | Y | Y | N |
| 9 Manton | N | N | N | N | N | Y | Y | N |
| 10 Schumer | N | N | Y | N | N | Y | Y | N |
| 11 Towns | N | N | Y | N | ? | # | Y | N |
| 12 Owens | N | N | N | N | N | Y | Y | N |
| 13 Solarz | N | N | Y | N | N | Y | ? | N |
| 14 ***Molinari*** | Y | N | Y | Y | Y | Y | N | Y |
| 15 ***Green*** | N | N | N | N | N | Y | N | Y |
| 16 Rangel | N | N | N | N | N | Y | Y | N |
| 17 Weiss | N | N | Y | N | N | Y | Y | N |
| 18 Serrano | N | N | Y | N | N | Y | Y | N |
| 19 Engel | N | N | N | N | N | Y | Y | N |
| 20 Lowey | N | N | N | N | N | Y | Y | N |
| 21 ***Fish*** | N | N | N | Y | Y | Y | N | N |
| 22 ***Gilman*** | Y | N | N | N | Y | Y | N | N |
| 23 McNulty | N | N | N | N | N | Y | Y | N |
| 24 ***Solomon*** | Y | N | Y | Y | Y | N | N | N |
| 25 ***Boehlert*** | N | N | Y | N | Y | Y | N | N |
| 26 ***Martin*** | N | Y | N | Y | Y | Y | N | Y |
| 27 ***Walsh*** | Y | N | Y | Y | Y | Y | N | N |
| 28 McHugh | N | N | N | N | N | Y | Y | N |
| 29 ***Horton*** | N | N | N | N | N | Y | N | Y |
| 30 Slaughter | N | N | N | N | N | Y | Y | N |
| 31 ***Paxon*** | Y | Y | Y | Y | Y | Y | N | Y |

| | 301 | 302 | 303 | 304 | 305 | 306 | 307 | 308 |
|---|---|---|---|---|---|---|---|---|
| 32 LaFalce | N | N | N | N | N | Y | Y | N |
| 33 Nowak | N | N | N | N | N | Y | Y | N |
| 34 ***Houghton*** | N | Y | Y | N | N | Y | N | Y |
| **NORTH CAROLINA** | | | | | | | | |
| 1 Jones | N | Y | N | N | N | Y | Y | N |
| 2 Valentine | Y | N | N | Y | Y | Y | N | N |
| 3 Lancaster | N | N | N | Y | N | Y | N | N |
| 4 Price | N | N | N | N | Y | N | Y | N |
| 5 Neal | ? | N | Y | Y | Y | Y | Y | N |
| 6 ***Coble*** | Y | Y | Y | Y | Y | N | N | Y |
| 7 Rose | N | Y | N | N | N | Y | Y | N |
| 8 Hefner | N | Y | N | Y | N | Y | Y | N |
| 9 ***McMillan*** | Y | Y | N | Y | Y | Y | N | Y |
| 10 ***Ballenger*** | Y | Y | Y | Y | Y | N | N | N |
| 11 ***Taylor*** | Y | Y | Y | Y | Y | Y | N | Y |
| **NORTH DAKOTA** | | | | | | | | |
| AL Dorgan | N | N | N | Y | Y | Y | N | N |
| **OHIO** | | | | | | | | |
| 1 Luken | Y | N | N | Y | Y | Y | Y | N |
| 2 ***Gradison*** | N | Y | N | Y | Y | Y | N | N |
| 3 Hall | Y | Y | N | N | N | Y | Y | N |
| 4 ***Oxley*** | Y | Y | Y | Y | Y | Y | N | Y |
| 5 ***Gillmor*** | N | Y | N | Y | Y | Y | N | Y |
| 6 ***McEwen*** | Y | Y | N | Y | Y | N | N | Y |
| 7 ***Hobson*** | ? | Y | N | Y | Y | Y | N | Y |
| 8 ***Boehner*** | Y | Y | Y | Y | Y | N | N | Y |
| 9 Kaptur | N | Y | N | N | N | Y | Y | N |
| 10 ***Miller*** | Y | Y | N | Y | Y | N | N | Y |
| 11 Eckart | N | N | N | Y | N | Y | Y | N |
| 12 ***Kasich*** | N | N | N | Y | Y | Y | N | N |
| 13 Pease | N | N | N | N | N | Y | Y | N |
| 14 Sawyer | N | N | N | N | N | Y | Y | N |
| 15 ***Wylie*** | N | N | Y | Y | Y | N | N | Y |
| 16 ***Regula*** | N | Y | N | Y | N | Y | N | Y |
| 17 Traficant | N | Y | N | N | N | Y | Y | N |
| 18 Applegate | Y | N | N | Y | N | Y | Y | N |
| 19 Feighan | ? | ? | ? | ? | ? | ? | ? | ? |
| 20 Oakar | N | Y | N | N | N | Y | Y | N |
| 21 Stokes | N | N | N | N | N | Y | Y | N |
| **OKLAHOMA** | | | | | | | | |
| 1 ***Inhofe*** | N | Y | Y | Y | Y | N | N | Y |
| 2 Synar | N | N | Y | N | N | Y | Y | N |
| 3 Brewster | N | Y | N | Y | Y | Y | Y | N |
| 4 McCurdy | N | N | N | Y | Y | Y | Y | N |
| 5 ***Edwards*** | Y | Y | N | Y | Y | N | N | N |
| 6 English | N | Y | N | Y | Y | Y | N | N |
| **OREGON** | | | | | | | | |
| 1 AuCoin | N | Y | N | N | N | Y | Y | N |
| 2 ***Smith*** | N | Y | Y | Y | Y | N | N | Y |
| 3 Wyden | N | Y | N | N | N | Y | Y | N |
| 4 DeFazio | N | Y | N | N | N | Y | Y | N |
| 5 Kopetski | — | + | — | — | — | Y | Y | N |
| **PENNSYLVANIA** | | | | | | | | |
| 1 Foglietta | N | N | N | N | N | Y | Y | N |
| 2 Blackwell | ? | N | N | N | N | Y | Y | N |
| 3 Borski | N | N | N | Y | N | Y | Y | N |
| 4 Kolter | ? | N | N | N | ? | Y | ? | ? |
| 5 ***Schulze*** | N | Y | Y | Y | Y | Y | N | N |
| 6 Yatron | N | N | Y | Y | N | Y | Y | N |
| 7 ***Weldon*** | Y | N | Y | Y | Y | Y | N | N |
| 8 Kostmayer | N | N | N | N | N | Y | Y | N |
| 9 ***Shuster*** | ? | Y | Y | Y | Y | Y | N | Y |
| 10 ***McDade*** | N | Y | N | Y | N | Y | N | ? |
| 11 Kanjorski | N | N | N | N | N | Y | Y | N |
| 12 Murtha | N | Y | N | N | N | Y | Y | N |
| 13 ***Coughlin*** | ? | ? | ? | ? | ? | ? | ? | ? |
| 14 Coyne | N | N | N | N | N | Y | Y | N |
| 15 ***Ritter*** | Y | Y | Y | Y | Y | Y | N | N |
| 16 ***Walker*** | Y | Y | Y | Y | Y | N | N | N |
| 17 ***Gekas*** | Y | Y | Y | Y | Y | N | N | N |
| 18 ***Santorum*** | Y | Y | N | Y | Y | N | N | N |
| 19 ***Goodling*** | N | Y | Y | Y | Y | Y | — | N |
| 20 Gaydos | N | N | N | N | N | Y | Y | N |
| 21 ***Ridge*** | N | N | Y | Y | Y | Y | N | N |
| 22 Murphy | Y | Y | N | Y | Y | N | N | N |
| 23 ***Clinger*** | N | Y | Y | Y | N | Y | N | Y |
| **RHODE ISLAND** | | | | | | | | |
| 1 ***Machtley*** | N | N | Y | N | N | Y | N | N |
| 2 Reed | N | N | N | Y | N | Y | Y | N |
| **SOUTH CAROLINA** | | | | | | | | |
| 1 ***Ravenel*** | N | N | Y | Y | Y | Y | N | N |
| 2 ***Spence*** | Y | N | Y | Y | Y | Y | N | N |
| 3 Derrick | N | Y | N | Y | N | Y | Y | N |
| 4 Patterson | Y | Y | Y | Y | Y | N | Y | N |
| 5 Spratt | N | Y | N | N | N | Y | Y | N |
| 6 Tallon | ? | ? | ? | ? | ? | ? | ? | ? |

| | 301 | 302 | 303 | 304 | 305 | 306 | 307 | 308 |
|---|---|---|---|---|---|---|---|---|
| **SOUTH DAKOTA** | | | | | | | | |
| AL Johnson | N | Y | Y | N | N | Y | Y | N |
| **TENNESSEE** | | | | | | | | |
| 1 ***Quillen*** | Y | Y | N | Y | N | Y | N | N |
| 2 ***Duncan*** | Y | Y | Y | Y | Y | N | N | Y |
| 3 Lloyd | Y | N | N | Y | Y | Y | Y | N |
| 4 Cooper | Y | Y | Y | Y | Y | Y | Y | N |
| 5 Clement | Y | N | N | Y | Y | Y | Y | N |
| 6 Gordon | N | N | N | Y | N | Y | Y | N |
| 7 ***Sundquist*** | Y | Y | N | Y | Y | N | N | N |
| 8 Tanner | Y | Y | N | Y | Y | Y | Y | N |
| 9 Ford | N | Y | N | N | Y | Y | N | N |
| **TEXAS** | | | | | | | | |
| 1 Chapman | ? | Y | N | Y | N | Y | Y | N |
| 2 Wilson | N | Y | N | Y | N | Y | Y | ? |
| 3 ***Johnson*** | Y | Y | Y | Y | Y | N | N | N |
| 4 Hall | N | Y | N | Y | Y | N | N | N |
| 5 Bryant | N | N | N | N | N | Y | Y | N |
| 6 ***Barton*** | Y | N | Y | Y | Y | N | N | Y |
| 7 ***Archer*** | Y | ? | Y | Y | Y | N | N | Y |
| 8 ***Fields*** | Y | Y | Y | Y | Y | N | N | Y |
| 9 Brooks | N | Y | N | N | N | Y | Y | N |
| 10 Pickle | Y | Y | N | N | N | Y | Y | N |
| 11 Edwards | Y | Y | N | Y | Y | Y | Y | N |
| 12 Geren | Y | N | N | Y | Y | Y | Y | N |
| 13 Sarpalius | Y | Y | N | Y | Y | N | Y | N |
| 14 Laughlin | N | Y | N | Y | N | Y | ? | ? |
| 15 de la Garza | N | Y | N | N | N | Y | Y | N |
| 16 Coleman | N | N | N | N | N | Y | Y | N |
| 17 Stenholm | Y | Y | Y | Y | Y | N | Y | N |
| 18 Washington | N | N | ? | N | N | Y | Y | ? |
| 19 ***Combest*** | Y | Y | Y | Y | Y | N | N | N |
| 20 Gonzalez | N | Y | N | N | N | Y | Y | N |
| 21 ***Smith*** | Y | Y | N | Y | Y | Y | N | Y |
| 22 ***DeLay*** | Y | Y | N | Y | Y | N | N | Y |
| 23 Bustamante | N | Y | N | N | N | Y | Y | N |
| 24 Frost | N | Y | N | Y | ? | Y | Y | N |
| 25 Andrews | Y | N | N | Y | Y | Y | Y | N |
| 26 ***Armey*** | Y | Y | Y | Y | Y | N | N | Y |
| 27 Ortiz | N | Y | N | Y | N | Y | Y | N |
| **UTAH** | | | | | | | | |
| 1 ***Hansen*** | # | ? | ? | ? | ? | X | ? | ? |
| 2 Owens | N | N | N | Y | N | Y | Y | N |
| 3 Orton | N | Y | N | Y | Y | N | Y | Y |
| **VERMONT** | | | | | | | | |
| AL *Sanders* | N | N | N | N | N | Y | Y | N |
| **VIRGINIA** | | | | | | | | |
| 1 ***Bateman*** | N | Y | N | Y | Y | Y | N | N |
| 2 Pickett | N | Y | N | Y | N | Y | Y | N |
| 3 ***Bliley*** | Y | Y | Y | Y | Y | Y | N | Y |
| 4 Sisisky | Y | Y | N | Y | N | Y | Y | N |
| 5 Payne | N | N | N | Y | Y | Y | Y | N |
| 6 Olin | N | Y | N | N | N | Y | Y | ? |
| 7 ***Allen*** | Y | Y | N | Y | Y | N | N | Y |
| 8 Moran | N | N | N | N | N | Y | Y | N |
| 9 Boucher | N | N | N | N | N | Y | Y | N |
| 10 ***Wolf*** | Y | Y | Y | Y | Y | Y | N | N |
| **WASHINGTON** | | | | | | | | |
| 1 ***Miller*** | N | Y | ? | Y | Y | N | N | Y |
| 2 Swift | N | Y | N | N | N | Y | Y | N |
| 3 Unsoeld | N | Y | N | N | N | Y | Y | N |
| 4 ***Morrison*** | N | Y | Y | Y | N | Y | N | N |
| 5 Foley | | | | | | | | |
| 6 Dicks | N | Y | N | N | N | Y | Y | N |
| 7 McDermott | N | Y | Y | N | N | Y | Y | N |
| 8 ***Chandler*** | N | Y | Y | Y | Y | Y | N | Y |
| **WEST VIRGINIA** | | | | | | | | |
| 1 Mollohan | N | Y | N | N | N | Y | Y | N |
| 2 Staggers | N | Y | N | Y | N | Y | N | N |
| 3 Wise | N | N | N | Y | N | N | Y | N |
| 4 Rahall | N | Y | N | N | N | Y | N | N |
| **WISCONSIN** | | | | | | | | |
| 1 Aspin | N | Y | Y | Y | Y | Y | Y | N |
| 2 ***Klug*** | Y | N | Y | Y | Y | N | N | Y |
| 3 ***Gunderson*** | Y | N | Y | Y | Y | Y | N | Y |
| 4 Kleczka | ? | ? | N | N | N | Y | Y | N |
| 5 Moody | N | N | Y | N | Y | Y | N | N |
| 6 ***Petri*** | Y | N | Y | Y | Y | N | N | N |
| 7 Obey | N | Y | N | N | N | Y | Y | N |
| 8 ***Roth*** | N | Y | Y | Y | Y | Y | N | N |
| 9 ***Sensenbrenner*** | Y | N | Y | Y | Y | N | N | N |
| **WYOMING** | | | | | | | | |
| AL ***Thomas*** | N | Y | N | Y | Y | N | N | ? |

Southern states - Ala., Ark., Fla., Ga., Ky., La., Miss., N.C., Okla., S.C., Tenn., Texas, Va.
Omitted votes are quorum calls, which CQ does not include in its vote charts.

**309. HR 4850. Cable Television Regulation/Miscellaneous.** Dingell, D-Mich., en bloc amendment to require cable operators to provide 30 days' notice of a rate increase over 5 percent; clarify protection for grandfathered rate regulation agreements between franchising authorities and cable companies; give channel positioning protections for local broadcasters; require an update of the nation's major television markets; indemnify local franchising authorities against discrimination claims; require a study of sports migration from broadcast to cable and pay-per-view services; and require cable providers to notify subscribers and allow blocking of premium channels carrying an X, R or NC-17 rating with charge. Adopted 403-2: R 157-2; D 245-0 (ND 172-0, SD 73-0); I 1-0, July 23, 1992.

**310. HR 4850. Cable Television Regulation/Program Access.** Manton, D-N.Y., substitute to the Tauzin, D-La., amendment, to prohibit video programmers controlled by cable operators from refusing to deal with other cable operators when such a refusal would unreasonably restrain competition. The Tauzin amendment would ban programmers affiliated with cable operators from dealing unreasonably in the price, terms and conditions of programming sold to satellite distributors and other potential competitors. Rejected 162-247: R 93-69; D 69-177 (ND 57-115, SD 12-62); I 0-1, July 23, 1992.

**311. HR 4850. Cable Television Regulation/Program Access.** Tauzin, D-La., amendment to give satellite distributors and other potential cable competitors lower-priced access to cable programming. Adopted 338-68: R 116-45; D 221-23 (ND 152-18, SD 69-5); I 1-0, July 23, 1992.

**312. HR 4850. Cable Television Regulation/Republican Substitute.** Lent, R-N.Y., substitute amendment to regulate rates for a basic level of cable service only. The substitute would also make other changes that would make the rate and program access regulation in the bill less stringent. Rejected 144-266: R 127-34; D 17-231 (ND 10-164, SD 7-67); I 0-1, July 23, 1992.

**313. HR 4850. Cable Television Regulation/Passage.** Passage of the bill to lower cable television rates and improve customer service by requiring the Federal Communications Commission (FCC) to set a nationwide price for basic cable service; allowing the FCC to regulate the rates for packages above the basic tier if there was a complaint by a state or local government or other type of franchising authority; and by other means. Passed 340-73: R 98-63; D 241-10 (ND 169-6, SD 72-4); I 1-0, July 23, 1992. A "nay" was a vote in support of the president's position.

**314. HR 4312. Voting Rights Language Assistance.** McCollum, R-Fla., substitute amendment to reduce the 15-year extension for voting rights language assistance for certain language-minority populations to five years; strike the provisions that augment the trigger mechanism that qualifies a jurisdiction to receive assistance; and require the Justice Department and Census Bureau to report on minority voting participation. Rejected 142-233: R 115-31; D 27-201 (ND 8-153, SD 19-48); I 0-1, July 24, 1992.

**315. HR 4312. Voting Rights Language Assistance/Costs.** Condit, D-Calif., amendment to require federal grants to cover the cost of providing bilingual voting assistance to counties that are required to provide assistance. Rejected 184-186: R 125-19; D 59-166 (ND 26-132, SD 33-34); I 0-1, July 24, 1992.

**316. HR 4312. Voting Rights Language Assistance/Request Requirement.** McCollum, R-Fla., amendment to require citizens to request bilingual aid in order to receive it. Rejected 141-230: R 120-25; D 21-204 (ND 7-152, SD 14-52); I 0-1, July 24, 1992.

## KEY

| | |
|---|---|
| Y | Voted for (yea). |
| # | Paired for. |
| + | Announced for. |
| N | Voted against (nay). |
| X | Paired against. |
| − | Announced against. |
| P | Voted "present." |
| C | Voted "present" to avoid possible conflict of interest. |
| ? | Did not vote or otherwise make a position known. |

Democrats **Republicans**
*Independent*

| | 309 | 310 | 311 | 312 | 313 | 314 | 315 | 316 |
|---|---|---|---|---|---|---|---|---|
| **ALABAMA** | | | | | | | | |
| 1 *Callahan* | Y | N | Y | Y | Y | ? | ? | ? |
| 2 *Dickinson* | Y | N | Y | N | Y | Y | Y | Y |
| 3 Browder | Y | N | Y | N | Y | Y | Y | N |
| 4 Bevill | Y | N | Y | N | Y | N | N | N |
| 5 Cramer | Y | N | Y | N | Y | Y | Y | N |
| 6 Erdreich | Y | N | Y | N | Y | Y | Y | Y |
| 7 Harris | Y | N | Y | N | Y | Y | Y | N |
| **ALASKA** | | | | | | | | |
| AL *Young* | Y | N | Y | Y | Y | Y | Y | Y |
| **ARIZONA** | | | | | | | | |
| 1 *Rhodes* | Y | Y | N | Y | N | Y | Y | Y |
| 2 Pastor | Y | Y | N | Y | N | N | N | N |
| 3 *Stump* | Y | Y | N | Y | N | Y | Y | Y |
| 4 *Kyl* | Y | Y | N | Y | N | Y | Y | Y |
| 5 *Kolbe* | Y | Y | N | Y | N | N | Y | Y |
| **ARKANSAS** | | | | | | | | |
| 1 Alexander | Y | N | Y | N | Y | N | N | N |
| 2 Thornton | Y | Y | Y | N | Y | N | N | N |
| 3 *Hammerschmidt* | Y | Y | Y | Y | Y | Y | ? | ? |
| 4 Anthony | ? | ? | ? | N | Y | ? | ? | ? |
| **CALIFORNIA** | | | | | | | | |
| 1 *Riggs* | Y | N | Y | Y | Y | # | # | # |
| 2 *Herger* | Y | Y | N | Y | N | Y | Y | Y |
| 3 Matsui | Y | Y | Y | N | Y | ? | ? | ? |
| 4 Fazio | Y | Y | Y | N | Y | N | N | N |
| 5 Pelosi | Y | Y | Y | N | Y | N | N | N |
| 6 Boxer | Y | Y | Y | N | Y | ? | X | ? |
| 7 Miller | Y | Y | Y | N | Y | N | N | N |
| 8 Dellums | Y | ? | Y | N | Y | N | N | N |
| 9 Stark | Y | N | Y | N | Y | N | N | N |
| 10 Edwards | Y | N | Y | N | Y | N | N | ? |
| 11 Lantos | Y | N | Y | N | Y | N | N | N |
| 12 *Campbell* | Y | N | Y | N | Y | N | Y | N |
| 13 Mineta | Y | N | Y | ? | N | N | N | N |
| 14 *Doolittle* | Y | Y | N | Y | Y | Y | Y | Y |
| 15 Condit | Y | N | Y | N | Y | Y | N | N |
| 16 Panetta | Y | Y | Y | N | Y | N | N | N |
| 17 Dooley | Y | Y | Y | N | Y | N | N | N |
| 18 Lehman | Y | N | Y | N | Y | N | N | N |
| 19 *Lagomarsino* | Y | Y | N | Y | N | Y | Y | Y |
| 20 *Thomas* | Y | N | Y | N | Y | Y | Y | Y |
| 21 *Gallegly* | Y | Y | Y | Y | Y | N | Y | Y |
| 22 *Moorhead* | Y | Y | Y | Y | Y | Y | Y | Y |
| 23 Beilenson | Y | N | Y | N | Y | N | N | N |
| 24 Waxman | Y | Y | Y | N | Y | N | N | N |
| 25 Roybal | Y | N | Y | N | N | N | N | N |
| 26 Berman | Y | Y | N | N | Y | N | N | N |
| 27 Levine | ? | ? | ? | ? | ? | ? | ? | ? |
| 28 Dixon | Y | N | N | N | N | N | N | N |
| 29 Waters | Y | N | Y | N | Y | X | N | N |
| 30 Martinez | Y | N | Y | N | Y | X | # | X |
| 31 Dymally | ? | ? | ? | ? | ? | ? | ? | ? |
| 32 Anderson | Y | N | Y | N | N | N | N | N |
| 33 *Dreier* | Y | N | Y | N | Y | Y | Y | Y |
| 34 Torres | Y | Y | N | N | Y | N | N | N |
| 35 *Lewis* | Y | Y | Y | Y | Y | N | Y | N |
| 36 Brown | Y | N | Y | N | Y | N | ? | ? |
| 37 *McCandless* | Y | N | Y | Y | Y | Y | Y | Y |
| 38 *Dornan* | Y | Y | N | Y | N | Y | Y | Y |
| 39 *Dannemeyer* | Y | Y | N | Y | N | Y | Y | Y |
| 40 *Cox* | Y | N | Y | Y | Y | Y | Y | Y |
| 41 *Lowery* | ? | Y | Y | Y | N | Y | Y | Y |

| | 309 | 310 | 311 | 312 | 313 | 314 | 315 | 316 |
|---|---|---|---|---|---|---|---|---|
| 42 *Rohrabacher* | Y | Y | N | Y | N | Y | Y | Y |
| 43 *Packard* | Y | N | Y | N | Y | Y | Y | Y |
| 44 *Cunningham* | Y | Y | N | Y | N | Y | Y | Y |
| 45 *Hunter* | N | Y | Y | Y | N | Y | Y | Y |
| **COLORADO** | | | | | | | | |
| 1 Schroeder | Y | Y | N | N | N | N | N | N |
| 2 Skaggs | Y | Y | N | N | N | N | N | N |
| 3 *Campbell* | Y | Y | N | Y | N | ? | ? | ? |
| 4 *Allard* | Y | Y | N | Y | N | ? | ? | ? |
| 5 *Hefley* | N | Y | N | Y | N | ? | ? | ? |
| 6 *Schaefer* | Y | Y | N | Y | N | Y | Y | Y |
| **CONNECTICUT** | | | | | | | | |
| 1 Kennelly | Y | N | Y | N | Y | N | N | N |
| 2 Gejdenson | Y | N | Y | N | Y | N | N | N |
| 3 DeLauro | Y | N | Y | N | Y | N | N | N |
| 4 *Shays* | Y | N | Y | N | Y | Y | Y | N |
| 5 *Franks* | Y | Y | N | Y | N | Y | Y | Y |
| 6 *Johnson* | Y | Y | Y | Y | N | Y | Y | Y |
| **DELAWARE** | | | | | | | | |
| AL Carper | Y | Y | Y | N | Y | N | N | N |
| **FLORIDA** | | | | | | | | |
| 1 Hutto | Y | N | Y | N | Y | Y | Y | Y |
| 2 Peterson | + | − | + | − | + | − | + | − |
| 3 Bennett | Y | N | Y | N | N | N | N | N |
| 4 *James* | Y | Y | Y | Y | Y | N | N | N |
| 5 *McCollum* | Y | Y | Y | Y | Y | Y | Y | Y |
| 6 *Stearns* | Y | Y | Y | Y | Y | Y | Y | Y |
| 7 Gibbons | Y | N | Y | N | N | N | N | N |
| 8 *Young* | Y | Y | Y | N | Y | Y | Y | Y |
| 9 *Bilirakis* | Y | Y | N | Y | Y | Y | Y | Y |
| 10 *Ireland* | Y | N | Y | N | Y | ? | ? | ? |
| 11 Bacchus | Y | N | Y | N | Y | ? | ? | ? |
| 12 *Lewis* | Y | Y | Y | Y | Y | Y | Y | Y |
| 13 *Goss* | Y | N | Y | Y | Y | Y | Y | Y |
| 14 Johnston | Y | Y | Y | N | N | N | N | N |
| 15 *Shaw* | Y | Y | Y | N | Y | Y | Y | Y |
| 16 Smith | Y | N | Y | N | Y | N | N | N |
| 17 Lehman | ? | ? | ? | ? | ? | N | N | N |
| 18 *Ros−Lehtinen* | Y | N | Y | N | N | N | N | N |
| 19 Fascell | Y | N | Y | N | Y | N | N | N |
| **GEORGIA** | | | | | | | | |
| 1 Thomas | ? | ? | ? | ? | ? | ? | ? | ? |
| 2 Hatcher | ? | ? | ? | ? | ? | ? | ? | ? |
| 3 Ray | ? | ? | ? | ? | ? | ? | ? | ? |
| 4 Jones | ? | N | Y | N | Y | N | N | N |
| 5 Lewis | Y | N | Y | N | N | N | N | N |
| 6 *Gingrich* | Y | Y | N | Y | N | Y | Y | Y |
| 7 Darden | Y | Y | Y | N | Y | Y | Y | N |
| 8 Rowland | Y | N | Y | N | Y | N | N | N |
| 9 Jenkins | Y | Y | N | Y | Y | Y | Y | N |
| 10 Barnard | Y | Y | N | Y | N | ? | ? | ? |
| **HAWAII** | | | | | | | | |
| 1 Abercrombie | Y | N | Y | N | Y | N | N | N |
| 2 Mink | Y | N | N | N | Y | N | N | N |
| **IDAHO** | | | | | | | | |
| 1 LaRocco | Y | N | Y | N | Y | N | N | N |
| 2 Stallings | Y | N | Y | N | Y | N | N | N |
| **ILLINOIS** | | | | | | | | |
| 1 Hayes | Y | N | Y | N | Y | N | N | N |
| 2 Savage | Y | N | Y | N | N | N | N | N |
| 3 Russo | Y | Y | Y | Y | ? | ? | N | N |
| 4 Sangmeister | Y | Y | Y | N | Y | N | N | N |
| 5 Lipinski | Y | N | Y | N | Y | Y | Y | N |
| 6 *Hyde* | ? | ? | ? | ? | ? | ? | ? | ? |
| 7 Collins | Y | N | N | N | N | N | N | N |
| 8 Rostenkowski | Y | N | Y | N | Y | N | N | N |
| 9 Yates | ? | ? | ? | X | ? | N | N | N |
| 10 *Porter* | Y | N | Y | Y | Y | Y | Y | Y |
| 11 Annunzio | Y | Y | Y | N | Y | N | N | N |
| 12 *Crane* | Y | N | N | Y | N | Y | Y | Y |
| 13 *Fawell* | Y | N | Y | N | Y | Y | Y | Y |
| 14 *Hastert* | Y | Y | Y | Y | Y | Y | Y | Y |
| 15 *Ewing* | Y | N | Y | Y | Y | Y | Y | Y |
| 16 Cox | Y | N | Y | N | Y | N | N | N |
| 17 Evans | Y | N | Y | N | N | N | N | N |
| 18 *Michel* | Y | Y | Y | N | Y | Y | Y | Y |
| 19 Bruce | Y | N | Y | N | Y | N | N | N |
| 20 Durbin | Y | N | Y | N | Y | N | N | N |
| 21 Costello | Y | Y | Y | N | Y | N | N | N |
| 22 Poshard | Y | N | Y | N | Y | N | N | N |
| **INDIANA** | | | | | | | | |
| 1 Visclosky | Y | N | Y | N | Y | N | N | N |
| 2 Sharp | Y | Y | Y | N | Y | N | ? | N |
| 3 Roemer | Y | N | Y | N | Y | N | Y | N |

| | 309 | 310 | 311 | 312 | 313 | 314 | 315 | 316 |
|---|---|---|---|---|---|---|---|---|
| 4 Long | Y | N | Y | N | Y | N | N | N |
| 5 Jontz | Y | N | Y | N | Y | N | N | N |
| 6 ***Burton*** | Y | Y | N | Y | N | Y | Y | Y |
| 7 ***Myers*** | Y | N | N | Y | N | Y | Y | Y |
| 8 McCloskey | Y | N | Y | N | Y | N | N | N |
| 9 Hamilton | Y | Y | Y | N | Y | N | N | N |
| 10 Jacobs | Y | N | Y | N | Y | N | N | N |
| **IOWA** | | | | | | | | |
| 1 ***Leach*** | Y | N | Y | N | Y | N | N | N |
| 2 ***Nussle*** | Y | N | Y | Y | Y | Y | Y | Y |
| 3 Nagle | Y | N | Y | N | Y | N | N | N |
| 4 Smith | Y | N | Y | Y | Y | N | N | N |
| 5 ***Lightfoot*** | Y | N | Y | N | Y | Y | Y | Y |
| 6 ***Grandy*** | Y | N | Y | N | Y | N | N | N |
| **KANSAS** | | | | | | | | |
| 1 ***Roberts*** | Y | N | Y | N | Y | Y | Y | Y |
| 2 Slattery | Y | N | Y | N | Y | N | N | N |
| 3 ***Meyers*** | Y | N | Y | N | Y | Y | Y | Y |
| 4 Glickman | Y | N | Y | N | Y | N | N | N |
| 5 ***Nichols*** | Y | N | Y | Y | Y | Y | Y | Y |
| **KENTUCKY** | | | | | | | | |
| 1 Hubbard | Y | N | Y | N | Y | N | Y | ? |
| 2 Natcher | Y | N | Y | N | Y | N | N | N |
| 3 Mazzoli | Y | N | Y | N | Y | N | N | N |
| 4 ***Bunning*** | Y | N | Y | N | Y | ? | ? | ? |
| 5 ***Rogers*** | Y | N | Y | Y | Y | Y | Y | Y |
| 6 ***Hopkins*** | Y | Y | N | Y | N | Y | Y | Y |
| 7 Perkins | Y | N | Y | N | Y | N | N | N |
| **LOUISIANA** | | | | | | | | |
| 1 ***Livingston*** | Y | Y | Y | Y | Y | Y | ? | ? |
| 2 Jefferson | Y | N | Y | N | Y | N | N | N |
| 3 Tauzin | Y | N | Y | N | Y | N | Y | Y |
| 4 ***McCrery*** | Y | N | Y | Y | N | Y | Y | Y |
| 5 Huckaby | Y | N | Y | N | Y | ? | ? | ? |
| 6 ***Baker*** | Y | N | Y | Y | N | Y | Y | N |
| 7 Hayes | Y | N | Y | N | Y | N | Y | ? |
| 8 ***Holloway*** | Y | Y | Y | Y | N | Y | ? | Y |
| **MAINE** | | | | | | | | |
| 1 Andrews | Y | N | Y | N | Y | N | N | N |
| 2 ***Snowe*** | Y | N | Y | N | Y | N | Y | N |
| **MARYLAND** | | | | | | | | |
| 1 ***Gilchrest*** | Y | Y | Y | N | Y | Y | Y | Y |
| 2 ***Bentley*** | Y | N | Y | Y | Y | Y | Y | Y |
| 3 Cardin | Y | N | Y | N | Y | N | N | N |
| 4 McMillen | Y | Y | Y | N | Y | N | Y | N |
| 5 Hoyer | Y | Y | Y | N | Y | N | N | N |
| 6 Byron | Y | N | Y | N | Y | Y | Y | Y |
| 7 Mfume | Y | N | Y | N | Y | N | N | N |
| 8 ***Morella*** | Y | Y | Y | N | Y | N | N | N |
| **MASSACHUSETTS** | | | | | | | | |
| 1 Olver | Y | N | Y | N | Y | N | N | N |
| 2 Neal | Y | N | Y | N | Y | N | Y | N |
| 3 Early | Y | N | ? | N | Y | ? | ? | ? |
| 4 Frank | Y | N | Y | N | Y | N | N | N |
| 5 Atkins | Y | N | Y | N | Y | ? | ? | ? |
| 6 Mavroules | Y | N | Y | N | Y | N | Y | N |
| 7 Markey | Y | N | Y | N | Y | ? | N | N |
| 8 Kennedy | Y | N | Y | N | Y | N | N | N |
| 9 Moakley | Y | N | Y | N | Y | N | N | N |
| 10 Studds | Y | N | Y | N | Y | N | N | N |
| 11 Donnelly | Y | N | Y | N | Y | N | Y | N |
| **MICHIGAN** | | | | | | | | |
| 1 Conyers | Y | Y | ? | N | Y | ? | ? | ? |
| 2 ***Pursell*** | Y | Y | Y | Y | N | Y | Y | Y |
| 3 Wolpe | Y | Y | Y | N | Y | N | N | N |
| 4 ***Upton*** | Y | Y | Y | Y | Y | N | Y | Y |
| 5 ***Henry*** | Y | Y | Y | N | Y | Y | Y | Y |
| 6 Carr | Y | Y | Y | N | Y | N | N | N |
| 7 Kildee | Y | Y | Y | N | Y | N | N | N |
| 8 Traxler | ? | ? | ? | ? | ? | N | ? | ? |
| 9 ***Vander Jagt*** | Y | Y | Y | Y | Y | Y | Y | Y |
| 10 ***Camp*** | Y | N | Y | Y | Y | Y | Y | Y |
| 11 ***Davis*** | Y | N | Y | Y | Y | Y | Y | N |
| 12 Bonior | Y | Y | N | N | Y | N | N | N |
| 13 Collins | Y | Y | Y | N | Y | N | N | N |
| 14 Hertel | Y | Y | Y | N | Y | N | N | N |
| 15 Ford | Y | ? | ? | N | Y | N | N | N |
| 16 Dingell | Y | Y | Y | N | Y | N | N | Y |
| 17 Levin | Y | Y | Y | N | Y | N | N | N |
| 18 ***Broomfield*** | Y | Y | Y | Y | Y | ? | ? | ? |
| **MINNESOTA** | | | | | | | | |
| 1 Penny | Y | N | Y | Y | N | N | Y | Y |
| 2 ***Weber*** | Y | Y | Y | ? | ? | Y | N | Y |
| 3 ***Ramstad*** | Y | Y | Y | N | Y | Y | Y | Y |
| 4 Vento | Y | N | Y | N | Y | N | N | N |
| 5 Sabo | Y | N | Y | N | Y | N | N | N |
| 6 Sikorski | Y | N | Y | N | Y | N | N | N |
| 7 Peterson | Y | N | Y | N | Y | N | Y | N |
| 8 Oberstar | Y | N | Y | N | Y | N | N | N |
| **MISSISSIPPI** | | | | | | | | |
| 1 Whitten | Y | N | Y | N | Y | ? | ? | N |
| 2 Espy | Y | Y | Y | N | Y | N | N | N |
| 3 Montgomery | Y | N | Y | N | Y | Y | Y | Y |
| 4 Parker | Y | Y | N | Y | N | Y | Y | Y |
| 5 Taylor | Y | N | Y | N | Y | Y | Y | Y |
| **MISSOURI** | | | | | | | | |
| 1 Clay | Y | N | Y | N | Y | N | N | N |
| 2 Horn | Y | N | Y | N | Y | N | N | N |
| 3 Gephardt | ? | Y | Y | N | Y | N | N | ? |
| 4 Skelton | Y | N | Y | N | Y | Y | N | N |
| 5 Wheat | Y | N | Y | N | Y | N | N | N |
| 6 ***Coleman*** | Y | N | Y | N | Y | ? | ? | ? |
| 7 ***Hancock*** | Y | Y | N | Y | Y | Y | Y | Y |
| 8 ***Emerson*** | Y | N | Y | Y | Y | Y | Y | Y |
| 9 Volkmer | Y | N | Y | N | Y | N | N | N |
| **MONTANA** | | | | | | | | |
| 1 Williams | Y | N | Y | N | Y | N | N | N |
| 2 ***Marlenee*** | Y | N | Y | Y | N | Y | Y | Y |
| **NEBRASKA** | | | | | | | | |
| 1 ***Bereuter*** | ? | N | Y | N | Y | Y | N | Y |
| 2 Hoagland | Y | N | Y | N | Y | N | N | N |
| 3 ***Barrett*** | Y | N | Y | Y | N | Y | Y | Y |
| **NEVADA** | | | | | | | | |
| 1 Bilbray | ? | N | Y | N | Y | N | N | N |
| 2 ***Vucanovich*** | Y | N | Y | N | Y | N | Y | N |
| **NEW HAMPSHIRE** | | | | | | | | |
| 1 ***Zeliff*** | Y | Y | N | Y | N | Y | Y | Y |
| 2 Swett | Y | Y | Y | N | Y | N | Y | N |
| **NEW JERSEY** | | | | | | | | |
| 1 Andrews | Y | Y | N | Y | Y | N | N | N |
| 2 Hughes | Y | N | Y | N | Y | N | N | N |
| 3 Pallone | Y | N | Y | N | Y | N | N | N |
| 4 ***Smith*** | Y | Y | Y | Y | Y | Y | Y | Y |
| 5 ***Roukema*** | Y | Y | N | Y | N | Y | Y | Y |
| 6 Dwyer | ? | N | Y | N | Y | ? | ? | ? |
| 7 ***Rinaldo*** | Y | Y | N | Y | Y | Y | Y | Y |
| 8 Roe | Y | N | Y | N | Y | N | N | N |
| 9 Torricelli | Y | N | Y | N | Y | N | N | N |
| 10 Payne | Y | N | Y | N | Y | N | N | N |
| 11 ***Gallo*** | Y | Y | Y | Y | Y | Y | Y | Y |
| 12 ***Zimmer*** | Y | Y | Y | Y | Y | Y | Y | Y |
| 13 ***Saxton*** | Y | Y | Y | Y | Y | Y | Y | Y |
| 14 Guarini | Y | N | Y | N | Y | N | N | N |
| **NEW MEXICO** | | | | | | | | |
| 1 ***Schiff*** | Y | Y | Y | Y | Y | N | N | Y |
| 2 ***Skeen*** | Y | N | Y | N | Y | N | Y | Y |
| 3 Richardson | Y | Y | Y | N | Y | N | N | N |
| **NEW YORK** | | | | | | | | |
| 1 Hochbrueckner | Y | N | Y | N | Y | N | Y | N |
| 2 Downey | Y | N | Y | N | Y | N | N | N |
| 3 Mrazek | Y | N | Y | N | Y | ? | N | ? |
| 4 ***Lent*** | Y | Y | N | Y | N | Y | Y | Y |
| 5 ***McGrath*** | Y | Y | N | N | Y | N | Y | Y |
| 6 Flake | Y | N | Y | N | Y | N | N | N |
| 7 Ackerman | Y | Y | Y | N | Y | N | N | N |
| 8 Scheuer | Y | Y | Y | N | Y | N | N | N |
| 9 Manton | Y | Y | Y | N | Y | N | N | N |
| 10 Schumer | Y | N | Y | N | Y | N | N | N |
| 11 Towns | Y | Y | Y | Y | Y | N | N | ? |
| 12 Owens | Y | Y | Y | N | Y | N | N | N |
| 13 Solarz | Y | ? | ? | ? | ? | N | N | N |
| 14 ***Molinari*** | Y | Y | N | Y | N | N | N | N |
| 15 ***Green*** | Y | Y | Y | Y | Y | N | N | N |
| 16 Rangel | ? | Y | Y | N | Y | N | N | N |
| 17 Weiss | Y | P | P | N | Y | N | N | N |
| 18 Serrano | Y | Y | Y | N | Y | N | N | N |
| 19 Engel | Y | Y | Y | N | Y | N | N | N |
| 20 Lowey | Y | Y | Y | N | Y | N | N | N |
| 21 ***Fish*** | Y | Y | N | Y | Y | N | N | N |
| 22 ***Gilman*** | Y | N | Y | N | Y | N | N | N |
| 23 McNulty | Y | Y | Y | N | Y | N | N | N |
| 24 ***Solomon*** | Y | Y | Y | N | Y | Y | Y | Y |
| 25 ***Boehlert*** | Y | Y | Y | N | Y | N | N | N |
| 26 ***Martin*** | Y | Y | Y | Y | Y | ? | ? | ? |
| 27 ***Walsh*** | Y | N | Y | N | Y | Y | Y | N |
| 28 McHugh | Y | Y | Y | N | Y | N | N | N |
| 29 ***Horton*** | Y | Y | N | Y | N | N | N | N |
| 30 Slaughter | Y | N | Y | N | Y | N | N | N |
| 31 ***Paxon*** | Y | Y | Y | Y | Y | Y | Y | Y |
| 32 LaFalce | Y | N | Y | N | Y | N | N | N |
| 33 Nowak | Y | Y | Y | N | Y | N | N | N |
| 34 ***Houghton*** | Y | N | Y | Y | Y | Y | N | Y |
| **NORTH CAROLINA** | | | | | | | | |
| 1 Jones | Y | ? | ? | ? | ? | N | N | N |
| 2 Valentine | Y | N | Y | N | Y | N | Y | Y |
| 3 Lancaster | Y | N | Y | N | Y | Y | Y | Y |
| 4 Price | Y | Y | Y | N | Y | N | Y | N |
| 5 Neal | Y | N | Y | N | Y | ? | N | N |
| 6 ***Coble*** | Y | Y | Y | Y | Y | Y | Y | Y |
| 7 Rose | Y | Y | Y | N | Y | N | N | N |
| 8 Hefner | Y | N | Y | N | Y | N | Y | N |
| 9 ***McMillan*** | Y | N | Y | Y | Y | Y | Y | Y |
| 10 ***Ballenger*** | Y | N | Y | Y | Y | Y | Y | Y |
| 11 ***Taylor*** | Y | Y | Y | Y | Y | Y | Y | Y |
| **NORTH DAKOTA** | | | | | | | | |
| AL Dorgan | Y | N | Y | N | Y | N | N | N |
| **OHIO** | | | | | | | | |
| 1 Luken | Y | Y | N | Y | N | N | Y | N |
| 2 ***Gradison*** | Y | Y | N | Y | Y | Y | Y | Y |
| 3 Hall | Y | Y | N | Y | Y | N | N | N |
| 4 ***Oxley*** | Y | Y | N | Y | N | Y | Y | Y |
| 5 ***Gillmor*** | Y | Y | Y | Y | N | Y | Y | Y |
| 6 ***McEwen*** | Y | N | Y | Y | Y | Y | Y | Y |
| 7 ***Hobson*** | Y | Y | N | Y | Y | Y | Y | Y |
| 8 ***Boehner*** | Y | Y | N | Y | N | ? | Y | Y |
| 9 Kaptur | Y | N | Y | N | Y | N | N | N |
| 10 ***Miller*** | Y | Y | N | Y | N | Y | Y | Y |
| 11 Eckart | Y | N | Y | N | Y | N | Y | N |
| 12 ***Kasich*** | Y | Y | Y | N | Y | N | Y | N |
| 13 Pease | Y | N | Y | N | Y | N | N | N |
| 14 Sawyer | Y | N | Y | N | Y | N | N | N |
| 15 ***Wylie*** | Y | N | Y | N | Y | Y | Y | Y |
| 16 ***Regula*** | Y | Y | Y | Y | Y | N | Y | Y |
| 17 Traficant | Y | N | Y | N | Y | ? | ? | ? |
| 18 Applegate | Y | N | Y | N | Y | N | Y | N |
| 19 Feighan | ? | ? | ? | ? | ? | ? | ? | ? |
| 20 Oakar | Y | N | Y | N | Y | N | N | N |
| 21 Stokes | Y | N | Y | N | Y | N | N | N |
| **OKLAHOMA** | | | | | | | | |
| 1 ***Inhofe*** | Y | N | Y | Y | Y | Y | Y | Y |
| 2 Synar | Y | N | Y | N | Y | N | N | N |
| 3 Brewster | Y | N | Y | N | Y | N | Y | N |
| 4 McCurdy | Y | N | Y | N | Y | N | Y | N |
| 5 ***Edwards*** | Y | Y | Y | Y | Y | ? | ? | ? |
| 6 English | Y | N | Y | N | Y | N | Y | N |
| **OREGON** | | | | | | | | |
| 1 AuCoin | Y | N | Y | N | Y | N | N | N |
| 2 ***Smith*** | Y | Y | Y | Y | N | Y | Y | Y |
| 3 Wyden | Y | N | Y | N | Y | N | N | N |
| 4 DeFazio | Y | N | Y | N | Y | ? | ? | ? |
| 5 Kopetski | Y | Y | N | N | Y | N | N | N |
| **PENNSYLVANIA** | | | | | | | | |
| 1 Foglietta | Y | N | Y | N | Y | N | N | N |
| 2 Blackwell | Y | N | ? | N | Y | N | N | N |
| 3 Borski | Y | Y | Y | N | Y | N | N | N |
| 4 Kolter | ? | ? | ? | ? | ? | ? | ? | ? |
| 5 ***Schulze*** | Y | N | Y | N | Y | Y | Y | Y |
| 6 Yatron | Y | N | Y | N | Y | ? | ? | ? |
| 7 ***Weldon*** | Y | Y | Y | Y | Y | Y | Y | N |
| 8 Kostmayer | Y | Y | N | N | Y | N | N | N |
| 9 ***Shuster*** | Y | Y | Y | Y | N | Y | Y | Y |
| 10 ***McDade*** | Y | N | Y | Y | Y | N | Y | Y |
| 11 Kanjorski | Y | N | Y | N | Y | Y | Y | Y |
| 12 Murtha | Y | N | Y | N | Y | N | N | N |
| 13 ***Coughlin*** | ? | ? | ? | ? | ? | ? | ? | ? |
| 14 Coyne | Y | N | Y | N | Y | N | N | N |
| 15 ***Ritter*** | Y | Y | Y | Y | N | Y | Y | N |
| 16 ***Walker*** | Y | Y | Y | Y | N | N | Y | Y |
| 17 ***Gekas*** | Y | Y | Y | Y | Y | Y | Y | Y |
| 18 ***Santorum*** | Y | Y | Y | Y | Y | Y | Y | Y |
| 19 ***Goodling*** | Y | Y | N | Y | N | Y | Y | Y |
| 20 Gaydos | Y | N | Y | N | Y | ? | ? | ? |
| 21 ***Ridge*** | Y | Y | Y | Y | Y | Y | Y | Y |
| 22 Murphy | Y | Y | Y | N | Y | Y | Y | N |
| 23 ***Clinger*** | Y | N | Y | Y | N | Y | Y | Y |
| **RHODE ISLAND** | | | | | | | | |
| 1 ***Machtley*** | Y | N | Y | N | Y | N | N | Y |
| 2 Reed | Y | N | Y | N | Y | N | N | N |
| **SOUTH CAROLINA** | | | | | | | | |
| 1 ***Ravenel*** | Y | N | Y | N | Y | N | Y | Y |
| 2 ***Spence*** | Y | N | Y | Y | Y | Y | Y | Y |
| 3 Derrick | Y | N | Y | N | Y | Y | N | Y |
| 4 Patterson | Y | N | Y | N | Y | Y | Y | N |
| 5 Spratt | Y | N | Y | N | Y | Y | N | N |
| 6 Tallon | ? | ? | ? | ? | ? | ? | ? | ? |
| **SOUTH DAKOTA** | | | | | | | | |
| AL Johnson | Y | N | Y | N | Y | Y | Y | Y |
| **TENNESSEE** | | | | | | | | |
| 1 ***Quillen*** | Y | N | Y | Y | Y | N | N | N |
| 2 ***Duncan*** | Y | N | Y | Y | Y | Y | Y | Y |
| 3 Lloyd | Y | N | Y | N | Y | ? | ? | ? |
| 4 Cooper | Y | N | Y | N | Y | N | N | N |
| 5 Clement | Y | N | Y | N | Y | Y | Y | Y |
| 6 Gordon | Y | N | Y | N | Y | N | N | N |
| 7 ***Sundquist*** | Y | N | Y | N | Y | ? | ? | ? |
| 8 Tanner | Y | N | Y | N | Y | N | Y | Y |
| 9 Ford | Y | Y | Y | N | Y | ? | ? | ? |
| **TEXAS** | | | | | | | | |
| 1 Chapman | Y | N | Y | N | Y | N | Y | N |
| 2 Wilson | ? | ? | ? | ? | Y | ? | ? | ? |
| 3 ***Johnson*** | Y | Y | N | Y | N | N | Y | Y |
| 4 Hall | Y | N | Y | N | Y | N | Y | N |
| 5 Bryant | Y | N | Y | N | Y | N | ? | ? |
| 6 ***Barton*** | Y | N | N | N | N | ? | ? | ? |
| 7 ***Archer*** | Y | Y | N | Y | N | Y | Y | Y |
| 8 ***Fields*** | Y | Y | N | Y | N | Y | Y | Y |
| 9 Brooks | Y | N | Y | N | Y | N | N | N |
| 10 Pickle | Y | Y | Y | N | Y | N | N | N |
| 11 Edwards | Y | N | Y | N | Y | N | N | N |
| 12 Geren | Y | N | Y | N | Y | N | Y | N |
| 13 Sarpalius | Y | N | Y | N | Y | N | N | N |
| 14 Laughlin | ? | ? | ? | ? | ? | ? | ? | ? |
| 15 de la Garza | Y | N | Y | N | Y | N | N | N |
| 16 Coleman | Y | N | N | N | Y | N | N | N |
| 17 Stenholm | Y | N | Y | N | Y | Y | Y | Y |
| 18 Washington | ? | N | Y | N | Y | N | N | N |
| 19 ***Combest*** | Y | N | Y | Y | N | Y | N | Y |
| 20 Gonzalez | Y | N | Y | N | Y | N | N | N |
| 21 ***Smith*** | Y | N | Y | Y | N | ? | ? | ? |
| 22 ***DeLay*** | Y | N | ? | Y | N | Y | Y | Y |
| 23 Bustamante | Y | N | Y | N | Y | N | N | N |
| 24 Frost | ? | ? | ? | ? | ? | ? | ? | ? |
| 25 Andrews | Y | N | Y | N | Y | ? | X | X |
| 26 ***Armey*** | Y | N | N | Y | N | Y | Y | Y |
| 27 Ortiz | Y | N | Y | N | Y | N | N | N |
| **UTAH** | | | | | | | | |
| 1 ***Hansen*** | ? | ? | ? | ? | ? | ? | ? | ? |
| 2 Owens | Y | N | Y | N | Y | N | N | N |
| 3 Orton | Y | Y | N | Y | N | N | Y | Y |
| **VERMONT** | | | | | | | | |
| AL *Sanders* | Y | N | Y | N | Y | N | N | N |
| **VIRGINIA** | | | | | | | | |
| 1 ***Bateman*** | ? | N | Y | N | Y | Y | Y | Y |
| 2 Pickett | Y | N | N | Y | N | Y | Y | Y |
| 3 ***Bliley*** | Y | Y | N | Y | N | Y | Y | Y |
| 4 Sisisky | Y | N | Y | N | Y | Y | Y | N |
| 5 Payne | Y | N | Y | Y | Y | N | Y | N |
| 6 Olin | Y | Y | N | Y | N | N | N | N |
| 7 ***Allen*** | Y | Y | Y | Y | Y | Y | Y | Y |
| 8 Moran | Y | N | Y | ? | Y | N | Y | N |
| 9 Boucher | Y | N | Y | N | Y | ? | ? | ? |
| 10 ***Wolf*** | Y | N | Y | N | Y | Y | Y | Y |
| **WASHINGTON** | | | | | | | | |
| 1 ***Miller*** | Y | Y | N | Y | N | N | Y | N |
| 2 Swift | Y | Y | Y | N | Y | N | N | N |
| 3 Unsoeld | Y | N | Y | N | Y | N | N | N |
| 4 ***Morrison*** | Y | Y | Y | Y | Y | ? | ? | ? |
| 5 Foley | | | | | | | | |
| 6 Dicks | Y | N | Y | N | Y | N | ? | ? |
| 7 McDermott | Y | N | Y | N | Y | N | N | N |
| 8 ***Chandler*** | Y | Y | Y | Y | N | ? | ? | ? |
| **WEST VIRGINIA** | | | | | | | | |
| 1 Mollohan | Y | N | Y | N | Y | N | N | N |
| 2 Staggers | Y | N | Y | N | Y | ? | ? | N |
| 3 Wise | Y | N | Y | N | Y | N | N | N |
| 4 Rahall | Y | N | Y | N | Y | N | N | N |
| **WISCONSIN** | | | | | | | | |
| 1 Aspin | Y | Y | N | N | Y | N | N | N |
| 2 ***Klug*** | Y | Y | N | Y | Y | Y | Y | Y |
| 3 ***Gunderson*** | Y | N | Y | Y | Y | N | Y | N |
| 4 Kleczka | Y | N | Y | N | Y | N | N | N |
| 5 Moody | Y | N | Y | N | Y | N | N | N |
| 6 ***Petri*** | Y | N | Y | N | Y | Y | Y | Y |
| 7 Obey | Y | N | Y | N | Y | N | ? | N |
| 8 ***Roth*** | Y | N | Y | Y | Y | Y | Y | Y |
| 9 ***Sensenbrenner*** | Y | N | Y | N | Y | Y | Y | Y |
| **WYOMING** | | | | | | | | |
| AL ***Thomas*** | ? | ? | ? | # | ? | # | ? | # |

Southern states - Ala., Ark., Fla., Ga., Ky., La., Miss., N.C., Okla., S.C., Tenn., Texas, Va.
Omitted votes are quorum calls, which CQ does not include in its vote charts.

## KEY

Y Voted for (yea).
\# Paired for.
\+ Announced for.
N Voted against (nay).
X Paired against.
− Announced against.
P Voted "present."
C Voted "present" to avoid possible conflict of interest.
? Did not vote or otherwise make a position known.

Democrats **Republicans**
*Independent*

---

**317. HR 4312. Voting Rights Language Assistance/Multiple Languages.** Rohrabacher, R-Calif., amendment to eliminate the extension in the bill that mandates counties to provide all election material in multiple languages, including ballots. Rejected 115-253: R 108-34; D 7-218 (ND 4-156, SD 3-62); I 0-1, July 24, 1992.

**318. HR 4312. Voting Rights Language Assistance/Recommittal.** McCollum, R-Fla., motion to recommit to the House Judiciary Committee the bill with instructions to report it back with an amendment to require federal grants to cover the cost of providing bilingual voting assistance to counties that are required to provide assistance. Motion rejected 172-195: R 128-16; D 44-178 (ND 16-142, SD 28-36); I 0-1, July 24, 1992.

**319. HR 4312. Voting Rights Language Assistance/Passage.** Passage of the bill to extend for 15 years through 2007 the provisions of law that require certain language-minority populations to be provided with language assistance to effectively participate in the electoral process. Passed 237-125: R 45-97; D 191-28 (ND 146-9, SD 45-19); I 1-0, July 24, 1992.

**320. HR 5677. Fiscal 1993 Labor, Health and Human Services, Education Appropriations/Funding Reduction.** Burton, R-Ind., amendment to reduce funding in the bill by 1.05 percent. Rejected 95-290: R 86-72; D 9-217 (ND 5-146, SD 4-71); I 0-1, July 28, 1992.

**321. HR 5677. Fiscal 1993 Labor, Health and Human Services, Education Appropriations/Motion to Rise.** Natcher, D-Ky., motion to rise from the Committee of the Whole and report the bill to provide $244,078,529,000 in new budget authority for the departments of Labor, Health and Human Services, Education, and related agencies. By defeating the motion to rise, Livingston, R-La., was able to offer an amendment, adopted by voice vote, to prohibit the Occupational Safety and Health Administration from enforcing workplace rules requiring seat belts and driver education programs. Rejected 181-215: R 2-158; D 178-57 (ND 129-28, SD 49-29); I 1-0, July 28, 1992.

**322. HR 5677. Fiscal 1993 Labor, Health and Human Services, Education Appropriations/Passage.** Passage of the bill to provide $244,078,529,000 in new budget authority for the Departments of Labor, Health and Human Services, Education, and related agencies in fiscal 1993, including $36.5 billion in fiscal 1994 and $272.3 million in fiscal 1995. The administration requested $244,419,291,000. Passed 345-54: R 108-53; D 236-1 (ND 159-0, SD 77-1); I 1-0, July 28, 1992.

**323. HR 5620. Fiscal 1992 Defense Supplemental Appropriations/Rule.** Bonior, D-Mich., motion to order the previous question (limiting debate and amendment) on the rule (H Res 527) to provide for House floor consideration of the bill to provide $7.5 billion in additional fiscal 1992 appropriations and rescind the remaining $12.5 billion from the U.S. funds appropriated to pay for Operation Desert Shield/Desert Storm. Motion agreed to 207-199: R 0-162; D 206-37 (ND 149-13, SD 57-24); I 1-0, July 28, 1992.

**324. HR 5620. Fiscal 1992 Defense Supplemental Appropriations/Rule.** Adoption of the rule (H Res 527) to provide for House floor consideration of the bill to provide $7.5 billion in additional fiscal 1992 appropriations and rescind the remaining $12.5 billion from the U.S. funds appropriated account to pay for Operation Desert Shield/Desert Storm. Adopted 230-174: R 7-154; D 222-20 (ND 153-9, SD 69-11); I 1-0, July 28, 1992.

| | 317 | 318 | 319 | 320 | 321 | 322 | 323 | 324 |
|---|---|---|---|---|---|---|---|---|
| **ALABAMA** | | | | | | | | |
| 1 *Callahan* | ? | ? | ? | Y | N | N | N | N |
| 2 *Dickinson* | Y | Y | N | Y | N | N | N | N |
| 3 Browder | N | Y | N | N | Y | Y | N | Y |
| 4 Bevill | N | Y | N | N | Y | Y | Y | Y |
| 5 Cramer | N | Y | N | N | Y | Y | N | Y |
| 6 Erdreich | N | Y | N | N | N | Y | N | Y |
| 7 Harris | N | Y | N | N | Y | Y | N | Y |
| **ALASKA** | | | | | | | | |
| AL *Young* | Y | Y | N | N | N | Y | N | N |
| **ARIZONA** | | | | | | | | |
| 1 *Rhodes* | Y | Y | N | Y | N | Y | N | N |
| 2 Pastor | N | N | Y | N | Y | Y | Y | Y |
| 3 *Stump* | Y | Y | N | Y | N | N | N | N |
| 4 *Kyl* | Y | Y | Y | Y | N | N | N | N |
| 5 *Kolbe* | Y | Y | Y | Y | N | Y | N | N |
| **ARKANSAS** | | | | | | | | |
| 1 Alexander | N | N | Y | N | Y | Y | Y | Y |
| 2 Thornton | N | N | Y | N | Y | Y | Y | Y |
| 3 *Hammerschmidt* | ? | ? | ? | N | N | Y | N | N |
| 4 Anthony | ? | ? | ? | N | N | Y | Y | Y |
| **CALIFORNIA** | | | | | | | | |
| 1 *Riggs* | ? | ? | X | N | N | Y | N | N |
| 2 *Herger* | Y | Y | N | Y | N | N | N | N |
| 3 Matsui | ? | ? | ? | ? | ? | ? | ? | ? |
| 4 Fazio | N | N | Y | N | Y | Y | Y | Y |
| 5 Pelosi | N | N | Y | − | + | + | + | + |
| 6 Boxer | ? | ? | ? | ? | ? | ? | ? | ? |
| 7 Miller | N | N | Y | N | Y | Y | Y | Y |
| 8 Dellums | N | N | Y | N | Y | Y | Y | Y |
| 9 Stark | N | N | Y | N | Y | Y | Y | Y |
| 10 Edwards | N | N | Y | N | Y | Y | Y | Y |
| 11 Lantos | N | N | Y | ? | ? | ? | ? | ? |
| 12 *Campbell* | N | Y | Y | ? | N | N | N | N |
| 13 Mineta | N | N | Y | N | Y | Y | Y | Y |
| 14 *Doolittle* | Y | Y | N | Y | N | N | N | N |
| 15 Condit | N | Y | N | Y | N | N | N | N |
| 16 Panetta | N | N | Y | N | Y | Y | Y | Y |
| 17 Dooley | N | N | Y | N | Y | Y | Y | Y |
| 18 Lehman | N | Y | N | N | Y | Y | Y | Y |
| 19 *Lagomarsino* | Y | Y | N | Y | N | N | N | N |
| 20 *Thomas* | Y | Y | N | Y | N | N | N | N |
| 21 *Gallegly* | Y | Y | Y | Y | N | N | N | N |
| 22 *Moorhead* | Y | Y | N | Y | N | N | N | N |
| 23 Beilenson | Y | N | N | N | Y | Y | Y | Y |
| 24 Waxman | N | N | Y | N | Y | Y | Y | Y |
| 25 Roybal | N | N | Y | N | Y | Y | Y | Y |
| 26 Berman | N | N | Y | N | Y | Y | Y | Y |
| 27 Levine | ? | ? | ? | ? | ? | ? | ? | ? |
| 28 Dixon | N | N | Y | N | Y | Y | Y | Y |
| 29 Waters | N | N | Y | N | Y | Y | Y | Y |
| 30 Martinez | ? | ? | ? | N | Y | Y | Y | Y |
| 31 Dymally | ? | ? | ? | ? | ? | ? | ? | ? |
| 32 Anderson | N | N | Y | ? | ? | ? | ? | ? |
| 33 *Dreier* | Y | Y | N | Y | N | N | N | N |
| 34 Torres | N | N | Y | N | Y | Y | Y | Y |
| 35 *Lewis* | Y | Y | N | N | N | N | N | N |
| 36 Brown | ? | ? | ? | N | Y | Y | ? | ? |
| 37 *McCandless* | Y | Y | N | Y | N | N | N | N |
| 38 *Dornan* | Y | Y | N | Y | N | N | N | N |
| 39 *Dannemeyer* | Y | Y | N | Y | N | N | N | N |
| 40 *Cox* | Y | Y | N | N | N | N | N | N |
| 41 *Lowery* | Y | Y | N | ? | N | Y | N | ? |

| | 317 | 318 | 319 | 320 | 321 | 322 | 323 | 324 |
|---|---|---|---|---|---|---|---|---|
| 42 *Rohrabacher* | Y | Y | N | Y | N | N | N | N |
| 43 *Packard* | Y | Y | N | N | N | N | N | N |
| 44 *Cunningham* | Y | Y | N | Y | N | N | N | N |
| 45 *Hunter* | ? | Y | N | Y | N | N | N | N |
| **COLORADO** | | | | | | | | |
| 1 Schroeder | N | N | ? | N | Y | Y | Y | N |
| 2 Skaggs | N | N | ? | N | Y | Y | Y | Y |
| 3 Campbell | ? | ? | ? | ? | ? | ? | ? | ? |
| 4 *Allard* | ? | ? | ? | Y | N | N | N | N |
| 5 *Hefley* | ? | ? | ? | Y | N | N | N | N |
| 6 *Schaefer* | Y | Y | ? | Y | N | N | N | N |
| **CONNECTICUT** | | | | | | | | |
| 1 Kennelly | N | N | Y | N | Y | Y | Y | Y |
| 2 Gejdenson | N | N | Y | N | Y | Y | Y | Y |
| 3 DeLauro | N | N | Y | N | Y | Y | Y | Y |
| 4 *Shays* | N | Y | N | N | Y | Y | N | N |
| 5 *Franks* | Y | Y | N | N | N | N | N | N |
| 6 *Johnson* | N | Y | N | N | Y | Y | N | N |
| **DELAWARE** | | | | | | | | |
| AL Carper | N | N | Y | N | Y | Y | N | N |
| **FLORIDA** | | | | | | | | |
| 1 Hutto | N | Y | N | N | Y | Y | Y | N |
| 2 Peterson | − | − | + | N | Y | Y | Y | Y |
| 3 Bennett | N | N | Y | Y | N | N | Y | Y |
| 4 *James* | Y | Y | N | N | N | N | N | Y |
| 5 *McCollum* | Y | Y | N | Y | N | N | N | N |
| 6 *Stearns* | Y | Y | N | N | N | N | N | N |
| 7 Gibbons | N | N | Y | N | Y | Y | N | Y |
| 8 *Young* | Y | Y | N | Y | N | N | N | N |
| 9 *Bilirakis* | Y | Y | N | Y | N | N | N | N |
| 10 *Ireland* | ? | ? | X | ? | ? | ? | N | N |
| 11 Bacchus | ? | ? | ? | N | Y | Y | N | Y |
| 12 *Lewis* | Y | Y | N | N | N | N | N | N |
| 13 *Goss* | Y | Y | N | N | N | N | N | N |
| 14 Johnston | N | N | Y | N | Y | Y | Y | Y |
| 15 *Shaw* | Y | Y | N | N | N | N | N | N |
| 16 Smith | N | N | Y | N | Y | Y | Y | Y |
| 17 Lehman | N | N | Y | ? | Y | Y | Y | Y |
| 18 *Ros−Lehtinen* | N | N | Y | N | N | N | N | N |
| 19 Fascell | N | N | Y | N | Y | Y | Y | Y |
| **GEORGIA** | | | | | | | | |
| 1 Thomas | ? | ? | ? | ? | ? | ? | ? | ? |
| 2 Hatcher | ? | ? | ? | ? | ? | ? | ? | ? |
| 3 Ray | ? | ? | ? | ? | ? | ? | N | N |
| 4 Jones | N | N | Y | N | Y | Y | Y | Y |
| 5 Lewis | N | N | Y | N | Y | Y | Y | Y |
| 6 *Gingrich* | N | Y | ? | ? | ? | ? | ? | ? |
| 7 Darden | N | Y | N | N | Y | Y | N | Y |
| 8 Rowland | N | Y | N | N | N | N | Y | Y |
| 9 Jenkins | N | Y | N | Y | Y | Y | N | Y |
| 10 Barnard | ? | ? | ? | ? | ? | ? | N | N |
| **HAWAII** | | | | | | | | |
| 1 Abercrombie | N | ? | Y | N | N | Y | Y | Y |
| 2 Mink | N | N | Y | N | Y | Y | Y | Y |
| **IDAHO** | | | | | | | | |
| 1 LaRocco | N | N | Y | N | Y | Y | N | N |
| 2 Stallings | N | N | Y | N | Y | N | N | N |
| **ILLINOIS** | | | | | | | | |
| 1 Hayes | N | N | Y | N | Y | Y | Y | Y |
| 2 Savage | N | N | Y | N | Y | Y | Y | Y |
| 3 Russo | N | N | Y | ? | ? | ? | ? | ? |
| 4 Sangmeister | N | Y | N | N | Y | Y | Y | Y |
| 5 Lipinski | Y | Y | N | N | Y | Y | Y | Y |
| 6 *Hyde* | ? | ? | ? | ? | ? | Y | Y | Y |
| 7 Collins | N | N | Y | N | Y | ? | Y | Y |
| 8 Rostenkowski | N | N | Y | N | Y | Y | Y | Y |
| 9 Yates | N | N | Y | N | Y | Y | Y | Y |
| 10 *Porter* | Y | Y | N | N | N | N | N | N |
| 11 Annunzio | N | N | Y | N | Y | Y | Y | Y |
| 12 *Crane* | Y | Y | N | Y | N | N | N | N |
| 13 *Fawell* | Y | Y | N | Y | N | N | N | N |
| 14 *Hastert* | Y | Y | N | N | N | N | N | N |
| 15 *Ewing* | Y | Y | N | N | N | N | N | N |
| 16 Cox | N | N | Y | N | Y | Y | N | N |
| 17 Evans | N | N | Y | N | Y | Y | Y | Y |
| 18 *Michel* | Y | Y | N | N | N | N | N | N |
| 19 Bruce | N | N | Y | N | Y | Y | Y | Y |
| 20 Durbin | N | N | Y | N | Y | Y | Y | Y |
| 21 Costello | N | N | Y | N | Y | Y | Y | Y |
| 22 Poshard | N | N | Y | N | N | Y | N | Y |
| **INDIANA** | | | | | | | | |
| 1 Visclosky | N | N | Y | N | Y | Y | Y | Y |
| 2 Sharp | N | Y | N | Y | N | Y | Y | Y |
| 3 Roemer | N | Y | N | N | Y | Y | Y | Y |

ND Northern Democrats    SD Southern Democrats

| | 317 | 318 | 319 | 320 | 321 | 322 | 323 | 324 |
|---|---|---|---|---|---|---|---|---|
| 4 Long | N | N | Y | N | Y | Y | Y | Y |
| 5 Jontz | N | N | Y | N | N | Y | Y | Y |
| 6 ***Burton*** | Y | Y | N | Y | N | N | N | N |
| 7 ***Myers*** | Y | Y | N | N | N | Y | N | Y |
| 8 McCloskey | N | N | Y | N | Y | Y | Y | Y |
| 9 Hamilton | N | N | Y | N | Y | Y | Y | Y |
| 10 Jacobs | N | N | Y | Y | Y | Y | N | Y |
| **IOWA** | | | | | | | | |
| 1 ***Leach*** | N | N | Y | N | N | Y | N | N |
| 2 ***Nussle*** | Y | Y | N | Y | N | N | N | N |
| 3 Nagle | N | N | Y | − | − | + | Y | Y |
| 4 Smith | N | N | Y | N | Y | Y | Y | Y |
| 5 ***Lightfoot*** | Y | Y | N | N | N | Y | N | N |
| 6 ***Grandy*** | N | N | Y | N | N | Y | N | N |
| **KANSAS** | | | | | | | | |
| 1 ***Roberts*** | Y | Y | N | Y | N | N | N | N |
| 2 Slattery | N | N | Y | N | N | Y | Y | Y |
| 3 ***Meyers*** | Y | Y | N | Y | N | Y | N | N |
| 4 Glickman | N | N | Y | N | N | Y | Y | Y |
| 5 ***Nichols*** | Y | Y | N | Y | N | N | N | N |
| **KENTUCKY** | | | | | | | | |
| 1 Hubbard | N | Y | Y | N | Y | Y | N | N |
| 2 Natcher | N | N | Y | N | Y | Y | Y | Y |
| 3 Mazzoli | N | N | Y | N | Y | Y | Y | Y |
| 4 ***Bunning*** | ? | ? | ? | Y | N | N | N | N |
| 5 ***Rogers*** | Y | Y | N | N | N | Y | N | Y |
| 6 ***Hopkins*** | Y | Y | N | Y | N | Y | N | N |
| 7 Perkins | N | N | Y | ? | ? | ? | ? | ? |
| **LOUISIANA** | | | | | | | | |
| 1 ***Livingston*** | ? | ? | X | Y | N | Y | N | N |
| 2 Jefferson | N | N | Y | ? | ? | Y | Y | Y |
| 3 Tauzin | N | ? | ? | N | N | Y | N | Y |
| 4 ***McCrery*** | Y | Y | N | Y | N | Y | N | N |
| 5 Huckaby | ? | ? | X | N | N | Y | N | N |
| 6 ***Baker*** | ? | ? | ? | Y | N | N | N | N |
| 7 Hayes | ? | ? | ? | N | N | Y | N | Y |
| 8 ***Holloway*** | Y | Y | N | Y | N | N | N | N |
| **MAINE** | | | | | | | | |
| 1 Andrews | N | N | Y | ? | Y | Y | Y | Y |
| 2 ***Snowe*** | N | Y | Y | N | N | Y | N | N |
| **MARYLAND** | | | | | | | | |
| 1 ***Gilchrest*** | N | Y | Y | N | N | Y | N | N |
| 2 ***Bentley*** | Y | Y | N | N | N | Y | N | N |
| 3 Cardin | N | N | Y | N | Y | Y | Y | Y |
| 4 McMillen | N | Y | Y | N | N | Y | N | Y |
| 5 Hoyer | N | N | Y | N | Y | Y | Y | Y |
| 6 Byron | N | Y | N | N | N | Y | Y | Y |
| 7 Mfume | N | N | Y | N | Y | Y | Y | Y |
| 8 ***Morella*** | N | N | Y | N | N | Y | N | N |
| **MASSACHUSETTS** | | | | | | | | |
| 1 Olver | N | N | Y | N | Y | Y | Y | Y |
| 2 Neal | N | N | Y | ? | Y | Y | Y | Y |
| 3 Early | ? | ? | ? | N | Y | Y | Y | Y |
| 4 Frank | N | N | Y | N | Y | Y | Y | Y |
| 5 Atkins | ? | ? | ? | ? | ? | ? | Y | Y |
| 6 Mavroules | N | N | Y | N | Y | Y | Y | Y |
| 7 Markey | N | N | Y | N | Y | Y | Y | Y |
| 8 Kennedy | N | N | Y | N | N | Y | Y | Y |
| 9 Moakley | N | N | Y | N | Y | Y | Y | Y |
| 10 Studds | N | N | Y | N | Y | Y | Y | Y |
| 11 Donnelly | N | Y | Y | ? | ? | ? | ? | Y |
| **MICHIGAN** | | | | | | | | |
| 1 Conyers | ? | ? | ? | ? | ? | ? | ? | ? |
| 2 ***Pursell*** | Y | Y | N | N | N | Y | N | N |
| 3 Wolpe | N | N | Y | N | Y | Y | Y | Y |
| 4 ***Upton*** | N | Y | Y | N | N | Y | N | N |
| 5 ***Henry*** | Y | Y | N | N | N | Y | N | N |
| 6 Carr | N | N | Y | N | Y | Y | Y | ? |
| 7 Kildee | N | N | Y | N | Y | Y | Y | Y |
| 8 Traxler | ? | ? | ? | N | Y | Y | Y | Y |
| 9 ***Vander Jagt*** | Y | Y | N | ? | N | Y | N | N |
| 10 ***Camp*** | N | Y | Y | Y | N | Y | N | N |
| 11 ***Davis*** | Y | Y | N | N | N | Y | N | N |
| 12 Bonior | N | N | Y | N | Y | Y | Y | Y |
| 13 Collins | ? | ? | ? | N | Y | Y | Y | Y |
| 14 Hertel | N | N | Y | N | Y | Y | Y | Y |
| 15 Ford | N | N | Y | N | Y | Y | Y | Y |
| 16 Dingell | N | N | Y | N | Y | Y | Y | Y |
| 17 Levin | N | N | Y | N | Y | Y | Y | Y |
| 18 ***Broomfield*** | ? | ? | ? | N | N | Y | N | N |
| **MINNESOTA** | | | | | | | | |
| 1 Penny | N | N | Y | Y | N | Y | N | N |
| 2 ***Weber*** | N | N | Y | N | N | Y | N | N |
| 3 ***Ramstad*** | Y | Y | N | N | N | Y | N | N |
| 4 Vento | N | N | Y | N | Y | Y | Y | Y |
| 5 Sabo | N | N | Y | N | Y | Y | Y | Y |
| 6 Sikorski | N | N | Y | N | N | Y | Y | Y |
| 7 Peterson | N | N | Y | N | Y | Y | Y | Y |
| 8 Oberstar | N | N | Y | N | Y | Y | Y | Y |
| **MISSISSIPPI** | | | | | | | | |
| 1 Whitten | N | N | N | N | Y | Y | Y | Y |
| 2 Espy | N | N | Y | N | Y | Y | Y | Y |
| 3 Montgomery | N | Y | N | N | Y | Y | Y | Y |
| 4 Parker | N | Y | N | N | N | Y | N | Y |
| 5 Taylor | Y | Y | N | N | Y | Y | Y | Y |
| **MISSOURI** | | | | | | | | |
| 1 Clay | N | N | Y | N | Y | Y | Y | Y |
| 2 Horn | N | N | Y | N | Y | Y | Y | Y |
| 3 Gephardt | ? | ? | ? | N | Y | Y | Y | Y |
| 4 Skelton | N | Y | N | N | N | Y | Y | Y |
| 5 Wheat | N | N | Y | N | Y | Y | Y | Y |
| 6 ***Coleman*** | ? | ? | ? | N | N | Y | N | N |
| 7 ***Hancock*** | Y | Y | N | Y | N | N | N | N |
| 8 ***Emerson*** | Y | Y | N | N | N | Y | N | N |
| 9 Volkmer | N | N | Y | N | N | Y | Y | Y |
| **MONTANA** | | | | | | | | |
| 1 Williams | N | N | Y | ? | Y | Y | Y | Y |
| 2 ***Marlenee*** | Y | Y | N | Y | N | Y | N | N |
| **NEBRASKA** | | | | | | | | |
| 1 ***Bereuter*** | N | N | N | N | N | Y | N | N |
| 2 Hoagland | N | N | Y | N | Y | Y | Y | Y |
| 3 ***Barrett*** | Y | Y | N | N | N | Y | N | N |
| **NEVADA** | | | | | | | | |
| 1 Bilbray | N | N | Y | N | Y | Y | N | Y |
| 2 ***Vucanovich*** | N | Y | Y | N | N | Y | N | N |
| **NEW HAMPSHIRE** | | | | | | | | |
| 1 ***Zeliff*** | Y | Y | N | Y | N | N | N | N |
| 2 Swett | N | Y | Y | N | N | Y | N | N |
| **NEW JERSEY** | | | | | | | | |
| 1 Andrews | N | N | Y | N | Y | Y | Y | Y |
| 2 Hughes | N | N | Y | N | Y | Y | Y | N |
| 3 Pallone | N | N | Y | N | Y | Y | Y | Y |
| 4 ***Smith*** | Y | Y | Y | N | N | Y | N | N |
| 5 ***Roukema*** | Y | Y | N | N | N | Y | N | Y |
| 6 Dwyer | ? | ? | ? | N | Y | Y | Y | Y |
| 7 ***Rinaldo*** | Y | Y | Y | Y | N | Y | N | N |
| 8 Roe | N | N | Y | N | ? | Y | Y | Y |
| 9 Torricelli | N | N | Y | ? | Y | Y | Y | Y |
| 10 Payne | N | N | Y | − | + | + | + | + |
| 11 ***Gallo*** | Y | Y | N | N | N | Y | N | N |
| 12 ***Zimmer*** | Y | Y | N | Y | N | Y | N | N |
| 13 ***Saxton*** | Y | Y | N | N | N | Y | N | N |
| 14 Guarini | N | N | Y | N | N | Y | Y | Y |
| **NEW MEXICO** | | | | | | | | |
| 1 ***Schiff*** | N | N | Y | N | N | Y | N | N |
| 2 ***Skeen*** | N | Y | Y | N | N | Y | N | N |
| 3 Richardson | N | N | Y | N | Y | Y | Y | Y |
| **NEW YORK** | | | | | | | | |
| 1 Hochbrueckner | N | N | Y | N | Y | Y | Y | Y |
| 2 Downey | N | N | Y | N | Y | Y | Y | Y |
| 3 Mrazek | ? | ? | ? | ? | ? | Y | Y | Y |
| 4 ***Lent*** | Y | Y | N | N | N | Y | N | N |
| 5 ***McGrath*** | N | Y | Y | N | N | Y | N | N |
| 6 Flake | N | N | Y | N | Y | Y | Y | Y |
| 7 Ackerman | N | N | Y | N | Y | Y | Y | Y |
| 8 Scheuer | N | N | Y | N | Y | Y | Y | ? |
| 9 Manton | N | N | Y | N | Y | Y | Y | Y |
| 10 Schumer | N | N | Y | N | Y | Y | Y | Y |
| 11 Towns | N | N | Y | ? | ? | ? | Y | Y |
| 12 Owens | N | N | Y | ? | Y | Y | Y | Y |
| 13 Solarz | N | N | Y | ? | ? | ? | ? | ? |
| 14 ***Molinari*** | N | N | Y | N | N | Y | N | N |
| 15 ***Green*** | N | N | Y | N | Y | Y | N | Y |
| 16 Rangel | N | N | Y | N | Y | Y | Y | Y |
| 17 Weiss | N | N | Y | N | Y | Y | Y | Y |
| 18 Serrano | N | N | Y | N | ? | Y | Y | Y |
| 19 Engel | N | N | Y | ? | ? | ? | ? | ? |
| 20 Lowey | N | N | Y | N | Y | Y | Y | Y |
| 21 ***Fish*** | ? | N | Y | N | N | Y | N | N |
| 22 ***Gilman*** | N | N | Y | N | N | Y | N | Y |
| 23 McNulty | N | N | # | N | Y | Y | Y | Y |
| 24 ***Solomon*** | Y | Y | N | Y | N | N | N | N |
| 25 ***Boehlert*** | N | N | Y | N | N | Y | N | N |
| 26 ***Martin*** | ? | ? | ? | N | N | Y | ? | ? |
| 27 ***Walsh*** | Y | Y | N | Y | N | Y | N | N |
| 28 McHugh | N | N | Y | N | Y | Y | Y | Y |
| 29 ***Horton*** | N | N | Y | N | N | Y | N | Y |
| 30 Slaughter | N | N | Y | N | Y | Y | Y | Y |
| 31 ***Paxon*** | Y | Y | N | N | N | Y | N | N |
| 32 LaFalce | N | N | Y | ? | Y | Y | Y | Y |
| 33 Nowak | N | N | Y | ? | Y | Y | Y | Y |
| 34 ***Houghton*** | Y | N | Y | N | N | Y | N | N |
| **NORTH CAROLINA** | | | | | | | | |
| 1 Jones | N | N | Y | N | Y | Y | Y | Y |
| 2 Valentine | N | Y | Y | N | Y | Y | N | N |
| 3 Lancaster | N | Y | N | N | N | Y | Y | Y |
| 4 Price | N | N | Y | N | Y | Y | Y | Y |
| 5 Neal | N | N | N | N | Y | Y | Y | Y |
| 6 ***Coble*** | Y | Y | N | Y | N | N | N | N |
| 7 Rose | N | N | Y | N | Y | Y | Y | Y |
| 8 Hefner | N | N | Y | N | N | Y | Y | Y |
| 9 ***McMillan*** | Y | Y | N | Y | N | Y | N | N |
| 10 ***Ballenger*** | Y | Y | N | Y | N | N | N | N |
| 11 ***Taylor*** | Y | Y | N | Y | N | Y | N | N |
| **NORTH DAKOTA** | | | | | | | | |
| AL Dorgan | N | N | Y | Y | Y | Y | N | Y |
| **OHIO** | | | | | | | | |
| 1 Luken | N | Y | Y | N | N | Y | N | N |
| 2 ***Gradison*** | Y | Y | Y | N | N | Y | N | N |
| 3 Hall | N | N | Y | N | Y | Y | Y | Y |
| 4 ***Oxley*** | Y | Y | N | Y | N | Y | N | N |
| 5 ***Gillmor*** | Y | Y | Y | N | N | Y | N | N |
| 6 ***McEwen*** | Y | Y | Y | Y | N | N | N | N |
| 7 ***Hobson*** | N | Y | Y | N | N | Y | N | N |
| 8 ***Boehner*** | Y | Y | N | Y | N | N | N | N |
| 9 Kaptur | N | N | Y | ? | ? | ? | ? | ? |
| 10 ***Miller*** | Y | Y | N | Y | N | N | N | N |
| 11 Eckart | N | N | Y | N | Y | Y | ? | Y |
| 12 ***Kasich*** | N | N | Y | N | N | Y | N | N |
| 13 Pease | N | N | Y | N | Y | Y | Y | Y |
| 14 Sawyer | N | N | Y | N | Y | Y | Y | Y |
| 15 ***Wylie*** | Y | Y | N | N | N | Y | N | N |
| 16 ***Regula*** | Y | Y | N | N | N | Y | N | N |
| 17 Traficant | ? | ? | ? | N | Y | Y | Y | Y |
| 18 Applegate | N | Y | Y | N | Y | Y | Y | Y |
| 19 Feighan | ? | ? | ? | N | Y | Y | Y | Y |
| 20 Oakar | N | N | Y | N | Y | Y | Y | Y |
| 21 Stokes | N | N | Y | N | Y | Y | Y | Y |
| **OKLAHOMA** | | | | | | | | |
| 1 ***Inhofe*** | Y | Y | N | Y | N | N | N | N |
| 2 Synar | N | N | Y | N | Y | Y | Y | Y |
| 3 Brewster | N | Y | N | N | N | Y | Y | Y |
| 4 McCurdy | N | Y | Y | N | N | Y | Y | Y |
| 5 ***Edwards*** | ? | ? | ? | ? | ? | ? | N | N |
| 6 English | N | Y | Y | N | N | Y | N | N |
| **OREGON** | | | | | | | | |
| 1 AuCoin | N | N | Y | N | Y | Y | Y | Y |
| 2 ***Smith*** | Y | Y | N | N | N | Y | N | N |
| 3 Wyden | N | ? | # | N | Y | Y | Y | Y |
| 4 DeFazio | ? | ? | ? | N | Y | Y | Y | Y |
| 5 Kopetski | N | N | Y | N | Y | Y | Y | Y |
| **PENNSYLVANIA** | | | | | | | | |
| 1 Foglietta | N | N | Y | ? | ? | Y | Y | Y |
| 2 Blackwell | N | N | Y | N | Y | Y | Y | Y |
| 3 Borski | N | N | Y | N | Y | Y | Y | Y |
| 4 Kolter | ? | ? | ? | N | Y | Y | Y | Y |
| 5 ***Schulze*** | Y | Y | Y | Y | N | Y | N | N |
| 6 Yatron | ? | ? | ? | N | Y | Y | Y | Y |
| 7 ***Weldon*** | N | Y | Y | Y | N | Y | N | N |
| 8 Kostmayer | N | N | N | N | N | Y | Y | Y |
| 9 ***Shuster*** | Y | Y | N | Y | N | N | N | N |
| 10 ***McDade*** | N | Y | Y | N | N | + | N | Y |
| 11 Kanjorski | Y | Y | N | N | Y | Y | Y | Y |
| 12 Murtha | N | N | Y | N | Y | Y | Y | Y |
| 13 ***Coughlin*** | ? | ? | ? | ? | ? | ? | ? | ? |
| 14 Coyne | N | N | Y | N | Y | Y | Y | Y |
| 15 ***Ritter*** | N | Y | Y | Y | N | Y | N | N |
| 16 ***Walker*** | N | Y | Y | Y | N | N | N | N |
| 17 ***Gekas*** | Y | Y | N | Y | N | Y | N | N |
| 18 ***Santorum*** | Y | Y | N | N | N | Y | N | N |
| 19 ***Goodling*** | Y | Y | N | N | N | Y | N | N |
| 20 Gaydos | ? | ? | ? | N | Y | Y | ? | Y |
| 21 ***Ridge*** | Y | Y | N | Y | N | Y | N | N |
| 22 Murphy | N | N | N | ? | Y | Y | Y | Y |
| 23 ***Clinger*** | Y | Y | N | N | N | Y | N | N |
| **RHODE ISLAND** | | | | | | | | |
| 1 ***Machtley*** | N | Y | Y | N | N | Y | N | N |
| 2 Reed | N | N | Y | N | Y | Y | Y | Y |
| **SOUTH CAROLINA** | | | | | | | | |
| 1 ***Ravenel*** | N | Y | N | Y | N | Y | N | N |
| 2 ***Spence*** | Y | Y | N | Y | N | Y | N | N |
| 3 Derrick | Y | Y | N | N | Y | Y | Y | Y |
| 4 Patterson | Y | Y | N | N | N | Y | Y | Y |
| 5 Spratt | N | N | Y | N | N | Y | Y | Y |
| 6 Tallon | ? | ? | ? | ? | N | Y | N | Y |
| **SOUTH DAKOTA** | | | | | | | | |
| AL Johnson | Y | Y | N | N | N | Y | Y | Y |
| **TENNESSEE** | | | | | | | | |
| 1 ***Quillen*** | N | N | Y | Y | N | Y | N | N |
| 2 ***Duncan*** | Y | Y | N | Y | N | Y | N | N |
| 3 Lloyd | ? | ? | ? | N | N | Y | Y | Y |
| 4 Cooper | ? | N | Y | N | Y | Y | Y | Y |
| 5 Clement | ? | ? | ? | N | Y | Y | N | Y |
| 6 Gordon | N | N | Y | N | N | Y | Y | Y |
| 7 ***Sundquist*** | ? | ? | ? | Y | N | N | N | N |
| 8 Tanner | N | Y | Y | N | N | Y | N | Y |
| 9 Ford | ? | ? | ? | ? | ? | ? | ? | ? |
| **TEXAS** | | | | | | | | |
| 1 Chapman | N | N | Y | N | Y | Y | Y | Y |
| 2 Wilson | ? | ? | ? | N | N | Y | Y | Y |
| 3 ***Johnson*** | Y | Y | N | Y | N | N | N | N |
| 4 Hall | N | Y | Y | N | N | Y | N | N |
| 5 Bryant | ? | ? | ? | N | Y | Y | Y | Y |
| 6 ***Barton*** | ? | ? | ? | Y | N | N | N | N |
| 7 ***Archer*** | Y | Y | N | Y | N | N | N | N |
| 8 ***Fields*** | Y | Y | N | Y | N | N | N | N |
| 9 Brooks | N | N | Y | N | Y | Y | Y | ? |
| 10 Pickle | N | ? | # | N | Y | ? | Y | Y |
| 11 Edwards | N | N | Y | N | N | Y | Y | Y |
| 12 Geren | N | Y | Y | N | N | Y | N | N |
| 13 Sarpalius | N | N | Y | Y | N | Y | Y | Y |
| 14 Laughlin | ? | ? | ? | N | N | Y | Y | Y |
| 15 de la Garza | N | N | Y | N | Y | Y | Y | Y |
| 16 Coleman | N | N | Y | N | Y | Y | Y | Y |
| 17 Stenholm | N | Y | N | Y | N | Y | N | N |
| 18 Washington | N | N | Y | N | Y | Y | Y | Y |
| 19 ***Combest*** | Y | Y | N | Y | N | N | N | N |
| 20 Gonzalez | N | N | Y | N | Y | Y | Y | Y |
| 21 ***Smith*** | ? | ? | ? | Y | N | Y | N | N |
| 22 ***DeLay*** | Y | Y | N | Y | N | N | N | N |
| 23 Bustamante | N | N | Y | N | Y | Y | Y | Y |
| 24 Frost | ? | ? | ? | N | Y | Y | Y | Y |
| 25 Andrews | ? | ? | ? | N | N | Y | N | Y |
| 26 ***Armey*** | Y | Y | N | Y | N | N | N | N |
| 27 Ortiz | N | N | Y | N | Y | Y | Y | Y |
| **UTAH** | | | | | | | | |
| 1 ***Hansen*** | ? | ? | ? | Y | N | N | N | N |
| 2 Owens | N | N | ? | N | N | Y | N | Y |
| 3 Orton | N | Y | N | Y | N | Y | N | N |
| **VERMONT** | | | | | | | | |
| AL *Sanders* | N | N | Y | N | Y | Y | Y | Y |
| **VIRGINIA** | | | | | | | | |
| 1 ***Bateman*** | Y | Y | N | N | N | Y | N | N |
| 2 Pickett | N | Y | N | N | Y | Y | Y | Y |
| 3 ***Bliley*** | Y | Y | N | Y | N | Y | N | N |
| 4 Sisisky | N | Y | Y | N | Y | Y | Y | N |
| 5 Payne | N | Y | Y | N | Y | Y | Y | Y |
| 6 Olin | N | N | Y | ? | Y | Y | Y | Y |
| 7 ***Allen*** | Y | Y | N | Y | N | N | N | N |
| 8 Moran | N | Y | Y | N | Y | Y | Y | Y |
| 9 Boucher | ? | ? | ? | N | Y | Y | Y | Y |
| 10 ***Wolf*** | Y | Y | Y | N | N | Y | N | N |
| **WASHINGTON** | | | | | | | | |
| 1 ***Miller*** | N | Y | Y | Y | N | Y | N | N |
| 2 Swift | N | N | Y | N | Y | Y | Y | Y |
| 3 Unsoeld | N | N | Y | N | Y | Y | Y | Y |
| 4 ***Morrison*** | ? | ? | ? | N | N | Y | N | N |
| 5 Foley | | | | | | | | |
| 6 Dicks | ? | ? | ? | ? | ? | ? | ? | ? |
| 7 McDermott | N | N | Y | N | Y | Y | Y | Y |
| 8 ***Chandler*** | ? | ? | ? | Y | N | Y | N | N |
| **WEST VIRGINIA** | | | | | | | | |
| 1 Mollohan | N | N | Y | ? | ? | ? | Y | Y |
| 2 Staggers | N | Y | Y | N | N | Y | Y | Y |
| 3 Wise | N | N | Y | − | + | + | + | + |
| 4 Rahall | N | N | Y | N | Y | Y | Y | Y |
| **WISCONSIN** | | | | | | | | |
| 1 Aspin | N | N | Y | N | Y | ? | Y | Y |
| 2 ***Klug*** | Y | Y | N | N | N | Y | N | N |
| 3 ***Gunderson*** | N | Y | Y | N | N | Y | N | N |
| 4 Kleczka | N | N | Y | N | Y | Y | Y | Y |
| 5 Moody | N | N | Y | N | N | Y | Y | Y |
| 6 ***Petri*** | Y | Y | N | Y | N | Y | N | N |
| 7 Obey | N | N | Y | N | Y | Y | Y | Y |
| 8 ***Roth*** | Y | Y | N | Y | N | N | N | N |
| 9 ***Sensenbrenner*** | Y | Y | N | Y | N | N | N | N |
| **WYOMING** | | | | | | | | |
| AL ***Thomas*** | ? | ? | # | Y | N | N | N | N |

Southern states - Ala., Ark., Fla., Ga., Ky., La., Miss., N.C., Okla., S.C., Tenn., Texas, Va.
Omitted votes are quorum calls, which CQ does not include in its vote charts.

1992 CQ ALMANAC — 79-H

**325. HR 5620. Fiscal 1992 Defense Supplemental Appropriations/Davis-Bacon.** Stenholm, D-Texas, amendment to strike a provision blocking Labor Department regulations to promote the use of helpers, or unskilled laborers, on Davis-Bacon construction projects. Rejected 172-242: R 136-24; D 36-217 (ND 3-169, SD 33-48); I 0-1, July 28, 1992. A "yea" was a vote supporting the president's position.

**326. HR 5620. Fiscal 1992 Defense Supplemental Appropriations/Passage.** Passage of the bill to provide $7.5 billion in additional fiscal 1992 appropriations and rescind the remaining $12.5 billion from the U.S. funds appropriated to pay for Operation Desert Shield/Desert Storm. The bill provided $3.2 billion to repair and refurbish equipment from the Persian Gulf War, $1.6 billion for military personnel pay, $500 million for a cost of living increase for veterans and $1 billion for environmental restoration of defense facilities. Passed 297-124: R 56-108; D 240-16 (ND 163-12, SD 77-4); I 1-0, July 28, 1992.

**327. HR 5645. Tax Exemption for Certain Sponsored Events/Passage.** Gibbons, D-Fla., motion to suspend the rules and pass the bill to clarify that in certain circumstances corporate contributions (including sponsorship of college football bowl games) to tax-exempt organizations, whether or not made in furtherance of the entities' exempt purpose, would remain tax-free. Motion agreed to 296-123: R 141-22; D 155-100 (ND 84-91, SD 71-9); I 0-1, July 28, 1992. A two-thirds majority of those present and voting (280 in this case) was required for passage under suspension of the rules.

**328. HR 5653. High-Speed Intercity Rail Tax-Exempt Bonds.** Gibbons, D-Fla., motion to suspend the rules and pass the bill to exempt tax-exempt bonds for government high-speed intercity rail facilities from a state's bond volume limitation and to require state and local governments to properly inform taxpayers about user fees not deductible from federal taxes. Motion rejected 48-369: R 4-159; D 44-209 (ND 33-140, SD 11-69); I 0-1, July 28, 1992. A two-thirds majority of those present and voting (278 in this case) was required for passage under suspension of the rules.

**329. HR 450. Stock-Raising Homestead Amendments.** Rahall, D-W.Va., motion to suspend the rules and pass the bill to establish new procedures for mining activities on stock-raising Homestead Act lands. Motion rejected 248-168: R 34-128; D 213-40 (ND 149-26, SD 64-14); I 1-0, July 28, 1992. A two-thirds majority of those present and voting (278 in this case) was required for passage under suspension of the rules. A 'nay' was a vote in support of the president's position.

**330. HR 5623. Waive Congressional Review Period for Certain D.C. Acts/Passage.** Passage of the bill to waive the required 30-day congressional review period and allow six bills to authorize the issuance of revenue bonds for nonprofit organizations and one bill to extend the life of a special hearing panel to become law. Passed 400-9: R 151-9; D 248-0 (ND 174-0, SD 74-0); I 1-0, July 29, 1992.

**331. HR 5679. Fiscal 1993 VA, Housing and Urban Development, Independent Agencies Appropriations/Previous Question.** Slaughter, D-N.Y., motion to order the previous question (thus limiting debate and the possibility of amendment) on adoption of the rule (H Res 529) to provide for House floor consideration of the bill to provide $86.8 billion in new budget authority for the departments of Veterans Affairs and Housing and Urban Development and for sundry independent agencies in fiscal 1993. Motion agreed to 237-180: R 0-162; D 236-18 (ND 170-7, SD 66-11); I 1-0, July 29, 1992.

**332. HR 5679. Fiscal 1993 VA, Housing and Urban Development, Independent Agencies Appropriations/Rule.** Adoption of the rule (H Res 529) to provide for House floor consideration of the bill to provide $86.8 billion in new budget authority for the departments of Veterans Affairs and Housing and Urban Development and for various independent agencies in fiscal 1993. Adopted 253-163: R 5-156; D 247-7 (ND 171-5, SD 76-2); I 1-0, July 29, 1992.

## KEY

| | |
|---|---|
| Y | Voted for (yea). |
| # | Paired for. |
| + | Announced for. |
| N | Voted against (nay). |
| X | Paired against. |
| − | Announced against. |
| P | Voted "present." |
| C | Voted "present" to avoid possible conflict of interest. |
| ? | Did not vote or otherwise make a position known. |

**Democrats** **Republicans**
*Independent*

| | 325 | 326 | 327 | 328 | 329 | 330 | 331 | 332 |
|---|---|---|---|---|---|---|---|---|
| **ALABAMA** | | | | | | | | |
| 1 *Callahan* | Y | N | Y | N | N | Y | N | N |
| 2 *Dickinson* | Y | N | Y | N | N | ? | N | N |
| 3 Browder | N | Y | Y | N | Y | Y | Y | Y |
| 4 Bevill | N | Y | Y | N | Y | Y | Y | Y |
| 5 Cramer | N | Y | Y | N | Y | Y | Y | Y |
| 6 Erdreich | N | Y | Y | N | ? | Y | Y | Y |
| 7 Harris | N | Y | Y | N | Y | Y | Y | Y |
| **ALASKA** | | | | | | | | |
| AL *Young* | N | Y | N | N | N | Y | N | N |
| **ARIZONA** | | | | | | | | |
| 1 *Rhodes* | Y | N | Y | N | N | Y | N | N |
| 2 Pastor | N | Y | Y | N | Y | Y | N | Y |
| 3 *Stump* | Y | N | Y | N | N | Y | N | N |
| 4 *Kyl* | Y | N | Y | N | N | Y | N | N |
| 5 *Kolbe* | Y | N | Y | N | Y | N | N | N |
| **ARKANSAS** | | | | | | | | |
| 1 Alexander | N | Y | Y | Y | Y | ? | Y | Y |
| 2 Thornton | N | Y | Y | N | Y | Y | Y | Y |
| 3 *Hammerschmidt* | Y | N | Y | N | N | N | N | N |
| 4 Anthony | Y | Y | Y | Y | Y | Y | Y | Y |
| **CALIFORNIA** | | | | | | | | |
| 1 *Riggs* | Y | N | Y | N | N | Y | N | N |
| 2 *Herger* | Y | N | Y | N | N | Y | N | ? |
| 3 Matsui | N | Y | Y | Y | Y | Y | Y | Y |
| 4 Fazio | N | Y | Y | Y | Y | Y | Y | Y |
| 5 Pelosi | N | Y | N | Y | Y | Y | Y | Y |
| 6 Boxer | ? | ? | ? | ? | ? | ? | ? | ? |
| 7 Miller | N | Y | N | Y | Y | Y | Y | Y |
| 8 Dellums | N | Y | N | Y | Y | Y | Y | Y |
| 9 Stark | N | Y | N | Y | Y | Y | Y | Y |
| 10 Edwards | N | Y | N | N | Y | Y | Y | Y |
| 11 Lantos | N | Y | Y | Y | Y | Y | Y | Y |
| 12 *Campbell* | Y | N | N | N | N | Y | N | N |
| 13 Mineta | N | Y | N | N | Y | Y | Y | Y |
| 14 *Doolittle* | Y | N | Y | N | N | Y | N | N |
| 15 Condit | N | N | N | N | Y | Y | Y | Y |
| 16 Panetta | N | Y | N | Y | Y | Y | Y | Y |
| 17 Dooley | N | Y | N | Y | Y | Y | Y | Y |
| 18 Lehman | N | Y | N | Y | Y | Y | Y | Y |
| 19 *Lagomarsino* | Y | N | N | N | N | Y | N | N |
| 20 *Thomas* | # | N | Y | N | N | Y | N | N |
| 21 *Gallegly* | Y | N | N | N | N | Y | N | N |
| 22 *Moorhead* | Y | N | N | N | N | Y | N | N |
| 23 Beilenson | N | Y | N | Y | Y | Y | Y | Y |
| 24 Waxman | N | Y | N | Y | Y | Y | Y | Y |
| 25 Roybal | N | Y | N | N | Y | Y | Y | Y |
| 26 Berman | N | Y | ? | Y | Y | Y | Y | Y |
| 27 Levine | N | Y | N | Y | Y | Y | Y | Y |
| 28 Dixon | N | Y | N | Y | ? | Y | Y | Y |
| 29 Waters | N | Y | N | Y | Y | Y | Y | Y |
| 30 Martinez | N | Y | N | Y | Y | Y | Y | Y |
| 31 Dymally | ? | ? | ? | ? | ? | Y | Y | Y |
| 32 Anderson | ? | Y | Y | N | Y | Y | Y | Y |
| 33 *Dreier* | Y | N | N | N | N | Y | N | N |
| 34 Torres | N | Y | N | N | Y | Y | Y | Y |
| 35 *Lewis* | Y | Y | Y | N | N | Y | N | N |
| 36 Brown | N | Y | Y | Y | Y | Y | Y | Y |
| 37 *McCandless* | Y | N | Y | N | N | Y | N | N |
| 38 *Dornan* | Y | N | Y | N | N | N | N | N |
| 39 *Dannemeyer* | Y | N | N | N | N | N | N | N |
| 40 *Cox* | Y | N | Y | N | N | N | N | N |
| 41 *Lowery* | Y | Y | Y | Y | N | Y | N | N |
| **COLORADO** | | | | | | | | |
| 1 Schroeder | N | Y | N | N | Y | Y | Y | Y |
| 2 Skaggs | N | Y | N | N | Y | Y | Y | Y |
| 3 Campbell | ? | Y | Y | N | Y | Y | Y | Y |
| 4 *Allard* | Y | N | N | N | N | N | N | ? |
| 5 *Hefley* | Y | N | Y | N | Y | N | N | N |
| 6 *Schaefer* | Y | N | Y | N | N | Y | N | N |
| **CONNECTICUT** | | | | | | | | |
| 1 Kennelly | N | Y | N | Y | Y | Y | Y | Y |
| 2 Gejdenson | N | Y | N | N | Y | Y | Y | Y |
| 3 DeLauro | N | Y | N | N | Y | Y | Y | Y |
| 4 *Shays* | N | Y | N | N | Y | Y | Y | Y |
| 5 *Franks* | Y | Y | Y | N | N | Y | N | Y |
| 6 *Johnson* | Y | N | Y | N | N | Y | N | N |
| **DELAWARE** | | | | | | | | |
| AL Carper | Y | N | N | N | Y | Y | Y | Y |
| **FLORIDA** | | | | | | | | |
| 1 Hutto | Y | Y | Y | N | Y | Y | Y | N |
| 2 Peterson | N | Y | Y | N | Y | Y | Y | Y |
| 3 Bennett | N | Y | Y | N | Y | Y | Y | Y |
| 4 *James* | Y | N | Y | N | N | N | N | N |
| 5 *McCollum* | Y | N | Y | N | N | N | N | N |
| 6 *Stearns* | Y | Y | Y | N | N | Y | N | N |
| 7 Gibbons | N | Y | Y | Y | Y | Y | Y | Y |
| 8 *Young* | Y | Y | Y | N | N | Y | N | N |
| 9 *Bilirakis* | Y | N | Y | N | N | Y | N | N |
| 10 *Ireland* | ? | N | Y | N | N | Y | N | N |
| 11 Bacchus | N | Y | Y | N | Y | Y | Y | Y |
| 12 *Lewis* | Y | N | Y | N | N | Y | N | N |
| 13 *Goss* | Y | N | Y | N | N | Y | N | N |
| 14 Johnston | N | Y | N | N | Y | Y | Y | Y |
| 15 *Shaw* | Y | Y | Y | N | N | Y | N | N |
| 16 Smith | N | Y | Y | Y | Y | Y | Y | Y |
| 17 Lehman | N | Y | ? | ? | ? | Y | Y | Y |
| 18 *Ros−Lehtinen* | Y | N | Y | N | N | Y | N | N |
| 19 Fascell | N | Y | Y | N | Y | Y | Y | Y |
| **GEORGIA** | | | | | | | | |
| 1 Thomas | ? | ? | ? | ? | ? | ? | ? | ? |
| 2 Hatcher | ? | ? | ? | ? | ? | ? | ? | ? |
| 3 Ray | Y | Y | Y | N | Y | Y | N | N |
| 4 Jones | N | Y | N | N | Y | ? | N | N |
| 5 Lewis | N | Y | Y | N | Y | Y | Y | Y |
| 6 *Gingrich* | ? | ? | ? | ? | ? | Y | N | N |
| 7 *Darden* | Y | Y | Y | N | Y | Y | — | — |
| 8 Rowland | Y | Y | Y | N | N | Y | — | — |
| 9 Jenkins | Y | Y | Y | Y | Y | Y | — | — |
| 10 Barnard | Y | Y | Y | Y | Y | Y | — | — |
| **HAWAII** | | | | | | | | |
| 1 Abercrombie | N | Y | N | Y | Y | Y | Y | Y |
| 2 Mink | N | Y | N | Y | Y | Y | Y | Y |
| **IDAHO** | | | | | | | | |
| 1 LaRocco | N | Y | N | Y | Y | Y | Y | Y |
| 2 Stallings | N | Y | N | N | N | ? | ? | ? |
| **ILLINOIS** | | | | | | | | |
| 1 Hayes | N | Y | N | N | Y | Y | Y | Y |
| 2 Savage | ? | Y | ? | ? | ? | ? | ? | ? |
| 3 Russo | ? | ? | ? | ? | ? | Y | Y | Y |
| 4 Sangmeister | N | Y | N | N | Y | Y | Y | Y |
| 5 Lipinski | N | Y | N | N | Y | Y | Y | Y |
| 6 *Hyde* | ? | ? | ? | ? | ? | ? | ? | ? |
| 7 Collins | N | Y | N | N | Y | Y | Y | Y |
| 8 Rostenkowski | N | Y | Y | Y | Y | Y | Y | Y |
| 9 Yates | N | Y | N | N | Y | Y | Y | Y |
| 10 *Porter* | Y | Y | Y | N | N | + | N | N |
| 11 Annunzio | N | Y | N | Y | Y | Y | Y | Y |
| 12 *Crane* | Y | N | N | N | N | N | N | N |
| 13 *Fawell* | Y | N | Y | N | N | N | N | N |
| 14 *Hastert* | Y | N | Y | N | N | N | N | N |
| 15 *Ewing* | Y | N | Y | N | N | N | N | N |
| 16 Cox | N | Y | N | Y | Y | Y | Y | Y |
| 17 Evans | N | Y | N | Y | Y | Y | Y | Y |
| 18 *Michel* | Y | N | N | N | N | Y | N | N |
| 19 Bruce | N | Y | N | N | Y | Y | Y | Y |
| 20 Durbin | N | Y | N | N | Y | Y | Y | Y |
| 21 Costello | N | Y | N | N | Y | Y | Y | Y |
| 22 Poshard | N | N | N | N | Y | Y | Y | Y |
| **INDIANA** | | | | | | | | |
| 1 Visclosky | N | Y | N | N | Y | Y | Y | Y |
| 2 Sharp | N | Y | N | N | Y | Y | Y | Y |
| 3 Roemer | N | Y | N | Y | Y | Y | Y | Y |

| | 325 | 326 | 327 | 328 | 329 | 330 | 331 | 332 |
|---|---|---|---|---|---|---|---|---|
| 42 *Rohrabacher* | Y | N | Y | N | N | Y | N | N |
| 43 *Packard* | Y | N | Y | N | N | Y | N | N |
| 44 *Cunningham* | Y | Y | Y | N | Y | N | N | N |
| 45 *Hunter* | Y | N | Y | N | N | Y | N | N |

| | 325 | 326 | 327 | 328 | 329 | 330 | 331 | 332 |
|---|---|---|---|---|---|---|---|---|
| 4 Long | N | Y | N | N | Y | Y | Y | Y |
| 5 Jontz | N | Y | N | N | Y | Y | Y | Y |
| 6 ***Burton*** | Y | N | Y | N | N | N | N | N |
| 7 ***Myers*** | Y | N | Y | N | N | Y | N | N |
| 8 McCloskey | N | Y | Y | N | Y | Y | Y | Y |
| 9 Hamilton | N | Y | Y | N | Y | Y | Y | Y |
| 10 Jacobs | N | N | Y | N | Y | Y | N | Y |
| **IOWA** | | | | | | | | |
| 1 ***Leach*** | Y | N | N | N | Y | Y | N | N |
| 2 ***Nussle*** | Y | N | N | N | N | Y | N | N |
| 3 Nagle | N | Y | N | N | N | Y | Y | Y |
| 4 Smith | N | Y | N | N | Y | Y | Y | Y |
| 5 ***Lightfoot*** | Y | N | Y | N | Y | Y | N | N |
| 6 ***Grandy*** | Y | N | Y | N | N | Y | N | N |
| **KANSAS** | | | | | | | | |
| 1 ***Roberts*** | Y | N | Y | N | N | Y | N | N |
| 2 Slattery | N | N | N | N | Y | Y | Y | Y |
| 3 ***Meyers*** | Y | N | Y | N | N | Y | N | N |
| 4 Glickman | N | N | N | N | Y | Y | Y | Y |
| 5 ***Nichols*** | Y | N | Y | N | N | Y | N | N |
| **KENTUCKY** | | | | | | | | |
| 1 Hubbard | N | N | Y | N | Y | Y | Y | Y |
| 2 Natcher | N | Y | Y | N | Y | Y | Y | Y |
| 3 Mazzoli | N | Y | N | Y | Y | Y | Y | Y |
| 4 ***Bunning*** | Y | N | Y | N | N | Y | N | N |
| 5 ***Rogers*** | Y | Y | Y | N | N | Y | N | Y |
| 6 ***Hopkins*** | Y | N | Y | N | N | Y | N | N |
| 7 Perkins | ? | ? | ? | ? | ? | Y | Y | Y |
| **LOUISIANA** | | | | | | | | |
| 1 ***Livingston*** | Y | Y | Y | N | N | Y | N | N |
| 2 Jefferson | N | Y | Y | N | Y | ? | ? | ? |
| 3 Tauzin | Y | Y | Y | N | Y | ? | ? | ? |
| 4 ***McCrery*** | Y | Y | Y | N | N | Y | N | N |
| 5 Huckaby | Y | Y | Y | N | N | Y | N | Y |
| 6 ***Baker*** | Y | N | Y | N | N | Y | N | N |
| 7 Hayes | Y | Y | Y | N | Y | ? | ? | ? |
| 8 ***Holloway*** | Y | N | Y | N | N | Y | N | N |
| **MAINE** | | | | | | | | |
| 1 Andrews | N | Y | N | Y | Y | Y | Y | Y |
| 2 ***Snowe*** | Y | Y | Y | N | Y | Y | N | N |
| **MARYLAND** | | | | | | | | |
| 1 ***Gilchrest*** | Y | Y | Y | N | Y | Y | N | N |
| 2 ***Bentley*** | Y | Y | Y | N | N | Y | N | N |
| 3 Cardin | N | Y | Y | Y | Y | Y | Y | Y |
| 4 McMillen | N | Y | N | Y | Y | Y | Y | N |
| 5 Hoyer | N | Y | Y | N | Y | Y | Y | Y |
| 6 Byron | Y | Y | Y | N | N | Y | N | Y |
| 7 Mfume | N | Y | N | N | Y | Y | Y | Y |
| 8 ***Morella*** | Y | Y | N | Y | Y | Y | N | N |
| **MASSACHUSETTS** | | | | | | | | |
| 1 Olver | N | Y | Y | N | Y | Y | Y | Y |
| 2 Neal | N | Y | Y | N | Y | Y | Y | Y |
| 3 Early | N | Y | Y | N | Y | Y | Y | Y |
| 4 Frank | N | Y | N | N | Y | Y | Y | Y |
| 5 Atkins | N | Y | N | N | Y | Y | Y | Y |
| 6 Mavroules | N | Y | N | N | N | Y | Y | Y |
| 7 Markey | N | Y | N | N | Y | Y | Y | Y |
| 8 Kennedy | N | Y | Y | N | Y | Y | Y | Y |
| 9 Moakley | N | Y | Y | N | Y | Y | Y | Y |
| 10 Studds | N | Y | N | N | Y | Y | Y | Y |
| 11 Donnelly | N | Y | Y | N | N | Y | Y | Y |
| **MICHIGAN** | | | | | | | | |
| 1 Conyers | ? | ? | ? | ? | ? | Y | Y | Y |
| 2 ***Pursell*** | Y | N | N | N | N | Y | N | N |
| 3 Wolpe | N | Y | N | N | Y | Y | Y | Y |
| 4 ***Upton*** | Y | N | Y | N | N | Y | N | N |
| 5 ***Henry*** | Y | N | N | N | N | Y | N | N |
| 6 Carr | N | Y | Y | N | N | Y | Y | Y |
| 7 Kildee | N | Y | N | N | Y | Y | Y | Y |
| 8 Traxler | N | Y | Y | ? | N | Y | Y | Y |
| 9 ***Vander Jagt*** | Y | Y | Y | N | N | Y | N | N |
| 10 ***Camp*** | Y | Y | Y | N | N | Y | N | N |
| 11 ***Davis*** | N | Y | Y | N | N | ? | N | N |
| 12 Bonior | N | Y | N | Y | Y | Y | Y | Y |
| 13 Collins | N | Y | N | Y | Y | Y | Y | Y |
| 14 Hertel | N | Y | Y | N | Y | Y | Y | Y |
| 15 Ford | N | Y | Y | N | Y | Y | Y | Y |
| 16 Dingell | N | Y | Y | N | Y | Y | Y | Y |
| 17 Levin | N | Y | Y | N | Y | Y | Y | Y |
| 18 ***Broomfield*** | Y | Y | Y | N | N | Y | N | N |
| **MINNESOTA** | | | | | | | | |
| 1 Penny | N | N | N | N | Y | Y | Y | Y |
| 2 ***Weber*** | Y | N | Y | N | N | Y | N | N |
| 3 ***Ramstad*** | Y | N | Y | N | N | Y | N | N |
| 4 Vento | N | Y | N | N | Y | Y | Y | Y |

| | 325 | 326 | 327 | 328 | 329 | 330 | 331 | 332 |
|---|---|---|---|---|---|---|---|---|
| 5 Sabo | N | Y | N | N | Y | Y | Y | Y |
| 6 Sikorski | N | N | N | N | Y | Y | Y | Y |
| 7 Peterson | N | Y | Y | N | Y | Y | Y | Y |
| 8 Oberstar | N | Y | Y | N | Y | Y | Y | Y |
| **MISSISSIPPI** | | | | | | | | |
| 1 Whitten | N | Y | Y | N | N | ? | Y | Y |
| 2 Espy | N | Y | N | N | N | Y | N | Y |
| 3 Montgomery | Y | Y | Y | N | Y | Y | Y | Y |
| 4 Parker | Y | Y | Y | N | Y | Y | Y | Y |
| 5 Taylor | N | Y | Y | N | Y | Y | Y | Y |
| **MISSOURI** | | | | | | | | |
| 1 Clay | N | Y | N | N | Y | Y | Y | Y |
| 2 Horn | N | Y | Y | N | Y | Y | Y | Y |
| 3 Gephardt | N | Y | Y | Y | Y | Y | Y | Y |
| 4 Skelton | N | Y | Y | N | N | Y | Y | Y |
| 5 Wheat | N | Y | Y | N | N | Y | Y | Y |
| 6 ***Coleman*** | Y | Y | Y | N | N | Y | N | N |
| 7 ***Hancock*** | Y | N | Y | N | Y | Y | N | N |
| 8 ***Emerson*** | Y | Y | Y | N | Y | Y | N | N |
| 9 Volkmer | N | Y | Y | N | N | Y | Y | Y |
| **MONTANA** | | | | | | | | |
| 1 Williams | N | Y | Y | N | N | Y | Y | Y |
| 2 ***Marlenee*** | Y | N | Y | N | N | N | N | N |
| **NEBRASKA** | | | | | | | | |
| 1 ***Bereuter*** | Y | N | Y | N | N | Y | N | N |
| 2 Hoagland | N | Y | N | Y | Y | Y | Y | Y |
| 3 ***Barrett*** | Y | N | Y | N | N | Y | N | N |
| **NEVADA** | | | | | | | | |
| 1 Bilbray | N | Y | Y | N | Y | Y | Y | Y |
| 2 ***Vucanovich*** | Y | Y | Y | N | N | Y | N | N |
| **NEW HAMPSHIRE** | | | | | | | | |
| 1 ***Zeliff*** | Y | N | N | N | N | Y | ? | ? |
| 2 Swett | N | Y | N | N | Y | Y | N | Y |
| **NEW JERSEY** | | | | | | | | |
| 1 Andrews | N | Y | N | ? | Y | Y | Y | Y |
| 2 Hughes | N | N | N | N | Y | Y | Y | Y |
| 3 Pallone | N | Y | N | N | Y | Y | Y | Y |
| 4 ***Smith*** | N | Y | Y | N | N | Y | N | N |
| 5 ***Roukema*** | Y | Y | Y | N | Y | Y | N | N |
| 6 Dwyer | N | Y | Y | N | Y | Y | Y | Y |
| 7 ***Rinaldo*** | N | Y | Y | N | Y | Y | N | N |
| 8 Roe | N | Y | Y | Y | Y | Y | Y | Y |
| 9 Torricelli | N | Y | Y | Y | Y | Y | Y | Y |
| 10 Payne | — | + | N | N | Y | Y | Y | Y |
| 11 ***Gallo*** | N | Y | N | N | N | Y | N | N |
| 12 ***Zimmer*** | Y | N | N | N | Y | Y | N | N |
| 13 ***Saxton*** | N | Y | N | N | ? | Y | N | N |
| 14 Guarini | N | N | Y | N | N | Y | Y | Y |
| **NEW MEXICO** | | | | | | | | |
| 1 ***Schiff*** | Y | Y | Y | N | Y | Y | N | N |
| 2 ***Skeen*** | Y | Y | Y | N | N | Y | N | N |
| 3 Richardson | N | Y | N | N | Y | Y | Y | Y |
| **NEW YORK** | | | | | | | | |
| 1 Hochbrueckner | N | Y | N | N | Y | Y | Y | Y |
| 2 Downey | N | Y | N | N | Y | Y | Y | Y |
| 3 Mrazek | N | Y | Y | N | Y | Y | Y | Y |
| 4 ***Lent*** | ? | Y | Y | N | Y | Y | N | N |
| 5 ***McGrath*** | N | Y | Y | Y | Y | Y | N | N |
| 6 Flake | N | Y | Y | N | Y | Y | Y | Y |
| 7 Ackerman | N | Y | Y | N | Y | Y | Y | Y |
| 8 Scheuer | N | Y | N | Y | Y | Y | Y | Y |
| 9 Manton | N | Y | Y | N | Y | Y | Y | Y |
| 10 Schumer | N | Y | N | N | Y | Y | Y | Y |
| 11 Towns | N | Y | N | N | Y | ? | ? | ? |
| 12 Owens | Y | Y | Y | N | Y | Y | Y | Y |
| 13 Solarz | ? | ? | ? | ? | ? | ? | ? | ? |
| 14 ***Molinari*** | Y | N | Y | N | N | Y | N | N |
| 15 ***Green*** | Y | Y | Y | N | N | Y | N | Y |
| 16 Rangel | N | Y | Y | Y | Y | Y | Y | Y |
| 17 Weiss | N | Y | N | Y | Y | ? | Y | Y |
| 18 Serrano | N | Y | N | N | Y | Y | Y | Y |
| 19 Engel | X | ? | Y | N | Y | Y | Y | Y |
| 20 Lowey | N | Y | N | N | Y | Y | Y | Y |
| 21 ***Fish*** | N | Y | Y | N | N | Y | N | N |
| 22 ***Gilman*** | N | Y | N | N | N | Y | N | Y |
| 23 McNulty | N | Y | Y | N | Y | Y | Y | Y |
| 24 ***Solomon*** | N | N | Y | N | N | Y | N | N |
| 25 ***Boehlert*** | N | Y | Y | N | Y | Y | N | N |
| 26 ***Martin*** | N | Y | Y | N | N | Y | N | N |
| 27 ***Walsh*** | N | Y | Y | N | N | Y | N | N |
| 28 McHugh | N | Y | N | N | Y | Y | Y | Y |
| 29 ***Horton*** | N | Y | Y | N | N | Y | N | N |
| 30 Slaughter | N | Y | N | N | Y | Y | Y | Y |
| 31 ***Paxon*** | Y | N | Y | N | N | Y | N | N |

| | 325 | 326 | 327 | 328 | 329 | 330 | 331 | 332 |
|---|---|---|---|---|---|---|---|---|
| 32 LaFalce | N | Y | Y | N | N | Y | Y | Y |
| 33 Nowak | N | Y | Y | N | N | Y | Y | Y |
| 34 ***Houghton*** | N | Y | Y | N | N | Y | N | N |
| **NORTH CAROLINA** | | | | | | | | |
| 1 Jones | N | Y | Y | N | N | Y | Y | Y |
| 2 Valentine | Y | Y | Y | N | Y | Y | Y | Y |
| 3 Lancaster | Y | Y | Y | N | Y | Y | Y | Y |
| 4 Price | Y | Y | Y | N | Y | Y | Y | Y |
| 5 Neal | Y | Y | Y | N | Y | Y | Y | Y |
| 6 ***Coble*** | Y | N | Y | N | N | N | N | N |
| 7 Rose | N | Y | Y | N | Y | Y | Y | Y |
| 8 Hefner | Y | Y | Y | N | N | Y | Y | Y |
| 9 ***McMillan*** | Y | N | Y | N | Y | Y | N | N |
| 10 ***Ballenger*** | Y | N | Y | N | N | Y | N | N |
| 11 ***Taylor*** | Y | N | Y | N | N | Y | N | N |
| **NORTH DAKOTA** | | | | | | | | |
| AL Dorgan | N | Y | N | N | Y | Y | Y | Y |
| **OHIO** | | | | | | | | |
| 1 Luken | N | N | Y | N | Y | Y | Y | Y |
| 2 ***Gradison*** | Y | N | N | N | N | Y | N | N |
| 3 Hall | N | Y | Y | N | Y | Y | Y | Y |
| 4 ***Oxley*** | Y | Y | Y | N | N | Y | N | N |
| 5 ***Gillmor*** | N | Y | Y | N | N | Y | N | N |
| 6 ***McEwen*** | Y | N | Y | N | N | Y | N | N |
| 7 ***Hobson*** | Y | Y | Y | N | N | Y | N | N |
| 8 ***Boehner*** | Y | N | Y | N | N | Y | N | N |
| 9 Kaptur | N | Y | Y | N | Y | Y | Y | Y |
| 10 ***Miller*** | Y | N | Y | N | N | Y | N | N |
| 11 Eckart | N | Y | N | Y | Y | Y | Y | Y |
| 12 ***Kasich*** | Y | Y | Y | N | N | Y | N | N |
| 13 Pease | N | N | N | Y | Y | Y | Y | Y |
| 14 Sawyer | N | Y | N | N | Y | Y | Y | Y |
| 15 ***Wylie*** | Y | N | Y | N | N | Y | N | N |
| 16 ***Regula*** | N | Y | Y | N | N | Y | N | N |
| 17 Traficant | N | Y | Y | N | N | Y | Y | Y |
| 18 Applegate | N | Y | Y | Y | N | Y | N | N |
| 19 Feighan | N | Y | Y | N | Y | Y | Y | Y |
| 20 Oakar | N | Y | Y | Y | Y | Y | Y | Y |
| 21 Stokes | N | Y | N | N | Y | Y | Y | Y |
| **OKLAHOMA** | | | | | | | | |
| 1 ***Inhofe*** | Y | N | Y | N | N | Y | N | N |
| 2 Synar | N | Y | N | N | Y | Y | Y | Y |
| 3 Brewster | N | Y | Y | N | Y | Y | Y | Y |
| 4 McCurdy | Y | Y | Y | N | Y | ? | ? | ? |
| 5 ***Edwards*** | Y | N | Y | N | N | ? | ? | N |
| 6 English | Y | Y | Y | N | Y | Y | N | Y |
| **OREGON** | | | | | | | | |
| 1 AuCoin | N | Y | N | N | Y | Y | Y | Y |
| 2 ***Smith*** | Y | N | N | N | N | Y | N | N |
| 3 Wyden | N | Y | N | N | Y | Y | Y | Y |
| 4 DeFazio | N | Y | N | Y | Y | Y | Y | Y |
| 5 Kopetski | N | Y | Y | N | Y | Y | Y | Y |
| **PENNSYLVANIA** | | | | | | | | |
| 1 Foglietta | N | Y | N | N | Y | Y | Y | Y |
| 2 Blackwell | N | Y | N | N | N | Y | Y | Y |
| 3 Borski | N | Y | Y | N | Y | Y | Y | Y |
| 4 Kolter | N | Y | Y | ? | ? | Y | Y | Y |
| 5 ***Schulze*** | ? | N | Y | N | N | Y | N | N |
| 6 Yatron | N | Y | Y | N | Y | Y | Y | Y |
| 7 ***Weldon*** | N | N | Y | N | N | Y | N | N |
| 8 Kostmayer | N | Y | N | N | Y | Y | Y | Y |
| 9 ***Shuster*** | Y | N | Y | N | N | Y | N | N |
| 10 ***McDade*** | N | Y | Y | N | N | Y | N | Y |
| 11 Kanjorski | N | Y | Y | N | Y | Y | Y | Y |
| 12 Murtha | N | Y | Y | N | N | Y | Y | Y |
| 13 ***Coughlin*** | Y | Y | ? | ? | ? | ? | ? | ? |
| 14 Coyne | N | Y | Y | Y | Y | Y | Y | Y |
| 15 ***Ritter*** | N | N | Y | N | N | Y | N | N |
| 16 ***Walker*** | Y | N | Y | N | N | Y | N | N |
| 17 ***Gekas*** | Y | N | Y | N | N | Y | N | N |
| 18 ***Santorum*** | N | N | Y | N | N | Y | N | N |
| 19 ***Goodling*** | Y | Y | Y | N | N | Y | N | N |
| 20 Gaydos | N | Y | Y | N | N | ? | Y | Y |
| 21 ***Ridge*** | N | N | N | N | N | Y | N | N |
| 22 Murphy | N | Y | Y | Y | N | Y | Y | Y |
| 23 ***Clinger*** | Y | N | Y | N | N | Y | N | N |
| **RHODE ISLAND** | | | | | | | | |
| 1 ***Machtley*** | Y | Y | Y | N | N | Y | N | N |
| 2 Reed | N | Y | N | N | Y | Y | Y | Y |
| **SOUTH CAROLINA** | | | | | | | | |
| 1 ***Ravenel*** | Y | Y | Y | N | Y | Y | N | N |
| 2 ***Spence*** | Y | Y | Y | N | N | Y | N | N |
| 3 Derrick | Y | Y | Y | Y | N | Y | Y | Y |
| 4 Patterson | Y | Y | N | N | Y | Y | Y | Y |
| 5 Spratt | Y | Y | Y | N | Y | Y | Y | Y |
| 6 Tallon | N | Y | Y | N | N | Y | Y | Y |

| | 325 | 326 | 327 | 328 | 329 | 330 | 331 | 332 |
|---|---|---|---|---|---|---|---|---|
| **SOUTH DAKOTA** | | | | | | | | |
| AL Johnson | N | Y | N | N | Y | Y | Y | Y |
| **TENNESSEE** | | | | | | | | |
| 1 ***Quillen*** | Y | N | Y | N | N | Y | N | Y |
| 2 ***Duncan*** | Y | N | Y | N | N | Y | N | N |
| 3 Lloyd | N | Y | Y | N | N | Y | Y | Y |
| 4 Cooper | Y | Y | Y | N | Y | Y | Y | Y |
| 5 Clement | N | Y | Y | N | Y | Y | Y | Y |
| 6 Gordon | N | Y | Y | N | Y | Y | Y | Y |
| 7 ***Sundquist*** | Y | N | Y | N | N | Y | N | N |
| 8 Tanner | Y | Y | Y | N | Y | Y | N | Y |
| 9 Ford | ? | ? | ? | ? | ? | ? | Y | Y |
| **TEXAS** | | | | | | | | |
| 1 Chapman | Y | Y | Y | N | N | Y | Y | Y |
| 2 Wilson | N | Y | Y | Y | Y | ? | Y | Y |
| 3 ***Johnson*** | Y | N | Y | N | N | Y | N | N |
| 4 Hall | Y | Y | Y | Y | Y | Y | Y | Y |
| 5 Bryant | N | Y | Y | N | Y | Y | Y | Y |
| 6 ***Barton*** | Y | N | Y | N | N | Y | N | N |
| 7 ***Archer*** | Y | N | Y | N | N | Y | N | N |
| 8 ***Fields*** | Y | N | Y | N | Y | Y | N | N |
| 9 Brooks | N | Y | Y | N | Y | Y | Y | Y |
| 10 Pickle | Y | Y | Y | Y | ? | Y | N | Y |
| 11 Edwards | N | Y | Y | N | Y | Y | Y | Y |
| 12 Geren | Y | N | Y | Y | Y | Y | Y | Y |
| 13 Sarpalius | N | Y | Y | Y | Y | Y | Y | Y |
| 14 Laughlin | N | Y | Y | N | Y | Y | Y | Y |
| 15 de la Garza | N | Y | Y | N | Y | Y | Y | Y |
| 16 Coleman | N | Y | Y | N | Y | Y | Y | Y |
| 17 Stenholm | Y | N | Y | N | Y | Y | N | Y |
| 18 Washington | N | Y | N | N | Y | Y | ? | ? |
| 19 ***Combest*** | Y | N | Y | N | Y | Y | N | N |
| 20 Gonzalez | N | Y | Y | N | Y | Y | Y | Y |
| 21 ***Smith*** | Y | N | Y | N | N | Y | N | N |
| 22 ***DeLay*** | Y | N | Y | N | N | Y | N | N |
| 23 Bustamante | N | Y | Y | N | Y | Y | ? | Y |
| 24 Frost | N | Y | Y | N | Y | Y | Y | Y |
| 25 Andrews | Y | Y | N | N | Y | Y | Y | Y |
| 26 ***Armey*** | Y | N | Y | N | N | N | N | N |
| 27 Ortiz | N | Y | Y | N | N | Y | Y | Y |
| **UTAH** | | | | | | | | |
| 1 ***Hansen*** | Y | N | Y | N | N | Y | N | N |
| 2 Owens | N | Y | N | N | Y | Y | Y | N |
| 3 Orton | N | N | Y | N | N | Y | Y | N |
| **VERMONT** | | | | | | | | |
| AL *Sanders* | N | Y | N | N | Y | Y | Y | Y |
| **VIRGINIA** | | | | | | | | |
| 1 ***Bateman*** | Y | Y | Y | N | N | Y | N | N |
| 2 Pickett | Y | Y | N | N | N | Y | Y | Y |
| 3 ***Bliley*** | Y | Y | Y | N | N | Y | N | N |
| 4 Sisisky | Y | Y | Y | N | Y | Y | N | Y |
| 5 Payne | Y | N | Y | N | Y | Y | N | Y |
| 6 Olin | N | Y | Y | N | Y | Y | Y | Y |
| 7 ***Allen*** | Y | N | Y | N | N | Y | N | N |
| 8 Moran | N | Y | N | N | Y | Y | Y | Y |
| 9 Boucher | N | Y | Y | N | Y | Y | Y | Y |
| 10 ***Wolf*** | Y | N | Y | N | Y | Y | N | N |
| **WASHINGTON** | | | | | | | | |
| 1 ***Miller*** | Y | N | Y | Y | N | Y | N | N |
| 2 Swift | N | Y | Y | Y | Y | Y | Y | Y |
| 3 Unsoeld | N | Y | N | N | Y | Y | Y | Y |
| 4 ***Morrison*** | N | Y | Y | N | N | Y | N | N |
| 5 Foley | | | | | | | | |
| 6 Dicks | N | Y | Y | N | Y | Y | Y | Y |
| 7 McDermott | N | Y | Y | Y | Y | Y | Y | Y |
| 8 ***Chandler*** | Y | Y | Y | N | N | Y | N | N |
| **WEST VIRGINIA** | | | | | | | | |
| 1 Mollohan | N | Y | N | N | Y | Y | Y | Y |
| 2 Staggers | N | Y | Y | N | Y | Y | N | Y |
| 3 Wise | N | Y | Y | N | Y | Y | Y | Y |
| 4 Rahall | N | Y | N | N | Y | Y | N | Y |
| **WISCONSIN** | | | | | | | | |
| 1 Aspin | N | Y | Y | N | Y | Y | Y | Y |
| 2 ***Klug*** | Y | N | N | N | Y | Y | N | N |
| 3 ***Gunderson*** | Y | N | Y | N | N | Y | N | N |
| 4 Kleczka | N | Y | Y | N | Y | Y | Y | Y |
| 5 Moody | N | Y | N | N | Y | Y | Y | Y |
| 6 ***Petri*** | Y | N | N | N | N | Y | N | N |
| 7 Obey | N | Y | N | N | Y | Y | Y | Y |
| 8 ***Roth*** | Y | N | N | N | N | Y | N | N |
| 9 ***Sensenbrenner*** | Y | N | N | N | N | Y | N | N |
| **WYOMING** | | | | | | | | |
| AL ***Thomas*** | Y | N | Y | N | N | Y | N | N |

Southern states - Ala., Ark., Fla., Ga., Ky., La., Miss., N.C., Okla., S.C., Tenn., Texas, Va.
Omitted votes are quorum calls, which CQ does not include in its vote charts.

**333. HR 5679. Fiscal 1993 VA, Housing and Urban Development, Independent Agencies Appropriations/ Administrative Cuts.** Dorgan, D-N.D., amendment to cut $19 million from the salaries and expenses for management and administration at the Department of Housing and Urban Development. Adopted 261-154: R 131-29; D 130-124 (ND 79-95, SD 51-29); I 0-1, July 29, 1992.

**334. HR 5679. Fiscal 1993 VA, Housing and Urban Development, Independent Agencies Appropriations/ Space Station Cuts.** Traxler, D-Mich., amendment to cut $1.2 billion of the $1.73 billion in the bill for NASA's space station *Freedom,* leaving $525 million for costs associated with closing down the program. Rejected 181-237: R 38-127; D 142-110 (ND 115-59, SD 27-51); I 1-0, July 29, 1992. A "nay" was a vote supporting the president's position.

**335. HR 5679. Fiscal 1993 VA, Housing and Urban Development, Independent Agencies Appropriations/ Classroom of the Future.** Hefley, R-Colo., amendment to cut the $1.8 million for the Classroom of the Future at Wheeling Jesuit College in West Virginia. Rejected 169-235: R 142-19; D 26-216 (ND 20-147, SD 6-69); I 1-0, July 29, 1992.

**336. HR 5679. Fiscal 1993 VA, Housing and Urban Development, Independent Agencies Appropriations/Draft Registration.** Atkins, D-Mass., amendment to eliminate the $28.6 million for the Selective Service System to register individuals for the draft. Rejected 96-310: R 11-151; D 84-159 (ND 78-90, SD 6-69); I 1-0, July 29, 1992.

**337. HR 5679. Fiscal 1993 VA, Housing and Urban Development, Independent Agencies Appropriations/ Aerospace Plane.** McCurdy, D-Okla., amendment to strike $1,000 from the bill in order to bring to the floor a directive to NASA to spend $33,499,000 on the national aerospace plane instead of the Consortium for International Earth Science Information Network, a network on global environmental data. Adopted 207-201: R 129-33; D 77-168 (ND 39-129, SD 38-39); I 1-0, July 29, 1992. The McCurdy vote was subsequently rejected after the Committee of the Whole House rose, and Traxler, D-Mich., requested a separate vote (vote 342).

**338. HR 5679. Fiscal 1993 VA, Housing and Urban Development, Independent Agencies Appropriations/ *Challenger* Planetarium.** Burton, R-Ind., amendment to cut $58 million from the bill: $8 million for a *Challenger* Center Planetarium at Delta College in University Center, Mich., and $50 million for a headquarters building in Saginaw, Mich., for the Consortium for International Earth Science Information Network, a network of global environmental data. Rejected 182-224: R 134-27; D 47-197 (ND 27-140, SD 20-57); I 1-0, July 29, 1992.

**339. HR 5679. Fiscal 1993 VA, Housing and Urban Development, Independent Agencies Appropriations/ ASRM.** Hansen, R-Utah., amendment to the Owens, D-Utah, amendment, to transfer $175 million from the Advanced Solid Rocket Motor (ASRM) program to the space station *Freedom,* cut an additional $90 million from the ASRM program and leave $50 million for continued development of the ASRM program. The Owens amendment cut $265 million from the ASRM program. Rejected 181-226: R 116-46; D 64-180 (ND 50-117, SD 14-63); I 1-0, July 29, 1992.

**340. HR 5679. Fiscal 1993 VA, Housing and Urban Development, Independent Agencies Appropriations/ ASRM.** Owens, D-Utah, amendment to cut $380 million from the Advanced Solid Rocket Motor (ASRM) program. Adopted 249-159: R 124-38; D 124-121 (ND 109-59, SD 15-62); I 1-0, July 29, 1992.

## KEY

| | 333 | 334 | 335 | 336 | 337 | 338 | 339 | 340 |
|---|---|---|---|---|---|---|---|---|
| **ALABAMA** | | | | | | | | |
| 1 *Callahan* | Y | N | Y | N | Y | Y | Y | N |
| 2 *Dickinson* | Y | N | Y | N | N | Y | Y | Y |
| 3 Browder | Y | N | N | N | N | N | N | N |
| 4 Bevill | Y | N | N | N | N | N | N | N |
| 5 Cramer | Y | N | N | N | N | N | N | N |
| 6 Erdreich | Y | N | N | N | N | N | N | N |
| 7 Harris | Y | N | N | N | N | N | N | N |
| **ALASKA** | | | | | | | | |
| AL *Young* | N | N | N | N | N | Y | Y | Y |
| **ARIZONA** | | | | | | | | |
| 1 *Rhodes* | N | N | N | N | Y | Y | Y | N |
| 2 Pastor | N | Y | N | N | N | N | N | N |
| 3 *Stump* | Y | N | Y | N | Y | Y | Y | Y |
| 4 *Kyl* | Y | N | Y | N | Y | Y | Y | Y |
| 5 *Kolbe* | Y | Y | Y | N | Y | Y | Y | Y |
| **ARKANSAS** | | | | | | | | |
| 1 Alexander | N | ? | ? | ? | ? | ? | ? | ? |
| 2 Thornton | Y | N | N | N | N | N | N | N |
| 3 *Hammerschmidt* | Y | N | Y | N | N | Y | Y | N |
| 4 Anthony | Y | Y | ? | ? | ? | ? | ? | ? |
| **CALIFORNIA** | | | | | | | | |
| 1 *Riggs* | Y | N | Y | N | Y | N | Y | Y |
| 2 *Herger* | Y | N | Y | N | Y | Y | Y | Y |
| 3 Matsui | N | N | N | Y | N | N | N | N |
| 4 Fazio | N | N | N | N | N | N | N | N |
| 5 Pelosi | N | Y | N | Y | N | N | N | N |
| 6 Boxer | ? | ? | ? | ? | ? | ? | ? | ? |
| 7 Miller | N | Y | N | N | N | N | N | N |
| 8 Dellums | N | N | N | Y | N | N | N | Y |
| 9 Stark | N | Y | ? | ? | ? | ? | ? | ? |
| 10 Edwards | N | N | N | Y | N | N | N | N |
| 11 Lantos | Y | Y | N | N | Y | N | Y | Y |
| 12 *Campbell* | Y | N | Y | N | Y | N | Y | Y |
| 13 Mineta | N | N | N | N | N | N | N | N |
| 14 *Doolittle* | Y | Y | Y | N | Y | Y | Y | Y |
| 15 Condit | Y | Y | Y | N | Y | Y | Y | Y |
| 16 Panetta | Y | Y | N | Y | N | N | N | Y |
| 17 Dooley | Y | Y | Y | Y | Y | Y | Y | Y |
| 18 Lehman | N | Y | N | N | N | N | N | N |
| 19 *Lagomarsino* | Y | N | Y | N | Y | Y | Y | Y |
| 20 *Thomas* | Y | N | N | N | Y | Y | Y | N |
| 21 *Gallegly* | Y | N | Y | N | Y | Y | Y | Y |
| 22 *Moorhead* | Y | N | Y | N | Y | Y | Y | Y |
| 23 Beilenson | N | Y | N | N | N | N | N | Y |
| 24 Waxman | N | N | Y | N | N | N | N | N |
| 25 Roybal | N | Y | N | N | N | N | N | N |
| 26 Berman | N | N | N | Y | N | ? | N | N |
| 27 Levine | N | N | Y | N | N | N | N | N |
| 28 Dixon | N | N | N | N | N | N | N | N |
| 29 Waters | Y | N | N | N | Y | N | N | Y |
| 30 Martinez | Y | N | N | Y | N | N | N | N |
| 31 Dymally | N | N | N | Y | N | N | N | N |
| 32 Anderson | Y | N | N | N | N | N | N | N |
| 33 *Dreier* | Y | N | Y | N | Y | Y | Y | Y |
| 34 Torres | N | N | N | N | N | N | N | N |
| 35 *Lewis* | Y | N | N | N | N | N | N | N |
| 36 Brown | Y | N | N | N | N | N | N | N |
| 37 *McCandless* | Y | N | Y | N | Y | Y | Y | Y |
| 38 *Dornan* | Y | N | Y | N | Y | Y | Y | Y |
| 39 *Dannemeyer* | Y | N | Y | N | Y | Y | Y | Y |
| 40 *Cox* | Y | N | Y | Y | Y | Y | Y | Y |
| 41 *Lowery* | N | N | N | N | N | N | N | N |

| | 333 | 334 | 335 | 336 | 337 | 338 | 339 | 340 |
|---|---|---|---|---|---|---|---|---|
| 42 *Rohrabacher* | Y | N | Y | N | Y | Y | Y | Y |
| 43 *Packard* | Y | N | Y | N | Y | Y | Y | Y |
| 44 *Cunningham* | Y | N | Y | N | Y | Y | Y | Y |
| 45 *Hunter* | Y | N | Y | N | Y | Y | Y | Y |
| **COLORADO** | | | | | | | | |
| 1 Schroeder | Y | Y | Y | Y | N | N | N | Y |
| 2 Skaggs | N | Y | Y | N | N | N | N | N |
| 3 *Campbell* | ? | ? | ? | ? | ? | ? | ? | ? |
| 4 *Allard* | Y | N | Y | N | Y | Y | Y | Y |
| 5 *Hefley* | Y | N | Y | N | Y | Y | N | Y |
| 6 *Schaefer* | Y | N | Y | N | Y | Y | Y | Y |
| **CONNECTICUT** | | | | | | | | |
| 1 Kennelly | N | N | N | N | N | N | N | Y |
| 2 Gejdenson | Y | N | N | N | N | N | N | Y |
| 3 DeLauro | Y | N | N | N | N | N | N | N |
| 4 *Shays* | Y | Y | Y | N | Y | N | Y | N |
| 5 *Franks* | Y | N | Y | N | Y | Y | Y | Y |
| 6 *Johnson* | N | N | Y | Y | Y | N | Y | N |
| **DELAWARE** | | | | | | | | |
| AL Carper | N | N | N | N | N | N | N | Y |
| **FLORIDA** | | | | | | | | |
| 1 Hutto | Y | N | N | Y | Y | Y | Y | Y |
| 2 Peterson | Y | N | N | N | Y | Y | N | N |
| 3 Bennett | Y | Y | N | N | Y | Y | Y | Y |
| 4 *James* | Y | N | Y | N | Y | Y | Y | Y |
| 5 *McCollum* | \# | N | Y | N | Y | Y | Y | Y |
| 6 *Stearns* | Y | N | N | N | Y | Y | Y | Y |
| 7 Gibbons | N | N | N | N | N | N | N | N |
| 8 *Young* | N | N | Y | N | Y | Y | Y | Y |
| 9 *Bilirakis* | N | Y | N | N | Y | Y | Y | Y |
| 10 *Ireland* | Y | N | Y | N | Y | Y | Y | Y |
| 11 Bacchus | Y | N | N | N | N | N | N | N |
| 12 *Lewis* | Y | N | Y | N | N | Y | Y | N |
| 13 *Goss* | Y | N | Y | N | Y | Y | Y | Y |
| 14 Johnston | Y | Y | N | N | N | N | N | Y |
| 15 *Shaw* | Y | N | Y | N | N | Y | Y | Y |
| 16 Smith | N | N | N | N | N | N | N | N |
| 17 Lehman | N | N | N | N | N | N | N | N |
| 18 *Ros—Lehtinen* | Y | Y | Y | N | Y | N | Y | N |
| 19 Fascell | N | N | N | N | N | N | N | N |
| **GEORGIA** | | | | | | | | |
| 1 Thomas | ? | ? | ? | Y | N | N | N | N |
| 2 Hatcher | ? | ? | ? | ? | ? | ? | ? | ? |
| 3 Ray | Y | Y | Y | N | Y | Y | Y | Y |
| 4 Jones | Y | Y | N | N | Y | Y | N | N |
| 5 Lewis | Y | N | N | N | N | N | N | N |
| 6 *Gingrich* | Y | N | Y | N | Y | Y | Y | Y |
| 7 Darden | Y | N | N | N | N | N | N | N |
| 8 Rowland | Y | N | N | N | N | N | N | N |
| 9 Jenkins | Y | N | N | N | N | N | N | N |
| 10 Barnard | Y | N | N | Y | Y | N | Y | N |
| **HAWAII** | | | | | | | | |
| 1 Abercrombie | N | Y | N | N | Y | N | N | Y |
| 2 Mink | Y | Y | N | Y | N | N | N | Y |
| **IDAHO** | | | | | | | | |
| 1 LaRocco | Y | Y | Y | Y | Y | N | Y | Y |
| 2 Stallings | ? | ? | ? | ? | ? | ? | ? | ? |
| **ILLINOIS** | | | | | | | | |
| 1 Hayes | Y | Y | N | Y | N | N | N | Y |
| 2 Savage | ? | ? | ? | ? | ? | ? | ? | ? |
| 3 Russo | Y | Y | N | N | Y | N | N | N |
| 4 Sangmeister | N | Y | N | N | N | N | N | N |
| 5 Lipinski | Y | N | N | N | N | N | N | N |
| 6 *Hyde* | ? | ? | ? | ? | ? | ? | ? | ? |
| 7 Collins | Y | Y | N | N | N | N | N | N |
| 8 Rostenkowski | N | N | N | N | N | N | N | N |
| 9 Yates | N | Y | N | N | N | N | N | N |
| 10 *Porter* | Y | Y | Y | N | N | Y | N | Y |
| 11 Annunzio | N | N | ? | ? | ? | ? | ? | ? |
| 12 *Crane* | Y | Y | Y | Y | Y | Y | Y | Y |
| 13 *Fawell* | Y | Y | Y | N | Y | Y | Y | Y |
| 14 *Hastert* | N | Y | Y | N | N | Y | Y | Y |
| 15 *Ewing* | Y | Y | Y | N | Y | Y | Y | Y |
| 16 Cox | Y | Y | Y | N | Y | N | Y | Y |
| 17 Evans | N | Y | N | N | N | N | N | N |
| 18 *Michel* | N | N | Y | N | Y | Y | N | N |
| 19 Bruce | Y | Y | N | N | N | Y | N | Y |
| 20 Durbin | N | Y | N | N | N | N | N | N |
| 21 Costello | N | Y | N | N | N | N | N | N |
| 22 Poshard | N | Y | N | N | N | Y | Y | N |
| **INDIANA** | | | | | | | | |
| 1 Visclosky | N | Y | N | N | N | N | N | N |
| 2 Sharp | Y | Y | Y | N | N | Y | N | Y |
| 3 Roemer | Y | Y | N | N | N | Y | Y | Y |

| | 333 | 334 | 335 | 336 | 337 | 338 | 339 | 340 |
|---|---|---|---|---|---|---|---|---|
| 4 Long | Y | Y | Y | Y | N | Y | Y | Y |
| 5 Jontz | Y | Y | N | Y | N | N | Y | Y |
| 6 ***Burton*** | Y | Y | Y | N | Y | Y | Y | Y |
| 7 ***Myers*** | Y | N | Y | N | N | N | Y | N |
| 8 McCloskey | Y | Y | N | N | N | Y | N | N |
| 9 Hamilton | Y | Y | Y | N | N | Y | Y | Y |
| 10 Jacobs | Y | Y | Y | N | N | Y | Y | Y |
| **IOWA** | | | | | | | | |
| 1 ***Leach*** | Y | Y | Y | N | N | Y | N | Y |
| 2 ***Nussle*** | Y | Y | Y | N | Y | Y | N | Y |
| 3 Nagle | N | N | N | N | N | N | Y | Y |
| 4 Smith | N | Y | N | N | N | N | N | N |
| 5 ***Lightfoot*** | N | N | N | N | N | Y | N | N |
| 6 ***Grandy*** | Y | Y | Y | N | Y | Y | N | Y |
| **KANSAS** | | | | | | | | |
| 1 ***Roberts*** | Y | N | Y | N | Y | Y | Y | Y |
| 2 Slattery | Y | N | N | N | Y | N | N | Y |
| 3 ***Meyers*** | Y | N | Y | N | Y | Y | Y | Y |
| 4 Glickman | Y | N | Y | N | Y | N | Y | Y |
| 5 ***Nichols*** | Y | N | Y | N | Y | Y | Y | Y |
| **KENTUCKY** | | | | | | | | |
| 1 Hubbard | Y | N | N | N | Y | Y | Y | Y |
| 2 Natcher | N | N | N | N | N | N | N | N |
| 3 Mazzoli | Y | Y | N | N | N | N | N | N |
| 4 ***Bunning*** | N | N | Y | N | Y | Y | Y | Y |
| 5 ***Rogers*** | Y | Y | Y | N | N | N | N | N |
| 6 ***Hopkins*** | Y | N | Y | N | Y | Y | Y | N |
| 7 Perkins | N | N | N | Y | N | N | N | N |
| **LOUISIANA** | | | | | | | | |
| 1 ***Livingston*** | N | N | Y | N | Y | N | N | N |
| 2 Jefferson | ? | ? | ? | ? | ? | ? | ? | ? |
| 3 Tauzin | ? | ? | ? | ? | ? | ? | ? | ? |
| 4 ***McCrery*** | Y | N | Y | N | Y | Y | Y | Y |
| 5 Huckaby | Y | N | N | N | Y | Y | N | N |
| 6 ***Baker*** | Y | N | Y | N | Y | Y | Y | Y |
| 7 Hayes | ? | ? | ? | ? | ? | ? | ? | ? |
| 8 ***Holloway*** | Y | N | Y | N | Y | Y | N | Y |
| **MAINE** | | | | | | | | |
| 1 Andrews | Y | Y | N | Y | N | Y | Y | Y |
| 2 ***Snowe*** | Y | Y | Y | N | N | Y | N | Y |
| **MARYLAND** | | | | | | | | |
| 1 ***Gilchrest*** | Y | N | Y | N | Y | Y | Y | Y |
| 2 ***Bentley*** | Y | N | Y | N | Y | Y | N | Y |
| 3 Cardin | Y | N | N | Y | N | N | Y | Y |
| 4 McMillen | Y | N | N | N | Y | N | N | N |
| 5 Hoyer | N | Y | N | N | N | N | N | N |
| 6 Byron | Y | N | N | N | Y | Y | N | Y |
| 7 Mfume | N | Y | N | Y | Y | N | Y | Y |
| 8 ***Morella*** | X | N | Y | N | N | Y | Y | Y |
| **MASSACHUSETTS** | | | | | | | | |
| 1 Olver | N | Y | N | Y | N | N | Y | Y |
| 2 Neal | N | N | N | Y | N | N | Y | Y |
| 3 Early | N | Y | N | Y | N | N | N | Y |
| 4 Frank | N | Y | N | Y | N | N | N | Y |
| 5 Atkins | N | Y | N | Y | ? | N | ? | ? |
| 6 Mavroules | N | N | N | N | N | N | N | Y |
| 7 Markey | N | Y | N | Y | N | N | N | Y |
| 8 Kennedy | N | Y | N | Y | N | N | N | Y |
| 9 Moakley | N | Y | N | Y | N | N | N | N |
| 10 Studds | N | Y | N | Y | N | N | N | Y |
| 11 Donnelly | N | Y | N | Y | N | N | N | Y |
| **MICHIGAN** | | | | | | | | |
| 1 Conyers | N | ? | ? | ? | ? | ? | ? | ? |
| 2 ***Pursell*** | N | Y | N | N | N | N | N | N |
| 3 Wolpe | N | Y | N | Y | N | N | Y | Y |
| 4 ***Upton*** | Y | Y | Y | N | N | N | Y | Y |
| 5 ***Henry*** | Y | Y | Y | N | N | N | N | Y |
| 6 Carr | N | N | N | Y | N | N | N | N |
| 7 Kildee | N | Y | N | Y | N | N | N | Y |
| 8 Traxler | N | Y | N | N | N | N | N | N |
| 9 ***Vander Jagt*** | Y | N | Y | N | N | N | Y | Y |
| 10 ***Camp*** | Y | Y | Y | N | N | N | N | Y |
| 11 ***Davis*** | N | N | ? | ? | ? | ? | ? | ? |
| 12 Bonior | N | N | N | N | N | N | N | N |
| 13 Collins | ? | ? | ? | ? | ? | ? | ? | ? |
| 14 Hertel | N | Y | ? | ? | ? | ? | ? | ? |
| 15 Ford | N | Y | N | Y | N | N | N | N |
| 16 Dingell | N | Y | N | Y | N | N | N | Y |
| 17 Levin | Y | Y | N | N | N | N | N | Y |
| 18 ***Broomfield*** | Y | N | Y | N | N | N | N | Y |
| **MINNESOTA** | | | | | | | | |
| 1 Penny | Y | Y | Y | N | Y | Y | N | Y |
| 2 ***Weber*** | N | N | Y | N | Y | N | Y | Y |
| 3 ***Ramstad*** | Y | Y | Y | N | N | Y | N | Y |
| 4 Vento | Y | Y | N | Y | N | N | N | Y |

| | 333 | 334 | 335 | 336 | 337 | 338 | 339 | 340 |
|---|---|---|---|---|---|---|---|---|
| 5 Sabo | N | Y | N | Y | N | N | N | N |
| 6 Sikorski | Y | Y | N | Y | N | N | N | Y |
| 7 Peterson | Y | Y | N | N | Y | N | N | N |
| 8 Oberstar | N | Y | N | Y | N | N | N | Y |
| **MISSISSIPPI** | | | | | | | | |
| 1 Whitten | N | N | N | N | N | N | N | N |
| 2 Espy | Y | Y | N | N | N | N | N | N |
| 3 Montgomery | N | Y | N | N | N | N | N | N |
| 4 Parker | N | Y | N | N | Y | N | N | N |
| 5 Taylor | Y | N | ? | N | Y | N | N | N |
| **MISSOURI** | | | | | | | | |
| 1 Clay | Y | Y | N | Y | N | N | N | Y |
| 2 Horn | Y | Y | Y | Y | Y | Y | Y | Y |
| 3 Gephardt | Y | N | ? | N | N | N | N | N |
| 4 Skelton | Y | Y | N | N | Y | N | N | N |
| 5 Wheat | N | Y | N | Y | N | N | Y | Y |
| 6 ***Coleman*** | Y | N | Y | N | Y | Y | Y | Y |
| 7 ***Hancock*** | Y | N | Y | N | Y | Y | Y | Y |
| 8 ***Emerson*** | Y | N | Y | N | Y | Y | Y | Y |
| 9 Volkmer | Y | N | N | N | Y | N | N | N |
| **MONTANA** | | | | | | | | |
| 1 Williams | Y | Y | Y | N | N | N | Y | Y |
| 2 ***Marlenee*** | Y | Y | Y | N | Y | Y | Y | Y |
| **NEBRASKA** | | | | | | | | |
| 1 ***Bereuter*** | N | Y | N | N | Y | Y | N | Y |
| 2 Hoagland | Y | Y | N | N | N | N | N | Y |
| 3 ***Barrett*** | Y | N | Y | N | Y | Y | Y | Y |
| **NEVADA** | | | | | | | | |
| 1 Bilbray | N | Y | N | N | N | N | Y | Y |
| 2 ***Vucanovich*** | Y | N | N | N | N | N | Y | Y |
| **NEW HAMPSHIRE** | | | | | | | | |
| 1 ***Zeliff*** | Y | N | Y | N | Y | Y | Y | Y |
| 2 Swett | Y | Y | Y | Y | Y | Y | Y | Y |
| **NEW JERSEY** | | | | | | | | |
| 1 Andrews | Y | N | N | N | N | N | Y | Y |
| 2 Hughes | Y | Y | Y | N | Y | N | Y | Y |
| 3 Pallone | Y | Y | N | N | Y | Y | Y | Y |
| 4 ***Smith*** | Y | N | N | N | Y | Y | Y | N |
| 5 ***Roukema*** | Y | Y | Y | N | Y | Y | N | Y |
| 6 Dwyer | N | Y | N | N | N | N | N | N |
| 7 ***Rinaldo*** | Y | Y | Y | Y | Y | N | N | Y |
| 8 Roe | Y | N | N | N | N | N | N | N |
| 9 Torricelli | Y | N | N | N | Y | Y | ? | N |
| 10 Payne | N | Y | N | Y | N | N | N | N |
| 11 ***Gallo*** | N | N | Y | N | N | N | N | N |
| 12 ***Zimmer*** | Y | Y | Y | Y | Y | Y | Y | Y |
| 13 ***Saxton*** | Y | N | Y | N | Y | N | Y | N |
| 14 Guarini | Y | N | N | N | N | N | Y | N |
| **NEW MEXICO** | | | | | | | | |
| 1 ***Schiff*** | Y | N | Y | N | Y | Y | Y | N |
| 2 ***Skeen*** | Y | N | Y | N | Y | N | Y | N |
| 3 Richardson | Y | N | N | N | N | N | Y | Y |
| **NEW YORK** | | | | | | | | |
| 1 Hochbrueckner | N | N | N | N | Y | N | N | Y |
| 2 Downey | N | N | N | N | Y | N | N | N |
| 3 Mrazek | N | N | N | Y | N | N | N | N |
| 4 ***Lent*** | Y | N | Y | N | Y | N | Y | N |
| 5 ***McGrath*** | Y | N | Y | N | N | Y | N | N |
| 6 Flake | N | Y | N | Y | Y | N | N | Y |
| 7 Ackerman | N | Y | N | Y | N | N | Y | Y |
| 8 Scheuer | N | Y | N | Y | Y | N | N | Y |
| 9 Manton | N | N | ? | ? | N | N | Y | Y |
| 10 Schumer | Y | Y | N | N | N | N | N | Y |
| 11 Towns | ? | ? | ? | ? | ? | ? | ? | ? |
| 12 Owens | Y | Y | N | Y | N | N | Y | Y |
| 13 Solarz | ? | ? | ? | ? | ? | ? | ? | ? |
| 14 ***Molinari*** | N | Y | Y | N | N | Y | N | Y |
| 15 ***Green*** | N | Y | N | Y | N | N | N | N |
| 16 Rangel | N | Y | N | Y | N | Y | N | Y |
| 17 Weiss | N | Y | N | Y | N | N | N | Y |
| 18 Serrano | N | Y | ? | ? | ? | ? | ? | ? |
| 19 Engel | N | N | N | N | N | N | N | Y |
| 20 Lowey | Y | Y | N | N | N | N | N | Y |
| 21 ***Fish*** | Y | Y | Y | N | N | Y | N | Y |
| 22 ***Gilman*** | Y | N | Y | N | N | Y | N | Y |
| 23 McNulty | N | N | N | N | N | N | N | N |
| 24 ***Solomon*** | Y | Y | Y | N | Y | Y | Y | Y |
| 25 ***Boehlert*** | Y | N | Y | N | N | Y | Y | Y |
| 26 ***Martin*** | N | N | Y | N | Y | Y | Y | Y |
| 27 ***Walsh*** | Y | N | Y | N | N | N | N | N |
| 28 McHugh | N | Y | N | N | N | N | N | N |
| 29 ***Horton*** | N | N | N | N | N | N | Y | N |
| 30 Slaughter | Y | Y | N | N | N | N | N | Y |
| 31 ***Paxon*** | Y | N | N | N | N | Y | Y | Y |

| | 333 | 334 | 335 | 336 | 337 | 338 | 339 | 340 |
|---|---|---|---|---|---|---|---|---|
| 32 LaFalce | Y | Y | N | N | N | N | N | N |
| 33 Nowak | N | Y | N | N | N | N | Y | N |
| 34 ***Houghton*** | Y | N | Y | N | Y | Y | Y | Y |
| **NORTH CAROLINA** | | | | | | | | |
| 1 Jones | N | N | ? | ? | ? | ? | ? | ? |
| 2 Valentine | Y | — | N | N | Y | N | N | N |
| 3 Lancaster | Y | Y | Y | N | Y | N | Y | Y |
| 4 Price | N | Y | N | N | N | N | N | N |
| 5 Neal | Y | Y | N | N | Y | N | Y | Y |
| 6 ***Coble*** | Y | Y | Y | N | Y | Y | Y | Y |
| 7 Rose | N | N | N | N | N | N | N | N |
| 8 Hefner | N | Y | ? | ? | ? | ? | ? | ? |
| 9 ***McMillan*** | Y | N | Y | N | Y | Y | N | Y |
| 10 ***Ballenger*** | Y | Y | Y | N | Y | Y | N | Y |
| 11 ***Taylor*** | N | N | Y | N | N | Y | Y | Y |
| **NORTH DAKOTA** | | | | | | | | |
| AL Dorgan | Y | Y | Y | N | Y | Y | N | N |
| **OHIO** | | | | | | | | |
| 1 Luken | Y | Y | N | N | Y | Y | N | Y |
| 2 ***Gradison*** | Y | N | Y | Y | Y | Y | N | N |
| 3 Hall | Y | N | N | N | Y | N | Y | N |
| 4 ***Oxley*** | Y | N | Y | N | Y | Y | Y | Y |
| 5 ***Gillmor*** | Y | N | Y | N | N | N | Y | Y |
| 6 ***McEwen*** | Y | N | Y | N | Y | Y | Y | Y |
| 7 ***Hobson*** | Y | N | Y | N | Y | Y | Y | Y |
| 8 ***Boehner*** | N | N | Y | N | Y | Y | Y | Y |
| 9 Kaptur | N | Y | N | N | N | N | N | N |
| 10 ***Miller*** | N | N | Y | N | Y | Y | N | N |
| 11 Eckart | Y | Y | N | Y | N | N | Y | Y |
| 12 ***Kasich*** | Y | Y | Y | N | Y | Y | N | Y |
| 13 Pease | N | Y | Y | N | N | Y | N | Y |
| 14 Sawyer | N | Y | N | N | N | N | N | Y |
| 15 ***Wylie*** | Y | N | Y | N | Y | Y | Y | Y |
| 16 ***Regula*** | N | N | Y | N | N | Y | N | N |
| 17 Traficant | N | N | N | N | N | N | N | N |
| 18 Applegate | N | N | N | N | N | N | N | N |
| 19 Feighan | Y | N | N | N | N | N | Y | Y |
| 20 Oakar | N | N | N | N | N | N | N | N |
| 21 Stokes | N | Y | N | Y | N | N | N | N |
| **OKLAHOMA** | | | | | | | | |
| 1 ***Inhofe*** | Y | N | Y | N | Y | Y | Y | Y |
| 2 Synar | Y | Y | N | Y | N | N | Y | Y |
| 3 Brewster | Y | N | N | N | Y | N | N | N |
| 4 McCurdy | Y | N | N | N | Y | Y | N | N |
| 5 ***Edwards*** | ? | N | Y | N | Y | Y | N | N |
| 6 English | Y | N | N | N | Y | N | N | N |
| **OREGON** | | | | | | | | |
| 1 AuCoin | Y | Y | N | Y | N | N | N | Y |
| 2 ***Smith*** | Y | N | Y | N | Y | Y | Y | Y |
| 3 Wyden | Y | Y | N | Y | Y | N | N | Y |
| 4 DeFazio | Y | Y | N | Y | Y | N | N | Y |
| 5 Kopetski | Y | N | N | Y | N | N | N | N |
| **PENNSYLVANIA** | | | | | | | | |
| 1 Foglietta | N | Y | N | Y | N | N | N | N |
| 2 Blackwell | N | Y | N | Y | N | N | N | N |
| 3 Borski | Y | N | N | N | N | N | N | Y |
| 4 Kolter | ? | N | ? | ? | ? | ? | ? | ? |
| 5 ***Schulze*** | Y | N | Y | N | Y | Y | Y | Y |
| 6 Yatron | N | N | N | N | N | N | Y | Y |
| 7 ***Weldon*** | Y | N | Y | N | Y | N | Y | Y |
| 8 Kostmayer | Y | Y | N | Y | N | N | N | Y |
| 9 ***Shuster*** | Y | Y | Y | N | Y | Y | Y | Y |
| 10 ***McDade*** | N | N | ? | ? | ? | ? | ? | ? |
| 11 Kanjorski | Y | Y | N | N | N | N | N | Y |
| 12 Murtha | N | Y | N | N | N | N | N | N |
| 13 ***Coughlin*** | N | N | ? | ? | ? | ? | ? | ? |
| 14 Coyne | N | Y | N | N | N | ? | N | Y |
| 15 ***Ritter*** | Y | N | N | N | Y | Y | Y | Y |
| 16 ***Walker*** | Y | N | Y | N | Y | Y | Y | N |
| 17 ***Gekas*** | Y | N | Y | N | Y | Y | Y | Y |
| 18 ***Santorum*** | Y | N | Y | N | Y | Y | Y | Y |
| 19 ***Goodling*** | Y | Y | ? | N | Y | Y | N | N |
| 20 Gaydos | N | N | N | N | N | N | N | N |
| 21 ***Ridge*** | Y | N | Y | N | Y | Y | N | N |
| 22 Murphy | Y | Y | N | Y | Y | Y | Y | Y |
| 23 ***Clinger*** | Y | N | N | N | Y | Y | Y | N |
| **RHODE ISLAND** | | | | | | | | |
| 1 ***Machtley*** | Y | Y | Y | N | Y | Y | N | Y |
| 2 Reed | Y | Y | N | N | N | N | N | Y |
| **SOUTH CAROLINA** | | | | | | | | |
| 1 ***Ravenel*** | Y | Y | Y | N | Y | Y | Y | Y |
| 2 ***Spence*** | Y | N | Y | N | Y | Y | Y | Y |
| 3 Derrick | Y | Y | N | N | N | N | N | N |
| 4 Patterson | Y | Y | Y | N | Y | Y | N | Y |
| 5 Spratt | Y | Y | N | N | N | Y | N | Y |
| 6 Tallon | Y | N | N | N | Y | Y | N | N |

| | 333 | 334 | 335 | 336 | 337 | 338 | 339 | 340 |
|---|---|---|---|---|---|---|---|---|
| **SOUTH DAKOTA** | | | | | | | | |
| AL Johnson | Y | Y | Y | N | Y | Y | Y | Y |
| **TENNESSEE** | | | | | | | | |
| 1 ***Quillen*** | Y | N | Y | N | N | N | Y | N |
| 2 ***Duncan*** | Y | Y | Y | N | Y | Y | Y | Y |
| 3 Lloyd | Y | N | N | N | N | N | N | N |
| 4 Cooper | Y | N | Y | N | Y | Y | N | N |
| 5 Clement | N | Y | N | N | N | N | N | N |
| 6 Gordon | Y | Y | N | N | N | N | N | N |
| 7 ***Sundquist*** | Y | N | Y | N | Y | Y | N | N |
| 8 Tanner | Y | N | N | N | Y | N | N | N |
| 9 Ford | N | Y | N | ? | N | N | N | Y |
| **TEXAS** | | | | | | | | |
| 1 Chapman | N | N | N | N | N | N | N | N |
| 2 Wilson | N | N | N | N | N | N | Y | N |
| 3 ***Johnson*** | Y | N | Y | N | Y | Y | Y | Y |
| 4 Hall | Y | N | N | N | N | Y | N | N |
| 5 Bryant | Y | N | N | N | Y | N | Y | N |
| 6 ***Barton*** | Y | N | N | N | Y | ? | Y | N |
| 7 ***Archer*** | Y | N | Y | N | Y | Y | Y | Y |
| 8 ***Fields*** | Y | N | Y | N | Y | Y | Y | Y |
| 9 Brooks | N | N | N | N | N | N | N | N |
| 10 Pickle | N | N | N | N | Y | Y | N | N |
| 11 Edwards | Y | N | N | N | Y | N | N | N |
| 12 Geren | Y | N | N | N | Y | Y | N | N |
| 13 Sarpalius | Y | N | N | N | N | N | N | N |
| 14 Laughlin | Y | N | N | N | Y | Y | N | N |
| 15 de la Garza | N | N | N | N | N | N | N | N |
| 16 Coleman | N | N | N | N | N | N | N | N |
| 17 Stenholm | Y | N | Y | N | Y | Y | N | Y |
| 18 Washington | N | Y | N | Y | N | N | N | Y |
| 19 ***Combest*** | Y | N | Y | N | Y | Y | Y | Y |
| 20 Gonzalez | N | Y | N | Y | N | N | N | N |
| 21 ***Smith*** | Y | N | Y | N | Y | Y | Y | N |
| 22 ***DeLay*** | Y | N | N | Y | Y | Y | Y | Y |
| 23 Bustamante | N | N | N | N | N | N | N | N |
| 24 Frost | Y | N | N | N | N | N | N | N |
| 25 Andrews | Y | N | N | N | Y | Y | Y | N |
| 26 ***Armey*** | Y | N | Y | N | Y | Y | Y | Y |
| 27 Ortiz | N | N | N | N | N | N | N | N |
| **UTAH** | | | | | | | | |
| 1 ***Hansen*** | Y | N | Y | N | Y | Y | Y | Y |
| 2 Owens | Y | Y | N | N | Y | N | Y | Y |
| 3 Orton | Y | Y | Y | Y | Y | Y | Y | Y |
| **VERMONT** | | | | | | | | |
| AL *Sanders* | N | Y | Y | Y | Y | Y | Y | Y |
| **VIRGINIA** | | | | | | | | |
| 1 ***Bateman*** | N | N | Y | N | Y | Y | Y | N |
| 2 Pickett | N | N | N | N | Y | N | N | N |
| 3 ***Bliley*** | Y | N | Y | N | Y | Y | Y | N |
| 4 Sisisky | Y | N | N | N | Y | N | N | N |
| 5 Payne | Y | Y | N | N | Y | N | N | Y |
| 6 Olin | N | Y | N | N | N | N | N | N |
| 7 ***Allen*** | Y | N | Y | N | Y | Y | Y | Y |
| 8 Moran | N | N | N | N | N | N | N | N |
| 9 Boucher | N | N | N | N | N | N | Y | N |
| 10 ***Wolf*** | Y | N | Y | N | Y | Y | Y | Y |
| **WASHINGTON** | | | | | | | | |
| 1 ***Miller*** | Y | N | Y | N | Y | Y | Y | Y |
| 2 Swift | N | N | N | Y | N | N | N | N |
| 3 Unsoeld | Y | Y | N | Y | N | N | N | Y |
| 4 ***Morrison*** | N | N | Y | N | Y | Y | N | Y |
| 5 Foley | | | | | | | | |
| 6 Dicks | N | N | N | N | N | N | N | Y |
| 7 McDermott | N | Y | N | Y | N | N | N | Y |
| 8 ***Chandler*** | Y | N | Y | N | Y | Y | Y | N |
| **WEST VIRGINIA** | | | | | | | | |
| 1 Mollohan | N | N | N | N | N | N | N | N |
| 2 Staggers | Y | Y | N | N | N | N | N | Y |
| 3 Wise | N | N | N | N | N | N | N | N |
| 4 Rahall | N | N | N | N | N | N | Y | Y |
| **WISCONSIN** | | | | | | | | |
| 1 Aspin | Y | N | N | N | Y | N | N | Y |
| 2 ***Klug*** | Y | N | Y | N | Y | Y | Y | Y |
| 3 ***Gunderson*** | Y | N | Y | N | Y | Y | Y | Y |
| 4 Kleczka | Y | Y | N | N | N | N | N | N |
| 5 Moody | Y | Y | N | N | Y | N | Y | Y |
| 6 ***Petri*** | ? | N | Y | N | Y | Y | Y | Y |
| 7 Obey | N | Y | N | Y | N | N | N | Y |
| 8 ***Roth*** | ? | N | N | N | N | N | Y | Y |
| 9 ***Sensenbrenner*** | Y | N | Y | Y | Y | Y | Y | N |
| **WYOMING** | | | | | | | | |
| AL ***Thomas*** | Y | N | Y | N | Y | Y | Y | Y |

Southern states - Ala., Ark., Fla., Ga., Ky., La., Miss., N.C., Okla., S.C., Tenn., Texas, Va.
Omitted votes are quorum calls, which CQ does not include in its vote charts.

**341. HR 5679. Fiscal 1993 VA, Housing and Urban Development, Independent Agencies Appropriations/ Potomac Yard Stadium.** Moran, D-Va., amendment to prohibit federal agencies from planning, financing, constructing or permitting a stadium at Potomac Yard in Alexandria, Va., until the Environmental Protection Agency conducts an environmental impact study. (Potomac Yard was the proposed site for a new stadium for the Washington Redskins.) Adopted 238-166: R 14-147; D 223-19 (ND 160-6, SD 63-13); I 1-0, July 29, 1992.

**342. HR 5679. Fiscal 1993 VA, Housing and Urban Development, Independent Agencies Appropriations/ Aerospace Plane.** Separate vote at the request of Traxler, D-Mich., on the McCurdy, D-Okla., amendment to strike $1,000 from the bill in order to bring to the floor a directive to NASA to spend $33,499,000 on the national aerospace plane instead of the Consortium for International Earth Science Information Network, a network of global environmental data. Rejected 189-219: R 123-40; D 65-179 (ND 32-136, SD 33-43); I 1-0, July 29, 1992.

**343. HR 5679. Fiscal 1993 VA, Housing and Urban Development, Independent Agencies Appropriations/ Recommittal.** Kolbe, R-Ariz., motion to recommit the bill to the House Appropriations Committee with instructions to report it back with an amendment to add $200 million for the Home Ownership for People Everywhere (HOPE) program for low-income individuals. Rejected 198-209: R 159-4; D 39-204 (ND 16-151, SD 23-53); I 0-1, July 29, 1992.

**344. HR 5679. Fiscal 1993 VA, Housing and Urban Development, Independent Agencies Appropriations/ Passage.** Passage of the bill to provide $85,902,665,000 in new budget authority for the departments of Veterans Affairs and Housing and Urban Development and for other independent agencies for fiscal 1993. The administration requested $90,145,976,810. Passed 314-92: R 89-74; D 224-18 (ND 150-16, SD 74-2); I 1-0, July 29, 1992.

**345. Procedural Motion.** Weldon, R-Pa., motion to adjourn. Motion rejected 11-366: R 8-138; D 3-228 (ND 3-154, SD 0-74); I 0-0, July 30, 1992.

**346. HR 5678. Fiscal 1993 Commerce, Justice and State Appropriations/Previous Question.** Frost, D-Texas, motion to order the previous question (thus limiting debate and the possibility of amendment) on adoption of the rule (H Res 530) to govern floor consideration of the bill to provide $22.3 billion in new budget authority for the Departments of Commerce, Justice and State, the judiciary, and related agencies in fiscal 1993. Motion agreed to 240-176: R 0-158; D 239-18 (ND 160-13, SD 79-5); I 1-0, July 30, 1992.

**347. HR 5678. Fiscal 1993 Commerce, Justice and State Appropriations/Rule.** Adoption of the rule (H Res 530) to govern floor consideration of the bill to provide $22.3 billion in new budget authority for the departments of Commerce, Justice and State, the judiciary and related agencies in fiscal 1993. Adopted 250-162: R 2-154; D 247-8 (ND 166-5, SD 81-3); I 1-0, July 30, 1992.

**348. Procedural Motion.** Dornan, R-Calif., motion to adjourn. Motion rejected 13-380: R 10-144; D 3-236 (ND 2-160, SD 1-76); I 0-0, July 30, 1992.

## KEY

| | |
|---|---|
| Y | Voted for (yea). |
| # | Paired for. |
| + | Announced for. |
| N | Voted against (nay). |
| X | Paired against. |
| − | Announced against. |
| P | Voted "present." |
| C | Voted "present" to avoid possible conflict of interest. |
| ? | Did not vote or otherwise make a position known. |

Democrats **Republicans** *Independent*

| | 341 | 342 | 343 | 344 | 345 | 346 | 347 | 348 |
|---|---|---|---|---|---|---|---|---|
| **ALABAMA** | | | | | | | | |
| 1 *Callahan* | N | Y | Y | N | N | N | N | N |
| 2 *Dickinson* | N | Y | Y | N | N | N | N | ? |
| 3 Browder | Y | Y | N | Y | N | Y | Y | N |
| 4 Bevill | Y | N | N | Y | N | Y | N | N |
| 5 Cramer | Y | N | N | Y | N | Y | Y | N |
| 6 Erdreich | N | Y | N | Y | N | N | Y | N |
| 7 Harris | N | N | N | Y | N | N | Y | N |
| **ALASKA** | | | | | | | | |
| AL *Young* | N | Y | Y | Y | ? | N | N | N |
| **ARIZONA** | | | | | | | | |
| 1 *Rhodes* | N | Y | Y | N | N | N | N | N |
| 2 Pastor | Y | N | N | Y | N | Y | Y | Y |
| 3 *Stump* | N | Y | Y | N | N | N | N | N |
| 4 *Kyl* | N | Y | Y | N | N | N | N | N |
| 5 *Kolbe* | N | Y | Y | N | N | N | N | N |
| **ARKANSAS** | | | | | | | | |
| 1 Alexander | ? | ? | ? | ? | N | Y | Y | N |
| 2 Thornton | Y | N | N | Y | N | Y | Y | N |
| 3 *Hammerschmidt* | N | Y | Y | Y | N | N | N | N |
| 4 Anthony | ? | ? | ? | ? | ? | Y | Y | N |
| **CALIFORNIA** | | | | | | | | |
| 1 *Riggs* | N | N | Y | Y | ? | N | N | N |
| 2 *Herger* | N | Y | Y | N | ? | N | N | N |
| 3 Matsui | Y | N | N | Y | N | Y | Y | N |
| 4 Fazio | Y | N | N | Y | N | Y | Y | N |
| 5 Pelosi | Y | N | N | Y | N | Y | Y | ? |
| 6 Boxer | ? | ? | ? | ? | ? | ? | ? | ? |
| 7 Miller | Y | N | N | Y | N | Y | Y | N |
| 8 Dellums | Y | N | N | Y | N | Y | Y | N |
| 9 Stark | ? | N | N | N | N | Y | Y | N |
| 10 Edwards | Y | N | N | Y | N | Y | Y | N |
| 11 Lantos | Y | Y | N | Y | N | Y | Y | N |
| 12 *Campbell* | N | Y | Y | N | N | N | N | N |
| 13 Mineta | Y | N | N | Y | N | Y | Y | N |
| 14 *Doolittle* | N | Y | Y | N | N | N | N | N |
| 15 Condit | Y | Y | N | N | ? | N | Y | N |
| 16 Panetta | Y | N | N | N | N | Y | Y | N |
| 17 Dooley | N | Y | N | Y | N | Y | Y | N |
| 18 Lehman | Y | N | Y | Y | ? | Y | Y | N |
| 19 *Lagomarsino* | N | Y | Y | N | N | N | N | N |
| 20 *Thomas* | N | Y | Y | N | N | N | N | N |
| 21 *Gallegly* | N | N | Y | N | N | N | N | N |
| 22 *Moorhead* | N | Y | Y | N | N | N | N | N |
| 23 Beilenson | Y | N | N | N | N | Y | Y | N |
| 24 Waxman | Y | N | N | Y | N | Y | Y | ? |
| 25 Roybal | Y | N | N | Y | N | Y | Y | N |
| 26 Berman | Y | N | N | Y | N | Y | ? | N |
| 27 Levine | Y | N | N | Y | N | Y | Y | N |
| 28 Dixon | Y | N | Y | ? | ? | N | Y | N |
| 29 Waters | Y | N | N | Y | N | Y | Y | N |
| 30 Martinez | Y | N | N | Y | N | Y | Y | N |
| 31 Dymally | Y | N | N | Y | ? | Y | Y | ? |
| 32 Anderson | Y | N | N | Y | N | N | Y | N |
| 33 *Dreier* | N | Y | Y | N | Y | N | N | Y |
| 34 Torres | Y | N | N | Y | ? | Y | Y | N |
| 35 *Lewis* | N | N | Y | N | N | N | N | N |
| 36 Brown | Y | Y | N | Y | N | Y | Y | N |
| 37 *McCandless* | N | Y | Y | N | N | N | N | ? |
| 38 *Dornan* | N | Y | Y | N | N | N | N | N |
| 39 *Dannemeyer* | N | Y | Y | N | N | N | N | N |
| 40 *Cox* | N | Y | Y | N | ? | N | N | Y |
| 41 *Lowery* | N | N | Y | Y | ? | ? | ? | ? |

| | 341 | 342 | 343 | 344 | 345 | 346 | 347 | 348 |
|---|---|---|---|---|---|---|---|---|
| 42 *Rohrabacher* | N | Y | Y | N | Y | N | N | N |
| 43 *Packard* | N | Y | Y | N | N | N | N | N |
| 44 *Cunningham* | N | Y | Y | N | N | N | ? | N |
| 45 *Hunter* | N | Y | Y | N | N | ? | N | ? |
| **COLORADO** | | | | | | | | |
| 1 Schroeder | Y | N | N | N | N | Y | Y | N |
| 2 Skaggs | N | N | N | Y | N | Y | Y | N |
| 3 Campbell | ? | ? | ? | ? | ? | Y | Y | N |
| 4 *Allard* | N | Y | Y | N | N | N | N | Y |
| 5 *Hefley* | N | Y | Y | N | Y | ? | ? | N |
| 6 *Schaefer* | N | Y | Y | N | N | N | N | N |
| **CONNECTICUT** | | | | | | | | |
| 1 Kennelly | Y | Y | Y | Y | N | Y | Y | N |
| 2 Gejdenson | Y | Y | N | Y | N | Y | Y | N |
| 3 DeLauro | Y | N | N | Y | N | Y | Y | N |
| 4 *Shays* | Y | N | Y | N | N | Y | Y | N |
| 5 *Franks* | N | Y | Y | N | N | N | N | N |
| 6 *Johnson* | N | Y | Y | N | N | N | N | N |
| **DELAWARE** | | | | | | | | |
| AL Carper | Y | N | N | ? | N | N | Y | N |
| **FLORIDA** | | | | | | | | |
| 1 Hutto | Y | Y | Y | Y | N | Y | N | N |
| 2 Peterson | N | Y | N | Y | N | Y | Y | N |
| 3 Bennett | Y | Y | Y | N | Y | N | Y | N |
| 4 *James* | N | Y | Y | N | Y | N | N | N |
| 5 *McCollum* | N | Y | Y | N | N | N | N | N |
| 6 *Stearns* | N | Y | Y | N | N | N | N | N |
| 7 Gibbons | Y | N | N | Y | N | Y | Y | N |
| 8 *Young* | N | Y | Y | N | N | N | N | N |
| 9 *Bilirakis* | N | Y | Y | N | N | N | N | N |
| 10 *Ireland* | ? | Y | Y | Y | ? | ? | ? | ? |
| 11 Bacchus | Y | Y | N | Y | N | Y | Y | N |
| 12 *Lewis* | N | Y | Y | N | N | N | N | N |
| 13 *Goss* | N | Y | Y | N | N | N | N | N |
| 14 Johnston | Y | N | N | Y | N | Y | Y | N |
| 15 *Shaw* | N | Y | Y | N | N | N | N | N |
| 16 Smith | Y | N | N | Y | N | Y | Y | N |
| 17 Lehman | ? | ? | ? | ? | N | Y | Y | N |
| 18 *Ros—Lehtinen* | N | Y | Y | N | N | N | N | N |
| 19 Fascell | Y | N | N | Y | N | Y | Y | N |
| **GEORGIA** | | | | | | | | |
| 1 Thomas | Y | N | N | Y | N | Y | Y | N |
| 2 Hatcher | ? | ? | ? | ? | ? | ? | ? | ? |
| 3 Ray | Y | Y | Y | Y | N | Y | Y | N |
| 4 Jones | Y | Y | Y | Y | N | Y | Y | N |
| 5 Lewis | Y | N | N | Y | N | Y | Y | N |
| 6 *Gingrich* | N | Y | Y | N | ? | N | N | N |
| 7 Darden | Y | Y | N | Y | N | Y | Y | N |
| 8 Rowland | Y | Y | Y | Y | N | Y | Y | N |
| 9 Jenkins | Y | Y | N | Y | ? | Y | Y | N |
| 10 Barnard | Y | N | N | N | N | Y | Y | N |
| **HAWAII** | | | | | | | | |
| 1 Abercrombie | Y | N | N | Y | N | Y | Y | N |
| 2 Mink | Y | N | N | Y | N | Y | Y | N |
| **IDAHO** | | | | | | | | |
| 1 LaRocco | Y | Y | N | Y | N | Y | Y | N |
| 2 Stallings | ? | ? | ? | ? | ? | ? | ? | ? |
| **ILLINOIS** | | | | | | | | |
| 1 Hayes | Y | N | N | Y | N | Y | Y | N |
| 2 Savage | ? | ? | ? | ? | ? | ? | ? | ? |
| 3 Russo | Y | N | N | Y | N | Y | Y | N |
| 4 Sangmeister | Y | N | N | Y | N | Y | Y | N |
| 5 Lipinski | Y | N | Y | Y | N | Y | Y | N |
| 6 *Hyde* | ? | ? | ? | ? | ? | ? | ? | ? |
| 7 Collins | Y | N | N | Y | N | Y | Y | N |
| 8 Rostenkowski | Y | N | Y | Y | N | Y | Y | N |
| 9 Yates | Y | N | N | Y | N | Y | Y | N |
| 10 *Porter* | N | N | Y | Y | ? | N | N | N |
| 11 Annunzio | ? | ? | ? | ? | N | Y | Y | N |
| 12 *Crane* | N | Y | Y | N | Y | N | N | Y |
| 13 *Fawell* | N | Y | Y | N | N | N | N | N |
| 14 *Hastert* | N | Y | Y | N | N | N | N | N |
| 15 *Ewing* | N | Y | Y | N | N | N | N | N |
| 16 Cox | Y | N | N | Y | N | Y | Y | N |
| 17 Evans | Y | N | N | Y | N | Y | Y | N |
| 18 *Michel* | N | Y | Y | N | N | N | N | N |
| 19 Bruce | Y | N | N | Y | N | Y | Y | N |
| 20 Durbin | Y | N | N | Y | N | Y | Y | N |
| 21 Costello | Y | N | N | Y | N | Y | Y | N |
| 22 Poshard | Y | N | N | Y | N | N | Y | N |
| **INDIANA** | | | | | | | | |
| 1 Visclosky | Y | N | N | Y | N | N | Y | N |
| 2 Sharp | Y | N | Y | N | Y | N | Y | N |
| 3 Roemer | Y | N | Y | N | Y | N | Y | N |

ND Northern Democrats    SD Southern Democrats

| | 341 | 342 | 343 | 344 | 345 | 346 | 347 | 348 |
|---|---|---|---|---|---|---|---|---|
| 4 Long | Y | N | N | Y | N | Y | Y | N |
| 5 Jontz | Y | N | N | Y | N | Y | Y | N |
| 6 ***Burton*** | N | Y | Y | N | N | N | N | N |
| 7 ***Myers*** | N | N | N | N | N | N | N | N |
| 8 McCloskey | Y | N | N | Y | N | Y | Y | N |
| 9 Hamilton | Y | N | N | Y | N | Y | Y | N |
| 10 Jacobs | Y | N | N | N | N | N | Y | N |
| **IOWA** | | | | | | | | |
| 1 ***Leach*** | Y | N | Y | N | N | N | N | N |
| 2 ***Nussle*** | N | Y | Y | N | N | N | N | N |
| 3 Nagle | Y | N | N | Y | N | Y | Y | N |
| 4 Smith | Y | N | N | Y | N | Y | Y | N |
| 5 ***Lightfoot*** | N | N | Y | Y | N | N | N | N |
| 6 ***Grandy*** | N | Y | Y | N | N | N | N | N |
| **KANSAS** | | | | | | | | |
| 1 ***Roberts*** | N | Y | Y | N | ? | N | N | N |
| 2 Slattery | Y | Y | N | Y | N | Y | Y | N |
| 3 ***Meyers*** | N | Y | Y | Y | N | N | ? | ? |
| 4 Glickman | Y | Y | N | Y | N | Y | Y | ? |
| 5 ***Nichols*** | N | Y | Y | N | N | N | N | N |
| **KENTUCKY** | | | | | | | | |
| 1 Hubbard | Y | Y | Y | Y | N | Y | Y | N |
| 2 Natcher | Y | N | N | Y | N | Y | Y | N |
| 3 Mazzoli | Y | N | N | Y | N | Y | Y | N |
| 4 ***Bunning*** | N | Y | Y | Y | N | N | N | N |
| 5 ***Rogers*** | N | N | Y | Y | N | N | N | N |
| 6 ***Hopkins*** | N | Y | Y | Y | N | N | N | N |
| 7 Perkins | N | N | N | Y | N | Y | Y | ? |
| **LOUISIANA** | | | | | | | | |
| 1 ***Livingston*** | N | N | Y | Y | N | N | N | N |
| 2 Jefferson | ? | ? | ? | ? | N | Y | Y | N |
| 3 Tauzin | ? | ? | ? | ? | ? | Y | Y | N |
| 4 ***McCrery*** | N | Y | Y | Y | ? | N | N | N |
| 5 Huckaby | N | Y | Y | Y | N | N | Y | N |
| 6 ***Baker*** | N | Y | Y | N | N | N | N | N |
| 7 Hayes | ? | ? | ? | ? | ? | Y | Y | N |
| 8 ***Holloway*** | N | Y | Y | Y | N | N | N | N |
| **MAINE** | | | | | | | | |
| 1 Andrews | Y | N | N | Y | N | Y | Y | ? |
| 2 ***Snowe*** | N | N | Y | Y | N | N | N | N |
| **MARYLAND** | | | | | | | | |
| 1 ***Gilchrest*** | N | Y | Y | Y | N | N | N | N |
| 2 ***Bentley*** | N | Y | Y | Y | N | N | N | Y |
| 3 Cardin | Y | N | N | Y | N | Y | Y | N |
| 4 McMillen | Y | Y | Y | Y | N | N | Y | N |
| 5 Hoyer | Y | N | N | Y | N | Y | Y | ? |
| 6 Byron | N | Y | N | Y | N | Y | Y | N |
| 7 Mfume | Y | Y | N | + | N | Y | Y | N |
| 8 ***Morella*** | N | N | Y | Y | N | N | N | N |
| **MASSACHUSETTS** | | | | | | | | |
| 1 Olver | Y | N | N | Y | N | Y | Y | N |
| 2 Neal | Y | N | N | Y | N | Y | Y | N |
| 3 Early | Y | N | N | Y | N | Y | Y | N |
| 4 Frank | Y | N | N | Y | N | Y | Y | N |
| 5 Atkins | ? | ? | N | Y | N | Y | Y | N |
| 6 Mavroules | Y | N | N | Y | N | Y | ? | ? |
| 7 Markey | Y | N | N | Y | N | Y | Y | N |
| 8 Kennedy | Y | N | N | Y | N | Y | Y | N |
| 9 Moakley | Y | N | N | Y | N | Y | Y | N |
| 10 Studds | Y | N | – | Y | N | Y | Y | N |
| 11 Donnelly | Y | N | N | Y | N | Y | Y | N |
| **MICHIGAN** | | | | | | | | |
| 1 Conyers | ? | ? | ? | ? | ? | ? | ? | ? |
| 2 ***Pursell*** | N | N | Y | Y | N | N | ? | N |
| 3 Wolpe | Y | N | N | Y | N | Y | Y | N |
| 4 ***Upton*** | N | N | Y | Y | N | N | N | N |
| 5 ***Henry*** | N | N | Y | N | N | N | N | N |
| 6 Carr | Y | N | N | Y | N | Y | Y | N |
| 7 Kildee | Y | N | N | Y | N | Y | Y | N |
| 8 Traxler | Y | N | N | Y | ? | ? | ? | ? |
| 9 ***Vander Jagt*** | N | N | Y | Y | N | N | N | N |
| 10 ***Camp*** | N | N | Y | Y | N | N | N | N |
| 11 ***Davis*** | ? | ? | ? | ? | N | N | N | N |
| 12 Bonior | Y | N | N | Y | N | Y | Y | N |
| 13 Collins | ? | ? | ? | ? | ? | ? | ? | ? |
| 14 Hertel | ? | ? | ? | ? | N | Y | Y | N |
| 15 Ford | Y | N | N | Y | N | Y | Y | N |
| 16 Dingell | Y | N | N | Y | N | Y | Y | N |
| 17 Levin | Y | N | N | Y | N | Y | Y | N |
| 18 ***Broomfield*** | N | N | Y | N | N | N | N | ? |
| **MINNESOTA** | | | | | | | | |
| 1 Penny | N | Y | N | N | N | N | Y | N |
| 2 ***Weber*** | Y | Y | Y | N | N | N | N | ? |
| 3 ***Ramstad*** | N | N | Y | N | N | N | N | N |
| 4 Vento | Y | N | N | Y | N | Y | Y | N |

| | 341 | 342 | 343 | 344 | 345 | 346 | 347 | 348 |
|---|---|---|---|---|---|---|---|---|
| 5 Sabo | Y | N | N | Y | N | Y | Y | Y |
| 6 Sikorski | Y | N | N | Y | N | Y | Y | N |
| 7 Peterson | Y | N | N | Y | N | Y | Y | N |
| 8 Oberstar | Y | N | N | Y | N | Y | Y | N |
| **MISSISSIPPI** | | | | | | | | |
| 1 Whitten | Y | N | N | Y | N | Y | Y | N |
| 2 Espy | Y | N | Y | Y | N | Y | Y | N |
| 3 Montgomery | Y | N | N | Y | N | Y | Y | N |
| 4 Parker | Y | N | N | Y | ? | Y | Y | N |
| 5 Taylor | Y | N | Y | Y | N | Y | Y | N |
| **MISSOURI** | | | | | | | | |
| 1 Clay | Y | N | N | Y | N | Y | Y | N |
| 2 Horn | Y | Y | N | Y | N | Y | Y | N |
| 3 Gephardt | Y | N | N | Y | N | Y | Y | N |
| 4 Skelton | Y | Y | N | Y | N | Y | Y | N |
| 5 Wheat | Y | N | N | Y | ? | Y | Y | N |
| 6 ***Coleman*** | N | N | Y | Y | N | N | N | N |
| 7 ***Hancock*** | N | Y | Y | N | Y | N | N | Y |
| 8 ***Emerson*** | N | Y | Y | Y | N | N | N | N |
| 9 Volkmer | Y | Y | Y | Y | N | Y | N | N |
| **MONTANA** | | | | | | | | |
| 1 Williams | Y | N | N | Y | ? | Y | Y | N |
| 2 ***Marlenee*** | N | Y | N | Y | ? | N | N | Y |
| **NEBRASKA** | | | | | | | | |
| 1 ***Bereuter*** | Y | Y | Y | Y | N | N | N | N |
| 2 Hoagland | Y | N | N | Y | N | Y | Y | N |
| 3 ***Barrett*** | N | Y | Y | Y | N | N | N | N |
| **NEVADA** | | | | | | | | |
| 1 Bilbray | Y | N | N | Y | N | N | Y | N |
| 2 ***Vucanovich*** | N | N | Y | Y | N | N | N | N |
| **NEW HAMPSHIRE** | | | | | | | | |
| 1 ***Zeliff*** | N | Y | Y | N | N | N | N | N |
| 2 Swett | Y | Y | N | Y | N | Y | Y | N |
| **NEW JERSEY** | | | | | | | | |
| 1 Andrews | Y | N | Y | Y | N | Y | Y | N |
| 2 Hughes | Y | Y | N | N | N | Y | Y | N |
| 3 Pallone | Y | Y | Y | N | N | N | Y | N |
| 4 ***Smith*** | N | Y | Y | Y | N | N | N | N |
| 5 ***Roukema*** | Y | Y | Y | N | N | N | N | N |
| 6 Dwyer | Y | N | N | Y | Y | Y | Y | N |
| 7 ***Rinaldo*** | N | Y | Y | Y | N | N | N | N |
| 8 Roe | Y | N | ? | ? | N | Y | Y | N |
| 9 Torricelli | Y | Y | N | Y | N | Y | Y | N |
| 10 Payne | Y | N | N | Y | N | Y | Y | N |
| 11 ***Gallo*** | N | N | Y | Y | N | N | N | N |
| 12 ***Zimmer*** | N | Y | Y | Y | N | N | N | N |
| 13 ***Saxton*** | N | N | Y | Y | N | N | N | N |
| 14 Guarini | Y | N | N | Y | N | Y | Y | N |
| **NEW MEXICO** | | | | | | | | |
| 1 ***Schiff*** | N | Y | Y | Y | N | N | N | ? |
| 2 ***Skeen*** | N | N | Y | Y | N | N | N | N |
| 3 Richardson | Y | N | Y | Y | N | Y | Y | N |
| **NEW YORK** | | | | | | | | |
| 1 Hochbrueckner | Y | Y | N | Y | N | Y | Y | N |
| 2 Downey | Y | N | N | Y | N | Y | Y | N |
| 3 Mrazek | Y | N | Y | Y | ? | ? | ? | ? |
| 4 ***Lent*** | N | Y | Y | Y | N | N | N | N |
| 5 ***McGrath*** | N | N | Y | Y | N | N | N | N |
| 6 Flake | Y | N | N | Y | N | Y | Y | N |
| 7 Ackerman | Y | N | N | Y | N | Y | Y | N |
| 8 Scheuer | Y | N | N | Y | N | Y | Y | N |
| 9 Manton | Y | N | N | Y | N | Y | Y | N |
| 10 Schumer | Y | N | N | Y | N | Y | Y | N |
| 11 Towns | ? | ? | ? | ? | ? | ? | ? | ? |
| 12 Owens | Y | N | N | Y | N | Y | Y | N |
| 13 Solarz | ? | ? | ? | ? | ? | ? | ? | ? |
| 14 ***Molinari*** | Y | N | Y | Y | N | N | N | N |
| 15 ***Green*** | Y | N | N | Y | N | N | Y | N |
| 16 Rangel | Y | N | N | Y | N | Y | Y | ? |
| 17 Weiss | Y | N | N | Y | ? | Y | Y | N |
| 18 Serrano | ? | ? | ? | ? | N | Y | Y | N |
| 19 Engel | Y | N | N | Y | N | Y | Y | N |
| 20 Lowey | Y | N | N | Y | N | Y | Y | N |
| 21 ***Fish*** | N | N | Y | Y | N | N | N | N |
| 22 ***Gilman*** | N | N | Y | Y | N | N | N | N |
| 23 McNulty | Y | N | N | Y | N | Y | Y | N |
| 24 ***Solomon*** | N | Y | Y | Y | N | N | N | N |
| 25 ***Boehlert*** | Y | N | Y | Y | N | N | N | N |
| 26 ***Martin*** | N | Y | Y | Y | ? | ? | ? | ? |
| 27 ***Walsh*** | N | N | Y | Y | N | N | N | N |
| 28 McHugh | Y | N | N | Y | N | Y | Y | N |
| 29 ***Horton*** | Y | N | Y | Y | N | N | N | N |
| 30 Slaughter | Y | N | N | Y | N | Y | Y | N |
| 31 ***Paxon*** | N | Y | Y | Y | N | N | N | N |

| | 341 | 342 | 343 | 344 | 345 | 346 | 347 | 348 |
|---|---|---|---|---|---|---|---|---|
| 32 LaFalce | Y | N | N | Y | N | Y | Y | N |
| 33 Nowak | Y | N | N | Y | N | Y | Y | N |
| 34 ***Houghton*** | N | N | Y | Y | N | N | N | N |
| **NORTH CAROLINA** | | | | | | | | |
| 1 Jones | ? | ? | ? | ? | N | Y | Y | ? |
| 2 Valentine | Y | Y | N | Y | N | Y | Y | N |
| 3 Lancaster | Y | Y | N | Y | N | Y | Y | ? |
| 4 Price | Y | N | N | Y | N | Y | Y | N |
| 5 Neal | Y | Y | N | Y | ? | Y | Y | N |
| 6 ***Coble*** | N | Y | Y | Y | N | N | N | N |
| 7 Rose | Y | N | N | Y | ? | Y | Y | N |
| 8 Hefner | ? | ? | ? | ? | N | Y | Y | N |
| 9 ***McMillan*** | N | Y | Y | Y | N | N | N | N |
| 10 ***Ballenger*** | N | Y | Y | Y | N | N | N | N |
| 11 ***Taylor*** | N | N | Y | Y | N | N | N | Y |
| **NORTH DAKOTA** | | | | | | | | |
| AL Dorgan | ? | Y | N | Y | N | N | Y | N |
| **OHIO** | | | | | | | | |
| 1 Luken | Y | Y | N | Y | N | Y | Y | N |
| 2 ***Gradison*** | N | Y | Y | N | N | N | N | N |
| 3 Hall | Y | Y | Y | Y | ? | Y | Y | ? |
| 4 ***Oxley*** | N | Y | Y | N | N | N | N | N |
| 5 ***Gillmor*** | N | Y | Y | Y | N | N | N | N |
| 6 ***McEwen*** | N | Y | Y | N | N | N | N | Y |
| 7 ***Hobson*** | N | Y | Y | Y | N | N | N | N |
| 8 ***Boehner*** | N | Y | Y | N | Y | N | N | N |
| 9 Kaptur | Y | N | N | Y | N | Y | Y | N |
| 10 ***Miller*** | N | Y | Y | N | N | N | N | N |
| 11 Eckart | Y | N | Y | Y | N | Y | Y | N |
| 12 ***Kasich*** | N | Y | Y | N | N | N | N | N |
| 13 Pease | N | N | N | N | ? | Y | Y | N |
| 14 Sawyer | Y | N | N | Y | N | Y | Y | N |
| 15 ***Wylie*** | N | Y | Y | Y | N | N | N | N |
| 16 ***Regula*** | N | N | Y | Y | N | N | N | N |
| 17 Traficant | Y | N | N | Y | N | Y | Y | N |
| 18 Applegate | Y | N | N | N | N | Y | Y | N |
| 19 Feighan | Y | N | N | Y | N | Y | Y | N |
| 20 Oakar | Y | N | N | Y | N | Y | Y | N |
| 21 Stokes | Y | N | N | Y | N | Y | Y | N |
| **OKLAHOMA** | | | | | | | | |
| 1 ***Inhofe*** | N | Y | Y | N | ? | N | N | N |
| 2 Synar | N | N | N | Y | N | Y | Y | N |
| 3 Brewster | Y | Y | Y | Y | N | Y | Y | N |
| 4 McCurdy | Y | Y | Y | Y | N | Y | Y | N |
| 5 ***Edwards*** | N | Y | Y | N | ? | N | N | N |
| 6 English | Y | Y | Y | Y | N | Y | N | N |
| **OREGON** | | | | | | | | |
| 1 AuCoin | Y | N | N | Y | N | Y | Y | N |
| 2 ***Smith*** | N | Y | Y | N | N | N | N | N |
| 3 Wyden | Y | Y | N | Y | N | Y | Y | N |
| 4 DeFazio | Y | Y | N | Y | Y | Y | Y | N |
| 5 Kopetski | Y | N | N | Y | N | Y | Y | N |
| **PENNSYLVANIA** | | | | | | | | |
| 1 Foglietta | Y | N | N | Y | N | Y | Y | N |
| 2 Blackwell | Y | N | N | Y | N | Y | Y | N |
| 3 Borski | Y | N | N | Y | N | Y | Y | N |
| 4 Kolter | ? | ? | ? | ? | ? | Y | Y | ? |
| 5 ***Schulze*** | N | Y | Y | N | N | N | N | N |
| 6 Yatron | Y | N | N | Y | N | Y | Y | N |
| 7 ***Weldon*** | N | Y | Y | Y | N | N | N | N |
| 8 Kostmayer | Y | N | N | Y | N | Y | Y | N |
| 9 ***Shuster*** | Y | Y | Y | N | N | N | N | N |
| 10 ***McDade*** | N | N | Y | Y | N | N | Y | N |
| 11 Kanjorski | Y | N | N | Y | Y | Y | Y | N |
| 12 Murtha | Y | N | N | Y | N | Y | Y | N |
| 13 ***Coughlin*** | ? | ? | ? | ? | ? | ? | ? | N |
| 14 Coyne | Y | N | N | Y | N | Y | Y | N |
| 15 ***Ritter*** | N | Y | Y | Y | N | N | N | N |
| 16 ***Walker*** | N | Y | Y | N | N | N | N | N |
| 17 ***Gekas*** | N | Y | Y | N | ? | N | N | N |
| 18 ***Santorum*** | N | Y | Y | N | N | N | N | N |
| 19 ***Goodling*** | N | Y | N | N | N | N | N | N |
| 20 Gaydos | ? | ? | ? | ? | N | Y | Y | N |
| 21 ***Ridge*** | N | Y | Y | Y | N | N | N | N |
| 22 Murphy | Y | Y | N | N | N | N | Y | N |
| 23 ***Clinger*** | N | Y | Y | Y | N | N | N | N |
| **RHODE ISLAND** | | | | | | | | |
| 1 ***Machtley*** | ? | Y | Y | Y | N | N | N | N |
| 2 Reed | Y | N | N | Y | ? | Y | Y | N |
| **SOUTH CAROLINA** | | | | | | | | |
| 1 ***Ravenel*** | Y | Y | Y | Y | N | N | N | N |
| 2 ***Spence*** | Y | Y | Y | Y | N | N | N | N |
| 3 Derrick | Y | N | N | Y | N | Y | Y | N |
| 4 Patterson | Y | Y | N | Y | N | Y | Y | N |
| 5 Spratt | Y | Y | N | Y | N | Y | Y | N |
| 6 Tallon | Y | N | N | Y | N | Y | Y | N |

| | 341 | 342 | 343 | 344 | 345 | 346 | 347 | 348 |
|---|---|---|---|---|---|---|---|---|
| **SOUTH DAKOTA** | | | | | | | | |
| AL Johnson | Y | N | Y | Y | N | N | Y | N |
| **TENNESSEE** | | | | | | | | |
| 1 ***Quillen*** | N | N | Y | Y | N | N | N | N |
| 2 ***Duncan*** | N | Y | Y | N | N | N | N | N |
| 3 Lloyd | N | N | N | Y | N | Y | Y | N |
| 4 Cooper | Y | Y | N | Y | N | Y | Y | N |
| 5 Clement | Y | N | N | Y | N | Y | Y | N |
| 6 Gordon | Y | N | N | Y | N | Y | Y | N |
| 7 ***Sundquist*** | N | Y | Y | N | N | N | N | N |
| 8 Tanner | Y | Y | Y | Y | N | N | Y | N |
| 9 Ford | Y | N | Y | Y | ? | Y | Y | Y |
| **TEXAS** | | | | | | | | |
| 1 Chapman | Y | N | N | Y | ? | Y | Y | N |
| 2 Wilson | Y | N | Y | Y | N | Y | Y | N |
| 3 ***Johnson*** | N | Y | Y | N | N | N | N | N |
| 4 Hall | Y | N | Y | Y | N | N | Y | N |
| 5 Bryant | Y | Y | N | Y | N | Y | Y | N |
| 6 ***Barton*** | N | Y | Y | N | ? | ? | ? | ? |
| 7 ***Archer*** | N | Y | Y | N | N | N | N | N |
| 8 ***Fields*** | N | Y | Y | N | N | N | N | N |
| 9 Brooks | Y | N | N | Y | N | Y | Y | N |
| 10 Pickle | N | Y | Y | Y | N | Y | Y | N |
| 11 Edwards | Y | N | N | Y | N | Y | Y | N |
| 12 Geren | Y | Y | N | Y | N | Y | Y | N |
| 13 Sarpalius | Y | N | N | Y | N | Y | Y | N |
| 14 Laughlin | N | N | N | Y | N | Y | Y | N |
| 15 de la Garza | Y | N | N | Y | N | Y | Y | N |
| 16 Coleman | Y | N | N | Y | N | Y | Y | N |
| 17 Stenholm | N | Y | Y | Y | N | Y | Y | N |
| 18 Washington | Y | N | N | Y | ? | Y | Y | ? |
| 19 ***Combest*** | N | Y | Y | N | N | N | N | N |
| 20 Gonzalez | Y | N | N | Y | N | Y | Y | N |
| 21 ***Smith*** | N | Y | Y | Y | N | N | N | N |
| 22 ***DeLay*** | N | Y | Y | N | ? | N | N | N |
| 23 Bustamante | Y | N | N | Y | N | Y | Y | N |
| 24 Frost | Y | N | N | Y | N | Y | Y | N |
| 25 Andrews | Y | Y | N | Y | N | Y | Y | ? |
| 26 ***Armey*** | N | Y | Y | N | Y | N | N | N |
| 27 Ortiz | Y | N | N | Y | N | Y | Y | N |
| **UTAH** | | | | | | | | |
| 1 ***Hansen*** | N | Y | Y | N | N | N | N | N |
| 2 Owens | Y | Y | N | Y | N | Y | Y | N |
| 3 Orton | N | Y | N | N | N | Y | N | N |
| **VERMONT** | | | | | | | | |
| AL *Sanders* | Y | Y | N | Y | ? | Y | Y | ? |
| **VIRGINIA** | | | | | | | | |
| 1 ***Bateman*** | N | Y | Y | Y | N | N | N | N |
| 2 Pickett | Y | Y | N | Y | N | Y | Y | N |
| 3 ***Bliley*** | N | Y | Y | Y | N | N | N | N |
| 4 Sisisky | N | Y | Y | Y | N | Y | Y | N |
| 5 Payne | N | Y | Y | Y | N | Y | Y | N |
| 6 Olin | Y | N | N | Y | N | Y | Y | ? |
| 7 ***Allen*** | Y | Y | Y | Y | N | N | N | N |
| 8 Moran | Y | N | Y | Y | N | Y | Y | N |
| 9 Boucher | N | N | Y | Y | N | Y | Y | N |
| 10 ***Wolf*** | Y | Y | Y | N | N | N | N | N |
| **WASHINGTON** | | | | | | | | |
| 1 ***Miller*** | N | Y | Y | Y | ? | N | N | N |
| 2 Swift | Y | N | N | Y | N | Y | Y | N |
| 3 Unsoeld | Y | N | N | N | N | Y | Y | N |
| 4 ***Morrison*** | N | Y | Y | Y | N | N | N | N |
| 5 Foley | | | | | | | | |
| 6 Dicks | Y | N | N | Y | N | Y | Y | N |
| 7 McDermott | Y | N | N | Y | N | Y | Y | N |
| 8 ***Chandler*** | N | Y | Y | Y | N | N | N | N |
| **WEST VIRGINIA** | | | | | | | | |
| 1 Mollohan | Y | N | N | Y | N | Y | N | N |
| 2 Staggers | Y | Y | Y | Y | ? | Y | N | N |
| 3 Wise | Y | N | N | Y | N | Y | Y | ? |
| 4 Rahall | Y | N | N | Y | N | Y | N | N |
| **WISCONSIN** | | | | | | | | |
| 1 Aspin | Y | Y | N | Y | N | Y | Y | N |
| 2 ***Klug*** | N | Y | Y | N | N | N | N | N |
| 3 ***Gunderson*** | N | Y | Y | N | N | N | N | N |
| 4 Kleczka | Y | N | N | Y | ? | Y | Y | N |
| 5 Moody | Y | Y | N | N | N | Y | Y | N |
| 6 ***Petri*** | N | Y | Y | N | N | N | N | N |
| 7 Obey | Y | N | N | Y | N | Y | Y | N |
| 8 ***Roth*** | N | N | Y | N | N | N | N | N |
| 9 ***Sensenbrenner*** | N | Y | Y | N | N | N | N | N |
| **WYOMING** | | | | | | | | |
| AL ***Thomas*** | N | Y | Y | N | Y | N | N | N |

Southern states - Ala., Ark., Fla., Ga., Ky., La., Miss., N.C., Okla., S.C., Tenn., Texas, Va.
Omitted votes are quorum calls, which CQ does not include in its vote charts.

**349. HR 5678. Fiscal 1993 Commerce, Justice and State Appropriations/Committee of the Whole House.** Smith, D-Iowa, motion that the House resolve itself into the Committee of the Whole House for consideration of the bill to provide $22.3 billion in new budget authority for the Departments of Commerce, Justice and State, the judiciary and related agencies in fiscal 1993. Motion agreed to 253-148: R 9-147; D 243-1 (ND 164-1, SD 79-0); I 1-0, July 30, 1992.

**350. HR 5678. Fiscal 1993 Commerce, Justice and State Appropriations/Economic Development Administration.** Burton, R-Ind., amendment to cut $235 million from the Economic Development Administration. Rejected 76-339: R 69-92; D 7-246 (ND 4-165, SD 3-81); I 0-1, July 30, 1992.

**351. HR 5678. Fiscal 1993 Commerce, Justice and State Appropriations/USIA Libraries.** Stark, D-Calif., amendment to cut 2 percent ($15.2 million) of the U.S. Information Agency (USIA) general operating budget, the amount to fund USIA overseas libraries in Organization for Economic Cooperation and Development countries (Western Europe, Japan, Australia and Canada). Adopted 345-63: R 145-15; D 199-48 (ND 124-40, SD 75-8); I 1-0, July 30, 1992.

**352. HR 5678. Fiscal 1993 Commerce, Justice and State Appropriations/TV Martí.** Alexander, D-Ark., amendment to cut all funding ($13 million) for TV Martí, the USIA television station that broadcasts to Cuba. Adopted 206-194: R 47-113; D 158-81 (ND 127-34, SD 31-47); I 1-0, July 30, 1992. A "nay" was a vote supporting the president's position. (The amendment was later rejected on a separate vote; see vote 353.)

**353. HR 5678. Fiscal 1993 Commerce, Justice and State Appropriations/TV Martí.** Separate vote at the request of Bliley, R-Va., on the Alexander, D-Ark., amendment to cut all funding ($13 million) for TV Marti, the USIA television station that broadcasts to Cuba. Rejected 181-215: R 35-124; D 145-91 (ND 121-39, SD 24-52); I 1-0, July 30, 1992. A "nay" was a vote supporting the president's position.

**354. HR 5678. Fiscal 1993 Commerce, Justice and State Appropriations/Passage.** Passage of the bill to provide $22.3 billion in new budget authority to the departments of Commerce, Justice and State, the judiciary and related agencies in fiscal 1993. The administration requested $23,571,683,000. Passed 242-153: R 33-124; D 208-29 (ND 140-20, SD 68-9); I 1-0, July 30, 1992. A "nay" was a vote supporting the president's position.

**355. HR 4318. Miscellaneous Tariff/Rule.** Adoption of the rule (H Res 532) to provide for House floor consideration of the bill to make almost 400 changes in various tariff schedules, most of them temporary reductions or eliminations. The bill also imposed a 25 percent tariff on imported minivans by overturning the Customs Service's designation of imported minivans as cars and classifying them as trucks. Cars were eligible for a 2.5 percent tariff. Adopted 243-150: R 16-141; D 226-9 (ND 149-7, SD 77-2); I 1-0, July 31, 1992.

**356. HR 4318. Miscellaneous Tariff/Motion To Recommit.** Archer, R-Texas, motion to recommit to the House Ways and Means Committee the bill, with instructions to report it back to the House with an appropriate source of offsetting revenue after removing provisions that would impose a 25 percent tariff on imported minivans by overturning the Customs Service's designation of imported minivans as cars and classifying them as trucks. Cars were eligible for a 2.5 percent tariff, whereas trucks were imported with a 25 percent tariff. Motion rejected 125-263: R 103-53; D 22-209 (ND 14-141, SD 8-68); I 0-1, July 31, 1992. A "yea" was a vote in support of the president's position.

## KEY

| | |
|---|---|
| Y | Voted for (yea). |
| # | Paired for. |
| + | Announced for. |
| N | Voted against (nay). |
| X | Paired against. |
| − | Announced against. |
| P | Voted "present." |
| C | Voted "present" to avoid possible conflict of interest. |
| ? | Did not vote or otherwise make a position known. |

*Democrats* **Republicans**
*Independent*

| | 349 | 350 | 351 | 352 | 353 | 354 | 355 | 356 |
|---|---|---|---|---|---|---|---|---|
| **ALABAMA** | | | | | | | | |
| 1 *Callahan* | N | Y | Y | N | N | N | N | Y |
| 2 *Dickinson* | ? | N | Y | Y | N | N | N | ? |
| 3 Browder | Y | N | Y | ? | ? | ? | Y | N |
| 4 Bevill | Y | N | Y | ? | ? | ? | Y | N |
| 5 Cramer | Y | N | Y | ? | ? | ? | Y | N |
| 6 Erdreich | Y | N | Y | N | N | N | Y | N |
| 7 Harris | Y | N | Y | ? | ? | ? | Y | N |
| **ALASKA** | | | | | | | | |
| AL *Young* | N | N | Y | N | N | N | Y | Y |
| **ARIZONA** | | | | | | | | |
| 1 *Rhodes* | N | Y | Y | N | N | N | N | Y |
| 2 Pastor | Y | N | Y | Y | Y | Y | Y | N |
| 3 *Stump* | N | Y | Y | N | N | Y | N | Y |
| 4 *Kyl* | N | Y | Y | N | N | N | N | Y |
| 5 *Kolbe* | N | Y | Y | Y | Y | Y | N | Y |
| **ARKANSAS** | | | | | | | | |
| 1 Alexander | Y | N | N | Y | Y | Y | Y | ? |
| 2 Thornton | Y | N | Y | Y | Y | Y | Y | N |
| 3 *Hammerschmidt* | N | N | N | N | N | Y | N | Y |
| 4 Anthony | Y | N | Y | Y | ? | Y | Y | N |
| **CALIFORNIA** | | | | | | | | |
| 1 *Riggs* | N | N | Y | N | N | N | N | Y |
| 2 *Herger* | N | N | Y | N | N | N | N | Y |
| 3 Matsui | ? | N | Y | Y | Y | Y | Y | N |
| 4 Fazio | Y | N | Y | ? | ? | # | Y | N |
| 5 Pelosi | Y | N | N | Y | Y | Y | ? | ? |
| 6 Boxer | ? | ? | ? | ? | ? | ? | ? | ? |
| 7 Miller | Y | N | Y | Y | Y | N | Y | N |
| 8 Dellums | Y | N | Y | Y | Y | Y | Y | N |
| 9 Stark | Y | N | Y | Y | Y | N | N | Y |
| 10 Edwards | Y | N | Y | Y | Y | Y | Y | N |
| 11 Lantos | Y | N | Y | Y | Y | Y | Y | N |
| 12 *Campbell* | N | N | N | N | N | N | Y | N |
| 13 Mineta | Y | N | Y | Y | Y | Y | Y | N |
| 14 *Doolittle* | N | Y | Y | N | N | N | N | Y |
| 15 Condit | Y | Y | Y | Y | Y | Y | Y | N |
| 16 Panetta | Y | N | Y | Y | Y | Y | Y | N |
| 17 Dooley | Y | N | Y | N | N | Y | Y | Y |
| 18 Lehman | Y | N | Y | Y | Y | Y | Y | N |
| 19 *Lagomarsino* | Y | N | Y | N | N | Y | N | Y |
| 20 *Thomas* | N | Y | Y | N | N | N | N | Y |
| 21 *Gallegly* | N | N | Y | N | N | N | N | Y |
| 22 *Moorhead* | N | Y | Y | N | N | N | N | Y |
| 23 Beilenson | Y | N | N | Y | Y | Y | Y | N |
| 24 Waxman | Y | N | Y | Y | Y | Y | Y | N |
| 25 Roybal | Y | N | Y | N | N | Y | Y | N |
| 26 Berman | Y | N | N | N | Y | Y | Y | Y |
| 27 Levine | Y | N | N | ? | ? | ? | ? | # |
| 28 Dixon | Y | N | Y | Y | Y | Y | Y | N |
| 29 Waters | Y | N | Y | Y | Y | Y | Y | N |
| 30 Martinez | Y | N | Y | ? | Y | Y | Y | N |
| 31 Dymally | Y | N | N | N | N | Y | Y | N |
| 32 Anderson | Y | N | Y | Y | Y | Y | Y | N |
| 33 *Dreier* | N | Y | N | N | N | N | N | Y |
| 34 Torres | Y | N | Y | N | N | Y | Y | N |
| 35 *Lewis* | Y | N | Y | N | N | Y | N | N |
| 36 Brown | Y | N | Y | Y | Y | Y | Y | ? |
| 37 *McCandless* | ? | N | Y | N | N | N | N | Y |
| 38 *Dornan* | N | Y | Y | N | N | N | N | Y |
| 39 *Dannemeyer* | N | Y | Y | N | N | N | N | Y |
| 40 *Cox* | N | Y | Y | N | N | N | N | Y |
| 41 *Lowery* | ? | ? | ? | ? | ? | ? | ? | # |

ND Northern Democrats    SD Southern Democrats

| | 349 | 350 | 351 | 352 | 353 | 354 | 355 | 356 |
|---|---|---|---|---|---|---|---|---|
| 42 *Rohrabacher* | N | Y | Y | N | N | N | N | Y |
| 43 *Packard* | N | Y | Y | N | N | N | N | Y |
| 44 *Cunningham* | N | Y | Y | N | N | N | N | Y |
| 45 *Hunter* | N | Y | Y | N | N | N | Y | N |
| **COLORADO** | | | | | | | | |
| 1 Schroeder | Y | N | Y | Y | Y | N | Y | N |
| 2 Skaggs | Y | N | N | Y | Y | Y | Y | Y |
| 3 Campbell | Y | N | ? | ? | ? | ? | ? | ? |
| 4 *Allard* | N | Y | Y | N | N | N | N | Y |
| 5 *Hefley* | N | Y | Y | N | N | N | N | Y |
| 6 *Schaefer* | N | Y | Y | N | N | N | N | Y |
| **CONNECTICUT** | | | | | | | | |
| 1 Kennelly | Y | N | Y | Y | Y | Y | Y | N |
| 2 Gejdenson | Y | N | Y | Y | Y | Y | Y | N |
| 3 DeLauro | Y | N | Y | Y | Y | Y | Y | N |
| 4 *Shays* | N | N | Y | N | N | N | N | Y |
| 5 *Franks* | N | N | Y | Y | Y | N | N | N |
| 6 Johnson | N | Y | Y | Y | Y | Y | N | N |
| **DELAWARE** | | | | | | | | |
| AL Carper | Y | N | Y | N | N | Y | Y | N |
| **FLORIDA** | | | | | | | | |
| 1 Hutto | Y | N | Y | N | N | N | Y | N |
| 2 Peterson | Y | N | Y | N | N | Y | Y | N |
| 3 Bennett | Y | N | Y | N | N | N | Y | N |
| 4 *James* | N | Y | Y | N | N | N | N | Y |
| 5 *McCollum* | N | Y | Y | N | N | N | N | Y |
| 6 *Stearns* | N | Y | Y | N | N | N | N | Y |
| 7 Gibbons | Y | N | Y | N | N | N | Y | N |
| 8 *Young* | N | Y | Y | N | N | N | N | Y |
| 9 *Bilirakis* | N | Y | Y | N | N | N | N | Y |
| 10 *Ireland* | ? | Y | Y | N | N | Y | N | Y |
| 11 Bacchus | Y | N | Y | N | N | Y | ? | ? |
| 12 *Lewis* | N | Y | Y | N | N | N | N | Y |
| 13 *Goss* | N | Y | Y | N | N | N | N | Y |
| 14 Johnston | Y | N | N | Y | Y | Y | Y | N |
| 15 *Shaw* | N | N | N | N | N | N | N | Y |
| 16 Smith | Y | N | N | N | N | Y | Y | N |
| 17 Lehman | Y | N | Y | N | N | Y | ? | ? |
| 18 *Ros-Lehtinen* | N | N | N | N | N | N | Y | N |
| 19 Fascell | Y | N | N | N | N | Y | Y | N |
| **GEORGIA** | | | | | | | | |
| 1 Thomas | Y | N | N | N | N | Y | Y | N |
| 2 Hatcher | ? | ? | ? | ? | ? | ? | ? | ? |
| 3 Ray | Y | N | Y | N | N | Y | Y | N |
| 4 Jones | Y | N | Y | N | N | Y | Y | N |
| 5 Lewis | Y | N | Y | Y | Y | Y | Y | N |
| 6 *Gingrich* | ? | Y | Y | N | N | N | N | Y |
| 7 Darden | Y | N | Y | N | N | Y | Y | N |
| 8 Rowland | Y | N | N | N | N | Y | Y | N |
| 9 Jenkins | Y | N | Y | N | N | Y | Y | N |
| 10 Barnard | Y | N | Y | N | N | Y | Y | N |
| **HAWAII** | | | | | | | | |
| 1 Abercrombie | Y | N | Y | Y | Y | Y | Y | N |
| 2 Mink | Y | N | N | Y | Y | Y | Y | N |
| **IDAHO** | | | | | | | | |
| 1 LaRocco | Y | N | Y | Y | Y | Y | Y | N |
| 2 Stallings | ? | ? | Y | Y | Y | Y | Y | N |
| **ILLINOIS** | | | | | | | | |
| 1 Hayes | Y | N | Y | Y | Y | N | Y | N |
| 2 Savage | ? | ? | ? | ? | Y | N | ? | N |
| 3 Russo | Y | N | Y | Y | Y | Y | Y | N |
| 4 Sangmeister | Y | N | Y | N | N | Y | Y | N |
| 5 Lipinski | Y | N | Y | Y | Y | Y | Y | N |
| 6 *Hyde* | ? | ? | ? | ? | ? | ? | ? | ? |
| 7 Collins | Y | N | Y | Y | Y | Y | Y | N |
| 8 Rostenkowski | Y | N | Y | Y | Y | Y | Y | N |
| 9 Yates | Y | N | Y | Y | Y | Y | Y | N |
| 10 *Porter* | N | Y | N | N | N | N | N | Y |
| 11 Annunzio | Y | N | Y | N | N | Y | Y | N |
| 12 *Crane* | N | Y | Y | N | N | N | N | Y |
| 13 *Fawell* | N | N | Y | N | N | N | N | Y |
| 14 *Hastert* | N | Y | Y | N | N | N | N | Y |
| 15 *Ewing* | N | Y | Y | N | N | N | N | Y |
| 16 Cox | Y | N | Y | Y | Y | Y | Y | N |
| 17 Evans | Y | N | Y | Y | Y | Y | Y | N |
| 18 *Michel* | N | N | Y | N | N | N | N | ? |
| 19 Bruce | Y | N | Y | Y | Y | N | + | − |
| 20 Durbin | Y | N | Y | Y | Y | Y | Y | N |
| 21 Costello | Y | N | Y | Y | Y | Y | Y | N |
| 22 Poshard | Y | N | Y | Y | Y | Y | Y | N |
| **INDIANA** | | | | | | | | |
| 1 Visclosky | Y | N | N | Y | Y | Y | Y | N |
| 2 Sharp | Y | N | Y | Y | Y | Y | Y | N |
| 3 Roemer | Y | N | Y | Y | Y | Y | Y | N |

| | 349 | 350 | 351 | 352 | 353 | 354 | 355 | 356 |
|---|---|---|---|---|---|---|---|---|
| 4 Long | Y | N | Y | Y | Y | Y | Y | N |
| 5 Jontz | Y | N | Y | Y | Y | N | Y | N |
| 6 ***Burton*** | N | Y | Y | N | N | N | N | N |
| 7 ***Myers*** | Y | N | Y | N | N | ? | ? | ? |
| 8 McCloskey | Y | N | Y | Y | Y | Y | Y | N |
| 9 Hamilton | Y | N | N | N | N | Y | Y | N |
| 10 Jacobs | Y | N | Y | Y | Y | N | N | N |
| **IOWA** | | | | | | | | |
| 1 ***Leach*** | N | N | N | N | N | N | N | Y |
| 2 ***Nussle*** | N | Y | Y | Y | Y | N | N | Y |
| 3 Nagle | Y | N | N | Y | Y | Y | Y | N |
| 4 Smith | Y | N | N | N | N | Y | Y | ? |
| 5 ***Lightfoot*** | N | N | Y | N | N | N | N | Y |
| 6 ***Grandy*** | N | N | Y | N | N | Y | N | Y |
| **KANSAS** | | | | | | | | |
| 1 ***Roberts*** | N | N | Y | N | N | N | N | Y |
| 2 Slattery | Y | N | Y | Y | Y | N | Y | N |
| 3 ***Meyers*** | N | N | N | Y | N | N | N | Y |
| 4 Glickman | Y | N | Y | Y | Y | N | Y | N |
| 5 ***Nichols*** | N | N | Y | N | N | N | N | Y |
| **KENTUCKY** | | | | | | | | |
| 1 Hubbard | Y | N | Y | N | N | N | N | Y |
| 2 Natcher | Y | N | Y | N | N | Y | Y | N |
| 3 Mazzoli | Y | N | Y | N | N | Y | Y | N |
| 4 ***Bunning*** | N | Y | Y | N | N | N | N | N |
| 5 ***Rogers*** | N | N | N | Y | Y | Y | N | N |
| 6 ***Hopkins*** | N | Y | Y | Y | N | N | N | Y |
| 7 Perkins | ? | N | Y | Y | Y | Y | Y | N |
| **LOUISIANA** | | | | | | | | |
| 1 ***Livingston*** | N | N | Y | N | N | N | N | Y |
| 2 Jefferson | Y | N | Y | Y | Y | Y | Y | N |
| 3 Tauzin | Y | N | Y | N | N | Y | Y | ? |
| 4 ***McCrery*** | N | N | Y | N | ? | ? | ? | ? |
| 5 Huckaby | Y | N | Y | ? | ? | ? | ? | ? |
| 6 ***Baker*** | N | Y | Y | N | N | N | N | Y |
| 7 Hayes | Y | N | Y | Y | Y | Y | Y | N |
| 8 ***Holloway*** | N | Y | Y | N | N | N | N | N |
| **MAINE** | | | | | | | | |
| 1 Andrews | Y | N | Y | Y | Y | Y | Y | N |
| 2 ***Snowe*** | N | N | Y | N | N | N | Y | N |
| **MARYLAND** | | | | | | | | |
| 1 ***Gilchrest*** | N | N | Y | Y | N | Y | N | Y |
| 2 ***Bentley*** | N | N | Y | N | N | Y | N | N |
| 3 Cardin | Y | N | Y | Y | Y | Y | Y | N |
| 4 McMillen | Y | N | Y | Y | Y | Y | Y | N |
| 5 Hoyer | Y | N | N | N | N | Y | Y | N |
| 6 Byron | Y | N | Y | Y | Y | Y | ? | ? |
| 7 Mfume | Y | N | Y | Y | Y | Y | N | N |
| 8 ***Morella*** | N | N | Y | Y | Y | Y | N | Y |
| **MASSACHUSETTS** | | | | | | | | |
| 1 Olver | Y | N | ? | Y | Y | Y | Y | N |
| 2 Neal | Y | N | Y | Y | Y | Y | Y | N |
| 3 Early | Y | N | ? | ? | ? | ? | ? | ? |
| 4 Frank | Y | N | Y | Y | Y | Y | Y | N |
| 5 Atkins | Y | Y | Y | Y | Y | Y | ? | X |
| 6 Mavroules | ? | ? | ? | ? | ? | ? | ? | ? |
| 7 Markey | Y | N | Y | Y | ? | ? | Y | N |
| 8 Kennedy | Y | N | N | Y | Y | Y | Y | N |
| 9 Moakley | Y | N | Y | Y | Y | Y | Y | N |
| 10 Studds | Y | N | Y | Y | Y | Y | Y | N |
| 11 Donnelly | Y | N | Y | Y | ? | ? | ? | ? |
| **MICHIGAN** | | | | | | | | |
| 1 Conyers | ? | ? | ? | ? | ? | ? | ? | ? |
| 2 ***Pursell*** | N | N | Y | Y | Y | N | N | N |
| 3 Wolpe | Y | N | N | Y | Y | Y | Y | N |
| 4 ***Upton*** | N | N | Y | Y | Y | N | N | N |
| 5 ***Henry*** | N | N | N | N | N | N | Y | N |
| 6 Carr | Y | N | N | Y | Y | Y | Y | N |
| 7 Kildee | Y | N | Y | Y | Y | Y | Y | N |
| 8 Traxler | ? | ? | ? | ? | ? | ? | ? | ? |
| 9 ***Vander Jagt*** | N | N | ? | N | N | N | N | Y |
| 10 ***Camp*** | N | N | Y | Y | Y | Y | Y | N |
| 11 ***Davis*** | N | N | Y | N | N | Y | ? | N |
| 12 Bonior | Y | N | Y | Y | Y | Y | Y | N |
| 13 Collins | ? | ? | ? | ? | ? | ? | ? | ? |
| 14 Hertel | Y | N | N | N | N | Y | Y | N |
| 15 Ford | Y | N | Y | Y | Y | Y | Y | N |
| 16 Dingell | Y | Y | Y | Y | Y | Y | Y | N |
| 17 Levin | Y | N | Y | Y | N | Y | Y | N |
| 18 ***Broomfield*** | ? | ? | ? | ? | ? | X | ? | X |
| **MINNESOTA** | | | | | | | | |
| 1 Penny | Y | Y | Y | Y | Y | Y | N | Y |
| 2 ***Weber*** | N | N | Y | N | N | N | N | Y |
| 3 ***Ramstad*** | N | Y | Y | Y | Y | N | N | Y |
| 4 Vento | Y | N | Y | Y | Y | Y | Y | N |
| 5 Sabo | Y | N | N | Y | Y | Y | Y | N |
| 6 Sikorski | Y | N | Y | Y | Y | Y | Y | N |
| 7 Peterson | Y | N | Y | Y | Y | N | Y | N |
| 8 Oberstar | Y | N | N | Y | Y | Y | Y | N |
| **MISSISSIPPI** | | | | | | | | |
| 1 Whitten | Y | N | N | N | N | Y | Y | N |
| 2 Espy | Y | N | Y | Y | Y | Y | Y | N |
| 3 Montgomery | ? | N | Y | Y | Y | N | Y | N |
| 4 Parker | Y | N | Y | N | N | Y | Y | N |
| 5 Taylor | Y | N | Y | Y | Y | N | Y | N |
| **MISSOURI** | | | | | | | | |
| 1 Clay | ? | N | Y | Y | ? | Y | Y | N |
| 2 Horn | Y | N | Y | Y | Y | Y | Y | N |
| 3 Gephardt | Y | N | ? | ? | ? | ? | Y | N |
| 4 Skelton | Y | N | Y | N | N | N | Y | N |
| 5 Wheat | Y | N | Y | N | N | Y | Y | N |
| 6 ***Coleman*** | N | N | Y | N | N | N | N | N |
| 7 ***Hancock*** | N | Y | Y | Y | N | N | N | Y |
| 8 ***Emerson*** | N | N | Y | N | N | N | N | N |
| 9 Volkmer | Y | N | Y | N | N | N | Y | N |
| **MONTANA** | | | | | | | | |
| 1 Williams | Y | N | Y | Y | Y | Y | Y | N |
| 2 ***Marlenee*** | N | N | Y | Y | Y | N | N | Y |
| **NEBRASKA** | | | | | | | | |
| 1 ***Bereuter*** | N | Y | Y | N | N | N | N | N |
| 2 Hoagland | Y | N | Y | N | N | Y | Y | N |
| 3 ***Barrett*** | N | Y | Y | Y | Y | N | N | Y |
| **NEVADA** | | | | | | | | |
| 1 Bilbray | Y | N | Y | Y | Y | Y | Y | N |
| 2 ***Vucanovich*** | N | N | Y | N | N | N | N | Y |
| **NEW HAMPSHIRE** | | | | | | | | |
| 1 ***Zeliff*** | N | N | Y | N | N | N | N | Y |
| 2 Swett | Y | N | Y | Y | N | Y | Y | N |
| **NEW JERSEY** | | | | | | | | |
| 1 Andrews | Y | N | Y | N | N | Y | Y | N |
| 2 Hughes | Y | N | Y | Y | Y | Y | Y | N |
| 3 Pallone | Y | N | Y | N | N | N | Y | N |
| 4 ***Smith*** | N | N | Y | N | N | N | N | N |
| 5 ***Roukema*** | ? | N | Y | Y | Y | N | N | N |
| 6 Dwyer | Y | N | ? | ? | ? | ? | ? | ? |
| 7 ***Rinaldo*** | N | N | Y | N | N | N | N | Y |
| 8 Roe | Y | N | Y | Y | N | Y | Y | N |
| 9 Torricelli | Y | N | N | N | N | Y | Y | N |
| 10 Payne | Y | N | Y | Y | Y | ? | Y | N |
| 11 ***Gallo*** | N | N | Y | N | N | Y | N | Y |
| 12 ***Zimmer*** | N | Y | Y | Y | Y | N | N | Y |
| 13 ***Saxton*** | N | N | Y | N | N | N | N | N |
| 14 Guarini | Y | ? | Y | N | N | Y | Y | N |
| **NEW MEXICO** | | | | | | | | |
| 1 ***Schiff*** | N | N | Y | N | N | Y | N | N |
| 2 ***Skeen*** | Y | N | Y | N | N | Y | N | Y |
| 3 Richardson | Y | N | Y | N | N | Y | Y | N |
| **NEW YORK** | | | | | | | | |
| 1 Hochbrueckner | Y | N | Y | Y | Y | Y | Y | N |
| 2 Downey | Y | N | N | Y | Y | Y | Y | N |
| 3 Mrazek | ? | ? | ? | ? | ? | ? | ? | ? |
| 4 ***Lent*** | N | N | Y | N | N | N | N | N |
| 5 ***McGrath*** | Y | N | Y | N | N | N | Y | N |
| 6 Flake | Y | N | Y | Y | Y | Y | Y | N |
| 7 Ackerman | Y | ? | ? | ? | ? | ? | ? | ? |
| 8 Scheuer | Y | N | N | Y | Y | Y | ? | ? |
| 9 Manton | Y | N | Y | Y | Y | Y | Y | N |
| 10 Schumer | Y | N | Y | Y | Y | Y | Y | Y |
| 11 Towns | ? | ? | ? | ? | ? | ? | ? | ? |
| 12 Owens | Y | N | Y | Y | Y | Y | Y | N |
| 13 Solarz | ? | ? | X | X | X | ? | ? | ? |
| 14 ***Molinari*** | N | N | Y | N | N | N | N | Y |
| 15 ***Green*** | N | N | N | Y | Y | Y | N | Y |
| 16 Rangel | ? | N | Y | Y | Y | Y | Y | N |
| 17 Weiss | Y | N | Y | Y | Y | Y | Y | N |
| 18 Serrano | Y | N | N | Y | Y | Y | Y | N |
| 19 Engel | Y | N | N | N | N | Y | Y | N |
| 20 Lowey | Y | N | Y | Y | Y | Y | Y | N |
| 21 ***Fish*** | N | N | Y | N | N | Y | N | Y |
| 22 ***Gilman*** | N | N | N | N | N | Y | Y | N |
| 23 McNulty | Y | N | Y | N | N | Y | Y | N |
| 24 ***Solomon*** | N | Y | Y | N | N | N | N | N |
| 25 ***Boehlert*** | N | N | Y | Y | Y | Y | Y | N |
| 26 ***Martin*** | ? | ? | ? | ? | ? | ? | ? | N |
| 27 ***Walsh*** | N | N | Y | N | N | N | Y | N |
| 28 McHugh | Y | N | N | Y | Y | Y | Y | N |
| 29 ***Horton*** | Y | N | Y | N | N | ? | Y | N |
| 30 Slaughter | Y | N | Y | Y | Y | Y | Y | N |
| 31 ***Paxon*** | N | N | Y | N | N | N | N | Y |
| 32 LaFalce | Y | N | N | N | N | Y | Y | N |
| 33 Nowak | Y | N | N | Y | Y | Y | Y | N |
| 34 ***Houghton*** | N | N | Y | N | N | Y | N | N |
| **NORTH CAROLINA** | | | | | | | | |
| 1 Jones | Y | N | Y | Y | Y | Y | Y | N |
| 2 Valentine | Y | N | Y | Y | Y | Y | Y | N |
| 3 Lancaster | ? | N | Y | N | N | Y | Y | N |
| 4 Price | Y | N | Y | N | N | Y | Y | N |
| 5 Neal | Y | N | N | Y | Y | Y | Y | N |
| 6 ***Coble*** | N | Y | Y | Y | Y | N | N | Y |
| 7 Rose | Y | N | Y | N | N | Y | Y | N |
| 8 Hefner | Y | N | Y | Y | N | Y | Y | N |
| 9 ***McMillan*** | N | N | Y | N | N | N | N | Y |
| 10 ***Ballenger*** | N | Y | Y | Y | N | N | N | N |
| 11 ***Taylor*** | N | Y | Y | Y | N | N | N | Y |
| **NORTH DAKOTA** | | | | | | | | |
| AL Dorgan | Y | N | Y | Y | Y | N | Y | N |
| **OHIO** | | | | | | | | |
| 1 Luken | Y | N | Y | Y | Y | N | Y | N |
| 2 ***Gradison*** | N | N | Y | Y | Y | N | N | Y |
| 3 Hall | ? | N | Y | Y | Y | Y | Y | N |
| 4 ***Oxley*** | N | Y | Y | N | N | Y | N | Y |
| 5 ***Gillmor*** | N | N | Y | N | N | N | N | N |
| 6 ***McEwen*** | N | N | Y | N | N | N | N | N |
| 7 ***Hobson*** | N | N | Y | Y | Y | N | N | N |
| 8 ***Boehner*** | N | N | Y | N | N | N | N | Y |
| 9 Kaptur | Y | N | Y | N | N | Y | Y | N |
| 10 ***Miller*** | N | N | Y | N | N | N | N | Y |
| 11 Eckart | Y | N | Y | Y | Y | N | ? | ? |
| 12 ***Kasich*** | Y | Y | Y | Y | N | N | N | N |
| 13 Pease | Y | N | N | Y | Y | Y | Y | N |
| 14 Sawyer | Y | N | N | Y | Y | Y | Y | N |
| 15 ***Wylie*** | N | Y | Y | Y | Y | N | N | N |
| 16 ***Regula*** | N | N | N | Y | Y | Y | Y | N |
| 17 Traficant | Y | N | Y | N | Y | Y | Y | N |
| 18 Applegate | N | N | N | Y | Y | N | Y | N |
| 19 Feighan | Y | N | N | N | N | Y | Y | N |
| 20 Oakar | Y | N | N | N | N | Y | ? | ? |
| 21 Stokes | Y | N | Y | Y | Y | Y | ? | ? |
| **OKLAHOMA** | | | | | | | | |
| 1 ***Inhofe*** | N | N | Y | N | N | N | N | N |
| 2 Synar | Y | N | Y | Y | Y | Y | Y | Y |
| 3 Brewster | Y | N | Y | N | N | Y | Y | N |
| 4 McCurdy | Y | N | N | N | N | Y | Y | Y |
| 5 ***Edwards*** | N | N | Y | ? | ? | ? | ? | ? |
| 6 English | Y | N | Y | N | N | N | Y | N |
| **OREGON** | | | | | | | | |
| 1 AuCoin | Y | N | Y | Y | Y | Y | Y | N |
| 2 ***Smith*** | N | Y | Y | Y | Y | N | N | Y |
| 3 Wyden | Y | N | Y | Y | Y | Y | Y | Y |
| 4 DeFazio | Y | N | Y | Y | Y | Y | Y | N |
| 5 Kopetski | Y | N | Y | Y | Y | Y | Y | Y |
| **PENNSYLVANIA** | | | | | | | | |
| 1 Foglietta | Y | N | Y | N | N | Y | Y | N |
| 2 Blackwell | Y | N | Y | Y | Y | Y | Y | N |
| 3 Borski | Y | N | Y | Y | Y | Y | Y | N |
| 4 Kolter | ? | N | Y | ? | ? | ? | Y | N |
| 5 ***Schulze*** | N | Y | N | N | N | N | N | ? |
| 6 Yatron | Y | N | ? | ? | ? | ? | ? | ? |
| 7 ***Weldon*** | N | N | Y | N | N | N | N | N |
| 8 Kostmayer | Y | N | Y | N | N | Y | Y | N |
| 9 ***Shuster*** | N | N | Y | Y | Y | N | N | N |
| 10 ***McDade*** | N | N | Y | N | N | Y | Y | N |
| 11 Kanjorski | Y | N | Y | Y | Y | Y | Y | N |
| 12 Murtha | ? | N | N | N | N | Y | Y | N |
| 13 ***Coughlin*** | N | N | Y | N | N | Y | N | N |
| 14 Coyne | Y | N | Y | N | N | Y | Y | N |
| 15 ***Ritter*** | N | N | Y | N | Y | N | Y | N |
| 16 ***Walker*** | N | Y | Y | N | N | N | N | Y |
| 17 ***Gekas*** | N | N | N | N | N | N | N | Y |
| 18 ***Santorum*** | N | N | Y | N | N | N | N | N |
| 19 ***Goodling*** | N | N | Y | Y | N | N | N | Y |
| 20 Gaydos | Y | ? | ? | ? | ? | ? | ? | ? |
| 21 ***Ridge*** | N | N | Y | N | N | N | N | N |
| 22 Murphy | Y | N | Y | Y | Y | N | Y | N |
| 23 ***Clinger*** | N | N | Y | N | N | Y | N | N |
| **RHODE ISLAND** | | | | | | | | |
| 1 ***Machtley*** | N | N | Y | N | N | Y | N | Y |
| 2 Reed | Y | N | Y | Y | Y | Y | Y | N |
| **SOUTH CAROLINA** | | | | | | | | |
| 1 ***Ravenel*** | N | N | Y | Y | N | N | N | Y |
| 2 ***Spence*** | N | N | Y | N | N | N | N | Y |
| 3 Derrick | Y | N | Y | Y | Y | Y | Y | N |
| 4 Patterson | Y | N | Y | Y | Y | Y | Y | N |
| 5 Spratt | Y | N | Y | Y | N | Y | Y | N |
| 6 Tallon | Y | N | Y | N | N | Y | Y | N |
| **SOUTH DAKOTA** | | | | | | | | |
| AL Johnson | Y | N | Y | Y | Y | Y | Y | N |
| **TENNESSEE** | | | | | | | | |
| 1 ***Quillen*** | Y | N | Y | Y | Y | N | N | Y |
| 2 ***Duncan*** | N | Y | Y | Y | Y | N | N | N |
| 3 Lloyd | Y | N | Y | N | N | Y | Y | Y |
| 4 Cooper | Y | N | Y | N | N | Y | Y | N |
| 5 Clement | Y | N | Y | Y | Y | Y | Y | ? |
| 6 Gordon | Y | N | Y | N | N | Y | Y | N |
| 7 ***Sundquist*** | N | N | Y | Y | Y | N | Y | N |
| 8 Tanner | Y | N | Y | Y | Y | Y | Y | Y |
| 9 Ford | Y | N | Y | ? | ? | ? | ? | ? |
| **TEXAS** | | | | | | | | |
| 1 Chapman | Y | N | Y | Y | N | Y | ? | ? |
| 2 Wilson | Y | N | Y | N | N | Y | Y | N |
| 3 ***Johnson*** | N | Y | Y | N | N | N | N | Y |
| 4 Hall | Y | Y | Y | N | N | N | Y | N |
| 5 Bryant | Y | N | Y | N | N | Y | Y | N |
| 6 ***Barton*** | ? | ? | ? | ? | ? | ? | N | Y |
| 7 ***Archer*** | N | Y | Y | N | N | N | Y | Y |
| 8 ***Fields*** | N | Y | Y | N | N | N | N | Y |
| 9 Brooks | Y | N | Y | N | N | Y | Y | N |
| 10 Pickle | Y | N | Y | Y | Y | Y | Y | N |
| 11 Edwards | Y | N | Y | N | N | Y | Y | N |
| 12 Geren | Y | N | Y | N | N | Y | Y | N |
| 13 Sarpalius | Y | N | Y | Y | N | N | Y | N |
| 14 Laughlin | Y | Y | Y | Y | N | Y | Y | N |
| 15 de la Garza | Y | N | Y | N | N | Y | Y | N |
| 16 Coleman | Y | N | N | N | N | Y | Y | N |
| 17 Stenholm | Y | N | Y | N | N | Y | Y | N |
| 18 Washington | ? | N | Y | Y | Y | Y | Y | N |
| 19 ***Combest*** | N | Y | Y | Y | Y | N | N | Y |
| 20 Gonzalez | Y | N | Y | Y | Y | Y | Y | N |
| 21 ***Smith*** | N | N | N | N | N | Y | N | Y |
| 22 ***DeLay*** | N | Y | Y | N | N | N | N | Y |
| 23 Bustamante | Y | N | Y | Y | Y | Y | Y | N |
| 24 Frost | Y | N | Y | N | N | Y | Y | N |
| 25 Andrews | Y | Y | Y | N | N | Y | Y | N |
| 26 ***Armey*** | N | Y | Y | N | N | N | N | Y |
| 27 Ortiz | Y | N | Y | N | N | Y | Y | N |
| **UTAH** | | | | | | | | |
| 1 ***Hansen*** | N | Y | Y | N | N | N | N | Y |
| 2 Owens | Y | N | Y | N | N | Y | ? | ? |
| 3 Orton | Y | N | Y | Y | Y | Y | Y | N |
| **VERMONT** | | | | | | | | |
| AL *Sanders* | Y | N | Y | Y | Y | Y | Y | N |
| **VIRGINIA** | | | | | | | | |
| 1 ***Bateman*** | N | N | Y | Y | Y | Y | N | Y |
| 2 Pickett | ? | N | Y | Y | Y | Y | Y | Y |
| 3 ***Bliley*** | N | N | Y | N | N | N | N | Y |
| 4 Sisisky | Y | N | Y | N | N | Y | Y | N |
| 5 Payne | Y | N | Y | N | N | Y | Y | N |
| 6 Olin | Y | N | ? | N | ? | ? | Y | N |
| 7 ***Allen*** | N | N | Y | N | N | N | N | Y |
| 8 Moran | Y | N | Y | Y | N | Y | Y | Y |
| 9 Boucher | Y | N | Y | Y | Y | Y | Y | N |
| 10 ***Wolf*** | N | N | Y | N | N | N | N | N |
| **WASHINGTON** | | | | | | | | |
| 1 ***Miller*** | N | Y | N | N | N | Y | N | Y |
| 2 Swift | Y | N | Y | Y | Y | Y | Y | N |
| 3 Unsoeld | Y | N | Y | Y | Y | Y | Y | N |
| 4 ***Morrison*** | Y | N | Y | Y | Y | Y | ? | ? |
| 5 Foley | | | | | | | | |
| 6 Dicks | Y | N | Y | Y | Y | Y | Y | Y |
| 7 McDermott | Y | N | Y | Y | Y | Y | Y | N |
| 8 ***Chandler*** | N | N | Y | N | N | N | N | Y |
| **WEST VIRGINIA** | | | | | | | | |
| 1 Mollohan | Y | N | N | Y | Y | Y | Y | N |
| 2 Staggers | Y | N | Y | Y | Y | Y | Y | N |
| 3 Wise | ? | N | Y | N | N | Y | Y | N |
| 4 Rahall | Y | N | # | # | # | ? | Y | N |
| **WISCONSIN** | | | | | | | | |
| 1 Aspin | Y | N | Y | N | N | Y | Y | N |
| 2 ***Klug*** | N | Y | Y | N | N | N | N | Y |
| 3 ***Gunderson*** | N | Y | Y | N | N | N | N | N |
| 4 Kleczka | Y | N | Y | Y | Y | Y | Y | N |
| 5 Moody | Y | N | Y | Y | N | Y | Y | N |
| 6 ***Petri*** | N | Y | Y | N | N | N | N | Y |
| 7 Obey | Y | N | N | Y | Y | Y | Y | N |
| 8 ***Roth*** | N | Y | Y | N | N | N | N | Y |
| 9 ***Sensenbrenner*** | N | Y | Y | Y | Y | N | N | Y |
| **WYOMING** | | | | | | | | |
| AL ***Thomas*** | N | N | Y | Y | Y | N | N | Y |

Southern states - Ala., Ark., Fla., Ga., Ky., La., Miss., N.C., Okla., S.C., Tenn., Texas, Va.
Omitted votes are quorum calls, which CQ does not include in its vote charts.

**357. HR 4318. Miscellaneous Tariff/Passage.** Passage of the bill to make almost 400 changes in various tariff schedules, most of them temporary reductions or eliminations. The bill would impose a 25 percent tariff on imported minivans by overturning the Customs Service's designation of imported minivans as cars and classifying them as trucks. Cars were eligible for a 2.5 percent tariff, whereas trucks were imported with a 25 percent tariff. Passed 273-112: R 66-89; D 206-23 (ND 141-11, SD 65-12); I 1-0, July 31, 1992. A "nay" was a vote in support of the president's position.

**358. HR 5191. Small Business Equity Enhancement.** Passage of the bill to make changes in a federal program that provides investment capital to small businesses through small-business investment companies (SBICs), including allowing pension funds and other institutional investors to invest in SBICs in an effort to improve their solvency. Passed 356-2: R 146-1; D 210-1 (ND 144-1, SD 66-0); I 0-0, July 31, 1992.

**359. HR 2782. Employee Retirement Income Security Act (ERISA) Apprenticeship Programs/Apprenticeship Standards.** Fawell, R-Ill., amendment to strike the provisions of the bill that allowed states to establish minimum standards for the certification or registration of apprenticeship or other training programs. Rejected 140-266: R 123-35; D 17-230 (ND 1-165, SD 16-65); I 0-1, Aug. 4, 1992.

**360. HR 5649. Repeal Occupational Taxes on the Liquor Industry.** Gibbons, D-Fla., motion to suspend the rules and pass the bill to phase out occupational taxes on liquor producers, distributors and retailers, and offset the resulting revenue loss by imposing the federal diesel fuel excise tax in the same manner as the tax on gasoline. Motion rejected 200-207: R 68-90; D 131-117 (ND 99-68, SD 32-49); I 1-0, Aug. 4, 1992. A two-thirds majority of those present and voting (272 in this case) was required for passage under suspension of the rules.

**361. HR 5475. Special Patent Term Extensions.** Hughes, D-N.J., motion to suspend the rules and pass the bill to develop stricter standards for congressional approval for patent term extensions and provide for patent term extension in the case of five product patents and four design patents. Motion agreed to 278-131: R 123-34; D 155-96 (ND 88-81, SD 67-15); I 0-1, Aug. 4, 1992. A two-thirds majority of those present and voting (273 in this case) was required for passage under suspension of the rules.

**362. HR 5334. Housing and Community Development/Order Previous Question.** Slaughter, D-N.Y., motion to order the previous question (thus limiting debate and the possibility of amendment) on adoption of the rule (H Res 537) to provide for House floor consideration of the bill to authorize $30.1 billion in fiscal 1993 for housing and community development programs. Motion agreed to 244-163: R 0-155; D 243-8 (ND 169-3, SD 74-5); I 1-0, Aug. 5, 1992.

**363. HR 5334. Housing and Community Development/Rule.** Adoption of the rule (H Res 537) to provide for House floor consideration of the bill to authorize $30.1 billion in fiscal 1993 for housing and community development programs. Adopted 251-154: R 6-150; D 244-4 (ND 165-4, SD 79-0); I 1-0, Aug. 5, 1992.

**364. HR 5334. Housing and Community Development/Disclosures for Mortgage Refinancing.** Torres, D-Calif., amendment to require Truth-in-Lending disclosures for mortgage refinancing to borrowers within three days of filing for application. Currently lenders have to provide such information only at the time of the original closing. Rejected 153-268: R 5-159; D 147-109 (ND 121-54, SD 26-55); I 1-0, Aug. 5, 1992.

## KEY

| | |
|---|---|
| Y | Voted for (yea). |
| # | Paired for. |
| + | Announced for. |
| N | Voted against (nay). |
| X | Paired against. |
| − | Announced against. |
| P | Voted "present." |
| C | Voted "present" to avoid possible conflict of interest. |
| ? | Did not vote or otherwise make a position known. |

Democrats  **Republicans**
*Independent*

| | 357 | 358 | 359 | 360 | 361 | 362 | 363 | 364 |
|---|---|---|---|---|---|---|---|---|
| **ALABAMA** | | | | | | | | |
| 1 *Callahan* | N | Y | Y | N | Y | N | N | N |
| 2 *Dickinson* | ? | ? | ? | ? | ? | ? | ? | ? |
| 3 Browder | Y | Y | N | N | Y | Y | Y | N |
| 4 Bevill | Y | Y | N | N | Y | Y | Y | N |
| 5 Cramer | Y | Y | N | N | Y | Y | Y | N |
| 6 Erdreich | Y | Y | N | N | Y | N | Y | N |
| 7 Harris | Y | Y | N | N | Y | N | Y | N |
| **ALASKA** | | | | | | | | |
| AL *Young* | N | Y | N | Y | Y | N | N | N |
| **ARIZONA** | | | | | | | | |
| 1 *Rhodes* | N | Y | Y | N | Y | N | N | N |
| 2 Pastor | Y | Y | N | Y | Y | Y | Y | Y |
| 3 *Stump* | N | Y | Y | N | Y | N | N | N |
| 4 *Kyl* | N | Y | Y | N | Y | N | N | N |
| 5 *Kolbe* | N | Y | Y | Y | N | N | N | N |
| **ARKANSAS** | | | | | | | | |
| 1 Alexander | ? | ? | N | N | Y | Y | Y | Y |
| 2 Thornton | Y | Y | N | ? | Y | Y | Y | N |
| 3 *Hammerschmidt* | N | Y | N | N | Y | N | N | N |
| 4 Anthony | Y | Y | N | N | Y | Y | Y | N |
| **CALIFORNIA** | | | | | | | | |
| 1 *Riggs* | N | Y | Y | Y | Y | N | N | N |
| 2 *Herger* | N | Y | Y | N | Y | N | N | N |
| 3 Matsui | Y | Y | N | Y | Y | Y | Y | Y |
| 4 Fazio | Y | Y | N | N | Y | Y | Y | Y |
| 5 Pelosi | ? | ? | N | Y | N | Y | Y | Y |
| 6 Boxer | ? | ? | N | Y | N | Y | Y | Y |
| 7 Miller | N | Y | N | Y | N | Y | Y | Y |
| 8 Dellums | Y | Y | N | Y | N | Y | Y | Y |
| 9 Stark | N | Y | N | Y | N | Y | Y | Y |
| 10 Edwards | Y | Y | N | Y | N | Y | Y | Y |
| 11 Lantos | Y | Y | N | Y | N | Y | Y | Y |
| 12 *Campbell* | N | Y | Y | N | P | N | N | N |
| 13 Mineta | Y | Y | N | Y | N | Y | Y | Y |
| 14 *Doolittle* | N | Y | Y | N | N | N | N | N |
| 15 Condit | Y | Y | N | N | Y | ? | ? | N |
| 16 Panetta | N | Y | N | Y | N | Y | Y | Y |
| 17 Dooley | N | ? | N | Y | N | Y | Y | Y |
| 18 Lehman | Y | Y | N | Y | N | Y | Y | Y |
| 19 *Lagomarsino* | N | Y | Y | C | N | Y | N | N |
| 20 *Thomas* | N | ? | Y | Y | N | N | N | N |
| 21 *Gallegly* | N | Y | Y | N | N | N | N | N |
| 22 *Moorhead* | N | Y | Y | N | Y | N | N | N |
| 23 Beilenson | Y | Y | N | Y | N | Y | Y | Y |
| 24 Waxman | Y | Y | N | Y | N | Y | Y | Y |
| 25 Roybal | Y | Y | N | Y | N | Y | Y | Y |
| 26 Berman | Y | ? | N | Y | N | Y | Y | Y |
| 27 Levine | X | ? | N | Y | N | Y | Y | Y |
| 28 Dixon | Y | Y | N | Y | N | Y | Y | Y |
| 29 Waters | Y | Y | N | P | N | Y | ? | Y |
| 30 Martinez | Y | Y | N | Y | N | Y | Y | Y |
| 31 Dymally | Y | ? | N | Y | N | Y | Y | Y |
| 32 Anderson | N | Y | N | Y | N | Y | Y | Y |
| 33 *Dreier* | N | Y | Y | N | Y | N | N | N |
| 34 Torres | Y | Y | N | Y | N | Y | Y | Y |
| 35 *Lewis* | N | Y | Y | N | Y | N | N | N |
| 36 Brown | ? | Y | N | Y | N | Y | Y | Y |
| 37 *McCandless* | Y | Y | Y | N | Y | N | N | N |
| 38 *Dornan* | N | Y | Y | N | N | N | N | N |
| 39 *Dannemeyer* | N | Y | Y | N | Y | N | N | N |
| 40 *Cox* | N | Y | Y | N | Y | N | N | N |
| 41 *Lowery* | X | ? | Y | Y | Y | ? | ? | N |

| | 357 | 358 | 359 | 360 | 361 | 362 | 363 | 364 |
|---|---|---|---|---|---|---|---|---|
| 42 *Rohrabacher* | N | Y | Y | N | Y | N | N | N |
| 43 *Packard* | N | Y | Y | Y | Y | N | N | N |
| 44 *Cunningham* | N | Y | Y | Y | Y | N | N | N |
| 45 *Hunter* | Y | Y | Y | N | Y | N | N | N |
| **COLORADO** | | | | | | | | |
| 1 Schroeder | ? | ? | N | N | N | Y | Y | Y |
| 2 Skaggs | Y | Y | N | N | Y | Y | Y | N |
| 3 *Campbell* | ? | ? | ? | ? | ? | Y | Y | ? |
| 4 *Allard* | N | Y | N | N | N | N | N | N |
| 5 *Hefley* | ? | ? | Y | N | N | N | N | N |
| 6 *Schaefer* | N | Y | Y | N | Y | N | N | N |
| **CONNECTICUT** | | | | | | | | |
| 1 Kennelly | Y | Y | N | N | Y | Y | Y | Y |
| 2 Gejdenson | Y | Y | N | N | Y | Y | Y | Y |
| 3 DeLauro | Y | Y | N | Y | Y | Y | Y | Y |
| 4 *Shays* | N | Y | N | N | Y | N | Y | Y |
| 5 *Franks* | Y | Y | Y | N | Y | N | N | N |
| 6 *Johnson* | Y | Y | N | N | N | N | N | N |
| **DELAWARE** | | | | | | | | |
| AL Carper | Y | Y | N | N | Y | Y | Y | Y |
| **FLORIDA** | | | | | | | | |
| 1 Hutto | N | Y | Y | N | Y | Y | Y | Y |
| 2 Peterson | Y | + | N | N | Y | Y | Y | Y |
| 3 Bennett | Y | Y | N | N | Y | Y | Y | N |
| 4 *James* | Y | Y | Y | Y | N | N | N | N |
| 5 *McCollum* | N | Y | Y | N | Y | N | N | N |
| 6 *Stearns* | N | Y | Y | N | N | N | N | N |
| 7 Gibbons | N | Y | N | Y | Y | Y | Y | Y |
| 8 *Young* | Y | Y | N | N | N | N | N | N |
| 9 *Bilirakis* | Y | Y | Y | N | Y | N | N | N |
| 10 *Ireland* | N | Y | N | Y | Y | ? | ? | N |
| 11 Bacchus | ? | ? | N | N | Y | Y | Y | Y |
| 12 *Lewis* | N | Y | N | N | Y | N | N | N |
| 13 *Goss* | N | Y | Y | N | N | N | N | N |
| 14 Johnston | Y | Y | N | Y | N | Y | Y | Y |
| 15 *Shaw* | N | Y | Y | N | Y | N | N | N |
| 16 Smith | Y | ? | N | Y | N | Y | Y | Y |
| 17 Lehman | ? | ? | N | Y | Y | Y | Y | Y |
| 18 *Ros-Lehtinen* | Y | Y | Y | N | N | N | N | N |
| 19 Fascell | Y | Y | Y | N | Y | Y | Y | Y |
| **GEORGIA** | | | | | | | | |
| 1 Thomas | Y | ? | N | N | Y | Y | Y | N |
| 2 Hatcher | ? | ? | ? | ? | ? | ? | ? | ? |
| 3 Ray | Y | Y | N | N | Y | Y | Y | N |
| 4 Jones | Y | Y | Y | N | Y | Y | Y | Y |
| 5 Lewis | Y | Y | N | Y | N | Y | Y | Y |
| 6 *Gingrich* | Y | Y | ? | N | N | N | N | N |
| 7 Darden | Y | Y | N | N | Y | Y | Y | N |
| 8 Rowland | Y | Y | N | N | Y | Y | Y | N |
| 9 Jenkins | Y | ? | Y | N | Y | Y | Y | N |
| 10 Barnard | Y | Y | N | Y | Y | ? | ? | N |
| **HAWAII** | | | | | | | | |
| 1 Abercrombie | Y | Y | N | Y | N | Y | Y | Y |
| 2 Mink | Y | Y | N | Y | N | Y | Y | Y |
| **IDAHO** | | | | | | | | |
| 1 LaRocco | Y | Y | N | N | Y | Y | Y | Y |
| 2 Stallings | Y | Y | N | N | N | Y | Y | N |
| **ILLINOIS** | | | | | | | | |
| 1 Hayes | Y | Y | N | Y | N | Y | Y | Y |
| 2 Savage | Y | Y | N | Y | N | Y | Y | Y |
| 3 Russo | Y | Y | Y | Y | Y | Y | Y | Y |
| 4 Sangmeister | Y | Y | N | N | Y | Y | Y | Y |
| 5 Lipinski | Y | Y | N | N | Y | Y | Y | N |
| 6 *Hyde* | ? | ? | Y | N | Y | N | N | N |
| 7 Collins | Y | Y | N | Y | N | Y | Y | Y |
| 8 Rostenkowski | Y | Y | N | N | Y | Y | Y | Y |
| 9 Yates | Y | Y | N | Y | N | Y | Y | Y |
| 10 *Porter* | N | Y | Y | Y | N | N | N | N |
| 11 Annunzio | Y | Y | N | N | Y | Y | Y | Y |
| 12 *Crane* | N | N | Y | N | N | N | N | N |
| 13 *Fawell* | N | Y | Y | N | N | N | N | Y |
| 14 *Hastert* | Y | Y | Y | N | N | N | N | N |
| 15 *Ewing* | Y | Y | N | N | Y | N | N | N |
| 16 *Cox* | Y | Y | Y | N | Y | N | N | N |
| 17 Evans | Y | Y | N | N | N | Y | Y | N |
| 18 *Michel* | ? | ? | Y | N | N | N | N | N |
| 19 Bruce | + | + | N | N | N | Y | Y | N |
| 20 Durbin | Y | Y | N | N | Y | Y | Y | N |
| 21 Costello | Y | Y | N | N | N | Y | Y | Y |
| 22 Poshard | Y | Y | N | N | Y | N | N | N |
| **INDIANA** | | | | | | | | |
| 1 Visclosky | Y | Y | N | N | N | Y | Y | N |
| 2 Sharp | Y | Y | N | N | N | Y | Y | N |
| 3 Roemer | Y | Y | N | N | N | Y | Y | N |

ND Northern Democrats   SD Southern Democrats

| | 357 | 358 | 359 | 360 | 361 | 362 | 363 | 364 |
|---|---|---|---|---|---|---|---|---|
| 4 Long | Y | Y | N | N | N | Y | Y | Y |
| 5 Jontz | Y | Y | N | N | N | Y | Y | Y |
| 6 ***Burton*** | Y | Y | Y | N | Y | N | N | N |
| 7 ***Myers*** | ? | ? | Y | N | N | N | N | N |
| 8 McCloskey | Y | ? | N | N | N | Y | Y | Y |
| 9 Hamilton | Y | Y | N | N | N | N | Y | N |
| 10 Jacobs | ? | Y | N | Y | N | N | N | Y |
| **IOWA** | | | | | | | | |
| 1 ***Leach*** | N | Y | Y | N | N | N | N | N |
| 2 ***Nussle*** | N | Y | Y | N | Y | N | N | N |
| 3 Nagle | Y | ? | N | N | Y | Y | Y | N |
| 4 Smith | ? | ? | N | N | Y | Y | Y | N |
| 5 ***Lightfoot*** | N | Y | Y | N | N | N | N | N |
| 6 ***Grandy*** | N | Y | Y | N | Y | N | N | N |
| **KANSAS** | | | | | | | | |
| 1 ***Roberts*** | N | Y | Y | N | Y | N | N | N |
| 2 Slattery | Y | Y | N | N | Y | Y | Y | N |
| 3 ***Meyers*** | Y | Y | ? | ? | ? | N | N | N |
| 4 Glickman | Y | Y | ? | N | Y | Y | Y | N |
| 5 ***Nichols*** | N | Y | ? | ? | ? | ? | ? | N |
| **KENTUCKY** | | | | | | | | |
| 1 Hubbard | N | Y | N | Y | Y | Y | Y | N |
| 2 Natcher | Y | Y | N | Y | Y | Y | Y | Y |
| 3 Mazzoli | Y | Y | N | Y | N | Y | Y | Y |
| 4 ***Bunning*** | Y | Y | Y | Y | Y | N | N | N |
| 5 ***Rogers*** | Y | Y | Y | Y | Y | N | N | N |
| 6 ***Hopkins*** | N | Y | Y | Y | Y | N | N | N |
| 7 Perkins | Y | Y | N | Y | Y | Y | Y | Y |
| **LOUISIANA** | | | | | | | | |
| 1 ***Livingston*** | N | Y | Y | N | Y | N | N | N |
| 2 Jefferson | Y | Y | N | Y | N | Y | ? | Y |
| 3 Tauzin | Y | Y | Y | N | Y | Y | Y | N |
| 4 ***McCrery*** | ? | ? | Y | N | N | N | N | N |
| 5 Huckaby | ? | ? | Y | N | N | N | Y | N |
| 6 ***Baker*** | Y | Y | Y | N | N | N | N | N |
| 7 Hayes | Y | Y | Y | N | Y | Y | Y | N |
| 8 ***Holloway*** | Y | Y | Y | N | Y | N | N | N |
| **MAINE** | | | | | | | | |
| 1 Andrews | Y | Y | N | Y | N | Y | Y | Y |
| 2 ***Snowe*** | Y | Y | Y | N | N | N | N | N |
| **MARYLAND** | | | | | | | | |
| 1 ***Gilchrest*** | N | Y | Y | N | Y | N | N | N |
| 2 ***Bentley*** | Y | Y | N | N | Y | ? | ? | N |
| 3 Cardin | Y | Y | N | Y | Y | Y | Y | Y |
| 4 McMillen | Y | Y | N | N | Y | Y | Y | Y |
| 5 Hoyer | Y | Y | N | Y | Y | Y | Y | N |
| 6 Byron | ? | ? | Y | N | N | Y | Y | Y |
| 7 Mfume | Y | Y | N | Y | N | Y | Y | Y |
| 8 ***Morella*** | N | Y | Y | Y | Y | N | N | N |
| **MASSACHUSETTS** | | | | | | | | |
| 1 Olver | Y | Y | N | N | Y | Y | Y | Y |
| 2 Neal | Y | Y | N | N | Y | Y | Y | Y |
| 3 Early | ? | ? | N | Y | Y | Y | Y | Y |
| 4 Frank | Y | Y | N | Y | Y | Y | Y | Y |
| 5 Atkins | # | ? | N | N | N | Y | Y | Y |
| 6 Mavroules | ? | ? | N | N | Y | Y | Y | Y |
| 7 Markey | Y | Y | N | Y | N | Y | Y | Y |
| 8 Kennedy | Y | Y | N | N | N | Y | Y | Y |
| 9 Moakley | Y | Y | N | N | Y | Y | Y | Y |
| 10 Studds | Y | Y | N | N | N | Y | Y | Y |
| 11 Donnelly | ? | ? | N | N | Y | Y | Y | Y |
| **MICHIGAN** | | | | | | | | |
| 1 Conyers | ? | ? | ? | ? | ? | ? | ? | ? |
| 2 ***Pursell*** | Y | Y | N | N | Y | N | N | N |
| 3 Wolpe | Y | Y | N | Y | Y | Y | Y | Y |
| 4 ***Upton*** | Y | Y | N | N | Y | N | N | N |
| 5 ***Henry*** | Y | Y | N | N | Y | N | N | N |
| 6 Carr | Y | Y | N | N | Y | Y | Y | N |
| 7 Kildee | Y | Y | N | Y | Y | Y | Y | Y |
| 8 Traxler | ? | ? | ? | ? | ? | ? | ? | ? |
| 9 ***Vander Jagt*** | N | Y | ? | ? | ? | ? | ? | N |
| 10 ***Camp*** | Y | Y | Y | N | Y | N | N | N |
| 11 ***Davis*** | Y | Y | N | N | Y | ? | ? | N |
| 12 Bonior | Y | Y | N | Y | Y | Y | Y | Y |
| 13 Collins | ? | ? | ? | ? | ? | ? | ? | Y |
| 14 Hertel | Y | Y | ? | ? | ? | ? | ? | ? |
| 15 Ford | Y | Y | N | Y | Y | Y | Y | ? |
| 16 Dingell | Y | Y | N | Y | Y | Y | Y | Y |
| 17 Levin | Y | Y | N | Y | Y | Y | Y | Y |
| 18 ***Broomfield*** | ? | ? | ? | ? | ? | ? | N | N |
| **MINNESOTA** | | | | | | | | |
| 1 Penny | N | N | N | N | N | Y | Y | N |
| 2 ***Weber*** | N | Y | Y | N | N | N | N | N |
| 3 ***Ramstad*** | N | Y | Y | Y | Y | N | N | N |
| 4 Vento | Y | Y | N | Y | N | Y | Y | Y |

| | 357 | 358 | 359 | 360 | 361 | 362 | 363 | 364 |
|---|---|---|---|---|---|---|---|---|
| 5 Sabo | Y | Y | N | Y | N | Y | Y | Y |
| 6 Sikorski | Y | Y | N | Y | N | Y | Y | Y |
| 7 Peterson | Y | Y | N | N | N | Y | Y | N |
| 8 Oberstar | Y | Y | N | N | Y | Y | Y | N |
| **MISSISSIPPI** | | | | | | | | |
| 1 Whitten | Y | ? | ? | ? | ? | ? | Y | N |
| 2 Espy | Y | Y | N | N | Y | Y | Y | N |
| 3 Montgomery | N | Y | Y | Y | Y | N | Y | N |
| 4 Parker | N | Y | Y | N | Y | Y | Y | N |
| 5 Taylor | Y | Y | Y | Y | Y | Y | Y | N |
| **MISSOURI** | | | | | | | | |
| 1 Clay | Y | Y | ? | ? | ? | Y | Y | Y |
| 2 Horn | Y | Y | N | Y | Y | Y | Y | N |
| 3 Gephardt | Y | Y | ? | N | Y | Y | Y | Y |
| 4 Skelton | Y | Y | N | N | Y | Y | Y | N |
| 5 Wheat | Y | Y | ? | ? | ? | Y | Y | Y |
| 6 ***Coleman*** | Y | Y | Y | N | Y | N | N | N |
| 7 ***Hancock*** | Y | Y | Y | N | Y | N | N | N |
| 8 ***Emerson*** | Y | Y | Y | N | Y | N | N | N |
| 9 Volkmer | Y | ? | ? | ? | ? | ? | ? | ? |
| **MONTANA** | | | | | | | | |
| 1 Williams | Y | Y | N | N | N | N | Y | N |
| 2 ***Marlenee*** | N | Y | Y | N | N | N | N | N |
| **NEBRASKA** | | | | | | | | |
| 1 ***Bereuter*** | Y | Y | Y | N | Y | N | N | N |
| 2 Hoagland | Y | Y | N | N | Y | Y | Y | N |
| 3 ***Barrett*** | N | Y | Y | N | Y | N | N | N |
| **NEVADA** | | | | | | | | |
| 1 Bilbray | Y | Y | N | Y | Y | Y | Y | N |
| 2 ***Vucanovich*** | N | Y | Y | Y | Y | N | N | N |
| **NEW HAMPSHIRE** | | | | | | | | |
| 1 ***Zeliff*** | N | Y | Y | Y | N | N | N | N |
| 2 Swett | Y | ? | N | Y | N | Y | Y | N |
| **NEW JERSEY** | | | | | | | | |
| 1 Andrews | Y | Y | N | Y | Y | Y | Y | Y |
| 2 Hughes | Y | Y | N | Y | Y | Y | Y | Y |
| 3 Pallone | Y | Y | N | Y | Y | Y | Y | Y |
| 4 ***Smith*** | Y | Y | N | Y | Y | N | N | N |
| 5 ***Roukema*** | Y | ? | Y | Y | Y | N | N | N |
| 6 Dwyer | ? | ? | N | Y | Y | Y | Y | Y |
| 7 ***Rinaldo*** | Y | Y | N | Y | Y | N | N | N |
| 8 Roe | Y | Y | N | ? | Y | Y | Y | N |
| 9 Torricelli | Y | Y | N | N | ? | ? | ? | ? |
| 10 Payne | Y | Y | N | N | Y | Y | Y | Y |
| 11 ***Gallo*** | N | Y | N | Y | Y | N | N | N |
| 12 ***Zimmer*** | N | Y | N | Y | N | N | N | N |
| 13 ***Saxton*** | Y | Y | N | Y | N | N | N | N |
| 14 Guarini | + | + | N | Y | Y | Y | Y | Y |
| **NEW MEXICO** | | | | | | | | |
| 1 ***Schiff*** | N | Y | N | N | Y | N | N | N |
| 2 ***Skeen*** | N | Y | Y | N | Y | N | N | N |
| 3 Richardson | Y | Y | N | N | Y | Y | Y | Y |
| **NEW YORK** | | | | | | | | |
| 1 Hochbrueckner | Y | Y | N | Y | Y | ? | ? | Y |
| 2 Downey | Y | Y | N | Y | Y | Y | Y | Y |
| 3 Mrazek | ? | ? | ? | ? | ? | Y | Y | Y |
| 4 ***Lent*** | Y | Y | Y | Y | Y | N | N | N |
| 5 ***McGrath*** | Y | ? | N | Y | Y | N | N | N |
| 6 Flake | Y | Y | N | Y | N | Y | Y | Y |
| 7 Ackerman | ? | ? | ? | ? | ? | Y | Y | Y |
| 8 Scheuer | ? | ? | N | Y | N | Y | Y | Y |
| 9 Manton | Y | Y | N | Y | Y | Y | Y | N |
| 10 Schumer | N | Y | N | Y | N | Y | ? | Y |
| 11 Towns | ? | ? | ? | ? | ? | ? | ? | Y |
| 12 Owens | Y | Y | N | Y | N | Y | ? | Y |
| 13 Solarz | ? | ? | N | Y | Y | Y | Y | Y |
| 14 ***Molinari*** | N | Y | N | Y | Y | N | N | N |
| 15 ***Green*** | N | Y | N | Y | N | N | N | Y |
| 16 Rangel | Y | Y | N | Y | N | Y | Y | Y |
| 17 Weiss | Y | Y | — | Y | N | Y | Y | Y |
| 18 Serrano | Y | Y | ? | ? | N | Y | Y | Y |
| 19 Engel | Y | Y | N | Y | Y | Y | Y | Y |
| 20 Lowey | Y | Y | N | Y | Y | Y | Y | Y |
| 21 ***Fish*** | N | ? | N | Y | Y | N | Y | N |
| 22 ***Gilman*** | Y | Y | N | Y | Y | N | Y | Y |
| 23 McNulty | Y | Y | N | N | Y | Y | Y | N |
| 24 ***Solomon*** | Y | Y | N | N | Y | N | N | N |
| 25 ***Boehlert*** | Y | Y | N | Y | Y | N | N | Y |
| 26 ***Martin*** | Y | Y | N | N | Y | N | N | N |
| 27 ***Walsh*** | Y | Y | N | N | Y | N | N | N |
| 28 McHugh | N | Y | N | N | Y | Y | Y | Y |
| 29 ***Horton*** | Y | Y | N | Y | Y | Y | Y | N |
| 30 Slaughter | Y | Y | N | Y | N | Y | Y | N |
| 31 ***Paxon*** | N | Y | Y | Y | Y | N | N | N |

| | 357 | 358 | 359 | 360 | 361 | 362 | 363 | 364 |
|---|---|---|---|---|---|---|---|---|
| 32 LaFalce | Y | Y | N | N | Y | Y | Y | N |
| 33 Nowak | Y | Y | N | N | Y | Y | N | N |
| 34 ***Houghton*** | Y | Y | N | N | Y | N | ? | N |
| **NORTH CAROLINA** | | | | | | | | |
| 1 Jones | Y | Y | N | Y | Y | Y | Y | Y |
| 2 Valentine | Y | Y | Y | N | Y | Y | Y | N |
| 3 Lancaster | Y | ? | N | N | Y | Y | Y | N |
| 4 Price | Y | Y | N | N | Y | Y | Y | N |
| 5 Neal | Y | Y | N | N | Y | ? | Y | N |
| 6 ***Coble*** | N | Y | Y | Y | Y | N | N | N |
| 7 Rose | Y | Y | N | N | Y | Y | Y | N |
| 8 Hefner | Y | Y | N | N | Y | Y | Y | N |
| 9 ***McMillan*** | N | Y | Y | Y | Y | N | N | N |
| 10 ***Ballenger*** | Y | Y | Y | Y | Y | N | N | N |
| 11 ***Taylor*** | N | + | Y | Y | Y | N | N | N |
| **NORTH DAKOTA** | | | | | | | | |
| AL Dorgan | Y | Y | N | N | N | Y | Y | N |
| **OHIO** | | | | | | | | |
| 1 Luken | Y | Y | N | N | Y | Y | Y | N |
| 2 ***Gradison*** | N | Y | Y | N | Y | N | N | N |
| 3 Hall | Y | Y | N | Y | Y | Y | Y | N |
| 4 ***Oxley*** | N | Y | Y | N | Y | N | N | N |
| 5 ***Gillmor*** | Y | Y | N | N | Y | ? | N | N |
| 6 ***McEwen*** | Y | Y | Y | Y | Y | N | N | N |
| 7 ***Hobson*** | Y | Y | Y | N | Y | N | N | N |
| 8 ***Boehner*** | N | Y | Y | N | Y | N | N | N |
| 9 Kaptur | Y | Y | N | N | N | Y | Y | N |
| 10 ***Miller*** | Y | Y | Y | N | N | N | N | N |
| 11 Eckart | ? | ? | N | Y | Y | Y | Y | Y |
| 12 ***Kasich*** | Y | Y | Y | N | Y | N | N | N |
| 13 Pease | Y | Y | N | Y | Y | Y | Y | Y |
| 14 Sawyer | Y | Y | N | Y | Y | Y | Y | Y |
| 15 ***Wylie*** | Y | Y | Y | N | Y | N | Y | N |
| 16 ***Regula*** | Y | Y | N | N | Y | N | N | N |
| 17 Traficant | Y | Y | N | Y | Y | Y | Y | Y |
| 18 Applegate | Y | Y | N | Y | Y | Y | Y | N |
| 19 Feighan | Y | Y | N | Y | Y | Y | Y | N |
| 20 Oakar | ? | ? | N | N | N | Y | Y | Y |
| 21 Stokes | # | ? | N | Y | N | Y | Y | Y |
| **OKLAHOMA** | | | | | | | | |
| 1 ***Inhofe*** | Y | Y | Y | Y | Y | N | N | N |
| 2 Synar | Y | ? | N | N | N | Y | Y | Y |
| 3 Brewster | Y | Y | N | Y | Y | Y | Y | N |
| 4 McCurdy | Y | Y | N | N | Y | Y | Y | N |
| 5 ***Edwards*** | ? | ? | Y | N | Y | ? | ? | N |
| 6 English | Y | Y | N | N | Y | Y | Y | N |
| **OREGON** | | | | | | | | |
| 1 AuCoin | Y | Y | N | N | Y | Y | Y | Y |
| 2 ***Smith*** | N | Y | Y | N | N | N | N | N |
| 3 Wyden | N | Y | N | N | N | N | Y | Y |
| 4 DeFazio | Y | Y | N | Y | N | Y | Y | Y |
| 5 Kopetski | N | Y | N | N | Y | Y | Y | N |
| **PENNSYLVANIA** | | | | | | | | |
| 1 Foglietta | Y | Y | N | Y | Y | Y | ? | Y |
| 2 Blackwell | Y | Y | N | Y | N | Y | Y | Y |
| 3 Borski | Y | Y | N | Y | N | Y | Y | Y |
| 4 Kolter | Y | ? | N | Y | Y | Y | Y | Y |
| 5 ***Schulze*** | ? | ? | ? | ? | ? | ? | ? | ? |
| 6 Yatron | ? | ? | N | Y | Y | Y | Y | N |
| 7 ***Weldon*** | Y | Y | N | Y | Y | N | N | N |
| 8 Kostmayer | Y | Y | N | Y | Y | Y | Y | Y |
| 9 ***Shuster*** | Y | Y | Y | N | Y | N | N | N |
| 10 ***McDade*** | Y | Y | N | N | Y | N | Y | N |
| 11 Kanjorski | Y | Y | N | Y | Y | Y | Y | N |
| 12 Murtha | Y | ? | N | N | Y | Y | Y | N |
| 13 ***Coughlin*** | Y | ? | ? | ? | ? | N | N | N |
| 14 Coyne | Y | Y | N | Y | Y | Y | Y | Y |
| 15 ***Ritter*** | Y | Y | N | Y | Y | N | N | N |
| 16 ***Walker*** | Y | Y | Y | N | Y | N | N | N |
| 17 ***Gekas*** | N | Y | Y | N | N | N | N | N |
| 18 ***Santorum*** | Y | Y | N | Y | Y | N | N | N |
| 19 ***Goodling*** | Y | Y | Y | N | Y | N | N | N |
| 20 Gaydos | ? | ? | N | Y | Y | Y | Y | N |
| 21 ***Ridge*** | Y | Y | N | Y | Y | N | N | N |
| 22 Murphy | Y | Y | N | Y | Y | Y | Y | N |
| 23 ***Clinger*** | Y | Y | Y | Y | Y | N | N | N |
| **RHODE ISLAND** | | | | | | | | |
| 1 ***Machtley*** | Y | Y | Y | Y | Y | N | N | N |
| 2 Reed | Y | Y | N | N | N | Y | Y | Y |
| **SOUTH CAROLINA** | | | | | | | | |
| 1 ***Ravenel*** | N | Y | Y | N | Y | N | N | N |
| 2 ***Spence*** | Y | Y | Y | N | Y | N | N | N |
| 3 Derrick | Y | Y | N | N | Y | Y | Y | Y |
| 4 Patterson | Y | Y | Y | N | Y | Y | Y | Y |
| 5 Spratt | Y | Y | N | N | Y | Y | Y | Y |
| 6 Tallon | Y | Y | N | N | Y | Y | Y | N |

| | 357 | 358 | 359 | 360 | 361 | 362 | 363 | 364 |
|---|---|---|---|---|---|---|---|---|
| **SOUTH DAKOTA** | | | | | | | | |
| AL Johnson | Y | Y | N | N | N | Y | Y | Y |
| **TENNESSEE** | | | | | | | | |
| 1 ***Quillen*** | N | Y | Y | Y | Y | N | N | N |
| 2 ***Duncan*** | Y | Y | Y | Y | Y | N | N | N |
| 3 Lloyd | N | ? | N | N | N | Y | Y | N |
| 4 Cooper | N | Y | N | N | Y | Y | Y | C |
| 5 Clement | ? | ? | N | Y | N | Y | Y | Y |
| 6 Gordon | Y | Y | N | Y | Y | Y | Y | N |
| 7 ***Sundquist*** | Y | ? | Y | Y | Y | N | N | N |
| 8 Tanner | Y | Y | N | N | Y | Y | Y | N |
| 9 Ford | ? | ? | ? | ? | ? | ? | ? | ? |
| **TEXAS** | | | | | | | | |
| 1 Chapman | ? | ? | N | N | Y | Y | Y | N |
| 2 Wilson | Y | Y | N | N | Y | Y | Y | N |
| 3 ***Johnson*** | N | Y | Y | N | Y | N | N | N |
| 4 Hall | N | Y | N | N | Y | Y | Y | N |
| 5 Bryant | Y | Y | N | N | Y | Y | Y | Y |
| 6 ***Barton*** | N | Y | Y | N | Y | N | N | N |
| 7 ***Archer*** | N | Y | Y | Y | Y | N | N | N |
| 8 ***Fields*** | N | + | Y | N | Y | N | N | N |
| 9 Brooks | Y | Y | N | Y | Y | Y | Y | N |
| 10 Pickle | N | Y | N | Y | Y | Y | Y | Y |
| 11 Edwards | Y | Y | N | N | Y | Y | Y | N |
| 12 Geren | N | ? | ? | Y | Y | Y | Y | N |
| 13 Sarpalius | Y | Y | Y | N | Y | Y | Y | N |
| 14 Laughlin | Y | Y | Y | N | Y | Y | Y | N |
| 15 de la Garza | Y | Y | N | N | Y | Y | Y | Y |
| 16 Coleman | Y | Y | N | Y | Y | Y | Y | Y |
| 17 Stenholm | N | Y | Y | N | N | Y | Y | N |
| 18 Washington | Y | ? | N | Y | N | Y | Y | Y |
| 19 ***Combest*** | N | Y | Y | N | Y | N | N | N |
| 20 Gonzalez | Y | Y | N | Y | Y | Y | Y | Y |
| 21 ***Smith*** | N | Y | Y | N | Y | N | N | N |
| 22 ***DeLay*** | N | Y | Y | N | N | N | N | N |
| 23 Bustamante | Y | Y | N | Y | Y | Y | Y | N |
| 24 Frost | Y | Y | N | Y | Y | Y | Y | N |
| 25 Andrews | Y | Y | N | Y | Y | Y | Y | N |
| 26 ***Armey*** | N | Y | Y | Y | Y | N | N | N |
| 27 Ortiz | Y | Y | N | Y | Y | Y | Y | Y |
| **UTAH** | | | | | | | | |
| 1 ***Hansen*** | N | Y | Y | N | Y | N | N | N |
| 2 Owens | ? | ? | N | N | N | Y | N | N |
| 3 Orton | N | Y | N | N | N | Y | N | N |
| **VERMONT** | | | | | | | | |
| AL *Sanders* | Y | ? | N | Y | N | Y | Y | Y |
| **VIRGINIA** | | | | | | | | |
| 1 ***Bateman*** | N | Y | Y | Y | Y | N | N | N |
| 2 Pickett | Y | Y | N | Y | Y | Y | Y | N |
| 3 ***Bliley*** | N | Y | Y | Y | Y | N | N | N |
| 4 Sisisky | Y | Y | N | Y | N | Y | Y | N |
| 5 Payne | Y | Y | Y | N | Y | Y | Y | N |
| 6 Olin | Y | ? | N | N | N | Y | Y | Y |
| 7 ***Allen*** | N | Y | Y | Y | Y | N | N | N |
| 8 Moran | Y | Y | N | Y | Y | ? | ? | N |
| 9 Boucher | N | Y | N | N | Y | Y | Y | N |
| 10 ***Wolf*** | Y | Y | Y | N | Y | N | N | N |
| **WASHINGTON** | | | | | | | | |
| 1 ***Miller*** | N | Y | Y | Y | N | N | N | N |
| 2 Swift | Y | Y | N | Y | N | Y | Y | Y |
| 3 Unsoeld | Y | Y | N | Y | N | Y | Y | Y |
| 4 ***Morrison*** | ? | ? | N | N | Y | N | N | N |
| 5 Foley | | | | | | | | |
| 6 Dicks | Y | Y | N | Y | Y | Y | Y | Y |
| 7 McDermott | Y | Y | N | Y | N | Y | Y | Y |
| 8 ***Chandler*** | N | Y | Y | N | Y | N | N | N |
| **WEST VIRGINIA** | | | | | | | | |
| 1 Mollohan | Y | Y | N | Y | Y | Y | Y | N |
| 2 Staggers | Y | Y | N | N | Y | ? | Y | N |
| 3 Wise | Y | Y | N | N | N | Y | Y | Y |
| 4 Rahall | Y | Y | N | N | N | Y | Y | N |
| **WISCONSIN** | | | | | | | | |
| 1 Aspin | Y | Y | N | N | Y | Y | Y | Y |
| 2 ***Klug*** | N | Y | Y | Y | Y | N | N | N |
| 3 ***Gunderson*** | Y | Y | N | N | Y | N | N | N |
| 4 Kleczka | Y | Y | ? | ? | ? | Y | Y | Y |
| 5 Moody | Y | Y | N | Y | N | Y | Y | Y |
| 6 ***Petri*** | N | Y | N | Y | Y | N | N | N |
| 7 Obey | Y | Y | N | N | Y | Y | Y | N |
| 8 ***Roth*** | N | Y | Y | Y | ? | N | N | N |
| 9 ***Sensenbrenner*** | N | Y | Y | Y | Y | N | N | N |
| **WYOMING** | | | | | | | | |
| AL ***Thomas*** | N | Y | Y | N | Y | N | N | N |

Southern states - Ala., Ark., Fla., Ga., Ky., La., Miss., N.C., Okla., S.C., Tenn., Texas, Va.
Omitted votes are quorum calls, which CQ does not include in its vote charts.

**365. HR 5334. Housing and Community Development/ Motion to Recommit.** Stearns, R-Fla., motion to recommit the bill to the Committee on Banking, Finance and Urban Affairs with instructions to report it back with a focus on the principles of the National Affordable Housing Act and additional funding for the Homeownership and Opportunity for People Everywhere (HOPE) program. Motion rejected 147-277: R 142-22; D 5-254 (ND 2-176, SD 3-78); I 0-1, Aug. 5, 1992.

**366. HR 5334. Housing and Community Development/ Passage.** Passage of the bill to authorize $28.8 billion in fiscal 1993 for housing and community development programs. Passed 369-54: R 111-52; D 257-2 (ND 176-2, SD 81-0); I 1-0, Aug. 5, 1992. A "nay" was a vote supporting the president's position.

**367. HR 4996. Overseas Private Investment Corporation Reauthorization/AID Funding.** Miller, R-Wash., amendment to reduce funding for the Office of Capital Projects in the Agency for International Development (AID) to a level of $100 million in fiscal 1992 and 1993, the level requested by the president, a reduction from the $650 million for fiscal 1992 and the $700 million for fiscal 1993 recommended in the bill. Rejected 184-230: R 122-37; D 62-192 (ND 41-134, SD 21-58); I 0-1, Aug. 5, 1992.

**368. HR 5237. Rural Electrification Administration Improvement.** De la Garza, D-Texas, motion to suspend the rules and pass the bill to improve electric and telephone service in rural areas. Motion agreed to 359-60: R 114-48; D 244-12 (ND 163-12, SD 81-0); I 1-0, Aug. 5, 1992. A two-thirds majority of those present and voting (280 in this case) was required for passage under suspension of the rules.

**369. HR 3603. Child Welfare and Nutrition Programs/ Order Previous Question.** Slaughter, D-N.Y., motion to order the previous question (thus limiting debate and the possibility of amendment) on adoption of the rule (H Res 543) to provide for House floor consideration of the bill to help abused and neglected children and lessen reliance on the foster-care system. The bill contained provisions aimed at alleviating child hunger by expanding eligibility for food stamps. Costs were to be paid by a 10 percent surtax on millionaires. Motion agreed to 247-166: R 0-160; D 246-6 (ND 170-2, SD 76-4); I 1-0, Aug. 6, 1992.

**370. HR 3603. Child Welfare and Nutrition Programs/ Rule.** Adoption of the rule (H Res 543) to provide for House floor consideration of the bill to help abused and neglected children and lessen reliance on the foster-care system. The bill contained provisions aimed at alleviating child hunger by expanding eligibility for food stamps. Costs were to be paid by a 10 percent surtax on millionaires. Adopted 220-196: R 1-159; D 218-37 (ND 161-14, SD 57-23); I 1-0, Aug. 6, 1992.

**371. HR 3603. Child Welfare and Nutrition Programs/ Motion to Recommit.** Archer, R-Texas, motion to recommit the bill to the Ways and Means Committee with instructions to report it back amended by a substitute to strike the 10 percent surtax on millionaires; eliminate the child hunger relief provisions of the bill; and replace entitlement for training and administrative expenses for foster care and adoption assistance with a capped entitlement program under which states could use the funding for any child welfare purpose. Motion rejected 191-230: R 159-3; D 32-226 (ND 10-169, SD 22-57); I 0-1, Aug. 6, 1992.

**372. HR 3603. Child Welfare and Nutrition Programs/ Passage.** Passage of the bill to help abused and neglected children and lessen reliance on the foster-care system; create a new child welfare entitlement; expand food stamp eligibility; and place a 10 percent surtax on millionaires. Passed 256-163: R 19-144; D 236-19 (ND 168-9, SD 68-10); I 1-0, Aug. 6, 1992. A "nay" was a vote supporting the president's position.

## KEY

| | |
|---|---|
| Y | Voted for (yea). |
| # | Paired for. |
| + | Announced for. |
| N | Voted against (nay). |
| X | Paired against. |
| − | Announced against. |
| P | Voted "present." |
| C | Voted "present" to avoid possible conflict of interest. |
| ? | Did not vote or otherwise make a position known. |

Democrats **Republicans**
*Independent*

| | 365 | 366 | 367 | 368 | 369 | 370 | 371 | 372 |
|---|---|---|---|---|---|---|---|---|
| **ALABAMA** | | | | | | | | |
| 1 *Callahan* | Y | Y | N | Y | N | N | Y | N |
| 2 *Dickinson* | ? | ? | ? | ? | ? | ? | ? | ? |
| 3 Browder | N | ? | Y | Y | Y | Y | N | Y |
| 4 Bevill | N | Y | N | Y | Y | Y | N | Y |
| 5 Cramer | N | Y | N | Y | Y | N | N | Y |
| 6 Erdreich | N | Y | N | Y | N | Y | Y | Y |
| 7 Harris | N | Y | N | Y | Y | N | Y | Y |
| **ALASKA** | | | | | | | | |
| AL *Young* | Y | Y | Y | Y | N | N | Y | N |
| **ARIZONA** | | | | | | | | |
| 1 *Rhodes* | Y | N | Y | N | Y | N | N | Y |
| 2 Pastor | N | Y | N | Y | Y | Y | N | Y |
| 3 *Stump* | Y | N | Y | N | N | N | Y | N |
| 4 *Kyl* | Y | N | Y | N | N | N | Y | N |
| 5 *Kolbe* | Y | Y | Y | Y | N | N | Y | N |
| **ARKANSAS** | | | | | | | | |
| 1 Alexander | N | Y | ? | Y | Y | Y | N | Y |
| 2 Thornton | N | Y | Y | Y | Y | Y | N | ? |
| 3 *Hammerschmidt* | N | N | Y | N | N | N | Y | N |
| 4 Anthony | N | Y | ? | Y | Y | Y | ? | ? |
| **CALIFORNIA** | | | | | | | | |
| 1 *Riggs* | Y | Y | Y | N | N | N | Y | N |
| 2 *Herger* | Y | Y | Y | N | N | N | Y | N |
| 3 Matsui | N | Y | N | Y | Y | Y | N | Y |
| 4 Fazio | N | Y | N | Y | Y | Y | N | Y |
| 5 Pelosi | N | Y | N | Y | Y | Y | N | Y |
| 6 Boxer | N | Y | N | Y | Y | Y | N | Y |
| 7 Miller | N | Y | N | Y | Y | Y | N | Y |
| 8 Dellums | N | Y | N | Y | Y | Y | N | Y |
| 9 Stark | N | Y | Y | Y | Y | Y | N | Y |
| 10 Edwards | N | Y | N | Y | Y | Y | N | Y |
| 11 Lantos | N | Y | N | Y | Y | Y | N | Y |
| 12 *Campbell* | Y | N | N | N | N | N | Y | N |
| 13 Mineta | N | Y | N | Y | Y | Y | N | Y |
| 14 *Doolittle* | Y | N | Y | N | N | N | Y | N |
| 15 Condit | N | Y | Y | Y | Y | N | Y | Y |
| 16 Panetta | N | Y | N | Y | Y | Y | N | Y |
| 17 Dooley | N | Y | N | Y | N | Y | N | Y |
| 18 Lehman | N | Y | N | Y | Y | Y | N | Y |
| 19 *Lagomarsino* | Y | Y | Y | N | N | N | Y | N |
| 20 *Thomas* | Y | Y | N | Y | N | N | Y | N |
| 21 *Gallegly* | Y | Y | Y | N | N | N | Y | N |
| 22 *Moorhead* | Y | N | Y | N | N | N | Y | N |
| 23 Beilenson | N | Y | N | Y | Y | Y | N | Y |
| 24 Waxman | N | Y | N | Y | Y | ? | N | Y |
| 25 Roybal | N | Y | N | Y | Y | Y | N | Y |
| 26 Berman | N | Y | N | Y | Y | Y | N | Y |
| 27 Levine | N | Y | Y | Y | ? | Y | N | Y |
| 28 Dixon | N | Y | N | Y | Y | Y | N | Y |
| 29 Waters | N | Y | N | Y | Y | Y | N | Y |
| 30 Martinez | N | Y | N | Y | Y | Y | N | Y |
| 31 Dymally | N | Y | N | Y | Y | Y | N | Y |
| 32 Anderson | N | Y | N | Y | Y | Y | N | Y |
| 33 *Dreier* | Y | N | Y | N | N | N | Y | N |
| 34 Torres | N | Y | N | Y | Y | Y | N | Y |
| 35 *Lewis* | Y | N | Y | N | N | N | Y | N |
| 36 Brown | N | Y | N | Y | Y | Y | N | Y |
| 37 *McCandless* | Y | Y | Y | N | N | N | Y | N |
| 38 *Dornan* | Y | N | Y | N | N | N | Y | N |
| 39 *Dannemeyer* | Y | N | Y | N | N | N | Y | N |
| 40 *Cox* | Y | N | Y | N | N | N | ? | N |
| 41 *Lowery* | Y | Y | Y | Y | N | N | Y | N |

| | 365 | 366 | 367 | 368 | 369 | 370 | 371 | 372 |
|---|---|---|---|---|---|---|---|---|
| 42 *Rohrabacher* | Y | N | Y | N | N | N | Y | N |
| 43 *Packard* | Y | N | Y | N | N | N | Y | N |
| 44 *Cunningham* | Y | N | Y | N | N | N | Y | N |
| 45 *Hunter* | Y | N | Y | N | Y | N | N | N |
| **COLORADO** | | | | | | | | |
| 1 Schroeder | N | Y | Y | Y | Y | Y | N | Y |
| 2 Skaggs | N | Y | Y | Y | Y | Y | N | Y |
| 3 Campbell | N | Y | N | Y | Y | Y | N | Y |
| 4 *Allard* | Y | N | Y | N | N | N | Y | N |
| 5 *Hefley* | Y | Y | Y | N | N | N | Y | N |
| 6 *Schaefer* | Y | N | Y | N | N | N | Y | N |
| **CONNECTICUT** | | | | | | | | |
| 1 Kennelly | N | Y | N | N | Y | Y | N | Y |
| 2 Gejdenson | N | Y | N | Y | Y | Y | N | Y |
| 3 DeLauro | N | Y | N | Y | Y | Y | N | Y |
| 4 *Shays* | Y | Y | N | N | N | N | N | Y |
| 5 *Franks* | Y | Y | Y | N | N | N | Y | N |
| 6 *Johnson* | Y | N | N | Y | N | N | Y | N |
| **DELAWARE** | | | | | | | | |
| AL Carper | N | Y | Y | Y | Y | N | Y | Y |
| **FLORIDA** | | | | | | | | |
| 1 Hutto | N | Y | N | Y | N | Y | N | Y |
| 2 Peterson | N | Y | Y | Y | Y | N | Y | Y |
| 3 Bennett | N | Y | Y | Y | Y | Y | N | Y |
| 4 *James* | Y | Y | Y | N | N | N | Y | N |
| 5 *McCollum* | Y | N | Y | N | N | N | Y | N |
| 6 *Stearns* | Y | N | N | N | N | N | Y | N |
| 7 Gibbons | N | Y | N | Y | Y | Y | N | Y |
| 8 *Young* | N | Y | N | Y | N | N | Y | N |
| 9 *Bilirakis* | N | Y | Y | Y | N | N | Y | N |
| 10 *Ireland* | Y | N | ? | N | N | N | Y | N |
| 11 Bacchus | N | Y | N | Y | Y | N | N | Y |
| 12 *Lewis* | Y | Y | Y | N | N | N | Y | N |
| 13 *Goss* | Y | N | Y | N | N | N | Y | N |
| 14 Johnston | N | Y | N | Y | Y | Y | N | Y |
| 15 *Shaw* | Y | Y | N | N | N | N | Y | N |
| 16 Smith | N | Y | N | Y | Y | Y | N | Y |
| 17 Lehman | N | Y | N | Y | Y | Y | N | Y |
| 18 *Ros−Lehtinen* | N | Y | N | Y | Y | Y | N | Y |
| 19 Fascell | N | Y | N | ? | Y | Y | N | Y |
| **GEORGIA** | | | | | | | | |
| 1 Thomas | N | Y | Y | Y | Y | N | N | Y |
| 2 Hatcher | ? | ? | ? | ? | ? | ? | ? | ? |
| 3 Ray | Y | Y | Y | Y | N | N | ? | N |
| 4 Jones | ? | Y | N | Y | Y | Y | N | Y |
| 5 Lewis | N | Y | N | Y | Y | Y | N | Y |
| 6 *Gingrich* | Y | Y | Y | N | N | N | Y | N |
| 7 Darden | N | Y | N | Y | Y | Y | N | Y |
| 8 Rowland | N | Y | N | Y | N | Y | N | Y |
| 9 Jenkins | N | Y | N | Y | Y | Y | N | Y |
| 10 Barnard | ? | ? | ? | ? | ? | ? | ? | ? |
| **HAWAII** | | | | | | | | |
| 1 Abercrombie | N | Y | N | Y | Y | Y | N | Y |
| 2 Mink | N | Y | N | Y | Y | Y | N | Y |
| **IDAHO** | | | | | | | | |
| 1 LaRocco | N | Y | N | Y | Y | Y | N | Y |
| 2 Stallings | N | Y | Y | Y | Y | N | N | Y |
| **ILLINOIS** | | | | | | | | |
| 1 Hayes | N | Y | N | Y | Y | Y | N | Y |
| 2 Savage | N | Y | N | Y | Y | Y | N | Y |
| 3 Russo | N | Y | N | Y | Y | Y | N | Y |
| 4 Sangmeister | N | Y | N | Y | Y | Y | N | Y |
| 5 Lipinski | Y | N | N | Y | Y | Y | N | Y |
| 6 *Hyde* | N | Y | Y | N | N | N | Y | N |
| 7 Collins | N | Y | N | Y | Y | Y | N | Y |
| 8 Rostenkowski | N | Y | Y | Y | Y | Y | N | Y |
| 9 Yates | N | Y | N | Y | Y | Y | N | Y |
| 10 *Porter* | Y | Y | Y | N | N | N | Y | N |
| 11 Annunzio | N | Y | N | Y | Y | Y | N | Y |
| 12 *Crane* | Y | N | N | N | N | N | Y | N |
| 13 *Fawell* | Y | Y | Y | N | N | N | Y | N |
| 14 *Hastert* | Y | Y | Y | N | N | N | Y | N |
| 15 *Ewing* | Y | Y | Y | N | N | N | Y | N |
| 16 Cox | N | Y | Y | N | N | N | Y | N |
| 17 Evans | N | Y | N | Y | Y | Y | N | Y |
| 18 *Michel* | Y | Y | N | N | N | N | Y | N |
| 19 Bruce | N | Y | N | Y | Y | Y | N | Y |
| 20 Durbin | N | Y | Y | Y | Y | Y | N | Y |
| 21 Costello | N | Y | N | Y | Y | Y | N | Y |
| 22 Poshard | N | Y | Y | Y | N | Y | N | Y |
| **INDIANA** | | | | | | | | |
| 1 Visclosky | N | Y | Y | Y | Y | Y | N | Y |
| 2 Sharp | N | Y | N | Y | Y | Y | N | Y |
| 3 Roemer | N | Y | N | Y | Y | Y | N | ? |

ND  Northern Democrats    SD  Southern Democrats

| | 365 | 366 | 367 | 368 | 369 | 370 | 371 | 372 |
|---|---|---|---|---|---|---|---|---|
| 4 Long | N | Y | N | Y | Y | Y | N | N |
| 5 Jontz | N | Y | Y | Y | Y | Y | N | Y |
| 6 ***Burton*** | Y | N | Y | Y | N | N | Y | N |
| 7 ***Myers*** | N | Y | Y | Y | N | N | Y | N |
| 8 McCloskey | N | Y | N | Y | Y | Y | N | Y |
| 9 Hamilton | N | Y | N | Y | Y | Y | N | Y |
| 10 Jacobs | N | Y | Y | N | N | Y | N | Y |
| **IOWA** | | | | | | | | |
| 1 ***Leach*** | N | Y | Y | Y | N | N | Y | Y |
| 2 ***Nussle*** | Y | Y | Y | Y | ? | N | Y | N |
| 3 Nagle | N | Y | N | Y | Y | Y | N | Y |
| 4 Smith | N | Y | N | Y | Y | Y | N | Y |
| 5 ***Lightfoot*** | Y | Y | N | Y | N | N | Y | N |
| 6 ***Grandy*** | Y | Y | N | Y | N | N | Y | N |
| **KANSAS** | | | | | | | | |
| 1 ***Roberts*** | Y | N | Y | Y | N | N | Y | N |
| 2 Slattery | N | Y | Y | Y | Y | Y | N | Y |
| 3 ***Meyers*** | Y | Y | N | N | N | N | Y | N |
| 4 Glickman | N | Y | Y | Y | Y | Y | N | Y |
| 5 ***Nichols*** | Y | N | Y | Y | N | N | Y | N |
| **KENTUCKY** | | | | | | | | |
| 1 Hubbard | N | Y | Y | Y | Y | N | Y | Y |
| 2 Natcher | N | Y | N | Y | Y | Y | N | Y |
| 3 Mazzoli | N | Y | Y | Y | Y | Y | N | Y |
| 4 ***Bunning*** | Y | Y | N | Y | N | N | Y | N |
| 5 ***Rogers*** | Y | Y | N | Y | N | N | Y | Y |
| 6 ***Hopkins*** | Y | N | Y | Y | N | N | Y | N |
| 7 Perkins | N | Y | N | Y | Y | Y | N | Y |
| **LOUISIANA** | | | | | | | | |
| 1 ***Livingston*** | Y | Y | N | Y | N | N | Y | N |
| 2 Jefferson | N | Y | N | Y | Y | Y | N | Y |
| 3 Tauzin | N | Y | N | Y | N | N | Y | Y |
| 4 ***McCrery*** | Y | Y | Y | Y | ? | ? | Y | N |
| 5 Huckaby | N | Y | Y | Y | Y | Y | N | N |
| 6 ***Baker*** | Y | Y | N | Y | N | N | Y | N |
| 7 Hayes | N | Y | Y | Y | N | N | Y | Y |
| 8 ***Holloway*** | Y | Y | Y | Y | N | N | Y | N |
| **MAINE** | | | | | | | | |
| 1 Andrews | N | Y | N | Y | ? | Y | N | Y |
| 2 ***Snowe*** | N | Y | Y | Y | N | N | Y | N |
| **MARYLAND** | | | | | | | | |
| 1 ***Gilchrest*** | Y | Y | Y | Y | N | N | Y | N |
| 2 ***Bentley*** | Y | Y | Y | N | N | N | N | Y |
| 3 Cardin | N | Y | N | N | Y | Y | N | Y |
| 4 McMillen | N | Y | N | Y | + | Y | N | Y |
| 5 Hoyer | N | Y | N | Y | Y | Y | N | Y |
| 6 Byron | N | Y | N | Y | Y | N | Y | Y |
| 7 Mfume | N | Y | N | Y | Y | Y | N | Y |
| 8 ***Morella*** | N | Y | N | Y | N | N | Y | Y |
| **MASSACHUSETTS** | | | | | | | | |
| 1 Olver | N | Y | N | Y | Y | Y | N | Y |
| 2 Neal | N | Y | N | Y | Y | Y | N | Y |
| 3 Early | N | Y | Y | Y | Y | Y | N | Y |
| 4 Frank | N | Y | N | N | Y | Y | N | Y |
| 5 Atkins | N | Y | Y | N | Y | Y | N | Y |
| 6 Mavroules | N | Y | N | Y | Y | Y | N | Y |
| 7 Markey | N | Y | N | Y | Y | Y | N | Y |
| 8 Kennedy | N | Y | N | Y | Y | Y | N | Y |
| 9 Moakley | N | Y | N | Y | Y | Y | N | Y |
| 10 Studds | N | Y | Y | Y | Y | Y | N | Y |
| 11 Donnelly | N | Y | Y | Y | Y | Y | N | Y |
| **MICHIGAN** | | | | | | | | |
| 1 Conyers | ? | ? | ? | ? | Y | Y | N | Y |
| 2 ***Pursell*** | Y | N | Y | N | N | N | Y | N |
| 3 Wolpe | N | Y | N | Y | Y | Y | N | Y |
| 4 ***Upton*** | Y | Y | Y | Y | N | N | Y | Y |
| 5 ***Henry*** | Y | N | N | N | N | N | Y | N |
| 6 Carr | N | Y | Y | Y | Y | Y | N | Y |
| 7 Kildee | N | Y | N | Y | Y | Y | N | Y |
| 8 Traxler | ? | ? | ? | ? | ? | ? | ? | ? |
| 9 ***Vander Jagt*** | Y | Y | ? | Y | N | N | Y | N |
| 10 ***Camp*** | Y | Y | Y | Y | N | N | Y | N |
| 11 ***Davis*** | Y | Y | Y | Y | ? | ? | Y | N |
| 12 Bonior | N | Y | N | Y | Y | Y | N | Y |
| 13 Collins | N | Y | N | Y | Y | Y | N | Y |
| 14 Hertel | N | Y | N | ? | Y | Y | N | Y |
| 15 Ford | N | Y | N | Y | Y | Y | N | + |
| 16 Dingell | N | Y | N | Y | Y | Y | N | Y |
| 17 Levin | N | Y | N | Y | Y | Y | N | Y |
| 18 ***Broomfield*** | Y | Y | ? | ? | N | N | Y | N |
| **MINNESOTA** | | | | | | | | |
| 1 Penny | Y | N | Y | Y | Y | Y | N | Y |
| 2 ***Weber*** | Y | Y | Y | Y | N | N | Y | N |
| 3 ***Ramstad*** | Y | Y | Y | Y | N | N | Y | N |
| 4 Vento | N | Y | Y | Y | Y | Y | N | Y |

| | 365 | 366 | 367 | 368 | 369 | 370 | 371 | 372 |
|---|---|---|---|---|---|---|---|---|
| 5 Sabo | N | Y | N | ? | Y | Y | N | Y |
| 6 Sikorski | N | Y | Y | Y | Y | Y | N | Y |
| 7 Peterson | N | Y | Y | Y | Y | Y | N | Y |
| 8 Oberstar | N | Y | N | Y | Y | Y | N | Y |
| **MISSISSIPPI** | | | | | | | | |
| 1 Whitten | N | Y | N | Y | Y | Y | N | Y |
| 2 Espy | N | Y | N | Y | Y | Y | N | Y |
| 3 Montgomery | N | Y | N | Y | Y | Y | Y | N |
| 4 Parker | N | Y | Y | Y | Y | Y | Y | Y |
| 5 Taylor | N | Y | N | Y | Y | N | Y | N |
| **MISSOURI** | | | | | | | | |
| 1 Clay | N | Y | N | Y | Y | Y | N | Y |
| 2 Horn | N | Y | Y | Y | Y | Y | N | Y |
| 3 Gephardt | N | Y | N | Y | Y | Y | N | Y |
| 4 Skelton | N | Y | N | Y | Y | N | Y | Y |
| 5 Wheat | N | Y | N | Y | Y | Y | N | Y |
| 6 ***Coleman*** | Y | Y | N | Y | N | N | Y | N |
| 7 ***Hancock*** | Y | N | Y | Y | N | N | Y | N |
| 8 ***Emerson*** | Y | Y | N | Y | N | N | Y | N |
| 9 Volkmer | ? | ? | ? | ? | Y | Y | N | Y |
| **MONTANA** | | | | | | | | |
| 1 Williams | N | Y | Y | Y | Y | Y | N | Y |
| 2 ***Marlenee*** | Y | N | Y | Y | N | N | Y | N |
| **NEBRASKA** | | | | | | | | |
| 1 ***Bereuter*** | N | Y | N | Y | N | N | Y | Y |
| 2 Hoagland | N | Y | Y | Y | Y | Y | N | Y |
| 3 ***Barrett*** | N | Y | Y | Y | N | N | Y | N |
| **NEVADA** | | | | | | | | |
| 1 Bilbray | N | Y | N | Y | Y | Y | N | Y |
| 2 ***Vucanovich*** | Y | Y | Y | Y | N | N | Y | N |
| **NEW HAMPSHIRE** | | | | | | | | |
| 1 ***Zeliff*** | Y | N | Y | Y | N | N | Y | N |
| 2 Swett | N | Y | N | Y | Y | Y | N | Y |
| **NEW JERSEY** | | | | | | | | |
| 1 Andrews | N | Y | N | Y | ? | ? | Y | N |
| 2 Hughes | N | Y | Y | Y | Y | Y | N | Y |
| 3 Pallone | N | Y | N | Y | Y | Y | Y | N |
| 4 ***Smith*** | Y | Y | N | Y | N | N | Y | N |
| 5 ***Roukema*** | N | Y | N | Y | N | N | N | Y |
| 6 Dwyer | N | Y | N | Y | Y | Y | N | Y |
| 7 ***Rinaldo*** | Y | Y | Y | N | N | N | Y | Y |
| 8 Roe | N | Y | ? | ? | ? | ? | N | Y |
| 9 Torricelli | ? | ? | N | Y | Y | Y | N | Y |
| 10 Payne | N | Y | N | Y | Y | Y | N | Y |
| 11 ***Gallo*** | Y | Y | N | Y | N | N | Y | N |
| 12 ***Zimmer*** | Y | N | Y | N | N | N | Y | N |
| 13 ***Saxton*** | Y | Y | Y | N | N | N | Y | N |
| 14 Guarini | N | Y | Y | Y | Y | Y | N | Y |
| **NEW MEXICO** | | | | | | | | |
| 1 ***Schiff*** | Y | Y | Y | Y | N | N | Y | N |
| 2 ***Skeen*** | N | Y | Y | Y | N | N | Y | N |
| 3 Richardson | N | Y | N | Y | Y | Y | N | Y |
| **NEW YORK** | | | | | | | | |
| 1 Hochbrueckner | N | Y | N | Y | Y | Y | N | Y |
| 2 Downey | N | Y | N | Y | Y | Y | N | Y |
| 3 Mrazek | N | Y | N | Y | Y | Y | N | Y |
| 4 ***Lent*** | Y | Y | Y | Y | N | N | Y | N |
| 5 ***McGrath*** | N | Y | N | Y | N | N | Y | N |
| 6 Flake | N | Y | N | Y | Y | Y | N | Y |
| 7 Ackerman | N | Y | N | Y | Y | Y | N | Y |
| 8 Scheuer | N | Y | Y | N | Y | Y | N | Y |
| 9 Manton | N | Y | N | Y | Y | Y | N | Y |
| 10 Schumer | N | Y | N | N | Y | Y | N | Y |
| 11 Towns | N | Y | N | Y | ? | ? | ? | ? |
| 12 Owens | N | Y | N | Y | Y | Y | N | Y |
| 13 Solarz | N | Y | N | Y | Y | Y | N | Y |
| 14 ***Molinari*** | Y | Y | Y | N | N | N | Y | N |
| 15 ***Green*** | N | Y | Y | Y | N | N | Y | Y |
| 16 Rangel | N | Y | N | Y | Y | Y | N | Y |
| 17 Weiss | N | Y | N | Y | Y | Y | N | Y |
| 18 Serrano | N | Y | ? | Y | Y | Y | N | Y |
| 19 Engel | N | Y | N | Y | Y | Y | N | Y |
| 20 Lowey | N | Y | N | Y | Y | Y | N | Y |
| 21 ***Fish*** | N | ? | Y | Y | N | N | Y | Y |
| 22 ***Gilman*** | N | Y | Y | Y | N | N | Y | Y |
| 23 McNulty | N | Y | N | Y | Y | Y | N | Y |
| 24 ***Solomon*** | Y | N | Y | N | N | N | Y | N |
| 25 ***Boehlert*** | Y | Y | Y | Y | N | Y | Y | N |
| 26 ***Martin*** | Y | Y | Y | Y | N | N | Y | N |
| 27 ***Walsh*** | N | Y | N | N | N | N | Y | N |
| 28 McHugh | N | Y | Y | Y | Y | Y | N | Y |
| 29 ***Horton*** | Y | Y | Y | Y | N | N | Y | Y |
| 30 Slaughter | N | Y | Y | N | Y | Y | N | Y |
| 31 ***Paxon*** | Y | Y | Y | Y | N | N | Y | N |

| | 365 | 366 | 367 | 368 | 369 | 370 | 371 | 372 |
|---|---|---|---|---|---|---|---|---|
| 32 LaFalce | N | Y | Y | Y | Y | Y | N | Y |
| 33 Nowak | N | Y | N | N | Y | Y | N | Y |
| 34 ***Houghton*** | Y | Y | N | Y | N | N | Y | N |
| **NORTH CAROLINA** | | | | | | | | |
| 1 Jones | N | Y | Y | Y | Y | Y | N | Y |
| 2 Valentine | N | Y | Y | Y | Y | N | Y | N |
| 3 Lancaster | N | Y | Y | Y | Y | N | Y | Y |
| 4 Price | N | Y | N | Y | Y | Y | N | Y |
| 5 Neal | N | Y | N | Y | Y | Y | N | Y |
| 6 ***Coble*** | Y | Y | Y | Y | N | N | Y | N |
| 7 Rose | N | Y | N | Y | Y | Y | N | Y |
| 8 Hefner | N | Y | N | Y | Y | Y | N | Y |
| 9 ***McMillan*** | Y | Y | N | Y | N | N | Y | N |
| 10 ***Ballenger*** | Y | Y | Y | Y | N | N | Y | N |
| 11 ***Taylor*** | N | N | Y | Y | N | N | Y | N |
| **NORTH DAKOTA** | | | | | | | | |
| AL Dorgan | N | Y | Y | Y | Y | Y | N | Y |
| **OHIO** | | | | | | | | |
| 1 Luken | N | Y | Y | Y | ? | ? | ? | ? |
| 2 ***Gradison*** | Y | Y | Y | N | N | N | Y | N |
| 3 Hall | N | Y | N | Y | ? | ? | N | Y |
| 4 ***Oxley*** | Y | Y | Y | Y | N | N | Y | N |
| 5 ***Gillmor*** | Y | Y | Y | Y | N | N | Y | N |
| 6 ***McEwen*** | Y | N | Y | Y | ? | ? | ? | ? |
| 7 ***Hobson*** | Y | Y | Y | Y | N | N | Y | Y |
| 8 ***Boehner*** | Y | Y | Y | Y | N | N | Y | N |
| 9 Kaptur | N | Y | Y | Y | Y | Y | N | Y |
| 10 ***Miller*** | Y | N | Y | N | N | N | Y | N |
| 11 Eckart | N | Y | N | Y | Y | Y | N | Y |
| 12 ***Kasich*** | Y | Y | Y | Y | N | N | Y | N |
| 13 Pease | N | Y | N | Y | Y | Y | N | Y |
| 14 Sawyer | N | Y | N | Y | Y | Y | N | Y |
| 15 ***Wylie*** | Y | Y | Y | N | N | N | Y | N |
| 16 ***Regula*** | Y | Y | N | Y | N | N | Y | Y |
| 17 Traficant | N | Y | N | Y | Y | Y | N | Y |
| 18 Applegate | N | Y | N | Y | Y | Y | N | Y |
| 19 Feighan | N | Y | N | Y | Y | Y | N | Y |
| 20 Oakar | N | Y | N | Y | Y | Y | N | Y |
| 21 Stokes | N | Y | N | Y | Y | Y | N | Y |
| **OKLAHOMA** | | | | | | | | |
| 1 ***Inhofe*** | Y | Y | Y | N | N | N | Y | N |
| 2 Synar | N | Y | N | Y | Y | Y | N | Y |
| 3 Brewster | N | Y | N | Y | Y | Y | N | Y |
| 4 McCurdy | N | Y | N | Y | Y | Y | N | Y |
| 5 ***Edwards*** | Y | Y | ? | ? | N | N | Y | N |
| 6 English | N | Y | N | Y | Y | N | Y | N |
| **OREGON** | | | | | | | | |
| 1 AuCoin | N | Y | Y | Y | Y | Y | N | Y |
| 2 ***Smith*** | Y | N | Y | Y | N | N | Y | N |
| 3 Wyden | N | Y | N | Y | Y | Y | N | Y |
| 4 DeFazio | N | Y | N | Y | Y | Y | N | Y |
| 5 Kopetski | N | Y | N | Y | Y | Y | N | Y |
| **PENNSYLVANIA** | | | | | | | | |
| 1 Foglietta | N | Y | N | Y | Y | Y | N | Y |
| 2 Blackwell | N | Y | N | Y | Y | Y | N | Y |
| 3 Borski | N | Y | N | Y | Y | Y | N | Y |
| 4 Kolter | N | Y | ? | ? | Y | Y | N | Y |
| 5 ***Schulze*** | ? | ? | ? | ? | ? | ? | ? | ? |
| 6 Yatron | N | Y | N | Y | Y | Y | N | N |
| 7 ***Weldon*** | Y | Y | Y | Y | N | N | Y | N |
| 8 Kostmayer | N | Y | N | Y | Y | Y | N | Y |
| 9 ***Shuster*** | Y | N | Y | Y | N | N | Y | N |
| 10 ***McDade*** | Y | Y | Y | Y | N | N | Y | Y |
| 11 Kanjorski | N | Y | Y | Y | Y | N | N | N |
| 12 Murtha | N | Y | N | Y | Y | Y | N | Y |
| 13 ***Coughlin*** | Y | Y | Y | N | N | N | Y | N |
| 14 Coyne | N | Y | N | Y | Y | Y | N | Y |
| 15 ***Ritter*** | Y | Y | Y | N | N | N | Y | N |
| 16 ***Walker*** | Y | N | Y | N | N | N | Y | N |
| 17 ***Gekas*** | Y | Y | Y | Y | N | N | Y | N |
| 18 ***Santorum*** | Y | Y | Y | N | N | ? | Y | N |
| 19 ***Goodling*** | Y | Y | N | Y | N | N | Y | N |
| 20 Gaydos | N | Y | ? | Y | ? | N | N | N |
| 21 ***Ridge*** | N | Y | Y | Y | N | N | Y | N |
| 22 Murphy | N | Y | N | N | N | N | N | Y |
| 23 ***Clinger*** | Y | Y | Y | Y | N | N | Y | N |
| **RHODE ISLAND** | | | | | | | | |
| 1 ***Machtley*** | Y | Y | Y | Y | N | N | Y | N |
| 2 Reed | N | Y | N | N | Y | Y | N | Y |
| **SOUTH CAROLINA** | | | | | | | | |
| 1 ***Ravenel*** | Y | Y | Y | Y | N | N | Y | N |
| 2 ***Spence*** | Y | Y | Y | Y | N | N | Y | N |
| 3 Derrick | N | Y | N | Y | Y | Y | N | Y |
| 4 Patterson | N | Y | Y | Y | Y | N | Y | N |
| 5 Spratt | N | Y | N | Y | Y | Y | N | Y |
| 6 Tallon | N | Y | N | Y | Y | Y | N | Y |

| | 365 | 366 | 367 | 368 | 369 | 370 | 371 | 372 |
|---|---|---|---|---|---|---|---|---|
| **SOUTH DAKOTA** | | | | | | | | |
| AL Johnson | N | Y | Y | Y | Y | Y | N | Y |
| **TENNESSEE** | | | | | | | | |
| 1 ***Quillen*** | Y | Y | N | Y | N | N | Y | N |
| 2 ***Duncan*** | N | N | N | N | N | N | Y | N |
| 3 Lloyd | N | Y | ? | Y | Y | Y | Y | Y |
| 4 Cooper | N | Y | N | Y | Y | Y | N | Y |
| 5 Clement | N | Y | N | Y | Y | Y | ? | ? |
| 6 Gordon | N | Y | N | Y | Y | Y | N | ? |
| 7 ***Sundquist*** | Y | Y | N | Y | N | N | Y | N |
| 8 Tanner | N | Y | Y | Y | Y | Y | N | Y |
| 9 Ford | ? | ? | ? | ? | ? | ? | ? | ? |
| **TEXAS** | | | | | | | | |
| 1 Chapman | N | Y | N | Y | ? | ? | N | Y |
| 2 Wilson | N | Y | N | Y | Y | Y | N | Y |
| 3 ***Johnson*** | Y | Y | Y | N | N | N | Y | N |
| 4 Hall | Y | Y | Y | Y | Y | N | Y | Y |
| 5 Bryant | N | Y | N | Y | Y | Y | N | Y |
| 6 ***Barton*** | Y | N | Y | Y | N | N | Y | N |
| 7 ***Archer*** | Y | N | Y | N | N | N | Y | N |
| 8 ***Fields*** | Y | N | Y | Y | N | N | Y | N |
| 9 Brooks | N | Y | N | Y | Y | Y | N | Y |
| 10 Pickle | N | Y | Y | Y | Y | Y | N | Y |
| 11 Edwards | N | Y | N | Y | Y | Y | N | Y |
| 12 Geren | N | Y | Y | Y | Y | N | Y | N |
| 13 Sarpalius | N | Y | Y | Y | Y | Y | Y | Y |
| 14 Laughlin | N | Y | N | Y | Y | N | N | Y |
| 15 de la Garza | N | Y | N | Y | Y | Y | N | Y |
| 16 Coleman | N | Y | N | Y | Y | Y | N | Y |
| 17 Stenholm | N | Y | Y | Y | Y | N | Y | Y |
| 18 Washington | N | Y | N | Y | ? | ? | N | Y |
| 19 ***Combest*** | Y | Y | Y | Y | N | N | Y | N |
| 20 Gonzalez | N | Y | N | Y | Y | Y | N | Y |
| 21 ***Smith*** | Y | Y | Y | Y | N | N | Y | N |
| 22 ***DeLay*** | Y | N | Y | N | N | N | Y | N |
| 23 Bustamante | N | Y | N | Y | Y | Y | N | Y |
| 24 Frost | N | Y | N | Y | Y | Y | N | Y |
| 25 Andrews | N | Y | N | Y | Y | Y | N | Y |
| 26 ***Armey*** | Y | N | Y | N | N | N | Y | N |
| 27 Ortiz | N | Y | N | Y | Y | Y | N | Y |
| **UTAH** | | | | | | | | |
| 1 ***Hansen*** | Y | N | Y | Y | N | N | Y | N |
| 2 Owens | N | Y | N | Y | Y | Y | N | Y |
| 3 Orton | N | Y | N | Y | Y | N | Y | N |
| **VERMONT** | | | | | | | | |
| AL *Sanders* | N | Y | N | Y | Y | Y | N | Y |
| **VIRGINIA** | | | | | | | | |
| 1 ***Bateman*** | Y | Y | Y | Y | N | N | Y | N |
| 2 Pickett | N | Y | N | Y | Y | Y | Y | N |
| 3 ***Bliley*** | Y | Y | Y | Y | N | N | Y | N |
| 4 Sisisky | N | Y | N | Y | Y | N | Y | Y |
| 5 Payne | N | Y | N | Y | Y | N | N | Y |
| 6 Olin | N | Y | N | Y | Y | Y | N | Y |
| 7 ***Allen*** | Y | N | Y | Y | N | N | Y | N |
| 8 Moran | N | Y | N | Y | Y | Y | N | Y |
| 9 Boucher | N | Y | N | Y | Y | Y | N | Y |
| 10 ***Wolf*** | Y | Y | N | Y | N | N | Y | N |
| **WASHINGTON** | | | | | | | | |
| 1 ***Miller*** | Y | N | Y | N | N | N | Y | N |
| 2 Swift | N | Y | N | Y | Y | Y | N | Y |
| 3 Unsoeld | N | Y | N | Y | Y | Y | N | Y |
| 4 ***Morrison*** | N | Y | ? | Y | N | N | Y | Y |
| 5 Foley | | | | | | | | |
| 6 Dicks | N | Y | Y | Y | Y | Y | N | Y |
| 7 McDermott | N | Y | Y | Y | Y | Y | N | Y |
| 8 ***Chandler*** | Y | Y | Y | Y | N | N | Y | N |
| **WEST VIRGINIA** | | | | | | | | |
| 1 Mollohan | N | Y | N | Y | Y | Y | N | Y |
| 2 Staggers | N | Y | N | Y | Y | Y | N | Y |
| 3 Wise | N | Y | N | Y | Y | Y | N | Y |
| 4 Rahall | N | Y | N | Y | Y | Y | N | Y |
| **WISCONSIN** | | | | | | | | |
| 1 Aspin | N | Y | N | Y | Y | Y | N | Y |
| 2 ***Klug*** | Y | Y | Y | Y | N | N | Y | N |
| 3 ***Gunderson*** | Y | Y | Y | Y | N | N | Y | N |
| 4 Kleczka | N | Y | N | Y | Y | Y | N | Y |
| 5 Moody | N | Y | N | Y | Y | Y | N | Y |
| 6 ***Petri*** | Y | N | Y | Y | N | N | Y | N |
| 7 Obey | N | Y | Y | Y | Y | Y | N | Y |
| 8 ***Roth*** | Y | N | N | Y | N | N | Y | N |
| 9 ***Sensenbrenner*** | Y | N | Y | N | N | N | Y | N |
| **WYOMING** | | | | | | | | |
| AL ***Thomas*** | N | Y | Y | Y | N | N | Y | N |

Southern states - Ala., Ark., Fla., Ga., Ky., La., Miss., N.C., Okla., S.C., Tenn., Texas, Va.
Omitted votes are quorum calls, which CQ does not include in its vote charts.

**374. HR 4547. Russian Aid.** Passage of the bill to provide aid to the former republics of the Soviet Union. The bill also increased the U.S. contribution to the International Monetary Fund by $12.3 billion and included numerous other measures to boost aid to the former republics. Passed 255-164: R 94-68; D 161-95 (ND 115-63, SD 46-32); I 0-1, Aug. 6, 1992. A "yea" was a vote in support of the president's position.

**375. S 323. Family Planning Amendments/Conference Report.** Adoption of the conference report to reauthorize Title X of the Public Health Service Act for five years through fiscal 1997. The bill overturned the administration's "gag rule" and thus allowed abortion counseling at federally funded family planning clinics. Adopted 251-144: R 48-102; D 202-42 (ND 147-22, SD 55-20); I 1-0, Aug. 6, 1992. A "nay" was a vote in support of the president's position.

**376. H Con Res 246. Free Trade Negotiations.** Adoption of the concurrent resolution to state that Congress would not approve a trade agreement, including one implementing ongoing multinational negotiations under the General Agreement on Tariffs and Trade or a North American Free Trade Area, that jeopardized U.S. health, safety, labor or environmental laws. Adopted 362-0: R 138-0; D 223-0 (ND 153-0, SD 70-0); I 1-0, Aug. 6, 1992.

**377. Procedural Motion.** Approval of the House Journal of Monday, Aug. 10. Approved 247-116: R 38-112; D 209-4 (ND 136-4, SD 73-0); I 0-0, Aug. 11, 1992.

**378. HR 3590. Private Bill for the Relief of Lloyd B. Gamble.** Approved 377-0: R 151-0; D 226-0 (ND 152-0, SD 74-0); I 0-0, Aug. 11, 1992.

**379. HR 5487. Fiscal 1993 Agriculture Appropriations/ Conference Report.** Adoption of the conference report on the bill to provide $60.5 billion in new budget authority for agriculture, rural development and related agencies for fiscal 1993. The conference report provided $38.4 billion for domestic food and nutrition programs, including $28.1 billion for the food stamps program and $2.9 billion for the Women, Infants and Children program; included $39 million for a new alcohol fuels credit guarantee program; and deleted funding for the Wetlands Reserve Program. Adopted 299-100: R 81-75; D 217-25 (ND 140-24, SD 77-1); I 1-0, Aug. 11, 1992.

**380. HR 5487. Fiscal 1993 Agriculture Appropriations/ Disadvantaged Farmers.** McHugh, D-N.Y., motion that the House recede from its disagreement and concur in the Senate amendment providing $1 million for outreach and assistance to socially disadvantaged farmers. Motion agreed to 249-144: R 28-124; D 220-20 (ND 154-9, SD 66-11); I 1-0, Aug. 11, 1992.

**381. HR 5021. New River Study.** Vento, D-Minn., motion to suspend the rules and pass the bill to include a segment of the New River in West Virginia and Virginia among the rivers chosen to be studied for possible inclusion in the National Wild and Scenic Rivers System. Motion agreed to 359-41: R 115-40; D 243-1 (ND 166-1, SD 77-0); I 1-0, Aug. 11, 1992. A two-thirds majority of those present and voting (267 in this case) was required for passage under suspension of the rules.

## KEY

| | |
|---|---|
| Y | Voted for (yea). |
| # | Paired for. |
| + | Announced for. |
| N | Voted against (nay). |
| X | Paired against. |
| − | Announced against. |
| P | Voted "present." |
| C | Voted "present" to avoid possible conflict of interest. |
| ? | Did not vote or otherwise make a position known. |

Democrats **Republicans**
*Independent*

| | 374 | 375 | 376 | 377 | 378 | 379 | 380 | 381 |
|---|---|---|---|---|---|---|---|---|
| **ALABAMA** | | | | | | | | |
| 1 *Callahan* | N | N | Y | Y | Y | Y | N | Y |
| 2 *Dickinson* | ? | ? | ? | ? | ? | ? | ? | ? |
| 3 Browder | Y | Y | Y | Y | Y | Y | Y | Y |
| 4 Bevill | ? | ? | Y | Y | Y | Y | Y | Y |
| 5 Cramer | Y | Y | Y | Y | Y | Y | Y | Y |
| 6 Erdreich | N | Y | Y | Y | Y | Y | N | Y |
| 7 Harris | N | Y | Y | Y | Y | Y | Y | Y |
| **ALASKA** | | | | | | | | |
| AL *Young* | Y | N | Y | N | Y | Y | Y | Y |
| **ARIZONA** | | | | | | | | |
| 1 *Rhodes* | Y | N | Y | N | Y | N | N | Y |
| 2 Pastor | N | Y | Y | Y | Y | Y | Y | Y |
| 3 *Stump* | N | N | Y | N | Y | N | N | N |
| 4 *Kyl* | N | N | Y | N | Y | N | N | Y |
| 5 *Kolbe* | Y | Y | Y | N | Y | N | N | Y |
| **ARKANSAS** | | | | | | | | |
| 1 Alexander | Y | Y | Y | ? | ? | Y | Y | ? |
| 2 Thornton | Y | Y | Y | ? | Y | Y | Y | Y |
| 3 *Hammerschmidt* | Y | N | Y | Y | Y | Y | N | Y |
| 4 Anthony | Y | Y | ? | Y | Y | ? | Y | Y |
| **CALIFORNIA** | | | | | | | | |
| 1 *Riggs* | Y | + | Y | N | Y | N | N | Y |
| 2 *Herger* | N | N | Y | N | Y | N | N | N |
| 3 Matsui | Y | Y | Y | Y | Y | Y | Y | Y |
| 4 Fazio | Y | Y | Y | Y | Y | Y | Y | Y |
| 5 Pelosi | Y | Y | Y | Y | Y | Y | Y | Y |
| 6 Boxer | N | Y | ? | ? | ? | ? | ? | ? |
| 7 Miller | N | Y | Y | Y | Y | N | Y | Y |
| 8 Dellums | N | ? | Y | Y | Y | Y | Y | Y |
| 9 Stark | N | Y | Y | Y | Y | N | Y | Y |
| 10 Edwards | Y | Y | Y | Y | Y | Y | Y | Y |
| 11 Lantos | Y | Y | Y | Y | Y | Y | Y | Y |
| 12 *Campbell* | Y | ? | ? | N | Y | N | N | Y |
| 13 Mineta | Y | Y | Y | Y | Y | Y | Y | Y |
| 14 *Doolittle* | N | N | Y | N | Y | N | N | N |
| 15 Condit | N | Y | Y | ? | ? | Y | N | Y |
| 16 Panetta | Y | Y | Y | Y | Y | Y | Y | Y |
| 17 Dooley | N | Y | Y | Y | Y | Y | Y | Y |
| 18 Lehman | N | Y | Y | Y | Y | Y | Y | Y |
| 19 *Lagomarsino* | Y | N | Y | N | Y | N | N | Y |
| 20 *Thomas* | Y | N | Y | N | Y | N | N | Y |
| 21 *Gallegly* | N | N | ? | N | Y | N | N | Y |
| 22 *Moorhead* | N | N | Y | N | Y | N | N | Y |
| 23 Beilenson | Y | Y | Y | Y | Y | N | Y | Y |
| 24 Waxman | Y | Y | Y | Y | Y | ? | ? | Y |
| 25 Roybal | N | Y | Y | Y | Y | Y | Y | Y |
| 26 Berman | Y | Y | Y | ? | ? | ? | ? | ? |
| 27 Levine | Y | Y | ? | Y | Y | Y | Y | Y |
| 28 Dixon | N | Y | Y | Y | Y | Y | Y | Y |
| 29 Waters | N | Y | Y | Y | Y | N | Y | Y |
| 30 Martinez | Y | Y | Y | ? | Y | Y | Y | Y |
| 31 Dymally | N | Y | Y | ? | ? | Y | Y | ? |
| 32 Anderson | Y | Y | Y | Y | Y | Y | Y | Y |
| 33 *Dreier* | N | N | Y | N | Y | N | N | Y |
| 34 Torres | Y | Y | Y | Y | Y | Y | Y | Y |
| 35 *Lewis* | Y | Y | Y | N | Y | N | N | Y |
| 36 Brown | Y | Y | Y | Y | Y | Y | Y | Y |
| 37 *McCandless* | N | Y | Y | N | Y | Y | N | N |
| 38 *Dornan* | N | N | Y | N | Y | N | N | Y |
| 39 *Dannemeyer* | N | N | Y | N | Y | N | N | Y |
| 40 *Cox* | N | N | ? | N | Y | N | N | Y |
| 41 *Lowery* | Y | N | Y | N | Y | N | Y | Y |

ND Northern Democrats   SD Southern Democrats

| | 374 | 375 | 376 | 377 | 378 | 379 | 380 | 381 |
|---|---|---|---|---|---|---|---|---|
| 42 *Rohrabacher* | N | N | ? | N | Y | N | N | N |
| 43 *Packard* | N | N | Y | N | Y | N | N | N |
| 44 *Cunningham* | N | N | Y | ? | ? | X | ? | ? |
| 45 *Hunter* | Y | N | Y | N | Y | ? | N | Y |
| **COLORADO** | | | | | | | | |
| 1 Schroeder | Y | Y | Y | N | Y | N | Y | Y |
| 2 Skaggs | Y | Y | Y | Y | Y | Y | Y | Y |
| 3 Campbell | N | Y | Y | ? | ? | ? | ? | Y |
| 4 *Allard* | N | N | Y | N | Y | N | N | Y |
| 5 *Hefley* | N | N | Y | N | Y | N | N | Y |
| 6 *Schaefer* | N | N | Y | N | Y | N | N | Y |
| **CONNECTICUT** | | | | | | | | |
| 1 Kennelly | Y | Y | Y | Y | Y | Y | Y | Y |
| 2 Gejdenson | Y | Y | ? | Y | Y | Y | Y | Y |
| 3 DeLauro | N | Y | Y | Y | Y | Y | Y | Y |
| 4 *Shays* | Y | Y | Y | N | Y | N | N | Y |
| 5 *Franks* | Y | Y | Y | N | Y | N | N | Y |
| 6 *Johnson* | Y | Y | Y | N | Y | N | N | Y |
| **DELAWARE** | | | | | | | | |
| AL Carper | Y | Y | Y | Y | Y | Y | Y | Y |
| **FLORIDA** | | | | | | | | |
| 1 *Hutto* | N | N | Y | Y | Y | Y | N | Y |
| 2 Peterson | Y | Y | Y | Y | Y | Y | Y | Y |
| 3 Bennett | Y | N | Y | Y | Y | Y | Y | Y |
| 4 *James* | Y | N | Y | N | Y | N | N | Y |
| 5 *McCollum* | N | Y | N | ? | ? | ? | ? | Y |
| 6 *Stearns* | N | N | Y | N | Y | N | N | N |
| 7 Gibbons | Y | Y | Y | N | Y | N | N | Y |
| 8 *Young* | N | N | Y | N | N | Y | N | Y |
| 9 *Bilirakis* | N | N | Y | N | Y | N | N | Y |
| 10 *Ireland* | Y | X | ? | N | Y | N | ? | Y |
| 11 Bacchus | Y | Y | Y | Y | Y | Y | Y | Y |
| 12 *Lewis* | N | X | ? | N | Y | N | N | Y |
| 13 *Goss* | N | N | Y | N | Y | N | N | Y |
| 14 Johnston | Y | Y | Y | Y | Y | Y | N | Y |
| 15 *Shaw* | Y | N | Y | N | Y | N | N | Y |
| 16 Smith | Y | # | ? | Y | Y | Y | Y | ? |
| 17 Lehman | Y | Y | ? | ? | Y | Y | Y | Y |
| 18 *Ros−Lehtinen* | N | N | Y | N | Y | N | N | Y |
| 19 Fascell | Y | Y | Y | Y | Y | Y | ? | Y |
| **GEORGIA** | | | | | | | | |
| 1 Thomas | Y | Y | Y | Y | Y | Y | Y | Y |
| 2 Hatcher | ? | ? | ? | ? | ? | ? | ? | ? |
| 3 Ray | N | N | Y | Y | P | Y | N | Y |
| 4 Jones | Y | Y | ? | Y | Y | Y | ? | Y |
| 5 Lewis | N | Y | Y | Y | Y | Y | Y | Y |
| 6 *Gingrich* | Y | N | Y | ? | ? | ? | N | Y |
| 7 Darden | N | Y | Y | Y | Y | Y | Y | Y |
| 8 Rowland | N | Y | Y | Y | Y | Y | Y | Y |
| 9 Jenkins | Y | Y | Y | Y | Y | Y | Y | Y |
| 10 Barnard | ? | ? | ? | ? | ? | ? | ? | ? |
| **HAWAII** | | | | | | | | |
| 1 Abercrombie | N | Y | Y | Y | Y | Y | Y | Y |
| 2 Mink | Y | Y | Y | Y | Y | Y | Y | Y |
| **IDAHO** | | | | | | | | |
| 1 LaRocco | Y | Y | Y | Y | Y | Y | Y | Y |
| 2 Stallings | Y | Y | Y | Y | Y | Y | Y | Y |
| **ILLINOIS** | | | | | | | | |
| 1 Hayes | N | Y | Y | Y | Y | Y | Y | Y |
| 2 Savage | N | Y | Y | Y | ? | Y | Y | Y |
| 3 Russo | Y | Y | Y | ? | Y | Y | Y | Y |
| 4 Sangmeister | N | Y | Y | Y | Y | Y | Y | Y |
| 5 Lipinski | N | N | Y | Y | Y | Y | Y | Y |
| 6 *Hyde* | Y | N | Y | ? | ? | ? | ? | ? |
| 7 Collins | N | Y | Y | ? | ? | Y | Y | Y |
| 8 Rostenkowski | Y | Y | Y | Y | Y | Y | Y | Y |
| 9 Yates | Y | Y | ? | Y | Y | Y | Y | Y |
| 10 *Porter* | Y | Y | Y | N | Y | N | N | Y |
| 11 Annunzio | Y | ? | ? | Y | Y | Y | Y | Y |
| 12 *Crane* | N | N | Y | N | Y | N | N | N |
| 13 *Fawell* | Y | Y | Y | N | Y | N | N | Y |
| 14 *Hastert* | N | − | + | N | Y | N | Y | N |
| 15 *Ewing* | Y | N | Y | N | Y | Y | N | N |
| 16 Cox | Y | Y | Y | Y | Y | Y | Y | Y |
| 17 Evans | N | Y | Y | Y | Y | Y | Y | Y |
| 18 *Michel* | Y | N | Y | N | Y | Y | ? | Y |
| 19 Bruce | Y | Y | Y | Y | Y | Y | Y | Y |
| 20 Durbin | N | Y | Y | Y | Y | Y | Y | Y |
| 21 Costello | N | N | Y | Y | Y | Y | Y | Y |
| 22 Poshard | N | N | Y | Y | Y | Y | Y | Y |
| **INDIANA** | | | | | | | | |
| 1 Visclosky | Y | Y | Y | Y | Y | Y | Y | Y |
| 2 Sharp | Y | Y | Y | Y | Y | Y | Y | Y |
| 3 Roemer | N | Y | Y | Y | Y | Y | Y | Y |

| | 374 | 375 | 376 | 377 | 378 | 379 | 380 | 381 |
|---|---|---|---|---|---|---|---|---|
| 4 Long | Y | Y | Y | Y | Y | Y | Y | Y |
| 5 Jontz | N | Y | Y | Y | Y | N | Y | Y |
| 6 ***Burton*** | N | N | Y | N | Y | N | N | N |
| 7 ***Myers*** | N | N | Y | Y | Y | Y | Y | Y |
| 8 McCloskey | Y | Y | Y | Y | Y | Y | Y | Y |
| 9 Hamilton | Y | Y | Y | Y | Y | Y | Y | Y |
| 10 Jacobs | N | Y | Y | N | Y | N | N | Y |
| **IOWA** | | | | | | | | |
| 1 ***Leach*** | Y | Y | Y | N | Y | Y | N | Y |
| 2 ***Nussle*** | Y | N | Y | N | Y | N | N | Y |
| 3 Nagle | Y | Y | Y | Y | Y | Y | Y | Y |
| 4 Smith | Y | Y | Y | Y | Y | Y | Y | Y |
| 5 ***Lightfoot*** | Y | N | Y | N | Y | Y | Y | Y |
| 6 ***Grandy*** | Y | N | Y | N | Y | N | Y | Y |
| **KANSAS** | | | | | | | | |
| 1 ***Roberts*** | Y | N | Y | N | Y | N | N | Y |
| 2 Slattery | Y | Y | Y | ? | ? | ? | N | Y |
| 3 ***Meyers*** | Y | Y | Y | N | Y | N | N | Y |
| 4 Glickman | Y | Y | Y | Y | Y | Y | N | Y |
| 5 ***Nichols*** | Y | Y | Y | Y | Y | N | N | N |
| **KENTUCKY** | | | | | | | | |
| 1 Hubbard | N | N | Y | Y | Y | Y | Y | Y |
| 2 Natcher | Y | N | Y | Y | Y | Y | Y | Y |
| 3 Mazzoli | N | N | Y | Y | Y | Y | Y | Y |
| 4 ***Bunning*** | N | N | Y | N | Y | Y | N | Y |
| 5 ***Rogers*** | N | N | Y | N | Y | Y | Y | Y |
| 6 ***Hopkins*** | Y | N | Y | N | Y | Y | N | Y |
| 7 Perkins | N | N | Y | Y | Y | Y | Y | Y |
| **LOUISIANA** | | | | | | | | |
| 1 ***Livingston*** | Y | N | Y | ? | Y | Y | N | Y |
| 2 Jefferson | N | ? | ? | Y | Y | Y | Y | Y |
| 3 Tauzin | N | N | Y | Y | Y | Y | N | Y |
| 4 ***McCrery*** | Y | ? | ? | N | Y | Y | N | Y |
| 5 Huckaby | N | Y | Y | Y | Y | Y | Y | Y |
| 6 ***Baker*** | N | N | Y | N | Y | Y | N | Y |
| 7 Hayes | N | N | Y | Y | Y | Y | Y | Y |
| 8 ***Holloway*** | N | N | Y | N | Y | Y | N | N |
| **MAINE** | | | | | | | | |
| 1 Andrews | Y | Y | Y | Y | Y | Y | Y | Y |
| 2 ***Snowe*** | N | Y | Y | Y | Y | Y | N | Y |
| **MARYLAND** | | | | | | | | |
| 1 ***Gilchrest*** | N | Y | Y | N | Y | Y | Y | Y |
| 2 ***Bentley*** | Y | Y | Y | N | Y | Y | N | Y |
| 3 Cardin | Y | Y | Y | Y | Y | Y | Y | Y |
| 4 McMillen | Y | Y | Y | Y | Y | Y | Y | Y |
| 5 Hoyer | Y | Y | Y | ? | Y | Y | Y | Y |
| 6 Byron | Y | Y | Y | Y | Y | Y | Y | Y |
| 7 Mfume | N | Y | Y | ? | ? | Y | Y | Y |
| 8 ***Morella*** | Y | Y | Y | N | Y | Y | N | Y |
| **MASSACHUSETTS** | | | | | | | | |
| 1 Olver | Y | Y | Y | Y | Y | Y | Y | Y |
| 2 Neal | N | Y | Y | ? | ? | N | Y | Y |
| 3 Early | N | Y | ? | ? | ? | ? | ? | ? |
| 4 Frank | Y | Y | ? | Y | Y | N | Y | Y |
| 5 Atkins | N | Y | Y | ? | ? | N | Y | Y |
| 6 Mavroules | Y | N | Y | ? | Y | Y | Y | Y |
| 7 Markey | Y | Y | Y | ? | ? | N | Y | Y |
| 8 Kennedy | Y | Y | Y | ? | ? | N | Y | Y |
| 9 Moakley | Y | Y | Y | Y | Y | Y | Y | Y |
| 10 Studds | Y | Y | Y | Y | Y | N | Y | Y |
| 11 Donnelly | N | N | Y | Y | Y | N | Y | Y |
| **MICHIGAN** | | | | | | | | |
| 1 Conyers | N | Y | Y | Y | Y | Y | Y | Y |
| 2 ***Pursell*** | N | ? | ? | Y | ? | N | N | N |
| 3 Wolpe | Y | Y | Y | Y | Y | Y | Y | Y |
| 4 ***Upton*** | Y | Y | Y | N | Y | N | Y | Y |
| 5 ***Henry*** | Y | N | Y | N | Y | N | N | Y |
| 6 Carr | N | Y | Y | Y | Y | Y | Y | N |
| 7 Kildee | Y | N | Y | Y | Y | Y | Y | Y |
| 8 Traxler | ? | ? | ? | ? | ? | ? | ? | ? |
| 9 ***Vander Jagt*** | Y | N | ? | Y | Y | N | N | Y |
| 10 ***Camp*** | N | N | Y | N | Y | Y | Y | Y |
| 11 ***Davis*** | Y | ? | ? | Y | Y | Y | Y | Y |
| 12 Bonior | Y | Y | Y | Y | Y | Y | Y | Y |
| 13 Collins | N | Y | Y | ? | ? | Y | Y | Y |
| 14 Hertel | Y | Y | ? | Y | Y | Y | Y | Y |
| 15 Ford | Y | Y | Y | Y | Y | Y | Y | Y |
| 16 Dingell | Y | Y | Y | Y | Y | Y | Y | Y |
| 17 Levin | Y | Y | Y | Y | Y | Y | Y | Y |
| 18 ***Broomfield*** | Y | N | ? | Y | Y | N | ? | ? |
| **MINNESOTA** | | | | | | | | |
| 1 Penny | Y | Y | Y | Y | Y | N | N | Y |
| 2 ***Weber*** | Y | ? | ? | ? | ? | ? | ? | ? |
| 3 ***Ramstad*** | N | Y | Y | N | Y | N | N | Y |
| 4 Vento | Y | Y | Y | Y | Y | N | Y | Y |

| | 374 | 375 | 376 | 377 | 378 | 379 | 380 | 381 |
|---|---|---|---|---|---|---|---|---|
| 5 Sabo | Y | Y | Y | Y | Y | Y | Y | Y |
| 6 Sikorski | Y | Y | Y | N | Y | N | N | Y |
| 7 Peterson | Y | N | Y | Y | Y | Y | Y | Y |
| 8 Oberstar | Y | N | Y | Y | Y | Y | Y | Y |
| **MISSISSIPPI** | | | | | | | | |
| 1 Whitten | Y | N | Y | Y | Y | Y | Y | Y |
| 2 Espy | N | Y | Y | ? | ? | Y | Y | Y |
| 3 Montgomery | Y | N | Y | Y | ? | Y | Y | Y |
| 4 Parker | Y | N | Y | Y | Y | Y | Y | Y |
| 5 Taylor | N | N | Y | Y | Y | Y | N | Y |
| **MISSOURI** | | | | | | | | |
| 1 Clay | N | Y | Y | ? | ? | ? | ? | ? |
| 2 Horn | Y | Y | Y | Y | Y | Y | Y | Y |
| 3 Gephardt | Y | Y | Y | Y | Y | Y | ? | Y |
| 4 Skelton | Y | N | Y | Y | Y | Y | Y | Y |
| 5 Wheat | N | Y | Y | Y | Y | Y | Y | Y |
| 6 ***Coleman*** | Y | Y | Y | N | Y | Y | Y | Y |
| 7 ***Hancock*** | N | N | Y | N | Y | N | N | N |
| 8 ***Emerson*** | Y | N | Y | N | Y | Y | Y | Y |
| 9 Volkmer | N | N | Y | Y | Y | Y | Y | Y |
| **MONTANA** | | | | | | | | |
| 1 Williams | N | Y | Y | ? | ? | Y | Y | Y |
| 2 ***Marlenee*** | N | N | Y | N | Y | N | N | N |
| **NEBRASKA** | | | | | | | | |
| 1 ***Bereuter*** | Y | Y | Y | N | Y | Y | Y | Y |
| 2 Hoagland | Y | Y | Y | Y | Y | Y | Y | Y |
| 3 ***Barrett*** | Y | N | Y | N | Y | Y | N | N |
| **NEVADA** | | | | | | | | |
| 1 Bilbray | Y | Y | Y | Y | Y | N | Y | Y |
| 2 ***Vucanovich*** | Y | N | ? | N | Y | Y | Y | N |
| **NEW HAMPSHIRE** | | | | | | | | |
| 1 ***Zeliff*** | Y | Y | Y | N | Y | N | N | N |
| 2 Swett | Y | Y | Y | Y | Y | N | Y | Y |
| **NEW JERSEY** | | | | | | | | |
| 1 Andrews | N | Y | Y | Y | Y | Y | Y | Y |
| 2 Hughes | N | Y | Y | Y | Y | Y | N | Y |
| 3 Pallone | Y | Y | Y | Y | Y | N | N | Y |
| 4 ***Smith*** | Y | N | Y | Y | Y | Y | N | Y |
| 5 ***Roukema*** | Y | Y | Y | N | N | N | N | Y |
| 6 Dwyer | # | # | ? | Y | Y | Y | Y | Y |
| 7 ***Rinaldo*** | Y | N | Y | Y | Y | Y | N | Y |
| 8 Roe | Y | N | Y | ? | Y | Y | Y | Y |
| 9 Torricelli | Y | Y | Y | Y | Y | Y | Y | Y |
| 10 Payne | N | Y | Y | Y | Y | Y | Y | Y |
| 11 ***Gallo*** | Y | Y | Y | N | Y | Y | N | Y |
| 12 ***Zimmer*** | N | Y | Y | N | Y | N | N | Y |
| 13 ***Saxton*** | Y | N | Y | N | Y | Y | N | Y |
| 14 Guarini | Y | Y | ? | Y | Y | Y | Y | Y |
| **NEW MEXICO** | | | | | | | | |
| 1 ***Schiff*** | Y | Y | Y | N | Y | Y | Y | Y |
| 2 ***Skeen*** | Y | Y | Y | Y | Y | Y | Y | Y |
| 3 Richardson | Y | Y | Y | Y | Y | Y | Y | Y |
| **NEW YORK** | | | | | | | | |
| 1 Hochbrueckner | Y | Y | Y | Y | Y | Y | Y | Y |
| 2 Downey | Y | Y | Y | Y | Y | Y | Y | Y |
| 3 Mrazek | Y | Y | Y | ? | ? | Y | Y | ? |
| 4 ***Lent*** | Y | N | Y | Y | Y | N | N | Y |
| 5 ***McGrath*** | Y | N | Y | Y | ? | N | N | Y |
| 6 Flake | N | Y | Y | ? | ? | ? | ? | ? |
| 7 Ackerman | Y | Y | ? | ? | ? | ? | ? | ? |
| 8 Scheuer | Y | Y | Y | Y | Y | N | Y | Y |
| 9 Manton | Y | N | Y | Y | Y | Y | Y | Y |
| 10 Schumer | Y | Y | Y | Y | Y | N | Y | Y |
| 11 Towns | N | Y | ? | ? | ? | ? | ? | ? |
| 12 Owens | N | Y | Y | ? | ? | Y | Y | Y |
| 13 Solarz | Y | # | ? | ? | ? | ? | ? | ? |
| 14 ***Molinari*** | Y | Y | Y | N | Y | N | N | Y |
| 15 ***Green*** | Y | Y | ? | Y | Y | Y | Y | Y |
| 16 Rangel | N | Y | ? | ? | Y | Y | Y | Y |
| 17 Weiss | Y | Y | Y | ? | ? | Y | Y | Y |
| 18 Serrano | N | Y | Y | ? | ? | # | Y | Y |
| 19 Engel | Y | Y | Y | Y | Y | Y | Y | Y |
| 20 Lowey | Y | Y | Y | Y | Y | Y | Y | Y |
| 21 ***Fish*** | Y | Y | Y | Y | Y | N | N | Y |
| 22 ***Gilman*** | Y | Y | Y | Y | Y | Y | + | Y |
| 23 McNulty | Y | Y | ? | Y | Y | Y | Y | Y |
| 24 ***Solomon*** | N | N | Y | ? | ? | ? | ? | ? |
| 25 ***Boehlert*** | Y | Y | Y | N | Y | Y | N | Y |
| 26 ***Martin*** | Y | ? | ? | ? | ? | Y | N | Y |
| 27 ***Walsh*** | N | N | Y | Y | Y | Y | N | Y |
| 28 McHugh | Y | Y | Y | Y | Y | Y | Y | Y |
| 29 ***Horton*** | Y | ? | ? | Y | Y | Y | Y | Y |
| 30 Slaughter | Y | Y | Y | Y | Y | Y | Y | Y |
| 31 ***Paxon*** | N | N | Y | ? | Y | Y | N | Y |

| | 374 | 375 | 376 | 377 | 378 | 379 | 380 | 381 |
|---|---|---|---|---|---|---|---|---|
| 32 LaFalce | Y | N | Y | ? | Y | Y | Y | Y |
| 33 Nowak | Y | N | ? | Y | Y | Y | Y | Y |
| 34 ***Houghton*** | Y | Y | Y | Y | Y | Y | N | Y |
| **NORTH CAROLINA** | | | | | | | | |
| 1 Jones | N | Y | ? | Y | Y | Y | Y | Y |
| 2 Valentine | N | Y | Y | Y | Y | Y | Y | Y |
| 3 Lancaster | Y | Y | Y | Y | Y | Y | Y | Y |
| 4 Price | Y | Y | Y | Y | Y | Y | Y | Y |
| 5 Neal | N | Y | Y | Y | Y | ? | Y | Y |
| 6 ***Coble*** | N | N | Y | N | Y | Y | N | N |
| 7 Rose | Y | Y | Y | Y | Y | Y | Y | Y |
| 8 Hefner | N | Y | Y | Y | Y | Y | Y | Y |
| 9 ***McMillan*** | ? | # | ? | Y | Y | Y | N | N |
| 10 ***Ballenger*** | N | Y | Y | N | Y | N | N | N |
| 11 ***Taylor*** | Y | N | Y | N | Y | N | N | N |
| **NORTH DAKOTA** | | | | | | | | |
| AL Dorgan | N | Y | ? | Y | Y | Y | Y | Y |
| **OHIO** | | | | | | | | |
| 1 Luken | ? | ? | ? | Y | Y | Y | Y | Y |
| 2 ***Gradison*** | Y | Y | Y | N | Y | N | N | Y |
| 3 Hall | Y | ? | ? | ? | Y | Y | Y | Y |
| 4 ***Oxley*** | Y | N | Y | N | Y | N | N | Y |
| 5 ***Gillmor*** | Y | N | Y | Y | Y | N | N | Y |
| 6 ***McEwen*** | ? | ? | ? | N | Y | N | N | Y |
| 7 ***Hobson*** | Y | Y | Y | N | Y | Y | Y | Y |
| 8 ***Boehner*** | Y | N | Y | N | Y | Y | N | N |
| 9 Kaptur | N | Y | Y | Y | Y | Y | Y | Y |
| 10 ***Miller*** | Y | N | Y | N | Y | N | N | Y |
| 11 Eckart | Y | Y | Y | Y | Y | Y | Y | Y |
| 12 ***Kasich*** | N | N | Y | Y | Y | Y | N | Y |
| 13 Pease | Y | Y | Y | Y | Y | Y | Y | Y |
| 14 Sawyer | Y | Y | Y | Y | Y | Y | Y | Y |
| 15 ***Wylie*** | Y | N | Y | Y | Y | N | N | Y |
| 16 ***Regula*** | Y | Y | Y | N | Y | N | N | Y |
| 17 Traficant | N | Y | Y | Y | Y | Y | Y | Y |
| 18 Applegate | N | N | Y | Y | Y | N | Y | Y |
| 19 Feighan | Y | Y | Y | ? | ? | ? | Y | Y |
| 20 Oakar | N | N | Y | ? | ? | ? | ? | ? |
| 21 Stokes | N | Y | Y | Y | Y | Y | ? | Y |
| **OKLAHOMA** | | | | | | | | |
| 1 ***Inhofe*** | N | N | Y | N | Y | N | N | N |
| 2 Synar | Y | Y | Y | Y | Y | Y | Y | Y |
| 3 Brewster | Y | Y | Y | Y | Y | Y | Y | ? |
| 4 McCurdy | Y | Y | Y | ? | Y | Y | Y | Y |
| 5 ***Edwards*** | N | N | ? | ? | ? | N | ? | ? |
| 6 English | N | Y | Y | Y | Y | Y | Y | Y |
| **OREGON** | | | | | | | | |
| 1 AuCoin | N | Y | Y | ? | Y | Y | Y | Y |
| 2 ***Smith*** | N | N | N | Y | N | Y | N | Y |
| 3 Wyden | Y | Y | Y | Y | Y | Y | Y | Y |
| 4 DeFazio | N | Y | Y | ? | ? | ? | ? | ? |
| 5 Kopetski | Y | Y | Y | Y | Y | Y | Y | Y |
| **PENNSYLVANIA** | | | | | | | | |
| 1 Foglietta | N | Y | Y | Y | Y | Y | Y | Y |
| 2 Blackwell | N | Y | Y | Y | Y | Y | Y | Y |
| 3 Borski | Y | N | Y | Y | Y | Y | Y | Y |
| 4 Kolter | Y | ? | ? | ? | ? | ? | Y | ? |
| 5 ***Schulze*** | ? | ? | ? | ? | ? | ? | ? | ? |
| 6 Yatron | Y | ? | ? | Y | Y | Y | Y | Y |
| 7 ***Weldon*** | Y | N | Y | N | Y | N | N | Y |
| 8 Kostmayer | Y | Y | Y | + | + | Y | Y | Y |
| 9 ***Shuster*** | N | N | ? | N | Y | N | N | Y |
| 10 ***McDade*** | Y | N | ? | N | Y | Y | Y | Y |
| 11 Kanjorski | N | N | Y | Y | Y | Y | Y | Y |
| 12 Murtha | Y | ? | ? | Y | Y | Y | Y | Y |
| 13 ***Coughlin*** | Y | Y | ? | ? | Y | Y | Y | ? |
| 14 Coyne | Y | Y | Y | Y | Y | Y | Y | Y |
| 15 ***Ritter*** | Y | N | Y | Y | Y | N | N | Y |
| 16 ***Walker*** | Y | N | Y | ? | ? | ? | ? | ? |
| 17 ***Gekas*** | Y | N | Y | N | Y | Y | N | N |
| 18 ***Santorum*** | N | N | Y | Y | Y | N | N | Y |
| 19 ***Goodling*** | N | N | Y | N | Y | Y | Y | N |
| 20 Gaydos | ? | ? | ? | Y | Y | Y | Y | Y |
| 21 ***Ridge*** | N | Y | Y | ? | ? | Y | N | Y |
| 22 Murphy | X | X | ? | N | Y | N | N | Y |
| 23 ***Clinger*** | Y | Y | Y | Y | Y | Y | N | Y |
| **RHODE ISLAND** | | | | | | | | |
| 1 ***Machtley*** | N | Y | Y | N | Y | N | N | Y |
| 2 Reed | N | Y | Y | Y | Y | Y | Y | Y |
| **SOUTH CAROLINA** | | | | | | | | |
| 1 ***Ravenel*** | Y | Y | Y | Y | Y | Y | N | Y |
| 2 ***Spence*** | N | N | Y | Y | Y | Y | N | Y |
| 3 Derrick | Y | Y | Y | Y | Y | Y | Y | Y |
| 4 Patterson | N | Y | Y | ? | Y | N | Y | Y |
| 5 Spratt | Y | Y | Y | Y | Y | Y | Y | Y |
| 6 Tallon | Y | N | Y | ? | ? | ? | ? | ? |

| | 374 | 375 | 376 | 377 | 378 | 379 | 380 | 381 |
|---|---|---|---|---|---|---|---|---|
| **SOUTH DAKOTA** | | | | | | | | |
| AL Johnson | Y | Y | Y | Y | Y | Y | Y | Y |
| **TENNESSEE** | | | | | | | | |
| 1 ***Quillen*** | N | X | ? | N | Y | Y | Y | Y |
| 2 ***Duncan*** | N | N | Y | N | Y | N | N | N |
| 3 Lloyd | N | Y | Y | Y | Y | Y | N | Y |
| 4 Cooper | Y | Y | Y | Y | Y | Y | Y | Y |
| 5 Clement | ? | ? | ? | Y | Y | Y | Y | Y |
| 6 Gordon | ? | ? | ? | Y | Y | Y | Y | Y |
| 7 ***Sundquist*** | N | N | Y | N | Y | Y | Y | Y |
| 8 Tanner | N | Y | Y | Y | Y | Y | Y | Y |
| 9 Ford | ? | ? | ? | ? | ? | ? | ? | ? |
| **TEXAS** | | | | | | | | |
| 1 Chapman | N | Y | Y | Y | Y | Y | Y | Y |
| 2 Wilson | ? | ? | ? | ? | ? | ? | ? | ? |
| 3 ***Johnson*** | Y | N | Y | N | Y | N | N | N |
| 4 Hall | N | N | Y | Y | Y | Y | N | Y |
| 5 Bryant | N | Y | ? | Y | Y | Y | Y | Y |
| 6 ***Barton*** | N | N | Y | N | Y | Y | N | N |
| 7 ***Archer*** | N | N | Y | Y | Y | N | N | Y |
| 8 ***Fields*** | N | N | Y | N | Y | Y | Y | N |
| 9 Brooks | Y | Y | Y | Y | Y | Y | Y | Y |
| 10 Pickle | Y | Y | Y | Y | Y | Y | Y | Y |
| 11 Edwards | Y | Y | Y | Y | Y | Y | Y | Y |
| 12 Geren | N | Y | Y | Y | Y | Y | N | Y |
| 13 Sarpalius | N | N | Y | Y | Y | Y | Y | Y |
| 14 Laughlin | Y | N | Y | Y | Y | Y | Y | Y |
| 15 de la Garza | Y | N | Y | Y | ? | Y | Y | Y |
| 16 Coleman | Y | Y | Y | Y | Y | Y | Y | Y |
| 17 Stenholm | Y | N | Y | Y | Y | Y | N | Y |
| 18 Washington | N | Y | Y | Y | Y | Y | Y | Y |
| 19 ***Combest*** | N | N | Y | Y | Y | Y | Y | N |
| 20 Gonzalez | N | Y | Y | Y | Y | Y | Y | Y |
| 21 ***Smith*** | Y | Y | Y | N | Y | Y | Y | Y |
| 22 ***DeLay*** | N | N | Y | Y | Y | N | N | N |
| 23 Bustamante | Y | Y | Y | Y | Y | Y | Y | Y |
| 24 Frost | Y | Y | Y | Y | Y | Y | Y | Y |
| 25 Andrews | Y | ? | Y | Y | Y | Y | N | Y |
| 26 ***Armey*** | N | N | Y | N | Y | N | N | N |
| 27 Ortiz | N | N | Y | Y | Y | Y | Y | Y |
| **UTAH** | | | | | | | | |
| 1 ***Hansen*** | Y | N | Y | ? | Y | N | Y | N |
| 2 Owens | Y | Y | ? | Y | Y | Y | Y | Y |
| 3 Orton | Y | N | Y | Y | Y | N | Y | Y |
| **VERMONT** | | | | | | | | |
| AL *Sanders* | N | Y | Y | ? | ? | Y | Y | Y |
| **VIRGINIA** | | | | | | | | |
| 1 ***Bateman*** | Y | N | Y | Y | Y | Y | N | Y |
| 2 Pickett | Y | Y | Y | Y | Y | Y | N | Y |
| 3 ***Bliley*** | Y | N | Y | N | Y | Y | N | Y |
| 4 Sisisky | Y | Y | ? | Y | Y | Y | Y | Y |
| 5 Payne | Y | Y | Y | Y | Y | Y | Y | Y |
| 6 Olin | Y | Y | Y | Y | Y | Y | Y | Y |
| 7 ***Allen*** | N | Y | Y | N | Y | N | N | Y |
| 8 Moran | Y | Y | Y | ? | Y | Y | Y | Y |
| 9 Boucher | Y | Y | Y | Y | Y | Y | Y | Y |
| 10 ***Wolf*** | Y | N | Y | N | Y | N | N | Y |
| **WASHINGTON** | | | | | | | | |
| 1 ***Miller*** | Y | Y | Y | N | Y | N | N | Y |
| 2 Swift | Y | Y | Y | Y | Y | Y | Y | Y |
| 3 Unsoeld | Y | Y | Y | Y | Y | Y | Y | Y |
| 4 ***Morrison*** | Y | Y | ? | Y | Y | Y | ? | Y |
| 5 Foley | Y | | | | | | | |
| 6 Dicks | Y | Y | Y | Y | Y | Y | Y | Y |
| 7 McDermott | Y | Y | Y | Y | Y | Y | Y | Y |
| 8 ***Chandler*** | Y | Y | Y | N | Y | Y | N | Y |
| **WEST VIRGINIA** | | | | | | | | |
| 1 Mollohan | Y | N | Y | Y | Y | Y | Y | Y |
| 2 Staggers | N | N | Y | Y | Y | Y | Y | Y |
| 3 Wise | Y | Y | Y | ? | Y | Y | Y | Y |
| 4 Rahall | N | N | Y | Y | Y | Y | Y | Y |
| **WISCONSIN** | | | | | | | | |
| 1 Aspin | Y | Y | Y | Y | Y | Y | Y | Y |
| 2 ***Klug*** | N | Y | Y | N | Y | Y | N | Y |
| 3 ***Gunderson*** | Y | N | Y | Y | Y | Y | Y | Y |
| 4 Kleczka | N | Y | Y | Y | Y | Y | Y | Y |
| 5 Moody | N | Y | Y | Y | Y | Y | Y | Y |
| 6 ***Petri*** | N | N | Y | Y | Y | N | N | N |
| 7 Obey | Y | ? | ? | Y | Y | Y | ? | Y |
| 8 ***Roth*** | N | N | Y | N | Y | Y | N | N |
| 9 ***Sensenbrenner*** | N | N | Y | N | Y | Y | N | N |
| **WYOMING** | | | | | | | | |
| AL ***Thomas*** | Y | Y | Y | N | Y | N | N | N |

Southern states - Ala., Ark., Fla., Ga., Ky., La., Miss., N.C., Okla., S.C., Tenn., Texas, Va.
Omitted votes are quorum calls, which CQ does not include in its vote charts.

**382. HR 4323. Neighborhood Schools Improvement Act/Rule.** Adoption of the rule (H Res 551) to provide for House floor consideration of the bill to authorize $800 million for grants to states to improve their education systems and to establish a National Education Goals Panel to oversee the development of voluntary national education standards. Adopted 232-153: R 1-149; D 230-4 (ND 158-3, SD 72-1); I 1-0, Aug. 12, 1992.

**383. HR 4323. Neighborhood Schools Improvement Act/Substitute.** Armey, R-Texas, amendment in the nature of a substitute to authorize $700 million in fiscal 1992 and such sums as necessary for fiscal years 1993 through 2001 for state and local school reform activities. The substitute would: require that 25 percent of a school district's grant be used for school choice programs that included private schools; allow school districts to use the grants to fund New American Schools, merit schools and site-based management that emphasized alternative certification; and require each governor to chair a state panel on education reform. But it would not formally create the National Education Goals Panel. Rejected 80-328: R 79-76; D 1-251 (ND 1-170, SD 0-81); I 0-1, Aug. 12, 1992.

**384. HR 4323. Neighborhood Schools Improvement Act/Substitute.** Goodling, R-Pa., amendment in the nature of a substitute to authorize $700 million in fiscal 1992 and such sums as necessary for fiscal years 1993 through 2001 for state and local school reform activities. The substitute would establish a National Education Goals Panel; create a council to coordinate voluntary national education standards; require each state to initiate an education reform plan; permit funding of school choice programs; and allow states and school districts to combine federal, state and local funds for reform plans. The substitute also would authorize $100 million in fiscal 1993 to fund the New American Schools program and separately would authorize $10 million in fiscal 1993 for a mentor program. Rejected 140-267: R 134-23; D 6-243 (ND 3-164, SD 3-79); I 0-1, Aug. 12, 1992. A "yea" was a vote in support of the president's position.

**385. HR 4323. Neighborhood Schools Improvement Act/Passage.** Passage of the bill to authorize $800 million in fiscal 1992 and such sums as necessary in fiscal years 1993 through 2001 for grants to states to improve their education systems (state matching funds would be required after the first year); establish a National Education Goals Panel; require each state to formulate an education reform plan; and provide a five-year demonstration program to determine whether waivers of certain federal and state laws enable schools to serve disadvantaged children more effectively. Passed 279-124: R 32-122; D 246-2 (ND 167-1, SD 79-1); I 1-0, Aug. 12, 1992. A "nay" was a vote in support of the president's position.

**386. HR 5466. Airline Competition Enhancement Act/Passage.** Passage of the bill to increase airline competition by regulating the computer reservation systems (CRS) used by travel agents; limiting the terms of contracts between a CRS and a travel agent to three years; and prohibiting a CRS from including certain restrictive provisions in contracts. Passed 230-160: R 65-90; D 164-70 (ND 130-27, SD 34-43); I 1-0, Aug. 12, 1992. A "nay" was a vote in support of the president's position.

**387. HR 4484. Maritime Administration Authorization.** Passage of the bill to authorize $765 million in fiscal 1993 for the operations of the Maritime Administration. Passed 331-48: R 106-45; D 224-3 (ND 149-2, SD 75-1); I 1-0, Sept. 9, 1992.

**388. Procedural Motion.** Approval of the House Journal of Wednesday, Sept. 9. Approved 260-109: R 41-104; D 218-5 (ND 148-5, SD 70-0); I 1-0, Sept. 10, 1992.

**389. S 5. Family Leave/Rule.** Adoption of the rule (H Res 560) to waive points of order against and provide for House floor consideration of the conference report to require companies with more than 50 employees to provide workers with up to 12 weeks of unpaid leave for family emergencies. Adopted 329-71: R 87-71; D 241-0 (ND 165-0, SD 76-0); I 1-0, Sept. 10, 1992.

## KEY

| | |
|---|---|
| Y | Voted for (yea). |
| # | Paired for. |
| + | Announced for. |
| N | Voted against (nay). |
| X | Paired against. |
| − | Announced against. |
| P | Voted "present." |
| C | Voted "present" to avoid possible conflict of interest. |
| ? | Did not vote or otherwise make a position known. |

*Democrats* **Republicans**
*Independent*

| | 382 | 383 | 384 | 385 | 386 | 387 | 388 | 389 |
|---|---|---|---|---|---|---|---|---|
| **ALABAMA** | | | | | | | | |
| 1 *Callahan* | N | Y | Y | N | N | Y | Y | N |
| 2 *Dickinson* | ? | Y | Y | N | Y | Y | ? | N |
| 3 Browder | Y | N | N | Y | N | Y | Y | Y |
| 4 Bevill | Y | N | N | Y | N | Y | Y | Y |
| 5 Cramer | Y | N | N | Y | Y | Y | Y | Y |
| 6 Erdreich | Y | N | N | Y | N | Y | Y | Y |
| 7 Harris | Y | N | N | Y | N | Y | Y | Y |
| **ALASKA** | | | | | | | | |
| AL *Young* | ? | N | Y | N | N | ? | ? | Y |
| **ARIZONA** | | | | | | | | |
| 1 *Rhodes* | N | N | Y | N | Y | ? | N | N |
| 2 Pastor | Y | N | N | Y | Y | Y | Y | Y |
| 3 *Stump* | N | Y | N | N | N | N | N | N |
| 4 *Kyl* | N | Y | Y | N | Y | N | N | N |
| 5 *Kolbe* | N | Y | Y | N | N | ? | N | Y |
| **ARKANSAS** | | | | | | | | |
| 1 Alexander | ? | N | N | Y | Y | ? | ? | ? |
| 2 Thornton | Y | N | N | Y | N | Y | Y | Y |
| 3 *Hammerschmidt* | N | Y | Y | N | Y | Y | Y | N |
| 4 Anthony | Y | N | N | Y | N | Y | Y | Y |
| **CALIFORNIA** | | | | | | | | |
| 1 *Riggs* | ? | N | Y | N | Y | Y | N | N |
| 2 *Herger* | N | Y | Y | N | N | Y | N | N |
| 3 Matsui | Y | N | N | Y | Y | Y | Y | Y |
| 4 Fazio | Y | N | N | Y | Y | Y | Y | Y |
| 5 Pelosi | Y | N | N | Y | Y | Y | Y | Y |
| 6 Boxer | Y | N | N | Y | ? | ? | Y | Y |
| 7 Miller | Y | N | N | Y | Y | Y | Y | Y |
| 8 Dellums | Y | N | N | Y | Y | Y | Y | Y |
| 9 Stark | ? | N | N | Y | Y | Y | Y | Y |
| 10 Edwards | Y | N | N | Y | Y | Y | Y | Y |
| 11 Lantos | Y | N | N | Y | Y | Y | Y | Y |
| 12 *Campbell* | N | Y | Y | N | N | N | N | Y |
| 13 Mineta | Y | N | N | Y | Y | Y | Y | Y |
| 14 *Doolittle* | N | Y | N | N | N | N | N | Y |
| 15 Condit | Y | N | N | Y | N | ? | ? | Y |
| 16 Panetta | Y | N | N | Y | Y | Y | Y | Y |
| 17 Dooley | Y | N | N | Y | Y | Y | Y | Y |
| 18 Lehman | Y | N | N | Y | ? | ? | Y | ? |
| 19 *Lagomarsino* | N | Y | N | N | Y | N | N | N |
| 20 *Thomas* | N | Y | N | N | N | N | N | Y |
| 21 *Gallegly* | N | Y | N | N | N | N | N | N |
| 22 *Moorhead* | N | Y | N | N | N | N | N | Y |
| 23 Beilenson | Y | N | N | Y | Y | Y | Y | Y |
| 24 Waxman | Y | N | N | Y | Y | Y | Y | Y |
| 25 Roybal | Y | N | N | Y | ? | Y | Y | Y |
| 26 Berman | Y | N | N | Y | Y | Y | Y | Y |
| 27 Levine | ? | N | N | Y | Y | ? | ? | ? |
| 28 Dixon | Y | N | N | Y | Y | Y | Y | Y |
| 29 Waters | Y | N | N | Y | Y | Y | Y | Y |
| 30 Martinez | Y | N | N | Y | Y | Y | Y | Y |
| 31 Dymally | ? | ? | ? | ? | ? | ? | ? | ? |
| 32 Anderson | Y | N | N | Y | Y | Y | Y | Y |
| 33 *Dreier* | N | Y | N | N | N | N | N | Y |
| 34 Torres | Y | N | N | Y | Y | Y | Y | Y |
| 35 *Lewis* | N | N | Y | N | N | ? | ? | ? |
| 36 Brown | Y | N | N | Y | Y | ? | Y | Y |
| 37 *McCandless* | N | N | Y | N | N | N | N | N |
| 38 *Dornan* | N | Y | N | N | N | N | ? | N |
| 39 *Dannemeyer* | N | Y | Y | N | N | N | N | N |
| 40 *Cox* | N | Y | N | N | Y | N | ? | Y |
| 41 *Lowery* | ? | Y | Y | N | N | Y | ? | Y |

| | 382 | 383 | 384 | 385 | 386 | 387 | 388 | 389 |
|---|---|---|---|---|---|---|---|---|
| 42 *Rohrabacher* | N | Y | N | N | N | N | Y | N |
| 43 *Packard* | N | Y | Y | N | N | N | Y | N |
| 44 *Cunningham* | ? | ? | ? | ? | ? | Y | N | N |
| 45 *Hunter* | N | ? | Y | N | Y | Y | ? | N |
| **COLORADO** | | | | | | | | |
| 1 Schroeder | Y | N | ? | Y | N | Y | N | Y |
| 2 Skaggs | Y | N | N | Y | Y | Y | Y | Y |
| 3 Campbell | ? | ? | ? | ? | ? | Y | ? | Y |
| 4 *Allard* | N | Y | Y | N | N | N | N | N |
| 5 *Hefley* | N | Y | N | N | N | N | N | N |
| 6 *Schaefer* | N | N | Y | N | N | Y | N | N |
| **CONNECTICUT** | | | | | | | | |
| 1 Kennelly | Y | N | N | Y | N | Y | Y | Y |
| 2 Gejdenson | Y | N | N | Y | Y | Y | Y | Y |
| 3 DeLauro | Y | N | N | Y | Y | Y | Y | Y |
| 4 *Shays* | N | N | N | N | Y | Y | N | Y |
| 5 *Franks* | N | Y | N | N | Y | Y | N | Y |
| 6 *Johnson* | N | N | Y | N | Y | Y | Y | Y |
| **DELAWARE** | | | | | | | | |
| AL Carper | Y | N | N | Y | Y | Y | ? | Y |
| **FLORIDA** | | | | | | | | |
| 1 Hutto | Y | N | Y | Y | Y | Y | Y | Y |
| 2 Peterson | Y | N | N | Y | Y | Y | Y | Y |
| 3 Bennett | Y | N | N | Y | Y | Y | Y | Y |
| 4 *James* | N | N | Y | N | N | Y | N | Y |
| 5 *McCollum* | ? | ? | # | X | ? | Y | N | N |
| 6 *Stearns* | N | Y | N | N | N | N | Y | N |
| 7 Gibbons | Y | N | N | Y | Y | Y | Y | Y |
| 8 *Young* | N | N | N | Y | N | Y | Y | Y |
| 9 *Bilirakis* | N | N | Y | N | Y | N | N | N |
| 10 *Ireland* | ? | ? | Y | ? | ? | Y | N | N |
| 11 Bacchus | ? | N | N | Y | Y | Y | Y | Y |
| 12 *Lewis* | N | Y | Y | N | Y | N | N | N |
| 13 *Goss* | N | Y | N | N | N | N | N | N |
| 14 Johnston | Y | N | N | Y | N | Y | Y | Y |
| 15 *Shaw* | N | Y | Y | N | Y | Y | N | Y |
| 16 Smith | ? | N | N | Y | Y | Y | Y | Y |
| 17 Lehman | Y | N | N | Y | Y | Y | Y | Y |
| 18 *Ros—Lehtinen* | N | Y | Y | N | N | N | N | Y |
| 19 Fascell | Y | N | N | ? | N | Y | ? | Y |
| **GEORGIA** | | | | | | | | |
| 1 Thomas | Y | N | N | Y | Y | ? | ? | ? |
| 2 Hatcher | ? | ? | ? | ? | ? | Y | Y | ? |
| 3 Ray | Y | N | N | Y | Y | Y | ? | Y |
| 4 Jones | Y | N | N | Y | Y | Y | ? | Y |
| 5 Lewis | Y | N | N | Y | Y | Y | Y | Y |
| 6 *Gingrich* | ? | ? | ? | ? | # | Y | N | Y |
| 7 Darden | Y | N | N | Y | Y | Y | Y | Y |
| 8 Rowland | Y | N | N | Y | Y | Y | Y | Y |
| 9 Jenkins | Y | N | N | Y | ? | Y | Y | Y |
| 10 Barnard | ? | ? | ? | ? | ? | Y | Y | Y |
| **HAWAII** | | | | | | | | |
| 1 Abercrombie | Y | N | N | Y | Y | Y | Y | Y |
| 2 Mink | Y | N | N | Y | Y | Y | Y | Y |
| **IDAHO** | | | | | | | | |
| 1 LaRocco | Y | N | N | Y | N | Y | Y | Y |
| 2 Stallings | Y | N | N | Y | N | Y | Y | Y |
| **ILLINOIS** | | | | | | | | |
| 1 Hayes | Y | N | N | Y | N | ? | Y | Y |
| 2 Savage | Y | N | N | Y | Y | Y | Y | Y |
| 3 Russo | Y | N | N | Y | Y | Y | Y | Y |
| 4 Sangmeister | Y | N | N | Y | Y | Y | Y | Y |
| 5 Lipinski | Y | Y | Y | N | Y | Y | Y | Y |
| 6 *Hyde* | ? | ? | ? | ? | ? | Y | Y | Y |
| 7 Collins | Y | N | N | Y | Y | Y | Y | Y |
| 8 Rostenkowski | Y | N | N | Y | Y | Y | Y | Y |
| 9 Yates | Y | N | N | Y | ? | ? | Y | Y |
| 10 *Porter* | N | N | N | Y | N | Y | N | Y |
| 11 Annunzio | Y | N | N | Y | Y | Y | Y | Y |
| 12 *Crane* | N | Y | N | N | ? | N | N | N |
| 13 *Fawell* | N | N | Y | N | N | N | N | N |
| 14 *Hastert* | N | N | N | N | N | N | N | N |
| 15 *Ewing* | N | N | Y | N | N | Y | N | N |
| 16 Cox | Y | N | N | Y | Y | Y | Y | Y |
| 17 Evans | Y | N | N | Y | Y | Y | Y | Y |
| 18 *Michel* | N | Y | N | N | Y | Y | N | Y |
| 19 Bruce | Y | N | N | Y | Y | Y | Y | Y |
| 20 Durbin | Y | N | N | Y | Y | Y | Y | Y |
| 21 Costello | Y | N | N | Y | Y | Y | Y | Y |
| 22 Poshard | Y | N | N | Y | N | Y | Y | Y |
| **INDIANA** | | | | | | | | |
| 1 Visclosky | Y | N | N | Y | N | Y | Y | Y |
| 2 Sharp | ? | N | N | Y | Y | Y | Y | Y |
| 3 Roemer | Y | N | N | Y | Y | Y | Y | Y |

ND Northern Democrats    SD Southern Democrats

| | 382 | 383 | 384 | 385 | 386 | 387 | 388 | 389 |
|---|---|---|---|---|---|---|---|---|
| 4 Long | Y | N | N | Y | Y | Y | Y | Y |
| 5 Jontz | Y | N | N | Y | Y | Y | Y | Y |
| 6 **Burton** | N | Y | Y | N | N | ? | N | N |
| 7 **Myers** | N | N | ? | ? | N | Y | Y | Y |
| 8 McCloskey | Y | N | N | Y | Y | Y | Y | Y |
| 9 Hamilton | Y | N | N | Y | Y | Y | Y | Y |
| 10 Jacobs | Y | N | N | Y | Y | N | N | Y |
| **IOWA** | | | | | | | | |
| 1 **Leach** | N | N | Y | Y | N | N | N | Y |
| 2 **Nussle** | N | Y | Y | N | Y | N | N | Y |
| 3 Nagle | ? | N | N | Y | Y | Y | ? | Y |
| 4 Smith | Y | N | N | Y | ? | ? | Y | Y |
| 5 **Lightfoot** | N | Y | Y | N | N | N | N | Y |
| 6 **Grandy** | N | Y | Y | N | N | N | N | Y |
| **KANSAS** | | | | | | | | |
| 1 **Roberts** | N | N | Y | N | Y | N | N | N |
| 2 Slattery | Y | N | N | Y | Y | Y | Y | Y |
| 3 **Meyers** | N | N | Y | Y | Y | N | ? | Y |
| 4 Glickman | Y | N | N | Y | Y | Y | Y | Y |
| 5 **Nichols** | N | N | N | N | Y | N | Y | N |
| **KENTUCKY** | | | | | | | | |
| 1 Hubbard | Y | N | N | Y | Y | Y | Y | Y |
| 2 Natcher | Y | N | N | Y | N | Y | Y | Y |
| 3 Mazzoli | Y | N | N | Y | Y | Y | Y | Y |
| 4 **Bunning** | N | Y | Y | N | Y | Y | N | N |
| 5 **Rogers** | N | N | Y | Y | N | Y | N | Y |
| 6 **Hopkins** | N | ? | Y | N | N | Y | N | N |
| 7 Perkins | ? | N | N | Y | Y | ? | Y | Y |
| **LOUISIANA** | | | | | | | | |
| 1 **Livingston** | N | Y | Y | N | N | Y | Y | Y |
| 2 Jefferson | Y | N | N | Y | Y | ? | Y | Y |
| 3 Tauzin | Y | N | N | Y | N | Y | Y | Y |
| 4 **McCrery** | N | Y | Y | N | N | Y | ? | N |
| 5 Huckaby | Y | N | N | Y | Y | Y | Y | Y |
| 6 **Baker** | N | Y | Y | N | N | Y | N | N |
| 7 Hayes | Y | N | N | Y | N | Y | ? | Y |
| 8 **Holloway** | N | Y | Y | N | N | Y | ? | ? |
| **MAINE** | | | | | | | | |
| 1 Andrews | Y | N | N | Y | Y | Y | Y | Y |
| 2 **Snowe** | N | N | N | Y | Y | Y | Y | Y |
| **MARYLAND** | | | | | | | | |
| 1 **Gilchrest** | N | Y | Y | Y | Y | Y | N | Y |
| 2 **Bentley** | N | N | Y | Y | Y | Y | N | Y |
| 3 Cardin | Y | N | N | Y | Y | Y | Y | Y |
| 4 McMillen | Y | N | N | Y | Y | Y | Y | Y |
| 5 Hoyer | Y | N | N | Y | Y | Y | Y | Y |
| 6 Byron | Y | N | Y | Y | N | Y | Y | Y |
| 7 Mfume | Y | N | N | Y | Y | Y | Y | Y |
| 8 **Morella** | N | N | N | Y | Y | Y | N | Y |
| **MASSACHUSETTS** | | | | | | | | |
| 1 Olver | Y | N | N | Y | Y | Y | Y | Y |
| 2 Neal | Y | N | N | Y | Y | ? | Y | Y |
| 3 Early | Y | N | N | Y | Y | ? | Y | Y |
| 4 Frank | Y | N | N | Y | Y | Y | Y | Y |
| 5 Atkins | ? | N | N | Y | Y | ? | ? | ? |
| 6 Mavroules | Y | N | N | Y | N | Y | ? | ? |
| 7 Markey | ? | ? | ? | ? | ? | Y | Y | Y |
| 8 Kennedy | Y | N | N | ? | Y | Y | Y | Y |
| 9 Moakley | Y | N | N | Y | Y | Y | Y | Y |
| 10 Studds | Y | N | N | Y | Y | ? | ? | ? |
| 11 Donnelly | Y | N | N | Y | Y | ? | ? | ? |
| **MICHIGAN** | | | | | | | | |
| 1 Conyers | ? | N | N | Y | Y | ? | ? | Y |
| 2 **Pursell** | N | N | Y | N | Y | ? | ? | ? |
| 3 Wolpe | Y | N | N | Y | Y | Y | Y | Y |
| 4 **Upton** | N | N | Y | N | Y | N | N | N |
| 5 **Henry** | N | Y | Y | N | Y | N | N | N |
| 6 Carr | Y | N | N | Y | Y | Y | Y | Y |
| 7 Kildee | Y | N | N | Y | Y | Y | Y | Y |
| 8 Traxler | ? | ? | ? | ? | ? | ? | ? | ? |
| 9 **Vander Jagt** | N | Y | Y | N | Y | Y | Y | N |
| 10 **Camp** | N | N | Y | N | Y | N | Y | Y |
| 11 **Davis** | N | N | N | Y | N | ? | Y | Y |
| 12 Bonior | Y | N | N | Y | Y | Y | Y | Y |
| 13 Collins | Y | N | N | Y | Y | ? | Y | Y |
| 14 Hertel | Y | N | N | Y | Y | ? | Y | Y |
| 15 Ford | Y | N | N | Y | Y | Y | Y | Y |
| 16 Dingell | Y | N | N | Y | Y | Y | Y | Y |
| 17 Levin | Y | N | N | Y | Y | Y | Y | Y |
| 18 **Broomfield** | N | Y | Y | N | N | Y | Y | Y |
| **MINNESOTA** | | | | | | | | |
| 1 Penny | N | N | N | N | Y | N | Y | Y |
| 2 **Weber** | ? | ? | ? | ? | ? | Y | N | N |
| 3 **Ramstad** | N | N | N | Y | Y | Y | N | Y |
| 4 Vento | Y | N | N | Y | ? | Y | Y | Y |
| 5 Sabo | Y | N | N | Y | Y | Y | Y | Y |
| 6 Sikorski | Y | N | N | Y | Y | Y | N | Y |
| 7 Peterson | Y | N | N | Y | Y | Y | Y | Y |
| 8 Oberstar | Y | N | N | Y | Y | Y | Y | Y |
| **MISSISSIPPI** | | | | | | | | |
| 1 Whitten | Y | N | N | Y | Y | Y | Y | Y |
| 2 Espy | Y | N | N | Y | Y | ? | Y | Y |
| 3 Montgomery | Y | N | N | Y | N | Y | Y | Y |
| 4 Parker | Y | N | N | Y | N | Y | Y | Y |
| 5 Taylor | Y | N | N | Y | N | N | Y | Y |
| **MISSOURI** | | | | | | | | |
| 1 Clay | ? | ? | ? | ? | ? | Y | N | Y |
| 2 Horn | Y | N | N | Y | Y | Y | Y | Y |
| 3 Gephardt | Y | N | N | Y | Y | Y | Y | Y |
| 4 Skelton | Y | N | N | Y | Y | Y | ? | Y |
| 5 Wheat | Y | N | N | Y | Y | Y | Y | Y |
| 6 **Coleman** | N | N | Y | N | Y | Y | N | Y |
| 7 **Hancock** | N | Y | Y | N | N | N | N | N |
| 8 **Emerson** | N | N | Y | N | Y | Y | N | Y |
| 9 Volkmer | Y | N | N | Y | Y | Y | Y | Y |
| **MONTANA** | | | | | | | | |
| 1 Williams | Y | N | N | Y | Y | Y | Y | Y |
| 2 **Marlenee** | N | N | Y | N | N | Y | N | N |
| **NEBRASKA** | | | | | | | | |
| 1 **Bereuter** | N | N | Y | N | Y | N | N | N |
| 2 Hoagland | Y | N | X | # | # | Y | Y | Y |
| 3 **Barrett** | N | N | Y | N | N | Y | N | Y |
| **NEVADA** | | | | | | | | |
| 1 Bilbray | Y | N | N | Y | N | Y | Y | Y |
| 2 **Vucanovich** | N | Y | Y | N | Y | Y | N | N |
| **NEW HAMPSHIRE** | | | | | | | | |
| 1 **Zeliff** | N | Y | Y | N | N | ? | ? | Y |
| 2 Swett | Y | N | N | Y | N | Y | Y | Y |
| **NEW JERSEY** | | | | | | | | |
| 1 Andrews | Y | N | N | Y | N | Y | Y | Y |
| 2 Hughes | Y | N | N | Y | Y | Y | Y | Y |
| 3 Pallone | Y | N | N | Y | Y | Y | Y | Y |
| 4 **Smith** | N | N | N | Y | Y | Y | Y | Y |
| 5 **Roukema** | N | N | N | N | Y | Y | N | Y |
| 6 Dwyer | Y | N | N | Y | ? | Y | Y | Y |
| 7 **Rinaldo** | N | N | N | Y | Y | Y | Y | Y |
| 8 Roe | Y | N | N | Y | Y | Y | Y | Y |
| 9 Torricelli | Y | N | N | Y | ? | Y | Y | Y |
| 10 Payne | Y | N | N | Y | Y | Y | Y | Y |
| 11 **Gallo** | N | N | N | Y | ? | Y | N | N |
| 12 **Zimmer** | N | Y | Y | N | N | N | N | Y |
| 13 **Saxton** | N | N | N | Y | N | Y | N | Y |
| 14 Guarini | Y | N | N | Y | Y | Y | Y | Y |
| **NEW MEXICO** | | | | | | | | |
| 1 **Schiff** | N | N | N | Y | N | ? | ? | ? |
| 2 **Skeen** | N | N | Y | N | N | Y | N | Y |
| 3 Richardson | Y | N | ? | ? | ? | Y | Y | Y |
| **NEW YORK** | | | | | | | | |
| 1 Hochbrueckner | Y | N | N | Y | N | Y | Y | Y |
| 2 Downey | Y | N | N | Y | Y | Y | ? | Y |
| 3 Mrazek | Y | N | N | Y | Y | ? | ? | ? |
| 4 **Lent** | N | N | Y | N | N | Y | Y | Y |
| 5 **McGrath** | N | N | Y | N | Y | Y | Y | Y |
| 6 Flake | ? | X | X | ? | ? | Y | ? | Y |
| 7 Ackerman | ? | ? | ? | ? | ? | ? | Y | Y |
| 8 Scheuer | Y | N | N | Y | Y | ? | Y | Y |
| 9 Manton | Y | N | N | Y | Y | Y | Y | Y |
| 10 Schumer | Y | N | N | Y | Y | Y | Y | Y |
| 11 Towns | ? | ? | ? | # | ? | ? | ? | ? |
| 12 Owens | Y | N | N | Y | Y | Y | Y | Y |
| 13 Solarz | ? | N | N | Y | Y | ? | ? | ? |
| 14 **Molinari** | N | N | N | N | Y | Y | N | Y |
| 15 **Green** | N | N | N | Y | N | Y | Y | Y |
| 16 Rangel | Y | N | N | Y | Y | Y | Y | Y |
| 17 Weiss | ? | ? | N | Y | Y | ? | ? | ? |
| 18 Serrano | Y | N | N | Y | Y | Y | Y | Y |
| 19 Engel | Y | N | N | Y | Y | ? | ? | Y |
| 20 Lowey | Y | N | N | Y | Y | Y | Y | + |
| 21 **Fish** | N | N | N | Y | N | N | Y | Y |
| 22 **Gilman** | Y | N | N | Y | Y | Y | Y | Y |
| 23 McNulty | Y | N | N | Y | N | Y | Y | Y |
| 24 **Solomon** | ? | ? | ? | ? | ? | Y | N | Y |
| 25 **Boehlert** | N | N | N | Y | Y | Y | N | Y |
| 26 **Martin** | N | N | Y | N | Y | Y | N | Y |
| 27 **Walsh** | N | N | N | Y | N | Y | Y | N |
| 28 McHugh | Y | N | N | Y | Y | Y | Y | Y |
| 29 **Horton** | N | N | N | Y | Y | Y | Y | Y |
| 30 Slaughter | Y | N | N | Y | Y | Y | Y | Y |
| 31 **Paxon** | N | Y | Y | N | N | Y | N | Y |
| 32 LaFalce | Y | N | N | Y | Y | Y | Y | Y |
| 33 Nowak | Y | N | N | Y | Y | Y | Y | Y |
| 34 **Houghton** | N | N | N | N | ? | Y | Y | Y |
| **NORTH CAROLINA** | | | | | | | | |
| 1 Jones | ? | N | N | Y | Y | ? | ? | ? |
| 2 Valentine | Y | N | N | Y | N | Y | Y | Y |
| 3 Lancaster | Y | N | N | Y | N | Y | Y | ? |
| 4 Price | Y | N | N | Y | N | Y | Y | Y |
| 5 Neal | ? | N | N | Y | N | Y | ? | Y |
| 6 **Coble** | N | Y | Y | N | N | Y | N | N |
| 7 Rose | Y | N | N | Y | N | Y | Y | Y |
| 8 Hefner | Y | N | N | Y | N | Y | ? | Y |
| 9 **McMillan** | N | Y | Y | N | N | ? | Y | Y |
| 10 **Ballenger** | N | Y | Y | N | N | Y | N | Y |
| 11 **Taylor** | N | Y | Y | N | Y | N | N | N |
| **NORTH DAKOTA** | | | | | | | | |
| AL Dorgan | Y | N | N | Y | Y | Y | Y | Y |
| **OHIO** | | | | | | | | |
| 1 Luken | Y | N | N | Y | Y | Y | Y | Y |
| 2 **Gradison** | N | Y | Y | N | N | Y | Y | Y |
| 3 Hall | Y | N | N | Y | Y | Y | ? | Y |
| 4 **Oxley** | N | Y | Y | N | N | Y | N | N |
| 5 **Gillmor** | N | N | Y | N | Y | Y | Y | Y |
| 6 **McEwen** | N | Y | Y | N | Y | Y | Y | N |
| 7 **Hobson** | N | N | Y | N | Y | Y | N | N |
| 8 **Boehner** | N | Y | Y | N | N | N | N | N |
| 9 Kaptur | ? | N | N | Y | Y | Y | Y | Y |
| 10 **Miller** | N | Y | Y | N | N | Y | N | Y |
| 11 Eckart | Y | N | N | Y | Y | Y | Y | Y |
| 12 **Kasich** | N | Y | Y | N | Y | Y | N | N |
| 13 Pease | Y | N | N | Y | Y | ? | ? | ? |
| 14 Sawyer | Y | N | N | Y | Y | Y | Y | Y |
| 15 **Wylie** | N | N | Y | ? | N | Y | Y | N |
| 16 **Regula** | N | N | Y | N | N | Y | N | Y |
| 17 Traficant | Y | N | N | Y | Y | Y | Y | Y |
| 18 Applegate | Y | N | Y | Y | Y | Y | Y | Y |
| 19 Feighan | Y | N | N | Y | Y | ? | Y | Y |
| 20 Oakar | Y | N | N | Y | Y | Y | Y | Y |
| 21 Stokes | Y | N | N | Y | Y | Y | Y | Y |
| **OKLAHOMA** | | | | | | | | |
| 1 **Inhofe** | N | Y | Y | N | N | Y | N | N |
| 2 Synar | Y | N | N | Y | N | ? | ? | ? |
| 3 Brewster | Y | N | N | Y | N | Y | Y | Y |
| 4 McCurdy | N | N | N | Y | N | Y | ? | ? |
| 5 **Edwards** | ? | N | Y | N | N | Y | ? | N |
| 6 English | Y | N | N | Y | N | Y | Y | Y |
| **OREGON** | | | | | | | | |
| 1 AuCoin | Y | N | N | Y | ? | # | ? | ? |
| 2 **Smith** | N | N | Y | N | N | X | ? | ? |
| 3 Wyden | Y | N | N | Y | Y | Y | Y | Y |
| 4 DeFazio | ? | ? | ? | ? | ? | ? | Y | Y |
| 5 Kopetski | Y | N | N | Y | Y | Y | Y | Y |
| **PENNSYLVANIA** | | | | | | | | |
| 1 Foglietta | Y | N | N | Y | Y | ? | Y | Y |
| 2 Blackwell | Y | N | N | Y | Y | Y | Y | Y |
| 3 Borski | Y | N | N | Y | Y | Y | Y | Y |
| 4 Kolter | ? | N | N | Y | Y | Y | ? | ? |
| 5 **Schulze** | ? | Y | Y | N | Y | Y | Y | N |
| 6 Yatron | Y | N | N | Y | ? | Y | Y | Y |
| 7 **Weldon** | N | N | Y | Y | Y | Y | N | Y |
| 8 Kostmayer | Y | N | N | Y | Y | Y | Y | Y |
| 9 **Shuster** | N | Y | Y | N | Y | N | N | Y |
| 10 **McDade** | ? | N | Y | N | Y | Y | N | Y |
| 11 Kanjorski | Y | N | N | Y | Y | Y | Y | Y |
| 12 Murtha | Y | N | ? | Y | ? | Y | Y | Y |
| 13 **Coughlin** | N | Y | Y | ? | Y | ? | N | Y |
| 14 Coyne | Y | N | N | Y | Y | Y | Y | Y |
| 15 **Ritter** | N | Y | Y | N | Y | Y | Y | Y |
| 16 **Walker** | ? | ? | ? | ? | ? | N | N | N |
| 17 **Gekas** | N | N | Y | N | Y | N | N | N |
| 18 **Santorum** | N | N | Y | N | Y | Y | Y | N |
| 19 **Goodling** | N | N | Y | N | Y | N | N | Y |
| 20 Gaydos | ? | N | ? | ? | ? | Y | ? | Y |
| 21 **Ridge** | N | N | Y | N | Y | Y | N | Y |
| 22 Murphy | Y | N | N | Y | Y | Y | Y | Y |
| 23 **Clinger** | N | Y | Y | N | Y | Y | Y | Y |
| **RHODE ISLAND** | | | | | | | | |
| 1 **Machtley** | N | N | N | Y | Y | Y | N | Y |
| 2 Reed | Y | N | N | Y | Y | Y | Y | Y |
| **SOUTH CAROLINA** | | | | | | | | |
| 1 **Ravenel** | N | Y | Y | Y | N | Y | Y | Y |
| 2 **Spence** | N | Y | Y | N | N | Y | Y | N |
| 3 Derrick | Y | N | N | Y | Y | Y | Y | Y |
| 4 Patterson | Y | N | N | Y | N | Y | Y | Y |
| 5 Spratt | Y | N | N | Y | Y | Y | Y | Y |
| 6 Tallon | ? | N | N | Y | Y | Y | ? | Y |
| **SOUTH DAKOTA** | | | | | | | | |
| AL Johnson | Y | N | N | Y | Y | Y | Y | Y |
| **TENNESSEE** | | | | | | | | |
| 1 **Quillen** | N | Y | Y | N | N | Y | Y | Y |
| 2 **Duncan** | N | Y | Y | Y | N | N | N | N |
| 3 Lloyd | Y | N | N | Y | Y | Y | Y | ? |
| 4 Cooper | Y | N | N | Y | N | Y | Y | Y |
| 5 Clement | Y | N | N | Y | N | Y | Y | Y |
| 6 Gordon | Y | N | N | Y | N | Y | Y | Y |
| 7 **Sundquist** | N | Y | Y | N | Y | N | N | N |
| 8 Tanner | Y | ? | ? | ? | ? | Y | Y | Y |
| 9 Ford | ? | N | N | Y | Y | ? | Y | Y |
| **TEXAS** | | | | | | | | |
| 1 Chapman | ? | N | N | Y | X | Y | ? | Y |
| 2 Wilson | ? | ? | N | Y | ? | ? | ? | ? |
| 3 **Johnson** | N | Y | N | N | N | N | ? | Y |
| 4 Hall | Y | N | Y | Y | N | Y | Y | Y |
| 5 Bryant | Y | N | N | Y | N | Y | Y | Y |
| 6 **Barton** | ? | # | # | X | X | Y | N | N |
| 7 **Archer** | N | Y | Y | N | Y | N | Y | Y |
| 8 **Fields** | N | N | Y | N | Y | Y | N | N |
| 9 Brooks | Y | N | N | Y | Y | Y | Y | Y |
| 10 Pickle | Y | N | N | Y | N | Y | Y | Y |
| 11 Edwards | Y | N | N | Y | N | Y | Y | Y |
| 12 Geren | Y | N | N | Y | N | Y | Y | Y |
| 13 Sarpalius | Y | N | N | Y | N | Y | Y | Y |
| 14 Laughlin | Y | N | N | Y | Y | Y | Y | Y |
| 15 de la Garza | Y | N | N | Y | Y | Y | Y | Y |
| 16 Coleman | Y | N | N | Y | N | Y | Y | Y |
| 17 Stenholm | Y | N | Y | N | ? | Y | Y | Y |
| 18 Washington | Y | N | N | Y | N | Y | Y | Y |
| 19 **Combest** | N | Y | Y | N | N | Y | Y | Y |
| 20 Gonzalez | Y | N | N | Y | N | Y | Y | Y |
| 21 **Smith** | N | Y | Y | N | Y | Y | N | N |
| 22 **DeLay** | N | Y | Y | N | Y | N | N | N |
| 23 Bustamante | Y | N | N | Y | N | Y | Y | Y |
| 24 Frost | Y | N | N | Y | N | Y | ? | Y |
| 25 Andrews | Y | N | N | Y | Y | Y | Y | Y |
| 26 **Armey** | N | Y | N | N | N | N | ? | N |
| 27 Ortiz | Y | N | N | Y | Y | Y | Y | Y |
| **UTAH** | | | | | | | | |
| 1 **Hansen** | N | Y | Y | N | Y | N | N | N |
| 2 Owens | N | N | N | Y | Y | ? | Y | Y |
| 3 Orton | N | N | N | Y | Y | Y | Y | Y |
| **VERMONT** | | | | | | | | |
| AL *Sanders* | Y | N | N | Y | Y | Y | Y | Y |
| **VIRGINIA** | | | | | | | | |
| 1 **Bateman** | N | N | Y | N | Y | Y | Y | Y |
| 2 Pickett | Y | N | N | Y | Y | Y | Y | Y |
| 3 **Bliley** | N | Y | Y | N | N | Y | N | N |
| 4 Sisisky | Y | N | N | Y | N | Y | Y | Y |
| 5 Payne | Y | N | N | Y | N | Y | Y | Y |
| 6 Olin | Y | N | N | ? | ? | Y | Y | Y |
| 7 **Allen** | N | Y | Y | N | N | Y | N | N |
| 8 Moran | Y | N | N | Y | Y | Y | Y | Y |
| 9 Boucher | Y | N | N | Y | Y | Y | ? | Y |
| 10 **Wolf** | N | Y | Y | N | N | Y | N | Y |
| **WASHINGTON** | | | | | | | | |
| 1 **Miller** | N | Y | Y | N | N | Y | ? | ? |
| 2 Swift | Y | N | N | Y | Y | Y | Y | Y |
| 3 Unsoeld | Y | N | N | Y | Y | Y | Y | Y |
| 4 **Morrison** | N | N | Y | Y | N | ? | ? | ? |
| 5 Foley | | | | | | | | |
| 6 Dicks | Y | N | N | Y | Y | Y | Y | Y |
| 7 McDermott | Y | N | N | Y | N | Y | Y | Y |
| 8 **Chandler** | N | Y | Y | N | Y | ? | ? | ? |
| **WEST VIRGINIA** | | | | | | | | |
| 1 Mollohan | Y | N | N | Y | Y | Y | Y | Y |
| 2 Staggers | ? | ? | ? | ? | ? | Y | Y | Y |
| 3 Wise | Y | N | N | Y | Y | ? | Y | Y |
| 4 Rahall | Y | N | N | Y | Y | Y | Y | Y |
| **WISCONSIN** | | | | | | | | |
| 1 Aspin | Y | N | N | Y | Y | Y | Y | Y |
| 2 **Klug** | N | N | Y | N | N | N | N | Y |
| 3 **Gunderson** | N | N | Y | Y | Y | Y | ? | Y |
| 4 Kleczka | Y | N | N | Y | Y | Y | Y | Y |
| 5 Moody | Y | N | N | Y | Y | ? | ? | ? |
| 6 **Petri** | N | N | Y | Y | Y | N | Y | Y |
| 7 Obey | Y | N | N | Y | Y | Y | Y | Y |
| 8 **Roth** | N | N | Y | N | N | N | Y | Y |
| 9 **Sensenbrenner** | N | N | Y | N | N | N | N | N |
| **WYOMING** | | | | | | | | |
| AL **Thomas** | N | N | Y | N | N | N | N | N |

Southern states - Ala., Ark., Fla., Ga., Ky., La., Miss., N.C., Okla., S.C., Tenn., Texas, Va.
Omitted votes are quorum calls, which CQ does not include in its vote charts.

**390. S 5. Family Leave/Conference Report.** Adoption of the conference report to require companies with more than 50 employees to provide workers with up to 12 weeks of unpaid leave for family emergencies. Employers would have to continue health care coverage and could not hire a permanent replacement. Adopted (thus cleared for the president) 241-161: R 37-119; D 203-42 (ND 157-12, SD 46-30); I 1-0, Sept. 10, 1992. A 'nay' was a vote in support of the president's position.

**391. HR 3724. Indian Health Care Amendments/Insurance Reimbursement.** Dannemeyer, R-Calif., amendment to require the Indian Health Service to pursue reimbursement for the costs associated with providing health care to Native Americans from private health-care insurance companies if the tribe or a tribal organization had private coverage or was self-insured. Rejected 165-199: R 140-13; D 25-186 (ND 8-134, SD 17-52); I 0-0, Sept. 15, 1992.

**392. HR 3724. Indian Health Care Amendments/Passage.** Passage of the bill to reauthorize Indian health-care programs through fiscal year 2000. The bill would also create minimum health standards for Indians, promote Indian recruitment in the health-care professions and develop a program to control Indian substance abuse. Passed 330-36: R 117-36; D 213-0 (ND 144-0, SD 69-0); I 0-0, Sept. 15, 1992.

**393. HR 5231. National Competitiveness/Previous Question.** Derrick, D-S.C., motion to order the previous question (thus limiting debate and the possibility of amendment) on adoption of the rule (H Res 563) to provide for House floor consideration of the bill designed to boost the global competitiveness of U.S. businesses through government programs. Motion agreed to 241-163: R 0-161; D 240-2 (ND 164-1, SD 76-1); I 1-0, Sept. 16, 1992.

**394. HR 5231. National Competitiveness/Rule.** Adoption of the rule (H Res 563) to provide for House floor consideration of the bill designed to boost the global competitiveness of U.S. businesses through government programs. Adopted 241-160: R 0-160; D 240-0 (ND 163-0, SD 77-0); I 1-0, Sept. 16, 1992.

**395. S 1699. Government Securities Reform.** Markey, D-Mass., motion to suspend the rules and pass the bill to strengthen the anti-fraud provisions of federal securities laws, extend the Security and Exchange Commission's authority to prescribe specific anti-fraud and anti-manipulation rules, require government securities brokers to develop internal controls, require reports of large concentrations of positions in the Treasury market, and take other measures to prevent false and misleading statements concerning the offerings of government securities. Motion rejected 124-279: R 22-138; D 102-140 (ND 73-92, SD 29-48); I 0-1, Sept. 16, 1992. A two-thirds majority of those present and voting (269 in this case) was required for passage under suspension of the rules. A 'nay' was a vote in support of the president's position.

**396. HR 5534. William O. Douglas Outdoor Classroom.** Vento, D-Minn., motion to suspend the rules and pass the bill to authorize the secretary of the Interior to enter into cooperative agreements with the William O. Douglas Outdoor Classroom, a nonprofit organization for environmental education. Motion rejected 243-154: R 45-113; D 197-41 (ND 143-19, SD 54-22); I 1-0, Sept. 16, 1992. A two-thirds majority of those present and voting (265 in this case) was required for passage under suspension of the rules.

**397. S 12. Cable Television Reregulation/Rule.** Adoption of the rule (H Res 571) to waive all points of order against and provide for House floor consideration of the conference report on the bill to cap basic cable rates and improve competition in the cable industry by having the Federal Communications Commission set rates for basic cable service and giving broadcasters the right to charge cable operators for the use of over-the-air signals. Adopted 263-134: R 33-126; D 229-8 (ND 156-7, SD 73-1); I 1-0, Sept. 17, 1992.

† *Ted Weiss, D-N.Y., died Sept. 14; Walter B. Jones, D-N.C., died Sept. 15. The last vote either was eligible for was 390.*

## KEY

Y  Voted for (yea).
#  Paired for.
+  Announced for.
N  Voted against (nay).
X  Paired against.
−  Announced against.
P  Voted "present."
C  Voted "present" to avoid possible conflict of interest.
?  Did not vote or otherwise make a position known.

Democrats  **Republicans**
*Independent*

| | 390 | 391 | 392 | 393 | 394 | 395 | 396 | 397 |
|---|---|---|---|---|---|---|---|---|
| **ALABAMA** | | | | | | | | |
| 1 *Callahan* | N | Y | Y | N | N | Y | N | Y |
| 2 *Dickinson* | N | Y | Y | N | N | N | N | N |
| 3 Browder | N | N | Y | Y | Y | N | Y | Y |
| 4 Bevill | Y | N | Y | Y | Y | N | Y | Y |
| 5 Cramer | N | N | Y | Y | Y | Y | Y | Y |
| 6 Erdreich | Y | N | Y | Y | Y | N | Y | Y |
| 7 Harris | N | Y | Y | Y | Y | Y | Y | Y |
| **ALASKA** | | | | | | | | |
| AL *Young* | Y | Y | Y | N | N | N | Y | ? |
| **ARIZONA** | | | | | | | | |
| 1 *Rhodes* | N | Y | Y | N | N | N | N | N |
| 2 Pastor | Y | N | Y | Y | Y | Y | N | Y |
| 3 *Stump* | N | Y | N | N | N | N | N | N |
| 4 *Kyl* | N | N | Y | N | N | N | N | N |
| 5 *Kolbe* | N | N | Y | N | N | N | N | N |
| **ARKANSAS** | | | | | | | | |
| 1 Alexander | ? | ? | ? | Y | ? | ? | ? | Y |
| 2 Thornton | Y | N | Y | Y | Y | N | N | Y |
| 3 *Hammerschmidt* | N | Y | Y | N | N | N | N | Y |
| 4 Anthony | Y | N | Y | ? | Y | Y | Y | ? |
| **CALIFORNIA** | | | | | | | | |
| 1 *Riggs* | N | Y | Y | N | N | N | N | N |
| 2 *Herger* | N | Y | Y | N | N | N | N | N |
| 3 Matsui | Y | N | Y | Y | Y | Y | Y | Y |
| 4 Fazio | Y | N | Y | Y | Y | Y | Y | Y |
| 5 Pelosi | Y | ? | ? | Y | Y | N | Y | Y |
| 6 Boxer | Y | ? | ? | ? | ? | ? | ? | ? |
| 7 Miller | Y | N | Y | Y | Y | N | Y | Y |
| 8 Dellums | Y | N | Y | ? | ? | N | Y | Y |
| 9 Stark | Y | N | Y | Y | Y | N | Y | Y |
| 10 Edwards | Y | N | Y | Y | Y | N | Y | Y |
| 11 Lantos | Y | ? | ? | ? | Y | N | Y | Y |
| 12 *Campbell* | Y | Y | Y | N | N | N | N | N |
| 13 Mineta | Y | N | Y | Y | Y | N | Y | Y |
| 14 *Doolittle* | N | Y | N | N | N | N | Y | N |
| 15 Condit | Y | Y | Y | Y | Y | N | N | Y |
| 16 Panetta | Y | N | Y | Y | Y | Y | Y | Y |
| 17 Dooley | Y | N | Y | Y | Y | N | Y | Y |
| 18 Lehman | Y | N | Y | Y | Y | ? | Y | Y |
| 19 *Lagomarsino* | N | Y | Y | N | N | N | N | N |
| 20 *Thomas* | N | Y | Y | N | N | N | Y | N |
| 21 *Gallegly* | N | ? | ? | N | N | N | N | N |
| 22 *Moorhead* | ? | Y | Y | N | N | Y | N | N |
| 23 Beilenson | Y | N | Y | Y | Y | N | Y | ? |
| 24 Waxman | Y | N | Y | Y | Y | Y | Y | Y |
| 25 Roybal | Y | ? | ? | Y | Y | N | Y | Y |
| 26 Berman | Y | N | Y | Y | Y | Y | Y | Y |
| 27 Levine | ? | ? | ? | ? | ? | Y | Y | Y |
| 28 Dixon | Y | N | Y | Y | Y | N | Y | Y |
| 29 Waters | Y | ? | Y | ? | ? | ? | ? | ? |
| 30 Martinez | Y | N | Y | Y | Y | N | Y | Y |
| 31 Dymally | ? | N | ? | Y | Y | N | Y | Y |
| 32 Anderson | Y | N | Y | Y | Y | N | Y | Y |
| 33 *Dreier* | N | N | N | N | N | N | N | N |
| 34 Torres | Y | N | Y | Y | Y | N | N | Y |
| 35 *Lewis* | X | Y | Y | N | N | N | N | N |
| 36 Brown | Y | N | Y | Y | Y | N | ? | Y |
| 37 *McCandless* | N | Y | Y | N | N | N | N | N |
| 38 *Dornan* | N | X | ? | X | X | ? | ? | N |
| 39 *Dannemeyer* | N | Y | N | N | N | N | N | N |
| 40 *Cox* | N | Y | Y | N | N | N | N | N |
| 41 *Lowery* | N | Y | Y | N | N | N | N | N |

| | 390 | 391 | 392 | 393 | 394 | 395 | 396 | 397 |
|---|---|---|---|---|---|---|---|---|
| 42 *Rohrabacher* | N | Y | N | N | N | N | N | N |
| 43 *Packard* | N | Y | Y | N | N | N | N | N |
| 44 *Cunningham* | N | Y | N | N | N | N | Y | N |
| 45 *Hunter* | N | Y | N | N | N | N | Y | N |
| **COLORADO** | | | | | | | | |
| 1 Schroeder | Y | Y | Y | Y | Y | Y | Y | N |
| 2 Skaggs | Y | N | Y | Y | Y | Y | Y | Y |
| 3 Campbell | Y | N | ? | Y | Y | N | Y | Y |
| 4 *Allard* | N | Y | N | N | N | N | N | N |
| 5 *Hefley* | N | Y | N | N | N | N | N | N |
| 6 *Schaefer* | N | N | Y | N | N | Y | N | N |
| **CONNECTICUT** | | | | | | | | |
| 1 Kennelly | Y | N | Y | Y | Y | Y | Y | Y |
| 2 Gejdenson | Y | N | Y | Y | Y | Y | Y | Y |
| 3 DeLauro | Y | N | Y | Y | Y | Y | Y | Y |
| 4 *Shays* | Y | Y | Y | N | Y | Y | Y | Y |
| 5 *Franks* | N | Y | N | N | N | N | N | N |
| 6 *Johnson* | Y | Y | Y | N | N | N | N | N |
| **DELAWARE** | | | | | | | | |
| AL Carper | Y | Y | Y | Y | Y | N | Y | Y |
| **FLORIDA** | | | | | | | | |
| 1 Hutto | N | Y | Y | Y | N | N | N | Y |
| 2 Peterson | Y | N | Y | Y | Y | N | Y | Y |
| 3 Bennett | Y | N | Y | Y | Y | Y | Y | Y |
| 4 *James* | Y | Y | N | N | N | N | N | N |
| 5 *McCollum* | N | Y | N | N | N | N | N | N |
| 6 *Stearns* | N | N | N | N | N | N | N | N |
| 7 Gibbons | Y | N | Y | Y | Y | N | Y | Y |
| 8 *Young* | Y | N | N | N | N | Y | N | N |
| 9 *Bilirakis* | N | N | N | N | N | Y | N | N |
| 10 *Ireland* | N | ? | ? | ? | ? | N | Y | ? |
| 11 Bacchus | Y | N | Y | Y | Y | Y | Y | Y |
| 12 *Lewis* | N | Y | Y | Y | Y | N | Y | Y |
| 13 *Goss* | N | Y | Y | N | N | N | N | N |
| 14 Johnston | Y | N | Y | Y | Y | Y | Y | Y |
| 15 *Shaw* | N | Y | N | N | N | N | N | N |
| 16 Smith | Y | N | Y | Y | Y | Y | Y | Y |
| 17 Lehman | Y | N | Y | Y | Y | N | Y | Y |
| 18 *Ros−Lehtinen* | Y | Y | Y | N | N | N | Y | N |
| 19 Fascell | Y | N | Y | ? | ? | ? | ? | ? |
| **GEORGIA** | | | | | | | | |
| 1 Thomas | ? | N | Y | Y | Y | N | Y | Y |
| 2 Hatcher | ? | ? | Y | Y | Y | N | Y | Y |
| 3 Ray | N | Y | Y | Y | Y | N | N | Y |
| 4 Jones | N | N | Y | Y | Y | N | Y | Y |
| 5 Lewis | Y | N | Y | Y | Y | N | Y | Y |
| 6 *Gingrich* | N | Y | N | N | N | N | N | N |
| 7 Darden | N | N | Y | Y | Y | Y | Y | Y |
| 8 Rowland | N | N | Y | Y | Y | N | Y | Y |
| 9 Jenkins | Y | N | Y | Y | Y | Y | Y | Y |
| 10 Barnard | X | ? | ? | ? | ? | ? | ? | ? |
| **HAWAII** | | | | | | | | |
| 1 Abercrombie | Y | N | Y | Y | Y | N | Y | Y |
| 2 Mink | Y | N | Y | Y | Y | N | Y | Y |
| **IDAHO** | | | | | | | | |
| 1 LaRocco | N | N | Y | Y | Y | N | Y | Y |
| 2 Stallings | N | N | Y | Y | Y | N | Y | Y |
| **ILLINOIS** | | | | | | | | |
| 1 Hayes | Y | N | Y | Y | Y | N | Y | Y |
| 2 Savage | Y | N | Y | Y | Y | Y | Y | ? |
| 3 Russo | Y | N | Y | Y | Y | Y | Y | Y |
| 4 Sangmeister | Y | N | Y | Y | Y | N | Y | Y |
| 5 Lipinski | Y | N | Y | Y | Y | N | Y | Y |
| 6 *Hyde* | Y | Y | Y | N | N | N | N | N |
| 7 Collins | Y | N | Y | Y | Y | Y | Y | Y |
| 8 Rostenkowski | Y | N | Y | Y | Y | Y | Y | Y |
| 9 Yates | Y | N | Y | Y | Y | Y | Y | Y |
| 10 *Porter* | N | Y | N | N | N | N | N | N |
| 11 Annunzio | Y | N | Y | Y | Y | N | Y | Y |
| 12 *Crane* | N | N | N | N | N | N | N | N |
| 13 *Fawell* | N | Y | N | N | N | N | N | N |
| 14 *Hastert* | N | Y | N | N | N | N | N | N |
| 15 *Ewing* | N | Y | N | N | N | N | N | N |
| 16 Cox | Y | N | Y | Y | Y | N | N | Y |
| 17 Evans | Y | N | Y | Y | Y | Y | Y | Y |
| 18 *Michel* | N | Y | N | N | N | N | N | N |
| 19 Bruce | Y | N | Y | Y | Y | Y | Y | Y |
| 20 Durbin | Y | N | Y | Y | Y | N | Y | Y |
| 21 Costello | Y | N | Y | Y | Y | N | Y | Y |
| 22 Poshard | Y | N | Y | Y | Y | N | N | Y |
| **INDIANA** | | | | | | | | |
| 1 Visclosky | Y | N | Y | Y | Y | N | Y | Y |
| 2 Sharp | Y | N | Y | Y | Y | N | Y | Y |
| 3 Roemer | Y | N | Y | Y | Y | N | N | Y |

ND  Northern Democrats  SD  Southern Democrats

| | 390 | 391 | 392 | 393 | 394 | 395 | 396 | 397 |
|---|---|---|---|---|---|---|---|---|
| 4 Long | Y | N | Y | Y | Y | Y | Y | Y |
| 5 Jontz | Y | N | Y | Y | Y | Y | Y | Y |
| 6 ***Burton*** | N | Y | N | N | N | N | N | N |
| 7 ***Myers*** | N | Y | Y | N | N | N | Y | N |
| 8 McCloskey | Y | N | Y | Y | Y | Y | Y | Y |
| 9 Hamilton | N | N | Y | Y | Y | Y | N | N |
| 10 Jacobs | Y | Y | Y | N | Y | Y | N | N |
| **IOWA** | | | | | | | | |
| 1 ***Leach*** | Y | Y | Y | N | N | N | Y | N |
| 2 ***Nussle*** | N | Y | Y | N | N | N | N | N |
| 3 Nagle | Y | N | Y | ? | Y | N | Y | Y |
| 4 Smith | Y | N | Y | Y | Y | N | Y | Y |
| 5 ***Lightfoot*** | N | Y | Y | N | N | N | N | N |
| 6 ***Grandy*** | N | Y | Y | N | N | N | N | Y |
| **KANSAS** | | | | | | | | |
| 1 ***Roberts*** | N | Y | Y | N | N | N | N | N |
| 2 Slattery | N | N | Y | Y | Y | Y | N | Y |
| 3 ***Meyers*** | N | Y | Y | N | N | N | N | N |
| 4 Glickman | N | Y | Y | Y | Y | Y | Y | Y |
| 5 ***Nichols*** | N | Y | Y | N | N | N | N | N |
| **KENTUCKY** | | | | | | | | |
| 1 Hubbard | Y | N | Y | Y | Y | N | Y | Y |
| 2 Natcher | Y | N | Y | Y | Y | N | Y | Y |
| 3 Mazzoli | Y | N | Y | Y | Y | N | Y | Y |
| 4 ***Bunning*** | N | Y | Y | N | N | N | N | N |
| 5 ***Rogers*** | N | Y | Y | N | N | N | N | Y |
| 6 ***Hopkins*** | N | Y | Y | N | N | N | N | N |
| 7 Perkins | Y | ? | ? | Y | Y | Y | Y | ? |
| **LOUISIANA** | | | | | | | | |
| 1 ***Livingston*** | N | Y | Y | N | N | N | N | N |
| 2 Jefferson | Y | ? | ? | Y | Y | N | Y | Y |
| 3 Tauzin | N | N | Y | Y | Y | Y | Y | Y |
| 4 ***McCrery*** | X | Y | Y | N | N | N | N | ? |
| 5 Huckaby | N | ? | ? | ? | ? | ? | ? | ? |
| 6 ***Baker*** | N | Y | Y | N | N | N | N | N |
| 7 Hayes | ? | ? | ? | ? | ? | ? | ? | ? |
| 8 ***Holloway*** | ? | ? | ? | N | N | N | N | N |
| **MAINE** | | | | | | | | |
| 1 Andrews | Y | N | Y | Y | Y | N | N | Y |
| 2 ***Snowe*** | Y | Y | Y | N | N | N | Y | N |
| **MARYLAND** | | | | | | | | |
| 1 ***Gilchrest*** | N | Y | Y | N | N | N | Y | N |
| 2 ***Bentley*** | N | Y | Y | N | N | N | ? | N |
| 3 Cardin | Y | N | Y | Y | Y | Y | ? | Y |
| 4 McMillen | Y | N | Y | Y | Y | Y | Y | Y |
| 5 Hoyer | Y | N | Y | Y | Y | Y | Y | Y |
| 6 Byron | N | N | Y | Y | Y | N | N | Y |
| 7 Mfume | Y | N | Y | Y | Y | N | Y | Y |
| 8 ***Morella*** | Y | Y | Y | N | N | Y | Y | ? |
| **MASSACHUSETTS** | | | | | | | | |
| 1 Olver | Y | N | Y | Y | Y | N | Y | Y |
| 2 Neal | Y | ? | ? | Y | Y | N | Y | Y |
| 3 Early | Y | ? | ? | Y | Y | Y | Y | + |
| 4 Frank | Y | N | Y | Y | Y | N | Y | N |
| 5 Atkins | ? | ? | ? | ? | ? | ? | ? | ? |
| 6 Mavroules | Y | ? | ? | ? | ? | ? | ? | Y |
| 7 Markey | Y | N | Y | Y | Y | Y | Y | Y |
| 8 Kennedy | Y | ? | ? | Y | Y | N | Y | ? |
| 9 Moakley | Y | ? | ? | Y | Y | N | Y | Y |
| 10 Studds | ? | ? | ? | Y | Y | Y | Y | Y |
| 11 Donnelly | ? | ? | ? | Y | Y | Y | Y | Y |
| **MICHIGAN** | | | | | | | | |
| 1 Conyers | Y | ? | ? | ? | ? | ? | ? | ? |
| 2 ***Pursell*** | X | Y | N | N | N | N | N | Y |
| 3 Wolpe | Y | N | Y | Y | Y | Y | Y | Y |
| 4 ***Upton*** | N | Y | N | N | N | N | N | N |
| 5 ***Henry*** | N | Y | N | N | N | N | N | Y |
| 6 Carr | N | N | Y | Y | Y | Y | N | Y |
| 7 Kildee | Y | N | Y | Y | Y | Y | Y | Y |
| 8 Traxler | ? | ? | ? | ? | ? | ? | ? | ? |
| 9 ***Vander Jagt*** | N | Y | Y | N | N | Y | N | N |
| 10 ***Camp*** | N | N | Y | N | N | N | N | N |
| 11 ***Davis*** | Y | Y | Y | N | N | N | Y | Y |
| 12 Bonior | Y | N | Y | Y | Y | Y | Y | Y |
| 13 Collins | Y | N | Y | Y | Y | Y | Y | ? |
| 14 Hertel | Y | N | Y | Y | Y | Y | Y | ? |
| 15 Ford | Y | N | Y | Y | Y | Y | Y | Y |
| 16 Dingell | Y | N | Y | Y | ? | Y | Y | Y |
| 17 Levin | Y | N | Y | Y | Y | Y | Y | Y |
| 18 ***Broomfield*** | N | Y | Y | N | N | N | Y | ? |
| **MINNESOTA** | | | | | | | | |
| 1 Penny | N | Y | Y | Y | Y | N | Y | Y |
| 2 ***Weber*** | N | Y | Y | ? | ? | ? | ? | ? |
| 3 ***Ramstad*** | Y | Y | Y | N | N | N | N | Y |
| 4 Vento | Y | N | Y | Y | Y | N | Y | Y |
| 5 Sabo | Y | ? | ? | Y | Y | N | Y | Y |
| 6 Sikorski | Y | ? | ? | ? | ? | ? | ? | Y |
| 7 Peterson | Y | N | Y | Y | Y | N | N | Y |
| 8 Oberstar | Y | N | Y | Y | Y | Y | Y | Y |
| **MISSISSIPPI** | | | | | | | | |
| 1 Whitten | Y | N | Y | Y | Y | N | ? | Y |
| 2 Espy | Y | ? | ? | Y | Y | Y | Y | Y |
| 3 Montgomery | N | Y | Y | Y | Y | N | N | Y |
| 4 Parker | N | Y | Y | Y | Y | N | N | Y |
| 5 Taylor | N | Y | Y | Y | Y | N | N | Y |
| **MISSOURI** | | | | | | | | |
| 1 Clay | Y | N | Y | Y | Y | N | Y | Y |
| 2 Horn | Y | N | Y | Y | Y | N | N | Y |
| 3 Gephardt | Y | N | Y | Y | Y | Y | Y | Y |
| 4 Skelton | N | Y | Y | Y | Y | N | N | Y |
| 5 Wheat | Y | N | Y | Y | Y | N | Y | Y |
| 6 ***Coleman*** | Y | Y | Y | N | N | Y | N | Y |
| 7 ***Hancock*** | N | Y | N | N | N | N | N | N |
| 8 ***Emerson*** | N | Y | Y | N | N | N | N | Y |
| 9 Volkmer | Y | N | Y | Y | Y | Y | N | Y |
| **MONTANA** | | | | | | | | |
| 1 Williams | Y | N | Y | Y | ? | N | N | Y |
| 2 ***Marlenee*** | N | N | Y | N | N | N | N | N |
| **NEBRASKA** | | | | | | | | |
| 1 ***Bereuter*** | N | Y | Y | N | N | N | Y | N |
| 2 Hoagland | Y | N | Y | Y | Y | N | Y | Y |
| 3 ***Barrett*** | N | Y | Y | N | N | N | N | N |
| **NEVADA** | | | | | | | | |
| 1 Bilbray | Y | Y | Y | Y | Y | N | Y | Y |
| 2 ***Vucanovich*** | N | Y | Y | N | N | N | Y | N |
| **NEW HAMPSHIRE** | | | | | | | | |
| 1 ***Zeliff*** | N | Y | Y | N | N | N | ? | N |
| 2 Swett | Y | N | Y | Y | Y | Y | Y | Y |
| **NEW JERSEY** | | | | | | | | |
| 1 Andrews | Y | N | Y | Y | Y | Y | Y | Y |
| 2 Hughes | Y | N | Y | Y | Y | N | Y | N |
| 3 Pallone | Y | N | Y | Y | Y | Y | Y | Y |
| 4 ***Smith*** | Y | Y | Y | N | N | N | Y | N |
| 5 ***Roukema*** | Y | ? | ? | N | N | N | N | N |
| 6 Dwyer | Y | N | Y | Y | Y | Y | Y | Y |
| 7 ***Rinaldo*** | Y | Y | Y | N | N | Y | N | Y |
| 8 Roe | Y | N | Y | Y | Y | Y | Y | Y |
| 9 Torricelli | Y | ? | ? | Y | Y | Y | Y | Y |
| 10 Payne | Y | N | Y | Y | Y | N | Y | Y |
| 11 ***Gallo*** | N | Y | Y | N | N | N | N | N |
| 12 ***Zimmer*** | Y | Y | Y | N | N | N | N | N |
| 13 ***Saxton*** | Y | Y | Y | N | N | N | Y | N |
| 14 Guarini | Y | N | Y | Y | Y | Y | Y | Y |
| **NEW MEXICO** | | | | | | | | |
| 1 ***Schiff*** | X | ? | ? | N | N | N | Y | N |
| 2 ***Skeen*** | N | ? | ? | N | N | N | Y | N |
| 3 Richardson | Y | N | Y | Y | Y | N | Y | N |
| **NEW YORK** | | | | | | | | |
| 1 Hochbrueckner | Y | N | Y | Y | Y | Y | Y | Y |
| 2 Downey | Y | N | Y | Y | Y | Y | Y | Y |
| 3 Mrazek | ? | ? | Y | Y | Y | N | Y | Y |
| 4 ***Lent*** | N | Y | Y | N | N | ? | ? | N |
| 5 ***McGrath*** | Y | Y | Y | N | N | Y | N | Y |
| 6 Flake | Y | ? | ? | Y | Y | N | Y | Y |
| 7 Ackerman | Y | ? | ? | Y | Y | N | Y | Y |
| 8 Scheuer | Y | N | Y | ? | ? | ? | ? | ? |
| 9 Manton | Y | ? | ? | Y | Y | Y | Y | Y |
| 10 Schumer | Y | N | Y | Y | Y | N | Y | Y |
| 11 Towns | # | ? | ? | ? | ? | ? | ? | ? |
| 12 Owens | Y | ? | ? | Y | Y | N | Y | Y |
| 13 Solarz | # | ? | ? | ? | ? | ? | ? | ? |
| 14 ***Molinari*** | Y | ? | ? | N | N | N | N | N |
| 15 ***Green*** | Y | Y | Y | N | N | N | Y | N |
| 16 Rangel | Y | ? | ? | Y | Y | N | Y | Y |
| 17 Weiss † | ? | | | | | | | |
| 18 Serrano | Y | ? | ? | Y | Y | ? | ? | Y |
| 19 Engel | Y | ? | ? | ? | ? | ? | ? | ? |
| 20 Lowey | Y | N | Y | Y | Y | Y | Y | Y |
| 21 ***Fish*** | Y | Y | Y | N | N | N | N | N |
| 22 ***Gilman*** | Y | Y | Y | N | N | N | Y | Y |
| 23 McNulty | Y | N | Y | Y | Y | Y | Y | Y |
| 24 ***Solomon*** | Y | Y | N | N | N | N | N | N |
| 25 ***Boehlert*** | Y | ? | ? | N | N | N | Y | N |
| 26 ***Martin*** | Y | Y | Y | N | ? | ? | N | N |
| 27 ***Walsh*** | N | N | Y | N | N | N | Y | Y |
| 28 McHugh | Y | N | Y | Y | Y | N | Y | ? |
| 29 ***Horton*** | Y | N | Y | N | N | Y | N | N |
| 30 Slaughter | Y | N | Y | Y | Y | N | Y | Y |
| 31 ***Paxon*** | N | Y | Y | N | N | N | N | N |
| 32 LaFalce | Y | N | Y | Y | Y | N | Y | Y |
| 33 Nowak | Y | N | Y | Y | Y | N | Y | Y |
| 34 ***Houghton*** | N | Y | Y | N | N | Y | Y | N |
| **NORTH CAROLINA** | | | | | | | | |
| 1 Jones † | ? | | | | | | | |
| 2 Valentine | N | Y | Y | Y | Y | N | N | Y |
| 3 Lancaster | N | N | Y | Y | Y | N | Y | Y |
| 4 Price | Y | N | Y | Y | Y | N | Y | Y |
| 5 Neal | N | N | Y | Y | Y | N | Y | Y |
| 6 ***Coble*** | N | Y | N | N | N | N | N | N |
| 7 Rose | Y | N | Y | Y | Y | N | Y | Y |
| 8 Hefner | Y | N | Y | Y | Y | N | Y | Y |
| 9 ***McMillan*** | N | N | Y | N | N | N | N | Y |
| 10 ***Ballenger*** | N | Y | Y | N | N | Y | N | N |
| 11 ***Taylor*** | N | Y | Y | N | N | N | N | N |
| **NORTH DAKOTA** | | | | | | | | |
| AL Dorgan | Y | N | Y | Y | Y | Y | Y | Y |
| **OHIO** | | | | | | | | |
| 1 Luken | N | ? | ? | Y | Y | N | N | Y |
| 2 ***Gradison*** | N | Y | Y | N | N | Y | N | N |
| 3 Hall | Y | N | Y | Y | ? | N | Y | Y |
| 4 ***Oxley*** | N | Y | Y | N | N | Y | N | N |
| 5 ***Gillmor*** | Y | Y | Y | N | N | N | Y | N |
| 6 ***McEwen*** | N | Y | N | N | N | N | N | N |
| 7 ***Hobson*** | N | Y | Y | N | N | N | Y | N |
| 8 ***Boehner*** | N | Y | N | N | N | N | N | N |
| 9 Kaptur | Y | ? | ? | Y | Y | N | Y | Y |
| 10 ***Miller*** | N | Y | N | N | N | Y | N | N |
| 11 Eckart | Y | N | Y | Y | Y | Y | Y | Y |
| 12 ***Kasich*** | N | Y | Y | N | N | N | N | Y |
| 13 Pease | ? | N | Y | Y | Y | N | Y | Y |
| 14 Sawyer | Y | N | Y | Y | Y | N | Y | Y |
| 15 ***Wylie*** | N | Y | Y | N | N | N | N | Y |
| 16 ***Regula*** | Y | Y | Y | N | N | N | N | N |
| 17 Traficant | Y | N | Y | Y | Y | N | Y | Y |
| 18 Applegate | Y | N | Y | Y | Y | N | Y | Y |
| 19 Feighan | Y | ? | Y | Y | Y | N | Y | Y |
| 20 Oakar | Y | N | Y | Y | Y | N | Y | N |
| 21 Stokes | Y | N | Y | Y | Y | N | Y | Y |
| **OKLAHOMA** | | | | | | | | |
| 1 ***Inhofe*** | N | Y | Y | N | N | N | N | Y |
| 2 Synar | # | # | ? | Y | Y | Y | Y | Y |
| 3 Brewster | N | N | Y | Y | Y | Y | N | ? |
| 4 McCurdy | ? | ? | ? | Y | Y | N | N | Y |
| 5 ***Edwards*** | N | Y | Y | N | N | ? | ? | N |
| 6 English | Y | N | ? | Y | Y | N | N | ? |
| **OREGON** | | | | | | | | |
| 1 AuCoin | # | ? | ? | # | ? | ? | ? | ? |
| 2 ***Smith*** | X | Y | Y | N | N | Y | N | N |
| 3 Wyden | Y | N | Y | Y | Y | Y | Y | Y |
| 4 DeFazio | Y | ? | ? | Y | Y | N | Y | Y |
| 5 Kopetski | Y | N | Y | Y | Y | Y | Y | Y |
| **PENNSYLVANIA** | | | | | | | | |
| 1 Foglietta | Y | ? | ? | Y | Y | N | Y | Y |
| 2 Blackwell | Y | N | Y | Y | Y | N | Y | Y |
| 3 Borski | Y | N | Y | Y | Y | Y | Y | Y |
| 4 Kolter | Y | N | Y | Y | Y | N | Y | Y |
| 5 ***Schulze*** | N | Y | Y | N | N | Y | N | N |
| 6 Yatron | Y | N | Y | Y | Y | N | Y | Y |
| 7 ***Weldon*** | Y | Y | Y | N | N | N | N | N |
| 8 Kostmayer | Y | ? | Y | Y | Y | Y | Y | Y |
| 9 ***Shuster*** | N | Y | N | N | N | N | N | N |
| 10 ***McDade*** | Y | Y | Y | N | N | N | N | N |
| 11 Kanjorski | Y | N | Y | Y | Y | N | Y | Y |
| 12 Murtha | Y | N | Y | Y | Y | ? | ? | Y |
| 13 ***Coughlin*** | Y | Y | Y | N | N | N | ? | N |
| 14 Coyne | Y | N | Y | Y | Y | Y | Y | Y |
| 15 ***Ritter*** | N | Y | N | N | N | Y | N | N |
| 16 ***Walker*** | N | Y | N | N | N | N | N | N |
| 17 ***Gekas*** | N | Y | N | N | N | N | N | N |
| 18 ***Santorum*** | N | Y | Y | N | N | N | N | N |
| 19 ***Goodling*** | N | Y | N | N | N | N | N | N |
| 20 Gaydos | Y | N | Y | Y | Y | N | Y | Y |
| 21 ***Ridge*** | N | Y | Y | N | N | N | N | N |
| 22 Murphy | Y | ? | ? | Y | Y | Y | Y | Y |
| 23 ***Clinger*** | N | Y | Y | N | N | N | N | N |
| **RHODE ISLAND** | | | | | | | | |
| 1 ***Machtley*** | Y | Y | Y | N | N | N | Y | Y |
| 2 Reed | Y | N | Y | Y | Y | Y | Y | Y |
| **SOUTH CAROLINA** | | | | | | | | |
| 1 ***Ravenel*** | Y | N | Y | N | N | N | Y | Y |
| 2 ***Spence*** | N | Y | Y | N | N | N | N | N |
| 3 Derrick | Y | ? | Y | Y | Y | N | Y | Y |
| 4 Patterson | N | N | Y | Y | Y | N | N | Y |
| 5 Spratt | Y | N | Y | Y | Y | N | Y | Y |
| 6 Tallon | Y | N | Y | Y | Y | N | Y | Y |
| **SOUTH DAKOTA** | | | | | | | | |
| AL Johnson | Y | N | Y | Y | Y | N | Y | Y |
| **TENNESSEE** | | | | | | | | |
| 1 ***Quillen*** | N | N | Y | N | N | N | N | Y |
| 2 ***Duncan*** | N | Y | N | N | N | N | N | N |
| 3 Lloyd | N | Y | Y | Y | Y | Y | N | Y |
| 4 Cooper | Y | N | Y | Y | Y | Y | N | Y |
| 5 Clement | Y | N | Y | Y | Y | Y | N | Y |
| 6 Gordon | Y | N | Y | Y | Y | N | N | ? |
| 7 ***Sundquist*** | N | Y | Y | N | N | N | N | Y |
| 8 Tanner | N | N | Y | Y | Y | Y | Y | Y |
| 9 Ford | Y | ? | ? | ? | ? | Y | Y | Y |
| **TEXAS** | | | | | | | | |
| 1 Chapman | Y | N | Y | Y | Y | N | Y | Y |
| 2 Wilson | # | N | Y | Y | Y | N | Y | N |
| 3 ***Johnson*** | N | Y | N | N | N | N | N | N |
| 4 Hall | N | Y | Y | N | Y | Y | N | Y |
| 5 Bryant | Y | ? | ? | Y | Y | Y | Y | Y |
| 6 ***Barton*** | N | Y | N | N | N | N | N | N |
| 7 ***Archer*** | N | Y | N | N | N | N | N | N |
| 8 ***Fields*** | N | Y | N | N | N | Y | N | Y |
| 9 Brooks | Y | N | Y | Y | Y | Y | Y | Y |
| 10 Pickle | Y | Y | Y | Y | Y | Y | N | ? |
| 11 Edwards | N | Y | Y | Y | Y | Y | Y | Y |
| 12 Geren | N | N | Y | Y | Y | N | N | Y |
| 13 Sarpalius | N | Y | Y | Y | Y | Y | N | Y |
| 14 Laughlin | N | Y | Y | Y | Y | Y | N | Y |
| 15 de la Garza | Y | N | Y | Y | Y | ? | ? | Y |
| 16 Coleman | Y | ? | ? | Y | Y | Y | Y | Y |
| 17 Stenholm | N | Y | Y | Y | Y | Y | N | Y |
| 18 Washington | Y | N | Y | ? | ? | N | Y | Y |
| 19 ***Combest*** | N | Y | Y | N | N | N | N | N |
| 20 Gonzalez | Y | N | Y | Y | Y | N | Y | Y |
| 21 ***Smith*** | Y | Y | Y | N | N | N | Y | N |
| 22 ***DeLay*** | N | Y | N | N | N | N | N | N |
| 23 Bustamante | Y | N | ? | Y | Y | N | Y | Y |
| 24 Frost | Y | N | Y | Y | Y | N | Y | Y |
| 25 Andrews | Y | N | Y | Y | Y | Y | Y | Y |
| 26 ***Armey*** | N | Y | N | N | N | N | N | N |
| 27 Ortiz | Y | N | Y | Y | Y | ? | ? | Y |
| **UTAH** | | | | | | | | |
| 1 ***Hansen*** | N | ? | ? | N | N | N | N | N |
| 2 Owens | Y | ? | ? | Y | Y | ? | ? | ? |
| 3 Orton | N | N | Y | Y | Y | N | N | Y |
| **VERMONT** | | | | | | | | |
| AL *Sanders* | Y | ? | ? | Y | Y | N | Y | Y |
| **VIRGINIA** | | | | | | | | |
| 1 ***Bateman*** | N | Y | Y | N | N | N | N | Y |
| 2 Pickett | N | Y | Y | Y | Y | N | Y | Y |
| 3 ***Bliley*** | N | Y | N | N | N | Y | Y | N |
| 4 Sisisky | N | Y | Y | Y | Y | N | N | Y |
| 5 Payne | N | ? | ? | Y | Y | N | Y | Y |
| 6 Olin | N | N | Y | Y | Y | N | Y | Y |
| 7 ***Allen*** | N | Y | N | N | N | N | N | N |
| 8 Moran | Y | N | Y | Y | Y | N | Y | Y |
| 9 Boucher | Y | Y | Y | Y | Y | Y | Y | Y |
| 10 ***Wolf*** | N | Y | Y | N | N | N | N | Y |
| **WASHINGTON** | | | | | | | | |
| 1 ***Miller*** | # | Y | Y | N | N | N | N | Y |
| 2 Swift | Y | N | Y | Y | ? | Y | Y | Y |
| 3 Unsoeld | Y | N | Y | Y | Y | N | Y | Y |
| 4 ***Morrison*** | ? | ? | ? | ? | ? | N | Y | Y |
| 5 Foley | | | | | | | | |
| 6 Dicks | Y | N | Y | Y | Y | N | Y | Y |
| 7 McDermott | Y | N | Y | Y | Y | N | Y | Y |
| 8 ***Chandler*** | ? | ? | ? | ? | ? | ? | ? | ? |
| **WEST VIRGINIA** | | | | | | | | |
| 1 Mollohan | Y | N | Y | Y | Y | Y | Y | Y |
| 2 Staggers | Y | N | Y | Y | Y | N | Y | Y |
| 3 Wise | Y | N | Y | Y | Y | Y | Y | Y |
| 4 Rahall | Y | N | Y | Y | Y | Y | Y | Y |
| **WISCONSIN** | | | | | | | | |
| 1 Aspin | N | ? | ? | Y | Y | ? | ? | Y |
| 2 ***Klug*** | Y | Y | Y | N | N | N | N | N |
| 3 ***Gunderson*** | N | ? | ? | N | N | N | Y | Y |
| 4 Kleczka | Y | N | Y | Y | Y | N | Y | Y |
| 5 Moody | ? | N | Y | Y | Y | Y | Y | Y |
| 6 ***Petri*** | N | Y | Y | N | N | N | Y | Y |
| 7 Obey | Y | N | Y | Y | Y | Y | Y | Y |
| 8 ***Roth*** | N | N | Y | N | N | N | Y | N |
| 9 ***Sensenbrenner*** | N | Y | N | N | N | N | N | N |
| **WYOMING** | | | | | | | | |
| AL ***Thomas*** | N | Y | Y | N | N | N | N | N |

Southern states - Ala., Ark., Fla., Ga., Ky., La., Miss., N.C., Okla., S.C., Tenn., Texas, Va.
Omitted votes are quorum calls, which CQ does not include in its vote charts.

## KEY

Y Voted for (yea).
\# Paired for.
+ Announced for.
N Voted against (nay).
X Paired against.
− Announced against.
P Voted "present."
C Voted "present" to avoid possible conflict of interest.
? Did not vote or otherwise make a position known.

Democrats    *Republicans*
*Independent*

**398. S 12. Cable Television Reregulation/Conference Report.** Adoption of the conference report on the bill to cap basic cable rates and improve competition in the cable industry by having the Federal Communications Commission set rates for basic cable service and giving broadcasters the right to charge cable operators for the use of over-the-air signals. Adopted 280-128: R 71-90; D 208-38 (ND 141-29, SD 67-9); I 1-0, Sept. 17, 1992. A "nay" was a vote in support of the president's position.

**399. HR 5373. Fiscal 1993 Energy and Water Development Appropriations/Conference Report.** Adoption of the conference report to provide $22,005,643,000 in new budget authority for energy and water development in fiscal 1993. The administration requested $22,419,288,000. Adopted 245-143: R 87-64; D 158-78 (ND 101-61, SD 57-17); I 0-1, Sept. 17, 1992.

**400. HR 5373. Fiscal 1993 Energy and Water Development Appropriations/Previous Question.** Bevill, D-Ala., motion to order the previous question (thus limiting debate and the possibility of amendment) on the Bevill motion to recede and concur in a Senate amendment with an amendment to provide $94.8 million for construction of 10 research facilities at various universities. Motion rejected 157-203: R 34-110; D 123-92 (ND 83-70, SD 40-22); I 0-1, Sept. 17, 1992.

**401. HR 5373. Fiscal 1993 Energy and Water Development Appropriations/Research Project Authorizations.** Brown, D-Calif., amendment to the Bevill, D-Ala., motion to recede and concur in a Senate amendment with an amendment to provide $94.8 million for construction of 10 research facilities at various universities, to make the projects in the Bevill motion contingent upon the authorization by the appropriate committees and subject to competitive selection by a merit-review board. Adopted 250-104: R 112-29; D 137-75 (ND 102-49, SD 35-26); I 1-0, Sept. 17, 1992.

**402. Procedural Motion.** Approval of the House Journal of Thursday, Sept. 17. Approved 226-120: R 28-115; D 197-5 (ND 136-5, SD 61-0); I 1-0, Sept. 18, 1992.

**403. H Res 572. Investigation of Rep. Gonzalez.** Bonior, D-Mich., motion to table (kill) the Combest, R-Texas, privileged resolution to direct the Committee on Standards of Official Conduct to investigate and report its findings on whether Henry B. Gonzalez, D-Texas, publicly disclosed classified information involving the administration's dealings with Iraq before the Persian Gulf War. Motion agreed to 216-150: R 0-150; D 215-0 (ND 148-0, SD 67-0); I 1-0, Sept. 18, 1992.

**404. HR 5006. Fiscal 1993 Defense Authorization/Close Conference.** Aspin, D-Wis., motion to close portions of the conference on the fiscal 1993 defense authorization. Motion agreed to 394-1: R 155-0; D 238-1 (ND 161-1, SD 77-0); I 1-0, Sept. 22, 1992.

**406. HR 5231. National Competitiveness/Discretion for Secretary.** Walker, R-Pa., en bloc amendment to give the secretary of Commerce discretion in implementing provisions of the bill by changing the programs from being mandatory to discretionary. Rejected 148-256: R 148-9; D 0-246 (ND 0-168, SD 0-78); I 0-1, Sept. 22, 1992.

| | 398 | 399 | 400 | 401 | 402 | 403 | 404 | 406 |
|---|---|---|---|---|---|---|---|---|
| **ALABAMA** | | | | | | | | |
| 1 *Callahan* | Y | Y | Y | N | N | N | Y | Y |
| 2 *Dickinson* | N | Y | N | Y | N | N | Y | Y |
| 3 Browder | Y | Y | Y | N | Y | Y | Y | N |
| 4 Bevill | Y | Y | Y | N | Y | Y | Y | N |
| 5 Cramer | Y | Y | Y | N | Y | Y | Y | N |
| 6 Erdreich | Y | Y | Y | N | Y | Y | Y | N |
| 7 Harris | Y | Y | Y | N | Y | Y | Y | N |
| **ALASKA** | | | | | | | | |
| AL *Young* | Y | Y | ? | ? | ? | N | Y | Y |
| **ARIZONA** | | | | | | | | |
| 1 *Rhodes* | N | Y | Y | Y | N | N | Y | Y |
| 2 Pastor | N | Y | N | N | Y | Y | Y | N |
| 3 *Stump* | N | N | N | Y | N | N | Y | Y |
| 4 *Kyl* | N | Y | N | Y | N | N | Y | Y |
| 5 *Kolbe* | N | Y | N | Y | N | N | Y | Y |
| **ARKANSAS** | | | | | | | | |
| 1 Alexander | Y | Y | ? | ? | ? | ? | Y | ? |
| 2 Thornton | Y | Y | Y | ? | Y | Y | Y | N |
| 3 *Hammerschmidt* | N | Y | Y | N | N | N | Y | Y |
| 4 Anthony | ? | ? | ? | ? | ? | ? | Y | N |
| **CALIFORNIA** | | | | | | | | |
| 1 *Riggs* | \# | ? | ? | ? | ? | ? | Y | Y |
| 2 *Herger* | N | Y | N | Y | N | N | Y | Y |
| 3 Matsui | N | Y | Y | Y | Y | Y | Y | N |
| 4 Fazio | N | Y | N | Y | Y | Y | Y | N |
| 5 Pelosi | Y | ? | Y | Y | Y | Y | Y | N |
| 6 Boxer | ? | ? | ? | ? | ? | ? | ? | ? |
| 7 Miller | Y | Y | N | Y | Y | Y | ? | N |
| 8 Dellums | Y | N | N | Y | Y | Y | Y | N |
| 9 Stark | Y | N | N | Y | ? | Y | Y | N |
| 10 Edwards | Y | N | Y | Y | Y | Y | Y | N |
| 11 Lantos | Y | N | Y | Y | Y | Y | Y | N |
| 12 *Campbell* | N | N | N | Y | N | N | Y | Y |
| 13 Mineta | Y | Y | N | Y | Y | Y | Y | N |
| 14 *Doolittle* | N | Y | N | Y | N | N | Y | Y |
| 15 Condit | Y | N | N | Y | Y | Y | Y | N |
| 16 Panetta | Y | N | Y | Y | Y | Y | Y | N |
| 17 Dooley | Y | Y | N | Y | ? | Y | Y | N |
| 18 Lehman | Y | Y | Y | Y | Y | Y | Y | N |
| 19 *Lagomarsino* | N | Y | N | Y | N | N | Y | Y |
| 20 *Thomas* | N | ? | ? | ? | ? | ? | Y | Y |
| 21 *Gallegly* | Y | Y | N | Y | N | N | Y | Y |
| 22 *Moorhead* | N | Y | N | Y | N | N | ? | Y |
| 23 Beilenson | Y | N | N | Y | Y | Y | Y | N |
| 24 Waxman | Y | N | ? | ? | Y | Y | Y | N |
| 25 Roybal | N | N | N | Y | Y | Y | Y | N |
| 26 Berman | N | Y | Y | Y | Y | Y | Y | N |
| 27 Levine | N | ? | ? | ? | ? | ? | ? | ? |
| 28 Dixon | N | Y | Y | N | ? | Y | Y | N |
| 29 Waters | ? | N | N | N | Y | Y | Y | N |
| 30 Martinez | Y | Y | N | Y | Y | Y | Y | N |
| 31 Dymally | Y | N | Y | ? | Y | Y | Y | N |
| 32 Anderson | Y | Y | Y | N | Y | Y | Y | N |
| 33 *Dreier* | N | N | N | Y | N | N | Y | Y |
| 34 Torres | N | Y | Y | Y | Y | Y | Y | N |
| 35 *Lewis* | N | Y | N | Y | N | N | Y | ? |
| 36 Brown | Y | Y | Y | Y | Y | Y | Y | N |
| 37 *McCandless* | N | Y | N | Y | N | N | Y | Y |
| 38 *Dornan* | N | Y | N | Y | N | N | Y | Y |
| 39 *Dannemeyer* | N | N | N | Y | N | N | Y | Y |
| 40 *Cox* | N | Y | N | Y | N | N | Y | Y |
| 41 *Lowery* | N | Y | ? | ? | N | N | Y | Y |

| | 398 | 399 | 400 | 401 | 402 | 403 | 404 | 406 |
|---|---|---|---|---|---|---|---|---|
| 42 *Rohrabacher* | N | Y | N | Y | N | N | Y | Y |
| 43 *Packard* | N | Y | N | Y | N | N | Y | Y |
| 44 *Cunningham* | N | Y | N | Y | N | N | Y | Y |
| 45 *Hunter* | N | Y | N | Y | N | N | Y | Y |
| **COLORADO** | | | | | | | | |
| 1 Schroeder | N | N | N | N | Y | Y | Y | N |
| 2 Skaggs | N | Y | N | Y | Y | Y | Y | N |
| 3 Campbell | N | ? | ? | ? | ? | ? | Y | N |
| 4 *Allard* | N | N | N | Y | N | N | Y | Y |
| 5 *Hefley* | N | N | N | Y | N | N | Y | Y |
| 6 *Schaefer* | N | Y | N | Y | N | N | Y | Y |
| **CONNECTICUT** | | | | | | | | |
| 1 Kennelly | Y | Y | Y | N | Y | Y | Y | N |
| 2 Gejdenson | Y | Y | Y | N | Y | Y | Y | N |
| 3 DeLauro | Y | Y | Y | N | Y | Y | Y | N |
| 4 *Shays* | Y | N | N | Y | N | Y | Y | N |
| 5 *Franks* | N | Y | Y | N | N | Y | Y | Y |
| 6 *Johnson* | N | Y | N | Y | N | N | Y | Y |
| **DELAWARE** | | | | | | | | |
| AL Carper | Y | Y | N | Y | Y | Y | Y | N |
| **FLORIDA** | | | | | | | | |
| 1 Hutto | Y | N | N | Y | Y | Y | Y | N |
| 2 Peterson | Y | Y | Y | N | Y | Y | Y | N |
| 3 Bennett | Y | N | N | Y | Y | Y | Y | N |
| 4 *James* | N | N | N | N | N | N | Y | Y |
| 5 *McCollum* | N | N | N | N | N | N | Y | Y |
| 6 *Stearns* | N | N | N | N | N | N | Y | Y |
| 7 Gibbons | N | Y | N | Y | Y | Y | Y | N |
| 8 *Young* | Y | Y | N | N | N | N | Y | Y |
| 9 *Bilirakis* | Y | Y | N | Y | N | N | Y | Y |
| 10 *Ireland* | N | ? | ? | ? | ? | N | ? | ? |
| 11 Bacchus | Y | Y | ? | Y | Y | Y | Y | N |
| 12 *Lewis* | Y | N | N | Y | N | N | Y | Y |
| 13 *Goss* | Y | N | N | Y | N | N | Y | Y |
| 14 Johnston | Y | N | ? | ? | Y | Y | Y | N |
| 15 *Shaw* | Y | ? | ? | ? | ? | ? | Y | Y |
| 16 Smith | Y | N | Y | Y | Y | Y | Y | N |
| 17 Lehman | Y | ? | ? | ? | ? | ? | Y | N |
| 18 *Ros—Lehtinen* | Y | Y | N | Y | N | N | Y | Y |
| 19 Fascell | ? | ? | ? | ? | ? | ? | Y | N |
| **GEORGIA** | | | | | | | | |
| 1 Thomas | Y | Y | ? | ? | Y | Y | Y | N |
| 2 Hatcher | Y | Y | ? | ? | Y | Y | Y | N |
| 3 Ray | Y | Y | Y | ? | ? | ? | N | N |
| 4 Jones | Y | ? | ? | ? | ? | ? | ? | ? |
| 5 Lewis | Y | N | N | Y | Y | Y | Y | ? |
| 6 *Gingrich* | N | ? | ? | N | N | N | Y | Y |
| 7 Darden | Y | Y | ? | Y | Y | Y | Y | N |
| 8 Rowland | Y | Y | ? | Y | Y | Y | Y | N |
| 9 Jenkins | Y | Y | ? | Y | Y | Y | Y | N |
| 10 Barnard | X | ? | ? | ? | ? | ? | ? | ? |
| **HAWAII** | | | | | | | | |
| 1 Abercrombie | Y | Y | Y | N | ? | Y | Y | N |
| 2 Mink | Y | Y | Y | N | Y | Y | ? | ? |
| **IDAHO** | | | | | | | | |
| 1 LaRocco | Y | Y | N | Y | Y | Y | Y | N |
| 2 Stallings | Y | Y | N | Y | Y | Y | Y | N |
| **ILLINOIS** | | | | | | | | |
| 1 Hayes | Y | N | N | Y | Y | Y | Y | N |
| 2 Savage | ? | Y | ? | ? | ? | ? | N | N |
| 3 Russo | N | Y | N | Y | ? | Y | Y | N |
| 4 Sangmeister | Y | Y | N | Y | Y | Y | Y | N |
| 5 Lipinski | Y | N | N | Y | Y | Y | Y | N |
| 6 *Hyde* | N | N | N | Y | N | N | Y | Y |
| 7 Collins | Y | N | N | Y | Y | Y | Y | N |
| 8 Rostenkowski | Y | N | Y | Y | Y | Y | Y | N |
| 9 Yates | Y | Y | N | Y | Y | Y | Y | N |
| 10 *Porter* | Y | N | N | Y | N | N | Y | Y |
| 11 Annunzio | Y | Y | ? | ? | ? | ? | Y | N |
| 12 *Crane* | N | N | N | N | N | N | Y | Y |
| 13 *Fawell* | N | Y | N | Y | N | N | Y | Y |
| 14 *Hastert* | N | N | N | N | N | N | Y | Y |
| 15 *Ewing* | Y | ? | N | Y | N | N | Y | Y |
| 16 Cox | Y | Y | Y | N | Y | Y | Y | N |
| 17 Evans | Y | N | Y | Y | Y | Y | Y | N |
| 18 *Michel* | Y | Y | Y | N | Y | N | Y | Y |
| 19 Bruce | Y | N | Y | Y | Y | Y | Y | N |
| 20 Durbin | Y | N | Y | Y | Y | Y | Y | N |
| 21 Costello | Y | N | Y | Y | Y | Y | Y | N |
| 22 Poshard | Y | N | Y | Y | Y | Y | Y | N |
| **INDIANA** | | | | | | | | |
| 1 Visclosky | Y | Y | Y | N | Y | Y | Y | N |
| 2 Sharp | Y | Y | Y | ? | Y | Y | Y | N |
| 3 Roemer | Y | Y | Y | N | Y | Y | Y | N |

ND Northern Democrats    SD Southern Democrats

| | 398 | 399 | 400 | 401 | 402 | 403 | 404 | 406 |
|---|---|---|---|---|---|---|---|---|
| 4 Long | Y | Y | Y | N | Y | Y | Y | N |
| 5 Jontz | Y | N | Y | Y | Y | Y | Y | N |
| 6 ***Burton*** | N | N | N | Y | N | N | Y | Y |
| 7 ***Myers*** | N | Y | Y | N | Y | N | Y | Y |
| 8 McCloskey | Y | Y | Y | N | Y | Y | Y | N |
| 9 Hamilton | Y | Y | Y | Y | Y | Y | Y | N |
| 10 Jacobs | Y | N | N | Y | N | Y | Y | N |
| **IOWA** | | | | | | | | |
| 1 ***Leach*** | Y | Y | N | Y | N | N | Y | Y |
| 2 ***Nussle*** | Y | N | N | Y | ? | N | Y | Y |
| 3 Nagle | Y | Y | Y | N | Y | Y | Y | N |
| 4 Smith | N | Y | Y | N | Y | Y | Y | N |
| 5 ***Lightfoot*** | Y | Y | Y | N | N | N | Y | Y |
| 6 ***Grandy*** | Y | Y | N | Y | N | N | Y | Y |
| **KANSAS** | | | | | | | | |
| 1 ***Roberts*** | Y | N | N | Y | N | N | Y | Y |
| 2 Slattery | Y | N | ? | ? | Y | Y | Y | N |
| 3 ***Meyers*** | Y | Y | N | Y | N | N | Y | Y |
| 4 Glickman | Y | N | N | Y | Y | Y | Y | N |
| 5 ***Nichols*** | Y | N | N | Y | N | N | Y | Y |
| **KENTUCKY** | | | | | | | | |
| 1 Hubbard | Y | Y | N | Y | Y | Y | Y | N |
| 2 Natcher | Y | Y | Y | N | Y | Y | Y | N |
| 3 Mazzoli | Y | Y | Y | N | Y | Y | Y | N |
| 4 ***Bunning*** | Y | Y | N | Y | ? | ? | ? | Y |
| 5 ***Rogers*** | Y | Y | Y | N | N | N | Y | Y |
| 6 ***Hopkins*** | N | Y | N | Y | N | N | Y | Y |
| 7 Perkins | ? | Y | Y | N | Y | Y | ? | ? |
| **LOUISIANA** | | | | | | | | |
| 1 ***Livingston*** | Y | Y | Y | N | N | N | Y | Y |
| 2 Jefferson | Y | Y | Y | N | ? | ? | ? | ? |
| 3 Tauzin | Y | Y | N | ? | Y | Y | Y | N |
| 4 ***McCrery*** | X | ? | ? | ? | ? | ? | ? | ? |
| 5 Huckaby | ? | ? | ? | ? | ? | ? | Y | N |
| 6 ***Baker*** | N | Y | Y | N | N | N | Y | Y |
| 7 Hayes | # | ? | ? | ? | ? | ? | ? | ? |
| 8 ***Holloway*** | N | ? | ? | ? | ? | N | Y | Y |
| **MAINE** | | | | | | | | |
| 1 Andrews | Y | N | N | Y | Y | Y | ? | N |
| 2 ***Snowe*** | Y | N | N | Y | N | N | Y | N |
| **MARYLAND** | | | | | | | | |
| 1 ***Gilchrest*** | Y | Y | N | Y | N | N | Y | Y |
| 2 ***Bentley*** | Y | Y | Y | Y | N | N | Y | Y |
| 3 Cardin | Y | Y | N | Y | Y | Y | Y | N |
| 4 McMillen | Y | Y | N | Y | Y | Y | Y | N |
| 5 Hoyer | Y | Y | Y | N | Y | Y | Y | N |
| 6 Byron | Y | Y | N | ? | Y | Y | Y | N |
| 7 Mfume | Y | N | N | Y | Y | Y | Y | N |
| 8 ***Morella*** | Y | N | N | Y | N | N | Y | N |
| **MASSACHUSETTS** | | | | | | | | |
| 1 Olver | Y | N | N | Y | Y | Y | Y | N |
| 2 Neal | Y | N | ? | ? | ? | ? | Y | N |
| 3 Early | Y | N | N | Y | Y | Y | Y | N |
| 4 Frank | N | N | ? | Y | Y | Y | Y | N |
| 5 Atkins | ? | ? | ? | ? | ? | ? | Y | N |
| 6 Mavroules | Y | ? | ? | ? | ? | ? | Y | N |
| 7 Markey | Y | N | N | Y | Y | Y | Y | N |
| 8 Kennedy | ? | ? | N | Y | Y | Y | ? | ? |
| 9 Moakley | Y | N | Y | Y | Y | Y | Y | N |
| 10 Studds | Y | N | ? | Y | Y | Y | Y | N |
| 11 Donnelly | Y | ? | ? | ? | ? | ? | Y | N |
| **MICHIGAN** | | | | | | | | |
| 1 Conyers | ? | ? | ? | ? | ? | ? | ? | ? |
| 2 ***Pursell*** | N | Y | Y | N | Y | N | Y | Y |
| 3 Wolpe | Y | N | N | Y | Y | Y | ? | ? |
| 4 ***Upton*** | Y | N | N | Y | N | N | Y | Y |
| 5 ***Henry*** | Y | N | N | Y | N | N | Y | N |
| 6 Carr | Y | Y | Y | N | Y | ? | ? | ? |
| 7 Kildee | Y | Y | Y | Y | Y | Y | Y | N |
| 8 Traxler | Y | ? | ? | ? | ? | ? | Y | N |
| 9 ***Vander Jagt*** | N | Y | N | ? | Y | N | Y | ? |
| 10 ***Camp*** | N | Y | N | Y | N | N | Y | Y |
| 11 ***Davis*** | Y | Y | ? | ? | ? | N | Y | N |
| 12 Bonior | Y | Y | Y | N | Y | Y | Y | N |
| 13 Collins | Y | N | N | Y | ? | ? | Y | N |
| 14 Hertel | Y | Y | Y | Y | ? | ? | Y | N |
| 15 Ford | Y | N | Y | Y | ? | ? | Y | N |
| 16 Dingell | Y | Y | Y | Y | Y | Y | N | N |
| 17 Levin | Y | N | N | Y | Y | Y | Y | N |
| 18 ***Broomfield*** | ? | ? | ? | ? | ? | ? | Y | Y |
| **MINNESOTA** | | | | | | | | |
| 1 Penny | N | N | N | Y | Y | Y | + | + |
| 2 ***Weber*** | ? | ? | ? | ? | ? | ? | Y | Y |
| 3 ***Ramstad*** | Y | N | N | Y | N | N | Y | Y |
| 4 Vento | Y | N | N | Y | Y | Y | Y | N |
| 5 Sabo | Y | Y | Y | N | Y | Y | Y | N |
| 6 Sikorski | Y | N | N | Y | N | Y | Y | N |
| 7 Peterson | N | Y | Y | Y | Y | Y | Y | N |
| 8 Oberstar | Y | Y | Y | Y | Y | Y | Y | N |
| **MISSISSIPPI** | | | | | | | | |
| 1 Whitten | Y | Y | Y | N | ? | Y | Y | N |
| 2 Espy | Y | Y | N | Y | Y | Y | Y | N |
| 3 Montgomery | Y | Y | Y | N | Y | Y | Y | N |
| 4 Parker | N | Y | Y | N | Y | Y | Y | N |
| 5 Taylor | Y | Y | Y | Y | Y | Y | Y | N |
| **MISSOURI** | | | | | | | | |
| 1 Clay | Y | N | N | Y | N | Y | Y | N |
| 2 Horn | Y | N | N | Y | Y | Y | Y | N |
| 3 Gephardt | Y | Y | ? | ? | ? | ? | ? | N |
| 4 Skelton | Y | Y | N | Y | Y | Y | Y | N |
| 5 Wheat | Y | N | N | Y | Y | Y | Y | N |
| 6 ***Coleman*** | Y | N | N | Y | N | N | ? | ? |
| 7 ***Hancock*** | N | N | N | Y | N | N | Y | Y |
| 8 ***Emerson*** | Y | Y | N | Y | N | N | Y | Y |
| 9 Volkmer | Y | Y | Y | Y | Y | Y | Y | N |
| **MONTANA** | | | | | | | | |
| 1 Williams | Y | Y | N | Y | ? | ? | Y | N |
| 2 ***Marlenee*** | Y | ? | N | Y | ? | ? | ? | ? |
| **NEBRASKA** | | | | | | | | |
| 1 ***Bereuter*** | Y | N | N | Y | N | N | Y | Y |
| 2 Hoagland | Y | N | Y | Y | Y | Y | Y | N |
| 3 ***Barrett*** | Y | N | N | Y | N | N | Y | Y |
| **NEVADA** | | | | | | | | |
| 1 Bilbray | Y | Y | Y | Y | Y | Y | Y | N |
| 2 ***Vucanovich*** | N | N | Y | N | N | N | Y | Y |
| **NEW HAMPSHIRE** | | | | | | | | |
| 1 ***Zeliff*** | N | N | N | ? | ? | ? | ? | Y |
| 2 Swett | Y | N | N | Y | Y | Y | Y | N |
| **NEW JERSEY** | | | | | | | | |
| 1 Andrews | N | Y | Y | N | Y | Y | Y | N |
| 2 Hughes | N | Y | Y | N | Y | Y | Y | N |
| 3 Pallone | Y | Y | Y | N | Y | Y | Y | N |
| 4 ***Smith*** | N | Y | Y | N | Y | N | Y | Y |
| 5 ***Roukema*** | N | N | N | Y | N | N | Y | Y |
| 6 Dwyer | Y | Y | Y | N | ? | ? | Y | N |
| 7 ***Rinaldo*** | Y | Y | ? | ? | Y | N | Y | Y |
| 8 Roe | Y | Y | Y | N | Y | Y | Y | N |
| 9 Torricelli | Y | Y | Y | Y | Y | Y | Y | N |
| 10 Payne | N | Y | Y | Y | Y | Y | Y | N |
| 11 ***Gallo*** | N | Y | Y | N | N | N | Y | Y |
| 12 ***Zimmer*** | N | N | N | Y | N | N | Y | Y |
| 13 ***Saxton*** | N | Y | Y | N | ? | ? | Y | Y |
| 14 Guarini | Y | Y | ? | ? | Y | Y | Y | N |
| **NEW MEXICO** | | | | | | | | |
| 1 ***Schiff*** | Y | Y | N | Y | N | N | Y | Y |
| 2 ***Skeen*** | Y | Y | Y | N | Y | N | Y | Y |
| 3 Richardson | N | ? | ? | ? | ? | ? | Y | N |
| **NEW YORK** | | | | | | | | |
| 1 Hochbrueckner | Y | Y | Y | Y | Y | Y | Y | N |
| 2 Downey | Y | Y | Y | Y | Y | Y | Y | N |
| 3 Mrazek | Y | ? | ? | ? | ? | ? | ? | N |
| 4 ***Lent*** | N | N | ? | ? | P | N | Y | Y |
| 5 ***McGrath*** | Y | N | N | Y | Y | N | Y | N |
| 6 Flake | Y | N | ? | ? | ? | ? | Y | N |
| 7 Ackerman | Y | Y | Y | Y | Y | Y | Y | N |
| 8 Scheuer | ? | ? | ? | ? | ? | ? | Y | N |
| 9 Manton | Y | ? | ? | ? | ? | ? | Y | N |
| 10 Schumer | Y | N | Y | Y | Y | Y | Y | N |
| 11 Towns | ? | Y | N | Y | ? | ? | Y | N |
| 12 Owens | Y | N | N | Y | Y | Y | Y | N |
| 13 Solarz | Y | ? | ? | ? | ? | ? | Y | N |
| 14 ***Molinari*** | Y | N | N | Y | N | N | Y | Y |
| 15 ***Green*** | Y | Y | ? | ? | ? | ? | Y | Y |
| 16 Rangel | Y | Y | Y | Y | Y | Y | Y | N |
| 17 Vacancy | | | | | | | | |
| 18 Serrano | Y | Y | N | Y | ? | Y | Y | N |
| 19 Engel | Y | Y | N | Y | Y | Y | ? | N |
| 20 Lowey | Y | Y | Y | Y | Y | Y | Y | N |
| 21 ***Fish*** | Y | N | N | Y | Y | N | ? | Y |
| 22 ***Gilman*** | Y | Y | N | Y | Y | N | Y | Y |
| 23 McNulty | Y | Y | Y | N | Y | Y | Y | N |
| 24 ***Solomon*** | N | N | N | Y | N | N | Y | Y |
| 25 ***Boehlert*** | Y | N | N | Y | N | N | Y | N |
| 26 ***Martin*** | N | N | ? | ? | ? | ? | Y | Y |
| 27 ***Walsh*** | Y | Y | Y | N | Y | N | Y | N |
| 28 McHugh | Y | Y | Y | N | Y | Y | Y | N |
| 29 ***Horton*** | N | ? | ? | ? | Y | N | Y | N |
| 30 Slaughter | Y | Y | Y | Y | Y | Y | Y | N |
| 31 ***Paxon*** | N | Y | N | Y | N | N | Y | Y |
| 32 LaFalce | Y | Y | Y | Y | Y | Y | Y | N |
| 33 Nowak | Y | Y | Y | Y | Y | Y | Y | N |
| 34 ***Houghton*** | Y | Y | Y | N | Y | N | Y | Y |
| **NORTH CAROLINA** | | | | | | | | |
| 1 Vacancy | | | | | | | | |
| 2 Valentine | Y | N | N | Y | Y | Y | Y | N |
| 3 Lancaster | Y | N | Y | Y | Y | Y | Y | N |
| 4 Price | Y | Y | Y | Y | Y | Y | Y | N |
| 5 Neal | Y | N | Y | Y | ? | Y | Y | N |
| 6 ***Coble*** | Y | N | N | Y | N | N | Y | Y |
| 7 Rose | Y | Y | Y | N | Y | Y | Y | N |
| 8 Hefner | Y | N | Y | Y | Y | Y | Y | N |
| 9 ***McMillan*** | Y | N | N | Y | N | N | Y | Y |
| 10 ***Ballenger*** | N | N | N | Y | N | N | Y | Y |
| 11 ***Taylor*** | Y | Y | N | Y | N | N | Y | Y |
| **NORTH DAKOTA** | | | | | | | | |
| AL Dorgan | Y | N | N | Y | Y | Y | Y | N |
| **OHIO** | | | | | | | | |
| 1 Luken | C | N | N | Y | Y | Y | Y | N |
| 2 ***Gradison*** | N | N | N | Y | Y | N | Y | Y |
| 3 Hall | N | Y | Y | ? | ? | ? | Y | N |
| 4 ***Oxley*** | N | N | N | Y | N | N | Y | Y |
| 5 ***Gillmor*** | N | N | N | Y | Y | N | Y | Y |
| 6 ***McEwen*** | N | N | N | Y | N | N | Y | Y |
| 7 ***Hobson*** | N | Y | Y | N | N | N | Y | Y |
| 8 ***Boehner*** | N | Y | N | Y | N | N | Y | Y |
| 9 Kaptur | Y | Y | Y | N | Y | Y | Y | N |
| 10 ***Miller*** | N | Y | Y | N | N | N | Y | Y |
| 11 Eckart | Y | N | Y | Y | Y | Y | Y | N |
| 12 ***Kasich*** | Y | Y | N | Y | Y | N | Y | Y |
| 13 Pease | Y | N | N | Y | Y | Y | Y | ? |
| 14 Sawyer | Y | N | N | Y | Y | Y | Y | N |
| 15 ***Wylie*** | Y | Y | Y | N | N | N | Y | Y |
| 16 ***Regula*** | N | Y | Y | N | N | N | Y | Y |
| 17 Traficant | Y | Y | N | Y | Y | Y | Y | N |
| 18 Applegate | Y | ? | Y | Y | Y | Y | Y | N |
| 19 Feighan | N | N | N | Y | ? | ? | Y | N |
| 20 Oakar | Y | Y | Y | N | Y | Y | ? | ? |
| 21 Stokes | Y | Y | Y | N | ? | ? | Y | N |
| **OKLAHOMA** | | | | | | | | |
| 1 ***Inhofe*** | Y | Y | N | Y | N | N | Y | Y |
| 2 Synar | Y | N | N | Y | Y | Y | Y | N |
| 3 Brewster | Y | Y | N | Y | ? | Y | Y | N |
| 4 McCurdy | Y | N | ? | Y | ? | ? | Y | N |
| 5 ***Edwards*** | N | Y | ? | ? | ? | ? | ? | Y |
| 6 English | Y | N | N | Y | Y | Y | Y | N |
| **OREGON** | | | | | | | | |
| 1 AuCoin | Y | ? | ? | ? | ? | ? | Y | N |
| 2 ***Smith*** | N | N | N | Y | N | N | Y | Y |
| 3 Wyden | Y | N | Y | N | Y | Y | Y | N |
| 4 DeFazio | Y | Y | Y | N | Y | Y | ? | ? |
| 5 Kopetski | N | Y | Y | N | Y | Y | Y | N |
| **PENNSYLVANIA** | | | | | | | | |
| 1 Foglietta | Y | N | Y | N | Y | Y | ? | ? |
| 2 Blackwell | Y | N | N | Y | ? | Y | Y | N |
| 3 Borski | N | Y | Y | N | Y | Y | Y | N |
| 4 Kolter | N | N | Y | Y | Y | Y | ? | N |
| 5 ***Schulze*** | Y | Y | ? | ? | Y | N | Y | Y |
| 6 Yatron | Y | ? | ? | ? | ? | ? | Y | N |
| 7 ***Weldon*** | N | N | N | Y | N | N | Y | Y |
| 8 Kostmayer | N | N | N | Y | Y | Y | Y | N |
| 9 ***Shuster*** | N | Y | N | ? | N | N | Y | Y |
| 10 ***McDade*** | N | Y | Y | N | N | N | Y | Y |
| 11 Kanjorski | N | N | Y | N | Y | Y | Y | N |
| 12 Murtha | ? | Y | Y | N | Y | Y | Y | N |
| 13 ***Coughlin*** | N | N | Y | N | N | N | Y | Y |
| 14 Coyne | Y | Y | Y | N | Y | Y | Y | N |
| 15 ***Ritter*** | N | N | N | Y | ? | ? | Y | N |
| 16 ***Walker*** | N | Y | N | Y | N | N | Y | Y |
| 17 ***Gekas*** | N | Y | N | Y | N | N | Y | Y |
| 18 ***Santorum*** | N | Y | N | Y | N | N | Y | Y |
| 19 ***Goodling*** | N | N | N | N | N | N | Y | Y |
| 20 Gaydos | Y | Y | ? | ? | ? | ? | Y | N |
| 21 ***Ridge*** | N | ? | N | Y | ? | ? | Y | Y |
| 22 Murphy | N | N | N | Y | N | Y | Y | N |
| 23 ***Clinger*** | N | Y | — | + | Y | N | Y | Y |
| **RHODE ISLAND** | | | | | | | | |
| 1 ***Machtley*** | Y | N | N | Y | N | N | Y | Y |
| 2 Reed | Y | N | N | Y | Y | Y | Y | N |
| **SOUTH CAROLINA** | | | | | | | | |
| 1 ***Ravenel*** | Y | N | N | Y | N | N | Y | Y |
| 2 ***Spence*** | Y | N | N | Y | N | N | Y | Y |
| 3 Derrick | Y | Y | Y | Y | Y | Y | Y | N |
| 4 Patterson | Y | N | N | Y | Y | Y | Y | N |
| 5 Spratt | Y | N | Y | Y | Y | Y | Y | N |
| 6 Tallon | Y | N | ? | ? | Y | Y | Y | N |
| **SOUTH DAKOTA** | | | | | | | | |
| AL Johnson | Y | Y | ? | ? | Y | Y | Y | N |
| **TENNESSEE** | | | | | | | | |
| 1 ***Quillen*** | Y | Y | Y | Y | N | N | Y | Y |
| 2 ***Duncan*** | Y | N | N | Y | N | N | Y | Y |
| 3 Lloyd | Y | Y | Y | Y | Y | Y | Y | N |
| 4 Cooper | Y | Y | N | Y | ? | ? | Y | N |
| 5 Clement | Y | N | Y | Y | Y | Y | Y | N |
| 6 Gordon | ? | ? | ? | ? | ? | ? | Y | N |
| 7 ***Sundquist*** | Y | Y | N | Y | N | N | ? | ? |
| 8 Tanner | Y | N | N | Y | Y | Y | Y | N |
| 9 Ford | Y | Y | ? | ? | ? | Y | Y | N |
| **TEXAS** | | | | | | | | |
| 1 Chapman | Y | Y | Y | N | ? | ? | Y | N |
| 2 Wilson | N | Y | Y | N | ? | Y | Y | N |
| 3 ***Johnson*** | N | N | N | Y | Y | N | Y | Y |
| 4 Hall | Y | Y | N | Y | Y | Y | Y | N |
| 5 Bryant | Y | Y | Y | N | Y | Y | Y | N |
| 6 ***Barton*** | N | Y | Y | Y | ? | N | Y | Y |
| 7 ***Archer*** | N | ? | ? | ? | Y | N | Y | Y |
| 8 ***Fields*** | N | Y | N | Y | N | N | Y | Y |
| 9 Brooks | N | Y | Y | N | ? | ? | Y | N |
| 10 Pickle | ? | # | ? | ? | ? | ? | Y | N |
| 11 Edwards | Y | Y | Y | N | Y | Y | Y | N |
| 12 Geren | Y | Y | N | Y | Y | Y | Y | N |
| 13 Sarpalius | Y | Y | Y | N | Y | Y | Y | N |
| 14 Laughlin | N | Y | Y | N | Y | Y | Y | N |
| 15 de la Garza | N | Y | Y | Y | Y | Y | Y | N |
| 16 Coleman | Y | Y | Y | Y | Y | Y | Y | N |
| 17 Stenholm | Y | Y | N | Y | Y | Y | Y | N |
| 18 Washington | Y | X | ? | ? | ? | ? | Y | N |
| 19 ***Combest*** | N | Y | N | Y | Y | N | Y | Y |
| 20 Gonzalez | Y | Y | Y | N | Y | Y | Y | N |
| 21 ***Smith*** | N | Y | N | Y | N | N | Y | Y |
| 22 ***DeLay*** | N | Y | N | Y | N | N | Y | Y |
| 23 Bustamante | N | Y | Y | N | Y | Y | Y | N |
| 24 Frost | Y | Y | Y | N | Y | ? | Y | N |
| 25 Andrews | Y | Y | N | Y | Y | Y | Y | N |
| 26 ***Armey*** | N | N | N | Y | N | N | Y | Y |
| 27 Ortiz | Y | Y | Y | N | Y | Y | Y | N |
| **UTAH** | | | | | | | | |
| 1 ***Hansen*** | N | Y | N | Y | N | N | ? | Y |
| 2 Owens | ? | ? | ? | ? | ? | ? | Y | N |
| 3 Orton | N | N | N | Y | Y | Y | Y | N |
| **VERMONT** | | | | | | | | |
| AL *Sanders* | Y | N | N | Y | Y | Y | Y | N |
| **VIRGINIA** | | | | | | | | |
| 1 ***Bateman*** | Y | Y | Y | N | Y | N | Y | Y |
| 2 Pickett | N | Y | Y | Y | Y | Y | Y | N |
| 3 ***Bliley*** | N | Y | Y | N | N | N | Y | Y |
| 4 Sisisky | Y | N | N | Y | Y | Y | Y | N |
| 5 Payne | Y | Y | N | Y | Y | Y | Y | N |
| 6 Olin | N | Y | Y | N | Y | Y | Y | N |
| 7 ***Allen*** | N | N | N | Y | N | N | Y | Y |
| 8 Moran | Y | Y | ? | ? | ? | Y | Y | N |
| 9 Boucher | Y | Y | Y | Y | Y | Y | Y | N |
| 10 ***Wolf*** | Y | N | Y | N | N | N | Y | Y |
| **WASHINGTON** | | | | | | | | |
| 1 ***Miller*** | Y | Y | N | Y | N | N | ? | ? |
| 2 Swift | Y | Y | Y | Y | Y | Y | Y | N |
| 3 Unsoeld | Y | Y | Y | N | Y | Y | Y | N |
| 4 ***Morrison*** | Y | Y | Y | Y | N | N | Y | Y |
| 5 Foley | | | | | | | | |
| 6 Dicks | Y | Y | Y | Y | Y | Y | ? | N |
| 7 McDermott | Y | Y | N | Y | Y | Y | Y | N |
| 8 ***Chandler*** | ? | ? | ? | ? | ? | ? | Y | ? |
| **WEST VIRGINIA** | | | | | | | | |
| 1 Mollohan | Y | Y | Y | N | Y | Y | Y | N |
| 2 Staggers | Y | N | N | Y | Y | Y | Y | N |
| 3 Wise | Y | Y | Y | N | Y | Y | ? | N |
| 4 Rahall | Y | Y | Y | N | Y | Y | Y | N |
| **WISCONSIN** | | | | | | | | |
| 1 Aspin | Y | Y | N | Y | ? | Y | Y | N |
| 2 ***Klug*** | Y | N | N | Y | N | N | Y | Y |
| 3 ***Gunderson*** | Y | N | N | Y | Y | N | Y | Y |
| 4 Kleczka | Y | Y | Y | Y | Y | Y | Y | N |
| 5 Moody | Y | Y | N | Y | Y | Y | Y | ? |
| 6 ***Petri*** | Y | N | N | Y | Y | N | Y | Y |
| 7 Obey | Y | N | Y | N | Y | Y | Y | N |
| 8 ***Roth*** | Y | N | N | Y | N | N | Y | Y |
| 9 ***Sensenbrenner*** | N | N | N | Y | N | N | Y | Y |
| **WYOMING** | | | | | | | | |
| AL ***Thomas*** | Y | Y | N | Y | N | N | Y | Y |

Southern states - Ala., Ark., Fla., Ga., Ky., La., Miss., N.C., Okla., S.C., Tenn., Texas, Va.
Omitted votes are quorum calls, which CQ does not include in its vote charts.

## KEY

Y   Voted for (yea).
\#   Paired for.
\+   Announced for.
N   Voted against (nay).
X   Paired against.
−   Announced against.
P   Voted "present."
C   Voted "present" to avoid possible conflict of interest.
?   Did not vote or otherwise make a position known.

Democrats    **Republicans**
*Independent*

**407. HR 5231. National Competitiveness/Manufacturing Centers.** Walker, R-Pa., amendment to strike the provisions that would extend expiring authorizations for manufacturing centers subsidized by government funds. Rejected 135-262: R 129-28; D 6-234 (ND 6-159, SD 0-75); I 0-0, Sept. 22, 1992.

**408. HR 5231. National Competitiveness/Critical Technology Development Program.** Walker, R-Pa., amendment to strike the section of the bill creating the Critical Technology Development Program, which would authorize $100 million in fiscal 1994 and 1995 for the Commerce Department to provide capital and development loans to U.S. high-technology companies. Rejected 131-257: R 130-23; D 1-234 (ND 1-158, SD 0-76); I 0-0, Sept. 22, 1992.

**409. HR 2194. Federal Facilities Compliance/Conference Report.** Adoption of the conference report to subject federal agencies to administrative orders and monetary penalties for failing to comply with federal, state, interstate and local solid and hazardous waste management and disposal requirements. Adopted 403-3: R 157-2; D 246-1 (ND 170-0, SD 76-1); I 0-0, Sept. 23, 1992.

**410. HR 5231. National Competitiveness/Reduce Funding.** Walker, R-Pa., en bloc amendment to cut the $2.2 billion authorization in the bill for fiscal 1994-97 by $1.5 billion, leaving an authorization of $700 million. Rejected 162-246: R 147-12; D 15-233 (ND 5-166, SD 10-67); I 0-1, Sept. 23, 1992.

**411. HR 5231. National Competitiveness/Recommital.** Walker, R-Pa., motion to recommit the bill to various committees, with instructions to report it back to the House with provisions to make American business more competitive. Motion rejected 161-248: R 159-2; D 2-245 (ND 2-169, SD 0-76); I 0-1, Sept. 23, 1992.

**412. HR 5231. National Competitiveness/Passage.** Passage of the bill to authorize $2.2 billion in fiscal 1994-97 for government programs designed to boost the global competitiveness of U.S. businesses. Passed 287-122: R 41-120; D 245-2 (ND 170-1, SD 75-1); I 1-0, Sept. 23, 1992.

**413. S 1330. National Competitiveness/Amend With House Bill.** Valentine, D-N.C., motion to strike all after the enacting clause and insert the text of HR 5231, a bill to authorize $2.2 billion in fiscal 1994-97 for government programs designed to boost the global competitiveness of U.S. businesses, as passed by the House. Motion agreed to 248-151: R 7-149; D 240-2 (ND 166-1, SD 74-1); I 1-0, Sept. 23, 1992.

**414. HR 5754. Water Resources Development/Rule.** Adoption of the rule (H Res 570) to provide for House floor consideration of the bill to authorize more than $2 billion for the Army Corps of Engineers water resource development projects. Adopted 269-141: R 23-136; D 245-5 (ND 165-5, SD 80-0); I 1-0, Sept. 23, 1992.

| | 407 | 408 | 409 | 410 | 411 | 412 | 413 | 414 |
|---|---|---|---|---|---|---|---|---|
| **ALABAMA** | | | | | | | | |
| 1 *Callahan* | Y | Y | Y | Y | Y | N | N | N |
| 2 *Dickinson* | Y | N | Y | Y | Y | Y | N | N |
| 3 Browder | N | N | Y | N | N | Y | Y | Y |
| 4 Bevill | N | N | Y | N | N | Y | Y | Y |
| 5 Cramer | N | N | Y | N | N | Y | Y | Y |
| 6 Erdreich | N | N | Y | N | N | Y | Y | Y |
| 7 Harris | N | N | Y | N | N | Y | Y | Y |
| **ALASKA** | | | | | | | | |
| AL *Young* | Y | Y | Y | Y | Y | N | N | Y |
| **ARIZONA** | | | | | | | | |
| 1 *Rhodes* | Y | Y | Y | Y | Y | N | N | N |
| 2 Pastor | N | N | Y | N | N | Y | Y | Y |
| 3 *Stump* | Y | Y | Y | Y | Y | N | N | N |
| 4 *Kyl* | Y | Y | Y | Y | Y | N | N | N |
| 5 *Kolbe* | Y | Y | Y | Y | Y | N | N | N |
| **ARKANSAS** | | | | | | | | |
| 1 Alexander | N | ? | ? | ? | ? | ? | ? | Y |
| 2 Thornton | N | N | Y | N | N | Y | Y | Y |
| 3 *Hammerschmidt* | N | Y | Y | Y | Y | N | N | Y |
| 4 Anthony | N | N | Y | N | N | Y | ? | Y |
| **CALIFORNIA** | | | | | | | | |
| 1 *Riggs* | Y | Y | Y | Y | Y | N | N | N |
| 2 *Herger* | Y | Y | Y | Y | Y | ? | N | N |
| 3 Matsui | N | N | Y | N | N | Y | Y | Y |
| 4 Fazio | N | N | Y | N | N | Y | Y | Y |
| 5 Pelosi | N | N | Y | N | N | Y | Y | Y |
| 6 Boxer | ? | ? | ? | ? | ? | ? | ? | ? |
| 7 Miller | N | N | Y | N | N | Y | Y | Y |
| 8 Dellums | N | N | Y | N | N | Y | Y | Y |
| 9 Stark | N | N | Y | N | N | Y | Y | Y |
| 10 Edwards | N | ? | Y | N | N | Y | Y | Y |
| 11 Lantos | N | N | Y | N | N | Y | Y | Y |
| 12 *Campbell* | Y | Y | Y | Y | Y | N | N | N |
| 13 Mineta | N | N | Y | N | N | Y | Y | Y |
| 14 *Doolittle* | Y | Y | Y | Y | Y | N | N | N |
| 15 Condit | N | N | Y | N | Y | N | Y | N |
| 16 Panetta | N | N | Y | N | N | Y | Y | Y |
| 17 Dooley | N | N | Y | N | N | Y | Y | Y |
| 18 Lehman | N | N | Y | N | N | Y | Y | Y |
| 19 *Lagomarsino* | Y | Y | Y | Y | Y | N | N | N |
| 20 *Thomas* | Y | Y | Y | Y | Y | N | N | N |
| 21 *Gallegly* | N | Y | Y | Y | Y | N | N | N |
| 22 *Moorhead* | Y | Y | Y | Y | Y | N | N | N |
| 23 Beilenson | N | N | Y | N | N | Y | Y | Y |
| 24 Waxman | N | N | Y | N | N | Y | Y | Y |
| 25 Roybal | N | N | Y | N | N | Y | Y | Y |
| 26 Berman | N | N | Y | N | ? | Y | ? | Y |
| 27 Levine | N | N | Y | N | N | Y | Y | Y |
| 28 Dixon | N | N | Y | N | N | Y | Y | Y |
| 29 Waters | N | N | Y | N | N | Y | Y | Y |
| 30 Martinez | N | N | Y | N | N | Y | Y | Y |
| 31 Dymally | N | N | Y | N | N | ? | Y | ? |
| 32 Anderson | N | N | Y | N | N | Y | Y | Y |
| 33 *Dreier* | Y | Y | Y | Y | Y | N | N | N |
| 34 Torres | N | N | Y | N | N | Y | Y | Y |
| 35 *Lewis* | Y | Y | Y | Y | Y | N | N | N |
| 36 Brown | ? | N | Y | N | N | Y | Y | Y |
| 37 *McCandless* | Y | Y | Y | Y | Y | N | N | N |
| 38 *Dornan* | Y | Y | Y | Y | Y | N | N | N |
| 39 *Dannemeyer* | Y | Y | Y | Y | Y | N | N | N |
| 40 *Cox* | Y | Y | Y | Y | Y | N | N | N |
| 41 *Lowery* | Y | Y | Y | Y | ? | ? | ? | N |

| | 407 | 408 | 409 | 410 | 411 | 412 | 413 | 414 |
|---|---|---|---|---|---|---|---|---|
| 42 *Rohrabacher* | Y | Y | Y | Y | Y | N | N | N |
| 43 *Packard* | Y | Y | Y | Y | Y | N | N | N |
| 44 *Cunningham* | Y | Y | Y | Y | Y | N | N | N |
| 45 *Hunter* | Y | N | Y | Y | Y | N | N | N |
| **COLORADO** | | | | | | | | |
| 1 Schroeder | N | N | Y | N | N | Y | Y | Y |
| 2 Skaggs | N | N | Y | N | N | Y | Y | Y |
| 3 Campbell | N | N | Y | N | N | Y | Y | Y |
| 4 *Allard* | Y | Y | Y | Y | Y | N | N | N |
| 5 *Hefley* | Y | Y | Y | Y | Y | N | N | N |
| 6 *Schaefer* | Y | Y | Y | Y | Y | N | N | N |
| **CONNECTICUT** | | | | | | | | |
| 1 Kennelly | N | N | Y | N | N | Y | Y | Y |
| 2 Gejdenson | N | N | Y | N | N | Y | Y | Y |
| 3 DeLauro | N | N | Y | N | N | Y | Y | Y |
| 4 *Shays* | Y | Y | Y | Y | Y | Y | Y | N |
| 5 *Franks* | Y | Y | Y | Y | Y | N | N | N |
| 6 Johnson | N | N | Y | N | N | Y | N | Y |
| **DELAWARE** | | | | | | | | |
| AL Carper | Y | N | Y | N | N | Y | Y | Y |
| **FLORIDA** | | | | | | | | |
| 1 Hutto | N | N | Y | Y | N | Y | Y | Y |
| 2 Peterson | N | N | Y | N | N | Y | Y | Y |
| 3 Bennett | N | N | Y | N | N | Y | Y | Y |
| 4 *James* | Y | Y | Y | Y | Y | N | N | N |
| 5 *McCollum* | Y | Y | Y | Y | Y | N | N | N |
| 6 *Stearns* | Y | Y | Y | Y | Y | N | N | N |
| 7 Gibbons | N | N | Y | N | N | Y | Y | Y |
| 8 *Young* | Y | Y | Y | Y | Y | N | N | N |
| 9 *Bilirakis* | Y | Y | Y | Y | Y | N | N | N |
| 10 *Ireland* | Y | ? | ? | Y | ? | N | ? | ? |
| 11 Bacchus | N | N | Y | N | N | Y | Y | Y |
| 12 *Lewis* | Y | Y | Y | Y | Y | N | N | N |
| 13 *Goss* | Y | Y | Y | Y | Y | N | N | N |
| 14 Johnston | N | N | Y | N | N | Y | Y | Y |
| 15 *Shaw* | Y | Y | Y | Y | Y | N | N | N |
| 16 Smith | N | N | Y | N | N | Y | Y | Y |
| 17 Lehman | N | N | Y | N | N | Y | Y | Y |
| 18 *Ros—Lehtinen* | Y | Y | Y | Y | Y | N | N | N |
| 19 Fascell | N | ? | Y | N | N | Y | Y | Y |
| **GEORGIA** | | | | | | | | |
| 1 Thomas | N | N | Y | N | N | Y | Y | Y |
| 2 Hatcher | N | N | Y | N | N | Y | Y | Y |
| 3 Ray | N | N | N | N | N | Y | Y | Y |
| 4 Jones | ? | ? | ? | ? | ? | ? | ? | ? |
| 5 Lewis | N | N | Y | N | N | Y | Y | Y |
| 6 *Gingrich* | Y | Y | Y | Y | Y | N | N | N |
| 7 Darden | N | N | Y | N | N | Y | Y | Y |
| 8 Rowland | N | N | Y | N | N | Y | Y | Y |
| 9 Jenkins | ? | N | Y | N | N | Y | Y | Y |
| 10 Barnard | ? | ? | ? | ? | ? | ? | ? | ? |
| **HAWAII** | | | | | | | | |
| 1 Abercrombie | N | N | ? | N | N | Y | Y | Y |
| 2 Mink | ? | ? | Y | N | N | Y | Y | Y |
| **IDAHO** | | | | | | | | |
| 1 LaRocco | N | N | Y | N | N | Y | Y | Y |
| 2 Stallings | N | N | Y | N | N | Y | Y | Y |
| **ILLINOIS** | | | | | | | | |
| 1 Hayes | N | N | Y | N | N | Y | Y | Y |
| 2 Savage | ? | ? | ? | ? | N | Y | Y | Y |
| 3 Russo | N | N | Y | N | N | Y | ? | Y |
| 4 Sangmeister | N | N | Y | N | N | Y | Y | Y |
| 5 Lipinski | N | N | Y | N | N | Y | Y | Y |
| 6 *Hyde* | Y | Y | Y | Y | Y | N | N | N |
| 7 Collins | N | N | Y | N | N | Y | Y | Y |
| 8 Rostenkowski | N | N | Y | N | N | Y | Y | Y |
| 9 Yates | N | N | Y | N | N | Y | Y | Y |
| 10 *Porter* | Y | Y | Y | Y | Y | N | N | N |
| 11 Annunzio | N | N | Y | N | N | Y | Y | Y |
| 12 *Crane* | Y | Y | Y | Y | Y | N | N | N |
| 13 *Fawell* | Y | Y | N | Y | Y | N | N | N |
| 14 *Hastert* | Y | Y | Y | Y | Y | N | N | N |
| 15 *Ewing* | Y | Y | Y | Y | Y | N | N | N |
| 16 Cox | Y | N | Y | N | Y | N | Y | Y |
| 17 Evans | N | N | Y | N | N | Y | Y | Y |
| 18 *Michel* | Y | Y | Y | Y | Y | N | N | N |
| 19 Bruce | N | N | Y | N | N | Y | Y | Y |
| 20 Durbin | N | N | Y | N | N | Y | Y | Y |
| 21 Costello | N | N | Y | N | N | Y | Y | Y |
| 22 Poshard | N | ? | Y | N | N | Y | Y | Y |
| **INDIANA** | | | | | | | | |
| 1 Visclosky | N | N | Y | N | N | Y | Y | Y |
| 2 Sharp | N | N | Y | N | N | Y | Y | Y |
| 3 Roemer | N | N | Y | N | N | Y | Y | Y |

ND Northern Democrats    SD Southern Democrats

| | 407 | 408 | 409 | 410 | 411 | 412 | 413 | 414 |
|---|---|---|---|---|---|---|---|---|
| 4 Long | N | N | Y | N | N | Y | Y | Y |
| 5 Jontz | N | N | Y | N | N | Y | Y | Y |
| 6 ***Burton*** | Y | Y | Y | Y | Y | N | N | N |
| 7 ***Myers*** | Y | Y | ? | ? | Y | N | N | Y |
| 8 McCloskey | N | N | Y | N | N | Y | Y | Y |
| 9 Hamilton | N | N | Y | N | N | Y | Y | Y |
| 10 Jacobs | Y | Y | Y | Y | Y | N | N | Y |
| **IOWA** | | | | | | | | |
| 1 ***Leach*** | Y | Y | Y | Y | Y | N | ? | N |
| 2 ***Nussle*** | Y | Y | Y | Y | Y | N | N | N |
| 3 Nagle | Y | ? | Y | ? | N | Y | Y | Y |
| 4 Smith | N | N | Y | N | N | Y | Y | Y |
| 5 ***Lightfoot*** | Y | Y | Y | Y | Y | N | N | N |
| 6 ***Grandy*** | Y | Y | Y | Y | Y | N | N | N |
| **KANSAS** | | | | | | | | |
| 1 ***Roberts*** | Y | Y | Y | Y | Y | N | N | N |
| 2 Slattery | N | N | Y | Y | N | Y | Y | Y |
| 3 ***Meyers*** | N | ? | Y | Y | Y | Y | Y | N |
| 4 Glickman | N | N | Y | N | N | Y | Y | Y |
| 5 ***Nichols*** | Y | Y | Y | Y | Y | N | N | N |
| **KENTUCKY** | | | | | | | | |
| 1 Hubbard | N | N | Y | N | N | Y | Y | Y |
| 2 Natcher | N | N | Y | N | N | Y | Y | Y |
| 3 Mazzoli | N | N | Y | N | N | Y | Y | Y |
| 4 ***Bunning*** | Y | Y | Y | Y | Y | N | N | N |
| 5 ***Rogers*** | Y | Y | Y | Y | Y | Y | N | N |
| 6 ***Hopkins*** | Y | Y | Y | Y | Y | N | N | N |
| 7 Perkins | ? | ? | ? | ? | ? | ? | ? | Y |
| **LOUISIANA** | | | | | | | | |
| 1 ***Livingston*** | Y | Y | Y | Y | Y | N | N | Y |
| 2 Jefferson | ? | ? | ? | ? | ? | ? | Y | Y |
| 3 Tauzin | N | N | Y | N | Y | N | Y | Y |
| 4 ***McCrery*** | ? | ? | Y | Y | Y | N | N | N |
| 5 Huckaby | N | N | ? | Y | N | Y | Y | Y |
| 6 ***Baker*** | Y | Y | Y | Y | Y | N | N | N |
| 7 Hayes | ? | ? | ? | ? | ? | ? | ? | ? |
| 8 ***Holloway*** | Y | Y | Y | Y | Y | N | N | N |
| **MAINE** | | | | | | | | |
| 1 Andrews | N | N | Y | N | N | Y | Y | Y |
| 2 ***Snowe*** | Y | N | Y | Y | Y | Y | N | N |
| **MARYLAND** | | | | | | | | |
| 1 ***Gilchrest*** | Y | Y | Y | Y | Y | Y | N | N |
| 2 ***Bentley*** | N | Y | Y | Y | Y | Y | N | N |
| 3 Cardin | N | N | Y | N | N | Y | Y | Y |
| 4 McMillen | N | N | Y | N | N | Y | Y | Y |
| 5 Hoyer | N | N | Y | N | N | Y | Y | Y |
| 6 Byron | ? | N | Y | Y | N | Y | Y | Y |
| 7 Mfume | N | N | Y | N | N | Y | Y | Y |
| 8 ***Morella*** | N | N | Y | N | Y | Y | Y | N |
| **MASSACHUSETTS** | | | | | | | | |
| 1 Olver | N | N | Y | N | N | Y | Y | Y |
| 2 Neal | N | N | Y | N | N | Y | Y | Y |
| 3 Early | N | N | Y | N | N | Y | Y | Y |
| 4 Frank | N | N | Y | N | N | Y | Y | Y |
| 5 Atkins | N | N | Y | N | N | Y | Y | N |
| 6 Mavroules | N | N | Y | N | N | Y | ? | ? |
| 7 Markey | N | N | Y | N | N | Y | ? | Y |
| 8 Kennedy | ? | ? | Y | N | N | ? | Y | Y |
| 9 Moakley | N | N | Y | N | N | Y | Y | Y |
| 10 Studds | N | N | Y | N | N | Y | Y | Y |
| 11 Donnelly | N | N | Y | N | N | Y | Y | Y |
| **MICHIGAN** | | | | | | | | |
| 1 Conyers | ? | ? | ? | ? | ? | ? | ? | ? |
| 2 ***Pursell*** | ? | ? | Y | Y | Y | N | ? | Y |
| 3 Wolpe | ? | ? | Y | N | ? | Y | Y | Y |
| 4 ***Upton*** | N | N | Y | Y | Y | Y | N | N |
| 5 ***Henry*** | N | N | Y | N | Y | Y | Y | N |
| 6 Carr | ? | ? | Y | N | N | Y | Y | Y |
| 7 Kildee | N | N | Y | N | N | Y | Y | Y |
| 8 Traxler | N | N | Y | N | N | Y | Y | Y |
| 9 ***Vander Jagt*** | N | Y | Y | Y | Y | N | ? | ? |
| 10 ***Camp*** | N | Y | Y | Y | Y | Y | N | N |
| 11 ***Davis*** | N | N | Y | ? | Y | Y | N | Y |
| 12 Bonior | N | N | Y | N | N | Y | Y | Y |
| 13 Collins | N | N | Y | N | N | Y | Y | Y |
| 14 Hertel | N | N | Y | N | N | Y | ? | Y |
| 15 Ford | N | N | Y | N | N | Y | Y | Y |
| 16 Dingell | N | N | Y | N | N | Y | Y | Y |
| 17 Levin | N | N | Y | N | N | Y | Y | Y |
| 18 ***Broomfield*** | N | Y | Y | Y | Y | Y | N | N |
| **MINNESOTA** | | | | | | | | |
| 1 Penny | + | + | + | + | + | − | − | + |
| 2 ***Weber*** | Y | Y | Y | Y | Y | N | N | N |
| 3 ***Ramstad*** | Y | Y | Y | Y | Y | N | N | N |
| 4 Vento | N | N | Y | N | N | Y | Y | Y |

| | 407 | 408 | 409 | 410 | 411 | 412 | 413 | 414 |
|---|---|---|---|---|---|---|---|---|
| 5 Sabo | N | N | Y | N | N | Y | Y | Y |
| 6 Sikorski | N | N | Y | N | N | Y | Y | Y |
| 7 Peterson | N | N | Y | N | N | Y | Y | Y |
| 8 Oberstar | N | N | Y | N | N | Y | Y | Y |
| **MISSISSIPPI** | | | | | | | | |
| 1 Whitten | N | N | Y | ? | N | Y | Y | Y |
| 2 Espy | N | N | Y | N | N | Y | Y | Y |
| 3 Montgomery | ? | N | Y | Y | N | Y | Y | Y |
| 4 Parker | N | N | Y | Y | N | Y | Y | Y |
| 5 Taylor | N | N | Y | N | N | Y | Y | Y |
| **MISSOURI** | | | | | | | | |
| 1 Clay | N | ? | Y | N | N | Y | Y | Y |
| 2 Horn | N | N | Y | N | N | Y | Y | Y |
| 3 Gephardt | N | N | Y | N | N | Y | Y | Y |
| 4 Skelton | ? | N | Y | N | N | Y | Y | Y |
| 5 Wheat | N | N | Y | N | N | Y | Y | Y |
| 6 ***Coleman*** | ? | ? | Y | Y | Y | Y | N | N |
| 7 ***Hancock*** | Y | Y | Y | Y | Y | N | N | N |
| 8 ***Emerson*** | N | N | Y | Y | Y | N | N | Y |
| 9 Volkmer | N | N | Y | N | N | Y | Y | Y |
| **MONTANA** | | | | | | | | |
| 1 Williams | N | N | Y | N | N | Y | Y | Y |
| 2 ***Marlenee*** | Y | Y | Y | Y | Y | N | N | N |
| **NEBRASKA** | | | | | | | | |
| 1 ***Bereuter*** | Y | Y | Y | Y | Y | Y | N | N |
| 2 Hoagland | N | N | Y | N | N | Y | Y | Y |
| 3 ***Barrett*** | Y | Y | Y | Y | Y | N | N | N |
| **NEVADA** | | | | | | | | |
| 1 Bilbray | N | N | Y | N | N | Y | Y | Y |
| 2 ***Vucanovich*** | Y | Y | Y | Y | Y | N | N | N |
| **NEW HAMPSHIRE** | | | | | | | | |
| 1 ***Zeliff*** | Y | Y | Y | Y | Y | N | N | N |
| 2 Swett | N | N | Y | N | N | Y | Y | Y |
| **NEW JERSEY** | | | | | | | | |
| 1 Andrews | N | N | Y | N | N | Y | Y | Y |
| 2 Hughes | N | N | Y | N | N | Y | Y | Y |
| 3 Pallone | N | N | Y | N | N | Y | Y | Y |
| 4 ***Smith*** | N | N | Y | N | Y | Y | N | Y |
| 5 ***Roukema*** | Y | N | Y | Y | Y | N | N | N |
| 6 Dwyer | N | ? | Y | N | N | Y | Y | Y |
| 7 ***Rinaldo*** | N | ? | Y | N | Y | Y | N | Y |
| 8 Roe | N | N | Y | N | N | Y | Y | Y |
| 9 Torricelli | N | N | Y | N | N | Y | Y | Y |
| 10 Payne | N | N | Y | N | N | Y | Y | Y |
| 11 ***Gallo*** | N | N | Y | Y | Y | N | N | N |
| 12 ***Zimmer*** | Y | Y | Y | Y | Y | N | N | N |
| 13 ***Saxton*** | N | N | Y | Y | Y | N | N | N |
| 14 Guarini | ? | N | Y | N | N | Y | Y | ? |
| **NEW MEXICO** | | | | | | | | |
| 1 ***Schiff*** | Y | Y | Y | N | Y | Y | N | N |
| 2 ***Skeen*** | Y | Y | Y | Y | Y | N | N | Y |
| 3 Richardson | N | N | Y | N | N | Y | Y | Y |
| **NEW YORK** | | | | | | | | |
| 1 Hochbrueckner | N | N | Y | N | N | Y | Y | Y |
| 2 Downey | — | N | Y | N | N | Y | Y | Y |
| 3 Mrazek | N | ? | Y | N | N | Y | Y | Y |
| 4 ***Lent*** | Y | Y | Y | Y | Y | N | ? | N |
| 5 ***McGrath*** | N | N | Y | Y | Y | Y | Y | ? |
| 6 Flake | N | N | Y | N | N | Y | Y | Y |
| 7 Ackerman | N | ? | Y | N | N | Y | Y | ? |
| 8 Scheuer | N | N | Y | N | N | Y | Y | Y |
| 9 Manton | N | N | Y | N | N | Y | Y | Y |
| 10 Schumer | N | ? | Y | N | N | Y | Y | Y |
| 11 Towns | N | N | Y | N | N | Y | Y | Y |
| 12 Owens | N | N | Y | N | N | Y | Y | Y |
| 13 Solarz | N | ? | Y | ? | ? | ? | Y | ? |
| 14 ***Molinari*** | Y | Y | Y | Y | Y | N | N | N |
| 15 ***Green*** | Y | Y | Y | Y | N | Y | N | N |
| 16 Rangel | N | N | Y | N | N | Y | Y | Y |
| 17 Vacancy | | | | | | | | |
| 18 Serrano | N | N | Y | N | N | Y | Y | Y |
| 19 Engel | N | N | Y | N | N | Y | Y | Y |
| 20 Lowey | N | N | Y | N | N | Y | Y | Y |
| 21 ***Fish*** | N | Y | Y | Y | Y | Y | N | N |
| 22 ***Gilman*** | Y | Y | Y | Y | Y | Y | N | Y |
| 23 McNulty | N | N | Y | N | N | Y | Y | Y |
| 24 ***Solomon*** | Y | Y | Y | Y | Y | N | N | N |
| 25 ***Boehlert*** | N | Y | N | Y | N | Y | N | Y |
| 26 ***Martin*** | Y | ? | Y | Y | Y | Y | N | N |
| 27 ***Walsh*** | N | N | Y | N | Y | Y | N | N |
| 28 McHugh | N | N | Y | N | N | Y | Y | Y |
| 29 ***Horton*** | N | N | Y | N | N | Y | N | Y |
| 30 Slaughter | N | N | Y | N | N | Y | Y | Y |
| 31 ***Paxon*** | Y | Y | Y | Y | Y | N | N | N |

| | 407 | 408 | 409 | 410 | 411 | 412 | 413 | 414 |
|---|---|---|---|---|---|---|---|---|
| 32 LaFalce | N | N | Y | N | N | Y | ? | Y |
| 33 Nowak | N | N | Y | N | N | Y | Y | Y |
| 34 ***Houghton*** | Y | Y | Y | Y | Y | Y | N | N |
| **NORTH CAROLINA** | | | | | | | | |
| 1 Vacancy | | | | | | | | |
| 2 Valentine | N | N | Y | N | N | Y | Y | Y |
| 3 Lancaster | ? | N | Y | N | N | Y | Y | Y |
| 4 Price | N | N | Y | N | N | Y | Y | Y |
| 5 Neal | N | N | Y | N | Y | N | Y | Y |
| 6 ***Coble*** | Y | Y | Y | Y | Y | N | N | N |
| 7 Rose | N | N | Y | N | N | Y | Y | Y |
| 8 Hefner | N | N | Y | N | N | Y | Y | Y |
| 9 ***McMillan*** | Y | Y | Y | Y | Y | N | N | N |
| 10 ***Ballenger*** | Y | Y | Y | Y | Y | N | N | N |
| 11 ***Taylor*** | Y | Y | Y | Y | Y | N | N | N |
| **NORTH DAKOTA** | | | | | | | | |
| AL Dorgan | N | N | Y | N | N | Y | Y | Y |
| **OHIO** | | | | | | | | |
| 1 Luken | N | N | Y | N | N | Y | Y | Y |
| 2 ***Gradison*** | Y | Y | Y | Y | Y | N | N | N |
| 3 Hall | N | N | Y | N | N | Y | Y | Y |
| 4 ***Oxley*** | Y | Y | Y | Y | Y | N | N | N |
| 5 ***Gillmor*** | Y | Y | Y | Y | Y | Y | N | N |
| 6 ***McEwen*** | Y | Y | Y | Y | Y | N | N | N |
| 7 ***Hobson*** | Y | Y | Y | Y | Y | N | N | N |
| 8 ***Boehner*** | Y | Y | Y | Y | Y | N | N | N |
| 9 Kaptur | N | N | ? | N | N | Y | Y | Y |
| 10 ***Miller*** | Y | Y | Y | Y | Y | N | N | Y |
| 11 Eckart | N | ? | Y | N | N | Y | Y | Y |
| 12 ***Kasich*** | Y | Y | Y | Y | Y | N | N | N |
| 13 Pease | N | N | Y | N | N | Y | Y | Y |
| 14 Sawyer | N | N | Y | N | N | Y | Y | Y |
| 15 ***Wylie*** | Y | Y | Y | Y | Y | N | N | N |
| 16 ***Regula*** | N | N | Y | Y | Y | Y | N | N |
| 17 Traficant | N | N | Y | N | N | Y | Y | Y |
| 18 Applegate | N | N | Y | N | N | Y | Y | Y |
| 19 Feighan | N | N | Y | N | N | Y | Y | Y |
| 20 Oakar | ? | ? | Y | N | N | Y | Y | Y |
| 21 Stokes | N | N | ? | ? | ? | ? | ? | Y |
| **OKLAHOMA** | | | | | | | | |
| 1 ***Inhofe*** | Y | Y | Y | Y | Y | N | N | N |
| 2 Synar | N | N | Y | N | N | Y | Y | Y |
| 3 Brewster | N | N | Y | N | N | Y | Y | Y |
| 4 McCurdy | N | N | Y | N | ? | ? | ? | Y |
| 5 ***Edwards*** | ? | ? | ? | ? | Y | N | ? | ? |
| 6 English | N | N | Y | N | N | Y | Y | Y |
| **OREGON** | | | | | | | | |
| 1 AuCoin | N | N | ? | ? | ? | ? | ? | ? |
| 2 ***Smith*** | Y | Y | Y | Y | Y | N | ? | N |
| 3 Wyden | N | N | Y | N | N | Y | Y | Y |
| 4 DeFazio | N | N | Y | N | N | Y | Y | Y |
| 5 Kopetski | N | N | Y | N | N | Y | Y | Y |
| **PENNSYLVANIA** | | | | | | | | |
| 1 Foglietta | ? | ? | ? | ? | ? | ? | ? | ? |
| 2 Blackwell | N | ? | ? | ? | ? | ? | ? | ? |
| 3 Borski | N | N | Y | N | N | Y | Y | Y |
| 4 Kolter | N | N | Y | N | N | Y | Y | Y |
| 5 ***Schulze*** | Y | Y | Y | ? | ? | ? | N | Y |
| 6 Yatron | N | N | Y | N | N | Y | Y | Y |
| 7 ***Weldon*** | Y | N | Y | Y | Y | Y | N | N |
| 8 Kostmayer | N | N | ? | N | N | Y | Y | Y |
| 9 ***Shuster*** | Y | Y | ? | ? | ? | ? | ? | ? |
| 10 ***McDade*** | Y | Y | ? | Y | Y | Y | N | Y |
| 11 Kanjorski | N | N | Y | N | N | Y | Y | Y |
| 12 Murtha | N | ? | Y | N | N | Y | Y | Y |
| 13 ***Coughlin*** | Y | ? | Y | Y | Y | N | N | N |
| 14 Coyne | N | N | Y | N | N | Y | Y | Y |
| 15 ***Ritter*** | N | N | Y | N | Y | Y | Y | N |
| 16 ***Walker*** | Y | Y | Y | Y | Y | N | N | N |
| 17 ***Gekas*** | Y | Y | Y | Y | Y | N | N | N |
| 18 ***Santorum*** | N | N | Y | N | Y | Y | N | N |
| 19 ***Goodling*** | Y | Y | + | Y | Y | N | N | N |
| 20 Gaydos | ? | N | Y | N | N | Y | Y | Y |
| 21 ***Ridge*** | N | Y | Y | N | Y | Y | N | N |
| 22 Murphy | N | N | Y | N | N | Y | Y | Y |
| 23 ***Clinger*** | Y | Y | ? | ? | ? | ? | ? | ? |
| **RHODE ISLAND** | | | | | | | | |
| 1 ***Machtley*** | Y | Y | Y | Y | Y | Y | N | N |
| 2 Reed | N | N | Y | N | N | Y | Y | Y |
| **SOUTH CAROLINA** | | | | | | | | |
| 1 ***Ravenel*** | ? | N | Y | Y | Y | Y | N | Y |
| 2 ***Spence*** | Y | N | Y | Y | Y | N | N | Y |
| 3 Derrick | N | N | Y | N | N | Y | Y | Y |
| 4 Patterson | N | N | Y | N | N | Y | Y | Y |
| 5 Spratt | N | N | Y | N | N | Y | Y | Y |
| 6 Tallon | N | N | Y | N | N | Y | Y | Y |

| | 407 | 408 | 409 | 410 | 411 | 412 | 413 | 414 |
|---|---|---|---|---|---|---|---|---|
| **SOUTH DAKOTA** | | | | | | | | |
| AL Johnson | N | N | Y | N | N | Y | Y | Y |
| **TENNESSEE** | | | | | | | | |
| 1 ***Quillen*** | Y | Y | Y | Y | Y | N | N | N |
| 2 ***Duncan*** | Y | Y | Y | Y | Y | N | N | N |
| 3 Lloyd | N | N | Y | N | N | Y | Y | Y |
| 4 Cooper | N | N | Y | N | N | Y | Y | Y |
| 5 Clement | N | N | Y | N | N | Y | Y | Y |
| 6 Gordon | N | N | Y | N | N | Y | Y | Y |
| 7 ***Sundquist*** | ? | ? | Y | Y | Y | N | N | N |
| 8 Tanner | N | N | Y | N | N | Y | Y | Y |
| 9 Ford | N | N | Y | N | N | Y | Y | Y |
| **TEXAS** | | | | | | | | |
| 1 Chapman | N | N | Y | N | N | Y | Y | Y |
| 2 Wilson | N | N | Y | N | N | Y | Y | Y |
| 3 ***Johnson*** | Y | Y | Y | Y | Y | N | N | N |
| 4 Hall | N | N | Y | Y | N | Y | Y | Y |
| 5 Bryant | N | N | Y | N | N | Y | Y | Y |
| 6 ***Barton*** | Y | Y | Y | Y | Y | N | N | N |
| 7 ***Archer*** | Y | Y | Y | Y | Y | N | N | N |
| 8 ***Fields*** | Y | Y | Y | Y | Y | N | N | N |
| 9 Brooks | N | N | Y | N | N | Y | Y | Y |
| 10 Pickle | N | N | Y | N | N | Y | Y | Y |
| 11 Edwards | N | N | Y | N | N | Y | Y | Y |
| 12 Geren | N | N | Y | N | N | Y | Y | Y |
| 13 Sarpalius | N | N | Y | N | N | Y | Y | Y |
| 14 Laughlin | N | N | Y | N | N | Y | Y | Y |
| 15 de la Garza | N | N | Y | N | N | Y | Y | Y |
| 16 Coleman | N | N | Y | N | N | Y | Y | Y |
| 17 Stenholm | N | N | Y | Y | N | Y | Y | Y |
| 18 Washington | N | N | Y | N | ? | ? | ? | Y |
| 19 ***Combest*** | Y | Y | Y | Y | Y | N | N | N |
| 20 Gonzalez | N | N | Y | N | N | Y | Y | Y |
| 21 ***Smith*** | Y | Y | Y | Y | Y | N | N | N |
| 22 ***DeLay*** | Y | Y | Y | Y | Y | N | N | N |
| 23 Bustamante | N | N | Y | N | N | Y | Y | Y |
| 24 Frost | N | N | Y | N | N | Y | Y | Y |
| 25 Andrews | N | N | Y | N | N | Y | Y | Y |
| 26 ***Armey*** | Y | Y | Y | Y | Y | N | N | N |
| 27 Ortiz | N | N | Y | N | N | Y | Y | Y |
| **UTAH** | | | | | | | | |
| 1 ***Hansen*** | Y | Y | Y | Y | Y | N | N | N |
| 2 Owens | Y | N | Y | N | N | Y | Y | Y |
| 3 Orton | Y | N | Y | N | Y | Y | Y | Y |
| **VERMONT** | | | | | | | | |
| AL *Sanders* | ? | ? | ? | N | N | Y | Y | Y |
| **VIRGINIA** | | | | | | | | |
| 1 ***Bateman*** | ? | N | Y | Y | Y | N | N | N |
| 2 Pickett | ? | N | Y | N | N | Y | Y | Y |
| 3 ***Bliley*** | Y | Y | Y | Y | Y | N | N | N |
| 4 Sisisky | N | N | Y | N | N | Y | Y | Y |
| 5 Payne | N | N | Y | N | N | Y | Y | Y |
| 6 Olin | N | N | Y | N | N | N | N | Y |
| 7 ***Allen*** | Y | Y | Y | Y | Y | N | N | N |
| 8 Moran | N | N | Y | N | N | Y | ? | Y |
| 9 Boucher | N | ? | Y | N | N | Y | Y | ? |
| 10 ***Wolf*** | N | Y | Y | Y | Y | N | N | N |
| **WASHINGTON** | | | | | | | | |
| 1 ***Miller*** | ? | ? | Y | Y | Y | N | N | N |
| 2 Swift | N | N | Y | N | N | Y | Y | Y |
| 3 Unsoeld | N | N | Y | N | N | Y | Y | Y |
| 4 ***Morrison*** | N | ? | Y | Y | Y | Y | N | Y |
| 5 Foley | | | | | | | | |
| 6 Dicks | N | N | Y | N | N | Y | Y | Y |
| 7 McDermott | N | N | Y | N | N | Y | Y | Y |
| 8 ***Chandler*** | ? | ? | Y | ? | Y | N | N | ? |
| **WEST VIRGINIA** | | | | | | | | |
| 1 Mollohan | N | N | Y | N | N | Y | Y | Y |
| 2 Staggers | N | N | Y | N | N | Y | Y | Y |
| 3 Wise | N | N | Y | N | N | Y | Y | Y |
| 4 Rahall | N | N | Y | N | N | Y | Y | Y |
| **WISCONSIN** | | | | | | | | |
| 1 Aspin | N | N | Y | N | N | Y | Y | Y |
| 2 ***Klug*** | Y | Y | Y | Y | Y | N | N | N |
| 3 ***Gunderson*** | Y | Y | Y | Y | Y | Y | N | N |
| 4 Kleczka | N | N | Y | N | N | Y | Y | Y |
| 5 Moody | N | N | Y | N | N | Y | ? | Y |
| 6 ***Petri*** | Y | Y | Y | Y | Y | N | N | N |
| 7 Obey | N | N | Y | N | N | Y | Y | Y |
| 8 ***Roth*** | Y | Y | Y | Y | Y | N | N | N |
| 9 ***Sensenbrenner*** | Y | Y | Y | Y | Y | N | N | N |
| **WYOMING** | | | | | | | | |
| AL ***Thomas*** | Y | Y | Y | Y | Y | N | N | N |

Southern states - Ala., Ark., Fla., Ga., Ky., La., Miss., N.C., Okla., S.C., Tenn., Texas, Va.
Omitted votes are quorum calls, which CQ does not include in its vote charts.

## KEY

Y   Voted for (yea).
#   Paired for.
+   Announced for.
N   Voted against (nay).
X   Paired against.
−   Announced against.
P   Voted "present."
C   Voted "present" to avoid possible conflict of interest.
?   Did not vote or otherwise make a position known.

Democrats   **Republicans**
*Independent*

**415. HR 5754. Water Resources Development/Auburn Dam.** Petri, R-Wis., amendment to strike the authorization of $456.2 million for the Auburn Dam project near Sacramento, Calif. Adopted 273-140: R 142-18; D 130-122 (ND 95-77, SD 35-45); I 1-0, Sept. 23, 1992.

**416. HR 5754. Water Resources Development/Authorization Ceilings.** Burton, R-Ind., amendment to reduce the bill's total authorization by $300 million by placing ceilings on annual authorizations for the general construction and flood control accounts. Rejected 104-303: R 87-73; D 17-229 (ND 12-159, SD 5-70); I 0-1, Sept. 23, 1992.

**417. HR 5754. Water Resources Development/Remove Projects.** Burton, R-Ind., amendment to strike the authorization for visitors' centers in Alton, Ill., and Mount Morris, N.Y., and a museum in Vicksburg, Miss. Rejected 125-282: R 101-56; D 24-225 (ND 16-155, SD 8-70); I 0-1, Sept. 23, 1992.

**418. HR 5754. Water Resources Development/Passage.** Passage of the bill to authorize more than $2 billion for the Army Corps of Engineers water resource development projects. Passed 326-87: R 86-75; D 239-12 (ND 161-11, SD 78-1); I 1-0, Sept. 23, 1992.

**419. HR 5504. Fiscal 1993 Defense Appropriations/Close Conference.** Murtha, D-Pa., motion to close portions of the conference on defense appropriations when issues of national security were to be considered. Motion agreed to 403-0: R 160-0; D 242-0 (ND 169-0, SD 73-0); I 1-0, Sept. 24, 1992.

**420. HR 5517. Fiscal 1993 District of Columbia Appropriations/Domestic Partnership.** DeLay, R-Texas, motion to recommit the conference report to conference. Proponents of the motion wanted the conference to include the Senate amendment to prohibit the District of Columbia from using any funds in the bill to extend employment, health or governmental benefits to homosexual or heterosexual unmarried couples ("domestic partners") on the same basis that such benefits were extended to legally married couples. Motion agreed to 235-173: R 144-16; D 91-156 (ND 38-137, SD 53-19); I 0-1, Sept. 24, 1992.

**421. HR 5419. International Dolphin Conservation.** Studds, D-Mass., motion to suspend the rules and pass the bill to authorize the secretary of State to enter into international agreements to establish a global moratorium to prohibit harvesting tuna with nets that ensnare dolphins or other marine mammals. Motion agreed to 389-15: R 144-14; D 244-1 (ND 171-1, SD 73-0); I 1-0, Sept. 24, 1992. A two-thirds majority of those present and voting (270 in this case) was required for passage under suspension of the rules.

**422. HR 5716. Reauthorization of Crime Control Programs.** Hughes, D-N.J., motion to suspend the rules and pass the bill to reauthorize for two years programs under the Justice Assistance Act that provide federal support to state and local law enforcement and anti-drug efforts. Motion agreed to 399-10: R 151-8; D 247-2 (ND 173-1, SD 74-1); I 1-0, Sept. 24, 1992. A two-thirds majority of those present and voting (273 in this case) was required for passage under suspension of the rules.

| | 415 | 416 | 417 | 418 | 419 | 420 | 421 | 422 |
|---|---|---|---|---|---|---|---|---|
| **ALABAMA** | | | | | | | | |
| 1 *Callahan* | Y | Y | N | Y | Y | Y | Y | Y |
| 2 *Dickinson* | Y | Y | Y | Y | Y | Y | Y | Y |
| 3 Browder | Y | N | N | Y | Y | Y | Y | Y |
| 4 Bevill | N | N | N | Y | Y | Y | Y | Y |
| 5 Cramer | Y | N | N | Y | Y | Y | Y | Y |
| 6 Erdreich | Y | N | N | Y | Y | Y | Y | Y |
| 7 Harris | Y | N | N | Y | Y | Y | Y | Y |
| **ALASKA** | | | | | | | | |
| AL *Young* | Y | N | N | Y | Y | Y | N | Y |
| **ARIZONA** | | | | | | | | |
| 1 *Rhodes* | Y | Y | Y | N | Y | Y | Y | Y |
| 2 Pastor | N | N | N | Y | N | Y | N | Y |
| 3 *Stump* | Y | Y | Y | N | Y | Y | N | N |
| 4 *Kyl* | Y | Y | Y | N | Y | Y | Y | Y |
| 5 *Kolbe* | Y | Y | Y | N | Y | N | Y | Y |
| **ARKANSAS** | | | | | | | | |
| 1 Alexander | ? | N | N | Y | ? | ? | Y | Y |
| 2 Thornton | N | N | N | Y | N | Y | N | Y |
| 3 *Hammerschmidt* | N | N | N | Y | Y | Y | N | Y |
| 4 Anthony | N | N | N | Y | ? | ? | ? | ? |
| **CALIFORNIA** | | | | | | | | |
| 1 *Riggs* | Y | N | N | Y | Y | Y | Y | Y |
| 2 *Herger* | Y | N | N | Y | Y | Y | Y | Y |
| 3 Matsui | N | N | N | Y | N | Y | N | Y |
| 4 Fazio | N | N | N | Y | N | Y | N | Y |
| 5 Pelosi | Y | N | N | Y | N | Y | N | Y |
| 6 Boxer | Y | ? | ? | Y | Y | N | Y | Y |
| 7 Miller | Y | N | N | Y | N | Y | ? | Y |
| 8 Dellums | Y | N | N | Y | N | Y | N | Y |
| 9 Stark | Y | N | N | Y | N | Y | N | Y |
| 10 Edwards | Y | N | N | Y | N | Y | N | Y |
| 11 Lantos | Y | N | N | Y | N | Y | N | Y |
| 12 *Campbell* | Y | Y | Y | N | Y | N | Y | Y |
| 13 Mineta | Y | N | N | Y | N | Y | N | Y |
| 14 *Doolittle* | Y | N | N | Y | Y | Y | Y | N |
| 15 Condit | N | Y | Y | Y | Y | Y | Y | Y |
| 16 Panetta | Y | N | N | Y | N | Y | N | Y |
| 17 Dooley | Y | N | Y | Y | N | Y | N | Y |
| 18 Lehman | N | N | N | Y | N | Y | N | Y |
| 19 *Lagomarsino* | Y | N | Y | Y | Y | Y | Y | Y |
| 20 *Thomas* | Y | Y | Y | Y | Y | Y | Y | Y |
| 21 *Gallegly* | Y | N | Y | Y | Y | Y | Y | Y |
| 22 *Moorhead* | Y | Y | Y | Y | Y | Y | Y | Y |
| 23 Beilenson | Y | N | N | Y | ? | N | Y | Y |
| 24 Waxman | Y | N | N | Y | N | Y | N | Y |
| 25 Roybal | N | N | ? | Y | Y | N | Y | Y |
| 26 Berman | Y | N | N | Y | N | Y | N | Y |
| 27 Levine | Y | N | N | Y | N | Y | N | Y |
| 28 Dixon | Y | N | N | Y | N | Y | N | Y |
| 29 Waters | N | N | N | Y | N | Y | N | Y |
| 30 Martinez | Y | N | N | Y | N | Y | N | Y |
| 31 Dymally | ? | ? | ? | ? | ? | Y | N | Y |
| 32 Anderson | N | N | N | Y | N | Y | N | N |
| 33 *Dreier* | Y | Y | Y | N | Y | Y | Y | Y |
| 34 Torres | N | N | N | Y | N | Y | N | Y |
| 35 *Lewis* | N | N | N | Y | Y | Y | Y | Y |
| 36 Brown | N | N | N | Y | N | Y | N | Y |
| 37 *McCandless* | Y | N | N | Y | Y | Y | Y | Y |
| 38 *Dornan* | Y | Y | Y | Y | Y | Y | Y | Y |
| 39 *Dannemeyer* | Y | Y | Y | N | Y | N | Y | N |
| 40 *Cox* | Y | ? | N | Y | N | Y | Y | Y |
| 41 *Lowery* | N | N | N | Y | Y | Y | ? | ? |

| | 415 | 416 | 417 | 418 | 419 | 420 | 421 | 422 |
|---|---|---|---|---|---|---|---|---|
| 42 *Rohrabacher* | Y | Y | Y | N | Y | N | Y | Y |
| 43 *Packard* | Y | Y | N | Y | Y | N | N | Y |
| 44 *Cunningham* | Y | Y | Y | Y | Y | Y | N | Y |
| 45 *Hunter* | Y | Y | Y | N | ? | Y | N | Y |
| **COLORADO** | | | | | | | | |
| 1 Schroeder | Y | N | N | Y | Y | N | Y | Y |
| 2 Skaggs | Y | N | N | Y | N | Y | N | Y |
| 3 Campbell | ? | ? | ? | ? | ? | ? | ? | ? |
| 4 *Allard* | Y | ? | Y | N | Y | Y | Y | Y |
| 5 *Hefley* | Y | Y | N | Y | N | Y | Y | Y |
| 6 *Schaefer* | Y | Y | Y | N | Y | Y | Y | Y |
| **CONNECTICUT** | | | | | | | | |
| 1 Kennelly | Y | N | N | Y | Y | N | Y | Y |
| 2 Gejdenson | Y | N | N | Y | N | Y | Y | Y |
| 3 DeLauro | Y | N | N | Y | N | Y | Y | Y |
| 4 *Shays* | Y | Y | Y | N | Y | N | Y | Y |
| 5 *Franks* | Y | Y | Y | N | Y | N | Y | Y |
| 6 *Johnson* | Y | N | N | N | Y | N | Y | Y |
| **DELAWARE** | | | | | | | | |
| AL Carper | Y | N | Y | Y | Y | Y | Y | Y |
| **FLORIDA** | | | | | | | | |
| 1 Hutto | Y | Y | N | Y | Y | Y | Y | Y |
| 2 Peterson | Y | N | N | Y | Y | N | Y | Y |
| 3 Bennett | N | N | N | Y | Y | Y | Y | Y |
| 4 *James* | Y | Y | N | Y | Y | Y | Y | Y |
| 5 *McCollum* | Y | Y | Y | N | Y | Y | Y | Y |
| 6 *Stearns* | Y | Y | N | Y | Y | Y | Y | Y |
| 7 Gibbons | N | N | N | Y | Y | N | ? | Y |
| 8 *Young* | Y | Y | Y | Y | Y | Y | Y | Y |
| 9 *Bilirakis* | Y | Y | N | Y | Y | Y | Y | Y |
| 10 *Ireland* | ? | ? | ? | N | ? | ? | ? | ? |
| 11 Bacchus | Y | N | N | Y | Y | N | Y | Y |
| 12 *Lewis* | Y | Y | N | Y | Y | Y | Y | Y |
| 13 *Goss* | Y | Y | Y | N | Y | Y | Y | Y |
| 14 Johnston | Y | N | N | Y | N | Y | N | Y |
| 15 *Shaw* | Y | N | N | Y | Y | Y | Y | Y |
| 16 Smith | N | N | N | Y | ? | N | Y | Y |
| 17 Lehman | N | ? | ? | ? | N | Y | Y | Y |
| 18 *Ros—Lehtinen* | Y | N | Y | Y | Y | Y | Y | Y |
| 19 Fascell | N | N | N | Y | N | Y | Y | Y |
| **GEORGIA** | | | | | | | | |
| 1 Thomas | N | N | N | Y | Y | Y | Y | Y |
| 2 Hatcher | N | ? | ? | Y | N | Y | Y | Y |
| 3 Ray | Y | N | N | Y | ? | # | Y | Y |
| 4 Jones | ? | ? | ? | ? | ? | ? | ? | ? |
| 5 Lewis | Y | N | N | Y | N | Y | Y | Y |
| 6 *Gingrich* | Y | Y | N | Y | N | Y | Y | Y |
| 7 Darden | Y | N | N | Y | Y | Y | Y | Y |
| 8 Rowland | Y | N | N | Y | Y | Y | Y | Y |
| 9 Jenkins | N | N | N | Y | ? | Y | Y | Y |
| 10 Barnard | ? | ? | ? | ? | ? | ? | ? | ? |
| **HAWAII** | | | | | | | | |
| 1 Abercrombie | Y | N | N | Y | Y | N | Y | Y |
| 2 Mink | Y | N | N | Y | N | Y | Y | Y |
| **IDAHO** | | | | | | | | |
| 1 LaRocco | Y | N | N | Y | Y | N | Y | Y |
| 2 Stallings | Y | N | N | Y | Y | Y | Y | Y |
| **ILLINOIS** | | | | | | | | |
| 1 Hayes | ? | N | N | Y | Y | N | Y | Y |
| 2 Savage | N | N | N | Y | ? | ? | ? | ? |
| 3 Russo | Y | N | N | Y | Y | Y | Y | Y |
| 4 Sangmeister | Y | N | N | Y | Y | Y | Y | Y |
| 5 Lipinski | Y | N | N | Y | Y | Y | Y | Y |
| 6 *Hyde* | Y | N | N | Y | Y | Y | Y | Y |
| 7 Collins | N | N | N | Y | N | Y | Y | Y |
| 8 Rostenkowski | N | N | N | Y | Y | N | Y | Y |
| 9 Yates | N | N | N | Y | N | Y | Y | Y |
| 10 *Porter* | Y | Y | Y | N | Y | Y | Y | Y |
| 11 Annunzio | N | N | N | Y | Y | N | Y | Y |
| 12 *Crane* | Y | Y | Y | N | ? | Y | Y | N |
| 13 *Fawell* | Y | Y | Y | N | Y | Y | Y | Y |
| 14 *Hastert* | Y | N | N | Y | Y | Y | Y | Y |
| 15 *Ewing* | Y | Y | Y | Y | Y | Y | Y | Y |
| 16 Cox | Y | N | Y | Y | Y | Y | Y | Y |
| 17 Evans | Y | N | N | Y | Y | N | Y | Y |
| 18 *Michel* | Y | Y | N | Y | ? | Y | Y | Y |
| 19 Bruce | Y | N | N | Y | Y | N | Y | Y |
| 20 Durbin | N | N | N | Y | Y | N | Y | Y |
| 21 Costello | N | N | N | Y | Y | Y | Y | Y |
| 22 Poshard | N | N | N | Y | Y | Y | Y | Y |
| **INDIANA** | | | | | | | | |
| 1 Visclosky | N | N | N | Y | N | Y | Y | Y |
| 2 Sharp | Y | N | N | Y | Y | N | Y | Y |
| 3 Roemer | Y | Y | Y | N | Y | N | Y | Y |

ND Northern Democrats    SD Southern Democrats

| | 415 | 416 | 417 | 418 | 419 | 420 | 421 | 422 |
|---|---|---|---|---|---|---|---|---|
| 4 Long | Y | N | N | Y | Y | N | Y | Y |
| 5 Jontz | Y | Y | Y | N | Y | N | Y | Y |
| 6 ***Burton*** | Y | Y | Y | N | Y | Y | Y | N |
| 7 ***Myers*** | N | N | N | Y | Y | Y | Y | Y |
| 8 McCloskey | Y | ? | N | Y | Y | N | Y | Y |
| 9 Hamilton | Y | N | Y | Y | Y | Y | Y | Y |
| 10 Jacobs | Y | Y | Y | ? | Y | N | Y | Y |
| **IOWA** | | | | | | | | |
| 1 ***Leach*** | Y | N | Y | Y | Y | N | Y | Y |
| 2 ***Nussle*** | Y | N | N | Y | Y | Y | Y | Y |
| 3 Nagle | N | N | N | Y | Y | N | Y | Y |
| 4 Smith | N | N | N | Y | Y | N | Y | Y |
| 5 ***Lightfoot*** | Y | N | N | Y | Y | Y | Y | Y |
| 6 ***Grandy*** | Y | N | N | Y | Y | Y | Y | Y |
| **KANSAS** | | | | | | | | |
| 1 ***Roberts*** | Y | Y | Y | N | Y | Y | Y | Y |
| 2 Slattery | Y | Y | Y | N | Y | Y | Y | Y |
| 3 ***Meyers*** | Y | Y | Y | N | Y | Y | Y | Y |
| 4 Glickman | Y | Y | Y | N | Y | Y | Y | Y |
| 5 ***Nichols*** | Y | Y | Y | N | Y | Y | ? | Y |
| **KENTUCKY** | | | | | | | | |
| 1 Hubbard | Y | N | Y | N | Y | Y | Y | Y |
| 2 Natcher | N | N | N | Y | Y | N | Y | Y |
| 3 Mazzoli | N | N | N | Y | Y | Y | Y | Y |
| 4 ***Bunning*** | Y | N | Y | N | Y | ? | Y | Y |
| 5 ***Rogers*** | N | N | N | Y | Y | Y | Y | Y |
| 6 ***Hopkins*** | Y | N | Y | Y | Y | Y | Y | Y |
| 7 Perkins | N | N | N | Y | Y | N | Y | Y |
| **LOUISIANA** | | | | | | | | |
| 1 ***Livingston*** | Y | N | N | Y | ? | ? | ? | ? |
| 2 Jefferson | N | N | N | Y | Y | N | Y | Y |
| 3 Tauzin | Y | N | N | Y | Y | Y | Y | Y |
| 4 ***McCrery*** | ? | N | Y | Y | Y | ? | ? | ? |
| 5 Huckaby | N | N | N | Y | Y | ? | ? | ? |
| 6 ***Baker*** | Y | Y | Y | Y | Y | Y | Y | Y |
| 7 Hayes | ? | ? | ? | ? | ? | ? | ? | ? |
| 8 ***Holloway*** | Y | Y | Y | Y | Y | Y | Y | Y |
| **MAINE** | | | | | | | | |
| 1 Andrews | Y | N | Y | Y | Y | N | Y | Y |
| 2 ***Snowe*** | Y | Y | Y | N | Y | Y | Y | Y |
| **MARYLAND** | | | | | | | | |
| 1 ***Gilchrest*** | Y | N | Y | Y | Y | Y | Y | Y |
| 2 ***Bentley*** | Y | N | N | Y | Y | Y | Y | Y |
| 3 Cardin | N | N | N | Y | Y | N | Y | Y |
| 4 McMillen | N | N | N | Y | Y | Y | Y | Y |
| 5 Hoyer | N | N | N | Y | Y | N | Y | Y |
| 6 Byron | N | Y | N | Y | Y | Y | Y | Y |
| 7 Mfume | N | N | N | Y | Y | N | Y | Y |
| 8 ***Morella*** | Y | N | Y | Y | Y | N | ? | ? |
| **MASSACHUSETTS** | | | | | | | | |
| 1 Olver | Y | N | N | N | Y | N | Y | Y |
| 2 Neal | Y | N | N | N | Y | N | Y | Y |
| 3 Early | N | N | N | Y | Y | N | Y | Y |
| 4 Frank | N | N | N | Y | Y | N | Y | Y |
| 5 Atkins | Y | Y | N | N | Y | N | Y | Y |
| 6 Mavroules | N | N | N | Y | Y | N | Y | Y |
| 7 Markey | Y | N | N | Y | Y | N | Y | Y |
| 8 Kennedy | Y | Y | Y | Y | Y | N | Y | Y |
| 9 Moakley | N | N | N | Y | Y | N | ? | Y |
| 10 Studds | Y | N | N | Y | Y | N | Y | Y |
| 11 Donnelly | Y | N | N | Y | Y | N | Y | Y |
| **MICHIGAN** | | | | | | | | |
| 1 Conyers | ? | ? | ? | ? | Y | N | Y | ? |
| 2 ***Pursell*** | Y | N | N | Y | Y | Y | Y | Y |
| 3 Wolpe | Y | N | N | Y | Y | N | Y | Y |
| 4 ***Upton*** | Y | Y | Y | N | Y | Y | Y | Y |
| 5 ***Henry*** | Y | Y | Y | N | Y | Y | Y | Y |
| 6 Carr | Y | N | N | Y | Y | N | Y | Y |
| 7 Kildee | Y | N | N | Y | Y | N | Y | Y |
| 8 Traxler | N | N | N | Y | Y | N | Y | Y |
| 9 ***Vander Jagt*** | Y | N | ? | Y | Y | Y | Y | Y |
| 10 ***Camp*** | Y | Y | Y | N | Y | Y | Y | Y |
| 11 ***Davis*** | N | N | N | Y | Y | Y | Y | Y |
| 12 Bonior | ? | N | N | Y | Y | N | Y | Y |
| 13 Collins | N | N | N | Y | Y | N | Y | Y |
| 14 Hertel | N | N | N | Y | Y | N | Y | Y |
| 15 Ford | Y | N | N | Y | Y | N | Y | Y |
| 16 Dingell | N | N | N | Y | Y | N | Y | Y |
| 17 Levin | Y | N | N | Y | Y | N | Y | Y |
| 18 ***Broomfield*** | Y | Y | Y | N | Y | Y | Y | Y |
| **MINNESOTA** | | | | | | | | |
| 1 Penny | + | + | + | + | Y | Y | Y | N |
| 2 ***Weber*** | ? | N | Y | N | Y | Y | Y | Y |
| 3 ***Ramstad*** | Y | Y | Y | N | Y | Y | Y | Y |
| 4 Vento | Y | ? | N | N | Y | N | Y | Y |

| | 415 | 416 | 417 | 418 | 419 | 420 | 421 | 422 |
|---|---|---|---|---|---|---|---|---|
| 5 Sabo | N | N | N | Y | Y | N | Y | Y |
| 6 Sikorski | Y | N | N | Y | Y | N | Y | Y |
| 7 Peterson | Y | N | N | Y | Y | Y | Y | Y |
| 8 Oberstar | Y | N | N | Y | Y | N | Y | Y |
| **MISSISSIPPI** | | | | | | | | |
| 1 Whitten | N | N | N | Y | Y | ? | Y | ? |
| 2 Espy | N | N | N | Y | Y | N | Y | Y |
| 3 Montgomery | Y | N | N | Y | Y | Y | Y | Y |
| 4 Parker | Y | N | N | Y | Y | Y | Y | Y |
| 5 Taylor | Y | N | N | Y | Y | Y | Y | Y |
| **MISSOURI** | | | | | | | | |
| 1 Clay | N | N | N | Y | Y | N | Y | Y |
| 2 Horn | N | N | N | Y | Y | N | Y | Y |
| 3 Gephardt | N | N | N | Y | Y | N | Y | Y |
| 4 Skelton | N | N | N | Y | Y | Y | Y | Y |
| 5 Wheat | N | N | N | Y | Y | N | Y | Y |
| 6 ***Coleman*** | Y | N | N | Y | Y | Y | Y | Y |
| 7 ***Hancock*** | Y | Y | Y | N | Y | Y | N | N |
| 8 ***Emerson*** | N | N | N | Y | Y | Y | Y | Y |
| 9 Volkmer | N | N | N | Y | Y | Y | ? | Y |
| **MONTANA** | | | | | | | | |
| 1 Williams | Y | N | N | Y | Y | N | Y | Y |
| 2 ***Marlenee*** | Y | Y | Y | Y | Y | Y | N | Y |
| **NEBRASKA** | | | | | | | | |
| 1 ***Bereuter*** | Y | Y | Y | N | Y | Y | Y | Y |
| 2 Hoagland | Y | N | N | Y | Y | N | Y | Y |
| 3 ***Barrett*** | Y | Y | Y | N | Y | Y | Y | Y |
| **NEVADA** | | | | | | | | |
| 1 Bilbray | N | N | N | Y | Y | Y | Y | Y |
| 2 ***Vucanovich*** | Y | Y | ? | Y | Y | Y | Y | Y |
| **NEW HAMPSHIRE** | | | | | | | | |
| 1 ***Zeliff*** | Y | N | N | Y | Y | Y | Y | Y |
| 2 Swett | Y | Y | Y | Y | Y | Y | Y | Y |
| **NEW JERSEY** | | | | | | | | |
| 1 Andrews | Y | N | N | Y | Y | N | Y | Y |
| 2 Hughes | Y | N | N | Y | Y | Y | ? | ? |
| 3 Pallone | Y | N | N | Y | Y | N | Y | Y |
| 4 ***Smith*** | Y | N | N | Y | Y | Y | Y | Y |
| 5 ***Roukema*** | N | N | N | Y | Y | Y | Y | Y |
| 6 Dwyer | N | N | N | Y | Y | N | Y | Y |
| 7 ***Rinaldo*** | N | N | N | Y | Y | Y | Y | Y |
| 8 Roe | N | N | N | Y | ? | N | Y | Y |
| 9 Torricelli | N | N | N | Y | Y | N | Y | Y |
| 10 Payne | N | N | N | Y | Y | N | Y | Y |
| 11 ***Gallo*** | N | N | N | Y | Y | Y | Y | Y |
| 12 ***Zimmer*** | Y | Y | Y | N | Y | Y | Y | Y |
| 13 ***Saxton*** | Y | N | N | Y | Y | Y | Y | Y |
| 14 Guarini | N | N | N | Y | Y | ? | Y | Y |
| **NEW MEXICO** | | | | | | | | |
| 1 ***Schiff*** | Y | Y | Y | Y | Y | Y | Y | Y |
| 2 ***Skeen*** | Y | N | N | Y | Y | Y | Y | Y |
| 3 Richardson | Y | N | N | Y | Y | N | Y | Y |
| **NEW YORK** | | | | | | | | |
| 1 Hochbrueckner | Y | N | N | Y | Y | N | Y | Y |
| 2 Downey | Y | N | N | Y | + | − | + | + |
| 3 Mrazek | N | N | N | Y | ? | N | Y | Y |
| 4 ***Lent*** | Y | N | N | Y | Y | Y | Y | Y |
| 5 ***McGrath*** | Y | ? | ? | ? | Y | Y | Y | Y |
| 6 Flake | N | N | N | Y | Y | N | Y | Y |
| 7 Ackerman | Y | N | N | Y | ? | X | ? | ? |
| 8 Scheuer | N | N | N | Y | Y | N | Y | Y |
| 9 Manton | N | N | N | Y | Y | N | Y | Y |
| 10 Schumer | Y | N | N | Y | Y | N | Y | Y |
| 11 Towns | N | N | N | Y | Y | N | Y | Y |
| 12 Owens | Y | N | N | Y | Y | N | Y | Y |
| 13 Solarz | Y | N | N | Y | Y | N | Y | Y |
| 14 ***Molinari*** | Y | N | N | Y | Y | Y | Y | Y |
| 15 ***Green*** | Y | N | N | Y | Y | N | Y | Y |
| 16 Rangel | N | N | N | ? | ? | N | Y | Y |
| 17 Vacancy | | | | | | | | |
| 18 Serrano | Y | N | N | Y | Y | N | Y | Y |
| 19 Engel | N | N | N | Y | Y | N | Y | Y |
| 20 Lowey | Y | N | N | Y | Y | N | Y | Y |
| 21 ***Fish*** | Y | N | Y | Y | Y | N | Y | Y |
| 22 ***Gilman*** | Y | N | Y | Y | Y | N | Y | Y |
| 23 McNulty | N | N | N | Y | Y | N | Y | Y |
| 24 ***Solomon*** | Y | Y | Y | N | Y | Y | Y | Y |
| 25 ***Boehlert*** | Y | N | N | Y | Y | N | Y | Y |
| 26 ***Martin*** | Y | N | N | Y | Y | Y | Y | Y |
| 27 ***Walsh*** | Y | N | N | Y | Y | Y | Y | Y |
| 28 McHugh | N | N | N | Y | Y | N | Y | Y |
| 29 ***Horton*** | N | ? | ? | ? | Y | N | Y | Y |
| 30 Slaughter | Y | N | N | Y | Y | N | Y | Y |
| 31 ***Paxon*** | Y | N | N | Y | Y | Y | Y | Y |

| | 415 | 416 | 417 | 418 | 419 | 420 | 421 | 422 |
|---|---|---|---|---|---|---|---|---|
| 32 LaFalce | N | N | N | Y | Y | N | Y | Y |
| 33 Nowak | N | N | N | Y | Y | N | Y | Y |
| 34 ***Houghton*** | Y | Y | N | Y | Y | N | Y | Y |
| **NORTH CAROLINA** | | | | | | | | |
| 1 Vacancy | | | | | | | | |
| 2 Valentine | Y | N | N | Y | Y | Y | Y | Y |
| 3 Lancaster | N | N | N | Y | Y | Y | ? | Y |
| 4 Price | N | N | N | Y | Y | N | Y | Y |
| 5 Neal | Y | N | Y | Y | Y | Y | Y | Y |
| 6 ***Coble*** | Y | Y | Y | N | Y | Y | Y | Y |
| 7 Rose | N | N | N | Y | Y | N | Y | Y |
| 8 Hefner | N | ? | N | Y | Y | Y | Y | Y |
| 9 ***McMillan*** | Y | Y | Y | Y | Y | Y | Y | Y |
| 10 ***Ballenger*** | Y | Y | Y | N | Y | Y | Y | Y |
| 11 ***Taylor*** | Y | Y | Y | N | Y | Y | Y | Y |
| **NORTH DAKOTA** | | | | | | | | |
| AL Dorgan | Y | N | N | Y | Y | Y | Y | Y |
| **OHIO** | | | | | | | | |
| 1 Luken | Y | N | N | Y | Y | Y | Y | Y |
| 2 ***Gradison*** | Y | N | N | N | Y | N | Y | Y |
| 3 Hall | N | N | N | Y | Y | Y | Y | Y |
| 4 ***Oxley*** | Y | Y | Y | N | Y | Y | Y | Y |
| 5 ***Gillmor*** | Y | N | N | Y | Y | Y | Y | Y |
| 6 ***McEwen*** | Y | Y | Y | Y | Y | Y | Y | Y |
| 7 ***Hobson*** | Y | N | N | Y | Y | Y | Y | Y |
| 8 ***Boehner*** | Y | Y | Y | N | Y | Y | Y | Y |
| 9 Kaptur | N | N | N | Y | ? | Y | Y | Y |
| 10 ***Miller*** | N | Y | Y | Y | Y | Y | Y | Y |
| 11 Eckart | Y | N | N | Y | Y | N | Y | Y |
| 12 ***Kasich*** | Y | N | Y | N | Y | Y | Y | Y |
| 13 Pease | Y | N | N | N | Y | N | Y | Y |
| 14 Sawyer | Y | N | N | Y | Y | N | Y | Y |
| 15 ***Wylie*** | Y | N | Y | N | Y | Y | Y | Y |
| 16 ***Regula*** | N | N | Y | Y | Y | Y | Y | Y |
| 17 Traficant | N | N | N | Y | Y | N | Y | Y |
| 18 Applegate | Y | N | N | Y | Y | N | Y | Y |
| 19 Feighan | N | N | ? | Y | Y | N | Y | Y |
| 20 Oakar | Y | N | N | Y | Y | N | Y | Y |
| 21 Stokes | N | N | N | Y | Y | N | Y | Y |
| **OKLAHOMA** | | | | | | | | |
| 1 ***Inhofe*** | Y | N | Y | Y | Y | Y | Y | Y |
| 2 Synar | Y | N | N | Y | Y | N | Y | Y |
| 3 Brewster | Y | N | N | Y | Y | Y | Y | Y |
| 4 McCurdy | Y | N | Y | Y | Y | Y | Y | Y |
| 5 ***Edwards*** | ? | ? | ? | ? | ? | Y | Y | Y |
| 6 English | Y | N | Y | Y | Y | Y | Y | Y |
| **OREGON** | | | | | | | | |
| 1 AuCoin | ? | ? | ? | ? | Y | N | Y | Y |
| 2 ***Smith*** | Y | Y | Y | N | Y | Y | Y | Y |
| 3 Wyden | Y | N | N | Y | Y | N | Y | Y |
| 4 DeFazio | Y | N | N | Y | Y | N | Y | Y |
| 5 Kopetski | N | N | N | Y | Y | N | Y | Y |
| **PENNSYLVANIA** | | | | | | | | |
| 1 Foglietta | ? | ? | ? | ? | ? | ? | ? | ? |
| 2 Blackwell | ? | ? | ? | ? | Y | N | Y | Y |
| 3 Borski | N | N | N | Y | Y | N | Y | Y |
| 4 Kolter | N | N | N | Y | Y | Y | Y | Y |
| 5 ***Schulze*** | Y | N | ? | ? | Y | Y | Y | Y |
| 6 Yatron | N | N | N | Y | Y | Y | Y | Y |
| 7 ***Weldon*** | Y | Y | Y | Y | Y | Y | Y | Y |
| 8 Kostmayer | Y | Y | Y | Y | Y | N | Y | Y |
| 9 ***Shuster*** | N | N | N | Y | Y | Y | Y | Y |
| 10 ***McDade*** | N | Y | N | Y | Y | Y | Y | Y |
| 11 Kanjorski | N | N | N | Y | Y | Y | Y | Y |
| 12 Murtha | N | N | N | Y | Y | N | Y | Y |
| 13 ***Coughlin*** | Y | N | N | Y | Y | Y | Y | Y |
| 14 Coyne | N | N | N | Y | Y | N | Y | Y |
| 15 ***Ritter*** | Y | Y | Y | N | Y | Y | Y | Y |
| 16 ***Walker*** | Y | Y | Y | N | Y | Y | Y | Y |
| 17 ***Gekas*** | Y | Y | Y | N | Y | Y | Y | Y |
| 18 ***Santorum*** | ? | N | N | Y | Y | Y | Y | Y |
| 19 ***Goodling*** | Y | Y | Y | N | Y | Y | Y | Y |
| 20 Gaydos | N | N | N | Y | Y | Y | Y | Y |
| 21 ***Ridge*** | Y | N | N | Y | Y | Y | ? | ? |
| 22 Murphy | Y | N | N | Y | Y | Y | Y | Y |
| 23 ***Clinger*** | Y | N | N | Y | Y | Y | Y | Y |
| **RHODE ISLAND** | | | | | | | | |
| 1 ***Machtley*** | Y | N | N | Y | Y | N | Y | Y |
| 2 Reed | Y | N | N | Y | Y | N | Y | Y |
| **SOUTH CAROLINA** | | | | | | | | |
| 1 ***Ravenel*** | Y | N | Y | Y | Y | Y | Y | Y |
| 2 ***Spence*** | Y | N | N | Y | Y | Y | Y | Y |
| 3 Derrick | Y | N | N | Y | Y | Y | Y | Y |
| 4 Patterson | Y | N | Y | Y | Y | Y | Y | Y |
| 5 Spratt | Y | N | N | Y | Y | Y | Y | Y |
| 6 Tallon | Y | N | N | Y | Y | Y | ? | Y |

| | 415 | 416 | 417 | 418 | 419 | 420 | 421 | 422 |
|---|---|---|---|---|---|---|---|---|
| **SOUTH DAKOTA** | | | | | | | | |
| AL Johnson | Y | N | N | Y | Y | Y | Y | Y |
| **TENNESSEE** | | | | | | | | |
| 1 ***Quillen*** | N | N | N | Y | Y | Y | Y | Y |
| 2 ***Duncan*** | Y | Y | Y | N | Y | Y | Y | Y |
| 3 Lloyd | Y | N | N | Y | Y | Y | Y | Y |
| 4 Cooper | Y | Y | N | Y | Y | N | Y | Y |
| 5 Clement | N | N | N | Y | Y | Y | Y | Y |
| 6 Gordon | Y | N | N | Y | Y | Y | Y | Y |
| 7 ***Sundquist*** | Y | N | Y | Y | Y | Y | Y | Y |
| 8 Tanner | N | N | N | Y | Y | Y | Y | Y |
| 9 Ford | N | N | N | Y | Y | ? | Y | Y |
| **TEXAS** | | | | | | | | |
| 1 Chapman | N | N | N | Y | ? | Y | Y | Y |
| 2 Wilson | N | ? | N | Y | Y | Y | Y | Y |
| 3 ***Johnson*** | Y | Y | Y | N | Y | Y | Y | N |
| 4 Hall | N | N | Y | Y | Y | Y | Y | Y |
| 5 Bryant | Y | N | N | Y | Y | Y | Y | Y |
| 6 ***Barton*** | Y | Y | Y | N | Y | Y | N | Y |
| 7 ***Archer*** | Y | Y | Y | N | Y | Y | Y | Y |
| 8 ***Fields*** | Y | Y | Y | N | Y | Y | N | Y |
| 9 Brooks | N | N | N | Y | Y | Y | Y | Y |
| 10 Pickle | Y | ? | N | Y | Y | Y | Y | Y |
| 11 Edwards | N | N | N | Y | Y | Y | Y | Y |
| 12 Geren | N | N | N | Y | Y | Y | Y | Y |
| 13 Sarpalius | N | Y | N | Y | Y | Y | ? | Y |
| 14 Laughlin | N | N | N | Y | Y | Y | Y | Y |
| 15 de la Garza | N | N | N | Y | Y | Y | Y | Y |
| 16 Coleman | N | N | N | Y | Y | Y | Y | Y |
| 17 Stenholm | Y | Y | Y | Y | Y | Y | Y | N |
| 18 Washington | Y | N | N | Y | ? | ? | ? | ? |
| 19 ***Combest*** | N | Y | Y | N | Y | Y | Y | Y |
| 20 Gonzalez | N | N | N | Y | Y | N | Y | Y |
| 21 ***Smith*** | Y | Y | Y | N | Y | Y | Y | Y |
| 22 ***DeLay*** | Y | Y | Y | N | Y | Y | N | Y |
| 23 Bustamante | N | N | N | Y | ? | ? | ? | ? |
| 24 Frost | N | N | N | Y | Y | Y | Y | Y |
| 25 Andrews | N | Y | Y | Y | Y | Y | Y | Y |
| 26 ***Armey*** | Y | Y | Y | N | Y | Y | N | N |
| 27 Ortiz | N | N | N | Y | Y | Y | Y | Y |
| **UTAH** | | | | | | | | |
| 1 ***Hansen*** | Y | N | Y | N | Y | Y | Y | Y |
| 2 Owens | Y | N | N | Y | Y | Y | Y | Y |
| 3 Orton | Y | Y | Y | N | + | Y | Y | Y |
| **VERMONT** | | | | | | | | |
| AL *Sanders* | Y | N | N | Y | Y | N | Y | Y |
| **VIRGINIA** | | | | | | | | |
| 1 ***Bateman*** | N | N | N | Y | Y | Y | Y | Y |
| 2 Pickett | N | N | N | Y | Y | Y | Y | Y |
| 3 ***Bliley*** | Y | N | Y | Y | Y | Y | Y | Y |
| 4 Sisisky | N | N | N | Y | Y | Y | Y | Y |
| 5 Payne | Y | N | N | Y | Y | Y | Y | Y |
| 6 Olin | N | ? | ? | Y | Y | N | Y | ? |
| 7 ***Allen*** | Y | Y | Y | N | Y | Y | Y | Y |
| 8 Moran | N | N | N | Y | Y | N | Y | Y |
| 9 Boucher | N | N | N | Y | Y | Y | Y | Y |
| 10 ***Wolf*** | Y | Y | Y | N | Y | Y | Y | Y |
| **WASHINGTON** | | | | | | | | |
| 1 ***Miller*** | Y | Y | Y | N | Y | Y | Y | Y |
| 2 Swift | N | N | N | Y | Y | N | Y | Y |
| 3 Unsoeld | Y | N | N | Y | Y | N | Y | Y |
| 4 ***Morrison*** | Y | N | N | Y | Y | Y | Y | Y |
| 5 Foley | | | | | | | | |
| 6 Dicks | Y | N | N | Y | Y | N | Y | Y |
| 7 McDermott | Y | N | N | Y | ? | N | Y | Y |
| 8 ***Chandler*** | ? | ? | ? | ? | ? | ? | ? | ? |
| **WEST VIRGINIA** | | | | | | | | |
| 1 Mollohan | N | N | N | Y | Y | Y | Y | Y |
| 2 Staggers | Y | N | N | Y | Y | N | Y | Y |
| 3 Wise | N | N | N | Y | Y | Y | Y | Y |
| 4 Rahall | Y | N | N | Y | Y | Y | Y | Y |
| **WISCONSIN** | | | | | | | | |
| 1 Aspin | N | N | N | Y | Y | N | Y | Y |
| 2 ***Klug*** | Y | Y | Y | N | Y | Y | Y | Y |
| 3 ***Gunderson*** | Y | N | N | Y | Y | N | Y | Y |
| 4 Kleczka | N | N | N | Y | Y | N | Y | Y |
| 5 Moody | Y | N | N | Y | Y | N | Y | Y |
| 6 ***Petri*** | Y | N | N | Y | Y | Y | Y | Y |
| 7 Obey | N | N | N | Y | Y | N | Y | Y |
| 8 ***Roth*** | Y | Y | Y | Y | Y | Y | Y | Y |
| 9 ***Sensenbrenner*** | Y | Y | Y | N | Y | Y | Y | N |
| **WYOMING** | | | | | | | | |
| AL ***Thomas*** | Y | Y | Y | N | Y | Y | Y | Y |

Southern states - Ala., Ark., Fla., Ga., Ky., La., Miss., N.C., Okla., S.C., Tenn., Texas, Va.
Omitted votes are quorum calls, which CQ does not include in its vote charts.

**423. HR 5323. Democracy in Cuba.** Torricelli, D-N.J., motion to suspend the rules and pass the bill to promote a peaceful transition to democracy in Cuba through a trade embargo against foreign subsidiaries of U.S. companies that trade or assist Cuba until it held free and fair elections and was moving toward a free-market economy. Motion agreed to 276-135: R 137-24; D 139-110 (ND 82-92, SD 57-18); I 0-1, Sept. 24, 1992. A two-thirds majority of those present and voting (274 in this case) was required for passage under suspension of the rules.

**424. HR 5938. Mammography Quality Standards.** Waxman, D-Calif., motion to suspend the rules and pass the bill to establish federal quality standards for mammograms to detect breast cancer. Motion agreed to 390-18: R 146-15; D 243-3 (ND 171-1, SD 72-2); I 1-0, Sept. 24, 1992. A two-thirds majority of those present and voting (272 in this case) was required for passage under suspension of the rules.

**425. HR 5673. Health-Care Policy and Research.** Waxman, D-Calif., motion to suspend the rules and pass the bill to reauthorize the Agency for Health Care Policy and Research to conduct health services research. Motion agreed to 397-8: R 151-7; D 245-1 (ND 170-1, SD 75-0); I 1-0, Sept. 24, 1992. A two-thirds majority of those present and voting (270 in this case) was required for passage under suspension of the rules.

**426. HR 3596. Consumer Credit Reporting Reform/Pre-emption of State Laws.** Gonzalez, D-Texas, amendment to strike the provisions of the bill that pre-empted all state laws that gave consumers additional protections from credit reporting agencies. Rejected 203-207: R 26-133; D 176-74 (ND 138-36, SD 38-38); I 1-0, Sept. 24, 1992.

**427. HR 3596. Consumer Credit Reporting Reform/Motion To Rise.** Torres, D-Calif., motion to rise from the Committee of the Whole during consideration of the bill to require that consumers be notified of action taken against them based on credit reports with no resolution thereon. Motion agreed to 228-177: R 8-150; D 219-27 (ND 160-10, SD 59-17); I 1-0, Sept. 24, 1992.

**428. HR 5517. Fiscal 1993 District of Columbia Appropriations/Death Penalty Referendum.** Gallo, R-N.J., motion to recede and concur in a Senate amendment with an amendment to place on the ballot in the District of Columbia within 90 days a referendum to establish a death penalty for first-degree murders. Motion agreed to 264-129: R 146-7; D 118-121 (ND 59-107, SD 59-14); I 0-1, Sept. 24, 1992.

**429. HR 5373. Fiscal 1993 Energy and Water Appropriations/Nuclear Testing Moratorium.** Aspin, D-Wis., motion to recede and concur in a Senate amendment with an amendment to impose a nine-month moratorium on nuclear testing until July 1, 1993; allow limited testing between July 1, 1993, and Jan. 1, 1997; require reports to Congress on the remaining weapons in the U.S. stockpile, proposed safety improvements and tests, and plans for a comprehensive test ban by Sept. 30, 1996; and, contingent upon certain factors, prohibit nuclear tests after Sept. 30, 1996, unless a foreign state conducted a nuclear test. Motion agreed to 224-151: R 28-122; D 195-29 (ND 150-7, SD 45-22); I 1-0, Sept. 24, 1992. A "nay" was a vote in support of the president's position.

**430. S 5. Family and Medical Leave Act/Postpone Veto Override.** Gephardt, D-Mo., motion to postpone consideration of a veto override until Wednesday, Sept. 30, 1992, on the bill to require companies with more than 50 employees to provide workers with up to 12 weeks of unpaid leave for family emergencies. Motion agreed to 239-139: R 15-134; D 223-5 (ND 156-1, SD 67-4); I 1-0, Sept. 25, 1992.

## KEY

Y  Voted for (yea).
#  Paired for.
+  Announced for.
N  Voted against (nay).
X  Paired against.
−  Announced against.
P  Voted "present."
C  Voted "present" to avoid possible conflict of interest.
?  Did not vote or otherwise make a position known.

Democrats **Republicans** *Independent*

| | 423 | 424 | 425 | 426 | 427 | 428 | 429 | 430 |
|---|---|---|---|---|---|---|---|---|
| **ALABAMA** | | | | | | | | |
| 1 Callahan | Y | N | ? | N | N | Y | N | N |
| 2 *Dickinson* | Y | Y | Y | N | N | Y | N | ? |
| 3 Browder | Y | Y | Y | N | N | Y | Y | Y |
| 4 Bevill | Y | Y | Y | N | Y | Y | Y | Y |
| 5 Cramer | Y | Y | Y | N | Y | Y | Y | Y |
| 6 Erdreich | Y | Y | Y | N | Y | Y | N | Y |
| 7 Harris | Y | Y | Y | N | N | Y | N | Y |
| **ALASKA** | | | | | | | | |
| AL *Young* | Y | Y | Y | N | N | Y | N | ? |
| **ARIZONA** | | | | | | | | |
| 1 *Rhodes* | Y | Y | Y | N | N | Y | N | N |
| 2 Pastor | N | Y | Y | Y | Y | N | Y | Y |
| 3 *Stump* | N | N | N | N | N | Y | N | N |
| 4 *Kyl* | Y | N | Y | N | N | Y | N | N |
| 5 *Kolbe* | N | Y | Y | N | N | Y | N | N |
| **ARKANSAS** | | | | | | | | |
| 1 Alexander | N | Y | Y | Y | Y | Y | Y | Y |
| 2 Thornton | Y | Y | Y | Y | Y | ? | Y | Y |
| 3 *Hammerschmidt* | Y | Y | Y | N | N | Y | N | N |
| 4 Anthony | ? | ? | ? | ? | ? | ? | ? | ? |
| **CALIFORNIA** | | | | | | | | |
| 1 *Riggs* | Y | Y | Y | N | N | Y | N | N |
| 2 *Herger* | Y | Y | Y | N | N | Y | N | N |
| 3 Matsui | Y | Y | Y | Y | Y | Y | Y | Y |
| 4 Fazio | Y | Y | Y | N | Y | ? | # | ? |
| 5 Pelosi | N | Y | Y | Y | Y | N | Y | Y |
| 6 Boxer | N | Y | Y | ? | ? | ? | ? | ? |
| 7 Miller | N | ? | Y | Y | Y | N | Y | Y |
| 8 Dellums | N | Y | Y | Y | N | Y | Y | Y |
| 9 Stark | N | Y | Y | Y | Y | N | Y | ? |
| 10 Edwards | N | Y | Y | Y | N | Y | Y | Y |
| 11 Lantos | Y | Y | Y | Y | Y | Y | Y | Y |
| 12 *Campbell* | N | Y | Y | N | N | N | N | N |
| 13 Mineta | N | Y | Y | Y | Y | N | Y | Y |
| 14 *Doolittle* | Y | Y | N | N | N | Y | N | N |
| 15 Condit | N | Y | Y | N | N | Y | Y | Y |
| 16 Panetta | N | Y | Y | Y | Y | Y | Y | Y |
| 17 Dooley | N | Y | Y | N | N | Y | Y | ? |
| 18 Lehman | Y | Y | Y | Y | Y | Y | Y | ? |
| 19 *Lagomarsino* | Y | Y | Y | N | N | Y | N | N |
| 20 *Thomas* | Y | Y | Y | N | N | Y | N | N |
| 21 *Gallegly* | Y | Y | Y | N | N | Y | N | N |
| 22 *Moorhead* | Y | Y | Y | N | N | Y | N | N |
| 23 Beilenson | N | Y | Y | Y | Y | N | Y | Y |
| 24 Waxman | Y | Y | Y | ? | N | ? | ? | ? |
| 25 Roybal | Y | Y | Y | Y | Y | N | Y | Y |
| 26 Berman | Y | Y | Y | Y | Y | N | Y | Y |
| 27 Levine | Y | Y | Y | Y | Y | N | Y | Y |
| 28 Dixon | Y | Y | Y | Y | Y | N | Y | Y |
| 29 Waters | N | Y | Y | Y | Y | N | ? | ? |
| 30 Martinez | Y | Y | Y | N | Y | N | Y | ? |
| 31 Dymally | N | Y | Y | ? | ? | ? | ? | Y |
| 32 Anderson | Y | Y | Y | Y | N | N | Y | Y |
| 33 *Dreier* | Y | Y | Y | N | N | Y | N | N |
| 34 Torres | N | Y | Y | Y | Y | N | Y | Y |
| 35 *Lewis* | Y | Y | Y | N | N | Y | N | N |
| 36 Brown | Y | Y | Y | Y | Y | N | Y | Y |
| 37 *McCandless* | Y | Y | Y | N | N | Y | N | N |
| 38 *Dornan* | Y | N | N | N | N | Y | N | N |
| 39 *Dannemeyer* | Y | N | N | N | N | Y | N | N |
| 40 *Cox* | Y | Y | Y | N | N | Y | N | N |
| 41 *Lowery* | ? | ? | ? | N | ? | Y | N | N |

| | 423 | 424 | 425 | 426 | 427 | 428 | 429 | 430 |
|---|---|---|---|---|---|---|---|---|
| 42 *Rohrabacher* | Y | Y | Y | N | N | Y | N | N |
| 43 *Packard* | Y | Y | Y | N | N | Y | N | N |
| 44 *Cunningham* | Y | Y | Y | N | N | Y | N | N |
| 45 *Hunter* | Y | Y | Y | N | N | Y | N | N |
| **COLORADO** | | | | | | | | |
| 1 Schroeder | Y | Y | Y | Y | Y | N | Y | Y |
| 2 Skaggs | N | Y | Y | Y | Y | Y | N | Y |
| 3 Campbell | ? | ? | ? | ? | ? | ? | ? | ? |
| 4 *Allard* | N | N | Y | N | N | Y | N | N |
| 5 *Hefley* | Y | Y | Y | N | N | Y | N | N |
| 6 *Schaefer* | Y | Y | Y | N | N | Y | N | N |
| **CONNECTICUT** | | | | | | | | |
| 1 Kennelly | N | Y | Y | Y | Y | Y | Y | Y |
| 2 Gejdenson | N | Y | Y | Y | Y | N | Y | Y |
| 3 DeLauro | N | Y | Y | Y | Y | Y | Y | Y |
| 4 *Shays* | Y | Y | Y | Y | Y | N | Y | Y |
| 5 *Franks* | N | Y | Y | N | N | Y | N | N |
| 6 *Johnson* | N | Y | Y | Y | Y | Y | Y | Y |
| **DELAWARE** | | | | | | | | |
| AL Carper | Y | Y | Y | N | Y | Y | Y | Y |
| **FLORIDA** | | | | | | | | |
| 1 Hutto | Y | Y | Y | N | N | Y | N | Y |
| 2 Peterson | Y | Y | Y | Y | Y | Y | Y | Y |
| 3 Bennett | Y | Y | Y | Y | Y | Y | Y | Y |
| 4 *James* | Y | Y | Y | N | N | Y | N | N |
| 5 *McCollum* | Y | Y | Y | N | N | Y | N | N |
| 6 *Stearns* | Y | Y | Y | N | N | Y | N | N |
| 7 Gibbons | Y | Y | Y | Y | Y | Y | Y | Y |
| 8 *Young* | Y | Y | Y | N | N | Y | N | N |
| 9 *Bilirakis* | Y | Y | Y | N | N | Y | N | N |
| 10 *Ireland* | ? | ? | ? | N | ? | N | ? | N |
| 11 Bacchus | Y | Y | Y | Y | Y | Y | Y | ? |
| 12 *Lewis* | Y | Y | Y | N | N | Y | N | N |
| 13 *Goss* | Y | Y | Y | N | N | Y | N | N |
| 14 Johnston | N | Y | Y | N | Y | N | Y | Y |
| 15 *Shaw* | Y | Y | Y | N | N | Y | N | N |
| 16 Smith | Y | Y | Y | Y | Y | Y | Y | Y |
| 17 Lehman | Y | Y | Y | Y | Y | ? | ? | ? |
| 18 *Ros—Lehtinen* | Y | Y | Y | Y | Y | N | Y | N |
| 19 Fascell | Y | Y | Y | Y | Y | ? | ? | ? |
| **GEORGIA** | | | | | | | | |
| 1 Thomas | Y | Y | Y | N | Y | Y | Y | Y |
| 2 Hatcher | Y | Y | Y | Y | Y | N | ? | Y |
| 3 Ray | ? | Y | Y | N | N | Y | N | Y |
| 4 Jones | ? | ? | ? | ? | ? | ? | ? | ? |
| 5 Lewis | N | Y | Y | Y | Y | N | Y | Y |
| 6 *Gingrich* | Y | Y | Y | N | ? | Y | N | N |
| 7 Darden | Y | Y | Y | N | N | Y | Y | Y |
| 8 Rowland | Y | Y | Y | N | N | Y | Y | Y |
| 9 Jenkins | Y | Y | Y | N | Y | Y | Y | Y |
| 10 Barnard | ? | ? | ? | X | ? | ? | ? | ? |
| **HAWAII** | | | | | | | | |
| 1 Abercrombie | N | Y | Y | Y | Y | ? | Y | Y |
| 2 Mink | N | Y | Y | Y | Y | N | Y | Y |
| **IDAHO** | | | | | | | | |
| 1 LaRocco | Y | Y | Y | Y | Y | Y | Y | Y |
| 2 Stallings | Y | Y | Y | N | N | Y | Y | Y |
| **ILLINOIS** | | | | | | | | |
| 1 Hayes | N | Y | Y | Y | Y | N | Y | Y |
| 2 Savage | ? | ? | ? | Y | Y | N | ? | ? |
| 3 Russo | Y | Y | Y | Y | Y | Y | Y | Y |
| 4 Sangmeister | N | Y | Y | Y | Y | Y | N | Y |
| 5 Lipinski | Y | Y | Y | Y | Y | Y | N | Y |
| 6 *Hyde* | Y | Y | N | Y | N | Y | N | N |
| 7 Collins | N | Y | Y | Y | Y | N | ? | Y |
| 8 Rostenkowski | Y | Y | Y | Y | Y | Y | Y | Y |
| 9 Yates | N | Y | Y | Y | ? | ? | ? | Y |
| 10 *Porter* | Y | Y | Y | N | N | Y | Y | N |
| 11 Annunzio | Y | Y | Y | Y | Y | Y | ? | Y |
| 12 *Crane* | Y | N | Y | N | N | Y | N | ? |
| 13 *Fawell* | Y | Y | Y | N | N | Y | N | N |
| 14 *Hastert* | Y | Y | Y | N | N | Y | N | N |
| 15 *Ewing* | N | Y | Y | N | N | Y | N | N |
| 16 Cox | N | Y | Y | N | N | N | Y | N |
| 17 Evans | N | Y | Y | Y | Y | N | Y | Y |
| 18 *Michel* | Y | Y | Y | N | N | Y | N | N |
| 19 Bruce | N | Y | Y | Y | Y | N | Y | Y |
| 20 Durbin | N | Y | Y | Y | Y | N | Y | Y |
| 21 Costello | N | Y | Y | Y | Y | Y | N | Y |
| 22 Poshard | N | Y | Y | Y | Y | Y | Y | Y |
| **INDIANA** | | | | | | | | |
| 1 Visclosky | Y | Y | Y | Y | Y | N | Y | Y |
| 2 Sharp | Y | Y | Y | Y | Y | N | Y | Y |
| 3 Roemer | Y | Y | Y | N | Y | Y | Y | Y |

ND Northern Democrats    SD Southern Democrats

| | 423 | 424 | 425 | 426 | 427 | 428 | 429 | 430 |
|---|---|---|---|---|---|---|---|---|
| 4 Long | N | Y | Y | Y | Y | Y | Y | Y |
| 5 Jontz | N | Y | Y | Y | Y | N | Y | Y |
| 6 ***Burton*** | Y | Y | N | N | N | Y | N | N |
| 7 ***Myers*** | Y | Y | Y | N | N | Y | ? | Y |
| 8 McCloskey | N | Y | Y | Y | Y | N | Y | Y |
| 9 Hamilton | Y | Y | Y | N | Y | Y | Y | Y |
| 10 Jacobs | Y | Y | Y | Y | Y | N | Y | Y |
| **IOWA** | | | | | | | | |
| 1 ***Leach*** | Y | Y | Y | N | N | N | Y | N |
| 2 ***Nussle*** | N | Y | Y | N | N | Y | Y | N |
| 3 Nagle | N | Y | Y | N | Y | N | Y | ? |
| 4 Smith | N | Y | Y | N | Y | N | Y | Y |
| 5 ***Lightfoot*** | N | Y | Y | N | N | Y | N | N |
| 6 ***Grandy*** | N | N | Y | N | N | Y | Y | N |
| **KANSAS** | | | | | | | | |
| 1 ***Roberts*** | N | Y | Y | N | N | Y | N | N |
| 2 Slattery | Y | Y | Y | N | N | N | Y | Y |
| 3 ***Meyers*** | Y | Y | Y | N | N | Y | N | N |
| 4 Glickman | Y | Y | Y | N | ? | Y | Y | Y |
| 5 ***Nichols*** | Y | Y | Y | N | N | Y | N | N |
| **KENTUCKY** | | | | | | | | |
| 1 Hubbard | Y | Y | Y | N | N | Y | N | Y |
| 2 Natcher | N | Y | Y | N | Y | N | Y | Y |
| 3 Mazzoli | Y | Y | Y | Y | Y | N | Y | Y |
| 4 ***Bunning*** | Y | Y | Y | N | N | Y | N | N |
| 5 ***Rogers*** | Y | Y | Y | N | N | Y | N | N |
| 6 ***Hopkins*** | Y | Y | Y | N | N | Y | N | N |
| 7 Perkins | N | Y | Y | Y | Y | Y | Y | ? |
| **LOUISIANA** | | | | | | | | |
| 1 ***Livingston*** | ? | ? | ? | ? | ? | ? | ? | ? |
| 2 Jefferson | N | Y | Y | Y | Y | N | Y | Y |
| 3 Tauzin | Y | Y | Y | Y | Y | Y | N | Y |
| 4 ***McCrery*** | ? | ? | ? | ? | ? | ? | ? | ? |
| 5 Huckaby | ? | ? | ? | ? | ? | ? | ? | ? |
| 6 ***Baker*** | Y | Y | Y | N | N | Y | N | N |
| 7 Hayes | ? | ? | ? | ? | ? | ? | ? | ? |
| 8 ***Holloway*** | Y | Y | Y | ? | ? | ? | ? | ? |
| **MAINE** | | | | | | | | |
| 1 Andrews | N | Y | Y | Y | Y | N | Y | Y |
| 2 ***Snowe*** | Y | Y | Y | Y | Y | Y | N | Y |
| **MARYLAND** | | | | | | | | |
| 1 ***Gilchrest*** | Y | Y | Y | N | N | Y | Y | N |
| 2 ***Bentley*** | Y | Y | N | N | N | Y | N | N |
| 3 Cardin | Y | Y | Y | Y | Y | N | Y | Y |
| 4 McMillen | Y | Y | Y | Y | Y | Y | Y | Y |
| 5 Hoyer | Y | Y | Y | Y | Y | N | Y | Y |
| 6 Byron | Y | Y | Y | N | Y | Y | N | Y |
| 7 Mfume | N | Y | Y | Y | Y | N | Y | Y |
| 8 ***Morella*** | N | Y | Y | Y | N | N | Y | ? |
| **MASSACHUSETTS** | | | | | | | | |
| 1 Olver | N | Y | Y | Y | Y | N | Y | Y |
| 2 Neal | N | Y | Y | Y | Y | N | Y | Y |
| 3 Early | N | Y | Y | Y | Y | Y | Y | Y |
| 4 Frank | N | Y | Y | Y | Y | N | ? | Y |
| 5 Atkins | N | Y | Y | Y | Y | N | Y | Y |
| 6 Mavroules | Y | Y | Y | Y | Y | N | Y | Y |
| 7 Markey | N | Y | ? | Y | Y | N | Y | Y |
| 8 Kennedy | N | Y | Y | Y | Y | N | Y | Y |
| 9 Moakley | N | Y | Y | Y | Y | N | Y | Y |
| 10 Studds | N | Y | Y | Y | Y | N | Y | Y |
| 11 Donnelly | Y | Y | Y | ? | ? | ? | ? | ? |
| **MICHIGAN** | | | | | | | | |
| 1 Conyers | N | Y | Y | Y | Y | N | Y | ? |
| 2 ***Pursell*** | Y | Y | Y | N | N | Y | Y | N |
| 3 Wolpe | N | Y | Y | Y | Y | N | Y | Y |
| 4 ***Upton*** | N | Y | Y | N | N | Y | Y | N |
| 5 ***Henry*** | Y | Y | Y | N | N | Y | Y | N |
| 6 Carr | Y | Y | Y | N | Y | Y | Y | Y |
| 7 Kildee | Y | Y | Y | Y | Y | N | Y | Y |
| 8 Traxler | Y | Y | Y | Y | Y | N | Y | Y |
| 9 ***Vander Jagt*** | Y | Y | Y | N | N | Y | N | ? |
| 10 ***Camp*** | N | Y | Y | N | N | Y | N | N |
| 11 ***Davis*** | Y | Y | Y | N | N | Y | N | Y |
| 12 Bonior | N | Y | Y | Y | Y | N | Y | Y |
| 13 Collins | N | Y | Y | Y | Y | N | Y | Y |
| 14 Hertel | Y | Y | Y | Y | Y | N | Y | Y |
| 15 Ford | Y | Y | Y | Y | Y | N | Y | Y |
| 16 Dingell | Y | Y | Y | Y | Y | N | Y | Y |
| 17 Levin | Y | Y | Y | Y | Y | Y | Y | Y |
| 18 ***Broomfield*** | Y | Y | Y | N | N | Y | ? | N |
| **MINNESOTA** | | | | | | | | |
| 1 Penny | N | N | N | N | Y | N | Y | N |
| 2 ***Weber*** | Y | Y | Y | N | N | Y | ? | N |
| 3 ***Ramstad*** | N | Y | Y | N | N | Y | N | Y |
| 4 Vento | N | Y | Y | Y | Y | N | Y | Y |

| | 423 | 424 | 425 | 426 | 427 | 428 | 429 | 430 |
|---|---|---|---|---|---|---|---|---|
| 5 Sabo | N | Y | Y | Y | Y | N | Y | Y |
| 6 Sikorski | N | Y | Y | Y | Y | N | Y | Y |
| 7 Peterson | N | Y | Y | N | Y | N | Y | Y |
| 8 Oberstar | N | Y | Y | Y | Y | N | Y | Y |
| **MISSISSIPPI** | | | | | | | | |
| 1 Whitten | Y | ? | ? | N | Y | N | Y | Y |
| 2 Espy | N | Y | Y | Y | Y | N | Y | Y |
| 3 Montgomery | Y | Y | Y | N | N | Y | N | Y |
| 4 Parker | Y | Y | Y | N | Y | Y | Y | ? |
| 5 Taylor | Y | Y | Y | Y | Y | Y | N | N |
| **MISSOURI** | | | | | | | | |
| 1 Clay | N | Y | Y | Y | ? | ? | ? | Y |
| 2 Horn | Y | Y | Y | Y | Y | N | Y | Y |
| 3 Gephardt | Y | Y | Y | Y | Y | N | Y | Y |
| 4 Skelton | Y | Y | Y | N | N | Y | ? | Y |
| 5 Wheat | N | Y | Y | Y | Y | ? | ? | Y |
| 6 ***Coleman*** | Y | Y | Y | N | N | Y | N | N |
| 7 ***Hancock*** | Y | N | N | N | N | Y | N | N |
| 8 ***Emerson*** | Y | N | Y | N | N | Y | N | N |
| 9 Volkmer | Y | Y | Y | N | Y | Y | Y | Y |
| **MONTANA** | | | | | | | | |
| 1 Williams | Y | ? | Y | N | Y | Y | Y | Y |
| 2 ***Marlenee*** | N | Y | Y | N | N | Y | N | N |
| **NEBRASKA** | | | | | | | | |
| 1 ***Bereuter*** | N | Y | Y | N | N | Y | N | N |
| 2 Hoagland | N | Y | Y | Y | Y | Y | Y | Y |
| 3 ***Barrett*** | N | Y | Y | N | N | Y | N | N |
| **NEVADA** | | | | | | | | |
| 1 Bilbray | Y | Y | Y | N | Y | Y | N | Y |
| 2 ***Vucanovich*** | Y | Y | Y | N | N | Y | N | N |
| **NEW HAMPSHIRE** | | | | | | | | |
| 1 ***Zeliff*** | Y | Y | Y | N | N | Y | N | N |
| 2 Swett | Y | Y | Y | Y | Y | N | ? | Y |
| **NEW JERSEY** | | | | | | | | |
| 1 Andrews | Y | Y | Y | Y | Y | N | N | Y |
| 2 Hughes | ? | Y | Y | Y | Y | N | Y | Y |
| 3 Pallone | Y | Y | Y | Y | Y | Y | Y | Y |
| 4 ***Smith*** | Y | Y | Y | Y | Y | N | Y | N |
| 5 ***Roukema*** | Y | Y | Y | N | N | N | Y | Y |
| 6 Dwyer | N | Y | Y | Y | Y | Y | Y | Y |
| 7 ***Rinaldo*** | Y | Y | Y | Y | Y | Y | ? | N |
| 8 Roe | Y | Y | Y | Y | Y | Y | Y | Y |
| 9 Torricelli | Y | Y | Y | Y | Y | Y | Y | Y |
| 10 Payne | N | Y | Y | Y | Y | N | Y | Y |
| 11 ***Gallo*** | Y | Y | Y | Y | Y | Y | N | N |
| 12 ***Zimmer*** | Y | Y | Y | N | N | Y | N | N |
| 13 ***Saxton*** | Y | Y | Y | Y | Y | Y | N | N |
| 14 Guarini | Y | Y | Y | Y | Y | Y | Y | ? |
| **NEW MEXICO** | | | | | | | | |
| 1 ***Schiff*** | Y | Y | Y | N | N | Y | N | N |
| 2 ***Skeen*** | Y | Y | Y | N | N | Y | N | N |
| 3 Richardson | P | Y | Y | Y | Y | Y | Y | ? |
| **NEW YORK** | | | | | | | | |
| 1 Hochbrueckner | N | Y | Y | Y | Y | N | Y | Y |
| 2 Downey | — | + | + | + | + | — | + | Y |
| 3 Mrazek | N | Y | ? | Y | Y | N | Y | Y |
| 4 ***Lent*** | Y | Y | Y | N | N | ? | N | N |
| 5 ***McGrath*** | Y | Y | Y | N | N | ? | N | N |
| 6 Flake | N | Y | Y | Y | Y | N | Y | Y |
| 7 Ackerman | ? | ? | ? | # | ? | ? | ? | Y |
| 8 Scheuer | N | Y | Y | Y | Y | N | Y | ? |
| 9 Manton | N | Y | Y | Y | Y | ? | ? | ? |
| 10 Schumer | N | Y | Y | Y | Y | ? | ? | Y |
| 11 Towns | N | Y | Y | Y | Y | N | Y | Y |
| 12 Owens | N | Y | Y | Y | Y | N | Y | Y |
| 13 Solarz | Y | Y | Y | Y | ? | N | Y | Y |
| 14 ***Molinari*** | Y | Y | Y | N | N | Y | N | Y |
| 15 ***Green*** | N | Y | Y | Y | N | N | Y | Y |
| 16 Rangel | N | Y | Y | Y | Y | N | ? | Y |
| 17 Vacancy | | | | | | | | |
| 18 Serrano | N | Y | Y | Y | Y | N | ? | Y |
| 19 Engel | Y | Y | Y | Y | Y | N | Y | Y |
| 20 Lowey | N | Y | Y | Y | Y | N | Y | Y |
| 21 ***Fish*** | Y | Y | Y | Y | N | N | Y | N |
| 22 ***Gilman*** | Y | Y | Y | Y | N | Y | Y | Y |
| 23 McNulty | Y | Y | Y | Y | Y | N | Y | Y |
| 24 ***Solomon*** | Y | Y | Y | Y | N | ? | ? | N |
| 25 ***Boehlert*** | Y | Y | Y | Y | N | Y | Y | Y |
| 26 ***Martin*** | Y | Y | Y | Y | N | Y | N | N |
| 27 ***Walsh*** | Y | Y | Y | Y | Y | N | Y | N |
| 28 McHugh | N | Y | Y | Y | Y | N | Y | Y |
| 29 ***Horton*** | Y | Y | Y | N | Y | ? | ? | ? |
| 30 Slaughter | Y | Y | + | Y | Y | N | Y | Y |
| 31 ***Paxon*** | Y | Y | Y | N | N | Y | N | N |

| | 423 | 424 | 425 | 426 | 427 | 428 | 429 | 430 |
|---|---|---|---|---|---|---|---|---|
| 32 LaFalce | Y | Y | Y | Y | Y | N | Y | Y |
| 33 Nowak | N | Y | Y | Y | Y | N | Y | Y |
| 34 ***Houghton*** | N | Y | Y | N | N | Y | N | N |
| **NORTH CAROLINA** | | | | | | | | |
| 1 Vacancy | | | | | | | | |
| 2 Valentine | N | Y | Y | ? | ? | ? | ? | Y |
| 3 Lancaster | Y | Y | Y | Y | Y | Y | N | Y |
| 4 Price | Y | Y | Y | Y | Y | Y | Y | Y |
| 5 Neal | Y | Y | Y | Y | Y | Y | Y | ? |
| 6 ***Coble*** | Y | Y | Y | N | N | Y | N | N |
| 7 Rose | Y | Y | Y | N | Y | Y | Y | Y |
| 8 Hefner | Y | Y | Y | Y | Y | Y | Y | Y |
| 9 ***McMillan*** | Y | Y | Y | N | N | Y | N | N |
| 10 ***Ballenger*** | Y | Y | Y | N | Y | Y | N | N |
| 11 ***Taylor*** | Y | Y | Y | N | N | Y | N | N |
| **NORTH DAKOTA** | | | | | | | | |
| AL Dorgan | Y | Y | Y | Y | Y | N | Y | Y |
| **OHIO** | | | | | | | | |
| 1 Luken | N | Y | Y | N | Y | N | Y | Y |
| 2 ***Gradison*** | N | Y | Y | Y | N | N | N | N |
| 3 Hall | Y | Y | Y | Y | ? | Y | Y | Y |
| 4 ***Oxley*** | Y | Y | Y | N | N | Y | N | N |
| 5 ***Gillmor*** | Y | Y | Y | N | N | Y | N | N |
| 6 ***McEwen*** | Y | Y | Y | N | N | Y | N | N |
| 7 ***Hobson*** | Y | Y | Y | N | N | Y | Y | N |
| 8 ***Boehner*** | N | Y | Y | N | N | Y | N | N |
| 9 Kaptur | Y | Y | ? | Y | Y | Y | Y | Y |
| 10 ***Miller*** | Y | Y | Y | N | N | Y | N | N |
| 11 Eckart | Y | Y | Y | N | Y | N | Y | Y |
| 12 ***Kasich*** | Y | Y | Y | ? | ? | ? | ? | N |
| 13 Pease | N | Y | Y | Y | Y | N | Y | Y |
| 14 Sawyer | N | Y | Y | Y | Y | N | Y | Y |
| 15 ***Wylie*** | Y | Y | Y | N | N | Y | N | N |
| 16 ***Regula*** | Y | Y | Y | N | N | Y | Y | N |
| 17 Traficant | Y | Y | Y | Y | Y | Y | Y | Y |
| 18 Applegate | Y | Y | Y | Y | Y | Y | Y | Y |
| 19 Feighan | Y | ? | Y | N | Y | N | Y | Y |
| 20 Oakar | Y | Y | Y | N | Y | Y | Y | ? |
| 21 Stokes | N | Y | Y | Y | Y | ? | Y | Y |
| **OKLAHOMA** | | | | | | | | |
| 1 ***Inhofe*** | Y | Y | Y | N | N | Y | N | N |
| 2 Synar | N | Y | Y | Y | Y | N | Y | Y |
| 3 Brewster | Y | ? | Y | N | Y | Y | N | Y |
| 4 McCurdy | Y | Y | Y | N | Y | Y | ? | Y |
| 5 ***Edwards*** | Y | Y | ? | N | N | Y | ? | ? |
| 6 English | N | Y | Y | N | Y | Y | Y | Y |
| **OREGON** | | | | | | | | |
| 1 AuCoin | Y | Y | Y | Y | Y | N | Y | Y |
| 2 ***Smith*** | Y | Y | Y | N | N | Y | N | N |
| 3 Wyden | N | Y | Y | Y | Y | N | Y | Y |
| 4 DeFazio | N | Y | Y | Y | Y | N | Y | Y |
| 5 Kopetski | N | Y | Y | N | Y | N | Y | Y |
| **PENNSYLVANIA** | | | | | | | | |
| 1 Foglietta | ? | ? | ? | ? | ? | ? | ? | ? |
| 2 Blackwell | N | Y | Y | Y | Y | N | Y | Y |
| 3 Borski | Y | Y | Y | Y | Y | Y | Y | ? |
| 4 Kolter | Y | Y | Y | Y | Y | Y | Y | Y |
| 5 ***Schulze*** | Y | Y | Y | N | N | ? | ? | ? |
| 6 Yatron | Y | Y | Y | Y | Y | Y | Y | ? |
| 7 ***Weldon*** | Y | Y | Y | N | N | Y | N | ? |
| 8 Kostmayer | Y | Y | Y | Y | Y | N | Y | Y |
| 9 ***Shuster*** | Y | Y | Y | N | N | Y | N | N |
| 10 ***McDade*** | Y | Y | Y | N | N | Y | N | N |
| 11 Kanjorski | N | Y | Y | N | N | Y | Y | Y |
| 12 Murtha | Y | ? | Y | N | Y | Y | N | Y |
| 13 ***Coughlin*** | Y | Y | ? | N | N | Y | N | N |
| 14 Coyne | N | Y | Y | Y | Y | N | Y | Y |
| 15 ***Ritter*** | Y | Y | Y | N | N | Y | N | Y |
| 16 ***Walker*** | Y | Y | Y | N | N | Y | N | N |
| 17 ***Gekas*** | Y | Y | Y | N | N | Y | N | N |
| 18 ***Santorum*** | N | Y | Y | N | N | Y | N | N |
| 19 ***Goodling*** | Y | Y | Y | N | N | Y | Y | N |
| 20 Gaydos | Y | Y | Y | Y | Y | Y | Y | ? |
| 21 ***Ridge*** | Y | Y | Y | Y | N | Y | Y | ? |
| 22 Murphy | Y | Y | Y | N | Y | Y | Y | Y |
| 23 ***Clinger*** | Y | Y | Y | N | N | Y | N | N |
| **RHODE ISLAND** | | | | | | | | |
| 1 ***Machtley*** | Y | Y | Y | Y | N | ? | ? | Y |
| 2 Reed | N | Y | Y | Y | Y | Y | Y | Y |
| **SOUTH CAROLINA** | | | | | | | | |
| 1 ***Ravenel*** | Y | Y | Y | Y | N | Y | N | Y |
| 2 ***Spence*** | Y | Y | Y | N | N | Y | N | N |
| 3 Derrick | Y | Y | Y | N | Y | Y | Y | Y |
| 4 Patterson | N | Y | Y | N | N | Y | N | Y |
| 5 Spratt | Y | Y | Y | Y | Y | Y | Y | Y |
| 6 Tallon | Y | Y | Y | N | N | Y | ? | Y |

| | 423 | 424 | 425 | 426 | 427 | 428 | 429 | 430 |
|---|---|---|---|---|---|---|---|---|
| **SOUTH DAKOTA** | | | | | | | | |
| AL Johnson | N | Y | Y | N | Y | Y | Y | ? |
| **TENNESSEE** | | | | | | | | |
| 1 ***Quillen*** | Y | Y | Y | N | N | Y | N | N |
| 2 ***Duncan*** | Y | N | Y | Y | N | Y | N | N |
| 3 Lloyd | Y | Y | Y | N | Y | Y | N | Y |
| 4 Cooper | Y | Y | Y | N | Y | N | ? | Y |
| 5 Clement | Y | Y | Y | N | N | Y | Y | Y |
| 6 Gordon | Y | Y | Y | N | N | Y | Y | Y |
| 7 ***Sundquist*** | Y | Y | Y | N | N | Y | N | N |
| 8 Tanner | Y | Y | Y | N | N | Y | Y | Y |
| 9 Ford | N | Y | Y | Y | N | N | Y | Y |
| **TEXAS** | | | | | | | | |
| 1 Chapman | Y | Y | Y | Y | Y | Y | Y | ? |
| 2 Wilson | Y | Y | Y | N | Y | Y | N | Y |
| 3 ***Johnson*** | Y | N | N | N | N | Y | N | N |
| 4 Hall | Y | N | Y | Y | N | Y | N | N |
| 5 Bryant | Y | Y | Y | Y | Y | Y | ? | Y |
| 6 ***Barton*** | Y | Y | Y | N | N | Y | N | N |
| 7 ***Archer*** | Y | Y | Y | N | N | Y | N | N |
| 8 ***Fields*** | Y | Y | Y | N | N | Y | N | N |
| 9 Brooks | Y | Y | Y | Y | Y | Y | Y | Y |
| 10 Pickle | Y | Y | Y | Y | Y | Y | Y | Y |
| 11 Edwards | Y | Y | Y | Y | Y | Y | Y | Y |
| 12 Geren | Y | Y | Y | N | N | Y | N | Y |
| 13 Sarpalius | N | Y | Y | Y | Y | Y | N | Y |
| 14 Laughlin | N | Y | Y | N | Y | Y | N | Y |
| 15 de la Garza | Y | Y | Y | Y | Y | Y | Y | Y |
| 16 Coleman | Y | Y | Y | Y | Y | Y | Y | Y |
| 17 Stenholm | N | N | Y | N | N | Y | N | Y |
| 18 Washington | ? | ? | ? | Y | Y | ? | ? | Y |
| 19 ***Combest*** | Y | N | Y | N | N | Y | N | N |
| 20 Gonzalez | N | Y | Y | Y | Y | N | Y | Y |
| 21 ***Smith*** | Y | Y | Y | N | N | Y | N | ? |
| 22 ***DeLay*** | Y | N | Y | N | N | Y | N | N |
| 23 Bustamante | ? | ? | ? | ? | ? | ? | ? | ? |
| 24 Frost | Y | Y | Y | N | Y | Y | Y | Y |
| 25 Andrews | Y | Y | Y | N | Y | Y | N | Y |
| 26 ***Armey*** | Y | N | Y | N | N | Y | N | N |
| 27 Ortiz | Y | Y | Y | Y | Y | Y | ? | Y |
| **UTAH** | | | | | | | | |
| 1 ***Hansen*** | Y | Y | Y | N | N | Y | N | ? |
| 2 Owens | Y | Y | Y | N | Y | N | Y | Y |
| 3 Orton | Y | Y | Y | N | N | Y | X | ? |
| **VERMONT** | | | | | | | | |
| AL *Sanders* | N | Y | Y | Y | Y | N | Y | Y |
| **VIRGINIA** | | | | | | | | |
| 1 ***Bateman*** | Y | Y | Y | N | N | Y | N | N |
| 2 Pickett | N | Y | Y | N | Y | Y | N | Y |
| 3 ***Bliley*** | Y | Y | Y | ? | ? | ? | ? | ? |
| 4 Sisisky | Y | Y | Y | N | Y | Y | N | N |
| 5 Payne | Y | Y | Y | N | Y | Y | Y | Y |
| 6 Olin | ? | ? | ? | ? | ? | N | ? | Y |
| 7 ***Allen*** | Y | Y | Y | N | N | Y | N | N |
| 8 Moran | Y | Y | Y | N | Y | Y | Y | Y |
| 9 Boucher | N | Y | Y | N | Y | N | Y | Y |
| 10 ***Wolf*** | Y | Y | Y | N | N | Y | N | N |
| **WASHINGTON** | | | | | | | | |
| 1 ***Miller*** | Y | Y | Y | N | N | Y | N | N |
| 2 Swift | Y | Y | Y | N | Y | N | Y | Y |
| 3 Unsoeld | N | Y | Y | N | N | N | Y | Y |
| 4 ***Morrison*** | N | Y | Y | N | N | Y | Y | N |
| 5 Foley | | | | | | | | |
| 6 Dicks | Y | Y | Y | Y | Y | Y | ? | Y |
| 7 McDermott | N | Y | Y | Y | Y | N | Y | Y |
| 8 ***Chandler*** | ? | ? | ? | ? | ? | ? | ? | ? |
| **WEST VIRGINIA** | | | | | | | | |
| 1 Mollohan | Y | Y | Y | N | Y | N | N | Y |
| 2 Staggers | Y | Y | Y | Y | Y | N | Y | Y |
| 3 Wise | Y | Y | Y | Y | Y | N | Y | Y |
| 4 Rahall | N | Y | Y | N | Y | Y | Y | Y |
| **WISCONSIN** | | | | | | | | |
| 1 Aspin | Y | Y | Y | Y | Y | Y | Y | Y |
| 2 ***Klug*** | Y | Y | Y | N | N | Y | Y | Y |
| 3 ***Gunderson*** | Y | Y | Y | N | N | Y | Y | N |
| 4 Kleczka | Y | Y | Y | Y | Y | N | Y | Y |
| 5 Moody | N | Y | Y | Y | Y | N | Y | Y |
| 6 ***Petri*** | Y | Y | Y | Y | N | Y | Y | N |
| 7 Obey | N | Y | Y | Y | Y | N | Y | Y |
| 8 ***Roth*** | Y | Y | Y | N | N | Y | Y | N |
| 9 ***Sensenbrenner*** | Y | Y | Y | N | N | Y | N | N |
| **WYOMING** | | | | | | | | |
| AL ***Thomas*** | Y | Y | Y | N | N | Y | N | N |

Southern states - Ala., Ark., Fla., Ga., Ky., La., Miss., N.C., Okla., S.C., Tenn., Texas, Va.
Omitted votes are quorum calls, which CQ does not include in its vote charts.

**431. HR 5679. Fiscal 1993 VA, Housing and Urban Development, Independent Agencies Appropriations/Rule.** Adoption of the rule (H Res 579) to provide for House floor consideration of the conference report to provide $86.9 billion for the departments of Veterans Affairs, Housing and Urban Development and independent agencies in fiscal 1993. Adopted 202-186: R 51-100; D 151-85 (ND 108-52, SD 43-33); I 0-1, Sept. 25, 1992.

**432. HR 5679. Fiscal 1993 VA, Housing and Urban Development, Independent Agencies Appropriations/Conference Report.** Adoption of the conference report to provide $86.9 billion in new budget authority for VA, HUD and independent agencies in fiscal 1993. The measure included $2.1 billion for the space station Freedom, $34.7 billion in VA funding and $23.8 billion for HUD. Adopted 286-97: R 97-54; D 188-43 (ND 123-35, SD 65-8); I 1-0, Sept. 25, 1992.

**433. HR 5679. Fiscal 1993 VA, Housing and Urban Development, Independent Agencies Appropriations/ Maryland, Utah Projects.** Traxler, D-Mich., motion to recede and concur in a Senate amendment to provide $12.5 million for the Christopher Columbus Center of Marine Research and Exploration in Baltimore, Md., and in an amendment to provide $5 million for a grant to the University of Utah for the design and construction of an intermountain regional network and scientific computation center. Adopted 208-168: R 31-119; D 177-48 (ND 133-20, SD 44-28); I 0-1, Sept. 25, 1992.

**434. HR 5679. Fiscal 1993 VA, Housing and Urban Development, Independent Agencies Appropriations/ Earth Observing System.** Rohrabacher, R-Calif., amendment to concur in a Senate amendment with an amendment to earmark funds for the development of the Earth Observing System, but to reduce the amount by $20 million, to $371 million. Rejected 87-279: R 71-74; D 16-204 (ND 4-146, SD 12-58); I 0-1, Sept. 25, 1992. (The House subsequently agreed by voice vote to concur in the Senate amendment to earmark $391 million for the Earth Observing System.)

**435. HR 5679. Fiscal 1993 VA, Housing and Urban Development, Independent Agencies Appropriations/Mission to Planet Earth.** Traxler, D-Mich., motion to recede and concur in a Senate amendment to establish an $8 billion dollar floor for the Mission to Planet Earth budget through fiscal 2000. Rejected 144-200: R 30-104; D 114-95 (ND 90-54, SD 24-41); I 0-1, Sept. 25, 1992.

**436. H J Res 512. Romania Most-Favored-Nation Status.** Rostenkowski, D-Ill., motion to suspend the rules and pass the joint resolution approving the extension of non-discriminatory (most-favored-nation) trade status to Romania. Motion rejected 88-283: R 54-94; D 34-189 (ND 18-137, SD 16-52); I 0-0, Sept. 30, 1992. A two-thirds majority of those present and voting (248 in this case) was required for passage under suspension of the rules.

**437. HR 6056. Fiscal 1993 District of Columbia Appropriations/Passage.** Passage of the bill to provide $624.9 million in new budget authority for a federal payment to the District of Columbia. This version of the bill included a prohibition on local funds being used for abortion that was not in HR 5517, vetoed by President Bush on Sept. 30. Passed 230-160: R 40-110; D 189-50 (ND 142-24, SD 47-26); I 1-0, Sept. 30, 1992.

**438. H J Res 553. Fiscal 1993 Continuing Resolution/Order Previous Question.** Moakley, D-Mass., motion to order the previous question (thus limiting debate and the possibility of amendment) on adoption of the rule (H Res 580) to provide for House floor consideration of the joint resolution to make continuing appropriations for fiscal 1993 through Oct. 5, or until the regular appropriations bills were signed into law. Motion agreed to 231-186: R 1-162; D 229-24 (ND 162-16, SD 67-8); I 1-0, Sept. 30, 1992.

## KEY

Y Voted for (yea).
\# Paired for.
+ Announced for.
N Voted against (nay).
X Paired against.
− Announced against.
P Voted "present."
C Voted "present" to avoid possible conflict of interest.
? Did not vote or otherwise make a position known.

Democrats  *Republicans*
*Independent*

| | 431 | 432 | 433 | 434 | 435 | 436 | 437 | 438 |
|---|---|---|---|---|---|---|---|---|
| **ALABAMA** | | | | | | | | |
| 1 *Callahan* | N | N | N | N | N | N | N | N |
| 2 *Dickinson* | ? | Y | N | N | ? | N | N | N |
| 3 Browder | N | Y | N | N | N | N | N | Y |
| 4 Bevill | Y | Y | Y | N | Y | N | N | Y |
| 5 Cramer | Y | Y | Y | N | N | N | N | Y |
| 6 Erdreich | N | Y | N | N | N | N | N | N |
| 7 Harris | N | Y | Y | N | N | N | N | Y |
| **ALASKA** | | | | | | | | |
| AL *Young* | N | Y | Y | N | N | ? | N | N |
| **ARIZONA** | | | | | | | | |
| 1 *Rhodes* | N | N | N | N | N | N | N | N |
| 2 Pastor | Y | Y | Y | N | Y | N | N | Y |
| 3 *Stump* | N | N | N | Y | N | N | N | N |
| 4 *Kyl* | N | N | N | Y | N | N | N | N |
| 5 *Kolbe* | N | Y | N | N | N | Y | N | N |
| **ARKANSAS** | | | | | | | | |
| 1 Alexander | Y | Y | ? | ? | ? | Y | Y | ? |
| 2 Thornton | Y | Y | Y | N | Y | Y | Y | Y |
| 3 *Hammerschmidt* | N | Y | N | Y | N | Y | N | N |
| 4 Anthony | ? | ? | ? | ? | ? | Y | Y | Y |
| **CALIFORNIA** | | | | | | | | |
| 1 *Riggs* | Y | Y | Y | N | Y | + | + | N |
| 2 *Herger* | N | N | N | Y | N | N | N | N |
| 3 Matsui | Y | Y | Y | N | Y | Y | Y | Y |
| 4 Fazio | # | # | # | ? | # | N | Y | Y |
| 5 Pelosi | Y | Y | Y | N | Y | N | Y | Y |
| 6 Boxer | ? | ? | ? | ? | ? | N | Y | Y |
| 7 Miller | Y | N | Y | N | N | N | Y | ? |
| 8 Dellums | N | Y | Y | N | N | N | Y | Y |
| 9 Stark | ? | ? | ? | ? | ? | N | Y | Y |
| 10 Edwards | Y | Y | Y | N | N | N | Y | Y |
| 11 Lantos | Y | Y | Y | N | N | N | Y | Y |
| 12 *Campbell* | N | N | N | Y | N | Y | N | N |
| 13 Mineta | Y | Y | Y | N | N | N | Y | Y |
| 14 *Doolittle* | N | N | N | Y | N | N | N | N |
| 15 Condit | N | N | N | N | ? | N | Y | N |
| 16 Panetta | Y | N | Y | N | N | Y | Y | Y |
| 17 Dooley | ? | ? | ? | ? | ? | N | Y | Y |
| 18 Lehman | ? | ? | ? | ? | ? | N | Y | Y |
| 19 *Lagomarsino* | N | Y | N | Y | N | Y | N | N |
| 20 *Thomas* | N | N | N | N | N | N | N | N |
| 21 *Gallegly* | N | Y | N | Y | N | N | N | N |
| 22 *Moorhead* | N | N | N | Y | N | N | N | N |
| 23 Beilenson | Y | N | Y | N | Y | Y | Y | Y |
| 24 Waxman | Y | Y | Y | N | ? | Y | Y | Y |
| 25 Roybal | Y | Y | Y | N | Y | Y | Y | Y |
| 26 Berman | Y | Y | Y | N | N | Y | Y | Y |
| 27 Levine | Y | Y | Y | N | Y | ? | ? | Y |
| 28 Dixon | ? | Y | Y | N | Y | N | Y | Y |
| 29 Waters | Y | Y | Y | ? | Y | N | Y | Y |
| 30 Martinez | ? | ? | ? | ? | ? | N | Y | Y |
| 31 Dymally | ? | ? | ? | ? | ? | ? | ? | ? |
| 32 Anderson | Y | Y | Y | N | N | N | Y | Y |
| 33 *Dreier* | N | N | N | Y | N | N | N | N |
| 34 Torres | Y | Y | Y | N | N | Y | Y | Y |
| 35 *Lewis* | Y | Y | Y | N | Y | N | N | Y |
| 36 Brown | Y | Y | Y | N | Y | N | Y | Y |
| 37 *McCandless* | N | N | N | Y | N | N | N | N |
| 38 *Dornan* | N | N | N | Y | N | N | N | N |
| 39 *Dannemeyer* | N | N | N | Y | N | N | N | N |
| 40 *Cox* | N | N | N | Y | N | N | N | N |
| 41 *Lowery* | Y | Y | Y | N | Y | N | Y | N |
| 42 *Rohrabacher* | Y | N | N | Y | N | N | N | N |
| 43 *Packard* | Y | N | N | Y | N | N | N | N |
| 44 *Cunningham* | N | Y | N | Y | N | N | N | N |
| 45 *Hunter* | N | N | N | ? | N | N | N | N |
| **COLORADO** | | | | | | | | |
| 1 Schroeder | N | N | N | N | N | N | N | Y |
| 2 Skaggs | Y | Y | Y | N | Y | N | Y | Y |
| 3 Campbell | ? | ? | ? | ? | ? | ? | N | Y |
| 4 *Allard* | N | N | N | Y | N | N | N | N |
| 5 *Hefley* | N | N | N | Y | N | N | N | N |
| 6 *Schaefer* | N | N | N | N | N | N | N | N |
| **CONNECTICUT** | | | | | | | | |
| 1 Kennelly | Y | Y | Y | N | Y | Y | Y | Y |
| 2 Gejdenson | Y | Y | Y | N | ? | N | Y | Y |
| 3 DeLauro | N | Y | Y | N | Y | N | Y | Y |
| 4 *Shays* | N | Y | N | N | N | Y | N | N |
| 5 *Franks* | N | Y | N | N | N | Y | N | N |
| 6 *Johnson* | Y | Y | Y | Y | ? | Y | N | N |
| **DELAWARE** | | | | | | | | |
| AL *Carper* | Y | Y | Y | N | Y | N | Y | Y |
| **FLORIDA** | | | | | | | | |
| 1 Hutto | N | Y | N | Y | N | ? | N | Y |
| 2 Peterson | N | Y | Y | N | N | Y | Y | Y |
| 3 Bennett | N | N | N | N | N | N | N | Y |
| 4 *James* | N | Y | N | Y | N | N | N | N |
| 5 *McCollum* | N | N | N | N | N | N | N | N |
| 6 *Stearns* | N | N | N | N | N | N | N | N |
| 7 Gibbons | Y | Y | Y | N | Y | N | Y | Y |
| 8 *Young* | N | Y | N | Y | N | N | N | N |
| 9 *Bilirakis* | N | Y | N | Y | ? | Y | N | Y |
| 10 *Ireland* | ? | ? | N | ? | ? | ? | ? | ? |
| 11 Bacchus | Y | Y | Y | Y | N | N | Y | N |
| 12 *Lewis* | X | X | X | ? | ? | Y | N | N |
| 13 *Goss* | N | N | N | N | N | N | N | N |
| 14 Johnston | Y | N | N | ? | ? | Y | Y | Y |
| 15 *Shaw* | N | Y | N | N | N | Y | N | N |
| 16 Smith | Y | Y | Y | N | ? | ? | ? | ? |
| 17 Lehman | ? | ? | ? | ? | ? | Y | Y | Y |
| 18 *Ros–Lehtinen* | N | Y | N | N | Y | ? | N | N |
| 19 Fascell | ? | ? | ? | ? | ? | Y | Y | Y |
| **GEORGIA** | | | | | | | | |
| 1 Thomas | Y | Y | Y | N | Y | Y | Y | Y |
| 2 Hatcher | Y | ? | ? | ? | ? | N | Y | Y |
| 3 Ray | N | N | N | Y | N | ? | ? | ? |
| 4 Jones | N | N | Y | N | Y | ? | ? | ? |
| 5 Lewis | Y | Y | Y | N | Y | Y | Y | Y |
| 6 *Gingrich* | Y | Y | Y | N | N | N | N | N |
| 7 Darden | N | Y | Y | N | Y | Y | N | N |
| 8 Rowland | N | N | Y | N | X | N | Y | Y |
| 9 Jenkins | N | Y | N | N | Y | Y | N | Y |
| 10 Barnard | ? | ? | ? | ? | ? | ? | X | ? |
| **HAWAII** | | | | | | | | |
| 1 Abercrombie | Y | Y | Y | N | Y | N | Y | Y |
| 2 Mink | Y | Y | Y | N | N | N | Y | Y |
| **IDAHO** | | | | | | | | |
| 1 LaRocco | N | N | N | N | N | N | N | Y |
| 2 Stallings | N | Y | N | N | N | N | N | N |
| **ILLINOIS** | | | | | | | | |
| 1 Hayes | Y | Y | Y | N | Y | N | Y | Y |
| 2 Savage | ? | ? | ? | ? | ? | Y | N | Y |
| 3 Russo | ? | ? | ? | ? | ? | N | Y | Y |
| 4 Sangmeister | N | N | Y | N | N | N | Y | Y |
| 5 Lipinski | N | N | Y | ? | ? | ? | ? | Y |
| 6 *Hyde* | N | Y | N | Y | ? | ? | Y | N |
| 7 Collins | Y | Y | Y | N | Y | N | Y | Y |
| 8 Rostenkowski | Y | Y | Y | Y | Y | Y | Y | Y |
| 9 Yates | Y | Y | Y | N | Y | N | Y | Y |
| 10 *Porter* | N | Y | N | Y | N | ? | Y | N |
| 11 Annunzio | Y | Y | Y | N | Y | Y | Y | Y |
| 12 *Crane* | ? | ? | ? | ? | ? | N | N | N |
| 13 *Fawell* | ? | N | ? | Y | N | N | N | N |
| 14 *Hastert* | N | Y | N | N | N | N | N | N |
| 15 *Ewing* | N | ? | ? | ? | ? | N | N | N |
| 16 *Cox* | N | Y | N | N | Y | N | N | N |
| 17 Evans | Y | Y | Y | N | Y | N | Y | Y |
| 18 *Michel* | N | Y | N | Y | ? | Y | Y | N |
| 19 Bruce | Y | Y | Y | N | N | N | Y | Y |
| 20 Durbin | Y | Y | Y | N | Y | N | Y | Y |
| 21 Costello | N | Y | Y | N | N | N | Y | Y |
| 22 Poshard | Y | Y | N | N | N | N | N | Y |
| **INDIANA** | | | | | | | | |
| 1 Visclosky | Y | Y | Y | N | Y | N | Y | Y |
| 2 Sharp | Y | Y | Y | N | ? | N | Y | Y |
| 3 Roemer | N | Y | N | N | N | N | N | Y |

| | 431 | 432 | 433 | 434 | 435 | 436 | 437 | 438 |
|---|---|---|---|---|---|---|---|---|
| 4 Long | N | Y | Y | N | N | N | Y | Y |
| 5 Jontz | N | N | Y | N | N | N | Y | Y |
| 6 ***Burton*** | N | N | N | Y | ? | N | N | N |
| 7 ***Myers*** | Y | Y | N | N | Y | Y | N | Y |
| 8 McCloskey | Y | Y | Y | N | Y | N | Y | Y |
| 9 Hamilton | Y | Y | N | N | N | Y | Y | Y |
| 10 Jacobs | Y | N | N | N | N | Y | Y | N |
| **IOWA** | | | | | | | | |
| 1 ***Leach*** | N | N | N | N | N | Y | N | N |
| 2 ***Nussle*** | N | N | N | N | N | Y | N | N |
| 3 Nagle | N | N | Y | N | N | ? | ? | Y |
| 4 Smith | Y | Y | Y | N | Y | Y | Y | Y |
| 5 ***Lightfoot*** | Y | Y | Y | N | Y | Y | N | N |
| 6 ***Grandy*** | N | N | Y | N | N | Y | Y | N |
| **KANSAS** | | | | | | | | |
| 1 ***Roberts*** | N | N | N | N | N | ? | ? | N |
| 2 Slattery | N | N | N | N | N | N | Y | Y |
| 3 ***Meyers*** | N | Y | N | Y | N | N | N | N |
| 4 Glickman | N | Y | N | Y | N | N | Y | Y |
| 5 ***Nichols*** | N | N | N | N | N | Y | N | N |
| **KENTUCKY** | | | | | | | | |
| 1 Hubbard | N | N | N | Y | N | N | Y | Y |
| 2 Natcher | Y | Y | Y | N | Y | N | Y | Y |
| 3 Mazzoli | Y | Y | Y | N | Y | N | Y | Y |
| 4 ***Bunning*** | N | Y | N | Y | N | N | N | N |
| 5 ***Rogers*** | N | Y | N | N | N | N | N | N |
| 6 ***Hopkins*** | N | N | N | N | ? | N | N | N |
| 7 Perkins | ? | ? | ? | N | Y | ? | ? | ? |
| **LOUISIANA** | | | | | | | | |
| 1 ***Livingston*** | ? | ? | ? | ? | ? | Y | N | ? |
| 2 Jefferson | Y | Y | Y | ? | N | ? | ? | ? |
| 3 Tauzin | Y | Y | N | N | N | N | N | N |
| 4 ***McCrery*** | ? | ? | ? | ? | ? | ? | ? | ? |
| 5 Huckaby | ? | ? | ? | ? | ? | ? | ? | ? |
| 6 ***Baker*** | Y | Y | Y | Y | N | ? | N | N |
| 7 Hayes | # | ? | ? | ? | ? | N | N | N |
| 8 ***Holloway*** | ? | ? | ? | ? | ? | ? | ? | N |
| **MAINE** | | | | | | | | |
| 1 Andrews | N | N | Y | N | ? | N | Y | Y |
| 2 ***Snowe*** | N | Y | Y | N | Y | N | N | N |
| **MARYLAND** | | | | | | | | |
| 1 ***Gilchrest*** | Y | Y | Y | N | N | Y | Y | N |
| 2 ***Bentley*** | N | Y | Y | Y | N | N | Y | N |
| 3 Cardin | Y | Y | Y | N | Y | N | Y | Y |
| 4 McMillen | Y | Y | Y | N | Y | N | Y | Y |
| 5 Hoyer | Y | Y | Y | N | Y | ? | # | Y |
| 6 Byron | N | Y | Y | N | Y | N | N | Y |
| 7 Mfume | Y | Y | Y | N | Y | N | Y | Y |
| 8 ***Morella*** | Y | Y | Y | N | N | N | Y | N |
| **MASSACHUSETTS** | | | | | | | | |
| 1 Olver | N | Y | Y | N | N | ? | N | Y |
| 2 Neal | N | Y | Y | N | ? | N | Y | Y |
| 3 Early | N | N | ? | N | Y | N | Y | Y |
| 4 Frank | Y | Y | Y | N | Y | N | N | Y |
| 5 Atkins | Y | Y | Y | N | Y | N | Y | Y |
| 6 Mavroules | Y | Y | Y | N | Y | N | Y | Y |
| 7 Markey | Y | Y | Y | N | N | N | N | Y |
| 8 Kennedy | Y | ? | ? | ? | ? | ? | Y | N |
| 9 Moakley | Y | Y | Y | N | Y | N | Y | Y |
| 10 Studds | Y | Y | Y | N | Y | N | N | Y |
| 11 Donnelly | ? | ? | ? | ? | ? | ? | ? | Y |
| **MICHIGAN** | | | | | | | | |
| 1 Conyers | N | Y | Y | N | Y | Y | Y | Y |
| 2 ***Pursell*** | Y | Y | Y | N | Y | N | N | N |
| 3 Wolpe | Y | # | ? | ? | ? | N | Y | Y |
| 4 ***Upton*** | Y | Y | N | N | Y | N | N | N |
| 5 ***Henry*** | Y | N | N | N | N | N | N | N |
| 6 Carr | Y | Y | Y | N | Y | N | Y | Y |
| 7 Kildee | N | Y | Y | N | Y | N | Y | Y |
| 8 Traxler | Y | Y | Y | N | Y | ? | Y | Y |
| 9 ***Vander Jagt*** | Y | Y | N | N | N | Y | Y | N |
| 10 ***Camp*** | Y | Y | N | N | Y | — | — | N |
| 11 ***Davis*** | Y | Y | Y | N | Y | N | Y | N |
| 12 Bonior | Y | Y | Y | N | Y | N | Y | Y |
| 13 Collins | Y | Y | Y | N | Y | N | Y | Y |
| 14 Hertel | Y | Y | Y | N | Y | ? | Y | Y |
| 15 Ford | Y | Y | Y | N | Y | N | Y | Y |
| 16 Dingell | Y | Y | Y | N | Y | N | Y | Y |
| 17 Levin | Y | Y | Y | N | N | N | Y | Y |
| 18 ***Broomfield*** | Y | Y | N | N | Y | Y | Y | N |
| **MINNESOTA** | | | | | | | | |
| 1 Penny | N | N | N | N | N | Y | N | N |
| 2 ***Weber*** | N | Y | N | Y | Y | ? | ? | N |
| 3 ***Ramstad*** | N | N | N | N | N | N | N | N |
| 4 Vento | Y | N | N | N | N | N | Y | Y |

| | 431 | 432 | 433 | 434 | 435 | 436 | 437 | 438 |
|---|---|---|---|---|---|---|---|---|
| 5 Sabo | Y | Y | Y | N | Y | N | Y | Y |
| 6 Sikorski | N | N | Y | N | N | ? | Y | Y |
| 7 Peterson | N | N | Y | N | ? | Y | N | Y |
| 8 Oberstar | Y | Y | Y | N | Y | N | Y | Y |
| **MISSISSIPPI** | | | | | | | | |
| 1 Whitten | Y | Y | Y | N | Y | Y | Y | Y |
| 2 Espy | Y | Y | Y | N | Y | ? | ? | Y |
| 3 Montgomery | N | Y | N | N | N | N | Y | Y |
| 4 Parker | N | Y | N | N | N | N | Y | Y |
| 5 Taylor | N | Y | N | Y | N | N | N | Y |
| **MISSOURI** | | | | | | | | |
| 1 Clay | ? | ? | ? | ? | ? | N | Y | Y |
| 2 Horn | N | N | Y | N | N | N | Y | Y |
| 3 Gephardt | Y | Y | ? | N | Y | N | Y | Y |
| 4 Skelton | Y | Y | N | N | Y | N | N | Y |
| 5 Wheat | Y | N | Y | N | Y | ? | Y | Y |
| 6 ***Coleman*** | Y | Y | N | ? | ? | N | N | N |
| 7 ***Hancock*** | N | N | N | Y | N | ? | N | N |
| 8 ***Emerson*** | N | Y | N | N | N | N | N | N |
| 9 Volkmer | Y | Y | N | N | Y | N | N | Y |
| **MONTANA** | | | | | | | | |
| 1 Williams | N | Y | N | N | Y | N | N | N |
| 2 ***Marlenee*** | N | Y | N | Y | ? | Y | N | N |
| **NEBRASKA** | | | | | | | | |
| 1 ***Bereuter*** | N | Y | N | Y | N | N | N | N |
| 2 Hoagland | N | N | Y | N | N | N | Y | Y |
| 3 ***Barrett*** | N | N | N | ? | ? | Y | N | N |
| **NEVADA** | | | | | | | | |
| 1 Bilbray | N | Y | Y | N | N | N | Y | Y |
| 2 ***Vucanovich*** | N | Y | Y | Y | N | Y | N | N |
| **NEW HAMPSHIRE** | | | | | | | | |
| 1 ***Zeliff*** | N | N | N | Y | N | N | N | N |
| 2 Swett | N | N | N | N | N | N | N | N |
| **NEW JERSEY** | | | | | | | | |
| 1 Andrews | N | Y | Y | N | Y | N | Y | Y |
| 2 Hughes | Y | N | Y | N | N | N | Y | Y |
| 3 Pallone | N | N | Y | N | Y | N | N | N |
| 4 ***Smith*** | N | Y | Y | N | N | Y | Y | N |
| 5 ***Roukema*** | N | Y | N | N | ? | N | N | N |
| 6 Dwyer | Y | ? | ? | ? | ? | N | Y | Y |
| 7 ***Rinaldo*** | Y | Y | Y | N | N | N | Y | N |
| 8 Roe | Y | Y | Y | N | ? | ? | ? | Y |
| 9 Torricelli | Y | Y | Y | Y | N | ? | ? | Y |
| 10 Payne | Y | Y | Y | N | Y | N | Y | Y |
| 11 ***Gallo*** | Y | Y | Y | N | Y | N | Y | N |
| 12 ***Zimmer*** | N | N | N | Y | N | N | N | N |
| 13 ***Saxton*** | Y | Y | N | N | N | N | N | N |
| 14 Guarini | Y | Y | Y | N | Y | Y | Y | Y |
| **NEW MEXICO** | | | | | | | | |
| 1 ***Schiff*** | N | Y | N | Y | N | Y | Y | N |
| 2 ***Skeen*** | Y | Y | Y | N | Y | N | Y | N |
| 3 Richardson | ? | ? | ? | ? | ? | N | Y | N |
| **NEW YORK** | | | | | | | | |
| 1 Hochbrueckner | Y | Y | Y | N | Y | N | Y | Y |
| 2 Downey | Y | Y | Y | N | Y | N | Y | Y |
| 3 Mrazek | Y | Y | Y | N | Y | Y | Y | Y |
| 4 ***Lent*** | Y | Y | Y | N | Y | Y | N | N |
| 5 ***McGrath*** | N | N | Y | N | Y | Y | Y | N |
| 6 Flake | Y | Y | Y | N | Y | N | Y | Y |
| 7 Ackerman | Y | Y | Y | ? | ? | N | Y | Y |
| 8 Scheuer | Y | Y | Y | N | N | N | Y | Y |
| 9 Manton | Y | Y | Y | N | Y | N | Y | Y |
| 10 Schumer | Y | Y | Y | N | Y | N | N | Y |
| 11 Towns | Y | Y | Y | N | Y | N | Y | Y |
| 12 Owens | Y | Y | Y | N | N | N | Y | Y |
| 13 Solarz | ? | Y | Y | N | Y | ? | ? | Y |
| 14 ***Molinari*** | N | Y | N | N | N | N | Y | N |
| 15 ***Green*** | Y | Y | Y | N | Y | N | Y | N |
| 16 Rangel | ? | Y | Y | N | Y | N | Y | Y |
| 17 Vacancy | | | | | | | | |
| 18 Serrano | Y | Y | Y | N | Y | N | Y | Y |
| 19 Engel | Y | Y | Y | N | N | ? | ? | Y |
| 20 Lowey | Y | Y | Y | N | Y | N | Y | Y |
| 21 ***Fish*** | Y | Y | N | N | Y | N | Y | N |
| 22 ***Gilman*** | N | Y | Y | N | Y | Y | ? | N |
| 23 McNulty | Y | Y | Y | N | Y | N | Y | Y |
| 24 ***Solomon*** | Y | Y | N | Y | N | N | N | N |
| 25 ***Boehlert*** | Y | Y | Y | N | ? | N | N | N |
| 26 ***Martin*** | Y | Y | N | N | N | Y | Y | N |
| 27 ***Walsh*** | Y | Y | Y | ? | ? | Y | Y | N |
| 28 McHugh | N | Y | Y | ? | ? | N | Y | Y |
| 29 ***Horton*** | ? | ? | ? | ? | ? | N | Y | N |
| 30 Slaughter | Y | Y | Y | N | Y | N | N | Y |
| 31 ***Paxon*** | N | Y | N | Y | N | N | N | N |

| | 431 | 432 | 433 | 434 | 435 | 436 | 437 | 438 |
|---|---|---|---|---|---|---|---|---|
| 32 LaFalce | Y | Y | Y | N | ? | ? | Y | Y |
| 33 Nowak | Y | ? | ? | ? | ? | N | Y | Y |
| 34 ***Houghton*** | Y | Y | Y | N | N | N | Y | N |
| **NORTH CAROLINA** | | | | | | | | |
| 1 Vacancy | | | | | | | | |
| 2 Valentine | Y | Y | N | Y | ? | N | N | Y |
| 3 Lancaster | N | Y | Y | N | Y | N | Y | Y |
| 4 Price | Y | Y | Y | N | Y | ? | Y | Y |
| 5 Neal | Y | Y | N | N | N | N | N | Y |
| 6 ***Coble*** | N | Y | N | Y | N | N | N | N |
| 7 Rose | Y | Y | Y | N | Y | Y | Y | Y |
| 8 Hefner | N | Y | Y | N | ? | N | ? | Y |
| 9 ***McMillan*** | Y | ? | N | N | N | Y | ? | N |
| 10 ***Ballenger*** | N | Y | N | Y | — | N | N | N |
| 11 ***Taylor*** | Y | Y | N | N | Y | N | N | N |
| **NORTH DAKOTA** | | | | | | | | |
| AL Dorgan | N | N | N | N | N | N | Y | N |
| **OHIO** | | | | | | | | |
| 1 Luken | Y | ? | ? | ? | ? | N | Y | Y |
| 2 ***Gradison*** | N | Y | N | N | N | Y | N | N |
| 3 Hall | Y | Y | Y | Y | Y | N | Y | Y |
| 4 ***Oxley*** | N | N | Y | N | N | Y | N | N |
| 5 ***Gillmor*** | Y | Y | N | N | N | Y | N | N |
| 6 ***McEwen*** | ? | ? | ? | ? | ? | N | N | N |
| 7 ***Hobson*** | N | Y | N | Y | N | N | N | N |
| 8 ***Boehner*** | N | N | N | Y | N | Y | N | N |
| 9 Kaptur | Y | Y | Y | N | Y | ? | Y | Y |
| 10 ***Miller*** | Y | Y | N | N | N | Y | N | N |
| 11 Eckart | Y | Y | Y | N | Y | N | Y | Y |
| 12 ***Kasich*** | N | Y | N | Y | N | ? | ? | N |
| 13 Pease | Y | N | N | N | N | Y | Y | Y |
| 14 Sawyer | Y | Y | Y | N | Y | N | Y | Y |
| 15 ***Wylie*** | Y | Y | N | N | ? | Y | Y | N |
| 16 ***Regula*** | N | Y | N | N | N | Y | Y | N |
| 17 Traficant | Y | Y | Y | N | N | N | Y | Y |
| 18 Applegate | N | N | Y | N | N | N | Y | Y |
| 19 Feighan | Y | Y | Y | N | N | Y | ? | Y |
| 20 Oakar | ? | ? | ? | ? | ? | Y | Y | Y |
| 21 Stokes | Y | Y | Y | N | Y | N | Y | Y |
| **OKLAHOMA** | | | | | | | | |
| 1 ***Inhofe*** | N | Y | N | Y | N | N | N | N |
| 2 Synar | N | Y | N | N | N | N | Y | Y |
| 3 Brewster | N | Y | Y | N | N | N | N | Y |
| 4 McCurdy | N | N | N | N | ? | N | Y | Y |
| 5 ***Edwards*** | N | Y | N | N | ? | N | ? | ? |
| 6 English | N | Y | N | N | Y | N | N | Y |
| **OREGON** | | | | | | | | |
| 1 AuCoin | Y | Y | Y | N | Y | N | Y | Y |
| 2 ***Smith*** | N | Y | N | Y | N | Y | N | N |
| 3 Wyden | N | N | ? | ? | ? | N | Y | Y |
| 4 DeFazio | N | N | Y | N | ? | N | N | Y |
| 5 Kopetski | Y | Y | Y | N | Y | ? | Y | Y |
| **PENNSYLVANIA** | | | | | | | | |
| 1 Foglietta | ? | ? | ? | ? | ? | ? | ? | Y |
| 2 Blackwell | N | Y | Y | N | N | N | Y | Y |
| 3 Borski | Y | Y | Y | N | Y | N | Y | Y |
| 4 Kolter | Y | Y | Y | ? | ? | N | Y | Y |
| 5 ***Schulze*** | ? | ? | ? | ? | ? | N | N | N |
| 6 Yatron | ? | ? | ? | ? | ? | N | Y | Y |
| 7 ***Weldon*** | ? | ? | ? | Y | N | N | N | N |
| 8 Kostmayer | N | Y | Y | N | N | N | N | Y |
| 9 ***Shuster*** | N | N | N | N | N | Y | N | N |
| 10 ***McDade*** | Y | N | Y | N | Y | Y | Y | N |
| 11 Kanjorski | Y | Y | Y | N | Y | N | Y | Y |
| 12 Murtha | Y | Y | Y | ? | ? | N | Y | Y |
| 13 ***Coughlin*** | Y | Y | ? | ? | ? | N | Y | N |
| 14 Coyne | N | Y | Y | N | Y | N | Y | Y |
| 15 ***Ritter*** | N | Y | N | Y | N | N | N | N |
| 16 ***Walker*** | Y | N | N | Y | N | N | N | N |
| 17 ***Gekas*** | Y | Y | N | N | Y | N | N | N |
| 18 ***Santorum*** | N | N | N | Y | N | ? | N | N |
| 19 ***Goodling*** | N | Y | N | Y | N | N | N | N |
| 20 Gaydos | ? | ? | ? | ? | ? | N | Y | Y |
| 21 ***Ridge*** | N | Y | N | Y | N | N | Y | N |
| 22 Murphy | N | N | Y | ? | ? | N | N | N |
| 23 ***Clinger*** | N | N | N | Y | Y | N | Y | N |
| **RHODE ISLAND** | | | | | | | | |
| 1 ***Machtley*** | Y | Y | N | N | N | N | Y | N |
| 2 Reed | Y | Y | Y | N | Y | N | Y | Y |
| **SOUTH CAROLINA** | | | | | | | | |
| 1 ***Ravenel*** | N | Y | N | Y | N | N | N | N |
| 2 ***Spence*** | N | Y | N | Y | N | N | N | N |
| 3 Derrick | Y | Y | Y | N | N | N | Y | Y |
| 4 Patterson | N | Y | N | N | N | — | N | Y |
| 5 Spratt | N | Y | N | N | N | ? | Y | Y |
| 6 Tallon | N | Y | N | N | N | Y | Y | Y |

| | 431 | 432 | 433 | 434 | 435 | 436 | 437 | 438 |
|---|---|---|---|---|---|---|---|---|
| **SOUTH DAKOTA** | | | | | | | | |
| AL Johnson | N | Y | Y | N | Y | Y | Y | Y |
| **TENNESSEE** | | | | | | | | |
| 1 ***Quillen*** | Y | Y | Y | N | Y | Y | N | N |
| 2 ***Duncan*** | N | N | N | Y | N | Y | N | N |
| 3 Lloyd | Y | Y | Y | N | Y | N | N | Y |
| 4 Cooper | Y | Y | Y | N | N | N | Y | Y |
| 5 Clement | N | Y | N | N | N | N | Y | Y |
| 6 Gordon | Y | Y | Y | N | N | N | Y | Y |
| 7 ***Sundquist*** | Y | Y | N | N | N | Y | N | N |
| 8 Tanner | Y | Y | Y | N | N | N | Y | Y |
| 9 Ford | Y | ? | Y | ? | ? | ? | ? | ? |
| **TEXAS** | | | | | | | | |
| 1 Chapman | Y | Y | Y | N | Y | N | N | Y |
| 2 Wilson | Y | Y | Y | N | Y | N | N | N |
| 3 ***Johnson*** | Y | N | N | Y | N | N | N | N |
| 4 Hall | N | Y | Y | Y | N | N | N | N |
| 5 Bryant | Y | Y | Y | N | N | N | Y | Y |
| 6 ***Barton*** | Y | N | N | Y | ? | Y | N | N |
| 7 ***Archer*** | Y | N | N | Y | N | Y | N | N |
| 8 ***Fields*** | N | Y | N | Y | N | N | N | N |
| 9 Brooks | Y | ? | Y | N | Y | N | Y | Y |
| 10 Pickle | N | Y | N | N | N | Y | Y | Y |
| 11 Edwards | Y | Y | N | N | N | N | N | Y |
| 12 Geren | Y | Y | N | Y | ? | N | N | N |
| 13 Sarpalius | N | Y | N | N | N | N | N | Y |
| 14 Laughlin | Y | Y | N | N | Y | N | Y | Y |
| 15 de la Garza | Y | Y | Y | N | N | N | N | Y |
| 16 Coleman | Y | Y | Y | N | Y | ? | ? | Y |
| 17 Stenholm | N | Y | N | Y | N | N | N | Y |
| 18 Washington | N | N | ? | ? | N | ? | N | Y |
| 19 ***Combest*** | N | N | N | Y | N | N | N | N |
| 20 Gonzalez | Y | Y | Y | N | Y | N | Y | Y |
| 21 ***Smith*** | ? | ? | ? | ? | ? | Y | N | N |
| 22 ***DeLay*** | Y | N | Y | Y | Y | Y | N | N |
| 23 Bustamante | ? | ? | ? | ? | ? | N | Y | Y |
| 24 Frost | Y | Y | Y | N | Y | N | Y | Y |
| 25 Andrews | Y | Y | N | N | N | N | N | Y |
| 26 ***Armey*** | N | N | N | Y | N | Y | N | N |
| 27 Ortiz | Y | Y | Y | N | N | N | Y | Y |
| **UTAH** | | | | | | | | |
| 1 ***Hansen*** | ? | ? | ? | ? | ? | Y | ? | N |
| 2 Owens | N | N | ? | N | N | N | Y | N |
| 3 Orton | X | X | ? | ? | ? | Y | N | N |
| **VERMONT** | | | | | | | | |
| AL *Sanders* | N | Y | N | N | N | ? | Y | Y |
| **VIRGINIA** | | | | | | | | |
| 1 ***Bateman*** | N | Y | N | N | Y | Y | Y | N |
| 2 Pickett | N | Y | Y | N | N | Y | N | Y |
| 3 ***Bliley*** | N | Y | N | N | N | N | Y | N |
| 4 Sisisky | N | Y | Y | Y | N | N | Y | Y |
| 5 Payne | N | N | Y | N | Y | Y | Y | Y |
| 6 Olin | Y | Y | ? | ? | ? | ? | ? | ? |
| 7 ***Allen*** | N | N | N | Y | N | Y | Y | N |
| 8 Moran | Y | Y | Y | N | Y | N | Y | Y |
| 9 Boucher | Y | Y | Y | N | Y | N | Y | Y |
| 10 ***Wolf*** | N | Y | Y | N | Y | Y | Y | N |
| **WASHINGTON** | | | | | | | | |
| 1 ***Miller*** | Y | Y | N | N | N | N | N | N |
| 2 Swift | Y | Y | Y | N | Y | N | Y | Y |
| 3 Unsoeld | N | Y | Y | N | Y | N | N | Y |
| 4 ***Morrison*** | N | Y | N | N | N | ? | Y | N |
| 5 Foley | | | | | | | | |
| 6 Dicks | Y | Y | Y | N | Y | N | Y | Y |
| 7 McDermott | Y | Y | Y | N | Y | N | Y | Y |
| 8 ***Chandler*** | ? | ? | ? | ? | ? | ? | N | N |
| **WEST VIRGINIA** | | | | | | | | |
| 1 Mollohan | Y | Y | Y | N | Y | N | Y | Y |
| 2 Staggers | N | N | Y | N | N | ? | ? | ? |
| 3 Wise | Y | Y | Y | N | Y | ? | Y | Y |
| 4 Rahall | N | Y | Y | N | Y | ? | ? | Y |
| **WISCONSIN** | | | | | | | | |
| 1 Aspin | Y | Y | Y | N | N | ? | ? | Y |
| 2 ***Klug*** | N | N | N | N | N | ? | ? | N |
| 3 ***Gunderson*** | N | Y | N | Y | N | N | N | N |
| 4 Kleczka | N | N | Y | N | N | N | Y | Y |
| 5 Moody | Y | N | Y | N | N | N | Y | Y |
| 6 ***Petri*** | N | N | N | Y | N | N | N | N |
| 7 Obey | N | N | ? | N | Y | N | Y | Y |
| 8 ***Roth*** | N | N | N | ? | ? | N | N | N |
| 9 ***Sensenbrenner*** | N | N | N | N | N | N | N | N |
| **WYOMING** | | | | | | | | |
| AL ***Thomas*** | Y | N | ? | ? | ? | N | N | N |

Southern states - Ala., Ark., Fla., Ga., Ky., La., Miss., N.C., Okla., S.C., Tenn., Texas, Va.
Omitted votes are quorum calls, which CQ does not include in its vote charts.

**439. H J Res 553. Fiscal 1993 Continuing Resolution/ Rule.** Adoption of the rule (H Res 580) to provide for House floor consideration of the joint resolution to make continuing appropriations for fiscal 1993 through Oct. 5, or until the regular appropriations bills were signed into law. Adopted 213-204: R 1-162; D 211-42 (ND 157-21, SD 54-21); I 1-0, Sept. 30, 1992.

**440. H J Res 553. Fiscal 1993 Continuing Resolution/ Passage.** Passage of the joint resolution to make continuing appropriations for fiscal 1993 through Oct. 5, or until the regular appropriations bills were signed into law. Passed 300-104: R 65-93; D 234-11 (ND 166-9, SD 68-2); I 1-0, Sept. 30, 1992.

**441. HR 5318. Conditional MFN for China in 1993/Veto Override.** Passage, over President Bush's Sept. 28 veto, of the bill to prohibit the president from waving the Jackson-Vanik amendment to the 1974 trade act and extending most-favored-nation status to products from Chinese state-owned enterprises in 1993 unless he certified that China had released and accounted for prisoners from the 1989 Tiananmen Square demonstrations and had made significant progress in adhering to standards for human rights and weapons non-proliferation. Passed (thus cleared for the Senate) 345-74: R 102-60; D 242-14 (ND 166-11, SD 76-3); I 1-0, Sept. 30, 1992. A two-thirds majority of those present and voting (280 in this case) was required to override a veto. A "nay" was a vote in support of the president's position.

**442. S 2. Neighborhood Schools Improvement/Recommit to Conference.** Goodling, R-Pa., motion to recommit to conference the report on the bill to authorize $800 million for grants to states and local education agencies for school improvement, with instructions to include language relating to the development of voluntary national school standards. Motion rejected 166-254: R 162-1; D 4-252 (ND 1-176, SD 3-76); I 0-1, Sept. 30, 1992.

**443. S 5. Family and Medical Leave/Veto Override.** Passage, over President Bush's Sept. 22 veto, of the bill to require companies with more than 50 employees to provide workers with up to 12 weeks of unpaid leave for family emergencies. Rejected 258-169: R 38-127; D 219-42 (ND 167-12, SD 52-30); I 1-0, Sept. 30, 1992. A two-thirds majority of those present and voting (285 in this case) was required to override a veto. A "nay" was a vote in support of the president's position.

**444. HR 3281. National Air and Space Museum Expansion Site Selection.** Frost, D-Texas, motion to suspend the rules and pass the bill to establish the National Air and Space Museum Expansion Site Advisory Panel to develop a national competition for the evaluation of expansion sites for the National Air and Space Museum. Motion rejected 106-317: R 16-147; D 90-169 (ND 72-106, SD 18-63); I 0-1, Sept. 30, 1992. A two-thirds majority of those present and voting (282 in this case) was required for passage under suspension of the rules.

**445. S 2681. Native Hawaiian Health Care.** Wyden, D-Ore., motion to suspend the rules and pass the bill to revise and extend the Native Hawaiian Health Care Act of 1988 through fiscal 2000. Motion rejected 228-194: R 16-145; D 211-49 (ND 165-14, SD 46-35); I 1-0, Sept. 30, 1992. A two-thirds majority of those present and voting (282 in this case) was required for passage under suspension of the rules.

**446. HR 2548. Lincoln Interpretive Center.** Vento, D-Minn., motion to suspend the rules and pass the bill to authorize $18 million for a visitor center at the Lincoln Home National Historic Site in Springfield, Ill. Motion agreed to 298-121: R 71-89; D 226-32 (ND 171-7, SD 55-25); I 1-0, Sept. 30, 1992. A two-thirds majority of those present and voting (280 in this case) was required for passage under suspension of the rules.

## KEY

| | |
|---|---|
| Y | Voted for (yea). |
| # | Paired for. |
| + | Announced for. |
| N | Voted against (nay). |
| X | Paired against. |
| − | Announced against. |
| P | Voted "present." |
| C | Voted "present" to avoid possible conflict of interest. |
| ? | Did not vote or otherwise make a position known. |

Democrats  *Republicans*
*Independent*

| | 439 | 440 | 441 | 442 | 443 | 444 | 445 | 446 |
|---|---|---|---|---|---|---|---|---|
| **ALABAMA** | | | | | | | | |
| 1 *Callahan* | N | N | N | Y | N | N | N | N |
| 2 *Dickinson* | N | Y | N | Y | N | N | N | N |
| 3 Browder | Y | Y | Y | N | N | N | N | N |
| 4 Bevill | Y | Y | Y | N | Y | N | N | Y |
| 5 Cramer | N | Y | Y | N | N | N | N | N |
| 6 Erdreich | N | Y | Y | N | N | N | N | N |
| 7 Harris | Y | Y | Y | N | N | N | N | N |
| **ALASKA** | | | | | | | | |
| AL *Young* | N | N | N | Y | N | Y | N | N |
| **ARIZONA** | | | | | | | | |
| 1 *Rhodes* | N | Y | Y | Y | N | N | N | Y |
| 2 Pastor | Y | Y | Y | N | Y | N | Y | Y |
| 3 *Stump* | N | N | N | Y | N | N | N | N |
| 4 *Kyl* | N | Y | Y | Y | N | N | N | N |
| 5 *Kolbe* | N | Y | N | Y | N | N | N | N |
| **ARKANSAS** | | | | | | | | |
| 1 Alexander | ? | ? | ? | N | Y | Y | Y | Y |
| 2 Thornton | Y | Y | N | Y | N | Y | N | Y |
| 3 *Hammerschmidt* | N | Y | N | Y | N | N | N | N |
| 4 Anthony | Y | Y | Y | N | Y | N | Y | Y |
| **CALIFORNIA** | | | | | | | | |
| 1 *Riggs* | N | N | Y | Y | N | N | ? | N |
| 2 *Herger* | N | N | Y | Y | N | N | N | N |
| 3 Matsui | Y | Y | Y | N | Y | Y | Y | Y |
| 4 Fazio | Y | Y | Y | N | Y | Y | Y | Y |
| 5 Pelosi | Y | Y | Y | N | Y | Y | Y | Y |
| 6 Boxer | Y | Y | Y | N | Y | Y | Y | Y |
| 7 Miller | Y | Y | Y | N | Y | Y | Y | Y |
| 8 Dellums | ? | Y | Y | N | Y | Y | Y | Y |
| 9 Stark | Y | Y | Y | ? | Y | N | Y | Y |
| 10 Edwards | Y | Y | Y | N | Y | Y | Y | Y |
| 11 Lantos | Y | Y | Y | N | Y | Y | Y | Y |
| 12 *Campbell* | N | Y | N | Y | N | N | Y | N |
| 13 Mineta | Y | Y | Y | N | Y | N | Y | Y |
| 14 *Doolittle* | N | N | Y | N | N | N | N | N |
| 15 Condit | N | Y | Y | N | N | N | N | N |
| 16 Panetta | Y | Y | Y | N | Y | Y | Y | Y |
| 17 Dooley | N | Y | Y | N | Y | N | Y | Y |
| 18 Lehman | N | Y | Y | N | Y | N | Y | Y |
| 19 *Lagomarsino* | N | N | Y | N | N | N | N | Y |
| 20 *Thomas* | N | N | N | Y | N | N | N | N |
| 21 *Gallegly* | N | Y | Y | Y | N | N | N | Y |
| 22 *Moorhead* | N | N | N | Y | N | N | N | N |
| 23 Beilenson | Y | Y | Y | N | Y | Y | Y | Y |
| 24 Waxman | Y | Y | Y | N | Y | Y | Y | Y |
| 25 Roybal | Y | Y | Y | N | Y | Y | Y | Y |
| 26 Berman | Y | Y | Y | N | Y | Y | Y | Y |
| 27 Levine | Y | Y | Y | N | Y | Y | Y | Y |
| 28 Dixon | Y | Y | Y | N | Y | N | Y | Y |
| 29 Waters | Y | Y | Y | N | Y | Y | Y | Y |
| 30 Martinez | Y | Y | Y | N | Y | N | Y | Y |
| 31 Dymally | ? | ? | ? | ? | # | ? | ? | ? |
| 32 Anderson | Y | Y | Y | N | Y | N | Y | Y |
| 33 *Dreier* | N | N | N | Y | N | N | N | N |
| 34 Torres | Y | Y | Y | N | Y | Y | Y | Y |
| 35 *Lewis* | N | N | N | Y | N | N | N | N |
| 36 Brown | N | ? | Y | N | Y | Y | Y | Y |
| 37 *McCandless* | N | N | N | Y | N | N | N | N |
| 38 *Dornan* | N | N | Y | N | N | N | N | Y |
| 39 *Dannemeyer* | N | N | Y | N | N | N | N | N |
| 40 *Cox* | N | N | Y | N | N | N | N | Y |
| 41 *Lowery* | N | Y | N | Y | N | ? | ? | ? |

| | 439 | 440 | 441 | 442 | 443 | 444 | 445 | 446 |
|---|---|---|---|---|---|---|---|---|
| 42 *Rohrabacher* | N | N | Y | Y | N | Y | N | N |
| 43 *Packard* | N | N | N | Y | N | Y | N | N |
| 44 *Cunningham* | N | N | Y | N | N | N | N | N |
| 45 *Hunter* | N | N | Y | Y | N | N | N | N |
| **COLORADO** | | | | | | | | |
| 1 Schroeder | N | N | Y | N | Y | Y | Y | Y |
| 2 Skaggs | Y | Y | Y | N | Y | Y | Y | Y |
| 3 Campbell | N | Y | Y | N | Y | Y | Y | Y |
| 4 *Allard* | N | N | N | Y | N | N | N | N |
| 5 *Hefley* | N | Y | Y | Y | N | N | N | N |
| 6 *Schaefer* | N | N | Y | Y | N | Y | N | N |
| **CONNECTICUT** | | | | | | | | |
| 1 Kennelly | Y | Y | Y | N | Y | N | Y | Y |
| 2 Gejdenson | Y | Y | Y | N | Y | Y | Y | Y |
| 3 DeLauro | Y | Y | Y | N | Y | Y | Y | Y |
| 4 *Shays* | N | N | Y | N | Y | N | Y | Y |
| 5 *Franks* | N | Y | Y | Y | N | N | N | Y |
| 6 *Johnson* | N | N | N | Y | N | N | N | Y |
| **DELAWARE** | | | | | | | | |
| AL Carper | Y | Y | Y | N | Y | N | Y | N |
| **FLORIDA** | | | | | | | | |
| 1 Hutto | N | Y | Y | N | N | N | N | N |
| 2 Peterson | Y | Y | Y | N | Y | N | Y | Y |
| 3 Bennett | N | Y | Y | N | Y | N | Y | Y |
| 4 *James* | N | Y | Y | Y | N | N | N | N |
| 5 *McCollum* | N | Y | Y | Y | N | N | N | N |
| 6 *Stearns* | N | N | Y | Y | N | N | N | N |
| 7 Gibbons | Y | Y | Y | ? | Y | Y | Y | Y |
| 8 *Young* | N | Y | Y | Y | N | Y | Y | Y |
| 9 *Bilirakis* | N | N | N | Y | N | N | N | N |
| 10 *Ireland* | N | ? | ? | Y | N | ? | ? | ? |
| 11 Bacchus | N | Y | Y | N | Y | N | Y | Y |
| 12 *Lewis* | N | N | N | Y | N | N | N | N |
| 13 *Goss* | N | N | N | Y | N | N | N | N |
| 14 Johnston | Y | Y | Y | N | Y | N | Y | Y |
| 15 *Shaw* | N | Y | Y | N | N | N | N | N |
| 16 Smith | # | ? | Y | N | Y | Y | Y | Y |
| 17 Lehman | Y | Y | Y | ? | Y | N | Y | ? |
| 18 *Ros—Lehtinen* | N | Y | Y | Y | N | N | N | N |
| 19 Fascell | Y | Y | Y | N | Y | N | Y | Y |
| **GEORGIA** | | | | | | | | |
| 1 Thomas | Y | Y | Y | N | N | N | N | Y |
| 2 Hatcher | Y | ? | Y | N | Y | N | Y | Y |
| 3 Ray | X | Y | Y | N | N | N | N | N |
| 4 Jones | Y | Y | Y | N | Y | Y | Y | Y |
| 5 Lewis | Y | Y | Y | N | Y | Y | Y | Y |
| 6 *Gingrich* | N | ? | Y | Y | N | N | N | Y |
| 7 Darden | Y | Y | Y | N | Y | N | Y | Y |
| 8 Rowland | Y | Y | Y | N | N | N | N | Y |
| 9 Jenkins | Y | Y | Y | N | Y | ? | ? | ? |
| 10 Barnard | ? | ? | ? | ? | X | ? | ? | ? |
| **HAWAII** | | | | | | | | |
| 1 Abercrombie | Y | Y | Y | N | Y | N | Y | Y |
| 2 Mink | Y | Y | Y | N | Y | N | Y | Y |
| **IDAHO** | | | | | | | | |
| 1 LaRocco | N | Y | Y | N | N | N | Y | Y |
| 2 *Stallings* | N | Y | Y | N | N | Y | Y | Y |
| **ILLINOIS** | | | | | | | | |
| 1 Hayes | Y | Y | Y | N | Y | Y | Y | Y |
| 2 Savage | Y | Y | Y | N | Y | Y | Y | Y |
| 3 Russo | Y | N | Y | N | Y | Y | Y | Y |
| 4 Sangmeister | Y | Y | Y | N | Y | N | N | Y |
| 5 Lipinski | Y | Y | Y | N | Y | N | N | Y |
| 6 *Hyde* | Y | Y | Y | N | N | N | N | Y |
| 7 Collins | Y | Y | Y | N | Y | Y | Y | Y |
| 8 Rostenkowski | Y | Y | Y | N | Y | N | Y | Y |
| 9 Yates | Y | Y | Y | N | Y | Y | Y | Y |
| 10 *Porter* | N | Y | Y | N | Y | N | Y | Y |
| 11 Annunzio | Y | Y | Y | N | Y | Y | N | Y |
| 12 *Crane* | N | N | Y | N | N | N | N | N |
| 13 *Fawell* | N | N | N | Y | N | N | N | N |
| 14 *Hastert* | N | N | N | Y | N | N | N | Y |
| 15 *Ewing* | N | N | N | Y | N | N | N | N |
| 16 Cox | Y | Y | Y | N | Y | N | Y | Y |
| 17 Evans | Y | Y | Y | N | Y | Y | Y | Y |
| 18 *Michel* | N | Y | Y | N | N | N | N | Y |
| 19 Bruce | N | Y | Y | N | Y | N | N | Y |
| 20 Durbin | Y | Y | Y | N | Y | Y | Y | Y |
| 21 Costello | Y | Y | Y | N | Y | N | N | Y |
| 22 Poshard | N | N | Y | N | N | N | N | Y |
| **INDIANA** | | | | | | | | |
| 1 Visclosky | Y | Y | Y | N | Y | Y | Y | Y |
| 2 Sharp | Y | Y | Y | N | Y | N | Y | Y |
| 3 Roemer | Y | Y | N | N | Y | N | N | N |

ND Northern Democrats    SD Southern Democrats

| | 439 | 440 | 441 | 442 | 443 | 444 | 445 | 446 |
|---|---|---|---|---|---|---|---|---|
| 4 Long | Y | Y | Y | N | Y | N | Y | Y |
| 5 Jontz | Y | Y | Y | N | Y | Y | Y | Y |
| 6 ***Burton*** | N | N | Y | N | Y | N | N | N |
| 7 ***Myers*** | N | Y | N | Y | N | N | N | Y |
| 8 McCloskey | Y | Y | Y | N | Y | N | Y | Y |
| 9 Hamilton | Y | Y | Y | N | N | N | Y | Y |
| 10 Jacobs | N | N | Y | N | Y | N | Y | Y |
| **IOWA** | | | | | | | | |
| 1 ***Leach*** | N | Y | N | Y | Y | N | N | Y |
| 2 ***Nussle*** | N | N | N | Y | N | N | N | N |
| 3 Nagle | Y | Y | Y | N | Y | ? | Y | Y |
| 4 Smith | Y | Y | N | N | Y | Y | Y | Y |
| 5 ***Lightfoot*** | N | Y | N | Y | N | N | N | Y |
| 6 ***Grandy*** | N | Y | N | Y | N | N | N | N |
| **KANSAS** | | | | | | | | |
| 1 ***Roberts*** | N | N | N | Y | N | N | N | Y |
| 2 Slattery | N | Y | Y | N | N | Y | Y | Y |
| 3 ***Meyers*** | N | Y | Y | Y | N | N | Y | N |
| 4 Glickman | Y | Y | Y | N | N | Y | Y | Y |
| 5 ***Nichols*** | N | N | N | Y | N | N | N | N |
| **KENTUCKY** | | | | | | | | |
| 1 Hubbard | Y | N | Y | Y | Y | N | N | N |
| 2 Natcher | Y | Y | Y | N | Y | Y | Y | Y |
| 3 Mazzoli | Y | Y | Y | N | Y | Y | Y | Y |
| 4 ***Bunning*** | N | N | Y | Y | N | N | N | N |
| 5 ***Rogers*** | N | Y | Y | Y | N | N | N | N |
| 6 ***Hopkins*** | N | N | Y | Y | N | N | N | N |
| 7 Perkins | ? | ? | Y | N | Y | N | Y | Y |
| **LOUISIANA** | | | | | | | | |
| 1 ***Livingston*** | ? | ? | N | Y | N | N | N | Y |
| 2 Jefferson | ? | Y | Y | N | Y | Y | Y | Y |
| 3 Tauzin | Y | ? | Y | N | N | N | Y | Y |
| 4 ***McCrery*** | ? | ? | ? | ? | ? | ? | ? | ? |
| 5 Huckaby | ? | ? | ? | ? | ? | ? | ? | ? |
| 6 ***Baker*** | N | N | N | Y | N | N | N | N |
| 7 Hayes | N | Y | Y | N | N | N | Y | Y |
| 8 ***Holloway*** | N | N | Y | Y | N | N | N | N |
| **MAINE** | | | | | | | | |
| 1 Andrews | Y | Y | Y | N | Y | N | Y | N |
| 2 ***Snowe*** | N | N | Y | Y | Y | N | N | N |
| **MARYLAND** | | | | | | | | |
| 1 ***Gilchrest*** | N | Y | Y | Y | N | Y | N | N |
| 2 ***Bentley*** | N | Y | Y | Y | N | Y | N | Y |
| 3 Cardin | Y | Y | Y | N | Y | Y | Y | Y |
| 4 McMillen | N | Y | Y | N | Y | Y | Y | Y |
| 5 Hoyer | Y | Y | Y | N | Y | Y | Y | Y |
| 6 Byron | N | Y | Y | Y | N | N | Y | Y |
| 7 Mfume | Y | Y | Y | N | Y | Y | Y | Y |
| 8 ***Morella*** | N | Y | Y | Y | Y | Y | Y | Y |
| **MASSACHUSETTS** | | | | | | | | |
| 1 Olver | Y | Y | Y | N | Y | N | Y | Y |
| 2 Neal | Y | Y | Y | N | Y | N | Y | Y |
| 3 Early | Y | Y | Y | N | Y | N | Y | Y |
| 4 Frank | Y | Y | Y | N | Y | Y | Y | N |
| 5 Atkins | Y | Y | Y | N | Y | Y | Y | Y |
| 6 Mavroules | Y | Y | Y | N | Y | N | Y | Y |
| 7 Markey | Y | Y | Y | N | Y | Y | Y | Y |
| 8 Kennedy | Y | Y | Y | N | Y | N | Y | Y |
| 9 Moakley | Y | Y | Y | N | Y | N | Y | Y |
| 10 Studds | Y | Y | Y | N | Y | N | Y | Y |
| 11 Donnelly | Y | Y | Y | N | Y | N | Y | Y |
| **MICHIGAN** | | | | | | | | |
| 1 Conyers | Y | Y | Y | N | Y | N | Y | Y |
| 2 ***Pursell*** | N | N | N | Y | N | N | N | N |
| 3 Wolpe | Y | Y | Y | N | Y | Y | Y | Y |
| 4 ***Upton*** | N | N | Y | Y | N | N | N | Y |
| 5 ***Henry*** | N | N | Y | Y | N | N | N | Y |
| 6 Carr | Y | Y | Y | N | N | N | N | Y |
| 7 Kildee | Y | Y | Y | N | Y | Y | Y | Y |
| 8 Traxler | Y | Y | Y | N | Y | Y | Y | Y |
| 9 ***Vander Jagt*** | N | N | N | Y | N | N | N | N |
| 10 ***Camp*** | N | N | Y | Y | N | N | N | N |
| 11 ***Davis*** | N | Y | N | Y | N | N | Y | Y |
| 12 Bonior | Y | Y | Y | N | Y | Y | Y | Y |
| 13 Collins | Y | Y | Y | N | Y | N | Y | Y |
| 14 Hertel | Y | Y | Y | N | Y | N | Y | Y |
| 15 Ford | Y | Y | Y | N | Y | N | Y | Y |
| 16 Dingell | Y | Y | Y | N | Y | N | Y | Y |
| 17 Levin | Y | Y | Y | N | Y | N | Y | Y |
| 18 ***Broomfield*** | N | N | N | Y | N | N | N | Y |
| **MINNESOTA** | | | | | | | | |
| 1 Penny | N | N | Y | N | N | N | N | N |
| 2 ***Weber*** | N | N | N | Y | N | N | Y | Y |
| 3 ***Ramstad*** | N | N | Y | Y | Y | N | N | N |
| 4 Vento | Y | Y | Y | N | Y | Y | Y | Y |

| | 439 | 440 | 441 | 442 | 443 | 444 | 445 | 446 |
|---|---|---|---|---|---|---|---|---|
| 5 Sabo | Y | Y | Y | N | Y | Y | Y | Y |
| 6 Sikorski | Y | Y | Y | N | Y | N | Y | Y |
| 7 Peterson | N | Y | N | N | Y | Y | N | Y |
| 8 Oberstar | Y | Y | Y | N | Y | N | Y | Y |
| **MISSISSIPPI** | | | | | | | | |
| 1 Whitten | Y | Y | Y | N | Y | Y | Y | Y |
| 2 Espy | Y | Y | Y | N | Y | N | Y | Y |
| 3 Montgomery | Y | Y | N | N | N | N | Y | Y |
| 4 Parker | Y | Y | Y | N | N | N | N | Y |
| 5 Taylor | Y | Y | Y | N | N | N | N | N |
| **MISSOURI** | | | | | | | | |
| 1 Clay | Y | Y | Y | N | Y | Y | Y | Y |
| 2 Horn | Y | Y | Y | N | Y | N | Y | Y |
| 3 Gephardt | Y | Y | ? | N | Y | Y | Y | Y |
| 4 Skelton | Y | Y | Y | N | N | N | Y | Y |
| 5 Wheat | Y | Y | Y | N | Y | N | Y | Y |
| 6 ***Coleman*** | N | Y | Y | Y | Y | N | N | Y |
| 7 ***Hancock*** | N | N | Y | Y | N | N | N | N |
| 8 ***Emerson*** | N | N | Y | Y | N | N | N | Y |
| 9 Volkmer | Y | Y | Y | N | Y | N | Y | Y |
| **MONTANA** | | | | | | | | |
| 1 Williams | Y | Y | N | N | Y | Y | Y | Y |
| 2 ***Marlenee*** | N | N | N | Y | N | N | N | N |
| **NEBRASKA** | | | | | | | | |
| 1 ***Bereuter*** | N | N | Y | Y | N | N | N | Y |
| 2 Hoagland | Y | Y | Y | N | Y | Y | Y | Y |
| 3 ***Barrett*** | N | N | N | Y | N | N | N | N |
| **NEVADA** | | | | | | | | |
| 1 Bilbray | N | Y | Y | N | Y | Y | Y | Y |
| 2 ***Vucanovich*** | N | Y | N | Y | N | Y | N | Y |
| **NEW HAMPSHIRE** | | | | | | | | |
| 1 ***Zeliff*** | N | N | Y | Y | N | N | N | ? |
| 2 Swett | Y | Y | Y | N | Y | N | N | Y |
| **NEW JERSEY** | | | | | | | | |
| 1 Andrews | Y | Y | Y | N | Y | N | N | Y |
| 2 Hughes | Y | Y | Y | N | Y | N | Y | Y |
| 3 Pallone | N | N | Y | N | Y | N | N | Y |
| 4 ***Smith*** | N | Y | Y | Y | Y | N | N | Y |
| 5 ***Roukema*** | N | Y | Y | Y | Y | N | N | Y |
| 6 Dwyer | Y | Y | Y | N | Y | N | Y | Y |
| 7 ***Rinaldo*** | N | Y | Y | Y | Y | N | N | Y |
| 8 Roe | Y | Y | N | N | Y | N | Y | Y |
| 9 Torricelli | Y | Y | Y | N | Y | Y | Y | Y |
| 10 Payne | Y | Y | Y | N | Y | Y | Y | Y |
| 11 ***Gallo*** | N | Y | Y | Y | N | N | N | Y |
| 12 ***Zimmer*** | N | N | Y | Y | Y | N | N | N |
| 13 ***Saxton*** | N | Y | Y | Y | Y | N | N | Y |
| 14 Guarini | Y | Y | Y | ? | Y | N | Y | Y |
| **NEW MEXICO** | | | | | | | | |
| 1 ***Schiff*** | N | Y | Y | Y | N | N | N | N |
| 2 ***Skeen*** | N | Y | Y | Y | N | N | N | Y |
| 3 Richardson | Y | Y | Y | N | Y | Y | Y | Y |
| **NEW YORK** | | | | | | | | |
| 1 Hochbrueckner | Y | Y | Y | N | Y | Y | Y | Y |
| 2 Downey | Y | Y | Y | N | Y | Y | Y | Y |
| 3 Mrazek | Y | Y | Y | N | Y | N | Y | Y |
| 4 ***Lent*** | N | Y | N | Y | N | N | N | Y |
| 5 ***McGrath*** | N | Y | Y | Y | Y | N | N | Y |
| 6 Flake | Y | Y | Y | N | Y | Y | Y | Y |
| 7 Ackerman | Y | Y | Y | N | Y | Y | Y | Y |
| 8 Scheuer | Y | Y | Y | N | Y | N | Y | Y |
| 9 Manton | Y | ? | Y | N | Y | N | Y | Y |
| 10 Schumer | Y | Y | Y | N | Y | Y | Y | Y |
| 11 Towns | Y | Y | Y | N | Y | N | Y | Y |
| 12 Owens | Y | Y | Y | N | Y | N | Y | Y |
| 13 Solarz | Y | Y | Y | N | Y | N | Y | Y |
| 14 ***Molinari*** | N | N | Y | Y | Y | N | N | Y |
| 15 ***Green*** | Y | Y | Y | Y | Y | N | Y | Y |
| 16 Rangel | Y | Y | Y | N | Y | Y | Y | Y |
| 17 Vacancy | | | | | | | | |
| 18 Serrano | Y | Y | Y | N | Y | N | Y | Y |
| 19 Engel | Y | Y | Y | N | Y | N | Y | Y |
| 20 Lowey | Y | Y | Y | N | Y | Y | Y | Y |
| 21 ***Fish*** | N | Y | Y | Y | Y | N | N | Y |
| 22 ***Gilman*** | N | ? | Y | Y | N | N | Y | Y |
| 23 McNulty | Y | Y | Y | N | Y | Y | Y | Y |
| 24 ***Solomon*** | N | N | Y | Y | Y | N | N | Y |
| 25 ***Boehlert*** | N | Y | Y | Y | Y | N | N | Y |
| 26 ***Martin*** | N | ? | N | Y | Y | N | N | Y |
| 27 ***Walsh*** | N | N | Y | Y | N | Y | N | Y |
| 28 McHugh | Y | Y | Y | N | Y | N | Y | Y |
| 29 ***Horton*** | N | Y | Y | Y | Y | N | Y | N |
| 30 Slaughter | Y | Y | Y | N | Y | N | Y | Y |
| 31 ***Paxon*** | N | N | Y | Y | N | N | N | Y |

| | 439 | 440 | 441 | 442 | 443 | 444 | 445 | 446 |
|---|---|---|---|---|---|---|---|---|
| 32 LaFalce | Y | Y | Y | N | Y | Y | Y | Y |
| 33 Nowak | Y | Y | Y | N | Y | N | Y | Y |
| 34 ***Houghton*** | N | Y | Y | Y | N | N | Y | N |
| **NORTH CAROLINA** | | | | | | | | |
| 1 Vacancy | | | | | | | | |
| 2 Valentine | N | Y | Y | N | N | N | N | N |
| 3 Lancaster | N | Y | Y | N | N | Y | Y | N |
| 4 Price | Y | Y | Y | N | Y | Y | Y | Y |
| 5 Neal | Y | Y | Y | N | N | N | N | N |
| 6 ***Coble*** | N | N | Y | Y | N | N | N | N |
| 7 Rose | Y | ? | Y | N | Y | Y | Y | Y |
| 8 Hefner | Y | Y | Y | N | Y | N | Y | Y |
| 9 ***McMillan*** | N | Y | Y | Y | N | N | N | N |
| 10 ***Ballenger*** | N | Y | Y | Y | N | N | N | N |
| 11 ***Taylor*** | N | N | Y | Y | N | N | N | N |
| **NORTH DAKOTA** | | | | | | | | |
| AL Dorgan | Y | Y | Y | N | Y | Y | Y | Y |
| **OHIO** | | | | | | | | |
| 1 Luken | Y | Y | Y | N | N | N | Y | Y |
| 2 ***Gradison*** | N | Y | N | Y | N | N | N | N |
| 3 Hall | Y | Y | Y | N | Y | N | Y | Y |
| 4 ***Oxley*** | N | Y | N | Y | N | N | N | N |
| 5 ***Gillmor*** | N | N | N | Y | Y | N | N | N |
| 6 ***McEwen*** | N | N | Y | Y | N | N | N | Y |
| 7 ***Hobson*** | N | N | Y | Y | N | N | Y | Y |
| 8 ***Boehner*** | N | N | N | Y | N | N | N | N |
| 9 Kaptur | Y | Y | Y | N | Y | N | Y | Y |
| 10 ***Miller*** | N | Y | N | Y | N | N | N | Y |
| 11 Eckart | Y | Y | Y | N | Y | N | Y | Y |
| 12 ***Kasich*** | N | Y | Y | Y | N | N | N | Y |
| 13 Pease | Y | N | Y | N | Y | N | Y | Y |
| 14 Sawyer | Y | Y | Y | N | Y | N | Y | Y |
| 15 ***Wylie*** | N | Y | N | Y | N | N | N | N |
| 16 ***Regula*** | N | Y | Y | Y | Y | N | N | Y |
| 17 Traficant | Y | Y | P | N | Y | Y | Y | Y |
| 18 Applegate | Y | Y | N | N | Y | N | Y | Y |
| 19 Feighan | Y | Y | Y | N | Y | N | Y | Y |
| 20 Oakar | Y | Y | Y | N | Y | Y | Y | Y |
| 21 Stokes | Y | Y | Y | N | Y | Y | Y | ? |
| **OKLAHOMA** | | | | | | | | |
| 1 ***Inhofe*** | N | N | Y | Y | N | N | N | N |
| 2 Synar | Y | Y | Y | N | Y | N | Y | Y |
| 3 Brewster | Y | Y | Y | N | N | N | Y | Y |
| 4 McCurdy | N | ? | ? | N | Y | N | N | Y |
| 5 ***Edwards*** | ? | ? | ? | ? | N | N | N | Y |
| 6 English | N | Y | Y | N | Y | N | N | Y |
| **OREGON** | | | | | | | | |
| 1 AuCoin | Y | Y | Y | N | Y | N | Y | Y |
| 2 ***Smith*** | N | N | N | Y | N | N | N | N |
| 3 Wyden | Y | Y | Y | N | Y | N | Y | Y |
| 4 DeFazio | Y | ? | Y | N | Y | Y | Y | Y |
| 5 Kopetski | Y | Y | N | N | Y | N | Y | Y |
| **PENNSYLVANIA** | | | | | | | | |
| 1 Foglietta | Y | Y | Y | N | Y | N | Y | Y |
| 2 Blackwell | Y | Y | Y | N | Y | N | Y | Y |
| 3 Borski | Y | Y | Y | N | Y | N | Y | Y |
| 4 Kolter | Y | Y | Y | N | Y | Y | Y | Y |
| 5 ***Schulze*** | N | N | Y | Y | N | N | N | Y |
| 6 Yatron | Y | + | Y | N | Y | N | Y | Y |
| 7 ***Weldon*** | N | N | Y | Y | Y | N | N | N |
| 8 Kostmayer | Y | Y | Y | N | Y | Y | Y | Y |
| 9 ***Shuster*** | N | N | N | Y | N | N | N | Y |
| 10 ***McDade*** | N | Y | N | Y | N | Y | Y | Y |
| 11 Kanjorski | Y | Y | Y | N | Y | N | Y | Y |
| 12 Murtha | Y | Y | Y | N | Y | Y | Y | Y |
| 13 ***Coughlin*** | N | Y | ? | Y | Y | N | Y | Y |
| 14 Coyne | Y | Y | Y | N | Y | N | Y | Y |
| 15 ***Ritter*** | N | N | Y | Y | N | N | N | N |
| 16 ***Walker*** | N | N | Y | Y | N | N | N | N |
| 17 ***Gekas*** | N | N | N | Y | N | N | N | N |
| 18 ***Santorum*** | N | Y | Y | Y | N | N | N | N |
| 19 ***Goodling*** | N | Y | Y | Y | N | N | Y | N |
| 20 Gaydos | Y | Y | N | N | Y | N | Y | Y |
| 21 ***Ridge*** | N | N | Y | Y | N | N | ? | N |
| 22 Murphy | Y | Y | Y | N | Y | N | Y | Y |
| 23 ***Clinger*** | N | Y | N | Y | N | N | Y | Y |
| **RHODE ISLAND** | | | | | | | | |
| 1 ***Machtley*** | N | Y | Y | Y | Y | N | Y | N |
| 2 Reed | Y | Y | Y | N | Y | N | Y | N |
| **SOUTH CAROLINA** | | | | | | | | |
| 1 ***Ravenel*** | N | Y | Y | Y | Y | N | N | N |
| 2 ***Spence*** | N | N | Y | Y | N | N | N | N |
| 3 Derrick | Y | Y | Y | N | Y | N | N | N |
| 4 Patterson | N | Y | Y | N | N | N | N | N |
| 5 Spratt | Y | Y | Y | N | Y | N | Y | Y |
| 6 Tallon | N | ? | Y | N | Y | N | N | N |

| | 439 | 440 | 441 | 442 | 443 | 444 | 445 | 446 |
|---|---|---|---|---|---|---|---|---|
| **SOUTH DAKOTA** | | | | | | | | |
| AL Johnson | N | Y | N | N | Y | N | Y | Y |
| **TENNESSEE** | | | | | | | | |
| 1 ***Quillen*** | N | N | N | Y | N | N | N | Y |
| 2 ***Duncan*** | N | N | Y | Y | N | N | N | N |
| 3 Lloyd | Y | Y | Y | N | N | N | N | N |
| 4 Cooper | N | Y | Y | N | Y | N | Y | Y |
| 5 Clement | N | Y | Y | N | Y | Y | Y | Y |
| 6 Gordon | Y | Y | Y | N | Y | N | Y | Y |
| 7 ***Sundquist*** | N | N | N | Y | N | N | N | Y |
| 8 Tanner | N | Y | Y | N | N | N | Y | N |
| 9 Ford | ? | ? | ? | ? | Y | N | N | N |
| **TEXAS** | | | | | | | | |
| 1 Chapman | Y | Y | Y | N | Y | N | N | N |
| 2 Wilson | N | Y | Y | N | Y | N | Y | Y |
| 3 ***Johnson*** | N | N | Y | Y | N | N | N | N |
| 4 Hall | Y | Y | Y | Y | N | N | N | N |
| 5 Bryant | Y | Y | Y | N | Y | N | Y | Y |
| 6 ***Barton*** | N | N | Y | Y | N | N | N | Y |
| 7 ***Archer*** | N | N | N | Y | N | N | N | N |
| 8 ***Fields*** | N | N | Y | Y | N | N | N | N |
| 9 Brooks | Y | Y | Y | N | Y | N | N | N |
| 10 Pickle | N | Y | Y | N | Y | Y | N | Y |
| 11 Edwards | Y | Y | Y | N | N | N | Y | Y |
| 12 Geren | N | Y | Y | N | N | N | N | N |
| 13 Sarpalius | Y | Y | Y | N | N | N | N | Y |
| 14 Laughlin | Y | Y | Y | N | N | N | N | N |
| 15 de la Garza | Y | Y | Y | N | Y | Y | Y | Y |
| 16 Coleman | Y | Y | Y | N | Y | N | Y | Y |
| 17 Stenholm | Y | Y | Y | N | N | N | N | N |
| 18 Washington | Y | ? | Y | N | Y | N | Y | Y |
| 19 ***Combest*** | N | Y | Y | Y | N | N | N | Y |
| 20 Gonzalez | Y | Y | Y | N | Y | N | Y | Y |
| 21 ***Smith*** | N | N | Y | Y | Y | N | N | Y |
| 22 ***DeLay*** | N | N | N | Y | N | N | N | Y |
| 23 Bustamante | Y | Y | Y | N | Y | N | Y | Y |
| 24 Frost | Y | Y | Y | N | Y | Y | Y | Y |
| 25 Andrews | N | Y | Y | N | Y | N | N | Y |
| 26 ***Armey*** | N | N | N | Y | N | N | N | N |
| 27 Ortiz | Y | Y | Y | N | Y | Y | Y | Y |
| **UTAH** | | | | | | | | |
| 1 ***Hansen*** | N | N | N | Y | N | N | N | Y |
| 2 Owens | N | Y | Y | N | Y | N | Y | Y |
| 3 Orton | N | Y | Y | N | N | N | N | Y |
| **VERMONT** | | | | | | | | |
| AL *Sanders* | Y | Y | Y | N | Y | N | Y | Y |
| **VIRGINIA** | | | | | | | | |
| 1 ***Bateman*** | N | Y | N | Y | N | N | N | Y |
| 2 Pickett | Y | N | N | N | N | N | N | Y |
| 3 ***Bliley*** | N | Y | Y | Y | N | N | N | N |
| 4 Sisisky | N | Y | Y | N | N | N | N | Y |
| 5 Payne | N | Y | Y | N | N | N | N | Y |
| 6 Olin | ? | ? | Y | N | N | N | N | Y |
| 7 ***Allen*** | N | N | Y | Y | N | N | N | N |
| 8 Moran | Y | Y | Y | N | Y | N | Y | Y |
| 9 Boucher | Y | ? | Y | N | Y | N | Y | Y |
| 10 ***Wolf*** | N | Y | Y | Y | N | N | N | Y |
| **WASHINGTON** | | | | | | | | |
| 1 ***Miller*** | N | N | Y | Y | Y | N | N | Y |
| 2 Swift | Y | Y | Y | N | Y | Y | Y | Y |
| 3 Unsoeld | Y | Y | Y | N | Y | N | Y | Y |
| 4 ***Morrison*** | N | Y | Y | Y | Y | N | Y | Y |
| 5 Foley | | | | | | | | |
| 6 Dicks | Y | Y | Y | N | Y | N | Y | Y |
| 7 McDermott | Y | Y | Y | N | Y | Y | Y | Y |
| 8 ***Chandler*** | N | ? | Y | ? | N | N | N | ? |
| **WEST VIRGINIA** | | | | | | | | |
| 1 Mollohan | Y | Y | Y | N | Y | N | Y | Y |
| 2 Staggers | ? | ? | ? | ? | # | ? | ? | ? |
| 3 Wise | Y | Y | Y | N | Y | N | Y | Y |
| 4 Rahall | Y | Y | Y | N | Y | N | N | N |
| **WISCONSIN** | | | | | | | | |
| 1 Aspin | Y | Y | Y | N | N | N | Y | Y |
| 2 ***Klug*** | N | Y | Y | Y | Y | N | N | N |
| 3 ***Gunderson*** | N | Y | Y | Y | N | N | N | N |
| 4 Kleczka | Y | Y | Y | N | Y | Y | Y | Y |
| 5 Moody | Y | Y | Y | N | Y | Y | Y | Y |
| 6 ***Petri*** | N | N | Y | Y | N | N | N | N |
| 7 Obey | Y | Y | Y | N | Y | N | Y | Y |
| 8 ***Roth*** | N | N | N | Y | N | N | N | Y |
| 9 ***Sensenbrenner*** | N | N | Y | N | N | N | N | N |
| **WYOMING** | | | | | | | | |
| AL ***Thomas*** | N | N | Y | Y | N | Y | N | ? |

Southern states - Ala., Ark., Fla., Ga., Ky., La., Miss., N.C., Okla., S.C., Tenn., Texas, Va.
Omitted votes are quorum calls, which CQ does not include in its vote charts.

**447. S 1528. Mimbres Culture Monument.** Vento, D-Minn., motion to suspend the rules and pass the bill to establish the Mimbres Culture National Monument and to establish an archaeological protection system for Mimbres sites in New Mexico. Motion rejected 179-243: R 8-153; D 171-89 (ND 137-42, SD 34-47); I 0-1, Sept. 30, 1992. A two-thirds majority of those present and voting (282 in this case) was required for passage under suspension of the rules. A "nay" was a vote in support of the president's position.

**448. HR 5678. Fiscal 1993 Commerce, Justice, State, Judiciary Appropriations/Conference Report.** Adoption of the conference report to provide $23,214,927,000 in new budget authority for fiscal 1993 for the departments of Commerce, Justice and State, the Judiciary and related agencies. The administration requested $23,858,164,000. Adopted 302-117: R 71-91; D 231-26 (ND 156-20, SD 75-6); I 0-0, Oct. 1, 1992.

**449. HR 5488. Fiscal 1993 Treasury, Postal Service Appropriations/Conference Report.** Adoption of the conference report to provide $22,562,042,000 for the Treasury Department, the U.S. Postal Service, the Executive Office of the President and certain independent agencies for fiscal 1993. The administration requested $22,374,481,000. Adopted 291-126: R 59-103; D 232-23 (ND 158-16, SD 74-7); I 0-0, Oct. 1, 1992.

**450. HR 5192. Veterans Health-Care Amendments/Tobacco Products.** Wise, D-W.Va., amendment to the Penny, D-Minn., amendment to allow the Department of Veterans Affairs (VA) to ban the sale of tobacco products at VA facilities but require those facilities to provide indoor designated smoking areas. (The Penny amendment would have struck provisions that would block the VA from banning the sale of tobacco products and require the VA to provide indoor designated smoking areas. The bill, as amended by the Wise amendment, subsequently was passed by voice vote.) Adopted 338-71: R 135-25; D 202-46 (ND 130-38, SD 72-8); I 1-0, Oct. 1, 1992.

**451. HR 5095. Fiscal 1993 Intelligence Authorization/Rule.** Adoption of the rule (H Res 587) to waive points of order against and provide for House floor consideration of the conference report to authorize a classified amount for U.S. intelligence and intelligence-related activities in fiscal 1993. Adopted 399-2: R 159-1; D 239-1 (ND 161-0, SD 78-1); I 1-0, Oct. 2, 1992.

**452. S 323. Family Planning Amendments/Veto Override.** Passage, over President Bush's veto Sept. 25, of the bill to reauthorize Title X of the Public Health Service Act through fiscal 1997. The bill would overturn the administration's "gag rule" and require women with unintended pregnancies to receive "non-directive counseling" on all options, including abortion. Rejected 266-148: R 56-107; D 209-41 (ND 145-24, SD 64-17); I 1-0, Oct. 2, 1992. A two-thirds majority of those present and voting (276 in this case) was required to override a veto. A "nay" was a vote supporting the president's position.

**453. HR 5427. Fiscal 1993 Legislative Branch Appropriations/Instruct Conferees.** Lewis, R-Calif., motion to instruct the House conferees on the fiscal 1993 legislative branch appropriations bill to accept the Senate amendment to reduce funding for the legislative branch by 15 percent over three years from the fiscal 1992 level. Motion agreed to 402-1: R 157-0; D 244-1 (ND 166-0, SD 78-1); I 1-0, Oct. 2, 1992.

**454. H Res 591. Expedited Consideration of Legislation.** Adoption of the rule (H Res 591) to waive certain rules for expedited consideration of legislation. The rule would waive the requirement of a two-thirds majority vote for rules considered the same day that they were reported, allow the consideration of legislation after two hours' notice and allow the Speaker to declare recesses at any time. Adopted 316-93: R 72-87; D 243-6 (ND 164-5, SD 79-1); I 1-0, Oct. 2, 1992.

## KEY

Y Voted for (yea).
# Paired for.
+ Announced for.
N Voted against (nay).
X Paired against.
− Announced against.
P Voted "present."
C Voted "present" to avoid possible conflict of interest.
? Did not vote or otherwise make a position known.

Democrats *Republicans*
*Independent*

| | 447 | 448 | 449 | 450 | 451 | 452 | 453 | 454 |
|---|---|---|---|---|---|---|---|---|
| **ALABAMA** | | | | | | | | |
| 1 *Callahan* | N | N | N | Y | Y | N | Y | N |
| 2 *Dickinson* | N | N | N | Y | Y | Y | Y | Y |
| 3 Browder | N | Y | Y | Y | Y | Y | Y | Y |
| 4 Bevill | N | Y | Y | Y | Y | Y | Y | Y |
| 5 Cramer | N | Y | Y | Y | Y | Y | Y | Y |
| 6 Erdreich | N | N | Y | Y | Y | Y | Y | Y |
| 7 Harris | N | Y | Y | Y | Y | Y | Y | Y |
| **ALASKA** | | | | | | | | |
| AL *Young* | N | N | Y | Y | ? | N | Y | Y |
| **ARIZONA** | | | | | | | | |
| 1 *Rhodes* | N | N | N | Y | Y | N | Y | N |
| 2 Pastor | Y | Y | Y | Y | Y | Y | Y | Y |
| 3 *Stump* | N | N | N | Y | N | N | Y | N |
| 4 *Kyl* | N | N | N | Y | N | N | Y | N |
| 5 *Kolbe* | N | Y | N | Y | Y | Y | Y | Y |
| **ARKANSAS** | | | | | | | | |
| 1 Alexander | Y | Y | Y | ? | Y | Y | ? | Y |
| 2 Thornton | Y | Y | Y | Y | Y | Y | Y | Y |
| 3 *Hammerschmidt* | N | Y | Y | Y | Y | N | Y | N |
| 4 Anthony | Y | ? | Y | Y | Y | Y | Y | Y |
| **CALIFORNIA** | | | | | | | | |
| 1 *Riggs* | N | Y | N | N | Y | Y | Y | N |
| 2 *Herger* | N | N | N | Y | N | Y | N | N |
| 3 Matsui | Y | Y | Y | ? | Y | Y | Y | Y |
| 4 Fazio | Y | Y | Y | Y | Y | Y | Y | Y |
| 5 Pelosi | Y | Y | Y | N | Y | Y | Y | Y |
| 6 Boxer | Y | Y | Y | ? | Y | Y | Y | Y |
| 7 Miller | Y | N | Y | N | Y | Y | Y | Y |
| 8 Dellums | Y | Y | Y | ? | Y | Y | Y | Y |
| 9 Stark | Y | N | N | N | Y | Y | Y | Y |
| 10 Edwards | Y | Y | Y | N | Y | Y | Y | Y |
| 11 Lantos | Y | Y | Y | Y | Y | Y | Y | Y |
| 12 *Campbell* | N | N | N | N | Y | Y | Y | N |
| 13 Mineta | Y | Y | Y | N | Y | Y | Y | Y |
| 14 *Doolittle* | N | N | N | N | Y | N | Y | N |
| 15 Condit | N | N | Y | Y | Y | Y | Y | Y |
| 16 Panetta | Y | Y | Y | Y | Y | Y | Y | Y |
| 17 Dooley | N | Y | Y | Y | Y | Y | Y | Y |
| 18 Lehman | N | Y | Y | Y | Y | Y | Y | Y |
| 19 *Lagomarsino* | N | N | N | Y | N | N | Y | N |
| 20 *Thomas* | N | N | N | Y | Y | Y | Y | Y |
| 21 *Gallegly* | N | N | N | Y | Y | N | Y | N |
| 22 *Moorhead* | N | N | N | Y | N | N | Y | N |
| 23 Beilenson | Y | Y | Y | N | Y | Y | Y | Y |
| 24 Waxman | Y | Y | Y | N | Y | Y | Y | Y |
| 25 Roybal | Y | Y | Y | N | Y | Y | Y | Y |
| 26 Berman | Y | Y | Y | Y | Y | Y | Y | Y |
| 27 Levine | Y | Y | Y | N | Y | Y | Y | Y |
| 28 Dixon | Y | Y | Y | ? | Y | Y | Y | Y |
| 29 Waters | Y | Y | Y | N | Y | Y | Y | Y |
| 30 Martinez | Y | Y | Y | Y | Y | Y | Y | Y |
| 31 Dymally | ? | ? | ? | ? | ? | ? | ? | ? |
| 32 Anderson | Y | Y | ? | Y | Y | Y | Y | Y |
| 33 *Dreier* | N | N | N | Y | N | N | Y | N |
| 34 Torres | Y | Y | Y | N | Y | Y | Y | Y |
| 35 *Lewis* | N | Y | Y | Y | Y | N | Y | Y |
| 36 Brown | Y | Y | Y | N | Y | Y | Y | Y |
| 37 *McCandless* | N | N | Y | N | Y | N | Y | Y |
| 38 *Dornan* | N | N | N | Y | N | N | Y | Y |
| 39 *Dannemeyer* | N | N | N | Y | N | N | Y | N |
| 40 *Cox* | N | N | ? | N | Y | N | Y | N |
| 41 *Lowery* | ? | Y | Y | Y | N | ? | Y | ? |

| | 447 | 448 | 449 | 450 | 451 | 452 | 453 | 454 |
|---|---|---|---|---|---|---|---|---|
| 42 *Rohrabacher* | N | N | N | Y | Y | N | Y | N |
| 43 *Packard* | N | N | N | Y | N | Y | N | N |
| 44 *Cunningham* | N | N | N | Y | Y | N | Y | N |
| 45 *Hunter* | N | N | N | Y | Y | N | Y | N |
| **COLORADO** | | | | | | | | |
| 1 Schroeder | Y | N | N | N | Y | Y | Y | Y |
| 2 Skaggs | N | Y | Y | Y | Y | Y | Y | Y |
| 3 Campbell | Y | N | N | Y | Y | Y | Y | Y |
| 4 *Allard* | N | N | N | Y | N | N | Y | N |
| 5 *Hefley* | N | N | N | Y | N | Y | N | N |
| 6 *Schaefer* | N | N | N | Y | Y | N | Y | N |
| **CONNECTICUT** | | | | | | | | |
| 1 Kennelly | N | Y | Y | N | Y | Y | Y | Y |
| 2 Gejdenson | Y | Y | Y | Y | Y | Y | Y | Y |
| 3 DeLauro | N | Y | Y | Y | Y | Y | Y | Y |
| 4 *Shays* | N | N | N | N | Y | Y | Y | Y |
| 5 *Franks* | N | Y | Y | Y | Y | Y | Y | N |
| 6 *Johnson* | N | Y | Y | N | Y | Y | Y | N |
| **DELAWARE** | | | | | | | | |
| AL Carper | Y | Y | Y | N | Y | Y | Y | Y |
| **FLORIDA** | | | | | | | | |
| 1 Hutto | N | Y | Y | Y | N | Y | Y | Y |
| 2 Peterson | N | Y | Y | Y | Y | N | Y | Y |
| 3 Bennett | Y | Y | Y | Y | N | Y | Y | Y |
| 4 *James* | N | N | N | Y | Y | N | Y | N |
| 5 *McCollum* | N | N | N | Y | Y | N | Y | N |
| 6 *Stearns* | N | N | N | Y | Y | N | Y | N |
| 7 Gibbons | Y | Y | Y | N | Y | Y | Y | Y |
| 8 *Young* | N | N | N | Y | Y | N | Y | N |
| 9 *Bilirakis* | N | N | N | Y | Y | N | Y | N |
| 10 *Ireland* | ? | Y | N | Y | N | Y | N | Y |
| 11 Bacchus | N | Y | Y | Y | Y | Y | Y | Y |
| 12 *Lewis* | N | N | N | Y | N | N | Y | N |
| 13 *Goss* | N | N | N | Y | N | N | Y | N |
| 14 Johnston | Y | Y | Y | N | Y | Y | Y | Y |
| 15 *Shaw* | N | Y | Y | Y | Y | N | Y | N |
| 16 Smith | Y | Y | Y | Y | Y | Y | Y | ? |
| 17 Lehman | Y | Y | Y | ? | Y | Y | Y | Y |
| 18 *Ros−Lehtinen* | N | Y | Y | Y | N | N | Y | N |
| 19 Fascell | Y | Y | Y | ? | Y | Y | Y | Y |
| **GEORGIA** | | | | | | | | |
| 1 Thomas | Y | Y | Y | Y | Y | Y | Y | Y |
| 2 Hatcher | N | Y | Y | Y | Y | Y | Y | Y |
| 3 Ray | N | Y | Y | Y | Y | Y | Y | Y |
| 4 Jones | Y | Y | Y | Y | Y | Y | Y | Y |
| 5 Lewis | Y | Y | N | Y | Y | Y | Y | Y |
| 6 *Gingrich* | ? | Y | N | Y | ? | N | Y | Y |
| 7 *Darden* | N | Y | Y | Y | Y | Y | Y | Y |
| 8 Rowland | N | Y | Y | Y | Y | Y | Y | Y |
| 9 Jenkins | ? | Y | Y | Y | Y | Y | Y | Y |
| 10 Barnard | ? | ? | ? | ? | ? | ? | ? | ? |
| **HAWAII** | | | | | | | | |
| 1 Abercrombie | Y | Y | Y | Y | Y | Y | Y | Y |
| 2 Mink | Y | Y | Y | Y | Y | Y | Y | Y |
| **IDAHO** | | | | | | | | |
| 1 LaRocco | Y | Y | Y | Y | Y | Y | Y | Y |
| 2 Stallings | N | N | Y | Y | Y | Y | Y | Y |
| **ILLINOIS** | | | | | | | | |
| 1 Hayes | Y | Y | Y | Y | Y | Y | Y | Y |
| 2 Savage | Y | Y | N | ? | Y | ? | Y | ? |
| 3 Russo | Y | Y | ? | Y | Y | Y | Y | ? |
| 4 Sangmeister | Y | Y | Y | Y | Y | Y | Y | Y |
| 5 Lipinski | N | ? | ? | ? | ? | ? | ? | ? |
| 6 *Hyde* | N | Y | ? | ? | Y | N | ? | N |
| 7 Collins | Y | Y | Y | Y | Y | Y | Y | Y |
| 8 Rostenkowski | Y | Y | Y | Y | Y | Y | Y | ? |
| 9 Yates | Y | Y | N | Y | Y | Y | Y | Y |
| 10 *Porter* | N | N | N | Y | Y | Y | Y | Y |
| 11 Annunzio | Y | Y | Y | Y | ? | N | Y | Y |
| 12 *Crane* | N | N | N | Y | N | N | Y | N |
| 13 *Fawell* | N | N | N | Y | Y | Y | Y | N |
| 14 *Hastert* | N | N | N | Y | N | N | Y | N |
| 15 *Ewing* | N | Y | N | Y | Y | N | Y | Y |
| 16 Cox | N | Y | Y | Y | Y | Y | Y | Y |
| 17 Evans | Y | Y | Y | Y | Y | Y | Y | Y |
| 18 *Michel* | N | Y | Y | Y | Y | N | Y | Y |
| 19 Bruce | Y | Y | Y | N | Y | Y | Y | Y |
| 20 Durbin | Y | Y | Y | Y | Y | Y | Y | Y |
| 21 Costello | N | Y | Y | Y | Y | N | Y | Y |
| 22 Poshard | Y | Y | Y | Y | Y | N | Y | Y |
| **INDIANA** | | | | | | | | |
| 1 Visclosky | Y | Y | Y | N | Y | Y | Y | Y |
| 2 Sharp | Y | N | Y | Y | Y | Y | Y | Y |
| 3 Roemer | N | N | N | Y | Y | N | Y | Y |

ND Northern Democrats   SD Southern Democrats

| | 447 | 448 | 449 | 450 | 451 | 452 | 453 | 454 |
|---|---|---|---|---|---|---|---|---|
| 4 Long | Y | Y | Y | Y | Y | Y | Y | Y |
| 5 Jontz | Y | N | N | Y | Y | Y | Y | Y |
| 6 Burton | N | N | N | Y | Y | N | Y | N |
| 7 Myers | N | Y | Y | Y | Y | N | Y | N |
| 8 McCloskey | Y | Y | Y | Y | Y | Y | Y | Y |
| 9 Hamilton | Y | Y | Y | Y | Y | Y | Y | Y |
| 10 Jacobs | N | N | N | N | Y | Y | Y | Y |
| **IOWA** | | | | | | | | |
| 1 Leach | N | N | N | Y | Y | Y | Y | Y |
| 2 Nussle | N | N | N | Y | Y | N | Y | N |
| 3 Nagle | N | Y | Y | Y | Y | Y | Y | Y |
| 4 Smith | N | Y | Y | Y | Y | Y | Y | Y |
| 5 Lightfoot | N | Y | Y | Y | Y | N | Y | Y |
| 6 Grandy | N | Y | Y | N | Y | N | Y | N |
| **KANSAS** | | | | | | | | |
| 1 Roberts | N | N | N | Y | Y | N | Y | N |
| 2 Slattery | N | Y | N | Y | Y | Y | Y | Y |
| 3 Meyers | N | Y | N | Y | Y | Y | Y | Y |
| 4 Glickman | N | N | Y | N | Y | Y | Y | Y |
| 5 Nichols | N | N | N | Y | Y | Y | Y | N |
| **KENTUCKY** | | | | | | | | |
| 1 Hubbard | N | N | N | Y | Y | Y | Y | Y |
| 2 Natcher | Y | Y | Y | Y | Y | Y | Y | Y |
| 3 Mazzoli | Y | Y | Y | N | Y | N | Y | Y |
| 4 Bunning | N | N | N | Y | Y | N | Y | N |
| 5 Rogers | N | Y | Y | Y | Y | N | Y | Y |
| 6 Hopkins | N | N | N | Y | Y | N | Y | N |
| 7 Perkins | Y | Y | Y | Y | ? | N | Y | Y |
| **LOUISIANA** | | | | | | | | |
| 1 Livingston | Y | Y | Y | Y | Y | N | Y | Y |
| 2 Jefferson | N | Y | Y | Y | Y | Y | Y | Y |
| 3 Tauzin | N | Y | Y | Y | Y | N | Y | Y |
| 4 McCrery | ? | ? | ? | ? | ? | X | ? | ? |
| 5 Huckaby | ? | ? | ? | ? | ? | ? | ? | ? |
| 6 Baker | N | N | N | Y | Y | N | Y | N |
| 7 Hayes | N | Y | Y | Y | Y | N | ? | Y |
| 8 Holloway | N | N | N | Y | Y | N | ? | ? |
| **MAINE** | | | | | | | | |
| 1 Andrews | N | Y | Y | Y | Y | Y | Y | Y |
| 2 Snowe | N | N | N | Y | Y | Y | Y | N |
| **MARYLAND** | | | | | | | | |
| 1 Gilchrest | N | Y | Y | Y | Y | Y | Y | Y |
| 2 Bentley | N | Y | Y | Y | Y | Y | Y | N |
| 3 Cardin | Y | Y | Y | N | Y | Y | Y | Y |
| 4 McMillen | N | Y | Y | Y | Y | Y | Y | Y |
| 5 Hoyer | Y | Y | Y | Y | Y | Y | Y | Y |
| 6 Byron | N | Y | Y | Y | Y | Y | Y | Y |
| 7 Mfume | N | Y | Y | Y | Y | Y | Y | Y |
| 8 Morella | Y | Y | Y | N | Y | Y | Y | Y |
| **MASSACHUSETTS** | | | | | | | | |
| 1 Olver | Y | Y | Y | N | Y | Y | Y | Y |
| 2 Neal | Y | Y | Y | Y | Y | Y | Y | Y |
| 3 Early | Y | Y | Y | Y | Y | Y | Y | Y |
| 4 Frank | Y | Y | Y | Y | Y | Y | Y | Y |
| 5 Atkins | Y | Y | ? | N | Y | Y | Y | Y |
| 6 Mavroules | Y | Y | Y | ? | ? | ? | Y | Y |
| 7 Markey | Y | Y | Y | Y | Y | Y | Y | Y |
| 8 Kennedy | Y | Y | Y | N | Y | Y | Y | Y |
| 9 Moakley | N | Y | Y | Y | Y | Y | Y | Y |
| 10 Studds | Y | Y | Y | Y | Y | Y | Y | Y |
| 11 Donnelly | Y | Y | Y | Y | Y | Y | Y | Y |
| **MICHIGAN** | | | | | | | | |
| 1 Conyers | Y | Y | Y | Y | Y | ? | Y | N |
| 2 Pursell | N | Y | Y | N | Y | Y | Y | Y |
| 3 Wolpe | Y | Y | Y | N | Y | Y | Y | Y |
| 4 Upton | N | Y | N | N | Y | Y | Y | N |
| 5 Henry | N | N | N | N | Y | N | ? | ? |
| 6 Carr | N | Y | Y | Y | Y | Y | Y | N |
| 7 Kildee | Y | Y | Y | Y | Y | N | Y | Y |
| 8 Traxler | Y | Y | Y | Y | ? | Y | ? | Y |
| 9 Vander Jagt | N | Y | Y | Y | Y | N | Y | N |
| 10 Camp | N | Y | N | Y | Y | N | Y | Y |
| 11 Davis | Y | Y | Y | Y | Y | ? | ? | Y |
| 12 Bonior | Y | Y | Y | Y | Y | Y | Y | Y |
| 13 Collins | Y | Y | Y | Y | Y | Y | Y | Y |
| 14 Hertel | Y | Y | Y | Y | Y | Y | Y | Y |
| 15 Ford | Y | Y | Y | Y | Y | Y | ? | Y |
| 16 Dingell | N | Y | Y | Y | Y | Y | Y | Y |
| 17 Levin | Y | Y | Y | Y | Y | Y | Y | Y |
| 18 Broomfield | N | Y | Y | N | Y | N | Y | Y |
| **MINNESOTA** | | | | | | | | |
| 1 Penny | N | N | Y | N | Y | Y | Y | Y |
| 2 Weber | N | Y | N | N | Y | N | Y | N |
| 3 Ramstad | N | N | N | Y | Y | Y | Y | N |
| 4 Vento | Y | N | N | N | Y | Y | Y | Y |

| | 447 | 448 | 449 | 450 | 451 | 452 | 453 | 454 |
|---|---|---|---|---|---|---|---|---|
| 5 Sabo | Y | Y | Y | Y | Y | Y | Y | Y |
| 6 Sikorski | Y | N | Y | Y | Y | Y | Y | Y |
| 7 Peterson | N | N | N | Y | Y | N | Y | Y |
| 8 Oberstar | Y | Y | Y | Y | Y | N | Y | Y |
| **MISSISSIPPI** | | | | | | | | |
| 1 Whitten | Y | Y | Y | Y | Y | N | Y | Y |
| 2 Espy | Y | Y | Y | Y | Y | Y | Y | Y |
| 3 Montgomery | N | Y | Y | Y | Y | N | Y | Y |
| 4 Parker | Y | Y | Y | Y | Y | N | Y | Y |
| 5 Taylor | N | Y | Y | Y | Y | N | Y | Y |
| **MISSOURI** | | | | | | | | |
| 1 Clay | Y | Y | Y | Y | ? | Y | Y | Y |
| 2 Horn | Y | Y | Y | Y | Y | Y | Y | Y |
| 3 Gephardt | Y | Y | Y | Y | Y | Y | ? | Y |
| 4 Skelton | N | Y | Y | Y | Y | N | Y | Y |
| 5 Wheat | Y | Y | Y | Y | Y | Y | Y | Y |
| 6 Coleman | N | N | N | Y | Y | Y | Y | N |
| 7 Hancock | N | N | N | Y | Y | N | Y | N |
| 8 Emerson | N | Y | Y | Y | Y | N | Y | N |
| 9 Volkmer | N | Y | Y | Y | Y | N | Y | Y |
| **MONTANA** | | | | | | | | |
| 1 Williams | Y | Y | N | Y | Y | Y | Y | Y |
| 2 Marlenee | N | N | N | Y | Y | N | Y | N |
| **NEBRASKA** | | | | | | | | |
| 1 Bereuter | Y | Y | Y | Y | Y | Y | Y | N |
| 2 Hoagland | Y | Y | Y | Y | Y | Y | Y | Y |
| 3 Barrett | N | Y | Y | Y | Y | N | Y | Y |
| **NEVADA** | | | | | | | | |
| 1 Bilbray | Y | Y | Y | Y | Y | Y | Y | N |
| 2 Vucanovich | N | Y | Y | Y | Y | N | Y | N |
| **NEW HAMPSHIRE** | | | | | | | | |
| 1 Zeliff | N | N | N | Y | Y | Y | Y | N |
| 2 Swett | N | Y | Y | Y | Y | Y | Y | Y |
| **NEW JERSEY** | | | | | | | | |
| 1 Andrews | N | Y | Y | Y | Y | Y | Y | Y |
| 2 Hughes | Y | Y | N | Y | Y | Y | Y | Y |
| 3 Pallone | Y | N | N | Y | Y | Y | Y | Y |
| 4 Smith | N | Y | Y | N | Y | N | Y | N |
| 5 Roukema | N | N | Y | Y | Y | Y | Y | Y |
| 6 Dwyer | Y | Y | Y | ? | Y | Y | Y | Y |
| 7 Rinaldo | N | Y | Y | ? | Y | N | Y | Y |
| 8 Roe | Y | Y | Y | Y | Y | N | Y | Y |
| 9 Torricelli | Y | Y | Y | ? | Y | Y | Y | Y |
| 10 Payne | Y | Y | Y | Y | Y | Y | Y | Y |
| 11 Gallo | N | Y | Y | Y | Y | Y | Y | Y |
| 12 Zimmer | N | N | N | Y | Y | Y | Y | N |
| 13 Saxton | N | ? | N | Y | Y | N | Y | Y |
| 14 Guarini | N | ? | Y | Y | ? | # | ? | Y |
| **NEW MEXICO** | | | | | | | | |
| 1 Schiff | N | Y | Y | Y | Y | Y | Y | N |
| 2 Skeen | N | Y | Y | Y | Y | Y | Y | Y |
| 3 Richardson | Y | Y | Y | Y | Y | Y | Y | Y |
| **NEW YORK** | | | | | | | | |
| 1 Hochbrueckner | Y | Y | Y | Y | Y | Y | Y | Y |
| 2 Downey | Y | Y | Y | N | Y | Y | Y | Y |
| 3 Mrazek | Y | Y | Y | N | Y | Y | Y | Y |
| 4 Lent | N | Y | Y | Y | Y | N | Y | Y |
| 5 McGrath | N | N | Y | Y | Y | N | Y | Y |
| 6 Flake | N | Y | Y | Y | ? | # | ? | ? |
| 7 Ackerman | Y | Y | Y | Y | Y | Y | Y | Y |
| 8 Scheuer | Y | Y | Y | N | Y | Y | Y | Y |
| 9 Manton | Y | Y | Y | Y | Y | N | Y | Y |
| 10 Schumer | Y | Y | Y | Y | Y | Y | Y | Y |
| 11 Towns | Y | Y | Y | Y | ? | # | Y | Y |
| 12 Owens | Y | Y | Y | Y | Y | Y | Y | Y |
| 13 Solarz | Y | Y | Y | Y | Y | Y | Y | Y |
| 14 Molinari | N | N | N | Y | Y | Y | Y | Y |
| 15 Green | N | Y | Y | Y | Y | Y | Y | Y |
| 16 Rangel | Y | Y | Y | Y | Y | Y | Y | Y |
| 17 Vacancy | | | | | | | | |
| 18 Serrano | Y | Y | Y | N | Y | Y | ? | Y |
| 19 Engel | Y | Y | Y | Y | Y | Y | Y | Y |
| 20 Lowey | Y | Y | Y | Y | Y | Y | Y | Y |
| 21 Fish | N | Y | N | Y | Y | Y | Y | Y |
| 22 Gilman | N | Y | Y | Y | Y | Y | Y | Y |
| 23 McNulty | Y | Y | Y | Y | Y | Y | Y | Y |
| 24 Solomon | N | N | Y | Y | Y | N | Y | Y |
| 25 Boehlert | N | Y | Y | Y | Y | Y | Y | Y |
| 26 Martin | N | Y | Y | Y | Y | Y | Y | Y |
| 27 Walsh | N | N | Y | Y | Y | N | Y | Y |
| 28 McHugh | Y | Y | Y | Y | Y | Y | Y | Y |
| 29 Horton | N | Y | Y | Y | Y | Y | Y | Y |
| 30 Slaughter | N | Y | Y | Y | Y | Y | Y | Y |
| 31 Paxon | N | Y | N | Y | Y | N | Y | N |

| | 447 | 448 | 449 | 450 | 451 | 452 | 453 | 454 |
|---|---|---|---|---|---|---|---|---|
| 32 LaFalce | Y | Y | Y | N | Y | N | Y | Y |
| 33 Nowak | Y | Y | Y | Y | Y | N | Y | ? |
| 34 Houghton | Y | Y | Y | ? | Y | Y | Y | Y |
| **NORTH CAROLINA** | | | | | | | | |
| 1 Vacancy | | | | | | | | |
| 2 Valentine | N | Y | Y | Y | Y | Y | Y | Y |
| 3 Lancaster | N | Y | Y | Y | Y | Y | Y | Y |
| 4 Price | Y | Y | Y | Y | Y | Y | Y | Y |
| 5 Neal | N | N | N | Y | Y | Y | Y | N |
| 6 Coble | N | N | N | Y | Y | N | Y | Y |
| 7 Rose | Y | Y | Y | Y | Y | Y | Y | Y |
| 8 Hefner | Y | Y | Y | Y | Y | Y | Y | Y |
| 9 McMillan | N | N | N | Y | Y | Y | Y | Y |
| 10 Ballenger | N | N | N | Y | Y | Y | Y | N |
| 11 Taylor | N | N | Y | Y | Y | N | Y | N |
| **NORTH DAKOTA** | | | | | | | | |
| AL Dorgan | N | N | N | Y | Y | Y | Y | Y |
| **OHIO** | | | | | | | | |
| 1 Luken | N | Y | N | N | Y | N | Y | Y |
| 2 Gradison | N | N | N | N | Y | Y | Y | Y |
| 3 Hall | Y | Y | N | Y | ? | ? | ? | ? |
| 4 Oxley | N | Y | N | Y | Y | N | Y | N |
| 5 Gillmor | N | Y | N | Y | Y | N | Y | N |
| 6 McEwen | N | N | N | Y | Y | N | Y | N |
| 7 Hobson | Y | N | N | Y | Y | N | Y | Y |
| 8 Boehner | N | N | N | Y | Y | N | Y | N |
| 9 Kaptur | Y | Y | Y | Y | ? | # | ? | ? |
| 10 Miller | N | N | N | Y | Y | N | Y | N |
| 11 Eckart | Y | Y | Y | N | Y | Y | Y | Y |
| 12 Kasich | N | N | N | N | Y | N | Y | Y |
| 13 Pease | Y | ? | Y | Y | Y | Y | Y | Y |
| 14 Sawyer | Y | Y | Y | Y | Y | Y | Y | Y |
| 15 Wylie | N | Y | N | N | Y | N | Y | Y |
| 16 Regula | N | Y | N | Y | Y | Y | Y | Y |
| 17 Traficant | Y | Y | Y | Y | Y | Y | Y | Y |
| 18 Applegate | N | Y | Y | ? | Y | N | Y | Y |
| 19 Feighan | Y | Y | ? | Y | ? | Y | Y | Y |
| 20 Oakar | Y | Y | Y | Y | Y | N | Y | Y |
| 21 Stokes | Y | Y | Y | Y | Y | Y | Y | Y |
| **OKLAHOMA** | | | | | | | | |
| 1 Inhofe | N | N | Y | Y | Y | N | Y | N |
| 2 Synar | Y | Y | Y | N | Y | Y | Y | Y |
| 3 Brewster | N | Y | N | Y | Y | Y | Y | Y |
| 4 McCurdy | N | Y | ? | N | Y | Y | Y | Y |
| 5 Edwards | N | Y | Y | ? | ? | N | ? | Y |
| 6 English | N | N | Y | Y | Y | Y | Y | Y |
| **OREGON** | | | | | | | | |
| 1 AuCoin | Y | Y | Y | Y | Y | Y | Y | Y |
| 2 Smith | N | N | N | Y | Y | N | Y | N |
| 3 Wyden | Y | Y | Y | N | Y | Y | Y | Y |
| 4 DeFazio | Y | Y | Y | Y | Y | Y | Y | Y |
| 5 Kopetski | Y | Y | Y | Y | Y | Y | Y | Y |
| **PENNSYLVANIA** | | | | | | | | |
| 1 Foglietta | Y | Y | Y | Y | ? | ? | ? | ? |
| 2 Blackwell | Y | Y | Y | Y | ? | ? | ? | ? |
| 3 Borski | Y | Y | Y | Y | Y | N | Y | Y |
| 4 Kolter | Y | Y | Y | Y | ? | ? | Y | Y |
| 5 Schulze | N | N | Y | Y | Y | N | Y | N |
| 6 Yatron | Y | Y | Y | Y | Y | N | Y | Y |
| 7 Weldon | N | N | N | Y | Y | N | Y | Y |
| 8 Kostmayer | Y | Y | Y | Y | Y | Y | Y | Y |
| 9 Shuster | N | ? | N | Y | Y | N | Y | Y |
| 10 McDade | N | Y | Y | Y | Y | N | Y | Y |
| 11 Kanjorski | N | Y | Y | Y | Y | N | Y | Y |
| 12 Murtha | Y | Y | Y | ? | Y | N | Y | Y |
| 13 Coughlin | N | Y | Y | Y | Y | Y | Y | ? |
| 14 Coyne | Y | Y | Y | Y | Y | Y | Y | Y |
| 15 Ritter | N | Y | N | Y | Y | N | Y | N |
| 16 Walker | N | N | N | Y | Y | N | Y | N |
| 17 Gekas | N | Y | N | Y | Y | Y | Y | N |
| 18 Santorum | N | N | N | Y | Y | N | Y | N |
| 19 Goodling | N | — | — | Y | Y | N | Y | N |
| 20 Gaydos | N | Y | Y | Y | ? | N | Y | Y |
| 21 Ridge | N | N | N | Y | Y | Y | Y | Y |
| 22 Murphy | Y | N | Y | Y | Y | N | Y | Y |
| 23 Clinger | N | Y | Y | Y | Y | Y | Y | Y |
| **RHODE ISLAND** | | | | | | | | |
| 1 Machtley | Y | Y | Y | N | Y | Y | Y | Y |
| 2 Reed | N | Y | Y | N | Y | Y | Y | Y |
| **SOUTH CAROLINA** | | | | | | | | |
| 1 Ravenel | N | Y | Y | Y | Y | Y | Y | Y |
| 2 Spence | N | Y | N | Y | Y | N | Y | N |
| 3 Derrick | N | Y | Y | Y | Y | Y | Y | Y |
| 4 Patterson | N | Y | N | Y | Y | Y | Y | Y |
| 5 Spratt | N | Y | Y | Y | Y | Y | Y | Y |
| 6 Tallon | N | N | N | Y | Y | N | Y | Y |

| | 447 | 448 | 449 | 450 | 451 | 452 | 453 | 454 |
|---|---|---|---|---|---|---|---|---|
| **SOUTH DAKOTA** | | | | | | | | |
| AL Johnson | Y | Y | Y | Y | Y | Y | Y | Y |
| **TENNESSEE** | | | | | | | | |
| 1 Quillen | N | Y | Y | Y | Y | N | Y | Y |
| 2 Duncan | N | N | N | Y | Y | N | Y | N |
| 3 Lloyd | N | Y | Y | Y | Y | Y | Y | Y |
| 4 Cooper | Y | Y | Y | Y | Y | Y | Y | Y |
| 5 Clement | N | Y | Y | Y | Y | Y | Y | Y |
| 6 Gordon | Y | Y | Y | Y | Y | Y | Y | Y |
| 7 Sundquist | N | Y | Y | Y | Y | N | Y | N |
| 8 Tanner | N | Y | Y | Y | Y | Y | Y | Y |
| 9 Ford | N | Y | Y | Y | Y | Y | Y | Y |
| **TEXAS** | | | | | | | | |
| 1 Chapman | N | Y | Y | Y | Y | Y | Y | Y |
| 2 Wilson | N | Y | Y | Y | Y | Y | Y | Y |
| 3 Johnson | N | N | N | Y | Y | N | Y | N |
| 4 Hall | N | Y | Y | Y | Y | N | Y | Y |
| 5 Bryant | N | Y | Y | Y | Y | Y | Y | Y |
| 6 Barton | N | N | N | Y | Y | N | Y | N |
| 7 Archer | N | N | N | Y | Y | N | Y | N |
| 8 Fields | N | N | N | Y | Y | N | Y | N |
| 9 Brooks | N | Y | Y | Y | Y | Y | Y | Y |
| 10 Pickle | N | Y | Y | Y | Y | Y | Y | Y |
| 11 Edwards | N | Y | Y | Y | Y | Y | Y | Y |
| 12 Geren | N | Y | Y | Y | Y | Y | Y | Y |
| 13 Sarpalius | N | N | N | Y | Y | N | Y | Y |
| 14 Laughlin | N | Y | Y | Y | Y | Y | Y | Y |
| 15 de la Garza | Y | Y | Y | Y | Y | N | Y | Y |
| 16 Coleman | Y | Y | Y | Y | Y | Y | Y | Y |
| 17 Stenholm | N | Y | Y | Y | Y | N | Y | Y |
| 18 Washington | Y | Y | Y | N | N | Y | N | Y |
| 19 Combest | N | N | N | Y | Y | N | Y | Y |
| 20 Gonzalez | Y | Y | Y | Y | Y | Y | Y | Y |
| 21 Smith | N | N | N | Y | Y | Y | Y | Y |
| 22 DeLay | N | N | N | Y | Y | N | Y | N |
| 23 Bustamante | Y | Y | Y | Y | ? | ? | ? | ? |
| 24 Frost | N | Y | Y | Y | Y | Y | Y | Y |
| 25 Andrews | Y | Y | Y | N | Y | Y | Y | Y |
| 26 Armey | N | N | N | Y | Y | N | Y | N |
| 27 Ortiz | Y | Y | Y | Y | Y | N | Y | Y |
| **UTAH** | | | | | | | | |
| 1 Hansen | N | N | N | N | Y | N | Y | Y |
| 2 Owens | Y | N | Y | ? | Y | Y | Y | Y |
| 3 Orton | N | N | N | N | Y | N | Y | Y |
| **VERMONT** | | | | | | | | |
| AL Sanders | N | + | + | Y | Y | Y | Y | Y |
| **VIRGINIA** | | | | | | | | |
| 1 Bateman | N | Y | Y | Y | Y | N | Y | Y |
| 2 Pickett | N | Y | Y | Y | Y | Y | Y | Y |
| 3 Bliley | N | Y | Y | Y | Y | N | Y | Y |
| 4 Sisisky | N | Y | Y | Y | Y | Y | Y | Y |
| 5 Payne | N | Y | Y | Y | Y | Y | Y | Y |
| 6 Olin | N | Y | Y | Y | Y | Y | Y | Y |
| 7 Allen | N | N | N | Y | Y | Y | Y | N |
| 8 Moran | Y | Y | Y | Y | Y | Y | Y | Y |
| 9 Boucher | Y | Y | Y | Y | Y | Y | Y | Y |
| 10 Wolf | N | Y | Y | Y | Y | N | Y | Y |
| **WASHINGTON** | | | | | | | | |
| 1 Miller | N | Y | N | Y | Y | Y | Y | Y |
| 2 Swift | Y | Y | Y | Y | Y | Y | Y | Y |
| 3 Unsoeld | Y | Y | Y | Y | Y | Y | Y | Y |
| 4 Morrison | N | Y | Y | Y | Y | Y | Y | Y |
| 5 Foley | | | | | | Y | | |
| 6 Dicks | Y | Y | Y | Y | Y | Y | Y | Y |
| 7 McDermott | Y | Y | Y | N | Y | Y | Y | Y |
| 8 Chandler | ? | Y | Y | N | ? | Y | ? | ? |
| **WEST VIRGINIA** | | | | | | | | |
| 1 Mollohan | Y | Y | Y | Y | Y | N | Y | Y |
| 2 Staggers | ? | ? | ? | ? | ? | ? | ? | ? |
| 3 Wise | Y | Y | Y | Y | Y | Y | Y | Y |
| 4 Rahall | Y | Y | Y | Y | Y | N | Y | Y |
| **WISCONSIN** | | | | | | | | |
| 1 Aspin | Y | Y | Y | Y | Y | Y | Y | Y |
| 2 Klug | N | N | N | Y | Y | Y | Y | ? |
| 3 Gunderson | N | Y | Y | Y | Y | N | Y | Y |
| 4 Kleczka | Y | Y | Y | Y | ? | Y | Y | Y |
| 5 Moody | Y | Y | Y | Y | Y | Y | Y | Y |
| 6 Petri | N | N | N | Y | Y | N | Y | Y |
| 7 Obey | Y | Y | Y | Y | Y | Y | Y | Y |
| 8 Roth | N | N | N | Y | Y | N | Y | N |
| 9 Sensenbrenner | N | N | N | N | + | X | + | — |
| **WYOMING** | | | | | | | | |
| AL Thomas | N | N | N | Y | Y | Y | Y | N |

Southern states - Ala., Ark., Fla., Ga., Ky., La., Miss., N.C., Okla., S.C., Tenn., Texas, Va.
Omitted votes are quorum calls, which CQ does not include in its vote charts.

**455. S 1696. Montana Wilderness/Passage.** Passage of the bill to designate 1.5 million acres in Montana as wilderness, restricting it from development or park use; release about 3.6 million acres for multiple-use activities; and create new wilderness study and national recreation areas. Passed 282-123: R 52-105; D 229-18 (ND 155-15, SD 74-3); I 1-0, Oct. 2, 1992. A 'nay' was a vote in support of the president's position.

**456. H Res 585. Investigation of Iranian Hostage Release.** Adoption of the resolution to provide for the completion of the activities of the task force to investigate allegations that the 1980 Reagan campaign conspired to delay the release of 52 American hostages in Iran until after the 1980 election so the Carter administration would be unable to benefit from a pre-election hostage release, or "October Surprise." The resolution would waive normal funding requirements for the task force and limit expenditures to $1.35 million. Adopted 221-181: R 0-153; D 220-28 (ND 162-9, SD 58-19); I 1-0, Oct. 2, 1992.

**457. HR 5677. Fiscal 1993 Labor, HHS, Education Appropriations/Conference Report.** Adoption of the conference report to provide $245,736,568,000 in new budget authority for the Departments of Labor, Health and Human Services, and Education and related agencies, $207.5 billion in fiscal 1993, $37.9 billion in fiscal 1994 and $292.6 million in fiscal 1995. The administration requested $244,419,291,000. Adopted 363-47: R 112-46; D 250-1 (ND 173-0, SD 77-1); I 1-0, Oct. 3, 1992.

**458. S 3144. Abortion in Military Medical Facilities/Passage.** Passage of the bill to allow military personnel and their dependents to receive abortions at overseas military facilities at their own expense. Passed (thus clearing the bill for the president) 220-186: R 35-121; D 184-65 (ND 129-44, SD 55-21); I 1-0, Oct. 3, 1992. A 'nay' was a vote in support of the president's position.

**459. HR 2164. Expedited Consideration of Proposed Rescissions.** Derrick, D-S.C., motion to suspend the rules and pass the bill to require the House to vote within 10 days on any rescission proposed by the president within three days of signing an appropriations bill. If the House approved the rescission, the Senate also would be required to vote. The requirement would be valid only during the 103rd Congress. The president could propose to rescind 100 percent of unauthorized programs and 25 percent of authorized programs. Motion agreed to 312-97: R 154-5; D 158-91 (ND 104-69, SD 54-22); I 0-1, Oct. 3, 1992. A two-thirds majority of those present and voting (273 in this case) was required for passage under suspension of the rules.

**460. S 2481. Indian Heath-Care Amendments.** Miller, D-Calif., motion to suspend the rules and pass the bill to reauthorize the programs and services of the Indian Health Care Service through fiscal 2000. Motion agreed to 335-74: R 93-67; D 241-7 (ND 173-0, SD 68-7); I 1-0, Oct. 3, 1992. A two-thirds majority of those present and voting (273 in this case) was required for passage under suspension of the rules.

**461. HR 5006. Fiscal 1993 Defense Authorization/Conference Report.** Adoption of the conference report to authorize $273.9 billion for defense programs in fiscal 1993, including $4.1 billion for the Strategic Defense Initiative and $2.7 billion to complete the B-2 bomber fleet at 20 planes. The bill would provide an authorization level less than the administration's proposal by $7 billion and the fiscal 1992 appropriated level by $16.4 billion. Adopted 304-100: R 119-40; D 185-59 (ND 118-51, SD 67-8); I 0-1, Oct. 3, 1992.

**462. S 2532. Russian Aid/Conference Report.** Adoption of the conference report to provide $1.4 billion in aid to the former republics of the Soviet Union. The bill also would increase the U.S. contribution to the International Monetary Fund by $12.3 billion. Adopted (thus clearing the bill for the president) 232-164: R 78-77; D 154-86 (ND 107-60, SD 47-26); I 0-1, Oct. 3, 1992. A "yea" was a vote in support of the president's position.

## KEY

| | |
|---|---|
| Y | Voted for (yea). |
| # | Paired for. |
| + | Announced for. |
| N | Voted against (nay). |
| X | Paired against. |
| − | Announced against. |
| P | Voted ''present.'' |
| C | Voted ''present'' to avoid possible conflict of interest. |
| ? | Did not vote or otherwise make a position known. |

**Democrats** *Republicans*
*Independent*

| | 455 | 456 | 457 | 458 | 459 | 460 | 461 | 462 |
|---|---|---|---|---|---|---|---|---|
| **ALABAMA** | | | | | | | | |
| 1 Callahan | N | N | N | N | Y | N | Y | N |
| 2 Dickinson | N | N | Y | Y | Y | Y | Y | N |
| 3 Browder | Y | N | Y | Y | Y | Y | Y | Y |
| 4 Bevill | Y | N | Y | N | N | Y | Y | N |
| 5 Cramer | Y | N | Y | Y | Y | Y | Y | Y |
| 6 Erdreich | Y | N | Y | N | Y | Y | Y | N |
| 7 Harris | Y | N | Y | N | Y | Y | Y | N |
| **ALASKA** | | | | | | | | |
| AL Young | N | N | Y | N | Y | Y | Y | Y |
| **ARIZONA** | | | | | | | | |
| 1 Rhodes | N | N | Y | N | Y | N | Y | Y |
| 2 Pastor | Y | Y | Y | Y | Y | Y | Y | N |
| 3 Stump | N | N | N | N | Y | N | N | N |
| 4 Kyl | N | N | N | N | Y | N | N | N |
| 5 Kolbe | N | N | Y | Y | Y | Y | Y | Y |
| **ARKANSAS** | | | | | | | | |
| 1 Alexander | Y | Y | Y | ? | ? | ? | ? | ? |
| 2 Thornton | Y | Y | Y | N | Y | Y | Y | Y |
| 3 Hammerschmidt | N | N | N | Y | N | Y | N | Y |
| 4 Anthony | ? | Y | Y | Y | Y | ? | Y | Y |
| **CALIFORNIA** | | | | | | | | |
| 1 Riggs | N | N | Y | N | Y | Y | Y | Y |
| 2 Herger | N | N | N | Y | N | Y | N | N |
| 3 Matsui | Y | Y | Y | Y | Y | Y | Y | Y |
| 4 Fazio | Y | Y | Y | Y | Y | Y | Y | Y |
| 5 Pelosi | Y | Y | Y | Y | Y | Y | ? | Y |
| 6 Boxer | ? | ? | ? | # | ? | ? | ? | ? |
| 7 Miller | Y | Y | Y | Y | Y | Y | N | N |
| 8 Dellums | Y | Y | Y | Y | N | Y | N | N |
| 9 Stark | Y | Y | Y | Y | N | Y | N | N |
| 10 Edwards | Y | Y | Y | Y | N | Y | N | Y |
| 11 Lantos | Y | Y | Y | Y | Y | Y | Y | Y |
| 12 Campbell | Y | N | N | Y | Y | Y | Y | Y |
| 13 Mineta | Y | Y | Y | Y | N | Y | Y | Y |
| 14 Doolittle | N | N | Y | N | Y | N | N | N |
| 15 Condit | Y | Y | Y | Y | Y | Y | Y | N |
| 16 Panetta | Y | Y | Y | Y | Y | Y | Y | Y |
| 17 Dooley | Y | Y | Y | Y | Y | Y | Y | Y |
| 18 Lehman | Y | Y | Y | Y | Y | Y | Y | Y |
| 19 Lagomarsino | N | N | N | N | Y | N | Y | Y |
| 20 Thomas | N | N | Y | Y | Y | Y | N | Y |
| 21 Gallegly | N | N | Y | Y | Y | N | Y | Y |
| 22 Moorhead | N | N | N | N | Y | N | Y | N |
| 23 Beilenson | N | Y | Y | Y | Y | Y | N | Y |
| 24 Waxman | N | Y | Y | Y | Y | N | Y | Y |
| 25 Roybal | Y | Y | Y | Y | N | Y | N | Y |
| 26 Berman | Y | Y | Y | Y | Y | Y | Y | Y |
| 27 Levine | Y | Y | Y | Y | Y | Y | Y | Y |
| 28 Dixon | Y | Y | Y | Y | Y | Y | Y | Y |
| 29 Waters | Y | Y | Y | Y | Y | N | Y | Y |
| 30 Martinez | Y | Y | Y | Y | N | Y | Y | N |
| 31 Dymally | Y | Y | Y | ? | N | Y | ? | ? |
| 32 Anderson | Y | Y | Y | Y | Y | ? | Y | N |
| 33 Dreier | N | N | N | N | N | N | N | N |
| 34 Torres | Y | Y | Y | Y | N | Y | N | Y |
| 35 Lewis | N | N | Y | N | Y | N | Y | Y |
| 36 Brown | Y | Y | Y | Y | N | Y | N | Y |
| 37 McCandless | N | N | Y | Y | Y | N | Y | N |
| 38 Dornan | N | N | N | N | Y | N | N | N |
| 39 Dannemeyer | N | N | N | N | N | N | N | N |
| 40 Cox | Y | N | Y | N | N | Y | N | N |
| 41 Lowery | N | N | Y | N | Y | Y | Y | Y |
| 42 Rohrabacher | N | N | N | N | Y | N | Y | N |
| 43 Packard | N | N | N | N | Y | N | N | N |
| 44 Cunningham | N | N | N | Y | N | Y | N | — |
| 45 Hunter | N | N | N | N | Y | N | Y | N |
| **COLORADO** | | | | | | | | |
| 1 Schroeder | Y | Y | Y | Y | Y | Y | Y | Y |
| 2 Skaggs | Y | Y | Y | Y | Y | Y | Y | Y |
| 3 Campbell | N | N | Y | Y | Y | Y | Y | Y |
| 4 Allard | N | N | N | N | Y | N | Y | N |
| 5 Hefley | N | N | N | N | Y | N | N | N |
| 6 Schaefer | N | N | N | N | Y | Y | Y | N |
| **CONNECTICUT** | | | | | | | | |
| 1 Kennelly | Y | Y | Y | Y | Y | Y | Y | Y |
| 2 Gejdenson | Y | Y | Y | N | Y | Y | Y | Y |
| 3 DeLauro | Y | Y | Y | N | Y | Y | Y | N |
| 4 Shays | Y | N | Y | Y | Y | Y | N | N |
| 5 Franks | N | N | Y | Y | Y | Y | N | N |
| 6 Johnson | N | N | Y | Y | Y | Y | Y | Y |
| **DELAWARE** | | | | | | | | |
| AL Carper | Y | Y | Y | Y | Y | Y | Y | Y |
| **FLORIDA** | | | | | | | | |
| 1 Hutto | Y | N | Y | N | Y | Y | Y | N |
| 2 Peterson | Y | Y | Y | N | Y | Y | Y | Y |
| 3 Bennett | Y | Y | N | N | Y | Y | Y | Y |
| 4 James | N | N | Y | N | Y | Y | Y | N |
| 5 McCollum | Y | N | N | N | Y | N | Y | N |
| 6 Stearns | N | N | Y | N | Y | N | Y | N |
| 7 Gibbons | Y | Y | Y | Y | Y | Y | Y | Y |
| 8 Young | Y | N | Y | N | Y | Y | Y | Y |
| 9 Bilirakis | Y | N | Y | N | Y | N | Y | N |
| 10 Ireland | ? | ? | N | ? | Y | N | Y | ? |
| 11 Bacchus | Y | Y | Y | Y | Y | Y | Y | N |
| 12 Lewis | Y | N | Y | N | Y | Y | Y | N |
| 13 Goss | Y | N | Y | N | Y | N | Y | N |
| 14 Johnston | Y | Y | Y | Y | Y | Y | Y | N |
| 15 Shaw | Y | N | Y | N | Y | N | Y | Y |
| 16 Smith | Y | Y | Y | Y | Y | Y | Y | N |
| 17 Lehman | ? | Y | Y | Y | N | Y | N | Y |
| 18 Ros−Lehtinen | Y | N | Y | N | Y | N | Y | N |
| 19 Fascell | Y | Y | Y | N | Y | N | Y | Y |
| **GEORGIA** | | | | | | | | |
| 1 Thomas | ? | ? | ? | ? | ? | ? | ? | ? |
| 2 Hatcher | Y | Y | Y | ? | ? | ? | Y | Y |
| 3 Ray | N | N | Y | N | Y | N | Y | N |
| 4 Jones | Y | Y | Y | N | Y | Y | Y | Y |
| 5 Lewis | Y | Y | Y | Y | N | Y | N | N |
| 6 Gingrich | N | N | N | Y | Y | Y | Y | N |
| 7 Darden | Y | Y | Y | Y | Y | Y | Y | N |
| 8 Rowland | Y | Y | Y | Y | N | Y | Y | N |
| 9 Jenkins | Y | Y | Y | Y | Y | Y | Y | Y |
| 10 Barnard | ? | ? | ? | ? | ? | ? | ? | ? |
| **HAWAII** | | | | | | | | |
| 1 Abercrombie | Y | Y | Y | Y | N | Y | Y | Y |
| 2 Mink | Y | Y | Y | Y | N | Y | Y | Y |
| **IDAHO** | | | | | | | | |
| 1 LaRocco | Y | Y | Y | Y | Y | Y | N | Y |
| 2 Stallings | N | N | Y | N | Y | Y | Y | Y |
| **ILLINOIS** | | | | | | | | |
| 1 Hayes | Y | Y | Y | Y | N | Y | N | N |
| 2 Savage | Y | Y | Y | Y | N | Y | N | N |
| 3 Russo | Y | Y | Y | N | Y | Y | ? | N |
| 4 Sangmeister | Y | N | Y | N | Y | Y | N | Y |
| 5 Lipinski | ? | ? | ? | ? | ? | ? | ? | ? |
| 6 Hyde | N | N | Y | N | Y | Y | Y | N |
| 7 Collins | Y | Y | Y | N | N | Y | N | N |
| 8 Rostenkowski | Y | Y | Y | Y | Y | Y | Y | Y |
| 9 Yates | Y | Y | Y | Y | N | Y | N | Y |
| 10 Porter | Y | N | Y | Y | Y | Y | Y | Y |
| 11 Annunzio | Y | Y | Y | N | Y | Y | # | ? |
| 12 Crane | ? | ? | N | N | Y | N | N | N |
| 13 Fawell | Y | N | Y | Y | N | Y | N | N |
| 14 Hastert | Y | N | Y | N | N | Y | Y | N |
| 15 Ewing | N | N | N | Y | N | Y | Y | Y |
| 16 Cox | Y | Y | Y | Y | Y | Y | Y | Y |
| 17 Evans | Y | Y | Y | Y | N | Y | Y | N |
| 18 Michel | N | N | N | Y | N | Y | Y | N |
| 19 Bruce | Y | Y | Y | Y | Y | Y | Y | N |
| 20 Durbin | Y | Y | Y | Y | N | Y | Y | N |
| 21 Costello | Y | Y | Y | N | Y | Y | Y | N |
| 22 Poshard | Y | Y | Y | N | Y | Y | Y | N |
| **INDIANA** | | | | | | | | |
| 1 Visclosky | Y | Y | Y | Y | N | Y | Y | Y |
| 2 Sharp | Y | Y | Y | Y | Y | Y | Y | Y |
| 3 Roemer | Y | Y | Y | N | Y | Y | Y | Y |

ND Northern Democrats    SD Southern Democrats

| | 455 | 456 | 457 | 458 | 459 | 460 | 461 | 462 |
|---|---|---|---|---|---|---|---|---|
| 4 Long | Y | Y | Y | Y | Y | Y | Y | Y |
| 5 Jontz | N | Y | Y | Y | Y | Y | Y | N |
| 6 ***Burton*** | N | N | N | N | Y | N | N | N |
| 7 ***Myers*** | N | N | Y | N | N | N | Y | N |
| 8 McCloskey | Y | Y | Y | Y | Y | Y | Y | Y |
| 9 Hamilton | Y | Y | Y | Y | Y | Y | Y | Y |
| 10 Jacobs | Y | Y | Y | Y | Y | Y | Y | N |
| **IOWA** | | | | | | | | |
| 1 ***Leach*** | Y | N | Y | Y | Y | Y | N | Y |
| 2 ***Nussle*** | N | N | N | N | Y | Y | N | Y |
| 3 Nagle | Y | Y | Y | Y | Y | Y | N | Y |
| 4 Smith | Y | Y | Y | Y | N | Y | Y | Y |
| 5 ***Lightfoot*** | N | N | Y | N | Y | Y | Y | Y |
| 6 ***Grandy*** | N | N | Y | N | Y | Y | Y | Y |
| **KANSAS** | | | | | | | | |
| 1 ***Roberts*** | N | N | N | N | Y | Y | N | Y |
| 2 Slattery | Y | Y | Y | Y | Y | Y | Y | Y |
| 3 ***Meyers*** | Y | N | Y | Y | Y | Y | Y | Y |
| 4 Glickman | Y | Y | Y | Y | Y | Y | Y | Y |
| 5 ***Nichols*** | N | N | N | Y | Y | Y | N | Y |
| **KENTUCKY** | | | | | | | | |
| 1 Hubbard | Y | N | Y | Y | Y | N | N | N |
| 2 Natcher | Y | Y | Y | N | N | Y | Y | Y |
| 3 Mazzoli | Y | Y | Y | N | Y | Y | Y | Y |
| 4 ***Bunning*** | N | N | N | N | Y | N | N | N |
| 5 ***Rogers*** | N | N | Y | N | Y | N | Y | N |
| 6 ***Hopkins*** | N | N | Y | N | Y | N | Y | Y |
| 7 Perkins | Y | Y | Y | N | N | Y | Y | N |
| **LOUISIANA** | | | | | | | | |
| 1 ***Livingston*** | ? | ? | ? | ? | ? | ? | ? | ? |
| 2 Jefferson | ? | ? | ? | ? | ? | ? | ? | ? |
| 3 Tauzin | Y | N | Y | N | Y | Y | Y | N |
| 4 ***McCrery*** | ? | ? | ? | ? | ? | ? | ? | ? |
| 5 Huckaby | ? | ? | ? | ? | ? | ? | ? | ? |
| 6 ***Baker*** | N | ? | ? | ? | ? | ? | ? | ? |
| 7 Hayes | ? | ? | ? | ? | ? | ? | ? | ? |
| 8 ***Holloway*** | ? | ? | ? | ? | ? | ? | ? | ? |
| **MAINE** | | | | | | | | |
| 1 Andrews | Y | Y | Y | Y | N | Y | Y | Y |
| 2 ***Snowe*** | Y | N | Y | Y | Y | Y | Y | N |
| **MARYLAND** | | | | | | | | |
| 1 ***Gilchrest*** | Y | N | Y | Y | Y | Y | Y | Y |
| 2 ***Bentley*** | N | N | Y | N | Y | Y | Y | Y |
| 3 Cardin | Y | Y | Y | Y | Y | Y | Y | Y |
| 4 McMillen | Y | Y | Y | Y | Y | Y | Y | Y |
| 5 Hoyer | Y | Y | Y | Y | Y | Y | Y | Y |
| 6 Byron | Y | N | Y | N | Y | Y | Y | Y |
| 7 Mfume | Y | Y | Y | Y | N | Y | N | N |
| 8 ***Morella*** | Y | N | Y | Y | Y | Y | N | Y |
| **MASSACHUSETTS** | | | | | | | | |
| 1 Olver | Y | Y | Y | Y | Y | Y | N | Y |
| 2 Neal | Y | Y | Y | N | Y | Y | N | N |
| 3 Early | Y | Y | Y | N | N | Y | N | N |
| 4 Frank | Y | Y | Y | Y | N | Y | N | Y |
| 5 Atkins | N | Y | Y | Y | Y | Y | N | Y |
| 6 Mavroules | Y | Y | Y | N | Y | Y | Y | Y |
| 7 Markey | Y | Y | Y | Y | ? | Y | N | Y |
| 8 Kennedy | N | Y | Y | Y | Y | Y | Y | Y |
| 9 Moakley | Y | Y | Y | N | Y | Y | Y | Y |
| 10 Studds | N | Y | Y | Y | Y | Y | N | Y |
| 11 Donnelly | Y | Y | Y | N | Y | Y | Y | N |
| **MICHIGAN** | | | | | | | | |
| 1 Conyers | # | Y | ? | Y | N | Y | N | N |
| 2 ***Pursell*** | N | N | Y | ? | Y | N | N | N |
| 3 Wolpe | Y | Y | Y | Y | Y | Y | Y | Y |
| 4 ***Upton*** | Y | N | Y | N | Y | N | Y | N |
| 5 ***Henry*** | ? | ? | Y | N | Y | Y | N | N |
| 6 Carr | Y | Y | Y | Y | N | Y | Y | N |
| 7 Kildee | Y | Y | Y | N | Y | Y | Y | Y |
| 8 Traxler | Y | Y | Y | N | N | Y | Y | N |
| 9 ***Vander Jagt*** | N | N | Y | N | Y | N | Y | ? |
| 10 ***Camp*** | Y | N | Y | N | Y | Y | Y | N |
| 11 ***Davis*** | Y | ? | ? | ? | ? | ? | ? | ? |
| 12 Bonior | Y | Y | Y | N | N | Y | Y | Y |
| 13 Collins | Y | Y | Y | Y | Y | Y | N | N |
| 14 Hertel | Y | Y | Y | N | N | Y | Y | Y |
| 15 Ford | Y | Y | Y | Y | Y | Y | Y | Y |
| 16 Dingell | Y | Y | Y | Y | N | Y | Y | Y |
| 17 Levin | Y | Y | Y | Y | Y | Y | Y | Y |
| 18 ***Broomfield*** | N | N | Y | N | Y | N | Y | Y |
| **MINNESOTA** | | | | | | | | |
| 1 Penny | N | N | Y | N | Y | Y | N | Y |
| 2 ***Weber*** | N | N | Y | N | Y | N | Y | Y |
| 3 ***Ramstad*** | Y | N | Y | Y | Y | Y | N | N |
| 4 Vento | Y | Y | Y | Y | N | Y | N | Y |

| | 455 | 456 | 457 | 458 | 459 | 460 | 461 | 462 |
|---|---|---|---|---|---|---|---|---|
| 5 Sabo | Y | Y | Y | Y | N | Y | Y | N |
| 6 Sikorski | N | Y | Y | Y | Y | Y | N | Y |
| 7 Peterson | Y | Y | Y | N | Y | Y | Y | Y |
| 8 Oberstar | Y | Y | Y | N | N | Y | N | Y |
| **MISSISSIPPI** | | | | | | | | |
| 1 Whitten | Y | Y | Y | N | N | Y | Y | Y |
| 2 Espy | Y | Y | Y | ? | N | Y | Y | N |
| 3 Montgomery | Y | N | Y | N | Y | N | Y | Y |
| 4 Parker | Y | N | Y | N | Y | N | Y | Y |
| 5 Taylor | Y | N | Y | N | Y | N | Y | N |
| **MISSOURI** | | | | | | | | |
| 1 Clay | Y | Y | Y | Y | N | Y | Y | N |
| 2 Horn | Y | Y | Y | Y | Y | Y | Y | Y |
| 3 Gephardt | Y | Y | ? | ? | ? | ? | Y | Y |
| 4 Skelton | Y | Y | Y | N | Y | Y | Y | Y |
| 5 Wheat | Y | Y | Y | Y | N | Y | N | N |
| 6 ***Coleman*** | N | N | Y | N | Y | N | Y | Y |
| 7 ***Hancock*** | N | N | N | N | Y | N | N | N |
| 8 ***Emerson*** | N | N | Y | N | Y | N | Y | Y |
| 9 Volkmer | Y | N | Y | N | Y | Y | Y | N |
| **MONTANA** | | | | | | | | |
| 1 Williams | Y | Y | Y | Y | Y | Y | Y | N |
| 2 ***Marlenee*** | N | N | Y | N | Y | Y | Y | N |
| **NEBRASKA** | | | | | | | | |
| 1 ***Bereuter*** | Y | N | Y | N | Y | Y | Y | Y |
| 2 Hoagland | Y | Y | Y | Y | Y | Y | Y | Y |
| 3 ***Barrett*** | N | N | Y | N | Y | Y | Y | Y |
| **NEVADA** | | | | | | | | |
| 1 Bilbray | Y | Y | Y | N | Y | Y | Y | Y |
| 2 ***Vucanovich*** | N | N | Y | N | Y | Y | Y | N |
| **NEW HAMPSHIRE** | | | | | | | | |
| 1 ***Zeliff*** | N | N | Y | Y | Y | Y | Y | Y |
| 2 Swett | Y | Y | Y | Y | Y | Y | Y | Y |
| **NEW JERSEY** | | | | | | | | |
| 1 Andrews | Y | Y | Y | Y | Y | Y | Y | N |
| 2 Hughes | Y | Y | Y | Y | Y | Y | N | N |
| 3 Pallone | Y | Y | Y | Y | Y | Y | + | Y |
| 4 ***Smith*** | Y | N | Y | N | Y | Y | Y | Y |
| 5 ***Roukema*** | Y | N | Y | Y | N | Y | X | ? |
| 6 Dwyer | ? | ? | Y | Y | N | Y | ? | ? |
| 7 ***Rinaldo*** | Y | N | Y | N | Y | Y | Y | ? |
| 8 Roe | Y | Y | Y | N | Y | Y | Y | Y |
| 9 Torricelli | Y | Y | Y | Y | Y | Y | Y | ? |
| 10 Payne | Y | Y | Y | Y | N | Y | N | N |
| 11 ***Gallo*** | Y | N | Y | Y | Y | Y | Y | Y |
| 12 ***Zimmer*** | Y | N | Y | Y | Y | Y | N | N |
| 13 ***Saxton*** | Y | N | Y | N | Y | Y | Y | Y |
| 14 Guarini | ? | ? | Y | ? | ? | ? | ? | ? |
| **NEW MEXICO** | | | | | | | | |
| 1 ***Schiff*** | N | N | Y | Y | Y | Y | Y | Y |
| 2 ***Skeen*** | N | N | Y | N | Y | Y | Y | Y |
| 3 Richardson | Y | Y | Y | Y | Y | Y | Y | Y |
| **NEW YORK** | | | | | | | | |
| 1 Hochbrueckner | Y | Y | Y | Y | Y | Y | Y | Y |
| 2 Downey | Y | Y | Y | Y | Y | Y | Y | Y |
| 3 Mrazek | Y | Y | Y | ? | ? | ? | Y | Y |
| 4 ***Lent*** | N | N | Y | N | Y | Y | Y | Y |
| 5 ***McGrath*** | N | N | Y | N | Y | Y | Y | Y |
| 6 Flake | Y | Y | ? | Y | N | Y | Y | N |
| 7 Ackerman | Y | Y | Y | Y | Y | Y | Y | Y |
| 8 Scheuer | Y | Y | Y | Y | N | Y | N | ? |
| 9 Manton | Y | Y | Y | N | Y | Y | Y | Y |
| 10 Schumer | Y | Y | Y | Y | Y | Y | N | Y |
| 11 Towns | Y | Y | Y | Y | N | Y | N | N |
| 12 Owens | Y | Y | Y | Y | N | Y | N | N |
| 13 Solarz | ? | Y | Y | Y | Y | Y | Y | Y |
| 14 ***Molinari*** | N | N | Y | Y | Y | Y | Y | Y |
| 15 ***Green*** | Y | N | Y | Y | Y | N | Y | Y |
| 16 Rangel | Y | Y | Y | Y | Y | Y | N | N |
| 17 Vacancy | | | | | | | | |
| 18 Serrano | Y | Y | Y | Y | N | Y | N | N |
| 19 Engel | Y | Y | Y | Y | N | Y | Y | Y |
| 20 Lowey | Y | Y | Y | Y | N | Y | Y | Y |
| 21 ***Fish*** | Y | N | Y | N | Y | Y | Y | Y |
| 22 ***Gilman*** | Y | N | Y | Y | Y | Y | Y | Y |
| 23 McNulty | Y | Y | Y | N | Y | Y | Y | Y |
| 24 ***Solomon*** | N | N | N | N | Y | N | Y | N |
| 25 ***Boehlert*** | Y | N | Y | Y | Y | Y | Y | Y |
| 26 ***Martin*** | N | N | Y | N | Y | Y | Y | Y |
| 27 ***Walsh*** | Y | N | Y | N | Y | Y | Y | N |
| 28 McHugh | Y | Y | Y | Y | N | Y | Y | Y |
| 29 ***Horton*** | Y | ? | Y | Y | Y | Y | Y | Y |
| 30 Slaughter | N | Y | Y | Y | Y | Y | Y | Y |
| 31 ***Paxon*** | N | N | Y | N | Y | Y | N | N |

| | 455 | 456 | 457 | 458 | 459 | 460 | 461 | 462 |
|---|---|---|---|---|---|---|---|---|
| 32 LaFalce | Y | Y | Y | N | Y | Y | Y | Y |
| 33 Nowak | Y | Y | Y | N | Y | Y | Y | Y |
| 34 ***Houghton*** | Y | N | Y | Y | Y | Y | Y | Y |
| **NORTH CAROLINA** | | | | | | | | |
| 1 Vacancy | | | | | | | | |
| 2 Valentine | Y | Y | Y | Y | Y | Y | Y | N |
| 3 Lancaster | Y | Y | Y | Y | Y | Y | Y | Y |
| 4 Price | Y | Y | Y | Y | N | Y | Y | Y |
| 5 Neal | Y | Y | Y | Y | Y | Y | Y | N |
| 6 ***Coble*** | N | N | Y | N | Y | N | Y | N |
| 7 Rose | Y | Y | Y | Y | N | Y | Y | Y |
| 8 Hefner | Y | Y | Y | Y | N | Y | Y | N |
| 9 ***McMillan*** | Y | N | Y | N | Y | Y | Y | Y |
| 10 ***Ballenger*** | N | N | N | N | Y | N | Y | N |
| 11 ***Taylor*** | N | N | Y | N | Y | N | Y | Y |
| **NORTH DAKOTA** | | | | | | | | |
| AL Dorgan | Y | ? | + | Y | Y | Y | Y | N |
| **OHIO** | | | | | | | | |
| 1 Luken | Y | Y | Y | N | Y | Y | N | Y |
| 2 ***Gradison*** | Y | N | Y | N | Y | Y | Y | Y |
| 3 Hall | ? | ? | Y | N | Y | Y | Y | Y |
| 4 ***Oxley*** | N | N | Y | N | Y | N | Y | Y |
| 5 ***Gillmor*** | Y | N | Y | N | Y | Y | Y | N |
| 6 ***McEwen*** | N | N | Y | N | Y | N | Y | N |
| 7 ***Hobson*** | Y | N | Y | N | Y | Y | Y | Y |
| 8 ***Boehner*** | N | N | N | N | Y | N | Y | Y |
| 9 Kaptur | Y | Y | Y | N | N | Y | Y | N |
| 10 ***Miller*** | N | N | N | N | Y | N | N | Y |
| 11 Eckart | Y | Y | Y | Y | Y | Y | ? | Y |
| 12 ***Kasich*** | N | N | Y | N | Y | Y | Y | N |
| 13 Pease | Y | Y | Y | Y | Y | Y | N | Y |
| 14 Sawyer | Y | Y | Y | Y | Y | Y | Y | Y |
| 15 ***Wylie*** | N | N | Y | N | Y | N | Y | Y |
| 16 ***Regula*** | Y | N | Y | N | Y | Y | Y | Y |
| 17 Traficant | Y | Y | Y | Y | N | Y | Y | N |
| 18 Applegate | Y | N | Y | N | N | Y | N | N |
| 19 Feighan | Y | Y | Y | Y | Y | Y | N | Y |
| 20 Oakar | Y | Y | Y | ? | ? | ? | Y | Y |
| 21 Stokes | Y | Y | Y | Y | N | Y | N | ? |
| **OKLAHOMA** | | | | | | | | |
| 1 ***Inhofe*** | N | N | Y | N | Y | Y | N | N |
| 2 Synar | N | Y | Y | Y | N | Y | N | Y |
| 3 Brewster | Y | Y | Y | Y | Y | Y | Y | Y |
| 4 McCurdy | Y | Y | Y | Y | Y | Y | Y | Y |
| 5 ***Edwards*** | N | N | ? | ? | Y | Y | Y | Y |
| 6 English | Y | Y | Y | N | Y | Y | Y | N |
| **OREGON** | | | | | | | | |
| 1 AuCoin | Y | Y | Y | Y | Y | Y | N | N |
| 2 ***Smith*** | N | N | Y | N | Y | Y | Y | N |
| 3 Wyden | Y | Y | Y | Y | Y | Y | N | Y |
| 4 DeFazio | Y | Y | ? | Y | Y | Y | N | N |
| 5 Kopetski | Y | Y | Y | Y | Y | Y | Y | Y |
| **PENNSYLVANIA** | | | | | | | | |
| 1 Foglietta | ? | ? | Y | Y | N | Y | Y | ? |
| 2 Blackwell | ? | Y | Y | Y | Y | Y | N | ? |
| 3 Borski | Y | Y | Y | N | N | Y | ? | ? |
| 4 Kolter | Y | Y | Y | N | Y | Y | Y | Y |
| 5 ***Schulze*** | N | N | Y | N | Y | Y | Y | Y |
| 6 Yatron | Y | Y | Y | N | Y | Y | Y | Y |
| 7 ***Weldon*** | Y | N | Y | N | Y | N | Y | N |
| 8 Kostmayer | N | Y | Y | Y | Y | Y | N | Y |
| 9 ***Shuster*** | N | N | N | N | Y | N | N | N |
| 10 ***McDade*** | N | N | Y | N | N | Y | Y | Y |
| 11 Kanjorski | Y | Y | Y | N | N | Y | Y | N |
| 12 Murtha | Y | Y | Y | N | N | Y | Y | Y |
| 13 ***Coughlin*** | N | N | Y | Y | Y | Y | Y | ? |
| 14 Coyne | Y | Y | Y | Y | N | Y | Y | Y |
| 15 ***Ritter*** | Y | N | Y | N | Y | N | Y | N |
| 16 ***Walker*** | N | N | N | N | Y | N | N | Y |
| 17 ***Gekas*** | N | N | Y | N | Y | N | Y | Y |
| 18 ***Santorum*** | N | N | Y | N | Y | N | Y | N |
| 19 ***Goodling*** | N | N | Y | N | Y | N | Y | N |
| 20 Gaydos | Y | Y | Y | N | N | Y | Y | N |
| 21 ***Ridge*** | Y | N | Y | Y | Y | Y | Y | N |
| 22 Murphy | Y | Y | Y | N | Y | Y | Y | N |
| 23 ***Clinger*** | N | N | Y | N | Y | Y | Y | Y |
| **RHODE ISLAND** | | | | | | | | |
| 1 ***Machtley*** | Y | ? | Y | Y | Y | Y | Y | N |
| 2 Reed | Y | Y | Y | Y | N | Y | Y | N |
| **SOUTH CAROLINA** | | | | | | | | |
| 1 ***Ravenel*** | Y | N | Y | N | Y | Y | Y | Y |
| 2 ***Spence*** | Y | N | Y | N | N | N | Y | N |
| 3 Derrick | Y | Y | Y | Y | Y | Y | Y | N |
| 4 Patterson | Y | N | Y | Y | Y | Y | Y | N |
| 5 Spratt | Y | Y | Y | Y | Y | Y | Y | Y |
| 6 Tallon | Y | Y | Y | Y | Y | Y | ? | ? |

| | 455 | 456 | 457 | 458 | 459 | 460 | 461 | 462 |
|---|---|---|---|---|---|---|---|---|
| **SOUTH DAKOTA** | | | | | | | | |
| AL Johnson | Y | ? | Y | Y | Y | Y | Y | Y |
| **TENNESSEE** | | | | | | | | |
| 1 ***Quillen*** | X | ? | ? | X | ? | N | Y | N |
| 2 ***Duncan*** | N | N | Y | N | Y | N | Y | N |
| 3 Lloyd | Y | N | Y | Y | Y | Y | Y | N |
| 4 Cooper | Y | Y | Y | Y | Y | Y | Y | Y |
| 5 Clement | Y | N | Y | Y | Y | Y | Y | Y |
| 6 Gordon | Y | Y | Y | Y | Y | Y | Y | Y |
| 7 ***Sundquist*** | N | N | Y | N | Y | Y | Y | N |
| 8 Tanner | Y | Y | Y | Y | Y | Y | Y | N |
| 9 Ford | Y | Y | Y | Y | N | Y | N | ? |
| **TEXAS** | | | | | | | | |
| 1 Chapman | Y | N | Y | Y | N | Y | Y | N |
| 2 Wilson | Y | ? | Y | Y | Y | Y | Y | Y |
| 3 ***Johnson*** | N | N | N | N | Y | N | Y | Y |
| 4 Hall | Y | Y | Y | N | Y | N | Y | N |
| 5 Bryant | Y | Y | Y | Y | Y | Y | Y | Y |
| 6 ***Barton*** | N | N | N | N | Y | N | Y | N |
| 7 ***Archer*** | N | N | N | N | Y | N | N | N |
| 8 ***Fields*** | N | N | N | N | Y | N | N | N |
| 9 Brooks | Y | Y | Y | Y | Y | Y | Y | Y |
| 10 Pickle | Y | Y | Y | Y | N | Y | Y | Y |
| 11 Edwards | Y | N | Y | Y | Y | Y | Y | Y |
| 12 Geren | Y | N | Y | Y | Y | N | Y | N |
| 13 Sarpalius | Y | Y | Y | N | Y | Y | Y | N |
| 14 Laughlin | Y | Y | Y | N | Y | Y | Y | Y |
| 15 de la Garza | Y | Y | Y | N | Y | Y | Y | Y |
| 16 Coleman | Y | Y | Y | Y | N | Y | Y | ? |
| 17 Stenholm | Y | N | Y | N | Y | Y | ? | ? |
| 18 Washington | Y | Y | Y | Y | N | Y | N | N |
| 19 ***Combest*** | N | N | N | N | Y | Y | Y | N |
| 20 Gonzalez | Y | Y | Y | Y | N | Y | Y | Y |
| 21 ***Smith*** | N | N | N | N | Y | Y | Y | Y |
| 22 ***DeLay*** | N | N | N | N | Y | N | N | N |
| 23 Bustamante | Y | Y | Y | Y | Y | Y | Y | Y |
| 24 Frost | Y | Y | Y | ? | ? | ? | ? | ? |
| 25 Andrews | Y | Y | Y | Y | Y | Y | Y | Y |
| 26 ***Armey*** | N | N | N | N | Y | N | N | N |
| 27 Ortiz | Y | Y | Y | N | N | Y | Y | N |
| **UTAH** | | | | | | | | |
| 1 ***Hansen*** | N | N | N | N | Y | Y | Y | Y |
| 2 Owens | N | Y | Y | Y | Y | Y | Y | Y |
| 3 Orton | N | Y | Y | N | Y | Y | N | Y |
| **VERMONT** | | | | | | | | |
| AL *Sanders* | Y | Y | Y | Y | N | Y | N | N |
| **VIRGINIA** | | | | | | | | |
| 1 ***Bateman*** | N | N | Y | N | Y | N | Y | Y |
| 2 Pickett | Y | Y | Y | Y | Y | N | Y | Y |
| 3 ***Bliley*** | N | N | Y | N | Y | N | Y | Y |
| 4 Sisisky | Y | Y | Y | Y | Y | Y | Y | Y |
| 5 Payne | N | Y | Y | Y | Y | Y | Y | Y |
| 6 Olin | Y | ? | Y | Y | N | Y | Y | Y |
| 7 ***Allen*** | N | N | N | N | Y | N | Y | N |
| 8 Moran | Y | Y | + | Y | Y | Y | Y | Y |
| 9 Boucher | Y | Y | Y | Y | Y | Y | Y | Y |
| 10 ***Wolf*** | N | N | Y | N | Y | Y | Y | Y |
| **WASHINGTON** | | | | | | | | |
| 1 ***Miller*** | Y | N | Y | Y | Y | Y | Y | Y |
| 2 Swift | Y | Y | Y | Y | Y | Y | Y | Y |
| 3 Unsoeld | Y | Y | Y | Y | N | Y | Y | Y |
| 4 ***Morrison*** | N | N | Y | Y | Y | Y | Y | Y |
| 5 Foley | | | | | | | | |
| 6 Dicks | Y | Y | Y | Y | Y | Y | Y | Y |
| 7 McDermott | Y | Y | Y | Y | N | Y | N | Y |
| 8 ***Chandler*** | ? | ? | ? | ? | ? | ? | ? | ? |
| **WEST VIRGINIA** | | | | | | | | |
| 1 Mollohan | Y | Y | Y | N | N | Y | Y | Y |
| 2 Staggers | ? | ? | ? | ? | ? | ? | ? | ? |
| 3 Wise | ? | ? | Y | Y | Y | Y | Y | Y |
| 4 Rahall | Y | Y | Y | N | N | Y | N | N |
| **WISCONSIN** | | | | | | | | |
| 1 Aspin | Y | Y | Y | Y | N | Y | Y | ? |
| 2 ***Klug*** | Y | N | Y | Y | Y | Y | N | N |
| 3 ***Gunderson*** | Y | N | Y | Y | Y | Y | Y | Y |
| 4 Kleczka | Y | Y | Y | N | Y | Y | Y | N |
| 5 Moody | Y | Y | Y | Y | Y | Y | N | Y |
| 6 ***Petri*** | Y | N | N | N | Y | Y | N | N |
| 7 Obey | Y | Y | Y | Y | N | Y | Y | Y |
| 8 ***Roth*** | N | N | N | N | Y | Y | N | N |
| 9 ***Sensenbrenner*** | — | — | N | N | Y | N | N | N |
| **WYOMING** | | | | | | | | |
| AL ***Thomas*** | N | N | N | N | Y | Y | Y | Y |

Southern states - Ala., Ark., Fla., Ga., Ky., La., Miss., N.C., Okla., S.C., Tenn., Texas, Va.
Omitted votes are quorum calls, which CQ does not include in its vote charts.

## KEY

Y Voted for (yea).
# Paired for.
+ Announced for.
N Voted against (nay).
X Paired against.
− Announced against.
P Voted "present."
C Voted "present" to avoid possible conflict of interest.
? Did not vote or otherwise make a position known.

Democrats **Republicans**
*Independent*

**463. HR 5427. Fiscal 1993 Legislative Branch Appropriations/Conference Report.** Adoption of the conference report to provide $2.3 billion in new budget authority for the activities of the legislative branch in fiscal 1993. Adopted 253-143: R 27-126; D 225-17 (ND 156-10, SD 69-7); I 1-0, Oct. 4, 1992.

**464. Procedural Motion.** Vucanovich, R-Nev., motion to adjourn. Motion rejected 83-316: R 81-75; D 2-240 (ND 2-163, SD 0-77); I 0-1, Oct. 4, 1992.

**465. HR 918. Mining Law Reform/Rule.** Adoption of the rule (H Res 574) to provide for House floor consideration of the bill to end the existing patenting system that allowed miners to take title to public land and impose fees as much as $25 an acre annually on mining claims with an 8 percent royalty on mineral receipts. Adopted 251-146: R 22-135; D 228-11 (ND 153-9, SD 75-2); I 1-0, Oct. 4, 1992.

**467. HR 918. Mining Law Reform/Increase Royalties.** DeFazio, D-Ore., amendment to raise the royalty on gross hard-rock mineral receipts in the bill from 8 percent to 12.5 percent. Rejected 161-237: R 19-138; D 141-99 (ND 116-49, SD 25-50); I 1-0, Oct. 4, 1992.

**468. HR 918. Mining Law Reform/Motion To Rise.** Vucanovich, R-Nev., motion to rise from the Committee of the Whole and report the bill back with no resolution thereon. Motion rejected 134-257: R 128-24; D 6-232 (ND 4-159, SD 2-73); I 0-1, Oct. 4, 1992.

**469. HR 918. Mining Law Reform/Delete Royalties.** Vucanovich, R-Nev., amendment to the Owens, D-Utah, amendment, to delete the royalty on gross hard-rock mineral receipts in the bill. The Owens amendment would lower the royalty on gross hard-rock mineral receipts from 8 percent to 5 percent. Rejected 136-254: R 120-32; D 16-221 (ND 7-157, SD 9-64); I 0-1, Oct. 4, 1992.

**470. HR 5368. Fiscal 1993 Foreign Operations Appropriations/Conference Report.** Adoption of the conference report to provide $26.26 billion for foreign aid in fiscal 1993. The administration requested $27.43 billion. The bill would provide $10 billion in loan guarantees for Israel and increase the U.S. contribution to International Monetary Fund by $12.3 billion. Adopted 312-105: R 104-58; D 208-46 (ND 152-20, SD 56-26); I 0-1, Oct. 5, 1992.

**471. HR 776. National Energy Policy/Rule.** Adoption of the rule (H Res 601) to waive points of order against and provide for House floor consideration of the bill to decrease U.S. energy dependence through increased domestic production and conservation. The bill would restructure the electric utility industry to increase competition; ease licensing for nuclear power plants; promote production of autos that ran on non-gasoline fuels; mandate greater energy efficiency; provide tax incentives for renewable energy and alternative fuels; change regulatory treatment of imported natural gas; and restructure the federal uranium enrichment program to decrease U.S. energy dependence through increased domestic production and conservation. Adopted 380-36: R 127-32; D 252-4 (ND 171-3, SD 81-1); I 1-0, Oct. 5, 1992.

| | 463 | 464 | 465 | 467 | 468 | 469 | 470 | 471 |
|---|---|---|---|---|---|---|---|---|
| **ALABAMA** | | | | | | | | |
| 1 *Callahan* | N | N | N | N | N | Y | N | Y |
| 2 *Dickinson* | N | N | N | N | N | Y | N | N |
| 3 Browder | Y | N | Y | N | N | N | Y | Y |
| 4 Bevill | Y | N | Y | N | N | N | Y | Y |
| 5 Cramer | Y | N | Y | N | N | N | Y | Y |
| 6 Erdreich | N | N | Y | N | N | N | Y | Y |
| 7 Harris | N | N | Y | N | N | N | Y | Y |
| **ALASKA** | | | | | | | | |
| AL *Young* | N | Y | N | N | Y | Y | Y | N |
| **ARIZONA** | | | | | | | | |
| 1 *Rhodes* | N | N | N | Y | N | Y | N | Y |
| 2 Pastor | Y | N | N | N | Y | N | Y | Y |
| 3 *Stump* | N | Y | N | N | Y | Y | N | Y |
| 4 *Kyl* | N | Y | N | N | Y | Y | Y | Y |
| 5 *Kolbe* | N | Y | N | N | Y | Y | Y | Y |
| **ARKANSAS** | | | | | | | | |
| 1 Alexander | ? | ? | ? | ? | ? | ? | Y | Y |
| 2 Thornton | Y | N | Y | N | N | N | Y | Y |
| 3 *Hammerschmidt* | N | N | N | N | N | N | N | N |
| 4 Anthony | # | ? | ? | ? | N | N | Y | Y |
| **CALIFORNIA** | | | | | | | | |
| 1 *Riggs* | Y | Y | N | N | Y | Y | Y | Y |
| 2 *Herger* | N | Y | N | N | N | Y | N | Y |
| 3 Matsui | Y | N | Y | N | N | Y | Y | Y |
| 4 Fazio | Y | N | Y | N | N | N | Y | Y |
| 5 Pelosi | Y | N | Y | N | N | Y | Y | Y |
| 6 Boxer | ? | ? | ? | ? | ? | ? | # | ? |
| 7 Miller | Y | N | Y | N | N | Y | Y | Y |
| 8 Dellums | Y | N | Y | N | Y | N | Y | Y |
| 9 Stark | Y | N | Y | N | N | Y | N | Y |
| 10 Edwards | Y | N | Y | N | N | Y | Y | Y |
| 11 Lantos | Y | N | Y | N | N | Y | Y | Y |
| 12 *Campbell* | N | N | N | N | Y | Y | Y | Y |
| 13 Mineta | Y | N | Y | N | Y | N | Y | Y |
| 14 *Doolittle* | N | Y | N | N | Y | Y | N | N |
| 15 Condit | Y | N | Y | N | N | N | N | Y |
| 16 Panetta | + | − | + | − | − | − | Y | Y |
| 17 Dooley | Y | N | Y | N | N | N | Y | Y |
| 18 Lehman | Y | Y | Y | N | N | N | N | Y |
| 19 *Lagomarsino* | N | Y | N | N | Y | Y | Y | N |
| 20 *Thomas* | N | Y | N | N | Y | Y | Y | N |
| 21 *Gallegly* | N | Y | N | N | Y | Y | N | Y |
| 22 *Moorhead* | N | Y | N | N | Y | Y | N | Y |
| 23 Beilenson | Y | N | ? | Y | N | N | Y | Y |
| 24 Waxman | Y | N | Y | N | N | Y | Y | ? |
| 25 Roybal | Y | N | Y | Y | N | Y | ? | Y |
| 26 Berman | Y | N | Y | N | N | Y | Y | Y |
| 27 Levine | ? | ? | ? | Y | N | N | Y | Y |
| 28 Dixon | Y | N | Y | N | N | Y | Y | Y |
| 29 Waters | Y | N | Y | Y | N | Y | Y | Y |
| 30 Martinez | Y | N | Y | N | N | N | Y | Y |
| 31 Dymally | Y | N | Y | N | N | Y | Y | Y |
| 32 Anderson | Y | N | Y | N | N | N | Y | Y |
| 33 *Dreier* | N | Y | N | N | Y | Y | N | Y |
| 34 Torres | Y | N | N | ? | N | ? | Y | Y |
| 35 *Lewis* | Y | Y | N | N | Y | N | Y | N |
| 36 Brown | Y | N | Y | N | N | N | Y | N |
| 37 *McCandless* | N | Y | N | N | Y | Y | N | Y |
| 38 *Dornan* | N | Y | N | ? | ? | N | Y | Y |
| 39 *Dannemeyer* | N | Y | N | N | ? | ? | N | Y |
| 40 *Cox* | N | Y | N | N | Y | Y | N | Y |
| 41 *Lowery* | Y | Y | N | ? | ? | Y | Y | ? |

| | 463 | 464 | 465 | 467 | 468 | 469 | 470 | 471 |
|---|---|---|---|---|---|---|---|---|
| 42 *Rohrabacher* | N | Y | N | N | Y | Y | N | N |
| 43 *Packard* | N | Y | N | N | Y | Y | N | N |
| 44 *Cunningham* | N | Y | N | N | Y | Y | N | N |
| 45 *Hunter* | N | Y | N | N | Y | Y | Y | Y |
| **COLORADO** | | | | | | | | |
| 1 Schroeder | Y | N | N | N | N | N | Y | Y |
| 2 Skaggs | Y | N | Y | N | N | N | Y | Y |
| 3 Campbell | N | N | N | N | Y | N | Y | Y |
| 4 *Allard* | N | Y | N | N | Y | Y | N | N |
| 5 *Hefley* | N | Y | N | N | Y | Y | Y | N |
| 6 *Schaefer* | N | Y | N | N | Y | Y | Y | ? |
| **CONNECTICUT** | | | | | | | | |
| 1 Kennelly | Y | N | ? | Y | N | N | Y | Y |
| 2 Gejdenson | Y | N | Y | N | N | Y | Y | Y |
| 3 DeLauro | Y | N | Y | N | N | N | Y | Y |
| 4 *Shays* | N | N | Y | N | N | Y | Y | Y |
| 5 *Franks* | N | Y | N | N | Y | Y | Y | Y |
| 6 *Johnson* | N | Y | N | N | Y | Y | Y | Y |
| **DELAWARE** | | | | | | | | |
| AL Carper | ? | ? | ? | ? | N | N | Y | Y |
| **FLORIDA** | | | | | | | | |
| 1 Hutto | Y | N | N | N | Y | N | Y | Y |
| 2 Peterson | Y | N | Y | N | N | N | N | Y |
| 3 Bennett | Y | N | Y | N | N | N | N | Y |
| 4 *James* | N | N | N | N | Y | Y | N | N |
| 5 *McCollum* | N | N | N | Y | Y | Y | N | Y |
| 6 *Stearns* | N | Y | N | Y | Y | ? | ? | ? |
| 7 Gibbons | Y | N | Y | N | N | N | N | Y |
| 8 *Young* | ? | ? | ? | N | Y | Y | N | Y |
| 9 *Bilirakis* | N | N | N | N | Y | Y | N | Y |
| 10 *Ireland* | N | N | N | ? | ? | ? | N | Y |
| 11 Bacchus | Y | N | Y | N | N | N | N | Y |
| 12 *Lewis* | N | N | N | N | Y | Y | N | N |
| 13 *Goss* | N | N | N | N | Y | N | N | N |
| 14 Johnston | Y | N | Y | N | Y | N | Y | Y |
| 15 *Shaw* | N | N | N | N | Y | Y | Y | ? |
| 16 Smith | Y | N | Y | N | N | Y | N | Y |
| 17 Lehman | Y | N | Y | N | ? | ? | Y | Y |
| 18 *Ros−Lehtinen* | N | N | Y | Y | N | Y | N | N |
| 19 Fascell | Y | N | Y | N | N | Y | Y | Y |
| **GEORGIA** | | | | | | | | |
| 1 Thomas | ? | N | Y | N | ? | N | Y | Y |
| 2 Hatcher | Y | N | Y | N | ? | ? | Y | Y |
| 3 Ray | Y | N | Y | N | N | N | N | Y |
| 4 Jones | Y | N | Y | N | N | N | Y | Y |
| 5 Lewis | Y | N | Y | N | N | N | Y | Y |
| 6 *Gingrich* | N | Y | N | N | Y | Y | Y | Y |
| 7 *Darden* | Y | N | Y | N | N | N | Y | Y |
| 8 Rowland | Y | N | Y | N | N | N | Y | Y |
| 9 Jenkins | Y | N | Y | N | N | ? | Y | Y |
| 10 Barnard | ? | ? | ? | ? | ? | ? | ? | ? |
| **HAWAII** | | | | | | | | |
| 1 Abercrombie | Y | N | Y | Y | N | N | Y | Y |
| 2 Mink | Y | N | Y | Y | N | N | Y | Y |
| **IDAHO** | | | | | | | | |
| 1 LaRocco | Y | N | N | N | Y | Y | Y | Y |
| 2 Stallings | N | N | N | Y | Y | Y | Y | Y |
| **ILLINOIS** | | | | | | | | |
| 1 Hayes | Y | N | Y | N | N | N | Y | Y |
| 2 Savage | ? | ? | ? | ? | ? | ? | N | Y |
| 3 Russo | Y | N | Y | N | N | N | N | Y |
| 4 Sangmeister | Y | N | Y | N | N | N | N | Y |
| 5 Lipinski | ? | ? | ? | ? | ? | ? | ? | ? |
| 6 *Hyde* | N | Y | N | N | Y | Y | Y | Y |
| 7 Collins | Y | N | Y | N | N | N | Y | Y |
| 8 Rostenkowski | Y | N | Y | N | N | ? | ? | Y |
| 9 Yates | Y | N | Y | Y | N | Y | Y | Y |
| 10 *Porter* | Y | N | Y | N | Y | N | Y | Y |
| 11 Annunzio | Y | N | Y | ? | ? | ? | Y | Y |
| 12 *Crane* | N | Y | N | N | Y | Y | N | N |
| 13 *Fawell* | N | N | N | N | Y | Y | Y | N |
| 14 *Hastert* | N | Y | N | N | Y | Y | Y | Y |
| 15 *Ewing* | N | Y | N | N | Y | Y | Y | Y |
| 16 Cox | Y | N | Y | N | N | Y | Y | Y |
| 17 Evans | Y | N | Y | N | N | N | Y | Y |
| 18 *Michel* | N | Y | N | N | Y | ? | ? | Y |
| 19 Bruce | Y | N | Y | N | N | N | Y | Y |
| 20 Durbin | Y | N | Y | N | N | N | Y | Y |
| 21 Costello | Y | N | Y | N | N | N | Y | Y |
| 22 Poshard | Y | N | N | N | N | N | Y | Y |
| **INDIANA** | | | | | | | | |
| 1 Visclosky | Y | N | Y | N | N | N | Y | Y |
| 2 Sharp | N | N | Y | N | N | N | Y | Y |
| 3 Roemer | N | N | Y | N | N | N | N | Y |

ND Northern Democrats   SD Southern Democrats

| | 463 | 464 | 465 | 467 | 468 | 469 | 470 | 471 |
|---|---|---|---|---|---|---|---|---|
| 4 Long | Y | N | Y | N | N | N | Y | Y |
| 5 Jontz | Y | N | Y | Y | N | N | N | Y |
| 6 ***Burton*** | N | Y | N | N | Y | Y | Y | N |
| 7 ***Myers*** | Y | Y | N | N | Y | Y | N | Y |
| 8 McCloskey | Y | N | Y | N | N | N | Y | ? |
| 9 Hamilton | Y | N | Y | N | N | N | Y | Y |
| 10 Jacobs | N | N | Y | Y | N | N | N | Y |
| **IOWA** | | | | | | | | |
| 1 ***Leach*** | N | N | N | Y | N | N | Y | Y |
| 2 ***Nussle*** | N | Y | N | N | Y | Y | N | Y |
| 3 Nagle | Y | N | Y | Y | N | N | Y | Y |
| 4 Smith | Y | N | Y | N | N | N | Y | Y |
| 5 ***Lightfoot*** | N | N | N | N | Y | Y | Y | Y |
| 6 ***Grandy*** | Y | N | N | N | Y | Y | Y | Y |
| **KANSAS** | | | | | | | | |
| 1 ***Roberts*** | N | Y | N | N | Y | Y | N | N |
| 2 Slattery | N | N | Y | Y | N | N | Y | Y |
| 3 ***Meyers*** | N | N | Y | Y | Y | N | Y | Y |
| 4 Glickman | N | N | Y | Y | N | N | Y | Y |
| 5 ***Nichols*** | N | N | N | N | Y | Y | N | Y |
| **KENTUCKY** | | | | | | | | |
| 1 Hubbard | N | N | N | N | Y | Y | N | Y |
| 2 Natcher | Y | N | Y | N | N | N | Y | Y |
| 3 Mazzoli | Y | N | Y | N | N | N | Y | Y |
| 4 ***Bunning*** | N | N | N | N | Y | Y | N | N |
| 5 ***Rogers*** | N | N | N | N | Y | Y | N | Y |
| 6 ***Hopkins*** | N | N | N | N | Y | Y | N | Y |
| 7 Perkins | Y | N | Y | N | N | N | N | Y |
| **LOUISIANA** | | | | | | | | |
| 1 ***Livingston*** | ? | ? | ? | N | Y | Y | Y | Y |
| 2 Jefferson | Y | N | Y | N | N | N | Y | Y |
| 3 Tauzin | Y | N | Y | N | N | Y | N | Y |
| 4 ***McCrery*** | ? | ? | ? | ? | ? | ? | Y | Y |
| 5 Huckaby | ? | ? | ? | ? | ? | ? | N | Y |
| 6 ***Baker*** | ? | ? | ? | N | Y | Y | N | Y |
| 7 Hayes | ? | ? | ? | ? | ? | ? | N | Y |
| 8 ***Holloway*** | ? | ? | ? | ? | ? | ? | N | Y |
| **MAINE** | | | | | | | | |
| 1 Andrews | Y | N | Y | Y | N | N | Y | Y |
| 2 ***Snowe*** | N | N | Y | Y | N | N | Y | Y |
| **MARYLAND** | | | | | | | | |
| 1 ***Gilchrest*** | N | Y | N | N | Y | N | Y | Y |
| 2 ***Bentley*** | Y | Y | N | N | Y | Y | Y | Y |
| 3 Cardin | Y | N | Y | ? | ? | ? | Y | Y |
| 4 McMillen | Y | N | Y | Y | N | N | Y | Y |
| 5 Hoyer | Y | N | Y | N | N | N | Y | Y |
| 6 Byron | Y | N | Y | N | N | N | Y | Y |
| 7 Mfume | Y | N | Y | Y | N | N | Y | Y |
| 8 ***Morella*** | Y | N | N | Y | Y | N | Y | Y |
| **MASSACHUSETTS** | | | | | | | | |
| 1 Olver | Y | N | Y | Y | N | N | Y | Y |
| 2 Neal | ? | ? | ? | Y | N | N | Y | Y |
| 3 Early | Y | N | Y | Y | N | N | Y | Y |
| 4 Frank | Y | N | Y | Y | ? | N | Y | Y |
| 5 Atkins | Y | N | Y | Y | N | N | ? | Y |
| 6 Mavroules | Y | N | Y | Y | ? | N | Y | Y |
| 7 Markey | Y | N | Y | Y | N | N | Y | Y |
| 8 Kennedy | ? | ? | ? | Y | N | N | Y | Y |
| 9 Moakley | Y | N | Y | Y | N | N | Y | Y |
| 10 Studds | Y | N | Y | Y | N | N | Y | Y |
| 11 Donnelly | Y | N | Y | Y | N | N | N | Y |
| **MICHIGAN** | | | | | | | | |
| 1 Conyers | Y | N | Y | Y | N | N | Y | Y |
| 2 ***Pursell*** | N | N | N | N | Y | ? | Y | Y |
| 3 Wolpe | Y | N | Y | Y | N | N | Y | Y |
| 4 ***Upton*** | N | Y | N | N | Y | N | Y | N |
| 5 ***Henry*** | N | Y | N | N | Y | Y | N | Y |
| 6 Carr | Y | N | Y | Y | N | N | Y | Y |
| 7 Kildee | Y | N | Y | Y | N | N | Y | Y |
| 8 Traxler | Y | N | Y | ? | ? | ? | Y | Y |
| 9 ***Vander Jagt*** | N | N | N | N | Y | Y | Y | N |
| 10 ***Camp*** | N | N | N | N | Y | Y | Y | Y |
| 11 ***Davis*** | ? | N | N | N | N | N | ? | Y |
| 12 Bonior | Y | N | Y | Y | N | N | Y | Y |
| 13 Collins | Y | N | Y | Y | N | N | Y | Y |
| 14 Hertel | Y | N | Y | Y | N | N | Y | Y |
| 15 Ford | Y | N | Y | N | N | N | Y | Y |
| 16 Dingell | Y | N | Y | Y | N | N | Y | Y |
| 17 Levin | Y | N | Y | Y | N | N | Y | Y |
| 18 ***Broomfield*** | N | N | N | N | Y | ? | Y | Y |
| **MINNESOTA** | | | | | | | | |
| 1 Penny | Y | N | Y | Y | N | N | Y | Y |
| 2 ***Weber*** | N | Y | N | N | ? | ? | Y | ? |
| 3 ***Ramstad*** | N | N | Y | Y | Y | N | Y | Y |
| 4 Vento | Y | N | Y | Y | N | N | Y | Y |

| | 463 | 464 | 465 | 467 | 468 | 469 | 470 | 471 |
|---|---|---|---|---|---|---|---|---|
| 5 Sabo | Y | N | Y | Y | N | N | Y | Y |
| 6 Sikorski | Y | N | Y | Y | N | N | ? | ? |
| 7 Peterson | Y | N | Y | Y | N | N | Y | Y |
| 8 Oberstar | Y | N | Y | Y | N | N | Y | Y |
| **MISSISSIPPI** | | | | | | | | |
| 1 Whitten | Y | N | Y | N | Y | ? | Y | Y |
| 2 Espy | Y | N | Y | ? | N | N | Y | Y |
| 3 Montgomery | Y | N | Y | N | N | Y | N | Y |
| 4 Parker | Y | N | Y | Y | N | N | Y | Y |
| 5 Taylor | Y | N | Y | N | N | Y | N | Y |
| **MISSOURI** | | | | | | | | |
| 1 Clay | Y | N | Y | Y | N | N | Y | Y |
| 2 Horn | Y | N | Y | Y | N | N | Y | Y |
| 3 Gephardt | Y | N | Y | N | N | N | Y | Y |
| 4 Skelton | Y | N | Y | N | N | N | Y | Y |
| 5 Wheat | Y | N | ? | Y | N | N | Y | Y |
| 6 ***Coleman*** | N | N | N | N | Y | Y | N | Y |
| 7 ***Hancock*** | N | Y | N | N | Y | Y | N | N |
| 8 ***Emerson*** | N | Y | N | N | Y | Y | Y | Y |
| 9 Volkmer | Y | N | Y | N | N | N | N | Y |
| **MONTANA** | | | | | | | | |
| 1 Williams | N | N | N | N | N | N | N | Y |
| 2 ***Marlenee*** | N | Y | N | N | Y | Y | N | N |
| **NEBRASKA** | | | | | | | | |
| 1 ***Bereuter*** | N | N | N | N | Y | Y | Y | Y |
| 2 Hoagland | Y | N | Y | Y | N | N | Y | Y |
| 3 ***Barrett*** | N | N | N | N | Y | Y | N | Y |
| **NEVADA** | | | | | | | | |
| 1 Bilbray | Y | Y | N | N | Y | Y | Y | N |
| 2 ***Vucanovich*** | N | Y | N | N | Y | Y | Y | N |
| **NEW HAMPSHIRE** | | | | | | | | |
| 1 ***Zeliff*** | N | Y | N | N | Y | Y | Y | Y |
| 2 Swett | Y | N | Y | N | N | N | Y | Y |
| **NEW JERSEY** | | | | | | | | |
| 1 Andrews | + | ? | ? | Y | N | N | Y | Y |
| 2 Hughes | N | N | Y | Y | N | N | Y | Y |
| 3 Pallone | N | N | Y | Y | N | N | Y | Y |
| 4 ***Smith*** | Y | N | Y | N | Y | N | Y | Y |
| 5 ***Roukema*** | X | ? | ? | ? | N | N | Y | Y |
| 6 Dwyer | ? | ? | ? | ? | ? | ? | Y | Y |
| 7 ***Rinaldo*** | Y | N | Y | Y | Y | N | Y | Y |
| 8 Roe | Y | N | Y | ? | ? | ? | Y | Y |
| 9 Torricelli | Y | N | Y | Y | N | N | Y | Y |
| 10 Payne | Y | N | Y | Y | N | N | Y | Y |
| 11 ***Gallo*** | Y | N | N | N | Y | Y | Y | Y |
| 12 ***Zimmer*** | N | Y | Y | Y | Y | N | Y | Y |
| 13 ***Saxton*** | N | N | Y | ? | ? | ? | Y | Y |
| 14 Guarini | Y | N | Y | N | N | N | X | Y |
| **NEW MEXICO** | | | | | | | | |
| 1 ***Schiff*** | Y | N | N | N | Y | Y | Y | Y |
| 2 ***Skeen*** | Y | Y | N | N | Y | Y | Y | Y |
| 3 Richardson | Y | N | Y | N | N | N | Y | Y |
| **NEW YORK** | | | | | | | | |
| 1 Hochbrueckner | Y | N | Y | Y | N | N | Y | Y |
| 2 Downey | Y | N | Y | Y | ? | N | Y | Y |
| 3 Mrazek | Y | N | Y | ? | N | N | ? | ? |
| 4 ***Lent*** | Y | N | N | N | Y | ? | Y | Y |
| 5 ***McGrath*** | Y | N | N | N | Y | Y | Y | Y |
| 6 Flake | ? | ? | ? | Y | N | N | Y | Y |
| 7 Ackerman | Y | N | Y | Y | N | N | Y | Y |
| 8 Scheuer | Y | N | Y | Y | N | ? | Y | Y |
| 9 Manton | Y | N | Y | N | N | N | Y | Y |
| 10 Schumer | Y | N | Y | Y | N | N | Y | Y |
| 11 Towns | ? | ? | ? | ? | ? | ? | Y | Y |
| 12 Owens | ? | ? | ? | ? | ? | ? | Y | Y |
| 13 Solarz | Y | N | Y | Y | N | ? | Y | Y |
| 14 ***Molinari*** | Y | Y | N | N | Y | Y | Y | Y |
| 15 ***Green*** | Y | N | Y | Y | N | N | Y | Y |
| 16 Rangel | Y | N | Y | Y | N | N | Y | Y |
| 17 Vacancy | | | | | | | | |
| 18 Serrano | Y | N | Y | Y | N | N | Y | Y |
| 19 Engel | Y | N | Y | Y | N | N | Y | Y |
| 20 Lowey | Y | N | Y | Y | N | N | Y | Y |
| 21 ***Fish*** | N | N | Y | Y | N | Y | Y | Y |
| 22 ***Gilman*** | N | N | Y | Y | N | Y | Y | Y |
| 23 McNulty | Y | N | Y | Y | N | N | Y | Y |
| 24 ***Solomon*** | N | N | N | N | Y | Y | N | Y |
| 25 ***Boehlert*** | Y | N | Y | Y | N | N | Y | Y |
| 26 ***Martin*** | Y | N | N | N | ? | ? | Y | Y |
| 27 ***Walsh*** | N | N | N | N | N | N | Y | Y |
| 28 McHugh | Y | N | Y | Y | N | ? | Y | Y |
| 29 ***Horton*** | Y | N | N | N | Y | N | Y | Y |
| 30 Slaughter | Y | N | Y | Y | N | N | Y | Y |
| 31 ***Paxon*** | N | Y | N | N | Y | Y | Y | Y |

| | 463 | 464 | 465 | 467 | 468 | 469 | 470 | 471 |
|---|---|---|---|---|---|---|---|---|
| 32 LaFalce | Y | N | Y | Y | N | N | Y | Y |
| 33 Nowak | Y | N | Y | N | N | N | Y | Y |
| 34 ***Houghton*** | Y | Y | N | N | Y | Y | Y | Y |
| **NORTH CAROLINA** | | | | | | | | |
| 1 Vacancy | | | | | | | | |
| 2 Valentine | Y | N | Y | Y | ? | N | N | Y |
| 3 Lancaster | Y | N | Y | Y | N | N | Y | N |
| 4 Price | Y | N | Y | Y | N | N | Y | Y |
| 5 Neal | Y | N | Y | Y | N | N | N | Y |
| 6 ***Coble*** | N | N | N | N | Y | Y | Y | Y |
| 7 Rose | Y | N | Y | N | N | ? | Y | Y |
| 8 Hefner | Y | N | Y | Y | N | N | N | Y |
| 9 ***McMillan*** | N | N | N | Y | Y | Y | Y | Y |
| 10 ***Ballenger*** | Y | Y | N | N | Y | Y | N | — |
| 11 ***Taylor*** | N | Y | N | N | Y | Y | Y | N |
| **NORTH DAKOTA** | | | | | | | | |
| AL Dorgan | Y | N | Y | Y | N | N | Y | N |
| **OHIO** | | | | | | | | |
| 1 Luken | Y | N | Y | Y | N | N | Y | Y |
| 2 ***Gradison*** | N | N | N | N | Y | Y | Y | Y |
| 3 Hall | Y | N | Y | Y | N | ? | Y | Y |
| 4 ***Oxley*** | N | N | N | N | Y | Y | N | Y |
| 5 ***Gillmor*** | Y | N | N | N | Y | N | Y | Y |
| 6 ***McEwen*** | N | Y | N | N | Y | Y | N | Y |
| 7 ***Hobson*** | N | N | N | N | N | Y | Y | Y |
| 8 ***Boehner*** | N | Y | N | N | Y | Y | Y | Y |
| 9 Kaptur | Y | N | Y | N | N | N | Y | N |
| 10 ***Miller*** | N | Y | N | N | Y | Y | N | Y |
| 11 Eckart | Y | N | Y | Y | N | N | Y | Y |
| 12 ***Kasich*** | ? | Y | N | N | N | N | Y | Y |
| 13 Pease | Y | N | Y | Y | N | N | Y | Y |
| 14 Sawyer | ? | ? | ? | Y | N | N | Y | Y |
| 15 ***Wylie*** | ? | ? | ? | N | N | N | Y | Y |
| 16 ***Regula*** | N | N | Y | N | N | N | Y | Y |
| 17 Traficant | Y | N | Y | N | N | N | N | Y |
| 18 Applegate | Y | N | Y | N | ? | N | N | Y |
| 19 Feighan | Y | N | Y | ? | N | N | Y | Y |
| 20 Oakar | Y | N | Y | N | N | N | Y | Y |
| 21 Stokes | Y | N | Y | Y | N | N | Y | Y |
| **OKLAHOMA** | | | | | | | | |
| 1 ***Inhofe*** | N | Y | N | N | Y | Y | Y | Y |
| 2 Synar | Y | N | Y | Y | N | N | Y | Y |
| 3 Brewster | Y | N | Y | N | N | N | Y | Y |
| 4 McCurdy | Y | N | Y | Y | N | N | Y | Y |
| 5 ***Edwards*** | Y | N | N | N | ? | ? | Y | ? |
| 6 English | Y | N | Y | N | N | N | N | Y |
| **OREGON** | | | | | | | | |
| 1 AuCoin | Y | N | Y | Y | N | N | Y | Y |
| 2 ***Smith*** | N | Y | N | N | Y | Y | N | Y |
| 3 Wyden | Y | N | Y | Y | N | N | Y | Y |
| 4 DeFazio | Y | N | Y | Y | N | N | N | Y |
| 5 Kopetski | Y | N | Y | Y | N | N | Y | Y |
| **PENNSYLVANIA** | | | | | | | | |
| 1 Foglietta | Y | N | Y | Y | N | N | Y | Y |
| 2 Blackwell | Y | N | Y | Y | N | N | Y | Y |
| 3 Borski | Y | N | Y | N | N | N | Y | Y |
| 4 Kolter | Y | N | Y | N | ? | N | Y | Y |
| 5 ***Schulze*** | N | N | N | ? | ? | Y | N | Y |
| 6 Yatron | Y | N | Y | N | N | N | Y | Y |
| 7 ***Weldon*** | N | N | N | Y | Y | N | N | Y |
| 8 Kostmayer | Y | N | Y | Y | N | N | Y | Y |
| 9 ***Shuster*** | N | N | N | N | Y | Y | N | Y |
| 10 ***McDade*** | ? | ? | ? | ? | ? | ? | Y | Y |
| 11 Kanjorski | Y | N | Y | N | N | N | N | Y |
| 12 Murtha | Y | N | Y | N | N | N | Y | Y |
| 13 ***Coughlin*** | ? | ? | N | N | ? | N | Y | Y |
| 14 Coyne | Y | N | Y | Y | N | N | Y | Y |
| 15 ***Ritter*** | Y | N | N | N | N | Y | Y | Y |
| 16 ***Walker*** | N | Y | N | N | Y | Y | N | Y |
| 17 ***Gekas*** | N | Y | N | N | Y | Y | N | Y |
| 18 ***Santorum*** | N | Y | N | N | Y | Y | Y | Y |
| 19 ***Goodling*** | N | Y | N | Y | Y | N | N | Y |
| 20 Gaydos | Y | ? | ? | N | N | N | N | Y |
| 21 ***Ridge*** | N | Y | N | N | Y | Y | Y | Y |
| 22 Murphy | Y | N | Y | Y | N | N | N | Y |
| 23 ***Clinger*** | N | Y | N | N | Y | Y | Y | Y |
| **RHODE ISLAND** | | | | | | | | |
| 1 ***Machtley*** | N | N | Y | N | N | N | Y | Y |
| 2 Reed | Y | N | Y | Y | N | N | Y | Y |
| **SOUTH CAROLINA** | | | | | | | | |
| 1 ***Ravenel*** | N | N | Y | Y | ? | N | Y | Y |
| 2 ***Spence*** | N | N | N | N | Y | Y | N | Y |
| 3 Derrick | Y | N | Y | N | N | N | Y | Y |
| 4 Patterson | Y | N | Y | Y | N | N | N | Y |
| 5 Spratt | Y | N | Y | Y | N | N | Y | Y |
| 6 Tallon | Y | N | Y | Y | N | N | Y | Y |

| | 463 | 464 | 465 | 467 | 468 | 469 | 470 | 471 |
|---|---|---|---|---|---|---|---|---|
| **SOUTH DAKOTA** | | | | | | | | |
| AL Johnson | Y | N | Y | N | N | Y | Y | Y |
| **TENNESSEE** | | | | | | | | |
| 1 ***Quillen*** | N | Y | Y | N | Y | Y | Y | Y |
| 2 ***Duncan*** | N | Y | N | N | Y | Y | N | N |
| 3 Lloyd | Y | N | Y | N | N | N | N | Y |
| 4 Cooper | Y | N | Y | N | N | N | Y | Y |
| 5 Clement | ? | ? | ? | ? | ? | ? | ? | ? |
| 6 Gordon | Y | N | Y | N | N | N | Y | Y |
| 7 ***Sundquist*** | N | Y | N | N | Y | Y | Y | Y |
| 8 Tanner | Y | N | Y | N | N | N | N | Y |
| 9 Ford | Y | N | Y | ? | N | N | Y | Y |
| **TEXAS** | | | | | | | | |
| 1 Chapman | Y | N | Y | N | N | N | N | Y |
| 2 Wilson | Y | N | Y | N | N | N | Y | Y |
| 3 ***Johnson*** | N | Y | N | N | Y | Y | Y | N |
| 4 Hall | N | N | Y | N | N | Y | N | Y |
| 5 Bryant | Y | N | Y | Y | N | N | Y | Y |
| 6 ***Barton*** | N | Y | N | N | Y | Y | N | Y |
| 7 ***Archer*** | N | N | N | N | Y | Y | N | Y |
| 8 ***Fields*** | N | Y | N | N | Y | Y | N | Y |
| 9 Brooks | Y | N | Y | Y | N | N | N | Y |
| 10 Pickle | Y | N | Y | N | N | N | Y | Y |
| 11 Edwards | Y | N | Y | N | N | N | Y | Y |
| 12 Geren | N | N | Y | N | N | Y | Y | Y |
| 13 Sarpalius | N | N | Y | N | N | N | N | Y |
| 14 Laughlin | Y | N | Y | N | N | N | Y | Y |
| 15 de la Garza | Y | N | Y | N | N | N | Y | Y |
| 16 Coleman | ? | ? | ? | ? | ? | ? | Y | Y |
| 17 Stenholm | Y | N | Y | N | N | Y | Y | Y |
| 18 Washington | Y | N | Y | Y | N | N | Y | Y |
| 19 ***Combest*** | N | Y | N | N | Y | Y | N | Y |
| 20 Gonzalez | Y | N | Y | N | N | N | N | Y |
| 21 ***Smith*** | N | Y | N | N | Y | Y | Y | Y |
| 22 ***DeLay*** | N | Y | N | N | Y | Y | N | Y |
| 23 Bustamante | Y | N | Y | N | N | N | Y | Y |
| 24 Frost | Y | N | Y | Y | N | N | Y | Y |
| 25 Andrews | Y | N | Y | N | N | N | Y | Y |
| 26 ***Armey*** | N | Y | N | N | Y | Y | N | N |
| 27 Ortiz | Y | N | Y | N | N | N | Y | Y |
| **UTAH** | | | | | | | | |
| 1 ***Hansen*** | N | Y | N | N | Y | Y | N | Y |
| 2 Owens | Y | N | Y | N | N | N | Y | ? |
| 3 Orton | Y | N | N | N | N | Y | Y | Y |
| **VERMONT** | | | | | | | | |
| AL *Sanders* | Y | N | Y | Y | N | N | N | Y |
| **VIRGINIA** | | | | | | | | |
| 1 ***Bateman*** | N | N | N | N | Y | Y | Y | Y |
| 2 Pickett | N | N | Y | N | N | N | Y | Y |
| 3 ***Bliley*** | N | N | N | N | Y | Y | Y | Y |
| 4 Sisisky | Y | N | Y | N | N | N | Y | Y |
| 5 Payne | Y | N | Y | Y | N | N | Y | Y |
| 6 Olin | Y | N | N | N | N | N | Y | Y |
| 7 ***Allen*** | N | Y | N | N | Y | Y | N | N |
| 8 Moran | Y | N | Y | Y | N | N | Y | Y |
| 9 Boucher | Y | N | Y | Y | N | N | N | Y |
| 10 ***Wolf*** | N | N | N | N | Y | N | Y | Y |
| **WASHINGTON** | | | | | | | | |
| 1 ***Miller*** | N | N | N | N | Y | N | Y | Y |
| 2 Swift | Y | N | Y | N | N | N | Y | Y |
| 3 Unsoeld | Y | N | Y | Y | N | N | Y | Y |
| 4 ***Morrison*** | Y | N | N | N | Y | Y | Y | Y |
| 5 Foley | | | | | | | | |
| 6 Dicks | Y | N | Y | N | N | N | Y | Y |
| 7 McDermott | Y | N | Y | Y | N | N | Y | Y |
| 8 ***Chandler*** | ? | ? | ? | ? | ? | ? | ? | ? |
| **WEST VIRGINIA** | | | | | | | | |
| 1 Mollohan | Y | N | Y | N | N | N | Y | Y |
| 2 Staggers | ? | ? | ? | ? | ? | ? | ? | Y |
| 3 Wise | Y | N | Y | N | N | N | Y | Y |
| 4 Rahall | Y | N | Y | N | N | N | N | Y |
| **WISCONSIN** | | | | | | | | |
| 1 Aspin | Y | N | Y | Y | N | N | Y | Y |
| 2 ***Klug*** | ? | ? | Y | Y | Y | N | Y | Y |
| 3 ***Gunderson*** | N | Y | N | N | Y | Y | Y | Y |
| 4 Kleczka | Y | N | Y | Y | N | N | N | Y |
| 5 Moody | Y | N | Y | Y | ? | N | Y | Y |
| 6 ***Petri*** | N | N | Y | N | N | Y | N | Y |
| 7 Obey | Y | N | Y | Y | N | N | Y | Y |
| 8 ***Roth*** | N | N | Y | N | N | Y | N | Y |
| 9 ***Sensenbrenner*** | N | N | Y | N | Y | Y | N | Y |
| **WYOMING** | | | | | | | | |
| AL ***Thomas*** | N | Y | N | N | Y | Y | N | Y |

Southern states - Ala., Ark., Fla., Ga., Ky., La., Miss., N.C., Okla., S.C., Tenn., Texas, Va.
Omitted votes are quorum calls, which CQ does not include in its vote charts.

**472. HR 5504. Fiscal 1993 Defense Appropriations/Rule.** Adoption of the rule (H Res 602) to waive points of order against and provide for House floor consideration of the conference report to provide $254 billion in new budget authority for the Department of Defense for the fiscal year ending Sept. 30, 1993. The administration requested $259 billion. The bill included $3.8 billion for the Strategic Defense Initiative (SDI). Adopted 250-171: R 61-102; D 188-69 (ND 132-44, SD 56-25); I 1-0, Oct. 5, 1992. (The conference report subsequently was adopted by voice vote.)

**473. HR 776. National Energy Policy/Nuclear Waste in Nevada.** Vucanovich, R-Nev., motion to recommit the conference report to the conference committee with instructions to report back after eliminating the provisions that could make it easier to open a nuclear waste dump at Yucca Mountain in Nevada. Motion rejected 102-323: R 53-110; D 48-213 (ND 42-137, SD 6-76); I 1-0, Oct. 5, 1992.

**474. HR 776. National Energy Policy/Conference Report.** Adoption of the conference report to decrease U.S. energy dependence through increased domestic production and conservation. The bill would restructure the electric utility industry to increase competition; ease licensing for nuclear power plants; promote production of cars that ran on non-gasoline fuels; mandate greater energy efficiency; provide tax incentives for renewable energy and alternative fuels; change regulatory treatment of imported natural gas; and restructure the federal uranium enrichment program. Adopted 363-60: R 123-40; D 239-20 (ND 164-13, SD 75-7); I 1-0, Oct. 5, 1992. A "yea" was a vote in support of the president's position.

**475. HR 5334. Housing and Community Development/Rule.** Adoption of the rule (H Res 603) to waive points of order against and provide for House floor consideration of the conference report to authorize $32.5 billion in fiscal 1993 and $34 billion in fiscal 1994 for housing and community development programs. Adopted 303-101: R 54-101; D 248-0 (ND 174-0, SD 74-0); I 1-0, Oct. 5, 1992.

**476. HR 5334. Housing and Community Development/Conference Report.** Adoption of the conference report to authorize $32.5 billion in fiscal 1993 and $34 billion in fiscal 1994 for housing and community development programs. Adopted 377-37: R 125-35; D 251-2 (ND 172-2, SD 79-0); I 1-0, Oct. 5, 1992.

**477. S 12. Cable Television Reregulation/Veto Override.** Passage, over President Bush's Oct. 3 veto, of the bill to cap basic cable rates and improve competition in the cable industry by having the Federal Communications Commission set rates for basic cable service and giving broadcasters the right to charge cable operators for the use of over-the-air signals. Passed (thus enacted into law) 308-114: R 77-85; D 230-29 (ND 156-22, SD 74-7); I 1-0, Oct. 5, 1992. Two-thirds of those present and voting (282 in this case) was required to override a veto. A "nay" was a vote in support of the president's position.

**478. HR 429. Western Water Bill/Order Previous Question.** Gordon, D-Tenn., motion to order the previous question (thus limiting debate and the possibility of amendment) on adoption of the rule (H Res 604) to waive points of order against and provide for House floor consideration of the conference report to reauthorize the Bureau of Reclamation dam and irrigation construction programs, including the authorization for the completion of the Central Utah Project and reforms for the Central Valley Project in California. Motion agreed to 230-182: R 26-134; D 203-48 (ND 151-21, SD 52-27); I 1-0, Oct. 5, 1992.

**479. HR 429. Western Water Bill/Rule.** Adoption of the rule (H Res 604) to waive points of order against and provide for House floor consideration of the conference report to reauthorize the Bureau of Reclamation dam and irrigation construction programs, including the authorization for the completion of the Central Utah Project and reforms for the Central Valley Project in California. Adopted 260-144: R 34-125; D 225-19 (ND 160-9, SD 65-10); I 1-0, Oct. 5, 1992.

## KEY

Y Voted for (yea).
\# Paired for.
\+ Announced for.
N Voted against (nay).
X Paired against.
− Announced against.
P Voted "present."
C Voted "present" to avoid possible conflict of interest.
? Did not vote or otherwise make a position known.

Democrats **Republicans**
*Independent*

| | 472 | 473 | 474 | 475 | 476 | 477 | 478 | 479 |
|---|---|---|---|---|---|---|---|---|
| **ALABAMA** | | | | | | | | |
| 1 *Callahan* | Y | N | Y | N | N | Y | N | N |
| 2 *Dickinson* | N | Y | Y | N | Y | N | N | N |
| 3 Browder | N | N | Y | Y | Y | Y | N | Y |
| 4 Bevill | Y | N | Y | Y | Y | Y | Y | Y |
| 5 Cramer | ? | N | Y | Y | Y | Y | Y | Y |
| 6 Erdreich | Y | N | Y | Y | Y | Y | Y | Y |
| 7 Harris | Y | N | Y | ? | Y | Y | N | Y |
| **ALASKA** | | | | | | | | |
| AL *Young* | Y | Y | Y | Y | Y | N | N | N |
| **ARIZONA** | | | | | | | | |
| 1 *Rhodes* | N | N | Y | N | N | Y | N | Y |
| 2 Pastor | Y | N | Y | Y | Y | N | Y | Y |
| 3 *Stump* | N | N | N | N | N | N | N | N |
| 4 *Kyl* | N | N | Y | N | N | N | N | Y |
| 5 *Kolbe* | N | N | Y | N | Y | N | Y | Y |
| **ARKANSAS** | | | | | | | | |
| 1 Alexander | Y | N | Y | ? | Y | Y | Y | Y |
| 2 Thornton | Y | N | Y | Y | Y | Y | Y | Y |
| 3 *Hammerschmidt* | N | N | Y | N | Y | N | N | N |
| 4 Anthony | Y | N | Y | Y | Y | N | Y | ? |
| **CALIFORNIA** | | | | | | | | |
| 1 *Riggs* | N | Y | Y | Y | Y | Y | Y | Y |
| 2 *Herger* | N | N | Y | N | N | N | N | N |
| 3 Matsui | Y | N | Y | Y | Y | N | Y | Y |
| 4 Fazio | Y | N | Y | Y | Y | Y | N | N |
| 5 Pelosi | Y | N | Y | Y | Y | Y | Y | Y |
| 6 Boxer | ? | ? | ? | ? | ? | ? | ? | ? |
| 7 Miller | Y | N | Y | Y | Y | Y | Y | Y |
| 8 Dellums | Y | N | Y | Y | Y | Y | Y | Y |
| 9 Stark | N | N | N | ? | Y | Y | Y | Y |
| 10 Edwards | N | N | Y | Y | ? | Y | Y | Y |
| 11 Lantos | Y | Y | Y | Y | Y | Y | Y | Y |
| 12 *Campbell* | N | Y | N | N | N | N | N | N |
| 13 Mineta | N | N | Y | Y | Y | Y | N | N |
| 14 *Doolittle* | N | Y | N | N | N | N | N | N |
| 15 Condit | N | N | Y | Y | Y | N | Y | Y |
| 16 Panetta | Y | N | Y | Y | Y | Y | Y | Y |
| 17 Dooley | N | N | Y | Y | Y | N | Y | Y |
| 18 Lehman | Y | N | Y | Y | Y | Y | N | N |
| 19 *Lagomarsino* | N | N | Y | N | N | N | N | N |
| 20 *Thomas* | N | Y | N | N | N | N | N | N |
| 21 *Gallegly* | N | N | Y | N | N | N | N | N |
| 22 *Moorhead* | N | N | Y | N | N | N | N | N |
| 23 Beilenson | N | N | Y | Y | Y | Y | N | N |
| 24 Waxman | N | Y | ? | Y | Y | Y | Y | Y |
| 25 Roybal | Y | N | Y | Y | Y | Y | Y | Y |
| 26 Berman | Y | Y | Y | Y | Y | Y | Y | Y |
| 27 Levine | Y | Y | Y | Y | Y | N | N | Y |
| 28 Dixon | Y | N | Y | Y | Y | N | Y | Y |
| 29 Waters | N | Y | Y | Y | Y | Y | Y | Y |
| 30 Martinez | Y | N | Y | Y | Y | Y | Y | Y |
| 31 Dymally | Y | N | Y | Y | Y | Y | Y | Y |
| 32 Anderson | N | N | Y | Y | Y | Y | N | Y |
| 33 *Dreier* | N | Y | N | N | N | N | N | N |
| 34 Torres | Y | N | Y | Y | ? | Y | Y | Y |
| 35 *Lewis* | N | Y | N | Y | N | Y | N | N |
| 36 Brown | N | N | Y | Y | Y | Y | Y | Y |
| 37 *McCandless* | N | N | Y | N | N | Y | N | N |
| 38 *Dornan* | N | Y | N | N | N | N | N | N |
| 39 *Dannemeyer* | N | N | Y | N | Y | N | N | N |
| 40 *Cox* | N | N | Y | N | N | N | N | N |
| 41 *Lowery* | Y | N | Y | N | Y | N | N | N |
| **COLORADO** | | | | | | | | |
| 1 Schroeder | N | Y | Y | Y | Y | Y | N | Y |
| 2 Skaggs | N | Y | Y | Y | Y | Y | N | Y |
| 3 Campbell | Y | Y | Y | Y | Y | Y | N | Y |
| 4 *Allard* | N | Y | N | N | N | N | N | N |
| 5 *Hefley* | N | N | N | N | N | N | N | N |
| 6 *Schaefer* | N | Y | Y | N | N | N | N | N |
| **CONNECTICUT** | | | | | | | | |
| 1 Kennelly | Y | N | Y | Y | Y | Y | Y | Y |
| 2 Gejdenson | Y | N | Y | Y | Y | Y | Y | Y |
| 3 DeLauro | Y | N | Y | Y | Y | Y | Y | Y |
| 4 *Shays* | N | N | Y | Y | Y | Y | Y | Y |
| 5 *Franks* | Y | N | Y | N | Y | N | N | N |
| 6 *Johnson* | N | N | Y | Y | Y | N | N | N |
| **DELAWARE** | | | | | | | | |
| AL Carper | Y | N | Y | Y | Y | Y | N | Y |
| **FLORIDA** | | | | | | | | |
| 1 Hutto | N | N | Y | Y | Y | Y | N | Y |
| 2 Peterson | Y | N | Y | Y | Y | Y | N | Y |
| 3 Bennett | N | N | Y | Y | Y | Y | Y | Y |
| 4 *James* | N | N | Y | N | Y | N | N | N |
| 5 *McCollum* | N | N | N | N | N | N | N | N |
| 6 *Stearns* | ? | ? | ? | ? | ? | ? | ? | ? |
| 7 Gibbons | Y | N | N | Y | N | Y | N | N |
| 8 *Young* | Y | N | Y | N | Y | N | Y | N |
| 9 *Bilirakis* | N | Y | N | ? | Y | N | N | N |
| 10 *Ireland* | N | Y | N | ? | N | ? | N | ? |
| 11 Bacchus | N | N | Y | Y | Y | Y | Y | Y |
| 12 *Lewis* | N | N | N | Y | Y | N | N | N |
| 13 *Goss* | N | Y | N | N | Y | N | N | N |
| 14 Johnston | Y | Y | Y | Y | Y | Y | Y | Y |
| 15 *Shaw* | N | Y | N | Y | N | N | N | N |
| 16 Smith | Y | N | Y | Y | Y | Y | Y | Y |
| 17 Lehman | Y | N | Y | Y | ? | ? | ? | ? |
| 18 *Ros—Lehtinen* | Y | Y | N | Y | Y | Y | Y | Y |
| 19 Fascell | Y | N | Y | Y | Y | Y | Y | Y |
| **GEORGIA** | | | | | | | | |
| 1 Thomas | Y | N | Y | Y | Y | Y | N | Y |
| 2 Hatcher | Y | N | Y | ? | Y | Y | ? | ? |
| 3 Ray | N | N | Y | Y | Y | Y | N | ? |
| 4 Jones | N | N | Y | Y | Y | Y | Y | Y |
| 5 Lewis | Y | N | Y | Y | Y | Y | Y | Y |
| 6 *Gingrich* | N | N | N | N | Y | N | N | N |
| 7 Darden | Y | N | Y | Y | Y | Y | Y | Y |
| 8 Rowland | Y | N | Y | Y | Y | Y | Y | Y |
| 9 Jenkins | Y | Y | Y | Y | Y | Y | Y | Y |
| 10 Barnard | ? | ? | ? | ? | ? | ? | ? | ? |
| **HAWAII** | | | | | | | | |
| 1 Abercrombie | Y | N | Y | Y | Y | Y | Y | Y |
| 2 Mink | Y | N | Y | Y | Y | Y | Y | Y |
| **IDAHO** | | | | | | | | |
| 1 LaRocco | N | Y | Y | Y | Y | Y | Y | Y |
| 2 *Stallings* | Y | Y | Y | Y | Y | Y | N | N |
| **ILLINOIS** | | | | | | | | |
| 1 Hayes | Y | N | Y | Y | Y | Y | Y | Y |
| 2 Savage | Y | Y | Y | Y | Y | Y | Y | Y |
| 3 Russo | Y | N | Y | Y | Y | Y | Y | Y |
| 4 Sangmeister | Y | N | Y | Y | Y | Y | Y | Y |
| 5 Lipinski | ? | ? | ? | ? | ? | ? | ? | ? |
| 6 *Hyde* | Y | N | Y | N | Y | N | N | N |
| 7 Collins | N | N | Y | Y | Y | Y | Y | Y |
| 8 Rostenkowski | Y | N | Y | Y | Y | Y | Y | Y |
| 9 Yates | N | Y | Y | Y | Y | Y | Y | Y |
| 10 *Porter* | N | N | Y | N | Y | N | Y | Y |
| 11 Annunzio | Y | N | Y | Y | Y | Y | ? | ? |
| 12 *Crane* | N | Y | N | N | N | N | N | N |
| 13 *Fawell* | N | Y | N | N | N | N | N | N |
| 14 *Hastert* | N | N | Y | N | Y | N | N | N |
| 15 *Ewing* | N | Y | Y | Y | Y | N | N | N |
| 16 Cox | Y | N | Y | Y | Y | Y | N | Y |
| 17 Evans | Y | Y | Y | Y | Y | Y | Y | Y |
| 18 *Michel* | N | Y | Y | N | Y | N | N | N |
| 19 Bruce | Y | N | Y | Y | Y | Y | Y | Y |
| 20 Durbin | Y | N | Y | Y | Y | Y | Y | Y |
| 21 Costello | N | N | Y | Y | Y | Y | Y | Y |
| 22 Poshard | N | N | Y | Y | Y | Y | Y | Y |
| **INDIANA** | | | | | | | | |
| 1 Visclosky | Y | N | Y | Y | Y | Y | Y | Y |
| 2 Sharp | Y | N | Y | Y | Y | Y | Y | Y |
| 3 Roemer | Y | N | N | Y | Y | Y | Y | Y |

ND Northern Democrats    SD Southern Democrats

| | 472 | 473 | 474 | 475 | 476 | 477 | 478 | 479 |
|---|---|---|---|---|---|---|---|---|
| 4 Long | Y | N | N | Y | Y | Y | Y | Y |
| 5 Jontz | N | Y | N | Y | Y | Y | Y | Y |
| 6 ***Burton*** | N | Y | N | N | N | N | N | N |
| 7 ***Myers*** | Y | Y | Y | Y | Y | N | N | N |
| 8 McCloskey | Y | N | Y | Y | Y | Y | N | Y |
| 9 Hamilton | Y | N | Y | Y | Y | Y | Y | Y |
| 10 Jacobs | N | N | Y | Y | Y | Y | N | Y |
| **IOWA** | | | | | | | | |
| 1 ***Leach*** | N | N | Y | Y | N | Y | Y | Y |
| 2 ***Nussle*** | N | N | Y | N | Y | Y | N | N |
| 3 Nagle | Y | Y | Y | Y | Y | Y | ? | ? |
| 4 Smith | Y | N | Y | Y | Y | N | Y | Y |
| 5 ***Lightfoot*** | N | N | Y | N | Y | Y | N | N |
| 6 ***Grandy*** | N | N | Y | N | Y | Y | Y | Y |
| **KANSAS** | | | | | | | | |
| 1 ***Roberts*** | N | N | Y | N | Y | Y | N | N |
| 2 Slattery | Y | N | Y | Y | Y | Y | Y | Y |
| 3 ***Meyers*** | N | N | Y | N | Y | Y | N | N |
| 4 Glickman | N | N | Y | Y | Y | Y | Y | Y |
| 5 ***Nichols*** | Y | N | Y | N | Y | Y | N | N |
| **KENTUCKY** | | | | | | | | |
| 1 Hubbard | N | N | Y | Y | Y | Y | N | N |
| 2 Natcher | Y | N | Y | Y | Y | Y | Y | Y |
| 3 Mazzoli | Y | N | Y | Y | Y | Y | Y | Y |
| 4 ***Bunning*** | N | N | Y | N | Y | Y | N | N |
| 5 ***Rogers*** | Y | N | Y | Y | Y | Y | N | N |
| 6 ***Hopkins*** | N | N | Y | N | N | N | N | N |
| 7 Perkins | Y | N | Y | Y | Y | Y | N | N |
| **LOUISIANA** | | | | | | | | |
| 1 ***Livingston*** | Y | N | Y | Y | Y | Y | N | N |
| 2 Jefferson | Y | N | Y | Y | Y | Y | Y | Y |
| 3 Tauzin | Y | N | Y | ? | Y | Y | N | N |
| 4 ***McCrery*** | Y | N | Y | N | Y | N | N | ? |
| 5 Huckaby | Y | N | Y | Y | Y | Y | N | N |
| 6 ***Baker*** | Y | N | Y | N | Y | N | N | N |
| 7 Hayes | N | N | Y | Y | Y | Y | N | Y |
| 8 ***Holloway*** | Y | N | Y | N | Y | N | N | N |
| **MAINE** | | | | | | | | |
| 1 Andrews | N | Y | N | Y | Y | Y | Y | Y |
| 2 ***Snowe*** | Y | Y | Y | Y | Y | Y | Y | Y |
| **MARYLAND** | | | | | | | | |
| 1 ***Gilchrest*** | N | Y | Y | N | Y | Y | Y | Y |
| 2 ***Bentley*** | N | Y | Y | N | Y | Y | N | N |
| 3 Cardin | Y | N | Y | Y | Y | Y | Y | Y |
| 4 McMillen | N | N | Y | Y | Y | Y | Y | Y |
| 5 Hoyer | Y | N | Y | Y | Y | Y | Y | Y |
| 6 Byron | Y | Y | Y | Y | Y | Y | N | Y |
| 7 Mfume | Y | Y | Y | Y | ? | Y | Y | Y |
| 8 ***Morella*** | Y | N | Y | Y | Y | Y | Y | Y |
| **MASSACHUSETTS** | | | | | | | | |
| 1 Olver | N | Y | Y | Y | Y | Y | Y | Y |
| 2 Neal | Y | N | Y | Y | Y | Y | Y | Y |
| 3 Early | N | N | Y | Y | Y | Y | Y | Y |
| 4 Frank | Y | N | Y | Y | Y | Y | Y | Y |
| 5 Atkins | Y | Y | Y | Y | Y | Y | Y | Y |
| 6 Mavroules | Y | N | Y | Y | Y | Y | Y | ? |
| 7 Markey | Y | N | Y | ? | Y | Y | Y | Y |
| 8 Kennedy | Y | N | Y | Y | Y | Y | Y | Y |
| 9 Moakley | Y | N | Y | Y | Y | Y | Y | Y |
| 10 Studds | Y | Y | Y | Y | Y | Y | Y | Y |
| 11 Donnelly | Y | N | Y | Y | Y | Y | N | Y |
| **MICHIGAN** | | | | | | | | |
| 1 Conyers | Y | Y | Y | Y | N | Y | Y | Y |
| 2 ***Pursell*** | N | N | Y | ? | Y | N | N | N |
| 3 Wolpe | N | Y | Y | Y | Y | Y | Y | Y |
| 4 ***Upton*** | N | N | Y | N | Y | Y | N | N |
| 5 ***Henry*** | N | N | Y | N | Y | Y | N | N |
| 6 Carr | Y | N | Y | Y | Y | Y | Y | Y |
| 7 Kildee | Y | N | Y | Y | Y | Y | Y | Y |
| 8 Traxler | Y | N | Y | Y | Y | Y | ? | ? |
| 9 ***Vander Jagt*** | Y | N | Y | ? | Y | N | N | N |
| 10 ***Camp*** | N | N | N | N | Y | N | N | N |
| 11 ***Davis*** | Y | N | Y | Y | Y | Y | ? | ? |
| 12 Bonior | Y | N | Y | ? | Y | Y | Y | Y |
| 13 Collins | Y | N | Y | Y | Y | Y | Y | Y |
| 14 Hertel | Y | N | Y | Y | Y | Y | Y | Y |
| 15 Ford | Y | N | Y | Y | Y | Y | Y | ? |
| 16 Dingell | N | N | Y | Y | Y | Y | Y | Y |
| 17 Levin | N | N | Y | Y | Y | Y | Y | Y |
| 18 ***Broomfield*** | Y | N | Y | N | Y | Y | N | N |
| **MINNESOTA** | | | | | | | | |
| 1 Penny | N | N | N | Y | N | N | Y | Y |
| 2 ***Weber*** | ? | Y | N | ? | Y | Y | N | N |
| 3 ***Ramstad*** | N | Y | Y | N | Y | Y | Y | Y |
| 4 Vento | N | Y | Y | Y | Y | Y | Y | Y |
| 5 Sabo | Y | N | Y | Y | Y | Y | Y | Y |
| 6 Sikorski | ? | Y | N | Y | Y | Y | Y | Y |
| 7 Peterson | Y | N | Y | Y | Y | Y | Y | Y |
| 8 Oberstar | Y | N | N | Y | Y | Y | Y | Y |
| **MISSISSIPPI** | | | | | | | | |
| 1 Whitten | Y | N | Y | Y | Y | Y | Y | Y |
| 2 Espy | Y | N | Y | Y | Y | Y | N | Y |
| 3 Montgomery | Y | N | Y | Y | Y | Y | N | Y |
| 4 Parker | Y | N | Y | Y | Y | N | Y | Y |
| 5 Taylor | Y | N | Y | Y | Y | Y | N | Y |
| **MISSOURI** | | | | | | | | |
| 1 Clay | Y | N | Y | ? | Y | Y | Y | Y |
| 2 Horn | N | N | Y | Y | Y | Y | Y | Y |
| 3 Gephardt | Y | N | Y | Y | Y | Y | Y | Y |
| 4 Skelton | Y | N | Y | Y | Y | Y | N | Y |
| 5 Wheat | Y | N | Y | Y | Y | Y | Y | Y |
| 6 ***Coleman*** | N | N | Y | Y | Y | Y | N | N |
| 7 ***Hancock*** | N | N | N | N | N | Y | N | N |
| 8 ***Emerson*** | N | N | Y | N | Y | Y | N | N |
| 9 Volkmer | Y | N | Y | Y | Y | Y | Y | N |
| **MONTANA** | | | | | | | | |
| 1 Williams | Y | N | Y | Y | Y | Y | Y | Y |
| 2 ***Marlenee*** | Y | Y | N | N | Y | Y | N | N |
| **NEBRASKA** | | | | | | | | |
| 1 ***Bereuter*** | N | N | Y | Y | Y | Y | Y | Y |
| 2 Hoagland | Y | N | Y | Y | Y | Y | Y | Y |
| 3 ***Barrett*** | N | Y | Y | N | Y | Y | N | N |
| **NEVADA** | | | | | | | | |
| 1 Bilbray | Y | Y | N | Y | Y | Y | N | Y |
| 2 ***Vucanovich*** | Y | Y | N | N | Y | N | N | Y |
| **NEW HAMPSHIRE** | | | | | | | | |
| 1 ***Zeliff*** | N | N | Y | N | N | N | N | N |
| 2 Swett | N | N | Y | Y | Y | Y | N | Y |
| **NEW JERSEY** | | | | | | | | |
| 1 Andrews | Y | N | Y | Y | Y | N | N | Y |
| 2 Hughes | Y | N | Y | Y | Y | N | Y | Y |
| 3 Pallone | Y | Y | N | Y | Y | Y | Y | Y |
| 4 ***Smith*** | Y | N | Y | Y | Y | N | N | Y |
| 5 ***Roukema*** | Y | N | Y | Y | Y | N | N | N |
| 6 Dwyer | Y | N | Y | Y | ? | Y | Y | Y |
| 7 ***Rinaldo*** | Y | N | Y | Y | Y | Y | N | Y |
| 8 Roe | Y | N | Y | Y | Y | Y | Y | Y |
| 9 Torricelli | Y | N | Y | Y | Y | Y | N | Y |
| 10 Payne | Y | N | Y | Y | Y | Y | Y | Y |
| 11 ***Gallo*** | Y | N | Y | Y | Y | N | N | N |
| 12 ***Zimmer*** | N | N | Y | N | N | N | Y | Y |
| 13 ***Saxton*** | Y | N | Y | ? | Y | N | N | N |
| 14 Guarini | Y | N | Y | Y | Y | Y | Y | Y |
| **NEW MEXICO** | | | | | | | | |
| 1 ***Schiff*** | Y | Y | Y | N | Y | Y | N | N |
| 2 ***Skeen*** | Y | Y | Y | Y | Y | Y | N | N |
| 3 Richardson | Y | Y | Y | Y | Y | N | Y | Y |
| **NEW YORK** | | | | | | | | |
| 1 Hochbrueckner | Y | N | Y | Y | Y | Y | Y | Y |
| 2 Downey | ? | N | Y | Y | Y | Y | Y | Y |
| 3 Mrazek | ? | N | Y | Y | Y | Y | Y | Y |
| 4 ***Lent*** | Y | N | Y | N | Y | N | N | N |
| 5 ***McGrath*** | Y | N | Y | Y | Y | Y | Y | Y |
| 6 Flake | Y | N | Y | Y | Y | Y | Y | Y |
| 7 Ackerman | Y | N | Y | Y | Y | Y | Y | Y |
| 8 Scheuer | Y | Y | Y | Y | Y | Y | Y | Y |
| 9 Manton | Y | N | Y | Y | Y | Y | Y | Y |
| 10 Schumer | Y | N | Y | Y | Y | Y | Y | Y |
| 11 Towns | Y | N | Y | Y | Y | Y | Y | Y |
| 12 Owens | N | N | Y | Y | Y | Y | Y | Y |
| 13 Solarz | Y | N | Y | Y | ? | Y | Y | Y |
| 14 ***Molinari*** | Y | N | Y | Y | Y | Y | Y | Y |
| 15 ***Green*** | Y | N | Y | Y | Y | Y | Y | Y |
| 16 Rangel | Y | Y | Y | Y | Y | Y | Y | Y |
| 17 Vacancy | | | | | | | | |
| 18 Serrano | Y | N | Y | Y | Y | Y | Y | Y |
| 19 Engel | N | N | Y | Y | Y | Y | Y | Y |
| 20 Lowey | Y | N | Y | Y | Y | Y | Y | Y |
| 21 ***Fish*** | Y | Y | Y | N | Y | Y | N | N |
| 22 ***Gilman*** | Y | Y | Y | Y | Y | Y | N | Y |
| 23 McNulty | Y | Y | Y | Y | Y | Y | Y | Y |
| 24 ***Solomon*** | N | N | N | N | N | N | N | N |
| 25 ***Boehlert*** | N | Y | Y | Y | Y | Y | Y | Y |
| 26 ***Martin*** | Y | N | Y | N | Y | N | N | N |
| 27 ***Walsh*** | Y | Y | Y | N | Y | Y | N | Y |
| 28 McHugh | Y | N | Y | Y | Y | Y | Y | Y |
| 29 ***Horton*** | Y | N | Y | Y | ? | N | N | N |
| 30 Slaughter | Y | N | Y | Y | Y | Y | Y | Y |
| 31 ***Paxon*** | Y | Y | Y | N | Y | N | N | N |
| 32 LaFalce | Y | N | Y | Y | Y | Y | Y | Y |
| 33 Nowak | Y | N | Y | Y | Y | Y | Y | Y |
| 34 ***Houghton*** | N | N | Y | Y | Y | Y | N | N |
| **NORTH CAROLINA** | | | | | | | | |
| 1 Vacancy | | | | | | | | |
| 2 Valentine | N | N | Y | Y | Y | Y | N | Y |
| 3 Lancaster | N | N | Y | Y | Y | Y | Y | Y |
| 4 Price | N | N | Y | Y | Y | Y | Y | Y |
| 5 Neal | N | N | Y | Y | Y | Y | Y | Y |
| 6 ***Coble*** | N | N | Y | N | Y | Y | N | N |
| 7 Rose | Y | N | Y | Y | Y | Y | ? | ? |
| 8 Hefner | Y | N | Y | Y | Y | Y | Y | ? |
| 9 ***McMillan*** | Y | N | Y | Y | Y | Y | N | N |
| 10 ***Ballenger*** | N | Y | Y | N | Y | N | N | N |
| 11 ***Taylor*** | N | N | Y | N | Y | Y | N | N |
| **NORTH DAKOTA** | | | | | | | | |
| AL Dorgan | N | N | Y | Y | Y | Y | ? | ? |
| **OHIO** | | | | | | | | |
| 1 Luken | N | N | Y | Y | Y | C | N | N |
| 2 ***Gradison*** | N | N | Y | Y | Y | Y | N | N |
| 3 Hall | Y | N | Y | Y | Y | N | Y | Y |
| 4 ***Oxley*** | Y | N | Y | Y | Y | N | N | N |
| 5 ***Gillmor*** | N | Y | Y | ? | Y | N | N | N |
| 6 ***McEwen*** | Y | Y | Y | Y | Y | N | N | N |
| 7 ***Hobson*** | Y | N | Y | Y | Y | N | N | N |
| 8 ***Boehner*** | N | N | Y | N | Y | N | N | N |
| 9 Kaptur | Y | Y | Y | Y | Y | Y | Y | Y |
| 10 ***Miller*** | Y | Y | Y | Y | N | N | N | N |
| 11 Eckart | N | N | Y | Y | Y | Y | Y | Y |
| 12 ***Kasich*** | Y | N | Y | Y | Y | Y | N | N |
| 13 Pease | N | N | Y | Y | Y | Y | Y | Y |
| 14 Sawyer | N | N | Y | Y | Y | Y | Y | Y |
| 15 ***Wylie*** | N | N | Y | Y | Y | Y | N | N |
| 16 ***Regula*** | Y | N | Y | Y | Y | N | N | N |
| 17 Traficant | Y | N | Y | Y | Y | Y | Y | Y |
| 18 Applegate | Y | N | Y | Y | Y | Y | Y | Y |
| 19 Feighan | N | N | Y | Y | Y | N | Y | Y |
| 20 Oakar | Y | N | Y | Y | Y | Y | Y | Y |
| 21 Stokes | Y | N | Y | Y | Y | Y | Y | ? |
| **OKLAHOMA** | | | | | | | | |
| 1 ***Inhofe*** | N | N | Y | N | Y | Y | N | N |
| 2 Synar | N | N | Y | Y | Y | Y | Y | Y |
| 3 Brewster | Y | N | Y | Y | Y | Y | Y | Y |
| 4 McCurdy | Y | N | Y | Y | ? | Y | N | N |
| 5 ***Edwards*** | N | N | Y | N | ? | ? | ? | ? |
| 6 English | N | N | Y | Y | Y | Y | Y | Y |
| **OREGON** | | | | | | | | |
| 1 AuCoin | Y | Y | Y | Y | Y | Y | Y | Y |
| 2 ***Smith*** | N | Y | Y | N | Y | N | N | N |
| 3 Wyden | Y | N | Y | Y | Y | Y | Y | Y |
| 4 DeFazio | Y | Y | N | Y | Y | Y | Y | Y |
| 5 Kopetski | Y | N | Y | Y | Y | N | Y | Y |
| **PENNSYLVANIA** | | | | | | | | |
| 1 Foglietta | Y | N | Y | Y | Y | Y | Y | Y |
| 2 Blackwell | Y | N | Y | Y | Y | Y | Y | Y |
| 3 Borski | Y | N | Y | Y | Y | N | Y | Y |
| 4 Kolter | Y | N | Y | ? | Y | Y | ? | ? |
| 5 ***Schulze*** | N | Y | Y | Y | Y | Y | N | N |
| 6 Yatron | Y | N | Y | Y | Y | Y | ? | ? |
| 7 ***Weldon*** | Y | N | Y | N | Y | N | Y | Y |
| 8 Kostmayer | Y | Y | N | Y | Y | N | Y | Y |
| 9 ***Shuster*** | Y | N | N | N | N | N | N | N |
| 10 ***McDade*** | Y | N | Y | ? | ? | ? | ? | ? |
| 11 Kanjorski | Y | N | Y | Y | Y | Y | Y | Y |
| 12 Murtha | Y | N | Y | Y | Y | Y | Y | Y |
| 13 ***Coughlin*** | N | N | Y | ? | Y | N | N | N |
| 14 Coyne | Y | N | Y | Y | Y | Y | Y | Y |
| 15 ***Ritter*** | N | N | Y | Y | Y | N | N | N |
| 16 ***Walker*** | N | N | N | N | N | N | N | N |
| 17 ***Gekas*** | Y | Y | N | N | Y | N | N | N |
| 18 ***Santorum*** | Y | N | Y | N | Y | N | N | N |
| 19 ***Goodling*** | Y | N | Y | Y | Y | N | N | N |
| 20 Gaydos | Y | N | Y | Y | Y | Y | ? | ? |
| 21 ***Ridge*** | N | N | N | Y | Y | N | N | N |
| 22 Murphy | Y | Y | Y | Y | Y | N | Y | Y |
| 23 ***Clinger*** | N | N | Y | Y | Y | N | N | N |
| **RHODE ISLAND** | | | | | | | | |
| 1 ***Machtley*** | Y | N | Y | Y | Y | Y | Y | Y |
| 2 Reed | Y | N | Y | Y | Y | Y | Y | Y |
| **SOUTH CAROLINA** | | | | | | | | |
| 1 ***Ravenel*** | N | N | Y | Y | Y | Y | Y | Y |
| 2 ***Spence*** | N | N | Y | Y | Y | Y | N | N |
| 3 Derrick | Y | N | Y | Y | Y | Y | Y | Y |
| 4 Patterson | N | N | Y | Y | Y | Y | Y | Y |
| 5 Spratt | Y | N | Y | Y | Y | Y | Y | Y |
| 6 Tallon | Y | N | Y | ? | Y | Y | N | Y |
| **SOUTH DAKOTA** | | | | | | | | |
| AL Johnson | N | N | Y | Y | Y | Y | Y | Y |
| **TENNESSEE** | | | | | | | | |
| 1 ***Quillen*** | Y | N | Y | Y | Y | Y | N | N |
| 2 ***Duncan*** | N | N | Y | N | N | Y | N | N |
| 3 Lloyd | Y | N | Y | Y | Y | Y | Y | Y |
| 4 Cooper | N | N | Y | Y | Y | Y | Y | Y |
| 5 Clement | ? | ? | ? | ? | ? | ? | ? | ? |
| 6 Gordon | Y | N | Y | Y | Y | Y | Y | ? |
| 7 ***Sundquist*** | Y | N | Y | Y | Y | Y | N | Y |
| 8 Tanner | N | N | Y | Y | Y | Y | N | N |
| 9 Ford | Y | N | Y | Y | Y | Y | Y | Y |
| **TEXAS** | | | | | | | | |
| 1 Chapman | Y | N | Y | Y | Y | Y | N | Y |
| 2 Wilson | Y | N | Y | Y | Y | Y | Y | Y |
| 3 ***Johnson*** | N | N | Y | N | Y | N | N | N |
| 4 Hall | N | N | Y | Y | Y | Y | N | N |
| 5 Bryant | Y | Y | Y | Y | Y | Y | Y | Y |
| 6 ***Barton*** | N | N | Y | N | N | N | N | N |
| 7 ***Archer*** | N | N | Y | N | N | N | N | N |
| 8 ***Fields*** | Y | N | Y | N | N | N | N | N |
| 9 Brooks | Y | N | Y | Y | Y | N | Y | Y |
| 10 Pickle | Y | N | Y | Y | Y | Y | Y | Y |
| 11 Edwards | Y | N | Y | Y | Y | Y | Y | Y |
| 12 Geren | Y | Y | Y | Y | Y | Y | N | N |
| 13 Sarpalius | Y | N | Y | Y | Y | Y | Y | Y |
| 14 Laughlin | N | N | Y | Y | Y | N | Y | Y |
| 15 de la Garza | Y | Y | Y | Y | Y | Y | Y | Y |
| 16 Coleman | Y | Y | Y | Y | Y | Y | Y | Y |
| 17 Stenholm | N | N | Y | Y | Y | Y | N | N |
| 18 Washington | N | Y | N | ? | Y | Y | Y | Y |
| 19 ***Combest*** | Y | N | Y | N | Y | N | N | Y |
| 20 Gonzalez | Y | N | Y | Y | Y | Y | Y | Y |
| 21 ***Smith*** | Y | Y | Y | N | Y | N | N | N |
| 22 ***DeLay*** | Y | Y | N | N | N | N | N | N |
| 23 Bustamante | Y | N | Y | Y | Y | Y | Y | Y |
| 24 Frost | Y | N | Y | Y | Y | Y | Y | Y |
| 25 Andrews | N | N | Y | Y | Y | Y | Y | Y |
| 26 ***Armey*** | N | N | N | N | N | N | N | N |
| 27 Ortiz | Y | N | Y | Y | ? | Y | Y | Y |
| **UTAH** | | | | | | | | |
| 1 ***Hansen*** | Y | Y | Y | Y | N | N | Y | Y |
| 2 Owens | N | Y | Y | Y | Y | Y | Y | Y |
| 3 Orton | N | Y | Y | Y | Y | N | Y | Y |
| **VERMONT** | | | | | | | | |
| AL *Sanders* | Y | Y | Y | Y | Y | Y | Y | Y |
| **VIRGINIA** | | | | | | | | |
| 1 ***Bateman*** | Y | N | Y | Y | Y | Y | N | N |
| 2 Pickett | Y | N | Y | Y | Y | N | N | Y |
| 3 ***Bliley*** | N | N | Y | N | Y | N | N | N |
| 4 Sisisky | Y | N | Y | Y | Y | Y | N | Y |
| 5 Payne | N | N | Y | ? | Y | Y | N | Y |
| 6 Olin | N | N | Y | ? | Y | N | N | N |
| 7 ***Allen*** | N | Y | N | N | Y | Y | N | N |
| 8 Moran | Y | N | Y | Y | Y | Y | Y | Y |
| 9 Boucher | Y | N | Y | Y | Y | Y | Y | Y |
| 10 ***Wolf*** | N | N | Y | N | Y | Y | N | N |
| **WASHINGTON** | | | | | | | | |
| 1 ***Miller*** | N | N | Y | N | N | Y | N | N |
| 2 Swift | Y | N | Y | Y | Y | Y | Y | Y |
| 3 Unsoeld | Y | N | Y | Y | Y | Y | Y | Y |
| 4 ***Morrison*** | N | N | Y | Y | Y | Y | N | N |
| 5 Foley | | | | | | | | |
| 6 Dicks | Y | N | Y | Y | Y | Y | Y | Y |
| 7 McDermott | Y | Y | Y | Y | Y | Y | Y | Y |
| 8 ***Chandler*** | ? | ? | ? | ? | ? | ? | ? | ? |
| **WEST VIRGINIA** | | | | | | | | |
| 1 Mollohan | Y | N | Y | Y | Y | Y | Y | Y |
| 2 Staggers | N | Y | Y | Y | Y | Y | Y | Y |
| 3 Wise | Y | N | Y | Y | Y | Y | Y | Y |
| 4 Rahall | Y | N | Y | Y | Y | Y | Y | Y |
| **WISCONSIN** | | | | | | | | |
| 1 Aspin | Y | N | Y | Y | Y | Y | Y | Y |
| 2 ***Klug*** | N | Y | Y | N | Y | Y | N | Y |
| 3 ***Gunderson*** | N | N | Y | Y | Y | Y | Y | Y |
| 4 Kleczka | Y | N | Y | Y | Y | Y | Y | Y |
| 5 Moody | N | Y | Y | Y | Y | Y | Y | Y |
| 6 ***Petri*** | N | N | N | Y | Y | Y | Y | Y |
| 7 Obey | N | Y | N | Y | Y | Y | Y | Y |
| 8 ***Roth*** | N | N | N | Y | Y | Y | N | N |
| 9 ***Sensenbrenner*** | N | N | N | N | N | N | N | N |
| **WYOMING** | | | | | | | | |
| AL ***Thomas*** | N | Y | Y | N | Y | Y | Y | Y |

Southern states - Ala., Ark., Fla., Ga., Ky., La., Miss., N.C., Okla., S.C., Tenn., Texas, Va.
Omitted votes are quorum calls, which CQ does not include in its vote charts.

**480. HR 429. Western Water Bill/Central Valley Project.** Thomas, R-Calif., motion to recommit to conference the conference report with instructions to report it back after deleting the reform of the Central Valley Project in California. Motion rejected 159-244: R 117-41; D 42-202 (ND 15-152, SD 27-50); I 0-1, Oct. 6, 1992 (in the session that began and the Congressional Record dated Oct. 5). (The conference report subsequently was adopted by voice vote.)

**481. HR 11. Tax Bill/Rule.** Adoption of rule (H Res 609) to provide for House floor consideration of the $27 billion conference report on the tax bill. Adopted 213-191: R 11-149; D 202-41 (ND 137-29, SD 65-12); I 0-1, Oct. 6, 1992 (in the session that began and the Congressional Record dated Oct. 5).

**482. HR 11. Tax Bill/Conference Report.** Adoption of the $27 billion conference report on the tax bill, including tax benefits for 25 inner-city and 25 rural-area enterprise zones; a restoration of tax breaks for individual retirement accounts (IRAs); penalty-free withdrawals from IRAs; a 12-month extension of a dozen expiring tax breaks, allowing the writeoff of intangible assets, including good will, over 14 years; passive loss deductions by real estate developers; new rules allowing real estate investment by pension funds; the repeal of luxury taxes; the permanent extension of the low-income housing and targeted jobs tax credits; the creation of a new child welfare capped entitlement; and provisions for other purposes. Adopted 208-202: R 39-122; D 169-79 (ND 119-51, SD 50-28); I 0-1, Oct. 6, 1992 (in the session that began and the Congressional Record dated Oct. 5).

**483. HR 5739. Export-Import Bank Reauthorization/Conference Report.** Adoption of the conference report to reauthorize the Export-Import Bank through fiscal 1997 to assist foreign countries in buying American-made goods and services through loans and loan guarantees. Adopted 332-44: R 118-37; D 213-7 (ND 142-5, SD 71-2); I 1-0, Oct. 6, 1992 (in the session that began and the Congressional Record dated Oct. 5).

**484. S 3100. Louisiana Land Conveyance/Motion To Suspend.** Vento, D-Minn., motion to suspend the rules and pass the bill to transfer about 162 acres of land in Cameron Parish, La., to the West Cameron Port Authority to be used as a public port facility. Motion agreed to 236-102: R 37-100; D 198-2 (ND 135-2, SD 63-0); I 1-0, Oct. 6, 1992 (in the session that began and the Congressional Record dated Oct. 5). A two-thirds majority of those present and voting (226 in this case) was required for passage under suspension of the rules.

**485. S 1704. National Park Service Employee Housing and Miscellaneous Public Lands/Motion To Suspend.** Motion to suspend the rules and pass the bill to improve the availability of housing for employees of the National Park Service, Forest Service, Bureau of Land Management, and Fish and Wildlife Service. Motion agreed to 237-107: R 47-90; D 189-17 (ND 137-6, SD 52-11); I 1-0, Oct. 6, 1992 (in the session that began and the Congressional Record dated Oct. 5.)

**486. Procedural Motion.** Kyl, R-Ariz., motion to adjourn. Motion rejected 97-250: R 94-35; D 3-214 (ND 3-143, SD 0-71); I 0-1, Oct. 6, 1992 (in the session that began and the Congressional Record dated Oct. 5).

**487. HR 6179. Delaware River Study/Motion To Suspend.** Kostmayer, D-Pa., motion to suspend the rules and pass the bill to authorize a study of 50 miles of Delaware River for inclusion in the Wild and Scenic River System. Motion agreed to 256-84: R 41-82; D 214-2 (ND 145-0, SD 69-2); I 1-0, Oct. 6, 1992 (in the session that began and the Congressional Record dated Oct. 5). A two-thirds majority of those present and voting (227 in this case) was required for passage under suspension of the rules.

## KEY

| | |
|---|---|
| Y | Voted for (yea). |
| # | Paired for. |
| + | Announced for. |
| N | Voted against (nay). |
| X | Paired against. |
| − | Announced against. |
| P | Voted "present." |
| C | Voted "present" to avoid possible conflict of interest. |
| ? | Did not vote or otherwise make a position known. |

**Democrats** *Republicans*
*Independent*

| | 480 | 481 | 482 | 483 | 484 | 485 | 486 | 487 |
|---|---|---|---|---|---|---|---|---|
| **ALABAMA** | | | | | | | | |
| 1 *Callahan* | Y | N | N | Y | N | N | Y | Y |
| 2 *Dickinson* | ? | N | N | N | N | N | Y | N |
| 3 Browder | Y | Y | Y | Y | ? | Y | N | Y |
| 4 Bevill | Y | Y | Y | Y | Y | Y | N | Y |
| 5 Cramer | N | Y | Y | Y | Y | Y | N | Y |
| 6 Erdreich | N | Y | Y | Y | Y | Y | N | Y |
| 7 Harris | Y | Y | Y | Y | Y | Y | N | Y |
| **ALASKA** | | | | | | | | |
| AL *Young* | Y | N | Y | Y | ? | ? | ? | ? |
| **ARIZONA** | | | | | | | | |
| 1 *Rhodes* | N | N | N | Y | N | N | Y | Y |
| 2 Pastor | N | N | Y | + | Y | Y | N | Y |
| 3 *Stump* | Y | N | N | N | N | N | Y | N |
| 4 *Kyl* | N | N | N | Y | N | N | Y | N |
| 5 *Kolbe* | N | N | N | Y | ? | ? | ? | ? |
| **ARKANSAS** | | | | | | | | |
| 1 Alexander | ? | ? | ? | ? | ? | ? | N | Y |
| 2 Thornton | N | Y | N | Y | Y | Y | N | Y |
| 3 *Hammerschmidt* | Y | N | N | Y | N | N | N | Y |
| 4 Anthony | N | Y | Y | Y | ? | ? | N | Y |
| **CALIFORNIA** | | | | | | | | |
| 1 *Riggs* | N | N | N | Y | ? | N | N | N |
| 2 *Herger* | Y | N | N | N | N | N | Y | N |
| 3 Matsui | N | Y | Y | Y | ? | ? | ? | ? |
| 4 Fazio | Y | Y | Y | Y | Y | Y | N | Y |
| 5 Pelosi | N | Y | Y | Y | ? | Y | N | Y |
| 6 Boxer | ? | ? | ? | ? | ? | ? | ? | ? |
| 7 Miller | N | Y | Y | Y | Y | Y | N | Y |
| 8 Dellums | N | Y | ? | ? | ? | ? | N | Y |
| 9 Stark | N | Y | Y | ? | ? | ? | ? | ? |
| 10 Edwards | N | Y | Y | Y | Y | Y | N | Y |
| 11 Lantos | N | Y | Y | Y | Y | Y | N | Y |
| 12 *Campbell* | Y | N | N | Y | N | N | N | Y |
| 13 Mineta | Y | Y | Y | Y | Y | Y | N | Y |
| 14 *Doolittle* | Y | N | N | N | N | Y | N | N |
| 15 Condit | Y | N | N | Y | ? | Y | N | Y |
| 16 Panetta | Y | N | Y | Y | Y | Y | N | Y |
| 17 Dooley | Y | N | N | ? | Y | Y | N | Y |
| 18 Lehman | Y | Y | Y | ? | Y | Y | N | Y |
| 19 *Lagomarsino* | N | N | N | Y | Y | Y | N | Y |
| 20 *Thomas* | Y | N | Y | ? | ? | Y | N | N |
| 21 *Gallegly* | Y | N | N | Y | N | Y | ? | ? |
| 22 *Moorhead* | Y | N | N | Y | Y | Y | N | Y |
| 23 Beilenson | N | Y | N | ? | ? | ? | ? | ? |
| 24 Waxman | N | Y | Y | Y | ? | Y | N | Y |
| 25 Roybal | N | Y | Y | Y | Y | Y | N | Y |
| 26 Berman | N | Y | Y | Y | ? | ? | ? | ? |
| 27 Levine | Y | Y | ? | ? | Y | Y | N | ? |
| 28 Dixon | N | Y | Y | ? | ? | ? | ? | ? |
| 29 Waters | N | Y | Y | ? | ? | ? | N | Y |
| 30 Martinez | N | Y | ? | ? | ? | N | ? | Y |
| 31 Dymally | N | Y | ? | ? | ? | N | ? | Y |
| 32 Anderson | N | Y | Y | ? | ? | Y | N | Y |
| 33 *Dreier* | Y | N | N | N | N | Y | Y | Y |
| 34 Torres | N | Y | Y | ? | ? | N | Y | Y |
| 35 *Lewis* | Y | N | N | N | N | N | Y | Y |
| 36 Brown | N | Y | Y | Y | Y | Y | N | Y |
| 37 *McCandless* | Y | N | Y | N | N | Y | N | N |
| 38 *Dornan* | Y | N | N | N | N | N | Y | N |
| 39 *Dannemeyer* | Y | N | N | N | N | N | Y | N |
| 40 *Cox* | Y | N | N | Y | N | Y | Y | Y |
| 41 *Lowery* | Y | N | N | Y | N | Y | N | Y |

| | 480 | 481 | 482 | 483 | 484 | 485 | 486 | 487 |
|---|---|---|---|---|---|---|---|---|
| 42 *Rohrabacher* | Y | N | N | N | N | N | Y | N |
| 43 *Packard* | Y | N | N | N | ? | N | Y | N |
| 44 *Cunningham* | Y | N | N | Y | Y | ? | ? | ? |
| 45 *Hunter* | Y | N | N | Y | N | ? | Y | N |
| **COLORADO** | | | | | | | | |
| 1 Schroeder | N | N | Y | Y | Y | Y | N | ? |
| 2 Skaggs | N | ? | Y | Y | Y | Y | N | Y |
| 3 Campbell | N | Y | Y | Y | Y | Y | N | Y |
| 4 *Allard* | Y | N | N | N | N | N | Y | Y |
| 5 *Hefley* | Y | N | Y | N | N | Y | Y | Y |
| 6 *Schaefer* | Y | N | N | N | N | N | Y | Y |
| **CONNECTICUT** | | | | | | | | |
| 1 Kennelly | N | Y | Y | Y | Y | Y | N | Y |
| 2 Gejdenson | N | Y | Y | Y | Y | Y | N | Y |
| 3 DeLauro | N | Y | Y | Y | Y | Y | N | Y |
| 4 *Shays* | N | N | N | Y | N | Y | N | Y |
| 5 *Franks* | Y | N | Y | Y | N | Y | N | Y |
| 6 *Johnson* | Y | Y | Y | Y | Y | N | N | Y |
| **DELAWARE** | | | | | | | | |
| AL Carper | N | N | Y | Y | Y | N | N | Y |
| **FLORIDA** | | | | | | | | |
| 1 Hutto | Y | N | N | Y | Y | N | N | Y |
| 2 Peterson | N | Y | Y | Y | Y | Y | N | Y |
| 3 Bennett | N | Y | N | Y | Y | Y | N | Y |
| 4 *James* | Y | N | N | N | N | N | Y | N |
| 5 *McCollum* | Y | N | N | N | N | N | Y | Y |
| 6 *Stearns* | ? | ? | ? | ? | ? | ? | ? | ? |
| 7 Gibbons | N | Y | Y | ? | ? | ? | N | Y |
| 8 *Young* | Y | N | N | N | N | N | N | N |
| 9 *Bilirakis* | Y | N | N | N | N | N | Y | Y |
| 10 *Ireland* | Y | N | N | N | N | N | ? | N |
| 11 Bacchus | N | Y | Y | Y | Y | N | ? | ? |
| 12 *Lewis* | Y | N | N | N | N | N | Y | Y |
| 13 *Goss* | Y | N | N | N | N | N | N | N |
| 14 Johnston | N | Y | Y | Y | Y | ? | ? | ? |
| 15 *Shaw* | Y | N | N | Y | ? | ? | ? | ? |
| 16 Smith | N | Y | Y | Y | Y | Y | N | Y |
| 17 Lehman | ? | ? | ? | ? | Y | Y | N | Y |
| 18 *Ros—Lehtinen* | N | N | N | Y | N | Y | N | Y |
| 19 Fascell | N | Y | Y | Y | Y | N | N | Y |
| **GEORGIA** | | | | | | | | |
| 1 Thomas | Y | Y | Y | Y | Y | Y | ? | ? |
| 2 Hatcher | ? | ? | ? | ? | ? | ? | ? | ? |
| 3 Ray | Y | N | N | Y | ? | N | ? | Y |
| 4 Jones | ? | ? | ? | Y | ? | N | ? | Y |
| 5 Lewis | N | Y | Y | Y | Y | Y | N | Y |
| 6 *Gingrich* | Y | N | N | N | N | N | N | Y |
| 7 Darden | N | Y | Y | Y | Y | Y | N | Y |
| 8 Rowland | N | Y | N | Y | Y | Y | N | Y |
| 9 Jenkins | N | Y | ? | ? | ? | ? | ? | ? |
| 10 Barnard | ? | ? | ? | ? | ? | ? | ? | ? |
| **HAWAII** | | | | | | | | |
| 1 Abercrombie | N | Y | Y | Y | Y | Y | N | Y |
| 2 Mink | N | Y | N | Y | Y | Y | N | Y |
| **IDAHO** | | | | | | | | |
| 1 LaRocco | N | Y | Y | Y | Y | Y | N | Y |
| 2 Stallings | Y | Y | N | Y | ? | ? | ? | ? |
| **ILLINOIS** | | | | | | | | |
| 1 Hayes | N | Y | Y | Y | Y | Y | N | Y |
| 2 Savage | N | ? | Y | ? | ? | ? | ? | ? |
| 3 Russo | N | Y | Y | Y | Y | Y | ? | ? |
| 4 Sangmeister | N | Y | N | Y | Y | Y | N | Y |
| 5 Lipinski | ? | ? | ? | ? | ? | ? | ? | ? |
| 6 *Hyde* | Y | N | N | Y | N | N | N | Y |
| 7 Collins | N | Y | Y | Y | ? | ? | N | Y |
| 8 Rostenkowski | N | Y | Y | Y | Y | Y | N | Y |
| 9 Yates | ? | ? | ? | ? | Y | Y | N | Y |
| 10 *Porter* | N | N | N | N | N | ? | ? | ? |
| 11 Annunzio | ? | ? | ? | ? | ? | ? | ? | ? |
| 12 *Crane* | Y | N | N | N | N | N | Y | N |
| 13 *Fawell* | Y | N | N | Y | N | N | N | Y |
| 14 *Hastert* | N | N | N | N | N | Y | Y | N |
| 15 *Ewing* | Y | N | N | N | Y | N | Y | Y |
| 16 Cox | N | Y | Y | Y | Y | Y | N | Y |
| 17 Evans | N | Y | Y | Y | Y | Y | N | Y |
| 18 *Michel* | Y | N | N | Y | N | N | N | Y |
| 19 Bruce | N | Y | Y | Y | Y | Y | N | Y |
| 20 Durbin | N | Y | Y | Y | Y | Y | N | Y |
| 21 Costello | N | Y | N | Y | Y | Y | N | Y |
| 22 Poshard | N | Y | N | Y | Y | Y | N | Y |
| **INDIANA** | | | | | | | | |
| 1 Visclosky | N | Y | N | Y | Y | Y | N | Y |
| 2 Sharp | ? | Y | Y | Y | Y | Y | N | Y |
| 3 Roemer | N | N | N | Y | Y | Y | N | Y |

ND Northern Democrats    SD Southern Democrats

| | 480 | 481 | 482 | 483 | 484 | 485 | 486 | 487 |
|---|---|---|---|---|---|---|---|---|
| 4 Long | N | Y | N | Y | Y | Y | N | Y |
| 5 Jontz | N | N | N | Y | Y | Y | N | Y |
| 6 ***Burton*** | Y | N | N | N | N | N | Y | N |
| 7 ***Myers*** | Y | ? | N | Y | Y | Y | N | N |
| 8 McCloskey | N | Y | Y | Y | Y | Y | N | Y |
| 9 Hamilton | N | Y | Y | Y | Y | Y | N | Y |
| 10 Jacobs | N | Y | Y | N | Y | Y | N | Y |
| **IOWA** | | | | | | | | |
| 1 ***Leach*** | N | N | Y | Y | Y | N | N | Y |
| 2 ***Nussle*** | Y | N | N | Y | N | N | Y | N |
| 3 Nagle | N | Y | Y | Y | Y | Y | N | Y |
| 4 Smith | N | Y | N | Y | Y | Y | ? | ? |
| 5 ***Lightfoot*** | Y | N | N | Y | N | N | Y | N |
| 6 ***Grandy*** | Y | N | Y | Y | ? | ? | ? | ? |
| **KANSAS** | | | | | | | | |
| 1 ***Roberts*** | Y | N | Y | Y | ? | ? | ? | N |
| 2 Slattery | N | N | N | Y | ? | N | N | Y |
| 3 ***Meyers*** | N | N | N | Y | Y | N | ? | ? |
| 4 Glickman | N | Y | Y | Y | Y | Y | N | Y |
| 5 ***Nichols*** | Y | N | N | Y | N | N | Y | N |
| **KENTUCKY** | | | | | | | | |
| 1 Hubbard | Y | N | N | Y | Y | N | N | N |
| 2 Natcher | N | Y | N | Y | Y | Y | N | Y |
| 3 Mazzoli | N | Y | Y | Y | Y | Y | N | Y |
| 4 ***Bunning*** | Y | N | Y | Y | ? | ? | Y | N |
| 5 ***Rogers*** | Y | N | N | Y | N | N | N | N |
| 6 ***Hopkins*** | N | N | N | Y | ? | ? | Y | N |
| 7 Perkins | Y | Y | N | Y | ? | ? | ? | ? |
| **LOUISIANA** | | | | | | | | |
| 1 ***Livingston*** | Y | N | N | Y | Y | N | Y | N |
| 2 Jefferson | N | Y | Y | Y | Y | Y | N | Y |
| 3 Tauzin | Y | Y | N | Y | ? | ? | ? | ? |
| 4 ***McCrery*** | Y | N | Y | Y | ? | ? | Y | Y |
| 5 Huckaby | Y | Y | Y | Y | Y | Y | N | Y |
| 6 ***Baker*** | Y | N | N | Y | Y | N | Y | N |
| 7 Hayes | N | Y | N | Y | Y | Y | N | Y |
| 8 ***Holloway*** | Y | N | N | N | Y | N | Y | N |
| **MAINE** | | | | | | | | |
| 1 Andrews | N | N | N | Y | Y | Y | N | Y |
| 2 ***Snowe*** | N | Y | Y | Y | Y | Y | N | Y |
| **MARYLAND** | | | | | | | | |
| 1 ***Gilchrest*** | N | N | Y | Y | Y | Y | Y | Y |
| 2 ***Bentley*** | Y | N | N | Y | N | Y | Y | N |
| 3 Cardin | N | Y | Y | Y | Y | Y | N | Y |
| 4 McMillen | N | Y | Y | Y | Y | Y | N | Y |
| 5 Hoyer | N | Y | Y | Y | Y | Y | N | Y |
| 6 Byron | Y | N | N | Y | Y | Y | N | Y |
| 7 Mfume | N | Y | Y | Y | Y | Y | N | Y |
| 8 ***Morella*** | N | N | Y | Y | Y | Y | Y | Y |
| **MASSACHUSETTS** | | | | | | | | |
| 1 Olver | N | Y | Y | Y | Y | Y | N | Y |
| 2 Neal | N | Y | Y | Y | Y | Y | N | Y |
| 3 Early | N | Y | Y | Y | Y | Y | N | Y |
| 4 Frank | N | Y | Y | Y | Y | Y | N | Y |
| 5 Atkins | N | N | Y | ? | ? | ? | ? | Y |
| 6 Mavroules | N | Y | Y | ? | ? | ? | N | Y |
| 7 Markey | N | Y | Y | Y | Y | Y | N | Y |
| 8 Kennedy | N | Y | Y | Y | Y | Y | N | ? |
| 9 Moakley | N | Y | Y | Y | Y | Y | N | Y |
| 10 Studds | N | Y | Y | Y | Y | Y | N | Y |
| 11 Donnelly | N | Y | Y | Y | ? | ? | ? | Y |
| **MICHIGAN** | | | | | | | | |
| 1 Conyers | N | Y | Y | ? | Y | Y | N | Y |
| 2 ***Pursell*** | Y | N | N | Y | N | N | ? | ? |
| 3 Wolpe | N | Y | Y | Y | Y | Y | N | Y |
| 4 ***Upton*** | N | Y | Y | N | Y | N | Y | Y |
| 5 ***Henry*** | Y | N | N | N | N | N | Y | Y |
| 6 Carr | N | N | N | Y | Y | Y | N | Y |
| 7 Kildee | N | Y | Y | Y | Y | Y | N | Y |
| 8 Traxler | ? | ? | ? | ? | ? | ? | N | ? |
| 9 ***Vander Jagt*** | Y | Y | Y | Y | N | Y | N | N |
| 10 ***Camp*** | Y | N | N | Y | N | N | Y | Y |
| 11 ***Davis*** | ? | N | Y | Y | Y | Y | N | ? |
| 12 Bonior | N | Y | Y | Y | Y | Y | N | Y |
| 13 Collins | N | Y | Y | Y | Y | Y | ? | ? |
| 14 Hertel | N | Y | N | Y | ? | ? | N | Y |
| 15 Ford | N | Y | N | ? | ? | Y | N | Y |
| 16 Dingell | N | Y | Y | Y | Y | Y | N | Y |
| 17 Levin | N | Y | Y | Y | Y | Y | N | Y |
| 18 ***Broomfield*** | Y | N | N | Y | ? | ? | ? | ? |
| **MINNESOTA** | | | | | | | | |
| 1 Penny | N | N | N | Y | Y | N | N | Y |
| 2 ***Weber*** | Y | N | N | Y | N | N | Y | N |
| 3 ***Ramstad*** | N | N | N | Y | N | N | Y | N |
| 4 Vento | N | Y | Y | Y | Y | Y | N | Y |

| | 480 | 481 | 482 | 483 | 484 | 485 | 486 | 487 |
|---|---|---|---|---|---|---|---|---|
| 5 Sabo | N | Y | Y | Y | Y | Y | N | Y |
| 6 Sikorski | N | Y | Y | Y | Y | Y | N | Y |
| 7 Peterson | N | Y | Y | Y | Y | Y | ? | ? |
| 8 Oberstar | N | Y | N | Y | Y | Y | N | Y |
| **MISSISSIPPI** | | | | | | | | |
| 1 Whitten | N | Y | ? | ? | ? | ? | N | Y |
| 2 Espy | Y | Y | Y | Y | ? | ? | N | Y |
| 3 Montgomery | N | Y | Y | Y | Y | Y | N | Y |
| 4 Parker | Y | Y | Y | Y | Y | Y | N | Y |
| 5 Taylor | Y | N | N | N | Y | N | N | Y |
| **MISSOURI** | | | | | | | | |
| 1 Clay | N | Y | Y | Y | Y | Y | ? | ? |
| 2 Horn | N | Y | Y | Y | Y | Y | N | Y |
| 3 Gephardt | N | Y | Y | Y | Y | Y | N | Y |
| 4 Skelton | Y | Y | N | Y | Y | Y | N | Y |
| 5 Wheat | N | Y | Y | Y | Y | Y | N | Y |
| 6 ***Coleman*** | Y | N | N | Y | Y | Y | ? | ? |
| 7 ***Hancock*** | Y | N | N | N | N | N | Y | N |
| 8 ***Emerson*** | Y | N | N | Y | N | Y | Y | N |
| 9 Volkmer | Y | Y | N | Y | Y | N | ? | ? |
| **MONTANA** | | | | | | | | |
| 1 Williams | N | Y | N | Y | Y | Y | N | Y |
| 2 ***Marlenee*** | Y | N | N | N | ? | ? | ? | N |
| **NEBRASKA** | | | | | | | | |
| 1 ***Bereuter*** | Y | N | N | Y | N | Y | N | Y |
| 2 Hoagland | N | Y | Y | Y | Y | Y | N | Y |
| 3 ***Barrett*** | Y | N | N | Y | N | N | Y | N |
| **NEVADA** | | | | | | | | |
| 1 Bilbray | N | Y | N | Y | Y | Y | N | Y |
| 2 ***Vucanovich*** | N | N | N | Y | N | N | ? | ? |
| **NEW HAMPSHIRE** | | | | | | | | |
| 1 ***Zeliff*** | Y | N | N | N | N | N | Y | N |
| 2 Swett | N | Y | N | Y | Y | Y | ? | ? |
| **NEW JERSEY** | | | | | | | | |
| 1 Andrews | N | N | N | Y | Y | Y | N | Y |
| 2 Hughes | N | N | N | Y | Y | Y | N | Y |
| 3 Pallone | N | Y | N | Y | Y | Y | N | Y |
| 4 ***Smith*** | N | Y | Y | Y | Y | Y | N | Y |
| 5 ***Roukema*** | N | N | Y | Y | Y | N | N | Y |
| 6 Dwyer | ? | ? | ? | ? | ? | ? | ? | ? |
| 7 ***Rinaldo*** | N | N | N | Y | N | Y | Y | Y |
| 8 Roe | N | ? | Y | ? | ? | ? | ? | Y |
| 9 Torricelli | N | N | Y | ? | Y | ? | N | Y |
| 10 Payne | N | Y | Y | Y | Y | Y | N | Y |
| 11 ***Gallo*** | Y | N | Y | Y | N | N | Y | ? |
| 12 ***Zimmer*** | N | N | N | N | Y | N | N | Y |
| 13 ***Saxton*** | Y | N | N | Y | Y | Y | Y | Y |
| 14 Guarini | N | N | Y | Y | # | # | N | Y |
| **NEW MEXICO** | | | | | | | | |
| 1 ***Schiff*** | Y | N | N | Y | N | N | N | N |
| 2 ***Skeen*** | Y | N | N | Y | N | N | ? | ? |
| 3 Richardson | N | Y | Y | Y | Y | Y | N | Y |
| **NEW YORK** | | | | | | | | |
| 1 Hochbrueckner | Y | Y | Y | Y | Y | Y | N | Y |
| 2 Downey | N | Y | Y | Y | Y | Y | N | Y |
| 3 Mrazek | N | Y | Y | Y | ? | ? | ? | ? |
| 4 ***Lent*** | Y | N | N | Y | ? | ? | ? | Y |
| 5 ***McGrath*** | N | N | Y | ? | ? | ? | ? | ? |
| 6 Flake | N | Y | Y | Y | Y | Y | N | Y |
| 7 Ackerman | N | Y | Y | Y | ? | ? | ? | ? |
| 8 Scheuer | N | Y | Y | Y | Y | Y | N | Y |
| 9 Manton | N | Y | Y | Y | ? | Y | N | Y |
| 10 Schumer | N | Y | Y | Y | Y | Y | N | Y |
| 11 Towns | N | Y | Y | Y | ? | ? | N | Y |
| 12 Owens | N | N | N | Y | ? | ? | N | Y |
| 13 Solarz | ? | ? | ? | ? | # | # | ? | Y |
| 14 ***Molinari*** | Y | N | N | Y | N | Y | Y | N |
| 15 ***Green*** | N | N | Y | Y | Y | Y | ? | ? |
| 16 Rangel | N | Y | Y | Y | Y | Y | N | Y |
| 17 Vacancy | | | | | | | | |
| 18 Serrano | N | Y | Y | ? | Y | Y | N | Y |
| 19 Engel | N | Y | Y | Y | Y | Y | N | Y |
| 20 Lowey | N | Y | Y | Y | Y | Y | N | Y |
| 21 ***Fish*** | Y | Y | Y | Y | Y | N | ? | Y |
| 22 ***Gilman*** | N | N | Y | Y | Y | Y | N | Y |
| 23 McNulty | N | Y | Y | Y | Y | Y | Y | Y |
| 24 ***Solomon*** | N | N | N | N | N | N | Y | N |
| 25 ***Boehlert*** | N | ? | Y | Y | Y | Y | N | Y |
| 26 ***Martin*** | Y | N | N | Y | ? | ? | Y | N |
| 27 ***Walsh*** | Y | N | N | Y | Y | Y | N | ? |
| 28 McHugh | N | N | N | Y | Y | Y | N | Y |
| 29 ***Horton*** | N | N | N | ? | Y | Y | N | Y |
| 30 Slaughter | N | Y | Y | Y | ? | Y | N | Y |
| 31 ***Paxon*** | Y | N | N | Y | N | N | Y | N |

| | 480 | 481 | 482 | 483 | 484 | 485 | 486 | 487 |
|---|---|---|---|---|---|---|---|---|
| 32 LaFalce | N | N | N | Y | ? | Y | N | Y |
| 33 Nowak | N | Y | Y | ? | Y | Y | N | Y |
| 34 ***Houghton*** | N | N | Y | Y | N | ? | Y | ? |
| **NORTH CAROLINA** | | | | | | | | |
| 1 Vacancy | | | | | | | | |
| 2 Valentine | Y | N | N | Y | Y | N | ? | ? |
| 3 Lancaster | N | Y | Y | Y | Y | Y | N | Y |
| 4 Price | N | Y | Y | Y | Y | Y | N | Y |
| 5 Neal | N | N | N | Y | Y | Y | N | Y |
| 6 ***Coble*** | Y | N | Y | N | N | N | Y | ? |
| 7 Rose | ? | Y | Y | Y | ? | ? | N | Y |
| 8 Hefner | N | Y | N | Y | Y | Y | ? | ? |
| 9 ***McMillan*** | Y | N | N | Y | N | Y | N | Y |
| 10 ***Ballenger*** | Y | N | N | + | N | N | + | — |
| 11 ***Taylor*** | Y | N | Y | N | N | N | Y | ? |
| **NORTH DAKOTA** | | | | | | | | |
| AL Dorgan | N | Y | Y | N | Y | Y | N | Y |
| **OHIO** | | | | | | | | |
| 1 Luken | Y | Y | Y | Y | Y | Y | ? | ? |
| 2 ***Gradison*** | Y | Y | Y | Y | N | Y | N | Y |
| 3 Hall | ? | Y | Y | ? | Y | Y | N | Y |
| 4 ***Oxley*** | Y | N | N | ? | ? | ? | Y | N |
| 5 ***Gillmor*** | Y | N | N | Y | ? | ? | Y | Y |
| 6 ***McEwen*** | Y | N | N | Y | ? | ? | ? | ? |
| 7 ***Hobson*** | Y | N | N | Y | N | Y | Y | N |
| 8 ***Boehner*** | Y | N | N | ? | N | N | Y | N |
| 9 Kaptur | N | N | N | Y | ? | ? | N | Y |
| 10 ***Miller*** | Y | N | — | Y | N | N | N | N |
| 11 Eckart | ? | Y | Y | N | Y | Y | N | Y |
| 12 ***Kasich*** | N | N | N | Y | N | Y | Y | N |
| 13 Pease | N | N | N | Y | Y | Y | N | Y |
| 14 Sawyer | N | Y | Y | Y | Y | Y | N | Y |
| 15 ***Wylie*** | Y | N | N | Y | N | N | N | N |
| 16 ***Regula*** | Y | N | N | Y | N | Y | Y | Y |
| 17 Traficant | N | Y | Y | Y | Y | Y | N | Y |
| 18 Applegate | N | Y | N | Y | N | N | N | Y |
| 19 Feighan | N | Y | Y | Y | ? | ? | N | Y |
| 20 Oakar | N | Y | Y | Y | ? | Y | N | Y |
| 21 Stokes | N | Y | Y | Y | ? | Y | N | Y |
| **OKLAHOMA** | | | | | | | | |
| 1 ***Inhofe*** | Y | N | N | Y | N | N | Y | N |
| 2 Synar | N | Y | N | Y | Y | Y | N | Y |
| 3 Brewster | N | Y | Y | Y | Y | Y | N | Y |
| 4 McCurdy | Y | N | N | Y | ? | ? | N | Y |
| 5 ***Edwards*** | ? | ? | ? | ? | ? | ? | Y | N |
| 6 English | Y | Y | N | Y | Y | Y | N | Y |
| **OREGON** | | | | | | | | |
| 1 AuCoin | N | Y | N | ? | ? | ? | ? | Y |
| 2 ***Smith*** | Y | N | N | Y | N | N | Y | N |
| 3 Wyden | N | Y | Y | Y | Y | Y | N | Y |
| 4 DeFazio | N | N | N | Y | Y | Y | N | Y |
| 5 Kopetski | N | Y | Y | Y | Y | Y | N | Y |
| **PENNSYLVANIA** | | | | | | | | |
| 1 Foglietta | ? | ? | Y | ? | ? | ? | ? | ? |
| 2 Blackwell | N | Y | N | Y | Y | Y | ? | Y |
| 3 Borski | N | Y | Y | Y | Y | Y | N | Y |
| 4 Kolter | ? | ? | ? | ? | Y | Y | N | Y |
| 5 ***Schulze*** | ? | N | Y | ? | N | N | ? | ? |
| 6 Yatron | ? | ? | ? | ? | Y | Y | ? | ? |
| 7 ***Weldon*** | N | N | N | Y | N | N | ? | ? |
| 8 Kostmayer | N | Y | N | Y | Y | Y | N | Y |
| 9 ***Shuster*** | Y | N | N | N | N | N | ? | ? |
| 10 ***McDade*** | ? | ? | ? | ? | ? | ? | ? | ? |
| 11 Kanjorski | N | N | Y | Y | Y | Y | N | Y |
| 12 Murtha | N | Y | Y | Y | ? | ? | ? | ? |
| 13 ***Coughlin*** | Y | N | N | Y | N | N | Y | N |
| 14 Coyne | N | Y | Y | Y | Y | Y | ? | ? |
| 15 ***Ritter*** | Y | N | Y | Y | ? | ? | ? | Y |
| 16 ***Walker*** | Y | N | N | N | N | N | Y | N |
| 17 ***Gekas*** | Y | N | N | Y | N | N | Y | N |
| 18 ***Santorum*** | N | N | N | Y | N | N | Y | N |
| 19 ***Goodling*** | ? | N | N | Y | N | N | Y | N |
| 20 Gaydos | ? | ? | ? | ? | Y | Y | ? | ? |
| 21 ***Ridge*** | Y | N | N | Y | ? | Y | Y | N |
| 22 Murphy | N | N | N | Y | N | N | Y | Y |
| 23 ***Clinger*** | Y | N | Y | Y | N | N | Y | N |
| **RHODE ISLAND** | | | | | | | | |
| 1 ***Machtley*** | N | N | Y | Y | Y | Y | N | ? |
| 2 Reed | N | Y | Y | Y | Y | Y | N | Y |
| **SOUTH CAROLINA** | | | | | | | | |
| 1 ***Ravenel*** | N | N | Y | Y | Y | Y | ? | ? |
| 2 ***Spence*** | Y | N | N | N | N | Y | N | N |
| 3 Derrick | N | Y | Y | Y | Y | Y | N | Y |
| 4 Patterson | N | N | N | Y | Y | N | N | Y |
| 5 Spratt | N | Y | Y | Y | Y | Y | N | Y |
| 6 Tallon | Y | Y | Y | Y | Y | N | N | Y |

| | 480 | 481 | 482 | 483 | 484 | 485 | 486 | 487 |
|---|---|---|---|---|---|---|---|---|
| **SOUTH DAKOTA** | | | | | | | | |
| AL Johnson | N | Y | Y | Y | Y | Y | N | Y |
| **TENNESSEE** | | | | | | | | |
| 1 ***Quillen*** | N | N | N | N | N | N | N | ? |
| 2 ***Duncan*** | Y | N | N | N | N | N | Y | N |
| 3 Lloyd | N | Y | N | Y | Y | Y | N | Y |
| 4 Cooper | N | Y | N | Y | Y | Y | N | Y |
| 5 Clement | ? | ? | ? | ? | ? | ? | ? | ? |
| 6 Gordon | N | Y | Y | Y | Y | Y | N | Y |
| 7 ***Sundquist*** | Y | N | Y | Y | N | N | Y | N |
| 8 Tanner | Y | Y | Y | Y | Y | Y | N | Y |
| 9 Ford | N | N | Y | Y | Y | Y | ? | Y |
| **TEXAS** | | | | | | | | |
| 1 Chapman | N | Y | N | ? | Y | Y | N | Y |
| 2 Wilson | N | Y | Y | ? | ? | ? | N | Y |
| 3 ***Johnson*** | Y | N | N | N | X | X | Y | N |
| 4 Hall | Y | N | N | Y | Y | N | N | N |
| 5 Bryant | N | Y | Y | Y | ? | ? | N | Y |
| 6 ***Barton*** | Y | N | N | Y | N | N | Y | N |
| 7 ***Archer*** | Y | N | N | Y | N | N | Y | N |
| 8 ***Fields*** | Y | N | N | + | — | — | ? | — |
| 9 Brooks | N | Y | N | Y | Y | Y | N | Y |
| 10 Pickle | N | Y | Y | Y | Y | Y | N | Y |
| 11 Edwards | Y | Y | N | Y | Y | Y | N | Y |
| 12 Geren | Y | N | N | Y | Y | N | N | Y |
| 13 Sarpalius | N | Y | Y | Y | Y | Y | N | Y |
| 14 Laughlin | N | Y | N | Y | Y | Y | N | Y |
| 15 de la Garza | N | Y | Y | Y | Y | Y | N | Y |
| 16 Coleman | Y | Y | Y | Y | Y | Y | N | Y |
| 17 Stenholm | Y | Y | Y | Y | Y | N | N | Y |
| 18 Washington | N | Y | Y | Y | ? | ? | ? | Y |
| 19 ***Combest*** | N | N | N | Y | ? | ? | ? | ? |
| 20 Gonzalez | N | Y | Y | Y | Y | Y | N | Y |
| 21 ***Smith*** | Y | N | N | N | N | N | Y | Y |
| 22 ***DeLay*** | Y | N | N | N | ? | N | Y | N |
| 23 Bustamante | N | Y | Y | Y | Y | Y | N | Y |
| 24 Frost | N | Y | Y | Y | ? | ? | ? | ? |
| 25 Andrews | N | Y | Y | Y | ? | ? | N | Y |
| 26 ***Armey*** | Y | N | N | N | N | N | ? | ? |
| 27 Ortiz | N | Y | N | Y | Y | Y | N | Y |
| **UTAH** | | | | | | | | |
| 1 ***Hansen*** | N | N | N | Y | N | Y | ? | N |
| 2 Owens | N | Y | Y | Y | Y | Y | N | Y |
| 3 Orton | N | Y | Y | Y | Y | Y | N | Y |
| **VERMONT** | | | | | | | | |
| AL *Sanders* | N | N | N | Y | Y | Y | N | Y |
| **VIRGINIA** | | | | | | | | |
| 1 ***Bateman*** | Y | N | Y | Y | Y | N | ? | ? |
| 2 Pickett | Y | Y | Y | Y | Y | N | N | Y |
| 3 ***Bliley*** | Y | N | N | Y | N | N | ? | ? |
| 4 Sisisky | Y | Y | Y | Y | Y | Y | N | Y |
| 5 Payne | Y | Y | Y | Y | Y | Y | N | Y |
| 6 Olin | Y | N | N | Y | Y | ? | N | Y |
| 7 ***Allen*** | Y | N | N | Y | N | N | Y | N |
| 8 Moran | N | Y | Y | Y | Y | Y | N | Y |
| 9 Boucher | N | ? | Y | ? | ? | Y | N | Y |
| 10 ***Wolf*** | Y | N | N | Y | N | Y | Y | Y |
| **WASHINGTON** | | | | | | | | |
| 1 ***Miller*** | N | N | N | Y | Y | Y | Y | ? |
| 2 Swift | N | Y | Y | Y | Y | Y | N | ? |
| 3 Unsoeld | N | Y | N | Y | Y | Y | N | Y |
| 4 ***Morrison*** | Y | Y | Y | Y | Y | Y | N | Y |
| 5 Foley | | | Y | | | | | |
| 6 Dicks | N | Y | Y | Y | Y | ? | N | Y |
| 7 McDermott | N | Y | Y | Y | Y | Y | ? | ? |
| 8 ***Chandler*** | ? | ? | ? | ? | ? | ? | ? | ? |
| **WEST VIRGINIA** | | | | | | | | |
| 1 Mollohan | N | Y | N | Y | Y | Y | N | Y |
| 2 Staggers | Y | Y | N | Y | Y | Y | N | Y |
| 3 Wise | N | N | N | Y | Y | Y | N | ? |
| 4 Rahall | N | N | N | N | Y | Y | N | Y |
| **WISCONSIN** | | | | | | | | |
| 1 Aspin | N | ? | ? | ? | Y | Y | N | Y |
| 2 ***Klug*** | N | Y | Y | Y | Y | Y | ? | ? |
| 3 ***Gunderson*** | N | N | Y | Y | Y | Y | Y | N |
| 4 Kleczka | N | Y | Y | Y | Y | Y | N | Y |
| 5 Moody | N | Y | Y | Y | Y | Y | N | Y |
| 6 ***Petri*** | N | Y | Y | N | Y | N | N | N |
| 7 Obey | N | N | N | Y | Y | Y | N | Y |
| 8 ***Roth*** | Y | Y | Y | Y | N | N | Y | N |
| 9 ***Sensenbrenner*** | Y | N | N | N | N | N | Y | N |
| **WYOMING** | | | | | | | | |
| AL ***Thomas*** | Y | N | N | Y | N | N | ? | ? |

Southern states - Ala., Ark., Fla., Ga., Ky., La., Miss., N.C., Okla., S.C., Tenn., Texas, Va.
Omitted votes are quorum calls, which CQ does not include in its vote charts.

**488. Procedural Motion.** Dannemeyer, R-Calif., motion to adjourn. Motion agreed to 268-38: R 99-17; D 168-21 (ND 119-13, SD 49-8); I 1-0, Oct. 6, 1992 (in the session that began and the Congressional Record dated Oct. 5).

## KEY

Y   Voted for (yea).
#   Paired for.
+   Announced for.
N   Voted against (nay).
X   Paired against.
—   Announced against.
P   Voted "present."
C   Voted "present" to avoid possible conflict of interest.
?   Did not vote or otherwise make a position known.

Democrats    **Republicans**
*Independent*

| | | 488 |
|---|---|---|
| **ALABAMA** | | |
| 1 | *Callahan* | Y |
| 2 | *Dickinson* | Y |
| 3 | Browder | ? |
| 4 | Bevill | Y |
| 5 | Cramer | Y |
| 6 | Erdreich | Y |
| 7 | Harris | Y |
| **ALASKA** | | |
| AL | *Young* | ? |
| **ARIZONA** | | |
| 1 | *Rhodes* | Y |
| 2 | Pastor | Y |
| 3 | *Stump* | Y |
| 4 | *Kyl* | Y |
| 5 | *Kolbe* | ? |
| **ARKANSAS** | | |
| 1 | Alexander | Y |
| 2 | Thornton | N |
| 3 | *Hammerschmidt* | ? |
| 4 | Anthony | Y |
| **CALIFORNIA** | | |
| 1 | *Riggs* | Y |
| 2 | *Herger* | Y |
| 3 | Matsui | ? |
| 4 | Fazio | Y |
| 5 | Pelosi | N |
| 6 | Boxer | ? |
| 7 | Miller | Y |
| 8 | Dellums | Y |
| 9 | Stark | ? |
| 10 | Edwards | Y |
| 11 | Lantos | Y |
| 12 | *Campbell* | N |
| 13 | Mineta | Y |
| 14 | *Doolittle* | Y |
| 15 | Condit | Y |
| 16 | Panetta | Y |
| 17 | Dooley | Y |
| 18 | Lehman | Y |
| 19 | *Lagomarsino* | Y |
| 20 | *Thomas* | Y |
| 21 | *Gallegly* | ? |
| 22 | *Moorhead* | Y |
| 23 | Beilenson | ? |
| 24 | Waxman | ? |
| 25 | Roybal | ? |
| 26 | Berman | ? |
| 27 | Levine | Y |
| 28 | Dixon | ? |
| 29 | Waters | ? |
| 30 | Martinez | N |
| 31 | Dymally | Y |
| 32 | Anderson | Y |
| 33 | *Dreier* | Y |
| 34 | Torres | ? |
| 35 | *Lewis* | ? |
| 36 | Brown | Y |
| 37 | *McCandless* | Y |
| 38 | *Dornan* | N |
| 39 | *Dannemeyer* | N |
| 40 | *Cox* | N |
| 41 | *Lowery* | N |

| | | 488 |
|---|---|---|
| 42 | *Rohrabacher* | Y |
| 43 | *Packard* | Y |
| 44 | *Cunningham* | ? |
| 45 | *Hunter* | Y |
| **COLORADO** | | |
| 1 | Schroeder | ? |
| 2 | Skaggs | Y |
| 3 | Campbell | Y |
| 4 | *Allard* | Y |
| 5 | *Hefley* | Y |
| 6 | *Schaefer* | Y |
| **CONNECTICUT** | | |
| 1 | Kennelly | Y |
| 2 | Gejdenson | Y |
| 3 | DeLauro | Y |
| 4 | *Shays* | N |
| 5 | *Franks* | Y |
| 6 | *Johnson* | N |
| **DELAWARE** | | |
| AL | Carper | Y |
| **FLORIDA** | | |
| 1 | Hutto | ? |
| 2 | Peterson | Y |
| 3 | Bennett | N |
| 4 | *James* | Y |
| 5 | *McCollum* | ? |
| 6 | *Stearns* | ? |
| 7 | Gibbons | Y |
| 8 | *Young* | Y |
| 9 | *Bilirakis* | Y |
| 10 | *Ireland* | Y |
| 11 | Bacchus | ? |
| 12 | *Lewis* | ? |
| 13 | *Goss* | N |
| 14 | Johnston | ? |
| 15 | *Shaw* | ? |
| 16 | Smith | ? |
| 17 | Lehman | ? |
| 18 | *Ros—Lehtinen* | N |
| 19 | Fascell | ? |
| **GEORGIA** | | |
| 1 | Thomas | ? |
| 2 | Hatcher | ? |
| 3 | Ray | Y |
| 4 | Jones | ? |
| 5 | Lewis | Y |
| 6 | *Gingrich* | Y |
| 7 | Darden | ? |
| 8 | Rowland | ? |
| 9 | Jenkins | ? |
| 10 | Barnard | ? |
| **HAWAII** | | |
| 1 | Abercrombie | Y |
| 2 | Mink | Y |
| **IDAHO** | | |
| 1 | LaRocco | N |
| 2 | Stallings | ? |
| **ILLINOIS** | | |
| 1 | Hayes | Y |
| 2 | Savage | ? |
| 3 | Russo | Y |
| 4 | Sangmeister | Y |
| 5 | Lipinski | ? |
| 6 | *Hyde* | N |
| 7 | Collins | Y |
| 8 | Rostenkowski | Y |
| 9 | Yates | Y |
| 10 | *Porter* | ? |
| 11 | Annunzio | ? |
| 12 | *Crane* | Y |
| 13 | *Fawell* | Y |
| 14 | *Hastert* | Y |
| 15 | *Ewing* | ? |
| 16 | Cox | Y |
| 17 | Evans | Y |
| 18 | *Michel* | Y |
| 19 | Bruce | Y |
| 20 | Durbin | Y |
| 21 | Costello | Y |
| 22 | Poshard | Y |
| **INDIANA** | | |
| 1 | Visclosky | Y |
| 2 | Sharp | ? |
| 3 | Roemer | Y |

ND   Northern Democrats      SD   Southern Democrats

| | | |
|---|---|---|
| 4 | Long | Y |
| 5 | Jontz | Y |
| 6 | *Burton* | Y |
| 7 | *Myers* | Y |
| 8 | McCloskey | Y |
| 9 | Hamilton | Y |
| 10 | Jacobs | Y |

**IOWA**

| | | |
|---|---|---|
| 1 | *Leach* | Y |
| 2 | *Nussle* | Y |
| 3 | Nagle | Y |
| 4 | Smith | ? |
| 5 | *Lightfoot* | Y |
| 6 | *Grandy* | ? |

**KANSAS**

| | | |
|---|---|---|
| 1 | *Roberts* | Y |
| 2 | Slattery | Y |
| 3 | *Meyers* | ? |
| 4 | Glickman | Y |
| 5 | *Nichols* | ? |

**KENTUCKY**

| | | |
|---|---|---|
| 1 | Hubbard | Y |
| 2 | Natcher | Y |
| 3 | Mazzoli | Y |
| 4 | *Bunning* | Y |
| 5 | *Rogers* | Y |
| 6 | *Hopkins* | N |
| 7 | Perkins | ? |

**LOUISIANA**

| | | |
|---|---|---|
| 1 | *Livingston* | Y |
| 2 | Jefferson | Y |
| 3 | Tauzin | ? |
| 4 | *McCrery* | Y |
| 5 | Huckaby | ? |
| 6 | *Baker* | Y |
| 7 | Hayes | ? |
| 8 | *Holloway* | Y |

**MAINE**

| | | |
|---|---|---|
| 1 | Andrews | Y |
| 2 | *Snowe* | Y |

**MARYLAND**

| | | |
|---|---|---|
| 1 | *Gilchrest* | Y |
| 2 | *Bentley* | Y |
| 3 | Cardin | ? |
| 4 | McMillen | Y |
| 5 | Hoyer | Y |
| 6 | Byron | Y |
| 7 | Mfume | N |
| 8 | *Morella* | Y |

**MASSACHUSETTS**

| | | |
|---|---|---|
| 1 | Olver | Y |
| 2 | Neal | Y |
| 3 | Early | N |
| 4 | Frank | Y |
| 5 | Atkins | Y |
| 6 | Mavroules | ? |
| 7 | Markey | Y |
| 8 | Kennedy | ? |
| 9 | Moakley | Y |
| 10 | Studds | N |
| 11 | Donnelly | Y |

**MICHIGAN**

| | | |
|---|---|---|
| 1 | Conyers | Y |
| 2 | *Pursell* | ? |
| 3 | Wolpe | Y |
| 4 | *Upton* | Y |
| 5 | *Henry* | ? |
| 6 | Carr | Y |
| 7 | Kildee | Y |
| 8 | Traxler | ? |
| 9 | *Vander Jagt* | Y |
| 10 | *Camp* | Y |
| 11 | *Davis* | ? |
| 12 | Bonior | Y |
| 13 | Collins | ? |
| 14 | Hertel | Y |
| 15 | Ford | Y |
| 16 | Dingell | Y |
| 17 | Levin | Y |
| 18 | *Broomfield* | ? |

**MINNESOTA**

| | | |
|---|---|---|
| 1 | Penny | Y |
| 2 | *Weber* | Y |
| 3 | *Ramstad* | N |
| 4 | Vento | ? |

| | | |
|---|---|---|
| 5 | Sabo | Y |
| 6 | Sikorski | Y |
| 7 | Peterson | ? |
| 8 | Oberstar | N |

**MISSISSIPPI**

| | | |
|---|---|---|
| 1 | Whitten | N |
| 2 | Espy | Y |
| 3 | Montgomery | Y |
| 4 | Parker | N |
| 5 | Taylor | Y |

**MISSOURI**

| | | |
|---|---|---|
| 1 | Clay | ? |
| 2 | Horn | Y |
| 3 | Gephardt | Y |
| 4 | Skelton | Y |
| 5 | Wheat | Y |
| 6 | *Coleman* | ? |
| 7 | *Hancock* | Y |
| 8 | *Emerson* | Y |
| 9 | Volkmer | ? |

**MONTANA**

| | | |
|---|---|---|
| 1 | Williams | Y |
| 2 | *Marlenee* | Y |

**NEBRASKA**

| | | |
|---|---|---|
| 1 | *Bereuter* | N |
| 2 | Hoagland | Y |
| 3 | *Barrett* | Y |

**NEVADA**

| | | |
|---|---|---|
| 1 | Bilbray | Y |
| 2 | *Vucanovich* | ? |

**NEW HAMPSHIRE**

| | | |
|---|---|---|
| 1 | *Zeliff* | Y |
| 2 | Swett | ? |

**NEW JERSEY**

| | | |
|---|---|---|
| 1 | Andrews | Y |
| 2 | Hughes | Y |
| 3 | Pallone | Y |
| 4 | *Smith* | Y |
| 5 | *Roukema* | ? |
| 6 | Dwyer | ? |
| 7 | *Rinaldo* | Y |
| 8 | Roe | Y |
| 9 | Torricelli | Y |
| 10 | Payne | Y |
| 11 | *Gallo* | ? |
| 12 | *Zimmer* | Y |
| 13 | *Saxton* | Y |
| 14 | Guarini | ? |

**NEW MEXICO**

| | | |
|---|---|---|
| 1 | *Schiff* | N |
| 2 | *Skeen* | Y |
| 3 | Richardson | Y |

**NEW YORK**

| | | |
|---|---|---|
| 1 | Hochbrueckner | Y |
| 2 | Downey | Y |
| 3 | Mrazek | ? |
| 4 | *Lent* | ? |
| 5 | *McGrath* | ? |
| 6 | Flake | ? |
| 7 | Ackerman | ? |
| 8 | Scheuer | Y |
| 9 | Manton | ? |
| 10 | Schumer | Y |
| 11 | Towns | Y |
| 12 | Owens | Y |
| 13 | Solarz | ? |
| 14 | *Molinari* | Y |
| 15 | *Green* | ? |
| 16 | Rangel | Y |
| 17 | Vacancy | |
| 18 | Serrano | Y |
| 19 | Engel | Y |
| 20 | Lowey | Y |
| 21 | *Fish* | Y |
| 22 | Gilman | Y |
| 23 | McNulty | Y |
| 24 | *Solomon* | Y |
| 25 | Boehlert | N |
| 26 | Martin | Y |
| 27 | Walsh | ? |
| 28 | McHugh | Y |
| 29 | *Horton* | Y |
| 30 | Slaughter | Y |
| 31 | *Paxon* | Y |

| | | |
|---|---|---|
| 32 | LaFalce | Y |
| 33 | Nowak | Y |
| 34 | *Houghton* | ? |

**NORTH CAROLINA**

| | | |
|---|---|---|
| 1 | Vacancy | |
| 2 | Valentine | ? |
| 3 | Lancaster | Y |
| 4 | Price | Y |
| 5 | Neal | Y |
| 6 | *Coble* | Y |
| 7 | Rose | N |
| 8 | Hefner | ? |
| 9 | *McMillan* | Y |
| 10 | *Ballenger* | + |
| 11 | *Taylor* | ? |

**NORTH DAKOTA**

| | | |
|---|---|---|
| AL | Dorgan | Y |

**OHIO**

| | | |
|---|---|---|
| 1 | Luken | ? |
| 2 | *Gradison* | Y |
| 3 | Hall | Y |
| 4 | *Oxley* | Y |
| 5 | *Gillmor* | Y |
| 6 | *McEwen* | Y |
| 7 | *Hobson* | Y |
| 8 | *Boehner* | Y |
| 9 | Kaptur | Y |
| 10 | *Miller* | N |
| 11 | Eckart | Y |
| 12 | *Kasich* | Y |
| 13 | Pease | Y |
| 14 | Sawyer | Y |
| 15 | *Wylie* | Y |
| 16 | *Regula* | Y |
| 17 | Traficant | Y |
| 18 | Applegate | Y |
| 19 | Feighan | Y |
| 20 | Oakar | Y |
| 21 | Stokes | Y |

**OKLAHOMA**

| | | |
|---|---|---|
| 1 | *Inhofe* | ? |
| 2 | Synar | ? |
| 3 | Brewster | Y |
| 4 | McCurdy | Y |
| 5 | *Edwards* | N |
| 6 | English | Y |

**OREGON**

| | | |
|---|---|---|
| 1 | AuCoin | N |
| 2 | *Smith* | Y |
| 3 | Wyden | Y |
| 4 | DeFazio | N |
| 5 | Kopetski | N |

**PENNSYLVANIA**

| | | |
|---|---|---|
| 1 | Foglietta | ? |
| 2 | Blackwell | N |
| 3 | Borski | N |
| 4 | Kolter | ? |
| 5 | *Schulze* | Y |
| 6 | Yatron | ? |
| 7 | *Weldon* | ? |
| 8 | Kostmayer | Y |
| 9 | *Shuster* | Y |
| 10 | *McDade* | Y |
| 11 | Kanjorski | Y |
| 12 | Murtha | ? |
| 13 | *Coughlin* | Y |
| 14 | Coyne | Y |
| 15 | *Ritter* | Y |
| 16 | *Walker* | Y |
| 17 | Gekas | Y |
| 18 | *Santorum* | Y |
| 19 | *Goodling* | Y |
| 20 | Gaydos | ? |
| 21 | *Ridge* | ? |
| 22 | Murphy | ? |
| 23 | *Clinger* | Y |

**RHODE ISLAND**

| | | |
|---|---|---|
| 1 | *Machtley* | ? |
| 2 | Reed | Y |

**SOUTH CAROLINA**

| | | |
|---|---|---|
| 1 | *Ravenel* | ? |
| 2 | *Spence* | Y |
| 3 | Derrick | Y |
| 4 | Patterson | Y |
| 5 | Spratt | Y |
| 6 | Tallon | Y |

**SOUTH DAKOTA**

| | | |
|---|---|---|
| AL | Johnson | Y |

**TENNESSEE**

| | | |
|---|---|---|
| 1 | *Quillen* | ? |
| 2 | *Duncan* | Y |
| 3 | Lloyd | Y |
| 4 | Cooper | Y |
| 5 | Clement | ? |
| 6 | Gordon | Y |
| 7 | *Sundquist* | Y |
| 8 | Tanner | Y |
| 9 | Ford | Y |

**TEXAS**

| | | |
|---|---|---|
| 1 | Chapman | Y |
| 2 | Wilson | Y |
| 3 | *Johnson* | Y |
| 4 | Hall | Y |
| 5 | Bryant | ? |
| 6 | *Barton* | Y |
| 7 | *Archer* | ? |
| 8 | *Fields* | ? |
| 9 | Brooks | Y |
| 10 | Pickle | Y |
| 11 | Edwards | Y |
| 12 | Geren | Y |
| 13 | Sarpalius | Y |
| 14 | Laughlin | Y |
| 15 | de la Garza | Y |
| 16 | Coleman | N |
| 17 | Stenholm | Y |
| 18 | Washington | ? |
| 19 | *Combest* | ? |
| 20 | Gonzalez | N |
| 21 | *Smith* | Y |
| 22 | *DeLay* | Y |
| 23 | Bustamante | Y |
| 24 | Frost | ? |
| 25 | Andrews | Y |
| 26 | *Armey* | ? |
| 27 | Ortiz | ? |

**UTAH**

| | | |
|---|---|---|
| 1 | *Hansen* | Y |
| 2 | Owens | ? |
| 3 | Orton | Y |

**VERMONT**

| | | |
|---|---|---|
| AL | *Sanders* | Y |

**VIRGINIA**

| | | |
|---|---|---|
| 1 | *Bateman* | ? |
| 2 | Pickett | Y |
| 3 | *Bliley* | Y |
| 4 | Sisisky | Y |
| 5 | Payne | Y |
| 6 | Olin | Y |
| 7 | *Allen* | Y |
| 8 | Moran | N |
| 9 | Boucher | Y |
| 10 | *Wolf* | ? |

**WASHINGTON**

| | | |
|---|---|---|
| 1 | *Miller* | ? |
| 2 | Swift | ? |
| 3 | Unsoeld | N |
| 4 | *Morrison* | Y |
| 5 | Foley | |
| 6 | Dicks | Y |
| 7 | McDermott | ? |
| 8 | *Chandler* | ? |

**WEST VIRGINIA**

| | | |
|---|---|---|
| 1 | Mollohan | Y |
| 2 | Staggers | N |
| 3 | Wise | Y |
| 4 | Rahall | Y |

**WISCONSIN**

| | | |
|---|---|---|
| 1 | Aspin | Y |
| 2 | *Klug* | ? |
| 3 | *Gunderson* | Y |
| 4 | *Kleczka* | ? |
| 5 | Moody | Y |
| 6 | *Petri* | Y |
| 7 | Obey | Y |
| 8 | *Roth* | Y |
| 9 | Sensenbrenner | Y |

**WYOMING**

| | | |
|---|---|---|
| AL | *Thomas* | ? |

Southern states - Ala., Ark., Fla., Ga., Ky., La., Miss., N.C., Okla., S.C., Tenn., Texas, Va.
Omitted votes are quorum calls, which CQ does not include in its vote charts.

CQ

# SENATE ROLL CALL VOTES

### KEY

|  |  |
|---|---|
| Y | Voted for (yea). |
| # | Paired for. |
| + | Announced for. |
| N | Voted against (nay). |
| X | Paired against. |
| − | Announced against. |
| P | Voted "present." |
| C | Voted "present" to avoid possible conflict of interest. |
| ? | Did not vote or otherwise make a position known. |

Democrats  *Republicans*

ND Northern Democrats    SD Southern Democrats

Southern states - Ala., Ark., Fla., Ga., Ky., La., Miss., N.C., Okla., S.C., Tenn., Texas, Va.

| State / Senator | 1 | 2 | 3 | 4 | 5 | 6 | 7 | 8 |
|---|---|---|---|---|---|---|---|---|
| **ALABAMA** | | | | | | | | |
| Heflin | Y | Y | Y | Y | N | Y | Y | N |
| Shelby | Y | Y | Y | Y | N | Y | Y | N |
| **ALASKA** | | | | | | | | |
| *Murkowski* | Y | Y | Y | Y | Y | Y | N | N |
| *Stevens* | Y | Y | Y | Y | Y | Y | N | N |
| **ARIZONA** | | | | | | | | |
| DeConcini | Y | Y | ? | ? | ? | ? | Y | N |
| *McCain* | Y | Y | Y | Y | Y | N | N | N |
| **ARKANSAS** | | | | | | | | |
| Bumpers | Y | Y | Y | N | N | N | N | N |
| Pryor | Y | Y | Y | N | N | Y | N | Y |
| **CALIFORNIA** | | | | | | | | |
| Cranston | Y | Y | Y | N | N | Y | Y | Y |
| *Seymour* | Y | Y | Y | Y | Y | N | N | N |
| **COLORADO** | | | | | | | | |
| Wirth | Y | Y | Y | N | N | Y | Y | Y |
| *Brown* | Y | Y | Y | Y | Y | N | N | N |
| **CONNECTICUT** | | | | | | | | |
| Dodd | Y | Y | Y | N | N | Y | N | N |
| Lieberman | Y | Y | Y | N | Y | Y | N | N |
| **DELAWARE** | | | | | | | | |
| Biden | Y | Y | Y | N | N | Y | Y | Y |
| *Roth* | Y | Y | Y | Y | Y | Y | N | N |
| **FLORIDA** | | | | | | | | |
| Graham | Y | Y | Y | N | N | Y | N | Y |
| *Mack* | Y | Y | Y | Y | Y | N | N | N |
| **GEORGIA** | | | | | | | | |
| Fowler | Y | Y | Y | N | N | Y | N | Y |
| Nunn | Y | Y | Y | N | Y | N | N | N |
| **HAWAII** | | | | | | | | |
| Akaka | Y | Y | Y | N | N | Y | Y | Y |
| Inouye | Y | Y | Y | N | N | Y | N | Y |
| **IDAHO** | | | | | | | | |
| *Craig* | ? | Y | Y | Y | Y | N | N | N |
| *Symms* | ? | Y | Y | Y | Y | N | N | N |
| **ILLINOIS** | | | | | | | | |
| Dixon | Y | Y | Y | N | N | Y | Y | Y |
| Simon | Y | Y | Y | N | N | Y | Y | Y |
| **INDIANA** | | | | | | | | |
| *Coats* | Y | Y | Y | Y | Y | N | N | N |
| *Lugar* | Y | Y | Y | N | Y | N | N | N |
| **IOWA** | | | | | | | | |
| Harkin | ? | ? | ? | ? | ? | ? | ? | ? |
| *Grassley* | Y | Y | Y | Y | Y | N | N | N |
| **KANSAS** | | | | | | | | |
| *Dole* | Y | Y | Y | Y | N | N | N | N |
| *Kassebaum* | Y | Y | Y | N | Y | Y | N | N |
| **KENTUCKY** | | | | | | | | |
| Ford | Y | Y | Y | Y | N | Y | N | N |
| *McConnell* | Y | Y | Y | Y | Y | N | N | N |
| **LOUISIANA** | | | | | | | | |
| Breaux | Y | Y | Y | Y | Y | N | N | Y |
| Johnston | Y | Y | Y | N | N | Y | N | Y |
| **MAINE** | | | | | | | | |
| Mitchell | Y | Y | Y | N | N | Y | Y | Y |
| *Cohen* | Y | Y | Y | N | N | Y | N | N |
| **MARYLAND** | | | | | | | | |
| Mikulski | Y | Y | Y | N | N | Y | Y | Y |
| Sarbanes | Y | Y | Y | N | N | Y | Y | Y |
| **MASSACHUSETTS** | | | | | | | | |
| Kennedy | Y | Y | Y | N | N | Y | Y | Y |
| Kerry | Y | Y | Y | N | N | Y | Y | Y |
| **MICHIGAN** | | | | | | | | |
| Levin | Y | Y | Y | N | N | Y | Y | Y |
| Riegle | Y | Y | Y | N | N | Y | Y | Y |
| **MINNESOTA** | | | | | | | | |
| Wellstone | Y | Y | Y | N | N | Y | Y | Y |
| *Durenberger* | Y | Y | Y | N | Y | Y | Y | N |
| **MISSISSIPPI** | | | | | | | | |
| *Cochran* | Y | Y | Y | Y | Y | N | N | N |
| *Lott* | Y | Y | Y | Y | Y | N | N | N |
| **MISSOURI** | | | | | | | | |
| *Bond* | ? | ? | ? | ? | ? | ? | N | N |
| *Danforth* | Y | Y | Y | N | Y | N | N | N |
| **MONTANA** | | | | | | | | |
| Baucus | Y | Y | Y | N | N | N | Y | Y |
| *Burns* | Y | Y | Y | Y | N | N | N | N |
| **NEBRASKA** | | | | | | | | |
| Exon | Y | Y | Y | N | N | N | Y | Y |
| Kerrey | ? | ? | ? | ? | ? | ? | ? | ? |
| **NEVADA** | | | | | | | | |
| Bryan | Y | Y | Y | N | N | Y | N | Y |
| Reid | Y | Y | Y | N | N | Y | N | Y |
| **NEW HAMPSHIRE** | | | | | | | | |
| *Rudman* | Y | Y | Y | N | Y | Y | N | N |
| *Smith* | Y | Y | Y | Y | Y | Y | N | N |
| **NEW JERSEY** | | | | | | | | |
| Bradley | Y | Y | Y | N | Y | Y | Y | Y |
| Lautenberg | Y | Y | Y | N | N | Y | Y | Y |
| **NEW MEXICO** | | | | | | | | |
| Bingaman | Y | Y | Y | N | N | N | Y | Y |
| *Domenici* | Y | Y | Y | N | N | N | Y | Y |
| **NEW YORK** | | | | | | | | |
| Moynihan | Y | Y | Y | N | N | Y | Y | Y |
| *D'Amato* | ? | Y | Y | ? | + | Y | N | N |
| **NORTH CAROLINA** | | | | | | | | |
| Sanford | Y | Y | Y | N | N | N | Y | Y |
| *Helms* | Y | Y | Y | Y | Y | ? | N | N |
| **NORTH DAKOTA** | | | | | | | | |
| Burdick | Y | Y | Y | N | N | Y | Y | Y |
| Conrad | Y | Y | Y | N | N | Y | Y | Y |
| **OHIO** | | | | | | | | |
| Glenn | Y | Y | Y | N | N | Y | Y | Y |
| Metzenbaum | Y | Y | Y | N | N | Y | Y | Y |
| **OKLAHOMA** | | | | | | | | |
| Boren | Y | Y | Y | N | N | N | N | N |
| *Nickles* | Y | Y | Y | Y | N | N | N | N |
| **OREGON** | | | | | | | | |
| *Hatfield* | Y | Y | Y | N | N | Y | Y | N |
| *Packwood* | Y | Y | Y | N | ? | Y | Y | N |
| **PENNSYLVANIA** | | | | | | | | |
| Wofford | Y | Y | Y | N | N | Y | Y | Y |
| *Specter* | Y | Y | Y | N | N | Y | Y | N |
| **RHODE ISLAND** | | | | | | | | |
| Pell | Y | Y | Y | N | N | Y | Y | Y |
| *Chafee* | Y | Y | Y | N | N | Y | Y | N |
| **SOUTH CAROLINA** | | | | | | | | |
| Hollings | Y | Y | Y | N | N | Y | N | Y |
| *Thurmond* | Y | Y | Y | N | Y | N | N | N |
| **SOUTH DAKOTA** | | | | | | | | |
| Daschle | Y | Y | Y | N | N | Y | Y | Y |
| *Pressler* | Y | Y | Y | Y | Y | N | N | N |
| **TENNESSEE** | | | | | | | | |
| Gore | Y | Y | Y | N | N | N | Y | Y |
| Sasser | Y | Y | Y | N | N | Y | N | Y |
| **TEXAS** | | | | | | | | |
| Bentsen | ? | Y | Y | Y | N | N | Y | Y |
| *Gramm* | ? | Y | Y | Y | Y | N | N | N |
| **UTAH** | | | | | | | | |
| *Garn* | Y | Y | Y | ? | + | ? | N | N |
| *Hatch* | Y | Y | Y | Y | Y | N | N | N |
| **VERMONT** | | | | | | | | |
| Leahy | Y | Y | Y | N | N | Y | Y | Y |
| *Jeffords* | Y | Y | Y | N | N | Y | Y | Y |
| **VIRGINIA** | | | | | | | | |
| Robb | Y | Y | Y | N | N | Y | Y | Y |
| *Warner* | Y | Y | Y | N | Y | Y | N | N |
| **WASHINGTON** | | | | | | | | |
| Adams | Y | Y | Y | N | N | Y | Y | Y |
| *Gorton* | Y | + | ? | ? | + | − | N | N |
| **WEST VIRGINIA** | | | | | | | | |
| Byrd | Y | Y | Y | N | N | Y | Y | Y |
| Rockefeller | Y | Y | Y | N | N | Y | N | Y |
| **WISCONSIN** | | | | | | | | |
| Kohl | Y | Y | Y | N | N | Y | Y | Y |
| *Kasten* | Y | Y | Y | Y | Y | Y | Y | N |
| **WYOMING** | | | | | | | | |
| *Simpson* | Y | Y | Y | Y | N | N | N | N |
| *Wallop* | Y | Y | Y | Y | Y | N | N | N |

**1. S 2. Elementary and Secondary Education/Cloture.** Mitchell, D-Maine, motion to invoke cloture (thus limiting debate) on the motion to proceed to the bill to authorize $850 million in fiscal 1992 for block grants to states for schools to compete for money to try new approaches to improving elementary and secondary education. The bill would allow the grants to be used for parental choice among public schools but not private schools. Motion agreed to 93-0: R 39-0; D 54-0 (ND 38-0, SD 16-0), Jan. 21, 1992. A three-fifths majority vote of the total Senate (60) is required to invoke cloture.

**2. S 2. Elementary and Secondary Education/New Public Schools.** Cochran, R-Miss., amendment to raise to 25 percent from 10 percent the percentage of block grant funds states would be allowed to allocate for new "break the mold" public schools. Adopted 96-0: R 41-0; D 55-0 (ND 38-0, SD 17-0), Jan. 23, 1992.

**3. S 2. Elementary and Secondary Education/Waivers.** Hatfield, R-Ore., amendment to allow up to 300 school districts in six states to obtain waivers from the secretary of Education to federal rules governing elementary and secondary education programs. Adopted 95-0: R 41-0; D 54-0 (ND 37-0, SD 17-0), Jan. 23, 1992. A "yea" was a vote in support of the president's position.

**4. S 2. Elementary and Secondary Education/School Prayer.** Helms, R-N.C., amendment to the Pressler, R-S.D., amendment, to express the sense of the Senate that the Supreme Court should reverse its earlier rulings prohibiting voluntary school prayer. Rejected 38-55: R 26-13; D 12-42 (ND 2-35, SD 10-7), Jan. 23, 1992.

**5. S 2. Elementary and Secondary Education/School Choice.** Hatch, R-Utah, amendment to authorize $30 million for six demonstration projects to provide low-income parents with money to pay for enrolling their child at the public or private school of their choice, including religious schools. Rejected 36-57: R 33-6; D 3-51 (ND 2-35, SD 1-16), Jan. 23, 1992. A "yea" was a vote in support of the president's position.

**6. S 2. Elementary and Secondary Education/Chapter One Formula.** Durenberger, R-Minn., motion to table (kill) the Hatch, R-Utah, amendment to base the Chapter One formula for the distribution of funds to states for helping educate disadvantaged children to a formula that relies on the number of students found to be in poverty rather than a formula that relies on state per pupil expenditures. Motion agreed to 55-37: R 15-23; D 40-14 (ND 32-5, SD 8-9), Jan. 23, 1992.

**7. S 2. Elementary and Secondary Education/Withholding Benefits.** Bentsen, D-Texas, motion to table (kill) the Nickles, R-Okla., amendment to allow states to withhold welfare benefits from parents of children who do not regularly attend school. Motion agreed to 55-43: R 6-37; D 49-6 (ND 36-2, SD 13-4), Jan. 28, 1992.

**8. S 2. Elementary and Secondary Education/Waive Budget Act.** Wirth, D-Colo., motion to waive the Budget Act to allow consideration of a Wirth amendment to express the sense of the Senate that the 1990 Budget Agreement (PL 101-508) should be amended to shift military spending into domestic programs including early child development, education and job training. Section 306 of the Budget Act prohibits consideration of any matter within the jurisdiction of the Budget Committee unless the committee reports the measure. Motion rejected 45-53: R 0-43; D 45-10 (ND 33-5, SD 12-5), Jan. 28, 1992. A three-fifths majority (60) of the total Senate is required to waive the Budget Act. (Subsequently, a Domenici, R-N.M., point of order was sustained and the Wirth amendment fell.)

| | 9 | 10 | 11 | 12 | 13 | 14 | 15 | 16 |
|---|---|---|---|---|---|---|---|---|
| **ALABAMA** | | | | | | | | |
| Heflin | Y | Y | Y | Y | N | Y | Y | Y |
| Shelby | Y | Y | Y | Y | Y | N | Y | Y |
| **ALASKA** | | | | | | | | |
| *Murkowski* | Y | N | Y | Y | Y | Y | Y | N |
| *Stevens* | Y | N | Y | Y | Y | N | N | Y |
| **ARIZONA** | | | | | | | | |
| DeConcini | Y | N | Y | Y | N | N | Y | Y |
| *McCain* | Y | N | Y | Y | N | Y | Y | Y |
| **ARKANSAS** | | | | | | | | |
| Bumpers | Y | Y | Y | Y | N | Y | Y | Y |
| Pryor | Y | Y | Y | Y | N | Y | Y | Y |
| **CALIFORNIA** | | | | | | | | |
| Cranston | Y | N | Y | Y | + | ? | ? | Y |
| *Seymour* | Y | N | Y | Y | Y | N | Y | Y |
| **COLORADO** | | | | | | | | |
| Wirth | Y | Y | Y | Y | Y | N | Y | Y |
| *Brown* | Y | N | Y | Y | Y | N | Y | N |
| **CONNECTICUT** | | | | | | | | |
| Dodd | Y | N | Y | Y | N | Y | Y | Y |
| Lieberman | Y | N | Y | Y | N | Y | Y | Y |
| **DELAWARE** | | | | | | | | |
| Biden | Y | Y | Y | Y | N | Y | Y | Y |
| *Roth* | Y | N | Y | Y | Y | N | Y | N |
| **FLORIDA** | | | | | | | | |
| Graham | Y | N | Y | Y | N | Y | Y | Y |
| *Mack* | Y | C | Y | C | C | C | Y | Y |
| **GEORGIA** | | | | | | | | |
| Fowler | Y | N | Y | Y | Y | Y | Y | Y |
| Nunn | Y | Y | Y | Y | N | Y | Y | Y |
| **HAWAII** | | | | | | | | |
| Akaka | Y | N | Y | Y | N | Y | Y | Y |
| Inouye | Y | N | Y | Y | N | Y | Y | ? |
| **IDAHO** | | | | | | | | |
| *Craig* | N | N | Y | Y | Y | N | Y | N |
| *Symms* | N | Y | Y | Y | # | N | N | N |
| **ILLINOIS** | | | | | | | | |
| Dixon | Y | Y | Y | Y | N | Y | Y | Y |
| Simon | Y | Y | Y | Y | N | Y | Y | Y |
| **INDIANA** | | | | | | | | |
| *Coats* | Y | Y | Y | Y | N | Y | Y | Y |
| *Lugar* | Y | N | Y | Y | N | Y | Y | Y |

| | 9 | 10 | 11 | 12 | 13 | 14 | 15 | 16 |
|---|---|---|---|---|---|---|---|---|
| **IOWA** | | | | | | | | |
| Harkin | ? | ? | ? | ? | ? | ? | ? | ? |
| *Grassley* | Y | N | Y | Y | N | Y | Y | Y |
| **KANSAS** | | | | | | | | |
| *Dole* | Y | N | Y | Y | Y | N | Y | Y |
| *Kassebaum* | Y | Y | Y | Y | Y | Y | Y | Y |
| **KENTUCKY** | | | | | | | | |
| Ford | Y | Y | Y | Y | N | Y | Y | Y |
| *McConnell* | Y | N | Y | N | Y | N | Y | Y |
| **LOUISIANA** | | | | | | | | |
| Breaux | Y | Y | Y | Y | # | Y | Y | Y |
| Johnston | Y | Y | Y | Y | Y | Y | Y | Y |
| **MAINE** | | | | | | | | |
| Mitchell | Y | N | Y | Y | N | Y | Y | Y |
| *Cohen* | Y | N | Y | N | Y | N | Y | Y |
| **MARYLAND** | | | | | | | | |
| Mikulski | Y | N | Y | Y | N | Y | Y | Y |
| Sarbanes | Y | N | Y | Y | N | Y | Y | Y |
| **MASSACHUSETTS** | | | | | | | | |
| Kennedy | Y | N | Y | Y | N | Y | Y | Y |
| Kerry | Y | N | Y | Y | Y | Y | Y | Y |
| **MICHIGAN** | | | | | | | | |
| Levin | Y | N | Y | Y | N | Y | Y | Y |
| Riegle | Y | N | Y | Y | X | + | Y | Y |
| **MINNESOTA** | | | | | | | | |
| Wellstone | Y | Y | Y | Y | N | Y | Y | Y |
| *Durenberger* | Y | Y | Y | Y | N | Y | N | Y |
| **MISSISSIPPI** | | | | | | | | |
| Cochran | Y | Y | Y | Y | Y | Y | Y | Y |
| *Lott* | Y | Y | Y | Y | Y | Y | Y | Y |
| **MISSOURI** | | | | | | | | |
| *Bond* | Y | N | Y | Y | X | + | Y | Y |
| Danforth | Y | N | Y | Y | N | Y | Y | Y |
| **MONTANA** | | | | | | | | |
| Baucus | Y | Y | Y | Y | N | Y | Y | Y |
| *Burns* | Y | Y | Y | Y | Y | N | Y | Y |
| **NEBRASKA** | | | | | | | | |
| Exon | Y | N | Y | Y | N | Y | Y | Y |
| Kerrey | ? | ? | ? | ? | ? | ? | ? | ? |
| **NEVADA** | | | | | | | | |
| Bryan | Y | N | Y | Y | Y | Y | Y | Y |
| Reid | Y | N | Y | Y | Y | N | Y | Y |

| | 9 | 10 | 11 | 12 | 13 | 14 | 15 | 16 |
|---|---|---|---|---|---|---|---|---|
| **NEW HAMPSHIRE** | | | | | | | | |
| *Rudman* | Y | N | Y | Y | Y | N | Y | Y |
| *Smith* | N | Y | Y | Y | Y | N | Y | Y |
| **NEW JERSEY** | | | | | | | | |
| Bradley | Y | Y | Y | ? | ? | ? | Y | Y |
| Lautenberg | Y | N | Y | Y | N | Y | Y | Y |
| **NEW MEXICO** | | | | | | | | |
| Bingaman | Y | N | Y | Y | N | Y | Y | Y |
| *Domenici* | Y | N | Y | Y | N | Y | Y | Y |
| **NEW YORK** | | | | | | | | |
| Moynihan | Y | N | Y | Y | N | Y | Y | Y |
| *D'Amato* | Y | N | Y | Y | Y | Y | Y | Y |
| **NORTH CAROLINA** | | | | | | | | |
| Sanford | Y | Y | Y | Y | N | Y | Y | Y |
| *Helms* | N | Y | Y | Y | Y | N | Y | N |
| **NORTH DAKOTA** | | | | | | | | |
| Burdick | Y | N | Y | Y | N | Y | Y | Y |
| Conrad | Y | N | Y | Y | N | Y | Y | Y |
| **OHIO** | | | | | | | | |
| Glenn | Y | N | Y | Y | N | Y | Y | Y |
| Metzenbaum | Y | N | Y | Y | N | Y | Y | Y |
| **OKLAHOMA** | | | | | | | | |
| Boren | Y | Y | Y | Y | ? | + | ? | Y |
| *Nickles* | Y | Y | Y | Y | Y | Y | Y | Y |
| **OREGON** | | | | | | | | |
| *Hatfield* | Y | N | Y | Y | Y | Y | Y | Y |
| *Packwood* | Y | N | Y | ? | Y | Y | Y | Y |
| **PENNSYLVANIA** | | | | | | | | |
| Wofford | Y | Y | Y | Y | ? | ? | Y | Y |
| *Specter* | Y | Y | Y | Y | Y | Y | Y | Y |
| **RHODE ISLAND** | | | | | | | | |
| Pell | Y | N | Y | Y | N | Y | Y | Y |
| *Chafee* | Y | N | Y | Y | Y | Y | Y | Y |
| **SOUTH CAROLINA** | | | | | | | | |
| Hollings | Y | N | Y | Y | N | Y | Y | Y |
| *Thurmond* | Y | N | Y | Y | Y | Y | Y | Y |
| **SOUTH DAKOTA** | | | | | | | | |
| Daschle | Y | Y | Y | Y | N | Y | Y | Y |
| *Pressler* | Y | N | Y | Y | N | Y | Y | N |
| **TENNESSEE** | | | | | | | | |
| Gore | Y | N | Y | Y | Y | Y | Y | Y |
| Sasser | Y | N | + | Y | N | Y | Y | Y |

| | 9 | 10 | 11 | 12 | 13 | 14 | 15 | 16 |
|---|---|---|---|---|---|---|---|---|
| **TEXAS** | | | | | | | | |
| Bentsen | Y | Y | Y | Y | N | Y | Y | Y |
| *Gramm* | Y | N | Y | Y | Y | N | Y | Y |
| **UTAH** | | | | | | | | |
| *Garn* | N | N | Y | Y | Y | N | N | N |
| *Hatch* | Y | N | Y | Y | Y | Y | Y | Y |
| **VERMONT** | | | | | | | | |
| Leahy | Y | N | Y | Y | N | Y | Y | Y |
| *Jeffords* | Y | N | Y | Y | Y | Y | Y | Y |
| **VIRGINIA** | | | | | | | | |
| Robb | Y | N | Y | Y | N | Y | Y | Y |
| *Warner* | Y | N | ? | Y | Y | Y | ? | ? |
| **WASHINGTON** | | | | | | | | |
| Adams | Y | N | Y | Y | N | Y | Y | Y |
| *Gorton* | Y | N | Y | Y | N | Y | Y | Y |
| **WEST VIRGINIA** | | | | | | | | |
| Byrd | Y | N | Y | Y | N | Y | Y | Y |
| Rockefeller | Y | N | Y | Y | N | Y | Y | Y |
| **WISCONSIN** | | | | | | | | |
| Kohl | Y | N | Y | Y | N | Y | Y | Y |
| *Kasten* | Y | Y | Y | Y | Y | Y | Y | Y |
| **WYOMING** | | | | | | | | |
| *Simpson* | Y | N | Y | Y | N | Y | Y | Y |
| *Wallop* | N | N | Y | Y | Y | N | Y | N |

ND Northern Democrats  SD Southern Democrats  Southern states - Ala., Ark., Fla., Ga., Ky., La., Miss., N.C., Okla., S.C., Tenn., Texas, Va.

**9. S 2. Elementary and Secondary Education/Passage.** Passage of the bill to authorize $850 million in fiscal 1992 for block grants to states for schools to compete for money to develop new approaches to improving education. The bill would allow the grants to be used for parental choice among public schools only. Passed 92-6: R 37-6; D 55-0 (ND 38-0, SD 17-0), Jan. 28, 1992.

**10. S 12. Cable Television Regulation/FCC Study.** Breaux, D-La., motion to table (kill) the Graham, D-Fla., amendment to the Breaux amendment, to require the Federal Communications Commission to conduct an inquiry to determine whether broadcast television stations whose programming consists predominantly of sales are serving the public interest. Motion rejected 33-64: R 13-29; D 20-35 (ND 9-29, SD 11-6), Jan. 29, 1992. (The Graham amendment was subsequently adopted by voice vote.)

**11. S Res 248. El Salvador Cease-Fire.** Adoption of the resolution to commend parties to negotiations that resulted in a cease-fire in El Salvador, and to express the sense of the Senate that the United States should provide appropriate assistance to promote reconstruction and democracy. Adopted 96-0: R 42-0; D 54-0 (ND 38-0, SD 16-0), Jan. 29, 1992.

**12. S 12. Cable Television Regulation/Offensive Programming.** Helms, R-N.C., amendment to require the Federal Communications Commission to issue regulations to limit the access of children to indecent programming and to allow cable operators to prohibit offensive programming. Adopted 95-0: R 41-0; D 54-0 (ND 37-0, SD 17-0), Jan. 30, 1992.

**13. S 12. Cable Television Regulation/Substitute Amendment.** Packwood, R-Ore., substitute amendment to regulate rates for basic service in cable markets where there is no effective competition; expand the areas in which telephone companies can provide cable service from rural areas with 2,500 residents to 10,000; remove restrictions on multiple ownership of broadcast stations; and for other purposes. Rejected 35-54: R 28-12; D 7-42 (ND 4-30, SD 3-12), Jan. 31, 1992.

**14. S 12. Cable Television Regulation/Passage.** Passage of the bill to allow cable rate regulation in areas absent effective competition; require national and regional cable programmers to deal fairly with competing multichannel video distributors; require cable systems to carry local broadcasts; give broadcasters rights controlling the retransmission of their signals; and enact other provisions to ensure competition and consumer protection in the cable market. Passed 73-18: R 27-14; D 46-4 (ND 31-3, SD 15-1), Jan. 31, 1992. A "nay" was a vote in support of the president's position.

**15. S 2166. National Energy Policy/Cloture.** Mitchell, D-Maine, motion to invoke cloture (thus limiting debate) on the motion to proceed to the bill to mandate that federal and private vehicle fleets use alternative fuels, to restructure electric utility regulations, to streamline the licensing process for nuclear power plants, and to enact other programs related to energy production and consumption. Motion agreed to 90-5: R 37-5; D 53-0 (ND 37-0, SD 16-0), Feb. 4, 1992. A three-fifths majority vote (60) of the total Senate is required to invoke cloture.

**16. S 2173. Unemployment Benefits Extension/Waive Budget Act.** Daschle, D-S.D., motion to waive the Budget Act with respect to a Brown, R-Colo., point of order and allow consideration of the bill to provide $2.7 billion to extend emergency unemployment benefits an additional 13 weeks for total emergency benefits of 33 weeks in high-unemployment states and 26 weeks in all other states. Motion agreed to 88-8: R 34-8; D 54-0 (ND 37-0, SD 17-0), Feb. 4, 1992. A three-fifths majority (60) of the total Senate is required to waive the Budget Act.

| | 17 | 18 | 19 | 20 | 21 | 22 | 23 | 24 |
|---|---|---|---|---|---|---|---|---|
| **ALABAMA** | | | | | | | | |
| Heflin | Y | Y | Y | Y | Y | N | Y | Y |
| Shelby | Y | Y | Y | Y | Y | N | Y | Y |
| **ALASKA** | | | | | | | | |
| *Murkowski* | Y | Y | Y | Y | Y | N | Y | Y |
| *Stevens* | Y | ? | ? | ? | Y | N | Y | Y |
| **ARIZONA** | | | | | | | | |
| DeConcini | Y | N | Y | N | Y | N | N | Y |
| *McCain* | Y | Y | Y | Y | Y | Y | Y | Y |
| **ARKANSAS** | | | | | | | | |
| Bumpers | Y | Y | Y | Y | Y | N | N | Y |
| Pryor | Y | Y | Y | Y | ? | N | N | Y |
| **CALIFORNIA** | | | | | | | | |
| Cranston | Y | N | Y | N | Y | Y | Y | N |
| *Seymour* | Y | Y | Y | N | Y | Y | Y | N |
| **COLORADO** | | | | | | | | |
| Wirth | Y | N | Y | Y | N | N | Y | Y |
| *Brown* | Y | Y | Y | Y | Y | N | Y | Y |
| **CONNECTICUT** | | | | | | | | |
| Dodd | Y | N | Y | N | Y | N | N | N |
| Lieberman | Y | N | Y | N | N | Y | N | N |
| **DELAWARE** | | | | | | | | |
| Biden | Y | Y | Y | Y | Y | N | Y | N |
| *Roth* | Y | Y | Y | Y | Y | N | Y | N |
| **FLORIDA** | | | | | | | | |
| Graham | Y | N | Y | N | Y | Y | N | N |
| *Mack* | Y | Y | Y | N | Y | N | N | N |
| **GEORGIA** | | | | | | | | |
| Fowler | Y | N | Y | N | Y | N | N | N |
| Nunn | Y | N | Y | Y | Y | N | N | N |
| **HAWAII** | | | | | | | | |
| Akaka | Y | Y | Y | N | Y | N | Y | N |
| Inouye | ? | ? | Y | # | ? | Y | Y | N |
| **IDAHO** | | | | | | | | |
| *Craig* | Y | Y | Y | Y | N | N | Y | Y |
| *Symms* | N | Y | Y | Y | N | N | Y | Y |
| **ILLINOIS** | | | | | | | | |
| Dixon | Y | N | Y | N | Y | Y | N | N |
| Simon | Y | N | Y | N | Y | Y | N | N |
| **INDIANA** | | | | | | | | |
| *Coats* | Y | Y | Y | Y | N | Y | Y | Y |
| Lugar | Y | Y | Y | N | N | N | Y | Y |
| **IOWA** | | | | | | | | |
| Harkin | ? | ? | ? | X | ? | ? | ? | ? |
| *Grassley* | Y | N | Y | N | N | Y | Y | Y |
| **KANSAS** | | | | | | | | |
| *Dole* | Y | Y | Y | Y | N | N | Y | Y |
| *Kassebaum* | Y | Y | Y | Y | Y | N | Y | N |
| **KENTUCKY** | | | | | | | | |
| Ford | Y | Y | Y | Y | Y | N | Y | Y |
| *McConnell* | Y | Y | Y | Y | Y | N | Y | N |
| **LOUISIANA** | | | | | | | | |
| Breaux | Y | Y | Y | Y | Y | N | Y | Y |
| Johnston | Y | Y | Y | Y | Y | N | Y | Y |
| **MAINE** | | | | | | | | |
| Mitchell | Y | N | Y | N | N | Y | N | N |
| *Cohen* | Y | N | Y | N | ? | Y | N | N |
| **MARYLAND** | | | | | | | | |
| Mikulski | Y | N | Y | N | N | N | Y | Y |
| Sarbanes | Y | N | Y | N | N | Y | N | N |
| **MASSACHUSETTS** | | | | | | | | |
| Kennedy | Y | N | Y | N | Y | Y | N | N |
| Kerry | Y | N | Y | N | Y | Y | N | N |
| **MICHIGAN** | | | | | | | | |
| Levin | Y | Y | Y | N | N | Y | N | N |
| Riegle | Y | Y | Y | ? | N | Y | Y | N |
| **MINNESOTA** | | | | | | | | |
| Wellstone | Y | N | Y | N | Y | Y | N | N |
| *Durenberger* | Y | Y | Y | N | Y | Y | N | N |
| **MISSISSIPPI** | | | | | | | | |
| *Cochran* | Y | Y | Y | Y | Y | N | Y | Y |
| *Lott* | Y | Y | Y | Y | Y | N | Y | Y |
| **MISSOURI** | | | | | | | | |
| *Bond* | Y | Y | Y | Y | Y | N | Y | Y |
| *Danforth* | Y | Y | Y | Y | Y | N | Y | Y |
| **MONTANA** | | | | | | | | |
| Baucus | Y | N | Y | Y | Y | N | Y | Y |
| *Burns* | Y | Y | Y | Y | Y | N | Y | Y |
| **NEBRASKA** | | | | | | | | |
| Exon | Y | N | Y | Y | Y | N | N | Y |
| Kerrey | ? | ? | ? | ? | ? | ? | ? | ? |
| **NEVADA** | | | | | | | | |
| Bryan | Y | N | Y | N | Y | N | N | N |
| Reid | Y | N | Y | N | Y | Y | N | N |
| **NEW HAMPSHIRE** | | | | | | | | |
| *Rudman* | Y | Y | Y | N | Y | N | Y | N |
| *Smith* | Y | Y | Y | Y | N | N | Y | N |
| **NEW JERSEY** | | | | | | | | |
| Bradley | Y | Y | Y | N | N | Y | N | N |
| Lautenberg | Y | N | Y | N | N | Y | N | N |
| **NEW MEXICO** | | | | | | | | |
| Bingaman | Y | Y | Y | Y | Y | N | N | Y |
| *Domenici* | Y | Y | Y | Y | Y | N | Y | Y |
| **NEW YORK** | | | | | | | | |
| Moynihan | Y | Y | Y | N | Y | Y | Y | N |
| *D'Amato* | Y | Y | Y | N | N | Y | N | N |
| **NORTH CAROLINA** | | | | | | | | |
| Sanford | Y | N | Y | N | Y | N | N | Y |
| *Helms* | N | Y | Y | Y | N | N | Y | Y |
| **NORTH DAKOTA** | | | | | | | | |
| Burdick | Y | Y | Y | Y | N | Y | N | Y |
| Conrad | Y | Y | Y | Y | N | N | Y | Y |
| **OHIO** | | | | | | | | |
| Glenn | Y | N | Y | N | N | Y | N | N |
| Metzenbaum | Y | N | Y | N | N | Y | N | N |
| **OKLAHOMA** | | | | | | | | |
| Boren | Y | Y | Y | N | Y | N | Y | Y |
| *Nickles* | Y | Y | Y | Y | Y | N | Y | Y |
| **OREGON** | | | | | | | | |
| *Hatfield* | Y | Y | Y | N | N | N | Y | Y |
| *Packwood* | Y | N | Y | N | N | N | Y | Y |
| **PENNSYLVANIA** | | | | | | | | |
| Wofford | Y | Y | Y | Y | Y | N | N | Y |
| *Specter* | Y | Y | Y | Y | N | Y | Y | N |
| **RHODE ISLAND** | | | | | | | | |
| Pell | Y | N | Y | N | N | Y | N | N |
| *Chafee* | Y | N | Y | N | N | N | Y | N |
| **SOUTH CAROLINA** | | | | | | | | |
| Hollings | Y | Y | Y | Y | N | N | N | N |
| *Thurmond* | Y | Y | Y | Y | Y | N | Y | Y |
| **SOUTH DAKOTA** | | | | | | | | |
| Daschle | Y | N | Y | N | Y | N | Y | Y |
| *Pressler* | Y | N | Y | Y | Y | N | Y | Y |
| **TENNESSEE** | | | | | | | | |
| Gore | Y | N | Y | N | N | Y | N | N |
| Sasser | Y | N | Y | Y | Y | N | Y | Y |
| **TEXAS** | | | | | | | | |
| Bentsen | Y | Y | Y | Y | Y | N | Y | Y |
| *Gramm* | Y | Y | Y | Y | Y | N | Y | Y |
| **UTAH** | | | | | | | | |
| *Garn* | Y | Y | Y | Y | N | N | Y | Y |
| *Hatch* | Y | Y | Y | Y | N | N | Y | Y |
| **VERMONT** | | | | | | | | |
| Leahy | Y | N | Y | N | Y | Y | N | N |
| *Jeffords* | Y | N | Y | N | Y | Y | N | N |
| **VIRGINIA** | | | | | | | | |
| Robb | Y | N | Y | N | Y | Y | N | N |
| *Warner* | ? | Y | Y | Y | Y | N | Y | Y |
| **WASHINGTON** | | | | | | | | |
| Adams | Y | N | Y | N | Y | Y | N | N |
| *Gorton* | Y | Y | Y | Y | Y | N | N | Y |
| **WEST VIRGINIA** | | | | | | | | |
| Byrd | Y | Y | Y | Y | N | Y | N | Y |
| Rockefeller | Y | N | ? | N | Y | N | Y | N |
| **WISCONSIN** | | | | | | | | |
| Kohl | Y | Y | Y | N | N | Y | N | Y |
| *Kasten* | Y | N | Y | N | N | Y | N | Y |
| **WYOMING** | | | | | | | | |
| *Simpson* | Y | Y | Y | Y | Y | N | Y | Y |
| *Wallop* | Y | Y | Y | Y | Y | N | Y | Y |

**KEY**

Y   Voted for (yea).
#   Paired for.
+   Announced for.
N   Voted against (nay).
X   Paired against.
—   Announced against.
P   Voted "present."
C   Voted "present" to avoid possible conflict of interest.
?   Did not vote or otherwise make a position known.

Democrats   *Republicans*

ND  Northern Democrats    SD  Southern Democrats         Southern states - Ala., Ark., Fla., Ga., Ky., La., Miss., N.C., Okla., S.C., Tenn., Texas, Va.

**17. HR 4095. Unemployment Benefits Extension/ Passage.** Passage of the bill (thus clearing the measure for the president) to provide $2.7 billion to extend unemployment benefits an additional 13 weeks for total emergency benefits of 33 weeks in high-unemployment states and 26 weeks in all other states and to change the expiration date of the emergency benefits from June 13 to July 4, 1992. Passed 94-2: R 40-2; D 54-0 (ND 37-0, SD 17-0), Feb. 4, 1992. A "yea" was a vote in support of the president's position.

**18. S 2166. National Energy Policy/Alternative Fuels.** Johnston, D-La., motion to table (kill) the Jeffords, R-Vt., amendment to require that by the year 2001, 10 percent of all fuels sold in the United States be replacement or alternative fuels. Motion agreed to 57-39: R 35-7; D 22-32 (ND 12-25, SD 10-7), Feb. 5, 1992.

**19. S 2166. National Energy Policy/Ozone Depletion.** Gore, D-Tenn., amendment to speed the phaseout of chemicals that deplete the ozone layer and to move to strengthen the 1987 Montreal Protocol to protect the ozone layer. Adopted 96-0: R 42-0; D 54-0 (ND 37-0, SD 17-0), Feb. 6, 1992.

**20. S 2166. National Energy Policy/NRC Hearings.** Johnston, D-La., motion to table (kill) the Graham, D-Fla., amendment to the Johnston amendment, to require the Nuclear Regulatory Commission to conduct full ajudicatory hearings before operation of new power reactors on serious new safety issues or major construction deficiencies. Motion agreed to 52-43: R 31-11; D 21-32 (ND 9-27, SD 12-5), Feb. 6, 1992.

**21. S 2166. National Energy Policy/Eminent Domain.** Johnston, D-La., motion to table (kill) the Craig, R-Idaho, amendment to require the Federal Energy Regulatory Commission to find in a separate proceeding that a specific public need is demonstrated before allowing private land to be confiscated under federal eminent domain laws for the expedited construction of natural gas pipelines. Motion agreed to 60-35: R 23-19; D 37-16 (ND 22-15, SD 15-1), Feb. 18, 1992.

**22. S 2166. National Energy Policy/Consumer Refunds.** Metzenbaum, D-Ohio, amendment authorizing the Federal Energy Regulatory Commission to require refunds for natural gas consumers if it determines that they have been overcharged. Rejected 41-57: R 11-32; D 30-25 (ND 27-11, SD 3-14), Feb. 19, 1992.

**23. S 2166. National Energy Policy/Industrial Efficiency Reporting.** Johnston, D-La., motion to table (kill) the Bryan, D-Nev., amendment to require the secretary of Energy to establish a voluntary program to compile information on energy consumption by corporations in major energy-consuming industries. Motion agreed to 58-40: R 36-7; D 22-33 (ND 12-26, SD 10-7), Feb. 19, 1992.

**24. S 2166. National Energy Policy/Florida Lease Moratorium.** Johnston, D-La., amendment to the Graham, D-Fla., amendment, to provide for a lease moratorium through Jan. 1, 2000, for oil and gas exploration of the outer continental shelf off the coast of southern Florida. The Graham amendment would have placed a moratorium on all leases anywhere off the coast of Florida. Adopted 53-45: R 29-14; D 24-31 (ND 13-25, SD 11-6), Feb. 19, 1992. (Subsequently, the Graham amendment, as amended, was adopted by voice vote.)

| | 25 | 26 | 27 | 28 | 29 | 30 | 31 | 32 |
|---|---|---|---|---|---|---|---|---|
| **ALABAMA** | | | | | | | | |
| Heflin | Y | Y | Y | Y | Y | Y | Y | Y |
| Shelby | Y | Y | Y | Y | Y | Y | N | Y |
| **ALASKA** | | | | | | | | |
| *Murkowski* | Y | Y | Y | Y | Y | Y | N | Y |
| *Stevens* | Y | Y | Y | Y | Y | Y | N | Y |
| **ARIZONA** | | | | | | | | |
| DeConcini | Y | Y | N | Y | Y | Y | Y | Y |
| *McCain* | Y | Y | Y | Y | Y | Y | N | Y |
| **ARKANSAS** | | | | | | | | |
| Bumpers | Y | Y | N | Y | Y | Y | Y | Y |
| Pryor | Y | Y | Y | Y | Y | Y | Y | Y |
| **CALIFORNIA** | | | | | | | | |
| Cranston | N | Y | N | Y | ? | Y | Y | Y |
| *Seymour* | N | Y | Y | Y | Y | Y | N | Y |
| **COLORADO** | | | | | | | | |
| Wirth | N | N | Y | Y | Y | Y | Y | Y |
| *Brown* | Y | Y | Y | Y | Y | Y | N | Y |
| **CONNECTICUT** | | | | | | | | |
| Dodd | N | N | Y | Y | Y | Y | Y | Y |
| Lieberman | N | N | Y | Y | Y | Y | Y | Y |
| **DELAWARE** | | | | | | | | |
| Biden | N | N | Y | Y | Y | Y | Y | Y |
| *Roth* | Y | Y | Y | Y | Y | Y | N | Y |
| **FLORIDA** | | | | | | | | |
| Graham | N | Y | N | N | Y | Y | Y | Y |
| *Mack* | N | Y | Y | Y | Y | Y | Y | Y |
| **GEORGIA** | | | | | | | | |
| Fowler | N | Y | N | Y | Y | ? | Y | Y |
| Nunn | N | Y | Y | Y | Y | Y | Y | Y |
| **HAWAII** | | | | | | | | |
| Akaka | N | N | Y | Y | Y | Y | Y | Y |
| Inouye | Y | N | N | Y | Y | Y | Y | Y |
| **IDAHO** | | | | | | | | |
| *Craig* | Y | Y | Y | Y | ? | ? | N | Y |
| *Symms* | Y | Y | Y | Y | Y | Y | N | Y |
| **ILLINOIS** | | | | | | | | |
| Dixon | N | N | N | Y | + | + | Y | Y |
| Simon | N | N | N | Y | Y | Y | Y | Y |
| **INDIANA** | | | | | | | | |
| *Coats* | Y | Y | Y | Y | Y | Y | N | Y |
| *Lugar* | Y | N | Y | Y | Y | Y | N | Y |

| | 25 | 26 | 27 | 28 | 29 | 30 | 31 | 32 |
|---|---|---|---|---|---|---|---|---|
| **IOWA** | | | | | | | | |
| Harkin | ? | ? | ? | ? | ? | ? | + | ? |
| *Grassley* | Y | Y | N | Y | Y | Y | N | Y |
| **KANSAS** | | | | | | | | |
| *Dole* | Y | Y | N | Y | Y | Y | N | Y |
| *Kassebaum* | N | Y | Y | Y | Y | Y | N | Y |
| **KENTUCKY** | | | | | | | | |
| Ford | Y | Y | Y | Y | Y | Y | Y | Y |
| *McConnell* | Y | Y | Y | Y | Y | Y | N | Y |
| **LOUISIANA** | | | | | | | | |
| Breaux | Y | Y | Y | Y | Y | Y | Y | Y |
| Johnston | Y | Y | Y | Y | Y | Y | N | Y |
| **MAINE** | | | | | | | | |
| Mitchell | N | N | Y | Y | Y | Y | Y | Y |
| *Cohen* | N | Y | N | Y | Y | Y | N | Y |
| **MARYLAND** | | | | | | | | |
| Mikulski | N | N | N | Y | Y | Y | Y | Y |
| Sarbanes | N | N | N | Y | Y | Y | Y | Y |
| **MASSACHUSETTS** | | | | | | | | |
| Kennedy | N | N | Y | Y | Y | Y | Y | Y |
| Kerry | N | N | N | Y | Y | Y | Y | Y |
| **MICHIGAN** | | | | | | | | |
| Levin | N | N | Y | Y | Y | Y | Y | Y |
| Riegle | N | N | Y | Y | Y | Y | Y | Y |
| **MINNESOTA** | | | | | | | | |
| Wellstone | N | N | N | N | Y | Y | Y | Y |
| *Durenberger* | N | Y | Y | N | Y | Y | N | Y |
| **MISSISSIPPI** | | | | | | | | |
| *Cochran* | Y | Y | Y | Y | Y | Y | N | Y |
| *Lott* | Y | Y | Y | Y | Y | Y | Y | Y |
| **MISSOURI** | | | | | | | | |
| *Bond* | Y | Y | Y | Y | Y | Y | Y | Y |
| *Danforth* | Y | Y | Y | Y | N | Y | N | Y |
| **MONTANA** | | | | | | | | |
| Baucus | N | N | Y | Y | Y | Y | N | Y |
| *Burns* | Y | Y | Y | Y | Y | Y | N | Y |
| **NEBRASKA** | | | | | | | | |
| Exon | Y | N | N | Y | Y | Y | Y | Y |
| Kerrey | ? | ? | ? | ? | ? | ? | + | ? |
| **NEVADA** | | | | | | | | |
| Bryan | N | N | N | Y | Y | Y | Y | Y |
| Reid | N | N | N | Y | Y | Y | Y | Y |

| | 25 | 26 | 27 | 28 | 29 | 30 | 31 | 32 |
|---|---|---|---|---|---|---|---|---|
| **NEW HAMPSHIRE** | | | | | | | | |
| *Rudman* | Y | Y | Y | Y | Y | N | N | Y |
| *Smith* | Y | Y | Y | N | Y | Y | Y | Y |
| **NEW JERSEY** | | | | | | | | |
| Bradley | N | N | Y | Y | Y | Y | Y | Y |
| Lautenberg | N | N | Y | Y | Y | Y | Y | Y |
| **NEW MEXICO** | | | | | | | | |
| Bingaman | N | N | Y | Y | Y | Y | Y | Y |
| *Domenici* | Y | Y | Y | Y | Y | Y | N | Y |
| **NEW YORK** | | | | | | | | |
| Moynihan | N | Y | N | Y | N | Y | Y | Y |
| *D'Amato* | N | Y | N | Y | Y | Y | N | Y |
| **NORTH CAROLINA** | | | | | | | | |
| Sanford | N | N | N | Y | Y | Y | Y | Y |
| *Helms* | Y | Y | Y | Y | Y | N | Y | Y |
| **NORTH DAKOTA** | | | | | | | | |
| Burdick | Y | Y | Y | Y | Y | Y | N | Y |
| Conrad | Y | Y | Y | Y | Y | Y | N | Y |
| **OHIO** | | | | | | | | |
| Glenn | Y | Y | N | Y | Y | Y | Y | Y |
| Metzenbaum | N | N | N | Y | Y | Y | Y | Y |
| **OKLAHOMA** | | | | | | | | |
| Boren | Y | Y | Y | Y | ? | ? | Y | Y |
| *Nickles* | Y | Y | Y | Y | Y | Y | N | Y |
| **OREGON** | | | | | | | | |
| *Hatfield* | Y | N | Y | Y | Y | Y | N | Y |
| *Packwood* | Y | Y | N | Y | Y | Y | N | Y |
| **PENNSYLVANIA** | | | | | | | | |
| Wofford | N | Y | Y | Y | Y | Y | Y | Y |
| *Specter* | N | Y | Y | Y | Y | Y | Y | Y |
| **RHODE ISLAND** | | | | | | | | |
| Pell | N | N | N | Y | Y | Y | Y | Y |
| *Chafee* | N | Y | N | Y | Y | Y | N | Y |
| **SOUTH CAROLINA** | | | | | | | | |
| Hollings | N | Y | Y | Y | Y | Y | Y | Y |
| *Thurmond* | Y | Y | Y | Y | Y | Y | N | Y |
| **SOUTH DAKOTA** | | | | | | | | |
| Daschle | N | Y | N | Y | Y | Y | Y | Y |
| *Pressler* | Y | Y | N | Y | Y | Y | Y | Y |
| **TENNESSEE** | | | | | | | | |
| Gore | N | N | N | Y | Y | Y | Y | Y |
| Sasser | Y | Y | N | Y | Y | Y | Y | Y |

| | 25 | 26 | 27 | 28 | 29 | 30 | 31 | 32 |
|---|---|---|---|---|---|---|---|---|
| **TEXAS** | | | | | | | | |
| Bentsen | Y | N | Y | Y | Y | Y | Y | Y |
| *Gramm* | Y | Y | Y | Y | Y | Y | N | Y |
| **UTAH** | | | | | | | | |
| *Garn* | Y | Y | Y | Y | Y | Y | N | Y |
| *Hatch* | Y | Y | Y | Y | Y | Y | N | Y |
| **VERMONT** | | | | | | | | |
| Leahy | N | N | N | Y | Y | Y | Y | Y |
| *Jeffords* | N | Y | N | Y | Y | Y | N | Y |
| **VIRGINIA** | | | | | | | | |
| Robb | N | Y | N | Y | Y | Y | Y | Y |
| *Warner* | Y | Y | Y | Y | Y | Y | N | Y |
| **WASHINGTON** | | | | | | | | |
| Adams | N | N | Y | Y | Y | Y | Y | Y |
| *Gorton* | Y | Y | Y | Y | Y | Y | Y | Y |
| **WEST VIRGINIA** | | | | | | | | |
| Byrd | Y | N | Y | Y | Y | Y | N | Y |
| Rockefeller | N | N | N | Y | Y | Y | Y | Y |
| **WISCONSIN** | | | | | | | | |
| Kohl | N | N | Y | Y | Y | Y | Y | Y |
| *Kasten* | Y | Y | Y | Y | Y | Y | N | Y |
| **WYOMING** | | | | | | | | |
| *Simpson* | Y | Y | Y | Y | N | Y | N | Y |
| *Wallop* | Y | Y | Y | Y | Y | Y | Y | Y |

ND Northern Democrats    SD Southern Democrats      Southern states - Ala., Ark., Fla., Ga., Ky., La., Miss., N.C., Okla., S.C., Tenn., Texas, Va.

**25. S 2166. National Energy Policy/Lease Cancellation.** Johnston, D-La., motion to table (kill) the Graham, D-Fla., amendment to require the secretary of Interior to cancel a lease for oil and gas exploration of the outer continental shelf if it has resulted in serious harm or poses a serious threat to the environment or national security. Motion agreed to 51-47: R 34-9; D 17-38 (ND 7-31, SD 10-7), Feb. 19, 1992.

**26. S 2166. National Energy Policy/Nuclear Safety Board.** Johnston, D-La., motion to table (kill) the Biden, D-Del., amendment to establish an independent Nuclear Safety Investigation Board to investigate safety-related incidents at civilian nuclear power facilities. Motion agreed to 63-35: R 41-2; D 22-33 (ND 8-30, SD 14-3), Feb. 19, 1992.

**27. S 2166. National Energy Policy/Alternative Fuels.** Johnston, D-La., motion to table (kill) the Grassley, R-Iowa, amendment to require the secretary of Energy to ensure that 10 percent of all motor fuels consumed in the United States by the year 2000 and 30 percent by the year 2010 are replacement and alternative fuels. Motion agreed to 64-34: R 35-8; D 29-26 (ND 19-19, SD 10-7), Feb. 19, 1992.

**28. S 2166. National Energy Policy/Passage.** Passage of the bill to mandate that federal and private vehicle fleets use alternative fuels, to restructure electric utility regulations, to streamline the licensing process for nuclear power plants and natural gas pipelines, and to enact other programs related to energy production and consumption. Passed 94-4: R 41-2; D 53-2 (ND 37-1, SD 16-1), Feb. 19, 1992. A "yea" was a vote in support of the president's position.

**29. S 1150. Higher Education Reauthorization/Veterans Hospitals.** Specter, R-Pa., amendment to block a joint project of the Departments of Veterans Affairs and Health and Human Services to use veterans hospitals to treat non-veterans in rural areas. Adopted 91-3: R 40-2; D 51-1 (ND 35-1, SD 16-0), Feb. 21, 1992.

**30. S 1150. Higher Education Reauthorization/Passage.** Passage of the bill to reauthorize the 1965 Higher Education Act for seven years through fiscal 1999 to provide college and trade school students with federal financial aid. Passed 93-1: R 41-1; D 52-0 (ND 37-0, SD 15-0), Feb. 21, 1992. A "yea" was a vote in support of the president's position.

**31. HR 2212. Conditional MFN for China in 1992/Conference Report.** Adoption of the conference report to prohibit the president from granting most-favored-nation (MFN) status to China for the 12-month period beginning July 3, 1992, unless he reports that China has accounted for and released prisoners detained because of 1989 pro-democracy protests ending in the June 3 crackdown in Tiananmen Square, and he reports that China has made significant progress in preventing human rights abuses, remedying unfair trade practices and limiting weapons proliferation. Adopted 59-39: R 9-34; D 50-5 (ND 35-3, SD 15-2), Feb. 25, 1992. A "nay" was a vote in support of the president's position.

**32. S 479. National Cooperative Research/Cloture.** Motion to invoke cloture (thus limiting debate) on the motion to proceed to the bill to broaden existing protections from antitrust laws for companies using joint ventures for research and development to include joint production ventures. Motion agreed to 98-0: R 43-0; D 55-0 (ND 38-0, SD 17-0), Feb. 25, 1992. A three-fifths majority vote (60) of the total Senate is required to invoke cloture.

| | 33 | 34 | 35 | 36 | 37 | 38 | 39 | 40 |
|---|---|---|---|---|---|---|---|---|
| **ALABAMA** | | | | | | | | |
| Heflin | N | Y | Y | Y | Y | Y | N | Y |
| *Shelby* | Y | Y | Y | Y | Y | Y | Y | Y |
| **ALASKA** | | | | | | | | |
| *Murkowski* | Y | Y | N | Y | Y | Y | Y | N |
| *Stevens* | N | Y | N | Y | Y | Y | Y | N |
| **ARIZONA** | | | | | | | | |
| DeConcini | N | Y | Y | Y | Y | N | N | N |
| *McCain* | Y | Y | N | Y | Y | Y | N | N |
| **ARKANSAS** | | | | | | | | |
| Bumpers | N | Y | Y | Y | Y | N | N | Y |
| Pryor | N | Y | Y | Y | Y | N | N | Y |
| **CALIFORNIA** | | | | | | | | |
| Cranston | N | Y | Y | + | Y | Y | N | Y |
| *Seymour* | Y | Y | N | Y | Y | Y | Y | N |
| **COLORADO** | | | | | | | | |
| Wirth | N | Y | Y | Y | Y | N | N | Y |
| *Brown* | Y | Y | N | Y | Y | Y | Y | N |
| **CONNECTICUT** | | | | | | | | |
| Dodd | N | Y | Y | Y | Y | Y | N | Y |
| Lieberman | N | Y | Y | Y | Y | Y | N | Y |
| **DELAWARE** | | | | | | | | |
| Biden | N | Y | Y | Y | Y | Y | N | Y |
| *Roth* | Y | Y | N | Y | Y | Y | Y | N |
| **FLORIDA** | | | | | | | | |
| Graham | Y | Y | Y | Y | Y | N | N | N |
| *Mack* | Y | Y | N | Y | Y | Y | N | N |
| **GEORGIA** | | | | | | | | |
| Fowler | N | Y | Y | Y | Y | N | N | Y |
| Nunn | N | Y | Y | Y | ? | N | N | Y |
| **HAWAII** | | | | | | | | |
| Akaka | N | Y | Y | Y | Y | N | N | Y |
| Inouye | N | Y | Y | Y | ? | ? | ? | # |
| **IDAHO** | | | | | | | | |
| *Craig* | Y | Y | N | N | N | Y | N | Y |
| *Symms* | Y | Y | N | Y | N | Y | Y | Y |
| **ILLINOIS** | | | | | | | | |
| Dixon | N | ? | ? | Y | ? | N | N | Y |
| Simon | N | Y | Y | Y | Y | N | N | N |
| **INDIANA** | | | | | | | | |
| *Coats* | Y | Y | N | Y | ? | Y | N | Y |
| *Lugar* | Y | Y | N | Y | ? | Y | Y | N |

| | 33 | 34 | 35 | 36 | 37 | 38 | 39 | 40 |
|---|---|---|---|---|---|---|---|---|
| **IOWA** | | | | | | | | |
| Harkin | ? | ? | ? | ? | ? | ? | ? | ? |
| *Grassley* | Y | Y | N | Y | Y | Y | Y | N |
| **KANSAS** | | | | | | | | |
| *Dole* | Y | Y | N | N | Y | Y | N | N |
| *Kassebaum* | Y | Y | N | Y | Y | Y | N | N |
| **KENTUCKY** | | | | | | | | |
| Ford | N | Y | Y | Y | Y | Y | N | Y |
| *McConnell* | Y | Y | N | Y | Y | Y | N | Y |
| **LOUISIANA** | | | | | | | | |
| Breaux | N | Y | Y | Y | Y | Y | N | Y |
| Johnston | N | Y | Y | Y | Y | Y | N | Y |
| **MAINE** | | | | | | | | |
| Mitchell | N | Y | Y | Y | Y | Y | N | Y |
| *Cohen* | N | Y | Y | Y | Y | N | N | N |
| **MARYLAND** | | | | | | | | |
| Mikulski | N | Y | Y | ? | Y | N | N | Y |
| Sarbanes | N | Y | Y | Y | Y | N | N | Y |
| **MASSACHUSETTS** | | | | | | | | |
| Kennedy | N | Y | Y | Y | Y | N | N | Y |
| Kerry | N | Y | Y | Y | Y | N | N | Y |
| **MICHIGAN** | | | | | | | | |
| Levin | N | Y | Y | Y | Y | N | N | N |
| Riegle | N | Y | Y | Y | Y | ? | − | + |
| **MINNESOTA** | | | | | | | | |
| Wellstone | N | Y | Y | ? | Y | N | N | Y |
| *Durenberger* | N | Y | N | Y | Y | N | N | Y |
| **MISSISSIPPI** | | | | | | | | |
| *Cochran* | N | Y | N | Y | ? | Y | Y | N |
| *Lott* | Y | Y | N | N | Y | Y | Y | N |
| **MISSOURI** | | | | | | | | |
| *Bond* | Y | Y | N | Y | Y | Y | Y | N |
| *Danforth* | Y | Y | N | Y | Y | Y | N | N |
| **MONTANA** | | | | | | | | |
| Baucus | N | Y | Y | Y | Y | Y | N | Y |
| *Burns* | Y | Y | N | Y | N | Y | Y | N |
| **NEBRASKA** | | | | | | | | |
| Exon | Y | Y | Y | Y | Y | Y | N | Y |
| Kerrey | ? | ? | ? | ? | Y | Y | N | Y |
| **NEVADA** | | | | | | | | |
| Bryan | N | Y | Y | Y | Y | N | N | Y |
| Reid | N | Y | Y | Y | Y | N | N | Y |

| | 33 | 34 | 35 | 36 | 37 | 38 | 39 | 40 |
|---|---|---|---|---|---|---|---|---|
| **NEW HAMPSHIRE** | | | | | | | | |
| *Rudman* | N | Y | N | Y | Y | Y | N | N |
| *Smith* | Y | Y | N | Y | Y | Y | Y | N |
| **NEW JERSEY** | | | | | | | | |
| Bradley | N | Y | Y | Y | Y | N | N | Y |
| Lautenberg | N | Y | Y | Y | Y | N | N | Y |
| **NEW MEXICO** | | | | | | | | |
| Bingaman | N | Y | Y | Y | ? | N | N | Y |
| *Domenici* | Y | Y | N | Y | Y | Y | N | Y |
| **NEW YORK** | | | | | | | | |
| Moynihan | N | Y | Y | Y | Y | Y | N | Y |
| *D'Amato* | Y | Y | N | Y | Y | Y | Y | N |
| **NORTH CAROLINA** | | | | | | | | |
| Sanford | N | Y | Y | Y | Y | N | N | Y |
| *Helms* | Y | Y | N | N | N | Y | Y | Y |
| **NORTH DAKOTA** | | | | | | | | |
| Burdick | N | Y | Y | Y | Y | N | N | Y |
| Conrad | Y | Y | Y | Y | Y | N | N | N |
| **OHIO** | | | | | | | | |
| Glenn | N | Y | Y | Y | Y | N | N | Y |
| Metzenbaum | N | N | Y | Y | Y | N | N | Y |
| **OKLAHOMA** | | | | | | | | |
| Boren | Y | Y | Y | Y | Y | N | N | N |
| *Nickles* | Y | Y | N | N | ? | Y | Y | ? |
| **OREGON** | | | | | | | | |
| *Hatfield* | N | Y | N | Y | Y | Y | Y | N |
| *Packwood* | Y | Y | Y | Y | ? | Y | Y | N |
| **PENNSYLVANIA** | | | | | | | | |
| Wofford | N | Y | Y | Y | Y | N | N | Y |
| *Specter* | Y | Y | N | Y | N | Y | N | Y |
| **RHODE ISLAND** | | | | | | | | |
| Pell | N | Y | Y | Y | Y | N | N | Y |
| *Chafee* | Y | Y | N | Y | Y | Y | N | Y |
| **SOUTH CAROLINA** | | | | | | | | |
| Hollings | Y | Y | Y | Y | Y | N | N | Y |
| *Thurmond* | Y | Y | N | Y | Y | Y | N | Y |
| **SOUTH DAKOTA** | | | | | | | | |
| Daschle | Y | Y | Y | Y | Y | N | N | Y |
| *Pressler* | Y | Y | N | Y | Y | Y | N | Y |
| **TENNESSEE** | | | | | | | | |
| Gore | N | Y | Y | Y | Y | N | N | Y |
| Sasser | N | Y | Y | Y | Y | N | N | Y |

| | 33 | 34 | 35 | 36 | 37 | 38 | 39 | 40 |
|---|---|---|---|---|---|---|---|---|
| **TEXAS** | | | | | | | | |
| Bentsen | N | Y | Y | Y | Y | N | N | Y |
| *Gramm* | Y | Y | N | Y | Y | Y | Y | Y |
| **UTAH** | | | | | | | | |
| *Garn* | Y | Y | N | Y | N | Y | N | Y |
| *Hatch* | Y | Y | N | Y | N | Y | N | Y |
| **VERMONT** | | | | | | | | |
| Leahy | N | Y | Y | Y | Y | N | N | Y |
| *Jeffords* | N | Y | Y | Y | ? | Y | N | Y |
| **VIRGINIA** | | | | | | | | |
| Robb | Y | Y | Y | Y | Y | N | N | Y |
| *Warner* | Y | Y | N | Y | ? | Y | Y | N |
| **WASHINGTON** | | | | | | | | |
| Adams | N | Y | Y | ? | Y | N | N | Y |
| *Gorton* | Y | Y | N | Y | Y | Y | Y | N |
| **WEST VIRGINIA** | | | | | | | | |
| Byrd | N | Y | Y | Y | Y | N | N | X |
| Rockefeller | N | Y | Y | Y | Y | N | N | Y |
| **WISCONSIN** | | | | | | | | |
| Kohl | N | Y | Y | Y | Y | N | N | N |
| *Kasten* | Y | Y | Y | Y | Y | Y | N | Y |
| **WYOMING** | | | | | | | | |
| *Simpson* | Y | Y | N | Y | Y | Y | Y | N |
| *Wallop* | Y | Y | N | N | N | Y | Y | N |

ND  Northern Democrats    SD  Southern Democrats    Southern states - Ala., Ark., Fla., Ga., Ky., La., Miss., N.C., Okla., S.C., Tenn., Texas, Va.

**33. S 479. National Cooperative Research/Line-Item Veto.** McCain, R-Ariz., motion to waive the Budget Act with respect to the Sasser, D-Tenn., point of order against the McCain amendment to give the president the power to veto appropriated funds by line item. Motion rejected 44-54: R 36-7; D 8-47 (ND 3-35, SD 5-12), Feb. 27, 1992. A three-fifths majority (60) of the total Senate is required to waive the Budget Act. (Subsequently, the Sasser point of order was upheld and the McCain amendment fell.)

**34. S 479. National Cooperative Research/Passage.** Passage of the bill to broaden existing protections from antitrust laws for companies using joint ventures for research and development to include joint production ventures. Passed 96-1: R 43-0; D 53-1 (ND 36-1, SD 17-0), Feb. 27, 1992.

**35. HR 1426. Lumbee Indian Tribe Recognition/Cloture.** Motion to invoke cloture (thus limiting debate) on the motion to proceed to the bill to give federal recognition to the Lumbee Tribe of Cheraw Indians of North Carolina. Motion rejected 58-39: R 4-39; D 54-0 (ND 37-0, SD 17-0), Feb. 27, 1992. A three-fifths majority vote (60) of the total Senate is required to invoke cloture. A "nay" was a vote in support of the president's position.

**36. S 1504. Corporation for Public Broadcasting Authorization/Cloture.** Mitchell, D-Maine, motion to invoke cloture (thus limiting debate) on the motion to proceed to the bill to authorize $1.1 billion for the Corporation for Public Broadcasting in fiscal 1994-96. Motion agreed to 87-7: R 36-7; D 51-0 (ND 34-0, SD 17-0), March 3, 1992. A three-fifths majority vote (60) of the total Senate is required to invoke cloture.

**37. S 792. Indoor Radon Abatement/Passage.** Passage of the bill to reauthorize and expand federal programs designed to reduce radon contamination in buildings. Radon is a natural radioactive gas that can damage lung tissue. Passed 82-6: R 30-6; D 52-0 (ND 36-0, SD 16-0), March 10, 1992. A "nay" was a vote in support of the president's position.

**38. HR 4210. 1992 Tax Bill/Prescription Drug Costs.** Bentsen, D-Texas, motion to table (kill) the Pryor, D-Ark., amendment to contain the cost of prescription drugs by denying certain tax breaks to drug companies that raise prices above the rate of inflation as reflected in the Consumer Price Index. Motion agreed to 61-36: R 41-2; D 20-34 (ND 11-26, SD 9-8), March 11, 1992.

**39. HR 4210. 1992 Tax Bill/Budget Waiver.** Packwood, R-Ore., motion to waive a point of order against the Packwood substitute amendment for not meeting pay-as-you-go requirements as scored by the Congressional Budget Office. The substitute would implement a plan that includes a cut in the capital gains rate, a $5,000 tax credit and penalty-free withdrawals from Individual Retirement Accounts for first-time home buyers, passive loss deductions for real estate developers, an increase in the rate of depreciation for business equipment, new rules encouraging real estate investment by pension funds, a more generous depreciation for companies under the alternative minimum tax and a repeal of all the 1990 luxury excise taxes. Motion rejected 37-60: R 36-7; D 1-53 (ND 0-37, SD 1-16), March 11, 1992. A three-fifths majority (60) of the total Senate is required to waive the Budget Act. (Subsequently, the point of order was sustained and the Packwood substitute fell.)

**40. HR 4210. 1992 Tax Bill/Child Credit.** Bentsen, D-Texas, motion to table (kill) the Levin, D-Mich., amendment to eliminate the $300-a-child tax credit for middle-income families and express the sense of the Senate that the savings be used for deficit reduction, job training and transportation infrastructure. Motion agreed to 57-38: R 9-33; D 48-5 (ND 32-4, SD 16-1), March 12, 1992.

| | 41 | 42 | 43 | 44 | 45 | 46 | 47 | 48 |
|---|---|---|---|---|---|---|---|---|
| **ALABAMA** | | | | | | | | |
| Heflin | Y | N | N | N | Y | N | Y | N |
| *Shelby* | Y | Y | N | Y | N | Y | Y | Y |
| **ALASKA** | | | | | | | | |
| *Murkowski* | Y | N | Y | Y | Y | N | N | Y |
| *Stevens* | Y | N | Y | Y | Y | N | Y | Y |
| **ARIZONA** | | | | | | | | |
| DeConcini | Y | N | Y | N | N | N | N | N |
| *McCain* | Y | N | Y | Y | Y | N | Y | Y |
| **ARKANSAS** | | | | | | | | |
| Bumpers | Y | N | N | N | N | N | N | N |
| Pryor | Y | N | ? | N | N | Y | Y | N |
| **CALIFORNIA** | | | | | | | | |
| Cranston | N | Y | N | N | Y | Y | Y | N |
| *Seymour* | Y | N | Y | Y | Y | N | Y | Y |
| **COLORADO** | | | | | | | | |
| Wirth | Y | N | N | N | N | N | N | N |
| *Brown* | Y | Y | Y | Y | Y | N | Y | Y |
| **CONNECTICUT** | | | | | | | | |
| Dodd | Y | N | N | N | N | N | N | N |
| Lieberman | Y | N | N | N | Y | N | N | N |
| **DELAWARE** | | | | | | | | |
| Biden | Y | N | N | N | Y | N | N | N |
| *Roth* | Y | N | N | Y | Y | N | Y | Y |
| **FLORIDA** | | | | | | | | |
| Graham | Y | N | N | N | N | N | N | N |
| *Mack* | Y | N | Y | Y | N | N | Y | Y |
| **GEORGIA** | | | | | | | | |
| Fowler | Y | N | N | N | N | N | N | N |
| Nunn | Y | Y | N | N | N | N | Y | N |
| **HAWAII** | | | | | | | | |
| Akaka | Y | N | Y | N | Y | Y | N | N |
| Inouye | ? | ? | ? | ? | ? | ? | N | N |
| **IDAHO** | | | | | | | | |
| *Craig* | Y | N | Y | Y | Y | N | Y | Y |
| *Symms* | Y | N | Y | Y | Y | N | Y | Y |
| **ILLINOIS** | | | | | | | | |
| Dixon | Y | N | N | N | N | Y | N | N |
| Simon | Y | N | Y | ? | ? | ? | N | N |
| **INDIANA** | | | | | | | | |
| *Coats* | Y | N | Y | Y | N | Y | N | Y |
| *Lugar* | Y | N | Y | Y | Y | N | Y | Y |

| | 41 | 42 | 43 | 44 | 45 | 46 | 47 | 48 |
|---|---|---|---|---|---|---|---|---|
| **IOWA** | | | | | | | | |
| Harkin | ? | ? | ? | ? | ? | ? | ? | ? |
| *Grassley* | Y | N | Y | Y | Y | N | N | Y |
| **KANSAS** | | | | | | | | |
| *Dole* | Y | Y | Y | Y | Y | N | N | Y |
| *Kassebaum* | Y | N | N | Y | Y | N | Y | Y |
| **KENTUCKY** | | | | | | | | |
| Ford | Y | N | N | N | N | Y | Y | N |
| *McConnell* | Y | Y | Y | Y | Y | N | Y | Y |
| **LOUISIANA** | | | | | | | | |
| Breaux | Y | N | N | N | N | Y | Y | N |
| Johnston | Y | Y | N | N | Y | N | N | N |
| **MAINE** | | | | | | | | |
| Mitchell | Y | N | N | N | N | Y | Y | N |
| *Cohen* | Y | N | Y | N | Y | N | Y | N |
| **MARYLAND** | | | | | | | | |
| Mikulski | Y | N | N | N | Y | N | N | ? |
| Sarbanes | Y | Y | N | Y | Y | Y | Y | N |
| **MASSACHUSETTS** | | | | | | | | |
| Kennedy | Y | Y | N | N | N | Y | Y | N |
| Kerry | Y | N | N | N | N | N | N | N |
| **MICHIGAN** | | | | | | | | |
| Levin | Y | Y | N | N | N | N | N | N |
| Riegle | ? | Y | N | ? | ? | ? | ? | ? |
| **MINNESOTA** | | | | | | | | |
| Wellstone | Y | Y | N | N | Y | N | N | N |
| *Durenberger* | Y | Y | Y | N | Y | Y | Y | N |
| **MISSISSIPPI** | | | | | | | | |
| *Cochran* | Y | N | Y | N | N | Y | Y | Y |
| *Lott* | Y | N | Y | Y | Y | N | Y | Y |
| **MISSOURI** | | | | | | | | |
| *Bond* | Y | Y | Y | Y | N | N | Y | Y |
| *Danforth* | Y | N | N | N | Y | N | Y | Y |
| **MONTANA** | | | | | | | | |
| Baucus | Y | Y | N | N | Y | Y | Y | N |
| *Burns* | Y | N | Y | Y | Y | N | Y | Y |
| **NEBRASKA** | | | | | | | | |
| Exon | Y | Y | N | N | Y | Y | Y | N |
| Kerrey | Y | Y | N | N | Y | Y | N | N |
| **NEVADA** | | | | | | | | |
| Bryan | Y | N | N | N | N | Y | N | N |
| Reid | Y | N | N | N | N | N | N | N |

| | 41 | 42 | 43 | 44 | 45 | 46 | 47 | 48 |
|---|---|---|---|---|---|---|---|---|
| **NEW HAMPSHIRE** | | | | | | | | |
| *Rudman* | Y | N | N | N | Y | N | Y | N |
| *Smith* | Y | N | Y | Y | Y | N | Y | N |
| **NEW JERSEY** | | | | | | | | |
| Bradley | Y | N | N | N | N | Y | Y | N |
| Lautenberg | Y | N | N | N | N | N | N | N |
| **NEW MEXICO** | | | | | | | | |
| Bingaman | Y | N | Y | N | N | N | N | N |
| *Domenici* | Y | N | Y | N | Y | N | Y | N |
| **NEW YORK** | | | | | | | | |
| Moynihan | Y | Y | N | N | N | Y | Y | N |
| *D'Amato* | Y | N | Y | Y | Y | N | N | Y |
| **NORTH CAROLINA** | | | | | | | | |
| Sanford | Y | Y | Y | N | N | N | N | N |
| *Helms* | Y | N | Y | Y | Y | N | Y | Y |
| **NORTH DAKOTA** | | | | | | | | |
| Burdick | Y | N | Y | N | Y | N | Y | N |
| Conrad | Y | N | N | N | N | N | N | N |
| **OHIO** | | | | | | | | |
| Glenn | Y | Y | N | N | N | N | N | N |
| Metzenbaum | Y | Y | N | N | N | N | N | N |
| **OKLAHOMA** | | | | | | | | |
| Boren | Y | Y | N | N | N | Y | N | N |
| *Nickles* | Y | N | Y | Y | Y | N | Y | Y |
| **OREGON** | | | | | | | | |
| *Hatfield* | Y | N | Y | N | N | N | Y | N |
| *Packwood* | Y | N | N | Y | Y | N | Y | N |
| **PENNSYLVANIA** | | | | | | | | |
| Wofford | Y | Y | N | N | N | Y | Y | N |
| *Specter* | Y | N | Y | Y | N | N | Y | N |
| **RHODE ISLAND** | | | | | | | | |
| Pell | Y | Y | N | N | Y | N | Y | N |
| *Chafee* | Y | Y | Y | N | Y | N | Y | Y |
| **SOUTH CAROLINA** | | | | | | | | |
| Hollings | Y | Y | N | Y | N | N | Y | N |
| *Thurmond* | Y | N | Y | Y | Y | N | Y | Y |
| **SOUTH DAKOTA** | | | | | | | | |
| Daschle | Y | N | Y | N | N | N | N | N |
| *Pressler* | Y | N | Y | Y | Y | N | Y | Y |
| **TENNESSEE** | | | | | | | | |
| Gore | Y | Y | N | Y | Y | Y | Y | N |
| Sasser | Y | Y | N | N | Y | Y | Y | N |

| | 41 | 42 | 43 | 44 | 45 | 46 | 47 | 48 |
|---|---|---|---|---|---|---|---|---|
| **TEXAS** | | | | | | | | |
| Bentsen | Y | Y | N | N | N | Y | Y | N |
| *Gramm* | Y | N | Y | Y | Y | N | Y | Y |
| **UTAH** | | | | | | | | |
| *Garn* | Y | N | Y | Y | Y | N | Y | Y |
| *Hatch* | Y | N | Y | Y | Y | N | Y | Y |
| **VERMONT** | | | | | | | | |
| Leahy | Y | Y | N | ? | ? | ? | ? | N |
| *Jeffords* | Y | Y | N | N | Y | N | Y | N |
| **VIRGINIA** | | | | | | | | |
| Robb | Y | Y | N | N | N | N | N | N |
| *Warner* | Y | N | Y | Y | Y | N | Y | Y |
| **WASHINGTON** | | | | | | | | |
| Adams | Y | N | N | N | N | N | N | N |
| *Gorton* | Y | N | Y | Y | Y | N | N | Y |
| **WEST VIRGINIA** | | | | | | | | |
| Byrd | N | N | N | N | N | N | N | N |
| Rockefeller | Y | Y | N | N | N | Y | N | N |
| **WISCONSIN** | | | | | | | | |
| Kohl | Y | N | N | N | N | Y | N | N |
| *Kasten* | Y | N | Y | Y | Y | N | N | Y |
| **WYOMING** | | | | | | | | |
| *Simpson* | Y | N | Y | Y | Y | N | Y | Y |
| *Wallop* | Y | N | Y | Y | Y | N | Y | Y |

ND   Northern Democrats    SD   Southern Democrats          Southern states - Ala., Ark., Fla., Ga., Ky., La., Miss., N.C., Okla., S.C., Tenn., Texas, Va.

**41. HR 4210. 1992 Tax Bill/House Bank Scandal.** Helms, R-N.C., amendment to express the sense of the Senate that no Senate bank with characteristics similar to those of the former House bank should ever be established. Adopted 95-2: R 43-0; D 52-2 (ND 35-2, SD 17-0), March 12, 1992.

**42. HR 4210. 1992 Tax Bill/Pension Funds.** Bentsen, D-Texas, motion to table (kill) the Reid, D-Nev., amendment to prohibit states from taxing the income from the pension or retirement funds of any individual who is not a current resident of the state. Motion rejected 36-62: R 7-36; D 29-26 (ND 18-20, SD 11-6), March 12, 1992. (Subsequently, the Reid amendment was adopted by voice vote.)

**43. HR 4210. 1992 Tax Bill/Budget Waiver.** McCain, R-Ariz., motion to waive a point of order against the McCain amendment for reducing revenue levels below the level set forth in the budget resolution. The McCain amendment would provide tax incentives for businesses locating on Indian reservations. Motion rejected 46-51: R 37-6; D 9-45 (ND 8-30, SD 1-15), March 12, 1992. A three-fifths majority (60) of the total Senate is required to waive the Budget Act. (Subsequently, the point of order was sustained and the McCain amendment fell.)

**44. HR 4210. 1992 Tax Bill/Budget Waiver.** McCain, R-Ariz., motion to waive the budget act with respect to the Sasser, D-Tenn., point of order against the McCain amendment for encroaching on jurisdiction of the Budget Committee. The McCain amendment would require 60 votes for legislation increasing taxes. Motion rejected 37-58: R 35-8; D 2-50 (ND 0-35, SD 2-15), March 13, 1992. Such a waiver requires 60 votes. (Subsequently, the Sasser point of order was sustained, and the McCain amendment fell.)

**45. HR 4210. 1992 Tax Bill/Highway Trust Funds.** Moynihan, D-N.Y., motion to table (kill) the Bumpers, D-Ark., amendment to express the sense of the Senate that pay-as-you-go requirements should be waived to authorize spending $10 billion in fiscal 1992-93 from Highway Trust Funds. Motion agreed to 53-42: R 37-6; D 16-36 (ND 11-24, SD 5-12), March 13, 1992.

**46. HR 4210. 1992 Tax Bill/Workfare Programs.** Bentsen, D-Texas, motion to table (kill) the D'Amato, R-N.Y., amendment to reduce by 10 percent welfare assistance to states that do not have workfare programs. Motion rejected 33-62: R 2-41; D 31-21 (ND 22-13, SD 9-8), March 13, 1992. (Subsequently, the D'Amato amendment was agreed to by voice vote.)

**47. HR 4210. 1992 Tax Bill/Child-Care Facilities.** Bentsen, D-Texas, motion to table (kill) the DeConcini, D-Ariz., amendment to establish a tax credit for employers who provide child-care facilities. Motion agreed to 62-35: R 37-6; D 25-29 (ND 12-25, SD 13-4), March 13, 1992.

**48. HR 4210. 1992 Tax Bill/Budget Waiver.** Kasten, R-Wis., motion to waive the budget act with respect to the Bentsen, D-Texas, point of order against the Kasten amendment for reducing revenue below the level set by the budget resolution. The Kasten amendment would strike tax increases, freeze discretionary spending and cut defense to levels in the president's budget. Motion rejected 36-61: R 35-8; D 1-53 (ND 0-37, SD 1-16), March 13, 1992. Such a waiver requires 60 votes. (Subsequently, the Bentsen point of order was sustained, and the Kasten amendment fell.)

| | 49 | 50 | 51 | 52 | 53 | 54 | 55 | 56 |
|---|---|---|---|---|---|---|---|---|
| **ALABAMA** | | | | | | | | |
| Heflin | Y | N | N | Y | N | N | Y | N |
| Shelby | Y | Y | N | N | N | N | Y | N |
| **ALASKA** | | | | | | | | |
| *Murkowski* | Y | Y | N | N | N | N | Y | N |
| *Stevens* | Y | Y | N | N | N | N | Y | N |
| **ARIZONA** | | | | | | | | |
| DeConcini | N | N | N | Y | Y | Y | Y | Y |
| *McCain* | N | Y | N | N | N | N | Y | Y |
| **ARKANSAS** | | | | | | | | |
| Bumpers | N | N | Y | Y | Y | Y | Y | Y |
| Pryor | N | N | Y | Y | Y | Y | Y | Y |
| **CALIFORNIA** | | | | | | | | |
| Cranston | N | N | Y | Y | Y | Y | Y | Y |
| *Seymour* | Y | Y | N | N | N | N | Y | N |
| **COLORADO** | | | | | | | | |
| Wirth | N | N | Y | Y | ? | ? | ? | N |
| *Brown* | Y | Y | N | N | N | N | Y | N |
| **CONNECTICUT** | | | | | | | | |
| Dodd | N | N | Y | Y | Y | Y | N | N |
| Lieberman | N | N | Y | Y | Y | Y | N | N |
| **DELAWARE** | | | | | | | | |
| Biden | N | N | Y | Y | Y | Y | Y | Y |
| *Roth* | Y | Y | N | N | N | N | N | N |
| **FLORIDA** | | | | | | | | |
| Graham | N | N | Y | Y | Y | Y | Y | Y |
| *Mack* | Y | Y | N | Y | N | N | Y | N |
| **GEORGIA** | | | | | | | | |
| Fowler | N | N | Y | Y | Y | Y | Y | Y |
| Nunn | N | N | Y | Y | Y | Y | Y | N |
| **HAWAII** | | | | | | | | |
| Akaka | N | N | Y | Y | Y | Y | N | Y |
| Inouye | N | N | Y | Y | Y | # | Y | Y |
| **IDAHO** | | | | | | | | |
| *Craig* | Y | Y | N | N | N | N | Y | N |
| *Symms* | Y | Y | N | N | N | N | Y | N |
| **ILLINOIS** | | | | | | | | |
| Dixon | N | N | Y | + | + | ? | ? | ? |
| Simon | N | N | Y | Y | Y | Y | Y | Y |
| **INDIANA** | | | | | | | | |
| *Coats* | Y | Y | N | N | N | N | Y | N |
| *Lugar* | Y | Y | N | N | N | N | Y | N |
| **IOWA** | | | | | | | | |
| Harkin | ? | ? | ? | Y | Y | Y | ? | + |
| *Grassley* | Y | Y | N | N | N | N | Y | N |
| **KANSAS** | | | | | | | | |
| *Dole* | Y | Y | N | N | N | N | Y | N |
| *Kassebaum* | N | Y | N | N | Y | N | Y | N |
| **KENTUCKY** | | | | | | | | |
| Ford | N | N | Y | Y | Y | Y | Y | Y |
| *McConnell* | Y | Y | N | N | N | N | Y | N |
| **LOUISIANA** | | | | | | | | |
| Breaux | N | N | Y | Y | N | Y | Y | Y |
| Johnston | N | N | Y | N | N | Y | Y | Y |
| **MAINE** | | | | | | | | |
| Mitchell | N | N | Y | Y | Y | Y | Y | Y |
| *Cohen* | N | Y | N | N | N | N | Y | N |
| **MARYLAND** | | | | | | | | |
| Mikulski | N | N | Y | Y | Y | Y | Y | Y |
| Sarbanes | N | N | Y | Y | Y | Y | N | Y |
| **MASSACHUSETTS** | | | | | | | | |
| Kennedy | N | N | Y | Y | Y | Y | Y | N |
| Kerry | N | N | Y | Y | Y | Y | Y | N |
| **MICHIGAN** | | | | | | | | |
| Levin | N | N | Y | Y | Y | Y | Y | Y |
| Riegle | ? | ? | # | Y | Y | Y | N | Y |
| **MINNESOTA** | | | | | | | | |
| Wellstone | Y | N | Y | Y | Y | Y | N | Y |
| *Durenberger* | N | Y | N | N | Y | N | Y | N |
| **MISSISSIPPI** | | | | | | | | |
| *Cochran* | Y | Y | N | N | N | N | Y | N |
| *Lott* | Y | Y | N | Y | N | N | Y | N |
| **MISSOURI** | | | | | | | | |
| *Bond* | Y | Y | N | N | N | N | Y | N |
| *Danforth* | Y | Y | N | N | N | N | Y | N |
| **MONTANA** | | | | | | | | |
| Baucus | N | N | Y | Y | Y | Y | Y | Y |
| *Burns* | Y | Y | N | N | N | N | Y | N |
| **NEBRASKA** | | | | | | | | |
| Exon | Y | N | Y | Y | Y | Y | Y | N |
| Kerrey | Y | N | N | Y | ? | ? | N | Y |
| **NEVADA** | | | | | | | | |
| Bryan | N | N | Y | Y | Y | Y | Y | Y |
| Reid | N | N | Y | Y | Y | Y | Y | Y |
| **NEW HAMPSHIRE** | | | | | | | | |
| *Rudman* | N | Y | N | N | N | N | Y | N |
| *Smith* | Y | Y | N | Y | N | N | Y | N |
| **NEW JERSEY** | | | | | | | | |
| Bradley | N | N | X | Y | Y | X | Y | Y |
| Lautenberg | N | N | Y | Y | Y | Y | Y | Y |
| **NEW MEXICO** | | | | | | | | |
| Bingaman | N | N | Y | Y | Y | Y | N | Y |
| *Domenici* | Y | Y | N | N | N | N | Y | N |
| **NEW YORK** | | | | | | | | |
| Moynihan | N | N | Y | Y | Y | Y | Y | Y |
| *D'Amato* | Y | Y | N | Y | N | N | Y | N |
| **NORTH CAROLINA** | | | | | | | | |
| Sanford | N | N | Y | Y | Y | Y | Y | Y |
| *Helms* | Y | Y | N | Y | N | N | Y | N |
| **NORTH DAKOTA** | | | | | | | | |
| Burdick | Y | N | Y | Y | Y | Y | Y | Y |
| Conrad | Y | N | Y | ? | Y | Y | Y | Y |
| **OHIO** | | | | | | | | |
| Glenn | N | N | Y | Y | Y | Y | N | Y |
| Metzenbaum | N | N | Y | Y | Y | Y | N | Y |
| **OKLAHOMA** | | | | | | | | |
| Boren | Y | N | Y | Y | Y | Y | N | Y |
| *Nickles* | Y | Y | N | N | N | N | Y | N |
| **OREGON** | | | | | | | | |
| *Hatfield* | N | Y | N | N | N | N | Y | N |
| *Packwood* | N | Y | N | N | N | N | Y | N |
| **PENNSYLVANIA** | | | | | | | | |
| Wofford | N | N | Y | Y | Y | Y | Y | Y |
| *Specter* | Y | Y | N | Y | N | N | Y | N |
| **RHODE ISLAND** | | | | | | | | |
| Pell | N | N | Y | Y | Y | Y | − | Y |
| *Chafee* | N | Y | N | Y | N | N | Y | N |
| **SOUTH CAROLINA** | | | | | | | | |
| Hollings | N | N | N | Y | N | Y | N | Y |
| *Thurmond* | Y | Y | N | N | N | N | Y | N |
| **SOUTH DAKOTA** | | | | | | | | |
| Daschle | Y | N | Y | Y | Y | Y | Y | Y |
| *Pressler* | Y | Y | N | Y | N | N | Y | N |
| **TENNESSEE** | | | | | | | | |
| Gore | N | N | Y | Y | Y | Y | N | Y |
| Sasser | N | N | Y | Y | Y | Y | N | Y |
| **TEXAS** | | | | | | | | |
| Bentsen | N | N | Y | Y | Y | Y | Y | Y |
| *Gramm* | Y | Y | N | N | N | N | Y | N |
| **UTAH** | | | | | | | | |
| *Garn* | Y | Y | N | N | N | − | Y | N |
| *Hatch* | Y | Y | N | N | N | N | Y | N |
| **VERMONT** | | | | | | | | |
| Leahy | Y | N | Y | Y | Y | Y | N | Y |
| *Jeffords* | N | N | N | N | Y | N | Y | N |
| **VIRGINIA** | | | | | | | | |
| Robb | N | N | Y | Y | Y | Y | Y | Y |
| *Warner* | Y | Y | N | N | ? | N | Y | N |
| **WASHINGTON** | | | | | | | | |
| Adams | N | N | Y | Y | Y | Y | Y | Y |
| *Gorton* | Y | Y | N | Y | N | Y | N | |
| **WEST VIRGINIA** | | | | | | | | |
| Byrd | N | N | Y | Y | Y | Y | Y | Y |
| Rockefeller | N | N | Y | Y | Y | Y | Y | Y |
| **WISCONSIN** | | | | | | | | |
| Kohl | Y | N | Y | Y | Y | Y | N | Y |
| *Kasten* | Y | Y | N | N | N | N | N | N |
| **WYOMING** | | | | | | | | |
| *Simpson* | Y | Y | N | N | N | N | Y | N |
| *Wallop* | Y | Y | N | Y | N | − | Y | N |

ND Northern Democrats    SD Southern Democrats    Southern states - Ala., Ark., Fla., Ga., Ky., La., Miss., N.C., Okla., S.C., Tenn., Texas, Va.

**49. HR 4210. 1992 Tax Bill/Budget Waiver.** Kasten, R-Wis., motion to waive the budget act with respect to the Bentsen, D-Texas, point of order against the Kasten amendment for reducing revenue below the level set by the budget resolution. The Kasten amendment would allow gains from the sale of farm assets to be rolled into individual retirement accounts. Motion rejected 45-53: R 34-9; D 11-44 (ND 8-30, SD 3-14), March 13, 1992. Such a waiver requires 60 votes. (Subsequently, the Bentsen point of order was sustained, and the Kasten amendment fell.)

**50. HR 4210. 1992 Tax Bill/Budget Waiver.** Seymour, R-Calif., motion to waive the budget act with respect to the Bentsen, D-Texas, point of order against the Seymour amendment for reducing revenue below the level set by the budget resolution. The Seymour amendment would strike provisions to create a bracket of 36 percent for high-income taxpayers. Motion rejected 43-55: R 42-1; D 1-54 (ND 0-38, SD 1-16), March 13, 1992. Such a waiver requires 60 votes. (Subsequently, the Bentsen point of order was sustained, and the Seymour amendment fell.)

**51. HR 4210. 1992 Tax Bill/Passage.** Passage of the $70.9 billion revenue bill that would create a top income tax rate of 36 percent, place a 10 percent surtax on millionaires, create a $300 child tax credit for families with taxable income of less than $47,500, reduce capital gains taxes with a graduated system, allow passive loss deductions for real estate developers, repeal certain luxury excise taxes and extend certain expiring tax breaks. Passed 50-47: R 0-43; D 50-4 (ND 36-1, SD 14-3), March 13, 1992. A "nay" was a vote supporting the president's position.

**52. HR 2212. Conditional MFN for China in 1992/Veto Override.** Passage, over President Bush's March 2 veto, of the bill to prohibit the president from granting most-favored-nation status to China for the 12-month period beginning July 3, 1992, unless certain conditions were met. Rejected 60-38: R 9-34; D 51-4 (ND 36-2, SD 15-2), March 18, 1992. A two-thirds majority of those present and voting (66 in this case) of both houses is required to override a veto. A "nay" was a vote supporting the president's position.

**53. HR 3371. Crime Bill/Cloture.** Mitchell, D-Maine, motion to invoke cloture (thus limiting debate) on the conference report to mandate a five-day waiting period and a background check for handgun purchases among other provisions. Motion rejected 54-43: R 4-38; D 50-5 (ND 37-1, SD 13-4), March 19, 1992. A three-fifths majority vote (60) of the total Senate is required to invoke cloture. A "nay" was a vote supporting the president's position.

**54. HR 4210. 1992 Tax Bill/Conference Report.** Adoption of the conference report to create a 20 percent tax credit against Social Security taxes paid by middle-income families to be replaced in 1994 by a permanent $300-a-child tax credit. Adopted 50-44: R 0-41; D 50-3 (ND 36-0, SD 14-3), March 20, 1992. A "nay" was a vote in support of the president's position.

**55. S 1696. Montana Wilderness/Passage.** Passage of the bill to designate 1.2 million acres in Montana as wilderness, restricting it from development or park use; release 4 million acres for multiple-use activities; and create wilderness study and national recreation areas. Passed 75-22: R 41-2; D 34-20 (ND 21-16, SD 13-4), March 26, 1992.

**56. S 2399. Eliminate Budget Fire Walls/Cloture.** Mitchell, D-Maine, motion to invoke cloture (thus limiting debate) on the motion to proceed to the bill to modify the 1990 Budget Enforcement Act (PL 101-508) to knock down the walls that prohibit the shifting of funds between defense and domestic appropriations. Motion rejected 50-48: R 3-40; D 47-8 (ND 35-3, SD 12-5), March 26, 1992. A three-fifths majority vote (60) of the total Senate is required to invoke cloture. A "nay" was a vote supporting the president's position.

**KEY**

Y Voted for (yea).
\# Paired for.
\+ Announced for.
N Voted against (nay).
X Paired against.
− Announced against.
P Voted ''present.''
C Voted ''present'' to avoid possible conflict of interest.
? Did not vote or otherwise make a position known.

Democrats   *Republicans*

| | 57 | 58 | 59 | 60 | 61 | 62 | 63 | 64 |
|---|---|---|---|---|---|---|---|---|
| **ALABAMA** | | | | | | | | |
| Heflin | Y | Y | N | Y | N | Y | Y | Y |
| Shelby | N | N | N | Y | N | Y | Y | Y |
| **ALASKA** | | | | | | | | |
| *Murkowski* | N | N | Y | N | Y | N | Y | N |
| *Stevens* | N | N | Y | Y | N | Y | Y | N |
| **ARIZONA** | | | | | | | | |
| DeConcini | Y | Y | N | Y | N | N | Y | Y |
| *McCain* | N | N | N | Y | Y | Y | Y | N |
| **ARKANSAS** | | | | | | | | |
| Bumpers | Y | Y | Y | N | Y | N | Y | Y |
| Pryor | Y | Y | N | Y | N | Y | Y | Y |
| **CALIFORNIA** | | | | | | | | |
| Cranston | ? | Y | Y | Y | N | Y | Y | Y |
| *Seymour* | N | Y | Y | Y | N | Y | Y | N |
| **COLORADO** | | | | | | | | |
| Wirth | Y | Y | Y | N | Y | N | Y | Y |
| *Brown* | Y | N | N | Y | N | Y | Y | N |
| **CONNECTICUT** | | | | | | | | |
| Dodd | Y | Y | Y | N | Y | N | Y | Y |
| Lieberman | Y | Y | Y | Y | N | Y | Y | Y |
| **DELAWARE** | | | | | | | | |
| Biden | Y | Y | Y | N | Y | N | Y | Y |
| *Roth* | N | N | Y | N | Y | N | Y | Y |
| **FLORIDA** | | | | | | | | |
| Graham | Y | Y | Y | N | Y | N | Y | Y |
| *Mack* | N | N | N | Y | N | Y | Y | N |
| **GEORGIA** | | | | | | | | |
| Fowler | Y | Y | Y | N | Y | N | Y | Y |
| Nunn | Y | Y | N | Y | N | Y | Y | Y |
| **HAWAII** | | | | | | | | |
| Akaka | Y | Y | N | Y | N | Y | Y | Y |
| Inouye | Y | Y | Y | Y | N | Y | Y | Y |
| **IDAHO** | | | | | | | | |
| *Craig* | N | N | N | Y | Y | Y | N | Y |
| *Symms* | ? | ? | ? | Y | Y | N | Y | N |
| **ILLINOIS** | | | | | | | | |
| Dixon | ? | ? | ? | Y | N | Y | Y | ? |
| Simon | Y | Y | N | Y | N | Y | Y | Y |
| **INDIANA** | | | | | | | | |
| *Coats* | N | N | N | Y | Y | Y | Y | N |
| *Lugar* | N | N | Y | Y | Y | Y | Y | ? |
| **IOWA** | | | | | | | | |
| Harkin | Y | Y | N | Y | N | Y | Y | Y |
| *Grassley* | N | Y | N | Y | Y | Y | Y | N |
| **KANSAS** | | | | | | | | |
| *Dole* | N | N | Y | Y | N | Y | N | Y |
| *Kassebaum* | N | N | N | Y | N | Y | Y | N |
| **KENTUCKY** | | | | | | | | |
| Ford | N | Y | Y | Y | Y | Y | Y | N |
| *McConnell* | N | N | N | Y | N | Y | Y | N |
| **LOUISIANA** | | | | | | | | |
| Breaux | Y | Y | Y | Y | N | Y | Y | Y |
| Johnston | N | Y | Y | Y | Y | Y | Y | Y |
| **MAINE** | | | | | | | | |
| Mitchell | N | Y | Y | Y | N | Y | Y | Y |
| *Cohen* | N | N | N | Y | N | Y | Y | Y |
| **MARYLAND** | | | | | | | | |
| Mikulski | Y | Y | N | Y | N | Y | Y | Y |
| Sarbanes | N | Y | Y | Y | N | Y | Y | Y |
| **MASSACHUSETTS** | | | | | | | | |
| Kennedy | ? | ? | ? | Y | N | Y | Y | Y |
| Kerry | Y | Y | Y | Y | N | Y | Y | Y |
| **MICHIGAN** | | | | | | | | |
| Levin | ? | ? | ? | Y | N | Y | Y | Y |
| Riegle | N | Y | Y | Y | N | Y | Y | Y |
| **MINNESOTA** | | | | | | | | |
| Wellstone | Y | Y | Y | N | Y | N | Y | Y |
| *Durenberger* | N | N | Y | Y | Y | Y | Y | Y |
| **MISSISSIPPI** | | | | | | | | |
| *Cochran* | ? | ? | ? | Y | Y | Y | Y | N |
| *Lott* | N | N | Y | Y | Y | N | Y | N |
| **MISSOURI** | | | | | | | | |
| *Bond* | N | N | N | Y | Y | Y | Y | Y |
| *Danforth* | N | N | Y | Y | N | Y | Y | Y |
| **MONTANA** | | | | | | | | |
| Baucus | Y | Y | N | Y | N | N | Y | Y |
| *Burns* | N | N | N | Y | Y | N | Y | N |
| **NEBRASKA** | | | | | | | | |
| Exon | Y | Y | N | Y | Y | Y | Y | N |
| Kerrey | Y | Y | N | Y | N | Y | Y | Y |
| **NEVADA** | | | | | | | | |
| Bryan | Y | Y | Y | N | Y | N | Y | Y |
| Reid | Y | Y | Y | N | Y | N | Y | Y |
| **NEW HAMPSHIRE** | | | | | | | | |
| *Rudman* | ? | ? | ? | Y | N | Y | Y | N |
| *Smith* | Y | N | N | N | Y | N | Y | N |
| **NEW JERSEY** | | | | | | | | |
| Bradley | Y | Y | N | Y | N | Y | Y | Y |
| Lautenberg | Y | Y | N | Y | N | Y | Y | Y |
| **NEW MEXICO** | | | | | | | | |
| Bingaman | N | Y | Y | Y | N | Y | Y | Y |
| *Domenici* | N | N | Y | Y | N | Y | Y | N |
| **NEW YORK** | | | | | | | | |
| Moynihan | Y | Y | Y | Y | N | Y | Y | Y |
| *D'Amato* | N | N | Y | Y | Y | N | Y | N |
| **NORTH CAROLINA** | | | | | | | | |
| Sanford | Y | Y | Y | N | Y | N | Y | Y |
| *Helms* | N | N | N | N | Y | N | Y | N |
| **NORTH DAKOTA** | | | | | | | | |
| Burdick | Y | Y | N | Y | N | N | Y | Y |
| Conrad | Y | Y | N | Y | N | N | Y | Y |
| **OHIO** | | | | | | | | |
| Glenn | N | Y | N | Y | N | Y | Y | Y |
| Metzenbaum | Y | Y | N | Y | N | Y | Y | Y |
| **OKLAHOMA** | | | | | | | | |
| Boren | Y | Y | Y | Y | N | Y | Y | Y |
| *Nickles* | Y | N | N | Y | N | Y | N | Y |
| **OREGON** | | | | | | | | |
| *Hatfield* | N | N | Y | N | Y | N | Y | Y |
| *Packwood* | N | Y | N | Y | N | Y | Y | N |
| **PENNSYLVANIA** | | | | | | | | |
| Wofford | Y | Y | N | Y | N | Y | Y | Y |
| *Specter* | N | Y | N | Y | N | Y | Y | N |
| **RHODE ISLAND** | | | | | | | | |
| Pell | Y | Y | Y | Y | N | Y | Y | + |
| *Chafee* | N | Y | Y | Y | N | Y | Y | Y |
| **SOUTH CAROLINA** | | | | | | | | |
| Hollings | Y | Y | N | Y | N | Y | Y | Y |
| *Thurmond* | N | N | Y | Y | N | Y | Y | Y |
| **SOUTH DAKOTA** | | | | | | | | |
| Daschle | Y | Y | N | Y | N | Y | Y | Y |
| *Pressler* | N | N | Y | Y | N | Y | Y | Y |
| **TENNESSEE** | | | | | | | | |
| Gore | N | Y | Y | Y | N | Y | Y | Y |
| Sasser | N | Y | Y | Y | N | Y | Y | Y |
| **TEXAS** | | | | | | | | |
| Bentsen | N | Y | Y | Y | N | Y | Y | Y |
| *Gramm* | N | N | N | Y | Y | Y | Y | N |
| **UTAH** | | | | | | | | |
| *Garn* | N | N | Y | Y | N | Y | Y | N |
| *Hatch* | N | N | Y | Y | Y | Y | Y | N |
| **VERMONT** | | | | | | | | |
| Leahy | Y | Y | N | Y | N | Y | Y | Y |
| *Jeffords* | N | N | Y | Y | N | Y | Y | Y |
| **VIRGINIA** | | | | | | | | |
| Robb | Y | Y | Y | N | Y | N | Y | Y |
| *Warner* | N | N | Y | Y | N | Y | Y | N |
| **WASHINGTON** | | | | | | | | |
| Adams | Y | Y | Y | N | Y | N | Y | Y |
| *Gorton* | N | N | Y | Y | N | Y | Y | N |
| **WEST VIRGINIA** | | | | | | | | |
| Byrd | Y | Y | N | Y | N | N | N | N |
| Rockefeller | Y | Y | N | Y | N | Y | Y | Y |
| **WISCONSIN** | | | | | | | | |
| Kohl | Y | Y | N | Y | N | Y | Y | Y |
| *Kasten* | N | N | N | Y | Y | N | Y | N |
| **WYOMING** | | | | | | | | |
| *Simpson* | N | N | Y | Y | N | Y | N | Y |
| *Wallop* | N | N | Y | Y | Y | N | Y | N |

ND Northern Democrats   SD Southern Democrats   Southern states - Ala., Ark., Fla., Ga., Ky., La., Miss., N.C., Okla., S.C., Tenn., Texas, Va.

**57. S 2482. RTC Funding/Budget Waiver.** Kerry, D-Mass., motion to waive the budget act with respect to the Garn, R-Utah, point of order against the Kerry amendment for violating Section 306 of the 1974 Congressional Budget Act and encroaching on the Budget Committee's jurisdiction. The Kerry amendment would require all money provided to the Resolution Trust Corporation (RTC) to be counted as direct spending toward the deficit and require that all grants and loans to the RTC be offset so as to be budget-neutral over a three-year period. Motion rejected 45-48: R 3-37; D 42-11 (ND 31-5, SD 11-6), March 26, 1992.

**58. S 2482. RTC Funding/'Clean Bill'.** Riegle, D-Mich., motion to table (kill) the Gramm, R-Texas, amendment to strike all language from the bill except for a provision that would provide approximately $42 billion in additional financing for the resolution of failed savings and loans by the Resolution Trust Corporation. Motion agreed to 58-36: R 5-35; D 53-1 (ND 37-0, SD 16-1), March 26, 1992.

**59. S 2482. RTC Funding/Passage.** Passage of the bill to provide the Resolution Trust Corporation with $42 billion to resolve failed savings and loan institutions by eliminating the April 1, 1992, expiration date on $25 billion provided in 1991 — of which $8 billion has been spent — and provide an additional $25 billion through April 1, 1993. Passed 52-42: R 23-17; D 29-25 (ND 17-20, SD 12-5), March 26, 1992. A "yea" was a vote supporting the president's position.

**60. HR 2507. National Institutes of Health Reauthorization/Cloture.** Mitchell, D-Maine, motion to invoke cloture (thus limiting debate) on the motion to proceed to the bill to reauthorize and amend the programs of NIH. The bill would lift the ban on fetal tissue transplant research, including fetal tissue obtained from induced abortions. Motion agreed to 98-2: R 41-2; D 57-0 (ND 40-0, SD 17-0), March 31, 1992. A three-fifths majority vote (60) of the total Senate is required to invoke cloture.

**61. HR 2507. National Institutes of Health Reauthorization/Fetal Tissue Research.** Hatch, R-Utah, amendment to replace the ban on fetal tissue transplant research provisions in the bill with provisions to establish a nonprofit registry of those desiring to participate in the creation of a nonprofit fetal tissue bank of tissue from spontaneous abortions and ectopic pregnancies. Rejected 23-77: R 20-23; D 3-54 (ND 1-39, SD 2-15), March 31, 1992. A "yea" was a vote supporting the president's position.

**62. H J Res 456. Fiscal 1992 Foreign Aid Continuing Appropriations/Passage.** Passage of the joint resolution to fund foreign aid for the remainder of the fiscal year through Sept. 30, 1992. Most programs would be funded at either the fiscal 1991 level or the level in the House-passed bill for fiscal 1992, whichever is lower. The bill does not include the loan guarantees for Israel but would provide an increase of $270 million for U.N. peacekeeping activities. Passed 84-16: R 33-10; D 51-6 (ND 36-4, SD 15-2), April 1, 1992. A "yea" was a vote supporting the president's position.

**63. S Res 277. Israeli Loan Guarantees/Adoption.** Adoption of the resolution to express the sense of the Senate that the U.S. government should support appropriate loan guarantees to Israel for refugee absorption. Adopted 99-1: R 43-0; D 56-1 (ND 39-1, SD 17-0), April 1, 1992.

**64. HR 2507. National Institutes of Health Reauthorization/Sexual Behavior Surveys.** Simon, D-Ill., amendment to require all NIH human sexual behavior surveys to meet the standard peer and ethical review process, be determined to provide information to reduce the incidence of sexually transmitted diseases and improve reproductive health. Adopted 57-40: R 6-36; D 51-4 (ND 36-2, SD 15-2), April 2, 1992.

## KEY

Y   Voted for (yea).
#   Paired for.
+   Announced for.
N   Voted against (nay).
X   Paired against.
−   Announced against.
P   Voted "present."
C   Voted "present" to avoid possible conflict of interest.
?   Did not vote or otherwise make a position known.

Democrats   *Republicans*

| State / Senator | 65 | 66 | 67 | 68 | 69 | 70 | 71 | 72 |
|---|---|---|---|---|---|---|---|---|
| **ALABAMA** | | | | | | | | |
| Heflin | Y | Y | Y | Y | N | N | N | Y |
| Shelby | Y | Y | Y | Y | N | N | N | Y |
| **ALASKA** | | | | | | | | |
| *Murkowski* | Y | Y | Y | Y | N | N | N | Y |
| *Stevens* | Y | Y | N | Y | N | N | N | Y |
| **ARIZONA** | | | | | | | | |
| DeConcini | N | Y | Y | Y | Y | Y | Y | Y |
| *McCain* | Y | Y | Y | Y | N | N | N | Y |
| **ARKANSAS** | | | | | | | | |
| Bumpers | Y | Y | ? | ? | Y | N | Y | N |
| Pryor | Y | Y | ? | ? | Y | N | Y | N |
| **CALIFORNIA** | | | | | | | | |
| Cranston | N | Y | Y | Y | Y | Y | N | N |
| *Seymour* | Y | Y | Y | Y | N | N | Y | Y |
| **COLORADO** | | | | | | | | |
| Wirth | N | Y | Y | ? | # | ? | ? | ? |
| *Brown* | Y | Y | Y | Y | N | N | Y | Y |
| **CONNECTICUT** | | | | | | | | |
| Dodd | N | Y | Y | Y | N | N | Y | N |
| Lieberman | N | Y | Y | Y | N | N | Y | Y |
| **DELAWARE** | | | | | | | | |
| Biden | N | Y | Y | Y | Y | Y | Y | Y |
| *Roth* | Y | Y | Y | Y | # | N | Y | Y |
| **FLORIDA** | | | | | | | | |
| Graham | Y | Y | Y | Y | N | N | Y | Y |
| *Mack* | Y | Y | Y | Y | N | N | Y | Y |
| **GEORGIA** | | | | | | | | |
| Fowler | Y | Y | Y | Y | N | N | Y | Y |
| Nunn | N | Y | Y | Y | N | N | Y | Y |
| **HAWAII** | | | | | | | | |
| Akaka | N | Y | Y | N | Y | Y | Y | N |
| Inouye | N | Y | Y | Y | N | N | Y | N |
| **IDAHO** | | | | | | | | |
| *Craig* | Y | N | N | Y | N | N | N | Y |
| *Symms* | Y | N | N | Y | N | N | N | Y |
| **ILLINOIS** | | | | | | | | |
| Dixon | ? | ? | Y | Y | N | Y | ? | ? |
| Simon | N | Y | Y | Y | Y | Y | Y | Y |
| **INDIANA** | | | | | | | | |
| *Coats* | Y | Y | Y | Y | N | N | Y | Y |
| *Lugar* | ? | ? | Y | Y | N | N | Y | Y |
| **IOWA** | | | | | | | | |
| Harkin | N | Y | Y | Y | Y | Y | Y | Y |
| *Grassley* | Y | Y | Y | Y | Y | N | Y | Y |
| **KANSAS** | | | | | | | | |
| *Dole* | Y | Y | N | Y | N | N | Y | Y |
| *Kassebaum* | Y | Y | Y | Y | N | N | N | Y |
| **KENTUCKY** | | | | | | | | |
| Ford | Y | N | Y | Y | N | Y | Y | Y |
| *McConnell* | Y | Y | Y | Y | N | N | Y | Y |
| **LOUISIANA** | | | | | | | | |
| Breaux | N | Y | Y | Y | N | Y | Y | Y |
| Johnston | N | Y | Y | Y | Y | N | Y | N |
| **MAINE** | | | | | | | | |
| Mitchell | N | Y | Y | Y | Y | N | N | N |
| *Cohen* | N | Y | Y | N | N | N | Y | Y |
| **MARYLAND** | | | | | | | | |
| Mikulski | N | Y | Y | Y | Y | Y | Y | Y |
| Sarbanes | N | Y | Y | Y | Y | Y | N | N |
| **MASSACHUSETTS** | | | | | | | | |
| Kennedy | N | Y | Y | Y | Y | Y | Y | Y |
| Kerry | N | Y | Y | Y | Y | Y | Y | N |
| **MICHIGAN** | | | | | | | | |
| Levin | N | Y | Y | Y | Y | Y | Y | N |
| Riegle | N | Y | Y | Y | Y | Y | N | N |
| **MINNESOTA** | | | | | | | | |
| Wellstone | N | Y | Y | Y | Y | Y | N | N |
| *Durenberger* | N | Y | Y | Y | N | N | Y | Y |
| **MISSISSIPPI** | | | | | | | | |
| *Cochran* | Y | Y | Y | Y | N | N | Y | Y |
| *Lott* | Y | Y | N | Y | N | N | Y | Y |
| **MISSOURI** | | | | | | | | |
| *Bond* | Y | N | Y | Y | N | N | Y | Y |
| *Danforth* | N | Y | Y | Y | N | N | Y | Y |
| **MONTANA** | | | | | | | | |
| Baucus | N | Y | Y | Y | N | N | Y | N |
| *Burns* | Y | N | N | Y | N | N | Y | Y |
| **NEBRASKA** | | | | | | | | |
| Exon | Y | Y | Y | Y | Y | N | Y | Y |
| Kerrey | N | Y | Y | Y | Y | Y | Y | N |
| **NEVADA** | | | | | | | | |
| Bryan | Y | Y | Y | Y | Y | N | Y | Y |
| Reid | Y | Y | Y | Y | Y | Y | Y | Y |
| **NEW HAMPSHIRE** | | | | | | | | |
| *Rudman* | Y | Y | Y | Y | N | N | Y | Y |
| *Smith* | Y | N | N | Y | N | N | Y | Y |
| **NEW JERSEY** | | | | | | | | |
| Bradley | N | Y | Y | Y | Y | Y | N | N |
| Lautenberg | N | Y | Y | Y | Y | Y | N | N |
| **NEW MEXICO** | | | | | | | | |
| Bingaman | N | Y | Y | N | Y | N | Y | N |
| *Domenici* | Y | Y | Y | Y | N | N | Y | Y |
| **NEW YORK** | | | | | | | | |
| Moynihan | N | Y | Y | Y | Y | Y | Y | N |
| *D'Amato* | Y | Y | Y | Y | N | N | Y | Y |
| **NORTH CAROLINA** | | | | | | | | |
| Sanford | N | Y | Y | Y | Y | N | N | Y |
| *Helms* | Y | N | N | Y | N | N | Y | Y |
| **NORTH DAKOTA** | | | | | | | | |
| Burdick | N | Y | Y | Y | Y | Y | Y | Y |
| Conrad | Y | Y | Y | N | Y | Y | Y | Y |
| **OHIO** | | | | | | | | |
| Glenn | N | Y | Y | Y | N | N | Y | N |
| Metzenbaum | N | Y | Y | Y | + | Y | N | N |
| **OKLAHOMA** | | | | | | | | |
| Boren | Y | Y | Y | Y | N | Y | Y | Y |
| *Nickles* | Y | Y | Y | Y | N | N | N | Y |
| **OREGON** | | | | | | | | |
| *Hatfield* | N | Y | Y | Y | Y | Y | N | N |
| *Packwood* | Y | Y | Y | Y | Y | Y | Y | Y |
| **PENNSYLVANIA** | | | | | | | | |
| Wofford | N | Y | Y | Y | Y | Y | Y | N |
| *Specter* | Y | Y | Y | Y | N | Y | Y | Y |
| **RHODE ISLAND** | | | | | | | | |
| Pell | − | + | Y | Y | X | Y | Y | Y |
| *Chafee* | N | Y | Y | Y | N | N | Y | Y |
| **SOUTH CAROLINA** | | | | | | | | |
| Hollings | Y | Y | Y | Y | N | N | Y | Y |
| *Thurmond* | Y | Y | Y | Y | N | N | Y | Y |
| **SOUTH DAKOTA** | | | | | | | | |
| Daschle | N | Y | Y | Y | Y | Y | Y | Y |
| *Pressler* | Y | N | Y | Y | N | N | Y | Y |
| **TENNESSEE** | | | | | | | | |
| Gore | N | Y | Y | Y | Y | N | Y | N |
| Sasser | Y | Y | Y | Y | Y | N | N | N |
| **TEXAS** | | | | | | | | |
| Bentsen | N | Y | Y | Y | Y | Y | N | Y | N |
| *Gramm* | Y | N | N | Y | N | N | ? | ? |
| **UTAH** | | | | | | | | |
| *Garn* | Y | Y | Y | Y | N | N | N | Y |
| *Hatch* | Y | N | Y | Y | N | N | Y | Y |
| **VERMONT** | | | | | | | | |
| Leahy | N | Y | Y | Y | Y | Y | Y | N |
| *Jeffords* | N | Y | Y | Y | Y | N | ? | ? |
| **VIRGINIA** | | | | | | | | |
| Robb | N | Y | Y | Y | Y | Y | Y | Y |
| *Warner* | Y | Y | Y | Y | N | N | Y | Y |
| **WASHINGTON** | | | | | | | | |
| Adams | N | Y | Y | Y | Y | Y | N | N |
| *Gorton* | Y | Y | Y | Y | N | N | Y | Y |
| **WEST VIRGINIA** | | | | | | | | |
| Byrd | Y | Y | Y | Y | Y | Y | Y | Y |
| Rockefeller | N | Y | Y | Y | Y | Y | N | N |
| **WISCONSIN** | | | | | | | | |
| Kohl | N | Y | Y | Y | Y | Y | Y | Y |
| *Kasten* | Y | Y | Y | Y | N | N | Y | Y |
| **WYOMING** | | | | | | | | |
| *Simpson* | Y | Y | N | Y | N | N | Y | Y |
| *Wallop* | Y | Y | N | Y | X | − | + | ? |

ND   Northern Democrats    SD   Southern Democrats    Southern states - Ala., Ark., Fla., Ga., Ky., La., Miss., N.C., Okla., S.C., Tenn., Texas, Va.

**65. HR 2507. National Institutes of Health Reauthorization/SHARP Survey.** Helms, R-N.C., amendment to prohibit funding for the SHARP survey of adult sexual behavior and the American Teenage Study of adolescent sexual behavior. Adopted 51-46: R 36-6; D 15-40 (ND 5-33, SD 10-7), April 2, 1992.

**66. HR 2507. National Institutes of Health Reauthorization/Passage.** Passage of the bill to reauthorize and amend the programs of NIH, including $2.2 billion for the National Cancer Institute and $1.5 billion for the Heart, Lung and Blood Institute. The bill would lift the ban on fetal tissue transplant research, including fetal tissue obtained from induced abortions. Passed 87-10: R 33-9; D 54-1 (ND 38-0, SD 16-1), April 2, 1992. A "nay" was a vote supporting the president's position.

**67. H Con Res 292. U.N. Conference on Environment Development/Adoption.** Adoption of the concurrent resolution to express the sense of Congress that the president should play a strong, active role in developing international agreements to enhance global environmental protection by supporting the U.N. Conference on Environment and Development. Adopted 87-11: R 32-11; D 55-0 (ND 40-0, SD 15-0), April 7, 1992.

**68. S Con Res 106. Fiscal 1993 Budget Resolution/Point of Order.** Bentsen, D-Texas, amendment to create a point of order under the 1974 Congressional Budget Act and require a 60-vote supermajority for any budget resolution that would decrease the excess of Social Security revenues over outlays. Adopted 94-3: R 43-0; D 51-3 (ND 36-3, SD 15-0), April 7, 1992.

**69. S Con Res 106. Fiscal 1993 Budget Resolution.** Exon, D-Neb., amendment to reduce the defense procurement accounts for smaller weapons projects by $8.8 billion in budget authority and $4.2 billion in outlays below the committee level for fiscal 1993. Rejected 45-50: R 4-37; D 41-13 (ND 32-5, SD 9-8), April 9, 1992.

**70. S Con Res 106. Fiscal 1993 Budget Resolution/Budget Act Waiver.** Bradley, D-N.J., motion to waive the 1974 Congressional Budget Act with respect to the Symms, R-Idaho, point of order against the Bradley amendment. The Bradley amendment would cut an additional $7 billion in budget authority for defense spending in fiscal 1993 and $11 billion over each of the next four years, with half the savings to go to education, health care and environmental clean-up and the rest to deficit reduction. Motion rejected 36-62: R 3-39; D 33-23 (ND 31-8, SD 2-15), April 9, 1992. Sixty votes are required to uphold a point of order. (Subsequently, the chair sustained the Symms point of order, and the Bradley amendment fell.)

**71. S Con Res 106. Fiscal 1993 Budget Resolution/Balanced Budget Amendment.** Byrd, D-W.Va., amendment to the Nickles, R-Okla., amendment, to express the sense of the Senate that it should adopt by June 5 a joint resolution proposing an amendment to the Constitution for a federal balanced budget, requiring the president to annually submit a balanced budget. Adopted 84-11: R 39-1; D 45-10 (ND 29-9, SD 16-1), April 9, 1992.

**72. S Con Res 106. Fiscal 1993 Budget Resolution/Balanced Budget Amendment.** Nickles, R-Okla., motion to waive the 1974 Congressional Budget Act with respect to the Sasser, D-Tenn., point of order against the Nickles amendment for not being germane. The Nickles amendment would express the sense of the Senate that it should adopt by June 5 a joint resolution proposing an amendment to the Constitution for a federal balanced budget. Motion agreed to 63-32: R 40-0; D 23-32 (ND 12-26, SD 11-6), April 9, 1992. Sixty votes were required to waive a point of order. (Subsequently, the chair ruled the Sasser point of order moot, and the Nickles amendment was adopted by voice vote.)

| | 73 | 74 | 75 | 76 | 77 | 78 | 79 | 80 |
|---|---|---|---|---|---|---|---|---|
| **ALABAMA** | | | | | | | | |
| Heflin | Y | Y | Y | Y | Y | N | N | N |
| Shelby | Y | Y | Y | Y | Y | N | N | N |
| **ALASKA** | | | | | | | | |
| *Murkowski* | Y | Y | Y | Y | N | Y | N | Y |
| *Stevens* | Y | Y | Y | Y | N | Y | N | Y |
| **ARIZONA** | | | | | | | | |
| DeConcini | Y | N | Y | Y | Y | Y | N | N |
| *McCain* | Y | Y | Y | Y | N | Y | N | N |
| **ARKANSAS** | | | | | | | | |
| Bumpers | N | Y | Y | Y | N | Y | Y | Y |
| Pryor | N | ? | ? | Y | Y | N | Y | Y |
| **CALIFORNIA** | | | | | | | | |
| Cranston | N | N | Y | Y | Y | N | N | Y |
| *Seymour* | Y | Y | Y | Y | N | Y | N | N |
| **COLORADO** | | | | | | | | |
| Wirth | ? | ? | ? | ? | ? | ? | ? | ? |
| *Brown* | Y | Y | N | Y | N | Y | Y | Y |
| **CONNECTICUT** | | | | | | | | |
| Dodd | Y | Y | Y | Y | Y | N | N | Y |
| Lieberman | Y | N | Y | Y | N | Y | N | Y |
| **DELAWARE** | | | | | | | | |
| Biden | N | N | Y | Y | Y | N | N | Y |
| *Roth* | Y | Y | N | Y | N | Y | Y | N |
| **FLORIDA** | | | | | | | | |
| Graham | Y | N | Y | Y | Y | N | Y | N |
| *Mack* | Y | Y | N | Y | N | Y | N | N |
| **GEORGIA** | | | | | | | | |
| Fowler | N | Y | Y | Y | ? | ? | ? | # |
| Nunn | Y | Y | N | Y | Y | Y | N | N |
| **HAWAII** | | | | | | | | |
| Akaka | Y | N | Y | Y | Y | N | N | N |
| Inouye | Y | N | Y | Y | Y | N | N | N |
| **IDAHO** | | | | | | | | |
| *Craig* | Y | Y | N | Y | N | Y | N | Y |
| *Symms* | Y | Y | N | Y | N | Y | Y | Y |
| **ILLINOIS** | | | | | | | | |
| Dixon | ? | ? | ? | ? | ? | ? | ? | ? |
| Simon | N | N | Y | Y | Y | N | Y | N |
| **INDIANA** | | | | | | | | |
| *Coats* | Y | Y | Y | Y | N | Y | N | Y |
| *Lugar* | Y | Y | N | Y | N | Y | N | Y |

| | 73 | 74 | 75 | 76 | 77 | 78 | 79 | 80 |
|---|---|---|---|---|---|---|---|---|
| **IOWA** | | | | | | | | |
| Harkin | N | N | Y | Y | Y | N | N | N |
| *Grassley* | Y | Y | Y | Y | N | Y | Y | Y |
| **KANSAS** | | | | | | | | |
| *Dole* | Y | Y | N | Y | N | Y | Y | Y |
| *Kassebaum* | Y | Y | N | Y | N | Y | Y | Y |
| **KENTUCKY** | | | | | | | | |
| Ford | Y | Y | Y | Y | Y | N | N | Y |
| *McConnell* | Y | Y | Y | Y | N | Y | N | Y |
| **LOUISIANA** | | | | | | | | |
| Breaux | ? | Y | Y | Y | Y | N | N | Y |
| Johnston | N | N | Y | Y | Y | N | N | Y |
| **MAINE** | | | | | | | | |
| Mitchell | N | N | Y | Y | Y | N | N | Y |
| *Cohen* | Y | Y | N | Y | N | N | N | Y |
| **MARYLAND** | | | | | | | | |
| Mikulski | N | Y | Y | Y | Y | N | N | Y |
| Sarbanes | N | N | Y | Y | Y | N | N | Y |
| **MASSACHUSETTS** | | | | | | | | |
| Kennedy | N | N | Y | Y | Y | N | N | Y |
| Kerry | N | N | Y | Y | Y | N | N | N |
| **MICHIGAN** | | | | | | | | |
| Levin | N | N | Y | Y | Y | N | N | Y |
| Riegle | N | N | Y | Y | Y | N | N | Y |
| **MINNESOTA** | | | | | | | | |
| Wellstone | N | N | Y | Y | Y | N | Y | N |
| *Durenberger* | Y | Y | N | Y | N | N | Y | N |
| **MISSISSIPPI** | | | | | | | | |
| Cochran | Y | N | N | Y | N | Y | N | N |
| *Lott* | ? | Y | N | Y | ? | ? | ? | ? |
| **MISSOURI** | | | | | | | | |
| *Bond* | Y | Y | N | Y | N | Y | N | Y |
| *Danforth* | Y | Y | N | ? | ? | ? | ? | ? |
| **MONTANA** | | | | | | | | |
| Baucus | N | N | Y | Y | Y | N | N | Y |
| *Burns* | Y | Y | Y | Y | N | Y | N | Y |
| **NEBRASKA** | | | | | | | | |
| Exon | N | Y | Y | Y | Y | N | N | N |
| Kerrey | N | Y | Y | Y | ? | ? | ? | ? |
| **NEVADA** | | | | | | | | |
| Bryan | Y | N | Y | Y | Y | N | Y | N |
| Reid | N | N | Y | Y | N | Y | N | Y |

| | 73 | 74 | 75 | 76 | 77 | 78 | 79 | 80 |
|---|---|---|---|---|---|---|---|---|
| **NEW HAMPSHIRE** | | | | | | | | |
| *Rudman* | Y | N | N | Y | N | Y | Y | Y |
| *Smith* | Y | Y | N | Y | N | Y | Y | N |
| **NEW JERSEY** | | | | | | | | |
| Bradley | N | ? | ? | ? | ? | ? | ? | ? |
| Lautenberg | N | N | Y | Y | Y | N | N | N |
| **NEW MEXICO** | | | | | | | | |
| Bingaman | N | N | N | Y | Y | N | N | N |
| *Domenici* | Y | Y | N | Y | N | Y | Y | Y |
| **NEW YORK** | | | | | | | | |
| Moynihan | N | Y | Y | Y | N | N | N | N |
| *D'Amato* | Y | Y | Y | Y | N | Y | N | N |
| **NORTH CAROLINA** | | | | | | | | |
| Sanford | N | N | Y | Y | Y | N | N | N |
| *Helms* | Y | Y | N | Y | N | Y | Y | N |
| **NORTH DAKOTA** | | | | | | | | |
| Burdick | N | N | Y | Y | Y | N | N | N |
| Conrad | N | N | Y | Y | Y | N | N | N |
| **OHIO** | | | | | | | | |
| Glenn | Y | N | Y | Y | Y | N | N | Y |
| Metzenbaum | N | N | Y | Y | Y | N | N | N |
| **OKLAHOMA** | | | | | | | | |
| Boren | N | Y | N | Y | Y | Y | N | Y |
| *Nickles* | Y | Y | N | Y | N | Y | Y | N |
| **OREGON** | | | | | | | | |
| *Hatfield* | N | N | N | Y | N | N | N | Y |
| *Packwood* | Y | Y | Y | Y | N | N | N | Y |
| **PENNSYLVANIA** | | | | | | | | |
| Wofford | N | Y | Y | Y | N | N | N | Y |
| *Specter* | Y | Y | Y | Y | N | N | N | Y |
| **RHODE ISLAND** | | | | | | | | |
| Pell | Y | N | Y | Y | Y | N | N | Y |
| *Chafee* | Y | Y | N | Y | N | N | N | Y |
| **SOUTH CAROLINA** | | | | | | | | |
| Hollings | Y | N | Y | Y | Y | N | N | Y |
| *Thurmond* | Y | Y | Y | Y | N | Y | Y | Y |
| **SOUTH DAKOTA** | | | | | | | | |
| Daschle | N | N | Y | Y | Y | N | N | N |
| *Pressler* | Y | Y | Y | Y | N | Y | Y | N |
| **TENNESSEE** | | | | | | | | |
| Gore | N | N | Y | Y | Y | N | N | Y |
| Sasser | N | N | Y | Y | Y | N | N | Y |

| | 73 | 74 | 75 | 76 | 77 | 78 | 79 | 80 |
|---|---|---|---|---|---|---|---|---|
| **TEXAS** | | | | | | | | |
| Bentsen | N | Y | Y | Y | Y | N | Y | N |
| *Gramm* | ? | ? | ? | ? | ? | ? | ? | ? |
| **UTAH** | | | | | | | | |
| *Garn* | Y | Y | ? | ? | ? | ? | ? | ? |
| *Hatch* | Y | Y | Y | Y | N | Y | Y | N |
| **VERMONT** | | | | | | | | |
| Leahy | N | N | Y | Y | Y | N | N | Y |
| *Jeffords* | ? | N | Y | Y | N | N | Y | Y |
| **VIRGINIA** | | | | | | | | |
| Robb | Y | N | Y | Y | N | Y | N | Y |
| *Warner* | Y | Y | N | Y | N | Y | N | Y |
| **WASHINGTON** | | | | | | | | |
| Adams | N | N | Y | Y | Y | N | N | X |
| *Gorton* | Y | N | N | Y | N | Y | N | N |
| **WEST VIRGINIA** | | | | | | | | |
| Byrd | N | N | Y | Y | Y | N | N | Y |
| Rockefeller | N | N | Y | Y | Y | N | N | Y |
| **WISCONSIN** | | | | | | | | |
| Kohl | N | Y | Y | Y | N | N | N | Y |
| *Kasten* | Y | Y | Y | Y | N | Y | Y | N |
| **WYOMING** | | | | | | | | |
| *Simpson* | Y | Y | N | Y | N | Y | Y | Y |
| *Wallop* | + | + | − | ? | − | + | + | − |

ND  Northern Democrats     SD  Southern Democrats          Southern states - Ala., Ark., Fla., Ga., Ky., La., Miss., N.C., Okla., S.C., Tenn., Texas, Va.

**73. S Con Res 106. Fiscal 1993 Budget Resolution/Defense Cuts.** Inouye, D-Hawaii, motion to table (kill) the Harkin, D-Iowa, amendment to reduce by $6 billion defense budget authority in fiscal 1993, and if the budget fire walls are eliminated, transfer the funds to programs for children, infrastructure, urban and rural economic development, and deficit reduction. Motion agreed to 53-40: R 38-1; D 15-39 (ND 8-30, SD 7-9), April 9, 1992.

**74. S Con Res 106. Fiscal 1993 Budget Resolution/Legislative Spending.** Seymour, R-Calif., amendment to reduce legislative branch expenditures by 25 percent over two years. Before being adopted, the Seymour amendment was amended by a Sasser, D-Tenn., amendment to include a similar reduction for the executive branch. Adopted 52-42: R 36-5; D 16-37 (ND 7-30, SD 9-7), April 9, 1992.

**75. S Con Res 106. Fiscal 1993 Budget Resolution/Entitlement Caps.** Mitchell, D-Maine, amendment to exempt veterans compensation from the entitlement caps and cuts contained in the Domenici, R-N.M., substitute amendment that would cap all mandatory spending, except for Social Security and interest on the debt, beginning in fiscal 1994. Adopted 66-28: R 16-24; D 50-4 (ND 36-1, SD 14-3), April 10, 1992. (Subsequently, the Domenici substitute amendment was withdrawn.)

**76. S Con Res 106. Fiscal 1993 Budget Resolution/WIC.** DeConcini, D-Ariz., amendment to express the sense of the Senate that the Supplemental Food Program for Women, Infants and Children (WIC) should be funded at $3 billion in fiscal 1993. Adopted 93-0: R 39-0; D 54-0 (ND 37-0, SD 17-0), April 10, 1992.

**77. S Con Res 106. Fiscal 1993 Budget Resolution/Movement of Recipients.** Moynihan, D-N.Y., point of order that the D'Amato, R-N.Y., amendment is unconstitutional for impinging on a citizen's constitutional right to travel freely from state to state. Point of order rejected 45-45: R 0-38; D 45-7 (ND 31-5, SD 14-2), April 10, 1992.

**78. S Con Res 106. Fiscal 1993 Budget Resolution/Welfare Benefits.** D'Amato, R-N.Y., amendment to lower the appropriate budget functions by $150 million over five years to lay the budget foundation for future legislation that would prohibit welfare recipients who move to a state to get higher benefits from receiving those higher benefits for one year. Rejected 43-47: R 31-7; D 12-40 (ND 6-30, SD 6-10), April 10, 1992.

**79. S Con Res 106. Fiscal 1993 Budget Resolution/Cargo Preferences.** Grassley, R-Iowa, motion to waive the 1974 Budget Act with respect to the Breaux, D-La., point of order against the Grassley amendment for not being germane. The Grassley amendment would express the sense of the Senate that cargo preference subsidies for the merchant marine should be eliminated, with the $416 million in domestic savings per year being transferred to children, welfare and education programs and the $310 million in defense savings going to establish a merchant marine reserve. Motion rejected 29-61: R 24-14; D 5-47 (ND 3-33, SD 2-14), April 10, 1992. A three-fifths majority (60) of the total Senate is required to waive such points of order. (Subsequently the chair sustained the Breaux point of order and the Grassley amendment fell.)

**80. H Con Res 287. Fiscal 1993 Budget Resolution/Adoption.** Adoption of the budget resolution to set budget levels for the fiscal year ending Sept. 30, 1993, as follows: budget authority, $1,514.3 billion; outlays, $1,500.5 billion; revenues, $1,173.4 billion; and deficit, $327.1 billion. Adopted 54-35: R 18-20; D 36-15 (ND 24-11, SD 12-4), April 10, 1992. (Before adoption the Senate struck everything after the resolving clause and inserted instead the language of S Con Res 106 as amended.)

| | 81 | 82 | 83 | 84 | 85 | 86 | 87 | 88 |
|---|---|---|---|---|---|---|---|---|
| **ALABAMA** | | | | | | | | |
| Heflin | Y | Y | N | Y | N | Y | Y | Y |
| Shelby | Y | N | N | N | N | Y | Y | N |
| **ALASKA** | | | | | | | | |
| *Murkowski* | Y | N | Y | N | Y | N | N | N |
| *Stevens* | Y | N | Y | N | N | N | N | N |
| **ARIZONA** | | | | | | | | |
| DeConcini | N | Y | N | N | Y | Y | Y | Y |
| *McCain* | ? | Y | Y | Y | N | N | N | Y |
| **ARKANSAS** | | | | | | | | |
| Bumpers | Y | Y | N | Y | Y | Y | Y | Y |
| Pryor | N | Y | N | N | Y | Y | Y | Y |
| **CALIFORNIA** | | | | | | | | |
| Cranston | N | Y | ? | ? | ? | Y | Y | Y |
| *Seymour* | Y | N | Y | Y | N | ? | N | N |
| **COLORADO** | | | | | | | | |
| Wirth | Y | Y | Y | Y | Y | Y | Y | Y |
| *Brown* | Y | N | Y | Y | N | N | N | N |
| **CONNECTICUT** | | | | | | | | |
| Dodd | Y | Y | N | Y | Y | Y | Y | Y |
| Lieberman | N | Y | N | N | Y | Y | Y | Y |
| **DELAWARE** | | | | | | | | |
| Biden | Y | Y | N | N | Y | Y | Y | Y |
| *Roth* | Y | N | Y | ? | N | N | N | N |
| **FLORIDA** | | | | | | | | |
| Graham | Y | Y | N | N | Y | Y | Y | Y |
| *Mack* | Y | N | Y | Y | N | N | N | N |
| **GEORGIA** | | | | | | | | |
| Fowler | N | Y | N | Y | Y | Y | Y | Y |
| Nunn | Y | Y | N | Y | Y | Y | Y | Y |
| **HAWAII** | | | | | | | | |
| Akaka | Y | Y | N | Y | Y | Y | Y | Y |
| Inouye | ? | Y | Y | N | Y | Y | Y | Y |
| **IDAHO** | | | | | | | | |
| *Craig* | Y | N | Y | N | Y | N | N | N |
| *Symms* | Y | N | Y | N | Y | N | N | N |
| **ILLINOIS** | | | | | | | | |
| Dixon | Y | Y | N | N | Y | Y | Y | Y |
| Simon | N | Y | N | Y | Y | Y | Y | Y |
| **INDIANA** | | | | | | | | |
| *Coats* | Y | N | Y | Y | N | N | N | N |
| *Lugar* | Y | N | Y | Y | N | N | N | N |

| | 81 | 82 | 83 | 84 | 85 | 86 | 87 | 88 |
|---|---|---|---|---|---|---|---|---|
| **IOWA** | | | | | | | | |
| Harkin | N | Y | N | N | Y | Y | Y | Y |
| *Grassley* | Y | N | Y | N | Y | N | N | N |
| **KANSAS** | | | | | | | | |
| *Dole* | Y | N | Y | Y | N | N | N | N |
| *Kassebaum* | Y | N | Y | N | N | N | N | N |
| **KENTUCKY** | | | | | | | | |
| Ford | Y | Y | N | N | Y | Y | Y | Y |
| *McConnell* | Y | N | Y | N | Y | N | N | N |
| **LOUISIANA** | | | | | | | | |
| Breaux | N | Y | N | N | Y | Y | Y | Y |
| Johnston | N | Y | N | N | Y | Y | Y | Y |
| **MAINE** | | | | | | | | |
| Mitchell | Y | Y | N | Y | Y | Y | Y | Y |
| *Cohen* | Y | N | Y | N | Y | N | N | N |
| **MARYLAND** | | | | | | | | |
| Mikulski | Y | Y | N | Y | Y | Y | Y | Y |
| Sarbanes | Y | Y | N | Y | Y | Y | Y | Y |
| **MASSACHUSETTS** | | | | | | | | |
| Kennedy | N | Y | N | N | Y | Y | Y | Y |
| Kerry | Y | Y | N | N | Y | Y | Y | Y |
| **MICHIGAN** | | | | | | | | |
| Levin | Y | Y | N | N | Y | Y | Y | Y |
| Riegle | Y | Y | N | N | Y | Y | Y | Y |
| **MINNESOTA** | | | | | | | | |
| Wellstone | N | Y | N | Y | Y | Y | Y | Y |
| *Durenberger* | Y | Y | Y | Y | N | Y | N | Y |
| **MISSISSIPPI** | | | | | | | | |
| *Cochran* | Y | N | Y | N | N | N | N | N |
| *Lott* | Y | N | Y | Y | N | N | N | N |
| **MISSOURI** | | | | | | | | |
| *Bond* | Y | N | Y | N | Y | N | N | N |
| *Danforth* | Y | N | Y | N | Y | N | N | N |
| **MONTANA** | | | | | | | | |
| Baucus | Y | Y | N | Y | Y | Y | Y | Y |
| *Burns* | Y | N | Y | N | Y | N | N | N |
| **NEBRASKA** | | | | | | | | |
| Exon | N | Y | N | N | Y | Y | Y | Y |
| Kerrey | Y | Y | N | N | Y | Y | Y | Y |
| **NEVADA** | | | | | | | | |
| Bryan | Y | Y | N | Y | Y | Y | Y | Y |
| Reid | N | Y | N | Y | Y | Y | Y | Y |

| | 81 | 82 | 83 | 84 | 85 | 86 | 87 | 88 |
|---|---|---|---|---|---|---|---|---|
| **NEW HAMPSHIRE** | | | | | | | | |
| *Rudman* | Y | N | Y | N | N | N | N | N |
| *Smith* | Y | N | Y | Y | N | N | N | N |
| **NEW JERSEY** | | | | | | | | |
| Bradley | Y | Y | Y | N | Y | Y | Y | Y |
| Lautenberg | Y | Y | N | N | Y | Y | Y | Y |
| **NEW MEXICO** | | | | | | | | |
| Bingaman | N | Y | Y | Y | Y | Y | Y | Y |
| *Domenici* | Y | N | Y | N | Y | N | N | N |
| **NEW YORK** | | | | | | | | |
| Moynihan | N | Y | N | N | Y | Y | Y | Y |
| *D'Amato* | Y | N | N | N | Y | N | N | N |
| **NORTH CAROLINA** | | | | | | | | |
| Sanford | N | Y | N | N | Y | Y | Y | Y |
| *Helms* | Y | N | Y | Y | N | N | N | N |
| **NORTH DAKOTA** | | | | | | | | |
| Burdick | Y | Y | N | Y | Y | Y | Y | Y |
| Conrad | Y | Y | Y | N | Y | Y | Y | Y |
| **OHIO** | | | | | | | | |
| Glenn | Y | Y | N | Y | Y | Y | Y | Y |
| Metzenbaum | N | Y | Y | Y | Y | Y | ? | ? |
| **OKLAHOMA** | | | | | | | | |
| Boren | Y | Y | N | N | Y | Y | Y | Y |
| *Nickles* | Y | N | Y | Y | N | N | N | N |
| **OREGON** | | | | | | | | |
| *Hatfield* | Y | N | Y | N | Y | Y | Y | Y |
| *Packwood* | Y | N | Y | N | N | Y | N | N |
| **PENNSYLVANIA** | | | | | | | | |
| Wofford | N | Y | N | N | Y | Y | Y | Y |
| *Specter* | ? | N | N | Y | N | N | Y | N |
| **RHODE ISLAND** | | | | | | | | |
| Pell | N | Y | N | N | Y | Y | Y | Y |
| *Chafee* | Y | N | N | N | Y | N | N | N |
| **SOUTH CAROLINA** | | | | | | | | |
| Hollings | N | N | N | N | Y | Y | Y | N |
| *Thurmond* | Y | N | Y | N | Y | N | N | N |
| **SOUTH DAKOTA** | | | | | | | | |
| Daschle | Y | Y | N | N | Y | Y | Y | Y |
| *Pressler* | Y | N | Y | N | Y | N | N | N |
| **TENNESSEE** | | | | | | | | |
| Gore | Y | Y | N | N | Y | Y | Y | Y |
| Sasser | Y | Y | Y | N | Y | Y | Y | Y |

| | 81 | 82 | 83 | 84 | 85 | 86 | 87 | 88 |
|---|---|---|---|---|---|---|---|---|
| **TEXAS** | | | | | | | | |
| Bentsen | Y | Y | Y | N | Y | Y | Y | Y |
| *Gramm* | Y | N | Y | Y | N | N | N | N |
| **UTAH** | | | | | | | | |
| *Garn* | Y | N | N | Y | N | N | N | N |
| *Hatch* | Y | N | Y | Y | N | N | N | N |
| **VERMONT** | | | | | | | | |
| Leahy | Y | Y | ? | N | Y | Y | Y | Y |
| *Jeffords* | Y | Y | N | Y | Y | Y | N | Y |
| **VIRGINIA** | | | | | | | | |
| Robb | Y | Y | N | N | Y | Y | Y | Y |
| *Warner* | Y | N | Y | Y | N | N | ? | N |
| **WASHINGTON** | | | | | | | | |
| Adams | N | Y | N | N | Y | Y | Y | Y |
| *Gorton* | Y | N | Y | Y | N | N | N | N |
| **WEST VIRGINIA** | | | | | | | | |
| Byrd | Y | Y | N | N | Y | Y | Y | Y |
| Rockefeller | N | Y | N | N | Y | Y | Y | Y |
| **WISCONSIN** | | | | | | | | |
| Kohl | Y | Y | Y | Y | Y | Y | Y | Y |
| *Kasten* | Y | N | N | N | N | N | N | N |
| **WYOMING** | | | | | | | | |
| *Simpson* | Y | N | Y | N | Y | N | N | N |
| *Wallop* | Y | N | Y | N | Y | N | N | N |

ND Northern Democrats    SD Southern Democrats    Southern states - Ala., Ark., Fla., Ga., Ky., La., Miss., N.C., Okla., S.C., Tenn., Texas, Va.

**81. HR 3337. Commemorative Coins/Conference Report.** Adoption of the conference report (H Rept 102-485) to mint coins in commemoration of the 200th anniversary of the White House and other events. Adopted (thus cleared for the president) 75-22: R 41-0; D 34-22 (ND 23-16, SD 11-6), April 28, 1992.

**82. S 3. Campaign Finance/Conference Report.** Adoption of the conference report to limit spending (H Rept 102-487) in congressional campaigns by providing incentives to candidates to agree to voluntary spending limits, restricting money that candidates can accept from political action committees (PACs) and restricting "soft money" raised and spent by state parties in federal elections. Adopted (thus cleared for the president) 58-42: R 3-40; D 55-2 (ND 40-0, SD 15-2), April 30, 1992. A "nay" was a vote supporting the president's position.

**83. S 2403. Fiscal 1992 Rescissions/Seawolf Submarine.** McCain, R-Ariz., amendment to the Byrd, D-W.Va., substitute amendment, to rescind, as proposed by the Bush administration, nearly $3 billion in funding for a second and third *Seawolf* nuclear submarine. Rejected 46-52: R 36-7; D 10-45 (ND 8-30, SD 2-15), May 5, 1992. A "yea" was a vote in support of the president's position.

**84. S 2403. Fiscal 1992 Rescissions/Administration Proposals.** Brown, R-Colo., amendment to include in the bill about $60 million in rescissions for 42 programs as proposed by the Bush administration but dropped by the Appropriations Committee. Rejected 43-55: R 34-8; D 9-47 (ND 6-33, SD 3-14), May 5, 1992. A "yea" was a vote in support of the president's position.

**85. S 2403. Fiscal 1992 Rescissions/Committee Substitute.** Senate Appropriations Committee amendment to rescind $8,287,546,644 in previously approved budget authority for fiscal 1992, including $7.2 billion in defense, $910 million in domestic programs and $172 million in foreign aid. Adopted 61-38: R 7-36; D 54-2 (ND 39-0, SD 15-2), May 6, 1992. A "nay" was a vote in support of the president's position.

**86. S 250. National Motor-Voter Registration/Cloture.** Mitchell, D-Maine, motion to invoke cloture (thus limiting debate) on the motion to proceed to the bill to require states to permit voter registration simultaneously with applying for public certificates such as a driver's license, marriage license or hunting permit., and require that forms be made available at numerous federal and state offices. Motion agreed to 61-38: R 4-38; D 57-0 (ND 40-0, SD 17-0), May 7, 1992. A three-fifths majority vote (60) of the total Senate is required to invoke cloture. A "nay" was a vote in support of the president's position.

**87. S 250. National Motor-Voter Registration/Cloture.** Motion to invoke cloture (thus limiting debate) on the committee substitute to the bill to require states to permit voter registration simultaneously with applying for public certificates such as a driver's license, marriage license or hunting permit. Motion rejected 58-40: R 3-39; D 55-1 (ND 38-1, SD 17-0), May 12, 1992. A three-fifths majority vote (60) of the total Senate is required to invoke cloture.

**88. S 3. Campaign Finance/Veto Override.** Passage, over President Bush's May 9 veto, of the bill to limit spending in congressional campaigns by providing incentives to candidates to agree to voluntary spending limits, restricting money that candidates can accept from political action committees (PACs) and restricting "soft money" raised and spent by state parties in federal elections. Rejected 57-42: R 3-40; D 54-2 (ND 39-0, SD 15-2), May 13, 1992. A two-thirds majority of those present and voting (66 in this case) of both houses is required to override a veto. A "nay" was a vote supporting the president's position.

## KEY

| | |
|---|---|
| Y | Voted for (yea). |
| # | Paired for. |
| + | Announced for. |
| N | Voted against (nay). |
| X | Paired against. |
| − | Announced against. |
| P | Voted "present." |
| C | Voted "present" to avoid possible conflict of interest. |
| ? | Did not vote or otherwise make a position known. |

Democrats   *Republicans*

| | 89 | 90 | 91 | 92 | 93 | 94 | 95 | 96 |
|---|---|---|---|---|---|---|---|---|
| **ALABAMA** | | | | | | | | |
| Heflin | Y | N | Y | Y | Y | Y | Y | Y |
| Shelby | Y | N | Y | Y | Y | Y | N | Y |
| **ALASKA** | | | | | | | | |
| *Murkowski* | N | Y | N | N | N | N | N | N |
| *Stevens* | N | Y | N | N | N | N | N | N |
| **ARIZONA** | | | | | | | | |
| DeConcini | Y | N | Y | Y | Y | Y | Y | Y |
| *McCain* | N | Y | N | N | Y | Y | N | Y |
| **ARKANSAS** | | | | | | | | |
| Bumpers | Y | N | N | Y | Y | Y | Y | N |
| Pryor | Y | N | Y | Y | Y | Y | Y | N |
| **CALIFORNIA** | | | | | | | | |
| Cranston | Y | ? | Y | Y | Y | Y | Y | Y |
| *Seymour* | N | Y | N | N | N | N | N | N |
| **COLORADO** | | | | | | | | |
| Wirth | Y | ? | Y | Y | Y | Y | Y | Y |
| *Brown* | N | Y | N | N | N | N | N | N |
| **CONNECTICUT** | | | | | | | | |
| Dodd | N | N | Y | Y | Y | Y | Y | Y |
| Lieberman | N | N | Y | Y | Y | Y | Y | Y |
| **DELAWARE** | | | | | | | | |
| Biden | Y | N | Y | N | Y | Y | Y | Y |
| *Roth* | N | N | N | Y | N | N | N | N |
| **FLORIDA** | | | | | | | | |
| Graham | Y | N | Y | Y | Y | Y | Y | Y |
| *Mack* | N | Y | ? | N | N | N | N | N |
| **GEORGIA** | | | | | | | | |
| Fowler | Y | N | Y | Y | Y | Y | Y | Y |
| Nunn | Y | N | ? | ? | Y | Y | Y | Y |
| **HAWAII** | | | | | | | | |
| Akaka | Y | N | Y | Y | Y | Y | Y | Y |
| Inouye | Y | N | Y | Y | Y | Y | Y | Y |
| **IDAHO** | | | | | | | | |
| *Craig* | N | ? | N | N | N | N | N | N |
| *Symms* | N | Y | N | N | N | N | N | N |
| **ILLINOIS** | | | | | | | | |
| Dixon | Y | N | Y | Y | Y | ? | ? | ? |
| Simon | Y | N | Y | Y | Y | Y | Y | Y |
| **INDIANA** | | | | | | | | |
| *Coats* | N | Y | N | N | N | N | N | N |
| *Lugar* | N | Y | N | N | N | N | N | N |

| | 89 | 90 | 91 | 92 | 93 | 94 | 95 | 96 |
|---|---|---|---|---|---|---|---|---|
| **IOWA** | | | | | | | | |
| Harkin | Y | ? | ? | ? | ? | ? | ? | ? |
| *Grassley* | N | Y | N | N | N | N | N | N |
| **KANSAS** | | | | | | | | |
| *Dole* | N | Y | N | N | N | N | N | N |
| *Kassebaum* | N | Y | N | N | N | N | N | N |
| **KENTUCKY** | | | | | | | | |
| Ford | Y | N | Y | Y | Y | Y | Y | Y |
| *McConnell* | N | Y | N | N | N | N | N | N |
| **LOUISIANA** | | | | | | | | |
| Breaux | Y | N | Y | Y | Y | Y | Y | Y |
| Johnston | Y | N | Y | Y | Y | Y | Y | Y |
| **MAINE** | | | | | | | | |
| Mitchell | Y | N | Y | Y | Y | Y | Y | Y |
| *Cohen* | N | Y | N | N | Y | N | N | N |
| **MARYLAND** | | | | | | | | |
| Mikulski | Y | N | Y | Y | Y | Y | Y | N |
| Sarbanes | Y | N | Y | Y | Y | Y | Y | Y |
| **MASSACHUSETTS** | | | | | | | | |
| Kennedy | Y | N | Y | Y | Y | Y | Y | Y |
| Kerry | Y | N | Y | Y | Y | Y | Y | Y |
| **MICHIGAN** | | | | | | | | |
| Levin | Y | N | Y | N | Y | Y | Y | Y |
| Riegle | N | N | Y | Y | Y | Y | Y | Y |
| **MINNESOTA** | | | | | | | | |
| Wellstone | Y | N | Y | Y | Y | Y | Y | Y |
| *Durenberger* | N | N | Y | Y | Y | Y | Y | Y |
| **MISSISSIPPI** | | | | | | | | |
| *Cochran* | N | Y | N | N | N | N | N | N |
| *Lott* | N | Y | N | N | N | N | N | N |
| **MISSOURI** | | | | | | | | |
| *Bond* | ? | Y | N | N | N | N | N | N |
| *Danforth* | N | Y | N | N | N | N | N | N |
| **MONTANA** | | | | | | | | |
| Baucus | Y | N | Y | Y | Y | Y | Y | Y |
| *Burns* | N | Y | N | N | N | N | N | N |
| **NEBRASKA** | | | | | | | | |
| Exon | Y | N | Y | Y | Y | Y | Y | Y |
| Kerrey | Y | N | Y | Y | Y | Y | Y | Y |
| **NEVADA** | | | | | | | | |
| Bryan | Y | N | Y | Y | Y | Y | Y | Y |
| Reid | Y | N | Y | Y | Y | Y | Y | Y |

| | 89 | 90 | 91 | 92 | 93 | 94 | 95 | 96 |
|---|---|---|---|---|---|---|---|---|
| **NEW HAMPSHIRE** | | | | | | | | |
| *Rudman* | N | Y | N | N | N | N | N | N |
| *Smith* | N | Y | N | N | N | N | N | N |
| **NEW JERSEY** | | | | | | | | |
| Bradley | Y | N | Y | Y | Y | Y | Y | Y |
| Lautenberg | Y | N | Y | Y | Y | Y | Y | Y |
| **NEW MEXICO** | | | | | | | | |
| Bingaman | Y | N | ? | ? | ? | ? | ? | ? |
| *Domenici* | N | Y | N | N | N | N | N | N |
| **NEW YORK** | | | | | | | | |
| Moynihan | Y | N | Y | Y | Y | Y | Y | Y |
| *D'Amato* | N | Y | N | N | N | N | N | N |
| **NORTH CAROLINA** | | | | | | | | |
| Sanford | Y | N | N | Y | N | Y | N | Y |
| *Helms* | N | Y | N | N | N | N | N | N |
| **NORTH DAKOTA** | | | | | | | | |
| Burdick | Y | N | Y | Y | Y | Y | Y | Y |
| Conrad | Y | N | Y | Y | Y | Y | Y | Y |
| **OHIO** | | | | | | | | |
| Glenn | Y | N | Y | Y | Y | Y | Y | Y |
| Metzenbaum | ? | ? | Y | Y | Y | Y | Y | Y |
| **OKLAHOMA** | | | | | | | | |
| Boren | N | N | Y | Y | Y | N | Y | N |
| *Nickles* | N | Y | N | N | N | N | N | N |
| **OREGON** | | | | | | | | |
| *Hatfield* | Y | N | Y | Y | Y | Y | Y | Y |
| *Packwood* | Y | N | Y | Y | Y | Y | Y | Y |
| **PENNSYLVANIA** | | | | | | | | |
| Wofford | Y | N | Y | Y | Y | Y | Y | Y |
| *Specter* | Y | Y | Y | N | Y | N | Y | Y |
| **RHODE ISLAND** | | | | | | | | |
| Pell | Y | − | Y | Y | Y | Y | Y | Y |
| *Chafee* | N | Y | N | N | N | N | Y | N |
| **SOUTH CAROLINA** | | | | | | | | |
| Hollings | Y | N | N | Y | N | N | N | N |
| *Thurmond* | N | Y | N | N | N | N | N | N |
| **SOUTH DAKOTA** | | | | | | | | |
| Daschle | Y | N | Y | Y | Y | Y | Y | Y |
| *Pressler* | N | Y | N | N | N | N | N | N |
| **TENNESSEE** | | | | | | | | |
| Gore | Y | N | Y | Y | Y | Y | Y | Y |
| Sasser | Y | N | Y | Y | Y | Y | Y | Y |

| | 89 | 90 | 91 | 92 | 93 | 94 | 95 | 96 |
|---|---|---|---|---|---|---|---|---|
| **TEXAS** | | | | | | | | |
| Bentsen | N | N | ? | ? | ? | ? | ? | ? |
| *Gramm* | N | Y | N | N | N | N | N | N |
| **UTAH** | | | | | | | | |
| *Garn* | N | Y | N | N | N | N | N | N |
| *Hatch* | N | Y | N | N | N | N | N | N |
| **VERMONT** | | | | | | | | |
| Leahy | Y | N | Y | Y | Y | Y | Y | Y |
| *Jeffords* | N | N | Y | Y | Y | Y | Y | Y |
| **VIRGINIA** | | | | | | | | |
| Robb | Y | N | Y | Y | Y | Y | Y | Y |
| *Warner* | N | Y | N | N | N | N | N | N |
| **WASHINGTON** | | | | | | | | |
| Adams | Y | N | Y | Y | Y | Y | Y | Y |
| *Gorton* | N | Y | N | N | N | N | N | N |
| **WEST VIRGINIA** | | | | | | | | |
| Byrd | Y | N | Y | Y | Y | Y | Y | Y |
| Rockefeller | Y | N | Y | Y | Y | Y | Y | Y |
| **WISCONSIN** | | | | | | | | |
| Kohl | N | N | Y | Y | Y | Y | Y | N |
| *Kasten* | N | Y | N | N | N | N | N | N |
| **WYOMING** | | | | | | | | |
| *Simpson* | N | Y | N | N | N | N | N | N |
| *Wallop* | N | Y | N | N | N | N | N | N |

ND  Northern Democrats    SD  Southern Democrats        Southern states - Ala., Ark., Fla., Ga., Ky., La., Miss., N.C., Okla., S.C., Tenn., Texas, Va.

**89. S 250. National Motor-Voter Registration/Product Liability.** Rockefeller, D-W.Va., motion to table (kill) the Kasten, R-Wis., amendment to lower the amount of awards that could be collected by plaintiffs in product-liability lawsuits by establishing a set of uniform standards under which businesses would be liable for injuries caused by their products. Motion agreed to 53-45: R 3-39; D 50-6 (ND 35-4, SD 15-2), May 14, 1992.

**90. S 250. National Motor-Voter Registration/Voluntary System.** Stevens, R-Alaska, substitute amendment to make the bill's provisions voluntary and authorize $25 million for fiscal 1992-94 to help states that want to implement such a registration system. The bill would make it mandatory for states to allow citizens to register to vote at the same time they apply for a driver's license or other public certificates and not authorize any funds to help states comply. Rejected 37-57: R 37-5; D 0-52 (ND 0-35, SD 0-17), May 14, 1992.

**91. S 250. National Motor-Voter Registration/Direct Financial Aid.** Ford, D-Ky., motion to table (kill) the McCain, R-Ariz., amendment to restrict government agencies from registering to vote people who receive direct financial aid from that agency. Motion agreed to 55-40: R 5-37; D 50-3 (ND 38-0, SD 12-3), May 19, 1992.

**92. S 250. National Motor-Voter Registration/Penalties.** Ford, D-Ky., motion to table (kill) the McConnell, R-Ky., amendment to raise the maximum penalty for voter fraud from the five years in the bill to 10 years. The amendment would also give federal officials more discretion in determining what constitutes voter fraud. Motion agreed to 57-39: R 6-37; D 51-2 (ND 36-2, SD 15-0), May 19, 1992.

**93. S 250. National Motor-Voter Registration/State Option.** Ford, D-Ky., motion to table (kill) the McConnell, R-Ky., amendment to allow a state to discontinue the programs established under the bill to increase voter participation if state voter participation in 1996 is not 2 percent greater than the 1992 level. Motion agreed to 61-36: R 7-36; D 54-0 (ND 38-0, SD 16-0), May 19, 1992.

**94. S 250. National Motor-Voter Registration/Federal Funds.** Ford, D-Ky., motion to table (kill) the Nickles, R-Okla., amendment to suspend the implementation of the bill until Congress enacts subsequent legislation to pay for the costs associated with the bill and incurred by the states. Motion agreed to 55-41: R 5-38; D 50-3 (ND 37-0, SD 13-3), May 19, 1992.

**95. S 250. National Motor-Voter Registration/Mandatory Minimum Penalties.** Ford, D-Ky., motion to table (kill) the Gramm, R-Texas, amendment to set mandatory minimum penalties for a person who commits voter fraud or voter intimidation of a fine of not more than $100,000 and jail sentences of one year for a private citizen, three years for a state or local registration official, and five years for elected officials. Motion agreed to 57-39: R 6-37; D 51-2 (ND 37-0, SD 14-2), May 19, 1992.

**96. S 250. National Motor-Voter Registration/Non-Citizens.** Ford, D-Ky., motion to table (kill) the Simpson, R-Wyo., amendment to suspend implementation of the bill until the attorney general certifies that sufficient procedures exist to prevent voting by non-citizens. Motion agreed to 54-42: R 6-37; D 48-5 (ND 35-2, SD 13-3), May 19, 1992.

| | 97 | 98 | 99 | 100 | 101 | 102 | 103 | 104 |
|---|---|---|---|---|---|---|---|---|
| **ALABAMA** | | | | | | | | |
| Heflin | Y | Y | Y | Y | Y | Y | N | Y |
| Shelby | Y | Y | Y | Y | Y | Y | Y | Y |
| **ALASKA** | | | | | | | | |
| *Murkowski* | N | N | Y | Y | N | Y | Y | Y |
| *Stevens* | N | N | Y | Y | N | Y | N | Y |
| **ARIZONA** | | | | | | | | |
| DeConcini | Y | Y | Y | Y | N | Y | Y | Y |
| *McCain* | N | N | Y | Y | N | Y | Y | Y |
| **ARKANSAS** | | | | | | | | |
| Bumpers | Y | Y | Y | Y | Y | N | Y | Y |
| Pryor | Y | Y | Y | Y | Y | ? | ? | Y |
| **CALIFORNIA** | | | | | | | | |
| Cranston | Y | Y | Y | Y | Y | N | N | Y |
| *Seymour* | N | N | Y | Y | N | N | Y | Y |
| **COLORADO** | | | | | | | | |
| Wirth | Y | Y | Y | Y | Y | Y | N | Y |
| *Brown* | N | N | Y | Y | N | Y | Y | Y |
| **CONNECTICUT** | | | | | | | | |
| Dodd | Y | Y | Y | Y | Y | N | N | Y |
| Lieberman | Y | Y | Y | Y | Y | N | Y | Y |
| **DELAWARE** | | | | | | | | |
| Biden | Y | Y | Y | Y | Y | N | N | Y |
| *Roth* | N | N | Y | Y | N | Y | Y | Y |
| **FLORIDA** | | | | | | | | |
| Graham | Y | Y | Y | Y | Y | Y | Y | Y |
| *Mack* | N | N | Y | Y | N | Y | Y | Y |
| **GEORGIA** | | | | | | | | |
| Fowler | Y | Y | Y | Y | Y | N | Y | Y |
| Nunn | Y | Y | Y | Y | Y | Y | Y | Y |
| **HAWAII** | | | | | | | | |
| Akaka | Y | Y | Y | Y | Y | N | Y | Y |
| Inouye | Y | Y | Y | Y | Y | N | Y | Y |
| **IDAHO** | | | | | | | | |
| *Craig* | N | N | Y | Y | N | Y | Y | Y |
| *Symms* | N | N | Y | Y | N | Y | Y | Y |
| **ILLINOIS** | | | | | | | | |
| Dixon | ? | Y | Y | Y | N | N | Y | Y |
| Simon | Y | Y | Y | Y | Y | N | Y | Y |
| **INDIANA** | | | | | | | | |
| *Coats* | N | N | Y | Y | Y | Y | Y | Y |
| *Lugar* | N | N | Y | Y | N | Y | Y | Y |
| **IOWA** | | | | | | | | |
| Harkin | ? | Y | Y | Y | Y | N | Y | Y |
| *Grassley* | N | N | Y | Y | N | Y | Y | Y |
| **KANSAS** | | | | | | | | |
| *Dole* | N | N | Y | N | Y | Y | Y | Y |
| *Kassebaum* | N | N | Y | Y | N | ? | ? | Y |
| **KENTUCKY** | | | | | | | | |
| Ford | Y | Y | Y | Y | Y | N | Y | Y |
| *McConnell* | N | N | Y | Y | N | Y | Y | Y |
| **LOUISIANA** | | | | | | | | |
| Breaux | Y | Y | Y | Y | Y | N | Y | Y |
| Johnston | Y | Y | Y | Y | Y | N | Y | Y |
| **MAINE** | | | | | | | | |
| Mitchell | Y | Y | Y | Y | Y | N | N | Y |
| *Cohen* | N | N | Y | Y | N | Y | Y | Y |
| **MARYLAND** | | | | | | | | |
| Mikulski | Y | Y | Y | Y | Y | Y | N | Y |
| Sarbanes | Y | Y | Y | Y | Y | N | N | Y |
| **MASSACHUSETTS** | | | | | | | | |
| Kennedy | Y | Y | Y | Y | Y | N | N | Y |
| Kerry | Y | Y | Y | Y | Y | N | N | Y |
| **MICHIGAN** | | | | | | | | |
| Levin | Y | Y | Y | Y | N | N | N | Y |
| Riegle | Y | Y | Y | Y | Y | N | Y | Y |
| **MINNESOTA** | | | | | | | | |
| Wellstone | Y | Y | Y | Y | Y | N | N | Y |
| *Durenberger* | Y | Y | Y | Y | N | Y | N | Y |
| **MISSISSIPPI** | | | | | | | | |
| *Cochran* | N | N | Y | Y | N | Y | Y | Y |
| *Lott* | N | N | Y | Y | N | Y | Y | Y |
| **MISSOURI** | | | | | | | | |
| *Bond* | N | N | Y | Y | N | Y | Y | Y |
| *Danforth* | N | N | Y | Y | N | N | Y | Y |
| **MONTANA** | | | | | | | | |
| Baucus | Y | Y | Y | Y | Y | Y | Y | Y |
| *Burns* | N | N | Y | Y | N | Y | Y | Y |
| **NEBRASKA** | | | | | | | | |
| Exon | Y | Y | Y | Y | Y | N | Y | Y |
| Kerrey | Y | Y | Y | Y | Y | N | N | Y |
| **NEVADA** | | | | | | | | |
| Bryan | Y | Y | Y | Y | Y | Y | Y | Y |
| Reid | Y | Y | Y | Y | Y | N | Y | Y |
| **NEW HAMPSHIRE** | | | | | | | | |
| *Rudman* | N | N | Y | Y | N | Y | N | Y |
| *Smith* | N | N | Y | Y | N | Y | Y | Y |
| **NEW JERSEY** | | | | | | | | |
| Bradley | Y | Y | Y | Y | Y | N | N | Y |
| Lautenberg | Y | Y | Y | Y | Y | N | N | Y |
| **NEW MEXICO** | | | | | | | | |
| Bingaman | ? | Y | Y | Y | N | Y | N | Y |
| *Domenici* | N | N | Y | Y | N | N | Y | Y |
| **NEW YORK** | | | | | | | | |
| Moynihan | Y | Y | Y | Y | Y | N | N | Y |
| *D'Amato* | N | N | Y | Y | N | Y | N | Y |
| **NORTH CAROLINA** | | | | | | | | |
| Sanford | Y | Y | Y | Y | Y | N | N | Y |
| *Helms* | N | N | Y | Y | N | Y | Y | Y |
| **NORTH DAKOTA** | | | | | | | | |
| Burdick | Y | Y | Y | Y | Y | Y | Y | Y |
| Conrad | Y | Y | Y | Y | Y | Y | Y | Y |
| **OHIO** | | | | | | | | |
| Glenn | Y | Y | Y | Y | Y | N | Y | Y |
| Metzenbaum | Y | Y | Y | Y | Y | N | Y | Y |
| **OKLAHOMA** | | | | | | | | |
| Boren | Y | Y | Y | Y | Y | N | Y | Y |
| *Nickles* | N | N | Y | Y | N | Y | Y | Y |
| **OREGON** | | | | | | | | |
| *Hatfield* | Y | Y | Y | Y | Y | N | N | Y |
| *Packwood* | Y | Y | Y | Y | N | Y | N | Y |
| **PENNSYLVANIA** | | | | | | | | |
| Wofford | Y | Y | Y | Y | Y | N | N | Y |
| *Specter* | N | Y | Y | Y | Y | N | N | Y |
| **RHODE ISLAND** | | | | | | | | |
| Pell | Y | Y | Y | Y | Y | N | N | Y |
| *Chafee* | N | N | Y | Y | N | Y | N | Y |
| **SOUTH CAROLINA** | | | | | | | | |
| Hollings | N | N | Y | Y | Y | Y | Y | Y |
| *Thurmond* | N | N | Y | Y | N | Y | Y | Y |
| **SOUTH DAKOTA** | | | | | | | | |
| Daschle | Y | Y | Y | Y | Y | N | Y | Y |
| *Pressler* | N | N | Y | Y | N | Y | Y | Y |
| **TENNESSEE** | | | | | | | | |
| Gore | Y | Y | Y | Y | Y | N | N | Y |
| Sasser | Y | Y | Y | Y | Y | N | N | Y |
| **TEXAS** | | | | | | | | |
| Bentsen | ? | ? | ? | ? | ? | ? | ? | ? |
| *Gramm* | N | N | Y | Y | N | Y | Y | Y |
| **UTAH** | | | | | | | | |
| *Garn* | N | N | Y | Y | N | Y | N | Y |
| *Hatch* | N | N | Y | Y | N | N | Y | Y |
| **VERMONT** | | | | | | | | |
| Leahy | Y | Y | Y | Y | Y | N | N | Y |
| *Jeffords* | Y | Y | Y | Y | Y | Y | N | Y |
| **VIRGINIA** | | | | | | | | |
| Robb | Y | Y | Y | Y | Y | N | N | Y |
| *Warner* | N | N | Y | Y | Y | Y | Y | Y |
| **WASHINGTON** | | | | | | | | |
| Adams | Y | Y | Y | Y | Y | N | N | Y |
| *Gorton* | N | N | Y | Y | N | Y | Y | Y |
| **WEST VIRGINIA** | | | | | | | | |
| Byrd | Y | Y | Y | Y | Y | N | Y | Y |
| Rockefeller | Y | Y | Y | Y | N | ? | ? | Y |
| **WISCONSIN** | | | | | | | | |
| Kohl | Y | Y | Y | Y | Y | Y | Y | Y |
| *Kasten* | N | N | Y | Y | N | Y | Y | Y |
| **WYOMING** | | | | | | | | |
| *Simpson* | N | N | Y | Y | N | Y | Y | Y |
| *Wallop* | N | N | Y | Y | N | Y | Y | Y |

ND   Northern Democrats    SD   Southern Democrats     Southern states - Ala., Ark., Fla., Ga., Ky., La., Miss., N.C., Okla., S.C., Tenn., Texas, Va.

**97. S 250. National Motor-Voter Registration/Undelivered Applications.** Ford, D-Ky., motion to table (kill) the Specter, R-Pa., amendment to require states to notify new registrants by mail and then reject applications if the mail notice is returned undelivered. Motion agreed to 56-40: R 4-39; D 52-1 (ND 37-0, SD 15-1), May 19, 1992.

**98. S 250. National Motor-Voter Registration/Passage.** Passage of the bill to require states to permit voter registration simultaneously with application for public documents such as a driver's license, marriage license or hunting permit. Passed 61-38: R 6-37; D 55-1 (ND 40-0, SD 15-1), May 20, 1992. A "nay" was a vote in support of the president's position.

**99. S Con Res 120. Recognition of the 27th Amendment to the Constitution/Adoption.** Adoption of the concurrent resolution to provide formal congressional recognition of the ratification by more than three-fourths of the states of the 27th Amendment to the Constitution, which provides that a congressional pay raise shall not take effect until an intervening election has occurred. Adopted 99-0: R 43-0; D 56-0 (ND 40-0, SD 16-0), May 20, 1992.

**100. S Res 298 Recognition of the 27th Amendment to the Constitution/Adoption.** Adoption of the resolution to provide formal Senate recognition of the ratification by more than three-fourths of the states of the 27th Amendment to the Constitution, which provides that a congressional pay raise shall not take effect until an intervening election has occurred. Adopted 99-0: R 43-0; D 56-0 (ND 40-0, SD 16-0), May 20, 1992.

**101. HR 5132. Fiscal 1992 Disaster Relief Supplemental Appropriations/Transportation Projects.** Lautenberg, D-N.J., amendment to waive in fiscal 1992 the 20 percent state matching requirement for transportation projects. Adopted 59-40: R 8-35; D 51-5 (ND 36-4, SD 15-1), May 20, 1992. A 'nay' was a vote supporting the president's position.

**102. HR 5132. Fiscal 1992 Disaster Relief Supplemental Appropriations/Offsets.** Graham, D-Fla., amendment to require all new appropriations authorized under the bill to be offset by rescissions of previously appropriated funds. Rejected 45-52: R 31-11; D 14-41 (ND 7-33, SD 7-8), May 20, 1992.

**103. HR 5132. Fiscal 1992 Disaster Relief Supplemental Appropriations/Riot Crimes.** Seymour, R-Calif., amendment to prohibit funds from going to any person under arrest, subject to a pending charge or convicted of a crime related to the riots in Los Angeles, Calif., between April 29 and May 9, 1992. Adopted 68-28: R 36-6; D 32-22 (ND 20-19, SD 12-3), May 20, 1992.

**104. S 2743. Yugoslavia Sanctions/Passage.** Passage of the bill to restrict U.S. assistance, multinational assistance and suspend air travel to Yugoslavia until Yugoslavia has met certain conditions, including recognizing the international borders of Croatia, Bosnia-Herzegovina and Macedonia. Passed 99-0: R 43-0; D 56-0 (ND 40-0, SD 16-0), May 21, 1992.

## KEY

- **Y** Voted for (yea).
- **#** Paired for.
- **+** Announced for.
- **N** Voted against (nay).
- **X** Paired against.
- **−** Announced against.
- **P** Voted "present."
- **C** Voted "present" to avoid possible conflict of interest.
- **?** Did not vote or otherwise make a position known.

Democrats   *Republicans*

| State / Member | 105 | 106 | 107 | 108 | 109 | 110 | 111 | 112 |
|---|---|---|---|---|---|---|---|---|
| **ALABAMA** | | | | | | | | |
| Heflin | N | N | N | Y | N | N | Y | N |
| Shelby | N | N | Y | Y | Y | N | Y | N |
| **ALASKA** | | | | | | | | |
| *Murkowski* | N | Y | Y | Y | N | N | Y | N |
| *Stevens* | N | Y | Y | Y | Y | Y | Y | N |
| **ARIZONA** | | | | | | | | |
| DeConcini | N | N | N | Y | N | − | Y | N |
| *McCain* | Y | Y | Y | N | N | N | Y | Y |
| **ARKANSAS** | | | | | | | | |
| Bumpers | N | N | N | Y | Y | Y | Y | N |
| Pryor | N | N | N | Y | Y | Y | Y | N |
| **CALIFORNIA** | | | | | | | | |
| Cranston | N | N | N | Y | Y | Y | Y | N |
| *Seymour* | Y | Y | Y | Y | Y | N | + | ? |
| **COLORADO** | | | | | | | | |
| Wirth | N | N | N | Y | Y | Y | Y | N |
| *Brown* | Y | Y | Y | Y | N | N | N | Y |
| **CONNECTICUT** | | | | | | | | |
| Dodd | N | N | N | Y | Y | Y | Y | N |
| Lieberman | N | N | Y | Y | Y | Y | Y | N |
| **DELAWARE** | | | | | | | | |
| Biden | N | N | N | Y | Y | Y | Y | N |
| *Roth* | Y | Y | Y | N | N | N | Y | Y |
| **FLORIDA** | | | | | | | | |
| Graham | N | Y | N | Y | N | Y | Y | N |
| *Mack* | Y | Y | Y | N | N | N | Y | Y |
| **GEORGIA** | | | | | | | | |
| Fowler | N | N | N | Y | Y | Y | Y | N |
| Nunn | N | N | Y | Y | Y | N | Y | N |
| **HAWAII** | | | | | | | | |
| Akaka | N | N | N | Y | Y | Y | Y | N |
| Inouye | N | N | N | Y | Y | ? | Y | N |
| **IDAHO** | | | | | | | | |
| *Craig* | Y | Y | Y | N | N | N | Y | Y |
| *Symms* | Y | Y | Y | N | N | N | Y | Y |
| **ILLINOIS** | | | | | | | | |
| Dixon | N | N | Y | Y | Y | ? | Y | N |
| Simon | N | N | N | Y | Y | Y | Y | N |
| **INDIANA** | | | | | | | | |
| *Coats* | Y | Y | Y | Y | N | N | Y | Y |
| *Lugar* | Y | Y | Y | N | N | Y | Y | N |
| **IOWA** | | | | | | | | |
| Harkin | N | N | N | Y | Y | N | Y | N |
| *Grassley* | Y | Y | Y | Y | N | Y | N | N |
| **KANSAS** | | | | | | | | |
| *Dole* | Y | Y | Y | Y | N | N | Y | Y |
| *Kassebaum* | Y | Y | Y | Y | N | Y | N | Y |
| **KENTUCKY** | | | | | | | | |
| Ford | N | N | Y | Y | Y | Y | Y | N |
| *McConnell* | Y | Y | Y | Y | N | N | Y | Y |
| **LOUISIANA** | | | | | | | | |
| Breaux | N | N | N | Y | Y | Y | Y | N |
| Johnston | N | N | N | Y | Y | Y | ? | ? |
| **MAINE** | | | | | | | | |
| Mitchell | N | N | N | Y | Y | Y | Y | N |
| *Cohen* | Y | Y | Y | Y | N | Y | Y | Y |
| **MARYLAND** | | | | | | | | |
| Mikulski | N | N | N | Y | Y | Y | Y | N |
| Sarbanes | N | N | N | Y | Y | Y | Y | N |
| **MASSACHUSETTS** | | | | | | | | |
| Kennedy | N | N | N | Y | Y | Y | Y | N |
| Kerry | N | N | N | Y | Y | N | Y | N |
| **MICHIGAN** | | | | | | | | |
| Levin | N | N | N | Y | Y | Y | Y | N |
| Riegle | N | N | N | Y | Y | Y | Y | N |
| **MINNESOTA** | | | | | | | | |
| Wellstone | N | N | N | Y | Y | Y | N | N |
| *Durenberger* | N | Y | N | N | Y | N | Y | N |
| **MISSISSIPPI** | | | | | | | | |
| *Cochran* | Y | Y | Y | Y | N | N | Y | Y |
| *Lott* | Y | Y | Y | Y | N | N | Y | Y |
| **MISSOURI** | | | | | | | | |
| *Bond* | Y | N | N | Y | Y | Y | + | Y |
| *Danforth* | Y | Y | N | Y | Y | Y | ? | Y |
| **MONTANA** | | | | | | | | |
| Baucus | N | N | N | Y | Y | Y | Y | N |
| *Burns* | Y | Y | Y | Y | Y | N | Y | N |
| **NEBRASKA** | | | | | | | | |
| Exon | N | N | N | Y | Y | Y | Y | N |
| Kerrey | N | N | N | Y | Y | N | Y | N |
| **NEVADA** | | | | | | | | |
| Bryan | N | N | N | Y | Y | Y | Y | N |
| Reid | N | N | N | Y | Y | Y | Y | N |
| **NEW HAMPSHIRE** | | | | | | | | |
| *Rudman* | Y | Y | Y | Y | N | Y | Y | N |
| *Smith* | Y | Y | Y | N | N | N | Y | Y |
| **NEW JERSEY** | | | | | | | | |
| Bradley | N | N | N | Y | Y | N | Y | N |
| Lautenberg | N | N | N | Y | Y | N | N | N |
| **NEW MEXICO** | | | | | | | | |
| Bingaman | N | N | N | Y | Y | N | Y | N |
| *Domenici* | Y | Y | Y | Y | N | Y | N | N |
| **NEW YORK** | | | | | | | | |
| Moynihan | N | N | N | Y | Y | Y | Y | N |
| *D'Amato* | N | N | Y | Y | Y | Y | Y | N |
| **NORTH CAROLINA** | | | | | | | | |
| Sanford | N | Y | N | Y | N | N | Y | N |
| *Helms* | Y | Y | Y | Y | N | N | + | + |
| **NORTH DAKOTA** | | | | | | | | |
| Burdick | N | N | N | Y | Y | Y | Y | N |
| Conrad | N | N | N | Y | Y | N | Y | N |
| **OHIO** | | | | | | | | |
| Glenn | N | N | N | Y | Y | Y | Y | N |
| Metzenbaum | N | N | N | Y | Y | N | Y | N |
| **OKLAHOMA** | | | | | | | | |
| Boren | Y | N | N | Y | Y | Y | Y | N |
| *Nickles* | Y | Y | Y | N | N | Y | Y | N |
| **OREGON** | | | | | | | | |
| *Hatfield* | N | N | N | Y | Y | Y | Y | N |
| *Packwood* | N | N | Y | Y | Y | Y | N | N |
| **PENNSYLVANIA** | | | | | | | | |
| Wofford | N | N | N | Y | Y | Y | Y | N |
| *Specter* | N | N | Y | Y | Y | Y | Y | N |
| **RHODE ISLAND** | | | | | | | | |
| Pell | N | N | N | Y | + | + | Y | N |
| *Chafee* | Y | Y | N | Y | ? | ? | Y | N |
| **SOUTH CAROLINA** | | | | | | | | |
| Hollings | N | N | Y | Y | Y | N | N | N |
| *Thurmond* | Y | Y | Y | Y | N | Y | N | N |
| **SOUTH DAKOTA** | | | | | | | | |
| Daschle | N | N | N | Y | Y | Y | Y | N |
| *Pressler* | Y | Y | Y | Y | N | N | Y | Y |
| **TENNESSEE** | | | | | | | | |
| Gore | N | N | N | Y | Y | Y | Y | N |
| Sasser | N | N | N | Y | Y | Y | Y | N |
| **TEXAS** | | | | | | | | |
| Bentsen | ? | ? | ? | ? | ? | ? | Y | N |
| *Gramm* | Y | Y | Y | N | N | N | Y | Y |
| **UTAH** | | | | | | | | |
| *Garn* | Y | Y | Y | N | N | N | Y | Y |
| *Hatch* | Y | N | Y | Y | Y | N | Y | Y |
| **VERMONT** | | | | | | | | |
| Leahy | N | N | N | Y | Y | Y | Y | N |
| *Jeffords* | Y | N | N | Y | N | ? | Y | N |
| **VIRGINIA** | | | | | | | | |
| Robb | N | N | N | Y | Y | Y | Y | N |
| *Warner* | Y | N | N | Y | Y | N | Y | N |
| **WASHINGTON** | | | | | | | | |
| Adams | N | N | N | Y | Y | Y | Y | N |
| *Gorton* | N | Y | N | Y | N | N | Y | N |
| **WEST VIRGINIA** | | | | | | | | |
| Byrd | N | N | Y | Y | Y | Y | Y | N |
| Rockefeller | N | N | N | Y | Y | Y | Y | N |
| **WISCONSIN** | | | | | | | | |
| Kohl | N | N | N | Y | Y | N | C | N |
| *Kasten* | Y | Y | Y | N | N | N | Y | Y |
| **WYOMING** | | | | | | | | |
| *Simpson* | Y | Y | Y | Y | N | Y | + | Y |
| *Wallop* | Y | Y | Y | N | N | N | N | Y |

ND Northern Democrats   SD Southern Democrats   Southern states - Ala., Ark., Fla., Ga., Ky., La., Miss., N.C., Okla., S.C., Tenn., Texas, Va.

**105. HR 5132. Fiscal 1992 Disaster Relief Supplemental Appropriations/Wage Standards.** Nickles, R-Okla., amendment to waive the provisions of the Davis-Bacon Act, which sets wage standards for federal contracts, with respect to any construction or repair project which receives funding under the bill. Rejected 36-63: R 35-8; D 1-55 (ND 0-40, SD 1-15), May 21, 1992.

**106. HR 5132. Fiscal 1992 Disaster Relief Supplemental Appropriations/Urban Programs.** Lott, R-Miss., amendment to strike the $1.45 billion in the bill that would be provided for summer youth employment, the "Weed and Seed" program to focus federal programs on high poverty and crime areas, a Head Start summer program for preschool children, and a Chapter I summer school program for elementary and secondary schools. Rejected 37-62: R 35-8; D 2-54 (ND 0-40, SD 2-14), May 21, 1992.

**107. HR 5132. Fiscal 1992 Disaster Relief Supplemental Appropriations/Anti-Riot Prosecution.** Judgment of the Senate on the germaneness of the Thurmond, R-S.C., amendment to allow for federal prosecution after a state prosecution for violations of federal anti-riot statutes, and increase penalties for killings, attempted killings and assaults resulting in serious bodily injury during a riot, including the death penalty for first-degree murder committed during a riot. Ruled non-germane 42-57: R 35-8; D 7-49 (ND 3-37, SD 4-12), May 21, 1992.

**108. HR 4990. Fiscal 1992 Rescissions/Adoption.** Adoption of the conference report to rescind $8,158,305,054 in previously approved budget authority for fiscal 1992, including $7.2 billion in defense, $761 million in domestic programs and $164 million in foreign aid. The bill would rescind $500 million for the B-2 bomber, $200 million for the Strategic Defense Initiative and terminate the third but not the second *Seawolf* nuclear submarine. The administration had requested rescissions of $7,862,772,690.

Adopted 90-9: R 34-9; D 56-0 (ND 40-0, SD 16-0), May 21, 1992.

**109. HR 5132. Fiscal 1992 Disaster Relief Supplemental Appropriations/Passage.** Passage of the bill to provide $1,944,185,000 in new budget authority in fiscal 1992, including $494.7 million for disaster assistance and loans to respond to the Los Angeles riots and the Chicago tunnel collapse and subsequent flooding, and $1.45 billion for summer youth employment, the "Weed and Seed" program to focus federal programs on high poverty and crime areas, a Head Start summer program, and a Chapter I summer program for elementary and secondary schools. Passed 61-36: R 11-31; D 50-5 (ND 37-2, SD 13-3), May 21, 1992.

**110. H Con Res 287. Fiscal 1993 Budget Resolution/Adoption.** Adoption of the conference report to set budget levels for the fiscal year ending Sept. 30, 1993: budget authority, $1.516 trillion; outlays, $1.500 trillion; revenues, $1.173 trillion; deficit, $327 billion. Adopted 52-41: R 16-25; D 36-16 (ND 25-11, SD 11-5), May 21, 1992.

**111. S 474. Sports Gambling.** Passage of the bill to prohibit state governments from sponsoring, operating, advertising, promoting, licensing or authorizing professional or amateur sports gambling. Passed 88-5: R 35-3; D 53-2 (ND 38-1, SD 15-1), June 2, 1992.

**112. S 1504. Corporation for Public Broadcasting Authorization/Funding Freeze.** Lott, R-Miss., amendment to freeze funding for the Corporation for Public Broadcasting by providing an authorization of $275 million in each of fiscal 1994, 1995 and 1996, instead of the $310 million in 1994, $375 million in 1995 and $425 million in 1996 as provided in the bill. Rejected 22-75: R 22-19; D 0-56 (ND 0-40, SD 0-16), June 3, 1992. A "yea" was a vote in support of the president's position.

| | 113 | 114 | 115 | 116 | 117 | 118 | 119 | 120 |
|---|---|---|---|---|---|---|---|---|
| **ALABAMA** | | | | | | | | |
| Heflin | Y | Y | Y | Y | Y | Y | Y | Y |
| Shelby | Y | Y | Y | Y | Y | Y | Y | Y |
| **ALASKA** | | | | | | | | |
| *Murkowski* | Y | Y | Y | N | Y | Y | Y | N |
| *Stevens* | Y | Y | Y | N | N | Y | N | Y |
| **ARIZONA** | | | | | | | | |
| DeConcini | Y | Y | Y | Y | Y | Y | Y | Y |
| *McCain* | Y | Y | Y | Y | N | N | Y | N |
| **ARKANSAS** | | | | | | | | |
| Bumpers | Y | Y | Y | Y | Y | Y | Y | N |
| Pryor | Y | Y | Y | Y | Y | Y | Y | N |
| **CALIFORNIA** | | | | | | | | |
| Cranston | Y | Y | Y | Y | Y | Y | Y | Y |
| *Seymour* | ? | \# | Y | Y | Y | Y | Y | N |
| **COLORADO** | | | | | | | | |
| Wirth | N | Y | Y | ? | ? | ? | ? | ? |
| *Brown* | Y | N | Y | N | N | Y | N | N |
| **CONNECTICUT** | | | | | | | | |
| Dodd | Y | Y | Y | Y | Y | Y | Y | Y |
| Lieberman | Y | Y | Y | Y | Y | Y | Y | Y |
| **DELAWARE** | | | | | | | | |
| Biden | Y | + | Y | N | Y | Y | Y | Y |
| *Roth* | Y | Y | Y | N | N | Y | N | N |
| **FLORIDA** | | | | | | | | |
| Graham | Y | Y | Y | N | N | Y | N | Y |
| *Mack* | Y | N | Y | N | N | N | N | N |
| **GEORGIA** | | | | | | | | |
| Fowler | Y | Y | Y | Y | Y | Y | Y | Y |
| Nunn | Y | Y | Y | Y | Y | Y | Y | Y |
| **HAWAII** | | | | | | | | |
| Akaka | Y | Y | Y | Y | Y | Y | Y | Y |
| Inouye | Y | Y | Y | Y | Y | Y | Y | Y |
| **IDAHO** | | | | | | | | |
| *Craig* | Y | N | N | Y | Y | N | Y | N |
| *Symms* | Y | N | N | Y | N | Y | N | N |
| **ILLINOIS** | | | | | | | | |
| Dixon | Y | Y | Y | Y | Y | Y | Y | Y |
| Simon | Y | Y | Y | Y | Y | Y | Y | Y |
| **INDIANA** | | | | | | | | |
| *Coats* | Y | N | N | Y | Y | Y | Y | N |
| *Lugar* | Y | Y | Y | Y | Y | Y | Y | N |

| | 113 | 114 | 115 | 116 | 117 | 118 | 119 | 120 |
|---|---|---|---|---|---|---|---|---|
| **IOWA** | | | | | | | | |
| Harkin | Y | Y | Y | Y | Y | Y | Y | Y |
| *Grassley* | Y | Y | Y | Y | Y | Y | Y | N |
| **KANSAS** | | | | | | | | |
| *Dole* | Y | N | Y | N | Y | Y | Y | N |
| *Kassebaum* | Y | Y | Y | Y | Y | Y | Y | N |
| **KENTUCKY** | | | | | | | | |
| Ford | Y | Y | N | Y | Y | Y | Y | Y |
| *McConnell* | Y | Y | Y | Y | Y | Y | Y | N |
| **LOUISIANA** | | | | | | | | |
| Breaux | Y | Y | Y | Y | Y | Y | Y | N |
| Johnston | ? | Y | Y | Y | Y | Y | Y | Y |
| **MAINE** | | | | | | | | |
| Mitchell | Y | Y | Y | Y | Y | Y | Y | Y |
| *Cohen* | Y | Y | Y | Y | Y | Y | Y | N |
| **MARYLAND** | | | | | | | | |
| Mikulski | Y | Y | Y | Y | Y | Y | Y | Y |
| Sarbanes | Y | Y | Y | Y | Y | Y | Y | Y |
| **MASSACHUSETTS** | | | | | | | | |
| Kennedy | Y | Y | Y | Y | Y | Y | Y | Y |
| Kerry | Y | Y | Y | Y | Y | Y | Y | Y |
| **MICHIGAN** | | | | | | | | |
| Levin | Y | Y | Y | Y | Y | Y | Y | Y |
| Riegle | Y | Y | Y | Y | Y | Y | Y | Y |
| **MINNESOTA** | | | | | | | | |
| Wellstone | Y | Y | Y | + | + | + | + | Y |
| *Durenberger* | Y | Y | ? | ? | ? | Y | Y | N |
| **MISSISSIPPI** | | | | | | | | |
| *Cochran* | Y | Y | Y | Y | Y | Y | Y | N |
| *Lott* | Y | Y | Y | Y | Y | Y | Y | N |
| **MISSOURI** | | | | | | | | |
| *Bond* | Y | Y | N | Y | Y | Y | Y | N |
| *Danforth* | Y | Y | Y | ? | ? | Y | Y | N |
| **MONTANA** | | | | | | | | |
| Baucus | Y | Y | Y | Y | Y | Y | Y | Y |
| *Burns* | Y | Y | N | Y | Y | Y | Y | N |
| **NEBRASKA** | | | | | | | | |
| Exon | Y | Y | Y | Y | Y | Y | Y | Y |
| Kerrey | Y | Y | Y | Y | Y | Y | Y | Y |
| **NEVADA** | | | | | | | | |
| Bryan | Y | Y | Y | N | N | Y | N | Y |
| Reid | Y | Y | Y | N | N | Y | N | Y |

| | 113 | 114 | 115 | 116 | 117 | 118 | 119 | 120 |
|---|---|---|---|---|---|---|---|---|
| **NEW HAMPSHIRE** | | | | | | | | |
| *Rudman* | ? | Y | Y | Y | Y | Y | Y | N |
| *Smith* | Y | N | N | Y | Y | Y | Y | N |
| **NEW JERSEY** | | | | | | | | |
| Bradley | Y | Y | Y | Y | Y | Y | Y | Y |
| Lautenberg | Y | Y | Y | Y | Y | Y | Y | Y |
| **NEW MEXICO** | | | | | | | | |
| Bingaman | Y | Y | ? | Y | Y | Y | Y | Y |
| *Domenici* | Y | Y | Y | Y | Y | Y | Y | N |
| **NEW YORK** | | | | | | | | |
| Moynihan | Y | Y | Y | Y | Y | Y | Y | Y |
| *D'Amato* | Y | Y | N | Y | Y | Y | Y | Y |
| **NORTH CAROLINA** | | | | | | | | |
| Sanford | Y | Y | Y | Y | Y | Y | Y | N |
| *Helms* | + | X | − | − | − | − | − | X |
| **NORTH DAKOTA** | | | | | | | | |
| Burdick | Y | Y | Y | Y | Y | Y | Y | Y |
| Conrad | Y | Y | Y | Y | Y | Y | Y | Y |
| **OHIO** | | | | | | | | |
| Glenn | Y | ? | Y | Y | Y | Y | Y | Y |
| Metzenbaum | N | Y | Y | Y | Y | Y | Y | Y |
| **OKLAHOMA** | | | | | | | | |
| Boren | Y | Y | Y | Y | Y | Y | Y | Y |
| *Nickles* | Y | N | N | Y | Y | Y | Y | N |
| **OREGON** | | | | | | | | |
| *Hatfield* | Y | Y | Y | Y | Y | Y | Y | Y |
| *Packwood* | Y | Y | Y | Y | Y | Y | Y | Y |
| **PENNSYLVANIA** | | | | | | | | |
| Wofford | Y | ? | Y | Y | Y | Y | Y | Y |
| *Specter* | Y | Y | Y | Y | Y | ? | ? | Y |
| **RHODE ISLAND** | | | | | | | | |
| Pell | Y | Y | Y | + | + | ? | + | Y |
| *Chafee* | Y | Y | Y | Y | Y | Y | Y | N |
| **SOUTH CAROLINA** | | | | | | | | |
| Hollings | Y | Y | Y | Y | Y | Y | Y | N |
| *Thurmond* | Y | Y | Y | Y | Y | Y | Y | N |
| **SOUTH DAKOTA** | | | | | | | | |
| Daschle | Y | Y | Y | Y | Y | Y | Y | Y |
| *Pressler* | Y | N | Y | Y | Y | Y | Y | N |
| **TENNESSEE** | | | | | | | | |
| Gore | Y | Y | Y | ? | ? | ? | + | \# |
| Sasser | Y | Y | Y | Y | Y | Y | Y | Y |

| | 113 | 114 | 115 | 116 | 117 | 118 | 119 | 120 |
|---|---|---|---|---|---|---|---|---|
| **TEXAS** | | | | | | | | |
| Bentsen | Y | Y | Y | N | Y | Y | Y | Y |
| *Gramm* | Y | N | N | N | N | N | N | N |
| **UTAH** | | | | | | | | |
| *Garn* | Y | N | Y | Y | Y | Y | Y | − |
| *Hatch* | Y | Y | N | Y | Y | Y | Y | N |
| **VERMONT** | | | | | | | | |
| Leahy | Y | Y | Y | Y | Y | Y | Y | Y |
| *Jeffords* | N | Y | Y | Y | Y | Y | Y | N |
| **VIRGINIA** | | | | | | | | |
| Robb | Y | Y | Y | N | Y | Y | Y | Y |
| *Warner* | Y | Y | Y | N | Y | Y | Y | N |
| **WASHINGTON** | | | | | | | | |
| Adams | Y | Y | Y | Y | Y | Y | Y | Y |
| *Gorton* | Y | Y | Y | Y | Y | Y | Y | N |
| **WEST VIRGINIA** | | | | | | | | |
| Byrd | Y | Y | Y | Y | Y | Y | Y | Y |
| Rockefeller | Y | Y | Y | Y | Y | Y | Y | Y |
| **WISCONSIN** | | | | | | | | |
| Kohl | Y | Y | Y | Y | Y | Y | Y | Y |
| *Kasten* | Y | Y | Y | Y | Y | N | Y | N |
| **WYOMING** | | | | | | | | |
| *Simpson* | Y | Y | Y | Y | Y | Y | Y | N |
| *Wallop* | Y | N | Y | Y | Y | Y | Y | N |

ND Northern Democrats   SD Southern Democrats        Southern states - Ala., Ark., Fla., Ga., Ky., La., Miss., N.C., Okla., S.C., Tenn., Texas, Va.

**113. S 1504. Corporation for Public Broadcasting Authorization/"Indecent" Programming.** Byrd, D-W.Va., amendment to extend the Federal Communications Commission's authority to prohibit radio and television stations from "indecent" broadcasts between 6 a.m. and midnight (10 p.m. for stations that go off the air by midnight). Adopted 93-3: R 39-1; D 54-2 (ND 38-2, SD 16-0), June 3, 1992. A "yea" was a vote in support of the president's position.

**114. HR 2977. Corporation for Public Broadcasting Authorization/Passage.** Passage of the bill to authorize $1.1 billion for the Corporation for Public Broadcasting in fiscal 1994-96. Passed 84-11: R 30-11; D 54-0 (ND 37-0, SD 17-0), June 3, 1992.

**115. HR 2507. National Institutes of Health Reauthorization/Conference Report.** Adoption of the conference report to reauthorize and amend the programs of the National Institutes of Health through fiscal 1996, including fiscal 1993 funding of $2.2 billion for the National Cancer Institute and $1.4 billion for the Heart, Lung and Blood Institute. The conference report would lift the ban on fetal tissue transplant research using fetal tissue obtained from induced abortions. Adopted 85-12: R 30-11; D 55-1 (ND 39-0, SD 16-1), June 4, 1992. A "nay" was a vote in support of the president's position.

**116. S 1306. Alcohol, Drug Abuse and Mental Health Administration Reorganization/Motion to Recommit.** Kennedy, D-Mass., motion to table (kill) the Graham, D-Fla., motion to recommit the conference report to reauthorize the federal substance abuse and mental health programs for fiscal 1993-94. Motion rejected 79-14: R 32-8; D 47-6 (ND 34-3, SD 13-3), June 9, 1992.

**117. S 1306. Alcohol, Drug Abuse and Mental Health Administration Reorganization/Cloture.** Mitchell, D-Maine, motion to invoke cloture (thus limiting debate) on the conference report to reauthorize the federal substance abuse and mental health programs for fiscal 1993-94. The bill would split the block grant for mental health and substance abuse services into two separate grants, transfer the research arms of the Alcohol, Drug Abuse and Mental Health Administration to the National Institutes of Health, and provide more money to rural areas under state funding formulas. Motion agreed to 84-9: R 34-6; D 50-3 (ND 35-2, SD 15-1), June 9, 1992. A three-fifths majority of the total Senate (60) is required to invoke cloture.

**118. Procedural Motion.** Mitchell, D-Maine, motion to instruct the sergeant at arms to request the attendance of absent senators. Motion agreed to 88-6: R 35-6; D 53-0 (ND 37-0, SD 16-0), June 9, 1992.

**119. S 1306. Alcohol, Drug Abuse and Mental Health Administration Reorganization/Conference Report.** Adoption of the conference report to reauthorize the federal substance abuse and mental health programs for fiscal 1993-94. The bill would split the block grant for mental health and substance abuse services into two separate grants, transfer the research arms of the Alcohol, Drug Abuse and Mental Health Administration to the National Institutes of Health, and provide more money to rural areas under state funding formulas. Adopted 86-8: R 36-5; D 50-3 (ND 35-2, SD 15-1), June 9, 1992.

**120. S 55. Striker Replacement Bill/Cloture.** Mitchell, D-Maine, motion to invoke cloture (thus limiting debate) on the bill to prohibit employers from permanently replacing striking workers. Motion rejected 55-41: R 5-36; D 50-5 (ND 39-0, SD 11-5), June 11, 1992. A three-fifths majority of the total Senate (60) is required to invoke cloture.

### KEY

| | |
|---|---|
| Y | Voted for (yea). |
| # | Paired for. |
| + | Announced for. |
| N | Voted against (nay). |
| X | Paired against. |
| − | Announced against. |
| P | Voted "present." |
| C | Voted "present" to avoid possible conflict of interest. |
| ? | Did not vote or otherwise make a position known. |

Democrats  *Republicans*

| | 121 | 122 | 123 | 124 | 125 | 126 | 127 | 128 |
|---|---|---|---|---|---|---|---|---|
| **ALABAMA** | | | | | | | | |
| Heflin | Y | N | Y | Y | N | Y | N | N |
| Shelby | Y | N | Y | Y | N | Y | N | N |
| **ALASKA** | | | | | | | | |
| *Murkowski* | N | N | Y | Y | N | N | N | Y |
| *Stevens* | Y | N | Y | Y | N | N | N | N |
| **ARIZONA** | | | | | | | | |
| DeConcini | Y | Y | Y | Y | N | N | N | N |
| *McCain* | N | N | Y | Y | N | N | N | N |
| **ARKANSAS** | | | | | | | | |
| Bumpers | N | Y | Y | Y | N | Y | N | N |
| Pryor | N | Y | Y | ? | N | Y | N | N |
| **CALIFORNIA** | | | | | | | | |
| Cranston | Y | Y | Y | Y | N | Y | N | N |
| *Seymour* | N | N | Y | Y | N | Y | N | Y |
| **COLORADO** | | | | | | | | |
| Wirth | Y | Y | Y | ? | Y | Y | N | N |
| *Brown* | N | Y | Y | Y | N | N | N | N |
| **CONNECTICUT** | | | | | | | | |
| Dodd | Y | Y | Y | Y | Y | Y | N | N |
| Lieberman | Y | Y | Y | Y | Y | Y | N | N |
| **DELAWARE** | | | | | | | | |
| Biden | Y | Y | Y | Y | Y | N | N | Y |
| *Roth* | N | N | Y | Y | ? | ? | ? | ? |
| **FLORIDA** | | | | | | | | |
| Graham | Y | Y | Y | Y | N | Y | N | N |
| *Mack* | N | N | Y | Y | N | N | N | Y |
| **GEORGIA** | | | | | | | | |
| Fowler | Y | N | Y | Y | N | Y | N | N |
| Nunn | Y | Y | Y | Y | N | Y | N | N |
| **HAWAII** | | | | | | | | |
| Akaka | Y | Y | Y | Y | Y | Y | N | N |
| Inouye | Y | Y | Y | Y | Y | Y | N | N |
| **IDAHO** | | | | | | | | |
| *Craig* | N | N | Y | Y | N | N | N | Y |
| *Symms* | N | N | ? | ? | N | N | Y | Y |
| **ILLINOIS** | | | | | | | | |
| Dixon | Y | Y | Y | Y | N | N | N | N |
| Simon | Y | Y | Y | N | Y | Y | N | N |
| **INDIANA** | | | | | | | | |
| *Coats* | N | N | Y | Y | N | N | N | N |
| *Lugar* | N | Y | Y | Y | N | N | N | N |
| **IOWA** | | | | | | | | |
| Harkin | Y | Y | Y | ? | Y | Y | N | N |
| *Grassley* | N | N | Y | Y | N | N | N | N |
| **KANSAS** | | | | | | | | |
| *Dole* | N | N | Y | Y | N | N | N | N |
| *Kassebaum* | N | Y | Y | ? | N | N | N | N |
| **KENTUCKY** | | | | | | | | |
| Ford | Y | Y | Y | N | N | N | N | N |
| *McConnell* | N | Y | Y | Y | N | N | N | N |
| **LOUISIANA** | | | | | | | | |
| Breaux | Y | Y | Y | Y | N | N | N | N |
| Johnston | Y | Y | Y | Y | N | N | N | N |
| **MAINE** | | | | | | | | |
| Mitchell | Y | Y | Y | Y | Y | Y | N | N |
| *Cohen* | N | Y | Y | Y | N | Y | N | N |
| **MARYLAND** | | | | | | | | |
| Mikulski | Y | Y | Y | Y | Y | Y | N | N |
| Sarbanes | Y | Y | Y | Y | Y | Y | N | N |
| **MASSACHUSETTS** | | | | | | | | |
| Kennedy | Y | Y | Y | Y | Y | Y | N | N |
| Kerry | Y | Y | Y | Y | Y | Y | N | N |
| **MICHIGAN** | | | | | | | | |
| Levin | Y | Y | Y | Y | Y | Y | N | N |
| Riegle | Y | Y | Y | Y | Y | Y | Y | Y |
| **MINNESOTA** | | | | | | | | |
| Wellstone | Y | Y | Y | Y | Y | N | N | N |
| *Durenberger* | N | Y | Y | ? | N | N | N | N |
| **MISSISSIPPI** | | | | | | | | |
| *Cochran* | N | N | Y | Y | N | N | N | N |
| *Lott* | N | N | Y | Y | N | N | N | N |
| **MISSOURI** | | | | | | | | |
| *Bond* | N | N | Y | Y | N | N | N | N |
| *Danforth* | N | Y | Y | Y | N | N | N | N |
| **MONTANA** | | | | | | | | |
| Baucus | Y | Y | Y | Y | Y | Y | N | N |
| *Burns* | N | N | Y | Y | N | N | N | N |
| **NEBRASKA** | | | | | | | | |
| Exon | Y | Y | Y | Y | Y | Y | N | N |
| Kerrey | Y | Y | Y | Y | Y | Y | N | N |
| **NEVADA** | | | | | | | | |
| Bryan | Y | Y | Y | Y | N | Y | N | N |
| Reid | Y | Y | Y | N | Y | N | N | N |
| **NEW HAMPSHIRE** | | | | | | | | |
| *Rudman* | N | Y | Y | Y | N | Y | N | Y |
| *Smith* | N | N | Y | Y | N | N | N | N |
| **NEW JERSEY** | | | | | | | | |
| Bradley | Y | Y | Y | Y | Y | Y | N | Y |
| Lautenberg | Y | Y | Y | Y | Y | Y | N | Y |
| **NEW MEXICO** | | | | | | | | |
| Bingaman | Y | Y | Y | Y | Y | Y | N | N |
| *Domenici* | N | N | Y | Y | N | N | N | N |
| **NEW YORK** | | | | | | | | |
| Moynihan | Y | Y | Y | Y | Y | Y | N | N |
| *D'Amato* | Y | N | Y | ? | N | ? | N | Y |
| **NORTH CAROLINA** | | | | | | | | |
| Sanford | N | Y | Y | ? | ? | ? | ? | ? |
| *Helms* | − | X | + | ? | − | − | + | + |
| **NORTH DAKOTA** | | | | | | | | |
| Burdick | Y | Y | Y | Y | Y | Y | N | N |
| Conrad | Y | Y | Y | Y | Y | Y | N | N |
| **OHIO** | | | | | | | | |
| Glenn | Y | Y | Y | Y | Y | Y | N | N |
| Metzenbaum | Y | Y | Y | Y | Y | Y | N | N |
| **OKLAHOMA** | | | | | | | | |
| Boren | N | + | Y | Y | N | Y | N | N |
| *Nickles* | N | N | Y | Y | N | N | N | N |
| **OREGON** | | | | | | | | |
| *Hatfield* | Y | # | + | + | N | N | N | N |
| *Packwood* | Y | N | Y | Y | N | N | N | N |
| **PENNSYLVANIA** | | | | | | | | |
| Wofford | Y | Y | Y | Y | Y | Y | N | N |
| *Specter* | Y | Y | Y | Y | N | Y | N | N |
| **RHODE ISLAND** | | | | | | | | |
| Pell | Y | Y | Y | Y | Y | Y | N | N |
| *Chafee* | N | Y | Y | ? | N | N | N | Y |
| **SOUTH CAROLINA** | | | | | | | | |
| Hollings | N | N | Y | Y | N | Y | N | N |
| *Thurmond* | N | N | Y | Y | N | N | Y | N |
| **SOUTH DAKOTA** | | | | | | | | |
| Daschle | Y | Y | Y | Y | Y | Y | N | N |
| *Pressler* | N | Y | Y | Y | N | N | N | N |
| **TENNESSEE** | | | | | | | | |
| Gore | Y | Y | Y | Y | Y | Y | N | N |
| Sasser | Y | Y | Y | Y | Y | Y | N | N |

| | 121 | 122 | 123 | 124 | 125 | 126 | 127 | 128 |
|---|---|---|---|---|---|---|---|---|
| **TEXAS** | | | | | | | | |
| Bentsen | Y | Y | Y | Y | N | Y | N | N |
| *Gramm* | N | N | Y | ? | N | N | N | N |
| **UTAH** | | | | | | | | |
| *Garn* | N | N | Y | Y | N | Y | Y | Y |
| *Hatch* | N | N | Y | Y | N | N | N | N |
| **VERMONT** | | | | | | | | |
| Leahy | Y | Y | Y | Y | Y | Y | N | N |
| *Jeffords* | N | Y | Y | ? | N | N | N | N |
| **VIRGINIA** | | | | | | | | |
| Robb | Y | Y | Y | Y | Y | Y | N | N |
| *Warner* | N | N | Y | Y | N | N | N | N |
| **WASHINGTON** | | | | | | | | |
| Adams | Y | Y | Y | Y | Y | Y | N | N |
| *Gorton* | N | N | Y | Y | N | Y | N | Y |
| **WEST VIRGINIA** | | | | | | | | |
| Byrd | Y | Y | Y | Y | Y | Y | N | N |
| Rockefeller | Y | Y | Y | Y | Y | Y | N | N |
| **WISCONSIN** | | | | | | | | |
| Kohl | Y | Y | Y | Y | Y | Y | N | N |
| *Kasten* | N | N | Y | Y | N | Y | N | N |
| **WYOMING** | | | | | | | | |
| *Simpson* | N | N | Y | Y | N | N | N | N |
| *Wallop* | N | N | Y | Y | N | N | Y | N |

ND  Northern Democrats    SD  Southern Democrats    Southern states - Ala., Ark., Fla., Ga., Ky., La., Miss., N.C., Okla., S.C., Tenn., Texas, Va.

**121. S 55. Striker Replacement/Invoke Cloture.** Mitchell, D-Maine, motion to invoke cloture (thus limiting debate) on the committee substitute to forbid employers from hiring permanent replacements for striking workers but allow employers to replace strikers if the employers agreed to accept a third-party mediation panel's recommendations and the workers rejected the recommendations. Motion rejected 57-42: R 5-37; D 52-5 (ND 40-0, SD 12-5), June 16, 1992. A three-fifths majority vote (60) of the total Senate is required to invoke cloture.

**122. S 1985. Bankruptcy Reform/Deficit Discussion.** Danforth, R-Mo., amendment to express the sense of the Senate that politicians should make proposals and engage in extensive substantive discussion and seek a mandate on reducing the deficit. The amendment says that the candidates for president should agree to a formal discussion entirely on the deficit. Adopted 65-32: R 13-28; D 52-4 (ND 40-0, SD 12-4), June 17, 1992.

**123. S 1985. Bankruptcy Reform/Passage.** Passage of the bill to establish a National Bankruptcy Review Commission to aid Congress in identifying and addressing problems found in the U.S. Bankruptcy Code; establish a pilot program to test how the bankruptcy code may more efficiently operate regarding small businesses; and make other changes to the bankruptcy code. Passed 97-0: R 40-0; D 57-0 (ND 40-0, SD 17-0), June 17, 1992.

**124. HR 5260. Unemployment Benefits Extension/Foreign Agricultural Workers.** Graham, D-Fla., amendment to retain the exemption for temporary foreign agricultural workers from unemployment tax. Adopted 84-3: R 34-0; D 50-3 (ND 36-2, SD 14-1), June 18, 1992.

**125. S 2733. Government-Sponsored Enterprises/Rail Strike.** Metzenbaum, D-Ohio, motion to table (kill) the Dole, R-Kan., amendment to the Riegle, D-Mich., substitute amendment to express the sense of the Senate that Congress needed to act immediately to forestall a railroad strike that was possible at midnight June 23. Motion rejected 39-58: R 0-41; D 39-17 (ND 36-4, SD 3-13), June 23, 1992. (The Dole amendment subsequently was adopted by voice vote; the Riegle amendment subsequently was adopted by voice vote.)

**126. S 2733. Government-Sponsored Enterprises/Superfund Lawsuits.** Lautenberg, D-N.J., motion to table (kill) the Chafee, R-R.I., amendment to the Riegle, D-Mich., substitute amendment to eliminate provisions that would exempt municipalities from liability lawsuits under the "superfund" hazardous waste cleanup law unless such suits were brought by the Environmental Protection Agency. Motion agreed to 52-44: R 6-34; D 46-10 (ND 34-6, SD 12-4), June 23, 1992.

**127. S 2733. Government-Sponsored Enterprises/Limited Partnership Roll-Ups.** Garn, R-Utah, motion to table (kill) the Dodd, D-Conn., amendment to the Riegle, D-Mich., substitute amendment to prohibit proxy solicitations or tender offers for stock shares in a limited partnership roll-up or reorganization, unless such actions were in accordance with rules promulgated by the Securities and Exchange Commission and designed to protect rights of affected limited partners. Motion rejected 10-87: R 9-32; D 1-55 (ND 1-39, SD 0-16), June 24, 1992. (The Dodd and Riegle amendments subsequently were adopted by voice vote.)

**128. S 2733. Government-Sponsored Enterprises/Interstate Thrift Branching.** Riegle, D-Mich., motion to table (kill) the Ford, D-Ky., amendment to the Riegle substitute amendment to place a 15-month moratorium on interstate branching by savings and loans associations. Motion rejected 15-82: R 9-32; D 6-50 (ND 6-34, SD 0-16), June 24, 1992. (The Ford and Riegle amendments subsequently were adopted by voice vote.)

**KEY**

| | |
|---|---|
| Y | Voted for (yea). |
| # | Paired for. |
| + | Announced for. |
| N | Voted against (nay). |
| X | Paired against. |
| − | Announced against. |
| P | Voted "present." |
| C | Voted "present" to avoid possible conflict of interest. |
| ? | Did not vote or otherwise make a position known. |

Democrats    *Republicans*

| State / Member | 129 | 130 | 131 | 132 | 133 | 134 | 135 | 136 |
|---|---|---|---|---|---|---|---|---|
| **ALABAMA** | | | | | | | | |
| Heflin | Y | N | Y | Y | N | N | Y | Y |
| Shelby | N | N | Y | Y | N | N | Y | Y |
| **ALASKA** | | | | | | | | |
| *Murkowski* | N | Y | N | Y | N | Y | N | Y |
| *Stevens* | N | Y | Y | Y | Y | N | Y | Y |
| **ARIZONA** | | | | | | | | |
| DeConcini | N | ? | ? | Y | Y | N | N | Y |
| *McCain* | N | Y | Y | N | Y | N | Y | Y |
| **ARKANSAS** | | | | | | | | |
| Bumpers | Y | Y | Y | ? | N | Y | N | N |
| Pryor | Y | Y | Y | Y | N | Y | N | N |
| **CALIFORNIA** | | | | | | | | |
| Cranston | Y | N | N | Y | N | Y | N | N |
| *Seymour* | Y | Y | Y | Y | Y | N | Y | Y |
| **COLORADO** | | | | | | | | |
| Wirth | Y | Y | Y | Y | N | Y | N | N |
| *Brown* | N | Y | N | Y | N | Y | N | N |
| **CONNECTICUT** | | | | | | | | |
| Dodd | Y | Y | Y | Y | N | Y | N | N |
| Lieberman | Y | Y | Y | Y | N | Y | N | N |
| **DELAWARE** | | | | | | | | |
| Biden | Y | N | N | Y | N | Y | N | N |
| *Roth* | ? | ? | ? | ? | ? | ? | ? | ? |
| **FLORIDA** | | | | | | | | |
| Graham | N | Y | Y | N | Y | N | Y | Y |
| *Mack* | N | Y | Y | Y | Y | N | Y | Y |
| **GEORGIA** | | | | | | | | |
| Fowler | Y | N | Y | Y | Y | N | Y | N |
| Nunn | Y | Y | Y | Y | N | Y | N | N |
| **HAWAII** | | | | | | | | |
| Akaka | Y | Y | Y | Y | N | Y | N | N |
| Inouye | Y | Y | Y | ? | N | Y | N | N |
| **IDAHO** | | | | | | | | |
| *Craig* | N | Y | Y | N | Y | N | Y | Y |
| *Symms* | N | Y | Y | Y | N | Y | N | Y |
| **ILLINOIS** | | | | | | | | |
| Dixon | Y | Y | Y | Y | N | N | Y | Y |
| Simon | Y | Y | Y | Y | N | N | Y | Y |
| **INDIANA** | | | | | | | | |
| *Coats* | N | Y | + | Y | Y | N | Y | Y |
| *Lugar* | N | Y | Y | Y | Y | N | Y | Y |
| **IOWA** | | | | | | | | |
| Harkin | Y | N | Y | Y | N | Y | N | N |
| *Grassley* | N | Y | Y | Y | Y | N | Y | Y |
| **KANSAS** | | | | | | | | |
| *Dole* | N | Y | Y | ? | Y | N | Y | Y |
| *Kassebaum* | N | Y | Y | Y | N | N | Y | Y |
| **KENTUCKY** | | | | | | | | |
| Ford | N | Y | Y | Y | N | N | N | N |
| *McConnell* | N | Y | Y | Y | Y | N | Y | Y |
| **LOUISIANA** | | | | | | | | |
| Breaux | N | Y | Y | Y | N | N | Y | N |
| Johnston | N | Y | Y | Y | N | Y | N | N |
| **MAINE** | | | | | | | | |
| Mitchell | Y | Y | Y | Y | N | Y | N | N |
| *Cohen* | Y | Y | Y | Y | N | N | Y | Y |
| **MARYLAND** | | | | | | | | |
| Mikulski | Y | Y | Y | ? | N | Y | N | N |
| Sarbanes | Y | Y | Y | Y | N | Y | N | N |
| **MASSACHUSETTS** | | | | | | | | |
| Kennedy | Y | Y | Y | Y | N | Y | N | N |
| Kerry | Y | Y | Y | Y | N | Y | N | N |
| **MICHIGAN** | | | | | | | | |
| Levin | Y | Y | Y | Y | N | Y | N | N |
| Riegle | Y | Y | Y | Y | N | Y | N | N |
| **MINNESOTA** | | | | | | | | |
| Wellstone | Y | N | N | Y | N | Y | N | N |
| *Durenberger* | N | Y | Y | Y | N | N | Y | Y |
| **MISSISSIPPI** | | | | | | | | |
| *Cochran* | N | Y | Y | Y | N | Y | N | Y |
| *Lott* | N | Y | Y | N | Y | N | Y | Y |
| **MISSOURI** | | | | | | | | |
| *Bond* | N | Y | Y | Y | N | Y | N | Y |
| *Danforth* | N | Y | Y | Y | N | N | Y | Y |
| **MONTANA** | | | | | | | | |
| Baucus | ? | Y | N | Y | N | Y | N | N |
| *Burns* | N | Y | Y | Y | Y | N | Y | Y |
| **NEBRASKA** | | | | | | | | |
| Exon | Y | N | Y | Y | N | N | N | N |
| Kerrey | Y | N | Y | Y | N | Y | N | N |
| **NEVADA** | | | | | | | | |
| Bryan | Y | Y | Y | Y | N | N | Y | Y |
| Reid | Y | Y | Y | Y | N | N | Y | Y |
| **NEW HAMPSHIRE** | | | | | | | | |
| *Rudman* | Y | Y | Y | Y | N | N | Y | Y |
| *Smith* | N | Y | Y | N | Y | N | Y | Y |
| **NEW JERSEY** | | | | | | | | |
| Bradley | Y | N | Y | ? | ? | + | X | X |
| Lautenberg | Y | N | Y | Y | N | Y | N | N |
| **NEW MEXICO** | | | | | | | | |
| Bingaman | Y | Y | Y | Y | N | Y | N | N |
| *Domenici* | N | Y | Y | Y | Y | N | Y | Y |
| **NEW YORK** | | | | | | | | |
| Moynihan | Y | Y | Y | Y | N | Y | N | N |
| *D'Amato* | Y | Y | Y | N | Y | N | Y | Y |
| **NORTH CAROLINA** | | | | | | | | |
| Sanford | ? | ? | ? | ? | ? | ? | ? | ? |
| *Helms* | − | ? | + | ? | + | − | + | + |
| **NORTH DAKOTA** | | | | | | | | |
| Burdick | Y | N | Y | Y | N | Y | N | N |
| Conrad | Y | N | Y | Y | N | Y | N | N |
| **OHIO** | | | | | | | | |
| Glenn | Y | Y | Y | Y | N | N | Y | Y |
| Metzenbaum | Y | Y | Y | Y | N | Y | N | N |
| **OKLAHOMA** | | | | | | | | |
| Boren | Y | ? | ? | ? | N | N | Y | N |
| *Nickles* | N | Y | Y | Y | Y | N | Y | Y |
| **OREGON** | | | | | | | | |
| *Hatfield* | N | N | Y | N | N | Y | N | N |
| *Packwood* | N | Y | Y | Y | N | N | Y | Y |
| **PENNSYLVANIA** | | | | | | | | |
| Wofford | Y | N | Y | Y | N | Y | N | N |
| *Specter* | Y | N | Y | ? | N | N | Y | Y |
| **RHODE ISLAND** | | | | | | | | |
| Pell | Y | Y | Y | Y | N | Y | # | # |
| *Chafee* | N | Y | Y | Y | N | N | Y | Y |
| **SOUTH CAROLINA** | | | | | | | | |
| Hollings | Y | Y | Y | Y | N | Y | N | Y |
| *Thurmond* | N | Y | Y | Y | Y | N | Y | Y |
| **SOUTH DAKOTA** | | | | | | | | |
| Daschle | Y | Y | Y | Y | N | Y | N | N |
| *Pressler* | N | Y | Y | Y | Y | N | Y | Y |
| **TENNESSEE** | | | | | | | | |
| Gore | Y | Y | Y | Y | N | Y | N | N |
| Sasser | Y | N | Y | Y | N | Y | N | N |
| **TEXAS** | | | | | | | | |
| Bentsen | Y | Y | Y | Y | N | Y | N | N |
| *Gramm* | N | Y | Y | N | Y | N | Y | Y |
| **UTAH** | | | | | | | | |
| *Garn* | Y | Y | Y | Y | N | Y | N | N |
| *Hatch* | N | Y | Y | Y | N | Y | N | Y |
| **VERMONT** | | | | | | | | |
| Leahy | Y | Y | Y | Y | N | Y | N | N |
| *Jeffords* | N | Y | Y | Y | N | Y | N | N |
| **VIRGINIA** | | | | | | | | |
| Robb | Y | Y | Y | Y | N | Y | N | N |
| *Warner* | N | Y | Y | Y | N | Y | N | Y |
| **WASHINGTON** | | | | | | | | |
| Adams | Y | N | N | Y | N | Y | N | N |
| *Gorton* | N | Y | Y | Y | N | Y | N | N |
| **WEST VIRGINIA** | | | | | | | | |
| Byrd | N | Y | Y | Y | N | Y | N | N |
| Rockefeller | N | Y | Y | Y | N | Y | N | N |
| **WISCONSIN** | | | | | | | | |
| Kohl | Y | Y | Y | Y | N | N | Y | N |
| *Kasten* | Y | Y | Y | N | Y | N | Y | Y |
| **WYOMING** | | | | | | | | |
| *Simpson* | N | Y | Y | Y | N | Y | N | Y |
| *Wallop* | N | + | ? | ? | Y | N | Y | Y |

ND   Northern Democrats    SD   Southern Democrats    Southern states - Ala., Ark., Fla., Ga., Ky., La., Miss., N.C., Okla., S.C., Tenn., Texas, Va.

**129. S 2733. Government-Sponsored Enterprises/Superfund Lawsuits.** Lautenberg, D-N.J., motion to table (kill) the Brown, R-Colo., amendment to proscribe the effective date of provisions in the Riegle, D-Mich., substitute amendment to exempt municipalities from liability lawsuits under the "superfund" hazardous waste cleanup law, unless such suits were brought by the Environmental Protection Agency. The provisions would be effective upon reauthorization of the superfund law. Motion agreed to 54-42: R 7-34; D 47-8 (ND 36-3, SD 11-5), June 24, 1992.

**130. H J Res 517. Railroad Labor Dispute/30-Day Cooling-Off Period.** Kennedy, D-Mass., motion to table (kill) the Wellstone, D-Minn., amendment to provide a 30-day cooling-off period during which all railroad employees would return to work. At the end of the 30-day period the parties would report to Congress on the progress of further negotiations. Motion agreed to 76-18: R 38-2; D 38-16 (ND 27-12, SD 11-4), June 25, 1992.

**131. H J Res 517. Railroad Labor Dispute/Passage.** Passage of the joint resolution to provide for a 38-day cooling-off and negotiating period for unresolved labor disputes between railroads and railroad employees. If there is no agreement, the parties must submit to an arbitrator their last best offers for rates of pay, rules and working conditions in the form of a contract. If agreement is not reached, the arbitrator will select one offer that will be binding on the parties. The president may reject the arbitrator's decision. Passed (thus clearing for the president) 87-6: R 38-1; D 49-5 (ND 34-5, SD 15-0), June 25, 1992. A "yea" was a vote in support of the president's position.

**132. Procedural Motion.** Mitchell, D-Maine, motion to instruct the sergeant-at-arms to request the attendance of absent senators. Motion agreed to 78-10: R 27-10; D 51-0 (ND 37-0, SD 14-0), June 26, 1992.

**133. S 2733. Government-Sponsored Enterprises/Supermajority for Tax Increases.** Kasten, R-Wis., amendment to the Seymour, R-Calif., amendment, to require a three-fifths majority vote of Congress to raise taxes beyond the rate of growth of national income. Rejected 33-63: R 31-10; D 2-53 (ND 0-39, SD 2-14), June 30, 1992.

**134. S 2733. Government-Sponsored Enterprises/Deficit-Reduction Plan.** Byrd, D-W.Va., amendment to the Seymour, R-Calif., amendment, to substitute for the balanced-budget amendment proposed by the Seymour amendment a statutory requirement that the president propose by this September an actual enforcement plan to balance the budget by fiscal 1998. Rejected 39-57: R 0-41; D 39-16 (ND 31-8, SD 8-8), June 30, 1992.

**135. S 2733. Government-Sponsored Enterprises/Cloture on Balanced-Budget Amendment.** Motion to invoke cloture (thus limiting debate) on the Seymour, R-Calif., amendment to propose a constitutional amendment that would prohibit deficit spending unless a three-fifths majority of both chambers of Congress approved a specific deficit amount or there is a declaration of war or a declaration of national military emergency enacted into law; require the president to submit a balanced budget each fiscal year; and require a three-fifths majority of both chambers of Congress to increase the public debt. Motion rejected 56-39: R 41-0; D 15-39 (ND 8-30, SD 7-9), June 30, 1992. A three-fifths majority of the total Senate (60) is required to invoke cloture.

**136. S 2733. Government-Sponsored Enterprises/Cloture on Balanced Budget Amendment.** Motion to invoke cloture (thus limiting debate) on the Seymour, R-Calif., amendment to propose a constitutional amendment limiting deficit spending and requiring a balanced budget. Motion rejected 56-39: R 41-0; D 15-39 (ND 8-30, SD 7-9), July 1, 1992. A three-fifths majority of the total Senate (60) is required to invoke cloture.

| | 137 | 138 | 139 | 140 | 141 | 142 | 143 | 144 |
|---|---|---|---|---|---|---|---|---|
| **ALABAMA** | | | | | | | | |
| Heflin | Y | Y | Y | Y | Y | Y | Y | Y |
| Shelby | Y | Y | Y | Y | Y | Y | Y | Y |
| **ALASKA** | | | | | | | | |
| *Murkowski* | Y | Y | N | Y | Y | Y | Y | Y |
| *Stevens* | N | Y | N | Y | Y | Y | Y | Y |
| **ARIZONA** | | | | | | | | |
| DeConcini | Y | Y | Y | Y | Y | Y | N | Y |
| *McCain* | N | Y | N | Y | Y | Y | N | Y |
| **ARKANSAS** | | | | | | | | |
| Bumpers | Y | Y | Y | Y | Y | Y | N | Y |
| Pryor | Y | Y | Y | + | Y | Y | Y | Y |
| **CALIFORNIA** | | | | | | | | |
| Cranston | Y | ? | N | N | Y | Y | Y | Y |
| *Seymour* | Y | Y | Y | Y | Y | Y | Y | Y |
| **COLORADO** | | | | | | | | |
| Wirth | Y | Y | N | Y | Y | Y | Y | Y |
| *Brown* | N | Y | N | Y | Y | N | Y | Y |
| **CONNECTICUT** | | | | | | | | |
| Dodd | Y | Y | N | Y | Y | Y | Y | Y |
| Lieberman | Y | Y | Y | Y | Y | Y | Y | Y |
| **DELAWARE** | | | | | | | | |
| Biden | Y | Y | N | Y | Y | Y | Y | Y |
| *Roth* | ? | ? | ? | ? | ? | ? | ? | ? |
| **FLORIDA** | | | | | | | | |
| Graham | Y | Y | N | Y | Y | Y | Y | Y |
| *Mack* | Y | Y | N | Y | N | N | Y | Y |
| **GEORGIA** | | | | | | | | |
| Fowler | Y | Y | Y | Y | Y | Y | N | Y |
| Nunn | Y | Y | N | Y | Y | Y | Y | Y |
| **HAWAII** | | | | | | | | |
| Akaka | Y | Y | N | Y | Y | Y | Y | Y |
| Inouye | Y | Y | N | Y | Y | Y | Y | Y |
| **IDAHO** | | | | | | | | |
| *Craig* | N | Y | Y | Y | Y | N | Y | Y |
| *Symms* | N | Y | Y | Y | Y | N | Y | Y |
| **ILLINOIS** | | | | | | | | |
| Dixon | Y | Y | Y | Y | Y | N | Y | Y |
| Simon | Y | Y | N | Y | Y | Y | Y | Y |
| **INDIANA** | | | | | | | | |
| *Coats* | N | Y | N | Y | Y | Y | Y | Y |
| Lugar | N | Y | N | Y | Y | Y | Y | Y |

| | 137 | 138 | 139 | 140 | 141 | 142 | 143 | 144 |
|---|---|---|---|---|---|---|---|---|
| **IOWA** | | | | | | | | |
| Harkin | Y | Y | N | Y | Y | Y | Y | Y |
| *Grassley* | Y | Y | N | Y | Y | N | Y | Y |
| **KANSAS** | | | | | | | | |
| *Dole* | N | Y | N | Y | Y | Y | Y | Y |
| *Kassebaum* | Y | Y | N | Y | Y | Y | Y | Y |
| **KENTUCKY** | | | | | | | | |
| Ford | Y | Y | Y | Y | Y | Y | Y | Y |
| *McConnell* | Y | Y | N | Y | Y | Y | Y | Y |
| **LOUISIANA** | | | | | | | | |
| Breaux | Y | Y | Y | Y | Y | Y | Y | Y |
| Johnston | Y | Y | N | N | Y | Y | Y | Y |
| **MAINE** | | | | | | | | |
| Mitchell | Y | Y | N | Y | Y | Y | Y | Y |
| *Cohen* | Y | Y | N | Y | Y | Y | Y | Y |
| **MARYLAND** | | | | | | | | |
| Mikulski | Y | Y | Y | Y | Y | Y | N | Y |
| Sarbanes | Y | Y | Y | Y | Y | Y | Y | Y |
| **MASSACHUSETTS** | | | | | | | | |
| Kennedy | Y | Y | N | Y | Y | Y | Y | Y |
| Kerry | Y | Y | N | Y | Y | Y | Y | Y |
| **MICHIGAN** | | | | | | | | |
| Levin | Y | Y | N | Y | Y | Y | Y | Y |
| Riegle | Y | Y | Y | Y | Y | Y | Y | Y |
| **MINNESOTA** | | | | | | | | |
| Wellstone | Y | Y | N | Y | Y | Y | Y | Y |
| *Durenberger* | N | Y | N | Y | Y | Y | Y | Y |
| **MISSISSIPPI** | | | | | | | | |
| Cochran | Y | Y | N | Y | Y | Y | Y | Y |
| *Lott* | Y | Y | N | Y | Y | N | Y | Y |
| **MISSOURI** | | | | | | | | |
| *Bond* | Y | Y | N | Y | Y | Y | Y | Y |
| *Danforth* | Y | Y | N | Y | Y | Y | Y | Y |
| **MONTANA** | | | | | | | | |
| Baucus | Y | Y | N | Y | Y | Y | Y | Y |
| *Burns* | N | Y | N | Y | Y | Y | Y | Y |
| **NEBRASKA** | | | | | | | | |
| Exon | Y | Y | N | Y | Y | Y | Y | Y |
| Kerrey | Y | N | N | Y | Y | Y | Y | Y |
| **NEVADA** | | | | | | | | |
| Bryan | Y | Y | N | Y | Y | Y | Y | Y |
| Reid | Y | Y | Y | Y | Y | Y | Y | Y |

| | 137 | 138 | 139 | 140 | 141 | 142 | 143 | 144 |
|---|---|---|---|---|---|---|---|---|
| **NEW HAMPSHIRE** | | | | | | | | |
| *Rudman* | Y | Y | N | Y | Y | Y | Y | Y |
| *Smith* | N | Y | Y | Y | Y | N | Y | Y |
| **NEW JERSEY** | | | | | | | | |
| Bradley | ? | ? | ? | ? | N | Y | ? | Y |
| Lautenberg | Y | Y | Y | Y | Y | Y | Y | Y |
| **NEW MEXICO** | | | | | | | | |
| Bingaman | Y | Y | N | Y | Y | Y | Y | Y |
| *Domenici* | N | Y | N | Y | Y | Y | Y | Y |
| **NEW YORK** | | | | | | | | |
| Moynihan | Y | Y | N | Y | Y | Y | Y | Y |
| *D'Amato* | Y | Y | Y | Y | Y | N | Y | Y |
| **NORTH CAROLINA** | | | | | | | | |
| Sanford | ? | ? | ? | ? | ? | ? | ? | ? |
| *Helms* | — | ? | + | + | ? | — | ? | ? |
| **NORTH DAKOTA** | | | | | | | | |
| Burdick | Y | Y | N | Y | Y | Y | Y | Y |
| Conrad | Y | Y | N | Y | Y | N | Y | Y |
| **OHIO** | | | | | | | | |
| Glenn | Y | Y | Y | Y | Y | Y | Y | Y |
| Metzenbaum | Y | Y | ? | ? | Y | Y | Y | Y |
| **OKLAHOMA** | | | | | | | | |
| Boren | Y | Y | N | Y | Y | Y | Y | Y |
| *Nickles* | N | Y | Y | Y | Y | N | Y | Y |
| **OREGON** | | | | | | | | |
| *Hatfield* | Y | Y | N | Y | Y | Y | Y | Y |
| *Packwood* | Y | Y | N | Y | Y | Y | Y | Y |
| **PENNSYLVANIA** | | | | | | | | |
| Wofford | Y | Y | Y | Y | Y | Y | Y | Y |
| *Specter* | Y | Y | Y | Y | Y | Y | Y | Y |
| **RHODE ISLAND** | | | | | | | | |
| Pell | Y | Y | N | Y | Y | Y | Y | Y |
| *Chafee* | N | Y | N | Y | N | Y | Y | Y |
| **SOUTH CAROLINA** | | | | | | | | |
| Hollings | Y | Y | Y | Y | Y | N | Y | Y |
| *Thurmond* | N | Y | N | Y | Y | Y | Y | Y |
| **SOUTH DAKOTA** | | | | | | | | |
| Daschle | Y | Y | N | Y | Y | Y | Y | Y |
| *Pressler* | N | Y | Y | Y | Y | N | Y | Y |
| **TENNESSEE** | | | | | | | | |
| Gore | Y | Y | Y | Y | Y | Y | Y | Y |
| Sasser | Y | Y | N | Y | Y | Y | Y | Y |

| | 137 | 138 | 139 | 140 | 141 | 142 | 143 | 144 |
|---|---|---|---|---|---|---|---|---|
| **TEXAS** | | | | | | | | |
| Bentsen | Y | Y | N | Y | Y | Y | Y | Y |
| *Gramm* | N | Y | Y | Y | N | Y | Y | Y |
| **UTAH** | | | | | | | | |
| *Garn* | Y | Y | N | Y | Y | Y | Y | Y |
| *Hatch* | Y | Y | N | Y | Y | Y | Y | Y |
| **VERMONT** | | | | | | | | |
| Leahy | Y | Y | N | Y | Y | N | Y | Y |
| *Jeffords* | Y | N | N | Y | Y | Y | Y | Y |
| **VIRGINIA** | | | | | | | | |
| Robb | Y | Y | N | Y | Y | Y | Y | Y |
| *Warner* | Y | Y | N | Y | Y | Y | Y | ? |
| **WASHINGTON** | | | | | | | | |
| Adams | Y | Y | Y | Y | Y | Y | Y | Y |
| *Gorton* | N | Y | N | Y | Y | Y | Y | Y |
| **WEST VIRGINIA** | | | | | | | | |
| Byrd | Y | Y | Y | Y | Y | Y | Y | Y |
| Rockefeller | Y | Y | N | Y | Y | Y | Y | Y |
| **WISCONSIN** | | | | | | | | |
| Kohl | Y | Y | Y | Y | Y | Y | Y | Y |
| *Kasten* | Y | Y | Y | Y | Y | N | Y | Y |
| **WYOMING** | | | | | | | | |
| *Simpson* | Y | Y | N | Y | Y | Y | Y | Y |
| *Wallop* | N | Y | Y | Y | Y | N | Y | Y |

## KEY

Y Voted for (yea).
# Paired for.
+ Announced for.
N Voted against (nay).
X Paired against.
— Announced against.
P Voted "present."
C Voted "present" to avoid possible conflict of interest.
? Did not vote or otherwise make a position known.

Democrats  *Republicans*

ND Northern Democrats  SD Southern Democrats  Southern states - Ala., Ark., Fla., Ga., Ky., La., Miss., N.C., Okla., S.C., Tenn., Texas, Va.

---

**137. S 2733. Government-Sponsored Enterprises/Passage.** Passage of the bill to create an independent regulatory agency within the Department of Housing and Urban Development to oversee the activities of the Federal National Mortgage Association and Federal Home Loan Mortgage Corporation. Passed 77-19: R 22-19; D 55-0 (ND 39-0, SD 16-0), July 1, 1992. A 'yea' was a vote in support of the president's position.

**138. S 2532. Aid for Former Soviet Republics/Credit Guarantees.** Leahy, D-Vt., amendment to strike the provisions easing the criteria for providing Commodity Credit Corporation guarantees to the republics of the former Soviet Union. Adopted 93-2: R 40-1; D 53-1 (ND 37-1, SD 16-0), July 1, 1992.

**139. S 2532. Aid for Former Soviet Republics/Russian Troops in Baltic States.** Pressler, R-S.D., motion to table (kill) the Pell, D-R.I., amendment to the DeConcini, D-Ariz., amendment, to provide a one-year grace period before imposing provisions of the DeConcini amendment that would suspend U.S. economic aid to Russia until the president certifies that Russia has made significant progress in withdrawing its armed forces from the Baltic States. Motion rejected 35-60: R 11-30; D 24-30 (ND 14-24, SD 10-6), July 1, 1992. A "nay" was a vote in support of the president's position. (The Pell amendment subsequently was adopted by voice vote.)

**140. S 2532. Aid for Former Soviet Republics/Russian Troops in Baltic States.** DeConcini, D-Ariz., amendment to prohibit U.S. economic aid to Russia until the president certifies that Russia has made significant progress in withdrawing its armed forces from the Baltic States. Suspension of the aid would not occur until one year after enactment of the bill. Adopted 92-2: R 41-0; D 51-2 (ND 37-1, SD 14-1), July 1, 1992.

**141. S 2532. Aid for Former Soviet Republics/LTV Sale.** Byrd, D-W.Va., amendment to express the sense of Congress in opposition to the sale of the LTV Aerospace and Defense Co. to any foreign-owned company. Adopted 93-4: R 38-3; D 55-1 (ND 39-1, SD 16-0), July 2, 1992.

**142. S 2532. Aid for Former Soviet Republics/International Monetary Fund.** Lugar, R-Ind., motion to table (kill) the Brown, R-Colo., amendment to limit the use of the United States' quota increase for the International Monetary Fund (IMF) to the United States' proportionate share of funding for new IMF programs for the independent states of the former Soviet Union. Motion agreed to 77-20: R 28-13; D 49-7 (ND 35-5, SD 14-2), July 2, 1992.

**143. S 2532. Aid for Former Soviet Republics/Defense Materials for Baltic States.** Byrd, D-W.Va., amendment to allow the Baltic States to receive non-lethal defense articles. Adopted 96-0: R 41-0; D 55-0 (ND 39-0, SD 16-0), July 2, 1992.

**144. S Res 324. Declassification of Materials Relating to POWs and MIAs.** Adoption of the resolution to express the sense of the Senate that the president should require all agencies to declassify and publicly release all documents, files and other materials pertaining to POWs and MIAs without compromising national security. Adopted 96-0: R 40-0; D 56-0 (ND 40-0, SD 16-0), July 2, 1992.

| | 145 | 146 | 147 | 148 | 149 | 150 | 151 | 152 |
|---|---|---|---|---|---|---|---|---|
| **ALABAMA** | | | | | | | | |
| Heflin | Y | Y | N | N | Y | Y | Y | N |
| Shelby | Y | N | N | N | N | Y | Y | N |
| **ALASKA** | | | | | | | | |
| *Murkowski* | Y | Y | Y | Y | Y | N | Y | - |
| *Stevens* | Y | Y | N | Y | ? | ? | ? | N |
| **ARIZONA** | | | | | | | | |
| DeConcini | Y | N | Y | N | Y | N | Y | N |
| *McCain* | Y | Y | Y | Y | Y | N | Y | ? |
| **ARKANSAS** | | | | | | | | |
| Bumpers | Y | Y | Y | N | N | Y | Y | N |
| Pryor | Y | N | Y | Y | N | Y | Y | N |
| **CALIFORNIA** | | | | | | | | |
| Cranston | Y | Y | Y | Y | Y | Y | Y | Y |
| *Seymour* | Y | N | N | N | ? | Y | Y | N |
| **COLORADO** | | | | | | | | |
| Wirth | Y | Y | Y | Y | ? | Y | Y | ? |
| *Brown* | N | Y | N | Y | Y | N | Y | N |
| **CONNECTICUT** | | | | | | | | |
| Dodd | Y | N | Y | N | Y | Y | Y | N |
| Lieberman | Y | Y | Y | Y | Y | Y | Y | N |
| **DELAWARE** | | | | | | | | |
| Biden | Y | Y | Y | Y | Y | Y | Y | Y |
| *Roth* | ? | ? | ? | ? | ? | ? | ? | N |
| **FLORIDA** | | | | | | | | |
| Graham | Y | N | Y | Y | Y | Y | Y | Y |
| *Mack* | Y | Y | Y | Y | Y | N | N | N |
| **GEORGIA** | | | | | | | | |
| Fowler | Y | N | Y | N | N | Y | Y | ? |
| Nunn | Y | Y | Y | Y | N | Y | Y | N |
| **HAWAII** | | | | | | | | |
| Akaka | Y | Y | Y | Y | Y | Y | Y | Y |
| Inouye | Y | N | Y | Y | Y | Y | Y | ? |
| **IDAHO** | | | | | | | | |
| *Craig* | N | Y | N | N | Y | N | Y | N |
| *Symms* | N | Y | N | Y | ? | X | N | |
| **ILLINOIS** | | | | | | | | |
| Dixon | Y | Y | Y | N | Y | Y | Y | Y |
| Simon | Y | Y | Y | Y | Y | Y | N | Y |
| **INDIANA** | | | | | | | | |
| *Coats* | Y | N | Y | N | Y | N | Y | N |
| *Lugar* | Y | Y | Y | Y | Y | N | Y | N |

| | 145 | 146 | 147 | 148 | 149 | 150 | 151 | 152 |
|---|---|---|---|---|---|---|---|---|
| **IOWA** | | | | | | | | |
| Harkin | Y | N | Y | Y | Y | Y | Y | Y |
| *Grassley* | Y | Y | N | Y | Y | Y | Y | N |
| **KANSAS** | | | | | | | | |
| *Dole* | Y | Y | Y | Y | Y | N | Y | N |
| *Kassebaum* | Y | Y | Y | Y | Y | N | Y | N |
| **KENTUCKY** | | | | | | | | |
| Ford | Y | N | Y | N | N | Y | Y | ? |
| *McConnell* | Y | Y | Y | Y | Y | N | Y | N |
| **LOUISIANA** | | | | | | | | |
| Breaux | Y | N | Y | N | N | Y | Y | N |
| Johnston | Y | Y | Y | Y | Y | Y | Y | N |
| **MAINE** | | | | | | | | |
| Mitchell | Y | N | Y | Y | Y | Y | Y | Y |
| *Cohen* | Y | Y | Y | Y | Y | N | Y | Y |
| **MARYLAND** | | | | | | | | |
| Mikulski | Y | N | N | N | Y | Y | Y | Y |
| Sarbanes | Y | N | Y | Y | Y | Y | Y | Y |
| **MASSACHUSETTS** | | | | | | | | |
| Kennedy | Y | Y | Y | Y | Y | Y | Y | Y |
| Kerry | Y | N | Y | Y | Y | Y | Y | Y |
| **MICHIGAN** | | | | | | | | |
| Levin | Y | Y | Y | Y | Y | N | Y | Y |
| Riegle | Y | N | Y | N | Y | Y | Y | Y |
| **MINNESOTA** | | | | | | | | |
| Wellstone | Y | N | Y | Y | Y | N | Y | N |
| *Durenberger* | Y | Y | N | Y | N | N | Y | N |
| **MISSISSIPPI** | | | | | | | | |
| *Cochran* | Y | Y | Y | Y | Y | N | Y | N |
| *Lott* | Y | Y | N | N | Y | N | Y | N |
| **MISSOURI** | | | | | | | | |
| *Bond* | Y | Y | Y | Y | Y | N | Y | ? |
| *Danforth* | Y | Y | Y | Y | Y | N | Y | N |
| **MONTANA** | | | | | | | | |
| Baucus | Y | Y | Y | Y | Y | Y | Y | N |
| *Burns* | Y | Y | N | Y | N | Y | N | N |
| **NEBRASKA** | | | | | | | | |
| Exon | Y | Y | Y | Y | N | Y | Y | Y |
| Kerrey | Y | Y | Y | Y | N | Y | Y | Y |
| **NEVADA** | | | | | | | | |
| Bryan | Y | N | Y | Y | N | Y | Y | ? |
| Reid | Y | N | Y | Y | N | Y | Y | N |

| | 145 | 146 | 147 | 148 | 149 | 150 | 151 | 152 |
|---|---|---|---|---|---|---|---|---|
| **NEW HAMPSHIRE** | | | | | | | | |
| *Rudman* | Y | Y | Y | Y | Y | N | Y | N |
| *Smith* | Y | Y | N | N | Y | N | Y | N |
| **NEW JERSEY** | | | | | | | | |
| Bradley | Y | N | Y | Y | Y | Y | Y | ? |
| Lautenberg | Y | N | Y | Y | Y | Y | Y | Y |
| **NEW MEXICO** | | | | | | | | |
| Bingaman | Y | Y | Y | Y | N | Y | Y | N |
| *Domenici* | Y | Y | Y | Y | N | N | Y | N |
| **NEW YORK** | | | | | | | | |
| Moynihan | Y | Y | Y | Y | Y | Y | Y | N |
| *D'Amato* | Y | Y | N | Y | Y | N | Y | - |
| **NORTH CAROLINA** | | | | | | | | |
| Sanford | ? | ? | ? | ? | N | Y | Y | ? |
| *Helms* | - | ? | - | - | ? | ? | + | - |
| **NORTH DAKOTA** | | | | | | | | |
| Burdick | Y | Y | Y | Y | ? | ? | ? | ? |
| Conrad | Y | Y | N | Y | N | Y | Y | N |
| **OHIO** | | | | | | | | |
| Glenn | Y | N | Y | N | N | Y | Y | Y |
| Metzenbaum | Y | N | Y | Y | Y | Y | Y | Y |
| **OKLAHOMA** | | | | | | | | |
| Boren | Y | Y | Y | Y | Y | N | Y | N |
| *Nickles* | Y | Y | N | N | N | Y | Y | N |
| **OREGON** | | | | | | | | |
| *Hatfield* | Y | Y | Y | Y | Y | N | Y | N |
| *Packwood* | Y | Y | Y | ? | ? | ? | ? | N |
| **PENNSYLVANIA** | | | | | | | | |
| Wofford | Y | Y | Y | Y | Y | Y | Y | Y |
| *Specter* | Y | N | N | Y | Y | N | Y | ? |
| **RHODE ISLAND** | | | | | | | | |
| Pell | Y | Y | Y | Y | Y | Y | Y | Y |
| *Chafee* | Y | Y | Y | Y | Y | N | Y | N |
| **SOUTH CAROLINA** | | | | | | | | |
| Hollings | Y | N | N | N | Y | Y | Y | N |
| *Thurmond* | Y | Y | N | Y | Y | N | Y | N |
| **SOUTH DAKOTA** | | | | | | | | |
| Daschle | Y | N | Y | Y | Y | Y | Y | Y |
| *Pressler* | Y | Y | N | Y | N | N | Y | N |
| **TENNESSEE** | | | | | | | | |
| Gore | Y | Y | Y | Y | ? | ? | ? | ? |
| Sasser | Y | N | Y | Y | N | Y | Y | N |

| | 145 | 146 | 147 | 148 | 149 | 150 | 151 | 152 |
|---|---|---|---|---|---|---|---|---|

### KEY

| | | |
|---|---|---|
| Y | Voted for (yea). | |
| # | Paired for. | |
| + | Announced for. | |
| N | Voted against (nay). | |
| X | Paired against. | |
| - | Announced against. | |
| P | Voted "present." | |
| C | Voted "present" to avoid possible conflict of interest. | |
| ? | Did not vote or otherwise make a position known. | |

Democrats  *Republicans*

| | 145 | 146 | 147 | 148 | 149 | 150 | 151 | 152 |
|---|---|---|---|---|---|---|---|---|
| **TEXAS** | | | | | | | | |
| Bentsen | Y | Y | Y | Y | ? | Y | Y | Y |
| *Gramm* | Y | Y | Y | Y | Y | N | Y | N |
| **UTAH** | | | | | | | | |
| *Garn* | Y | Y | Y | Y | Y | ? | ? | ? |
| *Hatch* | Y | Y | Y | Y | Y | - | # | N |
| **VERMONT** | | | | | | | | |
| Leahy | Y | Y | Y | Y | Y | Y | Y | Y |
| *Jeffords* | Y | Y | Y | Y | Y | N | Y | Y |
| **VIRGINIA** | | | | | | | | |
| Robb | Y | Y | Y | Y | Y | Y | Y | Y |
| *Warner* | ? | ? | ? | ? | Y | N | Y | N |
| **WASHINGTON** | | | | | | | | |
| Adams | Y | N | Y | Y | Y | Y | Y | Y |
| *Gorton* | Y | Y | Y | Y | Y | N | Y | N |
| **WEST VIRGINIA** | | | | | | | | |
| Byrd | Y | N | Y | N | N | Y | Y | Y |
| Rockefeller | Y | N | Y | N | Y | Y | Y | Y |
| **WISCONSIN** | | | | | | | | |
| Kohl | Y | Y | Y | Y | Y | Y | Y | Y |
| *Kasten* | Y | N | N | Y | N | N | Y | - |
| **WYOMING** | | | | | | | | |
| *Simpson* | Y | Y | Y | Y | Y | N | Y | N |
| *Wallop* | Y | Y | Y | Y | Y | N | Y | N |

ND   Northern Democrats     SD   Southern Democrats          Southern states - Ala., Ark., Fla., Ga., Ky., La., Miss., N.C., Okla., S.C., Tenn., Texas, Va.

**145. HR 5260. Extended Unemployment Benefits/Conference Report.** Adoption of the conference report to provide 20 or 26 weeks of extended unemployment benefits between July 4, 1992, and March 6, 1993, as long as the national unemployment rate stays above 7 percent. After March 6, 1993, states would have the option of using a new 6.5 percent total unemployment rate to trigger 13 weeks of extended benefits. Passed 93-3: R 37-3; D 56-0 (ND 40-0, SD 16-0), July 2, 1992. A "yea" was a vote in support of the president's position.

**146. S 2532. Aid for Former Soviet Republics/Domestic Spending.** Pell, D-R.I., motion to table (kill) the Riegle, D-Mich., amendment to require the president to match about $1 billion in the bill with similar support for domestic programs. Motion agreed to 64-32: R 36-4; D 28-28 (ND 20-20, SD 8-8), July 2, 1992.

**147. S 2532. Aid for Former Soviet Republics/Collateralized Loan System.** Pell, D-R.I., motion to table (kill) the Specter, R-Pa., amendment to establish a collateralized loan system under which, if the president finds that a republic is not properly repaying its loans, then the U.S. would support the use of petroleum or strategic materials as collateral until the International Monetary Fund loans were repaid. Motion agreed to 75-21: R 24-16; D 51-5 (ND 38-2, SD 13-3), July 2, 1992.

**148. S 2532. Aid for Former Soviet Republics/Passage.** Passage of the bill to provide aid to Russia and other former Soviet republics. Passed 76-20: R 33-7; D 43-13 (ND 34-6, SD 9-7), July 2, 1992. A "yea" was a vote in support of the president's position.

**149. S 2877. Interstate Transport of Municipal Waste/Differential Fees.** Baucus, D-Mont., motion to table (kill) the Reid, D-Nev., amendment to grant the governor of a state the authority to prohibit, limit or impose a differential fee on the disposal of out-of-state municipal waste. Motion agreed to 60-31: R 32-6; D 28-25 (ND 23-15, SD 5-10), July 22, 1992.

**150. HR 776. National Energy Policy/Cloture.** Motion to invoke cloture (thus limiting debate) on the motion to proceed to the bill to decrease U.S. energy dependence through increased domestic production and conservation. The bill would ease licensing for natural gas pipelines and nuclear power plants, promote cars that run on non-gasoline fuels, mandate greater energy efficiency, ban certain offshore drilling, provide tax incentives for renewable energy and alternative fuels, and provide tax relief for independent oil and gas drillers. The Senate Finance Committee also added a coal tax to help pay for health benefits for retired miners. Motion rejected 58-33: R 3-33; D 55-0 (ND 39-0, SD 16-0), July 23, 1992. A three-fifths majority of the total Senate (60) is required to invoke cloture.

**151. S 2877. Interstate Transport of Municipal Waste/Passage.** Passage of the bill to allow states to restrict the importation of municipal solid waste across their borders. Passed 89-2: R 35-1; D 54-1 (ND 38-1, SD 16-0), July 23, 1992. A "nay" was a vote in support of the president's position.

**152. S 3026. Fiscal 1993 Commerce, Justice, State, Judiciary Appropriations/Ruling by the Chair.** Judgment of the Senate to affirm the ruling of the chair that the Smith, R-N.H., amendment to repeal the District of Columbia's gun liability law, making manufacturers and distributors liable for crimes committed with semiautomatic firearms in the District, constituted legislation on an appropriations bill and was therefore not in order. Ruling of the chair rejected 32-50: R 2-33; D 30-17 (ND 26-8, SD 4-9), July 27, 1992. (The Smith amendment was subsequently adopted by voice vote.)

| | 153 | 154 | 155 | 156 | 157 | 158 | 159 | 160 |
|---|---|---|---|---|---|---|---|---|
| **ALABAMA** | | | | | | | | |
| Heflin | N | Y | Y | Y | Y | Y | Y | N |
| Shelby | Y | Y | Y | Y | Y | Y | Y | N |
| **ALASKA** | | | | | | | | |
| *Murkowski* | Y | Y | Y | Y | N | Y | Y | Y |
| *Stevens* | N | Y | Y | Y | Y | Y | Y | Y |
| **ARIZONA** | | | | | | | | |
| DeConcini | N | Y | Y | Y | Y | Y | N | N |
| *McCain* | Y | Y | N | Y | N | Y | Y | Y |
| **ARKANSAS** | | | | | | | | |
| Bumpers | N | Y | Y | Y | Y | Y | Y | N |
| Pryor | Y | Y | P | Y | Y | Y | Y | N |
| **CALIFORNIA** | | | | | | | | |
| Cranston | N | Y | N | Y | Y | Y | ? | ? |
| *Seymour* | Y | Y | N | Y | Y | Y | Y | Y |
| **COLORADO** | | | | | | | | |
| Wirth | Y | Y | N | N | N | N | Y | N |
| *Brown* | Y | Y | N | N | N | N | Y | Y |
| **CONNECTICUT** | | | | | | | | |
| Dodd | N | N | N | N | N | Y | N | N |
| Lieberman | N | N | N | N | N | Y | N | N |
| **DELAWARE** | | | | | | | | |
| Biden | N | Y | N | Y | N | Y | N | N |
| *Roth* | Y | Y | N | Y | Y | N | N | Y |
| **FLORIDA** | | | | | | | | |
| Graham | Y | Y | N | Y | Y | Y | Y | N |
| *Mack* | ? | ? | ? | Y | Y | Y | Y | Y |
| **GEORGIA** | | | | | | | | |
| Fowler | Y | Y | N | Y | Y | Y | N | N |
| Nunn | Y | Y | Y | Y | N | Y | N | N |
| **HAWAII** | | | | | | | | |
| Akaka | N | Y | Y | N | Y | Y | Y | N |
| Inouye | N | Y | Y | Y | Y | Y | Y | N |
| **IDAHO** | | | | | | | | |
| *Craig* | Y | Y | Y | Y | Y | Y | Y | Y |
| *Symms* | Y | Y | Y | Y | Y | N | Y | Y |
| **ILLINOIS** | | | | | | | | |
| Dixon | ? | Y | N | Y | Y | Y | Y | N |
| Simon | Y | Y | N | N | Y | Y | Y | N |
| **INDIANA** | | | | | | | | |
| *Coats* | Y | Y | N | Y | N | Y | Y | Y |
| *Lugar* | Y | Y | N | Y | N | Y | Y | Y |

| | 153 | 154 | 155 | 156 | 157 | 158 | 159 | 160 |
|---|---|---|---|---|---|---|---|---|
| **IOWA** | | | | | | | | |
| Harkin | Y | Y | N | Y | Y | Y | N | N |
| *Grassley* | Y | Y | N | Y | Y | Y | Y | Y |
| **KANSAS** | | | | | | | | |
| *Dole* | N | Y | Y | Y | Y | Y | Y | Y |
| *Kassebaum* | Y | Y | Y | Y | Y | Y | Y | N |
| **KENTUCKY** | | | | | | | | |
| Ford | Y | Y | Y | Y | Y | Y | Y | N |
| *McConnell* | Y | Y | Y | Y | N | Y | Y | Y |
| **LOUISIANA** | | | | | | | | |
| Breaux | N | Y | Y | Y | Y | Y | ? | ? |
| Johnston | N | Y | Y | Y | Y | Y | Y | N |
| **MAINE** | | | | | | | | |
| Mitchell | N | N | Y | N | Y | Y | N | N |
| *Cohen* | N | Y | N | N | N | Y | N | Y |
| **MARYLAND** | | | | | | | | |
| Mikulski | Y | Y | Y | N | Y | Y | N | N |
| Sarbanes | N | Y | Y | N | Y | Y | N | N |
| **MASSACHUSETTS** | | | | | | | | |
| Kennedy | N | Y | Y | Y | Y | Y | Y | N |
| Kerry | ? | Y | N | N | N | Y | N | N |
| **MICHIGAN** | | | | | | | | |
| Levin | Y | Y | N | Y | N | Y | N | N |
| Riegle | N | Y | Y | Y | Y | Y | Y | N |
| **MINNESOTA** | | | | | | | | |
| Wellstone | Y | Y | Y | Y | Y | Y | N | N |
| *Durenberger* | Y | N | Y | Y | Y | Y | N | Y |
| **MISSISSIPPI** | | | | | | | | |
| *Cochran* | N | Y | Y | Y | Y | Y | Y | N |
| *Lott* | Y | Y | Y | Y | Y | Y | Y | Y |
| **MISSOURI** | | | | | | | | |
| *Bond* | Y | Y | Y | Y | Y | Y | Y | Y |
| *Danforth* | Y | Y | N | Y | Y | Y | Y | Y |
| **MONTANA** | | | | | | | | |
| Baucus | N | Y | Y | Y | Y | Y | Y | N |
| *Burns* | Y | Y | Y | Y | Y | Y | Y | N |
| **NEBRASKA** | | | | | | | | |
| Exon | N | Y | Y | Y | Y | Y | Y | N |
| Kerrey | Y | Y | N | Y | Y | Y | Y | N |
| **NEVADA** | | | | | | | | |
| Bryan | Y | Y | N | N | N | N | N | N |
| Reid | Y | Y | Y | N | N | Y | N | N |

| | 153 | 154 | 155 | 156 | 157 | 158 | 159 | 160 |
|---|---|---|---|---|---|---|---|---|
| **NEW HAMPSHIRE** | | | | | | | | |
| *Rudman* | N | Y | Y | N | N | N | N | Y |
| *Smith* | Y | N | N | N | N | N | N | Y |
| **NEW JERSEY** | | | | | | | | |
| Bradley | ? | Y | N | N | N | Y | N | N |
| Lautenberg | N | Y | N | N | N | Y | N | N |
| **NEW MEXICO** | | | | | | | | |
| Bingaman | Y | Y | N | N | Y | Y | Y | N |
| *Domenici* | N | Y | Y | Y | N | Y | Y | Y |
| **NEW YORK** | | | | | | | | |
| Moynihan | N | Y | N | N | N | Y | Y | N |
| *D'Amato* | ? | Y | N | Y | N | Y | Y | Y |
| **NORTH CAROLINA** | | | | | | | | |
| Sanford | Y | Y | Y | Y | Y | Y | Y | N |
| *Helms* | + | + | + | ? | — | ? | + | + |
| **NORTH DAKOTA** | | | | | | | | |
| Burdick | ? | ? | ? | ? | ? | ? | ? | ? |
| Conrad | Y | Y | Y | Y | Y | Y | Y | Y |
| **OHIO** | | | | | | | | |
| Glenn | Y | Y | N | Y | N | Y | Y | N |
| Metzenbaum | Y | Y | N | N | N | N | N | N |
| **OKLAHOMA** | | | | | | | | |
| Boren | Y | Y | Y | Y | Y | Y | Y | N |
| *Nickles* | Y | Y | N | Y | N | Y | Y | Y |
| **OREGON** | | | | | | | | |
| *Hatfield* | N | Y | Y | Y | Y | Y | Y | Y |
| *Packwood* | N | Y | Y | Y | N | Y | N | N |
| **PENNSYLVANIA** | | | | | | | | |
| Wofford | Y | Y | N | Y | N | Y | Y | N |
| *Specter* | Y | Y | Y | Y | N | Y | Y | Y |
| **RHODE ISLAND** | | | | | | | | |
| Pell | N | N | Y | N | N | Y | N | N |
| *Chafee* | N | Y | N | Y | N | Y | Y | Y |
| **SOUTH CAROLINA** | | | | | | | | |
| Hollings | N | Y | Y | Y | N | Y | N | N |
| *Thurmond* | N | Y | Y | Y | Y | Y | Y | N |
| **SOUTH DAKOTA** | | | | | | | | |
| Daschle | Y | Y | Y | Y | Y | Y | Y | N |
| *Pressler* | Y | Y | Y | Y | Y | Y | Y | Y |
| **TENNESSEE** | | | | | | | | |
| Gore | ? | ? | ? | ? | ? | ? | ? | ? |
| Sasser | Y | Y | Y | Y | Y | Y | N | N |

| | 153 | 154 | 155 | 156 | 157 | 158 | 159 | 160 |
|---|---|---|---|---|---|---|---|---|
| **TEXAS** | | | | | | | | |
| Bentsen | N | Y | N | Y | Y | Y | Y | N |
| *Gramm* | N | Y | Y | Y | Y | Y | Y | Y |
| **UTAH** | | | | | | | | |
| *Garn* | N | Y | Y | Y | N | N | Y | Y |
| *Hatch* | Y | Y | Y | Y | Y | Y | Y | Y |
| **VERMONT** | | | | | | | | |
| Leahy | N | Y | Y | N | N | Y | N | N |
| *Jeffords* | N | N | Y | Y | Y | Y | N | Y |
| **VIRGINIA** | | | | | | | | |
| Robb | Y | Y | N | Y | N | Y | Y | Y |
| *Warner* | N | Y | N | Y | N | Y | Y | Y |
| **WASHINGTON** | | | | | | | | |
| Adams | N | Y | Y | Y | N | Y | N | N |
| *Gorton* | N | Y | Y | Y | N | Y | Y | Y |
| **WEST VIRGINIA** | | | | | | | | |
| Byrd | N | Y | Y | N | Y | Y | N | N |
| Rockefeller | N | Y | N | N | Y | Y | Y | N |
| **WISCONSIN** | | | | | | | | |
| Kohl | Y | Y | N | N | Y | Y | N | N |
| *Kasten* | Y | Y | Y | Y | N | Y | N | Y |
| **WYOMING** | | | | | | | | |
| *Simpson* | N | Y | N | Y | Y | Y | Y | N |
| *Wallop* | Y | Y | Y | Y | Y | N | Y | N |

ND   Northern Democrats      SD   Southern Democrats      Southern states - Ala., Ark., Fla., Ga., Ky., La., Miss., N.C., Okla., S.C., Tenn., Texas, Va.

**153. S 3026. Fiscal 1993 Commerce, Justice, State Appropriations/Overhead Spending.** Graham, D-Fla., amendment to reduce overhead spending for fiscal 1993 from $32,654,000 to $31,280,000, the fiscal 1992 level. Adopted 50-42: R 24-16; D 26-26 (ND 16-20, SD 10-6), July 28, 1992.

**154. HR 776. National Energy Policy/Cloture.** Mitchell, D-Maine, motion to invoke cloture (thus limiting debate) on the motion to proceed to the bill to decrease U.S. energy dependence through increased domestic production and conservation. The bill would ease licensing for natural gas pipelines and nuclear power plants, promote cars that run on non-gasoline fuels, mandate greater energy efficiency, ban certain offshore drilling and provide tax incentives for alternative fuels. The bill also contains a coal tax to help pay for health benefits for retired miners. Motion agreed to 93-3: R 38-3; D 55-0 (ND 39-0, SD 16-0), July 28, 1992. A three-fifths majority of the total Senate (60) is required to invoke cloture.

**155. HR 5487. Fiscal 1993 Agriculture Appropriations/Rural Electrification Administration.** Cochran, R-Miss., motion to table (kill) the Graham, D-Fla., amendment to cut funding for the Rural Electrification Administration. Motion agreed to 54-41: R 25-16; D 29-25 (ND 18-21, SD 11-4), July 28, 1992.

**156. HR 5487. Fiscal 1993 Agriculture Appropriations/Market Promotion Program.** Bumpers, D-Ark., motion to table (kill) the Bryan, D-Nev., amendment to reduce funding for the Market Promotion Program by $95.7 million to a level of $75 million. The Market Promotion Program is designed to encourage the development, maintenance and expansion of the export of U.S. agricultural products. Motion agreed to 74-23: R 38-4; D 36-19 (ND 20-19, SD 16-0), July 28, 1992. A "yea" was a vote in support of the president's position.

**157. HR 5487. Fiscal 1993 Agriculture Appropriations/Honey Price.** Daschle, D-S.D., motion to table (kill) the Brown, R-Colo., amendment to prohibit the use of funds to support the price of honey. Motion agreed to 56-41: R 21-21; D 35-20 (ND 22-17, SD 13-3), July 28, 1992.

**158. HR 5487. Fiscal 1993 Agriculture Appropriations/Passage.** Passage of the bill to provide $61,398,732,000 in new budget authority for agriculture, rural development, the Food and Drug Administration and related agencies in fiscal 1993 and for other purposes. The administration requested $60,381,222,000. Passed 88-9: R 35-7; D 53-2 (ND 37-2, SD 16-0), July 28, 1992.

**159. HR 776. National Energy Policy/Taxes.** Bentsen, D-Texas, motion to table (kill) the Bradley, D-N.J., amendment to strike the provisions of the bill providing a tax break for independent oil and gas producers by allowing them to calculate their alternative minimum tax without including the benefit of two specific tax breaks. Motion agreed to 63-32: R 35-7; D 28-25 (ND 16-22, SD 12-3), July 29, 1992.

**160. HR 776. National Energy Policy/Budget Act Waiver.** Specter, R-Pa., motion to waive the budget act with respect to the Bentsen, D-Texas, point of order against the Specter amendment to increase the access and affordability of health care for violating Section 311 of the 1974 Congressional Budget Act which prohibits consideration of legislation that would result in revenues falling below the revenue floor contained in the most recent budget resolution. Motion rejected 35-60: R 35-7; D 0-53 (ND 0-38, SD 0-15), July 29, 1992. (A three-fifths majority (60) of the total Senate is required to waive the budget act. Subsequently the chair upheld the Bentsen point of order, and the Specter amendment fell.)

## KEY

Y Voted for (yea).
\# Paired for.
\+ Announced for.
N Voted against (nay).
X Paired against.
— Announced against.
P Voted "present."
C Voted "present" to avoid possible conflict of interest.
? Did not vote or otherwise make a position known.

**Democrats** *Republicans*

| | 161 | 162 | 163 | 164 | 165 | 166 | 167 | 168 |
|---|---|---|---|---|---|---|---|---|
| **ALABAMA** | | | | | | | | |
| Heflin | Y | Y | Y | Y | N | Y | Y | Y |
| Shelby | Y | Y | Y | Y | N | Y | Y | Y |
| **ALASKA** | | | | | | | | |
| *Murkowski* | N | N | Y | Y | N | Y | Y | Y |
| *Stevens* | N | Y | Y | Y | N | Y | Y | Y |
| **ARIZONA** | | | | | | | | |
| DeConcini | Y | Y | Y | Y | N | Y | Y | Y |
| *McCain* | Y | N | Y | Y | N | Y | N | Y |
| **ARKANSAS** | | | | | | | | |
| Bumpers | Y | Y | Y | Y | N | N | N | Y |
| Pryor | Y | Y | Y | Y | N | N | Y | N |
| **CALIFORNIA** | | | | | | | | |
| Cranston | ? | ? | Y | N | Y | Y | Y | Y |
| *Seymour* | Y | Y | Y | Y | ? | + | ? | ? |
| **COLORADO** | | | | | | | | |
| Wirth | N | Y | Y | N | Y | N | Y | Y |
| *Brown* | N | Y | Y | Y | N | Y | N | Y |
| **CONNECTICUT** | | | | | | | | |
| Dodd | Y | Y | Y | N | Y | N | Y | N |
| Lieberman | Y | Y | Y | N | Y | N | Y | N |
| **DELAWARE** | | | | | | | | |
| Biden | Y | Y | Y | N | Y | N | Y | N |
| *Roth* | N | Y | Y | Y | N | Y | N | Y |
| **FLORIDA** | | | | | | | | |
| Graham | N | Y | Y | Y | Y | N | Y | Y |
| *Mack* | N | Y | Y | N | N | Y | N | Y |
| **GEORGIA** | | | | | | | | |
| Fowler | N | N | Y | Y | N | N | N | N |
| Nunn | N | Y | Y | Y | N | N | Y | N |
| **HAWAII** | | | | | | | | |
| Akaka | Y | Y | Y | N | Y | Y | Y | Y |
| Inouye | Y | Y | Y | Y | N | Y | Y | Y |
| **IDAHO** | | | | | | | | |
| *Craig* | N | Y | Y | Y | N | Y | N | Y |
| *Symms* | N | ? | ? | ? | ? | Y | N | Y |
| **ILLINOIS** | | | | | | | | |
| Dixon | Y | Y | Y | Y | N | + | + | ? |
| Simon | N | Y | Y | N | Y | Y | Y | Y |
| **INDIANA** | | | | | | | | |
| *Coats* | N | Y | Y | Y | N | N | N | Y |
| *Lugar* | Y | Y | Y | N | N | Y | N | Y |
| **IOWA** | | | | | | | | |
| Harkin | N | Y | Y | N | Y | N | Y | N |
| *Grassley* | N | Y | Y | Y | N | Y | Y | N |
| **KANSAS** | | | | | | | | |
| *Dole* | N | Y | Y | N | Y | N | Y | Y |
| *Kassebaum* | N | Y | Y | N | N | N | Y | N |
| **KENTUCKY** | | | | | | | | |
| Ford | Y | Y | Y | Y | N | Y | Y | Y |
| *McConnell* | N | N | Y | N | Y | Y | Y | Y |
| **LOUISIANA** | | | | | | | | |
| Breaux | ? | N | Y | N | Y | Y | Y | Y |
| Johnston | Y | Y | Y | Y | N | Y | Y | Y |
| **MAINE** | | | | | | | | |
| Mitchell | N | Y | Y | N | Y | N | Y | N |
| *Cohen* | N | Y | Y | N | Y | N | N | N |
| **MARYLAND** | | | | | | | | |
| Mikulski | N | Y | Y | N | ? | Y | Y | Y |
| Sarbanes | Y | Y | Y | N | Y | Y | Y | Y |
| **MASSACHUSETTS** | | | | | | | | |
| Kennedy | Y | Y | Y | N | Y | N | Y | N |
| Kerry | N | Y | Y | N | Y | N | Y | N |
| **MICHIGAN** | | | | | | | | |
| Levin | Y | Y | Y | N | Y | N | Y | N |
| Riegle | N | Y | Y | N | Y | N | Y | N |
| **MINNESOTA** | | | | | | | | |
| Wellstone | Y | Y | N | N | Y | N | Y | N |
| *Durenberger* | N | Y | N | N | N | N | N | Y |
| **MISSISSIPPI** | | | | | | | | |
| *Cochran* | N | Y | Y | N | Y | N | Y | N |
| *Lott* | N | N | Y | Y | N | Y | N | Y |
| **MISSOURI** | | | | | | | | |
| *Bond* | Y | Y | Y | N | N | Y | N | Y |
| *Danforth* | N | Y | Y | N | N | Y | Y | Y |
| **MONTANA** | | | | | | | | |
| Baucus | Y | Y | Y | N | Y | N | Y | Y |
| *Burns* | N | Y | Y | Y | N | Y | N | Y |
| **NEBRASKA** | | | | | | | | |
| Exon | N | Y | Y | Y | N | N | N | N |
| Kerrey | N | Y | Y | N | Y | Y | Y | Y |
| **NEVADA** | | | | | | | | |
| Bryan | N | Y | Y | Y | N | N | N | N |
| Reid | N | Y | Y | Y | N | Y | N | Y |
| **NEW HAMPSHIRE** | | | | | | | | |
| *Rudman* | N | Y | Y | Y | Y | Y | N | ? |
| *Smith* | Y | N | N | Y | N | N | N | N |
| **NEW JERSEY** | | | | | | | | |
| Bradley | Y | Y | Y | N | Y | N | Y | N |
| Lautenberg | Y | Y | Y | N | Y | N | Y | N |
| **NEW MEXICO** | | | | | | | | |
| Bingaman | N | Y | Y | N | Y | N | Y | Y |
| *Domenici* | N | Y | Y | Y | N | Y | N | Y |
| **NEW YORK** | | | | | | | | |
| Moynihan | N | Y | Y | N | Y | N | Y | N |
| *D'Amato* | N | Y | Y | Y | Y | Y | Y | Y |
| **NORTH CAROLINA** | | | | | | | | |
| Sanford | Y | Y | Y | N | Y | N | Y | Y |
| *Helms* | — | ? | ? | + | — | ? | ? | ? |
| **NORTH DAKOTA** | | | | | | | | |
| Burdick | ? | ? | ? | ? | ? | ? | ? | ? |
| Conrad | N | Y | Y | Y | ? | N | Y | N |
| **OHIO** | | | | | | | | |
| Glenn | Y | Y | Y | N | Y | Y | Y | Y |
| Metzenbaum | Y | Y | Y | N | Y | N | Y | N |
| **OKLAHOMA** | | | | | | | | |
| Boren | Y | Y | Y | Y | N | Y | Y | Y |
| *Nickles* | N | Y | Y | N | Y | N | Y | N |
| **OREGON** | | | | | | | | |
| *Hatfield* | Y | Y | Y | N | Y | Y | Y | Y |
| *Packwood* | Y | Y | Y | N | Y | Y | Y | Y |
| **PENNSYLVANIA** | | | | | | | | |
| Wofford | N | Y | Y | N | Y | N | Y | Y |
| *Specter* | N | Y | Y | Y | Y | Y | Y | Y |
| **RHODE ISLAND** | | | | | | | | |
| Pell | N | Y | Y | N | Y | Y | Y | Y |
| *Chafee* | N | Y | Y | N | Y | Y | Y | Y |
| **SOUTH CAROLINA** | | | | | | | | |
| Hollings | Y | Y | Y | Y | N | N | N | N |
| *Thurmond* | N | Y | Y | Y | N | Y | N | Y |
| **SOUTH DAKOTA** | | | | | | | | |
| Daschle | N | Y | Y | N | N | Y | Y | Y |
| *Pressler* | N | Y | Y | N | Y | Y | Y | N |
| **TENNESSEE** | | | | | | | | |
| Gore | ? | ? | Y | ? | ? | ? | ? | ? |
| Sasser | Y | Y | Y | N | N | N | Y | N |
| **TEXAS** | | | | | | | | |
| Bentsen | Y | Y | Y | Y | N | Y | Y | Y |
| *Gramm* | Y | N | Y | Y | N | Y | N | Y |
| **UTAH** | | | | | | | | |
| *Garn* | N | N | Y | N | Y | N | Y | N |
| *Hatch* | N | Y | Y | Y | N | + | — | + |
| **VERMONT** | | | | | | | | |
| Leahy | Y | Y | Y | N | Y | N | Y | N |
| *Jeffords* | N | ? | ? | ? | ? | N | Y | N |
| **VIRGINIA** | | | | | | | | |
| Robb | N | Y | Y | N | Y | Y | Y | Y |
| *Warner* | N | Y | Y | N | Y | N | N | N |
| **WASHINGTON** | | | | | | | | |
| Adams | N | Y | Y | N | Y | N | Y | Y |
| *Gorton* | N | Y | Y | N | Y | N | Y | N |
| **WEST VIRGINIA** | | | | | | | | |
| Byrd | Y | Y | Y | N | Y | N | Y | Y |
| Rockefeller | Y | Y | Y | N | Y | Y | Y | Y |
| **WISCONSIN** | | | | | | | | |
| Kohl | N | Y | Y | N | Y | N | Y | N |
| *Kasten* | N | N | Y | N | Y | N | Y | N |
| **WYOMING** | | | | | | | | |
| *Simpson* | Y | Y | Y | N | Y | N | Y | N |
| *Wallop* | Y | Y | Y | N | Y | N | Y | N |

ND Northern Democrats    SD Southern Democrats

Southern states - Ala., Ark., Fla., Ga., Ky., La., Miss., N.C., Okla., S.C., Tenn., Texas, Va.

**161. HR 776. National Energy Policy/Tax-Exempt Bonds.** Johnston, D-La., motion to table (kill) the Symms, R-Idaho, amendment to remove certain high-speed intercity rail facility bonds from the state volume cap for tax-exempt bond financing. Motion rejected 40-55: R 10-32; D 30-23 (ND 19-19, SD 11-4), July 29, 1992. (The Symms amendment was subsequently adopted by voice vote.)

**162. Procedural Motion.** Mitchell, D-Maine, motion to instruct the sergeant at arms to request the attendance of absent senators. Motion agreed to 84-10: R 32-8; D 52-2 (ND 38-0, SD 14-2), July 30, 1992.

**163. HR 776. National Energy Policy/Passage.** Passage of the bill to decrease U.S. energy dependence through increased domestic production and conservation. The bill would ease licensing for natural gas pipelines and nuclear power plants, promote cars that run on non-gasoline fuels, mandate greater energy efficiency, ban certain offshore drilling, provide tax incentives for renewable energy and alternative fuels, and provide tax relief for independent oil and gas drillers. Passed 93-3: R 38-2; D 55-1 (ND 38-1, SD 17-0), July 30, 1992. A "yea" was a vote in support of the president's position.

**164. HR 5517. Fiscal 1993 District of Columbia Appropriations.** Shelby, D-Ala., motion to table (kill) the Adams, D-Wash., amendment to the Shelby amendment, to place the provisions of the Shelby amendment on the ballot at the next District of Columbia general, special or primary election held at least 90 days after enactment of the bill. The Shelby amendment would provide for a federal death penalty for first-degree murders in the District of Columbia. Motion agreed to 50-45: R 29-11; D 21-34 (ND 9-30, SD 12-4), July 30, 1992.

**165. HR 5517. Fiscal 1993 District of Columbia Appropriations.** Adams, D-Wash., motion to table (kill) the Lott, R-Miss., amendment to prohibit the District of Columbia from using any funds in the bill to extend employment, health or governmental benefits to homosexual or heterosexual couples on the same basis that such benefits are extended to legally married couples. Motion rejected 41-51: R 8-31; D 33-20 (ND 28-9, SD 5-11), July 30, 1992.

**166. HR 5373. Fiscal 1993 Energy and Water Development Appropriations/Superconducting Super Collider.** Johnston, D-La., motion to table (kill) the Bumpers, D-Ark., amendment to terminate the superconducting super collider by cutting $516 million of the $550 million provided for the project. Motion agreed to 62-32: R 32-8; D 30-24 (ND 21-17, SD 9-7), Aug. 3, 1992. A "yea" was a vote in support of the president's position.

**167. HR 5373. Fiscal 1993 Energy and Water Development Appropriations/Nuclear Test Ban.** Hatfield, R-Ore., amendment to put a moratorium on U.S. nuclear tests until July 1993 unless a former republic of the Soviet Union conducts a nuclear test; require reports to Congress on plans for a comprehensive test ban by Sept. 30, 1996; and ban nuclear testing after Sept. 30, 1996, unless a former Soviet republic conducts a nuclear test. Adopted 68-26: R 17-23; D 51-3 (ND 36-2, SD 15-1), Aug. 3, 1992. A "nay" was a vote in support of the president's position.

**168. HR 5373. Fiscal 1993 Energy and Water Development Appropriations/Superconducting Super Collider.** Johnston, D-La., motion to table (kill) the Bumpers, D-Ark., amendment to prohibit funding for the superconducting super collider after June 1, 1993, unless the president certifies that the foreign contributions for the project meet or exceed $650 million in fiscal 1993, 1994 and 1995. Motion agreed to 62-31: R 30-9; D 32-22 (ND 22-16, SD 10-6), Aug. 3, 1992.

### KEY

Y Voted for (yea).
\# Paired for.
\+ Announced for.
N Voted against (nay).
X Paired against.
− Announced against.
P Voted "present."
C Voted "present" to avoid possible conflict of interest.
? Did not vote or otherwise make a position known.

Democrats    *Republicans*

| | 169 | 170 | 171 | 172 | 173 | 174 | 175 | 176 |
|---|---|---|---|---|---|---|---|---|
| **ALABAMA** | | | | | | | | |
| Heflin | Y | Y | N | N | Y | N | N | N |
| Shelby | Y | Y | Y | N | Y | N | N | N |
| **ALASKA** | | | | | | | | |
| *Murkowski* | Y | N | Y | N | Y | N | Y | N |
| *Stevens* | Y | N | Y | N | Y | Y | Y | N |
| **ARIZONA** | | | | | | | | |
| DeConcini | Y | Y | Y | N | ? | N | N | Y |
| *McCain* | Y | Y | N | N | Y | Y | N | N |
| **ARKANSAS** | | | | | | | | |
| Bumpers | Y | Y | Y | Y | Y | Y | N | Y |
| Pryor | Y | Y | Y | Y | Y | Y | N | Y |
| **CALIFORNIA** | | | | | | | | |
| Cranston | Y | Y | Y | Y | N | N | Y | Y |
| *Seymour* | Y | Y | Y | N | Y | Y | N | N |
| **COLORADO** | | | | | | | | |
| Wirth | Y | N | Y | N | N | N | Y | Y |
| *Brown* | Y | N | N | N | Y | Y | N | N |
| **CONNECTICUT** | | | | | | | | |
| Dodd | Y | N | Y | N | Y | N | N | Y |
| Lieberman | Y | N | Y | N | Y | N | N | Y |
| **DELAWARE** | | | | | | | | |
| Biden | ? | N | Y | Y | N | N | Y | Y |
| *Roth* | Y | N | N | Y | N | N | Y | Y |
| **FLORIDA** | | | | | | | | |
| Graham | Y | Y | N | N | N | N | Y | Y |
| *Mack* | Y | Y | N | N | Y | Y | N | N |
| **GEORGIA** | | | | | | | | |
| Fowler | Y | Y | Y | N | N | N | Y | Y |
| Nunn | Y | Y | N | N | N | N | Y | Y |
| **HAWAII** | | | | | | | | |
| Akaka | Y | N | Y | N | N | N | Y | Y |
| Inouye | Y | N | Y | N | N | N | Y | Y |
| **IDAHO** | | | | | | | | |
| *Craig* | Y | N | Y | N | Y | Y | Y | N |
| *Symms* | Y | N | Y | N | Y | Y | Y | N |
| **ILLINOIS** | | | | | | | | |
| Dixon | Y | N | Y | N | N | N | Y | Y |
| Simon | Y | N | Y | Y | N | N | Y | Y |
| **INDIANA** | | | | | | | | |
| *Coats* | Y | Y | N | N | Y | N | N | N |
| *Lugar* | Y | Y | N | N | Y | N | N | N |
| **IOWA** | | | | | | | | |
| Harkin | Y | N | Y | Y | ? | ? | ? | ? |
| *Grassley* | Y | N | Y | N | Y | N | N | Y |
| **KANSAS** | | | | | | | | |
| *Dole* | Y | Y | N | Y | N | Y | N | N |
| *Kassebaum* | ? | Y | Y | N | Y | N | N | N |
| **KENTUCKY** | | | | | | | | |
| Ford | Y | Y | Y | N | N | Y | N | Y |
| *McConnell* | Y | Y | Y | N | Y | Y | N | N |
| **LOUISIANA** | | | | | | | | |
| Breaux | ? | N | Y | N | N | N | N | Y |
| Johnston | Y | N | Y | Y | Y | Y | N | Y |
| **MAINE** | | | | | | | | |
| Mitchell | Y | N | Y | Y | N | N | Y | Y |
| *Cohen* | Y | N | Y | Y | N | N | N | Y |
| **MARYLAND** | | | | | | | | |
| Mikulski | Y | N | Y | N | Y | N | N | Y |
| Sarbanes | Y | N | Y | Y | N | N | Y | Y |
| **MASSACHUSETTS** | | | | | | | | |
| Kennedy | Y | N | Y | Y | N | N | Y | Y |
| Kerry | Y | N | Y | Y | N | N | Y | Y |
| **MICHIGAN** | | | | | | | | |
| Levin | Y | Y | N | Y | N | Y | N | Y |
| Riegle | Y | Y | Y | Y | Y | N | Y | Y |
| **MINNESOTA** | | | | | | | | |
| Wellstone | Y | N | Y | Y | N | N | Y | Y |
| *Durenberger* | Y | Y | Y | N | Y | Y | N | Y |
| **MISSISSIPPI** | | | | | | | | |
| *Cochran* | Y | Y | Y | N | Y | Y | N | N |
| *Lott* | Y | Y | Y | N | Y | Y | N | N |
| **MISSOURI** | | | | | | | | |
| *Bond* | ? | Y | N | N | Y | N | Y | N |
| *Danforth* | Y | Y | N | N | Y | Y | N | N |
| **MONTANA** | | | | | | | | |
| Baucus | Y | N | Y | N | Y | N | N | Y |
| *Burns* | Y | N | Y | N | Y | N | N | N |
| **NEBRASKA** | | | | | | | | |
| Exon | ? | N | Y | N | N | Y | N | N |
| Kerrey | Y | N | Y | N | Y | N | N | Y |
| **NEVADA** | | | | | | | | |
| Bryan | Y | N | Y | N | N | N | Y | Y |
| Reid | Y | N | Y | N | N | N | Y | Y |
| **NEW HAMPSHIRE** | | | | | | | | |
| *Rudman* | Y | N | Y | N | Y | Y | N | N |
| *Smith* | Y | N | N | N | N | Y | N | N |
| **NEW JERSEY** | | | | | | | | |
| Bradley | Y | N | Y | Y | N | N | Y | Y |
| Lautenberg | Y | N | Y | N | N | Y | Y | Y |
| **NEW MEXICO** | | | | | | | | |
| Bingaman | Y | N | N | N | N | N | N | Y |
| *Domenici* | Y | N | Y | N | Y | Y | N | N |
| **NEW YORK** | | | | | | | | |
| Moynihan | Y | N | Y | Y | N | N | Y | Y |
| *D'Amato* | Y | N | Y | N | Y | N | Y | N |
| **NORTH CAROLINA** | | | | | | | | |
| Sanford | Y | Y | Y | Y | Y | N | Y | Y |
| *Helms* | + | # | X | ? | ? | + | − | − |
| **NORTH DAKOTA** | | | | | | | | |
| Burdick | ? | ? | ? | ? | ? | ? | ? | ? |
| Conrad | ? | N | Y | N | N | N | N | Y |
| **OHIO** | | | | | | | | |
| Glenn | Y | Y | Y | Y | N | N | Y | Y |
| Metzenbaum | Y | Y | Y | Y | N | N | Y | Y |
| **OKLAHOMA** | | | | | | | | |
| Boren | Y | Y | N | N | N | N | Y | Y |
| *Nickles* | Y | Y | N | N | Y | Y | N | N |
| **OREGON** | | | | | | | | |
| *Hatfield* | Y | N | Y | N | Y | N | N | N |
| *Packwood* | Y | N | Y | Y | N | N | Y | N |
| **PENNSYLVANIA** | | | | | | | | |
| Wofford | Y | N | Y | N | N | N | Y | Y |
| *Specter* | Y | N | N | N | N | N | Y | Y |
| **RHODE ISLAND** | | | | | | | | |
| Pell | Y | N | Y | N | N | N | Y | Y |
| *Chafee* | ? | Y | Y | Y | Y | Y | Y | Y |
| **SOUTH CAROLINA** | | | | | | | | |
| Hollings | Y | N | Y | N | N | N | Y | Y |
| *Thurmond* | Y | N | Y | N | Y | Y | N | N |
| **SOUTH DAKOTA** | | | | | | | | |
| Daschle | Y | N | Y | N | Y | N | N | Y |
| *Pressler* | Y | N | Y | N | Y | Y | N | N |
| **TENNESSEE** | | | | | | | | |
| Gore | ? | ? | ? | ? | ? | ? | ? | ? |
| Sasser | Y | Y | Y | Y | N | N | Y | Y |
| **TEXAS** | | | | | | | | |
| Bentsen | Y | Y | Y | Y | Y | Y | N | Y |
| *Gramm* | Y | Y | N | N | Y | Y | N | N |
| **UTAH** | | | | | | | | |
| *Garn* | Y | N | Y | N | Y | Y | N | N |
| *Hatch* | + | X | # | − | + | + | − | − |
| **VERMONT** | | | | | | | | |
| Leahy | Y | N | Y | Y | N | N | Y | Y |
| *Jeffords* | Y | N | Y | Y | N | N | Y | Y |
| **VIRGINIA** | | | | | | | | |
| Robb | Y | Y | N | Y | N | N | Y | Y |
| *Warner* | Y | Y | N | Y | Y | Y | N | N |
| **WASHINGTON** | | | | | | | | |
| Adams | Y | N | Y | N | Y | N | N | Y |
| *Gorton* | Y | N | Y | N | Y | Y | N | N |
| **WEST VIRGINIA** | | | | | | | | |
| Byrd | Y | N | Y | N | Y | N | N | Y |
| Rockefeller | Y | N | Y | Y | N | N | Y | Y |
| **WISCONSIN** | | | | | | | | |
| Kohl | Y | Y | N | Y | N | N | Y | Y |
| *Kasten* | Y | Y | N | N | Y | N | N | Y |
| **WYOMING** | | | | | | | | |
| *Simpson* | Y | N | Y | N | Y | Y | N | N |
| *Wallop* | Y | N | N | N | Y | Y | N | N |

ND Northern Democrats    SD Southern Democrats    Southern states - Ala., Ark., Fla., Ga., Ky., La., Miss., N.C., Okla., S.C., Tenn., Texas, Va.

**169. HR 5503. Fiscal 1993 Interior Appropriations/Corporate Morality.** Domenici, R-N.M., amendment to express the sense of the Senate that individuals within corporations should be encouraged to insist on the acceptance of personal responsibility for the moral content and repercussions of the activities, products and services of their corporations. Adopted 89-0: R 38-0; D 51-0 (ND 36-0, SD 15-0), Aug. 4, 1992.

**170. HR 5518. Fiscal 1993 Transportation Appropriations/Highway Trust Fund Allocations.** Bond, R-Mo., amendment to increase the allocation from the Highway Trust Fund for states that contribute more to the fund in gasoline tax revenues than they receive in highway dollars. Rejected 39-57: R 19-22; D 20-35 (ND 7-32, SD 13-3), Aug. 5, 1992.

**171. HR 5518. Fiscal 1993 Transportation Appropriations/Passage.** Passage of the bill to provide $13.5 billion in new budget authority for the Department of Transportation and related agencies in fiscal 1993. The administration requested $12,951,362,569. Passed 74-22: R 27-14; D 47-8 (ND 36-3, SD 11-5), Aug. 5, 1992.

**172. HR 5503. Fiscal 1993 Interior Appropriations/Mining Law Revisions.** Bumpers, D-Ark., motion to table (kill) the Reid, D-Nev., amendment to the Bumpers amendment to revise the 1872 mining law to require individuals to pay market value for land instead of the current $2.50 to $5 an acre, to return land no longer used for mining to the federal government and to tighten requirements for restoring land after mining. The Bumpers amendment placed a one-year moratorium on patenting land for mining. Motion rejected 44-52: R 5-36; D 39-16 (ND 29-10, SD 10-6), Aug. 5, 1992. The Bumpers amendment, as amended by the Reid amendment, was subsequently adopted by voice vote.

**173. HR 5503. Fiscal 1993 Interior Appropriations/National Forest Service Funds.** Craig, R-Idaho, motion to table

(kill) the Fowler, D-Ga., amendment to reduce the Forest Service's National Forest System budget by $35 million to reflect a 25 percent reduction in below-cost timber sales. Motion agreed to 50-44: R 38-3; D 12-41 (ND 5-32, SD 7-9), Aug. 5, 1992.

**174. HR 5503. Fiscal 1993 Interior Appropriations/Forest Service Appeals.** Craig, R-Idaho, motion to table (kill) the Fowler, D-Ga., amendment to require the Agriculture secretary to establish a notice and comment process for proposed actions of the Forest Service. The amendment required an administrative appeals process with at least one level of administrative review and an automatic stay pending the appeal. Motion rejected 38-57: R 32-9; D 6-48 (ND 1-37, SD 5-11), Aug. 6, 1992.

**175. HR 5503. Fiscal 1993 Interior Appropriations/Forest Service Appeals.** Fowler, D-Ga., motion to table (kill) the Craig, R-Idaho, amendment to the Fowler amendment, to allow the right to appeal a decision of the Forest Service for people involved in the public comment process; disposition of an appeal included a meeting with Forest Service officials "in the vicinity" of the forest affected by the decision; the chief of the Forest Service would have the authority to override a stay pending the appeal if the chief determined an emergency existed. The Fowler amendment required an administrative appeals process with at least one level of administrative review and an automatic stay pending the appeal. Motion rejected 45-50: R 4-37; D 41-13 (ND 33-5, SD 8-8), Aug. 6, 1992. Subsequently, the Fowler amendment, as amended by the Craig amendment, was adopted by voice vote.

**176. HR 5503. Fiscal 1993 Interior Appropriations/Northern Spotted Owl Habitat.** Adams, D-Wash., motion to table (kill) the Gorton, R-Wash., amendment to allow salvage timber sales in the northern spotted owl's habitat unless such salvage adversely affected the spotted owl habitat as determined by the secretary of Agriculture. Motion agreed to 60-35: R 9-32; D 51-3 (ND 37-1, SD 14-2), Aug. 6, 1992.

### KEY

Y   Voted for (yea).
#   Paired for.
+   Announced for.
N   Voted against (nay).
X   Paired against.
−   Announced against.
P   Voted "present."
C   Voted "present" to avoid possible conflict of interest.
?   Did not vote or otherwise make a position known.

Democrats   *Republicans*

| State / Senator | 177 | 178 | 179 | 180 | 181 | 182 | 183 | 184 |
|---|---|---|---|---|---|---|---|---|
| **ALABAMA** | | | | | | | | |
| Heflin | Y | N | N | Y | Y | Y | Y | Y |
| Shelby | Y | N | N | Y | Y | Y | Y | Y |
| **ALASKA** | | | | | | | | |
| *Murkowski* | Y | N | Y | Y | Y | Y | Y | Y |
| *Stevens* | Y | N | Y | Y | Y | Y | Y | Y |
| **ARIZONA** | | | | | | | | |
| DeConcini | Y | N | N | Y | Y | N | Y | Y |
| *McCain* | Y | N | N | Y | Y | Y | Y | Y |
| **ARKANSAS** | | | | | | | | |
| Bumpers | N | Y | Y | N | Y | N | Y | Y |
| Pryor | Y | Y | Y | N | Y | N | Y | Y |
| **CALIFORNIA** | | | | | | | | |
| Cranston | N | N | N | Y | Y | N | Y | Y |
| *Seymour* | Y | N | Y | Y | Y | Y | Y | Y |
| **COLORADO** | | | | | | | | |
| Wirth | Y | ? | ? | ? | ? | ? | ? | Y |
| *Brown* | Y | Y | Y | Y | Y | Y | Y | Y |
| **CONNECTICUT** | | | | | | | | |
| Dodd | Y | N | N | Y | Y | N | Y | Y |
| Lieberman | N | N | N | Y | Y | N | Y | Y |
| **DELAWARE** | | | | | | | | |
| Biden | N | N | N | Y | Y | N | Y | Y |
| *Roth* | N | Y | Y | Y | Y | Y | Y | Y |
| **FLORIDA** | | | | | | | | |
| Graham | N | N | N | Y | Y | N | Y | Y |
| *Mack* | Y | Y | Y | Y | Y | Y | Y | Y |
| **GEORGIA** | | | | | | | | |
| Fowler | N | Y | Y | Y | Y | N | Y | Y |
| Nunn | N | N | N | Y | Y | Y | Y | Y |
| **HAWAII** | | | | | | | | |
| Akaka | N | N | N | Y | Y | N | Y | Y |
| Inouye | Y | N | N | Y | Y | Y | Y | Y |
| **IDAHO** | | | | | | | | |
| *Craig* | Y | Y | Y | N | Y | N | Y | Y |
| *Symms* | Y | Y | Y | N | N | Y | Y | Y |
| **ILLINOIS** | | | | | | | | |
| Dixon | N | N | N | Y | Y | Y | N | Y |
| Simon | N | N | N | Y | Y | N | Y | Y |
| **INDIANA** | | | | | | | | |
| *Coats* | N | Y | Y | N | Y | Y | ? | N |
| *Lugar* | N | Y | Y | N | ? | Y | Y | Y |
| **IOWA** | | | | | | | | |
| Harkin | ? | N | N | Y | Y | N | Y | Y |
| *Grassley* | Y | Y | Y | Y | Y | N | Y | Y |
| **KANSAS** | | | | | | | | |
| *Dole* | Y | Y | Y | Y | Y | Y | Y | Y |
| *Kassebaum* | N | N | N | Y | Y | N | Y | Y |
| **KENTUCKY** | | | | | | | | |
| Ford | Y | N | N | Y | Y | N | Y | Y |
| *McConnell* | Y | Y | Y | N | Y | Y | Y | Y |
| **LOUISIANA** | | | | | | | | |
| Breaux | ? | N | N | Y | Y | N | Y | Y |
| Johnston | Y | N | N | Y | Y | N | Y | Y |
| **MAINE** | | | | | | | | |
| Mitchell | N | N | N | Y | Y | N | Y | Y |
| *Cohen* | N | Y | Y | Y | Y | Y | Y | Y |
| **MARYLAND** | | | | | | | | |
| Mikulski | Y | N | N | Y | Y | N | Y | Y |
| Sarbanes | N | N | N | Y | Y | N | Y | Y |
| **MASSACHUSETTS** | | | | | | | | |
| Kennedy | N | N | N | Y | Y | N | Y | Y |
| Kerry | N | N | N | Y | Y | N | Y | Y |
| **MICHIGAN** | | | | | | | | |
| Levin | N | N | N | Y | Y | N | Y | Y |
| Riegle | N | N | N | Y | Y | N | Y | Y |
| **MINNESOTA** | | | | | | | | |
| Wellstone | N | N | N | Y | + | − | + | Y |
| *Durenberger* | Y | N | N | Y | Y | Y | Y | Y |
| **MISSISSIPPI** | | | | | | | | |
| *Cochran* | Y | Y | Y | N | Y | Y | Y | Y |
| *Lott* | Y | Y | Y | N | N | Y | Y | Y |
| **MISSOURI** | | | | | | | | |
| *Bond* | Y | Y | Y | N | Y | Y | Y | Y |
| *Danforth* | Y | Y | Y | N | Y | Y | Y | Y |
| **MONTANA** | | | | | | | | |
| Baucus | Y | Y | Y | N | Y | Y | Y | Y |
| *Burns* | Y | Y | Y | Y | Y | Y | Y | Y |
| **NEBRASKA** | | | | | | | | |
| Exon | N | N | N | Y | Y | Y | Y | ? |
| Kerrey | N | N | N | Y | Y | N | Y | Y |
| **NEVADA** | | | | | | | | |
| Bryan | Y | N | N | Y | Y | N | Y | Y |
| Reid | Y | N | N | Y | Y | N | Y | Y |
| **NEW HAMPSHIRE** | | | | | | | | |
| *Rudman* | N | Y | Y | N | Y | Y | Y | Y |
| *Smith* | N | Y | Y | N | Y | Y | Y | N |
| **NEW JERSEY** | | | | | | | | |
| Bradley | N | N | N | Y | Y | N | Y | Y |
| Lautenberg | N | N | N | Y | Y | N | Y | Y |
| **NEW MEXICO** | | | | | | | | |
| Bingaman | Y | N | N | Y | Y | Y | Y | Y |
| *Domenici* | Y | N | N | Y | Y | Y | Y | Y |
| **NEW YORK** | | | | | | | | |
| Moynihan | N | N | N | Y | Y | N | Y | Y |
| *D'Amato* | N | N | N | Y | Y | Y | Y | Y |
| **NORTH CAROLINA** | | | | | | | | |
| Sanford | N | N | N | Y | Y | N | Y | Y |
| *Helms* | + | # | # | X | ? | + | + | ? |
| **NORTH DAKOTA** | | | | | | | | |
| Burdick | ? | ? | ? | ? | ? | ? | ? | ? |
| Conrad | Y | Y | Y | N | Y | N | Y | Y |
| **OHIO** | | | | | | | | |
| Glenn | N | N | N | Y | Y | N | Y | Y |
| Metzenbaum | N | N | N | Y | Y | N | Y | Y |
| **OKLAHOMA** | | | | | | | | |
| Boren | Y | N | N | Y | Y | N | Y | Y |
| *Nickles* | Y | Y | Y | N | Y | Y | Y | Y |
| **OREGON** | | | | | | | | |
| *Hatfield* | Y | N | N | Y | Y | N | Y | N |
| *Packwood* | Y | N | N | Y | Y | Y | Y | Y |
| **PENNSYLVANIA** | | | | | | | | |
| Wofford | N | N | N | Y | Y | N | Y | ? |
| *Specter* | Y | N | N | Y | Y | Y | Y | Y |
| **RHODE ISLAND** | | | | | | | | |
| Pell | N | N | N | Y | Y | N | Y | Y |
| *Chafee* | N | N | N | Y | Y | N | Y | Y |
| **SOUTH CAROLINA** | | | | | | | | |
| Hollings | N | Y | Y | N | Y | Y | Y | Y |
| *Thurmond* | Y | Y | Y | N | Y | Y | Y | Y |
| **SOUTH DAKOTA** | | | | | | | | |
| Daschle | Y | N | N | Y | Y | N | Y | Y |
| *Pressler* | Y | Y | Y | N | Y | Y | Y | Y |
| **TENNESSEE** | | | | | | | | |
| Gore | ? | ? | ? | ? | ? | ? | ? | ? |
| Sasser | N | N | N | Y | Y | N | Y | Y |
| **TEXAS** | | | | | | | | |
| Bentsen | Y | N | N | Y | Y | Y | Y | Y |
| *Gramm* | Y | Y | Y | Y | Y | Y | Y | Y |
| **UTAH** | | | | | | | | |
| *Garn* | Y | Y | Y | N | Y | ? | ? | Y |
| *Hatch* | + | X | X | # | + | + | + | Y |
| **VERMONT** | | | | | | | | |
| Leahy | N | N | Y | Y | Y | N | Y | Y |
| *Jeffords* | N | N | N | Y | Y | N | Y | Y |
| **VIRGINIA** | | | | | | | | |
| Robb | N | N | N | Y | Y | N | Y | Y |
| *Warner* | Y | Y | Y | Y | Y | Y | Y | Y |
| **WASHINGTON** | | | | | | | | |
| Adams | Y | N | N | Y | Y | N | Y | Y |
| *Gorton* | Y | N | N | Y | Y | Y | Y | Y |
| **WEST VIRGINIA** | | | | | | | | |
| Byrd | Y | Y | N | N | Y | N | Y | N |
| Rockefeller | N | N | N | Y | Y | N | Y | Y |
| **WISCONSIN** | | | | | | | | |
| Kohl | N | N | N | Y | Y | N | Y | Y |
| *Kasten* | N | N | Y | Y | Y | + | + | Y |
| **WYOMING** | | | | | | | | |
| *Simpson* | Y | Y | Y | N | Y | Y | Y | Y |
| *Wallop* | Y | Y | Y | N | N | Y | Y | N |

ND   Northern Democrats      SD   Southern Democrats      Southern states - Ala., Ark., Fla., Ga., Ky., La., Miss., N.C., Okla., S.C., Tenn., Texas, Va.

**177. HR 5503. Fiscal 1993 Interior Appropriations/Grazing Fees.** Byrd, D-W.Va., motion to table (kill) the Jeffords, R-Vt., amendment to increase domestic livestock grazing fees on lands administered by the Bureau of Land Management by 25 percent to $2.40 per animal unit month. Motion agreed to 50-44: R 30-11; D 20-33 (ND 13-25, SD 7-8), Aug. 6, 1992.

**178. HR 4312. Bilingual Voting Assistance/Length of Extension.** Simpson, R-Wyo., amendment to reduce the 15-year extension for voting rights language assistance to five years; increase the benchmark for triggering the assistance from 10,000 voting-age citizens to 20,000; and require reports on voting participation rates and voting fraud. Rejected 32-63: R 25-16; D 7-47 (ND 3-35, SD 4-12), Aug. 7, 1992.

**179. HR 4312. Bilingual Voting Assistance/Federal Funding.** Simpson, R-Wyo., amendment to require the federal government to make grants to states to pay for the costs of complying with the bill. Rejected 35-60: R 29-12; D 6-48 (ND 2-36, SD 4-12), Aug. 7, 1992.

**180. HR 4312. Bilingual Voting Assistance/Passage.** Passage of the bill to extend for 15 years through 2007 the provisions of law that require certain language minority populations to be provided with language assistance to effectively participate in the electoral process. Passed 75-20: R 25-16; D 50-4 (ND 36-2, SD 14-2), Aug. 7, 1992.

**181. S 3114. Fiscal 1993 Defense Authorization/Defense Conversion Assistance.** Nunn, D-Ga., amendment to require the prompt implementation of the defense conversion and transition provisions in the bill; $1.2 billion is authorized for the assistance in fiscal 1993. Approved 91-2: R 38-2; D 53-0 (ND 37-0, SD 16-0), Aug. 7, 1992.

**182. S 3114. Fiscal 1993 Defense Authorization/Strategic Defense Initiative.** Warner, R-Va., motion to table (kill) the Sasser, D-Tenn., amendment to cut funding for the Strategic Defense Initiative (SDI) by $1 billion from the $4.3 billion in the bill to $3.3 billion. The administration had requested $5.4 billion. Motion rejected 43-49: R 34-5; D 9-44 (ND 4-33, SD 5-11), Aug. 7, 1992. A "yea" was a vote in support of the president's position.

**183. Carnes Nomination/Motion to Proceed.** Mitchell, D-Maine, motion to proceed to the confirmation of President Bush's nomination of Edward E. Carnes Jr. of Alabama to the 11th U.S. Circuit Court of Appeals. Motion agreed to 91-0: R 38-0; D 53-0 (ND 37-0, SD 16-0), Aug. 7, 1992.

**184. S Res 330. Multilateral Action in Bosnia-Herzegovina/Support for President.** Warner, R-Va., amendment to express the Senate's support for the six measures President Bush said Aug. 6 that the administration was taking to help resolve the Balkan crisis. Adopted 90-5: R 38-4; D 52-1 (ND 36-1, SD 16-0), Aug. 10, 1992.

| | 185 | 186 | 187 | 188 | 189 | 190 | 191 | 192 |
|---|---|---|---|---|---|---|---|---|
| **ALABAMA** | | | | | | | | |
| Heflin | Y | Y | Y | Y | N | Y | N | Y |
| Shelby | Y | Y | Y | Y | N | Y | N | Y |
| **ALASKA** | | | | | | | | |
| *Murkowski* | Y | N | Y | Y | N | ? | ? | Y |
| *Stevens* | Y | Y | N | Y | N | N | N | Y |
| **ARIZONA** | | | | | | | | |
| DeConcini | Y | Y | Y | N | N | Y | N | Y |
| *McCain* | Y | N | Y | Y | N | Y | Y | Y |
| **ARKANSAS** | | | | | | | | |
| Bumpers | Y | Y | Y | N | N | Y | Y | N |
| Pryor | Y | Y | Y | N | N | ? | ? | N |
| **CALIFORNIA** | | | | | | | | |
| Cranston | Y | Y | Y | N | Y | ? | ? | N |
| *Seymour* | ? | + | Y | Y | N | ? | ? | Y |
| **COLORADO** | | | | | | | | |
| Wirth | N | Y | Y | Y | N | Y | N | N |
| *Brown* | N | N | Y | Y | N | Y | Y | Y |
| **CONNECTICUT** | | | | | | | | |
| Dodd | Y | Y | Y | N | N | Y | N | Y |
| Lieberman | Y | Y | Y | N | Y | N | Y | N |
| **DELAWARE** | | | | | | | | |
| Biden | Y | Y | Y | N | Y | Y | ? | N |
| *Roth* | Y | N | Y | Y | N | ? | ? | Y |
| **FLORIDA** | | | | | | | | |
| Graham | Y | Y | N | N | N | Y | Y | Y |
| *Mack* | Y | Y | Y | Y | N | N | Y | Y |
| **GEORGIA** | | | | | | | | |
| Fowler | Y | Y | Y | N | N | Y | N | Y |
| Nunn | Y | Y | Y | N | N | Y | ? | Y |
| **HAWAII** | | | | | | | | |
| Akaka | Y | Y | Y | N | N | Y | N | Y |
| Inouye | Y | Y | Y | N | N | ? | ? | N |
| **IDAHO** | | | | | | | | |
| *Craig* | Y | N | Y | Y | N | N | N | Y |
| *Symms* | Y | Y | Y | Y | N | ? | ? | Y |
| **ILLINOIS** | | | | | | | | |
| Dixon | Y | Y | Y | N | N | Y | N | Y |
| Simon | Y | Y | N | Y | N | Y | Y | Y |
| **INDIANA** | | | | | | | | |
| *Coats* | N | N | Y | Y | N | Y | N | Y |
| *Lugar* | Y | Y | N | Y | N | Y | Y | Y |

| | 185 | 186 | 187 | 188 | 189 | 190 | 191 | 192 |
|---|---|---|---|---|---|---|---|---|
| **IOWA** | | | | | | | | |
| Harkin | Y | Y | Y | N | Y | Y | Y | N |
| *Grassley* | Y | Y | Y | Y | N | Y | Y | Y |
| **KANSAS** | | | | | | | | |
| *Dole* | Y | Y | N | Y | N | Y | N | Y |
| *Kassebaum* | Y | Y | N | Y | N | N | N | Y |
| **KENTUCKY** | | | | | | | | |
| Ford | Y | Y | Y | N | Y | N | Y | N |
| *McConnell* | N | N | Y | Y | N | N | N | Y |
| **LOUISIANA** | | | | | | | | |
| Breaux | Y | Y | Y | N | Y | N | Y | N |
| Johnston | Y | Y | Y | N | Y | N | Y | N |
| **MAINE** | | | | | | | | |
| Mitchell | Y | Y | Y | N | Y | N | N | N |
| *Cohen* | Y | N | N | N | N | Y | Y | Y |
| **MARYLAND** | | | | | | | | |
| Mikulski | Y | Y | Y | N | N | Y | N | N |
| Sarbanes | Y | Y | N | N | Y | Y | N | N |
| **MASSACHUSETTS** | | | | | | | | |
| Kennedy | Y | Y | Y | N | N | Y | N | N |
| Kerry | Y | Y | N | N | N | Y | N | N |
| **MICHIGAN** | | | | | | | | |
| Levin | Y | Y | Y | N | ? | Y | Y | N |
| Riegle | Y | Y | Y | N | N | Y | N | N |
| **MINNESOTA** | | | | | | | | |
| Wellstone | Y | Y | N | N | Y | Y | N | N |
| *Durenberger* | Y | N | N | N | N | Y | ? | Y |
| **MISSISSIPPI** | | | | | | | | |
| Cochran | Y | Y | Y | Y | N | N | N | Y |
| *Lott* | N | Y | Y | Y | N | Y | N | Y |
| **MISSOURI** | | | | | | | | |
| *Bond* | Y | Y | Y | Y | N | Y | N | Y |
| *Danforth* | Y | N | Y | N | N | Y | N | Y |
| **MONTANA** | | | | | | | | |
| Baucus | Y | Y | Y | N | N | Y | N | Y |
| *Burns* | Y | N | Y | Y | N | Y | Y | Y |
| **NEBRASKA** | | | | | | | | |
| Exon | N | Y | Y | N | Y | Y | Y | Y |
| Kerrey | N | N | N | N | N | Y | Y | Y |
| **NEVADA** | | | | | | | | |
| Bryan | Y | Y | Y | N | N | Y | Y | Y |
| Reid | Y | Y | Y | N | N | Y | Y | Y |

| | 185 | 186 | 187 | 188 | 189 | 190 | 191 | 192 |
|---|---|---|---|---|---|---|---|---|
| **NEW HAMPSHIRE** | | | | | | | | |
| *Rudman* | N | N | N | ? | N | Y | N | Y |
| *Smith* | N | N | Y | Y | N | Y | Y | Y |
| **NEW JERSEY** | | | | | | | | |
| Bradley | Y | Y | N | N | Y | Y | Y | N |
| Lautenberg | Y | Y | Y | N | Y | Y | Y | N |
| **NEW MEXICO** | | | | | | | | |
| Bingaman | Y | N | Y | N | N | Y | N | N |
| *Domenici* | Y | Y | N | N | N | Y | N | N |
| **NEW YORK** | | | | | | | | |
| Moynihan | Y | Y | Y | N | N | Y | N | N |
| *D'Amato* | Y | Y | Y | N | Y | N | Y | N |
| **NORTH CAROLINA** | | | | | | | | |
| Sanford | Y | Y | Y | N | N | Y | Y | Y |
| *Helms* | ? | ? | + | + | − | N | ? | Y |
| **NORTH DAKOTA** | | | | | | | | |
| Burdick † | ? | ? | ? | ? | ? | ? | | |
| Conrad | Y | Y | Y | N | N | Y | Y | Y |
| **OHIO** | | | | | | | | |
| Glenn | Y | Y | Y | N | N | Y | N | Y |
| Metzenbaum | Y | Y | N | Y | Y | Y | Y | N |
| **OKLAHOMA** | | | | | | | | |
| Boren | Y | Y | Y | N | N | Y | N | Y |
| *Nickles* | Y | Y | Y | ? | ? | Y | Y | Y |
| **OREGON** | | | | | | | | |
| *Hatfield* | N | N | Y | ? | − | Y | N | Y |
| *Packwood* | Y | N | N | N | N | Y | N | N |
| **PENNSYLVANIA** | | | | | | | | |
| Wofford | Y | Y | Y | N | N | Y | Y | N |
| *Specter* | ? | Y | Y | Y | Y | ? | ? | N |
| **RHODE ISLAND** | | | | | | | | |
| Pell | Y | Y | Y | N | Y | N | Y | # |
| *Chafee* | Y | Y | N | Y | N | Y | N | Y |
| **SOUTH CAROLINA** | | | | | | | | |
| Hollings | N | N | Y | N | N | Y | N | N |
| *Thurmond* | Y | Y | Y | Y | N | Y | Y | Y |
| **SOUTH DAKOTA** | | | | | | | | |
| Daschle | Y | Y | Y | N | N | Y | Y | Y |
| *Pressler* | Y | Y | Y | Y | N | Y | Y | Y |
| **TENNESSEE** | | | | | | | | |
| Gore | ? | ? | ? | ? | ? | ? | ? | X |
| Sasser | Y | Y | N | N | N | Y | N | ? |

| | 185 | 186 | 187 | 188 | 189 | 190 | 191 | 192 |
|---|---|---|---|---|---|---|---|---|
| **TEXAS** | | | | | | | | |
| Bentsen | Y | Y | Y | N | N | Y | N | Y |
| *Gramm* | Y | N | Y | Y | N | N | N | Y |
| **UTAH** | | | | | | | | |
| *Garn* | Y | Y | Y | N | N | Y | N | N |
| *Hatch* | Y | Y | Y | N | N | N | N | Y |
| **VERMONT** | | | | | | | | |
| Leahy | Y | Y | Y | N | N | Y | N | Y |
| *Jeffords* | Y | Y | N | N | N | Y | N | Y |
| **VIRGINIA** | | | | | | | | |
| Robb | Y | Y | Y | N | Y | Y | Y | N |
| *Warner* | Y | N | N | Y | N | Y | Y | Y |
| **WASHINGTON** | | | | | | | | |
| Adams | Y | Y | Y | N | N | Y | ? | N |
| *Gorton* | N | N | N | Y | N | Y | N | N |
| **WEST VIRGINIA** | | | | | | | | |
| Byrd | N | N | N | N | N | N | Y | N |
| Rockefeller | Y | Y | Y | N | N | Y | N | N |
| **WISCONSIN** | | | | | | | | |
| Kohl | Y | Y | Y | N | N | Y | N | Y |
| *Kasten* | Y | Y | Y | Y | N | ? | ? | Y |
| **WYOMING** | | | | | | | | |
| *Simpson* | Y | Y | N | Y | N | Y | N | Y |
| *Wallop* | Y | N | Y | Y | N | ? | Y | Y |

ND Northern Democrats    SD Southern Democrats        Southern states - Ala., Ark., Fla., Ga., Ky., La., Miss., N.C., Okla., S.C., Tenn., Texas, Va.

**185. S Res 330. Multilateral Action in Bosnia-Herzegovina/U.S. Funding.** Stevens, R-Alaska, amendment to express the sense of the Senate that the United States will provide necessary funds for U.S. participation in humanitarian and multilateral military action in Bosnia-Herzegovina. Agreed to 82-13: R 32-8; D 50-5 (ND 35-4, SD 15-1), Aug. 11, 1992.

**186. S Res 330. Multilateral Action in Bosnia-Herzegovina/Adoption.** Adoption of the resolution to express the sense of the Senate that the president should call upon the United Nations to authorize all means, including multinational military action, to ensure the flow of humanitarian relief in Bosnia-Herzegovina and to gain access for U.N. and International Red Cross personnel to refugee and war camps. Adopted 74-22: R 23-18; D 51-4 (ND 36-3, SD 15-1), Aug. 11, 1992.

**187. HR 11. Urban Aid and Tax Bill/Individual Retirement Accounts.** Bentsen, D-Texas, motion to table (kill) the Chafee, R-R.I., amendment to strike provisions that would provide all taxpayers a $2,000 exclusion from income for Individual Retirement Accounts while retaining provisions that provide penalty-free IRA withdrawals for certain expenses, such as house purchases, education or medical emergencies. Motion agreed to 72-25: R 28-14; D 44-11 (ND 30-9, SD 14-2), Aug. 11, 1992.

**188. HR 11. Urban Aid and Tax Bill/Budget Act Waiver for Capital Gains Tax Cut.** Mack, R-Fla., motion to waive the budget act with respect to the Bentsen, D-Texas, point of order against the Mack amendment for violating budget law provisions that prohibit consideration of legislation that would result in revenue falling below the revenue floor contained in the most recent budget resolution. The Mack amendment would have provided for a maximum long-term capital gains rate of 15 percent, among other things. Motion rejected 37-57: R 32-7; D 5-50 (ND 2-37, SD 3-13), Aug. 12, 1992.

**189. HR 11. Urban Aid and Tax Bill/Budget Act Waiver for Urban Initiatives.** Bradley, D-N.J., motion to waive the budget act with respect to the Bentsen, D-Texas, point of order against the Bradley amendment for violating budget law provisions that prohibit consideration of legislation within the Budget Committee's jurisdiction without its consent. The Bradley amendment would have eliminated certain tax provisions in the bill and authorized spending for four urban initiatives. Motion rejected 14-80: R 2-38; D 12-42 (ND 11-27, SD 1-15), Aug. 12, 1992.

**190. HR 5679. Fiscal 1993 VA, Housing and Urban Development, Independent Agencies Appropriations/Thrift Liability Claims.** Wirth, D-Colo., amendment to extend the statute of limitations on civil liability claims filed by the Resolution Trust Corporation against professionals at failed savings and loan institutions established in 1989 from three to five years except where state law authorizes a longer period. Adopted 78-10: R 26-10; D 52-0 (ND 37-0, SD 15-0), Sept. 8, 1992.

**191. HR 5679. Fiscal 1993 VA, Housing and Urban Development, Independent Agencies Appropriations/HUD Overhead.** Graham, D-Fla., amendment to cut appropriations for salaries and expenses at the Department of Housing and Urban Development (HUD) by $4,696,000. Rejected 37-47: R 17-18; D 20-29 (ND 15-20, SD 5-9), Sept. 8, 1992.

**192. Carnes Nomination/Cloture.** Motion to invoke cloture (thus limiting debate) on the confirmation of President Bush's nomination of Edward E. Carnes Jr. of Alabama to the 11th U.S. Circuit Court of Appeals. Motion agreed to 66-30: R 42-1; D 24-29 (ND 15-23, SD 9-6), Sept. 9, 1992. A three-fifths majority vote (60) of the total Senate is required to invoke cloture.

*† Quentin N. Burdick, D-N.D., died Sept. 8. The last vote he was eligible for was 189.*

## KEY

Y  Voted for (yea).
#  Paired for.
+  Announced for.
N  Voted against (nay).
X  Paired against.
−  Announced against.
P  Voted ''present.''
C  Voted ''present'' to avoid possible conflict of interest.
?  Did not vote or otherwise make a position known.

Democrats  *Republicans*

| | 193 | 194 | 195 | 196 | 197 | 198 | 199 | 200 |
|---|---|---|---|---|---|---|---|---|
| **ALABAMA** | | | | | | | | |
| Heflin | Y | N | Y | Y | N | N | N | Y |
| Shelby | Y | N | N | Y | N | N | N | Y |
| **ALASKA** | | | | | | | | |
| *Murkowski* | Y | N | Y | Y | Y | Y | Y | Y |
| *Stevens* | Y | N | Y | Y | Y | Y | Y | Y |
| **ARIZONA** | | | | | | | | |
| DeConcini | Y | Y | Y | Y | Y | Y | Y | Y |
| *McCain* | Y | N | N | Y | Y | Y | Y | Y |
| **ARKANSAS** | | | | | | | | |
| Bumpers | N | Y | N | ? | N | N | N | Y |
| Pryor | N | Y | N | Y | N | N | N | Y |
| **CALIFORNIA** | | | | | | | | |
| Cranston | N | N | N | Y | N | N | N | N |
| *Seymour* | Y | N | Y | Y | Y | Y | Y | Y |
| **COLORADO** | | | | | | | | |
| Wirth | N | N | ? | Y | N | N | N | N |
| *Brown* | Y | N | Y | Y | Y | Y | Y | N |
| **CONNECTICUT** | | | | | | | | |
| Dodd | N | N | N | Y | Y | Y | Y | Y |
| Lieberman | Y | N | N | Y | Y | Y | Y | Y |
| **DELAWARE** | | | | | | | | |
| Biden | N | ? | ? | + | N | N | N | N |
| *Roth* | Y | N | Y | N | Y | N | N | N |
| **FLORIDA** | | | | | | | | |
| Graham | Y | N | N | Y | N | N | N | Y |
| *Mack* | Y | N | Y | Y | Y | Y | Y | Y |
| **GEORGIA** | | | | | | | | |
| Fowler | N | Y | N | Y | X | ? | X | Y |
| Nunn | Y | Y | N | Y | Y | Y | Y | N |
| **HAWAII** | | | | | | | | |
| Akaka | Y | N | N | Y | N | N | N | Y |
| Inouye | N | N | N | Y | N | N | N | Y |
| **IDAHO** | | | | | | | | |
| *Craig* | Y | N | Y | Y | Y | Y | Y | N |
| *Symms* | Y | N | Y | Y | Y | Y | Y | N |
| **ILLINOIS** | | | | | | | | |
| Dixon | N | Y | N | Y | Y | Y | Y | N |
| Simon | N | Y | N | Y | N | N | N | Y |
| **INDIANA** | | | | | | | | |
| *Coats* | Y | N | N | Y | Y | Y | Y | N |
| *Lugar* | Y | N | N | Y | Y | Y | Y | Y |

| | 193 | 194 | 195 | 196 | 197 | 198 | 199 | 200 |
|---|---|---|---|---|---|---|---|---|
| **IOWA** | | | | | | | | |
| Harkin | N | Y | N | Y | N | N | N | Y |
| *Grassley* | Y | N | Y | Y | Y | Y | Y | Y |
| **KANSAS** | | | | | | | | |
| *Dole* | Y | N | Y | Y | Y | Y | Y | Y |
| *Kassebaum* | Y | N | Y | Y | Y | ? | Y | N |
| **KENTUCKY** | | | | | | | | |
| Ford | Y | Y | Y | Y | N | N | N | Y |
| *McConnell* | Y | N | Y | Y | Y | Y | Y | Y |
| **LOUISIANA** | | | | | | | | |
| Breaux | N | N | N | Y | N | N | N | Y |
| Johnston | Y | N | Y | Y | N | N | N | N |
| **MAINE** | | | | | | | | |
| Mitchell | N | Y | N | Y | N | N | N | Y |
| *Cohen* | Y | Y | N | Y | Y | Y | Y | N |
| **MARYLAND** | | | | | | | | |
| Mikulski | N | N | N | Y | N | N | N | Y |
| Sarbanes | N | N | N | Y | N | N | N | N |
| **MASSACHUSETTS** | | | | | | | | |
| Kennedy | N | Y | N | Y | N | N | N | Y |
| Kerry | N | Y | N | Y | N | N | N | N |
| **MICHIGAN** | | | | | | | | |
| Levin | N | Y | N | Y | N | N | N | N |
| Riegle | N | N | N | Y | Y | Y | Y | Y |
| **MINNESOTA** | | | | | | | | |
| Wellstone | N | Y | N | Y | N | N | N | Y |
| *Durenberger* | Y | N | N | Y | Y | Y | Y | N |
| **MISSISSIPPI** | | | | | | | | |
| *Cochran* | Y | N | Y | Y | Y | Y | Y | N |
| *Lott* | Y | N | Y | Y | Y | Y | Y | Y |
| **MISSOURI** | | | | | | | | |
| *Bond* | Y | N | Y | Y | Y | Y | Y | N |
| *Danforth* | Y | N | Y | Y | Y | Y | Y | N |
| **MONTANA** | | | | | | | | |
| Baucus | Y | Y | N | Y | N | N | N | N |
| *Burns* | Y | N | Y | Y | Y | Y | Y | Y |
| **NEBRASKA** | | | | | | | | |
| Exon | Y | Y | Y | Y | Y | Y | Y | Y |
| Kerrey | N | N | N | Y | # | N | # | N |
| **NEVADA** | | | | | | | | |
| Bryan | Y | Y | N | Y | N | N | N | Y |
| Reid | Y | Y | N | Y | N | N | N | Y |

| | 193 | 194 | 195 | 196 | 197 | 198 | 199 | 200 |
|---|---|---|---|---|---|---|---|---|
| **NEW HAMPSHIRE** | | | | | | | | |
| *Rudman* | Y | N | Y | Y | Y | Y | Y | N |
| *Smith* | Y | N | Y | N | Y | Y | Y | N |
| **NEW JERSEY** | | | | | | | | |
| Bradley | N | Y | N | Y | N | N | N | N |
| Lautenberg | N | Y | N | Y | Y | Y | Y | Y |
| **NEW MEXICO** | | | | | | | | |
| Bingaman | N | N | Y | N | Y | N | N | N |
| *Domenici* | Y | N | Y | Y | Y | Y | Y | Y |
| **NEW YORK** | | | | | | | | |
| Moynihan | N | N | N | Y | N | N | N | N |
| *D'Amato* | Y | N | N | Y | N | N | N | Y |
| **NORTH CAROLINA** | | | | | | | | |
| Sanford | Y | Y | N | Y | Y | Y | Y | Y |
| *Helms* | Y | N | Y | ? | Y | Y | Y | N |
| **NORTH DAKOTA** | | | | | | | | |
| Vacancy | | | | | | | | |
| Conrad | Y | Y | Y | Y | N | N | N | Y |
| **OHIO** | | | | | | | | |
| Glenn | N | N | N | Y | N | N | N | N |
| Metzenbaum | N | Y | N | Y | N | N | N | N |
| **OKLAHOMA** | | | | | | | | |
| Boren | Y | N | N | Y | Y | Y | Y | Y |
| *Nickles* | Y | N | Y | Y | Y | Y | Y | N |
| **OREGON** | | | | | | | | |
| *Hatfield* | Y | N | N | Y | Y | Y | N | N |
| *Packwood* | Y | N | Y | Y | N | N | N | N |
| **PENNSYLVANIA** | | | | | | | | |
| Wofford | N | N | N | Y | N | N | N | Y |
| *Specter* | N | Y | N | Y | Y | Y | Y | Y |
| **RHODE ISLAND** | | | | | | | | |
| Pell | N | N | N | Y | N | N | N | N |
| *Chafee* | Y | Y | N | Y | Y | Y | Y | Y |
| **SOUTH CAROLINA** | | | | | | | | |
| Hollings | N | Y | Y | N | Y | N | N | N |
| *Thurmond* | Y | N | Y | Y | Y | Y | Y | N |
| **SOUTH DAKOTA** | | | | | | | | |
| Daschle | N | Y | N | Y | Y | Y | Y | N |
| *Pressler* | Y | N | Y | Y | Y | Y | Y | N |
| **TENNESSEE** | | | | | | | | |
| Gore | ? | ? | ? | ? | ? | ? | ? | ? |
| Sasser | Y | Y | N | Y | N | N | N | Y |

| | 193 | 194 | 195 | 196 | 197 | 198 | 199 | 200 |
|---|---|---|---|---|---|---|---|---|
| **TEXAS** | | | | | | | | |
| Bentsen | Y | N | N | Y | Y | Y | Y | N |
| *Gramm* | Y | N | Y | Y | Y | Y | Y | N |
| **UTAH** | | | | | | | | |
| *Garn* | Y | N | Y | Y | Y | Y | Y | N |
| *Hatch* | Y | N | Y | Y | Y | Y | Y | Y |
| **VERMONT** | | | | | | | | |
| Leahy | N | Y | N | Y | N | N | N | N |
| *Jeffords* | Y | N | N | Y | Y | Y | Y | N |
| **VIRGINIA** | | | | | | | | |
| Robb | N | N | N | Y | Y | Y | Y | N |
| *Warner* | Y | Y | Y | Y | Y | Y | Y | N |
| **WASHINGTON** | | | | | | | | |
| Adams | N | N | N | Y | N | N | N | Y |
| *Gorton* | Y | N | Y | Y | Y | Y | Y | N |
| **WEST VIRGINIA** | | | | | | | | |
| Byrd | Y | Y | Y | Y | N | N | N | Y |
| Rockefeller | N | Y | Y | Y | Y | Y | Y | Y |
| **WISCONSIN** | | | | | | | | |
| Kohl | Y | Y | N | Y | Y | Y | Y | N |
| *Kasten* | Y | N | Y | N | Y | N | Y | N |
| **WYOMING** | | | | | | | | |
| *Simpson* | Y | N | Y | Y | N | N | N | Y |
| *Wallop* | Y | N | Y | N | Y | Y | Y | N |

ND  Northern Democrats    SD  Southern Democrats    Southern states - Ala., Ark., Fla., Ga., Ky., La., Miss., N.C., Okla., S.C., Tenn., Texas, Va.

**193. Carnes Nomination.** Confirmation of President Bush's nomination of Edward E. Carnes Jr. of Alabama to the 11th U.S. Circuit Court of Appeals. Confirmed 62-36: R 42-1; D 20-35 (ND 10-29, SD 10-6), Sept. 9, 1992. A "yea" was a vote in support of the president's position.

**194. HR 5679. Fiscal 1993 VA, Housing and Urban Development, Independent Agencies Appropriations/Space Station *Freedom*.** Bumpers, D-Ark., amendment to provide $500 million to terminate the space station *Freedom* and transfer from the space station account $200 million for veterans' health care and $62 million for veterans' medical research. Rejected 34-63: R 4-39; D 30-24 (ND 22-16, SD 8-8), Sept. 9, 1992. A "nay" was a vote in support of the president's position.

**195. HR 5679. Fiscal 1993 VA, Housing and Urban Development, Independent Agencies Appropriations/Safe Drinking Water Regulations.** Domenici, R-N.M., motion to table (kill) the Chafee, R-R.I., amendment to the Domenici amendment to place a moratorium on regulations concerning radon in drinking water, with the Environmental Protection Agency required to report on radon exposure and issue final regulations by Dec. 31, 1993, and to make recommendations on revision of the Safe Drinking Water Act within nine months. Motion rejected 43-53: R 33-10; D 10-43 (ND 6-31, SD 4-12), Sept. 9, 1992.

**196. HR 5679. Fiscal 1993 VA, Housing and Urban Development, Independent Agencies Appropriations/Passage.** Passage of the bill to provide $87.8 billion in new budget authority for the departments of Veterans Affairs and Housing and Urban Development and for other independent agencies in fiscal 1993. The administration requested $90,145,976,810. Passed 92-3: R 39-3; D 53-0 (ND 38-0, SD 15-0), Sept. 9, 1992.

**197. S 640. Product Liability/Cloture.** Motion to invoke cloture (thus limiting debate) on the motion to proceed to the bill to reduce lawsuits involving products that cause injuries to consumers by establishing nationwide standards on how victims should be compensated. Motion rejected 57-39: R 39-4; D 18-35 (ND 13-25, SD 5-10), Sept. 10, 1992. A three-fifths majority of the total Senate (60) is required to invoke cloture.

**198. S 640. Product Liability/Reconsideration.** Mitchell, D-Maine, motion to reconsider the vote (vote 197) on the motion to invoke cloture (thus limiting debate) on the motion to proceed to the bill to reduce lawsuits involving products that cause injuries to consumers by establishing nationwide standards on how victims should be compensated. Motion agreed to 57-39: R 39-3; D 18-36 (ND 13-26, SD 5-10), Sept. 10, 1992.

**199. S 640. Product Liability/Cloture.** Motion to invoke cloture (thus limiting debate) on the motion to proceed to the bill to reduce lawsuits involving products that cause injuries to consumers by establishing nationwide standards on how victims should be compensated. Motion rejected 58-38: R 40-3; D 18-35 (ND 13-25, SD 5-10), Sept. 10, 1992. A three-fifths majority of the total Senate (60) is required to invoke cloture.

**200. HR 5488. Fiscal 1993 Treasury-Postal Appropriations/"Notch Babies."** Sanford, D-N.C., motion to waive the budget act with respect to the Bentsen, D-Texas, point of order against the Sanford amendment to raise Social Security benefits for "notch babies," individuals born after 1916 and before 1927, at a cost of about $22 billion over five years. Motion rejected 49-49: R 16-27; D 33-22 (ND 21-18, SD 12-4), Sept. 10, 1992. A three-fifths majority of the total Senate (60) is required to waive the budget act.

**KEY**

- Y Voted for (yea).
- # Paired for.
- + Announced for.
- N Voted against (nay).
- X Paired against.
- − Announced against.
- P Voted "present."
- C Voted "present" to avoid possible conflict of interest.
- ? Did not vote or otherwise make a position known.

Democrats  *Republicans*

| | 201 | 202 | 203 | 204 | 205 | 206 | 207 | 208 |
|---|---|---|---|---|---|---|---|---|
| **ALABAMA** | | | | | | | | |
| Heflin | Y | N | Y | Y | N | Y | Y | N |
| Shelby | Y | Y | Y | Y | N | Y | Y | N |
| **ALASKA** | | | | | | | | |
| *Murkowski* | Y | Y | ? | ? | ? | ? | N | N |
| *Stevens* | Y | Y | Y | Y | N | Y | Y | N |
| **ARIZONA** | | | | | | | | |
| DeConcini | Y | Y | Y | Y | N | Y | Y | Y |
| *McCain* | Y | Y | Y | N | Y | Y | N | N |
| **ARKANSAS** | | | | | | | | |
| Bumpers | Y | Y | Y | Y | N | Y | Y | N |
| Pryor | N | Y | Y | Y | N | Y | Y | N |
| **CALIFORNIA** | | | | | | | | |
| Cranston | ? | ? | Y | Y | N | Y | Y | Y |
| *Seymour* | + | ? | ? | ? | Y | Y | N | N |
| **COLORADO** | | | | | | | | |
| Wirth | N | N | Y | Y | N | ? | Y | ? |
| *Brown* | Y | N | Y | Y | Y | N | N | N |
| **CONNECTICUT** | | | | | | | | |
| Dodd | Y | Y | ? | Y | N | Y | Y | N |
| Lieberman | Y | Y | Y | Y | N | Y | Y | N |
| **DELAWARE** | | | | | | | | |
| Biden | Y | Y | Y | Y | N | Y | ? | N |
| *Roth* | Y | N | Y | Y | Y | Y | Y | N |
| **FLORIDA** | | | | | | | | |
| Graham | Y | Y | Y | Y | Y | Y | Y | N |
| *Mack* | Y | Y | Y | Y | Y | Y | N | N |
| **GEORGIA** | | | | | | | | |
| Fowler | Y | Y | Y | Y | N | Y | Y | N |
| Nunn | N | Y | Y | Y | Y | Y | Y | N |
| **HAWAII** | | | | | | | | |
| Akaka | N | Y | Y | Y | N | Y | Y | Y |
| Inouye | N | Y | Y | Y | N | Y | Y | N |
| **IDAHO** | | | | | | | | |
| *Craig* | Y | N | N | N | Y | N | N | N |
| *Symms* | Y | N | N | N | Y | N | N | N |
| **ILLINOIS** | | | | | | | | |
| Dixon | N | Y | Y | Y | N | Y | Y | Y |
| Simon | N | Y | Y | Y | N | Y | Y | Y |
| **INDIANA** | | | | | | | | |
| *Coats* | Y | Y | Y | Y | Y | Y | N | N |
| *Lugar* | Y | Y | ? | ? | ? | ? | N | N |

| | 201 | 202 | 203 | 204 | 205 | 206 | 207 | 208 |
|---|---|---|---|---|---|---|---|---|
| **IOWA** | | | | | | | | |
| Harkin | Y | Y | Y | Y | N | Y | Y | Y |
| *Grassley* | Y | Y | Y | Y | Y | Y | N | N |
| **KANSAS** | | | | | | | | |
| *Dole* | N | Y | Y | Y | Y | Y | N | N |
| *Kassebaum* | N | Y | Y | Y | Y | Y | N | N |
| **KENTUCKY** | | | | | | | | |
| Ford | Y | Y | Y | Y | N | Y | Y | Y |
| *McConnell* | Y | Y | Y | N | Y | Y | N | N |
| **LOUISIANA** | | | | | | | | |
| Breaux | N | Y | Y | Y | N | Y | Y | N |
| Johnston | N | Y | Y | Y | N | Y | Y | N |
| **MAINE** | | | | | | | | |
| Mitchell | N | Y | Y | Y | N | Y | Y | Y |
| *Cohen* | N | Y | Y | Y | Y | Y | N | N |
| **MARYLAND** | | | | | | | | |
| Mikulski | Y | Y | Y | Y | N | Y | Y | Y |
| Sarbanes | N | Y | Y | Y | N | Y | Y | Y |
| **MASSACHUSETTS** | | | | | | | | |
| Kennedy | N | Y | Y | Y | N | Y | Y | Y |
| Kerry | N | Y | Y | Y | N | Y | Y | Y |
| **MICHIGAN** | | | | | | | | |
| Levin | N | Y | Y | Y | N | Y | Y | Y |
| Riegle | N | Y | Y | Y | N | Y | Y | Y |
| **MINNESOTA** | | | | | | | | |
| Wellstone | N | Y | Y | Y | N | Y | Y | Y |
| *Durenberger* | N | Y | Y | N | N | N | N | N |
| **MISSISSIPPI** | | | | | | | | |
| *Cochran* | Y | Y | Y | Y | Y | Y | N | N |
| *Lott* | Y | N | Y | N | Y | Y | N | N |
| **MISSOURI** | | | | | | | | |
| *Bond* | Y | Y | Y | N | Y | Y | N | Y |
| *Danforth* | N | Y | Y | Y | Y | Y | N | N |
| **MONTANA** | | | | | | | | |
| Baucus | N | N | Y | Y | N | Y | Y | N |
| *Burns* | Y | N | Y | Y | Y | Y | N | N |
| **NEBRASKA** | | | | | | | | |
| Exon | Y | Y | Y | Y | N | Y | Y | N |
| Kerrey | N | Y | Y | Y | N | Y | Y | Y |
| **NEVADA** | | | | | | | | |
| Bryan | Y | Y | Y | Y | N | Y | Y | Y |
| Reid | Y | Y | Y | Y | N | Y | Y | Y |

| | 201 | 202 | 203 | 204 | 205 | 206 | 207 | 208 |
|---|---|---|---|---|---|---|---|---|
| **NEW HAMPSHIRE** | | | | | | | | |
| *Rudman* | N | Y | ? | ? | Y | Y | N | N |
| *Smith* | Y | N | N | N | Y | N | N | N |
| **NEW JERSEY** | | | | | | | | |
| Bradley | N | Y | Y | Y | N | Y | Y | Y |
| Lautenberg | Y | Y | Y | Y | N | Y | Y | Y |
| **NEW MEXICO** | | | | | | | | |
| Bingaman | N | Y | Y | Y | N | Y | Y | Y |
| *Domenici* | N | Y | + | ? | ? | ? | N | N |
| **NEW YORK** | | | | | | | | |
| Moynihan | N | Y | Y | Y | N | Y | Y | N |
| *D'Amato* | Y | Y | Y | Y | N | Y | ? | Y |
| **NORTH CAROLINA** | | | | | | | | |
| Sanford | Y | Y | Y | Y | N | Y | Y | Y |
| *Helms* | ? | ? | N | N | Y | N | N | N |
| **NORTH DAKOTA** | | | | | | | | |
| Burdick * | | | | | | | | Y |
| Conrad | ? | Y | Y | Y | N | Y | Y | Y |
| **OHIO** | | | | | | | | |
| Glenn | N | Y | Y | Y | N | Y | Y | N |
| Metzenbaum | N | Y | Y | Y | N | Y | Y | Y |
| **OKLAHOMA** | | | | | | | | |
| Boren | N | Y | Y | Y | N | Y | Y | N |
| *Nickles* | Y | Y | Y | N | Y | N | N | N |
| **OREGON** | | | | | | | | |
| *Hatfield* | N | Y | Y | Y | N | Y | Y | N |
| *Packwood* | N | Y | Y | Y | N | N | N | N |
| **PENNSYLVANIA** | | | | | | | | |
| Wofford | Y | Y | Y | Y | N | Y | Y | Y |
| *Specter* | Y | Y | Y | N | N | Y | Y | Y |
| **RHODE ISLAND** | | | | | | | | |
| Pell | N | Y | Y | Y | N | Y | Y | Y |
| *Chafee* | N | Y | ? | ? | Y | Y | N | N |
| **SOUTH CAROLINA** | | | | | | | | |
| Hollings | Y | Y | Y | Y | N | Y | Y | Y |
| *Thurmond* | Y | Y | Y | Y | Y | Y | N | N |
| **SOUTH DAKOTA** | | | | | | | | |
| Daschle | Y | Y | Y | Y | N | Y | Y | Y |
| *Pressler* | Y | Y | Y | Y | Y | N | N | N |
| **TENNESSEE** | | | | | | | | |
| Gore | ? | ? | ? | ? | ? | ? | ? | ? |
| Sasser | N | Y | Y | Y | N | Y | Y | N |

| | 201 | 202 | 203 | 204 | 205 | 206 | 207 | 208 |
|---|---|---|---|---|---|---|---|---|
| **TEXAS** | | | | | | | | |
| Bentsen | N | Y | Y | Y | Y | Y | Y | N |
| *Gramm* | Y | Y | N | Y | Y | Y | N | N |
| **UTAH** | | | | | | | | |
| *Garn* | ? | ? | Y | Y | Y | Y | N | N |
| *Hatch* | Y | Y | Y | Y | Y | Y | N | N |
| **VERMONT** | | | | | | | | |
| Leahy | Y | Y | Y | Y | N | Y | Y | Y |
| *Jeffords* | Y | Y | Y | Y | Y | Y | ? | Y |
| **VIRGINIA** | | | | | | | | |
| Robb | N | Y | Y | Y | N | Y | Y | N |
| *Warner* | Y | Y | Y | Y | Y | N | N | N |
| **WASHINGTON** | | | | | | | | |
| Adams | N | Y | Y | Y | N | Y | Y | Y |
| *Gorton* | Y | Y | Y | Y | N | Y | N | N |
| **WEST VIRGINIA** | | | | | | | | |
| Byrd | N | Y | Y | Y | N | Y | Y | N |
| Rockefeller | N | Y | Y | N | Y | ? | N | N |
| **WISCONSIN** | | | | | | | | |
| Kohl | N | Y | Y | Y | N | Y | Y | Y |
| *Kasten* | Y | N | Y | N | Y | Y | N | N |
| **WYOMING** | | | | | | | | |
| *Simpson* | N | Y | Y | Y | N | Y | Y | N |
| *Wallop* | Y | N | N | N | Y | N | N | N |

ND  Northern Democrats    SD  Southern Democrats    Southern states - Ala., Ark., Fla., Ga., Ky., La., Miss., N.C., Okla., S.C., Tenn., Texas, Va.

**201. HR 5488. Fiscal 1993 Treasury-Postal Appropriations/Social Security Earnings Test.** McCain, R-Ariz., motion to waive the budget act with respect to the Bentsen, D-Texas, point of order against the McCain amendment to increase from $9,720 to $50,000 over five years the amount an individual between the ages of 65 and 69 could earn without having Social Security benefits reduced. Motion rejected 51-42: R 30-10; D 21-32 (ND 13-24, SD 8-8), Sept. 10, 1992. A three-fifths majority of the total Senate (60) was required to waive the budget act.

**202. HR 5488. Fiscal 1993 Treasury-Postal Appropriations/Passage.** Passage of the bill to provide $22.6 billion in new budget authority for the Treasury Department, the U.S Postal Service, the Executive Office of the President and certain independent agencies in fiscal 1993. Passed 82-12: R 31-9; D 51-3 (ND 36-2, SD 15-1), Sept. 10, 1992.

**203. S 2. Neighborhood Schools Improvement/Cloture.** Motion to invoke cloture (thus limiting debate) on the motion to disagree to House amendments and name conferees on the bill to authorize block grants to states for programs to improve education through teacher training, school construction or other local initiatives. Republicans tried to block a conference because neither chamber's bill contained President's Bush proposal to let the block grant money be used for private school choice. Motion agreed to 85-6: R 31-6; D 54-0 (ND 38-0, SD 16-0), Sept. 15, 1992. A three-fifths majority of the total Senate (60) was required to invoke cloture.

**204. Procedural Motion.** Mitchell, D-Maine, motion to instruct the sergeant-at-arms to request attendance of absent senators. Motion agreed to 80-12: R 25-12; D 55-0 (ND 39-0, SD 16-0), Sept. 15, 1992.

**205. HR 5620. Fiscal 1992 Defense and Disaster Supplemental Appropriations/Davis-Bacon Regulations.** Craig, R-Idaho, amendment to strike provisions that permanently prohibited the Department of Labor from implementing regulations to allow the use of low-wage, low-skill, non-union workers or helpers under the Davis-Bacon Act, which set wage standards for federal contracts. Rejected 37-58: R 33-7; D 4-51 (ND 0-39, SD 4-12), Sept. 15, 1992.

**206. HR 5620. Fiscal 1992 Defense and Disaster Supplemental Appropriations/Passage.** Passage of the bill to provide $10.46 billion in grants, direct assistance and loans to help the victims of Hurricane Andrew, Typhoon Omar and Hurricane Iniki. The bill also returned to the U.S. Treasury $14.7 billion of the original $15 billion appropriated for the U.S. share of Operation Desert Shield/Desert Storm and provide $500 million for urban aid assistance. Passed 84-10: R 30-10; D 54-0 (ND 38-0, SD 16-0), Sept. 15, 1992.

**207. HR 5677. Fiscal 1993 Labor, Health and Human Services, Education Appropriations/Cloture.** Motion to invoke cloture (thus limiting debate) on the motion to proceed to the bill to provide $240.9 billion in fiscal 1993 for the departments of Labor, Health and Human Services, and Education. Motion rejected 56-38: R 3-38; D 53-0 (ND 37-0, SD 16-0), Sept. 16, 1992. A three-fifths majority of the total Senate (60) was required to invoke cloture.

**208. HR 5677. Fiscal 1993 Labor, Health and Human Services, Education Appropriations/Budget Act Waiver.** Harkin, D-Iowa, motion to waive the Budget Act with respect to the Nunn, D-Ga., point of order against the Harkin amendment to transfer $4.1 billion from defense to domestic programs, including Head Start, the childhood immunization program and the Job Corps. Motion rejected 36-62: R 5-38; D 31-24 (ND 27-12, SD 4-12), Sept. 16, 1992. A three-fifths majority (60) of the total Senate was required to waive the Budget Act. A "nay" was a vote in support of the president's position.

*\* Jocelyn Birch Burdick, D-N.D., was sworn in Sept. 16 to replace her husband Quentin N. Burdick, D-N.D., who died Sept. 8. The first vote she was eligible for was vote 208. The last vote he was eligible for was vote 189.*

| | 209 | 210 | 211 | 212 | 213 | 214 | 215 | 216 |
|---|---|---|---|---|---|---|---|---|
| **ALABAMA** | | | | | | | | |
| Heflin | N | N | N | Y | N | N | Y | N |
| Shelby | N | Y | N | N | Y | N | N | N |
| **ALASKA** | | | | | | | | |
| *Murkowski* | N | Y | Y | N | Y | N | Y | N |
| *Stevens* | N | N | N | N | Y | N | Y | N |
| **ARIZONA** | | | | | | | | |
| DeConcini | N | N | Y | Y | N | Y | N | Y |
| *McCain* | N | Y | N | N | Y | N | Y | N |
| **ARKANSAS** | | | | | | | | |
| Bumpers | N | N | N | Y | N | Y | N | Y |
| Pryor | N | N | N | Y | N | Y | N | Y |
| **CALIFORNIA** | | | | | | | | |
| Cranston | Y | N | N | Y | N | Y | N | Y |
| *Seymour* | N | Y | Y | Y | Y | N | Y | N |
| **COLORADO** | | | | | | | | |
| Wirth | ? | ? | ? | ? | ? | ? | ? | ? |
| *Brown* | N | Y | N | Y | N | Y | Y | Y |
| **CONNECTICUT** | | | | | | | | |
| Dodd | N | N | N | Y | N | Y | N | Y |
| Lieberman | N | N | N | Y | N | Y | N | Y |
| **DELAWARE** | | | | | | | | |
| Biden | N | N | N | Y | Y | Y | N | Y |
| *Roth* | N | Y | Y | Y | Y | N | Y | N |
| **FLORIDA** | | | | | | | | |
| Graham | N | Y | N | Y | N | N | Y | Y |
| *Mack* | N | Y | N | Y | N | Y | N | Y |
| **GEORGIA** | | | | | | | | |
| Fowler | N | N | N | Y | N | Y | N | N |
| Nunn | N | N | N | Y | N | N | Y | N |
| **HAWAII** | | | | | | | | |
| Akaka | Y | N | Y | Y | N | Y | N | Y |
| Inouye | N | N | N | Y | N | N | Y | N |
| **IDAHO** | | | | | | | | |
| *Craig* | N | Y | N | N | Y | N | Y | N |
| *Symms* | N | Y | Y | N | Y | N | Y | N |
| **ILLINOIS** | | | | | | | | |
| Dixon | N | N | Y | Y | N | Y | N | Y |
| Simon | Y | N | Y | Y | Y | N | Y | N |
| **INDIANA** | | | | | | | | |
| *Coats* | N | Y | N | N | Y | N | Y | N |
| *Lugar* | N | Y | N | N | Y | N | Y | N |
| **IOWA** | | | | | | | | |
| Harkin | Y | N | Y | Y | N | Y | N | Y |
| *Grassley* | N | Y | N | N | Y | Y | N | Y |
| **KANSAS** | | | | | | | | |
| *Dole* | N | Y | N | N | N | N | Y | N |
| *Kassebaum* | N | Y | N | Y | Y | N | Y | N |
| **KENTUCKY** | | | | | | | | |
| Ford | N | N | Y | Y | Y | Y | Y | N |
| *McConnell* | N | Y | N | N | Y | N | Y | N |
| **LOUISIANA** | | | | | | | | |
| Breaux | N | N | N | Y | N | Y | N | N |
| Johnston | N | N | N | Y | N | Y | N | N |
| **MAINE** | | | | | | | | |
| Mitchell | Y | N | Y | Y | N | Y | N | Y |
| *Cohen* | N | N | N | Y | Y | Y | N | Y |
| **MARYLAND** | | | | | | | | |
| Mikulski | Y | N | Y | Y | N | Y | N | Y |
| Sarbanes | Y | N | Y | Y | N | Y | N | Y |
| **MASSACHUSETTS** | | | | | | | | |
| Kennedy | Y | N | Y | Y | N | Y | N | Y |
| Kerry | Y | N | Y | Y | N | Y | N | Y |
| **MICHIGAN** | | | | | | | | |
| Levin | N | N | N | Y | N | Y | N | Y |
| Riegle | N | Y | Y | Y | N | Y | N | Y |
| **MINNESOTA** | | | | | | | | |
| Wellstone | Y | N | Y | Y | N | Y | N | Y |
| Durenberger | N | N | N | Y | N | Y | N | N |
| **MISSISSIPPI** | | | | | | | | |
| *Cochran* | N | N | N | N | Y | N | Y | N |
| *Lott* | N | Y | N | N | Y | N | Y | N |
| **MISSOURI** | | | | | | | | |
| *Bond* | Y | Y | Y | Y | N | Y | N | Y |
| *Danforth* | N | Y | N | N | N | N | Y | N |
| **MONTANA** | | | | | | | | |
| Baucus | N | N | N | Y | N | Y | N | Y |
| *Burns* | N | Y | Y | N | Y | N | Y | N |
| **NEBRASKA** | | | | | | | | |
| Exon | N | Y | N | Y | N | Y | N | Y |
| Kerrey | Y | N | N | Y | N | Y | N | Y |
| **NEVADA** | | | | | | | | |
| Bryan | N | N | Y | Y | Y | Y | Y | N |
| Reid | Y | N | Y | Y | Y | Y | Y | N |
| **NEW HAMPSHIRE** | | | | | | | | |
| *Rudman* | N | N | N | Y | Y | N | Y | N |
| *Smith* | N | Y | N | N | Y | N | Y | N |
| **NEW JERSEY** | | | | | | | | |
| Bradley | Y | N | Y | Y | N | Y | N | Y |
| Lautenberg | Y | N | Y | Y | N | Y | N | Y |
| **NEW MEXICO** | | | | | | | | |
| Bingaman | N | N | N | Y | N | N | Y | ? |
| *Domenici* | N | N | N | N | Y | N | Y | N |
| **NEW YORK** | | | | | | | | |
| Moynihan | N | N | Y | Y | N | Y | N | Y |
| *D'Amato* | Y | Y | Y | Y | N | N | Y | N |
| **NORTH CAROLINA** | | | | | | | | |
| Sanford | Y | ? | ? | Y | Y | Y | N | N |
| *Helms* | N | Y | N | N | Y | N | Y | N |
| **NORTH DAKOTA** | | | | | | | | |
| Burdick | Y | N | Y | Y | N | Y | N | Y |
| Conrad | Y | N | Y | Y | Y | Y | N | N |
| **OHIO** | | | | | | | | |
| Glenn | ? | N | N | Y | N | Y | Y | Y |
| Metzenbaum | N | N | N | Y | N | Y | N | Y |
| **OKLAHOMA** | | | | | | | | |
| Boren | Y | Y | N | Y | N | N | Y | N |
| *Nickles* | N | ? | ? | N | Y | N | Y | N |
| **OREGON** | | | | | | | | |
| *Hatfield* | Y | N | Y | Y | N | Y | N | Y |
| *Packwood* | Y | Y | Y | Y | N | N | Y | Y |
| **PENNSYLVANIA** | | | | | | | | |
| Wofford | Y | N | Y | Y | N | Y | N | Y |
| *Specter* | Y | Y | Y | Y | N | N | Y | Y |
| **RHODE ISLAND** | | | | | | | | |
| Pell | Y | N | Y | Y | N | Y | N | Y |
| *Chafee* | N | Y | N | Y | N | Y | N | N |
| **SOUTH CAROLINA** | | | | | | | | |
| Hollings | Y | Y | Y | Y | N | Y | N | Y |
| *Thurmond* | N | Y | N | N | Y | N | Y | N |
| **SOUTH DAKOTA** | | | | | | | | |
| Daschle | Y | N | Y | Y | N | Y | N | Y |
| *Pressler* | Y | Y | Y | Y | N | Y | N | Y |
| **TENNESSEE** | | | | | | | | |
| Gore | ? | ? | ? | ? | ? | ? | ? | N |
| Sasser | N | N | N | Y | N | Y | N | Y |
| **TEXAS** | | | | | | | | |
| Bentsen | N | N | N | Y | N | Y | N | N |
| *Gramm* | N | Y | N | N | Y | N | Y | N |
| **UTAH** | | | | | | | | |
| *Garn* | N | Y | N | N | Y | N | Y | N |
| *Hatch* | N | Y | N | Y | N | Y | N | Y |
| **VERMONT** | | | | | | | | |
| Leahy | Y | N | Y | Y | N | Y | N | Y |
| *Jeffords* | N | N | N | Y | N | Y | N | Y |
| **VIRGINIA** | | | | | | | | |
| Robb | N | N | Y | Y | N | Y | N | Y |
| *Warner* | N | Y | Y | N | Y | N | Y | N |
| **WASHINGTON** | | | | | | | | |
| Adams | Y | N | Y | Y | N | Y | N | Y |
| *Gorton* | N | Y | Y | Y | N | N | Y | N |
| **WEST VIRGINIA** | | | | | | | | |
| Byrd | N | N | N | Y | Y | Y | N | Y |
| Rockefeller | N | N | Y | N | Y | N | Y | N |
| **WISCONSIN** | | | | | | | | |
| Kohl | N | N | N | Y | Y | Y | N | Y |
| *Kasten* | N | Y | N | N | Y | N | Y | N |
| **WYOMING** | | | | | | | | |
| *Simpson* | N | Y | N | N | Y | N | Y | N |
| *Wallop* | N | Y | N | N | Y | N | Y | N |

ND   Northern Democrats    SD   Southern Democrats          Southern states - Ala., Ark., Fla., Ga., Ky., La., Miss., N.C., Okla., S.C., Tenn., Texas, Va.

**209. HR 5677. Fiscal 1993 Labor, Health and Human Services, Education Appropriations/Budget Act Waiver.** Specter, R-Pa., motion to waive the Budget Act with respect to the Nunn, D-Ga., point of order against the Specter amendment to shift $2.9 billion from the Defense Department's procurement account to the Pell grant program for college students. Motion rejected 30-67: R 6-37; D 24-30 (ND 21-17, SD 3-13), Sept. 16, 1992. A three-fifths majority (60) of the total Senate was required to waive the Budget Act. A 'nay' was a vote in support of the president's position.

**210. HR 5677. Fiscal 1993 Labor, Health and Human Services, Education Appropriations/Enhanced Rescission Authority.** McCain, R-Ariz., motion to waive the Budget Act with respect to the Sasser, D-Tenn., point of order against the McCain amendment to grant the president enhanced authority to rescind individual spending items. Motion rejected 40-56: R 34-8; D 6-48 (ND 1-38, SD 5-10), Sept. 17, 1992. A three-fifths vote of the total Senate (60) was required to waive the Budget Act.

**211. HR 5677. Fiscal 1993 Labor, Health and Human Services, Education Appropriations/Breast Cancer Research.** D'Amato, R-N.Y., motion to waive the Budget Act with respect to the Stevens, R-Alaska, point of order against the D'Amato amendment to transfer $214 million from the Defense Department's research account to the National Cancer Institute for breast cancer research. Motion rejected 43-53: R 14-28; D 29-25 (ND 27-12, SD 2-13), Sept. 17, 1992. A three-fifths vote of the total Senate (60) was required to waive the Budget Act. A 'nay' was a vote in support of the president's position.

**212. HR 5677. Fiscal 1993 Labor, Health and Human Services, Education Appropriations/Needle Exchange Programs.** Kennedy, D-Mass., amendment to the Helms, R-N.C., amendment, to prohibit funding for the distribution of sterile needles to illegal drug users, unless the Surgeon General determined that such programs would help prevent the spread of AIDS and would not encourage the use of illegal drugs. The Helms amendment prohibited states that conducted clean needle programs from receiving funds under the bill, unless the president certified that such programs were effective. Adopted 69-29: R 14-29; D 55-0 (ND 39-0, SD 16-0), Sept. 17, 1992.

**213. HR 5677. Fiscal 1993 Labor, Health and Human Services, Education Appropriations/OSHA Regulations.** Lott, R-Miss., technical amendment to the Helms, R-N.C., amendment, to prohibit funding for the implementation of Occupational Safety and Health Administration (OSHA) regulations affecting mandatory seat belt use, mandatory motorcycle helmet use and mandatory employer driver safety awareness programs. Rejected 43-55: R 34-9; D 9-46 (ND 6-33, SD 3-13), Sept. 17, 1992.

**214. S 3114. Fiscal 1993 Defense Authorization/Strategic Defense Initiative.** Bumpers, D-Ark., amendment to provide $3.3 billion for the Strategic Defense Initiative in fiscal 1993. The committee bill would provide $4.3 billion; the administration requested $5.4 billion. Rejected 48-50: R 5-38; D 43-12 (ND 35-4, SD 8-8), Sept. 17, 1992. A "nay" was a vote in support of the president's position.

**215. S 3114. Fiscal 1993 Defense Authorization/Strategic Defense Initiative.** Nunn, D-Ga., amendment to provide $3.8 billion for the Strategic Defense Initiative in fiscal 1993. The committee bill would provide $4.3 billion; the administration requested $5.4 billion. Adopted 52-46: R 39-4; D 13-42 (ND 5-34, SD 8-8), Sept. 17, 1992.

**216. S 3114. Fiscal 1993 Defense Authorization/Stealth Bombers.** Leahy, D-Vt., amendment to cut $2,686,572,000 from the bill for production of additional B-2 stealth bombers, halting production of the B-2 fleet at 15 planes instead of the 20 planes requested by the administration. Rejected 45-53: R 8-35; D 37-18 (ND 31-7, SD 6-11), Sept. 18, 1992. A "nay" was a vote in support of the president's position.

| | 217 | 218 | 219 | 220 | 221 | 222 | 223 | 224 |
|---|---|---|---|---|---|---|---|---|
| **ALABAMA** | | | | | | | | |
| Heflin | N | Y | Y | Y | Y | Y | N | Y |
| Shelby | N | Y | Y | N | Y | N | N | Y |
| **ALASKA** | | | | | | | | |
| *Murkowski* | Y | Y | Y | Y | N | Y | N | N |
| *Stevens* | N | Y | Y | N | Y | N | N | Y |
| **ARIZONA** | | | | | | | | |
| DeConcini | Y | Y | Y | Y | Y | N | Y | Y |
| *McCain* | N | Y | Y | Y | Y | N | ? | N |
| **ARKANSAS** | | | | | | | | |
| Bumpers | Y | Y | Y | N | Y | N | Y | Y |
| Pryor | Y | Y | Y | N | ? | ? | Y | Y |
| **CALIFORNIA** | | | | | | | | |
| Cranston | Y | Y | Y | N | Y | N | Y | Y |
| *Seymour* | ? | ? | + | - | ? | ? | ? | Y |
| **COLORADO** | | | | | | | | |
| Wirth | ? | ? | ? | ? | ? | ? | Y | Y |
| *Brown* | N | Y | N | N | N | Y | N | N |
| **CONNECTICUT** | | | | | | | | |
| Dodd | Y | Y | Y | N | N | Y | Y | Y |
| Lieberman | Y | Y | Y | N | N | Y | N | Y |
| **DELAWARE** | | | | | | | | |
| Biden | Y | Y | Y | N | Y | Y | ? | Y |
| *Roth* | N | Y | N | Y | N | Y | N | Y |
| **FLORIDA** | | | | | | | | |
| Graham | Y | Y | Y | N | Y | N | N | Y |
| *Mack* | N | Y | Y | Y | Y | N | N | N |
| **GEORGIA** | | | | | | | | |
| Fowler | Y | Y | Y | N | Y | N | N | Y |
| Nunn | N | Y | Y | N | Y | N | N | Y |
| **HAWAII** | | | | | | | | |
| Akaka | Y | Y | Y | N | N | Y | N | Y |
| Inouye | Y | Y | Y | ? | ? | ? | N | Y |
| **IDAHO** | | | | | | | | |
| *Craig* | N | Y | N | Y | Y | N | N | Y |
| *Symms* | N | Y | N | Y | Y | N | N | N |
| **ILLINOIS** | | | | | | | | |
| Dixon | N | Y | Y | N | Y | N | N | Y |
| Simon | Y | Y | Y | N | N | Y | Y | Y |
| **INDIANA** | | | | | | | | |
| *Coats* | N | Y | Y | Y | Y | N | N | Y |
| *Lugar* | N | Y | Y | Y | Y | Y | N | Y |
| **IOWA** | | | | | | | | |
| Harkin | Y | Y | Y | ? | ? | ? | Y | Y |
| *Grassley* | Y | Y | Y | Y | Y | N | N | Y |
| **KANSAS** | | | | | | | | |
| *Dole* | N | Y | Y | Y | Y | N | N | Y |
| *Kassebaum* | Y | Y | Y | N | Y | Y | N | Y |
| **KENTUCKY** | | | | | | | | |
| Ford | Y | Y | Y | Y | Y | N | N | Y |
| *McConnell* | N | Y | Y | Y | Y | N | N | N |
| **LOUISIANA** | | | | | | | | |
| Breaux | N | Y | Y | Y | Y | N | N | Y |
| Johnston | N | Y | Y | Y | Y | N | N | Y |
| **MAINE** | | | | | | | | |
| Mitchell | Y | Y | Y | N | Y | N | Y | Y |
| *Cohen* | N | Y | Y | N | N | N | N | Y |
| **MARYLAND** | | | | | | | | |
| Mikulski | Y | Y | Y | N | Y | N | Y | ? |
| Sarbanes | Y | Y | Y | N | Y | N | Y | Y |
| **MASSACHUSETTS** | | | | | | | | |
| Kennedy | Y | Y | Y | N | Y | Y | Y | Y |
| Kerry | Y | Y | Y | N | Y | Y | N | Y |
| **MICHIGAN** | | | | | | | | |
| Levin | Y | Y | Y | N | Y | Y | Y | Y |
| Riegle | Y | Y | Y | N | Y | N | Y | Y |
| **MINNESOTA** | | | | | | | | |
| Wellstone | Y | Y | Y | N | Y | Y | Y | Y |
| *Durenberger* | N | Y | Y | Y | N | Y | N | Y |
| **MISSISSIPPI** | | | | | | | | |
| *Cochran* | N | Y | Y | N | Y | N | N | N |
| *Lott* | N | Y | N | Y | Y | N | N | N |
| **MISSOURI** | | | | | | | | |
| *Bond* | Y | Y | Y | Y | ? | ? | N | N |
| *Danforth* | Y | Y | Y | N | Y | N | N | N |
| **MONTANA** | | | | | | | | |
| Baucus | Y | Y | N | N | Y | Y | Y | Y |
| *Burns* | N | Y | Y | Y | Y | N | N | Y |
| **NEBRASKA** | | | | | | | | |
| Exon | Y | Y | Y | Y | Y | N | Y | Y |
| Kerrey | Y | Y | Y | N | Y | N | Y | Y |
| **NEVADA** | | | | | | | | |
| Bryan | N | Y | Y | N | Y | N | N | Y |
| Reid | N | Y | Y | Y | Y | N | N | Y |
| **NEW HAMPSHIRE** | | | | | | | | |
| *Rudman* | N | N | Y | N | ? | ? | N | Y |
| *Smith* | N | Y | N | Y | N | N | N | N |
| **NEW JERSEY** | | | | | | | | |
| Bradley | Y | Y | Y | N | Y | N | N | Y |
| Lautenberg | Y | Y | Y | N | Y | N | Y | Y |
| **NEW MEXICO** | | | | | | | | |
| Bingaman | ? | ? | ? | ? | ? | ? | Y | Y |
| *Domenici* | N | Y | Y | Y | Y | N | N | Y |
| **NEW YORK** | | | | | | | | |
| Moynihan | Y | Y | Y | N | Y | Y | Y | Y |
| *D'Amato* | Y | Y | Y | ? | ? | ? | ? | Y |
| **NORTH CAROLINA** | | | | | | | | |
| Sanford | Y | Y | Y | N | Y | N | Y | Y |
| *Helms* | N | Y | N | Y | ? | ? | ? | N |
| **NORTH DAKOTA** | | | | | | | | |
| Burdick | Y | Y | Y | N | Y | N | Y | Y |
| Conrad | Y | Y | N | N | Y | N | Y | Y |
| **OHIO** | | | | | | | | |
| Glenn | Y | Y | Y | N | Y | N | Y | Y |
| Metzenbaum | Y | Y | Y | N | Y | Y | Y | Y |
| **OKLAHOMA** | | | | | | | | |
| Boren | ? | ? | ? | ? | ? | ? | N | Y |
| *Nickles* | N | Y | Y | Y | N | N | N | Y |
| **OREGON** | | | | | | | | |
| *Hatfield* | Y | Y | Y | Y | Y | N | Y | Y |
| *Packwood* | Y | Y | Y | N | Y | N | Y | Y |
| **PENNSYLVANIA** | | | | | | | | |
| Wofford | Y | Y | Y | N | Y | Y | Y | Y |
| *Specter* | Y | Y | Y | N | N | N | ? | N |
| **RHODE ISLAND** | | | | | | | | |
| Pell | Y | Y | Y | N | Y | Y | Y | Y |
| *Chafee* | Y | Y | Y | N | N | Y | N | Y |
| **SOUTH CAROLINA** | | | | | | | | |
| Hollings | N | Y | Y | N | Y | N | N | Y |
| *Thurmond* | N | Y | Y | Y | Y | N | N | Y |
| **SOUTH DAKOTA** | | | | | | | | |
| Daschle | Y | Y | Y | N | N | Y | N | Y |
| *Pressler* | Y | Y | N | Y | Y | N | N | Y |
| **TENNESSEE** | | | | | | | | |
| Gore | ? | ? | ? | ? | ? | ? | ? | ? |
| Sasser | Y | Y | Y | N | N | Y | Y | Y |
| **TEXAS** | | | | | | | | |
| Bentsen | N | Y | Y | N | Y | N | Y | Y |
| *Gramm* | N | Y | N | Y | Y | N | N | N |
| **UTAH** | | | | | | | | |
| *Garn* | N | Y | N | Y | N | Y | N | N |
| *Hatch* | N | Y | Y | Y | Y | N | N | Y |
| **VERMONT** | | | | | | | | |
| Leahy | Y | Y | Y | N | Y | N | Y | Y |
| *Jeffords* | Y | Y | Y | N | ? | ? | N | Y |
| **VIRGINIA** | | | | | | | | |
| Robb | N | Y | Y | N | N | N | N | Y |
| *Warner* | N | Y | N | Y | N | Y | N | N |
| **WASHINGTON** | | | | | | | | |
| Adams | Y | Y | Y | N | Y | N | Y | Y |
| *Gorton* | N | Y | Y | N | Y | N | N | Y |
| **WEST VIRGINIA** | | | | | | | | |
| Byrd | Y | Y | Y | N | Y | N | N | Y |
| Rockefeller | Y | Y | Y | N | N | N | Y | ? |
| **WISCONSIN** | | | | | | | | |
| Kohl | Y | Y | Y | N | Y | N | Y | Y |
| *Kasten* | Y | Y | Y | ? | ? | ? | ? | ? |
| **WYOMING** | | | | | | | | |
| *Simpson* | N | Y | Y | ? | ? | ? | N | Y |
| *Wallop* | N | Y | N | Y | N | Y | N | N |

ND   Northern Democrats   SD   Southern Democrats          Southern states - Ala., Ark., Fla., Ga., Ky., La., Miss., N.C., Okla., S.C., Tenn., Texas, Va.

**217. S 3114. Fiscal 1993 Defense Authorization/Nuclear Testing Moratorium.** Hatfield, R-Ore., amendment to the Cohen, R-Maine, amendment. The Hatfield amendment imposed a nine-month moratorium on nuclear testing until July 1, 1993; allowed limited testing between July 1, 1993, and Jan. 1, 1997; required reports to Congress on the remaining weapons in the U.S. stockpile, proposed safety improvements and tests, and plans for a comprehensive test ban by Sept. 30, 1996; and, contingent upon certain factors, prohibited nuclear tests after Sept. 30, 1996, unless a foreign state conducted a test. The Cohen amendment imposed a three-month testing moratorium, allowed limited testing until 1998, and then imposed a test ban in 1998, with the proviso that the president could waive that ban for one year in order to negotiate a comprehensive test ban. Adopted 55-40: R 13-29; D 42-11 (ND 35-3, SD 7-8), Sept. 18, 1992. A "nay" was a vote in support of the president's position.

**218. HR 5677. Fiscal 1993 Labor, Health and Human Services, Education Appropriations/Dietary Supplement Regulations.** Hatch, R-Utah, amendment to prohibit funding to implement Health and Human Services' regulations for labeling of dietary supplement of vitamins, minerals, herbs or other similar nutritional substances. Adopted 94-1: R 41-1; D 53-0 (ND 38-0, SD 15-0), Sept. 18, 1992.

**219. HR 5677. Fiscal 1993 Labor, Health and Human Services, Education Appropriations/Passage.** Passage of the bill to provide $246,454,455,000 in new budget authority for the departments of Labor, Health and Human Services, and Education and related agencies for fiscal 1993. The administration requested $244,419,291,000. Passed 82-13: R 31-11; D 51-2 (ND 36-2, SD 15-0), Sept. 18, 1992. A "nay" was a vote in support of the president's position.

**220. S 3114. Fiscal 1993 Defense Authorization/**

**Abortions at Overseas Bases.** Coats, R-Ind., amendment to strike the provisions of the bill that would allow U.S. military personnel and their families to obtain abortions at U.S. military bases overseas at their own expense. Rejected 36-55: R 29-11; D 7-44 (ND 3-33, SD 4-11), Sept. 18, 1992. A "yea" was a vote in support of the president's position.

**221. S 3114. Fiscal 1993 Defense Authorization/Defense Sales.** Graham, D-Fla., motion to table (kill) the Dodd, D-Conn., amendment to the Graham amendment. Dodd's amendment authorized the president to extend $1 billion in loan guarantees for the sale of defense articles to NATO member nations, Israel, Australia, New Zealand and Japan. Motion agreed to 73-12: R 28-7; D 45-5 (ND 32-4, SD 13-1), Sept. 18, 1992.

**222. S 3114. Fiscal 1993 Defense Authorization/Cuba Sanctions.** Dodd, D-Conn., motion to table (kill) the Graham, D-Fla., amendment to incorporate into the bill the "Cuban Democracy Act," which placed sanctions against countries that assisted Cuba until Cuba held free elections and moved toward a free market economy. Motion rejected 24-61: R 6-29; D 18-32 (ND 16-20, SD 2-12), Sept. 18, 1992. The Graham amendment subsequently was adopted by voice vote.

**223. HR 5504. Fiscal 1993 Defense Appropriations/Intelligence Funding.** Bumpers, D-Ark., amendment to reduce funding for intelligence programs by $1 billion, $500 million from National Foreign Intelligence Program and $500 million from the Tactical Intelligence and Related Activities budget. Rejected 35-57: R 0-37; D 35-20 (ND 29-10, SD 6-10), Sept. 21, 1992.

**224. Procedural Motion.** Mitchell, D-Maine, motion to instruct the sergeant-at-arms to request the attendance of absent senators. Motion agreed to 83-13: R 29-13; D 54-0 (ND 38-0, SD 16-0), Sept. 22, 1992.

| | 225 | 226 | 227 | 228 | 229 | 230 | 231 | 232 |
|---|---|---|---|---|---|---|---|---|
| **ALABAMA** | | | | | | | | |
| Heflin | Y | Y | Y | Y | Y | N | N | N |
| *Shelby* | N | Y | Y | Y | Y | N | Y | N |
| **ALASKA** | | | | | | | | |
| *Murkowski* | Y | N | Y | Y | Y | N | N | Y |
| *Stevens* | N | N | Y | Y | Y | N | N | Y |
| **ARIZONA** | | | | | | | | |
| DeConcini | N | Y | N | Y | Y | Y | N | Y |
| *McCain* | Y | N | Y | Y | Y | N | N | Y |
| **ARKANSAS** | | | | | | | | |
| Bumpers | Y | Y | Y | Y | Y | N | N | Y |
| Pryor | Y | Y | Y | Y | Y | N | N | Y |
| **CALIFORNIA** | | | | | | | | |
| Cranston | N | Y | N | Y | Y | Y | Y | Y |
| *Seymour* | N | N | N | Y | ? | ? | ? | ? |
| **COLORADO** | | | | | | | | |
| Wirth | N | Y | ? | ? | ? | Y | Y | Y |
| *Brown* | N | N | Y | Y | N | N | N | N |
| **CONNECTICUT** | | | | | | | | |
| Dodd | Y | Y | N | Y | Y | Y | N | Y |
| Lieberman | Y | Y | N | Y | Y | Y | N | Y |
| **DELAWARE** | | | | | | | | |
| Biden | Y | Y | N | ? | Y | Y | Y | Y |
| *Roth* | Y | N | Y | Y | N | N | N | Y |
| **FLORIDA** | | | | | | | | |
| Graham | Y | Y | N | Y | Y | N | Y | Y |
| *Mack* | C | N | Y | Y | Y | N | N | N |
| **GEORGIA** | | | | | | | | |
| Fowler | N | Y | Y | Y | Y | N | N | Y |
| Nunn | Y | Y | Y | Y | ? | Y | ? | Y |
| **HAWAII** | | | | | | | | |
| Akaka | Y | Y | N | Y | Y | Y | N | Y |
| Inouye | Y | Y | N | Y | Y | Y | Y | Y |
| **IDAHO** | | | | | | | | |
| *Craig* | N | N | N | Y | Y | N | N | N |
| *Symms* | N | N | Y | ? | Y | N | N | N |
| **ILLINOIS** | | | | | | | | |
| Dixon | Y | Y | Y | Y | Y | N | N | Y |
| Simon | Y | Y | N | Y | Y | N | Y | Y |
| **INDIANA** | | | | | | | | |
| *Coats* | Y | N | Y | Y | Y | N | N | Y |
| *Lugar* | N | N | Y | Y | Y | N | N | N |
| **IOWA** | | | | | | | | |
| Harkin | Y | Y | N | Y | Y | Y | Y | Y |
| *Grassley* | Y | N | Y | Y | Y | Y | N | N |
| **KANSAS** | | | | | | | | |
| *Dole* | N | N | Y | Y | Y | N | N | N |
| *Kassebaum* | Y | N | N | Y | Y | Y | N | N |
| **KENTUCKY** | | | | | | | | |
| Ford | Y | Y | Y | Y | Y | N | Y | Y |
| *McConnell* | Y | N | Y | Y | Y | N | N | N |
| **LOUISIANA** | | | | | | | | |
| Breaux | Y | Y | Y | Y | Y | N | N | Y |
| Johnston | Y | Y | Y | Y | Y | Y | N | Y |
| **MAINE** | | | | | | | | |
| Mitchell | Y | Y | N | Y | Y | Y | N | Y |
| *Cohen* | Y | N | N | Y | Y | Y | N | Y |
| **MARYLAND** | | | | | | | | |
| Mikulski | Y | Y | N | Y | Y | Y | Y | Y |
| Sarbanes | Y | Y | N | Y | Y | Y | Y | Y |
| **MASSACHUSETTS** | | | | | | | | |
| Kennedy | Y | Y | N | Y | Y | Y | Y | Y |
| Kerry | Y | Y | Y | Y | Y | Y | Y | Y |
| **MICHIGAN** | | | | | | | | |
| Levin | Y | Y | N | Y | Y | N | Y | Y |
| Riegle | Y | Y | N | Y | Y | N | Y | Y |
| **MINNESOTA** | | | | | | | | |
| Wellstone | Y | Y | N | Y | N | Y | Y | Y |
| *Durenberger* | Y | Y | N | Y | Y | Y | Y | Y |
| **MISSISSIPPI** | | | | | | | | |
| *Cochran* | Y | N | Y | Y | Y | N | N | N |
| *Lott* | N | N | Y | Y | Y | Y | N | N |
| **MISSOURI** | | | | | | | | |
| *Bond* | Y | N | Y | Y | Y | Y | N | N |
| *Danforth* | Y | N | Y | Y | Y | Y | Y | N |
| **MONTANA** | | | | | | | | |
| Baucus | Y | Y | N | Y | Y | Y | N | Y |
| *Burns* | N | N | Y | Y | Y | N | N | N |
| **NEBRASKA** | | | | | | | | |
| Exon | Y | Y | N | Y | Y | Y | Y | Y |
| Kerrey | Y | Y | N | Y | Y | Y | Y | Y |
| **NEVADA** | | | | | | | | |
| Bryan | Y | Y | Y | Y | Y | Y | N | Y |
| Reid | N | Y | Y | Y | Y | Y | Y | Y |
| **NEW HAMPSHIRE** | | | | | | | | |
| *Rudman* | N | N | N | ? | Y | Y | N | N |
| *Smith* | N | N | Y | N | N | N | N | N |
| **NEW JERSEY** | | | | | | | | |
| Bradley | Y | Y | N | ? | N | Y | Y | Y |
| Lautenberg | Y | Y | N | Y | Y | Y | Y | Y |
| **NEW MEXICO** | | | | | | | | |
| Bingaman | Y | Y | N | Y | Y | Y | Y | Y |
| *Domenici* | Y | N | Y | Y | Y | N | N | N |
| **NEW YORK** | | | | | | | | |
| Moynihan | Y | Y | N | Y | Y | Y | Y | Y |
| *D'Amato* | Y | N | N | Y | Y | N | Y | Y |
| **NORTH CAROLINA** | | | | | | | | |
| Sanford | Y | Y | Y | Y | Y | N | N | Y |
| *Helms* | N | N | Y | ? | Y | N | N | N |
| **NORTH DAKOTA** | | | | | | | | |
| Burdick | Y | Y | N | Y | Y | Y | Y | Y |
| Conrad | Y | Y | Y | Y | Y | N | N | N |
| **OHIO** | | | | | | | | |
| Glenn | Y | Y | N | Y | Y | N | N | Y |
| Metzenbaum | Y | Y | N | Y | N | Y | Y | Y |
| **OKLAHOMA** | | | | | | | | |
| Boren | N | Y | N | Y | Y | N | N | Y |
| *Nickles* | N | N | Y | Y | Y | Y | Y | N |
| **OREGON** | | | | | | | | |
| *Hatfield* | Y | Y | N | Y | N | N | Y | Y |
| *Packwood* | N | Y | N | Y | N | Y | Y | Y |
| **PENNSYLVANIA** | | | | | | | | |
| Wofford | Y | Y | N | Y | Y | N | N | Y |
| *Specter* | Y | Y | N | Y | N | Y | Y | Y |
| **RHODE ISLAND** | | | | | | | | |
| Pell | Y | Y | N | Y | Y | N | Y | Y |
| *Chafee* | N | N | N | Y | Y | N | N | Y |
| **SOUTH CAROLINA** | | | | | | | | |
| Hollings | Y | N | Y | Y | Y | N | N | N |
| *Thurmond* | Y | N | Y | Y | N | N | N | N |
| **SOUTH DAKOTA** | | | | | | | | |
| Daschle | Y | Y | Y | Y | Y | Y | N | Y |
| *Pressler* | Y | N | Y | Y | Y | N | N | N |
| **TENNESSEE** | | | | | | | | |
| Gore | Y | Y | ? | ? | ? | ? | ? | Y |
| Sasser | Y | Y | N | Y | Y | Y | N | Y |
| **TEXAS** | | | | | | | | |
| Bentsen | Y | Y | Y | Y | Y | N | N | Y |
| *Gramm* | N | N | Y | Y | Y | N | N | N |
| **UTAH** | | | | | | | | |
| *Garn* | N | N | Y | N | Y | N | N | N |
| *Hatch* | Y | N | Y | N | Y | N | N | N |
| **VERMONT** | | | | | | | | |
| Leahy | Y | Y | N | Y | Y | N | Y | Y |
| *Jeffords* | Y | Y | N | Y | N | Y | N | Y |
| **VIRGINIA** | | | | | | | | |
| Robb | Y | Y | N | Y | Y | N | N | Y |
| *Warner* | Y | N | N | Y | Y | N | N | N |
| **WASHINGTON** | | | | | | | | |
| Adams | Y | Y | N | Y | Y | Y | Y | Y |
| *Gorton* | Y | N | Y | Y | Y | N | Y | N |
| **WEST VIRGINIA** | | | | | | | | |
| Byrd | Y | Y | Y | Y | Y | N | Y | Y |
| Rockefeller | Y | Y | N | Y | Y | N | N | Y |
| **WISCONSIN** | | | | | | | | |
| Kohl | Y | Y | N | Y | N | Y | Y | Y |
| *Kasten* | Y | Y | Y | Y | Y | N | N | N |
| **WYOMING** | | | | | | | | |
| *Simpson* | Y | N | Y | Y | Y | N | N | N |
| *Wallop* | N | N | Y | N | N | N | N | N |

**KEY**

| | |
|---|---|
| Y | Voted for (yea). |
| # | Paired for. |
| + | Announced for. |
| N | Voted against (nay). |
| X | Paired against. |
| − | Announced against. |
| P | Voted "present." |
| C | Voted "present" to avoid possible conflict of interest. |
| ? | Did not vote or otherwise make a position known. |

Democrats   *Republicans*

ND Northern Democrats    SD Southern Democrats    Southern states - Ala., Ark., Fla., Ga., Ky., La., Miss., N.C., Okla., S.C., Tenn., Texas, Va.

**225. S 12. Cable Television Reregulation/Conference Report.** Adoption of the conference report to cap basic cable rates and improve competition in the cable industry by having the FCC set rates for basic cable service and giving broadcasters the right to charge cable operators for the use of over-the-air signals. Adopted (thus cleared for the president) 74-25: R 24-18; D 50-7 (ND 36-4, SD 14-3), Sept. 22, 1992. A "nay" was a vote in support of the president's position.

**226. National Motor-Voter Registration/Veto Override.** Passage, over President Bush's July 2 veto, of the bill to require states to permit voter registration simultaneously with applying for public certificates such as a driver's license, marriage license or hunting permit. Rejected 62-38: R 6-37; D 56-1 (ND 40-0, SD 16-1), Sept. 22, 1992. A two-thirds majority of those present and voting (67 in this case) was required to override a veto. A "nay" was a vote in support of the president's position.

**227. HR 5504. Fiscal 1993 Defense Appropriations/Boy Scouts.** Helms, R-N.C., amendment to require the Office of Personnel Management to exclude from the Combined Federal Campaign, which collected and disbursed donations from federal employees to charities, any charity that withdrew support for the Boy Scouts of America because that organization disagreed with the Boy Scouts' admission policy barring homosexuals or atheists. Rejected 49-49: R 31-12; D 18-37 (ND 6-33, SD 12-4), Sept. 22, 1992.

**228. HR 5504. Fiscal 1993 Defense Appropriations/Breast Cancer Research.** Harkin, D-Iowa, amendment to cut the committee-recommended level for the Strategic Defense Initiative by $200 million to $3.6 billion in fiscal 1993. The amendment would increase by $185 million the amount earmarked for Army research on breast cancer. The administration requested $5.4 billion for SDI. Adopted 89-4: R 36-4; D 53-0 (ND 37-0, SD 16-0), Sept. 22, 1992.

Immediately after the amendment was adopted, it was amended by voice vote to restore the SDI appropriation to $3.8 billion while still adding the funds for cancer research.

**229. HR 5504. Fiscal 1993 Defense Appropriations/Passage.** Passage of the bill to provide approximately $250.5 billion in new budget authority for the Department of Defense for the fiscal year ending Sept. 30, 1993. The administration requested $259,212,724,000. Passed 86-10: R 37-5; D 49-5 (ND 34-5, SD 15-0), Sept. 23, 1992.

**230. HR 11. Tax Bill/Non-conventional Fuels.** Bradley, D-N.J., motion to table the Dole, R-Kan., amendment to extend for eight months the Section 29 tax credit for non-conventional drilling for natural gas. The amendment paid for it by shortening from 18 to 15 months the extension of other expiring tax breaks. Rejected 41-57: R 10-32; D 31-25 (ND 26-14, SD 5-11), Sept. 23, 1992. (The Dole amendment was subsequently adopted by voice vote.)

**231. HR 11. Tax Bill/Pilots' Pensions.** Packwood, R-Ore., amendment to strike provisions that gave non-unionized pilots the same exemption from pension law as unionized pilots, thereby allowing airlines to offer their pilots more generous pensions than they offered to other employees. Rejected 41-56: R 8-34; D 33-22 (ND 30-10, SD 3-12), Sept. 23, 1992.

**232. S 5. Family and Medical Leave/Veto Override.** Passage, over President Bush's Sept. 22 veto, of the bill to require companies with more than 50 employees to provide workers with up to 12 weeks of unpaid leave for family emergencies. Passed (thus cleared for House action) 68-31: R 14-28; D 54-3 (ND 40-0, SD 14-3), Sept. 24, 1992. A two-thirds majority of those present and voting (66 in this case) was required to override a veto. A "nay" was a vote in support of the president's position.

## KEY

Y Voted for (yea).
\# Paired for.
\+ Announced for.
N Voted against (nay).
X Paired against.
− Announced against.
P Voted "present."
C Voted "present" to avoid possible conflict of interest.
? Did not vote or otherwise make a position known.

Democrats    *Republicans*

| | 233 | 234 | 235 | 236 | 237 | 238 | 239 | 240 |
|---|---|---|---|---|---|---|---|---|
| **ALABAMA** | | | | | | | | |
| Heflin | Y | N | Y | N | Y | N | Y | N |
| Shelby | Y | Y | Y | Y | Y | N | Y | Y |
| **ALASKA** | | | | | | | | |
| *Murkowski* | N | N | Y | Y | Y | ? | ? | ? |
| *Stevens* | Y | N | N | Y | Y | Y | Y | Y |
| **ARIZONA** | | | | | | | | |
| DeConcini | N | C | Y | N | N | N | Y | N |
| *McCain* | N | Y | N | Y | Y | Y | N | Y |
| **ARKANSAS** | | | | | | | | |
| Bumpers | Y | Y | N | Y | N | Y | N | Y |
| Pryor | Y | N | N | N | Y | N | Y | N |
| **CALIFORNIA** | | | | | | | | |
| Cranston | N | Y | N | N | N | ? | ? | ? |
| *Seymour* | ? | ? | ? | ? | ? | ? | ? | ? |
| **COLORADO** | | | | | | | | |
| Wirth | N | N | ? | ? | ? | N | Y | N |
| *Brown* | Y | Y | Y | Y | Y | Y | N | Y |
| **CONNECTICUT** | | | | | | | | |
| Dodd | Y | Y | Y | N | Y | N | Y | N |
| Lieberman | Y | Y | Y | N | Y | N | Y | N |
| **DELAWARE** | | | | | | | | |
| Biden | N | Y | N | N | Y | N | Y | N |
| *Roth* | Y | Y | Y | Y | Y | Y | N | N |
| **FLORIDA** | | | | | | | | |
| Graham | Y | Y | Y | N | N | N | Y | N |
| *Mack* | Y | Y | Y | Y | Y | Y | N | Y |
| **GEORGIA** | | | | | | | | |
| Fowler | N | Y | N | Y | N | Y | N | Y |
| Nunn | N | Y | Y | N | Y | N | Y | N |
| **HAWAII** | | | | | | | | |
| Akaka | N | Y | N | Y | N | Y | N | Y |
| Inouye | N | N | Y | N | Y | N | Y | N |
| **IDAHO** | | | | | | | | |
| *Craig* | Y | N | Y | Y | Y | Y | Y | N |
| *Symms* | Y | N | Y | Y | Y | Y | Y | N |
| **ILLINOIS** | | | | | | | | |
| Dixon | Y | Y | Y | N | Y | Y | Y | N |
| Simon | N | Y | N | N | N | N | Y | N |
| **INDIANA** | | | | | | | | |
| *Coats* | Y | Y | N | Y | Y | Y | Y | N |
| *Lugar* | Y | Y | N | Y | Y | Y | Y | N |
| **IOWA** | | | | | | | | |
| Harkin | N | Y | N | N | Y | N | Y | N |
| *Grassley* | N | Y | N | Y | Y | Y | N | N |
| **KANSAS** | | | | | | | | |
| *Dole* | Y | N | Y | Y | Y | Y | N | Y |
| *Kassebaum* | Y | Y | Y | N | Y | Y | Y | N |
| **KENTUCKY** | | | | | | | | |
| Ford | Y | Y | Y | N | Y | N | Y | N |
| *McConnell* | N | Y | Y | Y | Y | Y | N | N |
| **LOUISIANA** | | | | | | | | |
| Breaux | Y | N | Y | N | Y | N | Y | N |
| Johnston | Y | X | Y | N | Y | N | Y | N |
| **MAINE** | | | | | | | | |
| Mitchell | Y | N | N | N | Y | N | Y | N |
| *Cohen* | Y | Y | N | Y | N | Y | N | N |
| **MARYLAND** | | | | | | | | |
| Mikulski | N | N | Y | N | N | Y | N | N |
| Sarbanes | N | Y | N | N | N | N | Y | N |
| **MASSACHUSETTS** | | | | | | | | |
| Kennedy | N | N | N | N | N | Y | N | N |
| Kerry | N | Y | N | N | N | N | Y | N |
| **MICHIGAN** | | | | | | | | |
| Levin | N | Y | N | N | N | Y | N | N |
| Riegle | N | Y | N | N | N | N | Y | N |
| **MINNESOTA** | | | | | | | | |
| Wellstone | N | Y | N | N | N | Y | N | N |
| *Durenberger* | Y | N | Y | N | Y | N | Y | Y |
| **MISSISSIPPI** | | | | | | | | |
| *Cochran* | Y | N | Y | Y | Y | Y | Y | N |
| *Lott* | Y | Y | Y | Y | Y | Y | Y | N |
| **MISSOURI** | | | | | | | | |
| *Bond* | N | Y | Y | Y | Y | ? | ? | ? |
| *Danforth* | Y | N | Y | N | Y | Y | Y | N |
| **MONTANA** | | | | | | | | |
| Baucus | Y | N | N | N | Y | N | Y | N |
| *Burns* | Y | Y | Y | Y | Y | Y | N | Y |
| **NEBRASKA** | | | | | | | | |
| Exon | N | Y | N | N | Y | N | Y | N |
| Kerrey | N | Y | N | N | Y | N | Y | N |
| **NEVADA** | | | | | | | | |
| Bryan | Y | Y | Y | N | Y | Y | Y | N |
| Reid | Y | Y | Y | N | Y | Y | Y | N |
| **NEW HAMPSHIRE** | | | | | | | | |
| *Rudman* | Y | N | Y | ? | Y | N | Y | N |
| *Smith* | Y | Y | Y | Y | Y | Y | Y | N |
| **NEW JERSEY** | | | | | | | | |
| Bradley | Y | Y | N | N | N | N | Y | N |
| Lautenberg | N | Y | N | N | N | N | Y | N |
| **NEW MEXICO** | | | | | | | | |
| Bingaman | N | Y | N | N | N | N | Y | N |
| *Domenici* | N | N | N | N | Y | Y | N | N |
| **NEW YORK** | | | | | | | | |
| Moynihan | Y | N | Y | N | N | N | Y | Y |
| *D'Amato* | N | Y | N | Y | Y | Y | Y | N |
| **NORTH CAROLINA** | | | | | | | | |
| Sanford | Y | \# | + | ? | ? | N | Y | N |
| *Helms* | Y | Y | Y | + | + | Y | N | Y |
| **NORTH DAKOTA** | | | | | | | | |
| Burdick | N | N | N | N | N | N | Y | N |
| Conrad | N | Y | Y | N | N | N | Y | N |
| **OHIO** | | | | | | | | |
| Glenn | N | Y | N | N | N | N | Y | N |
| Metzenbaum | N | Y | N | N | N | N | Y | N |
| **OKLAHOMA** | | | | | | | | |
| Boren | Y | ? | ? | ? | ? | ? | ? | ? |
| *Nickles* | N | Y | Y | Y | Y | Y | N | N |
| **OREGON** | | | | | | | | |
| *Hatfield* | Y | N | N | N | Y | N | N | Y |
| *Packwood* | Y | N | Y | N | Y | N | Y | N |
| **PENNSYLVANIA** | | | | | | | | |
| Wofford | ? | Y | N | N | Y | N | Y | N |
| *Specter* | N | Y | N | N | Y | N | Y | N |
| **RHODE ISLAND** | | | | | | | | |
| Pell | N | N | N | N | N | Y | N | N |
| *Chafee* | Y | N | N | N | Y | Y | Y | Y |
| **SOUTH CAROLINA** | | | | | | | | |
| Hollings | N | Y | Y | N | Y | N | Y | N |
| *Thurmond* | Y | N | Y | Y | Y | Y | N | Y |
| **SOUTH DAKOTA** | | | | | | | | |
| Daschle | Y | N | N | N | Y | N | Y | N |
| *Pressler* | N | N | Y | Y | Y | Y | N | Y |
| **TENNESSEE** | | | | | | | | |
| Gore | ? | ? | ? | ? | ? | ? | ? | ? |
| Sasser | N | N | Y | N | Y | N | Y | N |
| **TEXAS** | | | | | | | | |
| Bentsen | Y | N | Y | N | Y | N | Y | N |
| *Gramm* | Y | Y | Y | Y | Y | Y | N | Y |
| **UTAH** | | | | | | | | |
| *Garn* | Y | N | N | Y | Y | Y | N | Y |
| *Hatch* | Y | Y | Y | N | Y | Y | Y | N |
| **VERMONT** | | | | | | | | |
| Leahy | N | Y | N | N | N | N | Y | N |
| *Jeffords* | N | N | N | N | N | N | Y | Y |
| **VIRGINIA** | | | | | | | | |
| Robb | N | Y | N | Y | N | Y | N | N |
| *Warner* | Y | Y | Y | Y | Y | Y | N | Y |
| **WASHINGTON** | | | | | | | | |
| Adams | N | N | N | N | N | N | Y | N |
| *Gorton* | N | Y | Y | Y | Y | N | N | N |
| **WEST VIRGINIA** | | | | | | | | |
| Byrd | N | N | Y | N | N | N | Y | N |
| Rockefeller | ? | N | ? | N | Y | N | Y | N |
| **WISCONSIN** | | | | | | | | |
| Kohl | N | Y | N | N | Y | N | Y | N |
| *Kasten* | N | Y | Y | Y | Y | Y | ? | ? |
| **WYOMING** | | | | | | | | |
| *Simpson* | Y | N | Y | ? | Y | N | Y | N |
| *Wallop* | Y | Y | Y | Y | Y | Y | N | Y |

ND Northern Democrats    SD Southern Democrats    Southern states - Ala., Ark., Fla., Ga., Ky., La., Miss., N.C., Okla., S.C., Tenn., Texas, Va.

**233. HR 11. Tax Bill/Child Care Tax Credits.** Bentsen, D-Texas, motion to table (kill) the DeConcini, D-Ariz., amendment to provide tax credits to employers for providing on-site or near-site child care for their employees. Motion agreed to 50-46: R 29-13; D 21-33 (ND 10-28, SD 11-5), Sept. 24, 1992.

**234. HR 11. Tax Bill/Estimated Tax Payments.** Bumpers, D-Ark., motion to waive the Budget Act with respect to the Bentsen, D-Texas, point of order against the Bumpers amendment to strike certain provisions in the bill in order to keep estimated tax payments at 100 percent of what one earned in the previous year instead of 120 percent, as provided in the bill. Motion rejected 57-37: R 24-18; D 33-19 (ND 25-14, SD 8-5), Sept. 24, 1992. A three-fifths majority (60) of the total Senate was required to waive the Budget Act. (Subsequently, the chair upheld the Bentsen point of order and the Bumpers amendment fell.)

**235. HR 11. Tax Bill/Tobacco Advertising.** Ford, D-Ky., motion to table (kill) the Harkin, D-Iowa, amendment to reduce the tax deductibility on advertising for tobacco products from 100 percent to 80 percent with the revenue generated going to anti-smoking campaigns. Motion agreed to 56-38: R 28-14; D 28-24 (ND 16-22, SD 12-2), Sept. 24, 1992.

**236. HR 11. Tax Bill/Supermajority for Tax Increases.** McCain, R-Ariz., motion to waive the Budget Act with respect to the Sasser, D-Tenn., point of order against the McCain amendment to require three-fifths of the total Senate to pass a bill or amendment increasing taxes. Motion rejected 32-60: R 30-9; D 2-51 (ND 0-39, SD 2-12), Sept. 24, 1992. A three-fifths majority (60) of the total Senate was required to waive the Budget Act. (Subse-

quently, the chair upheld the Sasser point of order and the McCain amendment fell.)

**237. HR 11. Tax Bill/"Good Will."** Bentsen, D-Texas, motion to table (kill) the Simon, D-Ill., amendment to strike the provision to allow companies to write off future acquisitions of "good will" — the value of the company as a going concern. Motion agreed to 75-19: R 40-1; D 35-18 (ND 22-17, SD 13-1), Sept. 24, 1992.

**238. HR 11. Tax Bill/Deficit Reduction Tax Checkoff.** Smith, R-N.H., motion to waive the Budget Act with respect to the Sasser, D-Tenn., point of order against the Smith amendment to allow individuals to designate up to 10 percent of their income tax liability to reduce the public debt. Motion rejected 36-58: R 32-8; D 4-50 (ND 4-35, SD 0-15), Sept. 25, 1992.

**239. HR 11. Tax Bill/Presidential Campaign Tax Check-off.** Bentsen, D-Texas, motion to table (kill) the Gramm, R-Texas, amendment to repeal the Presidential Election Campaign Fund, which allowed individuals to designate $1 of their income taxes to the fund. Motion agreed to 62-31: R 8-31; D 54-0 (ND 39-0, SD 15-0), Sept. 25, 1992.

**240. HR 11. Tax Bill/Enterprise Zones.** Dole, R-Kan., amendment to eliminate provisions making permanent the existing cap on itemized deductions and the phaseout of the personal exemption for upper-income taxpayers, and to cut the number of tax enterprise zones from 125 to 30; limit the Individual Retirement Account deduction; and provide a 12-month extension for expiring tax provisions. Rejected 34-59: R 31-8; D 3-51 (ND 1-38, SD 2-13), Sept. 25, 1992. A "yea" was a vote in support of the president's position.

### KEY

Y Voted for (yea).
\# Paired for.
+ Announced for.
N Voted against (nay).
X Paired against.
– Announced against.
P Voted "present."
C Voted "present" to avoid possible conflict of interest.
? Did not vote or otherwise make a position known.

Democrats    *Republicans*

| | 241 | 242 | 243 | 244 | 245 | 246 | 247 | 248 |
|---|---|---|---|---|---|---|---|---|
| **ALABAMA** | | | | | | | | |
| Heflin | Y | N | Y | N | Y | Y | N | N |
| Shelby | Y | N | Y | N | Y | Y | N | N |
| **ALASKA** | | | | | | | | |
| *Murkowski* | ? | ? | ? | ? | ? | Y | N | N |
| *Stevens* | Y | Y | N | Y | N | Y | N | N |
| **ARIZONA** | | | | | | | | |
| DeConcini | Y | N | Y | N | Y | Y | N | N |
| *McCain* | Y | N | ? | ? | ? | Y | Y | Y |
| **ARKANSAS** | | | | | | | | |
| Bumpers | Y | N | ? | ? | ? | Y | N | N |
| Pryor | ? | ? | Y | N | Y | Y | N | N |
| **CALIFORNIA** | | | | | | | | |
| Cranston | ? | ? | ? | ? | ? | Y | N | N |
| *Seymour* | ? | ? | ? | ? | ? | Y | Y | Y |
| **COLORADO** | | | | | | | | |
| Wirth | ? | ? | ? | ? | ? | Y | N | N |
| *Brown* | Y | N | ? | ? | ? | Y | N | Y |
| **CONNECTICUT** | | | | | | | | |
| Dodd | N | N | Y | N | Y | Y | N | N |
| Lieberman | Y | N | Y | N | Y | N | N | N |
| **DELAWARE** | | | | | | | | |
| Biden | N | N | Y | N | Y | Y | N | N |
| *Roth* | N | N | N | N | Y | Y | N | N |
| **FLORIDA** | | | | | | | | |
| Graham | Y | N | Y | N | Y | Y | N | N |
| *Mack* | Y | Y | N | Y | N | Y | Y | N |
| **GEORGIA** | | | | | | | | |
| Fowler | Y | N | ? | ? | ? | Y | N | N |
| Nunn | Y | N | Y | N | Y | Y | N | N |
| **HAWAII** | | | | | | | | |
| Akaka | N | N | Y | N | Y | Y | N | N |
| Inouye | N | N | Y | N | Y | Y | N | N |
| **IDAHO** | | | | | | | | |
| *Craig* | Y | Y | N | Y | N | N | Y | Y |
| *Symms* | Y | Y | N | Y | N | N | Y | Y |
| **ILLINOIS** | | | | | | | | |
| Dixon | N | N | Y | N | Y | Y | N | N |
| Simon | N | N | Y | N | Y | Y | N | N |
| **INDIANA** | | | | | | | | |
| *Coats* | N | Y | N | Y | N | Y | Y | N |
| *Lugar* | N | Y | N | Y | N | Y | N | N |
| **IOWA** | | | | | | | | |
| Harkin | N | N | Y | N | Y | Y | N | N |
| *Grassley* | Y | N | N | Y | N | Y | N | N |
| **KANSAS** | | | | | | | | |
| *Dole* | Y | N | N | Y | N | Y | N | N |
| *Kassebaum* | N | Y | N | Y | N | Y | N | N |
| **KENTUCKY** | | | | | | | | |
| Ford | Y | N | Y | N | Y | Y | N | N |
| *McConnell* | Y | Y | N | N | Y | Y | N | N |
| **LOUISIANA** | | | | | | | | |
| Breaux | N | N | Y | Y | N | ? | N | N |
| Johnston | N | N | Y | # | N | Y | N | N |
| **MAINE** | | | | | | | | |
| Mitchell | Y | N | Y | N | Y | Y | N | N |
| *Cohen* | Y | N | ? | ? | ? | Y | N | N |
| **MARYLAND** | | | | | | | | |
| Mikulski | N | N | ? | ? | ? | Y | N | N |
| Sarbanes | Y | N | Y | N | Y | Y | N | N |
| **MASSACHUSETTS** | | | | | | | | |
| Kennedy | N | N | Y | Y | Y | Y | N | N |
| Kerry | Y | N | Y | Y | N | Y | N | N |
| **MICHIGAN** | | | | | | | | |
| Levin | N | N | Y | N | Y | Y | N | N |
| Riegle | Y | N | Y | N | Y | Y | N | N |
| **MINNESOTA** | | | | | | | | |
| Wellstone | N | N | + | – | + | Y | N | N |
| *Durenberger* | N | Y | ? | ? | ? | Y | N | N |
| **MISSISSIPPI** | | | | | | | | |
| Cochran | Y | Y | N | ? | N | Y | N | N |
| *Lott* | Y | Y | N | Y | N | Y | N | Y |
| **MISSOURI** | | | | | | | | |
| *Bond* | ? | ? | ? | ? | ? | ? | N | N |
| *Danforth* | N | Y | N | N | Y | Y | N | N |
| **MONTANA** | | | | | | | | |
| Baucus | N | N | Y | N | Y | Y | N | N |
| *Burns* | Y | N | N | Y | N | Y | N | Y |
| **NEBRASKA** | | | | | | | | |
| Exon | N | N | Y | N | Y | Y | N | N |
| Kerrey | Y | N | ? | ? | ? | Y | N | N |
| **NEVADA** | | | | | | | | |
| Bryan | Y | N | Y | N | Y | Y | N | N |
| Reid | Y | N | ? | ? | ? | Y | N | N |
| **NEW HAMPSHIRE** | | | | | | | | |
| *Rudman* | ? | N | N | Y | N | Y | N | N |
| *Smith* | Y | N | N | Y | N | N | N | Y |
| **NEW JERSEY** | | | | | | | | |
| Bradley | Y | N | Y | N | Y | Y | N | N |
| Lautenberg | Y | N | Y | Y | N | Y | N | N |
| **NEW MEXICO** | | | | | | | | |
| Bingaman | N | ? | Y | Y | N | Y | N | N |
| *Domenici* | Y | Y | N | Y | N | Y | N | N |
| **NEW YORK** | | | | | | | | |
| Moynihan | N | N | Y | N | Y | Y | N | N |
| *D'Amato* | Y | N | N | N | Y | Y | N | N |
| **NORTH CAROLINA** | | | | | | | | |
| Sanford | Y | N | ? | ? | ? | Y | N | N |
| *Helms* | + | + | – | ? | ? | N | Y | Y |
| **NORTH DAKOTA** | | | | | | | | |
| Burdick | ? | ? | ? | ? | ? | Y | N | N |
| Conrad | Y | N | Y | N | Y | Y | N | N |
| **OHIO** | | | | | | | | |
| Glenn | Y | N | Y | N | Y | Y | N | N |
| Metzenbaum | N | N | Y | N | Y | Y | N | N |
| **OKLAHOMA** | | | | | | | | |
| Boren | ? | ? | ? | ? | ? | Y | N | N |
| *Nickles* | Y | N | ? | ? | ? | Y | N | N |
| **OREGON** | | | | | | | | |
| *Hatfield* | N | Y | N | Y | N | Y | N | N |
| *Packwood* | Y | N | N | Y | N | Y | N | N |
| **PENNSYLVANIA** | | | | | | | | |
| Wofford | N | N | X | ? | ? | Y | N | N |
| *Specter* | N | N | Y | N | Y | ? | N | N |
| **RHODE ISLAND** | | | | | | | | |
| Pell | N | N | Y | ? | Y | Y | N | N |
| *Chafee* | N | N | N | Y | N | Y | N | N |
| **SOUTH CAROLINA** | | | | | | | | |
| Hollings | Y | N | Y | N | Y | Y | Y | Y |
| *Thurmond* | Y | N | N | Y | N | Y | Y | N |
| **SOUTH DAKOTA** | | | | | | | | |
| Daschle | Y | N | Y | N | Y | Y | N | N |
| *Pressler* | Y | N | Y | N | Y | N | Y | N |
| **TENNESSEE** | | | | | | | | |
| Gore | ? | ? | ? | ? | ? | ? | ? | ? |
| Sasser | N | N | Y | N | Y | Y | N | N |
| **TEXAS** | | | | | | | | |
| Bentsen | N | N | Y | N | Y | Y | N | N |
| *Gramm* | Y | Y | ? | ? | ? | ? | N | N |
| **UTAH** | | | | | | | | |
| *Garn* | Y | Y | ? | ? | ? | Y | Y | Y |
| *Hatch* | Y | Y | N | Y | N | Y | N | N |
| **VERMONT** | | | | | | | | |
| Leahy | N | ? | ? | ? | ? | + | N | N |
| *Jeffords* | N | N | N | Y | ? | Y | N | N |
| **VIRGINIA** | | | | | | | | |
| Robb | Y | N | Y | N | Y | Y | N | N |
| *Warner* | N | N | N | Y | N | N | N | N |
| **WASHINGTON** | | | | | | | | |
| Adams | N | ? | Y | Y | N | Y | N | N |
| *Gorton* | Y | N | Y | N | Y | N | N | N |
| **WEST VIRGINIA** | | | | | | | | |
| Byrd | Y | N | Y | N | Y | Y | N | N |
| Rockefeller | Y | N | Y | N | Y | Y | N | N |
| **WISCONSIN** | | | | | | | | |
| Kohl | N | N | Y | N | Y | Y | N | N |
| *Kasten* | ? | ? | ? | ? | ? | ? | N | N |
| **WYOMING** | | | | | | | | |
| *Simpson* | Y | N | N | Y | N | Y | Y | N |
| *Wallop* | Y | Y | N | Y | N | N | Y | Y |

ND Northern Democrats    SD Southern Democrats    Southern states - Ala., Ark., Fla., Ga., Ky., La., Miss., N.C., Okla., S.C., Tenn., Texas, Va.

**241. HR 11. Tax Bill/Income From Cuba.** Graham, D-Fla., motion to table (kill) the Harkin, D-Iowa, amendment to the Graham amendment to exempt food and medicine from the prohibition related to tax deductions from a Cuban source of income, unless the president determined that it was used for purposes other than those intended. The Graham amendment prohibited overseas subsidiaries of U.S. companies from deducting business expenses from doing business with Cuba. Motion agreed to 51-37: R 26-11; D 25-26 (ND 15-22, SD 10-4), Sept. 25, 1992. (The Graham amendment was subsequently adopted by voice vote.)

**242. HR 5679. Fiscal 1993 Veterans Affairs, Housing and Urban Development, Independent Agencies Appropriations/RTC.** Garn, R-Utah, motion to table (kill) the Metzenbaum, D-Ohio, amendment to extend from three years to five years the statute of limitations for certain legal actions brought by the Resolution Trust Corporation (RTC) against a failed savings association. Motion rejected 18-68: R 18-20; D 0-48 (ND 0-34, SD 0-14), Sept. 25, 1992. (The Metzenbaum amendment was subsequently withdrawn.)

**243. HR 11. Tax Bill/Adoption Expenses.** Bentsen, D-Texas, motion to table (kill) the Craig, R-Idaho, amendment to provide a $5,000 tax deduction per year per child for qualified adoption expenses. Motion agreed to 46-30: R 1-30; D 45-0 (ND 33-0, SD 12-0), Sept. 26, 1992.

**244. HR 11. Tax Bill/Minivans.** Packwood, R-Ore., motion to table (kill) the Riegle, D-Mich., amendment to express the sense of the Senate that multipurpose vehicles, such as minivans, should be classified as trucks for tariff purposes, making them subject to a 25 percent duty. Motion rejected 36-37: R 25-5; D 11-32 (ND 9-23, SD 2-9), Sept. 26, 1992.

**245. HR 11. Tax Bill/Minivans.** Riegle, D-Mich., amendment to express the sense of the Senate that multipurpose vehicles, such as minivans, should be classified as trucks for tariff purposes, making them subject to a 25 percent duty. Rejected 36-37: R 5-25; D 31-12 (ND 22-9, SD 9-3), Sept. 26, 1992.

**246. Treaty Docs 102-20, 102-32. Strategic Arms Reduction Treaty/Cloture.** Motion to invoke cloture (thus limiting debate) on the adoption of the resolution of ratification of the Strategic Arms Reduction Treaty (START), which would reduce by about one-third the arsenal of long-range missiles and bombers in the United States and former Soviet Union. Motion agreed to 87-6: R 33-6; D 54-0 (ND 39-0, SD 15-0), Sept. 29, 1992. A three-fifths majority vote (60) of the total Senate was required to invoke cloture.

**247. Treaty Docs 102-20, 102-32. Strategic Arms Reduction Treaty/ICBMs and Launchers.** Wallop, R-Wyo., amendment to require the president to certify that all intercontinental ballistic missiles (ICBMs) with multiple warheads and all launchers were eliminated. Rejected 16-83: R 15-28; D 1-55 (ND 0-40, SD 1-15), Sept. 29, 1992.

**248. Treaty Docs 102-20, 102-32. Strategic Arms Reduction Treaty/Non-Deployed Missiles.** Wallop, R-Wyo., amendment to require the president to certify that all non-deployed missiles for silo launchers of ICBMs, mobile launchers of ICBMs and launchers for submarine-launched ballistic missiles (SLBMs) were eliminated except for a verifiable finite number before the treaty could enter into force. Rejected 11-88: R 10-33; D 1-55 (ND 0-40, SD 1-15), Sept. 29, 1992.

| | 249 | 250 | 251 | 252 | 253 | 254 | 255 | 256 |
|---|---|---|---|---|---|---|---|---|
| **ALABAMA** | | | | | | | | |
| Heflin | Y | N | N | N | Y | Y | Y | Y |
| *Shelby* | N | N | Y | N | Y | Y | N | Y |
| **ALASKA** | | | | | | | | |
| *Murkowski* | Y | N | Y | N | Y | Y | N | Y |
| *Stevens* | Y | N | Y | N | Y | Y | N | Y |
| **ARIZONA** | | | | | | | | |
| DeConcini | Y | N | N | Y | Y | Y | Y | Y |
| *McCain* | N | Y | Y | Y | Y | N | N | N |
| **ARKANSAS** | | | | | | | | |
| Bumpers | Y | N | N | Y | Y | Y | Y | N |
| Pryor | Y | N | N | Y | Y | Y | Y | N |
| **CALIFORNIA** | | | | | | | | |
| Cranston | Y | N | N | N | Y | Y | Y | Y |
| *Seymour* | Y | Y | Y | Y | Y | Y | N | Y |
| **COLORADO** | | | | | | | | |
| Wirth | Y | N | N | N | Y | Y | Y | Y |
| *Brown* | N | N | Y | Y | Y | Y | Y | Y |
| **CONNECTICUT** | | | | | | | | |
| Dodd | Y | N | N | N | Y | Y | Y | Y |
| Lieberman | Y | N | N | N | Y | Y | Y | Y |
| **DELAWARE** | | | | | | | | |
| Biden | N | N | N | N | Y | Y | Y | Y |
| *Roth* | Y | N | Y | N | Y | Y | N | N |
| **FLORIDA** | | | | | | | | |
| Graham | Y | N | N | N | Y | Y | Y | Y |
| *Mack* | Y | N | Y | N | Y | N | Y | Y |
| **GEORGIA** | | | | | | | | |
| Fowler | Y | N | N | Y | Y | Y | Y | Y |
| Nunn | Y | N | N | Y | Y | Y | Y | Y |
| **HAWAII** | | | | | | | | |
| Akaka | Y | N | N | N | Y | Y | Y | Y |
| Inouye | Y | N | Y | N | Y | Y | Y | Y |
| **IDAHO** | | | | | | | | |
| *Craig* | N | Y | Y | Y | N | N | N | N |
| *Symms* | N | Y | Y | Y | N | N | N | N |
| **ILLINOIS** | | | | | | | | |
| Dixon | N | N | N | N | Y | Y | Y | Y |
| Simon | N | N | N | N | Y | Y | Y | Y |
| **INDIANA** | | | | | | | | |
| *Coats* | N | N | N | N | Y | Y | N | N |
| *Lugar* | N | N | N | N | Y | Y | N | Y |
| **IOWA** | | | | | | | | |
| Harkin | Y | N | N | N | Y | Y | Y | Y |
| *Grassley* | Y | N | Y | N | Y | N | N | Y |
| **KANSAS** | | | | | | | | |
| *Dole* | N | N | N | N | Y | Y | N | N |
| *Kassebaum* | N | N | N | N | Y | Y | N | Y |
| **KENTUCKY** | | | | | | | | |
| Ford | Y | N | N | Y | Y | Y | N | Y |
| *McConnell* | N | N | Y | Y | Y | Y | N | Y |
| **LOUISIANA** | | | | | | | | |
| Breaux | Y | N | Y | Y | Y | N | Y | Y |
| Johnston | Y | N | Y | N | Y | Y | N | Y |
| **MAINE** | | | | | | | | |
| Mitchell | Y | N | N | N | Y | Y | Y | Y |
| *Cohen* | Y | N | N | N | Y | Y | N | Y |
| **MARYLAND** | | | | | | | | |
| Mikulski | Y | N | N | N | Y | Y | Y | Y |
| Sarbanes | Y | N | N | N | Y | Y | Y | Y |
| **MASSACHUSETTS** | | | | | | | | |
| Kennedy | Y | N | N | N | Y | Y | Y | Y |
| Kerry | Y | N | N | N | Y | Y | Y | Y |
| **MICHIGAN** | | | | | | | | |
| Levin | Y | N | N | N | Y | Y | Y | Y |
| Riegle | Y | N | N | N | Y | Y | Y | Y |
| **MINNESOTA** | | | | | | | | |
| Wellstone | N | N | N | N | Y | Y | Y | Y |
| *Durenberger* | Y | N | N | N | Y | Y | Y | Y |
| **MISSISSIPPI** | | | | | | | | |
| *Cochran* | N | N | Y | N | Y | Y | N | N |
| *Lott* | N | Y | Y | Y | Y | N | N | Y |
| **MISSOURI** | | | | | | | | |
| *Bond* | Y | N | Y | N | Y | Y | Y | N |
| *Danforth* | Y | N | Y | N | Y | N | N | Y |
| **MONTANA** | | | | | | | | |
| Baucus | Y | N | N | Y | Y | Y | Y | Y |
| *Burns* | N | N | Y | Y | Y | Y | N | N |
| **NEBRASKA** | | | | | | | | |
| Exon | Y | N | N | N | Y | Y | Y | Y |
| Kerrey | Y | N | N | N | Y | Y | Y | Y |
| **NEVADA** | | | | | | | | |
| Bryan | Y | N | N | Y | Y | Y | Y | Y |
| Reid | Y | N | N | Y | Y | Y | Y | Y |
| **NEW HAMPSHIRE** | | | | | | | | |
| *Rudman* | N | N | N | N | Y | Y | N | Y |
| *Smith* | N | Y | Y | Y | N | N | Y | N |
| **NEW JERSEY** | | | | | | | | |
| Bradley | N | N | N | N | Y | Y | Y | Y |
| Lautenberg | Y | N | N | N | Y | Y | Y | Y |
| **NEW MEXICO** | | | | | | | | |
| Bingaman | Y | N | N | N | Y | Y | Y | Y |
| *Domenici* | Y | N | Y | N | Y | Y | Y | Y |
| **NEW YORK** | | | | | | | | |
| Moynihan | Y | N | N | N | Y | Y | Y | Y |
| *D'Amato* | Y | N | N | ? | Y | Y | Y | Y |
| **NORTH CAROLINA** | | | | | | | | |
| Sanford | Y | ? | ? | ? | Y | Y | Y | Y |
| *Helms* | N | + | Y | Y | N | N | Y | N |
| **NORTH DAKOTA** | | | | | | | | |
| Burdick | Y | N | N | Y | Y | Y | Y | Y |
| Conrad | Y | N | Y | Y | Y | Y | Y | N |
| **OHIO** | | | | | | | | |
| Glenn | Y | N | N | N | Y | Y | Y | Y |
| Metzenbaum | N | N | N | N | Y | Y | Y | Y |
| **OKLAHOMA** | | | | | | | | |
| Boren | Y | N | N | N | Y | Y | Y | Y |
| *Nickles* | Y | N | Y | Y | Y | N | N | Y |
| **OREGON** | | | | | | | | |
| *Hatfield* | Y | N | Y | N | Y | Y | N | Y |
| *Packwood* | Y | N | Y | N | Y | Y | N | Y |
| **PENNSYLVANIA** | | | | | | | | |
| Wofford | Y | N | N | N | Y | Y | Y | Y |
| *Specter* | Y | ? | ? | N | Y | Y | Y | Y |
| **RHODE ISLAND** | | | | | | | | |
| Pell | Y | N | — | — | Y | Y | Y | Y |
| *Chafee* | Y | N | Y | N | Y | Y | N | Y |
| **SOUTH CAROLINA** | | | | | | | | |
| Hollings | Y | Y | N | Y | N | Y | Y | N |
| *Thurmond* | Y | N | Y | Y | Y | N | Y | Y |
| **SOUTH DAKOTA** | | | | | | | | |
| Daschle | Y | N | N | N | Y | Y | Y | Y |
| *Pressler* | Y | Y | Y | Y | Y | N | N | N |
| **TENNESSEE** | | | | | | | | |
| Gore | ? | ? | ? | ? | ? | ? | ? | ? |
| Sasser | Y | N | N | N | Y | Y | Y | Y |
| **TEXAS** | | | | | | | | |
| Bentsen | Y | N | N | N | Y | Y | Y | Y |
| *Gramm* | N | N | Y | Y | Y | N | N | Y |
| **UTAH** | | | | | | | | |
| *Garn* | N | Y | Y | Y | Y | N | N | N |
| *Hatch* | N | N | Y | Y | Y | N | N | N |
| **VERMONT** | | | | | | | | |
| Leahy | N | N | N | Y | Y | Y | Y | Y |
| *Jeffords* | N | N | N | N | Y | Y | N | Y |
| **VIRGINIA** | | | | | | | | |
| Robb | Y | N | N | N | Y | Y | Y | Y |
| *Warner* | Y | N | Y | N | Y | Y | N | Y |
| **WASHINGTON** | | | | | | | | |
| Adams | Y | N | N | N | Y | Y | Y | Y |
| *Gorton* | N | N | Y | N | Y | Y | N | Y |
| **WEST VIRGINIA** | | | | | | | | |
| Byrd | Y | N | N | N | Y | Y | Y | N |
| Rockefeller | Y | N | N | N | Y | Y | Y | Y |
| **WISCONSIN** | | | | | | | | |
| Kohl | Y | N | N | N | Y | Y | Y | Y |
| *Kasten* | Y | N | Y | Y | Y | N | N | Y |
| **WYOMING** | | | | | | | | |
| *Simpson* | Y | N | N | N | Y | Y | N | Y |
| *Wallop* | N | Y | Y | Y | N | N | Y | N |

## KEY

| | |
|---|---|
| Y | Voted for (yea). |
| # | Paired for. |
| + | Announced for. |
| N | Voted against (nay). |
| X | Paired against. |
| − | Announced against. |
| P | Voted "present." |
| C | Voted "present" to avoid possible conflict of interest. |
| ? | Did not vote or otherwise make a position known. |

Democrats  *Republicans*

ND  Northern Democrats      SD  Southern Democrats      Southern states - Ala., Ark., Fla., Ga., Ky., La., Miss., N.C., Okla., S.C., Tenn., Texas, Va.

**249. HR 11. Tax Bill/Passage.** Passage of the $34 billion tax bill including tax benefits for enterprise zones in inner cities, a restoration of tax breaks for and penalty-free withdrawals from IRAs, provisions making permanent a limit on itemized deductions and the phaseout of the personal exemption for upper-income taxpayers, a tax credit for first-time home buyers, tax relief for companies under the alternative minimum tax, and for other purposes. Passed 70-29: R 22-21; D 48-8 (ND 33-7, SD 15-1), Sept. 29, 1992.

**250. Treaty Docs 102-20, 102-32. Strategic Arms Reduction Treaty/Mobile ICBMs.** Wallop, R-Wyo., amendment to require the president to certify that all mobile ICBMs and all launchers for mobile ICBMs were eliminated before the treaty could enter into force. Rejected 10-86: R 9-32; D 1-54 (ND 0-40, SD 1-14), Sept. 30, 1992.

**251. HR 5368. Fiscal 1993 Foreign Operations Appropriations/Morocco.** Kasten, R-Wis., amendment to the Kassebaum, R-Kan., amendment, to express the sense of the Senate that the U.N. secretary general's efforts to resolve conflict in the Western Sahara should be praised and the United States should encourage cooperation with the implementation of a U.N. referendum. The Kassebaum amendment limited funding to Morocco to $52 million unless the president certified that Morocco was cooperating with the U.N. for a self-determination plan for the people of Western Sahara. Rejected 40-56: R 33-9; D 7-47 (ND 4-35, SD 3-12), Sept. 30, 1992.

**252. HR 5368. Fiscal 1993 Foreign Operations Appropriations/Funding Reduction.** Helms, R-N.C., amendment to cut the budget authority in the bill by 10 percent with the savings going to deficit reduction. Rejected 38-58: R 22-20; D 16-38 (ND 8-31, SD 8-7), Sept. 30, 1992. A "nay" was a vote in support of the president's position.

**253. Treaty Docs 102-20, 102-32. Strategic Arms Reduction Treaty (START).** Adoption of the resolution of ratification of START to reduce by about one-third the arsenal of warheads on U.S. and Soviet long-range missiles and bombers. Adopted 93-6: R 38-5; D 55-1 (ND 40-0, SD 15-1), Oct. 1, 1992. A two-thirds majority of those present and voting (66 in this case) was required for adoption of resolutions of ratification. A "yea" was a vote in support of the president's position.

**254. S 323. Family Planning Amendments/Veto Override.** Passage, over President Bush's Sept. 25 veto, of the bill to reauthorize Title X of the Public Health Service Act for five years through fiscal 1997. The bill overturned the administration's "gag rule" and thus allowed abortion counseling at federally funded clinics. Passed (thus cleared for House action) 73-26: R 20-23; D 53-3 (ND 40-0, SD 13-3), Oct. 1, 1992. A two-thirds majority of those present and voting (66 in this case) was required to override a veto. A "nay" was a vote in support of the president's position.

**255. HR 5318. Conditional MFN for China/Veto Override.** Passage, over President Bush's Sept. 28 veto, of the bill to prohibit the president from waiving the Jackson-Vanik amendment to the 1974 Trade Act and extending most-favored-nation status to China in 1993 unless he certified that China had released and accounted for prisoners from the 1989 Tiananmen Square demonstrations and had made significant progress in adhering to standards for human rights and weapons non-proliferation. Rejected 59-40: R 8-35; D 51-5 (ND 37-3, SD 14-2), Oct. 1, 1992. A two-thirds majority of those present and voting (66 in this case) was required to override a veto. A "nay" was a vote in support of the president's position.

**256. HR 5368. Fiscal 1993 Foreign Operations Appropriations/Passage.** Passage of the bill to provide $26.5 billion in new budget authority for foreign assistance and related programs in fiscal 1993. The administration requested $27.3 billion. Passed 87-12: R 35-8; D 52-4 (ND 39-1, SD 13-3), Oct. 1, 1992.

### KEY

- Y  Voted for (yea).
- #  Paired for.
- +  Announced for.
- N  Voted against (nay).
- X  Paired against.
- −  Announced against.
- P  Voted ''present.''
- C  Voted ''present'' to avoid possible conflict of interest.
- ?  Did not vote or otherwise make a position known.

Democrats   *Republicans*

| | 257 | 258 | 259 | 260 | 261 | 262 | 263 | 264 |
|---|---|---|---|---|---|---|---|---|
| **ALABAMA** | | | | | | | | |
| Heflin | Y | N | N | Y | N | Y | Y | |
| Shelby | Y | N | Y | Y | Y | N | Y | N |
| **ALASKA** | | | | | | | | |
| *Murkowski* | Y | N | Y | Y | N | N | Y | N |
| *Stevens* | Y | N | Y | Y | N | N | Y | N |
| **ARIZONA** | | | | | | | | |
| DeConcini | N | N | Y | Y | Y | Y | Y | N |
| *McCain* | Y | N | Y | Y | N | N | Y | N |
| **ARKANSAS** | | | | | | | | |
| Bumpers | Y | N | Y | Y | Y | Y | Y | Y |
| Pryor | Y | N | Y | N | Y | Y | Y | Y |
| **CALIFORNIA** | | | | | | | | |
| Cranston | N | N | Y | Y | Y | Y | Y | N |
| *Seymour* | Y | N | N | Y | N | N | Y | N |
| **COLORADO** | | | | | | | | |
| Wirth | Y | N | Y | Y | Y | N | Y | Y |
| *Brown* | Y | N | N | N | N | N | Y | N |
| **CONNECTICUT** | | | | | | | | |
| Dodd | Y | N | Y | Y | Y | N | Y | Y |
| Lieberman | Y | N | Y | Y | Y | Y | Y | Y |
| **DELAWARE** | | | | | | | | |
| Biden | N | N | N | Y | Y | Y | Y | Y |
| *Roth* | Y | Y | N | N | N | N | Y | Y |
| **FLORIDA** | | | | | | | | |
| Graham | Y | N | Y | Y | Y | Y | Y | Y |
| *Mack* | Y | N | N | Y | N | N | Y | P |
| **GEORGIA** | | | | | | | | |
| Fowler | Y | N | N | Y | Y | Y | Y | N |
| Nunn | Y | N | Y | Y | Y | Y | Y | Y |
| **HAWAII** | | | | | | | | |
| Akaka | Y | N | Y | Y | Y | Y | Y | Y |
| Inouye | Y | N | Y | Y | Y | Y | Y | Y |
| **IDAHO** | | | | | | | | |
| *Craig* | Y | Y | N | N | N | N | N | N |
| *Symms* | Y | Y | N | N | N | N | N | N |
| **ILLINOIS** | | | | | | | | |
| Dixon | ? | ? | ? | ? | Y | Y | Y | Y |
| Simon | N | N | Y | Y | Y | Y | Y | Y |
| **INDIANA** | | | | | | | | |
| *Coats* | Y | N | N | N | N | N | N | Y |
| *Lugar* | Y | N | Y | Y | N | N | Y | N |
| **IOWA** | | | | | | | | |
| Harkin | N | N | Y | Y | Y | Y | Y | Y |
| *Grassley* | Y | N | Y | Y | N | N | Y | Y |
| **KANSAS** | | | | | | | | |
| *Dole* | Y | N | Y | Y | N | N | Y | N |
| *Kassebaum* | Y | N | Y | Y | N | Y | Y | Y |
| **KENTUCKY** | | | | | | | | |
| Ford | Y | N | Y | Y | Y | Y | N | Y |
| *McConnell* | Y | Y | N | Y | N | N | Y | Y |
| **LOUISIANA** | | | | | | | | |
| Breaux | Y | N | Y | Y | Y | Y | Y | Y |
| Johnston | N | N | Y | Y | Y | N | Y | Y |
| **MAINE** | | | | | | | | |
| Mitchell | Y | N | Y | Y | Y | Y | Y | Y |
| *Cohen* | Y | N | Y | Y | N | N | Y | Y |
| **MARYLAND** | | | | | | | | |
| Mikulski | Y | N | Y | Y | Y | Y | Y | Y |
| Sarbanes | N | N | Y | Y | Y | Y | Y | Y |
| **MASSACHUSETTS** | | | | | | | | |
| Kennedy | Y | N | Y | Y | Y | Y | Y | Y |
| Kerry | Y | N | Y | Y | Y | Y | Y | Y |
| **MICHIGAN** | | | | | | | | |
| Levin | Y | N | Y | Y | Y | Y | Y | Y |
| Riegle | Y | N | Y | Y | Y | ? | ? | Y |
| **MINNESOTA** | | | | | | | | |
| Wellstone | Y | N | Y | Y | Y | Y | Y | Y |
| *Durenberger* | Y | Y | Y | Y | ? | ? | ? | Y |
| **MISSISSIPPI** | | | | | | | | |
| *Cochran* | Y | N | Y | Y | N | N | Y | Y |
| *Lott* | Y | N | N | Y | N | N | Y | N |
| **MISSOURI** | | | | | | | | |
| *Bond* | Y | Y | Y | Y | N | N | Y | Y |
| *Danforth* | Y | Y | Y | Y | N | N | Y | Y |
| **MONTANA** | | | | | | | | |
| Baucus | Y | N | Y | Y | Y | Y | Y | Y |
| *Burns* | Y | N | Y | Y | N | N | N | N |
| **NEBRASKA** | | | | | | | | |
| Exon | Y | N | Y | Y | Y | Y | Y | Y |
| Kerrey | Y | N | Y | Y | Y | Y | Y | Y |
| **NEVADA** | | | | | | | | |
| Bryan | Y | N | Y | Y | Y | Y | Y | Y |
| Reid | Y | N | Y | Y | Y | ? | Y | N |
| **NEW HAMPSHIRE** | | | | | | | | |
| *Rudman* | Y | N | Y | Y | N | N | Y | N |
| *Smith* | Y | N | N | N | N | N | N | N |
| **NEW JERSEY** | | | | | | | | |
| Bradley | Y | N | Y | Y | Y | Y | Y | Y |
| Lautenberg | Y | N | Y | Y | Y | Y | Y | Y |
| **NEW MEXICO** | | | | | | | | |
| Bingaman | Y | N | Y | Y | Y | Y | Y | Y |
| *Domenici* | Y | N | Y | Y | N | N | Y | Y |
| **NEW YORK** | | | | | | | | |
| Moynihan | Y | N | Y | Y | Y | Y | Y | Y |
| *D'Amato* | Y | N | Y | Y | N | N | N | Y |
| **NORTH CAROLINA** | | | | | | | | |
| Sanford | Y | N | Y | Y | Y | Y | Y | Y |
| *Helms* | Y | N | N | N | N | N | N | N |
| **NORTH DAKOTA** | | | | | | | | |
| Burdick | Y | N | Y | Y | Y | Y | Y | Y |
| Conrad | Y | N | N | N | Y | Y | Y | Y |
| **OHIO** | | | | | | | | |
| Glenn | Y | N | Y | Y | Y | Y | Y | Y |
| Metzenbaum | Y | N | Y | Y | Y | Y | Y | Y |
| **OKLAHOMA** | | | | | | | | |
| Boren | Y | N | Y | Y | Y | Y | Y | N |
| *Nickles* | Y | N | N | N | N | N | N | N |
| **OREGON** | | | | | | | | |
| *Hatfield* | N | N | Y | Y | N | N | Y | Y |
| *Packwood* | Y | N | Y | Y | N | N | Y | N |
| **PENNSYLVANIA** | | | | | | | | |
| Wofford | Y | N | Y | Y | Y | Y | Y | Y |
| *Specter* | Y | N | N | Y | Y | Y | Y | Y |
| **RHODE ISLAND** | | | | | | | | |
| Pell | N | N | Y | Y | Y | Y | Y | Y |
| *Chafee* | Y | N | Y | Y | N | Y | Y | N |
| **SOUTH CAROLINA** | | | | | | | | |
| Hollings | Y | N | Y | Y | Y | Y | Y | Y |
| *Thurmond* | Y | N | Y | Y | N | N | Y | Y |
| **SOUTH DAKOTA** | | | | | | | | |
| Daschle | Y | Y | Y | Y | Y | Y | Y | Y |
| *Pressler* | Y | N | N | N | N | N | N | Y |
| **TENNESSEE** | | | | | | | | |
| Gore | ? | ? | ? | ? | Y | Y | ? | Y |
| Sasser | N | N | Y | Y | Y | Y | Y | Y |
| **TEXAS** | | | | | | | | |
| Bentsen | Y | Y | Y | Y | Y | Y | Y | Y |
| *Gramm* | Y | N | N | Y | N | N | N | N |
| **UTAH** | | | | | | | | |
| *Garn* | Y | N | N | Y | N | N | Y | N |
| *Hatch* | Y | Y | N | N | N | N | N | Y |
| **VERMONT** | | | | | | | | |
| Leahy | Y | N | Y | Y | Y | Y | Y | Y |
| *Jeffords* | Y | N | Y | Y | N | N | Y | Y |
| **VIRGINIA** | | | | | | | | |
| Robb | Y | N | Y | N | Y | Y | Y | Y |
| *Warner* | Y | N | Y | Y | N | N | Y | Y |
| **WASHINGTON** | | | | | | | | |
| Adams | Y | N | Y | Y | Y | Y | Y | Y |
| *Gorton* | N | N | Y | Y | N | N | Y | Y |
| **WEST VIRGINIA** | | | | | | | | |
| Byrd | N | N | Y | Y | Y | Y | Y | Y |
| Rockefeller | N | N | Y | Y | Y | Y | Y | Y |
| **WISCONSIN** | | | | | | | | |
| Kohl | Y | N | Y | Y | N | Y | Y | Y |
| *Kasten* | Y | N | N | Y | N | N | Y | Y |
| **WYOMING** | | | | | | | | |
| *Simpson* | Y | Y | Y | Y | N | N | Y | Y |
| *Wallop* | Y | Y | N | N | N | N | Y | N |

ND  Northern Democrats    SD  Southern Democrats    Southern states - Ala., Ark., Fla., Ga., Ky., La., Miss., N.C., Okla., S.C., Tenn., Texas, Va.

**257. HR 5427. Fiscal 1993 Legislative Branch Appropriations/Reduce Funding.** Seymour, R-Calif., amendment to reduce funding for the legislative branch by 15 percent over three years. Passed 85-13: R 41-2; D 44-11 (ND 30-9, SD 14-2), Oct. 1, 1992.

**258. HR 5427. Fiscal 1993 Legislative Branch Appropriations/Legal Fees.** Danforth, R-Mo., amendment to provide $1 million for legal fees incurred during Senate confirmation by presidential nominees to federal office. Rejected 11-87: R 10-33; D 1-54 (ND 0-39, SD 1-15), Oct. 1, 1992.

**259. HR 5427. Fiscal 1993 Legislative Branch Appropriations/Passage.** Passage of the bill to provide $2.2 billion in new budget authority for the operations of the legislative branch in fiscal 1993. Passed 75-23: R 24-19; D 51-4 (ND 37-2, SD 14-2), Oct. 1, 1992.

**260. HR 5678. Fiscal 1993 Commerce, Justice, State, Judiciary Appropriations/Conference Report.** Adoption of the conference report to provide $23,214,927,000 in new budget authority for fiscal 1993 for the departments of Commerce, Justice and State, the judiciary and related agencies. The administration requested $23,858,164,000. Adopted (thus clearing the bill for the president) 82-16: R 34-9; D 48-7 (ND 36-3, SD 12-4), Oct. 1, 1992.

**261. S 2. Neighborhood Schools Improvement/Cloture.** Motion to invoke cloture (thus limiting debate) on the motion to proceed to the conference report on the bill to authorize $800 million for grants to states and local education agencies to reform schools to improve student performance. The bill also provided for the development of educational content standards and increase flexibility in local schools by waiving federal and state regulations. The conference report did not include President Bush's proposals for increased parental choice of public and private schools. Motion rejected 59-40: R 2-40; D 57-0 (ND 40-0, SD 17-0), Oct. 2, 1992. A three-fifths majority vote of the total Senate (60) was required to invoke cloture.

**262. HR 3371. Crime Bill/Cloture.** Motion to invoke cloture (thus limiting debate) on the conference report to mandate a five-day waiting period and a background check for handgun purchases; authorize $3.3 billion for federal, state and local law enforcement; codify the "good faith" exception to the exclusionary rule; extend the federal death penalty to 53 crimes; and limit federal death row habeas corpus appeals to ones filed within one year from when a petitioner had exhausted all direct appeals. Motion rejected 55-43: R 3-39; D 52-4 (ND 39-0, SD 13-4), Oct. 2, 1992. A three-fifths majority vote (60) of the total Senate was required to invoke cloture. A "nay" was a vote in support of the president's position.

**263. S 2899. National Institutes of Health (NIH) Reauthorization/Cloture.** Motion to invoke cloture (thus limiting debate) on the motion to proceed to the bill to reauthorize and amend the programs of NIH through fiscal 1996, including funding for the National Cancer Institute and the Heart, Lung and Blood Institute. The bill continued the moratorium on fetal tissue transplant research using tissue obtained from induced abortions until May 19, 1993, after which the moratorium would be lifted under certain conditions. Motion agreed to 85-12: R 31-11; D 54-1 (ND 39-0, SD 15-1), Oct. 2, 1992. A three-fifths majority vote (60) of the total Senate was required to invoke cloture.

**264. S 12. Cable Television Reregulation/Veto Override.** Passage, over President Bush's Oct. 3 veto, of the bill to cap basic cable rates and improve competition in the cable industry by having the FCC set rates for basic cable service and giving broadcasters the right to charge cable operators for the use of over-the-air signals. Passed (thus cleared for House action) 74-25: R 24-18; D 50-7 (ND 36-4, SD 14-3), Oct. 5, 1992. A two-thirds majority of those present and voting (67 in this case) was required to override a veto. A "nay" was a vote in support of the president's position.

## KEY

Y Voted for (yea).
\# Paired for.
\+ Announced for.
N Voted against (nay).
X Paired against.
— Announced against.
P Voted "present."
C Voted "present" to avoid possible conflict of interest.
? Did not vote or otherwise make a position known.

Democrats  *Republicans*

| | 265 | 266 | 267 | 268 | 269 | 270 |
|---|---|---|---|---|---|---|
| **ALABAMA** | | | | | | |
| Heflin | N | Y | Y | Y | N | N |
| Shelby | Y | N | Y | N | N | N |
| **ALASKA** | | | | | | |
| *Murkowski* | Y | — | ? | ? | ? | ? |
| *Stevens* | Y | Y | Y | Y | Y | Y |
| **ARIZONA** | | | | | | |
| DeConcini | Y | Y | Y | Y | Y | Y |
| *McCain* | N | Y | Y | Y | N | N |
| **ARKANSAS** | | | | | | |
| Bumpers | Y | Y | Y | Y | Y | Y |
| Pryor | Y | Y | Y | Y | Y | Y |
| **CALIFORNIA** | | | | | | |
| Cranston | Y | Y | Y | Y | Y | Y |
| *Seymour* | N | Y | N | Y | N | Y |
| **COLORADO** | | | | | | |
| Wirth | Y | Y | Y | Y | Y | Y |
| *Brown* | N | Y | N | N | N | N |
| **CONNECTICUT** | | | | | | |
| Dodd | Y | Y | Y | Y | Y | Y |
| Lieberman | Y | Y | Y | Y | Y | Y |
| **DELAWARE** | | | | | | |
| Biden | Y | Y | Y | Y | Y | N |
| *Roth* | N | Y | Y | Y | Y | Y |
| **FLORIDA** | | | | | | |
| Graham | Y | N | Y | Y | Y | Y |
| *Mack* | N | Y | Y | Y | Y | Y |
| **GEORGIA** | | | | | | |
| Fowler | N | Y | Y | Y | Y | Y |
| Nunn | Y | Y | Y | Y | Y | Y |
| **HAWAII** | | | | | | |
| Akaka | Y | Y | Y | Y | Y | Y |
| Inouye | Y | Y | Y | Y | Y | Y |
| **IDAHO** | | | | | | |
| *Craig* | N | Y | N | N | N | N |
| *Symms* | N | Y | Y | Y | N | N |
| **ILLINOIS** | | | | | | |
| Dixon | Y | Y | Y | Y | N | N |
| Simon | Y | Y | Y | N | N | N |
| **INDIANA** | | | | | | |
| *Coats* | N | Y | Y | N | N | N |
| *Lugar* | Y | Y | Y | N | N | N |
| **IOWA** | | | | | | |
| Harkin | Y | Y | Y | Y | Y | Y |
| *Grassley* | N | Y | Y | Y | Y | Y |
| **KANSAS** | | | | | | |
| *Dole* | Y | Y | Y | Y | N | N |
| *Kassebaum* | N | Y | N | Y | N | N |
| **KENTUCKY** | | | | | | |
| Ford | Y | Y | Y | Y | Y | Y |
| *McConnell* | N | Y | Y | ? | ? | ? |
| **LOUISIANA** | | | | | | |
| Breaux | Y | Y | Y | Y | Y | Y |
| Johnston | Y | Y | Y | Y | Y | Y |
| **MAINE** | | | | | | |
| Mitchell | Y | Y | Y | Y | Y | Y |
| *Cohen* | N | Y | N | Y | Y | Y |
| **MARYLAND** | | | | | | |
| Mikulski | Y | Y | Y | Y | Y | Y |
| Sarbanes | Y | Y | Y | Y | Y | Y |
| **MASSACHUSETTS** | | | | | | |
| Kennedy | Y | Y | Y | Y | ? | Y |
| Kerry | Y | Y | Y | Y | Y | Y |
| **MICHIGAN** | | | | | | |
| Levin | Y | Y | Y | Y | Y | Y |
| Riegle | Y | Y | Y | Y | Y | Y |
| **MINNESOTA** | | | | | | |
| Wellstone | Y | N | Y | Y | N | N |
| *Durenberger* | Y | N | Y | Y | N | N |
| **MISSISSIPPI** | | | | | | |
| *Cochran* | Y | Y | Y | Y | N | Y |
| *Lott* | N | Y | Y | Y | N | N |
| **MISSOURI** | | | | | | |
| *Bond* | N | ? | ? | ? | ? | ? |
| *Danforth* | Y | Y | Y | Y | Y | Y |
| **MONTANA** | | | | | | |
| Baucus | Y | Y | Y | Y | Y | Y |
| *Burns* | N | Y | Y | Y | N | N |
| **NEBRASKA** | | | | | | |
| Exon | Y | Y | C | Y | Y | Y |
| Kerrey | Y | Y | Y | Y | Y | Y |
| **NEVADA** | | | | | | |
| Bryan | Y | N | Y | Y | Y | Y |
| Reid | Y | N | Y | ? | ? | ? |
| **NEW HAMPSHIRE** | | | | | | |
| *Rudman* | Y | Y | N | Y | N | N |
| *Smith* | N | Y | N | N | N | N |
| **NEW JERSEY** | | | | | | |
| Bradley | Y | Y | Y | Y | Y | N |
| Lautenberg | Y | Y | Y | Y | Y | Y |
| **NEW MEXICO** | | | | | | |
| Bingaman | Y | Y | Y | Y | Y | Y |
| *Domenici* | Y | Y | Y | Y | N | N |
| **NEW YORK** | | | | | | |
| Moynihan | Y | N | Y | Y | Y | Y |
| *D'Amato* | Y | Y | Y | Y | Y | Y |
| **NORTH CAROLINA** | | | | | | |
| Sanford | Y | ? | ? | ? | ? | ? |
| *Helms* | N | ? | ? | — | — | — |
| **NORTH DAKOTA** | | | | | | |
| Burdick | Y | Y | Y | Y | Y | \# |
| Conrad | N | Y | Y | Y | Y | Y |
| **OHIO** | | | | | | |
| Glenn | Y | Y | Y | Y | Y | Y |
| Metzenbaum | Y | Y | Y | N | N | N |
| **OKLAHOMA** | | | | | | |
| Boren | Y | Y | Y | Y | Y | Y |
| *Nickles* | N | Y | Y | Y | N | Y |
| **OREGON** | | | | | | |
| *Hatfield* | Y | Y | Y | Y | N | Y |
| *Packwood* | Y | Y | Y | Y | Y | Y |
| **PENNSYLVANIA** | | | | | | |
| Wofford | Y | Y | Y | Y | Y | Y |
| *Specter* | N | Y | Y | Y | Y | Y |
| **RHODE ISLAND** | | | | | | |
| Pell | Y | Y | Y | Y | Y | Y |
| *Chafee* | N | N | Y | Y | Y | Y |
| **SOUTH CAROLINA** | | | | | | |
| Hollings | Y | Y | Y | Y | Y | Y |
| *Thurmond* | Y | Y | N | Y | Y | Y |
| **SOUTH DAKOTA** | | | | | | |
| Daschle | Y | Y | Y | Y | Y | Y |
| *Pressler* | N | Y | Y | Y | Y | Y |
| **TENNESSEE** | | | | | | |
| Gore | ? | ? | ? | ? | ? | ? |
| Sasser | Y | Y | Y | Y | Y | Y |
| **TEXAS** | | | | | | |
| Bentsen | Y | Y | Y | Y | Y | Y |
| *Gramm* | N | Y | Y | Y | N | Y |
| **UTAH** | | | | | | |
| *Garn* | N | Y | Y | N | N | Y |
| *Hatch* | N | Y | Y | Y | N | Y |
| **VERMONT** | | | | | | |
| Leahy | Y | ? | ? | ? | ? | X |
| *Jeffords* | Y | ? | ? | ? | ? | ? |
| **VIRGINIA** | | | | | | |
| Robb | Y | Y | Y | Y | Y | Y |
| *Warner* | N | Y | Y | Y | Y | Y |
| **WASHINGTON** | | | | | | |
| Adams | Y | Y | Y | Y | Y | Y |
| *Gorton* | Y | Y | Y | Y | N | Y |
| **WEST VIRGINIA** | | | | | | |
| Byrd | Y | Y | Y | Y | Y | Y |
| Rockefeller | Y | Y | Y | Y | Y | Y |
| **WISCONSIN** | | | | | | |
| Kohl | N | Y | Y | Y | Y | Y |
| *Kasten* | ? | ? | ? | ? | ? | ? |
| **WYOMING** | | | | | | |
| *Simpson* | Y | Y | Y | Y | N | Y |
| *Wallop* | N | Y | Y | N | N | N |

ND Northern Democrats  SD Southern Democrats

Southern states - Ala., Ark., Fla., Ga., Ky., La., Miss., N.C., Okla., S.C., Tenn., Texas, Va.

**265. HR 5427. Fiscal 1992 Legislative Branch Appropriations/Conference Report.** Adoption of the conference report to provide $2,275,148,057 in new budget authority for the activities of the legislative branch in fiscal 1993. Adopted (thus cleared for the president) 68-30: R 16-26; D 52-4 (ND 38-2, SD 14-2), Oct. 5, 1992.

**266. HR 776. National Energy Policy/Cloture.** Motion to invoke cloture (thus limiting debate) on the conference report to decrease U.S. energy dependence through increased domestic production and conservation. The bill restructure the electric utility industry to increase competition; eased licensing for nuclear power plants; promoted production of cars that ran on non-gasoline fuels; mandated greater energy efficiency; provided tax incentives for renewable energy and alternative fuels; changed regulatory treatment of imported natural gas; and restructured the federal uranium enrichment program. Motion agreed to 84-8: R 36-2; D 48-6 (ND 35-4, SD 13-2), Oct. 8, 1992. A three-fifths majority vote (60) of the total Senate was required to invoke cloture. (The conference report subsequently was adopted by voice vote, clearing the bill for the president.)

**267. HR 429. Western Water Bill/Conference Report.** Adoption of the conference report to reauthorize the Bureau of Reclamation dam and irrigation construction programs, including the authorization for the completion of the Central Utah Project and reforms for the Central Valley Project in California. Adopted (thus clearing the bill for the president) 83-8: R 30-8; D 53-0 (ND 38-0, SD 15-0), Oct. 8, 1992.

**268. HR 11. Tax Bill/Cloture.** Motion to invoke cloture (thus limiting debate) on the $27 billion conference report on the tax bill, including tax benefits for 25 inner-city and 25 rural-area enterprise zones. Motion agreed to 80-10: R 30-7; D 50-3 (ND 36-2, SD 14-1), Oct. 8, 1992. A three-fifths majority vote (60) of the total Senate was required to invoke cloture.

**269. HR 11. Tax Bill/Waive Budget Act.** Bentsen, D-Texas, motion to waive the budget act with respect to the Brown, R-Colo., point of order against the conference report on the tax bill for violating Section 306 of the 1974 Congressional Budget Act and encroaching on the Budget Committee's jurisdiction. Motion agreed to 60-29: R 13-24; D 47-5 (ND 34-3, SD 13-2), Oct. 8, 1992. A three-fifths majority (60) of the total Senate was required to waive the budget act.

**270. HR 11. Tax Bill/Conference Report.** Adoption of the $27 billion conference report on the tax bill, including tax benefits for 25 inner-city and 25 rural-area enterprise zones; a restoration of tax breaks for individual retirement accounts (IRAs); penalty-free withdrawals from IRAs; a 12-month extension of a dozen expiring tax breaks, allowing the writeoff of intangible assets, including good will, over 14 years; passive loss deductions by real estate developers; new rules allowing real estate investment by pension funds; the repeal of luxury taxes; the permanent extension of the low-income housing and targeted jobs tax credits; the creation of a new child welfare capped entitlement; and provisions for other purposes. The bill increased taxes on securities firms and owners of commercial real estate, by increasing estimated taxes for individuals and corporations, capping deductions for business-related moving expenses, and limiting tax benefits to owners of failed thrifts, and through other measures. Adopted (thus clearing the bill for the president) 67-22: R 23-14; D 44-8 (ND 31-6, SD 13-2), Oct. 8, 1992.

# Appendix I

# INDEXES

# Bill Number Index

# Roll-Call Vote Index

# General Index